DEBRETT'S

Peerage

and Baronetage

Founded in 1769
Renamed Debrett in 1802

COMPRISES INFORMATION CONCERNING
THE ROYAL FAMILY, THE PEERAGE AND BARONETAGE

Edited by
Charles Kidd and David Williamson

DEBRETT'S PEERAGE LIMITED
LONDON

MACMILLAN

Copyright © Debrett's Peerage Limited and
Macmillan Reference Books 1995

Copyright © article Baronies by Writ and the Barony
of Grey of Codnor, its History and the Investigations
involved in having it called out of Abeyance, Thomas
Woodcock 1995

Copyright © article The Debrett Family: Ancestors
and Descendants of John Debrett, Frances-Jane
French 1995

Copyright © article A Rare Honour: British
Marquessates Through Six Centuries, Robert
Horley 1995

Published jointly 1995 by
DEBRETT'S PEERAGE LIMITED
73/77 Britannia Road London SW6 2JR and
MACMILLAN REFERENCE BOOKS
a division of Macmillan Publishers Limited
Cavaye Place, London SW10 9PG and Basingstoke
and in the United States of America by
ST MARTIN'S PRESS, INC.
175 Fifth Avenue, New York, NY 10010

Associated companies throughout the world

ISBN   UK: 0-333-41776-3
            0-333-62956-6 (leatherbound)
       US: 0-312-12557-7

A CIP catalogue record for this book is
available from the British Library and the Library of Congress
Library of Congress #85-648711

Typeset by Morton Word Processing Limited, Scarborough
Advertising: Macmillan Magazines Ltd
Printed and bound in Great Britain by BPC Hazell Books Ltd

CONTENTS

PREFACE

The 1995 edition of *Debrett* is the culmination of five years research and updating. Our daily sources of information remain, as one might expect, the birth, marriage and death columns of *The Times* and *The Daily Telegraph*, but we also receive a great deal of information from individual members of the peerage and baronetage, and their collaterals, who have taken on the role of family historian. The principal means of keeping our records accurate and up to date, however, lie in the mailing of proofs prior to each new edition, and the information volunteered in return. We aim to send a proof to every adult member of the peerage and baronetage families for whom we have an address, and this comes to an approximate total of 23,000.

Naturally we cannot rely on our entrants and the press to provide us with all the information we need, and, since the publication of the last *Debrett* in 1990, we have attempted a complete overhaul of the peerage section by making a comparative analysis of *Debrett* and *Burke*.

The objectives were principally to (a) trace the dates of death of female collaterals whose entries should probably have been removed years ago (b) trace the whereabouts of the descendants of "missing" male collaterals, and (c) re-instate entries for persons whose descendants are unknown, but who, if they exist, would be in remainder to a title.

As might be expected, this study highlighted many anomalies and contradictions between the two books, although these were often explained by their respective editorial policies. For example, *Debrett* adamantly excluded issue born out of wedlock, or born before a marriage had taken place (at least up until the 1960s). *Burke* had an altogether more relaxed attitude to this. *Debrett* usually limited its entries strictly to those who were in remainder to a peerage or baronetcy, whereas *Burke* often included lines of descendants who originated from an ancestor of the first peer or baronet (and were therefore not in remainder). *Debrett* has consistently included all living female issue (and their living descendants), and has given equal space to female heirs in cases where both males and females may inherit a title. *Burke* contains less female issue.

However, a very curious situation arose while comparing the respective articles on Earl Howe's family, which could not be explained by any of the above discrepancies. The entry in question was that of Henry Curzon, born 1899, about whom nothing else was known. A cursory study of the pedigree in *Burke's Peerage* 1970 indicated that Henry, if he were still living (or his senior male heir in the male line if he were deceased) would be the heir presumptive to the present peer.

The last edition of *Debrett* made no mention of Henry Curzon, who, according to *Burke*, was descended from the 4th son of the 1st Earl, and *Debrett* stated that the heir presumptive was Charles Mark Penn Curzon (born 1967), who was descended from the 6th son of the 1st Earl.

The obvious conclusion was that Henry Curzon had died unmarried or without issue, at which point his name would have been deleted from our pages. However, a search through the old editions of *Debrett* revealed that Henry had never been listed, nor indeed had his father's marriage ever been shown. Again according to *Burke*, Henry Curzon was the son of another Henry Curzon (1865-1912), of Graffham, Sussex, by his wife Ellen Hibberd.

Given *Debrett's* policy of not including issue born before the marriage, the next step was to obtain copies of the Curzon/Hibberd marriage certificate, and the birth certificate of the younger Henry. This done, the copies proved beyond doubt that Henry was born in wedlock.

After many fruitless letters and enquiries, and a visit to the village of Graffham, the only remaining course of action was to make a search of the marriage indexes at the General Register Office. Finally, a marriage was traced, and, from the information on the certificate it was quite simple to follow the trail. The bare facts stated that Henry Curzon (later Curzon-Howe), then aged 40 and a corporal in the RAF, married in 1940, Florence Jane Skinner, aged 28, who came from a Cornish farming family.

Two telephone calls were enough to contact Mrs Florence Curzon-Howe, Henry's widow, in Edinburgh. Sadly, Mrs Curzon-Howe confirmed that Henry had indeed died without issue in 1985 in Scotland.

Lord Howe took a lively interest in this research, and worked out that Henry had been his heir presumptive for about nine months, ie from the time of his succession to the title in May 1984 (upon the death of the 6th Earl Howe, son of the celebrated racing driver) until Henry's death in February 1985.

It is impossible not to conclude that family opposition to the marriage of Henry Curzon (senior) resulted in information being suppressed, which could in turn have led to a distinguished title going into abeyance as a result of a future heir's lack of sufficient evidence to prove his claim.

While attitudes to social morality, or "acceptability", have changed out of all recognition over the past 80 years, genealogists now face new problems in the form of privacy laws. In some places (for example the state of Victoria in Australia) the privacy laws have been tightened to such an extent that it is impossible to obtain a copy of a birth certificate of someone to whom one is not closely related. It is not difficult to imagine what sort of problems may ensue in attempting to sort out a disputed claim to a title when even such basic evidence is legally withheld.

Family disputes may frequently be the reason why some of our records are so incomplete, but the principal cause is geographical. At this point mention should be made of a number of genealogists or interested parties whose generous contributions have enabled us to trace many missing branches. Ted Rosvall, a Swedish genealogist and bookseller, has given us access to his extensive genealogical resources which have helped us to reach the Bagot family in the USA (last heard of in 1942), and a branch of the Earl of Guilford's family which had settled in India (last heard of in 1886). Shirley Veal and Mark Tapping gave us valuable assistance in South Africa with the Butler family (Baron Dunboyne), and the Lambart family (Earl of Cavan). Katherine Hamilton in Australia traced a branch of Lord Southampton's family, last heard of in 1907, and Alan Hustak, of Montreal, enabled us to reach a branch of Lord Massy's family in Canada (last heard of in 1920). Dr Morris Bierbrier must be thanked for his contributions to the Gardner pedigree, covering India, the UK and Australia.

In view of the amount of valuable information which has not appeared in print before, we have in some special cases deviated from our usual policy and have included deceased male and female issue in circumstances where they would normally have been deleted. We have also tried to reorganize the collateral branches by keeping them in strict order of seniority. This has meant that some deceased entrants have not been given new paragraphs, but have been kept in their previous positions and given a † before their names.

Further thanks are due to our heraldic artist, Jennifer Bush Kurzin, who has contributed over 80 new arms drawings against a formidable deadline; to Thomas Woodcock, Somerset Herald, Frances-Jane French and Robert Horley, who have written special articles; and Marlene Eilers for assisting us with the Royal Family section once more. Lydia Collins and Alwyn Arkle have put in a great deal of work in the editing and proof reading, and we also gratefully acknowledge the expertise and kindness of Patric Dickinson, Richmond Herald, and Sir Malcolm Innes of Edingight, Lord Lyon King of Arms. Finally we must thank Frances Johnston for keeping all the paperwork in immaculate order.

CHARLES KIDD

DAVID WILLIAMSON

BARONIES BY WRIT AND THE BARONY OF GREY OF CODNOR, ITS HISTORY AND THE INVESTIGATIONS INVOLVED IN HAVING IT CALLED OUT OF ABEYANCE

On 30 October 1989 Charles Legh Shuldham Cornwall-Legh took his seat in the House of Lords as 5th Baron Grey of Codnor. This terminated an abeyance which had lasted for 493 years since the death of Henry (Grey), 4th Baron Grey of Codnor, at Bytham in Lincolnshire on 8 April 1496.

The only peerages that can fall into abeyance are those deemed to have been created by a Writ of Summons to Parliament and a subsequent sitting in Parliament pursuant to that Summons. The doctrine that a dignity can be created in this way was formulated with authority in the early 17th century by Sir Edward Coke (1552-1634) in his *Institutes* (Part I 16B) and by the end of the seventeenth century it had been established that the Sovereign had a right to dispose of the dignity amongst the representatives of the coheirs. It was stated in the Report from the Select Committee on Peerages in Abeyance (1926) that the latest instance of a Barony created by Writ of Summons and sitting is that of Clifford in 1628. In that case Henry Clifford son and heir apparent of Francis (Clifford) 4th Earl of Cumberland was summoned to Parliament in 1628 in the lifetime of his father on the erroneous assumption that his father was Lord Clifford whereas that ancient Barony (now known as de Clifford) was subsequently held to have passed to Lady Anne Clifford the daughter and heir general of George (Clifford) 3rd Earl of Cumberland and first cousin of Henry Clifford. If his father had been Lord Clifford this would not have created a new peerage as a writ of acceleration summoning an eldest son in one of his father's subsidiary titles during the lifetime of the father does not create a new peerage. A more recent example is the Summons to Parliament and subsequent sitting in 1722 as Lord Percy of Algernon Seymour subsequently 7th Duke of Somerset on the erroneous belief that he had inherited a Barony of Percy from his mother. Apart from these odd instances English baronies created by Writs of Summons arose largely from Summonses to Parliament in the thirteenth, fourteenth and fifteenth centuries. At the time such Summonses were not considered to create Peerages. This concept arose as a result of decisions in individual cases from the seventeenth century onwards.

The alternative to a Barony created by Writ of Summons is one created by Letters Patent (Baronies by tenure were held to exist no longer in the Berkeley case of 1861 and although Dukedoms, Marquessates and Earldoms have been created by Act of Parliament usually by Royal Charter expressed to be made with the assent of Parliament the only Barony so created was that of Fanhope in 1432). The first Barony created by Letters Patent was that of Beauchamp of Kidderminster in 1387 which had a limitation to the heirs male of the body of the grantee. Baronies created by Patent in England were nearly always limited to heirs male of the body of the original grantee. By the end of the 15th century a Patent was the usual mode of creation of a Barony and the earliest surviving Barony created by Letters Patent is that of Stourton, which was created in 1448. Whereas a Barony created by Letters Patent descends according to the limitations in the Patent, a Barony by Writ descends to the heir general. Under English Law daughters rank equally and an abeyance arises when a Baron by Writ has more than one female heir such as daughters sisters or aunts and no male heir related in the same degree. An abeyance then arises as in England a dignity is impartible and remains in suspense among the coheirs either until all the lines but one are extinct when the senior descendant of that line takes the title as of right or when The Sovereign terminates the abeyance in favour of one of the coheirs. Abeyances do not arise in Scotland as in cases where Peerages can pass in the female line the eldest daughter inherits rather than ranking equally with her sisters. The present legal doctrine requires not only a Writ of Summons and sitting in Parliament pursuant to that Summons, but also that the Parliament must have the essential characteristics of a modern Parliament, ie it must have been an Assembly of the Three Estates of the Realm and latterly the Model Parliament of 1295 has usually been regarded as the earliest Parliament for Peerage purposes.

The first stage in calling a Peerage out of abeyance is a Petition from a person or persons who claim to be coheirs to a Barony in abeyance. This is presented to The Sovereign through the Home Secretary. Garter King of Arms is informally consulted as to whether the applicant makes out a *prima facie* case for his or her claim to be a coheir and whether there are other lines of coheirs. After receiving Garter's observations the Secretary of State formally refers the Petition to the Attorney-General. The Attorney-General submits a report to The Sovereign through the Secretary of State. If the Attorney-General reports that in his opinion the Petition should be referred to the House of Lords the Petition is endorsed "His (or Her) Majesty being moved upon this Petition is graciously pleased to refer the same to the Right Honourable The House of Peers to examine the allegations thereof as to what relates to the Petitioner's title therein mentioned, and to inform His (or Her) Majesty how the same shall appear to Their Lordships." The findings of the Committee for Privileges of the House of Lords are confirmed by a Resolution of the House of Lords and this is forwarded by the Clerk of the Parliaments to the Lord Chamberlain who lays it before The Sovereign and forwards it to the Prime Minister "for such advice as he may wish to tender." If the findings of the Committee are favourable the duty of advising The Sovereign as to whether to terminate an abeyance is therefore vested in the Prime Minister. If it is decided to call the Barony out of abeyance the Prime Minister informs the Home Secretary of The Sovereign's decision and the Home Secretary with the assistance of Garter King of Arms drafts a Warrant directing the issue of a Writ of Summons and when this has been signed by The Sovereign it is forwarded to the Lord Chancellor.

The practice of calling peerages out of abeyance began in the early 17th century. Following the death of Henry (Nevill) Lord Bergavenny in 1587 the title was claimed by his daughter Mary, wife of Sir Thomas Fane, as heir general and by his cousin Edward Nevill as heir male. The House of Lords avoided a formal decision and in 1604 it was agreed that suit should be made to the King for ennobling both parties by way of restitution. Dame Mary Fane was a coheir to the Barony of Despencer. The abeyance of this Barony which had lasted since 1461 was terminated in her favour by Letters Patent and as Edward Nevill had died his son, also Edward, became Baron Bergavenny. There were only three other cases in which it is now considered that abeyances were terminated in the seventeenth century namely Darcy (1641), Windsor (1660) and Ferrers of Chartley (1677). In the case of Darcy it was not until a subsequent claim in 1903 that the Committee for Privileges held that the events of 1641 when Conyers Darcy was summoned to Parliament had terminated an abeyance. In the reign of George III eight abeyances were terminated. Before then, discounting anomalous cases such as Despencer, no abeyances were terminated that had existed for more than thirty years. Close to the beginning of his reign in 1764 the Barony of Botetourt was called out of abeyance after 358 years. Thereafter Ros had been in abeyance for 199 years when the abeyance was terminated in 1806 and Zouche for 191 years when terminated in 1816. The law developed with the cases. The termination of the Barony of Braye in 1839 illustrates the point that a senior coheir does not rank above a coheir representing a younger sister as the Barony was terminated in favour of the descendant of the second of six sisters there being descendants of the eldest sister. The Zouche claim established that whilst all reasonable steps had to be taken to establish the identity of all the coheirs the failure to trace one line did not destroy a claim. In 1892 the claim of Mr John Chetwood Chetwood-Aiken to the Barony of de Wahull failed because he could not establish that his ancestors had sat in Parliament in response to summonses. Originally this cannot have been considered an impediment before the doctrine of abeyance developed as Elizabeth I created Lord Thomas Howard, Lord Howard de Walden by Writ of Summons dated 5 December 1597. This was used as the means of conferring a peerage quickly as the recipient was supposed to be at the point of death and not expected to survive the night and the Queen wished to benefit his infant son. In fact he recovered and survived till 1626. Lord Scrope was conducted in his place into the House of Lords on 7 December 1597 carrying Lord Howard de Walden's Writ. Had Lord Thomas Howard not survived the night of 5 December it would seem that it is only the subsequent interpretation of the law, which would not consider him to have been created a peer as there would only have been a Writ of Summons but no subsequent sitting.

In some cases a group of coheirs would join together to share the costs of pursuing a number of baronies. An example is C.M. Kenworthy, Dr R.G. Alexander and A.H. Leith who were three of the four coheirs of Sir William Brooke who would have been

Baron Cobham but for an attainder of 1603. The Committee for Privileges reported in 1912 that they were three of the four coheirs, but for the attainder, and at the same time that they were among a number of coheirs of the Barony of Burgh. In 1914 the Committee for Privileges further reported that they were among a number of coheirs of the Barony of Strabolgi. A membrane containing a record of the transactions of the King's Council was somehow inserted into the Parliament Roll of 1318 and the Committee for Privileges was persuaded that this conferred a Barony by Writ on David of Strathbogie, Earl of Atholl in Scotland, whose name appears on the membrane. An Act of Parliament in 1916 removed the effects of the Act of Attainder of 1603 so that the Barony of Cobham was no longer affected by this and shortly after this the baronies were called out of abeyance with each claimant or his heir receiving one of the three baronies.

In the first five years of the reign of Queen Victoria seven abeyances were terminated. Two of the seven abeyances (Clifford and Berners) had been of one year or less. The remaining five were abeyances of between 175 (Vaux) and 413 (Camoys) years. The Crown did not always terminate an abeyance even if the House of Lords reported that the Barony was in abeyance and the Petitioner for the termination of the abeyance was a coheir. An example is the Barony of Grandison where the House of Lords reported in 1858 that Sir Henry Bedingfeld, the Petitioner, was a coheir but no action was taken by The Crown. After the first five years of Queen Victoria's reign there were only seven terminations of abeyance for the rest of the century and the greatest length of abeyance was one hundred years (Mowbray and Segrave).

After the first decade of the twentieth century the number of abeyant peerage claims increased. Apart from the joint claim to the Baronies of Burgh, Cobham and Strabolgi, there were claims to the Baronies of Latymer (1911), Dudley (1914), Dynaunt, Fitzwaryn and Martin (1914), Wharton (1915), Strange of Knokin and Stanley (1920), Montagu, Monthermer, Montacute and Pole of Montagu (1921), Cromwell (1922) and Fitzwalter (1924). Peerage claims were taking up a considerable amount of time in the House of Lords as claims to abeyant Baronies were not the only peerage cases. For instance there was the disputed succession to the Dukedom of Somerset following the death of the 15th Duke in 1923. The case turned on the validity of the marriage of Colonel Francis Compton Seymour and Leonora Hudson in 1787. It was suggested that her first husband a seaman was still alive at the time of the marriage. In the Somerset case where the validity of the marriage was upheld there were 218 foolscap printed pages of evidence and proceedings and 192 printed pages of appendix containing copies of documents. This was much less than the normal abeyance cases where all the lines of coheirs had to be traced and printed with copies of the supporting documents.

On 24 June 1926 The House of Lords moved "that a select Committee of this House be set up to inquire into the subject of Peerages in Abeyance, and to report to the House on the matter". The Committee sat under the chairmanship of John Andrew (Hamilton) Baron Sumner who was created Viscount Sumner in 1927. Lord Sumner (1859-1934) was appointed a Lord of Appeal in Ordinary in 1913 when he was also created a Baron for life under the Appellate Jurisdiction Act of 1876. According to his obituary notice in *The Times* "The outstanding qualities of Lord Sumner's judgments are their exhaustiveness and lucidity, combined with a literary style unsurpassed in the Law Reports. When reading them ... one has a feeling of complete finality and that everything that can be said has been said and said supremely well. The ingrained cynicism with which he approached every subject ... made him less successful when dealing with the more human side of life."

As a result of the Report from the Select Committee an address was presented on 7 July 1927 to the King from the House of Lords "submitting to His Majesty that if it is His gracious pleasure to place some limitation on claims to peerages in abeyance, such limitation might be effected if His Majesty would be graciously pleased to issue an instruction to the Attorney General that if it should appear to him that a claim to a peerage in abeyance is affected by either of the following considerations: – (i) that the commencement of the existing abeyance occurred more than one hundred years before the presentation of the petition; or (ii) that the petitioner (not being a child of the last holder of the dignity or a descendant of a parent of the last holder) represents less than one third of the entire dignity, he should in his report to the Crown on such claim call attention to these circumstances, and that in such cases His

Majesty should be advised that no further proceedings should be taken except in the cases of petitions which have already been presented and in the absence of special circumstances or special reasons to the contrary; and that the attention of the Crown should also be called to any petitions for the introduction of Bills into the House of Lords for restoration in blood to qualify a claimant to the termination of an abeyance to enjoy the peerage where such claims are affected by the above-mentioned considerations; further submitting to His Majesty that where the Committee for Privileges of this House is satisfied that any arrangement, entered into between a petitioner for a peerage in abeyance and any co-heir is tainted with any impropriety, it would be desirable that the Committee should make no report to the House except that such arrangement is not shown to have been a proper one; and further submitting to His Majesty that in considering whether or not His Majesty should be advised to extend His Grace to the petitioner for a termination of an abeyance regard should be had to the character position and fitness of the petitioner." The King replied "I have received your Address submitting certain recommendations with a view to some limitation being placed on claims to peerages in abeyance. I will comply with your advice and will issue directions in accordance therewith.".

This put an end both to the peerage bar and to an area of work which had kept heralds occupied for two hundred years. As one of the conditions of claiming an abeyant peerage was proving the lines of descent of all the coheirs and providing documentary evidence to support each line there was a great deal of genealogical research needed for any claim to a peerage which had been in abeyance for a number of centuries.

The Select Committee met seven times between 7 July and 1 December 1926. The penultimate meeting was on 17 November 1926 after which a draft report was prepared for consideration by the Committee. On the same day (17 November 1926) the claim to the barony of Grey of Codnor can be considered to have begun with a letter of that date from A.T. Butler (1880-1946), then Portcullis Pursuivant subsequently Windsor Herald, addressed to C.H.G. Cornwall Legh Esq, High Legh Hall, Nr Knutsford, Cheshire. Butler has been described by Sir Anthony Wagner as probably the best working genealogist of his day (*English Genealogy* 3rd edition 1983 page 402). The letter reads as follows: "Dear Mr Legh, You are no doubt aware that since your uncle's death you have been a co-heir to the old barony of Grey, a barony which is descendible in the female line. There are several reasons why it is of importance just at the present time that you should take the steps necessary to safeguard the interests in the barony of yourself and your children, and if you could call and see me here when you are next in London, I shall be happy to explain the matter to you. Believe me yours very truly, A.T. Butler, Portcullis."

Charles Henry George Cornwall Legh (1876-1934), the recipient of the letter, was the son of Charles Walker and his wife Gertrude Mary Cornwall, one of the three sisters and coheirs of Henry Martin Cornwall Legh of High Legh who had died in 1904. On 19 October 1926 he had assumed the surname of Cornwall Legh in lieu of that of Walker by enrolled deed poll registered at the College of Arms. This had been arranged by A.G.B. Russell (1879-1955) Lancaster Herald, noted more as a collector of prints and drawings and an entomologist than as a genealogist. The coheirship to the barony of Grey of Codnor came through Anna Maria wife of George Legh of High Legh and only surviving child of Francis Cornwall of Burford, Shropshire. She died in 1741 aged 30 and her husband erected a monument to her memory in Rostherne church, Cheshire, which whilst not mentioning her coheirship to the Barony of Grey of Codnor does describe her as the "sole daughter and heir of Francis Cornwall Baron of Burford lineally descended from Richard Plantagenet Earl of Cornwall King of the Romans brother to Henry the third King of England." The Cornwall family were descended from an illegitimate son of Richard Plantagenet and although never summoned to Parliament were described as Barons of Burford as they held the manor of Burford in Shropshire from the King in chief by barony. This was not therefore a peerage title. The interest in the barony of Grey of Codnor came through the marriage of Thomas Cornwall and Elizabeth one of the two daughters who were (after the death of their brothers without issue) coheirs of Sir Roland Lenthall by his wife Lucy Grey, one of the three aunts and coheirs of Henry (Grey) Baron Grey of Codnor who died in 1496. Lucy Grey represented one third of the barony of Grey and her daughters one sixth each. As Anna Maria Cornwall was an only child the sixth share passed to the Legh family undivided and the only further division came on the death of Henry Martin Cornwall Legh in 1904 when his three sisters Gertrude Mary Cornwall wife of Charles Walker, Eveline Cornwall Legh and Frances Elinor wife of George Henry Brooks were his coheirs, each representing one eighteenth part of the barony of Grey of Codnor. On the death unmarried in 1919 of Eveline Cornwall Legh the fractional entitlement of Mrs Walker (who died in 1923) went up to one twelfth as did that of her nephew George William Desborough Cornwall Brooks whose mother Frances Elinor had died in 1914.

Mr C.H.G. Cornwall Legh was no doubt aware that he was a coheir to the barony of Grey of Codnor as entries of the family in Burke's *Landed Gentry* refer to quartering the arms of Grey. The Greys of Codnor descend from Henry de Grey who was in possession of the Manor of Codnor in Derbyshire in 1201 and died in 1219. His paternity is unknown. He had three sons Richard, John and William. The eldest son Sir Richard de Grey was of Codnor and Grays Thurrock in Essex which his father had acquired in 1199. John de Grey was the ancestor of the Greys of Wilton and Ruthin whose descendants include the Grey Dukes of Kent, Dorset and Suffolk, Marquesses of Dorset, Kent and de Grey, Earls of Kent, Harold, Stamford and Warrington and of Lady Jane Grey, daughter of Henry (Grey) Duke of Suffolk, proclaimed Queen at The Tower on 10 July 1553. William de Grey was the ancestor of the Greys of Sandiacre in Derbyshire. The Greys of Codnor have always been regarded as the senior representatives of Henry de Grey as they bore the arms Barry of six Argent and Azure undifferenced.

Sir Richard de Grey of Codnor was Steward of Gascony, Warden of the Channel Islands and one of the Commissioners, who ratified the Treaty between England and France in 1259. He died before 8 September 1271 and was succeeded by his son Sir John de Grey of Codnor who died shortly after his father and before 5 January 1271/ 2. His son Henry de Grey is described in printed sources such as *The Complete Peerage* as the 1st Baron Grey of Codnor as he was summoned to Parliament in 1299. However, neither knights nor burgesses were summoned so it was not held to be a properly constituted parliament for peerage purposes. He died in 1308 and was succeeded by his son Sir Richard de Grey sometime Steward of Gascony and Constable of Nottingham Castle and commonly described as 2nd Baron Grey of Codnor. He received many Writs of Summons and died shortly before 10 March 1334/ 5. His son and heir Sir John de Grey also received many Writs of Summons between 1335 and 1392 when he died and was succeeded by his grandson Richard de Grey (the son of his son Henry de Grey who predeceased his father). Sir John de Grey was in the Crécy Expedition and in 1371 was excused from attendance at parliaments and councils on account of old age and in consideration of his long service in the wars both overseas and in Britain. Despite the many Summonses to Parliament no evidence was produced that the so-called 2nd, 3rd and 4th Barons Grey of Codnor had sat in Parliament. The Solicitor-General on behalf of the Crown was satisfied that Richard de Grey had sat in Parliament following a Summons on 17 September 1397 and that this was a properly constituted Parliament. The Barony was therefore considered to have been established then and this Sir Richard de Grey who was a Knight of the Garter and at different times Admiral of the Fleet from the Mouth of the Thames to the North, the King's Chamberlain, Constable of Nottingham Castle and Master Forester of Sherwood died in 1418 and was the 1st Baron Grey of Codnor.

He was succeeded by his elder son John (Grey) 2nd Baron Grey of Codnor, who was appointed Lieutenant of Ireland for three years in 1427. He died in 1430 and was succeeded by his brother Henry (Grey), 3rd Baron Grey of Codnor who died in 1444 and was succeeded by his nine-year-old son Henry (Grey) 4th Baron Grey of Codnor who died in 1496 leaving three illegitimate sons. He had neither daughters nor sisters and his coheirs were his three aunts (or their descendants) the daughters of his grandfather Sir Richard de Grey, KG, 1st Baron Grey of Codnor. These daughters were Lucy, wife of Sir Roland Lenthall of Lenthall, Herefordshire, Eleanor wife of Sir Thomas Newport of High Ercall, Shropshire and Elizabeth wife of Sir John Zouche of Bulwick, Northamptonshire.

A.T. Butler's letter was inaccurate in the detail that Mr Cornwall Legh had become a coheir on the death of his uncle as his mother and aunts succeeded his uncle as coheirs and he became a coheir representing his mother's share on her death in 1923. It was accurate in foreseeing the conclusions of the Select Committee as after July

1927 the Attorney General would advise The Sovereign that no further proceedings should be taken in an abeyance where the petitioner (other than a child or a descendant of a parent of the last holder of the dignity) represented less than one third of the entire dignity (Mr Cornwall Legh represented one twelfth part) or where the abeyance had existed for more than one hundred years before the presentation of the petition (in 1927 the barony of Grey of Codnor had been in abeyance for 431 years).

The initial urgency and speed with which the case progressed is seen in that on Thursday 2 December, the day after the Select Committee sat for the last time and agreed the draft report, Mr C.H.G. Cornwall Legh's lawyers handed in his petition to the Home Office, two weeks and a day after Butler's original letter. The petition recites the petitioner's descent generation by generation from his Grey ancestors and also from Ralph (Basset) 1st Lord Basset of Sapcote whose younger daughter and coheir married Richard (Grey) Lord Grey of Codnor and was mother of Lucy wife of Sir Roland Lenthall. The petition concludes:

"That Your Petitioner's mother the said Gertrude Mary Cornwall Walker died on twenty one November 1923 whereupon Your Majesty's Petitioner became a co-heir of the ancient Baronies of Grey of Codnor and Basset of Sapcote. Your Petitioner therefore most humbly prays that Your Majesty will be graciously pleased to admit and allow his claim to be one of the right heirs to the said Baronies of Grey of Codnor and Basset of Sapcote and to .determine in favour of Your Petitioner the abeyance now existing in both or some one of the said Baronies by issuing to Your Petitioner a Writ of Summons to Parliament. And Your Majesty's Petitioner will ever pray, etc."

As there was a *prima facie* case the Home Secretary referred the Petition to the Attorney General on 7 January 1927. The report of the Attorney General (Sir Thomas Inskip, subsequently 1st Viscount Caldecote) to the King is dated the twentieth of July 1928. It followed a hearing in the Attorney General's room in the House of Commons on 5 July 1928. Counsel for the Petitioner was Mr A.H.M. Wedderburn as the original Counsel employed, Mr A.C. Fox-Davies, died aged 57 in May 1928. The Attorney General advised that no evidence had been produced to prove the existence of the barony of Basset of Sapcote, but that he was of opinion that the barony of Grey of Codnor was an ancient barony in fee in abeyance and that the petitioner was one of the coheirs. The report concludes "... inasmuch as the Petitioner presented his Petition to Your Majesty before Your Majesty had received the recent Address from the House of Peers in relation to the limitation on Claims to Peerages in Abeyance, and if Your Majesty, in the exercise of Your Royal Grace, should see fit therefore not to regard the consideration above mentioned in relation to the present petition only then upon the whole I humbly beg to Report That in my opinion, the present Petition, so far as it relates to the Barony of Grey of Codnor, should be referred by Your Majesty to the House of Peers."

Although the petition and report were referred to the House of Lords on 14 August 1928 it was not until 22 July 1930 that they were referred by the House of Lords to the Committee for Privileges.

It was, perhaps, fortunate that there was this delay of two years as the work obtaining evidence for the other lines of coheirs was proving difficult in parts and A.T. Butler wrote to the petitioner's solicitors Shelton & Co of New Square, Lincoln's Inn in May 1930 to say that he could not state definitely when the case would be completed. The Committee for Privileges could not consider the matter until a printed case had been lodged. Work was still in hand finding evidence to prove the lines of descent of all the coheirs when the petitioner died aged 58 in October 1934. In order to continue the claim, the petitioner's elder son and heir C.L.S. Cornwall Legh presented a further petition which the Home Secretary referred to the Attorney General on 24 April 1935. The latter advised in October 1936 that it should be referred to the House of Lords by The King. On 3 November 1936 King Edward VIII referred the petition to the House of Lords and as a result Mr C.L.S. Cornwall Legh was able to proceed with the benefit of his father's petition predating the change in the rules relating to abeyant peerages.

Work establishing the lines of the coheirs was delayed by the 1939-45 war. In 1945

A.T. Butler fell ill and passed his work to A.R. Wagner, Richmond Herald (subsequently Sir Anthony Wagner, Garter King of Arms 1961-78). In 1983 Sir Anthony Wagner, then Clarenceux King of Arms, lost his sight and passed his heraldic and genealogical work to T. Woodcock, Somerset Herald, who assumed responsibility at the College of Arms for the case. Shelton, Cobb & Sumpners, as successors of Shelton & Co, continued to deal with the case till 1972 when Mr Charles Green, who had worked on the case since 1960, took it with him to Denton Hall. A number of Counsel worked on the case, most notably G.D. Squibb, QC (1906-1994) Norfolk Herald Extraordinary, who was brought in by Sir Anthony Wagner in 1952. When the case was heard before the Committee for Privileges on 19 and 20 June 1989 Mr J. Fisher appeared on behalf of the petitioner.

The time between 1936 and 1989 was largely spent in establishing and producing evidence for the lines of coheirs. The successful claim to the barony of Zouche which was brought out of abeyance in 1816 established that whilst all reasonable steps had to be taken to establish the identity of all the coheirs the failure to trace one line did not destroy a claim. The coheirs to the barony of Zouche were also coheirs to the barony of Grey of Codnor as Katherine daughter of Sir Roland Lenthall was wife of the 6th Lord Zouche. In 1957 a petition was lodged in the Judicial Office of the House of Lords that Mr Cornwall Legh might be allowed to refer to the evidence and in the printed case to the proceedings in the case of Sir Cecil Bisshopp baronet claiming the Barony of Zouche of Haryngworth. Permission to do so facilitated the claim as it removed the need to produce new copies of all the evidence to prove each generation of the lines of coheirs descended from Katherine Zouche whose husband died in 1468. In earlier claims, petitioners had to print their evidence. Fortunately, the principal clerk in the Judicial Office of the House of Lords advised in June 1971 "the old day one hundred unbound copies of the case and twenty five copies bound in scarlet cloth are past. Today the Committee for Privileges would undoubtedly accept cases, evidence etc., in the same form as judicial cases in Appeals. These are type-litheod or photostated and bound in limp covers ... A total of fifteen or at the most twenty copies would suffice."

The genealogical research established that the claimant represented one twelfth of the dignity as did John Nicholas Hatfield Brooks a descendant of his great aunt. The descendants of the coheirs to the barony of Zouche represented a total of one sixth. Half of these namely the descendants of Mary daughter and coheir of Edward 11th Lord Zouche who married Thomas Leighton of Hanbury, Worcestershire in 1603 had not been traced in the early nineteenth century and still could not be traced. The fractional entitlements of the other Zouche coheirs were one forty-eighth each for the present Lord Zouche and John Fitzroy Pechell Somerset, one 288th part each for E.P. Donovan and his first cousin J.W. Spillane both resident in Australia, one 144th part for Mrs Sylvia Innis Hough also resident in Australia, one 72nd part for Reginald James Lashley who was resident in England and one 216th part each for three sisters living in Canada Mrs Phenix, Mrs Bigelow and Miss Howell. The above eleven coheirs were all descended from Lucy aunt of the last Lord Grey. Lucy had two sisters Eleanor wife of Thomas Newport and Elizabeth wife of John Zouche. The line of Eleanor whose descendants were the Newport Earls of Bradford divided into two in 1762 when Thomas (Newport) 4th Earl of Bradford died leaving the issue of two sisters as coheirs. One sister only had one child (The Earl of Mountrath) who died unmarried in 1802 when Orlando (Bridgeman) 2nd Baron Bradford of a new creation and subsequently 1st Earl of Bradford became the sole heir of Eleanor wife of Thomas Newport. His heir, the present Earl of Bradford as the sole heir of Eleanor Newport, represented one third of the dignity. The comparative size of a coheir's fractional representation before 1927 was not relevant. Thus in the de Ros case in 1806 the abeyance was terminated in favour of a coheir representing one quarter of the dignity whereas another coheir represented a half.

The final third of the representation was vested in the descendants of the third aunt of Henry Lord Grey of Codnor who died in 1496 namely Elizabeth wife of John Zouche. This line could be proved to the children of Sir John Zouche of Codnor and his wife Isabel Lowe. His will was proved in 1639 and it could be proved that a daughter Isabella married Robert Milward and had issue but no further. The coheirs who had been found therefore represented seven twelfths of the dignity, the missing coheirs being one twelfth from the heirs of Mary Leighton and four twelfths from the heirs of Sir John Zouche of Codnor, the heir of Elizabeth Zouche. A greater fraction had been found than in the Zouche case where coheirs representing only half the dignity were found. Despite this, the petitioner had to satisfy the Committee for Privileges that all reasonable steps had been taken to find the coheirs and affidavits were taken from those who worked on different aspects of the case detailing what they had done. In particular there were affidavits from four surviving genealogists at the College of Arms who had worked on the case, namely T. Woodard (b 1904), F. S. Andrus, Beaumont Herald Extraordinary (b 1915), J. R. Merton (b 1961), and N. J. de Somogyi (b 1963).

It was anticipated that the principal matters concerning the Committee for Privileges which sat on 19 and 20 June 1989 would be the fifty-three year delay since 1936 in bringing the case and the missing coheirs. The case took an unexpected turn when on 21 April 1989 Simon William Peel Vickers Fletcher (father of the actress Susannah York) submitted a petition praying for leave to oppose the petition of C.L.S. Cornwall Legh. Mr Fletcher claimed to be a coheir of Elizabeth Zouche and alleged that Sir John Zouche of Codnor and his wife Isabel Lowe had a son Thomas Zouche of Hengoed Llanarrow in Herefordshire from whom he was descended. Over sixty years work at the College of Arms had failed to produce any evidence to support the assertion that Thomas Zouche was a son of Sir John Zouche. Parts of Mr Fletcher's ancestry are recorded at the College of Arms and show his descent from Zouch Wilde of Codnor Castle a yeoman aged about 28 in 1626. His son Henry Wilde of the parish of Codnor is shown in the College of Arms record (Norfolk 41, 76) with a wife Mary whose paternity is not shown. Mr Fletcher alleged that she was the eldest daughter and coheir in her issue of Thomas Zouche of Hengoed Llanarrow. Mr Fletcher stated that he presented his petition at the request of the Treasury Solicitor and that he had not had time to trace and eliminate all potentially senior lines on his own pedigree. He also admitted that there were living issue of his father's elder half-brother Edward Fletcher who had surrendered their interest to him. Viscount Purbeck's case in 1678 established that an English peerage or dignity cannot be surrendered to the Crown or to another person.

The important and potentially fatal aspect of Mr Fletcher's petition was that he produced evidence which suggested that the last Lord Grey of Codnor did not have three aunts, but only one namely Elizabeth wife of John Zouche. Mr Cornwall Legh relied on an Inquisition Post Mortem in 1538 following the death of Sir Thomas Cornwall which recited that his great grandmother was one of the three aunts of Henry Lord Grey of Codnor who died in 1496. In addition, the last Lord Grey referred in his will to the "Lenthall part and Newport part of my land". One could not leave land by will although it could be settled in one's lifetime, so whilst the reference is consistent with a settlement on two cousins, it does not prove anything. On the other hand, Mr Fletcher produced the will dated 23 April 1445 of Elizabeth widow of Richard Lord Grey of Codnor and supposed mother of the three daughters. It only mentioned one Elizabeth wife of John Zouche. In addition, Star Chamber Proceedings were brought in 1530 by John Lord Zouche, Sir Thomas Cornwall and Thomas Newport against George Zouche in which they claimed to be coheirs with George, whereas he claimed to be sole heir of Henry Lord Grey. Only an interlocutory order relating to the case survives, so there is no conclusion. An Inquisition Post Mortem taken on the death of Sir John Zouche (or Souche) father of George Zouche in 1530 describes him as next and sole heir of Henry Lord Grey. A 1522 Inquisition Post Mortem following the death of Katherine widow of Henry Lord Grey held in Leicestershire found that the manor of Sapcote passed to John Zouche as "cousin and nearer heir of Henry Lord Grey". He is not described as sole heir and an Inquisition in the same year in Essex found that one half of the manor of Grays Thurrock passed to John Newport and the other half to Thomas Cornwall.

The Committee for Privileges met on Monday 19 June 1989 under the Chairmanship of Lord Wilberforce. The other members of the Committee were Lord Campbell of Alloway, Lord Elwyn-Jones, Lord Jauncey of Tullichettle and Lord Strabolgi. The Solicitor General (Sir Nicholas Lyell) opened the proceedings for The Crown and gave what he described as a brief overview of the matter. This was a detailed account of the law of abeyance and the relevance of various aspects to the case and he said "the existence or otherwise of three aunts as opposed to one aunt Elizabeth is probably certainly the main and possibly the only point which may deeply trouble your Lordships in this whole matter". He also recited the history of the barony and said that as far as The Crown was concerned there was no evidence that there had been a sitting in parliament as well as a summons before 1397. Mr Fletcher was next heard and as he could not establish his own interest as a coheir his petition to be heard in opposition to the claim was refused. Counsel for Mr Cornwall Legh however placed Mr Fletcher's material before the Committee so that it was given full consideration.

Mr Fisher then opened the case for the Petitioner and said that he was happy to accept 1397 rather than 1299 for the date of the commencement of the peerage. The next question was the delay in bringing the case. The principal clerk in the Judicial Office of the House of Lords had advised the Petitioner's solicitors in May 1971 that the normal judicial standing orders do not apply to peerage claims, nevertheless by 1989 53 years had passed. The Committee decided to admit Mr Cornwall Legh's petition and hear it on its merits as although 53 years had passed since the matter had been referred it appeared that the claimant had submitted to the Administrative Office of the House of Lords claims for prolongations, adjournments and extensions of time on a number of occasions from 1936 nearly up to 1989 which had been granted.

In the early months of 1989, with the knowledge of Mr Fletcher's material, a search was made to find evidence to support the contention that Richard Lord Grey of Codnor had three daughters not one. This produced two pieces of heraldic evidence. Both were in manuscripts in the College of Arms. One was a manuscript entitled Writhe's book numbered M10 and showed arms for Newport quartering Barry of six Argent and Azure, namely the arms of Grey of Codnor. This was a manuscript of John Writhe Garter King of Arms between 1478 and 1504. Writhe had a patent of appointment from The Crown and by a Writ of Aid in 1498 was empowered to check on all correct use of arms in England and Wales. The position was complicated by the fact that as paternal arms the arms of Ercall are shown rather than Newport. Thomas Newport who married Eleanor Grey was the son of an Ercall heiress. In the early fifteenth century before there was any systematic regulation of arms men occasionally assumed the arms of their mother's family. The Newport family succeeded to High Ercall and this must be why the arms of Ercall were favoured. Under the English Law of Arms one may only quarter the arms of a family if one is descended from an heraldic heiress of that family. This entry in Writhe's book is evidence that shortly after 1496 when Eleanor Newport became posthumously an heraldic heiress Mr Newport, as the entry is labelled, was recorded by Garter King of Arms as entitled to quarter the arms of Grey of Codnor, namely an undifferenced coat of Barry of Six Argent and Azure. In the arms of other branches of the Grey family there are additional charges.

The second piece of heraldic evidence was in a manuscript numbered I2 which is a book of Standards compiled in 1531 and 1532. It contains an entry for Sir Thomas Cornwall with a shield of arms. In the first quarter are the arms of Cornwall in the second Lenthall quartering Grey of Codnor. This means that a Cornwall had married a Lenthall heiress who was herself descended from a Grey heiress. This supports the 1538 Inquisition Post Mortem and the existence of Lucy daughter of Richard Lord Grey and wife of Sir Roland Lenthall. Although not compiled as an official record this manuscript was incorporated into a series of the Earl Marshal's books in the early seventeenth century.

The heraldic evidence was found by means of a card index of instances of arms in English heraldic sources before approximately 1530 begun by Sir Anthony Wagner in the early 1930s. The evidence was produced before the Committee for Privileges and the Solicitor General who had earlier cast doubt over the 1530 Inquisition of Sir John Zouche which described him as next and sole heir of Henry, Lord Grey, as it is only known from a seventeenth century copy described the heraldic evidence as impressive. Although no case of coheirship has ever been decided on the basis of heraldic evidence alone it did provide vital evidence in support of the petition.

After consideration of the evidence for the various lines of coheirs Lord Jauncey of Tullichettle produced an opinion with which Lord Wilberforce and Lord Elwyn-Jones concurred. This dealt in detail with the question as to whether there were three aunts or one and concluded that there were three. Additional research was done by a genealogist working for Somerset Herald after the hearing and this produced further evidence which proved conclusively the facts before the Committee for Privileges. Early Chancery Proceedings (PRO reference C1/6/162) show that Roland Leynthale, Knight and Luce his wife brought proceedings to obtain five hundred marks promised

GREY OF CODNOR CO-HEIRS

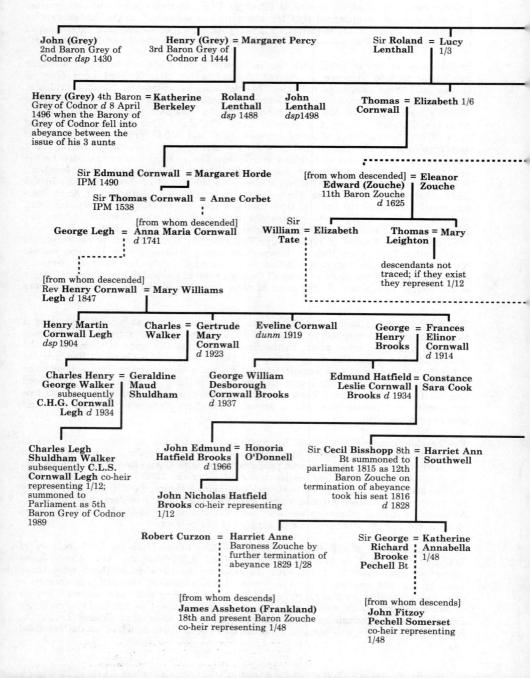

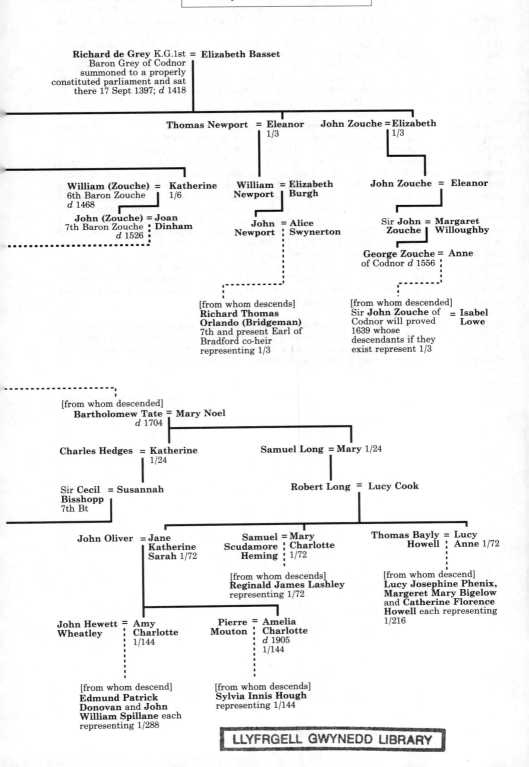

IPM – Inquisition Post Mortem
dsp – died without issue

Richard de Grey K.G.1st = **Elizabeth Basset**
Baron Grey of Codnor
summoned to a properly
constituted parliament and sat
there 17 Sept 1397; *d* 1418

Thomas Newport = **Eleanor** 1/3

John Zouche = **Elizabeth** 1/3

William (Zouche) = **Katherine** 1/6
6th Baron Zouche
d 1468

John (Zouche) = **Joan Dinham**
7th Baron Zouche
d 1526

William Newport = **Elizabeth Burgh**

John Newport = **Alice Swynerton**

[from whom descends]
Richard Thomas Orlando (Bridgeman)
7th and present Earl of Bradford co-heir
representing 1/3

John Zouche = **Eleanor**

Sir **John Zouche** = **Margaret Willoughby**

George Zouche = **Anne**
of Codnor *d* 1556

[from whom descended]
Sir **John Zouche** of = **Isabel Lowe**
Codnor will proved
1639 whose
descendants if they
exist represent 1/3

[from whom descended]
Bartholomew Tate = **Mary Noel**
d 1704

Charles Hedges = **Katherine** 1/24

Samuel Long = **Mary** 1/24

Sir **Cecil Bisshopp** = **Susannah**
7th Bt

Robert Long = **Lucy Cook**

John Oliver = **Jane Katherine Sarah** 1/72

Samuel Scudamore Heming = **Mary Charlotte** 1/72

Thomas Bayly Howell = **Lucy Anne** 1/72

[from whom descends]
Reginald James Lashley
representing 1/72

[from whom descend]
Lucy Josephine Phenix, Margaret Mary Bigelow and **Catherine Florence Howell** each representing 1/216

John Hewett Wheatley = **Amy Charlotte** 1/144

Pierre Mouton = **Amelia Charlotte** *d* 1905 1/144

[from whom descend]
Edmund Patrick Donovan and **John William Spillane** each representing 1/288

[from whom descends]
Sylvia Innis Hough
representing 1/144

to Luce in the will of her father Richard formerly Lord Grey payable on her marriage.

Lord Jauncey of Tullichettle's opinion concluded that he considered that the Barony of Grey of Codnor is an ancient barony in fee proved by the sitting of Richard de Grey on 17 September 1397, that it fell into abeyance in 1496 and was in abeyance between the named coheirs and possibly other unknown coheirs and that it is at Her Majesty's disposal. On 27 July 1989 Lord Wilberforce, after presenting the report of the Committee to the House of Lords and speaking in detail about the claim, moved that it be accepted by the House of Lords. The motion was agreed to and the judgment laid before Her Majesty. The duty of advising The Sovereign whether to terminate the abeyance is vested in the Prime Minister. A Writ of Summons to Parliament dated 4 October 1989 was sent to Charles Legh Shuldham Lord Grey of Codnor and on 30 October 1989 he took his seat.

There were many contributory factors to the success of the claim, not least of which was the perseverance of the claimant. Sixty years of detailed work had been done and in the opening stages of the case for The Crown the Solicitor General said: "Might I tell Your Lordships that in my own preparation of this case I have been hugely assisted by two things. One, if I may say so, not in any way anticipating Your Lordships' approach to the key questions that I shall identify to Your Lordships, the case has been beautifully prepared by those who act on behalf of the applicants. It has been prepared in masterly detail and I think that is a fair comment to make. Secondly, I have been hugely assisted by my learned junior Mr Lofthouse and by my instructing solicitor, Mr Turek, of the Treasury Solicitors Department, both of whom are not only expert lawyers but obviously antiquaries of some distinction for whom this has been a labour of love which will greatly assist My Lords." The reference to the preparation of the case was to the work of Lord Grey's solicitor Mr Charles Green and when he was examined Lord Wilberforce said to him: "I think that all we need to do is to thank you and congratulate you on the way in which this case has been presented, which is really very remarkable."

Sadly for heralds who enjoy working on such things, there will never be another case. In the words of Sir Nicholas Lyell, the Solicitor General, "it is highly unlikely, and that is probably an understatement, that a case like this – a classic abeyance case of this nature – will ever come before Your Lordships' Committee again."

THOMAS WOODCOCK, Somerset Herald

THE DEBRETT FAMILY: ANCESTORS AND DESCENDANTS OF JOHN DEBRETT

Note. *In this pedigree the surname has been repeated after each individual name as the spellings used vary constantly.*

According to family tradition this family of de Brett was related to a family of de Brett, or de Brette, living in the Limousin region of central France about 1528 and also in the town of Narbonne in the Rousillon region of southern France, near the Spanish border, where there had been a Protestant settlement in the Pyrenees since the time of the Reformation. The names of some descendants of these de Bretts or de Brettes appear on the Huguenot Roll of French Protestants.

JACQUES LOUYS (LOUIS) DE BRET: *m* Jeanne Permette Baud (or Band), and had issue,

JEAN LOUYS (LOUIS) DE BRET, who changed his name to JOHN DEBRETT on coming to England, is said to have been *b* in France in 1724. He was living in the parish of St James, Piccadilly in the 1750s, and in the parish of Melbury Sampford, Dorset in the 1780s and 1790s, when he was employed as a cook in the household of Elizabeth, Countess of Ilchester (widow of the 1st Earl), who, in her will dated 1 Dec 1786 left "my cook, Mr Debrett, £20"[1]: *m* at Melbury 14 April 1749, Rachel Panchaud (*b* 11 Oct, and *bapt* at the Tabernacle, Glasshouse Street and Leicester Fields, London 30 Oct 1732; *d* at Stoney Stoke, a hamlet in the parish of Shepton Montague, nr Bruton, Somerset 19 Feb 1765), sister of Paul Panchaud, of Portland Street, Soho, a Merchant Tailor, and 3rd da of Abel Panchaud, by his wife Marthe Calard (who were *m* at the Tabernacle 25 April 1721), and *d* in London April 1793 (*bur* graveyard of St James's, Piccadilly 17 April 1793; will, made at Melbury Sampford 16 May 1789, with codicil dated 26 Jan 1790, *pr* London 20 April 1793), having had issue,

1. JOHN FIELD DEBRETT, *of whom presently.*
2. Louis De Bret, *b* in the parish of St James, Piccadilly 3 Sept 1754, and *bapt* at La Patente de Soho (*alias* Le Temple Français Huguenot), Westminster 15 Sept 1754; *d* young.
3. George Debret, *b* 30 Jan 1763; probably *d* young.
1. Susannah Debret, *b* 7 Feb 1751/2; executrix of her father's will 1793; *d unm* June 1823.
2. Dianna (Diana) Debrett (Dobrett), *b* 1 Dec 1757, and *bapt* at St James's, Piccadilly 8 Jan 1758: *m* at St Mary's, Marylebone Road 12 Oct 1802, Henry Johnston, widower.

The eldest son,
JOHN FIELD DEBRETT, *b* in London 8 Jan, and *bapt* at St James's, Piccadilly 22 Feb 1753. In 1766 he was apprenticed to Robert Davis, bookseller of Piccadilly, for a premium of £10. On completing his apprenticeship in or about 1773, he remained in the employment of Davis as a journeyman bookseller and subsequently in the employment of Davis's son William until the latter's death in 1780. Debrett then moved to John Almon's Bookshop and Stationers opposite Burlington House, Piccadilly. When John Almon retired in 1781, he resigned his business to John Debrett. Almon had edited *The New Peerage*, which was printed for various members of the Davis family. The third edition appeared in 1784 with William Davis's name replaced by that of John Debrett (successor to John Almon), who was most probably the editor. The fourth edition, of which he was undoubtedly the editor, appeared in 1790 with his name on the title page. Between 1781 and 1791 Debrett continued to publish the series of Parliamentary Debates, which John Almon had started, as well as reprinting Almon's volumes. In 1801 Debrett got into financial difficulties and the 1802 volume was printed by assignment from the assignees of John Debrett for John Stockdale. Between 1784 and 1800 Debrett was the official publisher to the East India Company and published several calendars and almanacs, including *The Royal Kalendar*, *The American Kalendar* and *The East India Kalendar*, and later, between 1818 and 1822, edited *The British Imperial Calendar*, later renamed *The Civil Service List*. Debrett was twice declared bankrupt: on 31 Oct 1801 and again on 19 May 1804. His name does not appear in lists of London publishers or printers after 1803; but it is thought that he continued as a bookseller in Piccadilly until he retired in 1814. In conjunction with John Murray, Debrett was one of the founders of *The Globe* newspaper, first issued on 1 Jan 1803. The first edition of *The Correct Peerage* – the work with which John Debrett's name is universally associated – was published May 1802. It consisted of two small pocket volumes. In 1808 he added a pocket edition of *The Baronetage of England* in similar style. He continued to edit these works until his death. He was described as "a kindly man who had full opportunity of acquiring a large fortune but from too much confidence and easiness of temper he did not turn it to the best account."

John Debrett *m* at St James's, Piccadilly 27 April 1787, Sophia Granger (*b* at Deptford, Kent 17 June 1762; *d* at Linton Hill, nr Maidstone, Kent 18 Jan 1833; *bur* St Nicholas's Churchyard, Linton 2 Feb 1833), da of Capt John Granger, of the Maritime Service, HEIC, by his wife Sophia, da of William Spencely (or Spensley), of the City of Westminster[2]. John Debrett was found dead in his armchair at his lodgings at 11 Upper Gloucester Street, Regent's Park, 15 Nov 1822, and was *bur* in the churchyard of St James's, Piccadilly 22 Nov 1822. Admon of his will was granted to William Garlen, a creditor, 6 Dec 1822. He had issue,
1. JOHN EDWARD DEBRETT, *of whom presently.*
2. George Gibson Debrett (*alias* John George Debrett, *alias* John Gibson), *b* in

London 22 May, and *bapt* at St James's, Piccadilly 24 June 1792; Cadet 1807, arrived in India 14 Aug 1808, Ensign 19 Sept 1808, Lieut 18th Bengal Native Infantry 1811 served in Nepal War 1814-16, Cuttack insurrection and Khurda[3]; *d* "of a fever caught in the camp at Knordah" at Cuttack, E India 24 Dec 1817, *bur* Cuttack Cemetery (will dated 6 Jan 1816, *pr* Supreme Court of Jurisdiction, Fort William 14 May 1818).
3. Charles Field Debrett, *b* 5 Feb, and *bapt* at St James's, Piccadilly 20 Feb 1798; *d* 22 Aug, and *bur* at St James's, Piccadilly 28 Aug 1798.
4. Henry Symonds Debrett (Rev), *b* 5 Dec 1801, and *bapt* at St James's, Piccadilly 24 Jan 1802; *ed* Downing Coll, Camb (LLB 1827); ordained deacon 1825, priest 1826; Curate of Boughton Monchelsea, Kent 1825, Rector of Broughton, Lincs 1830-42; *d unm* at Broughton 26 Jan 1842.
1. Sophia Mirabella Debrett, *b* 12 Feb, and *bapt* at St James's, Piccadilly 5 March 1788; *m* at All Saints' Church, Chelsea (Chelsea Old Church) 3 Feb 1820, Rev Richard Samuel Butler Sandilands, Curate of Putney, Surrey, later Minister of Curzon Street Chapel, Mayfair 1827-45 and Rector of Croydon cum Clopton, Cambs 1845-64 (*b ca* 1791; *ed* Westminster, Ch Ch, Oxford (BA 1812, MA 1819), and Lincoln's Inn; *d* suddenly at Croydon Rectory 29 Feb 1864; *bur* with his wife in a vault in the churchyard of All Saints', Croydon), eldest son of Rev Richard Samuel Sandilands, of Lower Grosvenor Place, London, and *dsp* or *sps* 1859.
2. Maria Anne (*alias* Marie Amy) Debrett, *b* 13 April, and *bapt* at St James's, Piccadilly 17 May 1795; presumably joined her eldest brother in India, perhaps after the marriage of her sister; *d unm* at Calcutta 25 June 1826; *bur* South Park Street Burial Ground, Calcutta 26 June 1826.

The eldest son,
JOHN EDWARD DEBRETT (DE BRETT), *b* 15 Sept, and *bapt* at St James's, Piccadilly 1 Nov 1789; entered the Bengal Army as Cadet of Artillery 1806, Lieut 1808, Capt 1820; served in Nepal War 1814-15 and Third Mahratta War 1817-18; present at siege and capture of Chanda and at siege of Asirgarh; had charge of Expense Magazine Laboratory School at Dum-Dum; *m* at Chittagong, Bengal 31 Oct 1825, Martha Burrup (*b ca* 1794; returned to England after her husband's death and lived successively at Rugby, Cheltenham, and Bishopsteignton, Devon, where she *d* 17 Nov 1867; will and codicil dated 7 Jan 1862, *pr* London 24 Dec 1867), yst da of John Burrup, of 13 Grand Parade, Brighton, Sussex (will dated 16 Oct 1828, *pr* Sept 1829), and *d* of fever at Simla 10 May 1835, *bur* at Subathou Political Agency, Simla the same day, memorial in Mall Cemetery, Simla erected by his son 1865 (will dated Simla 8 May 1835, *pr* 11 Dec 1835). John Edward Debrett (de Brett) had issue,
1. Edward Richard Debrett, *b* at Agra 12

July, and *bapt* there 14 Oct 1829; *d* at Nasirabad 23 Aug 1831; *bur* there the same day.
2. William Allan Debrett, *b* 24 July, and *bapt* at Arbarabad (Delhi) 30 Oct 1832; *bur* at Fatehgarh 8 July 1833.
3. (EDWIN SANDILANDS) HARRY DEBRETT (DE BRETT), *of whom presently.*
1. Sophia Anne Debrett, *b* at Dum-Dum 1 Aug, and *bapt* at St Stephen's Church there 10 Dec 1826: *m* at St Andrew's Parish Church, Clifton, Bristol 3 July 1851, Rev Percival Richard Renorden Sandilands (*b* at Bodmin, Cornwall 1826; *ed* Tonbridge, and Jesus Coll, Camb (BA 1848, MA 1851); sometime Second Master of Crewkerne Gram Sch, Assist Master at Cheltenham Coll for ten years, then successively Curate of Chaffcombe, Curate of Seavington St Mary, Somerset, Vicar of Denford-with-Ringstead, Northants, and Vicar of Chudleigh Knighton, S Devon; *d* at Newton Abbot, Devon 26 Oct 1900; *bur* "in a plain earth grave" in Chudleigh Knighton Churchyard, "the choir singing the Nunc Dimittis and each member being presented with a new prayer book"; will dated 30 Jan 1887, *pr* Exeter by his widow 19 Dec 1900), eldest son of Rev George Percival Sandilands, Curate of St George's, Hanover Square, London (*d* 3 Jan 1836), and nephew of Rev Richard Samuel Butler Sandilands (*see above*). They had issue, at least 8 children (living 1912).
2. Maria Ellen Debrett, *b* at Dum-Dum 26 Nov 1827, and *bapt* at St Stephen's Church there 20 Feb 1828; *d* 22 Aug 1828; *bur* the same day at South Park Street Burial Ground, Calcutta.
3. Mary Isabella Debrett, *b* at Nasirabad 25 March, and *bapt* there 29 May 1831; returned to England with her mother; *d* at Rugby 8 June 1847.
4. Martha Sandilands Debrett, *b* (*posthumous*) at Calcutta 14 Dec 1835, and *bapt* at St Andrew's Church there 1 Jan 1836; returned to England with her mother and later lived at Clanoge, Bishopsteignton, Devon; *d unm* 6 March 1912; will dated 1 Aug 1903, *pr* Exeter 23 April 1912.

The only surviving son,
Major-General (EDWIN SANDILANDS) HARRY DE BRETT (which spelling he adopted), IA, of Sidcup Park, Kent, and later of 49 Earls Avenue, Folkestone, Kent, *b* at Fatehgarh 21 Aug, and *bapt* there 21 Oct 1834; returned to England with his mother and was *ed* Rugby and at Cheltenham Coll; Ensign 57th Bengal NI 1854, Brevet-Capt 1865, Capt Bengal SC 1866, Col 1883, Maj-Gen (ret) 1886; served in Indian Mutiny 1857 (medal with clasp), Naga Hills Expdn 1880 (medal with clasp), and Afghan War 1880 (medal): *m* in the Chapel of St Luke, parish of St Mary in the Marsh, Norwich, Norfolk 7 Aug 1866, Elizabeth Thomasine Müller (*b* at Calcutta 30 Sept, and *bapt* at St John's Cathedral there 12 Nov 1835; *d* 13 Feb 1929; will dated (she then of Fairhaven, Redhill Common, Surrey) 21 Jan 1916, *pr* with codicil 11 April 1929), da of Adolphus Gerrard Müller, of Frankfurt-

am-Main and Calcutta, merchant, by his wife Mary, da of William Blackhall Simonds (who *d* 17 Jan 1890, aged 100 years and 10 months), and *d* at Folkestone, Kent 2 Nov 1916 (will dated 15 April 1913, *pr* London 2 Jan 1917), leaving issue,

1. EDWARD ADOLPHUS DE BRETT, *of whom presently.*

2. Harry Symonds de Brett (Hon Brig-Gen), CB (1920), CMG (1917), DSO (1898), of Chelveshayes, Clyst Hydon, Cullompton, Devon, *b* at Gorakhpur, Burmah (NWP) 20 Sept, and *bapt* there 6 Nov 1870; *ed* Clifton, and RMA Woolwich; entered army 1889, Capt 1899, Major 1909, Lt-Col 1916, Col 1919; served NW Frontier Campaign with Tochi Field Force 1897-98 (first offr to receive DSO, medal with clasp), S African War 1899-1900 (medal with three clasps), China Expdny Force 1900-01 (medal), operations in Somaliland 1909-10 (medal with clasp), World War I 1914-18 (despatches, Bt Lt-Col, CMG, Bt Col, Belgian Croix de Guerre); cmd'd 3rd Air Defence Bde 1922-23, Woolwich Garrison and RA Depot 1923-27, ret 1927: *m* at Dunkeld Cathedral, Perthshire 1901, Alice Maud Davies (*b ca* 1870; trained as nurse at King's Coll Hosp and nursed wounded in Athens and at field hospitals in Turco-Greek War 1899; sometime Sister at Victoria Hosp, London and later nursed in S Africa under auspices of The Nat Soc for Aid to the Sick and Wounded in War; awarded medal and diploma by the Queen of the Hellenes; *d* at Bletchley, Bucks 6 Nov 1945; admon to husband at Llandudno 3 Jan 1946), 2nd da of Arthur Davies, by his wife, ..., da of .... Hemingway, an engineer involved in the construction of Cardiff Docks, and *d* at Exeter, Devon 25 Sept 1965 (cremated there 28 Sept 1965; will dated 10 Sept 1949, *pr* London 19 Nov 1965), leaving issue.

   1. Edward Simonds de Brett (Brig-Gen RE), of Honiton, Devon, *b* at Camberley, Surrey 15 Aug, and *bapt* in the Chapel of the Royal Military College, Sandhurst, Berks 15 Oct 1902; *ed* Wellington Coll, and RMA (Sword of Honour 1922); commn'd RE 1922; Shanghai Defence Force 1927; World War II 1939-45 in France and Egypt; Col 1947; Chief Engr N Midlands Dist 1948, West Africa 1950, SW Dist 1954, ret 1957: *m* at St Mary the Virgin, Newington, Kent 9 July 1929, Editha Margaret Webb (*b* at Newington 28 July 1907; *d* 26 Feb 1976), da of Arthur Sapte Webb, of The Manor House, Newington, nr Sittingbourne, Kent, by his wife Editha Elizabeth, *née* Gascoyne, and *d* 7 June 1994, leaving issue,

      (1) Harry Gascoyne de Brett, *b* at Gibraltar 14 Sept 1935; *ed* Wellington Coll, and Royal Coll of Mines; joined IBM UK Ltd 1956, instructor in computer programming, system engr and marketing specialist; System

Analysis Consultant: *m* at Surrey North Register Office 17 Aug 1956, Beryl Jean Ward (*b* at Chiswick, Middlesex 6 March 1936; *ed* Putney High Sch, Lycée Française de Londres, and London Univ; scenic artist and sculptor), da of Albert Henry Ward, of 5 Burlington House, Kings Road, Richmond, Surrey, by his wife Winifred Eliza, da of James George Brown, and has issue,

      1*a* Mark Nicholas de Brett, *b* at Chiswick, Middlesex 26 Dec 1956; *ed* Exeter Sch, and Univ of Wales Institute of Science and Technology; international transport executive: *m* at Richmond upon Thames Register Office 26 March 1983, Patricia Thelma Powick, *née* Wong (*b* at Sefton Park, Liverpool 17 March 1951; former Commonwealth Athlete, selected for 1968 Olympic Games, but did not compete because of injury), da of Clinton Archibald Wong, Flt Sergt RAF, by his wife Isabella Anastatia, *née* Pickavance, and has issue,

        1*b* Simon Edward de Brett, *b* at Kingston, Surrey 15 June 1984.

        1*b* Clara Louise de Brett, *b* at Kingston, Surrey 18 Nov 1986.

      2*a* Peter Guy de Brett, *b* at Teddington, Middlesex 27 June 1960; *ed* Hampton Sch; scenic artist and construction manager (film and television): *m* at the Parish Church, Farringdon, Devon 24 Aug 1991, Diana Frances Pentreath (*b* in London 1 Feb 1963; *ed* Twickenham Girls' Sch, and Univ of East Anglia; television editor), only da of Michael Richard Cadman Pentreath, of Danbow Farm, Farringdon, Devon, journalist, by his wife Barbara Anne, 2nd da of Lt-Col George Aubrey Howard-Vyse, JP, of Nutwith House, Masham, Ripon, Yorkshire, and has issue,

        1*b* Hugo Alexander de Brett, *b* at Chiswick, Middlesex 31 Jan 1992.

        2*b* Matthew Rufus de Brett, *b* at Chiswick, Middlesex 17 March 1994.

      3*a* Daniel Christopher James de Brett, *b* at Teddington, Middlesex 18 Sept 1964; *ed* Hampton Sch, and Southampton Univ; petroleum exploration geologist.

      (1) Tona Beatrice de Brett, *b* at Fleet, Hants 13 Feb 1961; *ed* Farnham Gram Sch, Cranborne Chase, and Dartington Hall;

singing teacher: *m* at the Parish Church of Clyst Hydon, Devon 10 April 1955, Charles Leonard West, of 42 Wood Vale, Highgate, London N10 (*b* at Sheffield 27 Aug 1927; actor and crime fiction writer), son of Leonard West, a potter, by his wife Beatrice, da of George Raynor, and has issue.

1. Beryl Frances de Brett, *b* at Naini Tal, Calcutta 25 Oct 1906; *m* 1st, in Malta 20 Nov 1930 (*m diss* 1941), Lieut Hugh Percival Brister, RN, and had issue, one son and one da. She *m* 2ndly, at Derby Register Office 21 July 1949, Adam Valentine Salter, formerly Szalaty (*b ca* 1904; *d* at Derby 18 Feb 1960), son of Adalbert Szalaty, head forester, and had further issue, two sons. She *m* 3rdly, at Blackpool Register Office 6 Sept 1971, William Snaddon, widower (*b* 28 Sept 1902; *d* at Blackpool 17 April 1987), son of Robert Snaddon.

1. Mary Helen de Brett, *b* 14 Sept 1868: *m* at St Mary Abbots Church, Kensington 31 July 1895, Rev Lancelot White Atkins (*b* at Bedhampton, Hants 1862; *ed* St John's Coll, Oxford; Diocesan Chaplain, Manchester 1894-95, Chaplain, God's House, Southampton 1895-1900, Rector of Puttenham, Herts 1900-09), eldest son of Rev Richard White Atkins, of Romansleigh Rectory, South Molton, Devon, and *dsp* or *sps*.

2. Beatrice Margaret de Brett, *b* 7 May 1873: *m* at Lincoln Cathedral 5 Oct 1904, Edmund Holmes Blakesley (*b* 7 Oct 1868; *ed* Charterhouse, and Ch Ch Oxford; Barrister-at-law, Lincoln's Inn 1896; ICS 1889-1914; Master of the Mercers' Co 1928-29; *d* ...... 19...), son of Very Rev Joseph William Blakesley, BD, Dean of Lincoln (*b* 6 March 1808; *d* 18 April 1885), by his wife Margaret Wilson Holmes (*d* 1880), da of Rev Thomas Holmes, of Brooke Hall, Norfolk, and *dsp* at Wrecclesham Grange, nr Farnham, Surrey 28 Aug 1957 (will dated 12 Feb 1948, *pr* London 11 Oct 1957).

3. Charlotte Minnie Lilian de Brett, *b* at Calcutta (?) 20 Dec 1875; *d* in infancy.

The elder son,
EDWARD ADOLPHUS DE BRETT, of Fairlawn, The Common, Redhill, Surrey, *b* at Mean Meer, Lahore 21 Jan 1867; *ed* Winchester, and New Coll, Oxford; joined ICS 1888, served in Central Provinces as Assist Commr and Settlement Offr at Wardha, Raipur, Bilaspur, Nagpur and Narsinghpur; Dep Commr at Mandasaur, Mandla, Jubbulpore, Chanda and Hoshangabad; Political Agent, Chhattisgarh, Feudatory States; Resident Sec to Chief Commr, Central Provinces, ret 1913; Lieut Royal Defence Corps 1915-19: *m* 1st, at Nagpur 1 Aug 1893, Francis (*sic*) Elizabeth Mary (Lilla) Stevens (*b* 1870; *d* 1894), eldest da of Sir John Foster Stevens, Judge of the High Court of Calcutta (*b* 9 July 1845; *d* 19 Sept 1925), by his wife Frances Louisa, da of Capt William H. Jeremie, IA, and had issue,

1. Doris (Dorie) de Brett, *b* at Tal Marchandy 28 April, and *bapt* at St John's Church, Naini Tal, Calcutta 10 June 1894; *d* of pneumonia 1 Nov, and was *bur* at Kandahar Cemetery, Nimar District, Central Provinces and Berar 2 Nov 1894.

Edward Adolphus Debrett *m* 2ndly, at Raipur 12 Jan 1910, Maude Helen Armit (*b ca* 1875; *d* in childbirth at Westgate, Kent 3 July 1913), yst da of Capt Robert Henry Armit, RN, by his wife Ellen, da of John Frederick Hilly, of Stoney, NSW, Australia, and by her had issue,

1. EDWARD MAURICE DE BRETT, of whom presently.

2. Rodney John Harry de Brett (Rev) *b* at Westgate, Kent 3 July 1913; *ed* Rugby, Ecole de Commerce, Lausanne, RMC Sandhurst, and (later) Wells Theological Coll; Lt-Col E Yorks Regt, later GP Capt RAF Regt; served in World War II with HQ 21st Army Gp, 2nd i/c Royal Welch Fus (wounded, despatches), Wing Cdr Air Ministry (Directorate of Ground Defence), ret 1963; ordained deacon 1964, priest 1965; Vicar of Stoke St Gregory with Burrowbridge and Lyng, Taunton, Somerset 1978-81, Rural Dean of Taunton, ret 1981: *m* at St Saviour's Church, Shanklin, Isle of Wight 16 March 1940, Diana Stirling Swinhoe (*b* at Shanklin 1 Jan 1918), da of Maj Lawrence Rodway Swinhoe, Royal Warwicks Regt, by his wife Katherine Helen Mackenzie Williams, da of Alexander Mackenzie Williams, of Cranbourne, Hants, and has issue,

1. Nicholas Edward de Brett, of Sydney, NSW, Australia, *b* at Shanklin, Isle of Wight 15 Oct 1944; *ed* Millfield; Australian Civil Service; Dir of Social Services, Liverpool, NSW: *m* 1st, at St Peter's Church, North Wootton, Somerset 16 Oct 1965 (*m diss* 1978), Susan Blake Thomas (*b* 1939), da of Adrian Blake Thomas, of Mosman, NSW, by his wife Madge Kellet and has issue,

(1) Simon de Brett, *b* 4 Oct 1972.

(1) Sarah Louise de Brett, *b* 25 Sept 1970.

Nicholas Edward de Brett *m* 2ndly, at Sydney, NSW 23 July 1987, Susan Bellamy (*b* at Worthing, Sussex 15 Nov 1953), da of Arthur Frederick Bellamy, of Ferring, Sussex, by his wife Katherine Clare, da of Harold Fairbrother.

2. Stephen John de Brett, *b* at Caterham, Surrey 19 Nov 1947; *ed* Millfield.

1. Jennifer Maude de Brett, *b* 23 Dec 1940: *m* at Exeter Register Office 16 April 1985, Stephen James McLynn, chemist (*b* at Dartford, Kent 14 Jan 1940; *ed* Downside, and Camb Univ), son of James Joseph McLynn, by his wife Sarah Goldstein.

2. Catherine Anne de Brett, *b* at Akrotiri, Cyprus 23 Sept 1953; Nurse, ARAMCO

American Hosp, Cyprus: *m* at Staunton Deane Register Office, Somerset 27 April 1974, Michael Anthony Chanter, son of Albert George Chanter. They have separated and she has resumed her maiden name.
3. Susan Helen de Brett, *b* 27 April 1958.

Edward Adolphus de Brett *m* 3rdly, at the Parish Church of St Mary Magdalene, Reigate, Surrey 1 Aug 1929, Phyllis Mary Worship Paine (*b* 4 June 1894; *d* at Horsham, Sussex 13 Jan 1983), da of William Worship Paine, of Mill Lane, Reigate, Surrey, solicitor and banker, by his wife Helen Edith Mary, da of William Worship, solicitor, and *d* at Reigate, Surrey 4 July 1957 (will dated 12 Feb 1948, *pr* London 30 Sept 1957).

The elder son,
EDWARD MAURICE DE BRETT (Lt-Col), *b* at Folkestone, Kent 7 Nov 1910; *ed* Winchester, and RMA Woolwich; served with RA in India and in World War II in Italy, Staff Coll, ret 1952; Civil Service, Ministry of Labour and National Service, later Dept of Employment, ret 1970: *m* at St Peter's Church, Withington, Herefordshire 25 Nov 1944, Dorothy Elizabeth Edwards (*b* at Sellack, Herefordshire 16 May 1910), da of Arthur Edwards, of Withington Court, Withington, Herefordshire, by his wife Ada Kate, *née* Little, and has had issue,
1. Margaret Elizabeth de Brett, *b* at Hereford 30 July 1946: *m* at St Nicholas's Church, Earls Croome, Worcs 21 Aug 1971, Maj Brian David Nichol, Gordon Highlanders (*b* at Glasgow 22 June 1946), son of Maj David Nichol, Highland Light Inf, by his wife Evangelie, da of Constantine Logiotasa, Greek diplomat, and *d* at Earls Croome, Worcs 19 Sept 1985, leaving issue, two das.
2. Rosemary Anne de Brett, *b* at Plymouth, Devon 1 May 1948: *m* at St Nicholas's Church, Earls Croome, Worcs 23 Nov 1968, Peter Jeremy Robinson (*b* at Macclesfield, Cheshire 29 March 1945; *ed* Shrewsbury, and Sidney Sussex Coll, Camb; computer programmer), son of Max Wilfred Robinson, by his wife Mona, *née* Crebbin, and has issue, two sons and one da.

NOTES

1 As Elizabeth, Countess of Ilchester died 15 Nov 1792 and her will was not proved until May 1793, one month after John Debrett's death, he never received this legacy which presumably passed to his heirs. The Countess was the sister and heiress of Thomas Strangways, formerly Horner, of Melbury Sampford, Dorset, and only da of Thomas Strangways-Horner, of Mells Park, Somerset, by Susanna, da and co-heiress of Thomas Strangways, of Melbury Sampford. It was through her that Melbury House passed to the Earls of Ilchester. Since John Debrett was employed as Lady Ilchester's cook and

must have been in her employment for some time to merit a legacy of £20 in her will made in 1786, it seems a reasonable inference that his time was divided between London and the west country estates. It is also interesting to note that the Ilchesters had a land agent in Somerset named Field and John Debrett gave his eldest son the middle name of Field. Mr Field as a fellow-servant may have stood godfather since it was customary in the eighteenth century, and indeed since, to name children after godparents who were not necessarily blood relations.
2 Following John Debrett's death, his widow had a draft petition prepared for a Royal Licence to change her name and that of her children from Debrett to Gibson. She claimed to be the heir at law of Mirabella Gibson, *née* Spencely. She was evidently also seeking the right to bear the arms of Spencely and Granger quarterly with those of Debrett, stating that she was the sole heiress of John Grainger (*sic*) and his wife Sophia Spencel(e)y, the only surviving issue of William Spencel(e)y. Garter considered her proofs to be insufficient and the matter was dropped. No Royal Licence was subsequenlty granted and no grant of arms made to any member of the Debrett family, although various sketches of possible arms for Debrett exist with the petition papers. (College of Arms MSS, *Bigland Collection*, Vol XLV, pp 72-96, made available by kind permission of Patric L. Dickinson, Richmond Herald.) However, Sophia Debrett's second son, George Gibson Debrett, who died unmarried in 1817, did significantly call himself "John Gibson" for a time.
3 The Indian Place names have been standardised as far as possible by using the general index to the *Imperial Gazetteer of India*, Vol XXVI, Atlas, new revised edition (Clarendon Press), Oxford, 1931.

ACKNOWLEDGEMENTS

With grateful acknowledgement for assistance to: the staff of The British Library, Oriental and India Office Collections; the staff of the Record Keeper's Department, Somerset House; the staff of the Public Record Office, Chancery Lane; the staff of the Public Search Room, St Catherine's House; Patric L. Dickinson, Richmond Herald, College of Arms; Dr Donal Begley, Chief Herald of Ireland, Genealogical Office, Dublin; the French Embassy, Dublin (cultural services) Ilchester Estate Papers; Mrs Mary Boucher for correspondence in French with The Huguenot Society in Paris; and various members of the de Brett family, especially the late Brigadier Edward Simonds de Brett.

FRANCES-JANE FRENCH, MA, MLitt.

A RARE HONOUR: BRITISH MARQUESSATES
THROUGH SIX CENTURIES

INTRODUCTION

Of all the degrees in the British peerage, that of marquess has received the least attention. Even *The Complete Peerage*, that great repository of all titles connected with the House of Lords, is sadly reticent on the degree. Compare, for instance, the study of dukedoms – an exhaustive appendix covering nearly 30 pages (Volume VIII, app A) – with that on marquesses, which covers less than 2 pages (Volume V, app H). It is hoped this article may help to redress the imbalance. It is, in fact, the *least* created hereditary honour and despite early unpopularity, has survived far better than any other degree.

Neither has it been solely the haunt of dukes' heirs and retired Viceroys. The six hundred years covered in these pages touch on much of our history: from early associations with Ireland and the cousins of kings, to an ill-fated Tudor consort, through the Civil Wars, great military victories and back, in our own times, to near royalty and the close relations of the newly-formed House of Windsor.

Selden[1] traces the origin of the title to very early times, but points out that such references were generally to princes or dukes and governors of territories. They were usually known by their higher, ruling titles, but were referred to as "Marckgraves" or "Margraves" when discussing the borders of their realm, as these terms denoted the "marks" or limits of the kingdom. He gives instances of its occurrence as a title on the continent some four centuries before introduction into England, and cites examples in Holland, Germany, Italy, Spain and France (where much later it was to be in common usage). It was probably from the last country, considering our monarchs' Norman associations, that the title prompted itself in the mind of King Richard II, although the margraviates of Brandenburg and Moravia, already vested in his wife's family, would have been familiar to him.

The bulk of this article will deal with **outright** creations and includes a complete list, with a table of creations according to country of origin and monarch. A second section will briefly discuss **submerged** titles and a final small piece on those titles said to have existed, but never having received official sanction.

OUTRIGHT CREATIONS

On exactly 100 occasions, the sovereign has seen fit to raise a subject to the dignity of Marquess. The first – and only life – creation was Dublin, in 1385 to Robert de Vere, 9th Earl of Oxford. He was a great favourite of the King, Richard II, a friendship described by the *Dictionary of National Biography* as one of "disgraceful origin". The modern interpretation is that the relationship was more fraternal than amorous[2]. There is no doubt that his fellow earls did not approve of this new distinction, placing Lord Oxford above all peers save dukes. The title was short lived, however, and within the year was surrendered and replaced with the Dukedom of Ireland. The next creation of this strange title was some twelve years later, when John Beaufort, Earl of Somerset – eldest of the legitimated sons of John of Gaunt by Catherine Swynford – was made a Marquess. His usual style is that of Dorset, although the Parliamentary charter gives him the same style as his earldom. Again, the title did not last long, since this peer was degraded of his honours upon the accession of Henry IV in 1399. Restoration came in 1402 and although his fellow peers petitioned that it should include the marquessate, he declined, saying the degree was one which was "strange in this realm". Lord Somerset was succeeded in his earldom by three sons, the last of whom, Edmund Beaufort, had been created Marquess of Dorset in 1443 (the third person to receive the rank). He was later (1448) created Duke of Somerset. He was succeeded by his son, Henry Beaufort, who fought on the losing side at the battle of Hexham and lost his head and all his honours in 1464[3].

---

[1] Selden, J; *Titles of Honour*, 3rd edition, 1672.
[2] Dublin had married Richard's cousin Philippa, a grand-daughter of Edward III in 1376.
[3] The attainder is reckoned to be continuous from 1461, although there was a period of restoration before his execution in 1464.

There were no holders of the title in the land (apart from William de la Pole – who as Duke, Marquess and Earl of Suffolk was known by his higher degree) until 1470, when John Neville was created Marquess of Montagu. This was in exchange for surrendering the earldom of Northumberland, which was restored to the Percy family. He died in the next year and was succeeded by his son, who – having already been made a duke[1] – never used the title. In any event the son was degraded of all his honours in 1478, being said not to have the "lifeload" to support such dignities and should henceforth be "neither duke, marquess, earl nor baron" and died a minor and unmarried in 1483. Again, this left one marquessate, that of Dorset, which had been created for Edward IV's step-son in 1475. Apart from the brief appearance in the Berkeley family of a title of the same name in 1489, which became extinct after three years, there were no creations until 1525 when Henry Courtenay, Earl of Devon was promoted to the marquessate of Exeter. This was one of 8 peerages created by Henry VIII on the same day. Lord Devon receiving the promotion from his cousin (he and Henry were both grandsons of Edward IV) to celebrate the creation of the King's natural son, Henry FitzRoy, Duke of Richmond. Both grantees' titles were short-lived, however, the Courtenay family suffering attainder in 1539.

In the meantime the only instance of a woman receiving the degree occurred. Anne Boleyn, in preparation for higher things, became Marchioness[2] of Pembroke in 1532. Having become Queen in the next year, the title may be said to have merged in the crown, or at any event became extinct upon her execution in 1536.

After 1539, Dorset was again left as the only marquessate. In 1547 Thomas Parr, Earl of Essex – brother of Henry VIII's last wife and a favourite step-uncle of the King, Edward VI – was promoted to the dignity of Marquess of Northampton. His enjoyment of this and his other titles ended shortly after his step-nephew's reign, as he suffered attainder for his involvement in the plot to divert the succession to Lady Jane Grey. Although threatened with execution, he survived into Elizabeth's reign and was restored to the Marquessate – but not his other honours – the title becoming extinct on his death in 1571. The degree had been saved from total extinction, however, as Thomas Paulet, Earl of Wiltshire, had been promoted to the marquessate of Winchester in 1551. This last title has now been in existence for nearly 450 years and is one of only a handful of peerages above the degree of baron to have survived from the Tudor or an earlier period. It is also an interesting instance of a commoner achieving the second highest degree within his own lifetime. In the space of 12 years he became a baron, earl and marquess. The last a reward for his assistance in the downfall of the Protector Somerset. Paulet was a great survivor at court, maintaining the office of Lord High Treasurer through three turbulent reigns, from 1550 until his death at the great age of 88 in 1572.

Although the grantees of early creations cannot be said to be especially of the blood royal, it is interesting to note that the first 10 holders of the rank were all fairly closely related to their monarchs and – therefore – to each other. They all descend from Henry III (Dublin directly from him, Suffolk, Dorset (cr 1475), Berkeley and Pembroke from Edward I and the others from Edward III). Some, as already noted, had closer royal associations.

Meanwhile, north of the border, the Scots monarchs had not been inactive. King James VI celebrated the christening of his daughter with the promotion of 2 earls: Huntly (surviving to this day) and Hamilton, both created in 1599. As James I he elevated the famous favourite Villiers to the marquessate of Buckingham (1618), on his way to a dukedom of the same name in 1623. Neither survived long, however, as the 2nd Duke died without issue in 1687.

James's successor, Charles I, was our second most prolific monarch, creating 10 marquesses, many as a result of the Civil Wars. Douglas (cr 1633), is another early Scots title to survive, albeit in a submerged capacity, as the 4th Marquess had already become Duke of Hamilton. The heirs apparent have used both Douglas and Clydesdale (see submerged section) as a courtesy title. Hertford (1641), Worcester (1643, and another survivor used as the courtesy style of the eldest sons of the Dukes

---

1 Bedford, in preparation for his marriage to King Edward IV's daughter, Elizabeth. The marriage never took place however, and she later married Henry VII and was ancestress of the Tudor dynasty.
2 The latin used in the patent makes it clear she was created a *marchioness*, not a marquess, although she was generally known as "the lady marquess" (*see* Miller, Dr. Helen; *Henry VIII and the English Nobility* (Blackwell, 1986) p24n).

of Beaufort). Newcastle on Tyne (1643), Montrose (1644, now submerged in the dukedom of that name – given to the 4th marquess in 1707) and Dorchester (1645). The first Irish titles appear in this reign. Ormonde (1642) becoming submerged in the dukedom of that name in 1661 (extinct 1758), Antrim (1645) and Clanricarde (1646) both extinct on the deaths of the grantees. Argyll (1641), described as a "small, wiry, squinting, blue eyed, red haired man, with a high forehead and a hooked nose", switched sides several times. Despite having been promised both a dukedom and the Garter by an exiled Charles II, he in fact lost all his honours – and his life – upon His Majesty's restoration. In an age when great store was set by beauty and fashion, his looks alone would have earned him a fall from grace! His son, restored to the earldom but not the higher title, fared little better and suffered attainder and death as a result of espousing the cause of Monmouth. The family fortunes were improved by the Marquess's grandson, this time switching from the losing (James II) to the winning (William III) monarch and finally achieving the dukedom they still enjoy.

Two Scots earls (Atholl and Queensberry) were promoted during Charles II's reign, along with his only English creation, that of Halifax in 1682. The last became extinct with the 2nd Marquess, although the 1st Marquess's illegitimate progeny flourished: a descendant being the actor Edmund Kean. Halifax was another of that rare breed: a commoner (4th baronet) who achieved high rank within a short number of years. James II's only creation in 1687, the Marquess of Powis, was a loyal Catholic subject and followed his master into exile where he received a Jacobite dukedom (see "Unofficial" titles).

Another commoner-baronet, Sir Thomas Osborne, attained the highest rank in the penultimate Stuart reign. From commoner to duke in the space of 20 years, passing four years as Marquess of Carmarthen (1689) before becoming Duke of Leeds in 1694. The marquessate was always used by the dukes' heirs apparent while they existed. Sadly, there were no heirs to succeed on the death of the 12th Duke in 1964, when all Sir Thomas's hard-earned honours became extinct. Among William III's other creations, both Tweeddale (1694) and Lothian (1701) survive to this day. The first was the just reward to a seventy year old man after a long and distinguished public career. The second, to ensure the Earl of Lothian's precedence over the Earl of Roxburghe and others. The triumph was short lived, however, as Lord Roxburghe acquired a dukedom in the next reign.

Of Queen Anne's creations, the Marquess of Kent (1706) was made duke of that name in the same reign. The Duke also took an unusual step by obtaining another marquessate – that of Grey – in the year of his death (1740), so that his granddaughter could succeed to high rank (the only woman known to have succeeded to the degree of marquess[1]). There is a wonderful portrait of this lady, referred to as Jemima, Marchioness Grey, still existing in the house of her husband's family, Wimpole Hall in Hertfordshire, which is now in the care of the National Trust. In spite of the Duke's efforts, this title expired on the death of Lady Grey in 1797 and her heirs are now represented by Lord Lucas of Crudwell.

George I created only three marquessates. This places him well down the table of regnal creations, but they are remarkable for another reason: they were all given to the same man! The 5th Baron and 1st Earl of Wharton received the British Marquessates of Malmesbury and Wharton on 15th February, 1715. On 12th April, 1715 he received the Irish title of Catherlough and died the same day! His son succeeded to this multitude of honours and was, as a minor, promoted to the dukedom of Wharton in 1718. He had previously flirted with the exiled court of James II, pressing for and obtaining some Jacobite peerages, including the "dukedom" of Northumberland. This young man squandered his fortune and vacillated between the Jacobites and his own government (at one point declaring himself "Prime Minister" of the former), and was eventually outlawed, although somewhat irregularly. Having made overtures to return to this country, which were rebuffed, he died abroad without male issue in 1731.

It was inevitable during George III's long reign, in which politicians played a major role in bestowing titles, that many of the creations should be of a political nature: most notable among them the promotion of Lansdowne, following his retirement as Prime Minister. Had succeeding retiring premiers followed this practice we may have

---

[1] The instance of Pembroke referred to earlier being a creation, not a succession.

seen a second woman receive the rank in our own time! There were also two creations for military exploits: Wellington, on his way to receiving one of the few non-royal dukedoms given by this monarch, and Anglesey – earned at Waterloo. Also, the first viceregal promotions occur: Cornwallis (for Bengal, later Canada): Wellesley (Bengal) and Hastings (India). Wellesley left no legitimate heirs and his title became extinct. He had, with other illegitimate issue, a daughter, Anne, from whom Queen Elizabeth The Queen Mother descends. George's other distinction is to have made six marquesses in the space of nine days (17-25 August, 1789). The first two, Clanricarde and Antrim, became extinct on the deaths of the grantees. The other four (Bath, Waterford, Downshire and Salisbury) are happily still with us.

Of George IV's three creations, Ailesbury is noticeable as the first marquessate created as a coronation honour. There have been five others, Ailsa, Breadalbane and Westminster for William IV's coronation, Normanby in Victoria's reign and Crewe when George V was crowned. Of Victoria's other creations, the Earls of Dalhousie, Dufferin and Zetland were either during or following viceregal terms of office. The former two commemorating Indian associations in their titles ("Dalhousie of Dalhousie Castle, co Edinburgh and of the Punjab" and "Dufferin and Ava in the county of Down and in the province of Burma") – doubtless a touch which much amused the Queen-Empress. Her other promotions were also earls, among them Lord Ripon, another descendant of Jemima, Marchioness Grey.

Edward VII and Edward VIII each created one marquessate, both at the end of viceregal terms of office. The former to Linlithgow (1902), the latter to another commoner by birth, Lord Willingdon, who rose from Baron to Marquess in the space of 26 years. George V achieves a high ranking in our regnal table, with 8 creations. To Crewe, already mentioned, may be added Lincolnshire, who had deputised in the office of Lord Great Chamberlain at the Coronation: and Aberdeen & Temair, Curzon of Kedleston and Reading – all holding or having held high office. The marquessates created for his relatives fall into a special category and follow the King's decision to "Anglicise" the royal house and family name (written of elsewhere in this volume). To his wife's brother he gave the title of Cambridge, and to his cousins he gave those of Milford Haven and Carisbrooke. Of these, only the middle title remains extant.

TABLE OF OUTRIGHT CREATIONS

NOTE: The following table lists all outright marquessate creations. Most of the headings are self explanatory. Countries of origin are abbreviated to one or two letters. The abbreviations in the last column refer to the current status of the title. These are: Attainted (Att), Degraded (Deg), Dormant (Dor), Extant, Extinct (Ex), Forfeited (For), Submerged (Sub), or Surrendered (Sur).

No.	TITLE & FAMILY NAME	DATE CREATED	ORIGIN	HOLDERS[1]	STATUS
1	Dublin (de Vere)	1 December, 1385	E	1	Sur 1386
2	Dorset/Somerset (Beaufort)	29 September, 1397	E	1	Deg 1399
3	Dorset (Beaufort)	24 June, 1443	E	1(1 Somerset)	Att, Sub 1461
4	Suffolk (de la Pole)	14 September, 1444	E	1(2 Suffolk)	Sur, Sub 1493
5	Montagu (Neville)	25 March, 1470	E	1(1 Bedford)	Deg, Sub 1478
6	Dorset (Grey)	18 April, 1475	E	2(1 Suffolk)	Att, Sub 1554
7	Berkeley (de Berkeley)	28 January, 1489	E	1	Ex 1492
8	Exeter (Courtenay)	18 June, 1525	E	1	Att 1539
9	Pembroke (Boleyn)	1 September, 1532	E	1	Ex 1536
10	Northampton (Parr)	16 February, 1547	E	1	Att 1553
11	Winchester (Paulet)	11 October, 1551	E	18	Extant
12	Northampton (Parr)	13 January, 1559	E	1	Ex 1571
13	Hamilton (Hamilton)	17 April, 1599	S	3(1 Hamilton)	Ex, Sub 1651
14	Huntly (Gordon)	17 April, 1599	S	13	Extant
15	Buckingham (Villiers)	1 January, 1618	E	1(1 Buckingham)	Ex, Sub 1687
16	Douglas (Douglas)	14 June, 1633	S	3(9 Hamilton)	Extant, Sub
17	Hertford (Seymour)	3 June, 1641	E	1(2 Somerset)	Ex, Sub 1675
18	Argyll (Campbell)	15 November, 1641	S	1	For 1661
19	Ormonde (Butler)	30 August, 1642	I	1(2 Ormonde)	Ex, Sub 1758
20	Worcester (Somerset)	2 March, 1643	E	3(10 Beaufort)	Extant, Sub
21	Newcastle on Tyne (Cavendish)	27 October, 1643	E	1(1 Newcastle &c)	Ex, Sub 1691
22	Montrose (Graham)	6 May, 1644	S	4(7 Montrose)	Extant, Sub
23	Antrim (MacDonnell)	26 January, 1645	I	1	Ex 1682
24	Dorchester (Pierrepont)	25 March, 1645	E	1	Ex 1680
25	Clanricarde (de Burgh)	21 February, 1646	I	1	Ex 1657
26	Atholl (Murray)	17 February, 1676	S	2(9 Atholl)	Extant, Sub
27	Queensberry (Douglas)	11 February, 1682	S	12	Extant
28	Halifax (Saville)	22 August, 1682	E	2	Ex 1700
29	Powis (Herbert)	24 March, 1687	E	3	Ex 1748

30	Carmarthen (Osborne)	9 April, 1689	E	1(11 Leeds)	Ex, Sub 1964
31	Normanby (Sheffield)	10 May, 1694	E	1(1 Buckingham &)	Ex, Sub 1735
32	Tweeddale (Hay)	17 December, 1694	S	13	Extant
33	Lothian (Kerr)	23 June, 1701	S	12	Extant
34	Annandale (Johnston)	24 June, 1701	S	3	Dor 1792
35	Kent (Grey)	14 November, 1706	E	1	Ex 1740
36	Lindsey (Bertie)	21 December, 1706	S	1(4 Ancaster & Kesteven)	Ex, Sub 1809
37	Dorchester (Pierrepont)	23 December, 1706	E	1(1 Kingston-on-Hull)	Ex, Sub 1773
38	Malmesbury (Wharton)	15 February, 1715	GB	2	Ex 1731
39	Wharton (Wharton)	15 February, 1715	GB	2	Ex 1731
40	Catherlough (Wharton)	12 April, 1715	I	2	Ex 1731
41	Grey (Grey)	19 May, 1740	GB	1(1 Kent)	Ex 1797
42	Rockingham (Watson-Wentworth)	19 April, 1746	GB	2	Ex 1782
43	Kildare (Fitzgerald)	3 March, 1761	I	1(7 Leinster)	Extant, Sub
44	Buckingham (Nugent-Temple-Grenville)	4 December, 1784	GB	2(2 Buckingham &c)	Ex, Sub 1889
45	Lansdowne (Petty)	6 December, 1784	GB	8	Extant
46	Stafford (Leveson-Gower)	1 March, 1786	GB	2(5 Sutherland)	Extant, Sub
47	Townshend (Townshend)	31 October, 1787	GB	7	Extant
48	Clanricarde (de Burgh)	17 August, 1789	I	1	Ex 1797
49	Bath (Thynne)	18 August, 1789	GB	7	Extant
50	Antrim (MacDonnell)	18 August, 1789	I	1	Ex 1791
51	Waterford (Beresford)	19 August, 1789	I	8	Extant
52	Downshire (Hill)	20 August, 1789	I	8	Extant
53	Salisbury (Cecil)	25 August, 1789	GB	6	Extant
54	Abercorn (Hamilton)	15 October, 1790	GB	2(4 Abercorn)	Extant, Sub
55	Donegall (Chichester)	4 July, 1791	I	7	Extant
56	Drogheda (Moore)	5 July, 1791	I	3	Ex 1892
57	Cornwallis (Cornwallis)	8 October, 1792	GB	2	Ex 1823
58	Hertford (Seymour-Conway)	5 July, 1793	GB	8	Extant
59	Bute (Stuart)	21 March, 1796	GB	7	Extant
60	Wellesley (Wellesley)	2 December, 1799	I	1	Ex 1842
61	Sligo (Browne)	29 December, 1800	I	11	Extant
62	Thomond (O'Brien)	29 December, 1800	I	3	Ex 1855
63	Headfort (Taylour)	30 December, 1800	I	6	Extant
64	Ely (Tottenham)	1 January, 1801	I	8	Extant
65	Exeter (Cecil)	4 February, 1801	UK	8	Extant
66	Camden (Pratt)	7 September, 1812	UK	6	Extant
67	Northampton (Compton)	7 September, 1812	UK	7	Extant
68	Wellington (Wellesley)	3 October, 1812	UK	1(7 Wellington)	Extant, Sub
69	Anglesey (Paget)	4 July, 1815	UK	7	Extant
70	Cholmondeley (Cholmondeley)	22 November, 1815	UK	7	Extant
71	Londonderry (Stewart)	13 January, 1816	I	9	Extant
72	Conyngham (Conyngham)	15 January, 1816	I	7	Extant
73	Ormonde (Butler)	January, 1816	I	1	Ex 1820
74	Hastings (Rawdon-Hastings)	13 February, 1817	UK	4	Ex 1868
75	Ailesbury (Brudenell-Bruce)	17 July, 1821	UK	8	Extant
76	Westmeath (Nugent)	12 January, 1822	I	1	Ex 1871
77	Ormonde (Butler)	5 October, 1825	I	7	Extant
78	Clanricarde (de Burgh)	26 November, 1825	I	2	Ex 1916
79	Bristol (Hervey)	30 June, 1826	UK	7	Extant
80	Cleveland (Vane)	5 October, 1827	UK	1(3 Cleveland)	Ex, Sub 1891
81	Ailsa (Kennedy)	10 September, 1831	UK	8	Extant
82	Breadalbane (Campbell)	12 September, 1831	UK	2	Ex 1862
83	Westminster (Grosvenor)	13 September, 1831	UK	3(5 Westminster)	Extant, Sub
84	Normanby (Phipps)	25 June, 1838	UK	5	Extant
85	Dalhousie (Broun-Ramsay)	25 August, 1849	UK	1	Ex 1860
86	Ripon (Robinson)	23 June, 1871	UK	2	Ex 1923
87	Abergavenny (Nevill)	14 January, 1876	UK	5	Extant
88	Breadalbane (Campbell)	11 July, 1885	UK	5	Ex 1922
89	Dufferin and Ava (Hamilton-Temple-Blackwood)	17 November, 1888	UK	5	Ex 1988
90	Zetland (Dundas)	22 August, 1892	UK	4	Extant
91	Linlithgow (Hope)	27 October, 1902	UK	4	Extant
92	Crewe (Milnes)	3 July, 1911	UK	1	Ex 1945
93	Lincolnshire (Wynn-Carrington)	26 February, 1912	UK	1	Ex 1928
94	Aberdeen and Temair (Gordon)	4 January, 1916	UK	6	Extant
95	Cambridge (Cambridge)	16 July, 1917	UK	2	Ex 1981
96	Milford Haven (Mountbatten)	17 July, 1917	UK	4	Extant
97	Carisbrooke (Mountbatten)	18 July, 1917	UK	1	Ex 1960
98	Curzon of Kedleston (Curzon)	28 June, 1921	UK	1	Ex 1925
99	Reading (Isaacs)	7 May, 1926	UK	4	Extant
100	Willingdon (Freeman-Thomas)	26 May, 1936	UK	2	Ex 1979

---

[1] The figures in parenthesis refer to those who have only ever been dukes (with the name of the dukedom), and therefore only held the marquessate in it's submerged capacity. The figures do not include titles which were temporarily submerged (such as Winchester and Queensberry), as the bulk of their existence has been as an independent title. The totals are correct to May 1994.

SUBMERGED CREATIONS

This section refers to those marquessates created *with* dukedoms, which therefore can never exist independently of the higher title. It is an oft-repeated fallacy that this was a common practice. The confusion probably arises from the fact that all dukes' eldest sons have the precedence of a marquess, placed between substantive holders of the rank and earls. In fact, of the 200 or so ducal creations and restorations, only 35 were ever granted with a marquessate as a second title. The practice was common during the reigns of Charles II, William and Mary, Anne and George I (a period of 66 years), who between them account for 27 courtesy marquessates.

About two thirds of the titles were created by Stuart monarchs, and the first 8 creations were all to Scots families. The first instance was in 1488, when James III (S) created his son Duke of Ross with the marquessate of Ormond. He died without issue in 1504, when all his honours became extinct. Ormond was used again for the second creation – this time with the dukedom of Albany, granted by James VI & I to the future King Charles I. He, in turn, created the dukedom of Hamilton with the marquessate of Clydesdale, titles still extant in the Hamilton family, the heir apparent using the second title usually combined with that of Douglas (see Outright Creations). Charles II created five dukedoms with marquessates. Four became extinct and are (with the dukedom in parenthesis): Clydesdale (for life with Hamilton, extinct 1694), March (Lauderdale, extinct 1682), Bambreich (Rothes, extinct 1681) and Huntly (Gordon, extinct 1836). The only title to survive is that of Dumfriesshire, vested in the dukes of Queensberry. It is not used as a courtesy title however, as the heirs of the marquesses of Bute usually take the title Earl of Dumfries, although the present peer's son uses the style of Lord Mount Stuart.

In William and Mary's reign, the marquessate of Harwich was twinned with the dukedom of Schomberg (extinct 1719), that of Alton with Shrewsbury (extinct 1718) and that of Clare with Newcastle (extinct 1711). Three further creations still exist and are used by heirs: Tavistock (with the dukedom of Bedford), Hartington (Devonshire) and Kintyre and Lorne (Argyll).

Queen Anne accounts for nine titles. She created her cousin, Prince George of Hanover, Duke and Marquess of Cambridge, titles which merged in the crown upon his accession as George II in 1727. Her other English creations were Blandford (with the dukedom of Marlborough), Granby (Rutland) – both still in use by heirs – and Monthermer, which became extinct on the death without issue of the 2nd Duke of Montagu. Her first Scots creation – Angus and Abernethy with the dukedom of Douglas – became extinct on the death of the grantee in 1761. Tullibardine (with the dukedom of Atholl), Graham & Buchanan (Montrose) and Bowmont & Cessford (Roxburghe) are all still extant and in use. Also, the first British peerages following the Act of Union were granted during this reign: the 2nd Duke of Queensberry being made Marquess of Beverley and Duke of Dover. The limitations were not as extensive as his Scottish honours, however, and did not survive his son's death in 1778.

George I gave his mistress, Ehrengard Melusine von der Schulenberg, the Irish earldom and marquessate of Dungannon with the dukedom of Munster for life in 1716. As if that were not enough, less than three years later he granted her the British dukedom of Kendal. Such lavish honours, it was said, were intended to encourage "the surrender of prudery in younger and handsomer subjects". History remains silent as to the effectiveness of this policy. It is certainly true that of several mistresses, her rewards were the greatest. His other six creations were British and all sadly, since the loss in 1990 of Titchfield with the dukedom of Portland, now extinct. The others were Clare (Newcastle, extinct 1768), Carnarvon (Chandos, extinct 1789) and Brackley (Bridgewater, extinct 1803). And the royal creations for two grandsons: Ely (with the dukedom of Edinburgh, merged in the crown 1760) and Berkhampstead (Cumberland, extinct 1765).

Monthermer (with the dukedom of Montagu) was revived in George III's reign, but did not survive the death of the grantee in 1790. This monarch's only other creation – Douro with the dukedom of Wellington – survives to this day and is in use by the current heir. George IV's only creation was Chandos, with the dukedom of Buckingham and Chandos, becoming extinct in 1889. Victoria created the last submerged marquessate (Macduff) in the same year, for her granddaughter's husband, who was also made Duke of Fife, both titles becoming extinct in 1912. Her other creation was Irish: Hamilton, still extant with the dukedom of Abercorn. The duke however uses an outright marquessate (also Abercorn) for his seat in the House of Lords.

"UNOFFICIAL" TITLES

There are five titles which are said to have existed, but for which no reliable authority, official sanction or regular usage can be found. They are: Billing (1645) to the 5th Earl of Thomond, Fife (1567, with the dukedom of Orkney) to the 4th Earl Bothwell, Kinneill (1604-25) used by the 2nd Marquess of Hamilton, Narbeth (1650) to Sir James Perrott, Bt, proved dead before 1637 and Wigtown (1602, with the dukedom of Kintyre) to the infant 3rd son of James VI (S), whose death a few months later did not allow time for the titles to pass the great seal.

The Jacobite "peerage" is extensively covered by the Marquis de Ruvigny in the work of that name. The 13 marquessates are briefly listed here: Beaufort (1740, with the dukedom of Fraser to Lord Lovat), Blair (1717, with the dukedom of Rannoch to the Duke of Atholl's heir), Borland (1717, with the dukedom of St. Albans to a foreign subject), Drummond (1701, with the dukedom of Perth to the earl of that name), Erskine (1715, with the dukedom of Mar to the earl of that name), Forth (1692, with the dukedom of Melfort to the earls of that name), Jamaica (1720, said to have been given to the Duke of Berwick's heir), Monck & Fitzhemom (1721, with the dukedom of Albemarle to Lord Lansdowne), Montgomery (1689, with the dukedom of Powis to the marquess of that name), Seaforth (1691, to the earl of that name), Trelissick (1715, to James Paynter), Tyrconnell (1689, with the dukedom of Tyrconnell to the earl of that name) and Woburn (1716, with the dukedom of Northumberland, to the Duke of Wharton).

REGNAL CREATIONS

The following table lists all marquessate creations by reign and country of origin (with the submerged titles in parenthesis). It is perhaps surprising to note that half of all outright titles were created by three monarchs: Charles I (10), George III (32) and George V (8).

MONARCH	ENGLAND	SCOTLAND	GREAT BRITAIN	UNITED KINGDOM	IRELAND	TOTALS
Richard II	2	–	–	–	–	2
Henry VI	2	–	–	–	–	2
Edward IV	2	–	–	–	–	2
Henry VII	1	–	–	–	–	1
Henry VIII	2	–	–	–	–	2
Edward VI	2	–	–	–	–	2
Elizabeth I	1	–	–	–	–	1
James VI & I	1	2(1)	–	–	–	3(1)
Charles I	4	3(1)	–	–	3	10(1)
Charles II	1	2(5)	–	–	–	3(5)
James II	1	–	–	–	–	1
William III & Mary II	2(5)	3(1)	–	–	–	5(6)
Anne	2(4)	1(4)	(1)	–	–	3(9)
George I	–	–	2(6)	–	1(1)	3(7)
George II	–	–	2	–	–	2
George III	–	–	10(1)	7(1)	15	32(2)
George IV	–	–	–	3(1)	3	6(1)
William IV	–	–	–	3	–	3
Victoria	–	–	–	7(1)	(1)	7(2)
Edward VII	–	–	–	1	–	1
George V	–	–	–	8	–	8
Edward VIII	–	–	–	1	–	1
James III (S)	–	(1)	–	–	–	(1)
TOTALS	23(9)	11(13)	14(8)	30(3)	22(2)	100(35)

So it can be seen that the degree of marquess has been used overwhelmingly for the promotion of existing peers. Nearly 90% of the outright creations have been to peers of at least second generation (over half, of five or more generations). This goes some way to explaining why so many have survived for so long, since families were already well-established in the peerage. Forty-four per cent of outright creations are still extant, including the nine titles currently held by dukes. Some families have not been fortunate, despite repeated attempts to obtain higher rank. Most notably the de Burghs (or Bourkes) with the thrice created and extinct title of Clanricarde, the

Campbells with Argyll (once) and Breadalbane (twice), although a descendant eventually achieved the dukedom referred to above, and the Butlers, who although currently enjoying the marquessate of Ormonde of the third creation, have no direct heirs to succeed.

We no longer govern a vast empire and politicians have long lost the gift of patronage on such an exalted scale. Although princes will continue to be made dukes and earls, it seems unlikely that a degree so little used in the history of royal titles will find favour in that quarter. As it may be that Willingdon will carry the distinction of being the last marquessate, it is sad to note that the title did not survive the death of the second holder in 1979.

ROBERT HORLEY

EARLY MARQUESS CREATIONS 1385–1547

Showing the close kinship between the early marquesses and their sovereigns

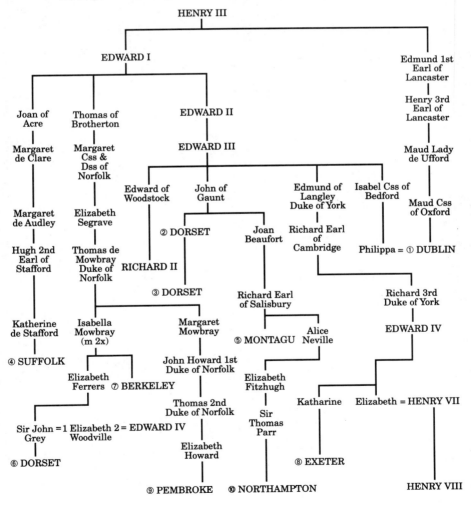

ABBREVIATIONS

AA Anti Aircraft, Architectural Association, and Automobile Association
AAA Amateur Athletic Association
AA & QMG Assistant Adjutant and Quartermaster-General
AACCA Associate of Association of Certified Corporate Accountants
AAG Assistant Adjutant-General
AAI Associate of Chartered Auctioneers' and Estate Agents' Institute
AAIM Associate of Australian Institute of Management
AAMC Australian Army Medical Corps
AASA Associate of Australian Society of Accountants
A & SH Argyll and Sutherland Highlanders
A/asia Australasia
ABCA Army Bureau of Current Affairs
ABCM Associate British College of Music
AC Companion of Order of Australia
ACA Associate of Institute of Chartered Accountants
ACAA Associate of Australian Institute of Cost Accountants
Acad Academy
ACCA Associate of the Association of Certified Accountants
ACCM Advisory Council for the Church's Ministry
ACCS Associate of Corporation of Secretaries
A/Cdre Air Commodore
ACGI Associate of City and Guilds of London Institute
ACIB Associate of the Corporation of Insurance Brokers
ACII Associate of Chartered Insurance Institution
ACIS Associate of Chartered Institute of Secretaries and Administrators
ACIT Associate of Chartered Institute of Transport
ACM Air Chief Marshal
ACMA Associate of Institute of Cost and Management Accountants
ACT Australian Capital Territory
ACWA Associate of Institute of Cost and Works Accountants
AD Dame of Order of Australia
ADC Aide-de-Camp
ADEME Assistant Director of Electrical and Mechanical Engineering
Adjt Adjutant
Adm Admiral
ADME Assistant Director of Mechanical Engineering
Admin Administrative, Administration, Administrator
ADMS Assistant Director of Medical Services
ADOS Assistant Director of Ordnance Services
AE Air Efficiency Award
AEGIS Aid for the Elderly in Government Institutions
AER Army Emergency Reserve
AEU Amalgamated Engineering Union
AFAIM Associate Fellow of Australian Institute of Management
AFC Air Force Cross
AFCIA Associate Fellow of Canadian Aeronautical Institute
AFGI Associate Fellow of Grocers' Institute
AFM Air Force Medal
AFRAeS Associate Fellow of Royal Aeronautical Society
A-G Adjutant-General
AGI Associate Member of Grocers' Institute
Agric Agriculture and Agricultural
AGSM Associate of Guildhall School of Music; Australian Graduate School of Management
AIAA Associate Architect Member of Incorporated Association of Architects and Surveyors
AIB Associate of Institute of Bankers
AICE Associate of Institution of Civil Engineers
AICS Associate of Institute of Chartered Shipbrokers
AIF Australian Imperial Forces
AIM Associate of Institute of Metallurgists (*now see* MIM)

AIMM Associate of Institute of Mining and Metallurgy
AInstP Associate of Institute of Physics
AIOB Associate of Institute of Building
AIWSP Associate of Institute of Work Study Practitioners
AK Knight of Order of Australia
AKC Associate of King's College, London
Ala Alabama (USA)
ALAS Associate of Land Agents Society
ALCM Associate of London College of Music
ALI Associate of the Landscape Institute
AM Albert Medal (now GM), Member of Order of Australia; Alpes Maritimes (France); Master of Arts (USA)
AMA Australian Medical Association
AMBIM Associate Member of the British Institute of Management
AMCT Associate of Manchester College of Science and Technology
AMet Associate of Metallurgy (Sheffield University)
AMF Australian Military Forces
AMICE Associate Member of Institution of Civil Engineers
AMIEA Associate Member of Institute of Engineers, Australia
AMIEE Associate Member of Institution of Electrical Engineers (*now see* MIEE)
AMIERE Associate Member of Institution of Electronic and Radio Engineers
AMI Ex Associate Member of Institute of Export
AMI Gas E Associate Member of Institution of Gas Engineers
AMIMechE Associate Member of Institution of Mechanical Engineers (*now see* MIMechE)
AMIMunE Associate Member of Institution of Municipal Engineers
AMInstPet Associate Member of Institute of Petroleum
AMInstW Associate Member of Institute of Welding
AMINucE Associate Member of Institution of Nuclear Engineers
AMIPM Associate Member of Institute of Personnel Management
AMIRSE Associate Member of Institution of Railway Signal Engineers
AMIStructE Associate Member of Institution of Structural Engineers
AMRAeS Associate Member of Royal Aeronautical Society
AMREF , African Medical and Research Foundation
AMRINA Associate Member of Royal Institution of Naval Architects
AMRTS Associate Member Royal Television Society
AMS Assistant Military Secretary
AMSE Associate Member of Society of Engineers
AMTPI Associate of Town Planning Institute
ante before
ANZAAS Australian and New Zealand Association for the Advancement of Science
AO Officer of Order of Australia
AOA Air Officer in Charge of Administration
AOC Air Officer Commanding
AOC-in-C Air Officer Commander in Chief
APEA Affiliate Physical Education Association
APM Assistant Provost Marshal
Apt Apartment
AQMG Assistant Quartermaster-General
ARA Associate of Royal Academy
ARAeS Associate of Royal Aeronautical So
ARAIA Associate of Royal Australian Institute of Architects
ARAM Associate of Royal Academy of Music
ARCA Associate Royal College of Art
ARCM Associate of Royal College of Music
ARCO Associate of Royal College of Organists
ARCS Associate of Royal College of Science
ARCST Associate of Royal College of Science and Technology (Glasgow)
ARCVS Associate of Royal College of Veterinary

Surgeons
ARIBA Associate of Royal Institute of British Architects
ARIC Associate of Royal Institute of Chemistry
ARICS Professional Associate of Royal Institution of Chartered Surveyors
Ariz Arizona (USA)
Ark Arkansas (USA)
Armd Armoured
ARPS Associate Royal Photographic Society
ARRC Associate Royal Red Cross
ARSA Associate of the Royal Scottish Academy
ARSM Associate of Royal School of Mines
ARTC Associate of Royal Technical College (Glasgow)
ARTS Associate of Royal Television Society
ASDA Associate Speech and Drama Australia
AS For Associate of the Royal Society of Foresters of Great Britain
ASH Anti-Smoking and Health
ASIA Associate of Society of Industrial Artists and Designers
Assist Assistant
Asso Association, Associate
AssocICE Associate of Institution of Civil Engineers
Assocn Association
ATAF Allied Tactical Air Force
ATC Air Training Corps
ATII Associate Member of Institute of Taxation
ATS Auxiliary Territorial Service
Aust Australia
Austn Australian
Av Avenue
AV-M Air Vice-Marshal
aws Graduate of RAF College of Air Warfare

B Baron
b born
BA Bachelor of Arts
BAC British Aircraft Corporation
BAFTA British Academy of Film and Television Arts
BAgr Bachelor of Agriculture
BAI Bachelor of Engineering
BAO Bachelor of Obstetrics
BAOR British Army of the Rhine
Bar Barrister
BArch Bachelor of Architecture
BASC British Association of Shooting and Conservation
Batn Battalion
BBC British Broadcasting Corporation
BC British Columbia
BCE Bachelor of Civil Engineering
BCh Bachelor of Surgery
BChir Bachelor of Surgery
BCL Bachelor of Civil Law
BCom Bachelor of Commerce
BComSc Bachelor of Commercial Science
BD Bachelor of Divinity
Bde Brigade
BDS Bachelor of Dental Surgery
BE Bachelor of Engineering (Australia)
BEA British European Airways
BEc Bachelor of Economics (Australia)
BEcon Bachelor of Economics
BEd Bachelor of Education
BEF British Expeditionary Force
BEM British Empire Medal
BEng Bachelor of Engineering
Berks Berkshire
BFI British Film Institute
BGS Brigadier General Staff
BL Bachelor of Law
BLitt Bachelor of Letters
BM Bachelor of Medicine
BMA British Medical Association
BME Bachelor of Mining Engineering
Bn Battalion
BNEC British National Export Council
BOAC British Overseas Airways Corporation
BPharm Bachelor of Pharmacy
BRCS British Red Cross Society
Brig Brigadier, Brigade
BS Bachelor of Surgery
BSc Bachelor of Science
Bt Baronet
Btss Baroness

Bty Battery
Bucks Buckinghamshire
BVSc Bachelor of Veterinary Science
By Barony

C Conservative, *c*, crowned
CA Member of Institute of Chartered Accountants of Scotland, and County Alderman
CAA Civil Aviation Authority
CAAV Central Association of Agricultural Valuers
Cal California (USA)
Camb Cambridge
Cambs Cambridgeshire
Capt Captain
Cav Cavalry
CB Companion of the Bath
CBE Commander of British Empire
CBI Confederation of British Industry
CBIM Companion of British Institute of Marketing
CC Companion of Order of Canada and County Councillor
CCRA Commander Corps Royal Artillery
C Chem Chartered Chemist
CD Canadian Forces Decoration
CDA College Diploma of Agriculture
Cdr Commander
CE Civil Engineer
CEI Council of Engineering Institutions
CEng Chartered Engineer
CENTO Central Treaty Organisation
CEO Chief Education Officer
CFMS Canadian Forces Medical Services
CFR Commander of Order of Federal Republic of Nigeria
cfs Qualified Central Flying School
CGeol Chartered Geologist
CGIA Insignia Award of City and Guilds of London Institute
CGM Conspicuous Gallantry Medal
CGS Chief of General Staff
CH Companion of Honour
Ch Chief
Chap Chaplain
Chap St J Chaplain of St John of Jerusalem
ChB Bachelor of Surgery
Ch Ch Christ Church
Ches Cheshire
Chm Chairman
ChM Master in Surgery
CI Lady of Imperial Order of the Crown of India, and Channel Islands
CIA Chemical Industries Association
CIE Companion of the Indian Empire
CIEE Companion of Institution of Electrical Engineers
CI Gas E Companion of Institution of Gas Engineers
CIGS Chief of Imperial General Staff
CIMarE Companion of Institute of Marine Engineers
CIMechE Companion of Institution of Mechanical Engineers
C in C Commander in Chief
CInstMC Companion Inst of Measurement and Control
CIOS International Committee for Scientific Management
CLA Country Landowners' Association
CLit Companion of Royal Society of Literature
Cllr Councillor
CM Master in Surgery and Member of Order of Canada
CMF Central Mediterranean Force and Commonwealth Military Forces
CMG Companion of St Michael and St George
CMM Commander of Order of Military Merit
CMS Church Missionary Society
CMZS Corresponding Member Zoological Society
CNAA Council for National Academic Awards
Co County, Company
COI Central Office of Information
Col Colonel
Coldm Gds Coldstream Guards
Coll College
Colls Collateral Branches
Colo Colorado (USA)
Com Commander
Comd Commander (Mil)

Comdg Commanding
Comdt Commandant
Com-in-Ch Commander-in-Chief
Commn Commission
commn'd commissioned
Commr Commissioner
Comp IEE Companion of Institution of Electrical Engineers
CompIERE Companion of Institution of Electronic and Radio Engineers
CON Commander of Order of the Niger (Nigeria)
Confedn Confederation
Conn Connecticut (USA)
Cos Counties, Companies
CP Cape Province (S Africa)
CPA Commonwealth Parliamentary Association; Chartered Patent Agent
CPM Colonial Police Medal for Gallantry and Colonial Police Medal for Meritorious Service
CQSW Certificate of Qualification in Social Work
cr creation
CRA Commander Royal Artillery
CRAC Commander Royal Armoured Corps
CRAeS Companion Royal Aeronautical Society
CRASC Commander Royal Army Service Corps
CRE Commander Royal Engineers
CREME Commander Royal Electrical and Mechanical Engineering
CSC Conspicuous Service Cross
CSI Companion of the Star of India
CSIRO Commonwealth Scientific and Industrial Research Organisation
CSO Chief Signal Officer
CStJ Commander of St John of Jerusalem
Cttee Committee
CV Cross of Valour
CVO Commander of Royal Victorian Order

d died
D Duke
da, dau daughter
DA Deputy Advocate, and Diploma in Anaesthesia
DA (Dundee) Diploma of Associate, Duncan of Jordanstone College of Art, Dundee
DA (Edin) Diploma of Associate, Edinburgh College of Art
DAA & QMG Deputy Assistant Adjutant and Quartermaster General
DAAG Deputy Assistant Adjutant-General
DA & QMG Deputy Adjutant and Quartermaster-General
DABR Diploma of American Board of Radiology
DACG Deputy Assistant Chaplain-General
DADMS Deputy Assistant Director of Medical Services
DADOS Deputy Assistant Director of Ordnance Services
DADST Deputy Assistant Director of Supplies and Transport
DAG Deputy Adjutant-General
DAMS Deputy Assistant Military Secretary
DAPM Deputy Assistant Provost Marshal
DAQMG Deputy Assistant Quartermaster-General
DAv Med Diploma in Aviation Medicine
DBE Dame Commander of Order of British Empire
DC District of Columbia (USA)
DCAe Diploma of College of Aeronautics
DCB Dame Commander of Order of the Bath
DCH Diploma in Child Health
DCL Doctor of Civil Law
DCLI Duke of Cornwall's Light Infantry
DCM Distinguished Conduct Medal
DCMG Dame Commander of Order of St Michael and St George
DCP Diploma in Clinical Pathology
DCSc Doctor of Commercial Science
DCVO Dame Commander of Royal Victorian Order
DD Doctor of Divinity
DDEME Deputy Director of Electrical and Mechanical Engineering
DDME Deputy Director of Mechanical Engineering
DDMS Deputy Director of Medical Services
DDOS Deputy Director of Ordnance Services
DDS Doctor of Dental Surgery
DDSc Doctor of Dental Science
DDST Deputy Director of Supplies and Transport
Del Delaware (USA)
DEME Director of Electrical and Mechanical Engineering

eering
DEng Doctor of Engineering
Dep Deputy
Derbys Derbyshire
DES Department of Education and Science
DesRCA Designer of the Royal College of Art
DFC Distinguished Flying Cross
DFH Diploma of Faraday House Engineering College
DGO Diploma in Gynaecology and Obstetrics
DHL Doctor of Hebrew Literature
DIC Diploma of Imperial College of Science
DIH Diploma in Industrial Health
DipAD Diploma in Art and Design
DipEd Diploma in Education
DipINSEAD Diploma in European Institute of Business Administration (L'Institut European d'administration des affaires)
Diplo Diplomatic
DipTP Diploma of Town Planning
Dir Director
Dist District
Div Division
DL Deputy Lieutenant
DLC Diploma Loughborough College
DLI Durham Light Infantry
DLit Doctor of Letters
DLitt Doctor of Letters
DLO Diploma in Laryngology and Otology
DM Doctor of Medicine
DME Director of Mechanical Engineering
DMilSc Doctor of Military Science
DMJ Diploma in Medical Jurisprudence
DMS Director of Medical Services
DMus Doctor of Music
DoE Department of the Environment
DObstRCOG Diploma Royal College of Obstetricians and Gynaecologists
DOMS Diploma in Ophthalmic Medicine and Surgery
DOS Director of Ordnance Services
DPA Diploma in Public Administration
DPH Diploma in Public Health
DPhil Doctor of Philosophy
DPM Deputy Provost Marshal, Diploma of Psychological Medicine
DPRM Diploma in Physical and Rehabilitation Medicine
DQMG Deputy Quartermaster-General
DRA Director of Royal Artillery
Drag Dragoon (Guards)
DrUniv Doctor of University
DSAO Diplomatic Service Administration Office
DSC Distinguished Service Cross
DSc Doctor of Science
DSIR Department of Scientific and Industrial Research
DSM Distinguished Service Medal
DSO Companion of Distinguished Service Order
dsp decessit sine prole (died without issue)
dspl decessit sine prole legitima (died without legitimate issue)
dspm decessit sine prole mascula (died without male issue)
dspms decessit sine prole mascula superstite (died without surviving male issue)
dsps decessit sine prole superstite (died without surviving issue)
dunm died unmarried
dvp decessit vita patris (died in the lifetime of the father)
dvm decessit vita matris (died in the lifetime of the mother)
DST Director of Supplies and Transport
DStJ Dame of St John of Jerusalem
DTD Dekoratie voor Trouwe Dienst (Decoration for Devoted Service)
DTech Doctor of Technology
DTM & H Diploma in Tropical Medicine and Hygiene
DVSM Diploma in Veterinary State Medicine
DVSc Doctor of Veterinary Science

E Earl or East
ECU English Church Union
ED Efficiency Decoration
ed educated
EDC Economic Development Committee

EEC European Economic Community
el eldest
EFTA European Free Trade Association
Eng Engineering
ERD Army Emergency Reserve Decoration
Estab Establishment
ext extinct
Extraor Extraordinary

FAA Fellow of Australian Academy of Science
FAAH Fellow of Australian Academy of the Humanities
FAAV Fellow of Central Association of Agricultural Valuers
FACCA Fellow of Association of Certified and Corporate Accountants
FACD Fellow of American College of Dentistry
FACE Fellow of Australian College of Education
FACMA Fellow of Australian College of Medical Administrators
FACOG Fellow American College of Obstetricians and Gynaecologists
FACP Fellow of American College of Physicians
FACS Fellow of American College of Surgeons
FACST Fellow of Australian College of Speech Therapists
FAHA Fellow of Australian Academy of the Humanities
FAI Fellow of Chartered Auctioneers and Estate Agents Institute
FAIAA Fellow of American Institute of Aeronautics and Astronautics
FAIAS Fellow of Australian Institute of Agricultural Science
FAIB Fellow of Australian Institute of Building
FAIM Fellow of Australian Institute of Management
FANY First Aid Nursing Yeomanry
FANZCA Fellow Australian and New Zealand College of Anaesthetists
FANZCP Fellow Australian and New Zealand College of Psychiatrists
FAO Food and Agricultural Organisation
FAPHA Fellow of American Public Health Association
FAPI Fellow of Australian Planning Institute
FARELF Far East Land Forces
FASA Fellow of Australian Society of Accountants
FBA Fellow of British Academy
FBCS Fellow of British Computer Society
FBHI Fellow of British Horological Institute
FBI Federation of British Industries
FBIM Fellow of British Institute of Management
FBIS Fellow British Interplanetary Society
FBOA Fellow of British Optical Association
FBPsS Fellow of British Psychological Society
FBS Fellow Building Societies Institute
FCA Fellow of Institute of Chartered Accountants
FCAA Fellow of Australasian Institute of Cost Accountants
FCANZ Fellow of Institute of Chartered Accountants in New Zealand
FCASI Fellow of Canadian Aeronautics and Space Institute
FCBA Fellow of Canadian Bankers Association
FCCA Fellow Association of Certified Accountants
FCCP Fellow of American College of Chest Physicians
FCCS Fellow of Corporation of Secretaries
FCGI Fellow of City and Guilds of London Institute
FCIB Fellow of Corporation of Insurance Brokers
FCII Fellow of Chartered Insurance Institute
FCIS Fellow of Chartered Institute of Secretaries and Administrators
FCIT Fellow of Chartered Institute of Transport
FCIV Fellow of Commonwealth Institute of Valuers (Australia)
FCMA Fellow of Institute of Cost and Management Accountants
FCO Foreign and Commonwealth Office
FCOG Fellow of College of Gynaecologists
FCP Fellow of College of Preceptors
FCRA Fellow of College of Radiologists of Australia
FCS Fellow of Chemical Society and Fellow College of Surgeons
FDS Fellow in Dental Surgery
FDS, RCPS Fellow in Dental Surgery, Royal College of Physicians and Surgeons (Glasgow)
Fedn Federation

FEng Fellow Royal Academy (formerly Fellowship) of Engineering
FEIS Fellow of Educational Institute of Scotland
FFA, RACS Fellow of Faculty of Anaesthetists, Royal Australasian College of Surgeons
FFA, RCS Fellow of Faculty of Anaesthetists, Royal College of Surgeons
FFA, RCSI Fellow of Faculty of Anaesthetists, Royal College of Surgeons in Ireland
FFAS Fellow, Faculty of Architects and Surveyors, London
FFA (SA) Fellow of Faculty of Anaesthetists, South Africa
FFB Fellow of Faculty of Building
FFCM Fellow of Faculty of Community Medicine
FFD, RCS Fellow of Faculty of Dentistry, Royal College or Surgeons
FFD, RCSIreland Fellow of Faculty of Dentistry, Royal College of Surgeons, Ireland
FFR Fellow of Faculty of Radiologists
FGI Fellow of Grocers' Institute
FGS Fellow of Geological Society
FGSM Fellow of Guildhall School of Music and Drama
FHA Fellow of Institute of Hospital Administrators
FHCIMA Fellow of Hotel Catering and Institutional Management Association
FIA Fellow of Institute of Actuaries
FIAL Fellow of International Institute of Arts and Letters
FIAM Fellow of International Academy of Management
FIArb Fellow of Institute of Arbitrators
FIAS Fellow of Institute of Aeronautical Sciences (US)
FIB Fellow of Institute of Bankers
FIBiol Fellow of Institute of Biology
FICD Fellow of Institute of Civil Defence
FICE Fellow of Institute of Civil Engineers
FICeram Fellow of Institute of Ceramics
FICM Fellow of Institute of Credit Management
FICS Fellow of Institute of Chartered Shipbrokers
FIEA Fellow of Institution of Engineers, Australia
FIEE Fellow of Institute of Electrical Engineers
FIEEE Fellow of Institute of Electrical and Electronics Engineers, USA
FIEI Fellow of Institution of Engineering Inspection
FIERE Fellow of Institution of Electronic and Radio Engineers
FIFST Fellow of Institute of Food Science and Technology
FIHE Fellow of Institute of Health Education
FIHM Fellow of Institute of Housing Managers
FIHVE Fellow of Institution of Heating and Ventilation Engineers
FIIP Fellow of Institute of Incorporated Photographers
FIL Fellow of Institute of Linguists
FIM Fellow of Institution of Metallurgists
FIMA Fellow of Institute of Mathematics and its Applications
FIMC Fellow of Institute of Measurement and Control (New Zealand), *formerly* Automatic Control and Instrumentation Society (New Zealand)
FIMechE Fellow of Institute of Mechanical Engineers
FIMgt Fellow of Institute of Management
FIMI Fellow of Institute of Motor Industry
FIMinE Fellow of Institution of Mining Engineers
FIMM Fellow of Institute of Mining and Metallurgy
FIMTA Fellow of Institute of Municipal Treasurers and Accountants
FIMunE Fellow of Institution of Municipal Engineers
FInstAM Fellow of Institute of Administrative Management
FInstD Fellow of Institute of Directors
FInstF Fellow of Institute of Fuel
FInstHE Fellow of Institute of Highways Engineers
FInstLEx Fellow of Institute of Legal Executives
FInstM Fellow of Institute of Marketing
FInstMet Fellow of Institute of Metals
FInst, Nav Fellow of Institute of Navigation
FInstP Fellow of Institute of Physics and Physical Society
FInstPet Fellow of Institute of Petroleum
FInstPS Fellow of Institute of Purchasing and Supply
FInstMSM Fellow of Institute of Marketing and

Sales Management
FInstW Fellow of Institute of Welding
FIO Fellow of Institute of Ophthalmology
FIOB Fellow of Institute of Building
FIPA Fellow of Institute of Public Administration
FIPlantE Fellow of Institution of Plant Engineers
FIPM Fellow of Institute of Personnel Management
FIPR Fellow of Institute of Public Relations
FIProdE Fellow of Institution of Production Engineers
FIQ Fellow of Institute of Quarrying
FIQA Fellow of Institute of Quality Insurance
FIREE (Aust) Fellow of Institution of Radio and Electronics Engineers (Australia)
FIStructE Fellow of Institution of Structural Engineers
FITD Fellow of Institute of Training and Development
FIWE Fellow of Institute of Water Engineers
FIWM Fellow of Institution of Works Managers
FIWSP Fellow of Institution of Work Study Practitioners
Fla Florida (USA)
FLAS Fellow of Chartered Land Agents Society
FLCM Fellow of London Coll of Music
Flints Flintshire (now Clwyd)
Fl Lt Flight Lieutenant
FLS Fellow of Linnean Society
FMA Fellow of Museums Association
FNI Fellow of the Nautical Institute
FNZIE Fellow of New Zealand Institution of Engineers
FNZIM Fellow of New Zealand Institute of Management
FNZSA Fellow of New Zealand Society of Accountants
F/O Flying Officer
FOIC Flag Officer in Charge
FPANZ Fellow Public Accountant of New Zealand
FPEA Fellow Physical Education Association
FPhysS Fellow of Physical Society
FPI Fellow of Plastics Institute
FPS Fellow of Pharmaceutical Society
FRACDS Fellow of Royal Australian College of Dental Surgeons
FRACGP Fellow of Royal Australian College of General Practitioners
FRACI Fellow of Royal Australian Chemical Institute
FRACMA Fellow of Royal Australian College of Medical Administrators
FRACP Fellow of Royal Australasian College of Physicians
FRACR Fellow of Royal Australasian College of Radiologists
FRACS Fellow of Royal Australasian College of Surgeons
FRAeS Fellow of Royal Aeronautical Society
FRAgS Fellow of Royal Agricultural Societies of Great Britain
FRAI Fellow of Royal Anthropological Institute
FRAIA Fellow of Royal Australian Institute of Architects
FRAM Fellow of Royal Academy of Music
FRANZCP Fellow of Royal Australian and New Zealand College of Psychiatrists
FRAPI Fellow of Royal Australian Planning Institute
FRAS Fellow of Royal Astronomical Society
FRASE Fellow of the Royal Agricultural Society of England
FRCGP Fellow of Royal College of General Practitioners
FRCA Fellow Royal College of Anaesthetists
FRCM Fellow of Royal College of Music
FRCO Fellow of Royal College of Organists
FRCOG Fellow of Royal College of Obstetricians and Gynaecologists
FRCP Fellow of Royal College of Physicians
FRCPC Fellow of Royal College of Physicians and Surgeons of Canada (formerly FRCSCan)
FRCPsych Fellow Royal College of Psychiatrists
FRCR Fellow of Royal College of Radiologists
FRCSEngland, FRCSEd, and FRCSI Fellow of Royal College of Surgeons of England, Edinburgh and Ireland respectively
FRCS(Glas) Fellow of Royal College of Surgeons of Glasgow
FRCVS Fellow of Royal College of Veterinary Surgeons

FREconS Fellow of Royal Economical Society
FRES Fellow of Royal Entomological Society of London
FRFPS Fellow of Royal Faculty of Physicians and Surgeons
FRGS Fellow of Royal Geographical Society
FRHistS Fellow of Royal Historical Society
FRHS Fellow of Royal Horticultural Society
FRIAS Fellow of Royal Incorporation of Architects in Scotland
FRIBA Fellow of Royal Institute of British Architects
FRIC Fellow of Royal Institute of Chemistry
FRICS Fellow of Royal Institute of Chartered Surveyors
FRIH Fellow of Royal Institute of Horticulture (NZ)
FRIN Fellow of Royal Institute of Navigation
FRINA Fellow of Royal Institute of Naval Architects
FRIPHH Fellow of Royal Institute of Public Health and Hygiene
FRMCM Fellow of Royal Manchester College of Music
FRMetS Fellow of Royal Meteorological Society
FRPS Fellow of Royal Photographic Society
FRS Fellow of Royal Society
FRSA Fellow of Royal Society of Arts
FRSAMD Fellow of Royal Scottish Academy of Music and Drama
FRSC Fellow of Royal Society of Canada
FRSCM Fellow of Royal School of Church Music
FRSE Fellow of Royal Society of Edinburgh
FRSGS Fellow of Royal Scottish Geographical Society
FRSH Fellow of Royal Society for Promotion of Health
FRSL Fellow of Royal Society of Literature
FRSM Fellow of Royal Society of Medicine
FRSNZ Fellow of Royal Society of New Zealand
FRSSA Fellow of Royal Society of South Africa
FRTPI Fellow Royal Town Planning Institute
FRTS Fellow Royal Television Society
FRVCM Fellow of Royal Victorian Coll of Music
FRZS (Scot) Fellow of Royal Zoological Society of Scotland
FSA Fellow of Society of Antiquaries
FSAA Fellow of Society of Incorporated Accountants and Auditors
FSAE Fellow of National Society for Art Education
FSE Fellow of Society of Engineers
FSFor Fellow of Society of Foresters of Great Britain
FSIA Fellow of Society of Industrial Artists and Designers
FSS Fellow of Royal Statistical Society
FSVA Fellow of Incorporated Society of Valuers and Auctioneers
FTCL Fellow of Trinity College of Music, London
FTIA Fellow of Taxation Institute of Australia
FWAAS Fellow of World Academy of Arts and Sciences
FWAG Farming and Wildlife Advisory Group
FZS Fellow of Zoological Society

Ga Georgia (USA)
GATT General Agreement of Tariffs and Trade
GBE Knight or Dame Grand Cross of British Empire
GC George Cross
GCB Knight or Dame Grand Cross of the Bath
GCFR Grand Commander of Order of Federal Republic of Nigeria
GCIE Knight Grand Commander of Indian Empire
GCMG Knight or Dame Grand Cross of St Michael and St George
GCON Grand Commander of the Order of Niger (Nigeria)
GCSI Knight Grand Commander of Star of India
GCStJ Bailiff or Dame Grand Cross of St John of Jerusalem
GCVO Knight or Dame Grand Cross of Royal Victorian Order
Gen General
GGSM Graduate in Music, Guildhall School of Music and Drama
GHQ General Headquarters
Glam Glamorgan
GLC Greater London Council

Glos Gloucestershire
GM George Medal
GMMG Grand Master of St Michael and St George
GOC General Officer Commanding
Gov Governor
Govt Government
GPMU Graphical, Paper and Media Union
GPO General Post Office
Gram Sch Grammar School
Gren Gds Grenadier Guards
GRNCM Graduate Royal Northern Coll of Music
GRO General Register Office
GRSM Graduate of Royal School of Music
GSO General Staff Officer
GTCL Graduate Trinity Coll of Music

ha heir apparent
HAA Heavy Anti Aircraft
HAC Honourable Artillery Company
Hants Hampshire
HCF Honorary Chaplain to the Forces
HDD Higher Dental Diploma
HEICS Honourable East India Company's Service
Herefords Herefordshire
Herts Hertfordshire
HG Home Guard
HGDH His or Her Grand Ducal Highness
HGV Heavy Goods Vehicles
HH His or Her Highness, His Holiness
HI&RH His or Her Imperial and Royal Highness
HIH His or Her Imperial Highness
HIllH His or Her Illustrious Highness
HLI Highland Light Infantry
HM His or Her Majesty
HMS His or Her Majesty's Ship
HMSO Her Majesty's Stationery Office
Hon Honourable, Honorary
HonGSM Honorary Guildhall School of Music
hp heir presumptive
HQ Headquarters
HRH His or Her Royal Highness
HSH His or Her Serene Highness
Hunts Huntingdonshire

IBA Independent Broadcasting Authority
IBERLANT Iberia Atlantic Area
ICI Imperial Chemical Industries, Ltd
ICS Indian Civil Service
idc Imperial Defence College
IDS Institute of Development Studies
IG Irish Guards
ILEA Inner London Education Authority
Ill Illinois (USA)
ILO International Labour Organisation
IMS Indian Medical Service
Inc Incorporated
Ind Independent or Indiana (USA)
Inf Infantry
Infra below
INSEAD (**Insead**) Institut Européen d'Administration des Affaires
Inst Institute
Instn Institution
IOM Isle of Man
IOW Isle of Wight
IPU Inter-Parliamentary Union
ISC Indian Staff Corps
ISO Companion of Imperial Service Order
ITN Independent Television News

JAG Judge Advocate-General
JD Doctor of Jurisprudence
JDipMA Joint Diploma in Management Accounting Services
Jnr Junior
JP Justice of the Peace
JSD Doctor of Juristic Science
jssc Joint Services Staff College

ka Killed in action; Killed on active service
Kan Kansas (USA)
KB Knight of the Bath (to 1814)
KBE Knight Commander of British Empire
KC King's Counsel
KCB Knight Commander of the Bath

KCH Knight Commander of the Hanoverian Order
KCIE Knight Commander of Indian Empire
KCMG Knight Commander of St Michael and St George
KCSG Knight Commander of St Gregory
KCSI Knight Commander of the Star of India
KCSS Knight Commander of the Order of St Silvester
KCVO Knight Commander of Royal Victorian Order
KG Knight of the Garter
KGFS King George's Fund for Sailors
KGStJ Knight of Grace of St John of Jerusalem
KJStJ Knight of Justice of St John of Jerusalem
Knt Knight
KOSB King's Own Scottish Borderers
KOYLI King's Own Yorkshire Light Infantry
KP Knight of St Patrick
KPFSM King's Police and Fire Service Medal
KPM King's Police Medal
KRRC King's Royal Rifle Corps
KSLI King's Shropshire Light Infantry
KSS Knight of the Order of St Silvester
KStJ Knight of St John of Jerusalem
KT Knight of the Thistle
Ky Kentucky (USA)

L Lord, and Lancers
L Liberal
La Louisiana (USA)
LAA Light Anti Aircraft
Lab Labour
LAB Licentiate of the Associated Board (Board being the combined Roy Coll of Music and Roy Acad of Music)
LAC Leading Aircraftsman
Lancs Lancashire
LCC London County Council
LCST Licentiate of College of Speech Therapists
LDS Licentiate of Dental Surgery
Leics Leicestershire
LG Life Guards; Lady of the Garter
LHD Literarum Humaniorum Doctor
LI Light Infantry
Lib Liberal
Lieut Lieutenant
Lieut-Col Lieutenant-Colonel
Lincs Lincolnshire
LitHum Literae Humaniores
LittD Doctor of Letters
LKQCP Licentiate of the King and Queen's College of Physicians, Ireland
LLB Bachelor of Laws
LLCM Licentiate London College of Music
LLCM (TD) Licentiate London College of Music (Teachers Diploma)
LLD Doctor of Laws
LLM Master of Laws
LM Licentiate in Midwifery
LMCC Licentiate, Medical Council of Canada
LMRTPI Legal Member Royal Town Planning Institute
LMSSA Licenciate in Medicine and Surgery of the Society of Apothecaries
Lp Lordship
LPEA Licentiate Physical Education Association
LRAM Licentiate of Royal Academy of Music
LRCP Licentiate of Royal College of Physicians
LRCPS Licentiate of Royal College of Physicians and Surgeons
LRCS Licentiate of Royal College of Surgeons
LRFPS Licentiate of Royal Faculty of Physicians and Surgeons, Glasgow
LRIBA Licentiate of Royal Institute of British Architects
LRPS Licentiate of Royal Photographic Society
LSA Licentiate of Society of Apothecaries
LSE London School of Economics
LSIA Licentiate of Society of Industrial Artists and Designers
Lt Lieutenant
Lt-Cdr Lieutenant Commander
LTCL Licentiate of Trin Coll of Music, London
Lt-Col Lieutenant-Colonel
Lt-Gen Lieutenant-General
LU Liberal Unionist
LVCM Licentiate of the Victoria College of Music
LVO Lieutenant of Royal Victorian Order, *formerly* MVO (Fourth Class)

Ly Lady

M Marquess
m married or marriage
MA Master of Arts
MACE Member of Australian College of Education
MACR Member of American College of Radiology
MAgr Master of Agriculture
MAI Master of Engineering
MAIME Member of American Institute of Mining and Metallurgical Engineers
Maj Major
Maj-Gen Major-General
MANZCP Member Australian and New Zealand College of Psychiatrists
MAO Master of Obstetric Art
MAP Ministry of Aircraft Production
MAPsS Member of Australian Psychological Society
MASME Member of American Society of Mechanical Engineers
Mass Massachusetts (USA)
MAusIMM Member of Australian Institute of Mining and Metallurgy
MB Bachelor of Medicine and Medal of Bravery
MBA Master of Business Administration
MBAOT Member of British Association of Occupational Therapists
MBCS Member British Computer Society
MBE Member of Order of British Empire
MBIM Member of British Institute of Management
MBOU Member British Ornithologists' Union
MC Military Cross
MCC Marylebone Cricket Club
MCE Master of Civil Engineering
MCh Master in Surgery
MChOrth Master of Orthopaedic Surgery
MCIP Member Canadian Institute of Planners
MCIT Member of Chartered Institute of Transport
MCL Master in Civil Law
MCom Master of Commerce (Scotland)
MCPA Member of College of Pathologists of Australia
MCPS Member of College of Physicians and Surgeons
MCSP Member of Chartered Society of Physiotherapists
Md Maryland (USA)
MD Doctor of Medicine
m diss marriage dissolved
MDS Master of Dental Surgery
Me Maine (USA)
ME Master of Engineering
MEC Member of Executive Council
MEcon Master of Economics
Med Medical
MEd Master of Education
MEIC Member of Engineering Institute of Canada
MELF Middle East Land Forces
MEng Master of Engineering
Met Metropolitan
MFCM Member of Faculty of Community Medicine
mfg manufacturing
MFH Master of Foxhounds
MGI Member of Grocers' Institute
Mgmnt Management
MHA Member of House of Assembly
MHR Member of House of Representatives
MIABTI Member International Association of Bomb Technicians and Investigators
MICE Member of Institution of Civil Engineers
MICFor Member Institute of Chartered Foresters
Mich Michigan
MIChemE Member of Institution of Chemical Engineers
Middx Middlesex
MIEA Member of Institution of Engineers, Australia
MIEE Member of Institution of Electrical Engineers
MIEI Member of Institution of Engineering Inspection
MIEIndia Member of Institution of Engineers in India
MIERE Member of Institution of Electronic and Radio Engineers
MIES Member of Institution of Engineers and Shipbuilders in Scotland
MIEx Member of Institute of Export
MIExpE Member Institute of Explosive Engineers
MI Gas E Member of Institution of Gas Engineers

MIHT Member of Institute of Highways and Transportation
MIIM Member of Institute of Industrial Management
Mil Military, Militia
MIM Member of Institute of Metallurgists
MIMarE Member of Institute of Marine Engineers
MIMC Member of Institute of Management Consultants
MIMechE Member of Institution of Mechanical Engineers
MIMI Member of Institute of Motor Industry
MIMinE Member of Institution of Mining Engineers
MIMM Member of Institute of Mining and Metallurgy
MIMTA Member of Institute of Municipal Treasurers and Accountants
MIMunE Member of Institution of Municipal Engineers
Min Minister or Ministry
MIN Member of Institute of Navigation
Minn Minnesota (USA)
MInstAM Member of Institute of Administrative Management
MInstF Member of Institution of Fuel
MInstHE Member of Institute of Highway Engineers
MInstM Member of Institute of Marketing
MInstMC Member of Institute of Measurement and Control
MInstMet Member of Institute of Metals
MInstNav Member of the Institute of Navigation
MInstPet Member of Institute of Petroleum
MInstPI Member of Institute of Patentees and Inventors
MInstPS Member of Institute of Purchasing and Supply
MInstW Member of Institute of Welding
MINucE Member of Institution of Nuclear Engineers
MIOB Member of the Institute of Building
MIPA Member of Institute of Public Administration
MIPlantE Member of Institution of Plant Engineers
MIPM Member of Institute of Personnel Management
MIPR Member of Institute of Public Relations
MIProdE Member of Institution of Production Engineers
MIQ Member of Institute of Quarrying
MIRSE Member of Institution of Railway Signal Engineers
MISM Member of Institute of Supervisory Management
Miss Mississippi
MIStructE Member of Institution of Structural Engineers
MITO Member Institution of Training Officers
MIWE Member of Institution of Water Engineers
MIWM Member of Institution of Works Managers
MIWSP Member of Institution of Work Study Practitioners
MLA Member of Legislative Assembly
MLC Member of Legislative Council
MLitt Master of Letters
MLitt Stud Master of Literary Studies (Australia)
MM Military Medal
MME Master of Mining Engineering
MMGI Master Member of Grocers' Institute
MMM Member of Order of Military Merit
MMSA Master of Midwifery of Society of Apothecaries
MNI Member of Nautical Institute
Mo Missouri (USA)
MO Medical Officer
MOD Ministry of Defence
Mon Monmouthshire (now Gwent)
Mont Montana (USA)
MP Member of Parliament
MPEA Member Physical Education Association
MPS Member of Pharmaceutical Society
MRAC Member of Royal Agricultural Society
MRCGP Member of Royal College of General Practitioners
MRCOG Member of Royal College of Obstetricians and Gynaecologists
MRCP Member of Royal College of Physicians
MRCPA Member of Royal College of Pathologists of Australia
MRCPEd Member of Royal College of Physicians,

Edinburgh
MRCPI Member of Royal College of Physicians, Ireland
MRCPsych Member of Royal College of Psychiatry
MRCS Member of Royal College of Surgeons
MRCVS Member of Royal College of Veterinary Surgeons
MRIA Member of Royal Irish Academy
MRICS Member of Royal Institution of Chartered Surveyors
MRIN Member of Royal Institute of Navigation
MRINA Member of the Royal Institution of Naval Architects
MRSC Member of Royal Society of Chemistry
MRSH Member of Royal Society for Promotion of Health
MRTPI Member Royal Town Planning Institute
MRTS Member Royal Television Society
MS Master of Surgery
MSAutE Member of Society of Automobile Engineers
MSc Master of Science
MSE Member of Society of Engineers
MSFor Member of the Society of Foresters of Great Britain
MSIAD Member of Society of Industrial Artists and Designers
MSIT Member Society of Instrument Technology
MSM Meritorious Service Medal
MStJ Member of St John of Jerusalem
MSW Master of Social Work (Canada)
Mt Mount
MusB Bachelor of Music
MusD Doctor of Music
MVO Member of Royal Victorian Order

N Nationalist
N North
NAAFI Navy, Army and Air Forces Institutes
nat natural
NATO North Atlantic Treaty Organisation
NC North Carolina (USA)
NDA National Diploma of Agriculture
NDak North Dakota
NDH National Diploma of Horticulture
Nebr Nebraska (USA)
NEDC National Economic Development Council
NEDO National Economic Development Office
Nev Nevada (USA)
New Mex New Mexico (USA)
NFU National Farmers' Union
NH New Hampshire (USA)
NI Northern Ireland
NJ New Jersey (USA)
NL National Liberal
NOIC Naval Officer in Charge
Northants Northamptonshire
Notts Nottinghamshire
NSPCC National Society for the Prevention of Cruelty to Children
NSW New South Wales
NUJ National Union of Journalists
NUR National Union of Railwaymen
NUT National Union of Teachers
NY New York
NZ New Zealand
NZEF New Zealand Expeditionary Force

OAM Medal of Order of Australia
OBE Officer of Order of British Empire
OC Officer Commanding and Officer of Order of Canada
ODA Overseas Development Administration
OECD Organisation for Economic Co-operation and Development
OEEC Organisation for European Economic Co-operation
OFS Orange Free State
OJ Order of Jamaica
Okla Oklahoma (USA)
OM Member of Order of Merit
OMM Officer of Order of Military Merit
Ont Ontario
Oreg Oregon (USA)
OSB Order of St Benedict
OStJ Officer of St John of Jerusalem
OTC Officers' Training Corps

Oxon Oxfordshire

Pa Pennsylvania (USA)
Parl Parliamentary
PC Privy Counsellor
PEI Prince Edward Island
PGCE Postgraduate Certificate in Education
PhC Pharmaceutical Chemist
PhD Doctor of Philosophy
PHAB Physically Handicapped and Able Bodied
Pl Place
Plen Plenipotentiary
PMRAFNS Princess Mary's Royal Air Force Nursing Service
P/O Pilot Officer
PPS Parliamentary Private Secretary
PQ Province of Quebec
PRA President of the Royal Academy
Preb Prebendary
Pres President
Presb Presbyterian
Prin Principal
PRO Public Records Office
Prof Professor
psc Passed staff college
Pt Point
ptr partner
Pty Proprietary
PWD Public Works Department

QAIMNS Queen Alexandra's Imperial Military Nursing Service
QALAS Qualified Associate of Land Agents' Society
QARANC Queen Alexandra's Royal Army Nursing Corps
QARNNS Queen Alexandra's Royal Naval Nursing Service
QC Queen's Counsel
QFSM Queen's Fire Service Medal
QGM Queen's Gallantry Medal
QHDS Queen's Honorary Dental Surgeon
QHNS Queen's Honorary Nursing Sister
QHP Queen's Honorary Physician
QHS Queen's Honorary Surgeon
QHVS Queen's Honorary Veterinary Surgeon
Qld Queensland
QMG Quartermaster-General
QOY Queen's Own Yeomanry
QPM Queen's Police Medal
QSM Queen's Service Medal, NZ
QSO Queen's Service Order, NZ

R Rector; Royal
RA Royal Artillery, Royal Academician
RAAF Royal Australian Air Force
RAAMC Royal Australian Army Medical Corps
RAAOC Royal Australian Army Ordnance Corps
RAASC Royal Australian Army Service Corps
RAC Royal Armoured Corps and Royal Automobile Club
RAC Royal Agricultural College (Cirencester)
RAChD Royal Army Chaplain's Dept
RACT Royal Australian Corps of Transport
RADA Royal Academy of Dramatic Art
RADC Royal Army Dental Corps
RAEC Royal Army Educational Corps
RAF Royal Air Force
RAFRO Reserve of Air Force Officers
RAFVR Royal Air Force Volunteer Reserve
RAM Member of Royal Academy of Music
RAMC Royal Army Medical Corps
RAN Royal Australian Navy
RANR Royal Australian Naval Reserve
RANVR Royal Australian Naval Volunteer Reserve
RAOC Royal Army Ordnance Corps
RAPC Royal Army Pay Corps
RARO Regular Army Reserve of Officers
RASC Royal Army Service Corps
RASE Royal Agricultural Society of England
RAuxAF Royal Auxiliary Air Force
RAVC Royal Army Veterinary Corps
RC Roman Catholic
RCAF Royal Canadian Air Force
rcds Royal College of Defence Studies
RCN Royal Canadian Navy
RCNC Royal Corps of Naval Architects

RCNVR Royal Canadian Naval Voluntary Reserve
RCS Royal College of Surgeons
RCT Royal Corps of Transport
Rd Road
RD Royal Naval Reserve Officer's Decoration
RDC Rural District Council
RDI Royal Designer for Industry
RE Royal Engineers
Regt Regiment
REME Royal Electrical and Mechanical Engineers
Ret Retired
Rev Reverend
RF Royal Fusiliers
RFA Royal Field Artillery, and Royal Fleet Auxiliary
RFC Royal Flying Corps
RFD Reserve Forces Decoration (Australia)
RFN Registered Fever Nurse
RFus Royal Fusiliers
RGA Royal Garrison Artillery
RGJ Royal Green Jackets
RGN Registered General Nurse
RHA Royal Horse Artillery; Royal Hibernian Academy
RHF Royal Highland Fusiliers
RHG Royal Horse Guards
RH G/D The Blues and Royals (Royal Horse Guards and 1st Dragoons)
RHR Royal Highland Regiment
RI Member of Royal Institute of Painters in Water Colour on Rhode Island (USA)
RIAC Royal Irish Automobile Club
RIAS Royal Incorporation of Architects in Scotland
RIBA Royal Institute of British Architects
RIIA Royal Institute of International Affairs
RIR Royal Irish Rangers
RLC Royal Logistic Corps
Rly Railway
RM Royal Marines; Registered Midwife
RMA Royal Marine Artillery; Royal Military Academy
RMC Royal Military College
RMLI Royal Marine Light Infantry
RMP Royal Military Police
RMR Royal Marine Reserve
RMS Royal Mail Steamer
RN Royal Navy
RNAS Royal Naval Air Service
RNC Royal Naval College
RNEC Royal Naval Engineering College
RNLI Royal National Lifeboat Institution
RNR Royal Naval Reserve
RNT Registered Nurse Tutor
RNVR Royal Naval Volunteer Reserve
RNZAC Royal New Zealand Armoured Corps
RNZAF Royal New Zealand Air Force
RNZAMC Royal New Zealand Army Medical Corps
RNZN Royal New Zealand Navy
ROI Royal Institute of Oil Painters
RoSPA Royal Society for the Prevention of Accidents
Roy Royal
Roy Signals Royal Corps of Signals
RP Member of Royal Society of Portrait Painters
RQMS Regimental Quartermaster Sergeant
RRC Lady of the Royal Red Cross
RRF Royal Regiment of Fusiliers
RRW Royal Regiment of Wales
RSA Royal Scottish Academician
RSAC Royal Scottish Automobile Club
RSCN Registered Sick Children's Nurse
RSF Royal Scots Fusiliers
RSignals Royal Signals
RSPCA Royal Society for the Prevention of Cruelty to Animals
RSSPCC Royal Scottish Society for Prevention of Cruelty to Children
RSW Member of Scottish Royal Society of Painters in Water Colours
Rt Right
Rt Hon Right Honourable
RTPI Royal Town Planning Institute
RTR Royal Tank Regiment
RWF Royal Welch Fusiliers
RWS Member of Royal Society of Painters in Water Colours

s succeeded

S South
Salop Shropshire
Sask Saskatchewan
SAS Special Air Service Regiment
SASO Senior Air Staff Officer
SBStJ Serving Brother of Order of St John of Jerusalem
SC Senior Counsel, Star of Courage, or South Carolina (USA)
ScD Doctor of Science
SCF Senior Chaplain to the Forces
Sch School
SCLI Somerset and Cornwall Light Infantry
SCM State Certified Midwife, and Student Christian Movement
SD Scientiae Doctor (Doctor of Science)
SEAC South East Asia Command
SEATO South East Asia Treaty Organisation
Sec Secretary
Ser Service
SG Scots Guards
SGM Sea Gallantry Medal
SHAEF Supreme Headquarters Allied Expeditionary Force
SHAPE Supreme Headquarters Allied Powers in Europe
SJ Society of Jesus
SJD Scientiae Juridicea Doctor (Doctor of Juridical Science)
SLI Somerset Light Infantry
SM Medal of Service, and Master of Science
Snr Senior
So Society
Soc Society
SOE Special Operations Executive
SOGAT Society of Graphical and Allied Trades
Som Somerset
SomLI Somerset Light Infantry
SOS Stars Organisation for Spastics
SPCK Society for Promoting Christian Knowledge
Sqdn Squadron
Sqdn-Ldr Squadron Leader
SR Supplementary Reserve
SRC Science Research Council
SRN State Registered Nurse
SSAFA Soldiers', Sailors' and Airmen's Families' Association
SSC Solicitor, Supreme Court (Scotland)
SSStJ Serving Sister of Order of St John of Jerusalem
St Street, Staffs, Staffordshire
STSO Senior Technical Staff Officer
Sup Superintendent and Supplementary
Supt Superintendent
Surg Surgeon
SWOAC Scottish Woodland Owners Association (Commercial)

TA Territorial Army
TA & VR Assocn Territorial Auxiliary and Volunteer Reserve Association
T & AF Assocn Territorial and Auxiliary Forces Association
T & AVR Territorial & Army Volunteer Reserve
TARO Territorial Army Reserve of Officers
Tas Tasmania
TD Efficiency (Territorial) Decoration
TEng (CEI) Technician Engineer (Council of Engineering Institutions)
Tenn Tennessee (USA)
Tex Texas (USA)
TF Territorial Force
Trin Trinity
TUC Trades Union Congress
Tvl Transvaal

U Unionist
UCLA University of California at Los Angeles (USA)
UDC Urban District Council
UK United Kingdom
UKAEA United Kingdom Atomic Energy Authority
UKLF United Kingdom Land Forces
UMIST University of Manchester Institute of Science and Technology
UN United Nations
UNA United Nations Association

UNESCO United Nations Educational, Scientific and Cultural Organisation
UNICEF United Nations Children's Fund
UNIDO United Nations Industrial Development Organisation
Univ University
UNO United Nations Organisation
UNRRA United Nations Relief and Rehabilitation Administration
UPNI Unionist Party of N Ireland
USAF United States Air Force
USPG United Society for the Propagation of the Gospel
USSR Union of Soviet Socialist Republics
UUUC United Ulster Unionist Coalition

V Vicar, Viscount, Volunteer
VA Lady of the Royal Order of Victoria and Albert
VAD Voluntary Aid Detachment
Va Virginia (USA)
Vt Vermont (USA)
VC Victoria Cross
VD Volunteer and Colonial Auxiliary Forces Officers' Decorations
Ven Venerable
Vet Veterinary
Vic Victoria
VMH Victoria Medal of Honour (Royal Horticultural Society)
Vol Volunteer(s)
VP Vice-President

VRD Royal Naval Volunteer Reserve Officer's Decoration
VUP Vanguard Unionist Party
Vy Viscountcy
W West
WAAF Women's Auxiliary Air Force
WAC(I) Womens' Army Corps, India
Wash Washington (State, USA)
WEU Western European Union
WG Welsh Guards
WHO World Health Organisation
Wing Cdr Wing Commander
Wis Wisconsin (USA)
WOI Warrant Officer Class I
WOII Warrant Officer Class 2
Worcs Worcestershire
WOSB War Office Selection Board
WRAC Women's Royal Army Corps
WRAF Women's Royal Air Force
WRNS Women's Royal Naval Service
WRVS Women's Royal Voluntary Service (formerly WVS)
WS Writer to the Signet
WVa West Virginia (USA)
WVS Women's Voluntary Services
Wyo Wyoming (USA)

Yeo Yeomanry
YMCA Young Men's Christian Association
Yorks Yorkshire
Yr Younger
Yst Youngest
YWCA Young Women's Christian Association

CLUBS REFERRED TO IN THE WORK

with addresses

Ladies' Clubs are marked *

All England Lawn Tennis Wimbledon.
Alpine 55 Charlotte Rd, EC2A 3QT.
American 95 Piccadilly, W1.
Army and Navy 36 Pall Mall, SW1Y 5JN.
Arts 40 Dover St, W1X 3RB.
Arts Theatre 50 Frith St, W1V 5TE.
Athenæum 107 Pall Mall, SW1Y 5ER.
Authors' 40 Dover St, W1X 3RB.

Beefsteak 9 Irving St, WC2 7AT.
Boodle's 28 St James's St, SW1A 1HJ.
Brooks's St James's St, SW1A 1LN.
Buck's 18 Clifford St, W1X 1RG.

Caledonian 9 Halkin St, SW1X 7DR.
Caledonian 32 Abercromby Pl, Edinburgh.
Canning 42 Half Moon St, W1Y 8DS.
Carlton 69 St James's St, SW1A 1PJ.
Cavalry and Guards' 127 Piccadilly, W1V 0PX.
Chelsea Arts 143 Old Church St, SW3 6EB.
City Livery Sion College, Victoria Embankment, EC4Y 0DN.
City of London 19 Old Broad St, EC2N 1DS.
City University 50 Cornhill, EC3V 3PD.
Constitutional c/o The Navy & Military Club, 94 Piccadilly, W1V 0BP.

East India, Devonshire, Sports and Public Schools 16 St James's Square, SW1Y 4LH.
English Speaking Union 37 Charles St, W1.
Europe House 1 Whitehall Place, SW1A 2HA.

Farmers' 3 Whitehall Court, SW1A 2EL.
Flyfishers' 24A Old Burlington St, W1X 1RG.

Garrick 15 Garrick St, WC2E 9AY.
Green Room 9 Adam St, WC2N 6AA.
Groucho 45 Dean St, W1V 5AP.

Hibernian United Service 8 St Stephen's Green North, Dublin.
Highland 39 High St, Inverness.
Hunters 3 London Wall Buildings, EC2M 5PD.
Hurlingham Ranelagh Gdns, SW6 3PR.

Jockey High Street, Newmarket.

Kennel 1-5 Clarges St, W1Y 8AB.
Kildare Street and University 17 St Stephen Green, Dublin 2.

Ladies' Caledonian 29 Queensferry St, Edinburgh 2.
Ladies' VAD 44 Great Cumberland Place, W1.
Lansdowne 9 Fitzmaurice Place, Berkeley Sq, W1X 6JD.
Leander Henley-on-Thames, and Putney, SW.

Manchester 50 Spring Gardens, Manchester.
Marylebone Cricket Club (MCC) St John's Wood, NW8 8QN.

National Liberal Whitehall Place, SW1A 2HE.
Naval 38 Hill St, W1X 8DP.
Naval and Military 94 Piccadilly, W1V 0BP.
New 86 Princes Street, Edinburgh.
New Cavendish 44 Great Cumberland Pl, W1H 8BS.

Oriental Stratford House, Stratford Place, W1N 0ES.

Portland 42 Half Moon St, W1Y 7RD.
Pratt's 14 Park Place, St James's, SW1A 1LP.
Press 76 Shoe Lane, EC4.

Puffin's c/o The Edinburgh Wine Bar, 110 Hanover St, Edinburgh.

Queen's Palliser Road, W Kensington, W14 9EQ.

Reform 104 Pall Mall, SW1 5EW.
Roehampton Roehampton Lane, SW15 5LR.
Royal Air Force 128 Piccadilly, W1V 0PY.
Royal Air Force Reserve 38 Hill St, W1.
Royal Air Force Yacht Hamble, Southampton.
Royal and Ancient St Andrews.
Royal Automobile 89 Pall Mall, SW1Y 5HS.
Royal Burnham Yacht Burnham-on-Crouch.
Royal Channel Islands Yacht Jersey.
Royal Cinque Ports Yacht Waterloo Cres, Dover.
Royal Commonwealth Society 18 Northumberland Avenue, WC2.
Royal Corinthian Yacht Burnham-on-Crouch, Essex.
Royal Dorset Yacht 6 Charlotte Row, Weymouth.
Royal Irish Automobile 55 South Mall, Dublin.
Royal Lymington Yacht Bath Rd, Lymington, Hants.
Royal Munster Yacht Crosshaven, co Cork.
Royal Naval and Royal Albert Yacht Pembroke Road, Portsmouth.
RNVR Now the Naval Club.
Royal Ocean Racing 20 St James's Place, SW1A 1NN.
Royal Over-Seas League Over-Seas House, Park Place, St James's, SW1A 1LR.
Royal Scottish Automobile 11 Blythswood Sq, Glasgow.
Royal Southern Yacht Hamble, Southampton.
Royal Thames Yacht 60 Knightsbridge, SW1X 7LF.
Royal Torbay Yacht Torquay.
Royal Ulster Yacht Bangor, co Down.
Royal Victoria Yacht 91 Fishbourne Lane, Fishbourne, Isle of Wight.
Royal Western Yacht The Hoe, Plymouth.
Royal Yacht Squadron Cowes, Isle of Wight.

St James's 7 Charlotte St, Manchester.
St John House 50 Eaton Place, SW1.
St Stephen's Constitutional 34 Queen Anne's Gate, SW1H 9AB.
Savage 1 Whitehall Place, SW1A 2HD.
Savile 69 Brook Street, W1Y 2ER.
Ski Club of Great Britain 118 Eaton Sq, SW1W 9AF.
Special Forces 8 Herbert Cres, SW1.
Stephen's Green 9 St Stephen's Green North, Dublin.

Thames Rowing Embankment, Putney SW15 1LB.
Travellers' 106 Pall Mall, SW1Y 5EP.
Turf 5 Carlton House Terr, SW1Y 5AQ.

Ulster 48 High St, Belfast.
Ulster Reform 4 Royal Avenue, Belfast BT1 1DA.
United Nursing Services 40 South Street, W1.
United Oxford and Cambridge University 71 Pall Mall, SW1Y 5HD.
United Service and Royal Aero 116 Pall Mall, SW1.
United Sports 4 Whitehall Court, SW1.
University Women's 2 Audley Sq, South Audley St, W1Y 6DB.

Victoria 1 North Court, Great Peter St, SW1P 3LL.
Victory Services 63-79 Seymour St, W2 2HF.

West Indian 4 Whitehall Court, SW1.
Western 32 Royal Exch Sq, Glasgow 1.
White's 37 St James's Street, SW1.
Wig and Pen 229-230 Strand, WC2R 1BA.

Yorkshire 17 Museum St, York.

HER MAJESTY'S OFFICERS OF ARMS

ENGLAND
College of Arms, Queen Victoria Street, London EC4V 4BT

EARL MARSHAL
His Grace the Duke of Norfolk, KG, GCVO, CB, CBE, MC

KINGS OF ARMS
Garter Sir Conrad Marshall John Fisher Swan, KCVO, PhD, FSA
Clarenceux Sir Anthony Richard Wagner, KCB, KCVO, DLitt, FSA
Norroy and Ulster John Philip Brooke Brooke-Little, CVO, FSA

HERALDS
Chester (and Registrar) David Hubert Boothby Chesshyre, LVO, FSA
Windsor Theobald David Mathew
Lancaster Peter Llewellyn Gwynn-Jones
Somerset Thomas Woodcock, FSA
Richmond Patric Laurence Dickinson
York Henry Edgar Paston-Bedingfeld

PURSUIVANTS
Rouge Dragon Timothy Hugh Stewart Duke
Bluemantle Robert John Baptist Noel
Portcullis William George Hunt, TD
Rouge Croix Vacant

HERALDS EXTRAORDINARY
New Zealand Phillippe Patrick O'Shea
Surrey (and Earl Marshal's Secretary) Sir Walter John George Verco, KCVO
Beaumont Francis Sedley Andrus, LVO
Maltravers John Martin Robinson, DPhil, FSA

PURSUIVANT EXTRAORDINARY
Howard Lt Cdr John Henry Bruce Bedells, JP, RN

SCOTLAND
Court of the Lord Lyon, HM New Register House, Edinburgh

THE RT HON THE LORD LYON KING OF ARMS
Sir Malcolm Rognvald Innes of Edingight, KCVO, WS, FSA Scot

HERALDS
Albany John Alexander Spens, RD, WS
Rothesay Sir Crispin Agnew of Lochnaw, Bt
Ross Charles John Burnett, FSA Scot

PURSUIVANTS
Kintyre John Charles Grossmith George, FSA Scot
Unicorn Alastair Lorne Campbell of Airds, yr, FSA Scot
Carrick Mrs Christopher Roads, MVO, FSA Scot

PURSUIVANTS OF EARLS
(Not forming part of Her Majesty's Household and not under the control of the Lord Lyon)
Pursuivants to the Earl of Erroll, the Countess of Mar and the Earl of Crawford

Slains Peter Drummond-Murray of Mastrick (Pursuivant to the Earl of Erroll)
Garioch David Gordon Allen d'Aldecamb Lumsden of Cushnie
(Pursuivant to the Countess of Mar)
Endure Hon Alexander Walter Lindsay (Pursuivant to the Earl of Crawford)

TABLE OF GENERAL PRECEDENCE

PEERS AND PEERESSES (in each degree) rank among themselves in the following order: those created (1) of England, (2) of Scotland, (3) of Great Britain, (4) of Ireland, and (5) of the United Kingdom and of Ireland created since the Union, according to the dates of their respective patents. BARONETS rank among themselves according to the dates of their respective patents *only*. PRECEDENCE OF LADIES is always derived from the father, or husband, except in the case of a Peeress in her own right.

Official precedence, such as that of the Great Officers of State, confers no corresponding precedence on their wives or daughters. The wives and issue of Archbishops and Bishops at present have no special precedence as such.

A Dowager Peeress, or widow of a Baronet, takes precedence of the wife of the incumbent of the title only while remaining a widow.

The children of a living Peer, or Baronet, have precedence above the children of the previous possessor, or possessors, of the title. If the daughter of a Peer marries a Peer she takes her husband's rank, but if she marries the eldest or younger son of a Peer she ranks either according to her own inherent precedence (*i.e.*, as the daughter of her father), or according to that of her husband (*i.e.*, as the wife of the eldest or younger son of a Duke, Marquess, Earl, etc), whichever happens to be the higher, no matter what the courtesy title may be.

Foreign titles of nobility borne by British subjects afford their holders no precedence in the United Kingdom.

PRECEDENCE IN ENGLAND
GENTLEMEN

The Duke of Edinburgh*
The Heir Apparent
The Sovereign's Younger Sons
The Sovereign's Grandsons
The Sovereign's Cousins
Archbishop of Canterbury
Lord High Chancellor
Archbishop of York
Prime Minister
Lord High Treasurer (when existing)
Lord President of the Council
Speaker of the House of Commons
Lord Privy Seal
Ambassadors and High Commissioners
Lord Great Chamberlain† ⎫
Lord High Constable (when existing) ⎬ Above all Peers of their own degree
Earl Marshal ⎪
Lord Steward of the Household ⎪
Lord Chamberlain of the Household ⎭
Master of the Horse
Dukes of England
Dukes of Scotland
Dukes of Great Britain
Dukes of Ireland
Dukes of UK and Ireland since the Union
Eldest Sons of Dukes of the Blood Royal
Marquesses of England
Marquesses of Scotland
Marquesses of Great Britain
Marquesses of Ireland
Marquesses of UK and Ireland since the Union
Eldest Sons of Dukes
Earls of England
Earls of Scotland
Earls of Great Britain
Earls of Ireland
Earls of UK and Ireland since the Union
Younger Sons of Dukes of the Blood Royal
Marquesses' Eldest Sons
Dukes' Younger Sons
Viscounts of England

*By Royal Warrant dated 18 September, 1952, it was declared that HRH the Duke of Edinburgh was henceforth to have Precedence next to HM the Queen, thus having place before the Heir Apparent.
†When in actual performance of official duty.

Viscounts of Scotland
Viscounts of Great Britain
Viscounts of Ireland
Viscounts of UK and Ireland since the Union
Earls' Eldest Sons
Marquesses' Younger Sons
Bishop of London
Bishop of Durham
Bishop of Winchester
Other English Diocesan Bishops according to seniority of consecration
Suffragan Bishops according to seniority of consecration
Secretaries of State, if of Baronial rank
Barons of England
Lords of Parliament, Scotland
Barons of Great Britain
Barons of Ireland
Barons of UK and Ireland since the Union, including Life Barons
Lords Commissioners of the Great Seal (when existing)
Treasurer of the Household
Comptroller of the Household
Vice-Chamberlain of the Household
Secretaries of State, being under Baronial rank
Viscounts' Eldest Sons
Earls' Younger Sons
Barons' Eldest Sons
Knights of the Garter
Privy Counsellors
Chancellor of the Exchequer
Chancellor of the Duchy of Lancaster
Lord Chief Justice of England
Master of the Rolls
President of the Family Division
Vice-Chancellor
Lord Justices of Appeal according to seniority of appointment
Judges of High Court of Justice, according to seniority of appointment
Viscounts' Younger Sons
Barons' Younger Sons
Sons of Life Peers and Lords of Appeal in Ordinary
Baronets, according to date of Patent
Knights of the Thistle*
Knights Grand Cross of the Bath
Knights Grand Commanders of the Star of India
Knights Grand Cross of St Michael and St George
Knights Grand Commanders of the Indian Empire
Knights Grand Cross of the Royal Victorian Order
Knights Grand Cross of the British Empire
Knights Commanders of the Bath
Knights Commanders of the Star of India
Knights Commanders of St Michael and St George
Knights Commanders of the Indian Empire
Knights Commanders of the Royal Victorian Order
Knights Commanders of the British Empire
Knights Bachelor
Circuit Judges in England and Wales, as follows:
(a) Vice-Chancellor of Co Palatine of Lancaster. (b) Circuit Judges who immediately before Jan 1st 1972, held office as Official Referees to Supreme Court (c) Recorder of London. (d) Recorders of Liverpool and Manchester, according to priority of appointment. (e) Common Serjeant. (f) Circuit Judges who immediately before Jan 1st, 1972 held office as Additional Judge of Central Criminal Court, Assistant Judge of the Mayor's and City of London Court, County Court judge, whole time Chm or whole time Dep Chm of courts of quarter sessions for Gtr London, Cheshire, Durham, Kent, and Lancs, according to priority of appointment. (g) Other Circuit Judges according to priority or order of their respective appointments
Companions of the Bath
Companions of the Star of India
Companions of St Michael and St George
Companions of the Indian Empire
Commanders of the Royal Victorian Order

*Knights of the Thistle have no relative precedence accorded to them by statute, but are customarily placed here. In Scotland they follow Knights of the Garter.

Commanders of the British Empire
Companions of the Distinguished Service Order
Lieutenants of the Royal Victorian Order
Officers of the British Empire
Companions of the Imperial Service Order
Eldest Sons of the Younger Sons of Peers
Eldest Sons of Baronets
Eldest Sons of Knights of the Garter
Eldest Sons of Knights of the Thistle*
Eldest Sons of Knights of the Bath§
Eldest Sons of Knights of the Star of India§
Eldest Sons of Knights of St Michael and St George§
Eldest Sons of Knights of the Indian Empire§
Eldest Sons of Knights of the Royal Victorian Order§
Eldest Sons of Knights of the British Empire§
Eldest Sons of Knights Bachelor
Members of the Royal Victorian Order
Members of the British Empire
Younger Sons of Baronets
Younger Sons of Knights
Esquires
Gentlemen

⁂ *Lord-Lieutenants and High Sheriffs of Counties have the first places in their own Counties during office, the Lord-Lieutenant taking precedence of the High Sheriff, but neither is assigned any place on the Official Scale of General Precedence. The Lord-Lieutenant has precedence within his jurisdiction over a Mayor, even within his own Borough, when present officially as the representative of the Crown. On all Municipal occasions, however, whether of business or entertainment, the Mayor should preside, or act as host.*

⁂ *Clergy (other than those mentioned above), Naval, Military and Air Force Officers, Members of the Legal and Medical Professions, Graduates of Universities, and Citizens and Burgesses have no precedence assigned to them, either by statute or by any fixed principle.*

LADIES
THE QUEEN
The Queen Mother
The Princess of Wales
The Duchess of York
The Sovereign's Daughter
The Sovereign's Sister
Wives of the Sovereign's Uncles
Wives of Dukes of the Blood Royal
Wives of Princes of the Blood Royal
The Sovereign's Cousin
Duchesses of England
Duchesses of Scotland
Duchesses of Great Britain
Duchesses of Ireland
Duchesses of UK and Ireland since the Union
Wives of the Eldest Sons of Dukes of the Blood Royal
Marchionesses of England
Marchionesses of Scotland
Marchionesses of Great Britain
Marchionesses of Ireland
Marchionesses of UK and Ireland since the Union
Wives of the Eldest Sons of Dukes
Daughters of Dukes
Countesses of England
Countesses of Scotland
Countesses of Great Britain
Countesses of Ireland
Countesses of UK and Ireland since the Union
Wives of the Younger Sons of Dukes of the Blood Royal
Wives of the Eldest Sons of Marquesses
Daughters of Marquesses
Wives of the Younger Sons of Dukes
Viscountesses of England
Viscountesses of Scotland
Viscountesses of Great Britain
Viscountesses of Ireland
Viscountesses of UK and Ireland since the Union
Wives of the Eldest Sons of Earls
Daughters of Earls
Wives of the Younger Sons of Marquesses
Baronesses of England

Ladies of Parliament, Scotland
Baronesses of Great Britain
Baronesses of Ireland
Baronesses of UK and Ireland since the Union, including Life Baronesses and Wives of Life Barons
Wives of the Eldest Sons of Viscounts
Daughters of Viscounts
Wives of the Younger Sons of Earls
Wives of the Eldest Sons of Barons
Daughters of Barons
Wives of Knights of the Garter
Privy Counsellors (Women)
Wives of the Younger Sons of Viscounts
Wives of the Younger Sons of Barons
Wives of Sons of Life Peers
Wives of Baronets, according to their husband's Patents
Wives of Knights of the Thistle
Dames Grand Cross of the Order of the Bath
Dames Grand Cross of the Order of St Michael and St George
Dames Grand Cross of the Royal Victorian Order
Dames Grand Cross of the British Empire
Wives of Knights Grand Cross of the Bath
Wives of Knights Grand Commanders of the Star of India
Wives of Knights Grand Cross of St Michael and St George
Wives of Knights Grand Commanders of the Indian Empire
Wives of Knights Grand Cross of the Royal Victorian Order
Wives of Knights Grand Cross of the British Empire
Dames Commanders of the Order of the Bath
Dames Commanders of the Order of St Michael and St George
Dames Commanders of the Royal Victorian Order
Dames Commanders of the British Empire
Wives of Knights Commanders of the Bath
Wives of Knights Commanders of the Star of India
Wives of Knights Commanders of St Michael and St George
Wives of Knights Commanders of the Indian Empire
Wives of Knights Commanders of the Royal Victorian Order
Wives of Knights Commanders of the British Empire
Wives of Knights Bachelor
Companions of the Order of the Bath
Companions of the Order of St Michael and St George
Commanders of the Royal Victorian Order
Commanders of the British Empire
Wives of Companions of the Bath
Wives of Companions of the Star of India
Wives of Companions of the St Michael and St George
Wives of Companions of the Indian Empire
Wives of Commanders of the Royal Victorian Order
Wives of Commanders of the British Empire
Wives of Companions of the Distinguished Service Order
Members of the Royal Victorian Order (4th class)
Officers of the British Empire
Wives of Members of the Royal Victorian Order (4th class)
Wives of Officers of the British Empire
Companions of the Imperial Service Order
Wives of Companions of the Imperial Service Order
Wives of the eldest sons of the Younger Sons of Peers
Daughters of the Younger Sons of Peers
Wives of the Eldest Sons of Baronets
Daughters of Baronets
Wives of the Eldest Sons of Knights of the Garter
Wives of the Eldest Sons of Knights
Daughters of Knights
Members of the Royal Victorian Order (5th class)
Members of the British Empire
Wives of Members of the Royal Victorian Order (5th class)
Wives of Members of the British Empire
Wives of the Younger Sons of Baronets
Wives of the Younger Sons of Knights
Wives of Esquires
Wives of Gentlemen

⁂ *Wives of the Clergy, Naval, Military and Air Force Officers, Members of the Legal and Medical Professions, Graduates of Universities, and Citizens and Burgesses have no precedence assigned to them, either by statute or by any fixed principle*

§Eldest sons of Knights Grand Cross take precedence of eldest sons of Knights of the 2nd degree

MAY

PRECEDENCE IN SCOTLAND

GENTLEMEN

The Duke of Edinburgh*
Lord High Commissioner to the General Assembly of
the Church of Scotland (during sitting of General
Assembly)
Duke of Rothesay (The Prince of Wales)
Sovereign's Younger Sons
Sovereign's Cousins
Lord-Lieutenants of Counties†
Lord Provosts of Cities being *ex-officio* Lord-Lieutenants
of Counties of Cities†
Sheriffs Principal†
Lord Chancellor of Great Britain
Moderator of General Assembly of Church of Scotland
(during office)
The Prime Minister
Keeper of the Great Seal of Scotland (the Secretary for
Scotland) (if a Peer)
Keeper of the Privy Seal of Scotland (if a Peer)
Hereditary High Constable of Scotland
Hereditary Master of the Household in Scotland
Dukes (as in English Table)
Eldest sons of Dukes of the Blood Royal
Marquesses (as in English Table)
Eldest Sons of Dukes
Earls (as in English Table)
Younger Sons of Dukes of the Blood Royal
Eldest sons of Marquesses
Younger Sons of Dukes
Keeper of the Great Seal (the Secretary for Scotland) (if
not a Peer)
Keeper of the Privy Seal (if not a Peer)
Lord Justice-General
Lord Clerk Register
Lord Advocate
Lord Justice-Clerk
Viscounts (as in English Table)
Eldest Sons of Earls
Younger Sons of Marquesses
Barons or Lords of Parliament (Scotland) (as in English
Table)
Eldest Sons of Viscounts
Younger Sons of Earls
Eldest Sons of Barons or Lords of Parliament
Knights of the Garter
Knights of the Thistle
Privy Counsellors
Senators of the College of Justice (Lords of Session),
including Chairman of Scottish Land Court
Younger Sons of Viscounts
Younger Sons of Barons or Lords of Parliament
Baronets
Knights Grand Cross and Knights Grand Commanders
of Orders (as in English Table)
Knights Commanders of Orders (as in English Table)
Solicitor-General for Scotland
Lyon King of Arms

*By Royal Warrant dated 18 September 1952, it was
declared that HRH the Duke of Edinburgh was
henceforth to have Precedence next to HM the Queen,
thus having place before the Lord High
Commissioner.
†During term of office, and within their respective
Counties, Cities, and Sheriffdoms.

Sheriffs Principal (when not within own county)‡
Knights Bachelor
Sheriffs
Companions of the Bath
Thence as in English Table

Lord-Lieutenants of Counties and of Counties of Cities
during their term of office and within the limits of
their jurisdiction have precedence before the Sheriffs
Principal having concurrent jurisdiction.

LADIES

The QUEEN
The Queen Mother
Duchess of Rothesay (The Princess of Wales)
Duchess of York
Sovereign's Daughter
Sovereign's Sister
Wives of Sovereign's Uncles
Wives of Dukes of the Blood Royal
Wives of Princes of the Blood Royal
Sovereign's Cousin
Duchesses (as in English Table)
Wives of the Eldest Sons of Dukes of the Blood Royal
Marchionesses (as in English Table)
Wives of Eldest Sons of Dukes
Daughters of Dukes
Wives of Younger Sons of Dukes of the Blood Royal
Wives of Eldest Sons of Marquesses
Daughters of Marquesses
Wives of Younger Sons of Dukes
Countesses (as in English Table)
Viscountesses (as in English Table)
Wives of Eldest Sons of Earls
Daughters of Earls
Wives of Younger Sons of Marquesses
Baronesses, or Ladies of Parliament (Scotland) (as in
English Table)
Wives of Eldest Sons of Viscounts
Daughters of Viscounts
Wives of Younger Sons of Earls
Wives of Eldest Sons of Barons or Lords of Parliament
Daughters of Barons or Lords of Parliament
Wives of Knights of the Garter
Wives of Knights of the Thistle
Privy Counsellors (women)
Wives of Younger Sons of Viscounts
Wives of Younger Sons of Barons
Wives of Baronets
Dames Grand Cross of Orders (as in English Table)
Wives of Knights Grand Cross and Knights Grand
Commanders of Orders (as in English Table)
Dames Commanders of Orders (as in English Tables)
Wives of Knights Commanders of Orders (as in English
Tables)
Wives of Knights Bachelor and Wives of Senators of the
College of Justice (Lords of Session) including the
wife of the Chairman of the Scottish Land Court§
Companions of the Order of the Bath
Thence as in English Tables

‡In Scotland Sheriffs exercise judicial functions.
§Taking precedence among themselves according to the
dates of their husbands' creation as Knights or
appointment as Senators of the College of Justice,
respectively.

FORMS OF ADDRESSING
PERSONS OF TITLE

Ecclesiastical and Services prefixes of rank are written before other titles. A High Officer of State or an official holding an important office, should be addressed by his official title when the communication refers to official business.

Eldest Sons of Dukes, Marquesses, and Earls bearing courtesy titles should not be styled "The Rt Hon" or "The" unless they themselves are Peers or Members of the Privy Council.

Formal conclusions to letters to Peers. The style "I am, my Lord, Your obedient servant" may be used (as applicable), but "Yours faithfully" and "Yours truly" are now more customarily adopted, except for letters to Members of the Royal Family. After the Lambeth Conference 1968 under the guidance of the Archbishop of Canterbury, a simplified form of address for the Clergy of the Church of England was announced.

Commanders, Companions, Officers or Members of any Order and recipients of Decorations and Medals are addressed according to their rank and are entitled to place the recognised initials after their names in the following order:-VC, GC, OM, VA, CI, CH, CB, CSI, CMG, CIE, CVO, CBE, DSO, MVO (4th class), OBE, QSO, ISO, MVO (5th class), MBE, RRC, DSC, MC, DFC, AFC, ARRC, DCM, CGM, GM, DSM, MM, DFM, AFM, SGM, CPM (for Gallantry), QGM, BEM, KPM, KPFSM, QPM, QFSM, CPM (for Meritorious Service), ERD, TD, ED, RD, VRD, AE, CD.

Succession to hereditary titles. By custom those who have succeeded to peerages and baronetcies are not so addressed until after their predecessor's funeral.

New honours. Knights and Dames of Orders of Chivalry may use their style of "Sir" and "Dame" and the appropriate letters after their names, and Knights Bachelor their style of "Sir" immediately their honours have been announced. Other recipients of honours may also use the appropriate letters. Peers may use their titles after the patent of creation has passed the Great Seal, when their respective Peerage titles will be announced.

Full details of Forms of Address are included in *Debrett's Correct Form*.

Air Efficiency Award   The Air Efficiency Award, introduced in 1942 to recognize meritorious Service in the Royal Auxiliary Air Force and the RAFVR, since 1975 including retired officers who have received the Award may place AE after their names.

Albert Medal   In Oct 1971, The Queen approved the exchange by which holders of the Albert Medal (AM) receive the George Cross. *See* George Cross.

Ambassador   (British) LETTERS *Superscription* (When in the country to which he is accredited only) "His Excellency (preceding all other ranks and titles), HM Ambassador to ———." *Commencement*, "Sir" or socially according to rank. *Conclusion*, "I have the honour to be Sir, Your Excellency's obedient servant." PERSONAL ADDRESS, "Your Excellency."

Ambassador's Wife   She is not entitled to the style "Her Excellency" and is referred to and addressed by name or conversationally as the Ambassadress.

Archbishop   LETTERS *Superscription*, "The Most Rev The Lord Archbishop of ———." *Commencement*, "Dear Archbishop." PERSONAL ADDRESS, "Your Grace" or "Archbishop." On retirement from office he reverts to the style of Bishop.

Archbishop's Wife   *As for* Wife of an Esquire.

Archdeacon   LETTERS *Superscription*,   "The Venerable the Archdeacon of (Ely)." *Commencement*, "Dear Archdeacon." The prefix of the Venerable is not retained after retirement unless the title of Archdeacon Emeritus has been conferred.

Baron   LETTERS *Superscription*, "The Right Hon the Lord ———" or socially "The Lord ———." *Commencement*, "My Lord" or socially "Dear Lord ———." PERSONAL ADDRESS, "My Lord."

Baroness   LETTERS *Superscription* if a Baroness in her own right "The Right Hon the Baroness ———," or socially "The Baroness ———," or "The Right Hon the Lady ———," or "The Lady ———." If the wife of a Baron "The Right Hon the Lady ———," or socially "The Lady ———." *Commencement*, "Madam" or socially "Dear Lady ———." PERSONAL ADDRESS, "Madam." (*See also* Baron's Widow).
*If a Baroness in her own right marry a commoner and has issue, the children have the same rank and are addressed as if their father were a Baron.

Baronet   LETTERS *Superscription*, "Sir (Charles) ———Bt." (The abbreviation "Bart." is also sometimes used). *Commencement*, "Sir." PERSONAL ADDRESS, "Sir" or socially "Dear Sir (Charles) Smith" or "Dear Sir (Charles)."

Baronet's Widow   *As for* Baronet's Wife if present baronet is unmarried. For widows where present incumbent of the title is married "Dowager". As to re-marriage, *see* Widows.

Baronet's Wife   LETTERS *Superscription*, if the daughter (i) of a commoner. "Lady ———"; (ii) of a Baron or a Viscount, "The Hon Lady ———"; (iii) of an Earl, a Marquess, or a Duke, "Lady (Emily) ———." *Commencement*, "Madam", or socially, "Dear Lady ———." PERSONAL ADDRESS, "Madam."

Baron's Daughter   LETTERS *Superscription*, if married (i) to an esquire, "The Hon Mrs. ———"; (ii) to a knight, or a baronet, "The Hon Lady ———"; (iii) to the son of a Baron, or Viscount, or to the younger son of an Earl, "The Hon Mrs. ———," or if her husband has a married brother, "The Hon Mrs. (William) ———"; (iv) to the younger son of a Marquess or a Duke, "Lady (Henry) ———." If unmarried, "The Hon (Mary) ———"; (v) to the eldest son of a Duke, Marquess, or Earl by his courtesy title. (*See also* "Duke's Daughter.") *Commencement*, "Madam." PERSONAL ADDRESS, "Madam," or socially if married to an esquire, "Dear Mrs. ———," or according to her husband's rank if a Peer.

Baron's Son   LETTERS *Superscription*, "The Hon (John) ———." *Commencement*, "Sir." PERSONAL ADDRESS, "Sir." or socially, "Dear Mr. ———." *See also* Master of ———.

Baron's Son's Widow   *As for* Baron's Son's Wife, so long as she remains a widow. As to re-marriage, *see* Widows.

Baron's Son's Wife   LETTERS *Superscription*, "The Hon Mrs. (Edward) ———," but if the daughter (i) of a Viscount or Baron, "The Hon Mrs. ———," (ii) of an Earl, a Marquess, or a Duke, "Lady (Ellen)." (*See also* "Duke's Daughter." *Commencement*, "Madam," or socially, if her father is an esquire "Dear Mrs. ———" or according to her father's rank, if a Peer. PERSONAL ADDRESS, "Madam."

Baron's Widow   *As for* Baroness, if present Baron is unmarried. For widows where present incumbent of title is married (*see* Dowager). As to re-marriage, *see* Widows.

Bishop (Diocesan)   LETTERS *Superscription*, "The Rt. Rev. the Lord Bishop of ———." *Commencement*, "Dear Bishop."

Bishop (Commonwealth, Church Overseas, Irish, Scottish   Episcopal,   Suffragan   and   Welsh LETTERS *Superscription*, "The Right Rev the Bishop of ———." Exceptions, The Bishop of Meath (Premier Bishop of Ireland), and the Primus of Scotland, who are styled "Most Rev." *Commencement*, "Dear Bishop."

(Bishop retired)   LETTERS commence "Dear Bishop," and are addressed "The Right Rev (John Smith) DD."

Bishop's Wife   *As for* Wife of Esquire.

Cabinet Ministers   Are   invariably   Privy Counsellors, *see Debrett's Distinguished People of Today*.

Canon LETTERS *Superscription,* "The Rev Canon (John Smith)." *Commencement,* "Dear Canon," or "Dear Canon (Smith)." On retirement from office he reverts to the style of other clergy unless he has been appointed a Canon Emeritus.

Chairman of Scottish Land Court, *As for* Lord of Session.

Circuit Judge *see* Judge, Circuit.

Clergy LETTERS *Superscription,* "The Rev. John ———." *Commencement,* "Dear Mr. (Smith)" or "Dear Father Smith." PERSONAL ADDRESS, "Sir." The Reverend precedes any title: The Rev the Hon. It is *incorrect* to write "The Hon and Rev." or "The Rev. *Mr.*" Christian name or initials should always be shown.

Consuls (British) LETTERS *Superscription,* "———, Esq, HM ('Consul-General,' 'Consul,' or 'Vice-Consul,' as the case may be) ———." In other respects as an Esquire.

Countess LETTERS *Superscription,* "The Rt Hon the Countess of ———," or socially "The Countess of ———." In other respects, as Baroness. (*See also* "Earl's Widow.") *Commencement,* formally "Madam," socially "Dear Lady ———." If a Countess in her own right marries a gentleman of lesser degree than herself, and has issue, the children would have the same rank and are addressed as if their father were an Earl.

Dames of Orders of Chivalry prefix "Dame" to their Christian names, adding the initials "GCB", "GCMG", "GCVO", "GBE", "DCB", "DCMG", "DCVO", or "DBE," as the case may be, after the surname. *Commencement,* formally "Madam" or socially "Dear Dame Edith ———" or "Dear Dame Edith." PERSONAL ADDRESS, "Dame Edith."

Dean LETTERS *Superscription,* "The Very Rev The Dean of ———." *Commencement,* "Dear Dean." PERSONAL ADDRESS, "Sir." The prefix of "The Very Rev." is not retained on retirement,

Degrees Those with doctorates of any faculty may be addressed by the appropriate abbreviations after their names following those of orders, decorations and medals conferred by the Crown. DD should always be included. Masters' and bachelors' degrees are not used in social correspondence. The order of letters signifying doctorates and degrees depends on the individual university which confers them.

Deputy Lieutenant The letters DL are usually put after name. They follow JP.

Divorced Ladies When a lady is divorced she loses any precedence which she gained by marriage. With regard to divorced Peeresses, the College of Arms, acting on an opinion of the Lord Chancellor, has long held that such persons cannot claim the privileges or status of Peeresses which they derived from their husbands. Divorced Peeresses are not summoned to a Coronation as Peeresses. The above remarks apply to ladies who have divorced their husbands as well as to those who have been divorced.

The correct style and description of divorced ladies who have not remarried, nor have taken steps to resume their maiden name with the prefix of Mrs, is as follows:

The former wife of a Peer or courtesy Peer,—— Mary, Viscountess ———.

The former wife of a Baronet or Knight,—— Mary, Lady ———.

The divorced wife of an "Honourable,"—The Hon Mrs John ———, or alternatively she may prefer to be known as Mrs Mary ———.

The divorced wife of a younger son of a Duke or Marquess,—— Lady John ———, or Mrs Mary ———.

The divorced wife of an untitled gentleman,—— Mrs Mary ——— or initials.

Doctorates *See* Degrees.

Dowager Lady is addressed according to her rank. Immediately a peer, or a baronet, marries the widow of the previous incumbent of the titles becomes "The Dowager"; but if there is more than one widow living of previous incumbents of a title, use must be made of the Christian name as a distinction, since the style of Dowager belongs to the senior of the widows for her lifetime. This prefix, however, is very much less used than formerly, use of the Christian name generally being preferred. In such cases ladies are addressed as Right

Hon (Mary) Countess of ———"; or socially as "(Mary), Countess of ———," etc, etc, if a peeress; or, as Ellen, Lady ———," if a Baronet's widow.

Duchess LETTERS *Superscription,* "Her Grace the Duchess of ———," or socially "The Duchess of ———." *Commencement,* formally "Madam," or socially "Dear Duchess of ———" or "Dear Duchess." PERSONAL ADDRESS, "Your Grace." (*See also* Duke's Widow, and for "Duchess of the Blood Royal" *see* Princess.)

Duke LETTERS *Superscription,* "His Grace the Duke of ———" or socially "The Duke of ———." The very formal style of "The Most Noble" is now rarely used. *Commencement,* "My Lord Duke," "Dear Duke of ———," or (more usual) "Dear Duke." PERSONAL ADDRESS, "Your Grace." (For "Duke of the Blood Royal" *see* Prince.)

Duke's Daughter LETTERS *Superscription,* "Lady (Henrietta) ———." *Commencement,* "Madam," or socially "Dear Lady Henrietta ———" or "Dear Lady Henrietta." PERSONAL ADDRESS, "Madam." *If the daughter of a Duke, a Marquess, or an Earl marry a Peer she is addressed according to the rank of her husband. If she marry the eldest son of a Duke, Marquess or Earl she is known by her husband's courtesy title, but if the daughter of a *Duke or Marquess* marry the eldest son of an Earl she is sometimes addressed by the courtesy title of her husband, but she may revert to the style of Lady (Mary) Stavordale, i.e. her own title, followed by her husband's courtesy title. His surname must never be used. This form is invariably used by such ladies after divorce.

Duke's Eldest Son, assumes by courtesy a secondary title of his father, and is addressed personally as if he were a Peer whatever 'The Most Hon.' or 'The Rt Hon.' *Superscription,* "Marquess of ———" (or as title adopted may be).

Duke's Eldest Son's Daughter is by courtesy addressed as if her father were a Peer.

Duke's Eldest Son's Eldest Son assumed by courtesy the third title of his grandfather, and is addressed personally as if he were a peer provided such courtesy title is the title of a Peerage vested in his grandfather. *Superscription,* "The Earl of ———" or "Lord ———" (or as title adopted may be).

Duke's Eldest Son's Younger Son is by courtesy addressed as if his father were a Peer.

Duke's Eldest Son's Widow *As for* Duke's Eldest Son's Wife, so long as she remains a widow. As to re-marriage, *see* Widows.

Duke's Eldest Son's Wife is known by his courtesy title, and is addressed as peeress without "The Most Hon" or "The Rt. Hon."

Duke's Widow *As for* Duchess, if present Duke is unmarried. For widows where present incumbent of title is married *see* Dowager. As to re-marriage, *see* Widows.

Duke's Younger Son LETTERS *Superscription,* "Lord (Robert) ———." *Commencement,* formally "My Lord," or socially "Dear Lord Robert ———," or "Dear Lord Robert." PERSONAL ADDRESS, "My Lord."

Duke's Younger Son's Widow *As for* Duke's Younger Son's Wife. As to re-marriage, *see* Widows.

Duke's Younger Son's Wife LETTERS *Superscriptiion,* "Lady (Thomas) ———." *Commencement,* "Madam," socially "Dear Lady Thomas ———," or "Dear Lady Thomas."

Earl LETTERS *Superscription,* "The Right Hon the Earl of ———," or socially "The Earl of ———." In other respects as Baron.

Earl's Daughter *As for* Duke's Daughter.

Earl's Eldest Son bears by courtesy a lesser (usually the second) title of his father, and is addressed as if he were a Peer but without 'The Rt. Hon.' *Superscription,* "Viscount ———."

Earl's Eldest Son's Daughter is by courtesy addressed as if her father were a Peer.

Earl's Eldest Son's Son is by courtesy addressed as if his father were a Peer. (If a Scottish Earldom, the eldest may be addressed as "The Master of ———." *See* Master.)

Earl's Eldest Son's Widow   *As for* Eldest Son's Wife, so long as she remains a widow. As to re-marriage, *see* Widows.

Earl's Eldest Son's Wife is usually known by his courtesy title (for exception *see* Duke's Daughter), and is addressed personally as if a Peeress but without 'The Rt Hon.'..

Earl's Widow   *As for* Countess if present Earl is unmarried. For widows where present incumbent of the title is married *see* Dowager.

Earl's Wife   *As for* Countess.

Earl's Younger Son   *As for* Baron's Son.

Earl's Younger Son's Widow   *As for* Baron's Son's Widow.

Earl's Younger Son's Wife *As for* Baron's Son's Wife.

Edward Medal   In Oct 1971, The Queen approved the exchange by which holders of the Edward Medal (EM) receive the George Cross. *See* George Cross.

Esquire   LETTERS *Superscription*, "(Edward) ——, Esq." *Commencement*, "Sir." PERSONAL ADDRESS, "Sir."

Esquire's Widow *As for* Esquire's Wife. She continues to use her late husband's christian name unless she re-marries. e.g. Mrs. John Smith *not* Mrs. Mary Smith.

Esquire's Wife   *Superscription* "Mrs. (Egerton)." or "Mrs. (John Egerton)." The former style is applicable if she is the wife of the head of the family, provided that there is no senior widow living, who retains the style for life or until re-marriage. LETTERS *Commencement*, "Madam." PERSONAL ADDRESS, "Madam."

Fire Service Medals   *see* Police Medals.

George Cross   The letters GC take precedence after VC, and before all other honours and decorations.

Governor of a Country within the British Commonwealth is styled "His Excellency" (preceding all other ranks and titles) while actually administering a Government and within its boundary (also an officer administering in his absence). If the Governor has not been knighted he is styled "His Excellency Mr. John Smith." Esquire should not be used with H.E.

Governor-General   The Style of His Excellency precedes all other titles and ranks, and is used while actually administering a Government and within the territory administered. LETTERS *Superscription*, "His Excellency (Sir John) ——, Governor-General of ——" (also an officer administering in his absence). In other respects as for Governor.

Governor-General's Wife   The style of "Her Excellency" has, since 1924, been confined to the wives of the Govs-Gen. of Countries of the Commonwealth within the country administered by her husband.

Governor's Wife   She is not accorded the style of "Her Excellency."

Grandchildren of Peers   If the eldest son of a peer predeceases his father and the grandson succeeds to the peerage held by his grandfather, a Royal Warrant is necessary (when such succession has eventuated) to grant to his younger brothers and his sisters, the "rank, title, place, pre-eminence, and precedence" which would have been due to them if their fathers had survived to inherit the Peerage.

High Commissioner   *Superscription*, "His Excellency (preceding all other ranks, and titles) the High Commissioner for ——." Otherwise as for an Ambassador.

"Honourable" in Commonwealth Countries   The title of "Honourable" is borne *for life* by all Members of the Queen's Privy Council in Canada, Member of the Canadian Senate and Premiers and Lieutenant-Governors of Canadian Provinces, and of the Executive Councils of the Commonwealth of Australia and of the States of Victoria and Tasmania. In Canada the title of "Honourable" is borne *during office* by the following categories of Judges in Canada—Judges of Supreme and Exchequer Courts of Canada the Chief Justices and Judges of the Supreme Courts of Ontario, Nova Scotia, New Brunswick, Alberta and Newfoundland, the Court of Queen's Bench and the Superior Court of Quebec, the Court of Appeal and the Court of Queen's Bench of Manitoba and Saskatchewan, the Court of Appeal and

the Supreme Court of British Columbia, the Supreme Court of Judicature of Prince Edward Island, and the Territorial Courts of NW Territories and Yukon Territory. They are eligible to be personally recommended by the Governor General for Her Majesty's permission to retain the title on retirement. Also in Commonwealth countries all Members of Executive Councils, all Members of Legislative Councils (other than Legislative Councils of Provinces of Canada), and by the Speaker of the Lower House of the Legislatures. It is also used locally by Members of the Executive and Legislative Councils of territories not possessing Responsible Government. The following in Commonwealth Countries are eligible to be recommended to retain the title of "Honourable" on retirement:—Executive Councillors who have served for at least three years as Ministers or one year as Prime Minister; Presidents of Senates and Legislative Councils and Speakers of Legislative Assemblies on quitting office after having served three years in their respective offices; Senators and Members of the Legislative Councils on retirement or resignation after a continuous service of not less than ten years.
(*See also* Judges in Commonwealth and Overseas Territories.)

Invitations   When sent jointly to married couples at their home address, the envelope should always be addressed to the wife.

Judge of City of London Court   As for Circuit Judge.

Judge in Commonwealth and Overseas Territories   The title of "The Right Honourable" is borne for life by the Chief Justice of Canada. The title of "Honourable" during tenure of office is borne by Chief Justices and Judges of the High Court of Australia, and the Supreme Courts of New South Wales, Vic, Queensland, S Aust, W Aust, Tasmania, NZ, and the Judges of the Supreme and Exchequer Courts, and the Chief Justices and Judges of certain other Courts in the provinces of Canada; also such Chief Justices and Judges of those Courts as may be specially permitted to bear it after retirement. *Superscription*, "The Hon the Chief Justice," or "The Hon Mr Justice ——." Judges of the Supreme Courts in Commonwealth Countries are styled "The Honourable."

Judge, Circuit   For the various appointments *see* Table of General Precedence.—LETTERS *Superscription*, "His Honour Judge ——." PERSONAL ADDRESS "Sir," but when on the Bench, "Your Honour." The prefix of "His Honour," but not "Judge," is retained after retirement from office, but personal address as "Judge" or "Judge Brown" may be continued unofficially in retirement.

Judge of High Court   LETTERS *Superscription* (official) "The Hon Mr Justice ——." (private) "Sir John ——." *Commencement*, "Sir." PERSONAL ADDRESS, "Sir," but when on the Bench, "My Lord," or, "Your Lordship." *See also* Lord Chief Justice of England, Master of the Rolls, Lord Justice of Appeal, *and* Lord of Appeal in Ordinary.

Judges of High Court, Ladies   LETTERS *Superscription* (official) "The Hon Mrs. Justice ——" (private) "Dame Mary Smith ——." *Commencement*, "Madam." PERSONAL ADDRESS, "Madam," but when on the Bench "My Lady" or "Your Ladyship."

Justice of the Peace   PERSONAL ADDRESS, When on the Bench, "Your Worship," and in other respects as an Esquire. The letters JP are usually put after name.

Knight Bachelor   LETTERS *Superscription*, "Sir (George) ——." In other respects same as Baronet. The letters KB should not be used.

Knight's Wife   *As for* Baronet's Wife. The wife of a clergyman of the Church of England who receives a Knighthood of an Order of Chivalry but consequently not the accolade, retains the style of "Mrs. ——."

Knight of an Order of Chivalry   *As for* Knight Bachelor, but adding to the superscription the recognised letters of the Order, such as "GCB," or "KCB". Clergymen of the Church of England and Honorary Knights do not receive the accolade, and consequently are addressed by the letters of the Orders but not the prefix "Sir."

Knight's Widow *As for* Knight's Wife so long as she remains a widow. As to remarriage, *see* Widows.

Lady (untitled) *As for* Esquire's wife and widow. Of unmarried daughters, the eldest of the senior generation is styled "Miss (Egerton)." A younger daughter is addressed as "Miss (Helen Egerton)."

Lady Mayoress *As for* Lord Mayor's Wife.

Lieutenant-Governor Isle of Man, Jersey and Guernsey, as for Governor. The style of a Lt-Gov of a Canadian Province is *"The Hon."* (borne for life).

Life Peer He is addressed as for an hereditary peer. *As for* "Baron."

Life Peer's Son *As for* Baron's Son.

Life Peer's Daughter *As for* Baron's Daughter.

Life Peeress *As for* Baroness.

Life Peeress in her own right. She is addressed as for an hereditary peeress. *As for* Baroness.

Lord, in Peerage of Scotland *As for* Baron.

Lord Advocate LETTERS *Superscription,* "The Rt Hon the Lord Advocate," or, "The Rt Hon (George) ———." In other respects as an esquire. (The prefix of Rt Hon. is not retained after retirement from office, unless a Member of the Privy Council.)

Lord Chancellor LETTERS *Superscription,* "The Rt Hon the Lord High Chancellor." In other respects as a peer according to his rank.

Lord Chief Justice LETTERS *Superscription,* "The Lord Chief Justice of England," or "To the Right Hon Lord ———, Lord Chief Justice of England." In other respects as a Judge, except when of noble rank, when he is addressed according to his degree.

Lord High Commissioner to General Assembly of Church of Scotland LETTERS *Superscription,* "To His Grace the Lord High Commissioner." *Commencement,* "Your Grace." PERSONAL ADDRESS, "Your Grace."

Lord Justice Clerk and Lord Justice General *See* Lord of Session, but addressed as "The Rt Hon the Lord Justice Clerk and the Rt Hon the Lord Justice General."

Lord Justice of Appeal LETTERS *Superscription,* "The Right Hon Lord Justice ———," or "To the Right Hon. Sir (Robert) ———." In other respects as a Judge of High Court.

Lord Mayor LETTERS The Lord Mayors of London, York, Belfast, and Cardiff have the privilege of being styled "The Rt Hon."; and permission to use this style has also been granted to the Lord Mayors of Sydney (NSW), Melbourne (Vic.), Adelaide (S. Aust.), Perth (W. Aust.), Brisbane (Queensland), and Hobart (Tasmania). *Superscription,* "The Rt. Hon. the Lord Mayor of ———." or "(Henry ———,) The Rt Hon. Lord Mayor of ———," (The prefix of Right Hon. is not retained after retirement from office. (See also "Lord Provost."). *Commencement,* "My Lord," or less formally, "Dear Lord Mayor." *Superscription* for other Lord Mayors "The Right Worshipful the Lord Mayor of ———."

Lord Mayor's Wife or Lady Mayoress LETTERS *Superscription,* "The Lady Mayoress." In other respects as Knight's or Esquire's wife.

Lord of Appeal-in-Ordinary *See* Baron.

Lord of Session, Scottish LETTERS *Superscription,* "The Hon. Lord ———." In other respects as a Baron, but children have no courtesy styles. *See also* Lord Justice Clerk *and* Lord Justice General.

Lord of Session's Wife or Widow LETTERS *Superscription,* "Lady ———." In other respects as Baron's wife.

Lord Provost LETTERS *Superscription,* The Lord Provosts of Edinburgh and Glasgow are addressed as "The Rt. Hon. the Lord Provost," while in office. The prefix may be placed before the name of the holder in the case of the Lord Provost of Edinburgh. In other respects as a Baron. The Lord Provost of Perth, Dundee and Aberdeen are styled "The Lord Provosts of ———."

Lord Provost's Wife *As for* the wife of an Esquire. The style of Lady Provost is incorrect.

Marchioness LETTERS *Superscription,* "The Most Hon. the Marchioness of ———," or socially, "The Marchioness of ———." In other respects as Baroness. *See also* Marquess's Widow.

Marquess LETTERS *Superscription,* "The Most Hon. the Marquess of ———," or less formally, "The Marquess of ———." In other respects as Baron.

Marquess's Daughter *As for* Duke's Daughter.

Marquess's Eldest Son *As for* Duke's Eldest Son. *Superscription,* "Earl of ———" (or as title adopted may be).

Marquess's Eldest Son's Daughter is by courtesy addressed as if her father were a peer.

Marquess's Eldest Son's Eldest Son *As for* Duke's Eldest Son. *Superscription,* "Viscount ———" (or as title adopted may be).

Marquess's Eldest Son's Younger Son is by courtesy addressed as if his father were a Peer, viz. "The Hon. ———."

Marquess's Eldest Son's Widow *As for* Duke's Eldest Son's Widow.

Marquess's Eldest Son's Wife is known by his courtesy title, and is addressed personally as a peeress without 'The Rt. Hon.'

Marquess's Widow *As for* Marchioness, if present Marquess is unmarried. For widows where present incumbent of title is married *see* Dowager. As to re-marriage, *see* Widows.

Marquess's Younger Son *As for* Duke's Younger Son.

Marquess's Younger Son's Widow *As for* Duke's Younger Son's Wife. As to re-marriage, *see* Widows.

Marquess's Younger Son's Wife *As for* Duke's Younger Son's Wife.

Master This title is borne in the *Peerage of Scotland* by the heir apparent or presumptive of a Peer. It is also used by *courtesy* by the eldest son of a Peer by courtesy. In the case of the heir apparent, "Master" is normally used by the eldest son of a Viscount and Lord, as the heirs of the senior grades of the Peerage normally use a courtesy title. He is styled "The Master of ———" (the appropriate title will be found under the Peerage article). If the heir be a woman, she is officially designated "The Mistress of ———" but this title is seldom used. A Master's wife is styled "The Hon. Mrs. (Donald Campbell)" or according to her husband's rank.

Master of the Rolls LETTERS *Superscription,* "The Right Hon. the Master of the Rolls," or "The Right Hon. ———, according to his rank." *Commencement,* as "Judge." PERSONAL ADDRESS, "Sir," but when on the Bench, "My Lord," or "Your Lordship."

Mayor (whether man or woman) LETTERS *Superscription* (if Mayor of a City), "The Right Worshipful the Mayor of ———" (if a Mayor of a Borough or Town Mayor. "The Worshipful the Mayor of ———." *Commencement,* "Sir (or Madam)." In other respects as an Esquire or an Esquire's Wife. The form "Dear Mr Mayor" may be used for a man or woman.

Members of the Executive and Legislative Councils *See* Honourable in Commonwealth Countries.

Members of Parliament According to rank, but adding the initials "MP" after title or name and honours.

Military Officers *See* "Naval, Military, and Air Force Officers."

Minister of the Crown If a Privy Counsellor, *see* that section or *Debrett's Handbook,* otherwise as Member of Parliament or Grade of Peerage. The social form of "Dear Secretary of State," or "Dear Minister" may be used if the matter concerns the Department.

Moderator of the General Assembly of Church of Scotland By Order in Council the Moderator has precedence in Scotland and at Court functions immediately after Bishops of the Church of England, and while in office is addressed as "Rt. Rev." Former Moderators, "Very Rev."

Naval, Military, and Air Force Officers Professional rank should always precede any titles, *e.g.,* "Adm. (the Right Hon.) the Earl of

————," "Gen. the (Right Hon.) Lord ————," "Air-Marshal Sir ————," but Lieutenants in the Army, and Flying Officers and Pilot Officers in the Air Force are addressed by their social and not their professional rank, e.g., "The Hon. Benjamin ————, Irish Guards," "George ————, Esq, 11th Hussars," or "William ————, Esq., RAF."

Peers and Peeresses by courtesy   As commoners they are not addressed as "Rt. Hon." or "The" but "Viscount (Brown)" or appropriate title.

Police and Fire Service Medals   The letters KPM, KPFSM, QPM, QFSM and CPM are now placed after the name. If the Colonial Police medal were awarded for gallantry the letters CPM are placed before BEM, and if for meritorious service after QFSM (see paragraph 4 at beginning of section).

Prebendary   As for Canon, but substituting the word Prebendary for Canon.

Prime Minister, The   See Privy Counsellors. The social form of "Dear (Mr.) Prime Minister" may be used if the matter concerns his office.

Prince   LETTERS Superscription, (i) the son of a Sovereign "His Royal Highness The Prince (Edward)"; (ii) other Princes "His Royal Highness Prince (Michael of Kent)"; (iii) Duke "His Royal Highness The Duke of (Gloucester)." Commencement, "Sir." Conclusion, "I have the honour to be, Sir, Your Royal Highness's most humble and obedient servant." PERSONAL ADDRESS, "Your Royal Highness," and henceforward as "Sir." (See also Royal Family.)

Princess   LETTERS Superscription, (i) the daughter of a Sovereign "Her Royal Highness The Princess Royal"; (ii) other Princesses "Her Royal Highness Princess (Alexandra), the Hon. Lady Ogilvy"; (iii) Duchess "Her Royal Highness The Duchess of (Kent)." Commencement, "Madam." Conclusion, "I have the honour to be, Madam, Your Royal Highness's most humble and obedient servant." PERSONAL ADDRESS, "Your Royal Highness," and henceforward as "Ma'am." (See also Royal Family.)

Privy Counsellors, also spelt PRIVY COUNCILLORS LETTERS Superscription, "The Right Hon. ————," but if a peer then as such, followed by the letters "PC," after all Orders and Decorations. Commencement, etc, according to the rank of the individual. Privy Counsellors of Northern Ireland, which are no longer created, are entitled to the prefix of Right Hon. and are included in this section. Members of the Privy Council of Canada are entitled to the style of "Hon." for life. Commencement, as for Esquire or appropriate rank.

Privy Counsellors, Wives of   They enjoy no special style or precedence as such.

Provost   As for Dean, but substituting the word Provost for Dean.

Queen Mother   LETTERS Superscription, for formal and state documents, "Her Gracious Majesty Queen Elizabeth The Queen Mother," otherwise "Her Majesty Queen Elizabeth The Queen Mother." Commencement, as for the Queen Regnant. Conclusion, "I have the honour to remain, Madam, Your Majesty's most humble and obedient servant." PERSONAL ADDRESS, as for the Queen Regnant.

Queen Regnant   LETTERS Superscriptions, for formal and state documents, "The Queen's Most Excellent Majesty." otherwise "Her Majesty The Queen," Commencement "Madam," or "May it please your Majesty." Conclusion, "I have the honour to remain

Madam, Your Majesty's most humble and obedient servant." PERSONAL ADDRESS, "Your Majesty," and henceforth as "Ma'am."

Queen's Counsel   LETTERS Superscription, "———— Esq., QC," In other respects as an Esquire. The letters are used after the name by Circuit Judges, but not by High Court Judges.

Rt Honourable   This prefix is borne by Privy Counsellors of Great Britain and Northern Ireland, the Governor General of Canada, and Prime Minister and Chief Justice of Canada for life; by Earls, Viscounts and Barons (except peers by courtesy) their wives and widows; and certain Lord Mayors (see Lord Mayors) and Provosts of Edinburgh and Glasgow (see Lord Provosts) while in office.

Royal Dukes   See Prince.

Royal Family   On Dec 11th, 1917, it was ordained that "The children of any Sovereign of the United Kingdom and the children of the sons of any such Sovereign and the eldest living son of the eldest son of the Prince of Wales, shall have and at all times hold and enjoy the style, title, or attribute of Royal Highness with their titular dignity of Prince or Princess prefixed to their respective Christian names, or with their other titles of honour; and that the grandchildren of the sons of any such Sovereign in the direct male line (save only the eldest living son of the eldest son of the Prince of Wales) shall have the style and title enjoyed by the children of Dukes." (See also Queen Regnant, Queen Mother, Prince, and Princess.)

Rural Deans   No special form of address.

Secretary of State   See Minister of the Crown and Privy Counsellors.

Sovereign, The   See Queen Regnant.

Titles just announced   See paragraph at commencement of this section.

Trinity House, Elder Bretheren of are entitled to be called "Captain," with precedence after Naval Captains.

Victoria Cross   The letters VC take precedence of all other honours and decorations.

Viscount   LETTERS Superscription, "The Right Hon. The Viscount ————," or socially "The Viscount ————." In other respects as Baron.

Viscountess   LETTERS Superscription, "The Right Hon. The Viscountess ————." or socially, "The Viscountess ————." In other respects as Baroness and Baron's widow. (See also Viscount's Widow).

Viscount's Son, and his Wife or Widow   As for Baron's.

Viscount's Daughter   As for Baron's.

Viscount's Widow   As for Viscountess if present Viscount is unmarried. For widows where present incumbent of title is married see Dowager. As to re-marriage, see Widows.

Wales, Prince of   See Prince and Royal Family.

Widows   A Widow who re-marries loses any title or precedence she gained by her previous marriage, and is not recognised as having any claim to bear the title of her deceased husband, e.g.: at a coronation or other State ceremonial, the widow of a peer would not be summoned as a peeress if she had subsequently married a commoner; and, if having espoused a peer of lesser degree than her former husband, she would only be recognised by the rank acquired by her last marriage. (See also Esquire's Widow.)

A GUIDE TO THE WEARING OF
ORDERS, DECORATIONS, MINIATURES AND MEDALS
WITH DRESS OTHER THAN UNIFORM

(By courtesy of The Secretary, Central Chancery of Orders of Knighthood, 1971)

1 Introduction

Members of the various Orders of Chivalry and all persons who have been awarded Decorations and Medals may, should they wish to do so, wear their Insignia on those occasions when the person responsible for a function deems it fitting for Decorations to be worn. This Memorandum gives guidance on the wearing of Orders, Decorations, Miniatures and Medals with Full Evening Dress, Dinner Jacket, Morning Dress, Lounge Suit and Overcoats and supersedes all previous instructions on this subject.

2 Full Evening Dress

(*a*) The occasions when Decorations may be worn can be divided into two categories:

(i) **When The Queen, The Queen Mother or a Member of the Royal Family who is a Royal Highness is present.** The host should ascertain from the Member of the appropriate Household whether it is desired that Decorations should be worn.

(ii) **On all other occasions.** The host should decide whether the nature or importance of the occasion makes it appropriate for Decorations to be worn and then issue instructions on the Invitation Cards.

On occasions when it is desired that Decorations be worn, Invitations should state "Evening Dress—Decorations".

(*b*) The method of wearing Orders, Decorations and Miniatures when "Decorations" are prescribed is as follows:

(i) **Knights of the Garter and Knights of the Thistle; Knights and Dames Grand Cross, Knights Grand Commanders.**
Broad Riband and Badge of the senior British Order, unless it is more appropriate on certain occasions to wear the Riband and Badge of a junior British or Foreign Order.
Up to four Stars may be worn on the left side of the coat or dress.
When wearing more than one Star the precedence of the position of each Star is (looking at the wearer):

Four Stars	*Three Stars*	*Two Stars*
1	1	1
2 3	2 3	2
4		

One neck Badge suspended on a ribbon (miniature width) of the Order is worn under the collar and hanging close up below the tie. Miniature Badges of all Orders and Medals are worn on a medal bar. (The Garter, Thistle, Order of Merit, Crown of India, Companion of Honour and Baronet's Badge are not worn in Miniature.)
Collars are not worn.

(ii) **Knights and Dames Commanders.** Up to four Stars may be worn on the left side of the coat or dress as in (i) above. One neck Badge suspended on a ribbon (miniature width) of the Order is worn under the collar and hanging close up below the tie. Miniature Badges of all Orders, Decorations and Medals are worn on a medal bar. (The Order of Merit, Crown of India, Companion of Honour and Baronet's Badge are not worn in Miniature). The Ladies' Badge is worn on a bow, below the Miniatures, on the left side.

(iii) **Companions and Commanders.** One neck Badge suspended on a ribbon (miniature width) of the Order is worn under the collar and hanging close up below the tie. Miniature Badges of all Orders, Decorations and Medals are worn on a medal bar. (The Order of Merit and Companion of Honour Badge are not worn in Miniature.) The Badges of a Companion of the Distinguished Service Order or Imperial Service Order are worn in Miniature on a medal bar and not as a neck Badge. The Ladies' Badge is worn on a bow, below the Miniatures, on the left side.

(iv) **Officers and Members.** Miniature Badges are worn on a medal bar.

(v) **Order of Merit, Companion of Honour.** These are neck Badges suspended on a ribbon (miniature width) of the Order worn under the collar and hanging close up below the tie. Only one neck Badge may be worn. Miniature Badges of all other Orders, Decorations and Medals are worn on a medal bar. (The Order of Merit and Companions of Honour Badges are not worn in Miniature). The Ladies' Badge is worn on a bow, below the Miniatures, on the left side.

(vi) **Baronet.** This Badge is worn as a neck Badge suspended on a ribbon (miniature width) worn under the collar and hanging close up below the tie. Miniature Badges of all other Orders, Decorations and Medals are worn on a medal bar. (The Baronet's Badge is not worn in Miniature.)

(vii) **Knight Bachelor.** This Badge is worn as an Order Star. Alternatively, in smaller dimensions as a neck Badge suspended on a ribbon (miniature width) worn under the collar and hanging close up below the tie. The Badge is also worn in Miniature on a medal bar in the same manner as Miniature Badges or Orders, Decorations and Medals.

(viii) **The Royal Victorian Chain.** This Chain is worn round the neck by men in place of a neck Badge and is adapted for wear by Ladies on a bow of the ribbon of the Order and worn on the left side above Miniatures.

At all times when "Evening Dress—Decorations" is prescribed, those not in possession of Full Evening Dress may wear a Dinner Jacket with Decorations as described in the next paragraph.

3   Dinner Jacket

(a) On occasions when it is desired that Dinner Jackets (and not Full Evening Dress) with Decorations are to be worn, Invitations should state "Dinner Jacket—Decorations".

In addition to Miniatures, only one Star (or the Badge of a Knight Bachelor) and one neck Badge may be worn.

(b) The method of wearing Orders, Decorations, Miniatures and Medals with a Dinner Jacket is as follows:

(i) **Knights of the Garter, Knights of the Thistle; Knights Grand Cross, Knights Grand Commanders.** One Star is worn on the left breast. Miniature Badges of all Orders, Decorations and Medals are worn on a medal bar. (The Garter, Thistle, Order of Merit, Crown of India, Companion of Honour and Baronet's Badge are not worn in Miniature.) Neither Collar nor Broad Riband and Badge will be worn.

(ii) **Knights Commanders.** One Star is worn on the left breast and one neck Badge suspended on a ribbon (miniature width) of the Order is worn under the collar and hanging close up below the tie. Miniature Badges of all Orders, Decorations and Medals are worn on the medal bar. (The Order of Merit, Crown of India, Companion of Honour and Baronet's Badge are not worn in Miniature.)

(iii) **Companions and Commanders.** One neck Badge suspended on a ribbon (miniature width) of the Order is worn under the collar and hanging close up below the tie. Miniature Badges of all Orders, Decorations and Medals are worn on a medal bar. (The Order of Merit and Companion of Honour Badge are not worn in Miniature.) The Badges of a Companion of the Distinguished Service Order or Imperial Service Order are worn in Miniature on a medal bar and not as a neck Badge.

(iv) **Officers and Members.** Miniature Badges are worn on a medal bar.

(v) **Order of Merit, Companion of Honour.** These are neck Badges suspended on a ribbon (miniature width) of the Order worn under the collar and hanging close up below the tie. Only one neck Badge may be worn. These Badges are not worn in Miniature.

(vi) **Baronet** This Badge is worn as a neck Badge suspended on a ribbon (miniature width) worn under the collar and hanging close up below the tie. This Badge is not worn in Miniature.

(vii) **Knight Bachelor.** This Badge is worn as an Order Star. Alternatively, in smaller dimensions as a neck Badge suspended on a ribbon (miniature width) worn under the collar and hanging close up below the tie. The Badge is also worn in Miniature on a medal bar in the same manner as Miniature Badges or Orders, Decorations and Medals.

(viii) **The Royal Victorian Chain.** The Chain may be worn round the neck in place of a neck Badge.

(c) **Ladies.** The regulations for the wearing of Orders, Decorations and Medals by Ladies are the same as in paragraph 2 (b) (ii) above.

4   Morning Dress

(a) The occasions when Orders, Decorations and Medals are worn with Morning Dress are comparatively rare. Such occasions may include special official public functions, religious Services connected with the Orders of Chivalry or Memorial Services. In each case the sponsor of the function or service should indicate whether the wearing of Decoratons would be appropriate. When Decorations are prescribed with Morning Dress not more than four Stars, one neck Badge and full size Medals should be worn. If a Star and neck Badge are worn they must be of different Orders.

Even so, on all such occasions the wearing of Insignia will be at the discretion of the holder.

(b) The method of wearing Orders, Decorations and Medals, when Decorations with Morning Dress are prescribed, is as follows:

(i) **Knights of the Garter, Knights of the Thistle; Knights and Dames Grand Cross, Knights Grand Commanders.** One Star only is worn on the left breast or, for Ladies, in a corresponding place on the dress. The Broad Riband and Badge is not worn. Collars are only worn with Morning Dress if ordered for a special occasion.

(ii) **Knights and Dames Commanders.** One Star only is worn on the left breast or, for Ladies, in a corresponding place on the dress. The neck Badge of a Knight Commander or the corresponding Badge of a Dame Commander may only be worn if belonging to a second Order. If worn with full-size Medals the Ladies' Badge, on a bow, is worn below the medal bar.

(iii) **Companions and Commanders.** One neck Badge suspended on a ribbon (miniature width) of the Order is worn under the collar. The Badge should hang three quarters of an inch below the tie knot in front of the tie. The Ladies' Badge is worn on a bow on the left side. If worn with full-size Medals the Badge is worn below the medal bar.

(iv) **Officers and Members.** The full-size Badge, whether worn singly or mounted on a medal bar, is worn on the left side in the same manner with civilian dress as with uniform. Companions of the Distinguished Service Order or Imperial Service Order wear their Insignia in this manner and not as a neck decoration. The Ladies' Badge, if worn separately, is worn on a bow on the left side of the dress. If worn with other Medals it is normally mounted on a medal bar and worn in the same manner with civilian dress as with uniform.

(v) **Order of Merit, Companion of Honour.** One neck Badge suspended on a ribbon (miniature width) of the Order is worn under the collar. The Badge should hang three quarters of an inch below the tie knot in front of the tie. The Ladies' Badge is worn on a bow on the left side. If worn with full-size Medals the Badge is worn below the medal bar.

(vi) **Baronet.** This Badge is worn as a neck Badge, suspended on a ribbon (miniature width) under the collar. The Badge should hang three quarters of an inch below the tie knot in front of the tie.

(vii) **Knight Bachelor.** This Badge is worn on the left breast as an Order Star. Alternatively, in smaller dimensions as a neck Badge suspended on a ribbon (miniature width) under the collar. The Badge should hang three quarters of an inch below the tie knot in front of the tie.

(viii) **The Royal Victorian Chain.** The Chain may be worn round the neck in place of a neck Badge.

5 Lounge Suit

(a) There are some occasions, such as Remembrance Sunday Services or Regimental gatherings, at which those attending are requested to wear Medals with lounge suits. On such occasions it is not customary to wear either Broad Ribands with Badges, Stars or the Royal Victorian Chain. One neck badge, suspended on a ribbon (miniature width) of the Order, worn under the collar and hanging close up below the tie knot in front of the tie; full-size Insignia mounted on a medal bar and worn on the left side as with uniform. On all such occasions the wearing of Insignia will be at the discretion of the holder.

(b) Appropriate strips of Ribbon, unattached to any Insiginia, of Orders, Decorations and Medals may be worn on all occasions with all forms of civilian dress at the discretion of the holder. If worn they should be sewn on the coat or dress or on to a medal bar and worn on the left hand side.

6 Overcoats

Full-size Medals may be worn on an overcoat, on the left hand side. No other insignia should be worn.

FOREIGN AND COMMONWEALTH ORDERS

A
Regulations concerning the Acceptance and Wearing by Persons in the Service of the Crown of Orders, Decorations and Medals conferred by Heads or Governments of Foreign States and by Members of the Commonwealth Overseas of which The Queen is not the Head of State.

(United Kingdom and Dependent Territories)

ORDERS AND DECORATIONS

1 No person in the service of the Crown may accept and wear the insignia of any Order or decoration without Her Majesty's permission.

2 Such permission, if granted, will be either
(a) unrestricted, allowing the insignia to be worn on any occasion; or
(b) restricted, allowing the insignia to be worn only on particular occasions associated with the country concerned.
The grant of both unrestricted and restricted permission will be conveyed by letter from Her Majesty's Private Secretary.

3 Full and unrestricted permission is contemplated in the case of Orders conferred:
(a) for distinguished services in saving or attempting to save life.
(b) on any officer in the Royal Navy, Army or Royal Air Force, or any United Kingdom official, in recognition of services (a) while lent to a Commonwealth Government or (b) while lent to a foreign Government provided that he is not in receipt of any emoluments from British public funds during the period of the loan.

4 Restricted permission is particularly contemplated in the case of Orders or decorations conferred in recognition of personal attention to a Head of State, or a member of the Royal Family of a foreign or Commonwealth country, on the occasion of State or official visits by such personages.

5 Restricted permission will also be given for the wearing of insignia of Orders and decorations conferred:
(1) on United Kingdom officials in connection with a State Visit by Her Majesty The Queen;
(2) on members of deputations of British regiments to Heads of States;
(3) on members of Special Missions when The Queen is represented at a Coronation, Wedding, Funeral, or similar occasion; or on any Diplomatic Representative, when specially accredited to represent Her Majesty on such occasions (but not on the members of his Staff).
Permission will *not* be given to:
(a) the Heads or other members of Her Majesty's Diplomatic or Consular establishments abroad, when leaving, whether on transfer or on final retirement;
(b) officers of British naval, military or air squadrons or units visiting foreign countries and Member countries of the Commonwealth overseas, except as provided at (2) above.

6 Applications for The Queen's permission, whether full or restricted, will be submitted to Her Majesty by Her Principal Secretary of State for Foreign and Commonwealth Affairs, who however shall be under no obligation to consider them unless, before the bestowal of the Order or decoration, the country concerned has ascertained through the British Diplomatic Representative there or through its Diplomatic Representative at Her Majesty's Court, that having regard to these Regulations the award would not give rise to any objection.
In no case can applications be considered in respect of Orders conferred more than five years previously, or offered in connection with events so long prior to the proposal to award them.

7 Permission will not be granted for the wearing of the insignia of Orders and decorations conferred otherwise than by the Heads or Governments of States recognised by Her Majesty as such.

MEDALS*

8 Medals with the exceptions specified below, and State decorations not indicating membership of an Order of Chivalry, are subject to the Regulations in the same manner as Orders. If granted, unrestricted permission is given by letter, restricted permission is given by certificate.

9 Medals for saving or attempting to save life whether conferred on behalf of the Head of Government of a foreign or Commonwealth State or by private Life-Saving Societies or Institutions, may be accepted and worn, subject only to the restrictions imposed by the Regulations for the Services concerned.

Applications for Her Majesty's permission to wear other medals conferred by Private Societies or Institutions cannot be entertained.

10 Applications for permission to wear medals gained in warlike operations will not be entertained if the grant of such permission would be at variance with considerations of general policy or public interest.

GENERAL

11 The wives of persons in the service of the Crown are regarded for the purposes of these Regulations as sharing the disabilities of their husbands concerning the acceptance of foreign or Commonwealth awards.

12 Persons employed in the commissioned or salaried service of the Crown on a temporary basis are subject to these Regulations in the same way as those employed on a permanent and pensionable basis.

B

Regulations concerning the Acceptance and Wearing by Persons NOT in the Service of the Crown of Orders, Decorations and Medals conferred by Heads or Governments of Foreign States and by Members of the Commonwealth Overseas of which The Queen is not the Head of State.

(United Kingdom and Dependent Territories)

ORDERS AND DECORATIONS

1 It is the Queen's wish that Her Majesty's subjects should not accept and wear the insignia of any Order or decoration without Her Majesty's permission.

2 Permission, if granted, will allow the insignia to be worn on any occasion, and will be conveyed by letter from Her Majesty's Private Secretary.

3 Permission will not be given:
(a) when considerations of general policy or public interest must be held to preclude it;
(b) in respect of Orders relating to services wholly rendered more than five years before the question of eligibility for permission is raised;
(c) unless authoritative evidence of the award is forthcoming, preferably in the form of a notification through one of the channels prescribed in Rule 4.

4 Applications for The Queen's permission will be submitted to Her Majesty by Her Principal Secretary of State for Foreign and Commonwealth Affairs, who however shall be under no obligation to consider them unless, before the bestowal of the Order, the Government of the foreign or Commonwealth country concerned has ascertained, through the British Diplomatic Representative there or through its Diplomatic Representative at Her Majesty's Court, that having regard to these Regulations the award would not give rise to any objection.

5 Permission will not be granted for the wearing of the insignia of Orders and decorations conferred otherwise than by the Heads or Governments of States recognised by Her Majesty as such.

MEDALS*

6 Medals, with the exceptions specified below, and State decorations not indicating membership of an Order of Chivalry, are subject to the Regulations in the same manner as Orders. No permission is needed for the acceptance of a foreign or Commonwealth medal if it is not designed to be worn.

7 Medals for saving or attempting to save life, whether awarded by the Head or Government of a foreign or Commonwealth State or by private Life-Saving Societies or Institutions, may be accepted and worn without permission; but such medals, if given by private organisations, should be worn on the right breast and not on the left with State awards, and not more than two awards in all should be worn in relation to one act of bravery.
Applications for Her Majesty's permission to wear other medals conferred by Private Societies or Institutions cannot be entertained.

8 Applications for permission to wear foreign or Commonwealth medals gained in warlike operations will not be entertained if the grant of such permission would be at variance with considerations of general policy or public interest.

GENERAL

9 The Regulations shall be regarded as applying, in the same way as to British subjects, to British-protected persons who are such by virtue of their connection with a Protectorate

or Trust Territory administered under the supervision of Her Majesty's Principal Secretary of State for Foreign and Commonwealth Affairs; they may also be regarded as applying in the same manner to British-protected persons who are such by virtue of their connection with a Protected State administered under the supervision of the said Principal Secretary of State, but Orders, decorations and medals conferred upon such British-protected persons by their Rulers are not regarded as falling within the scope of these Regulations.

Foreign and Commonwealth Office
April 1969

*These Regulations do not relate to awards of campaign or commemorative war medals.

LIST OF PRINCIPAL COMMONWEALTH AND FOREIGN ORDERS

Abu Dhabi
ORDER OF AL-NAHAYYAN

Afghanistan
ORDER OF ALMAR-E-A'LA
ORDER OF ALMAR-E-A'LI
ORDER OF SARDAR-E-A'LA
ORDER OF SARDAR-E-A'LI
ORDER OF STOR

Albania
ORDER OF FREEDOM
ORDER OF SKANDERBEG
ORDER OF THE FLAG
ORDER OF THE PARTISAN STAR
ORDER OF THE RED STAR

Argentina
ORDER OF LIBERATOR SAN MARTIN
ORDER OF MAY

Australia
ORDER OF AUSTRALIA

Austria
DECORATION OF HONOUR FOR SERVICES TO
  THE REPUBLIC OF AUSTRIA (Order of Merit)
DECORATION OF HONOUR FOR SCIENCE AND
  THE ARTS

Bahrain
ORDER OF KALIFIAH
ORDER OF BAHRAIN

Belgium
ORDER OF LEOPOLD
ORDER OF THE CROWN OF BELGIUM
ORDER OF LEOPOLD II

Bolivia
ORDER OF THE CONDOR OF THE ANDES

Botswana
PRESIDENTIAL ORDER OF MERITORIOUS
  SERVICE
PRESIDENTIAL ORDER OF HONOUR

Brazil
ORDER OF THE SOUTHERN CROSS
NATIONAL ORDER OF MERIT
ORDER OF RIO BRANCO
ORDER OF MILITARY MERIT
ORDER OF NAVAL MERIT
ORDER OF AERONAUTIC MERIT

Brunei
FAMILY ORDER
ORDER OF PAHLAWAN NEGARA
ORDER OF THE CROWN
STIA NEGARA

Bulgaria
ORDER OF GEORGI DIMITROV
ORDER OF PEOPLE'S REPUBLIC
ORDER OF 9TH SEPTEMBER 1944

ORDER OF PEOPLE'S FREEDOM
ORDER OF THE RED FLAG
ORDER OF THE RED FLAG OF LABOUR
ORDER OF BRAVERY
PEOPLE'S ORDER OF LABOUR
ORDER OF CYRIL AND METHODIUS

Burma
ORDER OF THUDHAMMA THINGAHA
ORDER OF PYIDAUNGSU SITHU THINGAHA

Cambodia
(See KHMER REPUBLIC)

Cameroon Republic
ORDER OF VALOUR
ORDER OF MERIT
ORDER OF CO-OPERATIVE MERIT

Canada
ORDER OF CANADA
ORDER OF MILITARY MERIT

Central African Republic
ORDER OF MERIT

Chile
ORDER OF MERIT
ORDER OF BERNARDO O'HIGGINS

China People's Republic
ORDER OF THE BRILLIANT STAR
ORDER OF THE PRECIOUS TRIPOD
ORDER OF NATIONAL GLORY
ORDER OF BLUE SKY AND WHITE SUN
ORDER OF LOYALTY AND BRAVERY
ORDER OF CLOUD AND BANNER
ORDER OF LOYALTY AND DILIGENCE
ORDER OF REJUVENATION
AIR FORCE ORDER OF GREAT UNITY
AIR FORCE ORDER OF HO-T'U
AIR FORCE ORDER OF THE ANCIENT SYMBOLS
AIR FORCE ORDER OF CH'LEN YUAN

Colombia
ORDER OF BOYACA
ORDER OF SAN CARLOS
ORDER OF ALMIRANTE PADILLA
ORDER OF ANTONIO RICAURTE
ORDER OF GENERAL JOSE MARIA CORDOBA
ORDER OF ANTONIO NARINO
ORDER OF JOSE FERNANDEZ MADRID
ORDER OF ESTRELLA DE LA POLICIA
ORDER OF MERITO INDUSTRIAL

Congo-Brazzaville (People's Republic of the Congo)
ORDER OF CONGOLESE MERIT

Cuba
ORDER OF CARLOS MANUEL DE CESPEDES
ORDER OF CARLOS J. FINLAY
ORDER OF LANUZA
ORDER OF JOSE MARIA HEREDIA
ORDER OF AGRICULTURAL AND INDUSTRIAL
  MERIT
ORDER OF COMMERCIAL MERIT
ORDER OF THE RED CROSS
ORDER OF MILITARY MERIT

ORDER OF NAVAL MERIT
ORDER OF POLITICAL MERIT

Czechoslovakia
ORDER OF MERIT
ORDER OF THE WHITE LION FOR VICTORY
ORDER OF THE WHITE LION
ORDER OF THE GOLD STAR
ORDER OF THE REPUBLIC
ORDER OF SOCIALISM
ORDER OF LABOUR

Denmark
ORDER OF THE ELEPHANT
ORDER OF THE DANNEBROG

Dominican Republic
ORDER OF MERIT OF JUAN PABLO DUARTE
ORDER OF CHRISTOPHER COLUMBUS

Ecuador
ORDER OF MERIT
ORDER OF ABDON CALDERON
ORDER OF SAN LORENZO

Egypt, Arab Republic of
ORDER OF THE NILE
ORDER OF THE REPUBLIC
ORDER OF MERIT
ORDER OF AL KAMAL
ORDER OF AGRICULTURE
ORDER OF SPORTS
ORDER OF COMMERCE AND INDUSTRY
ORDER OF SCIENCES AND ARTS

Finland
ORDER OF THE CROSS OF LIBERTY
ORDER OF THE WHITE ROSE
ORDER OF THE FINNISH LION

France
NATIONAL ORDER OF LEGION OF HONOUR
ORDER OF THE LIBERATION
NATIONAL ORDER OF MERIT
ORDER OF MARITIME MERIT
ORDER OF ACADEMIC PALMS
ORDER OF AGRICULTURAL MERIT
ORDER OF ARTS AND LETTERS

Gabon
ORDER OF EQUATORIAL STAR
ORDER OF THE GABONESE MERIT

Gambia, The
ORDER OF THE REPUBLIC

German Federal Republic
ORDER OF MERIT
ORDER OF MERIT FOR SCIENCE AND THE ARTS

Ghana
ORDER OF THE STAR OF GHANA
ORDER OF THE VOLTA

Greece
ORDER OF THE REDEEMER
ORDER OF THE PHOENIX
ORDER OF BENEVOLENCE
ORDER OF HONOUR

Guatemala
ORDER OF THE QUETZAL
ORDER OF THE REFORMER
ORDER OF MILITARY MERIT

Guyana
ORDER OF EXCELLENCE
ORDER OF SERVICE

Haiti
ORDER OF HONOUR AND OF MERIT
ORDER OF TOUSSAINT L'OUVERTURE

Holland
(see NETHERLANDS)

Holy See
ORDER OF CHRIST
ORDER OF THE GOLDEN SPUR
ORDER OF PIUS
ORDER OF ST. GREGORY THE GREAT
ORDER OF ST. SILVESTER
ORDER OF THE HOLY SEPULCHRE OF
    JERUSALEM

Honduras
ORDER OF MORAZAN

Hungary
ORDER OF HUNGARIAN PEOPLE'S REPUBLIC
ORDER OF THE RED BANNER
ORDER OF THE RED BANNER OF LABOUR
ORDER OF THE RED STAR
ORDER OF LABOUR
ORDER OF MERIT

Iceland
ORDER OF THE FALCON

Iran *(Suspended until further notice)*
ORDER OF PAHLAVI
ORDER OF ARYAMEHR (for ladies)
ORDER OF THE TAJ
ORDER OF HOMAYOON
ORDER OF THE KHORSHID (SUN)
ORDER OF THE HAFT PAYKAR (THE PLEIADES)

Italy
ORDER OF MERIT OF THE REPUBLIC
MILITARY ORDER OF ITALY
ORDER OF THE STAR OF ITALIAN SOLIDARITY
ORDER OF MERIT OF LABOUR

Ivory Coast
NATIONAL ORDER OF IVORY COAST

Jamaica
ORDER OF NATIONAL HERO
ORDER OF MERIT
ORDER OF JAMAICA
ORDER OF DISTINCTION

Japan
SUPREME ORDER OF THE CHRYSANTHEMUM
ORDER OF THE RISING SUN
ORDER OF THE PRECIOUS CROWN
ORDER OF THE SACRED TREASURE
ORDER OF CULTURE

Jordan, Kingdom of
ORDER OF EL HUSSEIN
ORDER OF EL NAHDA
ORDER OF EL KAWKAB
ORDER OF EL ISTIQLAL

Kenya
ORDER OF THE GOLDEN HEARTS
ORDER OF THE BURNING STAR

Khmer Republic
ORDER OF NATIONAL MERIT
ORDER OF MERIT FOR THE SERVANT OF THE
    STATE
ORDER OF THE REPUBLIC
ORDER OF SAHAMETREI

ORDER OF SOWATHARA
ORDER OF MONISARAPHON
ORDER OF INDUSTRIAL MERIT
ORDER OF MERIT FOR THE WORKER

Korea

GRAND ORDER OF MUGUNGHWA
ORDER OF MERIT OF NATIONAL FOUNDATION
ORDER OF MILITARY MERIT
ORDER OF CIVIL MERIT
ORDER OF SERVICE MERIT
ORDER OF DISTINGUISHED DIPLOMATIC
  SERVICE MERIT
ORDERS OF CULTURAL MERIT
ORDERS OF INDUSTRIAL SERVICE MERIT

Kuwait

ORDER OF MUBARAK THE GREAT

Lebanon

ORDER OF MERIT
ORDER OF THE CEDAR

Lesotho

ORDER OF MOSHOESHOE I
ORDER OF LESOTHO
DISTINGUISHED SERVICE ORDER
ORDER OF ACHIEVEMENT

Liberia

ORDER OF THE STAR OF AFRICA
ORDER OF HUMANE AFRICAN REDEMPTION
ORDER OF KNIGHTHOOD OF PIONEERS OF THE
  REPUBLIC
DISTINGUISHED SERVICE ORDER

Libya

ORDER OF COURAGE
ORDER OF THE REPUBLIC

Liechtenstein

ORDER OF MERIT

Luxembourg

ORDER OF THE GOLDEN LION OF HOUSE OF
  NASSAU
ORDER OF ADOLPHE OF NASSAU
ORDER OF THE OAK CROWN
ORDER OF MERIT

Malagasy Republic

NATIONAL ORDER OF THE MALAGASY REPUBLIC
ORDER OF MERIT
ORDER OF AGRICULTURAL MERIT

Malawi

GRAND ORDER OF THE LION

Malaysia

ORDER OF UTAMA KERABAT DI-RAJA (ROYAL
  FAMILY)
ORDER OF MAHKOTA NEGARA (THE CROWN)
ORDER OF PANGKUAN NEGARA (DEFENDER OF
  THE REALM)
ORDER OF SETIA MAHKOTA (THE CROWN)

Johore

ORDER OF DARJAH KARABAT (FAMILY ORDER)
ORDER OF DARJAH MAHKOTA (THE CROWN)

Kedah

ORDER OF DARJAH, KERABAT (FAMILY ORDER)
ORDER OF MERIT

Kelantan

ORDER OF AL-YUNUSI (FAMILY ORDER)
ORDER OF AL-MOHAMMADI (THE CROWN)
ORDER OF AL-ISMAILI (THE LIFE OF THE
  CROWN)
ORDER OF PAHLAWAN YANG AMAT GAGAH
  PERKASA (THE VALOROUS WARRIOR)

Perak

ORDER OF DARJAH KERABAT (FAMILY ORDER)
ORDER OF PADUKA MAHKOTA (THE CROWN)

Perlis

ORDER OF THE ROYAL FAMILY
ORDER OF THE CROWN OF PERLIS

Sabah

ORDER OF KINABALU

Sarawak

ORDER OF THE STAR OF SARAWAK

Selangor

ORDER OF DARJAH KERABAT (FAMILY ORDER)
ORDER OF PADUKA MAHKOTA

Trengganu

ORDER OF DARJAH KERABAT (FAMILY ORDER)
ORDER OF PADUKA MAHKOTA

Maldives

ORDER OF GHAZEE
ORDER OF IZZUDDIN
ORDER OF SHAHEED ALI
ORDER OF IBRAHIM
MILITARY ORDER

Mauritania

ORDER OF THE ISLAMIC REPUBLIC

Mexico

ORDER OF THE AZTEC EAGLE

Monaco

ORDER OF ST. CHARLES
ORDER OF THE CROWN OF MONACO
ORDER OF THE GRIMALDI
ORDER OF CULTURAL MERIT

Morocco

ORDER OF THE SHARIFIAN ALAOUITE HOUSE
ORDER OF RIDA
ORDER OF MOHAMMADI

Nepal

ORDER OF MAHENDRA-MALA
ORDER OF NEPAL-PRATAPA-BHASKARA
ORDER OF TRIBHUBAN - PRAJATANTRA
  SHREEPADA
ORDER OF NEPAL-SHREEPADA
ORDER OF NEPAL-TARA
ORDER OF OM-RAMA-PATTA
ORDER OF TRISHAKTI-PATTA
ORDER OF GORKHA-DAKSHINA-BAHU

Netherlands

MILITARY ORDER OF WILLEM
ORDER OF THE NETHERLANDS LION
ORDER OF ORANGE-NASSAU
ORDER OF THE HOUSE OF ORANGE
ORDER OF THE CROWN OF THE HOUSE OF
  ORANGE
ORDER OF THE GOLDEN ARK

New Zealand

QUEEN'S SERVICE ORDER

Niger
ORDER OF THE REPUBLIC

Nigeria
ORDER OF THE NIGER
ORDER OF THE FEDERAL REPUBLIC

Norway
ORDER OF ST. OLAV

Oman
ORDER OF OMAN
ORDER OF RENAISSANCE

Pakistan
ORDER OF PAKISTAN
ORDER OF SHUJAAT
ORDER OF IMTIAZ
ORDER OF QUAID-I-AZAM
ORDER OF KHIDMAT

Panãma
ORDER OF VASCO NUÑEZ DE BALBOA
ORDER OF MANUEL AMADOR GUERRERO

Paraguay
NATIONAL ORDER OF MERIT

Peru
ORDER OF THE SUN
ORDER OF AYACHUCO
ORDER OF MERIT
ORDER OF AGRICULTURAL MERIT
ORDER OF HIPOLITO UNANUE
ORDER OF PALMAS MAGISTERIALES
ORDER OF DANIEL A. CARRION
ORDER OF MILITARY MERIT
ORDER OF THE PERUVIAN CROSS FOR NAVAL
  MERIT
ORDER OF THE PERUVIAN CROSS FOR
  AERONAUTICAL MERIT
ORDER OF THE PERUVIAN CROSS FOR
  AGRICULTURAL MERIT

Philippines
ORDER OF SIKATUNA
ORDER OF THE GOLDEN HEART
LEGION OF HONOUR

Poland
ORDER OF THE BUILDERS OF PEOPLE'S POLAND
ORDER OF RESTITUTION OF POLAND (ORDER OF
  POLONIA RESTITUTA)
ORDER OF MILITARY VALOUR (ORDER OF
  VIRTURI MILITARI)
ORDER OF THE GRUNWALD CROSS
ORDER OF THE BANNER OF WORK
ORDER OF MERIT OF POLISH PEOPLE'S
  REPUBLIC

Portugal
ORDER OF THE TOWER AND SWORD
ORDER OF CHRIST
ORDER OF AVIZ
ORDER OF ST. JAMES OF THE SWORD
ORDER OF PRINCE HENRY THE NAVIGATOR
ORDER OF THE EMPIRE
ORDER OF PUBLIC INSTRUCTION
ORDER OF BENEMERENCIA
ORDER OF AGRICULTURAL AND INDUSTRIAL
  MERIT
ORDER OF ST MICHAEL OF THE WING

Romania
ORDER OF THE STAR OF THE SOCIALIST
  REPUBLIC
ORDER OF 23RD AUGUST
ORDER OF TUDOR VLADIMIRESCU

ORDER OF MOTHERLAND DEFENCE
ORDER OF SPECIAL SERVICES BROUGHT TO THE
  DEFENCE OF SOCIAL AND STATE SYSTEM
ORDER OF LABOUR
ORDER OF SCIENTIFIC MERIT
ORDER OF CULTURAL MERIT
ORDER OF MILITARY MERIT
ORDER OF SERVICES TO THE SOCIALIST
  MOTHERLAND
ORDER OF SPORTING MERIT

Rwanda
NATIONAL ORDER

San Marino
ORDER OF SAN MARINO
ORDER OF ST. AGATHA

Saudi Arabia
ORDER OF KING ABD AL-AZIZ

Senegal
NATIONAL ORDER OF SENEGAL
ORDER OF MERIT
ORDER OF 20TH OF AUGUST

Singapore
ORDER OF TEMASEK
DISTINGUISHED SERVICE ORDER

Soviet Union
ORDER OF LENIN
ORDER OF OCTOBER REVOLUTION
ORDER OF VICTORY
ORDER OF THE RED BANNER
ORDER OF SUVOROV
ORDER OF USHAKOV
ORDER OF KUTUZOV
ORDER OF NAKHIMOV
ORDER OF BOGDAN KHMELNITSKY
ORDER OF ALEXANDER NEVSKY
ORDER OF THE PATRIOTIC WAR
ORDER OF THE RED BANNER OF LABOUR
ORDER OF THE RED STAR
ORDER OF INSIGNIA OF HONOUR
ORDER OF GLORY
ORDER OF THE HEROINE MOTHER
ORDER OF THE GLORY OF MOTHERHOOD

Spain
ORDER OF THE GOLDEN FLEECE
ORDER OF ISABEL THE CATHOLIC
ORDER OF CARLOS III
ORDER OF MILITARY MERIT
ORDER OF CIVIL MERIT
ORDER OF ALFONSO X THE SABIO
ORDER OF MARIA LUISA (for ladies)

Sudan
ORDER OF HONOUR
ORDER OF THE REPUBLIC
ORDER OF THE TWO NILES
ORDER OF DISTINCTION
ORDER OF BRAVERY
ORDER OF MERIT

Swaziland
ORDER OF KING SOBHUZA II

Sweden
ORDER OF THE SERAPHIM
ORDER OF THE STAR OF THE NORTH
ORDER OF THE SWORD (no longer conferred)
ORDER OF VASA (no longer conferred)

Syria
ORDER OF OMAYYED
ORDER OF MILITARY HONOUR

ORDER OF INSTRUCTION
ORDER OF DEVOTION

Thailand

ORDER OF THE RAJAMITRABHORN
ORDER OF THE ROYAL HOUSE OF CHAKRI
ORDER OF THE NINE GEMS
ORDER OF CHULA CHOM KLAO
ORDER OF RAMA
ORDER OF THE WHITE ELEPHANT
ORDER OF THE CROWN OF THAILAND

Togo

NATIONAL ORDER OF BENIN

Trinidad and Tobago

ORDER OF TRINITY CROSS

Tunisia

ORDER OF THE REPUBLIC
ORDER OF INDEPENDENCE

Union of Soviet Socialist Republics

(see SOVIET UNION)
United States of America

LEGION OF MERIT

Venezuela

ORDER OF THE LIBERATOR
LEGION OF NATIONAL DEFENCE

ORDER OF FRANCISCO DE MIRANDA
ORDER OF MARSHAL SUCRE
ORDER OF GENERAL RAFAEL URDANETA
ORDER OF NAVAL MERIT

Vietnam

NATIONAL ORDER OF VIETNAM
ORDER OF KIM KHANH

Yugoslavia

ORDER OF THE NATIONAL HERO
ORDER OF LIBERTY
ORDER OF THE PARTISAN STAR
ORDER OF NATIONAL LIBERATION
ORDER OF SERVICE TO THE NATION
ORDER OF BROTHERHOOD AND UNITY
ORDER OF BRAVERY
ORDER OF LABOUR

Zaire

ORDER OF THE LEOPARD
ORDER OF THE ZAIRE

Zambia

ORDER OF DISTINGUISHED SERVICE

Independent Sovereign Order

SOVEREIGN MILITARY ORDER OF ST. JOHN OF
JERUSALEM, OF RHODES AND OF MALTA
(COMMONLY KNOWN AS KNIGHTS OF MALTA)

THE ROYAL FAMILY

THE SOVEREIGN'S OFFICIAL NAME

On succession, sovereigns choose the name under which they reign. This is a relatively recent development because until the end of the 17th century very few had more than one christian name. Although the Hanoverian kings all had more than one name they always chose the first as king, but when Queen Victoria, who had been christened Alexandrina Victoria, came to the throne, she chose the second of these. Her eldest son, Prince Albert Edward, also chose the second as Edward VII, because this was popular in English history, there having been three pre-Conquest and six subsequent kings of this name. Although Queen Victoria expressed her wish that all her male descendants should be christened Albert, this was disregarded after the Queen's death. George V and Edward VIII took their first names as kings; but after the Abdication of Edward VIII, he was succeeded by his brother Prince Albert, Duke of York, who chose his last name, reigning as George VI. It is possible, after the Abdication, that he wished to establish continuity with his father, and Albert, a foreign name, had strong associations with the Prince Consort. When the Queen succeeded it was a foregone conclusion that she would select her first name by which she has always been known.

NUMBERING OUR SOVEREIGNS

The first King of England to adopt enumeration on documents was Edward II, but "Henricus III" had appeared on the coins of Henry III, his grandfather. It is strange that, as Henry III particularly venerated Edward the Confessor and rebuilt Westminster Abbey, the three pre-Conquest Kings Edward were not included in the subsequent numbering, especially as William the Conqueror claimed the throne as the legitimate successor to Edward the Confessor.

In Scotland the first king to use numbering was Robert II who, in a preamble of a statute dated 1371-2, is described as "Secundus". The original does not exist but there is a contemporary text in *The Black Book*. He was also so described on 4 April 1373 in the Declaration of the Succession to the Scottish Throne, of which the original document survives. James IV introduced his numbering on coins, and James VI on Royal seals.

There was some difficulty with numbering when the thrones of England and Scotland were united in 1603. As this union did not unite the parliaments, which event did not take place until 1707, the Stuart kings continued the use of individual numbers for each country, such as James VI and VII in Scotland and James I and II in England. William III appeared as William II on the Scottish Royal seals. When Edward VII came to the throne a petition was sent from Scotland, which resulted in their letter boxes bearing ER instead of EVIIR. When the present Queen succeeded there was more intense feeling in Scotland on the matter, and it was announced that any subsequent sovereign whose number was different in England and Scotland would take the higher number, eg if we had another King James he would be known as James VIII instead of James III. The letter boxes in Scotland in the present reign now only bear a representation of the Scottish crown without any initials or numbers.

THE ROYAL SURNAME

The Queen declared in Council on 9 April 1952 that she and her children shall be styled and known as the House and Family of Windsor, as was her father King George VI. In this she followed the example, among others, of the Imperial Houses of Habsburg and Romanov and the Royal House of Orange. All these reigning Houses had passed through the female line to scions of the Houses of Lorraine, Holstein-Gottorp and Mecklenburg-Schwerin respectively. But, although the descendants belonged paternally to these Houses, in each case they continued the original House names of their predecessors in the female line. Despite the Queen's surname having been Mountbatten since her marriage in 1947 as Princess Elizabeth, this was then abandoned two months after her accession on the advice of Sir Winston Churchill.

On 8 February 1960 there was a declaration in Council that descendants of the Queen shall bear the surname of Mountbatten-Windsor, other than those bearing Royal attributes and female descendants who marry into other families. This followed a sermon by the Bishop of Carlisle (the Rt Rev Thomas Bloomer) delivered shortly before Prince Andrew's birth. The Bishop said that he did not like to think that any child born in wedlock should be deprived of his father's family name, a right and privilege that every other legitimate child possessed.

At the same time as the Queen's Declaration, the Press Secretary at Buckingham Palace issued a statement saying that "The Queen has always wanted, without changing the name of the Royal House established by her grandfather, to associate the name of her husband with her own and his descendants. The Queen has had this in mind for a long time and it is close to her heart".

The late Mr E. F. Iwi, an eminent constitutional lawyer, expressed the view that there was a distinction between the House and Family of Windsor collectively and members of the Royal Family as individuals. Consequently when, in 1973, Princess Anne married Captain Mark Phillips, her surname on her marriage certificate was shown as Mountbatten-Windsor. Thus the intention was to give a wider interpretation than that precisely stated in the 1960 Declaration.

A revised Declaration in Council to show that the family name is Mountbatten-Windsor would clarify the matter, because at present it is virtually impossible to be sure whether the Royal name is Windsor or Mountbatten-Windsor. That is, if the double name of Mountbatten-Windsor be adopted for both eventualities, (a) the Queen's descendants in the future who do not have royal styles and who are specially mentioned in the 1960 Declaration, and (b) a "hidden" surname for present members of the Royal Family, now occasionally used in certain official documents, there would no longer be such uncertainty as occurs at the present time. The first clause, which is already covered, will not come into effect until the birth of a great-grandchild to the Queen. The second clause, which is not covered, already occurs. A new Declaration would place the matter beyond all doubt.

It is unnecessary to add Mountbatten as the House name for the present Queen, for the reasons stated below (see Royal Houses).

The House and Family name of Windsor was adopted by King George V in 1917 on the suggestion of his Private Secretary, Lord Stamfordham, after many proposals had been rejected. This was a happy choice, for this Royal Castle has been a seat of the Royal Family since William the Conqueror. The Norman and early Plantagenet kings usually were known by nicknames or names bearing allusions to their parentage, such as William Rufus, Henry Beauclerc and Henry FitzEmpress. From the early 14th century it became customary to style members of the Royal Family by their birthplaces, such as Edward II, who was known as Edward of Caernarvon, Edward III and Henry VI who were known by their birthplace at Windsor and John of Gaunt who was born in Ghent.

It was only with the father of Edward IV that the name of Plantagenet as a surname came into being. The first recorded use of this name was in 1448. The origin goes back to Geoffrey, Count of Anjou, the father of Henry II, who was nicknamed Plantagenet from his adoption of a sprig of flowering broom or "Planta genista" as his badge.

The Tudors take their name from Henry VII's great-grandfather, Maredudd (Meredith) ap Tudur (Tudor). The Welsh did not have surnames at this time, sons bearing the qualification "ap" (meaning 'son of'), followed by their father's christian name. Henry VII's grandfather, Owen Tudor, son of Meredith, was also known sometimes as Owen Meredith. It is interesting to speculate that if the House had been known as Meredith instead of Tudor we would have a collection of "Ye Olde Meredith Tea Rooms".

Both the Bruces and Stewarts had these surnames before their succession to the Scottish throne. The Stewarts were so called from their hereditary office of High Steward of Scotland. In the time of Mary, Queen of Scots the French form of Stuart was first used, but her husband and kinsman, Henry, Lord Darnley, belonged to the Lennox branch of the Stewarts. Their son, James VI and I, also adopted the French spelling.

There has been controversy as to the surname of members of the Houses of Hanover and Saxe-Coburg and Gotha, but since both families were of ruling status before surnames came into being, they did not possess one. Nevertheless dynastic names, as distinct from surnames, came to be used. The House of Hanover is sometimes held to have the dynastic name of Guelph and sometimes that of Este. Their ancestors were lords of Este, a small feudal principality in Lombardy, from the 9th century. On marriage to a Bavarian heiress of the House of Guelph, they moved from Italy to Germany. The children of Queen Victoria's uncle, the Duke of Sussex, by a private marriage, used the name of d'Este, but another uncle, later William IV, was sometimes known as Guelph when he joined the Royal Navy. A former Clarenceux King of Arms dismissed as absurd the idea that the name was Guelph, and Queen Victoria sent a memo to dispute that this name should be used for an exhibition of treasures of the House of Hanover. Perhaps it would be more correct to term them Este-Guelph.

The family of Saxe-Coburg and Gotha has been traced to Thierry (Dietrich) of Buzici, a Thuringian noble living in 950, who founded the line of the Counts of Wettin, a small town on the banks of the river Saale in Saxony. The dynastic name of this family as Wettin thus cannot be regarded as a surname.

The Duke of Edinburgh belongs paternally to the House of Schleswig-Holstein-Sonderburg-Glücksburg which, in turn, is a branch of the House of Oldenburg. When the Duke of Edinburgh became a British subject in 1947, since he possessed no surname, one had to be selected. Old-castle from Oldenburg was suggested, but rejected. Eventually he chose Mountbatten, the anglicised form of his mother's name of Battenberg. The Battenbergs were descended from the Grand Ducal Family of Hesse from a morganatic marriage of Prince Alexander of Hesse and the Rhine to Countess Julie von Hauke, who was created Princess of Battenberg. The Grand Ducal Family of Hesse descends in the male line from Regnier, Count of Hainault, who died in 915. The Percys, Earls of Northumberland belonged to the same male stock until 1670, and the present Duke of Northumberland shares this lineage with Prince Philip in the female line.

ROYAL HOUSES

In common with other monarchies the British Royal Family may be divided into houses or dynasties. Normally the male stock of one dynasty is given an all-embracing house name, such as the House of Stuart and House of Hanover. A difficulty arises with the Plantagenets, of which the first English sovereign was Henry II. The early monarchs were known as Angevins, belonging to the House of Anjou. However, when Henry of Bolingbroke seized the crown from Richard II, he is often considered as the first of the House of Lancaster, although he was Richard's first cousin of the same male line. Similarly, when Edward IV gained the crown from Henry VI, he is often considered to have founded the House of York. This situation also occurred in France with the House of Capet, descended from Hugh Capet who became king in 987. The Capets continued as kings of France, with some interruptions, until Louis Philippe was dethroned in 1848. Even so, for convenience, the monarchs were divided into Houses such as Valois, Bourbon and Orleans.

It is customary for the name of a Royal House to continue until the death of a Queen Regnant born into that Royal House. Thus Queen Mary I, after her marriage to Philip of Spain, remained a member of the House of Tudor, Mary II and Queen Anne belonged to the House of Stuart, and Queen Victoria was the last of the House of Hanover.

TITLES AND PEERAGES OF THE PRINCE OF WALES

The Prince of Wales has inherited other honours in addition to his main title. He is also Earl of Chester and Duke of Cornwall in the Peerage of England, and Duke of Rothesay and Earl of Carrick in the Peerage of Scotland. His other Scottish titles are Baron of Renfrew, Lord of the Isles and Prince and Great Steward of Scotland.

Only two of these dignities have to be specially created for the heir apparent, that of Prince of Wales and Earl of Chester. Prince Charles received these in 1958 when he automatically became a Knight Companion of the Garter as a constituent part of the Order, but he was not invested and installed as Prince and Earl at Caernarvon Castle until 1968. The remainder of the titles passed to him, as heir apparent, the moment his mother succeeded as Queen. The first Duke of Cornwall (and the first instance of the creation of a duke in England) was Edward the Black Prince, son and heir of King Edward III. The dukedom was created "with remainder to his heirs being Kings of England" and Henry VI expressly stated that his first begotten son at the time of his birth was Duke of Cornwall. Thereafter, heirs apparent who are also the Sovereign's sons become Duke of Cornwall either at birth or immediately their parent succeeds to the Crown. The only heir apparent not to become Duke of Cornwall was George III, who was not "filius regis", being a grandson of his predecessor, George II.

The first Duke of Rothesay was David, eldest son of Robert III, King of Scots, who received this peerage in 1398. Rothesay, and Albany (which was given to his uncle), were the first dukes to be created in Scotland. Although the charter conferring the dukedom of Rothesay is not extant, Winton, a contemporary, stated that the Duke of Rothesay was to

> "haif yat Tityl ay.-
> And efter hym (as yet was done
> All tym) ye Kingis eldeste sone
> and his air suld be alway,
> Be titil, Duke cald of Rothesay."

It was confirmed by Act of Parliament in 1469 that the heir apparent and he alone, holds the title of Duke of Rothesay. When the Prince of Wales is in Scotland he is termed Duke of Rothesay. Since the union in 1603 of the Crowns of England and Scotland, the limitation of the Dukedom of Rothesay being identical to that of Cornwall, they descend together, as do the other Scottish honours.

The Earldom of Carrick was already in existence in about 1186 when Duncan, descendant of the Lords of Galloway, obtained from King William the Lion the district of Carrick. His grand-

BADMINTON SCHOOL BRISTOL

I.A.P.S. 5-11
GSA 11-18

Boarding and Day
360 Girls

Headmaster: C.J.T. Gould, M.A.

Most girls get 9 or 10 G.C.E.'s and 3 'A' Levels. 90% of the Sixth Form go on to degree courses, including Oxford and Cambridge. The school encourages a mature and friendly atmosphere and has a strong tradition in Music. Excellence and all round ability are equally valued.

Entrance and Scholarship Examinations

These take place in late January, with awards of up to half free for girls aged 11, 12 and 13 or entering the Sixth Form, and music scholarships at any age.

For further details please contact the Headmaster's Secretary:
BRISTOL BS9 3BA. TELEPHONE: (0117) 962 3141
Badminton is a registered charitable Trust providing education for children

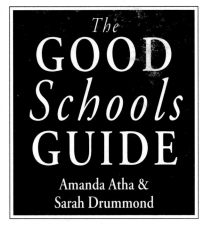

The "NOT FORGOTTEN" Association helps Ex-Service Disabled from all the Wars

There are almost 300,000 disabled ex-service men and women in this country. They have been injured in conflicts from 1914 to the present day.

Many of them earned decorations. Most had terrible experiences which they will never be able to forget. They all went to war knowing the risks, yet they accepted these courageously so that the rest of us could enjoy peace and freedom. Surely we owe them a debt of honour for the sacrifices they made.

Now most of them are elderly and often frail. Their essential needs may be provided for, but what we at the "Not Forgotten" Association do is to give them some of the "extras" which most of us take for granted - like television, holidays, outings, entertainments. In short, something to look forward to - something to make life worth living.

Please help us to make them feel that they matter - that they are "Not Forgotten".

Call us on (0171) 235 1951

Or write to
**The "NOT FORGOTTEN" Association
5 Grosvenor Crescent,
London SW1X 7EH**

Patron HRH the Duchess of Kent GCVO

Founded 1920

Registered Charity No 229666

CHARITIES

AN INSTRUMENT
THAT CAN IMPROVE THE QUALITY
OF LIFE FOR DEAF PEOPLE

In the right hands, the humble ballpoint pen can improve the quality of life for deaf people. It can provide residential care and vocational training for deaf people with special needs; communication support, such as sign language interpreters and lipspeakers; specialist telephone services and assistive products.

Please use it now to perform a sensitive operation. Sign your Will and leave a legacy to The Royal National Institute for Deaf People.

RNID

THE ROYAL NATIONAL INSTITUTE FOR DEAF PEOPLE

105 Gower Street London WC1E 6AH
Telephone 0171 387 8033 (Voice)   0171 383 3154 (Text)   0171 388 2346 (Fax)

QUALITY SERVICES FOR DEAF PEOPLE

Registered Charity No. 207720

THE GENERAL WELFARE OF THE BLIND

REGISTERED OFFICE
ASHBURTON GROVE, HOLLOWAY, LONDON N7 7DW
Telephone: 0171 609 0206/1238
Fax: 0171 607 4425

PRESIDENT H.R.H. THE DUCHESS OF GLOUCESTER

Dear Sir or Madam

Have you ever thought about work?

Yes, of course you have. It plays such an important place in everyone's life.

Now imagine if you were blind.

Blindness can creep up on you at anytime in life. You wouldn't be able to read this letter.

What would not being able to earn a living really mean?

Earning potential, but also the loss of your <u>independence; self-confidence; self-esteem</u> and <u>comradeship.</u>

THERE IS HOPE.

WE BELIEVE THAT DISABLED PEOPLE SHOULD BE GIVEN THE OPPORTUNITY TO LIVE LIFE AS FULLY AS POSSIBLE AND TO PLAY THEIR PART IN OUR SOCIETY.

Our aim is to provide employment for blind, partially sighted and disabled people, some of whom are severely disabled.

Help them to hold their own in life.

You too can contribute.

You can send a donation to "The General Welfare of the Blind". Or alternatively you can call for more information.

Thank you.

Yours sincerely

Brigitte Philippe

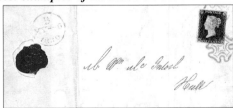

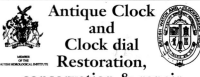

THIS IS JAYNE
a Kidney machine keeps her alive

With your help, The BKPA
make her life worth living

ANTIQUES,
FINE ARTS
AND
SPECIALIST SHOPS

daughter, who was Countess of Carrick in her own right, married Robert Bruce, and their son Robert Bruce, in 1306, became King of Scots as Robert I. Some of the later Earls of Carrick were heirs apparent, and by Act of Parliament in 1469 it was declared that the Earldom should be annexed forever to the first born prince of the King of Scots. Under the same Act of Parliament, the Barony of Renfrew was also settled upon him. The heir apparent is also Lord of the Isles. The Macdonalds were Lords of the Isles (the Irish annalists styled them kings), but after forfeitures, James IV, King of Scots annexed the Lordship of the Isles to the Crown, and from that time onwards the heirs to the Scottish throne and their successors have always held the title.

Walter Fitz Alan, forebear of the Stewarts, was High Steward of Scotland in the reigns of David I and Malcolm IV. In 1371 Robert, 7th High Steward of Scotland, succeeded his half-uncle, David II, as Robert II, the first Stewart king. The hereditary office of High Steward was confirmed by Act of Parliament in 1469 on the first born prince of the King of Scots forever.

PEERAGES OF OTHER MEMBERS OF THE ROYAL FAMILY

Once a peerage is conferred upon a member of the Royal Family and becomes extinct, it is then reserved for a later prince and is not available to a subject. The Dukedom of Edinburgh, conferred in 1947 upon Prince Philip, was first bestowed (spelt "Edenburgh" in the patent) on Frederick Lewis, grandson of George I, but a year later, after his father succeeded as George II,he was created Prince of Wales. This peerage passed to his son, the future King George III, on his death before being merged into the Crown. George III conferred the title, together with the Dukedom of Gloucester, upon his brother Prince William Henry, but as Gloucester was the senior title, this was normally used. Both became extinct in 1834 on the death of his son, nicknamed "Silly Billy". Queen Victoria made her son, Prince Alfred, Duke of Edinburgh, who like Prince Philip, was a "Sailor Prince". His Dukedom became extinct in 1900, and was not conferred again until it was given to the present Duke.

The Dukedom of York has usually been conferred upon the second son of our sovereigns since Edward IV in 1474 bestowed the title on his younger son, Richard. This was the younger of the Princes in the Tower, whose fate has exercised the credulity of historians ever since. Before this, in 1385, Edmund of Langley, a son of Edward III, became Duke of York and was ancestor of the House of York, who warred with Lancaster in the Wars of the Roses. The victor, Edward, Duke of York, who had only succeeded for two months, seized the Crown at the age of eighteen, becoming Edward IV.

Three second sons who became Duke of York, and ultimately kings, were Henry VIII (son of Henry VII), Charles I (son of James I), and James II (son of Charles I). With George I a slight difference in this pattern occurred when he gave it in 1716 to his youngest brother Ernest Augustus, in conjunction with the Dukedom of Albany; and the next two Hanoverian dukes likewise received both creations. The first was Prince Edward Augustus, brother of George III, who received the title in 1760, but he died unmarried two years later. George III later returned to the traditional style by giving it to his second son, Prince Frederick, later Commander-in-Chief. He was involved in the scandal over the selling of commissions, a racket organised by his mistress, Mary Anne Clarke, but in 1811, two years after his resignation, he was restored to the office which he held for the rest of his life. He is best known from the nursery rhyme "The Grand Old Duke of York". Bonnie Prince Charlie's younger brother, Henry, held the Jacobite Dukedom of York, and was generally known as Cardinal York.

Queen Victoria did not approve of her Hanoverian uncles' reputation, and departed from tradition by creating her second son Prince Alfred, Duke of Edinburgh. As she reached such a great age, she had two grandsons in the direct line who were adults. She reluctantly agreed to bestow the title of Duke of York on the younger of these, the future King George V, mainly under pressure from his father the Prince of Wales. In 1920, Prince Albert, second son of George V, became Duke of York, and the tradition was perpetuated when the Queen bestowed the title upon her second son, Prince Andrew, in 1986.

Like York, Gloucester has always been a Royal Dukedom. In 1385 the same day that the Dukedom of York was first created, Thomas of Woodstock, the youngest son of Edward III, was created Duke of Gloucester by his nephew Richard II. Subsequent Dukes were the Lancastrian Humphrey, "the Good Duke", brother of Henry V, and the Yorkist Richard, later Richard III. Charles I's youngest son, Henry, had the title, but he died unmarried of smallpox very shortly after the Restoration. The last Stuart creation was the pathetic little son of Anne, her only child to survive infancy. Although declared Duke of Gloucester, he was never formally so created, and died at the age of eleven before his mother became Queen.

After George III's brother, Prince William, became Duke of Gloucester and Albany, which died out with his son, the title was not re-created until 1928, when George V bestowed it upon his third son, Prince Henry. The Dukedom is now possessed by his son, Prince Richard.

Unlike these other Dukedoms, Kent was originally non-Royal, borne by the Greys, until this became extinct in 1797. Two years later, George III then gave it to his fourth son, Prince Edward, father of Queen Victoria, but it became extinct in 1820 on his death. The Dukedom was next conferred by George V in 1934 upon Prince George, his fourth son. His son, the present Duke, succeeded in 1942 following his father's death on active service.

Other titles reserved for members of the Royal Family include the Dukedom of Clarence, derived from the Honour of Clare in Suffolk. The first was Lionel of Antwerp, third son of Edward III, from whom the Yorkists eventually derived their claim to the throne. Some of the Dukes of Clarence have been unfortunate. George, brother of Edward IV and Richard III, was murdered after being found guilty of high treason. The method used, according to popular tradition, was drowning after being pushed headfirst into a butt of malmsey. The last Duke of Clarence, elder son of the future Edward VII, died unmarried of pneumonia at the age of twenty-eight, a few weeks after his engagement to Princess Mary of Teck, who later married his brother.

Both the Dukedoms of Cumberland and Albany were attainted as a result of their holders, being Germans, taking up arms against Britain in the First World War. Ernest, Duke of Cumberland, the most unpopular of Queen Victoria's uncles, succeeded William IV as King of Hanover, where Salic law operated. The Dukedom of Albany, bestowed on Queen Victoria's youngest son, passed to his son, who, as a boy, succeeded as Duke of Saxe-Coburg and Gotha. Since both peerages were merely suspended, they cannot be re-conferred, because theoretically they could be restored by an Act of Parliament. The most notorious Duke of Cumberland was William Augustus, second son of George II, who was in command of the Royal troops at the battle of Culloden, and earned the name of "Butcher Cumberland" as a result of his severe repression in the Highlands.

The Dukedom of Kendal was twice conferred upon sons of James II who died in infancy, and the Dukedoms of Sussex and Connaught were each conferred once: Sussex on Queen Victoria's uncle, and Connaught upon her third son. The former died out on the Duke's death, and Connaught on the death of the second Duke in 1943 in Canada. The Dukedom of Cambridge was occasionally brought into use at previous times, the last creation in 1801 was to a son of George III. This died out with his son, formerly the Commander-in-Chief, at his death in 1904, but was re-conferred as a Marquessate, to his maternal nephew the Duke of Teck upon relinquishing his German title, and became extinct on the death of the 2nd Marquess in 1981.

Another Royal Dukedom was that of Lancaster. The second Duke, but the best known, was John of Gaunt, made more famous by Shakespeare as "Time-honoured Lancaster" than as the hated uncle of the King against whom the fury of the Peasants' Revolt was directed. When Henry Duke of Lancaster dethroned, and later murdered, Richard II, thereby becoming the first Lancastrian king, the Dukedom merged in the Crown and has never been re-created, although the sovereign always succeeds to the Duchy of Lancaster. The loyal toast in the North remains "The Queen, Duke of Lancaster".

It has long been the custom for Royal scions to receive more than one peerage. The "Butcher" Duke of Cumberland, for example, was also Marquess of Berkhamsted, Earl of Kensington, Viscount Trematon and Baron of the Isle of Alderney.

It is possible that Prince Edward one day will receive the Dukedom of Sussex. Of the others, Connaught is a province of the Republic of Ireland and therefore unlikely to be revived. Kendal has somewhat unfortunate connotations, as the last time the Dukedom was conferred it was upon an unpopular mistress of George I, vulgarly called "the Maypole" from her extremely emaciated figure; and Clarence has an unfortunate history.

Some peerages were selected conjointly from England, Scotland and Ireland, such as the lesser peerages of the Duke of Kent, which are the Earldom of St Andrews and Barony of Downpatrick. The second senior peerage is thus available for use as a courtesy title for the eldest son and heir when the holder ceases to use Royal styles and titles. Otherwise heirs to Royal peerages have not used courtesy peerages; thus the late Prince William of Gloucester was never known as Earl of Ulster, but this was not always so, Edward IV being known as Earl of March when his father was Duke of York.

THE TITLES AND STYLES OF MEMBERS OF THE ROYAL FAMILY

King George V, by Letters Patent issued on 30 October 1917, declared that henceforward only the children, the children of sons of the Sovereign, and the eldest living son of the eldest son of the Prince of Wales, would be entitled to the style of Royal Highness and the titles of Prince and Princess. This meant that more distant descendants of the Royal Family had to give up Royal styles, thus HH Prince Alastair of Connaught (later the 2nd Duke of Connaught), who was a great-grandson of Queen Victoria, then became known as the Earl of Macduff, a courtesy title belonging to his mother, who was Duchess of Fife in her own right.

On the day before the Duke of Edinburgh's marriage to the present Queen, he was created

Royal Highness, but the children of the Dukes of Gloucester and Kent, as great-grandchildren of a sovereign, do not have Royal attributes. The sons and heirs of the Dukes of Gloucester and Kent therefore bear respectively the courtesy titles of Earl of Ulster and Earl of St Andrews, in the same way as the heirs of other dukes. The younger son and the daughter of the Duke of Kent are known as Lord Nicholas Windsor and Lady Helen Taylor, and the son and daughter of Prince Michael of Kent are known as Lord Frederick and Lady Gabriella Windsor, following the styles for younger sons and daughters of dukes as prescribed by further Letters Patent of 11 Dec 1917.

There has only been one example of children of a Princess and her non-Royal British husband receiving royal titles. When King Edward VII declared his eldest daughter to be Princess Royal, he instructed his Garter King of Arms to declare her two daughters Princesses. Garter is alleged to have told the King that this was impossible as there was no precedent. The King merely told him, "Do it." Accordingly, the two daughters, subsequently Princess Arthur of Connaught and the Countess of Southesk, were gazetted Princesses with the style of Highness and precedence immediately after all members of the Royal Family bearing the style of Royal Highness. The elder sister attained the style of Royal Highness on her marriage, but the younger ceased to use the style and title on her marriage without any specific declaration being made. It is believed this was to comply with the wishes of King George V, who had not approved of his father's action.

The case has never previously arisen when a grandson of a Sovereign has been untitled. Peter Phillips, the Queen's first grandchild, has no title, since neither of his parents has received a peerage, and there is no title to be passed on to their children. If a warrant of precedence could be given raising him to the rank of a son of a duke or marquess, Peter Phillips would at least be in the same position as the son of Prince and Princess Michael of Kent, by having the courtesy style of "Lord" before his name. There have been examples of such precedence being granted by previous sovereigns, such as Lady Katherine Brandram, previously Princess of Greece and Denmark, and Lady Valda Machell, formerly Countess Victoria Gleichen, daughter of Prince Victor of Hohenlohe-Langenburg and granddaughter of Admiral of the Fleet the Hon Sir George Francis Seymour. Brothers and sisters of peers, whose fathers never succeeded, may be given precedence as if their fathers had been peers.

THE ACT OF SETTLEMENT

The Act of Settlement, under which the Queen reigns, was passed in 1701 in the reign of William III. The Act was designed to ensure a Protestant succession to the throne. As the King was childless, the throne was to pass on his death to Queen Anne, whose only child to survive infancy had recently died. Then, in default of any issue, to the next Protestant descendant of the Royal House, the Electress Sophia of Hanover, niece of Charles I, and her descendants, being Protestants. This cut out the Roman Catholic descendants of James II. As Sophia predeceased Queen Anne, the Crown passed in 1714 to Sophia's son George I, first of the House of Hanover to ascend to the Throne.

The Act provides for a perpetual Protestant succession by debarring any person in line to the throne from reigning if he or she be a Roman Catholic or has married one. This question arose on the marriage of Prince Michael of Kent when he lost his right of succession through his marriage to a Roman Catholic, but according to the announcement from Buckingham Palace, their children and descendants remain in succession, provided that they are in communion with the Church of England.

THE ROYAL MARRIAGES ACT

The Royal Marriages Act was passed in 1772 following the marriages of the Dukes of Cumberland and Gloucester, which were considered unsuitable by their brother King George III. The Act provides that any descendant of George II, both male and female, is required to obtain the consent of the Sovereign, signified under the Great Seal and declared in Council, before any marriage is contracted. This does not apply to princesses, and their descendants, who marry into foreign families.

The Act also contains a proviso that princes and princesses, over the age of 25, are permitted to give notice to the Privy Council twelve calendar months before contracting such a marriage without the consent of the Sovereign. So far, this clause has never been utilised.

There have been marriages contracted by members of the Royal Family, for which the Sovereign's permission was not obtained, such as those of the Prince of Wales (later George IV) to Mrs Fitzherbert, and the marriages of his brother the Duke of Sussex and his nephew the Duke of Cambridge. These marriages, though presumably canonically valid, are legally null and void. There has been more than one attempt to repeal the Royal Marriages Act, and in 1967 a young constitutional lawyer, the late Mr Charles Farran, detected a flaw in it. He held that those descendants of princesses who married into foreign families who were therefore covered by the exemption clause, sometimes came to Britain to marry descendants of George II, who needed to seek permission to marry under the Act. It therefore followed that descendants of these marriages are also exempted, which was not foreseen when the Act was drawn up in 1772. Thus Princess Anne and Princess Alexandra, for example, are descended from Queen Alexandra who was herself descended from George II in the female line. Nearly all the Members of the Royal Family now fall into the category of being exempted.

THE SOVEREIGN, ROYAL FAMILY, PEERAGE, BARONETAGE AND OTHER DIGNITIES AND RANKS

Royal Crown as heraldically depicted

THE SOVEREIGN

THE SOVEREIGN is first in honour, dignity, and in power—and the seat and fountain of all three, possessing, according to Camden,

"Many rights and privileges peculiar to majesty termed by the learned lawyer, *sacra sacrorum*, that is, sacred and individual, or inseparable because they cannot be severed; and the ordinary royal prerogatives, termed the flowers of his crown, in which respect they affirm that the regal material crown is adorned with flowers. Some of these are held by positive or written law, others which, by right of custom, by a silent consent of all men without law, prescription of time has allowed, the king justly enjoys."

The Crown is held under the Act of Settlement (12 and 13 William III, cap. 2), the wording of which, with reference to succession is:—

"For default of issue of the said Princess Ann and of His Majesty respectively the crown and regall government of the said kingdoms of England France and Ireland and of the dominions thereunto belonging with the royall state and dignity of the said realms and all honours stiles and regalties prerogatives powers jurisdictions and authorities to the same belonging and appertaining shall be remain and continue to the said most excellent Princess Sophia (of Hanover) and the heirs of her body being Protestants."

Under the Statute of Westminster, 1931, any alteration in the law touching the Succession to the Throne or the Royal Style and Titles shall require the assent of the Parliaments of all the Dominions as well as of the Parliament of the United Kingdom. At present The Queen is Head of State of thirteen member countries of the Commonwealth. All member nations of the Commonwealth acknowledge The Queen as Head of the Commonwealth. Membership of the Commonwealth is subject to the approval of existing members.

Among the more clearly defined prerogatives of the British monarch are those of convoking, adjourning, removing, and dissolving Parliament, refusing assent to Bills, without which assent they cannot become law, increasing the number of Peers, declaring war at pleasure, choosing and appointing all commanders and officers by land, sea, and air, and all judges, councillors, officers of state, magistrates, Archbishops, Bishops, and high ecclesiastical dignitaries, bestowing all public honours, and pardoning criminals, besides exercising many other powers, by the advice of the Cabinet Ministers, who, however, alone are responsible, the theory of English law being that the Sovereign cannot commit wrong.

Another theory of our law is that the King (or Queen) never dies—substantially, that the throne is never vacant, the succession of the heir being instantaneous. A meeting of the Privy Council is held immediately after the Demise of the Crown (usually the next day) to give directions for proclaiming the new Sovereign. The proclamation takes place in London at St James's Palace, at Charing Cross, within the City Boundary at Temple Bar, and at the Royal Exchange, two or three days later. To this first meeting of the Privy Council of the new Reign, the Lord Mayor and Aldermen, etc, of London, although not themselves Privy Councillors, are invited. Since the Reform Act of 1867 Parliament does not dissolve at the Demise of the Crown, and, if at the time adjourned or prorogued, meets immediately, or, if dissolved, the old Parliament must meet at once and may serve for six months. The ceremony of a coronation, although essential, is a solemn recognition and confirmation of the royal descent and consequent right of accession, and is not necessary for the security of the title to the crown.

Before Edward I our Kings began to reign only after their coronations, being styled Duke of Normandy until that time.

Some of the styles of pre-Conquest kings were elaborate, such as King Edgar (957-975) call *Rex Anglorum* and *Basileus Anglorum*, and Edward the Martyr as *Gratia Dei Rex totius Albionis*. For styles since 1066, see "SOVEREIGNS"

It was not until Henry IV adopted the title of "Grace," that prefixes came into use. These prefixes were successively changed to "Excellent Grace," "High and Mighty Prince," and "Highness", until Henry VIII adopted those of "Majesty" and "Dread Sovereign."

The Sovereign's banner, commonly called the Royal Standard, is the personal flag of the Sovereign, and can only properly be flown over buildings or ships with Her Majesty's permission, which permission is only granted when the Queen is actually present in person, and not when Her Majesty is passing in processions.

THE QUEEN MOTHER

takes precedence amongst ladies immediately after the Queen, and has her own Household.

THE HEIR APPARENT TO THE CROWN

is next below the Sovereign in all honour and dignity—not as participating or comparing with the latter, who stands alone and supreme, but as enjoying the largest share of the honour which flows from the Crown; though in the present reign HRH the Duke of Edinburgh has ranked next to HM the Queen under the terms of a Royal Warrant dated 18 Sept 1952.

Plume of the Eldest Son of The Sovereign*

No person can hold this position save the son of the Sovereign, or, if the former be dead, his direct male descendant.

The Heir Apparent has, since the institution of the title by Edward I (who, in 1301, conferred it on his son, Edward, born at Caernarvon in 1284), usually but not invariably been *created* Prince of Wales. Since 1399, the Earldom of Chester has always been conferred, together with the Principality of Wales. There is no succession to this title, which, at every vacancy, becomes merged in the Crown, and is only renewed by the Sovereign's pleasure. Thus, had George IV died whilst Prince of Wales, his next brother, though heir apparent, would not have become the Prince of Wales without being so created.

The Sovereign's eldest son is Duke of Cornwall (peerage of England) and Duke of Rothesay (peerage of Scotland) from the moment of his birth or the Sovereign's accession, and becomes immediately entitled to the revenues of the Duchy of Cornwall. When there is no Duke of Cornwall, the Duchy is in the custody of, and the revenues are paid to, the Crown. The titles of Duke of Cornwall and Duke Rothesay, unlike that of Prince of Wales, do not become merged in the Crown on succession to the Monarchy or at death (unless the Sovereign has no son), but pass at once to the next heir apparent being the eldest living *son* of the Sovereign, to whom it is strictly limited.

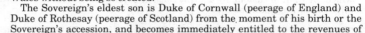

By course of the civil law the heir apparent sits at the right hand of the Sovereign in all solemn assemblies of state and honour; but he has no kingly prerogatives, and acknowledges reverence to his sovereign. He comes of age automatically on becoming Duke of Cornwall, however tender his years†. Thus he may take his seat in Parliament at the Sovereign's will.

A statute of Edward III enacts "that to compass or imagine the death of the King's eldest son and heir is *crimen læsæ majestatis*" (high treason).

In 1898 Letters Patent under the Great Seal were granted, declaring that the children of the eldest son of any Prince of Wales shall at all times have the title of "Royal Highness," but by further letters patent December 1917, this privilege was confined to the eldest living son only of the eldest son of the Prince of Wales.

Coronet of Eldest Son of The Sovereign

The Prince of Wales was invested at Caernarvon Castle on 1 July 1969, as the 21st Prince of Wales, and was introduced to the House of Lords on 11 Feb 1970.

MEMBERS OF THE ROYAL FAMILY

The rank and position of these are defined in the general
"Tables of Precedence"

The Latin *Princeps* signified "the first." Before the reign of Henry VIII the only prince was the Prince of Wales. As a courtesy title the style of Prince and Princess gradually superseded Lord and Lady—though the latter styles were in use as late as the reign of Charles II for his nieces and Frederick, Prince of Wales, in the reign of George II, expressed a wish that his sons and

---

*This plume of feathers, generally spoken of as "The Prince of Wales's feathers," is not in reality such, but is the badge of the Heir Apparent, in whom it is vested whether created Prince of Wales or not.
†Princes (The) Case 1606, 8 Co Rep 1a, 13b, and note to Blackstone's Commentaries Vol 1, 15th ed p 242.

daughters should be so styled, though they do not appear to have been. In Scotland the style of Prince of Scotland is borne by the eldest son of the Sovereign. The first charter is one granted by Robert III on 10 Dec 1404, in favour of his son James. Until the Reform Act, 1832, tenancy of 40s freehold from the Prince of Scotland was a qualification for a vote in Scottish counties.

The Royal Marriages Act prohibits the marriage of personages (descendants of George II) connected with the Blood Royal (except issue of Princesses who have married into Foreign Families) without the sanction of the Sovereign, but this is considerably modified by a conditional proviso, by which marriage contracted after the age of twenty-five is valid if a year's notice has been given to the Privy Council and both Houses of Parliament, and they have not interfered during that period expressing their disapprobation. Private marriages do not give the rank of the husband to the wife or issue of the marriage, and although duly solemnized and the issue legitimate, do not confer upon the children any right of succession to hereditary honours.

| *Coronet of the younger children of the Heir Apparent and of the daughters of the Sovereign's son* | *Coronet of the younger sons, daughters, brothers, and sisters of the Sovereign* | *Coronet of the grandsons (through younger sons) of the Sovereign* | *Coronet of the grandchildren (through daughters) of the Sovereign* |

Up to 1917 the Sovereign's sons, daughters, grandsons and granddaughters (being issue of sons), brothers, sisters, and uncles and aunts (on the Sovereign's side), the children of the eldest son of any Prince of Wales were all styled "Royal Highness." Grandchildren who were issue of daughters were sometimes granted by Royal Warrant the title of "Highness". Since that date the style of "Royal Highness" has been confined to the issue of any Sovereign and to issue of the sons of any Sovereign. The titles of "Prince" and "Princess" are similarly confined to *all* children of any Sovereign and to the children of the sons of any Sovereign. (See also under Heir Apparent.) The style of "Princess Royal," which is held for life, is customarily granted by declaration to the eldest daughter of the Sovereign after a vacancy has occurred. The first Princess so styled was the eldest daughter of Charles I.

ROYAL CORONETS

Members of the royal family use above their arms an heraldic representation of the coronets which they actually wear at coronations. Since the Restoration in 1660 the design of royal coronets has gradually become standardised into five types and these are worn with royal robes of purple velvet by ladies and with scarlet robes with capes semee of ermine by men. Ladies' coronets are a smaller version of those worn by men.

The five types of royal coronet are as follows:—

(1) The coronet of the heir apparent composed of alternate crosses patees and fleurs-de-lys, surmounted by a single arch topped with an orb and cross. The original coronet of this design forms part of the crown jewels exhibited at the Tower of London and was made for Frederick Louis, Prince of Wales, the son and heir of King George II*. It is often referred to incorrectly as the Prince of Wales's crown or coronet. However, as that title is only bestowed at the sovereign's pleasure, it would be better described as the Duke of Cornwall's coronet.

(2) The coronet of the younger sons, brothers, daughters and sisters of a sovereign is the same as the heir apparent's coronet with the omission of the arch. The eldest son of the heir apparent is also entitled to this coronet, but no other grandchildren of the sovereign use it. Originally exclusive to the sons and brothers of the sovereign, this type was extended by King Edward VII to his daughters, and King George VI approved its use by the Duke of Edinburgh.

(3) The coronet of younger children of the heir apparent and, since the time of Queen Victoria, of daughters of younger sons of the sovereign (oddly, the sons of younger sons use the next type) consists of two crosses patees, two strawberry leaves and four fleurs-de-lys. This type of coronet was also used by the daughters of sovereigns until King Edward VII allowed the use of the previous type to his daughters. Lady Patricia Ramsay continued to use her royal coronet even though she had renounced the title of Princess and style of Royal Highness on her marriage.

(4) The coronet of the sons of younger sons of a sovereign consists of alternate crosses patees and strawberry leaves. Until the reign of Queen Victoria all descendants in the male line with the style of Royal Highness bore this coronet, hence in 1902 the Duke of Cumberland and, it is presumed, his sister Princess Frederica, wore it at the coronation of King Edward VII. Queen Victoria promoted the daughters of younger sons to the preceding type, and King George V's exclusion of the German branches of the royal family after the first World War restricted its use to the present category.

*Two other coronets exist and are exhibited in the National Museum of Wales at Cardiff. They are the circlet of simple design made for the investiture of Edward, Prince of Wales in 1911, and the more elaborate interpretation in modern idiom of the single-arched crown or coronet made for the investiture of Prince Charles in 1969.

(5) A coronet composed of alternate fleurs-de-lys and strawberry leaves is generally stated to belong to the grandchildren of a sovereign through daughters. As Princesses generally married into other royal houses, this coronet first came into use for the daughters of the Princess Royal, Duchess of Fife. The Marquess of Carisbrooke was granted this type of coronet after renouncing his German titles and actually wore it at the 1937 coronation, lending it in 1953 to Lord Harewood, whose wife however wore the ordinary Countess's coronet since Lady Carisbrooke attended the coronation and there was only one lady's coronet of this type available. Since other grandchildren of sovereigns such as Princess Marie Louise (who, howe·er, used it heraldically) and the Hon Gerald Lascelles did not wear robes or coronets, it might be concluded that this type of coronet appertains to the sovereign's grandchildren through daughters provided such persons are peers or peeresses.

THE PEERAGE
LORDS SPIRITUAL

Lords Spiritual consist of the Archbishops of Canterbury and York and twenty-four Bishops (by rotation, but including always the Bishops of London, Durham, and Winchester). The sixteen Junior Bishops do not have seats in the House of Lords. The Bishop of Sodor and Man is unable to vote in the House of Lords, as he is a legislator in the Isle of Man. It has been the custom to bestow a barony on a retired Archbishop. A bishop on resigning his see ceases to be a peer of Parliament.

The Archbishop of Canterbury is the first peer of England next to the Royal Family, preceding not only all Dukes, but all the great officers of the Crown. The Bishop of London is his provincial Dean, the Bishop of Winchester his Chancellor, and the Bishop of Worcester his Chaplain. "It belongs to him to crown the King"; and the Sovereign and his or her Consort, wherever they may be located, are *speciales domestici parochiani Arch Cant* (parishioners of the Lord Archbishop of Canterbury).

The Archbishop of Canterbury is Primate of *all* England, is entitled to the prefix of "Your Grace," and styles himself "By Divine Providence, Lord Archbishop of Canterbury."

The Archbishop of York is the third peer in the United Kingdom, and precedes all secular peers, except the Lord High Chancellor. He is "Primate of England," and is perpetual chaplain of the Queen Consort. He is entitled to the prefix of "Your Grace," styles himself "By Divine Providence, Lord Archbishop of York," and possesses within his own province powers nearly equivalent to those exercised by the Archbishop of Canterbury within his. His precedence rests on an Act of Parliament in 31st year of Henry VIII.

An Archbishop's mitre is the same as that of a Bishop.

Diocesan Bishops of England, with the exceptions noted, are also peers of the kingdom and of Parliament, and take precedence of the temporal barons.

The Bishops of London, Durham, and Winchester have precedence over all the other bishops who rank according to the seniority of their consecration.

A Diocesan bishop is entitled to the prefix of Lord, and styles himself "Right Reverend Father in God, by Divine Permission, Lord Bishop of—."

The mitre, placed over the arms of a bishop, is a round cap, pointed and cleft at the top, from which hang two pendants, fringed at the ends, it is surmounted by a fillet of gold, set with precious stones. The mitre of the Bishop of Durham (as nominally Count Palatine of Durham) is represented as issuing out of a ducal crest coronet.

Archbishops and Bishops who are entitled to a seat in the House of Lords possess all the faculties and privileges of Peers of Parliament during the time they hold office.

A bishop impales his arms with those of the See, but he does not bear crest, supporters, or motto. The wives and children of bishops do not have any precedence as such.

PEERS

The degrees of the Peerage of England, Scotland, Ireland, Great Britain and the United Kingdom are five—viz, *Dukes, Marquesses, Earls, Viscounts*, and *Barons* (including Life Barons).

Scottish peers take precedence of British peers of the same rank created since the Union with Scotland. *Irish peers* created before the Union with Ireland, in like manner, take place of British peers created since. Irish peers of later creation than the Union, rank according to the dates of their patents, among the peers of Great Britain and Ireland. Peers holding only Scottish titles have been enabled to sit in the House of Lords since the passing of The Peerage Act 1963. By that Act, the enactments relating to the election of Scottish Representative Peers, by which they were elected by their fellow-Peers for one Parliament only, ceased to have effect.

Peers holding only Irish titles are not eligible to sit in the House of Lords. Representative Peers were (before establishment of the Irish Free State) elected by their fellow peers for life.

Irish peers are not disqualified from being elected as members in the House of Commons for any constituency in the United Kingdom, and to vote at elections for the House of Commons whether or not they be members of that House.

Peers of England, Scotland, Great Britain, and the United Kingdom are not entitled to sit in the House of Commons.

Since 1958 women have been admitted to the Upper House as Life Peeresses, and also since 1963, hereditary Peeresses of England, Great Britain, the United Kingdom, and Scotland.

Peers may not take their seats in the House of Lords until they are of age. If they then desire to do so they are required to prove their right of succession, after which a writ of summons is issued. Peerage patents are on parchment, and bear no signature, only the Great Seal.

The ceremony of admitting a peer into the House of Lords. He is introduced by two peers of his own degree, who conduct him to the Lord Chancellor. His patent is carried by Garter King of Arms. The new peer presents it together with his writ of summons to the Lord Chancellor, who directs the same to be read. The oaths are administered, the peer takes his seat, and then, rising, returns to the Chancellor, who congratulates him upon his elevation.

PRIVILEGES OF PEERS

The privileges enjoyed by peers were formerly numerous. Amongst those abolished is the privilege in cases of treason and felony of being tried by their peers only, who gave their verdict simply *upon their honour*, in a court specially fitted up at the expense of the Crown. This was discontinued under the Criminal Justice Act of 1948.

The privileges which continue are:—

Exemption from Jury Service.

Immunity from attachment, *ie* freedom from arrest in civil cases for a period of 40 days before and after a meeting of Parliament (a privilege shared with Members of Parliament, but it is wider for a Peer, since under Common Law "the person of a peer is forever sacred and inviolable.")

A peer (but not a peer by courtesy, with the following exception) is entitled to have Supporters granted to be borne with his arms, and to the use of the coronet of his rank. Heirs apparent of peers of Scotland are enabled to bear the peer's supporters, debruised with a three point label.

CLAIMS TO PEERAGES

Claims to dormant or abeyant Peerages or to Peerages whose succession is in dispute, are dealt with by the Committee for Privileges of the House of Lords on petition to the Crown, presented through the Home Secretary, who first refers the accompanying documents to the Attorney-General in order that he may report upon them to the Sovereign and advise in the matter.

These the Attorney-General passes to the Counsel for the Crown in Peerage claims, and he reports to the Attorney-General, who then, to obtain further particulars and elucidate any further details necessary, hears the petitioner and his counsel, after which the Attorney-General himself reports to the Home Secretary. If his report is unfavourable to the petitioner he advises that the petition shall not be referred to the Committee for Privileges. If on the contrary, he considers that the proofs and documents submitted at the hearing made out a *prima facie* case, he advises the House of Lords to refer it to their Committee for Privileges, which goes into the case in detail, the petitioner and any opposing claimant being represented by counsel, while the Crown is represented by the Attorney-General and the counsel for Peerage claims. The Committee for Privileges reports to the Sovereign the conclusions at which it arrives. Since 1977, claims to Scottish Peerages, and, in certain cases where there is a sufficient Scottish connection, claims to Peerages of Great Britain and of the United Kingdom, should be lodged with the Secretary of State for Scotland.

The Select Committee on Peerages in Abeyance 1926 made the general recommendations that, in the absence of special circumstances or special reasons to the contrary, no abeyance should be terminated, the first commencement of which occurred more than 100 years before the presentation of the committee, and no petition should be allowed to proceed where the petition represents less than one-third of the entire dignity.

ACCELERATED PROMOTION TO HOUSE OF LORDS

On occasions the eldest son of a peer has been summoned to the House of Lords during his father's lifetime in one of his father's minor titles, and in such cases if he predeceased his father the title and seat passed to his son (if any). The last instance of this practice occurred in 1992 when the eldest son of the 6th Marquess of Salisbury was called to the House of Lords in his father's Barony of Cecil.

SELECTION OF PEERAGE TITLES

The Sovereign, as the fountain of all honour, can bestow any title He or She may please, but in practice the following rules are usually observed.

Titles once conferred upon any member of the Royal Family are not again bestowed outside the Royal Circle. A title once extinct but subsequently revived, is rarely re-created in a lower rank than before, but this rule is not an invariable one.

Every peer below the rank of Earl must be described in his patent as "of—" (somewhere), usually the seat of the recipient, or some place with which he has a connection. Some peers are *created* with a territorial designation as actually *part of the title*, such as *Baron Ritchie of Dundee*, of Welders, Chalfont St Giles, *Baron Brassey of Apethorpe*, of Apethorpe, and *Baron Ponsonby of Shulbrede*, of Shulbrede. It will be noted that in such cases there is a double territorial designation.

Any semblance of duplication of titles is avoided as far as ever possible.

A surname, if desired, may *always* be adopted as a title, although another dignity of the same style be at the time in existence. In that case the recipients of all such similar (surname) titles of the same rank, except the first (then existing one) to be created, *must* add the territorial designation as an affix to the title by which they are commonly known. For instance, Baron Stanley (creation 1455); Baron Stanley (creation 1832) known as "Lord Stanley of Bickerstaff"; Baron Stanley (creation 1828) as "Lord Stanley of Alderley"; Baron Stanley (creation 1886) as "Lord Stanley of Preston." Again, Baron Curzon (creation 1794), and Baron Curzon (creation 1898) as "Lord Curzon of Kedleston."

In the case of Life Peers the surname is usually adopted.

The name of a county or county town is not as a rule permissible as a peerage title below the rank of earl (although exception may be made in favour of any one particularly eminent either as a statesman or in some other walk of life). Important towns are usually reserved for the higher steps in the peerage.

SIGNATURES

Peers sign by their titles only, as also do the eldest sons of peers bearing as a courtesy title one of their father's minor honours, but a peeress by marriage signs with her Christian name or initial prefixed to the title. A peeress in her own right, however, signs with the title only. Archbishops and Bishops sign with their Christian name, followed by province or see (in the cases of diocesan bishops the see is sometimes in Latin).

REMAINDERS TO PEERAGES

A peerage created by patent descends according to the limitation mentioned in the patent of creation, usually to the heir male of the body of the first peer, but special remainders are sometimes granted to others of the family (eg to daughters, brothers or sisters, etc, and the heirs male of their bodies). War leaders such as Nelson, Kitchener, Allenby, Mountbatten and Portal, if there was no male issue to inherit, were given special remainders for the peerages to have an extra chance of survival.

The complicated succession to Baronies which are held to have been created by a writ of summons to Parliament and the doctrine of abeyance have been discussed in detail in the Complete Peerage, Vol IV, Appendix H.

In the Peerage of Scotland remainders vary according to the limitation. The destination may be to heirs male whatsoever (ie to the senior male heir, despite the extinction of the male line descending from the first peer), heirs male of the body, heirs male of tailzie (entailed estates), heirs whatsoever (ie whether male or female), or a succession according to a series of named individuals. Some Scottish peerages were granted with "shifting remainders." An example is the Earldom of Selkirk. When a line of Earls became extinct, the next son of the Duke of Hamilton inherited. This occurred in 1885 and again in 1940. Until the Act of Union 1707, Scottish Peerages were capable of being surrendered to the Crown, who re-conferred them with different remainders.

In the Peerage of Ireland succession descends according to the limitation. Though the origin of the more ancient peerages is not always known, it is held that there are now only two which could pass in the female line. These are the Viscountcy of Massereene and the Barony of Loughneagh, created in the 16th century, with remainder, in default of issue male, to the heirs general. Both of these are held by Viscount Massereene and Ferrard.

Legitimated children are included in the Peerage articles, but are not normally in remainder to the peerage concerned, a possible exception being that persons of Scottish domicile may be in remainder to a Peerage of Scotland.

LIFE PEERS AND PEERESSES

Prior to the passing of the Life Peerages Act of 1958 the only Life Peers were the Lords of Appeal in Ordinary and no women sat in the House of Lords. Since then, however, men and women have been appointed peers or peeresses and rank as Barons or Baronesses for life. Each is entitled to a writ of summons to attend, and to sit and vote in the House of Lords.

The Life Barons' wives rank as Baronesses, and are entitled to the prefix of "Lady," while their children, and those of Life Baronesses, are styled "Hon" for life and hold special precedence.

Lords of Appeal in Ordinary hold office during good behaviour, notwithstanding the demise of the Crown, but may be removed from such office, on the address of both Houses or Parliament.

DISCLAIMING OF PEERAGES

The Peerage Act 1963, which received Royal Assent on 31 July 1963, authorised the disclaimer for life of certain hereditary peerages. The principal provisions are summarized below.

(1) *Disclaimer of certain hereditary Peerages*

A person subsequent to this Act who is already a peer or who succeeds to a peerage of England, Scotland, Great Britain or the United Kingdom may, by an instrument of disclaimer delivered to the Lord Chancellor, disclaim that peerage for life.

The instrument for one who succeeds to a peerage shall be delivered within the period of 12 months beginning with the day of succession to the peerage. If the person is under 21 on succession, the period of 12 months begins with the day he attains that age. No instrument shall be delivered in respect of a peerage by one who has applied for a writ of summons to attend the House of Lords.

The period for one who succeeded before the commencement of this Act is 12 months beginning with the commencement of the Act, or if under 21, 12 months beginning with the day he attains that age. An instrument of disclaimer may be delivered notwithstanding that he has applied before commencement of this Act, for a writ of summons to attend the House of Lords.

In either case, in reckoning the period for delivery of the instrument, no account shall be taken of time during which, to the satisfaction of the Lord Chancellor, the person is rendered by infirmity incapable of exercising or determining whether to exercise his rights.

(2) *Disclaimer by MPs and Parliamentary Candidates*

The period for an MP who succeeds to a peerage is one month beginning with the date of succession. Until that period expires he shall not, by virtue of that peerage, be disqualified from membership of the House of Commons, whether or not he has delivered an instrument of disclaimer, provided he does not sit or vote in the House of Commons whilst exempt from disqualification, or that he has not applied for a writ of summons to attend the House of Lords.

Where a person who succeeds to a peerage has been or is nominated at a Parliamentary election, held in pursuance of a writ issued before his succession, he shall not be disqualified by virtue of that peerage for election to the House of Commons at that election, unless he has applied for a writ of summons to the House of Lords. If he is elected, the above time limit will apply to him as if he had succeeded to the peerage immediately after the declaration of the result of the election.

Where an instrument of disclaimer is delivered by a person to whom this section applies, a copy shall be delivered by the Speaker.

In reckoning the period, no account shall be taken of any time during which (a) proceedings are pending on any parliamentary election petition in which the right to be elected or returned to the House of Commons is in issue (b) the person is shown to the satisfaction of the Speaker to have any infirmity as in Section 1 (c) Parliament is prorogued, or both Houses are adjourned for more than 4 days. If Parliament is dissolved during the period for delivery of disclaimer, the provisions of this section shall cease to apply to him in respect of the peerage in question.

(3) Effects of Disclaimer

The disclaimer of a peerage shall be irrevocable, and shall operate from the date by which the instrument is delivered to divest him, and his wife, of all right and interest to or in the peerage, and all titles, rights, offices, and privileges and precedence attaching thereto, and to relieve him of all obligations and disabilities (including any disqualification in respect of membership of the House of Commons and elections to that House) arising therefrom, but shall not accelerate the succession to that peerage nor affect its devolution on his death.

Where a peerage is disclaimed, no other hereditary peerage shall be conferred, and no writ of acceleration shall be issued in respect of that peerage to the person so entitled on his death.

STYLES AND PRECEDENCE OF THE CHILDREN OF PEERS WHO DISCLAIM THEIR PEERAGES

Statement issued by Garter King of Arms

Paragraph 4(b) of the Report of the Joint Committee on House of Lords Reform recommended that "the wife and descendants of a Peer who surrenders should not use the courtesy titles or enjoy the social precedence derived from such a Peer." The Peerage Act 1963, however, while dealing in terms with the effect of disclaimer on a disclaiming Peer himself and his wife, does not so deal with the effect on his children. This has, therefore, to be inferred and it might be argued on the one hand that the children of a Peer who disclaims are no longer the children of a Peer and so no longer enjoy the style and precedence which they would have enjoyed as such. Or it might be argued on the other hand that the Act does not deprive them of the styles and precedence they have enjoyed prior to their father's disclaimer and they may, therefore, still enjoy these just as the daughters of a peer continue to do so even if their father has died leaving no heir to his peerage."

The Home Office, which is concerned with precedence through the Home Secretary's responsibility for advising the Sovereign on Petitions for special precedence, has so far been unwilling to express a view on the point of law or to deal with the matter by recommending the issue of a Royal Warrant.

It is, therefore, necessary for the Earl Marshal, as the principal authority under The Crown for matters connected with style and precedence, to decide on a policy in the situation as it at present stands.

The Earl Marshal has been advised by Mr G. D. Squibb, QC, Norfolk Herald Extraordinary, that in his view the children of a disclaiming Peer retain their precedence as the children of a Peer and the same view has been expressed by the Lord Lyon King of Arms.

While, therefore, it is open to any child of a disclaiming Peer to say that he or she no longer wishes to be known by the courtesy title hitherto accorded him or her, in those cases where such children wish still to be accorded their courtesy titles the Earl Marshal and his Officers will so accord them.

PARLIAMENTARY QUALIFICATIONS OF SCOTTISH PEERS, IRISH PEERS, AND PEERESSES IN OWN RIGHT

The holder of a peerage in the peerage of Scotland shall have the same right to receive writs of summons to attend the House of Lords, and to sit and vote in that House, as the holder of a peerage in the peerage of the United Kingdom; and the enactments relating to the election of Scottish representative peers shall cease to have effect.

The holder of a peerage in the peerage of Ireland shall not by virtue of that peerage be disqualified—

(a) for being or being elected as a member of the House of Commons for any constituency in the United Kingdom, or

(b) for voting at elections for that House whether or not he is a Member of that House.

A woman who is the holder of an hereditary peerage in the peerage of England, Scotland, Great Britain or the United Kingdom shall (whatever the terms of the letters patent or other instrument, if any, creating that peerage) have the same right to receive writs of summons to attend the House of Lords, and to sit and vote in that House, and shall be subject to the same disqualifications in respect of membership of the House of Commons and elections to that House as a man holding that peerage.

DUKE This title (from Latin *Dux*, a leader) is the highest in our Peerage. As we have no "princes" outside the blood-royal, so pre-eminent in dignity is the ducal title that each royal prince, shortly after attaining his majority is usually created a Duke; the titular style of Prince, apart from the Prince of Wales, being one of courtesy. Thus, Prince Henry, son of King George V, was created *Duke* of Gloucester.

Duke's coronet

Since the title Duke signified Sovereign status, *eg* William the Conqueror was Duke of Normandy—it was not adopted until 1337, when Edward III conferred the Dukedom of Cornwall on his eldest son, the Black Prince. This was followed by Henry Duke of Lancaster in 1351. Both were created, in Parliament by the girding of the sword. Ceremonial attaching to the creation of this dignity was discontinued in 1615, and it now takes place by patent under the Great Seal.

The first subject to receive a dukedom who was not a member of the royal family, nor one nearly connected, was Sir William de la Pole, Marquess of Suffolk, who was created Duke of Suffolk in 1448.

There were no Dukedoms in existence during the reign of Elizabeth I, after the attainder of the Duke of Norfolk 1572, when the whole order according to Judge Blackstone "became utterly extinct." The Ducal order was revived in England by James I in the person of his favourite, George Villiers, Duke of Buckingham.

A Duke is styled *Most Noble* (or less formally *His Grace*), and by the Sovereign in public instruments, *Our right trusty and right entirely beloved cousin*, with the addition of *and counsellor* when a member of the Privy Council.

MARQUESS   The term *Marchio* was applied in the Norman period to the Earl or Baron guarding the Welsh or Scottish Marches, or border territories. Similarly in Germany the Count or Graf became known as the Markgraf, anglicised to Margrave. By

Marquess's
coronet

the twelfth century it had lost its territorial significance. It was introduced to England by Richard II, brother-in-law of the Margrave of Brandenburg, the honour being conferred upon Robert de Vere, Earl of Oxford, who became Marquess of Dublin in 1385. The precedence between Dukes and Earls caused great offence to the latter, and the patent was revoked in 1386 in favour of the Dukedom of Ireland. The next recipient did not appreciate the degree. When John Beaufort, Marquess of Dorset, was attainted and the House of Commons appealed to Richard II for its restoration, Beaufort begged the king not to restore this particular title "as the name of Marquess is a strange name in this realm."

The creation to this dignity was formerly attended with nearly the same ceremony as that of a duke.

The style of a marquess is *Most Honourable*. He is formally styled by the Sovereign, *Our right trusty and entirely beloved cousin* (*and counsellor* when of the Privy Council).

EARL   Before Canute an ealdorman administered a shire or province for the King. In Latin documents he was styled *Dux* or *Comes*, taking a place between the royal Atheling and the thegn. Under Canute the Danish equivalent of Earl was introduced.

Earl's coronet

Under the Normans the government of an earl was normally restricted to one county and became hereditary, though losing the functions of the King's representation in the county to the sheriff. An earl was usually invested with the third penny out of the sheriff's court of the county, of Anglo-Saxon origin.

The dignity was created by the girding on of the sword as a symbol of temporal authority, but this lost some of its significance when in 1328 Roger Mortimer was created Earl of March, derived neither from a county nor a city. The ceremony continued after earls were created by patent, and in the reign of Edward VI a cape of dignity and a golden circlet were added to the ceremony, but in 1615 such ceremonies ceased.

Earldoms were originally created in fee, but from the reign of Richard II they were either created for life or in tail male.

An Earl is styled *Right Honourable*, and is formally addressed by the Sovereign as *Our right trusty and entirely beloved cousin* (*and counsellor* when of the Privy Council.)

VISCOUNT   This title had its origin in the office of the deputy or the lieutenant (*Vice-Comes*) of a Count, which had become hereditary in the Empire by the beginning of the tenth century. It was also used as the Sheriff of a county. Henry VI, crowned King of England and France, created John Lord Beaumont in 1440 Viscount

Viscount's coronet

Beaumont in England and Viscount Beaumont in France (a title forfeited by the Duke of Alençon in 1415, and vacant on the death of the Duke of Bedford 1435), in order to integrate the titles of the two countries. The peerage title received precedence above all Barons, but it did not become popular until the seventeenth century. Viscounts were always created by patent.

A Viscount's style is *Right Honourable*. He is addressed by the King or Queen as *Our right trusty and well-beloved cousin* (*and counsellor* when of the Privy Council).

BARON   Barons were introduced into England by the Normans, most of whom held that rank in Normandy before the Conquest. Baron meant literally a man, being the King's tenant in chief, ie holding his land directly from him. The burgesses and leading citizens of London were also known collectively as Barons, and this style was allowed them by clerks who wrote the writs of William II and Henry I. The barons of the Cinque Ports are a parallel to the barons of

London (see "Norman London" by Sir Frank Stenton, and "Social Life in Early England" edited by Geoffrey Barraclough, 1960). In the thirteenth century they were summoned to the Counsel or Parliament, but at first this did not imply that a successor would necessarily also be summoned to subsequent Parliaments. The more important would probably be summoned, but by the reign of Edward III it became usual for successors to receive writs as a matter of course. Thus the Baronage emerged into an hereditary dignity of the Peerage.

Baron's coronet

The first baron created BY PATENT was John Beauchamp de Holt, created Baron Kidderminster, by Richard II in 1387 with remainder to his heirs male, but baronies by writ also continued to be created long after this date.

The succession to baronies by writ is not limited to heirs male, but is vested in heirs-general. In the event of the death without male issue of a baron by writ the title will fall into abeyance should he leave two or more daughters, and so will continue until only one daughter or the sole heir of one of the daughters survives. The Crown can, however, at any time terminate the abeyance in favour of any one of the co-heiresses, but it cannot alienate the barony from the representatives of the first baron.

When a baron is called to the House of Peers by writ of summons, the writ is in the Sovereign's name.

A baron is styled *Right Honourable* and formally by the Sovereign *Right trusty and well-beloved* (*and counsellor* when a Member of the Privy Council).

In Scotland, Sir George Mackenzie, Lord Advocate to Charles II, made it clear that the equivalent of Barons in England are Lords of Parliament in Scotland, as the word "Baron" in Scots law relates to Feudal Barons. This claim was immediately and correctly put forward by several Scottish Lords when they received summons as Barons to the House of Lords. Their protests were accepted and they were sent fresh summonses as Lords.

LORDS OF SESSION IN SCOTLAND

AND CHAIRMAN OF SCOTTISH LAND COURT

are the Senators of the College of Justice in Scotland, and on appointment to the Bench take the judicial title of Lord——, with the prefix of "The Hon", by which they are known and addressed (though they subscribe by their initials and surname), with the exception of the Lord Justice-General and Lord Justice-Clerk. Both of these are not usually described by the judicial title by which they take their seats but by their official designations, being primarily Officers of State.

By Royal Warrant granted in February 1905, Scottish Lords of Session who have retired are permitted to retain the title of "The Honourable Lord," while their wives are also granted the title of "Lady," to be retained after the decease of the husband, but during widowhood only.

Since 1912, a chairman of Scottish Land Court receives a Judicial title, by which he is always known both in office and retirement. He is treated as a Lord of Session.

BARONETS

The term baronet was first applied to the nobility who lost the right of individual summons to Parliament; and in this sense was used in a statute of Richard II. It is said that Sir Robert Cotton's discovery of William de la Pole's patent in the 13th year of Edward III, conferring upon him the dignity of a Baronet in return for a sum of money, suggested the revival of the Order.

The hereditary Order of Baronets in England was erected by Letters Patent by King James I on 22 May 1611, for the settlement of Ireland. He offered the dignity to 200 gentlemen of good birth, with a clear estate of £1,000 a year, on condition that each one should pay into the King's Exchequer in three equal instalments a sum equivalent to three years' pay to 30 soldiers at 8d per day per man. The first instalment was to be paid on the delivery of the patent. The Baronets form the sixth division of *Nobiles Majores*, following the five degrees of the Peerage.

The *Baronetage of Ireland* was erected on 30 September 1611; the *Baronetage of Scotland* or *Nova Scotia* on 28 May 1625, for the establishment of the plantation of Nova Scotia. After the union of England and Scotland in 1707 no further Baronets of England or Scotland were created, the style being changed to Baronet of Great Britain. With the union of Great Britain and Ireland in 1801, all Baronets subsequently created were under the style of the United Kingdom.

The Official Roll of Baronets was first gazetted 23 February 1914. By a further Royal Warrant dated 10 March 1922, anyone who considers he is entitled to be enrolled therein is at liberty to petition the Crown through the Home Secretary. Every person succeeding to a Baronetcy must exhibit his proofs of succession to the Secretary of State. Should the Secretary of State find any difficulty in advising the Crown as to any claim, he refers the matter to the Law Officers for their opinion, and further, may, on consideration of that opinion, direct that the matter be referred to the specially appointed Committee of the Privy Council for examination and advice to the Crown. The Roll is kept at the Home Office by the Registrar of the Baronetage.

The Standing Council of the Baronetage, was founded in 1898 to maintain the ancient rights and privileges of the Degree.

A baronet's wife is entitled to the prefix of either "Dame" (followed by christian name) or "Lady" without christian name, but the former style is now only used in legal and formal documents.

A baronet's helmet is depicted as for a knight.

Privileges　Under the first Letters Patent it was ordained that only two hundred Baronets of England were to exist at any one time. This limitation was soon withdrawn. No degree or dignity, etc, was ever to be created which would be superior or equal to the degree and dignity of Baronet.

Under the second Letters Patent it was stated that no person or persons should have place between Baronets and the younger sons of Viscounts and Barons. Privileges included the right of knighthood for Baronets and their eldest sons, and the addition of the Arms of Ulster as a canton or inescutcheon in armorial bearings, argent a sinister hand couped at the wrist and erect gules, known as the Badge of Ulster. A third Letters Patent, ratified and confirmed the above, and included the precedence of the eldest sons of Baronets before eldest sons of knights whatever the order, and with similar provisions respecting other sons. *Baronets of Ireland* have similar privileges except that in some cases the Baronets of Ireland have used a dexter hand for the Badge of Ulster. *Baronets of Scotland* or *Nova Scotia* were to enjoy the same privileges except the Ulster augmentation, and in addition grants of land in Nova Scotia, with plenary baronial rights and jurisdiction, and legislative powers in that plantation, but such grants ceased in 1683. They were given precedence above lesser Barons in Scotland, the addition of the Arms of Nova Scotia in armorial bearings, power to sit and vote by deputy in the Scottish Parliament when absent from the Kingdom, and the right to wear about the neck the badge of Nova Scotia, suspended by an orange-tawny ribbon. This consists of an escutcheon argent with a saltire azure thereon, an inescutcheon of the arms of Scotland, with an Imperial Crown above the escutcheon, and encircled with the motto *Fax mentis Honestae Gloria*. This Badge may be shown suspended by the ribbon below the shield of arms.

Badge of Ulster

Badge of Nova Scotia

Baronets of England and Ireland applied to Charles I for permission to wear a badge. Although a badge was worn in the 17th century, of which specimens still exist, it was not until 1929 that King George V granted permission to all baronets other than those of Scotland to wear round their necks a Badge. This was composed of the Arms of Ulster, on a silver field, a left hand gules, surmounted by an Imperial Crown, enamelled in proper colours, the whole enclosed by an oval border embossed with scroll work of (4) roses for baronets of England, (2) shamrocks for baronets of Ireland, (3) roses and thistles for baronets of Great Britain, and (4) roses, thistles and shamrocks combined for baronets of UK. The badge to be suspended from an orange riband with a narrow edge of dark blue on both sides, the total breadth to be 1¾ inches, and the breadth of each to be ¼ inch. The Badge may be shown suspended by its riband below the shield of arms. Baronets wishing to wear this badge may purchase it at their own expense. Application should be made to the Registrar of the Baronetage or the Standing Council of the Baronetage, if a Member of that body.

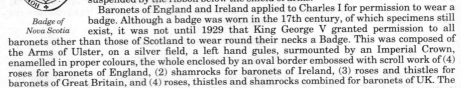

Baronets were accorded the courtesy title of Honourable from the erection of the degree, but this fell into disuse at the beginning of the 19th century. Despite petitions, this privilege has not been conceded by the Crown.

Badge of Baronets of the United Kingdom

George IV revoked the privilege of demanding knighthoods for the eldest sons or heirs apparent of Baronets upon attaining their majority, but without prejudicing Letters Patent granted before 19 December 1827. In 1874, Ludlow Cotter, son of Sir James Lawrence Cotter, 4th baronet of Rockforest, when 21 years of age, received the honour of knighthood. This is the latest instance of the privilege being exercised. Since then few claims have been made and they have all been refused, presumably on the ground that it was unconstitutional for a Sovereign to bind his successors to confer titles in the future on persons unborn.

REMAINDERS TO BARONETCIES

The destination of a baronetcy is in accordance with the limitation mentioned in the patent of creation. Though this is usually to the heirs male of the body of the first baronet, special remainders were sometimes granted (eg North of Southwell, 1920, failing heirs male of the body, to the male issue of daughters of the first baronet).

Baronetcies of Nova Scotia, or Scotland, were sometimes created with remainder to heirs male (ie the heir male of the first baronet, despite the extinction of his own descendants in the male line) and "heirs male and of tailzie". There are four existing Scottish baronets with the last remainder, whose descent, together with entail of estates, may pass to the heir general, viz Dalyell of the Binns, Dunbar of Hempriggs, Hope-Dunbar of Baldoon, and Stirling-Maxwell of Pollok, of whom the holder of the Dunbar of Hempriggs creation is a Baronetess.

Legitimated children are included in the Baronetage articles but are not normally in remainder to the baronetcy concerned. A possible exception is that a person of Scottish domicile may be in remainder to a Nova Scotia baronetcy.

KNIGHTS

Knighthood was a medieval institution of chivalry of both a religious and military character. Its birth and growth in Europe is obscure. It was conferred upon sovereigns, princes and others of noble rank, but not on ecclesiastics. The word has an affinity with horsemanship, a Roman knight, *eques*, a horseman, had held rank next below the Senatorial. The name thus indicates its original occupation as a military equestrian, hence the German Ritter and the French Chevalier. In old English *cnight* meant at first a youth or military follower, and later a trusted servant.

Knighthood was introduced to England at least as early as the reign of Alfred the Great, who made his grandson, Athelstan, a knight, and gave him a scarlet mantle set with precious stones and a sword with a golden scabbard.

With the arrival of the Normans, knights formed an integral part of the feudal system. In the Conqueror's time there were about 5,000 knights who served as fighting men under 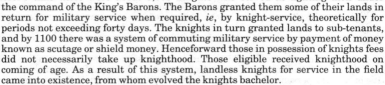 the command of the King's Barons. The Barons granted them some of their lands in return for military service when required, *ie*, by knight-service, theoretically for periods not exceeding forty days. The knights in turn granted lands to sub-tenants, and by 1100 there was a system of commuting military service by payment of money known as scutage or shield money. Henceforward those in possession of knights fees did not necessarily take up knighthood. Those eligible received knighthood on coming of age. As a result of this system, landless knights for service in the field came into existence, from whom evolved the knights bachelor.

Knight's helmet

In early times a knight was dubbed by his lord, his father or another knight. William Rufus was knighted by Archbishop Lanfranc. Matthew Paris recorded that the Earl of Gloucester invested his brother William with a military girdle, and Gilbert de Clare was knighted by Simon de Montfort. Kings used to send their sons to neighbouring courts to receive the honour of knighthood; thus Henry II sent to David I, King of Scots, and Malcolm IV, King of Scots to Henry II and Edward I to the King of Castile.

By the reign of Henry III reluctance for taking up knighthood became apparent, and in 1244 that King introduced distraints of knighthood and summons to those who qualified, with a fine for those who declined. Elaborate ceremonial and pageantry were then introduced, accompanied by feasting and jousting to make knighthood more attractive. From those who did not take up knighthood arose the esquire class.

Two main methods of conferring knighthood were used in the Middle Ages. The simpler form used on the battle-field was for the knight elect to kneel before the commander of the army who struck him with the sword on his back and shoulder with words such as "Avancez chevalier au nom de Dieu". The more elaborate method of knighting for which the dubbing became restricted to the King took place on special occasions. This included presentation of robes, arms and spurs, and was accompanied by vigil and bathing before being dubbed. This later evolved into the Knighthood of the Bath, of whom knights were created at coronations, royal marriages, etc. The first record of these knights is at the coronation of Henry IV, but they were not banded into any Society or Order such as the Garter, founded by Edward III about 1348, until the reign of George I.

Knights Banneret were created from personal distinction in battle rather than on feudal tenure, and were conferred on the field. All the greater nobility were entitled to bear banners, and on the creation of a banneret the points of his pennon were ceremoniously cut by the commander of the army. The last three Knights Banneret are believed to have been conferred by the Protector Somerset after the Battle of Pinkie, 1547, upon Sir Ralph Fane, Sir Francis Bryan and Sir Ralph Sadler.

See Orders of Knighthood for information concerning the various Orders of Chivalry.

The use of prefix "Sir" is not borne by honorary knights of these orders when, as is usually the case, the accolade has not been conferred and no special warrant has been granted permitting use of this appellation. This also applies to clerics of the Established Church, who likewise do not receive the accolade (their wives being entitled to precedence, but not to style of "Lady").

The Imperial Society of Knights Bachelor has its Registry at 21 Old Buildings, Lincoln's Inn, WC2.

The wife of a knight is entitled to the prefix of either "Dame" (followed by christian name), or "Lady" (without christian name), but the former style is now only used in legal documents.

A knight's helmet is depicted with visor up and without bars. The seventeenth century English rule that the helmet must be full faced may now be disregarded if inconvenient for the design of the crest.

In 1926 a Badge was granted for the use of Knights Bachelor. (See Orders of Knighthood.)

ESQUIRES

Esquire (Latin, *scutarius*, shield-bearer) was a personal attendant on a knight, which evolved into an apprentice knight, and later into a lord of a manor. The numbers were swelled by those of the knightly class who did not take up knighthood. By the 14th century an esquire (armiger) practically attained equality with a knight, both in function and privileges. With the rise of the use of the term gentleman as a rank, it became increasingly difficult to know where the lower limit should be drawn. Sir John Fearn, in his "Glory of Generositie" 1586, referred to four sorts of esquires; by creation, birth, dignity, and office. He commented that this title "is no less abused and profaned" than that of gentleman, and that "the degree of esquire is through custom tolerated to many other sorts of gentlemen, but they all, or most of them, are. . .in function of some offices of justice or government in the King's palace, as. . .annexed to the dignities of judges and barons of the benches and courts of justice; to the advocates and procurators of the sovereign; to the degree of sergeants at the coif; to the office of sheriff, escheator, and serjeant at arms; to the eldest born of a baron and peer of the realm or of a knight, besides many others. But that the same should descend from the father to the son, as the state of gentry doth, is mere fabulous. For the title of esquire of common right doth appertain to none, except that by creation he receives the same at the sovereign's hand, or else through the bearing of such an office as a dignity anent to the same, or else by right of birth as in cases aforesaid, and that through custom".

In 1580 Robert Glover, Somerset Herald drew up a list of those entitled and in 1681 an officer of arms, probably Dugdale, in a similar list, stated that heralds should only allow the title of esquire to 1, the heir male of the younger son of a nobleman; 2, the heir male of a knight; 3, those who by long prescription can show their lineal ancestors so styled; 4, sheriff of a county, a JP or those so styled in the King's commission (who cease to hold the title when the office ceases); 5, certain of the king's servants by reason of the office they bear, such as officers of arms, sergeants at arms, etc.

To these should now be added Royal Academicians (included by George III), Companions, Commanders, Officers and Members of Orders of Knighthood and Chivalry, Sergeants at law, Queen's Counsel, Deputy Lieutenants and Commissioners of Lieutenancy, Commissioners of the Court of Bankruptcy, Masters of the Supreme Court; also persons to whom the Sovereign grants arms with the title of Esquire, persons who are styled Esquires by the Sovereign in their patents, commissions or appointments, and officers of and above the rank of Lieutenant RN, Captain in the Army and Flight Lieutenant.

Esquire's helmet

An esquire's helmet is depicted with visor closed. The seventeenth century English rule that the helmet must be depicted in profile to the dexter may now be disregarded if inconvenient for the design of the crest. In Scotland the visor is garnished with gold.

Scottish Titles   Scottish law recognizes a number of special titles which fall under the jurisdiction of the Lord Lyon King of Arms, and are recognized by the Crown. Such recognized chiefly styles and territorial designations of chieftains (branch chiefs) and lairds are legally recorded as a part of the surname under Statute 1672, cap 47. A Scottish feudal baron is allowed the cap of dignity. Supporters are granted to chiefs of clans and ancient families, and feudal barons older than 1592.

GENTLEMEN

Originally gentlemen (Latin *gentilis*, Norman-French *gentil* and *gentilhomme*) meant no specific class but included barons, esquires and even franklins (free-tenants), *ie* all who were not ignoble. By the early 15th century it came to have a specific meaning. Sir George Sitwell contended that this arose from an Act of Parliament, 1413 (Statute I, Henry V, cap 5) that with all writs of action, personal appeals and indictments which involved processes of outlawry, the estate, degree or mystery of the defendant was to be stated. Thus in 1431, as printed in Feudal Aids, land-owners were classed as knights, esquires, gentlemen, yeomen, etc.

When gentlemen became regarded as a distinct order, they were associated with armigers, bearers of coats of arms. As late as the 15th century most of these were not granted in effect by the King, for the greater nobles maintained their own heralds and bestowed arms on their tenants. Sir George Sitwell asserted that heralds "were never authorised by the Crown to make a gentleman", but Sir Anthony Wagner, Garter King of Arms (in *Heralds and Heraldry in the Middle Ages*, 1939) points out that there are many references as early as the reign of Henry VIII to grants containing an ennobling clause. Though a right to arms became decisive evidence of gentility, it is apparent from the records of the High Court of Chivalry that there were those who were non-armigerous who were allowed the status for other reasons, such as military rank held, the fact that the father held a certain office, or that the individual had influential relations. It is also clear that the manner of living had some effect, for a yeoman could be more wealthy than a gentleman, though he lived in rougher style. In one family various members were frequently accorded the rank of gentlemen, yeomen and husbandmen. Fearn in 1586 included a student of common law, a groom of the Sovereign's Palace, a churl's son made priest or canon, those brought up in the service of a Bishop or Baron, governors of cities, etc. Commissioned officers below the rank stated under esquire are given the rank of gentleman. The helmet is as for an esquire, though in Scotland there is a distinction in that a gentleman's helmet is ungarnished. Prior to 1672, Scots gentlemen were allowed shields only.

FOREIGN TITLES

Foreign titles cannot be valued in comparison with British ones, according to their nominal rank. Their devolution is different from and often much wider than the British peerage. Titles of the Holy Roman Empire descend to all male descendants in the male line *ad infinitum*, and certain of those of the old Italian States can be given or left by will at the pleasure of the holder. It was the practice for the Crown, on the advice of the Secretary of State for the Home Department, to grant licences for the use of foreign titles by those domiciled in this country. In 1930 King George V decided that no more licences for the use of foreign titles in this country should be granted. In 1932 a Royal Warrant was issued revoking all licences then in force, with the exception of those issued for the life of the holder and his heir apparent. At that time there were 31 dignities which were allowed under the exception clause.

ORDERS OF
KNIGHTHOOD AND CHIVALRY

CENTRAL CHANCERY OF ORDERS OF KNIGHTHOOD

St James's Palace, SW1A 1BG

Secretary Maj-Gen Desmond Hind Garrett Rice, CVO, CBE.

On promotion to a higher class of an Order of Chivalry, the recipient should return the insignia of the lower class of that order to the Central Chancery, unless he or she has been honoured in both the Military and Civil Divisions of the same Order in which case the insignia of both Divisions may be worn and the post nominal letters of the senior class only may be used. The Orders of the Bath, Merit and the British Empire have a Military and Civil Division.

Collars are worn by KNIGHTS AND LADIES of the GARTER, THISTLE, and KNIGHTS AND DAMES GRAND CROSS OR GRAND COMMANDERS of the various Orders only on "Collar Days" and other special occasions, or when commanded by the Sovereign.

Collar Days are Easter Sunday, Ascension Day, Whit Sunday, Trinity Sunday, New Year's Day, Epiphany, Feb 6th (Accession Day), St. David, St. Patrick, Lady Day, April 21st (The Queen's Birthday), St George, St Philip and St. James, May 29th (Restoration of Royal Family), June 2nd (Coronation Day), 10th June (Duke of Edinburgh's Birthday), St John the Baptist, St. Peter, 4th Aug (Queen Elizabeth The Queen Mother's Birthday), St Michael and All Angels, All Saints, St. Andrew, and Christmas Day, and such other occasions of which due notification is given. Collars are also worn when attending the opening or prorogation of Parliament by the Sovereign, or when taking part in the Ceremony of an introduction of a Peer in the House of Lords, but not after sunset, nor when mounted on Ceremonial Parades, unless directions to that effect are specially given. With Uniform the Collar is placed under the shoulder board and is held in position by the pressure of the board. With Morning Dress the Collar is held in position by black cotton thread on a small gilt safety pin, the Collar hanging at equal distance back and front.

In the case of possessors of two or more Collars, only one should be worn at a time.

When the Collar (from which the Badge is suspended) is worn, the Riband with its Badge should not be worn, but it may be replaced by the Riband of another Order.

KNIGHTS AND LADIES of the GARTER, THISTLE, and KNIGHTS AND DAMES GRAND CROSS of the various Orders are entitled to bear Supporters to their Arms.

Instructions for the Wearing of Orders, Decorations, Miniatures with dress other than uniform will be found in the Preliminary Section. Instructions for wearing them with uniform is as laid down by the Service to which the recipient belongs or belonged. Ladies in uniform conform to the regulations for male holders.

THE MOST NOBLE ORDER OF THE GARTER

The Order of the Garter, constituted by King Edward III about August 1348, has, since June 28th, 1831, consisted of the Sovereign and twenty-four Knights Companions, such lineal descendants of

King George I, as may have been elected, and of Sovereigns and extra Knights who have been admitted by special statutes. The Prince of Wales is a constituent part of the original institution.

The Habit and Ensigns of the Order are (*i*) A GARTER of dark blue velvet, edged with gold, bearing the motto, *Honi soit qui mal y pense,* in gold letters, with a buckle and pendant of gold, richly chased. (It is worn on the left, below the knee) (*ii*) A MANTLE of dark blue velvet lined with white taffeta, with a representation of the Garter encircling the Cross of St George on an escutcheon argent embroidered on the left shoulder, the Sovereign having the star. (*iii*) A HOOD of crimson velvet. (*iv*) A SURCOAT of crimson velvet, lined with white taffeta. (*v*) A HAT of black velvet, lined with white taffeta, and fastened thereto a band of diamonds, a plume of white ostrich feathers. (*vi*) A COLLAR of gold (weighing thirty ounces, troy) consisting of twenty-four pieces, each in the form of a Garter surrounding the Tudor Rose, connected by twenty-four knots of chased gold, and pendent thereto (*vii*) the GEORGE, an enamelled figure of St. George on horseback, encountering the dragon. (*viii*) The LESSER GEORGE or BADGE of gold is worn pendent from a four-inch blue ribbon over the left shoulder. (*ix*) The STAR of eight points of silver, in the centre the Cross of St. George gules, encircled with the

Insignia of the Order of the Garter.

Garter. At death the Badge and Star are delivered up to Her Majesty by the Knight's male heir, the collar (with pendant Badge) and Garter being returned to the Central Chancery. The Queen's Royal Free Chapel of St George, Windsor Castle, is the chapel of the Order.

SOVEREIGN   HM The Queen

LADIES OF THE ORDER   HM Queen Elizabeth The Queen Mother, HRH The Princess Royal

ROYAL KNIGHTS COMPANIONS   HRH The Duke of Edinburgh, HRH The Prince of Wales, HRH The Duke of Kent

EXTRA KNIGHTS COMPANIONS AND LADIES OF THE ORDER   Princess Juliana of the Netherlands, Grand Duke of Luxembourg, Queen of Denmark, King of Sweden, King of Spain, Queen of the Netherlands

KNIGHTS COMPANIONS AND LADY OF THE ORDER   Sir Cennydd Traherne, Earl Waldegrave, Earl of Longford, Baron Shackleton, Marquess of Abergavenny, Baron Wilson of Rievaulx, Duke of Grafton, Baron Hunt, Sir Paul Hasluck, Duke of Norfolk, Baron Richardson of Duntisbourne, Baron Lewin, Baron Carrington, Baron Callaghan of Cardiff, Baron Hailsham of St Marylebone, Viscount Leverhulme, Lavinia Duchess of Norfolk, The Duke of Wellington, Baron Bramall, Sir Edward Heath, Baron Sainsbury of Preston Candover, Viscount Ridley, Sir Ninian Stephen, Baron Kingsdown, Baron Ashburton

Prelate   The Bishop of Winchester

Chancellor   The Marquess of Abergavenny, KG, OBE

Register   The Dean of Windsor

Garter Principal King of Arms   Sir Conrad Marshall John Fisher, KCVO, PhD, FSA

Usher of the Black Rod   Air Chief Marshal Sir John Gingell, GBE, KCB

Secretary   David Hubert Boothby Chesshyre, LVO, Chester Herald

THE MOST ANCIENT AND MOST NOBLE ORDER OF THE THISTLE

The date of the foundation of the Order of the Thistle is not known. When the Order was revived by King James VII and II in 1687 and by Queen Anne in 1703 it was narrated in the Royal Warrants that the Order had been instituted by "Achaius, King of Scots (of glorious memory)". This is now regarded as legendary. What seems more probable is that King Achaius instituted the veneration of St. Andrew who became the natural Patron Saint of

BADGE

STAR

THE COLLAR   AND BADGE.

Insignia of the Order of the Thistle.

the Order when in due time it was created. In "Les Souverains du Monde" (1722: Vol LV: P. 318) James II of Scotland is credited with "reviving" an Order of St Andrew in 1452 but it is to his eldest son and successor James III (1460-1488) that historical evidence now points as being the true founder of the the Most Ancient and Most Noble Order of the Thistle. The order consists of the Sovereign and sixteen Knights. Royal Knights and Extra Knights are admitted by special statutes in addition to the number of sixteen.

The insignia are (*i*) the STAR, consisting of a St. Andrew's cross of silver embroidery with rays emanating between the points of the cross; in the centre upon a field of gold, a Thistle of green heightened with gold, and surrounded by a circle of green, having thereon the motto in letters of gold, *Nemo me impune lacessit*. (It is worn affixed to the left breast.) (*ii*) The COLLAR of gold consists of thistles intermingled with sprigs of rue, pendant from the centre the St. Andrew of gold enamelled, with the gown green and the surcoat purple, bearing before him the cross enamelled white, and having round the image rays of gold going out from it in the form of a glory. (*iii*) The MANTLE is of green velvet bound with taffeta and tied with cords and tassels of green and gold; on the left shoulder is a representation of the Star of the Order. (*iv*) The BADGE (of gold enamelled) has on one side the image of St. Andrew with the cross before, enamelled as above described or cut in stone, and on the back enamelled a Thistle, gold and green, the flower reddish, with the before-mentioned motto round it, the Thistle on an enamelled green ground. (It is worn attached to a dark green ribbon passing over the left shoulder and resting on the right hip.) (*v*) The HAT is of black velvet, ornamented with white osprey plumes. At death the Badge and Star are delivered up to Her Majesty by the Knight's nearest male relative, the Collar (with pendant Badge) being returned to the Central Chancery. The Chapel of the Order is in St Giles's Cathedral, Edinburgh, and the Chancery at the Court of the Lord Lyon, HM New Register House, Edinburgh.

SOVEREIGN HM The Queen

LADY OF THE ORDER HM Queen Elizabeth The Queen Mother

ROYAL KNIGHTS HRH The Duke of Edinburgh, HRH The Duke of Rothesay (The Prince of Wales)

KNIGHTS Baron Home of the Hirsel, Earl of Wemyss and March, Earl of Dalhousie, Baron Clydesmuir, Sir Donald Cameron of Lochiel, Earl of Selkirk, Baron McFadzean, Hon Lord Cameron, Duke of Buccleuch, Earl of Elgin and Kincardine, Baron Thomson of Monifieth, Baron MacLehose of Beoch, Earl of Airlie, Capt Sir Iain Tennant, Viscount Whitelaw, Sir Fitzroy Maclean, Bt.

Chancellor Baron Home of the Hirsel, KT, PC

Dean The Very Rev Prof John McIntyre, CVO, MA, BD, DLitt, DD.

Secretary Sir Malcolm R. Innes of Edingight, KCVO, Lord Lyon King of Arms

Usher of the Green Rod Rear Adm David Arthur Dunbar-Nasmith, CB, DSC.

THE MOST HONOURABLE ORDER OF THE BATH

From Saxon times until the Coronation of King Charles II on great Royal occasions it was customary to confer "a degree of Knighthood" which, from the ceremonies associated with it, became known as the Knighthood of the Bath. Drawing on this ancient tradition, in 1725 King George I created a new military Order and called it the Order of the Bath. The Order was enlarged in 1815 and further extended in 1847, when new statutes regarding appointments were promulgated and the Civil branch established; the statutes were subsequently modified in 1905 and 1912. Under date of July 1925, all former statutes were repealed, and revised and consolidated statutes and ordinances were promulgated; these were further revised in 1930, 1936, 1939, 1969 and 1973. The Order now consists of three classes, each comprising two divisions (military and civil): (*i*) KNIGHTS AND DAMES GRAND CROSS. These Knights and Dames are entitled to receive a grant of supporters to their armorial bearings. (*ii*) KNIGHTS AND DAMES COMMANDERS. Each Knight of the Order is entitled to the distinctive appellation of knighthood. (*iii*) COMPANIONS. The Military division is open to Officers of the Navy, Army, and Air Force, and Naval, Military and Air Forces of the Commonwealth Countries. The Order consists of not more than 120 Knights and Dames Grand Cross (of whom the Great Master is the First and Principal), 355 Knights Commanders and Dames Commanders, and 1,870 Companions exclusive of Honorary Members and any Additional Members who may have been or may be appointed.

The Insignia are (*i*) the COLLAR of gold (weighing thirty ounces troy), composed of nine Imperial Crowns or and eight roses, thistles, and shamrocks, issuing from a gold sceptre, and

G.C.B. MILITARY. (STAR)

G.C.B. MILITARY. (COLLAR & BADGE)

K.C.B. MILITARY. (STAR)

K.C.B. MILITARY. (BADGE)

enamelled in their proper colours, linked together with seventeen knots enamelled argent, and having therefrom the Badge of the Order. (*ii*) The MILITARY KNIGHT AND DAME GRAND CROSS STAR is formed of rays of silver, charged with a Maltese cross or, in the centre whereof on the ground argent three Imperial Crowns, one and two or, the said three Imperial Crowns within a circle gules inscribed with the motto of the Order, *Tria juncta in uno*, in letters of gold, and the said circle encompassed by two branches of laurel proper, issuing from an escrol azure inscribed *Ich dien* in letters of gold. (*iii*) CIVIL KNIGHT AND DAME GRAND CROSS STAR is of rays of silver issuing from a centre and charged with three Imperial Crowns, one and two within a circle gules whereon is inscribed the motto of the Order in gold. The Collar and Badge are returned at death to the Central Chancery, but not so the investment Badge and Star. (*iv*) MILITARY KNIGHT AND DAME COMMANDER'S STAR is composed of four rays of silver, between each of which issues a smaller ray, also of silver, and has the same centre as the Knights Grand Cross, but without a gold Maltese cross thereon. (*v*) CIVIL KNIGHTS AND DAME COMMANDER'S STAR is of the same form and size, but without a laurel wreath round the circle containing the motto and the escrol, and without the words *Ich dien*

O.C.B. CIVIL (STAR)

O.C.B CIVIL (COLLAR & BADOB)

K.C.B. CIVIL (STAR)

K.C.B. CIVIL. (BADGE)

underneath. (The Crowns in the Stars, which formerly were of different designs for the Civil and Military Divisions, are now all of the same pattern.) (*vi*) MILITARY BADGE is a gold Maltese cross of eight points, enamelled argent, edged gold, and terminating with small gold balls having in each of the four angles a lion passant guardant or and in the centre on a ground argent, the rose, thistle, and shamrock, issuing from a sceptre between three Imperial Crowns, all or,

within a circle gules, thereon the motto of the Order, *Tria juncta in uno*, in gold letters and encompassed by two branches of laurel proper, issuant from an escrol azure inscribed *Ich dien* in letters of gold. (*vii*) CIVIL BADGE is of an oval shape, comprised of a rose, thistle, and shamrock, issuing from a sceptre between three Imperial Crowns, the whole pierced and encircled by the motto of the Order, all gold. The Badge is worn by Knights Grand Cross pendent from a four inch crimson riband, and by Dames Grand Cross pendent from a two and a quarter inch crimson riband passing from the

C.B. MILITARY. (BADGE)

C.B. CIVIL (BADGE)

right shoulder obliquely to the left side. Knights Commanders wear the Badge of a smaller size suspended from the neck by a crimson ribbon of miniature width and wear on their left side a Star. Dames Commanders wear the Badge on a Bow except with coats of military pattern, when the Badge is worn in the same manner as a Knight Commander. The Bow and Star are both worn on the left side. Gentlemen Companions wear the Badge of a smaller size, on a crimson ribbon of miniature width suspended from the neck. Lady Companions wear this Badge on a Bow except with a coat of military pattern when the Badge is worn suspended on a ribbon from the neck. The Badge and Star of a KCB and a DCB and the Badge of a CB are not returned after death, but the Collar and Badge of a GCB should be returned to the Central Chancery of the Orders of Knighthood. The MANTLE of a Knight and Dame Grand Cross is of crimson satin lined with white taffeta and tied with a cordon of white silk with two tassels of crimson silk and gold attached thereto, on the left side of the mantle below a white silk lace is embroidered a representation of the Star of a Knight Grand Cross. The HAT is of black velvet, high crowned and with an upright plume of white feathers in the front. Henry VII's Chapel in Westminster Abbey has been the Chapel of the Order since 1725.

SOVEREIGN   HM The Queen

Great Master and First or Principal Knight Grand Cross   HRH The Prince of Wales.

Dean   The Dean of Westminster.

Bath King of Arms   Air Chief Marshal Sir David Evans, GCB, CBE.

Secretary and Registrar   Air Marshal Sir Denis Crowley-Milling, KCB, CBE, DSO, DFC.

Genealogist   Sir Conrad Marshall John Fisher Swan, KCVO, PhD, FSA, Garter Principal King of Arms.

Gentleman Usher of the Scarlet Rod   Rear Adm D. E. Macey, CB.

Deputy Secretary   The Secretary of the Central Chancery of the Orders of Knighthood.

THE ORDER OF MERIT

This is a very exclusive Order (the Ordinary Members of which do not exceed 24 in number), instituted by King Edward VII on 23 June 1902, by letters patent, but carries with it no special title or personal precedence.

The BADGE of the Order consists of a cross of red and blue enamel of eight points, having the words "For Merit" (the motto of the Order) in gold letters within a laurel wreath on a blue enamel centre. The reverse of the badge shows the Royal and Imperial cipher in gold (two silver swords with gold hilts, placed saltirewise between the angles of the cross, being added in the case of members chosen for naval or military distinction) also within a laurel wreath, on a blue enamel centre; and the whole is surmounted by the Imperial Crown enamelled in colour, and suspended by a parti-coloured ribbon of Garter blue and crimson, two inches broad. The Sovereign's insignia, except, of course for the modifications necessary to distinguish the Royal dignity of the wearer, is similar to the insignia worn by the ordinary members of the Order. The Badge of the Order is always worn round the neck by gentlemen, and may be suspended from Armorial Bearings, is never worn in miniature, and is not returnable at death. Ladies wear the Badge on a bow on the left side except with coats of military pattern when the Badge is worn in the same manner as by a gentleman. The ceremony of investiture is from time to time conducted by the Sovereign as in the case of any other Order. Members of the Order are entitled to attach a facsimile of its badge and ribbon to their arms, and add the letters OM after their names, after GCB. The Seal of the Order is a facsimile of the badge, impaled with the Royal Arms, on a white ground, with the legend, "The Seal of the Order of Merit." June 23rd is the anniversary of the Order. The Secretary and Registrar, who wears, as his badge of office, a decoration similar to that worn by the members of the Order, with the addition of two silver pens placed saltirewise between the angles of the cross. The Chancery of the Order is in the Central Chancery of the Orders of Knighthood.

SOVEREIGN   HM The Queen.

Secretary and Registrar   Sir Edward Ford, KCB, KCVO, DL.

Members   HRH The Duke of Edinburgh, Dr Dorothy Hodgkin, Dame Veronica Wedgwood, Sir Isaiah Berlin, Sir George Edwards, Prof Sir Alan Hodgkin, Sir Ronald Syme, Baron Todd, Rev Prof Owen Chadwick, Sir Andrew Huxley, Sir Michael Tippett, Air Cdre Sir Frank Whittle, Frederick Sanger, Baron Menuhin, Prof Sir Ernst Gombrich, Dr Max Perutz, Dame Cicely Saunders, Prof Sir George Porter, Baroness Thatcher, Dame Joan Sutherland, Prof Francis Crick, Dame Ninette de Valois, Sir Michael Atiyah, Baron Jenkins of Hillhead, Lucien Freud.

THE MOST EXALTED ORDER OF THE STAR OF INDIA

The Order of the Star of India was instituted by Queen Victoria in 1861, and enlarged 1866, 1875, 1897, 1902, 1911, 1915, 1920, 1927, and 1939, and the dignity of Knight Grand Commander was conferred on Princes or Chiefs of India, or upon British subjects for important and loyal service rendered to the Indian Empire; the second and third classes were for services in the Indian Empire of not less than thirty years in the department of the Secretary of State for India. It consists of the Sovereign, the first class of Knights Grand Commanders, the second class of Knights Commanders, and the third class of Companions. No appointments to this Order have been made since 14 August, 1947.

The Insignia are (*i*) the COLLAR of gold, composed of the lotus flower of India, of palm branches tied together in saltire, of the united red and white rose, and in the centre an Imperial Crown; all enamelled in their proper colours and linked together by gold chains. (*ii*) The STAR OF A KNIGHT GRAND COMMANDER is composed of rays of gold issuing from a centre, having thereon a star of five points in diamonds resting upon a light blue enamelled circular riband, tied at the ends and inscribed with the motto of the Order, *Heaven's Light our Guide,* also in diamonds. That of a Knight Commander is somewhat different, and is described below. (*iii*) The BADGE, on onyx cameo having Her Majesty Queen Victoria's Royal effigy thereon, set in a perforated and ornamented oval, containing the motto of the Order in diamonds ensigned with a star of five points, composed of silver. (*iv*) The MANTLE of light blue satin lined with white, and fastened with a cordon of white silk with two blue and silver tassels. On the left side a representation of the star of the Order. The Ribbon of the Order (four inches wide for Knights Grand Commanders) is light blue, having a narrow white stripe towards either edge, and is worn from the right shoulder to the left side. A KNIGHT COMMANDER wears (*a*) around his neck a ribbon two inches in width, of the same colours and pattern as a Knight Grand Commander, and pendent therefrom a badge of a smaller size, (*b*) on his left breast a STAR composed of rays of silver issuing from a gold centre, having thereon a silver star of five points resting upon a light blue enamelled circular ribbon, tied at the ends, inscribed with the motto of the Order in diamonds. A Companion wears suspended from the neck a badge of the same form as appointed for a Knight Commander, but of a smaller size pendent to a like ribbon of the breadth of one and a half inches. Only the GCSI Collar and Badge appendant are returnable at death to the Central Chancery.

STAR G.C.S.I.

STAR K.C.S.I.

THE COLLAR   AND BADGE.

Insignia of the Order of the Star of India.

Secretary and Registrar   The Secretary of the Central Chancery of Orders of Knighthood.

THE MOST DISTINGUISHED ORDER OF ST MICHAEL AND ST GEORGE

Ordinary Membership of the Order of St Michael and St George, which was instituted in 1818, and enlarged and extended in 1868, 1879, 1887, 1901, 1911, 1915, 1927, 1935, 1937, 1939, 1948, 1953, 1954, 1960, 1965, 1969 and 1974 is conferred on subjects of the Crown of the United Kingdom and certain classes of British protected persons, who may hold, or have held high and confidential offices, or may render or have rendered extraordinary and important services (other than military) within or in relation to any part of the British Dominions or Territories under British Protection or Administration, and in reward for important and loyal services in relation to foreign affairs. The Order consists of not more than one hundred and twenty Knights Grand Cross and Dames Grand Cross (of whom the Grand Master is the First and Principal), three hundred and ninety Knights Commanders and Dames Commanders, and one thousand seven hundred and seventy five Companions, exclusive of Honorary members, and any Additional members who have been or may be appointed. The Knights Grand Cross and Dames Grand Cross are entitled to bear supporters, and to surround their coats of arms with the Collar, circle, and Motto of the Order, and to suspend therefrom the Badge of the Order. The Knights Commanders, Dames Commanders and Companions are permitted to surround their arms with the circle and motto, from which is suspended the ribbon and Badge of the Order.

The Insignia are: (i) the STAR of the Knight Grand Cross and Dame Grand Cross which is composed of seven rays of silver having a small ray of gold between each of them, and over all the Cross of St. George gules; in the centre is the representation of the Archangel St. Michael holding in his dexter hand a flaming sword and trampling upon Satan,

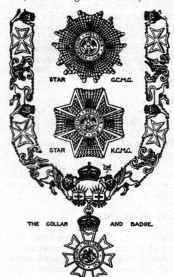

STAR G.C.M.G.

STAR K.C.M.G.

THE COLLAR   AND BADGE.

Insignia of the Order of St. Michael and St. George.

within a blue circle, inscribed with the motto, *Auspicium melioris aevi,* in letters of gold. The STAR for Dames being somewhat smaller than that for Knights. (ii) The COLLAR of gold, which is formed alternately of lions of England royally crowned, of Maltese crosses of white enamel, and of the cyphers S.M. and S. G. (also alternately), having in the centre the Imperial Crown over two winged lions, passant guardant, each holding in his fore paw a book and seven arrows; at the opposite end of the Collar are two similar lions, the whole linked together by small gold chains. The Chain for Dames is slightly smaller than that for Knights. (iii) The BADGE, which is a cross of fourteen points enamelled argent, edged gold, having in the centre on one side the Archangel St. Michael holding in his dexter hand a flaming Sword and trampling upon Satan, and on the other St. George on horseback and in armour with a spear encountering a dragon, each within a blue circle, on which is inscribed the motto of the Order in letters of gold; the Badge is ensigned by an Imperial Crown gold, and it is worn by the Knights Grand Cross and Dames Grand Cross (the Badge for Dames to be the same size as that for Knights Commanders) either attached to the Collar or to a four inch Saxon blue ribbon (for Knights Grand Cross) or to a two and one quarter inches ribbon (for Dames Grand Cross) with a scarlet central stripe, from the right shoulder to the left side. (iv) The MANTLE is of Saxon blue satin, lined with scarlet silk, tied with a cordon of blue and scarlet silk and gold, with two tassels of the same colours, and having on the left side an embroidered representation of the Star of the Order. Knight Commanders wear the Badge—one size smaller than the GCMG Badge—suspended on an Order ribbon of miniature width from the neck, and wear on their left side a STAR composed of four rays, thereon a small cross of eight points in saltire argent, surmounted by the Cross of St. George gules, and having the same centre as the Star of the Grand Crosses, while Dames Commanders wear a similar but slightly smaller Badge than Knights Commanders but tied in a bow and worn on the left shoulder, and they wear a slightly smaller Star. Companions wear the Badge or small Cross of the Order—smaller than the KCMG Badge—on an Order ribbon of miniature width, suspended from the neck; a Lady Companion wears the Badge on a bow one and three quarter inches wide and with an additional fitting on a ribbon suspended from the neck. The Chapel of the Order is in St. Paul's Cathedral, London. The Insignia of all classes of this Order are not returned at death, except in the case of the Collar of a Knight or Dame Grand Cross, provided it was awarded after 1948.

Sovereign HM The Queen

Grand Master HRH The Duke of Kent, KG, GCMG, GCVO, ADC.

Prelate The Rt Rev Simon Barrington-Ward, MA, Bishop of Coventry.

Chancellor The Rt Hon Lord Carrington, KG, GCMG, CH, MC.

Secretary The Permanent Under-Sec of State for the Foreign and Commonwealth Office.

Deputy Secretary The Secretary of the Central Chancery of the Orders of Knighthood.

King of Arms Sir (John) Oliver Wright, GCMG, GCVO, DSC.

Registrar Sir John Alexander Noble Graham, Bt, GCMG.

Gentleman Usher of the Blue Rod Sir John Oscar Moreton, KCMG, KCVO, MC.

Dean The Dean of St. Paul's.

Honorary Genealogist Sir Conrad Marshall John Fisher Swan, KCVO, PhD, FSA, Garter Principal King of Arms.

Chancery Central Chancery of the Orders of Knighthood, St. James's Palace, SW1A 1BG.

THE MOST EMINENT ORDER OF THE INDIAN EMPIRE

This Order, instituted by HM Queen Victoria, Empress of India, 31 Dec 1877, and enlarged in 1886, 1887, 1892, 1897, 1902, 1911, 1915, 1920, 1927, and 1939, was conferred for services rendered to the Indian Empire, and consists of the Sovereign, Grand Commanders, Knights Commanders, and Companions. No appointments to this Order have been made since 14 August 1947.

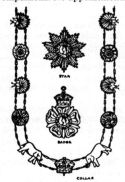

The Insignia are: (*i*) The COLLAR of gold, formed of elephants, lotus flowers, peacocks in their pride, and Indian roses, in the centre the Imperial Crown, the whole linked together with chains; (*ii*) The STAR of the Knight Grand Commander, comprised of five rays of silver, having a smaller ray of gold between each of them, the whole alternately plain and scaled, issuing from a gold centre, having thereon Her Majesty Queen Victoria's Royal Effigy, within a purple circle, inscribed *Imperatricis Auspiciis,* in letters of gold, the circle ensigned by an Imperial Crown, also gold; (*iii*) The BADGE, consisting of a rose enamelled gules, barbed vert, and having in the centre Her Majesty Queen Victoria's Royal Effigy, within a purple circle, inscribed *Imperatricis Auspiciis,* in letters of gold ensigned with an Imperial Crown, also gold; (*iv*) The MANTLE is of purple satin, lined with and fastened by a cordon of white silk, with purple silk and gold tassels attached. On the left side a representation of the Star of the Order.

The ribbon of a KNIGHT GRAND COMMANDER is of Imperial purple and four inches in width. A Knight Commander wears: (*a*) around his neck a riband two inches in width, of the same colour

Insignia of the Order of the Indian Empire.

(Imperial purple) and pattern as a Knight Grand Commander, pendent therefrom a badge of smaller size: (b) on his left breast a star, similar to that of the first class, but the rays of which are alternately bright and chipped.

Only the GCIE Collar is returnable at death to the Central Chancery.

A Companion wears suspended from the neck a badge (not returnable at death) of the same form as appointed for a Knight Commander, but of smaller size, pendent from a like ribbon of the breadth of one and a half inches.

Secretary and Registrar The Secretary of the Central Chancery of the Orders of Knighthood.

THE IMPERIAL ORDER OF THE CROWN OF INDIA

Instituted by Queen Victoria on 1 January 1878, to commemorate the assumption of the Imperial Title of Empress of India, and revised 14 May 1927, and 18 March 1939, this Order consists of the Sovereign, and of such of the Princesses of Her Majesty's Royal House, the wives or other female relatives of Indian Princes, and other Indian ladies, and of the wives or other female relatives of any of the persons who held the office of Viceroy and Governor-General of India, Governors of Madras, Bombay, or Bengal, or of Principal Secretary of State for India, or Commander-in-Chief in India. No appointments to this Order have been made since 14 August 1947.

The Order carries with it no title or precedence, but recipients are permitted to put the initials "CI" after their names, these being placed immediately before "GCVO".

The Badge of the Order consists of the Royal and Imperial Cypher of Queen Victoria, composed of the letters, V, R and I in diamonds, pearls, and turquoises, encircled by a border set with pearls, ensigned with the Imperial Crown jewelled and enamelled in proper colours, and is worn attached to a light blue watered riband, edged white, of an inch and a half in width, tied in a bow, on the left shoulder. The insignia is returnable at death to the Secretary of the Central Chancery of Orders of Knighthood, by whom the Register of the Order is kept.

SOVEREIGN HM The Queen

LADIES OF THE ORDER HM Queen Elizabeth The Queen Mother, HRH The Princess Margaret, Countess of Snowdon, HRH Princess Alice, Duchess of Gloucester.

THE ROYAL VICTORIAN ORDER

This Order, instituted by HM Queen Victoria, Empress of India, 21 April 1896, consists of the Sovereign, a Grand Master, Ordinary Members, and such Honorary Members as the

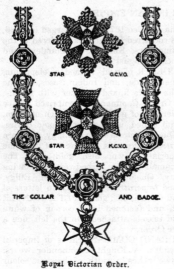

STAR   G.C.V.O.

STAR   K.C.V.O.

THE COLLAR   AND BADGE.

Royal Victorian Order.

Sovereign shall from time to time appoint, the Members being divided into five classes, and designated respectively: (1) Knights and Dames Grand Cross, (2) Knights and Dames Commanders, (3) Commanders, (4) Members of the Fourth Class (now styled Lieutenants), and (5) Members of the Fifth Class. Under date of 29 May 1936, a Warrant was issued consolidating the Statutes of the Order so as to permit of its bestowal upon women.

The persons to be admitted as Ordinary Members of this Order shall be such persons, being male or female subjects of the British Crown, who, having rendered extraordinary, or important, or personal service to the Sovereign, merit Royal favour; and the Honorary Members of the several classes consist of those Foreign Princes and persons upon whom the Sovereign may think fit to confer the honour of being received into the Order.

The Members of the several grades in the Order are to have place and precedence as follows:—Knights Grand Cross immediately after Knights Grand Commanders of the Order of the Indian Empire, Dames Grand Cross immediately before Dames Grand Cross of the Order of the British Empire, Knights Commanders immediately after Knights Commanders of the Order of the Indian Empire, Dames Commanders immediately before Dames Commanders of the Order of the British Empire, men who are Commanders immediately after Companions of the Order of the Indian Empire, women who are Commanders immediately before women who are Commanders of the Order of the British Empire, men who are Members of the Fourth Class (now Lieutenants) immediately after Companions of the Distinguished Service Order, women who are Members of the Fourth Class (now Lieutenants) immediately before women who are Officers of the Order of the British Empire, men who are Members (formerly of the Fifth Class) immediately after Companions of the Imperial Service Order, and women who are Members (formerly of the Fifth Class) immediately before women who are Members of the Order of the British Empire.

The number of the Members is unlimited, and the anniversary of the Order is the Twentieth day of June every year, being the day of Her late Majesty Queen Victoria's Accession to the Throne of these Realms.

The MANTLE of a Knight or Dame Grand Cross is of dark blue satin, edged with red satin two inches in width, the edging of the collar being half an inch wide, lined with white silk, the mantle being fastened by a cordon of dark blue silk and gold, having two dark blue silk and gold tassels attached thereto; on the left side of the mantle is embroidered a representation of the Star of a Knight or Dame Grand Cross of the Order. The COLLAR is of gold, composed of octagonal pieces and oblong perforated and ornamental frames alternately, linked together with gold; the said pieces edged and ornamented with gold, each containing upon a blue enamelled ground a gold rose jewelled with a carbuncle, and the said frames are of gold each containing a portion of the inscription "Victoria . . . Brit. Reg . . . Def Fid . . . Ind Imp" in letters of white enamel; in the centre of the collar, within a perforated and ornamental frame of gold, is an octagonal piece, enamelled blue, edged with red, and charged with a white saltire, thereon a gold medallion of Her late Majesty Queen Victoria's effigy, from which hangs the Cross of the Order (detachable).

The BADGE of Knights and Dames Grand Cross consists of white enamelled Maltese cross of eight points; on an oval centre of crimson enamel the Royal and Imperial cypher of Queen

Victoria (VRI) in gold, within a blue enamelled circle, thereon the motto of the Order, namely, "Victoria" in letters of gold, the circle being surmounted by an Imperial Crown enamelled in proper colours; and is worn over the right shoulder, suspended from a dark blue ribbon with a narrow edge either side of three stripes—red, white, and red—of the breadth of three inches in the case of Knights Grand Cross and of two inches and one quarter in the case of Dames Grand Cross, passing from the right shoulder to the left side.

The STAR of Knights and Dames Grand Cross consists of a silver chipped star of eight points; in the centre a representation of the Badge of the First Class of the Order.

G.C.V.O. and D.C.V.O. Badge.

The Knights Commanders wear around their necks a ribbon of miniature width of the same colours as that of the Knights Grand Cross, of the breadth of one inch and three-quarters, and pendent therefrom the badge, which is of the same pattern as, but of smaller size than, that of a Knight Grand Cross, whilst the Dames Commanders wear their badges attached to a Riband tied in a bow and worn on the left shoulder. The Star is composed of a Maltese cross in silver, with smaller rays issuing from the centre between the angles of the cross; in the centre the badge of the Order as before described, with the cross in frosted silver instead of white enamel.

Men who are Commanders wear around their necks the like riband and badge as that appointed for the Knights Commanders and women wear the bow and badge as appointed for Dames Commanders, but neither is entitled to wear the Star.

The Lieutenants (formerly Members of the Fourth Class) wear a badge of the same form and appearance as that appointed for the Commanders, but of smaller size, pendent from a ribbon of the same colours, of the breadth of an inch and a quarter, attached from the left breast in the case of men and tied in a bow and worn on the left shoulder in the case of women.

The Members wear, from their left breast or shoulder, the same riband and badge as that appointed for the Lieutenants, with the exception that the cross is of frosted silver instead of white enamel.

In uniform ladies wear their insignia in the same way as that adopted for male holders.

The collar is returnable at death or upon receipt of a Collar of an Order of Higher rank, but not the other Insignia.

The Queen's Chapel of the Savoy has been the Chapel of the Order since 1938.

("The Royal Victorian Medal" (silver-gilt, silver, or bronze, having on the obverse the Royal effigy, and on the reverse the Royal and Imperial cypher upon an ornamental shield within a wreath of laurel, in base a scroll, thereon the words "Royal Victorian Medal") was also instituted by Queen Victoria. This Medal is worn by men on the left breast of the coat or outer garment pendent from a ribbon of the breadth of one inch and a quarter of the same colour and pattern as that appointed for the members of the Royal Victorian Order, and by women from a ribbon tied in a bow on the left shoulder.)

SOVEREIGN   HM The Queen

Grand Master   HM Queen Elizabeth The Queen Mother.

Chancellor   The Lord Chamberlain.

Secretary   The Keeper of the Privy Purse.

Registrar   The Secretary of the Central Chancery of the Orders of Knighthood.

Chaplain Rev John Williams.

Hon Genealogist David Hubert Boothby Chesshyre, LVO, FSA, Chester Herald.

ROYAL VICTORIAN CHAIN

King Edward VII founded in Aug 1902 the "Royal Victorian Chain", which is only bestowed on special occasions, and, although forming no part of the Royal Victorian Order, may be worn on all occasions when other insignia of British Orders of Chivalry are worn; it is of a different and much lighter design than the Collar.

HOLDERS OF ROYAL VICTORIAN CHAIN

HM The Queen, HM Queen Elizabeth The Queen Mother, Queen of the Netherlands, King of Norway, King of Thailand, Crown Prince Asfa Wossen of Ethiopia, King of Jordan, King Mohamed Zahir Shah of Afghanistan, Rt Hon Roland Michener, Queen of Denmark, King of Nepal, King of Sweden, Baron Coggan, King Fahd of Saudi Arabia, King of Spain, HRH The Princess Margaret, Countess of Snowdon, Baron Runcie, François Mitterrand, Baron Charteris of Amisfield, King of Norway.

THE MOST EXCELLENT ORDER OF THE BRITISH EMPIRE

This Order, instituted by HM King George V in June 1917, extended Dec 1918, and altered March 1919, Dec 1922, June 1929, Nov 1933, March 1937, and Oct 1939, is conferred for important services rendered to the Empire, and is awarded to both men and women. It consists of the Sovereign and five classes:—(I) Knights Grand Cross and Dames Grand Cross, (II) Knights Commanders and Dames Commanders, (III) Commanders, (IV) Officers, (V) Members. Foreign persons upon whom the Order is conferred are "Honorary."

Further alterations to the Statutes of the Order were made in September 1959, May 1962, July 1964 and September 1969, limiting the numbers to be admitted to the Order in future, as follows:—

Knights and Dames Grand Cross (not to exceed Military 27, Civil 73), Knights and Dames Commanders (not to exceed Military 215, Civil 630), and Commanders (not to exceed Military 1,660, Civil 7,300), specifying the numbers of each of these Classes that may be appointed in a given period;

also Officers (Military not more than 713 in any year, Civil not more than 745 in any year); and Members (Military not more than 228 in any year, Civil not more than 1,256 in any year).

The above-mentioned limitation does not affect those already admitted to the Order prior to 29 December 1922, who are not to be included within the foregoing numbers allotted to each Class of the Order, nor additional appointments made by special statute in commemoration of special occasions.

Appointments are made on the recommendation of the Minister of Defence, the Secretary of State for Foreign and Commonwealth Affairs, and the appropriate Minister of State for Commonwealth Countries other than the United Kingdom, as regards the Military Division, and the Secretary of State for Foreign and Commonwealth Affairs as regards the Civil Division.

This Order ranks next to and immediately after the Royal Victorian Order; Knights Grand Cross have place and precedency next to and immediately after the Knights Grand Cross of the Royal Victorian Order; Dames Grand Cross next to and immediately after the Dames Grand Cross of the Royal Victorian Order, and may use the appellation and style of Dame before their Christian or first names; the Knights Commanders have place and precedency next to and immediately after the Knights Commanders of the Royal Victorian Order; Dames Commanders next to and immediately after the Dame Commanders of the Royal Victorian Order, and may use the appellation and style of Dame before their Christian or first names; men who are Commanders have place and precedency next to and immediately after the Commanders of the Royal Victorian Order and women who are

COLLAR OF THE ORDER.

commanders next to and immediately after women who are members of the Third Class of the Royal Victorian Order; Men who are Officers have place and precedency next to and immediately after Lieutenants of the Royal Victorian Order and women who are Officers next to and immediately after women who are Lieutenants of the Royal Victorian Order; Men who are Members have place and precedency next to and immediately after the Members of the Royal Victorian Order, and women who are Members next to and immediately after women who are Members of the Royal Victorian Order.

There are both Military and Civil Divisions of this Order; the Insignia for both is the same, but the Ribbon of the Military Division is distinguished by the narrow vertical pearl grey (formerly red) stripe in the centre which varies in width according to Class.

The COLLAR for Knights Grand Cross and Dames Grand Cross is of silver gilt composed of six medallions of the Royal Arms and six medallions of the Royal and Imperial Cypher of King George V alternately linked together with cables thereon the Imperial Crown between two sea-lions, from which hangs the Badge of the First Class of the Order. These Collars are returnable at death or upon receipt of a Collar of an Order of higher rank. The Mantle is of rose pink satin with pearl grey silk (originally purple satin lined with white silk) having the Grand Cross Star embroidered on the left side.

The Badge of the First Class of the Order consists of a cross patonce, enamelled pearl, fimbriated or, surmounted by a gold medallion bearing the crowned effigies of King George V, and Queen Mary combined with a circle gules inscribed with the motto, "For God and the Empire," in letters of gold ensigned with the Imperial Crown or, and on the reverse an engraving of the Royal and Imperial Cypher of King George V, the whole suspended from a rose pink riband edged with a pearl grey stripe (originally a purple riband) of the breadth of four inches for Knights Grand Cross, (with the addition, for Military Knights Grand Cross, of a vertical pearl grey stripe in the centre of a width of about one quarter of an inch), and two inches and one quarter for Dames Grand Cross, passing from the right shoulder to the left side, and on the left side of their coats or outer garments a Star (that for Dames being somewhat smaller than that worn by Knights), composed of chipped silver rays of eight points and charged with a medallion as above.

Knights Commanders wear around their necks a riband of miniature width of the same colour and pattern as that of Knights Grand Cross (the pearl grey stripe of Military Knights Commanders being about one sixteenth of an inch in width) and pendent therefrom the badge of the Knights Commanders of the Order, which shall be of a similar form and pattern to that appointed for Knights Grand Cross, but of smaller size, and also wear on the left side of their coats or outer garments a chipped silver Star composed of four greater and four lesser points, charged with a medallion as before, while Dames Commanders wear a badge of similar form and pattern as that appointed for Knights Commanders, attached to a riband, also similar to that worn by Knights Commanders, but tied in a bow and worn on the left shoulder, and they wear a like Star.

Commanders in the same manner wear the like riband and badge as that appointed for Knights or Dames Commanders, but are not entitled to wear the Star.

Officers wear a badge of similar form and pattern as that appointed for Commanders, but of a smaller size and of silver gilt, attached to a riband of the same colour and pattern of the breadth of one inch and a half (the vertical pearl grey stripe in the case of the Military Officers to be one sixteenth of an inch in width), attached to the left breast of their coats or outer garments by men, and tied in a bow on the left shoulder by women.

Members wear in like manner the same riband and badge as that appointed to Officers except that it is in silver.

The Insignia of all classes are, on promotion from a lower to a higher class in the same division, to be returned to the Registrar, but not at death except by Officials of the Order.

(There is a Military and Civil medal in connection with the Order which may be awarded to persons not Members of, or eligible for, any of its five classes, who render meritorious service. It is known as the BRITISH EMPIRE MEDAL, and entitles the recipients to place the letters "BEM" after their names.).

In 1957 it was decreed that appointments to and promotions in the Order of the British Empire and awards of the British Empire Medal, when granted for gallantry, should be distinguished by the wearing of an Emblem on the riband in crossed oak leaves, and in the announcement by an additional description "for gallantry." Gallantry awards in the Order continued until 19 June 1974, when The Queen's Gallantry Medal (QGM) was instituted.

SOVEREIGN   HM The Queen

Grand Master   HRH The Duke of Edinburgh, KG, KT, OM, GBE, AC, QSO, FRS.

Prelate   The Bishop of London.

King of Arms   Adm Sir Anthony Morton, GBE, KCB.

Registrar   The Secretary of the Central Chancery of the Orders of Knighthood.

Secretary   The Permanent Secretary to the Civil Service Department.

Dean   The Dean of St Paul's.

Gentleman Usher of the Purple Rod   Sir Robin Gillett, Bt, GBE, RD.

ORDER OF THE COMPANIONS OF HONOUR

Instituted on 4 June 1917 and altered 15 Oct 1919, consists of the Sovereign and not more than 65 Members (exclusive of Hon Members, and certain additional members appointed by special statute in commemoration of special occasions); it may be conferred on persons (women being eligible equally with men) for having done conspicuous national service, and for whom the distinction is deemed the most appropriate form of recognition, constituting as it does an honour dissociated either from acceptance of title or the classification of merit, and carrying with it no title or precedence, but recipients are permitted to put the initials "CH" after their names, these being placed subsequent to the initials "GBE." The Badge of the Order is oval, and consists of a gold medallion with representation of an oak tree and pendant from a branch a shield of the  Royal Arms; on the dexter a representation of a knight armed and in armour, mounted on a horse, the whole within a circle inscribed with the motto "In action faithful and in honour clear" in letters of gold ensigned with the Imperial Crown proper. Men suspend it around their necks from a carmine riband 1½ inches wide with a bordure interlaced gold; women wear it attached to a similar riband tied in a bow on the left shoulder. It is never worn in miniature, and is not returnable at death. A representation of the Badge may be suspended from an escutcheon of armorial bearings.

SOVEREIGN   HM The Queen

Secretary and Registrar   The Secretary of the Central Chancery of the Orders of Knighthood.

Members of the Order   Tunku Abdul Rahman, Viscount Watkinson, Baron Houghton of Sowerby, Sir John Gorton, Baron Goodman, Sir John Marshall, Viscount Whitelaw, Baron Hailsham of St Marylebone, Baron Ashley of Stoke, Prof Max Perutz, Baron Glenamara, Baron Cledwyn of Penrhos, Malcolm Fraser, Sir John Gielgud, James Jones, Michael Somare, Baron Healey, Sir Michael Tippett, Baron Thorneycroft, Frederick Sanger, Brian Talboys, Victor Pasmore, John Anthony, Dame Ninette de Valois, Prof Sir Karl Popper, Baron Carrington, Lucian Freud, Hon Sir Steven Runciman, Pierre Trudeau, Viscount Eccles, Sir Philip Powell, Prof Friedrich von Hayek, Sir Hugh Casson, Baron Joseph, Sydney Brenner, Baron Tebbit, Anthony Powell, George Rylands, Professor William Hawking, David Lange, Hon Peter Brooke, Kenneth Baker, Thomas King, Dame Elisabeth Frink (d 1993), Dr Joseph Needham, Sir Victor Pritchett, Charles Sisson, Dr Elsie Widdowson, Hon David Astor, Dame Janet Baker, Sir John Smith, Baron Owen.

Honorary Members   Lee Kuan Yew, Dr. Joseph Luns.

KNIGHTS BACHELOR

 The Word Knight is derived from the Saxon Cnyht, which signified a servant or attendant; and Knighthood is the most ancient title of honour known in this country, its origin dating back to Saxon times. The designation Knight Bachelor was in existence as long ago as the reign of King Henry III. Although for many centuries none but the Sovereign, or some person specially designated by him, has been able to create a Knight, originally both ecclesiastical and lay persons could confer the honour. Until 1926 Knights Bachelor had no insignia which they could wear, but in that year HM the King issued a Warrant authorising the wearing of a badge on all appropriate occasions. The Imperial Society of Knights Bachelor was founded for the maintenance and consolidation of the Dignity of Knights Bachelor in 1908, and obtained official recognition from the Sovereign in 1912. The Society keeps records of all Knights Bachelor, the interests of which its purpose is to maintain. The Knights Bachelor badge, which was approved in 1926, is worn on all appropriate occasions upon the left side of the coat or outer garment of those upon whom the degree of Knight Bachelor has been conferred. It measures 2⅜ inches in length and 1⅞ in width, is described as follows:—

"Upon an oval medallion of vermilion, enclosed by a scroll a cross-hilted sword belted and sheathed, pommel upwards, between two spurs, rowels upwards, the whole set about with the sword belt, all gilt".

In 1974 HM The Queen issued a further warrant authorising the wearing on appropriate occasions of a neck badge, slightly smaller in size, and in miniature. In 1988 a new certificate of authentication, a knight's only personal documentation, was designed by the College of Arms.

PATRON   HM The Queen

Knight Principal   Sir (Alexander) Colin Cole, KCVO, TD, FSA.
Hon Deputy Knights Principal   Sir Gilbert Inglefield, GBE, TD; Sir Arthur Driver.
Prelate   The Bishop of London.
Registrar   Sir Roger Falk, OBE.
Treasurer   Sir Peter Lane.
Clerk to the Council   Robert M. Esden.
Registry and Library   21 Old Buildings, Lincolns Inn, EC2 3UJ.

LIFE PEERS AND LAW LORDS

*LAW LORDS

*Baron Ackner
Baron Alexander of Weedon
Baron Allen of Abbeydale
Baron Alport
Baron Amery of Lustleigh
Baron Annan
Baron Archer of Sandwell
Baron Archer of Weston-super-Mare
Baron Armstrong of Ilminster
Baron Ashley of Stoke
Baron Attenborough
Baron Balniel (Earl of Crawford)
Baron Bancroft
Baron Banks
Baron Barber
Baron Barber of Tewkesbury
Baron Barnett
Baron Bauer
Baron Beaumont of Whitley
Baron Bellwin
Baron Beloff
Baron Benson
Baron Blake
Baron Blease
Baron Boardman
Baron Bonham-Carter
Baron Boston of Faversham
Baron Bottomley
Baron Bowden
Baron Boyd-Carpenter
Baron Braine of Wheatley
Baron Bramall
*Baron Brandon of Oakbrook
*Baron Bridge of Harwich
Baron Briggs
*Baron Brightman
Baron Brimelow
Baron Brookes
Baron Brooks of Tremorfa
*Baron Browne-Wilkinson
Baron Bruce of Donington
Baron Bullock
Baron Butterfield
Baron Butterworth
Baron Buxton of Alsa
Baron Callaghan of Cardiff
Baron Cameron of Lochbroom
Baron Campbell of Alloway
Baron Campbell of Croy
Baron Campbell of Eskan
Baron Carlisle of Bucklow
Baron Carmichael of Kelvingrove
Baron Carr of Hadley
Baron Carter
Baron Carver
Baron Cavendish of Furness
Baron Cayzer
Baron Chalfont
Baron Chapple
Baron Charteris of Amisfield
Baron Chelmer
Baron Chilver
Baron Chitnis
Baron Clark of Kempston
Baron Cledwyn of Penrhos
Baron Clinton-Davis
Baron Cockfield
Baron Cocks of Hartcliffe
Baron Coggan
Baron Collison
Baron Colnbrook
Baron Constantine of Stanmore
Baron Cooke of Islandreagh
Baron Craig of Radley
Baron Crickhowell
Baron Crohan
Baron Cudlipp
Baron Dacre of Glanton
Baron Dainton
Baron Dahrendorf
Baron Dean of Beswick
Baron Dean of Harptree
Baron Deedes
*Baron Denning
Baron Desai
Baron Diamond
Baron Dixon Smith
Baron Donaldson of Kingsbridge
Baron Donaldson of Lymington
Baron Donoghue

Baron Dormand of Easington
Baron Eatwell
Baron Eden of Winton
Baron Elliott of Morpeth
Baron Elis-Thomas
*Baron Elwyn-Jones
Baron Elystan Morgan
Baron Emslie
Baron Ennals
Baron Ewing of Kirkford
Baron Ezra
Baron Fanshawe of Richmond
Baron Fieldhouse
Baron Finsberg
Baron Fitt
Baron Flowers
Baron Foot
Baron Forte
Baron Fraser of Carmyllie
Baron Fraser of Kilmorack
Baron Gallacher
Baron Geraint
Baron Gibson
Baron Gibson-Watt
Baron Gilmour of Craigmillar
Baron Glenamara
*Baron Goff of Chieveley
Baron Goodman
Baron Goold
Baron Gormley
Baron Grade
Baron Graham of Edmonton
Baron Granville of Eye
Baron Gray of Contin
Baron Greene of Harrow Weald
Baron Greenhill of Harrow
Baron Gregson
Baron Grey of Naunton
*Baron Griffiths
Baron Griffiths of Fforestfach
Baron Grimond
Baron Hailsham of St Marylebone
Baron Hanson
Baron Harmar-Nicholls
Baron Harris of Greenwich
Baron Harris of High Cross
Baron Haskel
Baron Hartwell
Baron Harvington
Baron Haslam
Baron Hayhoe
Baron Healey
Baron Henderson of Brompton
Baron Hill-Norton
Baron Holderness
Baron Hollick
Baron Holme of Cheltenham
Baron Home of the Hirsel
Baron Hooson
Baron Houghton of Sowerby
Baron Howe of Aberavon
Baron Howell
Baron Howie of Troon
Baron Hughes
Baron Hunt
Baron Hunt of Tanworth
Baron Hutchinson of Lullington
Baron Ingrow
Baron Irvine of Lairg
Baron Jacques
Baron Jakobovits
*Baron Jauncey of Tullichettle
Baron Jay
Baron Jenkin of Roding
Baron Jenkins of Hillhead
Baron Jenkins of Putney
Baron John-Mackie
Baron Johnston of Rockport
Baron Joseph
Baron Judd
Baron Kagan
Baron Keith of Castleacre
*Baron Keith of Kinkel
Baron Kimball
Baron King of Wartnaby
Baron Kingsdown
Baron Kings Norton
Baron Kirkhill
Baron Kissin
Baron Knights

Baron Laing of Dunphail
*Baron Lane
Baron Lane of Horsell
Baron Lawson of Blaby
Baron Leonard
Baron Lever of Manchester
Baron Lester of Herne Hill
Baron Lewin
Baron Lewis of Newnham
*Baron Lloyd of Berwick
Baron Lloyd of Kilgerran
Baron Lovell-Davis
Baron Lowry
Baron McAlpine of West Green
Baron Macaulay of Bragar
Baron Macfarlane of Bearsden
Baron Mackay of Ardbrecknish
Baron McCarthy
Baron McCluskey
Baron McColl of Dulwich
Baron McFadzean
Baron McGregor of Durris
Baron McIntosh of Haringey
Baron MacKay of Clashfern
Baron Mackenzie-Stuart
Baron Mackie of Benshie
Baron MacLehose of Beoch
Baron Marlesford
Baron Marsh
Baron Marshall of Goring
Baron Mason of Barnsley
Baron Matthews
Baron Mayhew
Baron Mellish
Baron Menuhin
Baron Merlyn-Rees
Baron Mishcon
Baron Molloy
Baron Moore of Lower Marsh
Baron Moore of Wolvercote
Baron Morris of Castle Morris
Baron Morton of Shuna
Baron Moyola
Baron Mulley
Baron Murray of Epping Forest
Baron Murray of Newhaven
Baron Murton of Lindisfarne
Baron Mustill
Baron Nickson
*Baron Nolan
Baron Normand
Baron Northfield
Baron O'Brien of Lothbury
*Baron Oliver of Aylmerton
Baron Oram
Baron Orr-Ewing
Baron Owen
Baron Paget of Northampton
Baron Palumbo
Baron Parkinson
Baron Parry
Baron Pearson of Rannoch
Baron Pennock
Baron Perry of Walton
Baron Peston
Baron Peyton of Yeovil
Baron Pitt of Hampstead
Baron Plant of Highfield
Baron Plowden
Baron Plumb
Baron Plummer of St Marylebone
Baron Porter of Luddenham
Baron Prentice
Baron Prior
Baron Pritchard
Baron Prys-Davies
Baron Pym
Baron Quinton
Baron Rawlinson of Ewell
Baron Rayne
Baron Rayner
Baron Rees
Baron Rees-Mogg
Baron Reigate
Baron Renfrew of Kaimsthorn
Baron Renton
Baron Rhodes
Baron Richard
Baron Richardson
Baron Richardson of Duntisbourne

Baron Rippon of Hexham
Baron Rix
Baron Robens of Woldingham
Baron Rodger of Earlsferry
Baron Rodgers of Quarry Bank
Baron Roll of Ipsden
*Baron Roskill
Baron Ross of Marnock
Baron Ross of Newport
Baron Runcie of Cuddesdon
Baron Ryder of Eaton Hastings
Baron Sainsbury
Baron Sainsbury of Preston Candover
Baron St John of Fawsley
Baron Sanderson of Bowden
Baron Scanlon
*Baron Scarman
Baron Schon
Baron Shackleton
Baron Shawcross
Baron Sieff of Brimpton
Baron Simon of Glaisdale
Baron Skidelsky
Baron Slynn of Hadley
Baron Smith
Baron Soper
Baron Soulsby of Swaffham Prior
Baron Stallard

Baron Sterling of Plaistow
Baron Stevens of Ludgate
Baron Stewartby
Baron Stodart of Leaston
Baron Stoddart of Swindon
Baron Stokes
Baron Stonham
Baron Strauss
Baron Tanlaw
Baron Taylor of Blackburn
Baron Taylor of Gosforth
Baron Taylor of Gryfe
Baron Taylor of Hadfield
Baron Tebbit
*Baron Templeman
Baron Thomas of Gwydir
Baron Thomas of Swynnerton
Baron Thomson of Monifieth
Baron Todd
Baron Tombs
Baron Tordoff
Baron Tugendhat
Baron Varley
Baron Vinson
Baron Waddington
Baron Wade of Chorlton
Baron Wakeham
Baron Walker of Worcester

Baron Wallace of Campsie
Baron Wallace of Coslany
Baron Walton of Detchant
Baron Weatherill
Baron Wedderburn of Charlton
Baron Weidenfeld
Baron Weinstock
Baron Whaddon
Baron White of Hull
Baron Wigoder
*Baron Wilberforce
Baron Williams of Elvel
Baron Williams of Mostyn
Baron Willis
Baron Wilson of Langside
Baron Wilson of Rivaulx
Baron Wilson of Tillyorn
Baron Wolfson
Baron Wolfson of Sunningdale
*Baron Woolf
Baron Wright of Richmond
Baron Wyatt of Weeford
Baron Young of Dartington
Baron Young of Graffham
Baron Younger of Prestwick

LIFE PEERESSES

Baroness Birk
Baroness Blackstone
Baroness Blatch
Baroness Brigstocke
Baroness Brooke of Ystradfellte
Baroness Carnegy of Lour
Baroness Castle of Blackburn
Baroness Chalker of Wallasey
Baroness Cox
Baroness Cumberlege
Baroness David
Baroness Dean of Thornton-le-Fylde
Baroness Delacourt-Smith of Alteryn
Baroness Denington
Baroness Denton of Wakefield
Baroness Dunn
Baroness Eccles of Moulton
Baroness Elles
Baroness Faithfull
Baroness Falkender

Baroness Fisher of Rednal
Baroness Flather
Baroness Gardner of Parkes
Baroness Gould of Potternewton
Baroness Hamwee
Baroness Hilton of Eggardon
Baroness Hollis of Heigham
Baroness Hooper
Baroness Hylton-Foster
Baroness James of Holland Park
Baroness Jay of Paddington
Baroness Jeger
Baroness Llewelyn-Davies of Hastoe
Baroness McFarlane of Llandaff
Baroness Macleod of Borve
Baroness Mallalieu
Baroness Masham of Ilton
Baroness Miller of Hendon
Baroness Nicol
Baroness O'Cathain

Baroness Oppenheim-Barnes
Baroness Park of Monmouth
Baroness Perry of Southwark
Baroness Pike
Baroness Platt of Writtle
Baroness Robson of Kiddington
Baroness Ryder of Warsaw
Baroness Seccombe
Baroness Seear
Baroness Serota
Baroness Sharples
Baroness Stedman
Baroness Thatcher
Baroness Turner of Camden
Baroness Trumpington
Baroness Warnock
Baroness Williams of Crosby
Baroness White
Baroness Young

HEREDITARY PEERESSES IN THEIR OWN RIGHT

*of England †of Scotland ‡of The United Kingdom

*DACRE, Baroness
*DARCY DE KNAYTH, Baroness
*DUDLEY, Baroness
†DYSART, Countess of
†HERRIES OF TERREGLES, Lady
†KINLOSS, Lady
†LOUDOUN, Countess of
†MAR, Countess of

‡MOUNTBATTEN OF BURMA, Countess
†NAIRNE, Lady
†SALTOUN, Lady
†SEMPILL, Lady
*STRANGE, Baroness
†SUTHERLAND, Countess of
*WHARTON, Baroness
*WILLOUGHBY DE ERESBY, Baroness

PEERS WHO ARE MINORS

*and the dates when they are eligible to
sit in the House of Lords¶*

CRAVEN, Earl of. 12 June 2010.   GRETTON, Baron. 16 April 1996.

¶*Legally persons are deemed to obtain their majority, so far as sitting in the House of Lords is concerned, on
completion of their twenty-first year (i.e. on the day prior to the twenty-first anniversary of their birth)*

THE ROYAL HOUSEHOLDS

THE QUEEN'S HOUSEHOLD

Lord Chamberlain	The Earl of Airlie, KT, GCVO, PC
Lord Steward	The Viscount Ridley, KG, GCVO, TD
Master of the Horse	The Lord Somerleyton
Mistress of the Robes	The Duchess of Grafton, GCVO
Lords in Waiting	Lt-Col the Lord Charteris of Amisfield, GCB, GCVO, OBE, QSO, PC (Permanent)
	The Lord Moore of Wolvercote, GCB, GCVO, CMG, QSO
	The Viscount Boyne
	The Lord Camoys
	The Viscount Long
	The Lord Lucas of Crudwell
	The Lord Inglewood
Baronesses in Waiting	The Baroness Trumpington
	The Baroness Miller of Hendon, MBE
Captain, Gentlemen at Arms	The Lord Strathclyde
Captain, Yeomen of the Guard	The Earl of Arran
Treasurer of the Household	Gregory Knight, MP
Comptroller of the Household	David Lightbown, MP
Vice-Chamberlain of the Household	Sydney Chapman, MP
Ladies of the Bedchamber	The Countess of Airlie, CVO
	The Lady Farnham
Extra Lady of the Bedchamber	The Marchioness of Abergavenny, DCVO
Women of the Bedchamber	The Hon Mary Morrison, DCVO
	Lady Susan Hussey, DCVO
	Lady Dugdale, DCVO
	The Lady Elton
	The Hon Mrs van der Woude, CVO
	Mrs John Woodroffe, CVO
Extra Women of the Bedchamber	Lady Rose Baring, DCVO
	Mrs Michael Wall, DCVO
	Lady Abel Smith, DCVO
	Mrs Robert de Pass
Equerries	Lt-Col Sir Guy Acland, Bt, MVO
	Maj James Patrick
Temporary Equerry	Capt Edward Macfarlane

PRIVATE SECRETARY'S OFFICE

Private Secretary	The Rt Hon Sir Robert Fellowes, KCB, KCVO
Deputy Private Secretary	Sir Kenneth Scott, KCVO, CMG
Assistant Private Secretary	Robin Janvrin, CVO
Chief Clerk	Mrs Graham Coulson, MVO
Press Secretary	Charles Anson, LVO
Deputy Press Secretary	Geoffrey Crawford
Assistant Press Secretary	Miss Penelope Russell-Smith
Defence Services Secretary	Air Vice Marshal Peter Harding, CB, CBE, AFC

DEPARTMENT OF THE KEEPER OF THE PRIVY PURSE AND TREASURER TO THE QUEEN

Keeper of the Privy Purse and Treasurer to the Queen	Major Sir Shane Blewitt, KCVO
Director of Finance and Property Services	Michael Peat, CVO
Deputy Keeper and Deputy Treasurer	John Parsons, LVO
Chief Accountant and Paymaster	David Walker, LVO
Management Auditor	Ian McGregor
Personnel Officer	Miss Patricia Lloyd
High Almoner	The Bishop of St Albans (The Rt Rev John Taylor, MA, BTh)
Secretary, Royal Almonry	Peter Wright, CVO

MASTER OF THE HOUSEHOLD'S DEPARTMENT

Master of the Household	Maj-Gen Sir Simon Cooper, KCVO
Deputy Master of the Household	Lt-Col Sir Guy Acland, Bt, MVO
Chief Clerk	Michael Jephson, MVO

LORD CHAMBERLAIN'S OFFICE

Comptroller, Lord Chamberlain's Office	Lt-Col Malcolm Ross, CVO, OBE
Secretary, LCO	Peter Hartley, LVO
Assistant Secretary, LCO	Jonathan Spencer, MVO
State Invitations Assistant	John Hope
Marshal of the Diplomatic Corps	Vice Adm Sir James Weatherall, KBE
Vice-Marshal of the Diplomatic Corps	Anthony Figgis, CMG
First Assistant Marshal of the Diplomatic Corps	Robin Gorham
Assistant Marshal of the Diplomatic Corps	Maurice Dalton, LVO
Secretary, Central Chancery of the Orders of Knighthood, and Assistant Controller, LCO	Lt-Col Anthony Mather, OBE
Assistant Secretary	Miss Rachel Wells, MVO

Master of The Queen's Music	Malcolm Williamson, CBE, AO
Poet Laureate	Edward Hughes, OBE
Gentlemen at Arms: Lieutenant	Col Thomas Hall, OBE
Clerk of the Cheque and Adjutant	Lt-Col R. Mayfield, OBE
Yeomen of the Guard: Lieutenant	Colonel Greville Tufnell
Clerk of the Cheque and Adjutant	Colonel Shaun Longsden
Clerk of the Closet	The Bishop of Chelmsford (The Rt Rev John Waine)
Deputy Clerk of the Closet	The Rev William Booth
Dean of the Chapels Royal	The Bishop of London (The Rt Rev and Rt Hon David Hope)
Sub-Dean of the Chapels Royal	The Rev William Booth
Head of the Medical Household and Physician	Dr Richard Thompson, DM, FRCP
Apothecary to The Queen	Nigel Southward, LVO, MA, MB, BChir, MRCP
Serjeant Surgeon	Barry Jackson, MS, FRCS
Windsor Castle: Constable and Governor	Gen Sir Patrick Palmer, KBE
Superintendent	Major Barrie Eastwood, LVO, MBE
Heralds and Pursuivants	see HER MAJESTY'S OFFICERS OF ARMS

ROYAL MEWS DEPARTMENT

Crown Equerry	Lt-Col Seymour Gilbert-Denham, CVO
Superintendent, Royal Mews	Major Albert Smith, MBE

ROYAL COLLECTION DEPARTMENT

Director of the Royal Collection and Surveyor of the Queen's Works of Art	Sir Geoffrey de Bellaigue, KCVO, FBA, FSA
Surveyor of the Queen's Pictures	Christopher Lloyd
Deputy Surveyor of the Queen's Works of Art	Hugh Roberts, FSA
Director of Media Affairs	Richard Arbiter
Librarian, Royal Library	Oliver Everett, LVO
Curator of the Print Room, Royal Library	The Hon Mrs Roberts, MVO

HOUSEHOLD OF QUEEN ELIZABETH THE QUEEN MOTHER

Apothecary to the Household	Dr Nigel Southward, LVO, MA, MB BChir, MRCP
Clerk Comptroller to the Household	Malcolm Blanch, CVO
Equerries	Major Sir Ralph Anstruther, Bt, GCVO, MC
	Major Raymond Seymour, CVO
	Capt Sir Alastair Aird, KCVO
Temporary Equerry	Major Colin Burgess
Ladies of the Bedchamber	The Lady Grimthorpe, CVO
	The Countess of Scarbrough
	Dame Frances Campbell-Preston, DCVO
Women of the Bedchamber	The Lady Angela Oswald, LVO
	The Hon Mrs Rhodes
	Mrs Michael Gordon-Lennox
Lord Chamberlain	The Earl of Crawford and Balcarres
Page of Honour	Earl of Mornington
Information Officer	Mrs Roy Murphy, LVO
Private Secretary and Comptroller	Capt Sir Alastair Aird, KCVO
Apothecary to the Household at Royal Lodge, Windsor	Dr John Briscoe, MA, MB, BChir, MRCGP, DObst, RCOG
Treasurer	Major Sir Ralph Anstruther, Bt, GCVO, MC

HOUSEHOLD OF THE PRINCE PHILIP, DUKE OF EDINBURGH

Chief Clerk and Accountant to the Household	Graham Partington
Equerry	Major Charles Richards
	Capt Jonathan Walker
Temporary Equerries	Maj John Crosby, RM
	Capt Edward Bearcroft, REME
Treasurer	Sir Brian McGrath, KCVO
Private Secretary	Brigadier Miles Hunt-Davis, CBE

HOUSEHOLD OF THE PRINCE AND PRINCESS OF WALES

Apothecary to the Household	Dr Peter Wheeler, MB, BS, MRCP, MRCGP
Equerry to The Prince of Wales	Major Patrick Tabor
Temporary Equerry to The Prince of Wales	Capt Mark Dyer
	Miss Anne Beckwith-Smith, LVO
	Viscountess Campden
Ladies in Waiting	Mrs Max Pike
	Miss Alexandra Loyd
	Mrs James Lonsdale
Extra Lady in Waiting	The Lady Sarah McCorquodale
Private Secretary and Treasurer to The Prince of Wales	Cmdr Richard Aylard, CVO, RN
Deputy Private Secretary to The Prince of Wales	Stephen Lamport
Assistant Private Secretaries to The Prince of Wales	Matthew Butler
	Dr Manon Williams
Private Secretary to The Princess of Wales	Patrick Jephson

HOUSEHOLD OF THE DUKE AND DUCHESS OF YORK

Ladies in Waiting	Mrs John Spooner
	Mrs John Floyd
Extra Ladies in Waiting (temporary)	Miss Lucy Manners
	Mrs Harry Cotterell
Equerry	Capt David Thompson
Temporary Equerry	Major Elizabeth Towell, MBE
Private Secretary and Treasurer	Capt Neil Blair, RN
Comptroller and Assistant Private Secretary	Mrs Jonathan Mathias

HOUSEHOLD OF THE PRINCE EDWARD

Private Secretary	Lt-Col Sean O'Dwyer, Irish Guards
Assistant Private Secretary	Mrs Richard Warburton, MVO

HOUSEHOLD OF THE PRINCESS ROYAL

	Lady Carew Pole, LVO
	Mrs Andrew Feilden, LVO
	The Hon Mrs Legge-Bourke LVO
Ladies in Waiting	Mrs William Nunneley
	Mrs Timothy Holderness-Roddam
	Mrs Charles Ritchie
	Mrs David Bowes-Lyon
Extra Ladies in Waiting	Miss Victoria Legge-Bourke, LVO
	Mrs Malcolm Innes, LVO
	The Countess of Lichfield
Private Secretary	Lt-Col Peter Gibbs, LVO
Assistant Private Secretary	The Hon Mrs Louloudis

HOUSEHOLD OF THE PRINCESS MARGARET, COUNTESS OF SNOWDON

Apothecary to the Household	Dr Nigel Southward, LVO, MA, MB, BChir, MRCP
Comptroller and Equerry	Major the Lord Napier and Ettrick, KCVO
Lady in Waiting	The Hon Mrs Whitehead, LVO
	The Lady Elizabeth Cavendish, LVO
	Lady Aird, LVO
	Mrs Robin Benson, LVO, OBE
	The Hon Mrs Wills, LVO
Extra Ladies in Waiting	Mrs Jane Stevens, LVO
	The Lady Juliet Townsend, LVO
	The Lady Glenconner, LVO
	The Countess Alexander of Tunis, LVO
	Mrs Charles Vyvyan
Private Secretary	Major the Lord Napier and Ettrick, KCVO

HOUSEHOLD OF PRINCESS ALICE, DUCHESS OF GLOUCESTER

Apothecary to the Household	Dr Nigel Southward, LVO, MA, MB, BChir, MRCP
Comptroller and Equerry	Maj Nicholas Barne
Extra Equerry	Lt-Col Sir Simon Bland, KCVO
Ladies in Waiting	Dame Jean Maxwell-Scott, DCVO
	Mrs Michael Harvey
Private Secretary	Maj Nicholas Barne

HOUSEHOLD OF THE DUKE AND DUCHESS OF GLOUCESTER

Apothecary to the Household	Dr Nigel Southward, LVO, MA, MB, BChir, MRCP
Comptroller and Equerry	Maj Nicholas Barne
Extra Equerry	Lt-Col Sir Simon Bland, KCVO
	Mrs Michael Wigley, CVO
Ladies in Waiting	Mrs Euan McCorquodale, LVO
	Mrs Howard Page
	The Lady Camoys
Extra Lady in Waiting	Miss Jennifer Thomson
Assistant Private Secretary to the Duchess of GLoucester	Miss Suzanne Marland
Private Secretary	Maj Nicholas Barne

HOUSEHOLD OF THE DUKE AND DUCHESS OF KENT

Apothecary to the Household	Dr Nigel Southward, LVO, MA, MB, BChir, MRCP
Clerk Comptroller	Mrs Paul Christodoulou
Extra Equerry	Lt Cmdr Sir Richard Buckley, KCVO, RN
Temporary Equerry	Capt Alexander Tetley
	Mrs Colin Marsh, LVO
	Mrs Peter Troughton
Ladies in Waiting	Mrs Julian Tomkins
	Mrs Richard Beckett
	Fiona, Lady Astor of Hever
	Miss Helen Tughan
Extra Lady in Waiting	Mrs Fiona Henderson, CVO
Private Secretary	Nicolas Adamson, OBE
Personal Secretary to the Duchess of Kent	Miss Helen Tughan

HOUSEHOLD OF PRINCE AND PRINCESS MICHAEL OF KENT

Apothecary to the Household	Dr Nigel Southward, LVO, MA, MB, BChir, MRCP
Equerry	John Kennedy
Ladies in Waiting	Mrs Julian Fellowes
	Miss Anne Frost
	The Hon Mrs Sanders
Personal Secretary to Prince Michael of Kent	Miss Elise Moore-Searson
Personal Secretary to Princess Michael of Kent	Miss Philippa Leach

HOUSEHOLD OF PRINCESS ALEXANDRA, THE HON LADY OGILVY

Extra Equerry	Major Sir Peter Clarke, KCVO
Lady in Waiting	The Lady Mary Mumford, CVO
	Mrs Peter Afia
	The Lady Mary Colman
Extra Ladies in Waiting	The Hon Lady Rowley
	The Lady Nicholas Gordon Lennox
	Dame Mona Mitchell, DCVO
Private Secretary	Rear Adm Sir John Garnier, KCVO, CBE
Personal Secretary	Mrs Valerie Hampton

THE QUEEN'S HOUSEHOLD IN SCOTLAND

Hereditary Lord High Constable	The Earl of Erroll
Hereditary Master of the Household	The Duke of Argyll
Hereditary Standard Bearer for Scotland	The Earl of Dundee
Hereditary Bearer of the National Flag of Scotland	The Earl of Lauderdale
Hereditary Carver in Scotland	Maj Sir Ralph Anstruther, Bt, GCVO, MC
Hereditary Keepers:-	
Holyrood	The Duke of Hamilton and Brandon
Falkland	Ninian Crichton-Stuart
Stirling	The Earl of Mar and Kellie
Dunstaffnage	The Duke of Argyll
Dunconnel	Sir Fitzroy Maclean of Dunconnel, Bt, KT, CBE
Keeper of Dumbarton Castle	Brig A. S. Pearson, CB, DSO, OBE, MC, TD
Governor of Edinburgh Castle	Maj Gen Michael Scott, CBE, DSO
Dean of the Order of the Thistle	The Very Rev Gilleasbuig Macmillan, MA, BD
Dean of the Chapel Royal	Very Rev Dr William Morris, LLD, DD
Physicians in Scotland	Dr Peter Brunt, MD, FRCP
	Dr Alexander Muir, MD, FRCPEdin
Surgeons in Scotland	Jetmund Engeset, ChM, FRCS
	D. C. Carter, MD, FRCS
Apothecary to the Household at Balmoral	Dr Douglas Glass, MB, ChB
Apothecary to the Household at the Palace of Holyroodhouse	Dr John Cormack, MD, FRCPE, FRCGP
Royal Company of Archers:	
Capt-Gen and Gold Stick for Scotland	Col the Lord Clydesmuir, KT, CB, MBE, TD
Adjutant	Major The Hon Sir Lachlan Maclean, Bt
Heralds and Pursuivants	*see* HER MAJESTY'S OFFICERS OF ARMS

THE ORDER OF SUCCESSION

1   HRH The Prince of Wales.
2   HRH Prince William of Wales.
3   HRH Prince Henry of Wales.
4   HRH The Duke of York.
5   HRH Princess Beatrice of York.
6   HRH Princess Eugenie of York.
7   HRH The Prince Edward.
8   HRH The Princess Royal.
9   Peter Phillips.
10 Zara Phillips.
11 HRH The Princess Margaret, Countess of Snowdon.
12 Viscount Linley.
13 Lady Sarah Chatto.
14 HRH The Duke of Gloucester.
15 Earl of Ulster.
16 Lady Davina Windsor.
17 Lady Rose Windsor.
18 HRH The Duke of Kent.
19 Baron Downpatrick.
20 Lady Marina-Charlotte Windsor.
21 Lord Nicholas Windsor.
22 Lady Helen Taylor.
23 Columbus Taylor.
24 Lord Frederick Windsor.
25 Lady Gabriella Windsor.
26 HRH Princess Alexandra, The Hon Lady Ogilvy.
27 James Ogilvy.
28 Mrs Paul Mowatt.
29 Christian Mowatt.
30 Zenouska Mowatt.

THE ROYAL FAMILY

REIGNING SOVEREIGN

ELIZABETH II, BY THE GRACE OF GOD, OF THE UNITED KINGDOM OF GREAT BRITAIN AND NORTHERN IRELAND, AND OF HER OTHER REALMS AND TERRITORIES QUEEN, HEAD OF THE COMMONWEALTH, DEFENDER OF THE FAITH*.

Her Majesty ELIZABETH ALEXANDRA MARY, elder da of His late Majesty King George VI and of Lady Elizabeth Angela Marguerite Bowes-Lyon (*HM Queen Elizabeth The Queen Mother) (see page 104)*, da of 14th Earl of Strathmore and Kinghorne; *b* at 17 Bruton Street W1, 21 April 1926: ascended the throne 6 February 1952, proclaimed Queen 8 February 1952, and crowned at Westminster Abbey 2 June 1953; declared in Council 9 April 1952, that she and her children shall be styled and known as the House and Family of Windsor; and further 8 Feb 1960, that her descendants, other than descendants enjoying the style, title, or attribute of HRH and the titular dignity of Prince or Princess, and female descendants who marry, and their descendants shall bear the name of Mountbatten-Windsor; attended the Thanksgiving Service for her Silver Jubilee in St Paul's Cathedral with the Duke of Edinburgh, 7 June 1977; Hon BMus, London 1946; FRS 1947; Hon DCL,

*The Queen's style and titles used in the United Kingdom. Different forms are used by each Commonwealth Country of which the Queen is Sovereign.

Oxford 1948; Hon LLD, Edinburgh; Hon MusD, Wales 1949; Hon LLD, London 1951; Hon FRCS and FRCOG 1951; Lord High Adm of the United Kingdom, Col-in-Ch of Life Guards, Blues and Royals (R Horse Guards and 1st Dragoons), R Scots Dragoon Guards (Carabiniers and Greys), The Queen's R Lancers, R Tank Regt, RE, Grenadier Guards, Coldstream Guards, Scots Guards, Irish Guards, Welsh Guards, R Welch Fusiliers, Queen's Lancashire Regt, Argyll and Sutherland Highlanders (Princess Louise's), R Green Jackets, Adjutant Gen Corps, The Royal Mercian and Lancastrian Yeo, Corps of Roy Mil Police, Calgary Highlanders, Canadian Forces Mil Engineers Branch, King's Own Calgary Regt, R. 22e Regt, Gov-Gen's Foot Guards, Canadian Grenadier Guards, Le Régiment de la Chaudière, R New Brunswick Regt, 48th Highlanders of Canada, Argyll and Sutherland Highlanders of Canada (Princess Louise's), Royal Aust Engineers, Royal Aust Inf Corps, R Aust Army Ordnance Corps, R Aust Army Nursing Corps, RNZ Engineers, RNZ Inf Regt, RNZ Army Ordnance Corps, Malawi Rifles, R Malta Artillery, Capt-Gen RA, Hon Artillery Co, Combined Cadet Force, R Canadian Artillery, R Regt of Aust Artillery, RNZ Artillery, RNZ Armoured Corps, Air-Commodore-in-Chief, R Aux AF, RAF Regt, R Observer Corps, R Canadian Air Force Aux, Aust Citizen Air Force, Territorial Air Force of NZ, Hon Air Commodore RAF Marham, Comdt-in-Chief, RAF Coll, Cranwell, Hon Commr, R Canadian Mounted Police, Master of the Merchant Navy and Fishing Fleets. Head of the Civil Defence Corps; Sovereign of all British Orders of Knighthood, Order of Merit, R Order of Victoria and Albert, Order of Crown of India, Order of Companions of Honour, Distinguished Ser Order, Imperial Ser Order, and Order of Canada, Sovereign Head of the Order of the Hospital of St John of Jerusalem, Order of Australia, and The Queen's Ser Order of NZ§; received Freedom of Drapers' Co, and of R Borough of Windsor 1947, Burgess of R Burgh of Stirling, and Cities of London and Cardiff 1948, and Cities of Edinburgh and Belfast 1949; Order of the Elephant of Denmark 1947, Grand Cordon of Order of El Kemal of Egypt 1948, Grand Cross (or Cordon) of Legion of Honour of France 1948, Order of Ojaswi Rajanya of Nepal 1949, Grand Cross of Order of the Netherlands Lion 1950, Order of the Seraphim of Sweden 1953, Gold Collar of Order of Manuel Amador Guerrero of Panama 1953, Chain of Order of El-Hussein Ibn Ali of Jordan 1953, Grand Collar of Order of Idris I of Libya 1954, Chain and Collar of Order of the Seal of Solomon of Ethiopia 1954, Grand Cross, with Chain, of Order of St Olav of Norway 1955, Grand Sash and Cross of the Three Orders of Christ, Aviz and Santiago of Portugal 1955, Grand Order of the Hashimi, with Chain, of Iraq 1956, Chevalier, with Grand Cross and Grand Cordon, of Order of Merit of the Republic of Italy 1958, Special Grand Cross with Star of Order of Merit of Federal Republic of Germany 1958, Grand Cross with diamonds of Order of the Peruvian Sun 1960, Nishan-i-Pakistan 1960, Grand Collar of Order of the Liberator General San Martin of Argentina 1960, Order of Royal House of Chakri of Thailand 1960, Mahendra Chain of Nepal 1961, Grand Collar of Order of Independence of Tunisia 1961, Collar of Order of the White Rose of Finland 1961, Grand Cross of National Order of Senegal 1961, Grand Cordon of Order of Knighthood of the Pioneers of the Republic of Liberia 1961, Grand Cross of National Order of Ivory Coast 1961, Collar and Grand Cordon of Order of the Chrysanthemum of Japan 1962, Grand Band of Order of the Star of Africa of Liberia 1962, Grand Cross of Ordre de la Valeur Camerounaise 1963, Grand Cordon of the Order of Leopold of Belgium, 1963, Grand Cross of the Order of the Redeemer of Greece 1963, Grand Cross, with Chain, of Order of the Falcon of Iceland 1963, the Chain of Honour of Sudan 1964, Grand Collar of Order of Merit of Chile 1965, Grand Cordon of Austrian Order of Merit 1966, Grand Collar of Order of the Southern Cross of Brazil 1968, Grand Commander of National Order of The Niger (Nigeria) 1969, and Order of Al Nahayyan (First Class) of Abu Dhabi 1969, Grand Cross of The Equatorial Star of Gabon, Order of Supreme Sun of Afghanistan 1971, Order of Golden Lion of House of Nassau of Luxembourg 1972, Order of the Great Yugoslav Star 1972, Darjah Utama Seri Mahkota Negara of Malaysia 1972, Order of Temasek of Singapore 1972, Most Esteemed Family Order 1st Class (Darjah Kerabat Yan Amat Di-Homali Darjah Pertama) of Brunei 1972, Distinguished Order of Ghaazi of the Maldive Islands 1972, Order of the Golden Heart of Kenya 1972, Grand Collar of National Order of Aztec Eagle of Mexico 1973, Grand Cordon of National Order of the Leopard of Zaire 1973, Star of Indonesia (First Class) 1974, Grand Commander of Order of the Republic of the Gambia 1974, Chain of Order of Seraphim of Sweden 1975, Collar of the Order of the Nile of Egypt 1975, Order of the Star of the Socialist Republic of Romania 1st Class 1978, Great Collar of the Order of S Tiago da Espada of Portugal 1978, Necklace of Mubarak Al Kabir of Kuwait 1979, Order of the Khalifa Necklace of Bahrain 1979, Collar of the Order of King Abdul Aziz of Saudi Arabia 1979, Collar of Independence of Qatar 1979, Order of Oman 1st Class 1979, Order of the Lion of Malawi 1st Class 1979, Presidential Order of Botswana 1979, Collar of the Grand Cordon of the Most Venerable Order of Knighthood of the Pioneers of the Republic of Liberia 1979, Grand Cordon of the Order of the Republic of

§As Princess Elizabeth, Her Majesty was appointed a Member of Imperial Order of the Crown of India, a Lady of the Most Noble Order of the Garter, and a Dame Grand Cross of Order of St John of Jerusalem 1947.

Tunisia 1980, Collier de la Classe Exceptionelle of the Order of El Mohammedi of Morocco 1980, Order of Al Said of Oman 1982, Order of the Solomon Islands 1st Class 1982, and additional insignia (Sash and Badge) of the Order of Qeladet El-Hussein Ibn Ali (Jordan) 1984, Dominica Award of Honour 1985, The Trinity Cross Medal of the Order of Trinity (TC) (Gold) of Trinidad and Tobago 1985, Collar of the Order of Carlos III of Spain 1986, Grand Order of Mungunghwa of the Republic of Korea 1986, Order of the Golden Fleece of Spain 1988, Grand Star of the Federal Republic of Nigeria 1989, Chain of the Federation of the United Arab Emirates 1989, Grand Ribbon of the Order of Merit of the Republic of Poland 1991, Grand Cross of the Order of Merit (Hungary) 1991, Royal Family Order of the Sultan of Brunei 1992, Brunei Silver Jubilee Medal 1992, Grand Collar of the Order of Boyaca (Colombia) 1993. HM *m* at Westminster Abbey 20 Nov 1947, HRH The Prince Philip, Duke of Edinburgh, KG, KT, OM, GBE, AC, QSO, PC [see page 105], and has issue.

Residences—Buckingham Palace, SW1; Windsor Castle, Berkshire; Balmoral Castle, Aberdeenshire; Sandringham House, Norfolk.

Crown—A circle of gold, issuing therefrom four crosses patées and four fleurs-de-lis arranged alternately; from the crosses patées arise two golden arches ornamented with pearls, crossing at the top under a mound also gold, the whole enriched with precious stones. The cap is of crimson velvet, turned up ermine. **Royal Arms***—Quarterly: 1st and 4th, gules, three lions passant guardant in pale or, *England*; 2nd, or, a lion rampant within a double tressure flory counterflory gules, *Scotland*; 3rd, azure, a harp or, stringed argent, *Ireland*, the whole encircled with the Garter. **Crests**—*England*, upon the royal helmet the Royal crown proper, thereon statant guardant or, a lion imperially crowned also proper; *Scotland*, on the Crown proper a lion sejant affrontée gules crowned or, holding in the dexter paw a sword, and in the sinister a sceptre erect also proper; *Ireland*, on a wreath or and azure, a tower triple-towered of the first, from the portal a hart springing argent, attired and hoofed gold. **Supporters**—*Dexter*, a lion rampant guardant or, crowned as the crest; *sinister*, a unicorn argent, armed, crined, and unguled, or, gorged with a coronet composed of crosses patées and fleurs-de-lis, a chain affixed thereto, passing between the fore-legs, and reflexed over the back, of the last. **Badges**—*England*, the red and white rose united, slipped and leaved proper; *Scotland*, a thistle, slipped and leaved proper; *Ireland*, a shamrock leaf slipped vert, also a harp or stringed argent; *United Kingdom*, the Rose of England, the Thistle of Scotland, and the Shamrock of Ireland engrafted on the same stem proper, and an escutcheon charged as the Union Flag (all the foregoing ensigned with the Royal Crown); *Wales*, upon a mount vert a dragon passant wings elevated gules, and (Augmented Badge) within a circular riband argent fimbriated or, bearing the motto "Y Ddraig goch Ddyry Cychwyn" in letters vert, and ensigned with a representation of the Crown proper, an escutcheon per fesse argent and vert and thereon the Red Dragon passant; *The Royal House of Windsor*, on a mount vert the Round Tower of Windsor Castle argent mason Sable, flying thereon the Royal Standard, the whole within two branches of oak fructed or and ensigned with the Royal Crown.

The Arms of HRH The Prince Edward, HRH The Princess Royal, and HRH The Princess Margaret, Countess of Snowdon, are differenced by the following Labels—

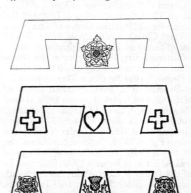

SONS LIVING

HRH PRINCE CHARLES PHILIP ARTHUR GEORGE, KG, GCB, AK, PC, ADC (*Prince of Wales*), *b* at Buckingham Palace 14 Nov 1948. (See page 107).

HRH Prince Andrew Albert Christian Edward (*Duke of York*), CVO, ADC, *b* at Buckingham Palace 19 Feb 1960. (See page 109).

HRH Prince Edward Antony Richard Louis, CVO, *b* at Buckingham Palace 10 March 1964; ed at Gordonstoun and Jesus Coll, Camb; 2nd Lieut RM 1983 (resigned 1987); Patron Nat Youth Theatre since 1987 Chm The Duke of Edinburgh's Award Special Projects Group; CVO 1989.

DAUGHTER LIVING

HRH Princess Anne Elizabeth Alice Louise (*The Princess Royal*), LG, GCVO, FRS, *b* at Clarence House 15 Aug 1950; ed at Benenden Sch; Chancellor of London Univ since 1981; Col-in-Ch 14th/20th King's Hussars, The Royal Scots (The Royal Regiment) Worcs and Sherwood Foresters Regt (29th/45th Foot) and 8th

---

*Scottish usage shows the Royal Arms with the Lion of Scotland in the 1st and 4th quarters, in conformity with the pattern prescribed for the Great Seal of Scotland, and appearing on Scottish official publications and on the tabards of the Scottish Officers of Arms.

Canadian Hussars (Princess Louise's), R Corps of Signals, Canadian Forces
Communications and Electronics Branch, Royal Aust Corps of Signals, RNZ Corps
of Signals, RNZ Nursing Corps, Grey and Simcoe Foresters Militia, The Royal
Regina Rifles, Royal Newfoundland Regt, Hon Col Univ of London Contingent, OTC;
Ch Comdt WRNS; Comdt in Chief Women's Transport Service (FANY), St John
Ambulance and Nursing Cadets; Hon Air Commodore RAF Lyneham; Hon Air
Commodore Univ of London Air Sqdn; Pres WRNS Benevolent Trust, British
Academy of Film and Television Arts, Save the Children Fund, Windsor Horse
Trials, Roy Sch for Daughters of Officers of Royal Navy and Royal Marines
(Haslemere), Missions to Seamen, Nat Agricultural Centre Rural Trust, Council for
National Academic Awards; Hon Pres Chartered Institute of Transport, Royal
Caledonian Hunt; Joint Pres Lowland Brigade Club; Vice-Pres Royal Bath and West
and Southern Counties Show; Patron All England Women's Lacrosse Association,
Royal Lymington Yacht Club, Butler Trust, Association of WRNS, Riding for the
Disabled Association (Australia), Home Farm Trust, Jersey Wildlife Preservation
Trust, The Royal Corps of Signals Institution, The Royal Signals Association, The
Canadian Communications and Electronic Branch Institution, The British School of
Osteopathy, The Royal Tournament, Spinal Injuries Association, The Army and
Royal Artillery Hunter Trials, Glos and N Avon Federation of Young Farmers'
Clubs, Royal Port Moresby Society for Prevention of Cruelty to Animals, Horse of
the Year Ball, Benenden Ball, National Union of Townswomen's Guilds, Canadian
Therapeutic Riding Association, College of Occupational Therapists, Association of
Combined Youth Clubs, Scottish Rugby Union, British Executive Service Overseas,
Australian Veterinary Association, Intensive Care Society, British Olympic Medical
Trust, The Royal Scots Club and The Flying Scot Club, British Women's
Gasherbrum II Expedition, William Lee Quatercentenary, World Student Debating
Championships 1990, The Cranfield Trust, Ulster Sports and Recreation Trust,
British Racing Schools Race Day, Home Farm Trust Development Trust, World
Junior Cycling Championships, National Association of Prison Visitors, Gateshead
National Garden Festival, Save the Children Fund Corporate Fund Raising Cttee,
Hong Kong, Univ of West Indies Relief and Development Fund, Glos Rugby Union,
British Nutrition Foundation, Animal Diseases Research Association (ADRA)
Equine Research and Grass Sickness Fund, and International Literacy Year 1990
(run under ALBSU); Vice-Patron, British Show Jumping Assocn; Commdt-in-Ch St
John Ambulance and Nursing Cadets; Life Member of R British Legion Women's
Section; Memb Internat Olympic Ctee since 1988; Member of Lloyd's 1989; received
Freedom of City of London 1976; Royal Bencher Inner Temple 1990; Hon Liveryman
Farriers' Co; Freeman of Fishmongers' Co; Hon Freeman, Farmers' Co, Loriners' Co,
Yeoman Saddlers' Co; Master of Carmen's Co; Hon Life Member, RNVR Officers'
Assocn; Hon Member, British Equine Veterinary Assocn; Visitor, Felixstowe Coll;
Variety Club's Internat Humanitarian Award (1987); FRS (1987); FRCVS (1986),
Hon FRCS (1986), Hon FIEE (1987), Hon FRCP (1990), *cr* GCVO 1974, Declared
The Princess Royal 13 June 1987, LG 1994; *m* 1st, at Westminster Abbey 14 Nov
1973 (*m diss* 1992), Capt Mark Anthony Peter Phillips, CVO, ADC(P) (*b* at Tetbury,
Glos 22 Sept 1948), only son of Maj Peter William Garside Phillips, MC, late 1st
King's Drag Guards; 2ndly, at Crathie Church 12 Dec 1992, Cmdr Timothy James
Hamilton Laurence, MVO, RN (*b* at Camberwell 1 March 1955), yr son of late Cmdr
Guy Stewart Laurence, RN, and has issue living (by 1st *m*): Peter Mark Andrew, *b*
at St Mary's Hosp, Paddington 15 Nov 1977; *ed* Gordonstoun—Zara Anne
Elizabeth, *b* at St Mary's Hosp, Paddington, 15 May 1981.

SISTER LIVING

HRH Princess Margaret Rose (*The Princess Margaret, Countess of Snowdon*), CI,
GCVO, *b* at Glamis Castle, Angus, 21 Aug 1930; Hon DMus London 1957; Hon LLD
Camb 1958; Hon DLitt Keele 1962; Hon LLD, Univ of BC 1958; Hon FRIBA 1953;
Hon FRSM 1957, Hon FRCS, England 1963, and Hon FRCOG 1966; Hon Life FZS; a
Bencher of Lincoln's Inn and Treasurer 1967; Col-in-Ch of R Highland Fusiliers
(Princess Margaret's Own Glasgow and Ayrshire Regt), 15th/19th King's R Hussars,
Princess Louise Fusiliers, Highland Fusiliers of Canada, QARANC, and WRAAC,
and Dep Col-in-Ch of R Anglian Regt Hon Air Commodore RAF Coningsby; Pres of
Scottish Children's League, Victoria League, R National Institute for the Blind, R
Ballet, National Soc for the Prevention of Cruelty to Children, R Scottish Soc for
Prevention of Cruelty to Children, Friends of the Elderly and Gentlefolk's Help,
Invalid Children's Aid Nationwide (also Chm of Council), Sadlers Wells Foundation,
English Folk Dance and Song Soc, Horder Centres for Arthritics, of Guides Assocn,
and of Chorleywood Coll for Girls with Little or No Sight; Joint-Pres of Lowland Bde
Club; Pres R Agricultural Soc of England 1966; Patron-in-Ch of English Harbour
Repair Fund; Patron of Light Infantry Club, QARANC Assocn, Barristers'
Benevolent Assocn, Bristol R Workshops for the Blind, British Sailors' Soc Ladies'
Guild, Friends of Southwark Cathedral, Friends of St John's, Mary Hare Gram Sch,
for the Deaf, National Pony Soc, Princess Margaret Rose Hosp, Edinburgh, Services
Sound and Vision Corporation, of R Coll of Nursing and National Council of Nurses
of UK, of Princess Margaret Hosp and Lodge Aux, Toronto, of The Mathilda and

Terence Kennedy Inst of Rheumatology, St Margaret's Chapel Guild, Edinburgh Castle, Scottish Assocn of Youth Clubs, Scottish Community Drama Assocn, Suffolk Regimental Assocn, Union of Schs for Social Ser, of W Indies Olympic Assocn, of Architects' Benevolent Soc, of Tenovus (Inst of Cancer Research), of Migraine Trust, of Zebra Trust, and of St Pancras Housing Assocn in Camden. Patron (temporary) of R Caledonian Ball since 1956; a CStJ; Grand President of St John Ambulance Assocn and Bde; Life Member of British Legion Women's Section, Hon Member of Automobile Assocn, Order of the Road, R Automobile Club, Cambridge Festival Assoc, Hallé Concerts Soc, Heart Disease and Diabetes Research Trut, Northern Ballet Theatre, Pottery and Glass Trades Benevolent Inst, The Scottish Ballet, R Anglian Regimental Assoc, and Sealyham Terrier Breeders' Assocn; Hon Member and Patron of Grand Antiquity Soc of Glasgow; Member of Haberdashers' Co 1966; received Freedom of City of London 1966 and of R Burgh of Queensferry 1972; Hon Life Mem of Century House Assoc (British Columbia); has Grand Cross of Order of Lion of the Netherlands 1948, Order of Brilliant Star of Zanzibar, first class 1956, Grand Cross of Order of Crown of Belgium 1960, Order of the Crown, Lion and Spear of Toro Kingdom, Uganda 1965, Order of Precious Crown of Japan first class 1971, and Grand Cross (1st class), Order of Merit of Federal Republic of Germany; cr CI 1947, GCVO 1953, Royal Victorian Chain 1990; m at Westminster Abbey 6 May 1960 (m diss 5 July 1978), 1st Earl of Snowdon, GCVO, and has issue:—

SON LIVING,—David Albert Charles (Viscount Linley), b at Clarence House 3 Nov 1961; ed Bedales; furniture designer: m at St Margaret's, Westminster 8 Oct 1993, Hon Serena Alleyne Stanhope, only da of Charles Henry Leicester, Viscount Petersham (see E Harrington).

DAUGHTER LIVING,—Lady Sarah Frances Elizabeth, b at Kensington Palace 1 May 1964; ed Bedales; principal bridesmaid to HRH The Princess of Wales: m at St Stephen's, Walbrook 14 July 1994, Daniel Chatto, yr son of late Thomas Chatto.

MOTHER LIVING (Widow of King George VI)

Her Majesty QUEEN ELIZABETH THE QUEEN MOTHER. See page 104

WIDOW LIVING OF SON OF KING GEORGE V

See Princess Alice, Duchess of Gloucester, page 110.

OTHER LIVING DESCENDANTS OF KING GEORGE V

Issue of Field Marshal HRH the late Prince Henry William Frederick Albert, KG, KT, KP, GCB, GCMG, GCVO, PC, 1st Duke of Gloucester, 3rd son of HM the late King George V, b 31 March 1900, d 10 June 1974; m 6 Nov 1935, Lady Alice Christabel Montagu-Douglas-Scott, GCB, CI, GCVO, GBE (GCStJ), 3rd da of 7th Duke of Buccleuch and Queensberry:—

See D Gloucester, page 110.

Issue of Air-Commodore HRH the late Prince George Edward Alexander Edmund, KG, KT, GCMG, GCVO, PC, RAF, 1st Duke of Kent, 4th son of HM the late King George V, b 20 Dec 1902, d (on active ser during European War) 25 Aug 1942; m 29 Nov 1934, HRH Princess Marina, CI, GCVO, GBE, who d 27 Aug 1968, da of HRH the late Prince Nicholas of Greece and Denmark, GCB, GCVO:—

See D Kent, page 111.

Issue of HRH the late Princess (Victoria Alexandra Alice) Mary (The Princess Royal), CI, GCVO, CBE, RRC, TD, CD, only da of HM the late King George V, b 25 April 1897, d 28 March 1965; declared Princess Royal 1 Jan 1932; m 28 Feb 1922, 6th Earl of Harewood, KG, GCVO, DSO, who d 24 May 1947:—

See E Harewood.

OTHER LIVING DESCENDANTS OF KING EDWARD VII

Grandson of HRH the late Princess Louise Victoria Alexandra Dagmar (The Princess Royal, Duchess of Fife), el da of King Edward VII, b 20 Feb 1867, d 4 Jan 1931; declared Princess Royal 28 Nov 1905: m 27 July 1889, 1st Duke of Fife, KG, KT, GCVO, who d 29 Jan 1912:—

Issue of HH the late Princess Maud Alexandra Victoria Georgina Bertha (Countess of Southesk), b 3 April 1893, d 14 Dec 1945; granted title of Princess, with style and attribute of "Highness" and precedence immediately after all members of Royal Family enjoying style of "Royal Highness", 1905; reverted to style of "Lady" after her marriage: m 12 Nov 1923, the 11th Earl of Southesk, KCVO:—

See D Fife.

Grandchildren of HM the late Maud Charlotte Mary Victoria (Queen of Norway), VA, CI, GCVO, youngest da of King Edward VII, b 26 Nov 1869, d 20 Nov 1938: m 22 July 1896, HRH Prince (Christian Frederik) Carl Georg Valdemar Axel of Denmark, KG, GCB, GCVO [elected King of Norway under style of HM Haakon VII 18 Nov 1905], who d 21 Sept 1957, second son of HM the late King Frederik VIII of Denmark, KG, GCB, GCVO:—

Issue of HM the late Olav V (Alexander Edward Christian Frederik) (*King of Norway*), KG, KT, GCB, GCVO, *b* 2 July 1903, *d* 17 Jan 1991: *m* 21 March 1929, HRH Princess Märtha Sophie Louise Dagmar Thyra of Sweden, who *d* 5 April 1954, da of HRH the late Duke (Oscar Carl Wilhelm) of Västergötland, GCVO:—

HM King Harald V (*King of Norway*), GCVO, *b* 21 Feb 1937; *ed* at Balliol Coll, **Norway** Oxford; Sovereign of Order of St Olav of Norway; Hon Gen British Army; has Grand Cross of Orders Elephant of Denmark, Seraphim of Sweden, Leopold of Belgium, Southern Cross of Brazil, White Rose of Finland, St George and St Constantine of Greece, Falcon of Iceland, Merit of Republic of Italy, Merit of Austria, Chula Chom Klao of Thailand, Star of Yugoslavia, Order of Merit of Federal Republic of Germany, and Chrysanthemum of Japan; GCVO (Hon) 1955, Royal Victorian Chain 1994: *m* 29 Aug 1968, Sonja, Grand Cross of St Olav of Norway and of Elephant of Denmark, da of Carl August Haraldsen, and has issue living, *HRH Prince* Haakon Magnus (*Crown Prince of Norway*), *b* 20 July 1973,——*HRH Princess* Märtha Louise, *b* 22 Sept 1971.——*Princess* Ragnhild Alexandra, *b* 9 June 1930; bears the name of Princess Ragnhild, Mrs Lorentzen: *m* 15 May 1953, Erling Sven Lorentzen, of Av Visc de Albuquerque 333, Bl B, apt 403, Rio de Janeiro, Brazil, and has issue living, Haakon, *b* 23 Aug 1954: *m* 14 April 1982, Martha Carvalho de Freitas, da of José Maria Gomes de Freitas, and has issue living, Olav Alexander *b* 11 July 1983, Christian Frederik *b* 23 May 1988, a da *b* 28 June 1994,——Ingeborg, *b* 27 Feb 1957: *m* 4 June 1982, Paulo César Ribeiro, son of Paulo César Ribeiro, and has issue living, Victoria Ragna *b* 19 Dec 1988,——Ragnhild Alexandra, *b* 8 May 1968.——*Princess* Astrid Maud Ingeborg, *b* 12 Feb 1932; bears the name of Princess Astrid, Mrs Ferner; *ed* at Lady Margaret Hall, Oxford; Grand Cross of Orders of St Olav of Norway and White Rose of Finland: *m* 12 Jan 1961, Johan Martin Ferner, of Oslo, Norway, and has issue living, Alexander, *b* 15 March 1965,——Carl-Christian, *b* 22 Oct 1972,——Cathrine, *b* 22 July 1962: *m* 9 Dec 1989, Arild Johansen, and has issue living, Sebastien *b* 9 May 1990, Madeleine *b* 7 March 1993,——Benedikte, *b* 27 Sept 1963: *m* 30 April 1994, Rolf Woods,——Elisabeth, *b* 30 March 1969: *m* 3 Oct 1992, Tom Folke Beckmann, son of Jann Beckmann.

OTHER LIVING DESCENDANTS OF QUEEN VICTORIA

Descendants of HRH the Duke of Edinburgh (Duke of Saxe-Coburg and Gotha), 2nd son of Queen Victoria

Grandchildren of HRH late Princess Marie Alexandra Victoria (*Queen of Roumania*), VA, CI, RRC (infra):—

Issue of HM the late King Carol II, KG, GCVO, *b* 16 Oct 1893, *d* 4 April 1953; renounced succession to the throne of Roumania 8 Dec 1925, subsequently proclaimed King as Carol II 8 June 1930; left Roumania 6 Sept 1940: *m* 1st, 31 Aug 1918 (*m diss* 8 Jan 1919), Joana Maria Valentina (Zizi), who *d* 11 March 1953, da of Col Constantin Lambrino; 2ndly, 10 March 1921 (*m diss* 21 June 1928), HRH Princess Helen, who *d* 28 Nov 1982, eldest da of HM King Constantine I of the Hellenes (infra); 3rdly, 3 July 1947, Elena (Magda), who assumed the style of HRH Princess Elena of Hohenzollern, who *d* 29 June 1977, da of Nicolas Lupescu (formerly Wolff), and formerly wife of Ion Tampeanu:—

(By 1st *m*) (Mircea Grigore) Carol (36 Doria Rd, SW6), *b* 8 Jan 1920; recognized as **Roumania** legitimate by French Courts at Paris 17 Dec 1955, when he assumed the name and style of HRH Prince Carol of Roumania: *m* 1st, 22 March 1944 (*m diss* 1960), Hélène Henriette, da of Paul Nagavitzine; 2ndly, 20 Dec 1960 (*m diss* 1977), (Thelma) Jeanne, who *d* 1988, da of Richard Williams, of Nashville, Tennessee, USA; 3rdly, 27 June 1984, Antonia, yr da of late Maj-Gen Edward Charles Colville, CB, DSO (*see* V Colville of Culross, colls), and formerly wife of Garry Lacon Jock Ropner (*see* Ropner Bt (cr 1904), colls), and has issue living, (by 1st *m*) Paul Philippe, *b* 13 Aug 1948; *ed* Gordonstoun and Millfield,——(by 2nd *m*) (Ion George Nicholas) Alexander, *b* 1 Sept 1961; *ed* Ampleforth.——(By 2nd *m*) HM King Mihai (Michael), GCVO, *b* 25 Oct 1921; reigned as King of Roumania (under regency) 20 July 1927-8 June 1930; re-ascended the throne on departure of his father 6 Sept 1940; deprived of the throne 30 Dec 1947; is Hon Air Ch Marshal, Roy Hellenic Air Force; a Ch Com of American Legion of Merit; has Grand Cross of Order of the Redeemer of Greece, Grand Cross of the Order of Leopold of Belgium, Orders of Victory of Russia, and of Annunciation of Italy, and French Legion of Honour; GCVO (Hon) 1938: *m* 10 June 1948, HRH Princess Anne Antoinette Françoise Charlotte, only da of HRH the late Prince René Charles Marie Joseph of Bourbon-Parma, and has issue living, *HRH Princess* Margarita, *b* 26 March 1949,——*HRH Princess* Helen, *b* 15 Nov 1950: *m* 24 Sept 1983 (*m diss* 1991), Dr (Leslie) Robin Medforth-Mills, son of Cyril Mills, and has issue living, Nicholas Michael DE ROUMANIE-MEDFORTH-MILLS *b* 1 April 1985, Elisabetta Karina DE ROUMANIE-MEDFORTH-MILLS *b* 4 Jan 1989,——*HRH Princess* Irina, *b* 28 Feb 1953: *m* 11 Feb 1984, John Kreuger, and has issue living, Michael Torsten *b* 25 Feb 1985, Angelica

Margareta Bianca *b* 29 Dec 1986,——*HRH Princess* Sophie, *b* 29 Oct 1957,——*HRH Princess* Maria, *b* 13 July 1964. *Residence* - 77 chemin Louis Degallier, CH-1290 Versoix, Geneva, Switzerland.

Granddaughter of Adm of the Fleet HRH late Prince Alfred Ernest Albert, KG, KT, KP, GCB, GCSI, GCMG, GCIE, GCVO, PC, Duke of Edinburgh (*cr* 1866), and reigning Duke of Saxe-Coburg and Gotha 1893-1900, 2nd son of Queen Victoria:—
Issue of HRH late Princess Marie Alexandra Victoria (*Queen of Roumania*), VA, CI, RRC, *b* 29 Oct 1875, *d* 18 July 1938: *m* 11 Jan 1893, HM King Ferdinand I of Roumania, KG, GCB, who *d* 20 July 1927:—

Austria †*HRH Princess* Ileana (*Mother Alexandra*), *b* 5 Jan 1909; an Orthodox nun: *m* 1st, 26 July 1931 (*m diss* 1954), HI & RH Archduke Anton Maria Franz Leopold Blanka Karl Joseph Ignaz Raphael Michael Margareta Nicetas of Austria, Prince of Tuscany, who *d* 22 Oct 1987; 2ndly, 19 June 1954 (*m diss* 1965), Dr Stefan Virgil Issarescu, and *d* 21 Jan 1991, leaving issue, (by 1st *m*) *HI & RH Archduke* Stefan; now known as Mr Stefan Habsburg-Lothringen (4684 Pine Eagles Drive, Brighton, Michigan 48116, USA), *b* 15 Aug 1932; US citizen: *m* 26 Aug 1954, (Mary) Jerrine, da of Charles B. Soper, of Boston, USA, and has issue living, Christopher *b* 26 Jan 1957: *m* 1 May 1987 (*m diss* 1991), Elysabeth Ann Blanchette, da of Larry Lee Popejoy (and has issue living, Stefan Christopher *b* 19 Jan 1990, Saygan Genevieve *b* 31 Oct 1987), Peter *b* 19 Feb 1959: *m* 1st, 27 June 1981 (*m diss* 1985 and annulled 1988), Shari Suzanne, da of William Marshall Reid; 2ndly, 17 June 1989, Lauren Ann, da of Martin John Klaus, Anton *b* 7 Nov 1964: *m* 5 Oct 1991, Ashley Byrd, da of Rev Dr William Douglas Carrell, Ileana *b* 4 Jan 1958: *m* 23 June 1979, David Scott Snyder (and has issue living, Nicholas David *b* 27 Feb 1987, Alexandra Marie *b* 18 Aug 1984), Constanza *b* 2 Oct 1960: *m* 16 Jan 1987, Mark Lee Matheson, son of Robert Kenneth Matheson,——*HI & RH Archduke* Dominic (San Stin 2368, I-30125 Venice, Italy), *b* 4 July 1937: *m* 11 June 1960, Engel, da of Friedrich Ditlev von Voss, of Houston, Texas, USA, and has issue living, Sandor *b* 13 Feb 1965, Gregor *b* 20 Nov 1968,——*HI & RH Archduchess* Alexandra, *b* 21 May 1935: *m* 1st, 31 Aug 1962 (*m diss* 1972 and annulled 1973), HRH Duke Eugen Eberhard Albrecht Maria Joseph Joan Rylski Robert Ulrich Philipp Odo Carl Hubert of Württemberg; 2ndly, 29 Dec 1973, Baron Victor Franz Clemens Raoul Emil Wilhelm von Baillou, of Hügelstrasse 9, D-6109 Muehltal/Traisa bei Darmstadt, Germany,——*HI & RH Archduchess* Maria Magdalena, *b* 2 Oct 1939: *m* 29 Aug 1959, Baron Hans Ulrich von Holzhausen, of Johann-Wolf-Strasse 6, Salzburg, Austria, and has issue living, *Baron* Johann Friedrich Anton *b* 29 July 1960, *Baron* Georg-Ferdinand *b* 16 Feb 1962: *m* 30 April (civ) and 22 May (relig) 1993, Countess Elena Maria Victoria Ingeborg, da of Count Reinhart Heinrich Hubertus Maria von und zu Hoensbroech, *Baroness* Alexandra Maria *b* 22 Jan 1963, *m* 2 July (civ) and 7 July (relig) 1985, Christoph Alexander Rudolf Michael Ferch, son of Rudolf Maria Ferch (and has issue living, Ferdinand Georg Botho *b* 17 Oct 1986, Leopold Anton David *b* 18 Aug 1988, Benedikt Peter *b* 2 March 1993),——*HI & RH Archduchess* Elisabeth, *b* 15 Jan 1942: *m* 31 July (civ) and 3 Aug (relig) 1964, Friedrich Josef Sandhofer, MD, of Gartnerweg 2, Salzburg, Austria, and has issue living, Anton Dominic Friedrich *b* 26 Oct 1966: *m* 28 May (civ) and 29 May (relig) 1993, Katarzyna Marta, da of Wlodzimierz Wojkowski (and has issue living, Dominik *b* 7 Jan 1994), Margareta Elisabeth *b* 10 Sept 1968: *m* 20 June 1992, Ernst Helmut Klaus Lux, son of Ernst Johann Karl Lux, Andrea Alexandra *b* 13 Dec 1969, Elisabeth Victoria Magdalena *b* 16 Nov 1971.

Grandson of HRH late Princess Marie (*Queen Marie of Yugoslavia*) (infra):—
Issue of HM late King Peter II of Yugoslavia (reigned 1934-45), *b* 6 Sept 1923, *d* 3 Nov 1970: *m* 20 March 1944, HRH Princess Alexandra, who *d* 30 Jan 1993, only da of HM late King Alexander I of the Hellenes (infra):—

Yugoslavia *HRH Prince* Alexander (*Crown Prince of Yugoslavia*) (Chancellery, 36 Park Lane, W1Y 3LE), *b* 17 July 1945; Lt 16th/5th The Queen's R Lancers: *m* 1st, 1 July 1972 (*m diss* 1985), HRH Princess Maria da Glória (Henriqueta Dolores Lucia Micaela Rafaela Gabriela Gonzaga), elder da of HRH Prince Dom Pedro Gastão of Orleans and Bragança; 2ndly, 21 Sept 1985, Katherine Clairy, da of Robert Batis, of Athens, and has issue living (by 1st *m*), *HRH Prince* Peter, *b* 5 Feb 1980,——*HRH Prince* Alexander, *b* 15 Jan 1982,——*HRH Prince* Philip, *b* (twin) 15 Jan 1982.

Grandsons of HRH late Princess Marie Alexandra Victoria (*Queen of Roumania*), VA, CI, RRC (ante):—
Issue of HRH late Princess Marie (*Queen Marie of Yugoslavia*), *b* 9 Jan 1900, *d* 22 June 1961: *m* 8 June 1922, HM King Alexander I of Yugoslavia, who *d* (assassinated) 9 Oct 1934:—
HRH Prince Tomislav, *b* 19 Jan 1928; *ed* Oundle, and Clare Coll, Camb: *m* 1st, 6 June 1957 (*m diss* 1982), HGDH Princess Margarita Alice Thyra Viktoria Marie Louise Scholastica, only da of HRH late Margrave Berthold of Baden (infra); 2ndly,

17 Oct 1982, Linda Mary, da of late Holbrook Bonney, and has issue living, (by 1st
m) *HRH Prince* Nikola, *b* 15 March 1958: *m* 30 Aug (civ) and 22 Nov (relig) 1992,
Ljiljana, da of Lazar Licánin, and has issue living, *HRH Princess* Maria *b* 4 Aug
1993,——*HRH Princess* Katarina, *b* 28 Nov 1959: *m* 5 Dec 1987, (George) Desmond
Lorenz de Silva, QC, KStJ, of 28 Sydney St, SW3, son of Edmund Frederick Lorenz
de Silva, and has issue living, Victoria Marie Esme Margarita *b* 6 Sept 1991,——(by
2nd *m*) *HRH Prince* George, *b* 25 May 1984,——*HRH Prince* Michael *b* 15 Dec
1985.——†*HRH Prince* Andrej, *b* 28 June 1929; *ed* Oundle, and Clare Coll,
Camb (BA 1950): *m* 1st, 1 Aug (civ) and 2 Aug (relig) 1956 (*m diss* 1962), HH
Princess Christina Margarete, da of HH late Prince Christoph Ernst August of
Hesse (infra); 2ndly, 18 Sept (civ) and 12 Oct (relig) 1963 (*m diss* 1972), HSH
Princess Kira-Melita Feodora Maria Viktoria Alexandra, da of HSH the 6th Prince
of Leiningen (infra); 3rdly, 30 March 1974, Eva Maria, da of Milan T. Andjelković,
and formerly wife of Dr Frank Lowe, and *d* 7 May 1990, leaving issue (by 1st *m*)
†*HRH Prince* Christopher, *b* 4 Feb 1960, *d* 14 May 1994 as the result of a motor
accident,——*HRH Princess* (Maria) Tatiana, *b* 18 July 1957: *m* 30 June 1990,
Gregory Per Edward Anthony Michael Thune Larsen, son of Knut Thune Larsen,
and has issue living, Sonia *b* 29 Oct 1992,——(by 2nd *m*) *HRH Prince* Karl Vladimir
Cyril Andrej, *b* 11 March 1964,——*HRH Prince* Dimitri Ivan Mihailo, *b* 21 April
1965. Prince Andrej and his second wife also formally adopted (15 Nov 1965) their
natural da, *HRH Princess* (se recognised by King Petar II of Yugoslavia 1965)
Lavinia Maria, *b* 18 Oct 1961: *m* 20 May 1989 (*m diss* 1993), Erastos Dimitrious
Sidiropoulos, and has issue living, Andrej Aristotle *b* 22 Feb 1990, Nadia-Marie *b* 11
Dec 1987.

Granddaughter of HRH late Princess Ileana of Roumania (ante):—
Issue of HI & RH late Archduchess Maria Ileana, *b* 18 Dec 1933, *d* 11 Jan
1959: *m* 7 Dec 1957, Count Jaroslav Franz Josef Ignaz Maria Kottulinsky,
who *d* (*k* in an air crash with his wife) 11 Jan 1959:—
Countess (Maria) Ileana, *b* 25 Aug 1958.

Grandson of HRH Prince Alfred Ernest Albert, Duke of Edinburgh
(ante):—
Issue of HRH late Princess Victoria Melita (Victoria Feodorovna) (*Grand
Duchess Kirill (Cyril) of Russia*), VA, CI, *b* 25 Nov 1876, *d* 2 March 1936: *m*
1st, 19 April 1894 (*m diss* 21 Dec 1901), HRH Grand Duke Ernst Ludwig
(Karl Albert Wilhelm) of Hesse and by Rhine, who *d* 9 Oct 1937 (infra); 2ndly,
8 Oct 1905, HIH Grand Duke Kirill (Cyril) Vladimirovitch of Russia (first
cousin of late Emperor Nicholas II), who *d* 13 Oct 1938:—
(By 2nd *m*) †*HIH Grand Duke* Vladimir Kirillovitch, *b* 30 Aug 1917; *ed* London   **Russia**
Univ; *s* his father as head of the Imperial House of Romanoff: *m* 13 Aug 1948,
Princess Leonida, da of late Prince George Alexandrovitch Bagration-Mukhransky,
and formerly wife of late Sumner Moore Kirby, and *d* 21 April 1992, leaving issue,
HIH Grand Duchess Maria Vladimirovna, *b* 23 Dec 1953: *m* 22 Sept 1976 (*m diss*
1986), HRH Prince Franz-Wilhelm (Viktor Christof Stefan) of Prussia (infra), and
has issue living, *HRH Prince* Georg, *b* 13 March 1981.

Grandchildren of HRH late Princess Victoria Melita (*Grand Duchess
Kirill of Russia*), VA, CI (ante):—
Issue of HIH late Grand Duchess Marie Kirillovna, *b* 2 Feb 1907, *d* 27 Oct
1951: *m* 24 Nov 1925, HSH the 6th Prince (Friedrich Karl Eduard Erwin) of
Leiningen, who *d* 2 Aug 1946:—
†*HSH Prince* Emich Kirill Ferdinand Hermann (*7th Prince of Leiningen*), *b* 18 Oct   **Leiningen**
1926: *m* 10 Aug 1950, HH Duchess Eilika Stephanie Elisabeth Thekla Juliana, da of
HRH Hereditary Grand Duke Nikolaus Friedrich Wilhelm of Oldenburg, and *d* 30
Oct 1991, leaving issue, *HSH Prince* Karl-Emich Nikolaus Friedrich Hermann (*8th
Prince of Leiningen*), *b* 12 June 1952: *m* 1st, 8 June (civ) and 16 June (relig) 1984,
HSH Princess Margarita Katharina Elisabeth, who *d* 27 Feb 1989, el da of HSH
Kraft Hans Konrad, 8th Prince of Hohenlohe-Öhringen, 5th Duke of Ujest; 2ndly, 24
May (civ) and 15 June (relig) 1991, Gabriele Renate Thyssen, da of Helmut-
Friedhelm Homey, and has issue living, (by 1st *m*) *HSH Princess* Cecilia Maria
Stephanie *b* 10 June 1988, (by 2nd *m*) *HSH Princess* Theresa Anna Elisabeth *b* 26
April 1992,——*HSH Prince* Andreas, *b* 27 Nov 1955: *m* 5 Oct (civ) and 11 Oct (relig)
1981, HRH Princess Alexandra Irene Margaretha Bathildis, da of HRH The Prince
of Hanover (infra), and has issue living, *HSH Prince* Ferdinand Heinrich Emich
Christian Karl *b* 8 Aug 1982, *HSH Prince* Hermann Ernst Johann Albrecht Paul *b*
13 Sept 1987, *HSH Princess* Olga Margarita Valerie Elisabeth Stephanie Alexandra
b 23 Oct 1984,——*HSH Princess* Melita Elisabeth Bathildis Helene Margarita, *b* 10
June 1951: *m* 14 April 1978, Horst Legrum, son of Jakob Legrum,——*HSH Princess*
Stephanie Margarita, *b* 1 Oct 1958. *Residence* - Odenwald 8762, Amorbach,
Bavaria, Germany.————†*HSH Prince* Karl Vladimir Ernst Heinrich, *b* 2 Jan
1928: *m* 14 Feb (civ) and 20 Feb (relig) 1957 (*m diss* 1968), HRH Princess Marie-
Louise, only da of HM late King Boris III of Bulgaria, and *d* 28 Sept 1990, leaving

issue, *HSH Prince* Karl Boris (Frank Markwart), *b* 17 April 1960, *m* 14 Feb 1987, Millena, da of Wladimir Manov, and has issue living, *HSH Prince* Nicholas Alexander Karel Friedrich *b* 25 Oct 1991,——*HSH Prince* Hermann Friedrich Roland Fernando, *b* 16 April 1963, *m* 16 May 1987, Deborah, da of Robert Cully, and has issue living, *HSH Princess* Tatiana Victoria Maureen *b* 27 Aug 1989, *HSH Princess* Nadia Christianne Ruth *b* 16 Dec 1991.———*HSH Prince* Friedrich Wilhelm Berthold, *b* 18 June 1938: *m* 1st, 9 July 1960 (*m diss* 1962), Karin Evelyne Goss; 2ndly, 23 Aug 1971, Helga, da of Hans Eschenbacher. *Residence* - Fürstl Palais, Amorbach, Bavaria, Germany. ———*HSH Princess* Kira-Melita Feodora Marie Viktoria Alexandra, *b* 18 July 1930: *m* 18 Sept (civ) and 12 Oct (relig) 1963 (*m diss* 1972), HRH Prince Andrej of Yugoslavia, and has issue living (ante).———*HSH Princess* Margarita Ileana Viktoria Alexandra, *b* 9 May 1932: *m* 3 Feb 1951, HH Prince Friedrich Wilhelm Ferdinand Josef Maria Manuel Georg Meinrad Fidelis Benedikt Michael Hubertus of Hohenzollern, and has issue living, *HSH Hereditary Prince* Karl Friedrich (Emich Meinrad Benedikt Fidelis Maria Michael Gerold), *b* 20 April 1952: *m* 15 June 1985, Alexandra, da of Clemens, Count Schenk von Stauffenberg, and has issue living, *HSH Prince* Alexander Friedrich *b* 16 March 1987, *HSH Princess* Philippa *b* 2 Nov 1988, *HSH Princess* Flaminia *b* 9 Jan 1992,——*HSH Prince* Albrecht Johannes Hermann Meinrad Stephan, *b* 3 Aug 1954,——*HSH Prince* Ferdinand Maria Fidelis Leopold Meinrad Valentin, *b* 14 Feb 1960. *Residence* - Landhaus Josefslust, Sigmaringen, Hohenzollern, Germany.———*HSH Princess* Mechtilde Alexandra, *b* 2 Jan 1936: *m* 25 Nov 1961, Karl Anton Bauscher, of 8600 Bamberg, Ohmstrasse 6, Germany, and has issue living, Ulf Karl Heinz Stephan Kraft, *b* 20 Feb 1963,——Berthold Alexander Eric, *b* 31 Oct 1965,——Johann Karl Joachim Fritz, *b* 2 Feb 1968.

Hohen-zollern

Issue of HIH late Grand Duchess Kira Kirillovna, *b* 9 May 1909, *d* 8 Sept 1967: *m* 2 May 1938, HI & RH Prince Louis Ferdinand Viktor Eduard Adalbert Michael Hubertus of Prussia (infra):—

Prussia

HRH Prince (Louis Ferdinand) Friedrich Wilhelm (Hubertus Michael Kirill) (Deliusweg 20, D-28359 Bremen, Germany), *b* 9 Feb 1939; renounced rights of succession for himself and his descendants 18 Sept 1967: *m* 1st, 22 Aug 1967 (*m diss* 1975), Waltraud, da of late Dr Alois Freydag, of Plön; 2ndly, 24 April 1976, Ehrengard Insea Elisabeth, da of Lt-Col Günther Ludwig Jobst Johann von Reden, and has issue living, (by 1st *m*) (*Prince*) Philipp Kirill Friedrich Wilhelm Moritz Boris Zdenko, *b* 23 April 1968,——(by 2nd *m*) (*Prince*) Friedrich Wilhelm (Louis Ferdinand Kirill), *b* 16 Aug 1979,——(*Prince*) Joachim Albert Bernhard Christian Ernst, *b* 26 June 1984,——(*Princess*) Viktoria-Luise Kira Ehrengard, *b* 2 May 1982.———*HRH Prince* (Wilhelm Heinrich) Michael (Louis Ferdinand Friedrich Franz Wilhelm) (Wümmehof, D-28357 Bremen, Germany), *b* 22 March 1940; renounced rights of succession for himself and his descendants 29 Aug 1966: *m* 1st 23 Sept 1966 (*m diss* 1982), Jutta, da of Otto Jörn; 2ndly, 23 June 1982, Birgitte, da of Hans Viktor Dallwitz-Wegner, and has issue living, (by 1st *m*) (*Princess*) Micaela Maria, *b* 5 March 1967,——(*Princess*) Nataly Alexandra Caroline, *b* 13 Jan 1970.———*HRH Prince* Christian Sigismund (Louis Ferdinand Kilian) (Wümmehof, D-28357 Bremen, Germany), *b* 14 March 1946: *m* 29 Sept 1984, Countess Nina Helene Lydia Alexandra, da of Count (Carl) Ludwig Erich Ernst Victor Christian Detlev Alexander zu Reventlow, and has issue living, *HRH Prince* Christian Ludwig (Michael Friedrich Ferdinand), *b* 16 May 1986,——*HRH Princess* Irina Maria Vera Kira *b* 4 July 1988: Prince Christian Sigismund has recognized (17 Dec 1969) his da by Christiane Grandmontagne, Isabella Alexandra VON PREUSSEN, *b* 18 Sept 1969.———*HRH Princess* Marie Cécile (Kira Viktoria Luise), *b* 28 May 1942: *m* 3 Dec 1965 (*m diss* 1989), HH Duke Friedrich August Wilhelm Christian Ernst of Oldenburg, and has issue living, *HH Duke* Paul Wladimir (Nikolaus Louis Ferdinand Peter Max Karl Emich), *b* 16 Aug 1969,——*HH Duchess* Rixa (Marie-Alix Kira Altburg), *b* 17 Sept 1970,——*HH Duchess* Bibiane (Maria Alexandra Gertrud), *b* 24 June 1974.———*HRH Princess* Kira (Auguste Viktoria Friederike), *b* 27 June 1943: *m* 10 Sept 1973 (*m diss* 1984), Thomas Frank Liepsner, and has issue living, Kira Marina, *b* 22 Jan 1977.———†*HRH Princess* Xenia (Sophie Charlotte Cecilie), *b* 9 Dec 1949: *m* 26 (civ) and 27 (relig) Jan 1973 (*m diss* 1978), Per-Edvard Lithander, and *d* 18 Jan 1992, leaving issue, Patrick Edvard Christian, *b* 25 June 1973,——Wilhelm Sebastian, *b* 21 Nov 1974.

Oldenburg

Grandchildren of HIH late Grand Duchess Kira Kirillovna (*Princess Louis Ferdinand of Prussia*) (ante):—

Issue of HRH late Prince Louis Ferdinand (Oskar Christian), *b* 25 Aug 1944, *d* 11 July 1977: *m* 24 May 1975, H Ill H Countess Donata Emma (who *m* 2ndly, 9 Feb 1991, HH Duke Friedrich August Wilhelm Christian Ernst of Oldenburg (ante)), only da of HSH Siegfried (Casimir Friedrich), 4th Prince zu Castell-Rüdenhausen:—

HRH Prince Georg Friedrich (Ferdinand), *b* 10 June 1976.———*HRH Princess* Cornelie-Cécile (Viktoria Irene), *b* (*posthumous*) 30 Jan 1978.

Grandchildren of HRH late Princess Alexandra Louise Olga Victoria (*Princess of Hohenlohe-Langenburg*) (infra):—
Issue of HSH late Prince Gottfried Viktor Hermann Alfred Paul Maximilian (*8th Prince of Hohenlohe-Langenburg*), b 24 March 1897, d 11 May 1960: m 20 April 1931, HRH Princess Margarita, who d 24 April 1981, da of HRH late Prince Andrew of Greece and Denmark, GCVO (infra):—

HSH Prince Kraft Alexander Ernst Ludwig Georg Emich (*9th Prince of Hohenlohe-Langenburg*), b 25 June 1935: m 1st, 5 June (civ) and 16 July (relig) 1965 (*m diss* 1990), HSH Princess Charlotte Alexandra Maria Clothilde, da of HSH Prince Alexander Georg Maria Josef Ignatius of Croy; 2ndly, 22 May 1992, Irma Gisela Christine, da of Eugen Pospesch, and has issue living (by 1st m), *HSH Hereditary Prince* Philipp Gottfried Alexander, b 20 Jan 1970,——*HSH Princess* Cecile Marita Dorothea, b 16 Dec 1967,——*HSH Princess* Xenia Margarita Anne, b 8 July 1972. *Residence* - D-74595 Schloss Langenburg, Württemberg, Germany.——*HSH Prince* (Georg) Andreas Heinrich (Tristanstrasse 18a, 80804 Munich, Germany), b 24 Nov 1938: m 14 Aug (civ) and 9 Sept (relig) 1968, HSH Princess Luise Pauline Amelie Vibeke Emma, da of HSH Prince Georg Ulrich of Schönburg-Waldenburg, and has issue living, *HSH Princess* Katharina Clementine Beatrix, b 21 Nov 1972,——*HSH Princess* Tatiana Louise, b 10 Feb 1975.——†*HSH Prince* Albrecht Wolfgang Christoph, b 7 April 1944: m 23 Jan 1976, Maria Hildegard, da of Max Willy Fischer, and d 23 April 1992, leaving issue, (*Prince*) Ludwig (Altensteinstrasse 38a, D-14195 Berlin, Germany), b 21 April 1976.——*HSH Princess* Beatrix Alice Marie Melita Margarita (Schloss Wolfsgarten, D-63225 Langen, Germany), b 10 July 1936.

Hohenlohe-Langen-burg

Issue of HSH late Princess Marie Melita Leopoldine Victoria Feodora Alexandra Sophie, b 18 Jan 1899, d 8 Nov 1967: m 15 Feb 1916, HH (Wilhelm) Friedrich Christian Günther Albert Adolf Georg, Duke of Schleswig-Holstein-Sonderburg-Glücksburg, who d 10 Feb 1965:—
HH Princess Marie Alexandra Caroline Mathilde Viktoria Irene, b 9 July 1927: m 22 July 1970, Douglas Barton Miller, of Schloss-strasse 1, D-88045 Friedrichschafen, Germany.

Grandchildren of HSH late Princess Marie Melita Leopoldine Victoria Feodora Alexandra Sophie (*Duchess of Schleswig-Holstein-Sonderburg-Glücksburg*):—
Issue of HH late Prince (Friedrich Ernst) Peter, Duke of Schleswig-Holstein-Sonderburg-Glücksburg, b 30 April 1922, d 30 Sept 1980: m 9 Oct 1947, HSH Princess Marie-Alix (Gut Bienebeck, Post Damp über Eckernförde, Germany), only da of HSH Prince Stephan Alexander Viktor of Schaumburg-Lippe:—

HH Prince Christoph (*Duke of Schleswig-Holstein-Sonderburg-Glücksburg*), b 22 Aug 1949: m 3 Oct 1981, HSH Princess Elisabeth, da of HSH Prince Alfred Karl of Lippe-Weissenfeld, and has issue living, *HH Prince* Friedrich-Ferdinand, b 19 July 1985,——*HH Prince* Constantin, b 14 July 1986,——*HH Princess* Sophie, b 9 Oct 1983.——*HH Prince* Alexander, b 9 July 1953.——*HH Princess* Marita, b 5 Sept 1948: m 23 May 1975, Baron Wilfrid von Plotho, of Sonnenweg 14, CH-4313 Möhlin bei Basel, Switzerland, and has issue living, *Baron* Christoph, b 14 March 1976,——*Baroness* Irina, b 28 Jan 1978.——*HH Princess* Ingeborg, b 9 July 1956: m 31 May (civ) and 1 June (relig) 1991, Nikolaus Albert Broschek, son of Curt Rudolph Broschek.

Schleswig-Holstein

Grandson of HRH Prince Alfred Ernest Albert, Duke of Edinburgh (ante):—
Issue of HRH late Princess Beatrice Leopoldine Victoria, VA, b 20 April 1884, d 13 July 1966: m 15 July 1909, HRH Prince Alfonso Maria Francisco Antonio Diego of Orleans, Infante of Spain, 5th Duke of Galliera, who d 10 Aug 1975:—

HRH Prince Alvaro Antonio Fernando Carlos Felipe (*6th Duke of Galliera*), b 20 April 1910; ed Winchester; is an AFRAeS and an AMIMechE: m 10 July 1937, Carla, el da of late Senator Leopoldo Girolamo Parodi-Delfino, and has issue living, *Don* Alvaro Jaime de Orléans, b 1 March 1947: m 24 May 1974, Donna Giovanna, yst da of Don Casimiro San Martino d'Aglie di San Germano, Marchese di San Germano, and has issue living, *Don* Andrés b 7 July 1976, *Don* Alois b 24 March 1979, *Doña* Pilar b 27 May 1975,——*Doña* Gerarda, b 25 Aug 1939: m 26 July 1963 (*m diss* 1977), Harry Freeman Saint, son of Ellis Chandler Saint, and has issue living, Marc b 20 March 1969: m 10 Dec 1990 (civ) and 6 July 1991 (relig), Dorothée Sophie, da of Michel André Horps, Carla b 22 May 1967: m 19 Sept 1992, John Stephen Lilly, son of Terence Lilly,——*Doña* Beatriz (*Marquesa de Torre Breva*), b 27 April 1943: m 25 April 1964 (*m diss* 1989), Dr Tomaso dei Conti Farini, Patrician of Ravenna, and has issue living, *Don* Gerardo Alfonso b 23 Nov 1967, Donna Elena b 27 Oct 1969.

Bourbon-Orleans

Grandsons of HRH Prince Alvaro Antonio Fernando Carlos Felipe of Orleans (*6th Duke of Galliera*) (ante):—

Issue of late Don Alonso of Orleans, *b* 23 Aug 1941, *d* 6 Sept 1975; was Spanish Consul at Houston, Texas, USA: *m* 12 Jan 1966, Donna Emilia, da of Don Vincenzo Ferrara-Pignatelli, 12th Principe di Strongoli:—
Don Alfonso, b 2 Jan 1968.———*Don Alvaro, b* 4 Oct 1969.

Descendants of Field Marshal HRH the Duke of Connaught and Strathearn, 3rd son of Queen Victoria.

Grandchildren of HRH late Princess Margaret Victoria Augusta Charlotte Norah (*Crown Princess of Sweden, Duchess of Skåne*) (infra):—
Issue of HRH late Prince Gustaf Adolf (Oscar Fredrik Arthur Edmund) (*Duke of Västerbotten*), GCVO, *b* 22 April 1906, *d* 26 Jan 1947: *m* 20 Oct 1932, HH Princess Sibylla Calma Marie Alice Bathildis Feodora, who *d* 28 Nov 1972, da of HRH Prince (Leopold) Charles Edward George Albert, 2nd Duke of Albany (Duke of Saxe-Coburg and Gotha) (infra):—

Sweden   *HM King* Carl XVI Gustaf (Folke Hubertus) (*King of Sweden*), KG (Royal Palace, S-11130 Stockholm, Sweden; Solliden Öland, Drottningholm), *b* 30 April 1946; *s* his grandfather King Gustaf VI Adolf 15 Sept 1973; Hon Adm RN 1975; has Orders of Seraphim of Sweden, Elephant of Denmark, Falcon of Iceland, Saint Olav of Norway, White Rose of Finland, Chrysanthemum of Japan; Roy Victorian Chain 1975, KG 1983: *m* 19 June 1976, Silvia Renate, da of Walther Sommerlath, of Heidelberg, and has issue living, *HRH Prince* Carl Philip (Edmund Bertil) (*Duke of Värmland*), *b* 13 May 1979,——— HRH Princess Victoria Ingrid Alice Désirée (*Crown Princess of Sweden, Duchess of Västergötland*), *b* 14 July 1977; Crown Princess of Sweden since 1 Jan 1980,———*HRH Princess* Madeleine Thérèse Amelie Josephine (*Duchess of Hälsingland and Gästrikland*), *b* 10 June 1982.———*HRH Princess* Margaretha Désirée Victoria, *b* 31 Oct 1934; has Order of Seraphim of Sweden: *m* 30 June 1964, John Kenneth Ambler (Knt Cdr RN Order of Vasa), of Chippinghurst Manor, Cuddesdon, Oxon, and has issue living, (Charles) Edward, *b* 14 July 1966,———James Patrick, *b* 10 June 1969,———Sybilla Louise, *b* 14 April 1965.———*HRH Princess* Birgitta Ingeborg Alice, *b* 19 Jan 1937; has Order of Seraphim of Sweden: *m* 30 May 1961, HSH Prince Johann Georg (Carl Leopold Eitel Friedrich Meinrad Maria Hubertus Michael) of Hohenzollern, and has issue living, *HSH Prince* Carl Christian (Friedrich Johannes Meinrad Maria Hubertus Edmund), *b* 5 April 1962,———*HSH Prince* Hubertus Gustav-Adolf Veit Georg Meinrad Maria Alexander, *b* 10 June 1966,———*HSH Princess* Désirée Margarethe Victoria Louise Sibylla Catharina Maria, *b* 27 Nov 1963: *m* 21 Sept (civ) and 6 Oct (relig) 1990, H Ill H Hereditary Count Heinrich Franz Josef Georg Maria of Ortenberg, eldest son of H Ill H Alram Karl Gottfried Hans Ladislaus, Count of Ortenberg, and has issue living, *H Ill H Count* Carl Theodor Georg Philipp Maria *b* 21 Feb 1992. *Residence* - Dr Maxstrasse 70, D-8022 Grünwald, Germany.———*HRH Princess* Désirée Elisabeth Sibylla (*Princess Désirée, Baroness Silfverschiöld*), *b* 2 June 1938; has Order of Seraphim of Sweden: *m* 5 June 1964, (Nils-August Otto Carl) Niclas, Baron Silfverschiöld, of Koberg, Sollebrunn, Sweden, and has issue living, *Baron* Carl Otto Edmund, *b* 22 March 1965,———*Baroness* Christina Louise (Ewa Madelaine), *b* 29 Sept 1966,———*Baroness* Hélène Ingeborg Sibylla, *b* 20 Sept 1968.———*HRH Princess* Christina Louise Helena (*Princess Christina, Mrs Magnuson*), *b* 3 Aug 1943; has Order of Seraphim of Sweden: *m* 15 June 1974, Tord Gösta Magnuson, of Beylon, Ulriksdal, S-171 71 Solna, Sweden, and has issue living, (Carl) Gustaf Victor, *b* 8 Aug 1975,——— (Tord) Oscar Fredrik, *b* 20 June 1977,———Victor Edmund Lennart, *b* 10 Sept 1980.

Grandchildren of FM HRH Prince Arthur William Patrick Albert, 1st Duke of Connaught and Strathearn, 3rd son of Queen Victoria:—
Issue of HRH late Princess Margaret Victoria Augusta Charlotte Norah (*Crown Princess of Sweden, Duchess of Skåne*), *b* 15 Jan 1882, *d* 1 May 1920: *m* 15 June 1905, HRH Crown Prince (Oscar Fredrik Wilhelm Olaf) Gustaf Adolf of Sweden, Duke of Skåne, GCB, GCVO, later HM King Gustaf VI Adolf, who *d* 15 Sept 1973:—
Count Sigvard Oscar Fredrik BERNADOTTE (af Wisborg) (Villagatan 10, S114 32 Stockholm, Sweden), *b* 7 June 1907; renounced right of succession, titles of Prince of Sweden and Duke of Uppland and style of HRH and assumed surname of Bernadotte 7 March 1934; *cr* Count Bernadotte af Wisborg by Grand Duchess of Luxembourg 2 July 1951; has Orders of North Star of Sweden and Elephant of Denmark: *m* 1st, 8 March 1934 (*m diss* 1943), Erika Maria Regina Rosalie, da of Anton Patzek; 2ndly, 26 Oct 1943 (*m diss* 1961), Sonja Helene, da of Robert Alexander Robbert, of Copenhagen, shipowner; 3rdly, 30 July 1961, (Gullan) Marianne, da of Helge Lindberg, of Helsingborg, and formerly wife of Gabriel Tchang, and has issue living, (by 2nd *m*) *Count* Michael Alexander Sigvard, *b* 21 Aug 1944: *m* 6 Feb 1976, Christine, da of Erwin Wellhöfer, and has issue living,

Countess Kajsa, *b* 12 Oct 1980.———*HRH Prince* Bertil Gustaf Oscar Carl Eugen (*Duke of Halland*), GCB, *b* 28 Feb 1912; Gen and Adm Roy Swedish Forces; was Assist Naval Attaché in London 1942-45; has Orders of Seraphim of Sweden and Elephant of Denmark; GCB (Hon Civil) 1956: *m* 7 Dec 1976, Lilian May, has Order of North Star of Sweden, da of William John Davies, of Swansea, and formerly wife of William Ian (Ivan) Sackville Craig. *Residence* - Villa Solbacken, Djurgårdsbrunn, Stockholm, Sweden.———*Count* Carl Johan (Arthur) BERNADOTTE (af Wisborg) *b* 31 Oct 1916; renounced right of succession, titles of Prince of Sweden and Duke of Dalecarlia and style of HRH and assumed surname of Bernadotte 22 Feb 1946; *cr* Count Bernadotte af Wisborg by Grand Duchess of Luxembourg 2 July 1951; has Order of North Star of Sweden: *m* 1st, 19 Feb 1946, (Elin) Kerstin Margareta, who *d* 11 Sept 1987, da of Dr Henning Wijkmark, and formerly wife of Axel Johnson; 2ndly, 29 Sept 1988, Countess Gunilla Märta Louise, da of Count Nils Claës Ludvig Wachtmeister, and widow of Carl-Herman Albert Gerhard Bussler. *Residence* - Kungsberga, Baåstad, Sweden.———*HRH Princess* Ingrid Victoria Sofia Louise Margareta (*HM Queen Ingrid, Queen Mother of Denmark*), *b* 28 March 1910: has Orders of the Elephant   **Denmark** of Denmark, Seraphim of Sweden, etc: *m* 24 May 1935, HM King Frederik IX of Denmark, KG, GCB, GCVO, who *d* 14 Jan 1972, and has issue living, *HM Queen* Margrethe II (Alexandrine Thorhildur Ingrid) (*Queen of Denmark*), LG, *b* 16 April 1940; *ed* Girton Coll, Camb; Roy Victorian Chain 1974, Lady of Order of the Garter 1979: *m* 10 June 1967, Henri Marie Jean André de Laborde de Monpezat (*HRH Prince Henrik of Denmark* from 10 June 1967), Knt Order of the Elephant, Chancellor Roy Danish Orders, Adm Roy Danish Navy and Gen de Brigade Roy Danish Army, and has issue living, *HRH Crown Prince* Frederik André Henrik Christian *b* 26 May 1968, *HRH Prince* Joachim Holger Waldemar Christian *b* 7 June 1969,———*HRH Princess* Benedikte Astrid Ingeborg Ingrid, *b* 29 April 1944: *m* 3 Feb 1968, HSH Richard Casimir Karl August Konstantin, 6th Prince of Sayn-Wittgenstein-Berleburg (5920 Bad Berleburg, Westfalen, Germany), and has issue living, *HSH Prince* Gustav Frederik Philip Richard (*Hereditary Prince of Sayn-Wittgenstein-Berleburg*) *b* 12 Jan 1969, *HSH Princess* Alexandra Rosemarie Ingrid Benedikte *b* 20 Nov 1970, *HSH Princess* Nathalie Xenia Margareta Benedikte *b* 2 May 1975,———*HRH Princess* Anne-Marie Dagmar Ingrid (*HM Queen of the Hellenes*), *b* 30 Aug 1946; has Grand Cross of Order of the Redeemer of Greece: *m*   **Greece** 18 Sept 1964, HM King Constantine II of the Hellenes (*infra*), and has issue living, *HRH Crown Prince* Paul *b* 20 May 1967, *HRH Prince* Nicholas *b* 1 Oct 1969, *HRH Prince* Philip *b* 26 April 1986, *HRH Princess* Alexia *b* 10 July 1965, *HRH Princess* Theodora *b* 9 June 1983.

Issue of late Lady (Victoria) Patricia Helena Elizabeth Ramsay, VA, CI, CD, *b* 17 March 1886, *d* 12 Jan 1974; renounced on her marriage by Roy permission the style and title of HRH and Princess and assumed that of Lady with precedence before Marchionesses of England: *m* 27 Feb 1919, Adm Hon Sir Alexander Robert Maule Ramsay, GCVO, KCB, DSO, who *d* 8 Oct 1972:—

See E Dalhousie, colls.

Descendants of HRH the Duke of Albany, 4th son of Queen Victoria.

Grandchildren of HRH late Prince (Leopold) Charles Edward George   **Saxe-**
Albert, 2nd Duke of Albany and reigning Duke of Saxe-Coburg and   **Coburg**
Gotha (*infra*):—   **and Gotha**
Issue of HH late Hereditary Prince Johann Leopold (Wilhelm Albert
Ferdinand Viktor):—
See Dukedom of Albany (*infra*).

Issue of HH late Princess Caroline Mathilde (Calma) Helene Ludwiga Auguste Beatrice, *b* 22 June 1912, *d* 5 Sept 1983: *m* 1st, 14 Dec 1931 (*m diss* 1938), H Ill H Count Friedrich Wolfgang (Otto) zu Castell-Rüdenhausen, who *d* (presumed killed in action) 11 June 1940; 2ndly, 22 June 1938, Capt Max Schnirring, German Air Force, who was *ka* 7 July 1944; 3rdly, 21 Dec 1946 (*m diss* 1949), Karl Otto (Jim) Andrée:—
(By 1st *m*) *H Ill H Count* Bertram Friedrich Wolfgang (Nibelungengasse 3/2/16, A-1110 Vienna, Austria), *b* 12 July 1932: *m* 10 Oct 1964, Countess Felizitas Anna Maria Elisabeth, only da of Count Hanno Herward Maria Josef Leo von Auersperg, and has issue living, *H Ill H Count* Dominik Dimitrij Johannes Friedrich, *b* 20 July 1965,———*H Ill H Count* Michael Alexej Wolfgang Friedrich, *b* 4 Nov 1967.———*H Ill H Count* Konradin Friedrich, *b* 10 Oct 1933: *m* 6 July 1961, Märta Catharina, da of Bjarne Lönegren, of Finland, and has issue living, *H Ill H Count* Carl-Eduard (Friedrich Hubertus), *b* 15 March 1964,———*H Ill H Countess* Anne Charlotte (Catharina Victoria), *b* 7 April 1962: *m* 4 July 1986, Martti Kalevi Rappu, and has issue living, Patrick Martin Conradin *b* 3 Sept 1987, Richard Valdemar *b* 1 May 1989, Fredrik Carl Anton *b* 7 Nov 1990; Countess Anne Charlotte also has natural issue, Henrik Mikael Frederik ZU CASTELL-RÜDENHAUSEN *b* 23 Dec 1982.———*H Ill H Countess* Victoria Adelheid Clementine Louise, *b* 26 Feb

1935: *m* 20 June 1960, (John) Miles Huntington-Whiteley, and has issue living (*see* Huntington-Whiteley, Bt).———(By 2nd *m*) Calma Barbara, *b* 18 Nov 1938: *m* 1st, 5 July 1961 (*m diss* 1973), Richard Darrell Berger; 2ndly, 15 May 1976, S. F. C. James Cook (132 Burnsdowne Road, Columbia, South Carolina 29210, USA), and has issue living, (by 1st *m*) Sascha Nikolaus Hubertus, *b* 22 Sept 1961: *m* 19 Nov 1982, Bonita Isabelle, da of James Olin Oden, and has issue living, Tristan Lee *b* 20 Nov 1984, Nicole Calma, *b* (twin) 20 Nov 1984,——— Richard Darrel, *b* 3 July 1962: *m* 1st, 9 Aug 1982 (*m diss* 1988), Gypsy Dianna, da of Donald Eugene Wheeler; 2ndly, 9 July 1990, Ronda Rae, da of (Roland) Roger Ross, and has issue living (by 1st *m*), Richard Jonathan Ross, *b* 31 Aug 1984,———Victor Dean, *b* 28 Sept 1963: *m* 15 Aug 1986, Sylvia Diane, da of LeRoy McKinney, and has issue living, Mary Katherine, *b* 11 June 1985,———Samuel Clinton, *b* 28 May 1965,———Wesley Martha, *b* 11 Oct 1967,——— David Charles, *b* 25 Sept 1968: *m* 29 Sept 1990, Constance Marie, da of Donald Albert Mueller.———Dagmar Sibylla, *b* 22 Nov 1940: *m* 26 Feb 1964, Heinrich Walz, and has issue living, (Maria) Valesca, *b* 14 Aug 1965,———Larissa, *b* 16 Sept 1967: *m* 23 July 1991, Takys Panajotakulos.

Granddaughters of HRH late Prince Leopold George Duncan Albert, KG, KT, GCSI, GCMG, PC, 1st Duke of Albany, 4th son of HM late Queen Victoria:—
Issue of HRH late Prince (Leopold) Charles Edward (George Albert):—
See Dukedom of Albany (infra).

Issue of HRH late Princess Alice Mary Victoria Augusta Pauline, VA, GCVO, GBE, *b* 25 Feb 1883, *d* 3 Jan 1981: *m* 10 Feb 1934, Maj-Gen 1st Earl of Athlone, KG, GCB, GCMG, GCVO, DSO, PC, who *d* 16 Jan 1957, 3rd son of HH Prince Francis, Duke of Teck, GCB, by his wife HRH Princess Mary Adelaide Wilhelmina Elizabeth, yr da of HRH the 1st Duke of Cambridge, son of King George III:—

Athlone   *See* E Athlone (ext).

Descendants of HRH Princess Victoria Adelaide Mary Louisa (Princess Royal), German Empress and Queen of Prussia, eldest da of Queen Victoria.

Grandson of HIM late (Friedrich) Wilhelm II (Viktor Albert), German Emperor and King of Prussia, eldest son of HIM Victoria Adelaide Mary Louisa, VA, CI, RRC (*The Princess Royal*), German Empress and Queen of Prussia, eldest da of Queen Victoria:—
Issue of HIH late Crown Prince (Friedrich) Wilhelm Viktor August Ernst of Prussia, *b* 6 May 1882, *d* 20 July 1951; renounced rights of succession to the thrones of the German Empire and of Prussia 1 Dec 1918; head of the Royal House of Prussia 1941-51: *m* 6 June 1905, HH Duchess Cecilie Auguste Marie, who *d* 6 May 1954, da of HRH Grand Duke Friedrich Franz III of Mecklenburg-Schwerin:—

Prussia   *HIH Prince* Louis Ferdinand (Viktor Eduard Adalbert Michael Hubertus), *b* 9 Nov 1907; Dr Phil 1931, formerly Lieut German Air Force: *m* 2 May 1938, HIH Grand Duchess Kira Kirillovna, who *d* 8 Sept 1967, da of HIH late Grand Duke Kirill Vladimirovitch of Russia, and has had issue (ante). *Residences* - Wümmehof, D-28357 Bremen, Germany; 9 Königsallee, Berlin-Grünewald, Germany.

Grandchildren of late Crown Prince (Friedrich) Wilhelm Viktor August Ernst of Prussia (ante):—
Issue of HRH late Prince Wilhelm Friedrich Franz Joseph Christian Olaf of Prussia, Lieut German Inf, *b* 4 July 1906, *ka* 26 May 1940; renounced his rights as first born son 1933: *m* 3 June 1933, Dorothea, who *d* 7 May 1972, only da of Alexander von Salviati:—
HRH Princess Felicitas Cecilie Alexandrine Helene Dorothea, *b* 7 June 1934: *m* 1st, 12 Sept 1958 (*m diss* 1972), Dinnies Friedrich Karl von der Osten; 2ndly, 27 Oct 1972, Jörg Hartwig von Nostitz-Wallwitz, and has had issue, (by 1st *m*) †Hartwig Dinnies Wilhelm Karl Alexander, *b* 15 Feb 1962, *d* 28 June 1989,———Hubertus Christoph Joachim Friedrich, *b* 5 May 1964,———Friederike Thyra Marion Wilhelmine Dorothea, *b* 14 July 1959: *m* 17 Aug 1984, Bernhard Ernst Dieter von Reiche, and has issue living, Felicitas Catharini Malina Johanna *b* 28 Oct 1986, Victoria Cecilie Alexandra Josephine *b* 19 Jan 1989, Donata Friederike Diana Sophie *b* 28 Jan 1992,———Cecilie Felicitas Katharina Sophie, *b* 12 March 1967,———(by 2nd *m*) Diana Renata Friederike, *b* 7 Oct 1974. *Residence* - 2055 Wohltorf, Lauenburg, Am Sachsenwald 3, Germany.———*HRH Princess* Christa Friederike Alexandrine Viktoria, *b* 31 Oct 1936: *m* 24 March 1960, Peter Paul Eduard Maria Clemens Maximilian Franz von Assisi Liebes, who *d* 5 May 1967. *Residence* - Bürklinstrasse 14, 8000 Munich 80, Germany.

Issue of HRH late Prince Hubertus Karl Wilhelm of Prussia, *b* 30 Sept 1909, *d* 8 April 1950: *m* 1st, 29 Dec 1941 (*m diss* 1943), Baroness Maria-Anna Sybilla Margarete, da of Baron Alexander Wilhelm Bernhard Ernst von Humboldt-Dachroeden; 2ndly, 5 June 1943, HSH Princess Magdalene Pauline (647 Büdingen, OHessen, Oberhof, Germany), el da of HSH Prince Heinrich XXXVI Reuss:—

(By 2nd *m*) *HRH Princess* Anastasia Viktoria Cecilie Hermine, *b* 14 Feb 1944: *m* 8 Nov 1965, HSH Prince Aloys-Konstantin (Karl Eduard Joseph Johann Konrad Antonius Gerhard Georg Benediktus Pius Eusebius Maria) of Löwenstein-Wertheim-Rosenberg, of 8764 Schloss Kleinheubach bei Miltenberg, Germany, and has issue living, *HSH Hereditary Prince* Carl Friedrich (Hubertus Georg Eduardo Paolo Nickolo Franz Alois Ignatius Hieronymus Maria), *b* 30 Sept 1966,——*HSH Prince* Hubertus Maximilian Gabriel Louis Franz Konstantin Dominik Wunibald Maria, *b* 18 Dec 1968,——*HSH Prince* Dominik-Wilhelm (Christian Nikolaus Sturmius Antonius Charles Benedikt Felix Maria), *b* 7 March 1983,——*HSH Princess* Christina-Maria (Johanna Caroline Magdalene Osy Cecilie Hermine Isidora Victoria Anastasia), *b* 4 April 1974.

Issue of HRH late Prince Friedrich Georg Wilhelm Christoph of Prussia, *b* 19 Dec 1911, *d* 20 April 1966; naturalised a British subject 1947 and acquired dual nationality by re-admission as a German subject 1953; assumed by deed poll 1951 the surname of von Preussen: *m* 30 July 1945, Lady Brigid Katharine Rachel Guinness (who *m* 2ndly, 3 June 1967, Maj Anthony Patrick Ness, who *d* 20 Aug 1993, of Patmore Hall, Albury, nr Ware, Herts), yst da of 2nd Earl of Iveagh, KG, CB, CMG, FRS:—

(*HRH Prince*) (Frederick) Nicholas, *b* 3 May 1946: *m* 27 Feb 1980, Hon Victoria Mancroft, elder da of 2nd Baron Mancroft, and has issue living, (*Prince*) Frederick Nicholas Stormont, *b* 11 June 1990,——(*Princess*) Beatrice Victoria, *b* 10 Feb 1981,——(*Princess*) Florence Jessica, *b* 28 July 1983 ,——(*Princess*) Augusta Lily, *b* 15 Dec 1986.——(*HRH Prince*) (William) Andrew, *b* 14 Nov 1947: *m* 2 Jan 1979, Alexandra BLAHOVA (formerly BLAHOVA-ALSBITT), da of Frantisek Blaha, and has issue living, (*Prince*) Frederick Alexander, *b* 15 Nov 1984,——(*Princess*) Tatiana Brigid Honor, *b* 16 Oct 1980.——(*HRH Prince*) Rupert Alexander Frederick (53 Redington Road, NW3), *b* 28 April 1955: *m* 5 Jan 1982, Ziba, da of Morteza Rastegar Javaheri, of Tehran, Iran, and has issue living, (*Princess*) Brigid Elizabeth Soraya, *b* 24 Dec 1983,——(*Princess*) Astrid, *b* 16 April 1985.——(*HRH Princess*) Victoria Marina Cecilie, *b* 22 Feb 1952: *m* 3 May 1976, Philippe Alphonse Achache, and has issue living, George Jean, *b* 8 June 1980,——Francis Maximilian Frederick, *b* 30 April 1982.——(*HRH Princess*) Antonia Brigid Elizabeth Louise (*Marchioness of Douro*), *b* (twin) 28 April 1955: *m* 3 Feb 1977, Arthur Charles Valerian Wellesley, Marquess of Douro, el son of 8th Duke of Wellington, MVO, OBE, MC, and has issue living (*see* D Wellington).

Issue of HRH late Princess Cecilie Viktoria Anastasia Zita Thyra Adelheid of Prussia, *b* 5 Sept 1917, *d* 21 April 1975: *m* 21 June 1949, Capt Clyde Kenneth Harris, US Army, who *d* 2 March 1958:—

Kira Alexandrine Brigid Cecilie Ingrid, *b* 20 Oct 1954: *m* 22 May 1982 (*m diss* 1993), John Mitchell Johnson, and has issue living, Philip Louis, *b* 18 Oct 1985.

Grandchildren of HRH late Prince Adalbert Berengar Ferdinand Viktor of Prussia, 3rd son of HIM late Emperor Wilhelm II (ante):—

Issue of HRH late Prince Wilhelm Victor (Freund Ernst Friedrich Georg Adalbert) of Prussia, *b* 15 Feb 1919, *d* 7 Feb 1989: *m* 20 July 1944, Countess Maria Antoinette (Franziska Ladislaja Josepha Paula Bernhardine Agnes) (8 Munich 81, Karl-Zuckmay, Germany), eldest da of Count Friedrich Heinrich Joseph Maria Gregor Kolumbus Hoyos-Sprinzenstein, Baron zu Stichsenstein:—

HRH Prince Adalbert-Adelhart (Alexander Friedrich Joachim Christian), *b* 4 March 1948: *m* 14 June 1981, Eva-Marie, da of Dr Günther Kudicke, and has issue living, (*Prince*) Alexander Markus Wilhelm-Victor, *b* 3 Oct 1984,——(*Prince*) Christian Friedrich Wilhelm Johannes, *b* 3 July 1986,——(*Prince*) Philipp Heinrich Adalbert Günther, *b* (twin) 3 July 1986.——*HRH Princess* Marie-Louise (Marina Franziska), *b* 18 Sept 1945: *m* 22 May 1971, Count Rudolf Maria Emil Franz Friedrich Hubertus Joseph Wenzel Michael von Schönburg-Glauchau, of Quinta Maria Luisa, Marbella, Malaga, Spain, and has issue living, *Count* Friedrich Wilhelm (Simeon Heinrich Dionysius Joachim Rudolf Maria Adalbert), *b* 27 April 1985,——*Countess* Sophie Anastasia Wilhelmine Marie Antoinette, *b* 17 May 1979.

Issue of HRH late Princess Victoria Marina, *b* 11 Sept 1917, *d* 21 Jan 1981; used the name of Countess Lingen: *m* 26 Sept 1947, Kirby William Patterson, of Springfield, Missouri, USA, who *d* 4 June 1984:—

Berengar Orin Bernhard, *b* 21 Aug 1948; BS.——Marina Adelaide Emily, *b* (twin) 21 Aug 1948: *m* 24 Sept 1982, John William Engel, of 11520 Potter St,

Norwalk, Cal 90650, USA, and has issue living, William John, *b* 17 Feb 1983.———— Dohna-Maria, *b* 7 Aug 1954: *m* 28 July 1974, Stephen Leroy Pearl.

Grandson of HRH late Prince August Wilhelm (Heinrich Günther Viktor) of Prussia, 4th son of HIM late Emperor Wilhelm II (ante):—
Issue of HRH late Prince Alexander Ferdinand (Albrecht Achilles Wilhelm Joseph Viktor Karl Feodor) of Prussia, *b* 26 Dec 1912, *d* 12 June 1985: *m* 19 Dec 1938, Irmgard, da of late Maj Friedrich Weygand, German Art, and formerly wife of Werner Rosendorff:—
(*Prince*) Stephan Alexander (Dieter Friedrich), *b* 30 Sept 1939: *m* 1st, 28 Feb 1964 (*m diss* 1976), Heide, da of Dr Ernst Arthur Julius Schmidt; 2ndly, 19 June 1981, Hannelore-Maria, da of Leo Kerscher, and has issue living (by 1st *m*), (*Princess*) Stephanie Viktoria-Luise Irmgard Gertrud, *b* 21 Sept 1966.

Issue of HRH late Prince Oskar Karl Gustav Adolf, 5th son of HIM late Emperor Wilhelm II (ante), *b* 27 July 1888, *d* 27 Jan 1958; Gd Master of Bailliage of Brandenburg of the Order of St John: *m* 31 July 1914, Countess Ina Marie (Helene Adele Elise) (*cr* Countess von Ruppin 27 July 1914, recognized as Princess of Prussia and HRH 26 Aug 1940), who *d* 17 Sept 1973, yr da of Count Karl Heinrich Ludwig von Bassewitz-Levetzow:—
HRH Prince Wilhelm-Karl (Adalbert Erich Detloff) (Einbeckerstrasse 21, 345 Holzminden, Germany), *b* 30 Jan 1922; Gd Master of Bailliage of Brandenburg of the Order of St John: *m* 1 March 1952, Armgard Else Helene, only da of Friedrich (Fritz) von Veltheim, and has issue living, *HRH Prince* Wilhelm-Karl (Oskar Friedrich), *b* 26 Aug 1955,———— *HRH Prince* Oskar Hans Karl Michael, *b* 6 May 1959: *m* 17 July (civ) and 3 Oct (relig) 1992, Auguste Therese Alexandra Hendrikje, da of Ralf Emil Eberhard Julek Hennig Zimmermann von Siefart, and has issue living, *HRH Prince* Oskar Julius Alvo Carlos, *b* 29 Nov 1993,———— *HRH Princess* Donata-Victoria (Ina-Marie Ottonie), *b* 24 Dec 1952.

Grandchildren of HRH late Prince Oskar Karl Gustav Adolf of Prussia (ante):—
Issue of HRH late Princess Herzeleide-Ina-Marie (Sophie Charlotte Else) of Prussia, *b* 25 Dec 1918, *d* 22 March 1989: *m* 16 Aug 1938, HSH Karl Peter Franz Andreas Alexander, Prince Biron von Curland, who *d* 28 Feb 1982:—
HSH Prince Ernst-Johann (Karl Oskar Franz Eitel-Friedrich Peter Burchard), *b* 6 Aug 1940; is a physicist: *m* 14 Aug (civ) and 15 Aug (relig) 1967, Countess Elisabeth Victoria Raimonda, yr da of Ludwig Joseph Albert Franz Heinrich Dieter, Count von Ysenburg-Philippseich.———— *HSH Prince* Michael Karl August Wilhelm (Rabenkopfstrasse 27, 8 Munich 90, Germany), *b* 20 Jan 1944; lawyer: *m* 1 July (civ) and 2 July (relig) 1969, Kristin, 2nd da of Joachim Leo Jürgen Karl Martin von Oertzen, and has issue living, *HSH Prince* Alexander, *b* 18 Sept 1972,———— *HSH Princess* Veronika, *b* 23 Jan 1970,———— *HSH Princess* Stephanie, *b* 24 Sept 1975.———— *HSH Princess* (Viktoria) Benigna Ina-Marie Cecilie Friederike-Luise Helene, *b* 2 July 1939: *m* 3 May (civ) and 6 May (relig) 1968 (*m diss* 19——), Baron John Christopher Robert von Twickel, and has issue living (*see* Throckmorton Bt).

Grandchildren of late Prince Joachim Franz Humbert of Prussia, 6th son of HIM Wilhelm II (ante):—
Issue of HRH late Prince (Karl) Franz Josef (Wilhelm Friedrich Eduard Paul), *b* 15 Dec 1916, *d* 23 Jan 1975: *m* 1st, 1 Oct 1940 (*m diss* 1946), Princess Henriette Hermine Wanda Ida Luise, who *d* 16 March 1972, yr da of Prince Johann Georg (Ludwig Ferdinand August) von Schoenaich-Carolath; 2ndly, 9 Nov 1946 (*m diss* 1959), Luise Dora, who *d* 23 April 1961, da of Max Emil Theodor Hartmann, and formerly wife of Fritz Simon; 3rdly, 20 July 1959, Eva Maria, who *d* 6 March 1987, da of Norberto Herrera, of Lima, Peru:—
(By 1st *m*) *HRH Prince* Franz Wilhelm (Victor Christoph Stephan) (Apartado 6097, E-28080 Madrid, Spain), *b* 3 Sept 1943: *m* 4 Sept 1976 (*m diss* 1986), HIH Grand Duchess Maria, only da of HIH late Grand Duke Vladimir Kirillovitch of Russia, and has issue living (ante).———— *HRH Prince* Franz Friedrich (Christian) (Reichskanzlerstrasse 4, 2000 Hamburg 52, Germany), *b* 17 Oct 1944: *m* 23 Oct 1970, Gudrun, da of Horst Winkler, and has issue living, (*Princess*) Christine, *b* 22 Feb 1968.———— (By 3rd *m*) (*Princess*) Alexandra Marie Auguste Juana Consuelo Eva, *b* 29 April 1960: *m* 28 April 1989, Juan Diego Martinez Lercari, son of Juan Martinez Garay.———— (*Princess*) Désirée Anastasia Maria Benedicta, *b* 13 July 1961: *m* 25 May 1983, Juan Carlos Gamarra y Skeels (Counsellor, Embassy of Peru in Madrid), son of Carlos Gamarra y Vargas, and has issue living, Juan Francisco, *b* 1 March 1987,———— Inés Désirée, *b* 28 April 1989.

Grandchildren of HIM Wilhelm II, (ante):—
Issue of HRH late Princess Viktoria Luise (Adelheid Mathilde Charlotte), *b* 13 Sept 1892, *d* 11 Dec 1980: *m* 24 May 1913, HRH Ernst August (Christian),

Duke of Brunswick and Lüneburg (1913-18), who *d* 30 Jan 1953, having assumed the title of Prince of Hanover 29 Aug 1931:—
See Dukedom of Cumberland and Teviotdale (infra.)

Grandchildren of HRH late Princess Viktoria Luise (Adelheid Mathilde Charlotte) of Prussia (*Duchess of Brunswick and Lüneburg*) (ante):—

Issue of HRH late Princess Friederike (Frederika) Luise Thyra Viktoria Margarete Sophie Olga Cecile Isabelle Christa (*Queen of the Hellenes*), *b* 18 April 1917, *d* 6 Feb 1981: *m* 9 Jan 1938, HM King Paul I of the Hellenes, who *d* 6 March 1964 (infra):—

HM King Constantine II (4 Linnell Drive, Hampstead Way, NW11), *b* 2 June 1940; **Greece** reigned as King of the Hellenes 6 March 1964-1 June 1973 (and nominally until 8 Dec 1974); Sovereign of Orders of the Redeemer, St George and St Constantine, George I, and the Phoenix of Greece, has Grand Cross of Order of the Elephant of Denmark, St Olav of Norway, of House of Orange of the Netherlands, and Grand Cordons of Legion of Honour of France and of King Idris I of Libya and Orders of Merit of Republic of Italy, of Golden Fleece of Spain, and of Annunciation of the House of Savoy; is Grand Officer of Order of St Charles of Monaco and Cdr of Legion of Merit of USA, Grand Cdr of Order of Dannebrog of Denmark, Collar of Order of the Nile of United Arab Republic, of Aztec Eagle of Mexico, and of Roy Order of Chakri of Thailand, and Grand Cross of Roy Order of Leopold of Belgium, of Seraphim of Sweden, of Al Nadha of Jordan, and Order of the Republic of Senegal: *m* 18 Sept 1964, HRH Princess Anne-Marie (Dagmar Ingrid), yst da of HM late King Frederik IX of Denmark, and has issue living (ante).———*HRH Princess* Sophie (Sofia) (*Queen of Spain*), *b* 2 Nov 1938; Hon LLD Cantab 1988, Hon Fellow Exeter **Spain** Coll, Oxford 1988: *m* 14 May 1962, HM King Juan Carlos I of Spain, KG (*infra*), and has issue living, *HRH Infante* Felipe Juan Pablo Alfonso y Todos los Santos (*Prince of the Asturias*), GCVO, *b* 30 Jan 1968; GCVO 1988,——*HRH Infanta* Elena Maria Isabel Dominga, *b* 20 Dec 1963,——*HRH Infanta* Cristina Federica Victoria Antonia, *b* 13 June 1965.———*HRH Princess* Irene, *b* 11 May 1942; has Grand Cross of Roy Order of St Olga and St Sophia of Greece.

Grandchildren of HRH late Grand Adm Prince (Albert Wilhelm) Heinrich of Prussia, 2nd son of HIM Victoria Adelaide Mary Louisa, VA, CI, RRC (*Princess Royal*), German Empress and Queen of Prussia (ante):—

Issue of HRH late Prince (Wilhelm Viktor Karl August Heinrich) Sigismund of Prussia, *b* 27 Nov 1896, *d* 14 Nov 1978: *m* 11 July 1919, HH Princess Charlotte Agnes (Ernestine Auguste Bathildis Marie Therese Adolfine), who *d* 16 Feb 1989, elder da of HH Duke Ernst II of Saxe-Altenburg:—

HRH Prince Alfred Friedrich Ernst Heinrich Konrad, of Apartado 856 Centro- **Prussia** Colon, 1007 San José de Costa Rica, *b* 17 Aug 1924: *m* 15 Dec 1984, Maritza, da of Julius Farkas de Zaladörgicse et Kiskapornok, and formerly wife of Dirke van Wilpe.———*HRH Princess* Barbara Irene Adelheid Viktoria Elisabeth Bathildis, *b* 2 Aug 1920: *m* 11 July 1954, HRH Duke Christian Ludwig (Ernst August Maximilian Johann Albrecht Adolf Friedrich) of Mecklenburg, of 2331 Hemmelmark bei Eckernförde, Schleswig-Holstein, Germany, and has issue living, *HH Duchess* Donata, *b* 11 March 1956: *m* 14 Aug (civil) and 19 Sept (relig) 1987, Alexander von Solodkoff, of 21 Clonmel Rd, SW6 5BL, son of George von Solodkoff and has issue living, Thora *b* 12 Oct 1989, Alix *b* 17 March 1992,——*HH Duchess* Edwina, *b* 25 Sept 1960.

Grandchildren of HRH late Princess Sophie Dorothea Ulrika Alice of Prussia, VA (*Queen of the Hellenes*) (infra):—

Issue of HM late King Alexander I of the Hellenes, *b* 1 Aug 1893, *d* 25 Oct 1920; reigned as King of the Hellenes 1917-20: *m* 4 Nov 1919, Aspasia, who *d* 7 Aug 1972 (having been recognized as Princess by Roy Decree 10 Sept 1922), da of Col Petros Mano:—

†*HRH Princess* Alexandra (*Queen of Yugoslavia*), *b* (*posthumous*) 25 March 1921; **Greece** had Grand Cross of Order of Star of Karadjordje of Yugoslavia and Orders of White Eagle and Crown of Yugoslavia: *m* 20 March 1944, HM King Peter II of Yugoslavia, who *d* 3 Nov 1970, and *d* 30 Jan 1993, leaving issue (ante).

Issue of HM late King Paul I of the Hellenes, KG, GCVO, *b* 14 Dec 1901, *d* 6 March 1964; reigned as King of the Hellenes 1947-64: *m* 9 Jan 1938, HRH Princess Friederike (Frederika) Luise Thyra Viktoria Margarete Sophie Olga Cecilie Isabelle Christa, who *d* 6 Feb 1981, only da of HRH late Prince Ernst August (Christian Georg) of Hanover, Duke of Brunswick and Lüneburg (ante).

Issue of HRH late Princess Helen of Greece and Denmark (*Queen Helen the Queen Mother of Roumania*), *b* 3 May 1896, *d* 28 Nov 1982: *m* 27 Oct 1921 (*m diss* 21 June 1928), HM King Carol II of Roumania, KG, GCVO, who *d* 4 April 1955 (ante).

Issue of HRH late Princess Irene of Greece and Denmark (*Duchess of Aosta*), *b* 13 Feb 1904, *d* 15 April 1974: *m* 1 July 1939, Adm HRH Prince Aimone Roberto Margherita Maria Giuseppe Torino of Savoy, Duke of Spoleto, later 4th Duke of Aosta, who *d* 30 Jan 1948:—

Savoy Aosta

HRH Prince Amedeo Umberto Constantino Giorgio Paolo Elena Maria Florenzio Zvonimir, 5th Duke of Aosta, Principe della Cisterna e di Belriguardo, Marchese di Voghera, Conte di Ponderano (Il Borro, San Giustino Valdarno, Prov d'Arezzo, Italy), *b* 27 Sept 1943: *m* 1st, 22 July 1964 (*m diss* 1982 and annulled 1987), HRH Princess Claude Marie Agnès Catherine of France, 5th da of HRH Prince Henri Robert Ferdinand Marie Louis Philippe of France, Comte de Paris, head of the Roy House of France; 2ndly, 30 March 1987, Donna Silvia, da of Don Vincenzo Paterno, Marchese di Regiovanni, Conte de Prades, Barone de Spedalotto, and has issue living (by 1st *m*), *HRH Prince* Aimone Umberto Emanuele Filiberto Luigi Amedeo Elena Maria Fiorenzo (*Duke of Apulia*), *b* 13 Oct 1967,——*HRH Princess* Bianca Irene Olga Elena Isabella Fiorenza Maria, *b* 2 April 1966: *m* 11 Sept 1988, Count Giberto Carbonello Tiberto Maria Arrivabene Valenti Gonzaga, son of Count Leonardo Arrivabene Valenti Gonzaga and has issue living, Viola Moreschina Nushi Adec Nicoletta Maria *b* 31 May 1991, Vera Clementina Verde Aimone Elena Maria *b* 18 Aug 1993,——*HRH Princess* Mafalda Giovanna Jolanda Shams Maria Fiorenza Isabella, *b* 20 Sept 1969.

Grandchildren of HIM late Victoria Adelaide Mary Louisa, VA, CI, RRC (*Princess Royal*), German Empress and Queen of Prussia (ante):—
Issue of HRH late Princess Sophie Dorothea Ulrika Alice, *VA* (*Queen of the Hellenes*), *b* 14 June 1870, *d* 13 Jan 1932: *m* 27 Oct 1889, HM King Constantine I of the Hellenes, who *d* 11 Jan 1923 (having reigned as King of the Hellenes 1913-17 and 1920-23):—
HRH Princess Katherine (*Lady Katherine Brandram*), *b* 4 May 1913; granted by Roy Warrant the rank of a Duke's daughter 25 Aug 1947; has Grand Cross of Order of St Olga and St Sophia of Greece: *m* 21 April 1947, Maj Richard Campbell Andrew Brandram, MC, TD, RA, who *d* 28 March 1994, and has issue living, (Richard) Paul George Andrew, *b* 1 April 1948: *m* 12 Feb 1975, Jennifer Diane, da of Lt-Col Robert Steele, of St Leonard's Grange, Beaulieu, Hants, and has issue living, Nicholas George *b* 23 April 1982, Sophie Eila *b* 23 Jan 1981, Alexia Katherine *b* 6 Dec 1985. *Residence* - Croft Cottage, Pound Lane, Marlow, Bucks.

Issue of HRH late Princess Margarethe Beatrice Feodora of Prussia (*Landgravine of Hesse*), *b* 22 April 1872, *d* 22 Jan 1954: *m* 25 Jan 1893, HRH Friedrich Karl (Ludwig Konstantin), who *d* 28 May 1940 (elected King of Finland Oct 1918, but withdrew acceptance Nov 1918):—
HH Prince Wolfgang Moritz, *b* (twin) 6 Nov 1896: *m* 1st, 17 Sept 1924, HGDH Princess Marie Alexandra (Thyra Viktoria Louise Carola Hilda), who *d* (killed in an air raid) 29 Jan 1944, only da of HGDH Prince Maximilian Alexander Friedrich Wilhelm of Baden; 2ndly, 7 Sept 1948, Ottilie, da of Ludwig Möller. Schloss Friedrichshof, 6242 Kronberg, Taunus, Germany.

Grandchildren of HRH late Princess Margarethe Beatrice Feodora of Prussia (*Landgravine of Hesse*) (ante):—
Issue of HRH late Landgrave Philipp of Hesse, head of all the House of Hesse 1968-80, *b* 6 Nov 1896, *d* 25 Oct 1980: *m* 23 Sept 1925, HRH Princess Mafalda Maria Elisabetta Anna Romana of Savoy, who *d* (in Buchenwald Concentration Camp) 27 Aug 1944, 2nd da of HM King Victor Emmanuel III of Italy: —

Hesse

HRH Landgrave Moritz Friedrich Karl Emanuel Humbert (*Landgrave of Hesse*), head of all the House of Hesse since 1980 (Schloss Friedrichshof, 6242 Kronberg i. Taunus, Germany), *b* 6 Aug 1926; adopted by his kinsman late Prince Ludwig of Hesse and by Rhine, head of the Grand Ducal House of Hesse (who *d* 30 May 1968): *m* 3 June 1964 (*m diss* 1974), HSH Princess Tatiana Louise Ursula Therese Elsa, 2nd da of HSH Gustav Albrecht, 5th Prince of Sayn-Wittgenstein-Berleburg, and has issue living, *HRH Prince* Heinrich Donatus Philipp Umberto, *b* 17 Oct 1966,——*HH Prince* Philipp Robin, *b* 17 Sept 1970,——*HH Princess* Mafalda Margarethe, *b* 6 July 1965,——*HH Princess* Elena Elisabeth Madeleine, *b* 8 Nov 1967.——*HH Prince* Heinrich Wilhelm Konstantin Victor Franz (Villa Polissena, Via San Filippo Martire 6, Rome, Italy; Villa la Falconara, Forio d'Ischia, Italy), *b* 30 Oct 1927; artist.——*HH Prince* Otto Adolf (S Marco 3366, 30124 Venice, Italy), *b* 3 June 1937; prehistorian: *m* 1st, 5 April (civ) and 6 April (relig) 1965 (*m diss* 1969), Angela Mathilde Agathe, da of Maj-Gen (Wilhelm Konrad Rodrigo) Bernd von Doering, and formerly wife of Hans Peter Schmeidler; 2ndly, 28 Dec 1988, Elisabeth Marga Dorothea, da of Wilhelm Wittler.——*HH Princess* Elisabeth Margarethe Elena Johanna Maria Jolanda Polyxene (Fasanenstrasse 24, 6078 Neu-Isenburg 2 (Gravensbruch), Germany), *b* 8 Oct 1940: *m* 28 Feb 1962, Count Friedrich Carl (Eduard Wilhelm Hans Franz Eusebius Michael Hubert Maria) von Oppersdorff, who *d* 11 Jan 1985, and has issue living, *Count* Friedrich Karl (Philipp Wilhelm Hans Moritz Maria), *b* 1 Dec 1962,——*Count* Alexander Wolfgang (Johannes Georg Victor Emanuel Maria), *b* 3 Aug 1965.

Issue of HH late Prince Christoph Ernst August of Hesse, *b* (twin) 14 May 1901, *d* 7 Oct 1943: *m* 15 Dec 1930, HRH Princess Sophie (who *m* 2ndly, 24 April 1946, HRH Prince Georg Wilhelm (Ernst August Friedrich Axel) of Hanover (ante)), da of HRH late Prince Andrew of Greece and Denmark (infra):—
HH Prince Karl Adolf Andreas, *b* 26 March 1937: *m* 18 April 1966, Countess Yvonne Margit Valerie, da of Count Béla Szapáry de Muraszombath, Széchysziget et Szapár, and has issue living, *HH Prince* Christoph, *b* 18 June 1969,——*HH Princess* Irina Verena, *b* 1 April 1971.——*HH Prince* Rainer Christoph Friedrich (Breitensteinstrasse 1, 8166 Neuhaus, Germany), *b* 18 Nov 1939; author.——*HH Princess* Christina Margarete, *b* 10 Jan 1933: *m* 1st, 1 Aug (civ) and 2 Aug (relig) 1956 (*m diss* 1962), HRH Prince Andrej of Yugoslavia (ante); 2ndly, 3 Dec 1962 (*m diss* 1986), Robert Floris van Eyck who *d* 19 Dec 1991, son of Pieter Nicolaus van Eyck, and has had issue, (by 1st *m*) (ante), (by 2nd *m*), Mark Nicholas, *b* 16 Feb 1966: *m* 12 June 1992, Joanne Marea, da of Michael John Green,—— Helen Sophie, *b* 25 Oct 1963: *m* 24 Jan 1986, Roderick Alan Harman, son of Douglas John Harman, and has issue living, Sascha Alexandra Sophia *b* 26 July 1986, Pascale Olivia *b* 19 March 1989.——*HH Princess* Dorothea Charlotte Karin, *b* 24 July 1934: *m* 31 March (civ) and 1 April (relig) 1959, HSH Prince Friedrich Karl Hugo Maximilian Maria Cyrillus Felix Hubertus zu Windisch-Graetz, and has issue living, *HSH Princess* Marina Margherita Sophia Leontina Christina, *b* 3 Dec 1960: *m* 28 May 1988, Gyula Lajos Jakabffy, son of Tamás Jakabffy, and has issue living, Réka Dorothea Sita *b* 17 Sept 1988, Sophia Magdolna *b* 27 Aug 1989,—— *HSH Princess* Clarissa Elisabetha Fiore, *b* 5 Aug 1966: *m* 16 Nov 1985, Eric Michel Jacques de Waele, son of Jean August de Waele, and has issue living, Michel Jean Henri *b* 18 May 1986, Alexander Federico Mark *b* 3 July 1987, Mathieu Paul Philippe *b* 16 Dec 1988. ——*HH Princess* Clarissa Alice (Clarisse de Hesse), *b* (posthumous) 6 Feb 1944: *m* 20 July 1971 (*m diss* 1976), Claude Jean Derrien. *Residence* - 108 rue Lepic, F-75118 Paris, France.

Descendants of HRH Princess Alice Maud Mary (Grand Duchess of Hesse and by Rhine), 2nd da of Queen Victoria.

Descendants of late George Louis Victor Henry Serge Mountbatten, 2nd Marquess of Milford Haven, GCVO, elder son of late Victoria Alberta Elizabeth Mathilde Marie, Marchioness of Milford Haven, VA (infra), eldest da of HRH late Princess Alice Maud Mary.
See M Milford Haven.

Descendants of late Louis Francis Albert Victor Nicholas Mountbatten, 1st Earl Mountbatten of Burma, KG, GCB, OM, GCSI, GCIE, GCVO, DSO, PC, FRS, yr son of late Victoria Alberta Elizabeth Mathilde Marie, Marchioness of Milford Haven, VA (infra), eldest da of HRH late Princess Alice Maud Mary.
See Cs Mountbatten.

Grandchildren of late Victoria Alberta Elizabeth Mathilde Marie, Marchioness of Milford Haven, VA (ante):—
Issue of HRH late Princess (Victoria) Alice Elizabeth Julia Marie, RRC, *b* 25 Feb 1885, *d* 5 Dec 1969: *m* 7 Oct 1903, HRH Prince Andrew of Greece and Denmark, GCVO, who *d* 3 Dec 1944:—
Greece HRH The Prince Philip, KG, KT, OM, GBE, AC, QSO, PC (*Duke of Edinburgh*), *b* 10 June 1921; *cr* Duke of Edinburgh 1947 (*see page 105*).——*HRH Princess* Sophie, *b* 26 June 1914: *m* 1st, 15 Dec 1930, HH Prince Christoph Ernst August of Hesse, who *d* 7 Oct 1943 (ante); 2ndly, 24 April 1946, HRH Prince Georg Wilhelm (Ernst August Friedrich Wilhelm Axel) of Hanover (ante).

Grandchildren of HRH late Princess (Victoria) Alice Elizabeth Julia Marie, RRC (*Princess Andrew of Greece and Denmark*) (ante):—
Issue of HRH late Princess Margarita of Greece and Denmark, *b* 18 April 1905, *d* 24 April 1981: *m* 20 April 1931, HSH Prince Gottfried Viktor Hermann Alfred Paul Maximilian, 8th Prince of Hohenlohe-Langenburg, who *d* 11 May 1960 (ante).

Issue of HRH late Princess Theodora of Greece and Denmark, *b* 30 May 1906, *d* 16 Oct 1969: *m* 17 Aug 1931, HRH Prince Berthold Friedrich Wilhelm Ernst August Heinrich Karl (*Margrave of Baden*), head of the Grand Ducal House of Baden 1929-63, who *d* 27 Oct 1963:—
Baden HRH Prince Maximilian (Max) Andrew Friedrich Gustav Ernst August Bernhard (*Margrave of Baden*) (Schloss Salem, D7777 Salem, Baden, Germany), *b* 3 July 1933; *ed* Gordonstoun; head of the Grand Ducal House of Baden since 1963: *m* 30 Sept 1966, HI & RH Archduchess Valerie Isabelle Marie Anna Alfonsa Desideria Brigitte Sophia Thomasia Huberta Josepha Ignatia, 7th da of HI & RH late Archduke Hubert Salvator (Rainer Maria Joseph Ignatius) of Austria, and has issue

living, *HRH Hereditary Prince* Bernhard Max Friedrich August Louis Kraft, *b* 27 May 1970,——*HGDH Prince* Leopold Max Christian Ludwig Clemens Hubert, *b* 1 Oct 1971,——*HGDH Prince* Michael Max Andreas, *b* 11 March 1976,——*HGDH Princess* Marie-Louise (Elisabeth Mathilde Theodora Cecilie Sarah Charlotte), *b* 3 July 1969.——*HGDH Prince* Ludwig Wilhelm Georg Ernst Christoph (Schloss Zwingenberg/N, D6931, Germany), *b* 16 March 1937: *m* 21 Sept 1967, HSH Princess Maria Anna (Marianne) Henriette Eleonore Gobertina, yst da of HSH Prince Karl Alain Maria Gobertus von Auersperg-Breunner, and has issue living, *HGDH Prince* Berthold Ernst-August Emich Rainer, *b* 8 Oct 1976,——*HGDH Princess* Sophie Thyra Josephine Georgine Henriette, *b* 8 July 1975,——*HGDH Princess* Aglaë Margareta Tatiana Mary, *b* 3 March 1981.——*HGDH Princess* Margarita Alice Thyra Viktoria Marie Louise Scholastica, *b* 14 July 1932: *m* 6 June 1957 (*m diss* 1982), as his 1st wife, HRH Prince Tomislav of Yugoslavia (ante).

Descendants of HRH Princess Beatrice Mary Victoria Feodore, 5th and yst da of Queen Victoria.

Grandson of late Alexander Albert Mountbatten, 1st Marquess of Carisbrooke, GCB, GCVO, el son of HRH late Princess Beatrice Mary Victoria Feodore, VA, CI, GCVO, GBE, RRC:—
Issue of late Lady Iris Victoria Beatrice Grace Mountbatten, *b* 13 Jan 1920, *d* 1 Sept 1982: *m* 1st, 15 Feb 1941 (*m diss* 1946), Maj Hamilton Joseph Keyes O'Malley, IG; 2ndly, 5 May 1957 (*m diss* 1957), Michael Neely Bryan, who *d* 20 Aug 1972; 3rdly, 11 Dec 1965, William Alexander Kemp, Canadian tv announcer, who *d* 12 Dec 1991:—
(By 2nd *m*) Robin Alexander, *b* 20 Dec 1957.

Grandson of HRH late Infante Jaime Luitpoldo Isabelino Enrique Alejandro Alberto Alfonso Victor Acacio Pedro Pablo Maria of Spain (*Duke of Segovia*) (infra):—
Issue of HRH late Don Alfonso Jaime Marcelino Manuel Victor Maria (*Duke of Cadiz*), *b* 20 April 1936; granted style of HRH 22 Nov 1972; *d* 30 Jan 1989: *m* 8 March 1972 (*m diss* 1983), Doña Maria del Carmen (Esperanza Alejandra de la Santisima Trinidad y de Todos los Santos) Martinez-Bordiu y Franco, da of Don Cristobal Martinez-Bordiu, 10th Marqués de Villaverde, by his wife Doña Maria del Carmen Franco, only da of Generalisimo Francisco Franco, Spanish Head of State (*Caudillo*) 1936-75:—
Don Luis Alfonso (Gonzalo Victor Manuel Marco), *b* 25 April 1974.

Grandson of HRH late Princess Victoria Eugenie Julia Ena (*Queen of Spain*) (infra):—
Issue of HRH late Infante Jaime Luitpoldo Isabelino Enrique Alejandro Alberto Alfonso Victor Acacio Pedro Pablo Maria of Spain (*Duke of Segovia*), *b* 23 June 1908; renounced all rights of succession to the throne of Spain for himself and his descendants 21 June 1933; *d* 20 March 1975: *m* 1st, 4 March 1935 (*m diss* in Roumania 6 May 1947; confirmed at Turin 3 June 1949), Donna (Victoria Jeanne Josephine Pierre Marie) Emanuela de Dampierre, da of late Vicomte Roger Richard Charles Henri Etienne de Dampierre, 2nd Duke of San Lorenzo; 2ndly, 3 Aug 1949, Charlotte Louise Auguste, who *d* 3 July 1979, da of Otto Eugen Tiedemann, ôf Königsberg, E Prussia, and formerly wife of — Hippler:—
Spain   (By 1st *m*) *Don* Gonzalo Victor Alfonso José Bonifacio Antonio Maria y Todos los Santos (79 Calle de Castello, Madrid 7, Spain), *b* 5 June 1937: *m* 1st, in Mexico 28 Jan 1983 (*m* not recognized in Spain), Carmen Harto Montealegre; 2ndly, 25 June (civil) and 30 June (religious) 1984 (*m diss* 1989), Maria de las Mercedes, er da of Don Luis Licer; 3rdly, 12 Dec 1992, Emmanuela Maria Lina, da of Vincenzo Pratolongo; has recognized a natural da, Stephanie Michelle de Borbón, *b* 19 June 1968.

Grandchildren of HRH late Princess Beatrice Mary Victoria Feodore, VA, CI, GCVO, GBE, RRC, *b* 4 April 1857, *d* 26 Oct 1944: *m* 23 July 1885, HRH Prince Henry Maurice of Battenberg, KG, PC, who *d* 20 Jan 1896:—
Issue of HRH late Princess Victoria Eugenie Julia Ena (*Queen of Spain*), VA, *b* 24 Oct 1887; granted style of HRH 3 April 1906; *d* 15 April 1969: *m* 31 May 1906, HM King Alfonso XIII of Spain, who *d* 28 Feb 1941 (having reigned as King of Spain from his birth 17 May 1886 until 14 April 1931, when he left the country):—
†*HRH Infante Don* Juan Carlos Teresa Silverio Alfonso (*Count of Barcelona*), *b* 20 June 1913; Midshipman RN 1933-35; appointed Hon Lieut 1936 and Hon Adm 1987; formally renounced his rights of succession to the Spanish throne in favour of his son the reigning King 14 May 1977: *m* 12 Oct 1935, HRH Princess Maria de las Mercedes Cristina Januaria Isabel Luisa Carolina Victoria, da of HRH late Prince Carlos Maria Francisco de Asis Pascual Ferdinando Antonio de Padua Francisco de

Paula Alfonso Andres Avelino Tancredo of Bourbon-Two Sicilies, Infante of Spain, and *d* 1 April 1993, leaving issue, *HM King* Juan Carlos I (Alfonso Victor Maria) of Spain, KG (Palacio de la Zarzuela, Madrid, Spain), *b* 5 Jan 1938; Hon LLD Cantab 1988; *s* as King of Spain 22 Nov 1975: *m* 14 May 1962, HRH Princess Sophie (Sofia) of Greece and Denmark, el da of HM late King Paul I of the Hellenes, and has issue living (ante),——*HRH Infanta* Maria del Pilar (Alfonsa Juana Victoria Luisa Ignacia y Todos los Santos) (*Duchess of Badajoz*), *b* 30 July 1936: *m* 5 May 1967, Don Luís Gómez-Acebo y Duque de Estrada, Vizconde de la Torre, who *d* 9 March 1991, and has issue living, *Don* Juan Filiberto (Nicolas) *b* 6 Dec 1969, *Don* Bruno Alejandro *b* 15 June 1971, *Don* (Luís) Beltrán Ataulfo, *b* 20 May 1973, *Don* Fernando Umberto *b* 13 Sept 1974, *Doña* (Maria de Fátima) Simoneta Luisa *b* 28 Oct 1968: *m* 12 Sept 1990, José Miguel Fernandez y Sastron, son of Jorge Fernandez y Menendez (and has issue living, *Don* Luís *b* 23 Sept 1991),——*HRH Infanta* Margarita Maria de la Victoria Esperanza Jacoba Felicidad Perpetua y Todos los Santos (*Duchess of Soria*), *b* 6 March 1939: *m* 12 Oct 1972, Don Carlos Zurita y Delgado, of Castellana 63, Madrid 4, Spain: and has issue living, *Don* Alfonso Juan Carlos *b* 9 Aug 1973, *Doña* Maria Sofia Emilia Carmen *b* 16 Sept 1975.——*HRH Infanta* Beatriz Isabel Federica Alfonsa Eugenia Cristina Maria Teresa Bienvenida Ladislàa, *b* 22 June 1909: *m* 14 Jan 1935, Don Alessandro Torlonia, 5th Principe di Civitella-Cesi, who *d* 12 May 1986, and has issue living, *Don* Marco Alfonso, 6th Principe di Civitella-Cesi (Palazzo Torlonia, 78 Via Bocca de Leone, Rome, Italy), *b* 2 July 1937: *m* 1st, 15 Sept 1960, Donna Orsetta, who *d* 10 March 1968, 2nd da of Don Adolfo Caracciolo dei Principi di Castagneto e Duchi di Melito; 2ndly, 9 Nov 1968 (*m diss* 1985), Philippa Catherine Blanche, da of John Linden McDonald, and formerly wife of Luc, Comte de Nanteuil; 3rdly, 11 Nov 1985, Blazena Anna Helena, da of Václav Jan Svitak, and has issue living, (by 1st *m*) *Don* Giovanni *b* 17 April 1962, (by 2nd *m*) *Donna* Victoria Eugenia Carolina Honor Paola Alexandra Maria *b* 8 May 1971, (by 3rd *m*) *Donna* Catarina Agnese *b* 14 June 1974,——*Don* Marino Ricardo Francesco Maria Giuseppe, *b* 13 Dec 1939,——*Donna* Sandra Vittoria, *b* 14 Feb 1936: *m* 20 June 1958, Conte Clemente Lequio di Assaba, who *d* 28 June 1971, and has issue living, *Conte* Alessandro Vittorio Eugenio Enrico *b* 20 June 1960: *m* 12 Oct 1987, Antonia Feodora, da of Donato Dell'Atte (and has issue living, Clemente Lorenzo *b* 2 April 1988; Conte Alessandro also has issue by Ana Garcia y Obregón, Alessandro Alfonso LEQUIO DI ASSABA Y OBREGÓN *b* 23 June 1992), *Contessa* Desideria Beatrice Elyse Francesca *b* 19 Sept 1962: *m* 11 Sept 1986, Count Oddone Paulo Tournon, son of Count Giovanni Felice Tournon (and has issue living, *Count* Giovanni Carlo Alberto Adriano Alessandro Costantino Demetrio Maria *b* 3 Sept 1991, *Count* Giorgio, *b* —Feb 1994),——*Donna* Olimpia, *b* 27 Dec 1943: *m* 26 June 1965, Paul-Annik Weiller, of 47 rue Vieille du Temple, 75004 Paris, France, son of Paul-Louis Weiller, and has issue living, (Aliki) Beatrice Victoria *b* 23 March 1967: *m* 23 June 1990, André Aranha Corrêa do Lago, son of Antonio Corrêa do Lago, Amb of Brazil, Sibilla Sandra *b* 12 June 1968, Cosima Marie Elisabeth Edmee *b* 18 Jan 1984, Domitilla Luise Marie *b* 14 June 1985.——*HRH Infanta* Maria Cristina (Teresa Alejandra Guadalupe Maria de la Concepción Ildefonsa Victoria Eugénia) (Via Giannone 10, Turin, Italy), *b* 12 Dec 1911: *m* 10 June 1940, Enrico Eugenio Francesco Antonio Marone-Cinzano, 1st Count Marone, who *d* 23 Oct 1968, and has issue living, *Donna* Vittoria Alfonsa Alberta Pilar Enrica Paola (Jesús Aprendiz 10, Madrid 28007, Spain), *b* 5 March 1941: *m* 12 Jan 1961 (*m diss* 19——), Don José Carlos Alvarez de Toledo y Gross, 8th Count of Villapaterna, and has issue living, *Don* Francisco de Borja *b* 27 March 1964, *Don* Marco Alfonso de Borja *b* 23 Jan 1966, *Don* Gonzalo *b* 1 Oct 1973, *Don* Vittoria Eugénia *b* 8 Oct 1961: *m* 29 Sept 1982, Don Alfonso Codorniu y Aguilar (and has issue living, *Don* Jaime *b* 15 Feb 1985, *Doña* Ana *b* 24 Jan 1987, *Doña* Carla *b* 5 July 1990),——*Donna* Giovanna Paola Gabriella (Julio Palacios 3, Madrid 28002, Spain), *b* 31 Jan 1943: *m* 1st, 24 July 1967 (*m diss* 1980), Don Jaime Galobert y Satrústegui; 2ndly, 4 Aug 1989, Don Luis Angel Sánchez Merlo y Ruiz, and has issue living (by 1st *m*), *Don* Alfonso Alberto *b* 12 April 1969,——*Donna* Maria Teresa (Beatrice) (Sor Angela de la Cruz 12, Madrid 28020, Spain), *b* 4 Jan 1945: *m* 22 April 1967 (*m diss* 1989), Don José Maria Ruiz de Arana y Montalvo, 5th Marqués de Brenes y (13th) de Castromonte, and has issue living, *Doña* Cristina Carmen Margarita *b* 24 March 1968, *Doña* Isabel Alfonsa Paola Maria Tommasa *b* 17 May 1970, *Doña* Inès Carla *b* 27 Dec 1973,——*Donna* Anna Sandra, *b* 21 Dec 1948: *m* 1st, 21 June 1969 (*m diss* 1985), Gian Carlo (Stavro) di Santarosa; 2ndly, 24 July 1986, Don Fernando Schwartz y Girón (Spanish Ambassador to the Netherlands), of Joaquìn Costa 15, Madrid 28006, Spain, and has issue living (by 1st *m*), Astrid Cristina Antonia *b* 24 April 1972, Yara Christiane *b* 29 June 1974.

HER MAJESTY QUEEN ELIZABETH
THE QUEEN MOTHER

Her Majesty ELIZABETH ANGELA MAR-GUERITE, LG, LT, CI, GCVO, GBE (*Queen Elizabeth The Queen Mother*), da of 14th Earl of Strathmore and Kinghorne; *b* in London 4 Aug 1900; Hon LLD, Queen's Univ, Belfast 1924, St Andrews 1929, Glasgow 1932, Edinburgh 1937, Cape Town 1947, Camb 1948, Manchester 1951, Leeds and Columbia Univ, NY 1954, Melbourne and Liverpool 1958, Auckland 1966, Halifax (Nova Scotia) and Dundee 1967; Hon DCL, Oxford 1931; HonDLitt London 1937 and W Indies 1965; HonLittD Keele 1965; HonDMus, Sheffield 1966; Hon FRCOG 1949; Hon FRCS England 1950; Hon FRCP Edinburgh 1953; FRCP 1962; Bencher Middle Temple 1944 (Treasurer 1949); FRS; Col-in-Ch 1st The Queen's Dragoon Guards, The Queen's Royal Hussars (The Queen's Own and Royal Irish), 9th/12th R Lancers (Prince of Wales's), King's Regt, R Anglian Regt, Light Inf, The Black Watch (R Highland Regt), The RAMC; Hon Col R Yeo, The London Scottish (The Gordon Highlanders) (TA), Col-in-Ch The Black Watch (R Highland Regt) of Canada, The Toronto Scottish Regt, CFMS, RAAMC, and RNZAMC; Comdt-in-Ch Women in The Royal Navy, Patron Women's Royal Army Corps Association, Comdt-in-Ch RAF Central Flying Sch and Women in the RAF; Comdt-in-Ch Nursing Corps and Divs, St John Ambulance Bde'; Hon Freeman of Grocers' Co, Butchers' Co, Merchant Taylors' Co, Shipwrights' Co, Musicians Co, and Barbers' Co; Hon Member of Lloyds; Pres of British Red Cross Soc 1937-52, since when Dept Pres; a GCStJ; has Grand Cross of Legion of Honour, and of Orders of the Lion of the Netherlands, of the Crown of Roumania, of St Olga and St Sophia of Greece, of St Sava of Serbia, of Lernor Ala of Afghanistan, of Sun of Peru, of Independence of Republic of Tunisia, and of Ojaswi Rajanya of Nepal; has French Red Cross Medal and Norwegian War Cross; received Freedom of City of Glasgow 1927, of Burghs of Stirling and Dunfermline 1928, of City of Perth 1935, of City of Edinburgh 1936, of Burgh of Inverness and of City of London 1953, of City of Dundee and of Borough of King's Lynn 1954, of Burghs of Forfar, Musselburgh, and Wick 1956, of City of Aberdeen 1959, and of City of St Albans 1961; Pres of R Highland and Agricultural Soc 1963-64; awarded gold Albert Medal of R Soc of Arts 1952; appointed Grand Master of R Victorian Order 1937; Pres of Univ Coll of Rhodesia and Nyasaland 1957-70; Chancellor of London Univ 1955-81, and first Chancellor of Dundee Univ 1967; Hon Fellow, Univ of London 1977, and of King's Coll London 1978; appointed Lord Warden and Admiral of the Cinque Ports and Constable of Dover Castle Sept 1978; received R Victorian Chain 1937; GBE (Civil) 1927, CI 1931, Lady of the Order of the Garter 1936, GCVO and Lady of the Order of the Thistle 1937: *m* at Westminster Abbey 26 April 1923, HM King George VI, who *d* 6 Feb 1952.

Arms—The Royal Arms, impaling quarterly 1st and 4th the arms of Bowes-Lyon; i.e. 1st and 4th argent, a lion rampant azure, armed and langued gules, within a double tressure flory-counterflory of the second, *Lyon*; 2nd and 3rd ermine, three bows, strings palewise proper, *Bowes*. **Supporters**—*Dexter*, that of the Sovereign; *sinister*, a lion per fesse or and gules, being one of the supporters of the Earls of Strathmore and Kinghorne.

Residences,—Clarence House, SW1; Royal Lodge, Windsor Great Park, Berks; Castle of Mey, Caithness.

DUKE OF EDINBURGH

His Royal Highness The Prince PHILIP, KG, KT, OM, GBE, AC, QSO, PC, 1st Duke, only son of HRH the late Prince Andrew of Greece and Denmark, GCVO, by HRH the late Princess (Victoria) Alice Elizabeth Julia Marie, RRC, da of 1st Marquess of Milford Haven; *b* at Mon Repos, Corfu 10 June 1921; ed at Cheam Sch, at Salem, Baden, at Gordonstoun, and at R Naval Coll, Dartmouth; 1939-45 War, with Mediterranean Fleet, in Home Waters, and with British Pacific Fleet in SE Asia and the Pacific [despatches, Greek War Cross, 1939-45, Atlantic, Africa, Burma (with Pacific rosette), and Italy Stars, War medal 1939-45 (with oak leaf) and French Croix de Guerre (with Palm)]; Hon LLD Wales 1949, London 1951, Edinburgh and Camb 1952, Karachi 1959, Malta 1964, and California 1966; Hon DCL Durham 1951, and Oxford 1964; Hon DSc Delhi 1959, Reading 1957, Salford (Lancs) and Southampton 1967; Hon DSc Univ of Victoria, BC, Canada 1969; Hon LLD Univ of Western Ontario 1983; Hon Degree, Univ of Jordan 1984; Hon Degree in Engineering, Lima 1962; Hon FRCP London 1952; Hon FRCSE, and Hon FRCS England; Hon Fellow Univ Coll, Oxford 1953; a Personal ADC to HM King George VI 1948; Adm of the Fleet, Field Marshal, Marshal of the RAF, Adm of the Fleet RAN, Field Marshal Aust Mil Forces, Field Marshal New Zealand Army, Marshal of the RAAF, Marshal of the RNZAF, Adm of the Fleet RNZ Navy, Capt Gen, R Marines, Dep Col-in-Ch Queen's Royal Hussars (The Queen's Own and Royal Irish), Col-in-Ch The Royal Gloucestershire, Berkshire and Wiltshire Regt Col-in-Ch The Highlanders (Seaforth, Gordons and Camerons), Intelligence Corps, Army Cadet Force, R Canadian Regt, Seaforth Highlanders of Canada, R Canadian Army Cadets, R Aust Electrical and Mechanical Engineers, Aust Cadet Corps, Corps of RNZ Electrical and Mechanical Engineers, Col of Grenadier Guards, Hon Col Edinburgh and Heriot-Watt Univs Officers' Training Corps, Trinidad and Tobago Regt; Air Commodore-in-Chief Air Training Corps, Air Commodore of the Air Sqdn since 1983, R Canadian Air Cadets, Hon Air Commodore RAF Kinloss, Cmdt-in-Ch and Extra Master, Merchant Navy; Ranger of Windsor Great Park since 1952, and Lord High Steward of Plymouth since 1960; Chancellor of Univs of Edinburgh since 1952, Camb since 1976, and Salford 1967-90; Visitor of Upper Canada Coll since 1955, Manchester Coll of Science and Technology since 1957, and Churchill Coll, Camb since 1959; Life Gov of King's Coll, London since 1954, Master of the Bench of Inner Temple since 1954; Elder Brother of Trin House since 1952 (Master since 1969) and Hon Brother of Hull Trin House since 1956; R Gov of Charterhouse since 1953; Pres R Nat Playing Fields Assoc 1949-84; Pres in Ch of British Racing Drivers' Club 1952-92 and Pres of British Amateur Athletic Board since 1952, Commonwealth Games Fedn 1955-90, British Sportsman's Club since 1958, Central Council of Physical Recreation since 1951, City and Guilds of London Inst since 1951, English-Speaking Union of the Commonwealth since 1952, Guinea Pig Club since 1960, Guards' Polo Club since 1955, R Agric Society of the Commonwealth since 1958, R Commn for Exhibition of 1851 since 1965, R Household Cricket Club since 1953, R Merchant Navy Sch since 1952, R Mint Advisory Cttee on design of seals, coins and medals since 1952, R Society of Arts since 1952, World Wild Life Fund 1961-82; Pres World Wild Life International (now World Wide Fund for Nature-International) since 1981; Pres Federation Equestre International 1964-84; Pres Maritime Trust since 1969; Grand Pres British Commonwealth Ex-Services League since 1974; Pres R Bath and West and Southern Counties Soc 1981; Pres Royal Windsor Horse Show 1991-94; Pres Windsor Park Equestrian Club since 1982; Vice-Pres Soc of the Friends of St George's and the Descendants of Knights of the Garter since 1948; FRS 1951; Permanent Fellow of Inst of Petroleum since 1963; Hon Fellow of R Soc of Canada since 1957, Australian Acad of Science since 1962, and R Zoological Soc of Scotland since 1963; Trustee of Nat Maritime Museum, Greenwich since 1948, and R Agric Soc of England since 1957; Patron and first Hon Fellow of Ghana Acad of Sciences since 1961 (Hon Pres 1959-61); Patron of R Inst of Navigation and Lord's Taverners (Pres of Council 1960-61, since when Twelfth Man), of Charities Aid Foundation, and Inst of Chemical Engineers; Patron and Trustee of The Duke of Edinburgh's Award; a Liveryman and Assist of Shipwrights' Co (Prime Warden 1954, Permanent Master since 1955), a Freeman and Liveryman of Fishmongers' Co

---

*By warrant dated 18 Sept 1952, the Duke was granted precedence next to HM The Queen except where otherwise provided by Act of Parliament.

(Prime Warden 1961, 4th Warden 1962-63), a Freeman and Liveryman of Mercers'
Co, Adm of the Master Mariners' Co, Grand Master of Guild of Air Pilots and Air
Navigators, a Guild Brother of Glasgow, of Craft Rank Qua Hammermen, Trades
House of Glasgow, Adm of Roy Yacht Squadron since 1953; Adm of House of Lords
Yacht Club, of R Motor Yacht Club, of RN Sailing Assocn, of R Southern Yacht Club,
of Bar Yacht Club, of Roy Dart Yacht Club, of R Gibraltar Yacht Club, of R Yacht
Club of Victoria, Australia; Commodore-in-Chief, Sandringham Yacht Club,
Victoria, since 1980, and of Great Navy of State of Nebraska, USA; received
Freedom of City of London, Greenwich and City of Edinburgh 1948, City of Belfast
1949, City of Cardiff 1954, City of Glasgow 1955, City of Melbourne 1956, City of
Dar-es-Salaam 1961, Hon Citizen of Montevideo 1962, City of Nairobi 1963, and
Cities of Guadalajara and Acapulco, Mexico, and Bridgetown, Barbados 1964 and
City of Los Angeles and Hon Citizen of Chicago 1966; Grand Cross Order of
Redeemer of Greece, Order of Phoenix of Greece, Grand Cross Order of George I
(with swords) of Greece, Order of St George and St Constantine (with swords) of
Greece (4th Class), Knight of Order of the Elephant of Denmark 1947, Grand Cross
of Order of St Charles of Monaco 1951, of Order of St Olav of Norway 1952, and of
Manuel Amador Guerrero of Panama 1953, Order of the Seraphim of Sweden, and
Chain of Most Exalted Order of the Queen of Sheba of Ethiopia 1954, Grand Cross of
Order of the Tower and the Sword (Civil) of Portugal 1955, of Order of King Faisal I
of Iraq 1956, and of the Legion of Honour of France 1957, Knight Grand Cross of
Order of Merit of the Italian Republic, Grand Cross of Order of the Lion of the
Netherlands, and of Order of Merit of Federal German Republic (1st Class) 1958,
Order of Ojaswi Rajanya of Nepal 1960, Knight Grand Band of Star of Africa of
Liberia 1961, Grand Cross of Order of San Martin of Argentina, of Order of the
Condor of Bolivia, and of National Order of Southern Cross of Brazil, Chain of
Chilean Order of Merit, Grand Cross Extraordinary of Order of Boyacá of Colombia,
Grand Cross of National Order of Merit of Ecuador, National Order of Merit of
Paraguay, and Great Cross of Order of the Sun, with Brilliants, of Peru, 1962,
Grand Cordon of Order of Leopold of Belgium and Order of the Brilliant Star of
Zanzibar (1st Class) 1963, and Decoration of Republic of Sudan (1st Class) and
Grand Cross of Order of the Icelandic Falcon 1964, and Collar of the Aztec Eagle of
Mexico 1964, Star and Riband of Order of Nahdah, Jordan 1966, Decoration of
Honour for Services to Republic of Austria, Grand Cordon 1966, Grand Commander
Order of Maritime Merit, San Francisco Port Authority 1968, Order of White Rose of
Finland 1969, Order of Superior Sun of Afghanistan 1971, Grand Cordon of
Supreme Order of Chrysanthemum of Japan 1971, Most Esteemed Family Order of
Brunei 1972, Chevalier Grand Cross Order of Golden Lion of Luxembourg 1972, a
Member of Distinguished Order of Izzuddin, of Republic of Maldives 1972, Hon
Member of Darjah Utama Temasek of Singapore 1972, Grand Cross Yugoslav Star
of Yugoslavia 1972, Grand Cordon of National Order of the Leopard (Mil) of Zaire
1973, Grand Collar of National Order of Infante Dom Henrique of Portugal 1973,
Commander of Order of the Golden Ark of the Netherlands 1979, First Class
(military) Order of Oman 1979, Collar of Order of Independence of Qatar 1979, 1st
class Order of Muhammadi of Morocco 1980, Companion of the Queen's Service
Order of New Zealand 1981, Canadian Forces Decoration 1982, Grand Cross of
Order of Carlos III of Spain 1986, Companion of the Order of Australia 1988, Grand
Ribbon of the Order of Merit of Poland 1991; King George VI Coronation Medal
(1937), and Queen Elizabeth II Coronation Medal (1953), Commemoration Medal of
New Zealand 1990, Sultan of Brunei Silver Jubilee Medal 1992, George Cross 50th
Anniversary Medal of Malta 1992; appointed Grand Master and First or Principal
Knt of Order of British Empire 1953; *cr.* KG, *Baron Greenwich*, of Greenwich co
London, *Earl of Merioneth*, and *Duke of Edinburgh* (peerage of United Kingdom)
1947, KT 1952, GBE (Mil) 1953, and OM 1968; naturalized a British subject and
adopted the surname of Mountbatten 28 Feb 1947; granted title, style and attribute
of Royal Highness 1947; introduced to PC 1951, and to PC Canada 1957; granted
style and titular dignity of a Prince of UK 1957: *m 20 Nov 1947, HM Queen
Elizabeth II, and has issue.

Arms—Quarterly; 1st, or, semee of hearts gules, three lions passant in pale azure
ducally crowned of the first; 2nd, azure, a cross argent; 3rd, argent, two pallets
sable; 4th argent, upon a rock proper a castle triple towered sable, masoned argent,
windows, port, turret caps, and vanes gules. Crest—A plume of five ostrich feathers
alternately sable and argent issuant from a ducal coronet or. Supporters—Dexter, a
representation of Heracles girt about the loins with a lion skin, crowned with a
chaplet of oak leaves and holding in the dexter hand a club proper; sinister, a lion
queue fourchee ducally crowned or and gorged with a naval coronet azure. Coronet A
coronet composed of crosses-patées and fleurs-de-lis alternately or.

Residences—Buckingham Palace, SW1; Windsor Castle, Berkshire; Balmoral
Castle, Aberdeenshire; Sandringham House, Norfolk.

*It was declared by Letters Patent of Oct 22nd, 1948, that the children of this marriage shall
enjoy the style of "HRH" and the titular dignity of Prince or Princess.

PRINCE OF WALES

His Royal Highness Prince CHARLES PHILIP ARTHUR GEORGE, KG, KT, GCB, AK, PC, *Prince of Wales and Earl of Chester, Duke of Cornwall and Rothesay, Earl of Carrick and Baron of Renfrew, Lord of the Isles and Great Steward of Scotland*, eldest son of HM Queen Elizabeth II; *b* at Buckingham Palace · 14 November 1948, ed at Cheam School, at Gordonstoun, at Geelong Grammar School, Trinity College, Cambridge (MA, Hon Fellow 1988), and University College of Wales, Aberystwyth; Bar Gray's Inn 1974, Hon Bencher 1975; Hon DCL Oxford Univ 1982; Personal ADC to HM since 1973; Capt RN since 1988; Colonel-in-Chief The Royal Regiment of Wales (24th/41st Foot) since 1969; Colonel Welsh Guards since 1974; Colonel-in-Chief The Cheshire Regiment since 1977; Colonel-in-Chief The Gordon Highlanders since 1977; Colonel-in-Chief Lord Strathcona's Horse (Royal Canadian) Regiment since 1977; Colonel-in-Chief The Parachute Regiment since 1977; Colonel-in-Chief The Royal Australian Armoured Corps since 1977; Colonel-in-Chief The Royal Regiment of Canada since 1977; Colonel-in-Chief 2nd King Edward VII Own Goorkhas since 1977; Colonel-in-Chief The Royal Winnipeg Rifles since 1977; Colonel-in-Chief Papua New Guinea 2nd Bn The Royal Pacific Islands Regt since 1984; Colonel-in-Chief Royal Canadian Dragoons since 1985; Colonel-in-Chief Army Air Corps since 1992; Colonel-in-Chief Royal Dragoon Gds since 1992; Group Capt RAF since 1988; Hon Air Commodore Royal Air Force Brawdy 1977-92; Hon Air Commodore RAF Valley since 1993; Air Commodore in Chief Royal New Zealand Air Force since 1977; Colonel-in-Chief Air Reserves Group of Air Command in Canada since 1977; President Society of Friends of St George's and Descendants of Knights of the Garter since 1975; Admiral Royal Thames Yacht Club since 1986; High Steward Royal Borough of Windsor and Maidenhead since 1975; President of The Royal Jubilee and Prince's Trusts since 1977; President of United World Colleges 1978-92; President of The Royal Agricultural Society 1990-91; Chairman of The Prince of Wales' Committee for Wales since 1977; Chancellor of The University of Wales since 1976; Patron of the National Gallery since 1986; Patron of the National Gallery Trust since 1993; Pres of Business in the Community, Scottish Business in the Community, Pres of The Prince of Wales Advisory Group on Disability, Pres of The Wildfowl Trust and Wetlands Trust since 1979; Pres Prince's Youth Business Trust and Prince's Scottish Youth Business Trust since 1986; Pres Prince of Wales Business Leaders Forum since 1990; Patron Royal Society for Nature Conservation since 1977; Patron of Ancient Monuments Society since 1990; Vice Patron British Council since 1984; Pres Royal Shakespeare Co since 1991; Pres The Prince of Wales's Institute of Architecture since 1992; Chm Royal Collection Trust since 1993; Pres King Edward VII Hospital Fund for London since 1986; Pres Royal Coll of General Practitioners 1991-92; represented HM at Memorial Service for Prime Minister of Australia 1967; at Independence Celebrations in Fiji 1970, at Requiem Mass for General Charles de Gaulle 1970, at Bahamas Independence Celebrations 1973, at Papua New Guinea Independence Celebrations 1975, at Coronation of King of Nepal 1975, at funeral of Sir Robert Menzies 1978, and at funeral of President of Kenya, Jomo Kenyatta 1978; Coronation Medal 1953; the Queen's Silver Jubilee Medal 1977; Grand Cross of the White Rose of Finland 1969; Grand Cordon of the Supreme Order of the Chrysanthemum of Japan 1971; Grand Cross of the House of Orange of the Netherlands 1972; Grand Cross of the Order of Oak Crown of Luxembourg 1972; Knight of the Order of Elephant of Denmark 1974; Grand Cross of the Order of Ojaswi Rajanya of Nepal 1975; Kt of the Order of the Seraphim of Sweden 1975; Grand Cross of the Order of the Southern Cross of Brazil 1978; Collar of the Republic of Egypt 1981; Gd Cross of the Order of Orange Nassau of the Netherlands 1982; Gd Cross Order of St Olav of Norway 1978; Offr Order of the Star of Ghana 1977; Grand Cross of the Legion of Honour of France 1984; Grand Cross of Order of Carlos III of Spain; Nepal Coronation Medal 1975; Grand Cross of Khalifiyyeh Order of Bahrain; Grand Cross of Order of the Lion of Malawi; Grand Cross of Order of Merit of Saudi Arabia; Papua New Guinea Independence Medal 1975; Fijian Independence Medal 1970; New Zealand Commemoration Medal 1990; Order of Merit of Qatar 1986; Order of Mubarak the Great of Kuwait 1993; created *Prince of Wales* and *Earl of Chester* 26 July 1958 (invested July 1st, 1969); KG 1958 (invested and installed 1968); KT 1977; Privy Counsellor 1977; GCB and Great Master of Order of the Bath 1975; Kt of the Order of Australia 1981; Extra Companion of Queen's Service Order of New Zealand 1983; received Freedom of City of Cardiff 1969, of Royal Borough of New Windsor 1970, of City of London 1971, of City of Chester 1973, of City of Canterbury 1978, of City of Portsmouth 1979, of City of Lancaster 1993, and of City of Swansea 1994; Liveryman of Fishmongers' Company 1971; a Freeman of Drapers' Company 1971, a Freeman Shipwrights' Company 1978; Honorary Member of the Honourable Company of Master Mariners 1977 (Master 1988-90), Liveryman of Gardeners' Company 1987, Master of Master Mariners' Company 1988; a Freeman of Goldsmiths' Company; Liveryman of Farmers' Company 1980; Liveryman of Pewterers' Company 1982; Liveryman of the Fruiterers' Company 1989; Liveryman of the Carpenters' Company 1992; Bencher Middle Temple 1988: *m* at St Paul's Cathedral, London 29 July 1981, Lady Diana Frances Spencer (Col-in-Ch Royal Hampshire Regt, Princess of Wales's Own Regt (Canada), and 13th/18th Royal Hussars (Queen Mary's Own)), yst da of 8th Earl Spencer, and has issue.

Arms—The Royal Arms, differenced by a label of three points argent, and in the centre an escutcheon of the arms of the Principality of Wales, viz, quarterly or and gules, four lions passant guardant counterchanged, ensigned by the coronet of his degree. Crest—The Royal crest, differenced with a label of three points argent, but with the coronets those of the Heir Apparent. Supporters—Same as the Royal Arms differenced by a label of three points argent, the *dexter* crowned with the Heir Apparent's coronet, and the *sinister* gorged with a coronet of fleurs-de-lis and crosses-pattées, a chain affixed thereto passing between the fore-legs and reflexed over the back, or. Badges—*Dexter*, a plume of three ostrich feathers argent, enfiled by a coronet, composed of fleurs-de-lis, and crosses-pattées or alternately with motto *Ich Dien*; *sinister*, a representation of the Badge of Wales, namely on a mount vert, a dragon passant gules, differenced as in the Crest with a label of three points argent. *Personal Flag in Wales*, Quarterly or and gules, four lions passant guardant counterchanged, over all an inescutcheon vert charged with the coronet of the Prince of Wales. Arms of Spencer— Quarterly argent and gules, in the 2nd and 3rd quarters a fret or, over all on a bend sable three escallops argent.
Residences—Highgrove House, nr Tetbury, Glos GL8 8TG; St James's Palace, SW1A 1BQ.

SONS LIVING

HRH Prince William Arthur Philip Louis OF WALES, *b* at St Mary's Hosp, Paddington 21 June 1982.

HRH Prince Henry (Harry) Charles Albert David OF WALES, *b* at St Mary's Hosp, Paddington 15 Sept 1984.

DUKE OF YORK

His Royal Highness The Prince Andrew Albert Christian Edward, CVO, 2nd son of HM The Queen and HRH The Duke of Edinburgh; *b* at Buckingham Palace 19 February 1960; *ed* at Gordonstoun, Lakefield Coll, Ontario, Canada, and RNC Dartmouth; Lt Cdr RN; served S Atlantic Campaign (1982) as helicopter pilot HMS *Invincible*; personal ADC to HM The Queen since 1984; Col-in-Ch Staffs Regt since 1989; Col-in-Ch The Canadian Airborne Regt since 1991; Col-in-Ch The Royal Irish Regt since 1992; Adm Sea Cadet Corps since 1992; visited St Helena to mark 150th anniversary of island becoming a Crown Colony 1984; visited Australia in HMS *Edinburgh* to be Reviewing Officer at Australian Bicentennial International Review 1988; visited Papua New Guinea to open 9th South Pacific Games 1991; assumed command of HMS *Cottesmore* 1993; received Freedom of City of York 1987; CVO 1979; *cr Baron Killyleagh, Earl of Inverness, and Duke of York* (UK) 1986: *m* at Westminster Abbey, 23 July 1986, Sarah Margaret (Chancellor of Salford Univ 1991-94), 2nd da of Maj Ronald Ivor Ferguson (*see* V Hampden, colls), and has issue.

DAUGHTERS LIVING

HRH Princess Beatrice Elizabeth Mary OF YORK, *b* at the Portland Hosp, London, 8 Aug 1988.

HRH Princess Eugenie Victoria Helena OF YORK, *b* at the Portland Hosp, London, 23 March 1990.

Residences - Buckingham Palace, London SW1; Sunninghill Park, Windsor, Berks.

𝔄rms—The Royal Arms, differenced by a label of three points argent, charged on the centre point with an anchor azure. 𝔠rest—On a coronet of crosses and fleurs-de-lys a lion statant guardant or, crowned with a like coronet and differenced by a label as in the Arms. 𝔖upporters—Same as the Royal Arms differenced by a like coronet and label. 𝔄rms of 𝔍erguson—Or issuant from a mound in base a thistle stalked and leaved and with three flowers, alighting upon that in chief a bumble bee all proper.

DUKE OF GLOUCESTER

His Royal Highness Prince RICHARD ALEXANDER WALTER GEORGE, GCVO; 2nd Duke; *b* at Northampton 26 Aug 1944; *s* 1974; ed at Eton, and Magdalene Coll, Camb (MA, Dip of Arch); RIBA; FSA; KStJ; Pres Inst of Advanced Motorists since 1971, of Cancer Research Campaign since 1973, of Nat Assocn of Boys' Clubs since 1974, of St Bartholomew's Hosp since 1975, and of British Consultants Bureau since 1978; Vice-Pres of British Leprosy Relief Assocn since 1971; Patron of ASH since 1974, of Society of Engineers since 1974, of Richard III Society since 1980, of Silver Jubilee Walkway Trust since 1978, and of Victorian Society since 1976; Ranger of Epping Forest since 1975; Queen's Trustee of British Museum since 1973; FRSA, 1976; Dep Col-in-Ch The Royal Gloucestershire, Berkshire and Wiltshire Regt since 1994, and The Royal Logistic Corps since 1993; Hon Col R Monmouthshire Royal Engineers (Militia) since 1977; Commodore of Royal Ulster Yacht Club since 1974, Gov Building Centre Trust since 1991, Hon Life Memb Friends of All Saints, Brixworth since 1991; Grand Prior, Order of St John of Jerusalem since 1975; Liveryman of Vintners' Co and Hon Freeman of Grocers' Co; Hon Freeman and Liveryman of Goldsmiths' Co; has Grand Cross Order of St Olav of Norway; GCVO 1974: *m* at Barnwell Parish Church, 8 July 1972, Birgitte Eva, GCVO (1989), DStJ (Dep Col-in-Ch The Adjutant General's Corps, Col-in-Ch Royal Australian Army Educational Corps since 1977, and Royal NZ Army Educational Corps since 1985, Pres of London Regions WRVS, of Roy Alexander and Albert Sch, of Royal Sch of Needlework, of Civil Service Sports Council, and of Royal School of Bath; Patron of Federation of Army Wives, Nat Asthma Campaign, Assoc for Spina Bifida and Hydrocephalus, Scottish Opera, Cheltenham International Music Festival, Bobath Centre and Foundation for the Study of Infant Deaths; Vice Patron The Queen's Club), yr da of late Asger Preben Wissing Henriksen, lawyer, of Odense, Denmark (by his 1st wife, Vivian, da of the late Waldemar Oswald van Deurs, whose name she assumed), and has issue.

Arms—The Royal Arms, differenced by a label of five points argent, the centre and two outer points charged with a cross gules, and the inner points with a lion passant guardant. **Crest**—On a coronet composed of four crosses-pattées alternated with four strawberry leaves, a lion statant guardant or, crowned with the like coronet, and differenced with the label as in the Arms. **Supporters**—The Royal Supporters, differenced with the like coronet and label. (By Royal Warrant dated 24 Feb, 1975, the arms which were assigned to a grandchild of a Sovereign became hereditary.)

Residences—Kensington Palace, W8 4PU; Barnwell Manor, Peterborough PE8 5PJ.

SON LIVING

ALEXANDER PATRICK GREGERS RICHARD   (*Earl of Ulster*), *b* at St Mary's Hosp, Paddington, 24 Oct 1974

DAUGHTERS LIVING

Lady Davina Elizabeth Alice Benedikte WINDSOR, *b* at St Mary's Hosp, Paddington, 19 Nov 1977

Lady Rose Victoria Birgitte Louise WINDSOR, *b* at St Mary's Hosp, Paddington 1 March 1980

WIDOW LIVING OF FIRST DUKE

Lady Alice Christabel Montagu-Douglas-Scott, GCB, CI, GCVO, GBE (*HRH Princess Alice, Duchess of Gloucester*), 3rd da of 7th Duke of Buccleuch and Queensberry; *b* in London, 25 Dec 1901; ed at St James's Sch, W Malvern and in Paris; Air Chief Marshal WRAF, Col-in-Ch KOSB, RACT, RNZ Army Ser Corps; Dep Col-in-Ch R Anglian Regt, and The King's Royal Hussars; a Member of Council British Red Cross Soc; Dep Comdt-in-Ch of Nursing Corps and Divs St John Ambulance Bde, since 1937; GCStJ; patron Crosby Hall; received Freedom of Cities of Edinburgh 1937, Gloucester 1939, and Belfast 1952; GBE (Civil) and CI 1937, GCVO 1948, GCB (Civil) 1975; *m* at Buckingham Palace, 6 Nov 1935, HRH The Prince Henry William Frederick Albert, KG, KT, KP, GCB, GCMG, GCVO, PC, 1st Duke of Gloucester, who *d* at Barnwell Manor, Northants, 10 June 1974, 3rd son of HM King George V.

Residences—Kensington Palace, W8 4PU; Barnwell Manor, Peterborough PE8 5PJ.

PREDECESSOR

[1] *HRH The Prince* HENRY WILLIAM FREDERICK ALBERT, KG, KT, KP, GCB, GCMG, GCVO, PC, 3rd son of his late Majesty King George V; *b* at York Cottage, Sandringham 31 March 1900; Field Marshal, and Marshal of RAF; Gov-Gen and C-in-C, Commonwealth of Australia 1944-47; received Roy Victorian Chain 1932; cr *Baron Culloden, Earl of Ulster,*and *Duke of Gloucester* (peerage of UK) 1928: *m* 6 Nov 1935, Lady Alice Christabel Montagu-Douglas-Scott, GCB, CI, GCVO, GBE, 3rd da of 7th Duke of Buccleuch and Queensberry, *d* 10 June 1974; *s* by his yr son [2] RICHARD ALEXANDER WALTER GEORGE, 2nd Duke, and present peer; also Earl of Ulster, and Baron Culloden.

DUKE OF KENT

Field Marshal His Royal Highness Prince EDWARD GEORGE NICHOLAS PAUL PATRICK, KG, GCMG, GCVO, ADC, 2nd Duke; *b* at 3 Belgrave Square, W1, 9 Oct 1935; *s* 1942; ed at Eton, in Switzerland, and at RMA, Sandhurst; Hon DCL Durham 1961; Maj-Gen (ret) R Scots Dragoon Gds (Carabiniers and Greys), and Dep Col-in-Chief since 1993; Col-in-Ch R Regt of Fusiliers, Devonshire and Dorset Regt, and Lorne Scots Regt (Canada); Col Scots Gds; acted as Special Representative of HM The Queen at Independence Celebrations in Sierra Leone 1961, Uganda 1962, The Gambia 1965, and Guyana and Barbados 1966, and at Coronation of King of Tonga 1967; personal ADC to HM since 1966; GSO II E Command 1966-58, and a Col Instructor, RMA, Sandhurst 1968-70, and in command C Sqdn R Scots Greys 1970-71; ret as Lt-Col 1976, promoted Maj-Gen 1983, Field Marshal 1993; Hon Air Cdre to RAF Leuchars 1993; Grand Master of United Grand Lodge of Freemasons of England and Grand Master of Order of St Michael and St George since 1967; Pres of Wellington Coll since 1969, of Commonwealth War Graves Commn since 1970, and of Scout Assocn since 1975; Vice-Chm of British Overseas Trade Board since 1976, Chm Duke of Edinburgh's Commonwealth Study Conference (UK Fund); Pres Royal Masonic Benevolent Inst, Royal Choral Soc, Imperial War Museum, Chest, Heart and Stroke Assocn, All England Lawn Tennis and Croquet Club, Wimbledon, and Engrg Council; Royal Patron Anglo-German Assoc since 1994, and The Help Poland Fund (Northern) since 1994; Pres Henley Soc since 1994; Chancellor of Univ of Surrey since 1977; Hon Fell of Royal Aeronautical Society 1993; Hon Freeman of Clothworkers' Co, Freeman Mercers' Co, and Hon Liveryman of Salters' Co and of Engineers' Co; received Hon Freedom of City of Georgetown, Guyana, 1966; has Orders of St George and St Constantine of Greece (1st Class), of Tri Shakti Patta of Nepal (1st Class), Grand Band of Order of the Star of Africa of Liberia, and Grand Cross of Order of Al-Nahda of Jordan; GCVO 1960, GCMG 1967, KG 1985: *m* at York Minster 8 June 1961, Katharine Lucy Mary, GCVO (Dep Col-in-Ch the Adjutant General's Corps since 1992, The Royal Dragoon Guards, and The Royal Logistic Corps; Pres Action Research since 1993, Royal Patron of Age Concern England since 1993, Patron ENABLE (formerly The Distressed Gentlefolks Association) and SCOPE (formerly The Spastics Society), Patron British Arts Festival Year 1995 since 1993, Patron Dyson Perrins Museum Appeal since 1993, of Nat Federation of Music Societies since 1993, of Ripon College, Cuddesdon since 1993; Hon Member of Royal Philharmonic Soc 1992, and Worshipful Company of Musicians 1993), only da of late Sir William Arthington Worsley, 4th Bt, and has issue.

Arms—The Royal Arms, differenced by a label of five points argent, the points charged with an anchor azure and a cross gules alternately. **Crests**—On a coronet of four crosses-pattées alternated with four strawberry leaves, a lion statant guardant or, crowned with the like coronet, and differenced with a label as in the Arms. **Supporters**—The Royal Supporters, differenced with the like coronet and label. (By Royal Warrant dated 24 Feb, 1975, the labels assigned to a grandchild of a Sovereign, except the eldest son of a Prince of Wales, became hereditary and are borne as part of the arms together with ordinary marks of difference when appropriate).

Residences—York House, St James's Palace, SW1; Nettlebed, Oxfordshire.

SONS LIVING

GEORGE PHILIP NICHOLAS (*Earl of St Andrews*), *b* at Coppins, Iver, Bucks 26 June 1962; ed at Eton, and Downing Coll, Camb: *m* at Leith 9 Jan 1988, Sylvana Palma, da of Maximilian Karl Tomaselli, and formerly wife of John Paul Jones, and has issue:—

 SON LIVING— Edward Edmund Maximilian George (*Baron Downpatrick*), *b* at St Mary's Hosp, Paddington, 2 Dec 1988.

 DAUGHTER LIVING— *Lady* Marina-Charlotte Alexandra Katharine Helen WINDSOR, *b* at The Rosie Hospital, Cambridge 30 Sept 1992.

Lord Nicholas Charles Edward Jonathan WINDSOR, *b* at King's College Hospital, London 25 July 1970.

DAUGHTER LIVING

Lady Helen Marina Lucy WINDSOR, *b* at Coppins, Iver, Bucks 28 April 1964: *m* at St George's Chapel, Windsor Castle 18 July 1992, Timothy Verner Taylor, eldest son of Cmdr Michael Verner Taylor, RN, and has issue living, Columbus George Donald, *b* 6 Aug 1994.

BROTHER LIVING

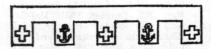

HRH *Prince* Michael George Charles Franklin OF KENT, KCVO, *b* at Coppins, Iver, Bucks 4 July 1942; ed at Eton, and at RMA Sandhurst; commn'd into 11th Hussars (PAO), later The Royal Hussars (PWO); Commodore RNR, member of HAC, Grand Master of the Lodge of Mark Master Masons, Hon Liverymnan of the Clothworkers' Co, Leathersellers' Co, Scientific Instrument Makers' Co, Coachmakers' and Coach Harness Makers' Co; represented HM The Queen at the Funeral of President Ahmed of India 1977, and the Funeral of President Makarios of Cyprus 1977, the Independence Celebrations in Belize 1981, the Funeral of King Sobhuza II of Swaziland 1982, and the Coronation of King Mswati III of Swaziland 1986; Commonwealth Pres of the Royal Life Saving Soc, Pres of the Royal Automobile Club, the Inst of the Motor Industry, SSAFA, Medical Commn on Accident Prevention, the Dogs' Home Battersea, the Royal Patriotic Fund Corporation, Nat Eye Research Centre, the Kennel Club, the Institute of Road Safety Officers, and the Society of Genealogists; Patron of the Museum of Army Flying, the Veteran Car Club of Great Britain, Thames Rowing Club, the Popular Flying Association, the David Shepherd Conservation Fund, the Carriage Foundation, the Brooklands Museum Trust Appeal, and the Bermuda Maritime Museum; Founder of the Prince Michael Road Safety Award Scheme; Fell of the Institute of the Motor Industry and the Royal Aeronautical Society; Trustee of the National Motor Museum; Chm of Advisory Board of House of Windsor; *m* at Vienna, 30 June 1978, Baroness Marie Christine (Agnes Hedwig Ida) (Patron Society of Women Artists), da of late Baron Günther Hubertus von Reibnitz, and formerly wife of Thomas Troubridge [*see* Troubridge, Bt] and has issue:—

SON LIVING,—*Lord* Frederick Michael David Louis WINDSOR, *b* at St Mary's Hosp, Paddington, 6 April 1979.

DAUGHTER LIVING,—*Lady* Gabriella (Ella) Marina Alexandra Ophelia WINDSOR, *b* at St Mary's Hosp, Paddington, 23 April 1981.

SISTER LIVING

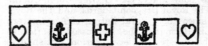

HRH *Princess* Alexandra Helen Elizabeth Olga Christabel OF KENT (*HRH Princess Alexandra, the Hon Lady Ogilvy*), GCVO, *b* at 3 Belgrave Square, SW1 25 Dec 1936; Hon LLD Queensland Univ, Australia 1959, Hong Kong 1961, and Mauritius 1974; Chancellor of Lancaster Univ 1964, Hon Fellow of R Faculty of Physicians and Surgs, Glasgow 1960 (known as Royal Coll since 1962), Faculty of Anaesthetists (known as Royal Coll since 1992), Royal Coll of Surgs of England since 1967, and of Royal Coll of Obstetricians and Gynaecologists since 1969; Col-in-Ch 17th/21st Lancers 1969-93, Queen's Own Rifles of Canada since 1960, The King's Own Border Regt since 1977, and The Canadian Scottish Regt (Princess Mary's) since 1977; Dep Col-in-Ch the LI since 1968, Dep Col-in-Ch The Queen's Royal Lancers since 1993, Dep Hon Col of Royal Yeo since 1975; Patron and Air Ch Comdt of Princess Mary's RAF Nursing Ser since 1966, Hon Comdt General Royal Hong Kong Police Force, and Royal Hong Kong Aux Police Force since 1969; acted as Special Representative of HM the Queen at Independence Celebrations in Nigeria 1960, at 150th Anniversary Celebrations of founding of Modern Singapore 1969, and at Independence Celebrations of St Lucia 1979; Patron of QARNNS, and People's Dispensary for Sick Animals; Pres Roy Commonwealth Soc for the Blind, Children's Country Holidays Fund, Queen Alexandra's House Assocn, Royal Star and Garter Home for Disabled Sailors, Soldiers and Airmen, Alexandra Rose Day,

British Sch at Rome, Royal Humane Soc, and World Wide Fund for Nature UK, Vice-Pres British Red Cross Soc; received Hon Freedom of City of Lancaster 1987; GCVO 1960: *m* at Westminster Abbey, 24 April 1963, Hon Sir Angus James Bruce Ogilvy, KCVO, 2nd son of 12th Earl of Airlie, and has issue living, James Robert Bruce, *b* at Thatched House Lodge, Richmond, Surrey, 29 Feb 1964: *m* 30 July 1988, Julia, eldest da of Charles Frederick Melville Rawlinson, of Arkesden, Essex,—Marina Victoria Alexandra, *b* at Thatched House Lodge, Richmond, Surrey, 31 July 1966: *m* 2 Feb 1990, Paul Julian Mowatt, son of David Mowatt, and has issue living, Christian Alexander *b* 4 June 1993, Zenouska May *b* 26 May 1990. *Residence*—Thatched House Lodge, Richmond Park, Surrey. *Office*—22, Friary Court, St James's Palace, SW1A 1BJ.

PREDECESSOR

[1] *HRH The Prince* GEORGE EDWARD ALEXANDER EDMUND, KG, KT, GCMG, GCVO, PC, 4th son of His late Majesty King George V; *b* at Sandringham House, Norfolk, 20 Dec 1902; Rear-Adm, Maj-Gen in the Army, and Air Commodore RAF, received Roy Victorian Chain 1936; cr *Baron Downpatrick, Earl of St Andrews, and Duke of Kent* (peerage of United Kingdom) 1934: *m* at Westminster Abbey, 29 Nov 1934, HRH Princess Marina, CI, GCVO, GBE, who *d* at Kensington Palace, 27 Aug 1968, youngest da of HRH late Prince Nicholas of Greece and Denmark GCB, GCVO; *d* (killed on active ser during European War) 25 Aug 1942; *s* by his el son [2] EDWARD GEORGE NICHOLAS PAUL PATRICK, 2nd Duke and present peer; also Earl of St Andrews and Baron Downpatrick.

DUKEDOM OF ALBANY (Duke UK 1881, suspended 1917)

Prince ERNST-LEOPOLD (EDUARD WILHELM JOSIAS) OF SAXE-COBURG AND GOTHA, in whom is vested the right to petition for restoration of the Dukedom of Albany; *b* 14 Jan 1935; *s* his father, *HH Hereditary Prince* JOHANN LEOPOLD (WILHELM ALBERT FERDINAND VIKTOR) as lineal representative of HRH the 1st Duke of Albany, 1972: *m* 1st, 3 Feb (civ) and 4 Feb (relig) 1961 (*m diss* 1963), Ingeborg, da of Richard Henig, of Herrenberg, Württemberg; 2ndly, 29 May 1963 (*m diss* 1985), Gertraude Maria Monika, da of Hermann Horst Pfeiffer; 3rdly, 20 Jan 1986, Sabine Margarete, da of Alfred Carl Biller, and has issue by 1st and 2nd *m*.

Residences - Hauptstrasse 75/1, 811 Garmisch-Partenkirchen, Germany.

SONS LIVING (By 1st marriage)

Prince HUBERTUS RICHARD ERNST LEOPOLD, *b* 8 Dec 1961.

(By 2nd marriage)

Prince Ernst-Josias Carl Eduard Hermann Leopold, *b* 13 May 1965.

Prince Carl-Eduard Wilhelm Josias, *b* 27 July 1966.

Prince Friedrich Ferdinand Georg Ernst Albert, *b* 14 Dec 1968.

DAUGHTERS LIVING (by 2nd marriage)

Princess Victoria Feodora Monika, *b* 7 Sept 1963: *m* 28 Nov 1986, Peter Jakob Schmidt, who has taken the name Prince of Coburg (Prinz von Coburg), and has issue living, Falk William Philip Albert Jakob, *b* 28 June 1990.

Princess Alice Sibylla Calma Beatrice, *b* 6 Aug 1974.

BROTHER LIVING

Prince Peter Albert Friedrich Josias, *b* 12 June 1939: *m* 11 May 1964, Roswitha Henriette, da of Robert Breuer, and has issue living, *Prince* Peter Karl Eduard Alexander, *b* 4 Oct 1964: *m* 1991, Kathrin, da of Dr Jan Kempin,——*Prince* Malte Georg Albert, *b* 6 Oct 1966.

SISTER LIVING

Princess (Caroline Mathilde Adelheid Sibylla) Marianne (Erika), *b* 5 April 1933: *m* 5 Dec 1953, Michael Adalbert Wilfried Nielsen, who *d* 20 Sept 1975, and has issue living, Margarete-Brigitte, *b* 31 Aug 1954: *m* 7 Dec 1988,——Renate Christine, *b* 1 April 1957: *m* 1st, 26 July 1978 (*m diss* 1981), (Wolfgang Willi) Reinhard Blechert, son of Willi August Blechert; 2ndly, 30 Sept 1986, Jörg Brackner, son of Erwin Günther Brackner.

UNCLE LIVING

HH Prince Friedrich Josias (Carl Eduard Ernst Kyrill Harald), *b* 29 Nov 1918; *s* as Head of the Ducal House of Saxe-Coburg and Gotha by virtue of the renunciation of his brother, HH Hereditary Prince Johann Leopold: *m* 1st, 25 Jan 1942 (*m diss* 1946), Countess Viktoria-Luise (Friederike Caroline Mathilde), da of Count Hans Georg of Solms-Baruth; 2ndly, 14 Feb 1949 (*m diss* 1964), Denyse Henriette, da of late Robert Gaston de Muralt, of Berne, Switzerland; 3rdly, 30 Oct 1964, Katrin Anna Dorothea, da of late Dietrich Carl Bremme, of Berlin, and has issue living, (by

1st *m*) *HH Prince* Andreas Michael Armin Siegfried Hubertus Friedrich Hans
(Elsasserstrasse 8, D8630 Coburg, Germany), *b* 21 March 1943: *m* 18 June 1971,
Carin, da of Adolf Wilhelm Martin Dabelstein, and has issue living, *Prince*
Hubertus Michael *b* 16 Sept 1975, *Prince* Alexander Philipp *b* 4 May 1977, *Princess*
Stephanie Sibylla *b* 31 Jan 1972,——(by 2nd *m*) *Prince* Adrian Vincenz Edward *b*
18 Oct 1955: *m* 20 Oct 1984, Lea, da of Marcel Rinderknecht, and has issue living,
Prince Simon *b* 10 March 1985, *Prince* Daniel *b* 26 Jan 1988,——*Princess* Maria
Claudia Sibylla, *b* 22 May 1949: *m* 17 March 1971, Gion Schäfer, of Suler, CH-7017
Flims-Dorf, Switzerland, and has issue living, Maria Christina Sibylla *b* 23 June
1972, Gianetta Antonia *b* 18 Feb 1975,——*Princess* Beatrice Charlotte, *b* 15 July
1951: *m* 11 June (civ) and 12 June (relig) 1977, Prince Friedrich Ernst Georg
Bernhard of Saxe-Meiningen, of 7117 Bitzfeld, Germany, and has issue living,
Prince Friedrich Constantin *b* 3 June 1980, *Princess* Marie Alexandra Elisabeth
Beatrice *b* 5 July 1978. *Residences* - Schloss Greinburg, Grein an der Donau,
Austria; Elsasserstrasse 8, D8630 Coburg, Germany.

WIDOW LIVING OF HH HEREDITARY PRINCE JOHANN LEOPOLD OF SAXE-COBURG AND GOTHA

MARIA THERESIA ELISABETH (*Theresia Erbprinzessin von Sachsen-Coburg und
Gotha*), da of Max Reindl, of Bad Reichenhall, and formerly wife of Werner Müller:
m 3 May (civ) and 5 May (relig) 1962, as his 2nd wife, HH Hereditary Prince Johann
Leopold of Saxe-Coburg and Gotha, who *d* 1972.

PREDECESSORS

[1] *HRH Prince* LEOPOLD GEORGE DUNCAN ALBERT, KG, KT, GCSI, GCMG, PC, 4th
son of Queen Victoria, *b* 7 April 1853; *cr* Baron Arklow, Earl of Clarence and Duke of
Albany, in the peerage of the United Kingdom, 24 May 1881: *m* 27 April 1882,
Helena Frederica Augusta, VA, CI, RRC, who *d* 1 Sept 1922, 3rd da of Georg Viktor,
Prince of Waldeck and Pyrmont; *d* 28 March 1884; *s* by his only son [2] (LEOPOLD)
CHARLES EDWARD (GEORGE ALBERT), 2nd Duke, KG (1902-15, when struck off the
Roll), *b* (posthumously) 19 July 1884; *s* his uncle as reigning Duke of Saxe-Coburg
and Gotha 30 July 1900; abdicated 14 Nov 1918; deprived of his peerages by the
Titles Deprivation Act 8 Nov 1917 and removed from the Roll of Peers by Order in
Council 28 March 1919: *m* 11 Oct 1905, Victoria Adelheid (Helene Luise Marie
Friederike), who *d* 3 Oct 1970, eldest da of Friedrich Ferdinand, Duke of Schleswig-
Holstein-Sonderburg-Glücksburg; *d* 6 March 1954; *s* by his eldest son [3] JOHANN
LEOPOLD (WILHELM ALBERT FERDINAND VIKTOR), Hereditary Prince of Saxe-Coburg
and Gotha, *b* 2 Aug 1906; renounced his rights to the Duchy of Saxe-Coburg and
Gotha but retained the right to petition for the restoration of the Dukedom of
Albany: *m* 1st, 14 March 1932 (*m diss* 1962), Feodora Maria Alma Margarete, who *d*
23 Oct 1991, da of Baron (Alfred Hermann) Bernhard von der Horst, and formerly
wife of Baron Wolf Sigismund Pergler von Perglas; 2ndly, 3 May 1962, Maria
Theresia Elisabeth, da of Max Reindl, and formerly wife of Werner Müller; *d* 4 May
1972; *s* by his eldest son [4] ERNST-LEOPOLD (EDUARD WILHELM JOSIAS), in whom is
vested the right to petition for restoration of the British peerages.

DUKEDOM OF CUMBERLAND AND TEVIOTDALE
(Duke GB 1799, suspended 1917)

His Royal Highness Prince ERNST AUGUST (ALBERT PAUL OTTO RUPPRECHT OSKAR
BERTHOLD FRIEDRICH-FERDINAND CHRISTIAN-LUDWIG) (*HRH The Prince of Hanover*),
Duke of Brunswick and Lüneburg, Prince of Great Britain and Ireland, head of the
Royal House of Hanover and Ducal House of Brunswick and Lüneburg since 1987;
in whom is vested the right to petition for restoration of the Dukedom of
Cumberland and Teviotdale; has Grand Cross Orders of St George, Guelph, and
Ernst August of Hanover, and Order of Henry the Lion of Brunswick; *b* 26 Feb 1954;
s his father, *HRH Prince* ERNST AUGUST (GEORG WILHELM CHRISTIAN LUDWIG FRANZ
JOSEF NIKOLAUS), 1987: *ed* Salem, RAC Cirencester, and Univ of Guelph, Canada: *m*
28 Aug (civ) and 30 Aug (relig) 1981, Chantal, da of Johann Gustav Hochuli, of
Zürich, Switzerland, and has issue.

Residences - Schloss Marienburg, D-30978 Nordstemmen, Germany; Calenberg, D-
30978 Pattensen, Germany; Königinvilla, A-4810 Gmunden, Austria; Hurlingham
Lodge, SW6.

SONS LIVING

HRH Prince ERNST AUGUST (ANDREAS PHILIPP KONSTANTIN MAXIMILIAN ROLF STEPHAN
LUDWIG RUDOLF), *b* 19 July 1983.

HRH Prince Christian Heinrich Clemens Paul Frank Peter Welf Wilhelm-Ernst
Friedrich Franz, *b* 1 June 1985.

BROTHER LIVING

HRH Prince Heinrich Julius (Christian Otto Friedrich Franz Anton Gunther), *b* 29 April 1961.

SISTERS LIVING

HRH Princess Marie Viktoria Luise Hertha Friederike, *b* 26 Nov 1952: *m* 5 June 1982, Count Michael Georg Botho von Hochberg, Baron zu Fürstenstein, only son of Count Konrad Eberhard Georg Botho von Hochberg, Baron zu Fürstenstein, and has issue living, *Count* Conrad Hans-Heinrich Ernst-August, *b* 17 June 1985,—— *Count* Georg Karl Albert, *b* 8 Oct 1987.

HRH Princess Olga Sophie Charlotte Anna, *b* 17 Feb 1958.

HRH Princess Alexandra Irene Margaretha Elisabeth Bathildis, *b* 18 Feb 1959: *m* 11 Oct 1981, HSH Prince Andreas of Leiningen, 2nd son of HSH Emich Cyril Ferdinand Hermann, 7th Prince of Leiningen, and has issue (*see* Leiningen ante).

UNCLES LIVING

HRH Prince Georg Wilhelm Ernst August Friedrich Axel (Georgi-Haus, D-8162 Neuhaus/Schliersee, Germany), *b* 25 March 1915; *ed* Marlborough, Vienna Univ, and Göttingen Univ (Dr jur 1948); late Maj 10th Cavalry Regt; late Headmaster of Salem Sch; Grand Cross of Order of the Redeemer of Greece: *m* 24 April 1946, HRH Princess Sophie, yst da of HRH late Prince Andrew of Greece and Denmark, and widow of HH Prince Christoph Ernst August of Hesse, and has issue living, *HRH Prince* Georg Paul Christian, *b* 9 Dec 1949: *m* 15 Sept 1973, Victoria Anne, yr da of Robert Bee, and has issue living, *HRH Princess* Vera Alice *b* 5 Nov 1976, *HRH Princess* Nora Sophie *b* 15 Jane 1979,—— *HRH Princess* Friederike Elisabeth Victoria Luise Alice Olga Theodora Helene, *b* 15 Oct 1954: *m* 17 Aug 1979, Jerry William Cyr, son of Gordon Paul Cyr, and has issue living, Jean-Paul Welf *b* 6 March 1985, Julia Emma *b* 17 Sept 1982.

HRH Prince Welf Heinrich Ernst August Georg Christian (Neuwiesenstrasse 22, 6 Frankfurt-am-Main-Niederrad, Germany), *b* 11 March 1923; *ed* Univs of Munich, Vienna and Göttingen (Dr jur 1953); Grand Cross of Order of the Redeemer of Greece: *m* 21 Sept 1960, HSH Princess Alexandra Sophie Cecilie Anna Maria Friederike Benigna Dorothea, only da of HSH Otto Friedrich Viktor Ferdinand Maximilian Gustav Richard Bogislav, 3rd Prince of Ysenburg and Büdingen.

STEPMOTHER LIVING

HRH Princess MONIKA (*HRH The Dowager Princess of Hanover*), da of H Ill H Count Georg Friedrich of Solms-Laubach: *m* 17 July 1981, as his 2nd wife, HRH Prince Ernst August, Prince of Hanover, Duke of Brunswick and Lüneburg, who *d* 9 Dec 1987.

COLLATERAL BRANCHES LIVING

Grandson of HRH the late Prince Ernst August of Hanover (*d* 1987):—
Issue of HRH the late Prince Ludwig Rudolph Georg Wilhelm Philipp Friedrich Wolrad Maximilian, *b* 21 Nov 1955, *d* 28 Nov 1988: *m* 27 Aug (civ) and 4 Oct (relig) 1987, Countess Isabella Maria, who *d* 28 Nov 1988, da of Count Ariprand Raimund Georg Alexander Maria Josef Fortunatus von Thurn und Valsassina-Como-Vercelli:—
HRH Prince Otto Heinrich Ariprand Georg Johannes Ernst August Vincenz Egmont Franz, *b* 13 Feb 1988.

Granddaughter of HRH Prince Georg Wilhelm (ante):—
Issue of HRH the late Prince Welf Ernst August Andreas Philipp Georg Wilhelm Ludwig Berthold, *b* 25 Jan 1947, *d* 10 Jan 1981: *m* 25 May 1969, Wibeke, da of Harry van Gunsteren:—
HRH Princess (Tania) Saskia Viktoria-Luise, *b* 24 July 1970: *m* 5 July 1990, as his 2nd wife, Michael Alexander Robert Naylor-Leyland (*see* Naylor-Leyland, Bt), and has issue living, Jake John, *b* 22 Sept 1993.

Granddaughters of HRH the late Duke of Brunswick (*d* 1953):—
Issue of HRH the late Prince Christian Oskar Ernst August Wilhelm Viktor Georg Heinrich, *b* 1 Sept 1919, *d* 10 Dec 1981: *m* 25 Nov 1963 (*m diss* 1976), Mireille, da of Armand Dutry:—
HRH Princess Caroline-Luise Mireille Irene Sophie, *b* 3 May 1965—— *HRH Princess* Mireille Viktoria Luise Sophie Friederike Danielle, *b* 3 June 1971.

PREDECESSORS

[1] *HRH Prince* ERNEST AUGUSTUS, KG, KT, GCB, GCH, 5th son of King George III, *b* 5 June 1771; *cr* Earl of Armagh, and Duke of Cumberland and Teviotdale, in the peerage of Great Britain, 24 April 1799; Field Marshal 1813; *s* his brother King William IV as King of Hanover 20 June 1837: *m* 29 May 1815, Friederike Caroline Sophie Alexandrine, who *d* 29 June 1841, 5th da of Karl, Grand Duke of Mecklenburg-Strelitz, and widow of Prince Friedrich Wilhelm of Solms-Braunfels and previously of Prince Ludwig of Prussia; *d* 18 Nov 1851; *s* by his only son [2] GEORG V (FRIEDRICH ALEXANDER KARL ERNST AUGUST), KING OF HANOVER (until that Kingdom was annexed by the Kingdom of Prussia 20 Sept 1866), 2nd Duke, KG, *b* 27 May 1819: *m* 18 Feb 1843, (Alexandrine) Marie Wilhelmine Katharina Charlotte Therese Henriette Louise Pauline Elisabeth Friederike Georgine, VA, who *d* 9 Jan 1907, eldest da of Joseph, Duke of Saxe-Altenburg; *d* 12 June 1878; *s* by his only son [3] ERNST AUGUST (WILHELM ADOLF GEORG FRIEDRICH), 3rd Duke, KG, GCH, *b* 21 Sept 1845; deprived of his peerages by the Titles Deprivation Act 8 Nov 1917 and removed from the Roll of Peers by Order in Council 28 March 1919: *m* 21 Dec 1878, Thyra Amelia Caroline Charlotte Anne, CI, who *d* 26 Feb 1933, yst da of Christian IX, King of Denmark; *d* 14 Nov 1923; *s* by his only surviving son [4] ERNST AUGUST (CHRISTIAN GEORG), Reigning Duke of Brunswick 1913-18, *b* 17 Nov 1887: *m* 24 May 1913, Viktoria Luise (Adelheid Mathilde Charlotte), who *d* 11 Dec 1980, only da of Wilhelm II, German Emperor and King of Prussia; *d* 30 Jan 1953; *s* by his eldest son [5] ERNST AUGUST (GEORG WILHELM CHRISTIAN LUDWIG FRANZ JOSEF NIKOLAUS), Prince of Hanover, *b* 18 March 1914; re-established his legal right to be a British subject 1955/6: *m* 1st, 4 Sept 1951, Ortrud Bertha Adelheid Hedwig, who *d* 6 Feb 1980, 2nd da of Prince Albert of Schleswig-Holstein-Sonderburg-Glücksburg; 2ndly, 17 July 1981, Monika, da of Count Georg Friedrich of Solms-Laubach; *d* 9 Dec 1987; *s* by his eldest son [6] ERNST AUGUST (ALBERT PAUL OTTO RUPPRECHT OSKAR BERTHOLD FRIEDRICH-FERDINAND CHRISTIAN-LUDWIG), in whom is vested the right to petition for restoration of the British peerages.

SOVEREIGNS OF ENGLAND, GREAT BRITAIN AND THE UNITED KINGDOM SINCE THE NORMAN CONQUEST

WILLIAM I *the Conqueror*, styled *Willelmus Rex Anglorum*; *b* at Falaise, Normandy 1027 or 1028; *s* his father as Duke of Normandy 1035; obtained the crown of England by conquest 14 Oct 1066; *c* 25 Dec 1066; *m* 1053, Matilda, *c* 11 May 1068 (*d* at Caen 2 Nov 1083; *bur* Church of Holy Trinity, Caen), da of Baldwin V, Count of Flanders (a direct descendant of Alfred *the Great*, King of the West Saxons); *d* at the Priory of St Gervais, nr Rouen 9 Sept 1087; *bur* Abbey of St Stephen, Caen; had 4 sons and 6 das; *s* in England by his 2nd son,

WILLIAM II *Rufus*, styled *Dei Gratia Rex Anglorum*; *b* in Normandy 1056/60; *c* 26 Sept 1087; *k* while hunting in the New Forest 2 Aug 1100; *bur* Winchester Cathedral; unm; *s* by his brother, the yst son of King William I,

HENRY I *Beauclerc*, styled the same as William II; *b* at Selby, Yorkshire *ca* Sept 1068; *c* 6 Aug 1100; *m* 1st, 11 Nov 1100, Matilda (formerly called Edith), *c* on her wedding day (*d* at Westminster 1 May 1118; *bur* Westminster Abbey; er da of Malcolm III *Canmore*, King of Scots; 2ndly, 29 Jan 1121, Adeliza, *c* 3 Feb 1121 (who *m* 2ndly, 1138, William d'Aubigny, 1st Earl of Arundel, and *d* at Afflighem, Flanders 23 March or April 1151; *bur* Afflighem), da of Godfrey I *the Bearded*, Duke of Lower Lorraine; *d* at St Denis-le-Fermont, nr Rouen 1 Dec 1135; *bur* Reading Abbey; had surviving issue (by 1st *m*) one son (*dvp*) and one da; *s* by his nephew, the 3rd son of Stephen, Count of Blois and Chartres, by his wife Adela, da of King William I,

STEPHEN, styled *Rex Anglorum, Dux Normannorum*; *b* at Blois *ca* 1096; *c* 26 Dec 1135; disputed the crown with his cousin Matilda, da of King Henry I, who finally renounced her claim in his favour for life with reversion to her son Henry; *m* 1125, Matilda, *suo jure* Countess of Boulogne, *c* 22 March 1136 (*d* at Hedingham Castle, Essex 3 May 1152; *bur* Faversham Abbey), only da and heiress of Eustace III, Count of Boulogne, by his wife Mary, yr da of Malcolm III *Canmore*, King of Scots; *d* at Dover 25 Oct 1154; *bur* Faversham Abbey; had 3 sons and 2 das; *s* by his first cousin once removed, the el son of Geoffrey V *Plantagenet*, Count of Anjou and Maine, by his wife Matilda, widow of the Emperor Henry V, and only da of King Henry I.

HENRY II *Curtmantle*, styled *Rex Angliae, Dux Normanniae et Aquitaniae et Comes Andegaviae*; *b* at Le Mans 5 March 1133; *c* 19 Dec 1154; *m* 18 May 1152, Eleanor, *suo jure* Duchess of Aquitaine, *c* with him (*d* at Fontévraud, Anjou 31 March/1 April 1204; *bur* Fontévraud Abbey), elder da and co-heiress of William X, Duke of Aquitaine, and formerly wife of Louis VII, King of France; *d* at Chinon, nr Tours 6 July 1189; *bur* Fontévraud Abbey; had 5 sons and 3 das; *s* by his 3rd, but eldest surviving, son,

RICHARD I *Coeur de Lion*, styled the same as Henry II; *b* at Beaumont Palace, Oxford 8 Sept 1157; *c* 3 Sept 1189; *m* 12 May 1191, Berengaria, *c* on her wedding day (*d* at L'Epau Abbey, nr Le Mans in or after 1230; *bur* there), da of Sancho VI *the Wise*, King of Navarre; *dsp* at Châlus, Aquitaine 6 April 1199; *bur* Fontévraud Abbey; *s* by his brother, the yst son of King Henry II,

JOHN *Lackland*, styled *Rex Angliae, Dominus Hiberniae, Dux Normanniae, et Dux Aquitaniae*; *b* at Beaumont Palace, Oxford 24 Dec 1167; *c* 27 May 1199; *m* 1st, 29 Aug 1189 (*m annulled* 1200), Isabella (who *m* 2ndly, 1213, Geoffrey de Mandeville, 5th Earl of Essex (*d* 1216); and 3rdly, *ca* Oct 1217, Hubert de Burgh, 1st Earl of Kent, and *dsp ca* 18 Nov 1217; *bur* Canterbury Cathedral), 3rd and yst da and co-heiress of William, Earl of Gloucester; 2ndly, 24 Aug 1200, Isabella, *c* 8 Oct 1200 (who *m* 2ndly, *ca* 1220, Hugh X de Lusignan, Count of La Marche, and *d* at Fontévraud 31 May 1246; *bur* there), only da and heiress of Aymer Taillefer, Count of Angoulême; *d* at Newark Castle 18/19 Oct 1216; *bur* Worcester Cathedral; had 2 sons and 3 das by 2nd *m*; *s* by his el son.

HENRY III, styled the same as John until 1259, then *Rex Angliae, Dominus Hiberniae et Dux Aquitaniae*; *b* at Winchester 1 October 1207; *c* (at Gloucester) 28 Oct 1216 and again (at Westminster) 17 May 1220; *m* 4 Jan 1236, Eleanor, *c* 20 Jan 1236 (*d* at Amesbury, Wilts 24 June 1291; *bur* there), 2nd da and co-heiress of Raymond Berenger V, Count of Provence; *d* at Westminster 16 Nov 1272; *bur* Westminster Abbey; had 6 sons and 3 das; *s* by his el son,

EDWARD I *Longshanks*, styled the same as Henry III; *b* at Westminster 17 June 1239; *c* 19 Aug 1274; *m* 1st, 13/31 Oct 1254, Eleanor, *c* with him (*d* at Herdeby, Lincs 24 Nov 1290; *bur* Westminster Abbey), da of (St) Ferdinand III, King of Castile and Leon; 2ndly, 10 Sept 1299, Margaret (*d* at Marlborough Castle, Wilts, 14 Feb 1317; *bur* Grey Friars Church, London), da of Philip III, King of France; *d* at Burgh-on-the-Sands, nr Carlisle 7 July 1307; *bur* Westminster Abbey; had (by 1st *m*) 4 sons and 11 das, (by 2nd *m*) 2 sons and 1 da; *s* by his 4th, but el surviving, son,

EDWARD II, styled the same as King Henry III; *b* at Caernarvon Castle 25 April 1284; *c* 25 Feb 1308; deposed by Parliament 20 Jan 1327; *m* 25 Jan 1308, Isabella, *c* with him (*d* at Castle Rising, Norfolk 22 Aug 1358; *bur* Grey Friars Church, London), el da of Philip IV, King of France; murdered at Berkeley Castle 21 Sept 1327; *bur* Gloucester Cathedral; had 2 sons and 2 das; *s* by his el son,

EDWARD III, styled the same as King Henry III until 1340, then *Rex Angliae et Franciae et Dominus Hiberniae*; *b* at Windsor Castle 13 Nov 1312; Keeper of the Realm 26 Oct 1326; proclaimed King 25 Jan 1327; *c* 2 Feb 1327; *m* 24 Jan 1328, Philippa, *c* 20 Feb 1328 (*d* at Windsor Castle 14 Aug 1369; *bur* Westminster Abbey), 3rd da of William, Count of Holland and Hainault; *d* at Sheen Palace, Surrey 21 June 1377; *bur* Westminster Abbey; had 7 sons and 5 das; *s* by his grandson, the only surviving son of Edward, Prince of Wales (who *dvp* 1376),

RICHARD II, styled the same as King Edward III; *b* at Bordeaux 6 Jan 1367; *c* 16 July 1377; deposed 29 or 30 Sept 1399; *m* 1st, 14 or 20 Jan 1382, Anne, *c* 22 Jan 1382 (*d* at Sheen Palace shortly before 3 June 1394; *bur* Westminster Abbey), da of Charles IV, Holy Roman Emperor and King of Bohemia; 2ndly, 1 Nov 1396, Isabelle, *c* 8 Jan 1397 (who *m* 2ndly, 29 June 1406, Charles, Duke of Orleans, and *d* at Blois 13 Sept 1409; *bur* Abbey of St Saumer, Blois, *re-bur* Paris *ca* 1624), 2nd da of Charles VI, King of France; *dsp* at Pontefract Castle, Yorkshire (supposedly murdered) 6 Jan 1400; *bur* Westminster Abbey; *s* on his deposition by his 1st cousin, the el surv son of John *of Gaunt*, Duke of Lancaster, KG, 4th son of King Edward III,

HENRY IV, styled the same as Edward III; *b* at Bolingbroke Castle, Lincs 4 April 1366; *c* 13 Oct 1399; *m* 1st, July 1380/March 1381, Mary (*d* at Peterborough Castle 4 July 1394; *bur* St Mary's Church, Leicester), yr da and co-heiress of Humphrey de Bohun, 7th Earl of Hereford, 6th Earl of Essex and 2nd Earl of Northampton, KG; 2ndly, 7 Feb 1403, Joan, *c* 26 Feb 1403 (*d* at Havering-atte-Bower, Essex 9 July 1437; *bur* Canterbury Cathedral), 2nd da of Charles II, King of Navarre, and widow of John V, Duke of Brittany; *d* in the Jerusalem Chamber, Westminster Abbey 20 March 1413; *bur* Canterbury Cathedral; had issue (by 1st *m*) 5 sons and 2 das; *s* by his el surv son,

HENRY V, styled the same as King Edward III until 1420, then *Rex Angliae, Haeres et Regens Franciae, et Dominus Hiberniae*; *b* at Monmouth 9 Aug 1387; *c* 9 April 1413; *m* 2 June 1420, Catherine, *c* 24 Feb 1421 (who *m* 2ndly, *ca* 1428, Owen Tudor, and *d* at Bermondsey Abbey 3 Jan 1437; *bur* Westminster Abbey), 6th and yst da of Charles VI, King of France; *d* at Bois de Vincennes, France 31 Aug 1422; *bur* Westminster Abbey; had one son, who *s* him as

HENRY VI, styled *Rex Angliae et Franciae et Dominus Hiberniae*; *b* at Windsor Castle 6 Dec 1421; *c* 6 Nov 1429; *c* King of France at Notre Dame Cathedral, Paris 16 Dec 1431; deposed 4 March 1461; regained the crown 3 Oct 1470; again deposed 11 April 1471; *m* 22 April 1445, Margaret, *c* 30 May 1445 (*d* at Château de Dampière, nr Saumur 25 Aug 1482; *bur* Angers), 2nd da of René, Duke of Anjou, titular King of Naples and Sicily; *d* at the Tower of London (supposedly murdered) 21 May 1471; *bur* Chertsey Abbey, *re-bur* St George's Chapel, Windsor; had issue, one son (*kvp* 1471); *s* on his deposition by the Yorkist claimant to the throne, the great-grandson of Edmund *of Langley* Duke of York, KG, 5th son of King Edward III, and also representative of Lionel *of Antwerp*, Duke of Clarence, KG, 3rd (but 2nd surv) son of King Edward III,

EDWARD IV, styled the same as King Henry VI; *b* at Rouen 28 April 1442; declared King in Parliament 4 March 1461; *c* 28 June 1461; deposed 3 Oct 1470 when Henry VI was restored; regained the crown 11 April 1471; *m* 1 May 1464, Elizabeth, *c* 26 May 1465 (*d* at Bermondsey Abbey 8 June 1492; *bur* St George's Chapel, Windsor), el da of Richard Woodville, 1st Earl Rivers, KG, and widow of Sir John Grey; *d* at Westminster 9 April 1483; *bur* St George's Chapel, Windsor; had issue, 3 sons and 7 das; *s* by his el son,

EDWARD V, styled the same as King Henry VI; *b* at Westminster 4 Nov 1470; never crowned; deposed by an assembly of Lords and Commons on the grounds of the supposed invalidity of his parents' marriage (King Edward IV having been contracted to Lady Eleanor Butler, who was still living at the time of his marriage to Lady Grey) 25 June 1483; confined in the Tower of London, where he was presumed to have been murdered (with his only surv brother Richard, Duke of York) in or after July 1483; *s* by his uncle, the brother of King Edward IV,

RICHARD III, styled the same as King Henry VI; *b* at Fotheringay Castle 2 Oct 1452; proclaimed King 26 June 1483; *c* 6 July 1483; *m* 12 July 1472, Anne, *c* with him (*d* at Westminster 16 March 1485; *bur* Westminster Abbey), yr da and co-heiress of Richard Nevill, 1st Earl of Warwick and 2nd Earl of Salisbury, KG, and widow of Edward, Prince of Wales (only son of King Henry VI); *k* fighting for his crown at Bosworth Field 22 Aug 1485; *bur* Grey Friars Abbey, Leicester; had issue, one son (who *dvp*); *s* by his rival Henry Tudor, Earl of Richmond, great-great-grandson of John *of Gaunt*, Duke of Lancaster, KG, 4th son of King Edward III, and grandson of Owen Tudor, by his wife Catherine, widow of King Henry V, who ascended the throne as

HENRY VII, styled the same as King Henry VI; *b* at Pembroke Castle 28 Jan 1457; *c* 30 Oct 1485; *m* 18 Jan 1486, Elizabeth, *c* 25 Nov 1487 (*d* at the Tower of London 11 Feb 1503; *bur* Westminster Abbey), el da of King Edward IV; *d* at Richmond Palace 21 April 1509; *bur* Westminster Abbey; had issue, 3 sons and 4 das; *s* by his 2nd (but only surv) son,

HENRY VIII, styled the same as King Henry VI until 1521, then *King of England and France, Defender of the Faith, Lord of Ireland, and of the Church of England on Earth Supreme Head* until 1542, then *King of England, France and Ireland, Defender of the Faith, and of the Church of England and also of Ireland in Earth the Supreme Head*; the first English sovereign to adopt the style of *Majesty*; *b* at Greenwich Palace 28 June 1491; *c* 24 June 1509; *m* 1st, 11 June 1509 (*m* declared null and void by Thomas Cranmer, Archbishop of Canterbury 23 May 1533 and "utterly dissolved" by Act of Parliament March 1534), Catherine, *c* with him (*d* at Kimbolton Castle, Hunts 7 Jan 1536; *bur* Peterborough Cathedral), da of Ferdinand II, King of Aragon (and V as King of Castile *jure uxoris*), and widow of his el brother Arthur, Prince of Wales; 2ndly, 25 Jan 1533 (*m* declared valid 28 May 1533 and invalid 17 May 1536), Anne, Marchioness of Pembroke (*cr* 1532), *c* 1 June 1533 (beheaded on Tower Green 19 May 1536; *bur* Chapel of St Peter ad Vincula in the Tower), da of Thomas Boleyn, 1st Earl of Wiltshire and Ormonde, KG; 3rdly, 30 May 1536, Jane (*d* at Hampton Court Palace 24 Oct 1537; *bur* St George's Chapel, Windsor), da of Sir John Seymour, Knt Banneret, of Wolf Hall, Savernake, Wilts; 4thly, 6 Jan 1540 (*m* annulled 9 July 1540), Anne (*d* at Chelsea 17 July 1557; *bur* Westminster Abbey), 2nd da of John III, Duke of Cleves; 5thly, 28 July 1540, Catherine (beheaded on Tower Green 13 Feb 1542; *bur* Chapel of St Peter ad Vincula in the Tower), da of Lord Edmund Howard, 3rd son of 2nd Duke of Norfolk; 6thly, 12 July 1543, Catherine (who *m* 4thly, April or May 1547, Thomas Seymour, 1st Baron Seymour of Sudeley, KG, Lord High Adm, brother of Queen Jane (see above), and *d* at Sudeley Castle, Glos 5 Sept 1548; *bur* Sudeley Castle Chapel), da of Sir Thomas Parr, of Kendal, Westmorland, and widow of (1) Hon Sir Edward Burgh, and (2) John Nevill, 3rd Baron Latimer; *d* at Whitehall Palace 28 Jan 1547; *bur* St George's Chapel, Windsor; and had living issue, (by 1st *m*) 2 sons and 1 da, (by 2nd *m*) 1 da, (by 3rd *m*) 1 son; *s* by his only surv son (by 3rd *m*),

EDWARD VI, styled the same as King Henry VIII; *b* at Hampton Court Palace 12 Oct 1537; *c* 20 Feb 1547; *d* at Greenwich Palace 6 July 1553; *bur* Westminster Abbey; *s* by his 1st cousin once removed, Lady Jane Dudley (el da of Henry Grey, 1st Duke of Suffolk, KG, by his wife Frances, da of Charles Brandon, 1st Duke of Suffolk, KG, by his wife Mary, 3rd da of King Henry VII), who had been declared heiress-presumptive 21 June 1553,

JANE, styled the same as King Henry VIII; *b* at Bradgate, Leics Oct 1537; proclaimed Queen 10 July 1553; dethroned in favour of the rightful heir Mary 19 July 1553; tried and condemned to death for high treason 13 Nov 1553; *m* 21 May 1553, Lord Guildford Dudley (beheaded on Tower Hill 12 Feb 1554; *bur* Chapel of St Peter ad Vincula in the Tower), 6th son of John Dudley, 1st Duke of Northumberland, KG; beheaded on Tower Green 12 Feb 1554; *bur* Chapel of St Peter ad Vincula in the Tower; *s* on her deposition by the el da of King Henry VIII (by his 1st *m*),

MARY I, styled the same as King Henry VIII until her marriage, then she and her husband were styled *Philip and Mary, by the Grace of God, King and Queen of England and France, Naples, Jerusalem and Ireland, Defenders of the Faith, Princes of Spain and Sicily, Archdukes of Austria, Dukes of Milan, Burgundy and Brabant*; *b* at Greenwich Palace 18 Feb 1516; *c* 1 Oct 1553; *m* 25 July 1554, as his 2nd wife, Philip, from 1555 Philip II, King of Spain (*d* at El Escorial, nr Madrid 13 Sept 1598; *bur* El Escorial), only son of the Emperor Charles V; *dsp* at St James's Palace 17 Nov 1558; *bur* Westminster Abbey; *s* by her half-sister (the da of King Henry VIII by his 2nd *m*),

ELIZABETH I, styled *Queen of England, France and Ireland, Defender of the Faith*; *b* at Greenwich Palace 7 Sept 1533; *c* 15 Jan 1559; *d* at Richmond Palace 24 March 1603; *bur* Westminster Abbey; *s* by her kinsman, James VI, King of Scots, great-grandson of Margaret, el da of King Henry VII (*see* SOVEREIGNS OF SCOTLAND),

JAMES I (Charles James), styled *King of England, Scotland, France and Ireland, Defender of the Faith*; *b* at Edinburgh Castle 19 June 1566; *s* his mother as King of Scots 24 July 1567; *c* King of Scots 29 July 1567; *c* as King of England, etc 25 July 1603; *m* 20 Aug 1589, Anne, *c* with him (*d* at Hampton Court Palace 4 March 1619; *bur* Westminster Abbey), 2nd da of Frederick II, King of Denmark and Norway; *d* at Theobalds Park, Herts 27 March 1625; *bur* Westminster Abbey; had living issue, 3 sons and 4 das; *s* by his 2nd but only surv, son,

CHARLES I, styled the same as King James I; *b* at Dunfermline 19 Nov 1600; *c* 2 Feb 1626; *c* King of Scots 18 June 1633; *m* 13 June 1625, Henrietta Maria (*d* at Colombe, nr Paris 31 Aug 1669; *bur* St Denis), yst da of Henry IV, King of France and Navarre; found guilty of high treason by a "High Court of Justice" appointed by Parliament and condemned to death 27 Jan 1649; beheaded outside Whitehall Palace 30 Jan 1649; *bur* St George's Chapel, Windsor; had issue, 4 sons and 5 das.

After the execution of King Charles I there was an interregnum entitled the Commonwealth. A republic was established and continued until 16 Dec 1653, when Oliver Cromwell was declared Lord Protector. He *d* 3 Sept 1658 and was *s* in the Protectorate by his son Richard, who held the office until April 1659, when a republic was re-established until 8 May 1660, when the 2nd, but el surv, son of King Charles I,

CHARLES II, was proclaimed by the same style as King James I, his reign having legally commenced on the death of his father; *b* at St James's Palace 29 May 1630; landed at Dover 29 May 1660 (Restoration Day); *c* 23 April 1661 (having been *c* King of Scots at Scone 1 Jan 1651); *m* 21 May 1662, Catherine Henrietta (*d* at Bemposta Palace, Lisbon 31 Dec 1705; *bur* Belém), da of John IV, King of Portugal; *dspl* at Whitehall Palace 6 Feb 1685; *bur* Westminster Abbey; *s* by his brother,

JAMES II (VII as King of Scots), styled the same as King James I; *b* at St James's Palace 14 Oct 1633; *c* 23 April 1685; declared by Act of Parliament (28 Jan 1689) to have abdicated the throne 11 Dec 1688, on which date he left the country; *m* 1st, 24 Nov 1659, Lady Anne Hyde (*d* at St James's Palace 31 March 1671; *bur* Westminster Abbey), el da of Edward Hyde, 1st Earl of Clarendon, PC, Lord High Chancellor of England; 2ndly, 30 Sept 1673, Mary Beatrice Eleonora, *c* with him (*d* at St Germain-en-Laye, France 7 May 1718; *bur* Convent of Chaillot), only da of Alfonso IV (d'Este), Duke of Modena; *d* at St Germain-en-Laye 6 Sept 1701; *bur* Church of the English Benedictines, rue St Jacques, Paris, later re-bur at St Germain-en-Laye; had issue (by 1st *m*), 4 sons and 4 das; (by 2nd *m*), 2 sons and 4 das.

After King James II was declared to have abdicated, the throne was offered by Parliament to his el da and son-in-law, who ascended it jtly as

WILLIAM III and **MARY II**, styled *King and Queen of England, Scotland, France and Ireland, Defenders of the Faith*; proclaimed 13 Feb 1689; *c* 11 April 1689. The Queen was *b* at St James's Palace 30 April 1662; *m* 4 Nov 1677, her 1st cousin, William Henry, Prince of Orange, Count of Nassau-Dillenburg, only son of William II, Prince of Orange, etc, by his wife Mary, Princess Royal, el da of King Charles I; *d* at Kensington Palace 28 Dec 1694; *bur* Westminster Abbey. The King was *b* at the Hague 14 Nov 1650; *dsp* at Kensington Palace 8 March 1702; *bur* Westminster Abbey; *s* by the sister of Queen Mary (2nd da of King James II),

ANNE, styled *Queen of England, Scotland, France and Ireland, Defender of the Faith* until the Act of Union with Scotland 6 March 1707, then *Queen of Great Britain, France and Ireland, Defender of the Faith*; *b* at St James's Palace 6 Feb 1665; *c* 23 April 1702; *m* 28 July 1683, Prince George of Denmark, KG, *cr* Duke of Cumberland 9 April 1689, Lord High Adm of England 20 May 1702, of Great Britain from 1707 (*d* at Kensington Palace 28 Oct 1708; *bur* Westminster Abbey), yr son of Frederick III, King of Denmark and Norway; *dsps* at Kensington Palace 1 Aug 1714; *bur* Westminster Abbey; had living issue, 2 sons and 3 das (and many stillborn children); *s* in accordance with the Act of Settlement of 1701 by her kinsman, the eldest son of Ernest Augustus, Elector of Hanover, by his wife Sophia, yst da of Frederick V, King of Bohemia and Elector Palatine of the Rhine, by his wife, Elizabeth, el da of King James I,

GEORGE I (George Louis), styled *King of Great Britain, France and Ireland, Duke of Brunswick-Lüneburg, Elector of Hanover, Defender of the Faith*; *b* at Hanover 28 May/7 June 1660; *c* 20 Oct 1714; *m* 21 Nov 1682 (*m diss* by a specially constituted tribunal of the Lutheran Church in accordance with Hanoverian law 28 Dec 1694), his 1st cousin, Sophia Dorothea (*d* at Ahlden 13 Nov 1726; *bur* Celle), only surv da and heiress of George William, Duke of Brunswick-Lüneburg and Celle, KG; *d* at Osnabrück 11 June 1727; *bur* Leineschloss Church, Hanover, re-bur Herrenhausen 1957; had issue, one son and one da; *s* by his only son,

GEORGE II (George Augustus), styled the same as King George I; *b* at Herrenhausen 30 Oct 1683; *c* 11 Oct 1727: *m* 22 Aug 1705, (Wilhelmina Charlotte) Caroline, *c* with him (*d* at St James's Palace 25 Nov 1737; *bur* Westminster Abbey), yst da of John Frederick, Margrave of Brandenburg-Ansbach; *d* at Kensington Palace 25 Oct 1760; *bur* Westminster Abbey; had (living) issue, 3 sons and 5 das; *s* by his grandson, the el son of Frederick Louis, Prince of Wales (*dvp* 20 March 1751),

GEORGE III (George William Frederick), styled the same as King George I until 1 Jan 1801, then *By the Grace of God, of the United Kingdom of Great Britain and Ireland, King, Defender of the Faith* (also Elector of Hanover until 12 Aug 1814, when that country was recognized by the Allied Powers as a Kingdom and he was proclaimed King of Hanover 12 Oct 1814); *b* at Norfolk House, St James's Square, London 4 June 1738; *c* 22 Sept 1761; *m* 8 Sept 1761, (Sophia) Charlotte, *c* with him (*d* at Kew Palace 17 Nov 1818; *bur* St George's Chapel, Windsor), yst da of Duke Charles Louis Frederick of Mecklenburg-Strelitz; *d* at Windsor Castle 29 Jan 1820; *bur* St George's Chapel, Windsor; had 9 sons and 6 das; *s* by his el son,

GEORGE IV (George Augustus Frederick), styled the same as King George III; *b* at St James's Palace 12 Aug 1762; Prince Regent of the United Kingdom from 5 Feb 1811 until his accession to the throne; *c* 19 July 1821; *m* 8 April 1795, Caroline Amelia Elizabeth (*d* at Brandenburg House, Hammersmith 7 Aug 1821; *bur* Brunswick), 2nd da of Charles William Ferdinand, Duke of Brunswick-Wolfenbüttel; *d* at Windsor Castle 26 June 1830; *bur* St George's Chapel, Windsor; had issue, one da (who *dvp* and *sps*); *s* by his brother, the 3rd son of King George III,

WILLIAM IV (William Henry), styled the same as King George III; *b* at Buckingham House (now Buckingham Palace) 21 Aug 1765; *c* 8 Sept 1831; *m* 11 July 1818, Adelaide Louisa Theresa Caroline Amelia, *c* with him (*d* at Bentley Priory, Middx 2 Dec 1849; *bur* St George's Chapel, Windsor), el da of George I, Duke of Saxe-Meiningen; *d* at Windsor Castle 20 June 1837; *bur* St George's Chapel, Windsor; had (living) issue, 2 das (who *d* in infancy); *s* in Great Britain and Ireland by his niece, the only da of Edward, Duke of Kent, 4th son of King George III, and in Hanover by his next surv brother, Ernest Augustus, Duke of Cumberland and Teviotdale.

VICTORIA (Alexandrina Victoria), styled the same as King George III until 1 Jan 1877, then *By the Grace of God, of the United Kingdom of Great Britain and Ireland, Queen, Defender of the Faith, Empress of India*; *b* at Kensington Palace 24 May 1819; *c* 28 June 1838; proclaimed Empress of India 1 Jan 1877; *m* 10 Feb 1840, HSH Prince (Francis) Albert Augustus Charles Emmanuel of Saxe-Coburg and Gotha, Duke of Saxony, *cr* HRH 7 Feb 1840 and Prince Consort 25 June 1857 (*d* at Windsor Castle 14 Dec 1861; *bur* Royal Mausoleum, Frogmore), yr son of Ernest I, Duke of Saxe-Coburg and Gotha; *d* at Osborne House, Isle of Wight 22 Jan 1901; *bur* Royal Mausoleum, Frogmore; had issue, 4 sons and 5 das; *s* by her el son,

EDWARD VII (Albert Edward), styled the same as Queen Victoria until 17 Aug 1901, then *By the Grace of God, of the United Kingdom of Great Britain and Ireland, and of the British Dominions beyond the Seas, King, Defender of the Faith, Emperor of India*; *b* at Buckingham Palace 9 Nov 1841; *c* 9 Aug 1902; *m* 10 March 1863, Alexandra Caroline Mary Charlotte Louisa Julia, *c* with him (*d* at Sandringham House, Norfolk 20 Nov 1925; *bur* St George's Chapel, Windsor), el da of Christian IX, King of Denmark; *d* at Buckingham Palace 6 May 1910; *bur* St George's Chapel, Windsor; had issue, 3 sons and 3 das; *s* by his 2nd, but only surv son,

GEORGE V (George Frederick Ernest Albert), styled the same as King Edward VII until 13 May 1927, then *By the Grace of God, of Great Britain, Ireland and the British Dominions beyond the Seas, King, Defender of the Faith, Emperor of India*; *b* at Marlborough House, London 3 June 1865; *c* 22 June 1911; assumed by Royal Proclamation on 17 July 1917 the name of Windsor for his

House and family; *m* 6 July 1893, (Victoria) Mary Augusta Louisa Olga Pauline Claudine Agnes, *c* with him (*d* at Marlborough House, London 24 March 1953; *bur* St George's Chapel, Windsor), only da of Francis Paul Charles Louis Alexander, Duke of Teck, by his wife Princess Mary Adelaide, yr da of Adolphus, Duke of Cambridge, 7th son of King George III; *d* at Sandringham House, Norfolk 20 Jan 1936; *bur* St George's Chapel, Windsor; had issue, 5 sons and 1 da; *s* by his el son,

EDWARD VIII (Edward Albert Christian George Andrew Patrick David), styled the same as King George V; *b* at White Lodge, Richmond Park, Surrey 23 June 1894; renounced the throne for himself and his descendants 10 Dec 1936 (confirmed by the Declaration of Abdication Act 11 Dec 1936); *cr* Duke of Windsor 8 March 1937; *m* 3 June 1937, (Bessie) Wallis Warfield (which surname she resumed by Deed Poll after her 2nd divorce) (*d* at Paris 24 April 1986; *bur* Frogmore), only child of Teackle Wallis Warfield, of Baltimore, Maryland, USA, and formerly wife of (1) Earl Winfield Spencer, and (2) Ernest Aldrich Simpson; *dsp* at Paris 28 May 1972 (*bur* Frogmore); *s* on his abdication by his brother,

GEORGE VI (Albert Frederick Arthur George), styled the same as King George V until 22 June 1948, when by Royal Proclamation he discontinued the style of Emperor of India; *b* at York Cottage, Sandringham 14 Dec 1895; *c* 12 May 1937; *m* 26 April 1923, Lady Elizabeth Angela Marguerite Bowes-Lyon, *c* with him, yst da of 14th Earl of Strathmore and Kinghorne, KG, KT, GCVO, TD; *d* at Sandringham House, Norfolk 6 Feb 1952; *bur* St George's Chapel, Windsor; had issue, 2 das; *s* by his el da,

ELIZABETH II (Elizabeth Alexandra Mary), styled the same as King George VI until 26 March 1953, then *By the Grace of God, of the United Kingdom of Great Britain and Northern Ireland, and of her other Realms and Territories, Queen, Head of the Commonwealth, Defender of the Faith.*

SOVEREIGNS OF SCOTLAND SINCE 1058

MALCOLM III *Canmore* (ie Great Head, or Chief), King of Scots, son of King Duncan I (*d* 1040); *b ca* 1031; *s* to the throne after the defeat and death of his rivals Macbeth and Lulach 17 March 1058; *c* at Scone 25 April 1058; *m* 1st, *ca* 1059, Ingibiorg (*d* in or before 1069), da of Finn Arnesson of Vrjar, Jarl of Halland, and widow of Thorfinn II, Earl of Caithness; 2ndly, *ca* 1069, St Margaret (*d* at Edinburgh Castle 16 Nov 1093; *bur* Dunfermline Abbey; canonized 1250), el da of Edward *the Atheling*, and grand-da of Edmund *Ironside*, King of England; *k* in battle at Alnwick, Northumberland 13 Nov 1093; *bur* Tynemouth, re-bur Dunfermline Abbey); had issue, (by 1st *m*) 3 sons, (by 2nd *m*) 6 sons and 2 das; *s* by his brother,

DONALD BANE, King of Scots; *b ca* 1033; chosen King by the people of Scotland; deposed by his nephew Duncan May 1094; regained the throne on the latter's death 12 Nov 1094; deposed and blinded by his nephew Edgar Oct 1097; *m* an unknown wife; *d* at Rescobie, Forfarshire 1099; *bur* Dunkeld, re-bur Iona; had issue, one da; *s* on his first deposition by his nephew, the el son of King Malcolm III,

DUNCAN II, King of Scots, *b ca* 1060; *m ca* 1090, Ethelreda (*bur* Dunfermline Abbey), da of Gospatrick, 1st Earl of Dunbar; *k* at Mondynes, Kincardineshire 12 Nov 1094; *bur* Dunfermline Abbey; had issue, one son; *s* by his uncle Donald Bane, who was again deposed and *s* by the 7th son of King Malcolm III (and 4th son of St Margaret),

EDGAR, King of Scots, *b ca* 1074; *d unm* at Edinburgh Castle 8 Jan 1107; *bur* Dunfermline Abbey; *s* by his next brother,

ALEXANDER I *The Fierce*, King of Scots, *b ca* 1077; *m* Sibylla (*d* on the island of Loch Tay 12 or 13 July 1122; *bur* Dunfermline Abbey), illegitimate da of Henry I, King of England; *dsp* at Stirling 23 April 1124; *bur* Dunfermline Abbey; *s* by his next brother,

DAVID I *The Saint*, King of Scots; *b ca* 1080; *c* 1124; *m ca* 1113/14, Matilda (*d* 1130/31; *bur* Scone), da and heiress of Waltheof, Earl of Huntingdon, and widow of Simon de St Liz; *d* at Carlisle 24 May 1153; *bur* Dunfermline Abbey; had issue, 2 sons and 2 das; *s* by his grandson, the son of Henry, Earl of Huntingdon (*dvp* 12 June 1152),

MALCOLM IV *The Maiden*, King of Scots; *b* 20 March 1142; *c* 1153; *d unm* at Jedburgh 9 Dec 1165; *bur* Dunfermline Abbey; *s* by his brother,

WILLIAM I *The Lion*, King of Scots; *b* 1143; *c* 24 Dec 1165; *m* 5 Sept 1186, Ermengarde (*d* 11 Feb 1234; *bur* Balmerino Abbey), da of Richard, Vicomte de Beaumont; *d* at Stirling 4 Dec 1214; *bur* Arbroath Abbey; had issue, 1 son and 3 das (and several illegitimate children, whose descendants were competitors for the crown in 1291); *s* by his only son,

ALEXANDER II, King of Scots; *b* at Haddington 24 Aug 1198; *c* 6 Dec 1214; *m* 1st, 19 June 1221, Joan (*d* at York 4 March 1238; *bur* Tarrant Crawford, Dorset), el da of John, King of England; 2ndly, 15 May 1239, Marie (who *m* 2ndly, before 6 June 1257, John de Brienne, son of John de Brienne, King of Jerusalem, and was *bur* at Newbottle), 2nd da of Enguerrand III, Baron de Coucy; *d* at Kerrera 8 July 1249; *bur* Melrose Abbey; had issue (by 2nd *m*), an only son,

ALEXANDER III, King of Scots; *b* at Roxburgh 4 Sept 1241; *c* 13 July 1249; *m* 1st, 26 Dec 1251, Margaret (*d* at Cupar Castle, Fife 26 Feb 1275; *bur* Dunfermline Abbey), el da of Henry III, King of England; 2ndly, 14 Oct 1285, Yolande (who *m* 2ndly, May 1294, Arthur II, Duke of Brittany, and *d* 1323), da of Robert IV, Comte de Dreux; *k* by a fall from his horse near Kinghorn 19 March 1286; *bur* Dunfermline Abbey; had issue (by 1st *m*), 2 sons (who *dvp*) and 1 da (also *dvp*); *s* by his grand-da, the only da of his da Margaret and Eric II, King of Norway,

MARGARET, Queen of Scots, called *The Maid of Norway*; *b* in Norway before 9 April 1283; *d* at Orkney on her voyage to Scotland *ca* 26 Sept 1290; *bur* Bergen.
    The death of Queen Margaret was followed by the First Interregnum, during which thirteen competitors submitted their claims to the throne to the arbitration of King Edward I of England, who pronounced at Berwick 17 Nov 1292 in favour of John Balliol, gt-grandson of David, Earl of Huntingdon, yr brother of Kings Malcolm IV and William the Lion, who ascended the throne as,

JOHN, King of Scotland (so styled); *b* 1249; *c* 30 Nov 1292; forced to abdicate at Brechin 10 July 1296; *m* before 7 Feb 1281, Isabella, da of John de Warenne, 7th Earl of Surrey; *d* at Bailleul-en-Gouffern, Normandy April 1313; probably *bur* in Church of St Waast there; had issue, 2 sons
    The abdication of John was followed by the Second Interregnum during which King Edward I of England assumed the government and attempted to treat Scotland as a conquered country. A long struggle for independence led first by Sir William Wallace and then by Robert Bruce, Earl of Carrick, ensued until the latter finally succeeded in establishing himself as,

ROBERT I *The Bruce*, King of Scots, gt-gt-grandson of David, Earl of Huntingdon; *b* at Writtle, nr Chelmsford, Essex 11 July 1274; chosen one of the Guardians of the Kingdom at Peebles 19 Aug 1299; *c* 27 March 1306; totally defeated the English at Bannockburn 24 June 1314, thereby restoring independence; *m* 1st, *ca* 1295, Isabella, da of Donald, 6th Earl of Mar; 2ndly, 1302, Elizabeth (*d* at Cullen 26 Oct 1327; *bur* Dunfermline Abbey), da of Richard de Burgh, 2nd Earl of Ulster; *d* at Cardross, Dumbartonshire 7 June 1329; *bur* Dunfermline Abbey; had issue, (by 1st *m*) 1 da, (by 2nd *m*) 2 sons and 2 das; *s* by his only surv son,

DAVID II, King of Scots; *b* Dunfermline 5 March 1324; *c* 24 Nov 1331; absent in France 1334-41; prisoner in England 1346-57; *m* 1st, 17 July 1328, Joan, *c* with him (*d* at Hertford 7 Sept 1362; *bur* Grey Friars Church, London), yr da of Edward II, King of England; 2ndly, *ca* 20 Feb 1364 (*m diss ca* 20 March 1370), Margaret (*d* soon after 31 Jan 1375), da of Sir Malcolm Drummond, and widow of Sir John Logie of that Ilk; *dsp* at Edinburgh Castle 22 Feb 1371; *bur* Holyrood Abbey; *s* by the son of his half-sister Marjorie and her husband Walter, High Steward of Scotland,

ROBERT II, King of Scots; *b* Paisley 2 March 1316; declared by Parliament heir to the crown in default of male issue of his maternal grandfather King Robert I 3 Dec 1318; *c* 26 March 1371; *m* 1st (dispensation dated 22 Nov 1347), Elizabeth (*d* before 1355), da of Sir Adam Mure of Rowallan; 2ndly (dispensation dated 2 May 1355), Euphemia, *c* 1372 (*d* 1387), da of Hugh, 4th Earl of Ross, and widow of John Randolph, 3rd Earl of Moray; *d* at Dundonald Castle, Ayrshire 19 April 1390; *bur* Scone Abbey; had issue, (by 1st *m*) 4 sons and 5 das, (by 2nd *m*) 2 sons and 2 das; *s* by his el son,

ROBERT III, King of Scots (originally named John); *b ca* 1337 (and legitimated by the subsequent marriage of his parents); declared by Parliament heir to the crown 27 March 1371; *c* 14 Aug 1390; *m ca* 1366-67, Annabella, *c* 15 Aug 1390 (*d* at Scone autumn 1401; *bur* Dunfermline Abbey), da of Sir John Drummond of Stobhall; *d* at Dundonald Castle 4 April 1406; *bur* Paisley Abbey; had issue, 3 sons and 4 das; *s* by his yst, but only surv, son,

JAMES I, King of Scots; *b* at Dunfermline Dec 1394; prisoner in England 1406-24; *c* 21 May 1424; *m* 2 Feb 1424, Lady Joan Beaufort (who *m* 2ndly, 1439, Sir James Stewart, "the Black Knight of Lorne", and *d* at Dunbar Castle 15 July 1445; *bur* Perth), el da of John Beaufort, 1st Duke of Somerset, KG (half-brother of Henry IV, King of England); assassinated at Perth by his uncle Walter Stewart, Earl of Atholl and others 21 Feb 1437; *bur* Carthusian Church, Perth; had issue, 2 sons and 6 das; *s* by his yr (twin), but only surv, son,

JAMES II, King of Scots, called "James of the Fiery Face" from a birthmark on his cheek; *b* at Holyrood 16 Oct 1430; *c* 25 March 1437; *m* 3 July 1449, Marie, *c* the same day (*d* at Edinburgh 1 Dec 1463; *bur* Collegiate Church of the Holy Trinity, Edinburgh), only da of Arnold, Duke of Gueldres; *k* by the accidental bursting of a cannon at the siege of Roxburgh Castle 3 Aug 1460; *bur* Holyrood Abbey; had issue, 4 sons and 2 das; *s* by his el son,

JAMES III, King of Scots; *b* at St Andrews Castle May 1452 (not at Stirling 10 July 1451 as formerly believed); *c* 10 Aug 1460; *m* 13 July 1469, Margaret (*d* at Stirling 14 July 1486; *bur* Cambuskenneth Abbey), only da of Christian I, King of Denmark; murdered after the battle of Sauchieburn at Milltown, nr Bannockburn 11 June 1488; *bur* Cambuskenneth Abbey; had issue, 3 sons; *s* by his el son,

JAMES IV *of the Iron Belt*, King of Scots; *b* 17 March 1473; *c* 26 June 1488; *m* 8 Aug 1503, Margaret (who *m* 2ndly, 6 Aug 1514 (*m diss* 1527), Archibald Douglas, 6th Earl of Angus; 3rdly, 1527, Henry Stewart, 1st Lord Methven, and *d* at Methven Castle 18 Oct 1541; *bur* Perth), el da of Henry VII, King of England; *k* at the Battle of Flodden 9 Sept 1513; *bur* Shene Abbey, Surrey; had issue, 4 sons and 2 das; *s* by his 3rd, but el surv, son,

JAMES V, King of Scots; *b* at Linlithgow 10 April 1512; *c* 21 Sept 1513: *m* 1st, 1 Jan 1537, Madeleine (*d* at Holyrood 7 July 1537; *bur* Holyrood Abbey), 3rd da of Francis I, King of France; 2ndly, 12 June 1538, Marie, *c* 22 Feb 1540, Queen Regent of Scotland 1554-60 (*d* at Edinburgh

Castle 10 June 1560; *bur* Rheims Cathedral), da of Claude I de Lorraine, Duke of Guise, and widow of Louis II, Duke of Longueville; *d* at Falkland Castle 14 Dec 1542, *bur* Holyrood Abbey; had issue, (by 2nd *m*) 2 sons (who *dvp*) and 1 da; *s* by his only da,

MARY, Queen of Scots; *b* Linlithgow 7 or 8 Dec 1542; *c* 9 Sept 1543; forced to abdicate 24 July 1567; prisoner in England 1568-87; *m* 1st, 24 April 1558, Francis II, King of France (*d* at Orleans 5 Dec 1560); 2ndly, 29 July 1565, Henry Stuart, Lord Darnley, *cr* Duke of Albany, Earl of Ross and Lord Ardmannoch 15 May 1565, proclaimed King 28 July 1565 (*d* (murdered) at Kirk o Field, Edinburgh 10 Feb 1567), 2nd son of Matthew Stuart, 4th Earl of Lennox, by his wife Margaret, da of Archibald Douglas, 6th Earl of Angus and Queen Margaret, widow of King James IV; 3rdly, 15 May 1567, James Hepburn, 4th Earl of Bothwell, *cr* Duke of Orkney 12 May 1567, Great Adm of Scotland (*d* at Draxholm, Norway 14 April 1578); beheaded at Fotheringay Castle, Northants 8 Feb 1587; *bur* Peterborough Cathedral, re-bur Westminster Abbey; *s* on her abdication by her only son (by her 2nd *m*),

JAMES VI (Charles James), King of Scots, who *s* Queen Elizabeth I as King of England 1603 (see SOVEREIGNS OF ENGLAND, etc).

THE PRINCES OF WALES

(1) 1301-1307   EDWARD *OF CAERNARVON*, 4th son of King Edward I, *b* at Caernarvon Castle 25 April 1284; became heir apparent on the death of his el brother Alfonso, Earl of Chester 19 Aug 1284; had a grant of the Principality of Wales and Earldom of Chester by charter 7 Feb 1301, and was summoned to Parliament by these titles 2 June 1302-3 Nov 1306; *s* his father as King Edward II 8 July 1307, when all his honours merged in the Crown.

(2) 1343-1376   EDWARD *OF WOODSTOCK*, el son of King Edward III, *b* at Woodstock 15 June 1330; heir apparent at birth; *cr* Earl of Chester 18 May 1333 and Duke of Cornwall 17 March 1337; *cr* Prince of Wales and invested at Westminster 12 May 1343; KG 1348: *m* 10 Oct 1361, his 1st cousin once removed, Joan, *suo jure* Countess of Kent (*d* at Wallingford Castle, Berks 8 Aug 1385; *bur* Stamford, Lincs), only da of Edmund *of Woodstock*, Earl of Kent (6th and yst son of King Edward I), and widow of Thomas de Holand, 1st Earl of Kent, KG; *dvp* at Westminster 8 June 1376; *bur* Canterbury Cathedral; known to posterity, though not to his contemporaries, as "The Black Prince"; had issue, two sons.

(3) 1376-1377   RICHARD *OF BORDEAUX*, yr, but only surv, son of the preceding, *b* at Bordeaux 6 Jan 1367; became heir apparent on the death of his father and was *cr* Prince of Wales, Duke of Cornwall and Earl of Chester 20 Nov 1376; invested at Westminster 25 Dec 1376; KG 23 April 1377; *s* his grandfather as King Richard II 21 June 1377, when all his honours merged in the Crown.

(4) 1399-1413   HENRY *OF MONMOUTH*, 2nd, but el surv, son of King Henry IV, *b* at Monmouth Castle 9 Aug 1387; became heir apparent on his father's accession 29 Sept 1399; *cr* Prince of Wales, Duke of Cornwall and Earl of Chester 15 Oct 1399; *s* his father as King Henry V 20 March 1413, when all his honours merged in the Crown.

(5) 1454-1471   EDWARD *OF WESTMINSTER*, only son of King Henry VI, *b* at Westminster Palace 13 Oct 1453; became heir apparent and Duke of Cornwall at birth; *cr* Prince of Wales and Earl of Chester 15 March 1454; invested at Windsor 9 June 1454: *m* Aug 1470, Anne (who *m* 2ndly, 12 July 1472, Richard, Duke of Gloucester, later King Richard III), yr da and co-heiress of Richard Neville, 1st Earl of Warwick and 2nd Earl of Salisbury, KG; *k* after the Battle of Tewkesbury 4 May 1471, *sp* and *vp*; *bur* Tewkesbury Abbey.

(6) 1471-1483   EDWARD *OF WESTMINSTER*, el son of King Edward IV, *b* in the Sanctuary at Westminster 4 Nov 1470; became heir apparent and Duke of Cornwall at his birth; *cr* Prince of Wales and Earl of Chester 26 June 1471; invested at Westminster 17 July 1471; KG 1475; *s* his father as King Edward V on 9 April 1483, when all his honours merged in the Crown.

(7) 1483-1484   EDWARD *OF MIDDLEHAM*, only son of King Richard III, *b* at Middleham Castle, Yorkshire *ca* Dec 1473; *cr* Earl of Salisbury (by his uncle King Edward IV) 15 Feb 1478; became heir apparent and Duke of Cornwall on his father's accession 26 June 1483; *cr* Prince of Wales and Earl of Chester 24 Aug 1483; invested at York Minster 8 Sept 1483; *dvp* at Middleham Castle 9 April 1484; *bur* Sheriff Hutton, Yorkshire.

(8) 1489-1502   ARTHUR TUDOR, el son of King Henry VII, *b* at Winchester Castle 19 Sept 1486; became heir apparent and Duke of Cornwall at birth; *cr* Prince of Wales and Earl of Chester and invested at Westminster 29 Nov 1489; KG 1491: *m* 14 Nov 1501, Catherine (who *m* 2ndly, 11 June 1509, her brother-in-law, King Henry VIII), da of Ferdinand II, King of Aragon (and V as King of Castile); *dsp* and *vp* at Ludlow Castle 2 April 1502; *bur* Worcester Cathedral.

(9) 1504-1509   HENRY TUDOR, 2nd son of King Henry VII and brother of the preceding, *b* at Greenwich Palace 28 June 1491; *cr* Duke of York and KB 31 Oct 1494; KG 1495; became heir apparent and Duke of Cornwall on the death of his brother Arthur 2 April 1502; *cr* Prince of Wales and Earl of Chester and invested at Westminster 18 Feb 1504; *s* his father as King Henry VIII 21 April 1509, when all his honours merged in the Crown.

(EDWARD TUDOR, DUKE OF CORNWALL, only surv son and heir of King Henry VIII (by his 3rd wife), was often styled Prince of Wales and was about to be formally *cr* Prince of Wales and Earl of Chester when his father *d* and he *s* as King Edward VI)

(10) 1610-1612   HENRY FREDERICK STUART, el son of King James I, *b* at Stirling Castle 19 Feb 1594; became heir apparent to the Scottish throne and Duke of Rothesay, etc at birth; became heir apparent to the English throne and Duke of Cornwall on his father's accession 24 March 1603; KG 1603; *cr* Prince of Wales and Earl of Chester and invested at Westminster 4 June 1610; *d unm* and *vp* at St James's Palace 6 Nov 1612; *bur* Westminster Abbey.

(11) 1616-1625   CHARLES STUART, 2nd son of King James I and brother of the preceding, *b* at Dunfermline 19 Nov 1600; *cr* Duke of Albany, Marquess of Ormond, Earl of Ross, and Lord Ardmannoch (in the peerage of Scotland) 23 Dec 1600 (the day of his baptism); KB 1605 and KG 1611; became heir apparent and Duke of Cornwall, Duke of Rothesay, etc, on the death of his brother Henry, Prince of Wales 6 Nov 1612; *cr* Prince of Wales and Earl of Chester and invested at Whitehall 4 Nov 1616; *s* his father as King Charles I 27 March 1625, when all his honours merged in the Crown.

(CHARLES JAMES STUART, DUKE OF CORNWALL, etc, el son of King Charles I, *b* and *d* at Greenwich 13 May 1629, was *bur* at Westminster Abbey as "Charles, Prince of Wales", but was never formally so created.)

(12)   *ca* 1638-1649   CHARLES STUART, 2nd, but el surv, son of King Charles I, *b* at St James's Palace 29 May 1630; became heir apparent and Duke of Cornwall at birth; declared Prince of Wales and Earl of Chester, although never formally so created, and styled as such from *ca* 1638; *s* his father as (*de jure*) King Charles II 30 Jan 1649, when all his honours merged in the Crown.

(13)   1688-1688   JAMES FRANCIS EDWARD STUART, 6th and yst, but only surv, son of King James II (by his 2nd wife), *b* at St James's Palace 10 June 1688; became heir apparent and Duke of Cornwall at birth; styled Prince of Wales (and by implication Earl of Chester) from 4 July 1688, but was never formally so created; went into exile with his parents Dec 1688; proclaimed King James III and VIII (following the death of his father) at St Germain-en-Laye 6 Sept 1701, when any honours he may have held may be deemed to have merged in the Crown; proclaimed in Scotland as King James VIII 6 Sept 1715 and again at Perth 1745; known to posterity as "The Old Pretender" and "The Chevalier de St George": *m* 3 Sept 1719, (Maria Casimire) Clementina (*d* at Rome 18 Jan 1735; *bur* St Peter's, Rome), 5th da of Prince James Louis Sobieski (el son of John III, King of Poland); *d* at Rome 1 Jan 1766; *bur* St Peter's Rome; had issue, two sons.

(CHARLES EDWARD (LOUIS JOHN CASIMIR SILVESTER MARIA) STUART, er son and heir apparent of the preceding, *b* at Rome 31 Dec 1720; styled Prince of Wales, etc, from his birth; held by his adherents to have *s* his father as King Charles III 1 Jan 1766, when all his hypothetical honours merged in the Crown; known to posterity as "The Young Pretender": *m* 17 April 1772, Louise Maximilienne Caroline Emanuele (*d* at Florence 29 Jan 1824; *bur* Church of Santa Croce, Florence), da of Gustavus Adolphus, Prince of Stolberg-Gedern; *dsp legit* at Rome 31 Jan 1788; *bur* St Peter's Rome.)

(14)   1714-1727   GEORGE AUGUSTUS, only son of King George I, *b* at Herrenhausen 30 Oct 1683; *cr* Baron of Tewkesbury, Viscount Northallerton, Earl of Milford Haven, and Marquess and Duke of Cambridge by Queen Anne 9 Nov 1706; became heir apparent and Duke of Cornwall, etc, on his father's accession 1 Aug 1714; *cr* Prince of Wales and Earl of Chester and invested at Westminster 27 Sept 1714; *s* his father as King George II 11 June 1727, when all his honours merged in the Crown.

(15)   1729-1751   FREDERICK LEWIS, el son of King George II, *b* at Hanover 20/31 Jan 1707; *cr* Baron of Snowdon, Viscount of Launceston, Earl of Eltham, Marquess of the Isle of Ely, and Duke of Edinburgh by his grandfather King George I 26 July 1726; became heir apparent and Duke of Cornwall, etc, on his father's accession 11 June 1727; *cr* Prince of Wales and Earl of Chester 8 Jan 1729: *m* 8 May 1736, Augusta (*d* at Carlton House, London 8 Feb 1772; *bur* Westminster Abbey), 6th and yst da of Frederick II, Duke of Saxe-Gotha; *dvp* at Leicester House, London 20 March 1751; *bur* Westminster Abbey; had issue, 5 sons and 4 das.

(16)   1751-1760   GEORGE WILLIAM FREDERICK, el son of the preceding, *b* at Norfolk House, St James's Square, London 4 June 1738; KG 1749; *s* his father as Duke of Edinburgh, etc, and became heir apparent to his grandfather King George II 20 March 1751; *cr* Prince of Wales and Earl of Chester 20 April 1751; *s* his grandfather as King George III 25 Oct 1760, when all his honours merged in the Crown.

(17)   1762-1820   GEORGE AUGUSTUS FREDERICK, el son of King George III, *b* at St James's Palace 12 Aug 1762; became heir apparent and Duke of Cornwall, etc, at birth; *cr* Prince of Wales and Earl of Chester 19 Aug 1762; KG 1765; PC 1783; *s* his father as King George IV 29 Jan 1820, when all his honours merged in the Crown.

(18)   1841-1901   ALBERT EDWARD, el son of Queen Victoria, *b* at Buckingham Palace 9 Nov 1841; became heir apparent and Duke of Cornwall, etc, at birth; *cr* Prince of Wales and Earl of Chester 8 Dec 1841; *cr* Earl of Dublin 17 Jan 1850; *s* his mother as King Edward VII 22 Jan 1901, when all his honours merged in the Crown.

(19)   1901-1910   GEORGE FREDERICK ERNEST ALBERT, 2nd, but only surv, son of King Edward VII, *b* at Marlborough House, London 3 June 1865; *cr* Duke of York, Earl of Inverness, and Baron Killarney by his grandmother Queen Victoria 24 May 1892; became heir apparent and Duke of Cornwall, etc, on his father's accession 22 Jan 1901; *cr* Prince of Wales and Earl of Chester 9 Nov 1901; *s* his father as King George V 6 May 1910, when all his honours merged in the Crown.

(20)   1910-1936   EDWARD ALBERT CHRISTIAN GEORGE ANDREW PATRICK DAVID, el son of King George V, *b* at White Lodge, Richmond Park 23 June 1894; became heir apparent and Duke of Cornwall, etc, on his father's accession 6 May 1910; *cr* Prince of Wales and Earl of Chester 23 June 1910; invested at Caernarvon Castle 13 July 1911; *s* his father as King Edward VIII 20 Jan 1936, when all his honours merged in the Crown.

(21)   1958-   CHARLES PHILIP ARTHUR GEORGE, el son of Queen Elizabeth II, *b* at Buckingham Palace 14 Nov 1948; became heir apparent and Duke of Cornwall, etc, on his mother's accession 6 Feb 1952; *cr* Prince of Wales and Earl of Chester 26 July 1958; invested at Caernarvon Castle 1 July 1969.

THE PEERAGE

THE PEERAGE

The scope of EACH ARTICLE IN THE PEERAGE is designed to include information concerning every *living* male descended in the male line from the first Peer and of all *living* females being issue of males so descended. Legitimated children are included, but are not normally in remainder, except for the Peerage of Scotland.

DECEASED FEMALE COLLATERALS and their issue are not generally included.

ISSUE, where both parents are mentioned in the work, will usually be found under the father's name.

CHRISTIAN NAMES OF THE HEIR apparent or heir presumptive are given in capital letters.

CREATIONS:— E.= England (prior to 1 May 1707).
                S.= Scotland (prior to 1 May 1707).
                  I.= Ireland.
         G.B.= Great Britain (1 May 1707 to 31 Dec. 1800).
         U.K.= United Kingdom (since 1 Jan. 1801).

ABERCONWAY, BARON (McLaren) (Baron UK 1911, Bt UK 1902)

CHARLES MELVILLE MCLAREN, 3rd Baron, and 3rd Baronet; *b* 16 April 1913; *s* 1953; *ed* Eton, and New Coll, Oxford (BA); Bar Middle Temple 1937; late RA; Chm of John Brown & Co Ltd 1953-78 (Pres 1978-85), of Sheepbridge Engineering Ltd 1961-79, and English China Clays Ltd 1963-84 (since when Pres); Dir National Westminster Bank (formerly National Provincial Bank) 1953-83; Dep Chm Sun Alliance & London Insurance Co Ltd 1976-85, and Westland Aircraft 1979-85; High Sheriff for Denbighshire 1950; Pres of Roy Horticultural Soc 1961-84 (since when Pres Emeritus); Commr Gen Internat Garden Festival Liverpool 1984: *m* 1st, 1941 (*m diss* 1949), Deirdre, da of John Knewstub; 2ndly, 1949, Ann Lindsay, only da of Mrs Alexander Lindsay Aymer, of New York City, USA, and formerly wife of Maj Robert Lee Bullard III, and has issue living by 1st and 2nd marriages.

Arms – Or, two chevronels invected gules between two shepherds crooks in chief and in base a castle triple towered and with flags flying sable. **Crest** – A representation of the Virgin Mary with the dexter arm uplifted vested azure, holding in the sinister arm the child Jesus. **Supporters** – On either side a wyvern argent, wings erect gules, each supporting a banner or charged with a horse-shoe sable.
Seat – Bodnant, Tal-y-Cafn, Colwyn Bay, N Wales LL28 5RE. *Town Residence* – 25 Egerton Terrace, SW3.

I am a son of the Church

SONS LIVING *(By 1st marriage)*

Hon (HENRY) CHARLES, *b* 26 May 1948; *ed* Eton, and Sussex Univ (BA): *m* 1981, Sally Ann, yr da of late Capt Charles Nugent Lentaigne, RN, of Hawkley Place, Hawkley, Liss, Hants, and formerly wife of Philip Charles Bidwell, and has issue living, Charles Stephen, *b* 27 Dec 1984, — Emily, *b* 1982.

(By 2nd marriage)

Hon Michael Duncan (27 Phillimore Gdns, W8), *b* 1958; *ed* Eton, and Christ's Coll, Camb (MA); Barrister-at-law (Middle Temple 1981): *m* 1985, Caroline Jane, elder da of late Air Chief Marshal Sir John Stacey, KCB, CBE, of Winchester, and has issue living, Angus John Melville, *b* 1987, — Hamish, *b* 1993, — Iona, *b* 1991.

DAUGHTERS LIVING *(By 1st marriage)*

Hon Julia Harriet (c/o UPI, Rome), *b* 1942; *ed* Grenoble Univ: *m* 1969, Charles Walter Hays Ridley, MC, late Capt The Reconnaissance Corps, and has issue living, Casper Charles, *b* 1977, — Emma Jane, *b* 1970, — Harriet Deirdre, *b* 1971.
Hon Caroline Mary SARGENT (Beaulieu Hall, Hemington, Oundle, Northants) *b* 1944; *ed* Imperial Coll, London (BSc, PhD, DIC, FLS); has resumed surname of Sargent: *m* 1st, 1962, Raimund Guernsey Sargent, of Massachusetts, USA; 2ndly, 1978, Graham Charles Steele, BSc, PhD, and has issue living (by 1st *m*), Dominic Fitzwilliam, *b* 1963; *ed* Blundell's Sch, and Trin Coll, Camb (organ scholar), — Orlando Gorham, *b* 1964; *ed* Blundell's Sch, and Sussex Univ.

BROTHER LIVING

Hon Christopher Melville (31 Upper Addison Gdns, W14 8AJ; *Club* – Boodle's), *b* 1934; *ed* Eton, and King's Coll, Camb (MA); Bar Inner Temple 1961; Chm of Govs and Chancellor South Bank Univ since 1992 (previously Chm of Govs South Bank Polytechnic): *m* 1973, Jane Elizabeth, da of James Barrie, and has issue living, Robert Melville, *b* 1974, — Lara Jane Christabel, *b* 1976.

SISTER LIVING

(Hon) Anne Laura Dorinthea McLAREN, DBE, *b* 1927; *ed* Lady Margaret Hall, Oxford (MA, DPhil); FRS 1975, FRCOG 1986; does not use courtesy title, or the style of Dame; Vice-Pres and Foreign Sec Royal Soc since 1992, Prin Research Associate Wellcome/Cancer Research Campaign Inst, and Research Fellow King's Coll, Camb since 1992, Pres British Assocn for the Advancement of Science 1993-94; *cr* DBE 1993: *m* 1952 (*m diss* 1959), Donald Michie, DPhil and has issue living, Jonathan Mark (19 Porson Rd, Cambridge CB2 9BD), *b* 1957: *m* 1st, 19— (*m diss* 19—), Ann Logan; 2ndly, 19—, Carolyn Downs, and has issue living, — Susan Fiona Dorinthea, *b* 1955: *m* 1981, Andrew Philip Drummond-Murray, and has issue (*see* B Rankeillour), — Caroline Ruth, *b* 1959. *Residence* – Flat 1, 40 Ainger Rd, Primrose Hill, NW3 3AT.

WIDOW LIVING OF SON OF SECOND BARON

Lady Rose Mary Primrose Paget, da of 6th Marquess of Anglesey: *m* 1940, S/Ldr *Hon* John Francis McLaren, RAF, who *d* 1953, and has issue living (*see* colls, infra). *Residence* – Old Bodnod, Eglwysbach, Colwyn Bay N Wales LL28 5RF.

COLLATERAL BRANCHES LIVING

Issue of late S/Ldr *Hon* John Francis McLaren, RAF, 2nd son of 2nd Baron, *b* 1919, *d* 1953: *m* 1940, Lady Rose Mary Primrose Paget (ante) da of 6th Marquess of Anglesey:—
Victoria Mary Caroline, *b* 1945: *m* 1966, Jonathan Jeremy Kirwan Taylor, of 42 Addison Rd, W14, yst son of Sir Charles Stuart Taylor, TD, DL, and has issue living, Arabella Lucy Kirwan, *b* 1969, — Lucinda Sophia Kirwan, *b* 1972, — Caroline Samantha Kirwan, *b* 1976, — Katharine Polly Kirwan, *b* 1979. —— Harriet Diana Christabel, *b* 1949: *m* 1972, Hugh John Reay Geddes, of 20 Gatcombe Rd, N19 (*see* B Geddes).

Grandchildren of *Hon* Francis Walter Stafford McLaren, yr son of 1st Baron —
Issue of late Maj Martin John McLaren, *b* 1914, *d* 1979, Gren Gds, Bar Middle Temple, MP for NW Div of Bristol (*C*) 1959-66, and 1970-74: *m* 1943, Nancy (Inkpen, Newbury, Berks; 30 Smith Sq, SW1), da of late Gordon Ralston, and of late Mrs Philip Cator:—
Richard Francis, *b* 1946; *ed* Eton, and Mansfield Coll, Oxford. —— †Francis Andrew, *b* 1949: *d* as the result of an accident 1960. —— †Patrick Andrew, *b* 1963; *ed* Eton, and Harvard Univ; *d* 1991.
Issue of late Guy Lewis Ian McLaren, *b* 1915, *d* 1978: *m* 1946, Maryse, who *d* 1987, da of late Alfred Jubin, of Lausanne, Switzerland:—
Michael (1 bis Rue du Printemps, 78 230 Le Pecq, France), *b* 1947; *ed* Eton, and St Andrew's Univ. —— Mary Caroline, *b* 1951: *m* 1971, Nicholas John Durlacher, of Archendines, Chapel Rd, Fordham, Colchester, Essex, and has issue living, David Michael, *b* 1976.

PREDECESSORS

PREDECESSORS – **(1)** *Rt Hon* CHARLES BENJAMIN BRIGHT McLaren, KC, 3rd son of late Duncan McLaren, of Newington House, Edinburgh (sometime MP for and Lord Provost of Edinburgh); *b* 1850; MP for Stafford (*L*) 1880-86, and for W, or Bosworth, Div of Leicestershire 1892-1910; *cr* a *Baronet* 1902, PC 1908, and *Baron Aberconway*, of Bodnant, co Denbigh (peerage of United Kingdom) 1911: *m* 1877, Laura, CBE, who *d* 1933, da of late Henry Davis Pochin, of Bodnant, Denbighshire; *d* 1934; *s* by his el son **(2)** HENRY DUNCAN, CBE, 2nd Baron; *b* 1879; was Parliamentary Private Sec to Pres of Board of Trade (Rt Hon D Lloyd George, MP) 1906-08, and Parliamentary Private Sec to Chancellor of the Exchequer (Rt Hon D Lloyd George, MP) 1908-10; sat as MP for Staffordshire, W Div (*L*) 1906-10, for Leicestershire, W, or Bosworth, Div 1910-18, and Bosworth Div 1918-22; Pres of Roy Horticultural Society 1931-53: *m* 1910, Christabel Mary Melville, who *d* 1974, da of late Sir Melville Leslie Macnaghten, CB (*see* Macnaghten, Bt, colls, 1972/73 Edn); *d* 1953; *s* by his eldest son **(3)** CHARLES MELVILLE, 3rd Baron and present peer.

ABERCORN, DUKE OF (Hamilton) Sits as MARQUESS OF ABERCORN (GB 1790) (Duke I 1868, Bt I 1660)

SOLA·NOBILITAS·VIRTUS

Virtue is the only nobility

JAMES HAMILTON, 5th Duke, and 15th Baronet; *b* 4 July 1934; *s* 1979; *ed* Eton, and RAC Cirencester; late Lt Gren Gds; MP for Fermanagh and S Tyrone (UU) 1964-70; DL co Tyrone (High Sheriff 1970), and Lord Lieut since 1987; Pres Building Societies Assocn since 1986: *m* 1966, Alexandra Anastasia, eldest da of late Lt-Col Harold Pedro Joseph Phillips, FRGS, Coldstream Gds (*see* Wernher, Bt, ext), and has issue.

Arms – Quarterly: 1st and 4th gules, three cinquefoils pierced ermine, *Hamilton;* 2nd and 3rd argent, an ancient ship or lymphad, with one mast, the sail furled and oars out sable, *Arran.* (Also claims, — over all an escutcheon azure, charged with three fleurs-de-lis or, surmounted by a French ducal coronet, *Chatelherault.*) **Crest** – Out of a ducal coronet or, an oak tree proper, fructed and penetrated through the stem transversely by a frame-saw proper, frame gold, the blade inscribed with the word "Through." **Supporters** – Two antelopes argent, horned, unguled, ducally gorged, hoofed, and the chains reflexed over their backs or.

Seat – Barons Court, Omagh, co Tyrone. *Town Residence* – 10 Little Chester St, SW1.

SONS LIVING

JAMES HAROLD CHARLES (*Marquess of Hamilton*), *b* 19 Aug 1969; a Page of Honour to HM The Queen 1982-84.
Lord Nicholas Edward Claud, *b* 1979.

DAUGHTER LIVING

Lady Sophia Alexandra, *b* 1973.

BROTHER LIVING

Lord (Claud) Anthony, *b* 1939; *ed* Eton; Lieut IG; DL co Fermanagh 1978, High Sheriff 1990, JP 1991: *m* 1982, Catherine Janet, eldest da of Dennis Faulkner, CBE, of Ringhaddy House, Killinchy, co Down, and has issue living, Alexander James, *b* 1987, — Anna Kathleen, *b* 1983. *Residence* – Killyreagh, Tamlaght, Enniskillen, co Fermanagh.

SISTER LIVING

Lady Moyra Kathleen, CVO, *b* 1930; a Maid of Honour to HM The Queen at Coronation 1953; appointed Lady-in-Waiting (temporary) to HRH Princess Alexandra of Kent 1954-64, a Lady-in-Waiting 1964-66 and an Extra Lady-in-Waiting 1966-69; CVO 1963: *m* 1966, Cdr Peter Colin Drummond Campbell, LVO, RN, of Hollybrook House, Randalstown, co Antrim, son of late Maj-Gen Sir (Alexander) Douglas Campbell, KBE, CB, DSO, MC, and has issue living, Rory Gerald Peter, *b* 1967, — Michael James Douglas, *b* 1970.

COLLATERAL BRANCHES LIVING

Granddaughter of late Rt Hon Lord George Francis Hamilton, GCSI, 3rd son of 1st Duke:—
Issue of late Ronald James Hamilton, OBE, *b* 1872, *d* 1958: *m* 1915, Florence Marguerite (the actress, Sarah Brooke), who *d* 1959, only da of late Major J Hanna:—
Maud Sarah, *b* 1917: *m* 1939 (*m diss* 1947), (Count) Manfred Maria Edmund Ralph Beckett Czernin, DSO, MC, DFC, Squadron Leader RAF, who *d* 1962, (*see* B Grimthorpe, 1962 Edn), and has issue living, (Manfred) Nicholas, *b* 1942; *ed* Harrow: *m* 1st, 1970 (*m diss* 1982), Danielle Alligier; 2ndly, 1987, Orapin Champanich, of Bangkok, and has issue living (by 1st wife), Nicholas *b* 1963, Sarah Moon *b* 1970, (by 2nd wife) Pawau Beckett *b* 1989, — Carolyn Lucile, *b* 1941: *m* 1966, Charles Norman George Peploe, of 54 Liberton Brae, Edinburgh EH16 6TF, and has issue living, Manfred Crispin David *b* 1969, Fergus Charles Nicolas *b* 1970. *Residence* – 50 Hartismere Rd, SW6.

(Not in remainder to the Dukedom)

Grandchildren of late Col Douglas James PROBY, who assumed by Royal Licence 1904, the surname of Proby in lieu of his patronymic, only son of Rt Hon Lord Claud Hamilton, MP, brother of 1st Duke:—
See Proby, Bt.

Descendants of late John Hamilton (son of late John Hamilton, son of late William Hamilton, brother of 6th Earl of Abercorn), who was cr *a Baronet* 1776:—
See Hamilton, Bt, cr 1776.

PREDECESSORS – (1) CLAUD Hamilton, *b* 1543, 4th son of James, 1st Duke of Chatelherault in kingdom of France, and 2nd Earl of Arran, in peerage of Scotland, was cr *Lord Paisley* 1578; *d* 1621; his son JAMES, cr *Lord Abercorn* (peerage of Scotland) 1603, and *Earl of Abercorn,* and *Lord Paisley, Hamilton, Mountcastell,* and *Kilpatrick* (peerage of Scotland) 1606; *d* March 1617, leaving with other issue (2) JAMES, 2nd Earl, and CLAUD, cr *Baron of Strabane* (peerage of Ireland) 1634, an honour that had been conferred in 1617 upon the 2nd Earl who, however, petitioned King Charles I to transfer the dignity to his next brother; JAMES was *s* by his 3rd son (3) GEORGE, 3rd Earl, who *d unm,* when the earldom devolved upon (4) CLAUD, PC, 4th Earl, who had previously *s* as 4th Baron Strabane; in 1691 he was outlawed and the estates and Barony of Strabane were forfeited; he was *s* in the Earldom by his brother (5) CHARLES, 5th Earl, who obtained a reversal of the attainder and restoration of the estates; *dsp* 1701, when the honours devolved upon (6) JAMES, 6th Earl, grandson of Hon Sir George Hamilton (cr a *Baronet* 1660), 4th son of 1st Earl; cr *Baron Mountcastle* and *Viscount Strabane* (peerage of Ireland) 1701; *d* 1734; *s* by his eldest son (7) JAMES, PC, FRS, 7th Earl; *d* 1744; *s* by his eldest son (8) JAMES, 8th Earl, cr *Viscount Hamilton* (peerage of Great Britain) 1785, with remainder to the son of his next brother John; *d unm* 1789: *s* by his nephew (9) JOHN JAMES, KG, 9th Earl, cr *Marquess of Abercorn* (peerage of Great Britain) 1790; *d* 1818; *s* by his grandson (10) JAMES KG, PC, DCL, LLD, 2nd Marquess; *b* 1811; was Groom of the Stole to late Prince Consort 1846-59, Viceroy of Ireland 1866-8 and 1874-6 Envoy Extraor upon a special mission to King of Italy 1878, Lord-Lieut of Donegal, Grand Master of Masonic Order in Ireland, Lieut-Gen of Royal Co of Archers, and Chancellor of Royal Univ of Ireland; in 1864 established his claim to the French Dukedom of Chatelherault (cr 1548), and assumed the title of *Duke of Châtelherault* which had been abeyant since 1651, and his right was not contested before the French tribunals, but Napoleon III granted a new creation of the same title to the 12th Duke of Hamilton; cr *Marquess of Hamilton* and *Duke of Abercorn* (peerage of Ireland) 1868: *m* 1832, Lady Louisa Jane Russell, VA, who *d* 1905, da of 6th Duke of Bedford; *d* 31 Oct 1885; *s* by his son **(11)** JAMES, KG, PC, CB, 2nd Duke; *b* 1838; a Lord of the Bedchamber to the Prince of Wales 1866-86, Groom of the Stole 1886-1910, and Lieut of co Donegal; MP for co Donegal (*C*) 1860-80; acted as High Constable of Ireland at Coronation of King George V 1911: *m* 1869, Lady Mary Anna Curzon, who *d* 1929, da of 1st Earl Howe; *d* 1913; *s* by his eldest son **(12)** JAMES ALBERT EDWARD, KG, KP, 3rd Duke; *b* 1869; was MP for Londonderry City (*C*) 1900-13, Treasurer of the Household 1903-5, and first Gov of N Ireland 1922-45; appointed a PC (Great Britain) 1945, and (N Ireland) 1946; bore Canopy at Coronation of King George VI: *m* 1894, Lady Rosalind Cecilia Caroline Bingham, DBE, LLD, who *d* 1958, da of 4th Earl of Lucan; *d* 1953; *s* by his eldest son **(13)** JAMES EDWARD, 4th Duke; *b* 1904; a Senator of N Ireland 1949-62; Lord-Lieut for co Tyrone 1950-79 and High Sheriff 1946; Co Councillor for Tyrone 1946-79; Chancellor of New Univ of Ulster 1970-70: *m* 1928, Lady Mary Kathleen Crichton, GCVO, who *d* 1990, sister of 5th Earl of Erne; *d* 1979; *s* by eldest son **(14)** JAMES, 5th Duke and present peer; also Marquess of Hamilton, Viscount Strabane, Baron of Strabane, Baron of Mountcastle, Marquess of Abercorn, Earl of Abercorn, Viscount Hamilton, Lord Paisley, Lord Abercorn, and Lord Paisley, Hamilton, Mountcastell, and Kilpatrick.

ABERDARE, BARON (Bruce) (Baron UK 1873)

MORYS GEORGE LYNDHURST BRUCE, KBE, PC, 4th Baron; *b* 16 June 1919; *s* 1957; *ed* Winchester, and New Coll, Oxford; Hon LLD (Wales); DL Dyfed 1985; late Major Welsh Gds; J. Arthur Rank Organisation 1947-49, BBC 1949-56, Min of State, Health and Social Security 1970-74, and Min without Portfolio 1974; Chm of Cttees, House of Lords 1976-92; Chm The Football Trust, Metlife (UK) Ltd, and Albany Life Assurance Co Ltd; Pres Nat Council of YMCAs of Wales, Kidney Research Unit for Wales Foundation, Tennis and Rackets Assocn, The Queen's Club; *cr* PC 1974, and KBE (Civil) 1984; Prior for Wales, OStJ 1958-88; GCStJ: *m* 1946, Maud Helen Sarah, only da of Sir John Lindsay Dashwood, 10th Bt (*cr* 1707), and has issue.

Arms – Or, a saltire gules, on a chief of the last a martlet of the field. **Crest** – A cubit arm in armour in bend, the hand holding a sceptre in bend sinister proper. **Supporters** – *Dexter*, a lion argent collared or, pendant therefrom an escutcheon of the arms of *Knight*, viz, paly of six argent and azure, on a canton of the last a spur rowel downwards leathered or; *sinister*, a lion azure, collared or, pendant therefrom an escutcheon charged with the arms.
Residence – 32 Elthiron Rd, SW5 4BW. *Clubs* – All England, Queen's, MCC.

SONS LIVING

Hon ALASTAIR JOHN LYNDHURST, *b* 2 May 1947; *ed* Eton, and Ch Ch Oxford: *m* 1971, Elizabeth Mary Culbert, da of John Foulkes, and has issue living, Hector Morys Napier, *b* 1974, — Sarah Katherine Mary, *b* 1976. *Residence* – 16 Beverley Rd, SW13 0LX.

Hon James Henry Morys, *b* 1948; *ed* Eton: *m* 1st, 1977, Grace, da of late Allen Jao Wu; 2ndly. 1991, Lucinda J., only da of Richard Temple West, and has issue living (by 1st *m*), Antonia Katherine Sarah, *b* 1979, — (by 2nd *m*) Robert Algernon Copley, *b* 1994, — Augusta Jane Sophia, *b* 1992.

Hon (Henry) Adam Francis, *b* 1962; *ed* Eton, and Trin Coll, Oxford: *m* 1992, Victoria Gillian, yr da of Maj Ivor Basil Ramsden, MBE, of Cosheston Hall, Pembroke (*see* V St Davids, colls, 1976 Edn).

Hon Charles Benjamin, *b* 1965; *ed* Eton: *m* 1990, Anna, da of late Bo Brannerydh, of Gävle, Sweden.

BROTHER LIVING

Hon Nigel Henry Clarence (Maitland Lodge, 21 The Causeway, Edinburgh EH15 3QA; Lansdowne Club), *b* 1921; *ed* Winchester, and New Coll, Oxford (MA); MSc, Dip SS; late Capt Welsh Gds and HM Diplomatic Service: *m* 1964, Catherine Marion, da of late Thomas Wolfe, and has issue living, Thomas, *b* 1965, — Sarah, *b* 1967.

SISTERS LIVING

Hon Rosalind Louise Balfour, *b* 1923; was in WRNS: *m* 1956, Benjamin Coote Heywood, and has issue living, Annabel Jane Louise, *b* 1958, — Olivia Sarah Rosalind, *b* 1961. *Residence* – 1 Elm Park Rd, SW3 6BD.

Hon Gwyneth Margaret, *b* 1928: *m* 1952, Robert McCheyne Andrew, of Hams Barton, Chudleigh, Newton Abbot TQ13 0DL, and has had issue, Robert Hugh Clarence, *b* 1954, — Caroline Margaret, *b* 1956, — Jennifer Anne Louise, *b* 1960; *d* 1984.

WIDOW LIVING OF SON OF SECOND BARON

Margaret Charlotte, da of Ernest Alfred Beechey, of The Old Vicarage, Hilgay, nr Downham Market, Norfolk: *m* 1941, as his 2nd wife, Hon Victor Austin Bruce, 4th son of 2nd Baron, who *d* 1978, and has issue (*see* colls infra). *Residence* – Cranmore, 1 Frog Grove Lane, Woodstreet Village, Guildford, Surrey.

COLLATERAL BRANCHES LIVING

Issue of late Hon John Hamilton Bruce, CBE, 3rd son of 2nd Baron, *b* 1889, *d* 1964: *m* 1923, Cynthia Juliet Grant Duff, who *d* 1977, da of late Julian Grant Duff Ainslie (who assumed the surname of Grant Duff) (*see* V Molesworth, colls, 1925 Edn):—

David Hamilton Grant Duff (Anker Far East, Dongwon Bldg Rm 603, 128-27 Dangjoo-Dong, Jongro-Gu, Seoul, Korea), *b* 1933; *ed* Winchester, and New Coll, Oxford; late Coldstream Gds: *m* 1960 (*m diss* 1965), Diana Rosemary, da of Douglas Sinclair Miller. —— Daphne Juliet, *b* 1928: *m* 1953, Baron Carlo Giuseppe Ando, and has issue living, Alexander Francis Carlo *b* 1955: *m* 1982, Lorenya Raponi, and has issue living, Edward Carlo George *b* 1986, Victoria Emanuela Eleanora *b* 1988, — Roderic David Clarence, *b* 1960. *Residences* – Corso Vittorio Emanuele II 252, Rome; Flat 3, 33 Caledonia Place, Clifton, Bristol.

Issue of late Hon Victor Austin Bruce, 4th son of 2nd Baron, *b* 1897, *d* 1978: *m* 1st, 1926 (*m diss* 1941), Mildred Mary, the aviatrix, racing driver, and speed-boat pilot, who *d* 1990, da of late Lawrence Joseph Petre (*see* B Petre, colls, 1990 Edn); 2ndly, 1941, Margaret Charlotte (ante), da of Ernest Alfred Beechey, of The Old Vicarage, Hilgay, nr Downham Market, Norfolk:—

(By 2nd *m*) Colin Michael Lyndhurst, *b* 1944. —— Margaret Jill, *b* 1943: *m* 1970, Thomas Richardson Hope, of Browes Close, Mickleton, nr Barnard Castle, co Durham, and has issue living, Christopher Victor John, *b* 1977, — Louise Margaret, *b* 1971, — Karen Anne, *b* 1972. —— Wendy Elizabeth, *b* 1948: *m* 1966, Richard Keith Grimmond, Inholms Farm, Woodstreet Green, Guildford, Surrey, and has issue living, Michael Richard, *b* 1971, — David Matthew, *b* 1984, — Nicola Jane, *b* 1966, — Caroline Anne, *b* 1967.

PREDECESSORS – (1) HENRY AUSTIN Bruce, GCB, PC, DCL, 2nd son of late John Bruce Pryce, of Duffryn, Glamorgan; *b* 1815; MP for Merthyr Tydfil (*L*) 1852-68, and Renfrewshire 1869-73; was Under-Sec for Home Depart 1862-4, Vice-Pres Education Board 1864-6, Second Church Estates Commr 1865-6, Sec of State for Home Depart 1868-73, and Lord Pres. of Council 1873-4; cr *Baron Aberdare*, of Duffryn, co Glamorgan (peerage of United Kingdom) 1873: *m* 1st, 1846, Annabella, who *d* 1852, da of late Richard Beadon, of Clifton; 2ndly, 1854, Norah Creina Blanche, who *d* 1897, da of late Gen Sir William Francis Patrick Napier, KCB; *d* 1895; *s* by his eldest son (2) HENRY CAMPBELL, 2nd Baron, *b* 1851; Vice-Lieut for Glamorgan: *m* 1880, Constance Mary, who *d* 1932, only da of late Hamilton Beckett; *d* 1929; *s* by his son (3) CLARENCE NAPIER, GBE, 3rd Baron; *b* 1885; Hon LLD Wales 1953; Bar Inner Temple 1911; Hon. Col 282nd (Welsh) Regt RA (TA) 1930-52; Chm of National Fitness Council 1937-9, and Pres of National Children's Playground Asso 1942-52; Prior of Priory for Wales of Order of St John of Jerusalem, Chm of National Asso of Boys' Clubs, and of Queen's Institute of Dist Nursing: *m* 1st, 1912, Margaret Bethune, who *d* 1950, da of Adam Black; 2ndly, 1957, Griselda Harriet Violet Finetta Georgiana, who *d* 1980, da of late Dudley Francis Amelius Hervey, CMG (*see* M Bristol, colls); *d* 1957; *s* by his eldest son (4) MORYS GEORGE LYNDHURST, 4th Baron and present peer.

ABERDEEN AND TEMAIR, MARQUESS OF (Gordon) (Marquess UK 1916 Earl S 1682, Bt S 1642)

Let fortune follow

ALASTAIR NINIAN JOHN GORDON, 6th Marquess, 12th Earl, and 14th Baronet; *b* 20 July 1920; *s* 1984; *ed* Harrow; a Member of British Section, Assocn Internationale des Critiques d'Art; Memb Bach Choir 1939-82; Chm Arts Club 1966-76; 1939-45 War as Capt Scots Gds: *m* 1950, Anne, da of late Lt-Col Gerald Barry, MC (*see* Barry, Bt, colls), and has issue.

Arms – Azure, three boars' heads couped or armed proper and langued gules within a double tressure flowered and counter-flowered interchangeably with thistles, roses, and fleurs-de-lys of the second. **Crest** – Two arms holding a bow and arrow straight upwards in a shooting posture and at full draught all proper. **Supporters** – *Dexter*, an Earl, and *sinister*, a Doctor of Laws, both habited in their robes proper. *Residence* – Quicks Green, Ashampstead, Berks RG8 8SN. *Clubs* – Arts, Puffins, and MCC

SON LIVING

ALEXANDER GEORGE (*Earl of Haddo*) (The Estate Office, Haddo House, Aberdeen; 22 Beauclerc Rd, W6 0NS), *b* 31 March 1955; *ed* Harrow: *m* 1981, Joanna Clodagh, da of late Maj Ian George Henry Houldsworth, TD (*see* E Morton, colls, 1963 Edn), and has issue:—

SONS LIVING — George Ian Alastair (*Viscount Formartine*), *b* 4 May 1983, — *Hon* Sam Dudley, *b* 1985, — *Hon* Charles David, *b* 1990.
DAUGHTER LIVING — *Lady* Anna Katharine, *b* 1988.

DAUGHTERS LIVING

Lady Emma Cecile, *b* 1953: *m* 1980, Dr Rodney Foale, eldest son of Maurice Spencer Foale, of Melbourne, Australia, and has issue living, Archie Alexander, *b* 1984, — Jamie, *b* 1986.
Lady Sophia Catherine, *b* 1960.

SISTER LIVING

Lady Jessamine Cecile Marjorie, *b* 1910: *m* 1937, (Stanley George) Michael St John Harmsworth, who *d* 1981, and has issue living, Andrew Vyvyan Michael Istvan St John (Revayah, Wester Quarff, Shetland), *b* 1939; late Capt 1st Queen's Own Highlanders: *m* 1967, Sarah Katherine Susan, eldest da of Col William Innes Moberly, CBE, RA, of Blackford, Yeovil, Somerset, and has issue living, Alasdair William Michael Gordon *b* 1971, Richard Andrew *b* 1981, Gideon David *b* 1985, Laura Jessamine *b* 1969, — Peter Michael Patrick John, *b* 1952, — Marigold Ishbel Geraldine Mary Jessamine, *b* 1940: *m* 1963, Rev (Victor) Francis Pym, of Bolney House, Bolney, Haywards Heath, W Sussex, and has issue living, Alexander Michael Francis *b* 1970, John Andrew Dudley *b* 1971, Rebekah Mary Jane *b* 1975, Victoria Naomi Jessamine *b* 1978, — Caroline Sophia, *b* 1946: *m* 1978, Petros Demetriades, of Tompazi 75, Nicosia, Cyprus, and has issue living, Anastasia Marjorie *b* 1980, Cecilia Laura *b* 1982, Myria Ishbel *b* 1986, Jessia Demetra Penelope *b* 1988, — Angela Mary Cecile, *b* 1949: *m* 1970, Donald Sinclair of Thrumster, of Thrumster Mains, Caithness, and has issue living, Peter Donald *b* 1973, Michael Douglas William *b* 1978, John *b* 1979, William *b* 1984, Fiona Gwendolen Isobel *b* 1970, — Islay Jane Winifred, *b* 1951: *m* 1976, Ruairidh

MacLeod, and has issue living, Andrew b 1978, Hamish b 1981, Catherine Mary b 1977, Elizabeth b 1979, Fiona Jane b 1987. *Residence* – Thrumster House, Caithness.

ADOPTED CHILDREN OF FOURTH MARQUESS

Andrew David, b 1950; ed Harrow: m 1982, Lucy Mary Frances, eldest da of Canon William John Milligan, of 29 Stirling Rd, SW9 9EF, and has issue living, William David, b 1988, — Rosie Kate Jessamine, b 1986, — Rachel Mary Ishbel, b 1991. *Residence* – Laverockbrae, Oldmeldrum, Aberdeenshire AB51 0DA.
James Drummond, b 1953; ed Harrow: m 1985, Marilyn, yr da of A. F. Sim, of Sompting, Lancing, Sussex. *Residence* – Drummond House, 62 Manor Rd, Worthing, Sussex.
Mary Katharine, b 1946: m 1968, Simon Piers Welfare, 2nd son of late Kenneth William Welfare, of The Old Doctor's House, Stradbroke, Suffolk, and has issue living, Toby William David, b 1973, — Hannah Mary, b 1969, — Alice Emily Ishbel, b 1971. *Residence* – Den of Keithfield, Tarves, Ellon, Aberdeenshire.
Sarah Caroline, b 1948: m 1st, 1969 (m diss 19—), Patrick John Raleigh Scott, elder son of late R. S. G. Scott, of The Hermitage, Peasmarsh, Sussex; 2ndly, 1993, Eric Norman Money, only son of G. E. Money, of N Mimms, Herts, and has issue living (by 1st m), Edward Gilbert Raleigh, b 1971, — Oliver Dickon Robert, b 1972, — Simon Gordon Thomas, b 1977, — Sasha Adam Quintus, b 1979, — Jody Timothy Fingal, b 1981, — Georgiana Morag June, b 1974. *Residence* – Scot's Float, Star Lock, Playden, nr Rye, Sussex.

WIDOW LIVING OF FOURTH MARQUESS

BEATRICE MARY JUNE, CBE (*June, Marchioness of Aberdeen and Temair*) (Haddo House, Aberdeen); Hon LLD Aberdeen, DStJ, FRCM, FRSE, DL of Aberdeenshire, CBE (Civil) 1989, da of late Arthur Paul Boissier, of Moretons, Harrow-on-Hill: m 1939, the 4th Marquess, who d 1974.

COLLATERAL BRANCHES LIVING

(In remainder to Earldom of Aberdeen)

Grandson of late Gen Hon Sir Alexander Hamilton Gordon, KCB, 2nd son of 4th Earl:—
Issue of late Lt-Gen Sir Alexander Hamilton Gordon, KCB, b 1859, d 1939: m 1888, Isabel, who d 1947, da of Maj-Gen George Newmarch, RE:—
Alan Herschel (Caixa Postal 499, Porto Allegre, Brazil), b 1898; ed Winchester; formerly Lieut RFA; entered Diplo Ser 1921; HM's Consul at Porto Alegre, Brazil, 1948-56; sometime Major and a GSO (Joint Intelligence Staff) War Cabinet Office: m 1933, Deenya Kovachevska, of Sofia, Bulgaria.

Grandchildren of late Caroline Augusta Gordon (who m 1885, Arthur John Lewis Gordon of Ellon, CMG, grandson of Alexander Gordon of Ellon, nat son of 3rd Earl of Aberdeen and Penelope Dering), 2nd da of late Gen Hon Sir Alexander Hamilton Gordon, KCB (ante):—
Issue of late Cosmo Alexander Gordon of Ellon, b 1886, d 1965: m 1914, Frances Gertrude, who d 1963, da of late Robert Chellas Graham of Skipness, Argyll:—
Arthur Hugh, b 1916; ed St Paul's, and Trin Coll, Camb: m 1941, Helen Bright, da of Arthur Bevington Gillett, and has issue living, Richard Ian Robert, b 1951, — Alexander William, b 1954: m 1977, Julia Hood, and has issue living, Naomi Tuesday b 1978, Charlotte Helen b 1979, — Jenepher, b 1944, — Margaret Penelope, b 1946. —— Albinia Susan Roope, b 1918: m 1941, Prof Philip George Houthem Gell, FRS, of Wychwood, Cranes Lane, Kingston, Cambridge, CB3 7NJ, and has issue living, Antony Francis, b 1945; ed Camb Univ (BA) and LSE (PhD): m 1974, Simeran Man Singh, — Teresa Elizabeth, b 1943: m 1964, John Hopkins, BA, and has issue living, Paul Cosmo b 1966, Matthew Philip b 1968, Simon Anthony b 1970, Janet Michelle b 1972. —— Joanna (33 Russell Court, Cambridge CB2 1HW), b 1923.

Descendants of late William Gordon (2nd son of late Hon Alexander Gordon, 4th son of 2nd Earl), who s his maternal uncle, Sir James Duff, 1st Bt, 1815, and assumed the additional surname of Duff.
See Duff-Gordon, Bt.

PREDECESSORS – (1) Sir GEORGE Gordon, of Haddo, 3rd *Baronet* of Nova Scotia (cr 1642), successively a Senator of the College of Justice, Pres of Court of Session, and Lord High Chancellor of Scotland, was cr *Lord Haddo, Methlic, Tarves*, and *Kellie, Viscount Formartine*, and *Earl of Aberdeen* (peerage of Scotland) 1682; d 1720; s by his only surviving son (2) WILLIAM, 2nd Earl, a Representative Peer for Scotland; d 1745; s by his eldest son (3) GEORGE, 3rd Earl, a Representative Peer for Scotland; d 1801; s by his grandson (4) GEORGE, KG, KT, PC, FRS, 4th Earl, eldest son of George, Lord Haddo; b 1784; was Lord-Lieut of Aberdeenshire, and a distinguished statesman who filled various high diplomatic and ministerial offices, and was First Lord of the Treasury and Prime Minister 1852-5; cr *Viscount Gordon* (peerage of United Kingdom) 1814; assumed by R licence 1818, the additional surname, arms, and supporters of Hamilton; d 1860; s by his eldest son (5) GEORGE JOHN JAMES, 5th Earl, b 1816; m 1840, Mary, who d 1900, da of late George Baillie, and sister of 10th Earl of Haddington; d 1864; s by his eldest son (6) GEORGE, 6th Earl, b 1841; having pursued a life of romantic adventure was accidentally drowned on 27 Jan 1870, off the coast of America when serving on board the *Hera*; s by his brother (7) Rt Hon JOHN CAMPBELL, KT, GCMG, GCVO, 7th Earl, b 1847; Lord-Lieut of Aberdeenshire 1880-1934, Lord High Commr to General Assembly of Church of Scotland 1881-5, and again 1915, Lord Lieut of Ireland, Jan to July 1886; Gov-Gen of Canada 1893-8, and again Lord-Lieut of Ireland 1905-15; cr *Earl of Haddo*, in co of Aberdeen, and *Marquess of Aberdeen and Temair*, in co of Aberdeen, in co of Meath, and in co of Argyll (peerage of United Kingdom) 1916: m 1877, Hon Ishbel Maria Marjoribanks, GBE, LLD, who d 1939, da of 1st Baron Tweedmouth; d 1934; s by his el son (8) GEORGE, OBE, 2nd Marquess, b 1879; Lord Lieut of Aberdeenshire 1934-59 m 1st, 1906, Mary Florence, who d 1937, da of late Joseph Clixby, of Owmby Cliff, Lincs, and widow of Edward Shepherd Cockayne, of Sheffield; 2ndly, 1940, Sheila, who d 1949 da of late Lt-Col John Foster Forbes, JP, DL, of Rothiemay Castle, Banffshire, and widow of Capt James William Guy Innes, CBE, DL, JP, RN (Innes, Bt colls); d 1965; s by his brother (9) DUDLEY GLADSTONE, DSO, 3rd Marquess, b 1883; Lt-Col Comdg 8th/10th and 5th Bns Gordon Highlanders: m 1st, 1907, Cecile Elizabeth, who d 1948, da of late George James Drummond (E Perth, colls) 2ndly, 1949, Margaret Gladys, ARRC, JP, who d 1990, only da of late Lt-Col Reginald George Munn, CMG; d 1972; s by his eldest son (10) DAVID GEORGE IAN ALEXANDER, CBE, TD, 4th Marquess, b 1908; Lord-Lieut for Aberdeenshire 1973-74; Prior of Order of St John of Jerusalem and KStJ: m 1939, Beatrice Mary June, MBE, da of late Arthur Paul Boissier, of Moretons, Harrow-on-the-Hill; d 1974; s by his brother (11) ARCHIBALD VICTOR DUDLEY, 5th Marquess, b 1913; writer and broadcaster; d 1984; s by his brother (12) ALASTAIR NINIAN JOHN, 6th Marquess and present peer; also Earl of Aberdeen, Earl of Haddo, Viscount Formartine, Viscount Gordon, and Lord Haddo, Methlic, Tarves, and Kellie.

Aberdour, Lord; son of Earl of Morton.

ABERGAVENNY, MARQUESS OF (Nevill) (Marquess UK 1876)

Form no mean wish

JOHN HENRY GUY NEVILL, KG, OBE, 5th Marquess; *b* 8 Nov 1914; *s* 1954; *ed* Eton and Trin Coll, Camb; Lt-Col late Life Gds; 1939-45 War in France (despatches), N-W Europe (OBE); Hon Col Kent and Co of London Yeo. 1948-62; a JP and DL for Sussex (Vice Lieut 1970-74; Lord-Lieut of E Sussex since 1974); KStJ; a Dir of Lloyds Bank plc (Chm SE Reg Board), and other Directorships; Member E Sussex Co Council 1947-54 (Alderman 1954-62); a Member of Nat Hunt Cttee since 1942 (Sen Steward 1955 and 63); Pres British Horse Soc 1970-71; a Trustee of Ascot Authority 1952-82; HM's Representative at Ascot 1972-82; Chancellor of The Order of the Garter since 1977; Hon LLD Sussex 1986; OBE (Mil) 1945, KG 1974: *m* 1938, (Mary) Patricia, DCVO, da of Maj John Fenwick Harrison, JP (*see* B Burnham, 1969 Edn), and has had issue.

Arms – Gules, a saltire argent, charged with a rose of the field. **Crest** – Out of a ducal coronet, or a bull's head proper, charged with a rose gules. **Supporters** – On either side a bull argent, pied sable, armed, unguled, collared, and chained or, the latter terminating in a staple. **Badges** – *Dexter*, a rose gules, barbed and seeded proper; *sinister*, a portcullis or.
Seat – Eridge Park, Tunbridge Wells TN3 9JT. *Town Residence* – Flat 2, 46 Pont St, SW1. *Club* – White's.

SON DECEASED

Henry John Montague (*Earl of Lewes*), *b* 2 Feb 1948; *ed* Eton; Page of Honour to HM 1962-64; *d* 2 April 1965.

DAUGHTERS LIVING

Lady Anne Patricia, *b* 1938: *m* 1971, Martin Frank Whiteley, who *d* 1984, and has issue living, Camilla Mary, *b* 1972, — Davina Marian Beatrice, *b* 1973, — Lucinda Jane, *b* 1978. *Residence* – Dalmar House, Culworth, nr Banbury, Oxon.
Lady Vivienne Margaret, *b* 1941: *m* 1962, Alan Lillingston, and has issue living, Luke, *b* 1963, — Andrew Harry, *b* 1972, — Georgina Patricia, *b* 1965: *m* 1988, Michael L. W. Bell, of Fitzroy House, Black Bear Lane, Newmarket, Suffolk, yr son of Capt Brian Bell, of Todenham Manor, Moreton-in-Marsh, Glos, and has issue living, Alexander Luke Wentworth *b* 1990, Amy Kitty Wentworth *b* 1991, — Sophie Susan, *b* 1967. *Residence* – Mount Coote, Kilmallock, co Limerick.
Lady Rose, *b* 1950: *m* 1990, George Mark Somerset Clowes, son of Archibald Somerset Clowes, of Ashlands, Billesdon, Leics, and has issue living, Toby Harry Somerset, *b* 1990, — Lucy Elizabeth, *b* 1992. *Residence* –

WIDOW LIVING OF SON OF FOURTH MARQUESS

Lady Anne Camilla Eveline Wallop (*Lady Rupert Nevill*) (Old House Farm, Glynde, Lewes, Sussex; 35 Upper Addison Gdns, W14), da of 9th Earl of Portsmouth: *m* 1944, Lord Rupert Charles Montacute Nevill, CVO, who *d* 1982, and has issue (*see* colls infra).

COLLATERAL BRANCHES LIVING

Issue of late Lord Rupert Charles Montacute Nevill, CVO, yr son of 4th Marquess, *b* 1923, *d* 1982: *m* 1944, Lady Anne Camilla Eveline Wallop (ante), da of 9th Earl of Portsmouth:—
†Guy Rupert Gerard, *b* 1945; *ed* Eton; a Page of Honour to HM 1958-61: *m* 1982, Lady Beatrix Mary Lambton (39 Basuto Rd, SW6; 251A Fulham Rd, SW3), 2nd da of Antony Claud Lambton (6th Earl of Durham until he disclaimed his title 1970), and *d* 1993. —— CHRISTOPHER GEORGE CHARLES (Sham Farm, Eridge Green, Kent), *b* 23 April 1955; *ed* Harrow: *m* 1985, Venetia J., elder da of Frederick Maynard, of 43 Bury Walk, SW3, and has had issue, George Rupert Gerard, *b* and *d* 1990, — Sophie Alice Augusta, *b* (twin) 1990. —— Angela Isabel Mary (7 Durham Place, SW3), *b* 1948: *m* 1994, William Keating. —— Henrietta Emily Charlotte (35 Upper Addison Gdns, W14), *b* 1964: *m* 1991, Capt Timothy J. Purbrick, 17/21st Lancers, son of William Purbrick.

(In remainder to Earldom and Barony of Abergavenny, and Viscountcy of Nevill only)

Grandsons of late Percy Llewelyn Nevill (infra):—
Issue of late Michael George Ralph Nevill, Lieut Scots Gds, *b* 1917, *ka* 1943: *m* 1940, Maureen Ethné David, JP (who *m* 2ndly, 1947, John Valentine Balfour, DSC, of Walnut Tree Farm, Birling, Maidstone, Kent (*see* Price, Bt, colls, 1950 Edn)), da of late Capt (Arthur) Tahu (Gravenor) Rhodes, MVO (*see* B Plunket, 1968 Edn):—
David Michael Ralph (Birling Place, Birling, Maidstone, Kent), *b* 1941; *ed* Bryanston: *m* 1972, Katherine Mary, da of Rossmore Derrick Westenra, of Halswell, Christchurch, NZ, and has issue living, Guy Michael Rossmore, *b* 1973, — Anna Louise, *b* 1976, — Georgina Rose, *b* 1981. —— Michael George Rathmore (*posthumous*), *b* 1943; *ed* Eton.

Granddaughter of Hon Ralph Pelham Nevill, 2nd son of 4th Earl:—
Issue of late Percy Llewelyn Nevill, *b* 1877, *d* 1927: *m* 1905, Marjorie, who *d* 1945, da of late Lord George Montacute Nevill (3rd son of 1st Marquess of Abergavenny):—
Cicely Rose, *b* 1915: *m* 1947, Peter Richard Nickols, who *d* 1990, and has issue living, two sons and one da. *Residence* – Pinewood Lodge, Spofforth, Harrogate, N Yorks.

PREDECESSORS – (1) *Sir* RALPH Nevill, KG, 6th son of 1st Earl of Westmorland, and 4th Baron Nevill, of Raby (cr 1294) (titles forfeited 13th Elizabeth I), a confidant of Edward IV, was summoned to the English Parliament as *Baron Bergavenny* 1450-75; *d* 1476; *s* by his son (2) *Sir* GEORGE, KB, 2nd Baron; was knighted at the battle of Tewkesbury; *d* 1492, and was *s* by his eldest son (3) *Sir* GEORGE, KG, KB, 3rd Baron; was companion in arms of Henry VIII in his French wars, and held high and important commands; *d* 1536; *s* by his eldest son (4) HENRY, 4th Baron; was committed to ward for striking the Earl of Oxford in the chamber of presence, but received special pardon within a month; was one of the peers who sat in judgement upon Mary, Queen of Scots; *d* 1586; at his decease the Barony was unsuccessfully claimed by his da Mary, wife of Sir Thomas Fane, who however, was subsequently granted the Barony of Le Despencer (cr by writ 1264), to which she was a co-heir; s by his cousin (5) EDWARD, 5th Baron, eldest son of Sir Edward Nevill, 2nd son of 2nd Baron; d 1589; s by his eldest son (6) EDWARD, 6th Baron; unsuccessfully claimed the Earldom of Westmorland; d 1622; s by his eldest son (7) HENRY, 7th Baron; d 1641; s by his eldest son (8) JOHN, 8th Baron; d 1660; s by his brother (9) GEORGE, 9th Baron; d 1666; s by his only son (10) GEORGE, 10th Baron, dsp 1694, when the barony reverted to his kinsman (11) GEORGE, 11th Baron, eldest son of Sir Christopher Nevill, 2nd son of 6th Baron; d 1720; s by his eldest son (12) GEORGE, 12th Baron; dsp 1723; s by his brother (13) EDWARD, 13th Baron; d 1724; s by his cousin (14) WILLIAM, 14th Baron, son of Edward Nevill, brother of 11th Baron; the first to be styled Lord Abergavenny (in lieu of Bergavenny); d 1745; s by his eldest son (15) GEORGE, 15th Baron; cr Viscount Nevill and Earl of Abergavenny (peerage of Great Britain) 1784; d 1785; s by his son (16) HENRY, KT, 2nd Earl; d 1843; s by his son (17) Rev JOHN, 3rd Earl; d 1845; s by his brother (18) Rev WILLIAM, 4th Earl, b 1792; m 1824, Caroline, who d 1873, da of Ralph Leeke, of Longford Hall, Salop; d 17 Aug 1868; s by his eldest son (19) WILLIAM, KG, 5th Earl, b 1826; Lord-Lieut of Sussex 1892-1905; cr Earl of Lewes and Marquess of Abergavenny (peerage of United Kingdom) 1876; m 1848, Caroline, who d 1892, sister of 1st Baron Derwent; d 1915; s by his eldest son (20) REGINALD WILLIAM BRANSBY, 2nd Marquess, b 1853; d 1927; s by his brother (21) HENRY GILBERT RALPH, 3rd Marquess, b 1854; m 1st, 1876, Violet, who d 1880, da of late Lieut-Col Henry Dorrien Streatfeild, of Chiddingstone Park, Kent; 2ndly, 1886, Maud Augusta, who d 1927, da of late William Beckett, MP (see B Grimthorpe, 1927 Edn); 3rdly, 1928, Mary Frances, who d 1954, da of late Hon Ralph Pelham Nevill, and widow of 3rd Viscount Hardinge; d 1938; s by his nephew (22) GUY TEMPLE MONTACUTE Larnach-Nevill (eldest son of late Lord George Montacute Nevill, 3rd son of 1st Marquess), 4th Marquess; b 1883; Capt Scots Guards; assumed by deed poll 1919 the additional surname of Larnach for himself and his wife only: m 1909, Isabel Nellie, who d 1953, only child of late James Walker Larnach: d 1954; s by his eldest son (23) JOHN HENRY GUY, 5th Marquess and present peer; also Earl of Abergavenny, Earl of Lewes, Viscount Nevill, and Baron Abergavenny (formerly Bergavenny).

ABERTAY, BARONY OF (Barrie) (Extinct 1940)

DAUGHTERS LIVING OF FIRST BARON

Hon June Jane Coupar, b 1928: m 1st, 1952 (m diss 1977), Col Alan Norman Breitmeyer, DL, High Sheriff of Cambs (1984), late Gren Gds; 2ndly 1977, Christopher Jeremy King Fordham, MA, FRICS, and has issue living (by 1st m), Timothy Hugh, b 1959; Maj Gren Gds: m 1985, Henrietta Beatrice Jane, yst da of Maj Jonathan Michael Herry Balcon, TD (see Hillingdon, By), and has issue living, Sophie Rebecca b 1987, Georgina Louise b 1990, — Patricia Anne, b 1954; m 1979, Rupert Edward Hanbury, and has issue living, James Antony b 1983, Charlotte Emma b 1981, Araminta Laura Elizabeth b 1992. Residence – Odsey Park, Ashwell, Herts.

Hon Rosemary Ethel Coupar, b 1931; JP Glos 1973: m 1952, John Stuart Maitland, and has issue living, John Andrew Charles, b 1954, — Robin Neil, b 1958: m 1988, Deborah, yr da of Watson Stuart, of Lower Grantsfield, Kimbolton, Herefords, and has issue living, Thomas Stuart b 1992, — Angus Kenneth, b 1963, — Fiona Romaire, b 1961: m 1990, Peter J. D. Leathart, yr son of Scott Leathart, of Overmead, Lower Heyford, Oxford. Residence – The Grange, Stancombe, Dursley, Glos.

Abingdon, Earl of; see Earl of Lindsey and Abingdon.

ABINGER, BARON (Scarlett) (Baron UK 1835)

He stands by his own strength

JAMES RICHARD SCARLETT, 8th Baron; b 28 Sept 1914; s 1943; ed Eton, and Magdalene Coll, Camb (BA); Lt-Col late RA; DL Essex 1968; Vice-Pres Byron Soc; KStJ: m 1957, Isla Carolyn, only da of late Vice-Adm James William Rivett-Carnac, CB, CBE, DSC (see Rivett-Carnac, Bt), and has issue.

Arms – Checky or and gules, a lion rampant ermine; on a canton azure, a castle, triple towered argent. Crest – A Tuscan column, checky, or and gules, supported on either side by a lion's jamb ermines, erased gules. Supporters – on either side an angel vested argent, tunic azure, wings or; in the exterior hand of each a sword in bend proper, pommel and hilt or.
Residences – 7 Cumberland St, SW1 VLS; Sheepcote House, Queen St, Castle Hedingham, Halstead, Essex CO9 3HA. Clubs – Carlton, Royal Automobile.

SONS LIVING

Hon JAMES HARRY, b 28 May 1959.
Hon Peter Richard, b 1961: m 1992, Sharon Elizabeth, da of Derek Turl, of Exeter, Devon.

BROTHER LIVING

Hon John Leopold Campbell, CBE, b 1916; ed Eton, and Magdalene Coll, Camb (BA 1938); formerly Maj RA; an Esquire of Order of St John of Jerusalem; cr CBE (Civil) 1973: m 1947, Bridget, da of late H. B. Crook, of 102 Stafford Court, W8, and has issue living, Hugh Lawrence, b 1953: m 1985, Dinah, da of Richard Pinsent, of Thora, NSW, Australia, — Felix James (83 FitzJohn's Av, NW3 6NY), b 1958: m 1991, Laura Stewart, only da of Edward Petrie, of Dundee, Tayside, and has issue living, Robert Campbell *b* 1992, Rory Maclaren *b* 1993, — Sarah Elizabeth, *b* 1954. *Residence* – Bramblewood, Castle Walk, Wadhurst, Sussex.

PREDECESSORS – (1) *Sir* JAMES Scarlett, PC, KB, DCL; called to the Bar 1791; sat successively as MP for Cockermouth, Peterborough, and Norwich, and was sometime Attorney-Gen; appointed Lord Chief Baron of the Exchequer 1834, and cr *Baron Abinger*, of Abinger, co Surrey (peerage of United Kingdom) 1835; *d* 1844; *s* by his eldest son (2) ROBERT CAMPBELL, 2nd Baron, *b* 1794; was a Barrister-at-Law: *m* 1824, Sarah, who *d* 1878, da of late George Smith, Chief Justice of Mauritius; *d* 24 June 1861; *s* by his eldest son (3) WILLIAM FREDERICK, CB, 3rd Baron, *b* 1826; Lieut-Gen in the Army: *m* 1863, Helen, who *d* 1915, da of Commodore George Allan Magruder, of the US Navy; *d* 1892; *s* by his son (4) JAMES YORK MACGREGOR, 4th Baron, *b* 1871; *d* 1903; *s* by his cousin (5) SHELLEY LEOPOLD LAURENCE (son of late Lieut-Col Leopold James Yorke Campbell Scarlett), son of late Hon Peter Campbell Scarlett, CB (3rd son of 1st Baron), 5th Baron, *b* 1872; Hon Com Roy Naval Vol Reserve; served during European War 1915-16: *m* 1899, Lila Lucy Catherine Mary, who *d* 1941 (having *m* 3rdly, 1921, Jean de Belot), da of late Rt Hon Sir William Arthur White, PC, GCB, GCMG, British Ambassador at Constantinople, and widow of Kammerherr Carl E de Geijer, Swedish Diplo Ser; *d* 1917; *s* by his brother (6) ROBERT BROOKE CAMPBELL, 6th Baron: *m* 1917, Jean Marguerite (Madame de Serignac), who *d* 1954, da of late Edouard Japy, and widow of Adolphe Steinheil, of Paris; *d* 1927; *s* by his brother (7) HUGH RICHARD, DSO, 7th Baron, *b* 1878; Lieut-Col RA (retired); S Africa 1900-1902; European War 1914-18 (DSO): *m* 1913, Marjorie Ursula, who *d* 1965, da of John MacPhillamy, of Blair Athol, Bathurst, NSW; *d* 1943; *s* by his eldest son (8) JAMES RICHARD, 8th Baron and present peer.

Aboyne, Earl of; son of Marquess of Huntly.

ACKNER, BARON (Ackner) (Life Baron 1986)

DESMOND JAMES CONRAD ACKNER, PC, son of Dr Conrad Ackner; *b* 18 Sept 1920; *ed* Highgate Sch, and Clare Coll, Camb (MA) Hon Fellow; Bar Middle Temple 1945, QC 1961, Bencher 1965; Chm Gen Council of Bar, and Vice-Pres Senate of Four Inns of Court 1968-70 (Pres 1980-82); Recorder of Swindon 1962-71, and Judge of Court of Appeal of Jersey and Guernsey 1967-71, Judge of High Court of Justice (Queen's Bench Div) 1971-80, Lord Justice of Appeal 1980-86; Treas Middle Temple 1984; a Lord of Appeal in Ordinary since 1986; *cr* Kt 1970, PC 1980, and *Baron Ackner*, of Sutton, W Sussex (Life Baron) 1986: *m* 1946, Joan, da of late John Evans, JP, and widow of K. B. Spence, and has issue.

Arms – Sable in fess issuant from a barrulet wavy azure fimbriated argent a representation of the bridge at Clare College Cambridge proper the whole between two whales spouting naiant counter naiant gold. **Crest** – Upon a helm with a wreath or and sable a short-eared owl proper crowned or supporting with the dexter claw a clarion azure. **Supporters** – Two otters each holding in the mouth a trout gold the compartment comprising a river bank with bulrushes growing therefrom proper. **Motto** – Non servimus justitiae silendo.
Residences – Browns House, Sutton, nr Pulborough, W Sussex; 7 Rivermill, 151 Grosvenor Rd, SW1.

SON LIVING

Hon Martin Stewart (Lands Farm, W Anstey, S Molton, Devon), *b* 1951; *ed* Oundle, and Birmingham Univ (BSc): *m* 1983, Janet, da of late C. W. Williamson.

DAUGHTER LIVING

Hon Claudia Madeleine, *b* 1954; *ed* Roedean, and Girton Coll, Camb (BA); Barrister-at-law: *m* 1978, Iain Hughes.

Lord Ackner has adopted his stepda, Moelwyn Ulva (da of late K. B. Spence), *b* 1943; *ed* St Michael's, Petworth, and Switzerland: *m* 1st, 19— (*m diss* 19—), J. K. Bouckley; 2ndly, 1980, Michael Healy, of Sylvan House, Goose Green, Gullane, E Lothian EH31 2AT, and has issue living (by 1st *m*), Joanna Helen Sarah Brooke, *b* 1969: *m* 1993, Simon William Young, twin son of Stephen Young, of Elgin.

ACTON, BARON (Lyon-Dalberg-Acton) (Baron UK 1869, Bt E 1644)

RICHARD GERALD LYON-DALBERG-ACTON, 4th Baron, and 11th Baronet; *b* 30 July 1941; *s* 1989; *ed* St George's Coll, Salisbury, Rhodesia, and Trin Coll, Oxford (BA 1963, MA 1988); Bar Inner Temple 1976; a Dir Coutts & Co 1971-74; Sr Law Officer, Zimbabwe Ministry of Justice, Legal and Parliamentary Affairs, 1981-85; writer; a Patrician of Naples, patron of one living (but, being a Roman Catholic, cannot present): *m* 1st, 1965, Hilary Juliet Sarah, who *d* 1973, da of Dr Osmond Laurence Charles Cookson, MB BS, MRCS, LRCP, of Perth, W Australia; 2ndly, 1974 (*m diss* 1987), Judith Garfield, writer, da of Hon Sir Garfield Todd, sometime PM of Southern Rhodesia, of Hokonui Ranch, PO Dadaya, Zimbabwe; 3rdly, 1988, Patricia, only da of late M. Morey Nassif, of Cedar Rapids, Iowa, USA, and has issue by 1st *m*.

Arms – Quarterly: 1st and 4th gules semée of cross-crosslets fitché or, two lions passant in pale argen:, *Acton*; 2nd quarterly, 1st and 4th azure, six fleurs-de-lis, three, two, and one argent, a chief dancettée of the last, 2nd and 3rd or, a cross patonce gules, over all an escutcheon of the first, thereon a tower argent, a chief dancettée of the last, *Dalberg*; 3rd azure, a lion passant or between three plates each charged with a griffin's head erased sable, *Lyon*. **Crest** – In front of a lion's head erased argent two hurts, *Lyon*. **Supporters** – On either side a lion guardant proper, gorged with a chain or, and charged with a cross patonce gules.
Residences – Marcham Priory, Abingdon, Oxon; 100 Red Oak Lane SE, Cedar Rapids, Iowa 52403, USA.

Deo adjurante
God assisting

SON LIVING *(By 1st marriage)*

Hon JOHN CHARLES FERDINAND HAROLD, *b* 19 Aug 1966; *ed* Winchester, and Balliol Coll, Oxford.

BROTHERS LIVING

Rev Hon John Charles (Westminster Diocesan Seminary, 28 Beaufort Street, SW3), *b* 1943; *ed* Gregorian Univ, Rome; Prof of Dogmatic Theology, Westminster Diocesan Seminary.
Hon Robert Peter (Rutland House, Saxton St, Newmarket, Suffolk), *b* 1946; stud mgr for Sheik Mohamed bin Rashid al Maktoum, Newmarket: *m* 1974, Michele, da of Henri Laigle, of 61 rue du Commerce, 92 Colombes, France, and has issue living, Christopher Richard Henri, *b* 1977, — Patrick John Pascal, *b* 1979, — William Benjamin, *b* 1986.
Hon Edward David Joseph (365 Unthank Rd, Norwich NR4 79G); *b* 1949; *ed* York Univ, and St Edmund's Coll, Camb; Prof of Modern European History, E Anglia Univ; author of *Alexander Herzen and the Role of the Intellectual Revolutionary* (1979), *Russia: the Present and the Past* (1986), *Rethinking the Russian Revolution* (1990), etc: *m* 1972, Stella Marie, da of late Henry Conroy, of 8 Stirling Rd, Bolton, and has issue living, Helen Marie, *b* 1974, — Natalie Elizabeth *b* 1977.
Hon Peter Hedley (Dancing Dicks, Blunts Hall Rd, Witham, Essex); *b* 1950; *ed* RAC Cirencester; Trainee Manager, Waterman & Ross: *m* 1981, Anne, da of James Sinclair, of Sanday, Orkney Is, and has issue living, Simon Richard, *b* 1981, — Emily, *b* 1989.

SISTERS LIVING

Hon Pelline Margot, *b* 1932: *m* 1953, Laszlo de Marffy von Versegh, of Ealing Farm, PO Box 29, Mvurwi, Zimbabwe, and has had issue, Denes (Rutland Lodge Stud, Saxon St, Newmarket, Suffolk), *b* 1954: *m* 1986, Rachel, da of Martin Lampard, of Tiverton, Devon, and has issue living, Edmond *b* 1988, — Miklos (Ealing Farm, PO Box 29, Mvurwi, Zimbabwe), *b* 1956: *m* 1986, Vibeke Jane, only da of Christopher Culley, of Gweru, Zimbabwe, and has issue living, Lucinda *b* 1988, — Joseph (364 Shenley Rd, Boreham Wood, Herts), *b* 1957: *m* 1987, Anne Margaret Elizabeth, da of Col Alexander W. D. Lewis, of Salcombe, S Devon, and Canberra, Australia and has issue living, Charles Alexander *b* 1989, — Paul (16A St Faith's Rd, W Dulwich, SE21), *b* 1958: *m* 1987, Lesley-Anne, da of Douglas Hall, of Bournemouth, and has issue living, Tamas *b* 1987, — Robert (Farming & Engineering, PO Box 918, Blantyre, Malawi), *b* 1962: *m* 1989, Katherine, da of Martin Graham, of Harare, Zimbabwe, — Stephen, *b* 1965, — Gabriella Mary, *b* 1960, *d* 1984.
Hon Catherine, *b* 1939: *m* 1960, Hon Joseph Mervyn Corbett (*see* B Rowallan). *Residence* – The Old Rectory, Coates, nr Cirencester, Glos.
Hon Jill Mary Joan, *b* 1947: *m* 1969, Nicholas Lampert (*see* V Ridley, colls, 1976 Edn), of 46 Clarence Rd, Moseley, Birmingham B13 9UH, and has issue living, Katherine, *b* 1969, — Frances, *b* 1971.
Hon Mary-Ann, *b* 1951: *m* 1972, Timothy John Sheehy, of 8 St Margaret's Rd, Oxford, and has issue living, Jane Elizabeth, *b* 1973, — Clare Anne, *b* 1975.
Hon Jane, *b* 1954: *m* 1st, 1975 (*m diss* 1982), Charles Thomas Pugh, who *d* 1989; 2ndly, 1983, Xan de Crespigny Smiley (*see* Smiley, Bt, colls), and has issue living (by 1st *m*), Charlotte, *b* 1978, — Rebecca, *b* 1979, — (by 2nd *m*) (*see* Smiley, Bt, colls). *Residence* – 36 Rectory Grove, SW4 0EB.

AUNTS LIVING *(daughters of 2nd Baron)*

Hon (Dorothy Elizabeth Anne) Pelline (18 Petersham House, Harrington Rd, SW7), *b* 1906: *m* 1928, Edward Joseph Eyre, who *d* 1962, and has issue living, Edward (The Field House, Gt Durnford, Salisbury, Wilts) *b* 1929; Bar Inner Temple 1957: *m* 1969, Ethel Mary, da of late Cdr Charles H. Drage, RN, of 38 Sheffield Terr, W8, and widow of Roderick Andrew Joseph Fraser (*see* L Lovat, colls), and has issue living, Robert Edward John *b* 1971, Mathilda Elizabeth Mary Pelline *b* 1970, Virginia Margaret Dorothy *b* 1974, Constance Rose Octavia *b* 1976, — *Sir* James Ainsworth Campden Gabriel, KCVO, CBE (Bockhampton Manor, Lambourn, Berks RG16 7LX), *b* 1930; Maj-Gen RHG/D; OBE 1975, CVO 1978, CBE 1980, KCVO 1986: *m* 1967, Monica Ruth Esther, da of late Michael Joseph Smyth, FRCS, MCh, of London, and has issue living, James Patrick *b* 1969; *ed* Ampleforth, and RMA Sandhurst; RHG/D, Annabelle Catherine *b* 1970. — John Michael Simon William (118 Prospect Hill Rd, Newport, RI, USA), *b* 1935: *m* 1960 (*m diss* 1979), Susan, da of Cdr Maxwell Cole, US Navy, and has issue living, Michael John *b* 1961, Christopher Maxwell *b* 1963, Giles Stephen *b* 1966, Julian Patrick *b* 1970, — Peter Gervaise Joseph (12 South Terr, SW7), *b* 1940; *ed* Downside; actor and dir, — Patrick Giles Andrew (twin), *b* 1940: *m* 1977,

Victoria Mary, only da of Charles Bathurst Norman (*see* B Wraxall), and formerly wife of Capt Raymond Edward Barthorp, — Dorothy Elizabeth Mary Pelline, *b* 1938: *m* 1972, Charles Gilbert Remmick, of 400 East 56 St, New York, NY 10022, USA, — Caroline Elisa Margaret (18 Petersham House, Harrington Rd, SW7), *b* 1945: *m* 1978 (*m diss* 1979), Alan Cooper, son of Albert Cooper.

Hon Helen Mary Grace (602 Park West, W2), *b* 1910: *m* 1933 (*m diss* 1958), Prince Guglielmo Camillo Carlo Rospigliosi, who *d* 1990, and has issue (*see* E Newburgh, colls)

Hon Joan Henrica Josepha Mary Clare (602 Park West, W2), *b* 1915.

Hon Margaret Mary Teresa (602 Park West, W2), *b* 1919.

Hon Ædgyth Bertha Milburg Mary Antonia Frances, OBE (Villa Ithaki, Twentydales Rd, Hatfield, Harare, Zimbabwe), *b* 1920; OBE (Civil) 1986: *m* 1949, John Alexander Callinicos, and has issue living, Alexander Theodore (45 King Henry's Walk, N1), *b* 1950; *ed* Balliol Coll, Oxford (PhD); lecturer at York Univ, and author of numerous philosophical works: *m* 1977, Joanna, da of late F. Seddon, of Dore, Sheffield, — Anastasius John (21 Parham Rd, Harare, Zimbabwe), *b* 1957; *ed* Exeter Univ: *m* 1985, Alice, da of Euan Robertson, of Harare, and has issue living, Michael Alexander *b* 1986, Helena Marie Immaculée *b* (twin) 1986, Marie-Madeleine Antonia *b* 1991.

WIDOW LIVING OF THIRD BARON

Hon DAPHNE STRUTT (*Dowager Baroness Acton*), da of 4th Baron Rayleigh: *m* 1931, the 3rd Baron, CMG, MBE, TD, who *d* 1989. *Residence* – 46 Clarence Rd, Moseley, Birmingham B13 9UH.

COLLATERAL BRANCHES LIVING   (*Male line of which is in remainder to Baronetcy only*)

Grandchildren of late Adm Baron Alfredo Acton (Hon KCB) (infra):—
Issue of late late Baron Ferdinando Amadeo Maria Acton, LLD, a Patrician of Naples, a 1st class Grandee of Spain, and 12th Prince of Leporano, *b* 1908, *d* 1979: *m* 1946, Emilia (a Dame Grand Cross of Constantinian Order of St George), only da of late Count Gioacchino del Balzo Presenzano:—
Baron Giovanni Alfredo Maria (*Prince of Leporano*), *b* 1948; a Patrician of Naples, 13th Prince of Leporano, and a Knt of Justice of Constantinian Order of St George. *Residences* – Palazzo Cellamare a Chiaja, Naples; 58 Via Panama, Rome; La Chiusa, nr Cittanova di Calabria, Italy; Cannavá, nr Gioia Tauro, Italy. —— Maria Eleanora Carlotta, *b* 1949; a Dame of Justice of Constantinian Order of St George: *m* 1972, Pier Luigi Taccone di Sitizano, a Patrician of Tropea, and a Knt of Justice of Constantinian Order of St George. *Residences* – Palazzo Cellences, Naples; Pizzo di Calabria, Italy.

Grandson of late Vice-Adm Ferdinando Acton, 6th son of late Commodore Charles Acton, eldest son of late Lt-Gen Joseph Edward Acton, brother of 6th baronet:—
Issue of late Adm Baron Alfredo Acton (Hon KCB; cr a Baron in Kingdom of Italy 1925), *b* 1867, *d* 1934: *m* 1907, Livia, who *d* 1963 (a Dame of Honour and Devotion of the Sovereign Order of Malta, and Dame Grand Cross of Constantinian Order of St George; Cross Pro Ecclesia et Pontifice), da of Giuseppe Giudice Caracciolo, 9th Prince of Villa and Cellamare, of Naples:—
Baron Francesco Eduardo Maria, *b* 1910; a Patrician of Naples Capt Italian Navy, a Knight of Sovereign Order of Malta, and a Knight Grand Cross of Constantinian Order of St George; cr a Baron of Kingdom of Italy 1940: *m* 1941, Marida (Dame of Justice of Constantinian Order of St George), only da of Baron Ameglio, and has had issue, Alfred, *b* 1942; *d* as a result of an accident 1946. *Residence* – Palazzo Cellamare a Chiaja, Naples, Italy.

Grandsons of late Paul Reginald Action (infra):—
Issue of late Richard Le Duc Acton, *b* 1913, *d* 1989: *m* 1933, Alberta Althea (27211-A Via Capote, San Juan Capistrano, Calif 92675, USA), da of late Francis Joseph Budwiser, of Dubuque, Iowa:—
Dennis Richard (8561 Martinique, Huntington Beach, Calif 92646, USA), *b* 1938: *m* 1st, 1961 (*m diss* 1971), Susan Caroline, da of Hartvige Rudolph Miklethum, of Minneapolis, Minn; 2ndly, 1973, Frances Lee, da of Harold Stark, of Huntington Beach, Calif, and has issue living (by 1st *m*), Christopher Michael, *b* 1962, — Paul Reginald, *b* 1968, — Julia Ann, *b* 1964. —— Paul Reginald, *b* 1943: *m* 1983, Suzzanne, da of Eugene Erickson, of Minneapolis, Minn.

Granddaughter of late Capt Richard George Acton, only son of late Maj Henry Acton, son of late Capt Henry Acton, 2nd son of late Lt-Gen Joseph Edward Acton (ante):—
Issue of late Paul Reginald Acton, *b* 1886, *d* 1951: *m* (Feb) 1907, Bertha Helen, who *d* 1973, da of Jules Le Duc of Stone County, Missouri, USA:—
Pauline Laura (Vera Cruz Rd, RFD No 1, Center Valley, Pa 18034, USA), *b* 1907: *m* 1929, Charles Henry Heiney, who *d* 1950.

PREDECESSORS – (1) Sir EDWARD Acton, of Aldenham Hall (10th in lineal descent from William de Acton Burnel, temp Edward III), cr a *Baronet*, for his fidelity to Charles I 1644; *d* 1659; *s* by his eldest son (2) Sir WALTER, MP; *d* 1665; *s* by his eldest son (3) Sir EDWARD, MP; *d* 1716; *s* by his eldest son (4) Sir WHITMORE; *d* 1731; *s* by his son (5) Sir RICHARD; *d* 1791; *s* by his kinsman (6) Sir JOHN FRANCIS EDWARD, great-grandson of Walter, 2nd son of 2nd Bt; was successively Com-in-Ch of the land and Sea forces in Naples, and Neapolitan Prime Minister; *d* 1811; *s* by his son (7) Sir FERDINAND RICHARD EDWARD, *b* 1801; assumed by R licence in 1833 the additional surname of Dalberg: *m* 1832, Marie Louise Pellina (who *m* 2ndly, 1840, 2nd Earl Granville, and *d* 1860), only child and heir of Emeric Joseph, Duke of Dalberg; *d* 1837; *s* by his son (8) Sir JOHN EMERICH EDWARD, KCVO, *b* 1834; MP for Carlow (L) 1859-65 and for Bridgnorth 1865-6; a Lord-in-Waiting to HM Queen Victoria 1892-5; Regius Professor of Modern History in Camb Univ 1895-1902; cr *Baron Acton* (peerage of United Kingdom) 1869: *m* 1865, Countess Marie, who *d* 1923, eldest da of Count Arco-Valley, of Munich; *d* 1902; *s* by his son (9) RICHARD MAXIMILIAN, KCVO, 2nd Baron, *b* 1870; a Lord-in-Waiting to King Edward VII. 1905-10, and to King George V 1910-15, and Envoy Extraor and Min Plen to Finland 1919-20; assumed by R licence the additional surname and arms of Lyon 1919: *m* 1904, Dorothy, who *d* 1923, only child of late Thomas Henry Lyon, JP, DL, of Appleton Hall, Cheshire, and Rutland Lodge, Rutland Gardens, SW; *d* 1924; *s* by his son (10) JOHN EMERICH HENRY, CMG, MBE, TD, 3rd Baron, *b* 1907; 1939-45 War as Maj Shropshire Yeo; Pres Rhodesian Royal Agric Soc 1960-64, Chm Gwebi Agric Coll 1958-62, and Chibero Agric Coll 1960-65, founding Chm Tattersalls Swaziland 1969: *m* 1931, Hon Daphne Strutt, da of 4th Baron Rayleigh; *d* 1989; *s* by his eldest son (11) RICHARD GERALD, 4th Baron and present peer.

ADDINGTON, BARON (Hubbard) (Baron UK 1887)

Seeking things above

DOMINIC BRYCE HUBBARD, 6th Baron; *b* 24 Aug 1963; *s* 1982; *ed* Hewett Comprehensive Sch, Norwich, and Aberdeen Univ (MA 1988).

ᴀrms – Vert, a chevron engrailed, plain cotised argent, between three eagles' heads erased of the second, each gorged with a collar fleurettée gules. Crest – In front of a fasces fessewise proper an eagle's head as in the arms. Supporters – On either side an eagle argent, wings addorsed, gorged with a collar fleurettée gules, and pendent therefrom an escutcheon ermine charged with a rose gules.
Residence – 9/11 Chalk Hill Rd, Thorpe Hamlet, Norwich NR1 1SC.

BROTHER LIVING

Hon MICHAEL WALTER LESLIE, *b* 7 July 1965; *ed* Hewett Comprehensive Sch, Norwich, Manchester Univ (BA), and Leicester Polytechnic (MA).

SISTERS LIVING

Hon Frances Linden, *b* 1962; *ed* Southampton Univ (BA); Journalist.
Hon Sally Anne, *b* 1966; *ed* Sch of Oriental and African Studies, London Univ (BA), and UCLA (MA).

UNCLE LIVING (*brother of 5th Baron*)

Peter, *b* 1932; *ed* Eastbourne Coll.

HALF-AUNT LIVING (*half-sister of 5th Baron*)

Nicolette, *b* 1926: *m* 1953, Richard Joseph Pike, of Little Rising, Queen Catherine Rd, Steeple Claydon, Buckingham MK18 2PY, and has issue living, James Eben, *b* 1955, — William Joseph Fitzgerald, *b* 1960.

MOTHER LIVING

Alexandra Patricia, da of late Norman Ford Millar, formerly of Glasgow and of Burma: *m* 1961 (*m diss* 1974), the 5th Baron, who *d* 1982. *Residence* – Thorpe Hamlet, Norwich.

COLLATERAL BRANCHES LIVING

Grandchildren of late Capt Gerald Napier Hubbard (infra):—
Issue of late Ralph Arthur Hubbard, *b* 1908, *d* 1981: *m* 1st, 1940 (*m diss* 1954), Hon Marion Woodruff, who *d* 1992, eldest da of 1st Baron Ashfield, and formerly wife of (i) James Hart Rutland, and (ii) James Henry Royds; 2ndly 1954, Elizabeth Gertrude, who *d* 1988, yr da of late Stephen Cozens, and formerly wife of (i) late Henry Reginald Gambier Colclough (ii) late Capt Michael Norton-Griffiths, RE (see Norton-Griffiths, Bt. colls), and (iii) George Paul Minchin Woodward:—
(By 1st *m*) Rosemary Jane, *b* 1942: *m* 1962, Andrew Peter Harold Parsons, Scots Gds, and has issue living, James Alastair Thomas, *b* 1964, — Edward Charles William, *b* 1968, — Annabel Jane, *b* 1969. — Angela Mary, *b* 1945: *m* 1st, 1965, (Luke Edward) Timothy Hue Williams; 2ndly, 1972, Peter Anthony Charles Mordaunt, of 9 Napier Av, SW6 3PS (*see* Mordaunt, Bt).
Issue of late S/Ldr Thomas Edward Hubbard, AuxAF 1939-43, *b* 1911, *d* 1985: *m* 1939 (*m diss* 1974), Bridget, da of late Charles Churchill Branch, OBE:—
Gerald Thomas Guy (19 Felden St, SW6), *b* 1947; *ed* Gordonstoun. —— Charles Benjamin (89 St Mark's Rd, W10 6JS), *b* 1950; *ed* Gordonstoun. —— Harriet Anne, *b* 1943: *m* 1972, Michael Frederick Bailey, of Great Dorweeke, Silverton, Exeter EX5 4BZ, and has issue living, Simon Douglas, *b* 1975, — Jessica Mary, *b* 1973.

Grandchildren of late Hon Arthur Gellibrand Hubbard, 4th son of 1st Baron:—
Issue of late Capt Gerald Napier Hubbard, *b* 1882, *d* 1939: *m* (Jan) 1908, Bertha Caroline, who *d* 1969, da of late Rev Edward Southwell Garnier, R of Quidenham, Attleborough:—
Derek, *b* 1920: *ed* Eton; 1939-45 Wars as Capt Sussex Yeo: *m* 1951, Joanne, da of late Donald D. Maclean, and has issue living, Rowan, *b* 1954: *m* 1978, Charles E. H. Collier-Wright, of 2 Burcote Rd, SW18 3LQ, and has issue living, Robert Edward *b* 1983, Emma *b* 1981, Frances Alexandra *b* 1986, — (Joanne) Candida, *b* 1957. *Residence* – Vine Cottage, Effingham, Surrey. —— Susan d'Esterre (12A The Hollies, Peter St, Shepton Mallet, Som), *b* 1914: *m* 1st, 1936 (*m diss* 1951), Edward Ernest Harrison; 2ndly, 1952, Capt Herbert John Tindall Carter, late RHG, who *d* 1980, and has issue living (by 1st *m*) Martin Edward (8 Ravenscourt Rd, W6; Brooks's Club), *b* 1937; *ed* Harrow, and Oriel Coll, Oxford: *m* 1965, Reziya Ahmad, and has issue living, Thomas Edward Henry *b* 1969; *ed* Westminster (Queen's Scholar), and Wadham Coll, Oxford, Frances Catherine Saida *b* 1966; *ed* Trin Hall, Camb, — (by 2nd *m*) Carolyn Rachel, *b* 1955: *m* 1st, 1982 (*m diss* 1986), Alan Laurence Kelly; 2ndly, 1991, John Richard House, of 1 Crown House, Catsash, Shepton Mallet, Som, and has issue living (by 1st *m*), John Laurence *b* 1983.

Grandchildren of late Eric Wyndham Hubbard (infra):—
Issue of late Evelyn Raymond WHEATLEY-HUBBARD, OBE, *b* 1921; assumed by deed poll 1949 the additional surname of Wheatley before his patronymic; *d* 1993: *m* 1949, Ann Christobel, OBE (The Dower House, Boyton, Warminster, Wilts), only child of late Col Charles Joshua Hirst Wheatley, of Berkswell Hall, Coventry:—
Thomas Henry, *b* 1952; *ed* Eton: *m* 1979, Caroline M. O., da of Col Hilary Lewis, of Reigny House, Newton Reigny, Penrith, Cumbria, and has issue living, Christopher Raymond, *b* 1982, — Andrew David, *b* 1984. —— Caroline Sophia, *b* 1950.

Grandchildren of late Hon Evelyn Hubbard, 5th son of 1st Baron:—
Issue of late Eric Wyndham Hubbard, *b* 1885, *d* 1946: *m* 1918, Edith Sylvia, who *d* 1977, da of Herbert Picton Morris, of 61 Pont St, SW:—
Jasper Picton, *b* 1923; *ed* Eton, and Ch Ch, Oxford: *m* 1951, Ethne Mary, only da of late Henry Charles Frederick Pelham-Clinton (*see* D Newcastle, colls), and has issue living, John Louis Pelham, *b* 1954, — Charlotte Anne, *b* 1952, — Rose Mary, *b* 1957. *Residence* – Hammonds, Lewes Heath, Horsmonden, Tonbridge, Kent TN12 8EE. —— Virginia, *b* 1919.

PREDECESSORS – (1) JOHN GELLIBRAND Hubbard, PC, son of late John Hubbard, of Stratford Grove, *b* 1805; sat as MP for Buckingham (*C*) 1859-68, and for City of London 1874-87; cr *Baron Addington*, of Addington, Bucks (peerage of United Kingdom) 1887: *m* 1837, Hon Maria Margaret, who *d* 1896, da of 9th Baron Napier; *d* 1889; *s* by his eldest son (2) EGERTON, 2nd Baron; *b* 1842; partner in firms of John Hubbard and Co, Russian Merchants, of London, and Egerton Hubbard and Co, of Petrograd; MP for Buckingham (*C*) 1874-80, and for N, or Buckingham, Div of Buckinghamshire 1886-9: *m* 1880, Mary Adelaide, who *d* 1933, da of Sir Wyndham Spencer Portal, 1st Bt; *d* 1915; *s* by his eldest son (3) JOHN GELLIBRAND, OBE, 3rd Baron; *b* 1883; British Custodian of Enemy Property in China 1923-28; *d* 1966; *s* by his brother (4) RAYMOND EGERTON, 4th Baron; *b* 1884; *d* 1971; *s* by his kinsman (5) JAMES (eldest son of Lt-Col John Francis Hubbard, OBE, eldest son of Hon Cecil John Hubbard, 3rd son of 1st Baron), 5th Baron; *b* 1930: *m* 1961 (*m diss* 1974), Alexandra Patricia, da of late Norman Ford Millar; *d* 1982; *s* by his elder son (6) DOMINIC BRYCE, 6th Baron and present peer.

ADDISON, VISCOUNT (Addison) (Viscount UK 1945)

WILLIAM MATTHEW WAND ADDISON, 4th Viscount; *b* 13 June 1945; *s* 1992; *ed* King's Sch, Bruton, and Essex Inst of Agric: *m* 1st, 1970 (*m diss* 19—), Joanna Mary, eldest da of late John Ivor Charles Dickinson, of Blyborough Grange, Gainsborough; 2ndly, 1991, Lesley Ann, da of George Colin Mawer, of Sudbeck Lane, Welton, Lincs, and has issue by 1st *m*.

Arms – Per chevron vert and or, in chief a snake embowed head debruised between two garbs of the last and in base an anchor sable. **Crest** – In front of two keys in saltire, wards upwards, a sword point downwards or. **Supporters** – On either side a Lincolnshire red bull proper, the headstall also proper charged with a sun in splendour or.
Residence – Church Barn, Oundle, Peterborough PE8 4AX.

To serve is to live

SON LIVING *(By 1st marriage)*

Hon PAUL WAND, *b* 18 March 1973; *ed* Rannoch Sch, Perthshire.

DAUGHTERS LIVING *(By 1st marriage)*

Hon Sarah Louise, *b* 1971.
Hon Caroline Amy, *b* 1979.

SISTERS LIVING

Hon Eleanor Brigit, *b* 1938: *m* 1972, Michael Girling. *Residence* – 16 Heatherwood, Midhurst, W Sussex GU29 9LH.
Hon Caroline Ruth, *b* 1942: *m* 1965, John Hollis Wearing, and has issue living, Patrick John, *b* 1969, — Jacalyn Ruth, *b* 1966. *Residence* – 12 Hill St North, Richmond, Nelson, NZ.

DAUGHTERS LIVING OF SECOND VISCOUNT

Hon Jacqueline Faith ADDISON, *b* 1944; has resumed her maiden name: *m* 1966 (*m diss* 1985), Jeremy Warren Payne, PhD, and has issue living, Katy Josephine, *b* 1972, — Christina Meriel, *b* 1975, — Anna Isabella, *b* 1978. *Residence* – 16A Bright's Crescent, Edinburgh EH9 2DB.
Hon Christine Gray, *b* 1946: *m* 1966, Terry Frederick Tidborough, of 2 Silver St, Willand, Cullompton, Devon.

WIDOW LIVING OF THIRD VISCOUNT

KATHLEEN (*Dowager Viscountess Addison*), only da of late Rt Rev and Rt Hon Bishop John William Charles Wand, KCVO, DD, formerly 110th Bishop of London: *m* 1936, the 3rd Viscount, who *d* 1992. *Residence* – Old Stables, Maplehurst, Horsham, Sussex.

PREDECESSORS – (1) Rt Hon Christopher Addison, KG, PC, MD, FRCS, son of late Robert Addison, of Hogsthorpe, Lincolnshire; *b* 1869; appointed Hunterian Professor and Examiner in Anatomy in Camb and London Univs 1901, Parliamentary Sec to Board of Education 1914, Sec to Min of Munitions 1915, Min of Munitions in National Ministry 1916, Min of Reconstruction 1917, Pres of Local Govt Board 1919, first Min of Health 1919 (with seat in the Cabinet from 1919), Min without Portfolio (with a seat in the Cabinet) April 1921 (resigned in July 1921), Parliamentary Sec to Min of Agriculture 1929, Min of Agriculture and Fisheries 1930 (resigned 1931), and Sec of State for Dominion Affairs (afterwards Commonwealth Relations) and Leader of House of Lords 1945; was Lord Privy Seal 1947-51 (also Paymaster-Gen 1948-49) and Lord Pres of the Council March to Oct 1951; elected Leader of Labour Party in House of Lords 1940; Chm of Med Research Council 1948-51; author of *Politics from Within*, etc, and numerous medical works; sat as MP for Hoxton Div of Shoreditch (*L*) 1910-18, for Shoreditch 1918-22, and for Swindon Div of Wilts 1929-31 and 1934-35; cr *Baron Addison*, of Stallingborough, co Lincoln (peerage of United Kingdom) 1937, and *Viscount Addison*, of Stallingborough, co Lincoln (peerage of UK) 1945: *m* 1st, 1902, Isobel, who *d* 1934, da of late Archibald Gray; 2ndly, 1937, Beatrice Dorothy, who *d* 1982, da of late F. Percy Low, of Thames View House, Staines, Middlesex; *d* 1951; *s* by his son (2) CHRISTOPHER, 2nd Viscount; *b* 1904: *m* 1928, Brigit Helen Christine, who *d* 1980, da of Ernest Edwin George Williams, Bar-at-law, of Wimbledon, SW; *d* 1976; *s* by his brother (3) MICHAEL, 3rd Viscount; *b* 1914; Chm Fulham (later Hammersmith) Borough Youth Cttee 1961-68, and Snr Lecturer Polytechnic of Central London Sch of Management Studies 1966-76; 1939-45 War as F/O (Intelligence) RAFVR: *m* 1936, Kathleen, only da of late Rt Rev and Rt Hon Bishop John William Charles Wand, KCVO, DD, late 110th Bishop of London; *d* 1992; *s* by his only son (4) WILLIAM MATTHEW WAND, 4th Viscount and present peer.

ADEANE, BARONY OF (Adeane) (Extinct 1984)

SON LIVING OF LIFE BARON

Hon George Edward, CVO (B4 Albany, Piccadilly, W1), *b* 1939; *ed* Eton and Magdalene Coll, Camb (BA); Bar Middle

Temple 1962; a Page of Honour to HM 1954-56; Private Sec to HRH The Prince of Wales 1979-85, and to HRH The Princess of Wales 1984-85; CVO (1985).

WIDOW LIVING OF LIFE BARON

HELEN (*Baroness Adeane*) (22 Chelsea Sq, SW3 6LF), da of late Richard Chetwynd-Stapylton (*see* V Chetwynd, colls): *m* 1939, Baron Adeane, GCB, GCVO, PC, FSA (Life Baron), who *d* 1984.

ADRIAN, BARON (Adrian) (Baron UK 1955)

To believe, not fear

RICHARD HUME ADRIAN, MD, FRCP, FRS, 2nd Baron, *b* 16 Oct 1927, *s* 1977; *ed* Westminster and Trin Coll, Camb; DL Cambs 1993; Professor of Cell Physiology, Camb Univ 1978-92; Fellow of Corpus Christi Coll 1956-60, and Fellow of Churchill Coll, Camb, 1960-81; Master Pembroke Coll, Camb 1981-92, and Vice-Chancellor of Camb Univ 1985-87; Trustee British Museum 1979-93; Member British Library Board 1987-93: *m* 1967, Lucy, elder da of Alban Douglas Rendall Caroe, of 15 Campden Hill Sq, W8.

Arms – Vert, three estoiles argent, on a chief of the last a lion passant sable. **Crest** – The astronomical sign of mercury or, between two roses gules, barbed and seeded proper. **Supporters** – On either side a lion sable semee of pentacles or. **Motto** – Non temere crede.
Residences – Frostlake Cottage, Malting Lane, Cambridge; Umgeni, Cley, Holt, Norfolk. *Club* – United Oxford and Cambridge.

SISTERS LIVING

Hon Anne Pinsent, *b* 1924: *m* 1945, Prof Richard Darwin Keynes, CBE, FRS, and has had issue, Adrian Maynard, *b* 1946; *ed* Marlborough, and Merton Coll, Oxford: *m* 1971, Rosemary Anne McKinley (who *m* 2ndly, 19—, W. A. Longworthy, of Colebrooke, Chelford, Cheshire), da of Dr Robert Young, and *d* 1974, leaving issue, Robert Geoffrey *b* 1974, — Randal Hume, OBE, *b* 1948; *ed* Marlborough, and New Coll, Oxford: *m* 1988, Zelfa, da of Cecil Amin Hourani, and has issue living, Alexander Amin Caspar *b* 1991, Soumaya Anne *b* 1989, — Roger John, *b* 1951; *ed* The Leys Sch, and Trin Coll, Camb: *m* 1st, 1975 (*m diss* 1983), Hilary Jane Ruth, only da of Lt-Col A. J. Lister, of Gooden Court, Harrow-on-the-Hill, Middx; 2ndly, 1993, Yasmina, da of Adel Kamal, of New York, USA, and has issue living (by 1st *m*), Oliver Adrian *b* 1978, Laura Margaret *b* 1979, — Simon Douglas, *b* 1952; *ed* The Leys Sch, and Trin Coll, Camb. *Residences* – 4 Herschel Road, Cambridge; Primrose Farm, Wiveton, nr Holt, Norfolk.
Hon Jennet Parker, *b* 1927: *m* 1953, Peter Watson Campbell, and has issue living, Richard John, *b* 1956: *m* 19—, Henrietta, da of John Wayne, and has issue living, Jocelyn *b* 1990, — Sally Anne, *b* 1958, — Emma Jane, *b* 1960. *Residence* – St Anthony in Roseland, Truro TR2 5EY, Cornwall.

PREDECESSORS – (1) EDGAR DOUGLAS ADRIAN, OM, son of late Alfred Douglas Adrian, CB, KC; *b* 1889; distinguished physiologist; Pres of Roy Soc 1950-55 and of British Assocn 1954; Master of Trin Coll, Camb 1951-65, Vice Chancellor Camb Univ 1957-59 and Chancellor 1968-75; cr OM 1942 and *Baron Adrian*, of Camb (peerage of UK) 1955: *m* 1923, Hester Agnes, DBE, BEM, who *d* 1966, da of late Hume Chancellor Pinsent; *d* 1977; *s* by his only son (2) RICHARD HUME, FRS, 2nd Baron and present peer.

AILESBURY, MARQUESS OF (Brudenell-Bruce) (Marquess UK 1821, Bt E 1611)

MICHAEL SYDNEY CEDRIC BRUDENELL-BRUCE, 8th Marquess and 14th Baronet; *b* 31 March 1926; *s* 1974; *ed* Eton; late Lt RHG (Res); a Member of London Stock Exchange: *m* 1st, 1952 (*m diss* 1961), Edwina Sylvia, da of Lt-Col Sir (Ernest) Edward de Winton Wills, 4th Bt (*cr* 1904); 2ndly, 1963 (*m diss* 1974), Juliet Adrienne Lethbridge, da of late Hilary Lethbridge Kingsford; 3rdly, 1974 (*m diss* 1992), Caroline Elizabeth, da of Cdr Owen Francis MacTier Wethered, RN (ret), and formerly wife of Simon Romilly, and has issue by 1st and 2nd *m*.

Arms – Quarterly: 1st and 4th or, a saltire and chief gules; on a canton argent, a lion rampant azure, *Bruce*; 2nd and 3rd argent, a chevron gules, between three caps of maintenance, their fronts turned towards the sinister, *Brudenell*. **Crest** – 1st, a lion statant, tail extended azure; 2nd a seahorse naiant proper. **Supporters** – Two savages proper wreathed about the temples and loins vert, each holding in his exterior hand a lance, thereon a banner of the arms of Bruce.
Residence – Luton Lye, Savernake Forest, nr Marlborough, Wilts.

SON LIVING (By 1st marriage)

DAVID MICHAEL JAMES (*Earl of Cardigan*) (Savernake Lodge, Savernake Forest, nr Marlborough, Wilts), *b* 12 Nov 1952; *ed* Eton, Rannoch, and RAC Cirencester; 31st Hereditary Warden of Savernake Forest (since 1987): *m* 1980, Rosamond Jane, eldest da of Capt W. R. M. Winkley, of Wyke Champflower Manor, Bruton, Somerset, and has issue:—
SON LIVING— Thomas James (*Viscount Savernake*), *b* 11 Feb 1982.

DAUGHTER LIVING— *Lady* Catherine Anna, *b* 1984.

DAUGHTERS LIVING *(By 1st marriage)*

Lady Sylvia Davina, *b* 1954: *m* 1987, Peter M. Gould, yst son of late R. C. L. Gould, of Grouville, Jersey. *Residence* – La Pulente, St Brelade, Jersey.
Lady Carina Doune BRUDENELL-BRUCE, *b* 1956; has resumed her maiden name: *m* 1982 (*m diss* 1988), Anthony Le Brun, only son of Basil Le Brun, of Beauchamp, Sion, Jersey. *Residence* – Le Perchoir, rue du Carrefour, Trinity, Jersey, CI.

(By 2nd marriage)

Lady Louise, *b* 1964.
Lady Kathryn Juliet, *b* 1965.

HALF-BROTHER LIVING

Lord Charles Adam, *b* 1951; *ed* Eton; late Lieut Royal Hus.

WIDOW LIVING OF SON OF SEVENTH MARQUESS

Nelida Garcia Otero (*Lady Piers Brudenell-Bruce*) (Cortijo de la Plata, Zahara de los Atunes, Cadiz, Spain), da of Mariano Garcia Villalba, of Madrid: *m* 1958, as his 2nd wife, Lord Chandos Gerald Piers Brudenell-Bruce, who *d* 1980, and has issue (infra).

WIDOW LIVING OF SEVENTH MARQUESS

JEAN FRANCES MARGARET (*Jean, Marchioness of Ailesbury*) (Bel au Vent, St Lawrence, Jersey), da of late John Addison Wilson, of Bodicote, Banbury, Oxon, and widow of Richard Williamson, MBE *m* 1950, as his 3rd wife, the 7th Marquess, who *d* 1974.

COLLATERAL BRANCHES LIVING

Issue of late Lord Chandos Gerald Piers Brudenell-Bruce, 2nd son of 7th Marquess, *b* 1929, *d* 1980: *m* 1st, 1951 (*m diss* 1957), Annie, only da of Henry Angelé, of Yamaa-el-Mokra, Tangier; 2ndly, 1958, Nelida Garcia Otero (ante), da of Mariano Garcia Villalba, of Madrid, Spain:—
(By 2nd *m*) Tamara Angela, *b* 1966. ——— Sandra Teresa *b* 1969.

Grandchildren of late Lord Robert Thomas Brudenell-Bruce, 4th son of 3rd Marquess:—
Issue of late George Lionel Thomas BRUDENELL, *b* 1880, *d* 1962, who assumed by Royal licence 1917, the surname and arms of Brudenell only: *m* 1923, Mary Julia, who *d* 1972, da of Stephen Schilizzi (*see* Ralli Bt, 1952 Edn):—
Edmund Crispin Stephen James George, *b* 1928; *ed* Harrow, and RAC Cirencester; DL Northants 1977: *m* 1955, Hon Marian Cynthia Manningham-Buller, eldest da of 1st Viscount Dilhorne, and has issue living, Robert Edmund, *b* 1956; *ed* Stanbridge Earls Sch, — Thomas Mervyn (twin), *b* 1956; *ed* Eton: *m* 1984, Venetia Jane, who *d* 1993, da of Maj Robert Patricius Chaworth-Musters, of Felley Priory, Jacksdale, Notts, and has issue living, Sophia *b* 1985, Victoria *b* 1987, — Anna Maria, *b* 1960; *ed* Benenden. *Seat* – Deene Park, Corby, Northants. *Town Residence* – 18 Laxford House, Ebury St, SW1.
Issue of late Col Robert Hanbury Brudenell-Bruce, DSO, Norfolk Regt, *b* 1881, *d* 1955: *m* 1st, 1913, Olive Vere, who *d* 1920, da of Charles H. Richardson, of Cedar Hurst, co Down; 2ndly, 1922, Judith Iris, who *d* 1981, da of late Maj Bertram William Arnold Keppel (*see* E Albemarle colls, 1980 Edn):—
(By 2nd *m*) †Chandos Robert Henry, *b* 1923: *m* 1949, Dana Moira Angela (Trainers House, Moulton Paddocks, Newmarket), da of Stanhope Joel, of Perots Island, Bermuda, and *d* 1993, leaving issue, Andrew Robert Joel, *b* 1951; *ed* Eton: *m* 1974, Sophie, da of Robert Stuart Malcolm Douglas Inch, of 32 Harmont House, 20 Harley St, W1, and has issue living, Henry Robert Woolf *b* 1976, Alice Marie Antoinette *b* 1974, Christabel Marie-Jeanne *b* 1981, Florence Anne-Marie *b* 1985, — Joanna Dana, *b* 1954: *m* 1st, 1975, Charles FitzRoy, who *d* 1975, eldest son of Hon Charles James FitzRoy (later 6th Baron Southampton); 2ndly, 1977, Paul Farrant, of The Chestnuts, Dunsfold, Surrey, and has issue living (by 2nd *m*), Thomas Robert Jack *b* 1986, Rebecca Dana *b* 1979, Francesca Joanna *b* 1981, — Sara Vivien *b* 1960: *m* 1985, Walter Hood, of Flint Barn, Snailwell, Newmarket, Suffolk.
Issue of late John Charles Brudenell-Bruce, MBE, *b* 1885, *d* 1960: *m* 1st, 1913 (*m diss* 1925), Else, da of Capt C. F. Dreschel, of Copenhagen; 2ndly, 1928, Sigrid Ellen, who *d* 1980, da of Anders Ammentorp, of Copenhagen:—
(By 2nd wife) David John, *b* 1927. ——— Simon Robert (47 Kings Rd, Paihia, NZ), *b* 1928: *m* 1st, 1964, Christine Muriel Heald, of Pokeno; 2ndly, 1986, Nina, da of Andreas Skjoth, of Kolding, Denmark, and has issue living (by 1st *m*), Peter Gregory, *b* 1965, — Barbara Ann, *b* 1967, — Penelope Jane, *b* 1970. ——— Barbara Karen *b* (twin) 1928: *m* 1953, Charles Zeese, of 60-64 69th Av, Ridgewood, NY; 1211 N Miller Rd, Scottsdale, Arizona; and Rt 9N, Springmeyer Hills, Silver Bay, NY, USA, and has issue living, Kevin Bruce (1657 Kenwood Av, Alexandria, Virginia 22302; Rt 9N, Springmeyer Hills, Silver Bay, NY, USA), *b* 1955: *m* 1976 (*m diss* 1994), Dina Smith, and has issue living, Alexander Bruce *b* 1983, Daniel Alfred *b* 1988, — Mark Charles (1672 Woodbine Av, Ridgewood, NY 11385, USA), *b* 1957: *m* 1989, Tatiana Taskova, and has issue living, Philip Taskova *b* 1994, Kristina Taskova *b* 1990, — Eve Ellen, *b* 1962: *m* 1988, Todd Stevens, of 67-76 Booth St, Forest Hills, NY 11375, and Rt 9N, Springmeyer Hills, Silver Bay, NY, USA, and has issue living, Sara Evelyn *b* 1991. ——— Diana Mary (Little Denmark, Tortola, BVI, W Indies), *b* 1936; has issue living, John Adam, *b* 1963. ——— Arabella Anne, *b* 1940: *m* 1st, 1962 (*m diss* 1969), Jack Ball, of Puerto Rico; 2ndly, 1972, Morgan J. Gatten, of 73-03 Bell Blvd, Bayside Apt 1-3J, New York 11364, USA, and has issue living (by 1st *m*) Robert J., *b* 1968, — Lesley Anne, *b* 1963, — Beth Sigrid, *b* 1965, — (by 2nd *m*) Michael J., *b* 1972.

Grandchildren of late John Charles Brudenell-Bruce, MBE (ante):—
Issue of late Marc Hadrian Brudenell-Bruce, *b* 1930, *d* 1965: *m* 1st, 1953 (*m diss* 1957); 2ndly, 1957, Rayna Ellen, da of Ernest Herbert Nicholas Howell, of Tayforth Rd, Westmere, Wanganui, NZ:—
(By 2nd *m*) Marc Raymond Christopher (38 Intrepid Drive, Mermaid Waters, Gold Coast, Qld, Australia), *b* 1962. ——— Keren Suzanne (1 Wainwright Av, Mt Roskill, Auckland, NZ), *b* 1958: *m* 1983, — Kempster, and has issue living, Fiona Rochelle, *b* 1981, — Jade Michelle, *b* 1984.

PREDECESSORS – (1) CHARLES Bruce, 4th Earl of Elgin, 3rd Earl of Ailesbury, and 6th Lord Kinloss; was the last male descendant of that branch of the Bruce family which settled in England circa 1603. He selected as his heir his nephew, Hon Thomas Brudenell, 4th son of 3rd Earl of Cardigan by Elizabeth Bruce; cr *Baron Bruce*, of Tottenham (peerage of Great Britain) 1746, with remainder to Hon Thomas Brudenell (ante); *d* 1747 without surviving male issue, when the Earldom of Ailesbury became ext, the Earldom of Elgin reverted to the 9th Earl of Kincardine, the Lordship of Kinloss became abeyant, and the Barony of Bruce devolved upon his nephew (ante) (2) THOMAS, 2nd Baron; inherited also the Wardenship of Savernake Forest in Wilts (an ancient office which became hereditary in the Esturmy family (1066-1427), passed thence into the Seymour family (see D Somerset)) and so in 1676 to the Bruces; he assumed the additional name and arms of Bruce; cr

Earl of Ailesbury (peerage of Great Britain) 1776; *d* 1814; *s* by his son **(3)** CHARLES, KT, 2nd Earl; *cr Viscount Savernake, Earl Bruce*, and *Marquess of Ailesbury* (peerage of United Kingdom) 1821: *m* 1st, 1793, Hon Henrietta Maria Hill, who *d* 1831, da of 1st Baron Berwick; 2ndly, 1833, Maria Elizabeth, who *d* 1893, da of Hon Charles Tollemache; *d* 1856; *s* by his elder son **(4)** GEORGE WILLIAM FREDERICK, KG, 2nd Marquess, *b* 1804; summoned to House of Lords in his father's Barony of Bruce 1839; was Lord-Lieut of Wilts and Master of the Horse 1868-74; *s* his kinsman, the 7th Earl of Cardigan, 1868 (see infra*): *m* 1837, Lady Mary Caroline Herbert, who *d* 1892, da of 11th Earl of Pembroke; *d* 6 Jan 1878; *s* by his brother **(5)** ERNEST AUGUSTUS CHARLES, PC, 3rd Marquess; was Lord-Lieut of Berks, MP for Marlborough (*C*) 1832-78, and Vice-Chamberlain to HM 1841-6, and 1852-8: *m* 1834, Hon Louisa Elizabeth Horsley-Beresford, who *d* 1891, da of 2nd Baron Decies; *d* 1886; *s* by his grandson **(6)** GEORGE WILLIAM THOMAS (son of George John Brudenell-Bruce, who *d* 1868, eldest son of 3rd Marquess), 4th Marquess, *b* 1863: *m* 1884, Dorothy Julia, who *d* 1917, da of Thomas Haseley, of Brighton; *d* 1894; *s* by his uncle **(7)** HENRY AUGUSTUS, 5th Marquess; *b* 1842; MP for N-W, or Chippenham, Div of Wiltshire (*C*) 1886-92: *m* 1870, Georgiana Sophia Maria, who *d* 1902, da of George Henry Pinckney, formerly of Tawstock Court, Barnstaple: *d* 1911: *s* by his son **(8)** GEORGE WILLIAM JAMES CHANDOS, DSO, TD, 6th Marquess; *b* 1873; late 3rd Batn Argyll and Sutherland Highlanders, R Wilts Yeo, Middlesex Yeo, Wilts. Regt, RASC and RFA (TA); S Africa 1899-1900 with Army Transports as DAAG (DSO), European War 1915-19 with Guards Div Train: *m* 1st 1903, Caroline Sydney Anne, who *d* 1941, da of late John Madden; 2ndly, 1945, Mabel Irene, who *d* 1954, da of late John Samuel Lindsay, of Wrexham; 3rdly, 1955, Alice Maude Emily, who *d* 1960, da of late Capt John Forbes Pinhey, and widow of (1) Col John Henry Arthur Boyce, (2) Col Francis Byrne Johnson, and (3) Col Rowland Money, OBE: *d* 1961; *s* by his son **(9)** CHANDOS SYDNEY CEDRIC, 7th Marquess; *b* 1904: *m* 1st, 1924, Joan Houlton, who *d* 1937, da of Stephen Salter, of Pondwell, Ryde, I of Wight; 2ndly, 1944 (*m diss* 1948) Joyce Frances, da of Charles Warwick-Evans, and formerly wife of Peter Quennell; 3rdly, 1950, Jean Frances Margaret, da of late John Addison Wilson, of Bodlicote, Oxon, and widow of Richard Williamson, MBE; *d* 1974; *s* by his elder son **(10)** MICHAEL SYDNEY CEDRIC, 8th Marquess and present peer; also Earl of Cardigan, Earl Bruce, Viscount Savernake, Baron Brudenell, and Baron Bruce.

*(1) Sir THOMAS Brudenell, a zealous supporter of the royal cause during the Civil War, suffered long imprisonment in the Tower; *cr* a *Baronet* 1611, *Baron Brudenell* (peerage of England) 1628, and *Earl of Cardigan* (peerage of England) 1661; *d* 1663; *s* by his eldest son **(2)** ROBERT, 2nd Earl; *d* 1703: *s* by his grandson **(3)** GEORGE, 3rd Earl; Master of the Buckhounds to Queen Anne; *d* 1732; *s* by his elder son **(4)** GEORGE, KG, 4th Earl; Gov to the Prince of Wales and Prince Frederick; *cr Marquess of Monthermer* and *Duke of Montagu* (peerage of Great Britain) 1776, and *Baron Montagu*, of Boughton (peerage of Great Britain) 1786, with remainder to his grandson Henry James, 2nd son of 3rd Duke of Buccleuch; *d* 1790 without surviving male issue, when the Marquessate and Dukedom became extinct, the Barony passed to his grandson (ante), and the Earldom devolved upon his brother **(5)** JAMES, 5th Earl; *dsp* 1811; *s* by his nephew **(6)** ROBERT, 6th Earl, son of Hon Robert, 3rd son of 3rd Earl; *d* 1837; *s* by his son **(7)** JAMES THOMAS, KCB, a Lieut-Gen in the Army and Col 11th Hussars; served with distinction in the Crimea; *dsp* 1868; *s* by his cousin **(8)** GEORGE WILLIAM FREDERICK, 2nd Marquess of Ailesbury (ante).

AILSA, MARQUESS OF (Kennedy) (Marquess UK 1831)

Consider the end

ARCHIBALD ANGUS CHARLES KENNEDY, 8th Marquess; *b* 13 Sept 1956; *s* 1994: *m* 1979 (*m diss* 1989), Dawn Leslie Anne, only da of David A. Keen, of 64 Rue Emeriau, Paris, and has issue.

𝔄rms – Argent, a chevron gules, between three cross crosslets fitchée sable, the whole within a double tressure flory counterflory of the second. 𝔠rest – A dolphin naiant, proper. 𝔖upporters – Two swans, wings inverted proper, beaked and membered gules.
Seat – Cassillis, Maybole, Ayrshire. *Club* – New (Edinburgh).

DAUGHTERS LIVING

Lady Rosemary Margaret, *b* 1980.
Lady Alicia-Jane Lesley, *b* 1981.

BROTHER LIVING

Lord DAVID THOMAS, *b* 3 July 1958; *ed* Strathallan Sch, and Berks Agric Coll: *m* 1991, Anne, da of Bernard Kelly, of Warwick, and has issue living, Katherine Jean, *b* 1993. *Residence* – Morriston Farm, Maidens, Maybole, Ayrshire KA19 8LB.

SISTER LIVING

Lady Elizabeth Helen, *b* 1955: *m* 1976, Rev Norman Walker Drummond, MA, BD, FRSA, Chap to HM in Scotland, Headmaster Loretto Sch, and has issue living, Andrew, *b* 1977, — Christian, *b* 1986, — Ruaraidh, *b* 1993, — Margaret, *b* 1980, — Marie Clare, *b* 1981. *Residences* – Pinkie House, Loretto School, Musselburgh, E Lothian EH21 7RE; Ach Nan Eun, Ellishader, Staffin, Isle of Skye.

WIDOW LIVING OF SEVENTH MARQUESS

MARY (*Marchioness of Ailsa*), da of late John Burn, of Amble, Northumberland: *m* 1954, Lt-Col the 7th Marquess, OBE, who *d* 1994. *Residence* – Cassillis, Maybole, Ayrshire.

COLLATERAL BRANCHES LIVING

    Grandchildren of late John Gilbert Kennedy, eldest son of late Lord Gilbert Kennedy, 5th son of late Archibald, Earl of Cassillis, elder son of 12th Earl of Cassillis (afterwards 1st Marquess):—
    Issue of late Capt Nigel Augustus Kennedy, *b* 1886, *d* 1957: *m* 1st, 1917 (*m diss* 1944), Gertrude Vera, da of late Brig-Gen Lionel Godolphin Brooke, CB (*see* V Brookeborough, colls); 2ndly, 1946, Dorothy Mary, who *d* 1962, da of William Henry Langley, of 1358 Victoria Av, Victoria, BC, Canada, and widow of Lt-Col Richard Clive Cooper, Canadian Inf:—
    (By 1st *m*) Ian Michael Godfrey, *b* 1921; European War 1941 as Pilot Officer RAF (invalided): *m* 1960, Josephine Helen, da of John Leslie Price, of Warham Court, Breinton, Hereford, and has issue living, Angus Michael David, *b* 1962; MRCP, — Virginia Anne Nicola, *b* 1964. *Residence* – The Camp Farm, Caynham, nr Ludlow, Shropshire. —— Lonia Hersey Joy, *b* 1924: *m* 1944 (*m diss* 1966), Donald MacLean, late Lt RCN, and has issue living, John Kennedy, *b* 1946: *m* 1983, Rosemary, yr da of F. P. Hillier, of Godalming, Surrey, — Alan Michael, *b* 1948: *m* 1971, Sandra, da of E. McDonald, of Vancouver, BC, and has issue living, Sarah Kennedy *b* 1978, Gillian Anne *b* 1983, — Brian William, *b* 1950.

Granddaughters of late Sir John Gordon Kennedy, KCMG, eldest son of late John Kennedy (infra):—
Issue of late Capt Aubrey Leo Kennedy, MC, *b* 1885, *d* 1965: *m* 1921, Sylvia Dorothy, who *d* 1968, da of late Arthur
Herbert Meysey-Thompson (*see* Meysey-Thompson, Bt, colls, 1968 Edn):—
Elizabeth Dorothy (4 Gordon Place, W8), *b* 1922: *m* 1st, 1945 (*m diss* 1958), Charles Russell Scarr; 2ndly, 1960, her cousin,
Jeremy John Le Mesurier (*see* Meysey-Thompson, Bt colls, 1972-73 Edn), and has had issue (by 1st *m*) (Aubrey) Mark
Kennedy MEYSEY-THOMPSON (Spellow Hill, Knaresborough, Yorks), *b* 1949; assumed by deed poll 1978 the surname of
Meysey-Thompson; Capt RGJ; TV prod: *m* 1975, Catharine Diana Jane Herdman-Newton, and *d* 1987, leaving issue, James
Leo Charles *b* 1979, Emma Catherine *b* 1978, — Caroline Sarah (64 Hatfield Rd, Chiswick, W4), *b* 1951. —— Horatia Clare,
b 1926: *m* 1969, Brian Huleatt Heddy, HM Dip Ser (ret), of Wynyards, Winsham, Chard, Somerset. —— Diana Helen
Marjorie, *b* 1929.

(In remainder to Earldom of Cassillis)

Grandchildren of Edward Briggs Kennedy, 3rd son of John Kennedy (infra):—
Issue of late Capt Edward Coverley Kennedy, RN; *b* 1879, *ka* 1939: *m* 1918, Rosalind Margaret Innes, who *d* 1977,
da of Sir Ludovic James Grant, 11th Bt:—
Ludovic Henry Coverley, *b* 1919; *ed* Eton, and at Oxford Univ; is a broadcaster, writer, and lecturer; author of *On My Way to
The Club* (1989); European War 1939-45 as Lieut RNVR: *m* 1950, Moira Shearer, the writer and former ballerina, da of late
Harold Charles King, and has issue living, Alastair Charles Coverley, *b* 1963, — Ailsa Margaret, *b* 1952, — Rachel Katharine,
b 1956: *m* 1988, Bill Hall, son of Prof Edward Thomas Hall, CBE, of Oxford, — Fiona Jane, *b* 1961. —— Morar Margaret, *b*
1926: *m* 1st, 1948 (*m diss* 1954), John Hamish Orr-Ewing; 2ndly, 1954, Royce Thomas Carlisle Ryton, of 10 Talbot Lodge,
West End Lane, Esher, Surrey KT10 8NE, and has issue living (by 1st *m*), Roderick Coverley Hugh, *b* 1951: *m* 1984, Elisabeth
Claire, only da of late Torolf Lyth, of 74 Princes House, Kensington Park Rd, W11, — Margaret, *b* 1950; *d* 1961, — (by 2nd
m) Charlotte Susan, *b* 1955. —— Katherine, *b* 1927: *m* 1947, Ion Melville Calvocoressi, MBE, MC, late Maj Scots Gds
(High Sheriff of Kent 1978), and has issue living, James Melville Ion, *b* 1948: *m* 1971, Richenda Victoria Hanson, eldest da of
late Peter Blandy, and has issue living, Matthew James *b* 1973, Rupert Benedict *b* 1976, Christopher John *b* 1988, — Richard
Edward Ion, *b* 1951: *m* 1976, Francesca, only da of late David Temple Roberts, and has issue living, Thomas David *b* 1977,
Natalia Katherine *b* 1980, Hermione Beatrice *b* 1984, — Andrew Matthew Ion, *b* 1953, — Iona Rosalind, *b* 1957: *m* 1980,
Richard James Priestley, yr son of James Priestley, of Upton Manor, Upton, Hants, and has issue living, Laura Katherine *b*
1982, Rosanna Victoria *b* 1985, Isabel Louise *b* 1988. *Residence* – Court Lodge, Westerham, Kent.

Granddaughter of Gilbert George Kennedy, 4th and yst son of John Kennedy, only son of Hon Robert
Kennedy, 3rd son of 11th Earl of Cassillis:—
Issue of late Judge John de Navarre Kennedy, OBE, *b* 1888, *d* 1979: *m* 1st, 1914, Elsie Margaret, who *d* 1969, da of
late Edwin Charles Pinks, of Lindsell, Essex; 2ndly, 1970, Marjorie Helen Troop (707 Weller St, Peterborough,
Ontario, Canada K9J 4X2), da of late Albert Morton, of Dudley, Worcs:—
(By 1st *m*) Anne Macomb, *b* 1930: *m* 1953, Frank Edward Dudas, of The Bothy, Victoria St, Bourton-on-the-Water, Glos
GL54 2DH, and has issue living, Edward Tibor, *b* 1959, — Linda Julianna Kennedy, *b* 1956, — Yone Anne Pinks, *b* 1962.

PREDECESSORS – **(1)** *Sir* GILBERT Kennedy, KB, cr *Lord Kennedy* (peerage of Scotland) 1452: was one of the six Regents
of the Kingdom during the minority of James III; *s* by his son **(2)** JOHN, 2nd Lord; *d* 1508; *s* by his son **(3)** DAVID, PC, 3rd
Lord; cr *Earl of Cassillis* 1509; *k* at Battle of Flodden 1513; *s* by his son **(4)** GILBERT, 2nd Earl; assassinated 1527 by Sir
Hugh Campbell, of Loudon, Sheriff of Ayr, and a supporter of the Angus faction, from whom he had unsuccessfully
attempted to rescue James V the previous year; *s* by his son **(5)** GILBERT, 3rd Earl, Lord High Treasurer of Scotland; *d* 1558;
s by his son **(6)** GILBERT, 4th Earl; *d* 1576; *s* by his son **(7)** GILBERT, 5th Earl, Lord Treasurer of Scotland; *d* 1615; *s* by his
nephew **(8)** JOHN, 6th Earl; *s* by his son **(9)** JOHN, 7th Earl; *d* 1701; *s* by his grandson **(10)** JOHN, 8th Earl; *dsp*, 1759, and in
1762 was by a resolution of House of Lords *s* by his kinsman **(11)** *Sir* THOMAS Kennedy, 4th Bt (cr 1682), of Culzean, 9th
Earl; *d* unmarried 1775; *s* by his brother **(12)** DAVID, 10th Earl; *dsp*, 1792, when the Baronetcy became ext, and the peerage
titles descended to the great-great-grandson of Hon Thomas, 2nd son of 3rd Earl **(13)** ARCHIBALD, 11th Earl, Capt RN; *d*
1794; *s* by his son **(14)** ARCHIBALD, KT, FRS, 12th Earl; cr *Baron Ailsa* (peerage of United Kingdom) 1806, and *Marquess of
Ailsa* (peerage of United Kingdom) 1831; *d* 1846; *s* by his grandson **(15)** ARCHIBALD, KT, 2nd Marquess, *b* 1816; Lord-Lieut
of Ayrshire: *m* 1846, Julia, who *d* 1899, da of Sir Richard Mounteney Jephson, 1st Bt; *d* 1870; *s* by his son **(16)** ARCHIBALD,
3rd Marquess, *b* 1847; Lord-Lieut of Ayrshire: *m* 1st, 1871, Hon Evelyn Stuart, who *d* 1888, 3rd da of 12th Baron Blantyre;
2ndly, 1891, Isabella, who *d* 1945, da of late Hugh McMaster, of Kausani, N-W Provinces, India; *d* 1938; *s* by his son **(17)**
ARCHIBALD, 4th Marquess, *b* 1872: *m* 1903, Frances Emily, who *d* 1949, da of Sir Mark John MacTaggart-Stewart, 1st Bt; *d*
1943; *s* by his brother **(18)** CHARLES, 5th Marquess, *b* 1875; Capt Ayrshire Yeo, and Lieut 3rd Batn, RSF: *m* 1st, 1925,
Constance Barbara, who *d* 1931, da of late Edward Clark of Avishays, Chard, and widow of Adm Sir John Kennedy Erskine
Baird, KCB; 2ndly, 1933, Helen Ethel, MBE, who *d* 1959, only da of late James McDouall, JP, DL, of Logan, and widow of
Major Richard John Cumminghame, MC, of Hensol, Kirkcudbrightshire; *d* 1956; *s* by his brother **(19)** ANGUS, 6th Marquess;
b 1882; formerly Capt RAF: *m* 1922; (Gertrude) Millicent, who *d* 1957, da of Gervas Weir Cooper, of Wordwell Hall, Bury St
Edmunds; *d* 1957; *s* by his son **(20)** ARCHIBALD DAVID, OBE, 7th Marquess, *b* 1925; Lieut Scots Guards, Lt-Col RSF (TA), DL
Ayrshire; Chm Anglo-Somali Soc: *m* 1954, Mary, da of late John Burn, of Amble, Northumberland; *d* 1994; *s* by his elder son
(21) ARCHIBALD ANGUS CHARLES, 8th Marquess and present peer; also Earl of Cassillis, Lord Kennedy, and Baron Ailsa.

AILWYN, BARONY OF (Fellowes) (Extinct 1988)

ADOPTED STEPDAUGHTER LIVING OF FOURTH BARON

Joan, da of Charles William Cudemore; *b* 1921; legally assumed surname of Fellowes in lieu of her patronymic upon adoption
1938: *m* 1942, Geoffrey Homer, FRCS, and has issue living, Garth, *b* 1944: *m* 1974, Penelope Saunders, and has issue, one
son and one da, — Keith, *b* 1947: *m* 1981, Dean Garrison, and has issue, two sons, — Bruce, *b* 1951. *Residence* – 3710
Cadboro Bay Rd, Victoria, BC V8P 5E1, Canada.

AIREDALE, BARON (Kitson) (Baron UK 1907, Bt UK 1886)

PALMAM QUI·MERUIT FERAT

Let him who merits bear the palm

OLIVER JAMES VANDELEUR KITSON, 4th Baron and 4th Baronet; *b* 22 April 1915; *s* 1958; *ed* Eton, and Trin Coll, Camb; Bar Inner Temple 1939; Maj Green Howards (ret); assumed by deed poll 1935, the additional forename of Vandeleur; appointed Dep Chm of Committees, House of Lords 1961, and Dep Speaker 1962.

𝔄rms – Or, on a pale azure, a pike hauriant of the first, on a chief of the second an annulet between two mill-rinds or. 𝔠rest – Issuant from a fence of paling proper, a demiunicorn argent, collared azure. 𝔖upporters – On either side an owl argent, gorged with a plain collar gules, pendent therefrom a shield of the arms.
Residence – Ufford Hall, Stamford, Lincolnshire.

SISTER LIVING

Hon Verona Vandeleur, OBE, TD, *b* 1920; Maj WRAC (TA); formerly Chm, Riding for the Disable Assocn, OBE (Civil) 1982, MBE (Mil) 1960. *Residence* – Pasture House, North Luffenham, Oakham, Leicestershire.

DAUGHTERS LIVING OF SECOND BARON

Hon Thelma Eirene, *b* 1902: *m* 1923, Noel Gordon Harris, MD, BS, MRCS, FRCP, DPM, who *d* 1963, son of Sir (Charles) Alexander Harris, KCMG, CB, CVO, and has issue living, James Gordon Shute (Mallet Court, Curry Mallet, Som TA3 6SY), *b* 1933: *m* 1978, Primrose Millicent Elaine Mallet, yr da of late Sir Philip Harvey du Cros, 2nd Bt, — Joyce Estelle, *b* 1924, RIBA: *m* 1953, Edward Fyfe Griffith, MRCS, LRCP, who *d* 1987, of Choughs, Trebetherick, Wadebridge, Cornwall, — Leslie Beryl, *b* 1926; MBAOT, FRVCM, AlDipR: *m* 1951, Michael Yate Johnson, MA, of 33 Beaumont Rd, Cambridge CB1 4PU, and has issue living, Martin Charles Yate *b* 1958: *m* 1985, Deborah Gillian Sack (and has issue living, Daniel Oliver Yate *b* 1987, Rupert Martin *b* 1989), Sally Yate *b* 1956: *m* 1982 (*m diss* 1986), Reginald Bernard Green (and has issue living, Gary Bernard Clifford *b* 1984), Jennifer Anne *b* 1957, — Jean Constance, *b* 1931: *m* 1952, James T. Arnot, of 9 Willifield Way, NW11, and has issue living, Keith James *b* 1955: *m* 1986, Louise Walker (and has issue living, Charles James *b* 1988, William Croasdale *b* 1991, Katherine Louise *b* 1993), Jacqueline Margaret *b* 1953. *Residence* – 28 Lyttelton Court, Lyttelton Rd, N2 0EB.
Hon Angela Estelle, *b* 1905: *m* 1927, George Herbert Goff, who *d* 1957, and has issue living, George Stephen, *b* 1928, — Jennifer Florence, *b* 1932: *m* 1st, 1954 (*m diss* 1965), Donald Iain Macaulay; 2nd, 1967, Brian Malcolm Richardson, and has issue living (by 1st *m*) Donald George Stuart *b* 1956, Angela Elisabeth Louise (20 Nelson Way, Stafford) *b* 1958: *m* 1982 (*m diss* 1990), Christopher John Hughes and has issue living, Siân Louise Jennifer *b* 1987. *Residence* – 20 Field Way, Broad Oak, Brede, E Sussex.

COLLATERAL BRANCH LIVING

Issue of late Hon Edward Christian Kitson, 3rd son of 1st Baron, *b* 1873, *d* 1922: *m* 1903, Mary Katharine (who *d* 1944, having *m* 2ndly, 1926, Walter John Burt, Bar-at-law, who *d* 1931), eldest da of Samuel Hirst, formerly of 3 The Crescent, Scarborough:—
Christine Annabel (3 Wilton Terrace, SW1), *b* 1908: *m* 1932. Cyril Alfred Roberts, CBE, DL, Bar-at-law, who *d* 1988, and has issue living, Francis Kitson (34 Quarrendon St, SW6 3SU), *b* 1935: *m* 1962, Joan Lena Lorna Dawes, and has issue living, Guy Francis Cyril *b* 1963, Philip Maurice Dawes *b* 1966, Cressida Lorna Joan *b* 1971, — David Christopher, *b* 1944: *m* 1973, Jane Roskill, — Geoffrey Michael, *b* 1947, — Penelope Christine Mary, *b* 1937: *m* 1961, Maj-Gen Thomas Anthony Boam, CB, CBE, late Scots Gds, and has issue living, Thomas Edward *b* 1964, Caroline Christine *b* 1962: *m* 1987, Nicholas Mann, Katharine Penelope *b* 1968.

PREDECESSORS – (1) JAMES KITSON, PC, son of late James Kitson, JP, of Elmet Hall, Leeds; *b* 1835; first Lord Mayor of Leeds 1896-7; MP for Yorkshire, W Riding, S Part, Colne Valley Div 1892-1907; cr a *Baronet* 1886, and *Baron Airedale*, of Gledhow, W Riding of co of York (peerage of United Kingdom) 1907: *m* 1st, 1860, Emily, who who *d* 1873, da of Joseph Cliff; 2ndly, 1881, Mary Laura, who *d* 1939, only da of late Edward Fisher Smith, of The Priory, Dudley; *d* 1911; *s* by his son (2) ALBERT ERNEST, 2nd Baron; *b* 1863; an Iron and Steel Manufacturer, a Director of London City and Midland Bank, Ltd, and a Member of Lloyds: *m* 1890, Florence, who *d* 1942, da of late Edward Schunck; *d* 1944; *s* by his half-brother (3) ROLAND DUDLEY, DSO, MC, 3rd Baron; *b* 1882; High Sheriff of co London 1928; late Capt Prince of Wales's Own (W Yorkshire Regt); European War 1914-18 (MC, DSO): *m* 1st 1913, Sheila Grace, who *d* 1935, da of late Frank E. Vandeleur, of 52 Evelyn Gardens, SW; 2ndly, 1937, Dorothy Christabel, who *d* 1970, da of late Rev Canon Raymond Percy Pelly (Pelly, Bt, colls), and widow of Hugh Mortimer Rowland; *d* 1958; *s* by his son (4) OLIVER JAMES VANDELEUR, 4th Baron and present peer.

AIREY OF ABINGDON, BARONY OF (Airey) (Extinct 1992)

SONS AND DAUGHTER OF LIFE BARONESS (*see* Neave, Bt, colls)

Hon (Richard) Patrick Sheffield NEAVE.
Hon William Robert Sheffield NEAVE.
Hon Marigold Elizabeth Cassandra WEBB.

AIRLIE, EARL OF (Ogilvy) (Earl S 1639)

To the end

DAVID GEORGE COKE PATRICK OGILVY, KT, GCVO, PC, 13th Earl, *b* 17 May 1926; *s* 1968; *ed* Eton; Capt Scots Gds (Res); DL Angus 1964, Lord Lieut Tayside Region, District of Angus, since 1989, JP; Lord Chamberlain HM's Household, and Chancellor Royal Victorian Order, since 1984; 2nd Bn Germany 1945, ADC to C-in-C, and High Commr Austria 1947-48; Chm, Schröders Ltd, Ashdown Investment Trust Ltd, Dep Chm, Gen Accident Fire and Life Assurance Corpn, Dir J Henry Schröder Wagg & Co Ltd, and other cos; Pres The Scout Assocn of Scotland; Hon LLD Dundee 1990; CStJ 1981; 1939-45 War; Malaya 1948-50; *cr* PC 1984, GCVO 1984 and KT 1985: *m* 1952, Virginia Fortune, CVO, da of John Barry Ryan, of Moorland Farm, Newport, Rhode Island, USA, and has issue.

Arms – Argent, a lion passant guardant gules crowned with an imperial crown and collared with an open one proper. *Crest* – A lady from the waist upwards affrontée azure holding a portcullis gules. *Supporters* – Two bulls sable, armed and unguled vert, and gored with a garland of flowers.
Seats – Cortachy Castle, and Airlie Castle, Kirriemuir, Angus. *Town Residence* – 5 Swan Walk, SW3.

SONS LIVING

DAVID JOHN (*Lord Ogilvy*), *b* 9 March 1958; *ed* Eton, and Ch Ch, Oxford (MA); a Page of Honour to HM 1971-72: *m* 1st, 1981 (*m diss* 1990), Hon Geraldine Theodora Mary Gabriel Harmsworth, eldest da of 3rd Viscount Rothermere; 2ndly, 1991, Tarka, da of John Kings, of Austin, Texas, USA, and has issue by 1st and 2nd *m*:—
SON LIVING (by 2nd m) — *Hon* David Huxley (*Master of Ogilvy*), *b* 11 Dec 1991.
DAUGHTER LIVING (by 1st m) — *Hon* Augusta, *b* 1981.
Residence – Airlie Castle, Kirriemuir, Angus.
Hon Bruce Patrick Mark, *b* 1959.
Hon Patrick Alexander, *b* 1971.

DAUGHTERS LIVING

Lady Doune Mabell, *b* 1953: *m* 1977, Hereward Charles Wake, of The Stables, Courteenhall, Northants, only son of Maj Sir Hereward Wake, 14th Bt.
Lady Jane Fortune Margaret, *b* 1955: *m* 1980, Francois Nairac, son of Paul Nairac, of Vacoas, Mauritius, and has issue living, Jessica Doune, *b* 1985, — Annabel Lydia, *b* 1988.
Lady Elizabeth Clementine, *b* 1965.

BROTHERS LIVING

Hon Sir Angus James Bruce, KCVO, *b* 1928; *ed* Eton, and at Trin Coll, Oxford; Scots Gds 1946-48, Member HM Body Guard for Scotland (Royal Company of Archers); Pres Imperial Cancer Research Fund since 1964, The Carr-Gomm Soc since 1983, and Youth Clubs UK (formerly Nat Assocn of Youth Clubs) 1969-89 (Chm 1964-69), Chm of Council Prince's Youth Business Trust since 1986; Patron Arthritis Care (formerly British Rheumatism & Arthritis Assocn) since 1978 (Chm 1963-69, Pres 1969-78), and Scottish Wildlife Trust since 1974 (Pres 1969-74); Vice Pres Friends of the Elderly & Gentlefolks' Help since 1969 (Treas 1952-63, Chm 1963-69), Vice Patron Nat Children's Homes since 1986; Member Gov Council of SPCK since 1984, and of Council of Business in the Community since 1984; Trustee Leeds Castle Foundn since 1975, and GB-Sasakawa Foundation since 1985, etc; Dir various public cos; Grand Officer of Order of the Lion of Finland, and of Order of the Oak Crown of Luxembourg, KCVO 1989: *m* 1963, HRH Princess Alexandra Helen Elizabeth Olga Christabel, GCVO, da of HRH 1st Duke of Kent (*see* ROYAL FAMILY), and has issue living, James Robert Bruce, *b* 1964: *m* 1988, Julia, eldest da of Charles Frederick Melville Rawlinson, of Arkesden, Essex, — Marina Victoria Alexandra, *b* 1966: *m* 1990, Paul Julian Mowatt, and has issue living, Christian Alexander *b* 1993, Zenouska May *b* 1990. *Residence* – Thatched House Lodge, Richmond Park, Surrey. *Club* – White's.
Hon James Donald Diarmid, *b* 1934; *ed* Eton; Scots Gds 1952-54, Member HM Body Guard for Scotland (R Company of Archers); a Partner, Rowe & Pitman 1964-86, Chm Rowan Investment Managers 1972-86, Chm Mercury Rowan Mullens, Vice-Chm Mercury Asset Management Ltd, Chief Exec Foreign & Colonial, and Dir of other Investment Cos; a Page of Honour to HM 1947-51: *m* 1st, 1959, Magdalen June Ruth, da of late Robert Ducas (*see* B Mowbray, colls); 2ndly, 1980, Lady Caroline Child-Villiers, da of 9th Earl of Jersey, formerly wife of (i) Viscount Melgund (later 6th Earl of Minto), and (ii) Hon John Douglas Stuart, son of 1st Viscount Stuart of Findhorn, and has issue living (by 1st *m*), Shamus Diarmid Ducas, *b* 1966, — Diarmid James Ducas, *b* 1970, — Laura Jane, *b* 1960: *m* 1990, Philippe G. Goffin, yr son of Jean Goffin, of Brussels, and has issue living, Sebastian *b* 1992, — Emma Louise, *b* 1962. *Residences* – 51 Eaton Sq, SW1; Sedgebrook Manor, Sedgebrook, Grantham, Lincs. *Club* – White's.

SISTERS LIVING

Lady Victoria Jean Marjorie Mabell (*Baroness Lloyd*), *b* 1918: *m* 1942, 2nd Baron Lloyd, MBE, who *d* 1985. *Residence* – Clouds Hill, Offley, Hitchin, Herts.
Lady Margaret Isla Marion, *b* 1920; formerly in WRNS: *m* 1946, Capt Sir Iain Mark Tennant, KT, DL, Scots Gds (*see* B Glenconner, colls). *Residence* – Lochnabo House, Elgin, Morayshire.

COLLATERAL BRANCH LIVING

Issue of late Hon Lyulph Gilchrist Stanley Ogilvy, DSO, 2nd son of 10th Earl, *b* 1861; *d* 1947: *m* 1902, Edith Gertrude Boothroyd, who *d* 1908, of Waterdale, Loveland, Colorado, USA:—
Jack David Angus, *b* 1903: *m* 1940, Dorothy Stanley, of Boulder, Colorado, USA. *Residence* – 1525 9th Street, Boulder, Colorado, USA.

PREDECESSORS – (1) *Sir* JAMES Ogilvy, KB; Ambassador from Scotland to Denmark 1491, was in that year cr *Lord Ogilvy of Airlie* (peerage of Scotland); *d* 1504; *s* by his eldest son (2) JOHN, 2nd Lord; he was *s* by his eldest son (3) JAMES, 3rd Lord; *s* by his eldest son (4) JAMES, 4th Lord, an Extraor Lord of Session; *d* 1554; *s* by his grandson (5) JAMES, 5th Lord; *d* 1606; *s* by his eldest son (6) JAMES, 6th Lord; *d* 1617; *s* by his son (7) JAMES, 7th Lord, a zealous partisan of Charles I; cr *Lord Ogilvy of Alyth and Lintrathen*, and *Earl of Airlie* (peerage of Scotland) 1639; *s* by his eldest son (8) JAMES, PC, 2nd Earl; being taken prisoner at the battle of Philipshaugh 1644, he was sentenced to death by the Parliament at St Andrew's, 26 Nov 1645, but escaped in his sister's clothes the night before his intended execution; pardoned by Act of Parliament 1649, and at the Restoration was sworn of the Privy Council; *s* by his son (9) DAVID, 3rd Earl; *d* 1717; his eldest son (10) JAMES, 4th Earl, assisted in the Earl of Mar's rising 1715, was attainted by Act of Parliament during his father's life, and afterwards pardoned; *d* 1731; *s* by his brother (11) JOHN, 5th Earl; *d* 1761; *s* by his son (12) DAVID, 6th Earl; he joined the Chevalier at Edinburgh 1745 at the head of 600 men, and was attainted by Act of Parliament; after the battle of Culloden he escaped to France where he commanded a Regiment of Foot, and attained the rank of Lt-Gen; in 1778 he received a pardon under the Great Seal; *d* 1803; *s* by his son (13) DAVID, 7th Earl; *d* unmarried; *s* by his uncle (14) WALTER, 8th Earl; *d* 1819; *s* by his eldest son (15) DAVID, 9th Earl, who had his honours confirmed by Act of Parliament 1826; was Lord-Lieut of Forfarshire and a Scottish Representative Peer; *d* 1849; *s* by his son (16) DAVID GRAHAM DRUMMOND, KT, 10th Earl, *b* 1826; a Representative Peer for Scotland, and Lord High Commr to Church of Scotland 1872-3: *m* 1851, Hon Henrietta Blanche Stanley, who *d* 1921, da of 2nd Baron Stanley of Alderley; *d* 25 Sept 1881; *s* by his eldest son (17) DAVID STANLEY WILLIAM, 11th Earl; *b* 1856: *m* 1886, Lady Mabell Frances Elizabeth Gore, GCVO, OBE, who *d* 1956, da of 5th Earl of Arran; *k* during S African War 1900; *s* by his son (18) DAVID LYULPH GORE WOLSELEY, KT, GCVO, MC, 12th Earl; *b* 1893; Col Scots Guards; Repres Peer for Scotland 1922-63; Lord-in-Waiting to HM 1926-29; Lord Chamberlain to HM Queen Elizabeth the Queen Mother 1937-65: *m* 1917, Lady Alexandra Marie Bridget Coke, who *d* 1984, da of 3rd Earl of Leicester; *d* 1968; *s* by his eldest son (19) DAVID GEORGE COKE PATRICK, 13th Earl and present peer; also Lord Ogilvy of Airlie, and Lord Ogilvy of Alyth and Lintrathen.

ALANBROOKE, VISCOUNT (Brooke) (Viscount UK 1946)

Glory the end

ALAN VICTOR HAROLD BROOKE, 3rd Viscount; *b* 24 Nov 1932; *s* 1972; *ed* Harrow; Capt (ret) RA.

Arms – Or, a cross engrailed per pale gules and sable, in the first quarter a crescent of the second. **Crest** – A brock, proper. **Supporters** – On either side an officer of the Royal Horse Artillery in full dress proper supporting with the exterior hand an escutcheon azure charged with seven barrulets wavy argent surmounted by a salmon rising gules.
Residence – Ferney Close, Hartley Wintney, Hants.

HALF-SISTER LIVING

Hon Rosemary, *b* 1918: *m* 1945, Capt Ronald Alastair Macdonald, RA, of Bottom Farm, Berkhamsted, Herts, and has issue living, Alastair Alan Graham, *b* 1947, — Ian Ronald, *b* 1952, — Janey Rosemary, *b* 1949.

PREDECESSORS – (1) *Field Marshal Sir* ALAN FRANCIS Brooke, KG, GCB, OM, GCVO, DSO, 6th son of Sir Victor Alexander Brooke, 3rd Bt (cr 1822) (*see* V Brookeborough); *b* 1883; late RA; Inspector of RA 1935-6, Dir of Mil Training War Office 1936-7, GOC, Mobile Div 1937-8, C-in-C, AA Command (TA) 1938-9, GOC-in-C, S Command 1939, GOC 2nd Corps 1939-40, C-in-C Home Forces 1940-41, CIGS 1941-6; Col Comdt RA 1939-57, RHA 1940-57, and Hon Artillery Co 1946-54, Master Gunner, St James's Park 1946-56, and Constable of Tower of London 1950-55; Lord High Constable of England at Coronation of HM Queen Elizabeth II: *m* 1st, 1914, Jane Mary, who *d* 1925, da of late Col John Mervyn Carleton Richardson; 2ndly, 1929, Benita Blanche, who *d* 1968, da of Sir Harold Pelly, 3rd Bt, and widow of Sir Thomas Evan Keith Lees, 2nd Bt (cr 1897); *d* 1963; *s* by his eldest son (2) THOMAS, 2nd Viscount; *b* 1920; *d* 1972; *s* by his half-brother (3) ALAN VICTOR HAROLD, 3rd Viscount and present peer.

ALBEMARLE, EARL OF (Keppel) (Earl E 1696)

Do not yield to misfortunes

RUFUS ARNOLD ALEXIS KEPPEL, 10th Earl; *b* 16 July 1965; *s* 1979; *ed* St Christopher Sch, Letchworth, Chelsea Sch of Art, and Central Sch of Art (BA).

Arms – Gules, three escallops argent. **Crest** – Out of a ducal coronet or, a swan's head and neck argent. **Supporters** – Two lions ducally crowned or.
Residence – 20A Pembroke Sq, W8 6PA.

HALF SISTERS LIVING (*Raised to the rank of an Earl's daughters,* 1980)

Lady Elizabeth Mairi, *b* 1941: *m* 1st, 1962 (*m diss* 1976), Alastair Michael Hyde Villiers (*see* D Roxburghe, 1968 Edn); 2ndly, 1980 (*m diss* 1988), 7th Baron Sudeley, and has issue living (by 1st *m*), Charles Alastair Hyde, *b* 1963: *m* 1994, Emma M. J., da of J. B. W. Goodall, of 11 Smith St, SW3, — Charlotte Mairi, *b* 1965.
Lady Rose Deirdre Margaret, *b* 1943: *m* 1975, Peter Lathrop Lauritzen, of Palazzo da Silva, Cannaregio 1468, Venice, Italy, and has issue living, Frederick Alexander Mark, *b* 1977.

AUNTS LIVING (*Daughters of 9th Earl by 1st marriage*)

Lady Cecilia Elizabeth, *b* 1910: *m* 1934, David McKenna, CBE, late Lt-Col RE (Cdr Order of Merit, France, Member of Br Rlys Board 1968, Past Chm Sadlers Wells Foundation and Bach Choir), son of late Rt Hon Reginald McKenna, and has issue living, Myee Miranda, *b* 1935: *m* 1958, John Francis Hyde Villiers (*see* E Clarendon, colls), — Pamela Primrose, *b* 1937: *m* 1961, Christopher James Folke Arnander (*see* E Crawford), of Old Wharf, Shillingford, Oxon, — Sophia Mary (Plas y Darren y Strafellte, Aberdare, Glamorgan), *b* 1944: *m* 1965 (*m diss* 1971), John Boyd Wilson. *Residences* – Rosteague, Portscatho, Truro, Cornwall; 13D Stuart Tower, Maida Vale, W9.

Lady Cynthia Rosalie, *b* 1918: *m* 1944, Prof Sir Michael Moissey Postan, FBA, who *d* 1981, Fellow of Peterhouse, Cambridge, and has issue living, Basil David, *b* 1946: *m* 1968, Maria, da of Samuel Carr, of Paultons Sq, SW3, — Alexander Henry Keppel, *b* 1948: *m* 1991, Jane, da of Dr J. Dillon, of Dublin.

HALF AUNT LIVING (*Daughter of 9th Earl by 2nd marriage*)

Lady Anne-Louise Mary, *b* 1932: *m* 1954, Maj Sir Hew Fleetwood Hamilton-Dalrymple, 10th Bt, KCVO. *Residence* – Leuchie, North Berwick, East Lothian EH39 5NT.

WIDOW LIVING OF SON OF NINTH EARL

Aline Lucy, da of late Brig-Gen John Harington, CB, CMG, DSO (*see* Harington, Bt, colls): *m* 1941, Lt-Cdr Hon Walter Arnold Crispian Keppel, DSC, RN, who *d* 1986, 2nd son of 9th Earl (by 1st *m*), and has issue (infra). *Residence* – Barton House, Meonstoke, Hants.

MOTHER LIVING

MARINA (*Viscountess Bury*); ARIBA, AA Dip (Piazza di Bellosguardo 10, Florence 50124, Italy), da of late Lt-Cdr Count Serge Orloff-Davidoff, RNVR (*see* B Howard de Walden and Seaford): *m* 1964, as his 2nd wife, Derek William Charles, Viscount Bury, who *d* 1968.

WIDOW LIVING OF NINTH EARL

Dame DIANA CICELY, DBE, DLitt, DCL, LLD, (*Countess of Albemarle*) (Seymours, Melton, Woodbridge, Suffolk), da of late Maj John A. Grove: *m* 1931, as his 2nd wife, the 9th Earl, MC, who *d* 1979.

COLLATERAL BRANCHES LIVING

Issue of late Lt-Cdr Hon Walter Arnold Crispian Keppel, DSC, RN, 2nd son of 9th Earl (by 1st *m*), *b* 1914, *d* 1986: *m* 1941, Aline Lucy (ante), da of late Brig-Gen John Harington, CB, CMG, DSO (*see* Harington, Bt, colls):—
CRISPIAN WALTER JOHN, *b* 29 Oct 1948; *ed* Eton: *m* 1990, Tina, elder da of Claus Ammann, of Stuttgart, Germany, and has issue living, Christin Alexa, *b* 1991. *Residence* – 15 Gresswell St, SW6 6PR. ——— Colin Rupert Harington, *b* 1951; *ed* Eton: *m* 1981, Frances May, da of late Cdr Francis Montagu Maxwell Ommanney, DSC, RN, of Droxford, Hants, and has issue living, Oliver George Rupert, *b* 1982, — William Richard Crispian, *b* 1986, — Isabel Frances Bridget, *b* 1984. ——— Judith Cynthia Aline KEPPEL, *b* 1942; has resumed her maiden name: *m* 1st, 1964 (*m diss* 1980), Desmond Leon Corcoran; 2ndly, 1985, Neil H. Shand, and has issue living (by 1st *m*), Alexander Martin Desmond, *b* 1968, — Sibylla Monacella, *b* 1966: *m* 1992, David J. Whitmore, yr son of John Whitmore, of Hartfield, Sussex, — Aline Rose, *b* 1972.

Granddaughters of late Col Edward George Keppel, MVO, son of late Rev William Arnold Walpole Keppel, son of late Rt Rev Hon Frederick Keppel, DD, Bishop of Exeter, 4th son of 2nd Earl:—
Issue of late Lt-Col Arnold Ramsay Keppel, *b* 1879, *d* 1930: *m* 1922, Launa Margaret, who *d* 1983 (having *m* 2ndly, 1961, Sir Richard Arthur Pease, 2nd Bt (*cr* 1920), who *d* 1969), da of Hughes Martin, formerly of Tullaghreine, co Cork:—
June Cecilia, *b* 1924: *m* 1st, 1946, Capt Edward Percy Canning Loyd, Coldstream Gds (*see* B Brabourne, 1967 Edn), who *d* 1977; 2ndly, 1990, Alexander K. H. Fletcher, of The Old Vicarage, Wighill, Tadcaster, N Yorks, and has issue living (by 1st *m*), David William Arnold (17 Larkhall Rise, SW4 6JB), *b* 1949; *ed* Eton: *m* 1985, Mrs Anabel Laura Dorothy Stapleton, only da of Hon Sir Charles Andrew Morrison, MP (*see* B Margadale), and has issue living, James Canning *b* 1988, Rupert Charles Percy *b* 1990, Tabitha Launa Mary *b* 1992, — Caroline Evelyn, *b* 1947: *m* 1968, Anthony Havelock Hudson, of Flat 3, Whittingstall Mansions, Whittingstall Rd, SW6, elder son of Sir Havelock Henry Trevor Hudson, of The Old Rectory, Stanford Dingley, Berks, and of Mrs Roger Houssemayne du Boulay, of Anstey House, nr Buntingford, Herts. ——— Bridget Anne (*Lady Martin Fitzalan Howard*), *b* 1925: *m* 1948, Capt Lord Martin Fitzalan Howard, late Gren Gds, of Brockfield Hall, York (*see* D Norfolk). ——— Lavinia Mary (*Hon Mrs Richard Beaumont*), *b* 1928: *m* 1971, Hon Richard Blackett Beaumont (*see* V Allendale), of Flat 1, 58 South Audley St, W1Y 5FB.

PREDECESSORS – (1) ARNOLD JOOST Van Keppel, KG, a Member of the Nobles in Holland, accompanied the Prince of Orange in his expedition 1688, and on the establishment of the Prince upon the throne of England was cr *Baron Ashford, Viscount Bury*, and *Earl of Albemarle* (peerage of England) 1696; *d* 1718; *s* by his son (2) WILLIAM ANNE, KG, 2nd Earl, a distinguished Gen and sometime Ambassador at the Court of Versailles; *d* 1754; *s* by his eldest son (3) GEORGE, KG, 3rd Earl, a Lt-Gen in the Army; Com-in-C Land Forces, engaged in combined expdn, with his brothers, Commodore Hon Augustus Keppel, First Lord of Admiralty (*cr* Viscount Keppel 1782, *ext* 1786), and Lt-Gen Hon William Keppel, which ended in the capture of Havanna, 1762; *d* 1772; *s* by his son (4) WILLIAM CHARLES, 4th Earl; *b* 1772: *m* 1792, Hon Elizabeth Southwell, who *d* 1817, da of 17th Baron Clifford; 2ndly, 1822, Charlotte Susannah, who *d* 1862, da of Sir Henry Hunloke, Bt; *d* 1849; *s* by his eldest son (5) AUGUSTUS FREDERICK, 5th Earl; *dsp* 1851, *s* by his brother (6) GEORGE THOMAS, 6th Earl, *b* 1799: served at Battle of Waterloo; MP for E Norfolk 1832-5, and for Lymington (*L*) 1847-50: *m* 1831, Susan, who *d* 1885, da of Sir Coutts Trotter, 1st Bt; *d* 1891; *s* by his eldest son (7) WILLIAM COUTTS, KCMG, PC, 7th Earl, *b* 1832; MP for Norwich (*L*) 1857-9, for Wick 1860-65, and for Berwick 1868-74; Treasurer of Queen Victoria's Household 1859 and Under-Sec of State for War 1878-80 and 1885-6; a Vol ADC to Queen Victoria; called to House of Lords during his father's lifetime as Baron Ashford 1876: *m* 1855, Sophia, who *d* 1917, da of Hon Sir Allan Napier Macnab, 1st Bt (*ext*), Prime Min of Canada; *d* 1894; *s* by his eldest son (8) ARNOLD ALLAN CECIL, GCVO, CB, VD, TD, 8th Earl, *b* 1858; Col in the Army; Vice-Lieut for Norfolk; S Africa 1900 (despatches, medal with four clasps, CB); an ADC to HM King Edward VII 1903-10 and King George V 1910-25, and a Lord-in-Waiting to HM Nov 1922-4; MP for Birkenhead (*C*) 1892-94: *m* 1881, Lady Gertrude Lucia Egerton, who *d* 1943, only child of 1st Earl Egerton of Tatton; *d* 1942; *s* by his eldest son (9) WALTER EGERTON GEORGE LUCIAN, MC, 9th Earl, *b* 1882; 1914-18 War as Lt-Cdr RN Div, and Maj Scots Gds (Machine Gun Co Cmdr) (despatches twice); ADC to Govs-Gen of Canada 1904-05 and India 1907-08, and to Gov of Orange River Colony 1907-08: *m* 1st, 1909, Lady Judith Sydney Myee Carrington, who *d* 1928, da of 1st Marquess of Lincolnshire (ext); 2ndly, 1931, Dame Diana Cicely, DBE, DLitt, DCL, LLD, da of late Maj John A. Grove; *d* 1979; *s* by his grandson (10) RUFUS ARNOLD ALEXIS (only son of late Derek William Charles, Viscount Bury, eldest son of 9th Earl), 10th Earl and present peer; also Viscount Bury, and Baron Ashford.

ALDENHAM, AND HUNSDON OF HUNSDON, BARON (Gibbs) (Baron UK 1896 and 1923)

VICARY TYSER GIBBS, 6th Baron Aldenham and 4th Baron Hunsdon of Hunsdon, *b* 9 June 1948; *s* 1986; *ed* Eton, Oriel Coll, Oxford, and RAC Cirencester; Liveryman Merchant Taylors' Co; Dir Montclare Shipping Co Ltd since 1986: *m* 1980, Josephine Nicola, elder da of John Fell, of Lower Bourne, Farnham, Surrey, and has issue.

Arms – Argent, three battle-axes erect within a bordure nebuly sable. **Crest** – In front of a rock a dexter arm embowed in armour, the hand gauntleted proper, bearing a battle-axe in bend sinister sable. **Supporters** – On either side a man habited in buff leather jerkin, gloves, and boots, armed with a three-barred helmet, long gorget, and sword, all proper, and holding in the exterior hand a battle-axe over the shoulder sable.
Residence – Aldenham Wood Lodge, Elstree, Herts.

Tenax propositi

Tenacious of purpose

SONS LIVING

Hon HUMPHREY WILLIAM FELL, *b* 31 Jan 1989.
Hon Thomas Antony John, *b* 1992.

DAUGHTER LIVING

Hon Jessica Juliet Mary, *b* 1984.

BROTHER LIVING

Hon George Henry Paul (The Old Sawmill, Middleton Stoney, Oxon OX6 8SH), *b* 1950: *m* 1st, 1973 (*m diss* 1989), Janet Elizabeth, da of Harold Leonard Scott; 2ndly, 1992, Elizabeth, da of late Prof Geoffrey Wingfield Harris, CBE, FRS, and has issue living (by 1st *m*), Piers Antony Scott, *b* 1973, — Corin William Tyser, *b* 1976.

SISTER LIVING

Hon Antonia Mary, *b* 1958: *m* 1989, Simon H. Johnson, son of E. A. Johnson, of Walmer, Kent, and has issue living, Edmund Antony Gibbs, *b* 1992, — Maud Eleanor Gibbs, *b* 1990. *Residence* – Manor Farm, Middle Chinnock, Som.

WIDOW LIVING OF SON OF FOURTH BARON ALDENHAM

Jean Frances, CVO, da of late Capt Angus Valdimar Hambro, MP; appointed a Lady-in-Waiting to HM when Princess Elizabeth 1945, and an Extra Woman of the Bedchamber to HM 1953; CVO 1953: *m* 1st, 1942, Capt Hon Vicary Paul Gibbs, Gren Gds, who was *ka* 1944; 2ndly, 1946, Rev Hon Andrew Charles Victor Elphinstone, who *d* 1975 (*see* L Elphinstone); 3rdly, 1980, Lt-Col John William Richard Woodroffe, who *d* 1990 (*see* E Ducie, colls, 1968 Edn) and has issue living (by 1st *m*) (*see* colls infra) (by 2nd *m*) (*see* L Elphinstone). *Residences* – Arnbarrow, Laurencekirk, Kincardineshire; Maryland, Worplesdon, Guildford, Surrey.

WIDOW LIVING OF SON OF FIRST BARON HUNSDON OF HUNSDON

Dame Molly Peel, DBE, CStJ, da of late John Peel Nelson, of Bulawayo: *m* 1934, Rt Hon Sir Humphrey Vicary Gibbs, GCVO, KCMG, OBE, who *d* 1990, and has issue (*see* colls infra). *Residence* – No 6 The Square, High St, Leigh, Kent TN11 8RJ; PO Box 30, Harare, Zimbabwe.

WIDOW LIVING OF FIFTH BARON

MARY ELIZABETH (*Mary, Baroness Aldenham*), only da of late Walter Parkyns Tyser, of Gordonbush, Brora, Sutherland: *m* 1947, the 5th Baron, who *d* 1986. *Residence* – Rathgar, The Avenue, Sherborne, Dorset DT9 3AH.

COLLATERAL BRANCHES LIVING

Issue of late Capt Hon Vicary Paul Gibbs, Gren Gds, eldest son of 4th Baron Aldenham, *b* 1921, *ka* 1944: *m* 1942, Jean Frances, CVO (ante) (who *m* 2ndly, 1946, Rev Hon Andrew Charles Victor Elphinstone, who *d* 1975 (*see* L Elphinstone); and 3rdly, 1980, Lt-Col John William Richard Woodroffe (*see* E Ducie, colls, 1968 Edn)), da of late Capt Angus Valdimar Hambro, MP:—
Jennifer Susan, *b* 1944; Lady-in-Waiting to HM Queen Elizabeth The Queen Mother since 1993: *m* 1974, Capt Michael Charles Gordon-Lennox, RN, of Fishers Hill, Iping, Midhurst, W Sussex (*see* D Richmond and Gordon, colls).

Issue of late Hon Sir Geoffrey Cokayne Gibbs, KCMG, 2nd son of 1st Baron Hunsdon of Hunsdon, *b* 1901, *d* 1975: *m* 1926, Helen Margaret, CBE, who *d* 1979, da of late Charles Frederick Henry Leslie, of Epcombs, Hertford:—
David Charles Leslie (21 William St, S Yarra, Melbourne, Australia), *b* 1927; *ed* Eton, and Ch Ch, Oxford; a Dir Australia and New Zealand Banking Group, and other cos: *m* 1965, Charmian Fleur, only da of Dalzell Pulteney Mein, of Toolang, Coleraine, Victoria, Australia, and has issue living, Hugo Dalzell, *b* 1967, — Justin Geoffrey, *b* 1969, — Emma Victoria, *b* 1966, — Arabella Sarah, *b* 1970. —— Stephen Cokayne (Dougarie, Isle of Arran, KA27 8EB), *b* 1929; *ed* Eton; late 2nd Lt KRRC; a Dir Vaux Group plc, and of other Cos: *m* 1972, Lavinia Winifred, da of Sir Edmund Castell Bacon, 13th Bt, KG, KBE, TD, and has issue living, James Edmund Geoffrey, *b* 1975, — William Stephen, *b* 1978, — Emily Anna Maria, *b* 1973. —— Julian Herbert, *b* 1932; *ed* Eton. —— Sir Roger Geoffrey (23 Tregunter Rd, SW10), *b* 1934; *ed* Eton, and Millfield; Dir Arsenal Football Club 1980, Chm Howard de Walden Estates 1993, Chm Gerrard and Nat Discount Co plc 1975-89, Gov The Wellcome Trust since 1983, and Chm since 1989; Ktd 1994. —— Christopher Henry (Manor House, Clifton Hampden, Abingdon, Oxon; L6 Albany, W1), *b* 1938; *ed* Eton, Stanbridge, and Univ of Poitiers; Trustee J. Paul Getty Jr Charitable Trust since 1985. —— Elizabeth Helen (twin), *b* 1938: *m* 1963, Valentine Patrick Fleming, of Stonewall Park, Chiddingstone Hoath, Edenbridge, Kent (*see* Borthwick, Bt, colls), and has issue living, Matthew Valentine, *b* 1964, — Harry Geoffrey, *b* 1966, — Rupert Michael, *b* 1969, — Thomas Mungo, *b* 1971.

Issue of late Rt Hon Sir Humphrey Vicary Gibbs, GCVO, KCMG, OBE, 3rd son of 1st Baron Hunsdon of Hunsdon, *b* 1902, *d* 1990; Gov of S Rhodesia 1959-69: *m* 1934, *Dame* Molly Peel, DBE, CStJ (ante), da of late John Peel Nelson, of Bulawayo:—

Jeremy Herbert (Upper Kennards, Leigh, Kent TN11 8RE), *b* 1935; *ed* Diocesan Coll, S Africa, and Ch Ch, Oxford (MA): *m* 1958, Alison Douglas, da of Col Douglas McCrone Martin, of Dunchattan, Troon, Ayrshire, and has issue living, Elizabeth Belinda, *b* 1959: *m* 1988, Ferrill D. Roll, of 92 Norwood Av, Upper Montclair, NJ 07043, USA, yst son of M. W. Roll, of New Mexico, USA, and has issue living, James Herbert *b* 1992, Helen Mary *b* 1990, Alice Elizabeth *b* 1993, — Barbara Anne Camilla, *b* 1961, — Lucinda Jane, *b* 1965, — Arabella Sophie, *b* 1967. —— Nigel Henry Vicary (Cyrene, Horcott, Fairford, Glos), *b* 1937; *ed* Ruzawi Sch, Marandellas, Diocesan Coll, Rondebosch, Prince Edward Sch, Salisbury, and RAC Cirencester: *m* 1967, Barbara Boitumelo, 2nd da of Rev Canon Edward George Paterson, and has issue living, Paul Humphrey Paterson, *b* 1968: *m* 1992, Claire Diane, only da of Peter Freeman, of Johannesburg, S Africa, — Douglas Robert Nigel, *b* 1972, — Mairi Rosalind Diana, *b* 1970. —— Timothy Durant (Silver Street House, S Cerney, Cirencester, Glos GL7 5TP), *b* 1938; *ed* Ruzawi Sch, Marandellas, and Diocesan Coll, Rondebosch: *m* 1978, Susan Heather, da of Graham Melville Rankine, and widow of Robert Duncan Bothwell Fleming, and has issue living, James Rankine Fleming, *b* 1979, — Caroline Rose, *b* 1981, — and two adopted children, David Alexander FLEMING-GIBBS, *b* 1974, — Sarah Victoria FLEMING-GIBBS, *b* 1977. —— Kenneth Richard (The Old Vicarage, Appledore, Kent), *b* 1941; *ed* Ruzawi Sch, Marandellas, Diocesan Coll, Rondebosch, and Cape Town Univ: *m* 1966, Mary Elizabeth Frances, only da of Francis Beamish, of E London, S Africa, and has issue living, Vicary James, *b* 1973, — Sara Jane, *b* 1970. —— Simon Humphrey (Brunswick Cottage, Church St, Kelvedon, Essex), *b* 1947; *ed* Peterhouse, Rhodesia, and Reading Univ: *m* 1974, Philippa Mary, da of Terence Astley Brand, and has issue living, Nicholas Geoffrey, *b* 1979, — Thomas Humphrey, *b* 1982, — Susannah Kate, *b* 1985.

(Male line in remainder to the Barony of Aldenham only)

Issue of late Ven Hon Kenneth Francis Gibbs, DD, 5th son of 1st Baron Aldenham, *b* 1856, *d* 1935: *m* 1894, Mabel Alice, who *d* 1953, da of Charles Edward Barnett (*see* B Ormathwaite, 1923 Edn):—
Bernard Vicary, TD, *b* 1905; *ed* Winchester; 1939-45 War as Maj Anti-Aircraft Regt, RA (TA). —— Andrew Antony, MBE, TD, *b* 1914; *ed* Winchester, and Ch Ch, Oxford (BA 1937, MA 1946); Maj Herts Regt (TA Res), a Dir of Barclays Bank 1962-84; 1939-45 War (despatches, MBE); MBE (Mil), 1945: *m* 1947, Elizabeth Joan, who *d* 1993, da of Major Eric Charles Montagu Flint, DSO, and widow of Capt Peter George William Savile Foljambe, Herts Regt (*see* E Liverpool), and has issue living, John Kenneth Andrew (The White Cottage, Old Heathfield, E Sussex), *b* 1948; *ed* Winchester; FCA, a Dir Balfour, Williamson & Co Ltd since 1988: *m* 1978, Julia Margaret, only da of Maurice Edwards, of Mullets, Piddletrenthide, Dorset, and has issue living, Simon Andrew Maurice *b* 1985, Emma Elizabeth *b* 1979, Louisa Mary *b* 1981, — Alan Francis (16 Edwardes Sq, W8), *b* 1953; *ed* Winchester, and Ch Ch, Oxford: *m* 1982, Francine Nicola, eldest da of Nicholas Preston, of Park Farm, Beverston, Tetbury, Glos, and has two children, Leo Antony Francis *b* 1988, Fleur Elizabeth *b* 1990. *Residence* – Kilvington Hall, Thirsk, Yorks. *Clubs* – Travellers', Pratt's.

Granddaughter of late Hon Henry Lloyd Gibbs, yst son of 1st Baron Aldenham:—
Issue of late Maurice Antony Crutchley Gibbs, *b* 1888, *d* 1974: *m* 1912 (*m diss* 1924), Elma, who *d* 1973, da of Sir William Gordon Gordon-Cumming, 4th Bt; 2ndly, 1933, Margaret Falkiner, who *d* 1964, only da of late Daniel Grant McBean, of Fairley Grange, NSW, and formerly wife of Reginald Francis Egerton, RN:—
(By 1st *m*) Daphne Marion, *b* 1912: *m* 1934, Percy Kirwan Agar, of La Haut, Dominica, and has issue living, Antony Edward (La Haut, Dominica), *b* 1936: *m* 1967, Madeleine Carmel, da of late Stephen Morrison, of Nova Scotia, and has issue living, Stephen Kirwan *b* 1968, Maurice Ashton *b* 1970, Madeleine Daphne *b* 1972, Francillia *b* 1975, — Elizabeth Anne *b* 1938: *m* 1958, Mark Varvill, of Lane End House, Ellanore Lane, W Wittering, W Sussex, and has issue living, Richard Antony *b* 1961, Katherine Mary *b* 1963.

PREDECESSORS – (1) HENRY HUCKS Gibbs, FSA, son of late George Henry Gibbs, of Aldenham House, Herts, and of Clifton Hampden, Oxon, *b* 1819; senior partner in the firm of Antony Gibbs and Sons, bankers and merchants, of 15 Bishopsgate Street Within, EC; a Director of the Bank of England 1853-1901 (Gov 1875-7); MP for City of London (*C*) 1891-2; cr *Baron Aldenham*, of Aldenham, co Hertford (peerage of United Kingdom) 1896: *m* 1845, Louisa Anne, who *d* 1897, da of William Adams, LLD, formerly of Thorpe, Chertsey, Surrey; *d* 1907; *s* by his eldest son (2) ALBAN GEORGE HENRY, 2nd Baron, *b* 1846; MP for City of London (*C*) 1892-1906: *m* 1873, Bridget, who *d* 1896, da of late Rt Hon Alexander James Beresford Beresford Hope, PC, of Bedgebury Park, Kent; *d* 1936; *s* by his only son (3) GERALD HENRY BERESFORD, 3rd Baron, *b* 1879, a partner in the firm of Antony Gibbs & Sons, merchants and bankers, of 22 Bishopsgate, EC: *m* 1905, Lillie Caroline, who *d* 1950, eldest da of late Rev William Thomas Houldsworth, of 44 Lennox Gardens, SW; *d* 1939; *s* by his cousin (4) WALTER DURANT, 4th Baron, 2nd Baron Hunsdon of Hunsdon (see infra *), *b* 1888; Chm of Antony Gibbs & Sons, 1939-65, and Westminster Bank 1950-61: *m* 1919, Beatrix Elinor, who *d* 1978, da of Herbert Woodfield Paul (*see* Mackworth, Bt, colls, 1924 Edn), and widow of Algernon Hyde Villiers (*see* E Clarendon, colls): *d* 1969; *s* by his yr son (5) ANTONY DURANT, 5th Baron, *b* 1922, 1939-45 War as Lt RNVR; Dir Antony Gibbs & Sons Ltd: *m* 1947, Mary Elizabeth, only da of late Walter Parkyns Tyser; *d* 1986, *s* by his eldest son (6) VICARY TYSER, 6th Baron and present peer; also 4th Baron Hunsdon of Hunsdon.
*(1) *Hon* HERBERT COKAYNE Gibbs, 4th son of 1st Baron Aldenham, *b* 1854; a partner in the firm of Antony Gibbs & Sons, bankers and merchants, of 22 Bishopsgate, EC; High Sheriff of Herts 1913; cr *Baron Hunsdon of Hunsdon*, of Briggens, co Hertford (peerage of United Kingdom) 1923: *m* 1885, Anna Maria, who *d* 1938, da of late Richard Durant, of High Canons, Herts, and Sharpham, Devon; *d* 1935; *s* by his eldest son (2) WALTER DURANT, 2nd Baron, who *s* as 4th Baron Aldenham 1939 (ante).

ALDINGTON, BARON (Low) (Baron UK, 1962)

Hope

TOBY (AUSTIN RICHARD WILLIAM) LOW, KCMG, CBE, DSO, TD, PC, 1st Baron, son of late Col Stuart Low, DSO (*see* B Atkin, 1957 Edn); *b* 25 May 1914; *ed* Winchester, and New Coll, Oxford (MA); Bar Middle Temple 1939; DL; Brig late The Rangers, KRRC (TA); Parl Sec to Min of Supply 1951-54, Min of State, Board of Trade 1954-57, and Dep Chm of Conservative Party Organization 1959-63; Chm GEC plc 1964-68 (Dep Chm 1968-84) Grindlays Bank Ltd 1964-76, Port of London Authority 1971-77, Gen Advisory Council BBC 1971-78, Cttee of Management, Inst of Neurology 1961-78, Sun Alliance and London Insurance plc 1971-85, Westland plc 1977-85, Nat Nuclear Corpn 1973-80; Dir Lloyds Bank plc 1967-85, Citicorp (USA) 1969-83; Chm Brain Research Trust 1971-86 (Pres 1986), and Leeds Castle Foundation 1984-94; Warden Winchester Coll 1979-87; Pres British Standards Instn 1986-89; 1939-45 War as Brig BGS 5 Corps Italy 1944-45, served Greece, Crete, Egypt, Libya, Tunisia, Sicily, Italy and Austria (despatches, DSO, MBE, CBE, French Croix de Guerre, Com of American Legion of Merit); MP for N Div of Blackpool (*C*) 1945-62; *cr* DSO 1941, MBE (Mil) 1944, CBE (Mil) 1945, PC 1954, KCMG 1957, and *Baron Aldington*, of Bispham, in Co Borough of Blackpool (peerage of UK) 1962: *m* 1947, Felicité Ann Araminta, da of late Sir Harold Alfred MacMichael, GCMG, DSO (*see* E Leven and Melville, colls, 1946 Edn), and formerly wife of Capt Paul Humphrey Armytage Bowman, Coldstream Gds (*see* Bowman, Bt, colls), and has issue.

Arms – Gules a pale ermine on a chief argent masoned sable three saffrons stalked and leafed proper. **Crest** – Out of the battlements of a tower or a cubit arm proper, the hand grasping a hurt. **Supporters** – *Dexter*, a stag proper; *sinister* a black Labrador dog proper; pendant from the neck of each by its own chains a portcullis or.
Residence – Knoll Farm, Aldington, Kent. **Clubs** – Carlton, Royal St George's Golf, Royal and Ancient.

SON LIVING

Hon CHARLES HAROLD STUART, *b* 22 June 1948; *ed* Winchester, New Coll, Oxford, and INSEAD (Fontainebleau); Man Dir Deutsche Bank AG, London Branch since 1988: *m* 1989, Regine, da of late Erwin von Csongrady-Schopf, of Bielefeld, Germany, and has issue living, Philip Toby Augustus, *b* 1 Sept 1990, — Louisa Charlotte Patience, *b* 1992, — Marie-Therese Sophie Araminta, *b* (twin) 1992. *Residence* – 59 Warwick Sq, SW1.

DAUGHTERS LIVING

Hon (Priscilla) Jane Stephanie, MVO, *b* 1949; *ed* Cranborne Chase Sch, Westfield Coll, London Univ, and Courtauld Inst of Art; Curator of Print Room, R Library, Windsor Castle since 1975; MVO 1985: *m* 1975, Hugh Ashley Roberts, son of Rt Rev Edward Roberts, sometime Bishop of Ely, and has issue living, Sophie Jane Cecilia, *b* 1978, — Amelia Frances Albinia, *b* 1982. *Residence* – Adelaide Cottage, Home Park, Windsor, Berks SL4 2JQ.
Hon (Lucy) Ann Anthea, *b* 1956; *ed* Cranborne Chase Sch, and Camberwell Sch of Arts and Crafts: *m* 1979, Alasdair North Grant Laing, and has issue (*see* E Stair, colls). *Residence* – Logie House, Forres, Morayshire IV36 0QN.

Alexander, Viscount; son of Earl of Caledon.

ALEXANDER OF HILLSBOROUGH, EARLDOM OF (Alexander) (Extinct 1965)

DAUGHTER LIVING OF FIRST EARL

Lady Beatrix Dora, *b* 1909; *ed* London Univ (BSc Econ 1932); a JP of Middlesex: *m* 1936, William Bernard Evison, BCom, and has issue living, Alexander Bernard, *b* 1948: *m* 1969, Joan Susan Hepworth, of Slaley, Northumberland, and has issue living, Deborah Claire *b* 1974, Carina Louise *b* 1976, Tanya Joan *b* 1978, — Jennifer Anne, *b* 1940; *ed* King's Coll, London (BSc and AKC 1962): *m* 1963, Wing Cdr Barry Charles Hunt, BSc, RAF, of 14 New Rd, Walters Ash, High Wycombe, Bucks, and has issue living, Geoffrey Alexander Waters *b* 1964; BEng: *m* 1990, Kelly Ann Vallee, of Seattle, Washington, USA, Toby Barry *b* 1966; BA (1966), Simon Charles *b* 1968; BSc (1968), Christopher Bernard *b* 1970. *Residence* – 101 Old Park Av, Enfield, Middx.

ALEXANDER OF POTTERHILL, BARONY OF (Alexander) (Extinct 1993)

SON LIVING OF LIFE BARON (By 2nd marriage)

Hon (Thomas) Bruce, *b* 1951; *ed* Oundle, and Clare Coll, Camb (MA): *m* 2ndly, 1984 (*m diss* 1993), Susan Joyce Allard, and has issue living, Thomas, *b* 1985. *Residence* – Suffolk House, Lidgate, nr Newmarket, Suffolk.

WIDOW LIVING OF LIFE BARON

JOAN MARY (*Baroness Alexander of Potterhill*), da of Robert Baxter Williamson, of Sheffield: *m* 1949, as his 2nd wife, Baron Alexander of Potterhill (Life Baron), who *d* 1993. *Residence* – 3 Moor Park Gdns, Pembroke Rd, Moor Park, Middlesex HA6 2LF.

ALEXANDER OF TUNIS, EARL (Alexander) (Earl UK 1952)

By land, by sea, by the stars

SHANE WILLIAM DESMOND ALEXANDER, 2nd Earl; *b* 30 June 1935; *s* 1969; *ed* Harrow, and Ashbury Coll, Ottawa; Lt Irish Gds (Res); Liveryman Mercers' Co; a Lord-in-Waiting to HM Jan to March 1974: *m* 1st, 1971 (*m diss* 1976), Hilary, only da of John van Geest; 2ndly, 1981, Hon Davina Mary Woodhouse, LVO (a Lady-in-Waiting to HRH Princess Margaret, Countess of Snowdon), yst da of 4th Baron Terrington, and has issue by 2nd *m*.

Arms – Per pale argent and sable, a chevron, and in base a crescent, all counterchanged; on a canton azure a harp or, stringed argent. **Crest** – An arm in armour, embowed, the hand holding a sword proper, hilt and pommel or. **Supporters** – *Dexter*, a piper of the Irish Guards holding under the interior arm a bagpipe; *sinister*, a sepoy of the 3rd/ 2nd Punjabi Regiment supporting with the exterior hand a rifle proper, each charged on the shoulder with an escutcheon barry nebuly of six argent and azure.
Residence – 59 Wandsworth Common, West Side, SW18 2ED.

DAUGHTERS LIVING (By 2nd marriage)

Lady Rose Margaret, *b* 1982.
Lady Lucy Caroline, *b* 1984.

BROTHER LIVING

Hon BRIAN JAMES, *b* 31 July 1939; *ed* Harrow; Lieut Irish Gds (Res). *Residence* – 11 The Little Boltons, SW10 9LJ.

SISTER LIVING

Lady Rose Maureen, *b* 1932; Vice-Chm Berwick-upon-Tweed Preservation Trust since 1989: *m* 1956, Lt-Col Humphrey Crossman, JP, DL, High Sheriff Berwick-on-Tweed 1990, and has issue living, David Lindisfarne Alexander, *b* (Nov) 1956: *m* 1985, Mrs Jane Lusk, da of S. J. Hamp-Adams, of Harare, Zimbabwe, and has issue living, Alice Patricia *b* 1986, Sophie Rose *b* 1988, — Emma Margaret, *b* 1959: *m* 1984, Christopher William Kennard Baldwin, of Twyssenden Manor, Goudhurst, Kent, son of late Peter Godfrey Kennard Baldwin, of Lindsay Hill, Parham, Antigua, WI, and has issue living, John Lindsay Alexander *b* 1989, Isabelle Rose *b* 1992. *Residence* – Cheswick House, Berwick-on-Tweed, Northumberland.

ADOPTIVE SISTER LIVING

Susan Mary, *b* 1948: *m* 1970, Andrew Paulet Hamilton, son of Capt Hubert Charles Paulet Hamilton, R Irish Fus (*see* Williams-Wynne, Bt, 1980 Edn), and has issue living, Alexander Caspar Paulet, *b* 1974, — Romany Celia Margaret, *b* 1971, — Imogen Laetitia Alice, *b* 1981. *Residence* – 8 Herondale Av, SW18.

PREDECESSORS – (1) FM Sir HAROLD RUPERT LEOFRIC GEORGE ALEXANDER, KG, GCB, OM, GCMG, CSI, DSO, MC, PC, 3rd son of 4th Earl of Caledon; *b* 1891; C-in-C British Forces in Burma 1942 and Middle East 1942-43, Dep C-in-C N Africa 1943, C-in-C 18th Army Group, N Africa 1943, C-in-C Allied Forces in Italy 1943-44 and Supreme Allied Comd Med 1944-45, Gov-Gen of Canada 1946-52, and Min of Defence 1952-54; Col Irish Gds 1947-69; cr *Viscount Alexander of Tunis*, of Errigal, co Donegal (peerage of UK) 1946, *Baron Rideau*, of Ottawa, and of Castle Derg, co Tyrone, and *Earl Alexander of Tunis* (peerage of UK) 1952: *m* 1931, Lady Margaret Diana Bingham, GBE, JP, who *d* 1977, da of 5th Earl of Lucan; *d* 1969; *s* by his eldest son (2) SHANE WILLIAM DESMOND, 2nd Earl and present peer; also Viscount Alexander of Tunis and Baron Rideau.

ALEXANDER OF WEEDON, BARON (Alexander) (Life Baron 1988)

ROBERT SCOTT ALEXANDER, QC, son of late Samuel James Alexander, of Newcastle, Staffs; *b* 5 Sept 1936; *ed* Brighton Coll, and King's Coll, Camb (BA 1959, MA 1963); Bar Middle Temple 1961, QC 1973, Bencher 1979, QC (NSW) 1983; Vice-Chm Bar Council 1984-85, Chm 1985-86; a Judge of Courts of Appeal of Jersey and Guernsey 1985-88; Chm Panel on Takeovers and Mergers 1987-89; Trustee Nat Gallery 1987-93; Non-Exec Dir RTZ Corpn plc since 1991, The London Stock Exchange 1991-93, Dep-Chm Securities and Investments Board since 1994, Member UK Panel on Sustainable Development; Chm Nat Westminster Bank plc since 1989; *cr Baron Alexander of Weedon*, of Newcastle-under-Lyme, co Staffs (Life Baron) 1986: *m* 1st, 1963 (*m diss* 1973), Frances Rosemary (*née* Pughe); 2ndly, 1978, Elizabeth (*née* Norman); 3rdly, 1985, Marie (*née* Sugrue), and has issue by 1st *m*.

𝕬rms – Per fess azure and gules between two swords in pale points upward argent hilts pommels and quillons or a tower argent pierced of a cross gules masoned proper and with a portcullis or infess with two towers each issuant in the flanks masoned and with a portal gold. 𝕮rests – Upon a chapeau gules encircled by a coronet rayonny or and turned up ermine a lion sejant or head and mane gules collared ermine supporting by its staff or spearheaded also or a banner of the arms fringed argent and gules. 𝕾upporters – *Dexter*, a lamb statant erect in trian aspect collared ermine unguled or; *Sinister*, a lion statant erect or head and mane in trian aspect gules collared ermine.
Residence – 28 Blomfield Rd, W9 1AA. *Club* – Garrick.

SONS LIVING *(By 1st marriage)*

Hon David Robert James, *b* 1964.
Hon William Richard Scott, *b* 1969.

DAUGHTER LIVING *(By 1st marriage)*

Hon Mary Frances Anne, *b* 1966.

ALINGTON, BARONY OF (Sturt) (Extinct 1940)

DAUGHTER LIVING OF THIRD BARON

Hon Mary Anna Sibell Elizabeth, OBE, *b* 1929; OBE (1980); High Sheriff Dorset 1989, DL 1989: *m* 1949, George Gosselin Marten, LVO, DSC, late Lt-Com RN (ret), son of late Vice-Adm Sir Francis Arthur Marten, KBE, CB, CMG, CVO, and has issue living, Napier Anthony Sturt, *b* 1959; a Page of Honour to HM 1973-75: *m* 1986, Virginie Charlotte, da of Alain R. E. Camu (*see* Crossley, Bt), and has issue living, Maximillian Augustus *b* 1988, Tobias *b* 1991, Constance Dorothea *b* 1987, — Victoria Mary, *b* 1950: *m* 1978, Ruaidhri McDonaugh, of 29 Regent's Park Rd, NW1 7TL, and has issue living, James Anthony *b* 1979, George Ruaidhri *b* 1981, Robert Francis *b* 1986, Hugo Napier *b* 1992, — Charlotte Diana, *b* 1952: *m* 1975, (Oswald) Alexander Mosley, and has issue (*see* B Ravensdale), — Georgina Elizabeth, *b* 1953: *m* 1st, 1973 (*m diss* 1980), Presley Francis Norton, of Ecuador; 2ndly, 1981, Augusto de Cruz, of The Galapagos Islands, and Quito, Ecuador, and has issue living (by 2nd *m*), Sebastian *b* 1982, Thomas *b* 1985, — Amabel Catherine, *b* 1954: *m* 1991, Ciaran Clarke, of Ardnamona House, Donegal, — Sophia Harriet, *b* 1962: *m* 1986, John Alexander, son of Peter Alexander, of 31 Rhenwyllan, Port St Mary, Isle of Man, and has issue living, Esmé Rose *b* 1992. *Residence* – Crichel, Wimborne, Dorset.

ALLAN OF KILMAHEW, BARONY OF (Allan) (Extinct 1979)

SON LIVING OF LIFE BARON

Hon Alexander Claud Stuart, *b* 1951: *m* 1978, Katie, da of Keith Clemson, NSW, Australia. *Residence* – Copse Hill Farm, Lower Froyle, Alton, Hants.

DAUGHTER LIVING OF LIFE BARON

Hon Jane Maureen, *b* 1952.

WIDOW LIVING OF LIFE BARON

MAUREEN (*Baroness Allan of Kilmahew*), da of late Harold Stuart Clark, of Singapore: *m* 1947, Baron Allan of Kilmahew (Life Baron), DSO, OBE, who *d* 1979.

ALLEN OF ABBEYDALE, BARON (Allen) (Life Baron 1976)

PHILIP ALLEN, GCB, yr son of late Arthur Allen, of Sheffield; *b* 8 July, 1912; *ed* King Edward VII Sch, Sheffield, and Queens' Coll, Camb (MA, Hon Fellow); Dep Chm Prison Commn 1950-52, Assist Under-Sec of State Home Office 1952-55, Dep Sec Min of Housing and Local Govt 1955-60, Dep Under-Sec of State Home Office 1960-62, Second Sec HM Treasury 1963-66, and Perm Under-Sec of State Home Office 1966-72; a Member of Security Commn 1973-91, and Chm of Gaming Board for Gt Britain 1977-85; cr CB (Civil) 1954, KCB (Civil) 1964, GCB (Civil) 1970, and *Baron Allen of Abbeydale*, of the City of Sheffield (Life Baron) 1976: *m* 1938, Marjorie Brenda, da of late Thomas John Colton Coe, of Sheffield.

𝔄rms – Barry of twelve azure and argent two swords in saltire points in base proper hilts pommels and quillons or surmounted by a representation of the tower of Beauchief Abbey proper. ℭrest – Within a wreath of holly proper a boar's head erased behind the ears argent holding in the jaws a dice gold. 𝔖upporters – On either side a tricolour cavalier King Charles spaniel the compartment comprising a grassy mount growing therefrom sprigs of holly all proper. 𝔐otto – Ad recta tende.
Residence – Holly Lodge, Englefield Green, Surrey, TW20 0JP.

ALLEN OF FALLOWFIELD, BARONY OF (Allen) (Extinct 1985)

SON LIVING OF LIFE BARON

Hon Lionel Paul (Raeburn Farm, Penton, Carlisle, Cumbria), *b* 1943: *m* 1981, Irene Lynwen (*neé* Morris).

DAUGHTER LIVING OF LIFE BARON

Hon Judith Felicity, *b* 1946: *m* 1973, Graham Tonge, of Orchard House, Innhams Wood, Crowborough, E Sussex TN6 1TE, and has issue living, Daniel Allen, *b* 1974, — Lucy Clare, *b* 1977.

WIDOW LIVING OF LIFE BARON

RUBY MILLICENT (*Baroness Allen of Fallowfield*) (83 Manley Rd, Sale, Cheshire), da of Albert Hounsell: *m* 1940, Baron Allen of Fallowfield, CBE (Life Peer), who *d* 1985.

ALLEN OF HURTWOOD, BARONY OF (Allen) (Extinct 1939)

DAUGHTER LIVING OF FIRST BARON

Hon Joan Colette (Polly) Clifford, *b* 1922. *Residence* – 10 Selwood Terrace, SW7.

ALLENBY, VISCOUNT (Allenby) (Viscount UK 1919)

With faith and work

MICHAEL JAFFRAY HYNMAN ALLENBY, 3rd Viscount; *b* 20 April 1931; *ed* Eton; *s* 1984; Lt-Col R Hus; CO R Yeo 1974-77; Dep Speaker House of Lords since 1993: *m* 1965, Sara Margaret, only da of Lt-Col Peter Milner Wiggin (*see* Wiggin, Bt, colls), and has issue.

𝕬rms – Per bend argent and gules, in the sinister three crescents, two and one of the second, and in the dexter, three horses' heads erased, one and two, of the first, all within a bordure azure. 𝕮rest – Issuant out of a crescent gules, a demi-lion proper. 𝕾upporters – *Dexter*, a horse reguardant or; *sinister*, a camel reguardant argent.
Residence – Newnham Lodge, Newnham, Basingstoke, Hants. *Club* – Cavalry and Guards'.

SON LIVING

Hon HENRY JAFFRAY HYNMAN, *b* 29 July 1968.

WIDOW LIVING OF BROTHER OF SECOND VISCOUNT

Barbara Marion (29 Hovedene, Cromwell Rd, Hove, Sussex BN3 3EH), da of John Hall, of Felpham, Sussex: *m* 1951, as his 2nd wife, Lt-Col *Hon* Claude William Hynman Allenby, who *d* 1975, having been raised to the rank of a Viscount's son 1939.

PREDECESSORS – (1) FM Sir EDMUND HENRY HYNMAN Allenby, GCB, GCMG, GCVO, son of late Hynman Allenby, of Felixstowe House, Felixstowe; *b* 1861; Bechuanaland Expedition 1884-5, Zululand 1888, S Africa 1899-1902, in command of a column (despatches, Brevets Lieut-Col and Col, CB), European War 1914-19, Comdg Cav Corps, and subsequently 5th Army Corps, 3rd Army, and Egyptian Expeditionary Force (despatches, KCB, Promoted Gen and Field-Marshal, Grand Cordons of the Nile, White Eagle of Serbia, Redeemer of Greece, Crown of Roumania, Wen Hu of China, Rising Sun of Japan (with flowers of Paulownia), El Nahda of the Hedjaz, and Michael the Brave of Roumania, Grand Officer of Legion of Honour, and Orders of Leopold of Belgium and Savoy of Italy, GCMG, American DSM, GCB, French and Belgian Croix de Guerre, thanked by Parliament, cr Viscount, granted £50,000); High Commr in Egypt 1919-25 (Arabic title— *Mandub es sami* (Very High Delegate)); received Grand Cordon of the Order of Mohamet Ali 1925, 1st class of Order of Al Rafidain of Iraq 1933, and Grand Cross (Mil) of Order of Leopold of Belgium 1935; Capt of Deal Castle 1925-7; elected Lord Rector of Edinburgh Univ 1935; cr *Viscount Allenby*, of Megiddo, and of Felixstowe. co Suffolk (peerage of United Kingdom) 1919, with remainder, in default of male issue, to his brother, Capt Frederick Claude Hynman Allenby, CBE, RN, and his male issue: *m* 1896, Adelaide Mabel, who *d* 1942, da of late Horace Edward Chapman, of Donhead House, Salisbury; *d* 1936; *s* by his nephew (2) DUDLEY JAFFRAY HYNMAN, son of late Capt Frederick Claude Hynman Allenby, CBE, RN (ante), 2nd Viscount, Lt-Col 11th Hus: *m* 1st, 1930 (*m diss* 1949), (Gertrude) Mary (Lethbridge), who *d* 1988, da of Edward Champneys, of Otterpool Manor, Sellindge, Kent; 2ndly, 1949, Daisy (CStJ), who *d* 1985, da of late Charles Francis Hancox, and formerly wife of (1) Carl Bendix, and (2) Capt Lionel George Cotterill Neame, Coldm Gds; *d* 1984; *s* by his only son (3) MICHAEL JAFFRAY HYNMAN, 3rd Viscount and present peer.

ALLENDALE, VISCOUNT (Beaumont) (Viscount UK 1911)

Trust, but see whom you trust

WENTWORTH HUBERT CHARLES BEAUMONT, 3rd Viscount; *b* 12 Sept 1922; *s* 1956; *ed* Eton; Flight-Lieut RAF Vol Reserve, Hon Air Commodore 3508 (co of Northumberland) Fighter Control Unit, Pres of Northumberland and Durham Asso of Building Sos, a DL for Northumberland, and an OStJ; Steward of Jockey Club 1963-65; ADC to Viceroy of India 1946; 1939-42 War (wounded, prisoner): *m* 1948 (*m diss* 198—), Hon Sarah Field Ismay, da of 1st Baron Ismay, and has issue.

𝕬rms – Gules, a lion rampant or, armed and langued azure, between eight crescents in orle of the second. 𝕮rest – A bull's head erased quarterly argent and gules, charged with a mullet sable. 𝕾upporters – *Dexter*, a lion argent, semée of crescents gules; *sinister*, a bull quarterly argent and gules, the horns of the first tipped or.
Residences – Bywell Hall, Stocksfield-on-Tyne, Northumberland; Allenheads Hall, Allenheads, Northumberland.

SONS LIVING

Hon WENTWORTH PETER ISMAY (Bywell Castle, Stocksfield-on-Tyne, Northumberland; Flat 7, 8 Draycott Place, SW3 2SB), *b* 14 Nov 1948; *ed* Harrow: *m* 1975, Theresa Mary Magdalene, 2nd da of late Francis Ambrose More O'Ferrall (*see* Jackson, Bt, *cr* 1869), and has issue living, Wentworth Ambrose Ismay, *b* 11 June 1979, — Lucy Harriet, *b* 1981, — Alice Theresa, *b* 1983, — Martha Rose, *b* 1986.

Hon Mark Henry (Dilston House, Corbridge, Northumberland), *b* 1950; *ed* Eton: *m* 1982, Diana Elizabeth, yst da of Lt-Col John Elliott Benson, of Chesters, Humshaugh, Northumberland, and has issue living, George Richard Benson, *b* 1987, — John Wentworth, *b* 1989.

Hon Charles Richard (Swallowship House, Hexham, Northumberland, NE41 1RJ), *b* 1954; *ed* Eton, and RAC Cirencester: *m* 1979, Charlotte Sybil, yst da of Lt-Col Richard Ian Griffith Taylor, DSO, MC, JP, DL (*see* B Buckland, 1973-74 Edn), and has issue living, Edward, *b* 1983, — Harry, *b* 1987, — Laura, *b* 1985.

BROTHERS LIVING

Hon Richard Blackett, *b* 1926; *ed* Eton; RNVR 1944, Sub-Lt 1946; Personal Assist to Sir Walter Monckton (later Viscount Monckton of Brenchley) Hyderabad 1947-48, ADC to Sir Donald MacGillivray, Malaya 1954-55; James Purdey & Sons 1949, Dir 1952, Chm 1971; Master Gunmakers' Co 1969 and 1985; author *Purdey's, The Guns and the Family* 1984: *m* 1971, Lavinia Mary, yst da of late Lt-Col Arnold Ramsay Keppel (*see* E Albemarle, colls). *Residence* – Flat 1, 58 S Audley St, W1.

Hon Sir (Edward) Nicholas Canning, KCVO, *b* 1929; *ed* Eton; Capt (ret) Life Gds; DL Berks 1982, Vice Lord Lieut 1989-94; Pres Baillie St John Ambulance Bde since 1988; LVO 1976, CVO 1986, KCVO 1994: *m* 1953, Jane Caroline Falconer, da of Alexander Lewis Paget Falconer Wallace, JP, of Candacraig, Strathdon, Aberdeen, and has issue living, Thomas Wentworth, *b* 1962, — Henry Alexander Nicholas, *b* 1966; a Page of Honour to HM Queen Elizabeth the Queen Mother 1979-82. *Residence* – Royal Enclosure Lodge, Ascot, Berks.

Hon Matthew Henry, *b* 1933; *ed* Bradfield: *m* 1st, 1959 (*m diss* 1972), Anne Christina Margaret, eldest da of Gerald John Hamilton (*see* M Bute, 1954 Edn); 2ndly, 1973, Belinda Jane Elizabeth, eldest da of late Harold David Cuthbert, of Beaufront Castle, Hexham, Northumberland (*see* Milnes Coates, Bt), and has issue living (by 1st *m*), Justin George Gerald, *b* 1960, — Charlotte Catherine Lucinda (*Lady Cardross*), *b* 1962: *m* 1987, Henry Thomas Alexander, Lord Cardross, elder son of 17th Earl of Buchan. *Residence* – Bearl House, Stocksfield, Northumberland NE43 7AJ.

SISTER LIVING

Hon Ela Hilda Aline (*Countess of Carlisle*), *b* 1925; an OStJ: *m* 1945, 12th Earl of Carlisle. *Residence* – Naworth Castle, Brampton, Cumbria.

COLLATERAL BRANCHES LIVING

Grandchildren of late Lt-Col Hon Ralph Edward Blackett Beaumont, CBE, TD (infra):—
Issue of late John Ralph Beaumont, *b* 1927, *d* 1992: *m* 1951, Audrey Lilian Christie (Plas Llwyngwern, Machynlleth, Powys SY20 9RP), yr da of late Edward Thomas Hickling, of York:—
Ralph Wentworth Christopher (Llwyngwern Farm, Machynlleth, Powys), *b* 1952; *ed* Peterhouse, Rhodesia: *m* 1979, Nicole Marie Blanche, da of R. J. Dubreuil, of Niort, France, and has issue living, Christopher Henry Louis, *b* 1982, — Aline Mary Helena, *b* 1985. —— Nigel Canning Vane, *b* 1954; *ed* Shrewsbury: *m* 1991, Nicola Carron Toy, da of late R. T. West, of Brighton, Sussex, and has issue living, Francesca Daisy, *b* 1992. —— Andrew John Blackett (12 Bishop's Mead, Laverstock, Salisbury, Wilts SP1 1PU), *b* 1956; *ed* Shrewsbury; Maj RWF: *m* 1988, Jane Margaret, only da of Colin Weedon, of Bournemouth, Hants, and has issue living, Henry George Canning, *b* 1993, — Lucinda Eleanor Christine, *b* 1991. —— Hugh Edward Stewart, *b* 1959; *ed* Shrewsbury: *m* 1988, Susan Elizabeth, da of Elfed Jones, of Wellington, Shropshire, and has issue living, Charlotte Louise Margaret, *b* 1991. —— Peter-John Tempest, *b* 1964; *ed* Wrekin: *m* 1993, Jill Nicola, only da of B. R. Rodgers, of Keighley, Yorks, and has issue living, Harry-John Tempest, *b* 1993. —— Louise Christine Winsmore, *b* (twin) 1956: *m* 1987, Allan N. Markham, only son of A. Markham, of Zambia, and has issue living, Lyon Frederick, *b* 1991, — Lily-Anne Winsmore, *b* 1988.

Issue of late Lt-Col Hon Ralph Edward Blackett Beaumont, CBE, TD, yr son of 1st Viscount, *b* 1901, *d* 1977: *m* 1926, Helena Mary Christine, who *d* 1962, da of Brig-Gen John Cecil Wray, CB, CMG, CVO, TD:—
David Christopher (Poolspringe, Much Birch, Herefordshire), *b* 1929: *m* 1st, 1954 (*m diss* 1974), Marion Edith, da of late H. J. Mallard, of 14 Stanbury Rd, Victoria Park, Bristol, and formerly wife of Thomas Harkness Davison; 2ndly, 1977, Valerie Margaret, da of late Talbot Wrigley Roberts, and has issue living (by 1st *m*), Timothy David, *b* 1955, — Sally Aline Christine, *b* 1956. —— Diana, *b* 1934: *m* 1954, Capt Brian Robert Outhwaite, RN, of Roseberry House, Westbourne, Emsworth, Hants, and has issue living, Mark Robert Canning, *b* 1957; *ed* Sherborne; Maj RTR (ret): *m* 1988, Sarah Elizabeth, only da of Michael Hipwell, of Affpuddle, Dorset, and has issue living, Catherine Rossana *b* 1992, — James Edward, *b* 1961; *ed* Stowe, — Charles Cedric, *b* 1965; *ed* Sherborne.

In remainder to the Barony only

Grandson of late Hon Hubert George Beaumont, 3rd son of 1st Baron:—
Issue of late Major Michael Wentworth Beaumont, TD, *b* 1903, *d* 1958: *m* 1st, 1924, Hon Faith Muriel Pease, who *d* 1935, da of 1st Baron Gainford; 2ndly, 1935, Doreen Christian (Harristown House, Brannockstown, co Kildare), da of Sir Herbert William Goff Davis-Goff, 2nd Bt:—
(By 1st *m*) *Rev* Timothy Wentworth, *b* 1928; *cr Baron Beaumont of Whitley* (Life Baron) 1967 (see that title).

PREDECESSORS – **(1)** Wentworth Blackett Beaumont, son of late Thomas Wentworth Beaumont; *b* 1829; MP for S Northumberland (*L*) July 1852 to Nov 1885, and for Tyneside Div of Northumberland July 1886 to July 1892; *cr Baron Allendale*, of Allendale and Hexham, co Northumberland (peerage of United Kingdom) 1906: *m* 1st, 1856, Lady Margaret Anne, who *d* 1888, da of 1st Marquess of Clanricarde; 2ndly, 1891, Edith Althea, who *d* 1927, da of late Maj-Gen Henry Meade Hamilton, CB, and widow of Maj-Gen Sir George Pomeroy Pomeroy-Colley, KCSI, CB, CMG; *d* 1907; *s* by his eldest son **(2)** Wentworth Canning Blackett, 2nd Baron, 1st Viscount, *b* 1860; Vice-Chamberlain to HM's Household Dec 1905 to Feb 1907, Capt of the Yeomen of the Guard 1907-11, and a Lord-in-Waiting to HM 1911-16; sat as MP for Hexham Div of Northumberland (*L*) 1895-1907; *cr Viscount Allendale*, of Allendale and Hexham, Northumberland (peerage of United Kingdom), 1911; *m* 1889, Lady Alexandrina Louisa Maud Vane-Tempest, who *d* 1945, da of 5th Marquess of Londonderry; *d* 1923; *s* by his eldest son **(3)** Wentworth Henry Canning, KG, CB, CBE, MC, 2nd Viscount; *b* 1890; Lieut-Col and Brevet Col Northumberland Yeo, and Lord Lieut for Northumberland; a Lord-in-Waiting to HM 1931-2, 1937-51, and 1952-4, and a Permanent Lord-in-Waiting 1954-6: *m* 1921, Violet Lucy Emily, who *d* 1979, da of Sir Charles Hilton Seely, 2nd Bt; *d* 1956; *s* by his eldest son **(4)** Wentworth Hubert Charles, 3rd Viscount, and present peer; also Baron Allendale.

ALLERTON, BARONY OF (Jackson) (Extinct 1991)

GRANDDAUGHTERS LIVING OF THIRD BARON

Issue of late Capt Hon Edward Lawies Jackson, RHG, only son of 3rd Baron; *b* 1928, *d* 1982: *m* 1st, 1953 (*m diss* 1971), Sally Moore, only da of Ian Moore Hezlett, of Cranbourne Corner, Ascot, Berks; 2ndly, 1971, Susannah Albinia (The Old Rectory, Cottisford, Brackley, Northants NN13 5SW), da of late (Alfred) Drewett Chaytor (*see* Chaytor, Bt, colls):—
(By 1st *m*) Susan Caroline Lawies, *b* 1954: *m* 1st, 1974 (*m diss* 1978), J. Nicholas H. Purvis; 2ndly, 1978, (Charles) Simon Treadwell, of Lower Highfield Farm, Thursley, nr Godalming, Surrey, eldest son of Charles James Treadwell, CMG, CVO, of Cherry Orchard Cottage, Buddington Lane, Midhurst, W Sussex, and has issue living (by 2nd m), (Charles) Timothy, *b* 1980, — James Edward, *b* 1983, — Katharine Claire, *b* 1986. —— Lavinia Jane Lawies, *b* 1957: *m* 1980, Robert James Hyde,

of 28 Christmas Pie Av, Normandy, Guildford, Surrey, son of J. Hyde, of The Dell, Woking, and has issue living, Nicholas John Edward, *b* 1986. —— (By 2nd *m*), Olivia Susannah, *b* 1975. —— Katharine Elizabeth, *b* 1978.

WIDOW LIVING OF SON OF THIRD BARON

Susannah Albinia (ante), da of late (Alfred) Drewett Chaytor (*see* Chaytor, Bt, colls): *m* 1971, as his 2nd wife, Capt Hon Edward Lawies Jackson, RHG (ante), who *d* 1982.

COLLATERAL BRANCH LIVING

　　　　Granddaughter of late Rt Hon Sir (Francis) Stanley Jackson, GCSI, GCIE, 2nd son of 1st Baron:—
　　Issue of late Maj Henry Stanley Lawies Jackson, *b* 1903, *d* 1963: *m* 1927, Grace Diana, who *d* 1974, da of Arthur Philip Beddard, MD:—
(Frances Harriet) Philippa (80 Melton Court, SW7), *b* 1947.

ALPORT, BARON (Alport) (Life Baron 1961)

CUTHBERT JAMES McCALL ALPORT, TD, PC, son of late Professor Arthur Cecil Alport; *b* 22 March 1912; *ed* Haileybury, and Pembroke Coll, Camb (MA) (Pres Camb Union 1935); Hon DCL; Bar Middle Temple 1944; DL Essex 1974; Assistant PMG 1955-7, Under-Sec of State Commonwealth Relations Office 1957-9, Min of State, Commonwealth Relations Office 1959-61, and British High Commr in Federation of Rhodesia and Nyasaland 1961-63; a Repres at Council of Europe 1964; Special Repres to Rhodesia 1967; High Steward of Colchester 1967, Hon Freeman of Colchester 1992; Master of Skinners' Co 1969 and 1982; Dep Speaker 1971-82, and since 1983; Pro-Chancellor City Univ, London 1972-79; 1939-45 War; Hon Lt-Col; MP for Colchester (*C*) 1950-61; PC 1960, and *Baron Alport*, of Colchester, co Essex (Life Baron) 1961: *m* 1945, Rachel Cecilia, who *d* 1983, da of late Lt-Col Ralph Charles Bingham, CVO, DSO, Coldstream Gds (E Lucan colls), and has issue.

Arms – Barry wavy argent and azure, on a bend or a Tudor Rose argent on gules between two oyster shells gules. **Crest** – a demi lion or gorged with a mural crown gules, within a Norman arch proper. **Supporters** – *Dexter*, a representation of a Roman centurion supporting a vexillum of the XXth Legion proper; *sinister*, a representation of an Ancient Briton proper.
Residences – The Cross House, Layer de la Haye, Colchester. *Clubs* – Farmers', Pratt's.

SON LIVING

Hon (Arthur) Edward Bingham, *b* 1954, *ed* Haileybury, and Exeter Univ (BSc); ACII (1979): *m* 1979, Anne Vivian, elder da of Patrick Alexander Grove-White, of Crown Piece, Wormingford, Colchester, and has issue living, Robert Michael Bingham, *b* 23 Aug 1983, — James Richard McCall, *b* 1989, — Catherine Rachel, *b* 1985. *Residence* – Huckleberry, Church St, Boxted, Colchester, Essex CO4 5SX.

DAUGHTERS LIVING

Hon Cecilia Alexandra Rose, *b* 1946: *m* 1969, Rev Geoffrey Wilfrid Francis Lang, of St Peter's Vicarage, 17 Ravenscourt Rd, W6 0UH, and has issue living, Oliver James Alport, *b* 1971, — Imogen Eileen Cecilia, *b* 1973.
Hon Lavender Lilias Carole, *b* 1950: *m* 1974, Ian Colin Taylor, MBE, MP, of 7 The Cooperage, Regents Bridge Gdns, SW8 1JR, and has issue living, Arthur Lawrence Alport, *b* 1977, — Ralph George Alport, *b* 1980.

Altamont, Earl of; son of Marquess of Sligo.

Althorp, Viscount; son of Earl Spencer.

ALTRINCHAM, BARONY OF (Grigg) (Baron UK 1945, disclaimed 1963)

SERVIRE·ET·SERVARE

To serve and to preserve

JOHN EDWARD POYNDER GRIGG, *b* 15 April 1924; *s* as 2nd Baron 1 Dec 1955; disclaimed his Peerage for life 31 July 1963; a writer; Editor of *National and English Review* 1954-60, Columnist for *The Guardian* 1960-70, with *The Times* 1986-93; Chm The London Library 1985-91; publications include: *The Young Lloyd George, Lloyd George: The People's Champion, Lloyd George: From Peace to War, Nancy Astor: Portrait of a Pioneer, 1943: The Victory that Never Was, The Thomson Years* (vol VI in the History of The Times); FRSL; 1943-45 War as Lieut Gren Gds: *m* 1958, (Marian) Patricia, da of H. E. Campbell, of Newcastle, co Down.

Arms – Sable, three owls argent, a chief azure, issuant from the base thereof a sun in splendour or. **Crest** – A grenade sable fired proper, between two roses argent barbed and seeded also proper. **Supporters** – (borne by Barons Altrincham), — On either side a lion gules gorged with a chain collar pendent therefrom a portcullis or, and supporting a date palm fructed proper.
Residence – 32 Dartmouth Row, SE10 8AW. *Clubs* – Garrick, Beefsteak.

BROTHER LIVING

Hon ANTHONY ULICK DAVID DUNDAS, *b* 12 Jan 1934; *ed* Eton, and New Coll, Oxford; late 2nd Lieut Gren Gds: *m* 1965, Eliane de Cassagne de Beaufort, da of the late Marquis de Miramon, of Paris, and has issue living, (Edward) Sebastian, *b* 1965: *m* 1993, Rachel Sophia, yr da of Laurence Kelly (*see* V Camrose), — Steven Thomas, *b* 1969, — Anne Casilda, *b* 1967. *Residence* – 11 Horbury Mews, W11 3NL.

PREDECESSORS – **(1)** *Rt Hon Sir* EDWARD WILLIAM MACLEAY Grigg, KCMG, KCVO, DSO, MC, PC, son of late Henry Bidewell Grigg, CIE, ICS; *b* 1879; was Mil Sec to HRH Prince of Wales during visits to Canada 1919 and Australia and New Zealand 1920, Private Sec to Prime Min (Rt Hon D Lloyd George) 1921-2, Gov and Com-in-Ch, Kenya 1925-30, Parliamentary Sec to Min of Information 1939-40, Financial Sec to War Office April to May, 1940, Joint Under-Sec of State for War 1940-2, and Min Resident in Middle East 1944-5; MP for Oldham (NL) 1922-5, and for Altrincham Div of Cheshire (*C*) 1933-45; cr *Baron Altrincham*, of Tormarton, co Gloucester (peerage of UK) 1945: *m* 1923, Hon Joan Alice Katherine Dickson-Poynder, who *d* 1987, da of 1st Baron Islington; *d* 1955; *s* by his eldest son **(2)** JOHN EDWARD POYNDER, 2nd Baron, until he disclaimed his Peerage 1963.

ALVINGHAM, BARON (Yerburgh) (Baron UK 1929)
(Name pronounced "Yarborough")

WHO WINS
DARES

ROBERT GUY EARDLEY YERBURGH, CBE, 2nd Baron; *b* 16 Dec 1926; *s* 1955; *ed* Eton; Maj-Gen late Coldm Gds; Dir of Army Quartering, Min of Defence 1978; OBE (Mil) 1972, CBE (Mil) 1977: *m* 1952, Beryl Elliott, da of late William D. Williams, of Hindhead, Surrey, and has issue.

Arms – Per pale argent and azure, on a chevron between three chaplets of roses counterchanged. **Crest** – A falcon close, belled or, preying on a mallard proper. **Supporters** – On either side a falcon, wings expanded, belled or, gorged with a chaplet of roses azure.
Residence – Bix Hall, Henley-on-Thames, Oxon.

SON LIVING

Hon ROBERT RICHARD GUY (Valley Farm House, Bix Bottom, Henley-on-Thames, Oxon), *b* 10 Dec 1956; *ed* Eton; late Capt 17th/21st Lancers; attached to Army Air Corps as Pilot 1979-83: *m* 1981 (*m diss* 1993), Vanessa Kelty, yr da of Capt Duncan Kinloch Kirk, and has issue living, Robert William Guy, *b* 16 Sept 1983, — Edward Alexander Henry, *b* 1986.

DAUGHTER LIVING

Hon Susannah Elizabeth, *b* 1953: *m* 1979, Edward I. J. G. Moss, 2nd son of late E. F. Moss, of The Gardens, Spotbrough, Yorks, and has issue living, Alice Elinor, *b* 1983, — Victoria Elizabeth, *b* 1986, — Theodora Katherine Rose, *b* 1992. *Residence* – 24 Rusham Rd, SW12 8TH.

SISTERS LIVING

Hon Dorothy Joan, *b* 1913: *m* 1934, Lt-Col William Aspinall Turner, late The Queen's Bays, and has issue living, Adrian Vernon Aspinall (The Old Rectory, Cheselbourne, Dorchester, Dorset) *b* 1946: *m* 1975, Jacquelyn Ann, eldest da of Wallace A. Seymour, of Summerfold, Child Okeford, Dorset, and has issue living, William Aspinall *b* 1980, Charles James Aspinall *b* 1982, Nicholas John Aspinall *b* 1988, — Caroline Sarah, *b* 1943: *m* 1965, Robin Gilman Arculus, of The Warren, Warren Row, Wargrave, Berks, and has issue living, James Edward Gilman *b* 1970, Henry William *b* 1974, Sophie Louise *b* 1972. *Residence* – Rectory Cottage, Cheselbourne, Dorchester, Dorset.

Hon Marjorie Elizabeth, *b* 1916: *m* 1st, 1938 (at Alexandria, Egypt), Abdul Hamid Mustafa Risk; 2ndly, 1952, Leon Setchim, and has issue living (by 2nd *m*) David Maurice, *b* 1952: *m* 1977, Marion Helena Grundy, of Dublin, and has issue living, James Ashley Yerburgh *b* 1983, — Richard Victor (15 North Rise, St George's Fields, W2 2YB), *b* 1954: *m* 1989, Elizabeth Mary, only da of H. F. Andrews, of Tilehurst, Reading, — (by 1st *m*) Diana, *b* 1940. *Residence* – 134 Lynton Rd, W3.

PREDECESSORS – **(1)** ROBERT DANIEL THWAITES Yerburgh, son of late Robert Armstrong Yerburgh, JP, DL (27 years MP for Chester), of Caythorpe Court, Lincolnshire (the Royal approval of a Peerage to whom had been signified in 1916, but who died before the patent was issued); *b* 1889; sat as MP for S Div of Dorset (*C*) 1922-9; cr *Baron Alvingham*, of Woodfold, co Lancaster (peerage of United Kingdom) 1929: *m* 1st, 1911, his cousin, Dorothea Gertrude, who *d* 1927, da of late John Eardley Yerburgh, of Wavendon Lodge, Bucks; 2ndly, 1936, Maud Lytton Grey, who *d* 1992, aged 99, da of late Charles Morgan, of Fairlight, Sussex, and formerly wife of R. E. Bright; *d* 1955; *s* by his son **(2)** ROBERT GUY EARDLEY, 2nd Baron and present peer.

Amberley, Viscount; son of Earl Russell.

AMERY OF LUSTLEIGH, BARON (Amery) (Life Baron 1992)

(HAROLD) JULIAN AMERY, PC, son of late Rt Hon Leopold Charles Maurice Stennett Amery, CH; *b* 27 March 1919; *ed* Eton, and Balliol Coll, Oxford; a Delegate to Consultative Assembly of Council of Europe 1950-53 and 1956, a Member of Round Table Conference on Malta 1955, Parly Under-Sec of State and Financial Sec War Office 1957-58, Parly Under-Sec of State Colonial Office 1958-60, Sec of State for Air 1960-62, Min of Aviation 1962-64, of Public Building and Works June-Oct 1970, and of Housing and Construction (Dept of Environment) 1970-72, Min of State FCO 1972-74; 1939-45 War as Fl Sgt RAF and as Capt Gen List in Egypt, Balkans and China; MP Preston N (*C*) 1950-66, and Brighton Pavilion (*C*) 1969-92; *cr* PC 1960, and *Baron Amery of Lustleigh*, of Preston, co Lancs, and of Brighton, co E Sussex (Life Baron) 1992: *m* 1950, Lady Catherine Macmillan, who *d* 1991, da of 1st Earl of Stockton, OM, PC, FRS, and has issue.
Residences – 112 Eaton Sq, SW1W 9AE; Forest Farm House, Chelwood Gate, Haywards Heath, Sussex.

SON LIVING

Hon Leopold Harold Hamar John, *b* 1956; *ed* Eton, and Balliol Coll, Oxford.

DAUGHTERS LIVING

Hon (Caroline) Louise Michelle, *b* 1951. *Residence* – Cahamuckee, Kealkil, Bantry, co Cork.

Hon Theresa Catherine Roxanne, *b* 1954: *m* 1984, John Harvey Boteler, yr son of late Lt-Cdr John Harvey Trevor Boteler, RN, of Frinton-on-Sea, Essex, and 68 Park St, W1, and has issue living, Jack Francis Clair, *b* 1987, — Catherine Audrey Roxanne, *b* 1989. *Residence* – 17 Colnbrook St, SE1.

Hon (Alexandra) Elizabeth Charmian, *b* (twin) 1956: *m* 1988, (Alan Simon) Mercury Hare, and has issue (*see* E Listowel). *Residence* – 11 Denbigh St, SW1.

AMHERST OF HACKNEY, BARON (Cecil) (Baron UK 1892)

One heart, one way

(WILLIAM) HUGH AMHERST CECIL, 4th Baron; *b* 28 Dec 1940; *s* 1980; *ed* Eton; Dir E. A. Gibson Shipbrokers Ltd: *m* 1965, Elisabeth, da of Hugh Humphrey Merriman, DSO, MC, TD, of Hazel Hall, Peaslake, Surrey, and has issue.

Arms – Quarterly: 1st and 4th, barry of ten argent and azure, six escutcheons, three, two and one sable, each charged with a lion rampant argent, a mullet for difference, *Cecil*; 2nd and 3rd, gules, three tilting spears, two and one or, headed argent, *Amherst* (also quartering Daniel, Tyssen, Auchmuty, Evering, Wayland, Sidnor, Morris, Earde, Babisford, and Leach). **Crest** – On a chapeau gules, turned up with ermine, a garb or, supported by two lions rampant, the dexter argent, the sinister azure. **Supporters** – Two herons proper, collared or. *Residence* – 25 Thurloe Sq, SW7. *Clubs* – Royal Yacht Sqdn, Royal Ocean Racing.

SON LIVING

Hon (HUGH) WILLIAM AMHERST, *b* 17 July 1968.

DAUGHTER LIVING

Hon Aurelia Margaret Amherst CECIL, *b* 1966; has resumed her maiden name: *m* 1990 (*m diss* 1993), Giles Wilson Mervyn Crewdson (*see* B Grimthorpe).

BROTHER LIVING

Hon Anthony Henry Amherst, *b* 1947; *ed* Eton: *m* 1st, 1969 (*m diss* 1974), Fenella Jane, da of David George Crichton, MVO (*see* E Erne, colls); 2ndly, 1974, Jane Elizabeth, da of late Philip Norman Elston Holbrook, and has issue living (by 2nd *m*), Henry Edward Amherst, *b* 1976, — Thomas Anthony Amherst, *b* 1981, — Georgiana Helen Amherst, *b* 1979. *Residence* – Bucks Farm, Shorwell, Isle of Wight.

SISTER LIVING

Hon Angela Margaret Amherst, *b* 1955: *m* 1980, (Gavin) Ian Reid, of Lower Dean, Watlington, Oxon, yr son of Col (Percy Fergus) Ivo Reid, OBE, DL, of The Glebe House, Marston St Lawrence, Banbury, Oxford, and has had issue, Nicholas Andrew, *b* 1985, — Susanna Claire, *b* and *d* 1987, — Jessica Mary, *b* 1988.

WIDOW LIVING OF THIRD BARON

MARGARET EIRENE CLIFTON (*Margaret, Baroness Amherst of Hackney*) (138 Cranmer Court, Sloane Av, SW3), yst da of late Brig-Gen Howard Clifton Brown, MP (*see* Brown, Bt, *cr* 1863, colls): *m* 1939, Maj the 3rd Baron, CBE, who *d* 1980.

COLLATERAL BRANCHES LIVING

Issue of late Hon Henry Kerr Auchmuty Cecil, Lieut Gordon Highlanders and Army Air Corps, brother of 3rd Baron, *b* 1914, *ka* 1942: *m* 1938, Elizabeth Rohays Mary (who *d* 1993, having *m* 2ndly, 1944, Capt Sir Cecil Boyd-Rochfort, KCVO, who *d* 1983), only da of Maj-Gen Sir James Lauderdale Gilbert Burnett of Leys, 13th Bt (cr 1626), CB, CMG, DSO:—
John Strongbow Amherst (The Old Rectory, Monk's Sherborne, nr Basingstoke, Hants), *b* 1939; *ed* Eton; Lt Scots Gds (Res): *m* 1966, Elizabeth Clare, da of C. Michael Hughes, of Penton Grafton, Andover, and has issue living, Richard Strongbow Amherst, *b* 1973, — Michael John Amherst, *b* 1977, — Miranda Elizabeth Rohays *b* 1974. —— James Comyn Amherst BURNETT OF LEYS (House of Crathes, Banchory, Kincardineshire), *b* 1941; *ed* Eton; recognized in the surname of Burnett of Leys by decree of Lyon Court 1966: *m* 1971, Fiona Mercedes, 2nd da of late Lt-Col Harold Pedro Joseph Phillips (*see* Wernher, Bt, ext), and has issue living, Alexander James Amherst, *b* 1973, — Victor Cecil Tobias, *b* 1982, — Eliza Amelia, *b* 1977. —— Henry Richard Amherst (*posthumous*) (Warren Place, Newmarket, Suffolk CB8 8QQ), *b* 1943; *ed* Canford; race-horse trainer: *m* 1st, 1966 (*m diss* 1990), Julia, da of late Sir (Charles Francis) Noel Murless; 2ndly, 1992, Natalie Payne, and has issue living (by 1st *m*), (Arthur) Noel Amherst, *b* 1973, — Katrina Henrietta Amherst, *b* 1971. —— David Henry Amherst (*posthumous*) (twin) (Cliff Stud, Helmsley, Yorks YO6 5HG), *b* 1943; *ed* Canford: *m* 1st, 1966 (*m diss* 1972), Hon Fiona Elizabeth Cameron Corbett, da of 2nd Baron Rowallan; 2ndly, 1973, Vanessa Josephine Bronislawna, da of late Wladyslaw Gallica, and has issue living (by 1st *m*), Rupert Lawrence Amherst, *b* 1967, — Benjamin David Amherst, *b* 1968, — (by 2nd *m*) Anoushka Henrietta Amherst, *b* 1975, — Sapphire Rose, *b* 1981.

Grandsons of late Hon Thomas James Amherst Cecil, 2nd son of Mary Rothes Margaret, Baroness Amherst of Hackney:—
Issue of late Barclay James Amherst Cecil, *b* 1913, *d* 1987: *m* 1st, 1941 (*m diss* 1950), Suzanne, da of Frederick Dennett, of Melbourne, Australia; 2ndly, 1972, Jessica Iliffe Lane (Upcross Hotel, Berkeley Av, Reading, Berks RG1 6HY), da of Rev Thomas Ernest Matthews, of Grantham, Lincs:—
(By 1st *m*) Timothy Dennett Amherst, *b* 1942. —— Jonathan Peter Hedworth, *b* 1944.

Issue of late Hon John Francis Amherst Cecil, 3rd son of Mary Rothes Margaret, Baroness Amherst of Hackney, *b* 1890, *d* 1954: *m* 1924 (*m diss* 1934), Cornelia, who *d* 1976, da of late George W. Vanderbilt, of USA:—
George Henry Vanderbilt (2 Arboretum Rd, Biltmore, N Carolina 28803, USA), *b* 1925: *m* 1955, Nancy, da of Charles Dexter Owen, of Biltmore, North Carolina, USA, and has issue living, John Francis Amherst Vanderbilt, *b* 1956: *m* 1993, Sarah, da of Thomas M. Mettler, of Palm Beach, Florida, and has issue living, Thomas Amherst Vanderbilt *b* 1994, — Christopher Henry Amherst, *b* 1965: *m* 1992, Ruth, da of William H. Taft, Jr, of Greenville, N Carolina, and has issue living, George Henry Vanderbilt II *b* 1994, — Edith Ann CECIL, *b* 1957; has resumed her maiden name: *m* 1983 (*m diss* 1991), Nicholas M. C. Stancioff, son of John Stancioff, and has issue living, Charlotte Eloïse *b* 1988, — Catherine Amherst, *b* 1959: *m* 1982, William M. Whitehouse, and has issue living, Timothy Amherst *b* 1984, Henry Meredith *b* 1986, Brooks Cecil *b* 1989, — Margaret Elizabeth, *b* 1961: *m* 1987, John B. Sinnott, of Pittsburgh, PA, and has issue living, Peter Cecil *b* 1991, David Stuyvesant *b* 1993, Mollie Amherst *b* 1989, — Louisa Owen (twin), *b* 1965: *m* 1994, W. W. Rodes Harrison, of New York, NY. —— William Amherst Vanderbilt (Biltmore Estate, Biltmore, N Carolina, USA), *b* 1928: *m* 1957, Mary Lee, da of late John J. Ryan, of New York, and has issue living, William Amherst Vanderbilt, *b* 1958: *m* 1983, Virginia Lee, da of late Robert A. Rott, of Asheville, N Carolina, and has issue living, Ryan Jordan Vanderbilt *b* 1987, Aubrey Lea Amherst *b* 1990, — and

an adopted da, Diana Marshall Ryan, *b* 1957 (adopted 1972): *m* 1985, George Wiley Pickering, son of George Wiley Pickering, of Black Mountain, N Carolina, USA, and has issue living, Chase Kennedy Cecil *b* 1987, Devon Lee Cecil *b* 1991.

Issue of late Hon Henry Mitford Amherst Cecil, OBE, RN, 4th son of Mary Rothes Margaret, Baroness Amherst of Hackney *b* 1893, *d* 1962: *m* 1923, Hon Yvonne Cornwallis, who *d* 1983, da of 1st Baron Cornwallis:—

Sir (Oswald) Nigel Amherst, KBE, CB (c/o C. Hoare & Co, 37 Fleet St, EC4), *b* 1925; *ed* RNC Dartmouth; Rear-Adm (ret); 1939-45 War; Naval ADC to HM The Queen 1975, Senior British Naval Officer, S Africa, and Naval Attaché, Cape Town 1971-73 (as Commodore), NATO Commander SE Mediterranean 1975-77, Commander British Forces, Malta, and Flag Officer, Malta 1975-79; Lieut-Gov of Isle of Man and Pres of Tynwald 1980-85; CB (Mil) 1977, KBE (Mil) 1979; OStJ (1973), KStJ (1980): *m* 1961, Annette (CStJ 1980), da of late Maj Robert Edward Barclay, TD, and has issue living, Robert Barclay Amherst, *b* 1965. —— Rachel Mary, *b* 1924: *m* 1954, Brig Mortimer Cecil Lanyon, MBE, MC, of Woodman's Farm House, W Meon, Hants, and has issue living, Robert Henry Mortimer, *b* 1962, — Charlotte Yvonne, *b* 1955: *m* 1977, Maj Paul Alistair Strutt (*see* B Rayleigh, colls), — Victoria Clare, *b* 1956: *m* 1987, Brig Angus I. Ramsay, RHF, of 7 Courtfield Gdns, SW5 0PA, son of late Col A.I. Ramsay, of Dalry, Kirkcudbright, and has issue living, James Ivor Iain *b* 1990, Alexandra Rachel Iona *b* 1988.

PREDECESSORS – (1) WILLIAM AMHERST Tyssen-Amherst, son of late William George Tyssen Tyssen-Amhurst, of Didlington, Norfolk; *b* 1835; assumed by Roy licence the surnames of Tyssen-Amherst in lieu of Tyssen-Amhurst 1877; MP for W Norfolk (*C*) 1880-85, and for S-W Div of Norfolk 1885-92; cr *Baron Amherst of Hackney*, in co London (peerage of United Kingdom) 1892, with remainder, in default of issue male, to his eldest da and her issue male: *m* 1856, Margaret Susan, who *d* 1919, only child and heiress of late Adm Robert Mitford, of Mitford, Northumberland, and Hunmanby Hall, York; *d* 1909, when the Barony devolved upon his eldest da (2) MARY ROTHES MARGARET, OBE, *b* 1857: *m* 1885, Lord William Cecil, CVO, who *d* 1943, 3rd son of 3rd Marquess of Exeter; *d* 1919; *s* by her grandson (3) WILLIAM ALEXANDER EVERING, CBE, eldest son of her eldest son, late Capt Hon William Amherst Cecil, MC, who was *ka* 1914, having *m* in 1910, Gladys (granted style and title of Baroness Amherst of Hackney 1920), da of Col Henry Charles Baggallay, 3rd Baron, *b* 1912; 1939-45 War as Maj R Horse Guards: *m* 1939, Margaret Eirene Clifton, yst da of late Brig-Gen Howard Clifton Brown, MP (*see* Brown, Bt, cr 1863, colls); *d* 1980; *s* by his son, (4) WILLIAM HUGH AMHERST, 4th Baron and present peer.

AMPTHILL, BARON (Russell) (Baron UK 1881)

What will be, will be

GEOFFREY DENIS ERSKINE RUSSELL, 4th Baron, CBE; *b* 15 Oct 1921; *s* 1973; *ed* Stowe; 1939-45 War as Capt Irish Gds; Gen Manager Fortnum and Mason 1947-51, Chm New Providence Hotel Co Ltd 1951-64, Man Dir of Theatre Owning and Producing Cos 1953-81; Dep Speaker House of Lords since 1983, Chm of Cttees House of Lords since 1992 (Dep Chm 1980-92); Chm Select Cttee on Channel Tunnel Bill 1987, Dep Chm Express Newspapers since 1989 (Dir since 1985), and United Newspapers since 1991 (Dir since 1981); he petitioned HM The Queen for a Writ of Summons as Baron Ampthill on the death of the 3rd Baron, and Cttee of Privileges, House of Lords, decided in his favour 1976; CBE (Civil) 1986: *m* 1st, 1946 (*m diss* 1971), Susan Mary Sheila, da of late Hon Charles John Frederic Winn (*see* B St Oswald, colls); 2ndly, 1972 (*m diss* 1987), Elisabeth Anne Marie, da of late Claude Henri Mallon, of Paris, and has had issue by 1st *m*.

Arms – Argent, a lion rampant gules, on a chief sable three escallops argent, a mullet or for difference. **Crest** – A goat statant, armed and unguled or, charged on the body with a mulletsable for difference. **Supporters** – *Dexter*, a lion gules, ducally gorged and charged on the shoulder with a mullet or; *sinister*, an heraldic antelope gules, armed, crined and tufted or, ducally gorged, and charged on the shoulder with a mullet also or.
Residence – 51 Sutherland St, SW1.

SONS LIVING AND DECEASED (*By 1st marriage*)

Hon DAVID WHITNEY ERSKINE (46 Ebury Mews, SW1W 9NY; *Clubs* – White's, Turf), *b* 27 May 1947; *ed* Stowe: *m* 1980, April McKenzie, yst da of Paul Arbon, of New York, and has issue living, Christabel Joan Susan, *b* 1981, — (Pauline Alexandra) Daisy, *b* 1983.

James Nicholas Geoffrey, *b* 1948; *d* 1969, in a motor accident.

Hon Anthony John Mark, *b* 1952; *ed* Stowe: *m* 1985, Christine L., elder da of John O'Dell, and has issue living, William Odo Alexander, *b* 1986.

DAUGHTER LIVING (*By 1st marriage*)

Hon Vanessa Mary Linda, *b* 1960: *m* 1983, Charles Ivor Angus Burt, of 21 Macaulay Rd, SW4 0QP, elder son of Ivor Burt, and has issue living, James Ivor Geoffrey, *b* 1984, — Emma Louise Victoria, *b* 1986.

HALF BROTHER LIVING

Hon John Hugo Trenchard (14 Brodrick Rd, SW17 7DZ; Ringstead Farm, Dorchester, Dorset DT2 8NF; *Club* – Turf), *b* 1950; *ed* Eton: *m* 1976, Susanna Helen, yr da of Peter Hugh Kennedy Merriam (*see* M Ailsa, 1985 Edn), and has issue living, Henry John Trenchard, *b* 1977, — James Peter Faber, *b* 1980, — Rose Susanna, *b* 1992.

HALF SISTER LIVING

Hon Georgiana Adeline Villiers, *b* 1953: *m* 1981, Charles Francis Hoare, who *d* 1991, son of Col Charles Edward Hoare.

AUNT LIVING *(Daughter of 2nd Baron)*

Hon Phyllis Margaret, OBE, *b* 1909; an OStJ; a temporary Lady-in-Waiting to HRH The Princess Royal 1963-65; 1939-45 War with British Red Cross Soc (despatches, OBE); OBE (Civil) 1946: *m* 1940 (marriage annulled on her petition 1942), Capt William George Preston Thorold, who *d* 1943 (Thorold, Bt, colls). *Residence* – 55 Ebury Mews, SW1.

WIDOWS LIVING OF SONS OF SECOND BARON

Hon (Helen) Elizabeth Blades *(Hon Lady Russell)*, da of 1st Baron Ebbisham: *m* 1939, Hon Sir Guy Herbrand Edward Russell, who *d* 1977, and has issue *(see* colls infra). *Residence* – Flat 8, 89 Onslow Sq, SW7 3LT.

Barbara (Tall Pines, 308 Hearthstone Ridge, Landrum, South Carolina 29356, USA; Pony's Point, Iona, CBI, Nova Scotia, Canada), da of late Baron Serge Alexandrovich Korff, of Russia: *m* 1st, 1941, Wing-Cdr Hon Edward Wriothesley Curzon Russell, OBE, RAFVR, who *d* 1982; 2ndly, 1988, Arthur Farwell, and has issue (by 1st *m*) *(see* colls infra).

WIDOW LIVING OF THIRD BARON

ADELINE MARY CONSTANCE *(Adeline, Baroness Ampthill)* (Flat 3, 75 Holland Park, W11), eldest da of Rev Canon Henry Evelyn Hone, late V of Godalming: *m* 1948, as his 3rd wife, the 3rd Baron, CBE, Capt RN, who *d* 1973.

COLLATERAL BRANCHES LIVING

Issue of late Adm Hon Sir Guy Herbrand Edward Russell, GBE, KCB, DSO, 2nd son of 2nd Baron, *b* 1898, *d* 1977: *m* 1939, Hon (Helen) Elizabeth Blades (ante), da of 1st Baron Ebbisham:—

James Rowland (Sheepcote, Harrow Court, Stockbury, nr Sittingbourne, Kent ME9 7UQ), *b* 1940; *ed* Radley, and Clare Coll, Camb (MA, MB, BChir, DObst RCOG); Surg-Lt RN: *m* 1965, Glenys Pearl, da of Herbert George Lofting, of Nairobi, and has issue living, Robert James, *b* 1966: *ed* Radley, and Middlesex Hosp; Capt RAMC: *m* 1994, Melanie Alexandra, da of late Bruce Cumming, of Chilham, Kent, — Katherine May, *b* 1968; *ed* Royal Ballet Sch; choreologist at Ballet Rambert, Elizabeth Sarah, *b* 1970; *ed* Gordonstoun, — Mary Glenys, *b* 1973. —— Oliver Henry (Ballindalloch Castle, Banffshire), *b* 1942; *ed* Radley, and Magdalene Coll, Camb; a Page of Honour to HM 1957-59, Member Queen's Body Guard for Scotland (Royal Company of Archers): *m* 1967, Clare Nancy, DL, da of Maj Sir Ewan George Macpherson-Grant, 6th Bt (ext), and has issue living, Guy Ewan, *b* 1968; a Page of Honour to HM 1981-83, — Edward Oliver, *b* 1970, — Lucy Clare Nancy, *b* 1972. —— Margaret Elizabeth, *b* 1945: *m* 1975, James Anthony Fowell Buxton, of Galhampton Manor, Yeovil, and has issue *(see* Buxton, Bt, colls).

Issue of late Wing-Cdr Hon Edward Wriothesley Curzon Russell, OBE, RAFVR, 3rd son of 2nd Baron, *b* 1901, *d* 1982: *m* 1941, Barbara (who *m* 2ndly, 1988, Arthur Farwell) (ante), da of late Baron Serge Alexandrovich Korff, of Russia:—

Diana, *b* 1943. —— Margaret Angela, *b* 1946: *m* 1992, Stephen Howell.

Issue of late Hon Sir Odo William Theophilus Villiers Russell, KCMG, KCVO, CB, 2nd son of 1st Baron, *b* 1870, *d* 1951: *m* 1910, Countess Marie Louise Ernestine, who *d* 1966, da of Count Rudolf Karl Caspar von Rex:—

Cosmo Rex Ivor (Parapet House, Lenham, Kent), *b* 1911; *ed* Eton, and Trin Coll, Oxford (MA); Dep Dir of Information, Council of Europe 1949-56, and Head, Political Studies Div, Secretariat-General of Council of Europe, 1956-63; a Public Relations Consultant 1963-71, since when a Reviser and Translator, European Commn; Maj Queen's Westminsters, KRRC (TA); sometime a Councillor of New Windsor, and a Co Councillor of Berks; Council of Europe Commemoration Medal; 1939-45 War (despatches, American Bronze Star Medal, Officer of Order of Orange Nassau of the Netherlands with swords): *m* 1941, Agnes Mary, da of late Rev Canon Richard Edward Parsons *(see* E Rosse, colls), and has issue living, Nicholas Odo Richard Desmond (3 Court Farm Cottages, Udimore, Sussex), *b* 1946; *ed* Strasbourg, Brickwall Sch, Northiam, and Munich Univ, overseas relief and development consultant: *m* 1982, Rashida Joan Anwar, — John Drummond Athelstan (The Hermitage, Peasmarsh, Rye, Sussex) *b* 1948; *ed* Strasbourg, and Brickwall Sch, Northiam; Lieut Irish Gds Res; Co Dir since 1979: *m* 1968, Toril, da of late Finn Tennfjord, of Norway, and has issue living, Rory Finn Cosmo *b* 1984, Maikki Natacha *b* 1969, Natacha Ann *b* 1971, Tatiana Agnes *b* 1973, — Cecilia Hester Marie Louise Constance, *b* 1942: *m* 1965, Peter Robert Nutting, of North Breache Manor, Ewhurst, Surrey *(see* Nutting, Bt, colls), — Jennifer Rose Ann, *b* 1945: *m* 1966, Julian Goldsmid, of 7 Phillimore Pl, W8, and has issue living, Tara Alexandra *b* 1970, — Theodosia Mary, *b* 1952: *m* 1976, Christopher Gouldstone, late Lieut Queen's Lancashire Regt, of Thorndene, Pluckley, Ashford, Kent, and has issue living, Edward Oliver *b* 1981, Emma Charlotte Elizabeth *b* 1979, — Katharine Agnes, *b* 1955. —— †Alaric Charles William, *b* 1912; *ed* Eton; formerly a Member of the London Stock Exchange, and Maj Queen's Westminsters KRRC (TA): *m* 1940, Iris Charmian (44 Linver Rd, SW6 3RD), da of Noel Van Raalte *(see* Graham, Bt, *cr* 1783, colls, 1976 Edn), and *d* 1986, leaving issue, Michael Noel (10A Highbury New Park, Islington, N5 2BD; *Club* – Pratt's) *b* 1941; *ed* Eton, — Amanda Charmian, *b* 1946: *m* 1966, Martyn Anthony Hedley, of 2 Milbourne Grove, SW10 9SN, elder son of Anthony Martyn Hedley, of Bailiff's Cottage, Crawley Down, Sussex. —— David Hastings Gerald, *b* 1915; late Lt RNVR: *m* 1940, Hester Clere, da of late Rev Canon Richard Edward Parsons *(see* E Rosse, colls), and has issue living, Wriothesley David Xavier *(Clubs* - Queen's, and Ski Club of Gt Britain), *b* 1941; *ed* Eton, and Trin Coll, Dublin: *m* 1992, Melissa Tan Hui Chui, — Rupert Edward Odo (Highleaze House, Oare, Marlborough, Wilts; *Clubs* – Buck's, Ski Club of Gt Britain), *b* 1944; *ed* Selwyn House Sch, Montreal, and Rannoch Sch, Perths; Solicitor 1973; a Member of Law Soc; Chm Cities of London and Westminster Conservative Assocn 1979-83 (Vice-Pres 1984): *m* 1981, Catherine Jill, da of William Gulliver, and formerly wife of 5th Baron Brougham and Vaux.

Issue of late Lt-Col Hon Victor Alexander Frederick Villiers Russell, CBE, 3rd son of 1st Baron, *b* 1874, *d* 1965: *m* 1905, Annora Margaret Bromley, who *d* 1949, da of late George Edward Martin, of Ham Court, Upton-on-Severn:—

Angela Irene, *b* 1912: *m* 1938, Robert Alexander Bennet Gosling, of Mutton Hall, Wetherden, Stowmarket, Suffolk *(see* M Lothian, 1956 Edn), and has issue living, Alexander Bennet (32 Auburn Grove, Hawthorn, Victoria 3123, Australia), *b* 1940: *m* 1st, 1963 (*m diss* 1987), Mary, yr da of Duncan Macrae, of 22 The Little Boltons, SW10; 2ndly 1989, Wirat Sukprem, and has issue living (by 1st *m*), Henrietta Mary *b* 1966: *m* 1990, Nicholas R. Worthington, of 90c Beaufort St, SW3, son of Philip Michael Worthington, of The Knoll House, Knossington, Leics (and has issue living, Victoria Mary *b* 1994), Louisa Katherine *b* 1968, — Andrew Edward (Osea Island, Maldon, Essex), *b* 1944: *m* 1st, 1966, Rosemary Ailsa, eldest da of Col John Lyon Corbett Winder, OBE, MC, of Vaynor Park, Berriew, Welshpool; 2ndly, 1977, Imogen Margaret, eldest da of Humphery Fisher Crosby Halahan, of Foxearth, Winterbourne Houghton, Blandford, and has issue living (by 1st *m*), Amanda Sophia Jane *b* 1968, Catherine Angela Rose *b* 1970, (by 2nd *m*) Matilda Ann *b* 1979, — Robert Anthony (Pulham Cottage, Wetherden, Stowmarket, Suffolk), *b* 1948: *m* 1969, Clarissa Beatrice, yr da of late Maj John Whitcombe, of The Malt House, Roundway Village, Devizes, Wilts *(see* E Halifax, colls), and has issue living. Richard Bennet *b* 1972, Charlotte Arabella Ida *b* 1974, — Annabel Victoria, *b* 1942: *m* 1965, Nathaniel Charles Sebag-Montefiore, of 180 Kensington Park Rd, W11 2ER, and has issue living, Matthew Oliver *b* 1971, Victoria Alice *b* 1969.

Issue of late Brig-Gen Hon Alexander Victor Frederick Villiers Russell (twin), CMG, MVO, 4th son of 1st

Baron, *b* 1874, *d* 1965: *m* 1909, Marjorie Gladys, who *d* 1949, da of late Claude Hume Campbell Guinness:—
William Rodney Villiers, MC (31A Morin Rd, Preston, Paignton, S Devon), *b* 1914; *ed* Wellington; Lt-Col (ret) Rifle Bde; 1939-45 War in Burma (MC): *m* 1950, Diana Marigold, da of Arthur Trafford, of Paignton, and has issue living, Rupert Alick Villiers, *b* 1951: *m* 1974, Laura Suzanne Golds, and has issue living, Christopher John *b* 1983, Elinor Kate *b* 1981, — Sarah Caroline Villiers, *b* 1956.

Grandchildren of late Brig-Gen Hon Alexander Victor Frederick Villiers Russell, CMG, LVO (ante):—
Issue of late Capt Stephen Alexander Villiers Russell, Black Watch, *b* 1916, *d* 1985: *m* 1945, Ailsa Mary (Godford Land, Honiton, Devon), 2nd da of William Hope Pilcher, of The Gows, Invergowrie, Dundee:—
John Alick Stephen Villiers (Godford Land Farm, Awliscombe, nr Honiton, Devon), *b* 1946; *ed* Wellington: *m* 1975 (*m diss* 1986), Verity Elizabeth Anne Murray, and has issue living, Alick Robin, *b* 1976, — Guy James Villiers, *b* 1983, — Rosie Alice Swallow, *b* 1978. —— Camilla Mary Louise, *b* 1949: *m* 1978, Robin Geoffrey Murray, and has issue living, Charles Tobias Heatley, *b* 1978. — William Barnaby Robin, *b* 1980. —— Lucy Marjorie Eileen, *b* 1954: *m* 1974, Christopher Nigel Gordon Smith, and has issue living, Ben Christopher Gordon, *b* 1979, — Flora Eileen Ailsa, *b* 1981.

PREDECESSORS – (**1**) *Lord* ODO WILLIAM LEOPOLD Russell, GCB, GCMG, PC, brother of 9th Duke of Bedford, *b* 1829; the eminent diplomatist; was Sec at Constantinople Washington, and Florence, and afterwards for twelve years HM's Representative at Rome; went on Special Mission to Versailles during Franco-Prussian War 1870; joint Plenipotentiary (with Earl of Beaconsfield and Marquess of Salisbury) at Berlin Congress 1878; was Ambassador to the German Empire 1871-84; cr *Baron Ampthill*, of Ampthill, co Bedford (peerage of United Kingdom) 1881: *m* 1868, Lady Emily Theresa Villiers, who *d* 1927, da of 4th Earl of Clarendon; *d* 1884; *s* by his son (**2**) OLIVER ARTHUR VILLIERS, GCSI, GCIE, 2nd Baron, *b* 1869; was Gov of Madras 1899-1906 (Viceroy and Gov-Gen of India *ad interim* 1904); European War 1914-19 (despatches thrice, Brevet Col): *m* 1894, Lady Margaret Lygon, CI, GCVO, GBE, who *d* 1957, da of 6th Earl Beauchamp; *d* 1935; *s* by his eldest son (**3**) JOHN HUGO, CBE, 3rd Baron, *b* 1896; Capt RN: *m* 1st, 1918 (*m diss* 1937), Christabel Hulme, who *d* 1976, da of Lt-Col John Hart, of Broadhurst, Heathfield, Sussex (Erskine, Bt, colls); 2ndly, 1937, Sibell Faithfull, who *d* 1947, da of Thomas Wilkinson Lumley; 3rdly, 1948, Adeline Mary Constance, eldest da of Rev Canon Henry Evelyn Hone, V of Godalming; *d* 1973; *s* by his eldest son (**4**) GEOFFREY DENIS ERSKINE, 4th Baron and present peer.

AMWELL BARON (Montague) (Baron UK 1947)

KEITH NORMAN MONTAGUE, 3rd Baron, *b* 1 April 1943; *s* 1990; *ed* Ealing Gram Sch, and Nottingham Univ (BSc); CEng, CGeol, FICE, FGS, MIHT: *m* 1970, Mary, only da of Frank Palfreyman, of Potters Bar, Herts, and has issue.

SONS LIVING

Hon IAN *b* 1973.
Hon Christopher, *b* 1977.

SISTER LIVING

Hon Sheila Elizabeth, *b* 1949.

AUNTS LIVING (*Daughters of 1st Baron*)

Hon Constance, *b* 1915: *m* 1938, Albert Henry Cecil Slade, and has issue living, David *b* 1943, — Lesley, *b* 1946, — Stephanie, *b* 1956. *Residence* – 24 Kershaw Rd, Swindon, Wilts.
Hon Betty, *b* 1920: *m* 1941, John Forbes Dudley, and has issue living, Lysbeth, *b* 1947: *m* 1972, Kenneth John Hall, of The Anchorage, The Chalks, Chew Magna, Bristol BS18 8SN. *Residence* – 76 Eastcourt Rd, Burbage, Wilts, SN8 3AG.

WIDOW LIVING OF SECOND BARON

KATHLEEN ELIZABETH (*Kathleen, Baroness Amwell*), da of Arthur Percival Fountain: *m* 1939, the 2nd Baron, who *d* 1990.

PREDECESSORS – (**1**) FREDERICK Montague, CBE, son of John Montague, of Clerkenwell, EC, *b* 1876; Under-Sec of State for Air 1929-31, Parl Sec Min of Transport 1940-41, and Min of Aircraft Production 1941-42; MP for W Islington (*Lab*) 1923-31, and 1935-47; cr *Baron Amwell*, of Islington, co London (peerage of UK) 1947: *m* 1911, Constance, who *d* 1964, da of James Craig, of Runcorn; *d* 1966; *s* by his only son (**2**) FREDERICK NORMAN, 2nd Baron, *b* 1912; ARAeS: *m* 1939, Kathleen Elizabeth, da of Arthur Percival Fountain; *d* 1990; *s* by his only son (**3**) KEITH NORMAN, 3rd Baron and present peer.

ANCASTER, EARLDOM OF (Heathcote-Drummond-Willoughby) (Earl UK 1892) (Extinct 1983)

DAUGHTER LIVING OF THIRD EARL

Lady (NANCY) JANE MARIE, *Baroness Willoughby de Eresby* (see that title).

DAUGHTERS LIVING OF SECOND EARL

(*see* Bs Willoughby de Eresby).

Ancram, Earl of; son of Marquess of Lothian.

Andover, Viscount; son of Earl of Suffolk and Berkshire.

ANGLESEY, MARQUESS OF (Paget) (Marquess UK 1815, Bt I 1730, Earl GB 1714, Baron E 1549)

By means of its own opposite

GEORGE CHARLES HENRY VICTOR PAGET, 7th Marquess, and 10th Baronet; *b* 8 Oct 1922; *s* 1947; *ed* Eton; Maj RHG; FSA 1952, FRSL 1969, Hon FRIBA 1971, FRHistS 1975, Hon DLitt Wales 1984; CC Anglesey 1951-67, JP 1959-68 and 1983-89, DL 1960, Vice Lieut 1960, Lord Lieut of Gwynedd since 1983; patron of four livings, and Lord of the Manor of Burton-on-Trent; Pres Anglesey Conservative Assocn 1948-83, Nat Museum of Wales 1962-68, Friends of Friendless Churches 1966-84, and Ancient Monuments Soc 1979-84; Member Historic Buildings Council for Wales since 1953 (Chm since 1977), Royal Fine Art Comm 1965-71, Redundant Churches Fund 1969-78, and Royal Commn on Historical Manuscripts since 1984; Trustee Nat Portrait Gallery since 1979, and Nat Heritage Memorial Fund 1980-92; Hon Fellow Royal Cambrian Acad and Freeman City of London; CStJ 1984; author: *m* 1948, Elizabeth Shirley Vaughan, DBE, LVO, a Trustee Theatres Trust since 1992, da of late Charles Morgan, LLD, and has issue.

𝕬rms – Sable, on a cross engrailed between four eagles displayed argent, five lions passant guardant, of the field. 𝕮rest – A demi heraldic tiger sable, maned, tufted, and ducally gorged argent. 𝕾upporters – Two heraldic tigers sable, maned, tufted, and ducally gorged argent.
Seat – Plas Newydd, Llanfair PG, Anglesey.

SONS LIVING

CHARLES ALEXANDER VAUGHAN (*Earl of Uxbridge*) *b* 13 Nov 1950; *ed* Eton, Exeter Coll, Oxford, and Sussex Univ (MA, DPhil); *m* 1986, Georganne Elizabeth Elliott, da of Col John Alfred Downes, MBE, MC, of Tudor Cottage, Whittlesford, Cambs, and has issue:—
      SON LIVING — Benedict Dashiel Thomas (*Lord Paget de Beaudesert*), *b* 11 April 1986.
      DAUGHTER LIVING — *Lady* Clara Elizabeth Isis, *b* 1988.
Lord Rupert Edward Llewellyn, *b* 1957; *ed* Westminster, and Oxford Air Training Sch: *m* 1982, Louise Victoria, yst da of Peter Hugh Youngman, of Charsfield Hall, Woodbridge, Suffolk, and has issue living, Jack William Kyffin, *b* 1989, — Lily Florence Angharad, *b* 1992. *Residence* – Plas Llanedwen, Llanfairpwll, Anglesey.

DAUGHTERS LIVING

Lady Henrietta Charlotte Eiluned, *b* 1949: *m* 1979, Timothy Megarry.
Lady (Elizabeth) Sophia Rhiannon, *b* 1954: *m* 1983, Robert D. Keir, son of James Dewar Keir, QC, of Crossways, High St, Dormansland, Surrey, and has issue living, (Owen) Samuel, *b* 1986, — (James) Oliver Dewar, *b* 1987. *Residence* – Lakelands Farm, Plaistow Rd, Kirdford, W Sussex RH14 0JR.
Lady Amelia Myfanwy Polly, *b* 1963: *m* 1984, Andrew M. Singleton, 2nd son of late Sir Edward Singleton, of 62 Queen's Gate, SW7 (*see* Scott, Bt, *cr* 1806, 1970 Edn), and has issue living, Henry Edward, *b* 1993, — Isobella Polly, *b* 1990.

SISTERS LIVING

Lady Mary Patricia Beatrice Rose, *b* 1918.
Lady Rose Mary Primrose, *b* 1919: *m* 1940, Hon John Francis McLaren, Squadron-Leader RAF (ret), who *d* 1953 (*see* B Aberconway). *Residence* – Old Bodnod, Eglwysbach, Colwyn Bay, N Wales LL28 5RF.
Lady Katharine Mary Veronica (twin), *b* 1922: *m* 1st, 1941 (*m diss* 1948), Lt-Col Jocelyn Eustace Gurney, DSO, MC, Welsh Gds, who *d* 1973, son of late Sir Eustace Gurney; 2ndly, 1949, Charles Farrell, MC, late Major Scots Gds, and HM Foreign Ser, and has issue living (by 1st *m*), Judith Marjorie Katherine, *b* 1942: *m* 1964, James Bowen, of Rishworth Hall Cottage, Sowerby Bridge, W Yorks, — (by 2nd *m*) Gerald Charles William, *b* 1956: *m* 1981, Joanna Rosemary, yr da of Col Philip Turner van Straubenzee, DSO, of Spennithorne House, Leyburn, N Yorks, and has issue living, Frederick Desmond Casimir *b* 1987, William *b* 1992, — Louisa Caroline Mary, *b* 1949: *m* 1970, Robin James Lane-Fox, 3rd son of late James Henry Lane-Fox, FRICS, of Middleton House, Middleton Cheney, Banbury, Oxon, and has issue living, Henry *b* 1975, Martha *b* 1973, — Diana (Dido) Eileen Mary, *b* 1958, — Marjorie Elizabeth Mary, *b* 1962. *Residence* – Cuttmill House, Watlington, Oxon.

COLLATERAL BRANCHES LIVING

Issue of late Capt Lord Victor William Paget, MC, brother of 6th Marquess, *b* 1889, *d* 1952: *m* 1st, 1913 (*m diss* 1921), Olive Mary (the actress, Miss Olive May), who *d* 1947, da of George Meatyard; 2ndly, 1922 (*m diss* 1932), Hon Bridget Colebrook, who *d* 1975, da of 1st Baron Colebrooke (ext; *see* 1973-74 Edn); 3rdly, 1935, May Beatrice (Mavis), who *d* 1977, da of William Crockford, and widow of Maj Herbert Dawson, MC:—
(By 1st *m*) Henry Alexander Reginald (Brick Hall, Gt Totham, Maldon, Essex), *b* 1914: *m* 1938, Sonia, da of late Count Paul Chatoulenco, and has issue living, Tessa Ann, *b* 1947: *m* 1967, Alexander Ramsay Hardman, and has issue living, Cameron Ramsay *b* 1971, Chouka Sonia *b* 1968. —— Peggy Hester Pauline, *b* 1913: *m* 1st, 1935, Nigel Arthur St George Gibbes, Lieut 8th Hus, who *d* of wounds received in action in the Middle East, 1942; 2ndly, 1944 (*m diss* 1950), Maj (Samuel) Peter Barrow, MC, RA, who *d* 1990; 3rdly, 1954, Ian Coward, who *d* 1988, in Malta, and has issue living (by 1st *m*), Michael Henry Arthur, *b* 1936; *ed* Eton, and ??? Coll, Camb: *m* 1961, Veronica Lillian, da of John Hamilton Mackenzie Ward, of SW15, and has issue living, Nigel Hamilton *b* 1967, Marina Jane *b* 1962, — (by 2nd *m*) Bryan Hugh Samuel (Weidweg 19, 8405 Winterthur, Switzerland), *b* 1946; *ed* Wellington Coll, and Newcastle Univ: *m* 1972, Vreni, da of Rudolf Kramer, of Winterthur, Switzerland, and has issue living, Janet Clare *b* 1973, Nadia Jane *b* 1975. —— (By 2nd *m*) Nicholas David (23 The Limes, 34-36 Linden Gdns, W2 4ET), *b* 1924: *m* 1st, 1952 (*m diss* 1956), Heather Betty (BEVIS), da of late Charles Smetham; 2ndly, 1956, Moya Lillian (HAYIM), who *d* 1962, da of Capt William John Enright, OBE, RD, RNR; 3rdly, 1962,

Ellen Bridget O'Neill, who d 1963, and has issue living (by 3rd m), John David b 1962, — Jane Bridget, b 1963. ——— Ann, b 1923.

Grandchildren of late Gen Rt Hon Sir Arthur Henry Fitzroy Paget, GCB, KCVO, eldest son of late Gen Lord Alfred Henry Paget, CB (infra):—
    Issue of late Capt Arthur Wyndham Louis Paget, MC, b 1888, d 1966: m 1928, Rosemary Victoria, who d 1970, da of late Brig-Gen Noel Armar Lowry-Corry, DSO (see E Belmore, colls, 1970 Edn):—
David Arthur Fitroy, b 1929; ed Eton, and Ch Ch Oxford. ——— Rosalind Louise (East Kennett Manor, Marlborough), b 1931: m 1958, Dr Clive Bremner Cameron, and has issue living, James Paget, b 1961, — Andrew Wyndham Armar, b 1965, — Sarah Louise, b 1959.

Grandchildren of late Gen Lord Alfred Henry Paget, CB, 5th son of 1st Marquess:—
    Issue of late Sir Almeric Hugh Paget, GBE, who was cr *Baron Queenborough* 1918 (see that title) (ext).

(In remainder to Earldom of Uxbridge and Barony of Paget de Beaudesert only)

Granddaughter of late Francis Edward Howard Paget, eldest son of late Howard Francis Paget, only son of Rev Francis Edward Paget, only son (by 1st m) of Gen Hon Sir Edward Paget (infra):—
    Issue of late Capt Edward Francis Howard Paget, Gren Gds, b 1910, d 1985: m 1948 (m diss 1972), Bridget, who d 1979, da of late Charles Harold Ellis, of Willington House, nr Maidestone:—
Caroline Charlotte, b 1950; BSc: m 1974, Hensel John Peters, of Jamestown, St Helena, S Atlantic Ocean, and has issue living, Howard Hensel, b 1974, — Nicole Maria, b 1982.

Granddaughters of late Salisbury Howard Paget, 2nd son of late Howard Francis Paget (ante):—
    Issue of late late John Henry Howard Paget, b 1925, d 1983: m 1948, Grace, da of E. Tunnicliffe, of Austrey, Warwicks:—
Deborah Ann, b 1952: m 1972, Norman Edward Sanford, and has issue living, Stephen Andrew, b 1980, — Michael Benjamin, b 1982. *Residence* – 69 Child Drive, Aurora, Ontario L4G 1Y8, Canada. ——— Kathryn Mary, b 1956: m 1979, William John Scrafton. *Residence* – 98 Connaught Av, Willowdale, Ontario M2M 1H2.

Grandchildren of late Hugh Arthur Paget, 2nd son of late Rev Edward Heneage Paget (infra):—
    Issue of late Clarence Arthur Edward Paget, b 1909, d 1991: m 1942, Cynthia Mary, who d 1977, da of late Herbert Hutchings:—
Hugh Charles Edward (27 Highbury Hill, N5 1SU), b 1946; ed Eton, and Merton Coll, Oxford: m 1977, Eleanor Mary, only da of late Rev Canon William Wallis, and has issue living, Francis Andrew Edward, b 1984, — Lucy Caroline Eleanor, b 1981. ——— Caroline Hermione, b 1942: m 1966, Dr Theodore Bennett Robbins, of Box 57, North Pomfret, Vermont 05053, USA. ——— Frances Catherine, b 1947. ——— Selina Mary, b 1950.

Granddaughter of late Rev Edward Heneage Paget, yst son (by 2nd m) of late Gen Hon Sir Edward Paget, GCB, 4th son of 1st Earl of Uxbridge:—
    Issue of late Eric Morton Paget, b 1867, d 1929: m 1904, Georgina Byng, who d 1916, da of late Herbert Byng Paget, of Darley House, Darley Dale, Derbyshire:—
Celia Mary (twin), b 1916: m 1st, 1942 (m diss 1946), Charles Cecil Patrick Kirwan; 2ndly, 1954, Arthur John Goodman, who d 1964, and has issue living (by 2nd m), Mark, b 1957, — Ariane, b 1955: m 1984, Andrew Dykes Scott Bankes, who d 1987 (see Spicer, Bt). *Residence* – 49 Grantchester St, Cambridge CB3 9HZ.

Grandchildren of late Leopold Cecil Paget, 2nd son of late Berkeley Paget, eldest son of late Capt Catesby Paget, 2nd son of late Hon Berkeley Thomas Paget (infra):—
    Issue of late Edward Catesby Paget, b 1903, d 1963: m 1940, Sibyl Gladys Rodney (who m 3rdly, 1963, Col Thomas Cromwell Williamson, DSO, of Casa Tabraza Apartado 46, San Pedro de Alcantara, (Malaga), Spain, who d 1987), da of late Col Charles Edward Duff, CB, and formerly wife of Col Robert Albert Glanville Bingley, CVO, DSO, OBE, 11th Hus, of Pegglesworth, Andoversford, Glos:—
(Anthony) Berkeley (c/o 8 Symons St, Sloane Sq, SW3 2TJ), b 1946: m 1st, 1976 (m diss 1979), Judith Mary Parry; 2ndly, 1981, Gabriele Mathilde Langer, of Munich, and has issue living (by 1st m), William Berkeley, b 1976, — (by 2nd m), Catesby Langer, b 1982, — Rodney Langer, b 1984. ——— Diana Jenefer, b 1943.

Grandchildren of late Lt-Col Cyril Nevil Paget, VD (infra):—
    Issue of late Richard Berkeley Paget, b 1928, d 1991: m 1965 (m diss 1986), Nicola Mary, eldest da of late Archibald Baird-Murray, of Old Park, Warninglid, Sussex:—
Edward Berkeley, b 1977. ——— Henrietta Elizabeth, b 1966. ——— Annabelle Mary, b 1968. ——— Charlotte Patricia, b 1971.

Granddaughters of late Com Claude Paget, RN, 2nd son of late Col Leopold Grimston Paget, 3rd son of Hon Berkeley Thomas Paget, 6th son of 1st Earl of Uxbridge:—
    Issue of late Lt-Col Cyril Nevil Paget, VD, b 1891, d 1980: m 1928, Eveleen Mary, who d 1983, da of late Barnaby Lanktree, of Cork:—
Mary Patricia, b 1931: m 1969, Lawrence Butterfield, TD, FRIBA, of Shepherds Wood, Sheffield Park, E Sussex. ——— Caroline Eve Mary (20 Hampstead Gdns, NW11), b 1935: m 1st, 1956 (m diss 1984), Anthony Aljoe; 2ndly, 1984, Francis J. B. Smith, and has issue living (by 1st m), Mark Coade, b 1959: m 1988, Sally Hancock.

Grandchildren of late Rev Cecil George Paget, 3rd son of Col Leopold Grimston Paget (ante):—
    Issue of late Bernard Leopold Paget, b 1892; d 1974: m 1935, Violet Gwendoline, da of late Lennox Robertson, FRIBA, of 14 Chargot Rd, Llandaff:—
Michael Robertson (207 Aldwick Rd, Bognor Regis, W Sussex), b 1936; ed King's Sch, Bruton; Composer and teacher; late Cpl Greenjackets Bde; Cyprus 1956-59: m 1960, Mrs Betty May Hobden, and has issue living, Gerardine Carol-Louise, b 1961, — Sarah Catherine, b 1963.
    Issue of late Felix Barnaby Paget, b 1904, d 1985: m 1st, 1932, Marjorie Therese, who d 1962, da of late Lt-Col Charles Seaver-Smith, RAMC; 2ndly, 1964, Dora Josephine Adams Clark, MRCS, LRCP, who d 1990:—
(By 1st m) Susan Jane Seaver, b 1937; dental surgeon: m 1957, J. Keith Wood, MSc, PhD, AMIEE, of 147 Prescot Rd, Aughton, Ormskirk, Lancs, and has issue living, Jonathan Piers Martin, b 1962, — Carolyn Jane, b 1965, — Elizabeth Anne, b 1967. ——— Carolyn Elizabeth, b 1935: m 1962, Arthur James Sanderson, ACII, who d 1986, of 3 Pedmore Court Rd, Pedmore, nr Stourbridge, Worcs, and has issue living, Helen Louise, b 1965, — Wendy Elizabeth, b 1967, — Clare Marjorie, b 1970.

Granddaughter of late Lieut-Col Arthur Leopold Paget, 5th son of late Col Leopold Grimston Paget (ante):—
    Issue of late Oswald Leopold Paget, Durham LI, b 1898, d 1955: m 1931, Barbara Mackintosh, who d 1968, da of Arthur Forman Balfour Paul, MC, FRIBA, of Peffermill, Craigmillar:—
Susan Blanche, b 1933: m 1956, Capt William Mitchell Miller, MVO, late Gren Gds, of Craighill, Kinellan Rd, Edinburgh, 12, and has issue living, Richard Neville, b 1964, — Anna Caroline, b 1959, — Victoria Jane, b 1961.

Grandchildren of late Mark John Paget, 9th and yst son of late Col Leopold Grimston Paget (ante):—
    Issue of late John Francis Paget, b 1903, d 1989: m 1932, Ann Millicent, who d 1981, da of Peter Arthur Blundell, formerly of Ridgelands, Cooparoo, Brisband, Australia:—
Peter Jeremy Valentine, RD (75 Little Walden Rd, Saffron Walden, Essex), b 1933; ed Malvern; Lt-Cdr RNR, and Master Mariner: m 1st, 1963, Helene Boye Hansen, who d 1978, of Ormoy, Stavangar, Norway; 2ndly, 19—, Mrs Sara Veronica Mills, only da of Mrs Joycella Colbourne, of 44 Gold St, Saffron Walden, Essex, and has issue living (by 1st m), Mark Sebastian Boye, b 1967, — Charles John Leopold, b 1974, — Caroline Elizabeth Astrid, b 1964. ——— Sarah Ann Victoria, b

1945; art therapist: *m* 1968, James Lewis, RIBA, of 101 High St, Marshfield, Chippenham, Wilts, and has issue living, Brett, *b* 1970: *m* 1992, John Benjamin Gardner, of Nailey Farm, St Catherine's, Bath, and has issue living, Benjamin James *b* 1993, — Kim, *b* 1973. —— Jane Melanie, *b* 1947: *m* 1967, Lt-Col Richard Seymour Corkran, Gren Gds, of Crockfords, Waltham St Lawrence, Berks, and has issue living, Claire Melanie, *b* 1973, — Alexandra Frances Louise, *b* 1976.

(In remainder to Baronetcy only)

Grandchildren of late Col Edward Richard Bayly, grandson of late Rev Edward Bayly, R of Killurin, son of late Lambert Bayly, 3rd son of 1st Bt:—

Issue of late Maj Edward Archibald Theodore Bayly, DSO, *b* 1877, *d* 1959: *m* 1921, Ileene Caroline Ethel Otway, who *d* 1960, da of late Major Arthur Augustus Hamlet Inglefield, of Old Church House, Beckington, Bath:—

Edward Archibald Richard (Ballyarthur, Arklow, co Wicklow), *b* 1922; *ed* St Columba's Coll, Trin Coll, Dublin, and Trin Coll, Oxford: *m* 1964, Rosemarie Evelyn Gisela Steins, only da of late Paul Heinrich Johann Minkley, of Frankfurt-on-Main, and has issue living, Edward Alexander Christian Lambart, *b* 1967, — Selina Ileene Suzanne Rosemarie, *b* 1965: *m* 1986, Robert J. Kavanagh, of Raheen, Beech Rd, Arklow, co Wicklow, and has issue living, Emma-Sarah Rosemarie Isabelle *b* 1988, — Catriona Louise Alicia Lucinda, *b* 1977. —— Adelaide Elizabeth Mary, *b* 1923: *m* 1955, Patrick Mullen, of Kilqueeney, Avoca, co Wicklow, and has issue living, Anthony Patrick Theodore, *b* 1956; *ed* De La Salle Coll, and Univ Coll, Dublin: *m* 1980, Aideen Mary, yst da of Frederick Shackleton, of 3 Kenure Lawns, Rush, co Dublin, and has issue living, Benjamin Anthony *b* 1983, Patrick William *b* 1984, Constance Elizabeth Joy *b* 1989, India Margaret Eileen *b* 1993, — Annabelle Sandra, *b* 1957. —— Rosabelle Ileene Zahra, *b* 1931: *m* 1957, Donald Brian Robinson, Gp Capt RAF (ret), of Green Acres, nr Chepstow, Gwent, and has issue living, Colan Denis, *b* 1958: *m* 1988, Jane Hilary Shrimpton, and has issue living, Matthew Conor *b* 1988, Anna Kirsten *b* 1990, — Timothy Rupert, *b* 1965, — Judith Sarah, *b* 1962.

PREDECESSORS – (1) *Sir* WILLIAM Paget, KG, PC, was summoned to Parliament of England as *Lord Paget de Beaudesert* 1549; *d* 1563; *s* by his eldest son (2) *Sir* HENRY, KB, 2nd Baron, *d* 1568; *s* by his brother (3) THOMAS, 3rd Baron, who was attainted by Parliament and his property confiscated; *d* 1589; *s* by his only son (4) WILLIAM, 4th Baron, who was restored to his rank and honours by Parliament; *d* 1629; *s* by his eldest son (5) WILLIAM, 5th Baron, Lord-Lieut of Bucks; *d* 1678; *s* by his son (6) WILLIAM, 6th Baron, Ambassador to the Sublime Porte; *d* 1713; *s* by his son (7) HENRY, 7th Baron, cr *Baron Burton* 1712, and *Earl of Uxbridge* (peerage of Great Britain) 1714; *d* 1743; *s* by his grandson (8) HENRY, 2nd Earl; *d* unmarried 1769, when the Barony of Burton and Earldom of Uxbridge became extinct, and the Barony of Paget devolved upon the son of Caroline, Lady Bayly, wife of Sir Nicholas Bayly, 2nd Bt, and da of Brig-Gen Thomas Paget, son of Henry, 2nd son of 5th Baron (9) HENRY, 9th Baron, assumed the surname and arms of Paget only; cr *Earl of Uxbridge* (peerage of Great Britain), 1784 *d* 1812; *s* by his son (10) *Field Marshal* HENRY WILLIAM, KG, GCB, GCH, 2nd Earl, a distinguished Cavalry officer in the Peninsular war, who at the head of the United British, Hanoverian and Belgian Horse, rendered exceptionally substantial aid at the battle of Waterloo, where he lost a leg; was Col of Royal Horse Guards, Lord-Lieut of cos Anglesey and Stafford, twice Lord-Lieut of Ireland, and Master-Gen of Ordnance, etc; cr *Marquess of Anglesey* (peerage of United Kingdom) 1815; *d* 1854; *s* by his eldest son (11) HENRY, PC, 2nd Marquess, *b* 1797; a Col in the Army and Lord-Lieut of Anglesey; summoned to House of Lords 1832 in his father's barony of Paget: *m* 1st, 1819, Eleanora, who *d* 1828, da of John Campbell, of Shawfield; 2ndly, Henrietta Maria, who *d* 1844, da of Rt Hon Sir Charles Bagot, GCB; 3rdly, 1860, Ellen Jane, who *d* 1874, da of George Burnand; *d* 1869; *s* by eldest son (12) HENRY WILLIAM GEORGE, 3rd Marquess; *dsp* 1880; *s* by his half-brother (13) HENRY, 4th Marquess, *b* 1835; *m* 1st, 1858, Elizabeth, who *d* 1873, da of Joseph Norman; 2ndly, 1874, Blanche Mary, who *d* 1877, da of Curwen Boyd, of Merton Hall, co Wigton; 3rdly, 1880, Mary Livingstone, who *d* 1931, da of J. P. King, of Sandhills, Georgia, USA, and widow of Hon Henry Wodehouse (E Kimberley); *d* 1898; *s* by his son (14) HENRY CYRIL, 5th Marquess, *b* 1875: *m* 1898, Lilian Florence Maud (who *d* 1962, having *m* 2ndly, 1909, Capt John Francis Grey Gilliat), da of Sir George Chetwynd, 4th Bt; *d* 1905; *s* by his cousin (15) CHARLES HENRY ALEXANDER, GCVO (son of late Lord Alexander Victor Paget, 3rd son of 2nd Marquess), 6th Marquess, *b* 1885; Lord-Lieut of Anglesey; Lord Chamberlain to HM Queen Mary 1922-47: *m* 1912, Lady Victoria Marjorie Harriet Manners, who *d* 1946, da of 8th Duke of Rutland; *d* 1947; *s* by his only son (16) GEORGE CHARLES HENRY VICTOR, 7th Marquess and present peer; also Earl of Uxbridge and Lord Paget of Beaudesert.

ANNALY, BARON (White) (Baron UK 1863)

My strength and valour

LUKE RICHARD WHITE, 6th Baron; *b* 29 June 1954; *s* 1990; *ed* Eton, RMA Sandhurst, and RAC Cirencester; Royal Hussars 1974-78, RAC Res 1978-86: *m* 1983, Caroline Nina, yr da of Col Robert Hugh Garnett, MBE, of Hope Bowdler Court, nr Church Stretton, Shropshire, and has issue.

𝔄rms – Argent, on a chevron engrailed gules, between three roses of the last, a cross crosslet or. 𝔠rest – A cubit arm, proper, charged with a chevron engrailed gules, thereon a cross crosslet or; in the hand three roses gules, slipped proper. 𝔖upporters – *Dexter*, a horse argent, caparisoned with the trappings of 14th regiment of Light Dragoons, proper; *sinister*, an Irish wolf-hound proper, gorged with an antique crown, and chained or.
Residence – Heath Farm, Fritwell, nr Bicester, Oxon OX6 9QS. *Club* – Cavalry and Guards'.

SON LIVING

Hon LUKE HENRY, *b* 20 Sept 1990.

DAUGHTERS LIVING

Hon Lavinia Marye, *b* 1987.
Hon Iona Elizabeth, *b* 1989.

HALF-SISTERS LIVING *(daughters of 5th Baron by 2nd marriage)*

Hon Doone Patricia, *b* 1961.
Hon Caroline Davina, *b* 1963.

AUNT LIVING (*daughter of 4th Baron*)

Hon Elizabeth Patricia, *b* 1923; European War 1942-45 in WAAF: *m* 1945, Lt-Cmdr (James) Osborne King, DSC, RNVR, and has issue living, James (Rademon, Crossgar, co Down), *b* 1952; *ed* Eton: *m* 1981, Sally Louisa, da of Alan Walker-Gray, of Nicholas Way Cottage, Northwood, Middx, and has issue living, James Charles Osborne *b* 1984, Dillon Alexander Jolyon *b* 1987, Justin Sheridan Vere *b* 1990, — Elizabeth Lavinia Sara (Riverview, Pallamallawa, NSW 2399, Australia), *b* 1946: *m* 1969 (*m diss* 1990), David Hugh Montgomery, son of late Maj Hugh Edward Montgomery, of Rosemount, Greyabbey, co Down (*see* E Carlisle, colls, 1940 Edn), and has issue living, Matthew Hugh *b* 1970, Alexander James *b* 1974, — Patricia Rose, *b* 1947: *m* 1970, Antony Douglas George North (PO Box 781336, Sandton 2146, S Africa), son of late William Douglas Herbert North, of Northdene, Rathfelder Av, Constantia, Cape Town, and has issue living, Christopher Douglas Antony *b* 1976, Richard James Patrick *b* 1978, Georgina Chloë Shallcross *b* 1972. *Residence* – 20 The Craig Rd, Downpatrick, co Down.

WIDOW LIVING OF FIFTH BARON

BEVERLEY ELISABETH (*Beverley, Baroness Annaly*), da of late William Maxwell, of Essex, and formerly wife of Michael Healy; Founder Anastasia Trust 'Sign' Campaign for Deaf People: *m* 1984, as his 3rd wife, the 5th Baron, who *d* 1990. *Residence* – 33 Chipstead St, SW6 3SR.

PREDECESSORS – (1) HENRY, son of late Luke White, MP for Leitrim, *b* 1790; Lord-Lieut of co Longford, and MP for Dublin (*L*) 1823-32, and for co Longford 1837-47 and 1857-63; cr *Baron Annaly* (peerage of United Kingdom) 1863: *m* 1828, Ellen, who *d* 1868, da of William S Dempster, of Skibo Castle, Sutherlandshire; *d* 1873; *s* by his eldest son (2) LUKE, KP, 2nd Baron, *b* 1829; sat as MP for Longford (*L*) 1861-2, and for Kidderminster 1862-6; was Lord-Lieut of co Longford 1873-4: *m* 1853, Emily, who *d* 1915, da of James Stuart; *d* 1888; *s* by his eldest son (3) LUKE, GCVO, 3rd Baron, *b* 1857; a Lord of the Bedchamber to Prince of Wales 1908-10, and Permanent Lord-in-Waiting to King George V 1910-21: *m* 1884, Hon Lilah Georgina Augusta Constance Agar-Ellis, who *d* 1944, da of 3rd Viscount Clifden; *d* 1922; *s* by his son (4) LUKE HENRY, MC, 4th Baron, *b* 1885; Maj 11th Hussars: *m* 1919, Lady Lavinia Emily Spencer, who *d* 1955, da of 6th Earl Spencer; *d* 1970; *s* by his son (5) LUKE ROBERT, 5th Baron, *b* 1927, F/O RAF 1944-48, Ptnr W. Greenwell & Co, and Member of London Stock Exchange, Freeman City of London: *m* 1st, 1953 (*m diss* 1957), Lady Marye Isabel Pepys, who *d* 1958, da of 7th Earl of Cottenham; 2ndly, 1960 (*m diss* 1967), Jennifer Margaret, only da of late Rupert Saumarez Carey, OBE, of East Hoe Manor, Hambledon, Hants; 3rdly, 1984, Mrs Beverley Elisabeth Healy, da of late William Maxwell; *d* 1990; *s* by his only son (6) LUKE RICHARD, 6th Baron and present peer.

ANNAN, BARON (Annan) (Life Baron 1965)

NOEL GILROY ANNAN, OBE, son of late James Gilroy Annan, of Bryanston Court, W1; *b* 25 Dec 1916; *ed* Stowe, and at King's Coll, Camb (Fellow 1944-56, Provost 1956-66); a Member of Academic Planning Board of Univ of E Anglia, and Chm of Academic Planning Board of Univ of Essex; Senior Fellow of Eton Coll 1956-66; a Gov of Stowe Sch 1945-66, and of Queen Mary Coll, London 1956-60; Univ Lecturer in Politics 1948-66, a Trustee of Churchill Coll, Camb since 1958, of British Museum 1963-78, Trustee Nat Gallery 1978-85, Pres London Library 1984; Provost of Univ Coll, London 1966-78, Vice-Chancellor of Univ of London 1978-81; 1939-45 War as Lt-Col with Mil Intelligence in War Cabinet Office in London, and in France and Germany; Cdr of Roy Order of King George I of the Hellenes; *cr* OBE (Mil) 1946, and *Baron Annan*, of Royal Burgh of Annan, co Dumfries (Life Peerage) 1965: *m* 1950, Gabriele, da of Louis Ferdinand Ullstein, of Berlin, and has issue.
Residence – 16 St John's Wood Rd, NW8 8RE.

DAUGHTERS LIVING

Hon Amanda Lucy, *b* 1952: *m* 1977, Spencer Thomas de Grey, of 56 Clapham Manor St, SW4 (*see* B Walsingham, colls).
Hon Juliet Louise, *b* 1955: *m* 1987, Dr James Richard Le Fanu, of 24 Grafton Sq, SW4 0DB, 2nd son of Richard Le Fanu, of 8 Malvern Terr, N1, and has issue living, Frederick James, *b* 1989, — Allegra Frances, *b* 1992.

ANNANDALE AND HARTFELL, EARL OF (Johnstone of Annandale and that Ilk) (Earl S by Charter 1662 with precedence 1643)

PATRICK ANDREW WENTWORTH HOPE JOHNSTONE OF ANNANDALE AND THAT ILK, 11th Earl; *b* 19 April 1941; *s* 1983 (claim to Earldom admitted by Committee for Privileges of House of Lords, and a writ issued summoning him to Parliament in the Upper House 1985); *ed* Stowe, and RAC Cirencester; Hereditary Steward of Annandale, Hereditary Keeper of Lochmaben Castle, Chief of Clan Johnstone; DL Nithsdale and Annandale and Eskdale Districts 1987; Chm Royal Jubilee and Prince's Trusts for Dumfries and Galloway 1984-88, Dir Murray Lawrence Members Agency, London, 1988-92, an Underwriting Memb of Lloyds since 1976: *m* 1969, Susan, only da of Col Walter John Macdonald Ross, CB, OBE, TD, JP, DL, of Netherhall, Castle Douglas, Kirkcudbrightshire, and has issue.

𝕬rms – Argent, a saltire sable, on a chief gules three cushions or. 𝕮rest – a winged spur or. 𝕾upporters – *Dexter*, a lion rampant argent armed and langued azure crowned with an imperial crown or. *Sinister*, a horse argent furnished gules. 𝕸otto – Nunquam non paratus (never unprepared).
Seat – Lochwood Castle, Dumfries-shire. *Residence* – Raehills, St Anns, Johnstonebridge, Lockerbie, Dumfries-shire.

SON LIVING

Hon DAVID PATRICK WENTWORTH (*Master of Annandale and Hartfell*; *Lord Johnstone*), *b* 13 Oct 1971; *ed* Stowe.

DAUGHTER LIVING

Lady Julia Claire, *b* 1974.

SISTER LIVING

Lady Eileen Elizabeth, *b* 1948: *m* 1969, Andrew Walter Bryce Duncan, of Newlands, Kirkmahoe, Dumfries-shire, son of Sir Arthur Bryce Duncan, and has issue living, John Walter Bryce, *b* 1971, — Edward James Bryce, *b* 1974, — Henry Andrew Bryce, *b* 1975.

HALF-AUNT LIVING (*Daughter of de jure 9th Earl by 2nd marriage*)

Lady Jean Evelyn, *b* 1917: *m* 1950, Maj Robert Philip Henry Elwes, MBE, MC, who *d* 1976, and has issue living, Sarah Jane, *b* 1951: *m* 1975, (Arthur) Guy Galbraith, of Newbold Revel, Haddington, E Lothian EH41 4HE, and has issue (*see* V Hampden, colls). *Residence* – Flat 4, 24 Collingham Gdns, SW5 0HL.

WIDOW LIVING OF DE JURE TENTH EARL

MARGARET JANE (*Dowager Countess of Annandale and Hartfell*), da of Herbert William Francis Hunter-Arundell, of Barjarg, Auldgirth, Dumfries-shire: *m* 1940, as his 2nd wife, the (*de jure*) 10th Earl, who *d* 1983. *Residence* – Blackburn House, Johnstonebridge, Lockerbie, Dumfries-shire.

COLLATERAL BRANCHES LIVING (*also in remainder, in male line, to Earldom of Hopetoun*)

Grandchildren of late Violet Constance, *b* 1881, *d* 1965, elder da of late Capt Percy Alexander Hope Johnstone, yr brother of John James Hope Johnstone (*de jure* 8th Earl of Annandale and Hartfell): *m* 1908, Capt Llewellyn Heywood Jones, late 5th Lancers, who *d* 19—:—
Issue of late Hugh HEYWOOD JONES, 10th Royal Hus and RAF, *b* 1909, *d* 1969: *m* 1937, Perena Grace, who *d* 1985, eldest da of late Sir Edward Ernest Pearson, JP (*see* Crofton, Bt, 1671, colls, 1971 Edn), and formerly wife of Capt Marcus George Roddick, 10th R Hus:—
Llewellyn HEYWOOD JONES (29 Flag Walk, Eastcote High Rd, Pinner, Middx), *b* 1937; *ed* Gordonstoun; Master Mariner, served Merchant Navy 1955-70, since when a civil servant with US Navy Mil Sealift Cmnd Office UK: *m* 1976, Irene Dorothy, SRN, da of late John Maurice Mark Andrews, of 18 Winchester Rd, Bexleyheath, Kent, and has issue living, Benjamin John, *b* 1980, — Perena, *b* 1978. —— Imogen Iris Heywood, *b* 1944: *m* 1965, Christopher Bowly, of Tulla Lodge, Emly, co Tipperary, and has issue living, Hamish, *b* 1966, — Samantha, *b* 1970.
Issue of late Olwen Heywood Jones, *b* 1911, *d* 1980: *m* 1940, Anthony Abel Smith, 10th R Hus (*see* B Sudeley, 1926 Edn), who *d* 1979:—
Timothy Bertram ABEL SMITH, *b* 1941; *ed* Eton: *m* 1965, Susanna Mary, eldest da of Douglas Collins (*see* Backhouse, Bt, 1980 Edn), and has issue living, Lucy, *b* 1969, — Julia, *b* 1971. *Residence* – 30 Dawson Place, W2.

Grandson of late Charles Cecil Gordon Hope Johnstone, elder son of George Gordon Hope Johnstone, 2nd son of John James Hope Johnstone (*de jure* 7th Earl):—
Issue of late George Wentworth Hope Johnstone, *b* 1872, *d* 1920: *m* 1900, Annie Eleanor, who *d* 1957, da of late Thomas Hack:—
George Ernest Gordon, *b* 1901: *m* 1st, 1926, Anna Dorothea Florence, who *d* 1959, only da of late Hon (Edward) Grenville Gore-Langton (*see* E Temple of Stowe, colls, 1959 Edn); 2ndly, 1940, Aileen Stephen, who *d* 1987, da of late Alfred Ewing, and has issue living (by 2nd *m*), John Wentworth Gordon (Town House 32, 4165 Fieldgate Dr, Mississauga, Ontario L4W 2M9, Canada), *b* 1944: *m* 1st, 19— (*m diss* 1975), Trudy, da of Dennis Delmar Dalquist; 2ndly, 1979, Patricia, da of Phillip Fisher, and has issue living (by 1st *m*), Jared *b* 1972, Jodi *b* 1974. *Residence* – 28 Roding Close, Elmbridge Village, Cranleigh, Surrey.

Grandsons of late George Granville Hope Johnstone, eldest son of late William James Hope Johnstone, yr son of George Gordon Hope Johnstone (ante):—
Issue of late Col William August Ludwig Vernon Alexander Hope Johnstone, *b* 1914, *d* 1993: *m* 1943 (*m diss* 1951), Pamela Maud, elder da of late Lt-Col John Murray Cobbold, of Glemham Hall, Suffolk (*see* D Devonshire, 1985 Edn):—

Philip William (Stud House, Easton, Woodbridge, Suffolk), *b* 1943; *ed* Radley, and RMA Sandhurst; late Maj 13/18th Royal Hus: *m* 1968 (*m diss* 1984), Antonia Jay, da of Jack Yuan Hutton-Potts, of Day Court, Elm Bridge Village, Cranleigh, Surrey, and has issue living, Thomas William, *b* 1974; *ed* Stowe,—Timothy Mark, *b* 1976; *ed* Stowe. —— Charles John Victor (Capel Hall, Trimley, Ipswich, Suffolk), *b* 1948; *ed* Radley, and Grenoble and Madrid Univs; Co Dir; Farmer.

> Granddaughter of late Capt William George Hope Johnstone, RN, son of Capt George James Hope John-stone, RN, yr brother of John James Hope Johnstone (*de jure* 7th Earl) (ante):—
> Issue of late Charles Henry Edmund Hope Johnstone, *b* 1867, *d* 1940: *m* 1st, 1901, Elizabeth, who *d* 1922, da of late George Samuel Wright, of Brunswick, NZ; 2ndly, 1929, Helen Muriel, who *d* 1954, da of late Thomas Revell, of Christchurch, NZ:—

(By 1st *m*) Evelyn Violet (158 Tawa Rd, Onehunga 6, Auckland, NZ), *b* 1906.

> Granddaughter (by 1st *m*) of late Charles Henry Edmund Hope Johnstone (ante):—
> Issue of late George William Hope Johnstone, *b* 1902, *d* 1985: *m* 1st, 1925 (*m diss* 1932), Dorothy Charity, da of Frederic Beasley-Hartley, of Birkhead, NZ; 2ndly, 1933 (*m diss* 1946), Amelia Daphne, da of Thomas Henry de Auvergue de Thierry, of Puniho, Taranaki, NZ; 3rdly, 1946, Helen Louisa, who *d* 1964, da of late William Taylor, of Howick, Scotland:—

(By 2nd *m*) Carolyn Ann, *b* 1938: *m* 1960, Gordon John Bracher, of 14 Reiman St, New Lynn, Auckland, NZ, and has issue living, Jonathan Charles, *b* 1963: *m* 1989, Sonia Claudette Mary, da of Edward John Galea Phipps, — Louise Jane, *b* 1961: *m* 1983, Geoffrey Stuart David Cooke, of Christchurch, NZ, and has issue living, Nathaniel David John *b* 1986, Sophia Jane *b* 1988, Elizabeth Ann *b* 1990, Juliette Rose *b* 1992.

> Grandchildren of late George William Hope Johnstone (ante):—
> Issue of late Graeme William Hope Johnstone, *b* 1934, *d* 1979: *m* 1961, Robin, da of late Edward Herbert, of Sydney, NSW:—

Gregory William, *b* 1963. —— Bruce Edward, *b* 1968. —— Trudy Anne (twin), *b* 1963: *m* 1989, Paul John Neave, RNZAF, and has issue living, Ryan Matthew, *b* 1993. —— Nerida Mae, *b* 1972.

> Granddaughter of late Charles Henry Edmund Hope Johnstone (ante):—
> Issue of late Charles James Hope Johnstone, *b* 1907, *d* 1964: *m* 1933, Ellen Sarah, da of Henry John Bennett Gason, of Temuka, S Canterbury, NZ:—

Robyn HOPE JOHNSTONE, *b* 1945; has resumed her maiden name: *m* 1954 (*m diss* 1992), Glen Douglas Ireland, of Kaiwaka, NZ, and has issue living, Kim Joanne, *b* 1967, — Gina Dianna, *b* 1969: *m* 1990, Matthew Harrison, — Jodi Hope, *b* 1971. *Address* – PO Box 101330, N Shore Mail Centre, NZ.

PREDECESSORS – JAMES JOHNSTONE, *b* 1602, cr *Lord Johnstone of Lochwood* 1633 (with limitation to his heirs male), and *Lord Johnstone of Lochwood, Moffatdale and Evandale*, and *Earl of Hartfell* 1643 (to him and his heirs male); *d* 1653; *s* by his elder son (1) JAMES, PC, 2nd Earl, *b* 1625, who by Letters Patent 1661 was also cr *Earl of Annandale* etc (with a direction that the titles should forever thereafter be named *Earl of Annandale and Hartfell*) with destination in the first instance to heirs male general; was further cr by Charter of 1662 *Earl of Annandale and Hartfell* (peerage of Scotland) with remainder to the heirs male of his body, whom failing to the eldest heirs female without division of his body and the heirs male of the body of such heirs female bearing the name and arms of Johnstone, whom all failing to his nearest heirs and assignees whomsoever; Hereditary Keeper of Lochmaben Castle and Hereditary Steward of Annandale: *m* (contract dated 1645), Henrietta, who *d* 1673, da of 1st Marquess of Douglas; *d* 1672; *s* by his eldest surv son (2) WILLIAM, KT, PC, 2nd Earl of Annandale and Hartfell, *b* 1664; thrice Lord Commr to Gen Assembly of Church of Scotland, Lord Privy Seal for Scotland May-Dec 1702 and 1715-21 (Great Seal for Scotland 1714-16), a Representative Peer for Scotland 1708-13 and 1715-21; cr *Lord Johnstone of Lochwood, Lochmaben, Moffatdale and Evandale, Viscount of Annand, Earl of Hartfell*, and *Marquess of Annandale* (Peerage of Scotland), with a destination to his heirs male whatsoever succeeding to his lands and estates, 1701: *m* 1st, 1682, Sophia, who *d* 1716, only da and heiress of John Fairholm, of Craigiehall, co Linlithgow; 2ndly, 1718, Charlotte Van Lore (who *m* 2ndly, Col John Johnstone (*see* B Derwent), who was *k* at Carthagena 1741), only da and heiress of John Vanden Bempde, of Hackness Hall, co York; *d* 1721; *s* by his eldest son (by 1st *m*) (3) JAMES, 2nd Marquess, who *dunm* 1730; *s* by his half-brother (4) GEORGE, 3rd Marquess, *b* 1720; declared to have been a lunatic by 1744 by an inquest in Chancery 1748; took the name of Vanden Bempde in accordance with the will of John Vanden Bempde by Act of Parliament 1744; *dunm* 1792, when the Marquessate and all the other honours became dormant; *s* (as 5th Earl according to the decision of the Committee for Privileges of House of Lords 1985*) by his kinsman (5) JAMES (son of 2nd Earl) of Hopetoun, who took the addl surname of Johnstone as stated in Charter of 1662, and grandson of 1st Earl of Hopetoun (by his wife, Lady Henrietta Johnstone, only surv da of 2nd Earl of Annandale and Hartfell), *de jure* 5th Earl of Annandale and Hartfell and 3rd Earl of Hopetoun (*see* M Linlithgow); *d* 1817; *s* by his eldest da (6) ANNE, *de jure* Countess of Annandale and Hartfell in her own right: *m* 1792, her 2nd cousin, Adm Sir William Hope, GCB (who took the addl surname of Johnstone before that of Hope); *d* 1818; *s* by her eldest son (7) JOHN JAMES, *de jure* 7th Earl, *b* 1796, MP for Dumfries-shire: *m* 1816, Alicia Anne, who *d* 1868, da of George Gordon, of Hallhead; *d* 1876; *s* by his grandson (8) JOHN JAMES, *de jure* 8th Earl, *b* 1842, MP for Dumfries-shire; *dunm* 1912; *s* by his nephew (9) EVELYN WENTWORTH, *de jure* 9th Earl, *b* 1879: *m* 1st, 1905, Eileen, who *d* 1909, da of Gustavus Villiers Briscoe, of Bellinter, co Meath; 2ndly, 1916 (*m diss* 1925), Marie Eleanor, who *d* 1969, da of Compton Charles Domvile; 3rdly, 1926, Mary Evelyn, who *d* 1962, da of late John Locke, of Kilbeggan, co West-meath, and formerly wife of John Beardmore Batten; *d* 1964; *s* by his only son (by 1st *m*) (10) PERCY WENTWORTH, *de jure* 10th Earl, *b* 1909, 16th/5th Queen's Royal Lancers, Maj RA (TA) Lanarkshire Yeo, served World War II 1939-42 (prisoner): *m* 1st, 1932, Phyllis Athena, only child of late Edgar Errol Napier MacDonell, CMG; 2ndly, 1940, Margaret Jane, da of Herbert William Francis Hunter-Arundell, of Barjarg, Auldgirth, Dumfries-shire; *d* 1983; *s* by his only son (by 2nd *m*) (11) PATRICK ANDREW WENTWORTH, 11th Earl and present peer; also Lord Johnstone.

*The many previous claimants to the Earldoms (between 1792-1879) founded their claims upon the Letters Patent of 1661 and were all rejected by the Committee for Privileges. The claimant of 1985 founded his claim not upon the Letters Patent but upon a Signature under the sign manual of King Charles II dated 23 April 1662 and the subsequent Charter. His contention that this Charter brought about the new creation of a separate Earldom in favour of the 1st Earl of Annandale and Hartfell, independent of the creation by Letters Patent, was accepted by the Committee of Privileges.

ANNESLEY, EARL (Annesley) (Earl I 1789)
(Name and Title pronounced Annsli)

From the love of valour

PATRICK ANNESLEY, 10th Earl; *b* 12 Aug 1924; *s* 1979; *ed* Strode's Gram Sch, Egham; late RN: *m* 1947, Catherine, only da of John Burgess, of Edinburgh, and has issue.

𝔄rms – Paly of six argent and azure, a bend gules. ℭrest – A Moor's head, couped at the shoulders, proper, wreathed round the temples argent and azure. 𝔖upporters – *Dexter*, a Roman soldier in armour or, tunic azure, helm of first, thereon three feathers argent and azure, resting his right hand on an antique shield or buckler proper; *sinister*, a Moorish prince in armour or, wreathed round the temples argent and azure, a quiver of arrows pendant from a belt over his left shoulder, and his left hand resting on a bow proper.

DAUGHTERS LIVING

Lady Jane Margaret, *b* 1948: *m* 1966, Vernon Hugh Gamester, of The Retreat, 23 Wendover Road, Staines, Middlesex TW18 3DE, and has issue living, Carl Vernon, *b* 1970, — Colette Louise, *b* 1967, — Juliet Dawn, *b* 1969.

Lady Nora Kathleen, *b* 1950: *m* 1969, John Bathurst Shaw Binning, of 6 Barons Way, Egham, Surrey, and has issue living, Gareth, *b* 1971, — Gavin Douglas, *b* 1977, — Madeleine Rachel, *b* 1969, — Carina Lorraine, *b* 1975.

Lady Patricia Catherine, *b* 1952: *m* 1974, David Sidney Morehead, of 133 Oriental Rd, Woking, Surrey, has issue living, Duncan Patrick David, *b* 1977, — George Sidney, *b* 1984, — Danielle Simone, *b* 1975.

Lady Frances Elizabeth, *b* 1957.

BROTHERS LIVING

Hon PHILIP HARRISON, *b* 29 March 1927; *ed* Strode's Gram Sch, Egham; late REME; Test and Calibration Engr Rediffusion Flight Simulation Ltd 1957, Systems Design Engr 1963, Systems Training Manager Hughes Rediffusion Simulation Ltd 1991: *m* 1951, Florence Eileen, only da of late John Arthur Johnston, of Gillingham, Kent. *Residence* – 17 Folly Mill Gdns, Bridport, Dorset DT6 3RN.

Hon Michael Robert, *b* 1933; *ed* Strode's Gram Sch, Egham; Warrant Officer RAF (ret); Asso Member Soc of Licenced Aircraft Eng and Technologists: *m* 1956, Audrey Mary, only da of Ernest Goodwright, of Dartford, Kent, and has issue living, Michael Stephen, *b* 1957: *m* 1983, Angela, 2nd da of David Matthews, of Chipping Norton, Oxon, and has issue living, Michael David *b* 28 Jan 1984, Zara Jane *b* (twin) 1984, — Robert Francis, *b* 1962: *m* 1992, Sharon Anne, 5th da of John Fraser, of Stevenage, Herts, — Sheila Marie, *b* 1961. *Residence* – 16 Coltash Rd, Furnace Green, Crawley, W Sussex.

COLLATERAL BRANCHES LIVING

Granddaughter of late Richard Grove Annesley, eldest son of late Lt-Gen Hon Arthur Grove Annesley, 3rd son of 2nd Earl:—

Issue of late Richard Arthur Grove Annesley, *b* 1879, *d* 1966: *m* 1907, Hilda Margaret, who *d* 1961, da of the Rt Hon Sir Francis Edmund Workman-Macnaghten, 3rd Bt:—

Diana Patricia (twin) (260 Snowden La, Princeton, New Jersey 08540, USA), *b* 1911: *m* 1932, (William) Martin Hill, CMG, former Asst Sec Gen UN, who *d* 1976, and has issue living, Colin Patrick Annesley Martin (104 Bayard Lane, Princeton, NJ 08540, USA), *b* 1941; *ed* Groton Sch, Princeton Univ (AB), and Trin Coll, Dublin (MLitt): *m* 1966, Margaret Lydia Faith, da of late Maj Charles Robert Purdon Coote (*see* Coote, Bt, colls) and has issue living, Sebastian Martin Coote *b* 1967, Brendan Colin Charles *b* 1970, Orlando William Eyre *b* 1980, Cordelia Diana Margaret *b* 1978.

Grandchildren of late Richard Arthur Grove Annesley (ante):—

Issue of late Richard Francis Michael Grove Annesley, *b* 1908, *d* 1979: *m* 1st, 1931 (*m diss* 1939), Elizabeth, da of J. Anderson, of Edinburgh; 2ndly, 1939, Elsie Susannah, da of Jacob Daniel Krige, of Stellenbosch, CP, and formerly wife of Reginald de Beer, of Johannesburg:—

(By 1st *m*) Diana Elizabeth Doreen, *b* 1932: *m* 1954, Robin Keitley Duff, of Box 67419, Bryanston, Transvaal, and has issue living, Hugh Robert Keitley, *b* 1955: — Margaret Jean Keitley, *b* 1955: *m* 1982, Nikola Vujovic, of Herceq, Yugoslavia. —— (By 2nd *m*) Richard David Fergus Robert Grove (Kensington Park, Adelaide, Australia), *b* 1940: *m* 1st, 1966 (*m diss* 19—), Marina Soares, of Salisbury, Rhodesia; 2ndly, 19—, Mary Hurley, of Durban, Natal, and has issue living (by 1st *m*), Michael Richard Edward Grove, *b* 1970, — Robert Patrick Sean, *b* 1971, — (by 2nd *m*) James Richard, *b* 1980, — Paul Daniel, *b* 1982. —— Rozanne Mary, *b* 1942: *m* 1967, David Worsley, of Rivermead, Henley-on-Klip, Transvaal, and has issue living, Nicolette Grace, *b* 1971, — Justine Elizabeth Mary, *b* 1975.

Issue of late Edmund Patrick Grove Annesley, OBE; *b* 1911; *d* 1975: *m* 1939, Ruth (Annes Grove, Castletownroche, co Cork), da of late Arthur Norman Rushforth, of Bouley Bay, Jersey:—

(Arthur) Noël Grove (Marlowe House, Dulwich Village, SE21; Brooks's Club), *b* 1941; *ed* Harrow, and Worcester Coll, Oxford; Dep Chm Christies Internat plc since 1992; Dir Christie's Internat plc: *m* 1968, Caroline Susan Aurea, da of late Thomas Henry Waldore Lumley, of 5 Robert Close, W9, and has issue living, Marcus Robert Grove, *b* 1972, — James Alexander Grove, *b* 1974. —— Francis Patrick Grove (Annes Grove, Castletownroche, co Cork), *b* 1943; *ed* Harrow, and Univ Coll, Oxford: *m* 1968, Jane Frances, da of late Egbert James Neville Holder, and has issue living, Melanie Jane Ruth, *b* 1969, — Cressida Mary Siobhan, *b* 1971.

Granddaughter of late Henry Robert Grove Annesley, 5th son of late Lt-Gen Hon Arthur Grove Annesley (ante):—

Issue of late Arthur Geoffrey Grove Annesley, *b* 1867, *d* 1954: *m* 1898, Mary Edith, who *d* 1972, da of late William J. Roe, of Landscape, Celbridge, co Kildare:—

Phyllis Kathleen Rhona, *b* 1907: *m* 1934, Brig Averell John Daniell, CBE, DSO, Col Comdt RA, and has issue living, Patrick John, CBE (Abbey Cottage, Itchen Abbas, Winchester, Hants), *b* 1939; Col RA (ret); CBE (Mil) 1987, — Michael Hugh, *b* 1946: *m* 1983, Susan Jane Winsor, and has issue living, Timothy Edward Winsor *b* 1988, Helena Rose Winsor *b* 1986, Esther Marianna Winsor *b* 1992, — Susan Mary, *b* 1937: *m* 1973, Guy Vivian Fennell Robinson, of 46 Carson Rd, W Dulwich, SE21, and has issue living, Thomas James Daniell *b* 1977, Philip Henry Guy *b* 1979. *Residence* – Oak Lodge, 21 Hillside St, Hythe, Kent CT21 5EJ.

Grandchildren of late Lt-Col Robert Michael Smith Annesley, 4th son of Capt Hon Francis Charles Annesley, RN 4th son of 2nd Earl:—

Issue of late Col Arthur Stephen Robert Annesley, CMG, *b* 1869, *d* 1939: *m* 1895, Kate Talbot, who *d* 1939, da of Gen William Howey:—

Vera Kathleen, *b* 1897: *m* 1921, Com Wilfrid Edmund Warner, DSC, RN, who *d* 1951, and has issue living, Elizabeth Vivienne Annesley, *b* 1921: *m* 1st, 1941, Loyzeleur Campbell Smith, who *d* 1949; 2ndly, 1952, Harold Basil Toller Foy, who *d* 1979, of Broxmead, Ewehurst Lane, Speldhurst, Kent, and has issue living (by 1st *m*), Heather Jane *b* 1944: *m* 1964, Roger Norman Alwen, of Great Budds, Mote Rd, Shipbourne, Kent TN11 9QD (and has issue living, Mark James *b* 1967, Jonathan David *b* 1977, Kate Annesley *b* 1969). *Residence* – Tunbridge Wells, Kent.

Grandchildren of late Capt William Robert Ewart Annesley, yr son of late Capt Hon William Henry Annesley, RN, 5th son of 2nd Earl:—

Issue of late Maj William Alan Cecil Annesley, RASC, *b* 1907, *d* 1976: *m* 1935, Dorothy Vaughan, who *d* 1971, da of late Frank Yewdall, ICS:—

David Robert Ewart (77 Park Av North, N8), *b* 1936; F/O RAF; sculptor: *m* 1st, 1960 (*m diss* 1968), Patricia, da of V. I. Jones, of London; 2ndly, 1992, Jane Victoria McLeod, elder da of Sir John Robert Whyte Ackroyd, 2nd Bt, and has issue living (by 1st *m*), Benjamin, *b* 1961, — (by 2nd *m*) William Harry McLeod, *b* 1992. —— William Gerald, *b* 1937. —— Simon Richard, *b* 1939: *m* 1961, Janine, da of late Ramand Varin, of France, and has issue living, Emanuel, *b* 1961. —— Sarah Elizabeth, *b* 1943: *m* 1962, Henry William Peter Thompson, of 34 Southam Rd, Greystone Park, Harare, Zimbabwe, and has issue living, Howard Luke, *b* 1964, — Paul David, *b* 1966.

PREDECESSORS – (1) WILLIAM, 6th son of Francis Annesley, 4th son of 1st Viscount Valentia, was cr *Baron Annesley*, of Castlewellan, co Down (peerage of Ireland) 1758, and *Viscount Glerawly*, of co Fermanagh (peerage of Ireland) 1766; *d* 1770; *s* by his eldest son (2) FRANCIS CHARLES, 2nd Viscount; cr *Earl Annesley*, of Castelwellan, co Down (peerage of Ireland) 1789; *d* 1802; under a special remainder was *s* by his brother (3) RICHARD, 2nd Earl; *d* 1824; *s* by his son (4) WILLIAM RICHARD, 3rd Earl, *b* 1772: *m* 1st, 1803 (*m diss* 1821), Lady Isabella St Lawrance, who *d* 1827, da of 2nd Earl of Howth; 2ndly, 1828, Priscilla Cecilia, da of Hugh Moore, of Eglantine, co Down; *d* 1838; *s* by his eldest son (5) WILLIAM RICHARD, 4th Earl, MP for Great Grimsby (*C*) 1852-7, and sometime a Representative Peer; *dsp* 1874; *s* by his brother (6) HUGH, 5th Earl, *b* 1831; a Representative Peer; Lieut-Col Scots Guards; MP for co Cavan (*C*) 1851-4: *m* 1st, 1877, Mabel Wilhelmina Frances, who *d* 1891, da of Col William Thomas Markham; 2ndly, 1892, Priscilla Cecilia, who *d* 1941, da of late William Armitage Moore, of Arnmore, co Cavan; *d* 1908; *s* by his son (7) FRANCIS, 6th Earl, *b* 1884; was a Sub-Lieut Roy Naval Reserve: *m* 1909, Evelyn Hester (Harrison), who *d* 1947, da of Alfred Edward Miller Mundy, of Shipley Hall, Derby; *ka* 1914, while serving with Royal Flying Corps; *s* by his cousin (8) WALTER BERESFORD (son of late Hon William Octavius Beresford Annesley, 6th son of 3rd Earl), 7th Earl, *b* 1861: *m* 1st, 1893, Maud Fleming, who *d* 1923, da of Haynes Bingham Higginson, of Glebe House, Walmer, Kent; 2ndly, 1924, Mabel Frances Aganoor, who *d* 1931, eldest da of late John Burnet; *d* 1934; *s* by his son (9) BERESFORD CECIL BINGHAM, 8th Earl; *b* 1894; sometime Lieut Roy Fusiliers: *m* 1st, 1921 (*m diss* 1941), Edith Constance, who *d* 1950, da of Major Alexander Albemarle Rawlinson, formerly of 4 Aldford Street, Park Lane, W1; 2ndly, 1945, Mrs Josephine Mary Repton, who *d* 1977; *d* 1957; *s* by his kinsman (10) ROBERT (son of late Arthur Albert O'Donel Valentia Annesley, grandson of late James Annesley, son of late Hon Robert Annesley, 2nd son of 2nd Earl), 9th Earl, *b* 1900; European Wars 1915-18 and 1939-44 in France and W Africa with R Corps of Signals: *m* 1922, Nora, who *d* 1992, yst da of Walter Harrison, of Sapperton, Cirencester, Glos; *d* 1979; *s* by his eldest son (11) PATRICK, 10th Earl and present peer; also Viscount Glerawly, and Baron Annesley of Castlewellan.

Anson, Viscount; son of Earl of Lichfield.

ANTRIM, EARL OF (McDonnell) (Earl I 1785)

Always ready

ALEXANDER RANDAL MARK McDONNELL, 9th Earl (*Viscount Dunluce*); *b* 3 Feb 1935; *s* 1977, but continues to be known as Viscount Dunluce; *ed* Downside, Ch Ch Oxford, and Ruskin Sch of Art; Keeper of Conservation, Tate Gallery since 1975, Head of Collection Sers 1990-93, since when Dir; Member Exec Cttee City and Guilds of London Art Sch, and of Court of R Coll of Art; Dir Ulster TV; FRSA: *m* 1st, 1963 (*m diss* 1974), Sarah Elizabeth Anne, 2nd da of St John Bernard Vyvyan Harmsworth (*see* Boothby, Bt, colls, 1980 Edn); 2ndly 1977, Elizabeth, da of late Michael Moses Sacher, and has issue by 1st and 2nd *m*.

Arms – Quarterly, 1st and 4th grand quarters, quarterly 1st or, a lion rampant gules; 2nd, or a dexter arm, issuant from the sinister fesse point, out of a cloud, proper, in the hand a cross crosslet fitchée, erect azure; 3rd argent, a ship, with sails furled sable; 4th per fesse azure and vert, a dolphin naiant in fesse proper, *McDonnell*; 2nd and 3rd grand quarters, quarterly, 1st and 4th, azure, a sun in splendour or, 2nd, gules on a chevron argent three mullets of the field, 3rd, sable on a chevron between three unicorns' heads, argent, as many mullets of the field, *Kerr*. **Crests** – First, A dexter arm embowed in fesse, coupled at the shoulder, vested or, cuffs argent, holding in the hand a cross crosslet fitchée erect azure *McDonnell*; 2nd, a sun in splendour or, *Kerr*. **Supporters** – *Dexter* a wild man wreathed about the temple and loins with ivy, all proper; *sinister*, a falcon, wings inverted, proper, beaked, membered and belled or.

Seat – Glenarm Castle, Glenarm, co Antrim. *Residence* – Deer Park Cottage, Glenarm, co Antrim. *Town Residence* – 35 Durand Gdns, SW9.

SON LIVING (By 1st marriage)

Hon RANDAL ALEXANDER ST JOHN, *b* 2 July 1967.

DAUGHTERS LIVING *(By 1st marriage)*

Lady Flora Mary, *b* 1963.
Lady Alice Angela Jane, *b* 1964: *m* 1991, Christian Gwinn, son of Richard Gwinn, of Philadelphia, USA, and has issue living, Louis, *b* 1991.

(By 2nd marriage)

Lady Rachel Frances, *b* 1978.

BROTHER LIVING

Hon Hector John (The Old Rectory, Glenarm, co Antrim), *b* 1947: *m* 1969 (*m diss* 1974), Catherine Elizabeth, da of Ronald Chapman, of Buttermilk Hall, Brill, Bucks, and has issue living, Colquitto Angus, *b* 1972, — Hannah Margaretta, *b* 1971.

UNCLE LIVING *(Son of 7th Earl)*

Hon James Angus Grey, *b* 1917; *ed* Eton; 2nd Lieut 7th Batn Roy Norfolk Regt (TA); European War 1939-40 (prisoner): *m* 1939, Jeanne Irene, da of late Col Stanley Leonard Barry, CMG, CBE, DSO (*see* Barry, Bt, colls), and has issue living, Sorley James, *b* 1940; *ed* Eton, — Louisa, *b* 1946. *Residence* – 36 Farley Court, Melbury Rd, W14.

AUNT LIVING *(Daughter of 7th Earl)*

Lady Jean Meriel, *b* 1914: *m* 1939, Hon William Speke Philipps, who *d* 1975 (*see* B Milford). *Residence* – Slebech Park, Haverfordwest, Pembrokeshire.

PREDECESSORS – **(1)** *Sir* RANDAL MACSORLEY MacDonnell, KB; cr *Viscount Dunluce* (peerage of Ireland) 1618 and *Earl of Antrim* (peerage of Ireland) 1620; *d* 1636, *s* by his eldest son **(2)** RANDAL, 2nd Earl, cr *Marquess of Antrim* (peerage of Ireland) 1644; *dsp* 1682, when the Marquessate became extinct, and the inferior dignities devolved upon his brother **(3)** ALEXANDER, PC, Col-proprietor of Antrim Regt 1688-91 in King James II's Irish Army; agent for Irish Catholic landowners 1692-99, and supporter of Confederation of Kilkenny; his titles were twice attainted and twice restored; *d* 1699; *s* by his son **(4)** RANDAL, 4th Earl; *d* 1721; *s* by his only son **(5)** ALEXANDER, 5th Earl; *d* 1775; *s* by his son **(6)** RANDAL WILLIAM, 6th Earl; cr *Viscount Dunluce* and *Earl of Antrim* (peerage of Ireland) 1785 with remainder to his daughters primogeniturely and their male issue, and *Marquess of Antrim* (peerage of Ireland) 1789; *d* (without male issue) 1791, when the Viscountcy of Dunluce (cr 1618), the Earldom of Antrim (cr 1620), and the Marquessate of Antrim (cr 1789) became extinct, while the Viscountcy of Dunluce and Earldom of Antrim (cr 1785) devolved upon his da **(7)** ANNE CATHERINE, 2nd holder of 2nd creation; *d* 1834; *s* by her sister **(8)** CHARLOTTE, 3rd holder of 2nd creation, wife of Adm Lord Mark Robert Kerr (M Lothian); *d* 1835; *s* by her son **(9)** HUGH SEYMOUR, 4th Earl of 2nd creation; assumed in 1836 the surname of McDonnell by R licence; *d* 1855; *s* by his brother **(10)** MARK, 5th Earl of 2nd creation; *b* 1814: *m* 1849, Jane Emma Harriet, da of Major Macan, of Cariff, co Armagh; *d* 10 Dec 1869; *s* by his eldest son **(11)** WILLIAM RANDAL, 6th Earl, *b* 1851: *m* 1875, Louisa Jane, VA, who *d* 1949, 3rd da of late Gen Hon Charles Grey; *d* 1918; *s* by his eldest son **(12)** RANDAL MARK KERR, 7th Earl, *b* 1878: *m* 1904, Margaret Isabel, who *d* 1974, da of late Rt Hon John Gilbert Talbot, DCI (E Shrewsbury, colls); *d* 1932; *s* by his son **(13)** RANDAL JOHN SOMERLED, 8th Earl, *b* 1911; Clerk in House of Lords 1933-35 and Chm National Trust 1965-77: *m* 1934, Angela Christina, who *d* 1984, da of Col Sir (Tatton Benvenuto) Mark Sykes (Bt cr 1783); *d* 1977; *s* by his son **(14)** ALEXANDER RANDAL MARK, 9th Earl of 2nd creation, and present peer; also Viscount Dunluce.

Apsley, Lord; son of Earl Bathurst.

ARBUTHNOTT, VISCOUNT OF (Arbuthnott) (Viscount S 1641)

Praise be to God

JOHN CAMPBELL ARBUTHNOTT, CBE, DSC, FRSE, 16th Viscount; *b* 26 Oct 1924; *s* 1966; *ed* Fettes, and Gonville and Caius Coll, Camb (MA); FRICS; Lord-Lieut Grampian Region (Kincardineshire) since 1977; Far East and Pacific 1944-45 with Fleet Air Arm (DSC) FRSA, FRICS, FRSE; Dir of the Aberdeen and N Marts 1973-91 (Chm 1986-91); Dir Britoil 1988-90, BP Scot Advisory Board since 1990, Clydesdale Bank 1985-92, Scottish Widows and Life Assur 1978-94 (Chm 1984-87), and Scottish Northern Investment Trust 1979-85; Pres of British Assoc for Shooting and Conservation 1973-92 and of RZS Scotland since 1976; Pres of Royal Scottish Geographic Soc 1982-85, Deputy Chm of Nature Conservancy Council 1980-85; Pres Highland Territorial and Volunteer Assocn 1984-89; HM Lord High Commr to Gen Assembly of Church of Scotland 1986 and 1987, a Member Royal Commn on Historical Manuscripts 1987-94; *cr* CBE (civil) 1986; KStJ 1982, Bailiff Grand Cross 1994, and Prior of the OStJ in Scot: *m* 1949, Mary Elizabeth Darley, eldest da of late Cdr Christopher Bernard Oxley, DSC, RN, and has issue.

Arms – Azure, a crescent between three mullets argent. *Crest* – A peacock's head, couped at the neck, proper. *Supporters* – Two wyverns, wings elevated, tails nowed vert, and vomiting flames proper. *Seat* – Arbuthnott House, by Laurencekirk, Kincardineshire.

SON LIVING

Hon (JOHN) KEITH OXLEY (*Master of Arbuthnott*) (Kilternan, Arbuthnott, Laurencekirk, Kincardineshire, AB3 1NA), *b* 18 July 1950; *ed* Fettes, and North Scotland Coll of Agric, Aberdeen (Higher Nat Diploma, and Diploma in Farm Business, Organisation and Management): *m* 1974, Jill Mary, eldest da of Capt Colin Farquharson, of Whitehouse, Alford, Aberdeenshire, and has issue living, Christopher Keith, *b* 20 July 1977, — Clare Anne, *b* 1974, — Rachel Sarah, *b* 1979.

DAUGHTER LIVING

Hon Susanna Mary, *b* 1954; *ed* Overstone, Northants; Dorset House Sch of Occupational Therapy, Oxford: *m* 1978, Hugh Turnbull Bradbridge Smith, of 52 Kings Road, Wimbledon SW19 8QW, yr son of Lewis Smith, of Darnlee, Melrose, Roxburghshire, and has issue living, Andrew Keith Turnbull, *b* 1981, — Emma Charlotte, *b* 1983.

BROTHERS LIVING

Hon (William) David, MBE, *b* 1927; *ed* Fettes; Col (ret) late Black Watch; Korea 1952-53, Kenya 1953-55, N Ireland 1974 (despatches); MBE (Mil) 1964: *m* 1955, Sonja Mary, eldest da of late Col Charles Newbigging Thomson, CBE, DSO, TD, of The Garden House, Panmure, Carnoustie, Angus, and has issue living, Charles Robert (Light House, Newtonairds, Dumfries DG2 0JL), *b* 1956; *ed* Fettes, and Silsoe Coll, Carnfield Inst of Technology (BSc (Engr)), *m* 1987, Patricia Diane, da of late Barrington Brooke, of Mukoko, Glendale, Zimbabwe, and has issue living, David Barrington *b* 1989, James Brooke *b* 1990, — Georgina Margaret, *b* 1964; *ed* Fettes, and St Andrew's Univ (MA), — Elizabeth Christian, *b* 1967. *Residence* – The Old Manse, Trochry, Dunkeld, Perthshire PH8 0DY.

Hon Hugh Sinclair, *b* 1929; *ed* Fettes, Gonville and Caius Coll, Camb (MA 1952), and Edinburgh Univ (LLB 1954); FCIS; late 2nd Lt 4th/5th Batn Black Watch; with Shell International Petroleum Co 1953-83: *m* 1963, Anne Rosamond, only da of late Charles Bentley Terdre, of Appledore, Cherry Walk, High Salvington, Worthing, and has issue living, Hugh James Hamilton, *b* 1967, — Katherine Anne, *b* 1970. *Residences* – 7 Birch Close, Boundstone Rd, Farnham, Surrey GU10 4TJ; Cairnhill, Forfar, Angus DD8 3TQ.

SISTER LIVING

Hon Christian Keith, *b* 1933; *ed* Edinburgh Univ (MA 1954): *m* 1954, Cdr Peter John Bing, OBE, CEng, FIMechE, FCIS, RN, of The Lodge, Church St, Edzell, Brechin, Angus DD9 7TQ, and has issue living, *Rev* Alan Charles (Mulberry Way, Round-swell, Barnstaple, Devon), *b* 1956; *ed* Christ's Hospital, and St Edmund Hall, Oxford (MA 1978); ordained priest 1992: *m* 1985, Wendy Margaret, eldest da of late Dennis Capstick, of Simonstone, Lancs, and has issue living, Alison Ursula *b* 1988, Emma Florence *b* 1990, Julia Margaret *b* 1993, — Robert Adrian (17 Grasmere Av, W3 6JT), *b* 1958; *ed* Christ's Hospital, and Magdalene Coll, Camb (MA 1980); ARICS 1982: *m* 1991, Sarah Frances, yst da of Laurence Greenwood, of Silvertrees, Coldwaltham, W Sussex, and has issue living, Henry Jarvis *b* 1992, — Andrew John Collingwood (Hudson Sq, Montrose, Angus), *b* 1960; *ed* Christ's Hospital, and Edinburgh Univ (MA 1984); Dip in Marketing 1985: *m* 1993, Isobel Donald (Zoë), da of John Wilson Muir, of Woodburn Gdns, Aberdeen, — Sarah Lucy *b* 1969; *ed* Marlborough, Edinburgh Univ (MA 1992), and Coll of Law, London.

COLLATERAL BRANCHES LIVING

Grandchildren of late Hugh Corsar Arbuthnott, yr son of late Lt-Col Hon Hugh Arbuthnott, 3rd son of 8th Viscount:—
Issue of late Lt-Col Hugh Arbuthnott, *b* 1896, *d* 1961: *m* 1923, Jess Agnes, who *d* 1978, da of Robert Henderson:—
Hugh John, *b* 1924; *ed* Sedbergh, and Camb Univ (BA hon 1950, MA 1955); late Capt RE; European War 1945 (wounded, despatches): *m* 1954, Dorothy Ferguson, who *d* 1991, only da of Sir William Lang Denholm, TD, of Glenmill, Kilmalcolm, Renfrewshire, and has issue living, Carolyn Ann, *b* 1955; *ed* St Andrew's Univ (BSc): *m* 1981, Hugh Alexander Normand, of Garden Cottage, Ardoch, Cardross, Dunbartonshire, and has issue living, William Alexander *b* 1984, Andrew John Charles *b* 1989, Margaret Catherine *b* 1986, — Sarah Jean, *b* 1957: *m* 1978, Jeremy Spencer James MacLehose, of Hop Garden Cottage, Westergate, nr Chichester, W Sussex, son of (Norman) Donald MacLehose, DSO (and nephew of Baron MacLehose of Beoch) and has issue living, Benjamin Donald Robert *b* 1981, Fergus Donald Hugh *b* 1988, Anna Margaret *b* 1983, — Susan Mary, *b* 1962: *m* 1983, Roger James Clegg, of Braeside, 257 Bangor Rd, Newtownards, co Down, and has issue living, James Hugh *b* 1988, Victoria Rebecca *b* 1986, — Christine Elizabeth, *b* 1966. *Residence* – Ardmoy, Rhu, Dunbartonshire. —— Mary, *b* 1926; BSc hons 1946: *m* 1949, Col Laurence MacLellan Young, MBE, MC, late RE, of Plovers, East Boldre, Brockenhurst, Hants, and has issue living, Alice Mary, *b* 1951: *m* 1972, Peter James Summerhayes, of The Paddock, Borthwood Lane, Sandown, Isle of Wight, and has issue living, Catherine Elizabeth *b* 1976, Christina Mary (twin) *b* 1976, Kirsty Alice *b* 1979, — Christina Jess, *b* 1954; *ed* Imp Coll, London, London Sch of Hygiene & Tropical Medicine (PhD): *m* 1978, David Peter Turner, of White Hart Cottage, Brinkley, Newmarket, Suffolk, and has issue living, James Peter *b* 1984, Catriona Jane *b* 1982. —— Marianne Jean Elspeth, *b* 1937: *m* 1967, William Richard Woods Ballard, of Oliver's Cottage, Capel St Mary, Ipswich (*see* V Molesworth, colls).
Issue of late Archibald Arbuthnott, MBE, ED, *b* 1898, *d* 1977: *m* 1931, Barbara Joan, who *d* 1988, yr da of late John Hughman Worters, of The White House, Chipstead:—
John (The Old Rectory, Llangynhafal, Denbigh, Clwyd), *b* 1933; *ed* Sedburgh, and Emmanuel Coll, Camb (MA), CEng, FRAeS: *m* 1956, Ann, yr da of late Arthur Garton, of Gwynn House, Lower Sloane St, SW1, and has issue living, Ian, *b* 1958; BSc: *m* 1986, Jane, da of Gary Redshaw, of Penllan, Stoney Lane, Llanbedr, Ruthin, Clwyd, and has issue living, Hannah *b* 1994, — David (Crenny, 15 Acorn Way, Shawbirch, Telford), *b* 1961; *ed* Aberdeen Univ (MA): *m* 1987, Dawn Grace, da of John Frederick Kirby, of Birmingham, and has issue living, Christopher John *b* 1991, Jennifer Ann *b* 1989, — Fiona, *b* 1957; MCSP: *m* 1984, Andrew Graham Sneddon, of Ty-Draw, Efenechtyd, Ruthin, Clwyd, and has issue living, John Andrew *b* 1986, Emily Fiona *b* 1988, Laura Alice *b* 1990, — Jane, *b* 1966; BA: *m* 1991, Robert Nicholas Shannon, of Crowborough, E Sussex, son of Robert Henry Shannon, of Belfast. —— Robert, CBE (Glazeley Old Rectory, nr Bridgnorth, Shropshire WV16 6AB), *b* 1936; *ed* Sedbergh, and Emmanuel Coll, Camb (MA); British Council 1960-93; late Lt The Black Watch; CBE (Civil) 1991: *m* 1962, Robina, el da of Robin Arthur Axford, of Benacre, Plummers Plain, Horsham, and has issue living, Robert Keith, *b* 1968; BA Cantab, — Alison Mary, *b* 1963; BSc Aberdeen — Catherine Anne, *b* 1965; MA St Andrews: *m* 1991, Owen A. Wheatley, of 182D Elm Rd, Kingston on Thames, Surrey KT2 6JB, elder son of Dr Garth Wheatley, of Lyddington, Rutland.

Grandson of late Hon David Arbuthnott, CSI, 4th son of 8th Viscount:—
Issue of late Donald Stuart Arbuthnott, CE, *b* 1860, *d* 1918: *m* 1892, Annie Elizabeth, who *d* 1944, da of James Brand, formerly of 10 Marchmont Terrace, Glasgow:—
Rev Canon Edmund Stephen (14 Westbrooke, Worthing), *b* 1909; *ed* Wimbledon Coll, and Camb Univ (MA); Canon of St George's Cathedral, Southwark (RC) since 1956.

Grandsons of late Cdr James Gordon Arbuthnott, RN (*infra*):—
Issue of late John Hyde Arbuthnott, *b* 1932; *d* 1981: *m* 1955, Patience Sarah (Hausse Cambe, 46700 Mauroux, France), da of Charles Wainman, of Hinton St George, Som:—
Anthony St John Gordon, *b* 1956: *m* 1980, Susan A., yr da of late George Humphreys, of Herts. —— Nicholas Charles, *b* 1958; *ed* Ampleforth, and CCC: *m* 1989 (*m diss* 1991), Tracey, yr da of Lesley Brett, of Eltham Park, Kent.

Grandchildren of late Donald Stuart Arbuthnott, CE (ante):—
Issue of late Cdr James Gordon Arbuthnott, RN, b 1894, d 1985: m 1931, Margaret Georgiana, who d 1993, da of John Woolley Hyde, of Seaview, Instow, N Devon:—
Hugh James, CMG (c/o Foreign & Commonwealth Office, King Charles St, SW1), b 1936; ed Ampleforth, and New Coll, Oxford; late 2nd Lt Black Watch; with Foreign Office since 1960, HM Ambassador to Romania 1986-89, to Portugal 1989-93, since when to Denmark; CMG (Civil) 1984: m 1964, Vanessa Rose, only da of Edward Dyer, and has had issue, Dominic Hugh, b 1965, — Justin Edward James, b 1967; ed Edinburgh Univ; drowned in a boating accident 1989, — Giles Sebastian, b 1970. —— Georgina Mary b 1940: m 1st, 1966 (m diss 1982), William Robert Sparling; 2ndly, 1988, Christian Toulet, of Touzinat, Orival, 16210 Chalais, France, and has issue living (by 2nd husband), Christophe Jean James Alexandre, b 1979, — Claire Margaret Suzanne, b 1984. —— Elizabeth Grace, b 1945: m 1967, Rupert Arthur Rees Evans, Barrister-at-law, of St Jacques, St Peter Port, Guernsey, CI, and has issue living, Marcus James Julius, b 1972, — Frances Imogen, b 1975, — Adelaide Grace, b 1978.
Issue of late Hugh Forbes Arbuthnott, b 1906, d 1982: m 1937, Janet Elizabeth, who d 1990, da of late Vice-Adm Herbert John Temple Marshall, of Gayton Hall, Ross, Herefordshire:—
Robert Marshall, b 1938. —— James Francis (Stone House Cottage, Kidderminster, Worcs), b 1940; Maj Black Watch: m 1974, Hon Louisa Nina Hughes-Young, yst da of 1st Baron St Helens, and has issue living, John Patrick, b 1977, — Albert Michael, b 1988, — Walter Francis, b 1991, — Elizabeth Nina, b 1980, — Florence Mary, b 1981. —— Simon David (Winterfold House, Chaddesley Corbett, Worcs), b 1942; ed Downside, and Ch Ch Oxford: m 1970, Suzanne Ruth, el da of Allen Mainwaring Parker, of Osmonds, Droitwich, and has issue living, Thomas James, b 1974, — Edward Alexander Hugh, b 1980, — Lucy Margaret, b 1972, — Katherine Anne, b 1976. —— Charles Philip (The Old Manse, Caputh, by Murthly, Perthshire), b 1946; ed Downside, and RMA Sandhurst: m 1983, Lindsay C., da of Angus Sillars, of Stuckenduff, Shandon, Dunbartonshire, and has issue living, Magnus Malcolm James, b 1989, a son b 1994, — Molly Victoria, b 1987. —— Hugh Andrew (13 Rosenau Rd, SW11), b 1948; ed Downside: m 1974, Elizabeth Jane, da of late Col Lionel James Showers, DSO, of The Old Rectory, Kington St Michael, Wilts, and has issue living, Hugh Frederick Archibald, b 1982, — Arabella Elizabeth, b 1979. —— Nicholas Octavius (10 Attwood Rd, W6), b 1952; ed Downside: m 1984, Vanessa Julie, da of Richard Mather, of The Ghyll, Kendal, Cumbria, and has issue living, George Arthur Harben, b 1986, — Edmund, b 1992, — Rose Elizabeth Marshall, b 1987, — Florence (Flora) Lily Nott, b 1990. —— Margaret Mary (Hon Mrs Hugh D. Donovan), b 1943: m 1968, Hon Hugh Desmond Donovan, of 40 Felden St, SW6, eldest son of Baron Donovan (Life Baron). —— Janet Felicity, b 1950: m 1980, William George McMorran, of 46 Holmewood, SW2, and has issue living, Donald Hugh, b 1983, — Roland Francis, b 1985, — Hugo Edmond, b 1988.

Descendants of Maj Hon Charles James Donald Arbuthnott, 6th son of 8th Viscount:—
Grandchildren of late David Arbuthnott, b 18—, d 19—: m 18—:—

PREDECESSORS – **(1)** Sir ROBERT Arbuthnott, was cr Lord Inverbervie and Viscount of Arbuthnott, with remainder to his heirs male (peerage of Scotland) 1641; d 1655; s by his eldest son **(2)** ROBERT, 2nd Viscount; d 1682, s by his eldest son **(3)** ROBERT, 3rd Viscount; d 1694; s by his eldest son **(4)** ROBERT, 4th Viscount; dsp 1710; s by his brother **(5)** JOHN, 5th Viscount; dsp 1756; s by his kinsman **(6)** JOHN, 6th Viscount, son of Hon John Arbuthnott, 2nd son of 2nd Viscount; d 1791; s by his eldest son **(7)** JOHN, 7th Viscount; d 1800; s by his eldest son **(8)** JOHN, 8th Viscount, b 1778; was Lord Lieut of Kincardineshire: m 1805, Margaret, who d 1870, da of Hon Walter Ogilvy (E Airlie); d 1860; s by his eldest son **(9)** JOHN, 9th Viscount, b 1806: m 1837, Lady Jean Graham Drummond Ogilvy, da of 8th Earl of Airlie; d 1891; s by his eldest son **(10)** JOHN, 10th Viscount, b 1843: m 1871, Anna Harriet, who d 1892, da of late Edmund Allen: d 1895; s by his brother **(11)** DAVID, 11th Viscount, b 1845; d 1914; s by his brother **(12)** WILLIAM, 12th Viscount, b 1849; d 1917; s by his cousin **(13)** WALTER CHARLES WARNER (son of late Capt the Hon Walter Arbuthnott, 2nd son of 8th Viscount), 13th Viscount, b 1847: m 1878, Emma Marion, who d 1930, da of late Rev John Hall Parlby, JP, of Manadon, near Plymouth; d 1920; s by his eldest son **(14)** JOHN OGILVY, 14th Viscount; b 1882; HM Lieut for Kincardineshire 1926-60; Convenor of Kincardineshire Co Council 1933; a Representative Peer for Scotland 1945-55: m 1914, Dorothy, OBE, who d 1990, yst da of late Adm Charles Lister Oxley, of The Hall, Ripon, Yorkshire; d 1960; s by his kinsman **(15)** ROBERT KEITH, CB, CBE, DSO, MC (son of John Campbell Arbuthnott, CIE, eldest son of late Lt-Col Hon Hugh Arbuthnott, 3rd son of 8th Viscount) 15th Viscount; b 1897; Maj-Gen late Black Watch (Col 1960-64); Lord Lt of Kincardineshire 1960-66: m 1924, Ursula, who d 1989, da of late Sir William Collingwood, KBE; d 1966; s by his eldest son **(16)** JOHN CAMPBELL, DSC, 16th Viscount and present peer; also Lord Inverbervie.

ARCHER OF SANDWELL, BARON (Archer) (Life Baron 1992)

PETER KINGSLEY ARCHER, PC, son of late Cyril Kingsley Archer, MM; b 20 Nov 1926; ed Wednesbury Boys' High Sch, Univ Coll, London (BA, LLB, Fellow 1978), and LSE (LLM); Bar Gray's Inn 1952, QC 1971, Bencher 1974, Recorder SE Circuit since 1982; Chm Council on Tribunals since 1992; PPS to Attorney Gen 1967-70, UK Delegation to UN Gen Assembly (Third Cttee) 1969, Chm Amnesty Internat (British Section) 1971-74, Chm Soc of Labour Lawyers 1971-74 and since 1980; Solicitor-Gen 1974-79; Opposition Frontbench Spokesman on Legal Affairs 1981-82, Trade 1982-83, and Shadow Sec NI 1983-87; author; MP Rowley Regis and Tipton (Lab) 1966-74, and Warley W 1974-92; cr PC 1977, and Baron Archer of Sandwell, of Sandwell, co W Midlands (Life Baron) 1992: m 1954, Margaret Irene, da of late Sydney John Smith, of London, Ontario, Canada, and has issue.
Residence – 7 Old School Court, Wraysbury, nr Staines, Middx.

SON LIVING

Hon John Kingsley, b 1962; ed Watford Gram Sch, and Corpus Christi, Camb.

ARCHER OF WESTON-SUPER-MARE, BARON (Archer) (Life Baron 1992)

JEFFREY HOWARD ARCHER, son of late William Archer; b 15 April 1940; ed Wellington Sch, Som, and Brasenose Coll, Oxford; Member GLC for Havering 1966-70, Dep Chm Conservative Party 1985-86; Pres Som Amateur Athletic Assocn 1973, Trustee RWS since 1989; FRSA 1973; author and playwright; MP Louth (C) 1969-74; cr Baron Archer of Weston-super-Mare, of Mark, co Somerset (Life Baron) 1992: m 1966, Mary Doreen, PhD, da of late Harold Norman Weeden, and has issue.

Residence – The Old Vicarage, Grantchester, Cambridge CB3 9ND. *Club* – MCC.

SONS LIVING

Hon William Harold, *b* 1972.
Hon James Howard, *b* 1974.

ARCHIBALD, BARON (Archibald) (Baron UK 1949, disclaimed 1975)

(GEORGE) CHRISTOPHER ARCHIBALD; FRSC, *b* 30 Dec 1926; *s* as 2nd Baron Archibald 25 Feb 1975; disclaimed his peerage for life 7 March 1975; *ed* King's Coll, Camb (MA) FRSC (1979), and London Sch of Economics (BSc Econ); formerly Prof of Economics, Univ of Essex, Lecturer in Economics, Otago Univ, NZ, and London Sch of Economics, and Leon Fellow, London Univ; Emeritus Prof of Economics, Univ of BC; Fellow Royal Society of Canada: *m* 1st, 1951 (*m diss* 1964), Liliana Leah, only da of Dr Noah Barou; 2ndly, 1971, Daphne May Vincent, da of George Henry Henham.
Address – c/o House of Lords, SW1.

PREDECESSOR – **(1)** GEORGE Archibald, CBE, son of George W. Archibald, of Glasgow; *b* 1898; Controller Min of Information 1944-45; Chm of Fedn of British Film Makers 1957-66; Dep Pres of Film Production of Gt Britain 1966-68; *cr Baron Archibald*, of Woodside, City of Glasgow (peerage of UK) 1949: *m* 1st, 1926, Dorothy Holroyd, who *d* 1960, da of George Henry Edwards, of Liverpool, 2ndly, 1961, Catherine Edith Mary, who *d* 1992, da of late Rt Hon Andrew Bonar Law, MP, and formerly wife of Kent Colwell; *d* 1975; *s* by his son **(2)** GEORGE CHRISTOPHER, 2nd Baron until he disclaimed his peerage.

Ardee, Lord; son of Earl of Meath.

ARDWICK, BARON (Beavan) (Life Baron 1970) (Extinct 1994)

Prepared in all things

JOHN COWBURN MORGAN BEAVAN, son of late Silas Morgan Beavan; *b* 19 April, 1910; *ed* Manchester Gram Sch; News Editor, *Manchester Evening News*, Manchester 1936-40, Assist Editor, Londoner's Diary, *Evening Standard*, and leader writer 1940-42, News Editor and Ch Sub *Observer* 1942-43, Editor, *Manchester Evening News* 1943-46, Dir *Manchester Guardian* and *Evening News* Ltd 1943-55, London Editor, *Manchester Guardian* 1946-55; Assit Dir Nuffield Foundation 1955-60; Editor *Daily Herald* 1960-62; Political Adviser to *Daily Mirror* Group 1962-75; a Member of European Parliament, Strasbourg 1975-79; *cr Baron Ardwick*, of Barnes, London Borough of Richmond upon Thames (Life Baron) 1970: *m* 1934, Gladys, da of late William Jones. Lord Ardwick *d* 18 Aug 1994.

Arms – Or a dragon passant between two roses gules, barbed and seeded proper, in chief and in base on a pile reversed gules, an owl argent. Crest – A cock criant standing upon a hand mirror proper, the frame and handle or. Supporters – On either side a representation of an angel holding in the superior hand a shepherd's crook proper.
Residence – 10 Chester Close, Queen's Ride, SW13. *Clubs* – Garrick, Roehampton.

ARGYLL, DUKE OF (Campbell) (Duke S 1701 and UK 1892, Bt (NS) 1627)

Forget not

IAN CAMPBELL, 12th Duke, and 14th Baronet; *b* 28 Aug 1937; *s* 1973; *ed* Le Rosey, Trin Coll, Glenalmond, and McGill Univ, Canada; late Capt Argyll and Sutherland Highlanders, Member Queen's Body Guard for Scotland, R Company of Archers; KStJ 1975; Hereditary Master of HM's Household in Scotland, Keeper of The Great Seal of Scotland, Keeper of Dunoon, Carrick, Dunstaffnage and Tarbert Castles, Adm of the Western Isles, and Hereditary Sheriff of Argyll: *m* 1964, Iona Mary, only da of Capt Sir Ivar Iain Colquhoun of Luss, 8th Bt, and has issue.

Arms – Quarterly: 1st and 4th gyronny of eight or and sable, *Campbell*; 2nd and 3rd argent a lymphad or ancient galley, sails furled, flags and pennants flying gules, and oars in action sable, *Lorne*; behind the shield are placed saltirewise a baton gules powdered with thistles or, ensigned with an Imperial crown proper thereon the Crest of Scotland (*Hereditary Great Master of Household in Scotland*), and a sword proper, pommel and hilt or (*High Justiciar of Scotland*). **Crest** – A boar's head fessewise, erased or, armed argent, langued gules. **Supporters** – Two lions guardant gules.
Seat – Inveraray Castle, Argyll. *Clubs* – White's, New (Edinburgh).

SON LIVING

TORQUHIL IAN (*Marquess of Lorne*), *b* 29 May 1968; a Page of Honour to HM 1981-83; *ed* Glenalmond, and RAC Cirencester.

DAUGHTER LIVING

Lady Louise Iona, *b* 1972.

BROTHER LIVING

Lord Colin Ivar, *b* 1946: *m* 1974 (*m diss* 1975), Georgia Ariana, da of Michael Ziadie.

HALF-SISTER LIVING

Lady Jeanne Louise, *b* 1928: *m* 1st, 1962 (*m diss* 1963), Norman Mailer, the writer; 2ndly, 1963, John Sergeant Cram, of Hopewell House, Irish Town, Jamaica, and has issue living (by 1st *m*), Kate, *b* 1962, — (by 2nd *m*) Cusi Charlotte Campbell Sergeant, *b* 1967.

WIDOW LIVING OF ELEVENTH DUKE

MATHILDA COSTER MORTIMER (*Mathilda, Duchess of Argyll*), (Lunga Tower, Ardfern, Argyll, and 6 Rue de Tournon, Paris VI), da of Stanley Mortimer, of Lichfield, Conn, USA, and formerly wife of Prof Clemens Heller, of Paris: *m* 1963, as his 4th wife, the 11th Duke, who *d* 1973.

COLLATERAL BRANCHES LIVING (*All in male line in remainder to Dukedom, Earldom and other titles in the Peerage of Scotland*)

Grandchildren of late Alexander Andrew Lochnell Campbell, 15th of Lochnell, son of late Archibald Argyll Lochnell Campbell, 13th of Lochnell, eldest son of Rev Colin Campbell, 4th son of Archibald Campbell, 11th of Lochnell, 8th in descent from John (Gorm) Campbell, 2nd son of 3rd Earl:—
Issue of late Alexander (Alasdair) Duncan Lochnell Campbell, 16th of Lochnell, *b* 1921, *d* 1993: *m* 1958, Rosemary Georgiana (Great House, Chipping Sodbury, Avon BS17 6PX), only da of Cdr Hugh Hope-Grant Begbie, RN:—
Alexander (Alick) Hugh Edward, *b* 1961; 17th of Lochnell; *ed* Radley, York Univ, and. RMA Sandhurst; late Capt 16th/5th The Queen's Royal Lancers; MBA (London Business Sch). —— Iain Charles Lochnell, *b* 1962. —— Caroline Irene Lochnell, *b* 1965.

Granddaughter of late Brig-Surg Alexander Dugald Campbell, MD, IMS, son of late Rear-Adm Donald Campbell, 5th of Achanduin, and 3rd of Barbreck, gt-grandson of Archibald Campbell, 1st of Achanduin, 3rd son of Colin Campbell, 5th of Lochnell, 4th in descent from John (Gorm) Campbell (ante):—
Issue of late Col James Donald Campbell, DSO, 10th of Achanduin and 8th of Barbreck, *b* 1884, *d* 1974: *m* 1911, Hazel, who *d* 1950, da of late Col Benjamin W. Marlow, CSI, CIE:—
Margaret Mary (87 Bedford Gdns, W8 7EQ), *b* 1915.

Grandchildren of late Lt-Col Geordie Osmond Lorne Mackie-Campbell, MC (infra):—
Issue of late Capt Peter Lorne Campbell, Rifle Bde, *b* 1925, *d* 1993: *m* 1954, Ann Gillian (Stonefield, Tarbert, Argyll), da of Ian Pountney Coats:—
†George Logan, *b* 1956; *d* 1986. —— Ileene, *b* 1958: *m* 19—, Dr Neil Duncan, and has issue living, Iain Campbell Duncan, *b* 1988, — Cara, *b* 1990.

Grandchildren of late Lt-Col Colin George Pelham Campbell, 6th of Stonefield, 8th in descent from Archibald Campbell, 4th son of Archibald Campbell, 2nd of Lochnell, son of John (Gorm) Campbell (ante):—
Issue of late Lt-Col Geordie Osmond Lorne Mackie-Campbell, MC, *b* 1896, *d* 1956: *m* 1921, Jessie Isobel, who *d* 1971, da of Sir Peter Jeffrey Mackie, 1st and last Bt (cr 1920):—
Colena Ileene, *b* 1922: *m* 1946, Iain Arthur Campbell, of Arduiane, Oban, Argyll, son of late Brig Sir Bruce Atta Campbell, KCB, CBE, TD, and has issue living, Nigel Bruce, *b* 1948, — Sheila Jean, *b* 1950. —— Patricia Isobel (Hillside House, Tinwell Rd, Stamford, Lincs PE9 3UB), *b* 1923: *m* 1946, Niall Campbell Macdiarmid, who *d* 1978, son of late Sir Allan Macdiarmid, and has had issue, Maunagh Elizabeth, *b* 1947; *d* 1973, — Fiona Jane, *b* 1949: *m* 1969, Roger Montague Prichard, son of Sir Montague Illtyd Prichard, CBE, MC, and has issue living, Duncan Montague *b* 1973, Cara Mae *b* 1971,

— Glenda Ileene, *b* 1954: *m* 1987, Lt-Col Gilbert Peter Kerruish, of Barnhaven, Apethorpe, Peterborough, Lincs PE8 5DP, son of Albert William Kerruish, and has issue living, Emma Campbell Rosalind *b* 1987, Holly Campbell Louise *b* 1989.

Descendants of Sir John (Ian) Campbell, 3rd son of 2nd Earl:—
Campbells of Cawdor (*see* E Cawdor), Ardchattan, Aros, and Clunes, and their cadets.

Descendants of Donald Campbell, 4th son of 2nd Earl:—
Campbells of Keithock, and their cadets.

Descendants of Thomas Campbell, 2nd son of 1st Earl:—
Campbells of Lundy, and their cadets.

Descendants of Colin Campbell, 1st son (by 2nd *m*) of 1st Lord Campbell:—
Campbells of Glenorchy (*see* E Breadalbane) and their cadets, including Campbell of Aberuchill Bt (*cr* 1668).

Descendants of Colin Campbell, 2nd son (by 2nd *m*) of 1st Lord Campbell:—
Campbells of Auchinbreck (*see* Campbell, Bt, *cr* 1628), Glencardel, Glensaddel, Kilduskland, Kilmorie Wester Kames, Kilberry, Dana, and their cadets.

Descendants of Neil Campbell, 4th son (by 2nd *m*) of 1st Lord Campbell:—
Campbells of Ormidale, Ellengreig, and their cadets.

PREDECESSORS – (1) Sir DUNCAN Campbell, of Lochow, assumed the designation of Argyll, and was cr *Lord Campbell* (peerage of Scotland) 1445; *d* 1453; *s* by his grandson (2) COLIN, 2nd Lord, Lord High Chancellor of Scotland, cr *Earl of Argyll* (peerage of Scotland) 1457, and *Lord Lorne* 1470; *d* 1493; *s* by his son (3) ARCHIBALD, 2nd Earl, killed at Flodden 1513; *s* by his son (4) COLIN, 3rd Earl, Hereditary High Sheriff of Argyllshire and Justice Gen of Scotland; *d* 1533; *s* by his son (5) ARCHIBALD, 4th Earl, the first important personage in Scotland who embraced the Protestant religion; *d* 1558; *s* by his eldest son (6) ARCHIBALD, 5th Earl, he espoused the cause of Queen Mary, and commanded HM's Forces at battle of Langside 1568; was subsequently Lord High Chancellor of Scotland; *d* 1575; *s* by his half-brother (7) Sir COLIN, PC, 6th Earl, Lord High Chancellor of Scotland; *d* 1584; *s* by his son (8) ARCHIBALD, 7th Earl, a distinguished military officer; *d* 1638; *s* by his eldest son (9) ARCHIBALD, 8th Earl, cr *Marquess of Argyll* (peerage of Scotland) 1641; was the first Commr from Scotland to the Parliament of England, and at the Coronation at Scone placed the crown upon Charles II's head; subsequently recognised Cromwell as Protector; upon the restoration of monarchy the Marquess repaired to London, but HM refused to see him and ordered his committal to the Tower; on 25 May 1661, he was tried for high treason and condemned to death, and on 27 May, he was beheaded at Edinburgh; *s* by his eldest son (10) ARCHIBALD, 9th Earl, who was restored to the Earldom; for refusing to subscribe to the Test Act was found guilty of high treason and condemned to death; he escaped, but was subsequently taken in an abortive attempt to invade Scotland, *temp* James II, and was beheaded 30 Jan 1685; *s* by his eldest son (11) ARCHIBALD, 10th Earl, in whom the *Baronetcy*, cr (NS) 1627, of Lundy (conferred upon Colin Campbell, grandson of 6th Earl of Argyll, with remainder to heirs male whatsoever), became vested in 1696 after the death of the 2nd Bt; cr in 1701 *Lord Inverary, Mull, Morvern, and Tiry, Viscount Lochow and Glenilla, Earl of Campbell and Cowal, Marquess of Kintyre and Lorne*, and *Duke of Argyll* (peerage of Scotland), with remainder to heirs male whomsoever; *d* 1703; *s* by his eldest son (12) JOHN, 2nd Duke, a Field Marshal in the Army, and a celebrated military commander; cr *Baron Chatham* and *Earl of Greenwich*, Kent (peerage of England) 1707, and *Duke of Greenwich* (peerage of Great Britain) 1719; *d* 1743 without male issue when the peerages of 1707 and 1719 became ext; *s* in Scottish titles by his brother (13) ARCHIBALD, 3rd Duke who in 1706 had been cr *Lord Oronsay, Dunoon and Arase, Viscount Ilay*, and *Earl of Ilay* (peerage of Scotland), which honours became extinct at his death 1761; *s* by his cousin (14) JOHN, 4th Duke, son of the Hon John Campbell, MP, 2nd son of 9th Earl; *d* 1770, *s* by his eldest son (15) JOHN, 5th Duke, cr *Baron Sundridge* (peerage of Great Britain) 1766, whose wife was cr *Baroness Hamilton* (peerage of Great Britain) 1776; *d* 1806; *s* by his eldest son (16) GEORGE WILLIAM, 6th Duke, who in 1790 had *s* to his mother's Barony of Hamilton; *d* 1839; *s* by his brother (17) JOHN DOUGLAS EDWARD HENRY, 7th Duke, *b* 1777: *m* 1st, 1802, Elizabeth, who *d* 1818, da of W. Campbell, of Fairfield; 2ndly, 1820, Joan, who *d* 1828, da of John Glassel, of Long Niddry; 3rdly, 1831, Anne Colquhoun, da of John Cunninghame; *d* 26 April 1847; *s* by his son (18) GEORGE DOUGLAS, KG, PC, KT, 8th Duke; *b* 1823; Lord Privy Seal 1853-5, 1859-66, and 1880-81; Postmaster-Gen 1855-8, and Sec of State for India 1868-74; Lord-Lieut of Argyllshire; cr *Duke of Argyll* (peerage of United Kingdom) 1892: *m* 1st, 1844, Lady Elizabeth Georgiana Sutherland-Leveson-Gower, who *d* 1878, eldest da of 2nd Duke of Sutherland, KG; 2ndly 1881, Amelia Maria, who *d* 1894, da of Right Rev Thomas Legh Claughton, DD (formerly Bishop of St Albans), of Danbury Palace, Essex, and widow of Col Hon Augustus Henry Archibald Anson, VC (*see* E Lichfield); 3rdly, 1895, Ina Erskine, VA, who *d* 1925, da of Archibald McNeil, of Colonsay; *d* 1900; *s* by his eldest son (19) JOHN DOUGLAS SUTHERLAND, KT, GCMG, GCVO, PC, 9th Duke; *b* 1845; MP for Argyllshire (*L*) 1868-78 and for Manchester, S Div (LU) 1898-1900; Private Sec to his father at India Office 1868-71, Gov-Gen of Canada and Com-in-Ch of Prince Edward Island 1878-83, and Gov and Constable of Windsor Castle 1892-1914; was Gov of Knights of Windsor, Lord-Lieut of Argyllshire, Hereditary Master of HM's Household in Scotland, Adm of the Western Isles, Chancellor of Order of St Michael and St George, Keeper of the Great Seal of Scotland, and Keeper of Dunoon, Carrick, and Dunstaffnage Castles: *m* 21 March 1871, HRH Princess Louise Caroline Alberta, VA, CI, GCVO, GBE, RRC, who *d* 1939, 4th da of HM Queen Victoria; *d* 1914; *s* by his nephew (20) NIALL DIARMID (only son of late Lord Archibald Campbell, 2nd son of 8th Duke), 10th Duke: *b* 1872; was Lord-Lieut of Argyllshire; *d* 1949; *s* by his kinsman (21) IAN DOUGLAS, TD (only son of late Douglas Walter Campbell, son of late Lord Walter Campbell, 3rd son of 8th Duke), 11th Duke; *b* 1903: *m* 1st, 1927 (*m diss* 1934), Hon Janet Gladys Aitken, who *d* 1988, da of 1st Baron Beaverbrook; 2ndly, 1935 (*m diss* 1951), Louise, who *d* 1970, da of late Henry Clews, of The Chateau of La Napoule, Alpes Maritimes, France, and formerly wife of late Hon Andrew Nicolas Armstrong Vanneck, MC (*B* Huntingfield); 3rdly, 1951 (*m diss* 1963), Margaret, who *d* 1993, da of late George Hay Whigham, and formerly wife of Charles Sweeny; 4thly, 1963, Mathilda Coster MORTIMER, da of Stanley Mortimer, of Lichfield, Conn, USA, and formerly wife of Prof Clemens Heller, of Paris; *d* 1973; *s* by his son (22) IAN, 12th Duke and present peer; also Marquess of Kintyre and Lorne, Earl of Argyll, Earl of Campbell and Cowal, Viscount Lochow and Glenilla, Lord Campbell, Lord Lorne, Lord Inverary, Mull, Morvern and Tiry, Baron Sundridge, and Baron Hamilton.

ARMSTRONG, BARONY OF (Watson-Armstrong) (Extinct 1987)

ADOPTED CHILDREN OF THIRD BARON

Francis William Paul, *b* 1965: *m* 1988, Sarah, elder da of Dr B. Gray, of Twyning, Glos.
Isabella Juliana Theresa, *b* 1970. *Residence* – Trewhitt Steads Farm, Thropton, Morpeth, Northumberland.

MARIA-TERESA (*Baroness Armstrong*), da of late Gen Conte Fabrizio Enea Chiodelli-Manzoni, and formerly wife of Baron Jean Marie Christian Colette Alphonse Jules du Four; *m* 1947, the 3rd Baron, who *d* 1987, when the title became ext. *Residence* – Bamburgh Castle, Northumberland.

ARMSTRONG OF ILMINSTER, BARON (Armstrong) (Life Baron 1988)

ROBERT TEMPLE ARMSTRONG, GCB, CVO, only son of late Sir Thomas Henry Wait Armstrong, of 1 East Street, Olney, Bucks; *b* 30 March 1927; *ed* Eton (Fellow 1979-94), and Ch Ch Oxford (Hon Student 1985); Hon Bencher Inner Temple 1986; entered Treasury 1950 (Assist Prin 1950-55, Prin 1955-64); Assist Sec Cabinet Office 1964-66; Assist Sec Treasury 1967-68, jt Prin Private Sec to Chancellor of the Exchequer 1968, Under Sec Treasury (Home Finance, 1968-70); Prin Private Sec to PM 1970-75; Home Office 1975-79 (Dep Under Sec of State 1975-77, Permanent Under Sec of State 1977-79); Sec of the Cabinet 1979-87, Head of Home Civil Ser 1981-87; Dir Royal Opera House 1988-93 (Sec to Dirs 1968-87), Dir RAM since 1975 (Hon Fellow 1985), Council of Management Royal Philharmonic Society, Rhodes Trust since 1975, Pilgrim Trust since 1987, D'Oyly Carte Opera Trust 1988-93, and Leeds Castle Foundn since 1988; Chm of Trustees Victoria and Albert Museum since 1988; Chm Biotechnology Investments Ltd since 1989, Chm Bristol and West Building Soc since 1993 (Dir since 1988) non-exec Dir Shell Transport and Trading plc, NM Rothschild & Sons Ltd, and other Cos since 1988; *cr* CB 1974, CVO 1975, KCB 1978, GCB 1983, and *Baron Armstrong of Ilminster,* of Ashill, co Somerset (Life Baron) 1988; *m* 1st, 1953 (*m diss* 1985), Serena Mary Benedicta, who *d* 1994, elder da of Sir Roger James Ferguson Chance, 3rd Bt, MC; 2ndly, 1985, (Mary) Patricia, only da of late Charles Cyril Carlow, and has issue by 1st *m*.
Address – House of Lords, SW1. *Clubs* – Athenaeum, Brooks's.

DAUGHTERS LIVING (*By 1st marriage*)

Hon Jane Orlanda, *b* 1954.
Hon Teresa Brigid, *b* 1957.

ARMSTRONG OF SANDERSTEAD, BARONY OF (Armstrong) (Extinct 1980)

SON LIVING OF LIFE BARON

Hon Peter William (20 Ravensbourne Gdns, W13), *b* 1943: *m* 1967 (*m diss* 1984), Kathleen Frances Widdicombe.

DAUGHTER LIVING OF LIFE BARON

Hon Janet Elizabeth, *b* 1947: *m* 1968, Malcolm Turnbull, of 62 Queens Rd, Swanage, Dorset.

WIDOW LIVING OF LIFE BARON

GWENDOLINE ENID (*Baroness Armstrong of Sanderstead*) (Pinewood House, Pleasure Pit Rd, Ashtead, Surrey), da of John Bennett, of Putney, SW15: *m* 1942, Baron Armstrong of Sanderstead, GCB, MVO, PC (Life Baron), who *d* 1980.

ARRAN, EARL OF (Gore) Sits as BARON SUDLEY (UK 1884) (Earl I 1762, Bt I 1662)

Under this sign thou shalt conquer

ARTHUR DESMOND COLQUHOUN GORE, 9th Earl and 11th Baronet; *b* 14 July 1938; *ed* Eton, and Balliol Coll, Oxford; late 2nd Lieut Gren Gds; Co-Chm Children's Country Holidays Fund; Under Sec of State, N Ireland Office, 1992-94, since when Under Sec of State, Dept of Environment: *m* 1974, Eleanor, elder da of Bernard van Cutsem (*see* E Fortescue), and has issue.

Arms – Gules, a fesse between three cross crosslets fitchée or. **Crest** – A wolf rampant argent collared gules. **Supporters** – Two horses argent. *Residence* – Crocker End House, Nettlebed, Henley-on-Thames, Oxon.

DAUGHTERS LIVING

Lady Laura Melissa, *b* 1975.
Lady Lucy Katherine, *b* 1976.

WIDOW LIVING OF EIGHTH EARL

FIONA BRYDE (*Fiona, Countess of Arran*), da of Sir Iain Colquhoun, 7th Bt, KT, DSO; first person to average 100 mph in an offshore boat (1980), awarded Segrave Trophy (1981): *m* 1937, the 8th Earl, who *d* 1983. *Residence* – Pimlico House, Hemel Hempstead, Herts.

COLLATERAL BRANCHES LIVING

Grandchildren of late Sir Francis Charles Gore, KCB, eldest son of Hon Charles Alexander Gore, brother of 4th Earl:—
Issue of late Charles Henry Gore, OBE, *b* 1881, *d* 1941: *m* 1st, 1911, Marguerite, who *d* 1918, da of Walter Langley; 2ndly, 1920, Hon Violet Kathleen Annesley, who *d* 1963, da of 11th Viscount Valentia:—
(By 2nd *m*) PAUL ANNESLEY, CMG, CVO (1 Burkitt Rd, Woodbridge, Suffolk), *b* 28 Feb 1921; *ed* Winchester, and Ch Ch, Oxford (MA); Capt late 16th/5th Lancers; Colonial Admin Ser 1948-65; cr CVO 1962, CMG 1964: *m* 1946, Gillian Mary, da of late Capt Tom Allen-Stevens, Dep Gov The Gambia 1962-65, and has had issue, †Charles Alexander, *b* 1947; *ed* Radley, and Southampton Univ: *m* 1st, 1970 (*m diss* 1973), Penelope, yr da of R. C. Caunce, of Maidenhead; 2ndly, 1984, Susan Diana, da of M. J. Hardy, and *d* 1985, — William Henry (106 Simpsons Rd, Bardon, Qld, Australia 4064), *b* 1950; *ed* Radley, and Lincoln Coll, Oxford: *m* 1st, 1980, Mrs Cecilia Nell McBean, who *d* 1990, da of R. Cox, of Brisbane, Australia; 2ndly 1993, Mrs Rosemary LINDHOLM, da of R. Payne, of Brisbane, Qld, and has issue living (by 1st *m*), Charles David *b* 1985, Letitia Sarah *b* 1982, — Nicholas David *b* 1952; *ed* Radley: *m* 1983, Christine Mary, da of H. W. Clothier, of Evercreech, Som, and formerly wife of C. B. Tilley, and has issue living, Alastair Mark *b* 1984, Robert William *b* 1986. —— Ursula Mary, *b* 1922: *m* 1947, Com Edward Graham Ducat-Hamersley, RN, who *d* 1987, and has issue living, Penelope Tara, *b* 1948: *m* 1973, Stephen Hayes, of 94 Sidney Rd, Walton-on-Thames, Surrey, and has issue living, Timothy *b* 1975, Kirsty *b* 1977, Rosemary *b* 1980, — Priscilla Rosemary, *b* 1951: *m* 1st, 1982, David Henderson, of Qld, Australia, who *d* 1989; 2ndly, 1994, Keith Nobes, of Qld, Australia, and has issue living (by 1st *m*), Nathan Edward Vivien *b* 1982, Kelly Letitia *b* 1984, Tara Gae *b* 1988, — Felicity, *b* 1954: *m* 1978, Gerald Brian O'Brien, of 55 Hyde Abbey Rd, Winchester, Hants, and has issue living, Katherine *b* 1983, Eleanor *b* 1987, — Joanna, *b* 1957: *m* 1st, 1980 (*m diss* 1983), Charles Robert Sindell; 2ndly, 1983 (*m diss* 1988), George Bentham Walker; 3rdly, 1990, Stephen Lockwood, of NSW, Australia, and has issue living (by 2nd *m*), Hugh Simon *b* 1985, (by 3rd *m*) Thomas Edward *b* 1990, Alice Sophie *b* 1992. *Residence* – 1 Brookside, Watlington, Oxon. —— Rosemary Kathleen, *b* 1924; formerly in WRNS: *m* 1945, Arthur Emerson Mabin, Lt (A) RNZNVR, who *d* 1986, and has issue living, Richard Peter, *b* 1965: *m* 1990, Elizabeth Katurah, yr da of James Doble, of Stony Stratton, Som, — Susan Kathleen, *b* 1946: *m* 1968, Leslie Howard Cook, and has issue living, Timothy Peter *b* 1972, Sarah Kathleen *b* 1974, Helen Ruth *b* 1976, — Caroline Ruth, *b* 1947, — Helen Rosemary, *b* 1950: *m* 1973, Alan Archibald Winwood, and has issue living, Derek Emerson *b* 1978, Christopher Alan *b* 1982, Thomas Willem *b* 1984, Joanna Rosemary *b* 1980, — Victoria Jane, *b* 1953; PhD: *m* 1st, 1983, Willem Louis Fritz van den Broek, who *d* 1984; 2ndly 1987, Christopher Mannings Sutton, PhD, of 8 Crofton Rd, Ngaio, Wellington, NZ, and has issue living (by 2nd *m*), Rebecca Jane *b* 1989, Emily Claire *b* 1991. *Residence* – 7 Manuka St, Nelson, NZ.
Issue of late John Francis Gore, CVO, TD, *b* 1885, *d* 1983: *m* 1926, Lady Janet Helena Campbell, who *d* 1982, da of 4th Earl Cawdor:—
Charles John (Port na Mine, Taynuilt, Argyll PA35 1HU), *b* 1932; *ed* Eton: *m* 1961, Jean, yr da of late Col Charles Ian Fraser, CBE, TD, of Reelig, Kirkhill, Inverness-shire, and has issue living, (Ian) Simon Francis, *b* 1965: *m* 1993, Sarah E., yr da of Colin Frizzell, of Chuffs House, Holyport, Berks, — John Alexander Charles, *b* 1971, — Helena Mary, *b* 1962: *m* 1992, Michael J. Bayler. —— Moyra, *b* 1927. —— Mary Elizabeth (*Lady Cave*), *b* 1929: *m* 1957, Sir Charles Edward Coleridge Cave, 4th Bt.

Grandchildren of late Spencer William Gore, 2nd son of Hon Charles Alexander Gore (ante):—
Issue of late George Pym Gore, *b* 1875, *d* 1959: *m* 1914, Alexandra Leila, who *d* 1970, da of late Rev Canon Frederick Alfred John Hervey, CVO (M Bristol, colls), and widow of Lt Sir Walter Clervaux Chaytor, RN, 5th Bt:—
Victoria Maud Lavinia Mary, *b* 1915: *m* 1944 (*m diss* 1955), Ian Alexander Kennedy, 16th/5th Lancers, and has issue living, Lavinia Susan, *b* 1948: *m* 1st, 1970 (*m diss* 1983), Timothy Scott Bigland, son of T. S. Bigland; 2ndly, 1984, as his 2nd wife, Richard Hugh Chaytor Vaux, late Maj RAPC (*see* Chaytor, Bt, 1973-74 Edn), and has issue living (by 1st *m*), Alexandra Rosalind *b* 1977, (by 2nd *m*) Philippa Clare Marisa *b* 1986, Lucinda Mary Diana *b* 1987.
Issue of late Spencer Frederick Gore, *b* 1878, *d* 1914: *m* 1912, Mary Joanna, who *d* 1968, da of Capt John Kerr:—
Frederick John Pym, CBE (Flat 3, 35 Elm Park Gdns, SW10), *b* 1913; *ed* Lancing Coll, and Trin Coll, Oxford; RA 1964; a Trustee of Imperial War Museum 1967-84; Head of Painting Dept, St Martin's Sch of Art, 1951-79, and Vice-Prin 1961-79; 1940-45 War as Maj RA; CBE (Civil) 1987: *m* 1st, 1945, Lili Reneé, da of L. Gaber; 2ndly, 19—, Constance Irene, da of W. H. Smith, of Brentford, Middx, and has issue living, (by 1st *m*) Georgiana Sarah, *b* 1950; PhD: *m* 19—, Laurent Christophe Michel Wierre, and has issue living, Natasha Anouk Eva *b* 1991, — (by 2nd *m*) Charles David (Flat 1, 2A Coleherne Mews, SW10), *b* 1954; BA, — Geraldine Lucy, *b* 1957; MA; has issue living, James Spencer *b* 1988. —— Margaret Elizabeth, *b* 1912: *m* 1940, Samuel Richard Cowie, who *d* 1979, and *d* 1994, leaving issue, Christopher Frederick (45 Wynn Rd, Tankerton, Kent), *b* 1941: *m* 1965, Corinna, da of Col H. V. Ewbank, R Sigs, and has issue living, Malcolm Ambrose *b* 1981, Charmian Philippa *b* 1969, — John Richard, *b* 1944; BA, — Martin George Charles GORE (c/o Kagoshima University, Kagoshima-Shi, Japan), *b* 1956; BA (Japan); has assumed the surname of Gore in lieu of his patronymic: *m* 1985, Yoko, da of

Tatsuo Matsumoto, of Kagoshima, and has issue living, Spencer Richard *b* 1989, Katherine Melissa *b* 1987, — Frances Mary (Oswalds Cottage, Watlington, Oxon), *b* 1947.

Grandson of late Arthur Saunders Gore, 3rd son of Ven John Ribton Gore, 4th son of Very Rev Hon George Gore, LLD, Dean of Killala, 3rd son of 2nd Earl:—
Issue of late Arthur Henry Baldwin Gore, *b* 1883, *d* 1953: *m* 1913, Jane Browne, who *d* 1975:—
Arthur Francis, MD, *b* 1914: *m* 1939, Helen Claire Mullen, of Omaha, Nebraska, USA, and has issue living, James Arthur, *b* 1950, — Judith Ann, *b* 1940: *m* 1964, Fernando Joseph Ramirez, of 8719 La Roca, Fountain Valley, Calif, USA, and has issue living, Jane Ellen *b* 1965, Anne Marie *b* 1969, — Nancy Jane, *b* 1942, — Margaret Francis, *b* 1946, — Pamela Elizabeth, *b* 1948: *m* 1969, Paul Everett Adkins, and has issue living, Jennifer Claire *b* 1975, — Jill Marie, *b* 1957, — Martha Jane, *b* 1959.

Grandchildren of late Arthur Henry Baldwin Gore (ante):—
Issue of late John Douglas Gore, *b* 1916, *d* 1976: *m* 1946, Evelyn Mae (Lyn) Wagner (who *m* 2ndly, 1978, Gerald Louis Artaud, who *d* 1979):—
John Douglas, *b* 1947. ——— Theresa Ann, *b* 1951: *m* 1973, Jon Patrick Ferguson, and has issue living, Stacy Ann, *b* 1975, — Dana Marie, *b* 1978. ——— Margaret Jane, *b* 1957: *m* 1978, John Fisher.

Grandson of late Major James Arthur Charles Gore, eldest son of late Gen Hon Sir Charles Gore, KH, GCB, 6th son of 2nd Earl:—
Issue of late Col Edward John Mounsey Gore, *b* 1863, *d* 1949: *m* 1899, Hon Emilia Herbert Fullerton Napier, who *d* 1932, da of 1st Baron Napier of Magdala:—
Humphry Gerard Napier, *b* 1916; *ed* Sherborne; Major (ret) late Roy Ulster Rifles: *m* 1948, Leslie Marshal Peabody, of New York, USA, and has issue living, Mark Staveley, *b* 1952; BA, — Brendon Bostwick, *b* 1955; BSc: *m* 1990, Helen Elizabeth, yst da of P. A. Merker, of Fleet, Hants, — Timothy Francis, *b* 1957; BA, BSc, ARICS: *m* 1989, Amanda S., twin da of P. F. Kingsley, of Sussex, and has issue living, Edward Charles Theodore *b* 1994 Emma Philippa *b* 1991, Celia Frances *b* 1992. *Residence* – The Red Cottage, South Park, Sevenoaks, Kent.

Grandchildren of late William Stuart Gore, 5th son of late Maj James Arthur Charles Gore (ante):—
Issue of late Erroll Napier Gore, *b* 1897, *d* 1968: *m* 1926, Alma Maude, who *d* 1978, da of William Edward Kessell:—
†William Erroll, *b* 1926: *m* 1951, Joan Hetherington, and *d* 1969, leaving issue, William Arran (1 Newcastle St, Stockton, NSW, Australia), *b* 1965, — Jennifer Louise, *b* 1957: *m* 1977, Jonathon Smith, and has issue living, Justin William *b* 1987, Jacqueline Louise *b* 1984, Jessica Ashleigh *b* 1991, — Susan Michelle, *b* 1959: *m* 1979, Steven Cole, and has had issue, Christopher Steven *b* 1980; *d* 1983, Mathew Dean *b* 1984, — Alyson Maree, *b* 1961: *m* 1991, Christopher John Gearing, and has issue living, Jack Ernest *b* 1993, — Catherine Anne, *b* 1968. ——— Stuart Maxwell, *b* 1929: *m* 1988, Leovegilda Marcos, and has issue living, Benjamin Laurence Stuart, *b* 1990, — Kylie-Anne Shirley, *b* 1989. ——— Ian Winn Bazalgette, *b* 1932; Maj Australian Staff Corps (ret): *m* 1961, Evelyne Phyllis, da of late Maj Charles William Sayers, of Melbourne, and has issue living, Robert Ian Charles, *b* 1966: *m* 1991, Tina Marie Kelly, and has issue living, Thomas Ian *b* 1992, — Belinda Jane, *b* 1967: *m* 1992, William Anthony Trewartha, and has issue living, William Ian Alexander *b* 1993. ——— Laurence James, *b* 1935. ——— Pamela Mary, *b* 1939: *m* 1961 (*m diss* 1967), Graham Richard Westwood, and has issue living, Nicholas Ian Richard, *b* 1964, — Jo-Anne Louise, *b* 1963.

Granddaughter of late William John Gore, son of late Capt Ralph Gore, RN, 2nd son of late Hon Paul Gore, 3rd son of 1st Earl:—
Issue of late Charles Arthur Gore, *b* 1845, *d* 1926: *m* 1st, 1883, Mary Goacher, who *d* 1894; 2ndly, 1907, Constance Gertrude (who *d* 1971, having *m* 3rdly, 1928, John James Sayers, who *d* 1955), da of John Burch, of 148 Ebury Street, SW1, and widow of Henry William Willis:—
(By 2nd *m*) Constance Joyce Gwendolen, *b* 1911; is a SRN: *m* 1937, Ernest Killingback, BSc, ARCS, who *d* 1939, and has issue living, Peter Gore (58 Highfields Dr, Loughborough, Leics LE11 3JT) *b* 1939; *ed* King Edward VI Gram Sch, Aston, London Sch of Pharmacy (BPharm), and Manchester Univ (MSc): *m* 1968, Janet Mary Reason, BSc, and has issue living, David Gore *b* 1971, Christopher Michael *b* 1975. *Residence* – 5 Orchard Cres, Enfield, Middx.

(In remainder to baronetcy only)

Descendants of late John Ralph ORMSBY-GORE (fourth in descent from late William Gore, MP, 3rd son of 1st Baronet), who was cr *Baron Harlech* 1876 (see that title).

PREDECESSORS – (1) *Sir* ARTHUR Gore, second son of Sir Paul Gore (who was cr a Baronet of Ireland 1621); cr a *Baronet* of Ireland 1662; *s* by his grandson (2) ARTHUR, 2nd Bt; MP for co Longford; *d* 1741; *s* by his eldest son (3) ARTHUR, 3rd Bt; cr *Baron Saunders* and *Viscount Sudley* (peerage of Ireland) 1758, and *Earl of Arran of Arran Islands* (peerage of Ireland) 1762; *d* 1773; *s* by his eldest son (4) ARTHUR SAUNDERS, KP, 2nd Earl; *d* 1809; *s* by his eldest son (5) ARTHUR SAUNDERS, 3rd Earl; *d* 1837; *s* by his nephew (6) PHILIP YORKE, KP, 4th Earl, *b* 1801: *m* 1838, Elizabeth Marianne, who *d* 1899, da of late Gen Sir William Francis Patrick Napier, KCB; *d* 25 June 1884; *s* by his son (7) ARTHUR SAUNDERS WILLIAM CHARLES FOX, KP, 5th Earl; *b* 1839; cr *Baron Sudley*, of Castle Gore, co Mayo (peerage of United Kingdom), 1884: *m* 1st, 1865, Hon Edith Jocelyn, who *d* 1871, da of Robert, Viscount Jocelyn, MP, and sister of 4th Earl of Roden; 2ndly, 1889, Winifred Ellen, who *d* 1921, da of late John Reilly, and widow of Hon John Montagu Stopford (*see* E Courtown, 1920 Edn), *d* 1901; *s* by his son (8) ARTHUR JOCELYN CHARLES, KP, PC, 6th Earl; *b* 1868: Brevet Major Roy Horse Guards; was HM Lieut and Custos Rotulorum for co Donegal 1917-20 and a KGStJ: *m* 1st, 1902, Mathilde Jacqueline Marie Beauclerk (a DGStJ), who *d* 1927, only da of Baron Huyssen van Kattendyke, of Kattendyke, Zeeland, Netherlands; 2ndly, 1929, Lilian Constance, who *d* 1961, da of late John Quick, of Crossdeep Place, Twickenham, and widow of Frank Browne, of Pyecroft Place, Chertsey; *d* 19 Dec 1958; *s* by his eldest son (9) ARTHUR PAUL JOHN CHARLES JAMES, *b* 1903; ADC to Gov-Gen of S Africa 1931; *d* 28 Dec 1958; *s* by his brother, (10) ARTHUR STRANGE KATTENDYKE DAVID ARCHIBALD, 8th Earl, *b* 1910; Attaché British Legation, Berne 1941-41, and British Embassy, Lisbon 1941-42, in Min of Information 1942-45 (Dir of Overseas Gen Div 1945), and in Central Office of Information 1945-49 (Dir of Secretariat); introduced in House of Lords, Sexual Offences Bill (now Act) (three times), and Badger Protection Bill (now Act); a Dir of *Daily Mail* and General Trust Ltd; Chm Children's Country Holidays Fund, and Hon Treas Moorfields Eye Hospital: *m* 1937, Fiona Bryde, eldest da of Sir Iain Colquhoun, 7th Bt, KT, DSO; *d* 1983; *s* by his only surv son (11) ARTHUR DESMOND COLQUHOUN, 9th Earl and present peer; also Viscount Sudley, Baron Saunders, and Baron Sudley.

Arundel and Surrey, Earl of; son of Duke of Norfolk.

ARUNDELL OF WARDOUR, BARONY OF (Arundell) (Extinct 1944)

DAUGHTER LIVING OF FIFTEENTH BARON

Hon Mary Isabella, *b* 1913: *m* 1935 (*m diss* 1955), Air Commodore Thomas Patrick Feltrim Fagan, RAF, who *d* 1985, and has issue living, Patrick Feltrim, CB, MBE (DG Mil Svy, Elmwood Av, Feltham, Middx TW13 7AH), *b* 1935; MBE (Mil) 1966, CB (Mil) 1990; Maj-Gen late RE: *m* 1967, Veronica, da of J. J. Lorant, and widow of Capt C. J. C. Thompson, RE, and has issue living, Daragh Patrick Feltrim *b* 1969, Rory Michael Feltrim *b* 1972, — Michael John, *b* 1940, — Deirdre Mairi, *b* 1937.

ARWYN, BARONY OF (Arwyn) (Extinct 1978)

SON LIVING OF LIFE BARON (*By 2nd marriage*)

Hon Arwyn Hugh Davies (Ewart, Ashley Rd, Bathford, Avon), *b* 1949; Bar Gray's Inn 1972: *m* 1977, Mary Elizabeth Gibson.

DAUGHTERS LIVING OF LIFE BARON (*By 1st marriage*)

Hon Mary Gwynne (28 Bloomfield Rd, Bath), *b* 1932: *m* 1954, Geoffrey James Webb, who *d* 1975, and has issue.
Hon Elisabeth Jocelyn, *b* 1938: *m* 1962, John Robb Macnab, of 186 Sedlescombe Road North, St Leonards-on-Sea, and has issue.

WIDOW LIVING OF LIFE BARON

BEATRIX EMILY (*Baroness Arwyn*) (Ormonde, Lostwithiel, Cornwall), da of Capt F. H. Organ of St Austell, Cornwall: *m* 1946, as his 2nd wife, Baron Arwyn (Life Baron), who *d* 1978.

ASHBOURNE, BARON (Gibson) (Baron UK 1885)

(EDWARD) BARRY GREYNVILLE GIBSON, 4th Baron; *b* 28 Jan 1933; *s* 1983; *ed* Rugby; Lt-Cdr RN (ret): *m* 1967, Yvonne Georgina, da of Mrs Flora Ham, and has issue.

Arms – Ermine, three keys fesswise in pale azure, and in chief as many trefoils slipped vert. **Crest** – A pelican in her piety on a bank of reeds proper. **Supporters** – *Dexter*, a female figure representing Mercy standing upon a fasces proper, habited argent, charged on the breast with a trefoil slipped vert, and resting her right hand on a sword point downwards proper, pommel or; *sinister*, a like figure representing Justice habited, charged and standing as the dexter, holding in her right hand a balance and in the left a sword erect proper. *Residence* – 107 Sussex Rd, Petersfield, Hants, GU31 4LB.

Open, oh, ye heavenly gates

SONS LIVING

Hon EDWARD CHARLES D'OLIER, *b* 31 Dec 1967.
Hon William Rodney Colles, *b* 1970.
Hon Patrick Mayne, *b* 1977.

AUNT LIVING (*Raised to the rank of a Baron's daughter* 1943)

Hon Kathleen Mary, *b* 1908: *m* 1930, James Hamilton Russell, who *d* 1981, and has issue living, Michael Anthony Hamilton (14 Courtlane Gdns, Dulwich Village, SE21), *b* 1932; MA Oxon; MB BS, MRCP Lond, MRCPsych: *m* 1962, Audrey Anne Timms, and has issue living, James Hamilton *b* 1974, Nicholas Hamilton *b* 1977, — Timothy Patrick HAMILTON-RUSSELL (Hamilton Russell Vineyards, PO Box 158, Hermanus 7200, Western Cape, S Africa), *b* 1934: *m* 1958, Athene Wendy Isobel, da of late William Aubrey Bindon, and has issue living, Anthony James *b* 1962: *m* 1990, Arabella Sabina Lilian, only da of late Hon David Anthony Lawrence Caccia (*see* By Caccia) (and has issue living, Olivia Sabina *b* 1992, Ella Maria *b* (twin) 1992), Patrick David *b* 1969, Bridgid Mary *b* 1960: *m* 1986, Scipion Vernede, Julia Kathleen *b* 1965: *m* 1992, Robert David Marshall (*see* Montagu-Pollock, Bt, colls), — Rt Rev David Patrick Hamilton (Bishopsbourne, 17 Durban St, Grahamstown 6140, S Africa), *b* 1938; Bishop of Grahamstown: *m* 1980, Dorothea Martha Madden, and has issue living, Sipho Matthew *b* 1981, Thabo Andrew *b* 1983, — Robin James (Brooke Hall, Flodden Rd, SE5 9LH), *b* 1947: *m* 1977 (*m diss* 1989), Imogene Veronica King, and has issue living, George *b* 1982, Thomas Richard Henry *b* 1984, Frances *b* 1977, Virginia *b* 1979, — Jill Mary, *b* 1935: *m* 1965, Anthony Ronald Hall, who *d* 19—, of 20 Unthank Rd, Norwich, Norfolk NR2, and has issue living, Catherine Sian *b* 1967, Marion Ruth *b* 1970, — Diana Elizabeth Hamilton (2432 Grant St, Berkeley, Calif 94703, USA), *b* (twin) 1938; *ed* Cape Town Univ (BA), LSE, and Harvard (MA, PhD); Prof Emerita of Sociology, Mills Coll. *Residence* – Fairmead Court, 6 College Rd, Rondebosch, Cape Town, S Africa.

WIDOW LIVING OF BROTHER OF THIRD BARON

Sabina (formerly Sabine), da of late Dr Ernest Landsberg, of Cape Town, S Africa: *m* 1947, Lt-Col Hon (William) David Gibson, OBE, TD (raised to the rank of a Baron's son 1943), who *d* 1993, and has issue (see colls, infra). *Residence* – Buckley Cottage, Batson, Salcombe, Devon.

WIDOW LIVING OF THIRD BARON

RETA FRANCES MANNING (*Reta, Baroness Ashbourne*), elder da of Ernest Manning Hazeland, of Hong Kong: *m* 1929, Vice-Adm 3rd Baron Ashbourne, CB, DSO, who *d* 1983. *Residence* – 18 St Peter's Court, Hylton Rd, Petersfield, Hants GU32 3HJ.

COLLATERAL BRANCHES LIVING

Issue of late Lt-Col Hon (William) David Gibson, OBE, TD (raised to the rank of a Baron's son 1943), yr brother of 3rd Baron, *b* 1914, *d* 1993: *m* 1947, Sabina (formerly Sabine) (ante), da of late Dr Ernest Landsberg, of Cape Town, S Africa:—
Celia Mary, *b* 1948: *m* 1977 (*m diss* 1993), Robert Sommers, and has issue living, Dominic Alexander, *b* 1977, — Abigail Jane, *b* 1980, — Jessica Sarah, *b* 1982. —— Monica Anne (13 Kingston Av, Stony Stratford, Milton Keynes, Bucks MK11 1DS), *b* 1951: *m* 1973, Andrew Vaughan Harding. —— Philippa Constance (Maes-y-Morfa, Llangrannog, Llandysul, Dyfed SA44 6RU), *b* 1953.

Issue of late Hon (Ernest) Victor Gibson, yst son of 1st Baron, *b* 1875, *d* 1922: *m* 1st, 1905, Mary Wood Salisbury, who *d* 1905, da of Joseph L. R. Wood, of New York; 2ndly, 1909, Caroline, who *d* 1952, da of Frederic de Billier, of New York:—
(By 2nd *m*) John Frederic, DSC, *b* 1919; is Lt RNVR; 1939-45 War (DSC): *m* 1st, 1941 (*m diss* 1946), Margaret A. Booth; 2ndly, 1947, Lorna M. Pickering, and has issue living (by 1st *m*), Victor Russell (Barn Hill House, 15 Parsonage Lane, Market Lavington, nr Devizes, Wilts), *b* 1943; *ed* Nautical Coll, Pangbourne: *m* 1968, Pamela Cherry, da of late Edward Cupitt-Eggleshaw, and has issue living, Geoffrey Andrew *b* 1971, Neil Henry *b* 1975, — (by 2nd *m*) Simon John (31844 Conrad Av, Clearbrook, BC, Canada V2T 2K3), *b* 1952: *m* 1976, Joy Beatrice, da of Walter Sidney Ridgway, of Vancouver, BC, and has issue living, Shari-Anne Joy *b* 1980, Alisa Julie *b* 1982, — Julia de Billier, *b* 1959: *m* 1985, Evert Van der Zee, of 15 Shawglen Place, SW Calgary, Alberta, Canada, and has issue living, Matthew James *b* 1988. *Residence* – 687 Erickson Rd, Campbell River, BC, Canada V9W 1S9.

PREDECESSORS – (1) *Rt Hon* EDWARD Gibson, LLD, son of late William Gibson, JP, of Merrion Square, Dublin; *b* 1837; Attorney-Gen for Ireland 1877-80, and Lord Chancellor of Ireland with a seat in the Cabinet 1885 to Jan 1886, July 1886 to Aug 1892, and June 1895 to Dec 1905 (many times acted as a Lord Justice of Ireland during absence of Lord-Lieut); MP for Dublin Univ (C) 1875-85; cr *Baron Ashbourne*, of Ashbourne, co Meath (peerage of United Kingdom) 1885: *m* 1868, Frances Maria Adelaide, who *d* 1926, da of late Henry Cope Colles; *d* 1913; *s* by his eldest son (2) WILLIAM, 2nd Baron; *b* 1868: *m* 1896, Marianne, who *d* 1953, da of Henri Roger de Monbrison, of Avenue de Jena, Paris; *d* 1942; *s* by his nephew (3) EDWARD RUSSELL, CB, DSO (eldest son of late Hon Edward Graves Mayne Gibson, 3rd son of 1st Baron), 3rd Baron, *b* 1901; Vice-Adm; served 1914-18 War in HMS *Superb*, *Dreadnought* and *Monarch*: *m* 1929, Reta Frances Manning, elder da of Ernest Manning Hazeland, of Hong Kong; *d* 1983; *s* by his only son (4) (EDWARD) BARRY GREYNVILLE, 4th Baron and present peer.

ASHBROOK, VISCOUNT (Flower) (Viscount I 1751)

DESMOND LLOWARCH EDWARD FLOWER, KCVO, MBE, 10th Viscount; *b* 9 July 1905; *s* 1936; *ed* Eton, and Balliol Coll, Oxford (BA); a DL for Cheshire (JP 1946-67, Vice-Lieut 1961-67); a Member of Council of Duchy of Lancaster 1957-77; formerly a Chartered Accountant; Chm of Country Gentleman's Assocn 1955-62; 1939-45 War as Maj RA (TA); MBE (Mil) 1945, KCVO 1977: *m* 1934, Elizabeth, elder da of late Capt John Egerton-Warburton (*see* Grey-Egerton, Bt, colls), and has had issue.

Arms – Quarterly: 1st and 4th argent, two chevronels between three ravens, each having an ermine spot in its beak, sable, and between the chevronels, three pellets; 2nd and 3rd gules, three towers argent. **Crest** – A raven, having an ermine spot in its beak. **Supporters** – Two tigers reguardant proper, ducally collared and chained or.
Residence – Woodlands, Arley, Northwich, Cheshire.

A mind conscious of rectitude

SON LIVING

Hon MICHAEL LLOWARCH WARBURTON, *b* 9 Dec 1935; *ed* Eton, and Worcester Coll, Oxford (MA); 2nd Lt Gren Gds 1955; Solicitor 1963; Partner Farrer and Co 1966-76, March, Pearson and Skelton, Manchester, since 1986; a DL and JP of Cheshire: *m* 1971, Zoë Mary, yst da of late Francis H. A. Engleheart, of The Priory, Stoke-by-Nayland, Suffolk, and has issue living, Rowland Francis Warburton, *b* 1975, — Harry William Warburton, *b* 1977, — Eleanor Filumena, *b* 1973.

DAUGHTER LIVING

Hon Jane Mary Elizabeth, *b* 1943; *ed* Lady Margaret Hall, Oxford (BA), and London Sch of Econ and Political Science (MSc): *m* 1967, Charles Francis Foster, of 18 Stanley Gdns, W11, and has issue living, Rupert Rowland, *b* 1970, — Antonia Elizabeth, *b* 1969, — Cordelia Rose, *b* 1974.

GRANDDAUGHTER LIVING

Issue of late Hon Anthony John Warburton Flower, yr son of 10th Viscount, *b* 1938, *d* 1991: *m* 1970, Bridget Karen (infra), yr da of J. Duncan:—
Alexandra Jane, *b* 1972.

WIDOW LIVING OF SON OF TENTH VISCOUNT

Bridget Karen, yr da of J. Duncan: *m* 1970, Hon Anthony John Warburton Flower, who *d* 1991, and has issue (ante).
Residence – Prouts Farm, Hawkley, Liss, Hants.

COLLATERAL BRANCH LIVING

Issue of late Hon Reginald Henry Flower, yr son of 8th Viscount, *b* 1871, *d* 1938: *m* 1901, Katherine Ella (Kate), who *d* 1957, da of Col Edward William Cuming, formerly of Crovar, co Cavan:—
Mollie Francis, *b* 1902: *m* 1st, 1929 (*m diss* 1945), John Albert Peacey; 2ndly, 1947, Maj Wilfrid Vincent Townshend Allen.

PREDECESSORS – (1) WILLIAM Flower, MP for co Kilkenny; *cr Baron Castle Durrow* (peerage of Ireland) 1733; *d* 1746; *s* by his son (2) HENRY, 2nd Baron; *cr Viscount Ashbrook* (peerage of Ireland) 1751; *d* 1752; *s* by his son (3) WILLIAM, 2nd Viscount; *d* 1780; *s* by his eldest son (4) WILLIAM, 3rd Viscount; *d* 1802; *s* by his brother (5) HENRY JEFFREY, 4th Viscount; *d* 1847; *s* by his son (6) HENRY JEFFREY, 5th Viscount, *b* 1806: *m* 1828, Frances, who *d* 1886, da of Sir John Robinson, 1st Bt; *d* 1871; *s* by his eldest son (7) HENRY JEFFREY, 6th Viscount; *d* 1882; *s* by his brother (8) WILLIAM SPENCER, 7th Viscount, *b* 1830: *m* 1861, Augusta Madeline Henriette, who *d* 1906, da of late George Marton, of Capernwray Hall, Lancaster; *d* 1906; *s* by his brother (9) ROBERT THOMAS, 8th Viscount, *b* 1836: *m* 1866, Gertrude Sophia, who *d* 1911, da of late Rev Sewell Hamilton, of Bath; *d* 1919; *s* by his eldest son (10) LLOWARCH ROBERT, 9th Viscount, *b* 1870: *m* 1899, Gladys Lucille, who *d* 1968, da of late Gen Sir George Wentworth Alexander Higginson, GCB, GCVO; *d* 1936; *s* by his son (11) DESMOND LLOWARCH EDWARD, 10th Viscount and present peer; also Baron Castle Durrow.

ASHBURTON, BARON (Baring) (Baron UK 1835)

Fortitude under difficulties

JOHN FRANCIS HARCOURT BARING, KG, KCVO, 7th Baron; *b* 2 Nov 1928; *s* 1991; *ed* Eton (Fellow 1982), and Trin Coll, Oxford (MA, Hon Fellow 1989), Hon Fellow Hertford Coll, Oxford 1976; Chm Baring Bros & Co Ltd 1974-89, Barings plc 1985-89 (non-exec Dir 1989-94), and Accepting Houses Cttee 1977-81; Chm British Petroleum Co plc since 1992 (Dir since 1982); Chm of Council Baring Foundation; Dir Pye Holdings Ltd 1967-79, Royal Insurance Co Ltd 1964-82 (Dep-Chm 1975-82), Trafford Park Estates Ltd 1964-77, Dunlop Holdings 1981-84; Chm Outwich Investment Trust 1965-86, and Baring Stratton Investment Trust plc since 1986; Member of President's Cttee CBI 1976-79, and a Vice-Pres Gen Council of British Bankers' Assocn 1977-81; Pres Overseas Bankers' Club 1977-78; Receiver-Gen Duchy of Cornwall 1974-90, since when Lord Warden of the Stannaries and Keeper of the Privy Seal of the Duchy; a Rhodes Trustee since 1970 (Chm since 1987), Trustee Royal Jubilee Trusts since 1979, National Gallery 1981-87, and The Police Foundation (Hon Treas) since 1989; Member Exec Cttee Nat Art-Collections Fund since 1989; High Steward Winchester Cathedral since 1991; *cr* CVO 1980, Knt 1983, KCVO 1990, KG 1994: *m* 1st, 1955 (*m diss* 1984), Hon Susan Mary Renwick, eldest da of 1st Baron Renwick; 2ndly, 1987, Mrs Sarah Crewe, da of late John George Spencer-Churchill (*see* D Marlborough, colls), and has issue by 1st *m*.

Arms – Azure, a fesse or, in chief a bear's head proper, muzzled and ringed of the second, differenced by a cross formy fitchy azure. **Crest** – A mullet erminois, between two wings, argent. **Supporters** – On either side a bear proper, muzzled, collared, and chained, or, charged on the shoulder with a cross patée fitchée of the last.
Residence – Lake House, Northington, Alresford, Hants. *Clubs* – Flyfishers', Pratt's.

SONS LIVING *(By 1st marriage)*

Hon MARK FRANCIS ROBERT, *b* 17 Aug 1958; *ed* Eton, and Ch Ch, Oxford: *m* 1983, Miranda Caroline, 2nd da of Capt Charles St John Graham Moncrieff, of Easter Elcho, Rhynd, Perth (*see* Peto, Bt, *cr* 1927, colls), and has issue living, Frederick Charles Francis, *b* 25 June 1990. — Aurea Rose, *b* 1988. *Residence* – 164 Mount Pleasant Rd, Singapore.
Hon Alexander Nicholas John, *b* 1964; *ed* Eton, and Oriel Coll, Oxford: *m* 1992, Lucy Caroline, yr da of Gen Sir David William Fraser, GCB, OBE (*see* Ly Saltoun).

DAUGHTERS LIVING *(By 1st marriage)*

Hon Lucinda Mary Louise, *b* 1956: *m* 1978, Hon Michael John Wilmot Malet Vaughan, 2nd son of 8th Earl of Lisburne. *Residence* – 44 Pembroke Sq, W8.
Hon Rose Theresa, *b* 1961.

BROTHER LIVING

Hon Robin Alexander, *b* 1931; *ed* Eton; late Sub-Lieut RNVR: *m* 1960, Ann Caroline Thalia, elder da of Maj Edward Fitzhardinge Peyton Gage (*see* V Gage, colls), and has issue living, Francesca Rhiannon, *b* 1963: *m* 1990, Stuart Douglas.

AUNT LIVING *(daughter of 5th Baron)*

Hon Angela Mildred, *b* 1893.

COLLATERAL BRANCHES LIVING

Grandchildren of late Lt-Col Hon Guy Victor Baring, MP, Coldstream Guards, 4th son of 4th Baron:—
Issue of late Simon Alexander Vivian Baring, *b* 1905, *d* 1962: *m* 1st, 1935 (*m diss* 1946), Jeanne, da of Felix Salmond, of London and New York; 2ndly, 1946, Pamela Rachel, who *d* 1985, da of late Sir Mark Beresford Russell Grant-Sturgis, KCB (*see* E Wharncliffe, 1968 Edn), and formerly wife of Allan Alexander Cameron:—
(By 1st *m*) Julian Guy Alexander (Manor Farm, Bradley, Alresford, Hants), *b* 1935: *m* 1971, Isla, da of late Sir Frank Samuel Tait, of Toorak, Melbourne, Victoria, Australia, and has issue living, Justin Frank Alexander, *b* 1971. — Rebecca Alexandra Viola, *b* 1973. —— (By 2nd *m*) Francis Esmond (Hill House, Monkwood, Alresford, Hants), *b* 1948: *m* 1978, Nicolette Mary Irving, yst da of late (Frederic) Alan (Irving) Muntz, of Les Hauts de Claires, Montauroux 83770, France, and has issue

living, Simon Esmond Charles, *b* 1983, — Sophie Edwina, *b* 1980. ——— Camilla Jane, *b* 1952; *ed* City and Guilds Coll of Art: *m* 1986, John Nicholas Robbins, and has issue living, Daniel John, *b* 1986, — William Francis, *b* 1987.

    Issue of late Amyas Evelyn Giles Baring, *b* 1910, *d* 1986: *m* 1st, 1935 (*m diss* 1949), Mona Montgomerie, who *d* 1988, da of Lt-Col Willoughby Brooking Mullins, of Ambersham House, Midhurst, Sussex, and formerly wife of Maj William Frederick Husband; 2ndly, 1949, Peggy Michell (Montana Cottage, West End, Southampton), da of late Surg Vice-Adm Sir Arthur Gaskell, KCB, OBE, FRCS, and formerly wife of George Clive Reeves:—
(By 1st *m*) Claire Leonora (7 Callow St, SW3; Villa Cetinale, Sovicille, Siena, Italy), *b* 1936: *m* 1956 (*m diss* 1974), Hon Peter Alastair Ward, and has issue (*see* E Dudley).

    Issue of late Sqd Ldr Aubrey George Adeane Baring, DFC, RAFVR, late Chm Twickenham Film Studios, *b* 1912, *d* 1987: *m* 1952, Marina, eldest da of Basil Bessel, of 22 Farley Court, W14, and formerly wife of Sir Charles Richard Andrew Oakeley, 6th Bt:—
Alexander Esmond, *b* 1953: *m* 1986, Zein El Guindi, and has issue living, Adam Alexander Aubrey, *b* 1988, — Lara Louise, *b* 1987. ——— Adrian Hugh Vasili, *b* 1962. ——— Louise Olivia, *b* 1955.

    Issue of late Lt-Col Esmond Charles Baring, OBE, *b* 1914, *d* 1963: *m* 1st, 1936 (*m diss* 1951), Zalia, who *d* 1986, da of late Sir Harold Edward Snagge, KBE (*see* B Avebury, colls, 1955 Edn); 2ndly, 1960, Judith (who *d* 1991, having *m* 3rdly, 1965, 3rd Marquess of Linlithgow, who *d* 1987), da of late Stanley Mathew Lawson, of Cincinnati, USA, and formerly wife of John Symonds Radway:—
(By 1st *m*) Oliver Alexander Guy (Deane House, Overton, Hants), *b* 1944: *m* 1967, Veronica, da of late Capt Ian Alexander Henderson (*see* B Faringdon, colls), and has issue living, Rupert Esmond Ian, *b* 1968, — Esmond Oliver Mark, *b* 1978, — Thomas Edward Joseph, *b* 1979, — Emma Rose, *b* 1970. ——— Guy Esmond, *b* 1945: *m* 1967, Raina, who *d* 1979, da of David Campbell, of Palerang, Bungendore, NSW, and has issue living, Ben, *b* 1970, — Ned, *b* 1975, — Samantha, *b* 1969. ——— Caroline Venetia, *b* 1937: *m* 1957, Henry Giles Francis Lascelles, of 119 Hambalt Rd, SW4 (*see* E Harewood, colls). ——— Patricia (*Hon Mrs Mark H. Wyndham*), *b* 1938: *m* 1st, 1965, Maj Henry Claude Lyon Garnett, CBE, who *d* 1990; 2ndly, 1986, as his 2nd wife, Hon Mark Hugh Wyndham (*see* B Egremont), of Newmans Cottage, Froxfield Green, Petersfield, Hants, and has issue living (by 1st *m*), Charles Henry Esmond, *b* 1966, — Henrietta Patricia, *b* 1968.

    Issue of late Hon Caryl Digby Baring, yst son of 4th Baron, *b* 1880, *d* 1956: *m* 1907, Ivy, who *d* 1971, da of late Humphrey Brooke Firman (formerly 16th Lancers), JP, of Stone Court, St Leonards-on-Sea:—
Denzil, *b* 1909; *ed* Eton; late Capt R Corps of Signals. *Residence* – 81 Cadogan Lane, SW1. ——— Leonora Jacqueline, *b* 1912.

PREDECESSORS – (1) The *Right Hon* ALEXANDER Baring, PC, DCL, 2nd son of Sir Francis Baring, 1st Baronet (B Northbrook), and cousin of Richard Dunning, 2nd Baron Ashburton (cr 1782, extinct 1823); cr *Baron Ashburton* (peerage of United Kingdom) 1835, was sometime Pres of Board of Trade and Master of the Mint; *d* 1848; *s* by his eldest son (2) WILLIAM BINGHAM, PC, 2nd Baron; was Sec of Board of Control 1841-5, Paymaster of the Forces and Treasurer of the Navy 1845-6, and seventeen years MP for various constituencies: *d* 1864; *s* by his brother (3) FRANCIS, 3rd Baron, *b* 24 May 1800; sat as MP for Thetford (*L*) 1832-41 and 1848-57: *m* 1832, Claire Hortense, who *d* 1882, da of the Duke of Bassano, Minister of Napoleon I; *d* 6 Sept, 1868; *s* by his son (4) ALEXANDER HUGH, 4th Baron: *b* 1835; sat as MP for Thetford (LC) 1857-67: *m* 1864, Hon Leonora Caroline, who *d* 1930, da of 9th Baron Digby: *d* 1889; *s* by his eldest son (5) FRANCIS DENZIL EDWARD, 5th Baron; *b* 1866: *m* 1st, 1889, Hon Mabel Edith Hood, who *d* 1904, da of 4th Viscount Hood; 2ndly, 1906, Frances, who *d* 1959, da of James Caryll Donnelly, of New York; *d* 1938; *s* by his only son (6) ALEXANDER FRANCIS ST VINCENT, KG, KCVO, 6th Baron; *b* 1898; Lieut Royal Scots Greys, and Group Capt AAF; Man Dir Baring Bros 1928-62, Dir 1962-68, etc; Lord Lieut and Custos Rotulorum Hants and Isle of Wight 1960-73, DL 1973, Receiver-Gen Duchy of Cornwall 1961-73, High Steward Winchester Cathedral 1967-78, etc; Trustee King George's Jubilee Trust 1949-68, Treasurer King Edward VII Hosp Fund for London 1955-64 (Gov 1971-75): *m* 1924, Hon Doris Mary Thérèse Harcourt, who *d* 1981, da of 1st Viscount Harcourt; *d* 1991; *s* by his elder son (7) JOHN FRANCIS HARCOURT, 7th Baron and present peer.

ASHBY, BARONY OF (Ashby) (Extinct 1992)

SONS LIVING OF LIFE BARON

Hon Michael Farries, FRS (51 Maids Causeway, Cambridge), *b* 1935; *ed* Campbell Coll, Belfast, and Queen's Coll, Camb (BA, PhD), Hon MA (Harvard); FRS; Prof of Engineering, Univ of Camb, Royal Society Prof since 1989: *m* 1962, Maureen, da of S. James Stewart, of White House, Montgomery, Powys.
Hon Peter (42 Bennington Heights Drive, Toronto, Ont M4G 1A6, Canada), *b* 1937; *ed* Campbell Coll, Belfast, and Queen's Univ, Belfast (MB, BCh, MD); Prof, Univ of Toronto: *m* 1967, Moya, da of Rear-Adm Maurice Henry Adams, CB, of Canberra, Rock, Cornwall.

WIDOW LIVING OF LIFE BARON

ELIZABETH HELEN MARGARET (*Baroness Ashby*), da of Francis Farries, of Castle Douglas, Kirkcudbrightshire: *m* 1931, Baron Ashby, FRS (Life Baron), who *d* 1992. *Residences* – 22 Eltisley Av, Cambridge; Norman Cottage, Brandon, Suffolk.

ASHCOMBE, BARON (Cubitt) (Baron UK 1892)

Happy is the prudent man

HENRY EDWARD CUBITT, 4th Baron, *b* 31 March 1924; *s* 1962; *ed* Eton; 1939-45 War with RAF: *m* 1st, 1955 (*m diss* 1968), Ghislaine, only da of Cornelius Willem Dresselhuys, of Long Island, New York, USA, and formerly wife of Maj Denis James Alexander, Irish Gds (later 6th Earl of Caledon); 2ndly, 1973 (*m diss* 1979), Hon Virginia Carington, yr da of the 6th Baron Carrington; 3rdly, 1979, (Mary) Elizabeth, da of Dr Henry Davis Chipps, of Lexington, Kentucky, USA, and widow of Geoffrey Mark Dent-Brocklehurst, of Sudeley Castle, Winchcombe, Cheltenham, Glos (*see* B Trevor, 1962 Edn).

𝕬rms – Checky or and gules, on a pile argent, a lion's head erased sable. 𝕮rest – A column proper, in front two scimitars in saltire argent, pommel and hilt or. 𝕾upporters – *Dexter*, a stonemason proper, habited in brown coat and hat, apron argent, in his right hand a mallet sable; *sinister*, a carpenter proper, habited in brown vest, apron argent, in his left hand a pair of compasses or.
Residences – Sudeley Castle, Winchcombe, Cheltenham, Glos; Flat 6, 53 Drayton Gdns, SW10 9RX. *Club* – White's.

SISTER LIVING

Hon Rosalind Maud, *b* 1921: *m* 1946, Major Bruce Middleton Hope Shand, MC, late 12th R Lancers, Vice Lord Lieut (E Sussex) 1974-92, and formerly Clerk of the Cheque, Queen's Body Guard of the Yeomen of the Guard, and has issue living, Mark Roland, *b* 1951; author of *Travels on My Elephant* (1991): *m* 1990, Clio, da of Edward René David Goldsmith, and of Comtesse Jean Baptiste de Monpezart, — Camilla Rosemary, *b* 1947: *m* 1973, Brig Andrew Henry Parker-Bowles, OBE, Blues & Royals (*see* E Macclesfield, colls), — Sonia Annabel, *b* 1949: *m* 1972, Simon John Elliot, of Stourpaine House, Blandford, Dorset, son of late Air Ch Marshal Sir William Elliot, GCVO, KCB, KBE, DFC, and has issue living, Benjamin William *b* 1975, Alice Rosalind *b* 1977, Catherine Camilla *b* 1981. *Residence* – The Laines, Plumpton, Lewes, E Sussex.

COLLATERAL BRANCHES LIVING

Issue of late Hon Jeremy John Cubitt, yr son of 3rd Baron, *b* 1927, *d* 1958: *m* 1952 (*m diss* 1957), Diana Edith, elder da of late Com Peter Du Cane, OBE, RN (*see* Pole, Bt, *cr* 1628, 1985 Edn):—
Sarah Victoria, *b* 1953: *m* 1975 (*m diss* 1981), David Gray Hutton, elder son of Thomas Hutton. *Residence* – Flat 3, 13 Cranley Gdns, SW7 3BB.

Grandsons of late Maj Hon Archibald Edward Cubitt (infra):—
Issue of late (Mark) Robin Cubitt, *b* 1936, *d* 1991; *m* 1962 (*m diss* 1984), Juliet Perpetua, da of Edward Corbet Woodall, OBE (*see* Crawley-Boevey, Bt, colls, 1964 Edn):—
MARK EDWARD, *b* 29 Feb 1964: *m* 1992, Melissa Mary, only da of Maj Charles Hay, of Boldre, Hants. *Residence* – 8 Hartismere Rd, SW6 7TT. —— David Antony, *b* 1966. —— Hugo John, *b* 1967.

Issue of late Maj Hon Archibald Edward Cubitt, 5th son of 2nd Baron, *b* 1901, *d* 1972: *m* 1st, 1926 (*m diss* 1933), Lady Irene Helen Pratt, who *d* 1976, da of 4th Marquess Camden; 2ndly, 1934 (*m diss* 1949), Sibell Margaret, da of Ronald Collet Norman (*see* E Bradford, 1936 Edn):—
(By 2nd *m*) Priscilla Margaret (*Countess of Harrington*), *b* 1941: *m* 1964, as his 3rd wife, 11th Earl of Harrington, of Greenmount, Patrickswell, co Limerick.

Issue living of late Col Hon (Charles) Guy Cubitt, CBE, DSO, TD, 6th and yst son of 2nd Baron, *b* 1903, *d* 1979: *m* 1927, Rosamond Mary Edith, who *d* 1984, da of Capt Sir Montague Aubrey Cholmeley, 4th Bt:—
Sir Hugh Guy, CBE (Chapel House, West Humble, Dorking, Surrey), *b* 1928; FRICS; *ed* RNC Dartmouth; JP; late Lieut RN; Lord Mayor of Westminster 1977-78; High Sheriff Surrey 1983; DL Greater London 1978; *cr* CBE (Civil) 1977, and Knt 1983: *m* 1958, Linda Ishbel, yst da of late Hon Angus Dudley Campbell, CBE (*see* B Colgrain, colls), and has issue living, Jonathan Guy, *b* 1962, — Joanna Mary, *b* 1960: *m* 1986, Charles William Smyth-Osbourne (*see* Ramsden, Bt), — Victoria Jane, *b* 1964: *m* 1987, Crispin Martin Harding-Rolls, of Rock Cottage, Buckingham Rd, S Holmwood, Dorking, Surrey RH5 4LB, yr son of Maj Christopher A. Harding-Rolls, of Pwll-y-Cwm, The Hendre, Monmouth, Gwent, and has issue living, George Christopher *b* 1992, Sophie Elizabeth *b* 1990. —— Sylvia Rosemary, *b* 1930: *m* 1951, Maj Ronald James Grant Dallas, 3rd Hus, of Glebe House, Shipton Moyne, Tetbury, Glos, and has had issue, Nigel Alexander, *b* 1962, — Caroline Rosamond, *b* 1952: *m* 1981, Philip T. Shearing, and *d* 1992, — Jenifer Mary, *b* 1954: *m* 1st, 1975 (*m diss* 1986), Philip S. W. Hawkins, son of Capt O. S. W. Hawkins, RN (ret); 2ndly, 1987, Roger Babington Hill; 3rdly, 1993, Simon King, of Southview, Sandford, nr Crediton, Devon. —— Celia Mary (*Baroness Carew*), *b* 1939: *m* 1962, 7th Baron Carew.

Granddaughters of late Maj Hon Archibald Edward Cubitt (ante):—
Issue of late Alick John Archibald Cubitt, *b* 1927; *d* 1983: *m* 1st, 1956, Priscilla Rosemary, who *d* 1957, elder da of Thomas Cecil Gouldsmith (*see* Laurie, Bt, colls, 1957 Edn); 2ndly, 1961, Jennifer Faith (Chetwode Manor, Buckingham) (who *m* 2ndly, 1986, J.E.H. (Tim) Collins), da of late Lt-Gen William Henry Ewart Gott, CB, CBE, DSO, MC:—
(By 2nd *m*) Amanda Jane, *b* 1966. —— Belinda Carey, *b* 1968.

PREDECESSORS – (1) GEORGE Cubitt, PC, son of late Thomas Cubitt, of Denbies, Surrey, *b* 1828: sat as MP for W Surrey (C) 1860-85, and for Mid, or Epsom, Div of Surrey Dec 1885 to June 1892; *cr* PC 1880, and *Baron Ashcombe*, of Dorking, co Surrey, and Bodiam Castle, Sussex (peerage of United Kingdom) 1892: *m* 1853, Laura, who *d* 1904, da of late Rev James Joyce, V of Dorking; *d* 1917; *s* by his son (2) HENRY, CB, TD, 2nd Baron; *b* 1867; sometime Lt-Col and Hon Col Comdg Surrey Yeo; Lord-Lt of Surrey 1905-39; MP for Surrey S-E or Reigate Div (C) 1892-1906: *m* 1890, Maud Mariamne, who *d* 1945, da of late Col Archibald Motteaux Calvert, of Ockley Court, Dorking; *d* 1947; *s* by his 4th but eldest surviving son (3) ROLAND CALVERT, 3rd Baron, *b* 1899: *m* 1st, 1920 (*m diss* 1947), Sonia Rosemary, OBE, who *d* 1986, da of late Lt-Col Hon George Keppel, MVO (E Albemarle, colls); 2ndly, 1948, Idina Joan (MILLS), who *d* 1954, da of late Col Robert Edward Myddelton, TD, DL, JP, of Chirk Castle, Denbighshire, and formerly wife of John Charles Trueman Mills; 3rdly, 1959, Jean, who was *k* in an air crash 1973, da of late Charles Tuller Garland, of Moreton Hall, Warwickshire, and formerly wife of (i) Arthur Turberville Smith-Bingham, (ii) Sir Robert George Maxwell Throckmorton, 11th Bt, and (iii) Greville Pollard Baylis; *d* 1962; *s* by his eldest son (4) HENRY EDWARD, 4th Baron and present peer.

ASHDOWN, BARONY OF (Silverstone) (Extinct 1977)

WIDOW LIVING OF LIFE BARON

LILLIAN NELL, CBE (*Baroness Ashdown*) (c/o Barclays Bank, 8 West Halkin St, SW1X 8JE) da of late Ralph and Mabel King; Member Westminster City Council 1957-65, of Nat Union of Conservative & Unionist Assocns' Exec Cttee 1963-79; Vice-Chm Women's Nat Advisory Cttee 1967-68, and Member Conservative Party Policy Cttee 1973-76; Gov Moorfields Eye Hosp since 1980; CBE (Civil) 1971: *m* 1937, Baron Ashdown (Life Baron), who *d* 1977.

Ashley, Lord; son of Earl of Shaftesbury.

ASHLEY OF STOKE, BARON (Ashley) (Life Baron 1992)

JACK ASHLEY, CH, PC, son of late John Ashley; *b* 6 Dec 1922; *ed* Ruskin Coll, Oxford, and Gonville and Caius Coll, Camb (Pres Union 1951); Shop Steward Convenor and Nat Exec Cttee Member Chemical Workers' Union 1946; Councillor Borough of Widnes 1946; BBC Radio Producer 1951-57, Sr TV Producer 1957-66, Member Gen Advisory Council BBC 1967-69 and 1970-74; PPS to Sec of State for Economic Affairs 1974-76, and to Sec of State for Dept of Health and Social SEcurity 1974-76; Member Lab Party Nat Exec Cttee 1976-78; author of *Journey into Silence* 1973; MP Stoke on Trent (*Lab*) 1966-92; *cr* CH 1975, PC 1979, and *Baron Ashley of Stoke*, of Widnes, co Cheshire (Life Baron) 1992: *m* 1951, Pauline Kay, da of Clarence Adley Crispin, of Liverpool, and has issue.
Address – c/o House of Lords, SW1.

DAUGHTERS LIVING

Hon Jacqueline, *b* 1954: *m* 1987, Andrew Marr, and has issue living, Harry Cameron, *b* 1989,—Isabel Claire, *b* 1991.
Hon Jane Elizabeth, *b* 1958: *m* 1992, Martin Rosenbaum, and has issue living, Ben, *b* 1992.
Hon Caroline, *b* 1966: *m* 1993, Richard Dewdney.

ASHTON OF HYDE, BARON (Ashton) (Baron UK 1911)

With faith and valour

THOMAS JOHN ASHTON, TD, 3rd Baron; *b* 19 Nov 1926; *s* 1983; *ed* Eton, and at New Coll, Oxford (MA); formerly Lieut 11th Hussars, and Maj R Glos Hus (TA); a JP of Oxon; Dir of Barclays Bank 1968-86: *m* 1957, Pauline Trewlove, eldest da of late Lt-Col Robert Henry Langton Brackenbury, OBE, of Yerdley House, Long Compton, Shipston on Stour, and has issue.

Arms – Sable, on a pile between two crescents in base argent, a mullet pierced of the first. **Crest** – On a mount vert, a mower proper, vested paly argent and sable, in the act of whetting his scythe also proper. **Supporters** – *Dexter*, a mower proper, vested paly argent and sable, holding in the exterior hand a scythe also proper; *sinister*, a boar argent semée of mullets sable pierced.
Residence – Fir Farm, Upper Slaughter, Bourton on the Water, Glos.
Club – Boodles.

SONS LIVING

Hon (THOMAS) HENRY, *b* 18 July 1958; *ed* Eton, and Trin Coll, Oxford; late Royal Hussars (PWO), Lieut Royal Wessex Yeo: *m* 1987, Emma Louise, da of Colin Allinson, of Bath, and has issue living, Harriet Emily, *b* 1990, — Isobel Louise, *b* 1992. *Residence* – Broadwell Hill, Moreton-in-Marsh, Glos. *Club* – Boodle's.
Hon John Edward, *b* 1966.

DAUGHTERS LIVING

Hon Charlotte Trewlove, *b* 1960: *m* 1987, Andrew D. Bartlett, only son of late D. W. Bartlett, and of Mrs J. D. Potts, of Macclesfield, Cheshire, and has issue living, Oliver William, *b* 1991.
Hon Katharine Judith, *b* 1962: *m* 1987, Douglas J. Lawson, son of Harry D. Lawson, of 58 Seafield Rd, Broughton Ferry, Dundee, and has issue living, James Alexander, *b* 1988, — Robert Douglas, *b* 1991.

PREDECESSORS – (1) THOMAS GAIR Ashton, son of late Thomas Ashton, JP, DL, of Hyde, Cheshire; *b* 1855; MP for Hyde Div of Cheshire (*L*) 1885-6, and for S, or Luton, Div of Bedfordshire 1895-1911; *cr Baron Ashton of Hyde*, co Chester (peerage of United Kingdom) 1911; *m* 1886, Eva Margaret, who *d* 1938, da of late John Henry James, of Kingswood, Watford, Herts: *d* 1933; *s* by his yr son (2) THOMAS HENRY RAYMOND, 2nd Baron, Maj R Glos Hus (TA); a JP and DL for Glos: *m* 1925, Marjorie Nell, who *d* 1993, da of late Hon Marshall Jones Brooks (*see* B Crawshaw, colls); *d* 1983; *s* by his only son (3) THOMAS JOHN, 3rd Baron and present peer.

ASHTOWN, BARON (Trench) (Baron I 1800)

Fortune is the companion of virtue

NIGEL CLIVE COSBY TRENCH, KCMG, 7th Baron; *b* 27 Oct 1916; *s* 1990; *ed* Eton, and Corpus Christi Coll, Camb; 1939-45 War as Maj KRRC (despatches); entered HM Foreign Ser (now Dip Ser) 1946; Counsellor Tokyo 1961-63, Washington 1963-67, and Cabinet Office 1967-69, HM Ambassador to Republic of Korea 1969-71, Assist Under-Sec Civil Ser Selection Board 1971-73, Ambassador to Portugal 1974-76; Member of Police, Prison and Fire Ser Selection Boards 1977-86; CMG 1966, KCMG 1976; Order of Diplomatic Service Merit, Rep of Korea, 1984; *m* 1939, Marcelle Catherine, who *d* 1994, yst da of Johan Jacob Clotterbooke Patyn van Kloetinge, of Zeist, The Netherlands, and has issue.

Arms – *Argent, a lion passant gules, between three fleurs-de-lis, azure, on a chief of the last a sun in splendour or.* **Crest** – *A dexter arm embowed in armour, the hand grasping a scimitar, all proper.* **Supporters** – *Dexter,* a lion gules, semée-de-lis, and ducally crowned or; *sinister,* a stag proper, attired, unguled, ducally collared and lined or. **Second Motto** – *Dieu pour la Tranche, qui contre ("God for the Trench, whoever may oppose!").*
Residence – 4 Kensington Court Gdns, W8 5QE. *Clubs* – MCC and Naval and Military.

SON LIVING

Hon RODERICK NIGEL GODOLPHIN, *b* 17 Nov, 1944; *ed* Eton, and Stanford Univ, USA: *m* 1st, 1967, Janet, who *d* 1971, da of Harold Hamilton-Faulkner, of Redwood City, Calif, USA; 2ndly, 1973, Susan Barbara, da of Lewis Frank Day, FRCS, DLO, of Cooden, Sussex, and formerly wife of Michael R. J. Wright, and has issue living (by 1st *m*), Timothy Roderick Hamilton, *b* 29 Feb 1968; *ed* Sherborne, and London Univ, — (by 2nd *m*) Victoria Susan, *b* 1977. *Residence* – Bassetts, Coggins Mill Lane, Mayfield, Sussex.

SISTER LIVING

Lois Eileen, *b* 1910: *m* 1937, Capt Charles Algernon Mackintosh-Walker, MBE, of Geddes, Nairn, and has issue living, Charles James (Geddes, Nairn), *b* 1939; *ed* Rugby: *m* 1967, Elizabeth Margaret, da of Charles Stewart, CMG, OBE, of The Cottage, Dunvegan, Skye, and has had issue, Ewen Charles *b* 1970; *d* 1980, Andrew Eneas *b* 1976, Maria Jane *b* 1968, Sarah Emily *b* 1972, — Serena Mary, *b* 1946: *m* 1st, 1968 (*m diss* 1976), Hugh Robert Norton, 2nd son of Leslie C. Norton; 2ndly, 1976, Dr Kenneth Mitchell Nuttall.

DAUGHTER LIVING OF FIFTH BARON

Hon Jacqueline Noël, *b* 1940: *m* 1966, Alastair Gordon Eadie; Dir Int Distillers and Vintners UK Ltd, of Bourne Orchard, Brickendon, Herts, and has issue living, James Alastair, *b* 1967, — Christopher John, *b* 1969, — Edward Charles, *b* 1972.

COLLATERAL BRANCHES LIVING (*male line in remainder to barony*)

Grandchildren of late Hon William Cosby Trench, brother of 3rd Baron:—
Issue of late Walter Frederick Oliver Trench, *b* 1899, *d* 1960: *m* 1st, 1921, Norah Maude, who *d* 1958, da of Ven John Richard Hedges Becher, Archdeacon of Ross; 2ndly, 1960, Marion Gwendolyn, da of Robert Young, of Woolley, Yorks:—
(By 1st *m*) Olga Ann Oliver (PO Box 377, Richmond, Natal), *b* 1922: *m* 1948 (*m diss* 19—), William Hugh Hindley, and has issue living, Michael Edward Oliver, *b* 1951: *m* 1977, Jane Mary Brimacombe, of Devizes, Wilts, and has issue living, Alexander William Oliver (John) *b* 1980, Lawrence Hugh John *b* 1982, Thomas Henry Walter *b* 1984, Caroline Jane *b* 1988, — Douglas William John, *b* 1963, — Sheila Rachel, *b* 1949: *m* 1981, Christopher Davis. —— Norah Susan Oliver, *b* 1936: *m* 1957, Walter Stuart Gash, MBE, of Rocklea, Mitchell Rd, Walliston, W Aust 6076, and has issue living, Maureen Susan, *b* 1959: *m* 1980, Gregory John Gittos, of 5 Cooper Ridge, Winthrop, W Australia 6150, and has issue living, Michael John *b* 1987, Lisa Marie *b* 1988, — Sheila Ann (Sydney, Australia), *b* 1960: *m* 1981 (*m diss* 1985), Kevin John McDowall.

Branch from 2nd brother of 1st Baron

Granddaughter of late Charles Steuart Trench, 2nd son of late Henry Trench (*b* 1806), 4th son of late Very Rev Thomas Trench, Dean of Kildare, 2nd brother of 1st Baron:—
Issue of late Henry Marryat Trench, *b* 1876, *d* 1948: *m* 1904, Juliet Benham, who *d* 1946, eldest da of late William Seaman, of Staten Island, New York, USA:—
Edith Katharine, *b* 1905: *m* 1930, Albert Irwin Dorr, who *d* 1947.

Granddaughters of late John Townsend Trench, son of William Steuart Trench, 5th son of late Very Rev Thomas Trench (ante):—
Issue of late Rev George Frederick Trench, *b* 1881, *d* 1966: *m* 1919, Muriel Leonore, who *d* 1974, da of late Leslie Stephen Robertson, MICE:—
Leonore Elisita, *b* 1920; *ed* Girton Coll, Camb (BA): *m* 1945, Henry Denis Whitwell Powell, FRCS, MB, ChB, of Old Fox Cottage, Heath End Rd, Gt Kingshill, Bucks HP15 6HS, and has issue living, John Denis Trench, *b* 1951, — Margaret Leonore, *b* 1945: *m* 1968, Frank William Taylor, and has issue living, Michael John *b* 1970, Peter Hugh *b* 1972, Christopher David *b* 1979, — Janet Elisita, *b* 1949: *m* 1972, Derek Peacock, and has issue living, Timothy Simon *b* 1978, Antony Robert *b* 1980, — Clare Louise, *b* 1954: *m* 1979, Philip Marshall Garside, and has issue living, Douglas Paul *b* 1982, Alan Nigel *b* 1984, Ian Richard *b* 1987. —— Bridget Wray, *b* 1928; a Member of Assocn of Occupational Therapists, and Canadian Occupational Therapy Assocn: *m* 1959, Robin Blakeway Dickens, of 18, 3144 Sherman Rd, Duncan, BC, Canada V9L 4B4, and has issue living, Mark Lester, *b* 1961, — Lynn Catherine, *b* 1963: *m* 1985, Mark Hayden Lane.

Branch from 3rd brother of 1st Baron

Granddaughter of late Louis Trench, yst son of late Rev Frederic Fitz-William Trench, son of late William Trench, 3rd brother of 1st Baron:—
Issue of late Geoffrey FitzLouis Trench, *b* 1885, *d* 1971: *m* 1927, Olive Muriel, who *d* 1984, da of George Constance:—
Joanna Mary, *b* 1937: *m* 1959, Timothy Francis Cox, of Priors Mesne, Aylburton, Lydney, Glos, and has issue living, Dermot Francis, *b* 1963: *m* 1989, Heather Ann, da of Anthony Jackson, of The Fields, Maesbury, Shropshire, — Miranda Josephine, *b* 1961: *m* 1985, Andrew Thomas Doran of The Manor House, Blockley, Glos, and has issue living, Dominic Henry *b* 1988, Fionnghuala Mary *b* 1987.

Branch from 2nd son of 5th brother of 1st Baron

Grandchildren of late Col Charles Chenevix Trench, 3rd son of late Most Rev and Rt Hon Richard Chenevix Trench, DD, 2nd son of late Richard Trench, 5th brother of 1st Baron:—
Issue of late Lt-Col Sir Richard Henry CHENEVIX TRENCH, CIE, OBE, IA, and Indian Political Ser, *b* 1876, *d* 1954: *m* 1913, Evelyn May, who *d* 1977, da of late Capt Harry Evelyn Stracy Pocklington, 15th Hus:—
Charles Pocklington, MC (Lisnamoe House, Ballymackey, Nenagh, co Tipperary), *b* 1914; *ed* Winchester, and Magdalen Coll, Oxford; Maj (ret) IA; author of *The Royal Malady* and other works; 1939-45 War in Italy (MC): *m* 1st, 1946, Patricia Jane, who *d* 1963, da of late Maj George Foster Gretton, of 62 Melton Court, SW7; 2ndly, 1954, Mary Elizabeth, da of Lt-Col George Kirkbride, of Mullion, Cornwall, and has issue living (by 1st *m*), Richard Hugh Roger, *b* 1949, — Charlotte Ann, *b* 1946, — Priscilla Jane, *b* 1947, — (by 2nd *m*) Lucy, *b* 1956: *m* 19—, Robert Collingwood, of 4 Luxembourg Gdns, W6 7EA, — Georgia, *b* 1959: *m* 1983, Prof Nicholas Gordon Martin, of 37 Burns Rd, Toowong, Qld 4066, Australia. —— (Evelyn) Jane Chenevix, *b* 1917: *m* 1950, Richard Christian Allhusen, and has issue living, Christian Henry (Manor House, Bradenham, Thetford, Norfolk IP25 7QU), *b* 1956: *m* 1986, Penelope Amanda, yr da of Colin G. C. Rae, of Fuller's House, Broxton, Cheshire, and has issue living, Benjamin Christian Thomas *b* 1989, Matthew John Oliver *b* 1991, Natasha Sophie Tamsin *b* 1993, — Richard Frederick (56 Denbigh St, SW1V 2EU), *b* 1960: *m* 1989, Katrina Jane, yr da of I. R. P. Haig, of Brockstone House, Dunley, Worcs, — Elizabeth Mary, *b* 1952: *m* 1977, William P. Durlacher, of Whalebone House, Langham, Colchester, Essex CO4 5PX, son of late Jack Durlacher, and has issue living, Emma Jane *b* 1980, Susanna Mary *b* 1982, — Rosalind Jane, *b* 1954: *m* 1985, Nicholas Charles Thoresby Pawson, only son of K. V. F. Pawson, and has issue living, Iona Elizabeth *b* 1988, Georgia Catherine *b* 1991. *Residence* – Bradenham Hall, Thetford, Norfolk.

Grandchildren of late Charles Godfrey Chenevix Trench, CIE (infra):—
Issue of late Christopher John CHENEVIX TRENCH, MBE, *b* 1911, *d* 1971: *m* 1936, Mary Elizabeth Catherine, who *d* 1990, eldest da of late G. H. Allen, of Branksome, Poole:—
Timothy Christopher John (196 Broom Rd, Teddington, Middx), *b* 1938; *ed* King's Sch, Canterbury, and Corpus Christi Coll, Oxford: *m* 1st, 1961 (*m diss* 1973), Penelope Mary Travers Walton; 2ndly, 1977, Stella-Maris Melhuish, da of late Edwin Samuel Henderson, Supt CID, Burma, and has issue living (by 1st *m*), Katherine Rae, *b* 1964: *m* 1984, Dr Robert Neil Summers Slater, of 25 Aldebrooke Rd, SW12, only son of Robert Slater, of Childswickham, Worcs, and has issue living, Thomas Alexander *b* 1986, — Alison Mary, *b* 1965: *m* 1983, Jonathan Robert Hill, son of Fl-Lt F. G. Hill, — Phillida Clare, *b* 1969. —— John Richard (Glenalmond Coll, Perthshire), *b* 1948: *m* 1970, Pauline, da of James Stephen Alexander, of 2 Sea-wood Place, Grange over Sands, Cumbria, and has issue living, Christopher Hamish, *b* 1977, — Alix (a da), *b* 1983. —— Elizabeth Mary *b* 1941: *m* 1964, Anthony Savile Stephen Rowe, of Woodtown, Sampford Spiney, Yelverton, Devon, and has issue living, Jonathan Stephen, *b* 1969, — James Benedict, *b* 1970, — Antonia Jane, *b* 1967: *m* 1993, Jonathan Katz.
Issue of late Lt-Cdr Richard Blakesley CHENEVIX TRENCH, RN, *b* 1912, *d* 1979: *m* 1939, Nancy Carey (21 Church Rd, Davenport Green, Wilmslow, Cheshire), only da of James Munro, of Shanghai:—
Fenella Anne, *b* 1943: *m* 1969, Richard Law Townsend, of 129 Broadleaf Cres, Ancaster, Ontario, Canada L9G 3T6, and has issue living, Simon Andrew, *b* 1974.
Issue of late Anthony CHENEVIX TRENCH, FRSE, FRSA, *b* 1919, *d* 1979: *m* 1953, Elizabeth Chalmers, who *d* 1991, da of Capt Sir Stewart Dykes Spicer, 3rd Bt, RN:—
Richard Thomas Chalmers (20 Hill Crest, 22 Plunketts Rd, The Peak, Hong Kong), *b* 1958: *m* 1985, Sarah Jane, eldest da of Raglan Charles Wykeham, of Northroyd, Crimphill, Englefield Green, Egham, Surrey, and has issue living, Harry Chalmers, *b* 1988, — James William Reynolds (by 1990, — Marcus, *b* 1993. —— Jonathan Charles Stewart, *b* 1961. —— Josephine Dykes, *b* 1954: *m* 1978, John George Richards Homfray, only son of Maj Herbert Franklen Richards Homfray, of Penllyn Court, Cowbridge, Glamorgan, and has issue living, Matthew Anthony, *b* 1980, — Thomas Richards, *b* 1983, — Virginia, *b* 1987.

Grandchildren of late Col Charles Chenevix Trench (ante):—
Issue of late Charles Godfrey CHENEVIX TRENCH, CIE, *b* 1877, *d* 1964: *m* 1910, Margaret May, who *d* 1981, eldest da of late John Holmes Blakesley, CE:—
Godfrey Maxwell, DSC (Kelling, Holt, Norfolk), *b* 1917; *ed* Shrewsbury; Cdr RN (ret); 1939-45 War (DSC and bar); history teacher: *m* 1945, Nancy Louise, da of Rev A. Clarkson Birch, of Cloughton, Scarborough, and has issue living, Juliet, *b* 1947: *m* 1973, Graham Duncan Campbell, of Perth, W Australia, and has issue living, Ian Neil *b* 1977, Duncan Alastair *b* 1981, — Frances Claire, *b* 1949: *m* 1972 (*m diss* 1985), Christopher Maurice White, and has issue living, Colin Stephen Maxwell, *b* 1974.
Issue of late Col Lawrence CHENEVIX TRENCH, CMG, DSO, *b* 1883, *d* 1958: *m* 1908, Winifred Ross, who *d* 1969, da of late Edward Henry Tootal:—
Katherine Anne, *b* 1912: *m* 1st, 1932, Lt-Col George William Frederic Leicester, Cheshire Regt, who *d* 1944 (*see* Leicester, Bt, colls, ext 1968); 2ndly, 1945, Lt-Col A. Frankland, who *d* 1969, and has issue (by 1st *m*) George Leicester, Bt, colls, ext 1968), — (by 2nd *m*) Philip, *b* 1946; *ed* Tonbridge, — John, *b* 1949; *ed* King's Sch, Canterbury: *m* 1975, Mary Faith Elizabeth Townsend, da of Lionel Becher Somerville-Large, MRIA, of Blackrock, co Dublin, and has issue living, William Becher Chenevix *b* 1983, Anna *b* 1978, — Sarah, *b* 1947: *m* 1969, Dr Peter Morris, of Ware, Herts, and has issue living, Patrick *b* 1982, Leila *b* 1980. *Residence* – The Gables, Hopton Cangeford, Ludlow, Shropshire.
Issue of late Brig Ralph CHENEVIX TRENCH, CB, OBE, MC, *b* 1885, *d* 1974: *m* 1916, Meriel Edith, who *d* 1985, da of late Rev George Edward Jelf, DD, Master of Charterhouse:—
John Gordon (Windmill Farm, Coleshill, Amersham, Bucks), *b* 1920; *ed* Wellington Coll; late Capt R Signals; FSA: *m* 1944, Ann Patricia, da of late Norman Moore, of 34 Jubilee Place, SW3, and has issue living, Maxwell John (26 Austen Walk, Bicester, Oxon), *b* 1952: *m* 1991, Chou Ern, da of Lam-Tai Lim, of Selangor, Malaysia, — Jessica, *b* 1949: *m* 1st, 1970 (*m diss* 1976), Jonathan Yardley; 2ndly, 1976, George Frederick Laurence, QC, and has issue living (by 1st *m*), Thomas James *b* 1974, (by 2nd *m*) Benjamin George *b* 1981, Catherine Ann *b* 1978. —— Susan Meriel, *b* 1925: *m* 1950, Oscar Patrick Wood, who *d* 1994, of Christ Church, Oxford, and has issue living, Charles William Chenevix, *b* 1955: *m* 1985, Mary Rose, da of Rex Cooper, of E Bergholt, Suffolk, and has issue living, Oscar Giles Chenevix *b* 1986, Amelia Claire Lucy *b* 1988, Georgia Charlotte *b* 1991, — Silas James London, *b* 1965, — Lucy Melesina, *b* 1956.
Issue of late Alfred Saward CHENEVIX TRENCH, MC, *b* 1887, *d* 1953: *m* 1st, 1920, Helen Winifred, who *d* 1945, da of George Fowler; 2ndly, 1949, Sylvia Mary Crawford, who *d* 1978, twin da of late Francis Crawford Caffin:—
(By 1st *m*) Dudley Alfred Chenevix, *b* 1928; *ed* Bradfield Coll; late Lieut RA: *m* 1955, Isobel Margaret Logie, da of William Low McDonald, of Port Elizabeth, S Africa, and has issue living, Jennifer Elizabeth Chenevix, *b* 1957, — Helen Winifred Chenevix, *b* 1959. —— Gillian Chenevix, *b* 1920: *m* 1947, Maj James Thomas Benedictus Notley, DSO, late Duke of Corn-

wall's LI, of Redcote, 48 Port Hill Gdns, Shrewsbury, and has issue living, Christopher John Marwood, *b* 1949; Maj 1st Bn LI: *m* 1st, 1977 (*m diss* 1982), Christine Louise, da of Patrick Hugh Ash, of Haughley, Suffolk; 2ndly, 1987, Alison Jane Leila, da of Colin Biggs, of IoW, — Helen Ann Hamilton, *b* 1950: *m* 1971 (*m diss* 1987), Timothy Rowland Hunt, and has issue living, Benjamin Rowland *b* 1973, Nina Kathryn *b* 1974.

Grandchildren of late Rev Herbert Francis Chenevix Trench, 6th son of late Most Rev and Rt Hon Richard Chenevix Trench, DD (ante):—
Issue of late Col Arthur Henry CHENEVIX TRENCH, CIE, *b* 1884, *d* 1968: *m* 1913, Dorothy Pauline, who *d* 1950, da of late Allan Gibson Steel, KC, Recorder of Oldham:—
Reginald Allan (Holly Tree House, Amberley, Arundel, Sussex), *b* 1920; Maj RE (ret): *m* 1957, Sophie Sybella Strathern, da of Air Chief Marshal Sir Douglas Claude Strathern Evill, GBE, KCB, DSC, AFC, RAF (ret) (*see* Kleinwort, Bt, 1980 Edn), and has issue living, Ivo Richard, *b* 1959: *m* 1982, Joelle, da of René Bézert, of Marseilles, France, and has issue living, Sophie Armella Françoise *b* 1982, — Angus, *b* 1960, — Katharine, *b* 1964, — Jessica Sophie, *b* 1966. —— Margaret Georgina (Farthings, School Lane, Fittleworth, Pulborough, W Sussex RH20 1JB), *b* 1915; formerly in FANY: *m* 1944, Patrick Millington Synge, late Maj Intelligence Corps, who *d* 1982, and has issue living, Arthur Hugh Millington, *b* 1951, — Robert Patrick, *b* 1957: *m* 1992, Susan Jean Frances Wixley. —— Dorothy Anne, *b* 1916; formerly in WRNS: *m* 1942, Roderick Peter Garratt Wilson, of Three Chimneys, Fittleworth, Pulborough, Sussex, son of Sir Roderick (Roy) Wilson, and has issue living, Sir Nicholas Allan Roy (*Hon Mr Justice Wilson*) (31 Sutherland Place, W2), *b* 1945; BA (Oxon); Bar Inner Temple 1967, QC and Recorder of Crown Court 1987-93, since when a Judge of High Court of Justice (Family Div); Ktd 1993: *m* 1974, Margaret (Bar Middle Temple 1966), da of late Reginald Francis Higgins, and has issue living, Matthew Roderick Benjamin *b* 1977, Camilla Jessica *b* 1981, — *Rev* Francesca Dorothy, *b* 1952: MA (Cantab), Dip Theol: *m* 1985, John Dudley Dixon, MBE, DSC.
Issue of late Maj Charles Reginald CHENEVIX TRENCH, *b* 1888, *ka* 1918: *m* 1915, Clare Cecily, who *d* 1989, da of late Henry Blunt Howard, of Bark Hart, Orpington, Kent;, —
Isabel Clare, *b* 1915; Dip Social Studies; London: *m* 1939, (Clarence) John Molyneux Fletcher, FSA, who *d* 1986, of 20 Tullis Close, Sutton Courtenay, Abingdon, Berks, and has issue living, *Prof* Anthony John (2 Bluecoat Court, Durham), *b* 1941; *ed* Wellington Coll, and Merton Coll, Oxford (MA): *m* 1967, Tresna Dawn, da of Charles Henry Railton Russell, of 25 Minchenden Crescent, Southgate, N4, and has issue living, Crispin Hilary Trench *b* 1970, Dickon Anthony Railton *b* 1972, — Martin Chenevix, *b* 1942: *m* 1972, Diana Cantillon, and has issue living, Nicholas Cantillon *b* 1975, Alison Chenevix *b* 1973, — Joanna Delle, *b* 1946: *m* 1992, Cmdr Robert Walker, RN (ret), — Hilary Clare, *b* 1951: *m* 1976, John Bennett, and has issue living, Peter David John *b* 1989, Charlotte Louise *b* 1981, Rowena Clare *b* 1982.
Issue of late Herbert CHENEVIX TRENCH, *b* 1892, *d* 1971: *m* 1922, Marjorie, who *d* 1962, da of R. C. Bell, of Melbourne, Vic, Australia:—
Frances Robina Chenevix, *b* 1925: *m* 1953, R. Raymond Lockyer, ARIBA, of The Old Manor Cottage, Broadwell, nr Lechlade, Glos, and has issue living, Sarah Frances Chenevix, *b* 1954: *m* 1982, Peter Hickman, son of W. J. Hickman, and has issue living, Emma Charlotte *b* 1985, Lucy Elizabeth *b* 1987, — Victoria Robina Chenevix, *b* 1957. —— Valerie Hester Chenevix, *b* 1929: *m* 1959, David McKie Kerslake, OBE, of Lime Tree Cottage, Yateley, Camberley, Surrey GU17 7SP, and has issue living, Michael John Chenevix, *b* 1962, — Caroline Julia Chenevix, *b* 1961.

Branch from 3rd son of 5th brother of 1st Baron

Grandchildren of late Richard Bayley Chenevix Trench, yst son of late Philip Charles Chenevix Trench, 3rd son of late Richard Trench (ante), 5th brother of 1st Baron:—
Issue of late Capt Hugo CHENEVIX TRENCH, *b* 1890, *d* 1965: *m* 1920 (*m diss* 1933), Emma Margaret Florence, who *d* 1948, da of Sir Robert McAlpine, 1st Bt:—
Brian Robert David (13 Holland Park, W11), *b* 1927: *m* 1st, 1956 (*m diss* 19—), Bridget, da of K. R. J. Saxon, of Boscombe, Hants; 2ndly, 1963, Elspeth Charlesworth, yr da of late Thomas Douglas Ross, OBE, of Stamford.
Issue of late Ivor CHENEVIX TRENCH, *b* 1892, *d* 1960: *m* 1918, Doris Mary, who *d* 1951, da of late John Francis Gaskell, of Cambus O'May, Aberdeenshire:—
Diana Doris, *b* 1920: *m* 1st, 1943 (*m diss* 1947), Capt Brodie Knight, WG; 2ndly, 1947, Gilbert Younghusband, late Capt RHG.
Issue of late Lionel CHENEVIX TRENCH, *b* 1901, *d* 1930: *m* 1925, Doris Maud (who *m* 2ndly, 1933, George Sweeting, who *d* 1956, and *d* 1980), da of late Charles D. Turrall, of Downes, Torrington, N Devon:—
(Keith Everard) George (The Old Mill, Worton, Devizes, Wilts), *b* 1926; *ed* Stowe; 1939-45 War as Sub-Lieut RNVR: *m* 1952 (*m diss* 1972), Bridget, da of Lt-Col K. R. O'Brien, MC, late R Ulster Rifles, and has issue living, Guy Charles, *b* 1955: *m* 1982, Sarah A., yr da of John Speakman, of Maldon, Essex, and has issue living, Olivia Katie *b* 1985, Poppy *b* 1987, — Rupert George, *b* 1957: *m* 1988, Susannah Rainey, da of Robert Craik, of The Old Rectory, Mawdesley, Lancs, and has issue living, Frederic George *b* 1989, Fleur Melesina *b* 1992.

Branch from 6th brother of 1st Baron

Granddaughters of late Wilbraham FitzJohn Trench (infra):—
Issue of late Patrick Mackenzie FitzJohn Trench, *b* 1905, *d* 1948: *m* 1st, 1926 (*m diss* 1930), Frances Cautley, who *d* 1982, da of late Cecil Cautley Baker; 2ndly, 1930, Evelyn, who *d* 1945, da of late John Hayden; 3rdly, 1948, Winifred Frances, who *d* 1992, da of late Arthur Edward Stidolph:—
(By 2nd *m*) Patricia Anne, *b* 1930: *m* 1954, Pierre Edouard Marie Ghislain Verstraete, and has issue living, Philippe, *b* 1957, — Jacques Michel, *b* 1962: *m* 1982, Lorraine Court, and has issue living, Maud *b* 1981, Zoë *b* 1983, — Catherine, *b* 1955: *m* 1977, Peter Carp, and has issue living, Benoit *b* 1983, Henri *b* 1986, Alain *b* 1988, Sara *b* 1981, — Brigide, *b* 1956: *m* 1984, Edouard Chanson, and has issue living, Sophie *b* 1984, Celine *b* 1986, Celine *b* 1988, — Anne, *b* 1960: *m* 1982, Patrice Droz, and has issue living, Olivier *b* 1985, Meryem *b* 1983, Nadège *b* 1990, Béatrice *b* 1991. *Residence* - Chemin des Oisillons 1, 1009 Pully, Switzerland. —— Eveline Mary, *b* 1932: *m* 1952 (*m diss* 1987), Thomas William Lane, and has issue living, William, *b* 1955: *m* 1980, Janet Ellinor, da of Thomas Merville de Blois, of Toronto, and has issue living, Helen Eilis de Blois *b* 1984, Heather Fiona de Blois *b* 1988, — Patricia Sheela, *b* 1954: *m* 1993, Kenneth Malcolm Maclure, of Victoria, BC, Canada, and has issue living, Troy Liam Chalmers Alexander *b* 1994. *Residence* - 190 Menhinick Dr, Fulford Harbour, BC, Canada. —— (By 3rd *m*) Bríd, *b* 19—: *m* 1962, Michael Frederick Strutt, son of Frederick Strutt, of Pontypool, Gwent, and has issue living, Patrick *b* 1962, — Catherine, *b* 1964, — Anna, *b* 1965, — Siân, *b* 1978.

Grandchildren of late John Alfred Trench, eldest son of late Rev Frederic FitzJohn Trench, eldest son of late John Trench, 6th brother of 1st Baron:—
Issue of late Wilbraham FitzJohn Trench, *b* 1873, *d* 1939: *m* 1903, Mary Alicia, who *d* 1930, eldest da of late Edward Cross, formerly Lieut RA, of Hollywood, Portishead, Somerset:—
Chalmers Edward FitzJohn, *b* 1909: *m* 1940, Beatrice Esther, who *d* 1980, da of late Charles St George Orpen, of Lisheens, Carrickmines, co Dublin, and has issue living, Fiachra Terence Wilbraham McMAHON TRENCH (Easton House, Delgany, co Wicklow), *b* 1941; M Mus Cincinnati; assumed additional surname of McMahon 1983: *m* 1st, 1965 (*m diss* 1980), Micaela Fredericka, da of late Edgar H. Maus, of Hamilton, Ohio, USA; 2ndly, 1983, Hanora Carmel, yst da of late Joseph McMahon, of Nenagh, co Tipperary, and has issue living (by 1st *m*), Michael Chalmers Wilbraham *b* 1966, (by 2nd *m*) Oisín Patrick *b* 1984, Rian Charles *b* 1986, — Brian Arthur Wilbraham, *b* 1945, — Patrick Chalmers Wilbraham (259 Lea Bridge Rd, E10), *b* 1955: *m* 1988, Julia Catherine, da of Dorian Cresswell Cooke, and has issue living, Liam Patrick Alexander *b* 1988, James Chalmers Dorian *b* 1991, — Beatrice Mary Wilbraham (18 Bellwood Av, Ottawa, Ontario, Canada), *b* 1948: *m* 1st, 1968 (*m*

diss 1976), Sydney Douglas Saunders; 2ndly, 1983, Gerald Adrian Bol, elder son of late Gerrit Bol, of Utrecht, Netherlands, and Essex, Ontario, and has issue living (by 2nd *m*), Kieran Gerrit *b* 1986. *Residence* – Killrian, Slane, co Meath.
—— Sheela Wilbraham FitzJohn, *b* 1907: *m* 1st, 1929, Diarmid Coffey, who *d* 1964; 2ndly, 1971, Erwin Strunz, of Clonmannon Village, Ashford, co Wicklow, and has issue living (by 1st *m*), Donal Manus George (Glendarragh Hill, Newtownmountkennedy, co Wicklow), *b* 1935: *m* 1959, Patricia Ann, da of late Daniel Taylor, of Glasgow, and has issue living, Aedan Diarmid Cailean *b* 1961, Fiona Ann Champagné *b* 1962, — Saive Frances Mary, *b* 1930, — Helen Dairine, *b* 1933.

Grandchildren of late Frederic Herbert Trench, elder son (but only son by 1st *m*) of late William Wallace Trench, 2nd son of late Rev Frederick FitzJohn Trench (ante):—
Issue of late Waldo Trench Fox, MC, *b* 1892, *d* 1954, having assumed by deed poll 1934 the names of Waldo Trench Fox in lieu of Wallace Talbot Trench: *m* 1933, Janet Mary Kennedy, who *d* 1987, da of MacIvor Bassett, of Lelant, Cornwall:—
Robert Trench FOX, CBE (Cheriton House, Alresford, Hants), *b* 1937; *ed* Winchester, and Univ Coll, Oxford (MA); CBE (Civil) 1993: *m* 1962, Lindsay Garrett, da of Sir Donald Forsyth Anderson, of The Manor, Notgrove, Glos, and has issue living, Barclay Trench, *b* 1971, — Caspar Lloyd, *b* 1972, — Fenella Garrett, *b* 1964: *m* 1990, John Francis Dernie, of Cirencester, — Tamara Forsyth, *b* 1967. —— Jill Trench, *b* 1935: *m* 1st, 1955, Lieut Rodney Francis Power Carne, RN, who *d* 1959; 2ndly, 1961, Capt Donald Barns Morison, RN, and has issue living (by 1st *m*), Rupert Barclay Power, *b* 1958, — Nicola Trench, *b* 1957: *m* 1985, Eric McClean, of co Tyrone, and has issue living, Angus Carne *b* 1990, Kirsten Valentine *b* 1988, — (by 2nd *m*) Barnaby Daniel Barns, *b* 1964, — Candida Trench, *b* 1963: *m* 1990, Robin Spencer, of The Wirral, and has issue living, Samuel Peter Nelson *b* 1992. *Residence* – Boskenna, St Martin in Meneage, Helston, Cornwall. —— Rachel Trench, *b* 1943: *m* 1965, Raymond Joseph Morin, of 52 Bellevue Av, Haverhill, Mass, USA.
Issue of late Desmond Patrick Trench, *b* 1893, *d* 1967: *m* 1st, 1916, Elfrida Mary Eliott, who *d* 1942, da of Rev Daniel Eliott Young, sometime V of St Mary's Penzance; 2ndly, 1947, Hilda Olive, who *d* 1993, da of A. A. J. Akhurst, of Lyncrest, Southbourne, Hants:—
(By 1st *m*) Anthony Barclay (c/o Trench Electrics Ltd, 390 Midwest Rd, Scarborough, Ontario, Canada M1P 3B5), *b* 1919; AMIEE (England); Consulting Engr, Ontario; 1939-45 War as Fl-Lieut RAFVR (prisoner): *m* 1st, 1940, Sheila Mary, da of Lawrence Lois Keith, of Hastings, Sussex; 2ndly, 1981, Doris Lynne, da of Alvin Radcliffe James, of St Elizabeth, Jamaica, and has issue living (by 1st *m*), Simon Patrick, *b* 1946. —— Heather Mavis, *b* 1925: *m* 1948, Robin Krohn Pooley, sometime Headmaster of Dane Court Sch, Pyrford, Woking, Surrey, and has issue living, Peter John (18 Rivermead Rd, St Leonards, Exeter, Devon EX2 4RL), *b* 1950; *ed* Bryanston: *m* 1986, Lynn Kimber, and has issue living, Alice Jane *b* 1990, — Catherine Susan (adopted da), *b* 1958: *m* 1984, Robert Darke, of Cour de la Bruyère, 27210 Manneville la Raoult Beuzeville, France, and has issue living, Jason Paul *b* 1980, Georgia *b* 1985, Jessica *b* 1989, Madeleine Barbara *b* 1991. *Residence* – Auburn, 48 Belmore Lane, Lymington, Hants SO41 9NN.

Granddaughters of late William Wallace Trench (ante):—
Issue of late Claud Llewellyn (Pomeroy) Trench, *b* 1881, *d* 1945: *m* 1911, Annie Elizabeth, who *d* 1972, eldest da of late William Charles Davis, of Cheltenham, Glos:—
Eileen Elizabeth, *b* 1917: *m* 1937, Cecil H. F. Knight, and has issue living, Bernard Cecil Frank, *b* 1939; Coldm Gds: *m* 1965, Jacqueline Ann, da of William John Rudkin, of 94 Heacham Drive, Leicester, and has issue living, Paul *b* 1968, — Elizabeth Ann (The Birches, 11A Willow Park Drive, Wigston, Leicester): *b* 1937: *m* 1956 (*m diss* 1973), John David Heighton, and has issue living, David Peter *b* 1957, Brian John *b* 1958: *m* 1977, Ellen Lucell Glover (and has issue living, Richard James Brian *b* 1981, Alexander Charles Luke *b* 1983, Claire Samantha Lucell *b* 1978), Suzanne Elizabeth *b* 1961, — Catherine Beryl, *b* 1945: *m* 1968, Patrick James Roddy, of 5 Highcroft, Husbands Bosworth, Leics, and has issue living, Christopher James *b* 1970, Paula Louise *b* 1972, — Hazel Mary, *b* 1949: *m* 1975, Martin Oliver, of 9 Dalby Rd, Anstey, Leics, and has issue living, Neil Edward Llewellyn *b* 1985, Heidi Joanne *b* 1974, Gwen Georgina *b* 1976, Jaqui Eve Marie *b* 1979, Ruth Christina *b* 1982. *Residence* – 51 Oadby Rd, Wigston Magna, Leicester LE18 3RP. —— Jean Olive, *b* 1922; is a registered Sick Children's Nurse: *m* 1944, Denis S. W. Foreman, RASC, and has two adopted children, Martin John (15 Midland Cottages, S Wigston, Leics LE8 2BU), *b* 1957: *m* 1989, Sarah J. M. Colbert, and has issue living, Ian James *b* 1990, — Jill Rosemary (47 Winford Crescent, Leicester LE13 1TA), *b* 1948: *m* 1st, 1973 (*m diss* 1980), Alan Egginton; 2ndly, 1990, Michael Andrew Wilcox, and has issue living (by 1st *m*), Robert John *b* 1975, David Paul *b* 1979. *Residence* – 61 Roehampton Drive, Wigston Fields, Leicester LE8 1HU.

Grandchildren of late Col Ernest Frederic Crosbie Trench, CBE, TD, eldest son of late George Frederick Trench (infra):—
Issue of late Dermot George Crosbie Trench, *b* 1904, *d* 1984: *m* 1938, Nancy Muriel (O'NEIL) (El Mirador, MG-CA19, Javea, Alicante, Spain), da of late Dr Stewart Arthur Smith, of Sydney, NSW:—
Anthony Crosbie, *b* 1941. —— Patricia Ann, *b* 1944: *m* 1976, Roger A. Nuttall, of 48 Grayton Rd, NW3, and has issue living, Tom Oliver, *b* 1977, — Peggy Ellen Nan, *b* 1980.
Issue of late Brian Morley Crosbie Trench, *b* 1908, *d* 1979: *m* 1938, Harriett Milward, who *d* 1981, da of late John Lyons Agnew, of Ontario:—
Jonathan Agnew (29 West Parade, Norwich), *b* 1939; *ed* Gordonstoun, and Ch Ch, Oxford (BA 1963): *m* 1969, Sarah, da of Don Cameron Williams, of Kansas City, USA, and has issue living, Mary Olivia, *b* 1972. —— Amanda Milward (184 Kensington Park Rd, WI1), *b* 1941: *m* 1961 (*m diss* 1979), Jonathan Radice, and has issue living, James Heneage, *b* 1961, — Daniel Brett, *b* 1967.
Issue of late Fl-Lieut Desmond Ernest Crosbie Trench, *b* 1911, *ka* 1941: *m* 1937, Dorothy Waugh (who *m* 2ndly, 1953, Maj William Spencer), da of late Maj H. C. Shewell, RGA:—
Josephine Crosbie, *b* 1938: *m* 1965, David McCowan, and has issue living, Jonathan David, *b* 1965, — Deborah Kate, *b* 1967. —— Kerry Deborah (*posthumous*), *b* 1941: *m* 1965, Michael Honnor, of Wilkeysmoor, Cornwood, Ivybridge, Devon, and has issue living, Julius Desmond, *b* 1973, — Seth Michael, *b* 1976.
Issue of late Peter Crosbie Trench, *b* 1912, *d* 1969: *m* 1st, 1941 (*m diss* 1946), Nan Dorice Hunter; 2ndly, 1947, Joy Seymour (26 Manor Drive, Wembley Park, Middx), da of late H. Shave, of Calcutta:—
(By 2nd *m*) Colin Crosbie, *b* 1949: *m* 1st, 1972 (*m diss* 1975), Susan Ann Saunders; 2ndly, 1976, Susan Wooldridge, and has issue living (by 2nd *m*), Jacqueline, *b* 1979, — Joanna, *b* 1984, — Michelle, *b* 1985.

Grandson of late George Frederick Trench, 3rd son of late Rev Frederic FitzJohn Trench (ante):—
Issue of late William Launcelot Crosbie Trench, CIE, *b* 1881, *d* 1949: *m* 1st, 1910, Margaret Zephanie, who *d* 1934, da of Rev W. P. Huddleston; 2ndly, 1935, Eileen Beatrice Cecil, who *d* 1980, da of Henry C. Marsh:—
(By 1st *m*) George Shan Crosbie (105 Walsall Rd, Four Oaks, Sutton Coldfield, Warwicks B74 4NP), *b* 1913; *ed* Stowe; Lt-Col RA (ret); 1939-45 War in Middle East (despatches): *m* 1945, Myrtle Sheila, da of H. Jerrett, of Meols, Cheshire, and has issue living, Barney George Crosbie (83 Rue Marie Therese, Brussels 1040), *b* 1947; *ed* St Edward's, Oxford, and St Catherine's Coll, Oxford (BA): *m* 1982, Marjorie (Midge) Shirley, — Margaret Felicity, *b* 1953.

Granddaughter of late William Launcelot Crosbie Trench, CIE (ante):—
Issue of late Sir David Clive Crosbie Trench, GCMG, MC, *b* 1915, *d* 1988: *m* 1944, Margaret, who *d* 1993, da of late Jay D. Gould, of New York, USA:—
Katherine Elizabeth, *b* 1956: *m* 1984, Christopher John Down, of 5a Bronsart Rd, SW6 6AJ, son of late Frederick William Down.

Granddaughter of late John Trench, 6th brother of 1st Baron:—
Issue of late James Currie Trench, b 1848, d 1936: m 1883, Annie Gertrude, who d 1944, elder da of late John Haughton, of Ardreigh, Athy, co Kildaire:—
Amy Feodora, b 1896: m 1922, James Alfred Stuart Watt, who d 1975, and has issue living, Lionel Robert (3 Ystrad Buildings, Trethomas, Newport, Mon), b 1924: m 1959, Elizabeth Maureen Buckley. Residence – 36 Castlwood Park, Rathmines, Dublin 6.

PREDECESSORS – (1) FREDERIC Trench, MP for Portarlington in the Irish Parliament, was cr Baron Ashtown (peerage of Ireland) 1800, with remainder to the heirs of his deceased father; d 1840; s by his nephew (2) FREDERIC MASON, 2nd Baron, b 1804: m 1st, Harriet, who d 1845, da of Thomas Phillips Cosby, of Stradbally Hall, Queen's co; 2ndly, 1852, Elizabeth, who d 1893, da and co-heir of Richard Oliver Gascoigne, of Parlington, Yorkshire; d 1880; s by his grandson (3) FREDERIC OLIVER (son of late Hon Frederic Sydney Charles Trench eldest son of 2nd Baron), 3rd Baron, b 1868; was a Representative Peer for Ireland 1908-15: m 1894, Violet Grace, who d 1945, yst da of Col Robert Ushworth Godolphin Cosby, of Stradbally Hall, Queen's co; d 1946; s by his eldest surviving son (4) ROBERT POWER, 4th Baron, b 1897: m 1st, 1926 (m diss 1938), Geraldine Ida, who d 1940, da of Sir Henry Foley Grey, 7th Bt; 2ndly, 1950, Oonah Anne, who d 1984, eldest da of late Brig-Gen Lewis Frederic Green-Wilkinson, CMG, DSO; d 1966; s by his brother (5) Dudley Oliver, OBE, 5th Baron, b 1901; Lt-Col KRRC; OBE (Civil) 1961: m 1st, 1932, Ellen Nancy, who d 1949, da of late William Garton, of Brixedon, Bursledon, Hants; 2ndly, 1955, Sheelah Adrienne Sarah, who d 1963, yr da of late Brig-Gen Lewis Frederic Green-Wilkinson, CMG, DSO; 3rdly, 1966, Frances Natalie, who d 1979, da of Maj Hermon Barker-Hahlo, and widow of Maj James Fenwick de Sales La Terriere; d 1979; s by his kinsman (6) CHRISTOPHER OLIVER (son of late Algernon Oliver Trench, 3rd son of late Hon William Cosby Trench, brother of 3rd Baron), 6th Baron, b 1931; Canadian Imperial Bank of Commerce 1950-57; dunm 1990; s by his kinsman (7) NIGEL CLIVE COSBY, KCMG (son of late Clive Newcome Trench, son of late Capt Hon Cosby Godolphin Trench, 2nd son of 2nd Baron), 7th Baron and present peer.

ASKWITH, BARONY OF (Askwith) (Extinct 1942)

DAUGHTER LIVING OF FIRST BARON

Hon Betty Ellen, b 1909; FRSL; author: m 1950, Keith Miller Jones who d 1978. Residence – 9/105 Onslow Sq, SW7.

Asquith, Viscount; son of Earl of Oxford and Asquith.

ASQUITH OF BISHOPSTONE, BARONY OF (Asquith) (Extinct 1954)

SON LIVING OF LIFE BARON

Hon Luke, b 1919; ed Winchester; 1939-45 War in N Africa, and Italy as GOC III and Liaison Officer 8th Army; a Company Dir: m 1954, (Ethel) Meriel, da of Maurice C. Evans, of Arrow Lawn, Eardisland, Herefordshire, and has issue living, Lucy, b 1962: m 1988, Nicholas John Troop, yr son of Robert Troop, of Barnes, SW, and has issue living, Vanessa Charlotte b 1990, Laura Alexandra b 1993, — Anne (Hon Mrs Roderick A. Cavendish), b 1965: m 1989, Hon Roderick Alexander Cavendish, only son of 7th Baron Waterpark, and has issue (see B Waterpark). Residence – The Paddock, Broad St, Alresford, Hants SO24 9AN.

DAUGHTER LIVING OF LIFE BARON

Hon Frances Rose (Hon Lady Stephenson), b 1925: m 1951, Rt Hon Sir John Frederick Eustace Stephenson (see E Shrewsbury, colls, 1960 Edn), and has issue living, David Guy, b 1954, — Daniel Paul, b 1960, — Mary, b 1952: m 1972, Philippe G. Wines, and has issue living, Daniel Philippe Glyn b 1983, Katharine Valerie Rose b 1972, Polly Victoria Jane b 1976, Lucy Helen Mary b 1979, — Laura Jane, b 1958: m 1st, 1980, D. J. Nicholas Bodington, son of late Maj W. J. Bodington, DFC, of Manor Farm, Beercrocombe, Som; 2ndly, 1987, Andrew F. Sykes, yr son of late Sir Richard Adam Sykes, KCMG, MC, of Wilsford-cum-Lake, Salisbury, Wilts, and has issue living (by 2nd m), Matthew John b 1991, Amelia Anne b 1989. Residence – 26 Doneraile St, SW6.

WIDOW LIVING OF SON OF LIFE BARON

Caroline Anne (41 Quarrendon St, SW6), yr da of Sir John Gawen Carew Pole, 12th Bt (cr 1628), DSO, TD: m 1963, as his 2nd wife, Hon Paul Asquith, who d 1984, and has issue (see E Oxford and Asquith, colls).

ASQUITH OF YARNBURY, BARONY OF (Bonham Carter) (Extinct 1969)

SONS LIVING OF LIFE BARONESS

Hon Mark Raymond, b 1922; cr Baron Bonham-Carter (Life Baron) 1986 (see that title).
Hon Raymond Henry (7 West Heath Av, NW11), b 1929; Lt Irish Gds: m 1958, Elena, da of late Don Eduardo Propper de Callejon, and has issue living, Edward Henry, b 1960, — Thomas David, b 1961: m 1990, Virginia Catherine Elizabeth, 2nd da of Nigel Sharp, of Brick House, Gt Bardfield, Essex, and has issue living, Freddy b 1990, Rose Violet b 1992, — Helena, b 1966; actress.

DAUGHTER LIVING OF LIFE BARONESS

(Hon) Helen Laura Cressida (does not use courtesy title) (Keeper's Cottage, Gt Bottom, Stockton, Warminster, Wilts), *b* 1917: *m* 1939, Jasper Alexander Maurice Ridley, Lt KRRC, who *d* on active ser in Italy 1943, and has issue (*see* V Ridley, colls).

ASTOR, VISCOUNT (Astor) (Viscount UK 1917)

To the stars

WILLIAM WALDORF ASTOR, 4th Viscount; *b* 27 Dec 1951; *s* 1966; *ed* Eton; a Lord in Waiting 1990-93; Dept of National Heritage 1992-93; Parly Under Sec, Dept of Social Security since 1993: *m* 1976, Annabel Lucy Veronica, da of Timothy Angus Jones (*see* B Clifford of Chudleigh, colls, 1985 Edn), and formerly wife of Reginald Adrian Berkeley Sheffield (now Sir Reginald Sheffield, 8th Bt), and has issue.

Arms – Or, a falcon resting on a dexter hand couped at the wrist, proper and gauntleted gules in chief two fleurs-de-lys of the last. **Crest** – From a mount vert a falcon rising proper, ensigned by three mullets gold. **Supporters** – *Dexter*, a North American Indian; *sinister*, a North American fur trapper; each habited, accoutred, and holding in the exterior hand a rifle, all proper.
Residences – Ginge Manor, Wantage, Oxon; 27 Egerton Gdns, SW3 2DE.

SONS LIVING

Hon WILLIAM WALDORF, *b* 18 Jan 1979.
Hon James Jacob, *b* 1981.

DAUGHTER LIVING

Hon Flora Katherine, *b* 1976.

HALF-SISTERS LIVING (*Daughter of 3rd Viscount by 2nd marriage*)

Hon Emily Mary, *b* 1956; photographer: *m* 1st, 1984, Alan McL. Gregory, elder son of Donald Gregory, of San Francisco, California, USA; 2ndly, 1988, as his 2nd wife, James Ian Anderson (*see* E Perth). *Residence* – 14 Shalcomb St, SW10 0HX.

(*Daughters of 3rd Viscount by 3rd marriage*)

Hon Janet Elizabeth (*Countess of March and Kinrara*), *b* 1961; *ed* New Coll, Oxford (BA), and King's Coll, London (MA): *m* 1991, as his 2nd wife, Charles Henry, Earl of March and Kinrara, only son of 10th Duke of Richmond. *Residences* – Goodwood, Chichester, W Sussex PO18 0PX; 7 Charles St, W1X 7HB.
Hon Pauline Marian, *b* 1964: *m* 1990, George C. V. Case, son of late Denis Case, of Marlow, Bucks, and has issue living, Magdalena Beatrice, *b* 1994. *Residence* – Turville Lodge, Turville Heath, Oxon.

UNCLES LIVING (*Sons of 2nd Viscount*)

Hon (Francis) David Langhorne, CH, *b* 1912; *ed* Eton, and Balliol Coll, Oxford; late Capt RM; Editor of *The Observer* 1948-75; 1939-45 War (Croix de Guerre) CH 1994: *m* 1st, 1945 (*m diss* 1951). Melanie, da of Philip Hauser, of Berne, Switzerland; 2ndly, 1952, Bridget Aphra, da of Maj Cyril Wreford, of Yew Tree House, Goosey, Faringdon, Berks, and has issue living (by 1st *m*), Frances Christine Langhorne, *b* 1947: *m* 1970, Dr Miles Frankel, of Kilbrack House, Doneraile, co Cork, — (by 2nd *m*), Richard David Langhorne, *b* 1955: *m* 1990, Sarah G. H., da of James Skinner, and has issue living, Bonny Jane *b* 1992, — Thomas Robert Langhorne, *b* 1962, — Alice Margaret Frances, *b* 1953: *m* 1st, 1972 (*m diss* 1985), Lawrence Woodward; 2ndly, 1987, Mark Thomas Luke Grindon-Welch, of Stockadon Farm, Loddiswell, Kingsbridge, Devon TQ7 4EQ, and has issue living (by 1st *m*), William Lawrence *b* 1978, Jessica Alice *b* 1980, (by 2nd *m*) Adam Thomas Richard *b* 1988, Rose Aphra Elizabeth *b* 1991, — Lucy Aphra Nancy, *b* 1958, — Nancy Bridget Elizabeth, *b* 1960: *m* 1990, Séan V. Naidoo, of 89 Carlton Mansions, Randolph Av, NW1 8UG, son of Stanley Naidoo, of Johannesburg, and has issue living, Cara Mary *b* 1992. *Residences* – 9 Cavendish Av, NW8 9JD; Manor House, Sutton Courtenay, Oxon.
Hon Sir John Jacob, MBE, *b* 1918; *ed* Eton, and New Coll, Oxford; late Maj Life Gds, and DL for Cambs; Chm, Agric Research Council 1968-78; N-W Europe 1944-45 (MBE, Legion of Honour, French Croix de Guerre); MP for Sutton Div of Plymouth (C) 1951-59; MBE (Mil) 1945; Kt 1978: *m* 1st, 1944 (*m diss* 1972), Ana Inez, who *d* 1992, da of late Senor Dr Don Miguel Angel Carcano, KCMG, KBE, sometime Argentine Ambassador in London; 2ndly, 1976, Mrs Susan Sheppard, da of late Maj Michael Eveleigh, 3rdly, 1988, Mrs Marcia de Savary, and has issue living (by 1st *m*), Michael Ramon Langhorne, *b* 1946: *m* 1979, Daphne, da of late Edward Mortimer Morris Warburg, of Westport, Conn, USA, — Stella (Cwm Hall, Clunton, Craven Arms, Shropshire), *b* 1949: *m* 1974 (*m diss* 19—), Martin Wilkinson, and has issue living, Matthew MiguelAngel *b* 1977, Alice AnaMaria *b* 1975. *Residence* – The Dower House, Hatley Park, Hatley St George, Sandy, Beds SG19 3HL.

MOTHER LIVING

Hon Sarah Katherine Elinor Norton (42 Melton Court, Old Brompton Rd, SW7 3JH), da of 6th Baron Grantley: *m* 1st, 1945 (*m diss* 1953), the 3rd Viscount, who *d* 1966; 2ndly, 1953 (*m diss* 1965), Maj Thomas Michael Baring, Derbyshire Yeo (*see* B Northbrook, colls).

WIDOW LIVING OF SON OF SECOND VISCOUNT

Judith Caroline Traill, da of Paul Innes, and formerly wife of John Moynihan (son of late Rodrigo Moynihan, CBE, portrait painter): *m* 1970, as his 3rd wife, Hon Michael Langhorne Astor, 3rd son of 2nd Viscount, who *d* 1980, and has issue (see colls infra).

WIDOW LIVING OF THIRD VISCOUNT

Janet Bronwen Alun (*Bronwen, Viscountess Astor*) (Tuesley Manor, Tuesley, Godalming, Surrey); psychotherapist; da of late His Honour Sir (John) Alun Pugh: *m* 1960, as his 3rd wife, the 3rd Viscount, who *d* 1966.

COLLATERAL BRANCHES LIVING

Descendants of late Hon John Jacob Astor, 2nd son of 1st Viscount, who was cr *Baron Astor of Hever* 1956 (see that title.)

Issue of late Hon Michael Langhorne Astor, 3rd son of 2nd Viscount, *b* 1916, *d* 1980: *m* 1st, 1942 (*m diss* 1961), Barbara Mary Colonsay, who *d* 1980, only da of late Capt Ronald Frank Rous McNeill; 2ndly, 1961 (*m diss* 1968), (Patricia David) Pandora, who *d* 1988, 2nd da of late Hon Sir Bede Edmund Clifford, GCMG, CB, MVO, FRGS (*see* B Clifford of Chudleigh, colls), and formerly wife of Timothy Angus Jones; 3rdly, 1970, Judith Caroline Traill (ante), da of Paul Innes, and formerly wife of John Moynihan (son of late Rodrigo Moynihan, CBE, portrait painter):—

(By 1st *m*) David Waldorf, CBE (Bruern Grange, Milton-under-Wychwood, Oxon), *b* 1943; *ed* Eton, and Harvard Univ; Chm Council for the Protection of Rural Eng; CBE 1994: *m* 1968, Clare Pamela, da of Cdr Michael Beauchamp St John, DSC, RN (*see* B St John of Bletso, colls), and has issue living, Henry Waldorf, *b* 1969, — Thomas Ludovic David, *b* 1972, — Joanna Colonsay Clare, *b* 1970, — Rose Nancy Langhorne, *b* 1979. —— James Colonsay Langhorne, *b* 1945; *ed* Eton: *m* 1972, Jane M. S., da of Charles de Chazal, of 11 Ossington St, W2, and has issue living, Tobias, *b* 1980, — Katharine Tamsin, *b* 1976. —— (Kathleen Nancy) Jane, *b* 1949. —— Georgina Mary, *b* 1952: *m* 1st, 1973 (*m diss* 1979), Hon Anthony Ramsay, 2nd son of 16th Earl of Dalhousie; 2ndly, 1979, (Thomas) Lorne Nelson, of Kilmaronaig, Connel, Argyll (*see* By Queenborough, 1990 Edn), and has issue living (by 1st *m*) (*see* E Dalhousie), — (by 2nd *m*) Thomas Michael, *b* 1979, — Alice Catherine, *b* 1981, — Clare Emma, *b* 1983. —— (By 3rd *m*) Polly Michael, *b* 1971. —— The Hon Michael Astor also adopted his stepson, Joshua Paul Michael Astor, *b* 1966.

PREDECESSORS – (1) WILLIAM WALDORF Astor, only son of John Jacob Astor, of New York; *b* 1848; United States Min to Italy 1882-5; naturalised 1899; cr *Baron Astor*, of Hever Castle, co Kent (peerage of United Kingdom) 1916, and *Viscount Astor*, of Hever Castle, co Kent (peerage of United Kingdom) 1917: *m* 1878, Mary Dahlgren, who *d* 1894, da of James W. Paul, of Philadelphia; *d* 1919; *s* by his eldest son (2) WALDORF, 2nd Viscount, *b* 1879; Chm of Directors of *The Observer*, and High Steward of Maidenhead; European War 1914-17 as temporary Major and Inspector of QMG Sers (despatches); Parliamentary Private Sec to Prime Min 1917-18, Parliamentary Sec to Min of Food 1918, and to Local Govt Board Jan to June 1919 (also Chm National Health Insurance Joint Committee Feb to June 1919), and first Parliamentary Sec to Min of Health 1919-21; appointed Hon Col Devon and Cornwall, Heavy Brig RA (TA) 1933; Chm of R Institute of International Affairs 1939-49, and of League of Nations Committee on Nutrition 1936-37; Lord Mayor of Plymouth 1939-44; MP for Plymouth (C) 1910-18, and for Sutton Div thereof 1918-19: *m* 1906, Nancy Witcher, CH, DLitt (first woman to sit in the House of Commons), who *d* 1964, da of late Col Chiswell Dabney Langhorne, of Mirador, Greenwood, Virginia, USA, and formerly wife of Robert Gould Shaw; *d* 1952; *s* by his eldest son (3) WILLIAM WALDORF, 3rd Viscount; *b* 1907; PPS to First Lord of the Admiralty 1936-37, and to Home Sec 1937-39; MP for E Fulham (C) 1935-45, and for Wycombe 1951-52: *m* 1st, 1945 (*m diss* 1953), Hon Sarah Katharine Elinor Norton, da of 6th Baron Grantley; 2ndly, 1955 (*m diss* 1960), Philippa Victoria, da of Lt-Col Henry Philip Hunloke (*see* D Devonshire, 1980 Edn); 3rdly, 1960, Janet Bronwen Alun, da of His Honour Sir (John) Alun Pugh; *d* 1966; *s* by his only son (4) WILLIAM WALDORF, 4th Viscount, and present peer; also Baron Astor.

ASTOR OF HEVER, BARON (Astor) (Baron UK 1956)

To the stars

JOHN JACOB ASTOR, 3rd Baron, *b* 16 June 1946; *s* 1984; *ed* Eton; Life Gds 1966-70: *m* 1st, 1970 (*m diss* 1990), Fiona Diana Lennox, da of Capt Roger Edward Lennox Harvey, of Parliament Piece, Ramsbury, Wilts (*see* Mainwaring, Bt, ext, 1990 Edn); 2ndly, 1990, Hon Mrs Elizabeth Constance Chagrin, yr da of 2nd Viscount Mackintosh of Halifax, and has issue by 1st and 2nd *m*.

Arms – Argent eight barrulets sable over all resting on a dexter hand couped at the wrist proper gauntleted gules a falcon also gules in chief two fleurs de lys of the last. **Crest** – Rising from a mount vert a falcon proper ensigned by three mullets or. **Supporters** – *Dexter*, the figure of Aesculapius, and *sinister*, that of Mercury, both proper.
Residence – Frenchstreet House, Westerham, Kent TN16 1PW. *Clubs* – House of Lords Yacht, Riviera Golf.

SON LIVING *(By 2nd marriage)*

Hon CHARLES GAVIN JOHN, *b* 10 Nov 1990.

DAUGHTERS LIVING *(By 1st marriage)*

Hon Camilla Fiona, *b* 1974.
Hon Tania Jentie, *b* 1978.

Hon Violet Magdalene, *b* 1980.

(by 2nd marriage)

Hon Olivia Alexandra, *b* 1992.

BROTHER LIVING

Hon Philip Douglas Paul, *b* 1959; *ed* Eton, and Ch Ch, Oxford. *Residence* – Flat 3, 6 Embankment Gdns, SW3 4LJ.

SISTERS LIVING

Hon Bridget Mary, *b* 1948: *m* 1st, 1980 (*m diss* 1986), Count Arthur Tarnowski, yr son of late Count Hieronim Tarnowski, of Rudnik nad Sanem, Poland; 2ndly, 1989, Geofrey Richard Smith, 4th son of late James William Smith, of Eywood House,

Titley, Hereford, and has issue living (by 1st husband), (John) Sebastian Gavin, b 1981, — Lucian Francis Philip, b 1984, — (by 2nd husband) Moya Morvenna Irene, b 1987. *Residence* – Sellack House, Sellack, Ross-on-Wye, Herefords HR9 6QP.

Hon (Elizabeth)˙ Louise, b 1951: m 1st, 1979 (m diss 1981), David John Shelton Herring; 2ndly, 1985, David Joseph Ward, FRCS, son of Joseph Ward, FRCOG, of Tancrey, Fordwich, Canterbury, Kent, and has issue living (by 2nd m), Oliver Gavin Joseph, b 1985, — Victoria Mary, b 1987. *Residence* – Sauvey Castle Farm, Withcote, Oakham, Leics LE15 8DT.

Hon Sarah Violet, b 1953: m 1975, Hon George Edward Lopes, and has issue (see B Roborough). *Residence* – Gnaton Hall, Yealmpton, Plymouth, Devon PL8 2HU.

UNCLES LIVING (Sons of 1st Baron)

Hon Hugh Waldorf, b 1920; ed Eton, and New Coll, Oxford; Dep Chm of Times Publishing Co Ltd 1959-66, a Dir of Hambro's Ltd 1960-91, Phoenix Assurance Co Ltd 1962-85, Winterbottom Trust Ltd 1961-86, and Olympia Ltd (Exec Vice Chm 1971-73); Dep Chm of Middlesex Hosp 1962-64; a Member of Fishmongers' Co (Prime Warden 1976-77) and a JP for Berks; High Sheriff of Berks 1963-64; a Gov of Bradfield Coll, and Greshams Sch (ret), a Trustee of Forte Ltd (Chm of Council of Trustees since 1971); 1939-45 War as Lt-Col Intelligence Corps: m 1950, Emily Lucy, da of Sir Alexander Davenport Kinloch, 12th Bt, and has issue living, Robert Hugh, b 1958: m 1991, Diana M., da of late Dr Louis Murray, of Johannesburg, — James Alexander Waldorf, b 1965, — Virginia Lucy (*Madam McGillycuddy of the Reeks*), b 1951: m 1984, Richard Denis Wyer McGillycuddy, The McGillycuddy of the Reeks, and has issue living, Tara Virginia b 1985, Sorcha Alexandra b 1990, — Rachel Mary (*Hon Mrs Nicholas Ward*), b 1955: m 1985, Hon (Edward) Nicholas Ward, yr son of 7th Viscount Bangor, and has issue (see V Bangor), — Jean Violet, b 1961: m 1982, John Maximilian Halford-Thompson, yr son of Lt-Col Peter Halford-Thompson, MC, of Manor Lodge, Longworth, Abingdon, and has issue living, Guy b 1986, Hugh Maximilian b 1988, Ralph Mark b 1993. *Residences* – Folly Farm, Sulhamstead, Berks RG7 4DF; 79 Ashley Gdns, Thirleby Rd, SW1P 1HG. *Clubs* – Brooks's, Buck's, Royal Yacht Squadron, Royal Ocean Racing.

WIDOW LIVING OF SON OF FIRST BARON

Penelope Eve, da of late Cdr George Francis Norton Bradford, RN, and formerly wife of late David Rolt: m 1982, as his 2nd wife, Hon John Astor, yst son of 1st Baron, who d 1987. *Residence* – Paxmere House, Peasemore, Newbury, Berks RG16 0JH.

WIDOW LIVING OF SECOND BARON

Lady IRENE VIOLET FREESIA JANET AUGUSTA HAIG (*Irene, Baroness Astor of Hever*), da of Field Marshal 1st Earl Haig, KT, GCB, OM, GCVO, KCIE: m 1945, the 2nd Baron, who d 1984. *Residences* – 11 Lyall St, SW1X 8DH; Hollytree House, Frenchstreet, Westerham, Kent, TN16 1PW.

COLLATERAL BRANCH LIVING

Issue of late Hon John Astor, yst son of 1st Baron, b 1923, d 1987: m 1st, 1950, Diana Kathleen, who d 1982, da of late George Henry Drummond (see E Perth, colls, 1980 Edn); 2ndly, 1982, Penelope Eve (ante), da of late Cdr George Francis Norton Bradford, RN, and formerly wife of late David Rolt:—
(By 1st m) (John) Richard, b 1953: m 1977, Katherine Mary, da of Brig Sir Jeffrey Lionel Darell, 8th Bt, MC, and has issue living, Charles John, b 1982, — Emily Mary, b 1980, — Tamara Sarah Diana, b 1989. *Residence* – Kirby House, Inkpen, nr Newbury, Berks. —— (George) David, b 1958: m 1983, Marianne Piroska Julia, only da of John Hurleston Leche, of Carden, Cheshire, and has issue living, Thomas David, b 1987, — Amy Violet, b 1989. —— Elizabeth Kathleen, b 1951.

PREDECESSORS – (1) *Hon* JOHN JACOB Astor, 2nd son of 1st Viscount Astor, b 1886; Ch Proprietor of *The Times Newspaper* 1922-66, Chm of Middx Hosp 1938-62, and of Middx Hosp Med Sch 1945-62; MP for Dover (U) 1922-45; cr *Baron Astor of Hever*, of Hever Castle, Kent (peerage of (UK) 1956): m 1916, Lady Violet Mary Elliot, who d 1965, da of 4th Earl of Minto, and widow of Maj Lord Charles George Francis Mercer-Nairne, CVO (M Lansdowne); d 1971; s by his eldest son (2) GAVIN, 2nd Baron, b 1918; Chm Times Publishing Co 1959-66, and Co-Chief Proprietor *The Times* 1962-66, Life Pres Times Newspapers Ltd 1967-84, Dir Alliance Assurance Co Ltd 1954-84, Pres of Council Commonwealth Press Union 1972-75 (Chm 1959-72), Chm of Council R Commonwealth Soc 1972-75; Lord Lieut of Kent 1972-82, High Sheriff of Sussex 1955-56, Seneschal of Canterbury Cathedral 1973-83, Prime Warden Worshipful Co of Goldsmiths 1981-82; 1939-45 War as Capt Life Gds: m 1945, Lady Irene Violet Freesia Janet Augusta Haig, da of FM 1st Earl Haig, KT, GCB, OM, GCVO, KCIE; d 1984; s by his elder son (3) JOHN JACOB, 3rd Baron and present peer.

ATHLONE, EARLDOM OF (Cambridge) (Extinct 1957)

DAUGHTER DECEASED OF FIRST EARL

Lady May Helen Emma (*Lady May Abel Smith*), b 23 Jan 1906; is a CStJ: m 24 Oct 1931, Col Sir Henry Abel Smith, KCMG, KCVO, DSO, late RHG, who d 24 Jan 1993 (see D Somerset, colls, 1951 Edn), and d 30 May 1994, leaving issue, Richard Francis Abel (Blidworth Dale, Ravenshead, Notts), b 11 Oct 1933; ed Eton; High Sheriff Notts 1978, Vice Lord Lieut 1991; late Capt RHG, cmd Sherwood Rangers Sqdn, Royal Yeo Regt 1967-69 (Hon Col 1979-89): m 28 April 1960, Marcia, High Sheriff Notts 1990, and DL 1993; da of late Maj-Gen Sir Douglas Anthony Kendrew, KCMG, CB, CBE, DSO, and has issue living, Katharine Emma (*Hon Mrs Hubert Beaumont*), b 11 March 1961: m 16 Oct 1980, Hon Hubert Wentworth Beaumont, eldest son of Baron Beaumont of Whitley (and has issue living, George Wentworth b 24 Aug 1985, Richard Christian b 27 May 1989, Michael b 23 April 1991, Amelia May b 12 Nov 1983), — Anne Mary Sibylla, b 28 July 1932: m 14 Dec 1957 (m diss 1982), David Ian Liddell-Grainger (see E Lindsey, 1976 Edn), and has issue living, Ian Richard Peregrine b 23 Feb 1959: m 31 Oct 1985, Jill, only da of (Ralph) Nicol Nesbit, of Greenlaw, Berwickshire (and has issue living, Peter Richard b 6 May 1987, Sophy Victoria b 27 Dec 1988, May Alexandra b 9 Sept 1992), Charles Montagu b 23 July 1960: m 23 Jan 1992, Karen Peta, only da of Peter Humphryes, of St Luke's St, SW3, Simon Rupert b 27 Dec 1962: m 26 Jan 1984, Romana Maria, only da of late Roman Emmanuel Anton Rogoshewski, of Montreal, Canada, and formerly wife of Philippe Guillaume Perrot, Malcolm Henry b 14 Dec 1967: m 1 Aug 1994, Helen J., elder da of Jeremy Bright, Alice Mary b 3 March 1965: m 13 Aug 1990, Pietro Panaggio, eldest son of Giuseppe Panaggio, of Castelvetere in Valfortore, Italy, — Elizabeth Alice, b 5 Sept 1936: m 29 April 1965 (m diss 1974), Peter Ronald Wise. *Residence* – Barton Lodge, Winkfield, Windsor.

ATHOLL, DUKE OF (Murray) (Duke S 1703)

GEORGE IAIN MURRAY, 10th Duke; *b* 19 June 1931; *ed* Eton, and Ch Ch, Oxford; *s* 1957; a Representative Peer for Scotland 1958-63; Chm Westminster Press 1974 and RNLI 1979-89; Vice Pres Nat Trust for Scot since 1977; Pres Internat Sheepdog Soc 1982-83, and 1988-89.

𝔄rms – Quarterly: 1st paly of six or and sable, *Atholl*: 2nd, or a fess checky azure and argent, *Stewart*: 3rd argent, on a bend azure three stags' heads cabossed or, *Stanley*: 4th, gules, three legs in armour proper, garnished and spurred or, flexed and conjoined in triangle at the upper part of the thigh, *Ensigns of Isle of Man*: over all an inescutcheon en surtout azure three mullets argent, within a double tressure flory, ensigned of a Marquess's coronet: *Chiefship of the name of Murray and Marquessate of Tullibardine*. 𝔈rests – 1st, a mermaid holding in her dexter hand a mirror, and in her sinister a comb, all proper, *Murray*, 2nd, a demi-savage proper, wreathed about the temples and waist with laurel, his arms extended, and holding in the right hand a dagger, in the left a key, all proper, *Atholl*; 3rd, a peacock's head and neck proper, accompanied on either side by two arms from the elbow proper, and vested in maunches azure doubled argent. 𝔖upporters – *Dexter*, a savage proper, wreathed about the temples and loins with juniper, his feet in fetters, the chain held in his right hand proper; *sinister*, a lion rampant gules, armed and langued azure, gorged with a plain collar of the last charged with three mullets argent. 𝔐ottoes – (above the crests) *Dexter*—Tout Prest (Chiefship of Name and Arms of Murray). *Centre*— Furth Fortune and Fill the Fetters (Dukedom of Atholl). *Sinister*—Praite.

Seat - Blair Castle, Blair Atholl, Perthshire. *Residence* - 31 Marlborough Hill, NW8. *Clubs* - Turf, White's and New (Edinburgh).

COLLATERAL BRANCHES LIVING

Granddaughter of late Rev George Edward Murray, eldest son of late Rt Rev George Murray, DD, Bishop of Rochester, 2nd son of late Rt Rev Lord George Murray, DD, Bishop of St David's, 2nd son of 3rd Duke:—
Issue of late Col Arthur Mordaunt Murray, CB, MVO, *b* 1852, *d* 1920: *m* 1st, 1895, Isabel, who *d* 1896, da of Richard Laurence Pemberton, formerly of Hawthorn Tower, Seaham Harbour, Durham; 2ndly, 1898, Mabel, who *d* 1964, eldest da of Frederick Francis Nicolson, formerly of Seaforth, Lancs.—
(By 2nd *m*) Olive Penelope, MBE (*Lady Norton*), *b* 1908; MBE (Civil) 1968: *m* 1st, 1928 (*m diss* 1942), Charles Russell Wood; 2ndly, 1948, Sir (Walter) Charles Norton, MBE, MC, Solicitor, who *d* 1974, and has issue living (by 1st *m*) Peter, *b* 1930. *Residences* - 23 Hans Place, SW1; Little Granthams, Chiddingfold, Surrey.

Granddaughters of late Col Arthur Mordaunt Murray, CB, MVO (ante):—
Issue of late Lt-Col Godfrey Pemberton Murray, DSO, Seaforth Highlanders, *b* 1901, *d* 1985: *m* 1934, Mary Isabel, da of J. Brownlee, of Middlesbrough:—
Susan Elizabeth, *b* 1935: *m* 1959, David Hill, of 95 Clarendon Rd, W11, son of Cdr George Walter Hill, RN, of Orlestone Grange, Ham St, Kent, and has issue living, Simon Sebastian, *b* 1961, — David Alexander, *b* 1964, — Tobias Hunter, *b* 1967. —— Mary Jennifer, *b* 1939: *m* 1964, James Vickers, of 45 Beever Rd, Ashford, Kent, and has issue living, Sandra, *b* 1965.

Granddaughters of late Col Walter Murray, OBE, MC, RE (infra):—
Issue of late Donald Stuart Murray, *b* 1917, *d* 1985: *m* 1948, Margaret Ann, da of Ernest Simmons, of The Glebe House, Boughton Aluph, Ashford, Kent:—
Elizabeth Anne, *b* 1949: *m* 1978, John Kneafsey Kelsey, and has issue living, Emily Jane, *b* 1981, — Victoria Louise, *b* 1983, — Henrietta Jean, *b* 1987. —— Jean Margaret, *b* 1951: *m* 1975, Nils Bertil Eidestedt, and has issue living, Richard Nils Donald, *b* 1987, — Jessica Maria, *b* 1976, — Karin Marie, *b* 1981.

Grandchildren of late Rev Douglas Stuart Murray, 3rd son of Rev George Edward Murray (ante):—
Issue of late Col Walter Murray, OBE, MC, RE, *b* 1882, *d* 1945: *m* 1911, Evelyn, who *d* 1976, da of William E. Adie, of The Rowans, Buxton, Derbyshire:—
Jean Pamela, *b* 1920: *m* 1947, Col James Andrew Fraser, MC, of Tomuaine, Tomich, by Beauly, Inverness-shire, and has issue living, Simon John, *b* 1950, — Donald James, *b* 1951, — Jean Catherine, *b* 1954: *m* 1973, Daniel Letts.
Issue of late Maj George Murray, *b* 1884, *ka* 1940: *m* 1928, Joan (Box 111, Louis Trichardt 0920, N Transvaal), da of late William Eastwood, of Buffelspoort, Mara, N Transvaal:—
JOHN, *b* 19 Jan 1929: *m* 1956, Margaret Yvonne, only da of late Ronald Leonard Leach, of Louis Trichardt, N Transvaal, and has issue living, Bruce George Ronald, *b* 1960: *m* 1984, Lynne Elizabeth, eldest da of Nicholas Andrew, of Bedfordview, S Africa, and has issue living, Michael Bruce John *b* 1985, David Nicholas George *b* 1986, Nicole *b* 1987, — Craig John, *b* 1963: *m* 1988, Inge, 2nd da of Auke Bakker, of Bedfordview, S Africa, and has issue living, Carl *b* 1993, — Jennifer, *b* 1958: *m* 1979 (*m diss* 1985), and has issue living, Grant Clive PURDON *b* 1981, Charlene PURDON *b* 1983. *Address* - PO Box 137, Haenertsburg 0730, S Africa.

Granddaughter of late Sir Herbert Harley Murray, KCB, 4th son of late Rt Rev George Murray, DD, Bishop of Rochester (ante):—
Issue of late Major Stewart Lygon Murray, *b* 1863, *d* 1930: *m* 1895, Harriet Sophia, who *d* 1948, da of late Col John Clark Kennedy, CB (*see* E Brownlow, colls, 1914 Edn):—
Christian Charlotte (1 Verandah Cottages, Cricket Green, Hartley Wintney, Hants), *b* 1904: *m* 1937, Ronald Peers Williams, who *d* 1968, and has issue living, Richard Murray, *b* 1947: *m* 1980, Linda, da of Dennis Akehurst, of Denbury, 199 Loxley Rd, Stratford-upon-Avon, and has issue living, David *b* 1983, Benjamin *b* 1984, — Jennifer Mary, *b* 1940: *m* 1965, Colin Willmott, of 43 Princess Rd, NW1, and has issue living, Giles Benedict Paddington *b* 1967, Victoria *b* 1965, — Susan *b* 1942, — Penelope Ann, *b* 1944: *m* 1971, Abraham Wax, of 219 E 69th St, New York 10021, NY, USA, and has issue living, David Israel *b* 1980, Rebecca *b* 1981.

Grandchildren of late Gerald Otway Hay Murray (infra) —
Issue of late Herbert Frederick Murray, *b* 1906, *d* 1971: *m* 1942, Doris Mary Rowsel (Grove Cottage, Stoke St Mary, nr Taunton):—
Kathleen Elizabeth (c/o Grove Cottage, Stoke St Mary, nr Taunton), *b* 1943: *m* 1969, Richard John May, Capt 2nd Bn LI, and has issue living, Amanda Jane, *b* 1969, — Emma Louise May, *b* 1972.

Issue of late Douglas Gerald Murray, *b* 1907, *d* 1980: *m* 1940, Brenda, who *d* 1986, da of Earle R. Waight:—
Julian Charles, *b* 1946. *Address* – c/o R South Australian Yacht Sqdn, Outer Harbour, S Australia 5018.
    Issue of late Stewart Hay Murray, *b* 1909, *d* 1988: *m* 1939, Freda Woodland (Folly House, Folly Lane, Lacock, Wilts):—
John Stewart (Houndall Wood, Sparkwell, Plymouth), *b* 1940: *m* 1970, Alison, da of Humphrey Trembath, of Reigate, and has issue living, Charles Humphrey Stewart, *b* 1971, — Jennifer Mary Ellen, *b* 1974. —— Peter Gerald Stewart (31 Priory Av, W4), *b* 1944: *m* 1967, Jane, da of Alexander Wood, of Ashtead, and has issue living, Rupert Hay, *b* 1969, — William Alexander, *b* 1972, — Sophie Elizabeth, *b* 19—, — Alice Adelaide, *b* 1981. —— Geoffrey Charles Stewart (46 Rylett Rd, W12 9ST), *b* 1948: *m* 1983, C. Lynne, da of Stewart Murray, of Ealing, and has issue living, James Stewart, *b* 1983, — George Andrew Stewart, *b* 1986.

        Grandsons of late Sir Herbert Harley Murray, KCB (ante):—
    Issue of late Gerald Otway Hay Murray, *b* 1868, *d* 1951: *m* 1905, Charlotte, who *d* 1944, yst da of Dudley George Cary-Elwes, formerly of Conway, Florida, USA:—
Arthur Frank (3 Androse Gdns, The Bickerley, Ringwood, Hants), *b* 1911: *m* 1937, Ruby Joyce Hooper, and has issue living, Ann Jennifer, *b* 1939: *m* 1959, Neil Jarman, of Bramley Cottage, 97 Gorley Rd, Ringwood, Hants BH24 1TN, and has issue living, Ian *b* 1960: *m* 1989, Elizabeth Caroline Foster (and has issue living, Stephen Andrew *b* 1994), Frances Ann *b* 1962: *m* 1989, Richard Allen (and has issue living, Jennifer Helen *b* 1992), Rebecca *b* 1965. —— Keith Robert (2 Windrush Place, Northmoor, Oxford), *b* 1912; formerly in RE: *m* 1941, Ellen Woodland, and has issue living, Andrew Keith, *b* 1946, — Joan Ursula, *b* 1945. —— Kathleen Margaret August (Grove Cottage, Stoke St Mary, Taunton), *b* 1916.

        Grandchildren of late Rev Frederick Auriol MURRAY-GOURLAY (who assumed additonal surname of Gourlay), eldest son of late Rev Frederick William Murray, yst son of Rt Rev George Murray, DD Bishop of Rochester (ante):—
    Issue of late (George) Ronald Auriol MURRAY-GOURLAY, *b* 1900, *d* 1961: *m* 1926, Phyllis, who *d* 1978, da of late Walter Langford Rowley, of Edgbaston, and Birlingham Grange, Worcs:—
Brian Austin Walter MURRAY-GOURLAY (The Old Smithy, School Lane, S Chard, Som), *b* 1927; late RN: *m* 1st, 1953 (*m diss* 1962), Margaret, yr da of William Bryant, of Elmsleigh, Cribbs Causeway, Glos; 2ndly, 1973, Patricia Mary, yr da of Daniel Eric Fewtrell, of Dudley, Worcs, and formerly wife of Charles Desmond Small, and has issue living (by 1st *m*), Hugh William Auriol (2 Vale View Cottages, Milton Lilbourne, Pewsey, Wilts), *b* 1960: *m* 1987, Fiona Joan, yst da of Capt John Rumble, of 88 Wroughton Rd, SW11, and of Lymington, Hants, and has issue living, Alice Auriol *b* 1992. —— Auriol Mary, *b* 1933: *m* 1957, Capt Frederick Ernest Herring, R Norfolk Regt, of The Dairy House, Watery Lane, Upwey, Weymouth, Dorset DT3 5QD, and has issue living, Jonathan James Auriol, *b* 1959, — Christopher John Murray, *b* 1962.

        Grandchildren of late Rev Charles Hay Murray, 2nd son of late Rev Frederick William Murray (ante):—
    Issue of late Sir (Francis) Ralph Hay Murray, KCMG, CB, *b* 1908, *d* 1983: *m* 1935, Countess Mauricette Vladimira (35 Vicarage St, Woburn Sands, Milton Keynes MK17 8RE), only child of late Count Bernhard Kuenburg, of Payerbach, Austria:—
Ingram Bernard Hay, TD (23 Dunton Rd, Stewkley, Leighton Buzzard, Beds), *b* 1937; *ed* Bedford Sch, and St Edmund Hall, Oxford; Lt-Col RE, TARO: *m* 1963, Juliet Anne Thackeray, da of late Capt J. M. T. Ritchie, and has issue living, Alistair James Hay, *b* 1968, — Xenia Margaret Thackeray, *b* 1966, — Francesca Helen Anne, *b* 1970. —— Nicholas Julyan Edward (The Old Vicarage, Aston Abbots, Aylesbury, Bucks), *b* 1939: *m* 1973, Caroline Anne, eldest da of Capt Alan McClintock, of Prospect House, Nenagh, co Tipperary, and has issue living, Anstice Aileen Thérèse, *b* 1981. —— Simon Anthony (46 St Leonard's Rd, Exeter, Devon), *b* 1948: *m* 1975, Lesley-Ann, JP, da of Robert Freeman-Wright, of Larks Cottage, Treen, Cornwall, and has issue living, Joshua Robert Darroch, *b* 1980, — Hannah Lisl, *b* 1982. —— Georgina Teresa, *b* 1942: *m* 1965, Roy Ashworth, of 55 Half Moon Lane, Dulwich, SE24, and has issue living, Simon, *b* 1966, — Jessica, *b* 1968.
    Issue of late Stephen Umfreville Hay Murray, RASC and ABCA, Capt (1938-46), actor (Stephen Murray), *b* 1912, *d* 1983: *m* 1937, Joanna Alestha, da of John Joseph Moy Butterfield, of London:—
Amanda, *b* 1942; actress: *m* 1975, George Tarry, of The Old Stables, Roeheath, Cinder Hill, Chailey, E Sussex BN8 4HR.

        Granddaughters of late Rev Frederick William Murray (ante):—
    Issue of late Rev Maurice William Murray, *b* 1870, *d* 1943: *m* 1909, Eva Margaret, who *d* 1958, da of Charles Hubback Watson, formerly of Stone Castle, Greenhithe, Kent:—
Kathleen Joan (Burwash Place, Burwash, E Sussex), *b* 1911: *m* 1958, Alfred E. Roberts, who *d* 1976. —— Ursula Mary (89 High St, Tenterden, Kent), *b* 1919: *m* 1941, Alan A. White, late Maj Border Regt, who *d* 1993, and has issue living, Christopher Douglas (11 Cornwall Mews South, Grenville Place, SW7 4RZ), *b* 1943: *m* 1987, Maria Eulalia Pessoa, and has issue living, Douglas Alan Pessoa *b* 1987, — David Ian (twin) (2 Balliol Cottages, Wadhurst, E Sussex), *b* 1943: *m* 1972, Margaret Ann Griffith, and has issue living, Jonathan Alan *b* 1974, Daniel Edmund *b* 1977.

        Grandsons of late Capt Rupert Auriol Conant Murray, Seaforth Highlanders, 4th son of late Col Charles Edward Gostling Murray (infra):—
    Issue of late Col Anthony Ian Rupert Murray, OBE, Seaforth Highlanders, *b* 1914, *d* 1993: *m* 1944, Alexandra Elizabeth Barbara Patience, who *d* 1991, only da of late Lt-Col Douglas William Alexander Dalziel Mackenzie, CVO, DSO, of Farr, Inverness:—
John Rupert (Old Cardinham, Bodmin, Cornwall PL30 4ED), *b* 1945: *m* 1977, Valerie Margaret, da of late Eric V. Sanders, and has issue living, Edward Ian, *b* 1977, — George John, *b* 1980. —— (Ian) James, *b* 1947; *ed* Eton, and RMA Sandhurst; Lt-Col Queen's Own Highlanders: *m* 1976, Christina Anne, yr da of late Arthur Carr, MC, and has issue living, Emma Juliette, *b* 1977, — Clare Patience Frances, *b* 1979, — Alice Christina, *b* 1983. —— Andrew Edward, *b* 1950; *ed* Gordonstoun, and Dijon Univ.

        Grandsons of late Col Charles Edward Gostling Murray, yr son of late Rev Edward Murray, 4th son of late Rt Rev Lord George Murray, DD, Bishop of St David's (ante):—
    Issue of late Stracey Montagu Atholl Murray, *b* 1888, *d* 1970: *m* 1926, Irene Margaretta, who *d* 1972, yr da of Capt William W. Waring:—
Edward William Atholl (Highfield, Derby Rd, Haslemere, Surrey), *b* 1927: *m* 1st, 1959, Anne Oakeley, who *d* 1972, da of late Maj Loraine Macgregor Kerr, MC (*see* Oakeley, Bt, 1967 Edn); 2ndly, 1974, Elizabeth Dawn, da of late H. D. Harman, MC, and has issue living (by 1st *m*), James Henry Atholl, *b* 1960, — Charlotte Melloney Loraine, *b* 1964. —— Fane Robert Conant (Park House Farm, Baldersdale, Barnard Castle, co Durham), *b* 1929: *m* 1962, Margaret Carsina, da of late Lt-Col Leslie George Gray-Cheape, MBE, JP, DL, of Carse Gray, Forfar, Angus, and has issue living, Rupert Charles, *b* 1963, — Emma Jane, *b* 1965.

        Grandson of late George Delmé-Murray, 3rd son of Vice-Adm James Arthur Murray, only son of Lord William Murray, 3rd son of 3rd Duke:—
    Issue of late Major George Arthur Delmé Murray, DSO, *b* 1879, *d* 1944: *m* 1906, Dorothea Emily Anne, who *d* 1938, da of late T. Alexander Webb, of Waynwern, Monmouthshire:—
George Philip Alexander DELMÉ MURRAY, DSO, MBE, *b* 1921; Lt-Col KSLI; formerly Maj IA; Burma 1943-45 (wounded, DSO); DSO 1945, MBE (Mil) 1966; *m* 1951, Alison Elizabeth, yr da of Col William John Beddows, MC, TD, JP, DL, of Ackleton House, nr Wolverhampton, and has issue living, Caroline Alison, *b* 1953: *m* 1979, John William Howson, of The Dingle,

Ditton Priors, Bridgnorth, Shropshire, and has issue living, William George Frederick *b* 1982, Edward James Philip *b* 1985, — Rosemary Janet, *b* 1956: *m* 1979, James Frederick Budgett, of Park Farm, Kirtlington, Oxon OX5 3JQ, and has issue living, Charles George Arthur *b* 1981, Georgina Patricia Alison *b* 1985 *Residence* – Yew Tree Cottage, Knowbury, Ludlow, Shropshire.

Granddaughters of late Rev Richard Paget Murray, eldest son of Col Henry Murray, RA (infra):—
Issue of late Capt Henry James Stewart Murray, RE, *b* 1874, *d* 1942: *m* 1919, Maude Amelia (who *d* 1974, having *m* 2ndly, 1947, Thomas Rosser-Dummer, of Cape Town, S Africa), yst da of George Jonathan Mills, of Norwich:—
Margaret Dorothea *b* 1926: *m* 1946, Stanley Alastair Miller, and has issue living, Pamela Ann (No 1 Shiraz, 26 Arum Rd, Bloubergrant, CP, S Africa), *b* 1949, — Sheila Frances, *b* 1950: *m* 1981, Anthony John Foxcroft, of Roodepoort, Transvaal, S Africa, and has issue living, Samantha Elizabeth *b* 1986, — Wendy Margaret, *b* 1954: *m* 1st, 1977 (*m diss* 1982), David Foxcroft; 2ndly, 1989, Mark Everingham, of 44 Slim St, Melville, Hamilton, NZ, and has issue living (by 1st *m*), Neil Alastair *b* 1979, Debrin Eileen *b* 1981, (by 2nd *m*) Katherine *b* 1991. *Residence* – La Tremouille, 104 Third Ave, Bredell, Transvaal 1623. *Address* – PO Box 14204, Bredell, Transvaal, S Africa.
Issue of late Rev Athole Evelyn Murray, *b* 1881, *d* 1962: *m* 1917, Ellen Emily, who *d* 1960, da of Henry Frederic Tiarks:—
Anne (67B High St, Codford, nr Warminster, Wilts), *b* 1920; BMus Durham: *m* 1954, John Edward Page, who *d* 1964, and has issue living, Edward John Atholl, *b* 1956, — Henry Stewart Murray (twin), *b* 1956, — Thomas Patrick Murray, *b* 1960, — Susan Margaret, *b* 1955: *m* 1974 (*m diss* 1986), Julian Marc Piers Bryant, and has issue living, Polly Louise *b* 1976, Sophie Katherine *b* 1978, Emma Charlotte *b* 1980.

Granddaughters of late Maj Henry Francis Farquharson Murray, Black Watch, only son of late Lt-Col Henry Murray, 2nd son of late Col Henry Murray, RA, only son of Lt-Col Richard Murray, only son of Lord Henry Murray, 4th son of 3rd Duke:—
Issue of late Lt-Col Ian Henry Murray, MC, RHF, *b* 1916, *d* 1990: *m* 1940, Eleanor Fownes, who *d* 1983, da of late Rev Geoffrey Lionel Porcher, formerly R of Weston-super-Mare:—
Alison Fownes, *b* 1947: *m* 1970, Oliver William Wilkins, of Victoria House, St Keyne, Liskeard, Cornwall PL14 4SG, and has issue living, Geoffrey James Murray, *b* 1976, — Andrea Caroline Fownes, *b* 1975. —— Jacqueline Dorothea Fownes (13 Wheatley Way, Chalfont St Peter, Bucks SL9 0JE), *b* 1942.

Grandchildren of late Rev Arthur Silver Murray, 6th son of late Col Henry Murray, RA (ante):—
Issue of late Arthur Evelyn Francis Murray, *b* 1888, *d* 1972: *m* 1927, Louise Isabelle (Amesbury Abbey, Amesbury, Wilts), da of Lt-Col Addis Delacombe, DSO, of Shrewton Manor, nr Salisbury:—
James Stewart, *b* 1941; *ed* Stellenbosch Univ (BSc Agric): *m* 1979, Susan Janet Elizabeth, widow of Air Vice Marshal Thomas James Hanlon, CB, CBE, and da of Wyndham John Williams, of Great Oak, Gwent, and has issue living, Duncan William, *b* 1980, — Henry Stewart, *b* 1983, — Angus Iain, *b* 1983 (twin). *Residence* – Lewtrenchard Manor, Lewdown, nr Okehampton, Devon. — Jean Evelyn Louise (White Lodge, Startley, Chippenham, Wilts), *b* 1932; *ed* Stellenbosch Univ (BA): *m* 1959, Maj Jonathan Beresford Oliphant, 7th Duke of Edinburgh's Own Gurkha Rifles (ret), and has issue living, Angus Laurence, *b* 1966, — Catriona Jane, *b* 1960, — Janet Elizabeth, *b* 1963.
Issue of late Douglas Vivian Murray, *b* 1905, *d* 1976: *m* 1st, 1932 (*m diss* 1958), Isabel Mary Farquhar, da of Dr Andrew Grierson Fausset-Farquhar, of Bridgeton House, St Cyrus, Kincardineshire; 2ndly, 1958, Beryl Violet (No 6 Courtmead Cottages, Southstoke, Bath BA2 7EB), da of Lt-Col John Henry Wybergh, Sherwood Foresters (ret), of Heath Brow, Ewshot, Farnham, Surrey:—
(By 2nd *m*) Hamish Douglas (136 Wellsway, Bath), *b* 1959; Merchant Navy: *m* 1993, Kate Watson. —— Andrew Vivian (No 2 Cottages, Newbarns, Inverkeilor, Arbroath, Angus), *b* 1961; RM: *m* 1988, Anne Towns, and has issue living, James Andrew, *b* 1988, — Claire Beryl, *b* 1991. —— Anne Beryl de la Trémoïlle, *b* 1963: *m* 1988, George Coronis, and has issue living, Douglas Michael, *b* 1990, — Clementine Aspasia, *b* 1989, — Portia Marie Violet, *b* 1993.

Grandchildren of late Hugh Percy Murray-Aynsley, son of John Murray-Aynsley, son of Very Rev Lord Charles Murray-Aynsley, 5th son of 3rd Duke:—
Issue of late Charles Percy Murray-Aynsley, *b* 1862, *d* 1936: *m* 1st, 1911, Ina Winifred, who *d* 1917, da of late H. H. Prins, MD; 2ndly, 1921, Gladys, who *d* 1959, da of late Francis Turnor:—
(By 2nd *m*) Francis Percy, *b* 1924: *m* 1950, Diana Gray, da of W. Gray Young, of Lowry Bay, Wellington, NZ, and has issue living, Charles William Percy, *b* 1955, — Susan Jane, *b* 1951, — Bridget Anne, *b* 1952. *Residence* – Wi Waka, Eketahuna, NZ. —— (By 1st *m*) Elizabeth, *b* 1912: *m* 1935, John Duncan Simpson, and has issue living, Charles William, *b* 1936, — Duncan Murray, *b* 1938: *m* 1961, Judith Margaret Mary, da of H. Simmons, of Hawkes Bay, NZ, and has issue living, Michael Paul *b* 1961, Toby Duncan *b* 1963, — Patricia Mary, *b* 1940. *Residence* – Dalvey, Turakina, New Zealand.

(In special remainder to Dunedom)

Descendants of Lord Charles Murray (2nd son of 1st Marquess), who was *cr* Earl of Dunmore (see that title).

PREDECESSORS – (1) Sir JOHN MURRAY, PC, 12th feudal Baron of Tullibardine, was *cr Lord Murray of Tullibardine* (peerage of Scotland) 1604, and *Earl of Tullibardine* (peerage of Scotland) 1606; *d* 1609; *s* by his eldest son (2) WILLIAM, 2nd Earl; appointed Hereditary Sheriff of Perthshire 1600 for rescuing the King at Perth from the attempt of the Earl of Gowrie; he *m* Lady Dorothea Stewart, da of John, 5th and last Earl of Atholl, Charles I having on petition agreed to revive the Earldom of Atholl on the issue of the Countess of Tullibardine, the Earl by consent of the crown resigned his dignities to his brother Patrick (see * infra); *d* 1626; *s* by his son (3) JOHN, *cr Earl of Atholl* (peerage of Scotland) 1629: *d* 1642; *s* by his son (4) JOHN, KT, 2nd Earl, who on the death of his cousin James in 1670 became 5th Earl of Tullibardine; *cr Marquess of Atholl, Earl of Tullibardine, Viscount of Balquhidder*, and *Lord Murray, Balvany and Gask* (peerage of Scotland with remainder to heirs male of his body) 1676; *d* 1703; *s* by his eldest son (5) JOHN, KT, 2nd Marquess; *cr* (in his father's lifetime) *Earl of Tullibardine, Viscount Glenalmond*, and *Lord Murray* (peerage of Scotland for life) 1696, *Lord Murray, Balvenie and Gask, Viscount of Baluhidder, Glenalmond, and Glenlyon, Earl of Strathtay and Strathardle, Marquess of Tullibardine* and *Duke of Atholl* (peerage of Scotland) 1703, with special remainder failing heirs male of his body to those of his father; his eldest surviving son having joined the Earl of Mar 1715, was charged with high treason, and attainted by Parliament; *d* 1724; *s* by his 2nd son (6) JAMES, KT, 2nd Duke, upon whom the family honours were settled by Act of Parliament; on the death of the 10th Earl of Derby, he *s* through his grandmother to the *Barony of Strange* (peerage of England, *cr* 1628), and the Sovereignty of the Isle of Man; *d* 1764, when the Barony of Strange and the Sovereignty of the Isle of Man devolved upon his da Charlotte, and the Scotch honours reverted to his nephew (eldest son of Lord George Murray, 5th son of the 1st Duke) (7) JOHN, KT, 3rd Duke, who *m* his cousin Charlotte, Baroness Strange (ante); the Duke and Duchess disposed of their Sovereignty in the Isle of Man to the British Govt for £70,000; *d* 1774; *s* by his eldest son (8) JOHN KT, 4th Duke, *cr Baron Murray of Stanley* and *Earl Strange* (peerage of Great Britain) 1786, and *s* to English Barony of Strange 1805; he disposed of his remaining property and privileges in the Isle of Man to the crown for £409,000; *d* 1830; *s* by his son (9) JOHN, 5th Duke; *d* 1846; *s* by his nephew (eldest son of James, 1st *Baron Glenlyon* (peerage of United Kingdom, *cr* 1821), 2nd son of 4th Duke) (10) GEORGE AUGUSTUS FREDERICK JOHN, KT, 6th Duke, *b* 1814; *s* his father as 2nd *Baron Glenlyon* 1837: *m* 1839, Anne, VA, who *d* 1897, da of late Henry Home Drummond, of Blair Drummond, Perth; *d* 1864; *s* by his son (11) JOHN JAMES HUGH HENRY, KT, 7th Duke, *b* 1840; in 1865 inherited *Barony of Percy* (*cr* by writ 1722, peerage of Great Britain) and registered at Lyon Court his assumption of the surname of Stewart before his patronymic; was Lord-Lieut of

Perthshire 1878-1917; in 1893 reverted to the original form of spelling the title ("Atholl" instead of "Athole"): *m* 1863, Louisa, who *d* 1902, eldest da of Sir Thomas Moncrieffe, 7th Bt; *d* 1917; *s* by his eldest son **(12)** JOHN GEORGE, KT, GCVO, CB, DSO, TD, PC, 8th Duke *b* 1871; Lord-Lieut of Perthshire; appointed Lord High Commr to Gen Assembly of Ch of Scotland 1918, 1919, and 1920; was Lord Chamberlain of the Household 1921-2; Nile Expedition 1898 (DSO), South Africa 1899-1902, in command of two Regts of Scottish Horse (which he raised) with rank of Lieut-Col, European War 1914-19 in Gallipoli and Egypt, with Regts of Scottish Horse (which he raised), and Comdg a Scottish Horse Brig, and subsequently 8th and 10th Cyclist Brigs (CB); an ADC to HM 1920-31; sat as MP for Perthshire, W Div (*C*) 1910-17: *m* 1899, Katharine Marjory, DBE, LLD, DCL, MP, who *d* 1960, da of Sir James Henry Ramsay, 10th Bt, of Banff; *d* 1942; *s* by his brother **(13)** JAMES THOMAS, 9th Duke; *b* 1879; formerly Major Queen's Own Cameron Highlanders; *d* 1957, when the Barony of Strange (peerage of England cr 1628) fell into abeyance (*see* Bs Strange); the Barony of Percy, cr by writ 1722 (peerage of Great Britain) passed to the Duke of Northumberland, and the Earldom of Strange (peerage of Great Britain) 1786, and the Baronies of Murray of Stanley (peerage of Great Britain) 1786, and of Glenlyon (peerage of UK), 1821, became ext; *s* in his other peerages by his kinsman **(14)** GEORGE IAIN, 10th Duke (son of late Lt-Col George Anthony Murray, OBE, RA, son of late Sir (George) Evelyn Pemberton Murray, KCB, grandson of late Rev George Edward Murray, grandson of Rt Rev Lord George Murray, DD, 2nd son of 3rd Duke), 10th Duke and present peer; also Marquess of Atholl, Marquess of Tullibardine, Earl of Atholl, Earl of Tullibardine, Earl of Strathtay and Strathardle, Viscount of Balwhidder, Glenalmond and Glenlyon, Lord Murray, Balvenie, and Gask, and Lord Murray of Tullibardine.

*****(1)** *Hon* PATRICK MURRAY was cr *Earl of Tullibardine* and *Lord Murray of Gask* (Peerage of Scotland) 1628, with remainder to his heirs male whatsoever, presumably with original precedence of 1606 and 1604 respectively, in consequences of resignation of that Earldom and Lordship by his brother, 2nd Earl of Tullibardine; *b* 15—: *m* Elizabeth, who *d* before 1656, da and co-heir of John Dent, of London, and widow of Francis Vere; *d* 1644; *s* by his son **(2)** JAMES, 4th Earl of Tullibardine, *b* 1617: *m* 1st, 1643, Lady Lilias Drummond, da of 2nd Earl of Perth; 2ndly, 1664, Lady Anne Murray, da of 1st Earl of Atholl (ante); 3rdly, 1667, Lilias (who *m* 2ndly, 16—, James Drummond, 4th Earl of Perth), da of Sir James Drummond of Machany; *d* 1670; *s* by his kinsman **(3)** JOHN Murray, 2nd Earl of Atholl (ante).

ATKIN, BARONY OF (Atkin) (Extinct 1944)

DAUGHTER LIVING OF LIFE BARON

Hon Elizabeth; Bar Gray's Inn 1955: *m* 1st, 1932, John Kennedy Cockburn Millar, Bar-at-Law, who *d* 1952; 2ndly, 1960, His Honour Judge Denis Hicks Robson, QC, who *d* 1983. *Residence* – Woodsford, Dreemskerry, I of Man.

ATTENBOROUGH, BARON (Attenborough) (Life Baron 1993)

RICHARD SAMUEL ATTENBOROUGH, CBE, son of late Frederick Levi Attenborough; *b* 29 Aug 1923; *ed* Wyggeston Gram Sch for Boys, Leicester, and at RADA; Hon DLitt Leicester 1970, Kent 1981, and Sussex 1987, Hon DCL Newcastle 1974, Hon LLD Dickinson Penn 1983, Fellow BAFTA 1983, BFI 1992 and King's Coll, London 1993; served RAF 1943-46 as Flt Sgt Airgunner and Cameraman; Actor, Film Producer and Dir; appeared in more than fifty films inc *In Which We Serve* 1942, *Brighton Rock* 1948, *The Angry Silence* 1959, *The Great Escape* 1962, *Seance on a Wet Afternoon* 1963, *Guns at Batasi* 1964, *The Flight of the Phoenix* 1965, *The Sand Pebbles* 1966, *10 Rillington Place* 1970, *Jurassic Park* 1992, and *Miracle on 34th Street* 1994; Producer *Whistle Down The Wind* 1961, *The L-Shaped Room* 1962, (and Dir) *Oh! What A Lovely War* 1969; Dir *Young Winston* 1972, *A Bridge Too Far* 1977, *Magic* 1978; Producer and Dir *Ghandi* 1980-81, *A Chorus Line* 1985, *Cry Freedom* 1987, *Chaplin* 1992, *Shadowlands* 1993; Chm BAFTA 1969-70 (Vice-Pres since 1971), RADA since 1970, Capital Radio 1972-92, Help A London Child since 1975, UK Trustees Waterford-Kamhlaba Sch, Swaziland since 1976, Duke of York's Theatre 1979-82, BFI 1982-92, Goldcrest Films and TV 1982-87, Channel 4 TV 1987-92; Dir Young Vic 1974-84, Gov National Film Sch 1970-81; Trustee Tate Gallery 1976-82, Tate Foundation since 1986, and Foundation for Sport and the Arts since 1991; Pro-Chancellor Sussex Univ since 1970; Freeman City of Leicester 1990; associated with many artistic and charitable fund-raising organisations; Cdr Ordre des Arts et des Lettres, Chevalier Légion d'Honneur, France; *cr* CBE (Civil) 1967, Knt 1976, and *Baron Attenborough*, of Richmond upon Thames in the London Borough of Richmond upon Thames (Life Baron) 1993: *m* 1945, Sheila Beryl Grant, JP (actress Sheila Sim), da of late Stuart Grant Sim, of Hove, Sussex, and has issue.

Clubs - Garrick, Beefsteak.

SON LIVING

Hon Michael John, *b* 1950; *ed* Westminster, and Sussex Univ (BA); Exec Producer and Dir RSC: *m* 1st, 1971 (*m diss* 1976), Jane (actress as Jane Seymour), da of late Benjamin John Frankenberg, MRCS, LRCP, FRCOG, of Hillingdon, Middx; 2ndly, 1984, Karen Esther, yr da of late Sydney Victor Lewis, of SW1, and has issue living (by 2nd *m*), Thomas Frederick Richard, *b* 1986, — William Grant Oliver, *b* 1991.
Address – c/o Royal Shakespeare Company, Barbican, EC2Y 8BQ.

DAUGHTERS LIVING

Hon Jane Mary, *b* 1955; *ed* Lady Eleanor Holles Sch, and Sussex Univ; arts admin: *m* 1982, Michael Holland, 2nd son of George Holland, of Heathfield, Sussex, and has issue living, Samuel George William, *b* 1984, — Alice Jane, *b* 1987, — Lucy Elizabeth, *b* 1989.
Hon Charlotte Isabel, *b* 1959; *ed* Lady Eleanor Holles Sch, and Bristol Univ; actress: *m* 1993, Graham Sinclair.

ATTLEE, EARL (Attlee) (Earl UK 1955)

Labour conquers all

JOHN RICHARD ATTLEE, 3rd Earl; *b* 3 Oct 1956; *s* 1991; *ed* Stowe: *m* 1993, Celia Jane, yst da of Dexter Plummer, of Bishops Stortford, Herts.

Arms – Azure, on a chevron, or, between three hearts of the last winged argent, as many lions rampant sable. **Crest** – On a mount vert two lions rampant addorsed or. **Supporters** – On either side a Welsh terrier sejant proper. *Address* – c/o House of Lords, SW1.

SISTER LIVING

Lady Jane Elizabeth, *b* 1959.

AUNTS LIVING (*daughters of 1st Earl*)

Janet Helen, *b* 1923; does not use courtesy title having taken American citizenship 1973: *m* 1947, Harold William Shipton, and has issue living, Ann Helen, *b* 1948: *m* 1969 (*m diss* 1994), Charles William Nandell, and has issue living, one son and four das. *Residence* – 4 North Kingshighway, St Louis, MO 63108, USA.
Lady Felicity Ann, *b* 1925: *m* 1955, John Keith Harwood, OBE, who *d* 1989, and has issue living, Richard James Attlee, *b* 1963, — Penelope Ann, *b* 1956: *m* 1990, Richard Charles Anthony Robertson, only son of late A. H. Robertson, of Strasbourg, France, and has issue living, Joseph Keith *b* 1993, — Joanna Patricia, *b* 1958: *m* 1st, 1979 (*m diss* 1984), Philip Michael Darcey Pinniger, yst son of late T. Keith Pinniger; 2ndly, 1988, Martin Roundell Greene, only son of late George Roundell Greene, of Beaconsfield, Bucks, and has issue living (by 1st *m*), Thomas George *b* 1981, (by 2nd *m*) Charles George *b* 1988, — Sally Alice Beatrice *b* 1990. *Residence* – Whinbury, 6 Hogback Wood Rd, Beaconsfield, Bucks HP9 1JR.
Lady Alison Elizabeth, *b* 1930: *m* 1952, Richard Lionel Lance Davis, and has issue living, Jennifer Alison, *b* 1953: *m* 1978, Christopher James Lochen, elder son of Harald Olaf Lochen, of Sevenoaks, Kent, — Tessa Meriel, *b* 1955: *m* 1976, Michael Robert Dormon, son of Jack Barrett Dormon, of Hadley Wood, Herts, — Belinda Jane, *b* 1957: *m* 1979, Atholl Christopher Johnston, yr son of Christopher Kitchen Johnston, of Belfast. *Residence* – Westcott, Beacon Rise, Sevenoaks, Kent TN13 2NJ.

MOTHER LIVING

Anne Barbara, eldest da of late James Henderson, CBE, of Bath; *m* 1955 (*m diss* 1988), as his 1st wife, the 2nd Earl, who *d* 1991.

WIDOW LIVING OF SECOND EARL

MARGARET DEANE (*Margaret, Countess Attlee*), only da of late Geoffrey Gouriet, CBE, of Paper House, Hampton Court, Middx: *m* 1988, as his 2nd wife, the 2nd Earl, who *d* 1991. *Residence* – 1 Cadet Way, Church Crookham, Aldershort, Hants GU13 0UG.

PREDECESSORS – (1) *Rt Hon* CLEMENT RICHARD Attlee, KG, OM, CH, PC, 4th son of Henry Attlee, Solicitor, of Westcott, Putney, SW; *b* 1883; MP for Limehouse (*Lab*) 1922-50, and W Walthamstow 1950-55; Leader of Labour Party 1935-55, Dep Prime Min 1943-45, Prime Min 1945-51, and Leader of Opposition 1951-55; cr *Earl Attlee*, and *Viscount Prestwood*, of Walthamstow, co Essex (peerage of UK) 1955: *m* 1922, Violet Helen, who *d* 1964, yst da of Henry Edward Millar, of Heathdown, Hampstead, NW; *d* 1967; *s* by his only son (2) MARTIN RICHARD, 2nd Earl, *b* 1927; late Merchant Navy; Assist Public Relations Officer S Region British Rail: *m* 1st, 1955 (*m diss* 1988), Anne Barbara, eldest da of late James Henderson, CBE, of Bath; 2ndly, 1988, Margaret Deane, only da of late Geoffrey Gouriet, CBE, of Paper House, Hampton Court, Middx; *d* 1991; *s* by his only son (3) JOHN RICHARD, 3rd Earl and present peer; also Viscount Prestwood.

AUCKLAND, BARON (Eden) (Baron I 1789 and GB 1793)

IAN GEORGE EDEN, 9th Baron; *b* 23 June 1926; *s* 1957; *m* 1954, Dorothy Margaret, JP, da of Henry Joseph Manser, of Beechwood, Friday Street, Eastbourne, and has issue.

Arms – Gules, on a chevron argent, between three garbs or, banded vert, as many escallops sable. **Crest** – A dexter arm embowed in armour proper, the hand grasping a garb or, the upper part of the arm encircled by an annulet gules. **Supporters** – *Dexter*, a horse guardant argent, charged on the shoulder with a fleur-de-lis or; *sinister*, a horse argent, charged on the shoulder with a tower or.
Address – c/o House of Lords, SW1. *Clubs* – Constitutional, City Livery, Epsom.

If there be but prudence

SON LIVING

Hon ROBERT IAN BURNARD, *b* 25 July 1962; *ed* Blundells: *m* 1986, Geraldine, da of —.

DAUGHTERS LIVING

Hon Margaret Fiona, *b* 1955: *m* 1979, Michael Shouler, yr son of J. R. Shouler, of Wollaton Nottingham, and has issue living, Benjamin, *b* 1987, — Elizabeth, *b* 1982, — Katherine, *b* 1983, — Abigail, *b* 1989.
Hon Rachel Audrey, *b* 1959: *m* 1981, Bramwell M. Paton, of 22 Penwortham Rd, Streatham, SW16 6RE, son of John B. Paton, of Maidenhead, Berks, and has issue living, Alexander Robert, *b* 1983, — Joe Bramwell, *b* 1986, — Charlotte Jane, *b* 1985.

BROTHER LIVING

Hon Ronald John, *b* 1931; *ed* Glenalmond, and Ch Ch Oxford; *m* 1957, Rosemary Dorothy Marion, da of late Sir John (Frederick) Ellenborough Crowder, MP, JP (*see* B Petre, colls, 1980 Edn), and has issue living, Henry Vane, *b* 1958: *m* 1988, Alicia Claire, yr da of Christopher James Blois Needham (*see* E Kilmorey, colls), and has had issue, Harry *b* and *d* 1989, Oliver *b* 1990, Roseanna *b* 1992, — Edward John, *b* 1959: *m* 1990, Victoria M. C., eldest da of Maj D. P. T. Deshon, of Hartley Mauditt House, Alton, Hants, and has issue living, William *b* 1991.

DAUGHTERS LIVING OF SEVENTH BARON

Hon Joan Edith, *b* 1920; JP of Essex: *m* 1st, 1941, Rev Alfred Lisinea Pond, V of Potten End and Nettleden, who *d* 1947; 2ndly, 1948, Rev Arthur Harrington Franklin, MBE, TD, and has issue living (by 1st *m*), Rosemary Jane, *b* 1942: *m* 1966, John Edward Rendall, of Sherborne Lodge, Adelaide Rd, Teddington, Middx, and has issue living, Angus Mark *b* 1975, Amelia Jane *b* 1969, Sophie Charlotte *b* 1971, — Sarah Joan, *b* 1945: *m* 1972, David Alexander Platts, of 6 Eddiscombe Rd, SW6 4UA, and has issue living, Charles Alexander *b* 1976, — (by 2nd *m*) Elizabeth, *b* 1949: *m* 1970, Dr Michael Peter Withycombe Lance, of 85 Ayer Rd, Williamsville, New York 14221, USA, and has issue living, Tom *b* 1979, Emma *b* 1977, — Caroline, *b* 1952: *m* 1979, Lt-Cdr Kenneth J. Leafe, RN, of Ivy House, Broughton, nr Huntingdon, Cambs, and has issue living, Alistair James Farquahar *b* 1984, Emily Jane *b* 1982, Charlotte Alice *b* 1993. *Residence* – Hea Corner, Mill Rd, Felsted, Dunmow, Essex.
Hon Elizabeth, *b* 1928: *m* 1954, Maj Frederic Edward Isdale (Robin) Mason, late 1st R Anglian Regt, and has issue living, Timothy Robin, *b* 1957, — Edward Geoffrey, *b* 1961: *m* 1987, Joanna Elizabeth, yr da of J. H. Beckly, of Manor Farm, Bowerchalke, Salisbury, Wilts, and has issue living, Georgina Sophie *b* 1991, — Catherine Elizabeth, *b* 1955: *m* 1989, Charles Robins Shelbourne, of 40 City Rd, Norwich, eldest son of G. R. Shelbourne, of Langore, Cornwall, and has issue living, Freya Anna *b* 1992. *Residence* – Reed Hall, Holbrook, nr Ipswich.

DAUGHTER LIVING OF SIXTH BARON

Hon Susan Constance, *b* 1918: *m* 1st 1942 (*m diss* 1956), Jose Diaz de Rivera; 2ndly, 1957, Guillermo Pakenham Bridges, OBE, HM's Hon Vice-Consul at Rio Grande, Argentina, who *d* 1980, and has issue living (by 1st *m*), Jose Diaz, *b* 1944; has assumed the christian names of Denis Pakenham in lieu of Jose Diaz, and the surname of Bridges in lieu of his patronymic.

COLLATERAL BRANCHES LIVING

Grandchildren of late William Annesley Eden, yr son of late Hon Robert Henley Shaw Eden, 4th son of 3rd Baron:—
Issue of late Edward Hildyard Eden, *b* 1898 *d* 1968: *m* 1942, Annie Sylvester who *d* 1981:—
Ernest John (RRH 2, Barrhead, Alberta, Canada), *b* 1943: *m* 1967, Allison Carolyne Wilde, and has issue living, Buckley John, *b* 1974, — Heidi Anne, *b* 1969: *m* 1991, Dereck Spence. —— William Edward (Box 13, Newbrook, Alberta, Canada), *b* 1945: *m* 1967, Maureen T. O'Hagan, and has issue living, Joseph Edward, *b* 1970.
Issue of late Maj George Henley Eden, TD, RA, *b* 1904: *d* 1982: *m* 1st, 1928 (*m diss* 1949), Avril Edith, who *d* 1966, da of late R. O. Simmons; 2ndly, 1951 (*m diss* 1974), Doreen Rosamund Averil Tobeason; 3rdly, 1974, Stella Frances, da of late W. H. Duplock:—
(By 1st *m*) Annesley Kathleen, *b* 1928: *m* 1949, David George Warre Yeats Brown, of 151 Oakwood Court, W14, and has issue living, Richard Andrew, *b* 1955, — Caroline, *b* 1950, — Sarah Kate, *b* 1961. —— Avril Jane, *b* 1930: *m* 1957, Peter Milne Horley (PO Box 65425, Benmore, Sandton, Transvaal), and has issue living, Rupert, *b* 1958. —— Sally Mabel Henley, *b* 1932: *m* 1964, Johann Leusink, and has issue living, Andrew Hamilton Henley, *b* 1968.
Issue of late Frederick Reeve Eden, *b* 1908, *d* 1989: *m* 1953, Beatrice Helena (Skimmersfield, Holmer Green, Bucks), da of late Montague Smith:—
Sarah Ursula, *b* 1954: *m* 1977, Michael Adam James Adams, of 91 The Common, Earlswood, Birmingham B94 5SJ, and has issue living, Ross Henley, *b* 1983, — Euan George, *b* 1986.

PREDECESSORS – (1) *Rt Hon* WILLIAM Eden, PC, 3rd son of Sir Robert Eden, 3rd Bt; *b* 1744; was Ch Sec for Ireland, and Ambassador to Versailles, Madrid, etc: *m* 1776, Eleanor, who *d* 1818, da of the Rt Hon Sir Gilbert Elliot, PC, 3rd Bt; cr *Baron Auckland* (peerage of Ireland) 1789, and *Baron Auckland* (peerage of Great Britain) 1793; *d* 1814; *s* by his eldest son (2) GEORGE, GCB, 2nd Baron; *b* 1784; Gov-Gen of India 1836-41; cr *Baron Eden* and *Earl of Auckland* (peerage of United Kingdom) 1839; *dsp* 1849, when the earldom became extinct; *s* in peerages of 1789 and 1793 by his brother (3) *Rt Rev* ROBERT JOHN, 3rd Baron, *b* 1799; was Lord Bishop of Sodor and Man 1847-54, and of Bath and Wells 1854-69: *m* 1825, Mary, who *d* 1872, eldest da of Francis Edward Hurt, of Alderwasley, co Derby; *d* 1870; *s* by his eldest son (4) WILLIAM GEORGE,

4th Baron, *b* 1829; in Diplo Ser 1847-61: *m* 1st, 1857, Lucy Walbanke, who *d* 1870, da of John Walbanke Childers, of Cantley, Yorkshire; 2ndly, 1872, Lady Mabel Emily Finch-Hatton, who *d* 1872, da of 11th Earl of Winchilsea; 3rdly, 1875, Edith, who *d* 1931, da of Sir William Eden, 6th Bt; *s* by his eldest son (5) WILLIAM MORTON, 5th Baron, *b* 1859: *m* 1891, Sybil Constance, who *d* 1955, eldest da of late George Morland Hutton, CB, *d* 1917; *s* by his only surviving son (6) FREDERICK COLVIN GEORGE, 6th Baron; *b* 1895; Flight-Lieut RAF Vol Reserve: *m* 1st, 1917 (*m diss* 1925), Susan Livingstone, only da of Augustus Griffin Hartridge, of Jacksonville, Florida, USA; 2ndly, 1939, Constance Caroline, who *d* 1946, da of Benno Hart, of San Francisco, California, USA; *d* as a result of enemy action during European War 1941; *s* by his cousin (7) GEOFFREY MORTON, MBE (son of late Hon George Eden 3rd son of 4th Baron), 7th Baron; *b* 1891; Capt RASC (retired); European War 1914-18 (despatches twice, MBE), European War 1939-41: *m* 1919, Dorothy Ida, who *d* 1964 da of Rev Francis Clyde Harvey, V of Hailsham, and Preb of Chichester; *d* 1955; *s* by his brother (8) TERENCE, MC, 8th Baron; *b* 1892; Major Roy Armoured Corps (TA); European War 1914-18 as Capt Machine Gun Corps (despatches, MC with Bar); European War 1939-41: *m* 1925, Evelyn Vane (DRUMMOND OF CROMLIX), who *d* 1971, da of late Col Arthur William Henry Hay Drummond; *d* 1957; *s* by his eldest son (9) IAN GEORGE, 9th Baron and present peer.

AUDLEY, BARON (Souter) (Baron E 1312-13)

RICHARD MICHAEL THOMAS SOUTER, 25th Baron, *b* 31 May 1914; *s* 1973; *ed* Uppingham; Lt RA: *m* 1941, Lily Pauline, da of Dallas Louis Eskell, and has issue.

Arms – not exemplified at time of going to press.
Residence – Friendly Green, Cowden, Edenbridge, Kent.

DAUGHTERS LIVING (*Co-heiresses presumptive*)

Hon PATRICIA ANN, *b* 10 Aug 1946: *m* 1969, Carey Leigh Mackinnon, of Tunbridge Wells, Kent, and has issue living, Angus-Carey, *b* 1974, — Tamsin Sarah, *b* 1976.
Hon JENNIFER MICHELLE, *b* 23 May 1948: *m* 1978, Michael William Carrington, and has issue living, Jesse Michael, *b* 1978, — Jonah David, *b* 1980, — Holly Rosina, *b* 1975.
Hon AMANDA ELIZABETH, *b* 5 May 1958.

STEP-MOTHER LIVING OF ROSINA LOIS VERONICA, BARONESS AUDLEY

Lillie Kathleen, da of late George Ross, of co Monaghan: *m* 1st, 1923, as his 2nd wife, Thomas Touchet Tuchet-Jesson, who *d* 1939, having assumed by deed poll 1937 the additional surname of Tuchet; 2ndly, 1941, George Wynter Gray, who *d* 1945.

COLLATERAL BRANCH LIVING

Issue of late Charlotte Pamela Souter, sister of 25th Baron, *b* 1916, *d* 1990: *m* 1954, William Francis Harvey:—
John Richard, *b* 1959. —— Katharine Mary, *b* 1955. —— Amelia Anne, *b* 1957.

PREDECESSORS – (1) NICHOLAS Audley, or Aldithley, of Heleigh, Staffordshire; *b* 1298; summoned to Parliament by writ as *Baron Audley* 1312-13: *m* 1312, Joan, only child of 1st Baron Martin, and widow of 6th Earl of Lincoln (cr circa 1147); *d* 1316; *s* by his son (2) JAMES, 2nd Baron; *b* 1313: *m* 1st, 13—, Joan, da of 1st Earl of March; 2ndly, 15—, Isabel, da of 5th Baron Strange of Knokin; *d* 1386; *s* by his son (3) NICHOLAS, 3rd Baron; *b* 13—: *m* 13—, Elizabeth, who *d* 1400, da of 1st Baron Beaumont; *d* 1391, when the Barony fell into abeyance between his sisters; this abeyance was terminated in 1405 in favour of his great-nephew (4) JOHN Tuchet (son of John Tuchet, son of Sir John Tuchet, by Joan, da of 2nd Baron), 4th Baron; *b* 1371: *m* 13—, Isabel, da of —; *d* 1408; *s* by his son (5) JAMES, 5th Baron; *b* 1398: *m* 1st, 14—, Margaret, da of 7th Baron de Ros; 2ndly, 14—, Eleanor, natural da of Thomas, Earl of Kent, by Constance, da of Edmund of Langley, Duke of York, 5th son of King Edward III; *d* 1459; *s* by his son (6) JOHN, PC, 6th Baron; *b* 14—; sometime Lord Treasurer: *m* 14—, Anne, who *d* 1498, a of Sir Thomas Echingham, and widow of John Rogers, of Bryanston, Dorset; *d* 1490; *s* by his son (7) JAMES, KB, 7th Baron; *b* 1463: *m* 1st, 14—, Margaret, da of Sir Richard Dayrell; 2ndly, 14—, Joan, who *d* 1532, da of Fulk, Lord Fitz-Warine; joined Cornish insurrection and was beheaded 1497, when the title became forfeited; *s* by his son (8) JOHN, 8th Baron; *b* 1483; secured restoration of the title 1512: *m* 15—, Mary, da of John Griffin, of Braybrooke, Northants; *d* *c* 1557; *s* by his son (9) GEORGE, 9th Baron; *b* 15—: *m* 1st, 15—, Elizabeth, da of Sir Brian Tuke; 2ndly, 1560, Joan Platt; *d* 1560; *s* by his son (10) HENRY, 10th Baron; *b* 15—: *m* 15—, Elizabeth, da of Sir William Sneyd, of Bradwell, Staffordshire; *d* 1563; *s* by his son (11) George, 11th Baron; *b* 1551; sometime Gov of Utrecht, Netherlands, and of Kells, co Meath; cr *Baron Audley*, of Orier, co Armagh, and *Earl of Castlehaven*, co Cork (peerage of Ireland) 1616: *m* 1st, 15—, Lucy, only da of Sir James Mervyn; 2ndly, 1611, Elizabeth (who *m* 2ndly, 1619, Sir Piers Crosby), da of Sir Andrew Noel; *b* 1617; *s* by his son (12) MERVYN, 2nd Earl; *b* 1593: *m* 1st, 1619, Elizabeth, da of Benedict Barnham, of London; 2ndly, 1624, Anne, who *d* 1647, da of 5th Earl of Derby, and widow of 5th Baron Chandos of Sudeley; convicted of felony and beheaded 1631, when the English Barony became forfeited; *s* (in the Irish Earldom and Barony) by his son (13) JAMES, 3rd Earl; *b* 16—; cr *Baron Audley* of Hely (with precedence of the former Barony (cr 1312-13)) 1633, subsequently confirmed by Act of Parliament 1678: *m* 1st, 16—, Elizabeth, who *d* 1679, da of 5th Baron Chandos of Sudeley; 2ndly, 1679, Elizabeth, da of —; *d* 1684; *s* by his brother (14) MERVIN, 4th Earl; *b* 16—: *m* 16—, Mary, da of Sir Francis Fortescue, and widow of 10th Earl of Shrewsbury; *d* 1686; *s* by his son (15) JAMES, 5th Earl; *b* 16—: *m* 16—, Anne, who *d* 1733, da of Richard Pelson, of St George's-in-the-Fields, Middlesex; *d* 1700: *s* by his son (16) JAMES, 6th Earl; *b* 16—: *m* 1722, Elizabeth, who *d* 1743, da of 4th Baron Arundell of Wardour; *d* 1740; *s* by his son (17) JAMES, 7th Earl; *b* 1723; *d* 1769; *s* by his brother (18) JOHN, 8th Earl; *b* 17—: *m* 17—, Susanna, who *d* 1789, da of Henry Drax, of Ellerton Abbey, Yorkshire, and widow of William Cracraft; *d* 1777, when the Earldom of Castlehaven, and the Barony of Audley of Orier, became extinct, and the Barony of Audley of Hely devolved upon his kinsman (19) GEORGE (son of Philip Thicknesse, by Elizabeth, da of 5th Earl), 19th Baron; *b* 1758; assumed by R licence 1783, the additional surname of Touchet after that of Thicknesse: *m* 1st, 1781, Elizabeth, who *d* 1785, da of Sir John Hussey Delaval, 1st Bt; 2ndly, 1792, Augusta Henrietta Catherina, who *d* 1844, yst da of the Rev André Boisdaune, and widow of Col Moorhouse; *d* 1818; *s* by his son (20) GEORGE JOHN, 20th Baron; *b* 1783: *m* 1816, Anne Jane, who *d* 1855, da of Vice-Adm Sir Ross Donnelly, KCB; *d* 1837; *s* by his son (21) GEORGE EDWARD, 21st Baron; *b* 1817: *m* 1st, 1857, Emily, who *d* 1860, da of Sir Thomas Livingstone Mitchell; 2ndly, 1868, Margaret Anne, who *d* 1888, widow of James William Smith; *d* 1872, when the Barony fell into abeyance between his two daughters, on the death of the yr of whom in 1937, the title devolved upon the elder (22) MARY, *b* 1858; *d* 1942; *s* by her kinsmen (23) THOMAS PERCY HENRY TOUCHET *Tuchet-Jesson*, MBE, son of late Thomas Touchet Tuchet-Jesson, son of late Thomas Jesson, by Charlotte Anna, da of late Hon John Nicholas Thicknesse-Tuchet, son of 20th Baron, *b* 1913; Maj Worcestershire Regt; assumed by deed poll 1937, the additional surname of Tuchet: *m* 1st, 1952 (*m diss* 1958), June Isabel, MBE, who *d* 1977, da of Lt-Col Reginald Chaplin, and formerly wife of Rudolph Edgar de Trafford, OBE (later Sir Rudolph de Trafford, 5th Bt), who *d* 1983: 2ndly, 1962, Hon Sarah Millicent Hermione Spencer-Churchill, who *d* 1982, da of Rt Hon Sir Winston Leonard Spencer-Churchill, KG, OM, CH, TD,

MP (D Marlborough, colls), and formerly wife of (i) Vic Oliver (né Victor von Samek), of Vienna; actor; and (ii) Antony Beauchamp, photographer; *d* 1963; *s* by his sister **(24)** ROSINA LOIS VERONICA, *b* 1911; assumed by deed poll 1937 additional surname of Tuchet; *m* 1943, John Archibald Joseph Macnamee; *d* 1973; *s* by her cousin **(25)** RICHARD MICHAEL THOMAS *Souter* (son of late Sir Charles Alexander Souter, KCIE, CSI, and his wife, late Charlotte Dorothy Jesson, aunt of 23rd Baron), 25th Baron and present peer.

AVEBURY, BARON (Lubbock) (Baron UK 1900, Bt UK 1806)

ERIC REGINALD LUBBOCK, 4th Baron, and 7th Baronet; *b* 29 Sept 1928; *s* 1971; *ed* Upper Canada Coll, Harrow and Balliol Coll, Oxford (BA); Lt Welsh Gds; MP for Orpington (*L*) 1962-70, and Liberal Ch Whip 1963-70: *m* 1st, 1953 (*m diss* 1983), Kina Maria, da of Count Joseph Henry O'Kelly de Gallagh, 2ndly, 1985, Lindsay Jean, da of Gordon Neil Stewart and of late Pamela Hansford Johnson (Lady Snow), writer, and has issue by 1st and 2nd *m*.

Arms – Argent, on a mount vert a stork close ermine, on a chief gules three estoiles of the field. **Crest** – A stork, wings elevated ermine, supporting an antique shield azure, bordered or, charged with a lion rampant-guardant argent. **Supporters** – Two storks, wings elevated ermine, each gorged with a chain or, and pendent therefrom an escutcheon gules charged with an estoile argent.

The author makes the value

SONS LIVING *(By 1st marriage)*

Hon LYULPH AMBROSE JONATHAN, *b* 15 June 1954: *m* 1977, Susan Carol MacDonald, and has issue living, Alexander Lyulph Robert, *b* 17 Jan 1985, — Vanessa Adelaide Felicity, *b* 1983. *Residence* – 53 Worlds End Lane, Orpington, Kent.
Hon Maurice Patrick Guy, *b* 1955: *m* 1982, Diana Rivia Tobin, and has issue living, Olivia Adelaide, *b* 1990.

(By 2nd marriage)

Hon John William Stewart, *b* 1985.

DAUGHTER LIVING *(By 1st marriage)*

Hon Victoria Sarah Maria, *b* 1959: *m* 1983, Alan Binney of 225 Evering Rd, E5 8AL, and has issue living, Archie, *b* 1983, — Alastair, *b* 1985.

SISTER LIVING

Alice Olivia Maureen (19 Beach Rd, Collaroy, NSW 2097, Aust), *b* 1926: *m* 1951 (*m diss* 1974), William Geoffrey Keighley, MLC, and has issue living, Francis Stephen, *b* 1953, — John William, *b* 1959, — Pamela Jane, *b* 1956, — Josephine Clare, *b* 1961.

DAUGHTER LIVING OF THIRD BARON

Hon Emma Rachel, *b* 1952: *m* 1977, Michael Charles Page, of Lepe House, Exbury, Southampton, and has issue living, Sophie Elizabeth, *b* 1982, — Natasha Diana, *b* 1984.

WIDOW LIVING OF THIRD BARON

BETTY GAY (*Betty, Baroness Avebury*), da of late William Oscar Ingham, and formerly wife of — Goode: *m* 1955, as his 3rd wife, the 3rd Baron, who *d* 1971.

COLLATERAL BRANCHES LIVING

(In remainder to Baronetcy only)

Grandchildren of late Maj Geoffrey Lubbock, 2nd son of late Henry James Lubbock, 2nd son of 3rd baronet:—
    Issue of late David Miles Lubbock, *b* 1911, *d* 1992: *m* 1939, Hon Helen Anne Boyd Orr (Newton of Stracathro, Brechin, Angus), da of 1st Baron Boyd Orr (ext):—
Geoffrey Orr (Marblehead, Mass, USA), *b* 1946; *ed* Eton, and Magdalene Coll, Camb: *m* 1981, Fiona Constance, yst da of Col Homer E. Harris, of Mass, USA, and has issue living, Francesca Eriminta Alessandra, *b* 1985, — Caroline Angelica, *b* 1989. —— John Nicholas Andrew (Harwood Mill, Bonchester Bridge, Hawick, Roxburghshire), *b* 1948; *ed* Eton: *m* 1977, Jane Louisa, da of Col Charles King, OBE, of Hale House, Cuckington, Som, and has issue living, Hamish Percy Elliot, *b* 1977, — James Alexander George, *b* 1982, — Sammie Elizabeth Ursula, *b* 1980. —— Kenneth Miles Boyd, *b* 1950; *ed* Eton: *m* 1975, Moira Baillie, of Helensburgh, Dunbartonshire, and has issue living, John Angus Elliot, *b* 1981, — Julia Janet Roxanne, *b* 1989. —— Ann Patricia, *b* 1941: *m* 1972, John Daniel Gooch, VRD, of The Schoolhouse, Oathlaw, Forfar, Angus, and has issue (*see* Gooch, Bt, colls, *cr* 1866).

Grandsons of late Henry James Lubbock (ante):—
    Issue of late Capt Rupert Egerton Lubbock, RN, *b* 1886, *ka* 1943: *m* 1912, Vera Isabel, who *d* 1962, da of G. R. Wingrove, of Shanghai:—
†Rupert James, *b* 1916; Capt 5th Batn Leics Regt (TA); 1939-45 War (prisoner): *m* 1954, Jeanette Patricia, who *d* 1976, only da of A. van Beugen Bik, of Broughton, Esher, Surrey, and *d* 1981, leaving issue, Rupert Guy Anthony, *b* 1956, — David Alexander, *b* 1958, — Fiona Jeanette Ariane, *b* 1960. —— Christopher William Stuart, *b* 1920; *ed* Charterhouse, and at Brasenose Coll, Oxford; 1939-45 War as Lieut RNVR: *m* 1947, Hazel Gordon Chapman, and has issue living, (Rupert) James Gordon (139 Ramsden Rd, SW12), *b* 1948: *m* 1982, Miranda Jane, eldest da of Stephen St Clair McNeile, of Redvers, Hinderclay, Diss, Norfolk, and has issue living, Richard Christopher Sinclair *b* 1983, Sophie Caroline *b* 1986, — Victoria Margaret, *b* 1950: *m* 1977, Geoffrey Richard Humphrey Edwards, of 44 St Barnabas Rd, Cambridge, and has issue living,

Charles David Christopher *b* 1979, Guy William Humphrey *b* 1983, Chloë Elizabeth Rose *b* 1981. *Residence* – New Barn House, Great Horkesley, Essex.

         Grandchildren of late Hugh Nevile Lubbock, 2nd son of late Sir Nevile Lubbock, KCMG, 3rd son of 3rd baronet:—
      Issue of late Ralph Hugh Lubbock, MC, *b* 1891, *d* 1961: *m* 1st, 1914 (*m diss* 1922), Adelaide Margaret Constance, who *d* 1940, da of late Samuel Hynman Montgomerie (*see* E Eglinton, 1940 Edn); 2ndly, 1923, Louise, who *d* 1987, da of James Charles Vogel, of Durban:—
(By 2nd *m*) John Ralph (Cavalry and Guards' Club), *b* 1925; *ed* Malvern; 1939-45 War as Lt Coldm Gds: *m* 1st, 1950 (*m diss* 1957), Patricia Helen Winifred, da of late Brig-Gen Hon Roger Brand, CMG, DSO (*see* V Hampden, colls); 2ndly, 1957 (*m diss* 1961), Jane Marjorie, da of Maj Evelyn Ronald Moncrieff Fryer, MC, Gren Gds (*see* E Peel, colls, 1985 Edn); 3rdly, 1963 (*m diss* 1966), Helene Gladys Frances, only da of late Maj William Ferguson Thomson; 4thly, 1967, Anne Elizabeth, da of late Frank Colville Pearce, and has had issue (by 1st *m*), †Hugh Roger, *b* 1951; *ed* Eton; *k* in a motor accident in Rio de Janeiro 1981, — (by 2nd *m*), Thomas Nevile, *b* 1957, — (by 4th *m*) Stephen Henry Ralph, *b* 1970, — Elizabeth Serena, *b* 1967. —— (By 1st *m*) Ursula Egidia, *b* 1919: *m* 1941, Peter Bellamy, of West End Cottage, Eythorne, nr Dover, and has issue living, Geraldine Anne, *b* 1943: *m* 1964, Michael Wyant, of Littlebourne, Canterbury, Kent.

         Grandchildren of late Frederic Lubbock, 6th son of 3rd baronet, *b* 1844, *d* 1927: *m* 1869, Catherine, who *d* 1934, only da of late John Gurney, of Earlham Hall, Norfolk:—
      Issue of late Brig-Gen Guy Lubbock, CMG, DSO, *b* 1870, *d* 1956: *m* 1912, Lettice Isabella, who *d* 1980, da of Robert Harvey Mason, of Necton Hall, Swaffham:—
Joseph Guy, *b* 1915; *ed* Eton, and Trin Coll, Camb (BA 1937); late Capt RE (TA): *m* 1941, Ruth Cecilia, da of Major Quintin Edward Gurney, of Bawdeswell Hall, Norfolk, and has issue living, Jennifer: *m* 1st, 1966 (*m diss* 1974), the Marchese Ciaralli-Parenzi; 2ndly, 1975, Michael Wynne-Parker, of 2 Rectory Lane, Mulbarton, Norwich, NR14 8AG (Carlton Club), and has issue living (by 1st *m*), Andrew *b* 1969, Elena *b* 1967 (by 2nd *m*), Sarah Ruth Isabella *b* 1978, Fiona Alice Elizabeth *b* 1981, — Catherine, *b* 1944: *m* 1968, Stuart Jennings, MB, BS, of The Moat House, Church St, Blackmore, Essex, and has issue living, Mark *b* 1970: *m* 1993, Sarah Louise Hesketh, Samuel *b* 1971, — Lucinda, *b* 1948: *m* 1st, 1974, Thomas Henry Carew, who *d* 1978 (*see* B Carew); 2ndly, 1983, John Martin Harkness, of Hill House, Geldeston, Beccles, Suffolk, and has issue living (by 1st *m*) (*see* B Carew) (by 2nd *m*), Edward John *b* 1984, Alice Elizabeth *b* 1986. *Residence* – High Elms, Waldringfield, Suffolk; Carlton Club.

         Grandchildren of late Cecil Lubbock (infra):—
      Issue of late Lt-Col Michael Ronald Lubbock, MBE, *b* 1906, *d* 1989: *m* 1st, 1929 (*m diss* 1956), Diana Beatrice, who *d* 1976, da of late Henry Ernest Crawley (*see* Crawley-Boevey, Bt, colls, 1976 Edn); 2ndly, 1957 (*m diss* 1975), Inga Olga, da of late Eugene Ivan de Rudez, of Zagreb, Jugoslavia, and widow of Col Geoffrey Moule; 3rdly, 1976, Elizabeth Christina (30/655 Richmond Rd, Ottawa, Ontario, Canada), da of John Sutherland, of Ontario, Canada:—
(By 1st *m*) Jeremy Michael (1390 Kelton Av, Apt 301, Los Angeles, CA 90024, USA), *b* 1931: *m* 1st, 1956 (*m diss* 1959), Jill Caroline, da of late Eric Nicholls; 2ndly, 1963, Shelagh Mary, da of Richard Lang, MB, of Kenilworth, Cape, S Africa; 3rdly, 1974 (*m diss* 1987), Philippa Harriet, da of Lt-Col Sir Charles Arthur Chadwyck-Healey, 4th Bt, OBE, TD (infra), and has issue living, (by 1st *m*), Justin Roger, *b* 1956, — (by 2nd *m*) Lindsay Brigid, *b* 1965, — (by 3rd *m*) Rowan Mark, *b* 1981, — Holly Andrée, *b* 1976. —— John David Peter (7 Warborough Rd, Shillingford, Oxon OX10 7SA), *b* 1945: *m* 1st, 1977 (*m diss* 1991), Eleanor Sloane; 2ndly, 1991, Christine Wilson Cairns, and has issue living (by 1st *m*), Daniel John, *b* 1978, — Patrick, *b* 1980, — (by 2nd *m*) Adam Thomas, *b* 1991, — Alexander Michael, *b* 1993. —— Judith Caroline Gurney, *b* 1934: *m* 1956, Martin Marriott, of Morris Farm House, Baverstock, nr Dinton, Salisbury, Wilts SP3 5EL, and has issue living, Charles John Phillip, *b* 1964, — Virginia Elizabeth, *b* 1958: *m* 1987, Patrick Francis O'Conor, of 51 Downs Park West, Westbury Park, Bristol, Avon, and has issue living, Harry Michael *b* 1993, Katherine Rosemary *b* 1989, Lucy Joanna *b* 1991, — Rebecca Jane, *b* 1960. —— Jessica Rose, *b* 1937: *m* 1961, Air Vice-Marshal David Brook, CBE, RAF, and has issue living, William, *b* 1965, — Julie Nicola, *b* 1961. —— Joanna, *b* 1941: *m* 1965, Michael Coleridge Seligman, of Crown Lodge, Newnham, Basingstoke, Hants RG27 9AN, and has issue living, Simon Michael Hugo, *b* 1966, — Thomas Reginald James, *b* 1975, — Kate Sophie, *b* 1968. —— (By 2nd *m*) Inga Cecilia, *b* 1957.

         Grandchildren of late Frederic Lubbock (*b* 1844) (ante):—
      Issue of late Cecil Lubbock, *b* 1872, *d* 1956: *m* 1898, Edith, who *d* 1960, 4th da of late Ven Charles Wellington Furse, Archdeacon of Westminster, of 1 Abbey Garden, Great College Street, SW1, and Halsdon House, N Devon:—
Viola (*Viola, Lady Chadwyck-Healey*), *b* 1912: *m* 1939, Lt-Col Sir Charles Arthur Chadwyck-Healey, 4th Bt, OBE, TD (ante), who *d* 1986. *Residence* – 38 Castle Court, River Park, Marlborough, Wilts SN8 1NH.
      Issue of late Samuel Gurney Lubbock, *b* 1873, *d* 1958: *m* 1915, Irene Scharrer, who *d* 1971:—
Rachel Gurney, *b* 1920; actress (as Rachel Gurney): *m* 1945 (*m annulled* 1950), Denys Gravenor Rhodes (*see* B Plunket, 1968 Edn), and has issue living, Sharon Gurney, *b* 1950: *m* 1970, Simon Peter Gough, of The Old Rectory, Baconsthorpe, Holt, Norfolk, son of Michael Gough, actor, and has issue living, Samuel Gurney *b* 1975, Dickon Graves *b* 1979, Tamasin Rachel *b* 1973, Daisy Diana *b* 1976.
      Issue of late Roy Lubbock, *b* 1892, *d* 1985: *m* 1919, Yvonne, who *d* 1987, da of late Sydney George Vernham:—
†Jocelyn Roy, *b* 1920; *ed* Eton, and Peterhouse, Camb (BA 1941, MA 1945, MusB 1946): *m* 1st, 1948 (*m diss* 1976), Frances Georgette Coningsby, da of late Capt George Ashmead-Bartlett, and formerly wife of George Derek Pepys Whiteley; 2ndly, 1976, Adriana Camarca, of via Lucrino 41, Rome 00199, Italy, and *d* 1992, leaving issue (by 1st *m*), Annina Nicolette Mary, *b* 1949. —— †Hubert Timothy, *b* 1923; *ed* Eton, and Peterhouse, Camb (MA 1948): *m* 1958, Barbara Anne Caruth (Beech Mount, Bircham Rd, Reepham, Norwich), and *d* 1991, leaving issue, Catherine Fiona, *b* 1960: *m* 1986, Neil Atkinson, of Lytham St Ann's, Lancs, and has issue living, Samuel Lawrence *b* 1990, Rebecca Louise *b* 1987, Elizabeth Anne *b* 1994, — Lucinda Anne, *b* 1964: *m* 1987, Christopher Copage, of Bawburgh, Norfolk.
      Issue of late Sir Alan Lubbock, *b* 1897, *d* 1990: *m* 1918, Helen Mary, who *d* 1987, only child of late John Bonham-Carter, of Adhurst St Mary, Petersfield, Hants:—
Roger John, DSC (Weatherall Lodge, Well Rd, NW3), *b* 1922; *ed* Eton, and King's Coll, Camb (MA); Lt-Cmdr RNR, served 1939-45 War (DSC): *m* 1955, Moyra, da of John Newton Mappin Fraser, and formerly wife of Maj Douglas Sutherland, and has issue living, Guy John, *b* 1957, — Paul Nigel, *b* 1960: *m* 1984, Lucinda, only da of late Ronald Simms, of St John's Wood, NW8, and has issue living, Oliver Guy *b* 1990, Alice Helen *b* 1988. —— Martin (Brown's Copse, Heyshott, Midhurst, Sussex), *b* 1925; *ed* Eton, and King's Coll, Camb; Lieut RNVR; European War 1943-45: *m* 1957, Elizabeth, da of Ronald Marshall, of W Kirby, Yorks, and formerly wife of late Rt Hon Selwyn Lloyd, MP (later Baron Selwyn-Lloyd), and has issue living, Toby Mark *b* 1959: *m* 1990, Bridget A., da of Geoffrey Sleddon, of Deopham, Norfolk, — Robin Alan, *b* 1961.

PREDECESSORS – (1) John Lubbock, *bapt* 1744, son of the Rev William Lubbock, R of Lammas, Norfolk; an opulent banker of the City of London; cr a *Baronet* 1806: *m* 1771, Elizabeth Christiana, da of Frederick Commerell, of Hanwell; *dsp* 1816; *s* by his nephew (2) John William, 2nd Bt, *b* 1773; an eminent banker: *m* 1799, Mary, da of James Entwistle, of Rusholme, Manchester; *d* 1840; *s* by his son (3) John William, 3rd Bt; *b* 1803; a banker, a distinguished scientific author, and Vice-Pres of R So: *m* 1833, Harriet, da of Lieut-Col George Gotham, of York; *d* 1865; *s* by his son (4) John, PC, DCL, LLD, 4th Bt; *b* 1834; cr *Baron Avebury*, of Avebury, Wilts (peerage of United Kingdom) 1900; was head of London banking firm of Robarts, Lubbock, and Co, of 15 Lombard Street, EC (now amalgamated with Coutts and Co), Pres of So of Antiquaries, of R Microscopical So, of Royal So, of Central Asso of Bankers, and of London Chamber of Commerce; sat as

MP for Maidstone (L) 1870-80, when he was defeated, and for the Univ of London 1880-1900: m 1st, 1856, Ellen Frances, who d 1879, da of late Rev Peter Horden, of Chorlton-cum-Hardy; 2ndly, 1884, Alice Augusta Laurentia, who d 1947, da of late Maj-Gen Augustus Henry Lane Fox-Pitt-Rivers; d 1913; s by his eldest son (5) JOHN BIRKBECK, 2nd Baron, b 1858; a Director of Coutts and Co, and of National Provincial and Union Bank of England; d 1929; s by his nephew (6) JOHN, son of late Capt Hon Harold Fox Pitt Lubbock (4th son of 1st Baron) ka 1918, 3rd Baron, b 1915: m 1st, 1938 (m diss 1945), Cicely Kathleen, da of late Dr N. A. K. Sparrow; 2ndly, 1946 (m diss 1955), Diana Mary Margaret Westcott, who d 1993, having m 2ndly, 1959 (m diss 1967), Charles Fletcher-Cooke, QC (later Sir Charles Fletcher Cooke), da of late Capt Edward Westcott King, RA; 3rdly, 1955, Betty Gay, da of late William Oscar Ingham, and formerly wife of — Goode; d 1971; s by his cousin (7) ERIC REGINALD (only son of late Hon Maurice Fox Pitt Lubbock, yst son of 1st Baron), 4th Baron and present peer.

AVON, EARLDOM OF (Eden) (Extinct 1985)

WIDOW LIVING OF FIRST EARL

CLARISSA (Countess of Avon) (32 Bryanston Sq, W1), only da of late Maj John Strange Spencer-Churchill, DSO (see D Marlborough, colls): m 1952, as his 2nd wife, the 1st Earl, who d 1977.

AVONMORE, VISCOUNTCY OF (Yelverton) (Dormant 1910)

This peerage has been dormant since the death of the 6th Viscount in 1910. The senior male descendant in the male line of Hon Augustus Yelverton, 3rd son of 2nd Viscount, presumably is heir to the title.

COLLATERAL BRANCHES LIVING

Grandsons of late Barry Augustus Yelverton (infra):—
Issue of late Barry Goring Yelverton, b 1923, d 1985: m 1950, Frances Winifred (28 Karamu St, Wanganui, New Zealand) (who m 2ndly, 1988, Alan Mangan), da of late William Francis Battersby, of Glasgow Terr, Feilding, New Zealand:—
Ian Foster (103 Torres St, Kurnell, NSW, Australia), b 1950; ed Palmerston North Boys High Sch: m 1985, Robyn Anne, da of late Aubrey Shearer, of 68 Tasman St, Kurnell, NSW, Australia, and has issue living, Lee Barry, b 1981, — Damian Talbot, b 1989, — Kursha May, b 1986. —— Avon Barry, b 1954: m 1983, Lisa Adele, da of William Johnstone, of Sandy Point, NSW, and has issue living, Nicholas William, b 1985, — Andrew Christion, b 1988, — Kimberley Rose, b 1990.

Grandson of late Foster Goring Yelverton (infra):—
Issue of late Barry Augustus Yelverton, b 1895, d 1960: m 1921, Margaret Ethel, who d 1970, da of John Thomas Green, of Christchurch, NZ:—
Michael Curran, b 1928: m 1949, Marjory Ruth, da of Arthur William Hall, of Gisborne, NZ, and has issue living, Kevin Barry (1 Aberdeen St, Geelong, Victoria, Australia), b 1949: m 1972, Cherry Belle, da of Rodger Thomas Keane, of Tauranga, NZ, and has issue living, John Mark b 1980, Tracey Anne b 1978, — Mark Amour (3 Ross St, Palmerston North, NZ), b 1961: m 1985, Siobhan, da of Barry Hannan, of Napier, — Sharon Anne, b 1950: m 1969, John Charles Meehan, of Kelvin Grove Rd, RD10, Palmerston North, NZ, and has issue living, Clive Richard b 1970, Richard John b 1978, Deborah Gay b 1972. *Residence* – 19 Coverdale St, Napier, NZ.
Issue of late Hermann Stratton Yelverton, b 1896, d 1973: m 1923, Janetta Ferguson, who d 1963, da of John McEwen, of Palmerston North, NZ:—
Stratton Barton (28 Strowan Rd, Strowan, Christchurch 5, NZ), b 1926: m 1st, 1962 (m diss 1981), Jill Marion, da of late Colin Fergus Tennent-Brown; 2ndly, 1988, Margaret Alxiere, MBE (who legally assumed the forename of Alxiere in lieu of Elsie 1992), da of late Lionel Gordon Malcolm, and has issue living (by 1st m), John Stratton, b 1962, — Andrew Colin, b 1964: m 1993, Karen Lee, da of L. M. Makings, — Bruce Avonmore, b 1966, — Sally Janetta, b 1969. —— June Avonmore, b 1924: m 1944, Charles Herbert Dudley Scantlebury, of 3 Bretton Terr, Hillcrest, Hamilton, NZ, and has issue living, Dudley Addison, b 1945: m 1976, Mary, da of Peter Shelling, of Nelson, NZ, — Gavin Stratton, b 1946: m 1971, Vivienne Mary, da of Wilfred John Westbury, of Adelaide, S Australia, and has issue living, Paul Gavin b 1974, Antoinette b 1973, — Gerald Avonmore, b 1955: m 1982, Angela Therese, da of George Osca McMonogle, of Waihi, NZ, and has issue living, Giselle Sara b 1983, — Mark Jonathan, b 1958: m 1978, Janet Anne, da of Douglas John Hemi, of Hamilton, NZ, and has issue living, Luke Douglas b 1980, John b 1987, Benjamin Samuel b 1993, Anna Jane b 1982, Sarah b 1984, — Rosamond Karen Jane, b 1948: m 1973, Lester Thur Banfield, and has issue living, Rhys Ewen b 1977, Aaron Lester b 1978, — Jennifer Marie, b 1956: m 1988, Raúl Casto Pardo, of Madrid, Spain, and has issue living, Sefora b 1990, Raquel b 1992. —— Matel, b 1928: m 1951, Raymond William Watson, 256/1 St Heliers Bay Rd, St Heliers Bay, Auckland, NZ, and has issue living, Christopher Raymond (11 Arthur Crescent, Takapuna, Auckland 9, NZ), b 1952: m 1978, Penelope Winifred St John, da of Stanley Raymond Worth, Lt Cmdr RN (ret), of Takapuna, NZ, and has issue living, James Christopher Avonmore b 1991, Katherine Fiona Matel b 1981, Alexandra Penelope Alice b (twin) 1981, — Nicholas Stratton (1 Iona St, Black Rock, Melbourne, Australia), b 1956: m 1980, Nella, da of Antonio Colasacco, of Melbourne, Australia, and has issue living, Renée Clare b 1984, Elisa Laura b 1987, — Nigel Alexander (10 Woodward St, Taupo, NZ), b 1963.

Granddaughter of Foster Goring Yelverton, son of Augustus Barrymore Yelverton, son of Hon Augustus Yelverton, 3rd son of 2nd Viscount:—
Issue of late Macey Goring Yelverton, b 1898, d 1980: m 1922, Pauline, who d 1986, da of Jarrett Owen Allen, of Nottingham:—
Enid, b 1929: m 1952, Arthur Joseph Byrne, of Maple Lodge, Knightwood Av, Lyndhurst, Hants, and has issue living, Stephen Martin, b 1953, — Carol Patricia, b 1954: m 1975 (m diss 1980), Richard Mortimer, of Beechgrange, Landford, Wilts, — Vanessa Elaine, b 1963: m 1990 (m diss 1994), and has issue living, Regan Melissa BYRNE b 1991.

AYLESFORD, EARL OF (Finch-Knightley) (Earl GB 1714)

To live with will unfettered

CHARLES IAN FINCH-KNIGHTLEY, 11th Earl; *b* 2 Nov 1918; *s* 1958; *ed* Oundle; Capt Black Watch, a JP for Warwickshire (Vice-Lieut 1964-74); Lord Lieut of W Midlands 1974-93; Warwickshire Co Commr for Boy Scouts Assocn 1949-74, since when Patron; a KStJ; a Member of Advisory Cttee World Wild Life Fund since 1970; 1939-45 War (wounded): *m* 1946, Margaret Rosemary, who *d* 1989, only da of late Maj Austin Arnold Tyer, MVO, TD, of Tunstall, Wadhurst, and has issue.

Arms – Argent, a chevron between three griffins passant sable. Crest – A griffin passant sable. Supporters – *Dexter*, a griffin sable, ducally gorged or; *sinister*, a lion or, ducally gorged azure.
Seat – Packington Old Hall, Meriden, Coventry, CV7 7HG.

SON LIVING

CHARLES HENEAGE (*Lord Guernsey*) (Packington Hall, Meriden, Coventry CV7 7HF) *b* 27 Mar 1947; *ed* Oundle, and Trin Coll, Camb: *m* 1971, Penelope Anstice, yr da of late Kenneth Arnold Gibbs Crawley, TD (*see* Crawley-Boevey, Bt, colls, 1968 Edn), and has issue:—

　　SON LIVING— *Hon* (Heneage) James Daniel, *b* 29 April 1985.
　　DAUGHTERS LIVING— *Hon* Rachel Louise, *b* 1974, — *Hon* Kate Pamela (twin), *b* 1974, — *Hon* Alexandra Rosemary, *b* 1977, — *Hon* Laura, *b* 1982.

DAUGHTERS LIVING

Lady Sarah Elizabeth Jane, *b* 1950: *m* 1974, Angus Nigel Garnet Maclean, 8th of Kilmoluaig, and has issue living, Angus Charles, *b* 1976, — Ian Andrew, *b* 1980.
Lady Clare Charlotte Rosemary, *b* 1959: *m* 1985, James Remington-Hobbs, son of C. Remington-Hobbs, of Normandy, France, and has issue living, Jonathan Ian, *b* 1986, — Alexander Charles, *b* 1988. *Residence* – 11a Porchester Terr, W2 3TH.

BROTHER LIVING

Hon Anthony Heneage, *b* 1920; *ed* Oundle; Lt and temp Capt Black Watch; a JP of Huntingdon; Middle East 1940-44 (despatches); Dep Chm of Huntingdon Bench; Pres Hunts Conservative Club: *m* 1948, Susan Mary, da of Maj-Gen Geoffrey Woodroffe Palmer, CB, CBE, and has issue living, Minette Jane FINCH-KNIGHTLEY, MBE, *b* 1950; has resumed her maiden name; MBE (Civil) 1990: *m* 1983 (*m diss* 1986), Nicholas Redfern, and has issue living, James Heneage Stuart *b* 1983, — Joanna Elizabeth, *b* 1954: *m* 1987, (Christopher) Paul Anthony, of Hillside Cottage, 109 High St, Hail Weston, Cambs PE19 4JS, 2nd son of Kenneth Anthony, of Oxted, Surrey, and has issue living, Harrington Arthur Heneage *b* 1992 Charlotte Susan *b* 1990. *Residence* – Broomleigh, Huntingdon Road, Brampton, Hunts.

COLLATERAL BRANCHES LIVING

　　Grandchildren of late Lt-Col Charles Arthur Wynne Finch, eldest son of late Charles Wynne Finch, MP, eldest son of late Charles Wynne Griffith-Wynne, eldest son of Hon Charles Finch, 2nd son of 3rd Earl:—
　　Issue of late Col John Charles Wynne Finch, CBE, MC, *b* 1891; *d* 1982: *m* 1914, Alice Mary Sybil, who *d* 1970, da of late Rt Rev Hon Edward Carr Glyn, DD (*see* B Wolverton, colls, 1970 Edn):—
Charles Edward Ifan (Cefnamwlch, Tudweiliog, Pwlheli, Caerns), *b* 1929; late Coldm Gds; Sheriff of Denbighshire: *m* 1967, Rosemary Dorothea, da of Lt-Col Clive Grantham Austin, JP, DL, RHA (*see* E Scarbrough, 1980 Edn), and has issue living, David Heneage, *b* 1970, — Mary Davina, *b* 1968, — Harriet Jane, *b* 1971. —— Elizabeth Jane Myfanwy, *b* 1918: *m* 1948, Alexander Dougal Malcolm, of Phillip's House, Much Marcle, Ledbury, and has issue living, James Ronald (457 E Crescent Av, Redlands, Calif 92373, USA), *b* 1951: *m* 1978, Sandra Lee, da of Charles Wilson Thomas, of Salt Lake City, Utah, USA, and has issue living, Peter Thomas *b* 1979, Lucy Caitlin *b* 1983, — Janet Mary, *b* 1949: *m* 1984, James Hume Greenfield, and has issue living, Harry Alexander Hume *b* 1985, Katharine Mary *b* 1987, — Elizabeth Anne, *b* 1960. —— Olwen Mary (The Bantam House, White Roding, Dunmow, Essex), *b* 1924: *m* 1944 (*m diss* 1969), Roger Wake (*see* Wake, Bt), who *d* 1988.

　　Granddaughter of late Edward Heneage Wynne Finch, yr son of late Charles Wynne Finch, MP (ante):—
　　Issue of late Arthur Wynne Finch, *b* 1878, *d* 1936: *m* 1926, Florence, who *d* 1978, da of late Very Rev Charles Thomas Ovenden, Dean of St Patrick's, Dublin:—
Anne, *b* 1927: *m* 1954 (*m diss* 1968), John Vavasour Earle, MB, BCh, and has issue living, Belinda Diana, *b* 1957, — Jenny Ruth, *b* 1959, — Polly Joan, *b* 1961. *Residence* – Beech Cottage, Carlton-in-Cleveland, Stokesley, Middlesbrough, Yorks.

PREDECESSORS – (1) *Rt Hon* HENEAGE Finch, PC, 2nd son of the 1st Earl of Nottingham and brother of 6th Earl of Winchilsea; was Solicitor-Gen 1678-86, when he was removed by James II, and MP for Oxford Univ 1678-9, and for Guildford 1685; cr *Baron Guernsey* (peerage of Great Britain) 1702, and *Earl of Aylesford* (peerage of Great Britain) 1714; *d* 1719; *s* by his eldest son (2) HENEAGE, 2nd Earl; *d* 1757; *s* by his son (3) HENEAGE, 3rd Earl, LLD; MP for Leicestershire 1732-41, and for Maidstone 1754; *d* 1777; *s* by his eldest son (4) HENEAGE, 4th Earl, Lord Steward of the Household; *d* 1812; *s* by his eldest son (5) HENEAGE, 5th Earl; *d* 1859; *s* by his eldest son (6) HENEAGE, 6th Earl, *b* 24 Dec 1824; was MP for Warwickshire South 1849-57: *m* 1846, Jane Wightwick, who *d* 1911, da of John W. Knightley, of The Bury, Leamington Spa; *d* 10 Jan 1871; *s* by his eldest son (7) HENEAGE, 7th Earl; *b* 1849: *m* 1871, Edith, who *d* 1897, da of late Lieut-Col Peers Williams, MP, of Temple House, Great Marlow; *d* 1885; *s* by his brother (8) CHARLES WIGHTWICK, 8th Earl; established his claim to the Earldom and Barony July 1885; *b* 1851: *m* 1st, 1873, Hon Georgina Agnes, who *d* 1874, da of 3rd Baron Bagot; 2ndly, 1879, Ella Victoria, who *d* 1939, da of late John Ross, of Benena, and widow of Capt J. H. Linton, of Hemingford Abbots, Hunts; *d* 1924; *s* by his grandson (9) HENEAGE MICHAEL CHARLES, son of late Capt Heneage Greville, Lord Guernsey, Irish Gds (eldest son of 8th Earl), *ka* 1914, 9th Earl; *b* 1908; Capt RA (TA): *m* 1940, Pamela Elizabeth (DUGDALE), who *d* 1990, da of late Col Hon John Charles Coventry; *ka* 1940; *s* by his uncle (10) CHARLES DANIEL FINCH-KNIGHTLEY (2nd son of 8th Earl), 10th Earl; *b* 1886; assumed the additional surname of Knightley 1912; late Capt Rifle Brig (Prince Consort's Own): *m* 1918, Aileen Jane Chartres, who *d* 1977, da of late William McCormac Boyle; *d* 1958; *s* by his eldest son (11) CHARLES IAN, 11th Earl and present peer; also Baron Guernsey.

AYLESTONE, BARON (Bowden) (Life Baron 1967)

HERBERT WILLIAM BOWDEN, CH, CBE, PC, son of Herbert Henwood Bowden, of Cardiff; *b* 20 Jan 1905; *ed* Canton High Sch, Cardiff; Member of Leicester City Council 1938-45, PPS to Postmaster-Gen 1947-49, a Lord Commr of the Treasury 1950-51, Dep Ch Opposition Whip 1951-55, Ch Opposition Whip 1955-64, Lord Pres of Council and Leader of the House, 1964-66, Sec of State for Commonwealth Affairs 1966-67; Dep Speaker House of Lords 1983-93; Chm of IBA (formerly ITA) 1967-75 (Gold Medal Royal Television Soc 1975); MP for S Leicester (*Lab*) 1945-50, and for SW Leicester 1950-67: served World War II RAF 1940-45; cr CBE (Civil) 1953, PC 1962, *Baron Aylestone*, of Aylestone, City of Leicester (Life Baron) 1967, and CH 1975: *m* 1st, 1928, Louisa Grace, da of William Brown of Cardiff; 2ndly, 1993, Vicki Clayton, and has issue by 1st *m*.

Address – c/o House of Lords, SW1.

DAUGHTER LIVING (*By 1st marriage*)

Hon Brenda Dolores, *b* 1929: *m* 1951 (*m diss* 1983), John Leonard Billingham, and has issue.

AYLMER, BARON (Aylmer) (Baron I 1718, Bt I 1662)

MICHAEL ANTHONY AYLMER, 13th Baron, and 16th Baronet; *b* 27 March 1923; *s* 1982; *ed* Trin Hall, Camb (Exhibitioner, BA 1944, LLB 1945, MA 1948); admitted Solicitor 1948: *m* 1950, Countess Maddalena Sofia Maria Gabriella Cecilia Stefania Francesca, da of late Count Arbeno Maria Attems di Santa Croce, of Aiello del Friuli (*see* By Pirbright, 1954 Edn), and has issue.

𝕬rms – Argent, a cross sable, between four Cornish choughs proper. 𝕮rest – Out of a ducal coronet or a Cornish chough rising proper. 𝕾upporters – Two marines vested with fur caps, brown jackets and blue breeches, their waists girt with bunting and dressed at all points like complete sailors, the *dexter* holding in his exterior hand a forestaff, and the *sinister* a deep-sea line, the plummet pendent, all proper. *Residence* – 42 Brampton Grove, NW4 4AQ.

SON LIVING

Hon (ANTHONY) JULIAN, *b* 10 Dec 1951; *ed* Westminster, and Trin Hall, Camb (MA); admitted Solicitor 1976: *m* 1990, Belinda Rosemary, only da of Maj Peter Henry Parker (*see* E Macclesfield, colls), and has issue living, Michael Henry, *b* 21 March 1991, — Rosemary Sofia, *b* 1993. *Residence* – 16 Edgarley Terrace, SW6.

DAUGHTER LIVING

Hon Gioia Francesca, *b* 1953: *m* 1991, Andrew Robert Shaw, and has issue living, Elizabeth Margaret Louise, *b* 1993. *Residence* – 25 Willow Drive, Southwold, Bicester, Oxon OX6 9XA.

DAUGHTER LIVING OF TWELFTH BARON

Hon Ann Kathleen *b* 1941: *m* 1972, Gregor Byron Miller, of 6-1701 Chesterfield Av, N Vancouver, BC, Canada V7M 2N9, and has issue living, Jonathan Brown Aylmer, *b* 1975.

WIDOW LIVING OF ELEVENTH BARON

HELEN COOPER (*Helen, Baroness Aylmer*) (RR3, Nelson, BC, Canada), da of late Thomas Hogg, of Toronto, Canada, and widow of Frederick Gordon Riseborough: *m* 1960, as his 2nd wife, the 11th Baron, who *d* 1977.

WIDOW LIVING OF TWELFTH BARON

ALTHEA (*Althea, Baroness Aylmer*), eldest da of late Lt-Col John Talbot, IA: *m* 1939, the 12th Baron, who *d* 1982. *Residence* – 601-1159 Beach Drive, Victoria, BC V8S 2N2, Canada.

COLLATERAL BRANCHES LIVING

Grandchildren of late Col Frederick Arthur Aylmer, 2nd son of late Maj-Gen Henry Aylmer, grandson of Rev Hon John Aylmer, 4th son of 2nd Baron:—
Issue of late Capt Edward Arthur Aylmer, DSC, RN, *b* 1892, *d* 1974: *m* 1925, Gwladys Phoebe, who *d* 1968, da of late David Evans, of Brecon:—
Gerald Edward (St Peter's Coll, Oxford), *b* 1926; *ed* Winchester, and Balliol Coll, Oxford (BA); served in RN 1944-47; Master of St Peter's Coll, Oxford Univ 1978-91; Pres R Historical Soc 1984-88, Chm R Commn on Historical MSS since 1989: *m* 1955, Ursula Adelaide, only da of late Maj Brian George Michael Frederick Nixon, and has two adopted children, Thomas Bartholomew, *b* 1962, — Emma Clare, *b* 1964. *Residences* - The Old Captains, Hereford Rd, Ledbury, Herefords HR8 2PX; 18 Albert St, Jericho, Oxford OX2 6AZ.
Issue of late Maj Henry Gerald Aylmer, *b* 1896, *d* 1978: *m* 1927, Nancy, who *d* 1991, da of late Drake Hollick, of The Old House, Sheering, Harlow, Essex:—
John Henry (Hilltop House, The Hill, Burford, Oxon OX18 4HX), *b* 1936; *ed* Radley: *m* 1st, 1959 (*m diss* 1970), Venetia Mary, el da of Ian Thomson Henderson (*see* Verner, Bt, 1962 Edn); 2ndly, 1971, Mrs Margaret Gillian Elliot, da of John Musker, and has issue living (by 1st *m*), Miranda Jane, *b* 1962: *m* 1987, Simon M. A. Webster, of 15 Harrison's Lane,

Ringmer, nr Lewes, E Sussex, eldest son of P. M. Webster, of Blackstone Grange, Henfield, W Sussex, and has issue living, Sophie Charlotte Monica *b* 1990, — Juliet Rose, *b* 1965. —— Rachel Moyra (*Lady Pauncefort-Duncombe*), *b* 1930: *m* 1951, Maj Sir Philip Digby Pauncefort-Duncombe, 4th Bt, Gren Gds (ret).

Issue of late Lt-Col Claud Aylmer, RA, *b* 1900, *d* 1952: *m* 1928, Margaret Victoria (Four Barns Hay, Old Marston, Oxford OX3 0PN) (who *m* 2ndly, 1954, Com John Rudolf Peronet Thompson, RN, who *d* 1965) (she subsequently resumed the surname of AYLMER by deed poll 1982), da of late Frank Hemming, of Franklyns, Great Waltham, Chelmsford:—

Richard Grenfell (Cromwell's House, 17 Mill Lane, Old Marston, Oxford OX3 0PY), *b* 1932; *ed* Wellington Coll, and London Univ (BA 1952); Capt (ret) RA: *m* 1964, Marelyn Joyce, only da of Sir James Miller, GBE, and has issue living, Christopher James, *b* 1966: *m* 1992, Cheryl Janice, yr da of Clive Perrett, of Stratford-upon-Avon, — Kenneth Malcolm, *b* 1970.

PREDECESSORS – (1) MATTHEW Aylmer, 2nd son of Sir Christopher Aylmer, 1st Bt (*cr* 1662); was MP for Portsmouth 1695-8, and for Dover 1698-1718, Gov of Deal Castle 1710, Com-in-Ch of the Fleet 1709, Master of Greenwich Hospital, and Rear-Adm of Great Britain, etc; *cr Lord Aylmer, Baron of Balrath* (peerage of Ireland) 1718; *d* 1720; *s* by his son (2) HENRY, 2nd Baron; *d* 1754; *s* by his son (3) HENRY, 3rd Baron, Capt RN; *d* 1766; *s* by his son (4) HENRY, 4th Baron, who *s* his kinsman as 7th Bt 1780; *d* 1785; *s* by his son (5) MATTHEW, GCB, 5th Baron; a Gen in the Army and Col 18th Foot; assumed 1825 by R licence the additional surname of Whitworth; was Gov Gen of Canada 1830-35; *dsp* 1850; *s* by his brother (6) FREDERICK WILLIAM, KCB, 6th Baron; was an Adm; *d* 5 Mar 1858; *s* by his cousin (7) UDOLPHUS (el son of Capt John Athalmer Aylmer, RN, el son of Adm John Aylmer, son of the Rev Hon John Aylmer, 4th son of 2nd Baron), 7th Baron; *b* 1814: *m* 1841, Mary Eliza, who *d* 1881, da of Edward Journeaux, of Melbourne, Canada; *d* 1901; *s* by his el son (8) MATTHEW, 8th Baron; *b* 1842; Maj-Gen; sometime A-G and Inspector-Gen Canadian Forces: *m* 1875, Amy Gertrude, who *d* 1935, da of late Hon John Young, of Montreal; *d* 1923; *s* by his el son (9)JOHN FREDERICK WHITWORTH, 9th Baron; *b* 1880: *m* 1928, Gertrude Emma, who *d* 1977, da of late Colin Black, CE, of Vic, BC; *d* 1971; *s* by his brother (10) KENNETH ATHALMER, 10th Baron; *b* 1883: *m* 1924, Eleanor Katharine, who *d* 1970, da of late John Francis Rogers, of Swanington, Norfolk; *d* 1974; *s* by his brother (11) BASIL UDOLPHUS, 11th Baron; *b* 1886; 1914-18 War as Capt Canadian Forces: *m* 1st, 1916, Bessie Irving, ARRC, who *d* 1956, da of late Joseph Watson, of Westward Park, Cumberland; 2ndly, 1960, Helen Cooper, da of late Thomas Hogg, of Toronto, and widow of Frederick Gordon Riseborough; *d* 1977; *s* by his kinsman (12) HUGH YATES (only son of Arthur Lovell Aylmer, grandson of Maj Gen Harry Aylmer, 2nd son of Adm John Aylmer, ante), 12th Baron, *b* 1907: *m* 1939, Althea, eldest da of Lt-Col John Talbot, IA; *d* 1982; *s* by his cousin (13) MICHAEL ANTHONY (only son of Christopher Aylmer, grandson of Maj-Gen Harry Aylmer, ante), 13th Baron and present peer.

BADEN-POWELL, BARON (Baden-Powell) (Baron UK 1929, Bt UK 1922)
(Name and Title pronounced "Bayden Poell")

ROBERT CRAUSE BADEN-POWELL, 3rd Baron, and 3rd Baronet; *b* 15 Oct 1936; *s* 1962; *ed* Bryanston; RN 1955-57; Ch Scouts Commr Scout Assocn 1963-82, since when Vice-Pres Scout Assocn, World Scout Foundation 1978-88; Pres Camping & Caravan Club since 1993: *m* 1963, Patience Hélène Mary, CBE, da of Maj Douglas Myers Batty, of Zimbabwe.

Arms – Quarterly: 1st and 4th, per fesse or and argent, a lion rampant guardant gules between two tilting spears erect proper, *Powell*; 2nd and 3rd, argent, a lion rampant proper, on the head a crown vallary or between four crosses patée gules and as many fleur-de-lis azure proper, *Baden*. **Crest** – 1st, a lion passant or, in the paw, broken tilting spear in bend proper, pendent therefrom by a riband gules and escutcheon resting on a wreath sable, charged with a pheon, or, *Powell*; 2nd, out of a crown vallary or a demi-lion rampant gules, on the head a like crown, charged on the shoulder with a cross patée argent, and supporting with the paws a sword erect proper, pommel and hilt gold, *Baden*. **Supporters** – *Dexter*, an officer of 13th/ 18th Hussars in full dress, his sword drawn over his shoulder proper; *sinister*, a boy scout holding a staff also proper.
Residence – Clandon Manor Farm, E Clandon, Guildford, Surrey GU4 7SA.

BROTHER LIVING

Hon DAVID MICHAEL (18 Kalang Rd, Camberwell, Victoria 3124, Australia), *b* 11 Dec 1940; *ed* Pierrepont House; a Member of Mercers' Co, and a Freeman of City of London: *m* 1966, Joan Phillips, da of late Horace William Berryman, of Camberwell, Melbourne, Australia, and has issue living, David Robert, *b* 6 Jan 1971, — Alexander Peter, *b* 1973, — Myles Warrington, *b* 1975.

SISTER LIVING

Hon Wendy Dorothy Lillian (4/16 Allambee Av, Camberwell, Victoria 3126, Australia), *b* 1944.

AUNT LIVING (*Daughter of 1st Baron*)

Hon Betty St. Clair, *b* 1917: *m* 1936, Gervas Charles Robert Clay, late Provincial Commr, Colonial Service, N Rhodesia, and has issue living, Robin Baden, *b* 1939: *ed* Michaelhouse, Natal, and Loughborough Coll: *m* 1971, Susan, el da of late Rev Charles de Candole, of Witchampton Rectory, Dorset, and has issue living, Toby *b* 1973, Annarella *b* 1975, — Nigel Gerard Arden, *b* 1943; *ed* Peterhouse, and Rhodesia Univ: *m* 1969, Elaine, da of late Albert Hughes, of Bournemouth, and has issue living, Gerard *b* 1970, Adam *b* 1975, Olivia *b* 1973, — Crispin David Powell, *b* 1944; *ed* Peterhouse, St David's Coll, Lampeter, and Univ of Wales: *m* 1973, Ortrud Wiese, of Windhoek, S-W Africa, and has issue living, Eric *b* 1974, — Gillian Ella St Clair, *b* 1937: *m* 1968, William Leigh Strudwick Clay, and has issue living, Rawley *b* 1971, Daphne *b* 1970. *Residence* - Ford Lodge, Wiveliscombe, Taunton, Som.

PREDECESSORS – The Powell family were resident in Suffolk until David Powell (*d* 1784) became a merchant in London. He *m* 1723, Susanna, da and heiress of Edward Thistlethwaite, Registrar to the Bishop of Salisbury, by Susanna, da and heiress of Andrew Baden, of Salisbury. His eldest son, David Powell, Treasurer St Luke's Hosp, London, *b* 1725: *m* 1761, Laetitia, who *d* 1801, da and heiress of John Clark, of St Botolph's, Bishopsgate, and *d* 1810, leaving issue, a yr son, Baden Powell, of Tunbridge Wells, Kent; High Sheriff Kent 1831; *b* 1767: *m* 1795, Hester, who *d* 1848, da of James Powell, of Clapton, and *d* 1844, leaving issue, three sons and two das. His eldest son, Rev Prof Baden Powell, was Vicar of Plumstead, Kent, and Savilian Prof of Geometry to Oxford Univ, FRGS, etc; *b* 1796, married thrice, and *d* 1860, leaving issue (by his 3rd wife, *m* 1846, Henrietta Grace, who *d* 1914, da of Vice-Adm W. H. Smyth), a 5th surv son **(1)** *Lieut-Gen Sir* ROBERT STEPHENSON SMYTH *Baden-Powell*, OM, GCMG, GCVO, KCB (assumed addl surname of Baden by Public Notice 1869, and the arms of Baden by Royal Licence 1902), *b* 1857; Lt-Gen late 13th Hussars; Afghanistan 1880-81, Zululand 1888, Ashanti Expedition 1895-96, in command of Native Contingent, which he raised, Matabeleland 1896, S Africa 1898-1900, raising Rhodesian Frontier Force, then Comdg troops defending Mafeking during memorable siege of that place; founded Boy Scouts Organization 1908, and Girl Guides Organization 1910; became Ch Scout of the World 1920; *cr* a *Baronet* 1922, and *Baron Baden-Powell*, of Gilwell, Essex (peerage of United Kingdom) 1929: *m* 1912, Olave St Clair, GBE, (World Ch Guide 1930-77), who *d* 1977, da of late Harold Soames, of Parkstone, Dorset; *d* 1941; *s* by his only son **(2)** ARTHUR ROBERT PETER, 2nd Baron, *b* 1913; in British S Africa Police 1934-37, and Native Affairs Dept, S Rhodesia 1937-45: *m* 1936, Carine, who *d* 1993, da of late Clement Hamilton Crause Boardman, of Johannesburg; *d* 1962; *s* by his el son **(3)** ROBERT CRAUSE, 3rd Baron and present peer.

BAGOT, BARON (Bagot) (Baron GB 1780, Bt E 1627)

Possessing antiquity

HENEAGE CHARLES BAGOT, 9th Baron, and 14th Baronet; *b* 11 June 1914; *s* 1979; *ed* Harrow; late Maj 6th Queen Elizabeth's Own Gurkha Rifles: *m* 1939, Muriel Patricia, da of late Maxwell James Moore Boyle, of Tullyvin House, co Cavan, and Lareen House, co Leitrim, and has issue.

Arms – Ermine, two chevronels azure. **Crest** – Out of a ducal coronet of five leaves or, a goat's head argent, armed gold. **Supporters** – Two goats argent, armed and bearded or.
Residences – Tyn-y-Mynydd, nr Llithfaen, Gwynedd, N Wales; 16 Barclay Rd, SW6.

SON LIVING

Hon CHARLES HUGH SHAUN (16 Barclay Rd, SW6), *b* 23 Feb 1944; *ed* Abbotsholme: *m* 1986, Mrs Sally A. Stone, da of D. G. Blunden, of Farnham, Surrey, and has issue living, Grace Lorina Kitty, *b* 1993.

DAUGHTER LIVING

Hon Caroline Patricia, *b* 1942: *m* 1st, 1962 (*m diss* 1985), Hugh Alexander James Cameron-Rose, who *d* 1993; 2ndly, 1991, Peter Garner-Clarke, and has issue living (by 1st *m*), Hugh Charles, *b* 1962, — Georgina Louise Stella, *b* 1968.

WIDOWS LIVING OF SIXTH AND SEVENTH BARONS

NANCY CONSTANCE BAGOT, da of late Francis Aldborough Spicer, of Sydney; resumed the surname of Bagot by deed poll 1971: *m* 1st, 1940, as his 2nd wife, the 6th Baron, who *d* 1961; 2ndly, 1965 (*m diss* 1972), George Kenneth Whitehead. *Residence* – Blithfield Hall, Rugeley, Stafford.

MARY FRANCES (*Dowager Baroness Bagot*) (8 Pembroke Place, W8), da of late Lt-Col George Frederick Hibbert, late 7th Fus, and widow of Lt-Col (Albert) Claud Hewitt, late R Fus: *m* 1972, as his 2nd wife, the 7th Baron, who *d* 1973.

COLLATERAL BRANCHES LIVING

Grandson of late Lt-Col Josceline FitzRoy Bagot, MP, of Levens Hall, Westmorland, who was nominated a *baronet* Jan 1913, but *d* March 1913 before the patent passed the Great Seal, grandson of late Rt Hon Sir Charles Bagot, GCB, 2nd son of 1st Baron:—
    Issue of late Dorothy Bagot, *b* 1886, *d* 1974: *m* 1905, Henry Melville Gaskell, JP, who *d* 1954:—
Oliver Robin BAGOT, TD (Levens Brow, Kendal, Cumbria), *b* 1914; *ed* Eton, and Trin Coll, Camb; JP Westmorland 1948, DL Cumbria 1967; Lieut 4th Bn Border Regt (TA); FRICS; 1939-45 War (prisoner); assumed by royal licence 1936 the surname of Bagot in lieu of his patronymic, and the arms of Bagot quarterly with those of Gaskell: *m* 1938, Annette Dorothy, da of Paymaster-Cdr F. R. Stephens, RN, of 2 Clarence Terr, Leamington Spa, and has issue living, Charles Henry (Levens Hall, Kendal, Cumbria), *b* 1946; FRICS; JP Cumbria 1991: *m* 1975, Susan Elizabeth, da of Ian Alexander Ross, of Aros Cottage, Gullane, E Lothian, and has issue living, Richard Alexander *b* 1981, Harry Josceline *b* 1983, Jessica Mary *b* 1977, Laura Elizabeth *b* 1979, — Priscilla, *b* 1939: *m* 1st, 1960 (*m diss* 1964), (Edward) Humphry Tyrrell Wakefield (afterwards 2nd Bt); 2ndly, 1967, Erik George Sebastian Smith, of Tithe Barn, Forde Abbey, Chard, Somerset TA20 4HN, and has issue living (by 2nd *m*), Miranda *b* 1968, Susanna *b* 1970, — Elizabeth Dorothy, *b* 1947: *m* 1967, Mark Roper, of Forde Abbey, Chard, Somerset (*see* E Lovelace, colls, 1985 Edn), and has issue living, Katherine Alice *b* 1968, Victoria Jane *b* 1970, Lucinda *b* 1972, — Lucinda Rose Mary (School House, Levens, Cumbria), *b* 1950: *m* 1969 (*m diss* 1993), Michael Victor Sclater, and has issue living, Josceline Mark *b* 1972, Henry Rupert *b* 1976.

    Grandchildren of late Cecil Villiers Bagot (*infra*):—
    Issue of late Lt-Col Charles Frederic Villiers Bagot, OBE, *b* 1912, *d* 1986: *m* 1939, Lucy Violet Kathleen de la

Cloche, who *d* 1972, da of late Harold Marriott, of 60 Great Cumberland Pl, Wl; 2ndly, 1975, Mrs Anne Elisabeth Dyke (DRABBLE) (The Red House, Brockdish, Diss, Norfolk), elder da of Arthur Calver, of Docking, Norfolk:—
(By 1st *m*) Richard Charles Villiers, *b* 1941. —— Julian William D'Arcy, *b* 1943. —— Harriet Anne Elizabeth, *b* 1951: *m* 1978, Julian Patrick Ashley Greene, only son of late Col J. S. Greene, OBE, MC, of Grange House, Long Melford, Suffolk, and has issue living, John Charles Henry, *b* 1985, — Lucy Diana Sylvia, *b* 1989. *Residence* – 27 Brockwell Park Gdns, SE24 9BJ. —— Patricia Mary, *b* 1953: *m* 1984, Terence B. A. Maguire. *Residence* – 87 Lea St, Kidderminster, W Midlands DY10 1SN.

Granddaughter of late Rev Frederic Bagot, DCL, 8th son of late Rt Rev Hon Richard Bagot, DD, Bishop of Bath and Wells, 3rd son of 1st Baron:—
Issue of late Cecil Villiers Bagot, *b* 1865, *d* 1940: *m* 1903, Ethel, who *d* 1944, yr da of late Jesse Garratt, of Wateringbury, Kent:—
Milicent Jessie Eleanor, CBE, *b* 1907; *ed* Lady Margaret Hall, Oxford (MA); formerly attached to Min of Defence; MBE (Civil) 1949; CBE (Civil) 1967. *Residence* – 5 Putney Heath Lane, SW15 3JG.

In remainder to baronetcy only

Grandsons of late Rev John Greville Chester, 4th son of late Lt-Col Charles Montagu Chester, 2nd son of late Rev William Chester, 3rd son of Charles Bagot-Chester (who assumed the surname of Chester in lieu of his patronymic 1755), 2nd son of 5th baronet:—
Issue of late Maj Anthony James Bagot Chester, MC, *b* 1892, *d* 1952: *m* 1924, Gladys Mabel, who *d* 1974, eldest da of late Rev Frederick Charles Stamer (*see* Stamer, Bt, colls, 1972-73 Edn):—
John Greville Bagot, MC, *b* 1925; 1939-45 War as Maj Coldstream Gds (MC); DL Bucks. *Residence* – The Old Rectory, N Crawley, Newport Pagnell, Bucks.
Issue of late Henry Montagu Bagot Chester, *b* 1896, *d* 1969: *m* 1924, Alyce Amy Maude Tranchell, who *d* 1934:—
Hugh Malcolm, *b* 1929: *m* 1972, Mrs Pauline Lillian Butt, da of late Thomas Nicholls, of Bishopsworth, Bristol, and formerly wife of Lionel Butt. *Residence* – 76 Aylesbury Crescent, Bedminster Down, Bristol BS3 5NN.

Grandchildren of late Reginald Warham Antony St Leger (*d* 1952), of New Dorp Beach, Staten Is, NY, yst son of late John St Leger (who assumed the surname of St Leger in lieu of his patronymic 1863), eldest son of late Lt-Gen John Chester, 4th son of Charles Bagot-Chester (ante):—
Issue of late Gaspard Douglas Anthony St Leger, *b* 1890, *d* 1974: *m* 1914, Ivy, who *d* 1945, da of late William S. West:—
†John Douglas, *b* 1920; *dunm* 1941. —— Ivy, *b* 1915: *m* 1939, Charles P. Leonard, of 23 Twin Hills Rd, Poughkeepsie, NY 12603, USA, and has issue living, Ann Carol, *b* 1940: *m* 1962, William Denno, and has issue living, Nicole *b* 1963, Lori *b* 1967. —— Virginia May, *b* 1922: *m* 1964, David Hunter, of 3616 Lone Wolf Trail, St Augustine, Florida 32086, USA.
Issue of late Geoffrey Bayard St Leger, *b* 1892, *d* 1961: *m* 1919, Grace Elizabeth, who *d* 1934, da of late Robert Baylor:—
Jean Mary, *b* 1923; *d* 1989. —— Claire Amy, *b* 1928: *m* 1952, H. Charles McNally, of 335 Old Army Rd, Basking Ridge, NJ 07920, USA, and has issue living, Robert Charles (20 Long Hill Rd, Long Valley, NJ 07853, USA), *b* 1953: *m* 1977, Jacqueline Port, and has issue living, Austin Charles *b* 1986, Ashley Jacqueline *b* 1983, Caroline Taylor *b* 1987, — Jan Barbara (51 Village Drive, Basking Ridge, NJ 07920, USA), *b* 1955, — Jane Hoefer, *b* 1959: *m* 1982, Douglas E. Brandt, of 354 S Maple Av, Basking Ridge, NJ 07920, USA.
Issue of late Roderic Craufurd St Leger, *b* 1894, *d* 1949: *m* 1916, Cora Irene, who *d* 1932, da of late Giles Curtis Gass:—
(Roderic) Harry (25 Dirks Terrace, Highland, NY 12528, USA), *b* 1919: *m* 1950, Doris J., da of late Eugene Geary, and has had issue, Thomas E., *b* and *d* 1951, — Nancy J. ST LEGER, *b* 1953; has resumed her maiden name: *m* 1978 (*m diss* 1990), Roy L. Post. —— Beverly Cora (25 Dirks Terrace, Highland, NY 12528, USA), *b* 1917: *m* 1955, George Howard Hurd, who *d* 1987.

Granddaughter of late Col Heneage Charles Bagot-Chester, yr son of late Lt-Gen John Chester (ante):—
Issue of late Capt Hugh Augustus Bagot-Chester, *b* 1876, *d* 1938: *m* 1st, 1895 (*m diss* 1908), Margaret Kathleen Julia, who *d* 1951, only da of late Col Richard E. Oakes, BSC; 2ndly, 1913, Clotilde Mary Hamilton, who *d* 1964, da of late Hon Arthur Henry Browne (*see* B Kilmaine, colls, 1963 Edn):—
(By 2nd *m*) Peggy Mary Clotilde, *b* 1914: *m* 1st, 1937 (*m diss* 1946), Wallace Stuart Finlayson, actor and stage dir (as Wallace Douglas), who *d* 1990; 2ndly, 1947 (*m diss* 1954), Edward Ralph Harley, CBE. *Residence* – 16 Swan Court, Flood St, Chelsea, SW3.

PREDECESSORS – This family descends from Bagod who held Bramshall, Staffs from Robert de Stafford at the time of the Domesday Survey in 1086. The Staffords, Dukes of Buckingham, descended from the same male stock, Hervey Bagot changing his name to Stafford in late 12th century as his mother was heiress of that family. (1) Sir HERVEY Bagot, Sheriff of Staffordshire 1626, a staunch loyalist; *cr* a Bt 1627; *d* 1660; *s* by his el son (2) Sir EDWARD, 2nd Bt, MP for Stafford in the Restoration Parliament; *d* 1673; *s* by his son (3) Sir WALTER, 3rd Bt, MP for Staffordshire in seven Parliaments; *d* 1704; *s* by his son (4) Sir EDWARD, 4th Bt, MP for co Stafford; *d* 1712; *s* by his son (5) Sir WALTER WAGSTAFFE, LLD, 5th Bt, successively MP for Newcastle-under-Lyme, Staffordshire, and Oxford Univ; *d* 1768; *s* by his el son (6) Sir WILLIAM, 6th Bt, MP for co Stafford 1754-80; *cr* Baron Bagot (peerage of Great Britain) 1780; *d* 1798; *s* by his el son (7) WILLIAM, LLD, 2nd Baron; distinguished for scientific attainments: *m* 1st, 1799, Hon Emily FitzRoy, who *d* 1800, da of 1st Baron Southampton; 2ndly, 1807, Lady Louisa Legge, who *d* 1816, da of 3rd Earl of Dartmouth; *d* 1856; *s* by his el son (8) WILLIAM, 3rd Baron; sat as MP for Denbighshire (C) 1835-52: *m* 1851, Hon Lucia Caroline Elizabeth Agar-Ellis, el da of 1st Baron Dover, and sister of 3rd Viscount Clifden; *d* 1887; *s* by his son (9) WILLIAM, 4th Baron, *b* 1857; a Gentleman Usher of Privy Chamber to HM Queen Victoria 1885-7, and a Lord-in-Waiting to HM Queen Victoria 1896-1901: *m* 1903, Lilian Marie, who *d* 1958, da of late Henry May, of Maryland, USA; *d* 1932; *s* by his cousin (10) GERALD WILLIAM (son of late Vice-Adm Henry Bagot, son of 3rd son of 1st Baron), 5th Baron, *b* 1866; *d* 1946; *s* by his cousin (11) CARYL ERNEST (son of late Rev Lewis Richard Charles Bagot, son of late Rev Charles Walter Bagot, 4th son of late Rt Rev the Hon Richard Bagot, DD, Bishop of Bath and Wells, 3rd son of 1st Baron), 6th Baron; *b* 1877; Lieut Irish Guards; European War 1914-19: *m* 1st, 1911, Margaret, who *d* 1937, da of James McMenemy; 2ndly, 1940, Nancy Constance, da of late Francis Aldborough Spicer of Sydney, NSW; *d* 1961; *s* by his cousin (12) HARRY ERIC (son of late Charles Frederick Heneage Bagot, 4th son of late Rev Charles Walter Bagot (ante)) 7th Baron; *b* 1894: *m* 1st, 1951, Kathleen Elizabeth Saddler, who *d* 1972, widow of Noel Murray Puckle, of Melbourne, Aust; 2ndly, 1972, Mary Frances, da of late Lt-Col George Frederick Hibbert, late 7th Fus, and widow of Lt-Col (Albert) Claud Hewitt, late R Fus; *d* 1973; *s* by his brother (13) REGINALD WALTER, 8th Baron; *b* 1887: *m* 1st, 1922 (*m diss* 1934), Winifred Gwyneth Bowen; 2ndly, 1934, Millicent Brenda, who *d* 1980, only da of late Henry White Bowden, of Mobwell House, Gt Missenden, Bucks; *d* 1979; *s* by his half-brother (14) HENEAGE CHARLES, 9th Baron and present peer.

BAILLIEU, BARON (Baillieu) (Baron UK 1953)

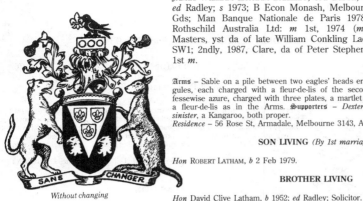

Without changing

JAMES WILLIAM LATHAM BAILLIEU, 3rd Baron; *b* 16 Nov 1950; *s* 1973; *ed* Radley; *s* 1973; B Econ Monash, Melbourne; late 2nd Lt Coldm Gds; Man Banque Nationale de Paris 1978-82, since when Man Rothschild Australia Ltd: *m* 1st, 1974 (*m diss* 1985), Cornelia Masters, yst da of late William Conkling Ladd, of 61 Cadogan Sq, SW1; 2ndly, 1987, Clare, da of Peter Stephenson, and has issue by 1st *m*.

𝕬rms – Sable on a pile between two eagles' heads erased or, three escutcheons gules, each charged with a fleur-de-lis of the second. 𝕮rest – Upon a billet fessewise azure, charged with three plates, a martlet sable, holding in the beak a fleur-de-lis as in the Arms. 𝕾upporters – *Dexter*, a yellow Labrador dog; *sinister*, a Kangaroo, both proper. *Residence* – 56 Rose St, Armadale, Melbourne 3143, Australia.

SON LIVING (By 1st marriage)

Hon ROBERT LATHAM, *b* 2 Feb 1979.

BROTHER LIVING

Hon David Clive Latham, *b* 1952; *ed* Radley; Solicitor.

UNCLES LIVING (Sons of 1st Baron)

Hon Robert Latham, MBE, TD, *b* 1917; *ed* Winchester, and Magdalen Coll, Oxford (MA); Solicitor 1954; formerly Dir Banque Belge Ltd, Man Dir of Henry Ansbacher Co Ltd, C. H. Goldrei, Foucard and Son Ltd, and View Forth Investment Trust Ltd; 1939-45 War as Major Middx Yeo (despatches, MBE); MBE (Mil) 1945: *m* 1949, Delphine Mary, yr da of late Edgar Hastings Dowler (*see* Reynolds, Bt, 1980 Edn), and has issue living, Simon, *b* 1951: *m* 1977, Jane Brebner, of Dunkeld, Johannesburg, and has issue living, James *b* 1982, Nicole *b* 1979, Karen *b* 1986, — Anthony Robert *b* 1956, *m* 1980 (*m diss* 1988), Clare Veronica, da of Richard Gubbins, of The Old Post House, Phoenix Green, Hartley Wintney, Hants, and has issue living, Emma Louise *b* 1986, — Mary Clare, *b* 1950: *m* 1974 (*m diss* 1985), James Neil Percival Cranston, and has issue living, Sophie *b* 1976, Georgina *b* 1978, — Celia Maria, *b* 1953: *m* 1977, William Bryant Style, and has issue (*see* Style Bt, colls), *Residences* – 9 Abingdon Court, Abingdon Villas, W8, and Little Barhams, Priors Way, Aldeburgh, Suffolk.

Hon Edward Latham, *b* 1919; *ed* Winchester, and Brasenose Coll, Oxford (BA 1942, MA 1947); formerly a Member of London Stock Exchange, Chm of Nat Mutual Life Assurance Assocn of Australasia (London Branch), Dir ANZ Bank, RTZ and other Cos; Dep Grand Master of United Grand Lodge of England; 1939-45 War as Capt RA and RHA (invalided): *m* 1942, Betty Anne Jardine, da of late Henry Leslie Jardine Taylor, of Crofton Lodge, Sunningdale, Berks, and has issue living, Christopher Latham, *b* 1949: *m* 1984, Jane E., only da of Robert Bowie, of Bayford, Somerset, and has issue living, Charles Latham *b* 1985, Edward Latham *b* 1990, Olivia Clare *b* 1987 , — Philip Latham, *b* 1958: *m* 1985, Lucinda Rosalie, el da of Francis Rokeby Black (*see* B Cadman), and has issue living, Sacha Frances *b* 1989, Francesca Caroline *b* 1994, — Annette Leslie, *b* 1955: *m* 1986, Christopher G. A. Aylwin, el son of late John Aylwin, FRCS, of Clos Nicolle, St Lawrence, Jersey, CI, and has issue living, Patrick John *b* 1990, Emma Alice *b* 1987, Camilla Louise *b* 1993.

AUNT LIVING (Daughter of 1st Baron)

Hon Yvette Latham, *b* 1922: *m* 1946, Robert Ruttan Wilson, of Durford Knoll, Upper Durford Wood, Petersfield, Hants (*see* Bs Berners, colls).

MOTHER LIVING

Anne Bayliss, el da of Leslie William Page, of Southport, Queensland, Australia: *m* 1st, 1945 (*m diss* 1961), Hon William Latham Baillieu, later 2nd Baron Baillieu, who *d* 1973; 2ndly, 1964, (Harry) Anthony Rupert Dodd, of Ridgewood, Parry Inlet, via Denmark, W Australia 6333, and of Ridgewood Manor, Uckfield, Sussex.

WIDOW LIVING OF SECOND BARON

DELIA MURIEL (*Delia, Baroness Baillieu*), da of —, and formerly wife of — Champion: *m* 1962, and his 2nd wife, the 2nd Baron, who *d* 1973.

PREDECESSORS – (1) *Sir* CLIVE LATHAM Baillieu, KBE, CMG, son of late Hon William Lawrence Baillieu, of Melbourne, Australia; *b* 1889; Dir-Gen British Purchasing Commn, Washington 1941-42; Head of British Raw Materials Mission, Washington, and British Repres on Combined Raw Materials Board 1942-43, Pres of FBI 1945-47, Chm of Dunlop Rubber Co 1949-57, and Pres 1957-67; *cr Baron Baillieu*, of Sefton Commonwealth of Australia and of Parkwood, co Surrey (peerage of UK) 1953: *m* 1915, Ruby Florence Evelyn, who *d* 1962, da of William Clark, of Windlesham Moor, Surrey; *d* 1967; *s* by his el son (2) WILLIAM LATHAM, 2nd Baron; *b* 1915: *m* 1st 1945 (*m diss* 1961), Anne Bayliss, el da of Leslie William Page, of Southport, Qld; 2ndly, 1962, Delia Muriel, Mrs Champion; *d* 1973; *s* by his elder son (3) JAMES WILLIAM LATHAM, 3rd Baron and present peer.

BAKER, BARONY OF (Baker) (Extinct 1985)

DAUGHTERS LIVING OF LIFE BARON

Hon Joanna MacAlister, *b* 1933: *m* 1962, Dr David Michael Ritchie Park, of 6 Saxe Coburg St, Edinburgh.
Hon Dinah, *b* 1936: *m* 1960, Nigel Esmond Recordon, of Bush Farm, Colwall, nr Malvern, Worcs.

Balcarres, Earl of; see Earl of Crawford and Balcarres.

BALDWIN OF BEWDLEY, EARL (Baldwin) (Earl UK 1937)

EDWARD ALFRED ALEXANDER BALDWIN, 4th Earl; *b* 3 Jan 1938; *s* 1976; *ed* Eton, and Trin Coll, Camb: *m* 1970, Sarah MacMurray, el da of Evan James, of Upwood Park, Abingdon, Berks, and has issue.

Arms – Argent, on a saltire sable a quatrefoil or. **Crest** – A cockatrice sejant, wings addorsed argent, combed, wattled, and beaked or, gorged with a crown vallary, lined and reflexed over the back gold and charged on the shoulder with a rose gules, barbed and seeded proper. **Supporters** – On either side a white owl proper, that on the sinister holding in the beak a sprig of broom also proper.
Residence – Manor Farm House, Godstow Rd, Upper Wolvercote, Oxford OX2 8AJ.

SONS LIVING

BENEDICT ALEXANDER STANLEY (*Viscount Corvedale*), *b* 28 Dec 1973; *ed* Bryanston. *Hon* James Conrad, *b* 1976. *Hon* Mark Thomas Maitland, *b* 1980.

PREDECESSORS – **(1)** *Rt Hon Sir* STANLEY Baldwin, KG, son of late Alfred Baldwin (MP for W, or Bewdley, Div of Worcestershire), of Wilden House, Stourport; *b* 1867; a Junior Lord of the Treasury Jan to June 1917; Joint Financial Sec to the Treasury 1917 to April 1921, Pres of Board of Trade April 1921 to Oct 1922, Chancellor of the Exchequer Oct 1922 to Aug 1923, Leader of the Conservative Party May 1923 to May 1937, Prime Min and First Lord of the Treasury May 1923 to Jan 1924, again Prime Min and First Lord of the Treasury Nov 1924 to June 1929, Lord Pres of the Council Aug 1931 to June 1935 (also Lord Privy Seal Sept 1932 to Jan 1934), and again Prime Min and First Lord of the Treasury June 1935 to May 1937; acted as a Counsellor of State during HM King George V's absence abroad 1925, and during HM's illness 1928-29; *cr Viscount Corvedale*, of Corvedale, co Salop, and *Earl Baldwin of Bewdley* (peerage of United Kingdom) 1937: *m* 1892, Lucy, GBE (a DGStJ), who *d* 1945, el da of late Edward Lucas J. Ridsdale, of Rottingdean, Sussex; *d* 1947; *s* by his son **(2)** OLIVER RIDSDALE, 2nd Earl; *b* 1899; an Author and Journalist; sometime Parliamentary Private Sec to Sec of State for War; was Gov and Com-in-Ch of Leeward Islands 1948-50; sat as MP for Dudley (*Lab*) 1929-31, and for Paisley 1945-47, *d* 1958; *s* by his brother **(3)** (ARTHUR) WINDHAM, 3rd Earl; *b* 1904: *m* 1936, (Joan) Elspeth who *d* 1980, yst da of late Charles Alexander Tomes, of New York; *d* 1976; *s* by his son **(4)** EDWARD ALFRED ALEXANDER, 4th Earl and present peer.

With the help of my God I leap over the wall

BALERNO, BARONY OF (Buchanan-Smith) (Extinct 1984)

SONS LIVING OF LIFE BARON

Rev the Hon Robert Dunlop (Eriska, Connel, Argyll; Caledonian Club), *b* 1936; *ed* Edinburgh Acad, Trin Coll, Glenalmond, Pembroke Coll, Camb (BA), New Coll, Edinburgh, and Princeton Theological Seminary, New Jersey (ThM); Min of Christ's Church, Dunollie, Oban, 1962-66; Chap to 8th Bn Argyll and Sutherland Highlanders 1963, and of 3rd Bn Argyll and Sutherland Highlanders, and of 51st Highland Volunteers 1967-68; Chap of St Andrew's Univ 1966-73, Preacher to USA for British Council of Churches 1968, Chancellor's Assessor, St Andrew's Univ 1981-85, and Dir Scottish Television since 1982: *m* 1966, Sheena Mary, da of late Alexander W. Edwards, and has issue.
Hon Jock Gordon (Pitcaple Farm, RR2, Cambridge, Ontario N3C 2V4, Canada; Royal Northern (Aberdeen) and Caledonian Clubs), *b* 1940; *ed* Trin Coll, Glenalmond, Aberdeen Univ, and Iowa State Univ, USA, PhD, Oklahoma; Lt Gordon Highlanders; TA (Res); Prof Univ of Guelph: *m* 1964, Virginia Lee, el da of John S. Maxson, of Dallas, Texas, and has issue.

DAUGHTER LIVING OF LIFE BARON

Hon Dame Mary Drummond, DBE, *b* 1927; *ed* St Denis, and Edinburgh Univ (MA 1949); Dep Ch Commr Girl Guides, Scotland 1972-77, Chm WRVS 1988-93, Member Parole Board for Scotland 1982-89, Chm Trustee Savings Bank Foundation, Scotland since 1994, Gov Fettes Coll since 1982, Memb Convocation Heriot Watt Univ since 1986, and Visiting Cttee Glenochil Young Offenders Inst since 1972; *cr* DBE 1993: *m* 1953, Col Charles Herbert Kenneth Corsar, LVO, OBE, TD, JP, DL, of Burg, Torloisk, Isle of Mull, and 11 Ainslie Pl, Edinburgh, and has issue.

WIDOWS LIVING OF SONS OF LIFE BARON

(Isobel Angela) Margaret, da of Edward Bowden, of Oxshott, Surrey, and widow of Stuart McIntosh: *m* 1961, Rev the Hon George Adam Buchanan-Smith, who *d* 1983. *Residence* – Woodhouselea, Milton Bridge, Pencuik, Midlothian.
Janet Delahoy, CBE, da of late Thomas Lawrie, CBE: *m* 1956, Rt Hon Alick Laidlaw Buchanan-Smith, MP, who *d* 1991. *Residence* – House of Cockburn, Balerno, Lothian.

BALFOUR, EARL OF (Balfour) (Earl UK 1922)

Virtue strives towards heaven

GERALD ARTHUR JAMES BALFOUR, 4th Earl; *b* 23 Dec 1925; *s* 1968; *ed* Eton; Master Mariner; Co Councillor (1960-74) and a JP for E Lothian; Merchant Navy (1944-53); farmer since 1969: *m* 1956, Mrs Natasha Georgina Lousada, da of late Capt George Anton, and formerly wife of late J. C. Lousada.

𝕬rms – (as recorded at Lyon Office), — Argent, on a chevron engrailed between three mullets sable as many otters' heads erased of the field. 𝕮rest – A palm tree proper. 𝕾upporters – Two otters proper, collared or.
Residence – Whittingehame Tower, Haddington, East Lothian EH41 4QA.

SISTERS LIVING

Lady Evelyn Jean Blanche, *b* 1929: *m* 1948 Michael William Brander, and has issue living, Andrew Michael, *b* 1949: *m* 1988, Mrs Donna Spielman, — Kathleen Jean, *b* 1950: *m* 1976, Ian McCall, and has issue living, Angus *b* 1979, Andrew *b* 1980, — Evelyn Ann, *b* 1952.
Lady Alison Emily, *b* 1934: *m* 1963, Thomas Kremer, MA, and has issue living, David Lytton, *b* 1964, — Amanda Lili, *b* 1966, — Kim Madeleine, *b* 1969. *Residence* – Widworthy Barton, Honiton, Devon.

AUNT LIVING (*Daughter of 2nd Earl*)

Lady Kathleen Constance Blanche (Woodhall Cottage, Pencaitland, E Lothian), *b* 1912; *ed* Newnham Coll, Camb (BA 1934, MA 1949): *m* 1933, Richard Charles Oldfield, who *d* 1972, and has issue living, Frances Elizabeth (164 Duke's Av, Muswell Hill, N10 2QB), *b* 1935; BSc, PhD: *m* 1963 (*m diss* 1983), Roderick Whitfield, MA, PhD, and has issue living, Aldus Francis *b* 1970, Martha Ming *b* 1965, Tanya Thisbe *b* 1967, — Margaret Cayley, *b* 1939; PhD: *m* 1960, Agbo Folarin, of Ife Univ, Nigeria, and has issue living, Oliver Abiola Raschid *b* 1973, Akinola Amos *b* 1978, Evelyn Adeola *b* 1970.

COLLATERAL BRANCH LIVING (*In special remainder*)

Issue of late Lt-Col Francis Cecil Campbell Balfour, CIE, CVO, CBE, MC, el son of Col Eustace James Anthony Balfour, yst brother of 1st Earl, *b* 1884, *d* 1965: *m* 1920, Hon Phyllis Evelyn Goschen, who *d* 1976, da of 2nd Viscount Goschen:—

EUSTACE ARTHUR GOSCHEN (Le Pavillon, Ancenis-les-Bois, 44440 Riaillé, France; Savignac, Nanteuil de Bourzac, 24320 Verteillac, France), *b* 26 May 1921; *ed* Eton; 1939-45 War as Capt Scots Gds in N Africa and Italy (wounded): *m* 1st, 1946 (*m diss* 1971), Anne, da of late Maj Victor Yule; 2ndly, 1971, Mrs Paula Susan Cuene-Grandidier, da of late John Maurice Davis, MBE, and has issue living (by 1st *m*), Roderick Francis Arthur (Burpham Lodge, Burpham, Arundel, Sussex; *Clubs* – White's, City of London, Hurlingham, Lord's Taverners), *b* 1948; *ed* Eton; Memb London Stock Exchange 1975-81, Dir Union Discount Co of London plc 1983-90, since when Dir Rothschild Trust Corpn Ltd; Liveryman Clothworkers' Co 1986: *m* 1971, Lady Tessa Mary Isabel Fitzalan Howard, el da of 17th Duke of Norfolk, and has issue living, Willa Anne *b* 1973, Kinvara Clare Rachel *b* 1975, Maria Alice Jubilee *b* 1977, Candida Rose *b* 1984, — Charles George Yule (15 Oakley St, SW3), *b* 1951; *ed* Eton; Man Dir NASDAQ Member Queen's Body Guard for Scotland (Royal Company of Archers): *m* 1st, 1978, Audrey Margaret, da of late Henry Peregrine Rennie Hoare, of Stourton, Wilts (*see* M Bristol, 1955 Edn); 2ndly, 1987, Reichsgräfin Svea Maria Cecily Lucrezia, elder da of Reichsgräf Ernst Friedrich von Goëss, of Staupitzhof, Carinthia, Austria, and has issue living (by 2nd *m*), George Eustace Charles *b* 1990, Eleanor Cecily Isabelle *b* 1989. *Clubs* – White's, Puffins.

PREDECESSORS – (1) Sir ARTHUR JAMES Balfour, KG, OM, PC, LLD, DCL, DPh, FRS, el son of late James Maitland Balfour, of Whittingehame, by his wife, Lady Blanche Mary Harriett Cecil, who *d* 1872, 2nd da of 2nd Marquess of Salisbury; *b* 1848; was employed on Special Mission of Lords Beaconsfield and Salisbury to Berlin 1878, Assist Private Sec to Sec of State for Foreign Affairs (Marquess of Salisbury) 1878-80, Pres of Local Govt Board June 1885 to Jan 1886, Sec for Scotland July 1886 to March 1887 (with a Seat in the Cabinet from Nov 1886), Ch Sec for Ireland March 1887 to Oct 1891, First Lord of the Treasury and Leader of the House of Commons Oct 1891 to Aug 1892, Leader of the Opposition 1892-5, again First Lord of the Treasury and Leader of the House of Commons 1895-1900 and 1900-1902, Prime Min, First Lord of the Treasury, and Leader of the House of Commons 1902-5 (also Lord Privy Seal 1902-3), Leader of the Opposition 1905-11, First Lord the the Admiralty May 1915 to Dec 1916 (also a Member of Cabinet War Council), Sec of State for Foreign Affairs in National Min 1916-19, Lord Pres of the Council 1919-22 and 1925-9, and Pres British Acad 1921-8; appointed a Member of Munitions of War Committee 1915, a British Representative at Peace Conference 1919, and British Delegate to Washington Conference 1921; Chm Med Research Council 1924-9; MP for Hertford (*C*) 1874-85, for E Div of Manchester 1885-1906, and for City of London Feb 1906 to April 1922; went as Head of Special Mission to USA 1917; a British Representative on League of Nations up to 1923; *cr Earl of Balfour*, and *Viscount Traprain*, of Whittingehame, co Haddington (peerage of United Kindom) 1922, with special remainder in default of heirs male of his body, to (1) his brother, *Rt Hon* Gerald William Balfour, and the heirs male of his body; (2) to his nephew, Francis Cecil Campbell Balfour, and the heirs male of his body; and (3) to his nephew, Oswald Herbert Campbell Balfour, and the heirs male of his body; *d* 1930; *s* under the special remainder by his brother (2) GERALD WILLIAM, who had been Ch Sec for Ireland 1895-1900, and Pres of Board of Trade 1900-1905; MP for Central Division of Leeds (*C*) 1885-1906: *m* 1887, Lady Elizabeth Edith Bulwer-Lytton, who *d* 1942, da of 1st Earl of Lytton; *d* 1945; *s* by his son (3) ROBERT ARTHUR LYTTON 3rd Earl; *b* 1902; Chm Scottish Div NCB 1946-51: *m* 1925, Jean Lily, who *d* 1981, da of late Rev John James Cooke-Yarborough (Cooke, Bt, colls); *d* 1968; *s* by his son (4) GERALD ARTHUR JAMES, 4th Earl and present peer; also Viscount Traprain.

BALFOUR OF BURLEIGH, LORD (Bruce) (Lord S 1607)

Every land is the home of a brave man
We have been

ROBERT BRUCE, 8th (de facto) (and 12th but for the attainder) Lord; *b* 6th Jan 1927; *s* 1967; *ed* Westminster; CEng; FIEE, FRSE 1986 (Treasurer 1989-94), Hon FRIAS; Chancellor Stirling Univ since 1988; Treas the Roy Scottish Corpn since 1967; a Dir of Bank of Scotland 1968-91 (Dep-Gov 1977-91), and The Scottish Investment Trust Ltd, Edinburgh since 1970; Chm of Scottish Arts Council 1970-78, and Viking Oil Ltd 1971-80; Commnr Forestry Commn 1971-74; Foreman and Supt The English Electric Co Ltd, Stafford & Liverpool 1952-57, Gen Manager The English Electric Co India, Ltd 1957-64, of English Electric Netherton Works 1964-66, and of D. Napier and Son, Ltd 1967-68; Dir Tarmac plc 1981-90, and Turing Inst 1983-92: *m* 1st, 1971 (*m diss* 1993), Jennifer, da of late E. S. Manasseh, and formerly wife of John Brittain Catlin; 2ndly, 1993, Dr Janet Morgan, da of Dr Frank Morgan, and has issue by 1st *m*.

Arms – Quarterly: 1st and 4th argent, on a chevron sable, an otter's head erased of the field, *Balfour*; 2nd and 3rd or, a saltire and chief gules, the latter charged with a mullet argent, *Bruce*. **Crest** – 1st, upon a rock a mermaid, holding in the dexter hand an otter's head, erased at the neck, and in the sinister hand a swan's head also erased, all proper; 2nd, a dexter arm in fesse, embowed, in armour, couped at the shoulder, the hand holding a sceptre in bend sinister, or. **Supporters** – *Dexter*, an otter proper; *sinister*, a swan also proper.
Residence – Brucefield, Clackmannan.

DAUGHTERS LIVING *(By 1st marriage)*

Hon VICTORIA, *b* 7 May 1973.
Hon Ishbel, *b* 1976.

BROTHER LIVING

(*Hon*) George John Done (does not use courtesy title) (6 Pembroke Walk, W8 6PQ; Athenaeum), *b* 1930; *ed* Westminster; Pres of Royal Soc of Portrait Painters.

SISTERS LIVING

Hon Lætitia Mary, *b* 1920; MB, ChB St Andrews 1946; Vice-Pres NE Council on Addictions since 1983, Pres W Northumberland Branch NSPCC since 1980; Memb Inst of Advanced Motorists, JP for Newcastle upon Tyne: *m* 1955, Dr Ian Metcalfe Telfer, MRCGP, JP, who *d* 1988, and has issue living, John Bruce, *b* 1956; BA, — George Metcalfe, *b* 1961; Dip RSA, MD: *m* 1992, Susan Elizabeth, da of Michael Bernard Allen, of Rose Cottage, 11 Stoneheads, Whaley Bridge, Stockport, — Mary Daubeny, *b* 1958; BSc, MSc: *m* 1990, Kenneth Francis Douthwaite, and has issue living, Matthew Geoffrey Ian *b* 1991, Christopher Robert *b* 1993. *Residence* – 5 Ruthven Court, Adderstone Crescent, Newcastle upon Tyne, NE2 2HH.
Katherine Gordon BRUCE (does not use courtesy title) (25 Kew Green, Kew, Richmond, Surrey TW9 3AA), *b* 1922; reverted by deed poll 1975 to the surname of Bruce: *m* 1946 (*m diss* 1961), Thomas Riviere Bland, MC, and has issue living, Charles Riviere, *b* 1949: *m* 1980, Julie Louise, da of Sir Edgar Charles Beck, CBE, and has issue living, William Riviere *b* 1990, Jemima Katherine Agnes *b* 1983, Daisy Prudence Harriet *b* 1986, — Susanna Katherine, *b* 1947: *m* 1986, Général Philippe Saint-Loubert Bié, and has issue living, Thomas Georges Bland *b* 1988, — Louise Margaret, *b* 1953.
Hon Jean, *b* 1924; formerly in WRNS: *m* 1st, 1949 (*m diss* 1971), John Shirley Ward, Jr; 2ndly, 1974, John Herbert Poole, of 1030, South El Molino Av, Pasadena, Cal 91106, USA, and has issue living (by 1st *m*), John Shirley, *b* 1960: *m* 1987 (*m diss* 1994), Monica Lanz, — Lætitia, *b* 1951: *m* 1980, Dr Paul Buehrens, and has issue living, Thomas *b* 1984, Daniel *b* 1986, — Reavis Mary, *b* 1955: *m* 1987, Gottfried Hilz Ward, and has issue living, Sonia *b* 1988, Christine *b* 1993.
Hon Margaret, *b* 1934: *m* 1967, David Graham Worthy, of Keepers Cottage, Hare Warren Hollow, Merrow Downs, Guildford, Surrey GU1 2HJ, and has issue living, Henry Jonathan David Bruce *b* 1971.

COLLATERAL BRANCHES LIVING

Descendants of Hon Mary Bruce, OBE, el da of 6th Lord, who *m* Sir John Augustus Hope, 16th Bt (*cr* 1628):—
See Hope, Bt (*cr* 1628).

Grandchildren of late Francis Balfour, elder son of late Maj Francis Walter Balfour, eldest son of Francis Balfour, great-grandson of Lt-Col Hon John Balfour, 2nd son of 3rd Lord:—
Issue of late Patrick Small Keir Balfour, *b* 1910, *d* 1967: *m* 1936, Lila Camilla (103 Greenleaf Gdns, Polgate, E Sussex BH6 6PH), da of Basil Edward Spicer:—
Robert William Keir (6 Millicent St, Leongatha, Vic 3953, Australia), *b* 1942: *m* 1964, Evelyn Mary Douglas, and has issue living, Michael Patrick Keir, *b* 1965. —— Frances Norah, *b* 1941: *m* 1965, Hugh Manning Tregarthen, of 10 Lawson St, Paddington, NSW 2021, Australia, and has issue living, Carolyn Mary, *b* 1967: *m* 1991, Stephen Noel Manns, and has issue living, Emelia Jean *b* 1994, — Sarah Jane, *b* 1970, — Susan Manning, *b* 1971. —— Sheila Katharine, *b* 1946: *m* 1st, 1966 (*m diss* 1975), Yan Owen Sikorski; 2ndly, 1989, Ronald Leslie Patterson, late RAAOC, of 67 Comer St, Henty, NSW 2658, Australia, and has issue living (by 1st *m*), Ian Patrick, *b* 1971, — Tanya Mary, *b* 1966: *m* 1988, Phillip Pitt, and has issue living, Christopher Leigh *b* 1983, Flynn Edward James *b* 1990, Kirsten Mary Marie *b* 1988, — Katharine Louise, *b* 1968.

PREDECESSORS – (1) Sir MICHAEL Balfour, KB, PC, Ambassador to the Duke of Tuscany and Lorraine, was *cr Lord Balfour of Burleigh* (peerage of Scotland) 1607; *d* 1619; *s* by his only da (2) MARGARET, who *m* Robert Arnot, who assumed the name of Balfour, and sat as Lord Balfour of Burleigh in the Scottish Parliament, of which he was President 1640-1; she *d* 1663; *s* by son (3) JOHN, 3rd Lord; *d* about 1696; *s* by his son (4) ROBERT, 4th Lord; *d* 1713; *s* by his son (5) ROBERT, 5th Lord, who previously to the death of his father had in 1709 been condemned to death for murder, but escaped from prison by exchanging clothes with his sister; he subsequently engaged in the rebellion of 1715, and in 1716 was attainted by Act of Parliament; *dsp* 1757; *s* (but for the attainder) by his sister (6) MARGARET, *b* 16— *d* 1769; *s* by her nephew (7) ROBERT (son of the Hon Mary Balfour, who *m* 1714, Brig-Gen Alexander Bruce of Kennet), *b* 1718; a Judge of Court of Session with title of *Lord Kennet* 1764: *m* 1754, Helen, who *d* 1786, da of George Abercromby of Tullibody; *d* 1785; *s* by his son **(8)** ALEXANDER, *b* 1755: *m* 1793, Hugh, who *d* 1851, da of Hugh Blackburn, of Glasgow; *d* 1808; *s* by his son **(9)** ROBERT, who claimed the lordship before the Committee for Privileges, House of Lords, but *d* before a decision was made; *b* 1794: *m* 1st, 1825, Anne, who *d* 1846, da of William Murray, of Touchadam; 2ndly, 1848, Jane Dalrymple Hamilton, who *d* 19—, da of Sir James Fergusson of Kilkerran, 4th Bt; *d* 1864; *s* by his son **(10)** ALEXANDER HUGH, KT, GCMG, GCVO, PC, 6th Lord, whose peerage was allowed by House of Lords 1868, the attainder of 1715 having been reversed by Act of Parliament 1869; *b* 1849; a Lord-in-Waiting to HM Queen Victoria 1887-88, Parliamentary Sec to Board of Trade 1888-92. Sec for Scotland with a seat in the Cabinet 1895-1903, and Lord Warden of the Stannaries and Rider and Master Forester of Dartmoor 1908-21; Capt Roy Co of Archers (HM Body Guard for Scotland): *m* 1876, Lady Katherine Eliza Gordon, who *d* 1931, da of 5th Earl of Aberdeen; *d* 1921; *s* by his son **(11)** GEORGE JOHN GORDON, 7th Lord, *b* 1883; Pres of Inst of Bankers 1948-49; Chm of Kensington Housing Trust 1926-49, of Medical Research Council 1936-48, of Cttee, of London Clearing Bankers 1950-52, and of Lloyds Bank 1946-54; a Representative Peer for Scotland 1922-63: *m* 1919, Violet Dorothy Evelyn, MBE, who *d* 1976, da of late Richard Henry Done, of Tarporley, Ches; *d* 1967; *s* by his el son **(12)** ROBERT, 8th Lord and present peer.

BALFOUR OF INCHRYE, BARON (Balfour) (Baron UK 1945)

God be with me

IAN BALFOUR, 2nd Baron; *b* 21 Dec 1924; *s* 1988; *ed* Eton, and Magdalen Coll, Oxford; European War 1942-45 with RN: *m* 1953, Josephine Maria Jane, da of late Morogh Wyndham Percy Bernard (*see* E Bandon, colls, ext), and has issue.

Arms – Argent, on a chevron indented sable between in chief a rose gules and in base a saltire couped azure, an otter's head erased of the first, a bordure engrailed of the third. **Crest** – A dexter hand grasping an olive branch, all proper. **Supporters** – *Dexter*, an otter per fess or and azure; *sinister*, a peregrine falcon proper, bells argent, jesses sable. *Residence* – 10 Limerston St, Chelsea, SW10 0HH.

DAUGHTER LIVING

Hon Roxane, *b* 1955: *m* 1978, Adrian Laird Craig, and has issue living, Robert Joseph, *b* 1982, — Mary Ann Josephine, *b* 1984, — Alethea Katharine, *b* 1986. *Residence* – 29 Regent Terr, Edinburgh EH7 5BS.

HALF SISTER LIVING

Hon Mary Ann, *b* 1949: *m* 1974, Hon Martin Dearman Sutherland Janson (*see* Cs Sutherland). *Residence* – Meadow Cottage, Christmas Common, Watlington, Oxon OX9 5HR.

WIDOW LIVING OF FIRST BARON

MARY AINSLIE (*Mary, Baroness Balfour of Inchrye*), da of late Baron Albert Profumo, KC: *m* 1947, as his 2nd wife, the 1st Baron, MC, PC, who *d* 1988. *Residence* – End House, St Mary Abbots Place, W8 6LS.

PREDECESSORS – **(1)** *Rt Hon* HAROLD HARINGTON Balfour, MC, son of Col Nigel Harington Balfour, OBE, of Belton, Camberley, Surrey; *b* 1897, European War 1914-19 with 60th Rifles, RFC, and RAF (MC and bar, 1914-15 star, two medals), was Parliamentary Under Sec of State for Air 1938-44, and Min Resident in W Africa 1944-45, Freeman City of London, MP for Isle of Thanet Div of Kent (*C*) May 1929-June 1945, *cr* PC 1941, and *Baron Balfour of Inchrye*, of Shefford, co Berks (peerage of United Kingdom) 1945: *m* 1st, 1921 (*m diss* 1946), Diana Blanche, who *d* 1982, da of Sir Robert Grenville Harvey, 2nd Bt (*cr* 1868, ext); 2ndly, 1947, Mary Ainslie, da of late Baron Albert Profumo, KC; *d* 1988; *s* by his only son **(2)** IAN, 2nd Baron and present peer.

Balgonie, Lord; son of Earl of Leven and Melville.

BALLANTRAE, BARONY OF (Fergusson) (Extinct 1980)

SON LIVING OF LIFE BARON

See Fergusson of Kilkerran, Bt.

Balniel, Lord; son of Earl of Crawford and Balcarres.

BALOGH, BARONY OF (Balogh) (Extinct 1985)

SONS LIVING OF LIFE BARON (By 1st marriage)

Hon Stephen Bernard, *b* 1946; *ed* Westminster, and Balliol Coll, Oxford.
Hon Christopher Thomas, *b* 1948; *ed* Westminster, and King's Coll, Camb.

DAUGHTER LIVING OF LIFE BARON (By 1st marriage)

Hon Penelope Kathryn Teresa, *b* 1957; *ed* Camden Sch for Girls, and Lancaster Univ: *m* 1988, Ian Henghes, only son of late Heinz Henghes, sculptor, and has issue living, Leo, *b* 1991.
5HE.

WIDOW LIVING OF LIFE BARON

CATHERINE, MRCS, LRCP (*Baroness Balogh*), da of late Arthur Cole, Fell of King's Coll, Camb, and formerly wife of Anthony Storr: *m* 1970, as his 2nd wife, Baron Balogh (Life Baron), who *d* 1985.

BANBURY OF SOUTHAM, BARON (Banbury) (Baron UK 1924, Bt Uk 1902)

I warn and I protect

CHARLES WILLIAM BANBURY, 3rd Baron and 3rd Baronet; *b* 29 July 1953; *s* 1981: *m* 1st, 1984 (*m diss* 1986), Lucinda Elizabeth Scarlett, elder da of John Frederick Edward Trehearne (*see* B Harvington); 2ndly, 1989, Mrs Inger Marianne Norton, da of — Wiegert, and has issue by 2nd *m*.

Arms – Ermine, a cross patée between five mullets of six points each within an annulet, three in chief and two in base, all gules. **Crest** – A demi-antelope proper, supporting between its feet a cross patée as in the arms and charged on the shoulder with a garb gules. **Supporters** – On either side a collie dog proper, each charged on the shoulder with a cross patée gules.
Residence – The Mill, Fossebridge, Cheltenham, Glos.

DAUGHTERS LIVING (By 2nd marriage)

Hon Charlotte Rosa, *b* 1990.
Hon Poppy Isobel, *b* 1991.

SISTERS LIVING

Hon Carolyn, *b* 1947: *m* 1977, Christopher (Kim) J. A. North, who was *k* in a motor accident 1988.
Hon Anna Josephine, *b* 1950: *m* 1970 (*m diss* 1981), Michael Gordon Croose Parry, and has issue living, Sophie Ruth Flora, *b* 1976.

AUNT LIVING (Raised to the rank of a Baron's daughter 1938)

Hon Mary Heritage, *b* 1914: *m* 1st, 1941, Siegfried Buchmayr; 2ndly, 1964, Richard D. Greenogh (120 East 79 St, New York NY 10026 USA), and has had issue (by 1st *m*), Siegfried Beale (137 Rowayton Av, Rowayton, Connecticut 06853, USA), *b* 1942: *m* 1987, Renée Bernier, and has issue living, Siegfried Brandon *b* 1987, Trevor Banbury *b* 1989, — Norbert Gant, *b* (triplet) 1942; *k* in a motor accident 1981, — Charles Rupert (403 Norwall Av, Norwall, Connecticut 06854, USA), *b* (triplet) 1942: *m* 19—, Katherine.

MOTHER LIVING

Hilda Ruth, da of late A.H.R. Carr, of Malone, Belfast: *m* 1st 1945 (*m diss* 1958), the 2nd Baron, who *d* 1981; 2ndly, 1959, Maj Robert O. G. Gardner, MC, who *d* 1987; 3rdly, 1988, as his 3rd wife, Richard Frederick Norman (*see* Collet, Bt, ext 1944, 1950 Edn).

PREDECESSORS – (1) *Rt Hon* FREDERICK GEORGE Banbury, PC, el son of late Frederick Banbury, of Shirley House, Surrey; *b* 1850; MP for Peckham Div of Camberwell (C) 1892-1906, and for City of London 1906-1924; *cr Baron Banbury of Southam*, of Southam, co Warwick (peerage of United Kingdom) 1924: *m* 1873, Elizabeth Rosa, who *d* 1930, da and co-heiress of late Thomas Barbot Beale, of Brettenham Park, Suffolk; *d* 1936; *s* by his grandson (2) CHARLES WILLIAM, son of late Capt Charles William Banbury, Coldstream Guards (only son of 1st Baron), *ka* 1914, 2nd Baron, *b* 1915; 1939-45 War (despatches): *m* 1945 (*m diss* 1958), Hilda Ruth (who *m* 2ndly, 1959, Maj Robert O. G. Gardner, MC, who *d* 1987, and 3rdly, 1988, as his 3rd wife, Richard Frederick Norman (*see* Collet, Bt, ext 1944, 1950 Edn)), da of late A. H. R. Carr, of Malone, Belfast; *d* 1981; *s* by his only son (3) CHARLES WILLIAM, 3rd Baron and present peer.

BANCROFT, BARON (Bancroft) (Life Baron 1982)

IAN POWELL BANCROFT, GCB, son of Alfred Ernest Bancroft; *b* 23 Dec 1922; *ed* Coatham Sch, Redcar, and Balliol Coll, Oxford (MA; Hon Fellow); served Rifle Bde WW11; PPS to Chancellor of the Exchequer and Lord Privy Seal 1953-57; Cabinet Office 1957-59; Principal Private Sec to successive Chancellors of the Exchequer 1964-66; Under-Sec HM Treasury 1966-68; Dep Chm HM Customs and Excise 1972-73; Second Permanent Sec Civil Service Dept 1973-75; Permanent Sec Dept of Enviroment 1975-77; Head of Home

Civil Service 1977-81; *cr* GCB 1979 (Civil), and *Baron Bancroft*, of Coatham, co Cleveland (Life Baron) 1982; Chm of Trustees Mansfield Coll Oxford since 1981; Memb of Bd of Management for Roy Hospital and Home, Putney since 1982 (Chm 1984-88); Memb Advisory Council on Public Records 1983-88; Dir Bass and The Rugby Group 1982-93, Grindlays Bank and Sun Life Assurance 1983-93, Vice-Pres Building Societies Assocn 1983-91, and Gov of Cranleigh Sch 1983-92; Pres Building Centre Trust 1987-92: *m* 1950, Jean Hilda Patricia, da of David Richard Swaine, and has issue.
Address – House of Lords, SW1.

SONS LIVING

Hon Simon Powell *b* 1953; *ed* Kings Coll Sch, Wimbledon, and LSE (BSc); Vice Pres of Swett and Crawford USA: *m* 1985, Vicki Lynn, da of Glenn Rosenquist, of Dallas, Texas, and has issue living, Nicholas Glenn Powell, *b* 1990, — Megan Louise, *b* (twin) 1990. *Residence* – 11231 Dwarfs Circle, Dallas, Texas 75229, USA.

Hon Adam David Powell (113 Pepys Rd, SW20); *b* 1955; *ed* Kings Coll Sch, Wimbledon, and LSE (BSc); wine merchant: *m* 1985, Amanda Claire, da of late A. J. McCance, of London SW19, and has issue living, Alexander Joseph Powell, *b* 1993, — Jessica Claire, *b* 1991.

DAUGHTER LIVING

Hon Emma Charlotte, *b* 1959; *ed* Canterbury Coll of Art (BA); graphic designer: *m* 1984, Jeremy Guy Minton Haines, of 24 Santos Rd, SW18, son of G. D. M. Haines, of Pippins, Duddleswell, Uckfield, Sussex, and has issue living, Louis George Bancroft, *b* 1990, — Oscar Edward Bancroft, *b* 1993, — Phoebe Alice Bancroft, *b* 1988.

BANDON, EARLDOM OF (Bernard) (Extinct 1979)

DAUGHTERS LIVING OF FIFTH EARL

Lady Jennifer Jane, *b* 1935. *Residence* – Castle Bernard, Bandon, co Cork.

Lady Frances Elizabeth, *b* 1943: *m* 1967, Paul Mark Carter, and has issue living, Philip Bernard, *b* 1979, — Emma Margaret, *b* 1969, — Annabelle Petrea, *b* 1971. *Residence* – Hill House, Birds Lane, Midgham, Reading, Berks RG7 5UL.

SISTER LIVING OF FIFTH EARL (*Raised to the rank of an Earl's daughter* 1925)

Lady Cynthia Lettice Margaret, *b* 1905: *m* 1st, 1925 (*m diss* 1936), Lt-Col Francis Christian Darby Tothill, Rifle Bde, who *d* 1992; 2ndly, 1947, A/Cdre Lionel Guy Stanhope Payne, CBE, MC, AFC, who *d* 1965, and has issue living (by 1st *m*), Betsann, *b* 1927: *m* 1947, Capt Matthew Page Page Wood, Coldstream Gds (*see* Page-Wood, Bt). *Residence* – 31 Halsey St, SW3.

WIDOW LIVING OF FIFTH EARL

Lois (*Countess of Bandon*) (Castle Bernard, Bandon, co Cork), da of Francis Russell, of Victoria, Australia, formerly wife of S/Ldr Frederick Arthur White, RAF: *m* 1946, as his 2nd wife, the 5th Earl, GBE, CB, CVO, DSO, who *d* 1979.

COLLATERAL BRANCH LIVING

Granddaughter of late Percy Brodrick Bernard, el son of late Rt Rev Hon Charles Brodrick Bernard, DD, Lord Bishop of Tuam, 2nd son of 2nd Earl:—
Issue of late Morogh Wyndham Percy Bernard, *b* 1902, *d* 1977: *m* 1929, Hon Diana Pearl Dundas, who *d* 1979, da of 7th Viscount Melville:—
Josephine Maria Jane (*Baroness Balfour of Inchrye*), *b* 1934: *m* 1953, 2nd Baron Balfour of Inchrye.

BANGOR, VISCOUNT (Ward) (Viscount I 1781)

Salvation beneath the Cross

WILLIAM MAXWELL DAVID WARD, 8th Viscount; *b* 9 Aug 1948; *s* 1993; *ed* Univ Coll, London: *m* 1976, Mrs Sarah Mary Malet Bradford, biographer, da of late Brig Hilary Anthony Hayes, DSO, OBE, and formerly wife of Anthony John Bradford, of Lisbon, Portugal.

𝕬rms – Quarterly: 1st and 4th azure, a cross patonce or, *Ward*; 2nd and 3rd gules, three cinquefoils ermine, on a chief of the second a man's heart of the first, *Hamilton*. 𝕮rest – A man's head couped at the shoulders affrontée proper, wreathed about the temples or and azure, and adorned with three ostrich feathers. 𝕾upporters – *Dexter*, a Knight in complete armour proper, charged on the breast with a cross moline gules, behind him a flowing crimson robe, a cross moline argent on its sinister side. On the helmet a plume of feathers of the last, his dexter hand resting on a drawn sword point downwards proper, pommel and hilt or; *sinister*, a Turkish prince vested in robes of blue and gold, white stockings, yellow sandals, gold sash and fringe round the waist, behind him a loose brown robe of fur, on the head a white turban with black feathers, and his hands in fetters proper. *Residence* – 31 Britannia Rd, SW6.

HALF-BROTHER LIVING

Hon (EDWARD) NICHOLAS, *b* 16 Jan 1953; *ed* Westminster, and Edinburgh Univ (MA); formerly Investment Analyst, Smith New Court Securities Ltd, since when an independent TV Prod: *m* 1985, Rachel Mary, da of Hon Hugh Waldorf Astor (*see* B Astor of Hever), and has issue living, Anna Roxelana, *b* 1987, — Zoë Rachel, *b* 1990. *Residence* – 9 Kildare Terrace, W2.

HALF-SISTER LIVING

Hon Sarah, *b* 1951; actress (as Lalla Ward): *m* 1st, 1980 (*m diss* 1982), Tom Baker, actor; 2ndly, 1992, Dr (Clinton) Richard Dawkins, DSc, of New College, Oxford. *Residences* – Savile House, Mansfield Rd, Oxford; 13 Durham Terrace, W2.

AUNTS LIVING (*Daughters of 6th Viscount*)

Hon Helen Elizabeth, *b* 1912. *Residence* – 7 Chelsea Lodge, 58 Tite St, SW3.
Hon Margaret Bertha Meriel (ERIC SMITH), *b* 1914: *m* 1st, 1938 (*m diss* 1947), Lt-Col Desmond Charles Forde, Coldstream Gds, who *d* 1961; 2ndly, 1947 (*m diss* 1962), Gavin Robert Sligh; 3rdly, 1969, Maj Dennis Eric Smith, of 17/21 Sloane Court West, SW3, and has issue living (by 1st *m*), Patrick Mathew Desmond (Seaforde, co Down), *b* 1940; *ed* Eton; JP and DL co Down: *m* 1965, Lady Anthea Geraldine Lowry-Corry, da of 7th Earl Belmore, and has issue living, Mathew Galbraith *b* 1967, Charles Patrick *b* 1972, Finnian Nicholas *b* 1982, Emily Louise *b* 1966, — Sylvia Helena (Flat 9, 110 Elm Park Gdns, SW10), *b* 1938.

COLLATERAL BRANCHES LIVING

Grandson of late Maj Bernard Maxwell Ward (infra):—
Issue of late Maj Bernard Maxwell Ward, LVO, late RHA, *b* 1921, *d* 1991: *m* 1948, Sunniva, who *d* 1962, elder da of Maj Sir Basil Hamilton Hebden Neven-Spence:—
Maxwell Colin Bernard, *b* 1949; *ed* Harrow, and St Catharine's Coll, Camb: *m* 1982, Sarah, yr da of late Lt-Col Peter William Marsham, MBE (*see* E Romney, colls), and has issue living, Charles Bernard Maxwell, *b* 1986, — Frederick Peter Neven, *b* 1989, — Laura Sunniva, *b* 1984, — Antonia Hersey, *b* 1993. *Residence* – Stobshiel House, Humbie, E Lothian EH36 5PD.

Grandson of late Lt-Gen Hon Bernard Matthew Ward, CB, 4th son of 3rd Viscount:—
Issue of late Maxwell William Bernard Ward, *b* 1889, *d* 1960: *m* 1st, 1919 (*m diss* 1931), Ruth Elizabeth, only da of late John Flasby Lawrance Whittingdale, OBE, MD, of Sherborne, Dorset, and Thornton-in-Lonsdale, Yorkshire; 2ndly, 1934, Josephine, yst da of Rev Hugh Robert Coulthard, Hon Canon of Truro, and V of Breage, Cornwall, and widow of Guy Nelson Brown:—
(By 1st *m*) John Maxwell *b* 1922; *ed* Sherborne; MRCS England, and LRCP London 1945: *m* 1948, Evelyn Millicent, da of J. P. Usher, and has issue living, Peter Evan, *b* 1949, — Michael John, *b* 1951, — Nicholas Crosbie, *b* 1956, — Philippa Jane, *b* 1957. *Address* – PO Box 72, Que Que, Zimbabwe.

Grandsons of late Edward Crosbie Ward, 2nd son of late Maj-Gen Sir Edward Wolstenholme Ward, KCMG (infra):—
Issue of late Maj John Crosbie Ward, S Wales Borderers, *b* 1911, *d* 1952: *m* 1935, Margaret Llewellyn, who *d* 1983, da of late Rev Llewellyn Christopher Watson Bullock, of Gt Wigborough, Colchester:—
Christopher John Robert Crosbie (The Old House, Longbridge Deverill, Warminster, Wilts BA12 7DJ), *b* 1937; *ed* Wellington Coll; Maj 2nd Goorkhas: *m* 1979, Caroline Fiona, da of late Maj James Alan Gerald Harley, MC, of Lower Lodge, Wyck Rissington, nr Cheltenham, Glos, and has issue living, Robert James Crosbie, *b* 1986, — Arabella Louise Crosbie, *b* 1980, — Sophie Ann Crosbie, *b* 1982. —— David Edward Crosbie (St Olaf, Sellafirth, Yell, Shetland), *b* 1941; *ed* Wellington Coll: *m* 1976, Christine Julia, da of late Travers Burnell Christopher Christie, of Nelson, NZ.

Granddaughter of late Maj-Gen Sir Edward Wolstenholme Ward, KCMG, eldest son of late Hon John Petty Ward, BCS (infra):—
Issue of late Lt-Col Guy Bernard Campbell Ward, DSO, Croix de Guerre with Palm, *b* 1875, *d* 1933: *m* 1904, Beatrice Constance Charlotte, who *d* 1959, da of late Hon Charles Lennox Butler (*see* B Dunboyne colls, 1959 Edn):—
Constance Isabel (7 Minford Gdns, W14 0AN) *b* 1905: *m* 1932, Charles Lawrence Mackness, Lieut The Buffs, who was *ka* 1943, and has issue living, Caroline Anne, *b* 1940: *m* 1968, John Sullivan, of Campagne Florent, 04280 Cereste, Alpes de Haute, Provence, France, and has issue living, Mercedes Emma *b* 1969.

Grandchildren of late John Petty Ward (*b* 1871) (infra):—
Issue of late Gen Sir Richard Erskine Ward, GBE, KCB, DSO, MC, *b* 1917, *d* 1989: *m* 1947, Stella Elizabeth (*Lady*

Ward) (Bellsburn, 18 Lower St, Rode, Somerset BA3 6PU), da of late Brig Philip Neville Ellis, RA, of Rhyllech, nr Pwlheli, Caerarvon:—
Anthony Richard Bangor (Lower Bowden House, Pangbourne, Berks RG8 8JL), *b* 1960: *m* 1989, Mrs Carolyn WALLACE, eldest da of Giles Walker, of IoM, and has issue living, Archie Erskine Bangor, *b* 1990, — Maximilian Richard Petty, *b* 1992. —— Jeremy Neville (266 Camberwell New Rd, SE5 0RP), *b* 1961: *m* 1984, Elizabeth, only da of Vernon Butterworth, of Thornton, Cleverlys, Lancs, and has issue living, Oliver Richard Xavier, *b* 1985, — Frederick, *b* 1988. —— Léonie, *b* 1949: *m* 1983, David James Chalmers Brown, of Berrycroft Farmhouse, Ashbury, Swindon, Wilts SN6 8LX, son of W. Chalmers Brown, of Balerno, Midlothian, and has issue living, Alexandra, *b* 1985, — Isobel, *b* 1988. —— Stephanie Rachel, *b* 1952: *m* 1981, John David Lace, of 58 Duke's Av, W4 2AF, and has issue living, William John Edward, *b* 1985, — Thomas Charles, *b* 1988, — Toby Richard, *b* (twin) 1988, — Jessica Elizabeth Rachel, *b* 1983.

Grandchildren of late Noel Edward Ward (infra):—
Issue of late Maj James Palmer Ward, *b* 1902, *d* 1976: *m* 1931, Yvonne Lockington (who *m* 2ndly, 1977, Arthur George Kelly, who *d* 1983), da of Cedric Lockington Flood, of Dublin:—
Michael James (20 Cluny Grove, Killiney, co Dublin), *b* 1934; *ed* Aldenham: *m* 1959, Jocelyn Mary, da of late Arthur George Kelly, of Athlone (ante), and has had issue, †Jeremy Charles Arthur James, *b* 1960; *ed* St Andrew's Univ; *d* 1983, — Alexandra Rowena, *b* 1963; *ed* Glengara Park, and Trin Coll, Dublin. —— Patrick Erskine, RD (57 Intwood Rd, Cringleford, nr Norwich NR4 6AA), *b* 1937: *ed* Nautical Coll, Pangbourne; Capt RNR (ret): *m* 1st, 1962 (*m diss* 1972), Eldrith Janet, da of John Bararis Delbridge, of Bulawayo; 2ndly, 1972, Sarah Elizabeth, da of late John Williams, of Ash, Bocking, Surrey, and has issue living (by 1st *m*), Richard Bangor, *b* 1967, — Julia, *b* 1963, — Jannette, *b* 1964, — (by 2nd *m*) James Julien Erskine, *b* 1977, — Timothy John, *b* 1979
Issue of late Jack Lionel Ward, OBE, *b* 1910, *d* 1986: *m* 1939, Beatrice Mary Caroline (Hope Cottage, Church Rd, Rotherfield, E Sussex TN6 3LE), da of George Austin Wareham, of King's Langley, Herts:—
Edward Nicholas (Hookwood House, Shipbourne, Tonbridge, Kent), *b* 1945; *ed* Winchester, and Trin Coll, Camb: *m* 1973, Felicity Lilian Beatrice, da of John Richard Gibbs, of Bromley, Kent, and has had issue, Lucy Beatrice Alice, *b* 1974; *ed* Sevenoaks, and St Andrews Univ, — Emily Charlotte Holly, *b* 1982, — Holly (twin), *b* and *d* 1982. —— Gillian Elizabeth, *b* 1939.

Grandchildren of late Sir William Erskine Ward, KCSI, 4th and yst son of late Hon John Petty Ward, BSC, 1st brother of 3rd Viscount:—
Issue of late John Petty Ward, *b* 1871, *d* 1956: *m* 1906, Rose Gladys May, who *d* 1937, da of Rev Richard Marsh Marsh-Dunn, V of St Nicholas', Shaldon, Devon:—
Myrtle Josephine, *b* 1907: *m* 1st 1929 (*m diss* 1972), Donald Stuart Denholm Fraser, who *d* 1986; 2ndly, 1972, Theodore Alfred Raymond, who *d* 1988, of Horizons Ord, Banff, Grampian, and has issue living (by 1st *m*), June, *b* 1930; ARCA: *m* 1963, Allen Hans Cull, of 5 Combemartin Rd, Southfields, SW18 5PP, and has issue living, Zoë Gail *b* 1970; BA, — Sally, *b* 1936: *m* 1971, Clive Freshwater, of The Hall, Kincraig, Inverness-shire, and has issue living, Duncan *b* 1971, Andrew *b* 1973, Jonathan *b* 1977, — Joanna (1021 Elliot Rd S, Lethbridge, Alberta, Canada), *b* 1950.
Issue of late Noel Edward Ward, *b* 1872, *d* 1944: *m* 1st, 1898 (*m diss* 1922), Jessie Mabel Wood, who *d* 1968, da of James B. Wood, of Woodbine Tea Estate, Assam; 2ndly, 1922, Muriel, who *d* 1983, da of Edward Dalton, of Leeds, Yorks:—
(By 2nd *m*) Noel Erskine (Penrowan, New Rd, Boscastle, N Cornwall), *b* 1925; *ed* Marlborough; a Co Dir: *m* 1st, 1948, June Margaret, da of Albert Ellerton-Long, of Gravesend; 2ndly, 1977, Mrs Jacqueline Ann Aylwin, who *d* 1990, da of James Cyril Lodge, and has issue living (by 1st *m*), Jonathan Philip (109a Tankerton Rd, Tankerton, Whitstable, Kent), *b* 1951; *ed* St Edmund's Sch: *m* 1980, Pauline, da of Howard Moore Gentry, and has issue living, Michael John *b* 1983, Sarah-Jane *b* 1981, — Graeme David, *b* 1953: RN: *m* 1977, Mrs Janet Gates, da of Sidney Brewer, and has issue living, Colin *b* 1977, Michelle *b* 1980.

Grandson of late Edward Robert Ward (infra):—
Issue of late Albert Edward Hamilton Ward, *b* 1902, *d* 1976: *m* 1932, Violet Kate, da of John Henderson Jones:—
John Albert, *b* 1933: *m* 1956, Judith Mary, da of Richard R. Lamdin, and has issue living, Stuart John, *b* 1964, — Fiona Maryon, *b* 1956.

Grandchildren of late John Hamilton Ward, 4th son of late Rev Hon Henry Ward, 2nd brother of 3rd Viscount:—
Issue of late Edward Robert Ward, *b* 1859, *d* 1941: *m* 1901, Edith Georgina, who *d* 1948, da of Albert George Sheriff:—
Robert Hamilton, *b* 1906. —— John Hamilton (14 Green Park Way, Chillington, Kingsbridge, S Devon), *b* 1907: *m* 1939, Peggy Elizabeth Louise, da of William Allen Hazeldine, and has issue living, Edward Hamilton (38 Cambridge Park, Twickenham, Middx) *b* 1944: *m* 1971, Jean Audrey, da of Alfred Hudson, — Roger Hamilton (42 Redruth House, Grange Rd, Sutton, Surrey), *b* 1947. —— Marcia Hamilton, *b* 1904; BA (Honours), London. *Residence* –

Granddaughters of late Thomas Lawrence Frederick Ward, 5th son of late Rev Hon Henry Ward (ante):—
Issue of late Frederic Valentine Ward, *b* 1878, *d* 1960: *m* 1908, Florence Grace, who *d* 1961, da of James Dalziel, of Auckland, NZ:—
Kathleen Florence Mary, *b* 1909: *m* 19—, William Samuel Hazlewood, of 3 Te Reinga View, Tawa, Wellington, NZ, and *d* 1989, leaving issue, Robert William, *b* 1940: *m* 1963, Mary Eagles, and has issue living, Mark *b* 1967, Anne *b* 1969, Lisa *b* 1971, — Barbara Grace (83 Castor Crescent, Porirua, Wellington, NZ), *b* 1944: *m* 1965, Gregory Burgoyne, who *d* 1993, of Melbourne, Australia, and has issue living, Debbie *b* 1966, Sharon *b* 1968, Wendy *b* 1972. —— Doreen Mabel Valerie, *b* 1915: *m* 1939, "Blondie" Henderson, of 15 Mason St, Lower Hutt, Wellington, NZ.

Granddaughter of late Francis Michael Ward, 7th son of late Rev Hon Henry Ward (ante):—
Issue of late Basil Edward Ward, *b* 1886, *d* 1953: *m* 1912, Hazel C. Smith, who *d* 1948:—
Caroline Anne (624 San Miguel Av, Berkeley, Calif 94707, USA), *b* 1914: *m* 1st, 1939, Robert Frederick McKean, who *d* 1966; 2ndly, 1967, Darrell Wiltse Walker, and has issue living (by 1st *m*), Robert Basil, *b* 1943: *m* 1967, — , and has issue living, Jacob Frederick *b* 1969, Aaron Robert *b* 1970, Nathaniel Basil *b* 1973, — Barbara Ann, *b* 1940: *m* 1960, Ray Donald Konig, and has issue living, Kathleen Ann *b* 1966, Colleen Ann *b* 1970, — Patricia Ann, *b* 1951: *m* 1979, Ramish Ramchandani, of 2503 Lincoln Av, Alameda, Calif 94501, USA.

Grandson of late Lt-Col Bernard Edward Ward, 2nd son of late Rev Bernard John Ward, 3rd son of late Col Rt Hon Robert Ward, 3rd son of 1st Viscount:—
Issue of late Capt Bernard John Hamilton Ward, OBE, RN, *b* 1875, *d* 1938: *m* 1908, Annie Lilias, who *d* 1978, da of late Ralph Dalyell, CB (*see* E Warwick, colls, 1924 Edn):—
Bernard Ralph Henry, OBE (Trotts Close, Trotts Lane, Westerham, Kent TN16 1SD), *b* 1911; Lt-Cdr RN (ret); entered Executive Class, Home Civil Ser 1957; OBE (Mil) 1946: *m* 1st, 1943 (*m diss* 1951), Tamara Estya Jasvoin; 2ndly, 1955, Marian Violet, who *d* 1958, da of late Capt Percy William Rimington, OBE, RN; 3rdly, 1961, Daphne Thalia, da of John Lumsden, MBE, Vice-Consul, Casablanca, and has issue living (by 3rd *m*), Nicholas Ralph Dalyell (5 Seaton Close, Highcliffe on Sea, Christchurch BH23 5HP), *b* 1964: *m* 1991, Victoria Anne, da of Leslie Francis Carr, of Highcliffe on Sea, and has issue living, Emily Stephanie *b* 1992, — Annie Christabel, *b* 1965: *m* 1992, Andrew Peter Forbes, of 70 Hillingdon Av,

Sevenoaks TN13 3RA, and has issue living, Frances Rose *b* 1988, Ruby Ann *b* 1993, — John Louis Frederic (adopted son), *b* 1959, *ed* Univ of E Anglia (BA 1981); Royal Hong Kong Police 1982: *m* 1985, Melanie Bayoneta, da of Salcedo Isidro, of Camalines Sur, Philippines, and has issue living, Louisa Marie Christabel *b* 1986, (and an adopted son, Dean Salcedo *b* 1984).

Grandchildren of late Capt John Richard Le Hunte Ward, CBE, RN, only son of late Adm Thomas Le Hunte Ward, CB, 3rd and yst son of late Rev Bernard John Ward (ante):—
Adopted daughters of late Lt-Col Edward Le Hunte Ward, *b* 1906, *d* 1987: *m* 1946, Flora (Linney Water, Eastern Rd, Ashburton, S Devon TQ13 7AP), da of late Capt William Balfour Macdonald, DSO, RN:—
Antonia Janet Elizabeth, *b* 1947: *m* 1975, Daryl George Youé, of Linney Water, Eastern Rd, Ashburton, S Devon, and has issue living, André, *b* 1978, — Dominic, *b* 1980. ——— Fynvola Mary Isabel, *b* 1949; (BA): *m* 1975, Carlo Angelo Bernabucci, of 28 via Anton Cechov Apt 10, Rome 00142, and has issue living, Ivan, *b* 1976, — Matteo, *b* 1978.

Grandchildren of late Maj Michael Bernard John Ward, yr son of late Capt John Richard Le Hunte Ward, CBE, RN (ante):—
Issue of late John Michael Barrie Ward, *b* 1945, *d* 1992: *m* 1974, Anne Christine Hotchkiss (The Victoria Tavern, Station Rd, Shrivenham, Swindon, Wilts):—
Thomas Edward Le Hunte, *b* 1980. ——— Charlotte Jane, *b* 1977. ——— Catherine Sophie, *b* 1979.

Grandchildren of late Maj Hamilton Frederick Ward (infra):—
Issue of late Capt John Frederick Ward, late Irish Gds, *b* 1923, *d* 1989: *m* 1950, Pamela Swinton (Kabazi, PO Box 153, Nakuru, Kenya), da of late Lt-Col George Archibald Swinton Home, of Soy, Kenya:—
Edward, *b* 1958. ——— Sarah, *b* 1953.

Granddaughter of late Lt Robert Frederick Ward, RN only son of late Vice-Adm James Hamilton Ward, 5th son of late Col Rt Hon Robert Ward (ante):—
Issue of late Maj Hamilton Frederick Ward, *b* 1880, *d* 1971: *m* 1913, Violet Enid Jane, who *d* 1972, da of late Sir Henry Conway Belfield, KCMG:—
Sheila Marie Jane, *b* 1914: *m* 1939, Alexander Frederick Reynard, of 675 Pretorius, St, Arcadia, Pretoria 0083, S Africa, and has issue living, Edward Anthony, *b* 1945: *m* 1969, Margaret Marian, da of Thomas Allan Fairbairn, of Millbrae Head, Kirkton Manor, Peebles, and has issue living, Iain Michael *b* 1971, Robert Neil *b* 1974, — John William, *b* 1947: *m* 1974 (*m diss* 1989), Sandra Dianne, da of Willacy Guy Goulding, of 273 Pasteur Rd, Rembrandt Park, S Africa, and has issue living, Angela Lynne *b* 1979, Jennifer Susan *b* 1983, — Monica Mary, *b* 1942: *m* 1983, Michael William Atkinson, Civil Engr, son of William Charles Atkinson, of Johannesburg.

Granddaughter of late William Robert Ward, 6th son of late Col Rt Hon Robert Ward (ante):—
Issue of late Lt-Col Edward Ward, MBE, *b* 1852, *d* 1929; *m* 1900, Harriette Caroline Adeline (Etta), who *d* 1937, da of late John Steuart Maconchy:—
Charlotte Hazel, *b* 1900. *Residence* – 54 Crossgar Rd, Saintfield, co Down.

PREDECESSORS – (1) BERNARD Ward, MP for co Down 1749-70; cr *Baron Bangor* (peerage of Ireland) 1770, and *Viscount Bangor* (peerage of Ireland) 1781; *d* 1781, and was *s* by his el son (2) NICHOLAS, 2nd Viscount; *dsp* 1827; *s* by his nephew, el son of Hon Edward Ward, 2nd son of 1st Viscount (3) EDWARD SOUTHWELL, 3rd Viscount: *m* 1826, Harriet Margaret, who *d* 1880, da of 6th Baron Farnham; *d* 1837; *s* by his el son (4) EDWARD, 4th Viscount, a Representative Peer; *dsp* 1881; *s* by his brother (5) HENRY WILLIAM CROSBIE, 5th Viscount, *b* 1828; a Representative Peer: *m* 1st, 1854, Mary, who *d* 1869, da of late Rev Henry King, of Ballylin, King's co; 2ndly, 1874, Elizabeth, who *d* 1919, da of late Major Hugh Eccles, of Cronroe, co Wicklow; *d* 1911; *s* by his son (6) MAXWELL RICHARD CROSBIE, PC, OBE, 6h Viscount, *b* 1868; a Representative Peer for Ireland; sometime Parliamentary Private Sec to Prime Min of N Ireland; was a Member of Senate, N Ireland 1921-50, and Speaker 1930-50: *m* (Jan) 1905, Agnes Elizabeth, who *d* 1972, da of late Dacre Mervyn Archdall Hamilton, *d* 1950; *s* by his son (7) EDWARD HENRY HAROLD, 7th Viscount, *b* 1905; Broadcaster and Journalist: *m* 1st, 1933 (*m diss* 1937), Elizabeth, who *d* 1969, da of Thomas Balfour, JP, of Wrockwardine Hall, Wellington, Shropshire; 2ndly, 1937 (*m diss* 1947), May Kathleen, who *d* 1969, da of William Middleton, of Shanghai; 3rdly, 1947 (*m diss* 1951), Leila Mary, who *d* 1959, da of David Rimington Heaton, DSO, of Brookfield, Crowhill, S Devon; 4thly, 1951, Marjorie Alice, who *d* 1991, da of late Peter Banks, of St Leonards-on-Sea, and formerly wife of Reginald Forbes Simpson; *d* 1993; *s* by his elder son (8) WILLIAM MAXWELL DAVID, 8th Viscount and present peer; also Baron Bangor.

BANKS, BARON (Banks) (Life Baron 1974)

DESMOND ANDERSON HARVIE BANKS, CBE, son of James Harvie Banks, OBE; *b* 23 Oct 1918; *ed* Univ Coll Coll Sch, Hampstead, NW3; Insurance Broker; Chm Liberal Party Exec 1961-63 and 1969-70, and Pres Liberal Party 1968-69; 1939-45 War as Maj RA in Middle East, Persia, Iraq and Italy; *cr* CBE (Civil) 1972, and *Baron Banks*, of Kenton, Greater London (Life Baron) 1974: *m* 1948, Barbara, da of Richard Taylor Wells, and has issue.
Residence – 58 The Ridgeway, Kenton, Harrow, Middx. *Club* – National Liberal.

SONS LIVING

Hon Alistair Richard Harvie, *b* 1950: *m* 1977, Loretta Ann Owen.
Hon Graham Thornton Harvie, *b* 1953.

BANNERMAN OF KILDONAN, BARONY OF (Bannerman) (Extinct 1969)

SONS LIVING OF LIFE BARON

Hon John Walter MacDonald, *b* 1932; MA (Hons) Glasgow; BA (Hons) Camb; PhD Camb; and has issue living, two sons and one da.
Hon Calum Ruairi Mundell, *b* 1936; BA Camb: *m* 1962, Mary (*neé* Parker), and has issue living, one son and two das.

DAUGHTERS LIVING OF LIFE BARON

Hon (Janet) Ray, MP, *b* 1934; LCST; MP (Lib Dem) Argyll and Bute since 1987: *m* 1957, Lt-Col Iain Michie, RAMC, of Tigh an Eas, Oban, Argyll, and has issue living, three das.
Hon Elizabeth Mary (The Braes, Uplawmoor, Renfrewshire), *b* 1938; resumed surname of Monro 1980: *m* 1st, 1960 (*m diss* 1971), D. S. Munro; 2ndly, 1972 (*m diss* 1980), Iain Buchanan Anderson; 3rdly, 1990, John Daniel Scott, and has issue living, one son and one da.

BARBER, BARON (Barber) (Life Baron 1974)

ANTHONY PERRINOTT LYSBERG BARBER, TD, PC, son of late John Barber, CBE; *b* 4 July 1920; *ed* Retford Sch, and Oriel Coll, Oxford (MA, Hon Fellow 1971); LLB London; 1939-45 War as Lt RA and pilot RAF (prisoner, despatches); a DL for W Yorks (1987); Bar Inner Temple 1948; PPS to Under-Sec of State for Air 1952-54, Govt Whip 1953-57, Lord Commr of Treasury 1957-58, PPS to PM 1958-59, Economic Sec to Treasury 1959-62, and Financial Sec to same 1962-63, and Min of Health 1963-64; Chm Conservative Party Orgn 1967-70; Chancellor of the Duchy of Lancaster June to July 1970, and Chancellor of the Exchequer 1970-74; Chm of Standard Chartered Bank 1974-87; Chm Council of Westminster Med Sch 1975-84; Member Franks Committee on Falklands 1982-83; British Member Eminent Persons Group on S Africa 1986; *cr* PC 1963, and *Baron Barber*, of Wentbridge, W Yorks (Life Baron) 1974: *m* 1st, 1950, Jean Patricia, who *d* 1983, da of Milton Asquith, of Wentbridge, W Yorks; 2ndly, 1989, Mrs Rosemary Surgenor (*née* Youens), formerly wife of John Surgenor, and has issue by 1st *m*.
Club - Carlton.

DAUGHTERS LIVING (By 1st marriage)

Hon Louise Patricia Lysberg, *b* 1951.
Hon Josephine Julia Asquith, *b* 1953: *m* 1989, William J. L. Bradby, son of James Bradby, of Spetisbury, Dorset. *Residence* – Hollesley Lodge, nr Woodbridge, Suffolk, IP12 3RT.

BARBER OF TEWKESBURY, BARON (Barber) (Life Baron 1992)

DEREK COATES BARBER, son of late Thomas Smith-Barber, of The Thatched House, nr Stradbroke, Suffolk; *b* 17 June 1918; *ed* RAC Circencester; Hon FRASE 1986; Hon DSc Bradford 1986; served 1939-45 War (invalided); Farmer and Land Consultant; Founder Member Farming & Wildlife Advisory Group 1969, Environment Consultant to Humberts, Chartered Surveyors, since 1972, Chm BBC's Central Agricultural Advisory Cttee 1974-80, Consultant to Humberts Landplan plc 1974-89, Chm RSPB 1976-81, and Pres 1990-91, Chm Countryside Commn 1981-91, Chm Booker plc Countryside Advisory Board since 1990, Pres Glos Naturalists' Soc since 1982, Patron Lancs Heritage Trust since 1990, Council Member Rare Breeds Survival Trust since 1987 (Pres since 1991), Pres Royal Agricultural Soc of England 1991-92, Chm New Nat Forest Advisory Board since 1991; author, and recipient of several agricultural and conservation awards; *cr* Kt Bach 1984, and *Baron Barber of Tewkesbury*, of Gotherington, co Glos (Life Baron) 1992: *m* 1st, 19- (*m diss* 1981), —, da of —, of —; 2ndly, 1983, Rosemary Jennifer Brougham, da of late Lt-Cdr Randolph Brougham Pearson, RN.
Residence – Chough House, Gotherington, Glos GL52 4QU. *Club* – Farmers'.

BARNARD, BARON (Vane) (Baron E 1698)

HARRY JOHN NEVILLE VANE, TD, 11th Baron; *b* 21 Sept 1923; *s* 1964; *ed* Eton; MSc Durham Univ; patron of 10 livings; JP co Durham 1961, DL 1956-70, Lord Lieut and Custos Rotulorum 1970-88; Lt-Col comdg Northumberland Hussars 1964-66, Hon Col 7th (Durham) Bn LI 1979-89; a Co Councillor for Durham 1952-61; Pres Durham County Branch BRCS 1969-87, Patron 1993, Vice-Chm of Council BRCS 1987-93 (Memb of Council 1982-85); Pres North of England TAVR Assocn 1974-77; KStJ; 1939-45 War as F/O RAFVR: *m* 1952 (*m diss* 1992), Lady Davina Mary Cecil, DStJ, el da of 6th Marquess of Exeter, and has issue.

𝕬rms – Azure, three sinister gauntlets or. 𝕮rest – A dexter hand in armour couped at the wrist grasping a sword in bend all proper, pommel and hilt or. 𝕾upporters – *Dexter*, a griffin argent, gorged with a collar azure thereon three sinister gauntlets or as in the arms; *sinister*, an antelope or, gorged with a collar azure, thereon three martlets or.
Seat – Raby Castle, PO Box 50, Staindrop, Darlington, co Durham, DL2 3AY. *Clubs* – Brooks's, Durham County, Northern Counties (Newcastle).

SON LIVING

Hon HENRY FRANCIS CECIL, *b* 11 March 1959, *ed* Eton, and Edinburgh Univ (BSc)

DAUGHTERS LIVING

Hon Carolyn Mary, *b* 1954; has issue living, Nicola Lauren VANE, *b* 1988.
Hon Elizabeth Anne, *b* 1956: *m* 1982, Glyn M. Deacon, elder son of late A. Deacon, and has issue living, Jessica Anne, *b* 1982, — Laura Sophie, *b* 1984.
Hon Sophia Rosalind, *b* 1962, *ed* Cobham Hall, and Westfield Coll, Univ of Lond (BSc): *m* 1986, Simon B. Phillips, yst son of late Peter J. Phillips, of Gustard Wood, Wheathampstead, Herts, and has issue living, Oliver John, *b* 1989, — Benjamin James, *b* 1994, — Emily Josephine, *b* 1992.
Hon Louise Cicely, *b* 1968; *ed* Cobham Hall, and Central St Martins' Sch of Art and Design (BA).

SISTER LIVING

Hon Rosemary Myra, *b* 1921; a Member of Barnard Castle RDC (Chm 1972-73); Chm Durham Co Fedn of Women's Insts: *m* 1948 (*m diss* 1954), Angus Josslyn Gore-Booth (later 8th Bt), and has issue (*see* Gore-Booth, Bt). *Residence* – The White House, Gainford, Darlington, DL2 3DN.

COLLATERAL BRANCH LIVING

Grandsons of late Col Hon William Lyonel Vane (*who was raised to the rank of a Baron's son* 1892), brother of 9th Baron:—
Issue of late William Morgan FLETCHER VANE, TD (*Baron Inglewood*) (see that title).

PREDECESSORS – (**1**) *Rt Hon* CHRISTOPHER Vane, *b* 1653, 5th and only surviving son of Sir Henry Vane, the younger, who was beheaded for treason 1662; *cr Baron Barnard*, of Barnard Castle, in the County Palatine of Durham (peerage of England) 1698; *d* 1723; *s* by his son (**2**) GILBERT, 2nd Baron, *b* 1678, *d* 1753; *s* by his son (**3**) HENRY, 3rd Baron, *b* 1705, successively MP for Launceston, St Mawes, Ripon, and co Durham, Paymaster in Ireland, a Lord of the Treasury, and Lord-Lieut and Vice-Adm of Durham; *cr Viscount Barnard* and *Earl of Darlington* (peerage of Great Britain) 1754; *d* 1758; *s* by his son (**4**) HENRY, 2nd Earl, *b* 1726, MP for Downton and for co Durham; Lord-Lieut and Vice-Adm of County Palatine of Durham, Master of the Jewel Office, and Gov of Carlisle; *d* 1792; *s* by his son (**5**) WILLIAM HARRY, KG, 3rd Earl, *b* 1766; Lord-Lieut and Vice Adm of Co Durham; MP for Totnes 1788-90 and for Winchelsea 1790-92; *cr Marquess of Cleveland* (peerage of United Kingdom) 1827 and *Baron Raby* and *Duke of Cleveland* (peerage of United Kingdom) 1833: *m* 1st, 1787, Lady Katharine Margaret Powlett, who *d* 1807, da and co-heir of Harry, 6th and last Duke of Bolton; 2ndly, 1813, Elizabeth, who *d* 1861, da of Robert Russell; *d* 1842; *s* by his el son (by 1st *m*) (**6**) HENRY, KG, 2nd Duke; *b* 1788; a Lieut-Gen in the Army; MP 1812-42; *dsp* 1864; *s* by his brother (**7**) WILLIAM JOHN FREDERICK, 3rd Duke; *b* 1792, assumed the surname of Powlett by R licence 1813, and resumed his patronymic, Vane, by R licence 1864; MP 1812-31 and 1846-57; *d* 1864; *s* by his brother (**8**) HARRY GEORGE, KG, 4th Duke, *b* 1803; MP for S Durham (*L*) 1841-59, and for Hastings 1859-64; assumed in 1864 the name and arms of Powlett in lieu of Vane: *m* 1854, Catherine Lucy Wilhelmina, who *d* 1901, da of 4th Earl Stanhope, and widow of Lord Dalmeny, el son of 4th Earl of Rosebery; *d* 1891, when all his honours became extinct with the exception of the Barony of Barnard, which devolved upon (**9**) HENRY DE VERE (son of Sir Henry Morgan Vane, a descendant of the 2nd Baron), who was adjudged 9th Baron by Cttee for Privileges, House of Lords, 1892; *b* 1854; DCL, Hon Col 4th Bn Durham LI: *m* 1881, Lady Catherine Sarah Cecil, who *d* 1918, da of 3rd Marquess of Exeter; *d* 1918; *s* by his son (**10**) CHRISTOPHER WILLIAM, CMG, OBE, MC, TD, 10th Baron, *b* 1888, Lt-Col and Brevet-Col 6th DLI; served World War I 1914-18 as Maj Westmorland and Cumberland Yeo; Lord-Lieut of co Durham 1958-64 and JP co Durham: *m* 1920, Sylvia Mary, who *d* 1993, da of Herbert Straker, late of Hartforth Grange, Richmond, Yorks; *d* 1964; *s* by his el son (**11**) HARRY JOHN NEVILLE, 11th Baron and present peer.

BARNETSON, BARONY OF (Barnetson) (Extinct 1981)

SON LIVING OF LIFE BARON

Hon (William) Denholm, *b* 1955.

DAUGHTERS LIVING OF LIFE BARON

Hon Astraea Joan Denholm, *b* 1941: *m* 1963, John R. D. Moore, of Nether Soonhope House, Peebles, and has issue living.
Hon Louise Jane Denholm, *b* 1952: *m* 1982 (*m diss* 1992), Bernard Rolfe, and has issue living.
Hon Julia Claire Denholm, *b* 1963: *m* 1990, Dr Timothy R. Cave, yr son of Maj Leslie Cave, of Eridge, Sussex.

WIDOW LIVING OF LIFE BARON

JOAN FAIRLEY (*Baroness Barnetson*) (Broom, Chillies Lane, Crowborough, Sussex), da of late William Fairley Davidson: *m* 1940, Baron Barnetson (Life Baron), who *d* 1981.

BARNETT, BARON (Barnett) (Life Baron 1983)

JOEL BARNETT, PC, son of late Louis Barnett, of Manchester; *b* 14 Oct 1923; *ed* Central High Sch, Manchester; Hon Visiting Fellow Strathclyde Univ (1980), Hon LLD Strathclyde 1983, Hon Fellow Birkbeck Coll 1993; FCCA; 1939-45 War; Consultant J. C. Allen & Co (now Hacker Young), Manchester (Sr Partner 1954-74); Chm Parl Labour Party Economic & Financial Gp 1967-70; Ch Sec HM Treasury 1974-79 (Cabinet Member 1977-79), Chm Public Accounts Cttee 1979-83; Member Cttee Hallé Society of Manchester 1982-93, Trustee Victoria and Albert Museum since 1983, Vice-Chm BBC 1986-93, Pres Royal Inst of Public Administrators 1988-92, Chm Birkbeck Coll Appeal Cttee since 1992, Chm Hansard Soc 1985-91; MP for Heywood and Royton Div of Lancs (*Lab*) 1964-83; *cr* PC 1975, and *Baron Barnett*, of Hey-

wood and Royton, in Greater Manchester (Life Baron) 1983: *m* 1949, Lilian Stella, da of Abraham Gold-stone, and has issue.
Residences – 7 Hillingdon Rd, Whitefield, Lancs M25 7QQ; Flat 92, 24 John Islip St, Westminster, SW1.

DAUGHTER LIVING

Hon Erica Hazel, *b* 1951.

BARRINGTON, VISCOUNTCY OF (Barrington) (Dormant or Extinct 1990)

SISTER LIVING OF ELEVENTH VISCOUNT

Priscilla Mary, *b* 1907.

COLLATERAL BRANCH LIVING

Granddaughter of late Hon Percy Evelyn Barrington, yst son of 9th Viscount:—
Issue of late Miguel O'Brien Shute Barrington, *b* 1909, *d* 1937: *m* 1935, Yvonne Guary-Dommergues, who *d* 1948, da of Madame Nebel, of Paris:—
Michaelle Susan (*posthumous*), *b* 1937; *ed* Somerville Coll, Oxford: *m* 1968, Renato Zanatta, of Savona, Italy.

BASING, BARON (Sclater Booth) (Baron UK 1887)
(Name pronounced "Slater Booth")

NEIL LUTLEY SCLATER BOOTH, 5th Baron; *b* 16 Jan 1939; *s* 1983; *ed* Eton, and Harvard Univ (BA); Dir Akroyd & Smithers Inc (New York City): *m* 1967, Patricia Ann, da of late George Bryan Whitfield, of 598 Prospect St, New Haven, Conn, USA, and has issue.

Arms – Quarterly; 1st and 4th gules a chevron, between in chief two bezants, and in base a portcullis chained or, *Booth*; 2nd and 3rd, argent a cross gules between two penguins proper in the first and fourth quarters, and two martlets azure in the second and third quarters, *Sclater*. **Crests** – *Dexter*, a horse's head erased proper, bridled and reined or, charged with a roundel argent, thereon a boar's head erect and erased sable, *Booth; sinister*, Between two sprigs of oak proper, fructed or, a woodcock's head erased proper, gorged with a collar argent, charged with a saltire azure, *Sclater*. **Supporters** – *Dexter*, winged a lion queue fourchee; *sinister*, an eagle sable; each gorged with a saltire azure affixed to the collar a chain reflexed over the back argent, the wings charged on the covert and secondary feathers with three cogwheels in chevron or.
Club – Harvard.

SONS LIVING

Hon STUART ANTHONY WHITFIELD, *b* 18 Dec 1969; *ed* The Collegiate Sch.
Hon Andrew Limbrey, *b* 1973; *ed* The Collegiate Sch.

DAUGHTERS LIVING OF THIRD BARON

Hon Diana Penelope Florence *b* 1925: *m* 1946, James Tennant Bailward, and has issue living, Christopher John (Horsington Manor, Horsington, Templecombe, Som), *b* 1949: *m* 1974, Anne, da of Lt-Col G. E. Gray, of Colehill, Wimborne, Dorset, and has issue living, James Richard *b* 1978, Thomas William *b* 1981, Robert John *b* (twin) 1981, Kate Louise *b* 1976, — Clare Penelope, *b* 1947: *m* 1973, Brian Jayes, of Wayside, Old Horsley Rd, Nailsworth, Glos, son of P. H. Hayes, of Lindfield, Sussex, and has issue living, Andrew Patrick Harris *b* 1977, Rosamund Sarah *b* 1974. *Residence* – Causeway House, Radipole, nr Weymouth, Dorset.
Hon Barbara Amy, *b* 1926: *m* 1961, Peter Michell Luttman-Johnson, and has issue living, William Michell (Waldegrave Farm, Hartest, Bury St Edmunds, Suffolk IP29 4EA), *b* 1963: *m* 1992, Lucilla Jane, eldest da of David Adams, of Earls Colne, Essex, — Anne Elizabeth, *b* 1962, — Catherine Mary, *b* 1966. *Residence* – Woodmancote, Lodsworth, Petworth, W Sussex.
Hon Gabrielle Mary, *b* 1929: *m* 1953, Cdr Martin Parnell Seth-Smith, RN, and has issue living Nicholas John, *b* 1961, — Imogen Gabrielle, *b* 1963. *Residence* – The Triangle, Wildhern, Andover.

COLLATERAL BRANCH LIVING

Issue of late Brig-Gen Hon Walter Dashwood Sclater-Booth, CB, CMG, DSO, late RA, yst son of 1st Baron, *b* 1869, *d* 1953: *m* 1913, Frances Mary, who *d* 1949, da of late Rowland Burdon, of Castle Eden, co Durham (*see* Slade, Bt, colls, 1930 Edn):—
Eleanor Mary, *b* 1914. *Residence* – 11 Elm Park Lane, SW3.

PREDECESSORS – (1) George Sclater, PC, el son of late William Lutley Sclater, of Hoddington House, Hants; *b* 1826; assumed by R licence 1856 the additional surname of Booth; MP for N Hants (C) 1857-85, and for Hants N, or Basingstoke, Div 1885-7; Parliamentary Sec to Poor Law Board 1867-8, Financial Sec to Treasury 1868, and Pres of Local Govt Board 1874-80; *cr Baron Basing* (peerage of United Kingdom) 1887: *m* 1857, Lydia Caroline, who *d* 1881, da of late Major George Birch, of Clare Park, Hants; *d* 1894; *s* by his el son (2) GEORGE LIMBREY, CB, *b* 1860; Lt-Col and Brevet-Col 1st (R) Dragoons, and Brig-Gen: *m* 1889, Mary, who *d* 1904, da of late John Hargreaves, of Maiden Erlegh Berks, and Whalley Abbey, Lancashire; *d* 1919; *s* by his only son (3) JOHN LIMBREY ROBERT, TD, 3rd Baron, *b* 1890: *m* 1924, Mary Alice Erle, who *d* 1970, da of late Lt-Col Richard Erle Benson, E Yorks Regt; *d* 1969, *s* by his cousin **(4)** GEORGE LUTLEY (son of Hon Charles Lutley Sclater Booth, 2nd son of 1st Baron), 4th Baron, *b* 1903: *m* 1st, 1938 (*m diss* 1944), Jeanette, who *d* 1957, da of late Neil Bruce MacKelvie, of New York; 2ndly, 1951, Cynthia, who *d* 1982, da of late Charles W. Hardy, of Salt Lake City, Utah, and widow of Carl H. Beal, of Los Angeles; *d* 1983; *s* by his only son **(5)** NEIL LUTLEY, 5th Baron and present peer.

BASNETT, BARONY OF (Basnett) (Extinct 1989)

WIDOW LIVING OF LIFE BARON

KATHLEEN JOAN MOLYNEAUX (*Baroness Basnett*): *m* 1956, Baron Basnett (*cr* Life Baron 1987), who *d* 1989, and has issue, two sons. *Residence* – Windrush, St John's Av, Leatherhead, Surrey.

BATH, MARQUESS OF (Thynn and Thynne) (Marquess GB 1789, Bt E 1641)
(Name pronounced "Thin")

I have good reason

ALEXANDER GEORGE THYNN, 7th Marquess, and 10th Baronet; *b* 6 May 1932; *s* 1992; *ed* Eton, and Ch Ch, Oxford (MA); formerly Lieut Life Guards and Royal Wilts Yeo; has reverted to spelling of Thynn since 1976; contested (Wessex Regionalist) Westbury 1974, Wells 1979; contested (Wessex Regionalist and European Federal Party) Wessex, European Election 1979; mural artist, and composer; author of *The Carry Cot*, *Lord Weymouth's Murals*, *A Regionalist Manifesto*, *The King is Dead*, *Pillars of the Establishment*, etc; Dir Longleat Enterprises 1964: *m* 1969, Anna (Anna Gael, actress and journalist), da of Laszlo Izsak Gyarmarthy, of Los Angeles, Calif, USA, and has issue.

Arms – Quarterly: 1st and 4th, barry of ten or and sable, *Botteville*; 2nd and 3rd argent, a lion rampat tail nowed and erect gules, *Thynne*. **Crest** – A reindeer statant or. **Supporters** – *Dexter*, a reindeer or, gorged with a plain collar sable: *sinister*, a lion tail nowed and erect gules. *Seat* – Longleat, Warminster, Wilts BA12 7NN.

SON LIVING

CEAWLIN HENRY LASZLO (*Viscount Weymouth*), *b* 6 June 1974; *ed* Kingsdown Comprehensve Sch, Warminster, Bedales, Cambridge Coll, Richmond Univ, Va, USA, and Univ Coll London.

DAUGHTER LIVING

Lady Lenka Abigail, *b* 1969; *ed* Kingsdown Comprehensive Sch, Warminster, and Univ Coll, Oxford.

BROTHER LIVING

Lord Christopher John, *b* 1934; *ed* Eton; late 2nd Lieut Life Guards: *m* 1968, Antonia Mary, da of Maj Sir Anthony Frederick Mark Palmer, 5th Bt (*cr* 1886), and has issue living, Sophie Emma, *b* 1968. *Residence* – Britmore House, Donhead St Andrew, Shaftesbury, Dorset SP7 9EB.

SISTER LIVING

Lady Caroline Jane (*Duchess of Beaufort*), *b* 1928; DL Avon 1986: *m* 1950, 11th Duke of Beaufort. *Residences* – Badminton House, Glos GL9 1DB; 90 Eaton Terrace, SW1.

HALF-SISTER LIVING

Lady Silvy Cerne, *b* 1958: *m* 1989, Iain McQuiston, only son of Iain McQuiston, of London, and has issue living, Milo Henry Cerne, *b* 1992, — Eve Iris, *b* 1990. *Residence* – 4 Argyle Rd, W8.

WIDOW LIVING OF SON OF SIXTH MARQUESS

Liese Maria (*Lady Valentine Thynne*), da of Kenneth William Dennis, of Bristol, and formerly wife of Karl Martin Weschke; is an artist: *m* 1977, as his 3rd wife, Lord Valentine Charles Thynne, who *d* 1979. *Residence* – 16 Bedford St, Bath BA1 6AF.

MOTHER LIVING

Hon Daphne Winifred Louise Vivian, da of 4th Baron Vivian: *m* 1st, 1926 (*m diss* 1953), 6th Marquess of Bath, ED, who *d* 1992; 2ndly, 1953 (*m diss* 1978), Maj Alexander (Xan) Wallace Fielding, DSO, who *d* 1991. *Residence* – Old Laundry, Badminton, Avon.

WIDOW LIVING OF SIXTH MARQUESS

VIRGINIA PENELOPE (*Dowager Marchioness of Bath*), da of late Alan Parsons, of The Baas, Broxbourne, Herts, and formerly wife of Hon David Francis Tennant (*see* B Glenconner, colls): *m* 1953, as his 2nd wife, the 6th Marquess, ED, who *d* 1992. *Residence* – Job's Mill, Crockerton, Warminster, Wilts.

COLLATERAL BRANCHES LIVING

Issue of late Lord Valentine Charles Thynne, yst son of 6th Marquess, *b* 1937, *d* 1979: *m* 1st, 1961 (*m diss* 1971), Veronica Ann, only da of Col G. E. Jackson, of Stratford, NZ; 2ndly, 1971 (*m diss* 1976), Susanne Caroline, da of Edgar Harold Alder, of Primrose Farm, Little Wilbraham, Cambs, and formerly wife of Christopher Hodgson Moore; 3rdly, 1977, Liese Maria (ante), da of Kenneth William Dennis, and formerly wife of Karl Martin Weschke:—
(By 1st *m*) Lucien, *b* 1965; *ed* Milton Abbey. —— Xenia Laura, *b* 1962: *m* 1989, Joshua David Mason, who *d* 1991, son of Richard Mason. *Residence* – 20 Ingate Terrace, SW8 3RR.

Grandchildren of late Col Ulric Oliver Thynne, CMG, CVO, DSO, TD, yst son of Rt Hon Lord Henry Frederick Thynne, 2nd son of 3rd Marquess:—
Issue of late Lt-Col Oliver St Maur Thynne, TD, *b* 1901, *d* 1978: *m* 1936, Mary Wroughton, who *d* 1992, formerly wife of Maj Richard Wale Gordon Dill, MC, and da of late Herbert Francis Morris:—
Sheridan Ulric (Eastfield Cottage, Whitchurch, nr Reading), *b* 1939; *ed* Eton; late Lt R Wilts Yeo: *m* 1964, Eve Clare, da of Lt-Cdr George Jameson Cardew, RN, of Beechwood, Upper Basildon, Berks, and has issue living, Piers Mark, *b* 1977, —— Louise Sarah, *b* 1965, — Marika Helen, *b* 1973, — Tamara Jane, *b* 1974.
Issue of late Group Capt Brian Sheridan Thynne, CBE, AFC, AE, RAAF, *b* 1907, *d* 1985: *m* 1st, 1940 (*m diss* 1948), Mrs Naomi BOURN, only da of C. E. Waters, of Sydney, Australia; 2ndly, 1952, Maria Fernanda Herrero, who *d* 1987, da of the Marques de Aledo, of Madrid:—
(By 1st *m*) Harriet Anne (General Gallegos 1, Madrid 28036), *b* 1941. —— (By 2nd *m*) Ulrica Maria Teresa, *b* 1954. —— Jane Georgiana, *b* 1955: *m* 1979, Javier Arzola, of Reno 4, Los Monteros, Marbella, Malaga, Spain, and has issue living, David, *b* 1981, — Raquel, *b* 1982, — Esther, *b* 1990.

Granddaughter of late Rt Hon Lord Henry Frederick Thynne (ante):—
Issue of late Col Ulric Oliver Thynne, CMG, CVO, DSO, TD, *b* 1871, *d* 1957: *m* 1st, 1899, Marjory, who *d* 1950, da of Edward Wormald; 2ndly, 1951, Elspeth Stiven, who *d* 1955, da of late David Tullis, of Rutherglen, and widow of 1st Baron Invernairn:—
(By 1st *m*) Ulrica Marjory, *b* 1911: *m* 1936 (*m diss* 1961), Maj George Anthony Murray Smith, late RHG (*see* B Belper, 1940 Edn), who *d* 1991. *Residence* – Gaddesby, Leics.

Grandson of late Francis John Thynne, 2nd son of Rev Lord John Thynne, DD, 3rd son of 2nd Marquess:—
Issue of late Capt George Augustus Carteret Thynne, late R N Devon Yeo, *b* 1869, *d* 1945: *m* 1915, Hon Gladys Isabel Annette Adderley, who *d* 1960, da of 2nd Baron Norton:—
John Grenville (Hays House, Shaftesbury, Dorset), *b* 1917; *ed* Stowe; late Maj RHG; European War 1939-45 in Iraq, Syria, Persia, Egypt, Italy, Holland, and Germany: *m* 1st, 1946, Baroness Marianne Madeleine, who *d* 1990, da of late Baron H. R. de Jenner, of Château de Landshut, Berne; 2ndly, 1991, Mrs Yvonne Watkins, da of late Maj Cuthbert Augustine Edward Chudleigh, of Rolandsfield, Bude, Cornwall, and has issue living (by 1st *m*), Bevil Grenville de Jenner, *b* 1947; *ed* Stowe: *m* 1970, Gertrude Dagnie, da of Arvid G. Ekman, of Skansen, Lodöse, Sweden, and has issue living, Christopher John Grenville *b* 1972, Richard Charles Grenville *b* 1977, — Richard George Grenville (Tads Cottage, Froxfield, Petersfield, Hants), *b* 1950: *m* 1st, 1973, Elizabeth Lydia Jill, da of Geoffrey Edward Courtney Barton, of Casa Nuevo, Aldosa, La Massana, Andorra; 2ndly, 1990, Mrs Penelope Jane Radmall, da of Cdr E. M. Halley, of Wickham, Hants, and has issue living (by 1st *m*), Piers James Carteret *b* 1976, Serena Katherine Nora *b* 1980, — Joanna Sybil Marcia, *b* 1949: *m* 1985, Graham Gordon, and has issue living, Edward Alexander *b* 1986, Jenna Elizabeth *b* 1988.

Granddaughter of late Rev Canon Arthur Christopher Thynne, 3rd son of Rev Lord John Thynne (ante):—
Issue of late Capt Hugh Edward Granville Thynne, RE, *b* 1881, *d* 1952: *m* 1907, Marguerite, who *d* 1964, da of W. Hearne:—
Grace Marian Granville, *b* 1913: *m* 1934, Kenneth Taylor Thomson, and has issue living, Peter Granville (Thrybergh Hall, Thrybergh, nr Rotherham, Yorks), *b* 1936: *m* 1962, Marion, da of Francis Harry Smith, of 39 Bank St, Ossett, Yorks, and has issue living, Christopher Granville *b* 1966, Sally Frances *b* 1964, — Jeremy Clayton (Hurworth Cottage, Hurworth-on-Tees, Darlington, co Durham), *b* 1938, — Robert Hugh, *b* 1942. *Residence* – Hanger Mill, Salcombe, Devon, TQ8 8LU.

PREDECESSORS – (1) *Sir* HENRY FREDERICK Thynne, *cra Baronet* 1641; *s* by his el son (2) *Sir* THOMAS, PC, 2nd Bt; Pres of Board of Trade 1702-7; sometime MP for Oxford University and Tamworth; inherited Longleat after the murder of his kinsman, and was *cr Baron Thynne of Warminster* and *Viscount Weymouth* (peerage of E) 1682, with remainder to his brother Henry Frederick; *d* 1714; *s* by his grand-nephew, grandson of Henry Frederick (ante) (3) THOMAS, 2nd Viscount; Ranger of Hyde and St James's Parks; *d* 1751; *s* by his son (4) THOMAS, KG, 3rd Viscount: was Lord of the Bedchamber 1760-63, Master of the Horse to Queen Charlotte 1765, Lord-Lieut of Ireland 1765, Sec of State for Northern Depart 1768, and Groom of the Stole 1782-96; *cr Marquess of Bath* (peerage of Great Britain) 1789; *d* 1796; *s* by his el son (5) THOMAS, KG, 2nd Marquess, Lord-Lieut of co Somerset; *d* 1837; *s* by his son (6) HENRY FREDERICK, 3rd Marquess, *b* 1797; Capt RN: *m* 1830, Hon Harriet, da of 1st Baron Ashburton; *d* 1837; *s* by his el son (7) JOHN ALEXANDER 4th Marquess, *b* 1831; Lord-Lieut of Wilts: *m* 1861, Hon Frances Isabella Catherine Vesey, who *d* 1915, el da of 3rd Viscount de Vesci; *d* 1896; *s* by his el son (8) THOMAS HENRY, KG, CB, TD, PC, 5th Marquess, *b* 1862; Lord-Lieut for Somerset; Under-Sec of State for India 1905; Chm of Wilts County Council 1906-46, and Master of the Horse 1922-4; MP for Frome Div of Somerset (C) 1886-92 and 1895-6: *m* 1890, Violet Caroline, who *d* 1928, da of Sir Charles Mordaunt, 10th Bt; *d* 1946; *s* by his son (9) HENRY FREDERICK, ED, 6th Marquess; *b* 1905; Major Royal Wilts Yeo, European War 1939-44 (wounded), Memb of Council of HRH the Prince of Wales 1933-36, MP Frome Div of Som (C) Oct 1931-Oct 1935: *m* 1st, 1926 (*m diss* 1953), Hon Daphne Winifred Louise Vivian, da of 4th Baron Vivian; 2ndly, 1953, Virginia Penelope, da of late Alan Parsons, of The Baas, Broxbourne, Herts, and formerly wife of Hon David Francis Tennant (*see* B Glenconner); *d* 1992; *s* by his eldest surviving son (10) ALEXANDER GEORGE, 7th Marquess and present peer; also Viscount Weymouth, and Baron Thynne of Warminster.

BATHURST, EARL (Bathurst) (Earl GB 1772)

Keep thy faith

HENRY ALLEN JOHN BATHURST, 8th Earl; *b* 1 May 1927; *s* 1943; *ed* Ridley Coll, Canada, Eton, and Ch Ch Oxford; Capt R Glos Hus (TA Res); DL Glos 1960-86; formerly Lieut 10th R Hus; appointed Gov of Hospital of St Lawrence, Cirencester 1944, and of RAC Cirencester 1948, and Chancellor of Primrose League 1959; a Lord-in-Waiting to HM 1957-61, and Joint Parl Under-Sec of State, Home Office 1961-2; a Member of Councils, Country Landowners' Assocn, and Timber Growers Orgn; Pres of R Forestry Soc 1976-78, Pres Institute of Sales and Marketing Management from 1981, and of the Assoc of Professional Foresters 1983: *m* 1st, 1959 (*m diss* 1976), Judith Mary, only da of late Amos Christopher Nelson; 2ndly, 1978, Gloria Wesley, only da of Harold Edward Clarry, of Vancouver, BC, and widow of David Rutherston, and has issue by 1st *m*.

꿔rms – Sable, two bars ermine, in chief three crosses patée, or. Crest – A dexter arm embowed, armed in mail, the hand, proper, grasping a spiked club or. Supporters – Two stags, argent, each gorged with a collar gemellé ermine.
Residence – Manor Farm, Sapperton, nr Cirencester, Glos. *Club* – White's.

SONS LIVING *(By 1st marriage)*

ALLEN CHRISTOPHER BERTRAM (*Lord Apsley*), *b* 11 March 1961: *m* 1986, Hilary Jane, yr da of John F. George, of Weston Lodge, Albury, Surrey, and has issue:—

SON LIVING — *Hon* Benjamin George Henry, *b* 6 March 1990.

DAUGHTER LIVING — *Hon* Rosie Meriel Lilias, *b* 1992.

Seat – Cirencester Park, Cirencester, Gos GL7 2BT.

Hon Alexander Edward Seymour, *b* 1965; *ed* Harrow, and RMA Sandhurst; Capt Royal Hussars (Prince of Wales's Own) (comm'd 1985): *m* 1992, Emma G., da of J. L. Sharpe, FRCS, and of Mrs Fiona Jackson. *Residence* – The Studio Cottage, Tarlton, Cirencester, Glos GL7 6PD.

DAUGHTER LIVING *(By 1st marriage)*

Lady Henrietta Mary Lilias, *b* 1962.

BROTHER LIVING

Hon George Bertram, *b* 1929, *ed* Eton, and Trin Coll, Oxford (MA); late Capt R Wilts Yeo; late Lt 10th Hus: *m* 1973, Susan, da of Malcolm Messer, of Tarlton, Glos, and has issue living, William Malcolm, *b* 1978. *Residence* – Hullasey House, Tarlton, Glos. *Club* – Cavalry and Guards'.

COLLATERAL BRANCH LIVING

Grandsons of late Lt-Col Hon (Allen) Benjamin Bathurst, 3rd son of 6th Earl:—
Issue of late Group Capt Peter Bathurst, *b* 1903, *d* 1970: *m* 1927, Lady Elizabeth Ann (12A Northanger Court, Grove St, Bath), da of late Capt Hon Chandos Graham Temple-Gore-Langton (*see* E Temple of Stowe):—
Sir (David) Benjamin, GCB (c/o Coutts & Co, 440 Strand, WC2; Army and Navy Club, and MCC), *b* 1936; *ed* Eton; Adm and C in C, Fleet, Allied C in C, Channel, and C in C Eastern Atlantic since 1989; Vice-Chief Defence Staff 1990-93, since when Chief of Naval Staff and First Sea Lord; *cr* KCB (Mil) 1987, GCB (Mil) 1991: *m* 1959, Sarah Christian Pandora, yst da of late Maj (Basil Arthur) John Peto (*see* Peto, Bt (*cr* 1927), colls), and has issue living, Benjamin John, *b* 1964, — Alice Patricia, *b* 1962, — Anna Christian, *b* 1968, — Lucilla Ruby, *b* 1970. — Timothy Seymour (College Farm, Tetbury Rd, Cirencester, Glos; Brooks's Club, and MCC), *b* 1939; *ed* Eton; late 2nd Lt Rifle Bde; a Dir of David Carritt Ltd and Artemis Fine Arts (UK) Ltd: *m* 1st, 1960 (*m diss* 1973), (Elizabeth) Mary, da of Philip Michael Armitage; 2ndly, 1973, Charlotte Anne, da of late Capt Richard Formby, RM, of Firwood, Formby, Lancs, and formerly wife of Richard Belloc Lowndes, and has issue living (by 1st *m*), Jonathan Chandos Seymour, *b* 1965, — Joanna Mary, *b* 1963: *m* 1989, Hugh Simon Nevile, of 50 Lonsdale Rd, W11 2DE (*see* B Mowbray, colls), — Elizabeth Sarah, *b* 1968: *m* 1993, Simon Dale Reid, of 10 Coulters Rd, W6 0BL, son of Hubert Reid, of The Old Rectory, Marton, Cheshire, — (by 2nd *m*) James Seymour, *b* 1976.

PREDECESSORS – *Sir* Benjamin Bathurst, MP, Gov of the HEIC 1688-9, Treasurer of the Household to Princess Anne, and on her accession Cofferer of the Household, had with other issue (1) ALLEN, PC; sat as MP for Cirencester 1705-11; *cr* *Baron Bathurst* (peerage of Great Britain) 1711, and *Earl Bathurst* (peerage of Great Britain) 1772; *d* 1775; *s* by his el son (2) HENRY, PC, who in 1771 had been appointed Lord High Chancellor and *cr* 1771 *Baron Apsley* (peerage of Great Britain); sat as MP for Cirencester 1735-54; was sometime a Justice of the Common Pleas and Lord Pres of the Council; *d* 1794; *s* by his son (3) HENRY, KG, PC, 3rd Earl; was Pres of Board of Trade 1807-12, Sec of War and Colonies 1812-27, and Pres of the Council 1828-30; *d* 1834; *s* by his el son (4) HENRY GEORGE, 4th Earl; was MP for Cirencester 1812-34, and a Commr of India Board 1812-18; *dsp* 1866; *s* by his brother (5) WILLIAM, 5th Earl; was Clerk of the Privy Council 1827-60; *dsp* 1878; *s* by his nephew (6) ALLEN ALEXANDER (son of Lt-Col Hon Seymour Thomas Bathurst, 3rd son of 3rd Earl), 6th Earl, *b* 1832; MP for Cirencester (C) 1857-78: *m* 1st, 1862, Hon Meriel Leicester Warren, who *d* 1872, da of 2nd Baron de Tabley; 2ndly, 1874, Evelyn, who *d* 1927, da of George James Barnard Hankey, of Fetcham Park, Leatherhead; *d* 1892; *s* by his el son (7) SEYMOUR HENRY, CMG, TD, 7th Earl, *b* 1864; Hon Col Gloucestershire Regt: *m* 1893, Hon Lilias Margaret Frances Borthwick, who *d* 1965, da of 1st Baron Glenesk (ext); *d* 1943; *s* by his grandson (8) HENRY ALLEN JOHN (son of late Lt-Col Allen Algernon Bathurst, DSO, MC, TD, MP, Lord Apsley (*ka* 1942), el son of 7th Earl), 8th Earl and present peer; also Baron Bathurst, and Baron Apsley.

BAUER, BARON (Bauer) (Life Baron 1983)

PETER THOMAS BAUER, son of Aladar Bauer who *d* 1944, of Budapest, Hungary; *b* 6 Nov 1915; *ed* Scholae Piae, Budapest, and Gonville and Caius Coll, Camb (MA); FBA; Reader in Agricultural Economics, Lond Univ 1947-48, Univ Lect in Economics, Camb Univ 1948-56, Smuts Reader in Commonwealth Studies, Camb Univ 1956-60, Prof of Economics at LSE, Lond Univ 1960-83, since when Prof Emeritus; author of *Indian Economic Policy and Development*, 1961; *Markets, Market Control and Marketing Reform* (co-author), 1968; *Dissent on Development*, 1972; *Aspects of Nigerian Development*, 1974; *Equality, The Third World of Economic Delusion*, 1981; *Reality and Rhetoric: Studies in the Economics of Development*, 1984, *The Development Frontier*, 1991; *cr Baron Bauer*, of Market Ward, City of Cambridge (Life Baron), 1983. *Address* – House of Lords, SW1. *Clubs* – Garrick, Beefsteak.

BEARSTED, VISCOUNT (Samuel) (Viscount UK 1925, Bt UK 1903)

Deeds, not words

PETER MONTEFIORE SAMUEL, MC, TD, 4th Viscount, and 4th Baronet; *b* 9 Dec 1911; *s* 1986; *ed* Eton, and New Coll, Oxford; Maj Warwickshire Yeo (TA); European War 1939-45 in Middle East (despatches, MC): *m* 1st, 1939 (*m diss* 1942), Deirdre du Barry; 2ndly, 1946, Hon Elizabeth Adelaide Cohen, who *d* 1983, da of late Baron Cohen (Life Baron), and widow of Capt Arthur John Pearce-Serocold, WG (Supplementary Res) (*see* B Sheffield, 1942 Edn); 3rdly, 1984, Nina Alice Hilary, da of Reginald John Hearn, of London, and widow of Carmichael (Michael) Charles Peter Pocock, CBE, and has issue by 2nd *m*.

Arms – Gules, on a chevron between two lions' heads erased in chief and in base a naval crown or, a heart gules. **Crest** – A dexter arm embowed proper, grasping a battle-axe argent, the head charged with two triangles interlaced sable. **Supporters** – *Dexter*, a horse argent; *sinister*, a dragon gules; each charged on the shoulder with a heart or.
Residences – Farley Hall, Farley Hill, nr Reading RG7 1UL; 9 Campden Hill Court, W8 7HX.

SONS LIVING (By 2nd marriage)

Hon NICHOLAS ALAN, *b* 22 Jan 1950; *ed* Eton, and New Coll, Oxford: *m* 1975, Caroline Jane, da of Dr David Sacks, and has issue living, Harry Richard, *b* 23 May 1988, — Eugenie Sharon, *b* 1977, — Natalie Naomi, *b* 1979, — Zoe Elizabeth, *b* 1982, — Juliet Samantha, *b* 1986. *Residence* – 9 Acacia Rd, NW8.

Hon Michael John, *b* 1952; *ed* Eton: *m* 1980, Julia Aline, yst da of James Edward Alexander Rundell Guinness, and has issue living, Benjamin Peter Marcus, *b* 1989, — Natasha Vivienne, *b* 1981, — Emily Elizabeth, *b* 1983, — Sophie Alexandra, *b* 1986. *Residence* – 24 Hyde Park Gate, SW7.

DAUGHTER LIVING (By 2nd marriage)

Hon Sarah Virginia, *b* 1947: *m* 1st, 1969 (*m diss* 1978), Duncan John Lloyd Fitzwilliams, yr son of late Charles Collinsplatt Fitzwilliams, TD, JP, DL, of Cilgwyn, Newcastle Emlyn, S Wales; 2ndly, 1980, Brian Mullins. *Residence* – Moorhill House, Brannockstown, Naas, co Kildare.

BROTHER LIVING

Hon Anthony Gerald, *b* 1917; *ed* Eton, and New College, Oxford; European War 1939-45 as Lt Intelligence Corps: *m* 1st, 1946 (*m diss* 1961), Mary Eve, da of late John Comyn Higgins, CIE, of Alford, Lincs; 2ndly, 1962 (*m diss* 1966), Jenifer, da of Major Kenneth Alfred Bridge Puckle, RM (ret) of Farnham: 3rdly, 1966, Mercy, da of Malcolm Charles Haystead, and has issue living (by 1st *m*), Jacqueline Eve (7212 Mulholland Drive, Los Angeles, Calif 90068, USA), *b* 1948: *m* 1st, 1978 (*m diss* 19—), Robert Rusk; 2ndly, 1988, Jack O'Halloran, of California, USA, and has issue living (by 2nd *m*), Slaine Aoife *b* 1988, — Daphne Lavinia (L'Europa Residence, Place des Moulins, MC 98000, Monaco), *b* 1951: *m* 1980 (*m diss* 1985), Leo Petro; and has issue living, Marco Antonio CERRETO *b* 1985. *Residences* – 29 St Leonard's Terr, SW3 4QG; Woodbury House, Longparish, Hants SP11 6PB. *Clubs* – White's, Anglers' (New York).

DAUGHTER LIVING OF THIRD VISCOUNT (By 1st marriage)

Hon Felicity Ann, *b* 1948: *m* 1975, Robert Bernard Waley-Cohen, and has issue (*see* Waley-Cohen, Bt). *Residence* – 18 Gilston Rd, SW10.

PREDECESSORS – (1)*Sir* MARCUS Samuel, 2nd son of late Marcus Samuel, of 18 Upper Bedford Place, W; *b* 1853; was a Shipowner and Merchant; Lord Mayor of London 1902-3 (Sheriff 1894-5); Founder (many years Chm) of Shell Transport and Trading Co (Limited); *cr* a *Baronet* 1903, *Baron Bearsted*, of Maidstone, co Kent (peerage of United Kingdom) 1921, and *Viscount Bearsted*, of Maidstone, co Kent (peerage of United Kingdom) 1925: *m* 1881, Fanny Elizabeth, who *d* 16 Jan 1927, only da of late Benjamin Benjamin; *d* 17 Jan 1927; *s* by his son (2) WALTER HORACE, MC, 2nd Viscount; *b* 1882; was a Trustee of National Gallery 1936-43 (Chm 1942-3), and again 1947-8, and of the Tate Gallery 1938-42: *m* 1908, Dorothea Montefiore, who *d* 1949, da of late Edward Montefiore Micholls, Bar-at-Law, of 11 Queen's Gate, SW; *d* 1948; *s* by his son (3) MARCUS RICHARD, 3rd Viscount, *b* 1909, DL Warwicks, served European War 1939-45 in Middle East (wounded) Chm Hill Samuel Gp 1948-66, etc: *m* 1st, 1947 (*m diss* 1966), Elizabeth Heather, who *d* 1993 (having *m* 2ndly, 1966, Sir Ronald Hugh Grierson), elder da of late Geoffrey Firmston-Williams, of Clunie House, Hans Pl, SW1; 2ndly, 1968, Jean Agnew, who *d*

1978, da of late Robert Agnew Wallace, of 10 Eton Terr, Edinburgh, and formerly wife of Maj John Somerville; *d* 1986; *s* by his brother **(4)** PETER MONTEFIORE, 4th and present peer; also Baron Bearsted.

BEATTY, EARL (Beatty) (Earl UK 1919)

Not by force but by art

DAVID BEATTY, 3rd Earl; *b* 21 Nov 1946; *s* 1972; *ed* Eton: *m* 1st, 1971 (*m diss* 1983), Anne, yr da of A. Please, of Wokingham, Berks; 2ndly, 1984, Anoma Corinne, da of Ray Wijewardene, of Colombo, Sri Lanka, and has issue by 1st *m*.

Arms – Azure, a beehive beset with nine bees volant or a chief argent charged with the Cross of St George gules. **Crest** – A demi-lion gules holding in the dexter paw a crescent or. **Supporters** – *Dexter*, a Sailor of the Royal Navy; *sinister*, a Soldier of the Royal Marines, both proper. *Address* – c/o House of Lords, SW1.

SONS LIVING *(By 1st marriage)*

SEAN DAVID (*Viscount Borodale*), *b* 12 June 1973.
Hon Peter Wystan, *b* 1975.

HALF-BROTHER LIVING *(Son of 2nd Earl by 4th marriage)*

Hon Nicholas Duncan, *b* 1961; *ed* Eton, and Exeter Univ (BA): *m* 1990, Laura Mary Catherine, da of Charles William Lyle Keen (*see* E Howe), and has issue living, David Brin Charles, *b* 1992.

HALF-SISTERS LIVING *(Daughter of 2nd Earl by 3rd marriage)*

Lady Diana Adrienne (*Viscountess Gage*), *b* 1952: *m* 1974, 8th Viscount Gage. *Residence* – The Cottage, Charwelton, Daventry, Northants.

(Daughter of 2nd Earl by 4th marriage)

Lady Miranda Katherine, *b* 1963: *m* 1989, (Iain) Alan Stewart, yst son of late Sir Dugald Leslie Lorn Stewart of Appin, KCVO, CMG, 16th Chief of Clan Stewart of Appin, and has issue living, Alexandra Katherine, *b* 1991, — Augusta Lileas, *b* 1994.

MOTHER LIVING

Dorothy Rita, da of late Michael James Furey, of New Orleans, and widow of Sgt Edward Bragg, RAF: *m* 2ndly, 1946 (*m diss* 1950), as his 2nd wife, the 2nd Earl, who *d* 1972; 3rdly, 1951, Abram Stevens Hewitt. *Address* – Mockingbird Hill, PO Box 254, Port Antonio, Jamaica, W Indies.

WIDOW LIVING OF SECOND EARL

DIANE, da of John Rutherford Blundell, of Havant, Hants, and adopted da of Capt Duncan Kirk: *m* 1st, 1959, as his 4th wife, the 2nd Earl, who *d* 1972; 2ndly, 1973, John Grenfell Nutting, of Chicheley Hall, Newport Pagnell, Bucks, el son of Rt Hon Sir (Harold) Anthony Nutting, 3rd Bt.

PREDECESSORS – **(1)** *Adm of the Fleet Sir* DAVID Beatty, GCB, OM, GCVO, DSO, PC, 2nd son of late David Longfield Beatty, of Borodale, Enniscorthy; *b* 1871; Dongola Expedition, 1896 (despatches DSO), Nile Expedition 1897 and 1898 (despatches twice, 4th class Order of Medjidie, promoted Com), China 1900 (despatches, wounded, promoted Capt), European War 1914-19, Comdg Battle Cruiser Squadron and Naval Forces in Heligoland Bight and Dogger Bank actions, and Battle Cruiser Fleet at battle of Jutland, and finally as Com-in-Ch of Grand Fleet (despatches, KCVO, GCB, Grand Cross of Order of Redeemer of Greece, Grand Officer Legion of Honour, GCVO, Mil Order of Savoy, Grand Cordon of Japanese Order of the Rising Sun (with Paulowina), Croix de Guerre, Orders of Leopold of Belgium and Star of Roumania, Grand Cordon (preciously brilliant) of Excellent Crop (China), Adm of the Fleet, thanked by Parliament, *cr* Earl, granted £100,000); was First Sea Lord of the Admiralty 1919-27; had 4th class of Russian Order of St George; elected Lord Rector of Edinburgh Univ 1917; *cr Earl Beatty, Viscount Borodale*, of Wexford, co Wexford, and *Baron Beatty*, of the North Sea, and of Brooksby, co Leicester (peerage of United Kingdom) 1919: *m* 1901, Ethel, who *d* 1932, da of Marshall Field, senr, of Chicago, USA; *d* 1936; *s* by his son **(2)** DAVID FIELD DSC, 2nd Earl; *b* 1905; Lt-Cdr RN (ret); PPS to Parl and Financial Sec of the Admiralty 1931-36, and Joint Under-Sec of State for Air 1945; MP for Peckham (*C*) 1931-36: *m* 1st, 1937 (*m diss* 1945), Dorothy Sands, who *d* 1966, da of Thomas Sarsfield Kent Power, of Va, USA, and formerly wife of late Harry Ester Reynolds Hall; 2ndly, 1946 (*m diss* 1950), Dorothy Rita da of late Michael James Furey, of New Orleans, and widow of Sgt Edward Bragg, RAF; 3rdly, 1951 (*m diss* 1958), Adelle, who *d* 1990 (having *m* 3rdly, 1960, Stanley Donen, film dir), da of M. Dillingham, of Oklahoma City, USA, and formerly wife of William V. O'Connor; 4thly, 1959, Diane (who *m* 2ndly, 1973, John Grenfell Nutting, el son of Rt Hon Sir (Harold) Anthony Nutting, 3rd Bt), da of John Rutherford Blundell, of Havant, Hants, and adopted da of Capt Duncan Kirk; *d* 1972; *s* by his el son **(3)** DAVID, 3rd Earl and present peer; also Viscount Borodale, and Baron Beatty.

BEAUCHAMP, EARLDOM (Lygon) (Extinct 1979)
(Title pronounced "Beecham" *Name Pronounced* "Liggon")

DAUGHTERS LIVING OF SEVENTH EARL

Lady Sibell, *b* 1907: *m* 1939, Flight-Lieut Michael Richard Bernard Rowley, AAF, who *d* 1952 (*see* Corbet, Bt, 1945 Edn). *Residence* – 1 Stable Cottages, Barton House, Guitting Power, nr Cheltenham, Glos GL54 5UH.
Lady Dorothy, *b* 1912; late Section Officer WAAF: *m* 1985, as his 2nd wife, Robert Vernon Heber-Percy (*see* D Northumberland, colls), who *d* 1987. *Address* – c/o Messrs C. Hoare & Co, 37 Fleet St, EC4P 4DQ.

WIDOW LIVING OF SON OF SEVENTH EARL

Patricia Janet (*Hon Mrs Richard E. Lygon*) (Pyndar House, Hanley Castle, Worcester), da of late Rev Thomas Kensit Norman: *m* 1939, Hon Richard Edward Lygon, who *d* 1970, and has issue living (*see* colls infra).

COLLATERAL BRANCHES LIVING

Issue of late Hon Richard Edward Lygon, yr son of 7th Earl, *b* 1916, *d* 1970: *m* 1939, Patricia Janet (ante), da of late Rev Thomas Kensit Norman:—
Lettice Patricia Mary, *b* 1940. —— Rosalind Elizabeth (*Hon Lady Morrison*), *b* 1946: *m* 1st, 1967 (*m. diss* 1984), Gerald John Ward (*see* E Dudley, colls); 2ndly, 1984, Hon Sir Charles Andrew Morrison, 2nd son of 1st Baron Margadale. *Seat* – Madresfield Court, Malvern, Worcs WR13 5AU.

Granddaughters of late Lt-Col Hon Robert Lygon, MVO, MC, Gren Gds, 3rd son of 6th Earl:—
Issue of late Reginald Arthur Lygon, *b* 1904, *d* 1976: *m* 1930, Agnes Mary Louise, who *d* 1969, da of late Rev George Fancourt Bell, V of Riverhead, Sevenoaks, and Hon Canon of Rochester:—
Margaret Annora Mary, *b* 1931: *m* 1955, Michael Richard West de Wend Fenton, of Ebberston Hall, Yorks (*see* E Buchan, colls, 1935 Edn), and has issue living, Jonathan Lygon West, *b* 1958: *m* 1988, Pamela Jane, yr da of G. A. Wood, of Ossett, W Yorks, and has issue living, William Osborne West *b* 1988, Lewis Charles Ross *b* 1992, Millicent Alexandra May *b* 1989, — Ross Mathew Mark, *b* 1960: *m* 1983, Helen Louise, elder da of Rev Charles Clifford Forster, of The Vicarage, Pudding Lane, Snainton, Scarborough, and has issue living, Charlotte Alice Rose *b* 1988, Amelia Jane *b* 1990, — Roselie Marye Margaret, *b* 1957: *m* 1981, Carlo Francis Tailleux, son of Francis Tailleux, of 27 rue de Longchamps, Neuilly sur Seine, and has issue living, Pierre Tancred *b* 1988, Tiphaine Eileen *b* 1984, — Clarissa Emily, *b* 1962: *m* 1986, Patrick Daulby, elder son of George Daulby, of Denmark Av, Wimbledon, and has issue living, Eleanor Clare *b* 1990. —— Anne Juliet (63A Primrose Mansions, Prince of Wales Drive, SW11), *b* 1938: *m* 1st, 1960 (*m diss* 1965), William James Cavendish-Bentinck, who *d* 1966 (*see* D Portland, colls, 1966 Edn); 2ndly, 1966, Robert Gore Langrishe (*see* Langrishe, Bt), who *d* 1982; 3rdly, 1983, Hugh Curran. *Residence* – 9 York Mansions, Prince of Wales Drive, SW11.

BEAUFORT, DUKE OF (Somerset) (Duke E 1682)

MUTARE·VEL·TIMERE·SPERNO

I scorn to change or to fear

David, *b* 1991, — Romy Caroline, *b* 1993.

DAVID ROBERT SOMERSET, 11th Duke; *b* 23 Feb 1928; *s* 1984; *ed* Eton; is Hereditary Keeper of Raglan Castle; late Lt Coldstream Gds; Pres British Horse Soc 1988-91: *m* 1950, Lady Caroline Jane Thynne, da of 6th Marquess of Bath, and has issue.

Arms – Quarterly, 1st and 4th azure, three fleurs-de-lis or, *France*; 2nd and 3rd gules, three lions passant guardant in pale or, *England*; all within a bordure compony argent and azure. **Crest** – A portcullis or, nailed azure, chains gold. **Supporters** – *Dexter*, a panther argent, flames issuing from his mouth and ears proper, plain collared and chained or, and semée of torteaux, hurts and pommes alternately; *sinister*, a wyvern, wings endorsed vert, in the mouth a sinister hand, couped at the wrist gules.
Seat – Badminton House, Gloucestershire, GL9 1DB. *Town Residence* – 90 Eaton Terrace, SW1. *Club* – White's.

SONS LIVING

HENRY JOHN FITZROY (*Marquess of Worcester*), *b* 22 May 1952; *ed* Eton: *m* 1987, Tracy Louise, yr da of Hon Peter Alistair Ward (*see* E Dudley), and has issue:—
SON LIVING— Robert (*Earl of Glamorgan*), *b* 20 Jan 1989.
DAUGHTER LIVING— *Lady* Isabella Elsa, *b* 1991.
Lord Edward Alexander, *b* 1958; *ed* Millfield: *m* 1982, Hon (Georgina) Caroline Davidson, 2nd da of 2nd Viscount Davidson, and has issue living, Francesca, *b* 1984, — a da, *b* 1992.
Lord John Robert, *b* 1964; *ed* King's Sch, Bruton: *m* 1990, Lady Cosima Maria Gabriella Fry, yr da of 9th Marquess of Londonderry, and has issue living, Lyle

DAUGHTER LIVING

Lady Anne Mary, *b* 1955; writer: *m* 1988, Matthew Xavier Maillard Carr (*see* Strickland-Constable, Bt, colls).

SISTER LIVING (*raised to the rank of a Duke's daughter* 1985)

Lady (Elizabeth) Anne, *b* 1929: *m* 1953, Maj David Alwyne Carne Rasch, Gren Gds, of Heale House, Woodford, Salisbury, and has issue (*see* Rasch, Bt).

COLLATERAL BRANCHES LIVING

Grandchildren of late Henry Plantagenet Somerset, 2nd son of late Col Charles Henry Somerset, CB, eldest son of late Lieut-Gen Sir Henry Somerset, KCB, KH, eldest son of Gen Lord Charles Henry Somerset, MP, 2nd son of 5th Duke:—
Issue of late Capt Charles William Henry Rollo Somerset, MC, *b* 1895, *d* 1936: *m* 1925, Glory Kathleen, who *d* 1973, da of late Frederick Albert Turner, of Glenbardi, Toogoolawah, Queensland (infra):—

Arthur Henry, *b* 1926; S-W Pacific 1944-5 with R Australian Navy: *m* 1950, Dorothy Joan, only da of William Harrison, of Brisbane, Queensland, and has issue living, Arthur Rollo Henry Plantagenet, *b* 1953; *ed* Queensland Univ (B Commerce): *m* 1979, Marion Lyle, da of D. V. Graham, of Brisbane, and has issue living, Katherine Lee *b* 1981, Victoria Anne *b* 1984, — John William Plantagenet, *b* 1965; *ed* Queensland Univ (B Commerce): *m* 1989, Margaret Judith, da of Ivan Bowen, of Brisbane, and has issue living, Justin Mitchell Plantagenet *b* 1993, — Andrea Helen, *b* 1957; BEd, Teaching Dip: *m* 1988, Andrew L. M. Todd, and has issue living, Phillip William Andrew *b* 1994, Naima Louise Somerset *b* (triplet) 1994, Rachelle Alexandra Somerset *b* (triplet) 1994. *Residence* – 31 Rangeview St, Aspley, Brisbane, Queensland 4034, Australia. —— Patricia Honor, *b* 1928: *m* 1953, Norman David Thomas Butler, and has issue living, Luke Norman, *b* 1954: *m* 1988, Margaret, el da of J. R. R. D. Field, of Brisbane, — Robert David, *b* 1957, — Glory Patricia, *b* 1962: *m* 1982, Trevor John Kennedy, and has issue living, Brendan James *b* 1986, Lachlan Gene *b* 1987. *Residence* – 110 Esplanade, Golden Beach, Caloundra, Queensland, Australia. —— Barbara Joan, *b* 1933.
       Issue of late Hereward Henry Plantagenet Somerset, *b* 1989: *m* 1923, Jean Castle, who *d* 1987, 2nd da of late Frederick Albert Turner, of Glenbardi, Toogoolawah, Qld (ante):—
Edward Plantagenet (79 Guy St, Warwick, Qld 4370, Australia), *b* 1924; European War 1942-44 with RAAF: *m* 1952, Elsie Joy, only da of Stanley Morrow, of Lismore, NSW, and has had issue, Richard John Plantagenet, *b* 1960: *m* 1982, Elizabeth Mary, da of Frank Neal, of Tara, Qld, and *d* 1991, leaving issue, Gillian Maree *b* 1985, Sarah Jane *b* 1987, Heidi Louise *b* 1990, — Pru-Ellen, *b* 1956: *m* 1976, Stuart Charles Barkla, of Rosscoe Downs, Cunnamulla, Qld 4490, and has issue living, Alina Jane *b* 1983, Zoë Ann *b* 1986. —— David Plantagenet (Peek-A-Doo, Taroom, Qld 4420, Australia), *b* 1926: *m* 1953, Margaret Pamela, 2nd da of David Victor Staines, of Jandowae, Qld, and has issue living, Jennifer Margaret, *b* 1954: *m* 1976, Stuart James Stirling, of Willwood, Pittsworth, Qld 4356, and has issue living, Jillian Elizabeth *b* 1978, Rebecca Lynn *b* 1981, Roslyn Ann *b* 1984, — Kerri Jane, *b* 1957, — Erica Jan, *b* 1959: *m* 1983, Harry Sibun Perrett, of Cattle Downs, Wandoan, Qld 4419, and has issue living, Edward Sibun *b* 1984, Hilary Elizabeth *b* 1986, Jessica Victoria *b* 1989, Sophie Jayne *b* 1993. —— Robert Plantagenet, AM (Caboonbah, Proston, Qld 4613, Australia), *b* 1930; AM 1992, JP: *m* 1952, Leslie Rawdon, only da of late Rawdon Briggs, JP, of Swindon, Mt Perry, Qld, and has had issue, Robert Plantagenet, *b* 1959: *m* 1990, Georgina Jane Persse, yst da of David Rokeby Robinson, of Lorraine, Longreach, Qld, — Leslie Ann, *b* 1953; JP: *m* 1974, Ian Robert Haselwood, of South Westgrove, Injune, Qld 4454, and has issue living, Georgina Leslie *b* 1984, — Katherine Nina, *b* 1957: *m* 1978, Lindsay George Joseph Marshall, of Yurunga Farms, Beechmont, via Nerang, Qld 4211, and has issue living, Lachlan Colvin *b* 1981, Adam Lindsay *b* 1983, — Victoria Joyce, *b* 1967, — Jane Elizabeth, *b* 1968, *d* 1973. —— William Plantagenet (Warra Willa, Brolga Rd, Beaudesert, Qld 4285, Australia), *b* 1934; late RAN: *m* 1961, Marion Helene, elder da of Maiben Hay Blackman, of Brisbane, and has issue living, Mark William Plantagenet, *b* 1965: *m* 1990, Anne Marie Murphy, 2nd da of Terrence Michael Murphy, of Dalby, Qld, and has issue living, Brent Michael John Plantagenet *b* 1991, — Steven Plantagenet, *b* 1968, — Christine Helene, *b* 1963: *m* 1988, Nicholas John Case, and has issue living, Stephanie Helene *b* 1988. —— Charles Plantagenet (Caraweena MS 612, Kingaroy, Qld 4610, Australia), *b* 1944: *m* 1978, Pamela Dorothy, da of Guy Oakes McIver, of Braeside Bell, Qld, and has issue living, Myles Plantagenet, *b* 1979, — Scott Plantagenet, *b* 1981. —— Susan Somerset (Cooranga MS 322, Gayndah, Qld 4625), *b* 1945: *m* 1969 (*m diss* 1991), Heath Hill Hassall, and has issue living, Rem Hill, *b* 1970, — Martine Dione, *b* 1974.

       Grandchildren of late Brig-Gen Charles Wyndham Somerset, CB, CMG, MVO, yr son of late Col Henry George Edward Somerset, 2nd son of late Lt-Gen Sir Henry Somerset, KCB, KH (ante):—
       Issue of late Major Alan Fitz Roy Somerset, *b* 1902, *d* 1940: *m* 1927, Nell Lauder, who *d* 1951, da of late Harold E. Pyman:—
Robin Fitzroy (91 Edgar Rd, Winchester), *b* 1930; *ed* Eton, and Balliol Coll, Oxford; late Capt Rifle Bde: *m* 1977, Sarah Marguerite, da of Vice-Adm Sir Charles Piercy Mills, KCB, CBE, DSC, and has issue living, Charles Fitzroy, *b* 1981, — Anne Marguerite, *b* 1978. —— Barbara Carol (Aldehaven, Leiston Rd, Aldeburgh, Suffolk), *b* 1933.

       Grandchildren of late Fitz Roy Maclean Henry Somerset, 3rd son of late Lt-Gen Sir Henry Somerset, KCB, KH, (ante):—
       Issue of late Fitz Roy Henry Somerset, *b* 1881, *d* 1946: *m* 1902, Martha Johanna, da of Philip Watermeyer, of Hanover, S Africa:—
Raglan Henry, *b* 1903; a boilermaker, Daggafontein Mines: *m* 1928, Hendrica Alida Van der Burg, of Bloemfontein, S Africa, and has issue living, Eugene, *b* 1929: *m* 1951, Valerie Rene Stewart, of Benoni, S Africa, and has issue living, Sharon *b* 1952, Geraldine *b* 1954, — John Fitzroy, *b* 1933, — Eunice, *b* 1931. —— Philip Arthur, *b* 1905. —— Harry Edward (1 Raydora Mansions, Roxburgh Rd, Selection Park, Springs 1568, S Africa), *b* 1914: *m* 1939, Muriel Elizabeth Watkins, and has issue living, Ronald Arthur (8 Raydora Mansions, Roxburgh Rd, Selection Park, Springs 1567, S Africa), *b* 1940: *m* 1966 (*m diss* 1973), Lesley Drummond, and has issue living, Grant Bradford Somerset *b* 1967, — Beryl Louise, *b* 1946: *m* 1966, Arie David de Lange, of 19 Rogers Rd, Selection Park, Springs 1567, S Africa, and has issue living, David Jon *b* 1969, Shaye Beryl *b* 1967. —— Lilian Blanche, *b* 1906: *m* 1st, 1933, Richard Flagg, who *d* 1940; 2ndly, 1949, Thomas Grieve, and has issue living (by 1st *m*), John Richard, *b* 1937, — Marjorie, *b* 1935. *Residence* – Floreat, 8 Paschendale Road, Delville, Germiston, S Africa. —— Winifred Mary, *b* 1925: *m* 1948, Derrick Egerton Moult, and has issue living, Adrian Thomas, *b* 1951, — Kathleen Dawn, *b* 1949.

       Granddaughter of late Maj Henry Calthorpe Somerset, elder son of late Col Henry George Edward Somerset (ante):—
       Issue of late Henry George FitzRoy Somerset, *b* 1885, *d* 1958: *m* 1913, Honore, who *d* 19—, da of J. Olive, of Ravenswood, Queensland:—
Margot, *b* 1916: *m* 1943, Donald Campbell, 9/11 Lovett St, Manly Vale, NSW, and has issue living, Bruce Ronald, *b* 1946, — Anne-Marie, *b* 1944.

       Granddaughter of Rev Henry Plantagenet Somerset, elder son of Rev Villers Henry Plantagenet Somerset, 3rd son of Gen Lord Charles Henry Somerset, MP (ante):—
       Issue of late Capt Noel Henry Plantagenet Somerset, *b* 1885, *d* 1921: *m* 1915, Helen Barbara, who *d* 1952, da of late Joseph Arderne Ormerod, MD, FRCP, of Greenhill, Upham, Hants, and 25 Upper Wimpole Street, W:—
Mary Arderne Frances (Lavenders, 151 Elsley Rd, Battersea, SW11), *b* 1920.

       Grandchildren of late William Francis Somerset (infra):—
       Issue of late Lionel Francis Somerset, *b* 1903, *d* 1981: *m* 1937, Wanda Gertrude (Box 422, Port Sydney, Muskoka, Ont, Canada), da of Arthur W. Clarke, of Port Sydney, Ontario:—
Lionel Vere (Box 295, Port Sydney, Muskoka, Ont, Canada POB 1LO), *b* 1938: *m* 1970, Janet Mary, da of Maj David Colin Heggie, MD, GM, of Brampton, Ont, and has issue living, Scott Edward, *b* 1973, — Steven Arthur, *b* 1975, — Tammy Lee, *b* 1978. —— Cyrle Henry, *b* 1940: *m* 1st, 1963 (*m diss* 1972), Bonnie Erin, da of Lloyd W. Wood, of Port Sydney; 2ndly, 1981, Gale Eileen, da of John William Russell, of Moncton, New Brunswick, and has issue living (by 1st *m*), Robin Marie, *b* 1964: *m* 1982, John Joseph Fiorini, of Shannon Hall, and has issue living, John Cyrle *b* 1984, Joey Michael *b* 1985, Matthew Dominic *b* 1988, Mikhele Erin *b* 1987, — (by 2nd *m*) Ashley Gale, *b* 1982. —— William John (Box 393, Port Sydney, Muskoka, Ont, Canada), *b* 1944: *m* 1978, Beverly Ann, da of George Robert Stewart, of 37 Wright Av, Toronto, Ont, and has issue living, Trevor John Stewart *b* 1985, Amanda Carol, *b* 1981.

       Grandchildren of late Vere Francis John Somerset, elder son of late Col Poulett George Henry Somerset, CB, MP, 4th son of late Gen Lord Charles Henry Somerset, MP (ante):—

Issue of late William Francis Somerset, *b* 1876, *d* 1942: *m* 1st, 1899, Laura Helen, who *d* 1926, da of W. H. Thoms, of Port Sydney, Muskoka, Ontario, Canada; 2ndly, 1927, Ann Margaret Vibert, who *d* 1955, da of C. V. Lawrence, of Allensville, Ontario, Canada:—
(By 1st *m*) Jessie Catherine, *b* 1907: *m* 1944, Brodie Kay, of Port Sydney, Muskoka, Ontario, Canada, and has issue living, William Douglas, *b* 1949: *m* 1979, Cynda Campbell, and has issue living, Courtney Eileon *b* 19—. —— Lenora Mary, *b* 1909: *m* 1936, George Simmens, who *d* 1973, and has issue living, Donald Wayne, *b* 1938: *m* 1970, Elaine Mary, da of Robert Bailey, of Cartier, Ontario, and has issue living, David Robert *b* 1974, Kirk William *b* 1976, Donald Glenn *b* 1980, — Norma Helen, *b* 1944. *Residence* – 129 Whitney Av, North Bay, Ontario, Canada.
Issue of late Charles Somerset, *b* 1878, *d* 1941: *m* 1913, Doris Amy (16 Allenby Rd, Dalkeith 6009, W Australia), da of Edward George Cronin:—
Henry Charles Fitzroy (16 Allenby Rd, Dalkeith 6009, W Australia), *b* 1919: *m* 1946, Patricia Barr, da of late Rudolph George Barr Goyder, and has issue living, Charles Nigel Fitzroy, *b* 1953, — Virginia Fitzroy, *b* 1947, — Suzette Fitzroy, *b* 1950, — Mary Ursula Fitzroy, *b* 1958, — Georgina Patricia Fitzroy, *b* 1963. —— Claud Edward Ralph, *b* 1925. —— Mary Poulett, *b* 1916. —— Diana, *b* 1918. —— Susette, *b* 1920. *Residence* – Ferndale, Balingup, W Australia.
Issue of late Vere Edward Somerset, MRCS, LRCP, *b* 1884, *d* 1961: *m* 1910, Gladys Mildred, who *d* 1980, da of Richard Baker, of Dolton, Devon:—
Vere Murielle Cecily Idina SOMERSET, *b* 1912; has resumed the surname of Somerset: *m* 1st, 1934, Fl-Lt Dudley Scorgie, AFC; 2ndly, 1959 (*m diss* 1978), Capt Alan Abraham, late RASC, and has issue living (by 1st *m*), Vere Roderick (27 Bicton St, Exmouth, Devon), *b* 1938, — Annette Idina, *b* 1939: *m* 1966, Alan Peter Crow, of Cherrington Manor, Newport, Salop, and has issue living, Christopher John *b* 1973, Timothy *b* 1975, Camille Bettina *b* 1970.

Granddaughter of late Capt Henry Charles FitzRoy Somerset, yr son of Col Poulett George Henry Somerset, CB, MP (ante):—
Issue of late Capt Charles Alexander Somerset, RA, *b* 1901; *d* 1981: *m* 1st, 1926, Audrey Vernon, who *d* 1935, 2nd da of George W. L. Thompson, of Olton, Warwicks; 2ndly, 1955, Winifred May (Little Hawks Grove, E Grimstead, Salisbury), 2nd da of late J. A. Helyar, of Windyridge, E Coker, Som:—
(By 1st *m*) Jessie Catherine, *b* 1954 (*m diss* 1960), Jeremy Paul Ellingham, and has issue living, Hugh Vere Alexander (Seal, Kent), *b* 1957; *ed* Marlborough, and Reading Univ (BSc), ARICS: *m* 1979, Angela, el da of late T. A. Jackson, of Lincoln, and has issue living, Marcus Charles Anthony *b* 1988, Luke William Alexander *b* 1990, Hugo Robert Vere *b* 1992, — (Charles Henry) Mark, *b* 1959; *ed* Marlborough, and Bristol Univ (BA): *m* 1991, Natania Maria, yst da of Dr Clifford Jansz, of London.

Grandson of late FitzRoy William Henry Somerset, 2nd son of late Col Henry Charles Capel Somerset, eldest son of late Rev Lord William George Henry Somerset, 6th son of 5th Duke:—
Issue of late Henry Charles FitzRoy Somerset, *b* 1870, *d* 1940: *m* 1920, Winifred Marion, da of late George Bartram, of London, N:—
Francis Charles, *b* 1921: *m* 1945, Sheila Marion, da of Aldred Davis, of Yass, NSW, and has issue living, Susan, *b* 1952.

Grandson of late Raglan Somerset (*b* 1872), yr son of late FitzRoy William Henry Somerset (ante):—
Issue of late Fitzroy Raglan Somerset, *b* 1901, *d* 1985: *m* 1924, Alma Lauderdale (81 Anthony St, Ascot, Brisbane 4007, Queensland, Australia), da of Henry Lauderdale Maitland, of Melbourne:—
Raglan Fitzroy, *b* 1925; MB BS: 1939-45 War in S-W Pacific with 2/10 Australian Commando Sqdn (despatches): *m* 1954, Lenore Beatrice, da of Oswald William Miller, of Brisbane, and has issue living, Stephen Raglan (112 Arundel St, Park Orchards, Victoria 3114), *b* 1956: *m* 1980, Antoinette Rose Briggs, and has issue living, Elise Ann *b* 1987, Olivia Rose *b* 1991. *Residence* – 67 Westering Rd, Christmas Hills, Victoria 3775, Australia.

Granddaughter of late Raglan Turberville Henry Somerset, 4th son of Rev William Somerset, 2nd son of Rev Lord William George Henry Somerset (ante):—
Issue of late Raglan Horatio Edwyn Henry Somerset, QC, *b* 1885, *d* 1956: *m* 1915, Adelaide Millicent Blanche Gwendolen, who *d* 1958, only da of late Arthur William FitzRoy Somerset (infra):—
Anna Millicent Horatia FitzRoy, OBE, *b* 1929: *m* 1950, William John Francis Tribe, and has issue living, William John Raglan Horatio, *b* 1955: *m* 1st, 1975 (*m diss* 1983), Maria Magdalena Hernas, of Wroclaw, Poland; 2ndly, 1983 (*m diss* 1987), Ana, da of Dr Janet Rutherford Esquivel; 3rdly, 1987, Ruth, da of Lawrence Corner, and has issue living (by 2nd *m*), Charles William Edward *b* 1986, — Raglan Horatio Andrew Harold, *b* 1961: *m* 1987, Susan Elizabeth, da of John Bennett, of Cheshire, — Mary Anna Kathleen Horatia, *b* 1958: *m* 1982, Ian Geoffrey Arthur, son of Colin Arthur, of Llangibby, Gwent, and has issue living, Rebecca Horatia Jean *b* 1988. *Residence* – Hill House, Raglan, Gwent.

Grandchildren of late Rev William Somerset (ante):—
Issue of late Charles Edward Henry Somerset, *b* 1862, *d* 1939: *m* 1908, Edith, who *d* 1932, da of Lionel Alexander Weatherly, MD, of Winsley House, Stourwood Bournemouth:—
Herbert Michael John Charles, *b* 1920. *Residence* – Ashbrook Hall, Hollington, St Leonards-on-Sea. —— Charlotte Georgiana Rose Mary (Hilliers Lodge, Bucklebury Common, Berks), *b* 1909; *ed* Oxford Univ (MA): *m* 1933, Jules Omer Malfroy, LLM, who *d* 1973, and has had issue, Jules Michael Charles Somerset (The Old School House, Boxworth, Cambridge), *b* 1939; *ed* Downside, and Fitzwilliam Coll, Camb (MA): ARICS, AMTPI: *m* 1967, Moira Gore, and has issue living, Benedict Charles Jules Somerset *b* 1976, Emma Charlotte Mary *b* 1968, Kate Emily Rose *b* 1971, — Deborah Mary Somerset, *b* 1934; MA Camb; Solicitor 1960; *d* 1987, — Louise Georgiana Somerset, *b* 1942; BSc St Andrews Univ: *m* 1965, Richard Kent Percival, BSc, of Stable Cottage, Dog Lane, Ashampstead, Berks, and has issue living, Richard Eyre Somerset *b* 1979, Charlotte Georgiana *b* 1970, Lucy Margaret *b* 1972, Alice Louise *b* 1977.

Grandchildren of late Charles Edward Henry Somerset (ante):—
Issue of late William Raglan Henry Guy Somerset, *b* 1912, *d* 1981: *m* 1st, 1932 (*m diss* 1950), Edna Margaret, da of Ernald Drybrough Smith, MD, FRCS, of Hastings: 2ndly, 1955, Evelyn, da of William Lee, of Bradford:—
(By 1st *m*) William Michael John Charles (Somerville, 9 Overslade Close, E Hunsbury, Northampton NN4 0RZ), *b* 1934: *m* 1967, Pearl Constance Langley, and has issue living, John Reginald, *b* 1970. —— Margaret Drybrough (Northfield, 44 North St West, Uppingham, Leics LE15 9S6), *b* 1933: *m* 1951, Herbert Paul Liquorish, RHG, and has had issue, Michael Paul, *b* 1952; RN; murdered in Antigua 1973, — Susan Carlotta Anne, *b* 1953, — Deri Jane, *b* 1957: *m* 1987, Tyrone Maloney, of St Peter's, Barbados, and has issue living, Antoine Michael Bevan *b* 1992, Tamara Chantel *b* 1985, Tiahra Charmain *b* 1986, — Cherillyn Mary, *b* 1959: *m* 1978 (*m diss* 1981), Terrance Carr, and has issue living, Cheryl Marie *b* 1978, — Karin Melinda, *b* 1963. —— (By 2nd *m*) Nicholas Anthony, *b* 1956, *d* 1981. —— Stephanie Lynn, *b* 1960. —— Amanda Jayne, *b* 1961, *d* 1971.

Grandchildren of late Arthur William FitzRoy Somerset, son of late Col FitzRoy Molyneux Henry Somerset, RE, 3rd son of late Rev Lord William George Henry Somerset (ante):—
Issue of late Arthur Plantagenet Francis Cecil Somerset, *b* 1889, *d* 1957: *m* 1916, Mary Frances Elizabeth (Hurst Manor, Martock, Somerset), el da of late Felton George Randolph (*see* Nepean, Bt, colls, 1950 Edn):—
John FitzRoy Pechell, *b* 1923; *ed* Wellington Coll, and London Univ (BSc 1949): is a qualified Asso of Chartered Land Agents So, and an ARICS; European War 1942-45 with King's Roy Rifle Corps (wounded): *m* 1952, Daphne Marigold, yr da of late Col Clement Topham, OBE, MC, and has issue living, Clement Charles FitzRoy (Longdean House, Clapham, nr Worthing,

Sussex), *b* 1956: *m* 1986, Sara Ann, da of Roy James Lally, of Worthing, Sussex, and has issue living, Georgina Katherine Ella *b* 1987, — Annabel Mary, *b* 1953: *m* 1979 Robert Matthew Smyth, of Altmover House, Dungiven, co Derry, and has issue living, Emily Margaret *b* 1980, — Philippa Margaret, *b* 1965. *Residence* – Holt Farm House, Clapham, nr Worthing, Sussex. —— Cecily Mary Adelaide, *b* 1919: *m* 1946, Maj Laurence James Howe-Ely, 60th Rifles, and has issue living, Christopher Laurence Somerset, *b* 1946: *m* 1984, Linda Gilbee, of Port Elizabeth, S Africa, and has issue living, Michael *b* 1987, — Michael James FitzRoy, *b* 1950: *m* 1980, Mary Anne, da of George Piers, of Pregrave Farm, Harare, Zimbabwe, and has issue living, Piers Lawrence *b* 1985, Caroline Louise *b* 1982, — Anne Diana Mary (25 Kew Dr, Highlands, Harare, Zimbabwe), *b* 1948: *m* 1972, George Constantine Papasavvas, who *d* 1983, and has issue living, Alexander Lawrence *b* 1979, Christina Helena *b* 1978, Georgina Zoe *b* 1983, Suzanna Cecily *b* (twin) 1983. *Residence* – Piras Gdns, Oxford Rd, Avondale, Zimbabwe.

Grandchildren of late Rev Boscawen Thomas George Henry Somerset, 5th son of late Rev Lord William George Henry Somerset (ante):—
Issue of late William Horace Boscawen Somerset, *b* 1880, *d* 1946: *m* 1921, Rubie Drummond-Nairne, who *d* 1977, da of late William Redston Warner:—
FitzRoy Douglas Boscawen (Thackit Eaves, Highclere, Newbury), *b* 1923; *ed* Marlborough, and Exeter Coll, Oxford (BA 1949, MA 1957); formerly Lt King's Shropshire LI; in Colonial Administrative Ser, Nigeria 1950-57, and Assist Adviser, Aden Protectorate 1957-68; Assist Master Cheam Sch 1970-86; 1939-45 War (wounded): *m* 1962, Sheila Jean, da of Dr D. J. B. Wilson, of High Wycombe, Bucks, and has issue living, Douglas William Boscawen, *b* 1965; *ed* Marlborough, Bristol Univ (BSc) and Queen's Coll, Oxford (PhD), — Eirene Helen Giffard *b* 1963; *ed* Downe House; RGN & RM. —— Helen Jane Boscawen, *b* 1925; *ed* Oxford Univ (MA 1950): *m* 1950, Henry Ensor Fossett Lock, of Winterborne, W Stafford, Dorchester, Dorset, and has issue living, Edward Henry Somerset, *b* 1953; *ed* Marlborough and London Univ (BA): *m* 1987, Caroline Metcalfe, and has issue living, Anthony Henry *b* 1989, Emma Ruth *b* 1991, — Charles John Somerset, *b* 1955; *ed* Marlborough and Keble Coll, Oxford (BA, PhD): *m* 1st, 1979 (*m diss* 1991), Helen Mogilansky; 2ndly, 1993, Nicoletta Isar, and has issue living (by 1st *m*), Nicholas Walter *b* 1981, Nadezhda Caroline *b* 1980, Persephone *b* 1987, — Richard Michael Somerset, *b* 1959; *ed* Marlborough and Balliol Coll, Oxford (BA): *m* 1991, Julia Bernhardt, — Amanda Mary Somerset, *b* 1966; *ed* Sherborne Sch for Girls.

Descendants of late Field Marshal Lord FitzRoy James Henry Somerset GCB (8th son of 5th Duke), who was *cr Baron Raglan* 1852 (see that title).

PREDECESSORS – (1) Sir CHARLES Somerset, KG, natural son of Henry Beaufort, 3rd Duke of Somerset, who was 3rd in descent from John of Gaunt and Catherine Swynford; Sir Charles was summoned to Parliament in right of his wife, as *Lord Herbert* (peerage of England, *cr* 1461); *cr Baron Herbert of Raglan, Chepstow and Gower* (peerage of England) 1506, and *Earl of Worcester* (peerage of England) 1513; appointed Lord Chamberlain for life; *d* 1526; *s* by his el son (2) HENRY, 2nd Earl; *d* 1549; *s* by his el son (3) WILLIAM, KG, 3rd Earl; *d* 1589; *s* by his son (4) EDWARD, KG, 4th Earl; was Master of the Horse 1601-15; his 3rd son, *cr Viscount Somerset*, was Master of the Horse to Queen Anne, consort of James I, the Earl *d* 1628; *s* by his el son (5) HENRY, 5th Earl; a devoted royalist; garrisoned Raglan Castle, and at his own expense held it for nearly four years against the Parliamentary forces; *cr Marquess of Worcester* (peerage of England) 1642; *d* 1646; *s* by his el son (6) EDWARD, 2nd Marquess; a zealous partisan of Charles I, who addressed him as *Earl of Glamorgan* before he *s* as Marquess; *d* 1667; *s* by his son (7) HENRY, KG, PC, 3rd Marquess; Lord Pres of Wales; *cr Duke of Beaufort* (peerage of England) 1682: on the accession of William and Mary he refused to take the oath of allegiance and afterwards lived in retirement; *d* 1699; *s* by his grandson (8) HENRY, KG, 2nd Duke; *d* 1714; *s* by his el son (9) HENRY, KG, 3rd Duke; *d* 1746; *s* by his brother (10) CHARLES NOEL, 4th Duke: *m* Elizabeth, sister of 4th Baron Botetourt; *d* 1756; *s* by his son (11) HENRY, KG, 5th Duke; was Master of the Horse to Queen Charlotte 1768-80; *s* as *Baron Botetourt* (see that title); *d* 1803; *s* by his el son (12) HENRY CHARLES, KG, 6th Duke, Lord-Lieut of cos Gloucester, Monmouth, and Brecon; *d* 1835; *s* by his son (13) HENRY, KG, 7th Duke; *b* 1792; served with distinction in Peninsula War: *m* 1st 1814, Georgiana Frederica, who *d* 1821, da of Hon Henry FitzRoy (B Southampton); 2ndly, 1822, Emily Frances, da of Culling Charles Smith; *d* 1853; *s* by his son (14) HENRY CHARLES FITZROY, KG, PC, 8th Duke, *b* 1824; Lord-Lieut of Monmouthshire; MP for E Gloucestershire (C) 1842-56; was Master of the Horse 1858-59 and 1866-8: *m* 1845, Lady Georgiana Charlotte Curzon, el da of 1st Earl Howe, GCH; *d* 1899; *s* by his el son (15) HENRY ADELBERT WELLINGTON FITZROY, 9th Duke, *b* 1847; High Steward of Gloucester and Bristol; bore Curtana at Coronation of King George V 1911: *m* 1895, Louise Emily, who *d* 1945, da of late William Henry Harford, JP, DL, of Oldtown, Tockington, and widow of Baron Carlo de Tuyll; *d* 1924; *s* by his only son (16) HENRY HUGH ARTHUR FITZROY, KG, GCVO, PC, 10th Duke, *b* 1900; Lord Lieut of Bristol and Gloucester; Master of the Horse to HM 1936-78, High Steward of Bristol and Gloucester and of Tewkesbury; founded Badminton Horse Trials 1949; Chm Masters of Foxhounds Assocn, Pres British Field Sports Soc: *m* 1923, Lady (Victoria Constance) Mary Cambridge, who *d* 1987, da of 1st Marquess of Cambridge; *d* 1984; *s* by his kinsman (17) DAVID ROBERT (only surv son of Capt Henry Robert Somers FitzRoy de Vere Somerset, DSO, only surv son of Henry Charles Somers Augustus Somerset, OBE, only son of Rt Hon Lord Henry Richard Charles Somerset, 2nd son of 8th Duke), 11th Duke and present peer; also Marquess of Worcester, Earl of Worcester, and Baron Herbert of Raglan, Chepstow and Gower.

BEAUMONT OF WHITLEY, BARON (Beaumont) (Life Baron 1967)

I can do no other

Rev TIMOTHY WENTWORTH BEAUMONT, son of late Maj Michael Wentworth Beaumont, TD (*see* V Allendale, colls), *b* 22 Nov 1928; *ed* Eton, Gordonstoun, and Ch Ch, Oxford (MA); V of Ch Ch Kowloon, Hong Kong 1957-59; resigned Holy Orders 1973 and resumed 1984, V of St Philip and All Souls, Kew, and St Luke's, Kew, 1986-91; Proprietor of *Prism* 1960-65 and *New Christian*, 1965-70, Chm of Studio-Vista Ltd 1963-68, Hon Treasurer of Liberal Party 1962-63, Head of Liberal Party Organisation 1965-66, Chm of Liberal Party 1967-68, and Pres 1969-70; Liberal Spokesman on Education, Arts and Environment 1971-85, and on Conservation and the Countryside since 1993; Member Liberal Democrat Federal Policy Cttee since 1992; Chm of Inst for Research into Mental Retardation 1972-74; Proprietor and Editor of *New Outlook* 1972-74; Pres British Fedn of Film Socs 1974-80; Leader of British Liberal Delegation to Parl Assemblies Council of Europe & Western European Union 1977-79; Vice-Chm Liberal Group, Council of Europe 1978; co-ordinator The Green Alliance 1977-80; *cr Baron Beaumont of Whitley*, of Child's Hill, Greater London, (Life Baron) 1967: *m* 1955, Mary Rose, da of Lt-Col Charles Edward Wauchope, MC, of Sandhill House, Rogate, Sussex, and has issue.

Arms – Gules, a lion rampant or, armed and langued azure, between eights crescents in orle of the second. **Crest** – A bull's head erased quarterly argent and gules, charged with a mullet sable. **Supporters** – *Dexter*, a phoenix; *sinister*, a pelican vulning herself proper.
Residence – 40 Elms Rd, SW4 9EX.

SON LIVING

Hon Hubert Wentworth (Harristown House, Brannockstown, Kildare), *b* 1956; *ed* Gordonstoun, and South Bank Polytechnic: *m* 1980, Katharine Emma, only da of Col Richard Francis Abel Smith, of Blidworth Dale, Notts (*see* E Athlone), and has issue living, George Wentworth, *b* 24 Aug 1985, — Richard Christian, *b* 1989, — Michael, *b* 1991, — Amelia May *b* 1983.

DAUGHTERS LIVING

Hon Atalanta Armstrong, *b* 1961: *m* 1987, Dr Stephen Francis Bungay, elder son of E. W. G. Bungay, of Chester, Cheshire, and has issue living, Felix Nicholas, *b* 1990, — Caspar Stephen, *b* 1994.
Hon Ariadne Grace, *b* 1963: *m* 1990, Mario Calvo-Platero, yr son of late Guido Calvo-Platero, of Milan, Italy, and has issue living, Oliver Guido, *b* 1991, — Milo Alaric, *b* 1992.

BEAVERBROOK, BARON (Aitken) (Baron UK 1917, Bt UK 1916)

Things for me, not I for things

MAXWELL WILLIAM HUMPHREY AITKEN, 3rd Baron and 3rd Baronet; *b* 29 Dec 1951; *s* 1985; *ed* Charterhouse, and Pembroke Coll, Camb; Chm Beaverbrook Foundation 1985-92; Lord in Waiting 1986-87; Dep Treas Conservative Party 1988-90, Treas 1990-92: *m* 1974, Susan Angela, el da of late Francis Ambrose Joseph More O'Ferrall (*see* Jackson, Bt, *cr* 1869), and has issue.

Arms – Argent, two barrulets wavy azure between in chief two maple leaves slipped and in base a thistle eradicated gules, a border sable charged with eight besants. **Crest** – Upon a drum proper a cock gules, wattled, armed and legged or. **Supporters** – On either side a beaver reguardant holding in the mouth a fish proper.
Residence – Denchworth Manor, Wantage, Oxon. *Club* – White's.

SONS LIVING

Hon MAXWELL FRANCIS, *b* 17 March 1977.
Hon Alexander Rory, *b* 1978.

DAUGHTERS LIVING

Hon Charlotte Susanna, *b* 1982.
Hon Sophia Violet Angela, *b* 1985.

HALF-SISTERS LIVING (*Daughters by 2nd marriage of 2nd Baron, who disclaimed the peerage for life 1964*)

Hon Kirsty Jane, *b* 1947: *m* 1st, 1966 (*m diss* 1973), Jonathan Derek Morley, yr son of late Brig Michael Frederick Morley, MBE, of Biddestone Manor, Chippenham, Wilts; 2ndly, 1975, Christopher Marten Smallwood, of 76 Hurlingham Rd, SW6, son of Canon Graham Marten Smallwood, of Brook House, Childswickham, Worcs, and has issue living (by 1st *m*), Dominic Max Michael, *b* 1967, — Sebastian Finch, *b* 1969: *m* 1993, Victoria Clare Helen, only da of Samuel Charles Whitbread (*see* B Clinton, colls), — (by 2nd *m*), Eleanor Bluebell, *b* 1982.

Hon Lynda Mary Kathleen, *b* 1948: *m* 1st, 1969 (*m diss* 1974), Nicholas Saxton, son of Robert Saxton, of La Jolla, Calif; 2ndly, 1977, Jonathan James Dickson, of 45 Broomwood Rd, SW11, and has issue living (by 2nd *m*), Joshua James, *b* 1977, — Leo Casper, *b* 1981.

SISTER LIVING

Hon Laura, *b* 1953; journalist; resumed her maiden name 1989: *m* 1st, 1984 (*m diss* 1989), David Victor Mark Mallet, yst son of late Sir Victor Alexander Louis Mallet, GCMG, CVO; 2ndly, 1992, Martin K. Levi, son of R. Levi, and has issue living (by 1st *m*), David Sonny Victor Maxwell, *b* 1984, — (by 2nd *m*) Lucci Violet, *b* 1993. *Residence* – The Prospect, 83 High St, Cowes, I of Wight.

WIDOW LIVING OF SON OF FIRST BARON

(Marie) Patricia, da of Michael Maguire, of Melbourne, Australia: *m* 1st, 1942, as his 2nd wife, Capt Hon Peter Rudyard Aitken, R Fus, who *d* 1947; 2ndly, 1948 (*m diss* 1956), Richard David Rafe Lycett Green, who *d* 1969 (*see* Green, Bt, *cr* 1886, colls), and has issue by 1st *m* (see colls, infra). *Residence* –

WIDOW LIVING OF FIRST BARON

MARCIA ANASTASIA (*Dowager Baroness Beaverbrook*) (Saint Andrews, New Brunswick, Canada), da of John Christoforides, of Leyswood, Groombridge, Sussex, and widow of Sir James Hamet Dunn, QC (*cr* 1921); Hon LLD Dalhousie; Chancellor of Dalhousie Univ since 1968: *m* 1963, as his 2nd wife, the 1st Baron, who *d* 1964.

WIDOW LIVING OF SECOND BARON (*who disclaimed the peerage for life* 1964)

VIOLET (*Lady Aitken*) (Mickleham Downs House, Dorking, Surrey), 3rd da of late Sir Humphrey Edmund de Trafford, 4th Bt, MC; Chancellor Univ of New Brunswick 1982-92 (Hon LLD), Chancellor Emeritus since 1992, Chm Beaverbrook Canadian Foundation: *m* 1951, as his 3rd wife, Sir Max (John William Maxwell) Aitken, 2nd Bt, DSO, DFC, who disclaimed the peerage for life 1964, and *d* 1985.

COLLATERAL BRANCH LIVING

Issue of late Capt Hon Peter Rudyard Aitken, R Fus, 2nd son of 1st Baron, *b* 1912, *d* 1947: *m* 1st, 1934 (*m diss* 1939), Janet Ruth Murrene, da of Prof Murray Macneill, of Dalhousie Univ, Halifax, Nova Scotia; 2ndly, 1942, (Marie) Patricia (ante), who *m* 2ndly, 1948 (*m diss* 1956), Richard David Rafe Lycett Green (*see* Green, Bt, *cr*, 1886, colls), da of Michael Maguire, of Melbourne, Australia:—

(By 2nd *m*) Timothy Maxwell *b* 1944; *ed* Repton, and McGill Univ; Chief Exec TV-am 1983-88: *m* 1972, Julie Ruth Filsted, and has issue living, Theodore Maxwell, *b* 1976. —— Peter Michael, *b* 1946; *ed* Malvern: *m* 1980 (*m diss* 1985), Hon (Joan) Elizabeth Rees-Williams, only da of 1st Baron Ogmore, and formerly wife of (i) Richard Harris, actor, and (ii) Rex Harrison (afterwards Sir Rex Harrison), actor. *Residence* – 14 Lowndes Sq, SW1. —— (By 1st *m*) Caroline Anne Christine, *b* 1935: *m* 1957, Conyers Collingwood Massy Baker, Lt, RCNR, of 28 Whitney Av, Toronto 5, Ontario, Canada, and has issue living, William Hugh Massy, *b* 1958, — Philip Massy, *b* 1960, — Jonathan Piers Massy, *b* 1967.

PREDECESSORS – **(1)** (WILLIAM) MAXWELL Aitken, CD, PC, son of Rev William Cuthbert Aitken Presbyterian Min of Newcastle, New Brunswick, Canada; *b* 1879; MP for Ashton-under-Lyne (*C*) 1910-16, with Canadian Expeditionary Force 1915, and Canadian Govt Representative at Front 1916, Chancellor of Duchy of Lancaster, and Min of Information 1918; formerly proprietor of *Daily Express*, *Sunday Express* (which he founded 1920), and *Evening Standard*; Min of Aircraft Production 1940, Min of State and Min of Supply 1941, a Member of War Cabinet 1940-42, Lord Privy Seal 1943-45; *cr* a *Baronet* 1916, and *Baron Beaverbrook*, of Beaverbrook, Prov of New Brunswick, Canada, and of Cherkley, co Surrey (peerage of UK) 1917: *m* 1st, 1906, Gladys, who *d* 1927, da of Brig-Gen Charles William Drury, CB, of Halifax, Nova Scotia; 2ndly, 1963, Marcia Anastasia, da of John Christoforides, of Leyswood, Groombridge, Sussex, and widow of Sir James Hamet Dunn, QC, 1st Bt (*cr* 1921); *d* 1964; *s* by his el son **(2)** JOHN WILLIAM MAXWELL, DSO, DSC, 2nd Baron (until he disclaimed his peerage for life 12 June 1964); Group Capt Aux Air Force, 1939-45 War (despatches, DFC, DSO, Czechoslavakian Mil Cross); Chm Beaverbrook Newspapers Ltd 1968-77, Life Pres 1977-85; MP for Holborn (*C*) 1945-50: *m* 1st, 1939 (*m diss* 1944), Cynthia Helen Glencairn, da of Col Hugh Glencairn Monteith, DSO, OBE; 2ndly, 1946 (*m diss* 1950), Ursula Jane, da of late Maj Robert Orlando Rudolph Kenyon-Slaney (*see* B Kenyon, colls), and formerly wife of late Lt-Col (David Ludovic) Peter Lindsay, DSO (*see* E Crawford, colls); 3rdly, 1951, Violet, da of late Sir Humphrey Edmund de Trafford, 4th Bt, MC; *d* 1985; *s* by his only son **(3)** MAXWELL WILLIAM HUMPHREY, 3rd Baron and present peer and 3rd Baronet.

Bective, Earl of; son of Marquess of Headfort.

BEDFORD, DUKE OF (Russell) (Duke E 1694)

What will be, will be

JOHN ROBERT RUSSELL, 13th Duke; *b* 24 May 1917; *s* 1953; European War 1939-40 in Coldstream Gds (invalided): *m* 1st, 1939, Clare Gwendolen, who *d* 1945, da of John Bridgman, and formerly wife of Maj Kenneth Chamney Walpole Hollway, MC; 2ndly, 1947 (*m diss* 1960), Hon Lydia Yarde-Buller, da of 3rd Baron Churston, and widow of Capt Ian Archibald de Hoghton Lyle, Black Watch, el son of Sir Archibald Moir Park Lyle, 2nd Bt, MC; 3rdly, 1960, Madame Nicole Milinaire, da of Paul Schneider, of Paris, and has issue by 1st and 2nd *m*.

Arms – Argent, a lion rampant gules; on a chief sable, three escallops of the first. **Crest** – A goat statant argent, armed and unguled or. **Supporters** – *Dexter*, a lion rampant gules, gorged with a collar argent, charged with three escallops sable; *sinister*, a goat argent, armed, unguled and bearded or.
Residence – Les Ligures, 2 rue Honoré Labande, MC98000, Monaco.

SONS LIVING *(By 1st marriage)*

HENRY ROBIN IAN (*Marquess of Tavistock*), *b* 21 Jan 1940; *ed* Le Rosey, and Harvard Univ; DL Beds 1985; Dir Trafalgar House Ltd 1977-92, United Racecourses Ltd since 1977, and Berkeley Govett & Co Ltd since 1986; Chm TR Property Invest Trust 1982-91, and Berkeley Development Capital Ltd 1984-92; Pres Woburn Golf Country Club since 1976; Chm of Trustees Kennedy Memorial Trust 1985-90: *m* 1961, Henrietta Joan, only da of Henry Frederic Tiarks, of Casa Ina, Finca Torres, Marbella, Malaga, Spain, and has issue:—

SONS LIVING — ANDREW IAN HENRY (*Lord Howland*), *b* 30 March 1962, — *Lord* Robin Loel Hastings, *b* 1963: *m* 1994, Stephanie, yst da of Kurt Niklas, of Beverly Hills, Calif, USA, — *Lord* James Edward Herbrand, *b* 1975.

Seat – Woburn Abbey, Bedfordshire MK43 0TP. *Clubs* – White's, Brook (New York)

Lord Rudolf, *b* 1944; *ed* Gordonstoun: *m* 1989, Farah, yr da of R. Moghaddam. *Residence* – Charlton Park House, Malmesbury, Wilts SN16 9DG.

(By 2nd marriage)

Lord Francis Hastings (13 George St, Woburn, Milton Keynes MK17 9PX), *b* 1950; *ed* Eton; BSc (Land Admin); ARICS: *m* 1971, Faith Diane, da of late Dr S. I. M. Ibrahim, of Singapore, and formerly wife of George Carrington, and has issue living, Czarina Lydia, *b* 1976.

BROTHER LIVING

Lord Hugh Hastings, *b* 1923: *ed* Christ's Coll, Camb; an ARICS: *m* 1957, Rosemary, yr da of late Keith Freeling Markby, of Treworder, Blisland, Bodmin, Cornwall, and has issue living, Mark Hugh (Churchtown Farm, Lanteglos-by-Fowey, Cornwall PL23 1NR), *b* 1960: *m* 1987, Charlotte E. A., da of late J. W. D. Stewart, of Kingston upon Thames, Surrey, and has issue living, Laurie Stewart *b* 1990, Chloe Ruth *b* 1988, Hester Mae *b* 1994, — Karen Diana, *b* 1961: *m* 1991, Hugh Yelverton Scott Barrett, son of John Scott Barrett, of Henfield, Sussex. *Residence* – The Bell House, Dolau, Llandrindod Wells, Powys.

COLLATERAL BRANCHES LIVING

Grandchildren of late Harold John Hastings Russell (*infra*):—
Issue of late Anthony Arthur Russell, *b* 1904, *d* 1978: *m* 1947, Alicia Charlotte (The Ridgeway, Shere, Guildford, Surrey), only da of late Seton Eustace, of Stoodwell, Merrow, Surrey:—
Francis Anthony, *b* 1948; *ed* Crookham Court, Newbury. —— Hugo Eustace Arthur, *b* 1951; *ed* Milton Abbey: *m* 1991, Caroline L., eldest da of late Donald Grant, OBE, of Molino de la Hoz, Las Rozas de Madrid, Spain, and has issue living, Arthur Donald Anthony, *b* 1994, — Catherine Lucy, *b* 1992. —— Julia Alicia, *b* 1950; *ed* Downe House, Newbury: *m* 1985, Dr Ian Rutherford Sanderson, of 6 Markham St, SW3 3NP, and has issue living, Vita Frances, *b* 1988. —— Victoria Evelyn Elizabeth, *b* 1953; *ed* Downe House, Newbury.

Grandchildren of late Lord Arthur John Edward Russell, next brother of 9th Duke:—
Issue of late Harold John Hastings Russell, *b* 1868, *d* 1926: *m* 1896, Lady Victoria Alberta Leveson-Gower, who *d* 1953, da of 2nd Earl Granville:—
Rachel Diana: *m* 1929, Hugh Noel Blakiston, who *d* 1984, and has issue living, Rachel Castalia (31 Edith Grove, SW10), *b* 1930: *m* 1951 (*m diss* 1968), James Gordon Akers Campbell, and has issue living, Julian James Noel *b* 1953: *m* 1971, Saundra Hale, Marcus George Akers *b* 1954, Benedict Robert Gordon *b* 1958: *m* 1986, Lynnette Caicco, Cosmo Thomas Aretas *b* 1960: *m* 1989, Brigitte Gürke, — Caroline Georgiana, *b* 1933: *m* 1970, Adam Russell Hunter, of 1 Dancer Rd, SW6, and has issue living, Adam Russell *b* 1970, Charlotte *b* 1972. *Residence* – 6 Markham Sq, SW3 4UY.
Issue of late Maj Gilbert Byng Alwyne Russell, *b* 1875, *d* 1942: *m* 1917, Maud Julia Augusta, who *d* 1982, da of late Paul Nelke:—
Martin Basil Paul, *b* 1918; *ed* Eton, and King's Coll, Camb (MA); with KRRC 1939-40; Assist Private Sec to Rt Hon Duff Cooper (later 1st Viscount Norwich), when Min of Information 1940-41, and to Brendan Bracken (later Viscount Bracken) 1941, and Private Sec to Rt Hon Duff Cooper when Chancellor of Duchy of Lancaster, on Mission to Far East 1941-42; HQ Ceylon Army Command 1942-43 and HQ Allied Land Forces SE Asia, Kandy and Singapore 1943-46, with rank of Capt; author of *The Art of George Keyt*, 1949; with British S Africa Co 1954-61, Minerals Separation 1961-63; Ionian Bank 1964-66; founded M. B. P. Russell & Co Ltd 1967; a Member of Council of R Soc for India, Pakistan and Ceylon; FRAS: *m* 1954, Anne Swinton (Croix de Guerre), da of late Brig Stanlake Swinton Lee, CBE, DSO, and has issue living, Julian Hugh (86 South Hill Park, NW3 2SN; Brooks's Club), *b* 1955; *ed* Harrow, — Stephen Raymond (twin), *b* 1955; *ed* Harrow, — Laura Diana, *b* 1959; *ed* Essex Univ (BA), and Way Colls of Biblical Research, USA: *m* 1989, Colin Beresford, and has issue living, Helen Anne *b* 1992, — Emily Esther, *b* 1962; *ed* Manchester Univ (BA). *Residence* – Dungrove Farm House, Tarrant Gunville, Blandford, Dorset DT11 8JS. *Clubs* – White's, Brooks's, Buck's, Travellers' (Paris).

Descendants of late Rt Hon Lord Odo William Russell, GCB, GCMG (yr brother of 9th Duke), who was *cr* *Baron Ampthill* 1881 (see that title).

Descendants of late Lord John Russell (3rd son of 6th Duke), who was *cr Earl Russell* 1861 (see that title).

Grandchildren of late Maj-Gen Sir Thomas Wentworth Russell, KBE, CMG, Pasha in Egypt, 2nd son (and co-heir to Baronies of Beauchamp and Mordaunt) of Rev Henry Charles Russell, son of Lt-Col Lord Charles James Fox Russell, 6th son of 6th Duke:—

Issue of late Sir John Wriothesley Russell, GCVO, CMG, sometime Amb to Ethiopia, Brazil and Spain, *b* 1914, *d* 1984: *m* 1945, Aliki (*Lady Russell*) (The Vine Farm, Northbourne, nr Deal, Kent; Flat 1, 48 Queen's Gate Gdns, SW7 5ND), da of George Diplarakos, of Athens, and formerly wife of Paul-Louis Weiller (*d* 1993):—

Alexander Charles Thomas Wriothesley, *b* 1950; *ed* Eton, and Trin Coll, Camb: *m* 1986, Elizabeth (Libby) Diana, el da of Lord John Manners, of Knipton, Grantham, Lincs (*see* D Rutland), and has issue living, Sophie Camilla Mary, *b* 1989, — Rose Isobel Aliki, *b* 1991. *Residence* – 48 Chester Row, SW1W 9DU. ⸺ Georgiana Alexandra (*Lady Boothby*), *b* 1947: *m* 1976, Sir Brooke Charles Boothby, 16th Bt, and has issue. *Residence* – Fonmon Castle, Barry, S Glamorgan CF6 9ZN.

PREDECESSORS – (1) JOHN Russell, KG, one of the most accomplished gentlemen of his time, attended the Archduke Philip of Austria (who had been stranded on the coast near Weymouth) to the Court of Henry VII, in 1506, where he was appointed a Gentleman of the Privy Chamber; accompanied Henry VIII in his French Wars, and having held various high appointments, was *cr Baron Russell* (peerage of England) 1539, and in 1540 obtained a grant of the site of Tavistock Abbey and of the extensive possessions belonging thereto; in 1550, *temp* Edward VI, he received a grant of the Monastery of Woburn and was *cr Earl of Bedford* (peerage of England); was Lord Privy Seal to Queen Mary, and went as Ambassador to Spain to conduct HM's royal consort, Philip II, into England; *d* 1555; *s* by his son (2) FRANCIS, KG, PC, 2nd Earl, a nobleman of great eminence, *temp* Elizabeth I; *d* 1585; *s* by his grandson (3) EDWARD, 3rd Earl; *dsp* 1627; *s* by his cousin, son of Sir William, *cr Baron Russell of Thornhaugh* (peerage of England) 1603, (4) FRANCIS, 4th Earl, who had previously *s* as 2nd Baron Russell; *d* 1641; *s* by his son (5) WILLIAM, KG, 5th Earl, *cr Marquess of Tavistock* and *Duke of Bedford* (peerage of England) 1694; his el son, William, the celebrated Lord Russell, was executed 21 July 1683, for high treason, as a participator in the Rye-House conspiracy; he *d* 1700, and the attainder upon Lord Russell having been annulled, he was *s* by his grandson (6) WRIOTHESLEY, KG, 2nd Duke; summoned to Parliament as *Baron Howland* (peerage of England) 1695; *d* 1711; *s* by his son (7) WRIOTHESLEY, 3rd Duke; *dsp* 1732; *s* by his brother (8) JOHN, KG, 4th Duke; successively Lord-Lieut of Ireland and Ambassador to France: *d* 1771; *s* by his grandson (9) FRANCIS, 5th Duke; *d* unmarried 1802; *s* by his brother (10) JOHN, KG, 6th Duke; *d* 1839; *s* by his son (11) FRANCIS, KG, 7th Duke; summoned to Parliament in his father's Barony of Howland 1833; *d* 1861; *s* by his son (12) WILLIAM, 8th Duke; *dsp* 1872; *s* by his cousin (13) FRANCIS CHARLES HASTINGS, KG, 9th Duke (el son of Maj-Gen Lord George William, GCB, 2nd son of 6th Duke, by Elizabeth Anne, da of Hon John Theophilus Rawdon, brother of 1st Marquess of Hastings), *b* 1819; MP for Bedfordshire (*L*) 1847-72 Lord-Lieut of Hunts: *m* 1844, Lady Elizabeth Sackville-West, VA, who *d* 1897, el da of 5th Earl De La Warr; *d* 1891; *s* by his el son (14) GEORGE WILLIAM FRANCIS SACKVILLE, 10th Duke, *b* 1852; MP for Bedfordshire (*L*) 1875-85: *m* 1876, Lady Adeline Marie Somers-Cocks, GBE, who *d* 1920, da of 3rd Earl Somers (*ext*); *d* 1893; *s* by his brother (15) HERBRAND ARTHUR, KG, KBE, 11th Duke; *b* 1858; was Lord-Lieut of Middlesex 1898-1926: *m* 1888, Dame Mary Du Caurroy, DBE, RRC, who *d* 1937, da of the Ven W. H. Tribe, formerly Archdeacon of Lahore; *d* 1940; *s* by his son (16) HASTINGS WILLIAM SACKVILLE, 12th Duke; *b* 1888; formerly Lieut 10th Batn Duke of Cambridge's Own (Middlesex) Regt: *m* 1914, Louisa Crommelin Roberta Jowitt, who *d* 1960, da of late Robert Jowitt Whitwell, of Thornbury Lodge, 70 Banbury Road, Oxford; *d* 1953; *s* by his el son (17) JOHN ROBERT, 13th Duke and present peer; also Marquess of Tavistock, Earl of Bedford, Baron Russell, and Baron Howland.

BEECHING, BARONY OF (Beeching) (Extinct 1985)

WIDOW LIVING OF LIFE BARON

ELLA MARGARET (*Baroness Beeching*), da of William J. Tiley, of Maidstone: *m* 1938, Baron Beeching (Life Baron), who *d* 1985. *Residence* – Barnlands, 97 High St, Lindfield, W Sussex RH16 2HN.

Belfast, Earl of; son of Marquess of Donegall.

BELHAVEN and STENTON, LORD (Hamilton) (Lord S 1647)

ROBERT ANTHONY CARMICHAEL HAMILTON, 13th Lord; *b* 27 Feb 1927; *s* 1961; *ed* Eton: *m* 1st, 1952 (*m diss* 1973), (Elizabeth) Ann, da of late Col Arthur Henry Moseley, DSO, of Hastings Rd, Warrawee, NSW; 2ndly, 1973 (*m diss* 1986), Rosemary, who *d* 1992, da of late Sir Herbert Geraint Williams, 1st Bt, MP (*cr* 1953), and formerly wife of late Sir Ian (John) Auld Mactaggart, 3rd Bt; 3rdly, 1986, Malgorzata Maria, da of Tadeusz Pobog Hruzik-Mazurkiewicz, of Batorego 11/8, Krakow, Poland, and has issue by 1st and 3rd *m*.

Arms – Quarterly, 1st and 4th, gules, a mullet argent between three cinquefoils ermine *Hamilton of Udston*; 2nd and 3rd gules, a man's heart proper, shadowed or, between three cinquefoils ermine, all within a bordure argent *Hamilton of Raploch*. **Crest** – A horse's head couped argent, bridled gules. **Supporters** – Two horses argent, bridled gules. *Residence* – 16 Broadwater Down, Tunbridge Wells, Kent, TN2 5NR.

SON LIVING *(By 1st marriage)*

Hon FREDERICK CARMICHAEL ARTHUR (*Master of Belhaven*), *b* 27 Sept, 1953; *ed* Eton: *m* 1st, 1981, Elizabeth Anne da of S. V. Tredinnick, of Naldretts Court, Wisborough Green, Sussex; 2ndly, 1991, Mrs Philippa Martha Gausel Collins, da of Sir Rowland John Rathbone Whitehead, 5th Bt, and has issue living (by 1st *m*), William Richard, *b* 30 Dec 1982, — James Frederick, *b* 1984, — (by 2nd *m*) Olivia Martha, *b* 1993.

DAUGHTERS LIVING *(By 1st marriage)*

Hon Julia Elizabeth Heather HAMILTON, *b* 1956; resumed her maiden name 1992: *m* 1st, 1975, Richard Newbury; 2ndly, 1979, Stephen Hobbs, and has issue living (by 2nd *m*), Sophie Louise Ann, *b* 1981, — Arabella Leonie, *b* 1983. *Residence* – 14 Westcroft Sq, W6 0TD.

(By 3rd marriage)

Hon Alexandra Maria, *b* 1987.

HALF-AUNTS LIVING *(Daughters of 11th Lord)*

Hon Margaret de Hauteville, *b* 1939: *m* 1st, 1964 (*m diss* 1981), C. Keith W. Schellenberg; 2ndly, 1983, James Frank Williams, of Udny Castle, Aberdeenshire, and has issue living (by 1st *m*), Nicholas Udny, *b* 1966, — Amy Julia Udny, *b* 1971, — Rose Camilla Joan Udny, *b* 1973.
Hon Victoria Edith, *b* 1941; PhD: *m* 1976, Nicholas Tufnell, of 990 Hanley Av, Los Angeles, Calif 90049, USA, and has issue living, Samuel, *b* 1978.

WIDOW LIVING OF TWELFTH LORD

CYRILLA MARY (Copper Cottage, New Galloway, Castle Douglas), da of late Raymund Louis Binns: *m* 1st, 1942, as his 2nd wife, the 12th Lord, who *d* 1961; 2ndly, 1969 (*m diss* 19—), Dennis Beaumont Vale, OBE.

COLLATERAL BRANCHES LIVING

Granddaughter of late Capt Henry George Hamilton, uncle of 10th Lord:—
Issue of late Adm Sir Frederick Tower Hamilton, GCVO, KCB, *b* 1856, *d* 1917: *m* 1889, Maria Walpole, who *d* 1952, da of late Adm of the Fleet Hon Sir Henry Keppel, GCB, OM (*see* E Albemarle, colls, 1952 Edn):—
Jean, *b* 1899. *Residence* – Mendham Lodge, Harleston, Norfolk IP20 0JB.

Grandchildren of late Arthur Richard Hamilton, uncle of 10th Lord:—
Issue of late Arthur Henry Hamilton, *b* 1872, *d* 1930: *m* 1906, Mabel, who *d* 1918 da of John Harrower, of Baldur, Manitoba:—
Gladys Dorothy, *b* 1908: *m* 1928, Walter Booth Jorgenson, who *d* 1978, and has issue living, Robert Arthur, *b* 1929, — Allen Edward, *b* 1932, — Lynda Dorothy, *b* 1940, — Ellen Jean, *b* 1942.
Issue of late Charles Augustus Hamilton, *b* 1874, *d* 1960: *m* 1906, Alice May, who *d* 1956, da of Benjamin Thorn, of Souris, Manitoba:—
Frederick William, MC (Lion's Manor, 320 Sherbrook St, Winnipeg, Manitoba R3B 2W6, Canada), *b* 1910; 1939-45 War as Maj R Canadian Engineers (MC): *m* 1945, Alice Elizabeth, who *d* 1969, da of George A. Stevenson, of Morris, Manitoba, and has issue living, Mary Ellen, *b* 1947: *m* 1st, 1969 (*m diss* 1982), Donald Keith Trueman, of Winnipeg, Canada; 2ndly, 1985, Michael Anthony Halligan, of 119 Balliol St, Toronto, Ontario, Canada MHS 1C2, and has issue living (by 1st *m*), Catherine Martha *b* 1973, — Catherine Alice, *b* 1949: *m* 1979, Robert Webster, and has issue, Paul Robert *b* 1981. —— Richard Terrick (Baldur, Manitoba), *b* 1912: *m* 1933, Muriel, da of John Mcleod, of Belmont, Manitoba, and has issue living, Betty Lorraine, *b* 1934: *m* 1961, W. Lexton Young, of Killarney, Manitoba, Canada, and has issue, Candis *b* 1961, Lana *b* 1963, Lisa *b* 1964, Jan *b* 1966, — Margaret Rose, *b* 1935: *m* 1955, Clare Vrooman, of Belmont, Manitoba, Canada, and has issue, Terry *b* 1956, Kevin *b* 1957, Dean *b* 1960, Patricia *b* 1958, Brenda *b* 1961, Kathy *b* 1962, Shelly *b* 1965, — Gertrude Joan, *b* 1936: *m* 1955, Neil Cline, of Wawanesa, Manitoba, Canada, and has issue, Bradley *b* 1956, Perry *b* 1959, Francis *b* 1965, Laurie *b* 1955, Pamela *b* 1958, — Joyce Elaine, *b* 1938: *m* 1956, Owen Vrooman, of Belmont, Manitoba, Canada, and has issue living, Darrel *b* 1956, Gordon *b* 1964, Debbie *b* 1957, Vicki *b* 1960. —— Rose Aileen, *b* 1908: *m* 1st, 1954, George Walter Easter, who *d* 1958; 2ndly, 1964, Rt Rev William Henry Howes Crump, DD, late Bishop of Saskatchewan.

Granddaughters of late Ven Anthony Hamilton (infra):—
Issue of late Clement Edward Hamilton, *b* 1854, *d* 1923: *m* 1898, Fanny, who *d* 1955, da of James Winch, JP, of Rochester:—
Eleanor Clara Roby, *b* 1902. —— Marjorie Francis Roby, *b* 1907.

Grandchildren of late Terrick Alfred Hamilton (infra):—
Issue of late Terrick Elyston Scott Hamilton, b 1881, d 1969: m 19—, Agnes, who d 1944, da of W. Lynch:—
Anthony Elyston John, b 1905: m 1928, Helen Margaret Doherty, and has issue living, Patrick, b 1928: m 1952, Dulcie Emily Hafey, and has issue living, Patrick William b 1953: m 1977, Maree Helen Fitzgerald, formerly wife of — Ward (and has issue living, Brendan James b 1979, Michelle Susan b 1978), Anthony John b 1955: m 1977, Suzanne Sylvia Heineman (and has issue living, Allison Madelene Natasha b 1975, Janie Leigh b 1978), Terrick Daniel b 1957: m 1979, Heather-Anne Watson, Dale Thomas b 1958, — Elyston William, b 1936: m 1960, Norma Merion Ilott, and has issue living, Jeanette b 1962, Kathleen b 1964, — Reginald John, b 1940: m 1962, Thelda Rose Park, and has issue living, Glen b 1963, Bradley b 1965, Ashley Reginald b 1969, Steven b 1971, — Margaret, b 1930: m 1st, 1951, Brian George Denny, who d 1959; 2ndly, 1966, Roy Palmer Carige, and has issue living (by 1st m), Annette Margaret b 1952: m 1971, Thomas William Kitchiner (and has issue living, Kellie Maree b 1974, Necia Ann b 1976, Suzanne b 1980), Denise b 1958: m 1975, Mark William Owttrim (and has issue living, Ryan Mark b 1981) (by 2nd m), Toni Maree b 1970, — Marjorie Jean, b 1935: m 1954, Donald Allan McKnight, and has issue living, Michael James b 1956: m 1980, Barbara Guascoine, Allan Douglas Thomas b 1967, Teresa Margaret b 1955, Tracy Ann b 1973, — Helen Margaret, b 1938: m 1957, Russell McQuie, and has issue living, Russell Scott b 1959: m 1981, Dana Cheree Mills, Larry b 1964, Wendy Ann b 1961, — Rita Grace, b 1941: m 1962, Allan Benjamin Park, and has issue living, Jenny Lorraine b 1964: m 1982, Neville Allen (and has issue living, Melissa Lorraine b 1981), Julie Maree b 1965, Allison Jane b 1969. —— Vernon Harvey, b 1914: m 1943, Gloria Volk, and has issue living, Ian Vernon, b 1944: m 1976, Patti Marie O'Neil, and has issue living, Roderick Joseph b 1969, Simon John b 1974, Ashley James b 1980, — Joy Agnes, b 1947: m 1967, Geoffrey Francis O'Neil, and has issue living, Lindsay Francis Louis b 1968, — Peter Sean b 1973, Renée Rose b 1975. —— John Edward, b 1917: m 1937, Olive Amy Florence Hannah Russell, and has issue living, Peter John, b 1939: m 1960, Joan Adele Kuln, and has issue living, Geoffrey b 1962, Peter Scott b 1966, — Alan Patrick, b 1952: m 1973, Marilyn Anne Ward, and has issue living, John Allan b 1976, Michael Frederick b 1981, Rosalea Anne b 1975, Jantelle Maree b 1978, — Margaret, b 1938: m 1st, 1957 (m diss 1969), Colin Miller; 2ndly, 1970 (m diss 19—), William John Dolgner, and has issue living (by 1st m), Kimberley Mark b 1957, Rodney John b 1961, Kara Lea b 1964, (by 2nd m) Jason Ashley b 1970, Clayton Scott b 19—, — Mary Rose, b 1948: m 1964, William John Eckel, and has issue living, William John b 1965, Raymond Francis b 1967. —— William Robert, b 1921: m 1947, Jean Elsie Higgins, and has issue living, Diane Carol, b 1946: m 1965, Daniel Cameron, and has issue living, Andreena Louise b 1978, — Maree Estelle, b 1947: m 1966 (m diss 1978), Dale McDonald, and has issue living, Michael John b 1967, — Lynda Agnes, b 1949: m 1969, Robert Sing, and has issue living, Sharlene Maree b 1971, Bronwyn Anne b 1981, — Mary Anne, b 1950: m 1978, John King, and has issue living, Aeron James b 1971, — Charmaine Lee, b 1962: m 1983, Steven Bailey. —— Julia Agnes, b 1908: m 1938, John Edward Whitman, of Hamilton, Rundle-Jardine Sts, Wandal, Rockhampton, Queensland, Australia, and has issue living, Barry John (Kerrigan St, N Rockhampton, Queensland, Australia), b 1944: m 1969, Margaret Collins, and has issue living, Mark John b 1975, Joanne Maree b 1970, Louise Margaret b 1977, — Michael John (Houlihan St, N Rockhampton, Queensland, Australia), b 1948: m 1971, Lynette Wallace, and has issue living, Karl Anthony b 1975, Clint Andrew b 1977, Luke Phillip b 1980, Emily May b 1983, — Paulanne Mary, b 1939: m 1961, Edward John Kelly, of 49 Blenheim St, Chermside West, Brisbane, Queensland, Australia, and has issue living, Chris James b 1965, Kim Edward b 1967, Lee Michael b 1969, Jason John b 1974, Julie Maree (twin) b 1974, — Julie Anne, b 1941; JP: m 1964, Phillip J. Walsh, of 129 Rundle St, Rockhampton, Queensland, Australia, and has issue living, Anthony John b 1965: m 1990, Verena Finocchiaro, Justin Philip b 1966, John Edward b 1969. —— Mary Alice, b 1911: m 1939, Thorwald Harold Widt, of 22 Boowgala Rd, Florida Gdns, Gold Coast, Quensland, Australia, and has issue living, Peter Anthony, b 1945: m 1969, Diane McCallum, and has issue living, Stephen Anthony b 1968, — Helen Margaret, b 1940. —— Eileen Marjorie, b 1925: m 1947, Roland Mervyn Smith, who d 1975, and has issue living, Terrick Elystan Scott, b 1953: m 1982, Yasmine Hartmann, — Lynda Ngaio, b 1949: m 1974, Sqdn Ldr Gordon Maxwell Bennett, — Ruth Bronwen, b 1954: m 1973, Capt Roland Francis Bagshaw, and has issue living, Kristi Leanne b 1973, Alison Louise b 1975, Veronica Lauren b 1978.

Grandson of late Edward William Terrick Hamilton, son of late Ven Anthony Hamilton (b 1778), Archdeacon of Taunton, great-uncle of 10th Lord:—
Issue of late Terrick Alfred Hamilton, b 1851, d 1925: m 1878, Alice, da of John Scott, of Newcastle, NSW:—
John Helenus, b 1888.

Grandchildren of late Charles Hamilton, b 1885, d 1961: m 1911, Olivia Abbott Palmer:—
Charles Clive, b 1919: m 19—, Nellie Olive Watson, and has issue living, Noel Peter, b 1953, — Judith Helen, b 1945, — Lexie Mae, b 1949. —— Olivia Jessie, b 1913: m 19—, Edmund Rockett, and has issue living, James Edward, b 1947. —— Margaret Jean, b 1915: m 1st, Ernest Henry Bellingham; 2ndly, 1965, William Edward McCulloch, and has issue living (by 1st m), Alan Ward b 1941: m 1966, Lynette Fawcett. —— Kepple Osborne, b 1917: m 19—, Dudley Halliwell Milton, and has issue living, Raymond Charles, b 1945.

Granddaughters of late Edward William Terrick Hamilton (ante):—
Issue of late Charles Gipps Hamilton, b 1857, d 1955: m 1892, Anna Gertrude Montgomerie, who d 1937, da of Hugh Morris Lang:—
Margaret Graham, MBE (Overstone House, Elvaston Rd, Hexham, Northumberland NE46 2HH), b 1895; MBE (Civil) 1946. —— Winifred Anna (Brown Knowe, Greenhaugh, Hexham, Northumberland), b 1905: m 1926, James Seymour Spencer, who d 1967, and has issue living, Antony James, b 1927; ed Eton: m 1956, Felicity Jacqueline, da of C. L. C. S. Baines, of Coneygore House, Penselwood, Wincanton, Som, and has issue living, Martin Antony b 1959, Philip Mark b 1961, Josephine Claudia b 1957, — Simon Charles (Redesmouth Hall, Redesmouth, Hexham, Northumberland NE48 2ER), b 1929; ed Eton: m 1965, Nancy Loveday, 2nd da of Edmund George Coryton, of Linkincorn House, Yelverton, S Devon (see Carew, Bt, colls, 1980 Edn), and has issue living, Charles James b 1966, Andrew George b 1968.

PREDECESSORS – (1) JOHN HAMILTON, of Broomhill (son of James Hamilton, of Broomhill, cr a Bt of Nova Scotia 1635), was cr Lord Belhaven and Stenton, of co Haddington (peerage of Scotland) 1647. In 1675 he surrendered his Lordship to the crown, and received a new patent with remainder to John Hamilton, of Pressmannan, husband of his granddaughter Margaret, and in failure of that line to his heirs male whatsoever; d 1679; s by his son-in-law (2) JOHN, 2nd Lord, a Lord of the Treasury 1704, and a zealous opponent of the Union; was imprisoned in the Tower of London as an ally of the Chevalier St. George; d 1708; s by his son (3) JOHN, 3rd Lord, a Representative Peer; having been appointed Gov of Barbados, was drowned in his passage out 1721; s by his son (4) JOHN, 4th Lord; dsp 1764; s by his brother (5) JAMES, 5th Lord; dsp 1777, when the title was incorrectly assumed by Capt. William Hamilton (descended from John Hamilton of Coltness, el great-uncle of 2nd Lord), who voted at the election of Scottish Peers in 1790; it was resolved by the Committee for Privileges 1793 that his vote was not valid, and the title in 1790 was determined in favour of (6-7) WILLIAM, 7th Lord, son of Robert Hamilton, of Wishaw (great-great grandson of William Hamilton, 2nd great-uncle of 2nd Lord) who was de jure 6th Lord, William d 1814; s by his (8) ROBERT MONTGOMERY, KT, 8th Lord; Lord-Lieutenant of Lanarkshire; cr Baron Hamilton, of Wishaw (peerage of United Kingdom) 1831; dsp 1868, when the barony of Hamilton became extinct, and the Lordship of Belhaven and Stenton became dormant, and remained so until 1875, when the House of Lords adjudged it to (9) JAMES, 9th Lord, (son of late Archibald Hamilton, Surgeon 92nd Regt), b 1822: m 1877, Georgina, who d 1940, da of Sir John Watson, Bt, of Earnock and Neilsland, Lanarkshire; d 1893, when the Lordship was claimed by (10) ALEXANDER CHARLES (son of late William John Hamilton, MP, a descendant of late William Hamilton (ante), through whom the 9th Lord was descended), b 1840; was served heir to his kinsman, voted at the election of Scottish Representative Peers, matriculated Arms at the Lyon Office as 10th Lord, and was elected a Representative Peer for Scotland in the House of Lords: m 1880, Georgina Katherine, who d 1932, da of late Legh Richmond; d 1920; s by his nephew (11) ROBERT EDWARD ARCHIBALD, CIE (son of late Archibald

William Hamilton, RN, yr brother of 10th Lord), 11th Lord, *b* 1871; Lieut-Col (ret) 4th Gurkhas (Indian Army); was Representative Peer for Scotland 1922-45; assumed the additional surname of Udny 1934: *m* 1st, 1898, Kathleen Gonville, who *d* 1935, da of Sir Benjamin Parnell Bromhead, CB, 4th Bt; 2ndly, 1938, Sheila de Hauteville, who *d* 1962, only da of Capt Algernon George Pearson, DSO, late Roy Berkshire Regt; *d* 1950; *s* by his son **(12)** ROBERT ALEXANDER BENJAMIN, 12th Lord; *b* 1903; Hon Lieut-Col, Roy Scots Fusiliers, an author, and an authority on S-W Arabia; was Political Officer Aden Protectorate 1934-9: *m* 1st, 1926 (*m diss* 1941), Heather Mildred Carmichael (who *d* 1992, having *m* 2ndly, 1944, Maj Basil William Seager, CMG, OBE, who *d* 1977, da of Lieut-Col Richard Carmichael Bell, DSO, OBE, late Central India Horse; 2ndly, 1942, Cyrilla Mary, who *m* 2ndly, 1969 (*m diss* 19—), Dennis Beaumont Vale, OBE, da of late Raymund Louis Binns; *d* 1961; *s* by his only son **(13)** ROBERT ANTHONY CARMICHAEL, 13th Lord and present peer.

BELLEW, BARON (Bellew) (Baron I 1848, Bt I, 1688)

All from above

JAMES BRYAN BELLEW, 7th Baron and 13th Baronet; *b* 5 Jan 1920; *s* 1981; late Lt IG: *m* 1st, 1942, Mary Elizabeth, who *d* 1978, el da of Rev Edward Eustace Hill; 2ndly, 1978, Gwendoline, da of late Charles Redmond Clayton-Daubeny, of Bridgwater, Som, and Bihar, India, and formerly wife of Maj P. Hall, and has issue by 1st *m*.

Arms – Sable, fretty or. **Crest** – An arm embowed, in armour, holding a sword proper. **Supporters** – *Dexter*, a leopard or, gorged with a mural crown azure; *sinister*, a wolf azure, gorged with a ducal coronet or. *Seat* – Barmeath Castle, Togher, Drogheda, co Louth.

SONS LIVING *(By 1st marriage)*

Hon BRYAN EDWARD, *b* 19 March 1943; *ed* Eton, and RMA Sandhurst; Maj IG (ret): *m* 1968, Rosemary Sarah, da of Maj Reginald Kilner Brasier Hitchcock, of Meers Court, Mayfield, Sussex, and has issue living, Patrick Edward, *b* 29 March 1969, — Anthony Richard Brooke, *b* 1972.
Hon Christopher James, *b* 1954; *ed* Eton, and Durham Univ (BA 1976): *m* 1984 (*m diss* 1991), Hon Rose Griselda Eden, yst da of 7th Baron Henley, and formerly wife of Stuart Ballin. *Residence* – 56 Margravine Gdns, W6.

DAUGHTER LIVING *(By 1st marriage)*

Hon Angela Mary, *b* 1944: *m* 1964, Capt Simon Hugh Walford, 17th/21st Lancers, of Summerstown House, Trim, co Meath, and has issue living, Jeanie Anne, *b* 1966: *m* 1993, Timothy Hugo Pollock (*see* B Londesborough), — Caroline Sarah, *b* 1968.

AUNT LIVING *(Raised to the rank of a Baron's daughter 1935)*

Hon Ada Kate (Jenkinstown House, Portarlington, co Offaly), *b* 1893: *m* 1st, 1917, Charles Barry Domvile, who *d* 1936; 2ndly, 1937, Lt-Col Hon Herbrand Charles Alexander, DSO, who *d* 1965 (*see* E Caledon), and has issue living (by 1st *m*), Denys Barry Herbert (Brook House, Sutton Courtenay, Oxon), *b* 1921; *ed* Eton, and Trin Coll, Oxford; Capt Life Gds, and Maj Inns of Court Regt: *m* 1958, Mary Elise, only child of Lt-Col Rowland Morrow Byers, DL, of Birchwood, Virginia Water, Surrey, and has issue living, Rowland Barry John *b* 1960, Katherine Lake *b* 1959: *m* 1986, Alexander Christie Stewart (*see* B Cochrane of Cults, colls), (Rosamund) Lucy *b* 1965: *m* 1988, W. Henry A. Forwood, of 9A Bedford Rd, SW4 7SH, son of William Forwood, of Woodstock, Newtownmountkennedy, co Wicklow.

WIDOW LIVING OF HALF-BROTHER OF SIXTH BARON *(Raised to the rank of a Baron's son 1935)*

Helen Carol, da of late Walter Clinton Louchheim, of New York: *m* 1954, as his 2nd wife, Hon Patrick Herbert Bellew, who *d* 1984. *Residence* – Litchfield, Conn, USA.

COLLATERAL BRANCHES LIVING

Issue of late Hon Sir George Rothe Bellew, KCB, KCVO, FSA, Garter Principal King of Arms 1951-61 (raised to the rank of a Baron's son 1935), half-brother of 6th Baron, *b* 1899, *d* 1993: *m* 1935, Ursula Kennard, who *d* 1994, da of late Anders Eric Knös Cull, of Warfield House, Berks:—
Richard George, *b* 1936; *ed* Eton; late 2nd Lieut Irish Guards; OStJ: *m* 1965, Shona, only da of late Col John Edward Mercer Ewart Clark Leask, MBE, IA, and formerly wife of Roderic Marshall Knowles, and has issue living, Henry Edward Courtenay, *b* 1973, — Aidan Nicholas, *b* 1980, — Serena Leonie Georgia, *b* 1969.

Issue of late Hon Patrick Herbert Bellew (raised to the rank of a Baron's son 1935), half-brother of 6th Baron, *b* 1905, *d* 1984: *m* 1st, 1936 (*m diss* 1947), Hon Catherine Moya de la Poer Beresford, who *d* 1967, da of 5th Baron Decies; 2ndly, 1954, Helen Carol (ante), da of late Walter Clinton Louchheim, of New York:—
(By 1st *m*) John Jeremy de la Poer, *b* 1937; *ed* Princeton Univ; Chase Manhattan Bank, NA 1961-87: *m* 1966, Cynthia Annette, da of Ernest J. Saunders, of Johannesburg, and has issue living, John Patrick, *b* 1966, — Catherine Moyra, *b* 1969.

(In remainder to Baronetcy only)

Sir Edward Bellew, 6th Bt, had eight brothers, Mathew, John, William, Patrick, Michael, Richard, Robert and Francis. Some of these married, and their male descendants, if any, are in remainder to the Baronetcy.

PREDECESSORS – **(1)** Sir PATRICK Bellew, son of Sir John Bellew, Knt, MP for co Louth 1639; *cr* a *Baronet* 1688; *d* 1716; *s* by his son **(2)** JOHN, 2nd Bt; *d* 1734; *s* by his son **(3)** EDWARD, 3rd Bt; *d* 1741; *s* by his el son **(4)** JOHN, 4th Bt; *d* 1750; *s* by his brother **(5)** PATRICK, 5th Bt; *d* 1795; *s* by his son **(6)** EDWARD, 6th Bt; *d* 1827; was *s* by his son **(7)** *Rt Hon* Sir PATRICK, PC, 7th Bt; *b* 1798; *cr* Baron Bellew (peerage of Ireland) 1848, was Lord-Lieut of co Louth: *m* 1829, Anna Femina, da of Don José Maria de Mendoza y Rios; *d* 1866; *s* by his son **(8)** EDWARD JOSEPH, 2nd Baron, *b* 1830: *m* 1853, Augusta Mary, who *d* 1904, da of Col George Bryan, of Jenkinstown, Kilkenny; *d* 1895, without having established his right to vote at the Elections of Irish Representative Peers; *s* by his el son **(9)** CHARLES BERTRAM, 3rd Baron, *b* 1855: *m* 1883, Mildred Mary Josephine, who *d* 1934, da of Sir Humphrey de Trafford, 2nd Bt, *d* 1911; *s* by his brother **(10)** GEORGE LEOPOLD Bryan, 4th Baron, *b* 1857; a Representative Peer for Ireland; sometime Major 10th Hussars and Yorkshire Regt (TF); Afghan War 1878-9, Nile Expedition 1884-5, S Africa 1900, European War 1914-18; assumed by R licence 1881 the surname of Bryan in lieu of his patronymic: *m* 1927, Elaine Carlisle, who *d* 1973, da of late John B. Leach, of Queenstown, S Africa, and widow of Herbert Lloyd-Dodd, of Johannesburg, Transvaal, *d* 1935: *s* by his nephew **(11)** EDWARD HENRY, MBE (son of late Hon Richard Eustace Bellew, 4th son of 2nd Baron), 5th Baron; *b* 1889: *m* 1912, Barbara Helen Mary, who *d* 1967, da of late Sir Henry Farnham Burke, KCVO, CB, Garter Principal King of Arms; *d* 1975; *s* by his brother **(12)** BRYAN BERTRAM, MC, 6th Baron, *b* 1890: *m* 1918, Jeanie Ellen Agnes, who *d* 1973, da of late James Ormsby Jameson, of Dolland, Clonsilla, co Dublin; *d* 1981; *s* by his son **(13)** JAMES BRYAN, 7th Baron and present peer.

BELLWIN, BARON (Bellow) (Life Baron 1979)

IRWIN NORMAN BELLOW, son of Abraham Bellow; *b* 7 Feb 1923; *ed* Leeds Grmr Sch, and Leeds Univ (LLB); DL W Yorks 1991; Parl Under Sec of State, Dept of the Environment 1979-83, Min of State for Local Gvt and Environmental Services since June 1983; Leeds City Council Leader 1975-79; Chm Leeds Housing Cttee 1967-72; an Alderman of Leeds City Council 1968-73; JP since 1969; Pres Moor Allerton Golf Club since 1979; *cr Baron Bellwin*, of the City of Leeds (Life Baron) 1979: *m* 1948, Doreen Barbara, da of Myer Saperia, and has issue.

Arms – Azure in chief two bellows argent garnished or and in base a rose argent barbed and seeded proper, a border or fetty azure. **Crest** – Upon a wreath an owl guardant azure beaked, legged, murally crowned and holding in the dexter claws a bell bendwise gold. **Supporters** – *Dexter*, A ram azure armed, langued and tailed or; *sinister*, a lion rampant azure armed, crined, langued and the tail tufted or, both with a collar argent, charged with triangles interlaced in pairs azure.
Residence – Woodside Lodge, Ling Lane, Scarcroft, Leeds LS14 3HX.

SON LIVING

Hon Stephen Jeremy (The Oval, 25a Bracken Park, Scarcroft, Leeds LS14 3HZ), *b* 1953; *ed* Leeds Gram Sch, and Leeds Poly: *m* 1974, Marilyn Stern, and has issue living, Adam, *b* 1989, — Milena, *b* 1986.

DAUGHTERS LIVING

Hon Frances Rochelle, *b* 1951: *m* 1971, Stephen Taylor, of Balboa, 12 Fern Chase, Scarcroft, Leeds LS14 3JL, and has issue living, Daniel Mark, *b* 1973, — Benjamin Paul, *b* 1974, — Edward David, *b* 1976.

Hon Linda Carol, *b* 1956: *m* 1st, 1976 (*m diss* 1988), Leslie Harris; 2ndly, 1990, Steven Porter, and has issue living (by 2nd *m*), Alexander, *b* 1993, — Robert, *b* 1993, — Eleanor, *b* 1992. *Residence* – 30 Ventnor Drive, Totteridge, N20 8BP.

BELMORE, EARL (Lowry-Corry) (Earl I 1797)

JOHN ARMAR LOWRY-CORRY, 8th Earl; *b* 4 Sept 1951; *s* 1960: *m* 1984, Lady Mary Jane Meade, 2nd da of 6th Earl of Clanwilliam, and has issue.

Arms – Quarterly: 1st grand quarter quarterly, 1st and 4th gules, a saltire argent, in chief a rose of the last, *Corry*: 2nd and 3rd sable, a cup argent, with a garland between two laurel branches issuing therefrom vert, *Lowry*; 2nd grand quarter gules, a saltire argent, on a bend azure, three buckles or, *Leslie*; 4th grand quarter or, a lion rampant gules, over all a bend sable, *Abernethy*. **Crest** – 1st, a cock proper; 2nd, a garland of laurel, between two branches of the same, all proper. **Supporters** – Two tiger cats, guardant proper, ducally collared and chained or.
Seat – Castle Coole, Enniskillen, co Fermanagh.

SONS LIVING

JOHN ARMAR GALBRAITH (*Viscount Corry*), *b* 2 Nov 1985.
Hon Montagu Gilford George, *b* 1989.

DAUGHTER LIVING

Lady Martha Catherine, *b* 1992.

SISTERS LIVING

Lady Anthea Geraldine, *b* 1942: *m* 1965, Patrick Mathew Desmond Forde, of Seaforde, co Down (*see* V Bangor).
Lady Sarah Lillian, *b* 1945: *m* 1979, Gary McNulty, of 4131, County Rd 103, Carbondale, Colorado 81623, USA.

AUNT LIVING (*Raised to the rank of an Earl's daughter, 1951*)

Lady Doreen Stella, *b* 1916; formerly 2nd Officer WRNS: *m* 1948, Rev John Gwinnett, MC, Chap to the Forces, who *d* 1977, and has issue living, Adrian John (28 Mayfield Av, Poole), *b* 1949: *m* 1971, Jane Elliot Allen, and has issue living, Giles Marcus *b* 1974, Verity Jane *b* 1977. *Residence* – Park Manor, Branksome, Dorset.

WIDOW LIVING OF SEVENTH EARL

GLORIA ANTHEA (c/o Army and Navy Club, Pall Mall, SW1), da of late Herbert Bryant Harker, of Melbourne, Australia: *m* 1st, 1939, the 7th Earl, who *d* 1960; 2ndly, 1963, Col Robert James Thompson Irwin, MC, R Inniskilling Fus, who *d* 1984.

COLLATERAL BRANCHES LIVING

Grandchildren of late Col Hon Henry William Lowry-Corry, 4th son of 3rd Earl:—
Issue of late Lt-Col Sir Henry Charles Lowry-Corry, MC, *b* 1887, *d* 1973: *m* 1920, Betty Alice Adeline, who *d* 1978, da of late Col Douglas James Proby (*see* D Abercorn, colls, 1976 Edn):—
Frederick Henry (Edwardstone Hall, Boxford, Suffolk), *b* 1926; *ed* Eton; Lt RN (ret); 1939-45 War: *m* 1949, Hon Rosemary Diana Lavinia Plumer, da of 2nd Viscount Plumer, and has issue living, Charles Frederick Armar, *b* 1951: *m* 1980, Elizabeth Jean, twin da of J. W. A. Andrews, of Ridge End, Highridge, Alton, Hants, and has issue living, Michael Henry Charles *b* 1983, Robert Galbraith *b* 1990, Joanna Elizabeth Louise *b* 1982, Angela Rosemary *b* 1987, — James Leopold Vincent, *b* 1955: *m* 1984, Judith, yr da of F. A. Lodge, of Overtrees, Foxhill, Leeds, Yorks, and has issue living, Charlotte *b* 1989. —— Elizabeth Margaret, *b* 1921. —— Edith (*Baroness Carver*), *b* 1923: *m* 1947, FM Baron Carver, GCB, CBE, DSO, MC (Life Baron), of Wood End House, Wickham, Hants, and has issue.

Granddaughter of late Brig-Gen Noel Armar Lowry-Corry, DSO (infra):—
Issue of late Montagu William Lowry-Corry, *b* 1907, *d* 1977: *m* 1st, 1929 (*m diss* 1938), Hon Mary Constance, who *d* 1991, da of 2nd Baron Biddulph; 2ndly, 1969, Jean Trefusis (Clover Farm, Shalden, Alton, Hants), da of late Hon Arthur Owen Crichton (*see* E Erne, colls), and widow of Lt-Col Eion James Henry Merry, MC:—
(By 1st *m*) Josephine Clare, *b* 1931: *m* 1957, HSH Prince Rupert Ludwig Ferdinand zu Löwenstein-Wertheim-Freudenberg (*see* By Pirbright, 1963 Edn), of Petersham Lodge, River Lane, Richmond, Surrey, and has issue living, *Prince* Rudolf Amadeus, *b* 1957, — *Prince* Konrad Friedrich Ferdinand Johannes Ottokar Sylvester, *b* 1958, — *Princess* Maria Theodora Marjorie, *b* 1966.

Granddaughter of late Armar Henry Lowry-Corry, son of Rt Hon Henry Thomas Lowry-Corry, MP, 1st Lord of the Admiralty, 2nd son of 2nd Earl:—
Issue of late Brig-Gen Noel Armar Lowry-Corry, DSO, *b* 1867, *d* 1935: *m* 1st, 1895, Rosalind Gertrude, who *d* 1903, da of Lt-Col Robert Hamilton Lloyd-Anstruther (Anstruther, Bt, colls); 2ndly, 1904, Hon Clare O'Brien, who *d* 1950, da of 14th Baron Inchiquin:—
(By 2nd *m*) Patricia, *b* 1905. *Residence* – 33 Wynnstay Gdns, Allen St, W8 6UT.

PREDECESSORS

– Galbraith Lowry, MP for co Tyrone; assumed in 1764 the additional surname of Corry; *d* 1769, having had with other issue (1) ARMAR, MP for co Tyrone, *cr Baron Belmore* 1781, *Viscount Belmore* 1789, and *Earl Belmore* (peerage of Ireland) 1797; *d* 1802; *s* by his son (2) SOMERSET, 2nd Earl; was Custos Rotulorum of co Tyrone; sometime MP for co Tyrone, Gov of Jamaica and a Representative Peer for Ireland; *d* 1841; *s* by his son (3) ARMAR, 3rd Earl, *b* 1801; was MP for co Fermanagh: *m* 1834, Emily Louise, who *d* 1904, da of William Shepherd, of Bradbourne, Kent; *d* 17 Dec 1845; was *s* by his son (4) SOMERSET RICHARD, GCMG, PC, MRIA, 4th Earl; *b* 1835; for fifty-six years a Representative Peer; Under-Sec of State for Home Depart 1866-7, Gov of NS Wales 1867-72, and one of the Lords Justices of Ireland during the absence of Lord-Lieut in 1885, 1890, 1891, 1895, 1896, 1897 and 1898; Lieut for co Tyrone 1892-1913: *m* 1861, Anne Elizabeth Honoria, who *d* 1919, 2nd da of late Capt John Neilson Gladstone, RN, MP; *d* 1913; *s* by his el son (5) ARMAR, 5th Earl; *b* 1870; Bar Inner Temple 1897; High Sheriff of co Fermanagh 1895, and of co Tyrone 1901; *d* 1948; *s* by his brother (6) CECIL, 6th Earl; *b* 1873,; was High Sheriff of co Tyrone 1916, and of co Fermanagh 1922, and Chm of Fermanagh Co Council 1943; *d* 1949; *s* by his cousin (7) GALBRAITH ARMAR (son of late Major Adrian Lowry-Corry, 5th son of late Adm Hon Armar Lowry-Corry, 2nd son of 3rd Earl), 7th Earl; *b* 1913; Major R Inniskilling Fusiliers, and a DL and JP for co Fermanagh: *m*

1939, Gloria Anthea, da of late Herbert Bryant Harker, of Melbourne, Australia; *d* 1960; *s* by his only son **(8)** JOHN ARMAR, 8th Earl and present peer; also Viscount Belmore, and Baron Belmore.

BELOFF, BARON (Beloff) (Life Baron 1981)

MAX BELOFF, son of late Simon Beloff; *b* 2 July 1913; *ed* St Paul's Sch, and Corpus Christi Coll, Oxford, MA, DLitt; Gladstone Prof of Govt and Public Admin, Oxford Univ 1957-74; Prin of Univ Coll, Buckingham 1974-79; Fellow of All Souls Coll, Oxford 1957-74, Emeritus Fellow since 1980; Supernumerary Fellow St Antony's Coll Oxford 1975-84; 1939-45 War Roy Signals; *cr* Knt 1980, and *Baron Beloff*, of Wolvercote, co Oxfordshire 1981: *m* 1938, Helen, da of Samuel Dobrin, and has issue.
Residence – Flat 9, 22 Lewes Crescent, Brighton BN2 1GB. *Club* – Reform.

SONS LIVING

Hon Michael Jacob, *b* 1942; *ed* Eton, and Magdalen Coll, Oxford; Bar Gray's Inn 1967; QC 1981; Recorder 1985; Bencher (Gray's Inn) 1988, Dep Judge of High Court 1989: *m* 1969, Judith Mary Arkinstall, and has issue living, Rupert, *b* 1973, — Natasha, *b* 1976. *Residence* – 38 Park Town, Oxford.
Hon Jeremy Benjamin, *b* 1943; *ed* Rugby, and Oxford Univ: *m* 1973, Carol Macdonald, and has issue living, Nicholas, *b* 1975, — Jonathan Max, *b* 1986, — Catherine, *b* 1978. *Residence* – Glenwood, Templewood Lane, Farnham Common, Bucks, SL2 3HW.

BELPER, BARON (Strutt) (Baron UK 1856)

(ALEXANDER) RONALD GEORGE STRUTT, 4th Baron, *b* 23 April 1912; *s* 1956; is Major Coldstream Gds, and patron of two livings; European War 1939-44 (wounded): *m* 1940 (*m diss* 1949), Zara Sophie Kathleen Mary, da of Sir Harry Stapleton Mainwaring, 5th Bt (ext), and has issue.

Arms – Per pale sable and azure, two chevronels engrailed, between three cross crosslets fitchée or. **Crest** – In front of rays of the sun proper, a cubit arm erect, vested, bendy of six or and sable, cuffed argent, in the hand a roll of paper proper. **Supporters** – On either side a leopard proper, gorged with a collar gemellé azure, therefrom pendant an escutcheon also azure, charged with a cross crosslet fitchée or.
Seat – Kingston Hall, Nottingham.

SON LIVING

Hon RICHARD HENRY (Slaughter Farm, Bourton-on-the-Water, Glos), *b* 24 Oct 1941; *ed* Harrow: *m* 1st, 1966 (*m diss* 19—), Jennifer Vivian, da of late Capt Peter Winser; 2ndly, 1980, Mrs Judith Mary de Jonge, da of James Twynam, of Kitemore House, Faringdon, Oxon, and has issue living (by 1st *m*), Michael Henry, *b* 1969, — Henrietta Lavinia, *b* 1970.

HALF-BROTHER LIVING

Hon Peter Algernon, MC, *b* 1924; *ed* Eton; Chm Tollemache & Cobbold Breweries Ltd, and Dir Britannia Building Soc; 1943-45 War as Lt Coldm Gds (MC); DL Suffolk 1988: *m* (Jan) 1953, Gay Margaret, da of Sir (Frank Guy) Clavering Fison, of Crepping Hall, Stutton, Suffolk, and has issue living, Henry Clavering Tollemache (Stutton Hall, Stutton, Ipswich), *b* (Dec) 1953: *m* 1979, Athena, only da of Jeremy Maas, of Suffolk House, Montpelier Row, Twickenham, and has issue living, Algy Jeremy Valentine *b* 1983, Leo Edward Orlando *b* 1988, Sam Jedediah *b* 1993, Scarlett *b* 1985, — Martin Andrew (100 Woodwarde Rd, Dulwich SE22), *b* 1958: *m* 1985, Mrs Emma Lithgow, da of late Jeremy John Holt and of Mrs Richard Cobbold, of Holbrook Lodge, nr Ipswich, Suffolk, and has issue living, Laurence *b* 1986, Luke *b* 1988, — Jane Mariota, *b* 1956: *m* 1979, Dr Murdoch Laing, and has issue living, Mungo Peter *b* 1984, Jash Murdoch (a son) *b* 1987, Tara *b* 1981, Alice Caitlin *b* 1982, — Elisabeth, *b* 1963. *Residence* – The Garden House, Stutton, Ipswich.

SISTER LIVING

Hon Lavinia Mary, LG, CBE (*Lavinia, Duchess of Norfolk*), *b* 1916; bore the Queen's Canopy at Coronation of King George VI; Lord Lieut W Sussex since 1975; CBE (Civil) 1971, LG 1990 (first non-royal woman to join the Order): *m* 1937, 16th Duke of Norfolk, who *d* 1975. *Residence* – Arundel Park, Sussex.

WIDOW LIVING OF SON OF THIRD BARON

Arielle (Catnip Corner, Bellevue Av, Newport, Rhode Island, USA), da of Joseph Washington Fraser, of Newport, Rhode Island, USA: *m* 1st, 1939, Hon Michael Strutt, P/O, RCAF, who was *ka* 1942; 2ndly, 1947 (*m diss* 1967), Eric Eweson.

WIDOW LIVING OF THIRD BARON

ANGELA MARIOTA, da of late Hon Douglas Alfred Tollemache (*see* B Tollemache colls): *m* 1st 1923, as his 2nd wife, the 3rd Baron, who *d* 1956; 2ndly, 1958, Rev (Harry) Norman Tollemache (formerly Wrigley). *Residence* – Bentley House, Ipswich.

COLLATERAL BRANCH LIVING

Issue of late Capt Hon (Desmond) Rupert Strutt, yr son (by 2nd *m*) of 3rd Baron, *b* 1926, *d* (27 Feb) 1993: *m* 1st, 1951 (*m diss* 1961), Jean Felicity, who *d* 1984, da of late Hon Francis Walter Erskine (*see* E Mar and Kellie, colls); 2ndly, 1964, Lucy Gwendolen, who *d* (16 Sept) 1993, only da of late Maj James William Stirling Home Drummond Moray, late Scots Guards (*see* D Buccleuch, colls):—
(By 1st *m*) Jeremy Bevil, *b* 1954; *ed* Eton: *m* 1979, Petrina, MP, twin da of late Peter Neville Smith, DFC, of Fir Tree Cottage, Henbury, Macclesfield, Cheshire, and has issue living, Toby Charles, *b* 1981, — Julian Rupert *b* 1983, — Rupert Peter, *b* 1987. —— Christopher Charles, *b* 1955. —— (By 2nd *m*) Dominick James, *b* 1966. —— James Edward, *b* 1969.

PREDECESSORS – (1) EDWARD Strutt, PC, FRS, LLD, son of William Strutt, of St Helen's House, Derby; *b* 1801; sat as MP (*L*) for Derby 1830-48, for Arundel 1851-2, and for Nottingham 1852-6; was Chancellor of Duchy of Lancaster 1852-4, and Lord-Lieut of Nottinghamshire 1864-80; *cr Baron Belper* (peerage of United Kingdom) 1856; *m* 1837, Amelia Harriet, da of late Right Rev William Otter, DD, Lord Bishop of Chichester; *d* 30 June 1880, and was *s* by his son (2) HENRY, PC, 2nd Baron; *b* 1840; MP for Derbyshire East (*L*), 1868-74, and for Berwick-on-Tweed in 1880; was Capt of HM's Corps of Gentlemen-at-Arms 1895-1906; *m* 1874, Lady Margaret Coke, who *d* 1922, da of 2nd Earl of Leicester; *d* 1914; *s* by his only son (3) ALGERNON HENRY, 3rd Baron; *b* 1883; Capt Household Cav and Major Reserve of Officers; *m* 1st, 1911 (*m diss* 1922), Hon Dame Eva Isabel Marian Bruce, DBE, JP, who *d* 1987, da of 2nd Baron Aberdare; 2ndly, 1923, Angela Mariota, who *m* 2ndly, 1958, Rev (Harry) Norman Tollemache (formerly Wrigley), da of late Hon Douglas Alfred Tollemache (*see* B Tollemache); *d* 1956; *s* by his el son (4) (ALEXANDER) RONALD GEORGE, 4th Baron and present peer.

BELSTEAD, BARON (Ganzoni) (Baron UK 1938, Bt UK 1929)

JOHN JULIAN GANZONI, PC, 2nd Baron and 2nd Baronet; *b* 30 Sept 1932; *s* 1958; *ed* Eton, and Ch Ch, Oxford; a JP of Ipswich, Lord Lieut Suffolk since 1994; a Parl Under-Sec of State, Depart of Education and Science 1970-73, and Parl Under Sec of State for N Ireland 1973-74; Chm of Governing Bodies Assocn since 1974; Under Sec of State, Home Office, 1979-82; Min of State, Foreign Office 1982-83, Min of Agriculture, Fisheries & Food 1983-87, Min of State, Dept of Environment, 1987-88; Deputy Leader House of Lords 1984-88, Leader of House of Lords and Privy Seal 1988-90, Min of State for N Ireland and Paymaster Gen 1990-92, since when Chm Parole Board; *cr* PC 1981.

Arms – Per fesse azure and argent a gentian plant, flowered and eradicated proper, between in chief a mullet and an increscent both or. **Crest** – A demi-lion or supporting a gentian plant as in the arms. **Supporters** – On either side a seahorse proper, gorged with a collar pendent therefrom a portcullis chained or.
Clubs – All England Lawn Tennis, MCC.

Fidelity overcomes

SISTER LIVING

Hon Mary Jill, *b* 1931; a DL Suffolk 1988; Memb Gen Synod of Church of England since 1970, a Church Commr 1978-93. *Residence* – Rivendell, Spring Meadow, Playford, nr Ipswich, Suffolk.

PREDECESSOR – (1) (FRANCIS) JOHN CHILDS Ganzoni, only son of late Julius Charles Ganzoni, of Prince's Gardens, SW7; *b* 1882; was Parliamentary Private Sec to Postmaster Gen 1924-9, temporary Chm of Committees, House of Commons 1932-34, and Chm of Private Bills Committee, House of Lords 1940-58; sat as MP for Ipswich (*C*) 1914-23, and 1924-37; *cr* a *Baronet* (UK, of Ipswich) 1929, and *Baron Belstead*, of Ipswich, Suffolk (peerage of UK) 1938: *m* 1930, Gwendolen Gertrude, who *d* 1962, el da of late Arthur Turner, of Ipswich; *d* 1958; *s* by his only son (2) JOHN JULIAN, 2nd Baron and present peer.

BENSON, BARON (Benson) (Life Baron 1981)

HENRY ALEXANDER BENSON, GBE, FCA, son of Alexander Stanley Benson; *b* 2 Aug 1909; Hon Master of the Bench, Inner Temple 1983; *ed* St. John's Coll, and Parktown High Sch, Johannesburg; Chartered Accountant; Senior Ptnr Coopers & Lybrand 1946-75; Pres of Inst of Chartered Accountants in England and Wales 1966; Adviser to Gov of Bank of England 1975-83; Chm of Royal Commn on Legal Services 1976-79, Chm of Executive Cttee of Accountants' Joint Disciplinary Scheme 1980-86; *cr* CBE (Civil) 1946, Kt 1964, GBE (Civil) 1971, and *Baron Benson*, of Drovers, co W Sussex (Life Baron) 1981: *m* 1939, Anne Virginia, da of Charles Macleod, and has issue.

Arms – Checky vert and argent on a fess gules between in chief two garbs and in base a trefoil slipped an abacus or. Crest – On a wreath argent and vert, a demi lion guardant argent murally crowned or supporting with the paws a hoop proper. Supporters – *Dexter*, a pheasant; *Sinister*, a halcyon proper.
Residence – 9 Durward House, 31 Kensington Court, W8 5BH. *Clubs* – Brook's, Royal Yacht Squadron and Jockey.

SONS LIVING

Hon Peter Macleod (22 Larpent Av, Putney, SW15), *b* 1940; *ed* Eton, and Edinburgh Univ (MA): *m* 1st, 1970 (*m diss* 1987), Hermione Jane Boulton; 2ndly, 1989, Maria de los Angeles Martin, da of Don Victoriano Martinez Latasa, and has issue living (by 1st *m*), Edward Henry, *b* 1975, — Candida Jane, *b* 1972, — Hermione Emily, *b* 1980.
Hon Michael D'Arcy (34 St. John's Av, SW15 6AN), *b* 1943: *m* 1969, Rachel Candia Woods, and has issue living, Charles D'arcy, *b* 1976, — Catherine Rachel, *b* 1971, — Harriet Anne, *b* 1974.

DAUGHTER LIVING

Hon Phyllida Anne, *b* 1943: *m* 1967, Simon John Dare, of 10 Bowerdean St, SW6.

BERKELEY, EARLDOM OF (Berkeley) (Extinct or dormant 1942)

Grandsons of late Capt Hastings George Fitzhardinge Berkeley, RN (not in remainder to Earldom as *b* before his parents' *m*), eldest son of late George Lennox Rawdon, 7th Earl of Berkeley, only surv son of Gen Sir George Henry Frederick Berkeley, KCB, eldest son of Adm Hon Sir George Cranfield Berkeley, GCB, 2nd son of 4th Earl:—
Issue of late Sir Lennox Randal Berkeley, CBE, *b* 1903, *d* 1989: *m* 1946, Elizabeth Freda (*Lady Berkeley*) (12 Hereford Mansions, Hereford Rd, W3 5BA), da of late Isaac Bernstein, of London:—
Michael Fitzhardinge (49 Blenheim Crescent, W11 2EF), *b* 1948; *ed* Westminster Cathedral Choir Sch, Oratory Sch and Royal Academy of Music; composer and broadcaster: *m* 1979, Deborah Jane, da of late Guy Coltman-Rogers, DL, of Stanage Park, Radnorshire, and has an adopted da, Jessica Rose, *b* 1986. —— Julian Lennox (Pottery Cottage, Ham Lane, Ramsdell, nr Basingstoke, Hants RG26 5SD), *b* 1950; *ed* Westminster Cathedral Choir Sch, Oratory Sch and Royal Coll of Music; partner, Berkeley Guard. —— Nicholas Eadnoth (Darby House, Burton Bradstock, Dorset), *b* 1956; *ed* Oratory Sch, and Bournemouth & Poole Coll of Art & Design; photographer and lecturer; has issue living (by Tessa Moffatt), Jack Hastings, *b* 1984, — Flora Eve, *b* 1979.

BERKELEY, BARON (Gueterbock) (Baron E 1421)

ANTHONY FITZHARDINGE GUETERBOCK, OBE, 18th Baron; *b* 20 Sept 1939; *s* 1992; *ed* Eton, and Trin Coll, Camb (MA); MICE; OBE (Civil) 1989: *m* 1965, Diana Christine (Dido), eldest da of Eric William John Townsend, MRCS, LRCP, and has issue.

Arms – Not exemplified at time of going to press.
Address – House of Lords, SW1.

SONS LIVING

Hon THOMAS FITZHARDINGE, *b* 5 Jan 1969; *ed* St Paul's.
Hon Robert William, *b* 1970; *ed* St Paul's, and Univ of Kent at Canterbury.

DAUGHTER LIVING

Hon Philippa Louise, *b* 1975; *ed* Godolphin & Latymer.

COLLATERAL BRANCHES LIVING

Grandsons of late Gen Sir (Frederick) Ivor Maxse, KCB, CVO, DSO, elder son of Adm Frederick Augustus Maxse, yr son of Lady Caroline FitzHardinge Berkeley (who *m* 1829, James Maxse), 2nd da of 5th Earl of Berkeley:—
Issue of late Maj John Herbert Maxse, Coldm Guards, *b* 1901, *d* 1978: *m* 1931, Dorinda Mary, who *d* 1988, da of William Hobart Houghton Thorne, a Judge of Mixed Courts of First Instance, Egypt:—
Anthony John MAXSE (Homestead Farm, Selborne, Alton, Hants), *b* 1932; *ed* Eton; late Capt Coldm Guards; ADC to Gov of Cyprus 1959-60: *m* 1961, Susan Jane, da of late Frederick James Emson, MC, and has issue living, John James Ivor, *b* 1968; *ed* Eton, — Georgina Anne, *b* 1962: *m* 1989, Hugh S. K. Knowles, of Paris, 2nd son of Keith Knowles, of Kensington, W8, and has issue living, Alicia *b* 1991, Claudia Rose *b* 1993, — Sarah Charlotte, *b* 1964: *m* 1990, George J. C. Bingham, of Hipley Farm, Hambledon, Hants, only son of late Cmdr George Edward Bingham, of Grenville House, Droxford, Hants, and has issue living, George *b* 1992. —— Martin William Frederick, LVO (Great Fisherton, Bishops Tawton, Barnstaple, N Devon; Boodle's, Pratt's), *b* 1935; *ed* Eton; late Col Coldm Guards; LVO 1977: *m* 1959, Penelope Ann, da of Maj Charles Chichester (*see* Fowke, Bt), and has issue living, Charles John Chichester, *b* 1962; *ed* Harrow, — Edward William, *b* 1969; *ed* Bradfield, — Clare Caroline, *b* 1960: *m* 1987, Capt Michael Patrick Campbell-Lamerton, SG, 2nd son of Col Michael John Campbell-Lamerton, of Shipston-on-Stour, Warwicks, and has issue living, Rory Patrick Chichester *b* 1989, William Michael John *b* 1991. —— Christopher James Ivor (King's Paddock, Meonstoke, Southampton; *Club* – Boodle's), *b* 1942; *ed* Eton, and Open Univ (BA).

Grandchildren of late Ella Henrietta Maxse (who *d* 1916, having *m* 1862, as his 2nd wife, Lt-Gen Hon Edward Thomas Gage, CB, who *d* 1889), da of Lady Caroline Fitz Hardinge Berkeley (who *m* 1829, James Maxse), 2nd da of 5th Earl of Berkeley:—
See V Gage, colls.

Grandchildren of late Mrs Winifred Laura Capel Fookes (*infra*):—
Issue of late Sydney Faber Fookes, *b* 1906, *d* 1983: *m* 1939, Lorna Kathleen Joblin:—
Timothy Faber FOOKES (48 Messines Rd, Karori, Wellington, NZ), *b* 1940; Bar and Solicitor: *m* 1972, Sandra Jane Field, and has issue living, Kate Faber, *b* 1974, — Jane Faber, *b* 1977. —— Sally Faber, *b* 1941: *m* 1965, Barrie Miles Owen, of 62 Matua Rd, Matua, Tauranga, NZ, and has issue living, Simon John, *b* 1972, — Angela Jane, *b* 1967, — Philippa Ann, *b* 1969.
Issue of late Kenneth Faber Fookes, *b* 1907, *d* 1984: *m* 1936, Constance Joyce Christian Boden:—
†Patrick Faber FOOKES, *b* 1937: *m* 1961, Anna Maree Tracy, and *d* 1982, leaving issue, John Faber *b* 1962, — Paul Faber, *b* 1966, — Stephen Faber, *b* 1967, — Joanna Tracy, *b* 1970. —— Alister Faber (4A Dunholme Rd, Remuera, Auckland, NZ), *b* 1941. —— Russell Faber, *b* 1947: *m* 1971, Margaret Edith Wilson, of 61 Dyers Pass Rd, Christchurch, NZ, and has issue living, Craig, *b* 1976, — Kerry, *b* 1975, — Megan Joy, *b* 1978. —— Jennifer Faber, *b* 1942: *m* 1964, David Aiken Olson, of 71 Rangitane St, Palmerston North, NZ, and has issue living, Carl David, *b* 1966, — Dean William, *b* 1969.

Granddaughter of late Capt Sydney Augustus Berkeley Capel, son of Lady Emily Elizabeth FitzHardinge Capel, 3rd da of 5th Earl of Berkeley:—
Issue of late Winifred Laura, *b* 1875, *d* 1927: *m* 1905, Dr Ernest Faber Fookes, who *d* 1948:—
Ernestine Emily Faber, *b* 1912: *m* 1940, Stuart Alexander Black, and has issue living, Anna Catherine, *b* 1946: *m* 19—, Orr. *Residence* – 31 Beach St, Fitzroy, New Plymouth, NZ.

Grandchildren of late Maude Harold Capel Nolan, yr da of late Capt Sydney Augustus Berkeley Capel (ante):—
Issue of late David Nolan, *b* 1912, *d* 1975: *m* 1940, Elsa Isabel Mooney:—
Robert Leslie NOLAN (11 Fairearth St, The Gap, Brisbane, Queensland 4061, Australian), *b* 1941: *m* 1967, Maureen Anne Heffernan, and has issue living Brent Robert, *b* 1972, — Kim Kathleen, *b* 1974. —— Susanne Margaret, *b* 1944: *m* 1970, David Thomas Thorp, of Mountain Rd, RD3, New Plymouth, NZ. —— Elizabeth Mary, *b* 1945: *m* 1969, Charles Miles Brown, of 13 Konini St, Riccarton, Christchurch, NZ. —— Catherine Ruth, *b* 1947: *m* 1971, Ian James Robinson, of York Rd, RD3, New Plymouth, NZ.
Issue of late Nina Leslie Nolan, *b* 1908, *d* 1992: *m* 1935, John Dixon Law, of 14 Takomaru St, New Plymouth, NZ:—
†Barry LAW, *b* 1936: *m* 1961, Faith Georgina Gordon Glassford, and *d* 1980, leaving issue, Michael Barry (129 Fisher Parade, Pakuranga, Auckland, NZ), *b* 1963, — Stephanie Jane, *b* 1968. —— John Berkeley (8 Cracroft St, New Plymouth, NZ), *b* 1941: *m* 1970, Janet Elizabeth Slater, and has issue living, Richard Berkeley, *b* 1973, — Catherine Muriel, *b* 1975. —— Janet Capel (450 Carrington, New Plymouth, NZ), *b* 1947: *m* 1969, Bryan Alexander Cleland, and has issue living, Scott Law, *b* 1971, — Sarah Law, *b* 1971, — Sarah Jane Capel, *b* 1974.

Descendants of late Hon Thomas Berkeley, 4th son of James, 1st Baron Berkeley:—

Grandchildren of Robert Valentine Berkeley (*infra*):—
Issue of late Capt Robert George Wilmot Berkeley, *b* 1898, *d* 1969: *m* 1927, Hon Myrtle Emmeline Theresa Dormer, who *d* 1982, da of 14th Baron Dormer:—
Robert John Grantley BERKELEY, TD (Berkeley Castle, Glos; Spetchley Park, Worcs), *b* 1931; *ed* Oratory Sch, and Magdalen Coll, Oxford; late Maj Queen's Own Warwicks and Worcs Yeo; late Lt 10th R Hus; JP Glos; and DL Hereford, Worcester and Glos, High Sheriff Worcs 1967, and Glos 1982; Joint Master Berkeley Foxhounds 1960-84: *m* 1967, Georgina Bridget, el da of late Maj Andrew Charles Stirling Home Drummond Moray, of Easter Ross, Comrie, Perthshire, and has issue living, Robert Charles, *b* 1968; *ed* Ampleforth, — Henry John Mowbray, *b* 1969; *ed* Ampleforth, and RMA Sandhurst; commn'd Queen's Own Hussars 1992. —— Rosalind Magdalen Ellen, *b* 1928; is a nun. —— Juliet Elizabeth Mary, *b* 1930.

Granddaughter of late Robert Berkeley (*b* 1823), el son of late Robert Berkeley (*b* 1794), 10th in descent from late Hon Thomas Berkeley (ante):—
Issue of late Robert Valentine Berkeley, *b* 1853, *d* 1940: *m* 1891, Rose, who *d* 1922, da of late Frederick Willmott, of Warley Place, Great Warley, Essex:—
Margaret Elizabeth, *b* 1902; is a nun. *Residences* – Spetchley Park, Worcs; Berkeley Castle, Glos.

Grandchildren of late Lt-Col Christopher Robert Berkeley, CMG, DSO, OBE, late Welch Regt, 2nd son of late Maj Henry William Berkeley, 3rd son of Robert Berkeley (*b* 1794) (ante):—
Issue of late Lt-Col Maurice Berkeley, RA, *b* 1921, *d* 1993: *m* 1950, Sylvia Mary Close (21 Chancellor House, Mount Ephraim, Tunbridge Wells, Kent TN4 8BT), da of late M. B. Tennant Maudsley:—
Hugh Christopher, *b* 1952; *ed* Stonyhurst. —— John Henry, *b* 1956; *ed* Worth, and LCP (BA): *m* 1980, Nina Elaine, yr da of A. R. S. Pritchard-Davies, of Tudor Cottage, Burford, Oxon, and has issue living, Luke Dominic, *b* 1981, — Milo Thomas, *b* 1983, — Benn Alexander, *b* 1986. —— Michael Frederick (14 Prebend Gnds, W4 1TW), *b* 1958; *ed* Worth, Magdalene Coll, Camb (MA), and SDA Bocconi, Milan (MBA): *m* 1989, Caroline Jane, elder da of Sydney Riddell, of 31 Belmont Gdns, Edinburgh, and has issue living, Oscar Frederick Robert, *b* 1991, — Thomas Bertram Maurizio, *b* 1993.
Issue of late Capt Edward Henry Berkeley, *b* 1923, *d* 1962: *m* 1951, Joyce Louise (who *m* 2ndly, 1965, Charles Michael Philips, of 63 Larkhall Rise, SW4), da of late D. C. Duncan, of Valparaiso, Chile:—
†Mowbray Thomas, *b* 1952; *ed* Stonyhurst; *d* 1970. —— Grantley William Andrew, *b* 1954; *ed* Stonyhurst, and Southampton Univ (LLB): *m* 1985, Sally Ann Stenson, da of late C. A. S. Webb, of Sutton Coldfield, Warwicks, and has issue living,

Edward Charles Mowbray, *b* 1986, — Alice Mary, *b* 1989, — Sophie Louise, *b* 1991. —— Wulstan Hubert, *b* 1956; *ed* Stonyhurst, and Worcester Coll, Oxford. —— Thurstan Timothy Edward (26 Ashland Av, Toronto, Ontario, Canada M4L 1KI), *b* 1961; *ed* Stonyhurst, and Hatfield Coll, Durham: *m* 1992, Karen Ann Theresa, eldest da of Norman Goodale, of Beaconsfield, Quebec, Canada. —— Fiona Maria Louise, *b* (twin) 1956; *ed* St Mary's, Ascot, and Bristol Univ: *m* 1990, Laurent Fauquex, of Geneva, Switzerland, and has issue living, Zoe, *b* 1990.

     Issue of late Capt Basil Robert Berkeley, IG, *b* 1925, *d* 1994: *m* 1953, Gillian Rosamond Wellesley (Highmoor House, Mayfield, E Sussex TN20 6PW), yst da of late Dr R. H. Spencer, of Alcester:—

Giles Robert (35 Grandison Rd, SW11 6LS), *b* 1959; *ed* Downside, and Durham Univ: *m* 1990, Alexandra Louise, yst da of Anthony Love, of Beggars Bush, Wadhurst, Sussex, and has issue living, Benedict Robert, *b* 1992, — Anthony Basil, *b* 1994. —— Roger Maurice (Hoggeshaws, Milstead, Sittingbourne, Kent ME9 0SA), *b* 1961; *ed* Downside: *m* 1986, Victoria, only da of John Russell Selmon, of Hemingfold Grange, Battle, E Sussex, and of Mrs William D. Hargraves, of Brickwall Bredgar, Sittingbourne, Kent, and has issue living, Rupert Charles, *b* 1988, — Robert Francis, *b* 1989.

PREDECESSORS – (1) Thomas de Berkeley, 6th Feudal Lord, was summoned to Parliament as a Baron 1295-1321: *d* 1321; *s* by his son (2) Maurice, summoned to Parliament of England as *Lord Berkeley*; having joined Thomas Plantagenet, Earl of Lancaster, he was imprisoned in Wallingford Castle, where he *d* 1326; *s* by his son (3) Thomas, summoned to Parliament 1329-60: was sometime Custodian of Edward II, and after the murder of that King was arraigned as a participator in the deed and honourably acquitted; *d* 1361; *s* by his son (4) Maurice, summoned to Parliament 1342; was wounded at Poitiers; *s* by his son (5) Thomas, *d* 1417; *s* by his nephew (6) James, summoned to Parliament by writ as *Baron Berkeley* 1421-61, *d* 1463; *s* by his el son (7) William, 2nd Baron; *cr Viscount Berkeley* 1481, *Earl of Nottingham* 1483, and *Marquess of Berkeley* (peerage of England) 1489; the castle, lands, and lordships composing the Barony of Berkeley he settled upon Henry VII and his heirs male, failing which to descend to his own rightful heirs, a circumstance that had its origin in his next brother having married the da of a Bristol Alderman; *d* 1491, when his own honours became extinct and his brother (8) Maurice *de jure* 3rd Baron was in consequence of the settlement referred to, deprived of the Barony; *d* 1506; *s* by his son (9) Sir Maurice *de jure* 4th Baron; *d* 1526; *s* by his brother (10) Sir Thomas *de jure* 5th Baron; *d* 1533; *s* by his son (11) Thomas, 6th Baron: summoned to Parliament 1534; *d* 1534; *s* by his son (12) Henry, 7th Baron, to whom the Barony and lands of Berkeley descended on the death of Edward VI, the last heir male of Henry VII; *d* 1613; *s* by his grandson (13) Sir George, 8th Baron; *d* 1658; *s* by his son (14) George, 9th Baron; *cr Viscount Dursley* and *Earl of Berkeley* (peerage of England) 1679; *d* 1698; *s* by his son (15) Charles, 2nd Earl, who in 1698 had been summoned to Parliament as Baron Berkeley; *d* 1710; *s* by his son (16) James, 3rd Earl, a distinguished naval officer, who in 1704 had been summoned to Parliament as Lord Dursley; *d* 1736; *s* by his son (17) Augustus, KT, 4th Earl; a distinguished military officer; *s* by his son (18) Frederick Augustus, 5th Earl; Lord Lieut of Gloucester: *m* 1796, Miss Mary Cole, who *d* 1844 (a previous *m* to the same lady in 1785 was unsuccessfully attempted to be proved in the House of Lords 1811); *d* 1810; *s* by his el son born after the marriage in 1796 (19) Thomas Moreton FitzHardinge, 6th Earl *de jure*; *d* 27 Aug 1882, *unm*, without having assumed the title or taken his seat in the House of Lords; at his decease the Earldom devolved upon his kinsman, George Lennox Rawdon Berkeley (upon the death of whose son, the Earldom became *ext* or dormant), and the Barony upon his niece (20) Louisa Mary Milman (only da of late Hon Craven Fitzhardinge Berkeley, 3rd son of 5th Earl of Berkeley), to whom the title was confirmed by Roy Warrant 1893; *b* 1840: *m* 1872, Maj-Gen Gustavus Hamilton Lockwood Milman, RA, who *d* 1915; *d* 1899; *s* by her da (21) Eva Mary Fitz-Hardinge, *b* 1875: *m* 1903, Col Frank Wigram Foley, CBE, DSO; R Berks Regt, who *d* 1949; *d* 1964, when the Barony fell into abeyance between her two daughters, Hon Mary Lalle Foley Berkeley and the Hon Mrs Cynthia Ella Gueterbock, and so continued until 1967, when the abeyance was terminated in favour of the elder (22) Mary Lalle Foley Berkeley; *b* 1905, assumed by deed poll 1951 the additional surname of Berkeley; *dunm* 1992; *s* by her nephew (23) Anthony FitzHardinge Gueterbock (son of late Hon Mrs Cynthia Ella Gueterbock, yr da of Eva Mary Fitz-Hardinge, Baroness Berkeley), 18th Baron and present peer.

Berkshire, Earl of; see Earl of Suffolk and Berkshire.

BERNERS, BARONY OF (Williams) (Baron E 1455) (Abeyant 1992)

Vera Ruby Williams, Baroness Berners, *d* 1992, when the Barony fell into abeyance between her two daughters.

DAUGHTERS LIVING OF VERA RUBY WILLIAMS, BARONESS BERNERS (15th holder of Barony) (*Co-heiresses to the Barony*)

Hon Pamela Vivien, *b* 30 Sept 1929: *m* 1952, Michael Joseph Sperry Kirkham, and has issue living, Rupert William Tyrwhitt, *b* 1953: *m* 1994, Lisa Carol (Judy), da of Col Edward Gibson Lipsey, USAF (ret), of Phoenix, Arizona, USA, and has issue living, Edward Michael Tyrwhitt *b* 1994, — Robin Raymond Tyrwhitt, *b* 1958: *m* 1992, Jennifer Anne, da of Eric Gaynor Eller, of Johannesburg, S Africa, — Caroline Rosemary Tyrwhitt, *b* 1956: *m* 1981, Robert Francis Gordon, of Aston End House, Coal Aston, Sheffield, and has issue living, John Francis *b* 1986, Sally Grace Tyrwhitt *b* 1984. *Residence* – Ashwellthorpe, Charlton Lane, Cheltenham, Glos.

Hon Rosemary Tyrwhitt, *b* 20 July 1931: *m* 1959, Kelvin Alexander Pollock, and has issue living, Simon Kelvin Tyrwhitt, *b* 1962, — Alastair Michael Tannahill, *b* 1964. *Residence* – Malt House, Hollingbourne, Kent.

COLLATERAL BRANCHES LIVING

     Grandchildren of late Hon Sibyl Grace Tyrwhitt (*m* 1895, James Volant Wheeler), da of Emma Harriet, Baroness Berners:—

     Issue of late W/Cdr Vashon James Wheeler, MC, DFC, *b* 1898, *ka* 1944: *m* 1930, Josephine Hermione, who *d* 1977, da of Maj John Charles Spencer-Phillips, DSO, of Ridley House, Kingswear, Devon:—

John Vashon Tyrwhitt Wheeler, *b* 1931; *ed* Eton, and Trin Coll, Camb (BA 1953, MA 1960): *m* 1st, 1957, Geraldine Noel, yr da of W. Noel Jones, of Little Gables, Glasllwch Lane, Newport, Gwent; 2ndly, 1978, Mrs Caroline Susan Chance, da of Patrick Edward Michael Holmes, of 47 Pittville Lawn, Cheltenham, and has issue living (by 1st *m*), James Vashon, *b* 1960, — Nicholas Charles Tyrwhitt, *b* 1965, — Justin Alexander Noel, *b* 1970, — Susan Verity, *b* 1958. *Residence* – Bitterley Court, Ludlow, Shropshire. —— Peter James, *b* 1933: *m* 1960, Eileen Mary, only da of A. E. Larcombe, of Brierley, Livesey Rd,

Ludlow, and has issue living, Gavin Vashon *b* 1972, — Karen Wanda Grace *b* 1970, — Amanda Hermione (twin), *b* 1972.
Residence – Llwyngoras, Velindre, nr Crymych, Pembs.
    Issue of late Lt-Cdr Hugh Volant Wheeler, DSC, RN, *b* 1901, *d* 1990: *m* 1st, 1938, Pauline Johnstone; 2ndly, 1947, Diana Joan (Little Calgary, 211 1st St, Voëlklip, CP 7203, S Africa), da of Maj Albert Herbert MacIlwaine, DSO, MC, of Larkhill, Marandellas, S Zimbabwe:—
(By 2nd *m*) David Hugh WHEELER (Calgary, PO Box 27, Harare, Zimbabwe), *b* 1949: *m* 1981, Tessa Mary Hunter, da of Prof Richard Hunter Chirstie, of Mapes Close, Mt Pleasant, Harare, and has issue living, Rory Vashon, *b* 1985, — Timothy Tyr-whitt, *b* 1986.
    Issue of late Col Gilbert Tyrwhitt Wheeler, DSO, *b* 1902, *d* 1984: *m* 1st, 1932, Beryl Audrey, who *d* 1974, da of H. J. Landon, of New England Hill, W Cobham; 2ndly, 1975, Kathleen, who *d* 1987, da of Herbert Sessions, of Quedgeley Court, Gloucester:—
(By 1st *m*) Audrey Julia, *b* 1933: *m* 1960, Capt William G. McC. Burn, RN, of 4 Clarence Crescent, Windsor, Berks, and has issue living, Peter William, *b* 1960: *m* 1993, Sandra Georgina Parker, — Hugh Tyrwhitt, *b* 1965, — Jenifer Julia, *b* 1962: *m* 1993, Clive Murray Norris. ——Jacqueline Mary, *b* 1935: *m* 1960, Don H. Olson, of 30 Forest St, Lexington, Mass, USA, and has issue living, Sven Tyrwhitt, *b* 1967, — Sonja Landon, *b* 1964.
    Issue of late A/Cdre Allen Henry Wheeler, CBE, RAF, *b* 1903, *d* 1984: *m* 1st, 1934, Ruth Margaret, da of George Ballard, of The Lowe, Stockton, Worcester; 2ndly, 1949, Barbara Agnes (Whistley Bridge Field, Twyford, Berks), da of Basil Alfred Slade, of Whistley Bridge House, Twyford, Berks:—
(By 1st *m*) Ardyn Margaret, *b* 1937: *m* 1972, Eric Griffin, who *d* 1980, of Conifer Cottage, Pipers End, Longdon, Tewkes-bury, Glos GL20 6AP, and has issue living, Robert, *b* 1974. —Meris Ann, *b* 1939.
    Issue of late Dorothy Sibyl Wheeler, *b* 1897, *d* 1977: *m* 1929, E. Brande Don:—
Volant Geoffrey Vincent DON, *b* 1930. *Residence* – No 1, Blake, 4 Avenue Rd, Wimborne, Dorset BH21 1BT.

        Grandchildren of late Oriana Mary Bracebridge Wilson (*m* 1894, Lt-Col Albert Finchett Garrard, VD, Australian Forces), da of late John Bracebridge Wilson, el son of Rev Edward Wilson, el son of Rev George Wilson, brother of 9th and 10th Barons:—
    Issue of late Edith Mary Bracebridge Garrard, *b* 1895, *d* 1992: *m* 1926, Harold Bruce Adair, Lieut Australian Army Med Corps, who *d* 1986:—
John Bracebridge Garrard ADAIR (21 Collins St, Werribee, Vic 3030, Australia), *b* 1933: *m* 1954, Joy Isabel Balcombe, and has issue living, Robyn Maree, *b* 1957: *m* 1978, Graeme Stephen Ball, and has issue living, Stephen John *b* 1981, David Graeme *b* 1985, Katherine Maree *b* 1983, — Tracey Anne, *b* 1960: *m* 1982, Rolando Carmine Milone, and has issue living, Daniel Robert *b* 1985, Kayla Rose *b* 1988, — Kerri Frances, *b* (twin) 1960: *m* 1982, Michael Clifford Newman, and has issue living, Maddison Adair *b* 1993, — Helen Therese, *b* 1965. ——Helen Becher Bracebridge, *b* 1930.

        Grandchildren of late Frederick Wilson, 10th son of Rev George Wilson (ante):—
    Issue of late Henry Fletcher Wilson, *b* 1852, *d* 1929: *m* 1890, Eugenie, who *d* 1959, da of Stephen Jauchler, of New Orleans, La, USA:—
Knyvet McDonald WILSON (241 Celeste Av, River Ridge, La, USA 70123), *b* 1909: *m* 1937, Ethel, da of James W. McKnight, of St. Louis, Mo, USA, and has issue living, Knyvet Robert (1810, Taylor St, Kenner, La, USA), *b* 1942: *m* 1967, Alice Ann, da of John Alexander Neely, of Anderson, SC, USA, and has issue living, Michael Patrick *b* 1969, Christine Suzanne *b* 1970, — Barbara Ethel, *b* 1938: *m* 1965, Robert Wayne Raley, of 804 Downing St, Richardson, Texas, and has issue living, Kevin Wayne *b* 1967, Craig Wade *b* 1968, Kathleen Elaine *b* 1971. ——Maude Alice, *b* 1899: *m* 1929, Hugh Francis Hart, of 2809 Law St, New Orleans, La, USA 70117, and has issue living, Gerard Hugh (610 Fos St, Harvey, La, USA), *b* 1930: *m* 1951, Lela, da of Wallace Chaisson, of Harvey, La, USA, and has issue living, Gerard Maurice *b* 1953, Stephen Francis *b* 1955, David Sidney *b* 1959, Susan Louise *b* 1957, Cindy Ann *b* 1965, — Maurice Henry (4616, Dreyfous Av, Metairie, La, USA), *b* 1932: *m* 1956, Audrey, da of Leonce Gaudet, of Paincourtville, La, USA, and has issue living, Brian David *b* 1959, Keith Michael *b* 1965, Jo Ann *b* 1957.

        Grandchildren of late Maj Arthur Knyvet Wilson (*b* 1860) (infra):—
    Issue of late Maj Arthur Knyvet Wilson, MC, *b* 1895, *d* 1979: *m* 1923, Dorothy Enid, da of late Lt-Col Walter W. Stewart:—
John Knyvet WILSON (339 Camelot Court, Burlington, Ont, Canada L7L 2G2), *b* 1933: *m* 1956, Marian Culham, and has issue living, David Knyvet, *b* 1961, — Peter John, *b* 1964. ——Nancy Margaret, *b* 1928: *m* 1953, William Arnold Parker, of 867 Montgomery Drive, Ancaster, Ont, Canada, and has issue living, Jeffrey Stewart, *b* 1955: *m* 1979, Katherine Beckett, of Ancaster, Ont, and has issue living, Wilson Beckett *b* 1985, James Thomas *b* 1987, Kelly Coburn *b* 1990, — Gregory, *b* 1957: *m* 1982, Sheilagh Ann O'Brien, of Halifax, NS, and has issue living, James O'Brien *b* 1986.
    Issue of late Archdale McDonald Wilson, *b* 1899, *d* 1960: *m* 1930, Norah Elizabeth (342-Providence Manor, 275 Sydenham St, Kingston, Ont, Canada K2K 1G7), da of Dr W. T. Connell, of Kingston, Ontario:—
Walter Archdale WILSON (158 Adie St, Sudbury, Ontario P3C 2C8, Canada), *b* 1936: *m* 1963, Freda Dian, da of late Wallace Frederick Bond Roberts, of Toronto. ——William Martin Connell (82 King St East, Bolton, Ont, Canada L7E 3G2), *b* 1942; a Member of Canadian Inst of Planners: *m* 1968, Sandra May, da of Elwood C. Bobzien, of 5995 Lincoln Court, Newfane, New York, and has issue living, Mark Alexander, *b* 1975.

        Grandson of late Frederick Wilson (ante):—
    Issue of late Archdale McDonald Wilson, *b* 1860, *d* 1944: *m* 1889, Elizabeth, who *d* 1942, da of Adam Cook, of Hamilton, Ontario:—
Roland Frederick WILSON, QC, LLB, *b* 1901; a Member of the legal firm of Day, Wilson, Campbell, of Toronto: *m* 1934, Adelaide Bernice Sill, da of Dr W. T. Langrill, of Hamilton, Ont, Canada, and has issue living, Donald Langrill (284 Ingle-wood Drive, Toronto 7, Canada) *b* 1935; a Member of Roy Arch Inst of Canada, and MArch, Harvard: *m* 1960, Judie Jean Arnold, da of R. F. Chisholm, of Toronto, and has issue living, Robert Frederick *b* 1962, Wendy Jean *b* 1964, — Stephen Roland *b* 1941; BA, W Ontario Univ; LLB Osgood Law Sch, and MBA Stanford; CA, — Frances Elizabeth, *b* 1939: *m* 1969, Todd John Edgar, BA, of 187 Glengrove Av W, Toronto, and has issue living, Wilson Gordon *b* 1973, Marnie Elizabeth *b* 1978.

        Grandsons of late Archdale McDonald Wilson (*b* 1860) (ante):—
    Issue of late Marion Alice Wilson, *b* 1893, *d* 1974: *m* 1920, Lt-Col Harold Brownlee Stuart, MBE, ED, RCE, who *d* 1946:—
Ronald Samuel STUART (26, Stratheden Rd, Toronto, Ont M4N 1E4, Canada), *b* 1927; BA 1950; MBA 1951; FCIS; formerly Lt RCN (Reserve): *m* 1954, Marjorie Irene, only da of Albert Parker Willis, of Mount Royal, Quebec, and has issue living, William Hugh Knyvet, *b* 1966, and two adopted children, Ronald Ian Knyvet, *b* 1964, — Marjorie Elizabeth Knyvet, *b* 1963; BA (1986).

        Grandson of late Alice (who *m* 1871, Charles J. S. Naftel), *b* 1845, *d* 1940, da of late Frederick Wilson (ante):—
    Issue of late Frederick John Naftel, *b* 1871, *d* 1943: *m* 1900, Caroline Mabel, who *d* 195—, da of R. J. Drummond:—
Frederick Robb Knyvet NAFTEL (182 Gillard Av, Toronto, Roslen, Ontario, Canada M4J 4N8), *b* 1903: Cdr RCN (ret); *b* 1903: *m* 1933, Ruth Short, and has issue living, William, *b* 1940, — Dorothy Carolyn Drummond NAFTEL (57 Withrow Av, Toronto,

Canada M4K IC8) (resumed maiden name 1975), *b* 1936: *m* 1964 (*m diss* 1975), M. E. Higgins, and has issue living, Benjamin *b* 1966.

Grandchildren of late Knyvett Eustace Naftel (infra):—

Issue of late Charles Knyvett Naftel, *b* 1910, *d* 1969: *m* 1937, Elizabeth, da of Cuthbert Bur:—
Paul NAFTEL (4006 Hill Av, Regina Saskatchewan, Canada S4S OX5), *b* 1939; *ed* Western Univ, London, Ontario (MSc): *m* 1967, Lillian Armbruster, of Prince Albert. —— Judith, *b* 1943: *m* 1965, David Mackintosh, CAF, and has issue living, Todd, *b* 1968, — Brian, *b* 1972.
    Issue of late James Eustace Naftel, *b* 1913, *d* 1983: *m* 1938, Pearl (19 St Vincent St, Goderich, Ontario, Canada), da of Thomas Sandy:—
Sandy James NAFTEL, *b* 1939. —— Kathryn, *b* 1943: *m* 1967, James Lachlan Carson.

Grandchildren of late Alice Naftel (ante):—

Issue of late Knyvett Eustace Naftel, *b* 1881, *d* 1951: *m* 1907, Marion Grace, who *d* 1966, da of Andrew Crawford:—
Leslie Roland NAFTEL, *b* 1917; *ed* Wayne State Univ, Detroit (BSc); Fl Lt (ret) RCAF; 1939-45 War (despatches, King's Commendation): *m* 1942, Anna Kathleen, da of William A. Logan, and has issue living, Logan, *b* 1943. —— Marion Alice Grace, *b* 1908: *m* 1930, Joseph L. Kulp, who *d* 1965, and has issue living, Joan Grace, *b* 1932: *m* 1952, Earl Roth, who *d* 1984, of 9274, Big Lake Rd, Clarkston, Mich 48016, USA, and has issue living, Lawrence Knyvet *b* 1953, Earl Lee *b* 1956, Leslie Ann *b* 1958; *ed* Michigan State Univ (BSc).

Grandsons of late Horace Alling Wilson, son of late John Coombe Wilson, 12th son of Rev George Wilson (ante):—

Issue of late Arthur Alling Wilson, *b* 1881, *d* 1934: *m* 1st, 1908, Lucie Nenon, who *d* 1924, el da of R. A. Ruttan, of Port Arthur, Ontario; 2ndly, 1926, Caroline Argyll (who *m* 2ndly, 1938, Julian Parks Hartley, of 351, East Main St, Grass Valley, Calif, USA), da of John Roberts Allen, of Kentucky and New York City, USA:—
(By 1st *m*) Robert Ruttan WILSON (Durford Knoll, Upper Durford Wood, Petersfield), *b* 1913: *m* 1946, Hon Yvette Latham Baillieu, only da of 1st Baron Baillieu, and has issue living, Nenon Baillieu, *b* 1948: *m* 1979 (*m diss* 1992), (George) Martin Antony Bonham, el son of Maj Sir Anthony Lionel Thomas Bonham, 4th Bt, — Elizabeth Ruttan, *b* 1950, — Merilyn Yvette, *b* 1953, — Deborah Baillieu, *b* 1955: *m* 1981, Philip Wingate Robert Carpenter, of Greenmead, Cumbers Lane, Rogate, nr Petersfield, Hants. —— (By 2nd *m*) Clarke Knyvet (2504 Delmar Drive, Plano, Texas 75075, USA) *b* 1929: *m* 1954, Sydney Ann Richardson, of Tacoma, Wash, USA, and has issue living, Robert Carroll, *b* 1962, — Loree Ann, *b* 1957, — Caroline Allen, *b* 1959.

Granddaughters of late Brereton Knyvet Wilson, yr son of late Rev Herbert Wilson, yst son of Rev George Wilson (ante):—

Issue of late Dorothy Beatrice Knyvet Wilson, *b* 1893, *d* 1979: *m* 1917, Lt-Col Henry Marshall, Royal Lincs Regt, who *d* 1952:—
Patricia Robena Knyvet, *b* 1918: *m* 1942, Maj David Young, MC, RA (ret), of Remenham Cottage, Remenham, Henley-on-Thames, Oxon, and has issue living, Julian David Young, *b* 1946, — Anthony Charles Mayne, *b* 1948; Lieut RN, — Simon John, MC, *b* 1950; Royal Green Jackets. —— Leslie Philippa Knyvet (11 Northfield Close, Henley-on-Thames, Oxon), *b* 1926; Maj (ret) QARANC.

PREDECESSORS – **(1)** *Sir* John Bourchier, KG, 4th son of *Sir* William Bourchier, Count of Eu, was summoned to the Parliament of England as John Bourchier *de Berners* 1455-72: *m* 14—, Margery, who *d* 1475, da of Sir Richard Berners, and widow of John Ferreby; *s* by his grandson **(2)** JOHN, 2nd Baron (son of Sir Humphrey Bourchier), *b* 14—; summoned to Parliament 1495-1529: *m* 14—, Lady Katharine Howard, who *d* 1536, da of 1st Duke of Norfolk; *s* by his only surviving da **(3)** JANE, *de jure* Baroness Berners, *b* 15—; did not assume the title: *m* 15—, Edmund Knyvet, of Ashwellthorpe, who *d* 1539; *d* 1561; *s* by her grandson **(4)** *Sir* THOMAS, *de jure* 4th Baron (son of John Knyvet), *b* 1539; obtained 1616 a certificate from the Commrs for the Office of Earl Marshal of his right to the Barony, but *d* before obtaining the King's confirmation: *m* 15—, Muriel, who *d* 1616, da of Sir Thomas Parry, Treasurer of the Household; *d* 1618; *s* by his grandson **(5)** THOMAS, *de jure* 5th Baron (son of Sir Thomas Knyvet), *b* 1596: *m* 1620, Katherine, who *d* 1658, da of 3rd Baron Burgh; *d* 1658; *s* by his el son **(6)** *Sir* JOHN, KB, *de jure* 6th Baron; *b* 16—: *m* 1655, Mary, who *d* 1713, el da of Sir Thomas Bedingfield; *d* 1673; *s* by his el son **(7)** THOMAS, *de jure* 7th Baron, *b* 1656; MP for Dunwich 1685-7, and for Eye 1689-90; *d* unm 1693, when the barony fell into abeyance between his sisters, Elizabeth, wife of Thomas Glenham, and Katharine, wife of John Harris, and so continued until 1711, when on the death without issue of Capt. Thomas Glenham, only child of Elizabeth Glenham, the barony devolved on **(8)** KATHERINE, Baroness Berners; *b* 1658; her title was confirmed by resolution of House of Lords 1720: *m* 1st, 1685, John Harris, who *d* 1686: 2ndly, 1696, Richard Bokenham, who *d* 1721: *d* 1743, when the Barony again fell into abeyance between the heirs of (i) Elizabeth Knyvet (wife of Henry Wilson, of Ashwellthorpe), and (ii) Lucy Knyvet (wife of Thomas Holt, and 2ndly, of John Field), granddaughters of John Knyvet, yr brother of *de jure* 6th Baron, and remained so until 1832, when the abeyance was terminated in favour of **(9)** ROBERT Wilson, 9th Baron, grandson of Elizabeth Knyvet (ante); *b* 1761, *d* unm 1838; *s* by his brother **(10)** *Rev* HENRY, 10th Baron, *b* 1762; summoned to Parliament by writ dated April 23rd, 1838: *m* 1788, Elizabeth, who *d* 1845, da of Thomas Sumpter; *d* 1851: *s* by his son **(11)** HENRY WILLIAM, 11th Baron, *b* 1797: *m* 1st, 1823, Mary Letitia, da and co-heir of Col George Crump, of Alexton Hall; 2ndly, 1857, Hon Henrietta Charlotte Cholmondeley, who *d* 1874, da of 1st Baron Delamere; *dsp* 27 June 1871; *s* by his niece **(12)** EMMA HARRIET, Baroness Berners, da of late Rev Hon Robert Wilson, R of Ashwellthorpe, by Harriet, widow of John Sheppard, of Campsey Ash, and da and co-heir of Col George Crump (ante), *b* 1835: *m* 1853, Sir Henry Thomas Tyrwhitt, 3rd Bt, who *d* 1894; *d* 1917; *s* by her el son **(13)** *Sir* RAYMOND ROBERT TYRWHITT-WILSON, 13th Baron, *b* 1885; assumed the additional surname of Wilson and the arms of Wilson only by R licence 1892, and had *s* as 4th Bt in 1894; *d* 1918; *s* by his nephew **(14)** GERALD HUGH, 14th Baron (son of late Capt Hon Hugh Tyrwhitt, CVO, CSI, RN, 3rd son of late Emma Harriet, Baroness Berners), *b* 1883; assumed by R licence 1919 the additional surname of Wilson and the arms of Wilson quarterly with those of Tyrwhitt; *d* 1950, when the Baronetcy became ext, and he was *s* in the Barony by his kinswoman **(15)** VERA RUBY, Baroness Berners (da of late Major Hon Rupert Tyrwhitt, 5th son of Emma Harriet, Baroness Berners), present peeress.

BERNSTEIN, BARONY OF (Bernstein) (Extinct 1993)

SON LIVING OF LIFE BARON (*By 2nd marriage*)

Hon David, *b* 19—.

DAUGHTERS LIVING OF LIFE BARON (*By 2nd marriage*)

Hon Charlotte, *b* 19—.
Hon Jane, *b* 1958: *m* 1986, Jonathan R. Wells, son of Arnold Wells, of New York, USA.

Berriedale, Baron; son of Earl of Caithness.

BESSBOROUGH, EARL OF (Ponsonby) Sits as BARON PONSONBY OF SYSONBY (GB 1749)
(Earl I 1739)
(Name Pronounced "Punsonby")

For the king, the law, and the people

ARTHUR MOUNTIFORT LONGFIELD PONSONBY, 11th Earl; *b* 11 Dec 1912; *s* 1993; *ed* Harrow, and Trin Coll, Camb (BA); served in World War II as Capt Welsh Gds 1940-46: *m* 1st 1939, Patricia, who *d* 1952, da of Col Fitzhugh Lee Minnigerode, of Virginia, USA; 2ndly, 1956 (*m diss* 1963), Anne-Marie (GALITZINE), da of late Lt-Gen Sir Rudolf Carl Slatin, Pasha (Baron von Slatin), GCVO, KCMG, CB; 3rdly, 1963, Madeleine Lola Margaret, da of late Maj-Gen Laurence Douglas Grand, CB, CIE, CBE, of Delaford Manor, Iver, and has issue by 1st and 3rd *m*.

ℑrms – Gules, a chevron between three combs argent. ℭrest – Out of a ducal coronet azure, three arrows, points downwards, one in pale and two in saltire, entwined at the intersection by a snake proper. Supporters – Two lions reguardant proper.
Residence – Roche Court, Winterslow, Wilts.

SONS LIVING *(By 1st marriage)*

MYLES FITZHUGH LONGFIELD (*Viscount Duncannon*) (6 Lyall Mews, SW1 8DJ; Broadreed, Stansted Park, Rowlands Castle, Hants PO9 6DX), *b* 16 Feb 1941; *ed* Harrow, and Trin Coll, Camb (MA); FCA: *m* 1972, Alison Marjorie, 3rd da of late William Storey, OBE, of Playford Mount, Gt Bealings, Suffolk, and has issue:—

SONS LIVING—*Hon* Frederick Arthur William, *b* 9 Aug 1974; *ed* Harrow, and E Anglia Univ.

Hon Henry Shakerley, *b* 1977; *ed* Harrow.

DAUGHTER LIVING—*Hon* Chloë Patricia, *b* 1975.

(By 3rd marriage)

Hon Matthew Douglas Longfield, *b* 1965; *ed* Marlborough, and Manchester Univ (BSc): *m* 1993, Jamilie Emett, eldest da of Graham Searle, of Thurloe Place, SW7. *Residence* – 281 New King's Rd, SW6 4RD.
Hon Charles Arthur Longfield, *b* 1967; *ed* Marlborough, and Downing Coll, Camb. *Residence* – 36 St Maur Rd, SW6 4DP.

DAUGHTER LIVING *(By 1st marriage)*

Lady Sarah, *b* 1943; painter and sculptress. *Residence* – Le Manoir du Moulin de Marolles, 14100 Lisieux, Calvados, France.

DAUGHTER LIVING OF TENTH EARL

Lady Charlotte Mary Roberte Paul, *b* 1949: *m* 1974, Yanni Petsopoulos, and has issue living, Alexis Anthony Frederick Ponsonby, *b* 1975; *ed* St Paul's, — Eric Demetri, *b* 1994. *Residence* – 43 Pembridge Villas, W11.

SISTER LIVING OF TENTH EARL

Lady Moyra Blanche Madeleine, DBE, *b* 1918; State Enrolled Nurse 1946; Chm, Hospitality Cttee, Victoria League 1956-62, and Vice-Chm, Central Council Victoria League 1961-65; Dep Supt-in-Ch, St. John Ambulance Bde 1964-70 (Supt-in-Ch 1970-83), Vice Pres R Coll of Nursing 1970-85, Nat Chm Support Group Research into Ageing 1987-93 (Gov since 1988); a DGStJ; OBE (Civil) 1962, DBE (Civil) 1977: *m* 1945, as his 2nd wife, Sir Denis John Wolko Browne, KCVO, FRCS, who *d* 1967, and has issue living, Desmond John Michael, QC (5 Raymond Buildings, Gray's Inn, WC1R 5BP), *b* 1947; *ed* Eton, and New Coll, Oxford; Bar Gray's Inn 1969; QC 1990: *m* 1973, Jennifer Mary, da of Frank Wilmore, of Brierfield, Lancs, and has issue living, Natasha Clare *b* 1974, Harriet Francesca *b* 1976, — Rosemary Anne Roberte (16 Wilton St, SW1X 7AX), *b* 1950: *m* 1974, Count Franco Aleramo Lanza, of Dronero, Italy, and has issue living, Aleramo Denis *b* 1979, Riccardo Vere (twin) *b* 1979. *Residence* – 16 Wilton St, SW1 7AX.

WIDOW LIVING OF TENTH EARL

MARY (*Dowager Countess of Bessborough*), da of Charles A. Munn, of New York, and of Paris: *m* 1948, the 10th Earl, who *d* 1993. *Residences* – Stansted Park, Rowlands Castle, Hants; 4 Westminster Gdns, SW1.

COLLATERAL BRANCHES LIVING

Grandchildren of late Violet Louise Ponsonby (Mrs Edward Archer Bolton Clive), only da of late John Henry Ponsonby-Fane, of Brympton d'Evercy, Som, eldest son of late Rt Hon Sir Spencer Cecil Brabazon Ponsonby-Fane, GCB, ISO (*infra*):—
Issue of late Nicholas Brabazon CLIVE-PONSONBY-FANE, *b* 1913, *d* 1963; assumed by Royal Licence 1935 the addl surname and arms of Ponsonby-Fane: *m* 1936, Petronilla (who *d* 1984, having *m* 2ndly, 1967, Walter Maurice Flower), only da of late Graham Eardley Dunsterville, Devonshire Regt (*see* Goldney, Bt, ext, 1980 Edn):—

Charles Edward Brabazon, *b* 1941; *ed* Harrow, l'Institut de Touraine, France, and RAC Cirencester; JP Som 1978, High Sheriff 1984: *m* 1974, Judy Barbara, da of Denis Bushby, of The Lodge, Unsted Park, Godalming, Surrey, and has issue living, Edward Nicholas Brabazon, *b* 1982, — Lisa Charlotte, *b* 1976, — Clementina Rose, *b* 1978. *Residence* – Little Brympton, Yeovil, Som BA22 8TD. —— Georgiana, *b* 1937: *m* 1958, (Donald) William Formby Tulloch, and has issue living, Frederick William, *b* 1969, — (Diana) Kishanda, *b* 1960: *m* 1991, Francis Christopher Fulford, of Great Fulford, Devon, and has issue living, Francis Arthur, *b* 1992, a son *b* 1994, Matilda Louisa, *b* (twin) 1992, — Catherine Serena, *b* 1961, — Louise Hermione, *b* 1964. *Residence* – Redlands Court, Highworth, Wilts. —— Helen, *b* 1940: *m* 1962, John David Hay Mackenzie, and has issue living, Graham Alexander, *b* 1963, — Charlotte, *b* 1964: *m* 1988, Theodore Anthony Koziarz, of Long Beach, NJ, USA. *Residence* – Baldromma House, Maughold Village, I of Man. —— Isobel Victoria, *b* 1944: *m* 1976, Simon Parkes, yr son of late Sir Roderick Parkes, KCMG, OBE, and has issue living, Roderick Henry Edward Alexander, *b* 1980, — Caroline Sophia Kerenhappuch, *b* 1978. *Residence* – Traiheen, Port Lewaigue, Maughold, I of Man IM7 4AG.

　　　　Grandchildren of late Robert Charles Ponsonby, 3rd son of Rt Hon Sir Spencer Cecil Brabazon Ponsonby-Fane, GCB, ISO, 6th son of 4th Earl:—
　　Issue of late Sir George Arthur Ponsonby, KCVO, *b* 1878, *d* 1969: *m* 1st, 1906, Julia Winifred Maitland (Sheila), who *d* 1918, da of late Phineas A. R. Oldfield; 2ndly, 1921, Elisa (Lady-in-Waiting to late Queen Maud of Norway), who *d* 1977, da of late Capt Hendrick Andreas Broch, of Oslo:—
(By 1st *m*) Robert Martin Dominic (172 Rivermead Court SW6), *b* 1911; Lt-Cdr (ret); 1939-45 War (despatches): *m* 1st, 1941 (*m diss* 1962), Dorothy Edith Jane, who *d* 1994, da of late John Henry Hervey Vincent Lane (*see* B Kensington, 1957 Edn), and formerly wife of Cholmeley Ranson Cuthbert; 2ndly, 1962, Jane Frances, who *d* 1993, da of late Thomas Hood Henderson Walker, LLD, JP, of Tigh-na-Muira, Monifieth, Angus, and widow of (i) Capt William Morris, and (ii) Maj George Reginald Benson, and has had issue (by 1st *m*), Hermione, *b* 1945: *m* 1975, Charles George, Viscount Raynham, son of 7th Marquess Townshend, and *d* 1985, in a motor accident, leaving issue. —— (By 2nd *m*), Maud Elisabeth, *b* 1922: *m* 1957, Lt-Cdr William Hutton-Attenborough, RN (32 Maidenhead Rd, Stratford-upon-Avon), and has issue living, George William, *b* 1958: *m* 1988, Julie, elder da of J. B. Davidge, of The Bryn, Pontllanfraith, Gwent, — John Frederick, *b* 1960: *m* 1987, Helen Louise, da of John T. Brewer, of Rickmansworth, Herts, and has issue living, Matthew George *b* 1993, Robert William *b* (twin) 1993, Emma Eileen Maud *b* 1988, Katherine Elisabeth *b* 1991. —— Victoria, *b* 1926: *m* 1947, Capt Rupert Mahaffy, late Irish Gds, of 95 Studdridge St, SW6 3TD (*see* V Dillon, 1959 Edn), and has had issue, Dominic John, *b* 1955; *d* 1956, — Henrietta Clare Elisabeth (Pine Cottage, Ealing Green, W5 5EN), *b* 1949: *m* 1979 (*m diss* 1990), Nicholas John Usherwood, of and has issue living, Theodore Patrick John *b* 1981, Constance Hazel Kate *b* 1985, — Sarah Georgiana, *b* 1952: *m* 1977, William Hugh Baker, of The Old Rectory, Scremby, Spilsby, Lincs PE23 5RP, and has issue living, Charles Frederick Benno *b* 1988, — Kate Alexandra Mary, *b* 1959: *m* 1983, Henry Melchior Marie Gerard, Marquis de Fayet de Montjoye, of 33 rue Georges Appay, 92150 Suresnes, France, and has had issue, Alexander Jacques Rupert *b* 1986, Clementine Marie *b* 1989, Emilie *b* and *d* 1991, Daisy Camille Marie *b* 1993, — Susanna Victoria, *b* 1963.

　　　　Descendants of late Gen Rt Hon Sir Henry Frederick Ponsonby, GCB, son of Maj-Gen Hon Sir Frederick Cavendish Ponsonby, GCMG, KCB, KCH, 2nd son of 3rd Earl:—
　　Issue of late Rt Hon Sir Frederick Edward Grey Ponsonby, GCB, GCVO, who was *cr Baron Sysonby* 1935 (see that title).

　　　　Issue of late Arthur Augustus William Harry, who was *cr Baron Ponsonby of Shulbrede* 1930 (see that title).
　　　　Descendants of late Hon William Francis Spencer Ponsonby (3rd son of 3rd Earl), who was *cr Baron de Mauley* 1838 (see that title).
　　　　Grandsons of late Chambré Brabazon Ponsonby, son of late Chambre Brabazon Ponsonby-Barker, grandson of 1st Viscount:—
　　Issue of late Thomas Brabazon Ponsonby, *b* 1878, *d* 1946: *m* 1909, Frances May, who *d* 1978, da of late Maj George Paynter, of Eaton Grange, Grantham, and 21 Belgrave Sq, SW:—
Chambré Brabazon (Low Port, Linlithgow, W Lothian), *b* 1911; Lt-Col (ret) 10th Hus; Comptroller to Gov-Gen of Australia 1936-37: *m* 1st, 1941, Merelina, who *d* 1993, only da of late Lt-Col James Tindal Ives Bosanquet; 2ndly, 1954, Diana Wray Hurt, of Reigate, Surrey, and has issue living (by 1st *m*), Merelina Karen (10 Lansdowne Gdns, S Lambeth, SW8 2EG), *b* 1946: *m* 1971 (*m diss* 1977), John Dymoke White, and has issue living, Merelina Rosanne *b* 1973, Lucinda Jane *b* 1974, — (by 2nd *m*), Richard Brabazon (9 Chess Close, Parkfield, Latimer, Chesham HP5 1UU), *b* 1955; BScEng(Hons); Capt RE (ret) (despatches): *m* 1978, Diana Louise, da of A. R. Moodie, of Bonnytown House, Linlithgow, and has issue living, Tristan *b* 1984, Lorna Anne *b* 1980, Marianne Jane *b* 1982, — Miles Chambré, *b* 1957: *m* 1987, Jane Elizabeth, yr da of (Oliver) Barrie Hopton, and has issue living, Simon Chambré *b* 1990, Jason Chambré *b* 1992. —— †George Thomas, MC, *b* 1913; Maj (ret) 17th/21st Lancers; 1939-45 War in N Africa and Italy (severely wounded, MC and bar): *m* 1948, Elizabeth Penelope Melville (Kilcooley Abbey, Thurles, co Tipperary), da of Capt Walter Douglas Melville Wills, CBE, and *d* 1984, leaving issue, Thomas Charles George (31 Ladbroke Gdns, W11 2PY), *b* 1950: *m* 1980 (*m diss* and annulled 1989), Elisabeth Marie Philippine, da of Jean Jules Marie Masurel, of 15 Avenue de Verzy, Paris 17, and has issue living, Sebastian Jean *b* 1983, — Henry Brabazon (Ballynatray, Youghal, co Cork), *b* 1952: *m* 1977, Elizabeth Fiona Mary, eldest da of Peter Bedford Brotchie, and has issue living, Thomas George Peter *b* 1981, Rose *b* 1988, — Peter Douglas (Kilcooley Abbey, Thurles, co Tipperary), *b* 1955: *m* 1982, Faith Primrose Orr, only child of Rev Canon Ernest Arthur Brandon, of The Rectory, Foulksmills, co Wexford, and has issue living, Emma Rebecca Brandon *b* 1984, Sarah Georgina Brandon *b* 1986, Julia Nicola Brandon *b* 1992. —— Henry Jeffrey, *b* 1930: *m* 1960, Rosemary Jane, da of Ernest Sydney Wells, of Buxted Sussex, and has issue living, Julian Henry, *b* 1963: *m* 1993, Patricia Lynn, da of Dr Robert Ingram, of Washington, USA, — Jane Frances, *b* 1965: *m* 1994, Simon D. Marsh, only son of Hugh Marsh, of Westmill, Buntingford, Herts, — Rosanna *b* 1966. *Residence* – Grove, Fethard, co Tipperary. —— Noreen de Vere, *b* 1917: *m* 1939, Brig Henry Lawrence Savill Young, DSO, late Irish Gds (*see* Young, Bt, *cr* 1769, colls). *Residence* – End House, Pilton, Som.

PREDECESSORS – (1) WILLIAM Ponsonby, PC, MP for co Kilkenny, *temp* Anne and George I, was *cr Baron Bessborough* 1721, and *Viscount Duncannon* 1722 (peerage of Ireland); *d* 1724; *s* by his el son (2) BRABAZON, 2nd Viscount; MP for co Kildare 1704 and for Newtown 1713-15; *cr Earl of Bessborough* 1739 (peerage of Ireland), and *Baron Ponsonby of Sysonby* 1749 (peerage of Great Britain); *d* 1758; *s* by his el son (3) WILLIAM, PC, 2nd Earl, successively MP for Kilkenny, Derby, Saltash and Harwich, a Lord of the Treasury and Joint Postmaster-Gen; *d* 1793; *s* by his son (4) FREDERICK, 3rd Earl, MP for Knaresborough, and a Lord of the Admiralty; *d* 1844; *s* by his son (5) JOHN WILLIAM, 4th Earl, *b* 1781, sometime Lord-Lieut of Ireland and Ch Commr of Woods and Forests: *m* 1805, Lady Maria Fane, da of 10th Earl of Westmorland, KG; *cr Baron Duncannon* (peerage of Great Britain) 1834; *d* 1847; *s* by his el son (6) JOHN GEORGE BRABAZON, 5th Earl; was Lord Lieut of co Carlow, Master of HM's Staghounds, and Lord Steward of the Household; *d* 1880; *s* by his brother (7) FREDERICK GEORGE BRABAZON, 6th Earl, *b* 1815; *dsp* 1895; *s* by his brother (8) *Rev* WALTER WILLIAM BRABAZON, 7th Earl, *b* 1821; R of Stutton, Ipswich 1884-94: *m* 1850, Lady Louisa Susan Cornwallis Eliot, who *d* 1911, da of 3rd Earl of St. Germans, GCB; *d* 1906; *s* by his son (9) EDWARD, KP, CB, CVO, 8th Earl, *b* 1851; Sec to Speaker of House of Commons 1884-95: *m* 1875, Blanche Vere, CBE, who *d* 1919, yst da of Sir Josiah John Guest, 1st Bt; *d* 1920; *s* by his el son (10) VERE BRABAZON, GCMG, PC, 9th Earl; *b* 1880; Gov-Gen and Com-in-Ch, Dominion of Canada 1931-5; sat as MP for Cheltenham (*C*) Jan-Nov 1910, for Dover 1913-18, and for Dover Div of Kent (*CoU*) 1918-20; *cr Earl of Bessborough* (peerage of United Kingdom) 1937: *m* 1912, Roberte, JP (a DGStJ) who *d* 1979, only da of Baron de Neuflize, of Paris; *d* 1956; *s* by his el son (11) FREDERICK EDWARD NEUFLIZE, 10th Earl, *b* 1913; Capt 98th (Surrey and Sussex Yeo), ADC to GOC 1st Canadian Corps, Field Brig RA (TA Reserve), DL W Sussex, HM Foreign Ser 1944, Merchant Banker 1950-56, Dir ATV Ltd 1955-60, etc, Parl Sec for Science 1963-64, etc, Member European Parl 1972-79, Vice-Pres and Dep Leader European Conservative Group 1973-77, Pres Chichester Festival

Theatre Trust and Playwright: *m* 1948, Mary, da of Charles A. Munn, of New York, and of Paris; *d* 1993, when the UK Earldom became ext, and he was *s* in his other titles by his cousin (**12**) ARTHUR MOUNTIFORT LONGFIELD (only son of late Maj Hon Cyril Myles Brabazon Ponsonby, MVO, Gren Gds, 2nd son of 8th Earl), 11th Earl and present peer; also Viscount Duncannon, Baron Duncannon, Baron Bessborough, and Baron Ponsonby of Sysonby.

BESWICK, BARONY OF (Beswick) (Extinct 1987)

SON LIVING OF LIFE BARON

Hon Frank Jesse, *b* 1949; *ed* Latymer Upper Sch. *Residence* – 28 Skeena Hill, SW18.

DAUGHTER LIVING OF LIFE BARON

Hon Patricia Ann (202 Lakedale Road, Plumstead, SE18), *b* 1939: *m* 1962, Anthony Woodbridge Atkinson, and has issue.

BETHELL, BARON (Bethell) (Baron UK 1922, Bt UK 1911)

I will keep faith

NICHOLAS WILLIAM BETHELL, 4th Baron, and 4th Baronet; *b* 19 July 1938; *s* 1967; *ed* Harrow, and Pembroke Coll, Camb; a Lord-in-Waiting to HM 1970-71; Member of European Parl, 1975-94, (elected rep June 1979): *m* 1st, 1964 (*m diss* 1971), Cecilia Mary Lothian, who *d* 1977, el da of Prof Alexander Mackie Honeyman, of Cowan's Rigg, St. Andrews; 2ndly, 1992, Bryony Lea Morgan, da of Brian David Griffiths, of Llanrhystyd, Dyfed, and Arguignac, France, and has issue by 1st *m*.

Arms – Or, a chevron azure charged with an estoile of the first, in chief two boars' heads couped of the second. **Crest** – Upon a rock proper a boar's head couped azure. **Supporters** – *Dexter*, a wolf proper charged on the shoulder with an estoile or; *sinister* a wolf proper charged with a portcullis or. *Residence* – 73 Sussex Sq, W2.

SONS LIVING (By 1st marriage)

Hon JAMES NICHOLAS, *b* 1 Oct 1967.
Hon William Alexander, *b* 1969.

SISTER LIVING

Sally Ann, *b* 1943: *m* 1965, Anthony Francis Wigram, of 16 Porchester Terr, W1, and has issue living, Maximilian John Lionel, *b* (March) 1966, — Camilla Ann, *b* (Dec) 1966: *m* 1989, Rupert Alister Peter John Cordle (*see* V Powerscourt, colls, 1985 Edn), and has issue living, Alexander Anthony *b* 1993, — Lucy Olga (twin), *b* (Dec) 1966: *m* 1990, Benjamin V. Sangster, son of Robert Sangster, of The Nunnery, Douglas, IoM, and of Mrs Ian Strathearn Gordon, of Angeston Grange, Uley, Glos, and has issue living, Eliza Camilla *b* 1992.

DAUGHTERS LIVING OF SECOND BARON

Hon Jennifer Mary, *b* 1930: *m* 1954, Edward Peter Moncrieff Brown, and has issue living, Alistair Peter, *b* 1955: *m* 1977, Eva Jacobsen, of Norway, and has issue living, Alexander *b* 1977, Charlotte *b* 1982, — Craig Edward, *b* 1957; *ed* Eton, and Bristol Univ; writer: *m* 1987, Frances J. M., only da of Colin Welch, of Aldbourne, Wilts, and has issue living, Silas *b* 1990, Tallulah *b* 1988, — James David, *b* 1959: *m* 1990, Tracey, yr da of John Gadd, of Torrington, Devon, and has issue living, Daisy *b* 1991, — David Francis, *b* 1960. *Residence* – St Anthony's Cottage, Duncton, Petworth, W Sussex GU28 0JY.
Hon Patricia Catherine, *b* 1933: *m* 1956, Michael William Nesbitt, DFC, and has issue living, William Patrick (The Bakehouse, Turkdean, nr Cheltenham, Glos), *b* 1963: *m* 1989, Caroline L., yr da of Dr D. Charlton-Smith, of Wellesbourne, Warwicks, and has issue living, Frederick William *b* 1993, Clementine Rose *b* 1991, — Anna Catherine, *b* 1957: *m* 1985, Kerry James McDonagh, of Manor Farmhouse, Wendlebury, nr Bicester, Oxon, elder son of James McDonagh, of Runcorn, Cheshire, and has issue living, Thomas *b* 1988, Edward *b* 1989, — Caroline Mary, *b* 1959. *Residence* – Rotherwood, Fittleworth, Pulborough, Sussex, RH20 1EW.

MOTHER LIVING

Ann Margaret Frances, only da of late Lt-Col Robert George Barlow, of The Holt, Ledbury, Herefordshire: *m* 1st, 1937 (*m diss* 1946), Hon William Gladstone Bethell, who *d* 1964, 3rd son of 1st Baron; 2ndly, 1946, John Rupert Dupree (*see* Dupree, Bt, colls), who *d* 1965; 3rdly, 1965, Roger Thornycroft, DSC, who *d* 1983, son of late Sir John Edward Thornycroft, KBE; 4thly, 1984, Stuart Warren Don. *Residence* – 113 Dovehouse St, SW3.

PREDECESSORS – (**1**) JOHN HENRY BETHELL, son of late George Bethell, of South Woodford, Essex; *b* 1861: a Director of Barclays Bank Ltd; sat as MP for S or Romford Div of Essex (*L*) 1906-18, and for N Div of East Ham 1918-22; *cr* a Baronet (UK of Park House) 1911, and *Baron Bethell*, of Romford, co Essex (peerage of UK) 1922: *m* 1895, Florence, who *d* 1957, da of James Woolley Wyles; *d* 1945; *s* by his el surviving son (**2**) JOHN RAYMOND, 2nd Baron; *b* 1902: *m* 1st, 1927 (*m diss* 1948), Veronica Eileen, who *d* 1981, da of late Hon Sir James Daniel Connolly; 2ndly, 1948, Joan, who *d* 1966, da of late Brig-Gen Norman William Webber, CMG, DSO, and widow of Lt-Cdr H. N. Reid, RN; *d* 1965; *s* by his only son (**3**) GUY ANTHONY JOHN, 3rd Baron; *b* 1928; *d* 1967; *s* by his cousin (**4**) NICHOLAS WILLIAM (only son of late Hon William Gladstone Bethell, 3rd son of 1st Baron), 4th Baron, and present peer.

BICESTER, BARON (Smith) (Baron UK 1938)
(Title pronounced "Bister")

TENAX·IN·FIDE

Steadfast in the faith

ANGUS EDWARD VIVIAN SMITH, 3rd Baron; *b* 20 Feb 1932; *s* 1968; *ed* Eton.

Arms – Or, a chevron cottised sable, between three demi-griffins couped of the last, the two in chief respecting each other. **Crest** – An elephant's head erased or, charged on the neck with three fleurs de lis, one and two azure. **Supporters** – On either side a griffin sable charged on the shoulder with a horse-shoe inverted or.

BROTHER LIVING

HUGH CHARLES VIVIAN, *b* 8 Nov 1934; *ed* Eton, and Worcester Coll, Oxford; late 2nd Lt RAC.

DAUGHTER LIVING OF SECOND BARON

Hon Jane Beatrix Randal, *b* 1928: *m* 1949 (*m diss* 1991), John Richard Daniel Green, and has issue living, John James Randal (Foxboro Hall, Melton, nr Woodbridge, Suffolk, IP12 1ND) *b* 1953: *m* 1980, Hon Claerwen Gibson-Watt, el da of Baron Gibson-Watt (Life Baron), and formerly wife of Enrique Ulvert, and has issue living, Toby James Ralph *b* 1982, Richard John Sebastian *b* 1984, David Peter Julian *b* (twin) 1984, — Elizabeth Jane, *b* 1950: *m* 1982 (*m diss* 1991), Ian Mackinnon, only son of late Maj C. N. Mackinnon, of Old Garth, Bembridge, Isle of Wight, — Amanda Carol, *b* 1957: *m* 1986, Charles Thomas Bunbury, 2nd son of Sir (John) William Napier Bunbury, 12th Bt. *Residence* – Appleshaw Manor, Appleshaw, Andover, Hants, SPL 9BH.

AUNT LIVING (*Daughter of 1st Baron*)

Hon Honor Mildred Vivian, OBE, *b* 1908; *ed* at London (BSc, BS, MD), and Oxford (MA) Univs; MRCS England and LRCP London 1940; MRCP 1954, FRCP 1965; OBE (Civil) 1962. *Residence* – Croft Lodge, Yarpole, Leominster, Herefords.

WIDOW LIVING OF SON OF FIRST BARON

Mabel, Mus Bac, da of late A. W. R. Lovering: *m* 1948, as his 2nd wife, Lt-Col Hon Stephen Edward Vivian Smith, late Coldm Gds, who *d* 1952. *Residence* – 6 Ravenscar Lodge, 22 The Downs, Wimbledon, SW20 8HT.

MOTHER LIVING

Elenor Anderson (Resides in USA), da of Edward Shepherd Hewitt, of New York City: *m* 1929 (*m diss* 1947), as his 1st wife, Lt-Col Hon Stephen Edward Vivian Smith, late Coldm Gds, who *d* 1952, 2nd son of 1st Baron.

COLLATERAL BRANCH LIVING

Issue of late Maj Hon Hugh Adeane Vivian Smith, MBE, 3rd son of 1st Baron Bicester, *b* 1910, *d* 1978: *m* 1933, Lady Helen Dorothy Primrose (The Old Rectory, Souldern Bicester, Oxon OX6 9HU), da of 6th Earl of Rosebery:—
George Harry Vivian, *b* 1934: *m* 1st, 1962, June Rose Jager, da of Basil William Foster-Towne, of S Africa; 2ndly, 1966, Susan Mary, da of Frank Goodfellow, of Johannesburg, and has issue living (by 1st *m*), Charles James Vivian, *b* 1963, — (by 2nd *m*) Sarah Helen, *b* 1968, — Amanda Mary, *b* 1972. —— Elizabeth Vivian, *b* 1939: *m* 1960, (Alexander) James Macdonald-Buchanan (*see* By Woolavington, 1985 Edn), and has issue living, Hugh James, *b* 1961, — James Iain Harry, *b* 1963, — Nicholas Mark, *b* 1967, — Charles Alexander, *b* 1970. *Residence* – Strathconon, Muir of Ord, Ross-shire.

PREDECESSORS – (1) VIVIAN HUGH Smith, son of late Hugh Colin Smith; *b* 1867; Chm of Morgan Grenfell, Ltd, and an Hon Freeman of Oxfordshire; was Lord-Lieut of Oxfordshire 1934-54; *cr Baron Bicester*, of Tusmore, co Oxford (peerage of United Kingdom) 1938: *m* 1897, Lady Sybil Mary McDonnell, who *d* 1959, da of 6th Earl of Antrim; *d* 1956; *s* by his el son (2) RANDAL HUGH VIVIAN, 2nd Baron; *b* 1898; High Sheriff of Oxon 1945: *m* 1922, Hon Dorothea Gwenllian James, who *d* 1974, da of 3rd Baron Northbourne; *d* 1968; *s* by his nephew (3) ANGUS EDWARD VIVIAN (2nd son of late Lt-Col Hon Stephen Edward Vivian Smith, 2nd son of 1st Baron), 3rd Baron, and present peer.

BIDDULPH, BARON (Maitland Biddulph) (Baron UK 1903)

Let us aim at loftier things

(ANTHONY) NICHOLAS COLIN MAITLAND BIDDULPH, 5th Baron; *b* 8 April 1959; *s* 1988; *ed* Cheltenham, and RAC Cirencester; an Armourer and Freeman of City of London; assumed addl surname of Maitland 1978: *m* 1993, Hon Sian Diana Gibson-Watt, yr da of Baron Gibson-Watt, MC, PC (Life Baron), and has issue.

Arms – Quarterly, 1st and 4th vert an eagle displayed and a canton argent (*Biddulph*); 2nd and 3rd or a lion rampant gules couped at all his joints of the field within a double tressure flory counterflory azure (*Maitland*). Crest – A wolf salient argent, charged on the shoulder with a trefoil slipped gules. Supporters – On either side a wolf argent, semée of trefoils slipped gules. *Seat* – Makerstoun, Kelso, Roxburghshire.

SON LIVING

Hon ROBERT JULIAN, *b* 8 July 1994.

BROTHER LIVING

Hon William Ian Maitland Biddulph, *b* 1963; *ed* Loretto; an Armourer and Freeman of City of London; assumed addl surname of Maitland 1978. *Residence* – Fair Oak, Ashford Hill, Newbury, Berks RG15 8BJ.

SISTER LIVING

Hon Fiona Mary, *b* 1961; *ed* Courtauld Inst; co-author of *Paris: Portrait of a City* 1994; assumed addl surname of Maitland 1981: *m* 1994, Anthony Henry Joseph Fraser (*see* L Lovat, colls). *Residence* – 4 Wilmington House, Highbury Crescent, Islington, N5 1RU.

UNCLE LIVING (*son of 3rd Baron*)

Hon Edward Sidney, *b* 1934; *ed* Eton; Lt RHG (ret). *Residence* – Ribston Lawn, Much Marcle, Ledbury, Herefords, HR8 2ND. *Club* – White's

AUNTS LIVING (*daughters of 3rd Baron*)

Hon Marjorie Amy, *b* 1927: *m* 1947, Thomas Ian Michael Walker-Munro, who *d* 1965 (*see* Munro, Bt, *cr* 1825, colls).
Hon Susan Louise, *b* 1929.

WIDOW LIVING OF FOURTH BARON

Lady MARY HELENA MAITLAND (*Lady Mary Biddulph*), da of late Ivor Colin James, Viscount Maitland, son of 15th Earl of Lauderdale: *m* 1958, the 4th Baron, who *d* 1988. *Residence* – Makerstoun, Kelso, Roxburghshire TD5 7PA. *Club* – Cavalry and Guards'.

COLLATERAL BRANCH LIVING

Grandchildren of late Hon Claud William Biddulph (*infra*):—
Issue of late Maj Anthony Biddulph, TD, *b* 1910, *d* 1984: *m* 1938, Mary Dearman, who *d* 1991, da of Maj Sir John Dearman Birchall, MP:—
Simon, TD (Rodmarton Manor, Rodmarton, Cirencester), *b* 1942; *ed* Eton: *m* 1970, Christina, da of George McCorquodale (*see* B Luke, 1990 Edn), and has issue living, John Simon, *b* 1971; *ed* Eton, — (Anthony) George, *b* 1973, — Sarah Rose, *b* 1980. —— (Anthony) Jasper (Manor Farm, Tarlton, Cirencester), *b* 1946; *ed* Eton: *m* 1975, Louise Perrett, da of William Sandeman Cox, of Coff's Harbour, NSW, and has issue living, James Jasper, *b* 1977, — Emily Selena Mary, *b* 1979. —— Clarissa Mary (28 Laxford House, Cundy St, SW1W 9JU), *b* 1939: *m* 1962, James Richard Ferard, and has issue living, Richard Anthony Agace, *b* 1963: *m* 1994, Lucilla Fleur Scott, elder da of late Hon (John) Greville Napier (*see* L Napier and Ettrick, colls), — (Charles) Edward, *b* 1970, — Susan Mary, *b* 1965.

Issue of late Hon Claud William Biddulph, yr son of 1st Baron, *b* 1871, *d* 1954: *m* 1906, Margaret, who *d* 1970, da of late Alfred John Howard (*see* E Carlisle, colls, 1970 Edn):—
Marjory Mary (*Lady Findlay*), *b* 1915: *m* 1st, 1938 (*m diss* 1962), as his 2nd wife, Maj Philip Wilfred Cripps, son of Maj Sir Frederick William Beresford Cripps, DSO; 2ndly, 1964, as his 2nd wife, Lt-Col Sir Roland Lewis Findlay, 3rd Bt, who *d* 1979, and has issue living (by 1st *m*), John Philip, *b* 1940; *ed* Eton: *m* 1975, Aileen Elizabeth, da of William Alexander Hamilton, — Diana Josephine, *b* 1953: *m* 1984, Richard P. Turner, yr son of John Turner, of Lound, Retford, Notts. *Residence* – Lyddington, Uppingham, Leics.

PREDECESSORS – (1) MICHAEL Biddulph, son of late Robert Biddulph, MP, of Ledbury; *b* 1834; a partner in London banking firm of Cocks, Biddulph and Co; MP for Herefordshire (*L*) July 1865 to Nov 1885, and S, or Ross, Div of Herefordshire (LU) 1885-1900; *cr Baron Biddulph*, of Ledbury, co Hereford (peerage of United Kingdom) 1903: *m* 1st, 1864, Adelaide Georgiana, who *d* 1872, da of late Gen Rt Hon Jonathan Peel, MP; 2ndly, 1877, Lady Elizabeth Philippa, VA, who *d* 1916, widow of Henry John Adeane, MP, and da of 4th Earl of Hardwicke; *d* 1923; *s* by his el son (2) JOHN MICHAEL GORDON, 2nd Baron, *b* 1869: *m* 1896, Marjorie Caroline Susan, who *d* 1961, da of late Col William Mure; *d* 1949; *s* by his el son (3) MICHAEL WILLIAM JOHN, 3rd Baron, *b* 1898: *m* 1925, Lady Amy Louise Agar, who *d* 1983, da of 4th Earl of Normanton; *d* 1972; *s* by his el son (4) ROBERT MICHAEL CHRISTIAN, 4th Baron, *b* 1931: a Tweed Commr: *m* 1958, Lady Mary Helena Maitland, da of late Ivor Colin James Viscount Maitland, son of 15th Earl of Lauderdale; *d* 1988; *s* by his elder son (5) (ANTHONY) NICHOLAS COLIN, 5th Baron and present peer.

Bingham, Baron; title of Earl of Lucan on Roll of HL

Bingham, Lord; son of Earl of Lucan.

Binning, Lord; son of Earl of Haddington.

BIRDWOOD, BARON (Birdwood) (Baron UK 1938, Bt UK 1919)

Calm in action

MARK WILLIAM OGILVIE BIRDWOOD, 3rd Baron, and 3rd Baronet; *b* 23 Nov 1938; *s* 1962; *ed* Radley, and Trin Coll, Camb (MA 1970); late 2nd Lt RHG; Chm Martlet Ltd since 1986, Dir Scientific Generics Ltd since 1989, Meta Generics Ltd, Chm Worthington & Co since 1994; Member Glaziers' Co: *m* 1963, Judith Helen, el da of Reginald Gordon Seymour Roberts, of Newton Aycliffe, co Durham, and has issue.

Arms – Azure, five martlets, two, two and one within an inescutcheon voided a representation of the Southern Cross, all argent. **Crest** – Out of a mural crown gules, a martlet argent between two branches of laurel proper. **Supporters** – *Dexter*, a Sergeant of the XIIth (Prince of Wales's Royal) Lancers, mounted on a bay horse; *sinister*, a Sikh Daffadar of the XIth (Prince of Wales's Own) Bengal Lancers mounted on a chestnut horse both habited and accoutred proper.
Residences – 5 Holbein Mews, SW1W 8NW; Russell House, Broadway, Worcs WR12 7BU. *Club* – Brooks's.

DAUGHTER LIVING

Hon Sophie Frederika (*Countess of Woolton*), *b* 1964: *m* 1987, 3rd Earl of Woolton, and has issue.

SISTER LIVING

Hon Sonia Gina Ogilvie, *b* 1933: *m* 1956, Geoffrey Thynne Valentine Archer, and has issue living, David Birdwood, *b* 1959: *m* 1984, Gwenyth Daphne, da of Ian Highley, of Stanford Dingley, Berks, — Sarah-Jane Birdwood, *b* 1957. *Residence* – Renson Mill, Ashwater, Devon EX21 5ER.

MOTHER LIVING

(Elisabeth) Vere Drummond, CVO, da of Lt-Col Sir George Drummond Ogilvie, KCIE, CSI, Indian Political Ser; MVO (5th class) 1958, CVO 1972: *m* 1931 (*m diss* 1954), the 2nd Baron, who *d* 1962. *Residence* – 11 Whitelands House, Cheltenham Terr, SW3.

WIDOW LIVING OF SECOND BARON

JOAN POLLOCK (*Dowager Baroness Birdwood*), da of Christopher Norman Graham, of Ealing: *m* 1954, as his 2nd wife, the 2nd Baron, who *d* 1962.

PREDECESSORS – (1) FM Sir WILLIAM RIDDELL Birdwood, GCB, GCSI, GCMG, GCVO, CIE, DSO, DCL, LLD, el surviving son of late Herbert Mills Birdwood, CSI, LLD, JP, ICS; *b* 1865; Field-Marshal; Hazara Expedition 1891 (medal with clasp), Isaza Expedition 1892, Tirah Expedition 1897-8 (despatches, medal with three clasps), S Africa 1899-1902, as Staff Officer, Brig Maj Mounted Brig (Natal) and DAAG, and Mil Sec to Com-in-Ch (Gen Lord Kitchener) (severely wounded, despatches five times, Queen's medal with six clasps. King's medal with two clasps, Brevets Major and Lieut-Col), Mohmand Expedition 1908, as Ch of Staff, present at action of Kargha (despatches, medal with clasp, DSO), European War 1914-18 with Mediterranean Expeditionary Force, first Comdg Australian and New Zealand Army Corps, then Com-in-Ch Mediterranean Expeditionary Force, and Comdg Dardanelles Army during Evacuation, and subsequently Comdg Australian and New Zealand troops and 5th Army in France (wounded, despatches many times, KCMG, Lieut-Gen, KCB, Grand Cordon of Legion of Honour, French Croix de Guerre with Palm, Belgian Order de la Couronne and Croix de Guerre, DSM of USA, Order of the Nile, Order of Aviz and of Christ and Grand Cordon of Tower and Sword of Portugal, 1st class of Orders of Rising Sun of Japan and Timsa of Persia, Order of Star of Nepal, GCMG, thanked by Parliament, *cr* Baronet, granted £10,000); was QMG, India May to Nov 1912, Sec to Govt of India, Army Depart, and a Member of Legislative Council of Gov-Gen of India 1912-14, Gen Officer Comdg Australian Imperial Forces 1915-20, ADC to King Edward VII 1906-10 and to King George V 1910-11, an ADC Gen to HM 1917-22, and Gen Officer Comdg-in-Ch, N Army, India 1920-24; acted as Com-in-Ch in India 1924, Com-in-Ch in India 1925-30, and Master of Peterhouse, Camb 1931-8; *cr* a *Baronet* (UK, of Anzac and Totnes) 1919, and *Baron Birdwood*, of Anzac, and of Totnes, co Devon (peerage of UK) 1938: *m* 1894, Janetta Hope Gonville, CI, who *d* 1947, el da of Col Sir Benjamin Parnell Bromhead, 4th Bt, CB; *d* 1951; *s* by his son (2) CHRISTOPHER BROMHEAD, MVO, 2nd Baron; *b* 1899; Lt-Col Probyn's Horse, Indian Army, a Commentator, Lecturer, and Author on International Affairs: *m* 1st, 1931 (*m diss* 1954), (Elisabeth) Vere Drummond, CVO, da of Lieut-Col Sir George Drummond Ogilvie, KCIE, CSI; 2ndly, 1954, Joan Pollock, da of Christopher Norman Graham; *d* 1962; *s* by his son (3) MARK WILLIAM OGILVIE, 3rd Baron and present peer.

BIRK, BARONESS (Birk) (Life Baroness 1967)

ALMA LILLIAN BIRK, FRS (1980), da of late Barnett Wilson, of London; *ed* South Hampstead High Sch, and London Sch of Economics (BSc Econ Hons); a JP since 1952; a Member of Fabian Soc since 1946, and of

Finchley Borough Council 1950-53, Sec of Fabian Soc Research Cttee on Marriage and Divorce 1951-52, and a Member of Hendon Group Hosp Management Cttee 1951-59; Chm of Health Education Council 1969-72; a Member of Howard League for Penal Reform since 1948; Asso Editor of *Nova* 1965-69; a Member of Youth Ser Development Council 1967-71, Stamford Hill Asso Clubs 1967-70, and Council for Children's Welfare 1968-75; Vice-Pres H. G. Wells Soc since 1967, and a Member of Panel of Pregnancy Advisory Ser since 1968, and of Redbridge Jewish Youth Centre since 1970; Vice-Pres of Divorce Law Reform Union since 1969; Gov British Film Inst 1981-87; Pres Assocn of Art Institutions, and Craft Art Design Assocn 1984-90, Vice-Pres Assocn of District Councils; a Member of Advisory Council of Birth Control Campaign; a Member of Hon Cttee of Albany Trust; a Gov of London Sch of Econ since 1971; a Baroness-in-Waiting to HM March to Oct 1974, Under-Sec of State, Dept of the Environment 1974-79, Front Bench Opposition Spokesman in House of Lords for the Environment 1979-86, and for Arts Heritage Broadcasting 1986-92; Trustee, York Sculpture Park, Health Promotion Research Trust, and The Theatres Trust; FRSA 1980; *cr Baroness Birk*, of Regent's Park, in Greater London (Life Baroness) 1967: *m* 1939, Ellis Samuel Birk, and has issue.
Residence – 3 Wells Rise, Regents Park, NW8 7LH.

SON LIVING

Dr the Hon David Barry Wilson (28 Charlbury Rd, Oxford OX2 6UU), *b* 1943: *ed* Clifton Coll, Jesus Coll, Camb, and Hull, London and Australian Nat Univs; PhD: *m* 1969, Kate, da of Joseph Green, of London, NW8, and has issue living, Rebecca, *b* 1970, — Antonia, *b* 1971, — Georgina, *b* 1974.

DAUGHTER LIVING

Hon Angela Felicity, *b* 1947; *ed* Camden Sch for Girls and London Univ; JP; *m* 1970, Richard Camber, of 28 Heath Drive, Hampstead, NW3, and has issue living, Thomas, *b* 1980, — Alice, *b* 1974, — Chloe, *b* 1980.

BIRKENHEAD, EARLDOM OF (Smith) (Extinct 1985)

SISTER LIVING OF THIRD EARL

Lady Juliet Margaret, LVO, *b* 1941; a Lady-in-Waiting to HRH The Princess Margaret, Countess of Snowdon 1965-71, since when an Extra Lady-in-Waiting; LVO (1981): *m* 1970, John Richard Townsend, of Newbottle Manor, Banbury, Oxon, and has issue living, Eleanor Mary, *b* 1971, — Alice Jane, *b* 1974, — Margaret Ann, *b* 1978.

BIRKETT, BARON (Birkett) (Baron UK 1958)

MICHAEL BIRKETT, 2nd Baron; *b* 22 Oct 1929; *s* 1962; *ed* Stowe, and Trin Coll, Camb; film producer; Dep Dir National Theatre since 1974; Dir Greater London Council Recreation and Arts since 1979: *m* 1960, Mrs Junia Crawford, who *d* 1973, da of Harold Elliott; 2ndly, 1978, Gloria, da of Thomas Taylor, of Queen's Gate, SW, and has issue by 2nd *m* .

Arms – Gules three full bottomed wigs argent. **Crest** – Between two wings gules a Viking ship proper charged on the sail with a raven close sable. **Supporters** – *Dexter*, a lion or semee of roses gules; *sinister*, a wolf sable semee of mullets gold.
Address – c/o House of Lords, SW1.

SON LIVING *(By 2nd marriage)*

Hon THOMAS, *b* 25 July 1982.

SISTER LIVING

Hon Linnea, *b* 1923: *m* 1949, Gavin Cliff Hodges, and has issue living, Marcus Birkett Adam, *b* 1959, — Victoria Françoise, *b* 1951, — Gabrielle, *b* 1953, — Charmian Sophie, *b* 1957: *m* 1981, Christopher John Allwright, of 17 East Common, Harpenden, Herts. *Residence* – Briar Cottage, Packers Hill, Holwell, Sherborne, Dorset DT9 5LN.

The Law is my light

PREDECESSORS – (1) WILLIAM NORMAN Birkett, PC, son of late Thomas Birkett, of Ulverston, Lancashire; *b* 1883; sat as MP for E Div of Nottingham (*L*) 1923-24, and 1929-31; Judge of High Court of Justice (King's Bench Div) 1941-50, and a Lord Justice of Appeal 1950-57; *cr Baron Birkett*, of Ulverston, co Palatine of Lancaster (peerage of UK) 1958: *m* 1920, Ruth, who *d* 1969, da of Emil Nilsson; *d* 1962; *s* by his son (2) MICHAEL, 2nd Baron and present peer.

BISHOPSTON, BARONY OF (Bishop) (Extinct 1984)

WIDOW LIVING OF LIFE BARON

WINIFRED MARY, JP; da of Frank Bryant, of Bristol: *m* 1945, Baron Bishopston, PC (Life Baron), who *d* 1984, leaving issue, four das. *Residence* – 11 Challoner Court, Merchants Landing, Redcliffe, Bristol BS1 4RG.

BLACK, BARONY OF (Black) (Extinct 1985)

DAUGHTER LIVING OF LIFE BARON

Hon Patricia Margaret, *b* 1919: *m* 1942, Leslie John Smyth, of Goudie's Farm, Lower Hamswell, Bath, Avon, and has issue.

BLACKETT, BARONY OF (Blackett) (Extinct 1974)

SON LIVING OF LIFE BARON

Hon Nicolas Maynard (18 Farquhar Rd, SW19), *b* 1928; *ed* Bristol Univ (BSc, PhD): *m* 1951, Patricia, da of Henry William Tankins, of Bristol, and has issue living, Peter, *b* 1962.

DAUGHTER LIVING OF LIFE BARON

Hon Giovanna, *b* 1926: *m* 1950, Kenneth Bloor, of 9 Queenston Rd, W Didsbury, Manchester M20.

BLACKFORD, BARONY OF (Mason) (Extinct 1988)

SISTER LIVING OF FOURTH BARON

Hon Elizabeth-Anne (St Luke St, SW3), *b* 1965.

BLACKSTONE, BARONESS (Blackstone) (Life Baroness 1987)

TESSA ANN VOSPER BLACKSTONE, da of late Geoffrey Vaughan Blackstone, CBE, GM, of Bures, Suffolk, by his wife Joanna, da of Maj Stanley Vosper; *b* 27 Sept 1942; *ed* Ware Gram Sch, and London Sch of Economics (BSc Soc, PhD); Associate Lect Enfield Coll 1965-66, Assist Lect, then Lect, Dept of Social Admin LSE 1966-75; Adviser Central Policy Review Staff, Cabinet Office, 1975-78; Prof of Educational Admin, Univ of London Inst of Educn, 1978-83; Dep Educn Officer (Resources), then Clerk and Dir of Educn, ILEA 1983-87; Master Birkbeck Coll since 1987; Dir Royal Opera House since 1987, and Chm Royal Opera House Ballet Board since 1991; Founder Memb and Chm of Trustees Inst for Public Policy Research since 1988; Trustee Natural History Museum since 1992; *cr Baroness Blackstone*, of Stoke Newington, Greater London (Life Baroness) 1987: *m* 1963 (*m diss* 1975), Tom Evans, and has issue. *Residence* – 2 Gower St, WC1E 6DP.

SON LIVING

Hon Benedict Blackstone, *b* 1963: *m* 1987, Suzi, da of Donal Godson, of Los Angeles, Calif, USA, and has issue living, Scarlet Eloise, *b* 1991.

DAUGHTER LIVING

Hon Liesel Morwenna, *b* 1966.

BLAKE, BARON (Blake) (Life Baron 1971)

ROBERT NORMAN WILLIAM BLAKE, FBA, son of William Joseph Blake, of Brundall, Norfolk; *b* 23 Dec 1916; *ed* King Edward VI Sch, Norwich, and Magdalen Coll, Oxford (MA, DLitt); Hon DLitt Glasgow, E Anglia, Westminster Coll, Fulton, Missouri, USA, and Buckingham; 1939-45 War as Capt, RA; N Africa 1942, POW Italy 1942-44, escaped 1944, despatches 1944; a JP of Oxford; a Member of Oxford City Council 1957-64; Lecturer in Politics Ch Ch Oxford 1946-47, Student and Tutor in Politics Ch Ch 1947-68; Censor 1950-55, Senior Proctor 1959-60; Ford's Lecturer in English History 1967-68; Provost of Queen's Coll, Oxford 1968-87, Pro-Vice-Chancellor of Oxford Univ 1971-87; Member of Board of Channel Four TV Co 1983-87; author of *The Private Papers of Douglas Haig* 1952, *The Unknown Prime Minister (Life of Andrew Bonar Law)* 1955, *Disraeli* 1966, *The Conservative Party from Peel to Churchill* 1970, *The Office of Prime Minister* 1975; ed, with John Patten, *The Conservative Opportunity* 1976, *A History of Rhodesia* 1977, *Disraeli's Grand Tour*

1982; ed *The English World* 1982, *The Decline of Power 1915-64* 1985, *The Conservative Party from Peel to Thatcher* 1985; ed *Dictionary of National Biography*; ed, with Roger Louis, *Churchill* 1993; Chm R Commn on Historical Manuscripts from 1982; Chm Rhodes Trust 1983-87; Trustee Brit Museum 1978-88; Prime Warden Dyers' Co 1976-77; High Steward of Westminster since 1989; *cr Baron Blake*, of Braydeston, co Norfolk (Life Baron) 1971: *m* 1953, Patricia Mary, el da of Thomas Richard Waters, of Great Plumstead, Norfolk, and has issue.
Residence – Riverview House, Brundall, Norwich, Norfolk. *Clubs* – Brooks's, Beefsteak, Pratt's, United Oxford and Cambridge University, and Norfolk County.

DAUGHTERS LIVING

Hon Deborah Cicelie, *b* 1955.
Hon Letitia Lindley, *b* 1960.
Hon Victoria Mary, *b* 1963.

BLAKENHAM, VISCOUNT (Hare) (Viscount UK 1963)

I hate whatever is profane

MICHAEL JOHN HARE, 2nd Viscount; *b* 25 Jan 1938; *s* 1982; *ed* Eton, and Harvard Coll, USA (AB Econ); late 2nd Lt Life Gds; Man Dir S Pearson 1979-83, Chm since 1983; Chm of RSPB since 1982; Pres Sussex Trust for Nature Conservation since 1983; Chm *Financial Times* since 1984: *m* 1965, his cousin, Marcia Persephone, da of Maj Hon Alan Victor Hare, MC (*see* E Listowel, colls), and has issue.

Arms – Gules, two bars and a chief indented or. **Crest** – A demi-lion rampant argent, ducally gorged or. **Supporters** – *Dexter*, a dragon ermine armed and langued gules; *Sinister*, a Guernsey cow proper.

SON LIVING

Hon CASPAR JOHN, *b* 8 April 1972.

DAUGHTERS LIVING

Hon Cressida, *b* 1966.
Hon Emily, *b* 1967.

SISTERS LIVING

Hon Mary Anne (Chipping Warden Manor, Banbury, Oxon) *b* 1936: *m* 1964, Timothy Mark Sergison-Brooke (*see* V Brookeborough, colls).
Hon Joanna Freda, *b* 1942: *m* 1967, Judge Stephen Breyer, of 12 Dunstable Rd, Cambridge, Mass, USA.

WIDOW LIVING OF FIRST VISCOUNT

Hon (BERYL) NANCY (*Nancy, Viscountess Blakenham*), da of 2nd Viscount Cowdray; *m* 1934, the 1st Viscount, who *d* 1982.

PREDECESSORS – (1) *Rt Hon* JOHN HUGH HARE, OBE, PC, 3rd son of 4th Earl of Listowel; *b* 1911; an Alderman LCC 1937-52, Chm of London Municipal Soc 1947-52, Vice-Chm of Conservative Party 1952-55; Min of State for Colonial Affairs 1955-56, Sec of State for War 1956-58, Min of Agriculture, Fisheries and Food 1958-60, Min of Labour 1960-63, and Chancellor of Duchy of Lancaster 1963-4, Dep Leader of House of Lords 1963-64, and Chm of Conservative Party Organisation 1963-5; Chm of Toynbee Hall 1966-82; Chm of Horticultural Soc 1970-82 (VMH 1974); Chm of Gov Peabody Donation Fund 1967-82; 1939-45 War in N Africa and Italy (despatches, MBE, OBE, Legion of Merit USA); MP for Woodbridge Div of E Suffolk (C) 1945-50, and for Sudbury and Woodbridge Div of E Suffolk 1950-63; *cr Viscount Blakenham*, of Little Blakenham, co Suffolk (peerage of UK) 1963: *m* 1934, Hon (Beryl) Nancy Pearson, da of 2nd Viscount Cowdray; *d* 1982; *s* by his only son (2) MICHAEL JOHN, 2nd Viscount and present peer.

BLANCH, BARON (Blanch) (Life Baron 1983) (Extinct 1994)

Rt Rev and Rt Hon STUART YARWOUTH BLANCH, PC, DD, son of late William Edwin Blanch; *b* 2 Feb 1918; *ed* Alleyns Sch, Dulwich, and St Catherine's Coll, and Wycliffe Hall, Oxford (MA); served World War II (1940-46) as Navigator RAF; V of Eynsham, Oxon 1952-57, Tutor and Vice-Prin of Wycliffe Hall Oxford 1957-60 (Chm of Council since 1967); Pro-Chancellor Hull Univ 1975-83, and York Univ 1977-83 (Council Member 1976); Hon LLD Liverpool, Hon DD Hull, Hon DD Toronto, Hon Doctor York Univ; Oriel Canon of Rochester and Warden Rochester Th Coll 1960-66; consecrated 5th Bishop of Liverpool 1966 and enthroned 94th Archbishop of York, Primate of England and Metropolitan 1975 (ret 1983); Chm Sandford St Martin Trust since 1988; author of *The World Our Orphanage, For all Mankind, The Christian Militant, The Burning Bush, Trumpet in the Morning, Ten Commandments,* and *Living by Faith*; Sub-Prelate, Order of the Hospital of St John of Jerusalem since 1975; *cr* PC 1975, and *Baron Blanch*, of Bishopthorpe, co N Yorks (Life Baron) 1983: *m* 1943, Brenda Gertrude, da of late William Arthur Coyte, and has had issue. Lord Blanch *d* 3 June 1994.

Arms – Argent on a pairle gules a rose argent barbed and seeded or between three cross crosslets fitchy towards the fess point argent floretty gold. **Crest** – Issuing from a circlet of double roses alternately gules on argent and argent on gules all barbed and seeded proper two lions' gambs gules armed or supporting between them a cross crosslet argent floretty gold. **Supporters** – On either side a Scottish sheepdog or charged on the breast with a heart gules enflamed proper.
Residence – Bryn Celyn, The Level, Shenington, nr Banbury, Oxon OX15 6NA.

SON LIVING

Hon Timothy Julian Yarworth, *b* 1953; *ed* King's Sch, Rochester, and Keble Coll, Oxford: *m* 1982, Monica Mary, da of late H. M. Keeble, and has issue living, Joseph Hugh, *b* 1987, — Rosa Katherine, *b* 1984. *Residence* – Ty Wrth Yr Eglwys, Glynogwr, Blackmill, nr Bridgend, Mid Glamorgan, S Wales.

DAUGHTERS LIVING AND DECEASED

Hon Susan Elizabeth, *b* 1946; *d* 1992.
Hon Hilary Jane, *b* 1948. *Residence* – 1 Chapel Cottages, Shutford, Oxon.
Hon Angela Francesca Hayward, *b* 1950: *m* 1974, Timothy Michael Ambrose, and has issue living, Bethany, *b* 1978, — Emily, *b* 1981. *Residence* – 7 Plewlands Av, Edinburgh.
Hon Alison Sarah, *b* 1955.

Blandford, Marquess of; son of Duke of Marlborough.

BLATCH, BARONESS (Blatch) (Life Baroness 1987)

EMILY MAY BLATCH, CBE, da of Stephen Joseph Triggs; *b* 24 July 1937; *ed* Secondary Sch for Girls, Prenton, Birkenhead, and Huntingdonshire Coll; Air Traffic Control Assist WRAF 1955-59, and A&AEE Boscombe Down 1959-63; Member Board of Peterborough Devpt Corpn since 1984, Cambs CC since 1977 (Leader 1981-85), ACC 1981-85, European Econ and Social Cttee 1986-87; Chm Anglo-American Community Relations Cttee RAF Alconbury since 1985; Baroness in Waiting since 1990, Min of State for Educn and Science since 1992; FRSA 1985; *cr* CBE 1983, and *Baroness Blatch*, of Hitchingbrooke, co Cambs (Life Baroness) 1987: *m* 1963, John Richard Blatch, AFC, and has issue (with one son deceased).
Residence – Red House, High St, Spaldwick, Cambridgeshire.

SONS LIVING

Hon James Richard, *b* 1967.
Hon Andrew Edward, *b* 1968.

DAUGHTER LIVING

Hon Elizabeth Anne, *b* (twin) 1968.

BLEASE, BARON (Blease) (Life Baron 1978)

WILLIAM JOHN BLEASE, son of William John Blease, *b* 28 May 1914; *ed* McClure Public Elementary Sch, New Univ of Ulster (Hon DLitt), and Queen's Univ, Belfast (Hon LLD); MBIM; Hon Fell BIM; N Ireland

Officer, Irish Congress of Trade Unions 1959-76; a Member of Standing Advisory Commn for Human Rights, N Ireland 1977-79, and of Indep Broadcasting Authority 1974-79; a Member of N Ireland Economic Council 1964-76; a JP for Belfast; *cr Baron Blease*, of Cromac, City of Belfast (Life Baron) 1978: *m* 1939, Sarah Evelyn, da of William Caldwell, and has issue.

SONS LIVING

Hon William Victor, *b* 1942: *m* 1969, Rose Mary, da of Alan Seaton, and has issue.
Hon Maurice Caldwell, *b* 1944: *m* 1967, Mary, da of Philip Carrol, and has issue.
Hon Paul Charles, *b* 1953: *m* 1979, Ann, da of Howard Jennings, and has issue.

DAUGHTER LIVING

Hon Gillian Sarah, *b* 1948: *m* 1972, John Compton, and has issue.

BLEDISLOE, VISCOUNT (Bathurst) (Viscount UK 1935)

Hold to thy faith

CHRISTOPHER HILEY LUDLOW BATHURST, QC, 3rd Viscount; *b* 24 June 1934; *s* 1979; *ed* Eton, and Trin Coll, Oxford; Bar Gray's Inn 1959; QC 1978; late Lt 11th Hus; Pres San Moritz Tobogganning Club since 1991; is Lord of the Manors of Lydney, Purton and Aylburton: *m* 1962 (*m diss* 1986), Elizabeth Mary, da of Sir Edward Walter Thompson, of Gatacre Park, Bridgnorth, Salop (*see* E Coventry, colls, 1968 Edn), and has issue.

Arms – Sable, two bars ermine, in chief three crosses-patée or. **Crest** – A dexter arm in mail embowed, the hand proper grasping a club with spikes or. **Supporters** – One either side a bull guardant, ringed and a line therefrom reflexed over the back or. *Seat* – Lydney Park, Gloucestershire. *Chambers*, Fountain Court, Temple, EC4. *Club* – Garrick.

SONS LIVING

Hon RUPERT EDWARD LUDLOW, *b* 13 March, 1964.
Hon Otto Benjamin Charles, *b* 1971.

DAUGHTER LIVING

Hon Matilda Blanche, *b* 1967.

WIDOW LIVING OF SECOND VISCOUNT

JOAN (*Viscountess Bledisloe*) (East Wing, Lydney Park, Glos; 14 Mulberry Walk, SW3), da of late Otto Krishaber: *m* 1933, the 2nd Viscount, QC, who *d* 1979.

WIDOW LIVING OF SON OF SECOND VISCOUNT

(Mary) Cornelia, da of Andrew Kirkwood McCosh, of Culter Allers, Biggar, Lanarkshire: *m* 1967, Hon David Charles Lopes Bathurst, who *d* 1992, and has issue (see colls, infra). *Residence* – South Lodge, East Heath Rd, NW3.

COLLATERAL BRANCH LIVING

Issue of late Hon David Charles Lopes Bathurst, yr son of 2nd Viscount, *b* 1937, *d* 1992: *m* 1967, (Mary) Cornelia (ante), da of Andrew Kirkwood McCosh, of Culter Allers, Biggar, Lanarkshire:—
Arabella Rose, *b* 1969. —— Lucy Celeste, *b* 1974. —— Flora Elizabeth, *b* 1977.

PREDECESSORS – **(1)** CHARLES BATHURST, GCMG, KBE, PC, son of late Charles Bathurst, of Lydney Park, Gloucestershire; *b* 1867; Bar Inner Temple 1892; was Parliamentary Sec, Min of Food 1916-17, Chm of Central Chamber of agriculture 1915, Director of Sugar Distribution 1918-19, Parliamentary Sec to Min of Agriculture 1924-28, Gov-Gen and Com-in-Ch of New Zealand 1930-35, and Pro-Chancellor of Bristol Univ 1934-47; *cr Viscount Bledisloe*, of Lydney, co Gloucester (peerage of United Kingdom) 1935: *m* 1st, 1898, Hon Bertha Susan Lopes, who *d* 1926, da of 1st Baron Ludlow; 2ndly, 1928, Hon Alina Kate Elaine (a DGStJ), who *d* 1956, da of 1st Baron Glentawe, and widow of Thomas Cooper-Smith; *d* 1958; *s* by his el son **(2)** BENJAMIN LUDLOW, 2nd Viscount, *b* 1899; QC and a Bencher Lincoln's Inn: *m* 1933, Joan, only da of late Otto Krishaber; *d* 1979; *s* by his el son **(3)** CHRISTOPHER HILEY LUDLOW, 3rd Viscount and present peer.

BLYTH, BARON (Blyth) (Baron UK 1907, Bt UK 1895)
(Name and Title pronounced "Bly")

ANTHONY AUDLEY RUPERT BLYTH, 4th Baron and 4th Baronet: *b* 3 June 1931; *s* 1977; *m* 1st, 1954 (*m diss* 1962), Elizabeth Dorothea, da of Robert T. Sparrow, of Vancouver, BC, Canada; 2ndly, 1963, Oonagh Elizabeth Ann, yr da of late William Henry Conway, of Dundrum, Dublin, and has issue by 1st and 2nd *m.*

Arms – Azure, on a mount vert a bull statant argent, ringed and chained or, on a chief arched of the fourth, a stag's head erased proper between two annulets gules. Crest – In front of a stag's head erased, gorged with a wreath of vine leaves proper, three roses argent. Supporters – Two stags proper, semée of annulets or, each gorged with a wreath of vine leaves, fructed proper.
Residences – Blythwood Estate, Athenry, co Galway; 79 Archer House, Vicarage Crescent, SW11 31G.

I hope for better things

SON LIVING *(By 1st marriage)*

Hon RILEY AUDLEY JOHN, *b* 4 March 1955; *ed* Portora Royal Sch: *m* 1979 (*m diss* 1984), Peggy, da of John Scanlon.

(By 2nd marriage)

Hon James Audley Ian, *b* 1970.

DAUGHTERS LIVING *(By 1st marriage)*

Hon Marcia Edna Dorothea, *b* 1956.
Hon Alexandra, *b* 1957.

(By 2nd marriage)

Hon Lucinda Audley Jane, *b* 1966.

BROTHER LIVING

Hon Adrian Ulrick Christopher David (Torwood, Maree, Oranmore, co Galway), *b* 1944; *ed* Sebright Sch, and Northants Coll of Agric, Engine Reconditioner: *m* 1966, Patricia Maureen, da of Desmond C. Southey, of Northampton, and has issue living, Mark Terence, *b* 1969, — Ian Christopher, *b* 1975, — Sarah Ursula, *b* 1967, — Verena Rosemary, *b* 1971, — Natasha Rachael, *b* 1973.

SISTERS LIVING

Hon Tanya Ormonde Audley, *b* 1929; SRN. *Residence* – Rockfield House, Athenry, co Galway.
Hon Barbara Edna Patricia, *b* 1936: *m* 1966, Aidan William Doyle, MRCVS, who *d* 1991, yst son of Martin E. Doyle, of Hill View, Athy, co Kildare, and has issue living, Nicholas Richard, *b* 1968, — Fiona Sarah, *b* 1971. *Residence* – Echo Gate, Friars Park, Trim, co Meath.
Hon Anne Shelagh Jennifer (twin), *b* 1936. *Residence* – Rockfield House, Athenry, co Galway.

PREDECESSORS – (1) JAMES Blyth, el son of late James Blyth, of Chelmsford, Essex by Caroline, da of late Henry Gilbey (Gilbey, Bt), of Bishop's Stortford, Herts; *b* 1841; was a Director of W. and A. Gilbey, wine merchants, of The Pantheon, Oxford Street, W, and Vice-Pres R So of Arts; deeply interested in agriculture and farming, and a recognized authority on vine culture and commerce connected therewith; *cr* a Baronet (UK, of Blythwood) 1895, and Baron Blyth, of Blythwood, Stansted Mountfitchet, co Essex (peerage of UK) 1907: *m* 1865, Eliza, who *d* 1894, da of William Mooney, of Clontarf, co Dublin; *d* 1925; *s* by his el son (2) HERBERT WILLIAM, 2nd Baron; *b* 1868: *m* 1927, Sylvia Mary (COLE), who *d* 1974 (having *m* 3rdly, 1947, Major Chave Charles Nainby Luxmoore, who *d* 1984), da of late Edwin E. Dennis; *d* 1943; *s* by his nephew (3) IAN AUDLEY JAMES (son of late Hon JAMES Audley Blyth, 2nd son of 1st Baron), 3rd Baron *b* 1905: *m* 1928, Edna Myrtle, who *d* 1952, da of Ernest Lewis, of Wellington, NZ; *d* 1977; *s* by his el son *b* (4) ANTHONY AUDLEY RUPERT, 4th Baron and present peer.

BLYTON, BARONY OF (Blyton) (Extinct 1987)

DAUGHTERS LIVING OF LIFE BARON

Hon Jane (139 Brockley Av, S Shields, Tyne and Wear), *b* 1920: *m* 1943, John Johansen, who *d* 1955, and has issue.
Hon Marion Rose, *b* 1926: *m* 1948, John Plank, of 36 Gerald St, S Shields, Tyne and Wear, and has issue.
Hon Rita, *b* 1930: *m* 1954, Andrew Scott, of 67 Australia Grove, S Shields, Tyne and Wear, and has issue.

BOARDMAN, BARON (Boardman) (Life Baron 1980)

THOMAS GRAY BOARDMAN, MC, TD, son of John Clayton Boardman; *b* 12 Jan 1919; *ed* Bromsgrove Sch; a DL for Northants since 1977; admitted a solicitor 1947; Min for Industry, Dept of Trade and Industry 1972-74; Chief Sec to Treasury 1974; Chm Chamberlain Phipps Ltd 1968-72; Dir Allied Breweries Ltd 1968-72 and 1974-1976 (Vice-Chm since 1975); Pres Assoc of British Chambers of Commerce 1977-80; Dir The Steetley Co Ltd 1975-83, Chm 1978-83; Dir National Westminster Bank plc since 1979 (Chm 1983-89); Dir MEPC Ltd 1980-89; Chm Cttee of London and Scottish Bankers 1987-89; Chm Heron International NV since 1993; Lt-Col Comdg Northants Yeo; served in NW Europe (MC 1944); MP (*C*) for Leicester SW 1967-74, and for Leicester S Feb-Sept 1974; *cr Baron Boardman*, of Welford, co Northants (Life Baron) 1980: *m* 1948, Norah Mary Deirdre, only da of late Hubert Vincent Gough, of Pangbourne, Reading, Berks, and widow of John Henry Chaworth-Musters, and has issue.

Arms – Azure on a fesse embattled between in chief two horses salient and in base a boar's head couped argent three roses gules barbed and seeded proper. **Crest** – A demi-horse argent maned crined and hooved or about its neck by the strings of a purse azure tasselled gold, mantled azure doubled or. **Supporters** – Dexter, a lion reguardant or head and mane gules gorged with a collar sable bezanty. Sinister, a horse rampant argent and maned crined and hooved or with a collar sable bezanty.
Residences – The Manor House, Welford, Northants NN6 6HX; 29 Tufton Court, Tufton St, London SW1P 3QH. *Club* – Cavalry and Guards.

SONS LIVING

Hon Anthony Hubert Gray (Lodge Farm, Hall Lane, Welford, Northants), *b* 1949; *m* 1977, Catherine, da of W. Penn, of Denton, Northants, and has issue, three das.
Hon Nigel Patrick Gray (Tufnell Park, N7), *b* 1950; *m* 1975, Sarah, da of T. A. Coslett, of Cambridge, and has issue, Hugo, *b* 1990, — Tamsin, *b* 1980, — Charlotte, *b* 1981, — Rebecca, *b* 1984, — Victoria, *b* 1985, — Cordelia, *b* 1987, — Elizabeth, *b* 1992.

DAUGHTER LIVING

Hon Grania Janet Gray, *b* 1955; *m* 1981, Capt Hon Rupert Edward Henry Law, late Coldm Gds, el son of 8th Baron Ellenborough.

BOLINGBROKE and ST JOHN, VISCOUNT (St John) (Viscount GB 1712, Bt E 1611)
(Name and Title pronounced "Bullingbrook and Sinjun")

Neither to seek nor to despise honours

KENNETH OLIVER MUSGRAVE ST JOHN, 7th Viscount, and 11th Baronet; *b* 22 March 1927; *s* 1974; *ed* Eton; patron of one living; a Fellow of Aust Inst of Travel; Pres of Travel Agents Assocn of NZ 1966-68; Dir of World Assocn of Travel Agencies 1968-75, and Chm of Australian Council of Tour Wholesalers 1972-74; Dir of Italian Importing Co: *m* 1st, 1953 (*m diss* 1972), Patricia Mary, da of B. J. McKenna, of Christchurch, NZ; 2ndly, 1972 (*m diss* 1987), Jainey Anne, da of the late Alexander Duncan McRae, of Timaru, NZ, and has issue by 1st and 2nd *m*.

Arms – Argent, on a chief gules two mullets or. **Crest** – On a mount vert, a falcon rising or, ducally gorged gules. **Supporters** – Dexter, a falcon, wings displayed, or, ducally gorged gules; sinister, an eagle, wings displayed, or, charged on the breast with the hames, an ancient badge of the family of Tregoze.
Residence – 15 Tonbridge Mews (PO Box 25.069), Shrewsbury St, Christchurch, NZ. *Club* – Christchurch (Christchurch, NZ).

SONS LIVING (By 1st marriage)

Hon HENRY FITZROY, *b* 18 May 1957.

(*By 2nd marriage*)

Hon Oliver John Beauchamp, *b* 1972.
Hon Nicholas Alexander Mowbray, *b* 1974.

BROTHER LIVING

Henry Ferdinand Musgrave (Newnham Corner, Newnham Green, Basingstoke, Hants), *b* 1928; *ed* Eton; late Lt LG: *m* 1956, Patricia Margaret Mary, da of Edward Ryan, of Exeter, Devon, and has had issue, Oliver Geoffrey, *b* 1958, *d* 1982.

SISTER LIVING

Antonia Josephine (c/o Midland Bank, 799 Fulham Rd, SW6), b 1933: m 1st, 1955 (m diss 1966), Henry Wilson; 2ndly, 1967, Peter Johnson, and has issue living (by 2nd m), Melanie Joanne, b 1967.

COLLATERAL BRANCHES LIVING

Grandchildren of late Maj John Henry St John, 2nd son of Hon Ferdinand St John (infra):—
Issue of late Henry Warren St John, b 1860, d 1931: m 1916, Justina Margaret, who d 1969, da of late Duncan
    Mackenzie, of Hill View, East Grinstead:—
Margaret Irene, b 1917: m 1939 (m diss 1947), Gerald Francis William Matthews, and has issue living, Texicia (Scatwell, 41
Brook Rd, Horsham, W Sussex), b 1940: m 1974, Tony Hodson, and has issue living, Caroline Rose b 1975, Sophie Louise b
1977, — Wendy (Flat C, 11 The Goffs, Eastbourne, Sussex), b 1941. Residence – Ibstock, Rowplatt Lane, Felbridge, nr East
Grinstead RH19 2NY.
Issue of late Walter Cecil Hompesch St John, b 1867, d 1955: m 1908, Maria Salome Rodrigues, who d 1930:—
Walter Warren (B° JM Paz-Ed 7-4° P-Dpto 27 (cp 1772), Villa Celina, Buenos Aires, Argentina), b 1921: m 1949, Lida
Goicoechea, and has issue living, Henry William (Juan J Paso 30-CP 1832, Lomas de Zamora, Prov Buenos Aires, Argentina),
b 1950: m 1977 (m diss 1981), Silvia Mazzoni, and has issue living, German Andres b 1980, — Alice, b 1950: m 1974,
Alejandro Funes Lorea, of Centenera 181, San Justo, Prov Buenos Aires, Argentina, and has issue living, Paulo b 1978, Clara
b 1976, Maria Guadalupe b 1980, Marianna b 1982. —— Lila Ramona del Rosario, b 1910: m 1935, Dr Ernesto Christensen,
of Entre Rios 166, Santiago del Estero, Argentina, and has issue living, Eduardo Ernesto (Entre Rios 166, Santiago del
Estero, Argentina), b 1936; an advocate: m 1974, Olga Vieyra, and has issue living, Alexander b 1976, Edward b 1979, —
Lilian Margarita, b 1943: m 1965, Rodolfo Diedrich, forest engr, of INTA Los Cerrillos, Salta, Argentina, and has issue living,
Rodolpho b 1967 Alejandro b 1973, Edwardo (twin) b 1973, Constanza b 1966, Cristina b 1971. —— Fanny del Valle, b 1912;
has Medal of Merit, Red Cross of Argentina: m 1938, Dr Ramon Bernardo Juarez, of Arturo Umberto Illia 316 Belgrano Sur,
CP 4200, Santiago del Estero, Argentina, and has had issue, Hugo Ramon, b 1939: m 1959, Maria Cristina Rodriguez (Arturo
Umberto Illia 316, Belgrano Sur, 4200 Santiago del Estero, Argentina), and d 1974, leaving issue, Hugo Walter b 1959,
Gustavo Alejandro b 1963, Monica Alicia b 1961: m 1981, Juan Failla (and has issue living, Alicia Veronica b 1982), — José
Enrique (Av Colón 4726-CP 5000, Córdoba, Argentina), b 1944: m 1969, Maria Virginia Espíndola Araoz, — Fanny Celina, b
1940: m 1965, Roberto Varela Vazquez, forest engr, of Las Retamas 427-CP 4400, Salta, Argentina, and has issue living,
Roberto Enrique b 1968, Sebastian Ernesto b 1972, Gabriela Celina b 1966. —— Margarita del Carmen, b 1913: m 1941, Luis
Frederico Quade, Engr, of Peru 161, Catamarca, Argentina, and has issue living, Josepha Margarita, b 1943: m 1965, José
Alberto Cisneros, engr, of Caseros 537, 4700 Catamarca, Argentina, and has issue living, José Maria b 1966, Luis Eduardo b
1967, Carlos Alberto b 1975, Marcela Inez b 1968, Maria Laura b 1971, — Luisa Celina b 1949: m 1974, Dr Raul Cardoso,
lawyer, of Ayacucho 636, 4700 Catamarca, Argentina, and has issue living, Maria Constanza b 1975. —— Rosa Pastora,
(Madero 755, CP 1408 Buenos Aires, Argentina), b 1916: m 1940, Ubaldo Casimiro García, agron engr (Inter-American Agric
Medal of OAS, Croix de Mérite Agric, France, Hon Agric Economist Texas Univ), and has issue living, Guillermo Ubaldo, b
1946; industrialist: m 1st, 1975 (m diss 1985), Norma Isabel Diez; 2ndly, 1985, Patricia Mónica Casto, and has issue living (by
2nd m), Christian Guillermo b 1989, Cintia Analía b 1986, — Graciela Salomé, b 1941: m 1970, Alfredo Pinto, of Cochicó 781,
CP 1408, Buenos Aires, and has issue living, Paula Marcela b 1971, María Alejandra b 1972, Natalia Virginia b 1973, María
Costanza b 1979, — María Rosa del Cármen, b 1942: m 1964, Guillermo Teijo, of Calle 16 No 785, Balcarce, Prov de Buenos
Aires, and has issue living, Alejandro b 1966, Esteban Guillermo b 1977, Alfonso Ezequiel b 1978, María Victoria b 1971, —
Teresa Pastora, b 1945: m 19—, Germán Aznar, Capitan de Fragata, Argentine Navy, who d 1986, of Cantílo 155, Haedo,
Prov de Buenos Aires, and has issue living, Germán Agustín b 1971, Federico b 1972, María Lidia b 1970, María Lucila b
1975.
Issue of late Edward Archibald St John, b 1876, d 1949: m 1922, Clare Esmeralda Magno, of 813 Calle Martinez,
    Capital, Buenos Aires, Argentina:—
Zeline Mabel Alice, b 1923. —— Gloria Alida, b 1924: m 19—, Prof Cesar Guerresi, and has issue living, a son, b 19—.

Grandchildren of late Sir Frederick Robert St John, KCMG, yst son of late Hon Ferdinand St John, 2nd
    son of 3rd Viscount:—
Issue of late Lt-Col Frederick Oliver St John, DSO, MC, b 1886, d 1977: m 1st, 1923 (m diss 1929), Dotie, da of late
    Sydney Bernard Burney, CBE; 2ndly, 1931, Elizabeth (Journeys End, East Looe, Cornwall), da of E. H. Pierce, of
    Peachland, BC:—
(By 2nd m) (Oliver) Peter (200 Dromore Av, Winnipeg 9, Manitoba, Canada), b 27 Feb 1938; hp to Earldom of Orkney; ed
Woodbridge Sch, Univ of BC (BA 1960), LSE (MSc 1963), and Lond Univ (PhD 1972); Lecturer, Univ Coll, Lond, 1963-64,
Univ of Manitoba 1964-66, Assist Prof 1966-72, Visiting Prof, Carleton Univ, 1981-82, Associate Prof of Political Science, Univ
of Manitoba, since 1972; Member Royal Inst of Internat Affairs since 1962, and Canadian Inst of Internat Affairs since 1964
(Pres Winnipeg Branch 1971-73); author: m 1st, 1963 (m diss 1985), Mary Juliet, da of late W. G. Scott-Brown, of 61 Harley
St, W1; 2ndly, 1985, Mrs Mary Barbara Huck, da of Dr David B. Albertson, of 4206 Cedar Glen Rd, Victoria, BC, and has
issue living (by 1st m), Oliver Robert, b 1969, — Juliet Elizabeth, b 1964, — Nicola Jane, b 1966, — Lucy Margaret, b 1972.
Prof St John has also adopted his stepson: Anthony Cameron ST JOHN, b 1969; has assumed the surname of St John in lieu
of his patronymic.
Issue of late Terence Alexander St John, b 1896; assumed by deed poll (enrolled at College of Arms) 1933, the
    surname of St John in lieu of his patronymic, but subsequently reverted to St John: d 1951: m 1st, 1923 (m diss
    1932), Simone Suzanne Marie Anne, only da of Jean Baptiste Guthmann, of Paris; 2ndly, 1947, Winifred Gladys, da
    of Charles Giles, and formerly wife of George Lewis Barry West:—
(By 1st m) Rosemary Anne, b 1927.

Granddaughters of late Major George Frederick Berkeley St John, 3rd son of late Gen Hon Frederick St
    John, 2nd son of 2nd Viscount:—
Issue of late Henry Augustus Bolingbroke St John, b 1847, d 1921: m 18—, Anna, da of late Maj — Henderson,
    HEICS:—
Mary Constance, b 1889. Residence – 1171 Newport Avenue, Victoria, British Columbia. —— Margaret, b 1896: m 1928,
Gordon Sweet.

Grandchildren of late Alexander Storey St John (infra):—
Issue of late Alexander Bolingbroke St John, b 1910, d 1968: m 1937, Gladys Spencer, who d 1981:—
Stewart Bolingbroke, b 1942. —— Janet Eleanor, b 1938: m 1962, Michael Stanley Hall, of 38 The Ridgeway, Tonbridge,
Kent TN10 4NJ, and has issue living, Stephen Philip St John, b 1969, — Wendy Deborah, b 1964, — Alison Judith, b 1967.

Granddaughter of late Frederick Charles St John, eldest son of late Charles William George St John, 5th
    and yst son of late Gen Hon Frederick St John (ante):—
Issue of late Alexander Storey St John, b 1867, d 1923: m 1906, Mabel Eleanor, who d 1928, 3rd da of late
    Inspector-Gen Sir Henry Frederick Norbury, KCB, MD, FRCS, RN, of St Margarets, Eltham, Kent:—
Stella Swithina Legge, b 1907. Address – Flat 9, 8 Newton St, WC2B 5EG.

Grandchildren of late Adm Henry Craven St John, 2nd son of late Charles William George St John (ante):—

Issue of late Vice-Adm Francis Gerald St John, CB, MVO, *b* 1869, *d* 1947: *m* 1st, 1898, Winifred Jessie, who *d* 1898, da of George Haward Trollope; 2ndly 1902, Emily Frances Louise, who *d* 1969, el da of late Allan Turner, of Bombay:—

(By 2nd *m*) Stratford Allan Gerald (Thornbury, Shamley Green, Guildford, Surrey), RN, *b* 1911; Capt 1956; European War 1939-44, operations off Norway and Sicily (despatches twice): *m* 1942, Honor Madeleine, da of Philip Smiles, of Belfast. —— Betty Allane, *b* 1905. —— Peggy Katharine Mary, *b* 1908: *m* 1st, 1939 (*m diss* 1948), Maj Leslie Fairfax d'Arch Smith; 2ndly, 1988, Colin Rosser Crickmay, of 2 Lynchen's Close, Bembridge, Isle of Wight, and has issue living (by 1st *m*), Nicola Lesley, *b* 1940: *m* 1962, Charles Quentin James, of Sandy Lane Farm, Parkmill, Swansea, W Glam, and has issue living, Andrew Thurstan Trewartha *b* 1965, Simon Charles Trewartha *b* 1969, Emma Charlotte *b* 1963: *m* 1994, Douglas Smith, Sophie Louise *b* 1971.

Descendants, if any, of Edward George St John (*b* 1870), only son of late Edward George St John (*b* 1840), of Nebraska, USA, 3rd son of late Charles William George St John (ante).

PREDECESSORS – OLIVER St John (a descendant of Oliver St John, second son of Sir Oliver St John of Bletso (*see* B St John of Bletso)), who obtained considerable renown in the wars of Elizabeth and James in Ireland, was *cr Viscount Grandison* 1620, in peerage of Ireland (with remainder to the issue of his niece Barbara, wife of Sir Edward Villiers), and *Baron Tregoze* (peerage of England) 1626; *dsp*, when the Barony became ext and the Viscountcy (now merged in the Earldom of Jersey) descended to William, son of Barbara (ante). His nephew (**1**) JOHN, brother of Barbara (ante), a zealous royalist, had three sons slain in fighting under the royal standard; *cr* a *Baronet* 1611; *s* by his grandson (**2**) Sir JOHN, 2nd Bt, *dsp* 1656; *s* by his uncle (**3**) Sir WALTER, 3rd Bt, MP for co Wilts; *d* 1708; *s* by his son (**4**) Sir Henry, 4th Bt; *cr Baron St John of Battersea* and *Viscount St John* (peerage of Great Britain) 1716, with remainder to his 2nd and 3rd sons, his el son Henry, a famous statesman and writer, having in 1712 been *cr Baron St John*, of Lydiard Tregoze, and *Viscount Bolingbroke* (peerage of Great Britain), with remainder to his father and his father's issue; in 1714 Viscount Bolingbroke was attainted, but in 1723 he was restored in blood, and in 1725 his estates were restored without his honours; Viscount St John *d* 1742, and was *s* by his 2nd son (**5**) JOHN, 2nd Viscount St John; *d* 1748; *s* by his son (**6**) FREDERICK, 3rd Viscount St John, who in 1751, on the demise of his uncle Henry without issue, *s* to the Barony of St John of Lydiard Tregoze and the Viscountcy of Bolingbroke; *d* 1787; *s* by his son (**7**) GEORGE RICHARD, 3rd Viscount Bolingbroke; *d* 1824; *s* by his son (**8**) HENRY, 4th Viscount Bolingbroke, *b* 1786: *m* 1812, Maria, da of Sir Henry Paulet St John Mildmay, 3rd Bt; *d* 1851; *s* by his son (**9**) HENRY MILDMAY, 5th Viscount Bolingbroke, *b* 1820: *m* 1893, Mary Emily Elizabeth, who *d* 1940, da of Robert Howard; *d* 1899; *s* by his son (**10**) VERNON HENRY, 6th Viscount Bolingbroke and St John, *b* 1896 (claim admitted by Cttee of Privileges of House of Lords 1922, and writ of summons issued April 1926): *m* 1950 (*m diss* 1952), Valenzina, da of late Frederick William Frohawk, of Sutton, Surrey; *d* 1974; *s* by his kinsman (**11**) KENNETH OLIVER MUSGRAVE (el son by 2nd *m* of Capt Geoffrey Robert St John, MC, el son of Henry Percy St John, el son of Rev Maurice William Ferdinand St John, DD, el son of Hon Ferdinand St John, 2nd son of 3rd Viscount), 7th Viscount and present peer; also Baron St John of Lydiard Tregoze, and Baron St John of Battersea.

BOLTON, BARON (Orde-Powlett) (Baron GB 1797)
(Name pronounced "Ord-Pawlett")

Love loyalty

RICHARD WILLIAM ALGAR ORDE-POWLETT, 7th Baron; *b* 11 July 1929; *s* 1963; *ed* Eton, and Trin Coll, Camb (BA 1951); JP N Riding of Yorks 1959-78; Chm, Yorks Branch, R Forestry Soc 1963-64; a Dir of Yorkshire General Life Assurance Ltd, late Chm of Waterers Group, and Yorks Soc of Agric: *m* 1st, 1951 (*m diss* 1981), Hon Christine Helena Weld-Forester, da of the 7th Baron Forester; 2ndly, 1981, Masha Anne, only da of Maj Francis Edward Hudson, TD, of Winterfield House, Bedale, Yorks; 3rdly, 1991, Mrs Lavinia Fenton, da of late William Edward Wright, and has issue by 1st *m*.

Arms – Sable: three swords in pile, points downwards argent, pommels and hilts or; on a canton argent, an escutcheon sable, charged with a salmon hauriant proper. **Crest** – A falcon rising or, ducally gorged azure, charged on the breast and on each wing with an estoile gules, and holding in the beak a salmon proper. **Supporters** – *Dexter*, a hind proper, ducally gorged or, and charged on the shoulder with a white rose; *sinister*, a Cornish chough proper, also charged on the shoulder with a white rose proper.

Seat – Bolton Hall, Leyburn, Yorkshire DL8 4UF. *Clubs* – Turf, Flyfishers', Central African Deep Sea Fishers', White's, Sloane.

SONS LIVING (By 1st marriage)

Hon HARRY ALGAR NIGEL (The Corner House, Wensley, Leyburn, N Yorks), *b* 14 Feb 1954; *ed* Eton: *m* 1977, Philippa A., da of Maj Peter L. Tapply, of Wanstead, Essex, and has issue living, Thomas, *b* 16 July 1979, — William Benjamin, *b* 1981, — Nicholas Mark, *b* 1985.

Hon Michael Brooke, *b* 1959: *m* 1985, Kate Mary, da of George William Laing, of Newsham, N Yorks, and has issue living, James Michael, *b* 1987, — Emma Katherine, *b* 1988. *Residence* – Hayes Barton, Jacobstowe, Okehampton, Devon.

DAUGHTER LIVING *(By 1st marriage)*

Hon Rosemary Victoria, *b* 1952: *m* 1974, (John) Richard Bentley North, of RMB 590 Boddington, W Australia 6390, and has issue living, Charles Richard, *b* 1975, — James William, *b* 1981, — Veronica Caroline *b* 1977.

BROTHER LIVING

Hon Patrick Christopher (Little Bordeaux, Little Chesterford, Saffron Walden, Essex), *b* 1931; *ed* Eton, and Jesus Coll, Camb (MA), ARICS; Council Member Timber Growers' Organisation, E England, until 1993; Partner J. Rothschild Partnership since 1994: *m* 1962, Elizabeth Jane, da of A. S. Kent, and has issue living, Rosamund Jane, *b* 1964, — Heather Victoria, *b* 1966.

PREDECESSORS – (1) *Rt Hon* THOMAS Orde, son of late John Orde, DL, of Morpeth: *m* 1778, Jean Mary Powlett, natural da of Charles, 5th Duke of Bolton *(see* M Winchester), and having *s* to his estates, assumed in 1795 by sign manual the additional surname of Powlett; *cr Baron Bolton* (peerage of Great Britain) 1797; *d* 1807; *s* by his el son (2) WILLIAM, 2nd Baron: *m* 1810, Hon Maria, who *d* 1863, da of 1st Baron Dorchester; *d* 1850; *s* by his nephew (3) WILLIAM HENRY, 3rd Baron (son of late Hon Thomas Orde-Powlett, 2nd son of 1st Baron), *b* 1818: *m* 1844, Letitia, who *d* 1882, da of Col Crawfurd, of Newfield, Ayrshire; *d* 1895; *s* by his el son (4) WILLIAM THOMAS, 4th Baron, *b* 1845: *m* 1868, Lady Algitha Frederica Mary Lumley, who *d* 1919, el da of 9th Earl of Scarbrough; *d* 1922; *s* by his son (5) WILLIAM GEORGE ALGAR, 5th Baron; *b* 1869; Lord-Lieut for N Riding of Yorkshire; MP for Yorkshire, N Riding, Richmond Div (C) 1910-18: *m* 1893, Hon Elizabeth Mary Gibson, who *d* 1943, da of 1st Baron Ashbourne, *d* 1944; *s* by his son (6) NIGEL AMYAS, 6th Baron; *b* 1900: *m* 1928, Victoria Mary, who *d* 1933, da of Henry Montagu Villiers, MVO (E Clarendon, colls); *d* 1963; *s* by his el son, (7) RICHARD WILLIAM ALGAR, 7th Baron and present peer.

BONHAM-CARTER, BARON (Bonham Carter) (Life Baron 1986)

MARK RAYMOND BONHAM CARTER, elder son of late Sir Maurice Bonham Carter, KCB, KCVO (*d* 1960), by his wife Lady (Helen) Violet Asquith, DBE (Baroness Asquith of Yarnbury) (*d* 1969), elder da of 1st Earl of Oxford and Asquith; *b* 11 Feb 1922; *ed* Winchester, Balliol Coll, Oxford, and Chicago Univ; served World War II 1940-45 in N Africa and NW Europe (despatches, prisoner 1943, escaped 1943); Chm Race Relations Board 1966-71, and Chm Community Relations Commn 1971-77, Vice-Chm and a Gov of BBC 1975-81, Chm of Govs of R Ballet since 1985; MP for Torrington Div of Devon (*L*) 1958-59; *cr Baron Bonham-Carter*, of Yarnbury, co Wilts (Life Baron) 1986: *m* 1955, Leslie, da of late Condé Nast, of New York, USA, and formerly wife of 2nd Baron St Just, and has issue.

Arms – Quarterly: 1st and 4th az two lions combatant or collared and lined gu supporting with their interior paws a mural crown gold, *Carter;* 2nd and 3rd gu a sword erect between in chief two cross crosslets fitchée arg over all a chevron of the last, *Bonham.* **Crests** – A lion's head erased or between two estoiles each within the horns of a crescent az, *Carter;* a dragon's head erased arg guttée de sang between two fountains, *Bonham.* **Motto** – Trusty to the end. *Residence* – 13 Clarendon Rd, W11 4JB.

DAUGHTERS LIVING

Hon Jane Mary, *b* 1957.

Hon Virginia Leslie, *b* 1959: *m* 1992, Charles David William Brand, of 1 Kingswood Av, NW6 6LA, and has issue *(see* V Hampden, colls).

Hon Elizabeth Cressida, *b* 1961.

Booth, see Baron Gore-Booth.

BOOTHBY, BARONY OF (Boothby) (Extinct 1986)

WIDOW LIVING OF LIFE BARON

WANDA (*Baroness Boothby*), da of Giuseppe Sanna, of Sardinia: *m* 1967, as his 2nd wife, Baron Boothby, KBE (Life Baron), who *d* 1986.
Residence – 1 Eaton Sq, SW1W 9DA.

Boringdon, Viscount; son of Earl Morley.

Borodale, Lord; son of Earl Beatty.

BORTHWICK, LORD (Borthwick of that Ilk) (Lord S ca 1450)

JOHN HENRY STUART BORTHWICK OF THAT ILK, TD, 23rd Lord; *b* 13 Sept 1905; *s* 1937 (claim to Lordship admitted by Lord Lyon 1986); *ed* Fettes; Baron of Heriotmuir, Midlothian, and Laird of Crookston; Hereditiary Falconer of Scotland to HM; one of the four representative Scottish barons in HM's post-Coronation State Visit to Edinburgh, carrying the Crown Canopy; Maj RA (TA), and a DL and JP for Midlothian; with Allied Mil Govt Staff 1944, Lt-Col 1946: *m* 1938, Margaret Frances, who *d* 1976, da of Alexander Campbell Cormack, and has issue.

𝕬rms – Argent, three cinquefoils sable. 𝕮rest – A moor's head couped proper wreathed argent and sable. 𝕾upporters – Two angels proper winged or. 𝕸otto – Qui conducit.
Seat – Borthwick Castle, Midlothian. *Residence* – Crookston, Heriot, Midlothian. *Club* – New (Edinburgh).

SONS LIVING

Hon JOHN HUGH (*Master of Borthwick*), *b* 14 Nov 1940; *ed* Gordonstoun: *m* 1974, Adelaide, only da of late Archy Birkmyre, of Lower Dalchonzie, Comrie, Perthshire (*see* Birkmyre, Bt, colls), and has issue living, Georgina, *b* 1975, — Alexandra, *b* 1977. *Residence* – The Neuk, Heriot, Midlothian. *Clubs* – New (Edinburgh), Carlton, Royal Canadian (Toronto).
Hon James Henry Alexander BORTHWICK OF GLENGELT, *b* (twin) 1940; *ed* Gordonstoun, and Heriot-Watt Univ: *m* 1972, Elspeth, da of Lt-Col Allan Dunn MacConachie, of Lauder, Berwicks (*see* V Molesworth, colls, 1990 Edn), and has issue living, Malcolm Henry, *b* 1973. *Residence* – Channelkirk Cottage, Oxton, Lauder, Berwicks TD2 6PT.

COLLATERAL BRANCH LIVING

Granddaughters of late Francis Borthwick, yst son of John Borthwick of Borthwick, 13th of Crookston, who repurchased Borthwick Castle 1812 to which, had it not been alienated, he would have *s* under a settlement of 1538, 12th in descent from John Borthwick, 2nd son of 1st Lord:—
Issue of late Francis John Gordon Borthwick, WS, *b* 1871, *d* 1948: *m* 1912, Eugenie Helen Franklyn, da of Edmund Stow Thompson:—
Mary Alice (*Hon Mrs Douglas D. E. Vivian*) (Monastery Garden, Edington, Westbury, Wilts): *m* 1943, Lt-Com Hon Douglas David Edward Vivian, DSC, RN (*see* B Vivian), who *d* 1973. —— Margaret Eugenie: *m* 1944, Maj Ian Rupert Farquhar, Gren Gds (*see* Farquhar, Bt, colls). *Residence* – Hamlyns, Chudleigh, S Devon.

PREDECESSORS – *Sir* William Borthwick of Borthwick, Knt, a substitute hostage for James I 1424-27, had a Crown Charter of the Lands of Borthwick 1410; his 3rd son Sir William Borthwick, 2nd of Borthwick, Knt, has a licence to build the Castle of Borthwick 1430; his son (1) Sir WILLIAM Borthwick, 3rd of Borthwick, *cr Lord Borthwick* in the Peerage of Scotland 1450-54, sat as Lord of Parliament 1455-57, was Commissioner to treat with England 1459; *d* 1483; *s* by his son (2) WILLIAM, 2nd Lord, knighted in his father's lifetime, Master of the Household to James III 1485; *d* 1503; *s* by his son (3) WILLIAM, 3rd Lord: *m* 1491, Margaret, da of John, Lord Hay of Yester; *k* at Battle of Flodden 1513; *s* by his son (4) WILLIAM, 4th Lord, to whom was entrusted the Castle of Stirling after Flodden; *d* 1543; *s* by his son (5) JOHN, 5th Lord, opposed Reformation of 1560: *m* before 1544, Isobel (who *m* 2ndly, George Preston, of Cameron, and *d* 1577), da of 8th Earl of Crawford; *d* 1566; *s* by his son (6) WILLIAM, 6th Lord; a zealous supporter of Mary, Queen of Scots: *m* before 1570, Grissel (who lodged a complaint against him for desertion and cruelty 1581, and *m* 2ndly, Walter Cairncross, of Colmslie), da of Sir Walter Scott, of Branxholm; *d* "of the French disease" 1582; *s* by his 2nd son (7) JAMES, 7th Lord, *b* 1570: *m* 1582, Margaret, el da of William, Lord Hay of Yester; *d* 1599; *s* by his son (8) JOHN, 8th Lord: *m* before 1616, Lilias, 5th da of 1st Earl of Lothian; *d* 1623; *s* by his son (9) JOHN, 9th Lord, *b* 1616; held the Castle of Borthwick against Protector Cromwell until he obtained terms of honourable surrender 1650: *m* 1649, Elizabeth, 2nd da of 3rd Earl of Lothian; *dsp* 1672, when the male line of the 4th Lord failed and his estates passed to his nephew, John Dundas, son of his sister, who was served as his heir; the title remained dormant until 1762, but the right of succession passed to the descendants of Alexander Borthwick, 3rd son of 2nd Lord, his cousin and heir male (10) WILLIAM, *de jure* 10th Lord, Major in the army: *m* 1665, Marion Moorhead; *d* ca 1687-90; *s* by his only son (11) WILLIAM, *de jure* 11th Lord, *bapt* 1666, Capt Cameronian Regt 1689, Col in the army: *m* Jean, da of Robert Ker, of Kersland; *dsp* being slain at battle of Ramillies 1706; *s* by his cousin (12) HENRY, *de jure* 12th Lord: *m* Mary, da of Sir Robert Pringle of Stitchill, 1st Bt; *d* of wounds received at battle of Ramillies 1706; *s* by his son (13) WILLIAM, *de jure* 13th Lord; *dsp* before 1723; *s* by his brother (14) HENRY, 14th Lord, his right to the title was admitted by the House of Lords 1762; *dsp* 1772, when the title again became dormant, the right of succession, however, passing to his cousin and heir male (15) PATRICK, *de jure* 15th Lord, a merchant in Leith: *m* Marian Scott; *d* 1772; *s* by his only son (16) ARCHIBALD, *de jure* 16th Lord, *b* 1732, a merchant in Christiansund, Norway, and afterwards a banker in Edinburgh: *m* 1777, Margaret Nicolson, who *d* 1833, da of James Scott, CS; *s* by his son (17) PATRICK, *de jure* 17th Lord, *b* 1779, sometime manager of National Bank of Scotland, Edinburgh; claimed the peerage 1816: *m* 1804, Ariana, who *d* 1836, 2nd da of Cunninghame Corbet, of Tolcross and of Glasgow; *d* 1840; *s* by his el son (18) ARCHIBALD, *de jure* 18th Lord, *b* 1811: *m* 1840, Mary Louisa, who *d* 1868, da of John Home Home, of Longformacus; *dspms* 1863; *s* by his brother (19) CUNNINGHAME, 19th Lord, *b* 1813; his claim to the Lordship was allowed 1870, a Representative Peer for Scotland: *m* 1865, Harriet Alice, who *d* 1911, da of Rev Thomas Hermitage Day, of Frinsbury, Kent; *d* 1885; *s* by his only son (20) ARCHIBALD PATRICK THOMAS, 20th Lord, *b* 1867, a Representative Peer for Scotland, and a JP for Wigtownshire: *m* 1901, Susanna Mary (DStJ) (who *m* 2ndly, 1916, as his 2nd wife, 18th Duke of Grafton (*d* 1930), and *d* 1961), da of Sir Mark John MacTaggart Stewart, 1st Bt; *d* 1910, when the title again became dormant, the right of succession, however, passing to his kinsman (21) WILLIAM HENRY, 15th of Crookston (14 in descent from Hon John Borthwick, 1st of Crookston, yr son of 1st Lord Borthwick), *de jure* 21st Lord, *b* 1832: *m* 1864, Rebecca, who *d* 1887, da of Robert Cathcart; *d* 1928; *s* by his el son (22) HENRY, *de jure* 22nd Lord, *b* 1868: *m* 1902, Melena Florence, who *d* 1962, 4th da of Capt James Thomas Pringle of Torwoodlee, RN: *d* 1937; *s* by his only son (23) JOHN HENRY STUART, 23rd Lord and present peer.

BORWICK, BARON (Borwick) (Baron UK 1922, Bt UK 1916)

It passes

JAMES HUGH MYLES BORWICK, MC, 4th Baron, and 4th Baronet; *b* 12 Dec 1917; *s* 1961; *ed* Eton; is Maj (ret) Highland LI; European War 1939-45 (MC): *m* 1954, Hyllarie Adalia Mary, da of late Lt-Col William Hamilton Hall Johnston, DSO, MC, DL, of Bryn-y-Groes, Bala, N Wales, and has issue.

Arms – Argent, three escarbuncles fesseways sable between three bears' heads erased of the last, muzzled or. **Crest** – Upon a mount proper, in front of a staff raguly erect azure, a stag browsing or, attired sable. **Supporters** – On either side a bear sable, muzzled and charged on the shoulder with an escarbuncle or. *Residence* – Leys Farm, Bircher, Leominster, Hereford HR6 0AZ. *Club* – Royal Ocean Racing.

DAUGHTERS LIVING

Hon Angela Jane BORWICK, *b* 1955; has resumed her maiden name: *m* 1988 (*m diss* 1991), Charles William Heathcoat Amory, yr son of late Lt-Col Sir William Heathcoat Amory, 5th Bt. *Residence* – Leys Farm, Bircher, Leominster, Hereford HR6 0AZ.

Hon Mary-Anne, *b* 1957.

Hon Diana, *b* 1959.

Hon Amanda Gwyneth Rosemary, *b* 1965: *m* 1987, Brian Wynn Parry, eldest son of P. Owen Parry, of Llandderfel, N Wales, and has issue living, Robert James William, *b* 1990, — Caroline Hyllarie Wynne, *b* 1988. *Residence* – 4 Bro Hafesb, Llandderfel, Bala, Gwynedd, N Wales.

HALF-BROTHERS LIVING

Hon GEORGE SANDBACH (Garrick Club), *b* 18 Oct 1922; *ed* Eton: *m* 1981, Esther, who *d* 1985, da of late Clarence de Sola, of Montreal, Canada, and widow of Sir John Reeves Ellerman, 2nd Bt (ext).

Hon Robin Sandbach, *b* 1927; *ed* Eton; late Lt The LG: *m* 1950, Hon Patricia Garnett, only da of Baron McAlpine of Moffat (Life Baron), and has issue living, (Geoffrey Robert) James (Jamie) (1 Love Lane, EC2), *b* 1955; *ed* Eton: *m* 1981, Victoria Lorne Peta, only da of late W/Cdr Roger Dennistoun Poore, of 33 Phillimore Gdns, W8 (*see* Poore, Bt, colls), and has issue living, Edwin Dennis William *b* 1984, Thomas James Robert *b* 1987, Alexandra Victoria *b* 1990, — Richard David, *b* 1960; *ed* Eton: *m* 1983, Nicole D., da of late S/Ldr Ronald M. Kerr, MVO, of Westwinds, Moulsford, Oxon, and has issue living, Christian *b* 1985, Summer Louise *b* 1987, Charlotte Alexandra *b* 1989, — Judith Patricia, *b* 1952: *m* 1971, Padraic Desmond Curry-Towneley-O'Hagan, 52 Mount Park Rd, W5 2RU (*see* B O'Hagan). *Residence* – Neptune House, Newells Lane, Bosham, Sussex PO18 8PS.

SISTERS LIVING

Hon Katharine Hilda, *b* 1914: *m* 1938, Ashton Jack Ulyate, and has had issue, Stanley Ian Robert Borwick (24 Burrawong Rd, Avalon, Sydney 2107, NSW, Australia), *b* 1939: *m* 1973, Margaret Mary Anne Morling, and has issue living, William Robert *b* 1975, James Ashton *b* 1976, — Raymond Grant (23 Park Rd, Glenfield, Auckland, NZ) *b* 1955: *m* 1979, Shelley Diana, da of Alfred Bryan Stent, of 34 Maygrane Dr, Orewa, Hibiscus Coast, NZ, and has issue living, Angus Bryan *b* 1985, Genevieve Kathryn *b* 1987, — Jacqueline Borwick, *b* 1942, *d* 1951, — Sandra Irene Borwick, *b* 1945: *m* 1972, Peter Leslie Berry, of 18 Phipson Rd, Scottsville, Pietermaritzburg 3201, Natal, S Africa, and has issue living, Cynthia Jacqueline *b* 1972, Bruce Sidney, *b* 1975. *Residence* – 48 High St, Glenholme, Rotorua, NZ.

Hon Phyllis Dorothy (16 Wood Lane, Falmouth, Cornwall), *b* 1916: *m* 1963, John A'Court Bergne, who *d* 1978.

PREDECESSORS – (1) ROBERT HUDSON Borwick, last surviving son of late George Borwick, of Morven, Torquay; *b* 1845; was a Director of George Borwick & Sons, Ltd, and a JP for co London; *cr* a *Baronet* 1916, and *Baron Borwick*, of Hawkshead, co Lancaster (peerage of United Kingdom) 1922: *m* 1872, Caroline Smith, who *d* 1936, da of late Richard Daniel Johnston, of Kurnool, Madras; *d* 1936; *s* by his el son (2) GEORGE, 2nd Baron, *b* 1880: *m* 1st, 1908 (*m diss* 1913), Mary Mason, da of Lewis Cruger Hassell, of New York; 2ndly, 1918 (*m diss* 1938), Dorothea Gertrude, who *d* 1986, da of late Charles Gray, of Anerley, SE; *d* 1941; *s* by his brother (3) ROBERT GEOFFREY, 3rd Baron; *b* 1886: *m* 1st, 1913 (*m diss* 1920), Irene Phyllis, who *d* 1969, da of late Thomas Main Patterson, of Littlebourne House, Canterbury; 2ndly, 1920, Margaret Elizabeth, who *d* 1969, da of late Gilbert Robertson Sandbach, of Stoneleigh, Rossett, Denbighshire; *d* 1961; *s* by his el son (4) JAMES HUGH MYLES, 4th Baron and present peer.

BOSSOM, BARONY OF (Bossom) (Extinct 1965)

SON LIVING OF LIFE BARON

Hon SIR CLIVE BOSSOM, 2nd Bt, who *s* to baronetcy (*cr* 1953), 1965 (*see* Bossom, Bt).

BOSTON, BARON (Irby) (Baron GB 1761, Bt E 1704)

TIMOTHY GEORGE FRANK BOTELER IRBY, 10th Baron, and 11th Baronet; *b* 27 March 1939; *s* 1978; *ed* Clayesmore Sch Dorset, and Southampton Univ (BSc): *m* 1967, Rhonda Anne, da of Ronald Albert Bate, of Balgowlah, NSW, and has issue.

𝔄rms – Argent, fretty sable, on a canton gules, a chaplet or. 𝔠rest – A Saracen's head in profile proper, wreathed round the temples argent and sable. 𝔖upporters – Two antelopes gules, each gorged with a chaplet or.
Residence – Cae'r Borth, Moelfre, Anglesey LL72 8NN.

Honour is the reward of fidelity

SONS LIVING

Hon GEORGE WILLIAM EUSTACE BOTELER, *b* 1 Aug 1971.
Hon Jonathan Charles Timothy, *b* 1975.

DAUGHTER LIVING

Hon Rebecca Frances Anne, *b* 1970.

HALF SISTER LIVING

Hon Anne Pauline, *b* 1927: *m* 1951, Sydney James Crews, MB, BChir, FRCSE, of 77 Wellington Rd, Edgbaston, Birmingham 15, and has issue living, Francis Robert, *b* 1953, — Emma Rosemary Joanna, *b* 1956, — Bridget Harriet, *b* 1963.

DAUGHTERS LIVING OF SEVENTH BARON

Hon Rachel Elizabeth Cecily, *b* 1914: *m* 1940, Lt Darsie Rawlins, RNVR, and has issue living, Adrian Drake, *b* 1942: *m* 1st, 1968 (*m diss* 1975), Julianna, da of Eugene Simor, of Budapest; 2ndly, 1980, Jill Catharine, da of Charles William Pays, of Gillingham, Kent, and has issue living (by 1st *m*), Titus Nicholas Gabriel *b* 1968, Alexander Francis Edward *b* 1971, — Anthony Irby, *b* 1944, — Diana Caroline Zoë, *b* 1949: *m* 1976, Colin Cyril Ind, of Langton Cottage, 78 Gretton Rd, Winchcombe, Glos GL54 5EL, and has issue living, Christopher Edward *b* 1980, Charlotte Emily *b* 1984, — Christina Elizabeth, *b* 1955: *m* 1st, 1983 (*m diss* 1991), Graham Joseph Tayar; 2ndly, 1992, Seamus Mulvihill, of 27 Ashmead Rd, SE8 4DY, and has issue living (by 2nd *m*), Thomas James Irby *b* 1992. *Residence* – 11 Framers Court, Lane End, High Wycombe HP14 3LL.
Hon Isobel Caroline, *b* 1917: *m* 1st, 1946 (*m diss* 1950), Major Vernon Owain Roberts, The Buffs; 2ndly, 1950, Edward Horatio Sales, who *d* 1988, and has issue living (by 2nd *m*), Christian Caroline (18 The Crescent, Barnes, SW13 0NN), *b* 1950: *m* 1973, David Wyndham Hughes, who *d* 1989, and has issue living, Alexander Wyndham *b* 1977, Ben Cressall *b* 1979, Alice Irby *b* 1982, Holly Irby *b* 1988, — Alexandra Josephine (27 Rowan Av, Hangleton, Hove, E Sussex), *b* 1952: *m* 1st, 1973 (*m diss* 1980), Daniel Sean Devaney; 2ndly, 1991, Martin Paul Doyle, who *d* 1993, and has issue living (by 1st *m*), Damian Julian *b* 1977, Fleur Josephine *b* 1978. *Residence* – 18 Fourth Av, Hove, E Sussex BN3 2PJ.
Hon Christian Florance, *b* 1921: *m* 1947, Etienne Humblet, who *d* 1971. *Residence* – 2510 Ocean Court, 83-85 Spring St, Bondi Junction, NSW 2022, Australia.

WIDOW LIVING OF BROTHER OF NINTH BARON (*who was raised to the rank of Baron's son* 1976)

Mrs Beryl Harrison, yst da of late Harold Mayman, of Bramsgore, Hants: *m* 1957, as his 2nd wife, Hon Anthony Paul Irby, TD, who *d* 1986. *Residence* – 44 Rosebank, Holyport Rd, SW6 6LQ.

COLLATERAL BRANCHES LIVING

Issue of late Hon Anthony Paul Irby, TD, brother of 9th Baron, *b* 1908, *d* 1986: *m* 1st, 1934, Countess Mary Apponyi, who *d* 1952, elder da of late Count Anton Apponyi; 2ndly, 1957, Mrs Beryl Harrison (ante):—
(By 1st *m*) Paul Anthony (Swaites Farm, Ecchinswell, Newbury, Berks RG15 8UN), *b* 1935; *ed* Eton; late 2nd Lieut KRRC: *m* 1982, Emma Mary, formerly wife of (i) Hugh Leopold Seymour (*see* M Hertford, colls), and (ii) John Laurence David Aschan, and only da of Robert Alister Henderson (*see* Lowther, Bt, *cr* 1824, colls), and has issue living, Rupert Paul Anthony, *b* 1983, — Harry Robert Paul Anthony, *b* 1985. ―― (George Anthony) Peter (Hill House, 64 Honor Oak Rd, SE23 3RZ), *b* 1942; *ed* Eton; late Maj RGJ: *m* 1981, Ginger Kay Patricia Wanda May, da of late Frank Edward Wallace, of Texas, USA, and has had issue, Edward Peter Anthony Wallace, *b* 1986, — Richard Peter Anthony Wallace, *b* 1988, *d* 1989, — Mary Charlotte Alexandra Wallace, *b and d* 1983, — Katharine Mary Louise Wallace, *b* 1984. ―― Charles Leonard Anthony (125 Blenheim Crescent, W11 2EQ), *b* 1945; *ed* Eton: *m* 1971, Sarah Jane, da of David Sutherland, and has issue living, Nicholas Charles Anthony, *b* 1975, — Caroline Sarah, *b* 1977.

Grandchildren of late Edward de Crespigny Irby, el son of late Edward Irby (*b* 1821), 4th son of Rev Hon Paul Anthony Irby, 5th son of 2nd Baron:—
Issue of late Francis Edward Irby, *b* 1877, *d* 1960: *m* 1925, Katie Lorna, who *d* 1981, da of late W. Tibbits, of Gilgandra, NSW:—
Edith Elizabeth (210 High St, Lismore, NSW, Australia), *b* 1927: *m* 1953, Richard E. Wratten, who *d* 1969, and has issue living, Nigel Richard Irby, *b* 1955. ―― Isla Frances, *b* 1930: *m* 1954, Wilfred Charles Tibbits, JP, of Cottage Green, Gilgandra, NSW, Australia, who *d* 1985.
Issue of late Paul Anthony Irby, *b* 1882: *d* 1968: *m* 1914, Mabel, who *d* 1960, da of Mrs Olive, of Casino, Sydney, NSW:—
Paul Anthony (2 Ray St, Bray Park, Murwillumbah, NSW 2484, Australia), *b* 1916; New Guinea and Solomon Islands 1944-45 with AIF: *m* 1948, Dorothy Mary, da of R. H. Hogg, of Wahroonga, Cecil Plains, Queensland, and has issue living, Paul Anthony Richard, *b* 1949; BEcon, — Ross James *b* 1959; BA, — Judith Jessie, *b* 1951: *m* 1982, Geoffrey Robert Williams, of 28 Carlton St, Highgate, Adelaide, and has issue living, Benjamin Robert *b* 1984, Courtney Jayne *b* 1987. ―― †Gordon Edward, *b* 1922: *m* 1950, Beryl Margaret (Weerona, Mooball, NSW, Australia), da of C. D. Mills, and *d* 1979, leaving issue living, Leonard Edward (12 Opal Place, Golden Links Estate, Murwillumbah, NSW, Australia 2484), *b* 1951: *m* 1981, Judith Ann, da of Robert B. Noble, of Murwillumbah, NSW, and has issue living, Mark Edward *b* 1983, Melissa Jan *b* 1986, Suzanne Marie *b* 1988, — Kenneth Francis, *b* 1954: *m* 1973, Robyn M. Shillan, and has issue living, Peter Richard *b* 1978, Felica Lea *b* 1974, — Stephen Victor, *b* 1960: *m* 1989, Robyn, da of Horace Alfred Martin, of 4 Ewing St, Murwillumbah,

NSW, and has issue living, Benjamin Anthony *b* 1992, Jacinta Elizabeth *b* 1990, — Robyn Joyce, *b* 1953, — Sharon Lea, *b* 1966: *m* 1989, Geoffrey David Grace, of Burringbar, NSW, Australia 2483. —— John Charles (Weerona, Mooball, NSW, Australia), *b* 1928: *m* 1952, Orene Ethel, da of W. D. Scott, of Burringbar, NSW, and has issue living, Douglas John (Greenvale Estate, Burringbar, NSW 2483), *b* 1953: *m* 1975, Barbara Anne, da of W. Murray, of Sydney, NSW, and has issue living, David John *b* 1978, Joanne Louise *b* 1977, Rachael Elizabeth *b* 1982, — Michael Anthony (43 Guildford Rd, Guildford, NSW 2161), *b* 1961: *m* 1994, Carolina, da of Manuel Baca, of Concord W, Sdyney, NSW, — Delmay Orene, *b* 1955, — Janelle May, *b* 1957: *m* 1984, John Butturini, of Mooball, NSW 2483, and has issue living, Matthew John *b* 1987, Nicholas James *b* 1989, Andrew Anthony *b* 1993, — Elsie Maree, *b* 1959: *m* 1986, Mark Richardson Clapham, of Lismore, NSW 2480, and has issue living, Thomas Anthony *b* 1991, Melanie Alice *b* 1988, — Shirley Ellen, *b* 1963: *m* 1987, Gregory Craig King, of Pottsville, NSW 2484, and has issue living, Lucas Scott *b* 1990, Stacey Mary *b* 1992. —— Florence Mabel, *b* 1919; a JP: *m* 1947, Dalley Leslie Griffin, JP, of 15, Napier Cres, N Ryde, 2113, NSW, Australia, and has issue living, David Leslie Paul, *b* 1947; JP: *m* 1978, Wendy, da of E. R. Raynor, of Manly, NSW, and has issue living, Jacqueline Lea *b* 1982, Lauren Jane *b* 1986, — Brian Arthur Charles, *b* 1948; BA; Aust Forces, 3rd Cav Regt, Vietnam; a JP: *m* 1972, Cheryl, da of K. Trescott, of Baulkham Hills, Sydney, NSW, and has issue living, Fiona Leigh *b* 1978, Kate Michelle *b* 1980, Sara Louise *b* 1984, — Elizabeth, Ann, *b* 1951; SRN. —— Nancy, *b* 1926: *m* 1946, Mervyn James Carthy, who *d* 1976, of Myponga, via Adelaide, S Australia 5202, and has issue living, Terry James, *b* 1947: *m* 1971, Maxine, da of K. Hutchinson of Myponga, S Australia, and has issue living, Todd Lee *b* 1978, Lisa Jane *b* 1975, — Peter, *b* 1949; served Austn Forces, Vietnam: *m* 1972, Wendy, da of Robert Rossiter, of Victor Harbour, S Australia, and has issue living, Meagan Emma *b* 1978, Belinda Abbie *b* 1980, — Graeme, *b* 1956, — Anne, *b* 1953: *m* 1973, Graham McKinley, of Jerramungup, W Australia, and has issue living, Ryan James *b* 1976, Amie Louise *b* 1978.

Grandchildren of late Edward de Crespigny Irby (ante):—
Issue of late Llewellyn George Irby, *b* 1883, *d* 1964: *m* 1914, Mary Louisa, el da of late Rev R. W. Stockdale, of Grafton, NSW:—

Kenneth Allan (1 Gibbons St, Wynward, Tasmania), *b* 1920; 1939-45 War in Middle East and S Pacific with RAAF: *m* 1948, Mary Rushton, da of the Rev E. E. Johnson, R of Carrick, Tas, and has issue living, Philip Anthony Kenelm, *b* 1951, — Judith Mary, *b* 1949: *m* 1971, Rev Ross Flint, of Wynyard, Tasmania, and has issue living, Andrew Mark *b* 1979, Janine Ruth *b* 1974, Natasha *b* 1976. —— Mary Edith (Rosemary) (Pond Farm, RMB 2545, Greens Rd, Upper Lurg, via Benalla, Victoria, Australia) *b* 1915: *m* 1943, George Philip MacDonell, who *d* 1980. —— Elspeth Douglas (3 Ivanhoe Court, Newcomb, Vic 3219 Australia), *b* 1917, late Sister in Australian Army Nursing Ser: *m* 1948, Rev Frederick Searle Ingoldsby, ThL, DipRE, who *d* 1976, and has issue living, James Douglas, *b* 1949; BA: *m* 1980, Leonie Christine Praetz, and has issue living, Sophie Sky *b* 1981, Liria Vida *b* 1982, — David Llewellyn, *b* 1954: *m* 1987, Rosemary Crosby, and has issue living, Jonathan Dale *b* 1990, Clare Elizabeth *b* 1988, — Marilyn Margaret, *b* 1950; BFA, — Pamela Jean, *b* 1952; BA: *m* 1974, Rev M. J. Vercoe, and has issue living, Stephen Philip *b* 1980, Alison Mary *b* 1982, — Janet Elspeth Irby, *b* 1959; BA: *m* 1981, Michael John Down, and has issue living, John Philip Frederick *b* 1982, Elizabeth Winsome Mary *b* 1984, Deborah Lyn Emily *b* 1986.

Grandson of late Charles Augustus Irby (infra):—
Issue of late Arthur Algernon Irby, *b* 1890, *d* 1927: *m* 1927, Mary Isabel Marsden, who *d* 1953:—

Brian Keith (3 Banyeena Place, Belrose 2085, Sydney, NSW, Australia), *b* 1931; JP: *m* 1952, June Eve Hutton, and has issue living, Peter Brian Edward, *b* 1956: *m* 1985, Ruth Helen Goven, and has issue living, Nicholas Roland *b* 1989, Cameron Peter *b* 1993, — Donna-Elizabeth, *b* 1953.

Grandsons of late Edward Irby (*b* 1821), 4th son of Rev Hon Paul Anthony Irby, 5th son of 2nd Baron (ante):—
Issue of late Charles Augustus Irby, *b* 1861, *d* 1941: *m* 1888, Eva Georgiana, da of Richard Roberts, of Sydney, NS Wales:—

Beverley Keith, *b* 1899: *m* 1942, Kathleen Pilley, of Mudgee. *Residence* – 7 Alfred St, Campsie, NSW, Australia. —— Richard Wilfred, *b* 1901: *m* 1939, Margery McMillan, of Bathurst, Australia, and has issue living, Jenny Eva, *b* 1942: *m* 1964, Raymond Thomas Connell, of 27 Hope St, Penrith, NSW, Australia. —— Roland Frank, *b* 1906: *m* 1938, Mary Brown. *Residence* – Kar-Mar, Wallacia, NSW, Australia.

Granddaughters of late Rev George Powell Irby, 7th son of Rev Hon Paul Anthony Irby (ante):—
Issue of late Lewis Michael Aubert Irby, *b* 1882, *d* 1974: *m* 1914, Isabel Kate, who *d* 1972, da of late G. M. Thornton:—

Audrey Cynthia Yvette, *b* 1915: *m* 1955, Christopher Lucian Chamberlin, TD, of Withybed Cottage, Butleigh Wootton, Glastonbury, Som BA6 8TX. —— Beryl Diana Noël, *b* 1919: *m* 1951, Henry John Bunting, of 5 Cambray Court, Cheltenham G50 1JU, and has issue living, George Irby, *b* 1952: *m* 1974, Julia Angela Davey, and has issue living, Samuel Charles *b* 1979, Timothy George *b* 1984, — James Walter Irby, *b* 1954: *m* 1982, Hisaka Margaret Hiraoka, and has issue living, Paul Shu *b* 1985, Mark Rhu *b* 1990, Sarah Mai *b* 1992, — Edward Irby, *b* 1959: *m* 1991, Boika Spasova, — Richard Irby, *b* 1962.

PREDECESSORS – **(1)** EDWARD Irby, son of late Anthony Irby; MP for Boston; *cr* a Baronet 1704; *d* 1718; *s* by his son **(2)** *Sir* WILLIAM, MP, 2nd Bt, Lord Chamberlain 1761; *cr* Baron Boston (peerage of Great Britain) 1761; *d* 1775; *s* by his son **(3)** FREDERICK, DCL, 2nd Baron, for fifty years a Lord of the Bedchamber to George III; *d* 1825; *s* by his son **(4)** GEORGE, 3rd Baron; *b* 1777; *d* 1856; *s* by his son **(5)** GEORGE IVES, 4th Baron; *b* 1802; *d* 1869: *m* 1st, 1830, Fanny Elizabeth, who *d* 1860, da of W. R. Hopkins-Northey; 2ndly, 1861, Hon Caroline Amelia, who *d* 1927, da of 3rd Baron de Saumarez; *d* 1869; *s* by his son **(6)** FLORANCE GEORGE HENRY, 5th Baron; *b* 1837: *m* 1859, Hon Augusta Caroline, who *d* 1929, da of 3rd Baron de Saumarez; *d* 1877; *s* by his son **(7)** GEORGE FLORANCE, 6th Baron; *b* 1860; a Lord-in-Waiting to HM Queen Victoria 1885-6; *m* 1890, Cecilia Constance, who *d* 1938, da of late Hon Augustus Anthony Frederick Irby; *d* 1941; *s* by his nephew **(8)** GREVILLE NORTHEY (son of late Hon Cecil Saumarez Irby, 2nd son of 5th Baron); *b* 1889; Hon Capt (ret) Oxford and Bucks LI; sometime Principal in Colonial Office: *m* 1st, 1913, Constance Beryl, who *d* 1969, da of late William Richard Lester, of Alderley, Llandudno; 2ndly, 1954, Irene Frances, who *d* 1987, da of late Francis Holt, of Ewell, Surrey, and widow of Harry Mills; *d* 1958; *s* by his brother **(9)** CECIL EUSTACE, MC, 8th Baron, *b* 1897, *d* 1972; *s* by his kinsman **(10)** GERALD HOWARD BOTELER, MBE (el son of Lt-Col Leonard Paul Irby, OBE, son of Lt-Col Leonard Howard Loyd Irby, son of Rear-Adm Hon Frederick Paul Irby, CB, 2nd son of 2nd Baron), 9th Baron, *b* 1897; 1914-18 War (MBE 1918); 1939-45 War as Maj RASC: *m* 1st, 1926 (*m diss* 1931), Katherine Gertude, da of Capt C. M. H. Edwards, RASC; 2ndly, 1936, Erica Nelly, who *d* 1990, da of T. H. Hill; *d* 1978: *s* by his son **(11)** TIMOTHY GEORGE FRANK BOTELER, 10th Baron and present peer.

BOSTON OF FAVERSHAM, BARON (Boston) (Life Baron 1976)

TERENCE GEORGE BOSTON, yr surviving son of late George Thomas Boston; *b* 21 March 1930; *ed* Woolwich Polytechnic Sch, and Kings Coll, Univ of London; Bar Inner Temple 1960, and Gray's Inn 1973; QC 1981; Fl Lt RAF 1950-52; BBC News Sub-Editor, External Sers 1957-60; Snr BBC Producer (Current Affairs) 1960-64; MP for Faversham, Kent (*Lab*) 1964-70; PPS to Min of Public Building and Works 1964-66, to Min of Power 1966-68, and to Min of Transport 1968-69; Assist Govt Whip 1969-70; UK Delegate to UN General Assembly 1976-78; Minister of State, Home Office 1979; Opposition Spokesman on Home Office Affairs 1979-84, on Defence 1984-86; Chm TVS (TVS Entertainment plc) 1980-90; Principal Dep Chm of Cttees and Chm Select Cttee on the European Communities, House of Lords, since 1992; *cr Baron Boston of Faversham*, of Faversham in co Kent (Life Baron) 1976; *m* 1962, Margaret Joyce, el da of late Rowley Henry Jack Head, and step-da of late Henry Fermin Winters, of Melbourne, Victoria, Australia.

Arms – per pale gules and azure a lion passant guardant dimidiated with a ship's hull or on a chief argent a duck-billed platypus statant proper between two cats' faces sable; **Crest** – a chapeau gules turned up ermine thereon a boar's head couped azure; **Supporters** – *Dexter*, a lion sejant erect guardant or; *Sinister*, a kangaroo guardant proper each resting the exterior foreleg on a fasces erect the axe facing outwards sable the whole upon a compartment comprising a grassy mount vert growing therefrom roses gules and argent barbed seeded slipped and leaved proper
Address – House of Lords, SW1A 0PW.

BOTETOURT AND HERBERT, BARONIES OF (Baron Botetourt, E 1305 and Baron Herbert, E 1461) (Abeyant 1984)

HENRY HUGH ARTHUR FITZROY SOMERSET, KG, KCVO, PC, 10th DUKE OF BEAUFORT, also 10th BARON BOTETOURT and 18th BARON HERBERT (*cr* 1461), *d* 1984, when the latter Baronies fell into abeyance between the descendants of his late sister Lady Blanche Linnie Somerset (infra).

CO-HEIRESSES TO BARONIES

Granddaughter of late Lady Rosemary Alexandra Eliot, el da of Lady Blanche Linnie Somerset (infra):—
Issue of late Davina Rosemary Enid NUTTING (see Nutting, Bt, colls, 1976 Edn), *b* 1940, *d* 1976, in a motor accident: *m* 1960 (*m diss* 1969), as his 2nd wife, John Martin Brentnall Cope, who *d* 1991:—
FREDERICA SAMANTHA MARY, *b* 1963; co-heir to Baronies of Botetourt and Herbert (quarter share); legally assumed forename of Frederica 1991. *Residence* – Flat H, 4 Chelsea Embankment, SW3 4LF.

Granddaughter of late Lady Blanche Linnie Somerset (infra):—
Issue of late Lady Rosemary Alexandra Eliot, *b* 1919, *d* 1963: *m* 1st, 1939, Capt Edward Christian Frederick Nutting, RHG, who *d* on active service 1943, 2nd son of late Sir Harold Stansmore Nutting, 2nd Bt; 2ndly, 1945 (*m* annulled 1949), Lt-Cdr David Frederick Hew Dunn, RN; 3rdly, 1949, Col Ralph Alexander Rubens, Sherwood Foresters:—
(By 3rd *m*) ALEXANDRA LOUISE, *b* 1951; co-heir to Baronies of Botetourt and Herbert (quarter share): *m* 1976, Daniel Augusto Peyronel (c/o 27 Gertrude Street, SW10 0JF), and has issue living, Jesse Alexander, *b* 1977.

Issue of late Lady Blanche Linnie Somerset, el da of 9th Duke of Beaufort, *b* 1897, *d* 1968: *m* 1st, 1918, 6th Earl of St Germans, who *d* 1922; 2ndly, 1924, Capt George Francis Valentine Scott Douglas, who *d* 1930 (see Douglas, Bt, *cr* 1786, 1969 Edn):—
(By 1st *m*) *Lady* CATHLEEN BLANCHE LILY, *b* 1921; co-heir to Baronies of Botetourt and Herbert (half share): *m* 1st, 1946 (*m diss* 1956), Capt John Seyfried, RHG; 2ndly, 1957, Sir Havelock Henry Trevor Hudson, of The Old Rectory, Stanford Dingley, Reading, Berks, and has issue by 1st and 2nd *m* (see E St Germans).

Botreaux, Barony of; see Loudoun, Countess of.

BOTTOMLEY, BARON (Bottomley) (Life Baron 1984)

ARTHUR GEORGE BOTTOMLEY, PC, OBE, son of George Howard Bottomley, of Tottenham, Middlesex; *b* 7 Feb 1907; *ed* Gamuel Road Council Sch, Walthamstow, and Toynbee Hall; mem Walthamstow Borough Council 1929-49, Mayor 1945-46; Dep Regional Commr, S Eastern Area 1941-45; MP for Chatham Divn of Rochester 1945-50, for Rochester and Chatham 1950-59, for Middlesbrough East 1962-74, and for Teesside (Middlesbrough) 1974-83; Parl Under-Sec of State for Dominion Affairs 1946-47; Sec for Overseas Trade 1947-51; Sec of State for Commonwealth Relations 1964-66; Min of Overseas Development 1966-67; Chm House of Commons Select Cttee on Race Relations and Immigration 1967-70; Hon Freeman of Chatham 1959; Freeman of City of London 1975, and of Middlesborough 1976; *cr* OBE (Civil) 1941, PC 1951, and

Baron Bottomley, of Middlesbrough, co Cleveland (Life Baron) 1984: *m* 1936, Bessie Ellen, DBE (1970), JP (1955) Essex, da of Edward Charles Wiles, of Walthamstow.
Residence – 19 Lichfield Road, Woodford Green, Essex.

BOURNE, BARONY OF (Bourne) (Extinct 1982)

SON LIVING OF LIFE BARON

Hon Michael Kemp (50 Bradbourne St, SW6), *b* 1937: *m* 1st, 1963 (*m diss* 1980), Penelope Jane, da of Capt H. W. Blyth, of Wyncombe Hill, Fittleworth, Sussex, 2ndly, 1985, Marian Lockhart, eldest da of Maj John Francis Leatham Robinson, MC (*see* Barran, Bt, colls), and has issue living (by 1st *m*) John Kemp, *b* 1969, — Amanda Caroline, *b* 1966: *m* 1987, Hugh Charles Gordon Garrod, son of Kenneth Garrod, of Whatton, Notts, and has issue living, George Charles *b* 1992, — Lucy Claire, *b* 1968.

DAUGHTER LIVING OF LIFE BARON

Hon Elizabeth Anne (Belmont House, Donhead St Mary, Shaftesbury, Dorset), *b* 1931: *m* 1952, Ian McKay Robertson, Maj Gordon Highlanders, who *d* 1984, and has issue four sons.

BOWDEN, BARONY OF (Bowden) (Extinct 1989)

SON LIVING OF LIFE BARON (By 1st marriage)

Hon Robin (19 Kirkbrae Av, Cults, Aberdeen AB1 9RF), *b* 1945; *ed* Old Swinford Hosp Sch, and Loughborough Univ; *m* 1978, Jess, da of W. MacPherson-Duncan, and has issue living, Alastair Robin, *b* 1982, — Lindsay Catherine, *b* 1979.

DAUGHTERS LIVING OF LIFE BARON (By 1st marriage)

Hon Mary Bowden (4 Martin Av, Dorval, H9S 3R3, Prov Quebec, Canada), *b* 1940; teacher of deaf children; has resumed her maiden name: *m* 1964 (*m diss* 19—), Dr Roger George Davey, and has issue, Lisa, *b* 1969, — Julie, *b* 1971.
Hon Virginia, *b* 1943; *ed* E Anglian Girls' Sch, and Reading and Manchester Univs: *m* 1967, David Ian Murray, of 61 Woburn Drive, Hale, Cheshire, and has issue living, Tanya, *b* 1973, — Louise, *b* 1976.

BOWLES, BARONY OF (Bowles) (Extinct 1970)

WIDOW LIVING OF LIFE BARON

Kathleen Amy (*Baroness Bowles*), (88 St James's St, SW1A 1PW; Naval and Military Club); el da of late Edward Hugh Musgrove, and widow of Air Commodore Edward Donald MacLulich Hopkins: *m* 1950, Baron Bowles (Life Baron), who *d* 1970.

Bowmont and Cessford, Marquess of; son of Duke of Roxburghe.

BOYD-CARPENTER, BARON (Boyd-Carpenter) (Life Baron 1972)

John Archibald Boyd-Carpenter, PC, only son of late Maj Sir Archibald Boyd Boyd-Carpenter, MP, River House, Walton-on-Thames; *b* 2 June 1908; *ed* Stowe, and Balliol Coll, Oxford (BA), Diploma Econ; Pres of Oxford Union 1930; Bar Middle Temple 1934; Financial Sec, Treasury 1951-54, Min of Transport and Civil Aviation 1954-55, Min of Pensions and Nat Insurance 1955-62, Ch Sec, Treasury and Paymaster Gen 1962-64, Opposition Spokesman on Housing and Land 1964-66, and Chm Public Accounts Cttee. 1964-70; Chm Orion Insurance Co 1968-72, and CLRP Investment Trust 1969-72, and a Dir of other Cos; Chm Carlton Club 1980-86; appointed High Steward of R Borough of Kingston upon Thames 1972; a DL of Greater London 1973; 1939-45 War served Scots Gds, (Maj 1943); MP for Kingston upon Thames (C) 1945-72; Chm of Civil Aviation Authority 1972-77; Chm Rugby Portland Cement Co Ltd 1976-84; *cr* PC 1954, and *Baron Boyd-Carpenter*, of Crux Easton, co Southampton (Life Baron) 1972: *m* 1937, Margaret Mary, da of the late Lt-Col George Leslie Hall, OBE, RE (ret) (*see* E Coventry, colls, 1976 Edn), and has issue.

Arms – Not exemplified at time of going to press.
Club - Carlton.

SON LIVING

Hon Sir Thomas Patrick John, KBE, *b* 1938; *ed* Stowe; Lieut-Gen, Dep Ch of Staff, Programmes, Min of Defence since 1992; MBE (Mil) 1973, KBE (Mil) 1993: *m* 1972, Mary Jean, da of John Elwes Duffield, BM, BCh, of The Tithe House, Church St, Marcham, Berks, and has issue.

DAUGHTERS LIVING

Hon Anne Mary, *b* 1942.
Hon Sarah Elizabeth Mary, *b* 1946: *m* 1968, Hon Douglas Martin Hogg, PC, MP (*see* B Hailsham of St Marylebone).

BOYD OF MERTON, VISCOUNT (Lennox-Boyd) (Viscount UK 1960)

SIMON DONALD RUPERT NEVILLE LENNOX-BOYD, 2nd Viscount; *b* 7 Dec 1939; *s* 1983; *ed* Eton, and Ch Ch, Oxford; Dep-Chm Arthur Guinness & Sons plc 1981-86; Chm Save the Children 1987-92, since when Chm Stonham Housing: *m* 1962, Alice Mary, High Sheriff of Cornwall 1987-88, da of late Maj Mersey George Dallas Clive (*see* E Longford), and has issue living.

Arms – Azure a fess chequy argent and gules, between an abbatical mitre simplex of the second filleted of the third in chief, and in base a rose of the second, seeded vert and barbed of the third **Crest** – A dexter hand erect in pale, having two fingers turned in and the rest pointing upwards proper the wrist habited in a close sleeve azure, with cuff chequy argent and gules. **Supporters** – Two squirrels proper, having collars chequy argent and gules.
Residences – 9 Warwick Sq, SW1; Wivelscombe, Saltash, Cornwall.

SONS LIVING

Hon BENJAMIN ALAN, *b* 21 Oct 1964; *ed* Millfield: *m* 1993, Mrs Sheila Mary Margaret Carroll, da of Harold Emmanuel George Williams, of 343 North Rd, W Plymouth, and formerly wife of Michael Carroll, of Saltash, Cornwall, and has issue living, Alan George Simon, *b* 11 March 1993, — Mary Alice, *b* 1994. *Residence* – South Broadmoor, Saltash, Cornwall.
Hon Edward George, *b* 1968; *ed* Eton, and Ch Ch, Oxford: *m* 1994, Tamsin, da of Antony Hichens. *Residence* – 3 Moreton Place, SW1.

DAUGHTERS LIVING

Hon Charlotte Mary, *b* 1963; *ed* Cheltenham Ladies Coll, and Univ Coll, London: *m* 1992, Charles C. J. Mitchell, eldest son of late James Mitchell, of Wilsford-cum-Lake, Wilts, and has issue living, Gwendolen Charlotte Julia, *b* 1994. *Residence* – 10 Essex Villas, W8.
Hon Philippa Patricia, *b* 1970; *ed* St Mary's, Calne. *Residence* – 38 Charlwood St, SW1.

BROTHERS LIVING

Hon Christopher Alan (42 Upper Brook St, W1; The Great House, Burford, Oxon), *b* 1941; *ed* Eton, and Ch Ch, Oxford.
Hon Mark Alexander, MP (3 Bloomfield Terr, SW1; Gresgarth Hall, Caton, Lancs), *b* 1943; *ed* Eton, and Ch Ch, Oxford; Bar Inner Temple 1968; MP for Morecambe and Lonsdale (*C*) 1979-83, since when MP for Morecambe and Lunesdale (*C*); PPS to Chancellor of Exchequer 1983-84, Assist Govt Whip 1984-86; Lord Commr of the Treasury 1986-88; PPS to Rt Hon Margaret Thatcher, Prime Minister, 1988-90, Parl Under-Sec, Foreign and Commonwealth Office 1990-92, since when Under-Sec of State, Dept of Foreign and Commonwealth Affairs: *m* 1974, Mrs Arabella Lacloche, only da of Piero Parisi, of Rome, and has issue living, Patricia Irene, *b* 1980.

WIDOW LIVING OF FIRST VISCOUNT

Lady PATRICIA FLORENCE SUSAN GUINNESS (*Patricia, Viscountess Boyd of Merton*), da of 2nd Earl of Iveagh: *m* 1938, the 1st Viscount, CH, PC, who *d* 1983. *Residences* – 2 Bloomfield Terr, SW1; Ince Castle, Saltash, Cornwall.

PREDECESSORS – ALAN TINDAL LENNOX-BOYD, CH, PC, son of Alan Walter Lennox-Boyd; *b* 1904; Parliamentary Sec to Min of Labour 1938-39, to Min of Home Security 1939, to Min of Food 1939-40, and to Min of Aircraft Production 1943-45; Min of State for Colonial Affairs 1951-52, Min of Transport and Civil Aviation 1952-54, and Sec of State for the Colonies 1954-59; Man Dir Arthur Guinness, Son & Co Ltd 1960-67, Joint Vice-Chm 1967-83; a Dir ICI; MP for Mid Div of Bedfordshire (*C*) Oct 1931-July 1960; *cr* PC 1951, and *Viscount Boyd of Merton,* of Merton-in-Penningham, co Wigtown (peerage of UK) 1960: *m* 1938, Lady Patricia Florence Susan Guinness, da of 2nd Earl of Iveagh; *d* 1983; *s* by his el son (2) SIMON DONALD RUPERT NEVILLE, 2nd Viscount and present peer.

BOYD-ORR, BARONY OF (Orr) (Extinct 1971)

DAUGHTERS LIVING OF FIRST BARON

Hon Elizabeth Joan Boyd, *b* 1916: *m* 1944, Lt-Col Kenneth Alfred John Barton, and has issue living, Robert John Orr, *b* 1944, — Kenneth Callum Orr, *b* 1949, — Elizabeth Jill Orr, *b* 1947. *Residence* – Rosehill, North Latch, Brechin, Angus.
Hon Helen Anne Boyd, *b* 1919: *m* 1939, David Miles Lubbock (*see* B Avebury, colls), who *d* 1992. *Residence* – Kapanda, Newton of Stracathro, Brechin, Angus DD9 7QQ.

Boyle, Viscount; son of Earl of Shannon.

Boyle of Marston, Baron; title of Earl of Cork and Orrery on Roll of HL.

BOYNE, VISCOUNT (Hamilton-Russell) Sits as BARON BRANCEPETH (UK 1866) (Viscount I 1717)

NEC·TIMEO · NEC · SPERNO

I neither fear nor despise

GUSTAVUS MICHAEL GEORGE HAMILTON-RUSSELL, 10th Viscount; *b* 10 Dec 1931; *s* 1942; *ed* Eton; KStJ; Lt (ret) Gren Gds, a JP and DL for Shropshire; Dep Chm Telford Development Corpn 1976-82, Dir Nat Westminster Bank 1976-90, and Private Patients Plan since 1986; Dir Ludlow Race Club; Lord in Waiting to HM since 1981: *m* 1956, Rosemary Anne, da of Sir Denis Frederick Bankes Stucley, 5th Bt, and has had issue.

Arms – Quarterly: 1st and 4th argent, between two chevronels a cinquefoil, the whole between three cross crosslets fitchée sable, *Russell*; 2nd and 3rd gules, three cinquefoils pierced ermine, *Hamilton*. **Crests** – 1st, a goat passant argent, collared gemelle, and charged on the body with an escallop sable, *Russell*; 2nd, out of a ducal crown, or, an oak tree fructed proper, and penetrated transversely in the main stem by a frame-saw proper, the frame gold, above the motto, "Through," *Hamilton*. **Supporters** – Two mermaids proper, hair dishevelled or, each holding in the exterior hand a mirror, of the last. **Seat** – Burwarton, Bridgnorth, Shropshire. *Club* – White's.

SON LIVING

Hon GUSTAVUS MICHAEL STUCLEY, *b* 27 May 1965; *ed* Harrow, and RAC Cirencester; ARICS: *m* 1991, Lucy, da of George Potter, of Foxdale, Bunbury, Cheshire, and has issue living, Emelia Rose, *b* 1994. *Residence* – Dingle Leys, Burwarton, Bridgnorth, Shropshire.

DAUGHTERS LIVING AND DECEASED

Hon Caroline Veronica, *b* 1957: *m* 1975 (*m diss* 1990), David George Fothergill Banks, FRICS, and has issue living, Richard George Fothergill, *b* 1977, — Georgina Emma, *b* 1980. *Residence* – Upper Norton, Bromyard, Herefords.
Hon Sara Emma, *b* 1959: *m* 1981 (*m diss* 1987), Nigel Anthony Twiston-Davies (*see* Archdale, Bt, colls), and *d* as the result of an accident 1989.
Hon Lucy Jane, *b* 1961: *m* 1st, 1983 (*m diss* 1986), Patrick James Bailey, yst son of Sir Derrick Thomas Louis Bailey, 3rd Bt; 2ndly, 1989, Simon E. H. Sherwood, son of Nathaniel Edward Carwardine Sherwood, of Easthorpe Hall, Colchester, Essex, and has issue living (by 2nd *m*), Jack Edward, *b* 1992, — Anna, *b* 1993. *Residence* – Summerdown, E Ilsley, nr Newbury, Berks.

UNCLE LIVING (*son of 9th Viscount*)

Hon Richard Gustavus, DSO, LVO, *b* 1909; *ed* Eton; Brig late 17th/21st Lancers; a Member of HM's Body Guard of Hon Corps of Gentlemen-at-Arms since 1956, Standard Bearer since 1977; High Sheriff Yorks 1968, and DL since 1973; 1939-45 War in N Africa and Italy (DSO and Bar); DSO 1943 (Bar 1944), LVO (4th class) 1977: *m* 1939, Hon Pamela Penelope Cayzer, who *d* 1987, da of 1st Baron Rotherwick, and has issue living, Brian Gustavus (c/o C. Hoare & Co, 37 Fleet St, EC4), *b* 1940; *ed* Eton; Col 17th/21st Lancers: *m* 1st, 1967, Lea, only da of Col Harry Noël Havelock Wild, of Shelley Court, Tite St, Chelsea; 2ndly, 1982, Sarah Julianne, da of late Reginald Waugh Harris, of Greenside Cottage, Wombleton, N Yorks, and formerly wife of Richard Jeremy Colebrook-Robjent, and has issue living (by 1st *m*), Henry William Gustavus *b* 1969, Victoria Essex Lea *b* 1976, — Richard Desmond (Mincinbury, Barley, Royston, Herts), *b* 1943; *ed* Eton; Commd 17th/21st Lancers: *m* 1965, Prudence Sophia, da of late Maj R. P. Pockney, of The Old Barn, Bishopthorpe, York, and has issue living, Charles Richard *b* 1965; Capt Queen's Royal Lancers: *m* 1993, Claire Fiona, da of Ian Dussek, of Little Allens, Plaxtol, Kent, Emma Sophia *b* 1968, Katharine Roseanna *b* 1972, — Veronica Anne, *b* 1949: *m* 1971, Nicholas Michael Houssemayne Jones, of 12 Paulton's St, SW3 5DR, and has issue living, Oliver Mark *b* 1977, Rowena Rose *b* 1975. *Residence* – South Hill House, Cornbury Park, Charlbury, Oxon.

AUNT LIVING (*Daughter of 9th Viscount*)

Hon Rosemary Katharine (*Lady Forbes*), *b* 1921: *m* 1942, 22nd Lord Forbes. *Residence* – Balforbes, Alford, Aberdeenshire.

COLLATERAL BRANCHES LIVING

Issue of late Major Hon John Hamilton-Russell, MC, 3rd son of 9th Viscount, *b* 1911, *ka* 1943: *m* 1937, Lady Diana Legge (who *d* 1970, having *m* 2ndly, 1946, Lt-Col A. L. Matthews), da of 7th Earl of Dartmouth:—
James Gustavus, MBE, *b* 1938; *ed* Eton; Col Household Cavalry (ret); MBE (Mil) 1976; FIMgt: *m* 1965, Alison, da of late Dr Sydney Haydn Heard, MBE, Lieut Bailiff and Jurat of R Court of Albecq, Guernsey, and has issue living, Mark John Gustavus, *b* 1969; *ed* Stowe, and RMA Sandhurst; commn'd RHG/D 1989, — Edward Haydn James (twin), *b* 1969; commn'd Life Guards 1990, — Julia Mary, *b* 1967.

Granddaughter of late Hon Claud Eustace Hamilton-Russell (*infra*):—
Issue of late Edric Claud Hamilton-Russell, *b* 1904, *d* 1984: *m* 1932, Helen Rosa (Cottage No 9, Headbourne Worthy House, Winchester, Hants SO23 7JG), da of late William Humble, of Skellow Grange, Doncaster:—

Ann Katharine, *b* 1933: *m* 1953, Lt-Col William Frank Philip Currie, Queen's R Irish Hus, of Rollington House, Redlynch, Salisbury, Wilts, and has issue living, Richard William, *b* 1955; Maj Queen's Royal Hussars, — Joanna, *b* 1959.

Issue of late Hon Claud Eustace Hamilton-Russell, 4th son of 8th Viscount, *b* 1871, *d* 1948: *m* 1899, Maria Lindsay, who *d* 1963, el da of Sir Lindsay Wood, 1st Bt (ext):—
Jean Katharine, *b* 1907: *m* 1931, Lt-Col Arthur Heywood Lonsdale, CBE, MC, Gren Gds, who *d* 1976 (*see* B Hamilton of Dalzell, 1930 Edn), and has issue living, Timothy Claud (The Old Laundry, Shavington, Market Drayton, Shropshire), *b* 1937: *m* 1964, Jennifer Elizabeth, only da of William Beck, of Tabley Grange, Knutsford, Cheshire, and has issue living, William Pemberton *b* 1970, Nichola Caroline *b* 1966. *Residence* – Shavington Grange, Market Drayton, Shropshire.

Granddaughters of late Maj Hon Arthur Hamilton-Russell, 5th son of 8th Viscount:—
Issue of late David Henry Gustavus Hamilton-Russell, *b* 1911, *d* 1988: *m* 1950, Pauline Albinia (103 Rowan House, Greycoat St, SW1P 2QD; 6 Torton Hill Rd, Arundel, W Sussex BN18 9LH), da of late George Penkivil Slade, KC, of St Michael's, Painswick, Glos:—
Marion Albinia, *b* 1952: *m* 1975, (Frederick) Simon Arden Armson, of Broad Oak, Hurley, Maidenhead, Berks SL6 5LW, and has issue living, Patrick David Arden, *b* 1982, — Meriel Albinia, *b* 1979, — Katherine Geraldine, *b* 1984. —— Georgiana Mary, *b* 1955: *m* 1983, John Kenrick Hayward, of 4 Herondale Av, SW18 3JL, 2nd son of late Surg-Col Edwin William Hayward, OBE, of Coln St Denis House, nr Cheltenham, Glos, and has issue living, Cicely Albinia, *b* 1985, — Edwina Mary, *b* 1987. —— Annette Katharine, *b* 1958: *m* 1989, Brian D. Lanaghan, of 100 Huron Rd, SW17 8RD, son of Richard Lanaghan, of Bath, and has issue living, James Henry David, *b* 1993, — Marina Katharine Albinia, *b* 1991. —— Margaret Louise, *b* 1960.

Issue of late Hon Eustace Scott Hamilton-Russell, OBE, 6th son of 8th Viscount, *b* 1878, *d* 1962: *m* 1906, Olive Mary, who *d* 1951, da of Col Francis Alexander Wolryche-Whitmore, formerly 3rd Batn Shropshire LI, of Dudmaston, Bridgnorth, Salop:—
Rachel Katharine (*Lady Labouchere*), *b* 1908: *m* 1st, 1930 (*m diss* 1940), Malcolm Findanus MacGregor, who *d* 1990 (*see* Mac-Gregor of MacGregor, Bt, colls); 2ndly, 1943, Sir George Peter Labouchere, GBE, KCMG, of Dudmaston, Bridgnorth, Salop.
Descendants, if any, of Henry Hamilton-Cox (*b* 1831), and his brother, Richard Sackville Hamilton-Cox (*b* 1834, *d* 1926, in USA), sons of Sackville Hamilton-Cox, 2nd son of Henry Hamilton-Cox (*d* 1821) (infra).
Descendants, if any, of Henry Alfred Hamilton-Cox (*b* 1842), and his brother, James Wellesley Hamilton-Cox (*b* 1844), both of Chicago, Illinois, USA, sons of Henry Wellesley Hamilton-Cox, 3rd son of Henry Hamilton-Cox (*d* 1821) (infra).

Granddaughters of late William Hamilton-Cox (infra):—
Issue of late Walter Hamilton-Cox, *b* 1915, *d* 1993: *m* 1938, Lola (2209 2nd St, Peru, Illinois, USA), da of Clarence Bradley:—
Carolyn Jane, *b* 1940: *m* 1964, Francis Donovan, and has issue living, Michael William, *b* 1970. —— Linda Jean, *b* 1947: *m* 1st, 1967, Charles Entwistle; 2ndly, 1981, James Krysiak, and has issue living (by 1st *m*), Scott Alan, *b* 1972, — Melissa Ann, *b* 1969.

Granddaughter of late Henry Augustus Hamilton-Cox, only son of William John Hamilton-Cox, yst son of Henry Hamilton-Cox (*d* 1821), grandson of Hon Henry Hamilton, 3rd son of 1st Viscount:—
Issue of late William Hamilton-Cox, *b* 1884, *d* 1970: *m* 1910, Caroline, who *d* 1977, da of late William Colling:—
Louise Rose, *b* 1918: *m* 1942, Clinton Carlton King, Horologist, of 1115 Herbert St, Peru, Illinois, USA, and has issue living, James Hamilton, MD, FACP (93 Victoria Av, Galesburg, Illinois 61401, USA), *b* 1944: *m* 1968, Mary, da of late Kenneth Gibson, and has issue living, John Hamilton *b* 1971, James Thaddeus *b* 1973.

Grandchildren of late Sackville Berkeley Hamilton, el son of Sackville Deane Hamilton, grandson of Rt Hon Sackville Hamilton, 3rd son of Hon Henry Hamilton, MP, 3rd son of 1st Viscount:—
Issue of late Col Sackville William Sackville Hamilton, DSO, MBE, *b* 1882, *d* 1956: *m* 1920, Margaret Dowell, who *d* 1993, da of S. C. Hester, of Laleham, Isle of Thanet:—
James Berkeley Sackville (The Old Rectory, Acklam, Malton, Yorks YO17 9RG), *b* 1923; *ed* King's Coll, Camb (MA); Lt-Col RE (ret) (despatches 1946); Bursar Pocklington Sch, nr York 1972-88: *m* 1947, Mary Grizel, da of late Col Cecil Alexander Boyle, CIE, DSO (*see* E Glasgow, colls), and has issue living, Charles Patrick Sackville (Thrussendale Farm, Acklam, Malton, N Yorks), *b* 1949; *ed* Wellington Coll; MA (Camb): *m* 1980, Heather, da of T. Goodwin, of Mow Cop, Staffs, — Andrew James Sackville (Colorado Univ, USA), *b* 1951; *ed* Wellington Coll; MA (Oxon), MSc (Liverpool), MSc (London), PhD (Virginia Univ, USA), FRAS: *m* 1978, Catherine Clare, da of Dr R. A. Davidson, of Mombassa, Kenya, and has issue living, Jamie Wildrose Sackville *b* 1988, Jessica Liberty Sackville *b* 1984, — Nigel Ruaraidh Sackville (Bronwydd, Cross St, Bow St, Dyfed), *b* 1953; *ed* Wellington Coll; MA, PhD (Camb): *m* 1983, Dr Charmian A. G., da of Col J. J. G. Hunter, of Middle Farm, Codford St Mary, Wilts, and has issue living, Henry James Sackville *b* 1989, Alice Charlotte Sackville *b* 1991, — Patricia Margaret Sackville (The Mount Farm, Burythorpe, N Yorks), *b* 1956; *ed* Tudor Hall: *m* 1982, Richard Hall, son of W. W. L. Hall, of Burythorpe, N Yorks, and has issue living, Jonathan *b* 1983, Nicholas *b* 1984. —— Anne Margaret Sackville, *b* 1925; MA Camb: *m* 1950, David MacEwen, and has issue living, Diana Cushla, *b* 1951, — Helen Margaret, *b* 1953, — Penelope Anne Georgina, *b* 1965. *Residence* – 5 Nelson House, Nelson Place West, Bath BA1 2BA.
Issue of late Maj Charles Sackville Hamilton, *b* 1885, *d* 1971: *m* 1918, Averina Jane, who *d* 1973, eldest da of William Richardson Oliver, of Kil-na-Mulla, Buttevant, co Cork:—
Patricia May Sackville (The Garden Cottage, Fritham Court, Lyndhurst, Hants SO43 7HH), *b* 1924; ARCA (London): *m* 1948, Lt Derek Richard Spooner, RN, who *d* 1978, and has issue living, Richard Hamilton (3 Green Hill, High Wycombe, Bucks), *b* 1952; *ed* The King's Sch, Ely; BA, ACA: *m* 1978, Susan Elizabeth Ann, yr da of John Rowntree, of Kidford, Sussex, and has issue living, Victoria Emily Barbara *b* 1985, Catherine Esmé Averina *b* 1987, Elizabeth Sackville *b* 1990, — Jane Rosemary Eleanor, *b* 1955: *m* 1979, Lt-Col John Malcolm Carmichael Watson, The Queen's Own Hus; elder son of John Watson, of Northallerton, Yorks, and has issue living, Anna Patricia Louise *b* 1983, Edwina Rose Jane *b* 1986, Fenella Margaret Grace *b* 1990.

PREDECESSORS – (1) Gustavus Hamilton, PC, son of the Hon Sir Frederick Hamilton, KB, youngest son of 1st Lord Paisley (D Abercorn), a distinguished military commander and MP for co Donegal 1703, was *cr Baron Hamilton of Stackallan* 1715, and *Viscount Boyne* 1717 (peerage of Ireland); *d* 1723, s by his grandson (2) Gustavus, PC, 2nd Viscount; sat as MP for Newport, I of W, 1735; *d* unmarried 1746; s by his cousin (3) Frederick, 3rd Viscount; *dsp* 1772; s by his brother (4) Richard, 4th Viscount; *d* 1789, s by his son (5) Gustavus, 5th Viscount; *d* 1826; s by his son (6) Gustavus, 6th Viscount; *d* 1855; s by his son (7) Gustavus Frederick, 7th Viscount; *b* 1797; assumed by R licence the additional surname of Russell, and was *cr Baron Brancepeth* (peerage of United Kingdom) 1866: *m* 1828, Emma Maria, da of Matthew Russell, MP, of Brancepeth Castle; *d* 1870; s by his son (8) Gustavus Russell, 8th Viscount, *b* 1830: *m* 1858, Lady Katherine Frances Scott, who *d* 1903, da of 2nd Earl of Eldon; *d* 1907; s by his son (9) Gustavus William, 9th Viscount, *b* 1864: *m* 1906, Lady Margaret Selina Lascelles, CBE, who *d* 1978, da of 5th Earl of Harewood; *d* 1942; s by his grandson (10) Gustavus Michael George , son of late Hon Gustavus Lascelles Hamilton-Russell, Lieut Gren Gds (el son of 9th Viscount), who was *ka* 1940, 10th Viscount and present peer; also Baron Hamilton of Stackallan, and Baron Brancepeth.

BRABAZON OF TARA, BARON (Moore-Brabazon) (Baron UK 1942)

IVON ANTHONY MOORE-BRABAZON, 3rd Baron, b 20 Dec 1946; s 1974; ed Harrow; a Lord-in-Waiting 1984-86; DL Isle of Wight 1993; Under-Sec for Transport (Min for Aviation and Shipping) 1986-89, Min of State Foreign and Commonwealth Office 1989-90, Min of State for Transport 1990-92; a Member of London Stock Exchange 1972-84: m 1979, Harriet Frances, da of Mervyn Peter de Courcy Hamilton, of Harare, Zimbabwe, and has issue.

Arms – Quarterly; 1st and 4th gules on a bend or three martlets sable, *Brabazon*; 2nd and 3rd azure on a chief per pale argent and or three mullets gules, *Moore*. **Crests** – 1st a falcon rising, belled or, *Brabazon*; 2nd issuant from a coronet composed of eight mullets set upon a rim or a Moor's head and shoulders proper wreathed about the temples argent and azure, *Moore*. **Supporters** – On either side a gull volant over water supporting the shield with its beak all proper.
Address – House of Lords, SW1A 0PW.
Clubs – White's, Royal Yacht Sqdn, Pratt's.

SON LIVING

My life is vowed

Hon BENJAMIN RALPH, b 15 March 1983.

DAUGHTER LIVING

Hon Anabel Mary, b 1985.

PREDECESSORS – (1) JOHN THEODORE CUTHBERT Moore-Brabazon, GBE, MC, PC, son of Col Arthur Henry Moore-Brabazon, of Tara Hall, co Meath; b 1884; pioneer in aviation; made first flight by any Briton in Great Britain 1909; received first pilot's certificate issued by Roy Aero Club; PPS to Sec of State for Air 1919-21, Parl Sec, Min of Transport 1923-27, Min of Transport 1940-41, and Min of Aircraft Production 1941-42; MP for Chatham Div of Rochester (U) 1918-29, and for Wallasey 1931-42: cr Baron Brabazon of Tara, of Sandwich, co Kent (peerage of UK 1942): m 1906, Hilda Mary, who d 1977, da of Charles Henry Krabbé, of Buenos Aires; d 1964, s by his el son (2) DEREK CHARLES, CBE, 2nd Baron, b 1910; Member of London Stock Exchange; Chm S Kensington Conservative Assocn 1952-54, and Pres Kensington Conservative Assocn 1966-74: m 1939, Henrietta Mary, who d 1985, da of late Sir (Alfred) Rowland Clegg, and widow of Ivor Krabbé; d 1974; s by his only son (3) IVON ANTHONY, 3rd Baron and present peer.

BRABOURNE, BARON (Knatchbull) (Baron UK 1880, Bt E 1641)
(Title pronounced "Braybn")

JOHN ULICK KNATCHBULL, CBE, 7th Baron, and 16th Baronet; b 9 Nov 1924; s 1943; ed Eton and Oxford Univ; a film and television producer; formerly Capt Coldstream Gds; Pres Kent Trust for Nature Conservation, formerly Chm Caldecott Community, Chm of Govs of Norton Knatchbull Sch, Gov Wye Coll, Gordonstoun Sch 1964-94, and United World Colls; Pro Chancellor, Univ of Kent; Dir Thames Television; Fellow and Gov BFI; Member British Screen Advisory Council; Trustee Science Museum, British Academy of Film & TV Arts, Vice-Pres Royal Soc for Nature Conservation; 1939-45 War in SE Asia (wounded); CBE (Civil) 1993: m 26 Oct 1946, Lady Patricia Edwina Victoria Mountbatten (*Countess Mountbatten of Burma* in her own right), elder da of 1st Earl Mountbatten of Burma, and has had issue.

Arms – Quarterly: 1st and 4th argent, on a mount vert, two boars' erect, respecting each other sable, their forelegs resting against an oak tree proper, *Hugessen*; 2nd and 3rd azure, three cross crosslets fitchée between two bendlets or, *Knatchbull*. **Crests** – 1st, an oak tree proper, between two wings elevated, pinions azure, feathered or, *Hugessen*; 2nd, on a chapeau azure, turned up ermine, an ounce statant argent, spotted sable, *Knatchbull*. **Supporters** – On either side a leopard argent pelletty, gorged with an oak wreath vert, fructed gold, and holding in the mouth a cross crosslet fitchée or.
Residences – Newhouse, Mersham, Ashford, Kent TN25 6NQ; 39 Montpelier Walk, SW7 1JH.

My glory is in the cross

SONS LIVING AND DECEASED

NORTON LOUIS PHILIP (*Lord Romsey*) (Broadlands, Romsey, Hants SO51 9ZD), *b* 8 Oct 1947; *ed* Gordonstoun, and Univ of Kent; High Steward of Romsey since 1980: *m* 20 Oct 1979, Penelope Meredith, only da of Reginald Eastwood, of Son Vida, Palma de Mallorca, Spain, and has had issue (*see* Ctss Mountbatten of Burma).

Hon Michael-John Ulick (9 Queen's Elm Sq, SW3 6ED), *b* 24 May 1950; *ed* Gordonstoun, and Reading Univ: *m* 1 June 1985, Melissa Clare, only da of Judge Sir John Owen, of Bickerstaff House, Idlicote, Shipston-on-Stour, Warwicks, and has issue (*see* Ctss Mountbatten of Burma).

Hon Philip Wyndham Ashley (41 Montpelier Walk, SW7 1JH), *b* 2 Dec 1961; *ed* Gordonstoun, and Kent Univ: *m* 16 March 1991, Mrs Atalanta Vereker, da of late John Cowan, and formerly wife of Hugo Dominic Charles Medlicott Vereker (*see* V Gort, colls), and has issue (*see* Ctss Mountbatten of Burma).

Hon Nicholas Timothy Charles, *b* 18 Nov 1964; *k* with his grandfather, Earl Mountbatten of Burma, 1979.

Hon Timothy Nicholas Sean, *b* (twin)18 Nov 1964; *ed* Gordonstoun, Atlantic Coll, and Christ's Coll, Camb.

DAUGHTERS LIVING

Lady Joanna Edwina Doreen, *b* 5 March 1955; *ed* Benenden, Atlantic Coll, Kent Univ, and Columbia Univ, USA: *m* 3 Nov 1984, Baron Hubert Henry François du Breuil, yr son of Baron Bertrand Pernot du Breuil, of 52 Avenue d'Iena, 75116 Paris, and has issue (*see* Ctss Mountbatten of Burma).

Lady Amanda Patricia Victoria, *b* 26 June 1957; *ed* Benenden, Gordonstoun, Kent Univ, Peking Univ, and Goldsmith Coll, London: *m* 31 Oct 1987, Charles V. Ellingworth, eldest son of William Ellingworth, of Laughton, Leics, and has issue (*see* Ctss Mountbatten of Burma).

COLLATERAL BRANCHES LIVING

Grandchildren of Hon Adrian Norton KNATCHBULL-HUGESSEN, QC (infra):—
Issue of late Edward Herrick KNATCHBULL-HUGESSEN, *b* 1923, *d* 1955: *m* 1947, Mary Louise, who *d* 1969, da of Walter Asahel Newton, of Montreal:—
Kenneth Norton (31 Russell Hill, Toronto, Ontario, Canada M4V 2S9), *b* 1949: *m* 1969, Karen, da of Olaf Wolff, of Montreal, and has issue living, Arlo Edward, *b* 1970. —— Kathleen Mary, *b* 1950. —— Patricia Margaret, *b* 1952: *m* 19—, — Osgoode.

Issue of late Hon Adrian Norton KNATCHBULL-HUGESSEN, QC, 3rd son of 1st Baron, *b* 1891, *d* 1976: *m* 1922, Margaret Cecilia Ross, who *d* 1980 da of George Herrick Duggan, of 3636 McTavish St, Montreal:—
Andrew John (5 Beacon Rd, Kirkland, Quebec, Canada), *b* 1926: *m* 1952, Jane Frances, da of Douglas Gilfillan Currie, of Montreal, Canada, and has issue living, Brian Andrew, *b* 1954, — John, *b* 1958, — Wendy Jane (twin), *b* 1954, — Martha, *b* 1960. —— *Hon* James Cornelius (31 Elmdale Av, Ottawa, Canada K1M 1A1; Rideau Club), *b* 1933; *ed* Balliol Coll, Oxford, and McGill Univ, Montreal; Bar Quebec 1958; Puisne Judge of Superior Court and Court of Queen's Bench, Quebec 1972-73, Asso Ch Justice, Superior Court of Quebec 1973-83, since when Puisne Justice of Federal Court of Appeal of Canada: *m* 1958, Mary Rosamond, da of R. Ewart Stavert, of Montreal, and has issue living, Jaime William, *b* 1959, — Alexander Ewart, *b* 1965, — Ross Adrian, *b* 1969, — Kathleen Jill, *b* 1960, — Alicia Mary, *b* 1962. —— Mary Cecelia, *b* 1929: *m* 1955, Stephen John Keynes, of 16 Canonbury Park South, N1, yr son of Sir Geoffrey Langdon Keynes, and has issue living, Gregory Robert Edward, *b* 1956, — Toby William, *b* 1959, — Zachary Edmund, *b* 1962, — Elizabeth Harriet, *b* 1957, — Martha Paganel, *b* 1961.

(In remainder to Baronetcy only)

Granddaughters of late Rev Reginald Bridges Knatchbull-Hugessen, 7th son of 9th baronet:—
Issue of late Major Everard Knatchbull-Hugessen; *b* 1871; *d* 1946: *m* 1908, Grace Marshall, who *d* 1937, da of James Arthur Hindmarsh, of Ayr:—
Mary, OBE (Leylands, Coleman's Hatch, Sussex), *b* 1909; formerly Regional Woman Fire Officer, Headquarters, National Fire Ser; a Serving Sister of Order of St John of Jerusalem; OBE (Civil) 1946: *m* 1932, William Paterson Keith, MVO, who *d* 1963. —— Pleasance Anne, *b* 1920: *m* 1948, John Stuart Comery, MC, of Home Farm, Upper Hayesden, Tonbridge, Kent, and has issue living, William Knatchbull, *b* 1952, — Patricia Mary, *b* 1950.
Issue of late Sir Hughe Montgomery Knatchbull-Hugessen, KCMG, *b* 1886, *d* 1971: *m* 1912, Mary, who *d* 1978, da of Brig-Gen Sir Robert Gordon Gilmour, 1st Bt, CVO, CB, DSO, *cr* 1926:—
Alethea (23 Emden House, Barton Lane, Old Headington, Oxford), *b* 1918.

Grandchildren of late Brig Gen George Wyndham Chichester Knatchbull, CMG, 4th son of late Lieut-Gen Reginald Edward Knatchbull (infra):—
Issue of late Lt-Col Wyndham Marsden Knatchbull, *b* 1901, *d* 1977: *m* 1934, Eileen Mary, who *d* 1986, el da of late Lt-Col William Chapman Croly, DSO, RAMC:—
Patrick Wyndham (16 Seafront Rd, Cultra, co Down BT18 OBB), *b* 1936; Cdr RD: *m* 1966, Mary, da of late L. F. Kelly, of Tile Hatch, Bishops Down Park Rd, Tunbridge Wells, and has issue living, Simon Marsden, *b* 1967, — Andrew Wyndham, *b* 1969, — Felicity Jane, *b* 1972. —— Michael Walter (Gambles Lodge, Upper Mountown, Dun Laoghaire, co Dublin) (twin), *b* 1936: *m* 1959, Rhona Dorothy, da of late John Sinclair Gunning, of Holywood, co Down, and has issue living, Richard Edward Walter, *b* 1971, — Mark Wyndham John, *b* 1978, — Fiona Bridgid, *b* 1962: *m* 1987, David Holmes, and has issue living, Philip Edward Knatchbull *b* 1993, Polly Amanda *b* 1991, — Lucy Rhona, *b* 1964: *m* 1988, Robert O'Riordan, and has issue living, Samson Robert *b* 1992, — Gillian Mary, *b* 1966. —— Bridget Eileen Mary, *b* 1943: *m* 1st, 1964 (*m diss* 1971), James Seymur Emerson (*see* Keane, Bt); 2ndly, 1974, Robert Ernest Somekh, of 6 Lyndewode Rd, Cambridge CB1 2HL.

Descendants, if any, of Reginald Edward Knatchbull (*b* 1893), late Capt IA Res of Officers, only son of Owen Edward Knatchbull, 6th and yst son of Lieut-Gen Reginald Edward Knatchbull, 8th son of 8th baronet.
Granddaughters of late Lt-Col Francis Knatchbull, 3rd son of Rev Wadham Knatchbull, LLD, 3rd son of 4th Bt:—
Issue of late Maj Wyndham Persse Knatchbull, *b* 1873, *d* 1967: *m* 1911, Sybil Mathilde, who *d* 1957, da of late Ulick Burke (Burke, Bt, colls):—
Angela Alice, *b* 1912: *m* 1948, Reginald Cyril Neville Owbridge, who *d* 1975, of 41 Stockens Green, Knebworth, Herts SG3 6DQ, and has issue living, Anthony Wyndham (26 Cherry Tree Rd, Chinnor, Oxford OX9 4QZ), *b* 1949: *m* 1972, Barbara Jean, only da of Lawrence Lacy, of Chesham, Bucks. —— Zara Eleanor (93 Livermore Green, Werrington, Peterborough PE4 5DQ), *b* 1920; 1939-45 War with ATS: *m* 1st, 1942 (*m diss* 1953), John Mackay; 2ndly, 1953, Christopher Jocelyn Lapage, who *d* 1990, and has issue living (by 2nd *m*) Fiona Anne, *b* 1954: *m* 1976, Hamdy Taha.

Grandsons of late Maj Wyndham Persse Knatchbull (ante):—
Issue of late Charles Norton Knatchbull, *b* 1918, *d* 1980: *m* 1940, Jacqueline Nora (Batch Farm, Kilmersdon, Bath), da of Henry Presland Veall, of Netley, Hants:—
Henry Norton (19 Riverside Rd, Westmoors, Ferndown, Dorset), *b* 1942; *ed* Stanbridge Earls Sch, Romsey: *m* 1988, Jenny Elizabeth, yst da of Roy Brown, of Ferndown, Dorset. —— Richard Wyndham (Batch Farm, Kilmersdon, Bath), *b* 1947; *ed*

Hurn Court, Christchurch: *m* 1970, Susan Ann Russle, only da of Arthur Candy, of Mells, Somerset, and has issue living, Paul Wyndham, *b* 1973, — James Wyndham, *b* 1975.

(Not in remainder to Baronetcy)

Grandchildren of Herbert Thomas KNATCHBULL-HUGESSEN, MP, 9th son of 9th baronet:—
Issue of late Paul Lionel Knatchbull-Hugessen, *b* 1874, *d* 1958: *m* 1906, Marie Blanche, who *d* 1945, yst da of Remi Poullin, of St Boniface, Manitoba:—
Herbert Clifford, *b* 1907: *m* 1936, Violet, el da of Samuel Oliver Emily Sutherland, of Edson, Alberta, Canada, and has issue living, Darolyn, *b* 1941.
Issue of late Edward Knatchbull-Hugessen, *b* 1877, *d* 1969: *m* 1920, Edith Elizabeth, who *d* 1957, da of Charles Edward Chatfield, of Bloomsbury:—
Christina Pauline (11 Greville Lodge, Avenue Rd, Highgate, N6 5DP), *b* 1931.
Issue of late George Knatchbull-Hugessen, *b* 1883, *d* 1966: *m* 1910, Jessie, who *d* 1961, da of John Downie Kay, of Brinkley, Newmarket, Suffolk:—
Peter Merrick (Ropley House, Ropley, Hants), *b* 1915; *ed* Wadham Coll, Oxford; late Capt RA; served World War II with 111th Field Regt, and 6th Indian Field Regt; formerly Headmaster Papplewick Sch, Ascot: *m* 1992, Anna-Rose, da of late Maj H. Bramwell, of The White House, Mallow, co Cork, and widow of Lord James Charles Crichton-Stuart (*see* M Bute).

Grandchildren of late Edward Knatchbull-Hugessen (ante):—
Issue of late Denis Norton Knatchbull-Hugessen, *b* 1923, *d* 1982: *m* 1947, Mavis Josephine, who *d* 1980, elder da of Henry Albert Peard, of Bath:—
Mark Wyndham (11 Frayslea, Cowley Rd, Uxbridge, Middx), *b* 1953. —— Bernice Simone, *b* 1949: *m* 1975, Raymond Charles Morley, of 112 Springdale Rd, Corfe Mullen, Wimborne, Dorset, and has issue living, Joseph Ronan Charles, *b* 1983, — Jessica Natasha, *b* 1985. —— Teresa Frances, *b* 1951: *m* 1971, Donald Pooley, of 145 Cowley Rd, Uxbridge, Middx, and has issue living, Matthew Lee, *b* 1970, — Damon Ross, *b* 1972.

Grandchildren of late George Knatchbull-Hugessen (ante):—
Issue of late Robin John Kay Knatchbull-Hugessen, *b* 1921, *d* 1986: *m* 1st, 1945 (*m diss* 1956), Enid Mabel, da of Thomas Marlow, of Highgate, N6; 2ndly, 1958, Barbara Anne Wilcox (Cilwern, Talley, Llandeilo, Dyfed):—
(By 1st *m*) Peter Wyndham, *b* 1947: *m* 1975 (*m diss* 1988), Henrietta Frances, da of Col John Ellis Spencer, of Hill Farm, Swalcliffe, Oxon, and has issue living, Thomas Michael, *b* 1977, — William Peter, *b* 1979, — Lydia Victoria, *b* 1982, — Holly Frances, *b* 1984. —— (By 2nd *m*) Simon Stephen (2 Rush House, Cedar Rd, Farnborough, Hants GU14 7AX), *b* 1960: *m* 1990, Tracy Helen, eldest da of G. Burns, of Hook, Hants. —— Sally Anne, MVO, *b* 1959; MVO 1989: *m* 1987, Dr Thomas P. O'Brien, of 616 Wyndhurst Av, Baltimore, Maryland 21210, USA, and has issue living, William Thomas Robin, *b* 1991. —— Jane Elizabeth, *b* 1962.

PREDECESSORS – (1) Rt Hon EDWARD HUGESSEN Knatchbull, PC, 6th son of the Rt Hon Sir Edward Knatchbull, MP, 9th Bt; *b* 1829; assumed by R licence the additional surname of Hugessen 1849; MP for Sandwich (*L*) 1857-80; was a Lord of the Treasury 1859-66, Under-Sec of State for Home Depart 1866, and 1868-71, and Under Sec for Colonies 1871-4; *cr Baron Brabourne*, of Brabourne, co Kent (peerage of United Kingdom) 1880: *m* 1st, 1852, Anna Maria Elizabeth, who *d* 1889, da of late Rev Marcus R. Southwell, of St Stephen's Herts; 2ndly, 1890, Ethel Mary, who *d* 1929, da of Col Sir George Gustavus Walker, KCB, of Crawfordton, Dumfriesshire, *d* 1893: *s* by his el son (2) EDWARD, 2nd Baron, *b* 1857; MP for Rochester (*L*) 1889-92; *m* 1880, Hon Amy Virginia Beaumont, who *d* 1949, da of 1st Baron Allendale: *d* 1909; *s* by his son, (3) WYNDHAM WENTWORTH, 3rd Baron; *b* 1885; Lt Gren Gds; *ka* 1915: *s* by his uncle (4) CECIL MARCUS, 4th Baron; *b* 1863; *s* in 1917 his cousin as 13th *Baronet* of Mersham Hatch (*cr* 1641): *m* 1893, Helena Regina Frederica, who *d* 1919, da of late Hermann von Flesch-Brunningen, Imperial Councillor of Vienna; *d* 1933: *s* by his only son (5) MICHAEL HERBERT RUDOLPH, GCSI, GCIE, MC, 5th Baron; *b* 1895; assumed by deed poll 1919, the surname of Knatchbull only; was MP for Ashford Div of Kent (*C*) 1931-3, and Gov of Bombay 1933-7, and of Bengal 1937-9 (acted as Viceroy of India, June-Sept 1938): *m* 1919, Lady Doreen Geraldine Browne, CI, who *d* 1979, da of 6th Marquess of Sligo: *d* 1939; *s* by his son (6) NORTON CECIL MICHAEL, 6th Baron: *b* 1922; Lt Gren Gds; served 1939-45 War (wounded, prisoner); *k* on active service (shot by the Germans after he had escaped from a prison train in N Italy and had been recaptured) 1943; *s* by his brother (7) JOHN ULICK, 7th Baron and present peer.

BRADBURY, BARON (Bradbury) (Baron UK 1925)

JOHN BRADBURY, 3rd Baron; *b* 17 March 1940; *s* 1994; *ed* Gresham's Sch, Holt, and Bristol Univ: *m* 1968, Susan, da of late William Liddiard, of E Shefford, Berks, and has issue.

Arms – Sable, a chevron ermine, between in chief two buckles and in base a fleur-de-lis argent **Crest** – In front of two ostrich feathers in saltire argent, a boar's head erect proper. **Supporters** – *Dexter*, a raven; *sinister*, a dove; both proper.
Residence – 10 Clifton Hill, NW8.

SONS LIVING

Hon JOHN, *b* 1973.
Hon Benjamin, *b* 1975.

SISTER LIVING

Hon Elizabeth Joan (twin), *b* 1940: *m* 1965, Warren Hansen, of 2 Sargent Pl, Waxahachie, Texas 75165, USA, and has issue living, Karl Geoffrey, *b* 1971, — Christine Joan, *b* 1967.

HALF-SISTER LIVING

Hon Anne, *b* 1947: *m* 1970, Alastair James Ker-Lindsay, and has issue living, James *b* 1972, — Mark *b* 1973, — John Alexander, *b* 1977, —

Justice, equity, and good faith

Adam, *b* 1979, — Laura, *b* 1985.

UNCLE LIVING (son of 1st Baron)

Hon Paul, *b* 1915; *ed* Westminster, and Brasenose Coll, Oxford: *m* 1940, Margaret Amy, da of late J. W. Stammers, of Purley, Surrey, and has issue living, Richard (Milcote House, Long Wood Drive, Jordans, Beaconsfield, Bucks), *b* 1941: *m* 1966, Elizabeth Mary Auchinleck, da of Douglas C. L. Love, of 3 Glenmore House, Richmond, Surrey, and has issue living, Clare *b* 1967, Jane (twin) *b* 1967, Philippa *b* 1972, — James (Barnford, Holy Cross, Clent, Worcs) *b* 1945: *m* 1967, Patricia Mary, da of late Hedley A. Funnell, of Bybrook House, Longdean, Yatton Keynell, Chippenham, Wilts, and has issue living, Anthony James *b* 1969, Jonathan Paul *b* 1971, Charlotte Ann *b* 1973, — David (Pencot, Tresham, Wotton-under-Edge, Glos), *b* 1950: *m* 1973, Janet Ann Salier, da of David H. Davidson, of Battramsley Cottage, Boldre, Lymington, Hants, and has issue living, Caroline Salier *b* 1978, Anna Sarah *b* 1980. *Residence* – Chelvey Batch, Brockley, Bristol, Avon.

MOTHER LIVING

Joan, only da of Walter Dingle Knight, of Darley, Addlestone Surrey: *m* 1939 (*m diss* 1946), Hon John Bradbury (later 2nd Baron Bradbury), who *d* 1994. *Residence* –

WIDOW LIVING OF SECOND BARON

GWERFYL (*Dowager Baroness Bradbury*), da of late E. Stanton Roberts, of Gellifor, nr Ruthin, Denbighshire: *m* 1946, as his 2nd wife, the 2nd Baron, who *d* 1994. *Residence* – 1 Irakl St, Engomi, Nicosia, Cyprus.

PREDECESSORS – (1) *Sir* JOHN SWANWICK Bradbury, GCB, son of late John Bradbury, of Winsford, Cheshire; *b* 1872; Under Treasurer of Natal 1904-5, Private Sec to Chancellor of Exchequer (Rt Hon Herbert H. Asquith, MP) 1905-8, Principal Clerk in the Treasury, and First Treasury Officer of Accounts 1908-11, Joint Permanent Sec to the Treasury 1913-19, Principal British Delegate to Reparation Commn (Paris) 1919-25, Chm of International Relief Credits Committee 1920, of National Food Council 1925-9, and of Bankers' Clearing House Committee and British Bankers' Asso 1929-30 and 1935-6; *cr* Baron Bradbury, of Winsford, co Chester (peerage of United Kingdom) 1925: *m* 1911, Hilda Maude, who *d* 1949, 2nd da of William Arthur Kirby, of Goldhurst Terrace, Hampstead, NW; *d* 1950; *s* by his son (2) JOHN, 2nd Baron, *b* 1914: *m* 1st, 1939 (*m diss* 1946), Joan, only da of Walter Dingle Knight, of Darley, Addlestone, Surrey; 2ndly, 1946, Gwerfyl, da of late E. Stanton Roberts, of Gellifor, nr Ruthin, Denbighshire; *d* 1994; *s* by his only son (3) JOHN, 3rd Baron and present peer.

BRADFORD, EARL OF (Bridgeman) (Earl UK 1815, Bt E 1660)

NEC·TEMERE·NEC·TIMIDE
Neither rashly nor timidly

RICHARD THOMAS ORLANDO BRIDGEMAN, 7th Earl, and 12th Baronet; *b* 3 Oct 1947; *s* 1981; *ed* Harrow, and Trin Coll, Camb; patron of five livings: *m* 1979, Joanne Elizabeth, el da of Benjamin Miller, of 42 Pembroke Road, W8, and has issue.

Arms – Sable, ten plates, four, three, two, and one; on a chief argent, a lion passant ermine. **Crest** – A demi-lion rampant argent, holding in the paws a wreath of laurel proper. **Supporters** – Two leopards guardant gules pelletée.
Seat – Weston Park, Shifnal, Shropshire. *Residence* – Woodlands House, Weston-under-Lizard, Shifnal, Shropshire TF11 8PX.

SONS LIVING

ALEXANDER MICHAEL ORLANDO (*Viscount Newport*), *b* 6 Sept 1980.
Hon Henry Gerald Orlando, *b* 1982.
Hon Benjamin Thomas Orlando, *b* 1987.

DAUGHTER LIVING

Lady Alicia Rose, *b* 1990.

BROTHER LIVING

Hon Charles Gerald Orlando (Albion Hayes Farm, Bomere Heath, Shrewsbury, Shropshire), *b* 1954; *ed* Harrow, Warwick Univ, and RAC Cirencester; ARICS 1993: *m* 1982, Nicola Marie-Thérèse, only da of Brian Sales, of Congleton, Cheshire, and has issue living, James Edward Charles Orlando, *b* 1978, — Robert Gerald Orlando, *b* 1983, — Nicholas, *b* 1991.

SISTERS LIVING

Lady Serena Mary BRIDGEMAN, *b* 1949; has resumed her maiden name: *m* 1978 (*m diss* 1989), Richard Arnold Andrew. *Residences* – Dell House, Whitebridge, Inverness-shire IV1 2UP; Flat 1, 3 Westgate Terr, SW10 9BT.
Lady Caroline Louise, *b* 1952: *m* 1974, Brian Martin Garnell, of 16 Holland Park Av, W11 3QU, and has issue living, Thomas Henry Michael *b* 1986, — Benedict Charles Orlando, *b* 1990, — Daniel Gerald Orlando, *b* 1993, — Tara Serena Clare, *b* 1983.

AUNT LIVING (Daughter of 5th Earl)

Lady Anne Pamela (*Lady Anne Cowdray*), *b* 1913: *m* 1939 (*m diss* 1950), 3rd Viscount Cowdray. *Residence* – Broadleas, Devizes, Wilts.

COLLATERAL BRANCHES LIVING

Issue of late Col Hon Henry George Orlando Bridgeman, DSO, MC, yst son of 4th Earl, *b* 1882, *d* 1972: *m* 1930, Joan, who *d* 1991, da of late Hon Bernard Constable-Maxwell (*see* L Herries of Terregles, colls):—
Peter Orlando Ronald, TD (Fallodon Hall, Embleton, Alnwick, Northumberland), *b* 1933; Lt-Col R Northumberland Fus (TA); TD 1968, DL Northumberland 1983; *m* 1967, Sarahjane, da of Patrick Corbett, of Silverlands, Boar's Head, Crowborough, and has issue living, Mark George Orlando, *b* 1968, — Emma Virginia, *b* 1969, — Davina Sacha, *b* 1972. —— John Henry Orlando (Boreland House, Lockerbie, Dumfriesshire), *b* 1938: *m* 1970, Susan Gay, da of late A. Leonard Hill, of Boreland of Dryfe, Lockerbie, Dumfriesshire, and has issue living, Camilla Jane, *b* 1971, — Alexandra Mary, *b* 1973. —— Mary Helena, *b* 1932: *m* 1960, William Simon Rodolph Kenyon-Slaney (*see* B Kenyon, colls). —— Alice Christina, *b* 1936: *m* 1967, Bruce Mckenzie, of Haselbech Hall, Northants NN6 9LG; Min of Agric, Kenya, and has issue living, Kim Alexander, *b* 1969, — James Malcolm, *b* 1971.

Grandchildren of late Brig-Gen Hon Francis Charles Bridgeman, 2nd son of 3rd Earl:—
Issue of late Reginald Francis Orlando Bridgeman, CMG, MVO, *b* 1884, *d* 1968: *m* 1923, Olwen Elizabeth, who *d* 1985, da of Maurice Jones, MPS:—
Henry Clive Orlando, *b* 1946; *ed* Harrow, and Trin Coll, Camb. —— Victoria Mary (71 Lauderdale Mansions, Lauderdale Rd, W9 1LX), *b* 1926: 1939-45 War with WRNS. —— Olwen Valery, *b* 1928: BA London: *m* 1962, Anthony Mark Barrington Golding, MB, FFPHM, of 12 Clifton Hill, NW8, and Keepers Cottage, Byworth, Petworth, Sussex, and has issue living, Richard Mark Orlando, *b* 1965; MEng & Man: *m* 1990 (*m diss* 1992), Sarah Dolman, and has issue living, Leo Dolman *b* 1992, — Rosemary Victoria Anne, *b* 1963; LLB; Solicitor, — Catherine Elizabeth Marian, *b* 1967; BMedSc, MB BS, — Charlotte Valery Patricia, *b* 1970.
Issue of late Com Francis Paul Orlando Bridgeman, RN, *b* 1888, *d* 1930: *m* 1922, Alice, who *d* 1979, da of Herman Greverus Kleinwort, of 45 Belgrave Square, SW1:—
Gerald William Paul Orlando, *b* 1929: *m* 1965, Mrs Rosemarie Ingrams, da of Willis Tomlinson. *Residences* – Dowdeswell Rookery, Andoversford, Glos; 43 Cheval Place, SW7; 51 Mixnam's Lane, Chertsey, Surrey. —— Jeannine Patricia, *b* 1923: *m* 1st, 1951 (*m diss* 1955), Alan Forde Scott, late Tanganyika Admin Ser; 2ndly, 1969, Rear Adm Josef Czeslaw Bartosik, CB, DSC, of Well House, Donnington, Moreton-in-Marsh, Glos, and of 33 Cheval Place, SW7. —— Marigold Helen, *b* 1925. *Residences* – Never End, Foxcote, Andoversford, Cheltenham, Glos GL54 4LP; 43 Cheval Place, SW7 1EW.

Grandchildren of late Maj Roger Orlando Bridgeman, only son of Charles George Orlando Bridgeman, yr son of Rev Hon George Thomas Orlando Bridgeman, 2nd son of 2nd Earl:—
Issue of late Richard Lynedoch Orlando Bridgeman, *b* 1931, *d* 1982: *m* 1965, Romayne Georgette Ord, who *d* 1985, only da of late Ingram Ord Capper, of The Mill, Polstead, Suffolk:—
(Leopold) Orlando, *b* 1968; *ed* Harrow. *Residence* – 8 Cranbourne Court, Albert Bridge Rd, SW11 4PE. —— Constantine Orlando, *b* 1970. *Residence* – 52 Ebury Mews, SW1. —— Celestine Victoria, *b* 1966: *m* 1988, Roger D. Bramley, of late Richard Bramley, of Unstone, Derbys, and has issue living, Cressida Romayne, *b* 1994. *Residences* – 40 Anhalt Rd, SW11 4NX; Chedglow Barn Cottage, Crudwell, Malmesbury, Wilts.

Grandsons of late Rev Hon John Robert Orlando Bridgeman, 3rd son of 2nd Earl:—
Issue of late Rt Hon William Clive Bridgeman, who was *cr Viscount Bridgeman* 1929 (see that title).

PREDECESSORS – (1) Sir ORLANDO Bridgeman, successively Lord Chief Baron of Exchequer, Lord Chief Justice of Common Pleas, and Lord Keeper of Great Seal; *cr* a *Baronet* 1660; *d* 1674; *s* by his son (2) Sir JOHN, 2nd Bt; *d* 1710; *s* by his son (3) Sir JOHN, 3rd Bt; *d* 1747; *s* by his son (4) Sir ORLANDO, 4th Bt, MP for Shrewsbury, who *m* Lady Ann Newport, da of Richard, 2nd Earl of Bradford (title extinct 1762, on death of 4th Earl); *d* 1764; *s* by his son (5) Sir HENRY, 5th Bt, *cr Baron Bradford* (peerage of Great Britain) 1794; *d* 1800; *s* by his son (6) ORLANDO, 2nd Baron, *cr Viscount Newport* and *Earl of Bradford* (peerage of United Kingdom) 1815; *d* 1825; *s* by his son (7) George Augustus Frederick Henry, 2nd Earl, *b* 1789: *m* 1st, 1818, Georgina Elizabeth, who *d* 1842, da of Sir Thomas Moncreiffe, 5th Bt; 2ndly, 1849, Helen, who *d* 1869, da of Æneas Mackay, of Scotston, and widow of Sir David Moncreiffe, 6th Bt; *d* 1865; *s* by his son (8) ORLANDO GEORGE CHARLES, PC, 3rd Earl, *b* 1819; sometime Lord-Lieut of Salop; MP for S Shropshire (C) 1842-65; Vice-Chamberlain of HM Queen Victoria's Household 1852 and 1858-9, Lord Chamberlain 1866-8, and Master of the Horse 1874-80 and 1885-6: *m* 1844, Hon Selina Louisa Forester, who *d* 1894, da of 1st Baron Forester: *d* 1898; *s* by his el son (9) GEORGE CECIL ORLANDO, 4th Earl, *b* 1845; Lieut 1st Life Guards 1864-7, and Capt Shropshire Yeo 1867; MP for N Shropshire (C) 1867-85: *m* 1869, Lady Ida Frances Annabella Lumley, who *d* 1936, 2nd da of 9th Earl of Scarbrough; *d* 1915; *s* by his el son (10) ORLANDO, 5th Earl; *b* 1873; was Assist Private Sec of State for Foreign Affairs (Marquess of Salisbury) 1898-1900, and to Prime Min (Marquess of Salisbury) 1902, Private Sec to Prime Min (Rt Hon A. J. Balfour, MP) 1902-5, and a Lord-in-Waiting to HM 1919-24: *m* 1904, Hon Margaret Cecilia Bruce, who *d* 1949, el da of 2nd Baron Aberdare; *d* 1957; *s* by his only son (11) GERALD MICHAEL ORLANDO, 6th Earl, *b* 1911; Vice-Lieut of Salop 1970-74; a Crown Estate Commr 1956-67; Pres of Country Landowners' Assocn 1955-57, and of Timber Growers Organisation 1962-64, and Chm of Forestry Cttee of Great Britain 1964-66; received Freedom of Shrewsbury 1957; 1939-45 War (despatches): *m* 1946, Mary Willoughby, who (*d* 1986), da of late Lt-Col Thomas Hassard Montgomery, DSO, of Cadogan House, Shrewsbury; *d* 1981; *s* by his el son (12) RICHARD THOMAS ORLANDO, 7th Earl and present peer; also Viscount Newport, and Baron Bradford.

BRAIN, BARON (Brain) (Baron UK 1962, Bt UK 1954)

I am, therefore I think

The mind the star of the brain

CHRISTOPHER LANGDON BRAIN, 2nd Baron and 2nd Baronet; *b* 30 Aug 1926; *s* 1966; *ed* Leighton Park Sch, and New Coll, Oxford (MA), ARPS: *m* 1953, Susan Mary, da of George Philip Morris, and has issue.

Arms – Per pale or and argent, three cats' heads erased gules. **Crest** – A falcon sable armed and belled or, supporting with the dexter claw a representation of the silver staff of office of the President of the Royal College of Physicians of London proper. **Supporters** – *Dexter*, a lion statant guardant or, gorged with a coronet composed of fleurs-de-lis argent, set upon a rim gobony silver and azure, holding in the interior paw a pomegranate slipped proper; *sinister*, a griffin gold beaked gules, gorged with a like coronet, holding in the interior claw a poppy slipped also proper.
Residence – The Old Rectory, Cross St, Moretonhampstead, Devon TQ13 8NL.

DAUGHTERS LIVING

Hon Nicola Dorothy, *b* 1955; MB, ChB, MRCP: *m* 1994, Dr Stephen Bashforth, elder son of G. P. Bashforth, of Norton, Sheffield.
Hon Fiona Janice, *b* 1958, BSc: *m* 1977, Rev Andrew John Proud, BD, of The Rectory, 136 Church Hill Rd, E Barnet, Herts EN4 8XD, and has issue living, Justin Dominic Edward, *b* 1979, — Emma Jane Chrysogen, *b* 1977.
Hon Naomi Melicent, *b* 1960; MA, MB BS: *m* 1990, Malcolm Hugh David Kemp, elder son of Prof C. D. Kemp, of St Andrews, Fife.

BROTHER LIVING

Hon MICHAEL COTTRELL, *b* 6 Aug 1928: *ed* Leighton Park Sch, and New Coll, Oxford (MA, BCh DM); FRCP, FRCP (C); late Cpt RAMC: *m* 1960, Dr Hon Elizabeth Ann Herbert, el da of late Baron Tangley (Life Baron), and has issue living, Thomas Russell, *b* 1965, — Hilary Catherine, *b* 1961: *m* 1986, Guido Dino de Luca, — Philippa Harriet, *b* 1963: *m* 1991, Armando Teves. *Residence* – 131 North Shore, Blvd E, Burlington, Ontario, Canada, L7T 4A4.

SISTER LIVING

Hon Janet Stella, *b* 1931; BA: *m* 1954, Leonard John Henry Arthur, MB, BCh, FRCP, who *d* 1983, of Royal Oak Cottage, Church Broughton, Derby (*see* Arthur, Bt, colls).

PREDECESSOR – (1) (WALTER) RUSSELL BRAIN, son of Walter John Brain, of Reading; *b* 1895; DM, FRCP, FRCPI, FRCPE; Pres of R Coll of Physicians 1950-57, and of British Assocn 1963-64; *cr* a Baronet (UK of Reading) 1954, *Baron Brain*, of Eynsham, co Oxford (peerage of UK) 1962: *m* 1920, Stella, who *d* 1993, da of Reginald Langdon Langdon-Down, MB, BCh; *d* 1966; *s* by his el son (2) CHRISTOPHER LANGDON, 2nd Baron, and present peer.

BRAINE OF WHEATLEY, BARON (Braine) (Life Baron 1992)

BERNARD RICHARD BRAINE, PC, son of late Arthur Ernest Braine, of Kew Gdns, Surrey; *b* 24 June 1914; *ed* Hendon County Gram Sch; DL Essex 1978; FRSA; 1939-45 War N Staffs Regt in W Africa, NW Europe and SE Asia, Camberley Staff Coll, Temp Lt-Col SEAC; Parly Sec Min of Pensions and Nat Insurance 1960-61, Under-Sec of State Commonwealth Relations 1961-62, Parly Sec Min of Health 1962-64, Chm Parly Cttee on Overseas Aid 1970-74, Dep-Chm Commonwealth Parly Assocn 1963-64 and 1970-74, Chm Nat Council on Alcohol 1974-82, British-German Parly Group 1970-92, British-Greek Parly Group 1979-92, UK Chapter Soc for Internat Development; Leader of several Parly Missions Abroad and Human Rights Mission to Soviet Union 1991; Father of the House of Commons 1987-92; Trustee and former Gov Commonwealth Inst, Visiting Prof Baylor Univ Texas; KStJ 1985, European Peace Medal 1979, Cdr Polonia Restituta (Polish Govt in Exile) 1983 (Grand Cross), Kt Cdr Order of Merit (W Germany) 1984, KCSG (Papal) 1987, Grand Cdr Order of Honour (Greece) 1987; MP Billericay (*C*) 1950-55, Essex SE 1955-83, and Castle Point 1983-92; *cr* Kt Bach 1972, PC 1985, and *Baron Braine of Wheatley*, of Rayleigh, co Essex (Life Baron) 1992: *m* 1935, Kathleen Mary, who *d* 1982, da of late Herbert William Faun, of E Sheen, Surrey, and has issue.
Residence – King's Wood, 67 Great Wheatley Rd, Rayleigh, Essex SS6 7AW.

SONS LIVING

Hon Richard Laurence, *b* 1939.
Hon Michael Rodney, *b* 1942.
Hon Brendan Timothy, *b* 1945.

BRAINTREE, BARONY OF (Crittall) (Extinct 1961)

DAUGHTERS LIVING OF FIRST BARON

Hon Valentine Ellen MacDermott, *b* 1918: *m* 1939, Karl Stewart Richardson, and has issue living, Peter Valentine, *b* 1942, — Jeremy Stewart, *b* 1946. *Residence* – Hungry Hall, Witham, Essex.
Hon Jane Olive, *b* 1921: *m* 1947, Thomas Anthony Inglis Hall, and has issue living, Barnaby Inglis, *b* 1948; photographer, — Thomas Valentine Inglis, *b* 1949, — Sophia Charlotte, *b* 1954. *Residence* – 6 Windsor Terrace, Clifton, Bristol.

Hon Mary Frances, *b* 1922: *m* 1950, Germano Facetti, and has issue living, Lucia Olivia Josephine, *b* 1954.

BRAMALL, BARON (Bramall) (Life Baron 1987)

EDWIN NOEL WESTBY BRAMALL, KG, GCB, OBE, MC, son of late Maj Edmund Haseldon Bramall, late RA, of 2 Symons St, Sloane Sq, SW3; *b* 18 Dec 1923; *ed* Eton; commn'd KRRC 1943; served NW Europe 1944-45 (MC 1945), occupation of Japan 1946-47, Instructor Sch of Inf 1949-51, psc 1952, Middle East 1953-58, Instructor Army Staff Coll 1958-61, on Lord Mountbatten's staff with responsibility for reorganization of MoD 1963-64, Comdg Officer 2nd Green Jackets, KRRC, Malaysia 1965-66, comd 5th Airportable Bde 1967-69, idc 1970, GOC 1st Div BAOR 1971-73, Lt-Gen 1973, Comdr British Forces Hong Kong 1973-76, Gen 1976, C-in-C UK Land Forces 1976-78, Vice-Chief of Defence Staff 1978-79, Chief of General Staff 1979-82, Chief of Defence Staff 1982-85; ADC (Gen) to HM 1979-82, Col Comdt 3rd Bn RGJ 1973-84, Col 2nd Goorkhas since 1976, Field Marshal 1982; Lord Lieut Greater London 1986; Trustee Imperial War Museum since 1983 (Chm 1989); Pres MCC 1988-89; Pres London Playing Fields Assocn since 1990, and Order of St John for London; *cr* OBE 1965, KCB 1974, GCB 1979, KG 1990, and *Baron Bramall*, of Bushfield, Hants (Life Baron) 1987: *m* 1949, Dorothy Avril Wentworth, only da of late Brig-Gen Henry Albemarle Vernon, DSO, late of Stoke Bruerne Park, Northants, and has issue.
Address – c/o National Westminster Bank, 34 Sloane Sq, SW3. *Clubs* – Travellers', Army and Navy, Pratts', MCC, I Zingari.

SON LIVING

Hon Nicolas, *b* 1952: *m* 1976 (*m diss* 1986), Janet Livingston, and has issue living, one son and one da.

DAUGHTER LIVING

Hon Sara, *b* 1951: *m* 1987, Dr Edwin R. Bickerstaff.

Brancepeth, Baron; title of Viscount Boyne on Roll of HL.

BRAND, BARONY OF (Brand) (Extinct 1963)

DAUGHTERS LIVING OF FIRST BARON

Hon Virginia (*Hon Lady Ford*), *b* 1918: *m* 1st, 1939, John Metcalfe Polk, who *d* 1948; 2ndly, 1949, Sir Edward William Spencer Ford, KCB, KCVO, ERD (E Shrewsbury, colls), and has issue living (by 1st *m*), John Robert, *b* 1942: *m* 1969, Benedetta Maryons, da of David Grose, of 49 Elystan St, SW3, and has issue living, James Metcalfe *b* 1973, Laura Elizabeth *b* 1971, Alice Victoria *b* 1981, — Robert Brand, *b* 1944: *m* 1979, Elizabeth Wells, only da of Alfred Lyndon Gibson, of Melbourne, Victoria, and has issue living, Edward John *b* 1980, Henry Brand *b* 1982, Thomas Robert *b* 1984, — (by 2nd *m*) Richard George, *b* 1951; Page of Honour to HM 1964-66: *m* 1986, Elisa Ann, only da of Michael Jeremy Kindersley Belmont (*see* Tate, Bt, colls), and has issue living, Jack *b* 1989, Katherine Ann *b* 1987, — Rose Virginia *b* 1990. — David Lionel, *b* 1952: *m* 1990, Margaret (Jubby), da of Richard Reid Ingrams (*see* Reid, Bt, *cr* 1897, colls), and has issue living, Samuel Christopher Valentine *b* 1992, Phoebe May *b* 1991. *Residence* – Canal House, 23 Blomfield Rd, W9 1AD.
Hon Dinah, *b* 1920: *m* 1st, 1943, Lyttleton Fox; 2ndly, 1953, Christopher Charles Cyprian Bridge, who *d* 1993, and has issue living (by 1st *m*), James Lyttleton, *b* 1945: *m* 1970, Valérie Mariane, da of Alain Lalonde, of 15 Rue de l'Universite, Paris VIII, and has issue living, Thomas Lyttleton *b* 1971, — Phyllis Langhorne, *b* 1944, — (by 2nd *m*) Charles Robert, *b* 1956: *m* 1980, Arabella Jane, da of David Bradstock, of Clanville Lodge, Andover, Hants, and has issue living, Oliver James Cyprian *b* 1983, Thomas Augustus William *b* 1987, Lucy Dinah *b* 1982, — Joanna, *b* 1954: *m* 1986, Graeme J. E. Jenkins, elder son of Kenneth Jenkins, and has issue living, Martha Nancy *b* 1989, Isabella Dinah *b* 1991. *Residence* – 18 The Street, Firle, nr Lewes, E Sussex BN8 6NR.

Brandon, Duke of; see Duke of Hamilton and Brandon.

BRANDON OF OAKBROOK, BARON (Brandon) (Life Baron 1981)

HENRY VIVIAN BRANDON, MC, PC; son of late Capt Vivian Ronald Brandon, CBE, RN, of Kensington, W8; *b* 3 June 1920; *ed* Winchester, and King's Coll, Camb; served 1939-45 War with RA in UK, Madagascar, India and Burma (Maj 1944); Barrister-at-law Inner Temple 1946, Member Bar Council 1951-53, QC 1961, Judge of High Court of Justice, Probate, Divorce and Admiralty Div 1966-71, and Judge of Family Div and Admiralty Court 1971-78, Judge of Commercial Court 1977-78, Lord Justice of Appeal 1978-81, a Lord of Appeal in Ordinary 1981-91; Member panel of Lloyd's arbitrators in salvage cases 1961-66, and of panel of Wreck Commrs 1963-66; *cr* Kt 1966, PC 1978 and *Baron Brandon of Oakbrook*, of Hammersmith, Greater

London (Life Baron) 1981: *m* 1955, Jeanette Rosemary, el da of late Julian Vivian Breeze Janvrin, and has issue.
Residence – 6 Thackeray Close, SW19.

SONS LIVING

Hon James Roderick Vivian, *b* 1956; LLB, ACA: *m* 1991, Amelia Mary Hungerford, elder da of Maj Peter Hungerford Jackson (*see* Jackson, Bt, *cr* 1815, colls). *Residence* – 50 Richmond Rd, SW20 0PQ
Hon Richard Henry, *b* 1961: *m* 1988, Jean Patricia, 2nd da of R. B. Horsfield, of Eccles, Manchester.
Hon William Roland, *b* 1964: *m* 1991, Polly Jennifer Miriam, da of Janos Nyiri.

DAUGHTER LIVING

Hon Juliet Mary, *b* 1958: *m* 1978, William Patrick Neill-Hall.

BRASSEY OF APETHORPE, BARON (Brassey) (Baron UK 1938, Bt UK 1922)

ARDUIS · SÆPE · METU · NUNQUAM
H·N·E.

Often in difficulties, never in fear

DAVID HENRY BRASSEY, OBE, 3rd Baron, and 3rd Baronet; *b* 16 Sept 1932; *s* 1967; *ed* Stowe; Maj (ret) Gren Gds; JP and DL Northants, OBE 1994; *m* 1st, 1958, Myrna Elizabeth, who *d* 1974, only da of Lt-Col John Baskervyle-Glegg, of 9 The Gateways, Chelsea, SW3; 2ndly, 1978, Caroline, da of late Lt-Col Godfrey Ariel Evill, and of the Dowager Lady Duntze, of 55 Elm Park Gdns, SW10, and has issue by 1st and 2nd *m*.

Arms – Quarterly; 1st, per fesse indented sable and argent, in the first quarter a mallard of the second; 2nd, gules, in chief three mullets argent, and in base a dexter hand apaumée couped at the wrist of the last; 3rd, sable, a chevron between three bulls' heads cabossed argent; 4th, argent, on a chevron gules, three trefoils slipped of the field. **Crest** – A mallard proper. **Supporters** – On either side a mallard holding in the beak an ear of wheat slipped and leaved proper.
Residence – The Manor House, Apethorpe, Peterborough.

SON LIVING *(By 1st marriage)*

Hon EDWARD, *b* 9 March 1964.

DAUGHTERS LIVING *(By 2nd marriage)*

Hon Zara, *b* 1980.
Hon Chloe, *b* 1982.

BROTHER LIVING

Hon Thomas Ian (The Coach House, Duncote, Towcester, Northants NN12 8AQ), *b* 1934; *ed* Stowe; formerly Lt Gren Guards: *m* 1960, Valerie Christine, da of Alan David Finlason, and has issue living, Thomas Hugh, *b* 1971, — Miranda, *b* 1963: *m* 1988, Andrew Robinson Rawlin, eldest son of Dr Michael Rawlin, of North Anston, Sheffield, Yorks, and has issue living, William Bradbury *b* 1994, — Louise, *b* 1964, — Davina Christine, *b* 1969: *m* 1994, Christopher Robert Merriman, yst son of late Patrick Merriman, of Rearsby House, Rearsby, Leics.

UNCLE LIVING (Son of 1st Baron)

Hon Peter Esmé (Pond House, Barnack, Stamford), *b* 1907; *ed* Eton, and Magdalene Coll, Camb; Bar Inner Temple 1930; is Lt-Col Northants Yeo, Lord Lieut of Cambs 1975-81; 1939-45 War as Lt-Col (wounded): *m* 1944, Lady Romayne Elizabeth Algitha Cecil, OBE, ARRC, da of 5th Marquess of Exeter, and has issue living, Henry Charles (Close House, Barnack, Stamford, Lincs, PE9 3DY) *b* 1947: *m* 1972, Linda, da of Geoffrey Pinnock, of Fern Cottage, Ripley, Surrey, and has issue living, Thomas Charles *b* 1974, Elizabeth Jane *b* 1978, — Richard Edwin (116 Lots Rd, SW6), *b* 1949: *m* 1st, 1971 (*m diss* 1979), Tania, da of Norman William Duckworth; 2ndly, 1986, Pamina, da of Robert Caruso, of New York, USA, and has issue living (by 1st *m*), Pikka (a da) *b* 1973, (by 2nd *m*) George Peter *b* 1987, — Rowena Jane, LVO, *b* 1945; a Lady-in-Waiting to HRH The Princess Royal since 1970; LVO 1974: *m* 1977, Andrew James Feilden, of The Old Manor House, Minster Lovell, Oxon (*see* V Hampden, colls).

WIDOW LIVING OF SECOND BARON

BARBARA (*Barbara, Baroness Brassey of Apethorpe*) (23 Bull Lane, Ketton, Stamford, Lincs), da of late Leonard Jorgensen, and formerly wife of Lt-Col Herbert Campbell Westmorland: *m* 1963, as his 2nd wife, the 2nd Baron, who *d* 1967.

PREDECESSORS – (1) (HENRY) LEONARD (CAMPBELL) Brassey, son of late Henry Arthur Brassey (formerly MP for Sandwich), of Preston Hall, Kent; *b* 1870; Major W Kent Yeo; Sheriff of Northants 1907; sat as MP for N Div of Northampton 1910-18, and for Peterborough Div thereof 1918-29; *cr* a Baronet 1922, and Baron Brassey of Apethorpe, of Apethorpe, co Northampton (peerage of United Kingdom) 1938: *m* 1894, Lady Violet Mary Gordon-Lennox, who *d* 1946, da of 7th Duke of Richmond and Gordon; *d* 1958; *s* by his 5th son (2) BERNARD THOMAS, MC, TD, 2nd Baron, *b* 1905: *m* 1st, 1931, Crystal Gloria, who *d* 1962, da of late Lt-Col Francis William George Gore (E Sondes); 2ndly, 1963, Mrs Barbara Westmorland, da of late Leonard Jorgenson; *d* 1967; *s* by his el son (3) DAVID HENRY, 3rd Baron, and present peer.

BRAYBROOKE, BARON (Neville) (Baron GB 1788)

Incline to nothing base

ROBIN HENRY CHARLES NEVILLE, 10th Baron; *b* 29 Jan 1932; *s* 1990; *ed* Eton, and Magdalene Coll, Camb; DL Essex 1980, Lord Lieut 1992; an Hereditary Visitor of Magdalene Coll, Camb; patron of three livings: *m* 1st, 1955 (*m diss* 1974), Robin Helen, only da of late Thomas Adolph Brockhoff, of Rose Bay, Sydney, NSW; 2ndly, 1974, Linda, 2nd da of Arthur Norman, of Saffron Walden, Essex, and has issue by 1st and 2nd *m*.

Arms – Quarterly: 1st and 4th gules, on a saltire argent, a rose of the field, barbed and seeded proper; 2nd and 3rd or, fretty gules; on a canton of the first a lymphad sable. **Crest** – A bull statant argent, collared and chained or. **Supporters** – Two lions reguardant argent, maned sable, and gorged with wreaths of olive proper.
Residence – Abbey House, Audley End, Saffron Walden, Essex. *Club* – Boodle's.

DAUGHTERS LIVING AND DECEASED (*By 1st marriage*)

Hon Amanda Muriel Mary, *b* 1962: *m* 1989, Stephen Christopher Jerningham Murray, only son of Christopher Mark Henry Murray, of La Glinette, St Aubin, Jersey, CI (*see* Jerningham, Bt (ext), 1955 Edn), and of late Mrs Michael P. Wyndham, and has issue living, Alexander Henry Jerningham, *b* 1992.
Hon Caroline Emma, *b* 1963.
Henrietta Jane, *b* 1965; *d* 1980.

Hon Victoria, *b* 1970.
Hon Arabella, *b* (twin) 1970.

(*By 2nd marriage*)

Hon Sara Lucy, *b* 1975.
Hon Emma Charlotte, *b* 1979.
Hon Lucinda Octavia, *b* 1984.

DAUGHTER LIVING OF SEVENTH BARON

Hon Catherine Dorothy, OBE (Asherne, Strete, Dartmouth, Devon), *b* 1922; OBE (Civil) 1993: *m* 1954, Gordon Alexander Egerton Ruck, who *d* 1977, and has issue living, Louise Dorothy Catherine, *b* 1959: *m* 1992, Richard Claude Newman (*see* Newman, Bt, *cr* 1836).

COLLATERAL BRANCHES LIVING

Grandchildren of late Adm Sir George Neville, KCB, CVO, 2nd son of late Ralph Neville-Grenville, MP, son of late Very Rev Hon George Neville-Grenville, 3rd son of 2nd Baron:—
Issue of late Capt Philip Lloyd Neville, CVO, RN, *b* 1888, *d* 1976: *m* 1942, Eleanor, who *d* 1972, da of Duncan Fellowes, of Toronto, Canada:—
GEORGE, *b* 23 March 1943; *ed* Eton: *m* 1972, Patricia, da of late Patrick Quinn, and has issue living, Richard Ralph, *b* 1977, — Eleanor Anne, *b* 1975. —— John (Welgoer, Poyntington, Sherborne, Dorset), *b* 1944; *ed* Eton, and McGill Univ (MBA 1971): *m* 1980, Frances Jane, da of John Stuart Lomax, and has issue living, Edward Grey, *b* 1982, — Cicely Georgia, *b* 1984.
Issue of late Brig Alfred Geoffrey Neville, CBE, MC, RA, *b* 1891, *d* 1955: *m* 1922, Philippa, who *d* 1981, da of late Vice-Adm Sir George Price Webley Hope, KCB, KCMG (*see* M Linlithgow, colls):—
Caroline Philippa (*Lady Newman*), *b* 1935: *m* 1960, Sir Gerard Robert Henry Sigismund Newman, 3rd Bt, who *d* 1987.
Residences – Burloes, Royston, Herts; 27 Bloomfield Terr, SW1.

Granddaughter of late Louis Neville, 4th son of late Ralph Neville-Grenville, MP (ante):—
Issue of late Bertram Neville, *b* 1880, *d* 1950: *m* 1919, Gertrude May Thompson:—
Edith Beryl, *b* 1925: *m* 1954, Derek George Rands, and has issue living, Margaret Elizabeth, *b* 1957, — Pauline Jane, *b* 1961.
Residence – 51 Wychwood Av, Luton, Bedfordshire.

PREDECESSORS – (1) *Field-Marshal Sir* John Griffin-Whitwell (heir-general of 3rd and last Baron Griffin of Braybrooke) was summoned to Parliament 1784 as 4th Baron Howard de Walden, and in 1788 was *cr Baron Braybrooke* (peerage of Great Britain), with remainder to Richard Neville-Aldworth, of Billingbere; *d* 1797, when the Barony of Howard de Walden fell into abeyance and the Barony of Braybrooke devolved upon (2) RICHARD Aldworth-Neville, 2nd Baron; *b* 1750; was Lord Lieut and Vice-Adm of Essex, Provost-Marshal of Jamaica, etc; assumed by R licence 1798 the additional and principal surname of Griffin: *m* 1780, Catherine, who *d* 1796, da of Rt Hon George Grenville, PC; *d* 1825; *s* by his son (3) RICHARD NEVILLE, LLD, 3rd Baron, *b* 1783; editor of the *Diary of Samuel Pepys*: *m* 1819, Lady Jane, who *d* 1856, da of 2nd Marquess Cornwallis; *d* 1858; *s* by his son (4) RICHARD CORNWALLIS, 4th Baron; *d* 1861; *s* by his brother (5) CHARLES CORNWALLIS, 5th Baron, *b* 1823: *m* 1849, Hon Florence Priscilla Alicia Maude, who *d* 1914, 3rd da of 3rd Viscount Hawarden; *d* 1902; *s* by his brother (6) *Rev* LATIMER, 6th Baron, *b* 1827: Master of Magdalene Coll Camb: *m* 1853, Lucy Frances, who *d* 1918, el da of John Le Marchant; *d* 1904; *s* by his el son (7) HENRY, 7th Baron; *b* 1855: *m* 1st, Emelie Pauline, who *d* 1912, da of late Antoine Gonin, of Château de Condemine, Mâcon; 2ndly, 1917, Dorothy Edith, who *d* 1973, yst da of late Sir George Lawson, KCB; *d* 1941; *s* by his el son (8) RICHARD HENRY CORNWALLIS, 8th Baron; *b* 1918; Lieut Gren Gds; *ka* 1943; *s* by his cousin (9) HENRY SEYMOUR (son of late Rev Hon Grey Neville, 2nd son of 6th Baron), 9th Baron, *b* 1897; European War 1915-19 as Flight-Com RNAS and Capt RAF; DL Essex: *m* 1st, 1930, Muriel Evelyn, who *d* 1962, da of late William Charles Manning, and widow of Euan C. Cartwright; 2ndly, 1963, Angela Mary, who *d* 1985, da of late William Herbert Hollis, and widow of John Ree; *d* 1990; *s* by his only son (10) ROBIN HENRY CHARLES, 10th Baron and present peer.

BRAYE, BARONESS (Aubrey-Fletcher) (Baron E 1529)

Beware. One alone.

MARY PENELOPE AUBREY-FLETCHER (*Baroness Braye*), *b* 28 Sept 1941; *s* 1985; High Sheriff of Northants 1983; heir-gen of the Earls Verney of Claydon (ext 1791): *m* 1981, as his 2nd wife, Lt-Col Edward Henry Lancelot Aubrey-Fletcher, Gren Gds (*see* Aubrey-Fletcher, Bt).

Arms – Quarterly, 1st and 4th azure, fretty argent *Cave*; 2nd and 3rd azure, on a cross argent five mullets gules, *Verney*. **Supporters** – Two lions guardant or, winged vaire. **Badge** – A Hemp-breaker.
Seat – Stanford Hall, Lutterworth, Leics, LE17 6DH.

Beware.

COLLATERAL BRANCH LIVING (*co-heiresses to the barony*)

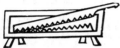

Badge of the Barons Braye

Granddaughters of late Hon Cecilia Violet (Hon Mrs von Gratzy), elder da of 5th Baron:—
Issue of late Vera Cecilia, *b* 1906, *d* 1981: *m* 1929, Claude Henry Browne (Foresters, Keeper's Walk, Virginia Water, Surrey):—
LINDA KATHLEEN CECILIA, *b* 2 May 1930: *m* 1965, Cdr Christopher Henry Fothergill, RN (*see* E Radnor, colls, 1966 Edn), of Otway House, Chobham, Surrey, and has issue living, Nicholas Henry, *b* 1965, — Alexander Verney Edmund, *b* 1967. —— THERESA BEATRICE, *b* 9 Aug 1934. *Residence* – Foresters, Keepers Walk, Virginia Water, Surrey.

PREDECESSORS – **(1)** *Sir* Edmund Braye, Knt, of Eaton Braye, co Bedford, nephew of Sir Reginald Braye, KG, Lord High Treas to Henry VII, summoned to Parl as a *Baron* of England 1529; *d* 1539; *s* by his son **(2)** JOHN, 2nd Baron, summoned to Parliament 1545-55; was Master of the Ordnance to Queen Mary; *d* without issue 1557, when the Barony became abeyant, and remained so until 1839, when it was terminated in favour of **(3)** SARAH, only da of Sir Thomas Cave, 6th Bt, of Stanford Hall, co Leicester, and wife of Henry Otway, she being the descendant of Elizabeth, 2nd da of the 1st Baron, and wife of Sir Ralph Verney, Knt, of Claydon; she resumed in 1819 by R licence the additional surname of Cave, and *d* 1862, leaving four das, among whom the title again remained abeyant until 13 May 1879, when it passed to the last survivor of them **(4)** HENRIETTA: *m* 1844, Edgell Wyatt-Edgell, who *d* 1888, 2nd son of late Edgell Wyatt-Edgell, of Milton Place, Egham, Surrey; *d* 14 Nov 1879; *s* by her son **(5)** ALFRED THOMAS TOWNSHEND, 5th Baron; *b* 1849; assumed in 1880 by R licence the surnames of Verney-Cave in lieu of Wyatt-Edgell: *m* 1873, Harriet Cecilia, who *d* 1935, da of late William Gerard Walmesley, of Westwood House, Wigan; *d* 1928; *s* by his son **(6)** ADRIAN VERNEY, 6th Baron; *b* 1874; Lieut-Com RNVR: *m* 1900, Ethel Mary, who *d* 1955, da of late Capt Edward Bouverie Pusey, RN; *d* 1952; *s* by his son **(7)** THOMAS ADRIAN, 7th Baron, *b* 1902; Maj 13th/18th R Hus, and formerly F/O RAF: *m* 1934, Dorothea, who *d* 1994, da of late Daniel C. Donoghue, of Philadelphia, USA; *d* 1985; *s* by his only da **(8)** MARY PENELOPE, Baroness Braye, present peeress.

BRAYLEY, BARONY OF (Brayley) (Extinct 1977)

DAUGHTERS LIVING OF LIFE BARON

Hon Avril Gay, *b* 19—: *m* 19—.

Hon Tessa Ann, *b* 1948: *m* 1st, 1967 (*m diss* 1974), Gerald Conway; 2ndly, 1974 (*m diss* 1978), Anthony Forrest; 3rdly, 1982 (*m diss* 1988), John Smart, and has issue living (by 1st husband), Gerrard Curtis, *b* 1966. *Residence* – Tree House, Stratford Rd, Wootton Wawen, Warwicks B95 6BY.

BREADALBANE AND HOLLAND, EARL OF (Campbell) (Earl S 1677, Bt S 1625)

(Name pronounced "Bredawlben")

JOHN ROMER BORELAND CAMPBELL, 10th Earl, and 14th Baronet; *b* 28 April 1919; *s* 1959; *ed* Eton; formerly Lieut Black Watch; European War 1939-42 in France (despatches, invalided): *m* 1949 (*m diss* 19—), Coralie, da of Charles Archer.

Arms – Quarterly: 1st and 4th gyronny of eight or and sable, *Campbell*; 2nd argent, a lymphad with sails unfurled and oars in action sable, *Lorn*; 3rd or, a fesse checky azure and argent, *Stewart of Lorn*. **Crest** – A boar's head erased proper. **Supporters** – Two stags proper, attired and unguled or.

COLLATERAL BRANCHES

Descendants, if any, of George Andrew Campbell, 2nd son of John Campbell of Boreland, great-uncle of 6th Earl, *b* 1791, *d* 1852: *m* 1830, Margaret, who *d* 1884, da of Col James Campbell, having issue, John Breadalbane Campbell, of Florida, *b* 1839, *d* 1918: *m* 1873, Katherine McDonald.

Descendants, if any, of late Colin Campbell, Surg 39th Regt, el son of Capt Robert Campbell, great-great-uncle of 6th Earl, *d* in Guadeloupe 1794.

Descendants, if any, of William Campbell (*d* before 30 Aug 1784) (4th son of Robert Campbell of Glenfalloch, great-great-uncle of 6th Earl), whose son Archibald, Sgt Middlesex Militia, had a son, Colin.

Descendants, if any, of Duncan Campbell, yst son of Robert Campbell of Glenfalloch (ante), of whom Colin Campbell went to America, and James Campbell was bookbinder to the Queen.

PREDECESSORS – (1) Sir DUNCAN Campbell, Knt (7th Laird of Glenorchy); was *cr* a *Baronet* 1631; was *s* by his son (2) Sir COLIN, 2nd Bt, who *d* without issue 1640; *s* by his brother (3)*Sir* ROBERT, 3rd Bt, MP for Argyllshire 1639-47: *d* 1657; *s* by his son (4) Sir JOHN, 4th Bt; *d* 1686; *s* by his son (5) Sir JOHN, PC; this gentleman being principal creditor of George, 6th Earl of Caithness, received from that nobleman an assignment of his Earldom, his whole estate, his heritable jurisdictions and titles of honour, and the right to assume the surname and arms of Sinclair; in return he became responsible for the Earl's debts, upwards of 1,000,000 marks, and after his lordship's death in 1676, he obtained in 1677 a patent creating him *Earl of Caithness*; however, in 1681, the Privy Council found that George Sinclair of Keiss, was heir male of the last Earl, and in consequence John Campbell relinquished his Earldom of Caithness, and in the same year was *cr Lord Glenorchy, Benederaloch, Ormelie and Weick, Viscount of Tay and Paintland*, and *Earl of Breadalbane and Holland* (peerage of Scotland) with precedency of 1677, and with remainder to (i) whichever of his sons (by his 1st m) he should designate in writing, (ii) to the heirs male of his body, and (iii) to his heirs whatsoever; *d* 1716; *s* by his 2nd son, whom in 1684 he had designated as heir, viz:—(6) JOHN, 2nd Earl; was Lord-Lieut of Perthshire, and a Representative peer; he *d* 1752, and was *s* by his son (7) JOHN, 3rd Earl; was MP for many years, and successively Master of the Horse to Princess Royal, Ambassador to Copenhagen and St Petersburg, a Lord of the Admiralty, Master of the Jewel Offices, a Representative Peer and Keeper of the Privy Seal in Scotland; *d* without surviving issue 1782, when the male line of 1st peer failed and the titles devolved upon the great-grandson of Colin, 3rd son of 3rd Bt (8) JOHN, 4th Earl; Maj-Gen in the Army and a Representative Peer; *cr Baron Breadalbane, Earl of Ormelie* and *Marquess of Breadalbane* (peerage of United Kingdom) 1806; *d* 1834; *s* by his son (9) JOHN, KT, 2nd Marquess, Lord-Lieut of Argyllshire; *d* 1862, when the English honours became extinct and the Scottish peerage devolved upon the great-great-grandson of William, 5th son of 3rd Bt (10) JOHN ALEXANDER GAVIN, 6th Earl: *b* 1824: *m* 1850, Mary Theresa, da of J. F. Edwards; *d* 1871; *s* by his son (11) GAVIN, KG, PC, 7th Earl; *b* 1851; *cr Baron Breadalbane*, of Kenmore, co Perth (peerage of United Kingdom) 1885; a Lord-in-Waiting to Queen Victoria 1873-4, Treasurer of Queen Victoria's Household 1880-85, Lord Steward of Queen Victoria's Household 1892-5, Lord High Commr to Gen Asembly of Church of Scotland 1893, 1894, and 1895, and Lord Keeper of Privy Seal of Scotland 1907-22: *m* 1872, Lady Alma Imogen Carlotta Leonora, who *d* 1932, da of 4th Duke of Montrose; *d* 1922, when the English honours became ext, and the Scottish peerages devolved upon his nephew (12) IAIN EDWARD HERBERT (son of late Capt Hon Ivan Campbell, 2nd son of 6th Earl), 8th Earl, *b* 1923; *s* by his kinsman (13) CHARLES WILLIAM, MC (son of late Maj-Gen Charles William Campbell of Boreland; a descendant of 5th son of 3rd Bt), 9th Earl; *b* 1889; a Representative Peer, Maj RHA, a Member of Queen's Body Guard of Scotland (R Company of Archers), and a Member of HM Hon Corps of Gentlemen-at-Arms; sometime Lieut-Col Comdg 8th Batn, Argyll and Sutherland Highlanders (TA): *m* 1918, Armorer Romer, who *d* 1987, da of Romer Williams, DL, JP, of Newnham Hall, Daventry, and widow of Capt Eric Nicholson, 12th R Lancers; *d* 1959; *s* by his only son (14) JOHN ROMER BORELAND, 10th Earl and present peer; also Viscount of Tay and Paintland, and Lord Glenorchy, Benederaloch, Ormelie and Weick.

Brecknock, Earl of; son of Marquess Camden.

BRECON, BARONY OF (Lewis) (Extinct 1976)

DAUGHTERS LIVING OF FIRST BARON

Hon Rosalind Helen Penrose, CBE, *b* 1938; *ed* Cheltenham Ladies' Coll; CBE 1994: *m* 1963, Arthur Leolin Price, QC, of 32 Hampstead Grove, NW3 6SR, and Moor Park, Llanbedr, Crickhowell, Powys NP8 1SS, and has issue living, Evan David Lewis, *b* 1976, — Thomas Leolin Alfred, *b* 1971, — Mary Ceridwen, *b* 1964, — Sophie Katharine, *b* 1966.

Hon Janet Mary Penrose, *b* 1944; *ed* Cheltenham Ladies' Coll: *m* 1969, Christopher John Foss, of Naish Hill House, Lacock, Wilts, and has issue living, Penrose Margaret Helen, *b* 1970, — Charlotte Sophia Louise, *b* 1975.

WIDOW LIVING OF FIRST BARON

MABEL HELEN, CBE (*Baroness Brecon*), (Greenhill, Cross Oak, Talybont-on-Usk, Powys, LD3 7UJ); a JP; High Sheriff of Breconshire 1971-72; CBE (Civil) 1964; da of late John McColville, of Abergavenny: *m* 1933, the 1st Baron, who *d* 1976, when the title became ext.

BRENTFORD, VISCOUNT (Joynson-Hicks) (Viscount UK 1929, Bt UK 1919)

CASSIS · TVTISSIMA · VIRTVS

Virtue is the safest helmet

CRISPIN WILLIAM JOYNSON-HICKS, 4th Viscount, 4th Baronet of Holmsbury and 2nd Baronet of Newick, *b* 7 April 1933; *s* 1983; *ed* Eton, and at New Coll, Oxford; Solicitor 1960; a partner in the legal firm of Taylor Joynson Garrett (formerly Joynson-Hicks); late Lt 9th Lancers: *m* 1964, Gillian Evelyn, el da of late Gerald Edward Schluter, OBE, of Nairobi, Kenya, and has issue.

Arms – Gules, on a fesse wavy between three fleurs-de-lis or, a portcullis sable, all within a bordure of the second. **Crest** – A stag's head proper gorged with a collar or, thereon five roses gules, and charged on the neck with a fleur-de-lis gold. **Supporters** – On either side a stag proper gorged with a collar or, thereon five roses gules and charged on the neck with a fleur-de-lis gold.
Residence – Cousley Place, Wadhurst, East Sussex, TN5 6HF.

SON LIVING

Hon PAUL WILLIAM, *b* 1971.

DAUGHTERS LIVING

Hon Emma Rosalie, *b* 1966.
Hon Rowena Phyllis, *b* 1967: *m* 1989, Simon J. Banks, yr son of M. J. Banks, of Bishop's Stortford, Herts.
Hon Amy Gillian, *b* 1978.

PREDECESSORS – (1) WILLIAM Joynson-Hicks, PC, son of late Henry Hicks, of Plaistow Hall, Kent; *b* 1865; founder of legal firm of Joynson-Hicks, solicitors; Parliamentary Sec (Overseas Trade Depart) to Board of Trade Oct 1922 to March 1923, Postmaster-Gen (also Paymaster-Gen) March to May 1923, Financial Sec to the Treasury (with a seat in the Cabinet), May to Sept 1923, Min of Health Sept 1923 to Jan 1924, and Sec of State for Home Depart Nov 1924 to June 1929; MP for NW Div of Manchester (C) April 1908 to Jan 1910, for Brentford Div of Middlesex March 1911 to Nov 1918, and for Twickenham Div thereof Dec 1918 to May 1929; *cr* a *Baronet* 1919, and *Viscount Brentford*, of Newick, Sussex (peerage of United Kingdom) 1929: *m* 1895, Grace Lynn, who *d* 1952, da of Richard Hampson Joynson, JP (whose surname he assumed), formerly of Chasefield, Bowdon, Cheshire; *d* 1932; *s* by his son (2) RICHARD CECIL, 2nd Viscount, *b* 1896; sometime on Staff of Gov of Jamaica: *m* 1st, 1920, Evelyn Mary Rothery, who *d* 1954, only da of late John F. McNellan, of Dollar, Clackmannanshire; 2ndly, 1955, Grace Esther, who *d* 1984, da of late A. E. A. Tothill, of Cape Town, and widow of D. S. T. McNellan, of Johannesburg, S Africa; *d* 1958; *s* by his brother (3) LANCELOT WILLIAM, 3rd Viscount, *b* 1902; solicitor 1926; Parliamentary Sec Min of Fuel and Power Nov 1951-Dec 1955; European War 1939-45 as acting Lt-Cdr RNVR; Senior Partner in the legal firm of Joynson-Hicks & Co 1938-66; Chm of Automobile Assocn 1957-74; MP for Chichester Div of W Sussex (C) May 1942-June 1958; *cr* a *Baronet* (of Newick) 1956: *m* 1931, Phyllis, who *d* 1979, only da of late Maj Herbert Allfrey, of Newnton House, Tetbury, Glos; *d* 1983; *s* by his only son (4) CRISPIN WILLIAM, 4th Viscount and present peer.

BRIDGE OF HARWICH, BARON (Bridge) (Life Baron 1980)

NIGEL CYPRIAN BRIDGE, PC, son of late Cdr Cyprian Dunscomb Charles Bridge, RN; *b* 26 Feb 1917; *ed* Marlborough; Bar Inner Temple 1947; Bencher 1964, Junior Counsel to HM Treasury in Common Law 1964-68, and a Judge of High Court of Justice (Queen's Bench Div) 1968-75; Presiding Judge, Western Circuit 1972-74; Lord Justice of Appeal 1975-80; Lord of Appeal in Ordinary since 1980; Member Security Commn 1977-82, Chm 1982-85; Treas Inner Temple 1986; 1939-45 War as Capt KRRC in Italy, France and Germany; *cr* Knt 1968, PC 1975, and *Baron Bridge of Harwich*, of Harwich, co Essex (Life Baron) 1980: *m* 1944, Margaret, da of Leonard Heseltine Swinbank, of Weybridge, Surrey, and has issue.

𝕬rms – Azure issuant from the centre of a bar wavy of water proper in the nombril point of a bridge of three arches embattled argent masoned sable the whole between as many sealions naiant guardant and each crowned with a mural crown gold. 𝕮rest – An eagle rising proper the beak or holding therein a sprig of lilac also proper. 𝕾upporters – *Dexter*, a winged horse in trian aspect argent hooved or resting the dexter hoof upon a portcullis chained also or; *sinister*, a sealion in trian aspect all argent resting the sinister forepaw on a portcullis chained gold, the compartment comprising a grassy mount growing therefrom on a rose gules barbed stalked and leaved proper another rose argent barbed and seeded also proper between on the dexter a rose argent and on the sinister a rose gules both barbed seeded stalked and leaved proper on the sinister side of the mount a flat rock proper.
Address – c/o House of Lords, SW1.

SON LIVING

Hon Charles Cyprian, *b* 1951: *m* 1971, Sheila Marie Street.

DAUGHTERS LIVING

Hon Jane Elizabeth, *b* 1944: *m* 1978, Prof J. M. Kister.
Hon Rachel Ann, *b* 1946: *m* 1975, Martin Pick.

BRIDGEMAN, VISCOUNT (Bridgeman) (Viscount UK 1929)

ROBIN JOHN ORLANDO BRIDGEMAN, 3rd Viscount; *b* 5 Dec 1930; *s* 1982; *ed* Eton; 2nd Lieut Rifle Bde 1950-51; CA 1958: *m* 1966, (Victoria) Harriet Lucy, da of Ralph Meredyth Turton, of Kildale Hall, Whitby (*see* V Chetwynd, colls), and has issue.

𝕬rms – Sable, ten plates, four, three, two, and one, on a chief argent, a lion passant ermines. 𝕮rest – A demi-lion rampant argent, holding in the paws a wreath of laurel proper. 𝕾upporters – On either side a leopard guardant gules pelletée, charged on the shoulder with a portcullis or.
Residences – Watley House, Sparsholt, Hants; 19 Chepstow Rd, W2 5BP.

SONS LIVING

Hon WILLIAM ORLANDO CASPAR, *b* 15 Aug 1968; *ed* Eton, and Bristol Univ.
Hon Luke Robinson Orlando, *b* 1971; *ed* Eton, and New Coll, Oxford.
Hon Esmond Francis Ralph Orlando, *b* 1974; *ed* Bryanston.
Hon Orlando Henry Geoffrey, *b* 1983.

SISTERS LIVING

Neither rashly nor timidly

Helena Mary, *b* 1932: *m* 1st, 1953 (*m diss* 1963), Hon Paul Asquith, who *d* 1984, son of Baron Asquith of Bishopstone, PC (Life Baron); 2ndly, 1963, James Francis Leslie Bayley, and has issue living (by 1st *m*) (*see* E Oxford and Asquith, colls), — (by 2nd *m*) Thomas Francis, *b* 1966, — Rachel Helena, *b* 1964.
Daphne, *b* 1940: *m* 1965, William Howard Clive Montgomery, and has issue living, Hugh Geoffrey Clive, *b* 1966, — Rose Evelyn, *b* 1968, — Frances Mary, *b* 1970, — Flora Anne Selina, *b* 1974. *Residence* – Grey Abbey, Newtownards, co Down.

DAUGHTERS LIVING OF SECOND VISCOUNT

Hon Anne Caroline Mary, *b* 1932: *m* 1955, Rev Nicolas David Stacey, and has issue living, David Robert, *b* 1958: *m* 1992, Annabel M. E., da of Maj Michael Edwards, of Norwood Farm, Corscombe, Dorset, — Caroline Jill, *b* 1956, — Mary Elizabeth, *b* 1961. *Residence* – The Old Vicarage, Selling, Faversham, Kent.
Hon Susan Elizabeth, *b* 1935; JP; was Lady-in-Waiting to Lady May Abel Smith, wife of H E Gov of Queensland 1958-60: *m* 1962, David Kenneth Dudley Foster, and has issue living, Robert Peter Dudley, *b* 1966, — Edward Kenneth Clive, *b* 1967, — Simon David Thomas, *b* 1969. *Residence* – Beech House, Shifnal, Salop.
Hon Mary Selina, *b* 1940; JP; *m* 1962, Jeremy David Bagot Bayliss, of Sheepbridge Court, Swallowfield, Reading, and has issue living, Jonathan Andrew Bagot (6 Netheravon Rd, W4 2NA), *b* 1964: *m* 1992, Sarah E., elder da of Richard Bowes, of Enton, Surrey, and has issue living, Walter Richard Bridgeman *b* 1993, — Richard Charles, *b* 1965, — Patrick Thomas Clive, *b* 1968.

COLLATERAL BRANCH LIVING

Issue of late Hon Sir Maurice Richard Bridgeman, KBE, yst son of 1st Viscount, *b* 1904, *d* 1980: *m* 1933, Diana Mary Erica, who *d* 1979, da of late Humphrey Minto Wilson, of 9 S Audley St, W1:—
Erica Jane (*Lady Harman*) (Brook House, Highclere, Newbury, Berks), *b* 1934: *m* 1960 (*m diss* 1987), Sir Jeremiah Le Roy Harman (Hon Mr Justice Harman), son of Rt Hon Sir Charles Eustace Harman, and has issue living, Charles Richard Le Roy, *b* 1963, — Toby John, *b* 1967: *m* 1992, Joanne L., da of Neville Boxer of Farnham Royal, Bucks, — Sarah Jane, *b* 1962: *m* 1993, Hugh Lewis Evans, only son of Maj-Gen John Alan Maurice Evans, CB, of Littletown, co Durham. —— Teresa Anne, *b* 1937: *m* 1960, Peter Baring, of 29 Ladbroke Sq, W11 (*see* B Revelstoke, colls). —— Elizabeth Caroline, *b* 1944: *m* 1971, Martin Dru Drury, of 3 Victoria Rise, SW4, and has issue living, Matthew Orlando Dru, *b* 1972, — Joseph Walter Richard Minto Dru, *b* 1977, — Augusta Daisy Elizabeth, *b* 1974. —— Rachel Diana, *b* 1947: *m* 1972, Philip Benjamin Hay, of Plummer, Tenterden, Kent, and has issue living, Thomas Alexander, *b* 1974, — Tara Caroline, *b* 1976.

PREDECESSORS – (**1**) *Rt Hon* WILLIAM CLIVE Bridgeman, PC, son of late Rev Hon John Robert Orlando Bridgeman, 3rd son of 2nd Earl of Bradford; *b* 1864; Chm of BBC, and of Govs of Shrewsbury Sch, a Fellow of Eton Coll and an Elder Brother of Trinity House; Assist Private Sec to Sec of State for Colonies 1889-92, Private Sec to Chancellor of Exchequer 1895-9, Junior Lord of the Treasury 1915-16, Assist Director, War Trade Depart 1916, Parliamentary Sec to Min of Labour 1916-18, and to Board of Trade 1919-20, Sec of Mines Aug 1920 to Oct 1922 Sec of State for Home Depart Oct 1922 to Jan 1924, and First Lord of the Admiralty Nov 1924 to June 1929; MP for Salop, W or Oswestry Div (*C*) 1906-29: *cr Viscount Bridgeman* of Leigh, co Salop (peerage of United Kingdom; 1929): *m* 1895, *Dame* Caroline Beatrix, DBE, who *d* 1961, da of late Hon Cecil Thomas Parker (E Macclesfield, colls); *d* 1935; *s* by his son (**2**) ROBERT CLIVE, KBE, CB, DSO, MC, 2nd Viscount, *b* 1896; Maj-Gen Rifle Bde (Prince Consort's Own); Lord Lieut for co Salop 1951-69, and Alderman of Salop Co Council 1951-75; Private Sec to his father when Parliamentary Sec to Min of Labour 1918; served in World Wars I and II; Dir-Gen Home Guard 1941-45, and DAG 1944-45: *m* 1930, Hon Mary Kathleen Lane Fox, JP, who *d* 1981, da of 1st Baron Bingley (ext); *d* 1982; *s* by his nephew (**3**) ROBIN JOHN ORLANDO, only son of late Brig Hon Geoffrey John Orlando Bridgeman, MC, MB, FRCS, LRCP, 2nd son of 1st Viscount, 3rd Viscount and present peer.

BRIDGES, BARON (Bridges) (Baron UK 1957)

To act without speaking

THOMAS EDWARD BRIDGES, GCMG, 2nd Baron; *b* 27 Nov 1927; *s* 1969; *ed* Eton, and New Coll, Oxford; HM Diplo Ser 1951-87 (ret); seconded as Private Sec for Overseas Affairs to Prime Min 1972-74; HM Ambassador to Italy 1983-87; CMG 1975, KCMG 1983, GCMG 1988: *m* 1953, Rachel Mary, yst da of Sir Henry Nöel Bunbury, KCB, and has issue.

Arms – Argent a cross sable charged with a wreath of laurel fructed of the field a chief chequy also sable and of the first. **Crest** – A man's head and shoulders couped proper wreathed about the temples argent the ribands gules, vested paly of six sable and argent. **Supporters** – On either side a swan wings elevated and addorsed proper gorged with a collar chequy sable and argent.
Residence – 56 Church St, Orford, Woodbridge, Suffolk IP12 2NT.

SONS LIVING

Hon MARK THOMAS (66 Lincolns Inn Fields, WC2A 3LH), *b* 25 July 1954; *ed* Eton, and Corpus Christi, Camb; solicitor (Partner Farrer & Co): *m* 1978, Angela Margaret, da of J. L. Collinson, of Mansfield, Notts, and has issue living, Miles Edmund Farrer, *b* 1 July 1992, — Venetia Rachel Lucy, *b* 1982, — Camilla Frances Iona, *b* 1985, — Drusilla Katharine Anne, *b* 1988.
Hon Nicholas Edward (103 Hemingford Rd, N1), *b* 1956; *ed* Eton, and Bath Univ; ARIBA; Partner, Blee Ettwein Bridges: *m* 1985, Susan, eldest da of Peter Guggenheim, of Woodbury Salterton, Devon, and has issue living, Matthew Orlando, *b* 1988, — Alice Clementine, *b* 1986.

DAUGHTER LIVING

Hon Harriet Elizabeth BRIDGES, *b* 1958; *ed* Bryanston, and York Univ; resumed her maiden name 1983: *m* 1981 (*m diss* 1983), John Charles Eells. *Residence* – 202 Mamanasco Rd, Ridgefield, Conn 06877, USA.

BROTHER LIVING

Hon Robert Oliver *b* 1930; *ed* Eton, Magdalen Coll, Oxford, and Architectural Assocn Sch of Architecture; an ARIBA: *m* 1963, Rosamund Theresa, yr da of late Roger C. V. de Wesselow, and has issue living, John Edward, *b* 1968, — James George Robert, *b* 1970. *Residence* – Goodmans Furze, Headley, Epsom, Surrey.

SISTERS LIVING

Hon Shirley Frances, *b* 1924: *m* 1957, Hilary Topham Corke, and has issue living, William Edward Orlando, *b* 1961, — Emma Lucy, *b* 1958, — Cicely Catharine, *b* 1960, — Georgiana Phoebe, *b* 1963.
Hon Margaret Evelyn, *b* 1932: *m* 1st, 1954 (*m diss* 1969), Trevor Henry Aston; 2ndly, 1971, Paul William Jex Buxton, of Castle House, Chipping, Ongar, Essex, and has issue (by 2nd *m*) (*see* Buxton, Bt, colls).

PREDECESSOR – (**1**) *Rt Hon Sir* EDWARD ETTINGDENE BRIDGES, KG, GCB, GCVO, MC, PC, FRS, son of late Robert Seymour Bridges, OM (Poet Laureate), (of Chilswell, Oxford); *b* 1892; Sec to the Cabinet 1938-46; Permanent Sec to HM Treasury and Head of Civil Ser 1945-56; Chm of British Council 1954-67; *cr Baron Bridges*, of Headley, co Surrey, and of St Nicholas at Wade, co Kent (peerage UK) 1957: *m* 1922, Hon Katharine Dianthe Farrer, who *d* 1986, da of 2nd Baron Farrer; *d* 1969; *s* by his son (**2**) THOMAS EDWARD, 2nd Baron and present peer.

BRIDPORT, VISCOUNT (Hood) (Viscount UK 1868)

ALEXANDER NELSON HOOD, 4th Viscount; *b* 17 March 1948; *s* 1969; *ed* Eton, and the Sorbonne; 7th *Duke of Bronte* in Sicily (*cr* 1799): *m* 1st, 1972 (*m diss* 1979), Linda Jacqueline, da of Lt-Col Vincent Rudolph Paravicini, of Nutley Manor, Basingstoke; 2ndly, 1979, Nina, da of Curt Lincoln, formerly wife of Phillip Martyn, and widow of Jochen Rindt, racing driver, and has issue by 1st and 2nd *m*.

Arms – Quarterly: 1st and 4th azure, a fret argent; on a chief or three crescents sable, *Hood;* 2nd and 3rd, or, a cross patonce sable, a bend gules surmounted of another engrailed of the field charged with three bombs fired proper, on a chief undulated argent, waves of the sea from which a palm tree issuant between a disabled ship on the dexter, and a battery in ruins on the sinister all proper, over all a fess wavy azure, thereon inscribed the word "Trafalgar" or, *Nelson.* Crest – A Cornish chough proper, the dexter foot resting on the fluke of an anchor in bend sinister or. Supporters – *Dexter*, a figure of Neptune, crowned with an Eastern crown or a green robe flowing round his loins, holding a trident in the left hand, and resting the right on an anchor, also or; *Sinister*, a sea lion argent, the back fin and top of the tail gules, resting the sinister paw on an anchor or.
Residence – Villa Jonin, Le Muids 1261, Vaud, Switzerland. *Club* – Brooks's

SONS LIVING *(By 1st marriage)*

Hon PEREGRINE ALEXANDER NELSON, *b* 30 Aug 1974.

(By 2nd marriage)

Hon Anthony Nelson, *b* 1983.

WIDOW LIVING OF THIRD VISCOUNT

SHEILA JEANNE AGATHA, (Via Plebiscito 107, Rome 00186, Italy), only da of late Johan Hendrik van Meurs, and widow of W/ Cdr J. H. Little, DFC, AuxAF: *m* 1946, the 3rd Viscount, who *d* 1969; 3rdly, 1988, Alexei V. Haieff.

PREDECESSORS – (1) *Adm Sir* ALEXANDER Hood, MP (yr brother of 1st Viscount Hood) a celebrated naval commander, was *cr Baron Bridport* (peerage of Ireland) 1794 with remainder to his great-nephew, Hon Samuel Hood, 2nd son of 2nd Viscount Hood, and in failure thereof to the heirs male of his uncle, Alexander Hood; *cr Baron Bridport*, of Cricket St Thomas, Som (peerage of GB) 1796, and *Viscount Bridport*, of Cricket St Thomas (peerage of GB) 1800; *d* without issue 1814, when the English honours expired, and the Irish peerage devolved upon his great-nephew (ante) (2) SAMUEL, 2nd Baron, *b* 1788: *m* 1810, Lady Charlotte Mary Nelson, Duchess of Bronte, who *d* 1873, only surviving child and heiress of 1st Earl Nelson; *d* 1868; *s* by his son (3) *Gen* ALEXANDER NELSON, GCB, 1st Viscount, *b* 1814; *cr Viscount Bridport* (peerage of United Kingdom) 1868; Groom-in-Waiting to HM Queen Victoria 1841-58, Clerk Marshal to late Prince Consort 1853-61, an Equerry to HM Queen Victoria 1858-84, a Lord-in-Waiting to HM Queen Victoria 1884-1901, and an Extra Equerry to HM Queen Victoria 1884-1901; was an Hon Equerry to HM King Edward VII: *m* 1838, Lady Mary Penelope Hill, who *d* 1884, da of 3rd Marquess of Downshire; *d* 1904; *s* by his son (4) Col ARTHUR WELLINGTON ALEXANDER NELSON, CB, 2nd Viscount, *b* 1839; MP for W Somerset (C) 1868-80: *m* 1872, Lady Maria Georgiana Julia Fox-Strangways, who *d* 1922, sister of 5th Earl of Ilchester; *d* 1924; *s* by his grandson (5) ROWLAND ARTHUR HERBERT NELSON (only son of late Lieut Hon Maurice Henry Nelson Hood, R Naval Div (*ka* 1915), 2nd son of 2nd Viscount), 3rd Viscount, *b* 1911; Lord-in-Waiting to HM 1939-40: *m* 1st, 1934 (*m diss* 1945), Pamela Aline Mary, only da of late Charles J. Baker; 2ndly, 1946, Sheila Jeanne Agatha (who *m* 3rdly, 1988, Alexei V. Haieff), only da of Johan Hendrik van Meurs, and widow of W/Cdr J. H. Little, DFC, AuxAF; *d* 1969; *s* by his son (6) ALEXANDER NELSON, 4th Viscount and present peer; also Baron Bridport.

BRIGGS, BARON (Briggs) (Life Baron 1976)

ASA BRIGGS, son of William Walker Briggs, of Keighley, Yorks; *b* 7 May 1921; *ed* Keighley Gram Sch, and Sidney Sussex Coll, Camb (MA); MA Oxford; BSc (Econ) London; Hon LLD York, Canada, New England, and Open University; Hon DLitt E Anglia, Strathclyde, Leeds, Liverpool, Bradford, Sussex, Birmingham Missouri, Cincinnati, and George Washington; FBA and Fellow American Academy; Hon Fellow, Sidney Sussex Coll and St Catharine's Coll, Camb, and Worcester Coll, Oxford; Hon DSc Florida Presbyterian; a Fellow of Worcester Coll, Oxford 1945-55, Prof of History, Leeds Univ 1955-61, Vice-Chancellor, Sussex Univ 1967-76, Provost of Worcester Coll, Oxford 1976-91, Chancellor, the Open Univ since 1979; Chm European Inst of Educn 1975; Chm Commonwealth of Learning 1988-93; *cr Baron Briggs*, of Lewes, in co of E Sussex (Life Baron) 1976: *m* 1955, Susan Anne, da of Donald William Banwell, of Keevil, Wilts, and has issue.
Residences – The Tower, Tyninghame House, Tyninghame, E Lothian; The Caprons, Keere St, Lewes, Sussex. *Clubs* – Beefsteak, Oxford and Cambridge.

SONS LIVING

Hon Daniel Nicholas, *b* 1958: *m* 1989, Anabel E. M., yst da of Harvey Ziegler, of Chiddingfold, Surrey, and has issue living, Henry Nathaniel, *b* 1994.
Hon Matthew William Banwell, *b* 1964.

DAUGHTERS LIVING

Hon Katharine Jane, *b* 1956: *m* 1980, David Robert Wheeler, of 30 Alexandra Rd, Epsom, Surrey, and has issue living, Timothy Robert, *b* 1985, — Caroline Jane, *b* 1982, — Charlotte Rose, *b* 1987, — Georgina May, *b* 1991.
Hon Judith Susanna, *b* 1961: *m* 1985, Philip G. F. Preston, only son of W. Preston, of Folkestone, Kent, and has issue living, Jonathan, *b* 1989, — Samuel, *b* 1993, — Thomas (twin), *b* 1993.

BRIGHTMAN, BARON (Brightman) (Life Baron 1982)

JOHN ANSON BRIGHTMAN, PC, son of William Henry Brightman, of St Albans, Herts; *b* 20 June 1911; *ed* Marlborough, and St John's Coll, Camb (Hon Fellow 1982); Bar Lincoln's Inn 1932, QC 1961, a Bencher 1966; Member Gen Council of the Bar 1955-60 and 1966-70; Attorney-Gen of Duchy of Lancaster, and Attorney and Serjeant within the County Palatine of Lancaster 1969-70; Judge of Nat Industrial Relations Court 1971-74; Judge of High Court of Justice 1970-79; Lord Justice of Appeal 1979-1982, a Lord of Appeal in Ordinary 1982-86; Able Seaman, Merchant Navy, 1939-40, RNVR as Lt-Cdr 1940-46; Assist Naval Attaché, Ankara 1944; *cr* Knt 1970, PC 1979, and *Baron Brightman*, of Ibthorpe, co Hants, 1982 (Life Baron): *m* 1945, Roxane, da of Gerasimo Ambatielo, of Cephalonia, and has issue.

Arms – Per fess wavy azure and argent in chief two dolphins naiant or and in base the stern of a man of war of circa 1805 proper. **Crest** – Upon a wreath argent and gules, a herring gull statant wings elevated and addorsed proper, supporting with the dexter foot a rose gules, barbed and seeded proper. **Supporters** – Two otters each on a grassy mount encircled by water proper and collared with a crown rayonny gold.
Residences – Ibthorpe, Hants SP11 0BY; 30 Onslow Gdns, SW7 3AH.

SON LIVING

Hon Christopher Anthony John, *b* 1948; *ed* Marlborough, and St John's Coll, Camb; MB, BChir, MSc: *m* 1975, Elisabeth, yr da of Jonkheer Willem de Beyer, and has issue living, Louisa, *b* 1978, — Justina, *b* 1980, — Eugénie, *b* 1982.

BRIGSTOCKE, BARONESS (Brigstocke) (Life Baroness 1990)

HEATHER RENWICK BRIGSTOCKE, da of Sqdn Leader John Renwick Brown, DFC; *b* 2 Sept 1929; *ed* Abbey Sch, Reading, and Girton Coll, Camb; Hon Bencher Inner Temple 1992; Classics Mistress Francis Holland Sch, SW1, 1951-53, and (part-time) Godolphin and Latymer Sch 1954-60, Latin Teacher Nat Cathedral Sch, Washington DC 1962-64, Headmistress Francis Holland Sch, NW1, 1965-74, and High Mistress St Paul's Girls' Sch 1974-89; Council Member London House for Overseas Graduates 1965-91 (Vice-Chm 1975-80), Middlesex Hosp Medical Sch 1971-80, Royal Holloway Coll 1977-85, City Univ 1978-83, Member The Royal Soc of Arts 1983-87, St George's House, Windsor, 1984-90, Modern Foreign Languages Working Group 1989-90, Museums and Galleries Commn since 1992, and Health Education Authority since 1989; Trustee National Gallery 1975-82, Kennedy Memorial Trust 1980-85, and City Technology Colls Trust since 1987; Pres Bishop Creighton House Settlement, Fulham, since 1977, and Girls' Schs Assocn 1980-81; Gov Wellington Coll 1975-87, The Royal Ballet Sch 1977-92, Forest Sch 1982-90, Museum of London 1986-92, and Gordonstoun Sch 1991-93; Chm English-Speaking Union of the Commonwealth since 1993; Non-Exec Dir LWT 1982-90, Member Programme Advisory Bd, LWT 1990-93; Chm Autistic Care & Training Devpt Appeal 1990, Trustees Geffrye Museum since 1990, Thames LWT Telethon Trust 1990, and The Menerva Educational Trust 1991-93; Independent Nat Dir The Times Newspaper Holdings since 1991; Member Governing Body Imperial Coll since 1991; Chm Landau Forte City Technology Coll, Derby since 1993 (Gov since 1992); Assoc Dir Great Universal Stores since 1993; Vice Pres City & Guilds of London Inst since 1993; Non-Exec Dir Burberrys since 1993; Cttee Member Automobile Assocn 1975-90; Special Advisor Kays 1989-90, and Burberrys 1989-92; *cr Baroness Brigstocke*, of Kensington, Royal Borough of Kensington and Chelsea (Life Baroness) 1990: *m* 1952, Geoffrey Brigstocke, who *d* 1974, and has issue.
Address – House of Lords, SW1A 0PW.

SONS LIVING

Hon David Hugh Charles, *b* 1953.
Hon Julian Renwick, *b* 1955.
Hon Thomas James Jefferson, *b* 1961.

DAUGHTER LIVING

Hon Emma Persephone, *b* 1957.

BRIMELOW, BARON (Brimelow) (Life Baron 1976)

THOMAS BRIMELOW, GCMG, OBE, son of late William Brimelow, of New Mills, Derbys; *b* 25 Oct 1915; *ed* New Mills Co Secondary Sch, and Oriel Coll, Oxford (BA; Hon Fellow 1973); Hon Fellow Queen's Coll, Oxford 1974; 1st Sec, Havana 1948, Counsellor Ankara 1954, Head of Northern Dept FO, 1956, Counsellor Washington 1960-63, Min British Embassy, Moscow 1963-66, Ambassador to Poland 1966-69, Dep Under-Sec of State FCO 1969-73, and Perm Under-Sec of State FO, and Head of Diplo Ser 1973-75; Member European Parliament 1977-78; Chm Occupational Pensions Bd 1978-82; *cr* OBE (Civil) 1954, CMG 1959, KCMG 1968, GCMG 1975, and *Baron Brimelow*, of Tyldesley, in co Lancs (Life Baron) 1976: *m* 1945, Jean E, who *d* 1993, da of late John William Underwood Cull, of Glasgow, and has issue.
Residence – 12 West Hill Court, Millfield Lane, N6 6JJ. *Club* – Athenaeum.

DAUGHTERS LIVING

Hon Alison Jane, *b* 1949.
Hon Elizabeth Anne, *b* 1951.

BRISTOL, MARQUESS OF (Hervey) (Marquess UK 1826)
(Name pronounced "Harvy")

I shall never forget

JE N'OUBLIERAI JAMAIS

FREDERICK WILLIAM JOHN AUGUSTUS HERVEY, 7th Marquess; *b* 15 Sept 1954; *s* 1985; *ed* Harrow; Hereditary High Steward of the Liberty of St Edmund, patron of thirty livings: *m* 1984 (*m diss* 1987), Francesca, da of Douglas H. Fisher, of Marbella, Spain, and formerly wife of Phillip Jones, of USA.

Arms – Gules, on a bend argent, three trefoils slipped vert. **Crest** – An ounce passant sable, spotted, ducally collared, and chain reflexed over the back or, holding in the dexter paw a trefoil slipped vert. **Supporters** – Two ounces sable, bezantée, ducally collared, and chain reflexed over the back or.
Seat – Ickworth, Bury St Edmunds, Suffolk.

HALF-BROTHERS LIVING (*Son of 6th Marquess by 2nd m*)

Lord (FREDERICK WILLIAM CHARLES) NICHOLAS WENTWORTH, *b* 26 Nov 1961.

(Son of 6th Marquess by 3rd m)

Lord Frederick William Augustus, *b* 1979.

HALF-SISTERS LIVING (*Daughters of 6th Marquess by 3rd m*)

Lady Victoria Frederica Isabella, *b* 1976.
Lady Isabella Frederica Louisa, *b* 1982.

MOTHER LIVING

Pauline Mary (Mesnil Warren, Newmarket, Suffolk), da of late Herbert Coxon Bolton: *m* 1st, 1949 (*m diss* 1959), as his 1st wife, Victor Frederick Cochrane Hervey, Earl Jermyn (afterwards 6th Marquess of Bristol), who *d* 1985; 2ndly, 1959, as his 2nd wife, Capt Edward George Lambton, RHG, who *d* 1983 (*see* E Durham, colls).

WIDOW LIVING OF SIXTH MARQUESS

YVONNE MARIE (*Marchioness of Bristol*) (Sun Tower, Square Beaumarchais, Monte Carlo, Monaco), only da of Anthony Sutton, of Woodstock, The Glen, Farnborough Park, Kent: *m* 1974, as his 3rd wife, the 6th Marquess, who *d* 1985.

COLLATERAL BRANCHES LIVING

    Granddaughter of late Sir George William Hervey, KCB, el son of late Lord William Hervey, CB, 3rd son of 1st Marquess:—
      Issue of late Claude Arthur Hervey, *b* 1891, *d* 1927: *m* 1920, Edith Kathleen, who *d* 1972, da of late Humphry B. Lamb, of Penn, Staffordshire:—
Cecilia Dora, *b* 1923: *m* 1945, John Quay, and has issue living, Jacqueline Teresa, *b* 1950. *Residence* – 48 Garden Wood Rd, East Grinstead, Sussex, RH19 1NL.

    Grandchildren of late Francis Arthur Hervey, yr son of late Lord William Hervey, CB (ante):—
      Issue of late Alec Francis Hervey, *b* 1885, *d* 1949: *m* 1st, 1912 (*m diss* 1924), Winifred Victoria (who *d* 1963), da of late Frederick George Cosens, of 7 Observatory Gdns, W, and Bacton, Norfolk; 2ndly, 1925, Edyth Cecilia, who *d* 1987, da of L Col John Charles Cowan, and formerly wife of Alexander Lockington:—
(By 1st *m*) Ronald Frederick William, *b* 1919: *m* 1st, 1943 (*m diss* 1948), Constance Mary (*dec*), da of late J. D. Bunce, and widow of Alexander Zatonski, Flying Officer RAF; 2ndly, 1958, Jeanne Patricia, da of late Rev A. W. Dowse, and has issue living (by 2nd *m*), Timothy Hugh (302 Victoria Drive, Eastbourne, E Sussex BN20 8XS), *b* 1960: *m* 1992, Susan Mary, da of Sidney Arthur Peacham, of Bexhill-on-Sea, E Sussex, and has issue living, Rebecca Maria *b* 1992, — Jennifer Charlotte, *b*

1962: *m* 1987, Kevin Allen Moon, of Church Farm Barn, Ninfield, E Sussex TN33 9JX. *Residence* – 16 Virginia Court, Virginia Water, Surrey. ——— Patricia Leila *b* 1914: *m* 1940, Capt Martin Edward Scobell Boissier, DSO, RN, who *d* 1964.

Granddaughter of Douglas George Hervey (infra):—
Issue of late Edward George Hervey, *b* 1917, *d* 1959: *m* 1956, Sheila Mary Howard (*Lady Sebright*), who *m* 2ndly, 1965, Sir Hugo Giles Edmund Sebright, 14th Bt, who *d* 1985, da of Walter Howard Rocke, of Salisbury, Rhodesia:—
Elizabeth Lepel Howard *b* 1957.

Grandchildren of late George Henry William Hervey, 2nd son of Rt Rev Lord Arthur Charles Hervey, DD, Lord Bishop of Bath and Wells, 4th son of 1st Marquess:—
Issue of late Douglas George Hervey, *b* 1880, *d* 1965: *m* 1913, Ida Constance, who *d* 1972, da of late Rev Edward Clowes, of Colworth, Bexhill-on-Sea:—
Constance Valentine, *b* 1920: *m* 1951, D. C. Lamsdale, who *d* 1993, of 51 Priory Rd, Hastings, E Sussex, and has issue living, Judith, *b* 1952, — Susan Sarah, *b* 1956. ——— Margery, MBE, *b* 1921: *m* 1945, Arthur Thomas Hingle, and has had issue, Michael, *b* 1949; *d* 1978, — Peter John Benedict, *b* 1956, — Jane, *b* 1947, — Gillian, *b* 1950, — Veronica Anne, *b* 1954, — Margaret Mary Bridget, *b* 1959. *Address* – PO Box 1067, Wimberley, Texas, USA.
Issue of late Gerald Arthur Hervey, Lieut (TF) RGA, *b* 1881, *ka* 1917: *m* 1912, Dorothy, who *d* 1949, da of late Alfred Symes, of Tendring, Essex:—
Anthony Gerald, *b* 1915; *ed* Marlborough, and Pembroke Coll, Camb: *m* 1948, Aileen Margaret, da of late Dr L. R. Pickett, of 167 Cooden Sea Road, Cooden, Sussex, and has issue living, Gerald Edward (12 Bucknalls Lane, Garston, Watford, Herts), *b* 1949: *m* 1974, Mary Agnes, da of late Michael Dore, of co Limerick, and has issue living, Simon Anthony *b* 1985, — Christopher Symes (5 Burlington Gds, W4), *b* 1952: *m* 1st, 1977 (*m diss* 1984), Christina Ann, da of Watson Failes, of Chorleywood, Herts; 2ndly, 1984 (*m diss* 1989), Nicole, da of Colin Charters, of Caterham, Surrey; 3rdly, 1992, Lesley, da of John Exley, of Stratford upon Avon, and has issue living (by 2nd *m*), Toby James Symes *b* 1987, Tanya Maria *b* 1985. *Residence* – 3825 Sarasota Golf Club Blvd, Sarasota, Florida, USA. ——— Elizabeth Mary (6 Bucklehaven, Stockton Close, Charlton Kings, Cheltenham, GL53 9JR), *b* 1913: *m* 1948, John Charles Jones, MBE, who *d* 1969.

Descendants of late Frederick Anne Hervey-Bathurst, next brother of late Felton Elwell Hervey-Bathurst (el son of late Felton Lionel Hervey, son of late Hon Felton Hervey, 8th son of 1st Earl of Bristol), who was *cr* a *Baronet* 1818, and whom he *s* (under special remainder) 1819:—
See Hervey-Bathurst, Bt.

PREDECESSORS – **(1)** John Hervey, of Ickworth, Suffolk, MP for Bury St Edmunds 1690-1 and 1695-1703, was *cr Baron Hervey of Ickworth* (peerage of England) 1703, and *Earl of Bristol* (peerage of GB)1714: *m* 1st, 1688, Isabella, who *d* 1693, da and heir of Sir Robert Carr, 3rd Bt; 2ndly, 1695, Elizabeth, who *d* 1741, da and co-heir of Sir Thomas Felton, 4th Bt, by Lady Elizabeth Howard, da and co-heir of 3rd Earl of Suffolk, and 3rd Lord Howard de Walden; his el son by 2nd *m*, John, who had been summoned to Parl as Lord Hervey 1733, *d* 1743, leaving, by his wife Mary Lepel, issue of whom three sons succeeded to the title; the Earl *d* 1751; s by his grandson **(2)** George William, 2nd Earl; Ambassador to Spain 1758-61; Lord Lt of Ireland 1766-67; *d unm* 1775; s by his brother **(3)** Augustus John, 3rd Earl, Vice-Adm of the Blue, and a Lord of the Admiralty in 1799; *dsp* 1779; s by his brother **(4)** Rt Rev Frederick Augustus, 4th Earl, *b* 1730; Bishop of Derry, who by descent from his grandmother *s de jure* to the Barony of Howard de Walden, which title was in 1806 confirmed upon his great-grandson, the 2nd Baron Seaford; the Bishop *m* 1752, Elizabeth, who *d* 1800, sister and heir of Sir Charles Davers, 5th Bt (and gt-grandda of 2nd Baron Jermyn); *d* 1803; s by his el surv son **(5)** Frederick William, 5th Earl; *cr Earl Jermyn and Marquess of Bristol* (peerage of UK) 1820; *m* 1798, Elizabeth Albana, who *d* 1844, da of 1st Baron Templetown, *d* 1859; s by his son **(6)** Frederick William, 2nd Marquess, *b* 1880; MP for Bury St Edmunds 1826-59; Treasurer of R Household 1841-46: *m* 1830, Lady Katharine Isabella Manners, who *d* 1848, da of 5th Duke of Rutland; *d* 1864; s by his son **(7)** Frederick William John, 3rd Marquess, *b* 1834; MP for W Suffolk (C) 1859-64, and Lord-Lt of Suffolk 1886-1907: *m* 1862, Geraldine Georgina Mary, who *d* 1927, da of Gen Hon George Anson; *d* 1907; s by his nephew **(8)** Frederick William Fane, MVO (son of Lord Augustus Henry Charles Hervey, MP, 2nd son of 2nd Marquess), 4th Marquess, *b* 1863; Rear-Adm; MP for Bury St Edmunds (C) 1906-07: *m* 1896, Alice Frances Theodora, who *d* 1957, da of George Edward Wythes, of Copt Hall, Epping; *d* 1951, s by his brother **(9)** Herbert Arthur Robert, 5th Marquess, *b* 1870; Min and Consul-Gen to Colombia 1919-23, and Min to Peru and Equador 1923-29: *m* 1st, 1914 (*m diss* 1933), Lady Jean Alice Elaine Cochrane, who *d* 1955, da of 12th Earl of Dundonald; 2ndly, 1952, Dora Frances Emblin, who *d* 1953, widow of Don Pedro de Zulueta; *d* 1960; s by his only son **(10)** Victor Frederick Cochrane, 6th Marquess, *b* 1915; Chancellor Monarchist League: *m* 1st, 1949 (*m diss* 1959), Pauline Mary, da of late Herbert Coxon Bolton; 2ndly, 1960 (*m diss* 1972), Lady Anne Juliet Dorothea Maud Wentworth Fitzwilliam, only child of 8th Earl Fitzwilliam; 3rdly, 1974, Yvonne Marie, only da of Anthony Sutton, of Woodstock, The Glen, Farnborough Park, Kent; *d* 1985; s by his el son **(11)** Frederick William John Augustus, 7th Marquess and present peer; also Earl of Bristol, Earl Jermyn, and Baron Hervey of Ickworth.

BROADBRIDGE, BARON (Broadbridge) (Baron UK 1945, Bt UK 1937)

PETER HEWETT BROADBRIDGE, 3rd Baron and 3rd Baronet; *b* 19 Aug 1938; *s* 1972; *ed* Hurstpierpoint, and St Catherine's Coll, Oxford (MA, BSc): *m* 1st, 1967 (*m diss* 1980), Mary, only da of W. O. Busch, of An Der Brücke, Dittershausen, Kassel, W Germany; 2ndly, 1989, Sally Frances Finn, and has issue by 1st *m*.

Arms – Gules, in chief two pens in saltire or and in base over water a stone bridge of a single span embattled proper. **Crest** – A dolphin hauriant argent between two gilly-flowers gules slipped and leaved vert. **Supporters** – On either side a dolphin proper charged with a sword erect gules.
Address – c/o House of Lords, SW1.

INDUSTRIA·ET·PERSEVERANTIA

By industry and perseverance

DAUGHTERS LIVING

Hon Jemima Louise, *b* 1970.
Hon Sophie Mary, *b* 1972.

UNCLE LIVING (*son of 1st Baron*)

Hon Howard Eustace (12 Texel, Alexandra Rd, Pietermaritzburg, Natal), *b* 1904: *m* 1935, Margaret Ada Marion, da of Capt H. H. Witherington, and has had issue, †George Witherington, *b* 1939; BSc: *m* 1962, Joan Margaret (Gablemere, Gable Road, Durban, Natal, S Africa), da of Cyril Ridge, of Pietermaritzburg, S Africa, and *d* 1968, leaving issue, Ann Magaret *b* 1967, — Sally Kathleen, *b* 1937: *m* 1966, Peter Jeremy Chadwick Horne, and has issue living, Lance Chadwick *b* 1969, Timothy George Chadwick *b* 1971.

WIDOWS LIVING OF SONS OF FIRST BARON

Anne Marjorie, da of J. Locke Elfick: *m* 1927, Hon Hugh Trevor Broadbridge, who *d* 1979, and has issue (*see colls infra*).
Margaret Anne, da of George S. Cumming, of Bloemfontein, S Africa: *m* 1948, Hon Rupert Guy Broadbridge, who *d* 19—, and has issue (*see colls infra*).

COLLATERAL BRANCHES LIVING

Issue of late Hon Ralph George Cameron Broadbridge, 2nd son of 1st Baron, *b* 1901; *d* 1983: *m* 1925, Emma Rose Hancock, who *d* 195-, da of Henry Van der Weydon:—
Enid Rose, *b* 1926: *m* 1948, Alexander Rolland, and has issue living, Andrew, *b* 1949, — Martin, *b* 1951, — Nigel, *b* 1955. —— June, *b* 1927. —— Anita, *b* 1928: *m* 1949, Dennis Robert Hutchins, and has issue living, Anthony David, *b* 1953, — Lucy Jane, *b* 1955.

Issue of late Hon Hugh Trevor Broadbridge, 3rd son of 1st Baron, *b* 1903, *d* 1979: *m* 1927, Anne Marjorie, da of J. Locke Elfck:—
MARTIN HUGH (The Old Candle House, Mill Lane, North Cave, E Yorks), *b* 29 Nov 1929: *m* 1954, Norma, da of late Maj Herbert Sheffield, MC; 2ndly, 1968, Elizabeth, da of J. E. Trotman, and has issue living (by 1st *m*), Richard, *b* 1959, — Katherine, *b* 1956. —— Jill, *b* 1932: *m* 1954, John Damment, RAF (c/o Lloyds Bank, 6 Pall Mall, SW1 5NH), and has issue living, Stephen, *b* 1957, — Helen, *b* 1956, — Deborah, *b* 1958, — Louise, *b* 1959, — Susan, *b* 1962.

Issue of late Hon Rupert Guy Broadbridge, 5th son of 1st Baron, *b* 1906, *d* 19—: *m* 1948, Margaret Anne, da of George S. Cumming, of Bloemfontein, S Africa:—
Beverley, *b* 1949: *m* 19—, Maurice Roger Descroizilles, and has issue living, Lee, *b* 1975, — Andrew Vivian, *b* 1977, — Corinne, *b* 1980.

PREDECESSORS – **(1)** *Sir* GEORGE Broadbridge, KCVO, son of late Henry Broadbridge, of Brighton; *b* 1869; an Alderman (Candlewick Ward) for City of London (Sheriff 1933-34), Lord Mayor of London 1936-37; sat as MP for City of London (*C*) 1938-45; *cr* a *Baronet* (UK, of Wargrave Place) 1937, and *Baron Broadbridge*, of Brighton, co Sussex (peerage of United Kingdom) 1945: *m* 1st 1895, Fanny Kathleen, who *d* 1928, da of late Richard Brigden, of Brighton; 2ndly, 1929, Clara Maud, who *d* 1949, da of late John Swornsbourne, of Bognor Regis, Sussex; *d* 1952, *s* by his el son **(2)** ERIC WILBERFORCE, 2nd Baron, *b* 1895: *m* 1924, Mabel Daisy, who *d* 1966, da of Arthur Edward Clarke; *d* 1972, *s* by his only son **(3)** PETER HEWETT, 3rd Baron and present peer.

Brocas, Viscount; son of Earl Jellicoe.

BROCK, BARONY OF (Brock) (Extinct 1980)

DAUGHTERS LIVING OF LIFE BARON

Hon Mary Rose, *b* 1933; *ed* Wycombe Abbey Sch: *m* 1959, Keith Vanstone, of Blakes Farm, Ashurst, Steyning, W Sussex, and has issue.
Hon Margaret Louise (Owl Cottage, Laurel Lane, Queen Camel, Som BA22 7NV), *b* 1936; *ed* Malvern Girls' Coll: *m* 1962 (*m diss* 1988) (John Alexander) Simon Cary Mayhew (*see* V Falkland, colls, 1990 Edn), and has issue living, Ella Rose Louise, *b* 1963, — Matilda Jane, *b* 1965: *m* 1990, James R. M. McMaster, son of Dr Brian Master, of W Coker, Som.

BROCKET, BARON (Nall-Cain) (Baron UK 1933, Bt UK 1921)

The cat stroked is meek

CHARLES RONALD GEORGE NALL-CAIN, 3rd Baron, and 3rd Baronet; *b* 12 Feb 1952; *s* 1967; *ed* Eton; late 14th/20th King's Hussars: *m* 1982, Isabell Maria only da of Gustavo Lorenzo, of Whaleneck Drive, Merrick, Long Island, New York, and has issue.

Arms – Quarterly: 1st and 4th argent, three salmon haurient gules, in chief an oak tree eradicated proper, *Cain*; 2nd and 3rd per chevron barry of six gules and or and of the first, in chief two stags' heads caboshed proper and in base a lion rampant guardant of the second, *Nall*. **Crest** – 1st, a cat salient guardant erminois holding between the paws a dexter hand couped gules, *Cain*; 2nd, within a leather garter buckled gules a bee or, *Nall*. **Supporters** – Two cats guardant erminois.
Residence – Brocket Hall, Welwyn, Herts.

SONS LIVING

Hon ALEXANDER CHRISTOPHER CHARLES, *b* 30 Sept 1984.
Hon William Thomas Anthony, *b* 1991.

DAUGHTER LIVING

Hon Antalya Stephanie Lauren, *b* 1987.

BROTHERS LIVING

(Raised to the rank of a Baron's sons 1969)

Hon Richard Philip Christopher (Potters Hall, Dane End, Ware, Herts SG12 0JU; MCC) *b* 1953; *ed* Eton; late Lieut 2nd Bn, RGJ: *m* 1978, Juliet Paula Vivian, da of J. E. V. Forester, of Villa Mont Gras d'Eau, St Brelade, Jersey, CI, and has had issue, Sam Christopher Philip, *b* and *d* 1987, — Rebecca Elizabeth Emily, *b* 1981, — Claire Antonia Louise, *b* 1982.
Hon David Michael Anthony (Attington Stud, Tetsworth, Oxon), *b* 1955; *ed* Harrow: *m* 1992, Albertine Hungerbühler.

UNCLE LIVING *(Son of 2nd Baron)*

Hon David Lawrence Robert (Ballacleator, St Judes, Isle of Man; Cavalry Club), *b* 1930; *ed* Eton, and Magdalene Coll, Camb (BA 1953, MA 1957), late 12th Roy Lancers and Derbyshire Yeo; FRICS; JP Cheshire 1964; Gov St Patrick's Hosp Dublin 1973-77: *m* 1958, Lady Katherine Elizabeth Palmer, sister of 4th Earl of Selborne, and has issue living, James Alexander, *b* 1961: *m* 1992, Sarah-Jane, elder da of Anthony Bremner, of Llorts, Andorra, — Caroline Davina, *b* 1959: *m* 1986, Paul David Cherry, yr son of Peter Harold Cherry, of Weston Manor, Hitchin, Herts, and has issue living, Alexander *b* 1988, Harriet *b* 1989, — Annabel Priscilla Angela (*Lady Anthony Hill*), *b* 1963: *m* 1992, Lord Anthony Ian Hill, yr son of 8th Marquess of Downshire.

AUNT LIVING *(Daughter of 2nd Baron)*

Hon Elizabeth Angela Veronica Rose, *b* 1938: *m* 1st, 1958 (*m diss* 1969), 6th Marquess of Headfort; 2ndly, 1970 (*m diss* 1987), William Murless Knight, and has issue living (by 1st *m*) (*see* M Headfort), — (by 2nd *m*), Peregrine Robert Christian Murless, *b* 1971. *Residence* – Thoodyn, Bay View, Ramsey, Isle of Man.

MOTHER LIVING

Elizabeth Mary, da of late R. J. Stallard, of Le Shakespeare, 12 Blvd Princess Charlotte, Monte Carlo, Monaco: *m* 1st, 1950, Hon Ronald Charles Manus Nall-Cain, who *d* 1961; el son of 2nd Baron; 2ndly, 1964, Colin John Richard Trotter, of Attington Stud, Tetsworth, Oxon.

PREDECESSORS

PREDECESSORS – The family of O'Cahan was settled in Northern Ireland from the earliest times, owning a large territory there called O'Cahan's country. The O'Cahans, who trace their descent from Niall of the Nine Hostages, King of Ulster in the 5th century (also ancestor of the O'Neills) were Lords of the Route and Princes of Limavady. They owned the fishing rights in the three rivers, Bann, Foyle, and Roe prior to the Plantation of Ulster, hence the three salmon in the Cain Arms, while the wild cat now used as a crest and supporters in the Arms is reputed to have been used on the shield of The O'Cahan in 850. Manus Cathan an Duin, Prince of Limavady, was killed in the Battle of Down in 1260. Sir Donall O'Cahan of Limavady was knighted in 1607. His grandson, Eanagh, was deprived of his lands on the Plantation of Ulster and settled in co Galway in 1631, Joseph O'Cahan, great-grandson of Eanagh, *d* in Ballybane, co Galway in 1756 and his 2nd son, William, *m* Catherine O'Malley, and was the father of James O'Cahan, *b* (in the parish of St Nicholas, Galway) 1787. James changed his name to Cain, joined the 88th Regiment of Foot (later the Connaught Rangers), and fought in the Penninsular War. He *m* Mary, da of Alexander Deane of Cork, and sister of Sir Thomas Deane, the well-known Architect and Lord Mayor of Cork. Their son, Robert Cain, *b* on Spike Island, Cork, 1826, emigrated to England in 1844: *m* 1848, Ann, da of James Newall, of Lowton. He founded the firm of Robert Cain & Sons, and had with other issue a 3rd son, William Ernest, *b* 1864, *cr* 1st Baronet of Wargrave, and a 4th **(1)** CHARLES ALEXANDER, *b* 1866; Chm of Walker Cain, Ltd, a JP and DL for Herts (High Sheriff 1925), Pres of Hitchin Dist of League of Mercy, and a KGStJ; assumed additional surname of Nall; *cr a Baronet* 1921, and *Baron Brocket*, of Brocket Hall, co Hertford (peerage of United Kingdom) 1933: *m* 1st, 1888, Florence, who *d* 1927, yst da of late William Nall, of Kegworth, Derbyshire; 2ndly, 1928, Anne Page, JP, who *d* 1949, da of late Richard Benyon Croft, JP, DL, of Fanhams Hall, Ware; *d* 1934; *s* by his son **(2)** ARTHUR RONALD NALL, 2nd Baron, *b* 1904; a JP for Herts; MP for Wavertree Div of Liverpool (C) 1931-34: *m* 1927, Angela Beatrix, who *d* 1975, yr da of late Rev Preb William Geoffrey Pennyman, of Ormesby Hall, Yorks (Walker, Bt, *cr* 1868), *d* 1967; *s* by his grandson **(3)** CHARLES RONALD GEORGE (el son of late Hon Ronald Charles Manus Nall-Cain, el son of 2nd Baron) 3rd Baron, and present peer.

BROCKWAY, BARONY OF (Brockway) (Extinct 1988)

SON LIVING OF LIFE BARON (By 2nd marriage)

Hon Christopher Fenner, *b* 1946: *m* 1st, 1974 (*m diss* 1979), — ; 2ndly, 1981, Sophie Marie-Luc, da of Luc Bernhard Niggli, of Switzerland, and has issue living (by 1st *m*), Steven, *b* 1974, — (by 2nd *m*) David Mehdi, *b* 1985, — Laylah Suzanne, *b* 1982.

DAUGHTERS LIVING OF LIFE BARON (By 1st marriage)

Hon Joan Vera, *b* 1921: *m* 1944, Capt Everett Samuel Pover, and has issue.
Hon Olive Fenner, *b* 1924: *m* 1944 (*m diss* 1986), Cecil Outrim, and has issue. *Residence* – Pass Christian, Hosey Hill, Westerham, Kent.

WIDOW LIVING OF LIFE BARON

EDITH VIOLET (*Baroness Brockway*), da of late Archibald Herbert King, of Catford, SE6: *m* 1946, as his 2nd wife, Baron Brockway (Life Baron), who *d* 1988.

Brooke, Lord; son of Earl Brooke and of Warwick (see Warwick)

Brooke and of Warwick, Earl (see Warwick)

BROOKE OF CUMNOR, BARONY OF (Brooke) (Extinct 1984)

SONS LIVING OF LIFE BARON

Rt Hon Peter Leonard, CH, MP (110A, Ashley Gdns, SW1; The Old Vicarage, W Lavington, Devizes, Wilts; *Clubs* – Brooks's, City Livery, I Zingari, MCC, St George's, Conservative), *b* 1934, *ed* Marlborough, Balliol Coll, Oxford and Harvard Business Sch, Assist Govt Whip House of Commons 1979-83; a Lord Commr of HM Treasury 1983, a Parliamentary Under Sec of State, Dept of Educn & Science, 1983-87, Paymaster Gen and Min of State 1987-89, Sec of State for N Ireland 1989-92, since when Sec of State for National Heritage, Chm Conservative Party 1987-89; MP for City of London and Westminster South (C) since 1977; PC 1988, CH 1992: *m* 1st, 1964, Joan, da of late Frederick George Smith, of São Paulo, Brazil; 2ndly, 1991, Mrs Lindsay Allinson, and has issue (by 1st *m*).
Hon Sir Henry (*Hon Mr Justice Brooke*), *b* 1936; *ed* Marlborough, and Balliol Coll, Oxford; a Judge of the High Court of Justice (Queen's Bench Div) since 1988; Chm Law Commn since 1993; Kt 1988: *m* 1966, Bridget Mary, da of Wilfrid George Kalaugher, of Appledene, Marlborough, and has issue, three sons and one da. *Address* – Royal Courts of Justice, Strand, WC2.

DAUGHTERS LIVING OF LIFE BARON

Hon Honor Leslie, *b* 1941: *m* 1966, Dr (Thomas) Nigel Miller, of Laurel Hill, Repton, Derby, and has issue.
Hon Margaret Hilary Diana, *b* 1944: *m* 1971, James Douglas Pulfer, c/o University of Papua New Guinea, and has issue.

WIDOW LIVING OF LIFE BARON

BARBARA MURIEL, Baroness Brooke of Ystradfellte (Life Baroness) (see that title).

BROOKE OF YSTRADFELLTE, BARONESS (Brooke) (Life Baroness 1964)

BARBARA MURIEL BROOKE, DBE, da of late Rev Canon Alfred Augustus Mathews, of Llanwern, Gwent; *b* 14 Jan 1908; *ed* Queen Anne's Sch, Caversham, and Glos Training Coll of Domestic Science; a Member of Hampstead Borough Council 1948-65, and Vice-Chm of Conservative Party Organization 1954-64; a Member of N-W Metropolitan Regional Hosp Board 1955-66; Chm of Governing Body of Godolphin and Latymer Sch since 1960, and of Exec Cttee of Queen's Inst of Dist Nursing 1961-71; a Member of Management Cttee, King Edward's Hosp Fund for London 1967-70; Hon Fellow of Westfield Coll; *cr* DBE (Civil) 1960, and *Baroness Brooke of Ystradfellte*, of Ystradfellte, co Brecknock (Life Baroness) 1964: *m* 1933, Baron Brooke of Cumnor, (Life Baron), who *d* 1984, and has issue (see that title, ext).
Residence – Romans Halt, Mildenhall, Marlborough, Wilts. *Club* – University Women's.

BROOKEBOROUGH, VISCOUNT (Brooke) (Viscount UK 1952 Bt UK 1822)

ALAN HENRY BROOKE, 3rd Viscount, and 7th Baronet; *b* 30 June 1952; *s* 1987; *ed* Harrow, and Millfield; DL co Fermanagh 1987; 17th/21st Lancers, Capt 4th Bn Ulster Defence Regt 1977, Maj 4th Bn UDR and Co Cmdr (part time) 1988, Lt-Col Royal Irish Regt 1993; Memb House of Lords EEC Agric Cttee 1988: *m* 1980, Janet Elizabeth, only da of John Cooke, of Ballyvoy Lodge, Doagh, co Antrim.

Arms – Or, a cross engrailed per pale gules and sable, a crescent for difference. **Crest** – A brock, or badger, passant argent. **Supporters** – *Dexter*, a dolphin sable; *sinister*, a lion double queued gules langued azure.
Seat – Colebrooke, Brookeborough, co Fermanagh. *Club* – Cavalry and Guards.

GLORIA FINIS

Glory is the end

Residence – Galgorm Castle, Ballymena, co Antrim.

BROTHER LIVING

Hon CHRISTOPHER ARTHUR, *b* 16 May 1954; *ed* Gordonstoun; Lt 5th Inniskilling Drag Gds: *m* 1990, Amanda M., da of G. N. R. Hodges, of Lowlands, Trinity, Jersey, CI, and has issue living, Archie Alan John, *b* 17 Dec 1991, — Henry Arthur Oliver, *b* 1993.

SISTERS LIVING

Hon (Rosalind) Juliana, *b* 1950: *m* 1st, 1973, Maj Nigel Cowie, who *d* 1991, 2nd son of Lt-Col Howard Elphinstone Cowie, of South Poorton, Powerstock, Bridport, Dorset; 2ndly, 1994, Christopher James Grose, only son of late Brig James Grose, of Bicknoller, Som, and has issue living (by 1st *m*), Alexander John, *b* 1975, — Rosalind Mary, *b* 1977. *Residence* – The Old Bakery, Aldsworth, Cheltenham, Glos.
Hon Melinda Charlotte, *b* 1958: *m* 1982, Nicholas Ronald Taylor, eldest son of Ronald Taylor, of Brighton Wood, Alresford, Hants, and has issue living, Christopher Martin John, *b* 1990, — Alice Melinda, *b* 1988. *Residence* – Bradley Fields Farm, Lillingstone Lovell, Buckingham MK18 5BH.
Hon Susanna Cynthia, *b* 1962: *m* 1989, Richard John Hamilton Stubber, 2nd son of late Col John Henry Hamilton Stubber, of Aughentaine, Fivemiletown, co Tyrone, and has issue living, Thomas Richard, *b* 1991, — Iona Rose, *b* 1993. *Residence* – Foley Hill, Aghalee, co Antrim BT67 0DZ.

WIDOW LIVING OF SECOND VISCOUNT

ROSEMARY HILDA (*Rosemary, Viscountess Brookeborough*), da of late Lt-Col Arthur O'Neill Cubitt Chichester, OBE, MC (*see* M Donegall, colls): *m* 1949, the 2nd Viscount, PC, who *d* 1987. *Residence* – Ashbrooke, Brookeborough, co Fermanagh.

COLLATERAL BRANCHES LIVING (*In remainder to Baronetcy only*)

Issue of late Sir Alan Francis Brooke, KG, GCB, OM, GCVO, DSO, 6th son of 3rd Baronet, who was *cr* Viscount Alanbrooke 1946 (see that title).

Granddaughters of late Col Arthur Brooke, IA, 2nd son of late Capt Sir Harry Vesey Brooke, KBE, 2nd son of 2nd baronet:—
Issue of late Maj Basil Arthur Brooke, MC, late Gordon Highlanders, *b* 1917, *d* 1992: *m* 1st, 1946, Mora Allison, da of late Col James Alexander Stewart Balmain, of Alford House, Somerset; 2ndly, 1968, Jane (Sussex Cottage, E Lavant, Chichester), da of — Lane, and widow of Howard Samuel:—
(By 1st *m*) Patricia Alison, *b* 1946. —— Sheelah Anne, *b* 1949. —— Diana Eva, *b* 1951.

Grandson of Arthur Basil Brooke, 3rd son of 2nd baronet:—
Issue of late Lt-Gen Sir Bertram Norman SERGISON-BROOKE, KCB, KCVO, CMG, DSO, *b* 1880, *d* 1967: *m* 1st, 1915, Prudence Ida Evelyn, who *d* 1918, da of late Capt Charles Warden Sergison, of Cuckfield Park, Sussex (*see* B Sudeley, 1911 Edn); 2ndly, 1923, Hilda, who *d* 1954, da of Mark Fenwick, of Abbotswood, Stow-on-the-Wold:—
(By 2nd *m*) Timothy Mark (Chipping Warden Manor, Banbury, Oxon), *b* 1924; *ed* Eton; 1939-45 War with Gren Gds: *m* 1964, Hon Mary Anne Hare, el da of 1st Viscount Blakenham, and has issue living, Nicholas Mark, *b* 1966, — Kate Constantia, *b* 1968.

Grandson of late Brig-Gen Henry Francis Brooke, el son of late George Augustus Frederick Brooke, 8th son of 1st baronet:—
Issue of late Maj George Cecil Brooke, *b* 1870, *ka* at Gallipoli 1915: *m* 1912, Barbara, who *d* 1979, only child of late Capt W. H. Allen, of Dhuarigle Castle, co Cork:—
Henry John Allen, MBE, DSC, RN, *b* 1913; *ed* Wellington Coll; Com; acting Capt and Senior Officer Reserve Ships, Portsmouth 1960-61; MOD (Navy Dept) 1961-79 (ret); Nyon Patrol, Spanish Civil War, 1937-38, 1939-45 War in Mediterranean, N African Landings, with Arctic Convoys OPs Norway, and in Pacific (despatches, DSC); MBE (Civil) 1974: *m* 1946, Lesley Mary, 2nd da of late Capt Eric Noble, of Harpsden Court, Henley-on-Thames, and has issue living, Michael Henry Hastings, OBE, *b* 1948; *ed* Pangbourne; Col, late RE; OBE (Mil) 1991: *m* 1971, Philippa Wendy, da of Brig Rupert Crowdy, OBE, and has issue living, Simon Mark Hastings *b* 1974, James Matthew Crowdy *b* 1976, — George John (45 Brookfield Av, Poynton, Stockport, Cheshire SK12 1JE), *b* 1952; *ed* Wellington Coll, St Peter's Coll, Oxford (MA); St John's Coll, Camb, and Claremont Graduate Sch, USA (PhD); staff of Salisbury & Wells Theo Coll 1978-84, Vice-Prin 1982, Lecturer Faculty Theo Manchester Univ 1984-94, since when Sr Lecturer: *m* 1976, Rev Rosemary Jane, da of Rev Dr Arthur R. Peacocke, MBE, DSc, DD, formerly Dean of Clare Coll, Camb, and has issue living, Peter George *b* 1979, David John *b* 1981, Rachel Mary *b* 1982, — Sarah Lesley, *b* 1949: *m* 1973, John Nigel Pointing, of 81 Spitalfield Lane, Chichester PO19 4SJ, son of late Leslie Arthur Pointing, and has issue living, Edward Hugh *b* 1983, Toby Richard *b* 1990, Clare Isabel *b* 1985, and two adopted children, Benjamin John *b* 1980, Jane Louise *b* 1978, — Mary Barbara, *b* 1954; BEd, MA. *Residence* – Benbow, Bosham, Chichester, W Sussex PO18 8QL. *Clubs* – Army and Navy, Civil Service; Royal Yacht Squadron.

Granddaughter of late George Augustus Frederick Brooke (ante):—

Issue of late Brig-Gen Lionel Godolphin Brooke, CB, *b* 1849, *d* 1931: *m* 1st, 1881, Emma, who *d* 1882, da of Lord John Henry Taylour (M Headfort); 2ndly, 1895, Gertrude Isabella, who *d* 1930, da of Col Henry Hills Goodeve (formerly RA), of Tower, near Tenby, S Wales:—
(By 2nd *m*) Gertrude Vera, *b* 1899: *m* 1st, 1917 (*m diss* 1944), Nigel Augustus Kennedy, late Capt Argyll and Sutherland Highlanders, who *d* 1957 (*see* M Ailsa, colls); 2ndly, 1944, Sidney Vanden Bergh.

Grandsons of late Lt-Col George Frank Brooke, DSO, elder son of late Rt Hon Frank (Francis) Theophilus Brooke, yst son of late George Augustus Frederick Brooke (ante):—
Issue of late Maj-Gen Frank Hastings Brooke, CB, CBE, DSO, *b* 1909; *d* 1982: *m* 1st, 1935, Helen Edith Mary, who *d* 1973, da of late Maj Rupert Berkeley; 2ndly 1974, Mrs Sheila N. Carson:—
(By 1st *m*) George Hugo Hastings, TD (Hawthorne Cottage, Biddestone, Chippenham, Wilts SN14 7DG), *b* 1936; *ed* Blundell's, and RMA Sandhurst; Maj (ret) late RTR: *m* 1st 1962 (*m diss* 1978), Sarah, yr da of late Robert Blackburn, of Bowcliffe Hall, Boston Spa; 2ndly, 1983, Mrs Elizabeth Paula Minty, da of late Herbert Edwin Foxwell Morris, and has issue living (by 1st *m*), Andrew Robert Hastings, *b* 1969, — Belinda Jane, *b* 1965, — (by 2nd *m*) Emily, *b* 1985, — Rebecca, *b* 1987. —— Nigel Francis, *b* 1937; *ed* Blundell's.

PREDECESSORS – (1) HENRY Brooke, son of Francis Brooke, of Whibrooke, Ireland, and Hanna, da of Henry Prittie, and sister of 1st Lord Dunally; *b* 1770; *d* 1834; *s* by his son (2) Sir ARTHUR BRINSLEY, 2nd Bt; *b* 1797; MP for Fermanagh (*C*) 1840-54: *m* 1841, Hon Julia Henrietta Anson, who *d* 1886, da of Gen Sir George Anson, GCB; *d* 1854; *s* by his son (3) Sir VICTOR ALEXANDER, 3rd Bt; *b* 1843: *m* 1864, Alice Sophia, who *d* 1920, da of Sir Alan Edward Bellingham, 3rd Bt; *d* 1891; *s* by his son (4) Sir ARTHUR DOUGLAS, 4th Bt; *b* 1865; a JP and DL for Fermanagh: *m* 1887, Gertrude Isabella, who *d* 1918, da of Stanlake Batson; *d* 1907; *s* by his son (5) Sir BASIL STANLAKE, 5th Bt, KG, CBE, MC, *b* 1888; Member of Senate NI 1921-29, MP for Lisnaskea (*U*) NI 1929-68; Min of Commerce and Production 1941-45 and PM 1943-63; *cr Viscount Brookeborough*, of Colebrooke, co Fermanagh (peerage of UK 1952): *m* 1st, 1919, *Dame* Cynthia Mary, DBE, who *d* 1970, da of late Capt Charles Warden Sergison (*see* B Sudeley, 1911 Edn); 2ndly, 1971, Sarah Eileen Bell, who *d* 1989, da of Henry Healey, of Belfast, and widow of Cecil Armstrong Calvert, FRCS, Dir of Neurosurgery, R Victoria Hosp, Belfast; *d* 1973; *s* by his only surv son (6) JOHN WARDEN, PC (NI) 1972, 2nd Viscount, *b* 1922; MP for Lisnaskea (*U*) NI 1968-72, Ch Whip and Min of State for Finance NI 1971-72, *cr* Member NI Assembly (UPNI) 1972-74, and of N Ireland Convention 1975-87, Chm Co Council co Fermanagh, High Sheriff 1955: *m* 1949, Rosemary Hilda, da of late Lt-Col Arthur O'Neill Cubitt Chichester, OBE, MC (*see* M Donegall, colls); *d* 1987; *s* by his elder son (7) ALAN HENRY, 3rd Viscount and present peer.

BROOKES, BARON (Brookes) (Life Baron 1975)

RAYMOND PERCIVAL BROOKES, son of William Percival Brookes, of W Bromwich, W Midlands; *b* 10 April, 1909; *ed* Kenrick Tech Coll, W Bromwich; Chm and Ch Exec Guest Keen & Nettlefolds Ltd, 1965-74, and Life Pres since 1975; *cr* Knt 1971, and *Baron Brookes*, of W Bromwich, co of W Midlands (Life Baron) 1975: *m* 1937, Florence Edna, da of Isaac William Sharman, and has issue.

Arms – Or, on a pale sable between in chief two crosses crosslet gules, a sword the point upwards and enfiling a Stafford knot the blade charged above with guard with a sun in splendour over all all or. **Crest** – a demi-bear rampant proper beside and resting its sinister paw on an anvil sable. **Supporters** – Dexter, a dragon sable, armed gules; *sinister*, a figure habited as Vulcan standing in front of an anvil resting his exterior hand on a hammer, all proper.
Residence – Mallards, Santon, Isle of Man.

SON LIVING

Hon John David (30425 South Greenbriar, Franklin, Mich 48025, USA), *b* 1940: *m* 1st, 1970, Faith, da of late John Rees Redman, of Blythe, Bidford on Avon, Warwicks; 2ndly, 1986, Susan Nemeth, and has issue.

BROOKS OF TREMORFA, BARON (Brooks) (Life Baron 1979)

JOHN EDWARD BROOKS, son of Edward George Brooks; *b* 12 April 1927; *ed* Coleg Harlech and Univ Coll, Cardiff; Field Officer, Council of Social Sers, Wales; Sec Cardiff SE, Constituency Labour Party; Leader of S Glamorgan County Council 1974-78; Chm of Labour Party Wales 1978-79; *cr Baron Brooks of Tremorfa*, of Tremorfa in the county of Glamorgan (Life Baron) 1979: *m* 1st, 1948 (*m diss* 1956); 2ndly, Margaret Pringle, and has issue by both *m*.
Residence – 46 Kennerleigh Rd, Rumney, Cardiff CF3 9BJ.

BROUGHAM and VAUX, BARON (Brougham) (Baron UK 1860)
(Name and Title pronounced "Broom")

MICHAEL JOHN BROUGHAM, 5th Baron; *b* 2 Aug 1938; *s* 1967; *ed* Lycée Jaccard, Lausanne, Millfield, and Northampton Inst of Agric; Pres Royal Soc for the Prevention of Accidents 1986-89 (Vice Pres since 1990), Chm Tax Payers' Soc 1989-91, and European Secure Vehicle Alliance since 1992, Co-Pres National Health & Safety Groups Council since 1994; a Dep Chm House of Lords since 1993: *m* 1st, 1963 (*m diss* 1967), Olivia Susan, only da of Rear-Adm Gordon Thomas Seccombe Gray, DSC; 2ndly, 1969 (*m diss* 1981), Catherine Jill, el da of William Gulliver, and has issue by 1st and 2nd *m.*

Arms – Gules, a chevron between three lucies hauriant argent. Crest – A dexter arm in armour embowed proper the hand holding a lucy fessewise argent, and charged on the elbow with a rose gules. Supporters – *Dexter*, a lion vert, armed and langued gules, gorged with a Vaux collar checky or and of the second; *sinister*, a stag argent, attired and unguled or, holding in the mouth a rose gules, barbed and seeded vert.
Residence – 11 Westminster Gdns, Marsham St, SW1P 4JA.

For the king, the law, and the people

SON LIVING *(By 2nd marriage)*

Hon CHARLES WILLIAM, *b* 9 Nov 1971.

DAUGHTER LIVING *(By 1st marriage)*

Hon Henrietta Louise, *b* 1965.

BROTHER LIVING

Hon David Peter (Folly House, Bampton, Oxon), *b* 1940; *ed* Sedbergh: *m* 1st, 1969 (*m diss* 1976), Moussie Christina Margareta Hallström, da of Sven Hörnblad, of Stockholm, Sweden; 2ndly, 1977, Caroline Susan, only da of Maj James Michael Heigham Royce Tomkin, MC, of Red House, Wissett, Halesworth, Suffolk (*see* Bunbury, Bt), and formerly wife of Julian Dixon, of Grantham, Lincs, and has issue living, (by 1st *m*) Henry Peter, *b* 1971, — (by 2nd *m*), Oliver Michael, *b* 1978.

WIDOW LIVING OF FOURTH BARON

EDITH ELLALINE (*Edith, Baroness Brougham and Vaux*), da of Leonard Teichman, and formerly wife of Richard Vaughan Hart-Davis: *m* 1942, as his 3rd wife, the 4th Baron, who *d* 1967.

COLLATERAL BRANCH LIVING

Grandsons of late Capt Henry Brougham, only son of 3rd Baron:—
Issue of late Hon Anthony Charles Brougham (raised to the rank of the son of a Baron 19—), *b* 1915, *d* 1981: *m* 1st, 1940 (*m diss* 1961), Sonya, who *d* 1970, da of late Ivan Salzman; 2ndly, 1961, Doreen Margaret, who *d* 1972, da of late Roland Billington, and formerly wife of Richard Francis Warren:—
(By 1st *m*) Christopher Anthony Henry, *b* 1941; *ed* privately, and Univ Coll of Rhodesia (BSc Econ): *m* 1967, Ann Elizabeth, el da of Cecil Goldridge, of 72 Savernake Road NW3, and has issue living, Benjamin Paul, *b* 1972, — Guy Christopher, *b* 1975. —— Adrian Charles, *b* 1945; *ed* Downside: *m* 1967, Jan, da of R. J. Westhorpe, of Lees Lane, Little Norton, Wirral, Cheshire.

PREDECESSORS – (1) *Rt Hon* HENRY Brougham, PC, an eminent statesman, orator philosopher and writer; Attorney-Gen for Queen Caroline 1820; successively MP for Camelford, Winchilsea, Knaresborough and Yorkshire, and Lord High Chancellor 1830-4 *cr Baron Brougham and Vaux* 1830, and *Baron Brougham and Vaux* (peerage of United Kingdom) 1860, with remainder to his brother; *d* 1868; *s* by his brother (2) WILLIAM, 2nd Baron, *b* 1795; sat as MP for Southwark 1835-40; *m* 1834, Emily Frances, who *d* 1884, da of Sir Charles William Taylor, 1st Bt; *d* 3 Jan 1886; *s* by his son (3) HENRY CHARLES, KCVO, 3rd Baron, *b* 1836; a Clerk in House of Lords 1857-70: *m* 1882, Adora Frances Olga, who *d* 1925, da of Peter Wells, of Forest Farm, Windsor Forest, and widow of Sir Richard Courtenay Musgrave, MP, 11th Bt: *d* 1927; *s* by his grandson (4) VICTOR HENRY PETER (son of late Capt Hon Henry Brougham, son of 3rd Baron), 4th Baron *b* 1909: *m* 1st (*m diss* 1934), 1931, Violet Valerie, da of late Lt-Col Hon Edward Gerald Fleming French, DSO (E Ypres); 2ndly, 1935 (*m diss* 1942), Jean, who *d* 1992, da of late Brig-Gen Gilbert Burrell Spencer Follet, DSO, MVO (E Dunmore); 3rdly, 1942, Edith Ellaline, da of Leonard Teichman, and formerly wife of Richard Vaughan Hart-Davis; *d* 1967; *s* by his elder surviving son (5) MICHAEL JOHN, 5th Baron, and present peer.

BROUGHSHANE, BARON (Davison) (Baron UK 1945)

Strength consists in action

PATRICK OWEN ALEXANDER DAVISON, 2nd Baron; *b* 18 June 1903; *s* 1953; *ed* Wincheser, and Magdalen Coll, Oxford; Bar Inner Temple 1926; 1939-42 War with Irish Gds; Assist Sec (Mil), War Cabinet 1942-5; has American Legion of Merit; *m* 1929, Bettine, da of the late Sir Arthur Edward Ian Montague Russell, 6th Bt (*cr* 1812), and has had issue.

Arms – Gules a stag trippant and in chief a celestial crown and a fleur-de-lis or. **Crest** – Upon a billet fessewise, a stag's head between two wings or. **Supporters** – On either side a stag, or gorged with a chain gules, and pendant therefrom torteau the dexter charged with a portcullis and the sinister with a grenade fired or.
Residence – 28 Fisher St, Sandwich, Kent. *Club* – White's.

GRANDDAUGHTERS LIVING

Issue of late Hon Alexander Davison, *b* 1936, *d* 1988: *m* 1st, 1961 (*m diss* 1966), Teresa Clare, only da of James Guy Bramwell (*see* Smith-Marriott, Bt, colls, 1990 Edn); 2ndly, 1970 (*m diss* 1977), Cecilia Ann, who *d* 1977, da of J. W. Ingrams, of Furlong, Patchings, Sussex; 3rdly, 1988, (Daphne) Bridget (infra), only da of late Thomas Walter Jones, of Cawston, Norfolk, and formerly wife of Anthony John

Nelson-Sullivan:—
(By 1st *m*) Emma Bettine, *b* 1962. —— Harriet Laura, *b* 1964. —— (By 2nd *m*) Arundell, *b* 1972.

BROTHER LIVING

Hon (WILLIAM) KENSINGTON, DSO, DFC (3 Godfrey St, SW3. *Club* – Garrick), *b* 25 Nov 1914; *ed* Shrewsbury, and Magdalen Coll, Oxford; Bar Inner Temple 1939; formerly W/Cdr RAF Vol Res; European War 1939-45 (DFC, DSO); DSO 1945.

SISTERS LIVING

Hon Joyce Margaret, *b* 1900: *m* 1922, Humphrey Bowstead Wilson, OBE, MB, and has issue living, Michael, *b* 1923, — Diana June, *b* 1926.
Hon Sheila Beatrice, *b* 1907: *m* 1936, Group Capt George Edward Gordon-Duff, CBE, who *d* 1966, and has issue living, Roderick, *b* 1940: *m* 1965, Patricia Anne, da of Bruce Watson, of Fishing Cottage, Littleton Panell, Wilts. *Residence* – 10 Jameson St, W8.

WIDOW LIVING OF SON OF SECOND BARON

Mrs (Daphne) Bridget Nelson-Sullivan, da of late Thomas Walter Jones, of Cawston, Norfolk: *m* 1988, as his 3rd wife, Hon Alexander Davison, who *d* 1988. *Residence* – 29 Queen St, King's Lynn, Norfolk.

PREDECESSOR – (1) WILLIAM HENRY DAVISON, KBE, only son of late Richard Davison, of Beechfield, Ballymena, co Antrim; *b* 1872; an Alderman of Roy Borough of Kensington (Mayor 1913-19), a FSA, Vice-Pres Roy So of Arts, a Gov of Foundling Hospital, a Freeman of City of London, a Member of Clothworkers' Co (Master 1941-42), and Pres Kensington Chamber of Commerce; during European War 1914-19 raised and equipped 22nd Batn R Fusiliers and assisted in raising 2 Territorial Batns; Chm of Metropolitan National Union of Conservative Assocns 1928-30; sat as MP for Kensington, S Div (C) 1918-45; *cr Baron Broughshane*, of Kensington, co London (peerage of United Kingdom) 1945: *m* 1st 1898 (*m diss* 1929), Beatrice Mary, who *d* 1971, da of late Sir Owen Roberts, DCL, LLD, FSA, DL; 2ndly, 1929, Louisa Mary Constance, who *d* 1971, da of late Maj Charles Frederick Mariott (B Stafford, colls), *d* 1953; *s* by his son (2) PATRICK OWEN ALEXANDER, 2nd Baron, and present peer.

BROWN, BARONY OF (Brown) (Extinct 1985)

SONS LIVING OF LIFE BARON (*By 2nd marriage*)

Hon Richard Banks Duncan, *b* 1942; *ed* Bryanston and Brunel Univ: *m* 1968, Gillian Mary, da of John Kennedy Cater, of Chichester, Berks, and has issue.
Hon Michael Colin Duncan, *b* 1944; *ed* Bryanston; AA, RIBA, Memb Chartered Soc of Designers: *m* 1970, Fenella, da of Peter Barnard, of White House, Rose Hill, Dorking. *Residence* – Palgrave House, Burnham Market, Norfolk PE31 8EJ.
Hon Angus John Duncan, *b* 1951; *ed* Bryanston, and Newcastle Univ: *m* 1974, Polonca, da of Janez Baloh, of Ljublijana, Yugoslavia, and has issue. *Residence* – 39 Clifton Rd, N8 8JA.

WIDOW LIVING OF LIFE BARON

MARJORIE HERSHELL (*Baroness Brown*), da of late John Hershell Skinner, Ealing, W5: *m* 1939, as his 2nd wife, Baron Brown, MBE, PC (Life Baron), who *d* 1985.

Brown, see Baron George-Brown.

BROWNE-WILKINSON, BARON (Browne-Wilkinson) (Life Baron 1991)

NICOLAS CHRISTOPHER HENRY BROWNE-WILKINSON, PC son of late Rev Canon Arthur Rupert Browne-Wilkinson, MC; *b* 30 March 1930; *ed* Lancing, and Magdalen Coll, Oxford (BA); Bar Lincoln's Inn 1953, QC 1972, Bencher 1977, a Judge of Courts of Appeal Jersey and Guernsey 1976-77, a High Court Judge Chancery Div 1977-83, Lord Justice of Appeal 1983-85, Vice-Chancellor Supreme Court 1985-91, since when a Lord of Appeal in Ordinary; Pres Senate of the Inns of Court and the Bar 1984-86; *cr* Knt 1977, PC 1983, and *Baron Browne-Wilkinson*, of Camden in the London Borough of Camden (Life Baron) 1991: *m* 1st, 1955, Ursula, who *d* 1987, da of Cedric de Lacy Bacon; 2ndly, 1990, Mrs Hilary Isabella Jane Tuckwell, da of Prof James Wilfred Warburton, and has issue by 1st *m*.
Address – Royal Courts of Justice, Strand, WC2

SONS LIVING *(By 1st marriage)*

Hon Adam, *b* 1957.
Hon Simon, *b* (twin)1957.
Hon Oliver, *b* 1962: *m* 1991, Carla R. da of Charles Smith, of Hong Kong.

DAUGHTERS LIVING *(By 1st marriage)*

Hon Henrietta, *b* 1960.
Hon Martha, *b* 1964.

BROWNLOW, BARON (Cust) (Baron GB 1776, Bt E 1677)

EDWARD JOHN PEREGRINE CUST, 7th Baron, and 10th Baronet: *b* 25 March 1936; *s* 1978; *ed* Eton; late Gren Gds; patron of ten livings; a Member of Lloyd's; a Dir of Hand-in-Hand Fire and Life Insurance Soc, and of Harris & Dixon (Underwriting Agencies) Ltd; High Sheriff of Lincs 1978-1979: *m* 1964, Shirlie, 2nd da of late John Yeomans, of Manor Farm, Hill Croome, Upton-on-Severn, Worcs, and has issue.

𝕬rms – Ermine, on a chevron sable, three fountains proper. 𝕮rest – A lion's head erased sable, gorged with a collar paly wavy of six, argent and azure. 𝕾upporters – Two lions reguardant argent, each gorged with a collar paly wavy of six argent and azure.
Residence – La Maison des Prés, St Peter, Jersey CI. *Club* – Whites.

SON LIVING

Hon PEREGRINE EDWARD QUINTIN, *b* 9 July 1974.

To be, rather than to seem

SISTER LIVING

Hon Caroline Elizabeth Maud (68 Scarsdale Villas, W8 6PP), *b* 1928: *m* 1954 (*m* diss 1973), John Arthur Partridge, and has issue living, Frank David Peregrine (7 Thurloe Sq, SW7 2TA), *b* 1955: *m* 1982, Susan Anne, yr da of Brig Charles Hince, of Stretton House, Benington, Herts, and has issue living, Charlotte Iris *b* 1985, Annabel Lucy *b* 1987, — Claude Edward, *b* 1962, — Sophia Josephine, *b* 1969: *m* 1993, Anthony John Waltham, elder son of Donald Waltham, of Fleet, Lincs.

COLLATERAL BRANCHES LIVING

Granddaughters of late Sir Lionel Henry Cust, KCVO, LittD, son of late Sir Reginald John Cust, son of late Rev Hon Henry Cockayne Cust, 2nd son of 1st Baron:—
Issue of late Col Sir (Lionel George) Archer Cust, CBE, *b* 1896, *d* 1962: *m* 1925, Margaret Violet Louisa, who *m* 2ndly, 1975, 5th Viscount Templetown (*d* 1981), and *d* 1988, el da of late Lt-Col Henry Arthur Clowes, 1st Life Gds (B Hatherton, colls):—
Elizabeth Jemima Mary (28 St Mary's Mead, Witan Way, Witney, Oxon), *b* 1926: *m* 1947, Jack Musson Benn, who *d* 1992, and has issue living, Anthony Christopher, *b* 1948, — Michael Robert, *b* 1950: *m* 1st, 1977 (*m diss* 1986), Zvia Silverman, of Israel; 2ndly, 1992, Bridene Forest, of Melbourne, Australia, and has issue living (by 1st *m*), Shandy *b* 1977, (by 2nd *m*) James Edward *b* 1993, — Elizabeth Philippa, *b* 1952: *m* 1970, Istvan Benedek de Ujfalussy, of Greenacres, New Rd, Shiplake, Henley-on-Thames, Oxon RG9 3LA, and has issue living, Nicholas *b* 1981, Catherine *b* 1970, Louisa *b* 1972, Andrea *b* 1984.
—— Margaret Sybil, *b* 1928: *m* 1950, (Paul) Oliver Ziegler, of Hightown Farm, Hightown Hill, Ringwood, Hants, and has issue living, Adam Charles (Restharrow, Hightown Hill, Ringwood, Hants), *b* 1952: *m* 1st, 1974 (*m diss* 1979), Christine Margaret Codling, of Ibsley, Hants; 2ndly, 1984, Trudi Lynette, da of Clayton William John Burt, and has issue living (by 1st wife), Nathaniel Oliver *b* 1977, (by 2nd wife) Amy Louise *b* 1983, Joanna Margaret *b* 1986, — William James Archer (Lords Oak Cottage, Landford, Salisbury, Wilts), *b* 1956: *m* 1979, Sarah Elizabeth, elder da of Com Ian Rochfort Johnston, RN (*see* B Vernon, colls), and has issue living, Polly Laura *b* 1983, Daisy Alice *b* 1985, Harriet Louise *b* 1988.

Grandchildren of late Rev William Arthur PUREY-CUST, el son of Very Rev Arthur Perceval PUREY-CUST, DD, 1st son of Hon William Cust, 4th son of the 1st Baron:—
Issue of late Brig Richard Brownlow PUREY-CUST, CBE, DSO, MC, *b* 1888, *d* 1958: *m* 1928, Gertrude Patricia Zoë, who *d* 1993, only da of late Francis Julian Laurence Birch:—
John Richard (c/o 12 Palliser Rd, Roseneath, Wellington, NZ), *b* 1934; *ed* Eton, and Edinburgh Univ (BSc). —— Veronica Caroline *b* 1937: *m* 1969, Herman Portmann, of C12, Site 3, RR7, Vernon, BC, Canada V1T 7Z3, and has issue living, Robert Purey, *b* 1974, — Heidi Patricia, *b* 1976.

Granddaughter of late Very Rev Arthur Perceval PUREY-CUST, DD (ante):—

Issue of late Adm Sir Herbert Edward PUREY-CUST, KBE, CB, *b* 1857; *d* 1938: *m* 1895, Alice Ella, who *d* 1949, da of late George Stuart Hepburn, of Smeaton, Victoria, Australia:—
Marjorie, *b* 1905.

PREDECESSORS – (1) RICHARD CUST, MP for co Lincoln 1635: *cr* a *Baronet* 1677; *d* 1700; *s* by his grandson (2) *Sir* RICHARD, 2nd Bt; *d* 1734; *s* by his son (3) *Sir* JOHN, PC, MP, 3rd Bt, was Speaker of House of Commons 1761-70; inherited the estates of his uncle Viscount Tyrconnel (*ext*); *d* 1770; *s* by his son (4) *Sir* BROWNLOW, 4th Bt; *cr Baron Brownlow* (peerage of United Kingdom) 1776; *d* 1807; *s* by his son (5) JOHN, 2nd Baron, *b* 1779; *cr Viscount Alford and Earl Brownlow* (peerage of United Kingdon) 1815; was Lord Lt of co Lincoln; his el son John Hume, Viscount Alford, MP, who *m* 1841, Lady Marian Margaret Compton, da of 2nd Marquess of Northampton, assumed by R licence the surname of Egerton, and pre-deceased him 1851; *d* 1853; *s* by his grandson (6) JOHN WILLIAM SPENCER, 2nd Earl; assumed by Roy licence 1853 the surname of Egerton, and in 1863 the additional surname of Cust; *d* 1867; *s* by his brother (7) ADELBERT WELLINGTON BROWNLOW, GCVO, PC, 3rd Earl; *b* 1844; Lord-Lt of Lincolnshire 1867-1921, Parliamentary Sec to Local Govt Board 1885-86, Paymaster-Gen 1887-89, and Under-Sec of State for War 1889-92: *m* 1868, Lady Adelaide Talbot, who *d* 1917, 3rd da of 18th Earl of Shrewsbury; *d* 1921, when the Earldom became ext, and the barony devolved upon his kinsman (8) ADELBERT SALUS-BURY COCKAYNE, 5th Baron (2nd son of late Capt Henry Francis Cockayne Cust, MP, grandson of 1st Baron), 5th Baron; *b* 1867; *m* 1895, Maud, who *d* 1936, da of late Capt S. Buckle, RE; *d* 1927; *s* by his son (9) PEREGRINE FRANCIS ADELBERT, 6th Baron; *b* 1899; Lt and Adjt Gren Gds, 1939-45 War as Sqdn-Ldr RAF VR; Mayor of Grantham 1934-35; Lord in Waiting (personal) to HM King Edward VIII July-Dec 1936; Lord Lieut Lincs; PPS to Min of Aircraft Production 1940-1941; *m* 1st, 1927, Dorothy, who *d* 1952, yr da of Brig-Gen Sir David Alexander Kinloch, 11th Bt, CB, MVO; 2ndly, 1954, Dorothy, who *d* 1966, yr da of Thomas Sarsfield Kent Power, of Norfolk, Virginia, USA, and formerly wife of (i) Harry Ester Reynolds Hall, (ii) 2nd Earl Beatty, DSC, (iii) John Gordon Baragwanath; 3rdly, 1969, Leila who *d* 1983, only da of late Maj Philip Guy Reynolds, DSO, formerly wife of late Maj John Dane Player, and widow of 2nd Baron Manton; *d* 1978; *s* by his son (10) EDWARD JOHN PEREGRINE, 7th Baron and present peer.

BROXBOURNE, BARONY OF (Walker-Smith) (Extinct 1992)

SON LIVING OF LIFE BARON

Hon Sir JOHN JONAH WALKER-SMITH, 2nd *Baronet*, *b* 1939 (*see* BARONETAGE).

DAUGHTERS LIVING OF LIFE BARON

Hon Deborah Susan, *b* 1941.
Hon Berenice Mary, *b* 1946 (*see* Walker-Smith, Bt).

WIDOW LIVING OF LIFE BARON

DOROTHY (*Baroness Broxbourne*) (*see* Walker-Smith, Bt).

Bruce, Lord; son of Earl of Elgin.

BRUCE OF DONINGTON, BARON (Bruce) (Life Baron 1974)

DONALD WILLIAM TREVOR BRUCE, son of the late William Trevor Bruce, of Norbury, Surrey: *b* 3 Oct 1912; *ed* Donington Gram Sch, Lincs; FCA; economist; 1939-45 War as Maj with R Signals (despatches); MP for N Portsmouth (*Lab*) 1945-50; PPS to Min of Health 1945-50; a Member of Min of Health delegation to Sweden and Denmark 1946, and of House of Commons Select Cttee on Public Accounts 1948-50; a Member of European Parl 1975-79; *cr Baron Bruce of Donington*, of Rickmansworth, Herts (Life Baron) 1974: *m* 1st, 1939 (*m diss* 1980), Joan Letitia, da of Hamilton Claude Butcher, of Maida Vale, W9; 2ndly, 1981, Mrs Cyrena Heard (*née* Shaw) and has issue by 1st *m*.
Address – 301/305 Euston Rd, NW1.

SON LIVING *(By 1st marriage)*

Hon Michael Gordon, *b* 1952.

DAUGHTERS LIVING *(By 1st marriage)*

Hon Ann, *b* 1942; *m* 19—, T. Samuels.
Hon Mary Trevor, *b* 1945: *m* 1968, Shuhada Hilmi.

BRUCE-GARDYNE, BARONY OF (Bruce-Gardyne) (Extinct 1990)

SONS LIVING OF LIFE BARON

Hon Thomas Andrew, *b* 1962; *ed* Marlborough.
Hon Adam George John, *b* 1967; *ed* Marlborough.

DAUGHTER LIVING OF LIFE BARON

Hon Roselle Sarah, *b* 1959; *ed* St Paul's Girls' Sch, Durham Univ, and INSEAD: *m* 1987, David Heckendorn, only son of C. H. Heckendorn, of Beaux Arts Village, Washington, USA, and has issue living, John Henry, *b* 1990, — Marianna Elizabeth, *b* 1993. *Residence* – 37 Fairfield Rd, Winchester SO22 6SG.

WIDOW LIVING OF LIFE BARON

SARAH LOUISA MARY (*Baroness Bruce-Gardyne*), only da of late Cmdr Sir John Francis Whitaker Maitland, RN, of Harrington Hall, Spilsby, Lincs: *m* 1959, Baron Bruce-Gardyne (Life Baron), who *d* 1990. *Residences* – 13 Kelso Place, W8; Illidge Green Farm, Brereton, Cheshire.

BRUNTISFIELD, BARON (Warrender) (Baron UK 1942, Bt GB 1715)

JOHN ROBERT WARRENDER, OBE, MC, TD, 2nd Baron, and 9th Baronet; *b* 7 Feb 1921; *s* 1993; *ed* Eton; DL Som 1965; Col RARO; Brig Queen's Body Guard for Scotland (Royal Company of Archers) (ret 1985), late Capt 2nd Dragoons, Royal Scots Greys; ADC to Gov of Madras 1946-48, and Comdg N Som Yeo 44th; Royal Tank Regt 1957-62 (OBE); 1939-45 War in Middle East, Italy and NW Europe (MC 1943); OBE (Mil) 1963: *m* 1st, 1948, Ann Moireen, who *d* 1976, 2nd da of late Lt-Col Sir Walter Fendall Campbell, KCIE, 2ndly, 1977, Mrs Shirley Crawley, who *d* 1981, da of J. L. Ross, and formerly wife of Jonathan James Crawley; 3rdly, 1985, Mrs Joanna (Jan) Kathleen Campbell Graham, da of late David Chancellor, of Pencaitland, E Lothian, and formerly wife of Capt Colin Hugh Campbell Graham (*see* Graham, Bt, *cr* 1906, colls), and has issue by 1st *m*.

Industry promotes

Arms – Quarterly: 1st and 4th, argent, on a bend wavy, between six roses gules, three plates, *Warrender*; 2nd, or, a lion rampant gules, couped in all joints of the field, within a double tressure flory counter flory azure, *Maitland*; 3rd grand quarter, counter-quartered 1st quarter 1st and 4th vert, a lion rampant argent; 2nd and 3rd argent, three papingoes vert, beaked and membered gules, *Hume*; 2nd quarter gyronny of eight gules and ermine, *Campbell of Cessnock*; third quarter azure, on a fesse between three mascles argent, as many cinquefoils of the first, *Purves of Purves*; 4th quarter, 1st and 4th gules, three piles engrailed argent, *Polwarth of that ilk*; 2nd and 3rd argent, a cross engrailed azure, *Sinclair of Hermiston*, on surtout of the grand quarter an inescutcheon argent charged with an orange imperially crowned and slipped all proper. **Crest** – A hare sejant proper. **Supporters** – Two lions reguardant argent. *Residence* – 18 Warriston Crescent, Edinburgh EH3 5LB. *Club* – New (Edinburgh).

SONS LIVING (By 1st marriage)

Hon MICHAEL JOHN VICTOR, *b* 9 Jan 1949; *ed* Downside, RMA Sandhurst, and Hatfield Coll, Durham (BA); Maj Irish Guards 1967-86; Dir Jardine Fleming Investment Mgmt Ltd since 1993: *m* 1978, Baroness Walburga, yr da of Baron Johannes von Twickel, of Schloss Lembeck, Lembeck, Germany.
Address – c/o Jardine Fleming Investment Management Ltd, PO Box 70, GPO Hong Kong. *Club* – White's.
Hon Jonathan James, *b* 1954; *ed* Downside, and Camberwell Sch of Art (BA); Artist: *m* 1979, Fiona Mary, yr da of late Alexander Grant Laing, MC, of Logie House, Forres, Moray (*see* E Stair, colls), and has issue living, George Alexander, *b* 1981, — Jonathan Hew, *b* 1985, — Alice Julian, *b* 1983. *Residence* – Minuntion, Pinmore, Girvan, Ayrshire KA26 0TE.

DAUGHTERS LIVING (By 1st marriage)

Hon Julian Mary, *b* 1950: *m* 1974, Francis Alexander Moreton Akers-Douglas, and has issue (*see* V Chilston, colls). *Residence* – Barnham Farmhouse, E Hoathly, Lewes, Sussex BN8 6QL.
Hon Sarah Jane, *b* 1952: *m* 1971, Anthony David Bune, and has issue living, Tertius Alexander, *b* 1978, — Eloise Anne Moireen, *b* 1977. *Address* – PO Box 467, Chapel Rd, Waccabuc, NY 10597, USA.

BROTHERS LIVING

Hon Simon George, DSC, *b* 1922: *ed* Eton, Co Director and Aviation Consultant, Founder and Chm Australian World Airways; Asso Royal Aeronautical Soc, Fellow British Interplanetary Sco, Consul for Uruguay in State of Victoria; late Lieut RNVR; 1939-45 War (DSC 1944), Star of Russia 1945-85: *m* 1950, Pamela, only da of late Sir Norman Myer, of Toorak, Victoria, Australia, and has had issue, Alexander Victor Simon, *b* 1955, *d* 1976, — Simon Hamilton Angus Norman, *b* 1962, — Edwina, *b* 1952, — Alicia Gizelle, *b* 1953. *Residence* – 35 Barkly Av, Armadale, Victoria 3143, Australia. *Clubs* – Bath, Turf, Royal Aero RNVR, Melbourne.
Hon Robin Hugh *b* 1927; *ed* Eton, and Trin Coll, Oxford: *m* 1951, Gillian Elizabeth, only da of Leonard Lewis Rossiter (*see* Oppenheimer, Bt, 1985 Edn), and has issue living, Hugh Mark, *b* 1968, — Carolyn Robin, *b* 1953: *m* 1985, Francis I. M. Hazeel, of 54 Alderney St, SW1V 4EX, yr son of late Capt Harry Hazeel, of 28 Ormonde Gate, SW3, and has issue living, James Albert Victor *b* 1989, Geordie Alexander Robin *b* 1993, — Annabel Rose (*Hon Mrs Alastair Campbell*), *b* 1956: *m* 1979, Hon Alastair Colin Leckie Campbell, of The Stables, Everlands, Sevenoaks, Kent, only son of 3rd Baron Colgrain, and has issue. *Residence* – Capps Lodge House, Fulbrook, Burford, Oxon OX18 4DB. *Clubs* – City of London, White's.

HALF-BROTHER LIVING

Hon Anthony Michael, *b* 1950; *ed* Eton, and Ch Ch Oxford; FCA: *m* 1st, 1976, Christine, da of Serge Semeneko, of Boston, Mass; 2ndly, 1983, Mrs Patricia Connors Kelly, da of Philip Connors, of Middleburg, Virginia, and has issue living (by 2nd *m*), Patrick Victor Anthony, *b* 1984. *Residence* – Little Cotland Farm, PO Box 1431, Middleburg, Virginia 22117, USA. *Clubs* – Turf, White's.

HALF-SISTER LIVING

Hon Victoria Isabella (*Lady Reay*), *b* 1952: *m* 1980, as his 2nd wife, 14th Lord Reay, and has issue. *Residences* – Kasteel Ophemert, Ophemert in Gelderland, Netherlands; 98 Oakley St, SW3.

WIDOW LIVING OF FIRST BARON

TANIA (*Dowager Baroness Bruntisfield*), da of late Dr Michel Kolin, of St Jacob, Dubrovnik, Yugoslavia: *m* 1948, as his 2nd wife, the 1st Baron, MC, who *d* 1993. *Residence* – Résidence le Village B1, CH-1837, Château-d'Oex, Switzerland.

PREDECESSORS – (1) GEORGE Warrender, son of late George Warrender; a Merchant and MP for Edinburgh 1715-21; *cr* a *Baronet* 1715: *m* 1st, 16—, Margaret Lawrie, of Edinburgh; 2ndly, Grizel, da of Hugh Blair of Edinburgh; *d* 1721; *s* by his el son (2) JOHN, 2nd Bt: *m* 1720, Henrietta, da of late Sir Patrick Johnston, MP, sometime Lord Provost of Edinburgh; *d* 1772; *s* by his only surviving son (3) PATRICK, 3rd Bt; *b* 1731; Lieut-Col 11th Dragoons; MP for Haddington Burghs 1768-74, and King's Remembrancer of Court of Exchequer 1771-91: *m* 1780, Miss H. Blair, who *d* 1838; *d* 1799; *s* by his el son (4) *Rt Hon* GEORGE, PC, 4th Bt *b* 1782: MP for Haddington Burghs 1807-12, for Truro 1812-18, for Sandwich 1818-26, for Westbury 1826-30, and for Honiton 1830-32; a Lord of the Admiralty 1812-22, and a Commr of Board of Control 1822-8: *m* 1810, Hon Anne Evelyn Boscawen, who *d* 1871, da of 3rd Viscount Falmouth; *d* 1849; *s* by his brother (5) JOHN, 5th Bt; *b* 1786; Capt in the Army: *m* 1st, 1823, Lady Julian Jane Maitland, who *d* 1827, da of 8th Earl of Lauderdale; 2ndly, 1831, Hon Frances Henrietta, who *d* 1852, da of 1st Baron Alvanley; *d* 1867; *s* by his only son (6) GEORGE, 6th Bt; *b* 1825; sometime Capt Coldstream Gds: *m* 1854, Helen, who *d* 1875, da of Sir Hugh Purves-Hume-Campbell, 7th Bt; *d* 1901; *s* by his el surviving son (7) GEORGE JOHN SCOTT, KCB, KCVO, 7th Bt; *b* 1860; Vice-Adm: *m* 1884, Lady Ethel Maud Ashley-Cooper, who *d* 1945, da of the 8th Earl of Shaftesbury; *d* 1917; *s* by his el son (8) VICTOR ALEXANDER GEORGE ANTHONY, MC, 1st Baron, *b* 1899; 2nd Lieut Gren Guards, European War 1917-18 (MC, Orders of St Stanislas and St Anne of Russia with Swords, Order of Star of Roumania); Vice-Chamberlain of the Household Sept 1932, Comptroller HM Household May 1935, Parl and Financial Sec to the Admiralty June 1935, Financial Sec to War Dept and a Member of Army Council Nov 1935, Parl Sec to Admiralty April 1940-July 1945; MP for Kesteven and Rutland, Grantham Div (*C*) Dec 1923-Feb 1942; *cr Baron Bruntisfield*, of Boroughmuir, City of Edinburgh (peerage of UK) 1942: *m* 1st, 1920 (*m diss* 1946), Dorothy Etta, who *d* 1975, da of late Col Richard Hamilton Rawson, MP (*see* E Lichfield, 1919 Edn); 2ndly, 1948, Tania, da of late Dr Michel Kolin, of St Jacob, Dubrovnik; *d* 1993; *s* by his eldest son (9) JOHN ROBERT, 2nd Baron and present peer.

BUCCLEUCH and QUEENSBERRY, DUKE OF (Montagu Douglas Scott) (Duke S 1663, Duke S 1684)

(Title pronounced "Buckloo")

I love

WALTER FRANCIS JOHN MONTAGU DOUGLAS SCOTT, KT, VRD, 9th Duke of Buccleuch, and 11th of Queensberry; *b* 28 Sept 1923; *s* 1973; *ed* Eton, and Ch Ch, Oxford; served RNVR and RNR 1942-46 Lt-Cdr, Hon Capt RNR 1988; Capt Queen's Body Guard for Scotland (Royal Company of Archers); Lord-Lieut of Roxburghshire 1974-75, of Selkirk 1975, since when of Roxburgh, Ettrick and Lauderdale; JP 1974, Roxburghshire CC 1958; PPS to Sec of State for Scotland 1962-64; Pres of Royal Highland and Agric Soc 1969-70; East of England Agric So 1976; Pres St Andrew's Ambulance Assocn since 1969, Pres Malcolm Sargent Cancer Fund for Children in Scotland, Commweath Forestry Assocn since 1979, and Royal Blind Asylum & School; Vice-Pres RSSPCC, and King George's Fund for Sailors; received Countryside Commn and Country Landowners' Assocn annual jt award 1983; Chm of Royal Assocn for Disability & Rehabilitation (CCD) 1973-93 (since when Pres), Buccleuch Heritage Trust since 1985, Living Landscape Trust since 1986, and Assocn of Lord Lieuts since 1990; Pres of Royal Scottish Agric Benevolent Instn, Royal Highland & Agric Soc of Scotland, Scottish Nat Instn for the War Blinded, and Vice-Pres Royal Scottish Forestry Soc since 1993 (Pres Elect 1994); Heritage Educn Trust Sandford Awards for Boughton 1989 and 1994, Drumlanrig 1991, and Bowhill 1994; Chancellor Order of the Thistle since 1992; MP for N Div of Edinburgh (*C*) 1960-73; 1939-45 War; KT 1978: *m* 1953, Jane, only da of late John McNeill, QC, of Drumavuic, Appin, Argyllshire, and has issue.

Arms – Quarterly: 1st *grandquarter for the Earldom of Doncaster,* quarterly 1st and 4th, quarterly (i) and (iv) azure, three fleur-de-lis or; (ii) and (iii) gules, three lions passant guardant in pale or; 2nd, or, a lion rampant gules within a double tressure flory-counter-flory of the second; 3rd, azure, a harp or; all debruised by a baton sinister argent; 2nd *grandquarter for the Dukedom of Argyll,* quarterly, 1st and 4th gyrony of eight or and sable (*Campbell*); 2nd and 3rd, argent, a lymphad, sails furled sable flags and pennons flying gules, and oars in action of the second (*Lorne*); 3rd *grandquarter for the Dukedom of Queensberry,* quarterly, 1st and 4th, argent, a human heart gules, crowned with an imperial crown or, on a chief azure three mullets of the field (*Douglas*); 2nd and 3rd azure, a bend between six cross crosslets fitchee or (*Mar*); the whole of this grandquarter within a border or, charged with a double tressure flory-counter-flory gules; 4th *grandquarter for the Dukedom of Montagu,* quarterly, 1st argent, three fusils conjoined in fess gules, a bordure sable (*Montagu*); 2nd, or a griffin displayed vert, beaked and membered gules (*Monthermer*); 3rd, sable, a lion rampant argent, on a canton of the last a cross gules (*Churchill*); 4th, argent, a chevron gules between three caps-of-maintenance, their fronts turned to the sinister azure, furred ermine (*Brudenell*); over the grandquarters, at the fess point an inescutcheon or, a bend azure mullet of six points between

two crescents of the field (*Scott*). **Crest** – A stag trippant proper, attired and unguled or. **Supporters** – Two female figures proper, habited from the waist downwards in kirtles azure gathered up at the knees, the arms and bosoms uncovered, around the shoulders flowing mantles as before suspended by the exterior hand, girdles and sandals gules, and their heads adorned with a plume of three ostrich feathers argent.
Seats – Bowhill, Selkirk; Boughton House, Kettering; Drumlanrig Castle, Thornhill, Dumfriesshire.

SONS LIVING

RICHARD WALTER JOHN (*Earl of Dalkeith*) (Dabton, Thornhill, Dumfriesshire), *b* 14 Feb 1954; *ed* Eton, and Ch Ch, Oxford; a Page of Honour to HM Queen Elizabeth the Queen Mother 1967-69; Member Queen's Body Guard for Scotland (Royal Company of Archers); DL Nithsdale, Annandale and Eskdale 1987; Council Memb Nature Conservancy Council 1989-91, Nature Conservancy Council for Scotland 1991-92, and Scottish Natural Heritage since 1992 (Chm SW Region since 1992); District Councillor Nithsdale 1984-90; Dir Border Television 1989-90, National Memb for Scotland Independent Television Commn since 1990, and Memb Millennium Commn since 1994; IBA 1990, ITC 1991: *m* 1981, Lady Elizabeth Marian Frances Kerr, yst da of 12th Marquess of Lothian, and has issue:—
> SONS LIVING— Walter John Francis (*Lord Eskdaill*) *b* 2 Aug 1984, — Hon Charles David Peter, *b* 1987.
> DAUGHTERS LIVING— *Lady* Louisa Jane Therese, *b* 1982, — *Lady* Amabel Claire Alice, *b* 1992.

Lord (William Henry) John, *b* 1957: *m* 1990, Mrs (Hafize) Berrin Torolsan, only da of Halil Torolsan, of Istanbul. *Residence* – Valikomaği Cad 62, Nişantäşi, Istanbul, Turkey.
Lord Damian Torquil Francis Charles, *b* 1969.

DAUGHTER LIVING

Lady Charlotte-Anne, *b* 1966: *m* 1991, Comte Bernard de Castellane, son of late Comte Albert de Castellane, of Brussels, and has issue living, Boniface Louis Albert Charles, *b* 1993.

SISTERS LIVING

Lady Elizabeth Diana (*Duchess of Northumberland*), *b* 1922; 1939-45 War in WRNS; Hon D Univ Newcastle Polytechnic (now Northumbria Univ) 1992; Hon Col 6th Bn Northumberland Fusiliers: *m* 1946, 10th Duke of Northumberland, who *d* 1988. *Residences* – Alnwick Castle, Northumberland; Syon House, Brentford, Middx TW8 8JF; Clive Lodge, Albury, Surrey.
Lady Caroline Margaret (*Baroness Gilmour of Craigmillar*), *b* 1927: *m* 1951, Baron Gilmour of Criagmillar, PC (Life Baron), of The Ferry House, Old Isleworth, Middx.

UNCLE LIVING (*son of 7th Duke*)

Lord George Francis John, *b* 1911; *ed* Eton, and Ch Ch, Oxford; is Brevet-Col (TA Reserve of Officers), Member of Queen's Body Guard for Scotland (Royal Company of Archers); formerly Maj 10th Hus, 23rd Hus, and Lt-Col, Northants Yeo; 1939-45 War in France, Belgium, Holland and Germany (despatches): *m* 1938, Mary Wina Mannin (Molly), only da of Lt-Col H. O. Bishop, of Harewood, Andover, Hants, and has issue living, David Henry George (19 Petworth St, SW11), *b* 1945: *m* 1967, Laura Jane, da of St John Bernard Vyvyan Harmsworth, of 25 Whitelands House, SW3 (*see* Boothby, Bt, colls, 1980 Edn), and has issue living, Lucy Rose *b* 1969, Harriet Mary *b* 1972, — Georgina Mary (*Baroness O'Neill*), *b* 1940: *m* 1963, 4th Baron O'Neill, of Shane's Castle, Antrim, — Charmian Rachel, *b* 1942: *m* 1st, 1964 (*m diss* 1977), Archibald Hugh Stirling, yr of Keir (*see* Stirling-Maxwell, Bt); 2ndly, 1987, Colin Guy Napier Campbell, of 2 Kildare Terr, W2 (*see* Campbell, Bt, *cr* 1815, colls). *Residences* – The Old Almshouse, Weekley, Kettering, Northants; 60 Glebe Pl SW3. *Club* – Cavalry and Guards'.

AUNTS LIVING (*Daughters of 7th Duke*)

Lady Alice Christabel, GCB, CI, GCVO, GBE (*HRH Princess Alice, Duchess of Gloucester*), *b* 1901, a GCStJ, Air Chief Marshal WRAF, Col-in-Ch of KOSB, Dep Col-in-Ch Royal Anglian Regt, and The King's Royal Hussars, and a Member of Council of British Red Cross Soc; received Freedom of City of Edinburgh 1937, of Gloucester 1939, and of Belfast 1952; GBE (Civil) and CI 1937, GCVO 1948, GCB (Civil) 1975: *m* 6 Nov 1935, HRH Prince Henry William Frederick Albert, 1st Duke of Gloucester, KG, KT, KP, GCB, GCMG, GCVO, PC, who *d* 10 June 1974, 3rd son of HM King George V (*see* ROYAL FAMILY). *Residences* – 1 Kensington Palace W8; Barnwell Manor, Peterborough.
Lady Angela Christine Rose, *b* 1906: *m* 1936, Vice-Adm Sir Peter Dawnay, KCVO, CB, DSC (*see* V Downe, colls), who *d* 1989. *Residence* – The Old Post Cottage, Wield, Alresford, Hants.

WIDOW LIVING OF SON OF SEVENTH DUKE

Lady Rachel Douglas-Home, da of 13th Earl of Home (*see* B Home of the Hirsel): *m* 1937, Lord William Walter Montagu Douglas Scott, who *d* 1958, and has issue (see colls infra). *Residence* – Beechwood, Melrose.

COLLATERAL BRANCHES LIVING

> Issue of late Lord William Walter Montagu Douglas Scott, MC, 2nd son of 7th Duke, *b* 1896, *d* 1958: *m* 1937, Lady Rachel Douglas-Home (ante), da of 13th Earl of Home (*see* B Home of the Hirsel):—
> Walter William, *b* 1946; *ed* Eton, and Keble Coll, Oxford: *m* 1991, Mrs Teresa Fisher, only da of Anatole Urbaniak, of Cape Town, S Africa. —— Margaret Elizabeth, *b* 1938. —— Frances Henrietta (*Baroness Cranworth*), *b* 1940: *m* 1968, 3rd Baron Cranworth. —— Rosemary Alice (twin), *b* 1940: *m* 1978, (Samuel Alexander) Mark Collins, son of late Sir William Collins, and has issue living, Sampson William Francis, *b* 1982, — Benjamin Mark Timothy, *b* 1984. —— Jean Louise (*Lady Tapps-Gervis-Meyrick*), *b* 1943: *m* 1968, Sir George Christopher Cadafael Tapps-Gervis-Meyrick, 7th Bt.

> Grandchildren of late Lt-Col Lord George William Montagu Douglas Scott, OBE (infra):—
> Issue of late Lt-Col John Henry Montagu Douglas Scott, MC, 9th Lancers, *b* 1911, *d* 1991: *m* 1954, Anne Peace Arabella (Arbell) (Kirklands, Ancrum), da of late Capt Angus Alexander Mackintosh, RHG (*see* D Devonshire, 1973-74 Edn), and formerly wife of Maj John Antony Warre, MC, 12th Royal Lancers:—
> James George, *b* 1959. —— (Elizabeth) Arabella, *b* 1956: *m* 1987, Peregrine J. Lewis, son of late Maj Raynard Lewis, 12th Royal Lancers, of Morden, Surrey, and has issue living, Merlin John Lewis, *b* 1991, — Arbell Eleanora, *b* 1993. *Residence* – Cotfield, Lilliesleaf, Melrose, Borders.

> Issue of late Lt-Col Lord George William Montagu Douglas Scott, OBE, 3rd son of 6th Duke, *b* 1866, *d* 1947: *m* 1903, Lady Elizabeth Emily Manners, who *d* 1924, da of 7th Duke of Rutland:—
> Claud Everard Walter, MC, *b* 1915; *ed* Eton, and Ch Ch, Oxford; formerly Lt-Col Lothians and Border Yeo (TA); is a Member of the Queen's Body Guard for Scotland (Royal Company of Archers); European War 1939-45 in N Africa and Italy (MC): *m* 1941, Margaret Francis, da of late Brig-Gen Lewis Francis Philips, CB, CMG, CBE, DSO (*see* E Ducie, colls, 1970 Edn), and has issue living, Thomas Walter, *b* 1943: *m* 1973 (*m diss* 1985), (Marion) Miranda, da of the Hon Claud Stephen

Phillimore (*see* B Phillimore), and has issue living, Alice *b* 1978, — Katharine Margaret, *b* 1946: *m* 1975, Robert Vere Spencer Bernard (*see* D Marlborough, colls). *Residence* – Bourton Hill House, Moreton-in-Marsh, Glos. —— Jeanetta Ruth (Arnbank, Abercairny, Crieff, Perthshire), *b* 1906: *m* 1937, Maj James William Stirling Home Drummond Moray, Scots Gds, who *d* 1968, and has had issue, William George (Abercairny, Crieff, Perthshire), *b* 1940: *ed* Eton: *m* 1st, 1969 (*m diss* 1991), (Angela) Jane, da of late Lt Cdr Michael John Baring, RN (*see* B Northbrook, colls); 2ndly, 1991, Emma Moyra, elder da of Capt James Silvester Rattray of Rattray (28th Chief), and has issue living (by 1st *m*), Anne Christian *b* 1971, Frances Tara *b* 1974, Georgina Jane *b* 1979, (by 2nd *m*) Caroline *b* 1992, — John Robert (Seggiebank Farm House, Milnathort, Kinross KY13 7RP), *b* 1943; *ed* Eton; Capt Scots Gds: *m* 1st, 1971 (*m diss* 1979), Meriel Frances, elder da of Peter Douglas Miller Stirling-Aird of Kippendavie, TD, of Kippenross, by Dunblane, Perthshire; 2ndly, 1981, Carole Ann, elder da of John N. Peniston, of Port Sarde, 1245 Collonge-Bellerive, Geneva, Switzerland, and has issue living (by 2nd *m*), Andrew James George *b* 1987, Susannah Laura *b* 1984, — David Maurice (Arnbank, Abercairny, Crieff, Perthshire), *b* 1945; *ed* Eton; Capt Scots Gds: *m* 1st, 1976 (*m diss* 1987), Amanda Mary, da of Ian Bayles, of Chatsworth Park, Tabilk, Victoria, Australia (*see* B Sherborne, colls); 2ndly, 1989, Iona, da of John Barber, of Majorca, and of Mrs Peter Mathis, of Perthshire, and has issue living (by 1st *m*), Edwina Alice *b* 1980, (by 2nd *m*) James Oliver *b* 1992, — Lucy Gwendolen, *b* 1939: *m* 1964, as his 2nd wife, Capt Hon (Desmond) Rupert Strutt who *d* (27 Feb) 1993, 4th son of 3rd Baron Belper, and *d* (16 Sept) 1993. —— Marjorie Katherine (twin), *b* 1906: *m* 1st, 1935, Maj Thomas Archibald Hacket Pain, Irish Gds, who was *ka* 1940; 2ndly, 1943, Adam Bell, who *d* 1984, and has issue living (by 2nd *m*), Charles James, *b* 1944; *ed* Eton; Member Queen's Body Guard for Scotland (Royal Company of Archers): *m* 1969, Caroline Jane, da of late Maj Peter Daniel Highton Fox, DSO, late Green Howards, and has issue living, Jonathan George *b* 1972; *ed* Eton, Susannah Katharine Janet *b* 1975, — Louisa, *b* 1947.

Grandchildren of late Lt-Col Lord Herbert Andrew Montagu Douglas Scott, CMG, DSO (infra):—
Issue of late Brig (Claud) Andrew Montagu Douglas Scott, DSO, *b* 1906, *d* 1971: *m* 1st, 1929 (*m diss* 1951), Lady Victoria Doris Rachel Haig, who *d* 1993, da of 1st Earl Haig; 2ndly, 1951, Zalia, who *d* 1986, yst (twin) da of Sir Harold Edward Snagge, KBE (*see* B Avebury, colls, 1955 Edn), and formerly wife of late Lt-Col Esmond Charles Baring, OBE (*see* B Ashburton):—
(By 1st *m*) Douglas Andrew, OBE (Halford House, Halford, nr Shipston-on-Stour, Warks), *b* 1930; late Capt IG; OBE (Civil) 1994: *m* 1st, 1954 (*m diss* 1977), Bridget Elizabeth, da of late Air Vice-Marshal Sir Robert Allingham George, KCVO, KBE, CB, MC; 2ndly, 1977, Daphne Maureen, only da of Dr Cyril de Vere Shortt, of Winchcome, Glos, and formerly wife of William George Fearnley-Whittingstall, and has had an adopted son, Adam, *b* 1961, *d* 1969, — and has two adopted das, Emily, *b* 1970, — Lucy Rosemary, *b* 1972. —— Henrietta (*Lady Griffin*), *b* 1934: *m* 1962, Maj Sir (Arthur) John Stewart Griffin, KCVO, of Barton's Cottage, Bushy Park, Teddington, Middx, and has issue living, Andrew Michael Stewart, *b* 1963: *m* 1989, Maria Diane Cordelia, da of Royston James Vavasseur-Williams, of Childwall, Liverpool L15 6US, and has issue living, Alexander William Michael Stewart *b* 1992, — Phillip Anthony Stewart, *b* 1965: *m* 1992, Heather A., elder da of late Gerald Kent, and of Mrs Malcolm Prescott, of Polstead, Suffolk. —— (By 2nd *m*) Nicholas Herbert, *b* 1954.

Issue of late Lt-Col Lord Herbert Andrew Montagu Douglas Scott, CMG, DSO, 5th son of 6th Duke, *b* 1872, *d* 1944: *m* 1905, Marie Josephine, who *d* 1965, da of late James Edwards, of Dovercourt, Essex:—
Marian Louisa (*Lady Elmhirst*) *b* 1908: *m* 1st, 1927, Col Andrew Henry Ferguson, late Life Gds, who *d* 1966 (*see* V Hampden, colls); 2ndly, 1968, Air Marshal Sir Thomas Walker Elmhirst, KBE, CB, AFC, who *d* 1982. *Residence* – No 2 Bungalow, Dummer Down Farm, Dummer, Basingstoke, Hants. —— Patricia Katharine (*Patricia, Countess of Dundee*), *b* 1910: *m* 1st, 1931, Lt-Col Walter Douglas Faulkner, MC, Irish Gds, who was *ka* (May) 1940; 2ndly (Sept) 1940, Lt Col (Hon) David Scrymgeour Wedderburn, DSO, Scots Gds, who *d* (of wounds received in action) 1944 (*see* E Dundee); 3rdly, 1946, 11th Earl of Dundee, who *d* 1983, and has had issue (by 1st *m*) David James, *b* 1932; Maj late IG: *m* 1958, Victoria Mary Rose (Haugh House, Longworth, Abingdon, Oxon), el da of late Robert James Buxton, MB, BChir, MRCS LRCP, DOMS (*see* Buxton, Bt, colls), and *d* 1993, leaving issue, John Douglas *b* 1959, Thomas Patrick *b* 1965, Matthew James *b* 1968, Robert David *b* 1970, Katharine Rose *b* 1960, — Hermione Patricia (*Lady Moncreiffe of that Ilk*), *b* 1937: *m* 1966, as his 2nd wife, Sir Rupert Iain Kay Moncreiffe of that Ilk, 11th Bt, CVO, QC, who *d* 1985, — (by 2nd and 3rd *m*) (*see* E Dundee). *Residence* – Coultra Farm House, Newport-on-Tay, Fife.

Issue of late Lt-Col Lord Francis George Montagu Douglas Scott, KCMG, DSO, yst son of 6th Duke, *b* 1879, *d* 1952: *m* 1915, Lady Eileen Nina Evelyn Sibell Elliot, who *d* 1938, da of 4th Earl of Minto:—
Moyra Eileen, *b* 1919; 1939-45 War with ATS (FANY) (despatches): *m* 1st, 1942, Maj Hugo Douglas Tweedie, Scots Gds, *ka* NE Europe 1945; 2ndly, 1947, Col David de Crespigny Smiley, LVO, OBE, MC, RHG (The Blues) (ret), of 30 Kensington Mansions, Trebovir Rd, SW5 9TQ (*see* Smiley, Bt), and has issue living (by 1st *m*), Gavin Hugo, *b* 1944; MA (Oxon); Maj The Blues & Royals (ret): *m* 1974, Philippa Mary, da of late Maj Michael Andrews, of Quarry House, Shepton Mallet, Som, and has issue living, Esmond Michael Xan *b* 1976, Alexander *b* 1978, — Anna Bridget Eileen, *b* 1942; MCSP: *m* 1971 (*m diss* 1986), Peter Robert McFerran, and has issue living, Hugo *b* 1975, Lucinda *b* 1972, — (by 2nd *m*) (*see* Smiley, Bt).

Issue of late Lord Henry John Douglas-Scott-Montagu, 2nd son of the 5th Duke of Buccleuch, who was *cr* *Baron Montagu of Beaulieu* 1885 (see that title).

PREDECESSORS - (1) Sir WALTER Scott, Knt, a powerful chieftain, and a military commander of renown in the Nether-lands under the Prince of Orange, was in 1606 *cr Lord Scott of Buccleuch* (peerage of Scotland); *d* 1611; *s* by his son (2) WALTER, 2nd Lord: *cr Lord Scott of Whitchester and Eskdaill* and *Earl of Buccleuch* (peerage of Scotland) 1619, with remainder to his heirs whatsoever; *d* 1633; *s* by his only son (3) FRANCIS, 2nd Earl; *d* 1651; *s* by his da (4) MARY, when 11 years of age she *m* Walter Scott (then 14 years old) afterwards Earl of Tarras for life; *d* without issue; *s* by her sister (5) ANNE: *m* 1st, 1663, James, KG, Duke of Monmouth, who assumed on his marriage the surname of Scott; in 1663 he and his wife were *cr Lord and Lady Scott of Whitchester and Eskdaill, Earl and Countess of Dalkeith*, and *Duke and Duchess of Buccleuch* (peerage of Scotland), with remainder to the heirs male whatsoever decending from the Dukes's body; the Duke was executed 15 July 1685, when all his honours were forfeited, but the honours vested in the Duchess were not attainted; Her Grace *m* 2ndly, Charles, 3rd Baron Cornwallis, by whom she had issue; *d* 1732; *s* by her grandson (6) FRANCIS, KT, 2nd Duke, son of James, Earl of Dalkeith, a Representative Peer; in 1743, was restored by Act of Parliament to the English honours of his grandfather, and became *Earl of Doncaster and Baron Scott of Tynedale* (peerage of England, *cr* 1663); *d* 1751; *s* by his grandson (7) HENRY, KG, KT, 3rd Duke; by the death, in 1810, of 4th Duke of Queensberry, he became, under a special remainder (granted in 1706), *Lord Douglas of Kinmont, Middlebie and Dornoch, Viscount of Nith, Thorthorwald and Ross, Earl of Drumlanrig and Sanquhar, Marquess of Dumfriesshire*, and *Duke of Queensberry* (peerage of Scotland); *d* 1812; *s* by his son (8) CHARLES WILLIAM, KT, 4th Duke of Buccleuch and 6th Duke of Queensberry; called up in his father's Barony of Tyne-dale 1807: *d* 1819; *s* by his son (9) WALTER FRANCIS, KG, PC, DCL, LLD, FRS, 5th Duke of Buccleuch and 7th Duke of Queensberry; *b* 1806; was Lord Privy Seal 1842-6, President of the Council 1846, Lord-Lieut of Midlothian and Roxburghshire, and Chancellor of Glasgow Univ: *m* 1829, Lady Charlotte Anne Thynne, VA, who *d* 1895, 3rd da of 2nd Marquess of Bath; *d* 16 April 1884; *s* by his son (10) WILLIAM HENRY WALTER, KG, KT, PC, 6th Duke of Buccleuch and 8th Duke of Queensberry; *b* 1831; MP for Edinburghshire (C) 1853-68 and 1874-80; Lord-Lieut of co Dumfries 1858-1914; *m* 1859, Lady Louisa Jane Hamilton, VA, who *d* 1912, da of 1st Duke of Abercorn, KG; *d* 1914; *s* by his el son (11) JOHN CHARLES, KT, GCVO, 7th Duke of Buccleuch, and 9th Duke of Queensberry; *b* 1864; MP for Roxburghshire (U) 1895- 1906; Lord Lieut of co Dumfries: *m* 1893, Lady Margaret Alice Bridgeman, who *d* 1954, da of 4th Earl of Bradford; *d* 1935; *s* by his el son (12) WALTER JOHN, KT, GCVO, TD, PC, 8th Duke of Buccleuch and 10th Duke of Queensberry, *b* 1894; Lord Steward of the Household 1937-40, Lord Clerk Register of Scotland, and Keeper of the Signet 1956-73, Capt-Gen Queen's Body Guard for Scotland (R Company of Archers), and Gold Stick for Scotland 1962-73, Chancellor of Order of Thistle 1966-73, MP for Roxburghshire and Selkirkshire (C) 1923-35, and Lord Lt of Roxburghshire 1932-73: *m* 1921, (Vreda Esther)

Mary, who *d* 1993, da of late Maj William Frank Lascelles (E Harewood, colls); *d* 1973; *s* by his son **(13)** WALTER FRANCIS JOHN, KT, VRD, 9th Duke of Buccleuch, and 11th Duke of Queensberry, present peer; also Marquess of Dumfriesshire, Earl of Dumfriesshire, Earl of Drumlanrig and Sanquhar, Earl of Buccleuch, Earl of Doncaster, Earl of Dalkeith, Viscount Nith, Thorthorwald and Ross, Lord Douglas of Kinmont, Middlebie and Dornoch, Lord Scott of Buccleuch, Lord Scott of Whitchester and Eskdaill, and Baron Scott of Tynedale.

BUCHAN, EARL OF (Erskine) (Earl S 1469)

MALCOLM HARRY ERSKINE, 17th Earl; *b* 4 July 1930; *s* 1984; *ed* Eton: *m* 1957, Hilary Diana Cecil, da of late Sir Ivan McLannahan Power, 2nd Bt, and has issue.

Arms – Quarterly of four; 1st azure, a barrulet en crancelin of four strawberry leaves between three garbs or *Buchan*; 2nd argent, a pale sable, in dexter canton a rose gules, barbed and seeded vert. *Erskine*; 3rd or, a lymphad sable, sails furled and oars in action and at the masthead a beacon all proper, surmounted of a fess chequy azure and argent charged with a mullet of the second, *Stewart of Buchan*; 4th argent, a lion passant guardant gules, crowned with an imperial and gorged with an open crown or, a label of three points of the second, the centre point charged with a crescent of the third, *Ogilvie of Auchterhouse*, on an inescutcheon en surtout gules, an eagle displayed or, armed and members azure, looking towards the sun in his splendour in dexter chief for lordship of *Cardross*. **Crest** – A dexter arm issuant from the wreath attired in a manche gules doubled ermine, the hand proper and grasping a club or. **Supporters** – Two ostriches proper, armed, beaked and membered or. *Residence* – Newnham House, Newnham, Basingstoke, Hants.

SONS LIVING

HENRY THOMAS ALEXANDER (*Lord Cardross*), *b* 31 May 1960: *m* 1987, Charlotte Catherine Lucinda, da of Hon Matthew Henry Beaumont (*see* V Allendale), and has issue:—
SONS LIVING- *Hon* Alexander, *b* 26 April 1990, —*Hon* Frederick Alastair, *b* 1992.
Hon Montagu John, *b* 1966.

DAUGHTERS LIVING

Lady Seraphina Mary, *b* 1961: *m* 1990, Steven K. Berry, elder son of Maj Roy Berry, of Witham, Essex, and has issue living, Katherine Aphra, *b* 1990, — Eleanor India, *b* 1994.
Lady Arabella Fleur, *b* 1969: *m* 1992, Francis Robin Charles Salvesen, eldest son of Robin Salvesen, of Eaglescairnie House, Haddington.

SISTERS LIVING

Lady Sarah Louisa (Redlands Row Cottage, Little Compton, Moreton-in-Marsh, Glos), *b* 1931: *m* 1957 (*m diss* 1972), Major Norman Neill-Fraser, and has issue living, James Montagu Nicholas, *b* 1959.
Lady Caroline Flower, *b* 1935: *m* 1963, John Robin William Lingard, of Semley Grange, Shaftesbury, Dorset, and has issue living, Christina Helen, *b* 1964, *m* 1st, 1981, Murad Teja, son of late M. P. Teja; 2ndly, 19—, Gawaine Maxwell, and has issue living (by 1st *m*), Alexandra Sophie *b* 1985, (by 2nd *m*) Jessica *b* 19—, Eloise Jane *b* 1990, — Victoria Margaret, *b* 1966.

COLLATERAL BRANCHES LIVING

Issue of late Hon (Richard) Alastair Erskine, yr son of 6th Baron Erskine, *b* 1901, *d* 1987: *m* 1933, Patricia, who *d* 1989, da of late Maj Paul FitzGerald Norbury, DSO, formerly of the Lench House, Stratford-on-Avon:—
Duncan FitzGerald (Little Cheesecombe, Hawkley, Liss, Hants GU33 6NB), *b* 1936; *ed* Malvern: *m* 1st, 1964 (*m diss* 1984), Jillian Lavinia Mary, da of Brig Vincent Alexander Prideaux Budge, CBE, MVO; 2ndly, 1986, Susan, da of late Maj Leslie Frederick Buckholt, and has issue living (by 1st *m*), Rory Alistair, *b* 1972, — Alexander FitzGerald *b* (quadruplet) 1972, — Charlotte Annabel, *b* (quadruplet) 1972. —— Melanie (adopted da), *b* 1938: *m* 1957 (*m diss* 1967), Sir John Patrick McLannahan Power, 3rd Bt, who *d* 1984.

Issue (by 2nd *m*) of late Capt Hon Albany Mar Stuart Erskine, 2nd son of 13th Earl, *b* 1852, *d* 1933: *m* 1st, 1878 (*m diss* 1900), Alice Ellen, who *d* 1902, da of late Alfred Keyser, of Cross Oak, Berkhamsted; 2ndly, 1909, Elizabeth Kate, who *d* 1965, da of George Samuel Craddock, of Melbourne, Australia:—
Rose Agnes Jessie Stuart (24 Carnwath Rd, Braehead, Forth, Lanark, ML11 BEY), *b* 1910. —— Gladys Evelyn Stuart, *b* 1916: *m* 1949, Johannes Adelbert Hopmann, of The Golliwogs, Windmill Rd, Mortimer, Berks.

Granddaughters of late Rev Thomas Erskine, son of Rt Hon Thomas Erskine, 3rd son of 1st Baron Erskine:—
Issue of late Col Henry Adeane Erskine, CB, CMG, CBE, VD, TD, *b* 1857, *d* 1953: *m* 1891, Florence Eliza Palmer, who *d* 1943, da of late Ven Frank Robert Chapman, formerly Archdeacon of Sudbury and Canon of Ely:—
Griselda Beatrice (Mount Pleasant, Castle Hill Lane, Mere, Wilts), *b* 1900: *m* 1921, Rev Canon George David Archer, who *d* 1971, and has issue living, Henry David, DFC, *b* 1922; W/Cdr RAF (ret) 1939-45 War (DFC): *m* 1957, Valda Mildred, who *d* 1978, da of late John Smart, of Wimbledon Park, SW, and has issue living, John David *b* 1958, Matthew George *b* 1962, Margaret Elizabeth *b* 1959, Charlotte Christian *b* 1961, — Richard George (Park Corner, Old Hollow, Worth, Sussex), *b* 1925: *m* 1956, Elizabeth Rosemary, da of late Kingsley Dykes, OBE, MC, of Ottinge Court, Kent, and has issue living, Caroline Griselda Erskine *b* 1959: *m* 1991, Charles Sussex, barrister, Elizabeth Georgiana *b* 1964, — Elizabeth Margaret Griselda, *b* 1923: *m* 1946, Lt Col Robert Kerr Montgomery MC, RE (ret), of Selwood House, Salisbury St, Mere, Wilts, and has issue living, Robert Michael *b* 1947: *m* 1979, Elizabeth Miles, of Stockbridge, Mass, USA, David Richard *b* 1949: *m* 1979, Gwynneth Owen, of Catcott, Som (and has issue living, Alexander Owen *b* 1984, Huw Thomas *b* 1986), — Alethea Mary, *b* 1926: *m* 1947, Cdr C. P. Evensen, DSC, RNVR, of Sherwoods, Staplehay, Trull, Taunton, Som, and has issue living, James Peter *b* 1951: *m* 1987, Robeena Holton, of Melbourne, Australia (and has issue living, Christian James *b* 1987, Nicolas Robin *b* 1989), Patricia Christian *b* 1948: *m* 1974, Alan Tucker, of Taunton, Som, Susan Alethea *b* 1950: *m* 1974, Donald Francis

Heather Bent, of The Corner House, Sandy Lane, Tilford, Farnham, Surrey (and has issue living, Simon Francis *b* 1979, Sarah Heather *b* 1976), Fiona Mary *b* 1952: *m* 1972, David Perratt, of Clavengers, E Nynehead, Wellington, Som (and has issue living, James Michael David *b* 1976, Diana Karen *b* 1974), — Mary Pamela, *b* 1929: *m* 1951, Capt Richard Ewen Hartley, RN, of 3 Newton Rd, Canford Cliffs, Poole Dorset, and has issue living, Christopher Richard (5 Bentley Close, Matlock, Derbys), *b* 1952: *m* 1976, Julia, da of Grenville Ball, of Sutton in Ashfield (and has issue living, David Richard *b* 1985, Katherine Mary *b* 1983), Michael Peter (4 Ashley Close, Charlton Kings, Cheltenham, Glos) *b* 1956: *m* 1985, Alison Mary, da of William Jacobs, of Ipswich, Suffolk (and has issue living, Caroline Alison *b* 1987, Charlotte Helen *b* 1990), Helen Mary *b* 1955: *m* 1979, Andrew George Alexander Wigmore, of 24 Chalfont Rd, Oxford (and has issue living, George Alexander *b* 1987, Hugh Richard *b* 1990), — Helen Christian, *b* 1935: *m* 1970, Alastair Nigel Courtney Bruce, of The Barn, Gt Durnford, Salisbury, and has issue living, Rowena Christian *b* 1970, Mary Courtney *b* 1972.

    Issue of late Thomas Edward Erskine, *b* 1859, *d* 1916: *m* 1888, Amy Gertrude, who *d* 1939, da of Lt-Gen Robert Bruce (Corbet, Bt, colls):—
Violet Amy (*Lady Seymour*), *b* 1894: *m* 1917, Sir Horace James Seymour, GCMG, CVO, who *d* 1978 (*see* M Hertford, colls). *Residence* – The Hut, Bratton, Westbury, Wilts.

    Grandchildren of Thomas Edward Erskine (ante):—
    Issue of late John Steuart Erskine, *b* 1900, *d* 1981: *m* 1928, Rachel (30 Tantramar Residences, Sackville, New Brunswick, Canada), da of Lt-Col Arthur Wilmot Rickman:—
David Steuart (71 Green Bush Rd, Willowdale, Ontario, Canada), *b* 1929; *ed* Acadia Univ (BSc 1948), and Toronto Univ (MA 1952): *m* 1957, Elizabeth Fyodorovna, da of late Fyodor Ivanovitch Kramarev, and has issue living, John David, *b* 1958, — Maria, *b* 1960: *m* 1981 (*m diss* 1990), Brian Clow, of Pickering, Ontario. —— Anthony John (PO Box 1327, Sackville, New Brunswick, Canada), *b* 1931; *ed* Acadia Univ (BSc 1952), Queen's Univ (MA 1955, PhD 1957), and BC Univ (MA 1960): *m* 1955, Janet Madeline Clarke, of Canning, Nova Scotia, and has issue living, Thomas Edward, *b* 1957: *m* 1981, Judith Rosemary, da of James Reynolds, of Woodstock, Ontario, and has issue living, Sarah Laurel *b* 1982, Bronwynn Rebecca *b* 1985, — Rachel Julia Andrée, *b* 1958: *m* 1988, Frank Collins, of Toronto, Canada, and has issue living, Julia Erskine *b* 1991, — Sally Eileen, *b* 1961: *m* 1980, Glenn Doucette, formerly of Hubbards Point, Nova Scotia, and has issue living, John Anthony Erskine *b* 1988, Madeleine Zoe *b* 1991, Clara Frances *b* 1993.

    Grandchildren of late John Steuart Erskine (ante):—
    Issue of late Roger Thomas Erskine, *b* 1933, *d* 1975: *m* 1956, Florence Elizabeth (RR3 Box 809, Bathurst, New Brunswick), da of late C. P. Taylor, of Windsor, Nova Scotia:—
Gerald Conrad, *b* 1957: *m* 1978, Carolyn, da of Clifford White, of Bathurst, New Brunswick, and has issue living, John Andrew, *b* 1981, — Ian Ross, *b* 1985. —— Neil Steuart, *b* 1960: *m* 1989, Ava, da of Stephen Czapalay, formerly of Barrington, Nova Scotia, and has issue living, Julian Benedict, *b* 1993. —— Joseph Christian, *b* 1962: *m* 1992, Donna Macdonald. —— Jane Elizabeth, *b* 1966.

    Grandchildren of late Edward John Erskine, yst son of late Rev Thomas Erskine (ante):—
    Issue of late Steuart Edward Erskine, *b* 1902, *d* 1992: *m* 1930, Marjorie Luxton Clendening, who *d* 1991:—
John Steuart (9448 Olympia Fields Drive, San Ramon, California 94583, USA), *b* 1937: *m* 1967, Sharyl Tomes, of Omaha, Nebraska, and has issue living, Karen, *b* 1968, — and an adopted da, LeAnn, *b* 1965 (adopted 1968). —— Patricia Louise (Le Petit Dixcart, Sark, Channel Islands), *b* 1934: *m* 1968, Stanley Falle, and has issue living, Marie Claire Erskine, *b* 1971.

    Grandchildren of late St Vincent Whitshed Erskine 2nd son of Maj Hon David Erskine, 21st Fus, 3rd son of 2nd Baron Erskine:—
    Issue of late Charles Howard Erskine, *b* 1871, *d* 1918: *m* 1900, Charlotte Mildred, who *d* 1947, da of William Wright Greathead:—
George St Vincent (961 Pershing Av, San José, California 95126, USA), *b* 1905: *m* 1936, Ruth Genevieve, who *d* 1992, da of Iver Nelson, and has issue living, Charles Nelson (9205 Jura Rd, RR2, Sidney, BC, Canada V8L 3S1), *b* 1938: *m* 1969, Linda Ruth, da of Thomas G. McReynolds, and has issue living, George Lindley *b* 1973, Gyneth Alice *b* 1971.
    Issue of late Maj Esmé Erskine, CMG, MC, *b* 1884, *d* 1962: *m* 1909, Elisabeth Susan Matilda, who *d* 1973, da of late Herman Reinders:—
Swanzie (*Lady Agnew of Lochnaw*), *b* 1916; *ed* Edinburgh Univ, (MA): *m* 1937, Sir Fulque Agnew of Lochnaw, 10th Bt, who *d* 1975.

    Grandsons of Maj Esmé Erskine, CMG, MC (ante):—
    Issue of late Esmé Stephenson Erskine, *b* 1914, *d* 1982: *m* 1941, Jean Meriel (Kingscliffe Farm, PO Glenside, 3477 Natal, S Africa), da of Harry Crawford Boyd, of Chobham, Surrey:—
Stephen St Vincent (Kingscliffe Farm, PO Glenside, 3477 Natal, S Africa), *b* 1947: *m* 1975, Bridget Grey, da of Derrick G. Norton, of Pietermaritzburg, Natal, and has issue living, Byron Thomas, *b* 1977, — Angela Jane, *b* 1979, — Paula Swanzie, *b* 1982. —— Andrew Stuart (Bosch Hoek, Balgowan, Natal, S Africa), *b* 1949: *m* 1972, Margaret Ann, da of Austin V. Johnson, of Howick, Natal, and has issue living, Stuart Graeme, *b* 1974, — Chad Esmé, *b* 1980, — Sarah Margaret, *b* 1976. —— David Boyd (335 Cowey Rd, Durban, Natal, S Africa), *b* 1954: *m* 1981, Marilyn-Gene, da of Harold Dodd, of Australia, and has issue living, Catherine Ann, *b* 1983, — Jennifer Lynn, *b* 1986.

(Not in remainder to the Earldom)

    Grandsons of late Capt Sir (Henry) David Erskine, KCVO, son of late James Erskine, el son of David Erskine, 3rd in descent from the Hon John Erskine, 3rd son of 2nd Lord Cardross:—
    Issue of late Col Sir Arthur (Edward) Erskine, GCVO, DSO, *b* 1881, *d* 1963: *m* 1921, Rosemary Freda, who *d* 1970, da of late Brig-Gen Edward William David Baird, CBE:—
Donald Seymour (Cleish House, Cleish, Kinross-shire). *Club* – New (Edinburgh), *b* 1925; *ed* Wellington Coll; FRICS; DL Kinross-shire, and a Member of Queen's Body Guard for Scotland (Royal Company of Archers); 1939-45 War as Capt RA: *m* 1953, Catharine Annandale, only da of late Kenneth McLelland, of Wester Housebyres, Melrose, Roxburghshire, and has issue living, James Malcolm Kenneth, *b* 1957; *ed* Wellington Coll; Maj The Black Watch (Royal Highland Regt); Memb Queen's Body Guard for Scotland (Royal Company of Archers): *m* 1987, Jennifer, elder da of Donald MacLellan, of Stockbridge, Symington, Ayrshire, and has issue living, Harry Charles David *b* 1988, Geordie James Donald *b* 1990, — Caroline Janet, *b* 1954: *m* 1982, Lt-Col Alan Keith McCulloch Miller, OBE, Argyll & Sutherland Highlanders, and has issue living, Kirstie Araminta Jane *b* 1983, Jennifer Catharine Susanne *b* 1985, Iona Caroline *b* 1988, — Fiona Catharine, *b* 1956: *m* 1991, Christopher Brendan Still, of Australia, and has issue living, Alexander Christopher *b* 1992, Harriet Angela *b* 1994, — Julia Rosemary, *b* 1962, — Joanna Christian, *b* 1968. —— Angus Bruce (16 Braid Farm Rd, Edinburgh EH10 6LF), *b* 1928; Cdr RN: *m* 1961, Alison Gillian, yr da of late Dr Comyn Duthie, of Welkom, Orange Free State, S Africa, and has issue living, Alexander David, *b* 1964, — Keith Malcolm, *b* 1967.

    Grandchildren of late Maj-Gen George Elphinstone Erskine, el son of Capt George Keith Erskine, 4th son of David Erskine (ante):—
    Issue of late Gen Sir George Watkin Eben James Erskine, GCB, KBE, DSO, *b* 1899, *d* 1965: *m* 1930, Ruby, who *d* 1974, da of Sir Evelyn Andros de la Rue, 2nd Bt:—

Philip Niel (Ida's Valley Homestead, PO Box 132, Stellenbosch, Cape, S Africa), 1933; Maj Scots Gds; Equerry to HRH Duke of Gloucester 1962-64: *m* 1960, Alice Fiona, da of late Maj Edward Copleston Radliffe, late 9th Lancers, of Lyndhurst House, Somerset West, Cape, S Africa, and has issue living, Rupert Alexander (The Auld House, Swellendam, Cape Prov, S Africa), *b* 1961: *m* 1986, Alida Maria, yr da of Gabriël Fagan, of Cape Town, — George Edward, *b* 1966, — Lucy Rose, *b* 1962. —— Robert Keith (Cliftonwood, Newbridge, Midlothian), *b* 1936: *m* 1991, Anne Nicola Parsons, and has issue living, Jonathan *b* 1994; author of *Business Management*: *m* 1964, Susan Morag, da of Sir Archibald Charles Edmonstone, 6th Bt, and has issue living, Hamish Robert Coll Charles, *b* 1967: *m* 1991, Anne Nicola Parsons, and had issue living, Jonathan *b* 1994, — Alexander William Ian Marshall, *b* 1970: *m* 1991, Carina Gustafsson, and has issue living, Carl *b* 1994, — Iona Mary, *b* 1965: *m* 1990, John Hunter Andrews, and has issue living, Morna *b* 1993. —— Elizabeth Polly, *b* 1945: *m* 1967, Paul L. H. Bristol, of La Metairie, Fabas 31230, Toulouse, France, and has issue living, Pollyanna, *b* 1969, — Sophy Louisa, *b* 1972, — Georgiana, *b* 1982.

PREDECESSORS – Buchan was one of the seven original Mormaerships (or Earldoms) of Scotland. In 1469 (1) Sir JAMES STEWART, 2nd son of Sir James Stewart of Lorn (the Black Knight of Lorn), by Joan, widow of James I of Scotland, was *cr Earl of Buchan* and *Lord Auchterhouse*; High Chamberlain of Scotland and Ambassador to France: *m* (before) 1466, Margaret, da of Sir Alexander Ogilvy, of Auchterhouse; *s* by his son (2) ALEXANDER, 2nd Earl; *d* 1505; *s* by his son (3) JOHN, 3rd Earl; *s* by his granddaughter (4) CHRISTIAN: *m* Robert Douglas, of Lochleven, who in right of his wife became Earl of Buchan; *s* by his son (5) JAMES, 5th Earl; *d* 1601; *s* by his da (6) MARY: *m* James Erskine, 2nd son of John, KG, 2nd Earl of Mar, who thereupon assumed the Earldom of Buchan; his wife resigned the dignity, and in 1617 she and her husband were *cr* by royal charter *Earl and Countess of Buchan* (peerage of Scotland), with remainder to the heirs-male of the marriage, whom failing, to the legitimate and nearest heirs-male and assignees of the Earl; in 1625 they had a further charter with similar limitation of the Earldom; in 1633 the precedency of the Earldom was established by Act of Parliament as 1469; the Countess *d* 1628, and the Earl 1640; *s* (under the charters of 1617 and 1625) by his son (7) JAMES, 7th Earl; *d* 1664; *s* by his son (8) WILLIAM, 8th Earl; *d* unmarried 1695; *s* by the heir male of 6th Earl (9) DAVID, PC, 9th Earl, and 4th Lord Cardross (see infra†), described in the Rolls of Parliament as 4th Earl of Buchan; right to this Earldom acknowledged by Parliament 1698; was a Representative Peer and Lord-Lieut of cos Stirling and Clackmannan; *d* 1745; *s* by his son (10) HENRY DAVID, 10th Earl; *d* 1767; *s* by his son (11) DAVID STEWART, 11th Earl: *d* 1829; *s* by his nephew (12) HENRY DAVID, 12th Earl; was *m* three times, 1st, 1809, to Elizabeth Cole who *d* 1828, da of Maj-Gen Sir Charles Shipley: he *d* 1857, and was *s* by his 2nd son by 1st *m* (13) DAVID STUART, 13th Earl, *b* 1815: *m* 1st, 1849, Agnes Graham who *d* 1875, da of James Smith, of Craigend Castle, Stirlingshire; 2ndly, 1876, Maria, da of William James, and widow of Jervoise Collas, of St Martin's House, Jersey; *d* 1898; *s* by his el son (14) SHIPLEY GORDON STUART, 14th Earl, *b* 1850: *m* 1876, Rosalie Louisa, who *d* 1943, da of late Capt Jules Alexandre Sartorius, of Hopsford Hall, Coventry; *d* 1934; *s* by his only son (15) RONALD DOUGLAS STUART MAR, 15th Earl; *b* 1878; formerly Lieut Argyll and Sutherland Highlanders, Scots Gds and E Riding Yeo; S Africa 1900-1902, European War 1915-17 in Egypt, Salonika and Palestine as Lieut RASC; *d* 1960; *s* by his kinsman (16) DONALD CARDROSS FLOWER, 7th Baron Erskine (see infra†), 16th Earl; Lt-Col 9th Lancers: *m* 1927, Christina, who *d* 1994, da of late Hugh Woolner, and adopted da of late Lloyd Harry Baxendale, JP, of Greenham Lodge, Newbury, Berks; *d* 1984; *s* by his only son (17) MALCOLM HARRY, 17th Earl and present peer; also Lord Cardross, Lord Auchterhouse and Baron Erskine.

*(1) JOHN, 2nd Earl of Mar, was *cr Lord Cardross* (peerage of Scotland) 1610, and acquired the right to assign the Lordship to whomsoever he might select, which privilege he exercised by Charter 1617 in favour of Henry, his 2nd son by his 2nd *m* ; *d* 1634; *s* by his grandson (2) DAVID, 2nd Lord *d* 1671; *s* by his son (3) HENRY, PC, 3rd Lord; suffered from religious persecution and was heavily fined and imprisoned; established a colony in Carolina, USA; was Gov of the Mint; *d* 1693; *s* by his son (4) DAVID, 4th Lord, afterwards 9th Earl of Buchan (ante).

†—(1) The *Hon* THOMAS ERSKINE, KT, 3rd son of 10th Earl of Buchan, having served both in Army and Navy was called to the English Bar and became a distinguished Advocate; Attorney-Gen to HRH the Prince of Wales 1783, Chancellor of Duchy of Cornwall 1802, and Lord High Chancellor 1806; *cr Baron Erskine*, of Restormel Castle, co Cornwall (peerage of United Kingdom) 1806: *m* 1st, 1770, Frances, who *d* 1805, da of David Moore, MP; 2ndly, 18—, Sarah Buck; *d* 1823; *s* by his son (2) DAVID MONTAGU, 2nd Baron *b* 1777: *m* 1st, 1799, Frances, who *d* (March) 1843, da of Gen John Cadwalader, of Philadelphia, USA; 2ndly (July), 1843, Ann Bond, who *d* 1851, da of late John Travis; 3rdly, 1852, Anna, who *d* 1886 (having *m* 3rdly, 1856, the Ven J. Sandford, BD, Archdeacon of Coventry), widow of Thomas Calderwood Durham, of Largo; *d* 1855; *s* by his el son (3) THOMAS AMERICUS, 3rd Baron, *b* 1802: *m* 1830, Louisa, who *d* 1867, da of G. Newnham, of New Timber Place, Sussex, and widow of Thomas Legh, of Adlington; *d* 1877; *s* by his brother (4) JOHN CADWALLADER, 4th Baron; *b* 1805; served in BCS 1826-53: *m* 1st, 1829, Margaret, who *d* 1862, da of John Martyn, of co Tyrone; 2ndly, 1865, Mary Louisa, who *d* 1889 (having *m* 2ndly, 1886, Philip Henry Egerton), da of Col Alexander Campbell, CB, KH, of Blackburn House, Ayrshire; *d* 28 Mar 1882; *s* by his son (5) WILLIAM MACNAGHTEN, 5th Baron, *b* 1841: *m* 1864, Caroline Alice Martha, who *d* 1922, da of late William Grimble; *d* 1913; *s* by his son (6) MONTAGU, 6th Baron; *b* 1865; formerly Lt-Cdr RNVR: *m* 1895, Florence, who *d* 1936, 4th da of Edgar Flower, JP, formerly of Middlehill Park, Broadway, Worcestershire, and The Hill, Stratford-on-Avon; *d* 1957; *s* by his el son (7) DONALD CARDROSS FLOWER, 7th Baron and afterwards 16th Earl of Buchan (ante).

Buckhurst, Lord; son of Earl De La Warr.

BUCKINGHAMSHIRE, EARL OF (Hobart-Hampden) (Earl GB 1746, Bt 1611)

(GEORGE) MILES HOBART-HAMPDEN, 10th Earl and 14th Baronet; *b* 15 Dec 1944; *s* 1983; *ed* at Clifton Coll, Exeter Univ (BA), and London Univ (MA): *m* 1st, 1968, Susan Jennifer, only da of late Raymond W. Adams, of Halesowen, Worcs; 2ndly, 1975, Alison Wightman, da of late William Forrest, of Edinburgh, and previously wife of late D. A. (Tim) Wishart, of Edinburgh.

ᴀʀᴍꜱ – Quarterly: 1st and 4th argent, a saltire gules, between four eagles displayed azure, *Hampden*: 2nd and 3rd sable, an estoile of six rays or, between two flaunches ermine, *Hobart*. ᴄʀᴇꜱᴛꜱ – 1st, a talbot statant ermine, collared and line reflexed thereto, tied in a knot over the back gules, *Hampden*; 2nd, a bull statant per pale sable and gules, bezantée, in the nose a ring or, *Hobart*. ꜱᴜᴘᴘᴏʀᴛᴇʀꜱ – *Dexter*, a buck; *sinister*, a talbot, both reguardant proper, each gorged with a radiant collar, and a line reflexed over the back or. ꜰɪʀꜱᴛ ᴍᴏᴛᴛᴏ – *Auctor pretiosa facit* (*The giver makes valuable*); ꜱᴇᴄᴏɴᴅ ᴍᴏᴛᴛᴏ – *Vestigia nulla retrorsum* (*No steps backward*). *Address* – House of Lords, SW1.

SISTER LIVING

Helen Moncreiff, *b* 1937: *m* 1962, Hugues Motteux, and has issue living, Thierry, *b* 1968, — Jean Paul, *b* 1973, — Nicole, *b* 1970. *Address* – Private Bag V7410, Mutare, Zimbabwe.

WIDOW LIVING OF NINTH EARL

MARGOT (*Margot, Countess of Buckinghamshire*) (c/o Barclays Bank, 6 Hanover Sq, W1), da of John Storey Rodger, of NSW, Australia, and widow of F. C. Bruce Hittman, MD, FRACS, of Sydney Australia: *m* 1972, the 9th Earl, who *d* 1983.

COLLATERAL BRANCHES LIVING

Granddaughter of late Capt Hon Charles Edward Hobart-Hampden, 4th son of 6th Earl:—
Issue of late Arthur Ernest Hobart-Hampden, *b* 1864; *d* 1952: *m* 1st, 1892, Henrietta Louisa, who *d* 1916, da of late Rev Thomas Orme Fetherstonhaugh, R of Moyne, co Wicklow; 2ndly, 1920, Cecilia Grace, who *d* 1929, da of late Sir Arthur Blackwood, KCB (Blackwood, Bt, colls); 3rdly, 1929, Bessie, RRC, who *d* 1960, da of late John West Stephenson:—
(By 1st *m*) Lucy Sybil (c/o Centennial Manor, Bancroft, Ontario, Canada), *b* 1898: *m* 1923, William Terence Webb McCarthy, MM, who was *ka* Italy 1944, and has issue living, Patrick Duniam (Bancroft, Ontario, Canada), *b* 1924; MD 1952: *m* 1952, Patricia, da of Archibald J. Stewart, of Toronto, — Elizabeth Sybil Ai-mei, *b* 1928.

Descendants of Sir Robert Henry Hobart KCVO, CB, *cr* a *Baronet* 1914, el son of Very Rev Hon Lewis Hobart, 4th son of 3rd Earl:—
Of whom *Sir* JOHN VERE HOBART, 4th *Baronet*, *b* 9 April 1945, is *hp* to the Earldom.

Grandchildren of late Charles Guy Reginald Vivian Beauchamp Hobart, yr son of late Charles Hobart (*b* 1842), eldest son of Lt-Col Charles Robert Hobart, 2nd son of Rev Henry Charles Hobart, only son of Hon Henry Hobart, yst son of 1st Earl:—
Issue of late John Bertram Hobart, *b* 1911, *d* 1982: *m* 1st, 1944 (*m diss* 1971), June Mary, da of Franklin George Barnes; 2ndly, 1972, Leone, da of —:—
(By 1st *m*) †Roger John *b* 1956; *d* as the result of a motor accident 1978. —— Hilary Rosamond (14 Stirling St, Kew, Victoria 3101, Australia), *b* 1958: *m* 1988, Carl Bethridge Topp, and has issue living, Matthew HOBART-TOPP, *b* 1987, — Annika Alexandra HOBART-TOPP, *b* 1990.
Issue of late Wallace Elliot Hobart, MB, BS, *b* 1922, *d* 1972: *m* 1st, 1946 (*m diss* 1956), Joyce Stella Hussey; 2ndly, 1957, Halina Zofia Bobinska, MB, ChB, of 86 Vida St, Essendon, Victoria 3040, Australia:—
(By 2nd *m*) Mark Michael (3 Derry St, Essendon, Victoria 3040, Australia), *b* 1958; *ed* Melbourne Univ (MB, BS): *m* 19—, Patricia Mildred Blair, and has issue living, Michael Wallace, *b* 1991, — Benedict Conrad William, *b* 1993. —— Pauline Ann, *b* 1960; BSc: *m* 1982, Bruce Twite, of 67 Research-Warrandyte Rd, Research, Victoria 3095, Australia, and has issue living, Adam Alexander, *b* 1988, — Elin Andrea, *b* 1990, — Hannah Gabrielle, *b* 1992.

Grandsons of late Rev William Henry Hobart, 4th and yst son of late Lt-Col Charles Robert Hobart (ante):—
Issue of late Rev Charles Hampden Hobart, *b* 1886, *d* 1961: *m* 1924, Alice, who *d* 1960, da of Samuel Plumbly, of Findon Valley, Worthing:—
John Hampden (Brandon, Buckland, Oxon SN7 8QW), *b* 1925; Maj (ret) late 5th R Inniskilling Drag Gds: *m* 1961, Maureen, da of Alfred Clowes, of Stoke-on-Trent, and has issue living, Andrew Hampden, *b* 1962, — Jeremy Charles, *b* 1963. —— Christopher Beauchamp (The Old Stables, The Coppice, Clifton Hampden, Oxon OX14 3DF), *b* 1927; *ed* St John's Leatherhead, and New Coll, Oxford: *m* 1st, 1953 (*m diss* 1970), Margaret, da of Gilbert Reed, of Lingfield, Surrey; 2ndly, 1970, Joanna Margaret, da of Rear Adm Anthony Davies, CB, CVO, of Witt's Piece, Aldbourne, Marlborough, Wilts, and has issue living (by 1st *m*), Richard Hampden, *b* 1960, — Simon Vere, *b* 1964, — (by 2nd *m*) Edward Andrew Beauchamp, *b* 1971, — Robert Anthony, *b* 1973, — John Henry *b* 1976.

PREDECESSORS – (1) Sir HENRY HOBART, successively MP for Norwich and Yarmouth, and Lord Chief Justice of the Common Pleas; was *cr* a *Baronet* 1611; *d* 1625; *s* by his son (2) Sir JOHN, MP, 2nd Bt; *d* 1647; *s* by his nephew (3) Sir JOHN, MP, 3rd Bt; *d* 1683; *s* by his el son (by his 1st *m* with Mary, da of the patriot John Hampden) (4) Sir HENRY, MP, 4th Bt; Equerry to King William III at the Battle of the Boyne 1690; killed in a duel by Oliver le Neve, 1698; *s* by his son (5) Sir JOHN, 5th Bt; *cr Baron Hobart* of Blickling (peerage of Great Britain) 1728, and *Earl of Buckinghamshire* (Peerage of Great Britain) 1746; *d* 1756; *s* by his son (6) JOHN, 2nd Earl; was Ambassador to Court of Russia 1762, and Viceroy of Ireland 1777; *d* 1793; *s* by his brother (7) GEORGE, 3rd Earl; *d* 1804; *s* by his son (8) ROBERT, PC, 4th Earl; was successively MP for Bramber, Sussex, and Armagh, Gov of Madras, Ch Sec for Ireland, Sec of State for War, and Sec of State for the Colonies, &c; summoned to Parliament as Baron Hobart 1797; *d* 1816; *s* by his brother (9) GEORGE ROBERT, 5th Earl (son of Hon George Vere Hobart by Jane, da of Horace Cataneo, Esq); sat as MP for St Michael 1812-3; assumed by R licence in 1824 the surname of Hampden in lieu of Hobart; *d* 1849; *s* by his brother (10) *Rev* AUGUSTUS EDWARD, 6th Earl; *b* 1793; assumed by R licence 1878 the additional surname of Hampden, *m* 1st, 1816, Mary, who *d* 1825, da of John Williams, King's Sergeant; 2ndly, 1826, Maria Isabella, who *d* 1873, da of Rev Godfrey Egremont; *d* 1885; *s* by his grandson (11) SIDNEY

CARR, OBE (son of Frederic John, Lord Hobart, 2nd son of 6th Earl, by Catherine Annesley, da of Rt Rev Thomas Carr, DD, formerly Bishop of Bombay), 7th Earl, *b* 1860; a Lord-in-Waiting to Queen Victoria 1895; assumed, by R licence 1903, the additional surnames of Mercer-Henderson for himself and issue: *m* 1888, Georgina Wilhelmina (authorised by R licence 1903, to use the surnames of Mercer-Henderson only and to subscribe herself by the surnames and title Mercer-Henderson-Buckinghamshire) who *d* 1937, da of late Hon Hew Adam Dalrymple Haldane Duncan-Mercer-Henderson; *d* 1930; *s* by his son **(12)** JOHN HAMPDEN, 8th Earl, *b* 1906; Dep-Chm of Cttees House of Lords 1952-4, and Dep Speaker House of Lords 1954-63; assumed by R licence 1938 the surname of Mercer-Henderson only in lieu of Hobart-Hampden-Mercer-Henderson; *d* 1963; *s* by his kinsman **(13)** VERE FREDERICK CECIL Hobart-Hampden (2nd son of late Arthur Ernest Hobart-Hampden, 2nd son of late Capt Hon Charles Edward Hobart-Hampden, 4th son of 6th Earl), 9th Earl *b* 1901; 1939-45 War with RAAF; *m* 1972, Margot Macrae, da of John Storey Rodger, of NSW, Aust, and widow of F. C. Bruce Hittman, MD, FRACS, of Sydney, Aust; *d* 1983; *s* by his kinsman **(14)** GEORGE MILES (only son of late Cyril Langel Hobart-Hampden, el son of Ernest Miles Hobart-Hampden, CMG, yst son of Hon George Augustus Hobart-Hampden, 5th son of 6th Earl), 10th Earl and present peer; also Baron Hobart.

BUCKMASTER, VISCOUNT (Buckmaster) (Viscount UK 1933)

MARTIN STANLEY BUCKMASTER, OBE, 3rd Viscount; *b* 11 April 1921; *s* 1974; *ed* Stowe; FRGS entered FO 1946, Political Officer, Abu Dhabi, 1955-58, First Sec (Information), British Embassy, Benghazi 1958-62, and Tripoli, 1962-63, First Sec (Political) Bahrain 1963-67, FO 1967-69; First Sec and British High Commn, Kampala 1969-71, British Embassy, Beirut 1971-73; FCO 1973-77, HM Chargé d'Affaires and Head of Chancery, Yemen Arab Republic, 1977-81 (ret); Capt R Sussex Regt (TA) 1939-46, served in Middle East; OBE (Civil) 1979.

Arms – Or, semée of fleurs-de-lis azure, a lion rampant of the last, on a chief of the second a portcullis of the first. **Crest** – A demi-lion azure, holding in the dexter paw a fleur-de-lis and charged on the shoulder with a portcullis, both or. **Supporters** – On either side a bulk proper, each gorged with a chain pendant therefrom a portcullis or.
Residence – 90 Cornwall Gdns, SW7 4AX.
Club – Travellers'.

BROTHER LIVING

Hon COLIN JOHN (Ryece Hall, Brettenham, Ipswich), *b* 17 April, 1923; *ed* Winchester; late Fl Lt RAF: *m* 1946, May only da of Charles Henry Gibbon, of The Lodge, Great Bentley, Essex, and has issue living, Adrian Charles, *b* 1949: *m* 1975, Dr Elizabeth M, only da of Norman Mark, MB, Bch, of Downings, Prinsted, Emsworth, Hants, and has issue living, Andrew Nicholas *b* 1980, Clare May *b* 1979, Nicola Mary *b* 1986, — Simon John, *b* 1956: *m* 1983, Emma Elizabeth, da of Field Marshal Sir John Wilfred Stanier, KCB, MBE, of Whitewater House, Dipley, Hartley Wintney, Hants, and has issue living, George John *b* 1984, Hugo Denis *b* 1987, Rachel May *b* 1988, — Michael Anthony Stanley, *b* 1959, — Ann Susan, *b* 1950: *m* 1976, Nicholas J. W. Tavener, and has issue living, Thomas Henry *b* 1980, Geoffrey John *b* 1985, Sarah Georgina *b* 1979, — Sarah Janet *b* 1952.

Equanimity, magnanimity

WIDOW LIVING OF SECOND VISCOUNT

DIANA CONSTANCE (Ringwold House, Middle Wallop, nr Stockbridge, Hants) da of late Maj Kenneth Arthur Seth-Smith, and formerly wife of Charles Stewart McDonnell Vane-Tempest (*see* M Londonderry, colls): *m* 1961, and 2nd wife, the 2nd Viscount, who *d* 1974; *m* 3rdly, 1982, as his 2nd wife, Roderick Edward Faure Walker.

PREDECESSORS – **(1)** *Rt Hon Sir* STANLEY OWEN Buckmaster, GCVO, PC, son of late John Charles Buckmaster, of Ashleigh, Hampton Wick; *b* 1861; sat as MP for Camb Borough (*L*) 1906-10, and for Keighley Div of N Part of W Riding of Yorkshire 1911-15; was Solicitor-Gen Oct 1913 to May 1915, and Lord High Chancellor of England May 1915 to Dec 1916; *cr Baron Buckmaster*, of Cheddington, Buckinghamshire (peerage of United Kingdom) 1915 and *Viscount Buckmaster*, of Cheddington, Buckinghamshire (peerage of United Kingdom) 1933: *m* 1889, Edith Augusta, who *d* 1935 da of S. R. Lewin, of Widford, Herts: *d* 1934: *s* by his son **(2)** OWEN STANLEY, 2nd Viscount, *b* 1890; Bar at law and underwriting member of Lloyds; Member of Cttee, London Stock Exchange 1938-42: *m* 1st, 1916 (*m diss* 1944), Joan, who *d* 1976, da of George Augustus Gary Simpson, MRCS; 2ndly, 1961, Diana Constance (VANE-TEMPEST) (who *m* 3rdly, 1982, as his 2nd wife, Roderick Edward Faure Walker), da of late Maj Kenneth Arthur Seth-Smith; *d* 1974; *s* by his el son **(3)** OWEN STANLEY, 3rd Viscount and present peer: also Baron Buckmaster.

BUCKTON, BARONY OF (Storey) (Extinct 1978)

SON LIVING OF LIFE BARON

Hon SIR RICHARD STOREY, 2nd Bt, who *s* to Baronetcy (*cr* 1960), 1978 (*see* BARONETAGE)

DAUGHTER LIVING OF LIFE BARON

Hon Jacquetta (*see* Storey, Bt)

BULLOCK, BARON (Bullock) (Life Baron 1976)

ALAN LOUIS CHARLES BULLOCK, FBA, son of Rev Frank Allen Bullock, of Bradford, Yorks; *b* 13 Dec 1914; *ed* Bradford Gram Sch, and Wadham Coll, Oxford (MD DLitt); Hon Fellow of St Catherine's Coll, New Coll, Merton Coll, Wadham Coll, Linacre Coll, and Wolfson Coll; Foreign Member of American Acad of Arts and Sciences; Hon Dr Univ Aix-Marseilles; Hon DLitt Bradford, Reading, Leicester, Sussex, Essex, Warwick, Newfoundland and Open University; Historian and Writer; FBA; Fellow, Dean and Tutor of New Coll, Oxford 1945-52, Censor of St Catherine's Soc Oxford 1952-60; Founding Master of St Catherine's Coll, Oxford 1960-80; Vice-Chancellor of Oxford Univ 1969-73; author of *Hitler, A Study in Tyranny* 1952, *The Liberal Tradition* 1956, *The Life and Times of Ernest Bevin* Vol I 1960, Vol II 1967, Vol III (*Ernest Bevin, Foreign Secretary*) 1983, *Hitler & Stalin: Parallel Lives* 1991 (revised edn 1993), and *The Twentieth Century* 1970, co-editor *Fontana Dictionary of Modern Thought* 1977 (2nd edn 1988), and *Fontana Biographical Companion to Modern Thought* 1983: *cr* Knt 1972, and *Baron Bullock*, of Leafield, co Oxfordshire (Life Baron), 1976: *m* 1940, Hilda Yates, da of Edwin Handy, of Bradford, and has issue.
Residence – The Old Manse, Leafield, Oxon.

SONS LIVING

Hon (Oliver) Nicholas Alan (King's College, Cambridge), *b* 1942: *m* 1st, 1967 (*m diss* 1972), — ; 2ndly, 1972 (*m diss* 1984), Ellen J. Blatt; 3rdly, 1984, Sally Todd, da of late Sinclair Holmes, of Bolden.
Hon Adrian Charles Sebastian (9 Wylie Close, Headington, Oxford OX3 7NH), *b* 1944: *m* 1st, 1970 (*m diss* 1984), Susan Elizabeth Swindlehurst; 2ndly, 1992, Bernadette Lucia Maria, da of James Ferry, of Glasgow.
Hon Matthew Peter Dominic, *b* 1949: *m* 1970, Anna-lena Margareta, da of Sven Hansson, of Uppsala, Sweden.

BURDEN, BARON (Burden) (Baron UK 1950)

PHILIP WILLIAM BURDEN, 2nd Baron; *b* 21 June 1916; *s* 1970; *ed* Raines Foundation Sch: *m* 1951, Audrey Elsworth, da of Maj Wilfred Elsworth Sykes, of Kirk Ella, Hull, and has issue.
Address – c/o Barclays Bank plc, 26-30 Regent St, Weston-super-Mare, Somerset BS23 1SH.

SONS LIVING

Hon ANDREW PHILIP, *b* 20 July 1959.
Hon Fraser William Elsworth, *b* 1964.
Hon Ian Stuart, *b* 1967.

DAUGHTERS LIVING

Hon Carol Mary, *b* 1952.
Hon Corynne Lesley, *b* 1955: *m* 1977, William D-Day Peters, of Greenland, Royston Water, Churchinford, Taunton, Som TA3 MEF, son of late Leonard Thomas Peters, and has issue living, Alexander, *b* 1983, — Lindsey Jane, *b* 1988.
Hon Adrienne Gail, *b* 1957.

PREDECESSOR – (1) THOMAS WILLIAM Burden, CBE, son of Thomas Burden, of Mile End, E; *b* 1885; 2nd Church Estates Commr 1945-50, a Member of House of Laity of Church Assembly 1947-50 and Lord in in Waiting to HM 1950-51; MP for Park Div of Sheffield (*Lab*) 1942-50; *cr Baron Burden*, of Hazlebarrow, co Derby (peerage of UK) 1950: *m* 1910, Augusta, who *d* 1976, da of David Sime, of Aberdeen; *d* 1970; *s* by his only son (2) PHILIP WILLIAM, 2nd Baron and present peer.

Burford, Earl of; son of Duke of St Albans.

BURGH, BARON (Leith) (E 1529)
(Title pronounced "Borough")

ALEXANDER PETER WILLOUGHBY LEITH, 7th Baron; *b* 20 March, 1935; *s* 1959; *ed* Harrow, and Magdalene Coll, Camb; formerly in RAF: *m* 1957 (*m diss* 1982), Anita Lorna, novelist (as Anita Burgh), da of late Frederick Clements Eldridge, of Gillingham, Kent, and has issue.

Arms – Quarterly, 1st and 4th or, a cross-crosslet fitchée sable between three crescents in chief and as many fusils in base barwise gules, all within a bordure azure, *Leith*; 2nd azure, three fleur-de-lis ermine, *Burgh*; 3rd, quarterly, 1st and 4th or, a lion rampant azure, armed and langued gules, *Percy*; 2nd and 3rd semée of six or and sable, *Strabolgi*. Crest – 1st, a cross-crosslet fitchée sable, *Leith*; 2nd, a falcon argent, beaked, legged and ducally gorged or, *Burgh*. Supporters – On either side a stag azure charged with three fleur-de-lis ermine in pale.
Address – c/o House of Lords, London SW1. *Residence* – Santa Cruz, California, USA.

SONS LIVING

Hon (ALEXANDER) GREGORY DISNEY, *b* 16 March 1958: *m* 1984, Catherine Mary, da of David Parkes, of The Old Rectory, Wrington, Bristol, and has issue living, Alexander James Strachan, *b* 11 Oct 1986. *Residence* – The White Hart, Nettlebed, Oxon RG9 5DD.

Hon Patrick Simon Vincent, *b* 1964.

DAUGHTER LIVING

Hon Rebecca Moraigh Eveleigh LEITH, *b* 1959; has resumed her maiden name: *m* 1978 (*m diss* 1983), David K. O. Brandler. *Residence* – 66 Cumberland Rd, Spike Island, Bristol BS1 6UF.

HALF-BROTHER LIVING

Hon John Barnabas (24 Gardiner Close, Abingdon, Oxon OX14 3YA), *b* 1947; *ed* Wellington Coll, and Exeter Univ: *m* 1970, Erica Jane, da of David M. Lewis, of Winchester, and has issue living, Alexander David Kalimat, *b* 1973, — Thomas Magnus Abad, *b* 1976, — Angharad Jane, *b* 1977.

WIDOW LIVING OF SIXTH BARON

JOYCE WATTS, da of W. Wilson Wilson, of 10 Curzon Road, Hoylake, Cheshire: *m* 1st, 1947, as his 2nd wife, the 6th Baron, who *d* 1959; 2ndly, 1960, Rupert Walter Westmacott. *Residence* – Little Roding, 35 Combeland Rd, Alcombe, Minehead, Somerset.

PREDECESSORS – (1) THOMAS Burgh, *de jure* 5th Baron Strabolgi, son of Sir Edward Burgh, MP for co Lincoln (who is held to have succeeded to the Barony of Strabolgi as 4th Baron in 1496); summoned to Parliament as Lord Burgh, of Gainsborough, co Lincoln 1529: *m* 1st, 1496, Agnes, da of Sir William Tyrwhitt; 2ndly, 15—, Alice, da of William London, and widow (1) of Sir Thomas Bedingfeld, and (2) of Edmund Rokewood; *d* 1550; *s* by his el surviving son (2) WILLIAM, 2nd Baron Burgh, and *de jure* 6th Baron Strabolgi; summoned to Parliament as Lord Burgh 1551-80: *m* 15—, Catherine, da of Edward, Earl of Lincoln; *d* 1584; *s* by his el surviving son (3) THOMAS, KG, 3rd Baron Burgh, and *de jure* 7th Baron Strabolgi; summoned to Parliament as Lord Burgh 1584- 97; Ambassador to Scotland 1593, and Lord Dep of Ireland 1597: *m* 15—, Frances, da of John Vaughan, of Sutton-on-Derwent, and his da Elizabeth *m* George Brooke (see B Cobham); *d* 1597; *s* by his el surviving son (4) ROBERT, 4th Baron Burgh, and *de jure* 8th Baron Strabolgi; *dsp* (about) 1600, when the Baronies fell into abeyance between his four sisters, among whose decendants they so remained until the abeyances were determined in 1916, the Barony of Burgh being called out of abeyance in favour of (5) ALEXANDER HENRY Leith, 5th Baron son of late Gen Robert William Disney Leith, CB, by Mary Charlotte Julia, who *d* 1926, da of Sir Henry Percy Gordon, 2nd Bt, FRS, *cr* 1818 (*ext*), by Lady Mary Agnes Blanche, da of 3rd Earl of Ashburnham, *b* 1866: also established his claim before Committee for Privileges of House of Lords as senior co-heir to the Baronies of Burgh and Cobham 1912, and to the Barony of Strabolgi 1914, and in 1916 the abeyance in the Barony of Burgh was determined in his favour: *m* 1st, 1893, Mildred Catherine, who *d* 1894, el da of late Gen Stuart Nicholson, CB: 2ndly, 1902, Phyllis, who *d* 1972, da of Col Mark Goldie, RE; *d* 1926: *s* by his son (6) ALEXANDER LEIGH HENRY, 6th Baron; *b* 1906; Lieut Black Watch: *m* 1st 1934 (*m diss* 1943), Elizabeth Rose, who *d* 1981, da of late Arthur Rose Vincent, CBE; 2ndly, 1947, Joyce Watts, (who *m* 2ndly, 1960, Rupert Walter Westmacott), da of W. Wilson Wilson, of 10 Curzon Road, Hoylake, Cheshire; *d* 1959: *s* by his el son (7) ALEXANDER PETER WILLOUGHBY 7th Baron and present peer.

Burghley, Lord; son of Marquess of Exeter.

Burlington, Earl of; grandson of Duke of Devonshire.

BURNHAM, BARON (Lawson) (Baron UK 1903, Bt UK 1892)

OF · OLD · I HOLD

HUGH JOHN FREDERICK LAWSON, 6th Baron, and 6th Baronet; *b* 15 Aug 1931; *s* 1993; *ed* Eton, and Balliol Coll, Oxford (MA); late Lieut Scots Guards: *m* 1955, Hilary Margaret, yr da of late Alan Hunter, of Huntingtowerfield House, Almondbank, Perthshire, and has issue.

Arms – Quarterly: 1st and 4th azure, three bars geme, argent, over all a winged morion or; 2nd and 3rd gules, a saltire double parted and fretted or between in fesse two rams' heads, couped in fesse argent. **Crests** – 1st, in, front of a terrestrial globe proper a winged morion or; 2nd a ram argent holding in the mouth a trefoil slipped vert and resting the dexter fore leg on a quatrefoil or. **Supporters** – *Dexter*, the figure of Clio, the Muse of history proper; *sinister*, the figure of Hermes vested argent, mantled azure; on the head a winged morion, on his heels wings, and in his exterior hand a caduceus or.
Residence – Woodlands Farm, Beaconsfield, Bucks HP9 2SF. *Clubs* – Garrick, Pratt's, Royal Yacht Squadron.

SON LIVING

Hon HARRY FREDERICK ALAN, *b* 22 Feb 1968; *ed* Eton.

DAUGHTERS LIVING

Hon Charlotte Ann, *b* 1960.
Hon Emma Lucia, *b* 1961.

DAUGHTERS LIVING OF FIFTH BARON

Hon Jenefer Anne, *b* 1949: *m* 1985, Andrew David Farncombe, son of George Frank Farncombe, of Ipswich, Suffolk, and has issue living, Frederick Alexander Edward, *b* 1987, — Joanna Abigail, *b* 1990. *Residence* – Little Hall Barn, Windsor End, Beaconsfield, Bucks HP9 2JW.
Hon Harriet Mary, *b* 1954: *m* 1984, Marino Sain, only son of Silvano Sain, of Trieste, Italy, and has issue living, Thomas Andrea, *b* 1987, — Giacomo Julian Lawson, *b* 1991, — Harry Benjamin, *b* 1994, — Teresa Anna, *b* (twin) 1994. *Residence* – via Rossini 16, Trieste, Italy 34100.
Hon Sarah Jane, *b* 1955; resumed her maiden name 1991: *m* 1st, 1982 (*m diss* 1991), Michael Ian Grade; 2ndly, 1992, David Patrick Maher. *Residences* – 2 Clarendon Close, W2 2NS; Newton Park, Wicklow.

SISTER LIVING

Hon Lucia Edith, (Hallin, 18 Burnham Av, Beaconsfield, Bucks HP9 2JA), *b* 1922; European War 1939-45 in France and Germany as Co Sergeant-Maj ATS (despatches): *m* 1st, 1946 (*m diss* 1953), Hon Roger David Marquis (later 2nd Earl of Woolton), who *d* 1969; 2ndly, 1966, John Whitehead, who *d* 1982.

WIDOW LIVING OF FIFTH BARON

ANNE (*Dowager Baroness Burnham*), 2nd da of late Maj George Gerald Petherick (*see* E Radnor, 1976 Edn); DL Bucks 1985: *m* 1942, Lt-Col the 5th Baron, who *d* 1993. *Residence* – Hall Barn, Beaconsfield, Bucks HP9 2SG.

PREDECESSORS – **(1)** *Sir* EDWARD Levy-Lawson, KCVO, son of late Joseph Moses Levy, JP, one of the principal founders of the Cheap Press in London; *b* 1833; was principal proprietor of the *Daily Telegraph*; assumed by R Licence 1875 the surname of Lawson in addition to and after that of Levy; *cr* a *Baronet* 1892, and *Baron Burnham*, of Hall Barn, Beaconsfield, Buckinghamshire (peerage of United Kingdom) 1903: *m* 1862, Harriette Georgiana, who *d* 1897, da of late Benjamin N. Webster, of Pen-y-craig, co Denbigh; *d* 1916; *s* by his eldest son **(2)** HARRY LAWSON WEBSTER, GCMG, CH, 2nd Baron, *b* 1862; sometime Principal Proprietor of the *Daily Telegraph*, and Chm of Newspaper Proprietors' Asso; Pres of Institute of Journalists 1910, and a Member of Indian Statutory Commn 1927-30; *cr Viscount Burnham*, of Hall Barn, co Buckingham (peerage of United Kingdom) 1919: *m* 1884, Olive, who *d* 1939, da of Gen Sir Henry Percival de Bathe, 4th Bt; *d* 1933, when the Viscountcy became ext and the Barony and Baronetcy passed to his brother **(3)** WILLIAM ARNOLD WEBSTER, DSO, 3rd Baron, *b* 1864; Capt Scots Guards and Lieut-Col and Brevet Col Bucks Yeo; S Africa 1900-1901 (DSO): *m* 1887 (*m diss* 1912), Sybil Mary, who *d* 1933, da of late Lieut-Gen Sir Frederick Marshall, KCMG; *d* 1943, *s* by his el son **(4)** EDWARD FREDERICK, CB, DSO, MC, TD, 4th Baron, *b* 1890; Maj-Gen TA; CRA 48th (S Midland Div) TA 1938-41, and GOC Yorkshire Div 1941-2, and Dir of Public Relations War Office and Senior Mil Adviser, Min of Information 1942-5: *m* 1920, Marie Enid, CBE, who *d* 1979, da of Hugh Scott Robson, of London, and Buenos Aires; *d* 1963; *s* by his el son **(5)** WILLIAM HARRY EDWARD, 5th Baron, *b* 1920; Lt-Col Scots Gds, comdg 1st Bn 1959-62; 1939-45 War in France, Middle East, N Africa and Italy; Malaya 1950-51 (despatches); DL Bucks: *m* 1942, Anne, 2nd da of late Maj George Gerald Petherick (*see* E Radnor, 1976 Edn); *d* 1993; *s* by his brother **(6)** HUGH JOHN FREDERICK, 6th Baron and present peer.

BURNTWOOD, BARONY OF (Snow) (Extinct 1982)

DAUGHTER LIVING OF LIFE BARON

Hon Harriet Louise Julia, *b* 1950.

BURTON, BARON (Baillie) (Baron UK 1897)

What is brighter than the stars?

MICHAEL EVAN VICTOR BAILLIE, 3rd Baron; *b* 27 June 1924; *s* 1962; *ed* Eton; late Lieut Scots Gds and Lovat Scouts: *m* 1st, 1948 (*m diss* 1977), Elizabeth Ursula Forster, who *d* 1993, da of late Capt Anthony Forster Wise; 2ndly, 1978, Coralie Denise, da of late Claud R. Cliffe, and has had issue by 1st *m*.

Seats – Dochfour, Inverness; The Gables, Rangemore, Burton-on-Trent. *Clubs* – Cavalry and Guards', Brooks's, New (Edinburgh) and Highland (Inverness).

𝕬rms – Quarterly, 1st and 4th azure, nine stars, three, three, two and one argent, within a border engrailed or, charged with six cinquefoils of the field, *Baillie*; 2nd and 3rd, gules on a chevron cottised argent between three plates each charged with a fleur-de-lys azure, a demi lion couped of the first, *Bass*. 𝕮rest – A boar's head couped argent, armed or, langued gules. 𝕾upporters – On either side a lion reguardant sable each charged on the shoulder with a plate thereon a fleur-de-lys azure and resting the inner hind leg on a stag's head caboshed proper.

SONS LIVING *(By 1st marriage)*

Hon EVAN MICHAEL RONALD *b* 19 March 1949; *ed* Harrow: *m* 1970, Lucinda, el da of Robert Law, of Turnpike House, Withersfield, Haverhill, Suffolk, and has issue living, James Evan, *b* 3 Dec 1975, — Hamish Michael, *b* 1979, — Emma Elizabeth, *b* 1977.
Hon Alexander James, *b* 1963.

DAUGHTERS LIVING AND DECEASED *(By 1st marriage)*

Hon Elizabeth Victoria, *b* 1950: *m* 1970, Hon Angus Grenfell Maclay, of Westruther Mains, Gordon, Berwickshire, and *d* 1986, leaving issue (*see* B Maclay).
Hon Philippa Ursula Maud, *b* 1951: *m* 1980, R. Ian McCowen, and has issue living, Ewan, *b* 1981, — Christopher Richard, *b* 1983. *Residence* – Polwarth Manse, Greenlaw, Berwickshire.
Hon Georgina Frances, *b* 1955.
Hon Fiona Mary, *b* 1957: *m* 1982, Alasdair Malcolm Douglas Macleod Hilleary (*see* D Hamilton and Brandon, 1985 Edn), and has issue living, Geordie, *b* 1991, — Flora Elizabeth Macleod, *b* 1985, — Rosannagh Catriona, *b* 1988. *Residence* – Greenhill House, Redcastle, Muir of Ord, Ross-shire.

BROTHER LIVING

(Raised to the rank of a Baron's son 1964)

Hon Peter Charles, *b* 1927; *ed* Eton; late Maj The Life Gds; a JP of Hants: *m* 1955, Jennifer Priscilla, da of late Com Harold Reginald Newgass, GC, of Winterborne, W Stafford, Dorset, and has issue living, Catriona Margaret, *b* 1956, — Elizabeth Mary Eilidh, *b* 1959: *m* 1982, Michael Halstead-Morton, of Oddfellows Cottage, Setley, Brockenhurst, Hants, and has issue living, Hannah Elizabeth *b* 1983, Emily Victoria *b* 1985, — Susan Jennifer, *b* 1960: *m* 1989, Capt Christopher Rushworth, RAOC, and has issue living, William Christopher *b* 1993, — Rachel Emma, *b* 1963. *Residence* – Wootton Hall, New Milton, Hants BH25 5SJ.

SISTER LIVING

(Raised to the rank of a Baron's daughter 1964)

Hon Judith Evelyn Maud, *b* 1925; formerly in ATS: *m* 1949, Lt-Col Angus Cameron, MC, Scots Gds, and has issue living, Angus Iain (Drummond, Dores, by Inverness), *b* 1952: *m* 1973, Candida, da of late Ronald T. Fryer Smith, of 8 Fulwood Park, Liverpool 17, and has issue living, Lorien *b* 1975, Fiona *b* 1978, — Hester Caroline, *b* 1950. *Residence* – Aldourie Castle, Inverness.

COLLATERAL BRANCH LIVING

Granddaughters of late Maj Hon Arthur Malcolm Augustus Baillie, yr son of late Nellie Lisa, Baroness Burton:—
Issue of late Lt-Col Ian Bruce Baillie, *b* 1928, *d* 1978: *m* 1962, June Marion Cloudesley (Congham Lodge, Hillington, King's Lynn, Norfolk PE31 6BZ), da of Arthur Cloudesley Smith, FRCS, and widow of (Arthur) Henry Bellingham (*see* Bellingham, Bt, colls):—
Katherine Victoria Harriet, *b* 1962: *m* 1990, (John) Malcolm Agnew Wallace, of 57 Shawfield St, SW3 4BA, only son of (John) Malcolm Agnew Wallace, of Lochryan, Stranraer, Wigtownshire (*see* B Bagot, colls, 1965 Edn), and has issue living, Alexander Ian Agnew, *b* 1992, — Hewie Malcolm Agnew, *b* 1993. —— Sarah Rosemary Caroline *b* 1964.

PREDECESSORS – (**1**) *Sir* MICHAEL ARTHUR BASS, KVCO, el son of late Michael Thomas Bass, MP for Derby 1848-83; *b* 1837; a Director of Bass, Ratcliff, Gretton and Co (Limited), of Burton-on-Trent; MP for Stafford (*L*) 1865-8, for E Staffordshire 1868-85, and for Burton Div of Staffordshire 1885-6; *cr* a *Baronet* 1882, *Baron Burton*, of Rangemore and Burton-on-Trent, co Stafford (peerage of United Kingdom) 1886, and *Baron Burton*, of Burton-on-Trent, and of Rangemore, co Stafford (peerage of United Kingdom) 1897, with special remainder, in default of issue male, to his da and her male issue: *m* 1869, Harriet Georgina, who *d* 1931, da of late E. Thornewill, of Dove Cliff, co Stafford; *d* 1909; when the Barony (*cr* 1896) became *ext*, the baronetcy passed to his nephew, William Arthur Hamar Bass, and the Barony (*cr* 1897) devolved under the special remainder upon his da and heir (**2**) NELLIE LISA, *b* 1873: *m* 1894, Col James Evan Bruce Baillie, MVO, RHA (TF), who *d* 1931; 2ndly 1932, Maj William Eugene Melles, who *d* 1953; *d* 1962; *s* by her grandson (**3**) MICHAEL EVAN VICTOR (son of late Brig Hon (George) Evan Michael BAILLIE, MC, TD, who *d* on active ser 1941), 3rd Baron and present peer.

BUTE, MARQUESS OF (Crichton-Stuart) (Marquess GB 1796, Bt S 1627)

JOHN COLUM CRICHTON-STUART, 7th Marquess, and 12th Baronet; *b* 26 April 1958; *s* 1993; *ed* Ampleforth; Hereditary Sheriff and Coroner of co Bute, Hereditary Keeper of Rothesay Castle, and patron of nine livings (but being a Roman Catholic cannot present); Racing Driver (as Johnny Dumfries), joint winner Le Mans 1988: *m* 1984 (*m diss* 1993), Carolyn, da of late Bryson Waddell, and has issue.

Arms – Quarterly: 1st and 4th or a fesse checky azure and argent, within a double tressure flory counterflory gules, and in dexter chief of the first quarter a canton of Nova Scotia, *Stuart*; 2nd and 3rd argent, a lion rampant azure, armed and langued gules, *Crichton*; behind the shield are placed in saltire a key or, having within its handle a fesse checky azure and argent, and a rod gules surmounted of a tower argent masoned sable, conically capped loopholes and port gules (*Insignia of Office of Heritable Keeper*) a coronet. **Crests** – 1st a dragon vert, crowned with an open crown of four strawberry leaves langued or, *Crichton*; 2nd, a demi-lion rampant gules, armed and langued azure *Stuart*; 3rd, argent and azure, a wyvern proper, holding in the mouth a sinister hand couped gules (*for the Lordship and Fief of Cardiff*). **Supporters** – *Dexter*, a stag proper, attired or, gorged with an Earls coronet also proper, having therefrom a chain reflexed over the back gules ; *sinister*, a horse argent, bridled gules.
Seat – Mount Stuart, Rothesay, Isle of Bute.

He flourishes in an honourable ancestry

SON LIVING

JOHN BRYSON (*Lord Mount Stuart*), *b* 21 Dec 1989.

DAUGHTERS LIVING

Lady Caroline, *b* 1984.
Lady Cathleen, *b* 1986.

BROTHER LIVING

Lord Anthony, *b* 1961; *ed* Ampleforth, and Durham Univ: *m* 1990, Alison J., yr da of Keith Bruce, of Highgate, NW6.

SISTERS LIVING AND DECEASED

Lady Sophia Anne, *b* 1956; resumed her maiden name 1988: *m* 1st, 1979 (*m diss* 1988), Jimmy Bain; 2ndly 1990, as his 2nd wife, Alexius John Benedict Fenwick (*see* B Lilford, colls), and has issue living (by 1st *m*), Samantha Ella, *b* 1981, — (by 2nd *m*) Georgia Jessie, *b* 1990.
Lady (Eileen) Caroline, *b* 1957; *k* in a motor accident 1984.

AUNT LIVING (*daughter of 5th Marquess*)

Lady (Caroline Moira) Fiona, *b* 1941: *m* 1959, Capt Michael Lowsley-Williams, 16/5th Lancers (*see* Makins, Bt, 1967 Edn), and has issue living, Patrick David Edward, *b* 1960, — Mark Ogden Francis, *b* 1961, — Paul John Fermin, *b* 1964, — Michael Charles Javier, *b* 1967.

GREAT AUNT LIVING (*Daughter of 4th Marquess*)

Lady Jean, *b* 1908; is a Dame Grand Cross of Honour and Devotion of Sovereign Mil Order of Malta: *m* 1928, Lt-Cdr Hon James Willoughby Bertie, RN, who *d* 1966 (*see* E Lindsey and Abingdon). *Residence* – Casa de Piro, Attard, Malta, GC.

WIDOWS LIVING OF SONS OF FIFTH MARQUESS

Helen (*Lady David Crichton-Stuart*) (Kames Court, Cronkbourne, Braddan, Isle of Man), da of William Kerr McColl: *m* 1972, Lord David Ogden Crichton-Stuart, who *d* 1977, and has issue (*see* colls infra).
Anna-Rose, da of late Maj H. Bramwell, of The White House, Mallow, co Cork: *m* 1st, 1970, as his 2nd wife, Lord James Charles Crichton-Stuart, who *d* 1982; 2ndly, 1992, Peter Merrick Knatchbull-Hugessen (*see* B Brabourne, colls), and has issue (by 1st *m*) (*see* colls infra). *Residence* – Ropley House, Ropley, Hants.

WIDOW LIVING OF SON OF FOURTH MARQUESS

Lady Janet Egidia Montgomerie (*Lady Robert Crichton-Stuart*) (Wards Cottage, Gartocharn, Dunbartonshire), da of 16th Earl of Eglinton and Winton: *m* 1934, Capt Lord Robert Crichton-Stuart, who *d* 1976, and has issue (*see* colls infra).

MOTHER LIVING

(Beatrice) Nicola Grace, only da of late Lt-Cdr Wolstan Beaumont Charles Weld-Forester, CBE, RN (*see* B Forester, colls): *m* 1955 (*m diss* 1977), as his 1st wife, the 6th Marquess of Bute, who *d* 1993.

WIDOW LIVING OF SIXTH MARQUESS

JENNIFER (*Marchioness of Bute*), da of John Brougham Home-Rigg, of Eastern Transvaal, and formerly wife of Gerald Percy (*see* D Northumberland, colls): *m* 1978, as his 2nd wife, the 6th Marquess of Bute, KBE, who *d* 1993.

COLLATERAL BRANCHES LIVING

Issue of late Lord David Ogden Crichton-Stuart, 2nd son of 5th Marquess, *b* (twin) 1933, *d* 1977: *m* 1972, Helen (ante), da of William Kerr McColl:—
Kenneth Edward David, *b* 1975. ―― Elizabeth Rose, *b* 1973.

Issue of late Lord James Charles Crichton-Stuart, 3rd son of 5th Marquess, *b* 1935, *d* 1982: *m* 1st, 1959 (*m diss* 1968), Sarah Frances, only da of Lt-Col Arthur Edward Croker-Poole, of 19 Launceston Place, W8;

2ndly, 1970, Anna-Rose (ante) (who *m* 2ndly, 1992, Peter Merrick Knatchbull-Hugessen) (*see* B Brabourne, colls), da of late Maj H. Bramwell, of The White House, Mallow, co Cork:—
(By 2nd *m*) William Henry, *b* 1971. —— Hugh Bertram, *b* 1973. —— Alexander Blane, *b* 1982.

Issue of late Capt Lord Robert Crichton-Stuart, 2nd son of 4th Marquess, *b* 1909, *d* 1976: *m* 1934, Lady Janet Egidia Montgomerie (ante), da of 16th Earl of Eglinton and Winton:—
†Ninian, *b* 1935; *d* 1992. —— Henry Colum (42 Beaufort Mansions, Beaufort Street, SW3), *b* 1938: *m* 1963 (*m diss* 19——), Patricia Margaret, only da of late Brig Hugh Ronald Norman, DSO, of Lower St Clere, Kemsing, Kent, and has issue living, Alexander Colum, *b* 1967, — Camilla, *b* 1964, — Serena, *b* 1965, — Teresa Clare, *b* 1971.

Issue of late Lord David STUART, 3rd son of 4th Marquess, *b* 1911; discontinued use of surname of Crichton by decree of Lord Lyon 1934; *d* 1970: *m* 1940, Ursula Sybil CLIFTON, who *d* 1989, formerly wife of Peter Thomas Clifton (*see* Bruce, Bt, *cr* 1904), and da of late Sir Edward Hussey Packe, KBE (By Colebrooke):—
Flora, *b* 1941.

Issue of late Lord Patrick Crichton-Stuart, 4th son of 4th Marquess, *b* 1913, *d* 1956: *m* 1st, 1937, Jane, who *d* 1944, da of Capt von Bahr, of Stockholm, Sweden; 2ndly, 1947, Linda Irene, who *d* 1974, only da of William Evans, of St Mellons, Monmouth:—
(By 1st *m*) Charles Patrick Colum Henry (16 Douglas Court, West End Lane, NW6), *b* 1939; *ed* Ampleforth; late RAF; Flying Instructor, London Sch of Flying, Elstree, and Racing Driver: *m* 1st, 1967 (*m diss* 19——), Shirley Ann Field, the actress; 2ndly, 1980, Jennifer A. A. Collie, and has issue living (by 1st *m*), Nicola Jane, *b* 1967, — (by 2nd *m*) Patrick James, *b* 1982, — Sophie, *b* 1980. —— Angela Mary Monica, *b* 1940: *m* 1963, Simon Mark Pilkington (*see* B Faringdon, colls).

Issue of late Capt Lord Rhidian Crichton-Stuart, RA, yst son of 4th Marquess, *b* 1917, *d* 1969: *m* 1939, Selina, who *d* 1985, da of Frederick Gerth Van Wijk, late Min Plen for the Netherlands in Paris:—
Frederick John Patrick (40 Fernyside Gdns, Gilmerton, Edinburgh), *b* 1940; a Kt of Sovereign Mil Order of Malta: *m* 1964, Elizabeth Jane Douglas, el da of Ernest J. Whitson, and has issue living, Rhidian Colum, *b* 1967, — Edward Neil James, *b* 1974, — Ione Jane, *b* 1965, — Amanda Mary, *b* 1968. —— (Jerome) Niall Anthony (5 Coldstream Gds, SW18), *b* 1948; Maj Scots Gds; a Kt of Sovereign Mil Order of Malta; Chevalier du Wissam Alouite (Royaume du Maroc): *m* 1971, Susan, el da of Prof Patrick Dwyer-Joyce, of Errislannan, Sandycove, co Dublin, and has issue living, Rhidian Charles Patrick, *b* 1974, — Niall Rollo Robert, *b* 1977, — Archie Michael John, *b* 1984. —— (Mary) Margot Patricia, *b* 1942: *m* 1962, Edward Henry Lovell, of 24 Hendrick Av, SW12, and has issue living, Peter Henry James, *b* 1965, *ed* Ampleforth, — Nicola Mary, *b* 1963, — Henrietta Margaret, *b* 1971.

Grandchildren of late Lt-Col Lord Ninian Edward Crichton-Stuart, MP, Welch Regt, 2nd son of 3rd Marquess:—
Issue of late Maj Michael Duncan David Crichton Stuart, MC, *b* 1915, *d* 1981: *m* 1941, Barbara, who *d* 1985, only da of late Lt-Col Sir (George) Stewart Symes, GBE, KCMG, DSO:—
Ninian John (Moncreiff House, High St, Falkland, Fife KY7 7BP), *b* 1957; Hereditary Keeper of Falkland Palace: *m* 1982, Anne Marie, da of Neil O'Donnell, of Dowanhill, Glasgow, and has issue living, Francis Paul, *b* 1984, — Christina Marie, *b* 1983. —— Elspeth Ann, *b* 1954: *m* 1981, Prof Thomas Puttfarken, of Annandale, Anglesea Rd, Wivenhoe, nr Colchester, Essex. —— The late Maj Michael D. D. Crichton Stuart also adopted two das, Mary (Marietta) Frances (4 Fitzwilliam Rd, Clapham Old Town, SW4), *b* 1951. —— Frances Elizabeth (6 Cadogan House, Beaufort St, SW3), *b* 1951; painter.

Grandchildren of late Capt Patrick James Crichton-Stuart, Gren Gds, only son of late Lt-Col James Frederick Dudley Crichton-Stuart, MP, Gren Gds, elder son of Lord Patrick James Herbert Crichton-Stuart, MP (who was granted the rank and precedence of the younger son of a Marquess 1817), 2nd son of John, Lord Mountstuart, eldest son of 1st Marquess:—
Issue of late Maj Patrick Dudley Crichton-Stuart, *b* 1909, *d* 1978: *m* 1948, Sheila Mary (1 Sloane Gdns, SW1), da of Lt Col James Douglas Kendall Restler, OBE:—
(Patrick) James (1 Sloane Gdns, SW1; *Club* – Turf), *b* 1954; *ed* Downside; Lieut Scots Gds (Res): *m* 1st, 1978 (*m diss* 1982), Amanda Mary Howell, eldest da of Michael Pollock Howell Williams, of Cosford House, Thursley, Surrey; 2ndly, 1991, Lady Rowena Katharine Meade, elder da of 7th Earl of Clanwilliam, and has issue living (by 1st *m*), Frederick James, *b* 1981, — Katherine Rose, *b* 1979. —— Caroline Mary Katherine, MVO, *b* 1949; MVO 1990: *m* 1993, Antony Frederick Gandolfi Hornyold, 4th Duke Gandolfi (*see* B Mowbray, colls).

Grandchildren of late Lt-Col Henry John Richard Villiers-Stuart, el son of Capt William Villiers-Stuart, MP, 2nd son of Lord Henry Stuart, 5th son of 1st Marquess:—
Issue of late Col John Patrick Villiers-Stuart, CB, DSO, OBE, *b* 1879, *d* 1958: *m* 1st, 1914, Phyllis Mary, who *d* 1933, da of late James Read; 2ndly, 1933, Eileen Nora (The Beeches, Catsfield, Battle, Sussex), da of late Col Alexander John Maunsell MacLaughlin, CIE, of Derryheen, Hook Heath, Woking:—
(By 1st *m*) Stella, *b* 1918; formerly Assist Section Officer, WAAF: *m* 1st, 1941, Squadron-Leader Donald Maitland Wellings, DFC, RAF (*ka* during 1939-45 War) 1944; 2ndly, 1949, Lt-Col Anthony Hamilton Gerald Barton, MC, late RA, of Manesty Cottage, The Green, Fernhurst, Haslemere, Surrey, and has issue living, (by 1st *m*) Donald James, *b* 1942, — (by 2nd *m*) Patrick Anthony Richard, *b* 1956: *m* 1980, Jennifer Ann, da of Anthony R. Lucas, of Moyles Wood, Farnham Lane, Haslemere, Surrey, and has issue living, Hamish Anthony *b* 1987, Angus Patrick *b* 1990, Sophie Caroline *b* 1993, — Julia Penelope Susan, *b* 1950.

Grandchildren of late Col John Patrick Villiers-Stuart, CB, DSO, OBE (ante):—
Issue of late Maj John Michael Villiers-Stuart, *b* 1927, *d* 1986: *m* 1960, Bridget Mary (Bestwall House, Wareham, Dorset), da of Lt-Col Patrick Grant, of Knockie, Whitebridge, Inverness-shire:—
Michael Patrick (34 Poets Rd, N5 2SE), *b* 1961: *m* 1986, Caroline Mary, elder da of David Richard Marsh, of Middleton-by-Youlgreave, Derbys, and has issue living, Archie James, *b* 1992, — Katharine Amelia, *b* 1990. —— Marianne Serena, *b* 1963: *m* 1st, 1986 (*m diss* 1993), Oliver John Nicholson; 2ndly, 1994, Michael Thomas Donnelly, and has issue living (by 1st *m*), Natasha Elizabeth, *b* 1986.

Granddaughter of late John Windsor Stuart, yr son of late Henry Stuart, only son of Rear-Adm Lord George Stuart, CB, 7th son of 1st Marquess:—
Issue of late Capt Henry Campbell Stuart, The Black Watch, *b* 1874, *d* 1953: *m* 1904, Eileene Barbara, who *d* 1969, da of Major H. G. Fenton Newall, of Hare Hill, Lancashire:—
Flora Emily Windsor, *b* 1910: *m* 1932, Group Capt Cyril Henry William Boldero, RAF, who *d* 1979, and has issue living, Ann Barbara Stuart, *b* 1933: *m* 1st, 1954 (*m diss* 1963), Peter Ingoldby; 2ndly, 1968, John Harris Burland, Capt 4th/7th Drag Gds (ret); 3rdly, 1982, Gwynne Douglas James, of Killiemore, Kirkcowan, Wigtownshire, and has issue living (by 1st *m*), Christopher Henry *b* 1955, Jane Patricia *b* 1957, (by 2nd *m*) James William *b* 1968, — Helen Cecilia Stuart, *b* 1936: *m* 1968, Robin Malcolm Anderson Howard, and has issue living, Alastair Charles Henry *b* 1969, Sarah Flora Margaret *b* 1970.
Residence – West Glen, Newton Stewart, Wigtownshire.

Grandchildren of late Com Dudley Charles Stuart, RN, elder son of late Henry Stuart (ante):—
Issue of late Com Evelyn Charles Henry Stuart, RN (ret), *b* 1875, *d* 1945: *m* 1906, Anna Knutzen Grane, who *d* 1944:—
Dudley Evelyn, *b* 1907. —— Amy Ingeborg Sybil Eda, *b* 1911.
Issue of late Eric Hoy Stuart, *b* 1890, *d* 1950: *m* 1918 (Dorothie) Primrose (who *m* 2ndly, 1958, as his 3rd wife, Hon Michael Scott, OBE, who *d* 1959 (*see* E Eldon) and 3rdly, 1969, Surg Vice-Adm Sir Clarence Edward Greeson, KBE, CB, who *d* 1979, and *d* 1982), da of Maj Murray-Stewart:—
(Patricia) Elizabeth *b* 1923: *m* 1st, 1946 (*m diss* 1950), Thomas Daniel; 2ndly, 1972, Lt-Cmdr Philip Baxendale, OBE, RD, who *d* 1986, and has issue living (by 1st *m*), Timothy Hugh, *b* 1946: *m* 1973, Sara Nancy Hood-Daniel, and has issue living, Hugo Charles *b* 1983, Emily Sara *b* 1975, Josephine Polly *b* 1977, Olivia Zoe *b* 1984.

In remainder to the Earldom of Bute only.
Descendants of late Rt Hon James Archibald STUART-WORTLEY (son of Hon James Archibald Stuart, 2nd son of 3rd Earl of Bute), who was *cr Baron Wharncliffe* 1820 (*see* E Wharncliffe).

In remainder to the Earldom of Dumfries only.
Grandchildren of late John Crichton Stuart McDouall, OBE (*b* 1878) (infra):—
Issue of late Maj John Crichton Stuart McDouall, R Sigs, *b* 1920, *d* 1951: *m* 1945, Dorothy Anne (who *m* 2ndly, 1954, Maj J. H. A. Bryden, RA, 61 Swanston Av, Edinburgh, EH10 7BZ), da of late Rev C. A. H. Going, of Shrewsbury:—
John Crichton Stuart (Flat 23, Block 8, Mansfield Rd, The Peak, Hong Kong), *b* 1950: Inspector R Hong Kong Police: *m* 1975, Susanna Sze Wing-Lai, and has issue living, John Crichton Stuart, *b* 1976, — Patrick, *b* 1978. —— Philip Lewis (twin) (c/o Lloyds Bank Ltd, 19 Obelisk Way, Camberley, Surrey), *b* 1950; Man Dir Tektronix, Toronto, Canada: *m* 1976, Marlis Bartels, and has issue living, Andrew Philip *b* 1977, — James Stephen, *b* 1979, — Joanna Marie, *b* 1984. —— Patricia Anne, *b* 1945: *m* 1971, James Downing, of 172 Homestead Cres, Edmonton, Alberta, Canada, and has issue living, Frederick James, *b* 1972, — Timothy John, *b* 1979, — Sarah Frances, *b* 1975. —— Elizabeth Jean, *b* 1947: *m* 1971, Jean Labaye, of 4 Impasse Tarantaise 69300, Lyons, France, and has issue living, Jean Simon, *b* 1972, — Georges-Antoine, *b* 1982, — Victoria Anne, *b* 1974.

Grandchildren of late Willoughby Crichton McDouall (*b* 1852), 5th son of John Crichton Stuart McDouall (*b* 1818), eldest son of Rev William M'Douall (*b* 1775), only son of John M'Douall, brother of 6th Earl of Dumfries:—
Issue of late John Crichton Stuart McDouall, OBE, *b* 1878; *d* 1941: *m* 1914, Marguerite Lavinia, who *d* 1950, da of Frank Garrett, of Highgate, N:—
Lewis Willoughby, *b* 1924: *m* 1964, Madeline, da of George Hall. *Address* – c/o Lloyds Bank, Sutton, Surrey. —— Marguerite Lavinia, *b* 1922: *m* 1941, Capt Ian Sibbald McCormick, MB, who *d* 1967, and has issue living, John Sibbald, *b* 1944: *m* 1975, Irene Marilyn, and has issue living, John Steven *b* 1981, David Charles *b* 1983, Jill Elaine *b* 1976, — Jennifer Anne, *b* 1943: *m* 1969, Kenneth Anthony Fleming, and has issue living, Stuart Kenneth *b* 1972, Andrew Michael *b* 1978, Anne Margaret *b* 1970, — Marguerite Lavinia, *b* 1948: *m* 1975, John Glen Abercromby, and has issue living, Andrew Frank *b* 1980, Jane *b* 1977, Carol Marguerite *b* 1983. *Residence* – 19 Durham Gdns, Lower Largo, Leven, Fife Y86 DU.

Grandchildren of late Rev Crichton Willoughby McDouall (infra):—
Issue of late John Crichton McDouall, CMG, *b* 1912, *d* 1979: *m* 1946, Kathleen Glover (Deep Well, Souldern, Oxon OX6 9JP), da of late Archibald Black Moir, of Isle of Wight:—
Brian John, *b* 1952: *m* 1978 (*m diss* 1989), Barbara May, da of Arnold Worth, of Manchester. —— Anne Glover (26 Barrett St, Oxford OX2 0AT), *b* 1948: *m* 1968 (*m diss* 1982), David Thomas Douglas James, PhD, and has issue living, Simon Alan, *b* 1969, — Annabel Louise, *b* 1971. —— Heather Crichton, *b* 1949: D Phil: *m* 1979, Robert Norman Swanson, PhD, of 106 Northfield Rd, Kings Norton, Birmingham, and has issue living, John Crichton Norman, *b* 1981, — Elizabeth Eleanor Crichton, *b* 1983.

Grandchildren of late Willoughby Crichton McDouall (*b* 1852) (ante):—
Issue of late Rev Crichton Willougby McDouall, *b* 1881, *d* 1966: *m* 1st, 1911, Florence Charlotte, who *d* 1923, da of late William Bampfield Cogan, of Bristol; 2ndly, 1935, Jessie Kentish, who *d* 1979, da of late George Rudolf Cole, of Sheffield:—
(By 1st *m*) Kenneth Willoughby (Greenways, 3 Mill Lane, Chinnor, Oxon OX9 4QU), *b* 1914; *ed* Monkton Combe; MA, Camb; CMS Sudan 1951-63: *m* 1958, Edith Joan Sears, and has issue living, Rhoda Mary, *b* 1959: *m* 1st, 1982 (*m diss* 1984), her 2nd cousin, Jeremy Stuart Stevenson, Lt RNZN (infra); 2ndly, 1992, Andrew Neil David Eagles. —— (By 2nd *m*) David Christopher (11 Chesterton Rd, Cambridge), *b* 1936; *ed* Radley, and Jesus Coll, Camb (MA): *m* 1969, Veronica Mary, da of H. Earl Heighway, of Wyre Piddle, Worcs, and has issue living, Jonathan Crichton Stuart, *b* 1976, — Sara Frances, *b* 1972, — Fiona Mary, *b* 1974.
Issue of late Philip Hastings McDouall, *b* 1884, *d* 1978: *m* 1917, Ivy Harrie, da of Henry Charles Sanders, formerly PWD India:—
Philip John (Blue Gentians, St Geroge's Well, Cullompton, Devon), *b* 1924: *m* 1950, Hazel Rosemary, who *d* 1992, da of Charles Frederick Bowring, late RN, and has issue living, Andrew Crichton, *b* 1951: *m* 1977, Katherine, da of Rey G. Hardy, — Janet Mary, *b* 1953, — Ellen Margaret, *b* 1963. —— Margaret Heather (Rua do Rio da Bica 7, S Pedro de Sintra, Portugal), *b* 1920: *m* 1946, Leonardo Rey Colaço de Castro Freire, who *d* 1970, and has issue living, Martin Anthony (Rua Alexandre Herculano 91, Tomar, Portugal), *b* 1952: *m* 1982, Filipa Macedo, and has issue living, Manuel Felipe *b* 1984, Martim Afonso *b* 1986, — Jorge Leonardo (Rua Garcia de Orta 70-3°, Lisbon, Portugal), *b* 1956: *m* 1979, Ana Simões Pinto, and has issue living, Diogo *b* 1986, — Alexander Anthony (Rua Garcia de Orta 70, Lisbon, Portugal), *b* 1959: *m* 1984, Paula Vieira, and has issue living, Carolina *b* 1986, — Philippa Maria, *b* 1949: *m* 1972, João Manuel Rocheta, of Rua Garcia de Orta 70-2°, Lisbon, Portugal, and has issue living, Gonçalo *b* 1975, Rita *b* 1978, — Catarina Maria *b* 1954. —— Mabel Frances Harrie (1 Woodlands, Budleigh Salterton, Devon), *b* 1926: *m* 1985, Peter Haynes.
Issue of late Eric Oldfield McDouall, *b* 1886, *d* 1918: *m* 1913, Elizabeth Carpenter, who *d* 1954, da of Richard Morrish, of Lincoln, Canterbury, New Zealand:—
Ella Barbara (72 Wiggins St, Sumner, Christchurch 8, NZ), *b* 1914: *m* 1937, Rev Henry Jackson Eaton, who *d* 1991 and has issue living, Michael McDouall (Mountford, Wapara, N Canterbury, NZ), *b* 1937; *ed* Univ of NZ (Diplo in Fine Arts); FRSA: *m* 1st, 1962, Lynne Eleanor, who *d* 1986, da of Lester Heyward; 2ndly, 1993, Elizabeth Savill, and has issue living (by 1st *m*), Jonathan Heyward McDouall *b* 1964; LLB: *m* 1994, Fiona Smith, Benjamin Herriot McDouall *b* 1967, Penelope Jane *b* 1962: *m* 1985, William David Thomas (and has issue living, James William Grigg *b* 1988, Georgina Lynne *b* 1988, Rosa Virginia *b* 1990), Sarah Lynne *b* 1969, — Rt Rev Derek Lionel, QSM, *b* 1941; MA, Dip Theol, TTC, Bishop of Nelson, NZ; QSM 1985: *m* 1964, Alice Janice, da of George Maslin, and has issue living, Simeon Michael *b* 1968, Stephen Daniel *b* 1969, Rebecca Ann *b* 1971: *m* 1992, Andrew Robert Burgess.
Issue of late Gerald William McDouall, *b* 1887, *d* 1969: *m* 1920, Dora Olive, who *d* 1975, da of Arthur Alexander McKinnon of Oamaru, NZ:—
Eric Willoughby (22 Greendale Rd, Glen Parva, Leicester), *b* 1921: *m* 1944, Marion Maud, da of J. Holder, of Tetbury, Glos, and has issue living Maurice Willoughby (PO Box 388, Caledon, Ont, Canada), *b* 1945; RN: *m* 1967, Bernice Towers, da of Lindon Towers Cunliffe, of Fareham, and has issue living, Fiona Bernice *b* 1968, Rebecca Jane *b* 1972, — Geraldine Ann, *b* 1950: *m* 1976, Martin Rex Challis, and has issue living, Christopher Martin *b* 1986, Kirsty Ann *b* 1983. —— Gerald Ian

Crichton, OBE (Freugh, 54 Oakland Av, Wanganui, NZ), *b* 1929; JP 1981, OBE 1984: *m* 1963, Shirley Maureen, da of late Thomas Sanson, of Wanganui, and has issue living, Gerald Andrew, *b* 1964; BCA: *m* 1992, Denys Ann, da of John Fotheringham, of Auckland, — Hamish Crichton, *b* 1968; BA, — Rachael Deborah, *b* 1963; BPharm: *m* 1994, Michael Patrick Hay, PhD, of Napier. —— Patricia Ellen, *b* 1923: *m* 1947, W/Cdr George Stuart Alexander Stevenson, DFC, RNZAF, who *d* 1993, of 43 Hamilton Av, Fendalton, Christchurch, NZ and has issue living, Hugh William, *b* 1951: *m* 1978, Jillian Margaret, da of late Melville James Pitt Glasgow, and has issue living, David James *b* 1985, Sarah Jane *b* 1983, — Jeremy Stuart (27 Rodney St, Howick, Auckland, NZ), *b* 1956 Lt RNZN: *m* 1st, 1982 (*m diss* 1984), his 2nd cousin, Rhoda Mary, da of Kenneth Willoughby McDouall (ante); 2ndly, 1990, Melinda Jane Ferguson, of Auckland, and has issue living (by 2nd *m*), Timothy Alexander Stuart *b* 1992, — Helen Patricia, *b* 1953: *m* 1st, 1982 (*m diss* 1984), Michael John Fowler, of Wellington, NZ; 2ndly, 1986, Robert Stephen Schaffel, of NJ, USA. —— Alison Crichton, *b* 1926: *m* 1957, Philip John Poulett Wells, of 14B Broadshard Lane, Ringwood, Hants BH24 1RR,and has issue living, Philip David Crichton (5 Collins Lane, Ringwood, Hants), *b* 1961: *m* 1990, Sally Henrietta, da of Peter Collings, of Denham, Middx, — Diana Jane, *b* 1958: *m* 1984, Richard David Trinick, of 17 Turnbury Av, Nailsea, Avon, and has issue living, Chester Michael *b* 1987, Robert John *b* 1989, Laurence James *b* 1990, — Elizabeth Joanna, *b* 1966.

Issue of late Alan Edward Crichton McDouall, *b* 1895, *d* 1962: *m* 1922, Doris Annie, who *d* 1984, da of Joseph Preston of Oamaru:—

Stuart Preston (28 Ure St, Oamaru, NZ), *b* 1922: *m* 1951, Winifred Edith Jones, who *d* 1985, and has issue living, Philip Stuart, *b* 1955: *m* 1978, Alison Nicholas, and has had issue, Daniel Stuart *b* 1980, James Murray *b* 1984, Timothy Philip *b* 1987, Melissa *b* 1982, *d* 1983, — Patricia Mary, *b* 1952: *m* 1973, Atholl Campbell, and has issue living, Hamish Iain *b* 1979, Sarah Leigh *b* 1976, — Judith Anne, *b* 1954: *m* 1976, Rex Ormandy, and has issue living, Michael Stuart *b* 1987, Haylee Jan *b* 1984, Lisa Jane *b* (twin) 1987, — Heather, *b* 1959: *m* 1981, Bruce Reilly, and has issue living, Megan Jayne *b* 1983, Anna Marie *b* 1985, Rachel Dawn *b* 1988. —— Willoughby Alan (PO Box 114, Kurow, N Otago, NZ), *b* 1935: *m* 1963, Pamela Anne Ruddock, and has issue living, John Alan Crichton *b* 1971, Fiona Mary *b* 1969, Joanna Louise *b* 1974. —— Doris Mary, *b* 1924: *m* 1947, Ernest Benjamin Lyons, of Woodbury RD21, Geraldine, NZ, and has had issue, Alan Mark, *b* 1950: *m* 1973, Vivienne Lorna McPhail of Wellington, NZ, and has issue living, Nathan John *b* 1979, — Valerie Anne *b* 1976, — John McDouall, *b* 1952: *m* 1982, Sue Hodgson, of Christchurch, NZ, and *d* 1991, leaving issue, Jai Douglas *b* 1985, Charlie John *b* 1987, — David Wayne, *b* 1954: *m* 1st, 1974 (*m diss* 1982), Frances Margaret O'Connell, of Invercargill, NZ; 2ndly, 1986, Margaret Shirley Bain, of Kawerau, NZ, and has issue living (by 1st *m*), Jeremy Rhys *b* 1974, Rachael Jane *b* 1978, Megan Aimee *b* 1980, (by 2nd *m*) Vanessa Lee *b* 1987, Samantha Renee *b* 19—, Amanda Kay *b* 1992, — Anthony Bruce, *b* 1956: *m* 1979 (*m diss* 1982), Gwen Haigh, of Perth, — Kenneth Brett, *b* 1957: *m* 1981 (*m diss* 1990), Jill Fowler, of Perth, — Susan Mary, *b* 1948: *m* 1972, Graeme Norris Sherwood, of Palmerston N, NZ, who *d* 1985, and has issue living, Jacalyn Anne *b* 1979, Joanne Lisa *b* 1982. —— Josephine Anne (16 Holly Rd, Christchurch, NZ) *b* 1926. —— Ellen Coverdale, *b* 1928: *m* 1952, James Bruce Anderson of Monuina, Tripp Settlement Rd, RD 21, Geraldine, S Canterbury, NZ, and has issue living, Duncan Bruce, *b* 1955, — Ian James, *b* 1959: *m* 1st, 1980 (*m diss* 1986), Carol Ruth Lynette Williams, of Geraldine, NZ; 2ndly, 1989, Rose-Marie Anne Birnie, of Oamaru, NZ, and has issue living (by 1st *m*), Steven Ian *b* 1984, Karen Lynette *b* 1984, Katherine Ruth (twin) *b* 1984, — Helen Mary, *b* 1954: *m* 1975, Halene Kupa Magatogia, of Alofi, Box 87, Niue Island, NZ, and has issue living, James Kupa *b* 1977, Charles Bruce Tali *b* 1979, Tani Mary Pua *b* 1981, — Barbara Ellen, *b* 1958: *m* 1981, Gerard Patrick Scott, of Kerrytown, RD4, Timaru, NZ, and has issue living, Finian Patrick *b* 1990, Lucy Bridget *b* 1984, Ingrid Jane *b* 1989, — Susan Grace, *b* 1960: *m* 1981, Geoffrey Ronald Taylor, of Taieri NZ; 2ndly, 1989, Brian John Close, of Oamaru, NZ, and has issue living (by 1st *m*), Scott James *b* 1981, Mark Ronald *b* 1984, (by 2nd *m*) Catherine Grace *b* 1990.

Granddaughters of late John Crichton Stuart McDouall (*b* 1818) (ante):—
Issue of late Herbert Crichton M'Douall, MRCS, LRCP, DPH, *b* 1860, *d* 1947: *m* 1899, Hester Maria Corry, who *d* 1942, da of late C. S. Hartigan, of Blackheath SE:—
Edith Isabella Stewart (Lourdes Retirement Village, Killara, NS Wales), *b* 1900: *m* 1926, Lindsay Fraser Single, who *d* 1988, and has issue living, Mark McDouall (19 View Sq, Wooloowin, Queensland), *b* 1930: *m* 1963, Jean Margaret, da of J. M. Vicars, of Lindfield, Sydney, and has issue living, Jane Margaret McDouall *b* 1965, — Marion Elizabeth McDouall, *b* 1928: *m* 1st, 1950, Douglas Lascelles Ryrie, who *d* 1959; 2ndly, 1966, Peter Cowper, of 180 Queen St, Woollahra, NSW, and has issue living (by 1st *m*), Mark Douglas *b* 1957. —— Penelope Crichton, *b* 1903. *Residence* – 3 Redleaf Apartments, 1630 Pacific Highway, Wahroonga, NSW 2076. —— Margaret Ellen Crichton, *b* 1907: *m* 1st, 1938, Harry G. Doyle, a planter in New Guinea, who *d* 1942; 2ndly, 1951, William Stanley Leslie, Headmaster of Barker Coll, Hornsby, NSW, who *d* 1957. *Residence* – 3 Redleaf Apartments, 1630 Pacific Highway, Wahroonga, NSW 2076. —— Mary Crichton Stuart, *b* 1909: *m* 1938, Alexander Bain, Master Mariner, of 25 Thomson Parade, Dalmeny, NSW, 2546, and has issue living, Roderick Alexander Crichton, *b* 1940, — John Herbert Crichton (28 Stapylton St, Holder, ACT), *b* 1944: BSc (New England), MSc (James Cook Univ, N Queensland): *m* 1969, Peta Jane, da of F. W. Holdsworth, of Somerton Park, Adelaide, S Aust, and has issue living, Scott James *b* 1971, Timothy Ross *b* 1974.

Granddaughter of late Rev William Sutherland M'Douall, 2nd son of Rev William M'Douall (*b* 1775) (ante):—
Issue of late Claud Hay M'Douall, *b* 1864, *d* 1905: *m* 1904, Alice May, who *d* 1955, da of George Redding:—
Joan Alma, *b* 1905: *m* 1931, Brian Miller, who *d* 1992, of Witches Moon, Stony Lane, Little Kingshill, Gt Missenden, Bucks HP16 0DS, and has issue living, Ian Claud (4 Fryer Close, Chesham, Bucks HP5 1RD), *b* 1932: *m* 1st, 1955, Violet Grace Waters, who *d* 1987; 2ndly, 1994, Hazel Gwendolyn Wray, and has issue living (by 1st *m*), Nicola Anne, *b* 1960: DPhil, — Peter Gerald (3 Nicolas Av, Glen Eden, Auckland 8, NZ), *b* 1934: *m* 1955, Patricia Ann Collins, and has issue living, Rogan Edward Oliver *b* 1966, Cameron Peter *b* 1970, Carolyn Jane *b* 1959, Philippa Jane *b* 1961.

Grandchildren of late Kenneth Gilbert M'Douall, 3rd son of late Rev William Sutherland M'Douall (ante):—
Issue of late Ferdinand Huth M'Douall, *b* 1905, *d* 1990: *m* 1931, Lillian Hall (Wensley House, Wensley Rd, Richmond, Nelson, NZ), da of late W. J. Saville:—
Kenneth Hugh (2 West St, Denbury, Newton Abbot, S Devon TQ12 6DP), *b* 1935: *m* 1964, Jean, only da of W. Leonard Crouch, and has issue living, Duncan Hugh, *b* 1969, — Justin Ian, *b* 1972. —— (Sidney) Morris (43c Wensley Rd, Richmond, Nelson, NZ), *b* 1944: *m* 1974, Virginia Helen, eldest da of M. N. Charters, of Rangiona, NZ, and has issue living, Michael Guy *b* 1977, — Simon Geoffrey *b* 1981. —— Evelyn Susan, *b* 1937: *m* 1st, 1962 (*m diss* 1968), Stuart Wallace Mac-Gregor; 2ndly, 1977, Andrew John Barr-Sim, of Blair House, 3 New St, Henley-on-Thames, Oxon, and has issue living (by 1st *m*), Fiona Judith, *b* 1964, — Alison Catherine, *b* 1966.

Grandchildren of late Alan Patrick M'Douall, 4th and yst son of late Rev William Sutherland M'Douall (ante):—
Issue of late Patrick Sutherland M'Douall, *b* 1904, *d* 1950: *m* 1941, Esther Mary (who *m* 2ndly 1952, George Black, of 3 Front Street, Cassop, Ferryhill, co Durham), da of late Jack William Albutt, of Newcastle:—
Alan Sutherland, *b* 1946: *m* 1970, Jennifer Ann Lingard, da of Kenneth John Jarvis, and has issue living, Alec Douglas Sutherland, *b* 1971, — Morwenna Jane, *b* 1973. —— Joy Mary, *b* 1942: *m* 1963, John Wilson, of 1 Tythe Pl, Fenstanton, Huntingdon, Cambs, and has issue living, Anthony John, *b* 1966, — Ian Patrick, *b* 1969.
Issue of late Alan Reeves M'Douall, *b* 1906, *d* 1971: *m* 1930, Hilma Hornfelt, who *d* 1994, of Saskatchewan:—
Katherine, *b* 1931; adopted the surname of McDouall 1961: *m* 1st, 1947 (*m diss* 1961), Raymond Frederick Flood; 2ndly, 1962, Royden Gilbert Young, of 956 Quadling Av, Coquitlam, New Westminster, BC, Canada, and has issue living (by 2nd *m*), Robert James *b* 1967, — Douglas Alan, *b* 1968. —— Audrey Ethel (105, 9295 122nd St, Surrey, BC, Canada V3V 4L4), *b* 1933: *m* 1st, 1955 (*m diss* 1969), Ronald O'Day; 2ndly, 1971 (*m diss* 1992), Fred Charlton, and has issue living (by 1st *m*),

Frederick Alan, b 1956, — Ronald Patrick (2491 11th Av, Port Alberni, BC, Canada V9Y 2S2), b 1957: m 1st, 1977 (m diss 1980), Shelley Mackenzie; 2ndly, 1989, Cheryl Eaglestad, and has issue living (by 1st m), Shane Ronald b 1978, Lucas b 1983, (by 2nd m) Cody Reeves b 1989, — Kathryn Rosanne, b 1958: m 1977, Steven Joseph Yaciw (Camp 37 Site 16, Kamloops, BC, Canada V2C 2J3, and has issue living, Angela Kristy b 1979, Lisa Marie b 1981, — Lorraine Janet, b 1959: m 1st, 1983 (m diss 1986), —; 2ndly, 1994, Dereck Ross Dawe (11352 Glenavon Drive, Surrey, BC, Canada V3R 4V5), and has issue living (by 2nd husband), Colton Frederick b 1990, Levi Dereck Ron b 1992, Kaileigh Andra b 1989, Allison Mary Barbara b 1993:—

Granddaughter of late Rev William Sutherland M'Douall (ante):—
    Issue of late Alan Patrick M'Douall, b 1872, d 1947: m 1902, Frances Ethel, who d 1968, da of late Edward Reeves, of Wellington, NZ:—
Mary Grace (Flat 5, Joan Nightingale House, Bolnore Rd, Haywards Heath, Sussex RH16 4AB), b 1908.

Grandchildren of late Rawdon M'Douall, 5th son of Rev William M'Douall (b 1775) (ante):—
    Issue of late Rawdon George Herbert M'Douall, b 1852, d 1919: m 1906, Mary Somerville Townshend, who d 1968:—
Rawdon Townshend, OAM, b 1907; OAM (1983), JP: m 1933, Elizabeth, who d 1983, da of late A. Cameron, of Glencoe, Narrabri, NSW, and has issue living, David Rawdon (Dunbeacon, Upper Horton, NSW 2347), b 1937: m 1962, Margaret Joan, da of Keith McDonald, of Strathallan Wirialda, NSW, and has issue living, Rawdon Angus b 1963: m 1987, Melinda Mary, da of Watkin Williams, of Wattombri, Garah, NSW (and has issue living, Thomas Rawdon b 1991, Polly Gwendoline b 1993), Ian Alexander b 1968, Helen Annette b 1964: m 1st, 1988 (m diss 1990), Timothy James Ross, of St Ives, NSW; 2ndly, 1992, Stephen Andrew Ninnes, of Ipswich, Qld. Residence – Doorah, Upper Horton, via Barraba, NSW. —— Lucy Katherine Shawford, b 1913: m 1946, Thomas Clark Capel, of The Oaks, Narrabri, NSW, who d 1986, and has issue living, Donald Gilbert, b 1949: m 19——, Jennifer Anne, da of Eric Bone, of Maitland, and has issue living, Angus Donald, b 1985, Louise Anne b 1983, — Katherine Shawford (Hon Mrs Alexander Erskine), b 1950: m 1977, Hon Alexander David Erskine, 2nd son of 13th Earl of Mar and Kellie, — Nancy Patricia, b 1953. — Patricia Hastings, b 1916: m 1954, Eric Limburg, of Windi, Bingara, NSW, and has issue living, Richard Eric b 1955: m 1988, Ann Margaret Simpson, — David Patrick Rawdon, b 1957: m 1981, Lea Ellen, da of Brian Forth, of Telarah, NSW, and has issue living, Nichole Ellen b 1983, Katrina Lea (twin) b 1983, Alyce Patricia b 1986, — Elizabeth Mary, b 1960: m 1981, Steven Mark Adams, of Gawler, S Australia, and has issue living, Kris b 1987, Naomi b 1984. —— Margaret Somerville, b 1918: m 1951, Jack Lattimore, who d 1988, of 21 Trelawney St, Thornleigh 2120, Sydney, NSW, and has issue living, Andrew Stuart, b 1958: m 1989, Bronwyn Gae Macpherson, da of Brig Brian Edwards, of Canberra, ACT, and has issue living, Jack Edward Macpherson b 1992, — Mary-Ann Elizabeth, b 1954: m 1979, Hugh Geoffrey Beecher, of Rosedale, Narrandera, NSW, and has issue living, Nicholas Hugh Lattimore b 1991, Emma Louise Lattimore b 1988, — Margaret Louise, b 1960: m 1991, Christopher Allan Murphy, who d 1992.

Granddaughters of late Daniel Crichton Stuart M'Douall (infra):—
    Issue of late Peter Crichton Stuart M'Douall, b 1933, d 1988: m 1959, Kay Margaret (Bald Hill, Narrabri, NSW), da of Kenneth Field Clemson, of Wyndella, Collarenebri, NSW:—
Sandra Anne, b 1961: m 1988, Richard Alexander Dillon, of Nass's Rd, Preston, Toowoomba, Qld. —— Nicki Jane, b 1963. —— Angela Susan, b 1967.

Grandchildren of late William Edward M'Douall (infra):—
    Issue of late Daniel Crichton Stuart M'Douall b 1905, d 1961: m 1930, Jean (4 Bowen St, Narrabri, NSW), da of P. A. McAlister, of Narrabri, NSW:—
Judith, b 1931: m 1954, Allan Richard McMaster, of Violet Downs, Narrabri 2390, NSW, and has issue living, Stuart Allan, b 1955: m 1979, Deborah, da of David Mackay, of Brisbane, Queensland, and has issue living, Richard Stuart b 1982, Alec Bruce b 1985, Abby Jane b 1981, — Margaret Jean, b 1957: m 1979, Stephen Leslie Frost, of Toowoomba, NSW, and has issue living, Samuel Allan b 1986, Melanie Alaire b 1980, Angela Judith b 1982, — Cathryn Mary, b 1960: m 1984, John Charles Edmondson, of Sydney, NSW, and has issue living, Allan Gordon b 1988.
    Issue of late Hastings Uchrid M'Douall, b 1907, d 1992: m 1938, Nancy May (Lowana, Upper Horton, Via Barraba, NSW 2347), da of Ernest Capel, of Burren Junction, NSW:—
Richard Hastings (Kildare, Upper Horton, NSW 2347), b 1940: m 1966, Susan Anne Etheridge, and has issue living, Stuart John, b 1966: m 1992, Jayne Vickery, — Graham Richard, b 1968. —— Donald Hastings (Boundary Creek, Bingara, NSW 2404), b 1946: m 1973, Bronwyn Lee, da of late W. Cupitt, of Bowral, NSW, and has issue living, Benjamin Donald, b 1975, — Samuel Hastings b 1977, — Serena Lee, b 1981. —— Pamela Hastings, b (twin) 1940: m 1st, 1963, Roderick Warren Scotton, MB BS, of Grafton, NSW, who d 1981; 2ndly, 1983, Fergus McMaster Fysh, of 4 Breimba St, Grafton, NSW 2460, and has issue living (by 1st m), Richard Stuart b 1966, — Peter Roderick, b 1969, — Sandra Louise, b 1965.

Grandchildren of late Rawdon M'Douall (ante):—
    Issue of late William Edward M'Douall, b 1865, d 1936: m 1904, May Edna, who d 1961, da of Robert Scholes:—
Robert William (Eungai, Upper Horton, NSW 2347), b 1909: m 1934, Nancy Spencer, and has issue living, William Robert b 1939: m 1963, Louise, da of Eric Lauric, of Walcher NSW, and has issue living, James William b 1965, Andrew Alexander (twin) b 1965, Jonathon Laurie b 1967, — Arthur Frank, b 1942: m 1963, Beverley Ann, da of Clive Pyke, of Inverell, NSW, and has issue living, Baden Robert b 1964, Gavin John b 1966, — Philippa Mary, b 1937: m 1957, Andrew Ellis Wauch, of Barraba, NSW, and has issue living, John Andrew Robert b 1958, Wendy Ann b 1959, Sally May b 1966. —— Noel Edward (Peri, Caroda, via Barraba, NSW, Australia), b 1911: m 1942, Amy Patricia Hawke, and has issue living, Malcolm Noel (50 Post Office Rd, Glenorie, NSW), b 1943: m 1968, Louise, da of late R. A. Pedlingham, of Pymble, NSW, and has issue living, Matthew Richard Stuart b 1970, — Jillian May, b 1946: m 1967 (m diss 1978), Michael Thomas Mahony, and has issue living, Jake Thomas b 1975, Camilla b 1972. Residence – 66 Liverpool St, Paddington, NSW, Australia. —— Harold Stuart (Ulumbarella, Upper Horton, Via Barraba, NSW 2347) b 1920; Fl-Lt (ret) RAAF: m 1st, 1947, Doris Marion, who d 1970, da of Maj W. Squires; 2ndly, 1974, Gloria Geraldine, da of late Capt W. G. F. Leadbeater, MN, and has issue living (by 1st m), Garry Stuart (Yarraman, Bingara, NSW 2404), b 1949: m 1971, Linda Anne, da of Richard Littlejohn, of The Meadows, Harden, NSW, and has issue living, Scott Stuart b 1978, Hamish Richard b 1981, — Michael William (Coolowie, Bingara, NSW 2404), b 1953: m 1982, Julie Kay, da of Dr E. S. Hughson, and has issue living, Cameron Stuart b 1983, Mich William b 1985, Jenna Marion b 1986, — Diane Marion, b 1950: m 1st, 1971 (m diss 1977), Peter Russell Jones; 2ndly, 1983, Phillip Arthur Kelly, of Blue Nobby, Cobbadah, NSW 2347, and has issue living (by 1st m), Heulwen b 1973, (by 2nd m) Dustin Phillip b 1986, Alana Mae b 1984, Kylie Elizabeth b 1988. —— Edna May, b 1918: m 1941, John Murray Bowman, of Tarpoly, Upper Manilla, NSW 2346, and has issue living, Roger Murray, b 1943: m 1973, Sara Wilkin Smith, and has issue living, Thomas Murray b 1976, Katherine Sara b 1974, Susan Wilkin b 1979, — Graham Edward, b 1945: m 1972, Nanette Mary Mahony, and has issue living, Luke Edward b 1974, Jonathan Graham b 1980, Anna Nannatte b 1977, — Christopher George, b 1953: m 1978, Sharron Hubbard, and has issue living, Samuel James b 1984, Laura Emily b (twin) 1984, Angela Jane b 1986, — Julie May, b 1950.
    Issue of late Frederick Crichton McDouall, b 1871, d 1932: m 1908, Florence Ethel Jackson, who d 1961:—
Joan Shawford (45 Congewoi Rd, Mosman 2088, NSW), b 1910: m 1936, Noel Peter Dawson, Maj AIF, who d 1981, and has issue living, Susanne Jane, b 1943: m 1970, Anthony Keith Wadey, Lt RANR, of 45 Congewoi Rd, Mosman, NSW 2088. —— Gwendolen Melville, b 1918: m 1936, Frederick Neville Griffiths, who d 1981, and has issue living, Frederick Ronald Neville, b 1936, — Richard John Neville, b 1941: m 1971, Margaret Ryan, of Sydney, and has issue living, Philip Andrew b 1974, Matthew David b 1976, Kathryn Louise b 1979, — Hugh Douglas, b 1951, — Elizabeth Joan, b 1943: m 1972, Ray

Johnson, MB, BS, and has issue living, Victoria Yvonne *b* 1972, Kathleen Elizabeth *b* 1974. *Residence* – 10 Emerald St, Cooroy, Queensland 4563.

PREDECESSORS – (1)*Sir* JAMES Stuart of Ardmaleish, Bute, 7th in descent from John Stuart, "The Black Stewart", natural son of Robert II, sided with Charles I; in 1640 his estates were sequestrated, but he was Commr for Bute 1643-8 and attended sittings in Parliament; dispossessed of custody of Rothesay Castle by Cromwell; *cr a Baronet of Nova Scotia 1627: m Grizel, da of Sir Dugall Campbell of Auchinbreck, 1st Bt: d 1662; s by his son* (2) *Sir* DUGAL, 2nd Bt: *m* 1658, Elizabeth, da of John Ruthven, of Dunglass; *d* 1670; *s* by his son (3) *Sir* JAMES, PC; a Commr to treat for a Union between Scotland and England; *cr Earl of Bute, Viscount Kingarth, Lord Mount Stuart, Cumra, and Inchmarnock* (peerage of Scotland) 1703, with remainder to heirs male whatsoever: *m* 1st, 1680, Agnes, da of Sir George MacKenzie of Rosehaugh; 2ndly, Christian, da of William Dundas of Kincavel; *d* 1710; *s* by his son (4) JAMES, 2nd Earl; Representative Peer 1715-23; Lord of the Bedchamber 1721-3: *m* 1711, Lady Anne Campbell (who *d* 1736, having *m* 2ndly, 1731, Alexander Fraser of Strichen), da of 1st Duke of Argyll; *d* 1723; *s* by his son (5) JOHN, KG, 3rd Earl; *b* 1713; Representative Peer 1737-41, and 1761-80; First Lord of the Treasury 1762-3: *m* 1736, Mary (*cr Baroness Mount Stuart of Wortley*, co York (peerage of Great Britain) 1761, with remainder to heirs male by her then marriage), who *d* 1794, da of Edward Wortley-Montagu; *d* 1792; *s* by his son (6) JOHN, 4th Earl, who in 1776 had been *cr Baron Cardiff*, of Cardiff Castle (peerage of Great Britain), and in 1796 was *cr Marquess of Bute, Earl of Windsor* and *Viscount Mountjoy*, of Isle of Wight, with remainder to heirs male of his body: *m* 1st, 1766, Charlotte Jane Windsor, who *d* 1800, da and heir of 2nd Viscount Windsor of Blackcastle, and Baron Mountjoy, of Isle of Wight (through whom the Welsh estates of the Earls of Pembroke passed to the House of Bute); 2ndly, 1800, Frances, who *d* 1832, da of Thomas Coutts, banker; *d* 1814; *s* by his grandson (7) JOHN, KT, (son of John, Viscount Mount Stuart by his wife Elizabeth Penelope, da and heir of 6th Earl of Dumfries), 2nd Marquess; *b* 1793; *s* his maternal grandfather as 7th Earl of Dumfries (see infra*); assumed in 1805 by Roy licence the additional surname of Crichton before Stuart: *m* 1st, 1818, Maria, who *d* 1841, el da of 3rd Earl of Guildford; 2ndly, 1845, Sophia, who *d* 1859, da of 1st Marquess of Hastings; *d* 1848; *s* by his only son (8) JOHN PATRICK, KT, LLD, 3rd Marquess; *b* 1847; Lord-Lieut of Buteshire: *m* 1872, the Hon Gwendolene Mary Anne Fitzalan-Howard, who *d* 1932, el da of 1st Baron Howard of Glossop; *d* 1900; *s* by his el son (9) JOHN, KT, 4th Marquess; *b* 1881: *m* 1905, *Dame* Augusta Mary Monica, DBE, who *d* 1947, da of Sir (Alan) Henry Bellingham, 4th Bt; *d* 1947; *s* by his son (10) JOHN, 5th Marquess; *b* 1907; Vice-Lieut for co Bute 1948-56: *m* 1932, Lady Eileen Beatrice Forbes, who *d* 1993, da of 8th Earl of Granard; *d* 1956; *s* by his el son (11) JOHN, KBE, 6th Marquess; *b* 1933; DL Bute 1961, Lord Lieut 1967-75, and Argyll and Bute 1990-93, Convenor Buteshire CC 1967-70, Lieut Scots Guards (Res), Member Countryside Commn for Scotland 1970-78, Chm Council and Exec Cttee National Trust for Scotland 1969-84 (Pres 1991-93), and Historic Buildings Council for Scotland 1983-88; FRSE, etc: *m* 1st, 1955 (*m diss* 1977), Beatrice Nicola Grace, only da of late Lt-Cdr Wolstan Beaumont Charles Weld-Forester, CBE, RN (*see* B Forester, colls); 2ndly, 1978, Jennifer, da of John Brougham Home-Rigg, and formerly wife of Gerald Percy (*see* D Northumberland, colls); *d* 1993; *s* by his elder son (12) JOHN COLUM, 7th Marquess and present peer; also Earl of Windsor, Earl of Dumfries, Earl of Bute, Viscount Mountjoy, Viscount Kingarth, Viscount of Air, Baron Mount Stuart of Wortley, Baron Cardiff, Lord Crichton, and Lord Mount Stuart, Cumra and Inchmarnock.

*****(1) *Sir* ROBERT CRICHTON, of Sanquhar, co Dumfries, probably descended from a son of Alexander Crichton of Crichton, co Edinburgh 1296; *cr Lord Crichton of Sanquhar* (peerage of Scotland) 1488: *m* 1st, Margaret Hay; 2ndly *c* 1457, Christian, da of Sir John Erskine of Kinnoull, and widow of John Crichton; *d* 1494-95; *s* by his grandson (2) ROBERT (son of Robert Crichton by Marion Stewart, da of 1st Earl of Lennox), 2nd Lord; *mc* 1491, Marion Maxwell; *d* 1513; *s* by his son (3) ROBERT, 3rd Lord: *m* Elizabeth, (who *m* 2ndly Herbert Maxwell), da of Cuthbert Murray of Cockpool; *d* 1516-20; *s* by his son (4) ROBERT, 4th Lord: *m ca* 1534, Elizabeth (who *m* 3rdly the 4th Earl of Glencairn), da and heir of John Campbell of W Loudoun, and widow of William Wallace of Craigie; *d* a minor *ca* 1535; *s* by his brother (5) WILLIAM, 5th Lord: *m ca* 1540, Elizabeth, da of 3rd Lord Fleming; *d* (stabbed by Robert, Master of Sempill) 1550; *s* by his son (6) ROBERT, 6th Lord: *m* Margaret, da of John Cunningham of Caprington, and widow of Gilbert Kennedy; *d* 1561; *s* by his brother (7) EDWARD, 7th Lord: *m* 1561, Margaret (who *m* 2ndly, 1571, 5th Earl of Menteith), da of Sir James Douglas of Drumlanrig; *d* 1569; *s* by his son (8) ROBERT, 8th Lord; *b ca* 1568; *d* 1608, Anne (who *d* 1675, having *m* 2ndly, 1615, 6th Earl of Thomond), da of Sir George Fermor, of Easton Neston, Northants; having connived at the murder of a fencing master John Turner, who had deprived him of the sight of an eye, was hanged in Great Palace Yard, Westminster, 1612; *s* by his kinsman (9) WILLIAM, (son of William, son of 5th Lord) 9th Lord; *cr Viscount of Air* and *Lord of Sanquhar* (peerage of Scotland) 1622, and *Earl of Dumfries, Viscount of Air*, and *Lord Crichton of Sanquhar and Cumnock* (peerage of Scotland) 1633, this creation with remainder to heirs male bearing the name and arms of Crichton: *m* 1st, Eupheme, da of James Seton of Touch, and widow of Patrick Hamilton; 2ndly, Ursula, da of Stephen Barnham, and widow of Sir Robert Swift; *d* 1642-3; *s* by his son (10) WILLIAM, PC (Scotland), 2nd Earl; resigned his honours to the Crown 1690, and obtained a new grant with same precedence, and with remainder to his grandson, then the four daughters of his deceased son Charles, Lord Crichton, failing whom to the latter's nearest heirs: *m* 1618, Penelope, da of Sir Robert Swift, and sister of 1st Viscount Carlingford; *d* 1691; *s* by his grandson (11) WILLIAM (son of Charles, Lord Crichton, by Sarah, da of 1st Viscount Stair), 3rd Earl; *d* young 1694; *s* by his sister (12) PENELOPE: *m* 1698, the Hon William Dalrymple, 2nd son of 1st Earl of Stair; *d* 1742; *s* by her son (13) WILLIAM Dalrymple- Crichton, KT (who also *s* as 4th Earl of Stair 1760: *m* 1st 1731, Lady Anne Gordon, who *d* 1755, da of 2nd Earl of Aberdeen; 2ndly, 1762, Anne, da of William Duff, of Crombie Advocate); *d* 1768; *s* in Earldom of Dumfries by his nephew (14) PATRICK MacDouall Crichton (son of Elizabeth Dalrymple-Crichton who *m* John MacDouall of Freugh); *b* 1726, Capt 3rd Foot Guards; Representative Peer 1790-1803: *m* 1771, Margaret, who *d* 1799, da of Ronald Crauford of Restalrig; *d* 1803; *s* by his grandson (15) JOHN, 2nd Marquess of Bute (ante) (son of Elizabeth Penelope, who *m* 1792, John Stuart, Viscount Mount Stuart, el son of 1st Marquess of Bute).

Butler of Mount Juliet, Baron; title of Earl of Carrick on Roll of HL.

BUTLER OF SAFFRON WALDEN, BARONY OF (Butler) (Extinct 1982)

SONS LIVING OF LIFE BARON

Hon Sir Richard Clive (Penny Pot, Halstead, Essex CO9 1RY), *b* 1929; *ed* Eton, and Pembroke Coll, Camb (MA); late 2nd Lt RHG; High Sheriff Essex 1969-70, DL Essex 1972; a Farmer; Pres NFU 1979-86 (Dep-Pres 1971-78, Vice-Pres 1970), and a Liveryman of Skinners' and Farmers' Cos; Dir Nat Westminster Bank plc, and NFU Mutual Insurance Soc Ltd, and other Cos; Kt Bach 1981: *m* 1952, Susan Anne Maud, only da of late Maj Patrick Bruce Walker, MBE, late RA, of Barry's Close, Long Crendon, Bucks (*see* Walker, Bt, *cr* 1868), and has issue living, (Richard) Michael (Froyz Hall, Halstead, Essex), *b* 1956: *m* 1984, Christina Anne, yst da of Robert B. Blackwell, of Gatehouse Farm, Earls Colne, Colchester, Essex, and has issue living, (Richard) Benjamin *b* 1986, Charles Robert *b* 1987, Rosie Olivia *b* 1993, — Christopher Patrick (twin), *b* 1956: *m* 1983, Tania G., 4th da of David Clarabut, of St Mary's Hoo, Kent, and has issue living, David Mark *b* 1987, Anna Louise *b* 1985, Kimberley Jane *b* 1988, — Antonia Mary, *b* 1954: *m* 1st, 1978 (*m diss* 1983), Nicholas Henry Seymour Lees; 2ndly,

1983, Timothy P. Finch, of Ruecastle, Lanton, Jedburgh, Roxburghshire, and has issue living (by 2nd *m*), Sophie Amanda *b* 1985, Lucy Charlotte *b* 1986.

Rt Hon Sir Adam Courtauld, FRSA (The Old Rectory, Lighthorne, Warwick CV35 0AR), *b* 1931; *ed* Eton and Pembroke Coll, Camb (BA); late 2nd Lt KRRC; DL Warwicks 1993; ADC to Gov-Gen of Canada 1954-55; with Courtaulds Ltd 1955-73, Dir H. P. Bulmer (Holdings) plc; an FRSA, and an Assist of Goldsmiths' Co; Chm Airey Neave Trust since 1990, Samuel Courtauld Trust, and Pres British Horse Soc 1990-92; a Conservative Whip 1974-75, PPS to Leader of Opposition (Rt Hon Margaret Thatcher) 1975-79; Min of State, Dept of Industry 1979-81, N Ireland Office 1981-84, and Defence Procurement 1984-85, MP for Bosworth (*C*) 1970-83, *cr* PC 1984, Kt 1986: *m* 1955, Felicity Sybil, only da of Guy Kemyel Molesworth-St Aubyn, of Larks Hill, Braughing, Ware, Herts (*see* Molesworth-St Aubyn, Bt), and has issue living, Samuel Montagu Guy, *b* 1957: *m* 1982, Amanda J., da of Anthony H. B. Hart, of Bagendon, Glos, and has issue living, George Percy Kemyel *b* 1985, Henry Courtauld *b* 1987, — Edward Adam, *b* 1962; Maj The Royal Green Jackets: *m* 1991, Sophie Caroline, yr da of Capt Alec Rose, RN, of Petersfield, Hants, and has had issue, Robin Augustus *b* 1994, Augusta Rose *b* and *d* 1993, — Alexandra Katharine *b* 1959: *m* 1st, 1985 (*m diss* 1988), Dominick James Alexander Ashe, son of Sir Derick Rosslyn Ashe, KCMG; 2ndly, 1990, Comte Charles-Henri du Luart, elder son of Comte Charles du Luart, of Paris, and has issue living (by 2nd *m*), Emily Marie-Madeleine *b* 1991, Eloise Jeanne Felicity *b* 1993.

Hon (Samuel) James (Gladfen Hall, Halstead, Essex), *b* 1936; *ed* Eton, and Pembroke Coll, Camb; late 2nd Lt RHG: *m* 1st, 1960 (*m diss* 1977), Lucilla Blanche, yr da of late Algernon Malcolm Borthwick, MC, TD, of Wethersfield Place, Braintree, Essex (*see* Borthwick, Bt, colls); 2ndly, 1986, Jennifer, only da of Dr George Gladston, of Almeria, NY, USA, and has issue living (by 1st *m*), Malcolm James *b* 1964, — George Victor, *b* 1969, — Sydney Louise, *b* 1962, — Fleur Josephine, *b* 1967: *m* 1991, Richard Selwyn Sharpe, son of Canon Roger Sharpe, — Lucilla Katherine Joan, *b* 1973, — Emily Rebecca (twin), *b* 1973.

DAUGHTER LIVING OF LIFE BARON

Hon Sarah Theresa Mary, *b* 1944: *m* 1969, Anthony John Willis Price, of Manor House, Snarestone, nr Burton-on-Trent, Staffs, and has issue living, Jack Jerome, *b* 1972, — Edward Mulligan, *b* 1973, — Theodore William, *b* 1979.

WIDOW LIVING OF LIFE BARON

MOLLIE (*Baroness Butler of Saffron Walden*) (Spencers, Gt Yeldham, Essex), da of late Frank Douglas Montgomerie, of Castle Hedingham, Essex (*see* L Napier and Ettrick, colls, 1985 Edn), and widow of Augustine Courtauld: *m* 1959, as his 2nd wife, Baron Butler of Saffron Walden, KG, CH, PC (Life Baron), who *d* 1982.

BUTTERFIELD, BARON (Butterfield) (Life Baron 1988)

(WILLIAM) JOHN HUGHES BUTTERFIELD, OBE, son of late William Hughes Butterfield; *b* 28 March 1920; *ed* Solihull Sch, Exeter Coll, Oxford (DM 1968, Hon Fell 1978), and John Hopkins Univ (MD 1951), MA, MD Cantab 1975; Hon Fell NY Acad Science 1962, NY Acad of Medicine 1987, Hon LLD Nottingham 1977, Hon DMedSci Keio Univ, Tokyo, 1983, Hon DSc Florida Internat Univ, Miami, 1985, Hon LLD Bristol 1994; late Maj RAMC; Medical Research Council 1946-58; Prof of Experimental Medicine Guy's Hosp 1958-63, Prof of Medicine Guy's Hosp Med Sch 1963-71; Prof Fell 1975-78, Master Downing Coll, Camb, 1978-87, Vice Chancellor Camb Univ 1983-85; Chm of many Medical, Scientific and Educational Cttees; Chm Jardine Educational Trust since 1982, and Health Promotion Research Trust since 1983; Trustee GB-Sasakawa Fndn 1991, Croucher Fndn, Hong Kong, since 1979, etc; Pres British Univs Sports Fedn, Council St George's House Windsor 1987-92; Visitor King Edward's Hosp Fund 1964-71, Examiner in Medicine Oxford Univ 1960-66, Univ of E Africa 1966, and Camb Univ 1967-75, etc; Visiting Prof Yale 1966, Harvard 1978; Rock Carling Fell, Royal Coll of Physicians 1968; Lecturer; FRSA 1971; *cr Baron Butterfield*, of Stechford, co W Midlands (Life Baron) 1988: *m* 1st, 1946, Ann, who *d* 1948, da of late Robert Sanders, of New York City, USA; 2ndly, 1950, Isabel-Ann, da of late Dr Foster Kennedy, of New York City, and has issue by 1st and 2nd *m*.

𝕬rms – Azure a pale ermine per fesse counterchanged on a fesse gules between three lozenges or a lion passant in trian aspect also or and between on the dexter a domed tower proper ensigned by an increscent argent and on the sinister a like tower ensigned by an estoile gold. 𝕮rest – A cubit arm vested azure semy of pentacles or the hand proper holding a pair of keys fesswise the bows interlaced gold. 𝕾upporters – *Dexter*, a greyhound statant erect argent gorged with an open crown or; *Sinister*, a griffin also statant erect gold.
Residence – 39 Clarendon St, Cambridge. *Clubs* – Athenaeum, MCC, Queen's.

SONS LIVING (By 1st marriage)

Hon Jonathan West Sanders, *b* 1948; BA; has issue living, two sons and one da. *Residence* – Dulwich, SE24.

(By 2nd marriage)

Hon Jeremy John Nicholas, *b* 1954; PhD, MA; has issue living, one son and one da. *Residence* – Jesus Coll, Cambridge.
Hon Toby Michael John, *b* 1965; BA; Bar Lincoln's Inn.

DAUGHTER LIVING *(By 2nd marriage)*

Hon Sarah Harriet Ann, *b* 1953; BSSc, ARIBA: *m* 1986, David Lindsay Willetts, MP, of Ashchurch Grove, W12, and has issue living, one son and one da.

BUTTERWORTH, BARON (Butterworth) (Life Baron 1985)

THE FEAR OF THE LORD IS THE BEGINNING OF WISDOM

JOHN BLACKSTOCK BUTTERWORTH, CBE, only son of John William Butterworth, by his wife, Florence, da of John Blackstock, of Dumfries; *b* 13 March 1918; *ed* Queen Elizabeth's Gram Sch, Mansfield, and The Queen's Coll, Oxford; Hon DCL Sierra Leone 1976, Hon DSc Aston Univ 1985, Hon LLD Warwick 1986; served RA 1939-46; Bar Lincoln's Inn 1947 (Hon Bencher 1989); Fellow New Coll, Oxford 1946-63, Faculty Fellow Nuffield Coll 1953-58, Managing Trustee Nuffield Foundation 1964-85; Chm Univs Cttee for Non-teaching Staffs 1970-85, Memb Board of British Council 1981-86; Vice Chancellor Warwick Univ 1963-85; Gov R Shakespeare Theatre since 1964, Memb Jarratt Cttee on Univ Efficiency since 1986, Crohan Cttee on review of Univ Grants Cttee since 1987, Univ Commr (under Educn Reform Act 1988) since 1988; a DL Warwicks 1967-74, since when W Midlands; JP City of Oxford 1962, and Coventry since 1963; *cr* CBE (Civil) 1982, and *Baron Butterworth*, of Warwick, co Warwick (Life Baron) 1985: *m* 1948, Doris Crawford, da of George Elder, of Edinburgh, and has issue.

Arms – Sable on a fess argent a representation of a DNA double helix spirals azure lined gules with connecting lines or and in chief two bears erect argent muzzled gules and in base an elephant also erect each standing against a ragged staff argent and collared and chained or the chain reflexed over the back round the foot of the staff and ending in a ring gold. **Crest** – Rising from a tree stock couped sable a phoenix or in flames proper grasping in the dexter claw a millrind sable. **Supporters** – Upon a compartment comprising a grassy mount strewn with buttercups proper on either side a little owl proper charged on the neck with a representation of a DNA double helix as in the arms.
. *Residence* – The Barn, Guiting Power, Glos GL54 5US. *Club* – Athenaeum.

SON LIVING

Hon John William Blackstock (5a Montpellier Grove, NW5), *b* 1952; *ed* Winchester, and New Coll, Oxford.

DAUGHTERS LIVING

Hon Anna Elizabeth Blackstock, *b* 1951; *ed* Benenden, and Lady Margaret Hall, Oxford: *m* 1983, Timothy Edward Hanson Walker, of 24 Old Park Av, SW12 8RH.
Hon Laura Blackstock, *b* 1959; *ed* Benenden, Dean Close Sch, Cheltenham, and Westfield Coll, London: *m* 1985, John Laughton Burley, of College Farm House, Millington, Pocklington, Yorks, son of John Burley, of Pocklington, York.

BUXTON, EARLDOM (Extinct 1934)

DAUGHTER LIVING OF FIRST EARL *(By 2nd marriage)*

Lady Alethea Constance Dorothy Sydney, *b* 1910: *m* 1934, Ven Peter Charles Eliot, MBE, TD, late Lt-Col RA (TA), of The Old House, Kingsland, Leominster, Herefordshire (*see* E St Germans, colls).

BUXTON OF ALSA, BARON (Buxton) (Life Baron 1978)

AUBREY BUXTON, MC, son of late Leland William Wilberforce Buxton (*see* Buxton, Bt, colls); *b* 15 July 1918; *ed* Ampleforth, and Trin Coll, Camb; Maj Sup Reserves; DL Essex 1975, High Sheriff 1972; Extra Equerry to HRH The Duke of Edinburgh since 1964; 1939-45 War (despatches, MC); Dir Anglia Television since 1958, Treas, London Zoological Soc 1977-83; British Vice-Pres World Wildlife Fund since 1968; Pres Royal Television Soc 1973-77; Ch Exec Anglia TV Group (Dir 1955-88, Chm 1986-88), Chm Independant TV News Ltd 1981-86; Chm UPITN Internat TV News Agency since 1981; Chm Survival Anglia since 1986; Member Countryside Commn, etc; *cr Baron Buxton of Alsa*, of Stiffkey, co Norfolk (Life Baron) 1978: *m* 1st, 1946, Pamela Mary, who *d* 1983, da of Sir Henry Ralph Stanley Birkin, 3rd Bt, and widow of Maj Samuel Luckyn Buxton, MC, 17th/21st Lancers (*see* Buxton, Bt, colls); 2ndly, 1988, Mrs Kathleen Peterson, of Maine, USA, and has issue by 1st *m*.

Arms – Argent a lion rampant the tail elevated and turned over the head between two mullets in fesse sable. **Crest** – A stag's head couped gules attired or gorged with a collar of the last pendent therefrom an escutcheon argent charged with a negro's head couped at the shoulders in profile proper. **Supporters** – *Dexter*, a crowned crane (Balearica Pavonina); *Sinister*, a flamingo proper.
Residence – Old Hall Farm, Stiffkey, Wells-next-the-Sea, Norfolk. *Club* – White's.

SONS LIVING (By 1st marriage)

Hon Timothy Leland (The Dairy, Castle Howard, York YO4 7BY), *b* 1948; *ed* Ampleforth: *m* 1st, 1972 (*m diss* 1986), Julie Mary, da of Lt-Cdr (John) Michael Avison Parker, CVO; 2ndly, 1994, Mrs Amanda Dickinson, da of A/Cdre Anthony Walkinshaw Fraser, and has issue living (by 1st *m*), Edward Leland, *b* 1976, — Alexandra Louise, *b* 1973.
Hon (Aubrey) James Francis (Church Farm, Carlton, Suffolk; *Club* – White's), *b* 1956; *ed* Ampleforth, and RAC Cirencester: *m* 1981, Melinda, da of Peter Henry Samuelson, of Ugley Hall, Ugley, Essex, and has issue living, Henry James Aubrey, *b* 1988, — Emma Lucie Maria, *b* 1984, — Olivia Louise, *b* 1986.

DAUGHTERS LIVING (By 1st marriage)

Hon Nicola Mary Caroline, *b* 1947: *m* 1970, Adrian William Guy Sykes, of Cook's Mill, Fordham Heath, Colchester, Essex, and has had issue, Samuel Adrian Aubrey, *b* 1974, — Eleanor Mary Fiona, *b* 1972, — Miranda Pamma Lucinda, *b* 1982, — Daisy Maria Hester, *b* and *d* 1985, — Pandora India Nicola, *b* 1987.
Hon Lucinda Catherine (The Old House, Langham, Holt, Norfolk), *b* 1950; Wildlife Photographer; FRGS.
Hon Veronica Frances *b* 1953: *m* 1975, William Robert Charles Williams-Wynne of Talybont, Tywyn, Gwynedd, and has issue (*see* Williams-Wynn, Bt, colls).
Hon Victoria Jane (Burntwalls Farm, Daventry, Northants), *b* 1960.

Buxton, see Baron Noel-Buxton.

BYERS, BARONY OF (Byers) (Extinct 1984)

SON LIVING OF LIFE BARON

Hon Charles William, *b* 1949; *ed* Westminster, and Ch Ch Oxford, Bar (Gray's Inn) 1973: *m* 1972, Suzan Mary, da of late Aubrey Kefford Stone, and has issue living, Jonathan Charles, *b* 1975, — George William, *b* 1977. *Residence* – 3 Clayford, Dormansland, Surrey.

DAUGHTERS LIVING OF LIFE BARON

Hon Elizabeth Frances, *b* 1941: *m* 1st, 1961 (*m diss* 1977), Charles Alasdair Ronald Malcolm; 2ndly, 1978, Peter Gaff, and has issue.
Hon (Ann) Luise, *b* 1946: *m* 1972, Dipak Nandy, of 38 Mauldeth Rd, Manchester 20, and has issue living, Francesca, *b* 1977, — Lisa, *b* 1979.
Hon Sara Margaret, *b* 1952: *m* 1979 (*m diss* 19—), Simon John Somers, and has issue living, Laura Sian, *b* 1982, — Amy Rowena, *b* 1984.

WIDOW LIVING OF LIFE BARON

JOAN ELIZABETH (*Baroness Byers*), da of late William Oliver: *m* 1939, Baron Byers, OBE, PC (Life Baron), who *d* 1984.

BYRON, BARON (Byron) (Baron E 1643)

ROBERT JAMES BYRON, 13th Baron; *b* 5 April 1950; *s* 1989; *ed* Wellington Coll, and Trin Coll, Camb; Bar Inner Temple 1974, Solicitor 1978, Ptnr Holman, Fenwick & Willan since 1984: *m* 1979, Robyn Margaret, da of John McLean, of Hamilton, NZ, and has issue.

𝕬rms – Argent, three bendlets enhanced gules. 𝕮rest – A mermaid proper. 𝕾upporters – Two horses of a brown bay colour unguled or. *Residence* – 19 Spencer Park, SW18.

SON LIVING

Hon CHARLES RICHARD GORDON, *b* 28 July 1990.

DAUGHTERS LIVING

Hon Caroline Anne Victoria, *b* 1981.
Hon Emily Clare, *b* 1984.
Hon Sophie Georgina, *b* 1986.

AUNT LIVING (*sister of 12th Baron*)

Sheila Margaret, *b* 1903: *m* 1st, 1923 (*m diss* 1929), James Roy Notter Garton, Capt KRRC, who *d* 1939; 2ndly, 1929, Edward William Standish, of Marwell Hall, Winchester, who *d* 1933; 3rdly, 1935, George Munro Kerr, who *d* 1970, and has issue living (by 2nd *m*), Anthony Edward Byron (Paternoster House, Ipplepen, S Devon), *b* 1931; *ed* Eton: *m* 1956, Diana Huguette, only da of late Dr Hugh Gordon, of 3 High St, Kirkcudbright, and has issue living, Miles Anthony *b* 1958, Alexander Hugh *b* 1959, Edward Pery *b* 1968: *m* 1992, Anna Margaret, yr da of John Raymond Perring, TD (*see* Perring, Bt), Caroline Lucy *b* 1963, — Susan Felicity, *b* 1929: *m* 1949, Capt Derek Russell de Courcy Trasenster, 4th/7th R Drag Gds, of Compton House, Upton Grey, Basingstoke, Hants, and has issue living, Mark William de Courcy, *b* 1954: *m* 1983, Elisabeth Ross (and has issue living, Sophie Georgina *b* 1984, Georgina Sarah *b* 1986, Sara Elisabeth *b* 1989, Cordelia Camilla de Courcy *b* 1991), Camilla de Courcy *b* 1951: *m* 1974, Brig Clendon Daukes, late 4th/7th R Drag Gds (and has issue living, Anthony Clendon, *b* 1976, Thomas Clendon *b* 1978, Rose-Anna *b* 1981). *Residence* – 52 Eresby House, Rutland Gate, SW7 1BG.

DAUGHTER LIVING OF ELEVENTH BARON

Hon (Isobel) Ann, *b* 1932: *m* 1st, 1951, Robert Reford Corr, who *d* 1980; 2ndly, 1983, Norman James Woods, son of late James Park Woods, VC, of W Australia, and has issue living, (by 1st *m*), John Byron Reford, *b* 1953: *m* 1982, Suzette Margaret Brackenridge, and has issue living, Alexandra Isobel *b* 1987, — Anthony Byron Reford, *b* 1956: *m* 1984, Joanne Lee Cruickshank, and has issue living, Louisa Ann *b* 1988, Alana May *b* 1991, — Helen Jane, *b* 1961. *Residence* – 55A Mayfair St, Mount Claremont, W Australia.

PREDECESSORS – (1) *Sir* JOHN Byron, KB, MP for Nottingham, a faithful adherent of Charles I, Gov to HRH the Duke of York, and FM Gen of the Forces is Worcester, Salop, Chester, and N Wales; was *cr Baron Byron*, of Rochdale, co Lancaster (peerage of England) 1643, with remainder to his brothers Richard, William, Thomas, Robert, Gilbert, and Philip; *dsp* 1652; *s* by his brother (2) RICHARD, KB, 2nd Baron, Gov of Appleby Castle, Westmorland, and of Newark: *d* 1679; *s* by his son (3) WILLIAM, 3rd Baron; *d* 1695; *s* by his son (4) WILLIAM, 4th Baron, gentleman of the Bedchamber to George, Prince of Denmark; *d* 1736; *s* by his son (5) WILLIAM, 5th Baron: having killed William Chaworth, Esq, in a duel, 26 Jan 1765, was arraigned before his peers and found guilty of manslaughter, but claiming the benefit of the statute of Edward VI, was discharged by simply paying the fees; *d* without surviving issue 1798; *s* by his great-nephew (6) GEORGE GORDON, 6th Baron, grandson of Hon John, 2nd son of 4th Baron; celebrated as a poet; *d* 1824, without male issue; *s* by his cousin (7) GEORGE ANSON, 7th Baron, an Adm and an Extra Lord-in-Waiting to HM Queen Victoria; *d* 1868; *s* by his son (8) GEORGE ANSON, 8th Baron: *m* 1844, Lucy Elizabeth Jane, who *d* 1912, da of late Rev William Westcomb, R of Langford; *dsp* 1870; *s* by his nephew (9) GEORGE FREDERICK WILLIAM, 9th Baron, *b* 1855: *m* 1901, *Dame* Fanny Lucy, DBE, who *d* 1936, da of late Thamas Radmall, of St Margarets, Twickenham (Brinckman, Bt), and formerly wife of Lt-Col Theodore Francis Brinckman (afterwards 3rd Bt) (she *m* 3rdly, 1924, Sir Robert Paterson Houston, 1st Bt, who *d* 1926); *d* 1917; *s* by his brother (10) *Rev* FREDERICK ERNEST CHARLES (son of Hon Frederick Byron, 2nd son of 7th Baron), 10th Baron, *b* 1861; sometime V of Thrumpton and R of Barton-in-Fabis: *m* 1921, Lady Anna Ismay Ethel, who *d* 1966, da of late Lord Charles Edward Fitzroy (D Grafton); *d* 1949; *s* by his kinsman (11) RUPERT FREDERICK GEORGE (son of late Col Wilfrid Byron, son of Rev Hon William Byron, 4th son of 7th Baron), 11th Baron, *b* 1903: *m* 1931, Pauline Augusta, who *d* 1993, da of late T. J. Cornwall, of Wagin, W Australia; *d* 1983; *s* by his kinsman (12) RICHARD GEOFFREY GORDON (son of late Col Richard Byron, DSO, son of late Maj-Gen John Byron, son of late Rev John Byron, son of Rear-Adm Richard Byron, CB, el son of Rev Hon Richard Byron, 3rd son of 4th Baron), 12th Baron, *b* 1899; Lt-Col 4th/7th R Drag Gds, European War 1939-45 in France (DSO 1944), ADC to Gov of Bombay 1921-22, Mil Sec to Gov-Gen and C-in-C New Zealand: *m* 1st, 1926 (*m diss* 1946), Margaret Mary, only da of late Francis Gerald Steuart, of Fyfhyde, Winchester, Hants; 2ndly, 1946, Dorigen Margaret, who *d* 1985, only da of Percival Kennedy Esdaile; *d* 1989; *s* by his yr son (his elder son, Hon Richard Noel Byron, *b* 1948, was *k* in an air accident in W Africa 1985, *unm*), (13) ROBERT JAMES, 13th Baron and present peer.

CACCIA, BARONY OF (Caccia) (Extinct 1990)
(Name pronounced "Catch-a")

SON DECEASED OF LIFE BARON

Hon David Anthony Lawrence, *b* 1936; *ed* Eton, and Trin Coll, Oxford; HM Foreign Ser: *m* 1962 (*m diss* 1973), Angela Margaret, da of Edward James Read, of Johannesburg, and *d* 1983, leaving issue, Alexander Orlando Harold (1 Phillimore Terr, Allen St, W8 6BJ), *b* 1963, — Arabella Sabina Lilian, *b* 1965: *m* 1990, Anthony James Hamilton-Russell, of Braemar House, P.O. Box 158, Hermanos, Cape, S Africa (*see* B Ashbourne).

DAUGHTERS LIVING OF LIFE BARON

Hon Clarissa Sabina, *b* 1939: *m* 1959, David Eugene Henry Pryce-Jones, of Pentwyn, Gwenddwr, Powys, and Phillimore Lodge, 1 Phillimore Terr, W8 6BJ, only son of Alan Payan Pryce-Jones, TD, and has had issue, Adam, *b* 1973, — Jessica, *b* 1961: *m* 1988, David Roderick Shukman, elder son of Prof Harold Shukman, of St Antony's Coll, Oxford, and has issue living, Jack Nicholas Oliver *b* 1989, Harold David *b* 1992, — Candida, *b* 1963: *m* 1989, Owen William Luxado Mostyn-Owen, elder son of William Mostyn-Owen, of Woodhouse, Rednal, Shropshire, and has issue living, Gemma Clare *b* 1992, — Sonia, *b* 1970, *d* 1972.
Hon Antonia Catherine Caccia (21 Westwood Rd, Barnes, SW13), *b* 1947; has resumed her maiden name: *m* 1970 (*m diss* 1974), Barton Midwood, and has issue living, Jacob Caccia, *b* 1972.

WIDOW LIVING OF LIFE BARON

Anne Catherine (Nancy) (*Baroness Caccia*), da of Sir George Lewis Barstow, KCB (*see* B Trevethin and Oaksey, 1970 Edn): *m* 1932, Baron Caccia, GCMG, GCVO (Life Baron), who *d* 1990. *Residence* – Abernant, Builth Wells, Powys LD2 3YR.

CADMAN, BARON (Cadman) (Baron UK 1937)

Always ready

John Anthony Cadman, 3rd Baron; *b* 3 July 1938; *s* 1966; *ed* Harrow, Selwyn Coll, Camb, and RAC Cirencester: *m* 1975, Janet, da of late A. Hayes, of Laneside, Walton Av, Bare, Lancs, and has issue.

Arms – Azure, three fleur-de-lys in pale between four endorses indented argent. **Crest** – A stork's head holding in the beak a sprig of columbine proper. **Supporters** – *Dexter* a stork, and *Sinister* a peacock agent beaked gules, each gorged with a collar azure charged with a fleur-de-lys also argent.
Residence – Heathcourt House, Ironmould Lane, Brislington, Bristol BS4 5RS.

SONS LIVING

Hon Nicholas Anthony James, *b* 18 Nov 1977.
Hon Giles Oliver Richard, *b* 1979.

BROTHER LIVING

Hon James Rupert, *b* 1944; *ed* Harrow.

UNCLE LIVING (Son of 1st Baron)

Hon Arthur Denys, *b* 1911; *ed* Harrow, and Harvard Univ: *m* 1933, Cary, da of Burke Baker, of Texas, USA, and has issue living, John Denys (QL 26 Conj 6 Casa 1, Lago Sul, Brasilia, Brazil 74665-165), *b* 1941; *ed* Princeton Univ (BSE), and Univ of California (MS, PhD): *m* 1st, 1964, Judith Ann, da of Warren Whittaker, and has issue living (by 1st *m*), Cynthia, *b* 1965, Cary Anne *b* 1968, — David Baker (1732 McSpadden, Vancouver, BC V5N 1L4, Canada), *b* 1948; *ed* Univ of The South, Sewanee, Tennessee (BA): *m* 1980, Marie, da of Henrick C. Orth-Pallavicini, of New York, and has issue living, Darcy Eryn *b* 1984, — Anne, *b* 1935: *m* 1957, John Edward McCrea Lawrence, of 98 Ruskin, Ottawa, Canada, and has issue living, Edward Burke *b* 1959, John Cadman *b* 1960: *m* 1980, Robyn Mooney (and has issue living, Jy Maya *b* 1989, Rohja Raina *b* 1991), Denys McCrea *b* 1962: *m* 1988, Mona Stiffler (and has issue living, Noah Denys *b* 1989), Cary Edwina *b* 1964: *m* 1992, Thomas Christopher Paul LaPierre, — Mary Betty, *b* 1937; BA Smith Coll, MDiv Trin Coll, Toronto Univ: *m* 1958, Robert Alexander Calvin, of 464 Oriole Parkway, Toronto, Canada, and has issue living, Robert Denys *b* 1960: *m* 1986, Barbara Patricia Lee (and has issue living, Graham Denys *b* 1992, Sarah Emily *b* 1990), John Collamer *b* 1962, Isobel Anne *b* 1965: *m* 1990, Justin Gray Bonar, — Cary, *b* 1945; BA, Chatham Coll, Pittsburgh, USA: *m* 1984, Robert A. Johnson, of 324 Elm St, Duxbury, Mass 02332, USA, and has issue living, Marlana Rose *b* 1988. *Residence* – 4100 Jackson Apt 503, Austin, Texas 78731, USA.

AUNT LIVING (Daughter of 1st Baron)

Hon Sybil Mary (Bryn-Dedwydd, Maerdy, Corwen, Clwyd LL21 9NY), *b* 1916: *m* 1st, 1938, Maj-Gen William Pat Arthur Bradshaw, CB, DSO late Scots Gds, who *d* 1966; 2ndly 1968, James Simon Cadman, who *d* 1986, and has issue living (by 1st *m*); Christopher Patrick Cadman (Blackbrook House, Dorking, Surrey), *b* 1941; *ed* Eton, and St Andrews Univ (BSc): *m* 1973,

Susan Elizabeth, da of D. W. Vasey, of Downways, Old Bosham, Sussex, and has issue living, Benjamin Patrick *b* 1975; *ed* Ardingly, Philippa Mary *b* 1977, Emma Judith *b* 1979, — (Francis) John Cadman, LVO (Rhagatt Hall, Carrog, Corwen, Clwyd LL21 9NY), *b* 1946; *ed* Pangbourne Nautical Coll; Cdr RN; LVO 1984: *m* 1981, Frances Mary Christine, only da of Col Robert Hugh Cuming, MBE (*see* B Robertson of Oakridge), and has issue living, Anna Mary Christine *b* 1983, Juliet Frances *b* 1985, Isabel Fiona *b* 1987, — Caroline *b* 1939: *m* 1959, Francis Rokeby Black, FCA, of The Old Vicarage, Wing, Bucks LU7 0NU, and has issue living, James Pat Rokeby *b* 1963; *ed* Eton, and Exeter Univ (BSc): *m* 1990, Susan Elizabeth Bone, Alexander William Francis *b* 1967; *ed* Harrow, and Exeter Univ (BSc), Lucinda Rosalie *b* 1960; *ed* Exeter Univ (BA): *m* 1985, Philip Latham Baillieu (*see* B Baillieu), Natasha Caroline *b* 1976, — Rosalie Annette *b* 1944: *m* 1965, David Bernard Butler Adams, of The Old Rectory, Holtby, York, YO1 3UD, and has issue living, William David *b* 1974; *ed* Rugby, Sophie Anne *b* 1966, Amanda Jane *b* 1968, Fiona Mary *b* 1972.

WIDOW LIVING OF SECOND BARON

MARJORIE ELIZABETH (*Marjorie, Baroness Cadman*) (Overlands, 157 Church Rd, Combe Down, Bath), da of Byron William Bunnis: *m* 1936, the 2nd Baron, who *d* 1966.

PREDECESSORS – (1) JOHN CADMAN, GCMG, DSc, FRS, son of the late James Cope Cadman, MICE, of Newcastle-under-Lyme; *b* 1877; a Mining Engineer and Petroleum Technologist; cr *Baron Cadman*, of Silverdale, co Stafford (peerage of United Kingdom) 1937: *m* 1907, Lilian Julia, who *d* 1963, da of the late John Harragin of Trinidad; *d* 1941; *s* by his son (2) JOHN BASIL COPE, 2nd Baron; *b* 1909: *m* 1936, Marjorie Elizabeth, da of Byron William Bunnis; *d* 1966; *s* by his son (3) JOHN ANTHONY, 3rd Baron, and present peer.

CADOGAN, EARL (Cadogan) (Earl GB 1800)
(Name pronounced "Caduggan")

QUI INVIDET MINOR EST

He who envies is the inferior

WILLIAM GERALD CADOGAN, MC, 7th Earl; *b* 13 Feb 1914; *s* 1933; *ed* Eton; late Capt Coldm Gds (Res), and Lt-Col R Wilts Yeo (TA); patron of four livings, and a DL; Mayor of Chelsea 1964; a Member of Chelsea Borough Council 1954-59; 1939-45 War in Middle East and Italy (MC): *m* 1st, 1936 (*m diss* 1959), Hon Primrose Lilian Yarde-Buller, who *d* 1970, da of 3rd Baron Churston; 2ndly, 1961, Cecilia, da of Maj Henry K. Hamilton-Wedderburn, OBE, and has issue by 1st *m*.

Arms – Quarterly: 1st and 4th gules, a lion rampant reguardant or, *Cadogan*: 2nd and 3rd argent, three boars' heads couped sable. **Crest** – Out of a ducal coronet or, a dragon's head vert. **Supporters** – *Dexter*, a lion reguardant or, gorged with a collar gemeflory counterflory gules; *sinister*, an eagle wings elevated sable, beaked, membered, and navally crowned or, gorged with a riband argent, fimbriated gules, pendent therefrom a representation of the cross of Imperial Austrian military order of Maria Theresa.
Residences – Snaigow, Dunkeld, Perthshire; 28 Cadogan Square, SW1. *Club* – White's.

SON LIVING (By 1st marriage)

CHARLES GERALD JOHN (*Viscount Chelsea*) (7 Smith St, SW3 4EE, and Marndhill, Ardington, Wantage, Oxon OX12 8PN; *Clubs* – White's, RAC), *b* 24 March 1937; *ed* Eton: *m* 1st, 1963, Lady Philippa Dorothy Bluett Wallop, who *d* 1984, da of 9th Earl of Portsmouth; 2ndly, 1989, Jennifer Jane Greig, da of J. E. K. Rae, and of Mrs S. Z. de Ferranti; 3rdly, 1994, Dorothy Ann, MVO, yr da of late Dr W. E. Shipsey, and has issue by 1st *m*:—

SONS LIVING—(by 1st *m*)— *Hon* Edward Charles, *b* 10 May 1966: *m* 1990, Katharina Johanna Ingeborg, da of Rear Adm Diether P. H. Hülsemann, German Navy, and has issue living, Philippa Katharina, *b* 1992. — *Hon* William John, *b* 1973.

DAUGHTER LIVING—(by 1st *m*)— *Hon* Anna-Karina, *b* 1964: *m* 1992, Gary Andrew Thomson.

DAUGHTERS LIVING (By 1st marriage)

Lady Sarah Primrose Beatrix (*Baroness Rockley*), *b* 1938: *m* 1958, 3rd Baron Rockley, of Lytchett Heath, Poole, Dorset BH16 6AE.
Lady Daphne Magdalen, *b* 1939: *m* 1961, David Malcolm Graham Bailey, of The Manor House, Dry Sandford, Abingdon, Oxon OX13 6JP, and has issue living, Alexander Graham (34 Twining Av, Twickenham, Middx TW2 5UR), *b* 1962: *m* 1986, Meriam Atsede Ambaye, and has issue living, Antony Francis Christopher Graham *b* 1987, Antoinette Catonia Mia Lydia Alga *b* (twin) 1987, — Kevin David, *b* 1964, — Leonie Daphne, *b* 1965: *m* 1988, Brian Sharrock, eldest son of Kevin Sharrock, of MacArthur, Victoria, Australia.
Lady Caroline Ann TAHANY *b* 1946 (assumed surname of Tahany 1981): *m* 1965 (*m diss* 1975), Euan Woodroffe Foster, and has issue living, Guy Peter Woodroffe, *b* 1968, — Hugo Woodroffe, *b* 1971. *Residence* – 11 Oakley Gdns, SW3.

SISTER LIVING

Lady Beatrix Lilian Ethel, *b* 1912: *m* 1st, 1931 (*m diss* 1941), (Henry Péregrine) Rennie Hoare (*see* M Bristol, 1955 Edn), who *d* 1981; 2ndly, 1942, Col Edward Leighton Fanshawe, who *d* 1982, el son of late Lt-Gen Sir Edward Arthur Fanshawe, KCB, and has issue living (by 1st *m*), Henry Cadogan, *b* 1931; *ed* Eton, and Trin Coll, Camb (MA): *m* 1st, 1959 (*m diss* 1970), Pamela Saxon, da of late Col George Francis Bunbury, OBE; 2ndly, 1977, Caromy, da of Robert Jenkins, CBE, and formerly wife of Donald Maxwell Macdonald (*see* E Ducie, colls), and has issue living (by 1st *m*), Henry Timothy *b* 1960, Nicholas

Colt *b* 1964, Arabella S. *b* 1968, — Melanie Beatrix, *b* 1937: *m* 1963, Charles Henry Petre (*see* B Petre, colls), — (by 2nd *m*) Ann Erika, *b* 1943, — Clodagh Frances, *b* 1945. *Residence* – 74 Cranmer Court, Sloane Av, SW3 3HF.

COLLATERAL BRANCHES LIVING

Issue of late Rt Hon Sir Alexander George Montagu Cadogan, OM, GCMG, KCB, yst son of 5th Earl, *b* 1884, *d* 1968: *m* 1912, Lady Theodosia Acheson, who *d* 1977, da of 4th Earl of Gosford:—
Ambrose Alec Patrick George (8 Wilton Road, Reading, Berks), *b* 1914: *m* 1955 (*m diss* 1961), Mrs Pamela Maud Hope-Johnstone, da of late Lt-Col John Murray Cobbold, Scots Gds (*see* D Devonshire, 1985 Edn). —— Patricia, *b* 1916: *m* 1939, Gerald Edward Coke, CBE, who *d* 1990 (*see* E Leicester, colls). —— Cynthia (*Lady Goschen*), *b* 1918; formerly Co Assist ATS: *m* 1946, Maj Sir Edward Christian Goschen, 3rd Bt, DSO. —— Gillian Moyra, *b* 1922: *m* 1948, Maj Patrick Henry Douglas Crichton, OBE, Berks Yeo (TA) (*see* E Erne, colls).

Grandchildren of late John Cecil Cadogan, 2nd son of late Hon Charles George Henry Cadogan, yst son of 4th Earl:—
Issue of late Erik Cadogan, *b* 1913, *d* 1990: *m* 1939, Caroline, da of Count Wachtmeister, of Malmö:—
Charles John, *b* 1954. —— (Caroline) Monica (*Hon Mrs Peter H. Lewis*), *b* 1942: *m* 1974, Maj Hon Peter Herbert Lewis, and has issue (*see* B Merthyr). —— Patricia Elisabeth, *b* 1945: *m* 1974, Simon Mark Corbett, and has issue living, Camilla Louise, *b* 1978, — Lucy Miranda, *b* 1980.
Issue of late Peter Cadogan, *b* 1918, *d* 1962: *m* 1st, 1940 (*m diss* 1955), Joan, who *d* 1979, only da of late Adm Frederick Arthur Frith Banbury; 2ndly, 1955, Pamela Mary, da of late Alexander Henry Burman, OBE:—
(By 1st *m*) Gerald (Culworth, Banbury, Oxon OX17 2AT), *b* 1942: *m* 1968, Lucy Dodd, da of Walter Ramberg, of Washington, DC, and has issue living, Leo, *b* 1975, — Nancy, *b* 1979. —— Sarah, *b* 1944: *m* 1st, 1966 (*m diss* 1970), Geoffrey Hugh Kenion; 2ndly, 1973, Robert Andrew Burns, CMG, c/o FCO, King Charles St, SW1A 2AH, and has issue living (by 1st *m*), Ella Jane, *b* 1968, — (by 2nd m) Robert Duncan, *b* 1975, — Thomas Alexander Luckwell *b* 1977.

Granddaughter of Cdr Francis Charles Cadogan, RN (infra):—
Issue of late Capt Christopher Michael Cadogan, R Berks Regt, *b* 1917, *ka* 1941: *m* 1940, Stella Irena (*Lady Wallinger*) (38 Perrymead St, SW6) (who *m* 2ndly, 1943 (*m diss* 1955), David Rhys Ellias, and 3rdly, 1958, Sir Geoffrey Arnold Wallinger, GBE, KCMG, who *d* 1979), da of late Konrad Zilliacus, MP:—
Catharine, *b* 1941.

Granddaughter of late Hon Charles George Henry Cadogan (ante):—
Issue of late Cdr Francis Charles Cadogan, RN, *b* 1885, *d* 1970: *m* 1913, Ruth Evelyn, who *d* 1962, da of late Sir (Edward) Stafford Howard, KCB (D Norfolk, colls), and widow of Gardner Sebastian Bazley (Bazley, Bt):—
Henriette Alice, DCVO (*Lady Abel Smith*) (The Garden House, Quenington, Glos) *b* 1914; JP; appointed a Lady-in-Waiting to HM The Queen when HRH Princess Elizabeth 1949, a Woman of the Bedchamber 1952, an Extra Woman of the Bedchamber 1953-73, since when again Woman of the Bedchamber; CVO 1964, DCVO 1977: *m* 1st, 1939, Maj Sir Anthony Frederick Mark Palmer, 4th Bt (*cr* 1886), RA, who was *ka* 1941; 2ndly, 1953, Brig Sir Alexander Abel Smith, TD, JP (D Somerset, colls), who *d* 1980, and has issue living (by 1st *m*), (*see* Palmer, Bt, *cr* 1886), — (by 2nd *m*) Christopher Abel, *b* 1954: *m* 19—, Catherine, da of Paul Berger, of Nancy, France, and has issue living, Lyam Paul Alexander *b* 1988, a da *b* 1985, — Juliet Sarah, *b* 1955: *m* 1979, Christopher Graham Stainforth, son of Maj-Gen Charles Herbert Stainforth, CB, OBE, of Powderham House, Dippenhall, Farnham, Surrey, and has issue living, Charles Alexander *b* 1989.

PREDECESSORS – (1) *Gen the Rt Hon Sir* WILLIAM CADOGAN, KT, PC, successively MP for Woodstock, Ambassador to Brussels, Master of the Robes, Ambassador to the States Gen, Master-Gen of the Ordnance and Com-in-Ch of HM's Forces, was cr *Baron Cadogan*, of Reading, co Berks (peerage of Great Britain) 1716, a *Baron Cadogan*, of Reading, co Berks with remainder to his brother Charles, and *Viscount Caversham* and *Earl Cadogan* (peerage of Great Britain) 1718; *d* 1726, without male issue, when the Barony of Cadogan of Reading 1716, and the Earldom and Viscountcy of 1718 became ext; *s* in Barony of Cadogan of Oakley by his brother (2) CHARLES, 2nd Baron; was a Gen of Horse, MP and Gov of Sheerness, etc; *d* 1776; *s* by his son (3) CHARLES SLOANE, 3rd Baron; was MP for Cambridge 1749-76, and Master of the Mint, etc; cr *Viscount Chelsea* and *Earl Cadogan* (peerage of Great Britain) 1800; *d* 1807; *s* by his son (4) CHARLES HENRY SLOANE, 2nd Earl; *d* 1832; *s* by his half-brother (5) GEORGE, CB, 3rd Earl, a distinguished Adm, who in 1831 had been cr *Baron Oakley*, of Caversham, co Oxford (peerage of United Kingdom); *d* 1864; *s* by his son (6) HENRY CHARLES, PC, 4th Earl, *b* 1812; was MP for Reading 1841-7 and for Dover 1852-7, and Capt of Yeomen of the Guard 1866-68; *m* 1836, his cousin, Mary Sarah who *d* 1873, da of late Rev Hon Gerald Valerian Wellesley, DD (E Cowley); *d* 8 June, 1873; *s* by his son (7) GEORGE HENRY, KG, PC, 5th Earl, *b* 1840; MP for Bath (*C*) 1873; Under-Sec. for War 1875-8, and for the Colonies 1878-80, Lord Privy Seal 1886-92, and Lord-Lieut. of Ireland with a Seat in the Cabinet 1895-1902; held Canopy at Coronation of King George V 1911: *m* 1st, 1865, Lady Beatrix Jane Craven, VA, who *d* 1907, da of 2nd Earl of Craven: 2ndly, 1911, Countess Adele Palagi, who *d* 1960, da of Lippo Neri, Count Palagi, a Florentine Patrician; *d* 1915, *s* by his third but el surviving son (8) GERALD OAKLEY, CBE, 6th Earl, *b* 1869; sometime Lt 1st Life Gds, and Capt 3rd Batn Suffolk Regt: *m* 1911, Lilian Eleanor Marie, who *d* 1973, da of George Steward Coxon, formerly of Craigleith, Cheltenham; *d* 1933, *s* by his son (9) WILLIAM GERALD CHARLES, 7th Earl and present peer; also Viscount Chelsea, Baron Cadogan of Oakley, and Baron Oakley.

CAIRNS, EARL (Cairns) (Earl UK 1878)

I flourish

SIMON DALLAS CAIRNS, CBE, 6th Earl; *b* 27 May 1939; *s* 1989; *ed* Eton, and Trin Coll, Camb; Receiver-Gen Duchy of Cornwall since 1990; CBE (Civil) 1992: *m* 1964, Amanda Mary, only da of late Maj Edgar Fitzgerald Heathcoat-Amory (*see* Heathcoat-Amory, Bt, colls), and has issue.

𝕬rms – Gules, three martlets, argent within a bordure of the second, charged with three trefoils slipped vert. 𝕮rest – A martlet argent, charged on the breast with a trefoil slipped vert. 𝕾upporters – On either side a hawk, wings expanded proper, collared belled and chained or, holding in its beak a trefoil slipped vert.
Residence – Bolehyde Manor, Allington, Chippenham, Wilts SN14 6LW.

SONS LIVING

HUGH SEBASTIAN (*Viscount Garmoyle*), *b* 26 March 1965; *ed* Eton, and Edinburgh Univ: *m* 1991, Juliet, only da of Andrew Eustace Palmer, CMG, CVO, of Little Missenden, Bucks, and has issue living, Hon Oliver David Andrew, *b* 7 March 1993.

Hon (David) Patrick, *b* 1967; *ed* Eton, and Bristol Univ: *m* 1993, Francesca L., da of Oliver Rena, of Little Venice, W2.

Hon Alistair Benedict, *b* 1969; *ed* Eton, and LSE.

BROTHER LIVING

Hon Hugh Andrew David (Knowle Hill Farm, Ulcombe, Maidstone, Kent), *b* 1942; *ed* Wellington Coll, and Dublin Univ: *m* 1966, Elizabeth, da of Lt-Col F. C. L. Bell, of Cross Glades, Chiddingfold, Surrey, and has issue living, Bertram Wilfrid Arthur, *b* 1972, — Katherine Frances, *b* 1974.

SISTER LIVING

Lady Elisabeth Olive, *b* 1944: *m* 1965, Capt Martin Ralph Lowe, 9th/12th R Lancers (ret), of Castle End, Ross-on-Wye, Herefords HR9 7JY, and has issue living, Alexander Charles, *b* 1970.

AUNT LIVING (*Daughter of 4th Earl*)

Lady Sheila Mary, *b* 1905: *m* 1930, Maj Charles Ivor Patrick Holroyd, late Rifle Bde, who *d* 1976, and has issue living, Charles John (Providence Cottage, Chute Cadley, Andover), *b* 1933; Lt-Col RGJ (ret): *m* 1969, Amanda Jane, da of Col Sir Richard Hamilton Glyn, 9th Bt, OBE, TD, MP, and has issue living, Charles Wilfrid *b* 1970; *ed* Eton, and New Coll, Oxford, George Alexander James *b* 1974; *ed* Eton, and Durham Univ, Joanna Mary Ursula *b* 1972; *ed* Sherborne, and Exeter Univ, — Richard Norton (Les Lausiers, Condillac, Montelimar, France), *b* 1946: *m* 1977, Karine, da of Raymond Phélip, and has issue living, Wilfrid Andrew *b* 1980, Alistair Hugo *b* 1985, Alexander Ivor *b* 1987, Annabel Juliette *b* 1983, — Alice Elizabeth, *b* 1936: *m* 1961, Ronald L. Lilburne, of Brook St, Renwick, Marlborough, NZ, and has issue living, David Milton *b* 1964, Linda Robyn *b* 1962, — Serena Jane, *b* 1939: *m* 1978, Dr Thomas D. Gledhill, of 5 Oakwood Rd, Henleaze, Bristol BS9 4NP, and has issue living, Stephen Mark *b* 1981, Sheona Grace *b* 1979, — Susan Virginia, *b* 1943. *Residence* – Meadow View, Lower Chute, Andover, Hants.

WIDOW LIVING OF SON OF FOURTH EARL

Barbara Mary Elisabeth (*Lady Hogg*), yr da of late Capt Arden Franklyn, of New Place, Shedfield, Hants: *m* 1st, 1936, Brig Viscount Garmoyle, DSO, late Rifle Bde, who was *ka* 1942; 2ndly, 1948, Sir John Nicholson Hogg, TD, of The Red House, Shedfield, Southampton (*see* Hogg, Bt, colls).

WIDOW LIVING OF FIFTH EARL

BARBARA JEANNE HARRISON (*Dowager Countess Cairns*), yst da of late Sydney H. Burgess, of Heathfield, Bowdon, Chesh: *m* 1936, Adm the 5th Earl, GCVO, CB, who *d* 1989. *Residence* – The Red House, Clopton, Woodbridge, Suffolk.

COLLATERAL BRANCH LIVING

Issue of late Hon Douglas Halyburton Cairns, 5th son of 1st Earl, *b* 1867, *d* 1936: *m* 1908, Lady Constance Anne Montagu Douglas Scott, who *d* 1970, da of 6th Duke of Buccleuch:—
Hugh William, MC, *b* 1911; Lt-Col late Cameron Highlanders; European War 1939-45 (wounded, MC): *m* 1939, Diana Soames, and has issue living, Peter Granville (11 St Mary Abbot's Court, W14), *b* 1940; *ed* Eton: *m* 1991, Mrs Ann Camilla Carlton, da of late J. B. Leworthy, of Beacon Hill, Westerham, Kent, — Francis John Hugh, *b* 1942; *ed* Eton, and Trin Coll, Camb: *m* 1983, Ulla Agneta, yr da of Sten Bylander, of Gothenburg, Sweden, and has issue living, Catriona Helen *b* 1984, — Celia Helen, *b* 1944: *m* 1968, David William Barclay, of Higham, Bury St Edmunds, and has issue living, Robin David *b* 1969, Katharine Elizabeth *b* 1971. *Residence* – Whitelee, St Boswells, Roxburghshire.

PREDECESSORS – (1) Rt Hon Sir HUGH MACCALMONT CAIRNS, DCL, LLD, 2nd son of late William Cairns, of Cultra, co Down; *b* 1819; sat as MP for Belfast (C) 1852-66; was Solicitor-Gen 1858-59, Attorney-Gen 1866, a Lord Justice of Appeal 1866-68, and Lord High Chancellor 1868 and 1874-80; cr *Baron Cairns*, of Garmoyle, co Antrim (peerage of United Kingdom) 1867, and *Viscount Garmoyle* and *Earl Cairns* (peerage of United Kingdom) 1878: *m* 1856, Mary Harriet, who *d* 1919, da of late John McNeile, of Parkmount, co Antrim; *d* 1885; *s* by his son (2) ARTHUR WILLIAM, 2nd Earl, *b* 1861: *m* 1887, Olivia Elizabeth, OBE, who *d* 1951, having *m* 2ndly, 1899, Major Roger Cyril Hans Sloane Stanley (*d* 1944), da of late Alexander Augustus Berens, of Castlemead, Windsor; *d* 1890; *s* by his brother (4) WILFRID DALLAS, CMG, 4th Earl; *b* 1865; sometime Capt Rifle Brig and Lt-Col Comdg London Rifle Brig; S Africa 1902, European War 1914-19 (CMG): *m* 1894, Olive, who *d* 1952, da of late J. P. Cobbold, MP, of The Cliffe, Ipswich; *d* 1946; *s* by his son (5) DAVID CHARLES, GCVO, CB, 5th Earl, *b* 1909; Rear Adm, Chm Naval Coll, Greenwich 1958-61, Marshal of Diplomatic Corps 1961-71, Prime Warden Fishmongers' Co 1972-73, Pres Navy League 1966-77, an Extra Equerry to HM 1972-89; 1939-45 War (despatches), DL Suffolk: *m* 1936, Barbara Jeanne Harrison, yst da of late Sydney H. Burgess, of Heathfield, Bowdon, Chesh; *d* 1989; *s* by his elder son (6) SIMON DALLAS, 6th Earl and present peer; also Viscount Garmoyle, and Baron Cairns.

CAITHNESS, EARL OF (Sinclair) (Earl S 1455, Bt S 1631)

MALCOLM IAN SINCLAIR, PC, 20th Earl and 15th Baronet; *b* 3 Nov 1948; *s* 1965; *ed* Marlborough, and RAC, Cirencester; FRICS; a Lord-in-Waiting to HM 1984-85, Under-Sec for Transport 1985-86, Min of State, Home Office 1986-88, Min of State, Dept of Environment 1988-89, Paymaster Gen 1989-90, Min of State, Foreign and Commonwealth Office 1990-92, since when Min of State for Transport 1992-94; PC 1990: *m* 1975, Diana Caroline, who *d* 1994, da of Maj Richard Lovel Coke, DSO, MC (*see* E Leicester, colls), and has issue.

Arms – Quarterly; 1st azure, a lymphad at anchor or, flagged gules sails furled argent oars erect in saltire, within a double tressure flory of the second, *Earldom of Orkney*, 2nd and 3rd or, a lion rampant gules armed and langued azure, *Sparr-Nithsdale*; 4th azure, a three-masted ship or, flagged gules under sail argent, *Earldom of Caithness*; over all dividing the quarters a cross engrailed and countercharged argent and sable, *Sinclair* **Crest** – A cock proper armed and beaked or. **Supporters** – Two griffins gules wings elevated, armed beaked and winged or.
Seat – Girnigoe Castle, Caithness. *Address* – c/o House of Lords, SW1.

SON LIVING

Alexander James Richard (*Lord Berriedale*), *b* 26 March 1981.

DAUGHTER LIVING

Lady Iona Alexandra, *b* 1978.

HALF-SISTERS LIVING

Lady Jean Elizabeth, *b* 1936; *m* 1961, David Peere Williams-Freeman, of Glendean Farm, Nottingham Rd, Natal, and has issue living, Andrew Frederick Peere, *b* 1962: *m* 1991, Fiona, da of Walter Hinds, of Nairobi, Kenya, — Juliet Margaret, *b* 1964: *m* 1994, Clive King, of Natal, S Africa, — Theresa Jean, *b* 1966: *m* 1991, Robert Wilson, of Howick, Natal, — Kim Jannette, *b* (twin) 1966: *m* 19—, Neil Roberts, of Shunigwi, Zimbabwe.
Lady Margaret Nicola, *b* 1937: *m* 1st 1959, Capt David Colin Kirkwood Brown, late Gordon Highlanders; 2ndly, 1983, John James Maxwell Glasse, of The Old Rectory, Milton Bryan, Beds, and has issue living (by 1st *m*), Nicola Jane Kirkwood, *b* 1960: *m* 1983, Duncan A. Clark, son of Michael Clark, CBE, of Braxted Park, Witham, Essex, — Olivia Grizel Kirkwood (*Hon Mrs Rupert Edwards*), *b* 1962: *m* 1990, Hon Rupert Timothy Guy Edwards, only son of Baron Crickhowell, PC (Life Baron).
Lady Fiona Catharine, *b* 1941: *m* 1969, Capt Michael Stephen Whitfield, late R Scots Drag Gds (*see* Renshaw, Bt), of PO Box 721, Marondera, Zimbabwe.

SISTER LIVING

Lady Bridget Sarah, *b* 1947: *m* 1976, Nicholas Anthony Oppenheim, of 46 Lysia St, SW6 6NG, son of Sir Duncan Morris Oppenheim, and has issue living, Christopher Duncan, *b* 1981, — Leonora Emily *b* 1977, — Zerlina Gabrielle, *b* 1979.

AUNTS LIVING (*Raised to the rank of an Earl's daughters* 1948)

Lady (Margaret) Alison, *b* 1910. *Residence* – Wych Elm, Kennington, Oxford.
Lady (Euphemia) Meredith, *b* 1915. *Residence* – 5a Mulberry Drive, Wheatley, Oxon.

DAUGHTER LIVING OF EIGHTEENTH EARL

Lady Lucy BUCHAN, *b* 1902: *m* 1928, Sir Thomas Innes of Learney, GCVO, LLD, FSA (Scot), who *d* 1971 (*see* Innes, Bt cr 1628, colls). *Residence* – The Laigh Riggs, Torphins, Aberdeenshire.

COLLATERAL BRANCH LIVING

Descendants of late James Sinclair (grandson of late Alexander Sinclair, youngest son of Hon George Sinclair, 3rd son of 4th Earl), who was cr a *Baronet* 1704.

PREDECESSORS – *Sir* William Sinclair, of Roslin, sat in the Scottish Parliament at Scone 1283-4; his great-grandson, *Sir* Henry Sinclair, was admitted to be Earl of Orkney in 1379, by Haakon VIth King of Norway, and his grandson (**1**) WILLIAM, 3rd Earl of Orkney, and Lord High Chancellor of Scotland, was cr *Earl of Caithness* (peerage of Scotland) 1455, and styled Earl of Orkney and Caithness; James III, having acquired the islands of Orkney in marriage with Margaret of Denmark, the Earl surrendered to the king the Earldom of Orkney in 1471; passing over his el son (ancestor of the Lords Sinclair), was *s* by his 2nd son (**2**) WILLIAM, 2nd Earl, slain at Flodden 1513; *s* by his son (**3**) JOHN, 3rd Earl; killed 1529 in attempting to take possession of the Orkneys, to which he asserted a right; *s* by his grandson (**4**) GEORGE, 4th Earl, who resigned his Earldom to James V, who in 1545 granted a charter thereof to John, the Earl's heir-apparent, with remainder to his heirs male and assigns, whom failing to his faither's heirs male whatever; *d* 1582; *s* by his grandson (**5**) GEORGE, 5th Earl; resigned Earldom and obtained a novodamus 1592 with remainder to his el son William (subsequently known as *Lord Berriedale*) and his heirs male and assigns whatsoever; in 1606 received charter of land forming Barony of Berriedale; *d* 1643; *s* by his great-grandson (**6**) GEORGE, 6th Earl; being heavily indebted to Sir John Campbell, 5th Bt, of Glenorchy, he assigned his estates and "Earldom of Caithness" (as held under a charter of apprizing) to that gentleman; *d* 1676, and Sir John Campbell (ante) was cr Earl of Caithness 1677, which honour he resigned 1681 (see E. Breadalbane), the apprizing and assignation carrying only the land of the Earldom, whilst the honours then passed to the rightful heir (**7**) GEORGE, 7th Earl, son of Francis (of Northfield), 2nd son of 5th Earl; *dsp* 1698; *s* by his kinsman (**8**) JOHN, 8th Earl, lineal descendant of 4th Earl; *d* 1706; *s* by his son (**9**) ALEXANDER, 9th Earl; *d* 1765; *s* by his kinsman (**10**) WILLIAM, 10th Earl, heir male of Sir John, grandson of 4th Earl; *d* 1779; *s* by his son (**11**) JOHN, 11th Earl; *d* 1789; *s* by his kinsman (**12**) *Sir* JAMES SINCLAIR (7th Bt, cr 1631, of Canisbay), 12th Earl, heir male of George, of Mey, youngest son of 4th Earl; Lord-Lieut of Caithness, a Representative Peer, and Postmaster-Gen of Scotland; *d* 1823; *s* by his son (**13**) ALEXANDER, 13th Earl; Lord-Lieut of Caithness; *d* 1855; *s* by his son (**14**) JAMES, FRS, 14th Earl, *b* 1821; Lord-Lieut and Vice-Adm of Caithness, and Lord-in-Waiting to HM Queen Victoria 1856 and 1859-66; cr *Baron Barrogill* (peerage of United Kingdom) 1866: *m* 1st, 1847, Louisa Georgiana, who *d* 1870, da of

Sir George Richard Philips, Bt; 2ndly 1872, Marie, who d 1895 (having been cr in her own right Duchess de Pomár by Pope Leo XIII in 1879), da of Don Antonio José de Mariategui, of Santa Catalina Macuriges, and widow of Gen the Count de Pomár; d 1881; s by his son **(15)** GEORGE PHILIPS ALEXANDER, 15th Earl, b 1858; Lord-Lieut of Caithness; d 1889, the title remaining dormant until 1890, when the nearest heir male of the 15th Earl was adjuged to be **(16)** JAMES AUGUSTUS (son of Lt-Col John Sutherland Sinclair, RA, a descendant of Robert Sinclair, of Durran, younger son of Sir James Sinclair, 1st Bt, of Mey), 16th Earl, b 1827: m 1855, Janet, da of Roderick Macleod, MD, of London; d 1891; s by his el son **(17)** JOHN SUTHER-LAND, 17th Earl, b 1857; d 1914; s by his brother **(18)** NORMAN MACLEOD, 18th Earl, b 1862; admitted a Solicitor 1887; a Representative Peer for Scotland 1918-29; Lieut-Col late Gordon Highlanders (TA); assumed 1911, the surname and arms of Buchan in lieu of his patronymic: m 1893, Lillian, who d 1933, da of late Higford Higford, of 23 Eaton Place, SW; d 1947; s by his nephew **(19)** (JAMES) RODERICK, CVO, CBE, DSO (son of late Rev Hon Charles Augustus Sinclair, 3rd son of 16th Earl), 19th Earl b 1906; a Representative Peer for Scotland 1950-63; Brig and Col Gordon Highlanders; Comdg Ceylon Army 1949-52; m 1st, 1933, Grizel Margaret, who d 1943, da of Sir George Miller-Cunningham, KBE, CB; 2ndly, 1946, Madeleine Gabrielle, who d 1990 (having m 3rdly, 1977, David Frederick Ewen, CBE, who d 1986), da of Herman Edward de Pury, and widow of Capt George Wareing Drewry Ormerod, RA; d 1965; s by his only son **(20)** MALCOLM IAN, 20th Earl and present peer; also Lord Berriedale.

CALDECOTE, VISCOUNT (Inskip) (Viscount UK 1939)

ROBERT ANDREW INSKIP, KBE, DSC, 2nd Viscount; b 8th Oct, 1917; s 1947; ed Eton (Fellow 1952-69), and King's Coll, Camb (MA, Fellow 1948-55); FRINA, Hon FIMechE, Hon FIEE, Hon FICE, FEng, Pres of Dean Close Sch 1960-90, a Vice-Pres of St Lawrence Coll, 1939-45 War as Lt-Cdr RNVR; DL Hants 1991; a Member of House of Laity, Church Assembly 1949-55, and of UK delegation to UN Assembly 1952; Vice-Pres of Eurospace 1961-68, Pres of Soc of British Aerospace Cos 1965-66, of AICMA 1966-68, and of Parl and Scientific Cttee 1966-69; Dir of English Elec Co 1955-69, and Dep Man Dir of British Aircraft Corpn 1960-67; Chm of EDC for Movements of Exports 1965-71, and of Export Council of Europe 1970-71; Exec Dir Delta Metal Co 1969-82 (Chm 1972), Dir Consolidated Goldfields, Ltd 1969-78, and of Lloyds Bank 1974-88, a Member of Review Board for Govt Contracts 1969-75, and of Inflation Accounting Cttee 1975-74; Dir of Legal and Gen Assurance of Soc 1976-80 (Chm 1977); Pro-Chancellor, Cranfield Inst of Technology 1976-84; Member British Rail Board 1979-85; Chm Investors in Industries Gp 1980-87; Chm Mary Rose Trust 1983-92; Dir W. S. Atkins Ltd 1985-92; KBE (1987): m 1942, Jean Hamilla, da of late Rear-Adm Hugh Dundas Hamilton, of Limes, Haddenham, Bucks, and has issue.

Arms – Per chevron azure and argent in chief two crosses pattée or and in base an eagle displayed of the first. **Crest** – Upon the battlements of a tower a grouse's leg erased proper. **Supporters** – Dexter, a talbot; sinister, a pegasus proper; each charged on the shoulder with a garb or.
Residence – Orchard Cottage, South Harting, Petersfield, Hants GU31 5NR. *Clubs* – Athenaeum Pratt's, Royal Ocean Racing, Royal Yacht Squadron.

SON LIVING

Hon PIERS JAMES HAMPDEN b 20 May 1947; ed Eton: m 1st, 1970, Susan Bridget, da of late W. P. Mellen, of Hill Farm, Gt Sampford, Essex; 2ndly, 1984, Kristine Elizabeth, da of Harvey Holbrooke-Jackson, of 12 Abbots Close, Ramsey, Cambs, and has issue living (by 2nd m), Thomas James, b 22 March 1985.

DAUGHTERS LIVING

Hon Serena Helen Christian, b 1943: m 1965 (m diss 1979), John Andrew Brodie Armit, and has issue living, Jerome Nathan, b 1971, — Vashti Imogen, b 1969.
Hon Antonia Jane Hamilla, b 1952: m 1972, Piers Rowlandson, and has issue living, Titus, b 1973.

PREDECESSORS – **(1)** Rt Hon Sir THOMAS WALKER HOBART Inskip, CBE, son of late James Inskip, of Clifton Park House, Bristol; b 1876; was Chancellor of Diocese of Truro 1920-22, Solicitor-Gen Oct 1922 to Jan 1924 and Nov 1924 to March 1928, Attorney-Gen March 1928 to June 1979, Solicitor-Gen in National Govt Sept 1931 to Jan 1932, again Attorney-Gen Jan 1932 to March 1936, Min for Co-ordination of Defence March 1936 to Jan 1939, Sec of State for Dominion Affairs Jan to Sept 1939, Lord High Chancellor Sept 1939 to May 1940, again Sec of State for Dominion Affairs (also Leader of the House of Lords) May to Oct 1940, and Lord Ch Justice of England 1940-46; MP for Central Div of Bristol 1918-29 and for Fareham Div of Hampshire 1931-9; cr *Viscount Caldecote*, of Bristol, co Gloucester (peerage of United Kingdom) 1939: m 1914, Lady Augusta Helen Elizabeth, who d 1967, da of 7th Earl of Glasgow, and widow of Charles Lindsay Orr-Ewing, MP; d 1947; s by his son **(2)** ROBERT ANDREW, 2nd Viscount and present peer.

Calder, see Baron Ritchie-Calder.

CALEDON, EARL OF (Alexander) (Earl I, 1800)

NICHOLAS JAMES ALEXANDER, 7th Earl, *b* 6 May 1955; *s* 1980; *ed* Gordonstoun; Lord Lieut co Armagh 1989: *m* 1st, 1979 (*m diss* 1985), Wendy Catherine, da of Spiro Nicholas Coumantaros, of Athens; 2ndly, 1989, Henrietta Mary Alison, elder da of John Francis Newman (*see* Newman, Bt, *cr* 1912), and has issue by 2nd *m*.

𝕬rms – Per pale argent and sable, a chevron, and in base a crescent counterchanged; on a canton azure, a harp or stringed argent. 𝕮rest – A dexter arm embowed in armour, the hand holding a sword proper. 𝕾upporters – *Dexter*, a mermaid with a mirror in her right hand proper; *sinister*, an elephant argent. *Seat* – Caledon Castle, co Tyrone.

By sea and by land

SON LIVING *(By 2nd marriage)*

FREDERICK JAMES (*Viscount Alexander*), *b* 15 Oct 1990.

DAUGHTER LIVING *(By 2nd marriage)*

Lady Leonora Jane, *b* 1993.

SISTER LIVING

Lady (Elizabeth) Jane, *b* 1962; resumed maiden name by deed poll 1987: *m* 1st, 1981 (*m diss* 1987), Rory F. A. Peck, a war cameraman, who was *k* in the Moscow riots 1993, son of Julian Peck, of Prehen House, co Londonderry; 2ndly, 1990, Richard Francis Andrew Dobbs, eldest son of Richard Arthur Frederick Dobbs, of Castle Dobbs, co Antrim, and has issue living (by 1st *m*), James Julian, *b* 1982, — Alexander Nicolas de Graevenitz, *b* 1984, — (by 2nd *m*) Louisa Valla Joan, *b* 1992. *Residence* – The Farm, Castle Dobbs, Carrickfergus, co Antrim.

HALF-SISTER LIVING

Lady Tana Marie, *b* 1945: *m* 1973, Paul Everard Justus Focke, QC, of 7 Cheyne Walk, SW3, and has issue living, Diana Natasha, *b* 1974, — Victoria Justine *b* 1976.

WIDOW LIVING OF SON OF FOURTH EARL

Hon Ada Kate, da of late Hon Richard Eustace Bellew (*see* B Bellew), and widow of Charles Barry Domvile: *m* 1937, as his 2nd wife, Lt-Col Hon Herbrand Charles Alexander, DSO, who *d* 1965. *Residence* – Jenkinstown House, Portarlington, co Leix.

WIDOW LIVING OF SIXTH EARL

MARIE ELISABETH BURTON (*Elisabeth, Countess of Caledon*), da of Maj Richard Burton Allen, and formerly wife of Maj Hon Iain Maxwell Erskine (later 2nd Baron Erskine of Rerrick): *m* 1964, as his 3rd wife, the 6th Earl, who *d* 1980.

COLLATERAL BRANCHES LIVING

Issue of late Harold Rupert Leofric George Alexander (*Earl Alexander of Tunis*), KG, GCB, OM, GCMG, CSI, DSO, MC, PC 3rd son of 4th Earl, *b* 1891, *d* 1969 (see that title).

Issue of late Col Hon William Sigismund Patrick Alexander, DSO, yst son of 4th Earl, *b* 1895, *d* 1972: *m* 1934, Jane Hermione, who *d* 1967, da of late Cdr Bernard Buxton, DSO (Buxton, Bt, colls):—
Alastair Patrick Lindsay (2665 Laguna St, San Francisco, California 94123, USA), *b* 1935; *ed* Eton; late Lt IG: *m* 1961, Evelyn, da of Massimimo Forte, of 28 Via San Sebastiano, Rome, and has issue living, Simone Eugenia, *b* 1962. —— Desmond Charles Bernard, *b* 1938; *ed* Eton, Univ of British Columbia (B Com), and Lancaster Univ (MA). —— Annabella Elizabeth Hero, *b* 1943.

Granddaughter of late Col Hon Walter Philip Alexander, 2nd son of 3rd Earl:—
Issue of late Capt Philip Sylvester Alexander, 8th Hus, *b* 1883, *d* 1953: *m* 1926, Violet, who *d* 1979, da of late H. Hendrick Aylmer, of Kerdiffstown, co Kildare:—
Patricia Margaret (*Lady Gray*), *b* 1929: *m* 1959, 22nd Lord Gray. *Residence* – Airds Bay House, Taynuilt, Argyll.

Granddaughters of Lt-Col Hon Charles Alexander, 3rd son of 3rd Earl:—
Issue of late Capt Conn Alexander, *b* 1883, *d* 1970: *m* 1st, 1906, Gladys Constance, who *d* 1944, da of late Thomas Wrigley Grimshaw, CB; 2ndly 1944, Doris Minnie, who *d* 1983, da of late Robert Pacey, of Hove:—
(By 1st *m*) Mona (Ayesha Castle, Killiney, co Dublin), *b* 1909: *m* 1939, Col Richard Michael Aylmer, who *d* 1975, and has issue living, Justin Michael, *b* 1940: *ed* Wellington: *m* 1981, Bridget Frances Georgina, elder da of Rev Canon George Alfred Salter, of St Luke's Rectory, Cork, and Lakka House, Castletownshend, co Cork, and has issue living, William George Algernon *b* 1984, Christopher Fenton Alexander *b* 1987, — Dennis Fenton (Valley House, Enniskerry, co Wicklow), *b* 1942; *ed* Wellington; Dir Lyons & Co (Ireland) Ltd: *m* 1976, Dorothy Margaret, da of Thomas Anthony Fleming, and has issue living, Richard Thomas *b* 1978, Elizabeth Mona *b* 1982. —— Marjorie (The Manor House, Rathlin I, co Antrim), *b* 1912: *m* 1931, Brig Richard Francis O'Donnell Gage, CBE, MC, who *d* 1973, and has issue living, Ezekiel Conn, *b* 1933; *ed* Wellington; Lt-Col RA: *m* 1965, Frances Elizabeth, elder da of Maj Frederick George Bolam, and has issue living, Matthew James George *b* 1967, Alexander Richard *b* 1972, Victoria Louise *b* 1968, — Patrick Richard, *b* 1938; *ed* Wellington; Cdr RN: *m* 1962, Annette Daphne, only da of late John Charles William Staveley, of Gloynes House, Yealmpton, Devon, and has issue living, Rory James *b* 1965, Nicola Jane *b* 1964, Lucinda Georgina *b* 1970.

PREDECESSORS – (1) JAMES Alexander (of whose family the Alexanders of Milford, co Carlow, are the senior branch), having filled several important offices in India, was cr *Baron Caledon*, of Caledon, co Tyrone (peerage of Ireland) 1790, *Viscount Caledon* (peerage of Ireland) 1797, and *Earl of Caledon* (peerage of Ireland) 1800; *d* 1802; *s* by his son (2) DU PRE, KP, 2nd Earl; first Gov of Cape of Good Hope; a Representative Peer; *d* 1839; *s* by his son (3) JAMES DU PRE, 3rd Earl, *b* 1812; a Representative Peer, Capt Coldstream Gds, and Col of Tyrone Militia: *m* 1845, Lady Jane Frederica Harriot Mary Grimston, VA, who *d* 1888, 4th da of 1st Earl of Verulam; *d* 1855; *s* by his son (4) JAMES, KP, 4th Earl, *b* 1846; a Representative Peer for Ireland: *m* 1884, Lady Elizabeth Toler, who *d* 1939, da of 3rd Earl of Norbury; *d* 1898; *s* by his elder son (5) ERIK JAMES DESMOND, 5th Earl; *b* 1885, *d* 1968; *s* by his nephew (6) DENIS JAMES (son of Lt-Col Hon Herbrand Charles Alexander, DSO, who *d* 1965), 6th Earl, *b* 1920; Maj Irish Gds and Ulster Defence Regt: *m* 1st, 1943 (*m diss* 1948),

Ghislaine, only da of Cornelius Willem Dresselhuys, of The Hague; 2ndly, 1952, Baroness Anne Louise, who *d* 1963, only child of late Baron Nicholas Werner Alexander de Graevenitz; 3rdly, 1964, Marie Elisabeth Burton, da of late Maj Richard Burton Allen, and formerly wife of Maj Hon Iain Maxwell Erskine (*see* B Erskine of Rerrick); *d* 1980; *s* by his only son **(7)**NICHOLAS JAMES, 7th Earl and present peer; also Viscount Caledon, and Baron Caledon.

CALLAGHAN OF CARDIFF, BARON (Callaghan) (Life Baron 1987)

(LEONARD) JAMES CALLAGHAN, KG, PC, son of late James Callaghan, Ch Petty Officer, of Portsmouth; *b* 27 March 1912; *ed* Portsmouth Sec (Northern) Sch; Visiting Fellow Nuffield Coll, Oxford 1959-67, Hon Life Fellow 1967, Hon Fellow Univ Coll Cardiff 1978, Portsmouth Univ 1981, and Swansea Univ Coll 1993, Hon LLD Wales Univ 1976, Sardar Patel Univ, India 1978, Birmingham Univ 1981, Meisei Univ, Japan, 1984, and Sussex Univ 1987; Parl Sec to Min of Transport 1947-50, Parl and Financial Sec to Admiralty 1950-51, Chancellor of the Exchequer 1964-67, and Home Office 1967-70, Sec of State for Foreign and Commonwealth Affairs 1974-76, Min of Overseas Dvpt 1975-76, Prime Minister and First Lord of the Treasury 1976-79; Leader of Labour Party 1976-80, Leader of Opposition 1979-80; Treasurer Labour Party 1967-76, Vice-Chm 1973, Chm 1974; Father of House of Commons 1983-87; Pres Univ Coll Swansea since 1986; Hon Bencher Inner Temple 1976, Hon Life Fell, Cardiff Inst of Higher Education 1991, Hon Freeman City of Cardiff 1974, City of Sheffield 1979, City of Portsmouth 1991, and City of Swansea 1993; Grand Cross 1st class Order of Merit of Federal Republic of Germany 1979; author of A House Divided: the dilemma of Northern Ireland (1973), Time and Chance (Memoirs) 1987; MP (*Lab*) S Cardiff 1945-50, SE Cardiff 1950-83, and Cardiff South and Penarth 1983-87; *cr* PC 1964, KG 1987, and *Baron Callaghan of Cardiff*, of the City of Cardiff, co S Glamorgan (Life Baron) 1987: *m* 1938, Audrey Elizabeth, da of Frank Moulton, of Loose, Kent, and has issue.

Arms – Quarterly vert and azure in the former a portcullis or in the latter a lymphad with an anchor at its prow and masted or the sail set argent and pennants flying gules overall a fess or to the sinister thereof a grassy mount with a hurst of oak trees and issuing therefrom passant to the dexter a wolf proper. **Crest** – A seadragon sejant gules langued and scaled or its tail of the last and scaled gules the dorsal fin also gules about the neck a mural crown or masoned gules and supporting to the front with the fin of the dexter foreleg a portcullis gold. **Motto** – Malo laborare quam languere.
Residences – Upper Clayhill Farm, Ringmer, E Sussex; 5 Temple West Mews, West Sq, SE11 4TJ.

SON LIVING

Hon Michael James, *b* 1945; *ed* Dulwich, Univ of Wales Cardiff, and Manchester Business Sch: *m* 1968, Jennifer Mary Morris, and has issue living, Joseph Edwin James, *b* 1981, — Kate Elizabeth, *b* 1970, — Sarah Jane, *b* 1972. *Residence* – 18 Brentwood Rd, Ingrave, Brentwood, Essex CM13 3QZ.

DAUGHTERS LIVING

Hon Margaret Ann (*Baroness Jay of Paddington*), *b* 1939; *cr* Baroness Jay of Paddington (Life Baroness) 1992: *m* 1961 (*m diss* 1986), Peter Jay, son of Rt Hon Douglas Patrick Thomas Jay (later Baron Jay, Life Baron), and has issue (*see* Bs Jay of Paddington). *Residence* – 44 Blomfield Rd, W9 2PF.
Hon Julia Elizabeth, *b* 1942: *m* 1967, Ian Hamilton Hubbard, and has issue living, Tobin James Hamilton, *b* 1970, — Tom Ian, *b* 1975, — Sam Jonathan, *b* 1976, — Joanna Jane, *b* 1971. *Residence* – Nettleslack Farm, Lowick Green, Ulveston, Cumbria.

Calne and Calstone, Viscount; grandson of Marquess of Lansdowne.

CALTHORPE, BARON (Gough-Calthorpe) (Baron GB 1796, Bt GB, 1728)

(Title pronounced "Callthorpe,") (Name pronounced "Goff-Callthorpe")

The same way by different Steps

PETER WALDO SOMERSET GOUGH-CALTHORPE, 10th Baron, and 11th Baronet; *b* 13 July 1927; *s* 1945; *ed* Stowe; formerly Lieut Welsh Gds: *m* 1st, 1956 (*m diss* 1971), Saranne Frances, who *d* 1984, only da of James Harold Alexander, of co Dublin; 2ndly, 1979, Elizabeth Sibyl, da of James Young, of Bandol, Cranley Rd, Guildford, Surrey.

Arms – Quarterly: 1st and 4th checky, or and azure a fesse ermine, *Calthorpe*, 2nd and 3rd gules, on a fesse argent, between three boars' heads couped or, a lion passant azure, *Gough*. Crests – 1st, a boar's head couped at the neck azure, *Calthorpe*; 2nd, a boar's head couped argent, pierced through the cheek with a broken spear, *Gough*. Supporters – Two wild men, wreathed about the temples and loins with oak, and each holding in his exterior hand a club erect or. *Address* – c/o Isle of Man Bank, Ltd, 2 Atholl St, Douglas, Isle of Man.

PREDECESSORS – (1) *Sir* Henry Gough, MP for Totnes 1732, and for Bramber; cr a *Baronet* 1728; *d* 1774; *s* by his son (2) *Sir* Henry, 2nd Bt; in 1788 inherited the Elvetham estates of his uncle, Sir Henry Calthorpe, KB, and assumed by R licence additional surname of Calthorpe; sat as MP for Bramber 1774-90; cr *Baron Calthorpe*, of Calthorpe, co Norfolk (peerage of Great Britain) 1796; *d* 1798; *s* by his eldest son (3) CHARLES, 2nd Baron, *d* 1807; *s* by his brother (4) GEORGE, 3rd Baron; *d* 1851; *s* by his brother (5) FREDERICK, 4th Baron; *b* 1790; assumed for himself in 1845 the name of Gough only: *m* 1823, Lady Charlotte Sophia Somerset, who *d* 1865, elder da of 6th Duke of Beaufort; *d* 1868; *s* by hs eldest son (6) FREDERICK HENRY WILLIAM, 5th Baron, *b* 1826; MP for E Worcestershire (*L*) 1859-68; *d* unm 1893; *s* by his brother (7) AUGUSTUS CHOLMONDELEY, 6th Baron, *b* 1829: *m* 1869, Maud Augusta Louisa, who *d* 1925, yst da of late Col Hon Octavius Duncombe: *d* 1910: *s* by his brother (8) SOMERSET JOHN, KCB, 7th Baron, *b* 1831; Lt-Gen in the Army; *m* 1862, Eliza Maria, who *d* 1919, only child of Capt Frederick Chamier, RN, and widow of Capt Frederick Crewe, *d* 1912; *s* by his elder son (9) SOMERSET FREDERICK, 8th Baron; *b* 1862: *m* 1891, Mary, who *d* 1940, da of late Ogden Hoffman Burrows, of Newport, Rhode Island, USA; *d* 1940; *s* by his grandson (10) RONALD ARTHUR SOMERSET (son of late Hon Frederick Somerset Gough-Calthorpe, only son of 8th Baron), 9th Baron, *b* 1924; Flying Officer RAF; *d* on active service 1945; *s* by his brother (11) PETER WALDO SOMERSET, 10th Baron and present peer.

CALVERLEY, BARON (Muff) (Baron UK 1945)

Labour conquers all

CHARLES RODNEY MUFF, 3rd Baron; *b* 2 Oct 1946; *s* 1971; *ed* Moravian Sch for Boys, Fulneck, Pudsey; Member of W Yorks Police (formerly City of Bradford Police): *m* 1972 Barbara Ann, da of Jonathan Brown, and has issue.

Arms – Azure, within two barrulets wavy argent between in chief a rose of the second barbed and seeded proper, and in base a fleece or, three ducal coronets of the last. Crest – In front of two miners' picks in saltire a miner's safety lamp all proper. Supporters – On either side a calf proper. *Residence* – 110 Buttershaw Lane, Wibsey, Bradford BD6 2DA.

SONS LIVING

Hon JONATHAN EDWARD, *b* 16 April 1975.
Hon Andrew Raymond, *b* 1978.

BROTHER LIVING

Hon Peter Raymond (Oakhurst, 377 Shadwell Lane, Leeds LS17 8AH), *b* 1953.

WIDOW LIVING OF SECOND BARON

MARY (*Mary, Baroness Calverley*), da of Arthur Farrar, of Halifax: *m* 1940, the 2nd Baron, who *d* 1971.

PREDECESSORS – (1) GEORGE MUFF, son of late George Muff, miner, of Bradford; *b* 1877; sat as MP for E Div of Kingston-upon-Hull (*Lab*) 1929-31, and 1935-45; cr *Baron Calverley*, of City of Bradford, W Riding of Yorkshire (peerage of United Kingdom) 1945: *m* 1909, Ellen Eliza, who *d* 1965, elder da of late Charles W Orford, of Bath; *d* 1955; *s* by his only son (2) GEORGE RAYMOND ORFORD, 2nd Baron *b* 1914: *m* 1940, Mary, da of Arthur Farrar, of Halifax; *d* 1971; *s* by his elder son (3) CHARLES RODNEY, 3rd Baron and present peer.

CAMBRIDGE, MARQUESSATE OF (Extinct 1981)

DAUGHTER LIVING OF SECOND MARQUESS

Lady Mary Ilona Margaret, *b* 1924; *m* 1950, Peter Whitley, only son of Sir Norman Henry Pownall Whitley, MC, and has issue living, Charles Francis Peter, *b* 1961: *m* 1991, Diana M., elder da of Mrs Diana Hewitt, of Hurtmore, Godalming, Surrey, — Sarah Elizabeth, *b* 1954: *m* 1982, Timothy J. F. Felton, and has issue living, Emily Ilona *b* 1985, Chlöe Amelia *b* 1987. *Residence* – Leighland House, Roadwater, Watchet, Som TA23 0RP.

CAMDEN, MARQUESS (Pratt) (Marquess UK 1812)

The judgement of my peers, or the law of the land

DAVID GEORGE EDWARD HENRY PRATT, 6th Marquess; *b* 13 Aug 1930; *s* 1983; *ed* Eton; late 2nd Lieut Scots Gds: *m* 1961 (*m diss* 1985), Virginia Ann, only da of Francis Harry Hume Finlaison, of Arklow Cottage, Windsor, Berks, and has issue.

Arms – Quarterly: 1st and 4th sable, on a fesse between three elephants' heads erased argent as many mullets of the field, *Pratt*; 2nd and 3rd sable, a chevron between three spears' heads argent, the points embrued, *Jeffreys*. **Crests** – 1st, an elephant's head erased argent; 2nd, a dragon's head erased vert,holding in the mouth a sinister hand couped at the wrist gules, and about the neck a gold chain, and pendant therefrom a portcullis or. **Supporters** – *Dexter*, a griffin sable; beak and claws gules, gorged with a plain collar argent, charged with three mullets sable; *sinister*, a lion or, collared as the dexter. *Residence* – Wherwell House, Andover, Hants.

SON LIVING

JAMES WILLIAM JOHN (*Earl of Brecknock*), *b* 11 Dec 1965; *ed* Eton.

DAUGHTER LIVING

Lady Samantha Carolina, *b* 1964.

HALF-BROTHER LIVING

Lord Michael John Henry, *b* 1946; *ed* Eton, and Balliol Coll, Oxford.

Residence – 16 Coulson St, SW3.

SISTER LIVING

Lady Mary Clementine, *b* 1921; is a DStJ: *m* 1st, 1940, Fl-Lt Hon (Herbert) Oswald Berry, who *d* 1952 (*see* V Kemsley); 2ndly, 1953, (Shafto) Gerald Strachan Pawle, who *d* 1991. *Residence* – Trehiven House, Madron, Penzance, Cornwall.

UNCLE LIVING (*Son of Fourth Marquess*)

Lord Roderic Arthur Nevill, *b* 1915; *ed* Eton, and Trin Coll, Camb (BA); Maj late Life Gds; 1939-45 War in Middle East, Italy, and Germany (wounded): *m* 1945, Ursula Eva, who *d* 1993, elder da of late Capt Hon Valentine Maurice Wyndham-Quin, RN (*see* E Dunraven), and has issue living, Adrian John Charles, *b* 1952; *ed* Eton; late Capt Blues and Royals; Man Dir British Equestrian Insurance Brokers since 1985, Memb of Lloyds since 1977: *m* 1984, Leanora R., da of Maj Peter Murray Lee, — Zara Elizabeth, *b* 1955: *m* 1988, John Weir Johnstone, of The Old Rectory, Lidgate, Newmarket, Suffolk, son of late Andrew Johnstone, of Bonshaw Mains, Kirtlebridge, Lockerbie, Dumfriesshire, and has issue living, Harry Andrew *b* 1989. *Residence* – The Garden House, Dewhurst, Wadhurst, E Sussex TN5 6QB.

WIDOW LIVING OF FIFTH MARQUESS

ROSEMARY CECIL (*Rosemary, Marchioness Camden*); artist; da of late Brig Hanbury Pawle, CBE, TD, DL, and formerly wife of (1) Gp-Capt Peter Wooldridge Townsend, CVO, DSO, DFC, and (2) John de Laszlo (*d* 1990): *m* 3rdly, 1978, as his 3rd wife, the 5th Marquess, who *d* 1983.

PREDECESSORS – (1) Sir CHARLES Pratt, Knt, MP for Downton, an eminent lawyer, was successively Attorney-Gen and Ch Justice of the Common Pleas; *cr* *Baron Camden*, of Camden Place, co Kent (peerage of Great Britain), 1765; appointed Lord High Chancellor 1766, and Lord Pres of the Council 1784; *cr* *Viscount Bayham* and *Earl Camden* (peerage of Great Britain 1786): *d* 1794; *s* by his son (2) JOHN JEFFREYS, KG, 2nd Earl; successively MP, a Lord of the Treasury, a Lord of the Admiralty, Viceroy of Ireland, and Chancellor of Univ of Camb; *cr* *Earl of Brecknock* and *Marquess Camden* (peerage of United Kingdom) 1812; *d* 1840; *s* by his son (3) GEORGE CHARLES, KG, 2nd Marquess; summoned to House of Lords 1835 as Baron Camden; *d* 1866; *s* by his son (4) JOHN CHARLES, 3rd Marquess; *b* 1840; MP for Brecon 1866: *m* 1866, Lady Clementine Augusta Spencer-Churchill, who *d* 1886, da of 6th Duke of Marlborough; *d* 1872; *s* by his son (5) JOHN CHARLES, GCVO, TD, 4th Marquess, *b* 1872; late Maj W Kent Yeo and Hon Col 58th (Kent) Brig RA (TA); Lord-Lieut for Kent 1905-43; *m* 1898, Lady Joan Marion Nevill, CBE, who *d* 1952, da of 3rd Marquess of Abergavenny; *d* 1943; *s* by his son (6) JOHN CHARLES HENRY, 5th Marquess, *b* 1899; 1939-45 War Comdg 45th Battery (which he raised), Maj Reserve of Officers Scots Gds Hon Col Light Anti-Aircraft Regt RA; a DL and JP for Kent; a member of Fedn Internationale des Automobiles, Patron of Coll of Automobile and Aeronautical Training, Chelsea, a Vice-Pres and Member of Cttee of Management of RNLI, Vice-Pres of Marine Motoring Assocn, Chm of Segrave Trophy Awarding Cttee, etc; a Gold Staff Officer at Coronation of King George VI: *m* 1st, 1920 (*m diss* 1941), Marjorie Minna, DBE, who *d* 1989, only child of Col Atherton Edward Jenkins, of Wherwell Priory, Andover; 2ndly, 1942, Averil, who *d* 1977, formerly wife of John Prescott Hallett, and elder da of late Col Henry Sidney John Streatfield, DSO, TD (E Lichfield); 3rdly, 1978, Rosemary Cecil, artist, formerly wife of (1) Gp-Capt Peter Wooldridge Townsend, CVO, DSO, DSC, and (2) John de Laszlo, and da of late Brig Hanbury Pawle, CBE, TD; *d* 1983; *s* by his elder son (7) DAVID GEORGE EDWARD HENRY, 6th Marquess and present peer; also Earl Camden, Earl of Brecknock, Viscount Bayham, and Baron Camden.

CAMERON OF BALHOUSIE, BARONY OF (Cameron) (Extinct 1985)

SON LIVING OF LIFE BARON

Hon Neil, *b* 1949; *ed* Dean Close Sch, London Univ (External, BA), and Bath Univ (Dip Ed).

DAUGHTER LIVING OF LIFE BARON

Hon Fiona Jane, *b* 1950; *ed* Birmingham Univ (MA).

WIDOW LIVING OF LIFE BARON

PATRICIA LOUISE (*Baroness Cameron of Balhousie*), da of late Maj Edward Asprey, RE: *m* 1947, Marshal of the RAF Baron Cameron of Balhousie, KT, GCB, CBE, DSO, DFC, AE (Life Baron), who *d* 1985.
Address – King's College, Strand, WC2.

CAMERON OF LOCHBROOM, BARON (Cameron) (Life Baron 1984)

KENNETH JOHN CAMERON, PC, son of Hon Lord (John) Cameron, KT, DSC, LLD (Scottish Lord of Session), of 28 Moray Place, Edinburgh, by his 1st wife, Eileen Dorothea, who *d* 1943, da of late Harry Milburn Burrell; *b* 11 June 1931; *ed* The Edinburgh Acad, Corpus Christi Coll, Oxford (MA) and Edinburgh Univ (LLB); admitted Faculty of Advocates 1958; QC (Scot) 1972; Hon Bencher Lincoln's Inn; Hon Fell Corpus Christi Coll, Oxford, Hon Fell RIAS, Fell RSE; Standing Junior to Dept of Transport 1964-71, to DoE 1971-72; Chm Industrial Tribunals in Scotland 1966-81; Advocate Depute 1981-84, Chm Pensions Appeal Tribunal (Scotland) 1975 (Pres 1976-84), Chm Cttee for Investigation in Scotland of Agricultural Marketing Schemes 1980-84, Lord Advocate 1984-89, since when Senator of Coll of Justice; served RN 1950-52 (comm'd RNVR 1951); *cr* PC 1984, and *Baron Cameron of Lochbroom*, of Lochbroom, in the District of Ross and Cromarty (Life Baron) 1984: *m* 1964, Jean Pamela, da of late Col Granville Murray, and has issue.

Arms – Gules, three bars Or, overall two flanches Ermine, at the honour point, also overall, a fleur de lys Sable. **Crest** – A kittiwake alighting wings expanded Proper. **Motto** – Et Regi Et Legi Servire.
Residence – 10 Belford Terr, Edinburgh EH4 3DQ. *Clubs* – Scottish Arts, New (Edinburgh).

DAUGHTERS LIVING

Hon Victoria Christian, *b* 1965: *m* 1991, James Annand Fraser, son of Sir Charles Annand Fraser, KCVO, DL, WS, of Shepherd House, Inveresk, Midlothian, and has issue living, Tabitha Christian Annand, *b* 1993.
Hon Camilla Louise, *b* 1967.

CAMOYS, BARON (Stonor) (Baron E 1383)

RALPH THOMAS CAMPION GEORGE SHERMAN STONOR, 7th Baron; *b* 16 April 1940; *s* 1976; *ed* Eton, and Balliol Coll, Oxford; a Lord in Waiting to HM since 1992; DL Oxon; Dep Chm Barclays de Zoete Wedd Holdings Ltd, and Sothebys Holdings Ltd, Dir National Provident Inst, formerly Member House of Lords EEC Select Cttee, Royal Commn on Historical MSS; formerly Chm Robert Jackson & Co Ltd, Man Dir Barclays Merchant Bank Limited, Chief Exec Barclays de Zoete Wedd Ltd, and Dir Barclays Bank plc; Consultor to the Patrimony of the Holy See; Order of Gorkha Dakshina Bahu, 1st Class (Nepal): *m* 1966, Elisabeth Mary Hyde, da of late Sir William Stephen Hyde Parker, Bt (cr 1681), and has issue.

Arms – 1st and 4th azure, two bars dancettée or, a chief argent, *Stonor;* 2nd and 3rd, or, on a chief gules, three bezants, *Camoys.* **Crest** – A falcon standing on a rock and regarding a projection of that rock argent, all semee of hurts, bezants, torteaux and pommeis, the rock tufted with grass vert and the falcon holding in his beak a ruby proper. **Supporters** – *Dexter*, a lion rampant or; *sinister*, a lion rampant sable.
Seat – Stonor Park, Henley-on-Thames, Oxon.

SON LIVING

Hon (RALPH) WILLIAM ROBERT THOMAS, *b* 10 Sept 1974; *ed* Eton.

DAUGHTERS LIVING

Hon Alina Mary, *b* 1967; *ed* St Mary's Convent, Ascot, and Balliol Coll, Oxford; ACA: *m* 1994, Simon Derek Barrowcliff, ARICS, of 4 Dunworth Mews, W11 1KE, yst son of Dr Derek Barrowcliff, and has issue living, Thomas Simon Marmaduke, *b* 1994.
Hon Emily Mary Julia, *b* 1969; *ed* St Mary's Convent, Ascot, and Durham Univ.
Hon Sophia Ulla, *b* 1971: *m* 1993, Hon James Alastair Stourton, yr son of 26th Baron Mowbray. *Residence* – 21 Moreton Place, SW1V 2NL.

SISTERS LIVING

Hon Julia Maria Cristina Mildred STONOR (90 Burnthwaite Rd, Fulham, SW6), *b* 1939; *ed* St Mary's Convent, Ascot, and Reading Technical Coll; resumed surname of Stonor by deed poll 1978: *m* 1963 (*m diss* 1977 and annulled 1978), Donald Robin Slomnicki Saunders, and has issue living, Alexander William Joseph STONOR SAUNDERS, *b* 1964; *ed* Worth, and St Andrew's Univ, — Frances Hélène Jeanne STONOR SAUNDERS *b* 1966; *ed* St Mary's Convent, Ascot, and St Anne's Coll, Oxford.
Hon Georgina Mary Hope (112 West St, Henley-on-Thames, Oxon RG9 2EA) *b* 1941; OstJ.
Hon Harriet Pauline Sophia, *b* 1943: *m* 1965, (Jonathan) Julian Cotterell, and has issue living, Edmund Julian Francis, *b* 1967: *m* 1993, Angelica I. L., eldest da of Humphrey Stone, of Lower Lawn House, Tisbury, Wilts, — Rupert Sherman John, *b* 1969, — Alice Ellinor Mary, *b* 1966: *m* 1992, Thomas Bernard Constable Maxwell (*see* L Herries, colls). *Residence* – Steeple Manor, Steeple, nr Wareham, Dorset.

AUNTS LIVING (*Daughters of 5th Baron*)

Hon (Pamela Sophia) Nadine, *b* 1917: *m* 1941, Lt-Col Charles Donald Leslie Pepys, King's Own Yorkshire LI (*see* E Cottenham, colls). *Residence* – 30 Lyefield Court, Kidmore End Rd, Emmer Green, nr Reading, Berks.
Hon (Mildred Sophia) Noreen, *b* 1922: *m* 1941, John R. Drexel, who *d* 1965, and has issue living, John Nicholas (IV), *b* 1945: *m* 1st, 1969 (*m diss* 1976), Pamela, da of Bernardo Rionda Braga; 2ndly, 1984, M. Jacqueline, da of John Jacob Astor, — Pamela Sandra Noreen (3685 Upton St NW, Washington DC 20008, USA), *b* 1942: *m* 1966 (*m diss* 1977), Bradford Hastings Walker, and has issue living, Andrew *b* 1968, James Drexel *b* 1971, — Noreen Elizabeth Mildred, *b* 1961. *Residence* – Stonor Lodge, Bellevue Av, Newport, Rhode Island 02840, USA.

COLLATERAL BRANCHES LIVING

Grandson of late Hon Edward Maurice Stonor, 2nd son of 4th Baron:—
Issue of late Betty Joyce Stonor, *b* 1910, *d* 1982: *m* 1938, Benjamin Rudolf Bonas, who *d* 1965:—
Benjamin Reginald Francis Stonor (16 Hereford Sq, SW7 4TS), *b* 1940; *ed* Marlborough, and Worcester Coll, Oxford: *m* 1967 (*m diss* 1994), Jacqueline A. J., eldest da of Jacques de Brabant, of Torcy, Seine-et-Marne, France, and has issue living, Charles Benjamin, *b* 1969, — Oliver Henry, *b* 1971.

Granddaughters of late Oswald Francis Gerard Stonor, CMG (infra):—
Issue of late Joan Florence Mary Stonor, *b* 1907, *d* 1956: *m* 1st, 1927 (*m diss* 1948), John Colburn Bennett, CMG, CBE, who *d* 1969; 2ndly, 1948, John Keith Macara, who *d* 19— (Macara, Bt):—
(By 1st *m*) Jill Mary (48 Peel St, W8 7PD), *b* 1929: *m* 1954 (*m diss* 1967), David Noel Templer Scott, who *d* 1989, and has issue living, John Andrew Templer (49 Telford Av, Streatham Hill, SW2 4XL), *b* 1960: *m* 1984, Catharine Frances, da of Cdr William John Macnamara Faulkner, RN (*see* de Trafford, Bt, colls), and has issue living, Rory David Templer *b* 1993, Alice Emily Cecilia *b* 1989, — Virginia Jane, *b* 1957: *m* 1985, Charles Leofric Thomas Temple-Richards, of 45 Mallinson Rd, SW11 1BW (*see* Temple, Bt, colls, 1990 Edn), and has issue living, Cornelia Florence *b* 1989, Juliana Virginia, *b* 1991. —— Veronica Anne (61a St Augustine's Rd, NW1 9RP), *b* 1942: *m* 1964 (*m diss* 1981), Michael Edward Rudman, and has issue living, Amanda Joan, *b* 1967, — Katherine Rose, *b* 1970.

Grandchildren of late Charles Joseph Stonor, only son of late Charles Henry Stonor, brother of 3rd Baron:—
Issue of late Oswald Francis Gerard Stonor, CMG, *b* 1872; *d* 1940: *m* 1906, Florence Mary Josephine, who *d* 1956, da of late Edward Talbot Wolseley (Wolseley, Bt, cr 1628, colls):—
Evelyn Mary, *b* 1911; *m* 1935 (*m diss* 1954), Com Denis Hugh Bryan Barrett, DSC, RN, CB (*see* B Kensington, 1935 Edn), and has issue living, Michael Patrick Denis, *b* 1937: *m* 1951 (*m diss* 19—), Kytia Buchs, — Bryan Nicholas, *b* 1940; Cdr RN: *m* 1964 (*m diss* 19—), Sally Lois, da of Arthur Maxwell Hankin, CMG, and has issue living, Claire Fiona *b* 1966, Georgina Mary *b* 1968.
Issue of late Charles Henry Joseph Stonor, *b* 1874, *d* 1930: *m* 1912, Hylda, who *d* 1968, da of Henry Lloyd-Carter, formerly of Bryn Seiont, Caernarvon:—
Henry Anthony, *b* 1926; *ed* Downside, and Shrewsbury; late Lt R Welch Fus. —— Beatrice Maude, *b* 1913: *m* 1949, Ralph Aldersey, who *d* 1971, and has issue living, William Ralph *b* 1950; *ed* Oswestry Sch. —— Pamela Mary, *b* 1915; OstJ Serving Sister, Brit Red Cross Soc (despatches). —— †Sheila Mary, *b* 1916: *m* 1946, Brig Ernest James Cholmeley Harrison, OBE, R Sigs, son of late Sir Charlton Scott Cholmeley Harrison, CIE, *d* 1994, leaving issue , James Hugh Cholmeley, *b* 1947, — Robert Mark Cholmeley, *b* 1950, — Sally Ann Monamie, *b* 1951. *Residence* – Afton Cottage, Lower Rd, Bemerton, Salisbury, Wilts. —— Anne, *b* 1929: *m* 1955, Peter B. Sawdy, of 18 Elm Park Rd, SW3 6VP, and has issue living, Caroline Ann, *b* 1957, — Susan Angela Lumley, *b* 1962.

Grandchildren of late Francis Cyril Stonor, 7th son of late Charles Joseph Stonor (ante):—
Issue of late Bernard Francis Stonor, *b* 1909; *d* 1982: *m* 1935, Elsie Graham:—
Mortimer (Bernie), *b* 1941: *m* 19—, Erika, da of —, and has issue living, Jamus, *b* 19—, — Brendon, *b* 19—, — Emily, *b* 19. —— Pride Cynthia (abandoned christian name of Anne), *b* 1935: *m* 1st, 1957, C. Killa, of Perth, W Australia; 2ndly, 1969, Douglas G. Maclean (PO Box 92, Margaret River, W Australia 6285), and has issue living (by 1st *m*), Deborah Anne, *b* 1958: *m* 1981, Bruce Wishart Smith, of Bressay, Shetland Islands, and has issue living, Jody Kimberley *b* 1985. —— Juliana, *b* 1938: *m* 1st, 1960 (*m diss* 1978), Michael Carter; 2ndly, 1981, Colin Keith Pember, of 18 Tropicana Way, Safety Bay, W Australia 6169, and has issue living (by 1st *m*), David Michael (14 Chadwin Place, Padbury, W Australia 6025), *b* 1961, — Brian John STONOR, *b* 1964; assumed surname of Stonor by deed poll 1986 in lieu of his patronymic: *m* 1989, Leah, only da of John Gadenne, — Jennifer Dawn, *b* 1962: *m* 1981, Allan Burke, of 3 Coral St, Scarborough, W Australia, and has issue living, Zara Sheree *b* 1982, Karleah Marie *b* 1985, — Tania Gaye, *b* 1971. —— Virginia, *b* 1946: *m* 19—, Desmond —, and has issue living, Stephen, *b* 19—, — Raelene, *b* 19—.

PREDECESSORS – (1) *Sir* THOMAS de Camoys, KG, an eminent warrior, commanded the left wing of the English army at Agincourt 1415; summoned to Parliament as a Baron of England 1383-1421; *d* 1421; *s* by his grandson (2) HUGH, 2nd Baron; *d* 1426, when the title went into abeyance between his sisters Margaret and Alianora, and it remained abeyant until 1839, when it was terminated in favour of the descendant of Margaret (3) THOMAS Stonor, 3rd Baron; sat as MP for Oxford 1832-3; was a Lord-in-Waiting to HM Queen Victoria 1846-52, 1853-8, 1859-66, and 1868-74; *d* 18 Jan 1881, and was *s* by his grandson (4) FRANCIS ROBERT, 4th Baron (son of late Hon Francis Stonor, 2nd son of 3rd Baron); *b* 1856; Lord-in-Waiting to HM Queen Victoria 1886 and 1892-5; *m* 1881, Jessie Philippa, who *d* 1928, 2nd da of late Robert Russell Carew, of Carpenders. Herts; *d* 1897; *s* by his elder son (5) RALPH FRANCIS JULIAN, 5th Baron; *b* 1884; *m* 1911, Mildred, who *d* 1961, da of late William Watts Sherman, of New York; *d* 1968; *s* by his only son (6) (RALPH ROBERT WATTS) SHERMAN, 6th Baron; *b* 1913: *m* 1938, Mary Jeanne, who *d* 1987, da of late Capt Herbert Marmaduke Joseph Stourton, OBE (B Mowbray colls); *d* 1976; *s* by his elder son (7) RALPH THOMAS CAMPION GEORGE SHERMAN, 7th Baron, and present peer.

Campbell, Baron see Baron Stratheden and Campbell.

CAMPBELL OF ALLOWAY, BARON (Campbell) (Life Baron 1981)

ALAN ROBERTSON CAMPBELL, QC, son of late John Kenneth Campbell; *b* 24th May 1917; *ed* Aldenham, and Trinity Hall, Camb. (MA); Bar Inner Temple 1939, QC 1965, Bencher 1972; Recorder of Crown Court 1976-89; Chm Legal Research Cttee of Soc of Conservative Lawyers 1968-80; Member of Management Cttee UK Assocn for European Law since 1975; commissioned Lieut RA (SR) 1939, served in France and Belgium (PoW Colditz 1940-45); *cr Baron Campbell of Alloway*, of Ayr, in the District of Kyle and Carrick (Life Baron) 1981: *m* 1957, Vivien da of late Comd A. H. de Kantzow, DSO, RN.
Chambers - 2 King's Bench Walk, Temple, EC4 7DE. *Clubs* – Carlton, Pratt's, Beefsteak.

CAMPBELL OF CROY, BARON (Campbell) (Life Baron 1974)

GORDON THOMAS CALTHROP CAMPBELL, MC, PC, son of late Maj-Gen James Alexander Campbell, DSO; *b* 8 June 1921; *ed* Wellington; Maj (ret) RA; 1939-45 War in NW Europe, OC 320 Field Bty, 15th (Scottish) Div 1942-45 (MC and Bar, wounded and disabled); Vice Lieut for Nairn since 1988; Diplo Ser 1946-57; UK Mission at UN New York 1949-52; Private Sec to Sec of Cabinet 1954-56, First Sec, Vienna 1956-57, Govt Whip 1961-63, Under-Sec of State for Scotland 1963-64, and Sec of State for Scotland 1970-74; Consultant to Chevron Cos 1975-94, Chm Stoic Insurance Services 1979-93, Dir Alliance Building Soc since 1983, and Alliance and Leicester Building Soc 1985-92; Chm for Scotland, Internat Year of Disabled People 1981; Pres Anglo-Austrian Soc since 1991; MP for Moray and Nairn (*C*) 1959-74; *cr* PC 1970, and *Baron Campbell of Croy*, of Croy, co Nairn (Life Baron) 1974; *m* 1949, Nicola Elizabeth Gina, da of late Capt Geoffrey Spencer Madan (*see* Noble, Bt, *cr* 1902, 1985 Edn), and has issue.

Arms – Gyronny of eight or and sable, overall on a fess ermine two pheons points upwards gules. **Crest** – Between two sprays of red roses barbed and leaved proper and tied in base with a riband or, a lyre sable. **Supporters** – Dexter an osprey and sinister a curlew both proper. *Residence* – Holme Rose, Cawdor, Nairn.

SONS LIVING

Hon Colin Ian Calthrop, *b* 1950; *ed* Eton (King's Scholar), and Trin Coll, Camb (Scholar).
Hon Alastair James Calthrop, *b* 1952; *ed* Eton, and Wadham Coll, Oxford (MA); commn'd Queen's Own Highlanders 1973, Lieut-Col 1991; a Member of Queen's Body Guard for Scotland (Royal Company of Archers); FRGS: *m* 1993, Primrose Felicia, elder da of William Henry Tugwell Palmer (*see* E Longford), of Nun Monkton, York, and has issue living, Ferdinand James Marc, *b* 1994. *Residence* – Holme Rose, Cawdor, Nairn.

DAUGHTER LIVING

Hon Christina Marjorie, *b* 1953: *m* 1980, Mark Michael Clarfelt, of 8 Vicarage Gdns, W8, son of Jack Clarfelt, of Linhay Meads, Timsbury, Romsey, Hants, and has issue living, Max, *b* 1986, — Alice Nicola Irene, *b* 1982, — Tessa, *b* 1984, — Harriet, *b* 1990.

CAMPBELL OF ESKAN, BARON (Campbell) (Life Baron 1966)

Do and hope

JOHN (JOCK) MIDDLETON CAMPBELL, son of late Colin Algernon Campbell, of Colgrain, Dunbartonshire, and Underriver House, Sevenoaks (Barrington, Bt, colls); *b* 8 Aug 1912; *ed* Eton, and Exeter Coll, Oxford (Hon Fellow 1973); D Univ, Open 1973; Chm Gvning Body of Imp Coll of Tropical Agriculture 1947-60; Pres of Booker McConnell Ltd 1967-80 (Chm 1952-66); Chm of Milton Keynes Development Corpn since 1967-83, and of Commonwealth Sugar Exporters' Assocn 1950-84; a Dir of Commonwealth Development Corpn, and a Trustee of Runnymede Trust and Chequers Trust since 1964; Chm of Statesman & Nat Publishing Co Ltd 1964-77 and New Towns Assocn 1975-77; Dir of London Weekend Television Ltd 1967-74 (Dep Chm 1969-73); Pres W India Cttee 1957-77; a Member of Community Relations Comm 1968-77 (a Dep Chm 1968-71); *cr* Knt 1957, and *Baron Campbell of Eskan*, of Camis Eskan, co Dunbarton (Life Baron) 1966: *m* 1st, 1938 (*m diss* 1948), Barbara Noel, da of late Leslie Arden Roffey; 2ndly, 1948, Phyllis Jacqueline Gilmour (Taylor), who *d* 1983, da of late Henry Boyd, CBE, and has issue by 1st *m*.

Arms – Gyronny of eight pieces or and sable, and in chief a mullet counterchanged of the field, all within a bordure embattled vert, charged with eight buckles of the first. **Crest** – A boar's head, erect and erased or. **Supporters** – Two jaguars proper, gorged of chaplets of bog-myrtle also proper. *Residence* – Lawers, Crocker End, Nettlebed, nr Henley-on-Thames, Oxon. *Club* – All England Lawn Tennis.

SONS LIVING *(By 1st marriage)*

Hon John Charles Middleton, *b* 1940; *ed* Eton: *m* 1965, Patricia Ann, elder da of late Tom Webster, and has issue, two das and one adopted da. *Residence* – 39 Gondar Gardens, NW6.
Hon Peter Mark Middleton, *b* 1946; *ed* Eton: *m* 1972 (*m diss* 1989), Anne Susan, da of John E. Cuthbert, of Enfield, Middx, and has issue, two sons and one da. *Residence* – 148 Bennerley Rd, SW11 6DY.

DAUGHTERS LIVING *(By 1st marriage)*

Hon Rosalind Leonora Middleton, *b* 1942. *Residence* – 13 Alma Green, Stoke Row, Henley-on-Thames, Oxon.
Hon Agneta Joanna Middleton, *b* 1944: *m* 1966 (*m diss* 1685), Jonathan Geoffrey William Agnew (*see* Agnew, Bt, colls, *cr* 1895). *Residence* – 4 Brookville Rd, SW6 7BJ.
Lord Campbell of Eskan is descended from Colin Campbell, 1st of Colgrain. 1st Baron Colgrain was elder son of George William Campbell, 6th son of Colin Campbell, 1st of Colgrain.

Campden, Viscount; son of Earl of Gainsborough.

CAMROSE, VISCOUNT (Berry) (Viscount UK 1941, Bt UK 1921)

Live with courage

(JOHN) SEYMOUR BERRY, TD, 2nd Viscount and 2nd Baronet; *b* 12 July 1909; *s* 1954; *ed* Eton, and Ch Ch, Oxford; Dep Chm of the *Daily Telegraph and Morning Post* (ret 1987); a Younger Brother of Trinity House; late Maj City of London Yeo, RA (TA); 1939-45 War in N Africa and Italy (despatches); MP for Hitchin Div of Herts (*C*) 1941-45: *m* 1986, Princess Joan Aly Khan, eldest da of 3rd Baron Churston, and formerly wife of (i) late W/Cdr (Thomas) Loel Evelyn Bulkeley Guinness, OBE (*see* B Ardilaun, ext, 1944 Edn), and (ii) late Prince Aly Khan.

Arms – Argent, three bars gules, over all a pile, ermine. **Crest** – A griffin sejant reguardant sable, collared or. **Supporters** – On either side a wolf proper gorged with a collar or, pendent therefrom an escutcheon sable, charged with two pens in saltire argent. *Seat* – Hackwood Park, near Basingstoke, Hants. *Town Residence* – 8a Hobart Pl, SW1W 0HH. *Clubs* – White's, Buck's, Beefsteak, Royal Yacht Squadron, MCC.

BROTHER LIVING

Hon (WILLIAM) MICHAEL, MBE, TD (*Baron Hartwell*), *b* 18 May 1911; *cr* Baron Hartwell (Life Peerage) 1968 (see that title).

SISTERS LIVING

Hon Mary Cecilia, *b* 1906: *m* 1930, Maj Ronald Guthrie McNair Scott, and has issue living Thomas Michael (Highfields House, Augerez, St Peter, Jersey), *b* 1935: *m* 1959, Susannah, who *d* 1993, da of Frederick Leslie Hodges, and has issue living, Simon Guthrie McNair *b* 1960: *m* 1988 (*m diss* 1991), Hon Camilla Birgitta Davidson, 3rd da of 2nd Viscount Davidson, Sarah *b* 1966: *m* 1990, Richard Byrd

Levett Haszard, of Milford Hall, Stafford ST17 0UL, son of Richard Haszard, of Milford Hall, Stafford (and has issue living, William Richard Levett b 1994, Francesca Rosamund Cecilia b 1991), — Nigel Guthrie, b 1945: m 1968, Anna Margaret, only da of late William Reginald Colquhoun, TD, of Cecily Hill House, Cirencester (see Greenwell, Bt cr 1906), and has issue living, Robert William b 1970, Alastair Nigel b 1972, David Ronald b 1973, Benjamin Guthrie b 1976, — Gillian Mary, b 1931: m 1951, Charles Ivor Mervyn Williams, MC, who d 1989, and has issue living, Oliver Mervyn b 1953, Richard Charles b 1955, (Samuel) Thomas Morgan b 1959: m 1983, his cousin, Mrs (Isabel) Tara Mary Gilroy, eldest da of late William Perine Macauley (infra) (and has issue, see infra), Lucinda Mary b 1956: m 1982, Philip Carspecken (and has issue living, Gabriel b 1983), — Alison Linda, b 1936: m 1963, Laurence Kelly, of 44 Ladbroke Grove, W11, yr son of late Sir David Victor Kelly, GCMG, MC, and has issue living, Nicolas Tara b 1967, Rosanna Mary b 1964, Rachel Sophia b 1965: m 1993, (Edward) Sebastian Grigg (see By Altrincham), — Valerie Susan b 1939: m 1964, Thomas Frank Dermot Pakenham, elder son of 7th Earl of Longford. Residence – Huish House, Old Basing, nr Basingstoke, Hants.

Hon Molly Patricia (Hon Lady Cotterell), b 1915: m 1st, 1936, Capt Roger Charles George Chetwode, who d 1940, only son of 1st Baron Chetwode; 2ndly, 1942 (m diss 1948), 1st Baron Sherwood; 3rdly, 1958, as his 2nd wife, Sir Richard Charles Geers Cotterell, 5th Bt, CBE, TD, who d 1978. Residence – Flat 1, 4 Eaton Place, SW1.

Hon Diana Phyllis, b 1924: m 1948, William Perine Macauley, who d 1990, and has issue living, William Francis b 1953: m 1992, Nicola Jane, elder da of Eric D. Thompson, of Shamley Green, Surrey, and has isue living, Nico (a son) b 1993, — Mark Justin, b 1956, — Rupert Timothy, b 1962: m 1989, Julie M., only da of Berkeley Baker, and has issue living, Alastair William Derby b 1991, Hamish Edward Dominic b 1992, — (Isabel) Tara Mary, b 1949: m 1st, 1972 (m diss 19—), Desmond Gilroy; 2ndly, 1983, her cousin, (Samuel) Thomas Morgan Williams (6 Dewhurst Road, W14 0EJ) (ante), and has issue living (by 1st m), Caspar Alexander b 1973, (by 2nd m) Francis Edward Morgan b 1988, Alice Rose b 1983, — Virginia Margaret Diana (Hon Mrs Alastair Hoyer Millar), b 1950: m 1974, Hon Alastair James Harold Hoyer Millar (see B Inchyra), — Mary Rosalind (Burway House, Ludlow, Shropshire), b (twin) 1953: m 1978, Dominic Sasse, poet, who was k in the Kathmandu air disaster 1992, and has issue living, Joshua Seymour b 1987, Lydia Nevis b 1982. Residence – Ballyward House, Blessington, co Wicklow.

WIDOWS LIVING OF SONS OF FIRST VISCOUNT

Susan Jenifer, da of William Arthur Fearnley-Whittingstall, TD, QC, of The Old Manor House, Melbourn, Cambs: m 1st, 1955, Hon Rodney Mathias Berry, TD, who d 1963; 2ndly, 1964 (m diss 1978), Henry Lambert Middleton (see Middleton, Bt, colls), and has an adopted da (by 1st m), Emma Louise, b 1961: m 1984, Jeremy N. Oakley, of Millbrook House, Burghclere, Hants, son of Capt Neville Oakley, of Golf Drive, Camberley, Surrey, and has issue living, Joshua b 1986, Georgia Alice b 1988. Residence – 7 Wedderburn House, Lower Sloane St, SW1W 8B2.

(Janet Frances) Denise, elder da of late Maj (John) Leslie Rowan-Thomson, of Sayers, Great Somerford, Wilts: m 1946, Col Hon Julian Berry, OBE, JP, DL, who d 1988, and has issue (see colls infra).

COLLATERAL BRANCH LIVING

Issue of late Col Hon Julian Berry, OBE, JP, DL, yst son of 1st Viscount, b 1920, d 1988: m 1946, (Janet Frances) Denise (The Old Rectory, Tunworth, nr Basinstoke, Hants), elder da of late Maj (John) Leslie Rowan-Thomson, of Sayers, Great Somerford, Wilts:—
Simon Ewert (Winslade Farm House, Winslade, Basingstoke, Hants RG25 2NE), b 1955; ed Eton: m 1981, Martha Davidson, yst da of Louis Davidson Sage, of New York City, and has issue living, Lucy Elizabeth b 1985, — Tara Edwina, b 1988, — Alexa Eloise, b 1992 . —— Caroline Denise, b 1948: m 1969, Jeremy James Wagg (see Horlick, Bt, 1969 Edn), and has issue living, Julian James, b 1972, — Katharine Denise, b 1974. Residence – 18 Eaton Mews South, Eccleston St, SW1.

PREDECESSOR – (1) WILLIAM EWERT BERRY, 2nd son of late Alderman John Mathias Berry, JP of Gwaelodygarth, Merthyr Tydfil; b 1879; a journalist and Newspaper Proprietor, Editor-in-Ch of Daily Telegraph and Morning Post, and Chm of Amalgamated Press Ltd; founder of Advertising world 1901, Editor-in-Ch Sunday Times 1915-36, Chm of Financial Times Ltd 1919-45, and of Allied Newspapers Ltd 1924-36: cr a Baronet 1921, Baron Camrose, of Long Cross, Surrey (peerage of United Kingdom) 1929, and Viscount Camrose, of Hackwood Park, co, Southampton 1941: m 1905, Mary Agnes, who d 1962, elder da of late Thomas Corns, of 2 Bolton St Piccadilly, W1; d 1954; s by his eldest son (2) (JOHN) SEYMOUR, 2nd Viscount and present peer; also Baron Camrose.

CARADON, BARONY OF (Foot) (Extinct 1990)

SONS LIVING OF LIFE BARON

Hon Paul Mackintosh (14 Canfield Gdns, NW6), b 1937; ed Univ Coll, Oxford; is a Journalist: m 1st, 1962 (m diss 1970), Monica, da of Dr Robert P. Beckinsale, of Oxford; 2ndly, 1971, Roseanne, da of Robert Harvey, and has issue living (by 1st m), John Mackintosh, b 1964, — Matthew Isaac, b 1966, — (by 2nd m) Tom, b 1979.

Hon Oliver Isaac, b 1947; ed Leighton Park Sch, RAC Cirencester, and Goddard Coll, Vermont, USA: m 1967 (m diss 1975), Nancy Foot, of New York City, USA, and has issue living, Jesse Isaac, b 1973, — Mary Rachel, b 1971.

Hon Benjamin Arthur, MBE, b 1949; ed Leighton Park Sch, and Univ Coll, Swansea; MBE (Civil) 1992: m 1981, Sally Jane, only da of late Maj Mark Francis Swain Rudkin, MC, and has issue living, Alexander Mark Isaac, b 1986, — Joanna Dingle, b 1983.

DAUGHTER LIVING OF LIFE BARON

Hon Sarah Dingle, b 1939: m 1961, Maj Timothy Nicholas Percival Winter Burbury, The Blues & Royals, and has issue living, Charles Alexander Winter, b 1964, — Camilla Jane Winter, b 1962: m 1988, Mark Lindfield, son of late Dr Robert Lindfield, of Pimlico, SW1.

CARBERY, BARON (Evans-Freke) (Baron I 1715, Bt I 1768)

Liberty

PETER RALFE HARRINGTON EVANS-FREKE, 11th Baron, and 7th Baronet; *b* 20 March 1920; *s* 1970; *ed* Downside; MICE; a Member of London Stock Exchange 1955-67; 1939-45 War as Capt RE in India and Burma: *m* 1941, Joyzelle Mary, only da of late Herbert Binnie, of Sydney, NSW, and has issue.

𝕬rms – Quarterly: 1st and 4th sable, two bars, and in chief three mullets or, *Freke*; 2nd and 3rd argent, three boars' heads couped sable, *Evans*. 𝕮rests – 1st, a bull's head couped at the back sable, collared and chained or, *Freke*; 2nd, a demi-lion rampant reguardant or, holding in the paws a boar's head sable, *Evans*. 𝕾upporters – Two lions reguardant or, ducally crowned azure. *Residence* – 2 Hayes Court, Sunnyside, Wimbledon SW19 4SH.

SONS LIVING

Hon MICHAEL PETER, *b* 11 Oct 1942; *ed* Downside, Ch Ch Oxford (MA), and Univ of Strathclyde (MBA): *m* 1967, Claudia Janet Elizabeth, only da of Capt Percy Lionel Cecil Gurney, of Little Chart, Penshurst, and has issue living, Dominic Ralfe Cecil, *b* 1969, — Richenda Clare, *b* 1971, — Isabel Lucy, *b* 1973, — Anna-Louise, *b* 1979.

Hon John Anthony (Lynturk Home Farm, Alford, Aberdeenshire AB33 8DU), *b* 1949; *ed* Downside, and RAC Cirencester; FRICS, formerly Agent to the Duke of Northumberland: *m* 1972, Veronica Jane, yst da of Maj Eric Williams, of House of Lynturk, Alford, Aberdeenshire, and has issue living, James Eric, *b* 1976, — Charles William Anthony, *b* 1981, — Flora Mary, *b* 1979.

Hon Stephen Ralfe (The Corner House, Norfolk, Conn 06058, USA; Casa Niños, 1320 Marlborough Rd, Hillsborough, Calif 94010, USA), *b* 1952; *ed* Downside, and Trin Coll, Camb (BA); Pres PaineWebber Devpt Corpn, etc (USA): *m* 1990, Valerie BEATTIE JOHNSON, eldest da of Russell Beattie, of Stonington, Conn, USA, and has issue living, Yorick Peter, *b* 1992, — Roland Charles Goodheart, *b* 1993.

DAUGHTERS LIVING

Hon Maura Clare, *b* 1946; formerly Admin Assist Roy Coll of Music: *m* 1966, Richard Henry William Fanshawe, of Rafters, Waldron, Heathfield, E Sussex TN21 0QY, and has issue (*see* E Lindsey and Abingdon, colls).

Hon Angela Mary, *b* 1954: *m* 1975, Martin David Tomlins, of 96 Wormholt Rd, W12, and has issue living, Alexander Peter David, *b* 1978, — William John Anthony, *b* 1981.

HALF SISTER LIVING

Anne Mary Elizabeth, *b* 1933: *m* 1957, Ross Young, of Easters, Sandhills, Cattistock, Dorchester, Dorset, DT2 0HQ, and has issue living, Paul Ralfe, *b* 1958, — Clare Elizabeth, *b* 1960: *m* 1986, Stephen Delevante, and has issue living, Andrew Edward *b* 1988, Patrick Ross *b* 1991, — Diana Mary, *b* 1967.

DAUGHTERS LIVING OF TENTH BARON

Hon Fabienne José, *b* 1916: *m* 1st, 1936 (*m diss* 1946), Com John Dudley Dowse-Finnemore, RN, who *d* 1971, having assumed by R licence 1938, the additional surname and arms of Finnemore; 2ndly, 1947, Philip Claridge, of Cloonagh, Monkstown, co Cork.

Juanita Virginia Sistare CARBERRY (does not use courtesy title), *b* 1925. *Residence* – Flat 5, Brunel House, 105 Cheyne Walk, SW10 0DF.

COLLATERAL BRANCHES LIVING

Issue of late Lt-Col Hon Percy Cecil Evans-Freke, 2nd son of 8th Baron, *b* 1871, *ka* 1915: *m* 1895, Eva, who *d* 1942, da of late Charles Kirwan, of Dalgan Park, co Mayo:—

Maida Cecil, *b* 1897: *m* 1927, Capt Edmund Michael Gordon Loeventhorpe Boyle, RN, who *d* 1982 (*see* E Cork, colls). *Residence* – Queen's Lodge, St Cross Rd, Winchester, Hants.

(Male line in special remainder to the Barony)

Grandchildren of late Eyre Frederick FitzGeorge Evans, eldest son of Maj George Thomas Evans, 3rd son of Eyre Evans (*b* 1773), only son of Eyre Evans, of Miltown Castle, co Cork, eldest son of Thomas Evans, MP, yr brother of 1st Baron:—

Issue of late Percy Evans, *b* 1871, *d* 1959: *m* 1916, Ethel Margaret, who *d* 1951, da of T. Dickson, formerly of Wanganui, NZ:—

Margaret Lees (113 Ingestre St, Wanganui, NZ), *b* 1925: *m* 1947 (*m diss* 1991), Clifford Roy Dewe.

Issue of late Savage Corry Evans, *b* 1878, *d* 1968: *m* 1st, 1902 (*m diss* 1920), Jane Ann, da of H. Healey, of Naseby, NZ; 2ndly, 1927, Alicia Madeleine Isabel Gifford, only da of late Charles Gifford Moore, of Oamaru, NZ; 3rdly, 19—, Lilian Amelia (20 Phrosso Rd, W Worthing, Sussex), da of Joseph Fair, of Headford, co Galway:—

(By 1st *m*) Trevor George Corry, OBE, TD (9 St Swithin's Close, Sherborne, Dorset), *b* 1910; *ed* abroad, and RAC Cirencester; JP, FRICS, formerly Chief Agent to Duke of Norfolk; 1939-45 War as Lt-Col Royal Sussex Regt; OBE (Mil) 1946: *m* 1937, Sara Gwendolyn, da of R. C. Drummond, of Masterton, NZ, and has issue living, Michael George Corry (10 Moor Lane, Clevedon, Avon BS8 4LJ), *b* 1938; *ed* Rugby, and RAC Cirencester, — Stephen Telford Eyre (c/o Border Farm, Closworth, Yeovil, Som BA22 9SZ), *b* 1939; *ed* Rugby, and RAC Cirencester: *m* 1970, Susan Biron, da of Michael Pallister Young, of Bishopsbourne, Kent, — Patrick Heugh Robert Eyre (Border Farm, Closworth, Yeovil, Som BA22 9SZ), *b* 1944; *ed* Nautical Coll, Pangbourne: *m* 1970, Jennifer Robin, da of late Capt Brian Granville White, RM, of Chaldon, Surrey, and has issue living, James Richard Eyre *b* 1975, Caroline Nicola Corry *b* 1974. —— Kathleen Ann, *b* 1906: *m* 1943, Capt Edward Copus, late RASC, of Spring Cottage, Harnett St, Sandwich, Kent CT13 9ES.

Grandchildren of late Rev Eric Evans (infra):—

Issue of late Rev Phillip Eyre Evans, *b* 1910, *d* 1980: *m* 1935, Florence Anne (15 Harrison Av, Burwood, Vic, Australia), da of Richard S. U. Reeves, of Melbourne:—

Rodger Eyre (13 Templemore Drive, Templestowe, Vic 3106, Australia), *b* 1937: *m* 1962, Noreen Lorraine, da of late James Alexander Cook, of Pascoe Vale South, Vic, and has issue living, Stephen Rodger Eyre, *b* 1970, — Robyn Anne, *b* 1963: *m* 1988, Rodney David Johnson, of 119 Glenvale Rd, Ringwood North, Vic, Australia, — Melinda Joy, *b* 1967: *m* 1993, Peter John McMullen, of 30 Glenvale Rd, N Victoria, Australia. —— Wendy Jillian, *b* 1940: *m* 1962, Dr Gilbert Wilson Turnbull, of

51 Harrison Av, Burwood, Vic 3125, Australia, and has issue living, Leeanne Jane, *b* 1963: *m* 1988, Andrew Graham Edwin Cooke, and has issue living, Benjamin Andrew *b* 1990, Elizabeth Anne *b* 1992, — Melissa Frances, *b* 1965: *m* 1991, Rodney Peter Endall, — Penelope Jillian, *b* 1967: *m* 1989, Timothy James Joyce, and has issue living, David George Gilbert *b* 1992, — Rosemary Ferelith, *b* 1969: *m* 1993, John Gerard Cincotta.

Grandchildren of late Eyre Frederick FitzGeorge Evans (ante):—
Issue of late Rev Eric Evans, *b* 1882, *d* 1970: *m* 1910, Dora Handforth, who *d* 1980, of Onerahi, Auckland, NZ:—
Lewellyn Handforth (62 Kernot St, Spotswood, Vic 3015, Australia), *b* 1913: *m* 1st, 1940, Ivy Edith, who *d* 1949, da of William Elliot, of Melbourne; 2ndly, 1951, Una Jessie, who *d* 1979, da of late Charles A. Drew, of Melbourne, and has issue living (by 1st *m*), Rev Peter Handforth (34 Cuba St, Petone, Wellington, NZ), *b* 1941: *m* 1967, Merlyne Leslie, da of Henry Graeme Chambers, of 41a Kirkbrae, 749 Mt Dandanong Rd, Kilsythe, Vic, and has issue living, Yona Leslie *b* 1968: *m* 1990, Michael Heyward, Megan Joan *b* 1970, — Corry Margrett, *b* 1942: *m* 1964, Peter Owen Skilbeck, of Lot 27 Juliet Crescent, Healesville, Vic 3777, Australia, and has issue living, Finlay Grant *b* 1969, Bryn Andrew *b* 1976, Trudy Anne *b* 1970: *m* 1992, Mark Edmondson, — Jean Rebecca, *b* 1949: *m* 1972, Bruce David Glover, of 6 Finlay Court, Lesmurdie 6076, W Australia, and has issue living, Katherine Grace *b* 1976, Leonie Joy *b* 1977. —— Raymond Austin (42 Jopling St, N Ryde, NSW 2113, Australia), *b* 1915: *m* 1958, Lucy Margaret, da of late Walter George Blomfield, of Killara, NSW, and has issue living, Bruce Raymond Blomfield, *b* 1962, — Kathryn Margaret, *b* 1959: *m* 1989, Murray Gerrard Wilson, of 57 Blue's Point Rd, McMahon's Point, Sydney, NSW 2060, and has issue living, Timothy Oliver *b* 1989, Sophia Kathryn *b* 1991. —— Denison Anthony (1 Gardiner Rd, Hawthorn, Vic 3122, Australia), *b* 1925: *m* 1962, Janette Relleen, da of Brian William Peacocke, of Hove, Sussex, and has issue living, Charles Anthony, *b* 1963: *m* 1989, Jane Spiers, — John Andrew, *b* 1966, — Sarah Louise, *b* 1965: *m* 1988, Mark Anderson. —— Rhoda Caroline, *b* 1916: *m* 1945, Joseph Emerson Gibson, of 1 Joyce St, Nunawading, Vic 3131, Australia, and has issue living, David Warwick (RMB 464, Smeaton, Vic 3364), *b* 1947: *m* 1st, 1969 (*m diss* ca 1984), Miriam Felicia, da of Rev Philip Neilson Simmons, of Box Hill, Vic; 2ndly, 1991, Ivy Virginia, da of William Gordon Lockhart, of Ballarat, Vic, and has issue living (by 1st *m*), Timothy James *b* 1970, Kathryn Ruth *b* 1972, Bronwyn Fiona *b* 1975, — Janet Katherine (1/10 Hotham St, Mont Albert, Vic 3127), *b* 1951.
Issue of late Thomas Charles Evans, *b* 1890, *d* 1960: *m* 1st, 1919, Elsa Phyllis Heckler, who *d* 1925, of Mangamahoe, NZ; 2ndly, 1925, Elsie Edith Smith, who *d* 1964, of Hawke's Bay, NZ:—
(By 1st *m*) Francis Eyre Ogilvie, *b* 1919: *m* 1942, Marjorie Ahradsen, and has issue living, David James Ogilvie, *b* 1953: *m* 1977, Helen Anne Cowie, and has issue living, Jeremy David Ogilvie *b* 1980, Gabrielle Helen *b* 1978, Miriam Elizabeth *b* 1982, Michaela Frances *b* 1987, — Christopher Paul Ogilvie, *b* 1947: *m* 1969, Dr James Robert Crush, of 1 Sheriff Place, Hillcrest, Hamilton, NZ, and has issue living, Alexandra Frances Hope *b* 1981, Stephanie Elizabeth Helen *b* 1985, — Elizabeth Frances, *b* 1948, *d* 1952. —— Thomas Corry Ogilvie (Forest Downs, RD2, Masterton, NZ), *b* 1921: *m* 1951, Marian Jean McIndoe, and has issue living, James Peter McIndoe, *b* 1958, — Corry Rhys Walter, *b* 1962, — Elsa Corrine *b* 1952: *m* 1973, Ian Vincent Morgan, of 129 Apollo Parade, Palmerston North, NZ, and has issue living, Craig Ian *b* 1973, Blair Evan *b* 1981, Deborah Corrine *b* 1974, — Marilyn Brenda, *b* 1953: *m* 1979, John Frederick David Peach, and has issue living, Isaac Corry John Enavold *b* 1984, Julia Nina Eileen *b* 1979, Olivia Hope Marion *b* 1980, Fleur Amy Charlotte *b* 1982, Genevieve Angelicia Marilyn *b* 1989, — Helen Jean, *b* 1956. —— William Phillip Ogilvie (Linden Downs, Rangitumau, Masterton, NZ), *b* 1924: *m* 1950, Fay St Clair Rawlins, and has issue, Lloyd Phillip, *b* 1955, — Stephen William, *b* 1958, *d* 1982, — Susan Phyllis, *b* 1952: *m* 1979, Graeme Edmond Millow, and has issue living, Belinda Jane, *b* 1982, — Hannah Susan, *b* 1987, — (By 2nd *m*) Ashley Ogilvie, *b* 1926: *m* 1950, Ruth Martin Napier, and has issue living, Neil Martin, *b* 1951, — Robert Denis, *b* 1954, — Philip Leslie, *b* 1958, — Allan Ashley, *b* 1960, — Bruce Raymond, *b* 1962. —— Lees Ogilvie, *b* 1932: *m* 1954, Rae Irene Anne Croudis, and has issue living, Laurence Thomas, *b* 1958, — Suzanne Mary, *b* 1955, — Cynthia Anne, *b* 1957, — Kathleen Pauline, *b* 1962, — Helen Lucy, *b* 1964, — Patricia Frances, *b* 1966. —— Olwyn Ogilvie, *b* 1927: *m* 1952, Eion John Davies, and has issue living, Garth Raynsley, *b* 1953, — Mark Thomas, *b* 1955, — Tracey Elizabeth, *b* 1958. —— José Ogilvie, *b* 1929. —— Fabienne Ogilvie, *b* (twin) 1932: *m* 1953, Neale Thomas Grenfell, and has issue living, Peter Andrew, *b* 1954, — Frank James, *b* 1956.

Grandchildren of late Eyre Waller D'Arcy-Evans (infra):—
Issue of late Eyre Henry D'Arcy-Evans, *b* 1892, *d* 1957: *m* 1923, Mary Eleanor, who *d* 1959, da of John Garmony, of Killylea, co Armagh:—
Trevor Wallace (Belgrove Farm, RMB 806, Jennapullin, W Australia 6401), *b* 1926: *m* 1952, Shirley June Lovatt, and has issue living, Andrew Thomas, *b* 1956, — Clive Hugh, *b* 1958, — Alan William, *b* 1959: *m* 1981, Gaye-Ann Michelle French, and has issue living, Simon *b* 1982, Belinda *b* 1984, Shona *b* 1987, — Christopher Michael, *b* 1960: *m* 1987, Marie Louise Caroline Schreurs, and has issue living, Luke *b* 1987, Brad *b* 1989. —— Joy, *b* 1924: *m* 1949, Dr Eric Brian Jeffcoat Smith, of 4 Kinnane Place, Attadale, W Australia 6156, and has issue living, Nicola, *b* 1953, — Deirdre, *b* 1955; BSc: *m* 1st, 1982, Leighton Brunn; 2ndly, 1988, Peter Baldock, of Margaret River, W Australia, — Vanessa, *b* 1960. —— Ethne Elizabeth, *b* 1931: *m* 1964, Ronald James Manton who *d* 1993, of 5 Deane St, Mosman Park, W Australia 6012.

Grandchildren of late John Wallace D'Arcy-Evans (infra):—
Issue of late John D'Arcy-Evans, *b* 19—, *d* 1990: *m* 19—, Christina, da of:—
Martin J. (1 MacLeod Rd, Applecross, Perth, W Australia 6015), *b* 19—; MB BS, MRCOG: *m* 19—, Lindy, da of, and has issue living, Elaine, *b* 19—. —— Anne, *b* 19—; MAPsS: *m* 19—, Rev John Patton.

Grandchildren of late John Wallace D'Arcy-Evans (infra):—
Issue of late John Wallace D'Arcy-Evans, *b* 1894, *d* 19—: *m* 19—, Anne Kaye Fairfield (57 Osborne Rd, E Fremantle, W Australia 6160):—
Eyre James (139 Moreing Rd, Attadale, W Australia 6156), *b* 19—: *m* 19—, da of, and has issue living, one son. —— Trevor Hugh, *b* 19—: *m* 1965, Priscilla Pang, and has issue living, Yergyeni Trevor, *b* 1965, — Mark Siegfried, *b* 1966. —— Ida, *b* 19—. —— A da, *b* 19—.

Grandson of late Capt George William Wallace D'Arcy-Evans (infra):—
Issue of late Cdr Hardress Waller Eyre D'Arcy-Evans, RN, *b* 1898, *d* 1962: *m* 1934, Mary Frideswide Leslie (39 Stanley Rd, Claremont, Cape, S Africa), da of late W. W. Jessopp Sharpe:—
John Hardress Waller (8 De Villiers Av, Rosebank 7700, S Africa), *b* 1938: *m* 1965, Janet Barbara, da of Francis Spencer Ware, and has issue living, Andrew Hardress Eyre, *b* 1966, — Stephen Elystan Waller, *b* 1973, — Jennifer Frances, *b* 1968. —— Wendy Nina Mary, *b* 1940: *m* 1970, Capt M. B. Fowkes, of Riverside, Lismore Av, Tokai, Cape, S Africa, and has issue living, Jeremy Matthew Michael, *b* 1973, — Sarah Isobel Mary, *b* 1970.

Grandsons of late Eyre Waller D'Arcy-Evans, son of late John D'Arcy-Evans (*b* 1817), 2nd son of James D'Arcy-Evans, of Knockaderry, co Limerick, 2nd son of Rev Thomas Waller Evans, LLD, Rector of Dunmanway, co Cork, 2nd son of Thomas Evans, MP (ante):—
Issue of late Capt George William D'Arcy-Evans, *b* 1898, *d* 1967: *m* 1923, Flora Eleanor Thorpe Edwardes:—
Peter (1 Interman Rd, Boronia 3155, Victoria, Australia), *b* 1924: *m* 1953, Isabel Blair, and has had issue, †Paul William, *b* 1955: *m* 1982, Catherine Kennedy, and *d* 1989, leaving issue, Simon *b* 1985, Kylie *b* 1987, — John, *b* 1959: *m* 1983, Margaret Borger, and has issue living, Nicholas John *b* 1990, Tara Kate *b* 1987, — Ian, *b* 1961: *m* 1987, Judith Hayes, and has issue living, Brendan *b* 1986, Tegen *b* 1988, Cassandra Jane *b* 1990, — Clare Louise, *b* 1966: *m* 1990, Frederick Grey Kohlman. —— John Eyre, *b* 1932: *m* 1959, Susan Kathleen, da of Henry Gerard de Visme Gipps, and has issue living, Guy William, *b* 1961, — Richard Henry, *b* 1962, — Patrick John, *b* 1965, — Jane, *b* 1968, — Kate, *b* 1971.

Issue of late Elystan Cecil D'Arcy-Evans, *b* 1906, *d* 1960: *m* 1953, Rosemonde Lovell Pryor Rainbird (Bland Rd, York, W Australia):—

Donald Hugh, *b* 1955: *m* 1982, Pamela Verena Hocking, and has issue living, Andrew Eyre, *b* 1983. *Residence* – 34 Stanley St, Morpeth Vale, S Australia 5136. —— Ainslie Jean, *b* 1957; BSc: *m* 1982, Michael John Slack-Smith, BSc, of Lot 7, Lyon Rd, Jandakot, W Australia, and has issue living, David, *b* 1986, — Matthew, *b* 1988.

PREDECESSORS – George Evans, Bar-at-law, a zealous promoter of the Revolution of 1688, was after the accession of William III sworn of the Privy Council, and returned as MP for Charleville, co Cork, and subsequently declined a peerage offered by George I, an honour however, that was accepted by his son (1) GEORGE, MP, cr *Baron Carbery*, of Carbery, co Cork (peerage of Ireland) 1715, with remainder to the male issue of his father; *d* 1749; *s* by his son (2) GEORGE, MP, 2nd Baron; *d* 1759; *s* by his son (3) GEORGE, 3rd Baron; *d* 1783; *s* by his son (4) GEORGE, 4th Baron, MP for Rutland, *dsp* 1804: *s* by his uncle (5) JOHN, 5th Baron (2nd son of 2nd Baron); *d* 1807, without surviving male issue; *s* by his kinsman (6) *Sir* JOHN EVANS-FREKE, 6th Baron (whose father, grandson of the 1st Baron, had been cr a *Baronet* (1) 1768, and assumed the additional surname of Freke); was a Representative Peer; *dsp* 1845; *s* by his nephew (7) GEORGE PATRICK, 7th Baron (son of Percy Evans-Freke, 3rd son of 1st Bt), by Dorothea, da of the Rev Christopher Harvey, DD, of Kyle, co Wexford, *b* 1807: *m* 1852, Harriet Maria Catherine, who *d* 1884, da of Lt-Gen Edward William Shuldham, HEIC, of Dunmanway, co Cork; *d* 1889; *s* by his brother (8) WILLIAM CHARLES, 8th Baron, *b* 1812; a Representative Peer for Ireland: *m* 1st, 1840, Lady Sophia Sherard, who *d* 1851, da of 5th Earl of Harborough (*ext*), and widow of Sir Thomas Whichcote, 6th Bt; 2ndly, 1866, Lady Victoria Cecil, who *d* 1932, da of 2nd Marquess of Exeter; *d* 1894; *s* by his elder son (9) ALGERNON WILLIAM GEORGE, 9th Baron, *b* 1868; *m* 1890, Mary, who *d* 1949, da of late Henry J. Toulmin, of The Prè St Albans; *d* 1898; *s* by his son (10) JOHN, 10th Baron, *b* 1892; assumed name of John Evans Carberry by deed poll in Nairobi 1920: *m* 1st, 1913 (*m diss* 1919), José, da of Evelyn James Metcalfe; 2ndly 1922, Maia Ivy, who *d* 1928, da of Alfred Anderson, of Nairobi; 3rdly, 1930, June Weir Mosley, who *d* 1980; *s* by his nephew (11) PETER RALFE HARRINGTON, only son of late Hon Ralfe Evans-Freke, MBE (*d* 1969), 2nd son of 9th Baron, 11th Baron and present peer.

Cardigan, Earl of; son of Marquess of Ailesbury.

Cardross, Lord; son of Earl of Buchan.

CAREW, BARON (Conolly-Carew) (Baron I 1834, and UK 1838)

To wonder at nothing

PATRICK THOMAS CONOLLY-CAREW, 7th Baron; *b* 6 March 1938; *s* 1994; *ed* Harrow; late Capt RHG: *m* 1962, Celia Mary, yr da of late Col Hon Charles Guy Cubitt, CBE, DSO, TD, DL (*see* B Ashcombe), and has issue.

Arms – Or, three lions passant in pale sable. **Crest** – An heraldic antelope passant sable, horned and tufted or. **Supporters** – Two heraldic antelopes gules, horned and tufted or.
Residence – Donadea House, Naas, co Kildare. *Clubs* – Cavalry and Guards', Kildare St, and University.

SON LIVING

Hon WILLIAM PATRICK, *b* 27 March 1973.

DAUGHTERS LIVING

Hon Virginia Mary, *b* 1965: *m* 1985, Neil S. McGrath, 3rd son of Dr Patrick McGrath, of Brownstown Stud Farm, Curragh, co Kildare, and has issue living, William James Thady, *b* 1987, — Christopher Neil, *b* 1990.
Hon Nicola Rosamond, *b* 1966: *m* 1991 (*m diss* 1992), Peter C. G. Schwerdt, eldest son of George Schwerdt, of Hants, and Mrs Diana Hutton, of Portbury, Bristol.
Hon Camilla Sylvia, *b* 1969.

BROTHER LIVING

Hon Gerald Edward Ian MAITLAND-CAREW (Thirlestane Castle, Lauder, Berwickshire), *b* 1941; Capt (ret) 15th/19th Hus; assumed by deed poll 1971 the surname of Maitland-Carew: *m* 1972, Rosalind Averil, da of Lt-Col Neil Hanning Reed Speke, MC, and has issue living, Edward Ian Conolly, *b* 1976, — a son, *b* 1979, — Emma Rosalind, *b* 1974.

SISTERS LIVING

Hon Diana Sylvia (*Baroness Alexis Wrangel*), *b* 1940: *m* 1985, Baron Alexis Wrangel, of Lone End, Oberstown Cross, Tara, co Meath.
Hon Sarah Catherine, *b* 1944: *m* 1966, Ian Arthur Cluny Macpherson, of Round Ash, E Worlington, Crediton, Devon EX17 4TZ, and has issue living, John Gavin, *b* 1967, — Caroline Emma Louisa, *b* 1969, — Katharine Heather Elizabeth, *b* 1974.

UNCLE LIVING (*son of 5th Baron*)

Hon Gavin George CAREW, MBE, TD (The Grove, Little Bealings, Woodbridge, Suffolk IP13 6LL), *b* 1906; *ed* Clifton; late Maj Co London Yeo; 1939-45 War in W Desert, Italy, Belgium, and Germany (despatches, MBE, Officer of American Legion of

Merit); MBE (Mil) 1945: *m* 1932, Aileen Hilda Frances, who *d* 1974, da of late Ean Francis Cecil (M Exeter, colls), and has issue living, Anne Hilda Catherine, *b* 1933: *m* 1953, John Dix, of Gellillyndu, Llanio, Tregaron, Dyfed, and has issue living, Stephen Gavin *b* 1955, Julia Anne *b* 1954, Anita Frances *b* 1957.

WIDOW LIVING OF SON OF FIFTH BARON

Barbara (Croft House, Great Bealings, Woodbridge, Suffolk), da of late Henry Wolley Leigh-Bennett (Price Bt, cr 1815, colls): *m* 1937, Lt-Cdr Hon Peter Cuthbert Carew, RN, who *d* 1980, and has issue living (*see* colls, infra).

COLLATERAL BRANCHES LIVING

Issue of late Lt-Cdr Hon Peter Cuthbert Carew, RN, yst son of 5th Baron, *b* 1908, *d* 1980: *m* 1937, Barbara (ante), da of late Henry Wolley Leigh-Bennett (Price, Bt, cr 1815, colls):—
David Edward, *b* 1942. —— Susan Catherine (*Lady Madel*), *b* 1944: *m* 1971, Sir (William) David Madel, MP, of 120 Pickford Rd, Markyate, Herts, and has issue living, Christopher William, *b* 1977, — Louise Iona, *b* 1975.

Granddaughter of late Lt-Cdr Hon Peter Cuthbert Carew, RN (ante):—
Issue of late Thomas Henry Carew, *b* 1947, *d* 1978: *m* 1974, Lucinda (who *m* 2ndly, 1983, John Martin Harkness, of Hill House, Geldeston, Beccles, Suffolk), yst da of Joseph Guy Lubbock (*see* B Avebury, colls):—
Rachel Catherine, *b* 1978 (*posthumous*).

PREDECESSORS – (1) ROBERT SHAPLAND Carew, Lord-Lt of co Wexford; cr *Baron Carew* (peerage of Ireland) 1834, and *Baron Carew*, of Castle Boro, co Wexford (peerage of United Kingdom) 1838; *d* 1856; s by his son (2) ROBERT SHAPLAND, KP, *b* 1818; Lord Lt of co Wexford, and MP for Waterford (*L*) 1840-7: *m* 1844, Emily Anne, da of Sir George Richard Philips, MP, 2nd Bt: *d* 1881; s by his son (3)ROBERT SHAPLAND GEORGE JULIAN, 3rd Baron; *b* 1860: *m* 1888, Julia Mary, who *d* 1922, da of late Albert Arthur Erin Lethbridge (Lethbridge, Bt colls); *d* 1923; s by his son (4) GEORGE PATRICK JOHN, 4th Baron; *b* 1863; *m* 1888, Maud Beatrice, who *d* 1955, da of late John Ramsay; *d* 1926; s by his cousin (5) GERALD SHAPLAND (son of late Hon Shapland Francis Carew, son of 1st Baron), 5th Baron; *b* 1860: *m* 1904, Catherine, who *d* 1947, only da of late Thomas Conolly, MP, of Castletown, co Kildare; *d* 1927 s by his eldest son (6) WILLIAM FRANCIS, CBE, 6th Baron; *b* 1905; Maj Duke of Cornwall's LI, served 1939-45 War (wounded), ADC to Gov and Com-in-Ch of Bermuda 1931-36; Nat Chm British Legion 1963-66, Trustee Irish Sailors and Soldiers Land Trust; assumed by deed poll 1938 the additional surname of Conolly: *m* 1937, Lady Sylvia Gwendoline Eva Maitland, who *d* 1991, da of 15th Earl of Lauderdale; *d* 1994; s by his elder son (7) PATRICK THOMAS, 7th Baron and present peer.

Carleton, Baron, title of Earl of Shannon on Roll of HL.

CARLISLE, EARL OF (Howard) (Earl E 1661)

I am willing, but not able

CHARLES JAMES RUTHVEN HOWARD, MC, 12th Earl; *b* 21 Feb 1923; *s* 1963, and *s* to Lordship of Ruthven of Freeland (Peerage of Scotland) 1982; *ed* Eton; FRICS; a Forestry Commr 1967-70; 1939-45 War as Lt Rifle Bde (twice severely wounded, MC); DL Cumbria 1984: *m* 1945, Hon Ela Hilda Aline Beaumont, only da of 2nd Viscount Allendale, and has issue.

Arms – Quarterly of six: 1st gules, a bend between six cross crosslets fitchée argent, on the bend an escutcheon or, charged with a demi-lion rampant, pierced through the mouth with an arrow, within a double tressure flory counterflory, all gules, and above the escutcheon a mullet sable, for difference, *Howard*; 2nd gules, three lions passant guardant or in pale, and in chief a label of three points argent, *Thomas of Brotherton*, son of Edward I; 3rd checky, or and azure, *Warren*, Earl Warren and Surrey; 4th gules, a lion rampant argent; *Mowbray*, Duke of Norfolk; 5th gules, three escallops argent, *Dacre*; 6th barry of six argent and azure over all, three chaplets gules proper, *Greystock*. Crest – On a chapeau gules, turned up ermine, a lion statant guardant, with the tail extended or, ducally gorged argent, a mullet sable for difference. Supporters – *Dexter*, a lion argent, charged with a mullet sable for difference; *sinister* a bull gules, armed unguled, ducally gorged and lined or.
Seat – Naworth Castle, Brampton, Cumberland.

SONS LIVING

GEORGE WILLIAM BEAUMONT (*Viscount Morpeth, Master of Ruthven*), *b* 15 Feb 1949; *ed* Eton, and Balliol Coll, Oxford (MA); Maj 9th/12th R Lancers (resigned commn 1987).
Hon Philip Charles Wentworth, *b* 1963; *ed* Eton, and Reading Univ.

DAUGHTERS LIVING (*In remainder to Lordship of Ruthven of Freeland*)

Lady Jane Annabelle, *b* 1947: *m* 1st, 1968 (*m diss* 1977), John David Vaughan Seth-Smith; 2ndly, 1983, Rodney S. Ledward, and has issue living (by 1st *m*), Gemma Bridget Annabel, *b* 1972, — (by 2nd *m*) Bertie Arthur Ruthven, *b* 1985. *Residence* – Beaulieu Cottage, The Riviera, Sandgate, Folkestone, Kent CT20 3AB.
Lady Emma Bridget, *b* 1952: *m* 1st, 1974 (*m diss* 1981), John Philip Charles Langton-Lockton; 2ndly, 1983 (*m diss* 1988), Robie Patrick Maxwell Uniacke; 3rdly, 1988, Guy Mark Sisson, and has issue living (by 1st *m*), Maximillian, *b* 1980, — Tabitha Jane, *b* 1978, — (by 2nd *m*) Robie Jonjo, *b* 1984, — (by 3rd *m*) Ned John Hamilton, *b* 1989. *Residence* – 28 Elms Rd, SW4.

SISTER LIVING (In remainder to Lordship of Ruthven of Freeland)

Lady Carolyn Bridget Dacre (16 Brunswick Rd, Penrith, Cumbria), *b* 1919; 1939-45 War as Subaltern ATS (transferred to FANY Ambulance Corps 1941).

HALF-SISTER LIVING (Not in remainder to Lordship of Ruthven of Freeland)

Lady Susan Ankaret, *b* 1948: *m* 1st 1967 (*m diss* 1978), Charles James Buchanan-Jardine (*see* Buchanan-Jardine, Bt); 2ndly, 1978, Count Hubert Charles de Meyer, of 50 Hasker St, SW3, and Tracey Farm, Great Tew, Oxon, and has issue living (by 1st *m*) (*see* Buchanan-Jardine, Bt), — (by 2nd *m*), Alexander Charles Benedict, *b* 1979.

WIDOW LIVING OF TENTH LORD RUTHVEN OF FREELAND

JUDITH GORDON (Denbigh, Foreland Rd, Bembridge, Isle of Wight), yr da of late Bertie E. Bell, of Guernsey: *m* 1st, 1953, as his 2nd wife, the 10th Lord, who *d* 1956; 2ndly, 1965, Maj Digby Robert Peel, MC, RA, who *d* 1971.

WIDOW LIVING OF ELEVENTH EARL

ESME MARY SHRUBB (*Esme, Countess of Carlisle*) (Duns Tew Manor, Oxon OX6 4JP), da of Charles Edward Iredell: *m* 1947, as his 2nd wife, the 11th Earl, who *d* 1963.

COLLATERAL BRANCHES LIVING

Grandchildren of late Hon Oliver Howard, 4th son of 9th Earl:—
Issue of late Hubert Arthur George Howard, *b* 1901, *d* 1986: *m* 1930, Moira, who *d* 1986, da of late Rev John Arthur Victor Magee, V of St Mark's, Hamilton Terr, W (Wilson, Bt, *cr* 1874):—
David Charles Hubert (Ranvilles Farm, nr Romsey, Hants), *b* 1940; *ed* Eton: *m* 1st, 1962 (*m diss* 1969), Pamela Mary, da of Frederick Thomas Rose, of Kenilworth; 2ndly, 1978, Norma Ellen, da of Norman William Sparks, of Bridgwater, Som, and has issue living (by 1st *m*), Susan Mary, *b* 1963, — Rosalind Emma, *b* 1966, — (by 2nd *m*) Oliver Charles Frederick, *b* 1980. —— Lavinia Moira, *b* 1944: *m* 1963, Christopher Thomas Bernard Turville-Constable-Maxwell (*see* L Herries of Terregles, colls).

Issue of late Hon Geoffrey William Algernon Howard, 5th son of 9th Earl, *b* 1877, *d* 1935: *m* 1915, Hon Ethel Christian, who *d* 1932, da of 3rd Baron Methuen:—
Dame Rosemary Christian, DBE, *b* 1916; Hon MA Lambeth; DBE (1986). *Residence* - Coneysthorpe, York.

Grandsons of late Hon Geoffrey William Algernon Howard (ante):—
Issue of late George Anthony Geoffrey Howard (*Baron Howard of Henderskelfe*), *b* 1920, *d* 1984; *cr* a Life Baron 1983: *m* 1949, Lady Cecilia Blanche Geneviève FitzRoy, who *d* 1974, da of 8th Duke of Grafton:—
Hon Henry Francis Geoffrey, *b* 1950. —— *Hon* Nicholas Paul Geoffrey, *b* 1952; *ed* Eton, and Oxford Univ: *m* 1st, 1983 (*m diss* 1990), Amanda Kate Victoria, only da of Derek Nimmo, actor, of Kensington; 2ndly, 1992, Victoria, da of Thomas E. Barnsley, OBE, of The Old Rectory, Llanelidan, N Wales, and has issue living (by 1st *m*), George Fulco Geoffrey, *b* 1985. *Residence* - 9 Kensington Place, W8. —— *Hon* Simon Bartholomew Geoffrey, *b* 1956; *ed* Eton: *m* 1983, Annette Marie, formerly wife of Spencer Douglas David, Earl Compton (later 7th Marquess of Northampton), and da of Charles Antony Russell Smallwood, of Storrington, Sussex. *Seat* - Castle Howard, York. —— *Hon* (Anthony) Michael Geoffrey, *b* 1958: *m* 1985, Linda Louise, yr da of Alexander McGrady, of Broughty Ferry, Angus, and has issue living, Arabella Blanche Geneviève, *b* 1986, — Grania Alexandra Louise, *b* 1988. *Residence* - Leyfield Farm, Coneysthorpe, York YO6 7DF.

Granddaughter of late Richard Fitzroy Howard (infra):—
Issue of late Richard Frederick Robert Howard, Capt Green Howards, *b* 1916, *d* 1978: *m* 1946, Jean McBride (Cottage 82, Doone Village, Pinetown 3610, S Africa), da of Cyril Taylor:—
Jane Anne McBride (8 Cleveland Rd, Westville, Durban, S Africa), *b* 1951: *m* 1969 (*m diss* 1984), Andrew Hugh Ross MacLennan, and has issue living, Angus Howard, *b* 1972, — Morag Jean, *b* 1970, — Shannon Fiona, *b* 1976.

Grandchildren of late Col Frederick Compton Howard, 3rd son of late Frederick John Howard, son of late Hon Frederick Howard, 3rd son of 5th Earl:—
Issue of late Richard Fitzroy Howard, *b* 1879, *d* 1962: *m* 1914, Elsie Anne, who *d* 1936, elder da of late Robert Clarkson, of Scarborough:—
George William, *b* 1924; CEng, FIMechE: *m* 1952, Barbara Enid, da of Reginald Edgar Everett, and has issue living, Katherine Margaret, *b* 1954; BA: *m* 1st, 19— (*m diss* 19—), Peter Kay; 2ndly, 1989, Thomas Idris Bowen, of Mrs Bird's Cottage, Sutton, Beds, — Lesley Jane, *b* 1957: *m* 1987, Stephen Hutty, of Elloughton, E Yorks, and has issue living, William Robert *b* 1988, Katharine Jane *b* 1990, Helen Rose *b* 1992, — Sarah Barbara, *b* 1960; MA Vet, MB MRCVS: *m* 1987, Geoffrey van-der-Walt, of Chiltington, Sussex. *Residence* - 109 Southella Way, Kirkella, E Yorks. —— Bertha Frances Grace (73 Silkham Rd, Oxted, Surrey), *b* 1914: *m* 1943 (*m diss* 1960), Douglas Haley, and has issue living, Ian Richard (30 Wellington Rd, Newark, Notts), *b* 1944: *m* 1965, Elizabeth Rose O'Reilly, of co Cavan, and has issue living, Damien Michael Douglas *b* 1974, Siobhan Geraldine *b* 1972, — Helen Veronica, *b* 1946: *m* 1974, Brian S. Liddell of 16 Pitford Rd, Woodley, Reading, and has issue living, Stephen *b* 1975, David *b* 1979. —— Kathleen Victoria, *b* 1918: *m* 1941, John Alan Lake, who *d* 1977, and has issue living, Ann Cecilia Mary, *b* 1942: *m* 1967, Stephen John Curtis, of Upton House, Beeford, Driffield, Yorks, and has issue living, Matthew John *b* 1968, Amelia Ann *b* 1971, Madeleine Ann *b* 1975, — Susan Margaret, *b* 1949: *m* 19—, David Christopher Lavender, of 2 Lea Way, Huntington, York, and has issue living, Rachael *b* 1970. *Residence* - 44 Alton Park, Beeford, Driffield, Yorks. —— Elsie Anne, *b* 1927: *m* 1951, William Byass Temple, and has issue living, Janet, *b* 1954: *m* 1977, Bjornsten, of Norwkapsgatan II, 163-55, Spånga, Stockholm, — Wendy, *b* 1956, — Diane, *b* 1962. *Residence* - Oak Wood, 19 Throxenby Lane, Newby, Scarborough, Yorks
Issue of late George Frederick Howard, *b* 1894, *d* 1957: *m* 1919, Jane Anne Scott, who *d* 1961, da of John Young Myrtle, of Edinburgh:—
Margaret Anne Myrtle, MB, ChB, DPH, *b* 1921; formerly Capt RAMC: *m* 1946, Ralph Kenyon Hardy, who *d* 1993, and has issue living, Christopher Nigel (15 St Mary's Rd, Ditton Hill, Surbiton, Surrey), *b* 1947: *m* 1977, Carol, 2nd da of Peter Barnes, of 3 Heathfield Rd, Hersham, Surrey, and has issue living, Gemma Elizabeth *b* 1980, Annabel Frances *b* 1984, — Peter Ralph Howard, *b* 1953. *Residence* - 13 Denleigh Gdns, Thames Ditton, Surrey.

Grandchildren of late Alfred John Howard, 4th son of late Frederick John Howard (ante):—
Issue of late Capt William Gilbert Howard, CBE, RN, *b* 1877, *d* 1960: *m* 1912, Hon Agnes Caroline Sophia Parnell, JP, who *d* 1968, da of 4th Baron Congleton:—
Frederick Henry, DSO, MC, *b* 1915; Lt-Col (ret) 3rd Hus; Palestine 1936 (MC); European War 1939-45 in N Africa and N-W Europe (Bar to MC, DSO); DSO 1946: *m* 1st, 1941 (*m diss* 1946), Estelle Georgette da of Capt Sharp, of Londjani Kenya; 2ndly, 1952, Hon Jean Margaret Parnell, da of 6th Baron Congleton, and has issue living (by 2nd *m*), Henry James, *b* 1956; *ed* Eton, and RMA; Capt R Scots Drag Gds; Capt Scottish Yeo, and Memb Queen's Body Guard for Scotland (Royal

Company of Archers): *m* 1983, Philippa Charlotte, 3rd da of Maj Lyon Balfour Paul, of Eskdale, Beauly, Inverness, and has issue living, William Henry *b* 1986, Kiloran Rose *b* 1988. — John Dugald, *b* 1958; *ed* Gordonstoun and RMA; 2nd Lt R Scots Drag Gds, — Rose, *b* 1953. *Residence* – Isle of Ulva, Aros, Mull, Argyll PA73 6LZ. *Clubs* – Naval and Military, Army and Navy, New (Edinburgh), Royal Highland Yacht. ——— †John William, *b* 1917; *ed* Gresham's, and Magdalene Coll, Camb (MA); Colonial Admin Ser, Kenya, 1939-63, etc; 1939-45 War in Abyssinia and Madagascar as Capt 5th King's African Rifles (despatches twice): *m* 1949, Elizabeth Bligh (Appletree Cottage, Staplecross, Robertsbridge, Sussex), yst da of Capt Robert Francis Veasey, RN (*see* E Darnley, colls, 1951 Edn), and *d* 1988, leaving issue, Jonathan Arthur Francis (Royal Oak, Donhead St Mary, Shaftesbury, Dorset), *b* 1955; *ed* Eton, and Nottingham Univ (BA); Maj Royal Hussars: *m* 1984, Louise Maria Theodora, elder da of late Richard Miles Backhouse (*see* Backhouse, Bt, colls), and has issue living, William Richard Michael *b* 1986, George Jonathan Henry *b* 1988, Henry John Arthur *b* 1989. — Sarah Elizabeth Anne, *b* 1951; BA London Univ; resumed maiden name 1978: *m* 1st, 1973 (*m diss* 1978), Robert James Rogers; 2ndly, 1989, Rev Charles Patrick Sherlock, elder son of late Niall Patrick Sherlock, of Ewhurst, Surrey, and has issue living (by 2nd *m*), Patrick John Howard *b* 1991, Francis Alexander Howard *b* 1994. — (Eva) Jane Agnes, *b* 1953: *m* 1979, Lt-Col Hugh Charles Gregory Willing, RGJ, and has issue living, Edward John David *b* 1982, Richard Hugh *b* 1984, Arabella Jane *b* 1987. ——— Mark Alfred, *b* 1919; is a Grazier; N Africa and Greece 1939-45 as Lt Australian Forces (prisoner): *m* 1950, Judith Ruth, da of F. E. Selwyn Scott, MBE, JP, of Scotsburn, Victoria, Australia, and has issue living, Michael Gilbert, *b* 1950; *ed* Geelong Gram Sch, and Australian Nat Univ (BA). — William Mark, *b* 1959; *ed* Geelong Gram Sch, and Glenormiston Agric Coll, — Margaret Jean, *b* 1952: *m* 1980, Colin McLeod Campbell, of Rockgedgiel, Quirinfdi, NSW, Australia, and has issue living, Henry Mark *b* 1982. *Residence* – Stonegate, Dunkeld, Victoria, Australia. *Clubs* – Naval and Military (Melbourne), Melbourne. ——— Margaret, *b* (twin) 1919; formerly Subaltern ATS: *m* 1945, Brig Christopher Charles Lloyd Browne, OBE, late RA, who *d* 1972, and has had issue, Andrew William Lloyd *b* 1948, *d* 1967, — Elizabeth, *b* 1947; *ed* London Univ (BSc): *m* 1978, Lt-Cdr Quentin Parker, RN, and has issue living, Jonathan *b* 1980, Charles Godfrey *b* 1981, — Felicity, *b* 1954: *m* 1974, Capt Charles William Granville Dobbie, KOSB, and has issue living, William Arthur Charles *b* 1980, George Galahad Christopher *b* 1986, Alice Felicity *b* 1982, — Carolyn, *b* 1958; BSc, PhD (Oxon). *Residence* – Dean House, W Dean, Salisbury, Wilts. ——— Agnes, *b* 1921; BA Open Univ; formerly Leading Wren WRNS: *m* 1945, Maj John Singleton Hattersley, RE, who *d* 1992, and has had issue, Charles William, *b* 1949; *ed* Marlborough, and Durham Univ (BA); FRGS; Lt-Cdr RN (ret): *m* 1988, Rebecca Jane, only da of David Smith, of Puttenham, Surrey, and has issue living, Elizabeth Maryse *b* 1989, Antonia Sarah *b* 1993, — Margaret Sarah, *b* 1950; *ed* Lond Univ (BA): late Capt WRAC: *m* 1979, John Martyn Ford, son of late Rev Basil Ford, and has issue living, Michael John *b* 1986, Alexandra Margaret *b* 1982, — Anne Agnes, *b* 1952, *d* 1974, — Victoria Vera, *b* 1955; *ed* Aberystwyth Univ (LLB): *m* 1985, Peter Francis Harris, — Helen Jean, *b* 1961; *ed* Sheffield Univ (BA). *Residence* – 17 Conference Way, Colkirk, Fakenham, Norfolk NR21 7JJ.

Issue of late Vice-Adm Ronald Howard, *b* 1878, *d* 1959: *m* (Jan) 1913, Ruth Evelyn, who *d* 1968, da of late William Coryton (Parker Bt, cr 1884, colls):—
†Michael William, MC, *b* 1917; Maj (ret) Devonshire Regt, 1939-45 War in Italy and NW Europe (MC and Bar): *m* 1949, Gillian Hester (Southern Wood, Peter Tavy, Devon), da of Sir John Frederick Shelley, 10th Bt (cr 1611), and *d* 1994. ——— Roger Alexander, TD (11 Knightsbridge Court, Sloane St, SW1), *b* 1919; Maj (ret) RAOC: *m* 1944, Jean, da of late Vice-Adm A. H. Alington, and has issue living, Alexandra Nancy, *b* 1946: *m* 1971, Christopher Skidmore Taylor, of Yorton House, Harmer Hill, Shrewsbury, and has issue living, Charles Argentine Weston, *b* 1981, Emily Clare *b* 1973, Alexia Lucy *b* 1974, — Miranda Jane *b* 1948: *m* 1973, Petar Djedovic, of 12 Sedlescombe Rd, SW6 1RD, and Petrovac Na Moru, Montenegro, Yugoslavia, and has issue living, Natasha Kate *b* 1975, — Elvina Lucy *b* 1949: *m* 1974, Peter Robert Siddons, of 49 Clarendon Rd, Holland Park, W11 4JD, and has issue living, Alastair Mark *b* 1978, Philippa Sarah *b* 1977, Melanie Sarah *b* 1980. ——— Millicent, *b* (Dec) 1913: *m* 1937, Col Charles Richard Spencer, OBE, DL, 12th R Lancers, of Elfordtown, Yelverton, S Devon, and has issue living, Edward Charles, *b* 1946: *m* 1974, Sarah Elizabeth Dewhurst, and has issue living, Oliver Charles Wyndham *b* 1978, Caroline Tana *b* 1976, Rebecca Victoria *b* 1983, — Elizabeth Janet (*Lady Kitson*), *b* 1938: *m* 1962, Gen Sir Frank Edward Kitson, GBE, KCB, MC, and has issue living, Catherine Alice *b* 1963, Rosemary Diana *b* 1966, Marion Ruth *b* 1969.

Grandsons of late Gerald Richard Howard (infra):—

Issue of late Bertram Marcus Howard, *b* 1890, *d* 1970: *m* 1924, Phyllis Maude, who *d* 1988, da of Robert James Lamb, of Surbiton, Surrey:—
Michael Cavendish (24 South View, Letchworth Garden City, Herts), *b* 1926; *ed* King's Coll, Taunton; C Chem MRSC; W Africa 1944-45 with REME: *m* 1st, 1956, Muriel, who *d* 1978, widow of W. T. Mullings, BSc, MD; 2ndly, 1980, Patricia Ellen Millicent Gwatkin, da of William James Sandiford, of Woodford, Essex. ——— Richard Cavendish (Pigeonhouse Barn, Dingle Rd, Brockamin, Leigh, Worcs WR6 5JX), *b* 1936; *ed* King's Coll, Taunton; MBIM, MIIM: *m* 1959 (*m diss* 1979), Diana Mary, da of Frank B. Wharton, of Lichfield, Staffs, and has issue living, Dale Robin Cavendish (6 Landsdowne Rd, East St Kilda, Melbourne 3183, Victoria, Australia), *b* 1960; BSc Manchester Univ: *m* 1993, Michelle Redman, — Timothy Richard Cavendish (139 Marley Fields, Leighton Buzzard, Beds LU7 8WJ), *b* 1962: *m* 1986, Anne Marcia, da of late Malcolm John McAlistair Bennett, of Harrogate, N Yorks, and has issue living, Daniel Timothy Cavendish *b* 1989, Ellen Francesca *b* 1988, — James David Cavendish (Rose Croft, 12 Haynes Close, Thorne, Doncaster, DN8 5HR), *b* 1968: *m* 1994, Leanda Ruston, — Angela Claire, *b* 1961: *m* 1992, Martin John Korchinsky, of 14 Empress Drive, Heaton Chapel, Stockport, SK4 2RW, and has issue living, Benjamin John *b* 1990, Josef James *b* 1993.

Granddaughter of late Frederick John Howard (ante):—

Issue of late Gerald Richard Howard, *b* 1853, *d* 1945: *m* 1886, Ada, who *d* 1937, da of late Charles Curtis:—
Blanche Esther Muriel (Chesterfield House, Feckenham, Worcs), *b* 1904: *m* 1928, Angelo Victor John de Rin (known in Italy as The Noble Angelo de Rin de Capodistria), who *d* 1944, and has issue living, Diana Maria, *b* 1930: *m* 1955, Hilary George Gosling, of Chesterfield House, Feckenham, Worcs, and has issue living, Oliver Angelo de Rin *b* 1958, Jane Dorothy Blanche *b* 1956: *m* 1983, Gerard John Cornwallis Sweeting, of 168 St Ann's Hill, SW18 (*see* Hawarden, V, colls, 1985 Edn) (and has issue living, Henry Donald Alfred Beauclerk *b* 1984, Frederick Humfry Oliver de Rin *b* 1987), Rosemary Agnes Pauline *b* 1961, Veronica Jean *b* 1963, — Victoria, *b* 1931: *m* 1959, David Lynn Pratt, CBE, FIMechE, FICE, of 6 Tite St, Chelsea, SW3, and Fox Lodge, Guildford, Surrey, and has issue living, Jonathan de Rin *b* 1960, James Lynn *b* 1963.

Grandchildren of late Capt John Henry Howard, RN, 2nd son of late Very Rev Hon Henry Edward John Howard, DD, Dean of Lichfield, 4th son of 5th Earl:—

Issue of late Cdr Robert John Howard, RN, *b* 1878, *d* 1965: *m* 1918, Violet Mary, who *d* 1930, da of late Thurstan Collins, of Newton Ferrers, Cornwall:—
John Thurstan Collins, MC (College Green Farm, East Pennard, Shepton Mallet, Som), *b* 1919; *ed* Eton; Lt-Col SCLI: *m* 1949, Margaret, only da of Col Edyvean, of Mawgan, Cornwall.

Issue of late Com Charles Wilbraham John Howard, RN *b* 1880, *d* 1959: *m* 1909, Dorothy Ida Leigh, who *d* 1968, da of Sir Thomas Leigh Hare, 1st Bt, MVO (cr 1905):—
Geoffrey Charles (Stow House, Great Somerford, Wilts SN15 5HU), *b* 1910; Maj (ret) Black Watch; 1939-45 War; *m* 1939, Katharine, da of late Adm Sir Eric John Arthur Fullerton, KCB, DSO (B Fisher). ——— Susan Elizabeth, *b* 1913. *Residence* – Wall, Broadwindsor, Beaminster, Dorset DT8 3LB.

Granddaughter of late Rev Henry Frederick Howard, 5th and yst son of late Very Rev Hon Henry Edward John Howard, DD (ante):—

Issue of late Major Bernard Henry Howard, *b* 1879, *ka* 1916: *m* 1909, Margaret Ellen Edith McLean, who *d* 1984, da of late Lt-Col Donat Edmund McMahon:—

Marjorie Isabella, *b* 1910: *m* 1st 1938, Lt-Cdr Robert Lampard, RN, who was *ka* 1941; 2ndly, 1945, Lt-Cdr Roger Hoyle, RN, who *d* 1988, and has issue living (by 2nd *m*) Hugo Charles John *b* 1949: *m* 1979, Susan Elizabeth Haynes, and has issue living, Joshua Roger *b* 1985, Sarah *b* 1984, —— Angela Felicity, *b* 1947. *Residence* – Swandown, Axford, Marlborough, Wilts.

(In remainder to Lordship of Ruthven of Freeland only.)

Issue of late Hon Alison Mary Ruthven, 3rd da of 10th Lord Ruthven; *b* 1902; *d* 1973: *m* 1929, Cdr Sir John Leighton Barran, 3rd Bt, RNVR, who *d* 1974:—
Sir John Napoleon Ruthven Barran, 4th Bt (see that title.)

Issue of late Hon Margaret Leslie Ruthven, 4th da of 10th Lord Ruthven; *b* 1902 (twin); *d* 1970: *m* 1932, Peter Llewelyn Davies, MC, who *d* 1960:—
Ruthven Barrie (Casa Romazelra, Monchique, Algarve, Portugal), *b* 1933; *ed* Eton; late Lt Life Gds: *m* 1960, Mary Bridget, da of late Dr John Musser Pearce, and Mrs S. M. R. Giddings, of New York City. —— George Caesar, *b* 1938; *ed* Eton. —— Peter Theodore (8550 Monchique, Algarve, Portugal), *b* 1940; *ed* Eton, and Trin Coll, Camb: *m* 1965, Frances Jane, da of — Carson.

Grandson of late Rt Hon Sir Alexander Gore Arkwright Hore-Ruthven, VC, GCMB, CB, DSO, PC (2nd son of 9th Lord), who was cr *Earl of Gowrie* 1945 (see that title.)
Issue of late Col Hon Christian Malise Hore-Ruthven, 3rd son of 9th Lord, *b* 1880; *d* 1969: *m* 1925, Hon Angela Margaret, RRC, who *d* 1970, da of 3rd Baron Manners:—
James John Malise (42 Westminster Gdns, Marsham St, SW1 4JD), *b* 1935; *ed* Eton: *m* 1965, Helen Dron, el da of John S. Craig, of Flat 1, Buckland Court, 37 Belsize Park NW3 4EB, and has issue living, Alexander Malise, *b* 1972, — Angela Dron, *b* 1976. —— Sarah Constance Anne, *b* 1930: *m* 1962, James Baynard-Smith, of 44 Sunderland Ave, Oxford, and has issue living, Peter James, *b* 1966: *m* 1993, Julia Woodley, — Christopher Ruthven, *b* 1972.

Granddaughters of late Hon Charles Edward Stewart Hore-Ruthven, OBE, brother of 8th Lord:—
Issue of late Charles Hore-Ruthven, *b* 1876, *d* 1963: *m* 1910, Elyned Rhona, who *d* 1965, da of late Thomas Wood (B Tollemache):—
Elcha Cecilia (Knoll House, Aylsham, Norwich), *b* 1912: *m* 1934 (*m diss* 1968), William Herbert Harrison, and has issue living, Rhona Moya, *b* 1936: *m* 1958, Edward Luddington (E Leicester), and has issue living, Christopher Mark *b* 1963, Andrew William *b* 1965, — Zara Carolyn *b* 1938: *m* 1962, Alastair Neil Campbell Harris, of Gattendon Lodge, Goring-on-Thames, and has issue living, James Neil *b* 1966: *m* 1992, Vanessa Hogan-Hern, Clare Louise *b* 1963, Lucinda Zara *b* 1968, — Susan Juliet, *b* 1945: *m* 1967, Charles Bannatyne Watson, of Kirkconnel, Ringford, Kirkudbrightshire, and has issue living, Adam Bannatyne *b* 1971, Sara Cecilia *b* 1969, — Susannah, *b* 1946: *m* 1975, Martin Woodnutt, and has issue living, Piers Mark *b* 1977, Emily Sophie, *b* 1979. — Elyned Barbara, MBE, *b* 1915; MBE (Mil) 1946: *m* 1940, John Allan Legh Barratt, TD, of Upgate House, Swannington, nr Norwich, and has had issue living, David John (Boat Barn Cottage, Blakeney, Norfolk), *b* 1947: *m* 1982, Penelope Constance Isabel Lloyd, and has issue living, Fergus Ralph Legh *b* 1984, Frederick David Nicholas *b* 1987, — Charles William Legh (Ollands Farm, Heydon, Norfolk), *b* 1949: *m* 1976, Caroline, da of Maj James Clifford Wilson, of Warren Farm, Ingoldisthorpe, Kings Lynn, and has issue living, William James *b* 1979, Samuel Charles Legh *b* 1982, — Anita Elyned, *b* 1952, *d* 19—.

PREDECESSORS – (1) CHARLES Howard, PC, great-grandson of Lord William Howard, 3rd son of 4th Duke of Norfolk; cr Viscount Howard of Morpeth by Oliver Cromwell 1657, and *Baron Dacre of Gillesland, Viscount Howard of Morpeth,* and *Earl of Carlisle* 1661; was subsequently Ambassador to the Czar of Muscovy and Gov of Jamaica; *d* 1686; *s* by his son (2) EDWARD, 2nd Earl; *d* 1692; *s* by his son (3) CHARLES, 3rd Earl; was First Lord of the Treasury, Constable of the Tower, and Gov of Windsor Castle; *d* 1738; *s* by his son (4) HENRY, KG; *d* 1758; *s* by his son (5) FREDERICK, KG, KT; Viceroy of Ireland 1780-2; *d* 1825; *s* by his son (6) GEORGE, KG, 6th Earl; *b* 1773; was Lord-Lieut of E Riding of York: *m* 1801, Lady Georgiana Dorothy Cavendish, da of 5th Duke of Devonshire; *d* 1848; *s* by his elder son (7) GEORGE WILLIAM FREDERICK, 7th Earl; was Ch Sec for Ireland 1835-41, Ch Commr of Woods and Forests 1846-50, Chancellor of Duchy of Lancaster 1850-2, and Lord-Lieut of Ireland 1855-8 and 1859-64; *d* unmarried 1864; *s* by his brother (8) WILLIAM GEORGE, 8th Earl, *b* 1808; R of Londesborough 1832-77; *d* unmarried 1889; *s* by his nephew (9) GEORGE JAMES (son of late Hon Charles Wentworth George Howard, MP, 5th son of 6th Earl), 9th Earl; *b* 1843; MP for E Cumberland (*L*) 1879-80, when he was defeated and 1881-5: *m* 1864, Hon Rosalind Frances, who *d* 1921, da of 2nd Baron Stanley of Alderley; *d* 1911; *s* by his son (10) CHARLES JAMES STANLEY, 10th Earl; *b* 1867; sat as MP for Birmingham, S Div (LU) 1904-11; *m* 1894, Rhoda Ankaret, who *d* 1957, da of Col Paget W. L'Estrange, formerly RA; *d* 1912; *s* by his only son (11) GEORGE JOSSLYN L'ESTRANGE, 11th Earl, *b* 1895; Chm of UK Commercial Corporation, Ankara, 1941-3; *m* 1st, 1918 (*m diss* 1947), Hon Bridget Helen Hore-Ruthven, CBE (who *s* as Lady Ruthven of Freeland 1956, and *d* 1982), da of 10th Lord Ruthven of Freeland; 2ndly, 1947, Esme Mary Shrubb, da of Charles Edward Iredell; *d* 1963; *s* by his only son (12) CHARLES JAMES RUTHVEN, 12th Earl and present peer; also Viscount Howard of Morpeth, and Baron Dacre of Gillesland; also Lord Ruthven of Freeland (see * infra).

*(1) Sir THOMAS Ruthven (great-grandson of William, 2nd Lord Ruthven, cr 1487-8, who was grandfather of 1st Earl of Gowrie), Col of Regt, a Commr for the Treaty of Ripon 1641, and a Commr of Exchequer 1649, was cr *Lord Ruthven of Freeland* (peerage of Scotland) 1651; the patent is stated to have been burnt with the house of Freeland in 1750, and the limitations are not accurately known, nevertheless as the dignity was retained (together with many extinct titles) on the Union Roll, it has been presumed that the honour was to heirs-general; *d* 1673; *s* by his son (2) DAVID, 2nd Lord; was a Lord of the Treasury in Scotland; *d* ummarried 1701, when the estates devolved by entail upon his yst sister (3) Jean, and at her death in April 1722 they passed to her nephew Sir William Cunningham, Bt (only son of her elder sister Anne, and also heir of line), who *d* Oct 1722, having assumed the surname of Ruthven upon the death of the 2nd Lord, but (living only six months after his accession to the estates) without ever having assumed the title; his cousin, however, (4) ISABELLA (da of Hon Elizabeth (2nd da and heir of line of 1st Lord) by her marriage with Sir Francis Ruthven, Knt), was summoned as a Lady to the Coronation of George II, and recognized in the Lordship of Ruthven of Freeland: *m* Col James Johnson, who assumed the name of Ruthven; *d* 1730; *s* by her son (5) JAMES, 5th Lord; *d* 1783; *s* by his son (6) JAMES, 6th Lord; *d* 1789; *s* by his son (7) JAMES, 7th Lord; *dsp* 1853; *s* by his sister (8) MARY ELIZABETH THORNTON: *m* 1806, Walter Hore, who assumed the additional surname of Ruthven *d* 1864; *s* by her grandson (9) WALTER JAMES, 9th Lord Ruthven of Freeland (*b* 1838), who, like his predecessors, voted at the Election of Representative Peers for Scotland, and was cr *Baron Ruthven of Gowrie* (peerage of United Kingdom) 1919: *m* 1869, Lady Caroline Annesley Gore, who *d* 1914, da of 4th Earl of Arran; *d* 1921; *s* by his elder son (10) WALTER PATRICK, CB, CMG, DSO, 10th Lord; *b* 1870; Maj-Gen late Scots Guards; commanded Bangalore Brig 1920-24, and London Dist 1924-8, and was Lieut-Gov of Guernsey 1929-34: *m* 1st, 1895, Jean Leslie who *d* 1952, da of late Norman George Lampson (Lampson Bt, colls); 2ndly, 1953, Judith Gordon (who *m* 2ndly, 1965, Maj Digby R. Peel), da of late Bertie E. Bell, of Guernsey; *d* 1956; *s* in the Barony of Ruthven of Gowrie (peerage of United Kingdom) by his great-nephew the 2nd Earl of Gowrie, and in the Lordship of Ruthven of Freeland by his elder da (11) BRIDGET HELEN, CBE, Lady Ruthven of Freeland, *b* 1896; her petition as heir of line and heir tailzie of 1st Lord allowed in Lyon Court 1967 and her *s* to Peerage recognised: *m* 1st, 1918 (*m diss* 1947), 11th Earl of Carlisle, who *d* 1963; 2ndly, 1947, as his 2nd wife, 1st Viscount Monckton of Brenchley, who *d* 1965; *d* 1982; *s* by her only son (12) CHARLES JAMES RUTHVEN, 12th Earl of Carlisle, and 12th Lord Ruthven of Freeland (ante).

CARLISLE OF BUCKLOW, BARON (Carlisle) (Life Baron 1987)

MARK CARLISLE, PC, QC, 2nd son of late Philip Edmund Carlisle; *b* 7 July 1929; *ed* Radley, and Manchester Univ (LLB); Bar Gray's Inn 1953, Bencher 1980 Northern Circuit, Judge of the Courts of Appeal of Jersey and Guernsey since 1990; Member Home Office Advisory Council on Penal System 1966-70, Recorder of Crown Court 1976-79 and since 1981; Joint Hon Sec Conservative Home Affairs Cttee 1965-69, Conservative Front Bench Spokesman on Home Affairs 1969-70, Parl Under-Sec of State Home Office 1970-72, Min of State Home Office 1972-74, Sec of State for Educn and Science 1979-81; Chm Conservative Home Affairs Cttee 1983-87, Parole Review Cttee 1987, Chm Criminal Injuries Compensation Bd since 1988; DL for Cheshire 1983; MP for Runcorn (*C*) 1964-83, and Warrington South 1983-87; QC 1971, PC 1979; *cr Baron Carlisle of Bucklow*, of Mobberley, co Cheshire (Life Baron) 1987: *m* 1959, Sandra Joyce, da of John Hamilton des Voeux, of St Ives, Cornwall, and has issue.
Residence – 3 Holt Gdns, Mobberley, Cheshire. *Club* – Garrick.

DAUGHTER LIVING

Hon Vanessa Lucy, *b* 19—.

Carlow, Viscount; son of Earl of Portarlington.

Carlton, Viscount; son of Earl of Wharncliffe.

CARMICHAEL OF KELVINGROVE, BARON (Carmichael) (Life Baron 1983)

NEIL GEORGE CARMICHAEL, son of James Carmichael, of Glasgow; *b* Oct 1921; *ed* Eastbank Acad, and Royal Coll of Science and Technology, Glasgow; PPS to Min of Technology 1966-67; Parl Under-Sec of State, Min of Transport 1967-69, Parl Sec, Min of Technology 1969-70, Parl Under-Sec of State, Dept of Environment 1974-75, and Dept of Industry 1975-76; Member Select Cttee on Transport since 1980; MP Woodside Div of Glasgow (*Lab*) 1962-74, and Kelvingrove Div of Glasgow (*Lab*) 1974-83; *cr Baron Carmichael of Kelvingrove*, of Camlachie, District of Glasgow (Life Peer) 1983: *m* 1948, Catherine McIntosh, da of John Dawson Rankin, of Glasgow, and has issue.
Residence – 53 Partickhill Rd, Glasgow G11 5AB.

DAUGHTER LIVING

Hon Sheena MacIntosh CARMICHAEL, *b* 1949; has resumed her maiden name: *m* 1974 (*m diss* 1988), Thomas Anthony Edward Sharpe, and has issue, one son and one da.

CARNARVON, EARL OF (Herbert) (Earl GB 1793)

One I will serve

HENRY GEORGE REGINALD MOLYNEUX HERBERT, KCVO, KBE, 7th Earl; *b* 19 Jan 1924; *s* 1987; *ed* Eton; late RHG; Hon Col 115th (Hampshire Fortress) Engineer Regt (TA) 1963; DL Hants 1965; appointed Racing Manager to HM 1970; KBE (Civil) 1976, KCVO (Civil) 1982: *m* 1956, Jean Margaret, da of Hon Oliver Malcolm Wallop (*see* E Portsmouth), and has issue.

Arms – Per pale azure and gules, three lions rampant argent, a crescent for difference. **Crest** – A wyvern, wings elevated, vert, in the mouth a sinister human hand couped at the wrist gules. **Supporters** – *Dexter*, a panther argent, incensed proper, spotted with hurts and torteaux alternately; *sinister*, a lion argent; both ducally gorged per pale azure and gules, with chain reflexed over the back or, and charged on the shoulder with an ermine spot sable.
Seat – Highclere Castle, Newbury, Berks, RG15 9RN. *Residence* – Milford Lake House, Newbury, Berks. *Clubs* – White's, Portland.

SONS LIVING

GEORGE REGINALD OLIVER MOLYNEUX (*Lord Porchester*), *b* 10 Nov 1956; *ed* Eton, and St John's Coll, Oxford; a Page of Honour to HM 1969-73: *m* 1989, Jayne M., eldest da of Kenneth A. Wilby, of Cheshire, and of Princess Prospero Colonna di Stigliano, of Ashford, co Wicklow, and has issue:—
  SON LIVING — *Hon* George, *b* 13 Oct 1992.
  DAUGHTER LIVING — *Hon* Saoirse, *b* 1991.
Residence – Dairy Cottage, Highclere Park, Newbury, Berks RG15 9RN.

Hon Henry Malcolm, *b* 1959; *ed* Eton: *m* 1992, Francesca (Chica) V., yr da of Jonathan Stuart Vaughan Bevan, of 17 Eaton Terr, SW1, and of Mrs Roger Dalzell, of W Wratting Hall, Cambridge, and has issue living, Chloe Victoria, *b* 1994. *Residence* – Field House, Highclere Park, Newbury, Berks RG15 9RN.

DAUGHTER LIVING

Lady Carolyn Penelope, *b* 1962: *m* 1985, John Frederick Rufus Warren, son of John Warren, of Harlow, Essex, and has issue living, Jakie James, *b* 1986, — Alexander Edward, *b* 1994, — Susanna, *b* 1988. *Residence* – The Priory, Moulton, Newmarket, Edmunds, Suffolk.

COLLATERAL BRANCHES LIVING

Issue of late Lt-Col Hon Aubrey Nigel Henry Molyneux Herbert MP, 2nd son of 4th Earl, *b* 1880, *d* 1923: *m* 1910, Hon Mary Gertrude Vesey, who *d* 1970, da of 4th Viscount De Vesci:—
Anne Brigit Domenica, *b* 1914: *m* 1935, Capt Allaster Edward George Grant, MC, late 9th Lancers (*see* E Malmesbury, 1909 Edn), who *d* 1947, and has had issue, Robert John David (Nutcombe Manor, Clayhanger, Tiverton, Devon), *b* 1942; *ed* Ampleforth, and New Coll, Oxford: *m* 1970, Harriet, da of late Markway Roope Reeve, of Lower Brook House, Kings Somborne, Hants, and has issue living, Charles Edward *b* 1971, Peter Mark Haddon *b* 1981, Katherine Bridget *b* 1972, Emma Philippa *b* 1973, — Mary Christina, *b* 1937: *m* 1962, Michael Edward Melotte, of Talfourd Rd, SE15 6NZ, and has issue living, Edward John *b* 1965; Capt IG, Victoria Mary *b* 1963: *m* 1985, Jonathan Clark, of 17 Crescent Grove, SW4, — Evelyn Elizabeth Anne, *b* 1938: *m* 1958, Ian James Fraser, CBE, MC (later Sir Ian Fraser), and *d* 1984, leaving issue (*see* L Lovat, colls).

Issue of late Hon Mervyn Robert Howard Molyneux Herbert, 3rd son of 4th Earl, *b* 1882, *d* 1929: *m* 1921, Mary Elizabeth, who *d* 1979, da of J. E. Willard, formerly Ambassador for USA at Madrid:—
Edward Alan Mervyn Henry Molyneux, *b* 1926; *ed* Eton; ARIBA; Bar Middle Temple 1952; late Capt Coldstream Gds: *m* 1966, Bridget Anne, who *d* 1976, da of Maj Hugh Washington Hibbert (*see* B Mowbray, colls), and has issue living, Alan Mervyn Edward Hugh, *b* 1971, — Mary Patricia, *b* 1967, — Elizabeth Anne, *b* 1968, — Penelope Gabrielle Serena, *b* 1969. *Residences* – Tetton House, Taunton: 37 Morpeth Mansions, SW1. —— Mary Elizabeth Catherine Gwendolen, *b* 1922; composer, singer and pianist: *m* 1st, 1946 (*m diss* 1957), Radu Tilea; 2ndly, 1970 (*m diss* 19—), Count Denys Halka Ledochowsky, who *d* 1980, and has issue living (by 1st *m*), Mary Catherine Ileana Camilla, *b* 1950: *m* 1978, Ian Henry Willis, of Chapel Barn, Goodworth Clatford, Andover, Hants, and has issue (*see* B Thurlow, colls), — Elizabeth Helen Rodica *b* 1953; *m* 1973, John Michael Darell Harrap, of 35 Kenway Rd, SW5, and has issue (*see* Darell, Bt). *Residence* – 193 Coleherne Court, Old Brompton Rd, SW5 9AD.

PREDECESSORS – Maj-Gen Hon William Herbert, 5th son of 8th Earl of Pembroke, MP for Wilton 1734-37; *d* 1756, leaving with other issue **(1)** HENRY; cr *Baron Porchester*, of High Clere, co Southampton (peerage of Great Britain), 1780, and *Earl of Carnarvon* (peerage of Great Britain) 1793; was Master of the Horse 1806; *d* 1811; *s* by his son **(2)** HENRY GEORGE, 2nd Earl, *d* 1833; *s* by his son **(3)** HENRY JOHN GEORGE, 3rd Earl; *b* 1800: *m* 1830, Henrietta Anna, who *d* 1876, da of Lord Henry Thomas Molyneux-Howard (D Norfolk); *d* 1849; *s* by his son **(4)** HENRY HOWARD MOLYNEUX, PC, 4th Earl, *b* 1831; Under Sec of State for colonies 1857-9, Sec of State thereof 1866-7 and 1874-8, and Lord-Lieut of Ireland 1885-6: *m* 1st, 1861, Lady Evelyn Stanhope, da of 6th Earl of Chesterfield; 2ndly, 1878, Elizabeth Catharine, who *d* 1929, elder da of late Henry Howard; *d* 1890; *s* by his elder son **(5)** GEORGE EDWARD STANHOPE MOLYNEUX, 5th Earl, *b* 1866; the discoverer, with Howard Carter, of Tutankhamun's tomb: *m* 1895, Almina Victoria Maria Alexandra, who *d* 1969 (having *m* 2ndly, 1923, Lt-Col Ian Onslow Dennistoun, MVO, who *d* 1938), da of late Frederick Charles Wombwell; *d* 1923; *s* by his son **(6)** HENRY GEORGE ALFRED VICTOR FRANCIS, 6th Earl *b* 1898; Lt-Col 7th (Queen's Own) Hus; European War 1916-19 in Mesopotamia: *m* 1st, 1922 (*m diss* 1936), Anne Catherine Tredick, who *d* 1977 (having *m* 2ndly, 1938, as his 2nd wife, Lt-Cdr Geoffrey Seymour Grenfell, RN, who was *ka* 1940, and 3rdly, 1950, Don Stuart Mommand), elder da of late Jacob Wendell, of New York; 2ndly, 1939 (*m diss* 1947), Ottilie (Tillie Losch, the dancer), who *d* 1975, da of Eugene Losch of Vienna, and formerly wife of late Edward Frank Willis James, of West Dean Park, Sussex; *d* 1987; *s* by his only son **(7)** HENRY GEORGE REGINALD MOLYNEUX, 7th Earl and present peer; also Baron Porchester.

Carnegie, Lord; grandson of Duke of Fife.

CARNEGY OF LOUR, BARONESS (Carnegy of Lour) (Life Baroness 1982)

ELIZABETH PATRICIA CARNEGY OF LOUR, elder da of late Lt-Col Ughtred Elliott Carnegy of Lour, DSO, MC, JP, DL, 12th of Lour (*see* Northesk, E, colls); *b* 28 April 1925; *ed* Downham Sch, Essex; DL Angus 1988; with Girl Guides Assoc since 1947; Co Commr Angus 1956-63; Training Adviser Scotland 1958-62, and Commonwealth HQ 1963-65, Pres Council for Scotland since 1979; Member Educn Cttee Angus CC 1967-75; Councillor Tayside Region 1974-82; Convenor Recreation and Tourism Cttee 1974-76; Educn Cttee 1976-82; Commr Manpower Services Commn 1979-82; Chm Working Party on Prof Training for Community Educn in Scotland 1975-77, of Manpower Services Commn Cttee for Scotland 1981-83, and of the Scottish Community Educn Council 1981-88, Member Scottish Economic Council 1981-83, Administrative Council Royal Jubilee Trusts 1984-88, Council Open Univ since 1984; Trustee Nat Museums of Scotland 1987-91; Member of Court, Univ of St Andrews since 1991; served in 1939-45 War in Cavendish Laboratory, Camb 1943-46; Hon Sheriff 1969-84; Hon LLD Dundee 1991; cr *Baroness Carnegy of Lour*, of Lour in the District of Angus (Life Baroness) 1982.

Spot without spot

Arms – Or, an eagle displayed azure, beaked and membered sable, within a bordure gules. **Crest** – A demi leopard rampant proper. **Supporters** – Dexter, a leopard proper having a collar argent charged with three torteaux. Sinister, a greyhound proper having a collar gules charged with three escallops argent.

Residence – Lour, by Forfar, Angus DD8 2LR. *Club* – Lansdowne.

CARNOCK, BARON (Nicolson of that Ilk) (Baron UK 1916, Bt NS 1629 and 1637)

DAVID HENRY ARTHUR NICOLSON OF THAT ILK, 4th Baron, 16th Baronet of Lasswade and 14th Baronet of Carnock; Chief of Clan Nicolson; *b* 10 July 1920; *s* 1982; *ed* Winchester, and Balliol Coll, Oxford, admitted a Solicitor 1949; European War 1940-45 R Devon Yeo, Artillery and Staff (Major); ptnr Clifford Turner 1955-86.

Arms – Or three falcons' heads erased gules armed argent in fess point an inescutcheon argent a saltire azure surmounted of an inescutcheon or charged with a lion rampant within a double tressure flory counterflory gules ensigned of an Imperial Crown proper being the addition of the arms of Nova Scotia as a Baronet. **Crest** – A lion issuant or armed and langued gules. **Supporters** – Two eagles or armed gules. **Mottoes** – (above the shield) - Generositate; (below the shield) - Nil sistere contra.
Residences – 90 Whitehall Court, SW1; Ermewood House, Harford, Ivybridge, Devon.
Clubs – Travellers', Beefsteak.

DAUGHTER LIVING OF FIRST BARON

Hon Clementina Gwendolen Catharine (*Dowager Baroness St Levan*), *b* 1896: *m* 1916, 3rd Baron St Levan, who *d* 1978. *Residence* – Avallon, Green Lane, Marazion, Cornwall.

Nothing to stand against

COLLATERAL BRANCH LIVING

Granddaughter of late Hon Sir Harold George Nicolson, KCVO, CMG (infra):—
Issue of late (Lionel) Benedict Nicolson, CBE, MVO, FBA, *b* 1914, *d* 1978: *m* 1955 (*m diss* 1962), Luisa, da of Prof Giacomo Vertova, of Florence:—
Vanessa Pepita Giovanna, *b* 1956: *m* 1991, Andrew Cunningham Churchill Davidson, son of Harry Churchill Davidson, of Hove, Sussex, and has issue living Elena Rose, *b* 1987, — Rosa Ilaria, *b* 1989. *Residence* – Horserace House, Sissinghurst, Cranbrook, Kent.

Issue of late Hon Sir Harold George Nicolson, KCVO, CMG, yst son of 1st Baron, *b* 1886, *d* 1968: *m* 1913, Hon Victoria Mary Sackville-West, CH, who *d* 1962, da of 3rd Baron Sackville:—
NIGEL, MBE (Sissinghurst Castle, Cranbrook, Kent), *b* 19 Jan 1917; *ed* Eton, and Balliol Coll, Oxford; 1939-45 War as Capt Gren Gds (despatches, MBE); MP for Christchurch and E Div of Bournemouth (*C*) 1952-59; MBE (Mil) 1945: *m* 1953: *m diss* 1970), Philippa Janet, who *d* 1987, da of Sir (Eustace) Gervais Tennyson-d'Eyncourt, 2nd Bt, and has issue living, Adam (Perch Hill Farm, Brightling, nr Battle, E Sussex), *b* 1957: *m* 1st, 1982 (*m diss* 1992), Olivia Mary Rokeby, eldest da of Lt Cdr Antony Charles Reynardson Fane, RN (*see* E Westmorland, colls); 2ndly, 1993, Sarah Clare, da of John Earle Raven, of King's Coll, Camb, and has issue living (by 1st *m*), Thomas *b* 1984, William *b* 1986, Benedict *b* 1988, (by 2nd *m*) Rose Raven *b* 1994, — Juliet, *b* 1954: *m* 1977, James Macmillan-Scott, of 15 East 77th St, New York, NY 10021, USA, and has issue living, Clementine *b* 1981, Flora *b* 1985, — Rebecca (*Hon Mrs Guy Philipps*), *b* 1963: *m* 1988, Hon Guy Wogan Philipps, of 68 Westbourne Park Rd, London W2 5PJ, eldest son of 3rd Baron Milford.

PREDECESSORS – Alexander Nicolson, by tradition from Isle of Skye, settled in Aberdeen 1444. From him descended John Nicolson, of Edinburgh, who *d* 1605, leaving issue four sons. Of these the eldest, John, was cr a *Baronet* (Nicolson of Lasswade) of Nova Scotia 1629, with remainder to heirs male whatsoever. Although this title was thought to have become extinct upon the death of the 7th Bt in 1743, the 4th Baron Carnock successfully petitioned the Lord Lyon to be recognised in the baronetcy of Nicolson of Lasswade, and as Chief of Clan Nicolson, and was so recognised in an interlocutor dated 3 Sept 1984. The 3rd son of John Nicolson of Edinburgh (ante) was **(1)** THOMAS Nicolson of Carnock, was cr a *Baronet* of Nova Scotia, with remainder to heirs-male whatsoever 1636; *d* 1646; *s* by his son **(2)** THOMAS, 2nd Bt, *d* 1664; *s* by his son **(3)** THOMAS, 3rd Bt, *d* 1670; *s* by his son **(4)** THOMAS, 4th Bt, *b* 1669; *s* as 4th Lord Napier of Merchistoun 1683; *d* 1686, when the peerage devolved upon his maternal aunt, and the baronetcy passed to his cousin and heir-male **(5)** THOMAS, 5th Bt, son and heir of Sir John Nicolson of Tillicoultry; *d* 1699; *s* by his son **(6)** GEORGE, 6th Bt (of Carnock) and *de jure* 8th Bt (of Lasswade) (ante), at which point the two baronetcies merged: *m* Charlotte Halkett; *d* 1771; *s* by his son **(9)** WALTER PHILIP, 9th and 7th Bt: *m* Helen Carpenter; *d* 1786; *s* by his brother **(10)** DAVID, 10th and 8th Bt; *d* 1808; *s* by his cousin and heir-male **(11)** WILLIAM, 11th and 9th Bt (only son of George Nicolson of Tarviston), *b* 1758; Maj-Gen in the Army: *m* 1804, Mary Russell; *d* 1820; *s* by his son **(12)** FREDERICK WILLIAM ERSKINE, 12th and 10th Bt; Adm, and sometime Chm Thames Conservancy Board: *m* 1st, 1847, Clementina Maria Marion, da of James Loch, of Drylaw; 2ndly, 1855, Augusta Sarah, da of Robert Cullington, and widow of Capt Hay; 3rdly, 1867, Anne, da of R. Cross; *d* 1899; *s* by his son **(13)** ARTHUR, GCB, GCMG, GCVO, KCIE, PC, 13th and 11th Bt, *b* 1849; was Assist Private Sec to Earl Granville at Foreign Office 1872-4; on Staff of Earl of Dufferin of Egypt 1882, acting Chargé d'Affaires at Athens 1882-5, Sec of Legation at Teheran, and Acting Chargé d'Affaires in Persia 1885-8, Consul-Gen for Hungary 1888-93, Sec of Embassy at Constantinople 1893-4, and Agent and Consul-Gen in Bulgaria 1894-5, Envoy Extraor and Min Plen at Tangier and Consul-Gen in Morocco 1895-1904, Ambassador Extraor and Plen to Spain 1904-5, and at St Petersburg 1906-10, and Permanent Under-Sec of State for Foreign Affairs 1910-16; British Representative at Algeciras Conference 1905-6; cr *Baron Carnock*, of Carnock co Stirling (peerage of United Kingdom) 1916: *m* 1882, Mary Catherine, who *d* 1951, da of late Archibald Rowan Hamilton of Killyleagh Castle, co Down; *d* 1928; *s* by his elder son **(2)** FREDERICK ARCHIBALD, MC, 2nd Baron; *b* 1883; Bar Inner Temple 1924; Major 15th King's Hussars; sometime ADC to Viceroy of India; *d* 1952; *s* by his brother **(3)** ERSKINE ARTHUR, DSO, 3rd Baron; *b* 1884; Capt RN: *m* 1919, Hon Katharine Frederica Albertha Lopes, who *d* 1968, da of 1st Baron Roborough; *d* 1982; *s* by his only surv son **(4)** DAVID HENRY ARTHUR, 4th Baron and present peer.

CARNWATH, EARLDOM OF (Dalzell) (Extinct or Dormant 1941)

DAUGHTER LIVING OF THIRTEENTH EARL

Lady Muriel Marjorie, *b* 1903: *m* 1927, Lt-Col John Norton Dalzell, IA, who *d* 1957 (only son of James Taylor, of Lisnamallard, co Tyrone), when they assumed by R licence the surname and arms of Dalzell in lieu of that of Taylor, and has issue living, John Victor Robert, *b* 1929. *Residence* – Sand House, Wedmore, Somerset.

CARR OF HADLEY, BARON (Carr) (Life Baron 1975)

(LEONARD) ROBERT CARR, PC, son of late Ralph Edward Carr; *b* 11 Nov 1916; *ed* Westminster and Gonville and Caius Coll, Camb (MA); PPS to Sir Anthony Eden, as Sec of State for Foreign Affairs 1951-55, and as PM 1955, Parl Sec to Min of Labour 1955-58; Sec for Tech Co-operation 1963-64; Sec of State for Employment and Productivity June to Oct 1970, for Employment 1970-72, Lord Pres of the Council and Leader of House of Commons April to Nov 1972, and Sec of State for Home Affairs 1972-74; MP for Mitcham (C) 1950-74, and Sutton (Carshalton) 1974-75; a Dir, Metal Closure Group 1959-63, and 1965-70 (Dep Chm 1958-63), Chm John Dale Ltd 1958-63, and 1965-70, Dir Securicor Ltd and Security Services plc 1961-63, 1965-70 and 1974-85, SGB Group plc 1974-86, Cadbury Schweppes plc 1979-87, Prudential Assurance Co Ltd 1976-85 (Dep Chm 1979-80, Chm 1980-85), and Prudential Corpn plc 1978-89 (Dep Chm 1979-80, Chm 1980-85); Pres Consultative Council of Professional Management Organisations since 1976; cr PC 1963, and *Baron Carr of Hadley*, of Monken Hadley in Greater London (Life Baron) 1975): *m* 1943, Joan Kathleen, da of Dr E. W. Twining, and has issue.
Address – c/o House of Lords, SW1. *Club* – Brooks's.

DAUGHTERS LIVING

Hon Susan Elizabeth, *b* 1947: *m* 1972, (Alun) Rhodri Bradley-Jones, of Gardener's Cottage, Kingscote, Glos.
Hon Virginia Sarah, *b* 1957: *m* 1984, Michael Frederick Fox.

Carpenter, see Baron Boyd-Carpenter.

CARRICK, EARL OF (Butler) Sits as BARON BUTLER OF MOUNT JULIET (UK 1912) (Earl I 1748)

Be steadfast

DAVID JAMES THEOBALD SOMERSET BUTLER, 10th Earl; *b* 9 Jan 1953; *s* 1992; *ed* Downside: *m* 1975, Philippa Janice Victoria, yr da of Wing Cmdr Leonard Victor Craxton, RAF (ret), of Mills Lydgate One, West Rd, Milford on Sea, Lymington, Hants, and has issue.

Arms – Or, a chief indented azure, a crescent for difference. Crest – Out of a ducal coronet or, a plume of ostrich feathers, and issuant therefrom a demi-falcon rising all argent. Supporters – *Dexter*, a falcon, wings inverted argent, beaked, membered, and belled, or; *sinister*, a male griffin argent, beaked, membered, armed, collared and chained, or; on each supporter a crescent for difference.
Residence – Pant yr Eos, Moelfre, Llansilin, Oswestry, Shropshire SY10 7QR.

SONS LIVING

(ARION) THOMAS PIERS HAMILTON (*Viscount Ikerrin*), *b* 1 Sept Jan 1975.
Hon Piers Edmund Theobald Lismalyn, *b* 1979.
Hon Lindsay Simon Turville Somerset, *b* (twin) 1979.

SISTER LIVING

Lady Juliana Mary Philomena, *b* 1960. *Residence* – 31 Greenbank Av, Saltdean, Brighton BN2 8QS.

WIDOW LIVING OF SON OF SEVENTH EARL

Dorothea, yst da of late Thomas Warwick Bennett, of 40 Bishop's Rd, E2: *m* 1957, as his 2nd wife, Maj Hon Pierce Alan Somerset David Butler, TD, who *d* 1964. *Residence* – .

WIDOW LIVING OF NINTH EARL

GILLIAN IRENE (*Gillian, Countess of Carrick*), da of Leonard Grimes: *m* 1986, as his 2nd wife, the 9th Earl, who *d* 1992. *Residence* – 10 Netherton Grove, SW10.

COLLATERAL BRANCHES LIVING

Issue of late Hon (Horace) Somerset Edmond Butler, CIE, 2nd son of 7th Earl, *b* 1903; *d* 1962: *m* 1928, Barbara, who *d* 1977, da of M. S. Jacomb-Hood:—
Georgina Carolin Eve (designer Gina Fratini), *b* 1931: *m* 1st, 1954, David Goldberg; 2ndly, 1961, Renato Fratini; 3rdly, 1969, James Allan Short (actor Jimmy Logan).

Issue of late Maj Hon Guy Somerset Lionel Butler, 3rd son of 7th Earl, *b* 1905; *d* 1983: *m* 1st, 1939 (*m diss* 1961), Mrs Patricia Anne (Paddianne) Tennant, who *d* 1982, da of late William Dunne; 2ndly, 1961, Mrs Janet Frances Parker, who *d* 1984, da of late Alexander Gordon Preston:—
(By 1st *m*) Rupert Lionel Somerset (Lily Bank Farm, Lily Bottom Lane, Parslows Hillock, Princes Risborough, Bucks HP27 0RN), *b* 1940, *ed* Tonbridge, Quintin Sch, and RAF Coll Cranwell: Fl-Lt RAF (ret) *m* 1968, Jenifer Mary, da of late Norman James Rush, FCA, of High Wood, Henley, Haslemere, Surrey, and has issue living, Piers Somerset Patrick, *b* 1970, — Eli Somerset James, *b* 1971, — Matthew Somerset Guy, *b* 1972, — Sebastian Somerset Lionel, *b* 1979. —— Dermot Somerset Launcelot (Prospect House, Newcastle, co Wicklow), *b* 1941; *ed* Tonbridge, and Quintin Sch: *m* 1st, 1970 (*m diss* 1983), Lorna Ailsa Graham, da of Maj Ian Graham Menzies; 2ndly, 1986, Mrs Victoria Marsland Nabarro, da of John Lloyd Owen, and has issue living (by 1st *m*), Tara Siobhan Somerset, *b* 1974.

Issue of late Maj Hon Pierce Alan Somerset David Butler, TD, 5th son of 7th Earl, *b* 1909, *d* 1964: *m* 1st, 1933 (*m diss* 1957), Leri, elder da of Dr G. Llywelyn-Jones, of Bryn Glas, Llangefni, Anglesey; 2ndly, 1957, Dorothea (ante), yst da of late Thomas Warwick Bennett:—
(By 1st *m*) David Llewelyn Somerset (Brook Farm, Wethersfield, Braintree, Essex), *b* 1937; *m* 1966, Anne, da of A. S. Haigh of White Roding, Essex, and has issue living, Michael Somerset, *b* 1969, — Hilary Mary, *b* 1971. —— Helen Sarah Ann (Fosters Buildings, Hartest, Bury St Edmunds, Suffolk), *b* 1936: *m* 1957 (*m diss* 1969), Anthony Thomas Colley.

Grandchildren of late Rev Pierce Rollo Butler (infra):—
Issue of late Theobald Rollo Pierce Butler, BEM, Detective Sgt, Metropolitan Police Force, *b* 1913, *d* 1983: *m* 1st, 1940 (*m diss* 1963), Christine Helen, da of Gilbert William Harding; 2ndly, 1964, Gwendoline May Emily (33 Dalinghoo Rd, Wickham Market, Woodbridge, Suffolk), formerly wife of Arthur Robert Lane, and da of Frederick George Jennings:—
(By 1st wife) Jeremy Somerset Pierce, *b* 1944. —— Charlotte Veronica, *b* 1942. —— (By 2nd wife) Mark Pierce (85 Beulah Rd, Walthamstow, E17 9LD), *b* 1960; serving Constable, Metropolitan Police: *m* 1983, Jane, da of Alfred Reginald Gill, and has issue living, Scarlett Frances, *b* 1986.
Issue of the late James Armar Cory Butler, *b* 1916, *d* 1973: *m* 1944, Marjorie Wells (140 Broom Rd, Teddington, Middx):—
Sandra Leigh, *b* 1945: *m* 19—, Charles Devine, and has issue living, Anthony Michael, *b* 1969, — Sarah Louise, *b* 1976. —— Melanie Ann, *b* 1949: *m* 1978, Terence Patrick Cook, and has had issue, Coralie Joanna, *b* 1979, *d* 1985, — Natalie Jane, *b* 1982, — Genevere Eloise, *b* 1987, — Daniella, *b* 1990.

Grandchildren of late Rev Pierce Armar Butler (infra):—
Issue of late Rev Pierce Rollo Butler, *b* 1885, *d* 1950: *m* 1911, Ethel Florence, who *d* 1943, da of Rev Thomas Legge Symes:—
Kenelm Somerset Priaulx, *b* 1917; late Lt-Col Falkland Islands Defence Force, and Admin Officer, S Georgia; formerly Capt R Sigs (TA): *m* 1954, Janet Cooper, da of James Gilmour. *Residence* – 16 Penny Lane, Durbanville, CP 7550, S Africa.
Issue of late Maj Hubert Blennerhassett Butler, *b* 1887, *d* 1986: *m* 1919, Sophie Marie, who *d* 1985, da of Jules Castravelli, of Bacos, Alexandria, Egypt:—

Marjorye Marie (Batchelors, Tyning, Heytesbury, Warminster, Wilts), *b* 1921: *m* 1944, Maj Peter Quentin Logan, S Staffordshire Regt, who *d* 1992, and has issue living, Michael Roderic Quentin, *b* 1947: *m* 1971 (*m diss* 1981), Gillian, da of Cdr J. McC. Rutherford, RNVR, of Henley-on-Thames, Oxon. —— Noreen May, *b* 1923: *m* 1944, Col Frank Hilary Bristowe, RM, of 18 Archery Sq, Walmer, Deal, Kent, and has issue living, Rosamund Gillian, *b* 1947: *m* 1969, Charles Vivian Parry, of 2 Queen's Terr, King's Rd, Windsor, Berks, — June Hilary, *b* 1949: *m* 1969, William Magnus Jamieson, of 53 Loxley Rd, SW18, and has issue living, Henry William Ashton *b* 1979, James Nicholas Rupert *b* 1986, Francesca Catherine Sophie *b* 1977, Leanda Georgina Hilary *b* 1983, — Nicola Catherine Diana, *b* 1960: *m* 1984, Courtenay Charles Ilbert Inchbald, of 10 Kempsford Gdns, SW5.

Granddaughter of late Rev Pierce Butler, 3rd son of late Lt-Gen Hon Henry Edward Butler, 2nd son of 2nd Earl:—

Issue of late Rev Pierce Armar Butler, *b* 1863, *d* 1924: *m* 1885, Emily, who *d* 1933, da of Capt W. J. Russwurm, W India Regt:—

Norah Veronica Pierce, *b* 1904. *Residence* – 7 Doric Place, Woodbridge, Suffolk.

PREDECESSORS – (1) *Sir* PIERCE Butler, Knt; Lt-Gen of the Irish Army under Lord Mountgarret, was cr *Viscount Ikerrin* (peerage of Ireland) 1629; *s* by son (2) PIERCE, 2nd Viscount; *s* by his son (3) JAMES, 3rd Viscount; *d* 1688; *s* by his son (4) PIERCE, 4th Viscount; *d* 1710; *s* by his son (5) JAMES, 5th Viscount; *d* a minor 1712; *s* by his uncle (6) THOMAS, 6th Viscount, Chaplain-Gen to Army in Flanders under James, Duke of Ormonde; *d* 1719; *s* by his son (7) JAMES, 7th Viscount; *d* 1721; *s* by his brother (8) SOMERSET HAMILTON, 8th Viscount; cr *Earl of Carrick* (peerage of Ireland) 1748; *d* 1774; *s* by his son (9) HENRY THOMAS, 2nd Earl; *d* 1813; *s* by his son (10) SOMERSET RICHARD, 3rd Earl; *b* 1779: *m* 1st, 1811, Anne, who *d* 1829, da of Owen Wynne, of Haslewood, co Sligo; 2ndly, 1833, Lucy, who *d* 1884, da of late Arthur French, of French Park; *d* 1838, *s* by his elder son (11) HENRY THOMAS, 4th Earl; *d* a minor 1846; *s* by his brother (12) SOMERSET ARTHUR, 5th Earl, *b* 1835; *d* 1901; *s* by his cousin (13) CHARLES HENRY SOMERSET (son of late Capt Charles George Butler, 86th Regt, grandson of 2nd Earl), 6th Earl, *b* 1851; present during repulse of an incursion of Fenians into Canada 1870: *m* 1st, 1873, Kathleen Emily Hamilton, who *d* 1888, da of Lieut-Col Albert Ernest Ross, 5th Fusiliers; 2ndly, 1896, Emily Codrington, who *d* 1915, da of late Mark Jones; *d* 1909; *s* by his son (14) CHARLES ERNEST ALFRED FRENCH SOMERSET, OBE, 7th Earl, *b* 1873; Comptroller of the Household to Lord-Lieut of Ireland 1913-15; cr *Baron Butler of Mount Juliet*, co Kilkenny (peerage of United Kingdom) 1912: *m* 1898, Ellen Rosamond Mary, who *d* 1946, da of late Lieut-Col Henry Gore Lindsay, *d* 1931; *s* by his son (15) THEOBALD WALTER SOMERSET HENRY, 8th Earl; *b* 1903; European War 1939-44 as acting Com RNVR, British Naval Liaison Officer in USA and Senior RN Officer: *m* 1st, 1930 (*m diss* 1938), Marion Caher (EDWARDS), who *d* 1973, da of Daniel C. Donoghue, of Philadelphia, USA; 2nd, 1938, Margaret (DRUM), who *d* (July) 1954, da of Charles B. Power, of Helena, Montana, USA; 3rdly, Oct 1954, Ruth, who *d* 1992, da of Francis T. M. McEnery, Chicago, Ill, USA, *d* 1957; *s* by his son (16) BRIAN STUART THEOBALD SOMERSET CAHER, 9th Earl; *b* 1931; Co Dir: *m* 1st, 1951 (*m diss* 1976), (Mary) Belinda, who *d* 1993, da of late Maj David Turville-Constable-Maxwell, TD, RA (see L Herries of Terregles, colls); 2ndly, 1986, Gillian Irene, da of Leonard Grimes; *d* 1992; *s* by his only son (17) DAVID JAMES THEOBALD SOMERSET, 10th Earl and present peer; also Viscount Ikerrin, and Baron Butler, of Mount Juliet.

CARRINGTON, BARON (Carington) (I 1796, GB 1797)

Persevering and faithful

PETER ALEXANDER RUPERT CARINGTON, KG, GCMG, CH, MC, PC, 6th Baron; *b* 6 June 1919; *s* 1938; *ed* Eton (Fellow 1966); Maj (ret) Gren Gds; Parl Sec Min of Agriculture and Fisheries 1951-54, Parl Sec Min of Defence 1954-56, High Commr for UK in Australia 1956-59, First Lord of the Admiralty 1959-63, Min without Portfolio and Leader of House of Lords 1963-64, Leader of the Opposition in House of Lords 1964-70, and 1974-79; Sec of State for Defence 1970-74, and Sec of State Dept of Energy Jan to Feb 1974; Min of Aviation Supply 1971-74; Chm of Conservative Party 1972-74; Sec of State, Foreign and Commonwealth Affairs and Min of Overseas Development 1979-82; Sec-Gen NATO 1983-88; a Dir Amalgamated Metal Corpn, Ltd, 1965-70, Hambros Bank 1967-70, Barclays Bank 1967-70, and 1974-79, Cadbury Schweppes, Ltd 1968-70, and 1974-79, Chm Christies 1988-92, Dir The Telegraph plc since 1990; Joint Dep Chm Aust & NZ Bank 1965-67, Chm 1967-69; a Dir Rio Tinto-Zinc Corpn 1974-79; Chm Trustees Victoria and Albert Museum since 1983; Pres The Pilgrims 1983, Trustee Tradescant Trust since 1990, Chm European Community Peace Conference on Yugoslavia 1991-92, since when Chancellor Reading Univ; Chancellor of the Order of St Michael and St George since 1984; 1939-45 War (MC); KCMG 1958, PC 1959, CH 1983, KG 1985, GCMG 1988: *m* 1942, Iona, da of Lt-Col Sir Francis Kennedy McClean, AFC, and has issue.

Arms – Or, a chevron cottised, between three demi-griffins, the two in chief respectant sable. **Crest** – An elephant's head erased or, eared gules, charged on the neck with three fleurs-de-lis, two and one azure. **Supporters** – Two griffins' wings elevated sable, the *dexter* charged with three fleurs-de-lis palewise or, the *sinister* with three trefoils slipped palewise of the last.
Seat – The Manor House, Bledlow, near Aylesbury, Bucks. *Town Residence* – 32A Ovington Square, SW3 *Clubs* – Pratt's, White's.

SON LIVING

Hon RUPERT FRANCIS JOHN, *b* 2 Dec 1948; *ed* Eton, and Bristol Univ: *m* 1989, Daniela, da of Flavio Diotallevi, of Madrid, and has issue living, Robert, *b* 7 Dec 1990, — Francesca, *b* 1993.

DAUGHTERS LIVING

Hon Alexandra, *b* 1943: *m* 1965, Maj Peter Noel de Bunsen, Coldm Gds (ret), eldest son of Charles de Bunsen (see Buxton, Bt, 1953 Edn), and has issue living, Charles Rupert, *b* 1970, — Peter James, *b* 1973, — Victoria, *b* 1968: *m* 1991, Andrew Falcon (see D Wellington, colls). *Residence* – The Old Rectory, Kirby Bedon, Norwich, Norfolk.

Hon Virginia CARINGTON, *b* 1946; has resumed her maiden name: *m* 1973 (*m diss* 1979), 4th Baron Ashcombe. *Residence* – 5 Rutland Gate Mews, SW7.

SISTER LIVING

Hon Elizabeth, *b* 1917: *m* 1943, William Lionel Dove, MB, ChB, MRCS, LRCP, and has issue living, Anthony Edward (Little House, Common Lane, Lower Stretton, Cheshire), *b* 1946: *m* 1st, 1983 (*m diss* 1988), Jane Susan, only da of A. H. Smith, of Dundrum, Queens Rd, Ilkley, Yorks; 2ndly, 19—, Julie Maria, da of G. Williams, of Warrington, Cheshire, — (John) Andrew, *b* 1951: *m* 1980 (*m diss* 1984), Jane Esther, da of Denis Horace Holland, of Park Farm, Lavenham, Sudbury, Suffolk. *Residence* – 6 Woolton Hill Rd, Liverpool, L25 6HX.

PREDECESSORS – (1) ROBERT Smith, MP for Nottingham 1779-96; cr *Baron Carrington*, of Bulcot Lodge (peerage of Ireland) 1796, and *Baron Carrington*, of Upton, Notts (peerage of Great Britain) 1797; *d* 1838; *s* by his son (2) ROBERT JOHN, 2nd Baron; *b* 1796; MP for Wendover 1818-20, Buckinghamshire 1820-30, and High Wycombe 1831-8; Lord-Lieut of Bucks; assumed surname of Carington in lieu of Smith by R licence 1839: *m* 1st, 1822, Hon Elizabeth Katherine, who *d* 1832, da of 1st Baron Forester; 2ndly, 1840, Hon Augusta Annabella Drummond-Willoughby, who *d* 1879, da of 21st Baron Willougbhy D'Eresby; *d* 1868; *s* by his son (3) CHARLES ROBERT, 3rd Baron; *b* 1843; Joint Hereditary Lord Great Chamberlain (appointed to act for Reign of King George V); sat as MP for Wycombe (*L*) 1865-8; surname of Carington confirmed by R licence 1880; subsequently granted R licence 1896 to assume the surnames of Wynn-Carrington; was Gov and Com-in-Ch of New South Wales 1885-90, Lord Chamberlain to Queen Victoria's Household 1892-5, Pres of Board of Agriculture Dec 1905 to Oct 1911, and Lord Privy Seal Oct 1911 to Feb 1912; bore St Edward's Staff at Coronation of King Edward VII; cr *Viscount Wendover*, of Chepping Wycombe, Bucks, *Earl Carrington* (peerage of United Kingdom) 1895, and *Marquess of Lincolnshire* (peerage of United Kingdom) 1912: *m* 1878, Hon Cecilia Margaret Harbord, elder da of 5th Baron Suffield; *d* 1928, when the Marquessate of Lincolnshire, the Earldom of Carrington, and the Viscountcy of Wendover became ext (his only son, Albert Edward Samuel Charles Robert, *Viscount Wendover*, *b* 1895; Lt RHG, *d* of wounds in action during WW I 1915), while the two Baronies of Carrington devolved upon his brother (4) RUPERT CLEMENT GEORGE Carington, CVO, DSO, 4th Baron, *b* 1852; MP for Buckinghamshire (*L*) 1880-85; surname of Carington confirmed by R licence 1880; *m* 1891, Edith, who *d* 1908, da of John S. Horsfall, of Widglewa, NS Wales; *d* 1929; *s* by his son (5) RUPERT VICTOR JOHN, 5th Baron, *b* 1891: *m* 1916, Hon Sybil Marion Colville, who *d* 1946, da of 2nd Viscount Colville of Culross; *d* 1938; *s* by his son (6) PETER ALEXANDER RUPERT, 6th Baron, and present peer.

CARRON, BARONY OF (Carron) (Extinct 1969)

DAUGHTERS LIVING OF LIFE BARON

Hon Hilary Mary, *b* 1933: *m* 1959, John Simon Weidemann, of The Gables, 27 Bromley Rd, SE6 2TS, and has issue.
Hon Patricia Ann, *b* 1945: *m* 1970 (*m diss* 1982), Victor Albert Hull, and has issue.

CARSON, BARONY OF (Carson) (Extinct 1935)

WIDOW LIVING OF SON OF LIFE BARON (*By 2nd marriage*)

Heather, da of late Frank Arthur Sclater, OBE, MC, of Milford, Surrey: *m* 1943, Hon Edward Carson, who *d* 1987. *Residence* – Crossways, Westfield, nr Hastings, Sussex.

CARTER, BARON (Carter) (Life Baron 1987)

DENIS VICTOR CARTER, son of late Albert William Carter; *b* 17 Jan 1932; *ed* Xaverian Coll, Brighton, E Sussex Agric Coll, Essex Coll of Agric, and Worcester Coll, Oxford (B Litt); agricultural consultant and farmer since 1957, founder AKC Ltd (agricultural accounting and management) 1957, partner Drayton Farms since 1975, and a Dir W.E. & D.T. Cave Ltd since 1976; Exec Prod Link TV (programmes for the disabled); Sgt RASC, in Central Zone, Egypt: cr *Baron Carter*, of Devizes, co Wilts (Life Baron) 1987: *m* 1957, Teresa Mary, da of late Cecil William Greengoe, and has had issue.
Address – c/o House of Lords, SW1. *Club* – Farmers'.

SON DECEASED

Andrew Peter, *b* 1963; *d* 1982.

DAUGHTER LIVING

Hon Catherine Mary, *b* 1959.

CARVER, BARON (Carver) (Life Baron 1977)

(RICHARD) MICHAEL POWER CARVER, GCB, CBE, DSO, MC, son of late Harold Power Carver; *b* 24 April 1915; *ed* Winchester, RMC Sandhurst; commd R Tank Corps 1935; GSO1, 7th Armd Div 1942; OC 1st RTR 1943; Cmd 4th Armd Bde 1944; GOC 3rd Div 1962-64; C-in-C Far East 1967-69; GOC Southern Command

1969-71; CGS 1971-73; Chief of Defence Staff 1973-76; Field Marshal 1973; British Commr designate for Rhodesia 1977; DSO 1943 (Bar 1944), CBE (Mil) 1945, CB (Mil) 1957, KCB (Mil) 1966, GCB (Mil) 1970; 1939-45 War in Middle East, Italy and NW Europe (despatches twice, MC, DSO and Bar, CBE); Kenya (despatches, CB); *cr Baron Carver*, of Shackleford, co Surrey (Life Baron) 1977: *m* 1947, Edith, da of late Lt-Col Sir Henry Lowry-Corry, MC (*see* E Belmore, colls) and has issue.
Residence – Wood End House, Wickham, Hants. *Clubs* – Cavalry & Guards, Anglo-Belgian.

SONS LIVING

Hon Andrew Richard (Bayswater Mill House, Headington, Oxford OX3 9SB), *b* 1950: *m* 1st, 1973, Anne Rosamunde, da of Brian Stewart, of the Broich, Crief, Perthshire; 2ndly, 1989, Patricia, da of Jack Taffe, of Marco Is, Florida, USA.
Hon John Antony, *b* 1961: *m* 1992, Susan E., only da of Alexander Graham, of Kirkcaldy, Fife.

DAUGHTERS LIVING

Hon Susanna Mary (57A Broughton Rd, SW6 2LE), *b* 1948.
Hon Alice Elizabeth (33 The Green, Brill, Aylesbury, Bucks HP18 9RU), *b* 1954: *m* 1976 (*m diss* 1989), Capt Claude Walters, Gren Gds.

CASEY, BARONY OF (Casey) (Extinct 1976)

SON LIVING OF LIFE BARON

Hon Donn (141 Newmarket Rd, Cambridge), *b* 1931; relinquished by deed poll 1970 the forenames Richard Charles.

DAUGHTER LIVING OF LIFE BARON

Hon Jane Alice Camilla (5 Darley Place, Darlinghurst, NSW 2010, Australia), *b* 1928: *m* 1955 (*m diss* 1981), Murray W. Macgowan.

CASTLE, BARONY OF (Castle) (Extinct 1979)

WIDOW LIVING OF LIFE BARON

BARBARA ANNE (*Baroness Castle of Blackburn*), PC; *cr Baroness Castle of Blackburn* (Life Baroness) 1990; da of Frank Betts: *m* 1944, Baron Castle (Life Baron), who *d* 1979.

CASTLE OF BLACKBURN, BARONESS (Castle) (Life Baroness 1990)

BARBARA ANNE CASTLE, PC, da of late Frank Betts; *b* 6 Oct 1910; *ed* Bradford Girls' Gram Sch, and St Hugh's Coll, Oxford (Hon Fellow 1966), Hon DTech Bradford 1968, and Loughborough 1969, Hon Fellow Bradford and Ilkley Community Coll 1985, Hon Fellow Umist 1991, Hon LLD Lancaster Univ 1991, Hon Fellow Humberside Polytechnic 1991, Hon Fellow York Univ 1992, Hon LLD Manchester Univ 1993; Cross of Order of Merit (Germany) 1990; Member Nat Exec Cttee of Labour Party 1950-85, Chm Labour Party 1959, Min of Overseas Devpt 1964-65, Min of Transport 1965-68, First Sec of State and Sec of State for Employment and Productivity 1968-70, Sec of State for Social Services 1974-76; Co-Chm Women's Nat Commn 1975-76; MP Blackburn (*Lab*) 1945-50, Blackburn East 1950-55, and Blackburn 1955-79, MEP Greater Manchester North 1979-84, and Greater Manchester West 1984-89; *cr* PC 1964, and *Baroness Castle of Blackburn*, of Ibstone, co Bucks (Life Baroness) 1990: *m* 1944, Edward Cyril Castle, who was *cr* Baron Castle (Life Baron) 1974, and who *d* 1979.
Address – House of Lords, SW1A 0PW.

CASTLEMAINE, BARON (Handcock) (Baron I 1812)

VIGILATE ET ORATE

Watch and pray

ROLAND THOMAS JOHN HANDCOCK, 8th Baron; *b* 22 April, 1943; *s* 1973; Maj Army Air Corps: *m* 1st, 1969, Pauline Anne, el da of John Taylor Bainbridge, of The Moat House, Burstow, Surrey; 2ndly, 1988, Lynne Christine, eldest da of Maj Justin Michael Gurney, RAEC, and has issue by 2nd *m*.

Arms – Ermine, on a chief sable, a dexter hand between two cocks argent, armed, crested, and jelloped gules. **Crest** – a demi-lion rampant azure, holding a lozenge argent, charged with a cock gules. **Supporters** – *Dexter*, a lion guardant azure; *sinister*, a cock, proper.
Address – Keepers Cottage, Winterbourne Stoke, Salisbury.

SON LIVING *(By 2nd marriage)*

Hon RONAN MICHAEL EDWARD, *b* 27 March 1989.

SISTERS LIVING

Hon Eileen Esther, *b* 1931: *m* 1959, Fl Lt Terence Frank Adams, RAF (ret), and has issue living, Patrick Joseph John, *b* 1960, — Niall Michael, *b* 1968, — Siobhan Mary, *b* 1962.
Hon Edith Deirdre, *b* 1936: *m* 1st 1957 (*m diss* 1974), Keith Moss, BEM; 2ndly, 1975, Terence Hook, and has issue living (by 1st *m*), Julian Duncan, *b* 1962.

COLLATERAL BRANCHES LIVING

Grandchildren of late Henry Handcock (infra):—
Issue of late Richard Henry Algernon Handcock, *b* 1895; *d* 1974: *m* 1943, Catherine, who *d* 1971, da of late Emmanuel Breham, of Pont de l'Arche, France, and widow of John Morgan Keeley Knight, Lt RFC:—
Clifford Marcel (Rancher, Beaconsfield Rd, Farnham Royal, Bucks), *b* 1925; late CQMS, KOSB; 1939-45 War with 1st Air-borne Div: *m* 1944, Joyce Morton, and has issue living, Linda, *b* 1945. —— Claude Desmond Richard, *b* 1928: *m* 1948, Enid Perry, and has issue living, Andre Patrick James, *b* 1950, — Peter Michael Roland, *b* 1951, — Teresa Catherine Rose, *b* 1954. —— Sheila Annette Kathleen, *b* 1927: *m* 19—, Brinley Aurelius, of 42 Humber Way, Langley, Bucks, and has issue living, Geoffrey, *b* 1955, — Heather, *b* 1947. —— Heather, *b* 1939: *m* 1961, Robert Henry Harvey, of 12 Clanfield Cres, Tilehurst, Reading, and has issue living, Sandra, *b* 1963.

Grandsons of late Hon Robert John Handcock, 2nd son of 3rd Baron:—
Issue of late Henry Handcock, *b* 1869, *d* 1917: *m* 1892, Charlotte, who *d* 1922, da of late Richard Cole:—
Terence Robin (53 Kidbrooke Park Rd, Blackheath, SE3 0EQ), *b* 1902: *m* 1933, Eva Mary, da of Charles Taylor, and has issue living, Michael Robin (The Annexe, 6 Pond Rd, Blackheath, SE3), *b* 1934: *m* 1961, Jean Anne, only da of J. T. Smoker, and has issue living, Jenny Samantha *b* 1969. —— Patrick Francis Denys (White Lodge, Restronguet Point, Feock, Truro, Cornwall), *b* 1913: *m* 1st, 1933, Kathleen Joan, who *d* 1972, da of Frederick Lyle; 2ndly, 1972, Hilary Maybelle, widow of Sqd-Ldr D. W. Willis, RAF, and has issue living (by 1st *m*), Patrick Michael, *b* 1934.

Grandson of late Rev John Harward Jessop Handcock, son of late Rev John Gustavus Handcock, 4th son of 2nd Baron:—
Issue of late Harward Devereux Handcock, *b* 1874, *d* 1944: *m* 1907, Eleanor Winifred, who *d* 1966, da of late Henry John Potts, of Glan-yr-afon, Mold, Flintshire, and Ollerton, Cheshire:—
John Harward (Anderida, Brook Green, Cuckfield, Sussex) *b* 1924: *m* 1949, Brenda Tenrill, da of Donald Stewart Alexander Simpson, and has issue living, Jeremy John, *b* 1953: *m* 1978, Effie, eldest da of H. Hallaschek, of Stuttgart, W Germany, and has issue living, Alexander John *b* 1981, Thomas William Heinz *b* 1983, — Timothy Charles, *b* 1964, — Fiona Elizabeth Jane, *b* 1956.

Grandchildren of late Robert Harris Temple Handcock, only son of Edward Stanley Handcock, yst son of late Lt-Col Hon Robert French Handcock, 8th son of 2nd Baron:—
Issue of late Cdr William Stanley Handcock, RN, *b* 1908, *d* 1964: *m* 1933, Joan Mary (Sparshott House, Hambledon, Hants), da of late Sir Ralph Molyneux Combe:—
Timothy Stannus (Holmwood Cottage, Stroud, Petersfield, Hants), *b* 1938. —— Deirdre Elizabeth, *b* 1935: *m* 1960, Capt Colin Prinsep James, MC, late Rifle Bde, of Cotleigh House, Honiton, Devon, and has issue living, Emma Louise, *b* 1962, — Belinda Anne Nonie, *b* 1964. —— Luleen Annette, *b* 1946: *m* 1st, 1977, Michael Poynder; 2ndly, 1981, Frederick Moseley Wanklyn, of Rose Cottage, PO Box N7776, Lyford Cay, Nassau, Bahamas.

PREDECESSORS – (1) WILLIAM Handcock, Constable and Gov of Athlone; *cr Baron Castlemaine*, of Moydrum, co West-meath (peerage of Ireland) 1812, with remainder to his brother and *Viscount Castlemaine* (peerage of Ireland) 1822; *d* 1839, when the Viscountcy became extinct; *s* in Barony by his brother (2) RICHARD, 2nd Baron; *d* 1840; *s* by his son (3) RICHARD, 3rd Baron; *b* 1791; a Representative Peer: *m* 1822, Margaret, da of Michael Harris, of Dublin; *d* 1869; *s* by his son (4) RICHARD, 4th Baron, *b* 1826; a Representative Peer, and Lord-Lieut of co Westmeath: *m* 1857, Hon Louisa Matilda, who *d* 1892, da of 2nd Baron Harris; *d* 1892; *s* by his el son (5) ALBERT EDWARD, 5th Baron; *b* 1863; a Representative Peer: *m* 1895, Annie Evelyn, who *d* 1955, da of late Col Thomas Joseph Barrington; *d* 1937; *s* by his brother (8) ROBERT ARTHUR, 6th Baron; *b* 1864; a DL for co Westmeath; European War 1914-19 as Lieut RASC; late 1894, Ethel Violet, who *d* 1934, da of late Col Sir Edmond Bainbridge, KCB, of Sheringham Norfolk; *d* 1954; *s* by his kinsman (7) JOHN MICHAEL SCHOMBERG STAVELEY (only son of late Robert John Handcock, 2nd son of late Hon Robert John Handcock, 2nd son of 3rd Baron), 7th Baron, *b* 1904: *m* 1930, Rebecca Ellen, who *d* 1978, only da of William T. Soady, RN; *d* 1973; *s* by his son (8) ROLAND THOMAS JOHN, 8th Baron and present peer.

Castlereagh, Viscount; son of Marquess of Londonderry.

CASTLE STEWART, EARL (Stuart) (Earl I 1800, BtS 1628)

ARTHUR PATRICK AVONDALE STUART, 8th Earl and 15th Baronet; *b* 18 Aug 1928; *s* 1961; *ed* Eton, and Trin Coll, Camb (BA 1950); late Lieut Scots Gds; is a Farmer; FBIM (1978): *m* 1952, Edna, da of William Edward Fowler, of Harborne, Birmingham, and has issue.

Arms – Quarterly of four: 1st the Royal arms of *Scotland*; 2nd or, a fesse checky azure and argent, and in chief a label of three points gules, *Stuart*; 3rd argent, a saltire between four roses gules, barbed and seeded proper, *Lennox*; 4th or, a lion rampant gules, *Macduff*; the whole within a bordure compony argent and azure. **Crest** – An unicorn's head couped at the neck argent, armed, crined, and tufted or. **Supporters** – Two wyverns, their tails, nowed or, armed proper and langued gules. *Seat* – Stuart Hall, Stewartstown, co Tyrone. *Residence* – Stone House, East Pennard, nr Shepton Mallet, Somerset.

SON LIVING

ANDREW RICHARD CHARLES (*Viscount Stuart*), (Combe Hayes Farm, Buckerell, nr Honiton, Devon), *b* 7 Oct 1953; *ed* Millfield: *m* 1973, Annie Yvette, da of Robert le Poulain, of 65 Av de Marville, St Malo, France, and has issue:—
> DAUGHTER LIVING— *Hon* Celia Elizabeth, *b* 1976.

DAUGHTER LIVING

Lady Bridget Ann (Stone House Farm, E Pennard, Shepton Mallet, Somerset) *b* 1957; *ed* Wynstones Sch, Whaddon, Glos; MHort (RHS) 1983; DMS 1989; lecturer in horticulture Kingston Maurward Coll, Dorset: *m* 1990, Robert W. Wadey, only son of Thomas Wadey, of 12 Marina Gdns, Brighton.

BROTHER LIVING

Hon Simon Walter Erskine (Windyridge, Wych Cross, Forest Row, Sussex RH19 5JP), *b* 1930; *ed* Eton, and Trin Coll, Camb (BA 1953, MA 1957); late 2nd Lt Scots Gds; an Assist Master at Haberdashers' Aske's Sch 1961-78 formerly at King's Canterbury, and Stowe, since when a writer: *m* 1973, Deborah Jane, da of late Michael Mounsey, of Backhouse, Murton, Appleby, Cumbria, and has issue living, Thomas Harry Erskine, *b* 1974, — Corin Edward Leveson, *b* 1975, — Tristram James Avondale, *b* 1977.

COLLATERAL BRANCHES LIVING

Granddaughter of late Richard Wingfield Stuart (infra)
Issue of late John William Wingfield Stuart, *b* 1901, *d* 1983: *m* 1930, Dorothy Eleanor, da of T. Baker Insoll, of Hamilton, NZ:—
Mary Rose Dorothy Wingfield, *b* 1931: *m* 1st, 1954, Leonard Russell Goggs, who *d* 1977; 2ndly, 1979, Percy Wilbur Collom, jr, of 19 Winchester St, St Peters, S Australia, and has issue living (by 1st *m*), Stephen John (19 Winchester St, St Peters, S Australia), *b* 1962: *m* 19—, Jillian, da of William Scrymgour, of 2 Violet Court, Novar Gdns, S Australia, — Brenda Margaret, *b* 1955: *m* 1976 (*m diss* 1990), Edmund John Attridge, and has issue living, Antony Hugh *b* 1986, Eleanor Charlotte *b* 1981, Sophie Irene *b* 1983, Vanessa Selina *b* 1985, — Catherine Mary, *b* 1956: *m* 1st, 1980 (*m diss* 1986), Peter Louis Baratosy; 2ndly, 1986, W/Cmdr Norman Melville Goodall, DFC, RAAF, of Paradale Too, Strathalbyn, S Australia, and has issue living (by 2nd *m*), Emma *b* 1986, — Ursula Anne, *b* 1958: *m* 1988, Alexander Edward Jeakins, of 48 Audley Rd, NW4 3EY, and has issue living, Adrian Edward *b* 1989, Humfrey Francis *b* 1990, — Sarah Louise, *b* 1963: *m* 1st, 1986 (*m diss* 1988), John Dostal; 2ndly, 1992, Graeme Russell George French, of 108 Toorak Rd, Rivervale, W Australia, and has issue living (by 2nd *m*), Hamish Russell Douglass *b* 1994.

Grandson of late Rev Hon Andrew Godfrey Stuart, 4th son of 2nd Earl:—
Issue of late Richard Wingfield Stuart, *b* 1843, *d* 1914: *m* 1st, 1869, Jeannie Miriam, who *d* 1889, da of John Macdermott, of Gayfield, Sydney; 2ndly, 1891, Isabel Clare, who *d* 1953, el da of Charles Lee, MLA of NS Wales for Tenterfield:—
(By 2nd *m*) Godfrey Richard Wingfield, *b* 1905. *Residence* – 19 Winchester St, St Peter's, S Australia.

Descendants, if any, of Andrew William Godfrey Stuart (*b* 1869), and his brother, George Sydney Stuart (*b* 1871), sons of Andrew Godfrey Stuart, of Hobart, Tasmania, eldest son of Andrew Thomas Stuart (infra).

Descendants, if any, of Arthur Burleigh Stuart (*b* 1876), only son of George Joseph Stuart, 2nd son of Andrew Thomas Stuart (infra).

Granddaughter of late Robert Walter Stuart, 3rd son of Andrew Thomas Stuart, eldest son of Hon Andrew Godfrey Stuart, 2nd son of 1st Earl:—
Issue of late Burleigh Stuart, *b* 1875, *d* 1912: *m* 1901, Helen Gertrude (who *d* 1956, having *m* 2ndly, 1913, John Martin Muir, of Sorell, Tasmania, who *d* 1943), da of Edward Mace, of Burnie, Tasmania:—
Sylvia Annie, *b* 1902.

Grandchildren of Walter Burleigh Stuart, eldest son of late Robert Walter Stuart (ante):—
Issue of late Burleigh Athol Stuart, *b* 1904, *d* 1982: *m* 1927, Winifred May, da of Ernest Kerrison, of Beaconsfield, Tasmania:—
Ernest Martin, *b* 1935: *m* 1965, June Rosalyn, da of Stanley Bastian, of Como, W Australia, and has issue living, Conway Athol, *b* 1968, — Kym Robina, *b* 1967. —— Claire Leila, *b* 1928: *m* 1951, Reginald Edward Johnston, of 19 Rialannah Rd, Mount Nelson, Hobart, Tasmania, and has issue living, Kent Reginald, *b* 1952: *m* 1975, Marlene Irene Baier, and has issue living, Nathan James, *b* 1975, Alycia Irene, *b* 1979, — Vivienne Claire, *b* 1955: *m* 1980, Kenneth Ross Watts, and has issue living, Emma Claire, *b* 1982, — Celia Anne, *b* 1963, — Dianne Ruth, *b* 1965. —— Winifred Ellen, *b* 1929: *m* 1950, John Robert Sinclair Mackey, of 460 Doran's Rd, Sandford, Tasmania 7020, and has issue living, Andrew John Sinclair (56 Terrina St, Lauderdale 7020, Tasmania), *b* 1956: *m* 1978, Debbie Lee Robson, and has issue living, Courtney Lee *b* 1986, Kurt Marcus Sinclair *b* 1992, — Denise Claire (c/o ANZ Banking Gp, 86 Collins St, Hobart, Tasmania), *b* 1952: *m* 19— (*m diss*

19—), Robert John Wells. —— Alma Elaine, *b* 1931: *m* 1955, James Maxwell Carter, of 1500 S Arm Rd, Clifton Beach, Tasmania 7020, and has issue living, Stuart James, *b* 1958: *m* 1984 (*m diss* 19—), Eleni Atzamoglou, — Michael Jackson, *b* 1960, — Lee Andrea, *b* 1956: *m* 1978, Ian Cameron Tremayne, and has issue living, Ben Cameron *b* 1981, Emma Kate *b* 1983.

Grandson of late Andrew Thomas Stuart (ante):—
Issue of late Audley Mervyn Stuart, *b* 1860, *d* 1942: *m* 1892, Alice Anne Rogers, of Hobart, Tasmania, who *d* 1897:—
Audley Andrew Mervyn, *b* 1897: *m* 1934, Beryl Elizabeth, da of Edward Alfred Irwin, of Hobart, Tasmania, and has issue living, Elizabeth Anne Castle *b* 1937, — Helen Christine Castle, *b* 1939, — Margaret Lyndsay Castle, *b* 1942.

Grandson of late Maj Burleigh William Henry Fitz-Gibbon Stuart, 4th son of Hon Andrew Godfrey Stuart (ante):—
Issue of late Maj Godfrey Richard Conyngham Stuart, CB, E Lancashire Regt, *b* 1866, *d* 1955: *m* 1899, Alice Mabel, who *d* 1936, yst da of late John Acheson Smyth, of Ardmore, co Londonderry:—
Godfrey Walter Burleigh (Glenwood, 3 Elmcroft, Datchet, Berks, SL3 9DS), *b* 1901; Lt-Col (ret) late E Lancs Regt: *m* 1933, Christine Valerie, da of late Col Stephen Simpson, TD, DL, of Bowerswood, nr Garstang, Lancashire, and has issue living, Jane Christine, *b* 1934: *m* 1st, 1960 (*m diss* 1972), Anthony Rossington Vickers; 2ndly, 1974, Herbert Jackson Daniel, who *d* 1974; 3rdly, 1982, Wayne Locksley Kines (head of World Media Inst Inc), of 549 Besserer St, Ottawa, Ont, Canada K1N 6C6, and has issue living (by 1st *m*), Robin Daniel Stuart *b* 1964: *m* 1988, Kathleen Nielsen, Helena Jane Stuart *b* 1969, — Wendy Mary STUART (Croft House, 19 Anderton Rd, Euxton, nr Chorley, Lancs PR7 6JA), *b* 1935; has resumed her maiden name: *m* 1st, 1955 (*m diss* 1972), William Joynson; 2ndly, 1983 (*m diss* 1990), John Remmett-Smith, and has issue living (by 1st *m*), Timothy William Stuart *b* 1958; BSc: *m* 1989, Linda Spencer, Nicholas George Stuart *b* 1960; MSc, MICE, CEng, Jeremy Duncan Stuart *b* 1963; BSc, Andrew Douglas Stuart *b* 1965; MEng.

Grandchildren of late Maj Godfrey Richard Conyngham Stuart, CB, (ante):—
Issue of late Lt-Col Robin Charles Burleigh Stuart, *b* 1907, *d* 1970: *m* 1939, Evelyn Alice, da of Harry Freegard, of Charlton Kings, Glos:—
Douglas Charles Burleigh, *b* 1940; *ed* Cheltenham, and Nautical Coll, Pangbourne; with Air Traffic Control, Melbourne; Pres Internat Fedn of Air Traffic Controllers: *m* 1st, 1962 (*m diss* 1990), Pamela, da of Gordon Sivyer, of Wembley, W Australia; 2ndly, 1993, Roslyn Harriet, da of late Roy Jennings, of Brighton, Vic, and has issue living (by 1st *m*), Andrew John Burleigh, *b* 1967; *ed* Eltham Coll, and Melbourne Univ (BComm), — Joanna Mary, *b* 1965; *ed* Eltham Coll, and Latrobe Univ (BA). *Residence* – 4 Loller St, Brighton, Vic 3186, Australia. . —— Rosemary Ann, *b* 1945: *m* 1967 (*m diss* 1984), Michael John Ridlington (*see* E Ilchester, colls, 1990 Edn). Brendon, Bradley Rd, Charlton Kings, Cheltenham, Glos.

Grandsons of late Maj Burleigh William Henry Fitz-Gibbon Stuart (ante):—
Issue of late Brig-Gen Burleigh Francis Brownlow Stuart, CB, CMG, *b* 1868, *d* 1952: *m* 1916, Evelyn Margaret, JP, who *d* 1970, da of Lt-Col Sir Edward Henry St Lawrence Clarke, 4th Bt, CMG, DSO (*cr* 1804, ext):—
John William Brownlow, MBE, MC (Corner Cottage, Radford, Inkberrow, Worcs WR7 4LR), *b* 1917; *ed* Rugby; Col Worcestershire Regt (ret); OC 1st Bn 1959-61; Palestine 1939 (MC), Sudan and Eritrea 1940-41 W Desert and Egypt 1941-43 (despatches), Italy 1944-45 (MBE), Kenya 1956-57 (Africa Gen Ser Medal with clasp); MBE (Mil) 1945: *m* 1954, Anthea Joan, who *d* 1977, el da of late Ashley Ernest Herman, OBE, FRCS, of Shipton Hill, Hambledon, Godalming. —— Burleigh Edward St Lawrence, *b* 1920; *ed* Rugby, Peterhouse, Camb and Trin Coll, Oxford (MA); Malayan Civil Ser 1951-52, E African High Commn (Forestry Research) 1952-56, Colonial Forest Ser, Kenya, 1956-63, and Commonwealth Forestry Bureau, Oxford 1964-76; formerly Capt Worcs Regt; India 1940-44, Burma 1944-45: *m* 1952, Joan Elizabeth, da of Col Matthew George Platts, CIE, OBE, MC, of The Down Wood, Blandford, Dorset, and has issue living, Edward John Burleigh (28 Sinnels Field, Shipton-under-Wychwood, Oxon), *b* 1953: *m* 1976, Alison Ann, yst da of James Steel, of Paddock Gate, Clanfield, Oxon, and has issue living, Simon Francis Brownlow, *b* 1980, Henry George Burleigh, *b* 1982, — Elizabeth Helen (*Countess Howe*), *b* 1955: *m* 1983, 7th Earl Howe, of Penn House, Amersham, Bucks, — Catherine Frances, *b* 1958: *m* 1982, Graham Ian Briggs, of Warwick House, Stewkley Rd, Wing, Leighton Buzzard, Beds. *Residence* – Hunter's Close, Ickford, Aylesbury, Bucks.

PREDECESSORS – (1) ANDREW Stuart, *cr* Lord Avondale (peerage of Scotland) 1459, was afterwards Chancellor of Scotland; *d* 1488; *s* by his nephew (2) ALEXANDER, 2nd Lord; one of the Lords Auditors; *d* 1489; *s* by his son (3) ANDREW, 3rd Lord; fell at Flodden 1513; *s* by his son (4) ANDREW, 4th Lord; exchanged his Lordship with Sir James Hamilton for that of Ochiltree, and by Act of Parliament 1542 was ordained to be styled *Lord Stuart of Ochiltrie*; *d* 1548; *s* by his son (5) ANDREW, 2nd Lord Stuart of Ochiltrie; *d* 1592; *s* by his grandson (6) ANDREW, 3rd Lord Stuart of Ochiltrie, a Lord of the Bedchamber to James I of England; resigned his title to his cousin, Sir James Stuart with the consent of the Crown, and was himself *cr Baron Castle Stuart* (peerage of Ireland) 1619, and received from the King considerable estates on Tyrone; *d* 1628; *s* by his son (7) Sir ANDREW, 2nd Baron, who in 1628 had been *cr a Baronet* (Nova Scotia): *d* 1639; *s* by his son (8) ANDREW, 3rd Baron; *d* 1650; *s* by his brother (9) JOSIAS, 4th Baron, *dsp* 1652. *s* by his uncle (10) JOHN, 5th Baron; *d* unmarried 1678, when the Peerage and Baronetcy became dormant, and remained so until 1774, when they were successfully claimed by (11) ANDREW THOMAS, 9th Baron, the descendant in the 4th generation of Col Hon Robert, 3rd son of 1st Baron; *cr Viscount Castle Stuart* (peerage of Ireland) 1793, and *Earl Castle Stewart* (peerage of Ireland) 1800; *d* 1809; *s* by his son (12) ROBERT, 2nd Earl; *d* 1854; *s* by his el son (13) EDWARD, 3rd Earl; *d* 1857; *s* by his brother (14) CHARLES KNOX, 4th Earl; *b* 1810: *m* 1835, Charlotte Raffles Drury, da of late Quintin Thompson; *d* 1874; *s* by his son (15) HENRY JAMES, 5th Earl, *b* 1837; assumed in 1867, by Roy licence, the additional surname of Richardson: *m* 1866, Augusta le Vicomte Massy Richardson, who *d* 1908, widow of Major Hugh Massy (85th Foot), yst da and heiress of late Major Richardson-Brady, of Drum Manor, co Tyrone; *d* 1914; *s* by his cousin (16) ANDREW JOHN (2nd son of late Rev Hon Andrew Godfrey Stuart, 4th son of 2nd Earl), 6th Earl; *b* 1841; in MCS: *m* 1876, Emma Georgiana, who *d* 1949, da of Maj-Gen Arthur Stevens; *d* 1921; *s* by his son (17) ARTHUR, 7th Earl; *b* 1889; Bar Inner Temple 1943; European War 1914-18 as Major Machine Gun Corps and a GSO (MC); sat as MP for Harborough Div of Leicestershire (*U*) 1929-33: *m* 1920, Eleanor May, who *d* 1992, da of Solomon R Guggenheim, of New York, USA; *d* 1961; *s* by his son (18) ARTHUR PATRICK AVONDALE, 8th Earl and present peer; also Viscount Castle Stuart, and Baron Castle Stuart.

CATHCART, EARL (Cathcart) (Lord S about 1452, Earl UK 1814)

ALAN CATHCART, CB, DSO, MC, 6th Earl; *b* 22 Aug 1919; *s* 1927; *ed* Eton, and Magdalene Coll, Camb; Maj-Gen; Lt Col Comdg Scots Gds 1960-62, Col AQ Scottish Command 1962-63, Imperial Defence Coll 1964, Commander 152nd Highland Inf Bde (TA) 1965-66, Brig Operations Div SHAPE 1967-69, GOC Yorks Dist 1969-70, and GOC Berlin (British Sector) 1970-73; ret 1973; Brig Queen's Body Guard for Scotland (R Company of Archers); Lord Prior Order of St John 1985-88; a Dep Chm of Cttees and Dep Speaker House of Lords 1976-89; NW Europe 1944-45 (despatches, MC, DSO), DSO 1945; CB (Mil) 1973: *m* 1st, 1946, Rosemary Clare Marie Gabrielle, who *d* 1980, da of late Air-Commodore Sir Henry Percy Smyth-Osbourne, CMG, CBE; 2ndly, 1984, Marie Isobel, da of late Hon William Joseph French (*see* B de Freyne, colls), and widow of Sir Thomas Brian Weldon, 8th Bt, and has issue by 1st *m*.

Arms – Azure, three cross crosslets fitchée issuing out of as many crescents argent. **Crest** – A dexter hand couped above the wrist and erect proper, grasping a crescent argent as in the arms. **Supporters** – Two parrots wings inverted proper.
Residence – Moor Hatches, W Amesbury, Salisbury, Wilts. *Clubs* – Brooks's, Royal Yacht Squadron.

SON LIVING (*By 1st marriage*)

CHARLES ALAN ANDREW (*Lord Greenock*), (Gateley Hall, Dereham, Norfolk; 18 Smith Terr, SW3), *b* 30 Nov 1952; *ed* Eton; late Scots Gds: *m* 1981, Vivien Clare, only da of Francis Desmond McInnes Skinner, of North Farm, Snetterton, Norfolk, and has issue:—
SON LIVING— *Hon* Alan George, *b* 16 March 1986.
DAUGHTER LIVING— *Hon* Laura Rosemary, *b* 1984.

DAUGHTERS LIVING (*By 1st marriage*)

Lady Louisa, *b* 1948: *m* 1975, Norman Kirkpatrick Cosgrave, of Totterdown Lodge, Inkpen, nr Hungerford, Berks, who *d* 1991.
Lady Charlotte Mary, *b* 1951: *m* 1972, Capt Anthony C. McCallum, late 1st The Queen's Drag Gds, and has issue living, Charles Colin, *b* 1973, — Anthony James, *b* 1977, — Sophie Charlotte, *b* 1975. *Residence* – Week Green Farm, Froxfield, Petersfield, Hants.

COLLATERAL BRANCHES LIVING

Grandchildren of late Maj Frederick Adrian Cathcart, el son of Hon Augustus Murray Cathcart (infra):—
Issue of late Alan Reginald Cathcart, *b* 1908, *d* 1967: *m* 1934, Daphne Victoria Catherine, who *d* 1993, da of late Maj-Gen John Archibald Henry Pollock, CB (*see* Montagu-Pollock, Bt, colls, 1990 Edn):—
Charles Alan (Culraven, Borgue, Kirkcudbright), *b* 1940: *m* 1973, Carol Ann, yr da of late A. E. Jenner, and has issue living, Daniel Edward, *b* 1974, — Emma Katherine, *b* 1976. —— Julia Mary, *b* 1936: *m* 1959, Angus George Millar, WS, of 24 Buckingham Terr, Edinburgh EH4 3AE, and has issue living, James George, *b* 1961: *m* 1992, Katharine Ann, yr da of late John Danielson, and has issue living, Hector George Danielson *b* 1994, — Charles Angus, *b* 1963, — Roderick Alan, *b* 1967.
Issue of late Lt-Col Charles Frederick Cathcart, DSO, *b* 1912, *d* 1971: *m* 1st, 1939 (*m diss* 1954), Pamela Violet, da of late Lt-Col Patrick Douglas Stirling, OBE, MC, JP, of Kippendavie, Kippenross, Dunblane, Perths; 2ndly, 1955, Pamela Vera, who *d* 1987, da of late Maj Harry Sebastian Garrard, of Welton Place, Daventry, and widow of Maj Sir Arthur Ralph Wilmot, 7th Bt:—
(By 1st *m*) Clovannis Jane, *b* 1942: *m* 1961, Maj Colin Berowald Innes, Black Watch (*see* Innes, Bt (*cr* 1628) colls). —— Miranda Jane, *b* (twin) 1942: *m* 1984, Anthony C. Henderson, of Sydney, NSW, Australia, and *dsp* 1987. —— (Sarah) Camilla (*Baroness Jauncey of Tullichettle*), *b* 1946: *m* 1977, Baron Jauncey of Tullichettle (Life Baron). *Residence* – Tullichettle, Comrie, Perthshire.

Granddaughter of Hon Augustus Murray Cathcart yr son of 2nd Earl:—
Issue of late Capt Augustus Ernest Cathcart, King's R Rifle Corps, *b* 1875, *ka* 1914: *m* 1913, Hilda Renée, who *d* 1958, da of late Maj Wiliam Frederick Lee, of Grove Hall, Knottingley:—
Eva Renée, OBE, *b* 1914; late ATS, raised Mauritius Womens Volunteer Corps 1945; is a JP for N Riding of Yorkshire; OBE (Civil) 1971. *Residence* – Warwick House, Aiskew, Bedale, Yorkshire.

PREDECESSORS – **(1)** Sir ALAN Cathcart, Knt, Warden of the West Marches and Master of Artillery, *cr Lord Cathcart* (peerage of Scotland) 1447; *d* 1499; *s* by his grandson **(2)** JOHN, 2nd Lord; *d* 1535; *s* by his grandson **(3)** ALAN, 3rd Lord; *k* at battle of Pinkie 1547; *s* by his son **(4)** ALAN, 4th Lord; *d* 1618; *s* by his grandson **(5)** ALAN, 5th Lord; *d* 1628; *s* by his son **(6)** ALAN, 6th Lord; *s* by his son **(7)** ALAN, 7th Lord; *d* 1732; *s* by his son **(8)** CHARLES, 8th Lord, a Representative Peer and a Lord of the Bedchamber to George II; appointed Com in Ch of the British Forces in America 1740, but *d* during the passage out; *s* by his son **(9)** CHARLES, KT, PC, 9th Lord, a Representative Peer, Lieut-Gen in the Army, First Lord of Police, Ambassador to Russia, etc; *d* 1776; *s* by his son **(10)** WILLIAM SCHAW 10th Lord, a Representative Peer, a Gen in the army, and Ambassador to St Petersburg 1805-06 and 1812-20; *cr Baron Greenock*, of Greenock, co Renfrew and *Viscount Cathcart*, of Cathart, co Renfrew (peerage of United Kingdom) 1807, and *Earl Cathcart* (peerage of United Kingdom) 1814; *d* 1843; *s* by his son **(11)** CHARLES MURRAY, GCB, 2nd Earl; *b* 1783; a Gen in the Army, and Gov-Gen and Com-in-Ch in British N America, etc; *m* 1818, Henrietta da of Thomas Mather, *d* 1859; *s* by his son **(12)** ALAN FREDERICK, 3rd Earl; *b* 1828; Chm of N Riding Quarter Sessions 1858-68: *m* 1850, Elizabeth Mary, who *d* 1902, el da and co-heiress of Sir Samuel Crompton, Bt (ext); *d* 1905; *s* by his **(13)** ALAN, 4th Earl, *b* 1856; *d* 1911; *s* by his brother **(14)** GEORGE, 5th Earl, *b* 1862: *m* 1919 (*m diss* 1922), Vera Estelle, who *d* 1993, da of late John Fraser, of Cape Town, and widow of Capt de Grey Warter, 4th Dragoon Guards; *d* 1927; *s* by his son **(15)** ALAN, 6th Earl and present peer; also Viscount Cathcart, Lord Cathcart, and Baron Greenock.

CATTO, BARON (Catto) (Baron UK 1936, Bt UK 1921)

STEPHEN GORDON CATTO, 2nd Baron, and 2nd Baronet; *b* 14 Jan 1923; *s* 1959; *ed* Eton, and Trin Coll, Camb; formerly Flt Lt RAF VR; a Member of Advisory Council of Export Credits Guarantee Dept 1959-65; a part-time Member of London Transport Board 1962-68; Pres Morgan Grenfell Group plc, Chm Yule Catto & Co plc, a Dir News International plc, and of other cos; Chm of RAF Benevolent Fund 1978-91: *m* 1st, 1948 (*m diss* 1965), Josephine Innes, el da of George Herbert Packer, of Alexandria, Egypt; 2ndly, 1966, Margaret, da of James Stuart Forrest, of Dilston, Tasmania, and has issue by 1st and 2nd *m*.

Arms – Or, on a chevron between three lymphads sable as many boars' heads couped of the field, Crests – A wild cat sejant proper, resting the dexter paw on a garb or. Supporters – On either side a tiger proper, charged on the shoulder with an ivy leaf or.
Residences – 41 William Mews, Lowndes Sq, SW1X 9HQ; House of Schivas, Ythanbank, Aberdeenshire.

SONS LIVING *(By 1st marriage)*

Hon INNES GORDON, *b* 7 Aug 1950. *Residence* – House of Schivas, Ythanbank, Ellon, Aberdeen AB4 0TN.

Hon Alexander Gordon, *b* 1952; *ed* Westminster: *m* 1981, Elizabeth Scott, twin da of Maj T. P. Boyes, of Brookvale Cottage, Whitford, Devon, and has issue living, Thomas Innes Gordon, *b* 1983, — Alastair Gordon, *b* 1986, — Charlotte Gordon, *b* 1988. *Residence* – 3 Edenhurst Av, SW6 3PD.

(By 2nd marriage)

Hon James Stuart Gordon, *b* 1966. *Residence* – Butlers Farmhouse, Colesbourne, Cheltenham, Glos GL53 9NS.

DAUGHTERS LIVING *(By 1st marriage)*

Hon Christian Victoria Gordon, *b* 1955: *m* 1983, Charles N. Menzies-Wilson, eldest son of W. N. Menzies-Wilson, of Holland Park, W11, and has issue living, Richard Napier, *b* 1988, — James Benedict, *b* 1991, — Cathryn Lucy, *b* 1986. *Residence* – Newport House, Newport Lane, Braishfield, nr Romsey, Hants SO51 0PL.

Hon Ariane Madeleine Gordon, *b* 1960.

(By 2nd marriage)

Hon Georgina Lucinda Gordon, *b* 1969: *m* 1993, Robert Alistair Newman, elder son of Alistair Newman, of Sutton Green, Guildford. *Residence* – Sandford House, Avening, Tetbury, Glos GL8 8NF.

SISTERS LIVING

Hon Isabel Ida Gordon, OBE (Holmdale, Holmbury St Mary, Surrey; 61 Cadogan Gdns, SW3), *b* 1912; a Gov of PNEU Schs; World Pres, YWCA 1955-63; Pres of YWCA of Gt Britain 1966-72; OBE (Civil) 1952.

Hon Ruth Gordon, *b* 1919: *m* 1947, Francis Ernest Herman Bennett, CBE, son of late Sir Ernest Nathaniel Bennett, MP, and has issue living, David Francis, *b* 1948: *m* 1980, Lynn D., da of Lt-Col Allan Burton, DSO, TD, of Limestone Hall, Milton, Ontario, Canada, and has issue living, Nicholas Gordon *b* 1982, Audrey Claire *b* 1984, — Adam Gordon Greverus, *b* 1954: *m* 1986, Zoë Diana, da of late Prof Terence John Bew Spencer, of Birmingham Univ, and has issue living, Oscar Francis *b* 1986, Isabel Diana *b* 1989, — Olivia Gay, *b* 1950.

PREDECESSORS – (1) *Rt Hon Sir* THOMAS SIVEWRIGHT CATTO, CBE, son of William Catto, of Peterhead, Aberdeenshire; *b* 1879; E India Merchant and Banker, and Managing Director of Morgan Grenfell & Co Ltd, of London, of Yule Catto & Co Ltd, of London, and of Andrew Yule & Co, of Calcutta; was Gov of Bank of England 1944-9; *cr* a Baronet 1921, and *Baron Catto*, of Cairncatto, co Aberdeen (peerage of UK) 1936: *m* 1910, Gladys Forbes, who *d* 1980, da of Stephen Gordon, of Elgin; *d* 1959; *s* by his son (2) STEPHEN GORDON, 2nd Baron and present peer.

CAVAN, EARL OF (Lambart) (Earl I 1647)

Prepared on every side

ROGER CAVAN LAMBART, 13th Earl (has not yet established his right to the Peerage); *b* 1 Sept 1944; *ed* Wilson's Sch, Wallington, Surrey.

𝕬rms – Gules, three gillieflowers pierced argent ℭrest – On a mount vert a centaur argent drawing a bow or. 𝕾upporters – Two knights in complete armour sable, garnished or, with an under habit gules, fringed of the second, the beaver up, and on the helmet seven plumes alternately of the third and argent. *Residence* – 34 Woodleigh Gdns, SW16.

HALF-SISTERS LIVING

Issue of late Frederick Cavan Lambart, *b* 1902, *d* 1963: *m* 1st, 1924 (*m diss* 1942), Adelaide Constance, da of late Ottywell Butler:—

Olivia Marianne (abandoned the christian name of Olive), *b* 1925: *m* 1950 (*m diss* 1970), Ernest Ephraim Corrett, and has issue living, Paul (2 Erskine Mews, Regent's Park, NW3), *b* 1952; *ed* Stowe: *m* 1984, Anne Margaret, da of late Ernest Joseph Ferridge, of 35 Dunbar Rd, N22, and has issue living, Catherine Marianne *b* 1986, — Graham, *b* 1954; *ed* Corona Stage Sch: *m* 1982 (*m diss* 1988), Kelly Elaine, da of late Seymour Arnold Hoppen, of 7 Egerton Place, SW3, and formerly of S Africa, and has issue living, Natasha *b* 1983.

Issue of late Frederick Cavan Lambart, *b* 1902, *d* 1963: *m* 3rdly, 1958, (Kathleen) Elizabeth (who *m* 2ndly, 1965, Frederick Rufus Lawrence, who *d* 1969; 3rdly, 1970, John Armstrong Wiggin, of The Anchor Hotel, Shepperton, Middx), elder da of Edward James Henry Darvill, of Port Vale House,

Hertford:—

Elizabeth, *b* 1959. *Residence* – .

DAUGHTERS LIVING AND DECEASED OF TWELFTH EARL

Lady Sarah Audrey, *b* 1948: *m* 1968, Capt Alistair Charles Sinclair, late 17th/21st Lancers, of The Walled Garden, Hinton Waldrist, Faringdon, Oxon SN7 8RN, and *d* 1981, leaving issue, Harry Charles Lambart, *b* 1972; *ed* Radley, — Rupert Alistair Grenville, *b* 1973; *ed* Radley.

Lady Jane Mary, *b* 1949; *d* 1954.

Lady Katherine Lucy LAMBART, *b* 1955; has resumed her maiden name: *m* 1978 (*m diss* 1986), Don Lorenzo Ruiz Barrero, yr son of Don Lorenzo Ruiz Jimenez, of Madrid, and has issue living, Lorenzo Cavan, *b* 1980, — Natasha Pepa, *b* 1982. *Residence* – 174 Broomwood Rd, SW11.

DAUGHTER LIVING OF ELEVENTH EARL

Lady Daphne Olive, *b* 1909: *m* 1944, Maj Kenneth Gordon Grierson, E Surrey Regt, who *d* 1976, and has issue living, William, *b* 1947; with BBC since 1967: *m* 1972, Barbara Edwina, da of late Edwin Locke, of Haywards Heath, Sussex, and has issue living, James Nicholas *b* 1981, Victoria Caroline *b* 1977. *Residence* – 24F Four Limes, Wheathampstead, Herts AL4 8PW.

DAUGHTERS LIVING OF TENTH EARL (By 2nd marriage)

Lady Elizabeth Mary (The Old Rectory, Todenham, Moreton-in-Marsh, Glos GL56 9PA), *b* 1924: *m* 1949, Mark Frederic Kerr Longman, who *d* 1972, and has issue living, Caroline Elizabeth, *b* 1951: *m* 1982, Peter J. Zevenbergen, son of Jan Zevenbergen, and has issue living, Frederick Christian Edmund *b* 1985, Raphael James *b* 1991, — Jane, *b* 1955, — Emma, *b* 1959: *m* 1980, Timothy James Hanbury, son of late James Robert Hanbury, of Burley-on-the-Hill, Oakham, Rutland (*see* Birkin, Bt, 1976 Edn), and has issue living, David Mark James *b* 1986, Marina Jane *b* 1982, Rose Sarah *b* 1984.

Lady Joanna, *b* 1929: *m* 1955, Maj Michael Godwin Plantagenet Stourton, Gren Gds (ret), of The Old Rectory, Great Rollright, Chipping Norton, Oxon (*see* B Mowbray).

GRANDDAUGHTER LIVING OF NINTH EARL

Issue of late Capt Hon Lionel John Olive Lambart, DSO, RN, 2nd son of 9th Earl, *b* 1873, *ka* 1940: *m* 1906, Adelaide Douglas, who *d* 1972, yr da of late Capt Arthur Randolph Randolph, 15th Hus, of Eastcourt, Wilts:—

Lady Edith Sybil, *b* 1918: raised to rank of an Earl's daughter 1947: *m* 1940 (*m diss* 1974), Ivan Cottam Foxwell Maj R Norfolk Regt (Res), film producer and screenwriter, and has issue living, Zia (Mill House, West Kington, Chippenham, Wilts SN14 7JQ), *b* 1940: *m* 1968 (*m diss* 1991), David Joseph Kruger, and has issue living, Patrick Gene *b* 1972, — Atalanta Edith, *b* 1956: *m* 1973, *Don* Stefano, Prince Massimo di Roccasecca dei Volsci, of Rome, and 44 Fernshaw Rd, SW10, and has issue living, *Don* Valerio Francesco *b* 1973, *Don* Cesare Camillo Alessandro *b* 1977, *Don* Tancredi Tara *b* 1986. *Residence* – 35 Seddlescombe Rd, SW6 1RE.

MOTHER LIVING

Audrey May, da of late Albert Charles Dunham: *m* 1942 (*m diss* 1948), as his 2nd wife, Frederick Cavan Lambart, who *d* 1963. *Residence* – 34 Woodleigh Gdns, SW16.

STEPMOTHER LIVING

(Kathleen) Elizabeth, elder da of Edward James Henry Darvill, of Port Vale House, Hertford: *m* 1st, 1958, as his 3rd wife, Frederick Cavan Lambart, who *d* 1963; 2ndly, 1965, Frederick Rufus Lawrence, who *d* 1969; 3rdly, 1970, John Armstrong Wiggin, of The Anchor Hotel, Shepperton, Middx.

WIDOW LIVING OF TWELFTH EARL

ESSEX LUCY (*Countess of Cavan*), only da of late Henry Arthur Cholmondeley (*see* B Delamere, colls): *m* 1947, Col the 12th Earl, TD, who *d* 1988. *Residence* – The Glebe House, Stockton, Shifnal, Salop T11 9EF.

COLLATERAL BRANCHES LIVING

Granddaughter of late Com Hon Octavius Henry Lambart, 5th son of 8th Earl:—
Issue of late Howard Frederick John Lambart, *b* 1880, *d* 1946: *m* 1st, 1908, Helen Marianne, who *d* 1932, da of late Samuel Shelley Wallbridge, LLB; 2ndly, 1938, May, who *d* 19—, da of late Hon Robert Bickerdike, of Montreal, Canada:—
(By 1st *m*) Evelyn Mary, *b* 1914. *Residence* – Mudgett Rd, RR No4, Sutton, Quebec J0E 2KO, Canada.

Granddaughter of late Maj Frederick Richard Henry Lambart, 2nd son of late Cdr Hon Oliver William Matthew Lambart, RN, 6th son of 7th Earl:—
Issue of late Capt Richard Frederick Lacon Lambart, DSO, *b* 1875, *d* 1924: *m* 1st, 1899 (*m diss* 1909), Enid, who *d* 1963, da of Spencer Brunton; 2ndly, 1913 (*m diss* 19—), Faith Bevan; 3rdly, 1922, Kitty (who *m* 2ndly, 1924 (*m diss* 19—), Herbert Alfred Rich; 3rdly, 1941, Capt Horace Lacy Bullimore, RQMS S Wales Borderers, who *d* 1969), da of Henry Edward Gibbens, of Stanmore, Essex:—
(By 3rd *m*) (Kathleen) Joy Lydia Lacon, *b* 1923. *Residence* – Canada.

Descendants, if any, of Arthur Oliver Reid Lambart (*b* 1909), only son of Ford Augustus Oliver Lambart, only son of Arthur Oliver Lambart, of E London, S Africa, 5th son of Cdr Hon Oliver William Matthew Lambart, RN (ante).

Grandchildren of late Cyril Henry Edward Lambart (infra):—
Issue of late Terence Edward William Lambart, *b* 1903, *d* 1965: *m* 1946, Valma Verdun Johnson, who *m* 2ndly, 1973, Philip John Richardson, of Coomera Gorge Drive, Tamborine Mountain, Queensland, Australia:—
Cavan Cyril Ernest (*presumed heir*) (19 Andrea St, Tarragindi, Brisbane, Qld 4121, Australia), *b* 27 March 1957; *ed* Queensland Inst of Technology (BE, MIEA): *m* 1989, Janita Sandona (BSc), and has issue living, Julian Stuart, *b* 26 Dec 1993, — Carla Thomasine, *b* 1991. —— Diana (21 Jersey St, Morningside, Qld 4170, Australia), *b* 1948: *m* 1968 (*m diss* 19—), Peter Athol McLauchlan, and has issue living, Fraser Burnett *b* 1968; BA, — Ashley Lambart, *b* 1970; BE, — Burnett Hunter, *b* 1972. —— Vivienne, *b* 1950; *ed* Queensland Univ (BA Hons; Dip Ed; M Litt Stud): *m* 1976, Donald William Muller, LLB, of 55 Sugars Rd, Bellbowrie, Brisbane, Queensland, and has issue living, Daniel Richard, *b* 1980, — Samuel Edward, *b* 1984, — Victoria Louise, *b* 1978. —— Rosalind, *b* 1952; *ed* Wollongong Univ (BCom): *m* 1973, Michael Angus Robinson (BSc, Dip Comp Sci), of Barton Place, Wombarra, NSW, and has issue living, Danielle, *b* 1983, — Emma, *b* 1986.
Issue of late Cyril Alwyn Lawrence Lambart, *b* 1910, *d* 1985: *m* 1940, Claire Gilmore, who *d* 1985:—
Charles Dennis (17 Bodalla St, Norman Park, Qld 4170, Australia), *b* 1943: *m* 1st, 1967, Mary Bambrick; 2ndly, 19—, Margaret Phyllis Beagrie, and has issue living (by 1st *m*), Sally Ann, *b* 1970, — Juliette, *b* 1972, — (by 2nd *m*) Charles James Cyril George, *b* 1992. —— Richard Gilmore, *b* 1947: *m* 1979, Michelle Pluskovits, and has issue living, Robin Stephen, *b* 1980, — Nicholas, *b* 1985, — Rebecca Kim, *b* 1981. —— Jacqueline Ann, *b* 1945: *m* 19—, Paul Grima, of Mena Creek, Innisfail, Qld 4860, Australia, and has issue living, Jason Paul, *b* 1973, — Matthew Thomas, *b* 1975, — David Julian, *b* 1977, — Tristan Jose, *b* 1980.

Grandson of late Gustavus William Lambart, 5th in descent from the Hon Oliver Lambart, MP, 2nd son of 1st Earl:—
Issue of late Cyril Henry Edward Lambart, *b* 1866, *d* 1955: *m* 1900, Ethel Caroline Annie, who *d* 1960, da of Albert Thomas Ward, of Newton Hall, Rosebery Topping, Yorks:—
George Desmond Richard (27 Richmond St, Chelmer, Brisbane, Queensland 4068, Australia), *b* 1912.

PREDECESSORS – **(1)** *Sir* Oliver Lambart, PC, Knt, Gov of Connaught 1601, and MP for co Cavan 1613, etc; *cr Lord Lambart, Baron of Cavan* (peerage of Ireland) 1617; *d* 1618; *s* by his son **(2)** Charles, PC, 2nd Baron, MP for Bossiney, Cornwall, 1625-7, and Com-in-Ch of Forces in City of Dublin 1642, etc; *cr Viscount Kilcoursie* and *Earl of Cavan* (peerage of Ireland) 1647; *d* 1660; *s* by his son **(3)** Richard, 2nd Earl; *s* by his son **(4)** Charles, 3rd Earl; *d* 1702; *s* by his son **(5)** Richard, 4th Earl; *d* 1741; *s* by his son **(6)** Ford, 5th Earl; *d* 1772; *s* by his cousin **(7)** Richard, 5th Earl, son of Hon Henry Lambart, 3rd son of 3rd Earl; *d* 1778; *s* by his son **(8)** Richard Ford William, 7th Earl; a Gen in the Army; commanded a Div under Sir Ralph Abercrombie in Egypt 1800; *d* 1837; *s* by his grandson **(9)** Frederick John William, 8th Earl, son of George Frederick Augustus, Viscount Kilcoursie, by Sarah, da of J. P. Coppin, of Cowley, Oxfordshire, *b* 1815: *m* 1838, Hon Caroline Augusta, who *d* 1892, da of 1st Baron Hatherton; *d* 1887; *s* by his el son **(10)** Frederick Edward Gould, KP, PC, 9th Earl, *b* 1839; Vice-Chamberlain of the Household 1886; served throughout siege of Sebastopol 1854; present at bombardment of Canton 1856, and with "forlorn hope" at attack of Pieho Forts 1858; MP for S Div of Somersetshire (*L*) 1885-92: *m* 1863, Mary Sneade, who *d* 1905, only child of late Rev John Olive; *d* 1900; *s* by his el son **(11)** Frederic Rudolph, KP, GCB, GCMG, GCVO, GBE, 10th Earl, *b* 1865; Field-Marshal; sometime Lieut of Tower of London; Ch of Imperial Gen Staff 1922-6; Capt of Hon Corps of Gentlemen-at-Arms 1929-31; S Africa 1899-1902 (despatches), European War 1914-19 in France and Comdg British Troops in Italy (despatches seven times, CB, KCB, GCMG, Orders of St Maurice and St Lazarus of Italy, Crown of Belgium and Wen Hu of China, Legion of Honour, Mil Order of Savoy, French and Italian Croix de Guerre): *m* 1st, 1893, Caroline Inez, who *d* 1920, da of late George Baden Crawley; 2ndly, 1922, Lady (Hester) Joan Byng, DBE, who *d* 1976, da of 5th Earl of Strafford, and widow of Capt Hon Andrew Edward Somerset Mulholland; *d* 1946; *s* by his brother **(12)** Horace Edward Samuel Sneade, 11th Earl; *b* 1878; Archdeacon Emeritus of Salop, Preb Emeritus and Provost of Denstone; sometime V of St Mary-the-Virgin, Shrewsbury: *m* 1907, Audrey Kathleen, who *d* 1942, da of late Alfred Basil Loder; *d* 1950; *s* by his son **(13)** Michael Edward Oliver, TD, 12th Earl *b* 1911; Lt-Col Shropshire Yeo (Comdg 1955-58), 1939-45 War (despatches), Vice Lord-Lieut for Salop 1975-87: *m* 1947, Essex Lucy, da of late Henry Arthur Cholmondeley (*see* B Delamere, colls); *d* 1988, *s* by his kinsman **(14)** Roger Cavan (only son of late Frederick Cavan Lambart, only son of late Maj Charles Edward Kilcoursie Lambart, 4th son of late Maj Frederick Richard Henry Lambart, 2nd son of late Com Hon Oliver Matthew Lambart, RN, 2nd son of 7th Earl), 13th Earl and present peer; also Viscount Kilcoursie, and Lord Lambart, Baron of Cavan.

CAVENDISH OF FURNESS, BARON (Cavendish) (Life Baron 1990)

(RICHARD) HUGH CAVENDISH, elder son of late Capt Richard Edward Osborne Cavendish (*see* D Devonshire, colls); *b* 2 Nov 1941; *ed* Eton; High Sheriff Cumbria 1978, DL 1988, Member Cumbria CC 1985-90, and Commn on Historic Buildings and Monuments (English Heritage) since 1992; a Lord in Waiting to HM 1990-92; Titular Abbot of Furness; Chm Holker Estate Group of Cos since 1971, Morecambe and Lonsdale Conservative Assocn 1975-78, and Chm of Govs St Anne's Sch, Windermere 1983-89; Dir UK Nirex Ltd since 1993; FRSA 1988; *cr Baron Cavendish of Furness*, of Cartmel (Life Baron) 1990: *m* 1970, Grania Mary, da of Brig Toby St George Caulfeild, CBE (*see* V Charlemont, colls), and has issue.

Arms – Sable, three bucks' heads cabossed argent. **Crest** – A serpent nowed proper.
Seat – Holker Hall, Cark-in-Cartmel, Cumbria LA11 7PL. *Clubs* – Brooks's, White's, Pratt's, Beefsteak.

SON LIVING

Hon Frederick Richard Toby, *b* 1972.

DAUGHTERS LIVING

Hon Lucy Georgiana, *b* 1973.
Hon Emily Moyra, *b* 1980.

CAWDOR, EARL (Campbell) (Earl UK 1827)

COLIN ROBERT VAUGHAN CAMPBELL, 7th Earl, and 25th Thane of Cawdor; *b* 30 June 1962; *s* 1993; *ed* Eton, and St Peter's Coll, Oxford.

Arms – Quarterly of four: 1st or, a stag's head cabossed sable attired gules, *Calder*; 3rd argent, a lymphad or ancient galley sable, *also Campbell*, 4th per fesse azure and gules, a cross or, *Lort*. **Crest** – A swan proper, crowned or. **Supporters** – *Dexter*, a lion guardant gules; *sinister*, a stag proper.
Seat – Cawdor Castle, Nairn.

BROTHER LIVING

Hon FREDERICK WILLIAM, *b* 29 July 1965; *ed* Eton, E Anglia Univ, and Heriot Watt Univ.

SISTERS LIVING

Lady Emma Clare, *b* 1958: *m* 1983, David Marrian, son of Peter Marrian, of Nairobi, and has issue living, Jack Alexander Wolf, *b* 1985, — Hunter James, *b* 1988, — Finlay David, *b* 1991. *Address* – PO Box 45465, Nairobi, Kenya.
Lady Elizabeth (Liza), *b* 1959: *m* 1990, William Robert Charles Athill, 3rd son of Maj Andrew Athill, Royal Norfolk Regt, of The Cottage, Morston, Norfolk, and has issue living, Atticus Ocean, *b* 1992, — Storm (a da), *b* 1990. *Residence* – 14 Almeric Rd, SW11.
Lady Laura Jane, *b* 1966.

UNCLE LIVING (*son of 5th Earl*)

Hon James Alexander (The Garden Cottage, 141 Bath Rd, Cheltenham, Glos), *b* 1942; *ed* Eton; ARCA: *m* 1st, 1964 (*m diss* 1973), Brigid Carol Dolben, da of late Capt Patrick Owen Lyons, RA; 2ndly, 1973 (*m diss* 1986), Ann Elizabeth, da of late Col Argyle Henry Gillmore, OBE, and has issue living (by 1st *m*), Slaine Catherine, *b* 1966, — Cara Jenny, *b* 1968, — (by 2nd *m*), Lucy Georgia Elizabeth, *b* 1973, — Sarah Ann, *b* 1977.

GREAT AUNT LIVING (*Daughter of 4th Earl*)

Lady Mary Agatha, *b* 1905: *m* 1931, Brig Henry Claude Warrington Eastman, DSO, MVO, RA, who *d* 1975, and has issue living, David William (Pandy Newydd, Halfway Bridge, Bangor, Gwynedd) *b* 1937: *m* 1969, Antonia Catherine, da of Anthony Dorman, of Mill House, Netherbury, Bridport, Dorset, — Sylvia, *b* 1935: *m* 1967, Peter Leth, who *d* 1987. *Residence* – Pandy Newydd, Halfway Bridge, Bangor, Gwynedd.

MOTHER LIVING

Cathryn, 2nd da of late Maj-Gen Sir (William) Robert Norris Hinde, KBE, CB, DSO, of Shrewton House, Shrewton, Salisbury, Wilts: *m* 1957 (*m diss* 1979), as his 1st wife, the 6th Earl, who *d* 1993. *Residences* – 30 Rawlings St, SW3 2LS; Kennt House, Ramsbury, nr Marlborough SN8 2QN.

WIDOW LIVING OF SIXTH EARL

Countess ANGELIKA (*Countess Cawdor*), da of Count Prokop Lazansky von Bukowa: *m* 1979, as his 2nd wife, the 6th Earl, who *d* 1993. *Residence* – Cawdor Castle, Nairn IV12 5RD.

COLLATERAL BRANCHES LIVING

Issue of late Lt-Col Hon Ralph Alexander Campbell, CBE, 3rd son of 3rd Earl, *b* 1877, *d* 1945: *m* 1st, 1906, Marjorie Theophila, who *d* 1911, da of Sir John Arthur Fowler, 2nd Bt; 2ndly, 1914, Marjorie Edith, who *d* 1984, da of Horace George Devas:—
(By 2nd *m*) David Archibald, CBE, TD, *b* 1915; *ed* Eton, and Trin Hall, Camb; FRICS; is Lt-Col and Brevet Col late Berks Yeo; OBE (Mil) 1954, CBE (Civil) 1988. *Residence* – Paxton House, Bucklebury, Reading, Berks. ——— Angus Mervyn, TD, *b* 1918; *ed* Eton; late Maj Surrey Yeo; 1939-45 War (despatches): *m* 1950, Rosemary Madeline Hamilton, only da of Hugh Alastair Hamilton Fraser (D Somerset, colls), and has issue living, Ian Angus Ralph (39 Grandison Rd, SW11), *b* 1951; *ed* Bradfield: *m* 1984, Jacqueline, da of John Jowett, and has issue living, Edward Alastair Ian *b* 1988, Frederick Hugh *b* 1990, — *Rev* James Malcolm (Endlebury, Bungay Rd, Scole, Diss, Norfolk IP21 4DX), *b* 1955; *ed* Eton, RAC Cirencester, and Wycliffe Hall, Oxford; ordained priest 1991: *m* 1984, Mary, eldest da of John Rolston, and has issue living, John (Jack) Alexander *b* 1990, Chloe Elizabeth *b* 1992, Alice Violet *b* 1994, — Catherine Rosemary, *b* 1964. *Residence* – Wasing Lodge, Aldermaston, Reading, Berks RG7 4LZ. ——— Rosemary Edith, *b* 1921. *Residence* – Pond Cottage, Padworth Common, Reading, Berks.

Issue of late Hon Elidor Ronald Campbell, 4th son of 3rd Earl, *b* 1881, *d* 1957: *m* 1913, Violet, who *d* 1975, da of Octavius Edward Bulwer-Marsh, of Bryngwyn Manor, Raglan, Monmouthshire:—
Fiona Mary, *b* 1925: *m* 1973, Iain Alastair MacDonald. *Residence* – 2 Blaen-y-Myarth, Llangynidr, nr Crickhowell, Powys.

Grandsons of late Capt Hon Ronald George Elidor Campbell, 2nd son of 2nd Earl:—
Issue of late Lt-Col Robert Campbell, DSO, *b* 1878, *d* 1945: *m* 1926, Mary Emelda, who *d* 1979, da of late William Robert Wood:—
Robin John Ronald, *b* 1927; *ed* Eton; Maj (ret) Queen's Own Highlanders; Malaya 1951 (despatches): *m* 1954, Alison Barbara Rose, da of late Major Horace Cave-Browne (*see* Cave-Browne-Cave, Bt, colls), and has issue living, Ian Robert, *b* 1956; *ed* abroad; Northern Constabulary, — James Farquhar Robin, *b* 1958; *ed* Gordonstoun; late Capt Queen's Own Highlanders: *m* 1985, Marina Caroline Vere, elder da of Maj Charles Pepler Norton, of Coldstone House, Ascott-under-Wychwood, Oxon (*see* Ogilvy, Bt, colls), and has issue living, Guy James Farquhar *b* 1991, Ishbel Elizabeth Rose *b* 1988. *Residence* – Kinrara, Aviemore, Inverness-shire. ——— Alan, *b* 1929; *ed* Eton; Lt-Col (ret) Queen's Own Highlanders (formerly The Cameronians) (Scottish Rifles); Malaya 1952 (despatches): *m* 1963, Sylvia, da of late Richard Hermon, CBE, and has issue living, Alexander, *b* 1964; *ed* Eton, — James, *b* 1967; *ed* Eton; Capt Queen's Own Highlanders: — Andrew, *b* 1969; *ed* Eton, — Nicholas, *b* 1971; *ed* The King's Sch, Ely, — Theresa Ann, *b* 1965. *Residence* – Crossways House, Bartlow, Cambridge.

Grandson of late Capt Hon Alexander Francis Henry Campbell, 3rd son of 2nd Earl:—
Issue of late Major Duncan Elidor Campbell, DSO, *b* 1880, *d* 1930: *m* 1914, Hon Florence Evelyne Willey, who *d* 1978, da of 1st Baron Barnby:—
Ian Robert, CB, CBE, AFC, *b* 1920; *ed* Eton; Air Vice-Marshal RAF (ret); Ch of Staff, No 18 Gp RAF 1973-75; 1939-45 War in Middle East and Italy (prisoner); CBE (Mil) 1964; CB (Mil) 1976: *m* 1st, 1953, Beryl Evelyn, who *d* 1982, da of late Brig Thomas Kennedy Newbigging, MC; 2ndly, 1984, Elisabeth, yst da of Maj Richard Kennedy Lingard-Guthrie (*see* B Maclean, colls, 1980 Edn), and has issue living (by 1st *m*), Alister Neil (69 Moore Park Rd, SW6 2HH), *b* 1955; *ed* Eton: *m* 1982, Ceril Diana, only da of A. Barnato-Kahan, of 12 Grove Court, Drayton Gardens, SW10, and has issue living, Rory Dominic Alexander *b* 1987, Arabella Louise Evelyn *b* 1984. *Residence* – Pike Farm, Fossebridge, Cheltenham, Glos. *Clubs* – Boodle's, RAF.

PREDECESSORS – Pryse Campbell, MP (a descendant of Sir John Campbell, 3rd son of 2nd Earl of Argyll), had with other issue (1) JOHN, MP for Nairnshire 1777-80 and for Cardigan 1780-96; *cr* **Baron Cawdor** (peerage of Great Britain) 1796; *d* 1821; *s* by his son (2) JOHN FREDERICK, FRS, DD, 2nd Baron; *b* 1790; *cr* **Viscount Emlyn** and **Earl Cawdor** (peerage of United Kingdom) 1827: *m* 1816, Lady Elizabeth Thynne, da of 2nd Marquess of Bath; *d* 1860; *s* by his son (3) JOHN FREDERICK VAUGHAN, 2nd Earl, *b* 1817, MP for Pembrokeshire (LC) 1841-59; Lord-Lieut of Carmarthenshire: *m* 1842, Sarah Mary, who *d* 1881, da of late Gen Hon Henry Frederick Compton Cavendish (D Devonshire); *d* 1898; *s* by his el son (4) FREDERICK ARCHIBALD VAUGHAN, PC, 3rd Earl, *b* 1847; Chm of Great Western Railway 1895-1905, and Lord-Lieut of Pembroke 1896-1911; MP for Carmarthenshire (C) 1874-85; First Lord of the Admiralty 1905: *m* 1868, Edith Georgina, who *d* 1926, el da of late Christopher Turnor, of Stoke Rochford; *d* 1911; *s* by his el son (5) HUGH FREDERICK VAUGHAN, 4th Earl, *b* 1870: *m* 1898, Joan Emily Mary, who *d* 1945, da of John Charles Thynne (*see* M Bath, colls); *d* 1914; *s* by his el son (6) JOHN DUNCAN VAUGHAN, 5th Earl, *b* 1900; Lt-Col Queen's Own Cameron Highlanders (TA); Chm Historic Buildings Council for Scotland; FSA: *m* 1st, 1929 (*m diss* 1961), Wilma Mairi, who *d* 1982, el da of late Vincent C. Vickers, of 38 Prince's Gate, SW7; 2ndly, 1961, Elizabeth, who *d* 1985, da of J. Topham Richardson, JP, of Harps Oak, Merstham, Surrey, and widow of Maj Sir Alexander Penrose Gordon Cumming, 5th Bt, MC; *d* 1970; *s* by his elder son (7) HUGH JOHN VAUGHAN, 6th Earl, *b* 1932; FSA, FRICS, FRSA, High Sheriff Carmarthenshire 1964: *m* 1st, 1957 (*m diss* 1979), Cathryn, 2nd da of late Maj-Gen Sir (William) Robert Norris Hinde, KBE, CB, DSO; 2ndly, 1979, Countess Angelika, da of Count Prokop Lazansky von Bukowa; *d* 1993; *s* by his elder son (8) COLIN ROBERT VAUGHAN, 7th Earl and present peer; also Viscount Emlyn, and Baron Cawdor.

CAWLEY, BARON (Cawley) (Baron UK 1918, Bt UK 1906)

I desire, I believe, I have

FREDERICK LEE CAWLEY, 3rd Baron and 3rd Baronet; *b* 27 July 1913; *ed* Eton, and New Coll, Oxford (MA); Bar Lincoln's Inn 1938; Capt RA (Leics Yeo), 1939-45 War (wounded); Dep Chm of Cttees, House of Lords 1958-67: *m* 1944, Rosemary Joan, da of late Reginald Edward Marsden (*see* V Dillon, 1990 Edn), and has issue.

Arms – Sable, three swans heads erased argent, guttée de poix, a chief arched or, thereon a rose gules, barbed and seeded proper, between two garbs azure. **Crest** – Upon a mount vert, a swan's head erased argent between six bullrushes stalked and leaved, three on either side, or. **Supporters** – On either side a swan, wings surgeant tergiant argent, guttée de poix, each standing upon a garb fessewise or.
Seat – Berrington Hall, Leominster. *Residence* – Bircher Hall Leominster, Herefordshire, HR6 0AX.

SONS LIVING

Hon JOHN FRANCIS (Castle Ground, Ashton, Leominster, Herefordshire HR60 DN), *b* 28 Sept 1946; *ed* Eton, *m* 1979, Regina Sarabia, el da of the late Marqués de Hazas, of Madrid, and has issue living, William Robert Harold, *b* 2 July 1981, — Thomas Frederick José-Luis, *b* 1982, — Andrew David, *b* 1988, — Susan Mary, *b* 1980.

Hon William Frederick, *b* 1947; *ed* Eton, and New Coll, Oxford (MA): *m* 1979 (*m diss* 1988), Philippa J., el da of Philip Hoare, DFC, of The Playle, Weycombe Rd, Haslemere, Surrey, and has issue living, Edward Frederick, *b* 1980, — Elizabeth Lena, *b* 1982.

Hon Richard Kenneth, *b* 1949; *ed* Eton, Durham Univ (BA), and City Univ Business Sch (MBA); MBIM: *m* 1976, Tsugumi, 2nd da of S. Ota, of Takarazuka, Japan.

Hon Justin Robert, *b* 1953; *ed* Milton Abbey Sch: *m* 1986, Margaret Lee Greatorex-Davies. *Residence* – 24 Malta Close, Popley, Basingstoke, Hants RG24 9PD.

Hon Charles Michael, *b* 1955; *ed* Milton Abbey Sch, and Manchester Univ (BA): *m* 1980 (*m diss* 1987), Justine J., da of J. F. B. Parry, of Hockley, Essex.

Hon Mark Andrew, *b* 1957; *ed* Eton, New Coll, Oxford (MA), and INSEAD (MBA).

DAUGHTER LIVING

Hon Vanessa Mary, *b* 1951; BA Open Univ: *m* 1971, Dr John Anthony Marston, of Gorwell House, Barnstaple, N Devon, and has issue living, Cicely Alice, *b* 1973, — Emma Elizabeth, *b* 1975, — Camilla Vere, *b* 1977, — Annabel Sarah, *b* 1979.

BROTHER LIVING

Hon Stephen Robert, *b* 1915; *ed* Eton, and New Coll, Oxford (BA 1937, BSc 1938, MA, 1946); 1939-45 War with R Sigs; JP Herefords and Worcs Supplemental 1974-78, Kidderminster (Active) 1978-83, and Surrey Supplemental since 1983; Prime Warden of Dyers' Co 1970-71: *m* 1952, Iris Edrica, da of late Reginald Edward Marsden (*see* V Dillon, 1990 Edn), and has issue living, Robin Alexander, *b* 1954: *m* 1982, Roslyn, only da of George Latham, of Newport, Gwent, — James Edward, *b* 1956: *m* 1984, Mary Fiona, only da of Lt-Cdr E. J. Wright, of Elm House, Ampleforth, York, and has issue living, Joseph Edward John *b* 1989, — Martin Harold, *b* 1959, — Yoland Diana, *b* 1957: *m* 1988, Mark Jonathan Dodgson. *Residence* – Woodhay, Tilford Rd, Hindhead, Surrey GU26 6QY.

PREDECESSORS – (1) *Rt Hon* FREDERICK Cawley, PC, son of late Thomas Cawley, of Priestland, Cheshire; *b* 1850; Chancellor of the Duchy of Lancaster in National Min 1916-18; MP for Prestwich Div of Lancashire (SE) (*L*) 1895-1918; *cr a* Baronet 1906, and *Baron Cawley*, of Prestwich, co Palatine of Lancaster (peerage of United Kingdom) 1918: *m* 1876, Elizabeth, who *d* 1937, da of John Smith, of Kynsal Lodge, Audlem; *d* 1930; *s* by his son (2) ROBERT HUGH, 2nd Baron, *b* 1877; S Africa 1900-01: *m* 1912, Vivienne, who *d* 1978 (aged 100), da of Harold Lee, of Broughton Park, Manchester; *d* 1954; *s* by his son (3) FREDERICK LEE, 3rd Baron and present peer.

CAYZER, BARON (Cayzer) (Life Baron 1981, Bt UK 1921)

Cautiously, but without fear

(WILLIAM) NICHOLAS CAYZER, *Life Baron* and 2nd *Baronet*, el son of late Lt-Cdr Sir August Bernard Tellefsen, 1st Bt, RN, *b* 21 Jan 1910; *ed* Eton, and Corpus Christi Coll, Camb; *hp* to his kinsman's Baronetcy (cr 1904); Chm Liverpool Steamship Owners Assoc 1944-45, Member Nat Dock Labour Board 1947-52, Pres The British Commonwealth Shipping Co PLC since 1958, Chm Gen Council of British Shipping, and Pres Chamber of Shipping of UK 1959; Pres Inst of Marine Engineers 1963-64 and Prime Warden of Shipwrights' Co 1969-70; *cr Baron Cayzer*, of St Mary Axe in the City of London (Life Baron) 1981: *m* 1935, Elizabeth Catherine, da of late Owain Williams, and has issue.

Arms – Per chevron azure and argent two estoiles or and an ancient ship with three masts sails furled sable colours flying gules on a chief of the third three fleurs-de-lys of the first. **Crest** – A sea lion erect proper porged with a naval crown holding in his dexter paw a fleur-de-lys gold. **Supporters** – Two golden retriever bitches sejant proper each having a collar azure buckled edged and garnished or and in the shoulder from between the forelegs a lilly reflexed behind the head also proper. **Motto** – Caute sed impavide.
Residences – 95 Eaton Sq, SW1; The Grove, Walsham-le-Willows, Suffolk.

DAUGHTERS LIVING

Hon Nichola, *b* 1937: *m* 1956, Michael Keith Beale Colvin, MP, late Lieut Gren Gds, and has issue living, James Michael Beale CAYZER-COLVIN, *b* 1965: *m* 1992, Esther Anne Mary, adopted da of Michael Tree, of Shute House, Donhead St Mary, Dorset (*see* D Devonshire), — Amanda, MBE, *b* 1957; MBE (Civil) 1990: *m* 1985, Rupert Spencer Ponsonby, 2nd son of Sir Ashley Charles Gibbs Ponsonby, 2nd Bt, KCVO, MC, and has issue (*see* Ponsonby, Bt), — Arabella Nichola, *b* 1960: *m* 1983, James Gaggero, only son of Joseph Gaggero, CBE, of King's Yard Lane, Gibraltar, and has issue living, Nicholas James *b* 1985, Alexander Charles *b* 1987. *Residences* – 73 Westminster Gdns, SW1; Tangley House, nr Andover, Hants.
Hon Elizabeth, *b* 1946: *m* 1992, Nigel Christopher Gilmour, MD.

Cecil, Baron; title of Viscount Cranborne on Roll of HL.

CHALFONT, BARON (Gwynne Jones) (Life Baron 1964)

Arms yield to the toga

ALUN ARTHUR GWYNNE JONES, OBE, MC, PC, son of Arthur Gwynne Jones, of Cwmbran, Newport, Mon; *b* 5 Dec 1919; *ed* W Monmouth Sch; Brevet Lt-Col (ret) S Wales Borderers (Regular Army Officer 1940-61); Defence and Mil correspondent, *The Times* 1961-64; Min of State, Foreign Office 1964-70, and British Permanent Representative to WEU 1969-70; 1939-45 War in Burma (MC); *cr*, OBE (Mil) 1961, PC 1964, and *Baron Chalfont*, of Llantarnam, co Monmouth (Life Baron) 1964: *m* 1948, Mona, MB, ChB, da of Harry Douglas Mitchell, of Grimsby.

Arms – Gules a sword point downwards proper pommel and hilt or within an orle of two branches of olive fructed gold. **Crest** – A dragon sejant gules supporting a column sable charged with nine bars argent, the capital also argent. **Supporters** – *Dexter*, a private of the Grenadier Company, 24th Foot (South Wales Borderers) in the uniform of circa 1751, supporting with the exterior hand a bamboo cane leaved proper; *sinister*, a herald vested in a tabard of the arms proper and holding in the exterior hand a sprig of olive fructed or.
Residence – 65 Ashley Gdns, SW1P 1QG. *Clubs* – Garrick, City Livery, MCC.

CHALKER OF WALLASEY, BARONESS (Chalker) (Life Baroness 1992)

LYNDA CHALKER, PC, da of late Sidney Henry James Bates; *b* 29 April 1942; *ed* Roedean, Heidelberg Univ, Westfield Coll, London, and Central London Poly; Statistician, Research Bureau Ltd (subsidiary of Unilever) 1963-69, Market Researcher Shell Mex and BP Ltd 1969-72, Chief Exec of Internat Div Louis Harris Internat 1972-74; Chm Greater London Young Conservatives 1969-70, National Vice-Chm 1970-71; Member BBC Gen Advisory Cttee 1975-79; Parly Under Sec of State Dept of Health and Social Security 1979-82, Transport 1982-83, Min of State Transport 1983-86, and FCO 1986, Dep Foreign Sec 1987-89, since when Min of State FCO and Min Overseas Devpt; MP Wallasey (*C*) 1974-92; *cr* PC 1987, and *Baroness Chalker of Wallasey*, of Leigh-on-Sea, co Essex (Life Baroness) 1992: *m* 1st, 1967 (*m diss* 1973), Eric Robert Chalker; 2ndly, 1981, Clive Landa.
Address – c/o House of Lords, SW1A 0PW.

CHAMPION, BARONY OF (Champion) (Extinct 1985)

DAUGHTER LIVING OF LIFE BARON

Hon Barbara, *b* 1931: *m* 1957, Trevor Chubb. *Residence* – 10 Salisbury Rd, Redland, Bristol, BF6 7AW.

WIDOW LIVING OF LIFE BARON

MARY EMMA (*Baroness Champion*) (22 Lanelay Terr, Pontypridd, Mid Glamorgan CF37 1ER), da of William Williams: *m* 1930, Baron Champion, PC (Life Baron), who *d* 1985.

CHANDOS, VISCOUNT (Lyttelton) (Viscount UK 1954)

Do what must be done, come what may

THOMAS ORLANDO LYTTELTON, 3rd Viscount; *b* 12 Feb 1953; *s* 1980; *ed* Eton, and Worcester Coll, Oxford (BA): *m* 1985, Arabella Sarah Lucy, da of John Adrian Bailey (*see* E Haddington), and has issue.

Arms – Argent, a chevron between three escallops sable a cross moline for difference. **Crest** – A Moor's head in profile couped at the shoulders proper, wreathed round the temples argent and sable. **Supporters** – On either side a merman proper holding in the outer hand a trident pendant from a rope around the inner shoulder an escutcheon or charged with a pile gules.
Residence – The Vine, Sherborne St John, Basingstoke, Hants

SONS LIVING

Hon OLIVER ANTONY, *b* 21 Feb 1986. —— *Hon* Benedict, *b* 1988.

DAUGHTER LIVING

Hon Rosanna Mary, *b* 1990.

BROTHER LIVING

Hon Matthew Peregrine Antony, *b* 1956; *ed* Eton, and Trin Coll, Camb (BA).

SISTERS LIVING

Hon Laura Katharine, *b* 1950; *ed* Cranborne Chase Sch, St Anne's Coll, Oxford (BA), and London Univ (BSc).
Hon Deborah Clare, *b* 1963.

UNCLE LIVING (*Son of 1st Viscount*)

Hon (Nicholas) Adrian Oliver, *b* 1937; *ed* Eton: *m* 1960, Margaret, who *d* 1993, da of late Sir Harold Hobson, the drama critic, and has issue living, Francis Sebastian Jasper, *b* 1967, — Celia Melissa Francesca, *b* 1960: *m* 1985, Dr Andrew Rae, eldest son of John Rae, of Brook House, Johannesburg. *Residence* – 30 Paulton's Sq, SW3.

AUNT LIVING (*Daughter of 1st Viscount*).

Hon Rosemary (*Viscountess Chaplin*), *b* 1922: *m* 1951, as his 2nd wife, 3rd Viscount Chaplin, who *d* 1981. *Residence* – 61 Ladbroke Rd, W11 3PN.

WIDOW LIVING OF SECOND VISCOUNT

CAROLINE MARY (*Hon Mrs David Erskine*), da of late Rt Hon Sir Alan Frederick Lascelles, GCVO, KCB, CMG, MC (*see* E Harewood, colls): *m* 1st, 1949, the 2nd Viscount, who *d* 1980; 2ndly, 1985, as his 2nd wife, Hon David Hervey Erskine, of Felsham House, Felsham, Bury St Edmunds, Suffolk, brother of 13th Earl of Mar and Kellie.

PREDECESSORS – (1) *Rt Hon* OLIVER LYTTELTON, KG, DSO, MC, PC, son of late Rt Hon Alfred Lyttelton, KC, MP, 8th son of 4th Baron Lyttelton (V Cobham), *b* 1893; Pres of Board of Trade 1940-41 and 1945, Min of State Cairo and Member of War Cabinet 1941, Min of Production 1942-45, and Sec of State for Colonies, of Aldershot, co Southampton (peerage of UK) 1954: *m* 1920, Lady Moira Godolphin Osborne, who *d* 1976, da of 10th Duke of Leeds; *d* 1972; *s* by his son (2) ANTONY ALFRED, 2nd Viscount, *b* 1920: *m* 1949, Caroline Mary, who *m* 2ndly, 1985, as his 2nd wife, Hon David Hervey Erskine, of Felsham House, Felsham, Bury St Edmunds, Suffolk (*see* E Mar and Kellie), da of late Rt Hon Sir Alan Frederick Lascelles, GCVO, KCB, CMG, MC (*see* E Harewood, colls); *d* 1980; *s* by his el son (3) THOMAS ORLANDO, 3rd Viscount and present peer.

CHAPLIN, VISCOUNTCY OF (Chaplin) (Extinct 1981)

DAUGHTERS LIVING OF THIRD VISCOUNT (*By 1st marriage*)

Hon (Oenone) Clarissa, *b* 1934: *m* 1958, Michael Charles Deane Luke, son of late Sir Harry Charles Luke, KCMG, and has issue living, Igor Charles de Zander, *b* 1965, — Chloe Oleanda Alvilde, *b* 1959, — Œnone Jemima, *b* 1960: *m* 1992, Richard C. Gladstone, of via Lombarda 355, Lammari, Lucca 55013, Italy, son of David Gladstone, of Menai Bridge, Anglesey, — Cressida Eugénie, *b* 1961. *Residence* – 22 Eaton Sq, SW1.

(*By 2nd marriage*)

Hon Miranda Amadea, *b* 1956: *m* 1980, Brian Corran, and has issue living, Hereward, *b* 1981.
Hon Christina Susanna, *b* 1958.

WIDOW LIVING OF THIRD VISCOUNT

Hon Rosemary (*Viscountess Chaplin*), da of 1st Viscount Chandos: *m* 1951, as his 2nd wife, the 3rd Viscount, who *d* 1981, when the title became ext. *Residence* – 61 Ladbroke Rd, W11 3PN.

CHAPPLE, BARON (Chapple) (Life Baron 1985)

FRANCIS (FRANK) JOSEPH CHAPPLE, son of Frank Chapple, of Shoreditch, by his wife Emily, da of Joseph Rook, of Hoxton; *b* Aug 1921; *ed* elementary sch; Member Electrical Trade Union Confederation 1937-83; Shop Steward and Branch Official; Member Exec Council 1958; Assist Gen Sec 1963-66; Gen Sec Electrical, Electronic, Telecommunication and Plumbing Union 1966-83; Member Gen Council of TUC 1971-83 (Chm 1982-83), Member Labour Party Exec; Gold Badge of Congress 1983; *cr Baron Chapple*, of Hoxton, Greater London (Life Baron) 1985: *m* 1944, Joan Jeanette, who *d* 1994, da of James Nicholls, and has issue.
Address – c/o Electrical, Electronic, Telecommunication and Plumbing Union, Hayes Court, West Common Rd, Bromley BR2 7AU.

SONS LIVING

Hon Roger Francis, *b* 1947; *ed* Brooke House Comprehensive Sch: *m* 1969, Susan Audrey, da of Charles F. W. Brown.
Hon Barry Joseph, *b* 1951; *ed* Hawes Down Comprehensive Sch: *m* 1980,

CHARLEMONT, VISCOUNT (Caulfeild) (Viscount I, 1665)
(Title pronounced "Char-le-mont")

DEO · DUCE · FERRO · COMITANTE

God my leader, the sword my companion

JOHN DAY CAULFEILD, 14th Viscount; *b* 19 March 1934; *s* 1985: *m* 1st, 1964, Judith Ann, who *d* 1971, da of James E. Dodd, of Islington, Ontario; 2ndly, 1972, Janet Evelyn, da of Orville R. Nancekivell, of Mount Elgin, Ontario, and has issue by 1st *m*.

𝕬rms – Quarterly, 1st and 4th, barry often argent and gules, on a canton of the second a lion passant guardant or, *Caulfeild*; 2nd and 3rd, or, a chevron checky argent and azure between three martlets sable. *Houston.* 𝕮rest – A dragon's head erased gules, gorged with a bar gemelle argent. 𝕾upporters – Two dragons gules, wings elevated, each gorged with a bar gemelle argent.
Residence – 39 Rossburn Drive, Etobicoke, Ontario, Canada M9C 2P9.

SON LIVING

Hon JOHN DODD, *b* 15 May 1966.

DAUGHTER LIVING

Hon Janis Ann, *b* 1968.

SISTER LIVING

Edith Jane, *b* 1941: *m* 1963, Edward John Cobean, of 106 Brown's Av, Walkerton, Ontario, Canada N0G 2V0, and has issue living, Robert Edward, *b* 1967, — Stephen John, *b* 1971, — Susan Jane, *b* 1966.

UNCLE LIVING (*Brother of 13th Viscount*)

Ven Arthur Edward Lampay, CD (23 Seaside Drive, St Andrews, New Brunswick EOE 2XO, Canada), *b* 1906; *ed* Bishop's Univ (BA); DD King's Coll, R of Trin Church, Saint John, New Brunswick 1957-73; Chap R Canadian Air Force 1941-51: *m* 1940, Emilie Kathleen Irene, da of Rev Edgar Frank Salmon, DD, of Philadelphia, USA, and has issue living, David Arthur, *b* 1942; BArch, MASc, MRAIC, PEng; architect: *m* 1965, Diane, da of late Frederick Parker Du Vernet, of Ottawa, and has issue living, Sean David *b* 1966, Derek Arthur *b* 1969, — Charles Patrick (883 Safari Rd, Kingston, Ontario K7M 6W2, Canada), *b* 1946; BEng: *m* 1968, Marjorie Agnes, da of late Robert Reid, of Saint John, New Brunswick.

DAUGHTERS LIVING OF TWELFTH VISCOUNT

Hon Dorothy Frances Lucy St George *Clubs* – (Overseas, St James's), *b* 1915: *m* 1945, Robert Hender Trowbridge, late Fl-Lt RAAF, who *d* 1993, of Drumcairn, Lane End, Elmstead Market, Essex C07 7BB, and has issue living, Mark Robert, *b* 1947, — Richard Keith Giles *b* 1950: *m* 1980, Pamela Mary, da of Philip N. Bradshaw, of Gt Driffield, NE Yorks, and has issue living, Laura Frances *b* 1986, Emma Kathryn *b* 1988.
Hon Alicia St George, *b* 1918: *m* 1939, Gp Capt Gordon Hackworth Stuart, MD, RAF, of 3 Lovel Hill, Windsor Forest, Berks, and has issue living, Colin, *b* 1940: *m* 1st, 1965 (*m diss* 1970), Jane Susan, da of Maj Dennis Mitchel, Kings African Rifles; 2ndly, 1981, Eve Lin-Yau, da of Yau Shan Shan, of Peking, and has issue living (by 2nd *m*), Alicia Frances Sarah, *b* 1983.

DAUGHTERS LIVING OF ELEVENTH VISCOUNT

Hon Constance Ada, *b* 1918: *m* 1943, Henry Edward Pearce, of 254 Mooroondu Rd, Thorneside, Queensland 4158, Aust, and has issue living, Edward Charles (44 Dawson Rd, Ormiston Heights, Queensland 4163), *b* 1943; AAIA: *m* 1967, Beverley Ellen Cooper, and has issue living, Rodney Edward *b* 1970, — Donald John, *b* 1947; BEng: *m* 1971, Rasa Janina Zvirblis, and has issue living, Scott Ramon *b* 1975, Kristie Louise *b* 1977, — Pamela Ann, 1946: *m* 1966, Hendrik Wouter Veenstra, of 18 Gallang St, Rochedale, Qld 4123, Australia, and has two adopted children, Wade Hendrick *b* 1971, Annelies Pamela *b* 1973, — Janet May, *b* 1950; BEd, — Wendy Roslyn, *b* 1958; DipT.
Hon Janie St George, *b* 1921: *m* 1942, David Dominic Moore, BSc; MIE (Aust), of 30 Maxwell St, Turramurra, Sydney, NSW, and has issue living, Colleen Janie, *b* 1944: *m* 1967, Alan Charles Watts, MB, ChB, LRCP, MRCS, and has issue living, Tracey Colleen *b* 1968, Kellie Mary Jane *b* 1972, Christine Judith *b* 1975, Sarra Alaine *b* 1979, — Margaret Louise, *b* 1947: *m* 1972, Keith Douglas Brodie, LLB, CA, of Sydney, NSW, and has issue living, Barry *b* 1977, Paula Louise *b* 1975, Claire Elizabeth, *b* 1980.

DAUGHTER LIVING OF NINTH VISCOUNT

Hon Patricia St George (55 New Rd, Lewes, E Sussex), *b* 1920; 1939-45 War as 3rd Officer WRNS.

WIDOW LIVING OF THIRTEENTH VISCOUNT

DOROTHY JESSIE (*Dowager Viscountess Charlemont*), da of late Albert Allan Johnston, of Ottawa, Canada: *m* 1930, the 13th Viscount, who *d* 1985. *Residence* – 2055 Carling Av, Apt No 915, Ottawa, Ontario, Canada K2A 1G6.

MOTHER LIVING

Edith Evelyn (43 Smithwood Drive, Islington, Ontario, Canada M9B 48I), da of Frederick William Day, of Ottawa: *m* 1933, Eric St George Caulfeild, who *d* 1975.

COLLATERAL BRANCHES LIVING

Granddaughter of late Francis John Rothe Toby St George Caulfeild, ISO, MICE, 6th son of Rt Rev Charles Caulfeild, DD, Bishop of Nassau, elder son of late Rev Hans Caulfeild (*d* 1854), son of late Rev Charles Caulfeild, 3rd son of late Rev Hon Charles Caulfeild, 5th son of 2nd Viscount:—
Issue of late Major Harry Frowd St George Caulfeild, *b* 1881, *d* 1961: *m* 1914, Geraldine Marguerite, who *d* 1922, da of Lt-Col Charles Purvis Boyd:—

Geraldine St George, *b* 1918: *m* 1st, 1947, Maj Peter Lawry Matthews, TD, RASC, who *d* 1970; 2ndly, 1975, Hugh Alan Mason, who *d* 1992, of Orchard Leigh, Prinsted, Emsworth, Hants, and has issue living (by 1st *m*), Toby St George, *b* 1950, — Helen Brontë, *b* 1953: *m* 1st, 1980 (*m diss* 1988), Charles Koller, of California, USA; 2ndly, 1989, Phillip Warren Kunz, and has issue living (by 2nd *m*), Sarah Kaitlyn *b* 1990.

Grandchildren of late Capt Alfred Hans Waring Caulfeild, MB, only son of late Hans James Caulfeild (infra):—
Issue of late Evan Michael St George Caulfeild, *b* 1918, *d* 1993: *m* 1948, Shirley Joyce (2 Clearside Place, Etobicoke, Ontario M9C 2G6, Canada), da of Harry Scutt Burt, of Richmond Hill, Ontario, Canada:—
Toby Michael Hans, *b* 1949; *ed* Univ of Toronto (BA and BEd).

Grandchildren of late Hans James Caulfeild, el son of late Hans Caulfeild, MD, 6th son of Rev Hans Caulfeild (*d* 1854) (ante):—
Issue of late (James) Gordon Caulfeild, *b* 1917, *d* 1975: *m* 1943, Olive (Irene), da of late Thomas Henry Bradley, of Goderich, Ontario:—
Roddy Terence, MD (Tavistock, Ontario, Canada N0B 2R0), *b* 1946; *m* 1969, Patricia Ann Rogers, and has issue living, Stephen Michael, *b* 1972, — Jonathan David, *b* 1975. —— Caroline Diane, *b* 1948: *m* 1969, Peter Stanley Wardell, of 74 Derby Court, Newmarket, Ontario, Canada L3Y 5Z9, and has issue living, Peter Alexander, *b* 1975, — Stephanie Suzanne, *b* 1978.

Grandchildren of late Edwin James Stuart Widdrington Caulfeild, only son (by 2nd *m*) of Cmdr Edwin Toby Caulfeild, RN, el son of Wade Toby Caulfeild (infra):—
Issue of late Edwin Vivian Stuart Caulfeild, *b* 1874, *d* 1958: *m* 1903, Edith Helen, who *d* 1966, aged 89, da of Claude L. Ferneley, formerly of Loughborough:—
Stewart Frederick Barry, *b* 1907. —— Leonore Alicia, *b* 1906.

Descendants, if any, of Charles St George Stewart Hanvey Caulfeild (*b* 1874), only son of late Charles Caulfeild, only son of late Rev Abraham St George Caulfeild, DD, Rector of Windsor, 7th son of Rev Hans Caulfeild (*d* 1854) (ante).
Grandchildren of late Vice-Adm Francis Wade Caulfeild, CBE, elder son of late Francis William Caulfeild, only son (by 2nd *m*) of Rev Edward Warren Caulfeild, yr son of Wade Toby Caulfeild, el son of Col William Caulfeild, 2nd son of Hon Toby Caulfeild, 3rd son of 1st Viscount:—
Issue of late Wade Toby Caulfeild, *b* 1902, *d* 1991: *m* 1935, Philippa Mary (Honeysuckle Cottage, Midhurst, Sussex), da of Capt H. C. R. Brocklebank, of Charlton House, Shaftesbury, Dorset:—
James Alexander Toby, *b* 1937; *ed* Eton, and New Coll, Oxford; late 2nd Lieut KRRC: *m* 1976, Diana Penelope, da of Col Martin Pound, RM, and has issue living, Harriet Katharine, *b* 1980, — Victoria Louise, *b* 1982, — Charlotte Frances, *b* 1984, — Sophie Elizabeth, *b* 1987. *Residence* – Hookland, Redford, Midhurst, Sussex. —— Charlotte Antonia, *b* 1939: *m* 1975, Rev David Burton Evans, Rector of St Michael's, Cornhill, EC3. *Residence* – 59 Walcot Sq, Kennington, SW11 4UB.

Grandchildren of late Col Robert Caulfeild, 2nd son of Lt-Col John Caulfeild, 2nd son of Col William Caulfeild (*d* 1831), el son of Ven John Caulfeild, 2nd son of Col William Caulfeild (ante):—
Issue of late Brig-Gen Francis William John Caulfeild, CBE, *b* 1859, *d* 1938: *m* 1897, Alys, who *d* 1950, da of James Hornidge Finnemor, formerly of Ounavarra, Gorey, Ireland:—
Joan (18 The Lindens, Farnham, Surrey), *b* 1903: *m* 1926, Capt Ludovic Ernest Porter, RN, who *d* 1976, and has had issue, Simon Hugh Ludovic (Stanley House, Stanley Hill, Ledbury, Herefords HR8 1HB), *b* 1934; *ed* Eton: *m* 1963, Patricia Anne, da of Maj Alfred Burges, and has issue living, Alison Joan *b* 1966, Rosemary Ann *b* 1967, — Jeremy Michael, *b* 1937; *ed* Eton; Capt RN: *m* 1966, Caroline Patricia, da of Maj Washington Hibbert (*see* B Mowbray, colls), and *d* 1985, leaving issue, James Robert *b* 1967, Toby Hugh Washington *b* 1969.
Issue of late Col Gordon Napier Caulfeild, DSO, *b* 1862, *d* 1922: *m* 1902, Mildred, who *d* 1963, yst da of Philip O'Reilly, DL, of Colamber, Westmeath:—
Irene Mildred, *b* 1909; a Nun at St Cecilia's Abbey, Ryde, Isle of Wight.

Granddaughter of late Brig-Gen Charles Trevor Caulfeild, CMG, 3rd son of late Col Robert Caulfeild (ante):—
Issue of late John Trevor Caulfeild, *b* 1908, *d* 1968: *m* 1948, Elisabeth Allie Madeleine, who *d* 1968, da of late Gerald de Mestral, of Berne and Mont sur Rolle, Switzerland:—
Catherine Norah (28 New Close, Knebworth, Herts SG3 6NU), *b* 1949: *m* 1985, Nicholas William Hall, yr son of Francis George Hall, of Sharmans How, Digswell, Hertfords, and has issue living, Andrew Nicholas Francis William, *b* 1988, — Clare Elisabeth Alexandra, *b* 1987.

Grandchildren of late Brig-Gen James Edward Wilmot Smyth Caulfeild, CMG, 2nd son of Rev William Caulfeild, only son of Commodore Thomas Gordon Caulfeild, 2nd son of the Ven John Caulfeild (ante):—
Issue of late Col St George Frederick Gordon Caulfeild, RM, *b* 1881, *d* 1973: *m* 1917, Eila Rosslyn, who *d* 1973, da of Reginald John, of Colombo:—
Toby St George, CBE (PO Box 11, Girne, Mersin 10, Turkey), *b* 1919; *ed* Wellington, Brig (reg), late RA; Instructor Staff Coll 1955-57, and OC, 7th Parachute Regt, RHA 1960-62; UK Nat Mil Repres SHAPE 1971-74; France 1939-40, SE Asia 1942-45, Korea 1952, Malaya 1958-59; MBE (Mil) 1952, CBE (Mil) 1974: *m* 1st, 1942 (*m diss* 1951), Mary, da of late Sir William Lindsay Murphy, KCMG; 2ndly, 1959, Agnes Sheila, da of Edward Buckmaster Robinson, of Tankerton, Kent, and has issue living (by 1st *m*), Toby John St George (Newlands Grange, Shotley Bridge, Consett, co Durham), *b* 1943: *m* 1st, 1967, Gillian, da of C. M. Rhead; 2ndly, 1980, Joanna, da of Arthur R. Yates Hunter, of Saskatoon, Canada, and has issue living (by 1st *m*), Patrick William St George *b* 1968, — Grania Mary (*Baroness Cavendish of Furness*), *b* 1947: *m* 1970, Baron Cavendish of Furness (Life Baron), of Holker Hall, Cark-in-Cartmel, Cumbria.
Issue of late Lt-Col Wilmot Smyth Caulfeild, MC, RA, *b* 1887, *d* 1980: *m* 1st 1923, Meredith de Lisle, who *d* 1924, yr da of late Reginald John, of Merryworth Lawn, Wrotham; 2ndly, 1928, Shellah, who *d* 1992, da of late John J. Bevan, of Dublin:—
(By 1st *m*) Pamela Ann de Lisle, *b* 1924; a JP of Shropshire: *m* 1st, 1944 (*m diss* 1970), Maj Philip Hugh Godsal, 52nd LI, who *d* 1982; 2ndly, 1970, Capt Walter Edward Browning Godsal, RN, of Edbrooke, Winsford, Som (yr brother of her 1st husband), and has issue living (by 1st *m*), Philip Caulfeild (Iscoyd Park, Whitchurch, Shropshire), *b* 1945; *ed* Eton; High Sheriff Clwyd 1993; FRICS; Land Agent: *m* 1st, 1969 (*m diss* 1985), Lucinda Mary, da of late Lt-Cdr Percival Royston Dancey, RNVR, of Old Shalesbrook, Forest Row, Sussex; 2ndly, 1986, Mrs Selina Baber, da of Thomas William Brooke-Smith, of Canford Cliffs, Dorset, and has issue living (by 1st *m*), Philip Langley *b* 1971, Benjamin Rupert Wilmot *b* 1976, Thomas Henry *b* 1977, Laura Sophie *b* 1973, — David Hugh, MBE, *b* 1947; *ed* Eton, and Exeter Univ (BA); Col late RGJ; MBE (Mil) 1983: *m* 1971, Tamsin Annette, da of Capt Thomas Keppel Edge-Partington, RN, of Arnoldsfield, Fairfield Rd, Quenington, Cirencester, Glos GL7 5RT, and has issue living, James Keppel *b* 1977, Jonathan Hugh *b* 1981, Nicola Jane *b* 1974, — Rupert Charles, *b* 1952; *ed* Eton; Dep Headmaster, Horris Hill Preparatory Sch, Newtown, Newbury, Berks, — Caroline Mary, *b* 1950: *m* 1974, Robert Thornewill Miller, of Stowbridge House, Moreton-in-Marsh, Glos, and has issue living, David Robert *b* 1982, Clare Serena *b* 1983, — Meredith Jane, *b* 1956: *m* 1981, Maj Adam H. C. MacMillan-Scott, KOSB, son of W. T. R. MacMillan-Scott, of 2 Grove Meadow, Sticklepath, Okehampton, Devon, and has issue living, Katherine Rachel Sarah *b* 1982, Charlotte Meredith Lucy *b* 1984, Isobel Sophie de Lisle *b* 1986. —— (By 2nd *m*) Eileen Ruth Morley, *b* 1929: *m* 1952,

Henry Edward Percy, who *d* 1985, and has issue (*see* D Northumberland, colls). *Residence* – Ballygate House, Beccles, Suffolk NR34 9ND. —— Barbara Joan Shellah, *b* 1932: *m* 1969, Preston Caradoc Hardinge Mostyn Prichard, of The Croft, Says Lane, Upper Langford, Bristol (*see* V Hardinge, colls, 1980 Edn), and has issue living, Julian Caulfeild Mostyn, *b* 1970; *ed* Milton Abbey, — Diana Mostyn, *b* 1973.

Grandchildren of late Capt George Blake Caulfeild, yr son of late George Caulfeild, 4th son of Lt-Gen James Caulfeild, CB, yst son of Ven John Caulfeild (*ante*):—
Issue of late Leslie Alexander Caulfeild, *b* 1902, *d* as a result of enemy action 1940: *m* 1930 (*m diss* 1936), Jennie Ida, da of late Charles Deering Manson:—
A son, *b* 193—.
Issue of late William Henry Caulfeild, *b* 1911, *d* on active service in Burma 1943: *m* 1935, Lorna (Flat 9, 26 Sussex Sq, Brighton BN2 5AB), da of late Cuthbert Wilkinson, of The Clock House, Nether Stowey, Som:—
Anne Marie, *b* 1941: *m* 1965, Rupert Alan Travis, of 97 Balham Park Rd, SW12 8EB, and has issue living, Benjamin William Norman, *b* 1973, — Toby Rupert Dale, *b* 1979, — Amanda Tiffany, *b* 1972.

PREDECESSORS – (1) *Rt Hon Sir* TOBY Caulfeild, PC, a distinguished soldier, MP for Armagh 1613, Master of the Ordnance 1614, &c, was *cr Lord Caulfeild, Baron of Charlemont* (peerage of Ireland) 1620, with remainder to his nephew Sir William Caulfeild, Knt; *d* unmarried 1627; *s* by his nephew (2) *Sir* WILLIAM, 2nd Baron: Master Gen of the Ordnance 1627-34; *d* 1640; *s* by his son (3) TOBY, 3rd Baron; when Governor of Charlemont, during the Rebellion of 1641, he was surprised and taken prisoner and subsequently shot by the order of Sir Phelim O'Neile; *d* unmarried; *s* by his brother (4) ROBERT, 4th Baron; *d* 1642, from an over-dose of opium; *s* by his brother (5) WILLIAM, 5th Baron; apprehended Sir Phelim O'Neile, and had him executed for the murder of his brother the 3rd Baron; *cr Viscount Charlemont* (peerage of Ireland) 1665; *d* 1671; *s* by his son (6) WILLIAM, 2nd Viscount; zealously opposed the cause of James II, by whose parliament he was attainted, but King William, after the rebellion was quelled, gave him a regt of foot and made him Gov of cos Tyrone and Armagh, &c; *d* 1726; *s* by his son (7) JAMES, 3rd Viscount, MP for Charlemont 1727; *d* 1734; *s* by his son (8) JAMES, KP, 4th Viscount; *cr Earl of Charlemont* (peerage of Ireland) 1763; was Com in Ch of Vol Army in Ireland 1779; *d* 1799; *s* by his son (9) FRANCIS WILLIAM, KP, 2nd Earl, *b* 1775; a Representative Peer; *cr Baron Charlemont* (peerage of United Kingdom) 1837, with remainder to his brother; *m* 1802, Anne, da and co-heir of William Bermingham, of Ross Hill, co Galway; *d* 1863; *s* by his nephew (10) JAMES MOLYNEUX, KP, 3rd Earl (son of Hon Henry, 2nd son of 1st Earl), *b* 1820; Lord-Lieut of co Tyrone; MP for Armagh co (*L*) 1847-67: *m* 1st, 1856, Hon Elizabeth Jane Somerville, who *d* 1882, da of 1st Baron Athlumney; 2ndly, 1883, Anna Lucy, who *d* 1925, da of the Rev Charles James Lambart; *d* 1892, when the Earldom (1763) and the Barony (1837) became extinct, and the Peerages of 1620 and 1665 devolved upon his cousin (11) JAMES ALFRED, CB (son of Edward Houston Caulfeild, great-grandson of Rev Hon Charles Caulfeild, 5th son of 2nd Viscount), 7th Viscount, *b* 1830; Capt Coldstream Guards; served in Crimean War 1854-6; Comptroller of Household to successive Viceroys of Ireland 1868-95; Usher of Black Rod to Order of St Patrick: *m* 1858, Hon Annette Handcock, who *d* 1888, da of 3rd Baron Castlemaine; *d* 1913; *s* by his nephew (12) JAMES EDWARD, PC (son of late Hon Marcus Piers Francis Caulfeild, brother of 7th Viscount), 8th Viscount, *b* 1880; Vice-Lieut for co Tyrone 1923-39; a Member of Senate of N Ireland 1925-37, and Min of Education and Leader of the Senate 1926-37: *m* 1st, 1914 (*m diss* April 1940), Evelyn, who *d* as a result of enemy action Oct 1940, da of Edmund Charles Pendleton Hull, of Park Gate House, Ham Common, Surrey; 2ndly, 1940, Hildegarde, who *d* 1969, da of Rodolphe Slock-Cottell, of Malstapel, Buysselede, Belgium; *d* 1949; *s* by his kinsman (13) CHARLES EDWARD ST GEORGE (only son of late Hans St George Caulfeild, 2nd son of late Rt Rev Charles Caulfeild, DD, Bishop of Nassau, el son of Rev Hans Caulfeild, grandson of Rev Hon Charles Caulfeild, 5th son of 2nd Viscount), 9th Viscount: *m* 1911, Mabel, who *d* 1965, el da of James Hawthorn; *d* 1964; *s* by his kinsman (14) ROBERT TOBY ST GEORGE (2nd son of late Henry St George Caulfeild, 1st son of late James Caulfeild, 2nd son of late Rev Hans Caulfeild (*ante*)), 10th Viscount; *b* 1881; *d* 1967; *s* by his brother (15) CHARLES ST GEORGE, 11th Viscount, *b* 1884: *m* 1915, Lydia Clara, who *d* 1973, da of Charles James Kingston, of Aramac; *d* 1971; *s* by his brother (16) RICHARD WILLIAM ST GEORGE, 12th Viscount, *b* 1887: *m* 1914, Dorothy Laura, who *d* 1961, da of Frank Giles, ICS; *d* 1979; *s* by his kinsman (17) CHARLES WILBERFORCE (el son of the Rev Wilberforce Caulfeild, Rector of St Mary, Kilkenny, 4th son of the Rev Hans Caulfeild (*ante*)), 13th Viscount, *b* 1899: *m* 1930, Dorothy Jessie, da of late Albert Allan Johnston, of Ottawa, Canada; *d* 1985; *s* by his nephew (18) JOHN DAY (son of late Eric St George Caulfeild), 14th Viscount and present peer; also Lord Caulfeild, Baron of Charlemont.

CHARLEVILLE, EARLDOM OF (Bury) (Extinct 1875)

COLLATERAL BRANCHES LIVING

Grandchildren of late Lady Beaujolois Eleanora Catherine Bury (who *m* 1853, Hastings Dent), da of 2nd Earl:—
Issue of late Alfred Robert Tighe Dent, *b* 1861, *d* 1922: *m* 1887, Ida M., da of Napoleon Richards, of Minneapolis, Minn, USA:—
Alfred Charles, *b* 1889: *m* 1913, Marion Tucker, and has issue living, Stephen Tucker (La Canada, Cal, USA), *b* 1917: *m* 1947, Clo O'Neal, — Peter Campbell (831 Ford St, Burbank, Cal 91505, USA), *b* 1925: *m* 1953, Constance Gillespie, and has issue living, Elena Marie, *b* 1955. —— Audrey Hope, *b* 1902: *m* 1926, William John Burke, of 1136 S Hudson Av, Los Angeles, Cal 90019, USA, and has had issue, Robert John (209 Calle Porto, San Clemente, Calif 92672, USA), *b* 1932: *m* 1st, 1953, Sarone Birdsell; 2ndly, 1963, Virginia Sue Parker, and has issue living (by 1st *m*), Kevin Patrick *b* 1958: *m* 1989, Leslie Allyn McPeak (and has issue living, Riley Dunavan *b* 1992, Liam Mackenzie *b* 1994), Kim Lorayne *b* 1957: *m* 1st, 1975, Rory Glenn Strahan; 2ndly, 1985, Robert Charles Weber, Jr (and has issue living (by 1st *m*), Brett Ryan *b* 1977, Scott Ryan *b* 1980), — Beaujolois Joan, *b* 1927: *m* 1963, Joseph Michael Phillips, of Bellevue, Washington, USA, and has issue living Michele Ann *b* 1964: *m* 1989, David Michael Tiffany, of Seattle, WA, USA, Madeleine Louise *b* 1965: *m* 1992, Scott Douglas Noe, — Connaught Marie, *b* 1929: *m* 1960, Earl Robert Lieberg, of Los Angeles, Cal, USA, and *d* 1992, leaving issue, Scott Robert *b* 1970, Laura Marie *b* 1961: *m* 1982, Mark Rivera, Robin Diane *b* 1965: *m* 1988, Jonathan Young, of Surrey, England (and has issue living, Natalie Chanel *b* 1989, Monique Brittany *b* 1992).

Grandchildren of late Alfred Robert Tighe Dent (*ante*):—
Issue of late Ronald Beaujolois Dent, *b* 1894, *d* 1947; legally relinquished the forename of Ardo (before that of Ronald): *m* 1916, Agnes Cecile Morris:—
Ronald Eden, *b* 1922: *m* 1946, Barbara LePage, and has issue living, Ronald Beaujolois, *b* 1947: *m* 1985, Mary Larson, — Suzanne Lorraine, *b* 1949: *m* 1st, 1971, Jaime Anijo; 2ndly, 1993, Rodney Luce, and has issue living (by 1st *m*), Michelle Ashley *b* 1972: *m* 1992, Paul Stevenson, — Janet Elizabeth, *b* 1951: *m* 1975, Frederick Curtiss Waits, and has issue living, Andrew Curtiss *b* 1983, Holly Janelle *b* 1977, Shannon Beaujolois *b* 1980, — Barbara Anne, *b* 1964: *m* 1987, Bruce Arneklev. —— Audrey Madeleine Beaujolois, *b* 1918: *m* 1944, Robert Patrick O'Hara, and has issue living, Patrick Joseph, *b* 1953: *m* 1990, Caterina Randolph, — Kevin Ronald, *b* 1955: *m* 1982, Jane Arleen Darrington, and has isssue living, Patrick Robert *b* 1984, Bryan Richard *b* 1987, — Kathleen Mary, *b* 1945: *m* 1970, Clayton Walker, and has issue living, Joseph Brian *b* 1973, — Anne Beaujolois, *b* 1951: *m* 1974, Stephen Leo Sandbo, and has issue living, Andrew O'Hara *b* 1979, Stephany Marie *b* 1976, Robyn Beaujolois (a da) *b* 1977, Kathryn Lisa *b* 1984, Emily Anne *b* 1985, Brittany Mary *b* 1987. —— Marianne

Cecile, *b* 1920: *m* 1946, John C. DiJoseph, and *d* 1991, having had issue, Thomas John, *b* 1947; *d* 1978, — Julie Mary, *b* 1948, — Theresa Ann, *b* 1950: *m* 1974, Craig John Sears, — Mary Elizabeth, *b* 1962: *m* 1980, Owen Scott Lawson, and has issue living, Jennifer Nicole *b* 1981, Holly Jean *b* 1984, Sarah Rose *b* 1989.

CHARTERIS OF AMISFIELD, BARON (Charteris) (Life Baron 1978)

Behold my charter

MARTIN MICHAEL CHARLES CHARTERIS, GCB, GCVO, QSO, OBE, PC, yr son of late Capt Hugo Francis Charteris, Lord Elcho, and brother of the 12th Earl of Wemyss and March; *b* 7 Sept 1913; *ed* Eton, and RMC Sandhurst; Lt-Col (ret) KRRC; Private Sec to HM the Queen when HRH Princess Elizabeth 1950-52; Assist Private Sec to HM 1952-72, and Private Sec and Keeper of the Queen's Archives 1972-77; an extra Equerry to HM 1956, and a permanent Lord in Waiting to HM since 1978; Provost of Eton Coll 1978-91; Chm Nat Heritage Memorial Fund 1980-92; a trustee Police Convalescence and Rehabilitation Trust since 1987; Pres Prayer Book Soc since 1987; Grand Officer of the Legion of Honour; 1939-45 War in Middle East; OBE (Mil) 1946, MVO (4th class) 1953, KCVO 1962, PC 1972, KCB (Civil) 1972, GCVO 1976, GCB (Civil) 1977, Royal Victorian Chain 1992; *cr Baron Charteris of Amisfield*, of Amisfield, E Lothian (Life Baron) 1978: *m* 1944, Hon (Mary) Gay Hobart Margesson, da of 1st Viscount Margesson, and has issue.

Arms – Quarterly; 1st and 4th, argent, a fess azure within a double tressure flory counterflory gules, *Charteris*; 2nd and 3rd, or, a lion rampant gules, armed and langued azure, *Wemyss*; over all at the fess point a crescent sable for difference. **Crest** – a dexter hand issuant paleways holding between the thumb and forefinger in bend sinister a pair of sulptor's callipers, all proper. **Supporters** – Dexter, a scribe soberly attired holding in his exterior hand a quill pen proper; *sinister*, an Officer of the King's Royal Rifle Corps in the uniform worn circa 1904, proper.
Residences – 11 Kylestrome House, Cundy St, SW1W 9JT; Wood Stanway House, Wood Stanway, Cheltenham, Glos GL54 5PE.

SONS LIVING

Hon Andrew Martin (11 Grove Rd, Hitchin, Herts), *b* 1947; *ed* Milton Abbey.
Hon Harold Francis (94 Talfourd Rd, SE15 5NZ), *b* 1950; *ed* Eton, and Pembroke Coll, Oxford: *m* 1984, Blandine Marie, elder da of Roger Desmons, of 14 rue Wilhelm, Paris 16me, and has issue living, Zoe France, *b* 1984, — Julia Marie, *b* 1985.

DAUGHTER LIVING

Hon Francesca Mary (*Baroness Pearson of Rannoch*), *b* 1945: *m* 1977, as his 2nd wife, Baron Pearson of Rannoch (Life Baron), and has issue. *Residence* – 3 Shepherd's Close, W1Y 3RT.

CHATFIELD, BARON (Chatfield) (Baron UK 1937)

For our altars and our hearths

ERNLE DAVID LEWIS CHATFIELD, 2nd Baron; *b* 2 Jan 1917; *s* 1967; *ed* Trin Coll, Camb; late Hon Lt RNVR; an ADC to Gov Gen of Canada 1940-45: *m* 1969, (Felicia Mary) Elizabeth, da of late Dr John Roderick Bulman, of Hereford.

Arms – Or, a griffin segreant sable, on a chief purpure an anchor between two escallops of the first. **Crest** – An heraldic antelope's head erased, argent, gorged with a naval crown or. **Supporters** – *Dexter*, an Admiralty Messenger holding in the exterior hand his staff; *sinister*, a Seaman Gunner of the Royal Navy resting the exterior hand on a shell all proper.
Address – 535 Island Rd, Victoria, BC V8S 2T7, Canada.

SISTER LIVING

Hon (Mary) Katharine Medina, OBE, *b* 1911; with Women's Vol Sers 1939-46; OBE (Civil) 1946: *m* 1947, Henry George Austen de L'Etang Herbert Duckworth, RA, who *d* 1992, son of late Sir George Herbert Duckworth, CB, FSA (*see* E Carnarvon, 1958 Edn), and has issue living, Sarah Margaret Katharine, *b* 1951: *m* 1974, Hector William Munro of Foulis (*see* Munro Bt, *cr* 1634, colls), — Harriet Angela Victoria (twin), *b* 1951: *m* 1979, Count Andreas Jean-Paul von Einsiedel, of 63 Wood Vale, SE23, son of Count Wittigo von Einsiedel, of Frankfurt, W Germany, and has issue living, (Count) Orlando Ernle Benedict *b* 1980, (Count) Evelyn *b* 1982, (Count) Robin *b* 1988, (Countess) Gwendolen *b* 1985. *Residence* – Dalingridge Place, Sharpthorne, Sussex.

PREDECESSOR – **(1)** *Adm of the Fleet Sir* (ALFRED) ERNLE MONTACUTE Chatfield, GCB, OM, KCMG, CVO, PC, son of late Adm Alfred John Chatfield, CB; *b* 1873; Present at actions of Heligoland Bight 1914, Dogger Bank 1915, and Jutland 1916, as Flag Capt HMS Lion, Third Sea Lord and Controller of Navy 1925-28, C-in-C Atlantic Fleet 1929-30; and Med Fleet 1930-32 First Sea Lord 1933-38, and Min for Co-ordination of Defence 1939-40; *cr Baron Chatfield*, of Ditchling, co Sussex (peerage of UK) 1937: *m* 1909, Lilian Emma (CStJ), who *d* 1977, da of late Maj George L. Matthews, TF; *d* 1967; *s* by his son **(2)** ERNLE DAVID LEWIS, 2nd Baron and present peer.

Chaworth, Baron; title of Earl of Meath on Roll of HL.

CHELMER, BARON (Edwards) (Life Baron 1963)

ERIC CYRIL BOYD EDWARDS, MC, TD, son of Col Cyril Ernest Edwards, DSO, MC, TD, DL, of Bullwood Hall, Hockley, Essex; *b* 9 Oct 1914; *ed* Felsted Sch, and London Univ (LLB 1937); Solicitor 1937; a Gen Commr of Taxes; Chm of Home Counties N Area of Conservative Party 1950-53, and Vice-Chm 1954 and 1955, Chm of National Union of Conservative Assocns 1956-65 and Pres 1966-67, Chm of National Union Exec Cttee 1957-63; Treas of Cons Party 1965-77; late Lt-Col Essex Yeo; DL of Essex; 1939-45 War (MC); *cr* Knt 1954, and *Baron Chelmer*, of Margaretting, co Essex (Life Baron) 1963: *m* 1939, Enid, da of Frank William Harvey, and has issue.

Arms – Sable a lion rampant or on a chief or two martlets sable. **Crest** – In front of a sun rising or a bull's head and neck gules armed or. **Supporters** – *Dexter*, a lion rampant proper; *Sinister*, a peacock in his pride proper.
Residence – Peacocks, Margaretting, Essex. *Clubs* – Carlton, Royal Ocean Racing.

SON LIVING

Hon Robin Ernest, *b* 1940: *m* 1967, Carol Mayes, and has issue.

CHELMSFORD, VISCOUNT (Thesiger) (Baron UK 1858, Viscount UK 1921)

Hope and fortune

FREDERIC JAN THESIGER, 3rd Viscount; *b* 7 March 1931; *s* 1970; late Lt Inns of Court Regt: *m* 1958, Clare Rendle, da of Dr George Rendle Rolston, of Bambers, Haslemere, Surrey, and has issue.

Arms – Gules, a griffin segreant or, within an orle of roses argent, barbed and seeded proper. **Crest** – A cornucopia fessewise, the horn or, the fruit proper, thereon a dove holding in the beak a sprig of laurel also proper. **Supporters** – On either side a griffin or, winged vaire.
Residence – 26 Ormonde Gate, SW3

SON LIVING

Hon FREDERIC CORIN PIERS, *b* 6 March 1962.

DAUGHTER LIVING

Hon Tiffany Gay, *b* 1968.

SISTERS LIVING

Hon Dawn Loraine (Hazelbridge Court, Chiddingfold, Surrey), *b* 1934.
Hon Philippa Merryn (Hazelbridge Court, Chiddingfold, Surrey), *b* 1939.

COLLATERAL BRANCHES LIVING (*In remainder to Barony only*)

Granddaughters of late Hon Percy Mansfield Thesiger, MBE, 2nd son of 2nd Baron:—
Issue of late Donald Adrian Wallace Thesiger, *b* 1901, *d* 1978: *m* 1927, Frances Nina, who *d* 1968, da of late Brig-Gen Sylvester Bertram Grimston, CMG:—

Nina Frances, b 1928. —— Zara Jane, b 1933: m 1969, Arthur Mark Farrer, of The Brick House, Finchingfield, Essex, and E12, Sloane Av Mansions, SW3, and has issue living, Lucy Frances, b 1971.

Granddaughters of late Capt Hon Wilfrid Gilbert Thesiger, DSO (infra):—
Issue of late Col Brian Peirson DOUGHTY-WYLIE, MC, who assumed the surname of Doughty-Wylie by deed poll 1933 in lieu of his patronymic, b 1911; d 1982: m 1937, Diana, who d 1976, only child of late Maj Vere de Hoghton (see de Hoghton, Bt, colls):—
Daphne Susan, b 1940: m 1st, 1961, Capt Jonathan Reeves, R Welch Fus; 2ndly, 1983, Jeremy David Michael Case, of New Marton Hall, New Marton, Oswestry, Shropshire, and has issue living (by 1st m), Thomas Somerville Thesiger, b 1969, —— Emma de Hoghton, b 1963: m 1988, Richard Charles Farquhar (see Farquhar, Bt, colls), —— Katherine Rebecca, b 1966. —— Philippa Vere Thesiger, b 1942: m 1964, Major John Lewarne Harvey, SCLI, of Halston, Whittington, Oswestry, Shropshire SY11 4NS, and has issue living, Rupert Lewarne, b 1965, —— James Thesiger, b 1969, —— Pippa Vere Karenza, b 1971, —— Joanna Demelza, b 1975.

Issue of late Capt Hon Wilfred Gilbert Thesiger, DSO, 3rd son of 2nd Baron, b 1871, d 1920: m 1909, Kathleen, CBE, who d 1973, having m 2ndly, 1931, as his 2nd wife, Reginald Basil Astley, who d 1942 (B Hastings, colls), da of late Thomas Mercer Cliffe Vigors, of Burgage, co Carlow (B Castlemaine, colls):—
Wilfred Patrick, CBE, DSO (15 Shelley Court, Tite St, SW3 4JB; Beefsteak, Travellers', Pratt's Clubs), b 1910, ed Eton, and Magdalen Coll, Oxford (MA); Hon DLitt Leics, and Bath 1992, Hon Fell British Acad 1982, Hon Fell Magdalen Coll, Oxford 1983; author of Arabian Sands, The Marsh Arabs, Desert, Marsh and Mountain, The Life of my Choice, Visions of a Nomad, My Kenya Days; Sudan Civil Ser 1935-44; 1939-45 War in Abyssinia as Bimbashi Sudan Defence Force, and in Middle East as Maj with Special Air Ser (despatches, DSO); attached to HRH the Duke of Gloucester's Mission to Ethiopia 1930 (Star of Ethiopia 3rd class); Founder's gold medal of R Geographical Soc, R Central Asian Soc's Lawrence of Arabia Medal, Livingstone Gold Medal of R Scottish Geographical Soc, R Soc of Literature Award, and R Asiatic Soc Burton Gold Medal; DSO 1941, CBE (Civil) 1968. —— Roderic Miles Doughty (Lucton, Leominster, Herefordshire), b 1915; ed Eton, and Ch Ch, Oxford (BA 1938); 1939-45 War as Capt Welsh Gds, and Parachute Regt (twice wounded): m 1st, 1940 (m diss 1946), Mary Rose, who d 1962, da of Hon Guy Lawrence Charteris (E Wemyss and March); 2ndly, 1946, Ursula Joan, da of Aymer William Whitworth (M Bristol, colls), and has issue living, (by 2nd m) Simon Dermot (Old Manor Cottage, Stapley, Taunton, Som), b 1950: m 1973, Concepción, da of Pérez Chavez, of Coyuca de Catalan, Mexico, and has issue living, a da b 1980, —— Sarah Elizabeth b 1947: m 1974, Christopher Simon Wintle, of 49 Stradella Rd, SE24, and has issue living, Alice Marina b 1977, Emily Miranda b 1981.

Grandson of late Lt-Col Hon Eric Richard Thesiger, DSO, yst son of 2nd Baron:—
Issue of late Osric Wilfrid Thesiger, b 1905, d 1977: m 1934, Cecily Mary, who d 1988, da of late F. Vandertaelen:—
Michael Eric (Ridgecrest, Church Rd, St John's, Redhill, Surrey), b 1936; ed Downside; FCA; Kt of Grace and Devotion of Sovereign Mil Order of Malta: m 1964, Patricia Low, da of G. Waddington, and has issue living, Edward Osric, b 1967; ed Downside, RMA Sandhurst, and Nottingham Univ (BA); commn'd RGJ 1992, —— Antony Martin, b 1968; ed Downside, and Oxford Polytechnic (BA), —— Justin Michael, b 1970; ed Downside, and Oxford Polytechnic (BSc), —— Robert Cedric, b (twin) 1970; ed Downside, and Exeter Univ (BA), —— Georgina Mary, b 1965: m 1993, David Charles Dowden, son of Lt-Col Ronnie Dowden, of Axminster, Devon.
Issue of late Cedric Paul Thesiger, b 1915, d 1987: m 1942, Barbara Cecilia (1/31 Dominion St, Takapuna, Auckland, NZ), da of late Maj Hubert Cecil Delacour Jarrett, IA:—
Peter Hubert (4934-2A Av, Delta, BC, Canada), b 1943; ed The Oratory, and Simon Fraser Univ (MBA 1977): m 1969, Jill Patricia, da of Lt-Cdr E. J. Worthy, RCN (ret), and has issue living, James Edward, b 1980, —— Julia Mary, b 1983. —— Richard Paul (Box 14-530, Panmure, Auckland, NZ), b 1945; ed The Oratory: m 1st, 1971 (m diss 1981), Susan, da of J. Sydes; 2ndly, 1981, Jennifer Diane, da of Jonathan David Sharp, RNZAMC, of 12 Stewart Av, Panmure, Auckland, NZ, and has issue living (by 1st m), Robin Bruce, b 1973, —— Clare Louise, b 1975. —— John Bede (9 Castleton St, Birkenhead, Auckland, NZ), b 1947; ed Blackfriars: m 1981, Christine Joyce, da of late G. A. Edmond, BEM, and has issue living, David George, b 1986, —— Kevin Ryan, b 1988.

Granddaughters of late Maj-Gen George Handcock Thesiger, CB, CMG, elder son of Lt-Gen Hon Charles Wemyss Thesiger, 2nd son of 1st Baron:—
Issue of late Sir Gerald Alfred Thesiger, MBE, b 1902; d 1981; Judge of High Court of Justice, Queen's Bench Div 1958-78: m 1932, Marjorie Eileen, who d 1972, da of late Raymond Guille, of Long Island NY:—
Oonah Caroline, b 1936: m 1957, Vincent Vine, of 16 Painted Cup Court, The Woodlands, Texas 77380, USA, and has issue living, Peter Gerald, b 1958, —— Juliet Mary, b 1960, —— Anita Oonah, b 1962. —— Juliet Elizabeth, b 1943: m 1st, 1966 (m diss 1977), Roderick Carl Warwick Neville; 2ndly, 1977, David Halliwell Sutcliffe, of The Firs, Churchtown Rd, Gerrans, Truro, Cornwall TR2 5DZ, and has issue (by 1st m), Roderick Thomas Gerald, b 1968: m 1993, Frances Johnson, —— Nicola Ingalisa, b 1967.

Grandchildren of His Honour late Arthur Lionel Bruce Thesiger (infra):—
Issue of late Lt-Col Richard Edward Knight Thesiger, OBE, b 1912, d 1984: m 1st, 1934 (m diss 1947), Carolin Sophie, da of Norman M. Grant, of New York; 2ndly, 1947, Eileen Alice, who d 1991 only da of late John Still:—
(By 1st m) David Arthur Grant (74 Herne Rd, Surbiton, Surrey KT6 5BP), b 1934; ed Winchester, and Trin Hall, Camb; solicitor 1965: m 1963, Margaret Evelyn, da of A. E. Thomas, and has issue living, Amanda Carolin Thomas, b 1964, —— Clare Margaret Thomas (Apt 401, 205 Boulevard Vincent Auriol, 75013 Paris), b 1966; has issue living, Madeleine Patience TILSON-THESIGER b 1992. —— (By 2nd m) John Still (7 Herne Rd, Surbiton, Surrey KT6 5BX), b 1948; ed Winchester, and Magdalen Coll, Oxford (MA); social worker (CQSW 1975): m 1979, Nefise Serpil, da of Mehmet Baybörü, of Küçükyali, Istanbul, and has issue living, Osman Richard Baybörü, b 1987, Hatice Emma b 1989. —— Anne Alice Florita, b 1951; ed Bristol Univ (BA): m 1973, Rev Paul Towner, of The Rectory, Hanwood, nr Shrewsbury, Shropshire SY5 8LJ, and has issue living, Andrew Paul John, b 1976, —— Katherine Anne, b 1975, —— Elizabeth Marjorie, b 1979. —— Frances Georgina (107 Upper Brook St, Winchester, Hants), b 1956.

Granddaughter of late Hon Sir Edward Peirson Thesiger, KCB, yst son of 1st Baron:—
Issue of His Honour late Arthur Lionel Bruce Thesiger, b 1872, d 1968: m 1902, Florita Maria Engracia, OBE, who d 1966, da of late Edward J. Knight of Tregroes, Pencoed, Glam:—
Patience Elizabeth Florita, MBE, TD (Eleven Plus, Hungershall Park, Tunbridge Wells), b 1908; a Borough Councillor; Mayor of R Tunbridge Wells 1969-70, Vice Chm Kent CC 1982-84; served ATS 1939-45; MBE (Civil) 1994.

PREDECESSORS – (1) Rt Hon Sir FREDERIC Thesiger, KB, DCL, FRS; b 1794; served as a Midshipman, RN, at battle of Copenhagen 1807; called to the bar at Gray's Inn 1818; became a KC 1834; was Solicitor-Gen 1844-5, Attorney-Gen 1845-6 and 1852, MP for Woodstock (C) 1840-4, for Abingdon 1844-52, and for Stamford 1852-8, and Lord High Chancellor 1858-9 and 1866-8; cr. Baron Chelmsford of Chelmsford, co Essex (peerage of United Kingdom) 1858: m 1822, Anna Maria, da of William Tinling, of Southampton, d 1878; s by his son (2) FREDERIC AUGUSTUS, GCB, GCVO, 2nd Baron; b 1827; a Gen in the Army, and Col 2nd Life Guards; served in Crimea, during Indian Mutiny, and in Abyssinia; commanded forces during Kaffir and Zulu Campaigns; an ADC to HM Queen Victoria 1868-77, and Lieut of Tower of London 1884-9: m 1867, Adria Fanny, who d 1926, da of late Maj-Gen Heath, Bombay Army; d 1905; s by his son (3) Rt Hon FREDERIC JOHN NAPIER, GCSI, GCMG, GCIE, GBE, 3rd Baron; b 1868; Gov of Queensland 1905-9, and of NS Wales 1909-13, Viceroy of India 1916-21, and First

Lord of the Admiralty Jan to Nov 1924; a KJStJ; *cr. Viscount Chelmsford*, of Chelmsford, co. Essex (peerage of United Kingdom) 1921: *m* 1894, Hon Frances Charlotte Guest, CI, GBE, who *d* 1957, da of 1st Baron Wimborne; *d* 1933; *s* by his son **(4)** ANDREW CHARLES GERALD, 2nd Viscount; *b* 1903: *m* 1927, Gillian, who *d* 1978, da of late Arthur Nevile Lubbock (B Avebury, colls); *d* 1970; *s* by his son **(5)** FREDERIC JAN, 3rd Viscount, and present peer; also Baron Chelmsford.

Chelsea, Viscount; son of Earl Cadogan.

CHELWOOD, BARONY OF (Beamish) (Extinct 1989)

DAUGHTERS LIVING OF LIFE BARON *(By 1st marriage)*

Hon Claudia Hamilton, *b* 1952.
Hon Andrea Tufton, *b* 1955: *m* 1985, Christopher C. Plowman.

WIDOW LIVING OF LIFE BARON

MARIA PIA *(Baroness Chelwood)*, da of Baron Ernest von Roretz, of Schloss Breiteneich, bei Horn, Austria, and formerly wife of Alan McHenry: *m* 1975, as his 2nd wife, Baron Chelwood, MC (Life Baron), who *d* 1989.

CHESHAM, BARON (Cavendish) (Baron UK 1858)

Secure by caution

Hon William George Gray, *b* 1980.

NICHOLAS CHARLES CAVENDISH, 6th Baron; *b* 7 Nov 1941; *s* 1989; *ed* Eton; ACA; Patron of two livings: *m* 1st, 1965 (*m diss* 1969), Susan Donne, eldest da of late Frederick Guy Beauchamp, MD, MRCS (*see* By North); 2ndly, 1973, Suzanne Adrienne, elder da of late Alan Gray Byrne, of Sydney, NSW, and has issue by 2nd *m*.

Arms – Sable three stags' heads cabossed argent. **Crest** – A snake, nowed proper. **Supporters** – *Dexter*, a buck proper, gorged with a chaplet of roses argent and azure; *sinister*, a greyhound argent gorged with a plain collar gules, thereon three buckles or.
Residence – Manor Farm, Preston Candover, nr Basingstoke, Hants RG25 2EN.
Clubs – Pratt's, Australian (Sydney).

SONS LIVING *(By 2nd marriage)*

Hon CHARLES GRAY COMPTON, *b* 11 Nov 1974; *ed* King's Sch, Parramatta, and Durham Univ.

BROTHER LIVING

Hon John Charles Gregory (Hall Farm, Farringdon, Alton, Hants), *b* 1952; *ed* Eton, and Jesus Coll, Camb: *m* 1976, Lucinda Mary, da of late Richard Hugh Corbett, of Manor Farm, Beauworth, Hants.

SISTERS LIVING

Hon Joanna Mary, *b* 1938: *m* 1960, Peter Henry Mabille Price, of Avington Manor Farm, Alresford Rd, Winchester, Hants, son of late Cmdr Maurice Price, RN, of Sutton, Surrey, and has issue living, Nicholas Henry Maurice, *b* 1971, — Caroline Mary, *b* 1967: *m* 1988, Christopher G. Marler, son of late Geoffrey Marler.
Hon Georgina Mary, *b* 1944: *m* 1967, (Michael) Wynne Tufnell, of High Dell Farmhouse, Bighton, Alresford, Hants, only son of late Capt Michael Neville Tufnell, DSC, RN (ret), of Curdridge Grange, Botley, Hants, and has issue living, Christopher Wynne, *b* 1969, — Michael Greville, *b* 1971, — Simon Charles *b* 1977.

WIDOW LIVING OF FIFTH BARON

MARY EDMUNDS *(Dowager Baroness Chesham)*, 4th da of late David Gregory Marshall, MBE, of White Hill, Cambridge: *m* 1937, the 5th Baron, TD, PC, who *d* 1989. *Residence* – Meadow House, Preston Candover, Basingstoke, Hants.

COLLATERAL BRANCH LIVING

Grandchildren of late Brig-Gen Hon William Edwin Cavendish, MVO 3rd of 2nd Baron:—
Issue of late Capt Evan George Charles Cavendish, OBE, RNVR, *b* 1891, *d* 1955: *m* 1923, Esmé Frances Sylvia IRBY, who *d* 1959, da of late Hon Gilbert Neville Smyth (B Boston, colls):—
Greville Adrian (Hope Town, Abaco, Bahamas; Moretown, Vermont, USA), *b* 1925; Lt-Cdr RN (ret): *m* 1st, 1952 (*m diss* 1974), Hazel Colleen Elizabeth, only da of late John Henry May, of Jersey; 2ndly, 1974, Gillian, da of late Leslie George Webb, of W. Hagley, Worcs, and has issue living (by 1st *m*), Rupert Edward Greville, *b* 1955, — Piers Antony Charles (58 St John's Hill Grove, SW11 2RG), *b* 1956: *m* 1986, (Rose Vivien) Louise, eldest da of late Gerard Dacres (Dickie) Olivier, and of Mrs Hester St John Ives, of Chain House, Modbury, S Devon, and has issue living, Patrick Alexander *b* 1990, Georgia Claire *b* 1989, — Kiloran Arabella, *b* 1959. —— Susan, *b* 1924: *m* 1st, 1951 (*m diss* 1955), David Murray Martin; 2ndly, 1955, Leslie Gordon Graham, and has issue living, (by 1st *m*) Trudy Carol, *b* 1952, — Amanda Jane, *b* 1954, — (by 2nd *m*) Sarah Frances, *b* 1956. *Residence* – Mount Farm, nr Ringwood, Hants.

PREDECESSORS – (1) *Hon* CHARLES COMPTON CAVENDISH, 4th son of 1st Earl of Burlington (*see* D Devonshire), MP for E Sussex (*L*) 1832-41, for Youghal 1841-47, and for Buckinghamshire 1847-57; *cr Baron Chesham* (Peerage of United Kingdom) 1858; *d* 1863; *s* by his son **(2)** WILLIAM GEORGE, 2nd Baron, *b* 1815; MP for Peterborough (*L*) 1847, and for Buckinghamshire 1857-63: *m* 1849, Henrietta Frances, who *d* 1884, da of late Right Hon William Saunders Sebright Lascelles (E Harewood); *d* 26 June 1882; *s* by his son **(3)** CHARLES COMPTON WILLIAM, 3rd Baron, KCB, PC, *b* 1850; Master of the Buckhounds 1900-1901, and a Lord of the Bedchamber to HRH the Prince of Wales 1901-7: *m* 1877, Lady Beatrice Constance Grosvenor, RRC, who *d* 1911, 2nd da of 1st Duke of Westminster; *d* 1907; *s* by his son **(4)** JOHN COMPTON, MC, 4th Baron; *b* 1894; Capt 10th Hussars and Squadron Leader RAF Vol Reserve: *m* 1st 1915 (*m diss* 1937), Margot, who *d* 1985, da of late John Layton Mills of Tansor Court, Oundle; 2ndly, 1938, Marion Caher (EDWARDS), who *d* 1973, da of Daniel C. Donoghue, of Philadelphia, USA, and formerly wife of 8th Earl of Carrick; *d* 1952; *s* by his only son **(5)** JOHN CHARLES COMPTON, TD, PC, 5th Baron, *b* 1916; Capt RA (TA); a Lord in Waiting to HM The Queen 1955-59, Joint Parl Sec Min of Transport 1959-64, Exec Vice-Chm RAC 1966-70, etc: *m* 1937, Mary Edmunds, 4th da of late David Gregory Marshall, MBE, of White Hill, Cambridge; *d* 1989; *s* by his elder son **(6)** NICHOLAS CHARLES, 6th Baron and present peer.

CHESHIRE, BARONY OF (Cheshire) (Life Baron 1991 Extinct 1992)

(GEOFFREY) LEONARD CHESHIRE, VC, OM, DSO, DFC, son of late Prof Geoffrey Chevalier Cheshire, DCL, of Grey Walls, Cothill, Abingdon, Berks; *b* 7 Sept 1917; *ed* Stowe, and Merton Coll, Oxford; joined Oxford Univ Sqdn (RAF) 1936, RAFVR 1937, served European War 1939-45 as Pilot Officer RAF 1939, Wing Cdr 1942, Gp Capt 1943 (ret 1946) (DSO 1940 and two bars 1942 and 1943, DFC 1941, VC 1944); founder Leonard Cheshire Foundation, co-founder Ryder-Cheshire Mission for the Relief of Suffering, Memorial Fund for Disaster Relief; Hon Master of Bench Gray's Inn 1983, Hon DCL Oxford, Hon LLD Liverpool 1973, Manchester Poly 1979, Nottingham Univ 1981, Bristol Univ 1985, and Kent Univ 1986; author; *cr* OM 1981, and *Baron Cheshire*, of Woodhall, co Lincs (Life Baron) 1991: *m* 1st, 1941, Constance Binney, of New York City; 2ndly, 1959, (Margaret) Susan (*Baroness Ryder of Warsaw*), CMG, OBE, da of late Charles Ryder, and *d* 31 July 1992, leaving issue by 2nd *m*.

SON LIVING *(By 2nd marriage)*

Hon Jeremy Charles, *b* 1960.

DAUGHTER LIVING *(By 2nd marriage)*

Hon Elizabeth Diana, *b* 1962.

CHESTERFIELD AND STANHOPE, EARLDOM OF (Scudamore-Stanhope) (Extinct 1967)

DAUGHTER LIVING OF TWELFTH EARL OF CHESTERFIELD

Lady (Evelyn) Patricia Mary, *b* 1917: *m* 1st, 1938 (*m diss* 1947), Lt-Cdr Ian McDonald, R Australian Navy; 2ndly 1947, as his 3rd wife, John Harford Stanhope Lucas-Scudamore, DL, who *d* 1976; 3rd, 1983, (Leckonby) John Alexander Phipps, and has issue living, (by 2nd *m*) John Edward Stanhope (Kentchurch Court, Hereford), *b* 1953: *m* 1983, Janice Claire Lyne, formerly wife of Terence Pascoe, and has issue living, Joselyn James Stanhope *b* 1983, Rosanna *b* 1985, — Charlotte Mary Frances, *b* 1949: *m* 1st 1971 (*m diss* 1977), Carlo Nardi Barbieri, of Florence; 2ndly, 1978, Gerald Francis Bruce Manley, of Bacton, Herefords, and has issue living (by 1st *m*), Carolina *b* 1972, Cammilla *b* 1973, (by 2nd *m*) Harry Rupert Scudamore *b* 1979. *Residence* – Newcote, Moccas, Hereford.

COLLATERAL BRANCHES LIVING

Descendants of Sir John Stanhope of Elvaston, Derbys, half-brother of 1st Earl of Chesterfield (*see* E Harrington).

CHETWODE, BARON (Chetwode) (Baron UK 1945, Bt E 1700)

CORONA MEA CHRISTUS

Christ is my crown

PHILIP CHETWODE, 2nd Baron and 8th Baronet; *b* 26 March 1937; *s* 1950; *ed* Eton; Capt (ret) RHG: *m* 1st, 1967 (*m diss* 1979), Susan Janet, el da of late Capt Voltelin James Howard Van der Byl, DSC, RN (ret) and formerly wife of Alwyn Richard Dudley Smith; 2ndly, 1990, Mrs Fiona Holt, da of late Christos Tsintsaris, of 15 Alexandrou Mihailidi, Thessaloniki, Greece, and has issue by 1st *m*.

𝕬rms – Quarterly argent and gules, four crosses patée counterchanged. Crest – Out of a ducal coronet or, a demi-lion rampant gules. 𝕾upporters – *Dexter*, a Crusader in chain armour and surcoat resting the exterior hand proper on a shield of the arms of Chetwode; *sinister*, an Officer of the 19th R Hus resting his exterior hand on the hilt of his sword proper.
Residence – The Mill House, Chilton Foliat, Hungerford, Berks.

SONS LIVING *(By 1st marriage)*

Hon ROGER, *b* 29 May 1968.
Hon Alexander, *b* 1969.

DAUGHTER LIVING *(By 1st marriage)*

Hon Miranda, *b* 1974.

BROTHER LIVING

(Raised to the rank of a Baron's son 1951)

Hon Christopher Roger (Hill House, Cheriton, Alresford, Hants), *b* 1940; *ed* Eton: *m* 1961, Hon Philippa Mary Imogen Brand, da of 5th Viscount Hampden, and has issue living, Michael Walhouse David, *b* 1962: *m* 1986, Louise Ann, da of R. W. Wood, of Maldon, Essex, and of Mrs Trevor R. Robins, of Bocking, Essex, and has issue living, George *b* 1992, Emma Louisa Patricia *b* 1987, Holly *b* 1989, Daisy *b* (twin) 1992, — Richard Christopher *b* 1964: *m* 1993, Sheelagh Maria, da of Desmond Francis Boylan, of Marion, Mas, USA (*see* O'Brien, Bt, 1980 Edn), — Charles Philip, *b* 1967, — William Robin, *b* 1973, — James Nicholas, *b* 1975.

MOTHER LIVING

Hon Molly Patricia Berry (*Hon Lady Cotterell*), da of 1st Viscount Camrose: *m* 1st, 1936, Capt Roger Charles George Chetwode, who *d* 1940; 2ndly, 1942 (*m diss* 1948), 1st Baron Sherwood; 3rdly, 1958, as his 2nd wife, Sir Richard Charles Geers Cotterell, 5th Bt, CBE, TD, who *d* 1978. *Residence* – Flat 1, 4 Eaton Place, SW1.

COLLATERAL BRANCHES LIVING *(In remainder to Baronetcy only)*

Granddaughter of late Adm Sir George Knightley Chetwode, KCB, CBE (*infra*):—
Issue of late Paymaster-Lt John Chetwode, RNR, *b* 1909, *ka* 1941: *m* 1934, Joan Muriel (who *d* 1951, having *m* 2ndly, 1947, Capt Joseph Anthony Collings, MBE, late N Somerset Yeo, who *d* 1954), da of Lt-Col Frederick George Glyn Bailey (E Inchcape):—
Janet Amanda Alice, *b* 1937; *ed* Westonbirt, and St Clare's Coll, Oxford. *Club* – Lansdowne.

Grandson of late Lt-Col Sir George Chetwode, 6th baronet:—
Issue of late Adm Sir George Knightley Chetwode, KCB, CBE, *b* 1877, *d* 1957, *m* 1st, 1908, Alice, who *d* 1937, da of late Maj Vaughan Hanning Vaughan-Lee, MP for W Div of Somersetshire; 2ndly, 1939, Elizabeth, who *d* 1979, da of Frederick Taylor, of Jericho, Queensland, and formerly wife of Capt Lionel Dawson, RN:—
(By 1st *m*) George David, MBE, *b* 1914; *ed* RNC Dartmouth, and RMC Sandhurst; Maj Coldsteam Gds; sometime ADC to Gov of Bombay; European War 1939-45 in N Africa and Italy (wounded, MBE); MBE (Mil) 1944: *m* 1946, Lady Willa Elliot, da of 5th Earl of Minto, and has issue living, Joshua Lariston Knightley, *b* 1967; *ed* Eton, and LSE, — Davina Marion (33 Summer St, Northampton, Mass 01060, USA), *b* 1947: *m* 1st, 1968 (*m diss* 1975), William John N. Moore, son of William Moore, of Thornhill House, Stalbridge, Dorset; 2ndly, 1977, Joshua Miller, son of Prof Irving Miller, of New York, and has issue living (by 1st *m*), Lucy *b* 1970 (by 2nd *m*), Carina Emily *b* 1979, Sophie Clare *b* 1983, — Sarah Alice (94 Cambridge Gdns, W10 6HS), *b* 1948: *m* 1969 (*m diss* 1983), Andrew Donald Cox, son of late Donald Cox, of Gourdie, Fife, and has issue living, Damian *b* 1975, Indiajane *b* 1970, Alice Dawn *b* 1972, Flora Eileen Gian *b* 1976, — Emma Bridget *b* 1950: *m* 1971, Simon Lindley Keswick, of Rockcliffe, Upper Slaughter, Cheltenham, Glos GL54 2JW, yst son of late Sir William Keswick, of Glenkiln, Shawhead, Dumfries (*see* By Lindley, 1950 Edn), and has issue living, Benjamin William *b* 1972, Archibald David *b* 1980, Poppy Teresa *b* 1978, Willa Mary China *b* 1984, — Willa Mary Gabriel (*Lady Elphinstone*), *b* 1954: *m* 1978, 18th Lord Elphinstone, — Georgina Caroline, *b* 1955: *m* 1983, Edward Charles Markes, of Au Pouceret, St Ost, Mirande 32300, France, 2nd son of late John Edward Markes, of Recess, co Galway, and has issue living, Dominic John *b* 1989, Gerard David *b* 1991, Araminta Victoria *b* 1987. *Residence* – Swiss Farm House, Upper Slaughter, Cheltenham, Glos GL54 2JP.

PREDECESSORS – (1) JOHN Chetwode, el son of late Philip Chetwode, of Oakley, Staffs, *b* 1666; *cr Baronet* 1700: *m* 1st, 1695, Mary, who *d* 1702, da of late Sir Jonathan Raymond, of Barton Court, Berks; 2ndly, 17—, Catherine, who *d* 1717, da of late John Tayleur, of Rodington, Shropshire; *d* 1733; *s* by his son (2) *Sir* PHILIP TOUCHET, 2nd Bt; *b* 1700: *m* 1727, Elizabeth, who *d* 1745, only da of late George Venables, of Agdon, Cheshire; *d* 1764; *s* by his el son (3) *Sir* JOHN, 3rd Bt; *b* 1732: *m* 1756, Dorothy, who *d* 1769, da of late Tobias Bretland, of Thorncliffe, Cheshire; *d* 1779; *s* by his only surviving son (4) *Sir* JOHN, 4th Bt; *b* 1764: *m* 1st, Lady Elizabeth Grey, who *d* 1826, da of 5th Earl of Stamford and 1st Earl of Warrington; 2ndly, 1827, Elizabeth, who *d* 18— (having *m* 2ndly, 1848, Andrew Kennedy Hutchinson, of Chester Square, Pimlico, SW); *d* 1845; *s* by his el son (5) *Sir* JOHN, 5th Bt; *b* 1788; assumed by R licence 1826 the additional surnames of Newdigate-Ludford: *m* 1st, 1821, Elizabeth Juliana, who *d* 1859, el da of late John Newdigate-Ludford, of Ansley Hall, Warwickshire; 2ndly, 1861, Arabella Phyllis, only child of late Samuel Denton, and widow of James Reade, of Lower Berkeley Street, W; *d* 1873; *s* by his nephew (6) *Sir* GEORGE (2nd son of late Rev George Chetwode, 2nd son of 4th Bt), 6th Bt; *b* 1823; Lt-Col 8th Hus: *m* 1868, Alice Jane, who *d* 1919, da of late Michael Thomas Bass, MP, of Rangemore, Staffs, *d* 1905: *s* by his el son (7) *Sir* PHILIP WALHOUSE, GCB, OM, GCSI, KCMG, DSO, 7th Bt; *b* 1869; became Field-Marshal 1933; Chin Hills Expedition 1892-3, S Africa 1899-1902 (despatches thrice, DSO), European War 1914-18 in France Comdg 5th Cav Brig (original) and 2nd Cav Div, in Sinai Comdg Desert Corps, and in Palestine and Syria Comdg 20th Army Corps which captured Jerusalem (wounded, despatches eight times, CB, promoted Maj-Gen and Lt-Gen KCMG, KCB); Assist Mil Sec, Aldershot 1906-8; commanded

London Mounted Brig, Territorial Force 1912-14; appointed Mil Sec to Sec of State for War, and Sec of Selection Board 1919, Dep Ch of Imperial Gen Staff and a Member of Army Council 1920, AG to the Forces 1922, Gen Officer Comdg-in-Ch, Aldershot Command 1923, Col R Scots Greys (2nd Drag) 1925, ADC-Gen to HM 1927, Ch of Gen Staff in India 1928, Col 8th King George's Own Light Cav (Indian Army) 1932, and Hon Col 2nd/10th Drags, Canadian Mil 1938; Com-in-Ch in India and a MEC 1930-35; Constable of Tower of London 1943-8; Col 15th/19th King's R Hus 1944-7; received Grand Cross of Orders of St Olav of Norway, and of George I of Greece, and Order of Brilliant Star of China with Grand Cordon; a Knight Grand Cross of Order of Orange-Nassau of the Netherlands; *cr Baron Chetwode*, of Chetwode, co Buckingham (peerage of United Kingdom) 1945: *m* 1899, Alice Hester Camilla, who *d* 1946, da of late Col Hon Richard Southwell George Stapleton-Cotton (*see* B Combermere, 1946 Edn); *d* 1950; *s* by his grandson **(8)** PHILIP (son of late Capt Roger Charles George Chetwode, son of 1st Baron), 8th Baronet and present peer.

CHETWYND, VISCOUNT (Chetwynd) (Viscount I 1717)

Probity is true honour

ADAM RICHARD JOHN CASSON CHETWYND, 10th Viscount; *b* 2 Feb 1935; *s* 1965; *ed* Eton; Lt Queen's Own Cameron Highlanders; New Business Man, The Prudential Assurance Co of SA Ltd, Harland House Branch, Johannesburg: *m* 1st, 1966 (*m diss* in Rhodesia 1974), Celia Grace da of Cdr Alexander Robert Ramsay, DSC, RNVR (*see* Ramsay, Bt, colls, *cr* 1806); 2ndly, 1975, Angela May, only da of Jack Payne McCarthy, of 21 Llanberis Grove, Aspley, Nottingham, and has issue by 1st *m*.

Arms – Azure, a chevron between three mullets or. **Crest** – A goat's head erased argent, horns gold. **Supporters** – Two unicorns argent, gorged with chaplets of roses gules, and having a chain of the same reflexed over their backs.
Address – c/o J. G. Ouvry, Esq, Lee Bolton & Lee, 1 Sanctuary, Westminster SW1P 3JT.

SONS LIVING *(By 1st marriage)*

Hon ADAM DOUGLAS, *b* 26 Feb 1969.
Hon Robert Duncan (twin), *b* 1969.

DAUGHTER LIVING *(By 1st marriage)*

Hon Emma Grace, *b* 1967.

SISTER LIVING

Hon Philippa Mary Agnes Joan, *b* 1930: *m* 1959, Major John Anthony Hawtrey Luard, Coldstream Gds, of Maidenford, Good-leigh, nr Barnstaple, Devon EX32 7NG, and has issue living, David Andrew John, *b* 1961, — Sophia Mary, *b* 1960: *m* 1982, Gianfranco Goddi, of 57 Oxford Gdns, W10, only son of Sra Mele-Goddi, of Rome, and has issue living, Lucrezia Ruth Jessica *b* 1983.

HALF-SISTERS LIVING

Hon Catherine Sophia Marianne, *b* 1956.
Hon Frances Diana Dorothea, *b* 1959.

AUNT LIVING *(Daughter of 8th Viscount)*

Hon (Mary Diana) Eve, *b* 1908. *Residence* – 6 Hulton Drive, Emberton, Olney, Bucks MK46 5BY.

COLLATERAL BRANCHES LIVING

Grandchildren of late Hon John Julian Chetwynd (*infra*):—
    Issue of late Richard Walter Chetwynd, *b* 1938, *d* 1990: *m* 1964, Judith Mary (Glebe House, Woodborough, nr Pewsey, Wilts), only da of late Capt Selwyn Victor Jephson, RN, of The Red House, Hambledon, Hants:—
Mark Richard, *b* 1972. —— Katharine Margaret, *b* 1965: *m* 1990, Michael William Toogood, eldest son of James Anthony Gordon Toogood, of Riversdale, Malmesbury, Wilts. —— Sarah Alexandra, *b* 1967.

    Issue of late Hon John Julian Chetwynd, 2nd son of 8th Viscount, *b* 1906, *d* 1966: *m* 1937, Margaret Agnes, who *d* 1993, da of late Maj-Gen Hugh Clement Sutton, CB, CMG (*see* Sutton, Bt, colls):—
John Hugh (South Hay Cottage, Kingsley, Borden, Hants), *b* 1942: *ed* Stowe: *m* 1st, 1966 (*m diss* 1971), Denyse Jacqueline, da of H. de Frisching, of Berne, Switzerland; 2ndly, 1973 (*m diss* 1977), Caroline, elder da of John Fitzwilliams; 3rdly, 1983, Mrs Lorna Butler (*née* Menzies), and has issue living (by 1st *m*), Hugh Nigel, *b* 1967, — Philip Mark, *b* 1969, — (by 3rd *m*) Fleur Alicia Camilla, *b* 1983.

    Granddaughter of late Capt Hon Henry Weyland Chetwynd, RN, 3rd son of 6th Viscount:—
    Issue of late Henry Goulburn Willoughby Chetwynd, AMICE, el brother of 8th Viscount, *b* 1858, *d* 1909: *m* 1893, Eva Constance Elizabeth Fanny, who *d* 1936, da of late Augustus Berney (Berney, Bt, colls):—
Sylvia Evelyn, *b* 1902: *m* 1931, Anthony Makower, who *d* 1984, and has issue living, Peter (2 Lillian Rd, Barnes, SW13), *b* 1932; *ed* Trin Coll, Camb, (MA); FRIBA; MRTPI: *m* 1960, Katharine, da of James Howarthe Paul Chadburn, MBE, and has had issue, Andrew *b* 1961, Timothy *b* 1965, Mary *b* 1963; *d* 1979, — Michael Stanley (Gogar House, Blairlogie, by Stirling), *b* 1936: *m* 1960, Selina Elizabeth, da of late Henry Vernon Flower Barran (*see* Barran, Bt, colls), and has issue living, Sophia Galiena *b* 1962, Janet Elizabeth Agnes *b* 1964, Margaret Eleanor *b* 1966, — *Rev Dr* Malory (Ludham House, 55 South Beach Parade, Gt Yarmouth, Norfolk), *b* 1938; *ed* Dublin Univ (MA), and St John Coll, Oxford (MA, DPhil): *m* 1967 (*m diss* 1987), Mary Noel, da of R. E. Stokes, and has issue living, Philip *b* 1969, William *b* 1976, Caroline *b* 1968, Sandra *b* 1972, — Anne (8 Richmond Hill, Monkstown, Dublin), *b* 1934, *ed* Dublin Univ (BA): *m* 1964, Christopher O'Connell Fitz-Simon, and has issue living, Adrian Christopher *b* 1967, Vanessa Una *b* 1965.

Grandsons of late Capt Hon Louis Wentworth Pakington Chetwynd, RN, brother of 8th Viscount:—
Issue of late Maj (Wentworth) Randolph Chetwynd, MBE, *b* 1903, *d* 1985: *m* 1st, 1931 (*m diss* 1964), Bridget, da of late Col Theobald Alfred Walsh, DSO; 2ndly, 1964, Mary, da of Francis Rosser:—
(By 1st *m*) Rupert Milo Talbot (The New Stables, Ingestre, nr Stafford), *b* 1934; *ed* Stowe: *m* 1st, 1956 (*m diss* 1970), Antonia, only child of late Denis Clark, DFC; 2ndly, 1970, Luciana Maria, el da of late Count Ernest Arrighi, and has issue living (by 1st *m*), Rupert Jonathan Richard, *b* 1957, — Dominic Jeremy, *b* 1959, — Crispin, *b* 1961, — Alexander Anthony, *b* 1964, — Persephone Catherine, *b* 1965, — (by 2nd *m*) Aaron St George Francesco Arrighi, *b* 1971, — Alalia, *b* 19—.
—— Tom Wentworth Guy (12 Mornington Terr, NW1), *b* 1938; 2nd Lieut RAC: *m* 1959, Helene, da of Baron Pierre de Bosmelet, and has issue living, Yolanda, *b* 1960, — Natasha, *b* 1961, — Bridget, *b* 1966.

Grandchildren of late Miles Chetwynd-Stapylton, yr son of late Henry Edward Chetwynd-Stapylton, el son of Maj Henry Richard Chetwynd-Stapylton, el son of Maj-Gen Hon Granville Anson Chetwynd-Stapylton, 2nd son of 4th Viscount:—
Issue of late Philip Miles Chetwynd-Stapylton, *b* 1889, *d* 1965: *m* 1920, Esmé, who *d* 1990, da of late W. G. Eveleigh:—
Henry Philip (8 Jubilee Terr, Chichester, W Sussex PO19 1XL), *b* 1921; *ed* Radley; late Capt IA (1939-45 War); B Arch 1952; an ARIBA, FRSA: *m* 1962, Elizabeth Bentinck, who *d* 1992, yst da of late E. E. Chambers, of Ringwood, Hants, and has issue living, (Henry) Edward, *b* 1966; *ed* Radley; BSc, Dip TP, FRGS, — Diana Rachel, *b* 1970. —— Esmé Elizabeth, *b* 1927: *m* 1954, Col Robert Edward Waight, OBE, late LI, and has issue living, Richard Edward Charles, *b* 1960; Maj LI, — Deborah Anne, *b* 1957. *Residence* – Charcroft, Maddington St, Shrewton, Wilts.

Grandchildren of late Lt-Gen Granville George Chetwynd-Stapylton, 2nd son of late Maj Henry Richard Chetwynd-Stapylton (ante):—
Issue of late Maj Granville Joseph Chetwynd-Stapylton, *b* 1871, *ka* 1914: *m* 1906, Elizabeth Grace, who *d* 1930, da of late Christopher Lethbridge, of 19 Chester Square, SW:—
Granville Richard (1a Shelton Fields, Shrewsbury), *b* 1909, *ed* Charterhouse; Lt-Col (ret) Somerset LI: *m* 1934, Emma, yst da of late Col W. A. Young, and has issue living, Richard Granville Hugh (Beckets House, Lapford, Crediton, Devon EX17 6PZ), *b* 1939; *ed* Charterhouse; Lt-Col (ret) LI: *m* 1968, Janet Mary Agnes, da of Cdr Alastair Shand Cumming, RN, and has issue living, Margot Emma *b* 1969, Polly Rose *b* 1971, — Sarah Elizabeth, *b* 1936: *m* 1962, Lt-Col Ian Guy Mathews (ret), SCLI, and has issue living, Nicola *b* 1963, Amanda *b* 1965. —— Barbara Mary Elizabth, *b* 1907: *m* 1934, Ronald Anthony Edward Birch, and has issue living, George Anthony, *b* 1935, — William *b* 1938, — John Montagu, *b* 1941.
Issue of late Col Bryan Henry Chetwynd-Stapylton, CBE, *b* 1873, *d* 1958: *m* 1905, Dorothy Constance, who *d* 1942, da of late Chambré Brabazon Ponsonby (E Bessborough, colls):—
Mary Blanche, *b* 1910: *m* 1936, Ralph Meredith Turton, of Kildale Hall, Whitby, N Yorks, who *d* 1988, and has issue living, Cecilia Mary, *b* 1936: *m* 1959, John Harold Vick Sutcliffe, of Chapelgarth, Gt Broughton, Middlesbrough, and has issue living, Andrew Harold Wentworth *b* 1960: *m* 1988, Emma Elisabeth, elder da of Sir Angus Duncan Æneas Stirling (*see* E Dunmore) (and has had issue, Ralph Andrew Æneas *b* 1991, *d* 1992, Rose Cecilia *b* 1990, Helena Grace *b* 1993), John Ralph Beaumont *b* 1964: *m* 1991, Marcella, yr da of Giovanni Pellegrino, of Milan (and has issue living, Francesca Renata *b* 1993), Mark David Chetwynd *b* 1967, Henrietta Cecilia *b* 1961: *m* 1987, Matthew Williams, elder son of Sir John Williams, of Hanging Langford, Wilts (and has issue living, Joshua John Ralph *b* 1989, Jonathan Frederick Matthew *b* 1991), — Lavinia Rose (*Lady Horsbrugh-Porter*), *b* 1939: *m* 1964, Sir John Simon Horsbrugh-Porter, 4th Bt, of Bowers Croft, Coleshill, Amersham, Bucks, — Victoria Harriet Lucy (*Viscountess Bridgeman*), *b* 1942; *ed* Trin Coll, Dublin (MA): *m* 1966, 3rd Viscount Bridgeman, of Watley House, Sparsholt, Hants, and 19 Chepstow Rd, W2, — Sylvia Dorothy, *b* 1947, *m* 1st, 1977, David Laurence (Jeremy) Booth; 2ndly, 1983, Martin Oakley, of 24 Warnborough Rd, Oxford, and has issue living (by 2nd *m*), Oliver Ronald *b* 1984, Edmund Ralph *b* 1986, Esther Amelia Blanche *b* 1990.

Granddaughter of late Maj Granville Joseph Chetwynd-Stapylton (ante):—
Issue of late Lt-Col Christopher George Chetwynd-Stapylton, RA, *b* 1913, *d* 1988: *m* 1952, Bridget, formerly wife of Ian Urquhart Wilson, and da of late Harry Selwyn Dixon-Spain, of Little Massingham Manor, King's Lynn, Norfolk:—
Elizabeth Alice, *b* 1954: *m* 1979, Lt-Col Michael Anthony Hart, MBE, QGM, The Cheshire Regt, elder son of late Maj R. F. S. Hart, of Gt Clacton, Essex, and has issue living, Christopher James Seymour, *b* 1984, — Rebecca Louise, *b* 1981.

Grandson of late Col Bryan Henry Chetwynd-Stapylton, CBE (ante):—
Issue of late Maj Edward Henry Chetwynd-Stapylton, *b* 1912, *d* 1992: *m* 1957, Priscilla (Ewelands House, Felixkirk, Thirsk, N Yorks), da of Maj Robert Gerald Wright, of Tunstall Grange, Richmond, N Yorks:—
Miles Edward, *b* 1958; *ed* Bradfield: *m* 1987, Caroline, da of late Jan Siwy, of Bedford Park, London, and has issue living, Rachel Caroline, *b* 1992. *Residence* – 51 Marston St, Oxford.

Grandchildren of late Edward Chetwynd-Stapylton, eldest son of Rev Canon William Chetwynd-Stapylton, 3rd son of Maj Henry Richard Chetwynd-Stapylton (ante):—
Issue of late Richard Chetwynd-Stapylton, *b* 1880, *d* 1945: *m* 1915, Vera Helen, who *d* 1959, da of late Andrew Coventry Maitland-Makgill-Crichton (E Lauderdale, colls):—
Edward Mark, *b* 1919; *ed* Winchester, and Magdalene Coll, Camb; formerly Maj KRRC; 1939-45 War in Middle East attached E Africa Reconnaissance Regt (despatches): *m* 1946, Anne Phillida (formerly WRNS), da of Sir Alfred Edward Pease, 2nd Bt (*cr* 1882), and has issue living, Judy Anne (5 Bridgefield Rd, Cheam, Surrey SM1 2DG), *b* 1948: *m* 1977, John Trevor Lambert, and has issue living, Sophie Alice Doanda *b* 1977, Hannah Madeleine Harriet *b* 1983, — Phillida Helen (9 Market St, Lewes, E Sussex BN7 2NB), *b* 1949, — Joanna Elizabeth (30 Lansdowne Pl, Lewes, E Sussex BN7 2JU), *b* 1951: *m* 1978 (*m diss* 1983), Kim Stephen Fuller, and has issue living, Jessie Alison *b* 1980. *Residence* – 110 Western Rd, Lewes, E Sussex BN7 1RR. —— Helen (*Baroness Adeane*) (22 Chelsea Sq, SW3), *b* 1916: *m* 1939, Baron Adeane, GCB, GCVO, who *d* 1984. —— Vera Rosemary (16 Dawn Gdns, Winchester, Hants), *b* 1924: *m* 1946 (*m diss* 1970), Maj Derek Leslie Lloyd, MC, 5th Fus (ret), who *d* 1990, and has issue living, Julian Richard Leslie (The Glebe, Leixlip, co Kildare), *b* 1947; *ed* Eton: *m* 1972, Hon Victoria Mary Ormsby-Gore, da of 5th Baron Harlech, and has issue living, Lester Guy Julian *b* 1982, Poppy Zita Aline *b* 1972, Zita Crystal Rosemary *b* 1974, — Carolyn Rosemary, *b* 1948: *m* 1978, John Derek Hall, of The Old Vicarage, Spreyton, Crediton, Devon EX17 5AL, son of late Sidney Hall, and has issue living, Jack Julian Bunker *b* 1980, Rosie Niamh *b* 1977, — Althea Victoria, *b* 1950: *m* 1977, Roderick David Alasdair Boyle, and has issue (*see* E Glasgow, colls).
Issue of late William Eric Chetwynd-Stapylton, *b* 1895, *d* 1978: *m* 1st, 1924, Vivienne, who *d* 1961, da of Harry Spurling, formerly of Upton Park, Slough; 2ndly, 1962, Audrey Margaret, who *d* 1983, da of Percival Hardy, of London, and widow of Ian T. B. Cash:—
(By 1st *m*) Violet Mary, *b* 1926; late WRNS: *m* 1955, Richard Nevill Vaughan Fairbank, TD, late Capt Hon Artillery Co, of Coopers Green, Windlesham, Surrey, and has issue living, David Richard Stapylton (Perry Leigh, Grove Rd, Selling, Faversham, Kent ME13 9RN), *b* 1956: *m* 1981, Clare Arabella, elder da of late Peter Leonard Eckersley, and has issue (*see* Hardy, Bt, colls), — Anthony William Vaughan, *b* 1963: *m* 1989, Harriet Caroline, elder da of Com Oliver Lascelles, MBE, DSC, RN (*see* E Harewood, colls), and has issue living, Emily Rose *b* 1991, Olivia Alice *b* 1992, — Victoria Mary Nevill, *b* 1959: *m* 1983, James Harman Thompson, late Major, Queen's Royal Irish Hussars, of Milton Bank Farm, Sandfield Lane, Acton Bridge, Northwich, Cheshire, and has issue living, William James Richard *b* 1986, Jack Peter *b* 1992, Rosanna Patricia Mary *b* 1988.

Granddaughters of late Granville Chetwynd-Stapylton, yst son of late Rev Canon William Chetwynd-Stapylton (ante):—

Issue of late Col Granville Brian Chetwynd-Stapylton, CB, OBE, TD, b 1887, d 1964: m 1922, Catherine, who d 1981, da of late Herbert Lyne, of Newport, Mon:—

Lucy (Jesus Fellowship Community, Festal Grange, Church Rd, Pattishall, nr Towcester, Northants), b 1923: m 1945 (m diss 1980), Paul Anthony Robinson, Fl-Lt late RAFVR, and has issue living, Nigel Anthony, b 1946: m 1971 (m diss 1986), Sandra Ann Coggs, and has issue living, Howard Charles b 1978, Suzanne Louise b 1974, — Jennifer Chetwynd, b 1949: m 1974, Malcolm Colin Bowden, and has issue living, David b 1981, Josephine b 1980. —— Bridget, b 1924: m 1st, 1948, Dennis Worsley Wilks, MB, BS, who d 1969; 2ndly, 1978, John Baron Sewter, of Harlequin Cottage, High St, Broughton, Stockbridge, Hants, and has had issue (by 1st m), David Michael Worsley, b 1949; MB, BS: m 1972 (m diss 1992), Patricia Dorothea Joyce, da of Charles Anthony Philip Hackforth, DSO, and has issue living, Anthony Peter Worsley b 1983, Philippa Carla b 1977, Nicola Catherine b 1980, — Peter Brian Chetwynd, b 1951; ed Exeter Coll, Oxford; d 1972, — John Richard Stapylton, b 1955; ed Balliol Coll, Oxford (MA, ARCM): m 1983, Suzan Jane Scothern, and has issue living, Naren Richard b 1985, — Nicholas Paul, b 1960; ed Ch Ch, Oxford (BA). —— Mary Elizabeth, b 1926: m 1949, Grahame Archer Nicholls, BSc, of 12A Lillington Av, Leamington Spa, Warwicks CV32 5UJ, and has issue living, Granville Richard, b 1952, — David Chetwynd, b 1957: m 1988, Karen Jane Hodgkinson, — Janet Archer, b 1950.

PREDECESSORS – (1) WALTER Chetwynd, son of late John Chetwynd; MP for boroughs of Stafford and Lichfield 1703-35, and sometime Ambassador at Turin and Master of the Stag hounds; cr Baron of Rathdown, co Dublin and Viscount Chetwynd, of Bearhaven, co Kerry (peerage of Ireland) 1717, with remainder to the issue male of his father; d 1735; s by his brother (2) JOHN, 2nd Viscount; Ambassador to Madrid 1717; d 1767; s by his brother (3) WILLIAM RICHARD, 3rd Viscount; Resident at Republic of Genoa 1708-12, MP 1714, Cmmr of the Admiralty 1717-27, and Master of the Mint 1727: d 1770; s by his son (4) JOHN, 4th Viscount, b 1721: m 1751: d 1791; s by his son (5) RICHARD, 5th Viscount: d 1821; s by his son (6) RICHARD WALTER, 6th Viscount, b 1800: m 1st, 1822, Mary, who d 1857, da of Robert Moss; 2ndly, 1861, Mary, who d 1901, da of late John Hussey; d 6 Dec 1879; s by his son (7) RICHARD WALTER, 7th Viscount, b 1823: m 1858, Harriet Johanna, who d 1898, da of late Walter Campbell; d 1911; s by his nephew (8) GODFREY JOHN BOYLE, CH (2nd son of late Capt Henry Weyland Chetwynd, RN, 3rd son of 6th Viscount), 8th Viscount, b 1863; was Managing Director of National Shell Filling Factory at Chilwell, Notts 1915-19: m 1st, 1893 (m diss —), Baroness Hilda von Alvensleben, da of Baron George von Alvensleben-Rusteberg; 2ndly, 1904, Hon Mary Eden, who d 1925, da of 4th Baron Auckland; d 1936; s by his son (9) ADAM DUNCAN, TD, 9th Viscount b 1904; a FSA, and Lt-Col RA: m 1st, 1928 (m diss 1951), Joan Gilbert (FINDLAY), and who d 1979, only child of late Herbert Alexander Casson, CSI; 2ndly, 1952, Dorothea Marianne, MBE, CStJ, who d 1990, da of Lt-Col Angus Colin Duncan-Johnstone, MBE, ED; d 1965; s by his only son (10) ADAM RICHARD JOHN CASSON, 10th Viscount and present peer; also Baron Rathdown.

Chewton, Viscount; son of Earl Waldegrave.

CHEYLESMORE, BARONY OF (Eaton) (Extinct 1974)

COLLATERAL BRANCH LIVING

Issue of late Hon Herbert Edward Eaton, 2nd son of 3rd Baron, b 1895, d 1962: m 1st, 1921 (m diss 1944), Sheila Marguerite, who d 1967, da of Alan Southey Dumbleton, of Victoria, BC, and formerly wife of John Aloysius Ashton Case; 2ndly, 1944, Barrie Kinghorn (WILLIAMS), who d 1972, da of Walter Grey, of Edinburgh:—

(By 1st m) Elizabeth Valerie EATON-CROSS, b 1922; 1939-45 War with WAAF: m 1949, Edward John Kynaston Cross, and has issue living, Richard Anthony Kynaston, b 1951: m 1978, Pauline Elizabeth, da of Herbert Leonard Tewkesbury, of Warnham, Sussex. Residence – 11 Holmbrook Gdns, Farnborough, Hants GU14 9SH.

CHICHESTER, EARL OF (Pelham) (Earl UK 1801, Bt E 1611)

The love of my country prevails

JOHN NICHOLAS PELHAM, 9th Earl and 14th Baronet; *b* (*posthumous*) 14 April 1944; *s* 1944: *m* 1975, Mrs June Marijke Hall, da of Group Capt E. D. Wells, DSO, DFC, of Marbella, Spain, and has issue.

Arms – Quarterly: 1st and 4th azure, three pelicans vulning themselves argent; 2nd and 3rd gules, two pieces of belts with buckles, erect in pale, the buckles upwards argent. **Crest** – A peacock in pride argent. **Badges** – The buckle of a belt or. **Supporters** – *Dexter*, a horse of a mouse dun colour; and *sinister*, a bear proper, each collared with a belt, buckle and pendant or.
Residence – Little Durnford Manor, Salisbury.

DAUGHTER LIVING

Lady Eliza Catherine, *b* 1983.

SISTER LIVING

Lady Georgina Jocelyn, *b* 1942: *m* 1974, Helios Alberto Caranci, of La Catalina, Diego de Alvear, Santa Fe, Argentina, son of Helios Jorge Caranci, of Arredondo 2015, Castelar, Buenos Aires, Argentina, and has issue living, Helios Nicolas, *b* 1983, — Cecilia Catalina, *b* 1976, — Ursula Claudia, *b* 1978.

COLLATERAL BRANCHES LIVING

Grandchildren of Hon Henry George Godolphin Pelham (infra):—
Issue of late Maj Anthony George Pelham, *b* 1911, *d* 1969: *m* 1938, Ann-Margret, who *d* 1990, da of late Axel Bergengren, of Borås, Sweden:—
RICHARD ANTHONY HENRY (Hisomley Farm House, Westbury, Wilts), *b* 1 Aug 1952; *ed* Eton: *m* 1987, Georgina, da of David Gilmour, of Ringshall Grange, Suffolk, and has issue living, Duncan James Bergengren, *b* 24 Nov 1987, — Christopher (Kit), *b* 1990. ⸺ Ella Christine, *b* 1940: *m* 1961, John Raymond Perring, of 21 Somerset Rd, Wimbledon, SW19, and has issue (*see* Perring, Bt). ⸺ Judith Henrietta, *b* 1943: *m* 1968, Christopher John Chetwood, of The Bell House, Ellisfield, Basingstoke, Hants, and has issue living, Thomas William, *b* 1970, — Henry Jonathan, *b* 1972, — Matthew James, *b* 1981, — Henrietta Rose, *b* 1983.

Issue of late Hon Henry George Godolphin Pelham, 2nd son of 5th Earl, *b* 1875, *d* 1949: *m* 1st, 1906, Agnes Lee, who *d* 1930, da of late T. J. Ollerhead, of Hillbury, Minehead, Somerset; 2ndly, 1938, Dorothy Mary, who *d* 1972, da of late George Bridger Shiffner (Shiffner, Bt, colls):—
(By 1st *m*) Joan Ursula, *b* 1907; is a JP for Surrey: *m* 1929, John Edward Sealy, who *d* 1968, and has issue living, Nicholas John Elliot (Timber Hill, Chobham, Surrey), *b* 1938; *ed* Eton; late Capt Rifle Bde: *m* 1971, Hon Lavinia Caroline Piercy, twin da of 2nd Baron Piercy, and has issue (*see* B Piercy), — Agnes Coral Pelham, *b* 1932: *m* 1954, James Gilbert Curwen, of Deep Ford Cottage, Chobham, Surrey, and has issue living, Henry James Gospatric *b* 1957, Simon Charles Edward *b* 1959: *m* 1984, Jane Kathrine, da of Robert Snell, of Dinas Powis, S Glam (and has issue living, Carolyn Sara *b* 1986, Nicola Helen *b* 1988), Philip Mark Ivo *b* 1963, Rachel Helen Vanessa *b* 1962, — Ann Pelham, *b* 1934: *m* 1957, Fereydoun Ala, MB, ChB, MRCPE, FRCP, and has issue living, a son *b* 1957, a son *b* 1960, a son *b* 1967. *Residence* – Hall Farm, Weatheroak Hill, Alvechurch, Birmingham B48 7EG. ⸺ Beryl Northup, *b* 1908: *m* 1940, Lawrence Swan, late Sqdn-Ldr RAFVR, of 6 Egley Drive, Mayford, Woking, Surrey.

Grandchildren of late Rev Walter Henry Pelham, only son of late Hon Thomas Henry William Pelham, CB, 3rd son of 3rd Earl:—
Issue of late Rev Thomas Bertram Pelham, *b* 1915, *d* 1984: *m* 1948, Gudrun Elisabeth (2 Upper Grange, Lovedays Mead, Stroud, Glos GL5 1XB), da of late Rev Uno Axel Valdemar Almgren, of Goteborg, Sweden:—
Philip Henry (15 Ethelbert Rd, Canterbury, Kent), *b* 1949; *ed* Lushington Boys Sch, Ootacamund, Malmesbury Gram Sch, and Sch of Herbal Medicine, Tunbridge Wells: *m* 1983, Mrs Jennifer B. Wellington, da of Col J. D. Power, of Tetherings, Mystole, nr Canterbury, Kent, and has issue living, Andrew Timothy, *b* 1984, — Annabel Claire, *b* 1985, — Elizabeth Rose, *b* 1990. ⸺ David Almgren (28 York Rd, Colwyn Bay, Clwyd), *b* 1950: *ed* Lushington Boys Sch, Ootacamund, Malmesbury Gram Sch, Derby Univ, and Rhodes Univ, Grahamstown, S Africa (MSc): *m* 1980, Julie Ann, da of D. G. Killingley, of 19 Trysull Gdns, Merry Hill, Wolverhampton, and has issue living, Thomas James, *b* 1982, — Lucy Jane, *b* 1985. ⸺ Peter Thomas (48 Leighton Hill Flats, 16 Link Rd, Happy Valley, Hong Kong), *b* 1952; *ed* Lushington Boys Sch, Ootacamund, Malmesbury Gram Sch, and Manchester Univ: *m* 1974 (*m diss* 1994), Linda Margaret, da of Capt P. H. Phillips, of Benallack, Grampound Rd, Truro, Cornwall, and has issue living, Henry William, *b* 1983, — and an adopted da Suyin, *b* 1985. ⸺ Erik John Christopher (12 Park Rd, Horncastle, Lincs), *b* 1954; *ed* Lushington Boys Sch, Ootacamund, Malmesbury Gram Sch, and Lancaster Univ: *m* 19—, Jane, da of John Souter Henley, and has issue living, Alexander *b* 1990, Joseph *b* 1992, Laura, *b* 1988. ⸺ (James) Richard (27 Hill Head, Glastonbury, Somerset), *b* (twin) 1955; *ed* Lushington Boys Sch, Ootacamund, and Bremilham Sch, Malmesbury; has issue (by Mary Chipper), Isaac Roy, *b* 1994. ⸺ Astrid Louisa, *b* (twin) 1955: *m* 1978, Richard Michael Flaye (formerly Fleay), of Kettlehouse, Chapel Lane, Belchford, Lincs, son of Martin Fleay, of Rydon Acres, Stoke Gabriel, Totnes, Devon, and has issue living, Thomas Charles, *b* 1983, — Tobias Pelham, *b* 1985, — Ella, *b* 1988. ⸺ Susan Margaret (1 Wraxhill Rd, Street, Somerset), *b* 1959; has issue, Robin David Pelham, *b* 1985, — (by Jonny Green) Maia, *b* 1992.
Issue of late Capt Robert Henry Pelham, RA, *b* 1919, *d* 1980: *m* 1951, Anne Farebrother Dalziel (8 Waterside, Rushford Warren, Mudeford, Bournemouth, Hants), da of Capt Geoffrey Dalziel Mayer, of Abinger, Surrey:—
Michael Henry, *b* 1953. ⸺ Sarah Mary, *b* 1955.

Grandsons of Sir (Edward) Henry Pelham, KCB (infra):—
Issue of late Maj Eric Thomas Pelham, WG, *b* 1915, *d* 1984: *m* 1940, Barbara Hilda, who *d* 1969, yst da of Henry John Fordham, of Therfield, Royston, Herts:—
Henry Thomas, *b* 1943; *ed* Harrow: *m* 1978, Sarah E., yr da of John Charlton, of Culworth Fields, Banbury, Oxon, and has issue living, Charles Thomas, *b* 1987, — Sophie, *b* 1980, — Clare, *b* 1981. ⸺ Richard John, *b* 1945; *ed* Harrow. ⸺ Charles Herbert, *b* 1947; *ed* Harrow: *m* 1st, 1972 (*m diss* 1979), Thérèse Annabella, elder da of Maj James Richard Edwards Harden, DSO, MC (*see* B Rayleigh, colls); 2ndly, 19—, Sarah, da of —, and has issue living (by 2nd *m*), Henry, *b* 1986, — Katharine, *b* 1984. ⸺ William Robert, *b* 1950; *ed* Harrow.

Granddaughters of late Henry Francis Pelham, Pres Trin Coll, Oxford, eldest son of Rt Rev Hon John Thomas Pelham, DD, Bishop of Norwich 1857-93, 4th son of 2nd Earl:—

Issue of late Sir (Edward) Henry Pelham, KCB, b 1876, d 1949: m 1905, Hon Irene Lubbock, who d 1961, da of 1st Baron Avebury:—

Irene Joan, b 1912: m 1961, Brig Maurice Leslie Hayne, CBE, who d 1971. *Residence* – 11 Heathfield Court, Crookham Rd, Fleet, Hants GU13 8DX. —— Susan, b 1918: m 1940, Air Vice-Marshal Cresswell Montagu Clementi, CB, CBE, who d 1981, only son of late Sir Cecil Clementi, GCMG, and has issue living, Christopher Pelham, b 1943; ed Bradfield: m 1976, Pamela Juliette Nollan, and has issue living, Richard Adam b 1978, — David Cecil, b 1949; ed Winchester, Lincoln Coll, Oxford, and Harvard Business Sch: m 1972, Sarah Louise, da of late Dr A. B. Cowley, of E Molesey, Surrey, and has issue living, Thomas Cowley b 1979, Anna Lucy b 1976, — Nancy, b 1946: m 1972, Peter Lambert Tribe, and has issue living, Mark Lambert b 1978, Howard Clementi b 1981, Natalie Clare b 1975. *Residence* – Navigator's Cottage, 44 Strand-on-the-Green, Chiswick W4.

PREDECESSORS – (1) THOMAS Pelham, MP for Sussex 1586, and Sheriff of Surrey and Sussex 1589; *cr* a *Baronet* 1611; *d* 1624; *s* by his son (2) Sir THOMAS, 2nd Bt, MP for Sussex; *d* 1654; *s* by his son (3) Sir JOHN, 3rd Bt, MP for Sussex in five parliaments; *d* 1703; *s* by his son (4) Sir THOMAS, 4th Bt, MP for many years; *cr Lord Pelham, Baron of Pelham*, of Laughton, co Sussex (peerage of Great Britain); *d* 1712; *s* by his son (5) THOMAS, KG, 2nd Baron, *cr Viscount Houghton* and *Earl of Clare*, co Suffolk (peerage of Great Britain) 1714, with remainder to his brother Henry; Marquess of Clare and Duke of Newcastle (peerage of Great Britain) 1715, with similar limitation; Duke of Newcastle-under-Lyme (peerage of Great Britain) 1756, with remainder to Henry, 9th Earl of Lincoln, who had *m* Catherine, da of his brother Henry (ante); and *Baron Pelham of Stanmer* (peerage of Great Britain) 1762, with remainder to his cousin Thomas, grandson of Henry, 3rd son of 3rd Bt; *d* without male issue 1768, when the peerages of 1712, 1714, 1715 became extinct, the dukedom of 1756 passed to the Earl of Lincoln, and the peerage of 1762 devolved upon his kinsman (6) THOMAS, PC, 2nd Baron Pelham; was successively MP for Sussex, Commr of Trade and Plantations, a Lord of the Admiralty, and Comptroller of the Household; *cr Earl of Chichester* 1801; *d* 1805; *s* by his son (7) THOMAS, 2nd Earl; *b* 1756; MP for Sussex 1780-90; was successively Sec to Lord-Lieut of Ireland, and Sec of State for Home Depart, Chancellor of Duchy of Lancaster, and Postmaster Gen; called to House of Lords in his father's barony 1801: *m* 1801, Mary Henrietta Juliana, who *d* 1862, da of 5th Duke of Leeds; *d* 1826; *s* by his son (8) HENRY THOMAS, 3rd Earl; *b* 1804; was Lord-Lieut of Sussex: *m* 1828, Lady Mary Brudenell, who *d* 1867, da of 6th Earl of Cardigan; *d* March 1886; *s* by his son (9) WALTER JOHN, 4th Earl; *b* 1838; MP for Lewes (*L*) 1865-74: *m* 1861, Elizabeth Mary, who *d* 1911, da of late Hon Sir John Duncan Bligh, KCB (*see* E Darnley, 1911 Edn); *d* 1902; *s* by his brother (10) *Rev* FRANCIS GODOLPHIN, 5th Earl; *b* 1844: *m* 1870, Hon Alice Carr Glyn, who *d* 1934, da of 1st Baron Wolverton; *d* 1905; *s* by his son (11) JOCELYN BRUDENELL, OBE, 6th Earl, *b* 1871; a Public Works Loan Commr 1904-26: *m* 1898, Ruth, da of late Francis William Buxton; *d* 14 Nov 1926; *s* by his el son (12) FRANCIS GODOLPHIN HENRY, 7th Earl, *b* 1905; *d* 22 Nov 1926: *s* by his brother (13) JOHN BUXTON, 8th Earl, *b* 1912; Capt Scots Guards: *m* 1940, Ursula, who *d* 1989, having *m* 2ndly, 1957 (*m diss* 1971), Ralph Gunning Henderson, da of late Walter de Pannwitz, of Hartekamp, Benebroek, Holland; *d* on active service 1944; *s* by his son (14) JOHN NICHOLAS, 9th Earl and present peer; also Baron Pelham of Stanmer.

Chichester, Viscount; grandson of Marquess of Donegall.

CHILSTON, VISCOUNT (Akers-Douglas) (Viscount UK 1911)

Wisdom and Truth

Hon Dominic, b 1979.

ALASTAIR GEORGE AKERS-DOUGLAS, 4th Viscount; *b* 5 Sept 1946; *s* 1982; *ed* Eton; patron of one living: *m* 1971, Juliet Anne, da of Lt-Col Nigel Lovett, of The Old Rectory, Inwardleigh, Okehampton, Devon, and has issue.

Arms – Quarterly: 1st and 4th argent, a man's heart gules, ensigned with an imperial crown and pierced by an arrow fessewise, the pheon to the dexter, proper; on a chief azure, three mullets of the field, *Douglas*; 2nd and 3rd, gules, three escallops or within a bordure argent, charged with eight acorns proper, *Akers*. **Crests** – 1st, an arm in armour embowed proper, garnished or, the gauntlet grasping a dagger also proper, *Douglas*; 2nd, an arm in armour embowed proper, garnished or, the gauntlet grasping a pennon barry of four azure and argent, *Akers*. **Supporters** – *Dexter*, a horse argent, supporting a banner azure charged with three mullets also argent; *sinister*, a like horse supporting a similar banner ermine, charged with a man's heart gules, ensigned with an imperial crown, and pierced by an arrow fesse wise, the pheon to the dexter, proper.
Seats – Chilston Park, Sandway, Maidstone, Kent; Craigs, near Dumfries. *Residence* – The Old Rectory, Twyford, Winchester, Hants.

SONS LIVING

Hon OLIVER IAN, b 13 Oct 1973.
Hon Alexander Hugh, b 1975.

SISTER LIVING

Diana, b 1948: m 1969, Simon Richard Harrap, and has issue (*see* Darell, Bt). *Residence* – Perryland, Bentley, Farnham, Hants.

HALF-SISTER LIVING

Jennifer, b 1938: m 1st, 1958, George David Henry Wiggin (*see* Wiggin, Bt, colls), who d 1990; 2ndly, 1993, Charles Arthur Smith-Bingham. *Residence* – Stag Cottage, Bagnor, Newbury, Berks.

MOTHER LIVING

Phyllis Rosemary, da of late Arthur David Clere Parsons (*see* E Rosse, colls): *m* 1st, 1945, as his 2nd wife, Capt Ian Stanley Akers-Douglas, who *d* 1952; 2ndly, 1965, John Anthony Cobham Shaw (*see* By Cobham). *Residence* – 18 Abbey Mews, Amesbury Abbey, Amesbury, Wilts.

COLLATERAL BRANCH LIVING

Grandchildren of late Lt-Col Hon George Alexander Akers-Douglas, Royal Fusiliers, 2nd son of 1st Viscount:—

Issue of late Maj Anthony George Akers-Douglas, late 13th/18th Royal Hussars, *b* 1914, *d* 1991: *m* 1941, Dorothy Louise (23 Mytten Close, Cuckfield, W Sussex RH17 5LN), da of late Brig-Gen Moreton Foley Gage, DSO (*see* V Gage, colls):—

Adrian Anthony (PO Box 257, Limassol, Cyprus), *b* 1943; *ed* Eton: *m* 1974, Janet (Penny), da of Sir Frederick Cecil Mason, KCVO, CMG, of The Old Forge, Ropley, Alresford, Hants, and has issue living, Lara Victoria, *b* 1983, — Nicola Antonia, *b* 1991. —— Francis Alexander Moreton (Barham Farmhouse, E Hoathly, Lewes, Sussex BN8 6QL), *b* 1948; *ed* Eton: *m* 1974, Hon Julian Mary Warrender, elder da of 2nd Baron Bruntisfield, and has issue living, Joseph Michael Aretas, *b* 1979, — James George, *b* 1989. —— Laura Dorothy, *b* 1957: *m* 1985, Nicholas James Bell, elder son of Dr Anthony Bell, of Woodruffs Farm, Fittleworth, Sussex, and has issue living, Joshua Anthony Fernie, *b* 1988, — Benedict William James *b* 1991, — Eliza Dorothy Thalia, *b* 1994.

PREDECESSORS – (1) ARETAS Akers-Douglas, GBE, PC, son of late Rev Aretas Akers, of Malling Abbey, Kent; *b* 1851; Patronage Sec to the Treasury June 1885 to Jan 1886, July 1889 to Aug 1892, and June to July 1895, First Commr of Works, with a seat in the Cabinet July 1895 to Aug 1902, and Sec of State for Home Depart Aug 1902 to Dec 1905; assumed in 1875, by Roy licence, the additional surname of Douglas; MP for E Kent (*C*) 1880-85, and for St Augustine's Div of Kent 1885-1911; *cr* Baron Douglas of Baads, co Midlothian, and *Viscount Chilston*, of Boughton Malherbe, co Kent (peerage of United Kingdom) 1911: *m* 1875, Adeline, who *d* 1929, da of Horatio Austen Smith, of Hayes Court, Kent; *d* 1926; *s* by his el son (2) ARETAS, GCMG, PC, 2nd Viscount, *b* 1876; was Envoy Extraor and Min Plen at Vienna 1921-28, and at Budapest 1928-33, and Ambassador at Moscow 1933-38: *m* 1903, Amy, who *d* 1962, da of J. R. Jennings Bramley, RHA; *d* 1947; *s* by his 2nd son (3) ERIC ALEXANDER, 3rd Viscount, *b* 1910: *m* 1955, Marion, who *d* 1970, da of late Capt Charles William Howard, RE; *d* 1982; *s* by his cousin (4) ALASTAIR GEORGE (son of late Capt Ian Stanley Akers-Douglas, el son of Lt-Col Hon George Alexander Akers-Douglas, yr son of 1st Viscount), 4th Viscount and present peer; also Baron Douglas of Baads.

CHILVER, BARON (Chilver) (Life Baron 1987)

(AMOS) HENRY CHILVER, FRS, eldest son of Amos Henry Chilver, of Southend-on-Sea, Essex; *b* 30 Oct 1926; *ed* Southend High Sch, and Bristol Univ; lectr Bristol Univ 1952-54, and Camb Univ 1956-61; Fell CCC 1958-61 (Hon Fell 1981); FRS (1982), FEng (1977), CBIM, Hon DSc Bath, Bristol, Leeds, Salford and Strathclyde Univs; Prof of Civil Engrg Univ Coll London 1961-69; Dir Centre for Environmental Studies 1967-69, Vice Chancellor Cranfield Inst of Technology 1970-89; Chm ECC Group plc since 1989, BASE Internat plc since 1988, and Milton Keynes Development Corpn since 1983, etc; author and contributor to various papers on structural theory in engineering journals; *cr* Kt 1978, and *Baron Chilver*, of Cranfield, co Beds (Life Baron) 1987: *m* 1959, Claudia Mary Beverley, only da of late Sir Wilfrid Grigson, CSI, of Pelynt, Cornwall, and has issue.

Residence – Lanlawren House, Trenewan, Looe, Cornwall PL13 2PZ. *Clubs* – Athenaeum, and United Oxford and Cambridge.

SONS LIVING

Hon John, *b* 1964; *ed* Bedford Sch.
Hon Mark, *b* 1965; *ed* Bedford Sch.
Hon Paul, *b* 1967; *ed* Bedford Sch.

DAUGHTERS LIVING

Hon Helen, *b* 1960: *m* 1979, Geoffrey Prentice.
Hon Sarah, *b* 1962.

CHITNIS, BARON (Chitnis) (Life Baron 1977)

PRATAP CHIDAMBER CHITNIS, son of late Chidamber Chitnis; *b* 1 May 1936; *ed* Stonyhurst, Birmingham Univ (BA), and Kansas Univ (MA); Head of Liberal Party Organisation 1966-69; Chief Exec Rowntree Social Ser Trust 1969-88; Member of Community Relations Comn 1971-77; *cr* Baron Chitnis, of Ryedale, co N Yorks (Life Baron) 1977: *m* 1964, Anne, da of Frank Mansell Brand, and had issue (one son deceased).

Address – Beverley House, Shipton Road, York.

CHOLMONDELEY, MARQUESS OF (Cholmondeley) (Marquess UK 1815)
(Name and Title pronounced "Chumley")

Virtue is the safest helmet

Kings Sutton, Banbury, Oxfordshire.

DAVID GEORGE PHILIP CHOLMONDELEY, 7th Marquess; *b* 27 June 1960; *s* 1990; *ed* Eton, and La Sorbonne; a Page of Honour to HM 1974-76; Joint Hereditary Lord Great Chamberlain of England (acting for reign of Queen Elizabeth II since 1990).

Arms – Gules, in chief two esquires' helmets argent, and in base a garb or. **Crest** – A demi-griffin segreant sable, beaked, winged, and membered or, holding between the claws a helmet as in the arms. **Supporters** – *Dexter*, a griffin sable, beaked, winged, and membered or, langued gules; *sinister*, a wolf or, collared vaire, armed and langued gules.
Seats – Cholmondeley Castle, Malpas, Cheshire; Houghton Hall, King's Lynn, Norfolk.

SISTERS LIVING

Lady Rose Aline, *b* 1948. *Residence* – 44 Bassett Rd, W10 6JL.
Lady Margot Lavinia, *b* 1950: *m* 1978, (Walter) Anthony Huston, only son of late John Huston, film director, of Las Caletas, Puerto Vallarta, Mexico, and has issue living, Matthew Horatio, *b* 1979, — Jack Alexander, *b* 1982, — Laura Sybil, *b* 1981. *Residence* – Village Farm, Houghton, King's Lynn, Norfolk.
Lady Caroline Mary, *b* 1952: *m* 1982, Rodolphe d'Erlanger, son of late Leo Frederic Alfred d'Erlanger, and has issue living, Leo Frederic Hugh, *b* 1983, — David Joshua Robert, *b* 1987. *Residence* – Grey Court,

AUNT LIVING *(daughter of 5th Marquess)*

Lady Aline Caroline, *b* 1916. *Residence* – 39 Eaton Sq, SW1.

WIDOW LIVING OF SON OF FIFTH MARQUESS

Maria Cristina (*Lady John Cholmondeley*), only da of late Giorgio Solari, of Genoa: *m* 1957, Lord John George Cholmondeley, who *d* 1986, and has issue (see colls infra). *Residence* – 22 Hyde Park Gdns, W2.

WIDOW LIVING OF SIXTH MARQUESS

LAVINIA MARGARET, DL (*Marchioness of Cholmondeley*), only da of late Lt-Col John Leslie, DSO, MC, of Brancaster, Norfolk (*see* Skipwith, Bt, colls, 1934 Edn); DL Cheshire 1992: *m* 1947, Maj the 6th Marquess, GCVO, MC, who *d* 1990. *Residences* – Cholmondeley Castle, Malpas, Cheshire; Houghton Hall, King's Lynn, Norfolk.

COLLATERAL BRANCHES LIVING

Issue of late Lord John George Cholmondeley, yr son of 5th Marquess, *b* 1920, *d* 1986: *m* 1957, Maria Cristina (ante), only da of late Giorgio Solari, of Genoa:—
CHARLES GEORGE, *b* 18 March 1959. —— Joanna Antonia, *b* 1958.

Issue of late Lord George Hugo Cholmondeley, OBE, MC, son of 4th Marquess, *b* 1887, *d* 1958: *m* 1st, 1911 (*m diss* 1921), Clara Elizabeth, who *d* 1925, da of Charles Henry Taylor, of Washington, USA, and formerly wife of Maj John Alexander Stirling, DSO, MC; 2ndly, 1921 (*m diss* 1948), Ina Marjorie Gwendoline, OBE, who *d* 1969, da of late Rev Canon Raymond Percy Pelly (Pelly, Bt, colls), and formerly wife of Maj Hon Christopher Lowther (*see* V Ullswater, 1935 Edn); 3rdly, 1948, Diana, who *d* 1965, da of late Hon Rupert Evelyn Beckett (*see* B Grimthorpe, colls, 1955 Edn), and widow of Albany Kennett Charlesworth, MC (*see* Laurie Bt, 1941 Edn):—
(By 1st *m*) Irene, *b* 1913: *m* 1947, Stanislaw Falkowski, MD, late Maj RAMC, who *d* 1986, having assumed 1949 the names of Stephen Falkland, and has issue living, Priscilla Susan, *b* 1948: *m* 1974, Robert A. I. Dicketts, of Rosemary Cottage, Wards Lane, Wallcrouch, Wadhurst, Sussex TN5 6HN, and has issue living, Oliver Simon *b* 1979.

PREDECESSORS – Robert Cholmondeley; *cr* a *Baronet* 1611, *Viscount Cholmondeley of Kells* (peerage of Ireland) 1628, *Baron Cholmondeley*, of Wiche Malbank (peerage of England) 1645 and *Earl of Leinster* (peerage of England) 1646; *dsp* 1659, when the honours became extinct and his estates passed to his nephew (1) ROBERT Cholmondeley; *cr Viscount Cholmondeley*, of Kells, 1661; *s* by his son (2) HUGH, 2nd Viscount; *cr Baron Cholmondeley*, of Namptwich (peerage of England) 1689, with remainder to his brother George, and *Viscount Malpas* and *Earl of Cholmondeley* (peerage of Great Britain) 1706, with similar remainder; *d* unmarried 1724; *s* by his brother (3) GEORGE, 2nd Earl, who had previously been *cr Baron Newborough*, of Newborough, co Wexford (peerage of Ireland) 1715, and *Baron Newburgh* in the Isle of Anglesey (peerage of Great Britain) 1716; a distinguished military officer; commanded Horse Guards at battle of the Boyne; *d* 1733; *s* by his son (4) GEORGE, KB, PC, 3rd Earl; MP for East Looe 1724 and Windsor 1727; successively Master of the Robes; Chancellor of Duchy of Lancaster, Keeper of Privy Seal, Paymaster Gen, and Treasurer of War for Ireland; *d* 1770; *s* by his grandson (5) GEORGE JAMES, KG, 4th Earl; *b* 1749; was Lord Steward of the Household; *cr Earl of Rocksavage* and *Marquess of Cholmondeley* (peerage of United Kingdom) 1815; *d* 1827; *s* by his son (6) GEORGE HORATIO, PC, 2nd Marquess; *b* 1792; summoned to House of Lords in his father's Barony of Newborough 1821; *s* his mother as Joint Hereditary Great Chamberlain of England 1838; *dsp* 1870; *s* by his brother (7) WILLIAM HENRY HUGH, 3rd Marquess; *b* 1800; sat as MP for Castle Rising 1822-32, and for S Hampshire (C) 1852-57; *d* 1884; *s* by his grandson (8) GEORGE HENRY HUGH (son of late Charles George Cholmondeley, by his wife, Susan Caroline, who *d* 1891, da of Sir George Dashwood, 4th Bt), 4th Marquess; *b* 1858; Joint Hereditary Lord Great Chamberlain (acted for reign of King Edward VII): *m* 1879, Winifred Ida, OBE, who *d* 1938, da of late Col Sir Robert Nigel Fitzhardinge Kingscote, KCB, of Kingscote, Wotton-under-Edge (E Howe); *d* 1923; *s* by his son (9) GEORGE HORATIO CHARLES, GCVO, 5th Marquess *b* 1883; Joint Hereditary Lord Great Chamberlain (acted for reign of King Edward VIII, and for reign of Queen Elizabeth II 1952-66): *m* 1913, Sybil Rachel Betty Cécile, CBE, who *d* 1989, da of Sir Edward Albert Sassoon, 2nd Bt (*cr* 1890) ext; *d* 1968; *s* by his son (10) (GEORGE) HUGH, GCVO, MC, 6th Marquess, *b* 1919; Joint Hereditary Lord Great Chamberlain (acted for reign of Queen Elizabeth II 1966-90): *m* 1947, Lavinia Margaret, only da of late Lt-Col John Leslie, DSO, MC, of Brancaster, Norfolk (*see* Skipwith, Bt, colls, 1934 Edn); *d* 1990; *s* by his only son (11)

DAVID GEORGE PHILIP, 7th Marquess and present peer; also Earl of Rocksavage, Earl of Cholmondeley, Viscount Malpas, Baron Cholmondeley, Baron Newborough, and Baron Newburgh.

CHORLEY, BARON (Chorley) (Baron UK 1945)

ROGER RICHARD EDWARD CHORLEY, 2nd Baron, *b* 14 Aug 1930; *s* 1978; *ed* Stowe, and Gonville and Caius Coll, Camb; Hon DSc Reading 1990, and Kingston 1992; Pres RGS 1987-90; Chm The National Trust since 1991: *m* 1964, Ann, yr da of A. S. Debenham, of Ingatestone, Essex, and has issue.

Arms – Per chevron argent and vert, in chief two blue-bottles proper and in base a fountain. **Crest** – In front of two torches in saltire or and inflamed, a teazle stalked and leaved proper. **Supporters** – On either side a buzzard proper. *Club* – Alpine.

SONS LIVING

Hon NICHOLAS RUPERT DEBENHAM, *b* 15 July 1966.
Hon Christopher Robert Hopkinson, *b* 1968.

BROTHER LIVING

Tenacious of purpose

Hon (Geoffrey) Patrick Hopkinson, *b* 1933; *ed* Stowe, and New Coll, Oxford: *m* 1st, 1955 (*m diss* 1972), Daria Antonia Maria, da of the Marquis de Merindol; 2ndly, 1975, May Amaryllis, da of Prof A. Ashmore, of 24 Pine Rd, Didsbury, Manchester, and has issue living (by 1st *m*), Alexandra (Asya) Maria, *b* 1956: *m* 1981, Hugh Bett, son of Cdr R. T. Bett, of Paxtons, E Lavant, Sussex, — Elizabeth Henrietta Marianne, *b* 1961. *Residence* – 7 Chalcot Cresc, NW1.

SISTER LIVING

Hon Gillian Theodora Marianne, *b* 1929; *ed* Liverpool Coll for Girls, and St Anne's Coll, Oxford; *m* 1965, F. Godfrey Goodwin of 29 Chalcot Sq, NW1, and has issue living, Robert Theodore Chorley, *b* 1969.

PREDECESSOR – (1) ROBERT SAMUEL THEODORE CHORLEY, QC, 1st Baron, son of Richard Fisher Chorley, of Kendal; *b* 1895; *cr Baron Chorley* of Kendal, co Westmorland (Peerage of UK) 1945; Bar Inner Temple 1920, QC 1961; a Principal, Home Office 1940-41, Assist-Sec Min of Home Security 1941-42, Dep Regional Commr for Civil Defence (NW Region) 1942-44; a Lord-in-Waiting to HM 1945-50: *m* 1925, Katharine Campbell, who *d* 1986, only da of Edward Hopkinson, DSc, of Alderley Edge, Cheshire; *d* 1978; *s* by his son (2) ROGER RICHARD EDWARD, 2nd Baron and present peer.

CHURCHILL, VISCOUNT (Spencer) (Viscount UK 1902)

VICTOR GEORGE SPENCER, 3rd Viscount; *b* (*posthumous*) 31 July 1934; *s* 1973; *ed* Eton, and New Coll, Oxford (MA); Lt Scots Gds 1953-55.

Arms – Quarterly argent and gules, in the 2nd and 3rd quarters a fret or, over all on a bend sable, three escallops of the first. **Crest** – Out of a ducal crest coronet or, a griffin's head, between two wings expanded argent, gorged with a bar gemelle gules. **Supporters** – *Dexter*, a griffin wings elevated per fesse argent and or, gorged with a collar or, charged with three escallops sable, line reflexed over the back also or; *sinister*, a wyvern wings elevated gules, gorged with a collar or, charged with three escallops sable. *Residence* – 6 Cumberland Mansions, George St, W1.

God defend the right

SISTER LIVING

Hon Sarah Faith Georgina, *b* 1931: *m* 1951, Richard John Palmer, JP, and has issue living, David Charles, *b* 1955: *m* 1989, Lucy Belinda, elder da of late Capt Patrick John Boteler Drury-Lowe (*see* Earle, Bt), and has issue living, George Richard Charles *b* 1992, Shamus Patrick John *b* 1993, — James Nicholas (49 Fernside Rd, SW12 8LN), *b* 1963: *m* 1988, Cybele I., da of Francis Bullock, of Egypt Farm, Hamptons, Kent, and has issue living, Oliver Victor George *b* 1990, — Christopher Richard, *b* 1967, — Caroline Mary, *b* 1952: *m* 1st, 1975 (*m diss* 1991), Maj Hon Richard Nicholas Bethell, MBE, elder son of 5th Baron Westbury; 2ndly, 1992, as his 2nd wife, Mark Chaytor Dickinson, of Newbrough Park, Newbrough, Hexham, Northumberland (*see* Chaytor, Bt, 1990 Edn). *Residence* – Queen Anne's Mead, Swallowfield, Berks.

COLLATERAL BRANCHES LIVING (*In remainder to Barony only*)

Granddaughter of late Col John Winston Thomas MUNRO-SPENCER, who assumed the additional surname of Munro 1911, son of late Lt-Col Hon George Augustus Spencer, 2nd son of 1st Baron:—
Issue of late Capt Almeric Stuart John Spencer, *b* 1885, *d* 1960: *m* 1912 (*m diss* 1928), Phyllis Margaret, who *d* 1971, da of late Charles Richard Rivers, of 20 Palmeira Square, Hove, and Orrell, Lancashire:—
Synolda Joan Margaret (Phoenix House, Hinton St George, Crewkerne, Somerset), *b* 1914: *m* 1949, Capt Cecil Campbell Hardy, DSO, RN, who *d* 1963, and has issue living, Charles Rupert Almeric, *b* 1951; *ed* Wellington Coll, and Magdalene Coll, Camb (BA); MBA (Insead): *m* 1982, Helen, da of Lt-Col R. C. Orgill, OBE, and has issue living, Robin Campbell Richard *b* 1984, Jack Spencer *b* 1986, Christopher Munro *b* 1992, — Theodora Margaret, *b* 1953; LCST: *m* 1989, Jeremy Gilson Lowe, and has issue living, Jessamy Synolda *b* 1991.

Grandsons of late Lt-Col Augustus Campbell Spencer (infra):—

Issue of late Col Richard Augustus Spencer, DSO, OBE, *b* 1888, *d* 1956: *m* 1925, Maud Evelyn, who *d* 1989, da of late Lieut-Col Henry Lushington Ramsay (*see* E Dalhousie, colls, 1990 Edn):—

RICHARD HARRY RAMSAY (The Old Vicarage, Vernham Dean, Hants), *b* 11 Oct 1926; hp to Barony of Churchill; late Lt Coldm Gds; ARIBA, AADipl: *m* 1958, Antoinette Rose-Marie, da of Godefroy de Charrière, of Perverenges, Lausanne, Switzerland, and has issue living, Michael Richard de Charrière, *b* 1960, — David Anthony, *b* 1970. —— Charles Geoffrey Campbell (Stokke Common, Marlborough, Wilts), *b* 1928; late Lt Coldm Guards; served in Malaya 1948-50, and Kenya 1954-56: *m* 1964, Cherry Elizabeth, da of William Carlyle Clarke.

Granddaughter of late Lt-Col Augustus Campbell Spencer, son of Gen Hon Sir Augustus Almeric Spencer, GCB, 3rd son of 1st Baron:—

Issue of late Lt-Col (Edward) Almeric Spencer, OBE, RA, *b* 1892, *d* 1984: *m* 1918, Elsie Winifred, who *d* 1969, da of Arthur Macan, DL, of Drumcashel, co Louth:—

Guinevere Elsie (Lower House, Ashley, Box, Corsham, Wilts), *b* 1920: *m* 1945 (*m diss* 1975), Charles Arthur Wellesley Williamson, MC, TD, late Maj Sherwood Foresters, and has issue living, Richard Almeric Spencer, *b* 1949; *ed* Winchester: *m* 1st, 1970 (*m diss* 1982), June, da of Wilfrid Mansfield; 2ndly, 1982, Aura Figueroa, and has issue living, (by 1st *m*) Sasha *b* 1971, Damian *b* 1974, Mischa *b* 1977, — Michael Anthony Wellesley, *b* 1952; *ed* Winchester, and Durham Univ (BA); ARCM: *m* 1981, Pascale Eyre, — Francis Charles Fitzroy, *b* 1959; *ed* Wellington Coll; MSc, — Patrick Alexander Campbell, *b* 1960; *ed* Wellington Coll, — Sarah Lavinia, *b* 1946: *m* 1976, Michael Danny, of The Manor House, Wellow, Bath, and has issue living, William *b* 1979, Christopher *b* 1981, Melissa *b* 1976.

Grandchildren of late Brig-Gen John Almeric Walter Spencer, CMG, DSO, son of late Capt William Francis Spencer, elder son of late Rev Hon William Henry Spencer, 4th son of 1st Baron:—

Issue of late Capt John Lawrence Spencer, DSO, MC, *b* 1917, *d* 1967: *m* 1943, Jane Lilian (Ghyllas, Sedbergh, Cumbria), da of late Col Granville Duff, MC, of Heydon, Norfolk:—

John William James, *b* 1957; *ed* Sedbergh, and Magdalene Coll, Camb: *m* 1st, 1982 (*m diss* 1987), Leonie Margaret, da of Ralph Jameson, 2ndly, 1987, Jane Elizabeth, da of late Andrew Young, and has issue living (by 2nd *m*), Charles William Alexander, *b* 1990, — Rosanagh Jane Katharine, *b* 1991. *Residence* – Ghyllas, Sedbergh, Cumbria. —— Caroline Mary, *b* 1948: *m* 1969, Robin Peter Sandys-Clarke, of Raff Yard House, Staindrop, Darlington, co Durham DL2 3AH, and has issue living, Peter Edward David, *b* 1981, — Jessica Jane, *b* 1975, — Lucinda Mary *b* 1977.

Granddaughter of late Col Almeric George Spencer, yr son of late Rev Hon William Henry Spencer (ante):—

Issue (by 2nd *m*) of late Lt-Col Almeric Arthur William Spencer, *b* 1874, *d* 1934: *m* 1st, 1907 (*m diss* 1927), Sybil da of Frederick William Lawson, formerly of Oaklands, Adel, Leeds; 2ndly, 1930, Charlotte (34 Ashgarth Court, Harrogate, N Yorks) (who *m* 2ndly, 1941, Cecil Trevor Hamilton Whiteside, MC, MRCS, who *d* 1965 (*see* L Belhaven, colls, 1980 Edn), da of late Rev John Lesley Parker, V of Lanteglos, Fowey:—

Ann Frances, *b* 1931; resumed her maiden name 1963: *m* 1st, 1957 (*m annulled* 1963), Rev Leslie Vandernoll Wright; 2ndly, 1979, Patrick Joseph Healy.

Grandson of late Col Francis Elmhirst Spencer, DSO, MC (infra):—

Issue of late Francis Tracey Spencer, *b* 1917, *d* 1989: *m* 1962, Rev Diana (Box 13, Ladysmith, BC, Canada VOR 2EO), eldest da of Dennis Haines, of Wattisfield Croft, Suffolk:—

Philip Henry (c/o Math Dept, Toronto, Univ, Canada), *b* 1966; *ed* Glenlyon Sch, Victoria, Univ of Victoria (BSc), and Harvard (PhD).

Granddaughter of late Lt-Col Charles Francis Henry Spencer, el son of late Rev Hon Charles Frederic Octavius Spencer, 8th son of 1st Baron:—

Issue of late Col Francis Elmhirst Spencer, DSO, MC, *b* 1881, *d* 1972: *m* 1916, Augusta (Vera), who *d* 1956, da of late Col Arthur Tracey, formerly RGA:—

Joan Elizabeth, *b* 1921; late QARNNS (Res): *m* 1949, Surg-Cdr Geoffrey Norman Shell, RN (ret), of Gomorin, Court Woods, Newton Ferrers, Plymouth, and has issue living, Peter Geoffrey, *b* 1951; *ed* Haileybury: *m* 1984, Marianne Jane, elder da of Paul Pierre Tissier, FRSS, of 97 Oxford Rd, Abingdon, — David Spencer, *b* 1954; *ed* Milton Abbey.

PREDECESSORS – (1) *Lord* FRANCIS ALMERIC Spencer, DCL, 2nd son of 4th Duke of Marlborough; *b* 1779; *cr Baron Churchill*, of Wychwood, co Oxford (peerage of United Kingdom) 1815: *d* 1845; *s* by his son (2) FRANCIS GEORGE, DCL, 2nd Baron; *b* 1802: *m* 1849, Lady Jane Conyngham, VA, who *d* 1900, da of 2nd Marquess Conyngham; *d* 24 Nov 1896; *s* by his son (3) VICTOR ALBERT FRANCIS CHARLES, GCVO, 3rd Baron, *b* 1864; was a Page of Honour to Queen Victoria 1876-81, and a Lord-in-Waiting to Queen Victoria 1889-92, and 1895-1901, and to King Edward VII, 1901-5; Chm of Great Western Railway Co, and of British Overseas Bank; Master of the Buckhounds 1900, Lord Chamberlain 1902, and Master of the Robes at Coronation of King George V 1911; KCVO 1900, GCVO 1902; *cr Viscount Churchill*, of Rolleston, co Leicester (peerage of United Kingdom) 1902: *m* 1st, 1887, Lady Verena Maude, VA, who *d* 1938 (from whom he had obtained a divorce for desertion in the Scottish Courts 1927), da of 3rd Earl of Lonsdale; 2ndly, 1927, Christine McRae, who *d* 1972, having *m* 2ndly, 1937 (*m diss* (Reno)) 1938), Lt-Col Ralph Heyward Isham, CBE, who *d* 1955, and 3rdly, 1939, Sir Lancelot Oliphant, KCMG, CB, who *d* 1965, da of William Sinclair; *d* 1934; *s* by his son (4) VICTOR ALEXANDER, 2nd Viscount, *b* 1890; FRAS: *m* 1st, 1916, Kathleen, who *d* 1943, da of late Hon Robert Beaven, formerly Premier of Victoria, BC, Canada, and widow of Capt Stanley Venn Ellis, RN; 2ndly, 1949, Joan, who *d* 1957, da of late Joseph Baron Black; *d* 1973; *s* by his half-brother (5) VICTOR GEORGE, 3rd Viscount and present peer; also Baron Churchill.

CHURSTON, BARON (Yarde-Buller) (Baron UK 1858, Bt GB 1790)

ΛQVILA NON CAPIT·MUSCAS

The eagle does not catch flies

JOHN FRANCIS YARDE-BULLER, 5th Baron and 7th Baronet; *b* 29 Dec 1934; *s* 1991; *ed* Eton; is patron of two livings; late 2nd Lieut RHG: *m* 1973, Alexandra Joanna, only da of Anthony Contomichalos, of 23 Eaton Place, SW1, and has issue.

𝕬rms – Quarterly; 1st and 4th sable, on a cross argent quarterly, pierced of the field, four eagles displayed of the first, *Buller*; 2nd and 3rd argent, a chevron gules, between three water-bougets sable, *Yarde*. 𝕮rest – A Saracen's head couped, proper. 𝕾upporters – *Dexter*, an ostrich proper, in the beak a horse-shoe or; *sinister*, an eagle sable. *Residence* – Yowlestone House, Puddington, Tiverton, Devon. *Clubs* – Buck's, White's.

SON LIVING

Hon BENJAMIN FRANCIS ANTHONY, *b* 13 Sept 1974; *ed* Eton.

DAUGHTERS LIVING

Hon Katherine Marina, *b* 1975.
Hon Francesca Elizabeth, *b* 1980.

SISTER LIVING

Hon Nicole, *b* 1936: *m* 1st, 1958 (*m diss* 1962), Richard Wilfred Beavoir Berens; 2ndly, 1963, Michael Russell, and has issue living (by 1st *m*), Thomas Richard, *b* 1960; *ed* Bishop Wordsworth Sch, — Jessica Primrose, *b* 1959; *ed* Cranbourne Chase; journalist, — (by 2nd *m*) Francis, *b* 1966; *ed* Harrow: *m* 1993, Penelope G., yr da of late Maj J. I. L. Syddall, of Puddletown, Dorset, — Alexander, *b* 1969; *ed* Eton, and Edinburgh Univ, — Lorna, *b* 1963; *ed* St Mary's Calne. *Residence* – Wilby Hall, Wilby, Norwich, Norfolk.

AUNTS LIVING (*daughters of 3rd Baron*)

Hon Joan Barbara (*Viscountess Camrose*), *b* 1908: *m* 1st, 1927 (*m diss* 1936), W/Cdr (Thomas) Loel Evelyn Bulkeley Guinness, OBE, Auxiliary Air Force (Res), who *d* 1988 (*see* By Audilaun, 1944 Edn); 2ndly, 1936 (*m diss* 1949), Aly Khan, who *d* in a motor accident 1960, son of HH late Rt Hon the Aga Khan, GCSI, GCIE, GCVO; 3rdly, 1986, 2nd Viscount Camrose, and has had issue (by 1st *m*), Patrick Benjamin (Tara), *b* 1931; *ed* Eton: *m* 1955, Countess Dolores Maria Agatha Wilhelmine Luisa (7 rue Crocus, 1074 Mollie Margaux, Switzerland), da of Count Franz Egon von Fürstenberg, and *d* in a motor accident 1965, leaving issue, Loel (Ave de Rumine 37, 1005 Lausanne, Switzerland) *b* 1957, Alexandra *b* 1956: *m* 1979, Count Foulques de Quatrebarbes, of Les Cassivettes, 1173 Fechy, Switzerland (and has issue living, Foulques Patrick *b* 1981, Laétitia *b* 1983, Aurelia *b* 1984, Olivia *b* 1985), Victoria *b* 1960: *m* 1984, Philippe Niarchos, of 2 rue de Chanaleilles, 75007 Paris, eldest son of Stavros Niarchos (and has issue living, Stavros *b* 1985, Eugeni *b* 1986), — (by 2nd *m*) HH Prince Karim (*HH the Aga Khan*) (Aiglemont, 60270 Gouvieux, France), *b* 1936; *ed* Le Rosey, and at Harvard Univ; *s* his grandfather as 4th Aga Khan 1957; is spiritual leader and Imam of Ismaili Muslims all over the world; received personal title of Highness 1957: *m* 1969, Sarah Frances, only da of Lt-Col A. E. Croker Poole, of 95 Eaton Sq, SW1, and formerly wife of Lord James Charles Crichton-Stuart (*see* M Bute), and has issue living, *Prince* Rahim *b* 1971, *Prince* Hussain *b* 1974, *Princess* Zahra *b* 1970, — *Prince* Amyn Mohamed (276 Route de Lausanne, 1292 Chambesy, Geneva, Switzerland; 69 rue de Lille, 75007 Paris), *b* 1937; *ed* Le Rosey, and at Harvard Univ. *Residences* – Hackwood Park, nr Basingstoke, Hants; 8a Hobart Place, SW1W 0HH.

Hon Denise Margaret *b* 1916: *m* 1941 (*m diss* 1954), as his 2nd wife, 5th Baron Ebury, who *d* 1957. *Residence* – Barton's Lodge, Eversholt, Bletchley, Bucks.

Hon Lydia, *b* 1917: *m* 1st, 1938, Capt Ian Archibald de Hoghton Lyle, Black Watch; who was *ka* 1942 in the Middle East, el son of Sir Archibald Moir Park Lyle, 2nd Bt, MC; 2ndly, 1947 (*m diss* 1960), 13th Duke of Bedford. *Residence* – Little Ribsden, Windlesham, Bagshot, Surrey.

WIDOW LIVING OF SON OF THIRD BARON

Guendolen, da of late Rev Charles Roots, of Heathfield, Sussex: *m* 1939, Hon John Reginald Henry Yarde-Buller, who *d* 1962, and has issue living (*see* colls, infra). *Residence* – Le Vallon, Mont Félard, Jersey.

COLLATERAL BRANCHES LIVING

Issue of late Hon John Reginald Henry Yarde-Buller, 2nd son of 3rd Baron, *b* 1915, *d* 1962: *m* 1939, Gwendolen (ante), da of late Rev Charles Roots, of Heathfield, Sussex:—
Roger Charles John, *b* 1942. —— Anthony Reginald Lawrence, *b* 1946.

Grandchildren of late Hon Geoffrey Yarde-Buller, brother of 2nd Baron:—
Issue of late Hon Geoffrey Yarde-Buller, *b* 1894, *d* 1993: *m* 1st, 1919, Hortensia Nab6ulet Pajot, who *d* 1957, da of Leon Nab6ulet, of Parana, Argentina; 2ndly, 19— (*m diss* 1972), Elsa Cejas:—
(By 1st *m*) Norberto (La Tribuna 1705, Castelar, Buenos Aires), *b* 1922: *m* 1946, Yolanda Adela, da of Carlos Devillier, of Florida, Argentina, and has issue living, Daniel Carlos, *b* 1954: *m* 1976, Elda Beatriz Martinez, and has issue living, Soledad Jorgelina *b* 1980, — Norberto Luis, *b* 1959: *m* 1987, Viviana Sandra Masseo, and has issue living, Alexis *b* 1988, Jimena *b* 1989, — Rita Adela, *b* 1947: *m* 1979, Ingeniero Jorge Daniel Balan, and has issue living, Gonzolo Daniel *b* 1992, — Susan Hortensia, *b* 1952: *m* 1985, Marcelo Esteban Gilberto. —— Eduardo (Luis Maria Campos 4029, Villa Insuperable, La Matanza, Buenos Aires), *b* 1926: *m* 1953, Isabel Esther, da of Francisco Hinojosa, of Buenos Aires, and has issue living, Eduardo Guillermo, *b* 1972, — Liliana Beatriz, *b* 1955: *m* 1976, Luciano Dal Cin, and has issue living, Mariano *b* 1983, Ignacio *b* 1985, Dario *b* 1988, Luciana *b* 1991, — Jaquelina Ines, *b* 1968: *m* 1985, Marcelo Romero, and has issue living, Federico *b* 1991, Maria Azul *b* 1987. —— Lilian (Arias 1955-5° Piso, Dto C, Buenos Aires), *b* 1920: *m* 1st, 1944, Osvaldo Federico Alizeri, who *d* 1962; 2ndly, 1968, Victor Antonio Olivera, Capitan de Corbeta de la Armada Argentina, and has had issue (by 1st *m*), Stella Maria, *b* 1945; *d* 1967, — Diana, *b* 1947: *m* 1973, Juan Jose Molero, and *d* 1980, leaving issue, Federico Jose *b* 1977, Enrique Marcelo *b* 1979. —— Delia (Av Maipu 1864-2° Piso, Vicente Lopez, Buenos Aires), *b* 1932: *m* 1949, Rafael Maria Parravicini Piaggio, who *d* 1967, and has issue living, Octavio Horacio, *b* 1950: *m* 1972, Raquel O. Melgarejo Dutra, and has issue living, Octavio Ovidio *b* 1976, Mercedes *b* 1980, Florencia Soila *b* 1985, Delmira Soita *b* (twin) 1985, — Rafael Guido, *b* 1952: *m* 1980, Ana Maria Liria Laurant, and has issue living, Alejo Andres *b* 1989, Lucia

Florencia *b* 1981, — Denise Oriental, *b* 1959. ——— Doris (Av Maipu 1468-2° Piso, Vicente Lopez, Buenos Aires), *b* 1934: *m* 1962, Jorge Gattino Cuesta, and has issue living, Gabriela Amalia, *b* 1965: *m* 1988, Ingeniero Leonardo Omar Lanzilotta. ——— Estela (Feliciano Chiclana 61, 1708 Morón, Buenos Aires), *b* 1939: *m* 1961, Prof Ismael Sabino Salvatierra, and has issue living, Alejandro Ismael, *b* 1962; Ingeniero, — Eduardo Pablo, *b* 1964; Prof: *m* 1993, Adrioma Marcela Viggiano, — Gustavo Fabian, *b* 1968, — Adriana Hortensia, *b* 1970. ——— (By 2nd *m*) Silvia Veronica, *b* 1966: *m* 1984, Luis Cosenza, and has issue living, Alexis, *b* 1985.

       Issue of late Edmond Yarde-Buller, *b* 1897, *d* 19—: *m* 19—, Adela Jmelnisky:—
Reinaldo Alberto (Avenida 9 de Julio 3260, Chajari (Entre Rios), Argentina), *b* 19—: *m* 19—, Martha Elena Melgar, and has issue living, Christian, *b* 1964. ——— Jorge, *b* 19—. ——— Anita Sofia, *b* 19—: *m* 19—, Rodolfo Juan Carlos Nux, of Gobernador Gregores, Santa Cruz, Argentina. ——— Cecilia Olegaria, *b* 19—: *m* 19—, Eduardo Tirado.

       Descendants, if any, of John Yarde-Buller (1893-1990), Henry Yarde-Buller (*b* 1899), Manuel Yarde-Buller (*b* 1901), Albert Yarde-Buller (*b* 1908), and Reginald Yarde-Buller (*b* 1911), sons of late Hon Geoffrey Yarde-Buller (*ante*).

(In remainder to Baronetcy only)

       Descendants of Sir Edward Manningham-Buller (who assumed the additional surname and arms of Manningham) 3rd son of 2nd Bt (*see* V Dilhorne).

PREDECESSORS – (1) Sir FRANCIS Buller, KB, KC, a very eminent lawyer and a Justice of the Common Pleas; *cr* a *Baronet* 1790; *d* 1800; *s* by his son (2) Sir FRANCIS, 2nd Bt, MP for Totnes; assumed the additional and final surname of Yarde by Roy licence 1800; *d* 1833; *s* by his son (3) JOHN, DCL, 3rd Bt; MP for S Devon (C) 1835-58; assumed the surname of Yarde-Buller by Roy licence 1860; *cr Baron Churston*, of Churston Ferrers, and Lupton, Devon (peerage of United Kingdom) 1858; *d* 1871; *s* by his grandson (4) JOHN, 2nd Baron, son of Hon John, el son of 1st Baron, by Charlotte, da of Edward Sacheverell Chandos-Pole, of Radborne, co Derby, *b* 1846: *m* 1872, Hon Barbara, who *d* 1924, da of late Adm Sir Hastings Reginald Yelverton, GCB, and of late Barbara (in her own right) Baroness Grey de Ruthyn, widow of 2nd Marquess of Hastings; *d* 1910; *s* by his son (5) JOHN REGINALD LOPES, MVO, OBE, 3rd Baron; *b* 1873; an ADC to Viceroy of India (Baron Curzon of Kedleston) 1902-3, and ADC to Inspector-Gen of the Forces (F-M HRH the Duke of Connaught) 1904-6; sometime Inspector of QMG Sers: *m* 1907 (*m diss* 1928), Jessie, who *d* 1960, only da of late Alfred Smither, *d* 1930; *s* by his son (6) RICHARD FRANCIS ROGER, VRD, 4th Baron, *b* 1910; Lt-Cdr RNVR; bore one of the Golden Spurs at the Coronations of King George VI and Queen Elizabeth II: *m* 1st, 1933 (*m diss* 1943), Elizabeth Mary (who *d* 1951, having *m* 2ndly, 1943, Maj Peter Laycock, who *d* 1978), da of late Lt-Col William Baring Du Pree, JP, DL, of Wilton Park, Beaconsfield, Bucks; 2ndly, 1949, Sandra, who *d* 1979, da of Percy Needham, and formerly wife of (i) Claud Harold Bertram Arthur Griffiths, and (ii) Jack Dunfee; 3rdly, 1981, Mrs Olga Alice Muriel Blair, who *d* 1992, natural da of 2nd Baron Rothschild (by Marie Barbara, da of Maximillian Fredenson, of Newton Sq, Bayswater, W2), and formerly wife of Bryce Evans Blair; *d* 1991; *s* by his only son (7) JOHN FRANCIS, 5th Baron and present peer.

CITRINE, BARON (Citrine) (Baron UK 1946)

Strive for right

NORMAN ARTHUR CITRINE, 2nd Baron; *b* 27 Sept 1914; *s* 1983; *ed* Univ Coll Sch; LLB London 1938; LLD London 1993 admitted a Solicitor 1937 (ret); is author of legal textbooks, technical and other works; was legal Adviser to Trades Union Congress 1946-51; Pres Devon and Exeter Law Soc 1971-72; Fell of Institute of Diagnostic Engineers 1990; European War 1940-45 as Lieut RNVR: *m* 1939, Kathleen Alice, da of late George Chilvers, of Saxmundham, Suffolk, and has issue.

Arms – Argent, on waves of the sea in base, an ancient three-masted ship in full sail proper, on a chief gules a Saxon crown between two seaxes points downwards or, the dexter in bend, the sinister in bend sinister. **Crest** – A cubit arm habited azure cuffed argent, the hand grasping a citrine proper. **Supporters** – *Dexter*, an alsatian wolfhound proper, on the shoulder a terrestial globe or, charged with a human heart; *sinister*, a lion proper, on the shoulder a torteau charged with a spade and pickaxe in saltire and pen-nib in pale or.
Residence – Casa Katrina, The Mount, Opua, Bay of Islands, New Zealand.

DAUGHTER LIVING

Hon Patricia Deirdre, *b* 1939.

BROTHER LIVING

Hon RONALD ERIC, MRCS, LRCP, *b* 19 May 1919; *ed* Univ Coll Sch, and Univ Coll London: *m* 1945, Mary, da of Reginald Williams, of Wembley, Middlesex. *Residence* – Paihia, Bay of Islands, North Island, NZ.

PREDECESSOR – WALTER MCLENNAN CITRINE, GBE, PC, 1st Baron, son of Alfred Citrine, of Wallasey, *b* 1887; *cr Baron Citrine*, of Wembley, co Middlesex (peerage of UK) 1946; was Gen Sec of Trades Union Congress 1926-46, Pres of Internat Fedn of Trade Unions 1928-45, and Pres of World Fedn of Trade Unions 1945-46; Pres World Anti-Nazi Council 1936-46; first Chm Central Electricity Authority 1947-57: *m* 1913, Doris Helen, who *d* 1973, da of Edgar Slade; *d* 1983; *s* by his el son (2) NORMAN ARTHUR, 2nd Baron and present peer.

CLANCARTY, EARL OF (Le Poer Trench) Sits as VISCOUNT (UK 1823) (Earl I 1803)

By counsel and prudence

WILLIAM FRANCIS BRINSELY LE POER TRENCH, 8th Earl, and Marquis of Heusden in The Netherlands; *b* 18 Sept 1911; *s* 1975, *ed* Nautical Coll, Pangbourne: *m* 1st, 1940 (*m diss* 1947), Diana Joan, da of Sir William Robert Younger, 2nd Bt; 2ndly, 1961 (*m diss* 1969), Wilma Dorothy Millen, da of S. R. Vermilyea, of USA, and formerly wife of William Robert Belknap, Jnr; 3rdly, 1974, Mrs Mildred Alleyn Spong, who *d* 1975, da of R. Bensusan; 4thly, 1976, Mary Agnes, da of E. Radonicich, and widow of Cdr Frank M. Beasley, RN (ret).

Arms – Quarterly: 1st and 4th argent, a lion passant gules, between three fleurs-de-lis azure, on a chief azure, a sun in splendour, *Trench*; 2nd and 3rd argent, a chief indented sable, *Le Poer*. Over all an escutcheon or, ensigned with the coronet of a Marquis of the Netherlands and charged with a wheel of six spokes gules. **Crest** – 1st, a dexter arm embowed in armour, the hand grasping a scimitar proper; 2nd, a lion rampant or, imperially crowned, holding in the dexter fore paw a naked sword argent, pommel and hilt gold, and in the sinister a sheaf of arrows also or; 3rd, a stag's head cabossed argent, attired or, and between the attires a crucifix. **Supporters** – *Dexter*, a lion gules, semée of fleurs-de-lis or; *sinister*, a stag guardant proper, attired or, between the attires a crucifix, and supporting with the sinister fore paw a lance resting bendwise over the shoulder proper, and thereon a banner of the arms of Le Poer.
Residence – Flat 2, 51 Eaton Sq, SW1X 8DE. *Club* – Buck's.

DAUGHTERS LIVING OF SIXTH EARL

Lady Maureen Isabel, *b* 1923: *m* 1949, Christopher Colin Cooper, and has issue living, Simon Richard Colin (Rectory Farm House, Bisley, nr Stroud, Glos GL6 7BB), *b* 1956; wood sculptor: *m* 1979, Julia C., yst da of E. B. Teesdale, of The Hogge House, Buxted, Sussex, — Claudia (Old Tannery, Donnington Village, Newbury, Berks RG13 2JT), *b* 1952; Univ lecturer, Sana'a Univ, S Yemen.

Lady Caragh Seymour LE POER TRENCH, *b* 1933; has resumed her maiden name: *m* 1st, 1953 (*m diss* 1961), Lt-Cdr John Anthony Lake, RN; 2ndly, 1961, Capt Arthur Jay Oken, USAF; 3rdly, 1966, Capt Donald Van Horn Lee, USAF; 4thly, 19—; 5thly, 19—, — Jefferson, and has issue living (by 1st *m*), Henry John Challoner, *b* 1955, — Catherine Challoner, *b* 1957, — Jean Challoner, *b* 1959. *Address* – PO Box 47788, San Antonio, Texas 78265, USA.

COLLATERAL BRANCH LIVING

Issue of late Hon Power Edward Ford Le Poer Trench, yst son of 5th Earl, *b* 1917, *d* 1975: *m* 1950, Jocelyn Louise Courtney, who *d* 1962:—
NICHOLAS POWER RICHARD (7 Guest Rd, Sheffield, S11 8U3), *b* 1 May 1952; *ed* Westminster Sch, Ashford Gram Sch, and Plymouth Polytechnic. —— Caroline Jessica Mary, *b* 1954; *ed* St Paul's Girls' Sch, and Wadham Coll, Oxford: *m* 1981 (*m diss* 1984), Alan Rodger.

PREDECESSORS – (1) WILLIAM POWER KEATING Trench, MP for Galway 1768-97; *cr Baron Kilconnel*, of Garbally, co Galway (peerage of Ireland) 1793, *Viscount Dunlo* (peerage of Ireland) 1801, and *Earl of Clancarty* (peerage of Ireland) 1803; *d* 1805; *s* by his son (2) RICHARD, GCB, 2nd Earl; *cr Baron Trench* (peerage of United Kingdom) 1815, and *Viscount Clancarty* (peerage of United Kingdom) 1823; appointed Ambassador to the Hague 1813; *cr Marquis of Heusden*, in the Kingdom of the Netherlands 1818, and in 1824 received the royal permission to bear the title in this country; *d* 1837; *s* by his son (3) WILLIAM THOMAS, 3rd Earl; *b* 1803: *m* 1832, Lady Sarah Juliana Butler, da of 3rd Earl of Carrick; *d* 1872; *s* by his son (4) RICHARD SOMERSET, 4th Earl, *b* 1834: *m* 1866, Lady Adeliza Georgiana Hervey, who *d* 1911, da of 2nd Marquess of Bristol; *d* 1891; *s* by his el son (5) WILLIAM FREDERICK, 5th Earl, *b* 1868: *m* 1st, 1889, Isabel Maude Penrice, who *d* 1906, da of John George Bilton, of Charlton, Kent; 2ndly, 1908, Mary Gwatkin, who *d* 1974, da of late W. F. Rosslewin Ellis, Bar-at-Law, of Fulford, Yorkshire; *d* 1929; *s* by his son (6) RICHARD FREDERICK JOHN DONOUGH, 6th Earl, *b* 1891: *m* 1st, 1915 (*m diss* 1918), Edith Constance, who *d* 1950, da of Maj Alexander Albemarle Rawlinson; 2ndly, 1919, Cora Marie Edith, who *d* 1993, aged 100, da of late H. H. Spooner, of Thornton Hall, Surrey; *d* 1971; *s* by his brother (7) GREVILLE SYDNEY ROCHFORT, 7th Earl; *b* 1902: *m* 1926, Beatrice Georgiana, who *d* 1979, yst da of late Capt James Gordon Miller, of Thurlow Hall, Suffolk; *d* 1975; *s* by his half-brother (8) WILLIAM FRANCIS BRINSLEY, 8th Earl and present peer; also Viscount Dunlo, Viscount Clancarty, Baron Kilconnel, and Baron Trench.

Clanfield, Viscount; son of Earl Peel.

CLANMORRIS, BARON (Bingham) (Baron I 1800)

SPES MEA CHRISTUS

Christ is my hope

SIMON JOHN WARD BINGHAM, 8th Baron; *b* 25 Oct 1937; *s* 1988; *ed* Downside, and Queens' Coll, Camb (MA); FCA: *m* 1971, Gizella Maria, only da of late Sandor Zverkó, of Budapest, and has issue.

Arms – Azure, a bend cottised or between six crosses-patée or. **Crest** – On a mount a falcon rising all proper. **Supporters** – Two lions azure. *Residence* – Sutherland House, Marloes Rd, W8 5LG.

DAUGHTER LIVING

Hon Lucy Katherine Gizella, *b* 1974.

SISTER LIVING

Hon Charlotte Mary Thérèse, *b* 1942; *ed* The Priory, Haywards Heath, and the Sorbonne, Paris; novelist and scriptwriter: *m* 1964, Terence Joseph Brady, writer and actor, of Hardway House, Hardway, Bruton, Som, and has issue living, Matthew Joseph Mulligan, *b* 1972, — Candida Marie Thérèse, *b* 1965: *m* 1994, Titus M Ogilvy.

COLLATERAL BRANCHES LIVING

Issue of late Lt-Col Hon (John) Denis Yelverton Bingham, DSO, 2nd son of 5th Baron, *b* 1880, *d* 1940: *m* 1926, Vera, who *d* 1972, da of late Major Norman Darbyshire, of Sefton Park, Liverpool:—

Elizabeth Rosemary, *b* 1927: *m* 1949, Maxwell John Denham, MBE, of Lock Farm, Tixall, Stafford ST18 0XR, and has issue living, (John) Alistair Campbell (19 Vanderbilt Rd, Earlsfield, SW18 3BG), *b* 1955, — Iain Maxwell (5 Gloucester Rd, Kew Green, Richmond, Surrey), *b* 1957: *m* 1988, Wendy Ann, da of Albert Edward Johnson, of Hastings, Sussex, and has issue living, Jonathan Maxwell *b* 1991, Jessica Sarah *b* 1989. —— (Mary) Mavourneen Denise, *b* 1931: *m* 1951, Albert Schiff, and has had issue, Robert John Denis, *b* 1958; *ed* Eton: *m* 1983, Lucinda Mary (who *m* 2ndly, 1992, Andrew Nigel Crosbie Bengough, of Church Farm House, Longparish, Hants, elder son of Col Sir Piers Henry George Bengough, KCVO, OBE DL (*see* Albu, Bt, 1980 Edn), of Great House, Canon Pyon, Herefords), elder da of Capt John Geoffrey Sherston, of Terry House, Warehorne, Ashford, Kent, and drowned 1990, leaving issue, Frederick John Albert *b* 1984, Maximilian Robert Denis *b* 1986, Robert Edmund Bingham *b* (*posthumous*) 1990, —— Miranda Caroline, *b* 1952: *m* 1980, Derek Hearn, of Muntins, The Gardens, Adstock, Bucks. *Residence* – Ambrose Farm House, Ramsbury, Wilts SN8 2PW.

Issue of late Rear-Adm Hon Edward Barry Stewart Bingham, VC, OBE, 3rd son of 5th Baron, *b* 1881, *d* 1939: *m* 1915 (*m diss* 1937), Vera, da of Edward Temple Patterson, formerly of 10 Culford Gardens, SW:—

Lavinia Mary, *b* 1921: *m* 1946, Simon Campbell (*see* V Hawarden, colls, 1973-74 Edn), and has issue living, Luke Bingham, *b* 1948; *ed* Lancing, — Julian Simon, *b* 1949; *ed* Lancing, — Roderick Barry, *b* 1951; *ed* Lancing, — Nicholas Edward Angus, *b* 1956, — Thomas Neil *b* 1961. *Residence* – Inchivore, Old Connaught Av, Bray, co Wicklow.

Issue of late Hon Hugh Terence de Burgh Bingham, 4th son of 5th Baron, *b* 1885, *d* 1957: *m* 1912, Dorothea Minnie, who *d* 1976, da of late J. A. Sinclair, Bar-at-Law, of Lahore:—

Elizabeth Maude, *b* 1922: *m* 1944, Jelle Roel Hogeveen Veenbaas, and has issue living, Peter Hans, *b* 1946: *m* 1978, Veronica Anne, da of Carl Christian Moore, of Warminghurst, Storrington, W Sussex. *Residence* – Erwarton Hall Farm, near Ipswich, Suffolk.

Grandchildren of Hon Hugh Terence de Burgh Bingham (ante):—

Issue of late John Peter Derrick Bingham, *b* 1913, *d* 1978: *m* 1st 1939 (*m diss* 1954), Mary Machen, el da of late Robert Morehead Rose, of Sydney, NSW; 2ndly, 1954, Jean, el da of late Robert Harold Hogarth, of Waverley, Tas:—

(By 1st *m*) Angela Rose, *b* 1944: *m* 1969, Anthony William Steyn, MB, BS, of Sydney, NSW.

Issue of late Capt Hugh Denis Sinclair Bingham, R Inniskilling Fus; *b* 1914, *d* 1946: *m* 1939, Margaret Douglas BINGHAM (she *m* 2ndly, 1948 (*m diss* 1953), George Lennox Barrow, resumed surname of Bingham by deed poll 1951, and *d* 1980, da of late Maj Robert Stevenson, DL, of Aloha, Dungannon, co Tyrone:—

ROBERT DEREK DE BURGH (Glevering House, Easton, nr Woodbridge, Suffolk IP13 0ET), *b* 29 Oct 1942; *ed* Stowe: *m* 1969, Victoria Mary, yr da of P. A. Pennant-Rea, of Laurel Tree Cottage, Guiting Power, Glos, and has issue living Alexandra Louise Clare, *b* 1974, — Georgina Mary Margaret, *b* 1976, — Rosamunde Jessica Elizabeth, *b* 1979. —— (Jane) Victoria (Clare) BINGHAM, *b* 1941; has resumed her maiden name: *m* 1966 (*m diss* 1985), Béla Peter de Daranyi, and has issue living, Imre Patrick Béla, *b* 1973, — Katherine Emma Margaret, *b* 1967: *m* 1991, Angus W. Macgregor Jurkschat, 2nd son of late Rudolf Jurkschat, — Sophie Jane Clare, *b* 1968.

PREDECESSORS – (1) JOHN Bingham, son of late Henry Bingham, of Newbrook, co Mayo; *b* 1762; *cr Baron Clanmorris*, of Newbrook, co Mayo (peerage of Ireland, 1800); *d* 1821; *s* by his son (2) CHARLES BARRY, 2nd Baron; *dsp* 1829; *s* by his brother (3) DENIS ARTHUR, 3rd Baron; *d* 1847: *m* 1825, Maria Helena, who *d* 1899, da of Robert Persse, of Roxborough; *s* by his son (4) JOHN CHARLES ROBERT, 4th Baron; *b* 1826: *m* 1849, Sarah Selina, who *d* 1907, da of Burton Persse, of Moyode Castle, co Galway; *d* 1876; *s* by his son (5) JOHN GEORGE BARRY, 5th Baron; *b* 1852; *d* 1878, (Maude) Matilda Catherine, who *d* 1941, only child and heiress of late Robert Edward Ward, of Bangor Catle, co Down; *d* 1916; *s* by his son (6) ARTHUR MAURICE ROBERT, 6th Baron; *b* 1879; Capt Lancers: *m* 1907, Leila, who *d* 1969, da of late Gordon Cloete, JP, of Rosebank, Cape Town, S Africa; *d* 1960; *s* by his son (7) JOHN MICHAEL WARD, 7th Baron, *b* 1908; spy and crime novelist (as John Bingham), author of *My Name is Michael Sibley*, *Five Roundabouts to Heaven*, *The Third Skin*, etc: *m* 1934, Madeleine Mary (biographer and novelist as Madeleine Bingham), who *d* 16 Feb 1988, da of late Clement Ebel, of Copyhold Place, Cuckfield, Sussex; *d* 6 Aug 1988; *s* by his only son (8) SIMON JOHN WARD, 8th Baron and present peer.

This family descends from the Binghams of Melcombe Bingham, Dorset. Sir George, 3rd son of Robert Bingham of Melcombe (*d* 1561), was father of Sir Henry Bingham, 1st baronet, ancestor of the Earls of Lucan, and of John Bingham of Foxford, co Mayo, ancestor of Barons Clanmorris.

CLANWILLIAM, EARL OF (Meade) Sits as BARON (UK 1828) (Earl I 1776 Bt I 1703)

Always ready

Hanging Langford, Salisbury, Wilts SP3 4NW.

JOHN HERBERT MEADE, 7th Earl and 10th Baronet; *b* 27 Sept 1919; *s* 1989; *ed* RNC Dartmouth: *m* 1956, Maxine, only da of late James Adrian Hayden Scott, and formerly wife of Michael John Willson Levien, and has issue.

Arms – Quarterly, 1st and 4th gules a chevron ermine between three trefoils slipped argent, *Meade*; 2nd and 3rd quarterly, 1st and 4th azure, three peewits argent, *Magill*, 2nd and 3rd per chevron argent and vert, three stags trippant proper, *Hawkins*. **Crest** – An eagle with two heads displayed sable, armed or. **Supporters** – *Dexter*, an eagle close sable; *sinister*, a falcon close proper, both plain collared and chained or.
Residence – Blundells House, Tisbury, Wilts. *Club* – Turf.

SON LIVING

PATRICK JAMES (*Lord Gillford*), *b* 28 Dec 1960: *m* 1989, Serena Emily, adopted da of Lt-Col Brian Joseph Lockhart, of Maugersbury, Glos (*see* L Gray, colls), and has issue:—
DAUGHTER LIVING *Hon* Tamara Louise, *b* 1990.

DAUGHTERS LIVING

Lady Rowena Katherine, *b* 1957: *m* 1991, as his 2nd wife, (Patrick) James Crichton-Stuart (*see* M Bute, colls). *Residence* – 1 Sloane Gdns, SW1.
Lady Tania Frances, *b* 1963: *m* 1989, as his 2nd wife, James Alwyne Compton (*see* M Northampton, colls). *Residence* – Coombe Cottage,

SISTER LIVING (*Raised to the rank of an Earl's daughter*, 1990)

Lady Jean Mary, *b* 1917: *m* 1943, Brig Michael James Babington Smith, CBE, TD, who *d* 1984, eldest son of late Sir Henry Babington Smith, GBE, CH, KCB, CSI (*see* E Elgin, 1944 Edn), and has issue living, Alan Babington, *b* 1946; *ed* Eton, and Trin Coll, Camb, — Louisa, *b* 1944: *m* 1967, Lt-Col James Richard Macfarlane, Coldm Gds, of Riverwood, Wickham, Hants PO1Y 5AY, and has issue living, Edward Michael Richard *b* 1969; Capt Coldm Gds, David Peter *b* 1970, — Susan Mary, *b* 1950: *m* 1979, John Henry Hemming, CMG, of 10 Edwardes Sq, W8, and has issue living, Henry Sebastian *b* 1979, Beatrice Margaret Louisa *b* 1981.

DAUGHTERS LIVING OF SIXTH EARL

Lady Selina Catherine, *b* 1950: *m* 1972, Nicholas George Lawrence Timpson, and has issue (*see* Houstoun-Boswall, Bt). *Residence* – Ardington Croft, Wantage, Oxon.
Lady Mary Jane (*Countess of Belmore*), *b* 1952: *m* 1984, 8th Earl of Belmore, of Castle Coole, Enniskillen, co Fermanagh, and has issue. *Residence* – Castle Coole, Enniskillen, co Fermanagh.
Lady Julia Elizabeth, *b* 1953: *m* 1985, as his 2nd wife, Robert Ralph Scrymgeour Hiscox, son of late Ralph Hiscox, CBE, and has issue living, Milo Edmund, *b* 1987, — Henry Charles, *b* 1989, — Sidney John, *b* 1993. *Residence* – Rainscombe Park, Oare, Marlborough, Wilts SN8 4HZ.
Lady Laura Louise, *b* 1957: *m* 1981, W. Scott B. Reid, son of Howard A. Reid, of Bronxville, New York, USA, and has issue living, Nicholas John Howard, *b* 1982, — Amelia Louise Catherine, *b* 1984, — Clementine Julia, *b* 1988.
Lady Katharine Anne, *b* 1959: *m* 1987, Christopher Aubrey Hamilton Wills, elder son of Hon Victor Patrick Hamilton Wills, and has issue (*see* B Dulverton). *Residence* – Litchfield Down, Whitchurch, Hants.
Lady Sophia Hester, *b* 1963: *m* 1990, Jonathan G. Heywood, son of Brig Anthony Heywood, of Monkton House, Monkton Deverill, Wilts, and has issue living, a son, *b* 1993.

WIDOW LIVING OF SIXTH EARL

CATHERINE (*Dowager Countess of Clanwilliam*), yst da of late Arthur Thomas Loyd, OBE, of Lockinge, Wantage, Berks: *m* 1948, Maj the 6th Earl, who *d* 1989. *Residence* – Maizley Cottage, Oare, Marlborough, Wilts SN8 4HZ.

COLLATERAL BRANCHES LIVING

Granddaughters of late Adm Hon Sir Herbert MEADE-FETHERSTONHAUGH, GCVO, CB, DSO (who assumed by Royal licence 1932 the surname of Fetherstonhaugh after Meade, and the arms quarterly), 3rd son of 4th Earl:—
Issue of late Richard James MEADE-FETHERSTONHAUGH, *b* 1913, *d* 1958: *m* 1948, Jean Phyllis (14 Limerston St, SW10; Uppark, Petersfield), da of late Maj Basil Falkner:—
Harriet Sarah, *b* 1949: *m* 1969, John de Bianchi Cossart, of Uppark, Petersfield, Hants, and 6 Darlan Rd, SW6 5BT, and has issue living, Charles Richard, *b* 1972, — Edward James, *b* 1984, — Henrietta-Maria *b* 1974. —— Emma Mary, *b* 1951: *m* 1976, Geoffrey Wanklyn Goad, of Deerkeepers, Uppark, Petersfield, Hants, and has issue living, Oliver Edward, *b* 1977, — Harry Frederick, *b* 1978, — Matilda Rose, *b* 1989. —— Sophia Theresa, *b* 1954: *m* 1985, Angus Warre, of Dalcross Castle, Croy, Inverness, eldest son of Maj John Antony Warre, MC, of Barrowden, Oakham, Rutland (*see* D Devonshire, 1973-74 Edn), and has issue living, Theodora, *b* 1986.

Grandchildren of late Sir Robert Henry Meade, GCB, 2nd son of 3rd Earl:—
Issue of late Charles Francis Meade, *b* 1881, *d* 1975: *m* 1913, Lady Aileen Hilda Brodrick, who *d* 1970, da of 1st Earl of Midleton:—
Simon Robert Jasper (Pen-y-lan, Meifod, Montgomeryshire), *b* 1928: *m* 1957, Lady Sophia Catherine Gathorne-Hardy, da of 4th Earl of Cranbrook, and has issue living, Jasper, *b* 1962, — Benjamin, *b* 1963, — Camilla, *b* 1958, — Rachel *b* 1965. —— Evelyn Clodagh, *b* 1916: *m* 1940, Colin Hercules Mackenzie, CMG, who *d* 1986, of Kyle House, Kyleakin, I of Skye, only son of late Maj-Gen Sir Colin John Mackenzie, KCB, and has issue living, Christian Fiona, *b* 1941: *m* 1966, (Charles) Nicholas Phipps, of Baldromma Christian, Onchan, Isle of Man (*see* D Buccleuch, 1990 Edn), and has issue living, Charles

Mackenzie *b* 1967, Alice Christian *b* 1969. —— Flavia Mary (*Baroness Ebbisham*), *b* 1920: *m* 1949, 2nd Baron Ebbisham, who *d* 1991.

Granddaughters of late Francis Henry Meade, CBE, only son of late Rev Hon Sidney Meade, 3rd son of 3rd Earl:—
Issue of late Lt-Col Robert Sidney Stuart Meade, *b* 1901, *d* 1971:*m* 1st, 1930, Veronica Augusta, who *d* 1968, da of Lt-Col Herbert Vere Wilbraham; 2ndly, 1970, Baroness Maria Elisabeth Johanna Rosalia Ottilia (The Hangingshaw, Selkirk), da of late Baron August Hermann Georg Victor Ramberg, Capt Imperial Austrian Navy, and widow of Count Ferdinand Zdenko Karl Emmerick Maria von Thun und Hohenstein:—
(By 1st *m*) Daphne Theresa, *b* 1936. —— Jane Cecilia (New English Art Club), *b* 1940: *m* 1967, Col David Henry George Corsellis, c/o Nat Westminster Bank, Bishops Stortford, Herts, and has issue living, Nicholas Robert Alexander, *b* 1968; Bar, Lincoln's Inn 1993. —— James Henry Merrick, *b* 1970.

Grandchildren of late Capt John Percy Meade, elder son of Capt John Meade, of Earsham Hall, Norfolk, and Burrenwood, co Down, yr son of Lt-Gen Hon Robert Meade, 2nd son of 1st Earl:—
Issue of Maj John Windham Meade, *b* 1894, *d* 1984: *m* 1932, Grace Dorothea, JP, who *d* 1977, da of late Sir Cecil Fane De Salis, KCB:—
John Michael (Manor Farm House, Hedenham, Bungay, Suffolk), *b* 1935; *ed* Stowe: *m* 1967, Princess Valentine, 2nd da of late Prince Nicholas Galitzine, and has issue living, Nicholas, *b* 1969, — Catherine, *b* 1968, — Tatiana, *b* (twin) 1968: *m* 1994, Prince Andrei Mikhailovitch Galitzine, son of Prince Mikhail V. Galitzine, of Moscow, — Elizabeth, *b* 1971. —— Francis Windham (Earsham Lodge, Bungay, Suffolk), *b* 1941; *ed* Stowe, and London Univ (BSc 1962). —— Theodosia Frances, *b* 1932.

PREDECESSORS – (1) Sir JOHN MEADE, KB; MP successively for Dublin Univ and co Tipperary, and Attorney-Gen to James, Duke of York; *cr* a *Baronet* of Ireland 1703; *d* 1711; *s* by his son (2) Sir PIERCE, 2nd Bt; *dsp*; *s* by his brother (3) Sir RICHARD, 3rd Bt; *d* 1744; *s* by his son (4) Sir JOHN, 4th Bt; *cr Baron Gillford* and *Viscount Clanwilliam* (peerage of Ireland) 1766, and *Earl of Clanwilliam* (peerage of Ireland) 1776; *d* 1800; *s* by his son (5) RICHARD, 2nd Earl; *d* 1805; *s* by his son (6) RICHARD, GCH, 3rd Earl; *b* 1795; Under-Sec for Foreign Affairs 1822, and Ambassador at Berlin 1823-8; *cr Baron Clanwilliam, co Tipperary* (peerage of United Kingdom) 1828: *m* 1830, Lady Elizabeth Herbert, who *d* 1858, da of 11th Earl of Pembroke; *d* 1879; *s* by his son (7) RICHARD JAMES, GCB, KCMG, 4th Earl; *b* 1832; an Adm of the Fleet; a Naval ADC to HM Queen Victoria 1872-6, and a Lord of the Admiralty 1874-80: *m* 1867, Elizabeth Henrietta, who *d* 1925, el da of late Sir Arthur Edward Kennedy; *d* 1907; *s* by his second son (8) ARTHUR VESEY, MC, 5th Earl, *b* 1873; was Capt and Adj Roy Horse Guards, and Assist Provost Marshal; S Africa 1900-02, European War 1914-18 (MC): *m* 1909, Muriel Mary Temple, MBE, who *d* 1952, da of Russell Stephenson and widow of Hon Oliver Howard (E Carlisle); *d* 1953; *s* by his only son (9) JOHN CHARLES EDMUND CARSON, 6th Earl; *b* 1914; Maj Coldm Gds, Lord Lieut co Down; European War 1939-45 in Middle East (despatches twice): *m* 1948, Catherine, yst da of late Arthur Thomas Loyd, OBE, of Lockinge, Wantage, Berks; *d* 1989; *s* by his cousin (10) JOHN HERBERT (yr son of late Adm Hon Sir Herbert Meade-Fetherstonhaugh, GCVO, CB, DSO, 3rd son of 4th Earl), 7th Earl and present peer; also Viscount Clanwilliam, Baron Clanwilliam, and Baron Gillford.

CLARENDON, EARL OF (Villiers) (Earl GB 1776)
(Name pronounced "Villers")

GEORGE FREDERICK LAURENCE HYDE VILLIERS, 7th Earl; *b* 2 Feb 1933; *s* 1955; *ed* Eton, and Madrid Univ; Page of Honour to HM King George VI 1948-49; Managing Dir of Seccombe, Marshall and Campion plc 1962-93 (and Chm 1985-93); Lt RHG (AER): *m* 1974, Jane Diana, da of Edward William Dawson, of Idmiston, Salisbury, Wilts, and has issue.

Arms – Argent, a cross gules, charged with five escallops or. **Crest** – A lion rampant argent ducally crowned or. **Supporters** – Two eagles, wings expanded and inverted sable, beaked, membered, and ducally crowned or, and charged on the breast with a plain cross argent.
Residences – 5 Astell St, SW3 3RT; Soberton Mill, Swanmore, Hants SO3 2QF.

The cross, the test of faith

SON LIVING

GEORGE EDWARD LAURENCE (*Lord Hyde*), *b* 12 Feb 1976; Page of Honour to HM The Queen 1988-90.

DAUGHTER LIVING

Lady Sarah Katherine Jane, *b* 1977.

SISTER LIVING (Raised to the rank of an Earl's daughter 1956)

Lady Rosemary Verena Edith (*posthumous*), *b* 1935: *m* 1959, Richard Hugh Jordan Steel, el son of Sir Christopher Eden Steel, GCMG, MVO (Buxton, Bt, colls), and has issue living, James Thomas Jordan (66 Manville Rd, SW17 8JL), *b* 1960: *m* 1989, Lindsay J., elder da of Michael Farrell, of Much Hadham, Herts, and has issue living, Frederick James Edward *b* 1993, Sophie Mary Verena *b* 1991, — Oliver George Nigel, *b* 1962: *m* 1992, Jacqueline E., yr da of Colin Quaife, of Lea, Wilts, — Arabella Rosemary Louise, *b* 1966. *Residence* – Glebe House, Notgrove, Cheltenham, Glos.

UNCLE LIVING (Son of 6th Earl)

Hon (William) Nicholas Somers Laurence Hyde, *b* 1916; *ed* Eton, and at New Coll, Oxford; Maj Gren Gds (SR), ERD; a JP for Hants, and an OStJ: *m* 1939, Mary Cecilia Georgina, da of Maj Hon Edric Alfred Cecil Weld-Forester, CVO (*see* B Forester), and has issue living, Caroline Jane (21 Glycena Rd, SW11 5TP), *b* 1940: *m* 1964 (*m diss* 1974), J. Kenneth Havard, — Nerena Anne Hyde (Old Posting House, Didmarton, nr Badminton, Glos), *b* 1941: *m* 1966 (*m diss* 1980), Timothy Congreve Stephenson (V Hawarden, colls), and has issue living Guy Congreve *b* 1969, Henry Frederick *b* 1978, Lucinda Mary Pamela *b* 1967, Henrietta Cecilia *b* 1975, — (Elizabeth) Georgina Gail, *b* 1952: *m* 1980, Edward R. R. Jewson, of Wacton House,

Norwich, Norfolk NR15 2UF, only son of late Col John Jewson, MC, of Mergate Hall, Norwich, and has issue living, Sophie Emily Josceline *b* 1987, Isobel Mary Elizabeth *b* 1988. *Residence* – Firs Farm, Milbourne, Malmesbury, Wilts.

COLLATERAL BRANCHES LIVING

Grandchildren of late Rt Hon Sir Francis Hyde Villiers, GCMG, CB, 4th son of 4th Earl:—
Issue of late Eric Hyde Villiers, DSO, Capt Highland LI, *b* 1881, *d* 1964: *m* 1928, Joan Ankaret, who *d* 1986, da of late John Edward Talbot (*see* E Shrewsbury, colls):—
Henry Hyde (Icknor House, South Green, Sittingbourne, Kent; *Club* – Boodle's), *b* 1931; *ed* Wellington Coll; JP Kent and High Sheriff 1992: *m* 1959 Mary Elizabeth Cavan, da of Robert Hugh Swan Corbett, of Yalding, Kent, and has issue living Charles James Hyde, *b* 1967, — Robert Henry Hyde, *b* 1969, — Charlotte Amelia, *b* 1961: *m* 1988, Christopher H. C. Figg, eldest son of Sir Leonard Clifford William Figg, KCMG, of Great Missenden, Bucks, and has issue living, Orlando *b* 1992, — Henrietta Barbara, *b* 1962: *m* 1986, Alastair Henderson Scott, son of Paul Henderson Scott, CMG, of 109 Keyes House, Dolphin Sq, SW1. —— James Michael Hyde (59 Maltravers St, Arundel, Sussex), *b* 1933; *ed* Wellington Coll; actor: *m* 1966 (*m diss* 1984), Patricia, da of William Victor Donovan, of Fern House, Pembroke. ——John Francis Hyde (21 Overstrand Mansions, Prince of Wales Drive, SW11 4EZ), *b* 1936; *ed* Winchester, and King's Coll, Camb (MA, PhD); Fellow Royal Asiatic Soc, and FRSA: *m* 1958 (Myee) Miranda, el da of Lt-Col David McKenna, CBE (*see* E Albemarle), and has issue living, Daniel James Hyde, *b* 1960, — Cecilia Ankaret, *b* 1962: *m* 1983, David Michael Holdsworth, of Vigeau, St Mézard, Lectoure, 32700 France, yr son of G. M. Holdsworth, of Seal, Kent, — Antonia Aniela, *b* 1965, — Susanna Sophia (twin), *b* 1965.

Grandchildren of late Algernon Hyde Villiers, Lieut Yeo, attached Machine Gun Corps (*ka* 1917), 3rd and yst son of late Rt Hon Sir Francis Hyde Villiers, GCMG, CB (ante):—
Issue of late Lt-Col Sir Charles English Hyde Villiers, MC, sometime Chm British Steel Corpn, *b* 1912, *d* 1992: *m* 1st, 1938, Pamela Constance, who *d* 1943, da of late Maj John Flower, 60th Rifles; 2ndly, 1946, Marie José (*Lady Villiers*) (Blacknest House, Sunninghill, Berks), da of Comte Henri de la Barre d'Erquelinnes, of Jurbise, Belgium:—
(By 1st *m*) Nicholas Hyde (St Leonard's Grange, Beaulieu, Hants), *b* 1939; *ed* Eton; late Lieut Gren Guards (AER): *m* 1983, Hon Mrs Catherine Mary Wilbraham, 2nd da of 1st Viscount De L'Isle, VC, KG, GCMG, GCVO, PC. —— (By 2nd *m*) Diana Mary, *b* 1947: *m* 1976, Ambassador John Dimitri Negroponte, US Foreign Ser. —— Anne Hyde, *b* 1950: *m* 1st, 1973, Paul Nuttall Kesterton; 2ndly, 1993, Thomas Martin, and has issue living (by 1st *m*), Toby, *b* 1977, — Lara Beatrice, *b* 1979.

Grandchildren of late Edward Ernest Villiers, only son of late Col Ernest Villiers, eldest son of Hon Edward Ernest Villiers, 3rd brother of 4th Earl:—
Issue of late Capt Algernon Edward Villiers, *b* 1892, *d* 1991: *m* 1924, Annie Augusta Merewether, who *d* 1978, da of late George Latham Massy, of Berridge, Sunningdale:—
George Edward, TD (73 Carlton Hill, NW8; *Club* – Boodle's), *b* 1931; *ed* Wellington Coll, and Brasenose Coll, Oxford (MA); late Maj Berks and Westminster Dragoons (TA), late Lieut RHA: *m* 1962, Anne Virginia, elder da of late Cuthbert Raymond Forster Threlfall, of Warstone House, Bewdley, Worcs, and has issue living, Edward Richard, *b* 1963, — Henry Raymond, *b* 1965, — Theresa Anne, *b* 1968. —— Elizabeth Anne, *b* 1925. —— Barbara Jane (Flat 17, 55 Shepherd's Hill, N6 5QP), *b* 1927.

Granddaughters of late Rev Henry Montagu Villiers (*b* 1837), el son of Rt Rev Henry Montague Villiers, Bishop of Durham, 4th and yst brother of 4th Earl:—
Issue of late Henry Montagu Villiers, MVO, *b* 1863, *d* 1948: *m* 1896, Carmen, who *d* 1953, da of late Dr Luhrsen, Envoy Extraor, and Min Plen for German Empire in Colombia, S America:—
Margaret Adelaide Rhoda, *b* 1913: *m* 1936, Rupert Huber, and has issue living, Anita Margaret, *b* 1939: *m* 1958, Eduard Bacher, of Wildbichl, Tirol, Austria, and has issue living, Hannes *b* 1959, Ewald *b* 1960, Tristan *b* 1964, Christoph *b* 1966, — Renate Krexentia, *b* 1941. *Residence* – Villa Hubertus, Kossen, Tyrol, Austria. —— Margaret Anne Theresa (twin), *b* 1913: *m* 1940, Ronald Basil Strickland, of Bow River, W Australia, and has issue living, John Montague, *b* 1940; Fl Cdr and Sqdn Ldr RAAF: *m* 1967, Elsa Rosen, — Mark Henry (Bull Creek, W Australia), *b* 1947: *m* 1972, Margaret Walker, and has issue living, Stuart *b* 1976, Margaret *b* 1974, — Neil William (Bedford, W Australia), *b* 1948: *m* 1968, Wendy Baker, and has issue living, Paulette *b* 1969, Cassandra *b* 1972, — Edward George (Canberra, Australia), *b* 1949, — Robert Clive, *b* 1956; BA W Australia Univ: *m* 1975, Linda Williams, — Tora Lillian, *b* 1944: *m* 1963, Terence McNamara, of Newman, W Australia, and has issue living, Michelle, *b* 1967, Marina *b* 1969, — Thea *b* 1973, — Ronda Christine, *b* 1951: *m* 1968, Robert Kemmers, of Girrawheen, W Australia, and has issue living, Robert *b* 1972, Catherine *b* 1968, — Terri Ann, *b* 1952: *m* 1970, Frank Ebbett, of Bow River, W Australia, and has issue living, Neil *b* 1975, Debra *b* 1971, Sandra *b* 1973.

Grandchildren of late Henry Montagu Villiers, MVO (*b* 1863) (ante):—
Issue of late Cdr George Dumba Villiers, RN, *b* 1900, *d* 1977: *m* 1926, Anne Hilda Whellens, who *d* 1990, da of late James Barton Hall, of Longframlington, Northumberland:—
Simon William George (8 Earl's Rd, Tunbridge Wells, Kent TN4 SE8), *b* 1927; Maj RA (ret), attached to Malay Regt, Malaya 1958 (despatches, Order of Ali Manghu Negra): *m* 1956, Patricia de Lacey, and has issue living, Clive Matthew George, *b* 1957, — Virginia Anne *b* 1959: *m* 1979, Nigel Mark Batchelor, of Parkfield, Wallaford Rd, Buckfastleigh, Devon, and has issue living, Matthew Joseph *b* 1979, Christopher Luke *b* 1981, — Moira Lillian (31 Bramley Hill, Mere, nr Warminster, Wilts BA12 6JX), *b* 1963: *m* 1983, Terence Michael Rodden, and has issue living, Sally Anne *b* 1985. —— Janet Mary (The Cottage, Aldersey Rd, Guildford) *b* 1929; formerly Head Mistress of Middle Sch, Tormead Sch for Girls, Guildford.
Issue of late Edmund Rollo Stanley Villiers, *b* 1909, *d* 1960: *m* 1st, 1934 (*m diss* 1957), Margit Cleland, da of late Robert Rogerson, of Marchmount, Dumfries; 2ndly, 1957, Christine Joan (13 Lowndes Square, SW1), da of late Com W. O. H. Lambert, RN, of The Toll, Buxted, Sussex:—
(By 1st *m*) Charles Russell (Wargrave Lodge, Wargrave-on-Thames, Berkshire), *b* 1938; *ed* Cheltenham, and Corpus Christi Coll, Camb (BA), MB, BCir, DMRD; FFR: *m* 1971, Barbara Clare, 3rd da of Fredwin R. McMaster, of Nottinghill, Belfast.

Grandchildren of late John Russell Villiers, 2nd son of late Rev Henry Montagu Villiers (*b* 1837) (ante):—
Issue of late Arthur Henry Villiers, MC, *b* 1894, *d* 1975: *m* 1919, Vera Adeline (who *d* 1976), da of late Charles Howe, of Durban, Natal:—
Peter William (13 Welbeck Rd, Harrow, Middx HA2 ORN), *b* 1922; *ed* Lancing Coll; late Lt KRRC; film producer: *m* 1st, 1945 (*m diss* 1958), June, only child of W. Friedhoff; 2ndly, 1959, Alice, da of A. J. Startup, and has had issue (by 1st *m*), Roger Peter, *b* 1946: *m* 1975, Julia Helen, da of A. S. Rymer, and has issue living, Mark Roger *b* 1980, Helen Fiona *b* 1977, — Jennifer Ann, *b* 1948, *d* 1970. —— Geoffrey Richard (1301 Jefferson St, Napa, Calif, USA), *b* 1924; *ed* Lancing Coll; 1939-45 War as Sub-Lt RNVR: *m* 1948, Janet Myra, da of Dr Leonard W. Trott, of Adelaide, S Aust, and has issue living, Mary Jane, *b* 1954, — Lisa Kathleen, *b* 1959: *m* 1988, George Emerson Smith, of 1815 Silverado Trail, Napa, Calif 94558. —— Christopher Nigel, *b* 1929; *ed* Lancing Coll: *m* 1953 (*m diss* 1964), Brenda Margaret, yr da of D. R. Penny, of Ferring, Sussex, and has issue living, Nigel Richard, *b* 1956: *m* 1980, Valerie Reeling, and has issue living, Kirstie June, *b* 1982, — Gillian Grace, *b* 1958: *m* 1977 (*m diss* 1984), Alan Lawrence, Sussex, and has issue living, Charlene Louise *b* 1978.
Issue of late Brig Richard Montagu Villiers, DSO, *b* 1905, *d* 1973: *m* 1932, Nancy (4 Orford Mews, Puddletown, Dorchester, Dorset DT2 8TL), el da of late Lt-Gen Sir Charles Alexander Campbell Godwin, KCB, CMG, DSO:—
Timothy Charles *b* 1943; *ed* Eton, and RMA; Lt-Col 15th/19th Hus: *m* 1971, Maureen, da of late Ven R. G. H. McCahearty, and has issue living, Nicholas Charles, *b* 1976, — Richard Henry *b* 1980, — Louise Elizabeth, *b* 1973. —— Judith Annette, *b*

1935: *m* 1960, Brig Rupert H. G. McCarthy, 15th/19th KRH, of Rew Cottage, Buckland Newton, Dorchester DT2 7DN, and has issue living, William Rupert, *b* 1963, — Sarah Victoria, *b* 1961, — Meriel Anne, *b* 1966. —— Victoria Belinda, *b* 1938: *m* 1963, Robert Quentin Yeatman, of 9 Clarendon Rd, Cambridge CB2 2BH, and has issue living, Catherine Victoria, *b* 1964, — Lucy Belinda, *b* 1966. — Rosanna Charlotte, *b* 1973. —— Carol Elspeth, *b* 1944: *m* 1st, 1965, Gerald Charles Mordaunt (*see* Mordaunt, Bt, colls); 2ndly, 1984, as his 3rd wife, Maj Charles Cyril Willmott Hammick (*see* Hammick, Bt, colls), who *d* 1990. *Residence* – Higher Waterston Farm, Dorchester, Dorset DT2 7SW.

Grandchildren of late Com Thomas Hyde Villiers, RN (*infra*):—
Issue of late Nicholas Lister Villiers, *b* 1926, *d* 1984: *m* 1954, Betty Midelton (Heatherlands, Orford Rd, Bromeswell, nr Woodbridge, Suffolk IP12 2PP), 2nd da of Sidney Ralph Midelton Barlow, of Wayside, Chalfont St Giles, Bucks:—
Derek Midelton Lister (Willows End, Orford Rd, Bromeswell, nr Woodbridge, Suffolk IP12 2PP), *b* 1958: *m* 1984, Deborah, da of Christopher John Randall, of 22 Glos Glanlliw, Pontlliw, Swansea, Glam, and has issue living, Nicholas Christopher Lister, *b* 1985, — George Alexander, *b* 1991, — Catriona Sarah, *b* 1987. —— Caroline Patricia (8 Ravenswood, New Town Rd, Colchester, Essex CO1 2EG), *b* 1960.

Grandson of Sir Thomas Lister Villiers, 3rd son of Rev Henry Montagu Villiers (*b* 1837) (*ante*):—
Issue of late Com Thomas Hyde Villiers, RN, *b* 1902, *d* 1955: *m* 1925, Eleanor, who *d* 1958, da of late Francis Edgar Croft (Croft, Bt, *cr* 1818, colls):—
Stephen Hyde (52 Church Road, Brightlingsea, Essex), *b* 1931; *ed* Eton: *m* 1958, Elizabeth Jill, da of John Stewart Jeffrey Chapple, of Clayton, Hadham Road, Bishop's Stortford, Herts, and has issue living, Harry Hyde, *b* 1959, — Timothy Stewart, *b* 1960, — Hugo James, *b* 1962, — Lucinda Victoria, *b* 1961.

Granddaughters of late Rev Henry Montagu Villiers (*b* 1837) (*ante*):—
Issue of late Godfrey Robert Randall Villiers, *b* 1877, *d* 1925: *m* 1967, Sylvia, who *d* 1926, da of late Dr James Moore Bennett, formerly of Princes Road, Liverpool:—
Sylvia Betty, *b* 1915: *m* 1934, Stavros Sirakos, and has issue living, Denise Catherine, *b* 1935: *m* 1961, Philippe Moulierac, and has issue living, Christopher *b* 1964, Pascale *b* 1967.
Issue of late Maj Paul Frederick Villiers, DSO, *b* 1884, *d* 1968: *m* 1912, Evelyn, who *d* 1973, da of late Edward Webb:—
Pauline Mary Lethbridge (8 St Lucia, West Parade, Bexhill on Sea, E Sussex TN39 3DT), *b* 1914: *m* 1936, Dennis Estyn Dunnill, MB BS, MRCS, LRCP, DA, who *d* 1986, and has issue living, Richard Paul Hyde (Dairy Farm House, Avon, nr Ringwood, Hants BH23 7BG), *b* 1945; MB BS, LRCP, MRCS, FFARCS; *ed* Charterhouse, and Guy's Hosp: *m* 1st, 1971 (*m diss* 1977), Rosamund Strange; 2ndly, 1978, Charlotte Gorter, and has issue living (by 1st *m*), Robert James Hyde *b* 1975, (by 2nd *m*) Charles William Hyde *b* 1981, Elizabeth Anna *b* 1979, Sarah Denise *b* 1986, — Veronica Mary, *b* 1937: *m* 1st, 1963 (*m diss* 1973), Timothy Mawdsley Welch; 2ndly, 1982, Andrew Charles Gottlieb, of 34 Boston Close, Sovereign Harbour, Eastbourne BN23 6RA, and has issue living (by 1st *m*), Andrew Ronald Mawdsley *b* 1968, Nicola Mary *b* 1966, — Angela Evelyn, *b* 1939; JP W Yorks: *m* 1966, William Raymond Barker, of 109 Tadcaster Rd, Dringhouses, York YO2 2XA, and has issue living, Christopher Paul Howard *b* 1967, Caroline Susan *b* 1969.
Issue of late Capt Gerald Berkeley Villiers, OBE, RN, *b* 1885, *d* 1959: *m* 1918, Rachel Joan, da of late Rev Henry Vernon Heber Percy (*see* D Northumberland, colls):—
Anthony Henry Heber, *b* 1921; Capt late Gren Gds; 1939-45 War: *m* 1948, Rosemary Elizabeth, da of late Maj (William) Bertram Bell, 12th Lancers (By Barrymore), and has had issue, (Anthony James) Valentine (The Kennels, Petworth Park, Petworth, W Sussex GU28 9LR), *b* 1949: *m* 1st, 1974, Sally Wilson; 2ndly, 1984, Sara A., da of Basil Gotto, of Willowhill House, Carrigaline, co Cork, and has issue living, (by 1st *m*) Henry Anthony Edward *b* 1978, (by 2nd *m*) Delia Dorothy *b* 1989, Geraldine Olive *b* 1990, — †Charles Henry, *b* 1954; *ed* Milton Abbey; *d* 1980, — (Rosemary) Henrietta Dorothy, *b* 1950: *m* 1st, 1973 (*m diss* 1983), (Nigel Graham Cedric) Peregrine Banbury; 2ndly, 1978, William Murray Lucas, who *d* 1982, and has an adopted da, Elizabeth Jacquetta *b* 1981, — Emma Helen, *b* 1963: *m* 1988, Richard Henry Ronald Benyon, and has issue (*see* Shelley, Bt, colls). *Residence* – The Old Priory, N Woodchester, Stroud, Glos. *Club* – Guards'.

Grandchildren of late Maj Oliver George Graham Villiers, DSO (*infra*):—
Issue of late W/Cdr David Hugh Villiers, DFC, *b* 1921, *d* 1962: *m* 1st, 1942 (*m diss* 1948), Patricia, only child of late Richard Payne; 2ndly, 1954, Elizabeth Barbara (who *m* 2ndly, 1992, Capt John B. Rumble, of White Horse Cottage, School St, Stoke-by-Nayland, Suffolk CO6 4QY) (assumed by deed poll 1949 the surname of Prideaux in lieu of her patronymic), da of late Horace Leonard Hobbins:—
(By 1st *m*) Robin Julian, *b* 1945: *m* 1974, Birgitte, da of Peter Stafford. —— (By 2nd *m*) Christopher Francis (100 Elsenham St, SW18 5NT), *b* 1958; actor: *m* 1985, Katherine, only da of William Threlfall, of SW6, and has issue living, Charles Sebastian, *b* 1987, — Frederick James, *b* 1988. —— Jonathan Paul, *b* 1961. —— Catherine Judith, *b* 1955.

Granddaughter of late Rev Henry Montagu Villiers (*b* 1837) (*ante*):—
Issue of late Maj Oliver George Graham Villiers, DSO, *b* 1886, *d* 1981: *m* 1918, Aleen Judith, who *d* 1976, da of late Rev Henry Vernon Heber-Percy (D Northumberland, colls):—
(Judith) Rosemary (3 West End, Spilsby, Lincs PE23 5ED), *b* 1919: *m* 1949, Peter George Locke-Wheaton, who *d* 1981, and has issue living, Henry George (17 Avebury Rd, Penhill, Swindon), *b* 1950: *m* 1973 (*m diss* 1986), Cynthia Jane, da of Eric Bagley, and has issue living, David George *b* 1983, Sarah Jane *b* 1977, Annabelle *b* 1980, — John Antony Charles (18 Evergreen Drive, Calcot, Reading, Berks), *b* 1952; MA (Cantab): *m* 1977, Margaret Patricia, da of late Rev George Clifford Hunt, and has issue living, Stephen Antony *b* 1983, Jennifer Anne *b* 1981, — Philip James (64 Baldwin Rd, Kidderminster, Worcs), *b* 1955: *m* 1980, Janet Rosemary, da of George Dakers, and has issue living, Daniel Philip *b* 1981, Luke Peter *b* 1983, Simon George *b* 1990, Naomi Janet *b* 1985, Miriam Rachel *b* 1988, — Richard Oliver (Mill Cottage, Toynton-all-Saints, Lincs), *b* 1957: *m* 1979, Janice Sheila, da of Peter Rothery, and has issue living, Christopher James *b* 1985, Nicola Claire *b* 1983, — (Henrietta) Mary-Anne, *b* 1951: *m* 1st, 1970 (*m diss* 1975), Richard Peter Noble; 2ndly, 1982, Graham Roy Elliker, of Robups, The Common, W Chiltington, W Sussex, and has issue living (by 1st *m*), Sarah Louise *b* 1974, (by 2nd *m*) Hallam Piers Oliver *b* 1983, Camilla Aleen *b* 1987, — Caroline Susan-Ann (76 Newmarket Rd, Bulwell, Nottingham), *b* 1953: *m* 1979 (*m diss* 1989), Capt Paul Hendy (Salvation Army), and has issue living, Stuart James *b* 1982, Corrine Louise *b* 1981.

Grandson of late Lt-Col Charles Walter Villiers, CBE, 2nd son of late Capt Frederick Ernest Villiers (*infra*):—
Issue of late Lt-Col (Francis) Berkeley Hyde Villiers, OBE, *b* 1906, *d* 1991: *m* 1938, Rose Marie (Stone House, Stone, nr Kidderminster, Worcs), da of Consul Gen von Passavant, of Vienna:—
Nicholas Hyde, *b* 1939; *ed* Eton. *Residence* – Stone House, Stone, nr Kidderminster, Worcs.

Grandchildren of late Capt Frederick Ernest Villiers, yr son of Rt Rev Hon Henry Montagu Villiers, DD, (*ante*):—
Issue of late Reginald Hyde Villiers, DSO, *b* 1876, *d* 1953: *m* 1906, Florence Marianne, who *d* 1937, da of Dr George Stockwell, formerly of Dunedin, New Zealand:—
Frederick Montagu Hyde (Braemar, 13 Dixon Rd, Buderim, Queensland 4556, Australia), *b* 1907; late Maj Ceylon LI: *m* 1st, 1936 (*m diss* 1947), Maisie Marguerite Hunt; 2ndly, 1948 (*m diss* 1959), Ann Sybella, da of Rev Nixon Chetwode Ram, of Petersfield, Hants, and formerly wife of Count Carl Otto Werner Schimmelmann, of Ahrensburg, Holstein; 3rdly, 1959, Sheila

Joyce, 3rd da of late Charles Alexander Squair, of Reigate, Surrey, and widow of Douglas Montague Baird, and has living issue (by 1st *m*), Judith Marianne, *b* 1937: *m* 1st, 1958 (*m diss* 1973), David Price; 2ndly, 1991, Geoffrey Alan Hill, of Hatfield Park, Limestone Rd, Yea, Victoria 3717, Australia, and has issue living (by 1st *m*), Brett Alexander Hyde (Bayswater, Melbourne, Victoria 3153, Australia) *b* 1960: *m* 1986, Lindy Sue Ferry (and has issue living, Maddison Hyde *b* 1988), James Stuart (Bayswater, Melbourne, Victoria 3153, Australia) *b* 1961: *m* 1987, Roslyn Anne Dimech (and has issue living, Brock David *b* 1987, Tamsin Jean *b* 1992).

Granddaughter of late Reginald Hyde Villiers, DSO (ante):—
Issue of late George Pelham Villiers, *b* 1909, *d* 1989: *m* 1st, 1937 (*m diss* 1945), Gladys Mildred Moehr, who *d* 1977; 2ndly, 1945, Ursula Alison Paterson, who *d* 1957, da of John Hodgson, of Kotapala, Ceylon; 3rdly, 1959, Kathleen Cooke, who *d* 1984:—
(By 1st *m*) Ursula Georgette Victoria Maria, *b* 1943: *m* 1st, 1965, Lieut John Philip Bear, RN, who *d* 1967; 2ndly, 1976, Capt Jonathan Alexander Burch, CBE, RN, and has issue living (by 1st *m*), Alexander George Philip Villiers, *b* 1966. *Residence* – 10 Pitman Court, Gloucester Rd, Lower Swainswick, Bath, Avon.

Grandchildren of late Evelyn Charles Arthur Villiers (infra):—
Issue of late Capt Robert Alexander Villiers, CBE, RN, *b* 1908, *d* 1990: *m* 1st, 1933, Leila Alexandra, who *d* 1938, eldest da of late Lt-Col William Alexander Victor Findlater, Royal Irish Fus, of The Croft, Tenterden, Kent; 2ndly, 1939 (*m diss* 1958), Elizabeth Mary, da of late Maj-Gen Arthur Leslie Irvine Friend, CB, CBE, MC, of Dynes Farm, Bethersden, Kent; 3rdly, 1960, (Irene) Mary (Robinsgreen, Warham, Sussex; 33 Ennismore Gdns, SW7), da of William Ellis-Jones, of W Kirby, Cheshire:—
(By 1st *m*) Diana Susan, *b* 1935: *m* 1963, Ian Buchanan Watt, CMG, who *d* 1988, of Kingswood House, 8 Lower Green Rd, Esher, Surrey, and has issue living, James Alexander Macdonald, *b* 1965, — Robert John Macdonald, *b* 1969, — Harriet Leila Elizabeth, *b* 1970. —— (By 2nd *m*) Michael Alexander (Woodhams Farm, Kings Worthy, Winchester, Hants SO23 7LB), *b* 1941; *ed* Eton, RMA Sandhurst, and Cranfield (MBA); commn'd 11th Hus 1959: *m* 1st, 1968 (*m diss* 1982), Vanessa Annabel, da of F. R. G. N. Sherrard, of South Lodge, Dorchester; 2ndly, 1989, Jean Annette Mary, da of late Brig Robert Angus Graham Binny, of Pitt Farm House, Skilgate, Taunton, Som (*see* E Coventry, colls, 1963 Edn), and formerly wife of Lt-Col William Robert Wilson FitzGerald, Royal Dragoons (*see* E Harrington, colls, 1941 Edn). —— Charles Nigel (8 Sutherland St, SW1), *b* (twin) 1941; *ed* Winchester, and New Coll, Oxford: *m* 1970, Sally Priscilla, da of late Capt D. H. Magnay, RN, and has issue living, Christopher Frederick Pelham, *b* 1976, — Caroline Harriet, *b* 1974. —— Sarah Jane Amanda, *b* 1956.

Granddaughter of late Capt Frederick Ernest Villiers (ante):—
Issue of late Evelyn Charles Arthur Villiers, *b* 1884, *d* 1968: *m* 1907, Dorothy Katherine, who *d* 1976, da of late Col George Howard Moore-Lane, CMG (*see* B Kinsale, colls, 1925 Edn):—
Marjorie Frances, *b* 1909: *m* 1932, Henry Samuel Malortie Hoare, and has issue living, Charles Antony Richard, *b* (Jan) 1934; *ed* King's Sch, Canterbury, and Merton Coll, Oxford (MA); Prof at Queen's Coll, Belfast, — Arthur Malortie, *b* (Dec) 1934; *ed* King's Sch, Canterbury, and Trin Coll, Oxford (MA, PhD), — Henry Ronald John, *b* 1936; *ed* King's Sch, Canterbury, and St John's Coll, Camb (BA, MSc), — Dorothy Ann Katherine, *b* 1945; *ed* St Hugh's Coll, Oxford (MA), — Janet Frances Mary, *b* 1948; *ed* St Aidan's Coll, Durham (BA). *Residence* – Sanctuary, Copers Cope Rd, Beckenham, KKent.

PREDECESSORS – (1) Rt Hon THOMAS Villiers, 2nd son of 2nd Earl of Jersey; successively Ambassador to Dresden, Poland, and Vienna, a Lord of the Admiralty, Joint Postmaster-Gen-Chancellor of the Duchy of Lancaster, and Ambassador to Berlin; *cr Baron Hyde*, of Hindon, Wilts (peerage of Great Britain) 1756, with remainder to the heirs male of his body by his then wife (Charlotte), da of 3rd Earl of Essex by Jane Hyde, da of 4th Earl of Clarendon (*cr* 1661), and in default to his said wife and the heirs male of her body, *Earl of Clarendon* (peerage of Great Britain) 1776, and a Baron of the Kingdom of Prussia 1782, which honour he received the Roy licence to enjoy; *d* 1786; *s* by his son (2) THOMAS, 2nd Earl; *d* unmarried 1824; *s* by his brother (3) JOHN CHARLES, 3rd Earl; *d* 1838; *s* by his nephew (4) GEORGE WILLIAM FREDERICK, KG, GCB, DCL, 4th Earl, el son of the Hon George, 3rd son of 1st Earl; *b* 1800; was First Commr of Excise 1824-33, Ambassador at Madrid 1833-9, Lord Privy Seal 1840-41, Pres of Board of Trade 1846-7, Viceroy of Ireland 1847-52, Sec. for Foreign Affairs 1853-8 and 1868-70, and Chancellor of Duchy of Lancaster 1864-5: *m* 1839, Lady Katherine Grimston, da of 1st Earl of Verulam, and widow of John Barham; *d* 27 June 1870; *s* by his el surviving son (5) EDWARD HYDE, GCB, GCVO, 5th Earl, *b* 1846; MP for Brecon (L) 1869-70; a Lord-in-Waiting to Queen Victoria 1895-1901, and Lord Chamberlain of the Household to King Edward VII 1901-5 and Lord-Lieut for Herts 1902-14: *m* 1st, 1876, Lady Caroline Elizabeth Agar, who *d* 1894, da of 3rd Earl of Normanton; 2ndly, 1908, Emma Mary Augusta, who *d* 1935, da of late Lt-Gen George Cliffe Hatch, CSI, and widow of Hon Edward Roden Bourke (E Mayo); *d* 1914; *s* by his el son (6) GEORGE HERBERT HYDE, KG, GCMG, GCVO, PC, 6th Earl; *b* 1877; Lord-in-Waiting to HM 1921-2, Ch Govt Whip in House of Lords, and Capt of HM Corps of Gentlemen-at Arms 1922-4 and 1924-5, Parliamentary Under-Sec of State for Dominion Affairs 1925-7, Chm British Broadcasting Corporation 1927-30, Gov-Gen and Com-in-Ch, Union of S Africa 1931-7, Lord Chamberlain of the Household and Chancellor of Roy Victorian Order 1938-52, Chancellor of Order of St Michael and St George 1942-55, and a permanent Lord-in-Waiting to HM 1952-5; *m* 1905, Adeline Verena Ishbel, LLLD, JP, who *d* 1963, da of late Herbert Haldane Somers-Cocks, and sister of 6th Baron Somers; *d* 1955; *s* by his grandson (7) GEORGE FREDERICK LAURENCE HYDE (son of late George Herbert Arthur Edward Hyde, Lord Hyde (*d* 1935) (who *m* 1932, Hon Marion Feodorovna Louise Glyn, DCVO, who *d* 1970, da of 4th Baron Wolverton), el son of 6th Earl), 7th Earl and present peer; also Baron Hyde.

CLARK, BARONY OF (Clark) (Extinct 1983)

SONS LIVING OF LIFE BARON

Rt Hon Alan Kenneth McKenzie (Saltwood Castle, Kent), *b* 1928: *ed* Eton, and Ch Ch, Oxford: Bar Inner Temple 1955; Gov St Thomas Hosp; Mil-Historian; Parliamentary Under Sec of State, Dept of Employment, 1983-86, Min for Trade 1986-90, Min for Defence 1990-92; MP for Plymouth, Sutton (C) Feb 1974-92; PC 1991; *m* 1958, Caroline Jane, da of Col Leslie Brindley Bream Beuttler, and has issue (*see* E Seafield, colls).
Hon Colin MacArthur (Paço da Glória, 4970 Arcos de Valdevez, Portugal), *b* 1932; *ed* Eton, and Ch Ch, Oxford: *m* 1st, 1961 (*m diss* 1969), Violette Verdy; 2ndly, 1971 (*m diss* 19——), Faith Beatrice, formerly wife of Julian Shuckburgh (*see* V Esher), and da of Sir Paul Hervé Giraud Wright; 3rdly, 1984, Helena Siu Kwan, da of late Cheung Wan Li, of Hong Kong, and has issue living (by 3rd *m*), Christopher Ming, *b* 1986.

DAUGHTER LIVING OF LIFE BARON

Hon Colette Elizabeth Dickson (twin), *b* 1932; *ed* Cheltenham Coll, and Lady Margaret Hall, Oxford (BA).

CLARK OF KEMPSTON, BARON (Clark) (Life Baron 1992)

WILLIAM GIBSON CLARK, PC, son of Hugh Clark, of Cautley Av, SW4; *b* 18 Oct 1917; *ed* in London; 1939-45 War in UK and India; Wandsworth Borough Cllr; Chm Clapham Conservative Assocn 1949-52, and Mid-Beds Conservative Assocn 1949-52, Nat Hon Dir Lord Carrington Conservative Appeal 1967-68, Joint Dep-Chm Conservative Party 1975-77 (Joint Treasurer 1974-75), Chm Conservative Finance Cttee since 1979; Chm Anglo-Austrian Soc since 1983; Pres City Cttee Smaller Companies (CISCO) since 1992; ACA 1941; Freeman City of London; Fellow Industry and Parliament Trust; Austrian Grand Gold Cross 1989; MP Nottingham S (*C*) 1959-66, E Surrey 1970-74, and S Croydon 1974-92; *cr* Kt Bach 1980, PC 1990, and *Baron Clark of Kempston*, of Kempston, co Beds (Life Baron) 1992: *m* 1944, Irene Dorothy Dawson, da of Edward Francis Rands, of Grimsby, Lincs, and has issue.

Arms – Erminois, on a pile azure between two quills pilewise points in base argent penned or, a portcullis chained in centre in chief or and five roundels in pile of the last. **Crest** – A demi unicorn azure winged, armed, crined and unguled or, collared chequy argent and azure and supporting with the forelegs a thistle plant flowered proper. **Supporters** – *Dexter*, a lion gules gorged with a collar chequy argent and azure, pendent therefrom by a cord or an escallop argent and resting the interior hind paw on a portcullis gold; *sinister*, an unicorn azure, winged, horned, unguled and crined or, gorged with a collar chequy argent and azure, pendent therfrom by a cord gold an escallop argent and resting the interior hoof on a bezant.

Residences – 3 Barton St, SW1; The Clock House, Box End, Bedford. *Clubs* – Buck's, Carlton.

SONS LIVING

Hon Richard Anthony, *b* 1947; *ed* Charterhouse, and Sorbonne; Solicitor: *m* 1973, Susan Kirstie Macgregor, da of late Hamish Edgar Donaldson Adamson, and has issue living, Oliver Hamish William, *b* 1978, — Lucy Caroline, *b* 1976, — Polly Catherine Isabel, *b* 1981. *Residence* – The Close, Pewsey, Wilts.

Hon David William Francis, *b* 1948; *ed* Charterhouse, and Sorbonne; FCA: *m* 1972, Elizabeth Grace, da of late Cdr Thomas Woodrooffe, and has issue living, Serena Elizabeth, *b* 1974, — Camilla Georgina Grace, *b* 1977. *Residence* – The Old Vicarage, Godmersham, Kent.

Hon Charles Edward Hugh, *b* 1959; *ed* Haileybury: *m* 1991, Nicoletta Luisa Caroline, da of Dr Mario Lentati, of Ave de Fabron, Nice, France. *Residence* – 5 Chelsea Embankment, SW5.

DAUGHTER LIVING

Hon Angela Margaret Grayson, *b* 1950: *m* 1st, 1971, Hugh Duncan Sinclair, who *d* 1987; 2ndly, 1992, Peter Thomas Labey, and has issue living (by 1st *m*), Hugh, *b* 1973, — Harriet Emily Margaret, *b* 1975. *Residence* – 5 Chelsea Embankment, SW5.

CLEDWYN OF PENRHOS, BARON (Hughes) (Life Baron 1979)

CLEDWYN HUGHES, CH, PC, son of late Rev Henry David Hughes; *b* 14 Sept 1916; *ed* Holyhead Gram Sch, and Univ Coll of Wales, Aberystwyth (LLB), Hon LLD Sheffield 1992; Pres Univ Coll of Wales, Aberystwyth 1975-84, Pro-Chancellor Univ of Wales since 1984; Solicitor 1940; Min of State for Commonwealth Affairs 1964-66, Sec of State for Wales 1966-68, Min of Agric, Fisheries and Food 1968-70; Chm of Parl Labour Party 1974-79; PM's Emissary to Southern Africa 1978; Opposition Leader of House of Lords 1982-92; MP for Anglesey (*Lab*) 1951-79; 1939-45 War as Fl Lt RAFVR; *cr* PC 1966, CH 1977, and *Baron Cledwyn of Penrhos*, of Holyhead in Isle of Anglesey (Life Baron) 1979: *m* 1949, Jean Beatrice, JP, da of Capt Jesse Hughes, and has issue.

Residence – Penmorfa, Trearddur, Anglesey. *Clubs* – Travellers, RAF.

SON LIVING

Hon Harri Cledwyn, *b* 1955: *m* 1986, Jennifer Meryl, da of R. P. Hughes, of Coedlys Valley, Anglesey, and has issue.

DAUGHTER LIVING

Hon Emily Ann, *b* 1950: *m* 1976, Peter Wright, and has issue.

CLIFDEN, VISCOUNTCY OF (Agar-Robartes) (Extinct 1974)

DAUGHTER LIVING OF EIGHTH VISCOUNT

Hon Rachel Mary, *b* 1922: *m* 1941, Capt Cromwell Felix Justin Lloyd-Davies, DSO, DSC, RN, and has issue living, Ann, *b* 1942: *m* 1964, Colin Victor Kenneth Williams, and has issue living, Andrew Nicholas Victor *b* 1967, Simon Justin Colin *b* 1972, Zara Alison *b* 1970.

CLIFFORD OF CHUDLEIGH, BARON (Clifford) (Baron E 1672)

Always ready

THOMAS HUGH CLIFFORD, 14th Baron, *b* 17 March 1948: *s* 1988; *ed* Downside; late Capt Coldm Guards: *m* 1980 (*m diss* 1993), (Muriel) Suzanne, da of Maj Campbell Austin, of The Old Rectory, Muff, co Donegal, and has issue.

Arms – Checky or and azure, a fease gules. **Crest** – Out of a ducal coronet or, a demi-wyvern gules. **Supporters** – Two wyverns purpure.
Seat – Ugbrooke Park, Chudleigh, S Devon TQ13 0AD.

SONS LIVING

Hon ALEXANDER THOMAS HUGH, *b* 24 Sept 1985.
Hon Edward George Hugh, *b* 1988.

DAUGHTER LIVING

Hon Georgina Apollonia, *b* 1983.

BROTHER LIVING

Hon Rollo Hugh, *b* 1954; *ed* Downside: *m* 1st, 1977, Fiona Margaret, only da of Richard Andrew Palethorpe Todd, OBE, actor; 2ndly, 1989, Mrs Caroline Peta (VERSEN), only da of Peter Marshall Roberts, of Sydney, Australia, and has issue living (by 1st *m*), Christopher Rollo, *b* 1982, — Alasdair Rollo, *b* 1986, — Elizabeth Alice, *b* 1981, — (by 2nd *m*) Sophie Katharine Rose, *b* 1991. *Residence* – Worthy Manor, Porlock Weir, Minehead, Som TA24 8PG.

SISTERS LIVING

Hon Cecilia Alice KIRBY CLIFFORD, *b* 1945: *m* 1968, Capt Nicholas Breakspear Kirby, RN, of Melbury Bubb, nr Dorchester, Dorset, and has issue living, Julian Breakspear Bede, *b* 1975, — Samantha Mary, *b* 1969, — Christina Mary Anna, *b* 1971, — Caroline Mary Julia, *b* 1977. *Residence* – 43 Wilson Rd, Blairgowrie, Victoria 3942, Australia.
Hon Sarah Amy, *b* 1956: *m* 1981, Robert Carwithen Richardson, of Greatcombe, Holne, Devonshire TQ13 7SP, 2nd son of Christopher Richardson, of Dartmouth, Devon, and has issue living, Amy Natasha, *b* 1984, — Jessie Katharine, *b* 1987.

AUNTS LIVING (*daughters of 12th Baron*)

Hon Mary, *b* 1919: *m* 1943, Major Jack Philip Albert Galvin Clifford Wolff, MBE and has issue living, Rosamund Elizabeth, *b* 1944: *m* 1966, John David Arnold Wallinger, of The Major House, Upton Grey, Basingstoke, Hants, son of late Sir Geoffrey Arnold Wallinger, GBE, KCMG, — Antoinette Mary, *b* 1946: *m* 1970, David Brian Parkes, of Ashcombe House, Tollard Royal, Wilts.
Hon Rosamund Ann (*Baroness Fisher*) (Marklye, Rushlake Green, Heathfield, Sussex); *b* 1924; formerly zoo director and author; *m* 1st, 1946 (*m diss* 1965), Geoffrey Forrester Fairbairn; 2ndly, 1970, 3rd Baron Fisher, and has issue living (by 1st *m*), James Clifford, *b* 1950: *m* 1979, Catherine Elizabeth, da of Prof E. K. Cruickshank, of Ore, Wilts, and has issue living, Paul *b* 1982, Julia *b* 1984, — Charles Marcus Clifford, *b* 1955: *m* 1984, Sarah Jane, da of P.A. Coveney, of Burgess Hill, Sussex, and has issue living, Rory Tobias *b* 1987, Chloe Rebecca *b* 1985, — Katrina Elizabeth, *b* 1947: *m* 1st, 1968 (*m diss* 1982), Robert Moss; 2ndly, 1986, Peter Laurence Wise, of 6 St Stephen's Av, W12 8JH, and has issue living (by 1st *m*), Pandora *b* 1971, Candida Rebecca *b* 1978, (by 2nd *m*) Serena Alice *b* 1988.

DAUGHTER LIVING OF ELEVENTH BARON

Hon Agnes Mary, *b* 1918: *m* 1944, Robert Weatherhead Stallybrass, and has had issue, Hugh Greville, *b* 1948; *ed* Downside: *m* 1969, Carey, da of L. R. Pullen, of Worthing, and *d* 1992, leaving issue, Alexander Hugh *b* 1978, Kate Helen *b* 1974, — Helen Hope, *b* 1945, — Emma Catherine, *b* 1951: *m* 1980, John Bowles, and has issue living, George David *b* 1981, Patrick William *b* 1987, Caroline Louise *b* 1984. *Residence* – The Old Laundry, Oakhill, nr Bath.

WIDOW LIVING OF THIRTEENTH BARON

Hon Katharine Vavasseur Fisher (*Katharine, Baroness Clifford of Chudleigh*), da of 2nd Baron Fisher: *m* 1945, Col the 13th Baron, OBE, who *d* 1988. *Residence* – Flat 3, The Care House, Les Blancs Bois, Rue Cohu, Guernsey, CI.

COLLATERAL BRANCHES LIVING

Issue of late Capt Hon Sir Bede Edmund Hugh Clifford, GCMG, CB, MVO, yst son of 10th Baron, *b* 1890: *d* 1969: *m* 1925, Alice Devin, who *d* 1980, da of John Murton Gundry, of Cleveland, Ohio, USA:—
Anne Frances May, *b* 1929: *m* 1952 (*m diss* 1985), 2nd Viscount Norwich. —— (Alice Devin) Atalanta, *b* 1932: *m* 1st, 1955, Richard Fairey, who *d* 1960, son of Sir (Charles) Richard Fairey, MBE; 2ndly, 1963, W/Cdr Timothy Ashmead Vigors, DFC; 3rdly, 1972, Michael Henry Dennis Madden, of 21A Barclay Rd, SW6 1EJ, and has issue living (by 1st *m*) Leanda Alice Devin Joan, *b* 1957, — (by 2nd *m*), Thomas Ashmead Merton, *b* 1969, — (by 3rd *m*) Henry George Bede, *b* 1973.

Descendants of late Sir Charles Clifford (el son of late George Lambert Clifford, 5th son of late Hon Thomas Clifford, 2nd son of 3rd Baron), who was *cr* a Baronet 1887:—
See Clifford, Bt, *cr* 1887.

PREDECESSORS – (1) *Rt Hon* THOMAS Clifford, PC; MP for Totnes, Comptroller of the Household 1666, Treasurer of the Household 1668, and Principal Sec of State and Lord High Treasurer 1672; *cr Baron Clifford of Chudleigh*, co Devon, 1672; *d* 1673; *s* by his son (2) HUGH, 2nd Baron; *d* 1730; *s* by his son (3) HUGH, 3rd Baron; *d* 1732; *s* by his son (4) HUGH, 4th Baron; *d* 1783; *s* by his el son (5) HUGH EDWARD HENRY, 5th Baron; *dsp* 1793; *s* by his brother (6) CHARLES, 6th Baron: *m* Hon Eleanor Mary (a Countess of the Holy Roman Empire), da of 8th Baron Arundell of Wardour; *d* 1831; *s* by his son (7) HUGH CHARLES, 7th Baron, and in right of his mother, a *Count of the Holy Roman Empire*; *d* 1858; *s* by his son (8) CHARLES HUGH, 8th Baron, *b* 1819: *m* 1845, Hon Agnes Catherine Louisa, who *d* 1891, da of 11th Baron Petre; *d* 1880; *s* by his son (9) LEWIS HENRY HUGH, 9th Baron, *b* 1851: *m* 1890, Mabel Anne, who *d* 1921, da of Col John Towneley, of Towneley, Lancashire; *d* 1916; *s* by his brother (10) WILLIAM HUGH, 10th Baron, *b* 1858: *m* 1st, 1886, Catherine Mary, who *d* 1943, da of R. Basset; 2ndly, (May) 1943, Grace Muriel, who *d* 1963, da of late W. St Clair Munro, of Glasgow; *d* (July) 1943; *s* by his el son (11) CHARLES OSWALD HUGH, 11th Baron; *b* 1887; Lieut 5th Batn Devon Regt (TA) and Sub-Lieut RNVR: *m* 1st, 1917, Dorothy, who *d* 1918, da of late Alfred Joseph Hornyold; 2ndly, 1940, Clare Mary, who *d* 1975, da of late Capt Jasper Graham Mayne, CBE, and widow of Charles Struthers White Ogilvie; *d* 1962; *s* by his brother, (12) LEWIS JOSEPH

HUGH 12th Baron; *b* 1889: *m* 1st, 1914, Amy, who *d* 1926 el da of John A. Webster, MD; 2ndly, 1934, Mary Elizabeth, da of late Rt Hon Sir Adrian Knox; *d* 1964; *s* by his only son (13) LEWIS HUGH, OBE, 13th Baron, *b* 1916, Col Devonshire Regt, Hon Col Devon Territorials (R Devon Yeo/1st Rifle Vol) T & AVR, Dep Hon Col Wessex Yeo RAC, TAVR, served European War 1939-45 (prisoner, escaped), ADC to HM 1964-69, DL Devon: *m* 1945, Hon Katharine Vavasseur Fisher, da of 2nd Baron Fisher; *d* 1988; *s* by his elder son (14) THOMAS HUGH, 14th Baron and present peer.

Clifton of Leighton Bromswold, Baron; title of Earl of Darnley on Roll of House of Lords.

Clifton of Rathmore, Lord; son of Earl of Darnley.

CLINTON, BARON (Fane Trefusis) (Baron E 1299)

GERARD NEVILE MARK FANE TREFUSIS, 22nd Baron; *b* 7 Oct 1934; *s* (on termination of abeyance) 1965; assumed by deed poll 1958 the surname of Trefusis after his patronymic; JP Bideford 1963, and DL Devon 1977: *m* 1959, Nicola Harriette, da of late Maj Charles Robert Purdon Coote (*see* Coote, Bt, colls), and has issue.

Arms – Argent semy of cross crosslets fitchy sable in a chief azure two mullets or pierced gules, *Clinton*, charged with a inescutcheon quarterly, 1st, argent, on a fess azure three dexter gauntlets appaumy or, *Fane*, 2nd, argent, a chevron between three spindles sable, *Trefusis*, 3rd, azure, three boars' heads couped argent, muzzled gules, a cross crosslet argent, for distinction, *Forbes of Pitsligo*, 4th, or, a bend gules, surmounted by a fess checky azure and argent, in chief a crescent azure, a canton ermine for difference, *Stuart*. **Crest** – A bull's head erased sable armed, and about the neck an ancient crown attached thereto a line or, in the mouth a rose gules barbed seeded slipped and leafed proper. **Supporters** – On either side a greyhound argent collared with line reflexed over the back gules, in the mouth a gauntlet as in the arms, *Clinton*.
Residence – Heanton Satchville, Okehampton, Devon EX20 3QE.

SON LIVING

Hon CHARLES PATRICK ROLLE, *b* 21 March 1962: *m* 1992, Rosanna E., yr da of (Alexander) John Rennie Izat, of High Cocklaw, Berwick upon Tweed, and has issue living, Edward Charles Rolle, *b* 26 Feb 1994. *Residence* – Kitts Hayes, Colaton Raleigh, nr Sidmouth, Devon EX10 0HY.

DAUGHTERS LIVING

Hon Caroline Harriet, *b* 1960.
Hon Henrietta Jane, *b* 1964.

SISTERS LIVING

Carol, *b* 1937: *m* 1959, Hugo Peter Charles Bevan, of The Old House, Little Everdon, Daventry, Northants, and has issue living, Rupert Charles, *b* 1965: *m* 1992, Sophie Louise, only da of Clement Michael Charles Royds, of Armathwaite, Cumbria, and has issue living, Orlando *b* 1994, — Georgina Lucy, *b* 1963: *m* 1991, Rupert Patrick Fordham, eldest son of late John Rupert Fordham, of 94 Portland Rd, W11, and has issue living, Patrick Hugo John *b* 1993, — Charlotte Adèle, *b* 1967, — Sophie Alexandra, *b* 1968.
Fiona, *b* 1939: *m* 1962, Sylvanus John Connolly, of The Long Barn, Monkton Deverill, Wilts, and has issue living, Daniel Charles, *b* 1970, — Nicola Jane, *b* 1964: *m* 1991, Michael Leslie John Beck, only son of Roger Beck, of Dinton, Wilts, — Alice Louise, *b* 1965, — Claudia Gay, *b* 1969.

UNCLE LIVING (Son of Hon Harriet Fane, elder da of 21st Baron)

John Henry Mark FANE, MBE (6 Ollivier St, Alderney, CI), *b* 1917; is Capt Green Howards; 1939-45 War (prisoner, escaped, MBE); MBE (Mil) 1944: *m* 1st, 1939 (*m diss* 1954), Catherine Adelaide Anne, only child of late Gabriel Noel Dyer (*see* Legard, Bt, colls, 1971 Edn); 2ndly 1954 (*m diss* 1962), Eleanor Sybil Ruth, da of late Albert Henry Archdeacon, of Hastings; 3rdly, 1964, Elizabeth, da of Kenneth W. Cowell, of Les Butes, Alderney, and has issue living, (by 2nd *m*) Simon John Nevile, *b* 1954, — Robert Trefusis, *b* 1958, — Harriet Jane, *b* 1956, — Briony Ann, *b* 1957.

AUNTS LIVING (Daughters of Hon Harriet Fane, elder da of 21st Baron)

Idonea Elizabeth, *b* 1912.
Etheldreda Flavia, *b* 1922.

COLLATERAL BRANCHES LIVING

    Granddaughter of late Hon Harriet Fane, elder da of 21st Baron:—
        Issue of late Anne Charmian Fane, *b* 1916, *d* 1990: *m* 1st, 1937 (*m diss* 1949), Maj Robert Henry Arthur Rivers-Bulkeley, Scots Guards (*see* E Wemyss, colls, 1985 Edn); 2ndly, 1949, Peter Richard Hampton, MC:—
(By 1st *m*) Miranda Jane, *b* 1938: *m* 1963, John Goglis (actor, as John Voglis), of Psaron 4, Glyfada, Athens, and has issue living, Dimitri, *b* 1965, — Robertos Nicholas, *b* 1969.

Issue of late Hon Fenella Hepburn-Stuart-Forbes-Trefusis, yr da of 21st Baron, *b* 1889, *d* 1966: *m* 1914, Hon
John Herbert Bowes-Lyon, who *d* 1930, 2nd son of 14th Earl of Strathmore:—
Katherine, *b* 1926.

Grandchildren of late Hon Fenella Hepburn-Stuart-Forbes-Trefusis (ante):—
Issue of late Anne Ferelith Fenella Bowes Lyon, *b* 1917, *d* 1980: *m* 1st, 1938 (*m diss* 1948), Maj Thomas William
Arnold, Viscount Anson, who *d* 1958; 2ndly, 1950, HH Prince Georg of Denmark, who *d* 1986:—
(By 1st *m*) (*see* E Lichfield)
Issue of late Diana Cinderella Bowes Lyon, *b* 1923, *d* 1986: *m* 1960, Peter Gordon Colin Somervell, who *d* 1993, of
Fettercairn House, Fettercairn, Kincardineshire, only surv son of Maj Sir Arnold Colin Somervell, OBE, DL:—
Katherine Elizabeth, *b* 1961: *m* 1991, Robert W. P. Lagneau, son of Michel Lagneau, and Mrs Jane Few Brown.

Grandchildren of late Maj Hon Henry Walter Hepburn-Stuart-Forbes-Trefusis, Scots Gds, 2nd son of 20th
Baron:—
Issue of late Henry Trefusis, late Lt Cdr RNVR, who relinquished the surnames of Hepburn-Stuart-Forbes by
statutory declaration 1939, *b* 1908, *d* 1975: *m* 1940, Sheila Margaret (20 Tregew, Flushing, Falmouth), da of late
Herman Bryan, of Lanthwaite, Eaton Hill, Norwich:—
Nicholas John Trefusis (Trefusis, Falmouth); *b* 1943; Lt-Cdr RN; JP for Cornwall: *m* 1973, Servane, yst da of late Louis
Mélénec, of Brest, and Landévennec, and has issue living, Jan Henry Nicholas, *b* 1977, — Tamara Jane *b* 1974.
—— Thomasine Mary, *b* 1942: *m* 1970, Philip Henry Faudel Heycock, of 62 Hamilton Park West, N5 1AB, and has issue
living, Thomas Henry Trefusis, *b* 1971, — Eleanor Rachel, *b* 1974, — Sarah Kerensa Faudel, *b* 1977. —— Morwenna Jane, *b*
1945: *m* 1973, Robin Orton, of 11 Radlett Av, SE26 4BZ, and has issue living, Magdalen Jane Dorothy, *b* 1975, — Ann Emily,
b 1977. —— (Ann) Kerensa, *b* 1949: *m* 1973, Andrew Michael Pearson, of 7 Gussiford Lane, Exmouth, and has issue living,
Timothy Mark, *b* 1977, — William Hugh, *b* 1979.

Issue of late Hon Robert Henry Hepburn-Stuart-Forbes-Trefusis, yst son of 20th Baron, *b* 1888, *d* 1958: *m*
1914, Lady Dorothy Marguerite Elizabeth, OBE, who *d* 1956, da of late Col Edward William Herbert, CB
(E Powis):—
Helen Beatrice Margaret, *b* 1917: *m* 1936, Maj Simon Whitbread, KRRC, of The Mallowry, Riseley, Bedford (*see* E Mayo,
colls, 1985 Edn), who *d* 1985, and has issue living, Samuel Charles (Southill Park, Biggleswade, Beds), *b* 1937; *ed* Eton, and
Trin Coll, Camb; a CC 1974-81, JP 1969-83, DL Beds, High Sheriff 1973-74, Lord Lieut since 1991; Chm Whitbread & Co
1984-92: *m* 1961, Jane Mary, da of Charles Hugh Hayter, and has issue living, Charles Edward Samuel *b* 1963: *m* 1991, Jane
Elizabeth, da of David Evans, of Warsash, Hants (and has issue living, Emily Victoria *b* 1992, Catherine Helen *b* 1994),
Henry George Simon *b* 1965: *m* 1994, Serena Caroline, da of Anthony J. Barclay, of Nineveh Farm, Nuneham Courtenay,
Oxon, William John Howard *b* 1966, Victoria Clare Helen, *b* 1969: *m* 1993, Sebastian Finch Morley (*see* B Beaverbrook), —
Elizabeth Anne (65 Eccleston Sq Mews, SW1), *b* 1939: *m* 1962, James Carthew Cavendish Bennett, Diplo Ser, who *d* 1969,
and has issue living, Nicholas James *b* 1964, Simon Patrick *b* 1965, Charles David *b* 1969.

Issue of late Hon Margaret Adela Hepburn-Stuart-Forbes-Trefusis, 3rd da of 20th Baron, *b* 1866, *d* 1939: *m*
1897, Rt Rev Leonard Jauncey White-Thomson, Bishop of Ely, who *d* 1933:—
(See 1939 Edn).

Issue of late Hon Harriet Margaret Hepburn-Stuart-Forbes-Trefusis, 6th and yst da of 20th Baron, *b* 1891, *d*
1975: *m* 1914, Lt-Col Eustace Widdrington Morrison-Bell, who *d* 1947:—
(See Morrison-Bell, Bt, *cr* 1905 colls).

Issue of late Katherine Helen Elizabeth Trefusis (who *m* 1906, Hon Arthur Owen Crichton), 3rd da of late
Col Hon Walter Rodolph Trefusis, CB, 3rd son of 19th Baron:—
(See E Erne, colls).

Issue of late Marion Gertrude Trefusis (who *m* 1905, 4th Earl of Leicester), 4th da of late Col Hon Walter
Rodolph Trefusis, CB (ante):—
(See E Leicester).

Grandchildren of late Margaret Harriet Trefusis (who *m* 1911, Lt-Col Edgar Hugh Brassey, MVO), 5th and
yst da of late Col Hon Walter Rodolph Trefusis, CB (ante):—
Issue of late Sir Hugh Trefusis Brassey, KCVO, OBE, MC, *b* 1915, *d* 1990: *m* 1939, Joyce Patricia (Manor
Farm, Little Somerford, Chippenham, Wilts), da of Capt Maurice John Kingscote (*see* B Gifford, 1947 Edn):—
Antony Hugh Owen Brassey (Morley Farm, Crudwell, Malmesbury, Wilts), *b* 1945; *ed* Eton; served Royal Scots Greys 1964-
67: *m* 1980, Mrs Sarah Sigri Burgoyne, da of late Robin Robsahm Fuglesang, of Laycock, Wilts, and has issue living, Hugo
Timothy, *b* 1982, — Louisa Fiona, *b* 1984. —— Kim Maurice (Trabbs Farmhouse, Seven Barrows, Lambourn, Newbury,
Berks), *b* 1955; financial consultant: *m* 1st, 1981, Alison Sarah, who *d* 1990, da of Edwin James Cracknell; 2ndly, 1992,
Joanna, da of late Capt Colin Gowans, MN, and has issue living (by 1st *m*), Fiona Elizabeth, *b* 1985, — Lily Patricia, *b* 1988,
— (by 2nd *m*) Jack William, *b* 1992, — Ellie *b* 1994. —— Fiona Gillian, *b* 1942; *d* 1958. —— Jane Margaret, *b* 1946: *m*
1971, John Morrison Rogers, of Riverhill House, Sevenoaks, Kent, son of late Maj David Morrison Rogers (*see* Morrison-Bell,
Bt, 1919 Edn), and has issue living, John Edward, *b* 1974, — Daniel Hugh, *b* 1976. —— Sarah Patricia, *b* 1949: *m* 1980,
John Moorehead, of 10 Egbert St, NW1, son of late Alan Moorehead, author and war correspondent, and has issue living,
Alexander Patrick, *b* 1979, — Benjamin Christopher, *b* 1982.
Issue of late Marjorie Eva Brassey, *b* 1911, *d* 1975: *m* 1933, Hugh Myddleton Peacock, TD, DL, of The Ferry,
Milton, Peterborough:—
Michael Hugh Peacock, *b* 1946; *ed* Eton: *m* 1974, Caroline Mary, yst da of Maj Robert Hoare, MC, of Hambleton Hall,
Oakham. —— Idina Caroline, *b* 1933: *m* 1957, Col James William Gordon Pirie, 60th Rifles, of 38 Kew Green, Richmond,
Surrey, and has issue living, James Hugh Pirie, *b* 1959, — Amanda Caroline, *b* 1962. —— Susan Margaret, *b* 1938: *m* 1964,
Michael Andrieus Jones, of 24 Sunswyck Rd, Darien, Connecticut 06820, USA, and has issue living, Philip Andrieus, *b* 1966:
m 1994, Susan Anne, da of Franklyn Ayres, of Winnetka, Illinois, USA, — Idina Maria, *b* 1968.

Granddaughter of late Col Hon John Schomberg Trefusis, CMG, 4th son of 19th Baron:—
Issue of late Elizabeth Katharine Mary Trefusis, *b* 1887, *d* 1976, Capt Garth Neville Walford, VC, RHA, who was *ka*
1915:—
Phyllida (Goonpiper House, Feock, Cornwall, TR3 6RA), *b* 1915: *m* 1944, Kenneth Ellis, who *d* 1972.

Grandson of Rt Rev Robert Edward Trefusis, DD (Bishop of Crediton), yr son of late Capt Hon George
Walpole Rolle Trefusis, RN, 3rd son of 17th Baron:—
Issue of late Maj George Rodolph Trefusis, *b* 1875, *d* 1927: *m* 1911, Elsie Jane, who *d* 1946, da of late James Start
Harrison of Sydney, NSW:—
Robert John Rodolph, *b* 1914; former Maj Scots Gds; CEng, MICE and FIMechE; HM's Foreign Ser 1946-54; Officer of
Order of Crown of Belgium: *m* 1955, Shirley Adeline Scott, da of late Charles Scott Barton, of Sullington, Sussex, and has

issue living, Charles Rodolph, *b* 1961: *m* 1989, Catherine, da of Brian Dudgeon, of Guildford, Surrey, and has issue living, Harriet Sarah Patricia *b* 1991, Charlotte Rosanna *b* 1993, — Rosemary Jane, *b* 1959: *m* 1988, Lt-Cdr David Richard Fry, RN, eldest son of Capt R. G. Fry, of Whitchurch, Canonicorum, Bridport, Dorset, and has issue living, Edward James *b* 1993, Emma Katherine *b* 1991. *Residence* – Longmeadows Lodge, Feniton, Honiton, Devon EX14 0BE. *Club* – Carlton.

PREDECESSORS – (1) JOHN de Clinton, summoned to Parliament of England 1299; his grandson (2) JOHN, 2nd Baron, summoned to Parliament 1332-35; *s* by his son (3) *Sir* JOHN, Knt, 3rd Baron, summoned to Parliament 1357-97; *d* 1397; *s* by his grandson (4) WILLIAM, 4th Baron; *d* 1432; *s* by his son (5) JOHN, 5th Baron; a staunch Yorkist, was attainted 1461, and subsequently restored; *d* 1464; *s* by his son (6) JOHN, 6th Baron; *d* 1488; *s* by his son (7) JOHN, 7th Baron; *d* 1514; *s* by his son (8) THOMAS, 8th Baron; *d* 1517; *s* by his son (9) EDWARD, KG, PC, 9th Baron, Lord High Adm; *cr Earl of Lincoln* (peerage of England) 1572; *d* 1585; *s* by his son (10) HENRY, KB, 2nd Earl; *d* 1616; *s* by his son (11) THOMAS, 3rd Earl; *d* 1618; *s* by his son (12) THEOPHILUS, KB, 4th Earl; *d* 1667; *s* by his grandson (13) EDWARD, 5th Earl; *dsp* 1692, when the Earldom devolved upon his cousin (*see* D Newcastle), and the barony became abeyant between the issue of his aunts; in 1721 the abeyance was terminated in favour of (14) HUGH Fortescue, 14th Baron; *cr Baron Fortescue*, of Castlehill, co Devon, with limitation to his half-brother Matthew, and *Earl of Clinton* (peerage of Great Britain) 1746, *dsp* 1751, when the Earldom of Clinton became extinct, the Barony of Fortescue passed to his half-brother (*see* E Fortescue), and the Barony of Clinton devolved upon his cousin (15) MARGARET, widow of 2nd Earl of Orford, and wife of Hon Sewallis Shirley (E Ferrers); *d* 1781; *s* by her son (16) GEORGE, 3rd *Earl of Orford* and 16th Baron Clinton; *dsp* 1791, when the Earldom passed to his nephew, and in 1794 the Barony of Clinton was sucessfully claimed by his cousin (17) ROBERT GEORGE WILLIAM Trefusis, 17th Baron, the descendant of Lady Arabella Rolle, 2nd da of 4th Earl of Lincoln; *d* 1797; *s* by his el son (18) ROBERT COTTON ST. JOHN, 18th Baron; a Lord of the Bedchamber to George III; *d* 1832; *s* by his brother (19) CHARLES RODOLPH, 19th Baron, *b* 1791: *m* 1831, Lady Elizabeth Georgiana Kerr, who *d* 1871, da of 6th Marquess of Lothian; *d* 1866; *s* by his son (20) CHARLES HENRY ROLLE, 20th Baron, *b* 1834; sat as MP for N Devon (LC) 1857-66; Under-Sec of State for India 1867-68, a Charity Commr 1874-80, and Lord-Lieut of Devonshire 1887-1904; assumed by Roy licence 1867, the additional surnames of Hepburn-Stuart-Forbes; *m* 1st, 1858, Harriet Williamina, who *d* 1869, da and heiress of Sir John Stuart Forbes, 8th Bt; 2ndly, 1875, Margaret, who *d* 1930, da of Sir John Walrond Walrond, 1st Bt; *d* 1904; *s* by his son (21) CHARLES JOHN ROBERT, GCVO, PC, 21st Baron; *b* 1863; High Steward of Barnstaple; was Joint Parliamentary Sec to Board of Agriculture and Fisheries 1918, a Member of Council of Cornwall (1911-33) and Keeper of the Privy Seal (1913-33) of HRH the Prince of Wales, and Lord Warden of the Stannaries 1921-33; Chm of Forestry Institute 1924-29, and of Forestry Commn 1927-29: *m* 1886, Lady Jane Grey McDonnell (a CStJ), who *d* 1953, da of 5th Earl of Antrim; *d* 1957, when the Barony fell into abeyance between his two daughters, Hon Harriet, who *d* 1958, having *m* Maj Henry Nevile Fane, and Hon Fenella, who *d* 1966, having *m* Hon John Herbert Bowes Lyon, and so continued until 1965, when the abeyance was terminated in favour of the senior co-heir (22) GERARD NEVILE MARK (only son of late Capt Charles Nevile Fane, el son of late Hon Harriet Fane), 22nd Baron and present peer.

CLINTON-DAVIS, BARON (Clinton-Davis) (Life Baron 1990)

STANLEY CLINTON-DAVIS, son of Sidney Davis; *b* 6 Dec 1928; *ed* Hackney Downs Sch, Mercers' Sch, and King's Coll, London; Parly Under Sec Trade 1974-79, Opposition Front Bench Spokeman Trade 1979-81, Foreign and Commonwealth Affairs 1981-83; Member Assocn of Professional, Executive, Clerical and Computer Staffs, Pres British Multiple Sclerosis Soc (Hackney Branch), Councillor (Hackney) 1959-71, Mayor Hackney 1968-69, Solicitor since 1953; Member Commn of European Communities 1985-89, Vice-Pres Soc of Lab Lawyers since 1987; Trustee Bernt Carlsson Trust, Hon Member Exec Council of Justice, Member UN Selection Cttee Sasakawa Environment Project since 1989; Dir Jewish Chronicle since 1989; Consultant on European Law and Affairs, S. J. Berwin & Co, since 1989, Senior Advisor on European Affairs with Hill & Knowlton Int since 1989; MP Hackney Central (*Lab*) 1970-83; assumed by deed poll 1990 the surname of Clinton-Davis in lieu of his patronymic; *cr Baron Clinton-Davis*, of Hackney, in the London Borough of Hackney (Life Baron) 1990: *m* 1954, Frances Jane, da of late Marcus Gershon Lucas, and has issue.

Residence – 22 Bracknell Gate, Hampstead, NW3.

SON LIVING

Hon Henry, *b* 1960.

DAUGHTERS LIVING

Hon Joanna, *b* 1955: *m* 19—, — Lavell.
Hon Susanna, *b* 1962: *m* 19—, — Fox.
Hon Melissa, *b* 1964.

CLITHEROE, BARON (Assheton) (Baron UK 1955, Bt UK 1945)

I am neither proud nor afraid

RALPH JOHN ASSHETON, 2nd Baron and 3rd Baronet; *b* 3 Nov 1929; *s* 1984; *ed* Eton (Oppidan Scholar), and Ch Ch, Oxford (Scholar, MA); late The Life Guards; DL Lancs 1986; Chm Yorkshire Bank plc since 1990, Dir Halliburton Co, Texas since 1987; formerly Dep Ch Exec RTZ Corpn plc, and Dir First Interstate Bank of California, of Touche Remnant Natural Resources, of American Mining Congress, of Chemical Industries Assocn, and other Cos; a Liveryman of Skinners' Co; Pres Assocn of Lancastrians in London 1990; FCIB, FRSA: *m* 1961, Juliet, da of Lt-Col Christopher Lionel Hanbury, MBE, TD, of Juniper Hill, Burnham, Bucks, and has issue.

Arms – Argent a mullet sable pierced of the field. Crest – On a cap of maintenance, a mower, vested and capped quarterly, argent and sable, sleeves and stockings counter changed, holding a scythe azure, handled or, the point of the blade towards the dexter. Supporters – *Dexter*, a Labrador dog sable; *sinister*, a bull argent armed or.
Residence – Downham Hall, Clitheroe, Lancs BB7 4DN. *Clubs* – Boodle's, Pratt's, RAC.

SONS LIVING

Hon RALPH CHRISTOPHER, *b* 19 March 1962; *ed* Eton; Lord of the Honor of Clitheroe.
Hon John Hotham, *b* 1964; *ed* Harrow: *m* 1989, Amanda E., da of Geoffrey Freeman, of Red Lion House, Nettlebed, Oxfordshire, and has issue living, William Hotham, *b* 1992.

DAUGHTER LIVING

Hon Elizabeth Jane, *b* 1968.

BROTHER LIVING

Hon Nicholas, *b* 1934; *ed* Eton, and Ch Ch, Oxford (MA); FSA; Lord of the Manor and Liberty of Slaidburn, Grindleton and Bradford; formerly Member of London Stock Exchange (Member of Council 1968-88), partner Montagu, Loebl, Stanley & Co 1960-87, Dep Chm Coutts & Co; a Liveryman of Vintners' Co; late 2nd Lt Life Gds, and Lt Inns of Court of Regt: *m* 1960, Jacqueline Jill, da of Marshal of the RAF Sir Arthur Travers Harris, 1st Bt, GCB, OBE, AFC, and has issue living, Thomas (Manor Farm, Longborough, Moreton-in-Marsh, Glos. *Clubs* – White's, Pratt's), *b* 1963; *ed* Eton, and Reading Univ (BSc); Capt Life Gds: *m* 1989, Katharine Sophie, da of David Alphy Edward Raymond Peake (*see* V Ingleby, colls), and has issue living, Noah Frederick *b* 1991, Molly *b* 1992, — Caroline, *b* 1961, — Mary Thérèse, *b* 1967; has issue living, Arthur Travers GORDON *b* 1994, Alice GORDON *b* 1988. *Residence* – 15 Hammersmith Terr, W6 9TS. *Clubs* – White's, Pratt's, City of London.

SISTER LIVING

Hon Bridget (*Hon Lady Worsley*), *b* 1926; late WRNS: *m* 1955, Sir (William) Marcus John Worsley 5th Bt. *Residence* – Hovingham Hall, York.

AUNT LIVING (*Daughter of 1st Baronet*)

Eleanor, CBE, *b* 1907; was Vice-Chm of the Yorkshire Provincial Area of National Union of Conservative and Unionist Assoc 1952-5; CBE (Civil) 1956: *m* 1926, Maj John Edward Evelyn Yorke, JP, and has issue living, David John (Hall Foot, Clitheroe, Lancs), *b* 1927; *ed* Eton, and Trin Coll, Camb (MA); late The Life Gds; FRICS; a JP and DL of Lancs: *m* 1957, Susan Alexandra, da of Lt-Col Scrope Arthur Francis Sutherland Egerton, Highland LI (ret) (*see* D Sutherland, colls), and has issue living, John Alexander *b* 1959; *ed* Eton, Charles Scrope Edward *b* 1965; *ed* Eton, Sophia Caroline Annabel *b* 1961: *m* 1984, Nicholas Anthony Bevil Acland, yr son of Sir Antony Arthur Acland, GCMG, GCVO (*see* Acland, Bt, *cr* 1890, colls), — Felicity Anne, *b* 1931: *m* 1955, James Patrick Ashley Cooper, son of Sir Patrick Ashley Cooper, of Hexton Manor, Hitchin, Herts, and has issue living, Patrick John Ashley *b* 1957; *ed* Eton, and Trin Hall, Camb: *m* 1989, Belinda Jane, da of Christopher Firth, of Brantingham Hall, Brough, E Yorks (and has issue living, Christopher Patrick Ashley *b* 1990, Thomas James Ashley *b* 1992), Edward James Ashley *b* 1966, Katharine Mary *b* 1956: *m* 1991, Dr Peter Foot (and has issue living, Sarah *b* 1993), Felicity *b* 1961. *Residence* – Halton Pl, Hellifield, Skipton, Yorks.

PREDECESSORS
– (1) Ralph Cockayne Assheton, son of late Ralph Assheton, MP, of Downham Hall, Clitheroe, Lancashire, and Cuerdale, Lancashire; *b* 1860; High Sheriff of Lancashire 1919; was a Co Councillor for Lancashire 1892-1902, and a Co Alderman 1902-49; *cr* a *Baronet* 1945: *m* 1898, Mildred Estelle Sybella, CBE, JP, who *d* 1949, da and co-heiress of John Henry Master, JP, of Montrose House, Petersham, Surrey; *d* (Sept) 1955; *s* by his only son (2) RALPH, 2nd Bt; *b* 1901; MP for Rushcliffe Div of Notts 1934-45, for City of London 1945-50 and for W Div of Blackburn 1950-55; Fin Sec to Treas 1942-44; *cr* PC 1944, *Baron Clitheroe*, of Downham, co Lancaster (peerage of UK) 1955, and KCVO 1977: *m* 1924, Hon Sylvia Benita Frances Hotham, FRICS, who *d* 1991, da of 6th Baron Hotham; *d* 1984; *s* by his elder son (3) RALPH JOHN, 2nd Baron and present peer, also 3rd Baronet.

Clive, Viscount; son of Earl of Powis

CLWYD, BARON (Roberts) (Baron UK 1919, Bt UK 1908)
(Title pronounced "Cloo-id")

(JOHN) ANTHONY ROBERTS, 3rd Baron and 3rd Baronet; *b* 2 Jan 1935; *s* 1987; *ed* Harrow, and Trin Coll, Camb; Bar Gray's Inn 1970: *m* 1969, (Linda) Geraldine, yr da of Charles Eugene Cannons, of Sanderstead, Surrey, and has issue.

𝕬rms – Per fesse azure and argent, a lion rampant between three ostrich feathers all counter-changed. 𝕮rest – A lion rampant per fesse argent and azure, holding in its paws on ostrich feather. 𝕾upporters – *Dexter*, a dragon proper, collared or; *sinister*, a sable bear, also collared or.
Residence – 24 Salisbury Av, Cheam, Surrey SM1 2DJ.

SONS LIVING

Hon (JOHN) MURRAY, *b* 27 Aug 1971.
Hon Jeremy Trevor, *b* 1973.
Hon Hugh Gerald Arthur, *b* 1977.

SISTER LIVING

Hon Alison de Bois, *b* 1939: *m* 1st, 1965 (*m diss* 1972), George Stricevic; 2ndly, 1972, Anthony H. Brown, of 9 Royal Terr, Glasgow, G3 7NT, and has issue living (by 1st *m*) Milorad, *b* 1967, — (by 2nd *m*) Barnaby Joseph, *b* 1973, — Benedict Joseph, *b* 1975, — Lionel Trevor, *b* 1978.

WIDOWS LIVING OF SONS OF FIRST BARON

Aileen Mary, da of late Charles Edward Burrow, of Sale, Cheshire: *m* 1936, Hon David Stowell Roberts, who *d* 1956, and has issue (see colls infra). *Residence* – 24 Long Ashton Rd, Long Ashton, Bristol BS18 9LB.
Eileen Margaret, da of late Alfred Thomas Easom, of Hillside, Abergele: *m* 1947, Hon (William Herbert) Mervyn Roberts, who *d* 1990, and has issue (see colls infra). *Residence* – 17 Wimblehurst Rd, Horsham, W Sussex RH12 2EA.

COLLATERAL BRANCHES LIVING

Issue of late Hon David Stowell Roberts, 2nd son of 1st Baron, *b* 1900, *d* 1956: *m* 1936, Aileen Mary (ante), da of late Charles Edward Burrow, of Sale, Cheshire:—
(Hugh) Martin (29 Chalfont Rd, Oxford OX2 6TL), *b* 1941; *ed* Christ's Hosp Sch, and Merton Coll, Oxford; Headmaster Cherwell Comprehensive Sch, Oxford: *m* 1966, Diana, da of Denis C. Cochran, of Cape Town, and has issue living, Thomas Owen, *b* 1973, — Sarah Megan *b* 1971. —— Peter Gareth (11 Sandford Rd, Hotwells, Bristol), *b* 1947; *ed* Christ's Hosp Sch, and Univ of E Anglia: *m* 1982, Susan Browne, and has issue living, Matthew Lewis, *b* 1984. —— Fenella (39 Drayton Gdns, SW10 9RY), *b* 1940: *m* 1968, Peter Rosenwald, and has issue living, David Joseph, *b* 1972, — Celia Janet, *b* 1974.

Issue of late Hon (William Herbert) Mervyn Roberts, 3rd and yst son of 1st Baron, *b* 1906, *d* 1990: *m* 1947, Eileen Margaret (ante), da of late Alfred Thomas Easom, of Hillside, Abergele:—
Catherine Angela, *b* 1950: *m* 1984, David James Arnold, of 17 Wimblehurst Rd, Horsham, W Sussex RH12 2EA.

PREDECESSORS – (1) JOHN HERBERT Roberts, el son of late John Roberts (sometime MP for Flint Dist) of Bryngwenallt, Abergele, N Wales; *b* 1863; Chm of Welsh Liberal Parliamentary Party 1912-18 (formerly Sec); MP for W Div of Denbighshire (L) 1892-1918; *cr* a *Baronet* 1908, and *Baron Clwyd*, of Abergele, co Denbigh (peerage of United Kingdom) 1919: *m* 1893, Hannah Rushton, who *d* 1951, da of late William Sproston Caine, MP, of 33 North Side, Clapham Common, SW; *d* 1955: *s* by his el son (2) (JOHN) TREVOR, 2nd Baron, *b* 1900, bar Gray's Inn; assist sec of Commons, Lord Chancellor's Dept, House of Lords 1949-61: *m* 1932, Joan de Bois, who *d* 1985, da of late Charles R. Murray, of Woodbank, Partickhill, Glasgow; *d* 1987; *s* by his only son (3) JOHN ANTHONY, 3rd Baron and present peer.

Clydesdale, Marquess of (Marquess of Douglas and Clydesdale); son of Duke of Hamilton and Brandon.

CLYDESMUIR, BARON (Colville) (Baron UK 1948)

I cannot forget

RONALD JOHN BILSLAND COLVILLE, KT, CB, MBE, TD, 2nd Baron; *b* 21 May 1917; *s* 1954; *ed* Charterhouse, and Trin Coll, Camb (BA); Hon LLD Strathclyde; Hon DSc Heriot-Watt; Hon Col 6th/7th (Territorial) Bn, The Cameronians (Scottish Rifles) 1967-71; Lieut of Queen's Body Guard for Scotland (Royal Company of Archers), Pres of Council (1974-81) and Pres of Lowlands of Scotland TA & VR Assocns 1968-73; Pres of Scottish Branch Nat Playing Fields Asscn; Gov Bank of Scotland 1972-81; a Dir of Scottish Provident Instn, of Caledonian Offshore Co Ltd; Chm of North Sea Assets Ltd; a Dir of British Steel Corpn Strip Mills Div, 1970-73; Chm of Exec Cttee, Scottish Council (Development and Industry) 1966-78; Pres Scottish Council (Development and Industry) since 1978; Lord High Commr to Gen Assembly of Church of Scotland 1971 and 1972; Lord Lieut for Lanarkshire since 1963; 1939-45 War (despatches); MBE (Mil) 1944, CB (Civil) 1965, KT 1972: *m* 1946, Joan Marguerita, da of Lt-Col Ernest Brabazon Booth, DSO, MD, and has issue.

Arms – Argent, a cross moline sable, on a chief of the last a thistle slipped proper between two bulls' heads also argent. **Crest** – A hind's head erased proper. **Supporters** – A roebuck and a doe, both proper. *Residence* – Langlees House, Biggar, Lanarkshire. *Clubs* – Caledonian, New (Edinburgh).

SONS LIVING

Hon DAVID RONALD, *b* 8 April 1949: *m* 1978, Aline Frances, el da of Peter Merriam, of Holton Lodge, Holton St Mary, Suffolk (*see* M Ailsa, 1985 Edn), and has issue living, Richard, *b* 21 Oct 1980, — Hamish, *b* 1989, — Rachel, *b* 1983, — Harriet, *b* 1985.

Hon Andrew John, *b* 1953; *ed* Harrow, and Magdalene Coll, Camb (MA); Solicitor 1976-80, since when a Merchant Banker: *m* 1978, Elaine Geneviève, yst da of E. G. Davy, of Corner Farm, Holton St Peter, Suffolk, and has issue living, Patrick Edwin Ronald, *b* 1988, — Emily Christine Rose, *b* 1986. *Residence* – 40 Pembroke Rd, W8.

DAUGHTERS LIVING

Hon Diana Mary, *b* 1947; temporary Lady in Waiting to HRH The Duchess of Gloucester 1980-83: *m* 1973, Christopher I. C. Munro, of 26 Pembroke Sq, W8 6PB, and has issue living, Andrew James William, *b* 1979, — Fiona Mary, *b* 1976.

Hon Elizabeth Anne *b* 1955: *m* 1983, Christopher J. V. R. Baker, son of late Maj Valentine Baker, and has issue living, Lucy Florence, *b* 1986.

SISTER LIVING

Hon Rosemary Anne Heather, *b* 1927: *m* 1954, Philip Arthur Whitcombe, of Green Cross Farm, Churt, Farnham, Surrey, and has issue living, Robert John, *b* 1955: *m* 1988, Sophie E., da of T. O. Roberts, of Petersfield, Hants, — Susan Anne Clare, *b* 1957: *m* 1985, Robin R. Marriott, yr son of Anthony Marriott, of Park View Farm, Headley, Hants.

PREDECESSOR – (1) *Rt Hon Sir* DAVID JOHN Colville, GCIE, TD, PC, son of late John Colville, MP, JP, of Cleland House, Lanarkshire; *b* 1894; was Parliamentary Sec to Depart of Overseas Trade 1931-5, Under-Sec of State for Scotland 1935-36, Financial Sec to the Treasury 1936-8, Sec of State for Scotland 1938-40 and Gov of Bombay 1943-48 (acted as Viceroy and Gov-Gen of India on four occasions); a Gov of British Broadcasting Corporation 1950-4 and National Gov for Scotland 1952-4; sat as MP for N Div of Midlothian and Peeblesshire (*U*) 1929-43; *cr Baron Clydesmuir*, of Braidwood, co Lanark (peerage of United Kingdom) 1948: *m* 1915, Agnes Anne, CI, who *d* 1970, da of Sir William Bilsland, 1st Bt, LLD, *d* 1954; *s* by his only son (2) RONALD JOHN BILSLAND, 2nd Baron and present peer.

COBBOLD, BARON (Lytton Cobbold) (Baron UK 1960)

Brave in adversity

DAVID ANTONY FROMANTEEL LYTTON COBBOLD, 2nd Baron; *b* 14 July 1937; *s* 1987; *ed* Eton, and Trin Coll, Camb (BA 1960); assumed by deed poll 1960 the additional surname of Lytton before his patronymic; DL Herts 1993; Fellow Assocn of Corporate Treasurers; BP Finance Internat 1979-87, Gen Manager Treasury, TSB England & Wales plc 1987-88, Dir Hill Samuel Bank Ltd 1988-89, Chm Lytton Enterprises Ltd since 1971, Hon Treasurer Historic Houses Assocn since 1988, Managing Dir Gaincorp UK Ltd since 1989, Dir Close Brothers Group plc since 1993, Pres Univ of Hertfordshire Development Cttee since 1992, Memb Board of Governors, Univ of Hertforshire since 1993, Trustee, The Pilgrim Trust since 1993, Chm Stevenage Community Trust since 1992: *m* 1961, Christine Elizabeth, 3rd da of Maj Sir Dennis Frederick Bankes Stucley, 5th Bt, and has issue.

Arms – Sable a chevron or between in chief two bezants and in base a lion passant guardant gold on a chief dancetty of the last two ducal coronets azure. **Crest** – A lion statant guardant argent crowned with a ducal coronet azure supporting with the dexter paw an escutcheon vert thereon three escutcheons also argent each having a bordure engrailed or. **Supporters** – On either side a yellow labrador dog proper each resting the interior hind foot on a battering ram fessewise the head inward also proper headed and garnished azure.

Seat – Knebworth House, Herts. *Town Residence* – 2d Park Place Villas, W2.

SONS LIVING

Hon HENRY FROMANTEEL, *b* 12 May 1962; *ed* Eton, and Kent Univ (BA 1983): *m* 1987, Martha Frances, da of James Buford Boone, Jr, of Tuscaloosa, Alabama, USA, and has issue living, Edward, *b* 23 April 1992, — Morwenna Gray, *b* 1989.

Hon Peter Guy Fromanteel, *b* 1964; *ed* Eton, and Durham Univ (BA 1986): *m* 1988, Ginette Elizabeth, da of Bernard Keigher, of Holland Park, W11, and has issue living, Frederick Alexander, *b* 1992.

Hon Richard Stucley Fromanteel, *b* 1968; *ed* Eton, and Bristol Univ; a Page of Honour to HM 1980-82.

DAUGHTER LIVING

Hon Rosina Kim, *b* 1971.

BROTHER LIVING

Hon Rowland John Fromanteel COBBOLD, *b* 1944; *ed* Eton, and Trin Coll, Camb (MA); Dir Cathay Pacific Airways Ltd since 1987: *m* 1969, Sophia Augusta, da of B. N. White-Spunner, of Lansdowne, Nenagh, co Tipperary, and has issue living, Patrick Alexander Fromanteel, *b* 1974, — Lorna Bridget, *b* 1971. *Residence* – 30 Astell St, SW3.

SISTER LIVING

Hon Susan Victoria, *b* 1933; High Sheriff Herts 1989: *m* 1957, S/Ldr Christopher Charles Blount, MVO, RAF and has issue living, James Hubert Rowland, *b* 1958, — Oliver Charles, *b* 1959, — Catherine Victoria Jane, *b* 1962: *m* 1988, Richard M. Glaister, 5th son of Thomas Glaister, of Crofthead, Kentmere, Kendal, Cumbria, and has issue living, Cosima Susan Ruth *b* 1990, Davina Millicent Jane *b* 1991, — Pamela Jane, *b* 1965: *m* 1991, Rupert A. W. Goodman, elder son of Nigel Goodman, of Eton Coll, Berks, and has issue living, Felix Christopher Woodward *b* 1993. *Residence* – Manor Farm, Barkway, Herts.

WIDOW LIVING OF FIRST BARON

Lady (Margaret) Hermione (Millicent) Lytton (*Lady Hermione Cobbold*), da of 2nd Earl of Lytton: *m* 1930, the 1st Baron, KG, GCVO, PC, who *d* 1987. *Residence* – Lake House, Knebworth, Herts.

PREDECESSORS – (1) *Rt Hon* CAMERON FROMANTEEL Cobbold, KG, GCVO, son of late Lt-Col Clement John Fromanteel Cobbold; *b* 1904, Lieut for City of London, DL for Herts, High Sheriff for Co of London 1946-47, Gov of Bank of England 1949-61, Chm Middx Hosp and Medical Sch Council 1963-74, Pres British Heart Foundation 1969-76, Lord Chamberlain of HM Household 1963-71, a Lord-in-Waiting to HM 1971-87; *cr* PC 1959, and *Baron Cobbold*, of Knebworth, co Herts (peerage of UK) 1960: *m* 1930, Lady (Margaret) Hermione (Millicent) Lytton, da of 2nd Earl of Lytton; *d* 1987; *s* by his elder son (2) DAVID ANTONY FROMANTEEL, 2nd Baron and present peer.

COBHAM, BARONY OF (Alexander) (Baron E 1312-13) (Abeyant 1951)

ROBERT DISNEY LEITH ALEXANDER, 13th Baron (16th but for the attainder), *s* his brother, GERVASE DISNEY ALEXANDER, 1933 (in whose favour the abeyance was determined 1916); *d* 1951, when the Barony again fell into abeyance.

WIDOW LIVING OF THIRTEENTH BARON

CHRISTINA JEAN (*Baroness Cobham*), da of Albert Edward Honeybone: *m* 1923 (*m diss* 1934), and whom she re-married 1949, the 13th Baron, who *d* 1951. *Address* – c/o 246 Metella Rd, Prospect, NSW 2149, Australia.

COLLATERAL BRANCHES LIVING

Issue of late Hon Mary Isabel Alexander, el sister of 13th Baron, *b* 1882, *d* 1978: *m* 1st, 1916, Capt John Leslie Morton Shaw, Duke of Wellington's (W Riding Regt), who *d* 1925; 2ndly, 1927, John Bazley Bazley-White, MC (*d* on active service 1940) (E Rothes):—
(By 1st *m*) John Anthony Cobham SHAW, MC (18 Abbey Mews, Amesbury Abbey, Amesbury, Wilts SP4 7EX), *b* 1917; *ed* Eton; 1939-45 War as Maj RA (MC and Bar): *m* 1st, 1945, Rhondda, who *d* 1964, da of late Brig-Gen Charles Herbert Rankin, CB, CMG, DSO (Rankin, Bt, *cr* 1898, colls); 2ndly, 1965, Phyllis Rosemary, da of late Arthur David Clere Parsons (*see* E Rosse, colls), and widow of late Capt Ian Stanley Akers-Douglas, Berks Yeo (*see* V Chilston, colls), and has issue living (by 1st *m*), Simon Rhys (40 James St, Oxford OX4 1ET), *b* 1949: *m* 1976, Christine, da of Alfred Morton Hind, — Veronica Mary (5 Dorchester Way, Greywell, Basingstoke, Hants), *b* 1946: *m* 19— (*m diss* 1988), Peter Kamerling, and has issue living, Henri Alexander *b* 1975, Henrietta Herina *b* 1978, Vancessa Johanna *b* 1980. —— Cynthia Mary, *b* 1920: *m* 1946, Sidney James Fulton, CMG, who *d* 1993, of The Old Farmhouse, Nailsbourne, Taunton, Somerset TA2 8AE, and has issue living, Robert Henry Gervase, *b* 1948: *m* 1975, Midge Free, and has issue living, James Anthony Gervase *b* 1977, Mark William Miller *b* 1980, — Ann Elizabeth, *b* 1947, — Jane Louisa, *b* 1954: *m* 1979, Denis Anthony Tocher, and has issue living, Alastair James *b* 1985, Lydia Josephine *b* 1987. —— Margaret Daphne, *b* 1923: *m* 1947, Charles Herbert Fowler Ransom, who *d* 1988, of Porter's Farm, Wyck Rissington, Cheltenham, Glos, and has issue living, Andrew Charles D'Oyley (35 Arlington Sq, N1), *b* 1948: *m* 1971, Elizabeth Magaret Gee, of Kingston-upon-Hull, E Yorks, — Mark Anthony (Church Farm, Idbury, Oxfordshire), *b* 1952: *m* 1979, Jane Eason, who *d* 1991, of Broadway, Worcs, and has issue living, three sons, — Jeremy Peter Scott (Church Farm Cottage, Idbury, Oxfordshire), *b* 1953: *m* 1984, Marie-Pierre Köhl, of Villeneuve-Loubet, France.

Issue of late Hon Muriel Helen Alexander, yr sister of 13th Baron, *b* 1887, *d* 1978: *m* 1916, Maj John Edmund Burnet Thornely, OBE, who *d* 1978:—
(Gervase) Michael (Cobham) THORNELY (High Stangerthwaite, Killington, Sedbergh, Cumbria), *b* 1918; *ed* Rugby, and Trin Hall, Camb (MA); Headmaster of Sedbergh Sch 1954-75: *m* 1954, Jennifer Margery, da of Sir (Charles) Hilary Scott, of Knowle House, Bishops Walk, Addington, Surrey, and has issue living, Richard Michael Gervase (Higher Hollowshaw Farm, Chinley, via Stockport, Cheshire SK12 6AW), *b* 1957: *m* 1987, Janet Anne, da of late Peter Francis Martin Turberville, of 16 Greenways, Beckenham, Kent, and has issue living, Michael Alistair *b* 1987, Andrew Peter *b* 1989, James Nicholas *b* 1994, — Charles William Alexander, *b* 1958, — Elizabeth Miranda, *b* 1960: *m* 1983, Edmund Nigel Ronald Hosker, and has issue living, Lucy Abigail *b* 1988, Josephine Rose *b* 1989, Katharine Amy *b* 1992, — Jacqueline Sarah, *b* 1965: *m* 1987, Bruce Andrew Walkom, and has issue living, Samuel Francis *b* 1990, Benjamin Oliver *b* (twin) 1990.

COBHAM, VISCOUNT (Lyttelton) (Viscount GB 1718, Bt E 1618)

One God, one king

JOHN WILLIAM LEONARD LYTTELTON, 11th Viscount, and 14th Baronet, *b* 5 June 1943; *s* 1977; *ed* Eton, Christ's Coll, NZ, and RAC Cirencester: *m* 1974, Penelope Ann, el da of Roy Cooper, of Moss Farm, Knutsford, Cheshire.

Arms – Argent, a chevron between three escallops sable. **Crest** – A Moor's head in profile couped at the shoulders proper, wreathed round the temples argent and sable. **Supporters** – Two mermen proper, each holding in the exterior hand a trident or.
Seat – Hagley Hall, Stourbridge, W Midlands DY9 9LG; 20 Kylestrome House, Cundy St, Ebury St, SW1.

BROTHERS LIVING

Hon CHRISTOPHER CHARLES (28 Abbey Gdns, NW8), *b* 23 Oct 1947; *ed* Eton: *m* 1973, Tessa Mary, da of late Col Alexander George Jeremy Readman, DSO (*see* Curtis, Bt, colls), and has issue living, Oliver Christopher, *b* 1976, — Sophie Emma, *b* 1978.
Hon Richard Cavendish (22 Baskerville Rd, SW18), *b* 1949; *ed* Eton: *m* 1971, Romilly, da of Michael Barker, of 14 Harley Gdns, SW10, and has issue living, Thomas Charles Henry, *b* 1986, — Mary Viola, *b* 1976.
Hon Nicholas Makeig, *b* 1951; *ed* Shiplake Court, Oxon: *m* 1980 (*m diss* 1993), June Carrington, and has issue living, David Charles, *b* 1981.

SISTERS LIVING

Hon Juliet Meriel, *b* 1944: *m* 1967, John Michael Dugdale, of Birch Farm, Kinlet, Bewdley, Worcs, DL12 3DS, son of John E. M. Dugdale, of Lower Cefn Perfa, Kerry, Newtown, Powys, and has issue living, Mark Rupert Marshall, *b* 1968, — Helen Riba, *b* 1970, — Clare Lucinda, *b* 1973, — Rowena Sarah, *b* 1976.
Hon (Elizabeth) Catherine (*Baroness Forester*), *b* 1946: *m* 1967, 8th Baron Forester, of Willey Park, Broseley, Salop.
Hon Lucy, *b* 1954: *m* 1980, Mark N. Kemp-Gee, of Beech Tree Cottage, Preston Candover, Basingstoke, Hants RG25 2EJ, yr son of late Bernard Kemp-Gee, of 16 Airlie Gdns, W8, and has issue Henry Alfred, *b* 1981, — Robert Arthur, *b* 1984, — John Andrew, *b* 1987.
Hon Sarah, *b* (twin) 1954: *m* 1976, C. Nicholas Bedford, of Armsworth Hill Cottage, Old Alresford, Hants, and has issue living, Minna Lucy, *b* 1978, — Olivia Alison, *b* 1982.

AUNTS LIVING (*Daughters of 9th Viscount*)

Hon Audrey Lavinia (Poplar Cottage, Fore St Hill, Budleigh Salterton, Devon), *b* 1918: *m* 1950, as his 3rd wife, David Edsell Thomas Lindsay, who *d* 1968 (*see* E Crawford, colls)
Hon Lavinia Mary Yolande (Cannon Cottage, Fore St, Budleigh Salterton, Devon), *b* 1921; Subaltern ATS 1941-45: *m* 1st, (Feb) 1945, Capt Cecil Francis Burney Rolt, 23rd Hus, who was *ka* April 1945; 2ndly, 1949, Maj John Edward Dennys, MC, who *d* 1973, and has issue living (by 2nd *m*), Nicholas Charles Jonathan, QC (The Old Rectory, Arborfield, Berks RG2 9HZ) *b* 1951; *ed* Eton, and Brasenose Coll, Oxford (BA); Bar, Middle Temple 1975; QC 1991: *m* 1977, Frances Winifred, da of Rev Canon Gervase William Markham, of Morland House, Penrith, and has issue living, Harriet *b* 1979, Sophie *b* 1981, Romilly Mary *b* 1984, Katharine *b* 1986.

COLLATERAL BRANCHES LIVING

Issue of late Hon George William Lyttelton, 2nd son of 8th Viscount, *b* 1883, *d* 1962: *m* 1919, Pamela Marie, who *d* 1975, da of late Charles Robert Whorwood Adeane, CB (B Leconfield, colls):—
Humphrey Richard Adeane, *b* 1921; musician and writer; Pres Soc for Italic Handwriting since 1990: *m* 1st, 1948 (*m diss* 1952), Patricia Mary Braithwaite, da of late J. Wellesley Gaskell; 2ndly, 1952, Elizabeth Jill, da of Albert F. Richardson and has issue living (by 2nd *m*), (Anthony) Stephen, *b* 1955: *m* 1989, Emma, da of J. de Vere Hunt, of Kensington, London, and has issue living, Charles *b* 1991, Oliver Stephen *b* 1993, Lucy Elizabeth *b* 1989, — David George, *b* 1958, — (by 1st *m*) Henrietta Marie, *b* 1949. — (by 2nd *m*), Georgina Pamela, *b* 1963. *Residence* – Alyn Close, Barnet Rd, Arkley, Herts. —— Diana Maud (*Viscountess Hood*), CVO, *b* 1920; was Assist Press Sec to HM late King George VI 1947-52, and to HM The Queen 1952-7; MVO (4th Class) 1952, CVO 1957: *m* 1957, 7th Viscount Hood. *Residences* – 67 Chelsea Sq, SW3; Loders Court, Bridport, Dorset. —— Helena Frances, *b* 1923: *m* 1940, Peter Stafford Hayden Lawrence, of Simeons, Little Milton, Oxford (*see* Lawrence, Bt, *cr* 1867, colls). —— Margaret Rose, *b* 1926: *m* 1949, Robert Morice Antony Bourne, an Assist Master at Eton 1947-84, of 25 Nine Mile Ride, Finchampstead, Wokingham, Berks, Dorset (*see* E Cairns, 1985 Edn), and has issue living, (Robert) Humphrey Lyttelton, *b* 1954, — George Julian, *b* 1960, — Harriet Madeline, *b* 1950, — Charlotte Elizabeth, *b* 1952, — Lucy Jane, *b* 1956, — Emily Hester, *b* 1963. —— Mary Pamela, *b* 1929: *m* 1953, Maj-Gen Arthur George Ernest Stewart Cox, DFC, RA, and has issue living, Rupert Lyttelton, *b* 1956: *m* 1984, Mary Catherine, yst da of J. M. Mitchell, of Tullymurdoch, Alyth, Perthshire, and has issue living, Georgina Helen *b* 1987, — Phoebe *b* 1991, — Jonathan May, *b* 1957, — Charles Arthur, *b* 1960. — Belinda Jane, *b* 1954. *Residence* – Long Mead, Brixton Deverill, Warminster, Wilts.

Issue of late Hon Richard Glynne Lyttelton, yst son of 8th Viscount, *b* 1893, *d* 1977: *m* 1931, Judith, who *d* 1993, da of late Lt-Col Percy Archer Clive, MP, Gren Gds:—
Spencer Clive, *b* 1939, *ed* Highgate; on staff of Guest, Keen & Nettlefold. —— Thomas Glynne (7 The Grove, Highgate Village, N6 6JU), *b* 1940; *ed* Eton, and Trin Coll, Camb; Assist Master, Eton Coll 1968-94.

Grandchildren of late Rt Rev Hon Arthur Temple Lyttelton, DD, 5th son of 4th Baron Lyttelton:—
Issue of late Cdr Stephen Clive Lyttelton, OBE, DSC, RN, *b* 1887, *d* 1959: *m* 1st, 1919 (*m diss* 1933), Maureen Nina, who *d* 1980, da of Harold Anthony Smith, formerly of 6 Dean's Yard, Westminster, SW; 2ndly, 1938, Mary Cicely, who *d* 1945, da of Brig-Gen Sir (Ernest) Frederick (Orby) Gascoigne, KCVO, CMG, DSO; 3rdly, 1947, Phoebe Hermione (3 The Croft, Old Headington, Oxford), da of A. K. Graham:—
(By 2nd *m*) Edward Gascoigne, *b* 1944; *ed* Eton, King's Coll, Camb, and Ripon Hall Theological Coll. *Residence* – 306 Delaware Av, Toronto, Ontario, Canada M6H 2T6. —— (By 1st *m*) Barbara Meriel, *b* 1921: *m* 1947, Charles Russell Fawcus, who *d* 1985, and has issue living, Mark Russell (22 Hill View Rd, Hildenborough, Kent), *b* 1951; *ed* Clifton: *m* 1975, Cynthia, da of Ronald Stephen Blair, and has issue living, Philip Russell *b* 1981, James Russell *b* 1989, — Meriel Clare, *b* 1949: *m* 1974, Benjamin J. I. Carver, of The Old Vicarage, Uppington, Telford, Shropshire, and has issue living, Annabel Jane *b* 1976, Victoria Meriel *b* 1978. *Residence* – High Drive House, Woldingham, Surrey. —— (By 2nd *m*) Mary Kathleen, *b* 1939: *m* 1970, Malcolm Robert Fraser of Reelig (Reelig House, Kirkhill, Inverness-shire). —— (By 3rd *m*) (Cicely Phoebe) Lavinia, *b* 1950: *m* 1979, Peter John Northrop, of Moor of Clunes, Kirkhill, Inverness, son of D. F. Northrop, of Teynham, Kent.

Descendants of late Rt Hon Alfred Lyttelton, KC, MP, 8th son of 4th Baron Lyttelton:—
Issue of late Rt Hon Oliver Lyttelton, DSO, MC, PC (*Viscount Chandos*), *b* 1893, *d* 1972:—
(*See* V Chandos).

PREDECESSORS – (1) *Sir* Richard Temple, 4th Bt, of Stowe, a military commander of renown under the 1st Duke of Marlborough, was *cr Baron Cobham*, of Cobham, Kent 1714, and *Baron Cobham*, Kent, and *Viscount Cobham* (peerage of Great Britain) 1718, with special remainder failing heirs male of his body, to his sister Hester, wife of Richard Grenville, MP, and her heirs male, and failing such to his 3rd sister, Christian, wife of Sir Thomas Lyttelton, 4th Bt (see infra), and her issue male; *d* 1740; *s* by his sister (2) HESTER GRENVILLE, *cr Countess of Temple* (peerage of Great Britain) 1749, with remainder to her heirs male; *d* 1752; *s* by her son (3) RICHARD, KG, 2nd Earl, a leading statesman, *temp* George III; *d* without issue 1779; *s* by his nephew (4) GEORGE, 3rd Earl; was Viceroy of Ireland 1782 and 1787: *m* Mary Elizabeth (who *d* 1812, having in 1800 been *cr Baroness Nugent* (peerage of Ireland), with remainder to her 2nd son George, who *d* 1850 without issue), da and heiress of Robert, Earl of Nugent, in the peerage of Ireland; assumed by R Licence the additional surnames of Nugent and Temple; was *cr Marquess of Buckingham* 1784, and in 1788 *s* by special remainder his father-in-law, as *Earl Nugent* (peerage of Ireland, *cr* 1776); *d* 1813; *s* by his son (5) RICHARD, KG, 2nd Marquess; assumed 1799, by R licence, the additional surnames of Brydges-Chandos; *cr Earl Temple* (with remainder to his grandda Anne Eliza Mary, afterwards wife of W. H. Powell Gore-Langton, Esq, MP), *Marquess of Chandos* and *Duke of Buckingham* (peerage of United Kingdom) 1822; *d* 1839; *s* by his son (6) RICHARD PLANTAGENET, KG, 2nd Duke; *d* 1861; *s* by his son (7) RICHARD PLANTAGENET CAMPBELL, 3rd Duke; *b* 1823: *m* 1st, 1851, Caroline, who *d* 1874, da of Robert Harvey, of Langley Hall, Bucks; 2nd, 1885, Alice Anne, who *d* 1931, el da of Sir Graham Graham-Montgomery, 3rd Bt; *d* 1889, when the Dukedom of Buckingham and the Earldoms of Temple (*cr* 1749) and Nugent became extinct, the Lordship of Kinloss (to which he had established his right in 1868) devolving on his el da, Lady Mary Morgan, the Earldom of Temple (*cr* 1822) on William Stephen Gore-Langton, and the Viscountcy of Cobham (under special remainder) as heir male of Christian, wife of Sir Thomas Lyttelton, 4th Bt, on (8) CHARLES GEORGE, 5th Baron Lyttelton (see *infra), 8th Viscount Cobham, *b* 1842; High Steward of Bewdley; MP for Worcestershire, E (*L*) 1868-74: *m* 1878, Hon Mary Susan Caroline Cavendish, who *d* 1937, da of 2nd Baron Chesham; *d* 1922; *s* by his son (9) JOHN CAVENDISH, KCB, TD, 9th Viscount, *b* 1881; Lt-Col RA (TA), High Steward of Bewdley, and Lord-Lieut for City and co of Worcester; Under-Sec of State for War 1939-40; MP for Worcestershire Mid or Droitwich Div (*U*) 1910-16: *m* 1908, Violet Yolande, who *d* 1966, da of Charles Leonard; *d* 1949; *s* by his son (10) CHARLES JOHN, KG GCMG, GCVO, TD, PC, 10th Viscount; *b* 1909; Lt-Col RA (TA); Hon Col (Warwicks and Worcs Yeo Sqdn), The Mercian Yeo 1972-77; Pres MCC 1954, Gov Gen NZ 1957-62; Lord Lieut Worcs 1963-74; Lord Steward of HM Household 1967-72, Chancellor of Order of the Garter 1972-77: *m* 1942, Elizabeth Alison (CStJ), who *d* 1986, da of John Reeder Makeig-Jones, CBE, late ICS; *d* 1977; *s* by his el son (11) JOHN WILLIAM LEONARD, 11th Viscount and present peer; also Baron Cobham, Lord Lyttelton, Baron of Frankley, and Baron Westcote.

*(1) *Sir* THOMAS Lyttelton, Knt; Sheriff of Worcester 1613, and MP for Worcestershire 1620-8 and 1639-40 (name spelt Littleton in records of Parliament); was a zealous partisan of Royalty during the Civil Wars, and suffered imprisonment in the Tower; *cr* a *Baronet* 1618; *d* 1650; *s* by his el son (2) *Sir* HENRY, 2nd Bt; was imprisoned in the Tower seventeen months for his attachment to the Royal cause; *dsp* 1703; *s* by his brother (3) *Sir* CHARLES 3rd Bt, also an active partizan of Royalty; was incarcerated in Colchester; *d* 1716; *s* by his son (4) *Sir* THOMAS, 4th Bt successively MP for Worcestershire and Camelford; a Lord of the Admiralty 1727-41: *m* Christian, da of Sir Richard Temple, Bt, of Stowe (see ante); *d* 1751; *s* by his son (5) *Sir* GEORGE, PC, 5th Bt, MP for Okehampton, Principal Sec to Prince of Wales 1737, a Lord of the Treasury 1744-55, Cofferer to the Household 1754-5, and Chancellor and Under Treasurer of Court of Exchequer 1755; *cr Lord Lyttelton, Baron of Frankley*, co Worcester 1756; *d* 1773; *s* by his son (6) THOMAS, 2nd Baron; *dsp* 1779, when the Barony became extinct, and the Baronetcy devolved upon his uncle (7) WILLIAM HENRY, 7th Bt; MP for Bewdley 1748-54, Gov of S Carolina 1755-60, Gov of Jamaica 1760-6, and Envoy Extraor to Portugal; *cr Baron Westcote*, of Balamere, co Longford (peerage of Ireland) 1766, and *Lord Lyttelton, Baron of Frankley* (peerage of England) 1794; *d* 1808; *s* by his son (8) GEORGE FULKE, 2nd Baron; *d* unmarried 1828; *s* by his half-brother (9) WILLIAM HENRY, 3rd Baron; was Lord-Lieut of co Worcester; *d* 1837; *s* by his son (10) GEORGE WILLIAM, KCMG, PC, FRS, 4th Baron; *b* 1817; was Lord-Lieut of co Worcester, Under Sec for Colonies 1846, and Ch Commr of Endowed Schools 1869-74: *m* 1st, 1839, Mary, who *d* 1857, da of Sir Stephen Richard Glynne, 8th Bt; 2ndly, 1869, Sybella

Harriet, who *d* 1900, da of George Clive, and widow of Humphrey Francis Mildmay; *d* 1876; *s* by his son (11) CHARLES GEORGE, 5th Baron, who *s* (under special remainder) as 8th *Viscount Cobham* 1889 (ante).

Cochrane, Lord; son of Earl of Dundonald.

COCHRANE OF CULTS, BARON (Cochrane) (Baron UK 1919)

(RALPH HENRY) VERE COCHRANE, 4th Baron; *b* 20 Sept 1926; *s* 1990; *ed* Eton, and King's Coll, Camb (MA); late Lieut RE, served 1945-48; Member Queen's Body Guard for Scotland (Royal Company of Archers); DL Fife: *m* 1956, Janet Mary Watson, da of late William Hunter Watson Cheyne, MB, MRCS, LRCP (*see* Cheyne, Bt, colls), and has issue.

Arms – Quarterly, 1st Argent, a chevron gules between three boars' heads erased azure, armed and langued of the second, within a bordure contre-ermine, *Cochrane*; 2nd, Gules, a fess ermine, in chief a stag's antler or, fessways, *Crawford of Kilbirnie*; 3rd, Gules, a fess chequy argent and azure, in chief three mullets of the second *Lindsay of the Byres*; 4th, Argent, on a saltire sable nine lozenges of the field, in centre chief a mullet gules, *Blair*, **Crest** – A horse passant argent, between two stag's attires gules. **Supporters** – Two ermines ermine.
Seat – Cults, Cupar, Fife KY15 5RD *Club* – New (Edinburgh).

SONS LIVING

By virtue of labour

Hon THOMAS HUNTER VERE, *b* 7 Sept 1957, *ed* Eton, and Exeter Univ; Bar Inner Temple 1980; ACII. *Clubs* – Royal and Ancient, New (Edinburgh).

Hon Michael Charles Nicholas, *b* 1959; *ed* Glenalmond, and RNC Dartmouth; Lt Cdr RN. *Clubs* – Naval and Military, Royal Yacht Sqdn.

BROTHER LIVING

Hon (John Douglas) Julian, *b* 1929; *ed* Eton: *m* 1965, Vaila Rose, da of late Cdr Robert Dalby, RN (ret), of Castle Donnington, Leics, and has issue living, John Colin, *b* 1969, — Julietta Anne, *b* 1966, — Alice Georgina, *b* 1974. *Residence* – Hopton, Derbys.

COLLATERAL BRANCHES LIVING

Issue of late Capt Hon Sir Archibald Douglas Cochrane, 2nd son of 1st Baron, GCMG, KCSI, DSO, RN, *b* 1885, *d* 1958: *m* 1926, Hon Julia Dorothy Cornwallis, CBE, who *d* 1971, da of 1st Baron Cornwallis:—
Douglas Fiennes, *b* 1928: *ed* Eton, and Trin Coll, Camb: *m* 1969 (*m diss* 1987), Patricia Ann, da of late Frank Renshaw, of Puddletown, Dorset, and has issue living, Alexander Douglas, *b* 1972, — James Archibald, *b* 1976. —— Mabel Dorothy, *b* 1932: *m* 1958, Col Geoffrey Douglas Gill, MBE, King's Regt, who *d* 1990, and has a son, Peter Geoffrey Fiennes, *b* 1966. *Residence* – Camino Son Toells 5, San Agustin, 07015 Palma de Mallorca, Spain.

Issue of late Air Ch Marshal Hon Sir Ralph Alexander Cochrane, GBE, KCB, AFC, 3rd son of 1st Baron, *b* 1895, *d* 1977: *m* 1930, Hilda Frances Holme, who *d* 1982, 3rd da of late Francis Holme Wiggin:—
John Alexander (Fairspear House, Leafield, Oxford, OX8 5NY), *b* 1935; *ed* Eton, and Balliol Coll, Oxford (BA): *m* 1966 Margaret Minna, da of late Sir Charles Henry Rose, 3rd Bt (*cr* 1909), and has issue living, Thomas Hugh, *b* 1973, — Phoebe Clare, *b* 1967, — Alexandra, *b* 1969, — Katherine Grizel Rose, *b* 1975. —— Malcolm Ralph (Grove Farmhouse, Shipton-under-Wychwood, Oxon), *b* 1938, *ed* Eton: *m* 1972, Mary Anne, da of Ralph Henry Scrope, JP (E Mexborough), and has issue living, William Ralph, *b* 1974, — Alice Anne, *b* 1976, — Harriet Mary, *b* 1979. —— Ann Grizel, *b* 1932: *m* 1953, Lt-Col Robert Christie Stewart, CBE, TD, Argyll and Sutherland Highlanders, HM Lord Lieut for Kinross-shire 1966-74 (*see* Lighton, Bt, 1980 Edn), and has issue living, Alexander Christie (Clarehaven, Newmarket, Suffolk), *b* 1955: *m* 1986, Katherine Lake, elder da of Denys Barry Herbert Domvile (*see* B Bellew), and has issue living, Archie Christie *b* 1989, Georgina Elizabeth *b* 1987, — John Cochrane, *b* 1957, — David Coldwells, *b* 1960: *m* 1989, Lucy, da of Maj Michael Paxton, — Catriona Ann, *b* 1954: *m* 1975, Julian Charles Marsham (*see* E Romney, colls), — Sara Jane, *b* 1966. *Residence* – Arndean, Dollar, Kinross-shire.

PREDECESSORS – (1) THOMAS HORATIO ARTHUR ERNEST Cochrane, yr son of 11th Earl of Dundonald; *b* 1857; Maj and Hon Lt-Col 4th Batn Princess Louise's (Argyll and Sutherland Highlanders), Lt-Col cmdg 2/7th Black Watch 1914-17; Parliamentary Private Sec of State for the Colonies 1895-1901, and Under Sec of State for the Home Depart 1902-1905; MP for Ayrshire, N Div (LU) 1892-1910; *cr Baron Cochrane of Cults*, of Crawford Priory, co Fife (peerage of United Kingdom) 1919: *m* 1880, Lady Gertrude Julia Georgina Boyle, OBE, who *d* 1950, da of 6th Earl of Glasgow; *d* 1951; *s* by his son (2) THOMAS GEORGE FREDERICK, DSO, 2nd Baron; *b* 1883; Maj Black Watch; 1914-18 War (DSO 1919): *m* 1st, 1920, Hon Elin Douglas-Pennant, who *d* 1934, da of 2nd Baron Penrhyn; 2ndly, 1948, Millicent Agnes Mary, who *d* 1981, da of late Alexander Duckham, PhD, and formerly wife of Wilfred Neill Foster; *d* 1968; *s* by his son (3) THOMAS CHARLES ANTHONY, 3rd Baron, *b* 1922; founder and trustee The Gardners' Memorial Trust; *d* 1990; *s* by his brother (4) (RALPH HENRY) VERE, 4th Baron and present peer.

COCKFIELD, BARON (Cockfield) (Life Baron 1978)

(FRANCIS) ARTHUR COCKFIELD, son of late Lt C. F. Cockfield; *b* 28th Sept 1916; *ed* Dover Gram Sch and LSE (LLB, BSc (Econ)); Hon LLD Fordham (NY), Hon LLD Sheffield, Hon DUniv Surrey; Bar Inner Temple 1942; Dir of Statistics and Intelligence, Board of Inland Revenue 1945-52, Commr of Inland Revenue, Member of Board of Inland Revenue 1951-52; Finance Dir, Boots Pure Drug Co Ltd 1953-61, and Man Dir and Chm, Exec Managing Cttee, 1961-67; Member NEDC 1962-64 and 1982-83, Pres, R Statistical Soc 1968-69; Adviser on Taxation Policy to Chancellor of the Exchequer 1970-73, and Chm Price Commn 1973-77; Min of State HM Treasury 1979-82; Sec of State for Trade 1982-83; Chancellor of Duchy of Lancaster 1983-84, Vice-Pres European Commn 1985-88; Grand Cross Order of Leopold II, Belgium; cr Knt 1973, PC 1983, and *Baron Cockfield,* of Dover, co Kent (Life Baron) 1978: *m* 19—, Aileen Monica Mudie, choreographer, who *d* 1992.
Address – House of Lords, SW1A 0PW.

COCKS OF HARTCLIFFE, BARON (Cocks) (Life Baron 1987)

MICHAEL FRANCIS LOVELL COCKS, PC, son of late Rev Harry F. Lovell Cocks, of Amersham, Oxon; *b* 19 Aug 1929; *ed* Bristol Univ; Assist Govt Whip 1974-76, Parl Sec to Treasury and Govt Whip 1974-79; MP (*Lab*) Bristol South 1970-87; *cr* PC 1976, and *Baron Cocks of Hartcliffe,* of Chinnor, co Oxfordshire (Life Baron) 1987: *m* 1st, 1954, Janet Macfarlane; 2ndly, 1979, Valerie Davis, and has issue, two sons and two das, by 1st *m*.
Address – c/o House of Lords, SW1.

COGGAN, BARON (Coggan) (Life Baron 1980)

Rt Rev and *Rt Hon* (FREDERICK) DONALD COGGAN, PC, DD, son of the late Cornish Arthur Coggan, of London; *b* 9 Oct 1909; *ed* Merchant Taylors' Sch, St John's Coll, Camb (MA), and Wycliffe Hall, Oxford; BD Toronto 1941; DD Lambeth 1957; Hon DD Toronto, Leeds, Cambridge, Hull, Aberdeen, Toyko, Saskatoon, Huron, and Manchester, Moravian Theol Seminary; HHD Westminster Choir Coll, Princeton, NJ, Hon D Litt Lancaster 1967, STD New York, Hon LLD Liverpool; Hon DCL Canterbury 1975; D Univ York 1975; Assist Lecturer in Semitic Languages and Literature, Manchester Univ 1931-34; Curate of St Mary's, Islington N 1934-37, Prof of New Testament, Wycliffe Coll, Toronto 1937-44, Prin of London Coll of Divinity 1944-56, and Examining Chap to Bishop of Lincoln 1944-56, to Bishop of Manchester 1951-56, to Bishop of Southwark 1954-56, and to Bishop of Chester 1955-56; select Preacher of Oxford Univ 1961; consecrated 3rd Bishop of Bradford 1956, enthroned 93rd Archbishop of York, Primate of England, and Metropolitan 1961, 101st Archbishop of Canterbury; Primate of All England and Metropolitan 1974-80; Sub-Prelate of Order of St John 1960 and Prelate 1967-90; Pro-Chancellor of York Univ 1962-74, and Hull Univ 1968-74 and Chm of Coll of Preachers; Chm exec cttee of Council of Christians and Jews 1983-87; author of *A People's Heritage* 1944, *The Ministry of the Word* 1945, *The Glory of God* 1950, *Stewards of Grace* 1958, *Five Makers of the New Testament* 1962, *Sinews of Faith* 1969, *Word and World* 1971, *Convictions* 1975, *Paul: Portrait of a Revolutionary* 1984, *The Sacrament of the Word* 1987, *Cuthbert Bardsley: Bishop, Evangelist, Pastor* 1989, *The Voice from the Cross* 1993, and *The Servant-Son* 1995; *cr* PC 1961 and *Baron Coggan,* of Canterbury and Sissinghurst, co Kent (Life Baron) 1980; received Royal Victorian Chain 1980: *m* 1935, Jean Braithwaite, da of Dr William Loudon Strain, and has issue.
Residence – 28 Lions Hall, St Swithun St, Winchester SO23 9HW. *Club* – Athenaeum.

DAUGHTERS LIVING

Hon Dorothy Ann, *b* 1938. *Residence* – 1 King Alfred Place, Hyde, Winchester.
Hon Ruth Evelyn, *b* 1940. *Residence* – 15 Plough Way, Badger Farm, Winchester.

COHEN, BARONY OF (Cohen) (Extinct 1973)

SON LIVING OF LIFE BARON

Hon Leonard Harold Lionel, *b* 1922; *ed* Eton, and New Coll, Oxford (BA 1945, MA 1946); Bar Lincoln's Inn 1948; European War 1941-45 with Rifle Brig (wounded): *m* 1949, Eleanor Lucy da of late Philip Q. Henriques, and has issue. *Residence* – Dovecote House, Swallowfield Park, nr Reading, Berks RG7 1TG. *Club* – White's.

WIDOW LIVING OF SON OF LIFE BARON

Jane, da of late Rt Hon Sir Seymour Edward Karminski (*see* Lewis, Bt, *cr* 1902, ext, 1955 Edn): *m* 1953, Hon Hugh Lionel Cohen, who *d* 1992, and has issue, three sons. *Residence* – Overbrook House, Devil's Highway, Crowthorne, Berks RGH 6BJ.

COHEN OF BRIGHTON, BARONY OF (Cohen) (Extinct 1966)

SON LIVING OF LIFE BARON (By 1st marriage)

Hon John Christopher Coleman, *b* 1940; *ed* Stowe, and McGill Univ (PhD): *m* 1965, Anne-Marie, da of Eugene Krauss, of Paris, and has issue.

DAUGHTERS LIVING OF LIFE BARON (By 1st marriage)

Hon Christine Coleman, *b* 1942: *m* 1965 (*m diss* 19—), David Maxwell Park, MRCP, and has issue, one da.
Hon Madeleine Coleman, *b* 1946; assumed by deed poll 19— the surname of Coleman in lieu of Coleman-Cohen: *m* 1978, Ross King, of 3222, 3rd Street SW, Calgary, Alberta T2S 1V3, Canada, and has issue, one son and one da.

Coke, Viscount; son of Earl of Leicester.

COLE, BARONY OF (Cole) (Extinct 1979)

SON LIVING OF LIFE BARON

Hon Jonathan Dare, *b* 1946; *ed* Eton, and Hertford Coll, Oxford.

DAUGHTER LIVING OF LIFE BARON

Hon Juliet Anthea, *b* 1951.

COLERAINE, BARON (Law) (Baron UK 1954)

JAMES MARTIN BONAR LAW, 2nd Baron; *b* 8 Aug 1931; *s* 1980; *ed* Eton, and Trin Coll, Oxford: *m* 1st, 1958 (*m diss* 1966), Emma Elizabeth, only da of late Nigel Richards; 2ndly, 1966, Anne Patricia, who accidentally drowned in Portugal 1993, yr da of Maj-Gen Ralph Henry Farrant, CB, of Wareham, Dorset, and has had issue by 1st and 2nd *m*.

Arms – Argent a saltire azure between four cocks proper. **Crest** – Issuant from a chaplet of maple leaves vert, a demi salmon proper. **Supporters** – *Dexter*, a Basenji dog; *Sinster*, a kid, both proper.
Residence – Flat 3, 5 Kensington Park Gdns, W11.

SON LIVING (By 2nd marriage)

Hon (JAMES) PETER BONAR, *b* 23 Feb 1975; *ed* Eton.

DAUGHTERS LIVING AND DECEASED (By 1st marriage)

Hon Elizabeth Mary, *b* 1961: *m* 1985, Hon Charles Edmund Grenville Ironside, only son of 2nd Baron Ironside.
Hon Sophia Anne, *b* 1964.

Thy law my thought

(By 2nd marriage)

Hon Henrietta Margaret, *b* 1968; accidentally drowned in Portugal 1993.
Hon Juliana Caroline Matilda, *b* 1971.

BROTHER LIVING

Hon Andrew Bonar, *b* 1933; *ed* Rugby, and Trin Coll, Dublin: *m* 1961, Joanna Margarette, da of Raymond Neill, of Fairview, Delgany, co Wicklow, and has issue living, Richard Pitcairn Bonar, *b* 1963, — Charlotte Mary de Montmorency Bonar, *b* 1964. *Residence* – Shankill Castle, Shankill, co Dublin.

PREDECESSOR – **(1)** *Rt Hon* RICHARD KIDSTON Law, PC, son of late Rt Hon Andrew Bonar Law, MP; Prime Minister 1922-23; *b* 1901; Min of State 1943-45, Min of Educn May-June 1945; Chm Standing Advisory Cttee on Pay of Higher Civil Service 1957-61, and Chm of Nat Youth Employment Council 1955-62; MP for SW Div of Kingston-upon-Hull (C) 1931-45, for S Div of Kensington 1945-50 and for Haltemprice Div of Kingston-upon-Hull 1950-54; *cr* PC 1943, and *Baron Coleraine*, of Haltemprice, E Riding of Yorks (peerage of UK) 1954: *m* 1929, Mary Virginia, who *d* 1978, yr da of late Abraham Fox Nellis, of Rochester, NY USA; *d* 1980; *s* by his el son **(2)** JAMES MARTIN BONAR, 2nd Baron and present peer.

COLERIDGE, BARON (Coleridge) (Baron UK 1873)

As life so the end

WILLIAM DUKE COLERIDGE, 5th Baron, *b* 18 June, 1937; *s* 1984; *ed* Eton; Maj Coldm Gds, served King's African Rifles and Kenya Army 1961-63, Commanded Guard's Independent Parachute Co 1970-72: *m* 1st, 1962 (*m diss* 1977), Everild Tania, only child of Lt-Col Beauchamp Hamborough, of Wispers Farm, Nairobi, Kenya; 2ndly, 1977, Pamela, da of George William Baker, CBE, VRD, and has issue by 1st and 2nd *m*.

Arms – Argent, on a mount vert in base an otter proper, a chief gules, charged with a dove of the first between two crosses patée fitchée or. **Crest** – On a mount vert therefrom issuing ears of wheat proper, in front of a cross gules an otter also proper. **Supporters** – *Dexter*, an otter proper; *sinister*, a lion sable; each gorged with a garland of roses gules, leaved vert.
Seat – The Chanter's House, Ottery St Mary, S Devon.

SON LIVING *(By 1st marriage)*

Hon JAMES DUKE, *b* 5 June 1967.

DAUGHTERS LIVING *(By 1st marriage)*

Hon Tania Rosamund, *b* 1966.
Hon Sophia Tamsin, *b* 1970.

(By 2nd marriage)

Hon Vanessa Leyla, *b* 1978.
Hon Katharine Suzannah, *b* 1981.

BROTHER LIVING

Hon Samuel John Taylor (43 Vogesenstrasse, 7570 Baden-Baden, W Germany), *b* 1942; *ed* Winchester, and Trin Coll, Oxford; Brig Gren Gds; attached Army Air Corps 1964-68, Mil Attaché Algiers and Tunis 1985-88: *m* 1973, Patricia Susan, yr da of John Basil Edwards, CBE, of Cradley, nr Malvern, Worcs, and has issue living, Jessica Alice Seymour, *b* 1974, — Clara Emily Taylor, *b* 1976.

COLLATERAL BRANCHES LIVING

Issue of late Hon (Ronald) James Duke Coleridge, yst son of 3rd Baron, *b* 1911, *d* 1972: *m* 1937, Ursula Mary, who *d* 1987, da of late Rev William Turner Long, of Cheltenham:—
Syndercombe James Duke, *b* 1941; *ed* King's Sch, Worcester, and RNC Dartmouth; Lt RN (ret): *m* 1st, 1964 (*m diss* 1969), Barbara June, da of F. L. Dawson, of Rio de Janeiro; 2ndly, 1969 (*m diss* 1972), Deborah Coburn, da of the Rev Marcus Brown Hall, of Vermount, USA; 3rdly, 1977, Susan Elizabeth, only da of Derrick Vernon Littlejohn, of St Alban's Mansions, Kensington, W8, and has issue living (by 1st *m*), Christina Joanne, *b* 1965, — (by 3rd *m*) Robert James Duke, *b* 1979, — Nicholas John, *b* 1981. —— Sara Louise Sidney, *b* 1945: *m* 1st, 1964, Alexander Arthur Luttrell Reid, PhD; 2ndly, 1988, Alexander Milne, and has issue living (by 1st *m*), Anna Louise, *b* 1965, — Katharine Louise, *b* 1967.

Grandchildren of late John Duke Coleridge, eldest son of late Hon Stephen William Buchanan Coleridge (infra):—
Issue of late Peter Duke Coleridge, *b* 1905, *d* 1958: *m* 1936 (*m diss* 1953), Sigrid Stahl Christensen:—
John Duke, MD, *b* 1940 (11644 N 52nd St, Scottsdale, Arizona 285254, USA); *ed* Univ of Göteborg Med Sch: *m* 1963, Carin Eva Christina, da of Karl Olaf Lennart Cassmark, and has issue living, Peter John, *b* 1966, — Christina *b* 1964, — Malin Charlotta, *b* 1970.
Issue of late Arthur Nicholas Coleridge, *b* 1915, *d* 1988: *m* 1941, Lady (Marguerite) Georgina Hay (33 Peel St, W8), da of 11th Marquess of Tweeddale:—
Frances Marguerite Katharine, *b* 1943: *m* 1964, Neil Lindsay Vaughan Smith, of Park Hill, Appledore, Kent, and has issue living, Julian Arthur Vaughan, *b* 1969, — Candida Louise Vaughan, *b* 1967: *m* 1992, Robert Machin.

Grandson of late Hon Stephen William Buchanan Coleridge, 2nd son of 1st Baron:—
Issue of late Paul Humphrey Coleridge, MC, *b* 1888, *d* 1955: *m* 1914, Margaret Frances, who *d* 1964, da of late George Campbell Giffard, JP, of Bulkeley House, Englefield Green:—
Antony Duke, *b* 1915; Capt late Queen's Bays; European War 1939-45 (despatches): *m* 1947, June Marian, da of George Frederick Charles Caswell, and has had issue, Jeremy Charles Duke, *b* 1949, *d* 1955, — Nicholas Antony, *b* 1955: *m* 1983, Gayl June, yr da of Clive O. J. Grove-Palmer, of 64 Staunton Rd, Oxford, and has issue living, Matthew Oliver Duke *b* 1984, Laura Claire May *b* 1986, — David George, *b* 1957: *m* 1981, Naomi Jean, 2nd da of Dr Harry Vere White, of 3 Elmfield Grove, Gosforth, Newcastle upon Tyne, and has issue living, Katherine Natasha *b* 1989, Hannah Lucy *b* 1991, — Geraldine Margaret, *b* 1948: *m* 1974, David Roger Leeming, and has issue living, Robert Antony Dundas *b* 1978, Toby Alexander David *b* 1981. *Residence* – Ottery, Harwood Rd, Marlow, Bucks.

Grandchildren of late Paul Humphrey Coleridge, MC (ante):—
Issue of late Maj James Bernard Coleridge, *b* 1919, *d* 1991: *m* 1946, Jane Evelina (85 Erpingham Rd, SW15), da of Campbell Walter Giffard, of 4 Melina Place, NW8:—
Paul James Duke, QC, *b* 1949; *ed* Cranleigh; Bar Middle Temple 1967, QC 1993: *m* 1973, Judith Elizabeth, da of Hugh Trenchard Rossiter, and has issue living, William Paul Hugh Duke, *b* 1976, — Edward James, *b* 1980, — Alice Evelina, *b* 1974. —— Susan Margaret Ethel, *b* 1947: *m* 1970, Peter John Cunard, and has issue living, Nicholas Peter, *b* 1971, — Sebastian James, *b* 1972, — Catherine Jane, *b* 1976. —— Lucy Veronica, *b* 1954: *m* 1977, Stuart John Selleck, and has issue living, Samuel George, *b* 1978, — Leo James, *b* 1986, — Georgina Jane, *b* 1980.
Issue of late Francis Stephen Coleridge, DSC, *b* 1920, *d* 1992: *m* 1st, 1948 (*m diss* 1973), Jane Dealtry, 3rd da of late Maj George Arthur Howson, MC; 2ndly, 1980, Mrs Jean Roberts McFadyean (*née* Ogden) (Sontut, Camino de San Vicente, Pollensa, Mallorca):—
(By 1st *m*) Stephen John, *b* 1953. —— Harriet Sibell, *b* 1959: *m* 1st 1988 (*m diss* 1994), Martin F. Wright; 2ndly, 1994 Alexander Victor Akoulitchev. *Residence* – Cherry Tree Pottery, Common Rd, Headley, Newbury, Berks.

PREDECESSORS – **(1)** *Rt Hon* JOHN DUKE Coleridge, PC, el son of late Rt Hon Sir John Taylor Coleridge; *b* 1820; MP for Exeter (*L*) 1865-73; Recorder of Portsmouth 1855-66, Solicitor-Gen 1868-71, Attorney-Gen 1871-3 Lord Ch Justice of Common Pleas 1873-80, and Lord Ch Justice of England 1880-94; *cr Baron Coleridge,* of Ottery St Mary, Devon (peerage of United Kingdom) 1873: *m* 1st, 1846, Jane Fortescue, who *d* 1878, da of Rev George Turner Seymour, of Farringford Hill, Isle of Wight; 2ndly, 1885, Amy Augusta Jackson, who *d* 1933, da of Henry Baring Lawford, BCS; *d* 1894; *s* by his el son **(2)** BERNARD JOHN SEYMOUR, 2nd Baron, *b* 1851; MP for Sheffield, Attercliffe Div (*L*) 1885-94; was a Judge of High Court of Justice 1907-23: *m* 1876, Mary Alethea, who *d* 1940, da of late Rt Rev John Fielder Mackarness, DD, sometime Lord Bishop of Oxford; *d* 1927; *s* by his son **(3)** GEOFFREY DUKE, 3rd Baron; *b* 1877; sometime Capt Devonshire Regt: *m* 1904, Jessie Alethea, who *d* 1957, da of late Evelyn Mackarness, of Lahard, co Cavan; *d* 1955; *s* by his son **(4)** RICHARD DUKE, KBE, 4th Baron, *b* 1905; Capt RN; French Gen Headquarters, Vincennes, France 1940, in War Cabinet Office 1940-41, Dep Sec to British Joint Staff and Combined Chiefs of Staff 1941-46, United Kingdom Sec, Mil Staff Committee of United Nations Organization, New York 1946-48, with British Joint Staff Mission, Washington, USA 1950-51, and Ch Staff Officer to Marshal of the RAF Lord Tedder 1950-51; represented British Chiefs of Staff on temporary Committee of Council of NATO Paris 1951, Exec Sec NATO 1952-70; attended Conferences of Washington, Quebec 1943/44, Cairo, Teheran 1943, Malta and Yalta 1945; DL of Devon; has American Legion of Merit; OBE (Mil) 1944, CBE (Mil) 1951, KBE (Civil) 1971: *m* 1936, Rosamund, who *d* 1991, el da of late Adm Sir William Wordsworth Fisher, GCB, GCVO; *d* 1984; *s* by his elder son **(5)** WILLIAM DUKE, 5th Baron and present peer.

COLGRAIN, BARON (Campbell) (Baron UK 1946)

FAC ET SPERA

Act and Hope

DAVID COLIN CAMPBELL, 3rd Baron; *b* 24 April 1920; *s* 1973; late 9th Lancers: *m* 1st 1945 (*m diss* 1964), Veronica Margaret, da of late Col William Leckie Webster, RAMC; 2ndly, 1973, Sheila, da of late Robert McLeod Mitchell, and formerly wife of M. M. Hudson, and has issue by 1st *m.*

𝕬rms – Gyronny of eight or and sable, on a chief azure a bezant between two crescents of the first. 𝕮rest – A boar's head erect and erased azure issuant from a wreath of myrtle leaved and flowered proper. 𝕾upporters – *Dexter,* a horse argent; *sinister,* a boar azure.
Residence – Bushes Farm, Weald, Sevenoaks, Kent.

SON LIVING *(By 1st marriage)*

Hon ALASTAIR COLIN LECKIE, *b* 16 Sept 1951; *ed* Eton, and Trin Coll, Camb: *m* 1979, Annabel Rose, yr da of Hon Robin Hugh Warrender, of Widcombe Manor, Church St, Bath (*see* B Bruntisfield), and has issue living, Thomas Colin Donald, *b* 9 Feb 1984, — Nicholas Robin, *b* 1986.

DAUGHTER LIVING *(By 1st marriage)*

Hon Virginia Charlotte Angela, *b* 1948: *m* 1973, Maj Jonathan Charles Mackay-Lewis, son of late Maj-Gen Kenneth Mackay-Lewis, CB, DSO, MC, of Stamps and Crows, Layer Breton, Essex, and has issue living, James Edward, *b* 1978, — George Mungo Pyne, *b* 1985, — Gemma Elizabeth, *b* 1977. *Residence* – Gattertop, Leominster, Herefords HR6 0JY.

BROTHERS LIVING

Hon Robert (Robin) Dudley, *b* 1921; late Scots Gds: *m* 1st, 1954 (*m diss* 1978), Cecilia Barbara, el da of late Cdr Alexander Leslie, RN (ret), of Old Manor Cottage, Lympne Hill, Kent; 2ndly, 1983, Mrs Muriel Anne Kandal, da of late George Tuson, RN, of Loughborough, Leics, and has issue living (by 1st *m*), Lenore Robina Cecilia, *b* 1957: *m* 1985, Michael C. Maynard, son of late Ronald Maynard, of Epping, Essex, and has issue living, Chantal Robina *b* 1987, Alexandra Samantha *b* 1992, — Zephyrine Alexandra, *b* 1967. *Residence* – Sharp's Place, Boughbeech, Edenbridge, Kent.

Hon Neil Donald, DSC, *b* 1922; late Lt RN: *m* 1951, Angela Louise Vereker, da of Rt Hon Sir Ronald Hibbert Cross, KCMG, KCVO, 1st Bt (ext), and has had issue, †Andrew Donald, *b* 1954; *ed* Harrow; *m* 1974, Dominique, eldest da of Peter Juul, of Copenhagen, and *d* 1980, having had issue, Claire *b* 1974; *d* 1978, — Roderick Hugo, *b* 1960: *m* 1988, Sophie Louise, da of Richard Hicks, and has issue living, Arthur Frederick *b* 1988, Edie Blanche *b* 1990, — Martin Emmott, *b* 1963, — Joanna Louise, *b* 1953: *m* 1st, 1980 (*m diss* 1987), Michael L. Wennink, yr son of Cornelis Wennink; 2ndly, 1992, Robert M. Tennant, son of late Cecil Tennant, and has issue living (by 1st *m*), Oliver Neil *b* 1981, (Jonathan Roelof) Donald *b* 1982, (by 2nd *m*), Hugh Campbell *b* 1992. *Residence* – Yorks Hill Farm, Ide Hill, Sevenoaks, Kent.

SISTER LIVING

Hon Gillian Margaret, *b* 1925: *m* 1951, Peter Scott Young, who *d* 1988, and has issue living, Robert James Campbell, *b* 1954: *m* 1986, Josynane Noelle, da of Jean Pierard, of Le Figueret, Flayosc, Haut-Var, France, and has issue living, Sam Peter Antoine *b* 1987, Yannick Robert Pierard *b* 1989, — Mark Peter, *b* 1961: *m* 1990, Andrea C. S., da of Maj Geoffrey Browne, MBE, of Jasmine Cottage, Harwell, Didcot, Oxon, and has issue living, Fergus Scott Antony *b* 1993, — Bridget Margaret, *b* 1952: *m* 1983, Patrick L. Macdougall, of 40 Stevenage Rd, SW6 6EJ, son of late J. A. Macdougall, of Midhurst, and has issue living, Laura Margaret Valerie, *b* 1984, Nicola Elizabeth Bridget *b* 1987, Vanessa Emily Hope *b* 1990, — Deborah Mary, *b* 1957: *m* 1983, Steven H. Hewlett, son of Maurice Hewlett, of 9 The Old Nurseries, Grange-over-Sands, Cumbria, and has issue living, Jacob (Jake) Robert *b* 1986, Adam James *b* 1988, Megan Ruth *b* 1991. *Residence* – Orchard House, Langton Green, Tunbridge Wells, Kent.

WIDOW LIVING OF SON OF FIRST BARON

Joan Esther Sybella, JP (Beech Cottage, 24 Cheerbrook Rd, Willaston, Nantwich, Cheshire), da of late Col Hercules Arthur Pakenham, CMG (*see* E Longford, colls): *m* 1926, Hon Angus Dudley Campbell, CBE, who *d* 1967, and has issue living (*see* colls, infra).

COLLATERAL BRANCH LIVING

Issue of late Hon Angus Dudley Campbell, CBE, yr son of 1st Baron, *b* 1895, *d* 1967: *m* 1926, Joan Esther Sybella, JP (ante), da of late Col Hercules Arthur Pakenham, CMG (*see* E Longford, colls):—
Judith Averil, *b* 1927: *m* 1954, Lt-Cdr Gerard St John Roden Buxton, RN, of Pitteadie House, Kirkcaldy, Fife (*see* Buxton, Bt colls). —— Fiona Mary, *b* 1930: *m* 1953, Donald Dundas Scott JP, DL, of Harsfold Manor, Wisborough Green, Sussex, and has had issue, Roderick (Rory) Arthur (53 Fentiman Rd, SW8 1LH), *b* 1958: *m* 1990, (Petrina) Jane, yr da of John Frederick Edward Trehearne (*see* B Harvington), and has issue living, Sebastian Angus Edward *b* 1993, Hannah Augusta *b* 1991, — Angus Malcolm, *b* 1964, — Arabella Joan, *b* and *d* 1955, — Henrietta Sara, *b* 1957: *m* 1982, William Eric Drake, of Twinstead Manor, Sudbury, Suffolk, yr son of Sir Eric Drake, CBE, and has issue living, Hector Donald Arthur *b* 1986, Milo Edmund Courtney *b* 1991, Edwina Margaret Fiona *b* 1987, — Rosanna Harriet, *b* 1962: *m* 1990, Rupert Jerome Dickinson, of 3 Beechmore Rd, SW11 4ET, 2nd son of Ian Dickinson, MC, of The Manor House, Riding Mill, Northumberland, and has issue living, Atalanta Bella *b* 1992. —— Linda Ishbel (*Lady Cubitt*), *b* 1934: *m* 1958, Sir Hugh Guy Cubitt, CBE, JP, of Chapel House, W Humble, Dorking, Surrey (*see* B Ashcombe).

PREDECESSORS – (1) Colin Frederick Campbell, son of George William Campbell; *b* 1866; Pres of British Bankers' Asso 1938-46, and a Director of National Provincial Bank, London Assurance, and other cos; *cr Baron Colgrain*, of Everlands, co Kent (peerage of United Kingdom) 1946: *m* 1890, Lady Angela Mary Alice Ryder, MBE, who *d* 1939, da of 4th Earl of Harrowby; *d* 1954; *s* by his eldest son (2) Donald Swinton, MC, 2nd Baron; *b* 1891; Chm of Grindlays Bank 1949: *m* 1917, Margaret Emily, who *d* 1989, da of late Percy William Carver, of Courtlands, W Hoathly, Sussex: *d* 1973; *s* by his eldest son (3) David Colin, 3rd Baron and present peer.

COLLISON, BARON (Collison) (Life Baron 1964)

Harold Francis Collison, CBE, *b* 10 May 1909; *ed* Hay Currie LCC Sch, Poplar, and Crypt Sch, Gloucester; a Farm Worker 1934-44, Dist Officer, National Union of Agricultural Workers 1944-46, and National Officer 1946-53, a Member of Pilkington Cttee on Broadcasting 1960-62; Gen Sec of National Union of Agricultural Workers 1953-59; a Member of Workers' Side of Agricultural Wages Board, and of Gen Council of TUC 1953-69 (Chm 1964-65), Chm of Social Insurance and Industrial Welfare Cttee of TUC 1957-68, British Delegate to International Labour Office 1957-69 (a Member of Gov Body 1960-69), a Member of Council on Tribunals 1959-69; Pres of International Federation of Plantation, Agricultural and Allied Workers 1960-76, a part-time Member of N Thames Gas Board 1961-69, a Member of Transport Consultative Cttee (re-elected) 1962-70, and of Agricultural Advisory Council 1962-80, Vice-Chm of Land Settlement Assocn 1964-69, Chm of Agric Apprenticeship Council 1968-74, and a Member of Roy Commn on Trades Unions and Employers' Assocn, of Home Grown Cereals Authority 1965-78, and Chm Supplementary Benefits Commn 1969-75; Pres Assocn of Agriculture 1976-84; a Member of Economic Development Council for Agric, of Industrial Health Advisory Cttee, of Industrial Safety Advisory Council, of National Insurance Advisory Cttee, of Industrial Consultative Approach to Europe, and of Oversea Labour Consultative Cttee; *cr* CBE (Civil) 1961, and *Baron Collison*, of Cheshunt, co Hertford (Life Baron) 1964: *m* 1946, Ivy Kate, da of Walter Hanks, of Burleigh, Glos.
Residence – Honeywood, 163 Old Nazeing Rd, Broxbourne, Herts.

COLNBROOK, BARON (Atkins) (Life Baron 1987)

Humphrey Eward Gregory Atkins, KCMG, PC, son of late Capt Edward Davis Atkins, of Nyeri, Kenya; *b* 12 Aug 1922; *ed* Wellington Coll; 1939-45 War as Lieut RN; PPS to Civil Lord of the Admiralty 1959-62, Opposition Whip 1967-70, Govt Deputy Chief Whip and Treas of HM Household 1970-73, Govt Chief Whip 1973-74, Opposition Chief Whip 1974-79, Sec of State for N Ireland 1979-81, Lord Privy Seal 1981-82, Chm Select Cttee on Defence 1984-87, Pres Nat Union of Conservative and Unionist Assocs 1985-86; MP (*C*) for Merton and Morden 1955-70 and for Spelthorne 1970-87; *cr* PC 1973, KCMG 1983 and *Baron Colnbrook*, of Waltham St Lawrence, co Berks (Life Baron) 1987: *m* 1944, Adela Margaret, da of late Maj Sir Robert Spencer-Nairn, 1st Bt, and has issue.

ᴀʀᴍꜱ – Per pale azure and or a fret on a bordure three anchors all counter-changed. Crest – An Indian elephant's head erased azure armed and holding aloft with the trunk a grapnel with three flukes or. Supporters – *Dexter*: a barrister at law in bands wig and gown; *Sinister*: a rating of the Women's Royal Naval Service in uniform circa 1944 both proper.
Residence – Tuckenhams, Waltham St Lawrence, Reading, Berks. *Club* – -Brooks's.

SON LIVING

Hon Charles Edward Spencer, *b* 1952; *ed* Eton: barrister-at-law; *m* 1980, Clare Margaret, da of Henry Neville Hemsley, and has issue living, Edward Oliver, *b* 1982, — Nicholas Charles, *b* 1985, — Matthew Spencer, *b* 1988, — Katherine Margaret Lucy, *b* 1992.

DAUGHTERS LIVING

Hon Sheila Kathleen, *b* 1944: *m* 1st, 1964 (*m diss* 1974), Peter Thornycroft Romer-Lee; 2ndly, 1975 (*m diss* 1978), Keith Allen Manners; 3rdly, 1982, Royston Joseph Schroeder, of Ellimore Farm, Lustleigh, Devon, and has issue living (by 1st *m*), Richard Peter, *b* 1965; *ed* Sherborne: *m* 1991, Kirsten, da of Col Richard Smith, — Anthony James, *b* 1967; *ed* Sherborne.
Hon Julia Margaret, *b* 1946; *m* 1st, 1966 (*m diss* 1972), David Charles Roderick; 2ndly, 1972, John Stanley Melville Keay, of Succoth, Dalmally, Argyll, and has issue living, (by 2nd *m*), Alexander John Melville, *b* 1973, — Samuel Michael Cosmo, *b* 1979, — Anna Julia, *b* 1974, — Nell Christina, *b* 1977.
Hon Sally Mary, *b* 1948: *m* 1970, William Field Clegg, of Homer House, Ipsden, Oxford, and has issue living, William Humphrey, *b* 1975, — Islay Mary, *b* 1973.

COLVILLE OF CULROSS, VISCOUNT (Colville) (Viscount UK 1902, Lord precedence S 1609)

I can not forget

JOHN MARK ALEXANDER COLVILLE, QC, 4th Viscount and 13th Lord (*cr* 1609); *b* 19 July 1933; *s* 1945; *ed* Rugby, and New Coll, Oxford (MA); Bar Lincoln's Inn 1960, QC 1978, a Bencher 1986; Chm Parole Board 1988-92; Recorder 1990, Circuit Judge 1993; Lt Gren Gds (Reserve), and a Member of Queen's Body Guard for Scotland (Royal Company of Archers); Member of Council, Univ of E Anglia 1968-72; Min of State Home Office 1972-74: *m* 1st, 1958 (*m diss* 1973), Mary Elizabeth, da of Col M. H. W. Webb-Bowen, RM; 2ndly, 1974, Margaret Birgitta (LLB King's Coll, Lond; JP Inner Lond), da of Maj-Gen Cyril Henry Norton, CB, CBE, DSO, and formerly wife of 2nd Viscount Davidson, and has issue by 1st and 2nd *m*.

Arms – Quarterly: 1st and 4th argent, a cross moline sable, *Colville*; 2nd and 3rd gules, a fesse, checky, argent and azure, *Lindsay*. **Crest** – A hind's head couped at the neck argent. **Supporters** – *Dexter*, a rhinoceros proper; *sinister*, a savage habited in a bearskin and supporting on his left shoulder with his exterior hand a club all proper.
Residence – Worlingham Hall, Suffolk NR34 7RA.

SONS LIVING *(By 1st marriage)*

Hon CHARLES MARK TOWNSHEND (*Master of Colville*), *b* 5 Sept 1959; *ed* Rugby, and Durham Univ (BA).
Hon (Richmond) James Innys, *b* 1961; *ed* Rugby, Bristol Univ (BSc), and London Univ (MSc); MB, BS: *m* 1993, (Aurea) Katharine, da of Sir Philip Manning Dowson, CBE, PRA (*see* Bacon, Bt).
Hon Alexander Fergus Gale, *b* 1964; *ed* Wellington Coll, and Nottingham Poly (BSc): *m* 1993, Elizabeth, yst da of John Desmond O'Hare, of Liverpool.
Hon Rupert George Streatfeild, *b* 1966; *ed* Milton Abbey.

(By 2nd marriage)

Hon Edmund Carleton, *b* 1978.

BROTHERS LIVING

Hon (Charles) Anthony (Rydes, Nevill Court, Tunbridge Wells, Kent), *b* 1935; *ed* Rugby, and Magdalen Coll, Oxford (BA); late Sub-Lt RNR; Solicitor 1969; Overseas Civil Ser, Kenya 1958-64: *m* 1965, Katherine, da of late Humphrey John Sankey, of Kinangop, Kenya, and has issue living, Robert Quintin Oxnam, *b* 1971, — Charles Alexander, *b* 1974.
Hon Angus Richmond, *b* 1939; *ed* Rugby; Lt Gren Gds (Res); FRICS. *Residence* – 1 Bedford Pl, Tavistock, Devon PL19 8AZ.

COLLATERAL BRANCHES LIVING

Grandchildren of late Adm Hon Sir Stanley Cecil James Colville (Vice Adm of UK), GCB, GCMG, GCVO, 2nd son of 1st Viscount:—
Issue of late Capt George Cecil Colville, CBE, RN, *b* 1903, *d* 1983: *m* 1935, Gabrielle, who *d* 1987, da of late Gen Sir Arthur Power Palmer, GCB, GCIE, and widow of Col Leger Livingstone-Learmonth, of Southover, Tolpuddle, Dorset:—
Rona Alice Gabrielle, *b* 1936: *m* 1959 (*m diss* 1975), Maj Hon Thomas Robin Valerian Dixon, MBE, Gren Gds (*see* B Glentoran). *Residence* – Gazebo, The Plantation, Curdridge, nr Southampton.
Issue of late Maj-Gen Edward Charles Colville, CB, DSO, *b* 1905, *d* 1982: *m* 1934, Barbara Joan, who *d* 1983, da of late Edward Henry Marland Denny, of Staplefield Place, Staplefield, Sussex:—
Jane, *b* 1936: *m* 1st, 1957 (*m diss* 1967), Sir Archibald Bruce Charles Edmondstone, 7th Bt; 2ndly, 1967, HSH Prince Martin Lubomirski, who *d* 1977; 3rdly, 1983, Capt John Holliday Bingham Hartley, late Coldm Gds, of 19 Cliveden Pl, SW1. —— Antonia (*Princess Carol of Roumania*), *b* 1939: *m* 1st, 1962 (*m diss* 1973) Garry Lacon Jock Ropner (*see* Ropner, Bt (*cr* 1904), colls); 2ndly, 1984, (HRH) Prince Carol of Roumania (*see* Royal Family), of 36 Doria Rd, SW6.
Issue of late Cdr (S) Sir Richard Colville, KCVO, CB, DSC, RN (ret), *b* 1907, *d* 1975: *m* 1933, Dorothy, who *d* 1972, da of Brig-Gen Halhed Brodrick Birdwood:—
Peter Alan (The Dairy House, Stalbridge Park, Stalbridge, Dorset), *b* 1935; late Lt RM: *m* 1964, Jane, el da of late Capt Thomas Harland, of Walton House, Kineton, Warwicks, and has issue living, James Richard, *b* 1976, — Julia Mary, *b* 1965, — Annabel Clare, *b* 1967, — Joanna Elizabeth, *b* 1969: *m* 1992, Nicholas Alexander Waite, of Spittlepond Cottage, Wambrook, Chard, Som TA20 3DE, elder son of Michael Waite, of E Coker, Som, — Sarah Dorothy Louise, *b* 1972. —— Anne Bridget (The Manse, Iden Green, nr Cranbrook, Kent), *b* 1939: *m* 1963 (*m diss* 19—), Oliver Spankie, late Capt RM, and has issue living, Hugh Nicholas, *b* 1967, — Rosemary Bridget, *b* 1964. —— June Claire, *b* 1948: *m* 1977, Anthony Barrington Prowse, of Rose Cottage, Coombe Shute, Stoke Gabriel, S Devon, and has issue living, Sebastian Irwin Barrington, *b* 1978, — Nicholas Richard Barrington, *b* 1982, — Alexandra Rose Adelaide Barrington, *b* 1979.

Grandchildren of late Hon George Charles Colville, MBE (*infra*):—
Issue of late David Richard Colville, *b* 1909, *d* 1986: *m* 1933, Lady Joan Child-Villiers (The Old Vicarage, Dorton, nr Aylesbury, Bucks), da of 8th Earl of Jersey:—

Robert John (Dorton, nr Aylesbury, Bucks; *Clubs* – Brooks's, Pratt's, Royal Yacht Sqdn), *b* 1941; *ed* Harrow. —— James Richard Charles (Melrose House, Minchinhampton, Glos), *b* 1952; *ed* Harrow: *m* 1982, (Mary) Virginia Louise, yr da of late Timothy Walter Horn (*see* E Carnarvon, colls, 1990 Edn), and has issue living, Charles David James, *b* 1987, — Edward Timothy George, *b* 1988, — Emma Virginia Anne, *b* 1987 (twin). —— Sarah Anne (*Sarah, Lady Pigot*), *b* 1933: *m* 1968, Maj-Gen Sir Robert Anthony Pigot, 7th Bt, CB, OBE, DL, of Wray House, Bembridge, I of Wight, who *d* 1986. —— Catherine, *b* 1935: *m* 1958, Cdr Warren Llewellyn Russell Euan Gilchrist, RN (ret), of Rook Hill, Monk Sherborne, Basingstoke, Hants, and has issue living, Charles Warren, *b* 1962, — David Warren, *b* 1967, — Catherine Anne, *b* 1960, — Julia Mary, *b* 1969. —— Mary Julia, *b* 1947: *m* 1969, Aubrey Francis Houston Bowden, of The Old Vicarage, Winkfield, Windsor, Berks (*see* Bowden, Bt).

      Issue of late Sir John Rupert Colville, CB, CVO, *b* 1915, *d* 1987: *m* 1948, Lady Margaret Egerton (The Close, Broughton, Stockbridge, Hants), da of 4th Earl of Ellesmere (*see* D Sutherland):—

Alexander George, *b* 1955; *ed* Harrow; a Page of Honour to HM 1968-71. —— Rupert Charles, *b* 1960; *ed* Harrow, and Trin Coll, Oxford (MA): *m* 1991, Sarah Catherine, da of Richard Russell, of Kidlington, Oxford. —— (Elizabeth) Harriet, *b* 1952; a Lady-in-Waiting to HRH The Princess Royal since 1990: *m* 1976, David James Bowes-Lyon (*see* E Strathmore, colls).

      Issue of late Hon George Charles Colville, MBE, 3rd son of 1st Viscount, *b* 1867; *d* 1943: *m* 1908, Lady (Helen) Cynthia Crewe-Milnes, DCVO, DBE, who *d* 1968, da of 1st Marquess of Crewe:—

Philip Robert, MBE, *b* 1910; *ed* Harrow, and Trin Coll: *m* 1656; *s* by his nephew N-W Europe 1944-45 (despatches, MBE); MBE (Mil) 1946. *Residence* – 4 Mulberry Walk, SW3. *Clubs* – Pratt's, White's, Royal Yacht Sqn.

PREDECESSORS – (1)*Sir* JAMES Colville, Knt; served with distinction in the French War under Henry of Navarre, afterwards Henry IV of France, and in 1589 received a charter of the Abbey of Culross as a feudal barony, and was *cr* (by charter and investiture) *Lord Colville of Culross* 1604 with remainder to his heirs male whatsoever; on the resignation of his kinsman the Commendator of Culross, the Abbey Estates were in 1609 re-erected with a Lordship and he was *cr Lord Colville of Culross* (peerage of Scotland) 1609, with remainder to heirs male whatsoever; *d* 1620; *s* by his son (2)JAMES, 2nd Lord, *d* 1624; *s* by his son (3) JOHN, 3rd Lord; *d* 1656; *s* by his brother (4) JOHN, 4th Lord; *s* by his kinsman (5)ALEXANDER, 5th Lord; *d* 1721; *s* by his son (6) JOHN, 6th Lord; in 1722, at the Gen Election of Scottish Peers his name was excluded from the Peers' Roll on the ground that it was not on the roll at the time of the Union; but on petition to the House of Lords, when the Charter of 1609 was the instrument acted on, he was declared, in 1723, to be entitled to the dignity, and his name was placed on the roll as *Lord Colville of Culross* next to Lord Cardross; *d* 1741; *s* by his eldest son (7) ALEXANDER, 7th Lord, a distinguished Vice-Adm; *d* 1770; *s* by his brother (8) JOHN, 8th Lord; *d* 1811; *s* by his son (9) JOHN; Adm of the White, and a Representative Peer; *d* 1849; *s* by his nephew (10) CHARLES JOHN (son of Gen Sir Charles Colville, GCB, 2nd son of 9th Lord), PC, KT, GCVO, 10th Lord, *b* 1818; Lord Chamberlain to Queen Alexandra 1873-1903; *cr Baron Colville of Culross* (peerage of United Kingdom) 1885, and *Viscount Colville of Culross*, co Perth (peerage of United Kingdom) 1902: *m* 1853, Hon Cecile Katherine Mary Carington, who *d* 1907, da of 2nd Baron Carrington; *d* 1903; *s* by his el son (11) CHARLES ROBERT WILLIAM, 2nd Viscount, *b* 1854; Lieut-Col late Grenadier Guards; was Mil Sec to Gov-Gen of Canada (Baron Stanley of Preston) 1888-92; Zulu War 1879 (despatches, medal with clasp): *m* 1885, Ruby, who *d* 1943, da of late Lt-Col Henry Dorrien Streatfeild, of Chiddingstone, Kent; *d* 1928; *s* by his son (12) CHARLES ALEXANDER, 3rd Viscount; *b* 1888; Com RN; European War 1914-19 (despatches), European War 1939-45: *m* 1931, Kathleen Myrtle, OBE, who *d* 1986, da of late Brig-Gen Henry Richmond Gale, CMG, RE; *k* in a flying accident on active service in the Azores 1945; *s* by his el son (13) JOHN MARK ALEXANDER, 4th Viscount and present peer; also Baron Colville of Culross, and Lord Colville of Culross.

COLWYN, BARON (Smith) (Baron UK 1917, Bt UK 1912)

I give thanks

IAN ANTHONY HAMILTON SMITH, CBE, 3rd Baron, and 3rd Baronet; *b* 1 Jan 1942; *s* 1966; *ed* Cheltenham, and London Univ (BDS), LDS RCS, CBE (Civil) 1989: *m* 1st, 1964 (*m diss* 1977), Sonia Jane, el da of P. H. G. Morgan, of Malvern, Worcs; 2ndly, 1977, Nicola Jeanne, da of Arthur Tyers, of The Avenue, Sunbury-on-Thames, Middx, and has issue by 1st and 2nd *m*.

Arms – Per chevron gules and argent, in chief two cocks of the second, in base a whale spouting proper. **Crest** – Upon a whale a cock, both as in the arms. **Supporters** – *Dexter*, a miner holding in his exterior hand and resting on his shoulder a pick-axe, suspended from his belt a miner's lamp, all proper; *sinister*, a female weaver holding in her exterior hand a shuttle also proper.

SON LIVING (By 1st marriage)

Hon CRAIG PETER, *b* 13 Oct 1968.

DAUGHTERS LIVING (By 1st marriage)

Hon Jacqueline Jane, *b* 1967.

(by 2nd marriage)

Hon Kirsten Antonia, *b* 1981.
Hon Tanya Nicole, *b* 1983.

BROTHER LIVING

Hon Timothy Hamilton (Diocesan Coll, Rondebosch 7700, Cape, S Africa), *b* 1944; *ed* Cheltenham; MA, Oxford: *m* 1967, Carolyn, da of late Bernulf Llewelyn Hodge, MRCS, LRCP, of The Old Cottage, Jac-na-Pare, Polperro, S Cornwall, and has issue living, Annabel, *b* 1972, — Fiona, *b* 1974.

AUNT LIVING (sister of 2nd Baron)

Elisabeth Joan Babette Hamilton (Ashcraig, The Croft, Bures, Essex), *b* 1919: *m* 1939, Lt-Col John Baddeley Bagot Ferguson,

R Tank Regt, and has issue, Nicholas John (Ashcraig, The Croft, Bures, Essex), b 1941: m 1965, Karen Elisabeth Svanso, and has issue living, James Fergus b 1966, Kate Elisabeth Venetia b 1967.

MOTHER LIVING

Miriam (Cantley, 32 Bafford Lane, Charlton Kings, Cheltenham), da of late Victor Bruce Ferguson, of Abbotsdene, Cheltenham: m 1940 (m diss 1951), the 2nd Baron, who d 1966.

COLLATERAL BRANCH LIVING

Issue of late Hon (Hubert) Constantine Smith, yr son of 1st Baron, b 1890, d 1956: m 1917, Majorie Methwold, OBE, who d 1984, da of late Arthur Birkett, of Langford Lodge, Southwold, Suffolk:—
Michael Constantine (Maes Nant, Pant Glas, Garndolbenmaen, Gwynedd), b 1919; is Capt RA: m 1st, 1945 (m diss 1970), Veronica, only da of Thomas Flanagan, of Tralee; 2ndly, 1970, Marie Therese, yr da of Patrick Stuart Martin, of Glasgow, and has issue living (by 1st m), Christopher Michael Constantine, b 1953, — Sally Constantine, b 1947, — Judy Jennifer Constantine, b 1951. —— Anthony Methwold Constantine, b 1923: m 1955, Susan Muriel, only da of Frederick B. Staveacre, of Braeside, Colwyn Bay, and has issue living, David Anthony Constantine, b 1962, — Caroline Constantine, b 1957, — Nicola Constantine, b 1959. —— Elizabeth Pamela Constantine, b 1918: m 1945, Michael William Malim, who d 1974, and has issue living, Flavia Constantine Eve, b 1949, — Lydia Elisabeth Constantine b 1952: m 1985, Nicholas David Umney, of 62 London Rd, Riverhead, Sevenoaks, Kent TN13 2DJ, and has issue living, Michael David b 1987, — Julia Pamela Constantine, b 1955, — Delia Constantine, b 1959. Residence – Little Court, High St, Stock, Ingatestone, Essex CM4 9BA.

PREDECESSORS – (1) Rt Hon FREDERICK HENRY Smith, el son of late Joshua Smith, JP, of Eccles; b 1859; was Dep Chm of Martin's Bank, Ltd, and a Director of Railway Cos; High Sheriff of Carnarvonshire 1917; cr a Baronet 1912, and Baron Colwyn, of Colwyn Bay, co Denbigh (peerage of United Kingdom) 1917: m 1882, Elizabeth Ann, who d 1945, da of late Hamilton Savage, of Eccles; d 1946; s by his grandson (2) FREDERICK JOHN VIVIAN (son of late Hon Frederick Henry Hamilton Smith, el son of 1st Baron), 2nd Baron; b 1914: m 1st, 1940 (m diss 1951), Miriam, da of late Victor Ferguson; 2ndly, 1952 (m diss 1954), Hermione Sophia O'Bryen, who d 1989, da of late Cyril Bertie Edward Hoare (Hoare, Bt, cr 1784); 3rdly, 1955, Beryl (who d 1987, having m 4thly, 1969, Sir George Taylor, FRS, who d 1993), da of the late Harvey Walker, formerly wife of Edward Chorley Cookson, and widow of Mortimer Reddington, FRCS; d 1966; s by his eldest son (3) IAN ANTHONY HAMILTON, 3rd Baron.

COLYTON, BARON (Hopkinson) (Baron UK 1956)

Look forward

HENRY LENNOX D'AUBIGNÉ HOPKINSON, CMG, PC, 1st Baron, el son of late Sir Henry Lennox Hopkinson, KCVO; b 3 Jan 1902; ed Eton, and at Trin Coll, Camb (BA honours 1923); appointed 3rd Sec, Washington 1924, 2nd Sec Foreign Office 1929 and Stockholm 1931, Assist Private Sec to Sec of State for Foreign Affairs 1932, 2nd Sec, Cairo 1934, 1st Sec there 1936, 1st Sec, Athens 1938, to War Cabinet Office 1939, Private Sec to Permanent Under-Sec for Foreign Affairs 1940, Counsellor 1941, and Diplo Adviser to Min of State, Cairo 1941, and Min Plen, Lisbon 1943; was Dep British High Commr, and Vice-Pres Allied Commn Italy 1944-6; resigned from Diplo Ser 1946; Head of Conservative Parliamentary Secretariat, and Joint Director of Conservative Research Dept 1946-49; Sec for Overseas Trade 1951-52, and Min of State for Colonial Affairs 1952-55, Delegate to Consultative Assembly of Council of Europe 1950-52, and to Gen Assembly of UN 1952-55, Chm Anglo-Egyptian Re-settlement Board 1957-60, Joint East and Central African Board 1960-65; Chm Tanganyika Concessions Ltd 1966-72; R Humane Soc's Award for Saving Life from drowning 1919; an OStJ; has Grand Cross of Order of Prince Henry the Navigator of Portugal, Grand Star Order Paduka Stia Negara of Brunei, Cdr of Order of Zaire of Zaire; MP for Taunton Div of Somerset (C) 1950-56; cr CMG 1944, PC 1952, and Baron Colyton, of Farway, co Devon, and Taunton, co Somerset (peerage of UK) 1956: m 1st, 1927, Alice Labouisse, who d 1953, da of Henry Lane Eno, of Bar Harbour, Maine, USA; 2ndly, 1956, Mrs Barbara Estella Addams, da of late Stephen Barb, of New York, USA, and has had issue by 1st m.

𝔄rms – Azure, on a chevron argent between three mullets of six points or as many mascles gules a bordure engrailed of the third. 𝔠rest – A demi-lion sable between two mullets of six points or. 𝔖upporters – On either side an angel proper habited azure winged or, the dexter holding in the exterior hand a Saxon Crown and the sinister likewise holding a trumpet gold. Residence – Le Formentor, Av Princess Grace, Monte Carlo, Monaco. Clubs – Buck's, White's, Beefsteak.

GRANDSONS LIVING

Issue of late Hon Nicholas Henry Eno Hopkinson, only son of 1st Baron, b 1932, d 1991: m 1957, Fiona Margaret (infra), only da of Sir (Thomas) Torquil Alphonso Munro, 5th Bt:—
ALISDAIR JOHN MUNRO, b 7 May 1958: m 1980, Philippa J., yr da of Peter J. Bell, of Harefield, Itchen Abbas, Hants, and has issue living, James Patrick Munro, b 1983, — Thomas Charles Robert, b 1985, — Kate Alice, b 1988. —— Charles Henry Kenneth, b 1960: m 1988, Karen Anne, eldest da of E. Snowdon, of Melbourne, Australia, and has issue living, Frederick Nicholas Hugo, b 1990, — Henry Jonathan Arthur, b 1992.

WIDOW LIVING OF SON OF FIRST BARON

Fiona Margaret, only da of Sir (Thomas) Torquil Alphonso Munro, 5th Bt: *m* 1957, Hon Nicholas Henry Eno Hopkinson, who *d* 1991. *Residence* – Drumleys, Lindertis, by Kirriemuir, Angus DD8 5NU.

COMBERMERE, VISCOUNT (Stapleton-Cotton) (Viscount UK 1826, Bt E 1677)
(Title pronounced "Cumbermeer")

Prepared in all circumstances

MICHAEL WELLINGTON STAPLETON-COTTON, 5th Viscount, and 10th Baronet; *b* 8 Aug 1929; *s* 1969; *ed* Eton, and King's Coll London Univ; BD, MTh London; Lecturer in Biblical and Religious Studies, Dept of Extra-Mural Studies, London Univ since 1972, Sr Lecturer in Religious Studies, Birkbeck Coll, London Univ, Centre for Extra Mural Studies since 1988; Chm World Congress of Faiths 1983-88; Fl Lt RAF (Reserve); served Palestine Police Force 1947-48 Roy Canadian Mounted Police 1948-50 and RAF 1950-58: *m* 1961, Pamela, Elizabeth, da of Rev Robert Gustavus Coulson, R of Stansted, Kent, and has issue.

Arms – Quarterly: 1st and 4th azure, a chevron between three hanks of cotton argent palewise, and in chief pendant from a ribbon gules, a representation of the medal and clasps presented to the 1st Viscount, *Cotton*; 2nd and 3rd argent, a lion rampant sable, *Stapleton*. **Crests** – 1st a falcon, wings expanded and inverted proper, beaked, membered, and belled or, holding in the dexter claw part of a belt proper, buckled gold; 2nd, on a mount vert, a dragoon of the 20th Regiment, mounted on a black horse, and in the act of charging, and over the crest in an escrol azure, the word "Salamanca", in gold letters; 3rd, out of a ducal coronet or, a Saracen's head couped at the shoulders affrontée wreathed round the temples, argent and sable. **Supporters** – Two falcons, wings expanded and endorsed proper, beaked, membered, and belled or, the *dexter* supporting a spear, also proper, therefrom flowing to the dexter a standard swallow-tailed vert, semée of estoiles or, streamers and tassels of the last, and the *sinister* supporting a like spear, therefrom flowing a yellow standard, swallow-tailed streamers and tassels of the last.
Residence – Vanners, Bucklebury, nr Reading, Berks RG7 6RU. *Club* – RAC

SON LIVING

Hon THOMAS ROBERT WELLINGTON, *b* 30 Aug 1969.

DAUGHTERS LIVING

Hon Tara Christabel, *b* 1961: *m* 1992, Laurent Saglio.
Hon Sophia Mary, *b* 1963.

BROTHER LIVING

Hon David Peter Dudley (The Old Buffers, Station Rd, Darling, Cape, S Africa), *b* 1932; *ed* Eton; Capt Life Gds (Res): *m* 1955, Susan Nomakepu, da of Sir George Werner Albu, 2nd Bt, and has issue living, Simon, *b* 1959: *m* 1993, Tessa, da of Dr John Cummings, of Cape Town, — Toby James, *b* 1966, — Nicola Caroline Louisa, *b* 1957: *m* 1994, Martin Street, son of Brian Street, of Evesham, Worcs, — Polly, *b* 1961: *m* 1990, Bernard John Harton, son of Mrs D. Barker, of Worcester.

COLLATERAL BRANCHES LIVING

(In remainder to Baronetcy only)

Grandchildren of late Capt Frederick Arthur Stapleton Cotton (infra):—
Issue of late Hugh Philip Stapleton Cotton, *b* 1913, *d* 1979: *m* 1938, Mary Josephine, da of Frederick Thomas Wheeler:—
Stephen Hugh Stapleton, *b* 1949; *ed* Tonbridge, and Reading Univ (BSc Estate Management); FRICS: *m* 1970, Josephine Katharina, da of Owen Eric Goddard, HM British Consul in Oporto, and has issue living, Rufus Tom Stapleton, *b* 1976, — Gabriele Pippa, *b* 1974, — Hannah Stephanie, *b* 1977, — Olivia Jo, *b* 19—. — Jennifer Mary (Whistle Cottage, Cowden, Edenbridge, Kent), *b* 1943: *m* 1964 (*m diss* 1983), Peter Ivan Chettle, and has issue living, Dominic Mark, *b* 1967, — Deborah Jane Emma, *b* 1970. —— Marilyn Elizabeth, *b* 1946; *ed* Sussex Univ (BEd), Dip RSA: *m* 1st, 1977 (*m diss* 1988), Christopher David Jones; 2ndly, 1989, Steven John Linehan, of 30 Stanford Av, Hassocks, W Sussex, and has issue living (by 1st *m*), Benjamin Kester, *b* 1973, — Daniel Ian, *b* 1975.

Granddaughter of late Rev James Stapleton Cotton, 2nd son of late Rev Henry James Cotton, elder son of late Very Rev James Henry Cotton, 2nd son of late Rev George Cotton, LLD, Dean of Chester, 3rd son of 4th Bt:—
Issue of late Capt Frederick Arthur Stapleton Cotton, *b* 1884, *d* 1927: *m* 1912, Evelyn Mary, who *d* 1968, da of late Col Samuel Ormsby Rogers, Army Ordnance Corps:—
Sheila Evelyn Ormsby, *b* 1915: *m* 1940, Maj Arthur Richard Burch, DSC, RM, who *d* 1964, and has issue living, Peter Ronald (760 San Mario Drive, Solana Beach, California, USA), *b* 1946; Lt Cdr RN (ret): *m* 1980, Mary Lou, da of Gordon Galligan, of

San Diego, and has issue living, Andrew Richard *b* 1986, Matthew David *b* (twin) 1986, Sarah Louise *b* 1983, — David John (Monastery House, Priory St, Newport Pagnell, Bucks), *b* 1949: *m* 1984, Pauline Heather, da of George Twitchen, and has issue living, Henry Arthur *b* 1987, Lucy Hester *b* 1985, Hazel Joan *b* 1989, — Sally Louise (43 Fortis Green Av, N2), *b* 1943: *m* 1972 (*m diss* 1980), David John North. *Residence* – Hilingdon House, Greta St, Saltburn-by-the-Sea, Cleveland.

    Grandchildren of late Charles Calveley Cotton, eldest son of late Charles Robert Cotton, son of late Henry Calveley Cotton (*b* 1750), 6th son of 4th Bt:—
    Issue of late Lt-Col Arthur Egerton Cotton, DSO, *b* (twin) 1876; *d* 1922; *m* 1909, Beryl Marie, who *d* 1966 (having *m* 2ndly, 1922, John Lee Brooker, JP, who *d* 1942), da of late Henry Jack Cumming, of Foston Hall, Derby:—
Diana Sara, *b* 1914: *m* 1936, Ernest Addenbrooke Crutchley, CBE, who assumed by deed poll 1945, the name of Brooke in lieu of his christian names of Ernest Addenbrooke, and has issue living, Edward Brooke, *b* 1950: *m* 1982, Eugenie Tsirmoula, and his issue living, James Edward Brooke *b* 1986, — Christopher Miles, *b* 1951, — Anna Maria, *b* 1954. *Residence* – 39 High Street, Great Shelford, Cambs.
    Issue of late Lt-Col Vere Egerton Cotton, CBE, TD, *b* 1888; *d* 1970: *m* 1922, Elfreda Helen, JP, who *d* 1992, aged 100, da of William Francis Moore:—
Simon Arthur (28 Sauncey Av, Harpenden, Herts) *b* 1924; *ed* Repton, and Magdalene Coll, Camb (Scholar, BA); Bar Gray's Inn 1951; JP: *m* 1960, Barbara Helen Ralston, da of late Albert James Sutcliffe, of Dodleston, Ches, and has issue living, William Andrew Calveley, *b* 1962; *ed* Radley, and Bristol Univ, — Emma Jane, *b* 1961; *ed* Sidney Sussex Coll, Camb (BA), — Helen Clare, *b* 1965; *ed* Durham Univ. —— Robert Charles (The Cherry Orchard, Badgemore, Henley on Thames), *b* 1925; *ed* Repton, and Magdalene Coll, Camb (MA): *m* 1954, Nicolette Anne, da of Capt Robert Lionel Brooke Cunliffe, CBE, RN (*see* Cunliffe, Bt, colls), and has issue living, Richard Robert (18 Edgar Rd, Winchester, Hants), *b* 1956; *ed* Bradfield, and E Anglia Univ (BA): *m* 1984, Corin, da of Carel Wevers, of The Hague, and has issue living, Oliver Charles *b* 1987, Anthony Vere *b* 1988, Pavinia Sarah *b* 1991, — Philip Egerton (11 Elms Rd, SW4), *b* 1960; *ed* Shiplake Coll: *m* 1987, Rosie Louise, da of Capt James Pack, OBE, RN, of Wickham, Hants and has issue living, Charles Egerton *b* 1989, — Penelope Clare, *b* 1957; *ed* Queen Anne's, Caversham, and Royal Free Med Sch (MB BS): *m* 1983, John Christopher Arnold, of The Cottage, Snitterfield, Warwicks, son of late Rev Eric Joseph Arnold, of Tiverton and has issue living, William Henry *b* 1991, Hugh James *b* 1993, — Caroline Harriet, *b* 1963; *ed* St Mary's, Calne, and Manchester Univ (BA): *m* 1992, Thomas Emlyn Jones, of 64 Churchway, NW1, son of J. H. Emlyn Jones, of Ivinghoe, Bucks, and has issue living, Kate *b* 1993.

    Grandchildren of late Lt-Col Vere Egerton Cotton, CBE, TD (ante):—
    Issue of late Henry Egerton Cotton, JP, Lord-Lieut Merseyside 1989-93; *b* 1929, *d* 1993: *m* 1955, (Elizabeth Margaret) Susan, JP, DL (Norwood, Grassendale Park, Liverpool 19), da of late Clifford James Peard, DSO, JP, of North Curry, Som:—
Timothy James Egerton, *b* 1958. —— Catherine Susan, *b* 1956.

    Grandchildren of late Maj Francis Egerton Cotton, 2nd son of Charles Robert Cotton, 5th son of Henry Calverley Cotton (*b* 1750) (ante):—
    Issue of late Maj Gilbert Francis Egerton Cotton, *b* 1880, *d* 1971: *m* 1913, Nora, who *d* 1956, da of Mathew Williams:—
Francis Brian Egerton (Low Houses, nr Brampton, Cumbria), *b* 1916; *ed* Eton; Maj (ret) RWF: *m* 1955, Ruth, MBE, da of late Richard Stratton, CBE, of Kingston Deverill, Wilts, and has issue living, Charles Egerton, *b* 1958. —— Helen Viola Egerton, *b* 1917: *m* 1st, 1940, Capt Sir John Hargreaves Pigott-Brown, 2nd Bt, Coldm Gds (*ka* 1942); 2ndly, 1948, Capt Charles Raymond Radclyffe, late R Scots Greys, of Lew, Oxon, and has issue living (by 1st *m*) (*see* Pigott-Brown, Bt), — (by 2nd *m*) Sarah (15 Shirlock Rd, NW3 2HR), *b* 1950; film producer.

    Granddaughter of late William Gordon Lynch Cotton, MICE, son of late Col Hugh Calveley Cotton, 6th son of Henry Calveley Cotton (*b* 1750) (ante):—
    Issue of late Hugh Gordon Cotton, *b* 1869, *d* 1942: *m* 1903, Gertrude Mary, da of late Charles Parsons:—
Vivien Mary, *b* 1903.

PREDECESSORS – **(1)** Sir ROBERT COTTON, MP for Cheshire; *cr* a Baronet 1677; *d* 1712; *s* by his son **(2)** Sir ROBERT SALUSBURY, 3rd Bt, MP for Cheshire; *dsp*; *s* by his brother **(4)** Sir LYNCH SALUSBURY, MP 4th Bt; *d* 1775; *s* by his son **(5)** Sir ROBERT SALUSBURY, 5th Bt, MP for Cheshire; *d* 1807; *s* by his son **(6)** Sir STAPLETON, GCB, GCH, KSI, *b* 1772; served with remarkable distinction in Peninsular War 1791-1814, and at siege of Bhurtpore 1826, when Com in Ch in India; was a Field-Marshal, Constable of the Tower, Lord-Lieut of Tower Hamlets, Gold Stick-in-Waiting, and Col 1st Life Guards; *cr* Baron Combermere, of Combermere, co Chester (peerage of United Kingdom) 1814, and *Viscount Combermere*, of Bhurtpore, E Indies, and of Combermere, co Chester (peerage of United Kingdom) 1827: *m* 2ndly, 1814, Caroline, da of William Fulke Greville; *d* 1865; *s* by his son **(7)** WELLINGTON HENRY, 2nd Viscount, *b* 1818; MP for Carrickfergus (*C*) 1847-57: *m* 1844, Susan Alice who *d* 1869, da of Sir George Sitwell, 2nd Bt; *d* 1891; *s* by his eldest son **(8)** ROBERT WELLINGTON, 3rd Viscount, *b* 1845: *m* 1st 1866 (*m diss* 1879), Charlotte Anne, only child of late J. Fletcher Ellis Fletcher, of Pool Hall, Lancashire; 2ndly, 1880, Isabel Marian, who *d* 1930, yst da of Sir George Chetwynd, 3rd Bt; *d* 1898; *s* by his only son **(9)** FRANCIS LYNCH WELLINGTON, 4th Viscount; *b* 1887: *m* 1st, 1913 (*m diss* 1926), Hazel Louisa, who *d* 1943, da of late Henry de Courcy Agnew (Agnew, Bt, *cr* 1629, colls); 2ndly, 1927, Constance Marie Katherine, who *d* 1968, da of late Lt-Col Sir Francis Dudley Williams-Drummond, KBE, of Hafodneddyn, Carmarthenshire (Williams-Drummond, Bt, colls): *d* 1969; *s* by his son **(10)** MICHAEL WELLINGTON, 5th Viscount and present peer; also Baron Combermere.

Compton, Earl; son of Marquess of Northampton.

CONGLETON, BARON (Parnell) (Baron UK 1841, Bt I 1766)

Honours have followed thee

CHRISTOPHER PATRICK PARNELL, 8th Baron, and 11th Baronet; *b* 11 March 1930; *s* 1967; *ed* Eton, and New Coll, Oxford: *m* 1955, Anna Hedvig, da of G. A. Sommerfelt, of Oslo, Norway, and has issue.

Arms – Gules: two Chevronels, and in chief three escallops argent. **Crest** – A boar's head erased or, between two wings gules, each charged with two chevronels argent. **Supporters** – *Dexter*, an angel vested argent, wings and the head radiated gold; *sinister*, a hermit vested, the exterior hand supporting his staff proper, the hat ensigned with an escallop or.
Residence – West End Farm, Ebbesbourne Wake, Salisbury, Wilts.

SONS LIVING

Hon JOHN PATRICK CHRISTIAN, *b* 17 March 1959: *m* 1985, Marjorie-Anne (Annie), only da of John Hobdell, of The Ridings, Cobham, Surrey, and has issue living, Christopher John Edward, *b* 1987, — Harry Gustav Willem, *b* 1990, — Phoebe Anna Hedvig, *b* 1992.
Hon Thomas David Howard, *b* 1963.

DAUGHTERS LIVING

Hon (Anne) Cathrine, *b* 1956: *m* 1980, (Michael) Robin Long, and has issue living, Richard Per, *b* 1981, — Willum Jan, *b* 1984.
Hon Elizabeth Dagny, *b* 1960.
Hon Mary-Clare, *b* 1965.

SISTERS LIVING

Hon Mary Elizabeth, *b* 1919: *m* 1956, Percy Purves Turnbull, who *d* 1976. *Residence* – 74 St Ann St, Salisbury, Wilts SP1 2DX. *Club* – Special Forces, New Cavendish.
Hon Jean Margaret, *b* 1922: *m* 1952, as his 2nd wife, Lt-Col Frederick Henry Howard, DSO, MC and bar, late 3rd Hus (*see* E Carlisle colls). *Residence* – Isle of Ulva, Aros, Mull, Argyll PA73 6LZ.
Hon Sheila Helen, *b* 1923: *m* 1959 (*m diss* 1979), Roger Henry Duvollet, and has had issue, Annette Frances, *b* 1961, *d* 1982.
Hon Ann Bridget, *b* 1927: *m* 1947 (*m diss* 1967), Maj Derek Campbell Russell, RE. *Residence* – Lyscombe, Piddletrenthide, Dorset.
Hon Heather Doreen, *b* 1929: *m* 1960, Robert Peter Mangin Bell, and has issue living, (Robert) Simon Parnell, *b* 1961: *m* 1986, Fiona J., MD, elder da of David Sanders, of Winchester, and has issue living, (Robert) Edward Sanders *b* 1989, Jack Digby *b* 1993, Alice Seymour *b* 1990, — Aidan William George, *b* 1967, — Penelope Edith, *b* 1963: *m* 1991, Peter M. Melville, elder son of Rev P. K. Melville, of Albury, NSW, Australia. *Residence* – Sarsen House, 5 Mead Rd, St Cross, Winchester.

COLLATERAL BRANCHES LIVING

> Grandchildren of late Bertram Damer Parnell, playwright, 2nd son of late Col Hon Arthur Parnell, 3rd son of 3rd Baron:—
>   Issue of late Desmond Damer Parnell, *b* 1900, *d* 1972: *m* 1930, Ivy Maude, who *d* 1972, da of late Mark Hunt Harding:—
> John Desmond (6 Gayton Court, Gayton Rd, Harrow, Middx), *b* 1930: *m* 1961, Barbara Jean, da of Laurence Chapell, of Leeds, and formerly wife of Coleson John King, and has issue living, Sally Dee, *b* 1966. —— Jean Pamela, *b* 1943: *m* 1976, Ronald James Johnson, of 59 Sutton Lane, Langley, Berks, and has issue living, Philip Andrew, *b* 1981, — Joanna, *b* 1976.

> Grandchildren of late Miles Bligh Damer FARMILOE (infra):—
>   Issue of late Michael John FARMILOE, *b* 1931, *d* (27 Feb) 1983: *m* 1953, Mary Elizabeth, who *d* 1980, only da of Vivian Ewart Berry, of 118 Berkeley Court, NW1:—
> Simon Charles FARMILOE, *b* 1961. —— Sarah Elizabeth, *b* 1959: *m* 1986, John Kiddell, son of Percy Edgar Kiddell, and has issue living, Jamie Michael, *b* 1992. *Residence* – 1 Cherrywood Close, Kingston upon Thames, Surrey.
>   Grandson of late Bertram Damer Parnell (ante):—
>   Issue of late Miles Bligh Damer FARMILOE (assumed surname of Farmiloe in lieu of his patronymic by deed poll 1929), *b* 1903, *d* (11 Oct) 1983: *m* 1929, Cynthia Joyce, who *d* 1990, da of Maj Henry Percy Holt:—
> Timothy Miles FARMILOE, *b* 1935; *ed* Winchester, and New Coll, Oxford (MA). *Residence* – Little Brookwood, 28 Woodfield Lane, Ashtead, Surrey KT21 2BE.

> Grandson of late Hon Lionel Charles Nugent Parnell, 7th son of 3rd Baron:—
>   Issue of late Harold Charles Stewart Parnell, *b* 1900, *d* 1973: *m* 1938, Marjorie J. Carvell, who *d* 1990:—
> Christopher Charles Stewart (213a Northfield Av, Ealing, W13 9QU), *b* 1946: *m* 1982, Joy E. Johnson.

PREDECESSORS – **(1)** JOHN PARNELL, MP for Maryborough 1761; *cr* a *Baronet* 1766; *d* 1782; *s* by his son **(2)** Sir JOHN, PC, 2nd Bt, MP for Queen's co 1783-1801, Chancellor of the Exchequer in Ireland 1787, and a Lord of the Treasury 1793-9; *d* 1801; *s* by his eldest son **(3)** Sir JOHN AUGUSTUS, 3rd Bt; *dsp* 1812; *s* by his brother **(4)** Sir HENRY BROOKE, 4th Bt; *s* to the paternal estates by special Act of Parliament 1789, upon the demise of his father; was MP for Maryborough 1797, Queen's co 1802-6, and Dundee (*L*) 1833-41, a Lord of the Treasury, Sec at War 1831-2. Paymaster-Gen of the Forces, and Treasurer of the Navy and Ordnance 1835-41; *cr Baron Congleton*, of Congleton, Cheshire (peerage of United Kingdom) 1841: *m* 1801, Lady Caroline Elizabeth Dawson, da of 1st Earl of Portarlington; *d* 1842; *s* by his eldest son **(2)** JOHN VESEY, 2nd Baron, *b* 1805: *d* 1883; *s* by his brother **(3)** HENRY WILLIAM, 3rd Baron, *b* 1809; present as Midshipman at battle of Navarino: *m* 1st, 1835, Sophia, who *d* 1846, da of late Col Hon William Bligh; 2ndly, 1851, Hon Caroline Margaret, who *d* 1912 (sometime a Maid of Honour to HM Queen Victoria), da of late Hon Lionel Charles Dawson; *d* 1896; *s* by his eldest surviving son **(4)** HENRY, CB, 4th Baron, *b* 1839; Maj-Gen in Army; served during Zulu Campaign 1879, Comdg 3rd Batn Buffs, *ed* Kent Regt (despatches, CB): *m* 1885, Elizabeth Peter, who *d* 1931, yst da of late Dugald Dove, of Nutshill, co Renfrew; *d* 1906; *s* by his son **(5)** HENRY BLIGH FORTESCUE, 5th Baron, *b* 1890; Lt Gren Gds; *ka* 1914 (despatches); *s* by his brother **(6)** JOHN BROOKE MOLESWORTH, 6th Baron, *b* 1892: *m* 1918, Hon Edith Mary Palmer Howard, who *d* 1979, da of late Baroness Strathcona and Mount Royal (in her own right); *d* 1932; *s* by his son **(7)** WILLIAM JARED, RN, 7th Baron, *b* 1925; *d* 1967; *s* by his brother **(8)** CHRISTOPHER PATRICK, 8th Baron and present peer.

CONSTANTINE, BARONY OF (Constantine) (Extinct 1971)

DAUGHTER LIVING OF LIFE BARON

Hon Gloria, *b* 1928; *ed* St Andrew's Univ (MA), and Inst of Education, London Univ (Dip Ed): *m* 1954, André Valère, barrister of 202A, Terrace Vale Rd, Goodwood Park, Point Cumana, Trinidad and Tobago, and has issue.

CONSTANTINE OF STANMORE, BARON (Constantine) (Life Baron 1981)

THEODORE CONSTANTINE, CBE, son of late Leonard Constantine, of London; *b* 15 March 1910; *ed* Acton Coll; High Sheriff and DL of Greater London 1967; Master of Worshipful Co of Coachmakers 1975; Freeman of City of London 1949, a Trustee of Sir John Wolstenholme Charity; Chm Nat Union of Conservative and Unionists Assocns since 1968 (Pres 1980); served in 1939-45 War with RAuxAF (AE 1945); DL Greater London; *cr CBE* (Civil) 1956; Kt 1964 and *Baron Constantine of Stanmore*, in Greater London (Life Baron) 1981: *m* 1935, Sylvia Mary, who *d* 1990, da of Wallace Henry Legge-Pointing, of London, and has issue. *Residence* – Hunters Beck, Uxbridge Rd, Stanmore, Middlesex.

SON LIVING

Hon Roy, *b* 1936. *Residence* – 11 Grove Park Terr, W4.

DAUGHTER LIVING

Hon Jill Diane, *b* 1938: *m* 1965, Geoffrey Murray, and has issue living, Guy John, *b* 1968, — Tracy Diane, *b* 1966. *Residence* – 46 Linskway, Northwood, Middlesex.

Conway of Ragley, Baron; grandson of Marquess of Hertford.

CONYNGHAM, MARQUESS (Conyngham) (Marquess I 1816) sits as BARON MINSTER (UK 1821)
(Title pronounced "Cunningham")

FREDERICK WILLIAM HENRY FRANCIS CONYNGHAM, 7th Marquess; *b* 13 March 1924; *s* 1974; *ed* Eton; late Capt Irish Gds; patron of one living: *m* 1st, 1950 (*m diss* 1970), Eileen Wren, da of Capt Clement Wren Newsam, of Ashfield, Beauparc, co Meath; 2ndly, 1971, Elizabeth Ann, yr da of late Frederick Molyneux Hughes, of Fareham, Hants, and formerly wife of David Sutherland Rudd; 3rdly, 1980, Daphne Georgina Adelaide, who *d* 1986, eldest da of R. C. Armour, formerly of Kenya, and formerly wife of C. P. V. Walker, of Nairobi; 4thly, 1987, (Emma Christianne) Annabel, only da of (Denys) Martin Agnew, of Grosvenor Court, 22 Grove Rd, East Cliffe, Bournemouth (*see* Agnew, Bt, *cr* 1895, colls), and has issue by 1st *m*.

Arms – Argent, a shake fork between three mullets sable. Crest – A unicorn's head erased argent, armed or crined and tufted sable. Supporters – *Dexter*, a horse argent, hoofs and mane or, and charged on the breast with an eagle displayed or; *sinister*, a stag, proper, attired, unguled and charged on the breast with a griffin's head erased or. *Residence* – Myrtle Hill, Andreas Rd, Ramsey, Isle of Man. *Clubs* – Boodle's, R St George Yacht.

SONS LIVING (by 1st marriage)

HENRY VIVIAN PIERPOINT (*Earl of Mount Charles*), *b* 23 May 1951; *ed* Harrow: *m* 1st, 1971 (*m diss* 1985), Juliet Ann, yr da of Robert R. B. Kitson, of Churchtown, Morval, Cornwall; 2ndly, 1985, Lady Iona Charlotte Grimston, yst da of 6th Earl of Verulam, and has issue by 1st and 2nd *m*:—
   SON LIVING (by 1st *m*) Alexander Burton (*Viscount Slane*), *b* 30 Jan 1975.
      DAUGHTERS LIVING (by 1st *m*) *Lady* Henrietta Tamara Juliet, *b* 1976, — (by 2nd *m*), *Lady* Tamara Jane, *b* 1991.
Seats – Slane Castle, co Meath; Beau Parc, Navan, co Meath. *Clubs* – Kildare Street and University.
Lord Simon Charles Eveleigh Wren (49 Oxberry Av, SW6), *b* 1953; *ed* Harrow: *m* 1st, 1978 (*m diss* 19—), Emma S., da of late W/Cdr F. W. Breeze; 2ndly, 1990, Mrs Carole Crossman Yorke, yst da of late Eldon F. le Poer Power, of Ashfield, Beauparc, co Meath, and formerly wife of Nicholas Roger Yorke (*see* E Hardwicke, colls), and has issue living (by 1st *m*), Chloe Wren, *b* 1980, — (by 2nd *m*) Frances, *b* 1991.

DEBRETT'S ILLUSTRATED PEERAGE

Lord (Frederick William) Patrick (North Wing, Severn End, Hanley Castle, Worcs), *b* 1959: *m* 1990, Charlotte Mary Temple Gordon, elder da of (Michael) Donald Gordon Black, MC, of Edenwood, Cupar, Fife.

WIDOW LIVING OF SON OF SIXTH MARQUESS

Olivia Phoebe (has reverted to her former style of *Lady John Conyngham*), da of late Capt Percy Neave Leathers, of Fayre Cottage, Robertsbridge, Sussex: *m* 1st, 1950, Lord John Victor Albert Blosse Conyngham, who *d* 1963; 2ndly, 1963, Hon Francis Alexander Innys Eveleigh-Ross-de-Moleyns, who *d* 1964 (*see* B Ventry). *Residence* – Windmill Cottage, Yapton Rd, Barnham, Bognor Regis, W Sussex.

COLLATERAL BRANCH LIVING

Descendants of late Lord Albert Conyngham, KCH, FRS (3rd son of 1st Marquess), was *cr Baron Londesborough* 1850 (see that title).

PREDECESSORS – (1) Rt Hon Henry Conyngham, PC, MP 1737-53, Vice-Adm, of Ulster and Gov of cos Donegal and Londonderry; *cr Baron Conyngham* (peerage of Ireland) 1953, *Viscount Conyngham* (peerage of Ireland) 1756, *Earl Conyngham* (peerage of Ireland) 1781, and *Baron Conyngham* (peerage of Ireland) 1781, with remainder to his nephew Francis Pierpont-Burton, MP; *d* 1781; *s* by his nephew (ante) (2) Francis Pierpont-Burton, 2nd Baron, who assumed by R licence the surname and arms of Conyngham; *d* 1787; *s* by his son (3) Henry, KP, 3rd Baron; was a Gen in the Army and a Representative peer for Ireland; *cr Viscount Conyngham* (peerage of Ireland) 1789, *Viscount Mount Charles*, and *Earl of Conyngham* (peerage of Ireland) 1797, *Viscount Slane, Earl of Mount Charles* and *Marquess Conyngham* (peerage of Ireland) 1816, and *Baron Minster* (peerage of United Kingdom) 1821; *d* 1832; *s* by his son (4) Francis Nathanial, KP, PC, GCH, 2nd Marquess; a Gen in the Army and Lord-Lieut of co Meath; *d* 1876; *s* by his son (5) George Henry, 3rd Marquess; *b* 1825; was a Lieut-Gen in the Army, a JP for Kent and Hon Col E Kent Yeo Cav: *m* 1854, Lady Jane St Maur Blanch Stanhope, da of 4th Earl of Harrington; *d* 2 June 1882; *s* by his son (6) Henry Francis, 4th Marquess, *b* 1857: *m* 1882, Hon Frances Elizabeth Sarah Eveleigh-de Moleyns, who *d* 1939, (having *m* 2ndly 1899, Major John Russell Bedford Cameron), da of 4th Baron Ventry; *d* 1897; *s* by his el son (7) Victor George Henry Francis, 5th Marquess, *b* 1883; *d* 1918; *s* by his brother (8) Frederick William Burton, 6th Marquess, *b* 1890: *m* 1st 1914 (*m diss* 1921), Elizabeth Alice, who *d* 1933, da of late William Andrew Tobin, of Australia; 2ndly, 1922, Antoinette Winifred, who *d* 1966, da of John William Howard Thompson; 3rdly, 1966, Stella, who *d* 1985, el da of late Francis Barrallier Thompson, MRCS, LRCP, and window of Robert Newton Tory; *d* 1974; *s* by his son (9) Frederick William Henry Francis, 7th Marquess and present peer; also Earl Conyngham, Earl of Mount Charles, Viscount Slane, Viscount Mount Charles, Viscount Conyngham, Baron Conyngham, and Baron Minster.

COOKE OF ISLANDREAGH, BARON (Cooke) (Life Baron 1992)

Victor Alexander Cooke, OBE, son of (Norman) Victor Cooke, of The Ingles, Greenisland, co Antrim; *b* 18 Oct 1920; *ed* Marlborough, and Trin Coll, Camb (MA); Lieut (E) RN 1940-46; DL co Antrim 1970; Henry R. Ayton Ltd, Belfast 1946-89 (Chm 1970-89), Chm Springvale EPS (formerly Polyproducts) Ltd since 1964, Belfast Savings Bank 1963, and Harland & Wolff Ltd 1980-81 (Dir 1970-87); Dir NI Airports 1970-85; Member of Senate NI Parliament 1960-68, NI Economic Council 1974-78; Commr Irish Lights since 1983 (Chm 1990-92); CEng, FIMechE; *cr* OBE (Civil) 1981, and *Baron Cooke of Islandreagh*, of Islandreagh, co Antrim (Life Baron) 1992: *m* 1951, Alison Sheila, only da of late Maj-Gen Francis Casement, DSO, of Craigtara, Ballycastle, co Antrim, and has issue.
Address – c/o House of Lords, SW1. *Club* – Naval.

SONS LIVING

Hon Michael John Alexander, *b* 1955; *ed* Marlborough, and Van Mildert Coll, Durham (BSc): *m* 1983, Anne Helen Madeleine, eldest da of late Maj Michael Henry Armstrong, MBE, DL, of Dean's Hill, co Armagh, and has issue living, Robert Michael James, *b* 1990. — Helen Frances Alice, *b* 1985, — Katharine Mary Elizabeth, *b* 1987, — Susannah Madeleine Jane, *b* 1993.
Hon James Victor Francis, *b* 1960; *ed* Marlborough, Trin Coll, Camb (MA), and Cranfield Business Sch (MBA).

DAUGHTER LIVING

Hon Victoria Sally, *b* 1956; *ed* Cobham Hall, Marlborough, and Edinburgh Univ (MA): *m* 1982, Nicholas Patrick Yonge, yst son of Cmdr Philip Evelyn Yonge, OBE, DSC, RN (ret), and has issue living, Cyprian Alexander, *b* 1990, — Charlotte Emma Rosaleen, *b* 1988.

COOPER OF STOCKTON HEATH, BARONY OF (Cooper) (Extinct 1988)

DAUGHTERS LIVING OF LIFE BARON (*By 1st marriage*)

Hon Brenda, *b* 1937: *m* 1st, 1958, (*m diss* 1967), John Abbott; 2ndly, 1968, Pereric Astrom. *Residence* – 9 Rathen Rd, Withington, Manchester M20 9QJ.
Hon Marjorie *b* 1941: *m* 1st 1959 (*m diss* 1969), Neville Finch; 2ndly, 1974 (*m diss* 1979), Robert Dennis Menpes, and has issue living, two sons and two das. *Residence* – 102 Douglas Rd, Esher, Surrey KT10 8BG.
Hon Jacqueline, *b* 1946: *m* 1972, J. Bradford Thomas, and has issue living, three sons. *Residence* – 54 Stanley Rd, East Sheen, SW14 7DZ.

WIDOW LIVING OF LIFE BARON

Joan (*Baroness Cooper of Stockton Heath*), fomerly wife of — Rogers: *m* 1969, as his 2nd wife, Baron Cooper of Stockton Heath (Life Baron), who *d* 1988. *Address* – 23 Kelvin Grove, Chessington, Surrey.

CORK and ORRERY, EARL OF (Boyle) Sits as BARON BOYLE OF MARSTON (GB 1711) (Earl I 1620)

PATRICK REGINALD BOYLE, 13th Earl *b* 7 Feb 1910; *s* 1967; *ed* Harrow, and RMC; Hereditary Life Gov and Chm of Exec Cttee of Christian Faith Soc, Pres and Chm of Exec Cttee, British Cancer Council 1973-77, and a Member of Council, Cancer Research Campaign 1973-77; a Dep Speaker and Dep Chm of Cttees House of Lords 1973-78; Dir St Christopher's Hospice, Sydenham, and of American Council for Cultural Exchange Inc 1973-78; 1939-45 War with R Ulster Rifles and Parachute Regt; S-E Asia 1941-45 with Burma Rifles and Cameronians (Scottish Rifles) in Special Force (Chindits) (severely wounded): *m* 1st, 1952, Mrs Dorothy Kate Scelsi, who *d* 1978, only da of late Robert Ramsden, of Meltham, Yorks; 2ndly, 1978, Mary Gabrielle, only da of late Louis Ginnett, and widow of Kenneth McFarlane Walker.

Arms – Per bend embattled argent and gules **Crest** – Out of a ducal coronet or, a lion's head per pale embattled, argent and gules. **Supporters** – Two lions the *dexter* per pale embattled, gules and argent; the *sinister*, per pale embattled, argent and gules. *Residence* – Flint House, Heyshott, Midhurst, Sussex.

BROTHER LIVING

(Raised to the rank of an Earl's son 1967)

Hon JOHN WILLIAM, DSC (Nether Craigantaggart, Dunkeld, Perthshire, PH8 0HQ), *b* 12 May 1916; *ed* Harrow, and King's Coll, London (BSc); FICE; 1939-45 War as Lt-Cdr RNVR (despatches twice, DSC): *m* 1943, Mary Leslie, da of late Gen Sir Robert Gordon Finlayson, KCB, CMG, DSO, and has issue living, John Richard (Lickfold House, Petworth, W Sussex GU28 9EY), *b* 3 Nov 1945; *ed* Harrow, and RNC Dartmouth; Lt Cdr RN (ret): *m* 1973, Hon Rebecca Juliet Noble, da of late Baron Glenkinglas (Life Baron), and has issue living, Rory Jonathan Courtenay *b* 10 Dec 1978, Cara Mary Cecilia *b* 1976, Davina Claire Theresa *b* (twin) 1978, — Robert William (30 Durand Gdns, SW9 0PP), *b* 1948; *ed* Harrow, and Ch Ch, Oxford (MA); FCA: *m* 1987, Fiona Mary, da of Hon (Oliver) Piers St Aubyn, MC (*see* B St Levan), and has issue living, Richard Piers *b* 1988, — (Charles) Reginald (6840 West 83rd St Terrace, Bloomington, MN 55438, USA), *b* 1957; *ed* Harrow and RMA; late Capt Coldm Gds: *m* 1987, Susan Shields, da of Philip Hoene, of Duluth, Minnesota, USA, and has issue living, Georgina Margaret *b* 1989.

COLLATERAL BRANCHES LIVING

Grandsons living of late Maj Charles John Boyle, 2nd son of Rev Hon Richard Cavendish Boyle, 4th son of 8th Earl:—

Issue of late Capt Richard Frederick Robert Pochin Boyle, Oxfordshire and Bucks LI, *b* 1888, *d* 1953: *m* 1918, Marion, who *d* 1969, da of late Maj-Gen Hill Wallace, CB:—

Richard Michael Charles, *b* 1918. *Residence* – Prospect, Birdswell Lane, Berrynarbor, Devon.

Issue of late Capt Edmund Michael Gordon Loeventhorpe Boyle, RN, *b* 1895, *d* 1982: *m* 1927, Maida Cecil (Queens Lodge, St Cross Rd, Winchester), da of late Lt-Col Hon Percy Cecil Evans-Freke (*see* B Carbery, colls):—

George Hamilton (Nozieres, 07270 Lamastre, France), *b* 1928; *ed* Canford, and Imp Coll, Lond (BSc); ARSM; High Sheriff Rutland 1964, and Leics and Rutland 1976, DL Leics: *m* 1953, Alathea Henriette Mary, da of John Adrian Frederick March Phillipps de Lisle, of Stockerston Hall, Leics, and has issue living, Robert Edmund John (Bisbrooke Hall, Uppingham, Rutland), *b* 1954; *ed* Eton, and RMA Sandhurst; late Capt Irish Gds: *m* 1985, Gabrielle Georgiana, only da of Patrick Tobias Telfer Smollett, MC, DL, of Bonhill, Cameron, Alexandria, Dunbartonshire (*see* Fox, Bt, ext 1959), and has issue living, Patrick *b* 1991, Albinia Mary *b* 1988, — Richard William (The Priory, Gt Milton, Oxford), *b* 1959; *ed* Gordonstoun, and Wanganui Coll: *m* 1990, Suzanna Jean, eldest da of Charles Bingham, of Tavistock, Devon, — Rupert Lancelot Cavendish (The Park House, Laxton, Northants), *b* 1960; *ed* Gordonstoun: *m* 1986, Sarah Daphne, eldest da of Simon Anthony Berry, of Cloggs Hall, Great Cornard, Suffolk, and has issue living, Angus Hugo Edmund *b* 1989, Christopher Simon Hamilton *b* 1992. —— Patrick Stephen Crispin, *b* 1935: *m* 1975, Heather Ann Williamson, and has issue living, Edmund Charles Thomas, *b* 1976, — Katharine Anna Cecil, *b* 1978. *Residence* – 5 Weech Rd, NW6.

Grandchildren of late Col Lionel Richard Cavendish Boyle, CMB, MVO, 2nd son of late Charles John Boyle, 2nd son of late Vice-Adm Hon Sir Courtenay Boyle, KCH, 3rd son of 7th Earl:—

Issue of late Capt Richard Courtenay Boyle, DSC, RN, *b* 1902, *d* 1986: *m* 1936, Guendolen Mabel Maclean (DL Herts) (14 Mandeville Close, Broxbourne, Herts EN10 7PN), da of late Lt-Col Edward Hugh Griffith, CBE:—

John Richard (40 Drayton Gdns, SW10), *b* 1938; *ed* Eton, and Trin Coll, Camb: *m* 1st, 1964 (*m diss* 1978), Jeannine Mary, da of Capt Timothy John Gurney, Coldm Gds, of The White House, Hare St, Buntingford, Herts (*see* De Bathe, Bt, ext); 2ndly, 1978, Mrs Lena Jupp, yst da of Maj G. B. Rahr, and has issue living (by 1st *m*), Richard Burlington, *b* 1966, — Charles Robert, *b* 1969, — Patrick William, *b* 1971, — (by 2nd *m*) Harry Courtenay, *b* 1979, — Olivia Mary, *b* 1982. —— William Robert Cavendish (21 Sussex St, SW1), *b* 1944; *ed* Eton: *m* 1994, Janet Ann, da of late John Bainbridge. — Belinda, *b* 1940: *m* 1963, Brig Thomas Neil McMicking, late The Black Watch, of Miltonise, New Luce, Wigtownshire DG8 0LY, elder son of late Maj-Gen Neil McMicking, CB, CBE, DSO, MC, and has issue living, Charles Neil, *b* 1965, — James Richard, *b* 1968, — Henrietta Sophia, *b* 1972.

PREDECESSORS – (1) *Rt Hon Sir* RICHARD BOYLE, PC, embarked for Ireland as an adventurer, and having eventually amassed considerable wealth, sat as MP for Lismore 1615; was knighted 1603, and *cr Baron Boyle of Youghal* (peerage of Ireland) 1616, and *Viscount Dungarvan* and *Earl of Cork* (peerage of Ireland) 1620, and was afterwards Lord High Treasurer of Ireland, and known as the "Great Earl;" Cromwell is reported to have said of him that "if there had been an Earl of Cork in every province, it would have been impossible for the Irish to have raised a rebellion"; *d* 1643; *s* by his son (2) RICHARD, 2nd Earl, who in 1642 had by special remainder *s* by his brother Lewis as 2nd *Baron of Bandon Bridge* and *Viscount Boyle of Kinalmeaky* (peerage of Ireland), *cr* 1627: *m* Elizabeth, da and heiress of Henry Clifford, 5th and last Earl of Cumberland, who had in 1628 been summoned by writ as Baron Clifford: he was *cr Baron Clifford*, of Lanesborough, co York (peerage of England) 1644, and *Earl of Burlington* (peerage of England) 1664; *d* 1697; *s* by his grandson (3) CHARLES, 3rd Earl; *d* 1703, *s* by his son (4) RICHARD, 4th Earl; an eminent patron of literature and the fine arts; claimed and was allowed the Barony of Clifford by writ, *cr* 1628; *d* 1753, without male issue, when the Barony of Clifford, of Lanesborough, devolved upon his da Charlotte, wife of William Marquess of Hartington, afterwards 4th Duke of Devonshire; the Barony of Clifford of Lanesborough, *cr* 1644, and the Earldom of Burlington became extinct, and the Irish honours reverted to his kinsman (5) JOHN, 5th Earl, who had in 1731 *s* as 5th *Earl of Orrery*, 5th *Lord Boyle, Baron of Broghill*, and 2nd *Baron Boyle of Marston* (see **infra*); *d* 1762; *s* by his son (6) HAMILTON, 6th Earl; *dsp* 1764: *s* by his half-brother (7) EDMUND, 7th Earl; *d* 1798; *s* by his son (8) EDMUND, KP; a Gen in the Army; *d* 1856; *s* by his grandson (9) RICHARD EDMUND ST LAWRENCE, KP, PC (son of Charles, Viscount Dungarvan, by Lady Katherine St Lawrence, da of 2nd Earl of Howth), 9th Earl; *b* 1829; Lord-Lieut Somerset; Master of the Buckhounds 1866, 1868, and 1880-85, and Master of the Horse 1886 and 1894-5: *m* 1853, Lady Emily Charlotte De Burgh, who *d* 1912, da of 1st Marquess of Clanricarde, KP; *d* 1904; *s* by his son (10) CHARLES SPENCER CANNING, 10th Earl, *b* 1861: *m* 1918, Rosalie Gray, who *d* 1930, da of William Waterman de Villiers, of Romsey, Hants; *d* 1925; *s* by his brother (11) ROBERT JOHN LASCELLES, 11th Earl, *b* 1864: *m* 1890, Josephine Catherine, who *d* 1953, da of J. P. Hale, of San Francisco, USA; *d* 1934; *s* by his kinsman (12) WILLIAM HENRY DUDLEY, GCB, GCVO, son of late Col Gerald Edmund Boyle (by Lady Elizabeth Theresa Pepys, da of 1st Earl of Cottenham), (grandson of 8th Earl), 12th Earl, *b* 1873; Adm of the Fleet; C in C Home Fleet 1933-35, and at Portsmouth 1937-39; commanded combined expedition for capture of Narvik 1940: *m* 1902, Lady Florence Cecilia Keppel, who *d* 1963, da of 7th Earl of Albemarle; *d* 1967, *s* by his nephew (13) PATRICK REGINALD (son of Maj Hon Reginald Courtenay Boyle, MBE, MC, by his wife, Violet, who *d* 1974, da of late Arthur Flower (*see* Pauncefort-Duncombe, Bt, 1936 Edn)) 13th Earl, and present peer; also Viscount Dungarvan, Viscount Boyle of Kinalmeaky, Baron Boyle of Youghal, Baron of Bandon Bridge, and Lord Boyle, Baron of Broghill, and Baron Boyle of Marston.

*(1) Sir ROGER BOYLE, PC, 3rd son of 1st Earl of Cork, *cr* when seven years of age *Baron Boyle of Broghill* (peerage of Ireland) 1621, with remainder to heirs of his father; was sometime MP for co Cork and for Arundel; substantially assisted to quell the rebellion in Ireland 1642-3, and after the death of Cromwell planned the restoration of Charles II in Ireland; *cr Earl of Orrery* (peerage of Ireland) 1660; *d* 1679; *s* by his son (2) ROGER, 2nd Earl; *d* 1682; *s* by his son (3) LIONEL, 3rd Earl; attainted by this Parliament of James II 1689; sometime MP for E Grinstead, Sussex; *dsp* 1703; *s* by his brother (4) CHARLES, KT, 4th Earl; and Lt-Gen in the Army, MP for Huntingdon 1700, Ambassador to Brabant and, Flanders, and a Lord of the Bedchamber to George I; *cr Baron Boyle of Marston*, Somerset 1711; in 1722 was imprisoned for six months in the Tower on suspicion of high treason; the astronomical instrument invented by George Graham was named "Orrery" after this peer: *d* 1731; *s* by his son (5) JOHN, 5th Earl, who *s* as 5th Earl of Cork (ante).

Cornwall, Duke of; title borne by the Prince of Wales.

CORNWALLIS, BARON (Cornwallis) (Baron UK 1927)

Virtue overcomes envy

FIENNES NEIL WYKEHAM CORNWALLIS, OBE, 3rd Baron; *b* 29 June, 1921; *s* 1982; *ed* Eton; formerly in Coldm Gds; Pres Nat Assocn of Agric Contractors 1958-63, and since 1986; Memb of Board of Trustees Chevening Estate since 1979; Chm Small Firms Council CBI 1978-81; DL; OBE (Civil) 1963: *m* 1st, 1942 (*m diss* 1948), Judith, only da of Lt-Col Lacy Scott, of Ashcroft, Wadhurst, Sussex; 2ndly, 1951, Agnes Jean, yr da of Capt Henderson Russell Landale, of Ewell Manor, W Farleigh, Maidstone, and has issue by 1st and 2nd *m*.

Arms – Quarterly 1st and 4th, sable, guttée d'eau, on a fesse argent three martlets of the field, *Cornwallis*; 2nd and 3rd, sable on a fesse embattled counter-embattled between three goats passant argent, as many pellets, *Mann*. **Crest** – On a mount vert, a stag lodged reguardant argent, attired or, vulned in the shoulder proper, and gorged with a wreath of laurel also proper. **Supporters** – On either side a stag argent, attired or and gorged with a chaplet of oak fructed vert. *Residences* – Ruck Farm, Horsmonden, Tonbridge, Kent; Dundurn, St Fillans, Perthshire; 25B Queen's Gate Mews, SW7.

SONS LIVING (By 1st marriage)

Hon (FIENNES WYKEHAM) JEREMY *b* 25 May, 1946; *ed* Eton, and RAC Cirencester: *m* 1969, Sara Gray de Neufville, da of Lt-Col Nigel Stockwell, of Benenden, Kent, and has issue living, (Fiennes) Alexander Wykeham Martin, *b* 25 Nov 1987, — Anna Julia Gray, *b* 1971, — Charlotte Louise, *b* 1972. *Residence* – 15 Mablethorpe Rd, SW6

(By 2nd marriage)

Hon (Patrick Wykeham) David (Hamnish Court, Hamnish, Leominster, Herefords) *b* 1952; *ed* Lancing, and Aiglon, Switzerland: *m* 1977, Susannah, da of William Edward Guest, of The Old Vineyard, Rufford Abbey, Notts, and widow of Stephen Thursfield, and has issue living, (Patrick Wykeham) James, *b* 1977, — Thomas Wykeham Charles, *b* 1980, — William Wykeham George, *b* 1982.

DAUGHTERS LIVING (By 2nd marriage)

Hon Cecily Mary Clare, *b* 1954: *m* 1980, Ian McCulloch, yr son of Mrs E. McCulloch, and has issue living, Ruari Alexander Fiennes, *b* 1982, — Rohan Grey, *b* 1984, — Fiennes, *b* 1989, — Skye, *b* 1987.
Hon Vanessa Rachel, *b* 1958: *m* 1986, H. Jeremy Middleton, of 104 Prince Albert Rd, Mosman, Sydney, NSW, Australia.
Hon (Susan Patricia) Rose, *b* 1963: *m* 1986, Scott Simon Crolla, designer, son of Romano Crolla, of Queen's Gate, London.

COLLATERAL BRANCH LIVING

Issue of late Capt Hon Oswald Wykeham Cornwallis, OBE, RN, yst son of 1st Baron; *b* 1894, *d* 1974: *m* 1923, Hon Venetia Jane Digby, who *d* 1956, da of 10th Baron Digby:—
Michael Wykeham (10 Ravelston House Rd, Edinburgh, EH4 3LW), *b* 1924: *ed* Eton; Lt-Cdr RN (ret): *m* 1953, Margaret Dorothy, da of late J. W. Cannon, MB, ChB, and has issue living, Richard Wykeham, *b* 1959, — Diana Margaret, *b* 1957: *m* 1991, David Casey, of 22 St Vincent Crescent, Alloway, Ayr KA7 4QW, son of A. Casey, of Dunblane, and has issue living,

Colin Wykeham b 1994. —— Venetia Mabel, b 1928: m 1956, Lt-Cdr Geoffrey Arthur George Brooke, DSC, RN, and has issue (see Brooke, Bt, colls cr 1903).

PREDECESSORS – (1) FIENNES STANLEY WYKEHAM Cornwallis, CBE, son of late Major Fiennes Cornwallis, of Chacombe Priory, near Banbury; b 1864; was Col late W Kent Imperial Yeo, a JP for Kent (Chm of County Council 1910-30), and MP for Maidstone (C) 1888-95 and 1898-1900; cr Baron Cornwallis of Linton, co Kent (peerage of United Kingdom) 1927: m 1886, Mabel, who d 1957, da of late Capt Oswald Peter Leigh, of Belmont Hall, Cheshire; d 1935; s by his son **(2)** WYKEHAM STANLEY, KCVO, KBE, MC, 2nd Baron, b 1892; Capt Scots Greys; Lord-Lieut of Kent 1944-72; Chm Co Council 1935-36, Lieut for City of London and Lord-Lieut for City and Co of Canterbury 1944-72; Pro-Chancellor Kent Univ 1965-72; Chm Kent War Agric Exec Cttee 1939-46; Pres MCC 1947-48; Hon Col 8th Bn (T) The Queen's Regt TAVR (W Kent); 1914-18 War in France and Belgium (wounded, despatches, MC, 1914 star, two medals): m 1st, 1917, Cecily Etha Mary, who d 1943, da of Sir James Heron Walker, 3rd Bt (cr 1868); 2ndly, 1948, Esme Ethel Alice, who d 1969, da of late Capt J. Montmorency de Beaumont, 5th Royal Irish Lancers, of Hove, Sussex, and widow of Maj Sir Robert James Milo Walker, 4th Bt (cr 1868); d 1982; s by his son **(3)** FIENNES NEIL WYKEHAM, and present peer.

Corry, Viscount; son of Earl of Belmore.

Corvedale, Viscount; son of Earl Baldwin of Bewdley.

COTTENHAM, EARL OF (Pepys) (Earl of UK 1850, Bt GB 1784 and UK 1801)
(Name pronounced "Pepp-iss")

MENS·CUJUSQUE·IS·EST·QUISQUE·

Mind makes the man

(KENELM) CHARLES EVERARD DIGBY PEPYS, 8th Earl, and 11th Baronet (cr 1784) and 10th (cr 1801); b 27 Nov 1948; s 1968; ed Eton: m 1975, Sarah, yr da of Capt Samuel Richard Le Hunte Lombard-Hobson, CVO, OBE, RN, and has issue.

𝕬rms – Sable, on a bend or, between two nags' heads erased argent, three fleurs-de-lis of the field. 𝕮rest – A camel's head erased or, bridled, lined, ringed, and gorged with a ducal coronet sable. 𝕾upporters – On either side a horse argent, bridled, and gorged with a ducal coronet sable; pendent therefrom an escutcheon or, charged with a fleur-de-lis of the second.
Residence – Priory Manor, Kington St Michael, Chippenham, Wilts.

SONS LIVING

MARK JOHN HENRY (Viscount Crowhurst), b 11 Oct 1983.
Hon Sam Richard, b 1986.

DAUGHTER LIVING

Lady Georgina Marye, b 1981.

SISTER LIVING

Lady Gillian Angela (Baroness McGowan), b 1941: m 1962, 3rd Baron McGowan. Residences – Highway House, Lower Froyle, Alton, Hants; 12 Stanhope Mews East, SW7.

DAUGHTERS LIVING OF SIXTH EARL

Lady Rose Edith Idina (Flat B, 101 Earls Court Rd, W8 6QS), b 1927.
Lady Paulina Mary Louise, b 1930: m 1973, Denis Bernard Hadley, of White Hill House, Upham, Hants, SO3 1JL.

COLLATERAL BRANCHES LIVING

Grandchildren of late Hon Henry Leslie Pepys, 3rd son of 1st Earl:—
Issue of late Lt-Col Arthur Guy Leslie Pepys, MC, Essex Regt, b 1875, d 1953: m 1915, Olive Grace, who d 1961, da of late John Frederick Starkey, JP, DL, of Bodicote House, Banbury:—
Iris Leslie, b 1918; late Flight Officer WRAF: m 1953, W/Cdr Norman Maxwell Boffee, DFC, RAF (ret), and has issue living, Mark Guy, b 1956: m 1982, Jean, da of Noshir Rumwalla, of Hounslow, Middx. Residence – 1B Little Green Lane, Chertsey, Surrey.

Issue of late Col Gerald Leslie Pepys, CB, DSO, b 1879, d 1936: m 1907, Charlotte Helen, who d 1965, da of late Charles W. Lambe Forbes, formerly of Auchrannie, Forfarshire:—
Charles Donald Leslie, b 1909: ed Radley; Lt-Col KOYLI: m 1941, Hon (Pamela Sophia) Nadine Stonor, da of 5th Baron Camoys. Residence – 30/31 Lyefield Court, Kidmore End Rd, Emmer Green, Reading, Berks RG4 8AP. Club – Naval and Military. —— Geraldine Mary Leslie, b 1908: m 1935, Lt-Col William Louis Barnard, Oxford and Bucks LI, who d 1953, and has issue living, Simon William Leslie (92B Underhill Rd, SE22), b 1938: m 1962, Joy, da of Thomas Frank Prior Pavely, and has issue living, Jonathan James b 1969, Emma Louise b 1966. Residence – 8 Royston Court, Burbage Rd, SE24.

Granddaughter of late Hon George Pepys, 4th son of 1st Earl:—
Issue of late George Digby Pepys, CBE, *b* 1868, *d* 1957: *m* 1902, Margaret Mary Humphry, who *d* 1954, da of late
George Walter Davidson, of 167 Queen's Gate SW:—
Anna Margaret, *b* 1906: *m* 1931, Peter Pryor, who *d* 1980, and has issue living, Roderick (Weston Lodge, Hitchin, Herts), *b*
1932: *m* 1959, Carolyn Vaughan, el da of late Donald Smith of Old Mill House, Sandwich, Kent, and has issue living, Peter
David *b* 1965: *m* 1993, Melanie Ruth, da of Malcolm Palmer, of Woodsford Sq, W14, Louise Margaret *b* 1960, Victoria Jane *b*
1962: *m* 1987, Denis Henry Clough, of 143 Elgin Cres, W11, son of Peter Clough, of Hampsthwaite, Yorks (and has issue
living, Hugh Peter *b* 1993, Alice Elanor *b* 1991), — George (Lady's Cottage, Melton Constable, Norfolk), *b* 1936: *m* 1960,
Virginia Anne, da of late Rev Charles M. Jones, of Chapel Hill, N Carolina, USA, and has had issue, Richard *b* 1965: *m* 19—,
Philippa, da of Colin Brannigan, OBE, Mark *b* 1967, Nicola *b* 1963, *d* 1965, Catherine Eleanor *b* 1970, — Clova Margaret, *b*
1935: *m* 1st, 1960 (*m diss* 1983), Glyn Tudor; 2ndly, 1990, David Elwyn Morris, of 42 Frenchay Rd, Oxford, son of late Rev
S. M. Morris, and has issue living (by 1st *m*), Adam *b* 1966, Anna Morwenna *b* 1962: *m* 1992, Marcel Goudsblom, of
Amersterdam, Gay Elizabeth *b* 1964, — Mary, *b* 1944: *m* 1969, Roy Hodges, of Newnham Grounds, Daventry, Northants
NN11 6EP, and has issue living, Jeremy George *b* 1972, Jonathan Francis *b* 1976. *Residence* – Weston Lodge, Hitchin, Herts.

Grandchildren of late Rev Charles Sidney Pepys, BD (infra):—
Issue of late Rt Rev (George) Christopher Cutts Pepys, Bishop of Buckingham, *b* 1914, *d* 1974: *m* 1947, Elizabeth
Margaret (who *m* 2ndly, 1991, Rt Rev Michael A. Mann, sometime Dean of Windsor, of Lower End Farm Cottage,
Eastington, Northleach, Glos), da of Maj-Gen Roger Gillies Ekin, CIE:—
(Charles) Richard Ekin (Thoke House, Hall Lane, Farringdon, Alton, Hants), *b* 1951; *ed* Winchester; BA: *m* 1979, Jane
Elizabeth Cracroft, da of late Lt-Cdr Gervis Frere-Cook, RN, of Exton, Hants (*see* Brown, Bt, colls), and has issue living,
(George) Oliver Frere, *b* 1982, — Suzannah Mary Elizabeth, *b* 1985, — Clemency Rosemary Eleanor, *b* 1987. —— Caroline
Elizabeth (53 Hayfield Rd, Oxford), *b* 1948. —— Sarah Priscilla, *b* 1950: *m* 1980, William Howard Davies, of Norcott, 68
Foreland Rd, Bembridge, Isle of Wight, and has issue living, William Christopher Pepys, *b* 1985, — Holly Pepys, *b* 1983.
—— Frances Mary (12A Clifford Gdns, NW10), *b* 1954. —— Anna Margaret, *b* 1956: *m* 1982, Robert Peter Agnew, of 1
Hogg End, Chipping Warden, Banbury, Oxon OX17 1LY, son of Dr Sydney Alexander Agnew, of South Molton, Devon, and
has issue living, Alexander Christian Pepys, *b* 1984, — Thomas Robert Pepys, *b* 1987, — Eleanor Josephine, *b* 1990.

Granddaughters of late Hon George Pepys (ante):—
Issue of late Rev Charles Sidney Pepys, BD, *b* 1875, *d* 1927: *m* 1913, Adelaide Mary Elizabeth, who *d* 1968, da of
late Charles Duncan Cutts, of Buenos Aires:—
Elizabeth Sidney, *b* 1915: *m* 1939, Rev Arthur Guy St John Daniel, and has had issue, (Arthur) Jeremy Pepys, *b* 1940; *ed* St
Paul's Sch; *d* as the result of a motor accident 1964, — Nicholas Guy, *b* 1942; *ed* St Paul's Sch: *m* 1st, 1974 (*m diss* 1983),
Menna Matthews; 2ndly, 1984, Susan Cartwright, — Timothy Peter Charles (3 Dundonald Rd, NW10), *b* 1944; *ed* St Paul's
Sch, and Bristol Univ: *m* 1974, Rosalie Horner. *Residence* – 2 Gervis Court, Penwerris Av, Osterley, Middx TW7 4QU.
—— (Phyllis) Ann Jennifer, *b* 1924: *m* 1947, Alexander Paton, MD, FRCP, and has had issue, Alexander, *b* 1948; *ed* Sebright
Sch, Wolverley: *m* 19—, Alison Kirkland McGilp, and has issue living, Rose *b* 1984, Eleanor *b* 1986, Anna *b* 1990, — Charles
Pepys, 1950; *ed* Solihull Sch; RN; *d* 1973, — Antony Grimwood, *b* 1954; *ed* Solihull Sch: *m* 1983, Pauline Marion Gibbins, and
has issue living, Benjamin Charles *b* 1985, Nicola Marion *b* 1990, — Clare Jennifer, *b* 1952: *m* 1st, 1972 (*m diss* 1983),
Terence Patrick Mead; 2ndly, 1988, George Albert Kitcher, and has issue living (by 1st *m*), Samuel James *b* 1979, Jessica
Ann *b* 1976, (by 2nd *m*) Nathan John *b* 1991, Naomi Mary *b* 1993, — Rachel Mary, *b* 1953. *Residence* – Knollbury,
Chadlington, Oxon. —— Alison Margaret, *b* 1927: *m* 1955, Peter Harold Edwin Courtenay, MB, BS, FRCS, and has issue
living, Stephen Harold Pepys, *b* 1956: *m* 1989, Mara Anna Gottler, — Simon Charles, *b* 1958: *m* 1991, Hélène Marie Claire
Dupuis, and has issue living, Maia Alison *b* 1992, — Michael Peter, *b* 1962, — Ann Elizabeth, *b* 1963. *Residence* – 9190
Canora Rd, Sidney, BC, Canada.

(In remainder to Baronetcy only)

Grandchildren of Herbert Frederick Pepys, eldest son of Rev Herbert George Pepys, yr son of Rt Rev
Henry Pepys, DD, Bishop of Worcester, 3rd son of 1st Baronet:—
Issue of late Frederick (Eric) Courtenay Pepys, *b* 1904, *d* 1983: *m* 1935, Mary Caroline Bradley (555 Santa Anita,
San Marino, California 91108, USA), of Los Angeles, California, USA:—
Eric Courtenay (jr) (526 S Bayfront, Newport Beach, California 92662-1039, USA), *b* 1936: *m* 1964, Shirley Ann Dietrich, and
has issue living, Noel Dietrich, *b* 1970, — Maximillian Paul, *b* 1972, — Renée Catherine, *b* 1964, — Tiffany Ann, *b* 1968.
—— Mark Bradley (6065 Via Sonoma, Rancho Palos Verdes, California 90274, USA), *b* 1937: *m* 1970, Anne Claire Bowden,
and has issue living, Craig Brian, *b* 1974, — Kirsten Anne, *b* 1976. —— Keith Alan (8223 Woodland Drive, Buena Bark,
California 90620, USA), *b* 1948. —— Christine (1816 Lark Ellen Drive, Fullerton, California 92635, USA), *b* 1939: *m* 1960,
Ronald Vincent Heusser, and has issue living, Melinda Christine, *b* 1965, — Noelle Pepys, *b* 1968, — Hilary Dawn, *b* 1971.
—— Mary Noel (Pier Nine, San Francisco, California, USA), *b* 1946; Attorney-at-Law.

PREDECESSORS – (1) William Weller Pepys, a Master in Chancery; *cr a Baronet* 801 of Wimpole Street; *d* 1825; *s* by his
son (2) William Weller, 2nd Bt; *dsp* 1845; *s* by his brother (3) Sir Charles Christopher, PC, KB, DCL, 3rd Bt; an eminent
lawyer, was Queen's Solicitor-Gen 1830, Solicitor-Gen 1834, Master of the Rolls 1834, High Commr of the Great Seal 1835,
and Lord High Chancellor 1836-41 and 1846-50; *cr Baron Cottenham* (peerage of United Kingdom) 1836; by special
remainder *s* by his cousin, Sir Henry (Pepys) Leslie, as 4th Bt, *cr* 1784 (of Upper Brook Street); *cr Viscount Crowhurst* and
Earl of Cottenham 1850: *m* 1821, Caroline Elizabeth, da of William Wingfield, QC; *d* 1851; *s* by his son (4) Charles Edward,
2nd Earl; *dsp* 1863; *s* by his brother (5) William John, 3rd Earl; *b* 1825: *m* 1870, Theodosia Selina, who *d* 1919, da of Sir
Robert Charles Dallas, 2nd Bt; *d* 1881; *s* by his son (6) Kenelm Charles Edward, 4th Earl; *b* 1874: *m* 1st 1899, Lady Rose
Nevill, who *d* 1913, da of 1st Marquess of Abergavenny; 2ndly, 1916, Patricia, who *d* 1962, da of late John Humphry Burke,
of Galway and California; *d* 1919; *s* by his el son (7) Kenelm Charles Francis, 5th Earl; *b* 1901, *d* 1922, *s* by his brother (8)
Mark Everard, 6th Earl; *b* 1903: *m* 1927 (*m diss* 1939), Sybil Venetia, da of Capt John Vickris Taylor, of North Aston Manor
Oxford; *d* 1943; *s* by his brother (9) John Digby Thomas, 7th Earl; *b* 1907: *m* 1933, Lady Angela Isabel Nellie Nevill, who *d*
1980, da of 4th Marquess of Abergavenny; *d* 1968; *s* by his son (10) Kenelm Charles Everard Digby, 8th Earl and present
peer; also Viscount Crowhurst, and Baron Cottenham.

COTTESLOE, BARON (Fremantle) (Baron UK 1874, Bt UK 1821)
(Title pronounced "Cotslo")

NEC PRECE NEC PRETIO

Neither by entreaty nor bribery

JOHN TAPLING FREMANTLE, 5th Baron, 5th Baronet, and a Baron of the Austrian Empire; *b* 22 Jan 1927; *s* 1994; *ed* Eton; Cdr RN (ret); High Sheriff Bucks 1969-70, Lord Lieut since 1984 Pres Bucks Co Scout Assocn, Royal British Legion, SSAFA and FHS, Bucks Branch CLA (Chm 1976-79), Bucks Historic Churches Trust, Bucks Council for Voluntary Ser, Bucks Assocn of Local Councils, Bucks Playing Fields Assocn, Bucks Record Soc, and Bucks Assocn for Care of Offenders; a Vice-Pres BASC, RASE, Eastern Wessex TAVR, The Hospital Saving Assocn, Bucks Co Show (Chm 1977-82, Pres 1983), and National Soc for Epilepsy; Manager Swanbourne; Ch of England First (Aided) Sch; Hon Treas Aylesbury Vale Assocn of Local Councils 1974-84; Vice-Chm CLA Game Fair 1971 and 1981, and of Winslow RDC 1971-74; a Gov Stowe Sch 1983-89, and a Radcliffe Trustee; Chm Oxon Bucks Div Royal Forestry Soc 1982-84; Memb Bucks Farming and Wildlife Advisory Group, Trustee Bucks Fedn of Young Farmers' Clubs, Bucks Military Museum Trust, and Bucks Assocn for the Blind; Hon DUniv Buckingham 1993; KStJ 1984: *m* 1958, Elizabeth Ann, elder da of late Lt-Col Henry Shelley Barker, DSO, of Walcote House, nr Rugby, and has issue.

Arms – Vert, three bars ermine, surmounted by a lion rampant gules, murally crowned or and in chief two plates. Crest – Out of a mural coronet or, a demi-lion gules, charged on the shoulder with a plate and holding in the paws a banner quarterly argent and vert. Supporters – Two eagles, wings expanded in inverted, sable.
Residence – The Old House, Swanbourne, Milton Keynes, Bucks MK17 0SH. *Clubs* – Travellers', RN, and Royal Albert Yacht (Portsmouth).

SON LIVING

Hon THOMAS FRANCIS HENRY, *b* 17 March 1966; *ed* St Edmund's Sch, Oxford, and RAC Cirencester.

DAUGHTERS LIVING

Hon Elizabeth (Betsy) Wynne, *b* 1959: *m* 1982, George Iain Duncan Smith, and has issue living, Edward St Alban, *b* 1987, — Alicia Cecilia, *b* 1989.
Hon Frances (Fanny) Ann, *b* 1961: *m* 1984, Shaun Richard Stanley (*see* B Haden-Guest, 1990 Edn), and has issue living, Joshua John, *b* 1988.

HALF-BROTHER LIVING

Hon Edward Walgrave, *b* 1961: *m* 1991, Sara E., da of late Lt Cmdr Harry Chillingworth, of Bembridge, I of Wight, and has issue living, Louisa Clare, *b* 1994.

SISTER LIVING

Hon Ann, *b* 1930: *m* 1951, Timothy Gerald Martin Brooks, and has issue (*see* B Crawshaw, colls). *Residence* – Wistow, Leicester.

HALF-SISTERS LIVING

Hon Elizabeth Cecilia Jane, *b* 1962; assumed additional forename of Elizabeth 1977; journalist: *m* 1991, Olivier Philippe Haguenauer, eldest son of Dr Pierre Haguenauer, of Neuilly-sur-Seine, France.
Hon Flora Catherine, *b* 1967: *m* 1993, Dan Miyonga, of Kisumu, Kenya.

AUNTS LIVING (*daughters of 3rd Baron*)

Hon Margaret Augusta (*Baroness Florey*), *b* 1904; *ed* Oxford Univ (MA, DM); Univ Lecturer in Pathology, Oxford Univ 1945-72, and a Fellow of Lady Margaret Hall, Oxford 1952-72: *m* 1st, 1930 (*m diss* 1946), Denys Arthur Jennings, BM, BCh; 2ndly, 1967, Baron Florey, OM, FRS (Life Baron), who *d* 1968. *Residence* – Longlands Nursing Home, Cassington, nr Oxford.
Hon Bride Faith Louisa, *b* 1910; *ed* Girton Coll, Camb (BA 1935, MA 1938): *m* 1936, John Berry, CBE, DL, LLD, PhD, DSc, FRSE, and has issue living, William (31 Stafford St, Edinburgh; Tayfield House, Newport-on-Tay, Fife), *b* 1939; *ed* Eton, St Andrews Univ (MA), and Edinburgh Univ (LLB), WS: *m* 1973, Elizabeth Margery, da of Sir Edward Redston Warner, KCMG, OBE, of Old Royal Oak, Blockley, Glos, and has issue living, John *b* 1976, Robert Edward Alexander *b* 1978, — Peter Fremantle (58 Pyrland Rd, N5), *b* 1944; *ed* Eton, and Lincoln Coll, Oxford (MA); Crown Agent 1988: *m* 1972, Paola, da of late Giovanni Padovani, and has issue living, Richard John *b* 1979, Sara *b* 1976, Anna *b* 1977, — Margaret Wilhelmina, *b* 1937; Dip Arch Edinburgh: *m* 1962, Ronald Lindsay Alexander, ARIBA, of 81 Balfour Rd, N5, and has issue living, Adam George *b* 1971; BA, Jane Louise *b* 1969; BA Oxon: *m* 1992, Duncan Arthur Spencer MacLaren. *Residence* – The Garden House, Tayfield, Newport-on-Tay, Fife DD6 8HA.
Hon Katharine Dorothy Honor, *b* 1919; *ed* Girton Coll, Camb (BA 1941); PhD London 1956. *Residence* – Dennelaan 48, Hollandsche Rading, Netherlands.

WIDOW LIVING OF SON OF THIRD BARON

Anne-Marie Huth (252 E 78th St, New York, NY 10021, USA), 2nd da of late Rt Hon Frederick Huth Jackson (*see* Jackson, Bt, colls): *m* 1930, Hon Christopher Evelyn Fremantle, who *d* 1979, and has issue (*see* colls infra).

WIDOW LIVING OF FOURTH BARON

GLORIA JEAN IRENE DUNN (*Dowager Baroness Cottesloe*), adopted da of late W. E. Hill, of Barnstaple, N Devon: *m* 1959, as his 2nd wife, the 4th Baron, GBE, TD, who *d* 1994. *Residence* – Oak House, Well Rd, Crondall, Surrey GU10 5PN.

COLLATERAL BRANCHES LIVING

Issue of late Hon Christopher Evelyn Fremantle, yst son of 3rd Baron, *b* 1906, *d* 1978: *m* 1930, Anne-Marie Huth (ante), 2nd da of late Rt Hon Frederick Huth Jackson (*see* Jackson, Bt, colls, cr 1869):—
Adam Augustus (178 East 93rd St, New York, NY 10128, USA), *b* 1934; *ed* Eton, and Balliol Coll, Oxford (MA), and Fordham Univ NYC (JD); Bar Inner Temple 1957: *m* 1963 (*m diss* 1978), Mary Christine, da of late Prince Paul Sapieha, and has issue living, Christopher Nicholas, *b* 1965; *ed* Worth, and Aberdeen Univ (MA, MLitt); Gov Dr Johnson's House Trust, Memb Children's Panel: *m* 1989, Gillian, yst da of Peter Hainey, of Bitterne, Southampton, — Paul Zachary (84 Addison Rd, Reading, Berks RG1 8EG), *b* 1968; *ed* Worth, and Balliol Coll, Oxford: *m* 1991, Jane Pamela, da of Rev John William Hunwicke, Chaplain of Lancing Coll. —— Richard Christian Wynne (via Matteo Palmieri 9, Florence 50122, Italy), *b* 1936; *ed* Portsmouth Priory, RI, and Columbia Univ, USA (MA): *m* 1971 (*m diss* 19—), Chloë Sarabella, yr da of Sir Geoffrey Cecil Ryves Eley, CBE (*see* Walker, Bt, colls, cr 1856). —— Dominic Christopher Hugh (252 E 78th St, New York, NY 10021, USA), *b* 1944; *ed* Georgetown Univ, USA.

Issue of late Hon Reginald Scott Fremantle, 2nd son of 2nd Baron *b* 1863, *d* 1956: *m* 1900, Hilda Lucy, who *d* 1953, da of late E. M. Barry, RA:—
Rosamund Beatrice, *b* 1902: *m* 1931, Thomas Gilbert Standing, who *d* 1942, of Education Dept, S Rhodesia, and Capt Nigeria Regt, and has issue living, Roderick Fremantle, *b* 1932, — Caspar Vernon, *b* 1933, — Lionel Gilbert *b* 1940. —— Joan Lucy, *b* 1904: *m* 1930, Caleb Henry Trevor, and has issue living, Malcolm Henry, *b* 1932. *Residence* – 72 Talbot Rd, Highgate, N6.

Grandchildren of late Sir Francis Edward Fremantle, OBE, TD, MD, MCh, FRCS, FRCP, DPH, MP, 4th son of Very Rev Hon William Henry Fremantle (Dean of Ripon) 2nd son of 1st Baron:—
Issue of late Lt-Col Francis David Eardley Fremantle, TD, *b* 1906, *d* 1968: *m* 1936, Emmeline Amy, who *m* 2ndly, 1973, Lt-Col Edward Peter Fletcher Boughey, OBE (*d* 1986) (*see* Boughey, Bt, colls), da of late Brig-Gen Vigant William de Falbe, CMG, DSO, of Whittington House, Lichfield:—
Edward Vigant Eardley (4 Sutherland St, SW1V 4LB), *b* 1942; *ed* Eton, and Balliol Coll, Oxford (MA): FCA: *m* 1973, Sarah Maud, yst da of Col William Henry Whitbread, TD, of Hazelhurst, Bunch Lane, Haslemere, Surrey, and has issue living, Anna Elizabeth, *b* 1981, — Katherine Fiona, *b* 1984. —— Thomas David (Wayside Cottage, E Markham, Newark, Notts), *b* 1944: *ed* Eton, and RNC Dartmouth; late Lt RN: *m* 1971, Alice Marian, da of late Cyril Reginald Egerton, of Hall Farm, New-market (*see* D Sutherland, colls), and has issue living, Mark Thomas, *b* 1975, — Christopher Richard, *b* 1978, — Emily Teresa Alice, *b* 1981. —— Richard Francis, *b* 1946; *ed* Eton, and Keble Coll, Oxford; *d* 1976. —— Marion Jane, *b* 1948: *m* 1972, David Christopher Hanbury, of The Old Rectory, Ruckinge, Ashford, Kent, and has issue living, Jonathan Christopher, *b* 1975, — Susannah Mary *b* 1977, — Caroline Jane, *b* 1981.

Grandson of late Ronald Aubrey Fremantle (infra):—
Issue of late Maj Maurice Alan Fremantle, *b* 1900, *d* 1972: *m* 1928, Ida Thelma Gordon, who *d* 1976, da of late Edward Reginald Stirling Bloxsome, of the Rangers, Copthorne, Sussex:—
Robin Patrick (Scatwell, Muir of Ord, Ross-shire), *b* 1930: *ed* Wellington Coll; Capt late 4th Queen's Own Hussars, and Ayrshire (ECO) Yeo (TA); Chm The Economic League since 1989-93; Principal Fremantle & Co since 1980: *m* 1st, 1962 (*m diss* 1980), June Helen, da of late Brig Ereld Boteler Winfield Cardiff, CB, CBE, of Easton Court, Ludlow, Shropshire; 2ndly, 1985, (Honor) Diana, yr da of late Sir (Coles) John Child, 2nd Bt, and widow of Noel H. Matterson, and has issue living (by 1st *m*), Charles Ereld Patrick, *b* 1964, — Serena Katherine, *b* 1967.

Granddaughters of late Hon Sir Charles William Fremantle, KCB, 3rd son of 1st Baron:—
Issue of late Ronald Aubrey Fremantle, *b* 1872, *d* 1947: *m* 1899, Eleanor Susan, who *d* 1946, da of Charles John Fletcher, of Dale Park, Madehurst, Arundel:—
Helen Antonia Theresa Susan, *b* 1914: *m* 1940, John Miller, who *d* 1988. *Residence* – Chilton House, Chilton, Aylesbury, Bucks HP18 9LR.

Grandchildren of late Sir Sydney Robert Fremantle, GCB, MVO, eldest son of late Adm Hon Sir Edmund Robert Fremantle, GCB, GCVO, CMG, 4th son of 1st Baron:—
Issue of late Cdr Edmund Seymour Denis Fremantle, DSC, RN, *b* 1904, *d* 1980: *m* 1st, 1928 (*m diss* 1944), Dorothy Clare Haldane, who *d* 1980, el da of Col W. M. Sinclair, OBE, RM; 2ndly, 1946, Edna Maud (Redlands, Hookhills Rd, Churston Ferrers, Paignton, Devon), da of late Albert John Tweed Cusselle, of Dartford, Kent, and formerly wife of James Richard Lyddon:—
(By 1st *m*) Charles Alan (Langley Corner, Langley Burrell, Chippenham, Wilts), *b* 1935; *ed* Sutton Valence, and RNC Dart-mouth; Cdr RN; Member Nautical Inst, N Wilts District Council 1987-91: *m* 1960, Caroline Mary, da of Cdr Sydney Andrew Boyd Morant, OBE, DSC, RN, and has issue living, Timothy Charles, *b* 1967; *ed* Plymouth Poly (BSc), — James Justin, *b* 1971; *ed* Portsmouth Univ (BA), — Naomi Juliet, *b* 1961; *ed* Keele Univ (BA): *m* 1990, Stuart John Hill, of Hammonds Cottage, Waltham Chase, Hants SO3 2LQ, son of Michael John Hill, of Eastleigh, Hants, and has issue living, Matthew Augustus Fremantle *b* 1992. —— Sydney Walter (4 Strafford Rd, Twickenham, Middx) *b* 1936; *ed* Sherborne, and Oriel Coll, Oxford (BA): *m* 1961, Susan Delia Aiton, da of the late Brig John Aiton Bell, CBE, and has had issue, Samuel Patrick, *b* 1967, — Joanna Mary Aiton, *b* 1964; *d* 1986. —— Ann Penelope, *b* 1931: *m* 1966, Sirio Morgia, of Summerfields, Via Tito Poggi 21, Via Ardeatina, Rome 00134. —— (By 2nd *m*) Richard William (40 Denmark Rd, W13), *b* 1948: *m* 1975, Alison, da of Arnold Cruse, and has issue living, Edmund Richard, *b* 1979, — Peter Thomas, *b* 1985, — Mary Grace, *b* 1980. —— Stephen Antony (9 Stavordale Way, Weymouth, Dorset), *b* 1950: *m* 1st, 1972 (*m diss* 1976), Hanna Elizabeth Fiona, da of K. Sierakowski, of Bickley, Kent; 2ndly, 1976, Patricia Mary, adopted da of Miss Margaret Lewin, and has issue living, (by 1st *m*) Melanie Leila, *b* 1973, — (by 2nd *m*) Holly, *b* 1978.
Issue of late Lt-Cdr David Robert Fremantle, RNVR, *b* 1906, *d* 1989: *m* 1st, 1939 (*m diss* 1951), Patience Ann, da of late Lt-Cdr Evelyn Culme-Seymour (*see* Culme-Seymour, Bt, colls); 2ndly, 1954 (*m diss* 1976), Mrs Rosabel Stewart-Liberty, da of late Arthur H. Fynn, of Helston, Cornwall, and formerly wife of late Arthur Ivor Stewart-Liberty, MC, TD:—
(By 1st *m*) Francesca Mary, *b* 1941; *ed* London Univ (PhD). *Residence* – 13 Child's St, SW5 9RZ.

Granddaughter of late Alfred Ernest Albert Fremantle, yst son of late Adm Hon Sir Edmund Robert Fremantle, GCB, GCVO, CMG (ante):—
Issue of late Maj Paris Oscar (Réné) Francesco Fremantle, *b* 1908, *d* of wounds 1944: *m* 1934, Rosamond Carnegie of 4 Ravens Court, St John's Rd, Eastbourne, who *m* 2ndly, 1947, Brig Gordon de Bruyne, OBE, late 60th Rifles (who *d* 1972), da of late Arthur Knox, of Fairfield, Wargrave, Berks:—
Valerie Rosamond Christina, *b* 1942. *Residence* – 39 Kensington Mansions, Trebovir Rd, SW5 9TQ.

PREDECESSORS – (1) *Rt Hon* THOMAS FRANCIS FREMANTLE, PC, son of Vice Adm Sir Thomas Francis Fremantle, GCB (*cr* Baron of Austrian Empire 1816); *b* 1798; sat as MP for Buckingham (*C*) 1827-46, and was successively Sec of the Treasury, Sec at War, Ch Sec for Ireland, and Chm of Board of Customs; received Royal licence for himself and issue to bear his father's Austrian title of Baron 1822; *cr* a *Baronet* 1821 (with remainder to his father's heirs), and *Baron Cottesloe*, of Swanbourne and Hardwick, co Bucks (peerage of UK) 1874: *m* 1824, Louisa Elizabeth, who *d* 1875, da of F-M Sir George Nugent, GCB, 1st Bt; *d* 1890; *s* by his el son (2) THOMAS FRANCIS, 2nd Baron; *b* 1830; MP for Buckinghamshire (*C*) 1876-85; sometime Chm of London, Brighton and South Coast Railway: *m* 1859, Lady Augusta Henrietta Scott, who *d* 1906, da of 2nd Earl of Eldon; *d* 1918; *s* by his el son (3) THOMAS FRANCIS, CB, VD, TD, 3rd Baron; *b* 1862; Hon Col (formerly Lieut-Col Comdg) Bucks Batn, Oxfordshire and Buckinghamshire LI; Assist Sec to Sec of State for War (Rt Hon W. St J. Brodrick, MP) 1900-1903; Lord Lieut of Bucks 1923-54: *m* 1896, Florence, who *d* 1956, da of late Thomas Tapling, of Kingswood, Dulwich; *d* 1956; *s* by his el surviving son (4) JOHN WALGRAVE HALFORD, GBE, TD, 4th Baron, *b* 1900; 1939-45 War as GSO (I), Sr Mil Liaison Officer and Lt-Col Comdg 20th Light Anti-Aircraft Regt RA (TA); Lt-Col RA (TA Reserve); DL co London 1951 (Chm of DL's Cttees in Bermondsey and Deptford), Memb LCC 1945-55, Port of London Authority 1949-67 (Vice-Chm 1955-67), etc; Trustee Tate Gallery 1953-60, Chm 1959-60, Chm Advisory Council and Reviewing Cttee on Export of Works of Art 1954-72, Chm Arts Council of GB 1960-65, Gov Old Vic and Sadler's Wells 1957-60, Chm South Bank Theatre Board 1962-77; Gov King Edward's Hosp Fund for London 1973-83, etc; Chm The Dogs Home, Battersea 1970-82: *m* 1st, 1926 (*m diss* 1944), Lady Elizabeth Harris, who *d* 1983, only da of 5th Earl of Malmesbury; 2ndly, 1959, Gloria Jean Irene Dunn, adopted da of late W.E. Hill, of Barnstaple, N Devon: *d* 1994; *s* by his elder son (5) JOHN TAPLING, 5th Baron and present peer.

COURTOWN, EARL OF (Stopford) Sits as BARON SALTERSFORD (GB 1796) (Earl I 1762)

Faithful to an unhappy country

JAMES PATRICK MONTAGU BURGOYNE WINTHROP STOPFORD, 9th Earl; *b* 19 March 1954; *s* 1975; *ed* Eton, Berkshire Coll of Agric, and RAC Cirencester; ARICS: *m* 1985, Elisabeth Dorothy, yr da of Ian Rodger Dunnett, of Broad Campden, Glos, and has issue.

Arms – Azure, semée of cross crosslets and three lozenges or. **Crest** – A wyvern, wings elevated proper. **Supporters** – Two stags proper, plain collared and chained, and each charged on the shoulder with a lozenge or. *Residence* – South Lawn, Leckhampton, Cheltenham, Glos.

SON LIVING

JAMES RICHARD IAN MONTAGU (*Viscount Stopford*), *b* 30 March 1988.

DAUGHTER LIVING

Lady Rosanna Elisabeth Alice, *b* 1986.

BROTHER LIVING

Hon Jeremy Neville, LVO *b* 1958; *ed* Eton; Capt Irish Gds; Temporary Equerry to HM Queen Elizabeth the Queen Mother 1982-84; LVO 1984: *m* 1984, Bronwen, da of Lt-Col David MacDonald Milner, of Ashford Hill, Newbury, Berks, and has issue living, Clementine Lucy Patricia, *b* 1986, — Matilda Rose Philippa, *b* 1988, — Violet Mary Renée, *b* 1992.

SISTER LIVING

Lady Felicity Aileen Ann, *b* 1951: *m* 1st, 1977 (*m diss* 1981), Leslie Edward Archer-Davis; 2ndly, 1982, John Andrew McIndoe, of 9 Franche Court Rd, SW17, and has issue living (by 2nd *m*), Harry James, *b* 1985.

HALF SISTERS LIVING

Lady Mary Christina, *b* 1936; JP, DStJ: *m* 1959, Geoffrey Jermyn Holborow, OBE, High Sheriff Cornwall 1977, and has issue living, Charles David Jermyn, *b* 1963, — Katharine Mary, *b* 1961: *m* 1990, Robert Anstey Preston Wild, of 22 Brackenbury Rd, W6 0BH, son of Anstey Wild, of The White Cottage, Brailsford, Derbys, and issue living, James *b* 1991, Madeleine *b* 1993. *Residence* – Ladock House, Ladock, Truro, Cornwall.
Lady Elizabeth Cameron, *b* 1939; High Sheriff Berks 1990; Chief Pres St John Ambulance since 1990: *m* 1962, Alan Anthony Colleton Godsal, and has issue living, Hugh Colleton, *b* 1965: *m* 1994, Samantha Jane, elder da of Ian Godsal, of El Campillo, Madrid, — Lucy Violet, *b* 1964: *m* 1992, Christopher J. Zeal, 2nd son of Michael Zeal, of Westcott, Surrey, — Laura Christina, *b* 1968. *Residence* – Haines Hill, Twyford, Berks.

UNCLE LIVING (*Son of 7th Earl*)

Hon Terence Victor (Lake End House, Dorney, Windsor, Berks), *b* 1918; *ed* Eton; Capt RN (ret); Assist Naval Advisor to UK High Commr in Canada 1959-60, Assist Dir of Underwater Weapons, Admiralty 1961-63, and Capt Inshore Flotilla Far East Fleet, and Cmdg HMS *Manxman* 1963-64; Ch of Staff to C-in-C Naval Home Command 1965-67, and Ch Staff Officer to Flag Officer Gibraltar 1967-69: Naval ADC to HM 1969: *m* 1951, Sheila Adèle, who *d* 1994, only da of late Philip Page, and has issue living, (Henry) Philip (Terence) (2 Ralston Rd, SW3 4DS), *b* 1953; *ed* Eton, Brunel (LLB), and Virginia Univ (LLM); Harkness Fellowship: *m* 1981, Michele Susan, da of Orlando Hyndman Lobo, of Bethesda, Maryland, USA, and has issue living, Philip Christian Andrew *b* 1983, Susannah Louise Adele *b* 1985, Alexandra Frances Ileara *b* 1991, — Robert Edward James, *b* 1958; *ed* Pangbourne: *m* 1987, Anne Louise, da of Lt-Cdr P. J. Patrick, of Bedford Lodge, Bourne End, — James Richard Hugh, *b* 1961; *ed* at Pangbourne; Maj Irish Gds: *m* 1989, Michelle, yr da of Michael N. Reeves, of St Catherines, Iver, and has issue living, Isabella Frances *b* 1992, — Catherine Mary Adéle, *b* 1965.

AUNTS LIVING (*Daughters of 7th Earl*)

Lady Patricia Mary, *b* 1906: *m* 1934, Maurice John Hayward, Malayan Civil Ser (ret), only son of late Sir Maurice Henry Weston Hayward, KCSI, and has issue living, Maurice Richard (28 Weymouth Bldgs, Four Oaks, Sutton Coldfield), *b* 1939: *m* 1968, Christina, da of Matthew Hyland, of the Glebe, Coolrain, co Leix, and has issue living, David Maurice *b* 1970, Philip Matthew *b* 1973, Jane Margaret *b* 1969, — Bridget Mary, *b* 1935: *m* 1964, John Everard Kitchin (18 Gloucester Rd, Hampton, Middx), and has issue living, Hugh Everard *b* 1965, Simon John *b* 1967, — Caroline Patricia, *b* 1936: *m* 1960, Myles Anthony Clive Saker, of Rose Cottage, Cuddington, Aylesbury, Bucks, and has issue living, John Anthony *b* 1962, Deborah Ann *b*

1967, — Sarah Elizabeth (Church Square Cottage, Islip, Oxon), *b* 1946. *Residence* – White Hart House, Haddenham, Aylesbury, Bucks.

Lady Moyra Charlotte, BEM *b* 1917: *m* 1943, Lt-Cdr David Henry Champion Streatfeild, RN, and has issue living, David Anthony (63 Roehampton Lane, SW15), *b* 1945: *m* 1971, Jill Katherine, da of late William Macfarlane, of The Old Cottage, Potters Lane, Send, Surrey and has issue living, James Anthony *b* 1973, Charles David *b* 1979, Katherine Moyra *b* 1975, — Timothy James (The Former Vicarage, North Stoke, Wallingford, Oxon), *b* 1947: *m* 1976, Jane, da of late Denis McVicar Merritt, MRCS, LRCP, of Grove House, Birchington, Kent, and has issue living, Rupert Champion *b* 1980, Anna Eleanor *b* 1978, — Peter Stopford (Royal Cottage, Kew Green, Kingston-upon-Thames, Surrey), *b* 1954: *m* 1981, Caroline J, da of D. S. M. (Roy) Webster, of Farnham, Surrey, and has issue living, Alexander David Stopford *b* 1988, Henry Peter Champion *b* 1990, — Cicely Mary, *b* 1950: *m* 1975, Dr Michael R. Smith, of Redlands, Clifton Rd, Chesham Bois, Bucks, son of Bryan Crossley Smith, CBE, of Wendover, Bucks, and has issue living, Harriet May Crossley *b* 1982, Lucy Patricia Streatfeild *b* 1985. *Residence* – Redberry House, Bierton, Aylesbury, Bucks.

Lady Cecilia Norah (twin), *b* 1917; formerly Junior Com ATS: *m* 1947, Cdr Thomas Philip Frederick Urquhart Page, RN, son of late Sir Leo Francis Page, and has issue living, Nicholas Leo Thomas (Shoelands, Grayswood, Haslemere, Surrey), *b* 1948: *m* 1971, Sarah June, el da of Leslie Bramhall, of Wheatsheaf Corner, Liphook, Hants, and has issue living, Thomas Leslie *b* 1973, Alexia Frances *b* 1976, — Victoria Cecilia, *b* 1951: *m* 1979, Robin E. Furber, son of Dr Stanhope Furber, of Somerton Cottage, Winkfield, Berks, and has issue living, George *b* 1986, Eleanor Primrose *b* 1988, — Juliet Mary, *b* 1955. *Residence* – Toller Porcorum, Dorchester, Dorset.

GREAT-AUNT LIVING (*Daughter of 6th Earl*)

Lady Marjorie Gertrude, *b* 1904. *Residence* – Bournemead, Herkomer Road, Bushey, Herts.

WIDOW LIVING OF SON OF SEVENTH EARL

Mrs Millicent DAVIES, elder da of late Geoffrey Watt, and previously wife of late Trevor Waterson: *m* 1978, as his 2nd wife, Hon Edward Richard Barrington Stopford, who *d* 1990. *Residence* – 8 Turner's Lane, N Ferriby, N Humberside HU14 3JP.

WIDOW LIVING OF EIGHTH EARL

Patricia (*Patricia, Countess of Courtown*) (Threeways, Jordans, Bucks), da of late Harry Stephen Winthrop, of Auckland, NZ: *m* 1951, as his 2nd wife, the 8th Earl, who *d* 1975.

COLLATERAL BRANCHES LIVING

Issue of late Hon Edward Richard Barrington Stopford, 2nd son of 7th Earl, *b* 1914, *d* 1990: *m* 1st, 1946, Ann Marie Elizabeth Douglas, who *d* 1976, only da of late Brig Harold Gordon Henderson, CBE, of Hyde House, Chalford, Glos; 2ndly, 1978, Mrs Millicent DAVIES (ante), previously wife of late Trevor Waterson, and elder da of late Geoffrey Watt:—

(By 1st *m*) Michael James Patrick (Pilgrim Cottage, Morchard Bishop, Devon), *b* 1950: *m* 1985, Mrs Prudence Jane Louise FAYERS, eldest da of late Noel Scott Unsworth, of Morchard Bishop, Devon. —— Christopher Gordon Edward, *b* 1953. —— Penelope Ann, *b* 1948: *m* 1977, Philip Henry Leigh, of 28 Great Cob, Chelmsford, Essex, and has issue living, Rosemary Ann, *b* 1980, — Alice Margaret, *b* 1983.

Grandson of late Capt Hon Edward Barrington Lewis Henry Stopford, 2nd son of 5th Earl:—
Issue of late Lt-Cdr Barrington George Dashwood Stopford, RN, *b* 1889, *d* 1930: *m* 1918, Muriel Florence Mary, who *d* 1980, el da of late Rev Nathaniel Nicholas Lewarne, formerly V of Yealmpton, S Devon:—
Brian Barrington Dashwood, LVO, *b* 1923; *ed* Stowe, and Trin Coll, Camb (BA); Solicitor 1948; Solicitor to Duchy of Cornwall 1954-72; LVO 1971: *m* 1st, 1948, Alison Honor, who *d* 1986, da of late Maurice Sylvester Gibb, CBE; 2ndly, 19—, Heather Mary Sally, da of John Basil Collingwood, and has issue living (by 1st *m*), Justin Montagu Dashwood (10 Lindop Rd, Hale, Altrincham, Cheshire), *b* 1949; *ed* Salford Univ: *m* 1972, Gillian, da of Eric Heatherington, and has issue living, Jeremy Lewis Dashwood *b* 1982, Nicola Louise *b* 1979, — Yolande Honor, *b* 1951; *ed* Dartford Coll of Ed: *m* 1982, Owen Arthur Reynolds, of Lower Ellenden Farm, Water Lane, Hawkhurst, Kent, and has issue living, Thomas *b* 1984, Oliver *b* 1986. *Residence* – 122 High St, Lewes, Sussex. *Club* – English-Speaking Union.

Grandchildren of late George Christian Noel Stopford (infra):—
Issue of late Edward Montagu Stopford, *b* 1917, *d* 1988: *m* 1941, Dora (Innisfail, Queensland, Australia), da of late T. W. Flood, of Warwick, Qld:—
Peter (PO Box 59, Innisfail 4860, Queensland, Australia), *b* 1942: *m* 1965, Lorraine Dawn, da of Percy Dinman Day, of Atherton, Qld, and has issue living, Mark Peter, *b* 1968, — Tracey Dawn, *b* 1966. —— Robin, *b* 1946. —— Wendy, *b* 1944: *m* 1965, Allan David Stephens, of Toowoomba, Qld, and has issue living, David Allan, *b* 1966, — Peter Brian, *b* 1974, — Christine Louise, *b* 1968.

Granddaughter of late Hon George Frederick William Stopford, 3rd son of 5th Earl:—
Issue of late George Christian Noel Stopford, *b* 1891, *d* 1969: *m* 1915, Mary Georgina, who *d* 1967, da of late Rev Canon Edward Newland, of Buncara, co Donegal:—
Claire, *b* 1922: *m* 1948, James Gordon McIlwraith, who *d* 1984, and has issue living, James Edward, *b* 1955: *m* 1990, Claire Elizabeth Davis, and has issue living, Jesse (a son) *b* 1989, — Duncan George, *b* 1956: *m* 1986, Yoshiko Hiramatsu, and has issue living, Ria Asuka *b* 1987, Ellie *b* 1989, — Margaret Anne (known as Annie Stopford), *b* 1951: *m* 1st, 1975, Dennis Morrison, who *d* 19—; 2ndly, 1989, Ayi Mensah, of Ghana, and has issue living (by 2nd *m*), Nii-ayitey (a son) *b* 1990, — Janet Claire, *b* 1953: *m* 1973, Roger O'Shannessy, and has issue living, Nye (a son) *b* 1974, Tristan *b* 1978, Keely (a da) *b* 1976, — Judith Pamela, *b* 1958: *m* 1987, Stuart Tutchen, and has issue living, Bradley (a son) *b* 1978, Duane (a son) *b* 1982, Shari (a da) *b* 1980. *Address* – Unit 10, Cascade Walk, 56 Burnett St, Buderim, Queensland 4556, Australia.

Grandchildren of late Rear-Adm Hon Walter George Stopford, 6th son of 4th Earl:—
Issue of late Rear-Adm Frederick Victor Stopford, CBE, *b* 1900; *d* 1982: *m* 1924, Mary Guise (Varndean House, St Leonards, Ringwood, Hants), da of Capt Frederick Charles Ulick Vernon-Wentworth, CB, RN (Guise Bt, colls):—
John Walter (Amberley, N Canterbury, NZ), *b* 1926; Capt R Canadian Armd Corps (ret): *m* 1960, Barbara, only da of Maj W. H. McHaffie, of Aberdour on Spey, and has issue living, Michael John, *b* 1966, — Susan Caroline, *b* 1961, — Jennifer Claire, *b* 1965. —— Robin Frederick (4 Park Homer Rd, Colehill, Wimborne, Dorset), *b* 1929: *m* 1960, Patricia Ann, el da of Lt-Col Leo Dominic Gleeson, DSO, and has issue living, Jonathan Paul Michael, *b* 1964, — Sarah Frances Ann, *b* 1969. —— Timothy Patrick (17 Allington Drive, Strood, Rochester, Kent), *b* 1935; co-author *A to Z of Royal Navy Ship's Badges 1919-89*. —— Catherine Jill, *b* 1939: *m* 1961, Capt (N) Garry Joseph Oman, CD, RCNR, of 1 Appledale Rd, Islington, Ont, Canada, and has issue living, Christopher David, *b* 1966, — Catherine Mary, *b* 1964, — Elizabeth Frances Anne, *b* 1972.

Grandson of late Rev Frederick Manners Stopford, son of late Lt-Col Hon Edward Stopford, 2nd son of 3rd Earl:—

Issue of late Walter Montagu Stopford, *b* 1874, *d* 1933: *m* 1919, Mary Josephine (Greenville, Enniscorthy, co Wexford), da of late Patrick O'Neill, of Enniscorthy, co Wexford:—
Lionel Frederick John, *b* 1921; European War 1944-5 in Welsh Gds: *m* 1950 (*m diss* 1960), Violet Eira, da of Harold Dart, of Cefn, Murch Road, Dinas Powis, Glamorgan, and has issue living, John Martin, *b* 1958, — Linda Mary, *b* 1951, — Wendy Margaret, *b* 1953. *Residence* – 153 Fraser St, Kenilworth Johannesburg, 2190, S Africa.

Grandson of late Maj-Gen Sir Lionel Arthur Montagu Stopford, KCVO, CB, son of Adm Hon Sir Montagu Stopford, KCB, 6th son of 3rd Earl:—
Issue of late Capt Lionel Montagu Phipps Stopford, Seaforth Highlanders, *b* 1897, *d* 1985: *m* 1934, Sheila Frances, MBE, who *d* 1978, da of Gen Sir Cecil Francis Romer, GCB, KBE, CMG:—
Robert Cecil Montagu (Kintail, Hobhole Bank, Old Leake, Boston, Lincs PE22 9RX), *b* 1935; *ed* Radley: *m* 1958, Elizabeth Ann, da of late Alexander Krott, and has issue living, Andrew Alexander Montagu (Zakres, Situ da Ribeira, S João da Boa Vista, 3420 Tabua, Portugal), *b* 1959, — Sara Elizabeth Fiona (2A Radbourne Av, off Little Ealing Lane, W5 4XD), *b* 1967.

Granddaughter of late Vice-Adm Frederick George Stopford, 4th son of Adm Robert Fanshawe Stopford, eldest son of Adm Hon Sir Robert Stopford, GCB, GCMG, 3rd son of 2nd Earl:—
Issue of late Robert Edward Wilbraham Stopford, *b* 1897, *d* 1982: *m* 1925, Alicia Ellen Saunders, who *d* 1967:—
Mona Alicia STOPFORD, *b* 1926; has resumed her maiden name: *m* 19— (*m diss* 19—), — Anderson, and has issue living, Robert Edward, *b* 1952, — Alec, *b* 1954, — Susan Jean STOPFORD, *b* 1956; assumed surname of Stopford by Court Order, — Ellen Pegeen STOPFORD, *b* 1960; assumed surname of Stopford by Court Order. *Address* – RR3, Tottenham, Ontario, Canada LOG 1WO.

Grandchildren of late Col Lionel Richard STOPFORD SACKVILLE, 2nd son of late William Bruce Stopford Sackville (who assumed by Royal Licence 1870 the additional surname and arms of Sackville), 4th son of late Rev Hon Richard Bruce Stopford, 4th son of 2nd Earl:—
Issue of late Col Nigel Victor Stopford Sackville, CBE, TD, *b* 1901: *m* 1st, 1929 (*m diss* 1943), Beatrix Helen Constance, who *d* 1990, da of late Col Hercules Arthur Pakenham, CMG (*see* E Longford, colls): 2ndly, 1946, Lilah Mary (The Weirs, Chilton Foliat, Hungerford, Berks), da of late Capt Percy Richard Hare (*see* E Listowel, colls), and formerly wife of Maj George Seton Wills, R Wilts Yeo (*see* Wills, Bt, *cr* 1904):—
(By 1st *m*) Lionel Geoffrey STOPFORD SACKVILLE (Drayton House, Lowick, Kettering) (*Clubs* - White's, Pratt's), *b* 1932 *ed* Eton; Chm of Union Jack Oil plc, Lowick Manor Farms Ltd, J. Goedhuis & Co Ltd; Dir of Mercury World Mining Trust plc, Dartmoor Investment Trust plc, Pantheon International Participations plc and Can Gold Resources Inc; FCA; Late Lt Northants Yeo; former Lt 14/20 Hus, served in Libya: *m* 1st, 1960, Susan J., only da of late Jenkin Coles, of the Abbey, Knaresborough, Yorks; 2ndly, 1980, Hon (Mary) Teresa Pearson, el da of 3rd Viscount Cowdray, TD, and has had issue (by 1st *m*), Charles Lionel, *b* 1961: *m* 1992, Shona, yst da of late Donald McKinney, CBE, of Nassau, Bahamas, and Mrs Philip Harari, of Cadogan Gdns, SW1, and has issue living, Luke Mordaunt *b* 1993, — Thomas Nigel *b* 1968, — Lucinda Mary, *b* 1963; *k* in a motor accident 1992, — (by 2nd *m*), Camilla Anne, *b* 1981. — Venetia Mary (50 Vera Rd, SW6), *b* 1930: *m* 1952 (*m diss* 1968), Maj Benjamin Robert Chetwynd Talbot, TD, and has issue living, Benjamin Simon Robert, *b* 1956, — Victoria Mary, *b* 1958.

Grandchildren of late Maj Heneage Frank Stopford, 4th son of James Sydney Stopford, 5th son of Rev Hon Richard Bruce Stopford (ante):—
Issue of late Capt James Coverley Stopford, OBE, RN, *b* 1909, *d* 1985: *m* 1936, (Katherine) Sheila Hope, who *d* 1986, da of late Capt G. C. S. MacLeod, Black Watch:—
Robert Heneage (Cool Bank Cottage, Winson, Cirencester, Glos), *b* 1945; *ed* Wellington. —— Serena Margaret, *b* 1939: *m* 1964, Christopher H. M. Holmes, Fl Lt RAF, of Allergarth, Burswell Villas, Hexham, Northumberland, eldest son of W/Cdr K. E. M. Holmes, RAF, of Great Leighs, Essex, and has issue living, Andrew David, *b* 1965, — Richard Mark, *b* 1967, — Bridget Constantia, *b* (twin) 1967.
Issue of late Edward Kennedy Stopford, CB, *b* 1911, *d* 1983: *m* 1952, Patricia Iona Mary, who *d* 1989, da of late W. Howard Carrick, and widow of Duncan George Stewart, CMG:—
Michael John (131 East 94th St, New York City, NY, USA), *b* 1953; *ed* Radley.

Grandchildren of the late Capt Wyndham Horace Stopford, 5th and yst son of James Sydney Stopford (ante):—
Issue of the late Wyndham Horace Stopford, *b* (*posthumous*) 1904, *d* 1984: *m* 1st 1928, May, who *d* 1967, da of Col John White Craig, of Manila, Philippine Islands; 2ndly, 1968, Charlotte, da of Rev James Graham Clark, of Barrhead, Glasgow:—
(By 1st *m*) Nevill Craig, *b* 1932: *m* 1963, (Helen) Alison, 2nd da of William Leslie Baty, of Cheviot View, Ponteland, Northumberland, and has issue living, Wyndham Leslie, *b* 1965, — Angus Craig, *b* 1967. —— Craig Leeson (Marbridge Foundation, Manchaca, Texas, USA), *b* 1939. —— Ann, *b* 1935: *m* 1959, Michael William Frewen Jenkin, 3rd son of the late Charles Oswald Frewen Jenkin, and has issue living, Andrew Wyndham, *b* 1960, — Richard Frewen, *b* 1962.

Grandchildren of late Lt-Col Horace Robert Stopford, only son of late Robert Stopford, 7th and yst son of Rev Hon Richard Bruce Stopford (ante):—
Issue of late Cdr Robert Maurice Stopford, DSC, RN, *b* 1890, *d* 1977: *m* 1920, Elsie, who *d* 1967, da of late Capt Francis William Lawson, Connaught Rangers:—
Michael Robert Horace (The Lodge, Tarrant Monkton, Blandford Forum, Dorset DT11 8RU), *b* 1921; Maj (ret) Queen's R Regt: *m* 1945, Megan, da of late Arthur Reyner Williams, and has had issue, Michael Hastings, *b* 1949; *ed* Downside: *m* 1st, 1976, Jennifer, da of late Maj J. H. Walmesley-Cotham; 2ndly, 1984, Alexandra E., da of Douglas G. Hartley, and has issue living (by 2nd *m*), Joshua Gordon *b* 1984, Benjamin Charles *b* 1986, Zoë Megan Patience *b* 1989, — Charles Michael Reyner, *b* 1950; *ed* Downside; Capt 9th/12th R Lancers (Prince of Wales's): *m* 1979, J. Clare (who *m* 2ndly, 1986, Jonathan J. Harris, of 50 Barclay Rd, SW6), yst da of late M. H. J. Villeneuve, of Byway House, Fordwich, Kent, and *d* 1980 as the result of a flying accident, — Laura Cecilia Mary, *b* 1947: *m* 1969, Capt Kenneth Andres Courtenay, RN, of Henstridge, Somerset, and has issue living, Edward Michael Andres *b* 1970, Tamsin Mary Andres *b* 1972, — Teresa Megan Marguerite, *b* 1955: *m* 1st, 1975, Nigel A. S. Healey; 2ndly, 1984, Anton D. Simon, of 8 Chepstow Villas, W11 2RB, 2nd son of Arthur G. Simon, of Portsmouth, and has issue living (by 2nd *m*), Charles Stephen *b* 1987, Harry Eugene *b* and *d* 1991, Eugene Michael *b* 1992. —— Stephen Robert Anthony, CB, MBE (c/o Child & Co, 1 Fleet St, EC4), *b* 1934; Maj-Gen late Scots DG; MBE (Mil) 1971, CB (Mil) 1988: *m* 1963, Vanessa, da of late Theodore Baron, of 18 Rex Pl, W1. —— Rosemary Dolores, *b* 1926: *m* 1963, John Walter Mills, TD, KSS, High Sheriff of Warwicks 1959-60.

PREDECESSORS – **(1)** JAMES Stopford, son of late James Stopford, MP, of Courtown, MP for co Wexford 1721-7, and for Fethard 1727-58; *cr Baron Courtown*, of co Wexford (peerage of Ireland) 1758, and *Viscount Stopford* and *Earl of Courtown* (peerage of Ireland) 1762; *d* 1770; *s* by his son **(2)** JAMES, 2nd Earl; *cr Baron Saltersford*, of Saltersford, co Chester (peerage of Great Britain) 1796; *d* 1810; *s* by his son **(3)** JAMES GEORGE, KP, PC, 3rd Earl; *d* 1835; *s* by his son **(4)** JAMES THOMAS, 4th Earl; *b* 1794: *m* 1st, 1822, Lady Charlotte Montagu-Scott, who *d* 1828, da of the 4th Duke of Buccleuch; 2ndly, 1850, Dora, who *d* 1859, da of late Right Hon Edward Pennefather, Ch Justice of the Queen's Bench in Ireland; *d* 1858; *s* by his son **(5)** JAMES GEORGE HENRY, 5th Earl; *b* 1823: *m* 1846, Hon Elizabeth Frances Milles, who *d* 1894, 2nd da of 4th Baron Sondes; *d* 1914; *s* by his el son **(6)** JAMES WALTER MILLES, 6th Earl, *b* 1853; High Sheriff of co Wexford 1877 and of co Carlow 1878, and Lieut for co Wexford 1901: *m* 1st, 1876, Hon Catherine Elizabeth Neville, who *d* 1884, da of 4th Baron Braybrooke; 2ndly, 1886, Gertrude, who *d* 1934, da of late Gen Charles James Conway Mills, of Cardington, Beds; *d* 1933; *s* by his el son **(7)** JAMES RICHARD NEVILLE, OBE, 7th Earl; *b* 1877; Major Gen List; S Africa 1900-1901, European War 1915-19, Mayor of Aylesbury 1927-8, DAAG, War Office 1941-7: *m* 1905, Cicely Mary, OBE, JP, who *d* 1973, yr da of late John Arden Birch; *d* 1957; *s* by his el son **(8)** JAMES MONTAGU BURGOYNE, OBE, TD, 8th Earl; *b* 1908; Lt Col and Brevet Col London Irish Rifles, R Ulster Rifles; N Africa 1943 and Italy 1943-45: *m* 1st, 1934 (*m diss* 1946), Christina Margaret, da of Adm John Ewen Cameron CB, MVO, of Brunton House, Christon Bank, Northumberland; 2ndly, 1951, Patricia, da of Harry Stephen Winthrop, of Auckland, NZ; *d* 1975; *s* by his el son **(9)** JAMES PATRICK MONTAGU BURGOYNE WINTHROP, 9th Earl, and present peer; also Viscount Stopford, Baron Courtown, and Baron Saltersford.

COUTANCHE, BARONY OF (Coutanche) (Extinct 1973)

SON LIVING OF LIFE BARON

Jurat the Hon John Alexander Gore, *b* 1925; Lt-Cdr RNR; Lieut Bailiff and Jurat of Royal Court, Jersey: *m* 1st, 1949, Jean Veronica, who *d* 1977, da of late Alexander Thomson Dawson, of Portelet House, Jersey; 2ndly, 1978, Gillian Margaret, da of late Brig John Douglas Fellowes Fisher, CBE, of Ravenscroft, Val de la Mare, Jersey, and has issue living by 1st *m*. *Residence* – Clos Des Tours, St Aubin, Jersey.

COVENTRY, EARL OF (Coventry) (Earl E 1697)

Candidly and constantly

GEORGE WILLIAM COVENTRY, 11th Earl; *b* 25 Jan 1934; *s* 1940; *ed* Eton; late 2nd Lt Gren Gds: *m* 1st 1955 (*m diss* 1963), Marie Farquhar, da of late William Sherman Medart, of St Louis, USA; 2ndly, 1969 (*m diss* 1975), Ann, da of Frederick William James Cripps, of Bickley, Kent; 3rdly, 1980 (*m diss* 1988), Valerie Anne Birch; 4thly, 1992, Rachel Wynne, da of Jack Mason, and has issue by 1st *m*.

Arms – Sable, a fesse ermine, between three crescents or. **Crest** – A cock gules, comb, wattles, and legs or, standing on a garb fesse-wise or. **Supporters** – Two eagles, wings expanded and inverted argent, beaked and membered or.
Seat – Earls Croome Court, Earls Croome, Worcester WR8 9DE.

SON LIVING (By 1st marriage)

EDWARD GEORGE WILLIAM OMAR (*Viscount Deerhurst*), *b* 24 Sept 1957.

SISTERS LIVING

Lady Anne Donne, *b* 1922.
Lady Maria Alice COVENTRY (Levant Lodge, Earls Croome, Worcester), *b* 1931: *m* 1954 (*m diss* 1968), John Richard Lewes.

WIDOW LIVING OF TENTH EARL

Hon NESTA DONNE PHILIPPS, TD, da of 1st Baron Kylsant (ext); a DL of Carmarthenshire; 1939-45 War as Ch Com ATS: *m* 1st, 1921, the 10th Earl, who was *ka* 1940; 2ndly, 1953, Maj Terrance Vincent Fisher-Hoch, RA, who *d* 1978.

COLLATERAL BRANCHES LIVING

Issue of late Col Hon Charles John Coventry, 2nd son of 9th Earl, CB, *b* 1867, *d* 1929: *m* 1900, Lily, who *d* 1970, yr da of late Fitz Hugh Whitehouse, of Eastbourne Lodge, Newport, USA:—
Francis Henry, *b* 1912; *ed* Eton, and New Coll, Oxford (BA 1934); is Lt-Cdr RNVR; formerly Lieut Worcestershire Yeo (TA): *m* 1945, Yolande Lucienne, da of P. di Benedetto, of Alexandria and has issue living, Patricia Caroline Mary, *b* 1950: *m* 1st, 1969 (*m diss* 1984), Antonio Morisani; 2ndly, 1986, Raymond P. Bianchi, of Castel S Pietro, and has issue living (by 1st *m*), Gian-Marco *b* 1970. *Residence* – 6987 Caslano, Switzerland.

Issue of late Hon Sir Reginald William Coventry, KC, 4th son of 9th Earl, *b* 1869, *d* 1940: *m* 1st, 1911, Gwenllian Pascoe, who *d* 1925, da of Edward Vaughan Morgan, formerly of 22 Harrington Gardens, SW; 2ndly, 1926, Frances Constance, who *d* 1943, widow of Walter P. Jeffreys, of Cynghordy:—
(By 1st *m*) Mary Gwenllian, *b* 1912: *m* 1935, George Albert Finegan, LRCPI, LRCSI, who *d* 1965, and has issue living, Barbara Jane, *b* 1936, — Sonia Mary, *b* 1939. *Residence* – 274 Cooden Drive, Bexhill, Sussex.

Issue of late Hon Thomas George Coventry, yst son of 9th Earl, *b* 1885, *d* 1972: *m* 1910, Alice, who *d* 1961, da of Thomas Ward, of Hasketon, Woodbridge, Suffolk:—
†William Thomas, *b* 1911: *m* 1st, 1940, Gwendolyn V. Burton; 2ndly, 1950, Irene Muriel Shay, and *d* 1993. —— Victor Gerald, CD (1739-148 A St, Surrey, BC, Canada V4A 6G5), *b* 1917; Lt (QW) Cdn Militia, Sup Customs-Excise, Govt of Canada (ret): *m* 1943, Constance Hilda, da of late Henry Edward Green, of S Tottenham, N15, and has had issue, †John Stephen, *b* 1949; *d* 1972, — Angela Barbara, *b* 1944: *m* 1974, Robert Arthur Chapman, of 553 Schoolhouse, Coquitlam, BC, V3J 5P2, Canada, and has issue living, Lloyd Steven *b* 1979, Susan Teresa *b* 1977.

Granddaughter of late Hon Thomas George Coventry (ante):—

Issue of late Flight-Lieut Robert George Coventry, RAF, *b* 1913, *ka* 1940: *m* 1936, Olga, who *d* 1985, only da of late John Henry Warhurst:—
Monica Anne (c/o National Westminster Bank, 27 Cannon St, EC4), *b* 1939: *m* 1967, James Stuart Underhill.

Granddaughter of late Henry Robert Beauclerk Coventry, only son of late Capt Henry Amelius Beauclerk Coventry, son of late Hon Henry Amelius Coventry, 2nd son of 8th Earl:—
Issue of late Capt Arthur Beauclerk Coventry, OBE, DSC, RN, *b* 1900, *d* 1971: *m* 1928, Muriel Ethel Francis, who *d* 1986, da of late Hugh B. Craven, of Wheathills House, Kirk Langley, Derbys:—
Auriol Susan, *b* 1932: *m* 1966, Wallace McMillan Reid, of 36 Peter's Sq, W6, and has issue living, Caspar James Beauclerk, *b* 1971, — Frances Elizabeth, *b* 1967.

Grandson of late Gilbert William Coventry (infra):—
Issue of late Cdr Cecil Dick Bluett Coventry, DSC, RD, RNR, *b* 1905, *d* 1952: *m* 1939, Anne Josephine Hale, who *d* 1974, da of late Maj H. J. Sherwood, RE:—
George William (21 Malvern Rd, Hampton, Middx), *b* 1939; *ed* Prince of Wales Sch, Nairobi: *m* 1965, Gillian Frances, da of late Frank W. R. Randall, of Wyke Regis, Weymouth, Dorset, and has issue living, Diana Elizabeth Sherwood, *b* 1980.

Grandchildren of late Cdr Cecil Dick Bluett Coventry, DSC, RD, RNR (ante):—
Issue of late Peter Harold Sherwood Coventry, *b* 1941, *d* 1985: *m* 1969, Kay Sandra (Hillsborough, Bere Ferrers, Yelverton, Devon), da of late Lt-Cdr Roy S. Baker-Falkner:—
David Duncan Sherwood, *b* 1973. —— Lynn Karen Sherwood, *b* 1970.

Grandchildren of late Gilbert William Coventry (infra):—
Issue of late Arthur John Clifford Coventry, *b* 1909, *d* 1965: *m* 1st, 1937 (*m diss* 1947), Dulcie Alice Saxon; 2ndly, 1952, Margaret Nancy, who *d* 1986, only da of W. E. Gell, of Gosford, NSW:—
(By 1st *m*) Gilbert John Henry (15 Queen St, Guildford, NSW 2161, Australia), *b* 1939: *m* 1961, Patricia Anne, da of Reginald Charles Deeley, of Balgowaie, NSW, and has issue living, Wesley John, *b* 1965, — Anne Maree, *b* 1962: *m* 1993, Xavier Hogan, — Robyne Michelle, *b* 1971; has issue living, Justin Alan COVENTRY *b* 1992. —— †Geoffrey Robert, *b* 1941: *m* 1964, Lynette, da of Patrick Salmon, of Corrimal, NSW, and *d* 1964. —— Margaret Elaine, *b* 1943: *m* 1964, Barrie Robert Stanford, of 10 Jennifer Crescent, Thirroul, NSW 2515, Australia, and has issue living, Cheryn Lee, *b* 1968: *m* 1992, Charles Goudman, — Karlyn Leslie, *b* 1970: *m* 1992, Sean Johns. —— (By 2nd *m*) Richard William (29 Munro Rd, Queanbeyan, NSW 2620, Australia), *b* 1953: *m* 1st, 19—, —; 2ndly, 1984, Carolyn, da of William John Dray, of 11-13 Frederick St, Marburg, Qld, and has issue living (by 1st *m*), Richard John, *b* 1972, — (by 2nd *m*), Sarah Margaret, *b* 1986. —— Elizabeth Nancy, *b* 1955: *m* 1986, Colin Hickey, of 9 Marston Close, Macarthur, ACT 2905, Australia; has issue living, Penelope Lee COVENTRY, *b* 1973.

Grandchildren of late William George Coventry, eldest son of late Hon William James Coventry, 4th son of 7th Earl:—
Issue of late Gilbert William Coventry, *b* 1868; *d* 1947: *m* 1st, 1902, Georgina Blanche, who *d* 1922, da of late Major William H. P. G. Bluett (formerly Lincolnshire Regt), of Paignton; 2ndly, 1923, Margaret Charlotte, who *d* 1981, widow of Major G. D'Arcy Elliott-Cooper:—
(By 1st *m*) (Gilbert) Hugo Gordon (Fermoy Cottage, Vermont Drive, E Preston, Sussex), *b* 1911; formerly Lt-Cdr R Indian Navy; sometime Rubber Planter; formerly Manager of Eng Kee Kundong Estates, Tangkah, Johore, Malaysia: *m* 1st, 1948 (*m diss* 1953), Alice, widow of Frank Tabrum; 2ndly, 1959, Mary, who *d* 1991, widow of Gordon Graham, of Mile End House, Aberdeen. —— (By 2nd *m*) Anne, *b* 1925: *m* 1951, Stanley A. Peter Keevil, and has issue living, Sarah Anne, *b* 1952: *m* 1975, Paul Kane, of Three Oaks, 65 Worthing Rd, Horsham, Sussex, — Charlotte Fiona, *b* 1956: *m* 1990, Anthony Ferens, of Château de Béysserat, Monségur, 33580 Gironde, France. *Residence* – The Barn, W Ogwell, Newton Abbot, Devon.

Grandchildren of late Rev Henry William Coventry, 2nd son of Hon William James Coventry (ante):—
Issue of late Fulwar Cecil Ashton Coventry, OBE, *b* 1874, *d* 1944: *m* 1917, Lorna Mary, who *d* 1965, da of late Capt Peregrine H. T. Fellowes, Ch Constable of Hants:—
Digby Colquitt, *b* 1919; 1939-45 War (despatches, Chevalier of Order of Leopold with palm, Belgian Croix de Guerre with palm): *m* 1946, Marina, formerly wife of Willie Gosse, and only da of Wilhelm Georg Viktor von Wahl, and has issue living, Sebastian, *b* 1946: *m* 1965, Helene Kozlow, of Paris, and has issue living, Adrian *b* 1967, Alexandra *b* 1966, Christine *b* 1971, Catherine *b* 1976, — Mark, *b* 1952, — Elizabeth, *b* 1947: *m* 1967, Henry J. C. Pauwels, — Xenia, *b* 1949. —— Lorna Peggy Maria, *b* 1922.

Grandchildren of late Harry Coventry (infra):—
Issue of late St John Coventry, *b* 1901, *d* 1963: *m* 1930, Caroline Gertrude, da of John David Hocking:—
Henry John (149 Moores Valley Rd, Lower Hutt, NZ), *b* 1932; BCA Victoria; Sqdn-Ldr RNAZF; Queen's Commendation 1964: *m* 1958, Rev Frances Winifred, da of Marcus Davenport Clarke, and has issue living, Simon St John, *b* 1963, — David Henry Halford, *b* 1969, — Rosalyn Barbara, *b* 1959; BA Victoria: *m* 1989, Rev Dr Uili Feleterika Nokise, — Adrienne Claire, *b* 1960: *m* 1988, Niel Douglas Brown, — Anna Louise *b* 1967; BA Canterbury. —— Roger Michael (Merrivale, Battersea Line, Greytown, NZ), *b* 1934; Asso of RSH: *m* 1961, Margaret Ann Cooke, and has issue living, Geoffrey Alan, *b* 1969, — Jennifer Beryl, *b* 1965: *m* 1988, Bill Biber, — Sylvia Ann, *b* 1967, — Marilyn Gay, *b* 1968. —— Alan Francis (22 Lynmore Av, Rotorua, NZ), *b* 1940; a Radio Technician: *m* 1st, 1961 (*m diss* 1972), Patrina Rathbride, da of Patrick Francis Dwan; 2ndly, 1972, Alison Leslie, da of Dallas Evans, and has issue living (by 1st *m*), Charles Raymond St John, *b* 1963: *m* 19—, Pauline Wendy Dyer, and has issue living, Sean James St John *b* 1985, Benjamin St John *b* 1987, Alyson Patrina *b* 1983, — Andrew Patrick Francis, *b* 1964: *m* 1988, Irene Florence, da of David Alan Parr, — Charmaine Louise, *b* 1961: *m* 19—, Andrew Bryan Duxfield, and has issue living, Michael Thomas *b* 1984, Timothy Edward *b* 1986, Amy Georgiana *b* 1988, — (by 2nd *m*) Richard Alan Penrose, *b* 1971, — Katherine Margaret, *b* 1973. —— Bernadine Helen Mary, *b* 1945: *m* 1964, Enda Francis McBride, of 27 Tennyson St, Trentham, Upper Hutt, NZ, and has issue living, Lenore Frances, *b* 1965: *m* 1989, Michael Cunningham, — Joanna Claire, *b* 1967: *m* 1988, Robert Stuart Nicol.

Grandchildren of late Henry Halford Coventry, CE, yst son of late Frederick Coventry, el son of late Hon John Coventry, 2nd son of 6th Earl:—
Issue of late Harry Coventry, *b* 1858, *d* 1943: *m* 1896, Evangeline who *d* 1963, da of Gustav August Hermann Hohenzollern (Rockel), of Carnarvon, Feilding, NZ:—
Frederick Halford, *b* 1905: *m* 1940, Dolores Rosamund Christine, yr da of late Léon Dominic Ashton, of Cairo, Egypt, and has issue living, Edward Bernard Halford St John, *b* 1943; Bsc London, — Elizabeth Mary Hephzibah, *b* 1947; Dip AD: *m* 1st, 1968 (*m diss* 1980), Terence Carville; 2ndly, (Jan) 1981, John Henry Brierley, and has issue living (by 2nd *m*), Alexandra Frances Mary, *b* (Dec) 1981. *Residence* – 125 Ipswich Rd, Woodbridge, Suffolk IP12 4BY.

Grandchildren of late John Coventry (*b* 1845), eldest son of late Rev John Coventry (*b* 1819), eldest son of late John Coventry (*b* 1793) (infra):—
Issue of late John Joseph Coventry, *b* 1882, *d* 1950: *m* 1910, Margaret Camilla (who *d* 1958, having *m* 2ndly, 1955,

Adrian Leonard Moreton, MS, FRCS, of Wilton House, Hungerford, Berks), da of Carlyle Henry Hayes Macartney, formerly of Foxhold, Newbury:—

Barbara Mary St John, MBE, b 1912; MRCS England 1952, and LRCP London 1952, MB and BS London 1952; 1939-45 War as Junior Com ATS (MBE); MBE (Mil) 1945. *Residence* – 1 Back Lane, East Bridge, Leiston, Suffolk. —— Catherine Margaret Mary, b 1915: m 1936, Herbert Alan Jones, and has issue living, Charles Alan (10 Rodway Rd, SW15), b 1937: m 1961, Margaret Elizabeth Cowper, and has issue living, Timothy Charles b 1963, Nicholas Alan b 1967, Patricia Margaret b 1965, — Celia Margaret, b 1948. *Residence* – 4 Earls Court Gdns, SW5. —— Dorothea Olivia, b 1918: m 1937 (m diss 1952), Adrian Charles Enthoven, and has issue living, Stephen Andrew (15 Ladbroke Sq, W11 3NA), b 1939: m 1965, Fiona Valerie Maclean, and has issue living, Thomas Samuel Donald b 1974, John Henry William b 1978, — John Christopher, b 1945: m 1968, Valerie Kathleen Roberts, and has issue living, Andrew James b 1975, Alexandra Louise b 1973.

Issue of late Bernard Seton Coventry, b 1887, d 1965: m 1910, Annie, who d 1960, da of late James Cunningham, MICE, of Cyprus:—

Rev John Joseph Seton (114 Mount St, W1Y 6AH), b 1915; ed Oxford Univ (MA); in Holy Orders Roman Catholic Church.

Grandson of Bernard Seton Coventry (ante):—

Issue of late Anthony James Seton Coventry, b 1913, d 1955: m 1942, Mollie Rosina (Seton, 20 St Anne's Gdns, Lymington, Hants SO4 9HT), who m 2ndly, 1961, Harold J. Hayles, who d 1972, da of J. Grummett, of St Abbs Head, Coldingham, Berwickshire:—

John James Seton, b 1955. *Residences* – 62 Eastbury Grove, Chiswick, W4; Little Petherton, Middle Winterslow, Salisbury, Wilts. —— The late Anthony James Seton Coventry also had an adopted da, Margaret Elizabeth, b 1946: m 1978, Nigel James Brooks, of Shilton House, Pitmore Lane, Lymington, Hants, son of late Lt-Cdr F. L. Brooks, MBE, RD, RN, of Lymington, Hants, and has issue living, Richard John, b 1981, — Anthony James, b 1982, — Nicola Kate, b 1985.

Granddaughter of late John Coventry (b 1793), 2nd son of late Hon John Coventry (ante):—

Issue of late Francis Martin Coventry, b 1863, d 1917: m 1896, Amy Maud, who d 1949, da of Henry W. J. Hill, formerly of 17 Cleveland Square, W, and Turcoliah, Bengal:—

Catherine Nora, b 1906: m 1926, Hubert de Burgh Williams, who d 1949, and has issue living, Evan John, b 1926: m 1952, Janet, da of Boyd Hill, of Ross-on-Wye, and has issue living, Alan Christopher b 1956, Sheila Anne b 1954, — Hubert Michael, b 1927. *Residence* – 71 Castle Rd, Colchester, Essex CO1 1UN.

Grandchildren of late Gilbert Walter Coventry, 4th son of late Thomas William Coventry, only son of late Hon Thomas William Coventry, 3rd son of 6th Earl:—

Issue of late Francis Gilbert Coventry, b 1892, d 1960: m 1929, Clara Dorothy, who d 1970, da of late Robert Charles Brown:—

Noel, b 1933: m 1960, Nola Elsie May, da of Robert Archibald Lindsay. *Residence* – 72 Station Rd, Paeroa, New Zealand. —— Francis Henry, b 1934: m 1961, Shirley Ann, da of late Thomas Henry Lionel Turner.

Issue, if any, of late Arthur Roger Coventry, b 1894, d 1975: m 19—, Alma Rale, who d 1980.

PREDECESSORS – (**1**) *Sir* THOMAS Coventry, KB (whose ancestor John Coventry was Lord Mayor of London 1426), Recorder of London 1615, Solicitor and Attorney-Gen 1616, and Lord Keeper of the Great Seal 1625; *cr Baron Coventry*, of Aylesborough, co Worcester (peerage of England) 1628; *d* 1640; *s* by his son (**2**) THOMAS, 2nd Baron; *d* 1661; *s* by his son (**3**) GEORGE, 3rd Baron; *s* by son (**4**) JOHN, 4th Baron; *d* unmarried 1687; *s* by his uncle (**5**) THOMAS, 5th Baron, 2nd son of 2nd Baron; *cr Viscount Deerhurst* and *Earl of Coventry* (peerage of England) 1697, with limitation to the grandson of Walter, yst brother of 1st Baron; *d* 1699; *s* by his son (**6**) THOMAS, 2nd Earl; *d* 1710; *s* by his son (**7**) THOMAS, 3rd Earl *d* a minor 1712; *s* by his uncle (**8**) GILBERT, 4th Earl, 2nd son of 1st Earl; *dsp* 1719, when the Barony became extinct, and the other honours reverted to his kinsman (**9**) WILLIAM, PC, 5th Earl, grandson of Walter Coventry (ante); successively a Clerk of the Green Cloth, MP for Bridport, and Lord-Lieut of Worcestershire; *d* 1751; *s* by his son (**10**) GEORGE WILLIAM, 6th Earl, *d* 1809; *s* by son (**11**) GEORGE WILLIAM, 7th Earl, Recorder of Worcester and High Steward of Tewkesbury; *d* 1831; *s* by his son (**12**) GEORGE WILLIAM, 8th Earl; Lord-Lieut of Worcestershire; *d* 1843; *s* by his grandson (**13**) GEORGE WILLIAM, PC (son of George William, Viscount Deerhurst, el son of 8th Earl), 9th Earl *b* 1838; Capt and Gold Stick of Corps of Gentlemen at Arms 1877-80 and 1880-85, Master of the Buckhounds 1886-92 and 1895-1890, and Lord-Lieut of Worcestershire 1891-1903: *m* 1865, Blanche, who *d* 1930, da of 2nd Earl of Craven, *d* 1930; *s* by his grandson (**14**) GEORGE WILLIAM REGINALD VICTOR (son of late George William, Viscount Deerhurst, el son of 9th Earl), 10th Earl, *b* 1900: *m* 1921, Hon Nesta Donne Philipps (who *m* 2ndly, 1953, Major Terrance Vincent Fisher-Hoch), da of 1st Baron Kylsant (ext); *ka* 1940; *s* by his only son (**15**) GEORGE WILLIAM, 11th Earl and present peer, also Viscount Deerhurst.

COWDRAY, VISCOUNT (Pearson) (Viscount UK 1917, Bt UK 1894)

WEETMAN JOHN CHURCHILL PEARSON, TD, 3rd Viscount and 3rd Baronet; *b* 27 Feb 1910; *s* 1933; *ed* Eton, and at Ch Ch, Oxford; formerly Capt 98th (Surrey and Sussex) Field Regt RA (TA); formerly DL Sussex; European War 1939-40 (severely wounded); was Parliamentary Private Sec to Under-Sec of State for Air 1941-42: *m* 1st, 1939 (*m diss* 1950), Lady Anne Pamela Bridgeman, da of 5th Earl of Bradford; 2ndly, 1953, Elizabeth Georgiana Mather, 2nd da of Sir Anthony Henry Mather Mather-Jackson, 6th Bt (*cr* 1869), and has issue by 1st and 2nd *m*.

Arms – Per fesse indented gules and or, in chief two suns in splendour and in base a demi-gryphon couped, all counter-changed. **Crest** – In front of a demi-gryphon gules holding between its claws a millstone proper thereon a mill-rind sable, a sun in splendour. **Supporters** – *Dexter*, a diver holding in his exterior hand his helmet; *sinister* a Mexican peon; both proper.
Seats – Cowdray Park, Midhurst, W Sussex GU29 0AX; Dunecht House, Dunecht, Skene, Aberdeenshire AB32 7DD. *Address* – 17th Floor, Millbank Tower, Millbank, SW1P 4QZ.

SONS LIVING *(By 1st marriage)*

Hon MICHAEL ORLANDO WEETMAN (Les Acacias, 18 Boulevard des Moulins, Monte Carlo 98000, Monaco), *b* 17 June 1944; *ed* Gordonstoun: *m* 1st, 1977 (*m diss* 1984), Ellen (Fritzi), da of late Hermann Erhardt, of Munich; 2ndly, 1987, Marina Rose, 2nd da of John Howard Cordle, of Malmesbury House, The Close, Salisbury, Wilts (*see* V Powerscourt, colls, 1985 Edn), and has issue living (by 2nd *m*), Eliza Anne Venetia, *b* 1988, — Emily Jane Marina, *b* 1989, — Catrina Sophie Lavinia, *b* 1991.

(By 2nd marriage)

Hon Charles Anthony (14 Markham Square, SW3), *b* 1956: *m* 1992, Baroness Benedicte Blixen-Finecke, da of Ifver Iuul, of Fyn, Denmark, and of Mrs Gerald Barry, of Cookham, Berks, and has issue living, Carinthia Alexandra, *b* 1993.

DAUGHTERS LIVING *(By 1st marriage)*

Hon Mary Teresa, *b* 1940: *m* 1980, as his 2nd wife, Lionel Geoffrey Stopford Sackville, and has issue (*see* E Courtown, colls).
Hon Liza Jane, *b* 1942: *m* 1967, Malcolm MacNaughton, of Old Law House, 395 Miramontes Rd, Woodside, Cal 94062, USA, and has issue living, Justin John, *b* 1972, — Natasha Anne, *b* 1969.

(By 2nd marriage)

Hon Lucy, *b* 1954: *m* 1st, 1972 (*m diss* 1978), Luis Hector Juan Sosa Basualdo, of Buenos Aires; 2ndly, 1988, Charles Torquil de Montalt Fraser, late The Life Guards, elder son of Maj Michael Quintin Fraser, late 7th Hussars (*see* B Molesworth, colls, 1958 Edn), and has issue living (by 1st *m*), Rupert Peregrine PEARSON, *b* 1976, — Charlotte PEARSON, *b* 1974, — (by 2nd *m*) Emerald Chloe, *b* 1989, — Iona Violet, *b* 1991, — Iolanthe Maude, *b* 1993. *Residence* – The Old Poor House, Sutton End, Petworth, W Sussex RH20 1PY.
Hon Rosanna, *b* 1959: *m* 1988, Palma Taylor, of Jamaica, and has issue living, Annie Glennah, *b* 1990.

SISTERS LIVING

Hon (Beryl) Nancy (*Nancy, Viscountess Blakenham*), *b* 1908: *m* 1934, 1st Viscount Blakenham, who *d* 1982.
Hon (Helena) Daphne, *b* 1918: *m* 1939, Lt-Col John Lakin, TD, late Warwickshire Yeo, who *d* 1989 (*see* Lakin, Bt colls).
Residence – Hammerwood House, Iping, Midhurst, Sussex.

COLLATERAL BRANCHES LIVING

Issue of late Hon (Bernard) Clive Pearson, 2nd son of 1st Viscount, *b* 1887, *d* 1965: *m* 1915, Hon Alicia Mary Dorothea Knatchbull-Hugessen, who *d* 1974, da of 1st Baron Brabourne:—
Elisabeth Dione (*Baroness Gibson*), *b* 1920: *m* 1945, Baron Gibson (Life Baron), of Penn's Rocks, Groombridge, Sussex.

Issue of late Hon Francis Geoffrey Pearson, 3rd son of 1st Viscount, *b* 1891, *ka* 1914: *m* 1909, Ethel Elizabeth PEARSON (who *m* 2ndly, 1918 (*m diss* 1926), Air-Commodore Henry John Francis Hunter, CBE, MC, RAF (B Dormer), and *d* 1982, having resumed the surname of Pearson 1928), da of John Lewis, of Hove:—
Joan Cinetta, *b* 1912: *m* 1932, William Antony Acton, who *d* 1993, and has issue living, Caroline Jane (*Lady Dawson*) (11 Burton Court, Franklin's Row, SW3), *b* 1933: *m* 1955, Maj Sir Hugh Halliday Trevor Dawson, 3rd Bt (*cr* 1920), late Scots Gds, who *d* 1983. *Address* – Post Box 31, Poste Restante, Corfu, Greece.

PREDECESSORS – **(1)** *Right Hon Sir* WEETMAN DICKINSON Pearson, GCVO, PC, son of late George Pearson, of Brickendonbury, Hertford; *b* 1856; was Pres of the firm of S Pearson & Son Ltd, of Westminster, SW, and High Steward of Colchester 1897-1927; Pres of Air Board Jan to Nov 1917; MP for Colchester (Lib) 1895 to 1910; Lord Rector of Aberdeen Univ 1918-21; Hon Freeman of Aberdeen and Colchester; *cr* a *Baronet* 1894, *Baron Cowdray*, of Midhurst, co Sussex (peerage of United Kingdom) 1910, and *Viscount Cowdray*, of Cowdray, Sussex (peerage of United Kingdom) 1917: *m* 1881, Annie, GBE, who *d* 1932, da of late Sir John Cass, of Bradford, Yorkshire; *d* 1927; *s* by his son **(2)** WEETMAN HAROLD MILLER, 2nd Viscount, *b* 1882; MP for N-E or Eye, Div of Suffolk (Lib) 1906-18: *m* 1905, Agnes Beryl, who *d* 1948, da of late Lord Edward Spencer-Churchill; *d* 1933; *s* by his only son **(3)** WEETMAN JOHN CHURCHILL, 3rd Viscount and present peer; also Baron Cowdray.

COWLEY, EARL (Wellesley) (Earl UK 1857)

GARRET GRAHAM WELLESLEY, 7th Earl; *b* 30 July 1934; *s* 1975, *ed* Univ of S California (BS), and Harvard Univ (MBA); US Army Counter-Intelligence Corps, France 1957-60; Investment Analyst, Wells Fargo Bank, San Francisco 1962-64, Investment Counsel Dodger Cox 1964-66, Research Dir, Wells Fargo Bank 1966-67, Vice-Pres, Investment Council, Thorndike, Doran, Paine & Lewis, Los Angeles 1967-69; Sr Vice-Pres (Dir securities, real estate and acquisitions), Shareholders Capital Corpn, Los Angeles 1969-74; Sr Vice-Pres (Investment Mgr), Bank of America, San Francisco 1974-78; Gp Vice-Pres (Man Dir), Internat Investment Management Service, Bank of America, London 1978-84, Ch Investment Offr (Private Banking Div), Bank of America, London 1978-85: Dir Bank of America Internat Ltd 1978-83, etc; Inv Partner, Thos. R. Miller & Son (Bermuda) since 1990; Member Assocn of Conservative Peers: *m* 1st, 1960 (*m diss* 1967), Elizabeth Suzanne, da of late Haynes Lennon, of S Carolina; 2ndly, 1968 (*m diss* 1981), Isabelle O'Bready, of Sherbrooke, Quebec, Canada; 3rdly, 1981, Paige Deming, of Reno, Nevada, USA, and has issue by 1st *m*.

Arms – Quarterly: 1st and 4th gules, a cross argent, between twenty plates, five in each quarter saltirewise, *Wellesley*; 2nd and 3rd or, a lion rampant gules, ducally gorged gold, *Cowley*. **Crest** – Out of a ducal coronet or, a demi-lion rampant gules, holding a spear erect proper, and thereon flowing a pennon argent, charged with the cross of St George. **Supporters** – Two lions, gules, ducally gorged and chained or, and charged on the shoulder with an annulet for difference.
Address – c/o House of Lords, SW1A 0PW.

Moreover, one thing is necessary

SON LIVING *(By 1st marriage)*

GARRET GRAHAM (*Viscount Dangan*), *b* 30 March 1965: *m* 1990, Claire L., only da of Peter W. Brighton, of Stow Bridge, Norfolk, and has issue living, *Hon* Henry Arthur Peter, *b* 3 Dec 1991. *Club* – Brooks's.

DAUGHTER LIVING *(By 1st marriage)*

Lady Tara Lennon, *b* 1962.

BROTHER LIVING

Hon Brian Timothy (115 32nd Av NE, Fargo, N Dakota 58102, USA), *b* 1938; *ed* Arizona State Coll, Denver Univ, Colorado, and Nevada Univ (BS); Dir of Internal Revenue Service, US Treasury Dept, N Dakota: *m* 1st, 1961 (*m diss* 1964), Patricia Tribbey; 2ndly 1966 (*m diss* 1980), Karen Elizabeth Bradbury, of Reno, Nevada, USA; 3rdly, 1988, Katherine Samaniego, of New Mexico, USA.

SISTER LIVING

Lady Colleen, *b* 1925: *m* 1945, Paul A. Hanlon, MD, late Capt US Army, and has issue living, Paul Christian, *b* 1946, — Gavin Edward, *b* 1948, — Christopher Peter, *b* 1951, — Timothy Patrick, *b* 1955, — Richard Francis, *b* 1957, — Colleen Patricia, *b* 1958, — Jennifer Mary, *b* 1960. *Residence* – 543 Westmoreland Avenue, Kingston, Pennsylvania, USA.

DAUGHTERS LIVING OF SIXTH EARL

Lady Alexia Anne Elizabeth, *b* 1973.
Lady Caroline Maria Frances *b* (*posthumous*), 1976.

WIDOW LIVING OF SON OF THIRD EARL

Valerie Rose (Priestown House, Mulhuddart, co Dublin), 2nd da of late Christian Ernest Pitman, CBE, of Doynton House, Doynton, nr Bath: *m* 1969, as his 4th wife, Hon Henry Gerald Valerian Francis Wellesley, 2nd son of 3rd Earl, who *d* 1981, and has issue (*see colls infra*).

MOTHER LIVING OF SIXTH EARL

Elizabeth Anne, da of late Lt-Col Pelham Rawstorn Papillon, DSO, of Crowhurst, Sussex, and widow of Fl-Lt Stephen Alers Hankey, RAF: *m* 2ndly, 1944 (*m diss* 1950), Denis Arthur, Viscount Dangan (later the 5th Earl), who *d* 1968; 3rdly, 1953, Freeman Winslow Hill. *Address* – PO Box 285, Paget, Bermuda.

WIDOWS LIVING OF FOURTH, FIFTH AND SIXTH EARLS

MARY (ELSIE) MAY HIMES (*Elsie, Countess Cowley*), of San Francisco, California, USA: *m* 1933, the 4th Earl who *d* 1962. *Residence* – 3201 Plumas St, Reno, Nevada 89509, USA.
JANET ELIZABETH MARY, da of late Ramiah Doraswamy Aiyar, FRCS, of Ystrad, Denbigh, N Wales: *m* 1st, 1961, as his 3rd wife, the 5th Earl, who *d* 1968; 2ndly, 1976 (*m diss* 1981), Piers (Pierson John Shirley) Dixon, son of late Sir Pierson Dixon, GCMG, CB.
MARIA DELIA (5 Stanhope Gdns, SW7 5RG), yr da of Enrique Buenaño, of Vicente Lopez, 2602 7° A, Buenos Aires: *m* 1st, 1971, the 6th Earl, who *d* 1975; 2ndly, 1980, as his 2nd wife, Maj Robin James Stirling Bullock-Webster, OBE, Irish Gds.

COLLATERAL BRANCHES LIVING

Issue of late Hon Henry Gerald Valerian Francis Wellesley, 2nd son of 3rd Earl, *b* 1907; *d* 1981: *m* 1st, 1929 (*m diss* 1953), Sabia, da of late Edward Robert Kennedy; 2ndly, 1954 (*m diss* 1955), Nancy Joan, only da of late Bentley Collingwood Hilliam, of The White Cottage, Bank, Lyndhurst, Hants; 3rdly, 1957 (*m diss* 1969), Marina Isobel Sherlock, da of late Capt Rowland Francis Eustace, of Doric House, Bath, formerly wife (i) Capt George James Wellwood Moncreiffe, and (ii) Cmdr John Bremer Richards Horne, DSC, RN, and widow of Lt Robert Charles Dundas; 4thly, 1969, Valerie Rose (Priestown House, Mulhaddart, co Dublin), 2nd da of late Christian Ernest Pitman, CBE, of Doynton House, Doynton, nr Bristol:—
(By 4th *m*) Henry Arthur Winston Butler, *b* 1970. —— Richard Valerian, *b* 1972.

(In remainder to Barony of Cowley of Wellesley)

Grandson of late Gerald Edward Wellesley, son of late Hon William Henry George Wellesley, 2nd son of 1st Baron Cowley of Wellesley;—
Issue of late Capt Gerald Valerian Wellesley, MC, *b* 1885, *d* 1961: *m* 1931, Elizabeth Thornton, (who *m* 3rdly, 1965, Basil Harvey, and *d* 1981), da of Otho Ball, of Chicago, USA, and formerly wife of Quintin Holland Gilbey:—
Julian Valerian, *b* 1933: *m* 1965, Elizabeth Joan, da of Cyril Stocken, and formerly wife of David Hall, and has issue living, William Valerian, *b* 1966, — Kate Elizabeth, *b* 1970. *Residence* – Tidebrook Manor, Wadhurst, Sussex.

PREDECESSORS – (1) *Hon Sir* HENRY Wellesley, GCB, 5th son of 1st Earl of Mornington, and brother of Marquess Wellesley and 1st Duke of Wellington: *b* 1773: an eminent diplomatist; *cr Baron Cowley of Wellesley* (peerage of United Kingdom) 1828: *m* 1st, 1803 (*m diss* 1810), Lady Charlotte Cadogan, who *d* 1853; she *m* 2ndly, 1810, (1st Marquess of Anglesey), da of 1st Earl Cadogan; 2ndly, 1816, Lady Georgiana Charlotte Augusta Cecil, who *d* 1860, da of 1st Marquess of Salisbury; *d* 1847; *s* by his son (2) HENRY RICHARD CHARLES, 2nd Baron, KG, GCB, PC, DCL; *b* 1804; was Min Plen in Switzerland 1848-49; Envoy Extraor, and Min Plen at Frankfort 1849-51, and to Germanic Confederation 1851-52, and Ambassador Extraor, and Min Plen to France 1852-67; *cr Viscount Dangan* and *Earl Cowley* (peerage of United Kingdom) 1857: *m* 1833, Hon Olivia Cecilia Fitzgerald de Ros, who *d* 1885, da of Charlotte (in her own right), Baroness de Ros; *d* 15 July 1884; *s* by his son (3) WILLIAM HENRY WELLESLEY, 2nd Earl, *b* 1834; Lieut-Col Coldstream Guards: *m* 1863, Emily Gwendolin, who *d* 1932, da of Col Thomas Peers Williams, MP, of Temple House, Great Marlow; *d* 1895; *s* by his son (4) HENRY ARTHUR MORNINGTON, 3rd Earl, *b* 1886: *m* 1st, 1889 (*m diss* 1897), Lady Violet Nevill, who *d* 1910, da of 1st Marquess of Abergavenny; 2ndly, 1905 (*m diss* 1913), Hon Millicent Florence Eleanor, da of the 1st Baron Nunburnholme, and formerly wife of Sir Charles Edward Cradock-Hartopp, 5th Bt; 3rdly, 1914, Clare Florence Mary, who *d* 1949, da of Sir Francis George Stapleton, 8th Bt; *d* 1919; *s* by his son (5) CHRISTIAN ARTHUR, 4th Earl, *b* 1890: *m* 1st (in New York, USA), 1914 (*m diss* 1933), Mae Pickard (an actress), of Memphis, Tennessee, USA, who *d* 1946; 2ndly (at Reno, Nevada) 1933, Mary (Elsie) May HIMES, of San Francisco, Calif, USA; *d* 1962; *s* by his son (6) DENIS ARTHUR, BEM, 5th Earl, *b* 1921; Chm and Managing Dir of City Prudential Building Soc 1962-65: *m* 1st, 1944 (*m diss* 1950), Elizabeth Anne, da of late Pelham Rawstorn Papillon, DSO, of Crowhurst, Sussex, and widow of Fl-Lt Stephen Alers Hankey, RAF; 2ndly, 1950, Mrs Annette Nancy Doughty Simmonds, who *d* as the result of a motor accident 1959, da of Maj J. J. O'Hara; 3rdly, 1961, Janet Elizabeth Mary (who *m* 2ndly, 1976 (*m diss* 1981), Piers Dixon), da of Ramiah Doraswamy Aiyar, FRCS, of Ystrad, Denbigh, N Wales; *d* 1968; *s* by his only son (7) RICHARD FRANCIS, 6th Earl, *b* 1946: *m* 1971, Maria Delia (who *m* 2ndly, 1980, Maj Robin James Stirling Bullock-Webster), yr da of Enrique Buenaño, of Vicente Lopez, 2602 7° A, Buenos Aires; *d* 1975; *s* by his uncle (8) GARRET GRAHAM, 7th Earl, and present peer; also Viscount Dangan, and Baron Cowley of Wellesley.

COX, BARONESS (Cox) (Life Baroness 1982)

CAROLINE ANNE COX, da of late Robert John McNeill Love, of Sewards, Brickendon, Hertford; *b* 7 July 1937; *ed* Channing Sch, Highgate, and Lond Univ (BSc Hons Sociology, MSc Economics); Head of Sociology Dept, N Lond Polytechnic, 1974-77, Dir Nursing Educn Research Unit, Chelsea Coll, Lond Univ 1977-84; a Baroness in Waiting April-Aug 1985; *cr Baroness Cox*, of Queensbury, in Greater London (Life Baroness) 1982: *m* 1959, Murray Newell Cox, and has issue.

Arms – Azure a sword in fess the blade couped at the point argent the hilt pommel and quillons to the sinister or between two ancient lamps also or enflamed proper. Supporters – *Dexter*, a horse argent crined and hoofed or: *sinister*, an unicorn argent its horn or crined and unguled gold.
Residences – The White House, Wyke Hall, Gillingham, Dorset SP8 4NS; 1 Arnellan House, 144-146 Slough Lane, Kinsbury, NW9. *Club* – Royal Commonwealth Society.

SONS LIVING

Hon Robin Michael COX McNEILL LOVE, *b* 1959; *ed* Kingsbury High Sch, and The Royal Free Hosp Sch of Medicine (MB BS); Surg Lt Cdr RN, Prin Med Officer HMY Britannia: *m* 1985, Penelope Jane, da of Dr Richard Michael Griffin, of 64 Warwick Rd, Bishops Stortford, Herts.
Hon Jonathan Murray, *b* 1962; *ed* Kingsbury High Sch.

DAUGHTER LIVING

Hon Philippa Ruth Dorothy, *b* 1965; *ed* Channing Sch, Highgate.

COZENS-HARDY, BARONY OF (Cozens-Hardy) (Extinct 1975)
(Name and Title pronounced "Kuzzens-Hardy")

DAUGHTERS LIVING OF THIRD BARON

Hon Beryl Gladys, OBE, *b* 1911; formerly JP for Norfolk; Chm of World Cttee, World Assocn of Girl Guides and Girl Scouts 1972-75; OBE (Civil) 1971. *Residence* – The Glebe, Letheringsett, Holt, Norfolk NR25 7YA.

Hon Helen Rosemary, *b* 1918: *m* 1953, Brig Douglas Vandeleur Phelps, TD, JP, DL, who *d* 1988, and has an adopted son and da, John Edward Vandeleur, *b* 1961, — Laura Douglas, *b* 1959. *Residence* – Grove Farm House, Langham, Holt, Norfolk NR25 7BU.

CRAIG OF RADLEY, BARON (Craig) (Life Baron 1991)

DAVID BROWNRIGG CRAIG, GCB, OBE, son of late Maj Francis Brownrigg Craig, of Dublin; *b* 17 Sept 1929; *ed* Radley, and Lincoln Coll, Oxford; Commn'd RAF 1951, AOC No 1 Gp RAF Strike Command 1978-80, Vice-Chief of Air Staff 1980-82, AOC-in-C Strike Command and C-in-C UKAF 1982-85, Chief of Air Staff 1985-88, Chief of Defence Staff 1988-91, and Marshal of the RAF 1988; *cr* OBE 1967, CB 1978, KCB 1980, GCB 1984, and *Baron Craig of Radley*, of Helhoughton, co Norfolk (Life Baron) 1991: *m* 1955, Elisabeth June, da of late Charles James Derenburg, of W Byfleet, Surrey, and has issue.

Arms – Ermine, an arrow in bend gules feathered or, the point upwards proper, transfixing a mullet vert, over all on a chevron sable three delta figures argent. **Crest** – Rising from an astral crown or a knight on horseback in full armour, his dexter hand holding a broken tilting spear, all proper, his helm surmounted by three ostrich plumes gules, argent and sable. **Supporters** – On either side a double-headed eagle wings displayed per pale gules and azure, beaked and legged or, that to the dexter charged on the breast with two keys in saltire wards upwards also gold and that to the sinister charged on the breast with a rose argent barbed and seeded proper; a compartment comprising a grassy mount traversed palewise by a runway both proper bordered by four crosses formy gules.
Address – House of Lord, SW1A 0PW.

SON LIVING

Hon Christopher Charles Brownrigg, *b* 1957; *ed* Radley, and Jesus Coll, Camb: *m* 1981, Marilyn Ashmead. *Address* – c/o Royal Bank of Scotland, 9 Pall Mall, SW1Y 5LX.

DAUGHTER LIVING

Hon Susan Elisabeth, *b* 1960.

CRAIGAVON, VISCOUNT (Craig) (Viscount UK 1927, Bt UK 1918)
(Title pronounced "Craigavvon")

JANRIC FRASER CRAIG, 3rd Viscount, and 3rd Baronet; *b* 9 June 1944; *s* 1974; *ed* Eton, and London Univ (BA, BSc); FCA.

Arms – Gules, a fesse ermine between three bridges of as many arches proper. **Crest** – A demi-lion rampant per fesse gules and sable, holding in the dexter paw a mullet or. **Supporters** – *Dexter*, a Constable of the Ulster special Constabulary, his hand resting on a rifle; *sinister* a Private of the Royal Ulster Rifles, armed and accoutred, both proper.
Address – House of Lords, London SW1.

SISTERS LIVING

Hon Janitha Stormont, *b* 1940: *m* 1965, Gordon Robert MacInnes, ICSA, and has issue living, Avila, *b* 1967, — Córdova, *b* 1971, — Jimena, *b* 1975.

Hon Jacaranda Fiona (23 Kelso Place, W8 5QG), *b* 1949: *m* 1972 (*m diss* 1983), Dudley Francis MacDonald, and has issue living, Toby James Francis, *b* 1975, — Rose Carole, *b* 1978.

WIDOW LIVING OF SECOND VISCOUNT

(ANGELA) FIONA (*Viscountess Craigavon*), da of late Percy Tatchell, MRCS, LRCP: *m* 1939, the 2nd Viscount, who *d* 1974.

COLLATERAL BRANCH LIVING

Issue of late Maj Hon (Patrick William) Dennis Craig, MBE, yr son of 1st Viscount, b 1906, d 1972: m 1st, 1931 (m diss 1935), Aline Margaret Mary McLaren, da of late J. Cumming; 2ndly, 1947, Marjorie Joy, who d 1974, da of Algernon Cecil Newton, RA, and formerly wife of late Igor Vinogradoff:—
(By 1st m) Deirdre, b 1931: m 1st, 1951 (m diss 1959), Jonathan Craven, late 9th Lancers; 2ndly, 1959, Cyril Vernon Connolly, CBE, writer, who d 1974; 3rdly, 1977, Peter Chad Tigar Levi, Prof of Poetry at Oxford Univ since 1984, of Austin's Farm, Stonesfield, Oxford, and has issue living (by 1st m), Simon James (Shepherd's Cottage, Tilton Farm, W Firle, Lewes, Sussex), b 1954; ed Eton, — Sarah, b 1952: m 1973 (m diss 1983), Martin J. Bradbury, and has issue living, Arthur John b 1976, Jack Daniel b 1978, — (by 2nd m), Matthew Vernon, b 1970, — Cressida Louisa Vernon, b 1960; journalist: m 1st, 1982 (m diss 1983), Adrian A. Gill; 2ndly, 1985, Charles Alexander Burnell Hudson, of Wick Manor, Wick, Pershore, Worcs, and has issue living, Gabriel Charles More b 1994, Violet Isobel Connolly b 1988, Ellen Rose b 1990.

PREDECESSORS – (1) JAMES CRAIG, PC, LLD, DCL, DL, 6th son of late James Craig, JP, of Craigavon and Tyrella, co Down; b 1871; was Treasurer of HM Household 1916-18, Parliamentary Sec to Min of Pensions 1919-20, Financial Sec to Admiralty 1920-21, and Prime Min of N Ireland 1921-40; sat as MP for E Down Div of Down Co (U and Tariff Reformer) 1906-18, and for Mid Div thereof 1918-21, and for Down co (U) in Parliament of N Ireland 1921-29, and for N Down Div of Down co 1929-40; cr a Baronet 1918, and Viscount Craigavon, of Stormont, co Down (peerage of United Kingdom) 1927: m 1905, Dame Cecil Mary Nowell Dering, DBE, who d 1960, da of late Sir Daniel Alfred Anley Tupper, MVO, formerly Assist Comptroller of Lord Chamberlain's Depart and Sergeant-at-Arms to HM King George V; d 1940; s by his son (2) JAMES, 2nd Viscount; b 1906: m 1939, (Angela) Fiona da of late Percy Tatchell, MRCS, LRCP; d 1974; s by his son (3) JANRIC FRASER, 3rd Viscount and present peer.

CRAIGMYLE, BARON (Shaw) (Baron UK 1929)

Mercy, Fidelity, Right

THOMAS DONALD MACKAY SHAW, 3rd Baron; b 17 Nov 1923; s 1944; ed Eton, and Trin Coll, Oxford; 1939-45 War as Sub-Lt (A) RNVR; Kt Grand Cross of Obedience, Sovereign Mil Order of Malta (Pres British Assocn 1989-95); Kt Cmdr with Star, Order of Pius IX 1993 KStJ: m 1955, Anthea Esther Christine Theresa, da of late Edward Charles Rich, of 31 Yeomans Row, SW3, and has issue.

Arms – Ermine, a fir tree issuing out of a mount in base proper, between two piles azure, issuing from a chief gules charged with a scroll argent, its seal pendant proper between two lymphads or. Crest – A demi-savage holding in his dexter hand a club resting on his shoulder proper. Supporters – Dexter, a lion rampant gules; sinister, a kangaroo proper.
Residences – 18 The Boltons, SW10 9SY; Scottas, Knoydart, Inverness-shire PH41 4PL.

SONS LIVING

Hon THOMAS COLUMBA, b 19 Oct 1960: m 1987, (Katharine) Alice, 2nd da of David Floyd, OBE, of Priory Close, Combe Down, Bath, and has issue living, Alexander Francis, b 1 July 1988, — Finnian Donald, b 1990, — Calum Edward, b 1993. Residence – Court Farm, St Catherine, Bath BA1 8HA.
Hon Justin Edward Magnus, b 1965; ed Eton, and Gonville and Caius Coll, Camb. Residence – 32 Thurloe Sq, SW7 2SD.
Hon (Alexander) Joseph (Ranald), b 1971; ed Ampleforth, and St Benet's Hall, Oxford.

DAUGHTERS LIVING

Hon Alison Margaret, b 1956; ed Harvard Univ (BA 1979), and Antioch Univ (MA 1991). Residence – 6/6 Collingham Gdns, SW5 0HW.
Hon Catriona (Kate) Mary, b 1958: m 1986, Dr Brian Irial Patrick MacGreevy, elder son of late Dr Brian MacGreevy, of Onslow Sq, SW7, and has issue living, Ivo Alexander Patrick, b 1987, — Hubert Donald Brian, b 1989, — Christabel Elizabeth Anthea, b 1991, — Flora Catherine Mary, b 1993. Residence – 1 Fernshaw Rd, SW10 0TB.
Hon Madeleine Claire, b 1963.

SISTERS LIVING

Hon (Margaret) Jean, b 1915: m 1949, Shirl Mussell, who d 1956, and has issue living, Anabel Margaret, b 1954: m 1978, Francisco Parra, — Lisabel Jean, b 1956. Residence – Dyke Croft, Ravenglass, Cumbria CA18 1RN.
Hon Thalia Mary, b 1918: m 1939, Winton Basil Dean, and has issue living, Stephen Nicholas Winton (Fairnilee, Galashiels, Selkirkshire TD1 3PR), b 1946; ed Seaford Coll, and Kent Univ, — Diana Rosamund Thalia (adopted da), b 1955: m 1978, Michael William Bracewell, of 49 Windsor Rd, Kew, Surrey TW9 2EJ. Residence – Hambledon Hurst, Godalming, Surrey GU8 4HF.
Hon Elspeth Ruth, b 1921: m 1945, Archibald James Florence Macdonald, JP, who d 1983, and has issue living, Michael Christopher Archibald, b 1947; ed Univ Coll Sch, and Merton Coll, Oxford: m 1979 (m diss 1989), C. Ann, da of Rodney G. Searight, — Ian Alexander James (Coldred Court Cottage, Coldred, nr Dover, Kent CT15 5AQ), b 1950; ed Univ Coll Sch, and Atlantic Coll. Residence – 22 Heath Drive, Hampstead, NW3 7SB.

PREDECESSORS – (1) Rt Hon THOMAS SHAW, PC, KC, LLD, son of Alexander Shaw, of Dunfermline, Fifeshire; b 1850; was Solicitor-Gen for Scotland 1894-5, and Lord Advocate 1905-9: MP for Hawick Dist (L) 1892-1909; became a Lord of Appeal in Ordinary with title of Baron Shaw, of Dunfermline, co Fife (Life Baron) 1909; cr Baron Craigmyle, of Craigmyle, co Aberdeen (Peerage of United Kingdom) 1929: m 1879, Elsie Stephen, who d 1939, da of George Forrest, of Ludquharn, Aberdeenshire; d 1937; s by his son (2) ALEXANDER, 2nd Baron; b 1883; sat as MP for Kilmarnock Dist (L) 1915-18, and for Kilmarnock Div of Buteshire and Ayrshire 1918-23; m 1913, Lady Margaret Cargill Mackay, who d 1958, el da of 1st Earl of Inchcape; d 1944; s by his son (3) THOMAS DONALD MACKAY, 3rd Baron and present peer.

CRAIGTON, BARONY OF (Browne) (Extinct 1993)

WIDOW LIVING OF LIFE BARON

EILEEN HUMPHREY (*Baroness Craigton*), da of Henry Whitford Nolan, of London: *m* 1950, as his 2nd wife, Group Capt Baron Craigton, CBE, PC, who *d* 1993. *Residence* – Friary House, Friary Island, Wraysbury, Bucks.

Cranborne, Viscount; son of Marquess of Salisbury.

CRANBROOK, EARL OF (Gathorne-Hardy) (Earl UK 1892)
(Name pronounced "Gaythorn-Hardy")

Armed with hardy faith

GATHORNE GATHORNE-HARDY, 5th Earl; *b* 20 June 1933; *s* 1978; *ed* Eton, and Corpus Christi Coll, Camb (BA, MA), PhD Birmingham 1960, Hon DSc Aberdeen 1989; late Lt RA (TA); OStJ, FLS, FZS, C Biol; DL Suffolk; Assist Sarawak Museum 1956-58, and Fellow Jajasan Siswa Lokantara, Indonesia 1960-61, and Lect in Zoology, Univ of Malaya, Kuala Lumpur 1961-70; editor of *Ibis* 1973-80; Suffolk Coastal District Councillor 1976-83; Chm Panel of Enquiry into Shooting and Angling 1976-79; Pres Suffolk Trust for Nature Conservation since 1979, Member R Commn on Environmental Pollution 1981-92; author of *Mammals of Borneo*, *Wild Mammals of Malaya*, *Riches of the Wild: Mammals of SE Asia*, ed *Key Environments: Malaysia*, and co-author of *Birds of the Malay Peninsula*, vol 5, and *Belalong: a tropical rainforest*; Trustee BM (Nat Hist) 1982-86; Member Natural Environmental Research Council 1982-88, Board of Anglian Water since 1987, Broads Authority since 1988, and Harwich Haven Authority since 1989: *m* 1967, Caroline, da of late Col Ralph George Edward Jarvis, of Doddington Hall, Lincoln (E Clanwilliam, colls), and has issue.

Arms – Quarterly, 1st and 4th argent, on a bend invected plain, cottised gules, three catherine wheels or; on a chief of the second as many leopards' faces of the third, *Hardy;* 2nd and 3rd, per pale argent and or, a bend company azure and gules between two pellets, each within an annulet sable, *Gathorne.* **Crest** – 1st, a dexter arm embowed in armour proper, garnished or entwined with a branch of oak vert, charged with two catherine wheels, the one above and the other below the elbow gules, the hand grasping a dragon's head erased proper, *Hardy;* 2nd, in front of a wolf's head erased argent, a staff reguly fessewise or, *Gathorne.* **Supporters** – On either side a leopard guardant proper, gorged with a collar gules, therefrom suspended an escutcheon of the last, charged with a catherine wheel or.
Address – c/o House of Lords, SW1A 0PW.

SONS LIVING

(JOHN) JASON (*Lord Medway*), *b* 26 Oct 1968; *ed* Woodbridge Sch, and Pembroke Coll, Oxford (BA).
Hon Argus Edward, *b* 1973; *ed* Woodbridge Sch, Gresham's Sch, King's Coll, London, and Trin Coll, Dublin.

DAUGHTER LIVING

Lady Flora, *b* 1971; *ed* Woodbridge Sch, Bryanston, and Emmanuel Coll, Cambridge (BA).

BROTHER LIVING

Hon Hugh, *b* 1941; *ed* Eton and Corpus Christi Coll,Camb (MA): *m* 1971, Caroline Elisabeth, da of William Nigel Ritchie, of Mariners, Bradfield, Berks (*see* B Ritchie of Dundee, colls), and has issue living, Frederick Jasper, *b* 1972, — Alfred, *b* 1978, — Alice, *b* 1974, — Daisy, *b* 1977. *Residence* – The Hall Farm, Great Glemham, Saxmundham, Suffolk.

SISTERS LIVING

Lady Juliet (The White House, Rooks Hill, Underriver, Sevenoaks, Kent), *b* 1934: *m* 1958 (*m diss* 1970), Charles Colin Simpson, TD, and has issue living, Charles Duncan, *b* 1962, — Edward Colin, *b* 1965, — Fidelity Anne, *b* 1960, — Amanda Juliet, *b* 1964.
Lady Sophia Catherine, *b* 1936: *m* 1957, Simon Robert Jasper Meade, of Pen-y-lan, Meifod, Powys, and has issue (*see* E Clanwilliam, colls).
Lady Christina, *b* 1940: *m* 1967, Stanley Edward Letanka, MRCS, LRCP, of Pepsall End, Pepperstock, Luton, and has issue living, Peter Edward, *b* 1974, — Stella, *b* 1968, — Florence Ruth, *b* 1969.

AUNT LIVING (*daughter of 3rd Earl*)

Lady Anne Catherine Dorothy, *b* 1911: *m* 1938, George Heywood Hill, of Snape Priory, Saxmundham, Suffolk (*see* Johnstone, Bt, colls, 1959 Edn), who *d* 1986, and has issue living, Harriet, *b* 1943: *m* 1st, 1963 (*m diss* 1981), Timothy John Behrens;

2ndly, 1985, Simon Frazer, and has issue living (by 1st *m*), Algernon Kenneth *b* 1966, Charlie Corrado Heywood *b* 1979, Frances Anne *b* 1963, — Rabea (Lucy), *b* 1946: *m* 1970, Abdul Azis (George James) Redpath, of The Tithe Barn, Stoke Holy Cross, Norwich, and has issue living, Justin Abd'Allah *b* 1971, Abdul Razzaq *b* 1977, Hafidha *b* 1975, Aisha Iman *b* 1983, Khayria *b* 1985.

WIDOW LIVING OF SON OF THIRD EARL

Mary Catherine (21 Cranebrook, Manor Rd, Twickenham, Middx), da of late Bernard Joseph Smartt: *m* 1974, as his 2nd wife, Cdr Hon Antony Gathorne Gathorne-Hardy, MB, ChB, who *d* 1976 (infra).

WIDOW LIVING OF FOURTH EARL

FIDELITY (*Dowager Countess of Cranbrook*), OBE, JP (Red House Farm, Great Glemham, Saxmundham, Suffolk), da of Hugh Exton Seebohm, JP, of Poynders End, Hitchin: *m* 1932, as his 2nd wife, the 4th Earl, CBE, JP, DL, who *d* 1978.

COLLATERAL BRANCHES LIVING

Issue of late Cdr Hon Antony Gathorne Gathorne-Hardy, MB, ChB, RN, yst son of 3rd Earl, *b* 1907, *d* 1976: *m* 1st 1931, Ruth Elizabeth, who *d* 1973, da of Cdr Arthur Penton Napier Thorowgood, DSO, RN (*see* Hunter-Blair, Bt, colls, 1936 Edn); 2ndly, 1974, Mary Catherine (ante), da of late Bernard Joseph Smartt:—
(By 1st *m*) Jonathan Gathorne (31 Blacksmith's Yard, Binham, Fakenham, Norfolk NR21 0AL) *b* 1933: writer: *m* 1st, 1963 (*m diss* 1977), Sabrina Viola, da of late Hon David Francis Tennant, of El Palomar, Mijas, Malaga, Spain (*see* B Glenconner, colls); 2ndly, 1985, Nicolette, da of Dr Kenneth William Cripps Sinclair-Loutit, MBE, and has issue living (by 1st *m*), Benjamin, *b* 1967: *m* 1992, Philippa, yr da of David Heimann, and of Mrs Desmond Corcoran, — Jenny, *b* 1965. —— Samuel Gathorne (Old Bullock Sheds, Great Glemham, Saxmundham), *b* 1936: *m* 1965, Grace D'Cruz, and has issue living, Robert Dee, *b* 1973, — Lydia, *b* 1964, — Penelope Rose, *b* 1965. —— Elizabeth Rose, *b* 1949: *m* 1974, Ian Richmond Battye, MB, BS, and has issue living, Thomas Gathorne, *b* 1975, — Nell Aurore, *b* 1977.

Issue of late Lt-Col Hon Nigel Charles Gathorne-Hardy, DSO, yst son of 2nd Earl, *b* 1880, *d* 1958: *m* 1910, Doris Cecilia Featherston, who *d* 1973, da of late Hon Sir Charles John Johnston, MLC, of Karori, Wellington, New Zealand:—
Margaret Doris (*Lady Cameron of Lochiel*), *b* 1913: *m* 1939, Col Sir Donald Hamish Cameron of Lochiel, KT, CVO, TD, late Comdg Lovat Scouts (*see* D Montrose, 1976 Edn), and has issue living, Donald Angus yr of Lochiel, *b* 1946; *ed* Harrow, and Ch Ch, Oxford; DL Lochaber, Inverness, and Badenoch and Strathspey since 1986: *m* 1974, Lady Cecil Nennella Therese Kerr, el da of 12th Marquess of Lothian, and has issue living, Donald Andrew John *b* 1976, Catherine Mary *b* 1975, Lucy Margot Therese *b* 1980, Emily Frances *b* 1986, — John Alastair Nigel, *b* 1954: *m* 1982, Julia R., da of R. C. Wurtzburg, of Kensington Court Place, W8, and has issue living, Hamish *b* 1985, Robert Andrew *b* 1991, Kirsty Anne *b* 1987, — Margaret Anne, *b* 1942: *m* 1968, Timothy E. Nott-Bower, of Buckwood, Chisbury Lane, nr Marlborough, Wilts, son of late Sir John Reginald Hornby Nott-Bower, KCVO, and has issue living, John William *b* 1972, Katherine Margot *b* 1970, — Caroline Marion, *b* 1943: *m* 1967, Blaise Noel Anthony Hardman, of Farley House, Farley Chamberlayne, Romsey, Hants, son of Air Ch Marshal Sir (James) Donald Innes Hardman, GBE, KCB, DFC, and has issue living, Thomas *b* 1977, Jane *b* 1969, Annabel *b* 1971, Elizabeth *b* 1974, Rosanna *b* 1979. *Residence* – Achnacarry, Spean Bridge, Inverness-shire.

PREDECESSORS – (1) *Right Hon* GATHORNE Hardy, GCSI, PC, DCL, LLD, third son of late John Hardy, MP; *b* 1814; Under-Sec of State for Home Depart 1858-9, Pres of Poor Law Board 1866-7, Sec of State for Home Depart 1867-8, for War 1874-8, and for India 1878-80, and Lord Pres of the Council 1885-6 and 1886-92; assumed in 1878, by Roy licence, the additional surname of Gathorne; MP for Leominster (C) 1856-65, and for Univ of Oxford 1865-78; GCSI 1880; cr. *Viscount Cranbrook*, of Hemsted, co Kent (peerage of United Kingdom) 1878, and *Earl of Cranbrook* and *Baron Medway*, of Hemsted, co Kent (peerage of United Kingdom) 1892: *m* 1838, Jane, CI, who *d* 1897, da of James Orr, of Hollywood House, co Down; *d* 1906: *s* by his el son (2) JOHN STEWART, 2nd Earl, *b* 1839; MP for Rye (C) 1868-80, for Mid-Kent 1884-5, and for Kent, Mid, or Medway, Div 1885-92: *m* 1867, Cicely Marguerite Wilhelmina, who *d* 1931, da and heiress of late Joseph Ridgway, of Fairlawn, Kent: *d* 1911: *s* by his el son (3) GATHORNE, 3rd Earl; *b* 1870: *m* 1899, Lady Dorothy Montagu Boyle, who *d* 1968, da of 7th Earl of Glasgow; *d* 1915; *s* by his el son (4) JOHN DAVID, CBE, JP, DL, 4th Earl, *b* 1900; Trustee of British Museum (Natural History), and Member of Nature Conservancy: *m* 1st, 1926 (*m diss* 1931), his cousin, Bridget Cicely, DBE, who *d* 1985, da of Rupert D'Oyly Carte, impressario (*see* E Cranbrook, 1976 Edn); 2ndly, 1932, Fidelity, OBE, JP, da of Hugh Exton Seebohm, JP, of Poynders End, Hitchin; *d* 1978; *s* by his el son (5) GATHORNE, 5th Earl and present peer; also Viscount Cranbrook, and Baron Medway.

Cranley, Viscount; son of Earl of Onslow.

CRANWORTH, BARON (Gurdon) (Baron UK1899)

Virtue flourishes in dangers

PHILIP BERTRAM GURDON, 3rd Baron; *b* 24 May 1940; *s* 1964; *ed* Eton, and Magdalene Coll, Camb; late Lt R Wilts Yeo: *m* 1968, Frances Henrietta, da of late Lord William Walter Montagu Douglas Scott, MC (*see* D Buccleuch, colls), and has issue.

Arms – Sable, three leopards' faces jessant-de-lis or **Crest** – A goat climbing up a rock, all proper. **Supporters** – On either side a rock thereon a goat proper, collared gemelle or
Seat – Grundisburgh Hall, Woodbridge, Suffolk.

SONS LIVING

Hon (SACHA WILLIAM) ROBIN, *b* 12 Aug 1970.
Hon Brampton Charles, *b* 1975.

DAUGHTER LIVING

Hon Louisa-Jane, *b* 1969.

SISTER LIVING

(Raised to the rank of a Baron's daughter 1964)

Hon Jeryl Marcia Sarah, DL (*Hon Lady Smith-Ryland*), *b* 1932; DL Warwicks 1990; CStJ 1981, DStJ 1990: *m* 1952, Sir Charles Mortimer Tollemache Smith-Ryland, KCVO, who *d* 1989, of Sherbourne Park, Warwick, and has issue (*see* B Tollemache, colls).

PREDECESSORS – (1) ROBERT THORNHAGH Gurdon, el son of late Brampton Gurdon, MP, of Letton Hall, Norfolk, and Grundisburgh, Suffolk; *b* 1829; MP for S Norfolk (*L*) 1880-85, and for Norfolk Mid Div (*L*) 1885-6, and (LU) 1886-92 and April to July 1895; *cr Baron Cranworth*, of Letton and Cranworth, co Norfolk (peerage of UK) 1899: *m* 1st, 1862, Harriott Ellin, who *d* 1864, da of Sir William Miles,MP, 1st Bt; 2ndly, 1874, Emily Frances, who *d* 1934, da of Robert Boothby Heathcote; *d* 1902; *s* by his son (2) BERTRAM FRANCIS, KG, MC, 2nd Baron; *b* 1877; Vice-Lieut for Suffolk 1947-64: *m* 1903, Vera Emily, CBE, who *d* 1966, el da of late Arthur William Ridley (V Ridley, colls); *d* 1964; *s* by his grandson (3) PHILIP BERTRAM (yr son of late Hon Robert Brampton Gurdon, who was *ka* in Libya 1942), 3rd Baron, and present peer.

CRATHORNE, BARON (Dugdale) (Baron UK 1959, Bt UK 1945)

By persevering

CHARLES JAMES DUGDALE, 2nd Baron and 2nd Baronet; *b* 12 Sept 1939; *s* 1977; *ed* Eton, and Trin Coll, Camb (MA); FRSA; DL Cleveland 1983; Assist to Pres Parke-Bernet, New York 1965-69; James Dugdale & Associates, London, Independent Fine Art Consultancy Service, since 1969; James Crathorne & Associates since 1980; Member, Productions Cttee Georgian Theatre, Richmond since 1969, and Yorks Regional Cttee Nat Trust 1978-84, and since 1988; Member Court of Leeds Univ since 1985, Conservative Advisory Group on Arts and Heritage since 1988, and Chm The Georgian Group since 1990, etc; Trustee Captain Cook Trust since 1978, and Nat Heritage Memorial Fund since 1992; Dir Blakeney Hotels Ltd since 1981, and Woodhouse Securities Ltd since 1989; author *Edouard Vuillard* (1967), and co-author *Tennant's Stalk* (1973), and *History of Crathorne* (1989): *m* 1970, Sylvia Mary, yr da of Brig Arthur Montgomery, OBE, TD (*see* Montgomery, Bt, colls) and has issue.

Arms – Ermine a cross moline gules between four hurts. **Crest** – A gryphon's head ermine wings endorsed erminois gorged with a collar azure therefrom pendant a cross moline gules. **Supporters** – *Dexter*, a crow sable beaked and membered or in the beak a sprig of blackthorn flowered proper; *sinister*, a stag also sable attired unguled and gorged with a mural crown gold charged on the shoulder with a thistle slipped and leaved also proper.
Residence – Crathorne House, Yarm, Cleveland.

SON LIVING

Hon THOMAS ARTHUR JOHN, *b* 30 Sept 1977.

DAUGHTERS LIVING

Hon Charlotte Patricia, *b* 1972.
Hon Katharine Feodora Nicola, *b* 1980.

BROTHER LIVING

Hon David John (Park House, Crathorne, Yarm, Cleveland), *b* 1942; *ed* Eton, and Trin Coll, Camb (MA): *m* 1972, Susan Louise, yr da of late Lewis A. Powell, and has issue living, Jonathan William Shaun, *b* 1980, — Clare Nancy Louise, *b* 1978.

PREDECESSOR – **(1)** *Rt Hon Sir* THOMAS LIONEL DUGDALE, TD, PC, son of James Lionel Dugdale, of Crathorne, Yorks; *b* 1897; PPS to Rt Hon Sir Philip Cunliffe-Lister, MP 1931-35 and to Rt Hon Stanley Baldwin, MP 1935-37, a Junior Lord of the Treasury 1937-40, Dep Ch Govt Whip and Vice-Chm of Conservative Party Orgn 1941-42 and Chm 1942-44, Min of Agric and Fisheries 1951-54, and UK Member of Gen Assembly, Council of Europe 1958-59 and 1961-65 (Vice-Pres 1962-64); MP for Richmond Div, N Riding of Yorks (*C*) 1929-59; *cr* a Baronet 1945, PC 1951 and *Baron Crathorne*, N Riding of Yorks (peerage of UK) 1959: *m* 1936, Nancy (GATES), OBE, who *d* 1969, da of Sir Charles Tennant, 1st Bt (B Glenconner); *d* 1977; *s* by his el son **(2)** CHARLES JAMES, 2nd Baron, and present peer.

CRAVEN, EARL OF (Craven) (Earl GB 1801)

BENJAMIN ROBERT JOSEPH CRAVEN, 9th Earl; *b* 13 June 1989; *s* 1990.

Arms – Argent, a fesse, between six cross crosslets fitchée, gules. **Crest** – On a chapeau gules, turned up ermine, a griffin statant wings elevated ermine, beaked and membered or. **Supporters** – Two griffins, wings elevated ermine, beaked and membered or.

AUNT LIVING (*daughter of 6th Earl by 2nd marriage*)

Lady Ann Mary Elizabeth, *b* 1959; *ed* — Univ (BA): *m* 1978, Dr Lionel Tarassenko, MA, DPhil, CEng, MIEE, of 2 The Glebe, Cumnor, Oxford, elder son of Sergei Tarassenko, of Swanage, Dorset, and has issue living, Luke Ivan Thomas, *b* 1988, — Simon Robert Serge, *b* 1991, — Naomi Rachel Elizabeth, *b* 1989.

HALF-AUNT LIVING (*daughter of 6th Earl by 1st marriage*)

Lady Sarah Jane, *b* 1940: *m* 1961, David John Trail Thomson Glover, of La Gratitude, 6 De Villiers St, Cape Province 7130, S Africa, and has had issue, Suzanne Gwendoline, *b* 1964, — Priscilla, *b* 1967, *d* 19—, — Vanessa Kate, *b* 1972.

WIDOW LIVING OF SIXTH EARL

ELIZABETH GWENDOLEN TERESA, da of late Robert Sholto Johnstone-Douglas (*see* M Queensberry, colls): *m* 1st, 1954, as his 2nd wife, the 6th Earl, who *d* 1965; 2ndly, 1966, Kenneth Harmood Banner, of Peelings Manor, Pevensey, Sussex.

WIDOW LIVING OF EIGHTH EARL

Virtue consists in action

TERESA MARIA BERNADETTE (*Countess of Craven*), da of Arthur John Downes, of Black Hall, Clane, co Kildare: *m* 1988, the 8th Earl, who *d* 1990, following a motor accident. *Residence* – Hawkwood House, Hawkhurst Lane, Waldron, E Sussex.

COLLATERAL BRANCHES LIVING

Issue of late Major Hon Rupert Cecil Craven, OBE, 2nd son of 3rd Earl, *b* 1870, *d* 1959: *m* 1st, 1898 (*m diss* 1908), Inez, da of George Broom; 2ndly, 1925, Josephine Marguerite, who *d* 1971, da of José Reixach, and widow of Capt Charles William Banbury (B Banbury):—
(By 2nd *m*) RUPERT JOSE EVELYN (Swordly, Bettyhill by Thurso, Caithness KW14 7TA), *b* 22 March 1926; Lt-Cdr RN: *m* 1955, Margaret Campbell, who *d* 1985, da of Alexander Smith, MBE, of Glasgow, and Alness.

Granddaughter of late William George Craven, el son of Hon George Augustus Craven, yr son of 1st Earl:—
Issue of late Augustus William Craven, *b* 1852, *d* 1929: *m* 1st, 1880, Florence Champagné, who *d* 1899, da of Gen Corbet Cotton (V Combermere); 2ndly, 1900, Lilian, da of John Hearn:—
(By 2nd *m*) Violet Lilian Mary (Lullington Manor, Alfriston, Sussex), *b* 1906: *m* 1935, Roland Crosley Wimbush, who *d* 1964, and has issue living, Jennifer, *b* 1940: *m* 1965, James Charles Tempest Bouskell, and has issue living, James Henry Tempest *b* 1968, Louisa Jane *b* 1967: *m* 1994, James Richard Symington.

(In Special remainder to Barony only)

Grandchildren of late Edmund Filmer Craven, grandson of late Fulwar Craven (*b* 1782), grandson of late Charles Craven, brother of 2nd Baron:—
Issue of late Fulwar Craven, *b* 1873, *d* 1956: *m* 1916, Elizabeth A. Wheatley:—
Edmund Filmer (11 Buckley Av, Mount Isa 4825, Cloncurry, Queensland, Australia), *b* 1917; late RAAF: *m* 1944, Ada Clemence Adelaide, da of C. Richardson, of Cloncurry, Queensland, Australia, and has issue living, John Edmund (Unit 2 No 471 6th Av, Kedron 4031, Queensland, Australia), *b* 1946: *m* 1980 (*m diss* 1987), Julie Ann Airie, and has issue living, Jillian Lee *b* 1980. —— Evelyn Caroline, *b* 1929: *m* 1952, Donald Leslie Whitehouse, who *d* 1981, of 58 Alma Rd, Clayfield, Brisbane 4011, Queensland, Australia, and has had issue, Gregory Thomas, *b* 1954: *m* 1990, Kerryn Wilson, and has issue living, Edward Anthony *b* 1991, — Jennifer Lynette, *b* 1953: *m* 1976, Clive Baylis, of London, and *dsp* 1979.

PREDECESSORS – **(1)** *Sir* WILLIAM Craven, Knt, a soldier of renown in the Netherlands under Henry, Prince of Orange, under Gustavus Adolphus, King of Sweden, and in the service of the States of Holland, was a zealous partisan of Charles I and Charles II; *cr Baron Craven*, of Hamstead Marshall, co Berks (peerage of England) 1626, with remainder to his brothers, John and Thomas, *Viscount Craven*, of Uffington, co Berks, with remainder to Sir William Craven, Knt, and Sir Anthony Craven, *Earl of Craven* (peerage of England), 1663, and *Baron Craven*, of Hamstead Marshall, Berks, 1665, with remainder to Sir William Craven, Knt, of Combe Abbey, Warwickshire, son of Thomas Craven, brother of Sir Anthony (ante); *d* unmarried 1697, when all the peerages became extinct except the *cr* of 1665, which devolved upon **(2)** WILLIAM, 2nd Baron, son of Sir William, Knt (ante); *d* 1711; *s* by his son **(3)** WILLIAM, 3rd Baron; *dsp* 1739; *s* by his brother **(4)** FULWAR, 4th Baron; *d* unmarried; *s* by his cousin **(5)** WILLIAM, 5th Baron, son of John, 2nd son of 2nd Baron; *d* 1769; *s* by his nephew **(6)** WILLIAM, 6th Baron; *d* 1791; *s* by his son **(7)** WILLIAM, 7th Baron; a Maj-Gen in the Army, and Lord-Lieut of

Berks; *cr Viscount Uffington* and *Earl of Craven* (peerage of Great Britain) 1801; *d* 1825; *s* by his son **(8)** WILLIAM, 2nd Earl; *b* 1809; Lord-Lieut of Warwickshire; *d* 1866; *s* by his son **(9)** GEORGE GRIMSTON, 3rd Earl; *b* 1841; Lord-Lieut of Berks: *m* 1867, Hon Evelyn Laura, da of 7th Viscount Barrington; *d* 1883; *s* by his son **(10)** WILLIAM GEORGE ROBERT, 4th Earl; *b* 1868; Lord-Lieut of Warwickshire: *m* 1893, Cornelia, who *d* 1961, da of late Bradley Martin, of New York, USA; *d* 1921; *s* by his son **(11)** WILLIAM GEORGE BRADLEY, 5th Earl, *b* 1897; European War 1915-18, as Lieut Hampshire Regt (wounded): *m* 1916, Wilhelmina Mary, who *d* 1974, da of William George, OBE, JP, Town Clerk of Invergordon, Scotland; *d* 1932; *s* by his son **(12)** WILLIAM ROBERT BRADLEY, 6th Earl, *b* 1917: *m* 1st, 1939 (*m diss* 1954), Irene, da of late Ferdinand Richard Holmes Meyrick, MD, of 59 Kensington Court, W8; 2ndly, 1954, Elizabeth Gwendolen Teresa (who *m* 2ndly, 1966, Kenneth Harmood Banner), da of late Robert Sholto Johnstone-Douglas (*see* M Queensberry, colls); *d* 1965; *s* by his el son **(13)** THOMAS ROBERT DOUGLAS, 7th Earl, *b* 1957; *dspl* 1983; *s* by his brother **(14)** SIMON GEORGE, 8th Earl, *b* 1961; student nurse: *m* 1988, Teresa Maria Bernadette, da of Arthur John Downes, of Black Hall, Clane, co Kildare; *d* 1990, following a motor accident; *s* by his only son **(15)** BENJAMIN ROBERT JOSEPH, 9th Earl and present peer; also Viscount Uffington, and Baron Craven.

CRAWFORD and BALCARRES, EARL OF (Lindsay) (Earl S 1398 and 1651)

Suffer bravely

ROBERT ALEXANDER LINDSAY, PC, 29th Earl of Crawford (Premier Earl on Union Roll of Scotland), and 12th Earl of Balcarres; *b* 5 March, 1927; *s* 1975; *ed* Eton, and Trin Coll, Camb; late Lt Gren Gds; PPS to Financial Sec to the Treasury 1955-57, and to Min of Housing and Local Govt 1957-59, Prin Opposition Front Bench Spokesman on Health and Social Security 1967-70; Min of State, Defence 1970-72, and Min of State for Foreign and Commonwealth Affairs 1972-74; Lord Chamberlain to HM Queen Elizabeth the Queen Mother since 1992; MP for Hertford Div of Herts (*C*) 1955-74, and for Welwyn and Hatfield Feb to Oct 1974; Pres Rural Dist Councils Assocn for England and Wales 1959-65; Chm National Assocn of Mental Health 1963-70, Lombard North Central Ltd, and Historic Buildings Council for Scotland 1976-83; a Dir of National Westminster Bank Ltd 1975-88, Vice-Chm Sun Alliance and London Insurance Group since 1975, and Dir of Scottish American Investment Trust 1978-88; First Crown Estate Commissioner 1980-85, Chm Royal Commn on Ancient and Historical Monuments of Scotland since 1985, Crown Trustee and Chm of Board of Nat Library of Scotland since 1990; *cr* PC 1972, and *Baron Balniel, of Pitcorthie, co Fife* (Life Baron), 1974: *m* 1949, Ruth Beatrice, da of Leo Meyer-Bechtler, of 49 Keltenstrasse, Zürich, Switzerland, and has issue.

Arms – Quarterly: 1st and 4th gules, a fesse checky argent and azure, *Lindsay;* 2nd and 3rd or, a lion rampant gules, debruised of a ribbon in bend sable, *Abernethy.* **Crest** – Out of an antique ducal coronet a swan's neck and wings proper. **Supporters** – Two lions rampant guardant gules.
Seat – Balcarres, Colinsburgh, Fife.

SONS LIVING

ANTHONY ROBERT (*Lord Balniel*) (6 Pembridge Place, W2 4XB; *Club* – New (Edinburgh)), *b* 24 Nov 1958; *ed* Eton, and Edinburgh Univ: *m* 1989, Nicola A., yst da of Antony Bicket, of Derwas, Dolwen, N Wales, and has issue:—
    SONS LIVING— *Hon* Alexander Thomas (*Master of Lindsay*), *b* 5 Aug 1991.
    Hon James Antony, *b* 1992.
Hon Alexander Walter, *b* 1961; *ed* Eton; Endure Pursuivant to his father. *Residence* – Studio 5, Neckinger Mills, 162 Abbey St, SE1.

DAUGHTERS LIVING

Lady Bettina Mary, *b* 1950: *m* 1975, Peter Charles Hay Drummond-Hay, of 86 Rowayton Av, Rowayton, Conn 06853, USA, and Le Pestou, Castelsagrat, France (*see* E Kinnoull, colls).
Lady Iona Sina, *b* 1957: *m* 1983, Charles Gerard Mackworth-Young, of 18 The Chase, SW4 0NH (*see* Young, Bt, *cr* 1813, colls).

BROTHER LIVING

Hon Thomas Richard, *b* 1937; *ed* Eton; late 2nd Lieut Scots Gds: *m* 1961, Sarah Virginia, only da of George Nigel Capel Cure, TD, JP, DL (*see* Barry, Bt, colls), and has issue living, Ivan James, *b* 1962: *m* 1992, Julie, da of Mads Gad, of Rolighedsvej 11, 2942 Skodsborg, Denmark, and has issue living, Maximilian James *b* 1993, — Constantine David, *b* 1966, — Jason Richard, *b* 1968, — Alexandra Mary, *b* 1964: *m* 1990, Marcus Basil Ziani de Ferranti (*see* E Eglinton, 1990 Edn), and has issue living, a son *b* 1994, Polly *b* 1992, — Sophia Victoria, *b* 1971. *Residence* – The Old Rectory, Ashmore, Salisbury, Wilts, SP5 5AG. *Club* – Brook's.

UNCLE LIVING (Son of 27th Earl)

Hon James Louis, *b* 1906; *ed* Eton, and Magdalen Coll, Oxford; formerly Maj King's R Rifle Corps; unsuccessfully contested S-E Div of Bristol (*C*) Nov 1950, and Oct 1951; sat as MP for N Div of Devon May 1955 to Sept 1959; defeated there Oct 1959: *m* 1933, Hon Bronwen Mary Scott-Ellis, da of 8th Baron Howard de Walden, and has issue living, Hugh John Alexander (The Old Rectory, Litton Cheney, Dorchester, Dorset DT2 9AH), *b* 1934; *ed* Eton, and Magdalen Coll, Oxford;

Chartered Accountant; late 2nd Lt Black Watch: *m* 1961, Constance Carolyn, yr da of Sir Charles James Buchanan, 4th Bt, and has issue living, David Charles (26 Avondale Park Gdns, W11) *b* 1962; *ed* Eton, and Southampton Univ; CA, Alastair James (11 Barlby Gdns, W10) *b* 1964; *ed* Eton, and Southampton Univ; CA: *m* 1992, Heather J., da of Denis Adair, of New-townabbey, co Antrim, Robert Hugh *b* 1967; *ed* Eton, and Reading Univ; Capt Scots Gds, Serena Clare *b* 1970; *ed* St Andrews Univ, and Homerton Coll, Camb, — Alexander Thomas (Cavalry Club), *b* 1936; *ed* Eton, and Magdalen Coll, Oxford; Col 17th/21st Lancers: *m* 1966, Jessie Miranda Cecilia, da of Col John Anthony Tristram Barstow, DSO, TD, DL, and has issue living, James Alexander Tristram *b* 1968; *ed* Eton, Roderick Charles *b* 1970; *ed* Eton, Felix Thomas *b* 1973; *ed* Eton, — Stephen James (Invermoidart, Acharacle, Argyll), *b* 1940; *ed* Eton; Lt-Col Black Watch: *m* 1966, Margaret Ann, da of late Maj J. H. C. Powell, and has issue living, Richard Stephen *b* 1969; *ed* Eton, and St Catherine's Coll, Oxford, Charles Ludovic *b* 1974; *ed* Eton, and St Andrews Univ, Andrew James Ronald *b* 1977; *ed* Eton, Jane Margaret *b* 1966; *ed* Edinburgh Univ: *m* 1991, Charles R. S. Graham, of 43 Moreton Terrace, SW1V 2NS, son of Maj Stephen Graham, of Flint House, Goodworth, Clatford, Andover, Hants, — Julia Margaret, *b* 1941: *m* 1963, Peter Barton, of 3 Aubrey Rd, W8 7JJ, and has issue living, Henry James *b* 1967; *ed* Eton, and Durham Univ, Christopher Charles *b* 1970; *ed* Eton, and Durham Univ, Fenella Jane *b* 1965; *ed* Exeter Univ. *Residence* – Sutton Manor, Sutton Scotney, nr Winchester, Hants S021 3JX.

AUNTS LIVING (*Daughters of 27th Earl*)

Lady (Cynthia) Anne, *b* 1904: *m* 1st, 1931, Per Erik Folke Arnander, who *d* 1933, 1st Sec, Swedish Legation, Rome; 2ndly, 1934, Giovanni Fummi, who *d* 1970, and has issue living (by 1st *m*) Christopher James Folke (Old Wharf, Shillingford, Oxon), *b* 1932: *m* 1961, Pamela Primrose, da of David McKenna, CBE (*see* E Albemarle), and has issue living, Conrad David Folke *b* 1963, Michael Theodore Per *b* 1964, Magnus William Thomas *b* 1970, Katharine Louise *b* 1967, — (by 2nd *m*) Francesca Giovanna Maria, *b* 1935; *ed* St Andrew's Univ (MA): *m* 1961, Christopher Robin St Quintin Wall, of The Apple Orchard, Bradenham, High Wycombe, Bucks (*see* E Peel, colls, 1972-73 Edn), and has issue living, Dominic John St Quintin *b* 1964, Camilla Mary *b* 1962: *m* 1990, Charles Ranfurly Plunkett-Ernle-Erle-Drax, of High Fogrigg, Bardon Mill, Hexham, Northumberland (*see* B Dunsany, colls). *Residence* – 10 Lochmore House, Cundy St Flats, Ebury St, SW1.
Lady Mary Lilian (*Dowager Viscountess Dilhorne*), *b* 1910: *m* 1930, 1st Viscount Dilhorne, who *d* 1980. *Address* – 6 King's Bench Walk, Temple, EC4.
Lady Barbara, *b* 1915: *m* 1939, Col Richard Lumley Hurst, R Sussex Regt TA, Bar-at-law, who *d* 1962, son of Sir Cecil James Barrington Hurst, GCMG, KCB, and has issue living, Robert Andrew, *b* 1945: *m* 1977, Cristina, el da of J. J. Couper Edwards, of Rusper Nunnery, Horsham, W Sussex, and has issue living, Andrew *b* 1981, Sarah *b* 1978, Mary *b* 1982, — Elizabeth, *b* 1940: *m* 1967, Angus Hugh Gilroy, Member Queen's Body Guard for Scotland (Royal Company of Archers), of Grainingfold, Five Oaks, Billingshurst, W Sussex, and has issue living, Fergus Hugh *b* 1969, Margaret Cecilia *b* 1970, — Cecilia Barbara, *b* 1944: *m* 1968, Rt Hon Alastair Robertson Goodlad, MP, of Common Farm, Rhuddal Heath, Tarporley, Cheshire, and has issue living, Magnus James *b* 1972; *ed* Eton, and Oriel Coll, Oxford, William Duff *b* 1974; *ed* Eton and Pembroke Coll, Oxford, — Katharine Constance, *b* 1948: *m* 1st, 1975, Donald M. Corbett, who *d* 1987; 2ndly, 1991, as his 2nd wife, (Peter) Noel (Houldsworth) Gibbs (*see* B Dulverton, colls), of Combend Manor, Elkstone, Cheltenham, Glos GL53 9PT, and has issue living (by 1st *m*), Alexander James *b* 1977, Clare Barbara *b* 1978. *Residence* – Porters Farm, Rusper, Horsham, Sussex, RH12 4QA.

WIDOW LIVING OF SON OF TWENTY-EIGHTH EARL

Lady Amabel Mary Maud YORKE (*Lady Amabel Lindsay*) (12 Lansdowne Rd, W11), eldest da of 9th Earl of Hardwicke: *m* 1955, Hon Patrick Lindsay, who *d* 1986, and has issue (see colls infra).

WIDOW LIVING OF TWENTY-EIGHTH EARL

MARY KATHARINE (*Mary, Countess of Crawford and Balcarres*), (Balcarres, Colinsburgh, Fife), da of late Col Rt Hon Lord Richard Frederick Cavendish, CB, CMG (*see* D Devonshire, colls): *m* 1925, the 28th Earl, who *d* 1975.

COLLATERAL BRANCHES LIVING

Issue of late Hon Patrick Lindsay, 2nd son of 28th Earl of Crawford, *b* 1928, *d* 1986: *m* 1955, Lady Amabel Mary Maud Yorke (ante), eldest da of 9th Earl of Hardwicke:—
Ludovic Alexander, *b* 1957. —— James Richard, *b* 1961. —— Valentine, *b* 1962: *m* 1990, Hayley, elder da of Rex Whittome, of Willowhayne House, Sutton, nr Wansford, Peterborough. —— Laura Mary, *b* 1956.

Granddaughter of late Hon Walter Patrick Lindsay, 2nd son of 26th Earl of Crawford:—
Issue of late Kenneth Andrew Lindsay, *b* 1903, *d* 1970: *m* 1928, Kathleen Mary, who *d* 1975, da of H. E. Lovemore, formerly of Queenstown, S Africa:—
Patricia Jane, *b* 1932: *m* 1956, Noël Gwynne Harpur, of 19 Surrey St, Claremont, Cape Town 7700, and has issue living, Patrick Leslie Gwynne, *b* 1957, — Colin Andrew Lindsay, *b* 1959.

Issue of late Maj Hon Robert Hamilton Lindsay, 3rd son of 26th Earl of Crawford, *b* 1874, *d* 1911: *m* 1903, Mary Janet, who *d* 1960, da of Sir William John Clarke, 1st Bt:—
Robert William Ludovic, OBE (Edzell, Mount Macedon, Victoria 3441, Australia), *b* 1905; *ed* Eton, and RMC Sandhurst; Gren Gds 1925-45, Trans-Jordan Frontier Force 1932-34 (ret as Maj); a Member of House of Representatives of Australia 1954-66; ret 1966; OBE (Civil) 1971: *m* 1946, Rosemary Catherine Marion, only da of Sir Robert Wilson Knox (*see* Clarke, Bt, *cr* 1882, 1963 Edn), and has had issue, Robin David, *b* 1947, *d* 1965, — Andrew William Michael, *b* 1949, — Ian Alexander, *b* 1957, — James Malcolm, *b* 1961. *Clubs* – Guards, Melbourne (Vic). —— Joyce Emily (40 Ladbroke Rd, W11 3PH), *b* 1904: *m* 1932 (*m diss* 1967), Sir Martin Alexander Lindsay, 1st Bt, CBE, DSO, who *d* 1981.

Issue of late Hon Lionel Lindsay, MC, 6th and yst son of 26th Earl of Crawford, *b* 1879, *d* 1965: *m* 1921, Kathleen Yone, who *d* 1970, da of late Sir John Gordon Kennedy, KCMG (M Ailsa, colls):—
Colin Paul (Hambrook House, Chichester, W Sussex PO18 8UD; *Club* – Royal Ocean Racing), *b* 1922; *ed* Eton, and at New Coll, Oxford; is a FCA: *m* 1955, Jennifer Ann, da of late Capt Thomas Marcus Brownrigg, CBE, DSO, RN (ret), and has issue living, Christopher Ronald, *b* 1957: *m* 1986, Anna Giulia, da of Andrea Orsini Baroni, of Via della Scala, Florence, and has issue living, Giulia *b* 1988, Francesca *b* 1993, — Andrew Mark, *b* 1962.

Grandchildren of late Lt-Col Henry Edith Arthur Lindsay, OBE, 4th and yst son of Col Hon Charles Hugh Lindsay, CB, 3rd son of 24th Earl of Crawford:—
Issue of late Lt-Col (David Ludovic) Peter Lindsay, DSO, *b* 1900, *d* 1971: *m* 1st, 1940 (*m diss* 1946), Ursula Jane, da of late Robert Orlando Rodolph Kenyon-Slaney (*see* B Kenyon, colls); 2ndly, 1950, Barbara J. (Méribel, Les Allues, Savoie, France), da of Edward Dunn:—
(By 2nd *m*) David Michael, *b* 1956: *m* 1991, Sarah Jane, eldest da of Anthony Poat, of Salisbury. *Residence* – Chivers Farm, Stoke St Michael, Bath BA3 5LD. —— Jane Caroline, *b* 1951. —— Sarah Jacqueline (*Hon Mrs James Jauncey*), *b* 1952: *m* 1988, as his 2nd wife, Hon James Malise Dundas Jauncey, elder son of Baron Jauncey of Tullichettle (Life Baron).

Grandson of late Maj Francis Howard Lindsay, 4th son of late William Alexander Lindsay, CVO, KC (infra):—

Issue of late Major John Stewart LINDSAY-MacDOUGALL, DSO, MC, Argyll and Sutherland Highlanders, b 1911, d (of wounds while a prisoner in Italy) 1943, having assumed the additional surname of MacDougall 1932: m 1934, Sheila Marion Roma (6 Laverockbank Rd, Edinburgh EH5 3DG) (who m 2ndly, 1949, Lt-Col Aubrey Wynter Gibbon, OBE, Argyll and Sutherland Highlanders, who d 1978), da of late Capt J. W. L. Sprot, Black Watch:—

Colin John Francis (Lunga, Ardfern, Lochgilphead, Argyll), b 1939; ed Radley: m 1961 (m diss 1978), Hon Frances Phœbe, da of late Capt Hon Anthony Francis Phillimore (see B Phillimore), and has issue living, James Alexander, b 1964, — Lucien Coll, b 1966, — Aidan John, b 1968, — Antonia Frances, b 1961, — Joanna Theresa, b 1962.

Granddaughter of late William Alexander Lindsay, CVO, KC, el son of late Hon Colin Lindsay, 4th son of 24th Earl of Crawford:—

Issue of late Maj Francis Howard Lindsay, b 1876; ka 1916: m 1910, Helen Margaret, who d 1941, el da and co-heir of the late Lt-Col Stewart MacDougall, Gordon Highlanders (formerly Maj Argyll and Sutherland Highlanders), one of HM's Corps of Gentlemen-at-Arms, of Lunga, Ardfern, Argyll:—

Katherine Frances LINDSAY-MacDOUGALL, b 1915; ed St Hilda's Coll, Oxford (MA, BLitt, Dip Archive Admin); Curator of Manuscripts, Nat Maritime Museum, Greenwich 1949-59; educational work in Zambia 1964-69; 1939-45 War as 1st Officer WRNS; assumed the additional surname of MacDougall 1949. Residence – Innisaig, Ardfern, Argyll.

Grandchildren of late Maj Sir George Humphrey Maurice BROUN LINDSAY, DSO, only son of late Alfred Lindsay, 3rd son of late Hon Colin Lindsay (ante):—

Issue of late Colin George BROUN LINDSAY, b 1926, d 1989: m 1952, Countess Beatrice Marie Thérèse Ferdinande Yvonne Ghislaine (Madam Broun Lindsay) (Colstoun, Haddington), da of Count Conrard Marie Joseph Gaspard Melchior Baltasar Ghislain d'Ursel, of Château de Moulbaix, Belgium:—

Ludovic David, b 1954; ed Ampleforth. Residence – Colstoun, Haddington. —— Christian Georgeana, b 1956.

Grandsons of late Capt Claud Frederic Thomas Lindsay, RFA, 2nd son of late Col Henry Edzell Morgan Lindsay, CB, eldest son of late Lt-Col Henry Gore Lindsay (infra):—

Issue of late Maj George Morgan Thomas Lindsay, b (posthumous) 1918, d 1990: m 1954, Jennifer Mary (Glanmor, Southerndown, nr Bridgend, Glamorgan; Lane End Cottage, Porton, Salisbury), only da of late Col John Geoffrey Ferry, RA (ret), of Wymering Lodge, Farnborough, Hants:—

David Charles Thomas, b 1955; ed Wellington Coll: m 1987, Alexandra Wendy, da of late Robert Emmas. —— William George Thomas, b 1958; ed Wellington Coll.

Grandchildren of late Col Henry Edzell Morgan Lindsay, CB (ante):—

Issue of late David Edzell Thomas Lindsay, b 1910, d 1968: m 1st, 1933 (m diss 1939), Kathleen Mary, yr da Austin Green; 2ndly, 1940 (m diss 1947), Eleanor Margaret, da of Kenneth Campbell, of Foxcote House, Andoversford, Glos; 3rdly, 1950, Hon Audrey Lavinia Lyttelton (Poplar Cottage, Fore St Hill, Budleigh Salterton, Devon), da of 9th Viscount Cobham:—

(By 1st m) David Claud (38 Bassingham Rd, SW18 3AG), b 1934; ed Eton: m 1964, Sheela Mary, da of late Michael Edward FitzGerald, of Brougham House, Newcastle, co Galway. —— (By 3rd m) † Hugh Charles Lyttelton, MVO, b 1953; ed Millfield; Maj 9th/12th Lancers (Prince of Wales's); Equerry to HM 1984: m 1987, Sarah Patricia, MVO (39 Hanover Gdns, SE11 5TN), da of Brian J. Brennan, MC, of Weybank House, Godalming, Surrey, and d in a skiing accident 1988, leaving issue, Alice Rose Lyttelton, b (posthumous), 1988. —— Andrew Edzell Thomas (38 Durdham Park, Bristol BS6 6XB), b 1956: m 1991, Patricia May, da of David Thesen, of Bude, Cornwall. —— Emma Katrina, b 1955: m 1986, Lt-Col Ian M. Daniell, RE, elder son of Dr B. L. Daniell, of Farnham, Surrey, and has issue living, Tobias Hugh, b 1989, — Amy Meriel, b 1987.

Granddaughters of late Lt-Col Henry Gore Lindsay, 2nd son of late George Hayward Lindsay, 4th son of late Rt Rev Hon Charles Dalrymple Lindsay, Bishop of Kildare, 6th son of 5th Earl of Balcarres:—

Issue of late Maj David Balcarres Lindsay, b 1863, d 1943: m 1898, Grace Maud, who d 1945, da of George Miller, of Brentry House, Westbury-on-Trym:—

Madeline, b 1899: m 1936, Thomas Morgan, and has issue living, John Patrick (12 Maidenerlegh Drive, Earley, Reading RG6 2HP), b 1937: m 1968, Raine, da of G. F. Tredwell, and has issue living, James Christopher b 1984, Edward Patrick b 1987, — Bernard Lawrence, b 1938: m 1st, 1960 (m diss 1976), Chong Siew Yong, of Kuala Lumpur, Malaysia; 2ndly, 1977, Monique Huart, of Lumumbashi, Zaire, and has issue living (by 1st m), Michael Gary b 1963, David b 1965, Susan Jane b 1961, (by 2nd m) Michael David b 1978, Philip b 1979. Residence – Ivy Lodge, Letcombe Bassett, Berks. —— Winifred Laura, b 1907. Residence – Newtown Anner, Clonmel, co Tipperary.

Issue of late Maj-Gen George Mackintosh Lindsay, CB, CMG, CBE, DSO, b 1880, d 1956: m 1907, Constance, who d 1974, da of George Stewart Hamilton:—

Joan Mary, b 1911: m 1938, Charles Holwell Thomas, OBE, who d 1990 (see E Lauderdale, colls, 1968 Edn), and has had issue, Robert Heriot Lindsay, b 1941, — David Charles Morgan, b 1942: m 1970, Ann Tresina, da of R. H. B. Benger, of Johannesburg, and d 1987, leaving issue living, Rupert James Morgan b 1972; k in a motor accident 1992, Camilla Jane Beringer b 1976, — George Francis Maitland b 1944: m 1976, Geraldine, da of Adrian van der Kwast, of Curacao, Netherlands Antilles, and has issue living, Morgan Adrian Maitland b 1979, Georgiana Elaine Lindsay b 1980, — Sarah Elizabeth Lindsay, b 1946: m 1971, Henry Charles Alfred Rowe, of Winfrith House, Winfrith Newburgh, Dorset, and has issue living, Charles Edward Kingsley b 1973, Louise Arabella Lindsay b 1975, Serena Elizabeth Henrietta b 1977. Residence – Southwick House, Kirkcudbrightshire.

PREDECESSORS – (1) WALTER de Lindesay (1113); s by his son, or brother (2) WILLIAM, of Ercildun, 2nd Lord of his name, s by his son (3) WALTER, 3rd Lord; s by his son (4) WILLIAM, 4th Lord; s by his son (5) WALTER, 5th Lord (Lord of Lamberton); s by his son (6) WILLIAM, 6th Lord (1247); s by his son (7) WALTER, 7th Lord; s by his son (8) WILLIAM, 8th Lord (1282); s by his kinsman (9) Sir ALEXANDER, 9th Lord (grandson of Sir David of Brenevil and the Byres, a Regent of Scotland 1255), companion of King Robert Bruce, and a Baron 1308; s by his son (10) Sir DAVID, 10th Lord, one of the Barons who signed the famous letter to Pope John XXII asserting the independence of Scotland; s by his son (11) Sir JAMES, 11th Lord; s by his son (12) Sir JAMES, 12th Lord, High Justiciary of Scotland; s by his cousin (13) Sir DAVID, 13th Lord, a valiant knight, was cr, proclaimed and belted Earl of Crawford (peerage of Scotland) at Perth, April 21, 1398, his lordship being at the same time erected into a regality; was Ambassador to England 1406; s by his son (14) ALEXANDER, 2nd Earl; a Commr to treat for the release of James I; was detained as a hostage for his ransom 1424-7; s by his son (15) DAVID, 3rd Earl; k 1446 while endeavoring to prevent the Battle of Arbroath; s by his son (16) ALEXANDER, 4th Earl; Hereditary Sheriff of Aberdeenshire; fought in rebellion at Battle of Brechin 1452; was attainted and afterwards restored; s by his son (17) DAVID, 5th Earl; having held numerous high offices, was cr Duke of Montrose (peerage of Scotland) 1488, a dignity that has not since been assumed by any of his successors; d 1495; s by his 2nd son (18) JOHN, 6th Earl; accused of murdering his el brother, but was killed at Flodden before the accusation was heard; s by his uncle (19) ALEXANDER, 7th Earl; s by his son (20) DAVID, 8th Earl; his son Alexander being found guilty of constructive parricide, was by the law of Scotland attainted; s by his kinsman (21) DAVID, 9th Earl, grandson of Walter, son of 3rd Earl; by consent of the crown he reconveyed his earldom to the son of Alexander (ante), but in failure of his issue the title to be in remainder to his son, Sir David (Lord Edzell), a Lord of Session; John, the 2nd son of this peer, Lord Menmuir, a Lord of Session, had issue, David, cr 1st Lord Lindsay of Balcarres (infra): s by his kinsman (22) DAVID, 10th Earl; a faithful adherent of Queen Mary's cause;

s by his son **(23)** DAVID, 11th Earl; *s* by his son **(24)** DAVID, 12th Earl, who alienated the greater portion of the estates; *s* by his uncle **(25)** HENRY, 13th Earl, son of 10th Earl; *s* by his son **(26)** GEORGE, 14th Earl; *s* by his half-brother **(27)** ALEXANDER, 15th Earl; *s* by his brother **(28)** LUDOVIC, 16th Earl; during the Civil Wars commanded a Regt of Horse, and fought at Marston Moor, Philiphaugh, and Newcastle, where he was taken prisoner, and in exchange, it is supposed, for his liberty, resigned with the sanction of the Crown, his Earldom to Charles I for a re-grant (failing his own issue) to John, 10th Earl of Lindsay, with remainder to his own collateral heirs; *dsp*, when the Earldom passed to John, 10th Earl of Lindsay, in whose family it continued until 1808, when the line failed (see E Lindsay). **(29)** DAVID, son of Lord Menmuir (refer to 9th Earl), was *cr Lord Lindsay of Balcarres* (peerage of Scotland) 1633; *s* by his son **(30)** ALEXANDER, 2nd Lord; rendered valuable service to the royal cause; *cr Lord Lindsay and Balniel* and *Earl of Balcarres* (peerage of Scotland) 1651; for taking part with the Earl of Glencairn his estates were sequestrated; *s* by his son **(31)** CHARLES, 2nd Earl of Balcarres; *d* unm 1662; *s* by his brother **(32)** COLIN, a staunch Royalist; *s* by his son **(33)** ALEXANDER, 4th Earl of Balcarres; became in 1744, on the death of David Lindsay of Edzell, *de jure* Lord Lindsay of Crawford, and Chief of his house: *m* 1718, Elizabeth, who *d* 1768, da of David Scott, of Scotstarvet; *d* 1746; *s* by his brother **(34)** JAMES, 5th Earl of Balcarres; *d* 1768; *s* by his son **(35)** ALEXANDER, 6th Earl of Balcarres; a Representative Peer, a Gen in the Army and Gov of Jamaica; in 1808, *s* as 23rd Earl of Crawford; *d* 1828; *s* by his son **(36)** JAMES, 24th Earl of Crawford and 7th of Balcarres; *b* 1783: *m* 1811, Hon Maria Margaret Frances Pennington, who *d* 1850, da of 1st Baron Muncaster; *cr Baron Wigan*, of Haigh Hall, co Lancaster (peerage of United Kingdom) 1826, and had Earldom of Crawford and Lordship of Lindsay confirmed to him 1848; *d* 1869; *s* by his son **(37)** ALEXANDER WILLIAM CRAWFORD, 25th Earl of Crawford and 8th of Balcarres, and 33rd Lord Lindsay of Crawford; *b* 1912: *m* 1846, Margaret, who *d* 1909, da of Lt-Gen James Lindsay, of Balcarres; *d* 1880; *s* by his son **(38)** JAMES LUDOVIC, KT, LLD, FRS, 26th Earl of Crawford and 9th of Balcarres; *b* 1847; MP for Wigan **(C)** 1874-80; acted as Dep for Great Steward of Scotland at Coronations of King Edward VII, and King George V: *m* 1869, Emily Florence, who *d* 1934, da of late Col Hon Edward Bootle-Wilbraham; *d* 1913; *s* by his el son **(39)** DAVID ALEXANDER EDWARD, KT, PC, DCL, 27th Earl of Crawford and 10th of Balcarres; *b* 1871; was a Junior Lord of the Treasury 1903-5, Pres of Board of Agriculture and Fisheries July to Dec 1916, Lord Privy Seal 1916-19, Chancellor of Duchy of Lancaster 1919-21, First Commr of Works 1921-2 and Min of Transport 1922; MP for Lancashire (N), Chorley Div **(C)** 1895-1913: *m* 1900, Constance Lilian, who *d* 1947, da of Sir Henry Carstairs Pelly, MP, 3rd Bt; *d* 1940; *s* by his el son **(40)** DAVID ALEXANDER ROBERT, KT, GBE, FSA, 28th Earl of Crawford and 11th Earl of Balcarres; *b* 1900; Chm of National Gallery 1938-41, and again 1945-49, Roy Fine Art Commn 1943-57, National Trust 1945-65, National Art Collections Fund 1945-70, National Gallery of Scotland 1952-72, and National Library of Scotland 1944-74; R of St Andrews Univ 1952-55; MP for Lancs, Lonsdale Div **(U)** 1924-40: *m* 1925, Mary Katherine, da of late Col Rt Hon Lord Richard Frederick Cavendish, CB, CMG (D Devonshire); *d* 1975; *s* by his el son **(41)** ROBERT ALEXANDER, PC, 29th Earl of Crawford, and 12th Earl of Balcarres and present peer; also Lord Lindsay (of Crawford), Lord Lindsay of Balcarres, Lord Lindsay and Balniel, Baron Wigan, and Baron Balniel (Life Peer).

CRAWSHAW, BARON (Brooks) (Baron UK 1892, Bt UK 1891)

Consider the end

WILLIAM MICHAEL CLIFTON BROOKS, 4th Baron and 4th Baronet; *b* 25 March 1933; *s* 1946; *ed* Eton, and Ch Ch, Oxford; DL Leics 1992; Lord of the Manor of Long Whatton; Treasurer Loughborough Div Conservative Assocn 1954-8, since when Co Commr, Leics Boy Scouts.

Arms – Argent, three bars wavy azure, a cross fleury erminois, in chief a fountain. **Crest** – A demi-lion proper, maned argent, charged on the shoulder with a fountain, and holding in the paws a pheon in bend sinister proper, stringed or. **Supporters** – *Dexter*, a stag argent; *sinister*, a horse argent; each collared wavy azure, and suspended from the collar an escutcheon erminois charged with a fountain.
Seat – Whatton, Loughborough, Leicestershire.

BROTHERS LIVING

Hon DAVID GERALD (Little Riste Farm, Long Whatton, Loughborough, Leics), *b* 14 Sept 1934; *ed* Eton, and RAC, Cirencester: *m* 1970, Belinda Mary, da of George Burgess, of 14 Kirkwood Av, Sandringham, Melbourne, Aust, and has issue living, Susanna Jane, *b* 1974, — Amanda, *b* 1975, — Elisabeth, *b* 1976, — Katharine, *b* 1978.

Hon John Patrick (25 Cadogan St, SW3), *b* 1938; *ed* Loughborough Coll: *m* 1967, Rosemary Vans Agnew, only da of late C. Vans Agnew Frank, of Greenways, Hunmanby, E Yorks, and has issue living, Edward Samuel, *b* 1969, — Caroline Miranda, *b* 1972.

SISTER LIVING

Hon Mary Altheia, *b* 1931.

COLLATERAL BRANCHES LIVING

Grandchildren of late Hon Herbert William Brooks (infra):—
Issue of late Capt Christopher John Brooks, Coldm Gds, *b* 1925, *d* 1991: *m* 1st, 1951 (*m diss* 1957), Patricia Evelyn Beverley, who *d* 1992, el da of John William Matthews, of Heathercroft, Hertford Heath, Herts; 2ndly, 1958, Gwendoline Helen (10 Tonsley Rd, SW18 1BG), el da of Louis D. Evans:—
(By 1st *m*) Sarah Jane, *b* 1956: *m* 1988, Maj Harry St John Holcroft, The Blues and Royals, yst son of late Oliver Holcroft, of Upton-on-Severn, Worcs, and has issue living, Harry Christopher Esmond, *b* 1990, — Christopher Nicholas, *b* 1991.
—— (By 2nd *m*) Timothy Allan William, *b* 1962: *m* 1986, Christine, da of Leonard Pugh, of Adelaide, Australia.
—— Georgina Helen, *b* 1960: *m* 1985, Peter Myrtle, of 115 Golfers Drive, Covington, Louisiana 70433, USA, son of Giles Myrtle, of Dalreagle, Wigtownshire, and has issue living, Frederick Giles Christopher, *b* 1988, — Christopher Thomas John, *b* 1992, — Victoria Gwendoline Virginia, *b* 1987.

Issue of late Hon Herbert William Brooks, yr son of 2nd Baron, *b* 1890, *d* 1974: *m* 1922, Hilda Muriel, who *d* 1967, da of late A. G. Steel, KC:—
Timothy Gerald Martin (Wistow, Leicester), *b* 1929; NDA; JP Leics 1960, High Sheriff 1980, DL 1984, Lord Lieut 1989: *m* 1951, Hon Ann Fremantle, da of 4th Baron Cottesloe, and has issue living, Richard Allan Halford, *b* 1958: *m* 1985, Diana Elizabeth, yr da of Sir Godfrey Michael David Thomas, 11th Bt (*cr* 1694), and has issue living, Charles John Halford *b* 1989, Michael *b* 1994, Sabrina *b* 1991, — Andrew Herbert John, *b* 1966, — Michael Julian, *b* 1969, — Lucinda Jane, *b* 1953: *m*

1978, Keith Charlton, and has issue living, two sons and two das, — Nicola Frances, *b* 1955: *m* 1978, Gerald A. Michel, and has issue living, two das.

Grandchildren of late Hon Marshall Jones Brooks, yr son of 1st Baron:—
Issue of late Lt-Col Thomas Marshall Brooks, MC, TD; *b* 1893; *d* 1967: *m* 1920, Evelyn Sylvia, who *d* 1967, da of Rev Hon Archibald Parker, Preb of Lichfield (E Macclesfield, colls):—
Ronald Marshall (Heath Hill, Bourton-on-the-Water, Glos), *b* 1924; *ed* Eton; 1939-45 War as Lt Queen's Bays: *m* 1950, Dorothy Valerie, da of Geoffrey Freer, of Ditchford Hill, Moreton-in-Marsh, Glos.
Issue of late Maj Noel Brand Brooks, MC, TD, *b* 1896, *d* 1984: *m* 1921, Joan Margaret, JP, who *d* 1984, da of Brig-Gen Sir Edward Thomas Le Marchant, 4th Bt, CB, CBE:—
Anne, *b* 1922. —— Betty Rosamond, *b* 1924: *m* 1950, Maj Nigel Steuart Kearsley, late Welsh Gds (Ramsay, Bt, *cr* 1806, colls), of The Old Vicarage, Asthall, nr Burford, Oxon, and has issue living, Rosamond Joanna, *b* 1955, — Grania Anne, *b* 1957: *m* 1983, Maj Patrick John Tabor, The Blues and Royals, and has issue, two sons and one da.

Grandchildren of Maj Noel Brand Brooks, MC, TD (ante):—
Issue of late Robert Noel Brand Brooks, *b* 1927, *d* 1976: *m* 1955, Caroline Diana (Castle Barn, Churchill, Oxon), only da of Brig George Herbert Norris Todd, MC, DL, of Court House, Stretton-on-Fosse, Moreton-in-Marsh, Glos:—
Christopher George, *b* 1959: *m* 1989, Miranda, eldest da of John Sergeant, of Phoenix Farm, Widford, nr Ware, Herts. —— Charles Patrick Evelyn, *b* 1963. —— Annabel Joan, *b* 1958: *m* 1981, Damian David Harris (*see* B Ogmore).

PREDECESSORS – (1) THOMAS BROOKS, son of late John Brooks, of Crawshaw Hall, Lancashire, *b* 1825; High Sheriff of Lancashire 1884; *cr* a *Baronet* 1891, and *Baron Crawshaw*, of Crawshaw, co Lancaster and of Whatton, co Leicester (peerage of the United Kingdom) 1892: *m* 1851, Catherine, who *d* 1917, da of late John Jones, of Kilsall Hall, Shropshire; *d* 1908; *s* by his son (2) WILLIAM, 2nd Baron, *b* 1853: *m* 1882, Mary Ethel, who *d* 1914, da of Sir Michael Hicks-Beach, 8th Bt; *d* 1929; *s* by his son (3) GERALD BEACH, 3rd Baron, *b* 1884: *m* 1930, Marjory Sheila, da of late Lieut-Col Percy Robert Clifton, CMG, DSO, TD; *d* 1946; *s* by his son (4) WILLIAM MICHAEL CLIFTON, 4th Baron and present peer.

CRAWSHAW OF AINTREE, BARONY OF (Crawshaw) (Extinct 1986)

WIDOW LIVING OF LIFE BARON

AUDREY FRANCES (*Baroness Crawshaw of Aintree*), da of Francis Augustine Lima, of Liverpool: *m* 1960, Baron Crawshaw of Aintree, OBE (Life Baron), who *d* 1986. *Residence* – The Orchard, Aintree Lane, Liverpool L10 8LE.

CREWE, MARQUESSATE OF (Crewe-Milnes) (Extinct 1945)

DAUGHTER LIVING OF FIRST MARQUESS (*By 2nd marriage*)

Lady Mary Evelyn Hungerford, *b* 1915; bore the Queen's Canopy at Coronation of King George VI: *m* 1935 (*m diss* 1953), 9th Duke of Roxburghe, who *d* 1974. *Residence* – 15 Hyde Park Gardens, W2.

Crichton, Viscount; son of Earl of Erne.

CRICKHOWELL, BARON (Edwards) (Life Baron 1987)

(ROGER) NICHOLAS EDWARDS, PC, son of late (Herbert Cecil) Ralph Edwards, CBE, FSA, of Suffolk House, Chiswick Mall, W4, and of Pont Esgob Mill; *b* 25 Feb 1934; *ed* Westminster, and Trin Coll, Camb (MA 1968); Pres Univ of Wales Coll of Cardiff; a Member of Lloyds since 1965, Dir Wm Brandts Sons & Co Ltd 1974-76, and Chief Exec Brandts Insurance Div; Chm Nat Rivers Authority, Dir HTV Group plc, Associated British Ports Holdings plc, Anglesey Mining plc and Member of Cttee of Automobile Assocn; Opposition Spokesman on Welsh Affairs 1975-79, Sec of State for Wales 1979-87; MP for Pembroke (*C*) 1970-87; *cr* PC 1979, and *Baron Crickhowell*, of Pont Esgob in the Black Mountains and co of Powys (Life Baron) 1987: *m* 1963, Ankaret, da of William James Healing, of Kinsham House, nr Tewkesbury, Glos, and has issue.
Residences – Pont Esgob Mill, Fforest, Abergavenny NP7 7LS; 4 Henning St, SW11 3DR.

SON LIVING

Hon Rupert Timothy Guy, *b* 1964; *ed* Radley, and Trin Coll, Camb: *m* 1990, Olivia Grizel Kirkwood, yr da of Capt David Colin Kirkwood Brown (*see* E Caithness), and has issue living, Joshua James, *b* 1991, — Camilla Sophie, *b* 1994.

DAUGHTERS LIVING

Hon Sophie Elizabeth Ankaret, *b* 1966.
Hon Olivia Caroline, *b* 1970.

CROFT, BARON (Croft) (Baron UK 1940, Bt UK 1924)

To be rather than to seem

MICHAEL HENRY GLENDOWER PAGE CROFT, 2nd Baron, and 2nd Baronet; *b* 20 Aug, 1916; *s* 1947; *ed* Eton, and at Trin Hall, Camb (BA); Bar Inner Temple 1952; OStJ; FRSA; 1939-45 War; Hon Capt RASC: *m* 1948, Lady Antoinette Fredericka Hersey Cecilia Conyngham, who *d* 1959, da of 6th Marquess Conyngham, and has issue.

Arms – Quarterly per fesse indented azure and argent; in the 1st quarter a lion passant guardant or. Crests – 1st, a lion passant guardant argent; 2nd, a wyvern sable vulned in the side gules. Supporters – *Dexter*, a lion rampant quarterly per fesse indented azure and argent; *sinister*, a wyvern sable, vulned in the side gules.
Seat – Croft Castle, Leominster, Herefordshire HR6 9PW. *Residence* – 19 Queens Gate Gdns, SW8 51Z. *Clubs* – Athenaeum, Bath.

SON LIVING

Hon BERNARD WILLIAM HENRY PAGE, *b* 28 Aug 1949; *ed* Stowe, and Wales Univ (BSc Econ). *Residence* – 5 Comeragh Mews, Comeragh Rd, W14 9HW.

DAUGHTER LIVING

Hon Charlotte Elizabeth Ann, *b* 1952; *ed* Benenden: *m* 1975, Emrys Thomas Devonald, of Enderley, Stony Lane, Little Kingshill, Great Missenden, Bucks, and has issue living, James Emrys, *b* 1979, — Jennifer Ann, *b* 1977.

SISTERS LIVING

Hon Hilda Elizabeth Mary, *b* 1909: *m* 1934, Richard Hayter Bayford, Bar-at-Law, Capt R Berks Regt, who *d* 1982, and has issue living, Robert Michael Croft, *b* 1936, — Gillian Sara Carolyn *b* 1935: *m* 1958, Flight-Lieut Michael Holmes, RAF, — Mary Elizabeth, *b* 1944. *Residence* – Croft Lodge, Goring on Thames, Oxon.
Hon Nancy Diana Joyce, *b* 1912: *m* 1936, Manfred Uhlman, who *d* 1985, and has issue living, Francis Raymond Croft *b* 1943, — Caroline Ann, *b* 1940: *m* 1966 (*m diss* 19—), Albert Charles Compton, and has issue living, Tristram Ludovic Archer *b* 1968, Sarah Harriet *b* 1972. *Residence* – Croft Castle, Leominster, Herefords HR6 9PW.
Hon Anne Rosemary Dorothea, *b* 1918: *m* 1946, Flight-Lieut Herbert Edmund Poole, RAF, who *d* 1984, and has issue living, Herbert Benyon, *b* 1947, — Jeremy Henry Borwick, *b* 1949; — Hugo Edmund, *b* 1952: *m* 1st, 1977 (*m diss* 1992), Christina Susan de Jong Cleyndert; 2ndly, 1992, Anne Margaret Lovell, and has issue living (by 1st *m*), Charlotte Annalika *b* 1979, Jessica Margery Anne *b* 1981, Kate Antonia *b* 1982. *Residence* – Dower House, 17A Knight St, Sawbridgeworth, Herts.

PREDECESSOR – **(1)** *Rt Hon Sir* HENRY PAGE Croft, CMG, TD, PC, son of late Richard Benyon Croft, of Fanhams Hall, Ware (see Croft, Bt, *cr* 1671, colls); *b* 1881; European War 1914-16 as Brig-Gen late Herts Regt (CMG); was Joint Under-Sec of State for War 1940-45; sat as MP for Christchurch (C) 1910-18, and for Bournemouth 1918-40; *cr* a *Baronet* 1924, and *Baron Croft*, of Bournemouth, co Southampton (peerage of United Kingdom) 1940: *m* 1907, Hon Nancy Beatrice Borwick, who *d* 1949, yst da of 1st Baron Borwick; *d* 1947; *s* by his son **(2)** MICHAEL HENRY GLENDOWER PAGE, 2nd Baron and present peer.

CROFTON, BARON (Crofton) (Baron I 1797, Bt I 1758)

God gives the increase

GUY PATRICK GILBERT CROFTON, 7th Baron and 10th Baronet; *b* 17 June 1951; *s* 1989; *ed* Theresianistische Akademie, Vienna, and at Midhurst Gram Sch; Lt-Col 9th/12th R Lancers (POW): *m* 1985, Gillian Susan Burroughs, only da of Harry Godfrey Mitchell Bass, CMG, of Reepham, Norfolk, and has issue.

Arms – Per pale indented or and azure, a lion passant guardant counterchanged. **Crest** – Seven ears of wheat growing on one stalk or. **Supporters** – *Dexter*, a lion azure: *sinister*, a stag proper. *Address* – c/o Drummond's Bank, 49 Charing Cross, SW1A 2DX. *Club* – Cavalry and Guards'.

SONS LIVING

Hon (EDWARD) HARRY (PIERS), *b* 23 Jan 1988.
Hon (Charles) Marcus (George), *b* (twin) 1988.

BROTHER DECEASED

Hon Arthur Blaise Adrian, *b* 1957; *d* 1987.

SISTER LIVING

Hon Georgiana Ann CROFTON, *b* 1955; has resumed her maiden name: *m* 1980 (*m diss* 1986), Brent Hutchinson, son of Ivan Hutchinson, and has issue living, Blaise, *b* 1982, — Louisa, *b* 1981. *Address* – c/o The Red House, Inistioge, co Kilkenny.

DAUGHTER LIVING OF SIXTH BARON

Hon Freya Charlotte, *b* 1983.

WIDOW LIVING OF SON OF FOURTH BARON

Madeleine Barbara (PRATT), da of late William James Heath, of London: *m* 1951, as his 4th wife, Hon (Arthur) Marcus (Lowther) Crofton, Maj Irish Guards, who *d* 1962. *Residence* – 401, 1430 Newport Av, Victoria, BC, Canada.

MOTHER LIVING

Ann Pamela TIGHE, elder da of Gp Capt Charles Herbert Tighe, OBE, DFC, RAF (ret), of The Red House, Inistioge, co Kilkenny; has resumed her maiden name: *m* 1st, 1948 (*m diss* 1963), 5th Baron Crofton, who *d* 1974; 2ndly 1964 (*m diss* 1972), Robert Thomas Francis Flach, Bar-at-law, of London; 3rdly, 1973 (*m diss* 1976), Guy Brooke, of New York City. *Residence* – The Red House, Inistioge, co Kilkenny.

WIDOW LIVING OF FIFTH BARON

MARY (*Mary, Baroness Crofton*), eldest da of late Maj James Irvine Hatfeild Friend, OBE, MC, DL, of Northdown, Thanet, Kent: *m* 1st, 1951 (*m diss* 1963), Robert Thomas Francis Flach, Bar-at-law (ante), of London; 2ndly, 1964, as his 2nd wife, the 5th Baron, who *d* 1974. *Residence* – Flat 1, 123 Gloucester Terr, W2.

WIDOW LIVING OF SIXTH BARON

MAUREEN JACQUELINE (*Maureen, Baroness Crofton*), da of Stanley James Bray, of Taunton, Som: *m* 1976, the 6th Baron, who *d* 1989. *Residence* – Briscoe Cottage, Ford St, nr Wellington, Somerset.

COLLATERAL BRANCHES LIVING (*In remainder to Barony and Baronetcy*)

Grandchildren of late Capt Hon Francis George Crofton, RN, yr brother of 3rd Baron:—
    Issue of late George Crofton, *b* 1881, *d* 1943: *m* 1910, Elina, da of late K. Smith:—
Francis George, *b* 1915.
    Issue of late Alfred Gerald Crofton, *b* 1882, *d* 1942: *m* 1903, Frances Nona, who *d* 1951, da of the Rev Edward Wilson:—
Dermott Kenneth (Winfrith, Ganges, BC, Canada), *b* 1904: *m* 1934, Doris Livingstone, el da of late J. W. Taylor, of Belfast, and has issue living, Patrick Dermott (Ballymurry Farm, 4010 Prospect Lake Rd, RR7, Victoria, BC, Canada V8X 3X3), *b* 1935; Lt-Cdr (S) CAF (ret): *m* 1958, Patricia Judith Mary, only da of Capt Trevor Williams, of Folly, The Walled Garden, Wargrave, Berks, and has issue living, Marietta Susan Annette *b* 1959, Virginia Margaret Adele *b* 1961, Susanne Catherine Mary *b* 1962, Tessa Penelope Sarah *b* 1965, — Marcus Livingstone, *b* 1937; Lt Cdr CAF: *m* 1966, Elizabeth Jane, da of Lt-Col G. A. Churchill, of Victoria, BC, and has issue living, Dermott Marcus Churchill *b* 1970, Geoffrey Patrick *b* 1973, Laura Elizabeth *b* 1967, Jenny Livingstone *b* 1969, — Sharron Diana, *b* 1940: *m* 1964 (*m diss* 1970), Robert Montagu Scott, and has issue living, Ian Dermott Montagu *b* 1967, Andrea Gillian *b* 1966. —— Donovan Patrick (10672 Madrona Drive, RR1, Sidney, BC, Canada V8L 3R9), *b* 1915; Italy and NW Europe 1943-45 as Maj Princess Patricia's Canadian LI (despatches): *m* 1946, Anne B., da of Harry Marshall Erskine Evans, OBE, of Edmonton, Alberta, and has issue living, Cameron P. L., *b* 1947, — Barry Gerald, *b* 1953. —— Doreen Sheila, *b* 1911: *m* 1939, Frederick A. E. Morris, and has issue living, Robert Frederick, *b* 1942, — James R., *b* 1949, Wendy P., *b* 1940. —— Denise Frances, *b* 1913.

Grandchildren of late Alfred Gerald Crofton (ante):—
    Issue of late Lt-Col Desmond Gerald Crofton, ED, *b* 1905, *d* 1977: *m* 1st, 1925, Ida, who *d* 1970, da of late Frank Hardcastle, DL, JP, and widow of Maj F. Harvey Corbett, MC, RFA; 2ndly, 1971, Dorothea Herriet (Roscommon, PO Box 432, Ganges, BC, Canada V0S 1EO), yst da of Arthur George Wilson, and widow of Keith Edward Hook:—
(By 1st *m*) John Edward, *b* 1925; Lt-Col CAF: *m* 1950, Marie White, and has issue living, Desmond, *b* 1951, — Kevin, *b* 1954, — Neil, *b* 1956. —— Sylvia Ida, *b* 1928, *m* 1954, Maj Arthur Leake Gale, CD, Princess Patricia's Canadian LI, and has issue living, Reginald Derek Leake, *b* 1956, — Rupert Arthur Leake, *b* 1962, — Deirdre Sylvia Leake, *b* 1957.

Grandson of late Capt Hon Francis George Crofton (ante):—
Issue of late Francis Lowther Crofton, *b* 1883, *d* 1971: *m* 1st, 1917, Annie Rebecca, MM, who *d* 1956, da of late
Robert Colhoun, of Londonderry; 2ndly, 1957, Nancy Esten, da of H. H. Nash, and widow of F. Arthur Inglis:—
(By 1st *m*) Francis David, *b* 1919; *ed* McGill Univ (MD); late Capt RCAMC: *m* 1948, Marguerite, da of Earl Hines, of
Halifax, Nova Scotia, and has issue living, Catherine Elizabeth Ellen, *b* 1950.

(In remainder to Baronetcy only)

Granddaughters of late Frederick Norris Lowther Crofton, elder son of Maj George Lowther Crofton, only
son of Frederick Charles Edward Lowther Crofton, elder son of Frederick Lowther Crofton, grandson of
Capt John Frederick Crofton, 4th son of 1st baronet:—
Issue of late George Lowther Crofton, *b* 1905, *d* 1976: *m* 1928, Nea, who *d* 1981, da of Rev A. P. Cameron,
Moderator of Church of Scotland, NSW, of The Manse, Glen Innes, NSW:—
Judith Mary, *b* 1932: *m* 1st, 1957 (*m diss* 1968), Les Hayna; 2ndly, 1970, Edgar Allen, of M/S 108 Windermere Rd,
Bundaberg, Queensland 4670, Australia, and has issue living (by 1st *m*), Christine Nea (PO Box 620, Bundaberg, Qld 4670),
b 1957: *m* 1977, Wayne Olsen, of Bundaberg, Queensland, and has issue living, Timothy Malcolm *b* 1981, Daniel Christopher
b 1985, Kerri-Ann *b* 1977, — (by 2nd *m*) Geoffrey Edgar Howell, *b* 1971, — William George John, *b* (twin) 1971. —— Clare
Edith, *b* 1936: *m* 1st, 1956 (*m diss* 1982), Alex Barry Mitchell; 2ndly, 1986, Desmond Fourro, of Bundaberg, Qld, and has
issue living (by 1st *m*), Steven George, *b* 1957: *m* 1989, Lynette Mary Baker, of Mackay, Qld, and has issue living, Kirsty
Leeanne *b* 1982, Kylie Marie *b* (twin) 1982, — Brian Alec, *b* 1961: *m* 1985, Jacqueline Davies, of Mackay, Queensland, and
has issue living, Hayden Rhys *b* 1992, Kylie Nicole *b* 1986, Leah Suzanne *b* 1988, — Glenn Cameron, *b* 1965; has issue living
(by Sharon Dawn McLean), Jias Nathan Braid *b* 1993, — Jennifer Jeanie, *b* 1959: *m* 1984 (*m diss* 1986), Guus Hoogland, of
Mackay, Queensland; has issue living (by Wayne Robert King, of Mackay, Qld), Michelle Cori *b* 1991.

PREDECESSORS – (1) Catherine, da of Sir Edward Crofton, MP, 4th Bt, of the Mote (which title, *cr* 1661, became extinct
on the death of the 5th Bt 1780): *m* MARCUS Lowther, MP for Roscommon, who assumed the surname of Crofton and was *cr*
a Bt 1758; *d* 1774; *s* by his son (2, 3) *Sir* Edward, 2nd Bt; MP for co Roscommon: *m* Anne, da and heir of Thomas Croker,
of Baxtown, co Kildare; *d* 30 Sept 1797, having a short time before his death been offered a peerage; on 1 Dec of the same
year his widow ANNE, was *cr Baroness Crofton* (peerage of Ireland); she *d* 1817, and was *s* by her grandson; Sir Edward was
s by his son (4) EDWARD, 3rd Bt; *d* 1816; *s* by his son (5) EDWARD, 4th Bt, *b* 1806; *s* his grandmother as 2nd Baron 1817; a
Representative Peer, and a Lord-in-Waiting to HM Queen Victoria: *m* 1833, Lady Georgiana Paget, da of 1st Marquess of
Anglesey; *d* 1869; *s* by his son (6) EDWARD HENRY Churchill, 3rd Baron; *b* 1834; a Representative Peer; Gentleman of the
Bedchamber (1866-8) and State Steward (1880) to Viceroy of Ireland; *d* 1912; *s* by his nephew (7) ARTHUR EDWARD Lowther,
4th Baron, *b* 1866; a Representative Peer: *m* 1893, Jessie Castle, who *d* 1923, da of J. Hewitson and widow of Neville Paddon;
d 1942; *s* by his grandson (8) EDWARD BLAISE (son of late Hon Edward Charles Crofton, el son of 4th Baron), 5th Baron, *b*
1926: *m* 1st, 1948 (*m diss* 1963) Ann Pamela, elder da of Gp Capt Charles Herbert Tighe, OBE, DFC, RAF (ret); 2ndly, 1964,
Mary, el da of late Maj James Irvine Hatfeild Friend, OBE, MC, DL, and formerly wife of Robert Thomas Francis Flach; *d*
1974; *s* by his el son (9) CHARLES EDWARD PIERS, 6th Baron, *b* 1949; Ship Master, Member Nautical Inst: *m* 1976, Maureen
Jacqueline, da of Stanley James Bray, of Taunton, Som; *d* 1989, *s* by his brother (10) GUY PATRICK GILBERT, 7th Baron and
present peer.

CROHAM, BARON (Allen) (Life Baron 1977)

Always ready

DOUGLAS ALBERT VIVIAN ALLEN, GCB, son of late Albert John Allen; *b*
1917; *ed* Wallington County Boys, and LSE (BScEcon); Perm Sec,
Dept of Economic Affairs 1966-68, Perm Sec, Treasury 1968-74, and
Perm Sec, Civil Service Dept, and Head of Home Civil Ser 1974-77;
Advisor to Gov of Bank of England 1978-83; Chm British Nat Oil
Corpn 1982-86, and Guiness Peat Gp plc 1983-89; 1939-45 War as
Capt RA, AA Command; *cr* CB 1963, KCB 1967; GCB 1973, and
Baron Croham, of London Borough of Croydon (Life Baron) 1977: *m*
1941, Sybil Eileen, da of late John Marco Allegro, and has issue.

Arms – Argent on a base checky or and azure an oak tree proper fructed or,
the trunk supported by two crows respectant proper beaked and legged gold.
Crest – An alaunt proper gorged with a crown or reposing its dexter paw upon
a purse azure corded and tasselled the cords tied over the paw in a bow or.
Supporters – Dexter, a griffin azure semy of roundels or and argent winged
beaked legged and tufted or. Sinister, a pantheon azure semy of mullets of six
points or and argent winged and hooved or.
Residences – 9 Manor Way, South Croydon; Ashcroft, Crowborough Rd, Nutley,
Sussex.

SONS LIVING

Hon John Douglas (Westfields, 23 Quaker Rd, Sileby, Leics), *b* 1945: *m* 1969, Sheila, only da of Dr A. J. Ward, of
Hemingford Grey, Cambs, and has issue living, two sons and one da.
Hon Richard Anthony (2 Mount Close, Kenley, Surrey), *b* 1950: *m* 1st, 1980 (*m diss* 1986), Karen, only da of F. Hughes, of
Whetstone, London; 2ndly, 1988, Gillian, only da of R. Harraway, of Huddersfield, Yorks.

DAUGHTER LIVING

Hon Rosamund Sybil, *b* 1942: *m* 1974, Stephan Sulyák, of 8A Harewood Rd, S Croydon, Surrey CR2 7AL, son of late Laszló
Sulyák, of Kunszentmartón, Hungary, and has issue living, Veronica Claire, *b* 1976.

CROMARTIE, EARL OF (Mackenzie) (Earl UK 1861)

I shine not burn

JOHN RUARIDH GRANT MACKENZIE, 5th Earl, *b* 12 June 1948; *s* 1989; *ed* Rannoch Sch, and Strathclyde Univ; recognized by Lord Lyon as Chief of Clan Mackenzie; discontinued the use of the forename and surname of Blunt 1962; author of *Selected Climbs in Skye*, etc; MIExpE: *m* 1st, 1973 (*m diss* 1983), Helen, da of John Murray; 2ndly, 1985, Janet Clare, da of Christopher James Harley, of Strathpeffer, Ross-shire, and has issue by 2nd *m*.

ⁱⁱⁱⁱ **Arms** – Quarterly, 1st; or a mountain azure in flames proper (*Macleod of Lewis*); 2nd, azure a buck's head cabossed or (*Mackenzie*); 3rd, gules three legs of a man armed proper, conjoined in the centre at the upper part of two of the thighs, flexed in triangle, garnished and spurred, or (*Isle of Man*); 4th, argent, on a pale sable an Imperial Crown proper, within a double tressure flowered and counter-flowered with fleur-de-lys gules (*Erskine of Innerteall*). **Crest** – The sun in his splendour. **Supporters** – *Dexter*, a wild man wreathed about the loins with oak, holding a club resting on the exterior shoulder proper; *sinister*, a greyhound argent, collared gules.
Seat – Castle Leod, Strathpeffer, Ross and Cromarty. *Clubs* – Army and Navy, Pratt's, Scottish Mountaineering.

SONS LIVING *(By 2nd marriage)*

COLIN RUARIDH (*Viscount Tarbat*), *b* 7 Sept 1987.
Hon Alasdair Kenelm Stuart, *b* 1989.

HALF-SISTERS LIVING

Lady (Sibell Anne) Julia MACKENZIE, *b* 1934; has resumed her maiden name: *m* 1st, 1953 (*m diss* 1961), Francis Edward Lascelles-Hadwen; 2ndly, 1974, Apputhurai Jeyarama Chandran, and has issue living (by 1st *m*), James Brian Mackenzie, *b* 1957, — Georgina Frances, *b* 1959, — (by 2nd *m*) Anita Anne Dorothy, *b* 1977.
Lady Gilean Frances MACKENZIE-WELTER, *b* 1936: *m* 1959 (*m diss* 1973), Rene Eugene Welter, and has issue living, Michael George, *b* 1964, — Nadia (Nadine) Christine, *b* 1960. *Residence* – 52 South Edwardes Sq, W8.

AUNT LIVING *(daughter of Sibell Lilian, Countess of Cromartie)*

Lady Isobel, *b* 1911: *m* 1947, Capt Oscar Linda. *Residence* – Assynt House, Evanton, Ross-shire.

WIDOW LIVING OF SON OF SIBELL LILIAN, COUNTESS OF CROMARTIE

Mary, da of Theophilus Dan Hix, of Holbech, Lincs: *m* 1st, 1946, as his 2nd wife, Hon Walter Osra Blunt-Mackenzie, who *d* 1951; 2ndly, 1964, Maj Clement Victor Palmer, who *d* 1969; 3rdly, 1982, Sijbren Tijmstra, and has issue living (by 1st *m*) (see colls, infra). *Address* – PO Box 14, White River, E Transvaal, S Africa.

MOTHER LIVING

Olga, da of late Stewart Laurance, and of Mme Ziv, of 27 Rue des Sablons, Paris, and formerly wife of Peter Mendoza: *m* 1947 (*m diss* 1962), as his 2nd wife, Maj Roderick Grant Francis, Viscount Tarbat, MC (later 4th Earl of Cromartie), who *d* 1989. *Residence* – Ludshott Manor, Bramshott, Hants.

WIDOW LIVING OF FOURTH EARL

LILIAS JANET GARVIE (*Dowager Countess of Cromartie*), MB, ChB Leeds, da of Prof James Walter McLeod, OBE, FRS, and formerly wife of Lt-Col D. S. Richard, MBE: *m* 1962, as his 3rd wife, Maj the 4th Earl, MC, TD, who *d* 1989. *Residence* – Castle Leod, Strathpeffer, Ross and Cromarty.

COLLATERAL BRANCHES LIVING

Issue of late Hon Walter Osra Blunt-Mackenzie, 2nd son of Sibell Lilian, Countess of Cromartie, *b* 1906, *d* 1951: *m* 1st, 1934 (*m diss* 1940), Pamela Lilian Ursula, da of Mr Justice Oliver; 2ndly, 1946, Mary (ante) (who *m* 2ndly, 1964, Maj Clement Victor Palmer, who *d* 1969, and 3rdly, 1982, Sijbren Tijmstra), da of Theophilus Dan Hix, of Holbech, Lincs:—
(By 2nd *m*) Roderick BLUNT-MACKENZIE, *b* 1947: *m* 1969, Yvonne, da of Bernard Arthur (Bill) Lemmon, of White River, S Africa, and has issue living, Craig Walter, *b* 1973, — Jacquelyn, *b* 1970. — Lara, *b* 1971, — Sarah Jane, *b* 1978. *Address* – 21 Crowned Eagle Way, Oak Park, Pietermaritzburg 3201, S Africa.
Descendants of late Lady Florence Leveson-Gower, eldest da of Anne, Duchess of Sutherland (Countess of Cromartie) *b* 1855, *d* 1881: *m* 1876, Rt Hon Henry Chaplin, afterwards 1st Viscount Chaplin (see that title, and Cs Sutherland, colls).
PREDECESSORS – (1) ANNE, VA, only child of John Hay Mackenzie of Cromartie, in direct descent from the 3rd Earl of Cromartie who was attainted in 1746: *m* 1849, 3rd Duke of Sutherland, and was cr *Countess of Cromartie, Viscountess Tarbat of Tarbat Baroness Castlehaven, of Castlehaven, and Baroness MacLeod, of Leod* (peerage of United Kingdom 1861), with remainder (1) to her second surviving son, Francis, and the heirs male of his body, (2) to each other of her yr sons in like manner in priority of birth, (3) to said Francis and the heirs of his body, (4) to each other her yr sons in like manner in priority of birth, (5) to her daughter Florence and the heirs of her body, and (6) to each other of her daughters (in like manner in priority of birth); she *d* 1888, when the Earldom of Cromartie devolved, in accordance with the special remainder, upon her second surviving son (2) FRANCIS, *b* 1852: *m* 1876, Hon Lilian Janet, who *d* 1926, da of 5th Baron Macdonald; *d* 1893, when the title fell into abeyance between his two surviving das, Sibell Lilian and Constance, and so remained until the abeyance was terminated in 1895 in favour of his eldest da and the heirs of her body, when the honours were confirmed to (3) SIBELL LILIAN, as Countess of Cromartie in her own right; *b* 1878: *m* 1899, Lieut-Col Edward Walter Blunt, DL, who *d* 1949, having assumed the additional surname of Mackenzie 1905; she subsequently discontinued the surname of Blunt; *d* 1962; *s* by her eldest son (4) RODERICK GRANT FRANCIS, MC, TD, 4th Earl, *b* 1904; Maj Seaforth Highlanders (TA), served N Ireland, India and European War 1939-45 as Maj 4th Bn in France (prisoner 1940-45), Hon Sheriff Ross and Cromarty, Convenor 1971-75, FSAS; discontinued surname of Blunt, recognised as Chief of Clan Mackenzie by Lord Lyon 1979: *m* 1st, 1933 (*m diss* 1945), Dorothy (PORTER), da of Grant Butler Downing, of Kentucky, USA; 2ndly, 1947, Olga (MENDOZA), da of

Stewart Laurance, and formerly wife of Peter Mendoza; 3rdly, 1962, Lilias Janet Garvie (RICHARD), MB, ChB Leeds, da of Prof James Walter McLeod, OBE, FRS, and formerly wife of Lt-Col D. S. Richard; *d* 1989; *s* by his son (5) JOHN RUARIDH BLUNT GRANT, 5th Earl and present peer, also Viscount Tarbat, Baron Castlehaven, and Baron Macleod.

CROMER, EARL OF (Baring) (Earl UK 1901)

By probity and industry

EVELYN ROWLAND ESMOND BARING, 4th Earl; *b* 3 June 1946; *s* 1991; *ed* Eton; Man Dir Inchcape (China) Ltd, and Inchcape Vietnam Ltd, Dep-Chm Motor Transport Co of Guangdong & Hong Kong Ltd (China), and Land-Ocean Inchcape Container Transport Co Ltd (China): *m* 1st, 1971 (*m diss* 1992), Plern, da of late Dr Charanpat Isarangkul na Ayudhya, of Thailand; 2ndly, 1993, Shelley Hu, da of Hu Guo-qin, of Shanghai, and has issue by 2nd *m*.

Arms – Quarterly, 1st and 4th azure, a fesse or, in chief a bear's head proper, muzzled and ringed or, differenced by an escallop azure; 2nd and 3rd gules, a cross-patée fitchée or between three fish haurient argent within an orle of eight cross-crosslets of the second. **Crest** – A mullet erminois between two wings argent. **Supporters** – Two bears proper, muzzled or, the dexter collared checky, argent and azure and charged on the shoulder with a lion's head erased or, the sinister collared azure, and charged on the shoulder with an escallop or.
Residence – Drayton Court, Drayton, Somerset. *Address* – GPO Box 36, Hong Kong. *Clubs* – Oriental, White's, Hong Kong.

SON LIVING *(By 2nd marriage)*

ALEXANDER ROWLAND HARMSWORTH (*Viscount Errington*), *b* 5 Jan 1994.

BROTHER LIVING

Hon Vivian John Rowland, *b* 1950; *ed* RAC Cirencester; Dir Northcliffe Newspapers Group Ltd; Chm of St John Ambulance Council, Kent 1985-87, Chm Council, Glos 1989-93: *m* 1974, Lavinia Gweneth, an Extra Lady-in-Waiting to HRH the Princess of Wales 1981-92, eldest da of late Maj Sir Mark Baring, KCVO (*see* colls infra), and has issue living, Rowley Mark Thomas, *b* 1977; a Page of Honour to HM 1989-91, — Thomas Patrick Vivian, *b* 1979, — Camilla Rose, *b* 1985. *Residence* – The Stone House, Lower Swell, Stow on the Wold, Glos GL54 1LQ. *Clubs* – White's, Royal Yacht Squadron.

SISTER DECEASED

Lady Lana Mary Gabriel, *b* 1943: *m* 1963, Anthony James Gray, of 5 Ranelagh Av, SW6, son of late Prof Sir James Gray, CBE, MC, FRS, and *d* 1974, leaving issue, Ashley James Rowland, *b* 1964; *ed* Grenville Coll, Devon: *m* 1990, Annabel, yst da of John Ludovici, of East Woodhay, Berks, and has issue living, Lily Lana Patricia *b* 1993, — Tamara Mary Gabriel, *b* 1966.

AUNT LIVING *(daughter of 2nd Earl)*

Lady Rosemary Ethel, *b* 1908; FRGS; *m* 1932, Lt-Col John David Hills, MC, formerly Headmaster of Bradfield Coll, and has issue living, John Evelyn Baring (Priory Cottage, Long Newnton, Tetbury, Glos), *b* 1939; *ed* Eton; Maj 17/21st Lancers, Col Royal Wessex Yeo (TA), Hon ADC to HM since 1990; High Sheriff Glos 1990, DL 1989: *m* 1964, Katherine Adrian, yr da of late G. F. Alderson-Smith, of Bishopric Court, Horsham, Sussex, and has issue living, John George Baring *b* 1966; *ed* Bradfield, Veronica Adrian Harriet *b* 1968, — Jean Adini (Buckhold Farm, Pangbourne, Berks RG8 8QB), *b* 1933: *m* 1955 (*m diss* 1990), Brig Hon (Henry Ernest) Christopher Willoughby, Coldm Gds, and has issue (*see* B Middleton), — Margaret Ruby, *b* 1934: *m* 1960, Michael Giles Neish Walker, of Shanwell House, Kinross-shire (*see* Nairn, Bt, 1980 Edn), and has issue living, Simon Giles David *b* 1961; *ed* Eton: *m* 1991, Corinne Rawstorne (and has issue living, a da *b* 1993), Geordie Michael *b* 1966; *ed* Strathallan, Nicola Margaret *b* 1965. *Residence* – Buckhold Farm, Pangbourne, Berks RG8 8QB.

WIDOW LIVING OF THIRD EARL

Hon ESME MARY GABRIEL HARMSWORTH, CVO, da of 2nd Viscount Rothermere: *m* 1st, 1942, 3rd Earl of Cromer, KG, GCMG, MBE, PC, who *d* 1991; 2ndly, 1993, as his 2nd wife, (Reinier) Gerrit Anton van der Woude, late Capt Gren Guards. *Residences* – Heronden, Eastry, Sandwich, Kent CT13 0ET; 1 Douro Place, W8.

COLLATERAL BRANCHES LIVING

Issue of late Hon Windham Baring, 2nd son of 1st Earl, *b* 1880, *d* 1922: *m* 1913, Lady Gweneth Frida Ponsonby (who *d* 1984, having *m* 2ndly, 1926, Col Ralph Henry Voltelin Cavendish, CBE, MVO (*see* D Devonshire, colls, 1968 Edn), who *d* 1968), da of 8th Earl of Bessborough:—
Robin Windham, *b* 1914, TD; *ed* Eton, and at Trin Coll, Camb; is a Member of London Stock Exchange, and an OStJ; 1939-45 War in N Africa, Italy and NW Europe as Capt RA (TA): *m* 1954, Anne Elizabeth, JP, el da of Maj William Frederick Husband, and has issue living, James Windham, *b* 1957: *m* 1st, 1985, Suzy, da of John Barry Prendergast, of Oyster Bay, New York, and of Mrs Barbara Barnard, of North Lodge, Odiham, Hants; 2ndly, 1991, Mrs Angela P. Clarke, eldest da of Peter Halstead, of Cranmer Court, SW3, and has issue living (by 2nd *m*), Clementine Lara *b* 1992, — Clarissa, *b* 1955: *m* 1987, Michael Charles David Pilkington, eldest son of Ronald Charles Leslie Pilkington, of Stanstead Abbotts, Herts, and has issue living, Grace Cristabel Alice *b* 1987, Eleanor Scarlett Rose *b* 1989, Silvy Emerald Isabelle *b* 1993, — Rosemary Anne, *b* 1960: *m* 1989, Anthony M. Standing, of The Old Rectory, Sharrington, Melton Constable, Norfolk NR24 2PG, son of late Michael Frederick Cecil Standing, CBE, and has issue living, Michael Frederick Oliver *b* 1990, Archie Jonathan Guy *b* 1992, — Katherine Claire, *b* 1963: *m* 1992, Alexander T. H. Slack, yr son of Tom Slack, of Mousehole, Cornwall, and of Chelsea, SW3. *Residence* – Went House, West Malling, Kent.

Granddaughters of late Hon Windham Baring (ante):—
Issue of late Maj Sir Mark Baring, KCVO, *b* 1916, *d* 1988: *m* 1949, Victoria Winifred (*Lady Baring*) (66 Melton Court, SW7 3JH), da of late Col Reginald Edmund Maghlin Russell, CVO, CBE, DSO, of Hurst House, Church Crookham, Hants:—

Lavinia Gweneth (*Hon Mrs Vivian Baring*), *b* 1951; an Extra Lady in Waiting to HRH the Princess of Wales 1981-92: *m* 1974, Hon Vivian John Rowland Baring (ante). —— Juliet Victoria (22 Chester Square, SW1), *b* 1953: *m* 1984, Gavin Adrian Alexander Henderson (*see* B Faringdon, colls), who *d* 1991.

Issue of late Hon Sir Evelyn Baring, KG, CMG, KCVO (who was *cr Baron Howick of Glendale* 1960), yst son of 1st Earl (see that title).

PREDECESSORS – (1) Rt Hon Sir EVELYN Baring, GCB, OM, GCMG, KCSI, CIE, yr son of late Henry Baring, MP (see B Northbrook, colls); was Commr of Egyptian Public Dept 1877-9, Comptroller-Gen in Egypt 1879-80, Financial Member of Council of Viceroy of India 1880-83, and Agent and Consul-Gen in Egypt and a Min Plen in Diplo Ser 1883-1907 (granted £50,000 by Parliament); *cr Baron Cromer*, of Cromer, co Norfolk (peerage of United Kingdom) 1892, *Viscount Cromer*, co Norfolk (peerage of United Kingdom) 1899, and *Viscount Errington*, of Hexham, co Northumberland, and *Earl of Cromer*, co Norfolk (peerage of United Kingdom) 1901: *m* 1st, 1876, Ethel Stanley, who *d* 1898, da of Sir Rowland Stanley Errington, 11th Bt; 2ndly, 1901, Lady Katherine Georgiana Louisa Thynne, who *d* 1933, da of 4th Marquess of Bath; *d* 1917; *s* by his eldest son (2) ROWLAND THOMAS, GCB, GCIE, GCVO, PC, 2nd Earl, *b* 1877; in Diplo Ser 1900-11; Private Sec to successive Permanent Under-Secs of State for Foreign Affairs (Lord Hardinge of Penshurst, and Lord Carnock) 1907-11, ADC to successive Viceroys and Govs-Gen of India (Lord Hardinge of Penshurst, and Viscount Chelmsford) 1915-16, Equerry and Assist Private Sec to HM 1916-20, and an Extra Equerry 1920-53; Ch of Staff to HRH the Duke of Connaught during visit to India 1920-21 (KCIE), and to HRH the Prince of Wales during tour of India 1921-22; Lord Chamberlain of the Household 1922-38; a Permanent Lord-in-Waiting 1938-53; Pres of Marylebone Cricket Club 1934-35; Chm Joint Red Cross and St John War Organisation 1939-40; Receiver-Gen of Order of St John of Jerusalem 1943-47; a British Govt Director of Suez Canal 1926-50: *m* 1908, Lady Ruby Florence Mary Elliot (a GCStJ), who *d* 1961, da of 4th Earl of Minto; *d* 1953; *s* by his only son (3) GEORGE ROWLAND STANLEY, KG, GCMG, MBE, PC, 3rd Earl, *b* 1918; Sr Partner and Man Dir Baring Brothers & Co Ltd, 8 Bishopsgate, EC2 1948-60 and 1967-70, Dir Daily Mail & General Trust Ltd 1948-58, and many other Cos, Chm IBM United Kingdom Ltd 1967-70 and 1974-79, Economic Min and Head of UK Treasury and Supply Delegation, Washington 1959-61, UK Exec Dir International Monetary Fund, International Bank for Reconstruction and Development, and International Finance Corporation 1959-61, Gov Bank of England 1961-66, HM Ambassador to Washington 1971-74; Trustee King George's Jubilee Trust, Dep Chm Queen's Jubilee Appeal Council, and Treas Canterbury Cathedral Appeal; HM Lieut City of London 1961, DL Kent 1968-79: *m* 1942, Hon Esme Mary Gabriel Harmsworth, CVO (who *m* 2ndly, 1993, as his 2nd wife, (Reinier) Gerrit Anton van der Woude, late Capt Gren Guards), da of 2nd Viscount Rothermere; *d* 1991; *s* by his elder son (4) EVELYN ROWLAND ESMOND, 4th Earl and present peer; also Viscount Cromer, Viscount Errington, and Baron Cromer.

CROMWELL, BARON (Bewicke-Copley) (Baron E 1375)

I conquer by the cross

GODFREY JOHN BEWICKE-COPLEY, 7th Baron; *b* 4 March 1960; *s* 1982; *ed* Eton, and Camb Univ: *m* 1990, Elizabeth A., da of John Hawksley.

Arms – 1st and 4th, argent, a chief gules, over all a bend azure, *Cromwell*; 2nd and 3rd, chequy or and gules, a chief ermine, *Tateshall*; on an escutcheon of pretence, quarterly, 1st and 4th, argent a cross-moline sable, *Copley*; 2nd and 3rd, argent five lozenges conjoined in fesse gules, each charged with a mullet of the field, between three bears' heads erased sable, *Bewicke*. Crest – 1st, out of a ducal coronet or five ostrich feathers argent, *Copley*; 2nd, a goat's head erased at the neck argent, armed, maned and gorged with a mural crown gules, *Bewicke*. Supporters – On either side a lion sable charged on the shoulder with a representation of the Treasurer's Purse (being the Badge of Ralph, 3rd Baron Cromwell).
Residence – Warren Farm, Lutterworth, Leics LE17 4HP.

BROTHER LIVING

Hon THOMAS DAVID, *b* 6 Aug 1964; *ed* Eton; actor (as Percy Copley).

SISTERS LIVING

Hon Anne Elizabeth, *b* 1955: *m* 1982, David James McNaught Runciman, yst son of late Dr J. B. M Runciman, of Langbank, Renfrewshire, and has issue living, Findlay Redfers, *b* 1990. — Ruth Vivian, *b* 1987.
Hon Davina Mary, *b* 1958: *m* 1991, Anthony William Savile Birkbeck, and has issue (*see* B Somerleyton).

AUNT LIVING (*daughter of 5th Baron*)

Hon Philippa Selina (*Hon Lady Mather*), *b* 1925: *m* 1951, Lt-Col Sir (David) Carol (MacDonell) Mather, MC, MP, Welsh Gds (ret), and has issue living, Nicholas David, *b* 1958: *m* 1985, Susan Alexandra, da of H. B. Thomas, of the Old Rectory, Harnhill, Glos, and has issue living, Toby Montgomery William *b* 1993, Leila Isabella Nadežhda *b* 1990, — Selina Jane, *b* 1952: *m* 1980, Maj Alastair Alexander Linton Watson, The Black Watch, elder son of Maj-Gen Andrew Linton Watson, CB, of Royal Hospital, Chelsea, and has issue living, Harry William George *b* 1988, Sophia Arabella *b* 1981, Alice Selina *b* 1985, — Rose Amabel, *b* 1954: *m* 1986, David Benjamin Shepherd-Cross, elder son of late Maj Peter Shepherd-Cross, of Compton Bassett, Wilts, and has issue living, Max *b* 1989, a son *b* 1991, — (Alice) Victoria, *b* 1960: *m* 1988, Edward Mortimer Harley, elder son of Christopher Charles Harley, of Brampton Bryan Hall, Herefordshire, and has issue living, (Leonora) Brilliana *b* 1992, a da *b* 1994. *Residence* – Oddington House, Moreton-in-Marsh, Glos.

WIDOW LIVING OF SIXTH BARON

(DORIS) VIVIAN (*Dowager Baroness Cromwell*) (The Oranges, Sherborne, Northleach, Glos), yst da of Hugh de Lisle Penfold, of Isle of Man: *m* 1954, the 6th Baron, who *d* 1982.

PREDECESSORS – (1) RALPH de Cromwell; summoned to Parliament 1375-97: *m* 1366, Maud, da of John Bernake, of Tattershall; *d* 1398; *s* by his son (2) RALPH, 2nd Baron; summoned to Parliament 1399-1417: *m* a widow (Joan), who *d* 1434; *d* 1417; *s* by his son (3) RALPH, PC, 3rd Baron; summoned to Parliament 1422-55; Lord High Treasurer 1433-43, Master of the Kings' Mews and Falcons 1436, and Constable of Nottingham Castle 1444-5: *m* 1424, Margaret, da of John, Lord Deincourt; *d* 1454, when the Barony fell into abeyance between the co-heirs, his nieces Maud, widow of Robert, Lord Willoughby de Broke, and Joan, wife of Sir Humphrey, Bourchier; on the death of the latter without issue in 1490, the

Barony devolved upon the former **(4)** MAUD; *dsp* 1497, when the Barony again passed into abeyance between co-heirs descendants of the das of the 1st Baron, and so remained until 1922, when the Committee for Privileges of the House of Lords reported in favour of the petition of Selina Frances, wife of Brig-Gen Sir Robert Calverley Alington Bewicke-Copley, KBE, CB, who *d* 1923 (she was da of Sir Charles Watson Copley, 3rd Bt (Watson, Bt, cr 1700), and one of the co-heirs of William Fitzwilliam, sole heir of Maud, wife of Sir William Fitzwilliam, of Sprotborough, and a da of the 1st Baron), for the determination of the abeyance; she *d* 1923, and the Barony was in July 1923 called out of abeyance in favour of her son **(5)** ROBERT GODFREY WOLSELEY Bewicke-Copley, DSO, MC, 5th Baron, *b* 1893; Lord Lieut of Leics 1949-65: *m* 1925, Freda Constance who *d* 1979, da of Maj Frederick William Beresford Cripps, DSO, of Ampney Park, Glos; *d* 1966; *s* by his only son **(6)** DAVID GODFREY, 6th Baron, *b* 1929; Barrister-at-law, Inner Temple, 1956, Senior Govt Broker 1981-82: *m* 1954, Doris Vivian, yst da of Hugh de Lisle Penfold, of Isle of Man; *d* 1982; *s* by his elder son **(7)** GODFREY JOHN, 7th Baron and present peer.

CROOK, BARON (Crook) (Baron UK 1947)

DOUGLAS EDWIN CROOK, 2nd Baron; *b* 19 Nov 1926; *s* 1989; *ed* Whitgift Sch, Croydon, and Imp Coll of Science and Technology; BSc (Eng) 1947, ACGI, DIC, MICE: *m* 1954, Ellenor, da of late Robert Rouse, and has issue.

Arms – Or, on a bend vert between in chief two Tudor roses barbed and seeded proper, and in base a sprig of oak slipped and fructed of the second, a shepherd's crook of the field. **Crest** – Two crooks in salt-ire or, surmounted by a Tudor rose barbed and seeded proper. **Supporters** – *Dexter*, an antelope gorged with a collar of Tudor roses leaved proper; *sinister*, a greyhound argent collared or, with line reflexed over the back, the collar charged with three cross crosslets gules.
Residence – Ridgehill Barn, Etchinghill, Folkestone, Kent CT18 8BP.

SON LIVING

Hon ROBERT DOUGLAS EDWIN (21 Doncella St, The Gap, Qld 4060, Australia), *b* 29 May 1955: *m* 1981, Suzanne Jane, da of Harold Robinson, of Farnsfield, Notts, and has issue living, Matthew Robert, *b* 28 May 1990, — James Nicholas, *b* 1992.

DAUGHTER LIVING

The cross a shield

Hon Catherine Hilary CROOK, *b* 1960; resumed her maiden name 1993: *m* 1984, Christopher John Ramsdale, of Quebec House, Lutmans Haven, Knowl Hill, Berks RG10 9YN, son of C. Ramsdale, of Coventry.

PREDECESSORS – **(1)** REGINALD DOUGLAS Crook, *b* 1901; Chm National Dock Labour Board 1951-65; *cr Baron Crook*, of Carshalton, co Surrey (peerage of UK) 1947: *m* 1922, Ida Gertrude, who *d* 1985, da of Joseph Haddon; *d* 1989; *s* by his only son **(2)** DOUGLAS EDWIN, 2nd Baron and present peer.

CROSS, VISCOUNT (Cross) (Viscount UK 1886)

ASSHETON HENRY CROSS, 3rd Viscount; *b* 7 May 1920; *s* 1932; *ed* Shrewsbury, and at Magdalene Coll, Camb; formerly Capt Scots Guards: *m* 1st, 1952 (*m diss* 1957), Patricia Mary, eldest da of Edward Pearson Hewetson, of The Craig, Windermere, Westmorland; 2ndly, 1972 (*m diss* 1977), Mrs Victoria Webb; 3rdly, 1983 (*m diss* 1987), Mrs Patricia J. Rossiter, widow of John Rossiter, and has issue (by 1st *m*).

Arms – Gules, a cross flory argent, charged with five passion nails sable, a bordure of the second. **Crest** – A griffin's head, erased argent, gorged with a double chain gold, therefrom pendant a mullet pierced sable, in the beak a passion nail also sable. **Supporters** – On either side a pegasus argent, holding in the mouth a passion nail sable, the dexter gorged with a chain or, therefrom pendant a cross flory gules, the sinister gorged with a double chain or, therefrom pendant a mullet pierced sable.

Trust in the Cross

Residence – Wildwood, Itchenor, Sussex. *Club* – Guards'.

DAUGHTERS LIVING *(By 1st marriage)*

Hon Venetia Clare, *b* 1953: *m* 1986, Rev Norman Hill, son of late Charles Hill, of Sheffield. *Residence* – 6 Egmere Rd, Walsingham, Norfolk.
Hon Nicola, *b* 1954: *m* 1992, Audley George Parry Burnett, son of Lt-Col G. P. Burnett, of Winchester, Hants.

WIDOW LIVING OF SON OF SECOND VISCOUNT

Sybil Anne, da of late Thomas Prain Douglas Murray, MBE, TD, DL, JP, of Templewood, Brechin, Angus: *m* 1st, 1950, Hon John Michael Inigo Cross, who *d* 1951; 2ndly, 1956, Lt-Cdr James Parker-Jervis, RN (ret) (*see* V St Vincent, colls), and has issue living (by 1st *m*) (*see* colls infra). *Residence* – Templewood, Brechin, Angus DD9 7PT.

COLLATERAL BRANCH LIVING

Issue of late Hon John Michael Inigo Cross, 3rd son of 2nd Viscount, *b* 1923, *d* 1951: *m* 1950, Sybil Anne (ante); she *m* 2ndly, 1956, Lt-Cdr James Parker-Jervis, RN (ret) (*see* V St Vincent, colls), da of late Thomas Prain Douglas Murray, MBE, TD, DL, JP, of Templewood, Brechin, Angus:—

Mary Beatrice (*posthumous*) (*Lady Jardine of Applegirth*), *b* 1951: *m* 1982, Sir Alexander Maule Jardine of Applegirth, 12th Bt. *Residence* – Ash House, Millom, Cumbria.

PREDECESSORS – (1) *Rt Hon Sir* RICHARD ASSHETON Cross, GCB, GCSI, PC, DCL, LLD, FRS, 3rd son of late William Cross, DL, of Red Scar, Preston; *b* 1823; Sec of State for Home Depart 1874-80 and 1885-6, one of the Committee of Council on Education in Scotland Aug 1885 to Jan 1886, Sec of State for India July 1886 to Aug 1892, and Lord Privy Seal June 1895 to Oct 1900; MP for Preston (*C*) 1857-62, for SW Lancashire 1868-85, and for Newton Div of SW Lancashire 1885-6; cr *Viscount Cross*, of Broughton-in-Furness (peerage of United Kingdom) 1886: *m* 1852, Georgiana, CI, who *d* 1907, da of late Thomas Lyon, JP, DL, of Appleton Hall, Cheshire; *d* 1914; *s* by his grandson (2) RICHARD ASSHETON, 2nd Viscount (only son of late Hon William Henry Cross, MP, 2nd son of 1st Viscount), by Mary da of late William Lewthwaite, JP, DL of Broadgate, Cumberland, *b* 1882; acted as Private Sec to successive Permanent Secs to the Treasury 1912-17, and was a Principal there 1917-32: *m* 1918, Maud Evelyn Inigo (who *d* 1976, having *m* 2ndly, 1944, as his second wife, Guy Hope Coldwell, who *d* 1948), da of late Maj-Gen Inigo Richmond Jones, CVO, CB; *d* 1932; *s* by his son (3) ASSHETON HENRY, 3rd Viscount and present peer.

CROSS OF CHELSEA, BARONY OF (Cross) (Extinct 1989)

DAUGHTER LIVING OF LIFE BARON

Hon Julia, *b* 1953: *m* 1st, 1973 (*m diss* 19—), Barney Walker; 2ndly, 19—, David Openshaw, and has issue living.

WIDOW LIVING OF LIFE BARON

MILDRED JOAN (*Baroness Cross of Chelsea*), da of late Lt-Col Theodore Eardley-Wilmot, DSO (*see* Eardley-Wilmot, Bt, colls): *m* 1952, Baron Cross of Chelsea, PC (Life Baron), who *d* 1989. *Residence* – The Bridge House, Leintwardine, Craven Arms, Shropshire.

Crowhurst, Viscount; son of Earl of Cottenham.

CROWTHER, BARONY OF (Crowther) (Extinct 1972)

SONS LIVING OF LIFE BARON

Hon Charles Worth (Bourne Bank, Bourne End, Bucks), *b* 1939: *m* 1963, Barbara, yr da of Prof Norman Merrett Hancox, MD, of Barn End, Moorside Lane, Neston, Wirral, Cheshire, and has issue, one son and da.
Hon David Richard Geoffrey, *b* 1943: *m* 1974, Martina, da of Martin Menn-Fink, of Ilanz, Switzerland.

DAUGHTERS LIVING OF LIFE BARON

Hon Anne Hallowell, *b* 1937: *m* 1958, Jonathan Sofer, Bar-at-Law, of 46 Regent's Park Rd, NW1, and has issue, two sons and one da.
Hon Felicity Margaret, *b* 1947: *m* 1978, Colin Rochfort Luke, of 18 Regent's Park Rd, NW1 7TX, and has issue, two sons and one da.
Hon Nicola Mary, *b* 1950.

CROWTHER-HUNT, BARONY OF (Crowther-Hunt) (Extinct 1987)

DAUGHTERS LIVING OF LIFE BARON

Hon Elizabeth Anne, *b* 1947; *ed* Headington Sch, Oxford, and Newnham Coll, Camb; Dir The Prince's Trust Volunteers since 1990: *m* 1976, Peter John Coulson, of 37 Deodar Rd, Putney, SW15 2NP, and has issue.
Hon Rosamund Shirley, *b* 1950: *m* 1978, John Christopher Hill, of 5 Aldwincle Rd, Thorpe Waterville, Kettering, Northamptonshire, and has issue.
Hon Penelope Carol, *b* 1955: *m* 1988, Andrew A. Barr, elder son of W. G. Barr, of Oxford, and has issue. *Residence* – 30 Upland Park Rd, Oxford.

WIDOW LIVING OF LIFE BARON

JOYCE (*Baroness Crowther-Hunt*), da of late Rev Joseph Stackhouse, of Walsall Wood, Staffs; Pres Oxfordshire Guides 1990, Lazo de Dama de Isabel la Católica 1991; DL Oxon: *m* 1944, Baron Crowther-Hunt (Life Baron), who *d* 1987. *Residence* – 14 Apsley Rd, Oxford.

CUDLIPP, BARON (Cudlipp) (Life Baron 1974)

HUGH KINSMAN CUDLIPP, OBE, son of William Cudlipp, of Cardiff; *b* 28 Aug 1913; *ed* Howard Gardens Sch, Cardiff; 1939-45 War; Features Editor *Sunday Chronicle*, London, 1932-35; Features Editor *Daily Mirror* 1935-37; Editor *Sunday Pictorial* 1937-40, and again 1946-49; Man Editor *Sunday Express* 1950-52; Joint Man Dir *Daily Mirror* and *Sunday Pictorial* 1959-63 (Editorial Dir 1952-63), Chm Odhams Press Ltd 1961-63, of Daily Mirror Newspapers Ltd 1963-68, of Internat Publishing Corpn 1968-73 (Dep Chm 1964-68), and of Internat Publishing Corpn Newspaper Div 1970-73; Dep Chm (editorial) Reed Internat Board 1970-73; a Dir of Asso Television Ltd 1956-72; adviser to PM on Counter-inflation Policies 1976; author of *Publish and be Damned!* 1955, *At Your Peril* 1962, *Walking on the Water* 1976, *The Prerogative of the Harlot* (*Press Barons and Power*); *cr* OBE (Civil) 1945, Knt 1973, and *Baron Cudlipp*, of Aldingbourne, co W Sussex (Life Baron) 1974: *m* 1st, 1938; 2ndly, 1945, Eileen Ascroft, who *d* 1962; 3rdly, 1963, Jodi, da of late John L. Hyland, of Palm Beach, Fla, USA.
Residence – 14 Tollhouse Close, Avenue de Chartres, Chichester, W Sussex PO19 1SF.

CULLEN OF ASHBOURNE, BARON (Cokayne) (Baron UK 1920)

CHARLES BORLASE MARSHAM COKAYNE, MBE, 2nd Baron; *b* 6 Oct 1912; *s* 1932; *ed* Eton; is Major Roy Corps of Signals (TA); a Lord in Waiting to HM 1979-82, and a Lieut of City of London; MBE (Mil) 1945: *m* 1st, 1942, Valerie Catharine Mary, da of late W. H. Collbran; 2ndly, 1948, Patricia Mary, el da of late Col S. Clulow-Gray, and has issue by 1st *m*.

Arms – Argent, three cocks gules, armed crested, and jelloped sable. **Crest** – A cock's head erased gules, beaked, crested, and jelloped sable. **Supporters** – *Dexter*, a lion guardant party per fesse or and argent; *sinister*, an ostrich argent holding in its beak a horseshoe proper; each gorged with a collar pendant therefrom an escutcheon argent, charged with two bars vert.
Residence – 75 Cadogan Gardens, SW3.

DAUGHTER LIVING (By 1st marriage)

Hon Julia Collbran, *b* 1943: *m* 1968 (*m diss* 1989), Don Francesco Costa Sanseverino di Bisignano; 2ndly, 1991, Michael G. M. Groves, and has issue living (by 1st *m*), Edoardo, *b* 1969, — Alessandro, *b* 1971, — Sveva, *b* 19—. *Residences* – The Poplars, Landican, Wirral, Merseyside L49 5LJ; 9 Prothero Rd, SW6 7LY.

Courage in Adversity

BROTHERS LIVING

Hon EDMUND WILLOUGHBY MARSHAM (Box 1254, Irvine Av, Merritt, BC, Canada VOK 2B0), *b* 18 May 1916; *ed* Eton; late Fl Lt RAF: *m* 1943, Janet (MANSON), da of late William Douglas Watson, of Canterbury.
(*Hon*) John O'Brien Marsham (does not use courtesy title), *b* 1920; *ed* Eton: *m* 1948, Anne Frances, who *d* 1971, da of late Bertram Clayton, of Wakefield, Yorks, and has issue living, Michael John, *b* 1950: *m* 1st, 1976 (*m diss* 1985), Baudilia Medina Negrin, of Caracas, Venezuela; 2ndly, 1986, Yvette Santana. *Residence* – 14 St Omer Rd, Cowley, Oxford OX4 3HB.

SISTERS LIVING

Hon Barbara Mary, *b* 1905: *m* 1929, Maj Gilbert Edgar Francis Vandernoot, late Irish Gds, who *d* 1981, and has issue living, Anthea Caroline (22 Byfields Rd, Kingsclere, Newbury, Berks RG15 8TG), *b* 1936: *m* 1963, John Michael Ryan, who *d* 1990. *Residence* – Oak Cottage, Hartley Wintney, Hants.
Hon Ruth Margaret (c/o M. M. Acland Hood, 9 Fentiman Rd, SW8 1LD), *b* 1909: *m* 1st, 1939, Capt Robert William Alfred Moore, RA, who was *ka* 1940; 2ndly, 1949, Rev David Henry Aitcheson Williams, who *d* 1955, and has issue living, (by 1st *m*) Elizabeth Virginia (*posthumous*), *b* 1940: *m* 1973, Donald Franklin Hoover, of Telkwa, BC, Canada.

PREDECESSOR – (1) *Sir* BRIEN IBRICAN Cokayne, KBE, son of late George Edward Cokayne, FSA, Clarenceux King of Arms; *b* 1864; a partner in the firm of Anthony Gibbs and Sons, merchants and bankers; appointed a Director of the Bank of England 1902, and was Dep Gov 1915-18, and Gov 1918-20; *cr Baron Cullen of Ashbourne*, of Roehampton, co Surrey (peerage of United Kingdom) 1920: *m* 1904, Grace Margaret, who *d* 1971, da of late Rev the Hon John Marsham (E Romney); *d* 1932; *s* by his son (2) CHARLES BORLASE MARSHAM, 2nd Baron and present peer.

CUMBERLEGE, BARONESS (Cumberlege) (Life Baroness 1990)

JULIA FRANCES CUMBERLEGE, CBE, da of Dr Lambert Ulrich Camm, of Appleton, Newick, Sussex; *b* 27 Jan 1943; *ed* Convent of the Sacred Heart, Kent; JP 1973-85, DL E Sussex 1986, Vice Lord Lieut 1991; Member Lewes District Council 1966-79 (Leader 1977-78), E Sussex CC 1974-85 (Chm Social Services Cttee 1979-82), E Sussex Area Health Authority 1977-81; Chm Brighton Health Authority 1981-88, Nat Assocn of Health Authorities 1987-88, and SW Thames Regional Health Authority 1988-92; Member NHS Policy Bd since 1989, Council of St George's Medical Sch, Press Council 1977-83, and Appointments Commn since 1984; Chm Review of Community Nursing for England 1985, Vice-Pres Royal Coll of Nursing since 1988; Under-Sec of State, Dept of Health since 1992; *cr* CBE (Civil) 1985, and *Baroness Cumberlege*, of Newick,

co E Sussex (Life Baroness) 1990: *m* 1961, Patrick Francis Howard Cumberlege (*see* Gibbons, Bt), and has issue.
Residence – Vuggles Farm, Newick, Lewes, E Sussex BN8 4RU.

SONS LIVING

Hon (Christopher) Mark, *b* 1962; *ed* Sutton Valence.
Hon Justin Francis, *b* 1964; *ed* Haileybury.
Hon Oliver Richard, *b* 1968; *ed* Lancing.

CUNLIFFE, BARON (Cunliffe) (Baron UK 1914)

Faithfully

ROGER CUNLIFFE, 3rd Baron; *b* 12 Jan 1932; *s* 1963; *ed* Eton, and at Trin Coll, Camb (MA), Architectural Assocn (AA Dipl), and Open Univ; RIBA, MIMgt; Assist, Goldsmiths' Co: *m* 1957, Clemency Ann, el da of late Maj Geoffrey Benyon Hoare, of Clover House, Aldeburgh, Suffolk, and has issue.

Arms – Per chevron or and sable, three conies courant counterchanged. **Crest** – Upon a rock a greyhound sejant sable, collared or. **Supporters** – On either side a figure habited as a Gate Porter of the Bank of England, supporting in the exterior hand his staff of office. *Residence* – The Broadhurst, Brandeston, Woodbridge, Suffolk IP13 7AG.

SONS LIVING

Hon HENRY, *b* 9 March 1962, *ed* Eton; Freeman Goldsmiths' Co.
Hon Luke, *b* 1965, *ed* Eton, and Bransons Coll; Freeman, Goldsmiths' Co: *m* 1992, Penelope A., da of Cmdr P. S. Wilson, RN (ret), of Chipstead, Surrey, and of Mrs J. H. Grantham, of Hampstead, London.

DAUGHTER LIVING

Hon Rachel Henrietta, *b* 1960; *ed* N London Collegiate Sch, Felsted Sch, Camb Univ (BA), Manchester Univ (MEd), and Arizona Univ; Freeman, Goldsmiths' Co: *m* 1987, Roger David Hardesty, son of late R. D. Hardesty, of Belle Mead, NJ, USA.

BROTHER LIVING

Hon Merlin (Wills Rd, Dixon's Creek, Vic 3775, Aust), *b* 1935; *ed* Eton: *m* 1st, 1960 (*m diss* 19—), Deborah Rutherford Grimwade; 2ndly, 1978, Mrs Amanda June Foster, da of Samuel Rogers, and has had issue (by 1st *m*), Tamsin Elizabeth, *b* 1963; *d* 1982, — Sophia Catherine, *b* 1966.

SISTERS LIVING

Hon Shirley Cynthia, *b* 1926: *m* 1959, Alan Desmond Wilson, and has issue living, Matthew Crispin, *b* 1961, — Richenda Catherine, *b* 1963. *Residence* – Ashbrook, Aston Tirrold, Didcot, Oxon OX11 9DL.
Hon Corinna, *b* 1929: *m* 1957, Frederick Starr Wildman, and has issue living, Tarik Charles, *b* 1959: *m* 1993, Susan O'Reilly. *Address* – The Applehouse, RR1 Box 979, Dorset, Vermont 05251, USA.

COLLATERAL BRANCHES LIVING

Grandchildren (by 1st *m*) of late Hon Geoffrey Cunliffe (infra):—
Issue of late Peter Cunliffe, *b* 1925, *d* 1987: *m* 1955, Barbara Marion (5 Grouville Park, Jersey, CI), da of H. F. Phillips, of Sous La Hougue, of Jersey, CI:—
Robert, *b* 1958. —— Christopher, *b* 1960. —— Oliver, *b* 1966.

Issue of late Hon Geoffrey Cunliffe, 2nd son of 1st Baron, *b* 1903, *d* 1982: *m* 1st, 1922, Patrick Sidney, who *d* 1940, da of late Robert Benjamin Frend, of Ardsallagh, co Tipperary; 2ndly, 1941 (*m diss* 1947), Gavrelle, da of William Arthur Thomas, and widow of Christopher Hobhouse; 3rdly, 1947, Barbara Waring, who *d* 1990, da of Dr J. A. Gibb, of Maidstone, Kent, and formerly wife of Laurence A. Evans:—
(By 2nd *m*) Adam (17 Dorset Rd, Leeds 8, W Yorks), *b* 1946; *ed* Wellington Coll. —— Carol (7 Orchard St, Mendham, NJ 07945, USA), *b* 1944: *m* 1st, 1966 (*m diss* 1985), Joseph Francis Logan; 2ndly, 1992, Jay K. Dilley.

PREDECESSORS – (1) Sir WALTER Cunliffe, GBE, son of late Roger Cunliffe, of Tyrrells Wood, Surrey; *b* 1855; was head of the firm of Cunliffe Bros (afterwards Goschens and Cunliffe), of 12 Austin Friars, EC; Dep-Gov of Bank of England 1911-13, and Gov 1913-18; *cr Baron Cunliffe*, of Headley, co Surrey (Peerage of United Kingdom) 1914: *m* 1st, 1890, Mary Agnes, who *d* 1893, da of late Robert Henderson, of Randalls Park, Leatherhead; 2ndly, 1896, Edith Cunningham, who *d* 1965, da of Col Robert Tod Boothby, of St Andrews Fife; *d* 1920; *s* by his el son (2) ROLF, *b* 1899; Wing-Cdr RAFVR: *m* 1st, 1925 (*m diss* 1952), Joan Catherine, who *d* 1980, da of late Cecil Lubbock (B Avebury, colls); 2ndly, 1952, Kathleen Elsie, who *d* 1990, da of Ernest Brownfield Pope, of Wargrave, Berks, and widow of Capt Philip Robinson, RAMC, of Manor House, Wendover, Bucks (*ka* 1944); *d* 1963; *s* by his el son (3) ROGER, 3rd Baron and present peer.

CURZON OF KEDLESTON, MARQUESSATE OF (Curzon) (Extinct 1925)

DAUGHTER LIVING OF FIRST MARQUESS

(*See* B Ravensdale)

DACRE, BARONESS (Douglas-Home) (Baron E 1321)

RACHEL LEILA DOUGLAS-HOME (*Baroness Dacre*); *b* 24 Oct 1929; da of 4th Viscount Hampden; *s* (on termination of abeyance) 1970: *m* 1951, Hon William Douglas-Home, who *d* 1992 (*see* B Home of the Hirsel), and has issue.

Arms – Not exemplified at time of going to press.
Residence – Derry House, Kilmeston, nr Alresford, Hants.

SON LIVING

Hon JAMES THOMAS ARCHIBALD, *b* 16 May 1952: *m* 1979, Christine, da of William Stephenson, of The Ridings, Royston, Herts, and has issue living, Emily, *b* 7 Feb 1983.

DAUGHTERS LIVING

Hon Sarah, *b* 1954: *m* 1977, Nicholas Charles Dent, yst son of Maj J. C. Dent, of 51 Addison Rd, W14, and has issue living, a da, *b* 1982.
Hon Gian Leila, *b* 1958.
Hon Dinah Lilian, *b* 1964: *m* 1989, Harry Marriott, 2nd son of John Marriott, of Gt Milton, Oxfordshire, and has issue living, a son, *b* 1994.

SISTER LIVING

Hon Tessa Mary, *b* 1934: *m* 1956, Julian Ogilvie Thompson, of Froome, Froome Rd, Athol Extension, Johannesburg, S Africa, and has issue living, Christopher William, *b* 1958: *m* 1984, Kathleen Jean, da of Alastair Blackstock, of Blairgowrie, Johannesburg, and has issue living, James Alastair *b* 1988, Luke Julian *b* 1991, — Anthony Thomas, *b* 1964, — Rachel Amanda, *b* 1960: *m* 1985, Richard Miles Keene, of The Oast House, Mill Court, Upper Froyle, Hants, son of Douglas Keene, of Littlehampton, W Sussex, and has issue living, Harold Thomas *b* 1988, Justin Frederick *b* 1989, Oliver Stephen *b* 1993, — Leila Katharine, *b* 1965: *m* 1990, Hilton A. Barnett, of 36a Parktown North, Johannesburg 2193, son of G. G. Barnett, of Bryanston, Johannesburg.

COLLATERAL BRANCHES LIVING (*See* V Hampden).

PREDECESSORS – **(1)** Sir RANDOLF de Dacre, son and heir of Sir William de Dacre of Dacre, Cumberland; summoned to Parliament 1321-38, whereby he is held to have become Lord Dacre: *m* Margaret, da and heir of Thomas de Multon, of Gilsland, Cumberland; *d* 1339; *s* by his son **(2)** WILLIAM, 2nd Baron: *m* Katherine, da of Sir Ralph Neville, of Raby, co Durham; *d* 1361; *s* by his brother **(3)** RANDOLF, 3rd Baron; *b* about 1322; murdered 1375; *s* by his brother **(4)** HUGH, 4th Baron: *m* 1354/55, Elizabeth, widow of Sir William Douglas, Earl of Atholl; *d* 1383; *s* by his son **(5)** WILLIAM, 5th Baron: (said to have married first, Joan Douglas): *m* Mary; *d* 1399; *s* by his son **(6)** THOMAS, 6th Baron; *b* 1387: *m* Philippa, da of Ralph Neville, Earl of Westmorland; *d* 1458; *s* by his grand-da **(7)** JOAN (da of Sir Thomas Dacre): *m* 1446, Sir Richard Fiennes, who was summoned to Parliament as Baron Dacre 1459; he *d* 1483 and his widow *d* 1486; he was *s* by his grandson, **(8)** THOMAS (son of Sir John Fiennes), 8th Baron; KB 1494: *m* about 1492, Anne, da of Sir Humphrey Bourchier; *d* 1533; *s* by his grandson **(9)** THOMAS (son of Sir Thomas Fiennes), 9th Baron: *m* 1536, Mary, da of George Nevill, Lord Abergavenny; having taken part in a deer hunt at Laughton Park, Sussex, when a park keeper was killed, he was found guilty of murder, hanged at Tyburn 1541, and his honours forfeited; his son **(10)** GREGORY, 10th Baron (whose elder brother Thomas, *d* 1553, aged 15, would have succeeded but for his father's forfeiture) was restored to his honours 1558: *m* about 1558, Anne Sackville, sister of 1st Earl of Dorset; *d* 1594; *s* by his sister **(11)** MARGARET, *b* 1541: *m* 1564, Sampson Lennard, who *d* 1615; *d* 1612; *s* by her son **(12)** HENRY, 12th Baron; *b* 1570: *m* 1589, Chrysogona, da of Sir Richard Baker of Sissinghurst; *d* 1616; *s* by his son **(13)** RICHARD, 13th Baron; *b* 1596: *m* 1st, 1617, Elizabeth, da of Sir Arthur Throckmorton; 2ndly, 1625, Dorothy North, da of 3rd Lord North; *d* 1630; *s* by his son **(14)** FRANCIS, 14th Baron; *b* 1619: *m* 1641, Elizabeth Bayning (who was *cr* Viscountess of Sheppey for life 1680), da of Paul 1st Viscount Bayning of Sudbury; *d* 1662; *s* by his son **(15)** (THOMAS, 15th Baron) *b* 1654; *cr Earl of Sussex* 1674: *m* 1684, Anne Palmer or FitzRoy, da of Barbara Duchess of Cleveland; *d* 1715, when the Earldom became ext and the Barony of Dacre fell into abeyance between his two das, until 1741, when the yr **(16)** ANNE *s* on the death without issue of her sister Barbara; *b* 1684: *m* 1st, 1716, Richard Barrett, of Belhus, Essex, who *d* 1716; 2ndly, 1718, Henry Roper, 8th Baron Teynham, who *d* 1723; 3rdly, 1725, Hon Robert Moore, son of 3rd Earl of Drogheda, who *d* 1762; she *d* 1755; *s* by her son **(17)** THOMAS Barrett-Lennard, 17th Baron; *b* 1717: *m* 1739, Anna Maria, sister of 1st Earl Camden; *d* 1786; *s* by his nephew **(18)** TREVOR CHARLES Roper (son of Hon Charles Roper), 18th Baron; *b* 1745: *m* 1773, Mary, da and heir of Sir Thomas Fludyer, of Lee, Kent; *d* 1794; *s* by his sister **(19)** GERTRUDE; *b* 1750: *m* 1771, Thomas Brand, who *d* 1794; *d* 1819; *s* by her son **(20)** THOMAS, 20th Baron; *b* 1774: *m* 1819, Barbarina, da of Adm Sir Chaloner Ogle, 1st Bt, who *d* 1854; *d* 1851; *s* by his brother **(21)** HENRY OTWAY Trevor, 21st Baron; *b* 1777; Gen in the Army; assumed by R licence 1824 the surname of Trevor in lieu of Brand: *m* 1806, Pyne Crosbie, sister and co-heir of William, 4th Baron Brandon; *d* 1853; *s* by his son **(22)** THOMAS CROSBIE WILLIAM Trevor, 22nd Baron; *b* 1808; assumed by R licence 1851 the surname of Trevor in lieu of Brand: *m* 1837, Hon Susan Sophia Cavendish, da of 1st Baron Chesham; *d* 1890; *s* by his brother **(23)** HENRY BOUVERIE WILLIAM, GCB, PC, 23rd Baron; Speaker of the House of Commons, who in 1884 was *cr Viscount Hampden*, of Glynde, Sussex (peerage of UK); from that time the Barony of Dacre descended with the Viscountcy of Hampden **(25-27)** until the death of the 4th Viscount and 27th Baron in 1965, when the Barony fell into abeyance between his two das, Hon Mrs Rachel Leila Douglas-Home, and Hon Mrs Tessa Mary Ogilvie Thompson, and so continued until 1970, when the abeyance was terminated in favour of the el **(28)** RACHEL LEILA, present peeress.

DACRE OF GLANTON, BARON (Trevor-Roper) (Life Baron 1979)

Prof HUGH REDWALD TREVOR-ROPER, son of late Bertie William Trevor-Roper, MB, MRCS (*see* B Teynham, colls); *b* 15 Jan 1914; *ed* Charterhouse, and Ch Ch Oxford; Regius Prof of Modern History, Oxford 1957-1980; Master of Peterhouse, Camb 1980-87; *cr Baron Dacre of Glanton*, of Glanton, co Northumberland (Life Baron) 1979: *m* 1954, Lady Alexandra Henrietta Louisa, da of 1st Earl Haig, and formerly wife of Rear Adm Clarence Dinsmore Howard-Johnston, CB, DSO, MC.

Arms – Quarterly: *1st and 4th*, per fesse azure and or, a pale and three roebuck's heads erased counterchanged for *Roper*; *2nd and 3rd*, per bend sinister ermine and ermines a lion rampant or, and for distinction a canton sanguine, thereon an escallop argent charged with a cross flory of the fourth for *Trevor*. **Crests** – 1st, a lion rampant sanguine holding in his right paw a ducal coronet or for *Roper*; 2nd, on a chapeau gules turned up ermine a wyvern wings elevated sanguine and for distinction on the breast an escallop charged as in the arms.
Residence – The Old Rectory, Didcot, Oxon OX11 7EB.

DAHRENDORF, BARON (Dahrendorf) (Life Baron 1993)

RALF DAHRENDORF, KBE, son of late Gustav Dahrendorf; *b* 1 May 1929; *ed* Hamburg Univ (DPhil), and LSE (PhD), Hon DLitt Reading and Dublin, Hon LLD Manchester, Wagner Coll, NY, York (Ontario), and Columbia, NY, Hon DHL Kalamazoo Coll, and John Hopkins Univ Baltimore, Hon DSc Ulster, Bath and Bologna, Hon DUniv Open Univ, Maryland and Surrey, Hon Dr Université Catholique de Louvain, Hon DSSc Queen's Belfast and Birmingham, etc; Hon Fellow Imperial Coll and LSE; formerly Prof of Sociology at Hamburg, Tübingen and Konstanz Univs; Member EEC Commn Brussels 1970-74, Dir LSE 1974-84; Non-Exec Dir Glaxo Holdings plc 1984-92; Warden St Antony's Coll, Oxford, since 1987, Dir and Chm Newspaper Publishing plc 1992-93; FBA, FRSA; *cr* KBE 1982, and *Baron Dahrendorf*, of Clare Market, in the City of Westminster (Life Baron) 1993: *m* 1980, Ellen Joan, da of James Krug, of New York.
Residence – St Antony's College, Oxford OX2 6JT. *Clubs* – Reform, Garrick.

DAINTON, BARON (Dainton) (Life Baron 1986)

FREDERICK SYDNEY DAINTON, son of late George Whalley Dainton; *b* 11 Nov 1914; *ed* Central Secondary Sch, Sheffield, St John's Coll, Oxford (MA, BSc, Hon Fellow 1968), and Sidney Sussex Coll, Camb (PhD, ScD); Hon Fellow St Catherine's Coll, Camb 1961, Goldsmiths' Coll, Queen Mary Coll, London, Birkbeck Coll, London, Hon FRCP, Hon FRSC, Hon FRCR, Hon FLA, Hon ScD Lódź and Dublin, Hon DSc Bath, Loughborough, Heriot-Watt, Warwick, Strathclyde, Exeter, Queen's Univ, Belfast, Manchester, E Anglia, Leeds, McMaster, Uppsala, Liverpool, Salford and Kent, Hon LLD Nottingham, Aberdeen, Sheffield, Cambridge and London, Hon DCL Oxford, Hon DLitt Council for Nat Academic Awards, etc; Prof of Physical Chemistry Leeds Univ 1950-65, Vice-Chancellor Nottingham Univ 1965-70; Dr Lee's Prof of Chemistry, Oxford Univ 1970-73; Chm Univ Grants Cttee 1973-78, since when Chancellor Sheffield Univ; Chm: Assocn for Radiation Research 1964-66, Nat Libraries Cttee 1968-69, British Library Board, Nat Radiological Protection Board 1978-85, Edward Boyle Memorial Trust since 1982, etc; Member of Council, Royal Postgraduate Medical Sch since 1980; Trustee: Natural History Museum 1974-84, and Wolfson Foundn 1978-88, etc; Prime Warden Goldsmiths' Co 1982-83; FRS 1957; *cr* Kt 1971, and *Baron Dainton*, of Hallam Moors, S Yorkshire (Life Baron) 1986: *m* 1942, Barbara Hazlitt, JP, PhD, Hon DSc, only da of late Dr W. B. Wright, of Manchester, and has issue.
Residence – 36 Charlbury Road, Oxford OX2 6UX. *Club* – Athenaeum.

SON LIVING

Hon John Bourke, *b* 1947. *Residence* – Westcroft, 30 Oldfield Rd, Heswall, Wirral, Merseyside L60 6SF.

DAUGHTERS LIVING

Hon Mary Crawford, *b* 1950: *m* 1981 (*m diss* 1988), David Whitehead, and has issue living, two children. *Residence* – 7 Veronica Rd, Didsbury, Manchester M20 0ST.
Hon Rosalind Hazlitt, *b* 1952: *m* 1981, Christopher Conway. *Residence* – 58 Trinity St, Belle Vue, Shrewsbury SY3 7PQ.

DALHOUSIE, EARL OF (Ramsay) (Earl S 1633)

Pray and labour

SIMON RAMSAY, KT, GCVO, GBE, MC, 16th Earl; *b* 17 Oct 1914; *s* 1950; *ed* Eton, and Ch Ch, Oxford; Lord-Lieut of Angus, and a KStJ; late Major 4th/5th Batn Black Watch (TA); Gov-Gen of Federation of Rhodesia and Nyasaland 1957-63; Lord Chamberlain to HM Queen Elizabeth the Queen Mother 1965-92, Lord Lieut co Angus (later Tayside Region) 1967-89 and Chancellor of Dundee Univ since 1977; Hon LLD Dalhousie Univ, Halifax, Nova Scotia, and Dundee; 1939-45 War (MC); an additional Conservative Whip 1946-50; MP for Forfarshire (*C*), 1945-50; GBE (Civil) 1957; KT 1971; GCVO 1978: *m* 1940, Margaret Elizabeth Mary, da of late Brig-Gen Archibald Stirling of Keir (*see* Stirling-Maxwell, Bt, colls), and has issue.

Arms – Argent, an eagle displayed sable, beaked and membered gules. **Crest** – An unicorn's head, couped at the neck argent, armed, maned, and tufted or. **Supporters** – *Dexter*, a griffin argent; *sinister*, a greyhound argent, gorged with a collar gules, charged with three escallops of the first.
Seats – Brechin Castle, Brechin, Angus, DD9 68H; Dalhousie Castle, Bonnyrigg, Midlothian. *Clubs* – White's and Puffin's.

SONS LIVING

JAMES HUBERT (*Lord Ramsay*) (Dalhousie Lodge, Edzell, Angus; 3 Vicarage Gdns, W8), *b* 17 Jan 1948; *ed* Ampleforth; late 2nd Lt Coldm Gds; DL Angus 1993: *m* 1973, Marilyn Davina, da of Maj Sir David Henry Butter, KCVO, MC (*see* Wernher, Bt, ext), and has issue:—
    SON LIVING— *Hon* Simon David, *b* 18 April 1981.
    DAUGHTERS LIVING— *Hon* Lorna Theresa, *b* 1975, — *Hon* Alice Magdalene, *b* 1977.
Hon Anthony, *b* 1949; *ed* Ampleforth, and Magdalen Coll, Oxford: *m* 1st, 1973 (*m diss* 1979), Georgina Mary, da of late Hon Michael Langhorne Astor (*see* V Astor); 2ndly, 1984, Vilma, da of late Raphael Salcedo, of Santa Martha, Colombia, and has issue living (by 1st *m*), Alexander Simon, *b* 1977, — (by 2nd *m*) Zoë Mary, *b* 1985, — Isabella, *b* 1987. *Residence* – 37 Anhalt Rd, SW11 4N2.
Hon John Patrick, *b* 1952; *ed* Ampleforth: *m* 1981, Louisa Jane, only da of late Robert Erland Nicolai d'Abo, of West Wratting Park, W Wratting, Cambs (*see* D Rutland), and has issue living, Christopher, *b* 1984, — Lucy Emma, *b* 1985. *Residence* – 1 Kassala Rd, SW11.

DAUGHTERS LIVING

Lady Elizabeth (*Countess of Scarbrough*), *b* 1941: *m* 1970, 12th Earl of Scarbrough. *Residence* – Sandbeck Park, Maltby, Rotherham S66 8PF.
Lady Sarah, *b* 1945: *m* 1966, Sir (John) Chippendale (Lindley) Keswick, of 1A Ilchester Place, W14, and Auchendolly House, Old Bridge of Urr, Castle Douglas, Kirkcudbrightshire, 2nd son of late Sir William Keswick, of Glenkiln, Shawhead, Dumfries (*see* Lindley, By, 1950 Edn), and has issue living, David, *b* 1967, — Tobias, *b* 1968, — Adam, *b* 1973.

SISTER LIVING

Lady Jean Maule, *b* 1909: *m* 1945, Lt-Col David McNeil Campbell Rose, DSO, Black Watch, and has issue living, Hugh Ramsay, *b* 1946; Maj Black Watch (ret): *m* 1977, Flora Margaret, el da of Lt-Col W. J. C. Adamson, of Careston Castle, Brechin, — Mary Janet, *b* 1948: *m* 1976, Maj Anthony James Herber Davies, RE (ret). *Residence* – Jezreel, 17 Leegomery Rd, Wellington, Shropshire TF1 3BP.

COLLATERAL BRANCHES LIVING

Granddaughter of late Hon Sir Patrick William Maule Ramsay, KCMG, 2nd son of 13th Earl, *b* 1879, *d* 1962: *m* 1917, Cynthia, who *d* 1957, da of late Brig-Gen Sir Herbert Conyers Surtees, CB, and widow of Christopher Cecil Tower, of Weald Hall, Essex:—
Issue of late David Patrick Maule Ramsay, *b* 1919, *d* 1978: *m* 1948 (*m diss* 19—), Hélène (who *d* 1980, having *m* 2ndly, John Tod Horton), da of Leonidas Arvanitidi, of Paris:—
Sylvia Patricia (5617 South Dorchester Av, Chicago, 60637-1749 Illinois, USA), *b* 19—.

Issue of late Adm Hon Sir Alexander Robert Maule Ramsay, GCVO, KCB, DSO, 3rd son of 13th Earl, *b* 1881, *d* 1972: *m* 1919, HRH Princess (Victoria) Patricia Helena Elizabeth, VA, CI, CD, GCStJ, who *d* 1974 (who on her marriage renounced by Royal permission the style and title of "HRH" and "Princess", and adopted the style of "Lady", with precedence before Marchionesses of England), yr da of Field Marshal HRH the 1st Duke of Connaught and Strathearn (*see* ROYAL FAMILY):—
Alexander Arthur Alfonso David Maule RAMSAY OF MAR (Cairnbulg Castle, Fraserburgh, Aberdeenshire AB43 5TN; c/o Mar Estate Office, Braemar, Aberdeenshire; Flat 8, 25 Onslow Sq, SW7 3NJ; *Clubs* – Cavalry & Guards', New (Edinburgh), Puffin's (Edinburgh), Turf); *b* 21 Dec 1919; *ed* Eton, and Trin Coll, Oxford (MA); FRICS; DL (Aberdeenshire); Baron of Kellie; Capt Gren Gds (ret); served 1938-47 (wounded Tunisia 1943); an ADC to HRH the Duke of Gloucester whilst Gov-Gen of Australia 1944-47; a Page of Honour at Coronation of King George VI; Chm of Exec Cttee of Scottish Life Boat Council, RNLI since 1965; Vice-Patron of RNMDSF, and of Braemar Royal Highland Soc: *m* 6 Oct 1956, Hon Flora Marjory Fraser (*Lady Saltoun* in her own right), da of 19th Lord Saltoun, and has issue (*see* L Saltoun).

Granddaughters of Capt Archibald Henry Maule Ramsay (*infra*):—
Issue of late Robert John Maule Ramsay, *b* 1920, *d* 1978: *m* 1st, 1948 (*m diss* 1961), Theodora Jean (2 Cliffield, Shalford, Essex CM7 5HP), da of Martyn Hewlett, of Cranham Hall, Little Waltham; 2ndly, 1961, Elizabeth Frances, who *d* 1972, da of A. F. Bultitude:—
(By 1st *m*) Theodora Alice Maule (8-2 Hailsland Grove, Wester Hailes, Edinburgh EH14 3BW), *b* 1950. —— Christian Ismay Maule (10 Braintree Rd, Shalford, nr Braintree, Essex CM7 5HG), *b* 1952: *m* 1972, Juan Carlos Torres, of Santiago de

Compostela, Spain, and has issue living, Aaron *b* 1976. —— Charlotte Maule, *b* 1954: *m* 1976, John Gentry, of 275 Peach Tree Lane, Newnan, Georgia 30263, USA, and *d* 1992, leaving issue, Nathan, *b* 1975, — Mathew, *b* 1982, — Andrew, *b* 1989.

Grandsons of late Lt-Col Henry Lushington Ramsay (infra)—
Issue of late Capt Archibald Henry Maule Ramsay, *b* 1894, *d* 1955: *m* 1917, Hon Ismay Lucretia Mary, who *d* 1975, da of 14th Viscount Gormanston, and widow of Lord Ninian Edward Crichton-Stuart (M Bute):—

George Patrick Maule (The Old School House, The Square, Elham, Kent), *b* 1922; *ed* Eton; Col late Scots Gds: *m* 1st, 1947 (*m diss* 1977), Patricia Mary, da of Dr J. J. Morrin; 2ndly, 1980, Mrs Bridget Kelly, da of late Ronald Thomas Dyson Hornby, of 25 Elm Tree Green, Gt Missenden, Bucks, and formerly wife of late Capt Edward Kelly, and has issue living (by 1st *m*), Alexander John Patrick Maule (Flat A, 38 Dafforne Rd, SW17), *b* 1948, — Patrick William Maule (40 Elmbourne Rd, SW17 8JR), *b* 1951: *m* 1984, Fiona, da of Peter Stoddart, of North Rye House, Moreton-in-Marsh, Glos GL56 0XU, and has issue living, Nicholas George *b* 1992, Emily May *b* 1986, Katie Olivia *b* 1988, — Catherine Mary Maule (The Stone House, Wyck Rissington, Cheltenham, Glos GL54 2PN), *b* 1950: *m* 1972 (*m diss* 1991), Capt Sir Peter Ralph Leopold Walker-Okeover, 4th Bt, Blues and Royals, — Diana Mary Maule, *b* 1957: *m* 1983, as his 2nd wife, Timothy J. P. Coghlan, of Weedon Lodge Cottage, Everdon, nr Daventry, Northants NN11 6BQ, son of late A. F. Coghlan, of Ludwell Grange, Horsted Keynes, Sussex, and has issue living, Louise Mary *b* 1985, Elizabeth Mary *b* 1987, — Fiona Elisabeth Maule, *b* 1964: *m* 1987, Robert Algernon Radcliffe Boyle, Maj Irish Gds (ret) (*see* E Shannon, colls). —— Rev John Charles Maule (St Philomena's, Niddry Rd, Winchburgh, Broxburn EH52 6RY), *b* 1926; *ed* Eton, and at Pontifical Beda Coll, Rome; late Maj Scots Gds; Roman Catholic priest.

Granddaughter of late Gen the Hon Sir Henry Ramsay, KCSI, CB, brother of 12th Earl:—
Issue of late Lieut-Col Henry Lushington Ramsay, *b* 1854, *d* 1928: *m* 1893, Sophia, who *d* 1946, da of late J. P. Thomas, of Warneford Place, Wilts, and Calcutta:—

Vera Edith (5 Manor Court, Swan Road, Pewsey, Wilts SN9 5DW), *b* 1990.

PREDECESSORS – (1) *Sir* GEORGE Ramsay of Dalhousie, Knt; on his own resignation had a charter of the Barony of Dalhousie; also of the Barony of Melrose on the resignation of John Ramsay, Earl of Holderness; *cr Lord Ramsay of Melrose* (peerage of Scotland) by charter 1618, but not liking the title obtained a letter from James VI to change it to *Lord Ramsay of Dalhousie* (with precedence of 1618); *d* 1629; *s* by his el son **(2)** WILLIAM, 2nd Lord; raised a Regt in Army of the Covenant, which he commanded at Marston Moor and Philliphaugh; *cr Lord Ramsay of Keringtoun*, and *Earl of Dalhousie* (peerage of Scotland) 1633; *d* 1674; *s* by his son **(3)** GEORGE, 2nd Earl; *d* 1675; *s* by his son **(4)** WILLIAM, 3rd Earl; 2nd in command of Earl of Mar's Regt at Bothwell Brig 1679; *d* 1682; *s* by his son **(5)** GEORGE, 4th Earl; (killed in a duel) 1696 unmarried; *s* by his brother **(6)** WILLIAM, 5th Earl; Col Scots Guards; (while on active ser in Spain during War of Succession) 1710; *s* by his kinsman **(7)** WILLIAM, 6th Earl, son of John 2nd son of 1st Earl; *d* 1739; *s* by his grandson **(8)** CHARLES, 7th Earl; *d* 1764 unmarried; *s* by his brother **(9)** GEORGE, 8th Earl; an Advocate; Lord High Commr to Gen Assembly of Church of Scotland 1777-82, and a Representative Peer 1774-87 (his 2nd son, William, *cr Baron Panmure*, peerage of United Kingdom 1831, assumed the surname and arms of Maule of Panmure, and *d* 1852); *d* 1787; *s* by his el son **(10)** GEORGE, GCB, 9th Earl; a Gen in the Army; served with distinction in Peninsular War, and commanded 7th and 6th Divs at Vittoria; Gov-Gen of Canada 1819-28, and Com-in-Ch in India 1829-32; *cr Baron Dalhousie*, of Dalhousie Castle, co Edinburgh (peerage of United Kingdom) 1815; *d* 1838; *s* by his son **(11)** JAMES ANDREW, KT, PC, 10th Earl; Gov-Gen of India 1847-56, Constable of Dover Castle, Lord Warden of the Cinque Ports, etc; assumed the additional surname of Broun of Coulstoun on succession to the Coulstoun estate; *cr Marquess of Dalhousie*, of Dalhousie Castle, co Edinburgh, and of the Punjab (peerage of United Kingdom) 1849; *d* 1860, when the UK Barony of Dalhousie and the Marquessate became ext; *s* in Scottish honours by his cousin **(12)** FOX, KT, GCB, PC, 11th Earl, who had in 1852 *s* his father as 2nd Baron Panmure; was an Under-Sec of State 1835-41, Vice-Pres of Board of Trade 1841, Sec at War 1846-52 and 1855-8, Lord-Lieut of co Forfar, and Keeper of the Privy Seal of Scotland, etc, assumed the surname and arms of Ramsay of Dalhousie after that of Maule; *dsp* 1874, when the UK Barony of Panmure expired; *s* by his cousin **(13)** GEORGE, CB, 12th Earl, son of Hon John Ramsay, 4th son of 8th Earl, *b* 1806; was an Adm; *cr Baron Ramsay*, of Glenmark, co Forfar (peerage of United Kingdom) 1875: *m* 1845, Sarah Frances, da of William Robertson, of Logan House, NB; *d* 1880; *s* by his son **(14)** JOHN WILLIAM, KT, PC, 13th Earl, *b* 1847: *m* 1877, Lady Ida Louisa Bennett, who *d* 1887, da of 6th Earl of Tankerville: *d* 1887; *s* by his el son **(15)** ARTHUR GEORGE MAULE, 14th Earl, *b* 1878; Capt Scots Guards, and Hon Col RGA (TA): *m* 1903, Lady Mary Adelaide Heathcote-Drummond-Willoughby, who *d* 1960, yst da of 1st Earl of Ancaster; *d* 1928; *s* by his son **(16)** JOHN GILBERT, 15th Earl; *b* 1904; *d* 1950; *s* by his brother **(17)** SIMON, 16th Earl and present peer; also Lord Ramsay of Dalhousie, Lord Ramsay of Keringtoun, and Baron Ramsay of Glenmark.

Dalkeith, Earl of; son of Duke of Buccleuch.

Dalmeny, Lord; son of Earl of Rosebery.

Dalrymple, Viscount; son of Earl of Stair.

DARCY DE KNAYTH, BARONESS (Ingrams) (Baroness E 1332)

DAVINA MARCIA INGRAMS (*Baroness Darcy de Knayth*), *b* 10 July 1938; *s* 1943; a Member Gen Advisory Council IBA 1987-90: *m* 1960, Rupert George Ingrams, who *d* 1964 (*see* Reid, Bt *cr* 1897, 1964 Edn), and has issue

Arms – Per pale azure and gules, three lions rampant argent. **Supporters** – *Dexter*, an heraldic tiger argent; *sinister*, a bull sable. *Residence* – Camley Corner, Stubbings, Maidenhead, Berks SL6 6QW.

SON LIVING

Hon CASPAR DAVID, *b* 5 Jan 1962.

DAUGHTERS LIVING

Hon Miranda, *b* 1960.
Hon Catriona, *b* 1963.

AUNT LIVING (*Daughter of 4th Earl of Powis*)

Lady Hermione Gwladys, *b* 1900: *m* 1924, Roberto Lucchesi Palli, 11th Duke della Grazia, and 13th Prince of Campofranco; Bailiff Grand Cross of the Sovereign Mil Order of Malta, who *d* 1979, and has issue living, Violet Maria Carolina Sidonie, *b* 1930.

Residence – Villa Rovera Molina, Via Lunga 57, 21020 Barasso, Varese, Italy.

WIDOW LIVING OF SEVENTEENTH BARON

VIDA, only da of late Capt James Harold Cuthbert, DSO, Scots Gds; is an OStJ; appointed a Lady-in-Waiting to HRH the Duchess of Gloucester 1944: *m* 1st, 1934, the 17th Baron (also Viscount Clive), who was *ka* 1943; 2ndly, 1945, Brig Derek Shuldham Schreiber, MVO, who *d* 1972 (*see* B Faringdon, 1946 Edn). *Residences* – Fir Hill, Droxford, Hants; 59 Cadogan Pl, SW1.

COLLATERAL BRANCHES LIVING

See 1969 and earlier edns.

PREDECESSORS – **(1)** JOHN DARCY DE KNAYTH was summoned to Parliament of England as *"Johanni Darcy le Cosin"* 1332; *d* 1347; *s* by his son **(2)** JOHN; summoned to Parliament as *Lord Darcy de Knayth*: *m* Elizabeth, in her own right *Baroness Meinill* (who *d* 1368), only child of Nicholas, Lord Meinill; *d* 1356, and was *s* by his son **(3)** JOHN, 3rd Baron; *d* unmarried, and *vita matris*; *s* by his brother **(4)** PHILIP, Lord Darcy de Knayth and Meinill; *d* 1398; *s* by his son **(5)** JOHN; *d* 1411; *s* by his el son **(6)** PHILIP, Lord Darcy de Knayth and Meinill, at whose death in 1418 the Baronies of Darcy de Knayth and Meinill fell into abeyance between his das, of whom the yr, Margery, *m* Sir John Conyers, of Hornby, and had a son Sir John Conyers, of Hornby, who *m* Alice, da and co-heir of William Nevill, Earl of Kent, and Lord Fauconberg (by Joan his wife *suo jure* Baroness Fauconberg); they had issue William, 1st Lord Conyers (*see* By of Fauconberg and Conyers), whose great-great-grandson **(7)** CONYERS DARCY (son of Thomas Darcy by Elizabeth, da and co-heir of the 3rd Baron Conyers) received in 1641 Letters Patent determining in his favour the abeyances then existing in the Baronies of Darcy de Knayth and Conyers; *d* 1653; *s* by his son **(8)** CONYERS, Baron Darcy de Knayth and Conyers; *cr Earl of Holderness* 1682; *d* 1688; *s* by his son **(9)** CONYERS, 2nd Earl; *d* 1692; *s* by his grandson **(10)** ROBERT 3rd Earl; *d* 1722; *s* by his son **(11)** ROBERT 4th Earl; *d* 1778, when the Earldom became ext, but the Baronies passed to his da **(12)** AMELIA, wife of 5th Duke of Leeds; *d* 1784; *s* by her son **(13)** GEORGE WILLIAM FREDERICK, 6th Duke; *d* 1838; *s* by his son **(14)** FRANCIS GODOLPHIN DARCY, 7th Duke; *d* 1859; *s* by his nephew **(15)** SACKVILLE GEORGE (son of Sackville Walter Lane Fox, Esq, MP), *b* 1827: in 1859 established his right to Barony of Conyers only, and was known by that title, his right to the Barony of Darcy de Knayth being established postumously in 1903: *m* 1860, Mary, Lady Darcy de Knayth and Conyers, who *d* 1921, el da of Reginald Curteis, of Windmill Hill, Sussex; *d* 1888, when the Baronies fell into abeyance, this being determined as to the Barony of Conyers in 1892 in favour of the elder da Marcia Amelia Mary, Countess of Yarborough (in whose favour also the abeyance existing in the Barony of Fauconberg was determined 1903), and as to the Barony of Darcy de Knayth in 1903 in favour of the yr da **(16)** VIOLET IDA EVELYN, Countess of Powis, *b* 1865: *m* 1890, 4th Earl of Powis, who *d* 1952; *d* 1929; *s* by her yr son **(17)** MERVYN HORATIO, 17th Baron; *b* 1904; Squadron-Leader RAF: *m* 1934, Vida, only da of late Capt James Harold Cuthbert, DSO; *ka* 1943; *s* by his only child **(18)** DAVINA MARCIA, present peeress.

DARESBURY, BARON (Greenall) (Baron UK 1927, Bt UK 1876)

I seek to rise

(Title pronounced "Darsbury")

EDWARD GILBERT GREENALL, 3rd Baron, and 4th Baronet; *b* 27 Nov 1928; *s* 1990; *ed* Eton; Chm Randall and Vautier Ltd, Grunhalle Lager Internat: *m* 1st, 1952 (*m diss* 1986), Margaret Ada, yst da of late Charles John Crawford (*see* Anson, Bt, 1954 Edn); 2ndly, 1986, Mary Patricia, da of late Lewis Parkinson, and has issue by 1st *m*.

Arms – 1st and 4th or, on a bend benuly vert three bugle-horns stringed of the field, *Greenall*; 2nd and 3rd argent, five pallets sable, the centre pallet charged with an ermine spot of the field, *Griffith*. **Crest** – Between two wings or, a pomme surmounted by a bugle-horn as in the arms. **Supporters** – *Dexter*, a bull proper; *sinister*, a bay mare, mane and tail sable, charged on the shoulder with a sprig of two oak leaves or.
Residence – Crossbow House, Trinity, Jersey, CI.

SONS LIVING *(By 1st marriage)*

Hon PETER GILBERT, *b* 18 June 1953; *ed* Eton; High Sheriff Cheshire 1992, DL 1994: *m* 1982, Clare Alison, only da of Christopher Nicholas Weatherby, of Whaddon House, Whaddon, Bucks (*see* E Erne, colls), and has issue living, Thomas Edward, *b* 6 Nov 1984, — Oliver Christopher, *b* 1986, — Toby Peter, *b* 1988, — Jonathan James, *b* 1992. *Residence* – Hall Lane Farm, Daresbury, Warrington, Cheshire WA4 4AF.

Dr the Hon Gilbert, CBE, *b* 1954; *ed* Eton; MB, ChB, MBA; CBE (Civil) 1993: *m* 1983, Sarah Elizabeth, elder da of Ian C. Mouat, of Stetchworth, Suffolk, and formerly wife of Robert Greville Kaye Williamson, and has issue living, Gilbert Edward, *b* 1984, — Frederick John, *b* 1986, — Alexander, *b* 1988, — Amelia Frances, *b* 1990. *Residence* – Bromesborrow Place, Ledbury, Herefordshire HR8 1RZ.

Hon John Edward, *b* 1960; *ed* Fettes; BSc Econ: *m* 1985, Gabrielle, da of Stephen James, of Lymington, Hants, and has issue living, James Edward, *b* 1988, — Katie Laura, *b* 1986. *Residence* – Lullington House, Lullington, Burton-on-Trent, Staffs DE12 8EG.

DAUGHTER LIVING *(By 1st marriage)*

Hon Susan Rosemary, *b* 1956: *m* 1st, 1978 (*m diss* 1989), David St Clare Oswald Bruton; 2ndly, 1989, Anthony St John Haden-Taylor, son of late Frank Pacey Haden-Taylor, of Broughton Gifford, Wilts, and has had issue (by 1st *m*), Alastair Edward Oswald, *b* 1985, — Natasha Charlotte, *b* 1983, — (by 2nd *m*) Pandora Eleanor Christine, *b* 1989, *d* 1990. *Residence* – Bledisloe House, Coates, nr Cirencester, Glos GL7 6NH.

WIDOW LIVING OF ELDER SON OF FIRST BARON

Betty Isobel, el da of late J. S. Crawford, of Thorpe Satchville Hall, Melton Mowbray, *m* 1st, 1924, the Hon Gilbert Greenall, Lieut The Life Guards, who *d* 1928; 2ndly, 1933, Reginald Arthur Farquhar, who *d* 1937 (*see* Farquhar, Bt, 1937 Edn). *Residence* – Ardsallagh, Fethard, co Tipperary.

PREDECESSORS – (1) GILBERT Greenall, 6th son of late Edward Greenall, of Wilderspool, co Chester, *b* 1806; MP for Warrington (C) 1847-68, 1874-80 and 1885-92; *cr* a Baronet 1876, *m* 1st, 1836, Mary, who *d* 1861, da of David Claughton, of Haydock, Lancashire; 2ndly, 1864, Susannah, who *d* 1896, da of John Louis Rapp; *d* 1894; *s* by his only son (2) *Sir* GILBERT, CVO, 2nd Bt, *b* 1867; High Sheriff for Cheshire 1907; *cr* Baron Daresbury of Walton, co Chester (peerage of United Kingdom) 1927: *m* 1900, Frances Eliza, JP, who *d* 1953, da of late Capt Edward Wynne Griffith, formerly 1st R Dragoons; *d* 1938; *s* by his only surviving son (3) EDWARD, 2nd Baron, *b* 1902; Lieut Res of Officers, late Life Guards, Jt Master Belvoir Hounds 1934-47, Master co Limerick Hounds 1947-89: *m* 1st, 1925, Joan Madeline, who *d* 1926, elder da of late Capt Robert Thomas Oliver Sheriffe, of Goadby Hall, Melton Mowbray; 2ndly, 1927, Josephine, who *d* 1958, yst da of late Brig-Gen Sir Joseph Frederick Laycock, KCMG, DSO (*see* E Listowel, colls, 1952 Edn); 3rdly, 1966, Lady Helena Albreda Marie Gabriella, who *d* 1970, da of 7th Earl Fitzwilliam, and formerly wife of late Maj Chetwode Charles Hamilton Hilton-Green; *d* 1990; *s* by his only son (4) EDWARD GILBERT, 3rd Baron and present peer.

DARLING, BARON (Darling) (Baron UK 1924)

ROBERT CHARLES HENRY DARLING, 2nd Baron; *b* 15 May 1919; *s* 1936; *ed* Wellington Coll; Major (ret) Somerset LI; DL for Avon: *m* 1942, (Bridget) Rosemary Whishaw, da of Rev Francis Cyprian Dickson, formerly V of Emery Down, Lyndhurst, Hants, and has issue.

Arms – Argent, on a chevron engrailed between three flesh-pots sable a stirrup leathered or. **Crest** – In front of a dexter cubit arm proper holding in the hand a heart gules a chaplet of laurel vert. **Supporters** – On either side a Pegasus argent, charged on each wing with a chevron engrailed sable. **Badge** – A sprig of heather and a sprig of gorse in saltire proper, enfiled by a Baron's coronet.
Residence – Puckpits, Limpley Stoke, Bath, Avon.

SON LIVING

Hon (ROBERT) JULIAN HENRY (Intwood Hall, Norwich), *b* 29 April 1944; *ed* Wellington Coll, and RAC Cirencester; FRICS: *m* 1970, Janet Rachel, yr da of Mrs D. M. E. Mallinson, of Richmond, Yorks, and has issue living, Robert James Cyprian, *b* 1972, — Henry Thomas Unthank, *b* 1978, — Rachel Pollyanna Margaret, *b* 1974.

DAUGHTERS LIVING

The gift of God

Hon Anna Josephine Bridget, *b* 1946: *m* 1971, Anthony Robert Pardoe, of Sharow Cottage, Sharow, Ripon, N Yorks, and has issue living, David Hugh Charles, *b* 1974, — Georgina Rosemary Jane, *b* 1977.
Hon Lucinda Mary Joan, *b* 1958: *m* 1982, Rory P. A. Macdiarmid, only son of late Col Peter Macdiarmid, and has issue living, George Peter Robert, *b* 1985, — Fergus Charles Ian, *b* 1987, — Philippa Rosemary Kate, *b* 1990.

PREDECESSOR – (1) Rt Hon Sir CHARLES JOHN Darling, PC, el son of late Charles Darling, of Langham Hall, Essex; *b* 1849; MP for Deptford (C) 1888-97; Judge of the High Court of Justice 1897-1923; *cr Baron Darling*, of Langham, Essex (peerage of United Kingdom) 1924: *m* 1885, Mary Caroline, who *d* 1913, el da of late Maj-Gen Wilberforce Harris Greathed, CB; *d* 1936; *s* by his grandson (2) ROBERT CHARLES HENRY (son of late Maj Hon John Clive Darling, DSO, only son of 1st Baron), 2nd Baron and present peer.

DARLING OF HILLSBOROUGH, BARONY OF (Darling) (Extinct 1985)

SON LIVING OF LIFE BARON

Hon Peter George, *b* 1950.

DAUGHTER LIVING OF LIFE BARON

Hon Isabel, *b* 1948.

DARNLEY, EARL OF (Bligh) Sits as BARON CLIFTON OF LEIGHTON BROMSWOLD (E 1608)
(Earl I 1725)
(Name pronounced "Bly")

ADAM IVO STUART BLIGH, 11th Earl; *b* 8 Nov 1941; *s* 1980; *ed* Harrow, and Ch Ch Oxford; Vice-Chm of the Govs of Cobham Hall Sch since 1991: *m* 1965, Susan Elaine, JP, da of late Sir Donald Forsyth Anderson (*see* Llewellyn, Bt, *cr* 1922), and has issue.

Arms – Azure, a griffin segreant or, armed and langued gules, between three crescents argent. **Crest** – A griffin's head erased or. **Supporters** – Two griffins, wings expanded or, ducally gorged and chained azure.
Residence – Netherwood Manor, Tenbury Wells, Worcs WR15 8RT.

SON LIVING

Look to the end

IVO DONALD STUART (*Lord Clifton of Rathmore*), *b* 17 April 1968; *ed* Marlborough, and Edinburgh Univ.

DAUGHTER LIVING

Lady Katherine Amanda, *b* 1971; *ed* St Mary's Sch Calne, Marlborough Coll, and St Edmund Hall, Oxford.

SISTERS LIVING

Lady Melissa Geraldine Florence, *b* 1945: *m* 1st, 1965, Don Manuel Torrado y de Fontcuberta, who *d* 1980; 2ndly, 1985, Rev Colin Russell Levey and has issue living (by 1st *m*), Manuel Ivo (7 St George's Close, Ogbourne St George, Marlborough, Wiltshire), *b* 1966: *m* 1991, Audrey Elizabeth, da of Andrew Perratt, — Maria Melissa, *b* 1968, — Victoria Irene, *b* 1973. *Residence* – The Vicarage, Orton, Cumbria C10 3RQ.

Lady Harriet Esme Ghislaine, *b* 1949; *ed* Cobham Hall, and Somerville Coll, Oxford. *Residence* – Meadow House Cottage, Cobham, Gravesend, Kent DA12 3B2.

HALF-SISTERS LIVING *(Daughter of 9th Earl by 1st marriage)*

Lady Marguerite Rose (52 Redcliffe Gdns, SW10), *b* 1913: *m* 1st, 1934 (*m diss* 1941), Claud Dobrée Strickland, F/O AAF, who *d* *ka* Oct 1941 (*see* Strickland-Constable, Bt, colls); 2ndly, 1942 (*m diss* 1951), W/Cmdr Gordon Stanley Keith Haywood, RAF; 3rdly, 1951 (*m diss* 1963), as his 2nd wife, Nigel Trevithick Tangye, who *d* 1988, and has issue living (by 2nd *m*), Gareth Peter, *b* 1943: *m* 1965 (*m diss* 1969), Zehra Ipek, da of Prof Semseddin Talip Diler, of Taksmin, Istanbul, — Lucinda March (twin) (74 Ifield Rd, SW10), *b* 1943: *m* 1964 (*m diss* 1983), James Hilary Glyn (see B Wolverton, colls).

(Daughter of 9th Earl by 2nd marriage)

Lady Rose Amanda (*Lady Rose Hare*), *b* 1935: *m* 1961, Sir Thomas Hare, 5th Bt, who *d* 1993, of Stow Bardolph, King's Lynn, Norfolk PE34 3HU, and has issue (*see* Hare, Bt).

WIDOW LIVING OF SON OF EIGHTH EARL

Mrs Kathleen Weatherill Strickland (5 Sloane Gate Mansions, D'Oyly St, SW1): *m* 1973, as his 3rd wife, Lt-Col Hon Noel Gervase Bligh, DSO, who *d* 1984.

WIDOW LIVING OF NINTH EARL

ROSEMARY, da of late Basil Potter: *m* 1st, 1940, as his 3rd wife, the 9th Earl, who *d* 1955; 2ndly, 1963, as his 2nd wife, Pierre Trasenster, who *d* 1968. *Residence* – Meadow House, Cobham, Gravesend, Kent DA12 3BZ.

COLLATERAL BRANCH LIVING

Grandchildren of late Major Lodovick Edward Bligh, son of Rev Hon Edward Vesey Bligh, 2nd son of 5th Earl:—

Issue of late Algernon Stuart Bligh, *b* 1888, *d* 1952: *m* 1st, 1922 (*m diss* 1937), Dora Joan, da of T. Lovelace, of Bratton Court, Minehead; 2ndly, 1938, Dorothy (Amberley, Lower Park, Minehead, Som), da of late J. F. V. Larway:—

(By 1st *m*) Noel Edward, *b* 1926; late Capt RASC, and Lt RN: *m* 1961, Jane Mary, da of Trevor Seymour-Smith, and has issue living, Victoria Joan, *b* 1962. *Residence* – Weeks Park, High Bickington, Umberleigh, N Devon. —— Audrey Diana, *b* 1924: *m* 1947, John Sefton Spencer Hawkins, and has issue living, Nigel Bligh Spencer, *b* 1954, — David Stuart Spencer, *b* 1956. *Residence* – Osbornes, Upper Dicker, Hailsham, Sussex. —— (By 2nd *m*) Jennifer Wendy, *b* 1942: *m* 1st, 1963 (*m diss* 1974), Ronald Colin Board Webber; 2ndly, 1975 (*m diss* 19—), Alan Thomas Wormell; 3rdly, 1982, Peter MacDonell Prior-Wandesforde, of Well Farm, Timberscombe, Minehead, Som, and has issue living (by 1st *m*), Katrina Jane, *b* 1964: *m* 1991, Capt J. P. Stanhope-White. —— Heather Rosalind, *b* 1945: *m* 1st, 1968 (*m diss* 1977), Arthur Keith Amor; 2ndly, 1983, Christopher James Dunn, of Staple Fitzpaine Manor, Staple-Fitzpaine, Taunton, Som and has issue living (by 1st *m*), Jason Keith Bligh, *b* 1970, — Lucinda Jane Bligh, *b* 1969, — (by 2nd *m*), Harry James Bligh, *b* 1984.

PREDECESSORS – **(1)** JOHN BLIGH, MP for Athboy 1709-21; *cr Baron Clifton of Rathmore* (peerage of Ireland) 1721, *Viscount Darnley* (peerage of Ireland) 1723, and *Earl of Darnley* (peerage of Ireland) 1725; *d* 1728; *s* by his son **(2)** EDWARD, 2nd Earl, who in 1722 had *s* his mother as *Baron Clifton of Leighton Bromswold* (peerage of England) by writ of summons 1608; *d* unmarried 1747; *s* by his brother **(3)** JOHN, 3rd Earl; MP for Maidstone; *d* 1781; *s* by his son **(4)** JOHN, 4th Earl; in 1829 claimed as heir-gen the Scottish Dukedom of Lennox, but the House of Lords did not come to any decision; *d* 1831; *s* by his son **(5)** EDWARD, 5th Earl; *b* 1795; sat as MP for Canterbury 1818-30; was Lord Lieut of co Meath: *m* 1825, Emma Jane, who *d* 1884, da of 1st Baron Congleton; *d* 1835; *s* by his son **(6)** JOHN STUART, 6th Earl, *b* 1827: *m* 1850, Lady Harriet Mary Pelham, who *d* 1905, el da of 3rd Earl of Chichester; *d* 1896; *s* by his el son **(7)** EDWARD HENRY STUART, 7th Earl, *b* 1851: *m* 1899, Miss Jemima Adeline Blackwood; *d* 1900, when the Barony of Clifton of Leighton Bromswold passed to his da and only child Elizabeth Adeline Mary (see infra *), while he was *s* in the Earldom by his brother **(8)** IVO FRANCIS WALTER, 8th Earl; *b* 1859; a Representative Peer for Ireland: *m* 1884, Dame Florence Rose, DBE, who *d* 1944, da of late Stephen Morphy, of Beechworth, Victoria; *d* 1927; *s* by his son **(9)** ESME IVO, 9th Earl; *b* 1886: *m* 1st, 1912 (*m diss* 1920), Daphne Rachel, who *d* 1948, da of late Hon Alfred John Mulholland; 2ndly, 1923 (*m diss* 1936), Nancy, who *d* 1991, da of late Capt Glen Kidston, 3rd Batn Black Watch; 3rdly, 1940, Rosemary (who *m* 2ndly, 1963, as his 2nd wife, Pierre Trasenster, who *d* 1968, da of late Basil Potter; *d* 1955; *s* by his el son **(10)** PETER STUART, 10th Earl; *b* 1915; *d* 1980; *s* by his half-brother **(11)** ADAM IVO STUART, 11th Earl and present peer; also Viscount Darnley, Baron Clifton of Rathmore, and Baron Clifton of Leithton Bromswold.

*(1)** Sir GERVASE Clifton, son of Sir John Clifton, of Barrington, Somerset, was summoned to Parliament as *Baron Clifton of Leighton Bromswold* (peerage of England) 1608: *d* 1618; *s* by his da **(2)** CATHERINE: *m* Lord Esme Stuart who was *cr Baron Stuart* of Leighton Bromswold (in her right), and *Earl of March* 1619, and *s* as 3rd Duke of Lennox, 1624; *d* 1637; *s* by her son **(3)** JAMES, 4th Duke of Lennox; *d* 1655; *s* by his son **(4)** ESME, 5th Duke; *d* 1660; *s* by his sister **(5)** MARY Butler, Countess of Arran; *d* 1667; *s* by her cousin **(6)** CHARLES, 6th Duke of Lennox; *d* 1672; *s* by his sister **(7)** CATHERINE O'Brien (wife of Henry, el son of 7th Earl of Thomond), who claimed and was allowed the barony in 1674 as grand-da of Catherine, da of 1st Baron; she *m* 2ndly, Sir Joseph Williamson; *d* 1702; *s* by her da **(8)** CATHERINE Hyde, Viscountess Cornbury; *d* 1706; *s* by her son **(9)** EDWARD, Viscount Cornbury; *d* 1712; *s* by his sister **(10)** THEODOSIA: *m* John Bligh, of Rathmore, co Meath, who was *cr Baron Clifton of Rathmore* (peerage of Ireland) 1721, *Viscount Darnley* (peerage of Ireland) 1723, and *Earl of Darnley* (peerage of Ireland) 1725; *d* 1722; *s* by her son **(11)** EDWARD, 2nd Earl of Darnely, who in 1722 had *s* his mother as *Baron Clifton of Leighton Bromswold* (peerage of England) by writ of summons 1608; *d* unmarried 1747; *s* by his brother **(12)** JOHN, 3rd Earl; MP for Maidstone; *d* 1781; *s* by his son **(13)** JOHN, 4th Earl; in 1829 claimed as heir-gen the Scottish Dukedom of Lennox, but the House of Lords did not come to any decision; *d* 1831; *s* by his son **(14)** EDWARD, 5th Earl; *b* 1795; sat as MP for Canterbury 1818-30; was Lord-Lieut of co Meath: *m* 1825, Emma Jane, who *d* 1884, da of 1st Baron Congleton; *d* 1835; *s* by his son **(15)** JOHN STUART, 6th Earl; *b* 1827: *m* 1850, Lady Harriet Mary Pelham, who *d* 1905, el da of 3rd Earl of Chichester; *d* 1896; *s* by his el son **(16)** EDWARD HENRY STUART, 7th Earl; *b* 1851: *m* 1899, Miss Jemima Adeline Blackwood; *d* 1900, when the Earldom of Darnley passed to his brother, while he was *s* in the Barony of Clifton of Leighton Bromswold by his da and only child **(17)** ELIZABETH ADELINE MARY, Baroness Clifton of Leighton Bromswold; *b* 1900; *d* 1937; *s* by her cousin **(18)** ESME IVO 9th Earl of Darnley (ante).

DARTMOUTH, EARL OF (Legge) (Earl GB 1711)

GERALD HUMPHRY LEGGE, 9th Earl; *b* 26 April 1924; *s* 1962; *ed* Eton; FCA (ret); Grand Official, Order of Cruzeiro do Sul (Brazil); Hon LLD Dartmouth Coll; Italy 1944-5, as Capt Coldstream Guards (despatches): *m* 1st, 1948 (*m diss* 1976), Raine, da of late Alexander George McCorquodale, of The White Lodge, Speen, Berks; 2ndly, 1980, Mrs Gwendoline May Seguin, da of late Charles René Seguin, and has issue by 1st *m*.

Arms – Azure, a buck's head cabossed argent. **Crest** – Out of a ducal coronet or, a plume of five ostrich feathers argent and azure alternately. **Supporters** – *Dexter*, a lion argent semée of fleurs-de-lis sable, ducally crowned or, and issuing from the coronet a plume of five ostrich feathers argent and azure, alternately; *sinister*, a stag argent, unguled or, and semée of mullets gules. *Residence* – The Manor House, Chipperfield, Kings Langley, Herts.

Virtue rejoices in trial

SONS LIVING *(By 1st marriage)*

WILLIAM (*Viscount Lewisham*), *b* 23 Sept 1949; *ed* Eton, and Ch Ch, Oxford.

Hon Rupert, *b* 1951; *ed* Eton, and Ch Ch Oxford (MA); Bar Inner Temple 1975; author of *The Children of Light* (1986), *Playing With Fire* (1993), etc: *m* 1984, M. Victoria S., da of Lionel Edward Bruce Ottley, of Tichborne Park Cottage, Alresford, Hants (*see* Avebury, B, colls, 1955 Edn), and has issue living, Edward Peregrine, *b* 1986, — Claudia Rose *b* 1989. *Residence* – Hamswell House, nr Bath, Avon BA1 9DG.

Hon Henry, *b* 1968.

DAUGHTER LIVING *(By 1st marriage)*

Lady Charlotte, *b* 1963: *m* 1990, Duca Don Alexander Paternò Castello di Cárcaci, 13th Duca di Cárcaci, of 25 Holland Park Gdns, W14 (*see* E Inchcape, 1973-74 Edn).

SISTER LIVING

Lady Heather Margaret Mary (*Baroness Herschell*), *b* 1925: *m* 1948, 3rd Baron Herschell, *Residence* – Westfield House, Ardington, Wantage, Berks.

DAUGHTERS LIVING OF SEVENTH EARL

Lady Mary Cecilia, *b* 1906: *m* 1929, Cdr Noel Charles Mansfeldt Findlay, RN, who *d* 1976, son of Sir Mansfeldt de Cardonnel Findlay, GBE, KCMG, CB, and has issue living, Jonathan Mansfeldt (Eden Lodge, Droxford, Hants), *b* 1933; Cdr RN: *m* 1962, Jutta, da of Gen Karl von Graffen, and has issue living, Christopher Mansfeldt Karl *b* 1967, Caroline Ilse *b* 1962, Angela Mary *b* 1964, — Martin Charles (Ledburn Manor, Leighton Buzzard, Beds), *b* 1935: *m* 1966, Davina Margaret, da of Maj Sir Thomas Calderwood Dundas, MBE, 7th Bt (*cr* 1898) (ext), and has issue living, Mark Simon *b* 1967, Adam James *b* 1969, — Jane Elizabeth, *b* 1930: *m* 1961, Jeremy Debenham, of Reeds Farm, Sayers Common, Hassocks, Sussex, and has issue living, Catherine Mary *b* 1962, Henrietta Jane *b* 1965: *m* 1991 Oliver George Curtis, Susannah Elizabeth *b* 1968. *Residence* – 2 South Close, The Precincts, Canterbury, Kent CT1 2EJ.

Lady Elizabeth, DCVO (67 Cottesmore Court, Stanford Rd, W8), *b* 1908; appointed an Extra Woman of the Bedchamber to HM Queen Elizabeth the Queen Mother 1955; CVO 19—, DCVO 1989: *m* 1931, Ronald Lambart Basset, who *d* 1972 (*see* Salusbury-Trelawny, Bt, 1947 Edn), and has issue living, Bryan Ronald, CBE (Quarles, Wells-next-the-Sea, Norfolk NR23 1RY), *b* 1932: *m* 1960, Lady Carey Elizabeth Coke, da of 5th Earl of Leicester, and has issue living, David Francis *b* 1961, Michael James *b* 1963, James Bryan *b* 1968; formerly a Page of Honour to HM.

Lady Barbara, *b* 1916; formerly in First Aid Nursing Yeo: *m* 1945, Adam Kwiatkowski, Lieut Polish Army, and has issue living, Jan Witold (Tantallon Terrace, North Berwick, E Lothian), *b* 1945: *m* 1968, Sarah Hope, da of Christopher Challis, of Pineways, Grays Park, Stoke Poges, Bucks, and has issue living, Adam Witold *b* 1972, Daniel Christopher *b* 1974, William *b* 1977, Alexander George *b* 1979, — Marek William, *b* 1947: *m* 1977, Belinda Mary Graham, el da of Maj John Cecil Graham Moon (*see* Moon, Bt *cr* 1855, colls), and has issue, Stefan Marek *b* 1981, — Christopher (The Stables, Patshull, Albrighton, Salop), *b* 1951: *m* 1978, Allison Porter, el da of R. P. Yates, of Hinnington Grange, Shifnal, Salop, and has issue living, Marek *b* 1987, Anna *b* 1989, — Michael Andrew Adam, *b* 1955: *m* 1978 (*m diss* 1981), Scylla Nina Antoinette, yst da of late Roderick W. Parkyn, of Pen-y-Lan, Hardwicke, Herefordshire. *Residence* – The Bothy, Patshull Park, Burnhill Green, Wolverhampton.

Lady Josceline Gabrielle (*Marchioness of Donegall*), *b* 1918; is in First Aid Nursing Yeo: *m* 1946, 7th Marquess of Donegall, *c/o* Wexford. *Residence* – Dunbrody Park, Arthurstown, co Wexford.

WIDOW LIVING OF EIGHTH EARL

ROMA ERNESTINE (*Roma, Countess of Dartmouth*) (15B, Bedford Towers, Brighton), da of Sir Ernest Burford Horlick, 2nd Bt: *m* 1923, the 8th Earl, who *d* 1962.

COLLATERAL BRANCHES LIVING

Grandchildren of late Nigel Walter Henry LEGGE-BOURKE, only son of late Col Hon Sir Henry Charles Legge, GCVO, 2nd son of 5th Earl:—
Issue of late Maj Sir (Edward Alexander) Henry Legge-Bourke, KBE, DL, MP, *b* 1914, *d* 1973: *m* 1938, Catherine Jean (*Lady Legge-Bourke*) (121 Dovehouse St, SW3 6JZ), da of Col Sir Arthur Grant of Monymusk, 10th Bt, CBE, DSO:—
William Nigel Henry (Penmyarth, Glanusk Park, Crickhowell, Powys), *b* 1939; *ed* Eton, and Magdalene Coll Camb (MA); late Capt RHG (The Blues): *m* 1964, Hon (Elizabeth) Shân (Josephine) Bailey, LVO, da of 3rd Baron Glanusk, and has issue living, Harry Russell, *b* 1972; a Page of Honour to HM The Queen 1985-87; commn'd WG 1992, — Alexandra Shân, *b* 1965, — Zara Victoria, *b* 1966: *m* 1985, Capt Richard Grosvenor Plunkett-Ernle-Erle-Drax (*see* B Dunsany, colls). —— Heneage (*c/o* 121 Dovehouse St, SW3 6JZ; 17 rue du Stade, Paucaurt, Louiret 45200, France), *b* 1948; a Page of Honour to HM The Queen 1963-64: *m* 1978, Maria Clara, da of late Vasco de Sá-Carneiro, of Lisbon, and has issue living, Edward Alexander Heneage, *b* 1984, — Eleanor Jean Maria, *b* 1980. —— Victoria Lindsay, LVO (21 Eccleston Sq, SW1V 1NS), *b* 1950; a Lady in Waiting to HRH The Princess Royal since 1974; LVO 1986.

Grandchildren of late Rev Hugh Legge, 3rd son of late Rev Hon George Barrington Legge, 2nd son of 4th Earl:—
Issue of late Maj John Barrington Legge, b 1918, d 1989: m 1940, Gertrude Sarah (The Porch House, Dodford, Northants), da of Frederick Wood, of Little Preston Capes, Northants:—
Hugh, b 1945; ed Haileybury; late Lieut RA: m 1977, Julia, da of J. H. Taylor, of Newcastle, Staffs, and has issue living, Robin Francis, b 1980, — Colin Brendan, b 1982. —— Jane, b 1941: m 1977, John Grace Day. —— Hannah, b 1947; d 1987.

Granddaughter of late Lt-Col the Hon Edward Henry Legge, 3rd son of 4th Earl:—
Issue of late John Douglas Legge, MC, b 1886, d 1954: m 1917, Haroldine, who d 1970, da of late Harold S. Peck, of Chicago, USA:—
Virginia Lois (Hon Mrs Nial A. R. O'Neill), (Crowfield House, Crowfield, Ipswich, Suffolk IP6 9TP), b 1922: m 1966, Maj Hon Nial Arthur Ramleh O'Neill, who d 1980 (see B Rathcavan).

Grandchildren of late Rt Rev Hon Augustus Legge, DD, Bishop of Lichfield, 5th son of 4th Earl:—
Issue of late Francis Augustus Legge, b 1880, d 1966: m 1909, Mabel Clara Arden, who d 1963, da of late Charles Lucena, of Westwick, Easthampstead:—
Christopher Augustus Sackville (c/o 1013 Mass Ave NE, Washington DC 20002, USA), b 1911; ed Eton, and Worcester Coll, Oxford (MA); Bar Inner Temple 1936: m 1st, 1952, Kari, who d 1971, da of the late Walther Brebeck, Pres of Senate, of Eutin, Germany; 2ndly, 1979, Signe White, and has issue living (by 1st m) Christopher Walter, b 1955, — Barbara Ingrid, b 1960. — Fanny Angela Mary (Little Stoke, Meonstoke, Hants), b 1912: m 1940, Lt-Col Philip Lewis, SLI, who d 1968, and has issue living, Christopher Julian Arden (Lone Barn, East Garston, nr Newbury, Berks), b 1941: m 1972, Caroline Dyson, — Lavinia Zaria, b 1943: m 1969, Lt-Col (Murray Bernard) Neville Cyprian Howard, Coldm Gds (see D Norfolk, colls).

Grandchildren of late Hon Charles Gounter Legge, 6th son of 4th Earl:—
Issue of late Brig-Gen William Kaye Legge, CMG, DSO, b 1869, d 1946: m 1902, Constance Adeline, who d 1964, da of late Hon James David Palmer, of Bloemfontein, Orange Free State Province, S. Africa:—
Peter, b 1910; ed Wellington Coll; Wing-Cdr (ret) RAF; 1939-45 War (despatches twice): m 1st, 1937 (m diss 1953), Mary Claire, da of William Dwyer, of Elmville, Rushbrooke, co Cork; 2ndly, 1955, Violet Bertha, da of late George Wallace, and has issue living (by 1st m), Michael William, b 1938; ed Downside: m 1965 (m diss 19—), Kim Hoang, and has issue living, Julian b 1969, Nicola b 1967, — David Anthony, b 1941; ed Downside: m 1966, Mary Roden, and has issue living, Christopher Dermot b 1970, Thomas David b 1974, Andrew b 1976, Jennifer Claire b 1968, Anna Constance b 1972, — Susan Noelle Ann, b 1943: m 1966, Paul Dempsey, and has issue living, Karen Jane b 1967, Joanna Ruth b 1969, Sophie Ann b 1972, Emma Claire b 1973, Rachel b 1978.
Issue of late Lt-Cdr John Augustus Legge, RD, RNR, b 1871, d 1945: m 1908, Grace Margaret, who d 1957, da of late Alexander Henderson Dunsmure, of 46 Egerton Crescent, SW3:—
John Michael Derek, b 1913; ed Eton: m 1945, Esmé Edith, da of the late Vice-Adm Cyril St Clair Cameron, CBE, and has issue living, Derek Rupert Spicer, b 1949: m 1990, Jacqueline Ann Hollaway, and has issue living, Henry Rupert Cameron b 1993, Victoria Alice b 1990, — Elizabeth Angela, b 1946. Residence – Little Combe, Whatley, Frome, Som. —— David Alexander Keppel, CBE, b 1916; ed Eton; Col R Fus (ret); 1939-45 War (wounded); MBE (Mil) 1953, CBE (Mil) 1970: m 1944, Patria, da of late Lt-Col C.B.R. Hornung, DL, JP, of Ivorys, Cowfold, and has issue living, Richard Charles Gounter (Furneaux Farmhouse, Whatfield, Ipswich, Suffolk) b 1948: m 1972, Lesley Mayfield Finch, da of Frederick Ledger, of Brompton House, Malvern, and has issue living, Jonathan Alexander Heneage b 1979, Thomas Henry Finch b 1983, — Anthea Frances, b 1946: m 1969, Richard Charles Roundell, of Dorfold Hall, Nantwich, Cheshire (Cs Dysart, colls), and has issue living, Charles Henry b 1975, Laura Ann b 1972. Residence – Sandwell, Marston Magna, Yeovil, Som. —— Margaret Elizabeth, b 1908. Residence – Tutton Hill House, Colerne, Wilts.
Issue of late Thomas Charles Legge, b 1872, d 1949: m 1904, Ivy Emily, who d 1961, yst da of J. Reid, of Zeerust, Transvaal:—
Mary Charlotte Lois, b 1905; BCom: m 1934, George Wilson Low, Colonial Vet Ser. Address – Cramond, Vipingo, via Mombasa, Kenya.

Grandson of late Thomas Charles Legge (ante):—
Issue of late (Gounter Heneage) Hugh Legge, b 1909, d 1992: m 1936, Joyce Kathleen, who d 19—, yst da of late Thomas Angus Brown:—
Traver Francis Hugh (20 Cherry Glebe, Mersham, Ashford, Kent TN25 6NL), b 1942; assumed the christian name of Traver in lieu of Thomas; ed Witwatersrand Univ (BSc(Eng)), and Imperial Coll, London (DIC, MSc): m 1972, Helen Dorothy, da of John Downie, of Johannesburg, and has issue living, Angela Claire, b 1975, — Janet Helen, b 1980.

Grandchildren of late Capt Ronald George Legge, 7th son of late Hon Charles Gounter Legge (ante):—
Issue of late Major Rupert Mortimer Legge, Roy Fusiliers, b 1911, ka in Italy 1944: m 1940, Anne, who d 1982, da of late Sir James Adam, CBE, KC:—
Rupert James (Woodend Garden Cottage, Thirsk, Yorks YO7 4DP), b 1944; ed Wellington Coll: m 1968, Jacqueline Hope, da of late Maj E. T. H. Ubsdell, and has issue living, Edward James b 1971, — Philippa Georgina b 1972. —— (Christian Anne) Victoria, b 1942: m 1973 (m diss 1993), Christopher T. Sharman, and has issue living, Matthew Rupert Derek b 1975, — Thomas Christopher James b 1977, — Patrick William Adam b 1979.

PREDECESSORS – (1) Rt Hon George Legge, an eminent naval commander, and Col of a regt of Foot; founded the Roy Fus; Gov of Portsmouth, Master of the Ordnance, and Master of the Horse and Gentleman of the Bedchamber to James, Duke of York, etc; cr Baron Dartmouth, of Devon (peerage of England) 1682; during the reign of James II held several important offices, but falling with his party at the Revolution, and having been suspected of plotting against William III, was imprisoned in the Tower, where he d 1691; s by his son (2) Rt Hon William, 2nd Baron; Sec of State 1710; Lord Privy Seal 1713, and after the death of Queen Anne, one of the Lords Justice of Great Britain; cr Viscount Lewisham and Earl of Dartmouth (peerage of Great Britain) 1711; d 1750; s by his grandson (3) William, 2nd Earl; Sec of the Colonies; sponsor of Dartmouth Coll, Hanover, New Hampshire 1769; d July 1801; s by his son (4) George, KG, 3rd Earl, summoned to Parliament in his father's barony June 1801; d 1810; s by his son (5) William, FRS, DCL, 4th Earl; b 1784: m 1st, 1821, Lady Frances Charlotte, who d 1823, da of 2nd Earl Talbot; 2ndly, Hon Frances, who d 1849, da of 5th Viscount Barrington; d 22 Nov 1853; s by his son (6) William Walter, 5th Earl, b 1823; MP for S Staffordshire (C) 1849-53; Lord-Lieut of Staffordshire: m 1846, Lady Augusta Finch, who d 1900, el da of 5th Earl of Aylesford; d 1891; s by his el son (7) Rt Hon William Heneage, GCVO, KCB, VD, TD, 6th Earl; b 1851; Vice-Chamberlain of HM Queen Victoria's Household 1885-6, and 1886-91, and Lord-Lieut of Staffs 1891-1927; MP for W Kent (C) 1878-85, and for Lewisham 1885-91: m 1879, Lady Mary Coke, CBE, who d 1929, da of 2nd Earl of Leicester; d 1936; s by his el son (8) William, GCVO, TD, 7th Earl; b 1881; Co Councillor for London, 1907-10, Hon Col Duke of Wellington's (W Riding) Regt and Staffordshire Yeo; MP for West Bromwich (C) 1910-18; upon death of Marquess of Lincolnshire appointed 1928 by HM King George V to execute office of Lord Great Chamberlain for remainder of his reign: m 1905, Lady Ruperta Wynn-Carrington, who d 1963, da of 1st Marquess of Lincolnshire; d 1958; s by his brother (9) Humphry, CVO, DSO, 8th Earl; b 1888; Cdr RN; present at Jutland 1916; Assist Ch Constable of Staffs 1929-32, and Ch Constable of Berks 1932-54: m 1923, Roma Ernestine, da of Sir Ernest Burford Horlick, 2nd Bt; d 1962; s by his only son (10) Gerald Humphry, 9th Earl and present peer; also Viscount Lewisham and Baron Dartmouth.

DARWEN, BARON (Davies) (Baron UK 1946)

ROGER MICHAEL DAVIES, 3rd Baron; *b* 28 June 1938; *s* 1988; *ed* Bootham Sch, York: *m* 1961, Gillian Irene, da of Eric G. Hardy, of Valley View, Leigh Woods, Bristol, and has issue.
Residence – Labourer's Rest, Green St, Pleshey, Chelmsford, Essex.

SONS LIVING

Hon PAUL *b* 1962.
Hon Benjamin, *b* 1966.

DAUGHTERS LIVING

Hon Sarah, *b* 1963.
Hon Naomi, *b* 1965.
Hon Mary, *b* 1969.

BROTHERS LIVING

Hon Stephen Humphrey, *b* 1945: *m* 1968, Kathleen Prestwood, and has issue living, Timothy Prestwood, *b* 1970, — Peter, *b* 1980, — Ruth Mary, *b* 1972, — Rachel, *b* 1976.
Hon Philip Cedric Mark, *b* 1951.

SISTER LIVING

Hon Catherine Joy, *b* 1948; *ed* Cardiff Univ (BA, PGCE), lecturer in Eng Lit and Lang: *m* 1st, 1970 (*m diss* 1976), Robert Nienhuis; 2ndly, 1976, Richard George Tipping, of Coombe Cottage, 44 Worcester Rd, Droitwich, Worcs, and has issue living, (by 2nd *m*) Damian Richard George, *b* 1977, — Gregory Luke Darius, *b* 1980.

UNCLES LIVING (*sons of 1st Baron*)

Hon Thomas Barratt (56 Old St, Upton-upon-Severn, Worcs), *b* 1916; *ed* Bootham Sch, Coll of Art, Liverpool: *m* 1941, Doreen, da of Arthur James Allen, and has issue living, Alan John Barry, *b* 1949, — Barbara Jean, *b* 1944, — Frances Hilary, *b* 1947, — Judith Anne (twin), *b* 1949.
Hon (Francis) Ronald, *b* 1920; *ed* Bootham Sch, and Queen's Coll, Oxford (BA 1942, MA 1946); Bar Gray's Inn 1948: *m* 1942, Margaret Phyllis, da of John George Cocksworth, and has issue living, Daniel Watson, *b* 1948, — John Russell, *b* 1950, — Helen Bronwen, *b* 1954: *m* 1979, Peter Johnson. *Residence* – 39 Parkside, Mill Hill, NW7.

AUNTS LIVING (*daughters of 1st Baron*)

Hon Joan Kathleen, *b* 1917: *m* 1940, Walter Higham Brindle, MBE, TD, and has issue living, Michael Patrick, *b* 1943, — Alison Lesley, *b* 1947. *Residence* – 27 Abbotsford Court, Colinton Road, Edinburgh EH10 5EH.
Hon Marjorie Heather, *b* 1923; a JP for Ilkeston, Derbys: *m* 1944, Frederick Joseph Adams, CBE, and has issue living, Christopher Stephen, *b* 1946. *Residences* – 2 Beaumont Close, Belper, Derbys DE5 0ED; 4 Redwood Close, Boverton, Llantwit Major, S Glam CF6 9UT.

WIDOW LIVING OF SECOND BARON

KATHLEEN DORA (*Kathleen, Baroness Darwen*), da of George Sharples Walker *m* 1934, the 2nd Baron, who *d* 1988. *Residence* – White Lodge, Sandelswood End, Beaconsfield, Bucks.

PREDECESSORS – (1) JOHN PERCIVAL Davies, son of late Thomas Pearce Davies, of Heatherfield, Darwen, and Pengarth, Grange-over-Sands; *b* 1885; a Cotton Manufacturer; a Lord-in-Waiting to HM 1949-50; *cr Baron Darwen*, of Heys-in-Bowland, W Riding of Yorkshire (peerage of UK) 1946: *m* 1914, Mary Kathleen, who *d* 1964, da of Alfred Kemp Brown, BD; *d* 1950; *s* by his son (2) CEDRIC PERCIVAL, 2nd Baron, *b* 1915 *m* 1934, Kathleen Dora, da of George Sharples Walker; *d* 1988; *s* by his elder son (3) ROGER MICHAEL, 3rd Baron and present peer.

DAVENTRY, VISCOUNT (FitzRoy Newdegate) (Viscount UK 1943)

FRANCIS HUMPHREY MAURICE FITZROY NEWDEGATE, 3rd Viscount, *b* 17 Dec 1921; *s* 1986; *ed* Eton; formerly Capt Coldm Gds (wounded); ADC to Viceroy of India 1946-48; JP 1960, DL 1970, High Sheriff of Warwicks 1970, Vice Lord Lieut 1974-90, since when Lord Lieut; KStJ 1991: *m* 1959, Hon Rosemary Norrie, da of 1st Baron Norrie, and has issue.

Arms – Quarterly 1st and 4th, gules three lion's gambs two and one argent, *Newdegate*; 2nd and 3rd grand quarters quarterly: 1st and 4th, France and England quarterly; 2nd Scotland, 3rd Ireland; the whole debruised by a baton sinister compony argent and azure, *FitzRoy*. **Crests** – 1st, a fleur-de-lys argent, *Newdegate*; 2nd, on a chapeau gules, turned up ermine, a lion statant guardant or, ducally crowned azure, and gorged with a collar counter compony argent and azure, *FitzRoy*. **Supporters** – *Dexter*, a lion rampant guardant or crowned azure; *Sinister*, a greyhound argent; both gorged with a collar gobony ermine and azure a mullet argent in the azure, each collar edged also azure.
Residence – Temple House, Arbury, Nuneaton, Warwicks.

SONS LIVING

Hon JAMES EDWARD, *b* 27 July 1960; *ed* Milton Abbey, and RAC Cirencester.
Hon Hugh Francis, *b* 1962; *ed* Eton.

DAUGHTER LIVING

Hon Joanna Norrie, *b* 1964: *m* 1990, Nicholas Yvone John Kirkpatrick (*see* Loder, Bt, colls).

SISTERS LIVING (*raised to the rank of a Viscount's daughters 1988*)

Hon Lucia Anne, *b* 1920: *m* 1942, Maj Timothy Stuart Lewis, R Scots Greys, of Inchdura House, N Berwick, and has had issue, Michael Humphrey Stuart, *b* 1943; *ed* Trin Coll, Glenalmond; *d* as the result of a motor accident 1963, — Caroline Anne, *b* 1946: *m* 1st, 1967 (*m diss* 1994), Sir (Frederick Douglas) David Thomson, 3rd Bt, 2ndly; 1994, as his 2nd wife, James Henry Denison-Pender (*see* B Pender, colls).
Hon Jocelyne, *b* 1929: *m* 1st, 1952 (*m* annulled 1953), Richard John Barton; 2ndly, 1957 (*m diss* 1980), Maj Henry John Allfrey, OBE, RA (ret), and has issue living (by 2nd *m*), Henry David, *b* 1959; *ed* Wellington Coll; Maj Scots DG: *m* 1985, Fiona Jean Hamilton, only da of Gen Sir Edward Burgess, KCB, OBE, and has issue living, Henry Edward *b* 1991, Olivia *b* 1988, — Charles John, *b* 1963; *ed* Eton; Capt The Royal Hus (Prince of Wales's Own) (ret): *m* 1989, Caroline Margaret Violet, elder da of Sir Alastair Sturgis Aird, KCVO (*see* Aird, Bt, colls), — Lucia Susan *b* 1961: *m* 1988, Maj David St John Homer, MBE, RGJ, elder son of G/Capt Derek Homer, MVO, of Harpenden, Herts, and has issue living, Thomas David William *b* 1990. *Residence* – 3 New Cottages, Alnport, Andover, Hants.

DAUGHTERS LIVING OF SECOND VISCOUNT

Hon Katherine Susan (PO Box 1284, Kelvin 2054, Transvaal, S Africa) *b* 1923; late Cadet Ensign First Aid Nursing Yeo: *m* 1st, 1945 (*m diss* 1958), Phil John Turner; 2ndly, 1958, Anthony Woodington Boardley, who *d* 1967, and has issue living (by 2nd *m*), Kevan Anthony FitzRoy, *b* 1961.
Hon Barbara Helen, *b* 1928: *m* 1952, Major Peter Charles Ormrod, MC, 8th King's R Irish Hus, JP 1958, High Sheriff of Clwyd 1962, DL (1972), and has issue living, Emma Jane Caroline, *b* 1958: *m* 1980, Julian Pendrill Warner Holloway, of 64 Alderbrook Rd, SW12 8AB, and Pen-y-Lan, Ruabon, Wrexham, Clwyd, yr son of A. G. W. Holloway, of Boscobel, Burleigh, Stroud, Glos, and has issue living, James Oliver Pendrill *b* 1986, Thomas Henry Charles *b* 1988, Alexander Hugh George *b* 1991, Lavinia Sophie Olivia *b* 1984, — Alice Amelia, *b* 1964: *m* 1991, (Roger) James St George Hedley, of The Smithy, Selattyn, Oswestry, Shropshire, son of Maj Roger St George Hedley, late Royal Fusiliers, of Corton, Wilts, and has issue living, Barbara Jane *b* 1992, Lilian Grace *b* 1994. *Residence* – Bridge Lodge, Pen-y-Lan, Ruabon, Wrexham, Clwyd.
Hon Amelia Grace (Bridge Cottage, Stoke Charity, Winchester, Hants), *b* 1930: *m* 1950 (*m diss* 1978), Capt David Charles George Jessel, Coldstream Guards, and has issue (*see* Jessel, Bt), who *d* 1985.

PREDECESSORS – **(1)** Muriel, CBE, da of late Lt-Col Hon Archibald Charles Henry Douglas-Pennant (*see* B Penrhyn, colls), *b* 1869; *cr* Viscountess Daventry, of Daventry, co of Northampton (peerage of UK) 1943: *m* 1891, Capt Rt Hon Edward Algernon FitzRoy, MP (Speaker of House of Commons 1928-43), who *d* 1943 (two months before he was to have received a Viscountcy) (*see* B Southampton, colls); *d* 1962; *s* by her el son **(2)** (ROBERT) OLIVER, 2nd Viscount *b* 1893, Capt RN, High Sheriff of Rutland 1956, European Wars 1914-18, and 1939-45 (despatches): *m* 1916, Grace Zoe, who *d* 1978, da of late Claude Hume Campbell Guinness (E Westmeath, colls); *d* 1986; *s* by his nephew **(3)** FRANCIS HUMPHREY MAURICE (only son of late Cdr Hon John Maurice FitzRoy Newdegate, RN), *b* 1897, *d* 1976, who assumed by R Licence 1936, the addl surname and arms of Newdegate, by his wife, Lucia Charlotte Susan, OBE, who *d* 1982, da of late Sir Francis Alexander Newdegate-Newdegate, GCMG (*see* B Bagot, 1940 Edn), 3rd Viscount and present peer.

DAVID, BARONESS (David) (Life Baroness 1978)

NORA RATCLIFF DAVID, da of George Blockley Blakesley; *b* 23 Sept 1913; *ed* Ashby-de-la-Zouch Girls' Gram Sch, St Felix, Southwold, and Newnham Coll, Camb (MA, Hon Fellow 1986), Cambridge City Councillor 1964-67, and 1968-74; Cambs Co Councillor 1974-78; Member of Board, Peterborough Development Corpn 1976-78; Baroness-in-Waiting to HM 1978-79; JP Cambridge City; *cr* Baroness David, of Romsey, City of Cambridge (Life Baroness) 1978: *m* 1935, Richard William David, CBE, who *d* 1993, and has issue.
Residences – 50 Highsett, Cambridge CB2 1NZ; Cove, New Polzeath, Cornwall PL27 6UF.

SONS LIVING

Hon Nicholas Christopher (Dept of Archaeology, Univ of Calgary, Canada), *b* 1937: *m* 1st, 1962 (*m diss* 1975), Hilke Hennig; 2ndly, 1977 (*m diss* 1982), Iva Williams; 3rdly, 1985, Judy Sterner.
Hon (Richard) Sebastian David (Box 820, Fort Macleod, Alberta, Canada), *b* 1940: *m* 1963, Eva Ross.

DAUGHTERS LIVING

Hon Teresa Katherine (50 Clarence Road, Moseley, Birmingham B13 9UH), *b* 1944: *m* 1967, Llewelyn Anthony Davies.
Hon Elizabeth Sarah, *b* 1947: *m* 1st, 1966 (*m diss* 1977), Martin Anthony Potter; 2ndly, 1979, John Forder.

DAVIDSON, VISCOUNT (Davidson) (Viscount UK 1937)

Light out of darkness

JOHN ANDREW DAVIDSON, 2nd Viscount; *b* 22 Dec 1928; *s* 1970; *ed* Westminster, and Pembroke Coll, Camb; Capt Yeomen of the Guard (Dep Chief Whip) 1986-91, and since 1992: *m* 1st, 1956 (*m diss* 1974), Margaret Birgitta, da of late Maj-Gen Cyril Henry Norton, CB, CBE, DSO; 2ndly, 1975, Mrs Pamela Joy Dobb, da of John Vergette, and has issue by 1st *m*.

Arms – Argent, on a fesse sable between in chief two pheons azure and in base a boar's head erased of the second a portcullis chained or. **Crest** – A lion passant gules charged on the shoulder with a pheon or and holding in the dexter paw a torch inflamed proper. **Supporters** – *Dexter*, a horse argent charged on the shoulder with a rose gules, barbed and seeded proper; *sinister*, a horse sable charged on the shoulder with a martlet or.
Residence – 25 Cliveden Place, SW1.

DAUGHTERS LIVING *(By 1st marriage)*

Hon Alexandra Frances Margaret, *b* 1957: *m* 1982, Richard John Oldfield, only son of late Christopher Charles Bayley Oldfield, of 5 Ovington Gdns, SW3, and has issue living, Christopher, *b* 1986, — Henry, *b* 1991, — Leonora, *b* 1985.
Hon (Georgina) Caroline (*Lady Edward Somerset*), *b* 1958: *m* 1982, Lord Edward Alexander Somerset, 2nd son of 11th Duke of Beaufort.
Hon Camilla Birgitta, *b* 1963: *m* 1988 (*m diss* 1991), Simon Guthrie McNair Scott (*see* V Camrose).
Hon Kristina Louise (twin), *b* 1963.

BROTHER LIVING

Hon MALCOLM WILLIAM MACKENZIE, *b* 28 Aug 1934; *ed* Westminster, and Pembroke Coll, Camb: *m* 1970, Mrs Evelyn Ann Carew Perfect, yr da of William Blackmore Storey (M Queensberry, colls), and previously wife of late Alan Perfect, WS, and has issue living, John Nicolas Alexander, *b* 1971, — Sophie Ann Frances, *b* 1973. *Residence* – Las Cuadras, Monte de la Torre, Los Barrios, Prov de Cadiz, Spain. *Clubs* – Travellers', Pratt's.

SISTERS LIVING

Hon Margaret Joan, *b* 1922: *m* 1943, Ven Benjamin George Burton Fox, MC, TD, Archdeacon of Wisbech, who *d* 1978, and has issue living, *Rev* Colin George, TD (The Rectory, Church Street, Pewsey, Wilts SN9 5DL), *b* 1946: *m* 1975, Bridget Andrea Louise Willan, and has issue living, George Hugh *b* 1977, Henry Benjamin Andrew *b* 1983, Alice Frances *b* 1979, — Elizabeth Angela, *b* 1943 CStJ: *m* 1973, Prof Anthony R. Mellows, TD, GCStJ, LLD, of 22 Devereux Court, Temple Bar, WC2R 3JJ, — Catherine Anne, *b* 1950: *m* 1977, James Lemon, who *d* 1992, — Penelope Margaret, *b* 1953: *m* 1979, Jonathan Hay Marland, of The Cottage, Morlys Lane, Gislingham, nr Eye, Suffolk, — Rosemary Marjorie (twin), *b* 1953: *m* 1978, Michael Swiney of Twofold Cottage, Cock Hall Lane, Langley, Macclesfield, Cheshire SK11 0DE. *Residence* – Tudor House, Terling, N Chelmsford, Essex CM3 2PH.
Hon Jean Elizabeth, *b* 1924; late Capt WRAC (TA): *m* 1952, Hon Charles Richard Strutt, who *d* 1981 (*see* B Rayleigh). *Residence* – Berwick Place, Hatfield Peverel, Chelmsford, Essex.

PREDECESSOR – **(1)** *Rt Hon Sir* JOHN COLIN CAMPBELL Davidson, GCVO, CH, CB, PC, son of the late Sir James Mackenzie Davidson, MB, *b* 1889; MP for Hemel Hempstead (*U*) 1920-23 and 1924-37; Chancellor of Duchy of Lancaster 1923-24 and 1931-37; Chm of Conservative and Unionist Party Organisation 1927-30; *cr Viscount Davidson*, of Little Gaddesden, co Hertford (peerage of UK) 1937: *m* 1919, Hon Dame Frances Joan Dickinson, DBE (*Baroness Northchurch*), who *d* 1985, da of 1st Baron Dickinson; *d* 1970; *s* by his el son **(2)** JOHN ANDREW, 2nd Viscount, and present peer.

DAVIES, BARON (Davies) (Baron UK 1932)

DAVID DAVIES, 3rd Baron, *b* 2 Oct 1940; *s* 1944; *ed* Eton, and King's Coll, Camb: *m* 1972, Beryl, da of W. J. Oliver, and has issue.

Arms – Or, a lion rampant gules, between two fleurs-de-lis in fesse azure; on a chief azure, two pickaxes fessewise. **Crest** – An arm embowed proper, vested to the elbow argent, holding in the hand a miner's safety lamp proper.
Seat – Plas Dinam, Llandinam, Powys.

SONS LIVING

Hon DAVID DANIEL, *b* 23 Oct 1975.
Hon Benjamin Michael Graham, *b* 1985.

DAUGHTERS LIVING

Hon Eldrydd Jane, *b* 1973.
Hon Lucy, *b* 1978.

BROTHER LIVING

Hon Jonathan Hugh (Stonehill House, Abingdon, Oxon), *b* 1944; *ed* Eton, and Univ Coll, Oxford; a Member of Museums and Galleries Commn since 1985: *m* 1966, Mary Veronica, da of Sir (William) Godfrey Agnew, KCVO, of Pinehurst, S Ascot, Berks, and has issue living, Michael Edward, *b* 1968, — Alexander William, *b* 1972: *m* 1994, Sophia Mary Clare, only da of (John) Robin

Thistlethwayte, of Sorbrook Manor, Adderbury, Oxon, — Ruth Gwendoline, b 1969, — Gwendoline Christianne Mary, b 1975, — Christianne Eldrydd, b 1976, — Mary Theresa Ruth, b 1982.

UNCLES LIVING

Hon Edward David Grant, b 1925; ed Gordonstoun, and King's Coll, Camb; late RAF: m 1st, 1949, Patricia Elizabeth, da of Clifford Roberts Musto, of Salisbury, Rhodesia; 2ndly, 1975, Shirley, da of Le Grew Harrison, and formerly wife of John Gaze, and has issue living (by 1st m), David Edmund Clifford, b 1958: m 1988, Nicola D. M., yst da of John Walter Maxwell Miller Richard, of Edinburgh, — Mary Ann Margaret, b 1949: m 1970, Martin Lovegrove, of Boarden House, Hawkenbury, Headcorn, Kent, and has two children, Thomas b 1983, Amy b 1979, — Patricia Jean, b 1951: m 1977, Toby Douglas Everett, of Woodhill Farm, Frensham, Farnham, Surrey, and has issue living, James Douglas b 1980, Emma Patricia b 1978, Polly Victoria b 1986, — Penelope Eldrydd, b 1955: m 1983, Maj Peter Geoffrey Scrope, 13th/18th R Hus (Queen Mary's Own) (see E Mexborough, 1972-73 Edn), of Langbaurgh Hall, Gt Ayton, Middlesbrough, N Yorks TS9 6QQ, and has issue living, Edward Ralph William b 1989, Alexandra Beatrice Mary b 1985, Victoria Emily Louise b 1986, Henrietta Perpetua Agnes b 1991. *Residences* – 30 Southacre, Hyde Park Crescent, W2.

Hon Islwyn Edmund Evan, b 1926; ed Gordonstoun; is a JP for Montgomeryshire, and a DL for Powys: m 1959, Camilla Anne, el da of late Col L. W. Coulden, of 14 Portsea Place, W2, and has issue living, Robin David, b 1961: m 1988, Julie Hughes, — Christopher William, b 1963: m 1988, Wendy Jones, — Richard Edward, b 1965. *Residence* – Perth-y-bu, Sarn, Newtown, Powys SY16 4EP.

AUNTS LIVING

Hon Mary Myfanwy, b 1923; formerly in Women's Roy Canadian Naval Ser; is a CStJ: m 1958 (m diss 1979), Hugh MacAskill Noble and has three sons, Robert David, b 1961, — Andrew Jonathan, b 1962: m 1992, — Hugh James, b 1965.

Hon Gwendoline Rita Jean, b 1929: m 1950 (m diss 1979), John McRae Cormack, AFC, and has had issue, Michael John, b 1962, d as the result of an accident 1980, — Shara Jane, b 1955: m 1983, Anthony J. Leonard, of 5 Montana Rd, SW20, son of Hon Sir John Leonard, and has issue living, Olivia Mary b 1985, Stephanie Emma b 1989, — Amanda Caroline, b 1957: m 1982, Edward John Weston, of The Malt House, Coln St Aldwyns, Glos, and has issue living, Ruth Medina b 1984, Ella Jane b 1986, — Teresa Mary (*Hon Mrs Henry Tennant*), b 1959: m 1983, Hon Henry Lovell Tennant, who d 1990, 2nd son of 3rd Baron Glenconner, and has issue (see B Glenconner).

PREDECESSORS – (1) DAVID Davies, on Plâs Dinam, Llandinam; b 1880; a Director of Great Western Railway, and of Midland Bank; sat as MP for Montgomeryshire (L) 1906-29; cr Baron Davies, of Llandinam, co Montgomery (peerage of United Kingdom), 1932; m 1st, 1910, Amy, who d 1918, da of L. T. Penman, of Broadwood Park, Lanchester, and Gateshead; 2ndly, 1922, Henrietta Margaret, who d 1948, da of late James Grant Fergusson, of Baledmund; d June 1944; s by his son (2) DAVID MICHAEL, 2nd Baron; b 1915; Maj R. Welch Fusiliers (TA): m 1939, Ruth Eldrydd, who d 1966, da of late Maj W. M. Dugdale, of Glanyrafon Hall, Llanyblodwell, Salop; ka Sept 1944; s by his son (3) DAVID, 3rd Baron and present peer.

DAVIES OF LEEK, BARONY OF (Davies) (Extinct 1985)

DAUGHTER LIVING OF LIFE BARON

Hon Harriet Olivia, b 1930; BScEcon London: m 1950, Derek Shephard, of 36 Clevenden Mansions, Lissenden Gdns, NW5.

DAVIES OF PENRHYS, BARONY OF (Davies) (Extinct 1992)

SONS LIVING OF LIFE BARON

Hon Gwynfor, b 1942: m 1969, Linda, da of late Anthony Henry, of Port Talbot, Glam, and has issue.
Hon David Daniel, b 1944: m 1969, Cheryl, da of Thomas Herbert, of Tylorstown, Rhondda, and has issue, one son.

DAUGHTER LIVING OF LIFE BARON

Hon Beryl, b 1947: m 1965, Colin James Powell, of Maesgwyn, Ton Pentre, Rhondda, and has issue one son.

WIDOW LIVING OF LIFE BARON

GWYNETH (*Baroness Davies of Penrhys*), da of Daniel Rees, of Trealaw, Rhondda: m 1940, Baron Davies of Penrhys, who d 1992. *Residence* – Maes-y-Ffrwd, Ferndale Rd, Tylorstown, Rhondda, Mid-Glam.

Davies, see Baron Llewelyn-Davies.

Davies, see Baron Lovell-Davies.

Dawick, Viscount; son of Earl Haig.

DAWSON OF PENN, VISCOUNTCY OF (Dawson) (Extinct 1945)

DAUGHTERS LIVING OF FIRST VISCOUNT

Hon Ursula Margaret (*Hon Lady Bowater*), *b* 1907: *m* 1927, Lt-Col Sir Ian Frank Bowater, GBE, DSO, RA (TA), who *d* 1982, (*see* Bowater, Bt, *cr* 1939). *Residence* – 38 Burton Court, Franklin's Row, SW3 4SZ.
Hon Rosemary Monica (*Hon Lady Wrightson*), *b* 1913: *m* 1939, Col Sir John Garmondsway Wrightson, 3rd Bt, DL, Durham LI (TA), who *d* 1983. *Residence* – Stud Yard House, Neasham, near Darlington.

DEAN OF BESWICK, BARON (Dean) (Life Baron 1983)

JOSEPH JABEZ DEAN, son of John Dean, of Manchester; *b* 3 June 1922; Leader Manchester City Council; Party Private Sec to Min of State, Civil Service Dept 1974-77; an Assist Gvt Whip 1978-79; Lab Party Pairing Whip 1982-83; MP for Leeds West (*Lab*) 1974-83; *cr Baron Dean of Beswick*, of West Leeds, co West Yorks (Life Baron) 1983: *m* 1945, Helen, da of Charles Hill, and has issue.
Address – c/o House of Lords, SW1A 0AA.

DEAN OF HARPTREE, BARON (Dean) (Life Baron 1993)

(ARTHUR) PAUL DEAN, PC, son of late Arthur Dean, of Weaverham, Cheshire; *b* 14 Sept 1924; *ed* Ellesmere Coll, and Exeter Coll, Oxford (MA, BLitt); served 1939-45 War as Capt WG, ADC to Cdr 1 Corps BAOR; formerly a farmer; Resident Tutor Swinton Conservative Coll 1958-64, Assist Dir Conservative Research Dept 1962-64; Parl Under-Sec Dept of Health and Social Security 1970-74, Chm Conservative Health and Social Security Cttee, and Memb Commons Services Select Cttee 1979-82, 2nd Dep Chm House of Commons, and Dep Chm Ways and Means 1982-87, 1st Dept Chm Ways and Means, and Dep Speaker 1987-92; Dir Charterhouse Pensions, and Watney Mann and Truman Holdings, Gov Commonwealth Inst 1981-89, and former Gov BUPA, Pres Oxford Univ Conservative Assocn; MP N Som (*C*) 1964-83, and Woodspring 1983-92; *cr* Knt 1985, PC 1991, and *Baron Dean of Harptree*, of Wedmore, co Somerset (Life Baron) 1993: *m* 1st, 1957, Doris Ellen, who *d* 1979, da of late Frank Webb, of Sussex; 2ndly, 1980, Peggy Parker.
Address – House of Lords, SW1A 0AA. *Clubs* – Oxford Carlton, Oxford and Cambridge.

DEAN OF THORNTON-LE-FYLDE, BARONESS (McDowall) (Life Baroness 1993)

BRENDA DEAN, da of Hugh Dean, of Thornton, Cleveleys, Lancs; *b* 29 April 1943; *ed* St Andrews, Eccles, and Stretford Gram Sch; Hon MA Salford 1986, Hon Fellow Lancashire Poly 1991, Hon Law Degree City Univ, London 1993; Admin Sec Manchester Branch SOGAT 1959-71, Assist Branch Sec 1971, Sec 1976, Pres SOGAT 1983-85, Gen Sec 1985-91, Dep Gen Sec GPMU 1991-92; Memb Women's National Commn NEDC 1985-92 (Co-Chm 1975-78), BBC Gen Advisory Council 1985-89, TUC Gen Council 1985-92, TUC Econ Cttee 1987-92, City Univ Council since 1991; Gov Ditchley Foundation since 1992; Chm ICSTIS since 1993, Memb Press Complaints Commn since 1993, Memb Broadcasting Complaints Commn since 1993, non-exec dir Inveresh plc; *cr Baroness Dean of Thornton-le-Fylde*, of Eccles, co Greater Manchester (Life Baroness) 1993: *m* 1988, Keith Desmond McDowall, CBE.
Address – c/o House of Lords, SW1A 0AA.

DECIES, BARON (de la Poer Beresford) (Baron I 1812)
(Title pronounced "Deeshies")

Nothing without the Cross

MARCUS HUGH TRISTRAM DE LA POER BERESFORD, 7th Baron, *b* 5 Aug 1948; *s* 1992; *ed* St Columba's Coll, and Dublin Univ (M Litt): *m* 1st, 1970 (*m diss* 1974), Sarah Jane, only da of Col Basil Gunnell; 2ndly, 1981, Edel Jeannette, da of late Vincent Ambrose Hendron, of Dublin, and has issue by 2nd *m.*

ᴀrms – Quarterly: 1st and 4th argent semée or cross-crosslets fitchée, three fleurs-de-lis within a bordure engrailed, all sable, *Beresford;* 2nd and 3rd argent, a chief indented sable, *de la Poer;* a mullet argent for difference. ℭrest – A dragon's head erased azure, transfixed in the neck with a broken tilting spear or, the point broken off argent transfixing the upper jaw, charged with a mullet for difference. ꙅupporters – Two angels proper, vested argent, crined and winged or, each holding in the exterior hand a sword erect of the first, pommel and hilt gold and charged on the breast with a mullet for difference. *Residence* – Straffan Lodge, Straffan, co Kildare.

SONS LIVING *(By 2nd marriage)*

Hon ROBERT MARCUS DUNCAN DE LA POER, *b* 14 July 1988.
Hon David George Morley Hugh de la Poer, *b* 1991.

DAUGHTER LIVING *(By 2nd marriage)*

Hon Louisa Katherine de la Poer, *b* 1984.

SISTERS LIVING

Hon Sarah Ann Vivien de la Poer, *b* 1949: *m* 1st, 1975 (*m diss* 1982), Joerg B. Schnapka, son of Dr Herbert Schnapka, of Bochum, W Germany; 2ndly, 1992, Andrew McMeekan, and has issue living (by 1st *m*), Roland Rufus, *b* 1976. *Residence* – 12A Malcolm Rd, Wimbledon, SW19 4AS.
Hon Clare Antoinette Gabrielle de la Poer, *b* 1956: *m* 1986, Jorge Koechlin, son of late Jose Edmondo Koechlin, of Lima, Peru, and has issue living, Michael Joseph Tristram, *b* 1986. *Address* – c/o Coutts & Co, 1 Old Park Lane, W1.

WIDOW LIVING OF SON OF THIRD BARON

Ida Kaye: *m* 1941, as his 4th wife, Hon William Arthur Horsley-Beresford, who *d* 1949, and has issue (see colls, infra).

WIDOW LIVING OF SIXTH BARON

DIANA (*Dowager Baroness Decies*), da of late W/Cdr George Turner-Cain, of Marsh House, Wells, Norfolk, and widow of Maj David W. A. Galsworthy, The Royal Fus: *m* (Sept) 1945, as his 2nd wife, the 6th Baron, who *d* 1992. *Residence* – Little Barwick, Stanhoe, King's Lynn, Norfolk.

COLLATERAL BRANCHES LIVING

Grandchildren of late Hon William Arthur de la Poer Horsley-Beresford (infra):—
Issue of late George Graham Horsley-Beresford, *b* 1903, *d* 1974: *m* 1938, Sherman (Frederiksted, Isle of St Croix, US Virgin Islands), da of Frank Olmsted of New York, NY, USA:—
Marcus Hughes (Frederiksted, St Croix, US Virgin Islands), *b* 1943; late Capt USAF; Pilot Eastern Airlines: *m* 1st, 1962 (*m diss* 19-), Lynne Green, of East Millstone, NJ, USA; 2ndly, 1979, Diane Armstrong, and has issue living (by 1st *m*), Marcus Tyler de la Poer, *b* 1963, — Teresa Leigh, *b* 1965, — (by 2nd *m*) Julia Victoria de la Poer, *b* 1983. —— Peter Graham de la Poer, *b* 1956. —— Holley Audrey, *b* 1939.

Issue of late Hon William Arthur de la Poer Horsley-Beresford, yst son of 3rd Baron, *b* 1878; *d* 1949: *m* 1st, 1901 (*m diss* 1919), Florence, who *d* 1969, da of Gardner L. Miller, MD, of Providence, Rhode Island, USA; 2ndly, 1919 (*m diss* 1928), Laura, who *d* 1958, da of late Capt St John Halford Coventry (E Coventry, colls); 3rdly, 1933 (*m diss* 1940), Georgina Leonora, who *d* 1969, only da of late Richard Frederik Hendrik Mosselmans, of the Hague, and formerly wife of Count Fernand de Bertier de Sauvigny; 4thly, 1941, Ida Kaye (ante):—
(By 1st *m*) John Duncan (3510 Front St, San Diego, California, USA), *b* 1904: *m* 1934, Aina, who *d* 1974, da of Blaine R. Richard, of Miami Beach, Flor, USA, and has had issue, Sheila Kathleen, *b* 1941; *d* 1986. —— (By 2nd *m*) Patrick, *b* 1924: *m* 1st, 1953 (*m diss* in USA 1956), Miriam Morton, of Philadelphia, USA; 2ndly, 1959, Leslie Yvonne, who *d* 1985, da of late Leslie Robert McCaskey, of Wellington, NZ, and has issue living (by 2nd *m*) Marcus Dominic St John (Via dei Tirreni 16, 01015 Sutri (VT) Italy), *b* 1960: *m* 1984, Rossana, da of Angelo Zeppa, of Viterbo, Italy, and has issue living, Morgan J. R. *b* 1985, Jordan M. L. *b* 1988. —— Hazel (Springfield, 32 Park Avenue, Old Basing, Basingstoke, Hants RG24 0HT), *b* 1920: *m* 1940, Gerald Herbert Incledon, who *d* 1990, and has had issue, Jonathan Guy, *b* 1963, — Margaret Anne, *b* 1941: *m* 1961, Anthony E. Hodson, of Spring Lanes, Holly Spring Lane, Bracknell, Berks, and has issue living, Christopher James *b* 1963, Lucy Alice *b* 1967, — Heather, *b* 1943: *m* 1966, Christopher C. E. Stamford, of Grassmere, Mid St, S Nutfield, Surrey, and has issue living, Daniel Charles *b* 1967, Charlotte Anne *b* 1970, Louisa Emma *b* 1975, — Susan Amber *b* 1945: *m* 1st, 1968 (*m diss* 1976), David Ellis Green, MBE, R Regt Fus; 2ndly, 1979, Christopher Norman (Merton House, 7 Bath Rd, Camberley, Surrey), and *d* 1993, leaving issue (by 1st *m*), Rebecca Claire *b* 1973, (by 2nd *m*) Annabel Sarah *b* 1983, — Amanda Elizabeth, *b* 1947: *m* 1983, Richard Bailey, of 38 Robert Cecil Av, Swaythling, Southampton, Hants, — Moya Catherine, *b* 1956: *m* 1976, Charles Mellor, of 5 Sandpiper Close, Marchwood, Hants, and has issue living, Stephen Andrew *b* 1981, Gillian Leigh *b* 1984, Joanna *b* (twin) 1984. —— (By 4th *m*) Peter, *b* 1945; *ed* Emanuel Sch, and Univ Coll, Oxford (BA). —— Maureen, *b* 1942.

Grandchildren of late Henry Tristam Beresford, son of Rev George Hamilton de la Poer Beresford, 3rd son of Rev Hon George Beresford, 2nd son of 1st Baron:—
Issue of late Maj-Gen Sir George de la Poer Beresford, CB, MC, *b* 1885, *d* 1964: *m* 1916, Margaret Ethel Granville, who *d* 1963, da of late Rev Arthur Christopher Thynne (M Bath, colls):—

Benedict Henry de la Poer (3 Cambridge Cottages, Kew, Richmond, Surrey), *b* 1917; 1939-45 War with RAC: *m* 1949, Dorothy Kate, da of George Cooper, of Gt Bedwyn, Wilts, and has issue living, Margaret Jane, *b* 1963.
   Issue of late William Coventry de la Poer Beresford, *b* 1887, *d* 1938: *m* 1921, Jessie, who *d* 1931, da of J. Rowling, of NSW:—
(Charles) Marcus Tristram de la Poer (Deepdene, Coonabarabran, NSW), *b* 1923; 1942-45 War with RAAF: *m* 1st, 1948, Mary Frances, who *d* 1972, da of Hugh Buckingham Loveband, of Blenheim, Coonabarabran, NSW; 2ndly, 1973, Gwen Cornwell, and has issue living (by 1st *m*), Roslyn de la Poer, *b* 1949, — Julia de la Poer, *b* 1952. —— Patricia de la Poer, *b* 1922: *m* 1953, R. S. Meares, of 51 Bishop St, Goulburn, NSW, and has issue living, Richard Grant, *b* 1955, — Philip Marcus, *b* 1960.
   Issue of late Marcus Gervais de la Poer Beresford, *b* 1888, *d* 1967: *m* 1927, Susan Mildred (3 Hovel St, Manuka, ACT 2603, Aust), da of late Edward Charles Campbell:—
Barrington Henry de la Poer (9 Melrose Av, Sylvania, NSW), *b* 1928: *m* 1952, Fleur Marie, da of late John Crisp, of Corowa, NSW, and has issue living, Sean Anthony de la Poer, *b* 1962, — Amanda de la Poer, *b* 1956.

   Granddaughters of late Maj-Gen Sir George de la Poer Beresford, CB, MC (ante):—
   Issue of late Lieut-Cdr Stephen Marcus de la Poer Beresford, DSC, RN, *b* 1920, *d* 1982: *m* 1952, Susan Wendy (c/o PO Cooma, NSW 2630, Australia), da of late Maj Tom Lees Dearbergh, of Hollywood Cottage, Lymington, Hants:—
Diana Margaret, *b* 1976, Henry James Harmer, of 46 Blackborough Rd, Reigate, Surrey, and has issue living, Nicholas Benjamin, *b* 1983, — Claire Susan, *b* 1981, — Amy Diana, *b* 1986. —— Angela Susan, *b* 1953 (twin).

PREDECESSORS – **(1)** *Rev Hon* WILLIAM Beresford, 3rd son of 1st Earl of Tyrone and brother of 1st Marquess of Waterford; Bishop of Dromore 1780-2, Bishop of Ossory 1782-94, and Archbishop of Tuam 1794-1819; *cr Baron Decies* (peerage of Ireland) 1812; *d* 1819; *s* by his son **(2)** JOHN, 2nd Baron; *b* 1773: *m* 1810, Charlotte Philadelphia, only da and heiress of Robert Horsley, of Bolam House, Morpeth, when he assumed the additional surname of Horsley; *d* 1 March 1855; *s* by his son **(3)** WILLIAM ROBERT JOHN DE LA POER, 3rd Baron, *b* 1811: *m* 1860, Catherine Anne, who *d* 1941, da of William Hedley-Dent, of Shortflatt Tower, Belsay; *d* 1893; *s* by his el son **(4)** WILLIAM MARCUS DE LA POER, 4th Baron, *b* 1865: *m* 1901, Maria Gertrude, who *d* 1939, da of Sir John Pollard Willoughby, 4th Bt; *d* 1910; *s* by his brother **(5)** JOHN GRAHAM HOPE DE LA POER, PC, DSO, 5th Baron, *b* 1866; Major (ret) 7th Hussars; Matebeleland 1896, S Africa 1902, Somaliland 1903-4 (DSO); Ch Press Censor in Ireland 1916-19: *m* 1st, 1911 Helen Vivien, who *d* 1931, da of late George Jay Gould, of New York USA; 2ndly, 1936, Elizabeth, who *d* 1944, da of George Drexel, and widow of Henry Symes Lehr; *d* 1944; *s* by his son **(6)** ARTHUR GEORGE MARCUS DOUGLAS DE LA POER, 6th Baron, *b* 1915; European War 1938-45 as Flying Officer RAFVR (American DFC): *m* 1st, 1937, Ann Christina, who *d* (March) 1945, da of late Sidney Walter Trevor, of Camperdown, Vic, Australia; 2ndly, (Sept) 1945, Diana, da of late W/Cdr George Turner-Cain, of Marsh House, Wells, Norfolk, and widow of Maj David W. A. Galsworthy, The Royal Hus; *d* 1992; *s* by his only son **(7)** MARCUS HUGH TRISTRAM DE LA POER, 7th Baron and present peer.

DE CLIFFORD, BARON (Russell) (Baron E 1299)

JOHN EDWARD SOUTHWELL RUSSELL, 27th Baron; *b* 8 June 1928; *s* 1982; *ed* Eton, and RAC Cirencester: *m* 1959, Bridget Jennifer, yst da of Duncan Robertson, of Llantysilio Hall, Llangollen, Denbighshire (*see* Williams-Wynn, Bt).

Arms – Argent, a lion rampant gules, on a chief sable three escallops of the first. **Crest** – A goat statant argent, armed and unguled or. **Supporters** – *Dexter*, a wyvern gules; *Sinister*, a monkey proper, ringed round the loins and lined or. *Residence* – Riggledown, Pennymoor, Tiverton, Devon EX16 8LR.

BROTHER LIVING

Hon WILLIAM SOUTHWELL (Gilboa Farmhouse, Brokenborough, Malmesbury, Wiltshire SN16 0HX), *b* 26 Feb 1930; *ed* Eton, and King's Coll, Camb: *m* 1961, Jean Brodie, da of Neil Brodie Henderson, of Glebe House, Little Hormead, Buntingford, Herts (*see* Madden, Bt, 1980 Edn), and has issue living, Miles Edward Southwell, *b* 1966, — Mary-Jane Sophia, *b* 1963: *m* 1991, Matthew G. Howe, elder son of Philip Howe, of Sydney, Australia, — Joanna Clare, *b* 1965.

What will be, will be

WIDOW LIVING OF TWENTY-SIXTH BARON

MINA MARGARET (*Mina, Baroness de Clifford*), only da of George Edward Sands: *m* 1973, as his 2nd wife, Col 26th Baron, who *d* 1982.

COLLATERAL BRANCHES LIVING

   Issue of late Hon Diana Katharine Russell, only da of 25th Baron, *b* 1909, *d* 1978: *m* 1st, 1933 (*m diss* 1948), Mervyn Hesseltine Taylor; 2ndly, 1948, His Honour Judge Thomas Elder-Jones, who *d* 1988:—
(By 1st *m*) Christopher John TAYLOR (East Cottage, Bourton on the Hill, Morton-in-Marsh, Glos), *b* 1934: *m* 1st, 1959 (*m diss* 1971), Sarah Mary, only da of late Ewan Mews; 2ndly, 1972, Jane Seymour, yst da of late George Macdonald Brown, and has issue living (by 1st *m*), Vernon Edmund Christopher, *b* 1965, — Claire Virginia Mary, *b* 1962. —— Virginia Carol EDLER-JONES, *b* 1945; adopted by her mother and stepfather, whose name she assumed 1956.

   Descendants of Frances Sophia Cholmondeley (da of George James Cholmondeley, by Hon Mary Elizabeth, da of John Thomas Townshend, 2nd Viscount Sydney, by his 1st wife, Hon Sophia Southwell, da of 20th Baron): *m* 1846, Rev Charles Riddell, of whom Rev John Charles Riddell was father of 11th Bt:—
(*see* Riddell, Bt).

   Descendants of Robert Marsham-Townshend, only son of 2nd Earl of Romney, by his 2nd wife, Hon Mary Elizabeth Townshend, da of 2nd Viscount Sydney, and widow of George James Cholmondeley (ante):—
(*see* E Romney, colls).

   Descendants of Hon Elizabeth Southwell, da of 20th Baron: *m* 1792 as his 1st wife, the 4th Earl of Albemarle:—
(*see* E Albemarle).

PREDECESSORS – **(1)** ROGER de Clifford: *m* Isabel, el da and co-heiress of Robert de Vipont, Lord of Westmorland, and in 1277 acknowledged the service of two fees and a half, for a moiety of the Barony of Westmorland; *d* 1282; *s* by his son **(2)** ROBERT, 2nd Lord of Westmorland, and *1st Baron de Clifford*; summoned to Parliament of England 1299-1313; Earl Marshal of England 1307, Warden of Scotland 1308; killed at Bannockburn 1314; *s* by his son **(3)** ROGER, 2nd Baron ; *dsp* 1327; *s* by his brother **(4)** ROBERT, 3rd Baron; *d* 1344; *s* by his son **(5)** ROBERT, 4th Baron; *dsp* 1362; *s* by his brother **(6)** ROGER, 5th Baron; *d* 1390; *s* by his son **(7)** THOMAS, 6th Baron ; *d* 1392; *s* by his son **(8)** JOHN, 7th Baron; *d* 1422; *s* by his son **(9)** THOMAS, 8th Baron; *d* 1455; *s* by his son **(10)** JOHN, 9th Baron; *d* 1461; *s* by his son **(11)** HENRY, 10th Baron; *d* 1524; *s* by his son **(12)** HENRY, 11th Baron; *cr Earl of Cumberland* (peerage of England) 1525; obtained large grants out of the monastic spoliations and had a principal command in the army which invaded Scotland; *d* 1543; *s* by his son **(13)** HENRY, KB, 2nd Earl; *d* 1569; *s* by his son **(14)** GEORGE, KG, 3rd Earl, an eminent naval commander and an ardent sportsman; *d* 1605, leaving issue one da **(15)** ANNE, wife of Richard Sackville, 2nd Earl of Dorset; in 1628 the Countess of Dorset claimed the title, but the House of Lords postponed the hearing, and the Barony remained dormant until 1691, when it was allowed to **(16)** NICHOLAS, 15th Baron, and 3rd Earl of Thanet, son of John, 2nd Earl of Thanet, by Lady Margaret, da of Anne, Countess of Dorset (ante); *s* by his brother **(17)** JOHN, 16th Baron, and 4th Earl of Thanet: *s* by his brother **(18)** RICHARD, 17th Baron, and 5th Earl of Thanet; *s* by his brother **(19)** THOMAS, 18th Baron, and 6th Earl of Thanet; *d* 1721, when the Earldom of Thanet devolved upon his nephew, and the Barony of de Clifford went into abeyance between his five das, and remained so until 1734, when the crown terminated it in favour of the 3rd da **(20)** MARGARET, wife of Thomas Coke, 1st Baron Lovel, who in 1744 was *cr* Earl of Leicester; *d* 1775, when the Barony again became abeyant, and it remained so until 1776, when it was terminated in favour of **(21)** EDWARD Southwell, 20th Baron (MP for co Gloucester), son of Edward Southwell, by the Hon Catherine, da of Edward, Viscount Sondes (el son of 1st Earl of Rockingham) and Lady Catherine, el da of 6th Earl of Thanet; *d* 1777; *s* by his son **(22)** EDWARD, 21st Baron; *dsp* 1832, when the Barony became abeyant between his sisters, and remained so until 1833, when it was terminated in favour of the surviving issue of his el sister Catherine, by Col George Coussmaker, viz **(23)** SOPHIA, wife of Capt John Russell, RN *(see* D Bedford, colls); *d* 1874, *s* by her son **(24)** EDWARD SOUTHWELL, 23rd Baron; *b* 1824; MP for Tavistock *(L)* 1847-58: *m* 1853, Harriet Agnes, who *d* 1896, da of late Adm Sir Charles Elliot, KCB; *d* 1877; *s* by his son **(24)** EDWARD SOUTHWELL, 24th Baron; *b* 1855: *m* 1879, Hilda, who *d* 1895, da of Charles Balfour, of Easthampstead, Berks; *d* 1894; *s* by his son **(25)** JACK SOUTHWELL, 25th Baron; *b* 1884: *m* 1906, Evelyn Victoria Anne, who *d* 1979, having *m* 2ndly, 1913, Capt Arthur Roy Stock *(d* 1915), of Glenapp Castle, Ballantrae, Ayrshire, and 3rdly, 1922, George Vernon Tate, MC *(d* 1955) *(see* Tate, Bt, colls) da of Walter Robert Chandler; *d* 1909; *s* by his son **(26)** EDWARD SOUTHWELL, OBE, 26th Baron *b* 1907; Col REME, R Gloucestershire Hussars (TA) *m* 1st 1926 *(m diss* 1973), Dorothy Evelyn, who *d* 1987, da of Ferdinand Richard Holmes Meyrick, MD, of 59 Kensington Court, W8; 2ndly 1973, Mina Margaret, only da of George Edward Sands; *d* 1982; *s* by his el son **(27)** JOHN EDWARD SOUTHWELL RUSSELL, 27th Baron and present peer.

DEEDES, BARON (Deedes) (Life Baron 1986)

WILLIAM FRANCIS DEEDES, MC, PC; *b* 1 June 1913, only son of late Herbert William Deedes, of Galt, Hythe, Kent, and formerly of Sandling Park and Saltwood Castle, Kent *(see* B Ashtown, colls, 1966 Edn); *ed* Harrow; Hon DCL (Univ of Kent at Canterbury 1988); Parliamentary Sec, Min of Housing and Local Govt 1954-55, Joint Parliamentary Under-Sec of State Home Office, 1955-57, and Min without Portfolio 1962-64; Editor, The Daily Telegraph 1974-86; served 1939-45 War as Maj KRRC (TA); a DL of Kent; MP for Ashford Div of Kent *(C)* 1950-74; *cr* PC 1962, and *Baron Deedes*, of Aldington, co Kent (Life Baron) 1986: *m* 1942, Evelyn Hilary, da of Clive Branfoot, of Stonegrave, Yorks, and has had issue.
Residence – New Hayters, Aldington, Kent. *Club* – Carlton.

SONS LIVING AND DECEASED

Hon Jeremy Wyndham, *b* 1943; *ed* Eton; journalist and Editorial Director The Daily Telegraph since 1986: *m* 1973, Anna Rosemary, da of late Maj Elwin Clive Gray, Seaforth Highlanders, of Aldington, Kent, and has issue living, George William, *b* 1976, — Henry Julius, *b* 1978. *Residence* – Hamilton House, Compton, Newbury, Berks. *Club* – Boodle's.

Julius Brook, *b* 1947; journalist; *dunm* 1970.

DAUGHTERS LIVING

Hon Juliet Evelyn Mary, *b* 1948: *m* 1990, Robert Dale Means, eldest son of Robert Means, of Blythe, Calif. *Residence* – 92 North Rd, Hythe, Kent.

Hon Victoria Frances Jill, *b* 1950: *m* 1982, Jonathan Edward Southey, 3rd son of Sir Robert Southey, AO, CMG, of Mount Eliza, Australia, and has issue living, Samuel William Robert, *b* 1984, — Simon Raymond Julius, *b* 1986. *Residence* – Maben House, Llaneast St, Malvern 3144, Victoria, Australia.

Hon Lucy Rose, *b* 1955: *m* 1978, Hon Crispin James Alan Nevill Money-Coutts, son of 8th Baron Latymer, and has issue. *Residence* – Church House, Stopham, W Sussex.

Deerhurst, Viscount; son of Earl of Coventry.

DE FREYNE, BARON (French) (Baron UK 1851)

MALO MORI QUAM FOEDARI

I had rather die than be dishonoured

FRANCIS ARTHUR JOHN FRENCH, 7th Baron; *b* 3 Sept 1927; *s* 1935; is a Knight of Sovereign Order of Malta: *m* 1st, 1954 (*m diss* 1978), Shirley Ann, da of late D. R. Pobjoy; 2ndly 1978, Sheelin Deirdre, da of late Col Henry Kane O'Kelly, DSO, of co Wicklow, and widow of William Walker Stevenson and has issue by 1st *m*.

Arms – Ermine, a chevron sable. **Crest** – A dolphin embowed proper. **Supporters** – *Dexter*, an ancient Irish warrior habited, supporting with his dexter hand a battle-axe, head downwards and bearing on his sinister arm a shield, all proper; *sinister*, a female figure vested proper and scarf flowing argent.
Address – c/o House of Lords, Westminster SW1.

SONS LIVING *(By 1st marriage)*

Hon FULKE CHARLES ARTHUR JOHN, *b* 21 April 1957: *m* 1986, Julia Mary, only da of Dr James H. Wellard, of Hampstead, NW3, and has issue living, Alexander James Charles, *b* 22 Sept 1988, — William Rory Francis, *b* 1991. *Residence* – 26 Oakhill Rd, SW15 2QR.
Hon Patrick Dominick Fitzstephen Jude, *b* 1969.

DAUGHTER LIVING *(By 1st marriage)*

Hon Vanessa Rose Bradbury, *b* 1958: *m* 1991, Richard Leslie Phillips, of 16 Mablethorpe Rd, SW6.

SISTER LIVING

Hon Patricia Mary (4 Linley Court, Rouse Gdns, W Dulwich, SE21), *b* 1917: *m* 1941, Reginald Johnson, who *d* 1958, and has issue living, Michael Reginald (56 Pymers Mead, SE21), *b* 1943: *m* 1982, Marta Jablonska, and has issue living, Patrick Martin *b* 1983, Mark Conrad Eric *b* 1986, — Diana Mary, *b* 1942: *m* 1972, Frederick Robert Robinson, of 111 Gatley Ave, Westewell, Surrey, and has issue living, Nicholas Frederick *b* 1980, Victoria Jane *b* 1977.

WIDOW LIVING OF SON OF FOURTH BARON

Mary Frances (Stychfield, Stychens Lane, Bletchingley, Redhill, Surrey), da of Charles Hasslacher, of 3 Kensington Park Gdns, W8: *m* 1937, the Hon Hubert John French, who *d* 1961, and has issue (see colls, infra).

COLLATERAL BRANCHES LIVING

Issue of late Capt Hon William Joseph French, 3rd son of 4th Baron, *b* 1885, *d* 1974: *m* 1920, Victoria Louise, who *d* 1989, da of late William Dalglish Bellasis, JP:—
Marie Isobel (*Countess Cathcart*), *b* 1923: *m* 1st, 1942, Capt Sir Thomas Brian Weldon, 8th Bt, who *d* 1979; 2ndly, 1984, as his 2nd wife, 6th Earl Cathcart. *Residence* – Moor Hatches, W Amesbury, Salisbury, Wilts. —— Eleanor Mary, *b* 1925: *m* 1946, Capt Patrick Munro of Foulis (*see* Munro Bt, *cr* 1634), Seaforth Highlanders, of Foulis Castle, Evanton, Ross-shire.

Issue of late Hon Louis Richard French, 5th son of 4th Baron, *b* 1888, *d* 1952: *m* 1922, Margaret Eleanor, who *d* 1972, da of late Capt Maurice Kirk, 4th King's Own (Roy Lancaster) Regt:—
Sheila Mary, MBE, *b* 1924; MBE (Civil) 1987: *m* 1948, John Benedict Stilwell, Lieut Coldstream Guards (ret), and has had issue, Mark Andrew (Quinta de Alcalar, Alvor, Portimão, Portugal), *b* 1949: *m* 1974, Viviane de Gheldere, and has issue living, John Philip *b* 1975, Alexandra Mary *b* 1978, — Christopher John (21 Monte da Bemposta, Portimão, Portugal), *b* 1952: *m* 1982, Dr Ana Luiza Mendes Victor, and has issue living, John William *b* 1983, — John William, *b* 1954: *d* 1983, — Charles Louis (Brackenwood, 5 Plymouth Rd, Barnt Green, Worcs B45 8JE), *b* 1957: *m* 1986, Mary Elizabeth Baker, and has issue living, Simon Benedict *b* 1989, Christian Louis *b* 1992, Andrew Charles *b* (twin) 1992, — Philippa Ann, *b* 1950: *m* 1973, João Carlos Zilhão, of 41 Avenida do Restelo, Lisbon, Portugal, and has issue living, João Miguel *b* 1974, Antonio Carlos *b* 1976, Francisco *b* 1989, Ana Felipa *b* 1981. *Residence* – Casa dos Arcos, Tapada da Penina, Portimão, Portugal.

Issue of late Hon Hubert John French, 8th son of 4th Baron, *b* 1896, *d* 1961: *m* 1937, Mary Frances (ante), da of Charles Hasslacher, of 3 Kensington Park Gardens, W8:—
Christopher John (Brewerstreet Farm, Bletchingley, Surrey), *b* 1943: *m* 1966, Sacha, da of late Robert Wild, of 5 Ivy Mill Lane, Godstone, Surrey, and has issue living, Philip John, *b* 1968, — Julia Winifred, *b* 1971. —— Richard Charles, *b* 1945: *m* 1969, Hilda Mary Felicity, el da of Lt-Col J. J. Pearson, of Tandridge, Surrey, and has issue living, Charles Peter, *b* 1974, — Helen Mary Luise, *b* 1969, — Suszanna Frances (twin), *b* 1974. —— Jane Mary, *b* 1938: *m* 1966, Donald John Lawlor, of 2 Elsenwood Crescent, Camberley, Surrey, and has issue living, Bernard John, *b* 1969, — Timothy Charles, *b* 1970, — Stephen Andrew, *b* 1976, — Elizabeth Mary, *b* 1967. —— Sarah Anne, *b* 1940 (6281 Lightpoint Place, Columbia, Md 21045, USA), *b* 1940; BA (Oxon), MPhil, MEd, PhD: *m* 1971, Clement Henry Lutterodt, PhD, and has issue living, Tobias Henry *b* 1973, — Isabelle Anne, *b* 1975, — Justine Frances, *b* 1979.

Issue of late Hon Bertram Leo French, 9th son of 4th Baron, *b* 1900, *d* 1941: *m* 1927, Maud Mary, who *d* 1974, only da of late Edmund FitzLaurence Dease (*see* B Stafford, colls):—
Maurice Aloysius, MBE (71 East St, Warminster, Wilts), *b* 1930; Maj R Regt Fus; Korea 1952 (despatches), MBE (Mil) 1976: *m* 1st (*m diss* 1965), Heather, da of late A. C. Tarbutt; 2ndly, 1965, Lavinia Mary, da of late Maj Patrick Henry Anthony Burke, of Stackalan, co Meath, and has issue living, (by 1st *m*) Dominic Arthur, *b* 1959: *m* 1987, Miranda, da of late Philip Howden, and has issue living, Richard Maurice *b* 1988, James Philip *b* (twin) 1988, — Nicola Anne, *b* 1960: *m* 1984, David Stogdale, and has issue living, Sam Patrick *b* 1987, Will Benedict *b* 1994, Abigail Gaynor *b* 1990, — (by 2nd *m*), Patrick Rollo, *b* 1966; MA, FRGS: *m* 1992, Abigail Digna Joanna, da of Cmdr Eoin Ashton-Johnson, of East Orchard, Dorset, and has issue living, Thomas Tenzin *b* 1994, — Gerald Hugh, *b* 1975, — Claudia Rosemary, *b* 1973, — Emily Mary Lucia (twin), *b* 1975. —— Arthur Edmund, *b* 1933; ed Trin Coll, Camb (BA 1957); Bar Inner Temple 1962; late Lt Irish Gds (Reserve): *m* 1986, Charlotte Mary, 2nd da of Sir Simon Peter Edmund Cosmo William Towneley, KCVO, of Dyneley, Burnley, Lancs (*see* E Lindsey and Abingdon, colls), and has issue living, Edmund Peter *b* 1989, — Alice Cecilia, *b* 1987. —— Lavinia Marie, *b* 1928: *m* 1971, Maj John Norman Pembroke Watson, late RHG, of Pannett's, Shipley, Horsham, Sussex.

PREDECESSORS – (B)(1) ARTHUR French, MP, great-grandson of late Arthur French, of French Park, who *d* 1769; *cr* *Baron de Freyne*, of Artagh (peerage of United Kingdom) 1839, and *Baron de Freyne*, of Coolavin (peerage of United Kingdom) 1851, with remainder to his brothers; *d* 1856, when the 1st peerage expired; *s* in Barony of 1851 by his brother (2) *Rev* JOHN, 2nd Baron; *d* 1863; *s* by his brother (3) CHARLES, 3rd Baron: *m* 1851, by a Roman Catholic priest, to Catherine, da of Luke Maree; a question having arisen as to the validity of that marriage, she being a Roman Catholic and he a Protestant, they were again married in 1854 in the Established Church, having at that time had issue, Charles, MP for co Roscommon 1873-80, *b* 1851 (who *d* 1925), John *b* 1853 (who *d* 1916), and William *b* 1854 (who *d* 1929 in USA); *s* by his el son born after the marriage of 1854 (4) ARTHUR, 4th Baron; *b* 1855: *m* 1st, 1877, Lady Laura Octavia Dundas, who *d* 1881, sister of 3rd Earl of Zetland; 2ndly, 1882, Marie Georgiana, who *d* 1923, da of late Richard Westbrook Lamb, of West Denton, Northumberland; *d* 1913; *s* by his son (5) ARTHUR REGINALD, 5th Baron; *b* 1879; Capt 3rd Batn S Wales Borderers: *m* 1902, Annabel, who *d* 1962, da of William Angus; *ka* 1915 (despatches); *s* by his half-brother (6) FRANCIS CHARLES, 6th Baron, *b* 1884: *m* 1916, Lina Victoria, who *d* 1974, da of Sir John Alexander Arnott, 2nd Bt; *d* 1935; *s* by his son (7) FRANCIS ARTHUR JOHN, 7th Baron and present peer.

DELACOURT-SMITH, BARONY OF (Delacourt-Smith) (Extinct 1972)

SON LIVING OF LIFE BARON

Hon Stephen DELACOURT-SMITH (73 Athenlay Rd, SE15), *b* 1946.

DAUGHTERS LIVING OF LIFE BARON

Hon Carolyn DELACOURT-SMITH, *b* 1944: *m* 1969, Roger Martin Pudney, of Tanglewood, Manor Park, Hazlemere, Bucks and has issue, a son, *b* 1977, — a da, *b* 1975.
Hon Lesley DELACOURT-SMITH (6 Herrick Rd, N5), *b* 1948.

WIDOW LIVING OF LIFE BARON

MARGARET ROSALIND (*Baroness Delacourt-Smith of Alteryn*) (56 Aberdare Gdns, NW6), da of Frederick James Hando of Newport, Mon; *cr* a Life Baroness 1974: *m* 1st, 1939, Baron Delacourt-Smith (Life Baron) who *d* 1972; 2ndly, 1978, Prof Charles Stuart Blackton.

DELACOURT-SMITH OF ALTERYN, BARONESS (Blackton) (Life Baroness 1974)

MARGARET ROSALIND DELACOURT-SMITH, da of Frederick James Hando, of Newport, Mon; *b* 5 April 1916; *ed* Newport High Sch, and St Anne's Coll, Oxford (MA); Councillor of Roy Borough of New Windsor 1962-65, and a JP 1962-67; *cr Baroness Delacourt-Smith of Alteryn*, of Alteryn, in co of Gwent (Life Baroness) 1974: *m* 1939, Baron Delacourt-Smith (Life Baron) who *d* 1972, and has issue (see that title); 2ndly, 1978, Prof Charles Stuart Blackton.
Residence – 56 Aberdare Gdns, NW6.

DELAMERE, BARON (Cholmondeley) (Baron UK 1821)
(Name pronounced "Chumley")

Virtue is the safest helmet

HUGH GEORGE CHOLMONDELEY, 5th Baron; *b* 18 Jan 1934; *s* 1979; *ed* Eton, and Magdalene Coll, Camb (MA): *m* 1964, Ann Willoughby, only da of late Sir Patrick Muir Renison, GCMG, of Freeman's Farm House, Mayfield, Sussex, and formerly wife of Michael Patrick Tinné, and has issue.

Arms – Gules, two esquires' helmets in chief proper, and in base a garb or. **Crest** – A demi-griffin sejeant sable, beaked, membered, ducally gorged, and wings elevated or, holding between the claws a helmet, as in the arms. **Supporters** – Two griffins sable, beaked, membered, and wings elevated, ducally gorged and chained or.
Residence – Soysambu, Elmenteita, Kenya.

SON LIVING

Hon THOMAS PATRICK GILBERT, *b* 19 June 1968.

SISTER LIVING

Hon Anne Jeanetta Essex, *b* 1927: *m* 1951, Conrad Peter Almeric Garnett, and has had issue, Jeremy Paul, *b* 1953, — David Michael, *b* 1956, *d* 1981. *Residence* – Burnside House, Easter Balgedie, Kinross-shire KY13 7HQ.

COLLATERAL BRANCHES LIVING

Granddaughters of late Hon Thomas Grenville Cholmondeley, 2nd son of 1st Baron:—
Issue of late Brig-Gen Hugh Cecil Cholmondeley, CB, CBE, *b* 1852, *d* 1941: *m* 1st, 1885, Mary Stewart, who *d* 1929, da of late Horace Payne Townshend; 2ndly, 1931, Violet Maud, JP, who *d* 1993, aged 100, da of late Rev Hon Archibald Parker (*see* E Macclesfield, colls):—
(By 2nd *m*) (Violet) Essex, *b* 1932: *m* 1964, Maj William James Pinney, 11th Hussars, and has issue living, Hugh Charles William, *b* 1966. *Residence* – Lee Old Hall, Ellesmere, Shropshire SY12 9AE.
Issue of late Henry Arthur Cholmondeley, *b* 1855, *d* 1952: *m* 1920, Helen Mary, who *d* 1923, da of Harold Wrigley, of Ganton Hall, Scarborough:—
Essex Lucy (*Countess of Cavan*), *b* 1921: *m* 1947, 12th Earl of Cavan, who *d* 1988. *Residence* – The Glebe House, Stockton, Shifnal, Salop.

Granddaughters of late Maj Henry Reginald Cholmondeley, DSO, son of late Rev Hon Henry Pitt Cholmondeley, 3rd son of 1st Baron:—
Issue of late Maj Anthony Pitt Cholmondeley, *b* 1908, *d* 1986: *m* 1936, Monica Irene, da of late Rev Albert Ernest Snow:—
Anne, *b* 1938. —— Gillian, *b* 1951. —— Faith, *b* 1953: *m* 1978, Nicholas John Vann.

PREDECESSORS – (1) THOMAS Cholmondeley; *b* 1767; *cr Baron Delamere*, of Vale Royal, co Chester (peerage of United Kingdom) 1821: *m* 1810, Henrietta Elizabeth, da of Sir Watkin Williams-Wynn, 4th Bt; *d* 1855; *s* by his son (2) HUGH, 2nd Baron, *b* 1811; sat as MP for Denbighshire (C) 1840-1, and for Montgomery 1841-7: *m* 1st, 1848, Lady Sarah Hay, who *d* 1859, da of 10th Earl of Kinnoull: 2ndly, 1860, Augusta Emily, who *d* 1911, el da of late Rt Hon Sir George Hamilton Seymour, GCB, GCH, PC; *d* 1887; *s* by his son (3) HUGH, KCMG, 3rd Baron; *b* 1870; sometime a MLC of Kenya Colony: *m* 1st, 1899, Lady Florence Anne Cole, who *d* 1914, da of 4th Earl of Enniskillen: 2ndly, 1928, Gwladys Helen, who *d* 1943, da of Hon Rupert Evelyn Beckett; *d* 1931; *s* by his son (4) THOMAS PITT HAMILTON, 4th Baron, *b* 1900; Capt Welsh Gds: *m* 1st, 1924 (*m diss* 1944), Phyllis Anne, who *d* 1978, el da of late Lord George William Montagu-Douglas-Scott, OBE (*see* D Buccleuch, colls); 2ndly, 1944 (*m diss* 1955), Hon (Ruth) Mary Clarisse, who *d* 1986, yr da of 1st Baron Mount Temple (ext), and formerly wife of (i) Capt Alec Stratford Cunningham-Reid, DFC (*d* 1987), (ii) Maj (Ernest) Laurie Gardner; 3rdly, 1955, Diana, who *d* 1987, yr da of late Seymour Caldwell, and formerly wife of (i) Vernon Motion (*d* 1980); widow of Sir (Henry John) Delves Broughton, 11th Bt, and formerly wife of (ii) Gilbert de Préville Colvile (*d* 1966) (*see* B de Clifford, 1972-73 Edn); *d* 1979; *s* by his only son (5) HUGH GEORGE, 5th Baron and present peer.

DE LA WARR, EARL (Sackville) (Earl GB 1761)
(Title pronounced "De la Ware")

Day of my life!

WILLIAM HERBRAND SACKVILLE, 11th Earl; *b* 10 April 1948; *s* 1988; *ed* Eton; patron of four livings; *m* 1978, Anne Pamela, eldest da of Arthur Edmund Leveson, OBE, of Hall Place, Ropley, Hants, and formerly wife of Adrian John Charles, Earl of Hopetoun (later 4th Marquess of Linlithgow), and has issue.

Arms – Quarterly, 1st, argent, a fesse dancettée sable, *West*; 2nd, azure, three leopards' heads reversed jessant de lys or, *Cantelupe*; 3rd gules erusilly and a lion argeut, *la Warr*; 4th, quarterly or and gules, a bend vaire, *Sackville*. **Crest** – 1st, issuant from a ducal coronet or a griffin's head azure, beaked and eared gold. *West*; 2nd, upon a coronet composed of fleurs-de-lis or, an estoile argent, *Sackville*. **Supporters** – Dexter, a wolf coward argent gorged with a collar or; sinister, a cockatrice or, winged azure. **Badge** – A Crampet or, he inside per pale azure and gules, charged with the letter R.
Seat – Buckhurst Park, Withyham, Sussex. *Town Residence* – 14 Bourne St, SW1. *Clubs* – White's, Turf.

SONS LIVING

WILLIAM HERBRAND THOMAS (*Lord Buckhurst*) *b* 13 June 1979.
Hon Edward Geoffrey Richard, *b* 1980.

BROTHER LIVING

Hon Thomas Geoffrey, *b* 1950; *ed* Eton, and Lincoln Coll, Oxford (BA); Under-Sec of State, Dept of Health since 1992; MP (C) for Bolton West since 1983; merchant banker: *m* 1979, Catherine, da of late Brig James Windsor Lewis, and has a son and da, Arthur Michael, *b* 1983, — Savannah Elizabeth, *b* 1986.

SISTER LIVING

Lady Arabella Avice Diana SACKVILLE, *b* 1958; has resumed her maiden name: *m* 1981 (*m diss* 1988), Conte Giovanni Emo Capodilista Maldura, son of Conte Gabriele Emo Capodilista Maldura, of Palazzo Grazioli, Rome (*see* E Newburgh, colls).

AUNT LIVING (*daughter of 9th Earl*)

Lady Katharine Pamela, *b* 1926: *m* 1946, Frank Thomas Robertson Giles, and has issue living, (Henry Frank) Sebastian, *b* 1952; *ed* Westminster: *m* 1988, Sarah, elder da of Brian Palmer, of Highgate Village, N6, and has issue living, Maxwell Joseph W. *b* 1989, Lucas Charles O. *b* 1992, — Sarah Elizabeth, *b* 1972 (*m diss* 1976), Rodolphe d'Erlanger, son of late Leo Frederic Alfred d'Erlanger, — Belinda Susan Mary, *b* 1958; *ed* Girton Coll, Camb: *m* 1982, Christopher Simon Sykes, and has issue (*see* Sykes, Bt, 1783). *Residence* – 42 Blomfield Rd, W9 1AH.

WIDOW LIVING OF TENTH EARL

ANNE RACHEL (*Anne, Countess De La Warr*), only da of late Capt Geoffrey Charles Devas, MC (*see* E Cawdor, colls, 1924 Edn): *m* 1946, the 10th Earl, who *d* 1988.

COLLATERAL BRANCHES LIVING

Descendants of Lt-Col Hon William Edward SACKVILLE-WEST, 6th son of 5th Earl, *b* 1830, *d* 1905: *m* 1860, Georgina, who *d* 1883, da of late George Dodwell, of Kevinsfort, Sligo (*see* B Sackville).

Descendants of Hon Leonard West, 5th son of 8th Baron De La Warr (*cr* 1342) (*not in remainder to Earldom and Barony of De La Warr cr* 1570):—

See 1969 and earlier edns.

PREDECESSORS – **(1)** Sir THOMAS West, Knt, accompanied Edward III to France 1329, and also in the wars with David Bruce, King of Scotland; summoned to Parliament of England as *Baron West* 1342; *d* 1342; *s* by his son **(2)** THOMAS, 2nd Baron; was not summoned to Parliament; served at Crecy 1346; *s* by his son **(3)** THOMAS, 3rd Baron; summoned to Parliament 1402; *d* 1405; *s* by his son **(4)** THOMAS, 4th Baron; took a distinguished part in the French wars of Henry V; *dsp* 1415; *s* by his brother **(5)** REGINALD, 5th Baron; summoned to English Parliament as 6th *Baron De La Warr* on the death of his uncle 1426 (see note *infra*); *d* 1451; *s* by his son **(6)** RICHARD, 7th Baron, a staunch supporter of the House of Lancaster in the War of the Roses; *d* 1497; *s* by his son **(7)** THOMAS, 8th Baron; *d* 1525; *s* by his son **(8)** THOMAS, 9th Baron; not having male issue he adopted as his heir William, son of his half-brother Sir George West; his nephew, however, having attempted to poison his uncle was debarred by Act of Parliament from succeeding to his uncle's honours or estates; *d* 1554, when the baronies of West and De La Warr fell into abeyance. **(9)** WILLIAM West (ante), nephew of the 9th Baron, having served in the English Army at Picardy, was knighted Feb 1568, fully restored in blood by Act of Parliament in March following, and *cr Baron De La Warr* 1570; *d* 1595; *s* by his son **(10)** THOMAS, 11th Baron; restored to the place and precedence of his ancestors; *s* by his son **(11)** THOMAS, 12th Baron; Gov and Capt-Gen of Virginia; *d* 1618; *s* by his son **(12)** HENRY, 13th Baron; *d* 1628; *s* by his son **(13)** CHARLES, 14th Baron; *s* by his son **(14)** JOHN, 15th Baron; *d* 1723; *s* by his son **(15)** JOHN, KB, PC, 16th Baron; a Gen in the Army, Lord of the Bedchamber to George I, Gov and Capt-Gen of New York; *cr Viscount Cantelupe* and *Earl De La Warr* (peerage of Great Britain) 1761; *d* 1766; *s* by his son **(16)** JOHN, 2nd Earl; a Lt-Gen in the Army, Master of the Horse, and Vice-Chamberlain to the Queen; *d* 1777; *s* by his el son **(17)** WILLIAM AUGUSTUS, 3rd Earl; *d* unmarried 1783; *s* by his brother **(18)** JOHN RICHARD, 4th Earl; *d* 1795; *s* by his son **(19)** GEORGE JOHN, PC, DCL, 5th Earl; *b* 1791; Lord Chamberlain 1858-9; assumed by Roy licence 1845 the additional surname of Sackville: *m* 1813, Lady Elizabeth Sackville, who *d* 1870, yr da and co-heir of 3rd Duke of Dorset (title extinct); this lady was in 1864 *cr Baroness Buckhurst*; of Buckhurst, co Sussex (peerage of United Kingdom), with remainder to her yr sons and their male issue, but with a proviso that upon any Baron Buckhurst succeeded to the Earldom of Delawarr, the said Barony should devolve upon the heir next entitled to succeed, as if the person having so succeeding to the Earldom of De La Warr had died without male issue; *d* 1869; *s* by his son **(19)** CHARLES RICHARD, KCB, 6th Earl; a Maj-Gen in the Army distinguished himself in India and in the Crimea; *d* unmarried 1873, *s* by his brother **(20)** Rev REGINALD WINDSOR, 7th Earl, who *d* 1870 had *s* his mother as 2nd Baron Buckhurst, but a claim to that Barony under the above-mentioned proviso by his next brother was unsuccessful, and it has remained merged in the Earldom; *b* 1817; assumed by Roy licence 1871 the surname of Sackville only in lieu of Sackville-West: *m* 1867, Hon Constance Mary Elizabeth, who *d* 1929, el da of 1st Baron Lamington; *d* 1896; *s* by his second son **(21)** GILBERT GEORGE REGINALD, 8th Earl; *b* 1869: *m* 1st, 1891 (*m diss* 1902), Lady Muriel Agnes, who *d* 1930, da of 1st Earl Brassey; 2ndly, 1903, Hilda Mary Claverin (who *d* 1963, having *m* 2ndly, 1922, John William Dennis, sometime MP), da of late Col C. Lennox Tredcroft, of Glen Ancrum, Guildford; *d* while on active service as Lieut RNVR 1915; *s* by his only son **(22)** HERBRAND EDWARD DUNDONALD BRASSEY, GBE, PC, 9th Earl; *b* 1900; Lord-in-Waiting to HM 1924 and 1929-30; Parl Under-Sec of State for the Colonies 1936-37, Lord Privy Seal 1937-38, Pres of Board of Education 1938-40, First Commnr of Works 1940, and PMG 1951-55: *m* 1st, 1920, Diana, who *d* 1966, da of late Capt Henry Gerard Leigh (*see* Antrobus, Bt, colls); 2ndly, 1968, Dame Sylvia Margaret, DBE, who *d* 1992, da of William Harrison, of Liverpool, and widow of 1st Earl of Kilmuir; *d* 1976; *s* by his son **(23)** WILLIAM HERBRAND, 10th Earl, *b* 1921, served 1939-45 war as Capt Parachute Regt, Hon Col Sussex ACF, a DL for E Sussex: *m* 1946, Anne Rachel, only da of late Capt Geoffrey Charles Devas, MC, of Hunton Court, Maidstone, Kent (*see* E Cawdor, colls, 1924 Edn); *d* 1988; *s* by his elder son **(24)** WILLIAM HERBRAND, 11th Earl and present peer; also Viscount Cantelupe, Baron De La Warr, and Baron Buckhurst.

*ROGER La Warr, summoned to English Parliament 1299-1311; *d* 1329; *s* by his son **(2)** JOHN, KB, 2nd Baron, a valiant soldier; summoned to Parliament of England 1307-47; *d* 1347; *s* by his son **(3)** ROGER, 3rd Baron; a renowned soldier, was present at Poitiers when John, King of France, surrendered to him and Sir John Pelham, in commemoration of which the crampet, or chape, of the king's sword was given to him as a badge: *m* 2ndly, Alianore, da of John, 2nd Baron Mowbray, and had an only da, Joanna, wife of 3rd Baron West, who had issue Thomas 4th Baron West, and Richard 5th Baron West and 6th Baron De La Warr; *d* 1370; *s* by his son **(4)** JOHN, 4th Baron, summoned to Parliament 1370-97; *d* 1398; *s* by his brother **(5)** THOMAS, 5th Baron; Rector of the Parish Church of Manchester; *d* 1426; *s* by his half-sister's son **(6)** REGINALD, 5th Baron West (ante).

DELFONT, BARON (Delfont) (Life Baron 1976) (Extinct 1994)

BERNARD DELFONT, son of Isaac Winogradsky; *b* 5 Sept 1909; former Chm and Ch Exec EMI Film and Theatre Corpn 1969-80; Chm and Ch Exec Trusthouse Forte Leisure 1981-82; Chm and Ch Exec First Leisure Corpn, 1983-88, Chm 1988-92, Pres since 1992; Pres Entertainment Artists Benevolent Fund; Asso OStJ; *cr* Knt 1974, and *Baron Delfont*, of Stepney in Greater London (Life Baron) 1976: *m* 1946, Helen Violet Carolyn, actress, as Carole Lynne, da of Victor Cecil Haymen, and formerly wife of Derek Farr, actor, who *d* 1986, and has issue. Lord Delfont *d* 28 July 1994.

Arms – Per pale or and gules two haunches and three mullets in fess all counterchanged. **Crest** – A billet fesswise or thereon a large elephant hawk moth displayed proper. **Supporters** – Pierrot and Pierrette both proper vested and capped argent with pompoms gules.
Address – 7 Soho St, Soho Sq, W1V 5FA.

SON LIVING

Hon David Stephen, *b* 1953; *ed* Millfield: *m* 1981, Sarah, da of Peter Edgington, and has issue living, Joseph, *b* 1983, — Alexander, *b* 1985.

DAUGHTERS LIVING

Hon Susan Jane, *b* 1947; stills photographer for films and TV: *m* 1982, Mark Derek Meddings, and has issue, one son and one da.
Hon Jennifer, *b* 1949: *m* 1974, Andrew Morse, and has issue, two sons.

DE L'ISLE, VISCOUNT (Sidney) (Viscount UK 1956, Bt UK 1806 and 1818)
(Title pronounced "De Lyle")

PHILIP JOHN ALGERNON SIDNEY, MBE, 2nd Viscount, and 10th Baronet of Castle Goring (*cr* 1806) and 8th Baronet of Penshurst Place (*cr* 1818); *b* 21 April 1945; *s* 1991; *ed* Tabley House; late Maj Grenadier Guards; Hon Col 5th Bn Princess of Wales Royal Regt since 1992; Freeman City of London, and Liveryman Goldsmiths' Co; MBE (Mil) 1977: *m* 1980, Isobel Tresyllian, yst da of late Sir Edmund Gerald Compton, GCB, KBE, and has issue.

Arms – Quarterly: 1st and 4th or, a pheon azure, *Sidney*; 2nd and 3rd sable, on a fesse engrailed, between three whelk shells or, a mullet for difference, *Shelley*. **Crests** – 1st, a porcupine statant azure, quills, collar, and chain or; 2nd, a griffin's head erased argent, ducally gorged or. **Supporters** – *Dexter*, a porcupine azure, quills, collar, and chain or; *sinister*, a lion queue fourchée vert.
Seat – Penshurst Place, Tonbridge, Kent.

SON LIVING

Hon PHILIP WILLIAM EDMUND, *b* 2 April 1985.

DAUGHTER LIVING

Hon Sophia Jacqueline Mary, *b* 1983.

Whither the Fates call me

SISTERS LIVING

Hon Elizabeth Sophia, *b* 1941: *m* 1st, 1959 (*m diss* 1966), George Silver Oliver Annesley Colthurst (*see* Colthurst, Bt); 2ndly, 1966 (*m diss* 1971), Sir (Edward) Humphry Tyrrell Wakefield, 2nd Bt; 3rdly, 1972 (*m diss* 1989), Capt James Silvester Rattray of Rattray, 28th Chief; 4thly, 1989, (Robert) Samuel Clive Abel Smith (*see* Buxton, Bt, colls, 1957 Edn), and has issue living (by 1st *m*) (*see* Colthurst, Bt), — (by 2nd *m*) (*see* Wakefield, Bt), — (by 3rd *m*) Robert, *b* 1972; *ed* Milton Abbey. *Residence* – The Old Hall, Langham, Oakham, Leics.
Hon Catherine Mary, *b* 1942: *m* 1st, 1964 (*m diss* 1983), (Martin) John Wilbraham; 2ndly, 1983, Nicholas Hyde Villiers (*see* E Clarendon, colls), and has issue living (by 1st *m*), Alexander John, *b* 1965; *ed* Eton, — Rupert Edward Robert, *b* 1967; *ed* Eton, — Jocelyn Thomas Ralph, *b* 1970; *ed* Eton. *Residence* – St Leonard's Grange, Beaulieu, Hants.
Hon Anne Marjorie, *b* 1947: *m* 1967, David Alexander Harries, elder son of late Rear Adm David Hugh Harries, CB, CBE, and has issue living, (David) Henry, *b* 1970; *ed* Eton, — James Hugh, *b* 1972; *ed* Eton, — Alexandra Victoria Corinna, *b* 1968; *ed* Benenden, and Somerville Coll, Oxford. *Residence* – Lower Woolwich, Rolvenden, Cranbrook.
Hon Lucy Corinna Agneta, *b* 1953: *m* 1974, Hon Michael Charles James Willoughby, eldest son of 12th Baron Middleton, MC, and has issue (*see* B Middleton). *Residence* – North Grimston House, Malton, N Yorks.

WIDOW LIVING OF FIRST VISCOUNT

MARGARET ELDRYDD (*Dowager Viscountess De L'Isle*), da of late Maj-Gen Thomas Herbert Shoubridge, CB, CMG, DSO; High

Sheriff Powys 1977: *m* 1st, 1942, as his 2nd wife, 3rd Baron Glanusk, DSO, who *d* 1948; 2ndly, 1966, as his 2nd wife, 1st Viscount De L'Isle, VC, KG, GCMG, GCVO, PC, who *d* 1991. *Residence* – Glanusk Park, Crickhowell, Powys.

COLLATERAL BRANCH LIVING

Granddaughter of late Capt George Ernest Shelley, brother of 5th Baronet:—
Issue of late Maj George Edward Shelley, MBE, *b* 1891, *d* 1961: *m* 1st, 1920 (*m diss* 1935), Cicely Alice Colquhoun, who *d* 1954, el da of late Lt-Col Lionel Arthur Bosanquet; 2ndly, 1935 (*m diss* 1941), Hon Lucy Gwen, who *d* 1957, da of Baron Atkin (Life Peer); 3rdly, 1951, Freda Victoria (OHLSON), who *d* 1977, yr da of late F. H. L. Jeffery:—
(By 1st *m*) Iris Gwendolin, *b* 1927: *m* 1954, Maj Philip Gordon Tanner, RA, Church Farm, Pulham St Mary, Diss, Norfolk, IP21 4YH, and has issue living, Nicholas Shelley (The Coach House, Ampney Crucis, Glos GL7 5RY), *b* 1955: *m* 1980, Melanie Anne, elder da of late A. F. Challis, and has had issue, George William *b* 1982; *d* 1989, William Archie Bowen *b* 1988, Olivia *b* 1990, Isabel *b* 1993, — Clare Theresa, *b* 1958: *m* 1987, Keith Evans, elder son of L. Evans and has issue living, Christopher *b* 1990, Daniel *b* 1992.

PREDECESSORS – (1) *Sir* JOHN Shelley-Sidney; *cr* a *Baronet* 1818; assumed additional surname of Sidney by Roy licence 1793 on succeeding to the estate of his maternal grandmother, Elizabeth (who *m* William Perry), da of Hon Thomas Sidney, 4th son of 4th Earl of Leicester; *d* 1849; *s* by his son (2) PHILIP CHARLES, GCH, DCL, who had in 1835 been *cr Baron De L'Isle and Dudley* (peerage of United Kingdom); *b* 1800; discontinued the surname of Shelley: *m* 1825, Lady Sophia Fitzclarence, natural da of King William IV, and sister of 1st Earl of Munster: *d* 4 March 1851; *s* by his son (3) PHILIP, 2nd Baron, *b* 1828: *m* 1st, 1850, Mary, who *d* 1891, da of Sir William Foulis, 8th Bt; 2ndly, 1893, Emily Frances, who *d* 1926, el da of late William Fermor Ramsay; *d* 1898; *s* by his el son (4) PHILIP, 3rd Baron, *b* 1853: *m* 1902, Hon Elizabeth Maria, da of 4th Viscount Gort, and widow of William Harvey Astell, JP, DL, (sometime Grenadier Guards), of Woodbury Hall, Beds; *d* 1922; *s* by his brother (5) ALGERNON, 4th Baron, *b* 1854; sometime Lieut-Col and Brevet Col RA; *d* April 1945; *s* by his brother (6) WILLIAM, 5th Baron, *b* 1859; Bar Inner Temple 1886; Mayor of Chelsea 1906 and 1907 and a County Councillor for London 1922-34: *m* 1905, Winifred Agneta Yorke, who *d* 1959, da of late Roland Yorke Bevan, *d* June 1945; *s* by his son (6) WILLIAM PHILIP, VC, KG, GCMG, GCVO, PC, 1st Viscount, *b* 1909, Capt Grenadier Guards (Reserve), 1939-45 War in France and Italy (VC), DL Kent, Parl Sec to Min of Pensions May-July 1945, Sec of State for Air 1951-55, Gov-Gen of Australia 1961-65, MP for Chelsea (C) Oct 1944-June 1945, Chm of Trustees Winston Churchill Memorial Trust, and sometime Chm Phoenix Assurance Co, Dir Phoenix Assurance Co of New York, Yorkshire Bank Ltd, and other Cos, Chm Board of Trustees of the Armouries 1983-86; *cr Viscount De L'Isle*, of Penshurst, co Kent (peerage of United Kingdom) 1956: *m* 1st, 1940, Hon Jacqueline Corinne Yvonne Vereker, who *d* 1962, da of F-M 6th Viscount Gort, VC, GCB, CBE, DSO, MVO, MC; 2ndly, 1966, Margaret Eldrydd, da of late Maj-Gen Thomas Herbert Shoubridge, CB, CMG, DSO, and widow of 3rd Baron Glanusk; *d* 1991; *s* by his only son (7) PHILIP JOHN ALGERNON, 2nd Viscount and present peer; also Baron De L'Isle and Dudley (see infra *).

*(1) *Sir* BYSSHE Shelley, of Castle Goring, Sussex son of Timothy Shelley, 7th in descent from Edward Shelley of Worminghurst Park, Sussex, yr son of John Shelley, of Michelgrove (*d* 1526) (*see* Shelley Bt, *cr* 1611); *b* 1731; *cr a Baronet* 1806: *m* 1st, Mary Catherine, who *d* 1760, da and heir of the Rev Theobald Mitchell; 2ndly, 1769, Elizabeth Jane Sidney, who *d* 1781, da and heir of William Perry by Elizabeth Sidney, heir of Penshurst Place, Kent; *d* 1815; *s* by his el son (2) Sir TIMOTHY, 2nd Bt, *b* 1753: *m* 1791, Elizabeth, da of Charles Pilfold, of Effingham, Surrey; *d* 1844; *s* by his grandson (3) *Sir* PERCY FLORENCE, 3rd Bt (son of Percy Bysshe Shelley the poet, who was drowned 1822); *b* 1819: *m* 1848, Jane, who *d* 1899, da of Thomas Gibson, and widow of Hon Charles Robert St John; *d* 1889; *s* by his cousin (4) *Sir* EDWARD, 4th Bt; *b* 1827; Capt 16th Lancers: *m* 1866, Mary, who *d* 1886, da of Henry Mitchell Smyth; *d* 1890; *s* by his brother (5) *Sir* CHARLES, 5th Bt; *b* 1838; Lt-Col Scots Fus Guards: *m* 1869, Lady Mary Jane Jemina Stopford, who *d* 1937, da of 3rd Earl of Courtown; *d* 1902; *s* by his el son (6) Sir JOHN COURTOWN EDWARD, 6th Bt, *b* 1871; Capt Scots Guards: *m* 1898, Hon Eleanor Georgiana Rolls, who *d* 1961, da and heir of 1st and last Baron Llangattock; they assumed by Royal Licence 1917, the additional name and arms of Rolls; *d* 1951; *s* by his brother (7) Sir PERCY BYSSHE, 7th Bt, *b* 1872; *d* 1953; *s* by his brother (8) Sir SIDNEY PATRICK, 8th Bt; Capt Hampshire Yeo; *d* 1965; *s* by his kinsman (9) 1st Viscount De L'Isle, descendant of Sir John Shelley-Sidney, 1st Bt (*cr* 1818), only son of 1st Bt (*cr* 1806) by his 2nd wife (ante).

Delvin, Lord; son of Earl of Westmeath.

DE MAULEY, BARON (Ponsonby) (Baron UK 1838)
(Name pronounced "Punsonby")

For the king, the law, and the people

GERALD JOHN PONSONBY, 6th Baron; *b* 19 Dec 1921; *s* 1962; *ed* Eton, and Ch Ch, Oxford (BA 1941, MA 1947); Bar Middle Temple 1949; formerly Lieut Leicestershire Yeo, and Capt RA; European War 1939-45: *m* 1954, Helen Alice, da of late Hon Charles William Sholto Douglas (*see* E Morton), and widow of Lt-Col Bryan Lynch Leslie Abdy Collins, OBE, MC, RE.

Arms – Gules, a chevron between three combs argent. **Crest** – Out of a ducal coronet or three arrows, points downwards, one in pale and two in saltire, entwined at the intersection by a snake proper. **Supporters** – *Dexter*, a lion reguardant proper; *sinister*, a bull sable, armed, unguled, tufted, and ducally gorged or.
Residence – Langford House, Little Faringdon, Lechlade, Glos.

BROTHER LIVING

Hon THOMAS MAURICE, TD, *b* 2 Aug 1930; *ed* Eton; Lt-Col The Wessex Yeo; Brevet Col TA; DL for Glos; High Sheriff of Glos 1978: *m* 1956, Maxine Henrietta, da of late William Dudley Keith Thellusson, and has issue living, Rupert Charles, *b* 1957, — Ashley George, *b* 1959. *Residence* – The Common, Little Faringdon, Lechlade, Glos.

SISTER LIVING

Hon June Mary (*Baroness Grimston of Westbury*), *b* 1924: *m* 1949, 2nd Baron Grimston of Westbury. *Residence* – The Old Rectory, Westwell, Burford, Oxon.

COLLATERAL BRANCHES LIVING

Grandchildren of late Hon Edwin Charles William Ponsonby, 5th son of 2nd Baron:—
Issue of late Col Sir Charles Edward Ponsonby, Bt TD, *b* 1879; *d* 1976; *cr* a Baronet 1956 (*see* Baronetage).
Issue of late Rev Maurice George Jesser Ponsonby, MC, *b* 1880, *d* 1943: *m* 1918, Lady Phyllis Sydney Buxton, OBE, who *d* 1942, da of 1st Earl Buxton:—
Elizabeth, *b* 1922: *m* 1952, John Lionel Clay, TD, Circuit Judge, and has issue living, Andrew John Buxton, *b* 1962, — Fiona Elizabeth, *b* 1954: *m* 1982, Rev John Alexander Taylor, — Catriona Mary, *b* 1955: *m* 1983, John Kendall Bush, — Joanna Penelope, *b* 1958. *Residence* – Newtimber Place, Hassocks, Sussex. —— Mary Veronica, *b* 1927: *m* 1961, William Peter Ward Barnes, HM Civil Service, 2nd son of Rt Rev Ernest William Barnes, Bishop of Birmingham, and has issue living, Peter Denis Ponsonby, *b* 1962, — Thomas William Ponsonby, *b* 1965, — Susanna Barbara, *b* 1963: *m* 1987, Ian Hardy, of 25 Farringford Close, Chiswell Green, St Albans, Herts, and has issue James William Barnes *b* 1992, Christina Louise *b* 1990. *Residence* – 21 Rona Rd, NW3 2HY.
Issue of late Capt Victor Coope Ponsonby, MC, *b* 1887, *d* 1966: *m* 1923, Gladys Edith, who *d* 1964, da of late Godfrey Walter, of Malshanger, Basingstoke:—
Myles Walter, CBE (The Old Vicarage, Porton, Salisbury, Wilts SP4 0LH), *b* 1924; *ed* Eton; late Capt KRRC; HM Consul-Gen at Hanoi 1964-65; Ambassador to Mongolian People's Republic 1974-77; 1939-45 War; CBE (Civil) 1966: *m* 1950, Ann Veronica Theresa, da of late Brig Francis Herbert Maynard, CB, DSO, MC, and has issue living, John Maurice Maynard, *b* 1955; Sqdn-Ldr RAF: *m* 1980, Marie Jose (Cé) Antoinette, eldest da of W. M. van Huizen-Husselson, of Knoll House, Kilmersdon, nr Radstock, Bath, and has issue living, Luke Myles William *b* 1986, Charlotte Emma *b* 1982, Francesca Sarah *b* (twin) 1986, — Belinda Mary, *b* 1951: *m* 1973, John Mitchell, of 28 Lancaster Grove, NW3, and has issue living, Jonathan Myles *b* 1976, Charles Edward *b* 1978, — Emma Christina, *b* 1959: *m* 1981, Capt Bryn St Pierre Parry, RGJ, elder son of late Lt-Col R. G. R. Parry, MC, and has issue living, Thomas Robin St Pierre *b* 1985, Sophie Laura *b* 1983, Louisa Mary *b* 1987. —— Sheila Mary (Bathurst Cottage, Teffont Magna, Salisbury SP3 5QP, Wilts), *b* 1927: *m* 1st, 1952 (*m diss* 1975), Cdr Michael Edward St Quintin Wall, RN (*see* E Peel, colls, 1972-73 Edn); 2ndly, 1976, Giles Aubrey Cartwright, who *d* 1988 (*see* Buxton, Bt, colls, 1990 Edn), and has issue living (by 1st *m*), Hugo St Quintin, *b* 1954, — Sarah Fenella, *b* 1955: *m* 1981 Michael Hugh Warwick Bampfylde, and has issue (*see* B Poltimore).

Grandchildren of late Claude Ashley Charles Ponsonby, el son of late Capt Hon Ashley George John Ponsonby, 2nd son of 1st Baron:—
Issue of late Harold Ashley Curzon Ponsonby, *b* 1891, *d* 1950: *m* 1941, Ruth Margaret, only da of James Miller, of Chippenham, Wilts:—
John Ashley Charles, *b* 1948. —— Sarah Haller, *b* 1944: *m* 1971, Phillip James Hilton, of Winishill, Nibley Lane, Yate, Bristol. —— Jane Caroline, *b* 1946: *m* 1966 (*m diss* 1969), Stephen Thornton Parr, and has issue living, Sally Jane Thornton, *b* 1965.

PREDECESSORS – (1) *Hon* WILLIAM FRANCIS SPENCER Ponsonby, 3rd son of 3rd Earl of Bessborough, *b* 1787: *m* 1814, Lady Barbara Ashley-Cooper, da of 5th Earl of Shaftesbury (a co-heir to Barony of Mauley *cr* 1295); *cr Baron de Mauley*, of Canford, co Dorset (peerage of United Kingdom) 1838; *d* 1855; *s* by his son (2) CHARLES FREDERICK ASHLEY COOPER, 2nd Baron, *b* 1815; MP for Poole (*L*) 1837-47 and for Dungarvan 1851-2: *m* 1838, Lady Maria Jane Elizabeth Ponsonby, da of 4th Earl of Bessborough; *d* 1896; *s* by his el son (3) WILLIAM ASHLEY WEBB, 3rd Baron; *b* 1843; *d* 1918; *s* by his brother (4) *Rev* MAURICE JOHN GEORGE, 4th Baron, *b* 1846; sometime V of Wantage: *m* 1875, Hon Madeleine Emily Augusta Hanbury-Tracy, who *d* 1938, da of 2nd Baron Sudeley; *d* 1945; *s* by his son (5) HUBERT WILLIAM, 5th Baron; Capt Gloucester Yeo, 1914-18 War: *m* 1920, Elgiva Margaret, who *d* 1987, da of late Hon Cospatrick Thomas Dundas (*see* M Zetland, colls); *d* 1962; *s* by his son (6) GERALD JOHN, 6th Baron and present peer.

DENBIGH AND DESMOND, EARL OF (Feilding) (Earl E 1622)

WILLIAM RUDOLPH MICHAEL FEILDING, 11th Earl; *b* 2 Aug 1943; *s* 1966; *ed* Eton: *m* 1965, Caroline Judith Vivienne, da of Lt-Col Geoffrey Cooke, and has issue.

Arms – Argent, on a fesse azure, three lozenges or. **Crest** – A nuthatch pecking at a hazel branch, all proper. **Supporters** – Two stags proper, attired and unguled or.
Residence – Newnham Paddox, Monks Kirby, Rugby CV23 0RX.

Honour is the reward of virtue

SON LIVING

ALEXANDER STEPHEN RUDOLPH (*Viscount Feilding*), *b* 4 Nov 1970.

DAUGHTERS LIVING

Lady Samantha Clare Barbara, *b* 1966: *m* 1990, Guy John Desmond Hurley, elder son of David Hurley, of Ballydaheen, Port Salon, co Donegal, and has issue living, Charlotte Lauren Sasha, *b* 1992.
Lady Louisa Helen, *b* 1969.

SISTER LIVING

Lady (Imelda) Clare, *b* 1941: *m* 1st, 1966 (*m diss* 1979), David Rodney Doig; 2ndly, 1984, Jack Levon Simonian, of Harrogate, and has issue living (by 1st *m*) Andrew William David, *b* 1969, — Rowena Helen, *b* 1967, — Zoe Claire *b* 1971. *Residence* – Grounds Farm, Monks Kirby, Rugby CV23 0RH.

UNCLE LIVING

Hon Hugh Richard, *b* 1920; *ed* Ampleforth; FCA; late Sqd Ldr RAF VR; 1939-45 War (despatches): *m* 1944, Sheila Katharine, only da of late Brig Charles Arthur Bolton, CBE, and has issue living, John Henry Christopher, *b* 1945; *ed* Ampleforth: *m* 1971, Veronica, 2nd da of John Farmer, of 36 Iverna Gdns, W8, and has issue living, Michael John Richard *b* 1975, Andrew Francis Alexander *b* 1977, Natasha Frances Katharine *b* 1973, Alexandra *b* 1981. *Residence* – Home Farm, Bainton, Driffield, E Yorks. *Club* – RAF.

WIDOWS LIVING OF BROTHERS OF TENTH EARL

Rosemary (The Park Cottage, Monks Kirby, Rugby), da of late Cdr (Frederick) Neville Eardley-Wilmot, RN (ret) (*see* Eardley-Wilmot, Bt): *m* 1939, Capt Hon Basil Egerton Feilding, who *d* 1970, and has issue (see colls infra).
Dunia Maureen (The Manor House, Pailton, nr Rugby), da of Gordon Spencer, MD; *m* 1950, Capt Hon Henry Anthony Feilding, MC, who *d* 1994, and has issue (see colls infra).

WIDOW LIVING OF TENTH EARL

VERENA BARBARA (*Betty, Countess of Denbigh and Desmond*) (Newnham Paddox, nr Rugby), da of William Edward Price, and widow of Lt-Col Thomas Paget Fielding Johnson: *m* 1940, the 10th Earl, who *d* 1966.

COLLATERAL BRANCHES LIVING

Issue of late Hon David Charles Feilding (2nd son of late Lt-Col Rudolph Edmund Aloysius, Viscount Feilding, CMG, DSO, el son of 9th Earl), *b* 1913, *d* 1966: *m* 1938, Elizabeth Alice, who *d* 1990, da of late William Fletcher, of Cumberland:—
William David (Oristano Great House, Bluefields, PO Box 1, Westmoreland, Jamaica), *b* 1939; *ed* Downside; artist: *m* 1980, Lydia Sarah, da of Martin Harding, of Chelsea. —— Michael Henry (107 Hartfield Rd, Wimbledon, SW19 3TJ), *b* 1946; *ed* Downside, and Oxford Univ (BSc): *m* 1970, Linnet, da of William Hale, of The Island, Hurstbourne Priors, Hants, and has issue living, Emily Linnet, *b* 1973, — Melissa Anne, *b* 1976. —— Charles Richard (47 Vista Barranca, Rancho Santa Margarita, California 92688, USA), *b* 1949; *ed* Downside, and Fordham Univ, New York: *m* 1972, Jeanne, da of Eugene Tanzillo, of New York.

Issue of late Capt Hon Basil Egerton Feilding (3rd son of late Lt-Col Rudolph Edmund Aloysius, Viscount Feilding, CMG, DSO, el son of 9th Earl), *b* 1916, *d* 1970: *m* 1939, Rosemary (ante), da of late Cdr (Frederick) Neville Eardley-Wilmot, RN (ret) (*see* Eardley-Wilmot, Bt):—
Peter Rudolph (Highfields, 11 Marlow Rd, High Wycombe, Bucks HP11 1TA), *b* 1941; *ed* Ampleforth; FCA: *m* 1968, Diana Mourne, only da of C. C. Cox, TD, of 16 Albany House, Albany Court, Lansdown Rd, Cheltenham, Glos, and has issue living, Basil James, *b* 1974, — Chloë Louise, *b* 1972. —— Giles Anthony STEUART-FEILDING (The Manor House, Arnesby, Leics), *b* 1950; assumed surname of Steuart-Feilding in lieu of his patronymic by deed poll 1981: *m* 1977, Sara Jane, da of late Cdr D. E. Barton, MVO, DSC, RN, of 47 St Mary Abbot's Terr, W14, and has issue living, Thomas Assheton Henry, *b* 1980, — Imogen Clare, *b* 1978. —— Crispin Everard, *b* 1960. —— Jennifer Mary, *b* 1947: *m* 1st 1968 (*m diss* 1971), Graham F. Bond; 2ndly, 1974, Charles Eliot Crawley, and has issue living (by 2nd *m*) Tobias, *b* 1978. —— Imelda Jane, *b* 1958: *m* 1981, Piers L. Rendell, of Little Thatch, Woolage Green, Canterbury, Kent CT4 6SF, son of Brig D. B. Rendell, of West Street House, Selsey, and has issue living, Hugo Anthony, *b* 1983, — Sebastian James, *b* 1985.

Issue of late Capt Hon Henry Anthony Feilding (yst son of late Lt-Col Rudolph Edmund Aloysius, Viscount Feilding, CMG, DSO, el son of 9th Earl), *b* 1924, *d* 1994: *m* 1950, Dunia Maureen (ante), da of late Gordon Spencer, MD, of Putley, nr Ledbury, Herefordshire:—
Jasper Simon (Falstaff House, 33 Sheep St., Shipston-on-Stour, Warwicks), *b* 1953; *ed* Ampleforth, and RAC, Cirencester: *m* 1980, Diana Margaret, only da of Maj E. D. Lloyd-Thomas, of Maes-y-Crochan House, St Mellons, Cardiff, and has issue living, Katherine Louisa, *b* 1982, — Tessa Caroline, *b* 1985. —— Penelope Dunia, *b* 1954: *m* 1976, Maj Robert Hugh Power Goodwin, RGJ, of 6 Church Rd, Aspley Heath, Woburn Sands, Beds MK17 8TA, yst son of Lt-Gen Sir Richard Elton Goodwin, KCB, CBE, DSO, and has issue living, Lucy Dunia, *b* 1980, — Clare Penelope, *b* 1982, — Alice Elizabeth, *b* 1985.

Grandchildren of late Percy Henry Feilding, yr son of late Gen Hon Sir Percy Robert Basil Feilding, KCB, 2nd son of 7th Earl:—

Issue of late Basil Percy Terence Feilding, b 1907, d 1986: m 1931, Margaret Mary (Beckley Park, Oxford), da of Lt-Col Rowland Charles Feilding, DSO (infra):—
Jocelyn Rupert Roland Geoffrey (37 Elvaston Place, SW7), b 1940; ed Downside: m 1963 (m diss 1983), Rowena Marion, da of Capt Simon Harvey Combe, MC, of the Manor House, Burnham Thorpe, Norfolk (see E Leicester), and has issue living, Emma Mary Clothilde, b 1964, — Lucy Silvia Margaret, b 1966. —— Julia Felicity Maria Gabrielle, b 1933; Dip Arch Oxford, ARIBA: m 1st, 1957 (m diss 1963), Leslie Rebanks; 2ndly, 1963, Donald Rhind Morrison, ARIBA, of Bridge End House, Dorchester-on-Thames, and has issue living (by 1st m), Leander Piers John, b 1960, — Alexander Basil, b 1961, — (by 2nd m) Justin Guy Stuart Feilding, b 1964, — Zuleika Jane Feilding, b 1963. —— Chloë Mary Antonia (16 London Pl, Oxford), b 1936: m 1962 (m diss 1973), David Coombes, and has issue living, Rowland William Sebastian, b 1967, — Victoria Roque-Rebecca, b 1963, — Connemara Alice Mary, b 1965. —— Amanda Claire Marion, b 1943.

Grandchildren of late John Basil Feilding, eldest son of Rev Hon Charles William Alexander Feilding (infra):—
Issue of late Rev Charles Rudolph Feilding, STD, b 1902, d 1978: m 1935, Ann (Suite 803, 10 Avoca Av, Toronto M4T 2B7, Canada), only da of late Ernest Truslow, of Southport, Conn, USA:—
Geoffrey Truslow (655 Grosvenor Av, Westmount, Quebec), b 1939: m 1966, Martha Anne, da of John S. Corrigan, of Toronto, and has issue living, Charles Corrigan, b 1968, — Jonathan Corrigan, b 1970. —— Goodith Mary (550, Gilmour St, Peterborough, Ont K9H 2K2), b 1936: m 1956, Rev Brian Heeney, DPhil, who d 1983, Vice-Pres, Trent Univ, Peterborough, Ontario, Canada, and has issue living, Michael Feilding, b 1957: m 1982, Hilary Meredith, and has issue living, Henry Meredith b 1988, Frances Meredith b 1991, — Timothy Charles, b 1966: m 1991, Shuna Baird, — Matthew Macleod, b 1968, — Ann, b 1961: m 1987, Richard Johnston, and has issue living, Rachel Margaret Heeney b 1991.

Granddaughters of late Rev Hon Charles William Alexander Feilding, 4th son of 7th Earl:—
Issue of late Lt-Col Rowland Charles Feilding, DSO, b 1871, d 1945: m 1903, Edith Mary, who d 1961, da of late Frederick Stapleton-Bretherton, of The Hall, Rainhill, Lancs (B Petre):—
Margaret Mary, b 1908: m 1931, Basil Percy Terence Henry Feilding (ante), who d 1986. —— Prunella Mary Patricia, b 1916; late Junior Com ATS: m 1942, Charles Neil Howard, MC, late Major Black Watch, who d 1975, and has issue living, Simon Neil (11 Crescent Mansions, 122 Elgin Crescent, W11 2JN), b 1951, — Caroline Edith Mary (Lodge Farm, Stowood, nr Beckley, Oxford OX3 9SR), b 1947: m 1st, 1966 (m diss 1989), David Hugh Craig, MA; 2ndly, 1990 Simon Lachlan Gordon-Duff (see Baird, Bt, cr 1809), and has issue living (by 1st m), Nicholas Charles David b 1977, — Harriet Prunella Mary, b 1948. Residence – The Cottage, Lodge Farm, Stowood, Beckley, Oxon.

Grandchildren of late Allen Fielding, son of late Rev Henry Fielding, el son of late Rev Allen Fielding (son of the famous novelist), grandson of the late Rev Hon John Fielding, DD, son of 1st Earl of Desmond and brother of 3rd Earl of Denbigh:—
Issue of late Geoffrey Kenmil Fielding, b 1884, d 1960: m 1917, Elsie, who d 1986, da of late John Edward Watkins, of Shrewsbury:—
Allen Henry (5/60 Pennington Terr, N Adelaide, S Australia 5006), b 1919; ARIBA, ARAIA; served 1939-46 War as Capt Royal Sussex Regt: m 1943, Estelle Teague, of The Old Hall, Builth Wells, and has issue living, David Henry, b 1944, — Barbara Ann, b 1950: m 1972, William Henderson, of P.O. Box 38 Clare, South Australia 5453, and has issue living, Andrew William Fielding b 1987. —— John Henry (twin), b 1919; 1939-45 War as Capt RA: m 1st, 1948, Pamela Mary, who d 1986, only da of John Alfred Spurde Barnard; 2ndly, 1988, Grace McInnes, da of William Collins, of Glasgow, and has issue living (by 1st m), Simon Henry (100 Beaconsfield Rd, Leicester), b 1949, — Geoffrey John (The Old Farmhouse, St Mary's Rd, Wrotham, Kent), b 1950. Residence – 113 Woodbrook Rd, Sidmouth, Devon.

Grandchildren of late Rev George Frederick Marshall Fielding, eldest son of late George Fielding (b 1827) (infra):—
Issue of late George Basil Fielding, b 1889, d 1959: m 1st, 1918 (m diss 1932), Esmé, who d 1961, da of late Outram Kellie McCallum; 2ndly, 1932, Gertrude, who d 1983, widow of G. A. Vickers:—
(By 1st m) Cecil Dolores, b 1922: m 1944, Maj Charles William Auchmuty, late Indian Army, of Pond Cottage, Portsmouth Rd, Liphook, Hants GU30 7EE, and has issue living, Susan Ann Esmé, b 1950: m 1972, David André Wavre, of 6 Shalford Rd, Guildford, Surrey, and has issue living, Robert André Auchmuty b 1975, Thomas Marc b 1978, Natalie Chantal b 1982, — Jane Dolores, b 1955: m 1977, Richard David Lee Crowe, of 2 Hillclose Av, Darlington, co Durham DL3 9BH, and has issue living, David William b 1979, James Andrew b 1981.
Issue of late Henry Armitage Fielding, b 1892, d 1965: m 1914, Ethel Mary Baldock, who d 1975:—
Henry George (89 Chapel Lands, Alnwick, Northumberland NE66 1ES), b 1916: m 1st, 1940, Anne Scargill, who d 1965; 2ndly, 1965, Eirene Helen, only da of late George Sydney Sell, of Northumberland, and has issue living, (by 1st m) Henry Michael Clive, MSc (33 Woodstock Rd, Carlingford, Sydney, NSW 2188), b 1944: m 1971, Lorraine Patricia Kirton, and has issue living, Zoë Anne Clare b 1977, Sorrel Elizabeth May b 1979, Imogen Olivia Heather b 1981, — George Peter Keith (20 Ashwell Rd, Bygrave, Baldock, Herts SG7 5DT), b 1945; Lt RN (ret): m 1968, Gillian Margaret Stearn, and has issue living, James Marcus b 1977, Sarah Anne b 1970, Emma Jade b 1972, — John David Barry (19 Arnold Av, Camden, Sydney, NSW 2570), b 1946: m 1968, Pamela Margaret Cann, and has issue living, Maxine Anne b 1969, Chelsea Louise b 1974, — Anthony Robert Max, b 1948; Lt RN (ret): m 1st, 1977 (m diss 1978), Stephanie Ann Johnson; 2ndly, 1980, Mrs Rachael Jane Thompson, da of Frederick Dodge, of Somerset, and has issue living (by 2nd m), Henry Lawrence Max b 1983, Amelia Anne b 1981. —— Barbara Jean, b 1917: m 1st, 1940 (m diss 1952), Frank St Omer; 2ndly, 1952, Godfrey Walter Allen Sweet, of 606 Rochester Way, Eltham, SE9 1RL, and has issue living, (by 1st m) Judy Mary (28 Grange Rd, Gravesend, Kent DA11 0EU), b 1942: m 1970 (m diss 1984), Martin Moseling, and has issue living, Mark Christian b 1973, Emma Jane b 1972, — (by 2nd m) John Simon (171 Tuckers Rd, Loughborough, Leics LE11 2PH), b 1954: m 1981, Kathleen Susan Cornell, and has issue living, Robbie John Dylan b 1993.

Grandchildren of late Percy Fielding, 4th son of late George Fielding (b 1827), 2nd son of late Rev Charles Fielding, LLB, 3rd son of late Rev Allen Fielding (ante):—
Issue of late George Rudolph Fielding, b 1889, d 1969: m 1926, Marya Nagazina, who d 1973:—
Ernest Rudolf (439 Willowdale Crescent SE, Calgary, Alberta, Canada T2J 1K2), b 1927: m 1956, Audrey Madge, da of Alex Mackie, of Calgary, and has issue living, Douglas Ernest (204 Woodmont Court SW, Calgary, Alberta, Canada T2W 4X1), b 1957: m 1985, Mary Ann Dibulskis, and has issue living, Mark Antantas b 1989, — Grant Alexander, b 1964, — Karen Lea, b 1962. —— Rosa Alice, b 1926: m 1944, John Boyd, of Box 843, Rosedale, Alberta, Canada T0J 2V0, and has issue living, Bryan Alexander, b 1955, — Kathleen Anne, b 1945, — Gloria Jean, b 1947. —— Vera Mary, b 1929: m 1946, John Mackenzie Adamson, of 3213 19th Av SE, Calgary, Alberta, Canada T2B 0A4, and has issue living, Gary Wesley (50 Sandringham Way NW, Calgary, Alberta, Canada), b 1951: m 1986, Catherine Elizabeth Kirkham, — Carol Anne, b 1948: m 1968, Larry Alexander Jones, of 2815 Dover Ridge Drive SE, Calgary, Alberta, Canada T2B 2L2.

Granddaughters of late Sir Charles William Fielding, KBE, only son of late Thomas Mantell Fielding, 3rd son of late Rev Charles Fielding, LLB (ante):—
Issue of late Rudolph Burton Fielding, b 1902, d 1970: m 1939, Frances Adelaide (Okehurst, Billingshurst, W Sussex RH14 9HS), da of George Greene, of Dublin:—
Daphne Claire, b 1942; MA, MRCS, LRCP: m 1980, Timothy Hugh Drabble, and has issue living, Oliver John Fielding, b

1981. —— Jean Eleanora Leckie, *b* 1946: *m* 1966, Terence Michael O'Flynn, and has issue living, Caspar Michael, *b* 1969, — Emma Frances, *b* 1966. *Residence* – Wyneshore House, West Lavington, Devizes, Wilts SN10 4LW.

Grandson of late Rev George Hanbury Fielding, son of late Rev George Fielding, son of late Rev Allen Fielding (ante):—

Issue of late Major George Rudolf Fielding, Sherwood Foresters (Notts and Derbyshire Regt), *b* 1881, *ka* 1915: *m* 1914, Evelyn Carlota, da of Edward Jewell, formerly of Clifton Court, Bournemouth:—

George Rudolf Hanbury, DSO, *b* 1915: *ed* Shrewsbury; Major (ret) 3rd King's Own Hussars; European War 1939-45; DSO 1945: *m* 1940, Beatrice Georgina, da of Maj Maurice Pope, and has issue living, Martin George Rudolf (East Hall Gate Cottage, Middleton Tyas, nr Richmond, N Yorks DL10 6RE) *b* 1945; *ed* Eton; Capt (ret) The Queen's Own Hussars; ARICS, FAAV: *m* 1992, Mrs Erica Mackay Agace, yr da of late Acland Mackay Geddes, of Cuesta de la Villa, Tenerife, Canary Is, — Sarah Georgina (*Hon Mrs Guy B. Norrie*), *b* 1947: *m* 1968, Hon Guy Bainbridge Norrie, of Old Church Farm, Broughton, nr Stockbridge, Hants SO20 8AA (*see* B Norrie). *Address* – Val d'Ogoz, 1837, Château d'Oex, Vaud, Switzerland.

PREDECESSORS – (1) *Sir* WILLIAM Feilding, Knt, was *cr Baron Feilding*, of Newnham Paddox, Warwickshire, *Viscount Feilding* (peerage of England) 1620, and *Earl of Denbigh* (peerage of England) 1622; a faithful adherent of Charles I; killed in a skirmish near Birmingham 1643; his 2nd son Sir George, KB, was in 1622 *cr Baron Feilding*, of Lecaghe, *Viscount Callan* and *Earl of Desmond* (peerage of Ireland); *s* by his el son (2) BASIL, 2nd Earl, was one of the most eminent of the Parliament's Mil Commanders; *cr* after the restoration of the monarchy *Baron St Liz* 1663, with remainder to the male issue of his father; *dsp* 1675: *s* by his nephew (3) WILLIAM, 3rd Earl, who had in 1665 *s* his father George (ante) as 2nd Earl of Desmond; *d* 1685; *s* by his son (4) BASIL, 4th Earl; *d* 1717; *s* by his son (5) WILLIAM 5th Earl; *d* 1755; *s* by his son (6) BASIL, 6th Earl, *b* 1719: *m* 1957, Mary, who *d* 1782, 3rd da of Sir John Bruce Cotton, 6th Bt; *d* 1800; *s* by his grandson (7) WILLIAM BASIL PERCY, DCL (el son of William Robert Basil, Viscount Feilding, el son of 6th Earl), 7th Earl, *b* 1796; Master of the Horse to Queen Adelaide: *m* 1822, Mary Elizabeth Kitty, who *d* 1842, el da of 1st Earl of Ducie; *d* 1865; *s* by his son (8) RUDOLPH WILLIAM BASIL, 8th Earl, *b* 1823: *m* 1st, 1846, Louise, who *d* 1853, da of David Pennant, of Downing, Flint; 2ndly, 1857, Mary, who *d* 1901, da of Robert Berkeley; *d* 1892; *s* by his son (9) RUDOLPH ROBERT BASIL ALOYSIUS AUGUSTINE, GCVO, 9th Earl, *b* 1859; Col TA (ret); a Lord-in-Waiting to HM Queen Victoria 1897-1901 and to HM King Edward VII 1901-1905: *m* 1st, 1884, the Hon Cecilia Mary Clifford, who *d* 1919, da of 8th Baron Clifford of Chudleigh; 2ndly, 1923, Kathleen, who *d* 1952, da of late Thomas Addis Emmet, of New York, USA; *d* 1939; *s* by his grandson (10) WILLIAM RUDOLPH STEPHEN (el son of late Lieut-Col Rudolph Edmund Aloysius, Viscount Feilding, CMG, DSO, el son of 9th Earl), 10th Earl of Denbigh and 9th Earl of Desmond, *d* 1912: *m* 1940, Verena Barbara, da of William Edward Price, and widow of Lt-Col Thomas Paget Fielding Johnson; *d* 1966; *s* by his only son (11) WILLIAM RUDOLPH MICHAEL, 11th Earl of Denbigh and 10th Earl of Desmond and present peer; also Viscount Callan, Viscount Feilding, Baron Feilding, and Baron St Liz.

DENHAM, BARON (Bowyer) (Baron UK 1937, Bt England 1660 and UK 1933)

BERTRAM STANLEY MITFORD BOWYER, KBE, PC, 2nd Baron, 10th Baronet of Denham, and 2nd Baronet of Weston Underwood; *b* 3 Oct 1927; *s* to the Barony and Baronetcy of Bowyer of Weston Underwood (*cr* 1933) 1948, and to the Baronetcy of Bowyer of Denham (*cr* 1660) 1950; *ed* Eton, and King's Coll, Camb; a Lord-in-Waiting to HM 1961-64, and again 1970-71; Capt Yeomen of the Guard and Dep Chief Whip House of Lords 1971-74; Opposition Dep Chief Whip 1974-78, and again 1978-79, Capt Gentlemen at Arms (Chief Whip) 1979-92; Countryside Commr since 1993; author of *The Man Who Lost His Shadow* (1979), *Two Thyrdes* (1983) and *Foxhunt* (1988); PC 1980, KBE (Civil) 1991: *m* 1956, Jean, only da of Kenneth McCorquodale, MC, TD, of Fambridge Hall, White Notley, Essex, and has issue.

Arms – Or, a bend vaire cottised sable. **Crest** – A falcon rising, belled or. **Supporters** – *Dexter*, a golden retriever; *sinister*, a black greyhound proper, each charged on the shoulder with portcullis or.
Residence – The Laundry Cottage, Weston Underwood, Olney, Bucks.
Clubs – White's, Buck's, Pratt's.

Contentment surpasses riches

SONS LIVING

Hon RICHARD GRENVILLE GEORGE, *b* 8 Feb 1959: *m* 1988, Eleanor, only da of A. Sharpe, of Truemans Heath, Worcs.

Hon Henry Martin Mitford, *b* 1963.
Hon George Philip Paul, *b* 1964.

DAUGHTER LIVING

Hon Jocelyn Jane, *b* 1957.

SISTER LIVING

Hon Peggy, *b* 1925: *m* 1947 Cdr John David Latimer Repard, OBE, DSC, RN, and has issue living, Jennifer Ann, *b* 1948: *m* 1970, Peter William Allen, of Chearsley, Bucks, and has issue living, William John Kenneth *b* 1974, John Peter Clarkson *b* 1977, — Susan Elisabeth, *b* 1950: *m* 1976, Richard G. Algeo, son of late Sir Arthur Algeo, CBE, and has issue living, Nicholas Arthur *b* 1978, Jonathon Henry *b* 1985, Lucy Catharine *b* 1978, — Melinda Louise, *b* 1955: *m* 1993, Gerald Stone. *Residence* – Bridleway Cottage, Leafy Lane, Tring, Herts HP23 6JS.

WIDOW LIVING OF FIRST BARON

Hon DAPHNE FREEMAN-MITFORD (*Dowager Baroness Denham*), da of 1st Baron Redesdale: *m* 1919, the 1st Baron, who *d* 1948. *Residence* – Dunsland, Shrublands Rd, Berkhamsted, Herts.

COLLATERAL BRANCHES LIVING (*In remainder to Baronetcy of Bowyer of Denham* (*cr* 1660) *only*)

Grandchildren of late Lt-Cdr John Francis Bowyer, CB, RN (infra):—
Issue of late Maj Hugh Edward Wentworth Bowyer, Rifle Bdle, *b* 1921, *d* 1985: *m* 1942, Suzette (The Pantiles, 12 Fountain Hill, Budleigh Salterton, Devon EX9 6AR), da of Capt Peter Longton, of Heatherwold, Burghclere, Newbury:—
James David Ross (9 Fairview Gdns, Woodford Green, Essex G98 7DG), *b* 1949; *ed* Harrow: *m* 1993, Susan Rymond. —— Sally Anne, *b* 1945: *m* 1967, Brig Robert Stewart Tailyour, RM, of Boxfield, 15 Knowle Rd, Budleigh Salterton, Devon EX9 6AR, and has issue living, Helen Caroline, *b* 1971, — Georgina Anne, *b* 1977.

Grandchildren of late Lt-Col Wentworth Grenville Bowyer, 2nd son of late Rev William Henry Wentworth Atkins-Bowyer, 2nd son of late Maj William Atkins-Bowyer, el son of late Richard Atkins-Bowyer, 5th son of 3rd baronet of Denham:—
Issue of late Lt-Cdr John Francis Bowyer, CB, RN (Emergency List), *b* 1893, *d* 1974: *m* 1919, Violet (1 Avenue Lodge, Avenue Rd, NW8), da of Maj-Gen George Robert James Shakespear, Indian Army, and widow of Maj Egerton Lowndes Wright, MC:—
John Robert Patrick, *b* 1924: *m* 1948, Diana, da of late J. P. Longland, of Olney, Bucks, and has issue living, David Hugh, *b* 1950, — Sabrina Violet, *b* 1949, — Sarah Joy, *b* 1958, — Diana Jane, *b* 1965. —— Michael Christopher (14 Exeter House, Putney Heath, SW15 3SU), *b* 1926: *m* 1952, Elizabeth Anne, da of Cdr Stuart J. Layton Bennett, RN. —— Penelope Rosemary Joy MOUNTLANGEN (twin), *b* 1926; assumed by deed poll 1968, the surname of Mountlangen: *m* 1955 (*m diss* 1963), Derek Langenberg.

PREDECESSORS – (1) GEORGE EDWARD WENTWORTH Bowyer, MC, son of late Lieut-Col Wentworth Grenville Bowyer, el son of late Rev William Henry Wentworth Atkins-Bowyer, great-grandson of 3rd Bt of Denham (*cr* 1660); *b* 1886; Major late Oxfordshire and Bucks LI; Parliamentary Private Sec (unpaid) to Pres of Board of Trade 1921-24; Conservative Party Whip in House of Commons 1925-35, Vice-Chm Conservative and Unionist Party Organization 1930-36, a Junior Lord of the Treasury 1926-29, Comptroller of HM's Household June to Dec 1935, and Parliamentary Sec to Min of Agriculture and Fisheries 1939-40; a Conservative Whip in House of Lords 1945-47; European War 1914-18 (wounded, despatches, MC); sat as MP for Buckingham Div of Buckinghamshire (*U*) 1918-37; *cr* a Knt 1929, a *Baronet* 1933, and *Baron Denham* of Weston Underwood, co Buckingham (peerage of United Kingdom) 1937: *m* 1919, Hon Daphne Freeman-Mitford, da of 1st Baron Redesdale; *d* 1948; *s* by his son (2) BERTRAM STANLEY MITFORD, 2nd Baron and present peer.

*(1) *Sir* WILLIAM Bowyer, el son of Sir Henry Bowyer, of Denham Court, Bucks; *b* 1612; MP for Bucks 1659-60, and 1661-79 (Sheriff 1646-47); *cr* a Baronet 1660: *m* 1634, Margaret, who *d* 1678, da of John Weld, of Arnolds, Edmonton, Middlesex; *d* 1679; *s* by his el son (2) WILLIAM, 2nd Bt; *b* 1639: *m* 1679, Hon Frances, who *d* 1723, da of Charles Cecil, Viscount Cranborne, son of 2nd Earl of Salisbury; *d* 1722; *s* by his grandson (3) WILLIAM (el son of late Cecil Bowyer, el son of 2nd Bt), 3rd Bt; *b* 1710: *m* 1733, Anne who *d* 1785, da of Rt Hon Sir John Stonehouse, MP, 7th and 4th Bt of Radley, Berks; *d* 1767; *s* by his el son (4) WILLIAM 4th Bt, *b* 1736; Capt The Guards: *m* 1776, Anne, who *d* 1802, da of — Carey, and widow of Capt James Baker, RN; *d* 1799; *s* by his brother (5) GEORGE, 5th Bt, *b* 1739; Adm; MP for Queenborough 1784-90; distinguished himself in Lord Howe's naval victory over the French, 1 June 1794, for which he was rewarded with an annual pension of £1,000, and was *cr* a *Baronet* 1794 (of Radley, Berks): *m* 1st, 1768, Margaret, who *d* 1778, da of Rev — Price, curate of Barrington, Gloucestershire, and widow of Sir Jacob Garrard Downing, 4th Bt; 2ndly, 1782, Henrietta, who *d* 1845, da of Adm Sir Piercy Brett, of Beckenham, Kent; *d* 1799; *s* by his el son (6) GEORGE, 6th Bt, *b* 1783; MP for Malmesbury 1807-10, and for Abingdon 1811-18: *m* 1808, Anne Hammond, who *d* 1844, da of Capt Sir Andrew Snape Douglas, RN; *d* 1860; *s* by his son (7) GEORGE, 7th Bt, *b* 1811; MP (*L*) for Dundalk 1852-68, and for Wexford 1874-80; *d* 1883; *s* by his brother (8) WILLIAM, 8th Bt, *b* 1812: *m* 1857, Ellen Sarah, who *d* 1899, da of Shirley Foster Woolmer, Bar-at-law; *d* 1893; *s* by his nephew (9) GEORGE HENRY (only son of late Henry George Bowyer, yst son of 6th Bt), 9th Bt; *b* 1870; Lieut Cheshire Mil: *m* 1899 (*m diss* 1900), Ethel, da of Francis Hawkins; *d* 1950; *s* by his kinsman (10) BERTRAM STANLEY MITFORD (ante).

DENINGTON, BARONESS (Denington) (Life Baroness 1978)

EVELYN JOYCE DENINGTON, DBE, da of late Philip Charles Bursill, of Woolwich; *b* 9 Aug 1907; *ed* LCC Schs, Blackheath High Sch (GPDST), and Bedford Coll, London; Hon FRIBA, and Hon MRTPI: Journalist 1927-31, and Teacher 1933-45; Gen Sec, Nat Assocn of Labour Teachers 1938-47; a Member of St Pancras Borough Council 1945-59, Chm Staff Cttee, Planning Cttee and GP Cttee LCC 1946-65 (Vice-Chm Housing Cttee 1949-60, Chm Development and Management Sub Cttees 1949-60, Chm, New and Expanding Towns Cttee 1960-65); a Member of GLC 1964-77 (Chm 1975-76, and of Housing Cttee 1964-67); Dep Leader (Lab) opposition GLC 1967-73; Chm Transport Cttee 1973-75; a Member SE Economic Planning Council 1966-79 (Dep Chm 1971-79); Member of Stevenage Development Corpn 1950-80 (Chm 1965-80); Chm New Towns Chm's Conference 1973-75, Memb Minister's Central Housing Advisory Cttee 1955-73, Sub Cttee producing Parker-Morris Report, and Our Older Homes, Memb N British Housing Assocn 1976-87, Sutton Dwellings Housing Trust 1976-82, etc; Gov of Schs in St Pancras and Islington 1945-73, Memb and Chm of Govs Coll for the Garment Trades (renamed Coll of Fashion), Ardale Senior Boys Approved Sch, etc; Vice-Chm Town and Country Planning Assocn; Freeman City of London; *cr* CBE (Civil) 1966, DBE (Civil) 1974, and *Baroness Denington*, of Stevenage, co Herts (Life Baroness) 1978: *m* 1935, Cecil Dallas Denington, son of Richard Denington, of Wanstead.
Residence – Flat 3, 29 Brunswick Square, Hove BN3 1EJ. *Club* – Arts.

DENMAN, BARON (Denman) (Baron UK 1834, Bt UK 1945)

CHARLES SPENCER DENMAN, CBE, MC, 5th Baron, and 2nd Baronet (of Staffield, co Cumberland); *b* 7 July 1916; *s* as 2nd Bt 1957, and as 5th Baron, 1971; *ed* Shrewsbury; late Maj DCLI (TA); 1939-45 War in Middle East (MC); CBE (Civil) 1976; Chm Arundell House Securities, Dir Close Bros, and Marine and Gen Mutual Life Assurance; Vice Pres of Middle East Assoc, Member Cttee of Middle East Trade, and of British Invisible Export Council: *m* 1943, Sheila Anne, who *d* 1987, da of late Lt-Col Algernon Bingham Anstruther Stewart, DSC (*see* E Galloway, colls), and has issue.

Arms – Argent, on a chevron between three lions' heads erased gules, as many ermine spots or. **Crest** – A raven rising proper, in the beak an annulet or. **Supporters** – On either side a lion gules, charged on the body with five ermine spots in cross or. *Address* – c/o House of Lords. *Club* – Brooks's.

SONS LIVING

Hon RICHARD THOMAS STEWART, *b* 4 Oct 1946; *ed* Milton Abbey: *m* 1984, (Lesley) Jane, da of John Stevens, of 2 Shakespeare Drive, Hinckley, Leics, and has issue living, Natasha Anne, *b* 1986, — Philippa Jane, *b* 1987, — Louisa Clare, *b* 1993. *Club* – Brooks's.

Hon James Stewart, *b* 1954; *ed* Stowe: *m* 1989, Philippa Jane Emma, da of late Lewis Ronald Frederick Trowbridge, of Falfield, Winchester, Hants, and has issue living, Olivia Anne Stewart, *b* 1992. *Residence* – 14 Prairie St, SW8 3PU.

Hon (Christopher) John, *b* 1955; *ed* Millfield: *m* 1984, Jenny Bridget, MVO, only da of Rupert Allen, of Head Hedgeside, Headley, Hampshire, and has issue living, Nicholas Thomas Stewart, *b* 1988, — Charles Rupert Pendarves, *b* 1990, — Thomas Oliver Pelham, *b* 1993. *Residence* – Hurston Street Farm, Hurston Lane, Storrington, W Sussex RH20 4HF.

DAUGHTER LIVING

Hon Gillian Patricia, *b* 1944: *m* 1971, William K. McCall, of Upper Old Park Farm, Farnham, Surrey, and has issue (*see* Laurie, Bt, colls).

BROTHERS LIVING

Harold (East Heath Barn, Stream Lane, Hawkhurst, Kent TN18 4RD), *b* 1922; *ed* Repton, and Balliol Coll, Oxford (BA); 1939-45 War with RA: *m* 1976, Lady Frances Esmé Curzon, da of 5th Earl Howe, and formerly wife of Derek Alan Whiting, and has issue living, Roland Sebastian Richard, *b* 1977.

George (Stratton House, Stoney Stratton, Shepton Mallet, Somerset BA4 6EA), *b* 1925; 1939-45 War with Border Regt: *m* 1960, Linda Louisa, yr da of David Fortune Landale, of Dalswinton, Dumfries, and has issue living, Louisa Anne, *b* 1961, — Carola Jane, *b* 1963: *m* 1993, James Alexander Moffat Bain Campbell, elder son of Sir Colin Moffat Campbell, 8th Bt, MC, — Davina, *b* 1968.

SISTERS LIVING

Phyllis (Penberth, 41 Oakfield Rd, Ashtead, Surrey KT21 2RD), *b* 1919; MRCS England and LRCP London.

Catherine (Cherwell House, Old Kidlington, Oxford OX5 2EG), *b* 1920: *m* 1957, Philip Musgrave Cowburn, who *d* 1989, and has issue living, Stephen Denman, *b* 1959, — Anne Clare, *b* 1962: *m* 1986, Ieuan D. Hemlock.

COLLATERAL BRANCHES LIVING

(Not in remainder to the Baronetcy)

Grandchildren of late Sir Arthur Denman, 2nd son of late Rt Hon George Denman, 4th son of 1st Baron:—
   Issue of late Lieut-Col Roderick Peter George Denman, Roy Corps of Signals, *b* 1894, *ka* 1941: *m* 1922, Charlotte Marie Mathilde, MBE, who *d* 1980, da of late Baron Raphael d'Erlanger (*see* Blennerhassett, Bt, 1963 Edn):—
Peter Frederick Arthur, *b* 1923; *ed* Eton, and Trin Coll, Camb (BA 19—): *m* 1957, Cornelia Rowena (JANSON), da of late Hon (Oscar) Montague Guest (*see* V Wimborne, colls), and has issue living, Philip, *b* 1961, — Benedict Raphael, *b* 1970, — Francesca Marie-Carola, *b* 1959. *Residence* – Duke's House, 23 Lawrence St, SW3. —— Carol Antonia Rosaline, *b* 1928.
   Issue of late Henry du Bourg Denman, *b* 1918, *d* 1938: *m* 1936, (Evelyn) Joy (who *m* 2ndly, 1947, William Herbert Hooper, barrister-at-law, who *d* 1974, of 75 Mill Lane, Herne Bay, Kent), da of late George Henry Hatton:—
Carol Julian du Bourg (son), *b* 1938. *Residence* – 70 Fiddlers Folly, Fordham Heath, Colchester, Essex.

Grandchildren of late Lewis William Eden Denman, son of late Rev Hon Lewis William Denman, 5th son of 1st Baron:—
   Issue of late Joseph Alban Denman, *b* 1890, *d* 1965: *m* 1919, Annie Mary, who *d* 1954, da of Thomas Spicer, of Sask, Canada:—
George Lewis, *b* 1920: *m* 1st, 1949, Emily Woodgate who *d* 1956; 2ndly, 1963, Catherine Woodgate, da of W. A. C. Batchelor, of Water Valley, Alberta, and has issue living, (by 1st *m*) Robert John, *b* 1952, — Ronald Dean, *b* 1954, — Dorothy Louisa, *b* 1951: *m* 1971, Robert Honeyman. —— David Keith (Box 20, RR1, Prince George, BC, Canada), *b* 1937: *m* 1957, Helen Balko, and has issue living, Stephen Lawrence, *b* 1961, — Stacey Eldon, *b* 1968, — Shaun Lewis Eden, *b* 1973, — Debra Ann, *b* 1958, — Denise Josephine, *b* 1965. —— Joan Gwendoline, *b* 1925: *m* 1959, Maurice J. Parfitt, and has issue living, Dennis Lee, *b* 1946: *m* 1966, Lynn Stoddard, and has issue living, Michelle Lee *b* 1970: *m* 1991, Jacques Pelletier (and has issue living, Brandon Dennis Rudolphe *b* 1993), — Sydney Robert, *b* 1947: *m* 1969, Susan Strom, and has issue living, Rachael Andrea *b* 1971, Kirsten Jane *b* 1973, — Lee Roy, *b* 1949, — Gordon Douglas, *b* 1952: *m* 1973, Brenda Erickson, and has issue living, Spencer James *b* 1976, Amy Olan *b* 1978. *Residence* – RR#8, Site 5, Comp 3A9, Prince George, BC, Canada V2N 4M6.

PREDECESSORS – (1) *Sir* THOMAS Denman, *b* 1779; MP for Nottingham, Attorney-Gen 1830-2 and Lord Ch Justice of England 1832-50; *cr Baron Denman*, of Dovedale (peerage of United Kingdom) 1834: *m* 1804, Theodosia Anne, da of late Rev Richard Vevers, Rector of Saxby; *d* 1854; *s* by his son (2) THOMAS, 2nd Baron, *b* 1805; Bar Lincoln's Inn 1833; Marshal and Associate to his father 1832-50; assumed by Roy licence 1876 the additional surname of Aitchison: *m* 1st, 1829, Georgiana, who *d* 1871, el da of late Rev Thomas Roe; 2ndly, 1871, Marion, who *d* 1902, el da and co-heiress of James Aitchison, of Alderston and Morham, NB; *d* 1894; *s* by his great nephew (3) THOMAS, GCMG, KCVO, PC (el son of late Richard Denman, grandson of 1st Baron), 3rd Baron; *b* 1874; was a Lord-in-Waiting to King Edward VII 1905-7, Capt of HM's Hon Corps of

Gentlemen-at-Arms 1907-11, Dep Speaker in House of Lords, 1909, and Gov-Gen of Commonwealth of Australia 1911-14: *m* 1903, Hon *Dame* Gertrude Mary Pearson, GBE, who *d* 1954, da of 1st Viscount Cowdray; *d* 1954; *s* by his only son **(4)** THOMAS, 4th Baron; *b* 1905; *d* 1971; *s* by his cousin **(5)** CHARLES SPENCER (el son of the Hon Sir Richard Douglas Denman, who was *cr* a *Baronet* (UK) 1945), 5th Baron, and present peer.

DENNING, BARON (Denning) (Life Baron 1957)

ALFRED THOMPSON DENNING, PC, son of late Charles Denning, of Whitchurch, Hants; *b* 23 Jan 1899; *ed* Magdalen Coll, Oxford (Hon Fellow 1948); Hon LLD Ottawa 1955, Glasgow and Southampton 1959, London 1960, Camb 1963, Leeds 1964, McGill 1967, Dallas 1969, Dalhousie 1970, Wales 1973, Exeter 1976, Columbia (New York) 1976, Tilburg (Netherlands) 1977, W Ontario and British Columbia 1979, Sussex 1980, Buckingham 1983, and Nottingham 1984; Hon DCL Oxford, 1965; Hon Bencher Middle Temple 1972, Gray's Inn 1979, Inner Temple 1982; Bar Lincoln's Inn 1923, a KC 1938, and a Bencher 1944; Chancellor of Diocese of Southwark 1937-44, and of London 1942-44, Recorder of Plymouth 1944; a Judge of the High Court of Justice 1944-48, a Lord Justice of Appeal 1948-57, and a Lord of Appeal in Ordinary 1957-62, Master of the Rolls 1962-82; conducted Profumo Inquiry 1963; Treas, Lincoln's Inn 1964; 1914-18 War in France with RE; *cr* Knt 1944, PC 1948, and *Baron Denning*, of Whitchurch, co Southampton (Life Baron) 1957: *m* 1st, 1932, Mary, who *d* 1941, da of late Rev F. N. Harvey, R of Fawley, Hants; 2ndly, 1945, Joan Daria, who *d* 1992, da of John Vinings Elliott Taylor, and widow of John Matthew Blackwood Stuart, CIE, and has issue by 1st *m*.

Arms – Per bend or and gules a bar wavy between two lions' heads erased in chief and a lion's face in base all counter-changed. **Crest** – On a chapeau gules turned up ermine a dexter glove argent grasping a scroll fesswise proper. **Supporters** – On either side a representation of a Chief Justice of the King's Bench in judicial robes the dexter circa 1780 and the sinister circa 1580
Residence – The Lawn, Whitchurch, Hants. *Club* – Athenaeum.

SON LIVING *(By 1st marriage)*

Hon Robert Gordon, *b* 1938; *ed* Winchester, and Magdalen Coll, Oxford (Fellow 1968): *m* 1967, Elizabeth Carlyle Margaret, da of E. R. Chilton, of Oxford, and has issue.

DENTON OF WAKEFIELD, BARONESS (Denton) (Life Baroness 1991)

JEAN DENTON, CBE, da of Charles Moss, of Wakefield, W Yorks; *b* 29 Dec 1935; *ed* Rothwell Gram Sch, and LSE (BSc); Information Exec BBC News Div (Home and Overseas) 1958, Communications Exec Proctor & Gamble 1959-61, Marketing Consultant and Assist Ed Retail Business Economist Intelligence Unit 1961-64, Women's Magazine Div IPC 1964-66, Hotel and Catering Dept Surrey Univ 1966-68, Professional Racing and Rally Driver 1968-71; Marketing Dir Huxford Group 1971-78, Heron Motor Group 1978-80, Man Dir Herondrive 1980-85 (voted Female Exec of the Year 1983); Dir External Affairs Austin Rover Group 1985-86, Dir Burson-Marsteller since 1986, Dep Chm Black Country Development Corpn since 1987; Board Member British Nuclear Fuels plc, Triplex Lloyd plc, London & Edinburgh Insurance Group, and Think Green 1988-91; Member Interim Advisory Cttee on Teachers Pay and Conditions, The Engineering Council, The Royal Soc of Arts Council, and School Teachers Review Body since 1991; Board Member North West TV since 1991; Chm FORUM UK, Women on the Move Against Cancer, and formerly Chm Marketing Group of GB; Member of Worshipful Co of Marketors, Freeman City of London 1982; Baroness in Waiting 1991-92; Under-Sec of State, Dept of Trade and Industry 1992-94, since when Under-Sec N Ireland Office; FCInstM 1972, FIMI 1974, FRSA 1987, CBIM 1988; *cr* CBE (Civil) 1990, and *Baroness Denton of Wakefield*, of Wakefield, co W Yorks (Life Baroness) 1991: *m* 19—, — Denton.

Clubs – Reform, British Women Racing Drivers.

DERAMORE, BARON (de Yarburgh-Bateson) (Baron UK 1885, Bt UK 1818)

We fly by night

RICHARD ARTHUR DE YARBURGH-BATESON, 6th Baron, and 7th Baronet; *b* 9 April 1911; *s* 1964; *ed* Harrow, and at St John's Coll, Camb (MA); 1939-45 War as Fl-Lt RAFVR; ARIBA: *m* 1948, Janet Mary (served 1939-45 War as 3rd Officer WRNS), da of late John Ware, MD, of Nether Close, Askam-in-Furness, and has issue.

Arms – Quarterly, 1st and 4th grand quarters, 1st and 4th argent, three bats' wings erect sable, on a chief gules, a lion passant or, *Bateson*; 2nd and 3rd per pale argent and azure, a chevron between three chaplets counter-changed, *de Yarburgh*, 2nd and 3rd grand quarters, argent three lions dormant in pale sable between two flaunches of the last, each charged with three mullets palewise of the first, *Lloyd*. **Crests** – 1st, a bat's wing as in the arms; 2nd, a falcon close or, belled gold, preying on a mallard proper. **Supporters** – Two lions or, each gorged wth a collar gemel gules, and pendant therefrom an escutcheon ermine, that on the dexter charged with a bat's wing as in the arms, and that on the sinister wth a raven proper. **First Motto** – "Nocte volamus" (*We fly by night*). **Second Motto** – "Non est sine pulvere palma" (*The prize is not won without dust*).
Residence – Heslington House, Aislaby, Pickering, Yorks. *Clubs* – RAF and RAC

DAUGHTER LIVING

Hon Ann Katharine, *b* 1950: *m* 1982, Jonathan Henry Maconchy Peel, elder son of Walter Peel, of Knockdromin, Lusk, co Dublin (*see* Rugge-Price, Bt, colls, 1969 Edn), and has issue living, Nicholas Richard Yarburgh, *b* 1987, — Katharine Diana, *b* 1985. *Residence* – Sturdy Cottage, High Street, Thornborough, Bucks.

DAUGHTER LIVING OF FIFTH BARON

Hon Jane Faith (*Baroness Mowbray, Segrave and Stourton*), *b* 1933: *m* 1952, 26th Baron Mowbray, Segrave and Stourton. *Residences* – 23 Warwick Sq, SW1; Marcus, by Forfar, Angus.

PREDECESSORS – **(1)** ROBERT BATESON; MP for Londonderry (*C*) 1830-42; *cr* a Baronet 1818; *b* 1782: *m* 1811, Catherine, da of late Samuel Dickson, of Ballynaguile, Limerick; *d* 1863; *s* by his son **(2)** Sir THOMAS, 2nd Bt, who was *cr* Baron Deramore, of Belvoir, co Down (peerage of United Kingdom) 1885, with remainder to his younger brother, George William Bateson de Yarburgh; *b* 1819; sat as MP for Londonderry (*C*) 1844-57, and for Devizes 1864-85; a Lord of the Treasury 1852: *m* 1849, Hon Caroline Elizabeth Anne Rice-Trevor, who *d* 1887, da of 4th Baron Dinevor; *d* 1890; *s* by his brother **(3)** GEORGE WILLIAM, 2nd Baron; *b* 1823; assumed by Roy Licence 1876, the additional surname of de Yarburgh, and in 1892 the surname of Bateson after, instead of before, that of de Yarburgh: *m* 1862, Mary Elizabeth, who *d* 1884, da of George John Yarburgh, of Heslington Hall, York; *d* 1893; *s* by his el son **(4)** ROBERT WILFRID, TD, 3rd Baron; *b* 1865; Lord-Lieut for E Riding of Yorkshire, and Lieut-Col late Yorkshire Hussars Yeo: *m* 1st, 1897, Lucy Caroline, who *d* 1901, da of late William Henry Fife, of Lee Hall, Northumberland; 2ndly, 1907, Blanche Violet, who *d* 1972, el da of Col Philips Saltmarshe, formerly RA, of Saltmarshe, East Yorkshire; *d* 1936; *s* by his brother **(5)** GEORGE NICHOLAS, 4th Baron: *b* 1870; *m* 1900, Muriel Katharine, who *d* 1960, da of late Arthur Grey; *d* 1943, *s* by his el son **(6)** STEPHEN NICHOLAS, 5th Baron, *b* 1903: *m* 1929, Nina Marion, OBE, who *d* 1979, da of late Alastair Macpherson-Grant; *d* 1964, *s* by his brother **(7)** RICHARD ARTHUR, 6th Baron and present peer.

DE RAMSEY, BARON (Fellowes) (Baron UK 1887)

Patience and perseverance with magnanimity

JOHN AILWYN FELLOWES, 4th Baron; *b* 27 Feb 1942; *s* 1993; *ed* Winchester; patron of four livings; DL Cambs 1993; Pres Country Landowners' Assocn 1991-93 Crown Estate Commr since 1994; Pres Assocn Drainage Authorities since 1992: *m* 1st, 1973 (*m diss* 1983), Phyllida Mary, yr da of Philip Athelstan Forsyth, MRCS, LRCP, of The Poplars, Wickhambrook, Suffolk; 2ndly, 1984, Alison Mary, elder da of Sir Archibald Birkmyre, 3rd Bt, and has issue by 1st and 2nd *m*.

Arms – Azure, a fesse dancettée ermine between three lions' heads erased or, murally crowned argent. **Crest** – A lion's head as in the arms, charged with a fesse dancettée ermine. **Supporters** – On either side a ram proper gorged with a chain or, pendant therefrom and escutcheon ermine charged with a ram's eye also proper.
Seat – Abbots Ripton Hall, Huntingdon, Cambs.

SONS LIVING *(By 1st marriage)*

Hon FREDDIE JOHN, *b* 31 May 1978; *ed* Eton.

(By 2nd marriage)

Hon Charles Henry, *b* 1986.

DAUGHTERS LIVING *(By 2nd marriage)*

Hon Daisy Lilah, *b* 1988.
Hon Flora Mary, *b* 1991.

BROTHER LIVING

Hon Andrew Edward (36 Charolais Crescent, Ben Owa, Qld 4217, Australia), *b* 1950: *m* 1974, Anne Mary, da of Roy Tweedy, of Mungle, North Star, NSW, and has issue living, Robert Andrew, *b* 1978, — Katherine Jane, *b* 1976, — Rachael Julie, *b* 1982.

SISTERS LIVING

Hon Sarah, *b* 1938: *m* 1972, Peter Shelton, of Es Moli Nou de Canet, Es Glayeta, Mallorca, and has issue living, David, *b* 1977, — Fay, *b* 1973.
Hon Jennifer Julia FELLOWES (Hall Farm, Abbots Ripton, Huntingdon), *b* 1940; has resumed her maiden name: *m* 1964 (*m diss* 1986), John Frederick Moxon, and has issue living, Simon John, *b* 1965, — Matthew Sebastian, *b* 1967, — Christian Frederick, *b* 1974, — Alice Lavinia, *b* 1966: *m* 1989, Anthony Cripps, of 96 Terry St, Rozelle, Sydney 2039, NSW, Australia, and has issue living, William John *b* 1990, Henry Anthony *b* 1992, — Emily Faith Martha, *b* 1972.

HALF-UNCLE LIVING *(half-brother of 3rd Baron)* *(raised to the rank of a Baron's son 1933)*

Hon (John) David Coulson (Flat 3, 117 Elgin Cres, W11), *b* 1915; *ed* Eton, and Univ Coll, Oxford (BA); late 2nd Lt Rifle Bde; 1939-45 War in France (wounded, despatches, prisoner): *m* 1st, 1946 (*m diss* 1962), Louise, who *d* 1975, da of Lt Sir James Henry Domville, 5th Bt RN, and formerly wife of Leslie Alexander Mackay; 2ndly, 1963, Joan Lynette, who *d* 1965, only da of Edgar G. Rees, of Llanelli, and formerly wife of Richard Dewar Neame; 3rdly, 1977, Mervyn, da of late Reinold de Toll, and formerly wife of Peter Sherwood, and has issue living, (by 1st *m*) Peter Reginald (134 Belsize Rd, NW6), *b* 1948: *m* 1980, Alison Elizabeth, 2nd da of Dr John Vance, of 173 Rivermead Court, SW6, and has issue living, Charles Oliver Vance *b* 1983, Daisy Louise *b* 1984, — Jacqueline Denise, *b* 1955: *m* 1982, Michael Humfrey, of Cedar Cottage, Coney Weston Rd, Barningham, nr Bury St Edmunds, Suffolk.

COLLATERAL BRANCH LIVING

Issue of late Hon Reginald Ailwyn Fellowes, 2nd son of 2nd Baron, *b* 1884, *d* 1953: *m* 1919, Marguerite Severine Philippine, who *d* 1962, da of 4th Duc Decazes, and widow of Prince Jean de Broglie:—
Rosamond Daisy FELLOWES (7 Eliza St, Thornhill, Ontario, Canada), *b* 1921; resumed her maiden name by deed poll 19—: *m* 1st, 1941 (*m diss* 1945), James Gustavus Gladstone, Lieut King's Own Scottish Borderers (*see* E Shrewsbury, colls, 1949 Edn): 2ndly, 1952 (*m diss* 19—), Tadeusz Maria Wiszniewski, and has issue living (by 1st *m*), Reginald James (Marsh Benham House, Newbury, Berks), *b* 1943; *ed* Eton; journalist: *m* 1st, 1965, Mary Valentine, da of late Leslie Alexis Chiodetti, of Crondall, Surrey; 2ndly, 1993, Jane Doxford, and has issue living (by 1st *m*), Alexander *b* 1969, Benedict Hugh *b* 1973, — (by 2nd *m*) Diana Marguerite, *b* 1953: *m* 1978, Robert Shaw, of 106 Coon's Rd, Oak Ridges, Ontario, Canada, and has issue living, James Robert *b* 1983, Jennie Marguerite *b* 1981.

PREDECESSORS – (1) EDWARD Fellowes, *b* 1809; MP for Huntingdonshire (*C*) 1837-80; *cr Baron De Ramsey*, of Ramsey Abbey, Huntingdon (peerage of United Kingdom), 5 July 1887: *m* 1845, Hon Mary Julia Milles, el da of 4th Baron Sondes; *d* 9 Aug 1887; *s* by his el son (2) WILLIAM HENRY, 2nd Baron, *b* 1848; MP for Huntingdonshire (*C*) 1880-85, and for N, or Ramsey, Div of Huntingdonshire 1885-7; a Lord-in-Waiting to Queen Victoria 1890-92: *m* 1877, Lady Rosamond Jane Frances Spencer-Churchill, who *d* 1920, da of 7th Duke of Marlborough, KG; *d* 1925; *s* by his grandson (3) AILWYN EDWARD, KBE (son of late Capt Hon Coulson Churchill Fellowes, 1st Life Guards, el son of 2nd Baron), 3rd Baron, *b* 1910; Capt RA (TA), served 1939-45 War (prisoner), Lord-Lieut Hunts 1947-65, and Huntingdon and Peterborough 1965-68: *m* 1937, Lilah Helen Suzanne, who *d* 1987, da of late Francis Anthony Labouchere (*see* Stirling, Bt, *cr* 1800 (ext), 1940 Edn); *d* 1993; *s* by his elder son (4) JOHN AILWYN, 4th Baron and present peer.

DERBY, EARL OF (Stanley) (Earl E 1485, Bt E 1627)

EDWARD JOHN STANLEY, MC, 18th Earl, and 12th Baronet; *b* 21 April 1918; *s* 1948; *ed* Eton, and Oxford Univ; late Maj Gren Gds (Res); Hon Col 5th/8th (Vol) Bn, King's Regt (Comdg) 5th Bn 1947-51, Hon Col 1951-67 and 4th (Vol) Bn, Queen's Lancashire Regt TAVR Hon Col 1st and 2nd Bn Lancastrian Vols 1967-75; Hon Capt Mersey Div, RNR; Hon LLD Liverpool and Lancaster, Pres of Merseyside Chamber of Commerce 1972, Lord-Lt of co Lancaster 1951-68; Pro-Chancellor of Univ of Lancaster 1964-71; Pres of N-W Prov Area Council of National Union of Conservative Assocns 1969-72; Constable of Lancaster Castle since 1972; 1939-45 War in Italy (MC): *m* 1948, Lady Isabel Milles-Lade, who *d* 1990, sister of 4th Earl Sondes.

Arms – Argent, on a bend azure, three bucks' heads, cabossed or. **Crest** – On a chapeau gules, turned up ermine, an eagle wings extended, or, preying on a child proper, swaddled gules, in a cradle laced or. **Supporters** – *Dexter*, a griffin, wings elevated, or, ducally collared, and line reflexed over the back azure; *sinister* a stag, or, collared and lined as the dexter.
Seats – Knowsley, Prescot, Merseyside L34 4AF; Stanley House, Newmarket, Suffolk CB8 7DF.

Without changing

WIDOWS LIVING OF GRANDSONS OF SEVENTEENTH EARL

Mary, da of late Maj Vyvian Alfred Tylor, MC, of Sussex, formerly wife of W/Cdr P. H. M. Richey, DFC, and widow of William Herbert Harrison: *m* 1979, as his 2nd wife, Capt Hon Richard Oliver Stanley, who *d* 1983. *Residence* – Barn House, Ledwell, Chipping Norton, Oxon OX7 7AN.
Mary Rose, da of Charles Francis Birch, of Rhodesia: *m* 1st, 1961, Hon Hugh Henry Montagu Stanley, who *d* 1971; 2ndly, 1973, A. William A. Spiegelberg, of Oulton Park House, Tarporley, Cheshire CW6 9EE, and has issue (by 1st *m*) (see colls infra).

COLLATERAL BRANCHES LIVING

Grandsons of late Rt Hon Edward Montagu Cavendish Stanley, MC (*Lord Stanley*), el son of 17th Earl:—
Issue of late Hon Hugh Henry Montagu Stanley, *b* 1926, *d* 1971: *m* 1961, Mary Rose (ante) (who *m* 2ndly, 1973, A. William A. Spiegelberg), da of Charles Francis Birch, of Rhodesia:—
EDWARD RICHARD WILLIAM (90 Old Church St, Chelsea, SW3), *b* 10 Oct 1962; *ed* Eton, and RAC Cirencester; commn'd Gren Guards 1982-85; Merchant Banker, Fleming Private Asset Management Ltd. —— Peter Hugh Charles (New England Stud, Newmarket, Suffolk CB8 0XB), *b* 1964; *ed* Eton: *m* 1990, Hon Frances Caroline Burke Roche, only da of 5th Baron Fermoy, and has issue living, Richard Hugh Edward, *b* 1993.

Grandsons of late Rt Hon Oliver Frederick George Stanley, MC, MP (infra):—
Issue of late Capt Michael Charles Stanley, MBE, *b* 1921, *d* 1990: *m* 1951, (Aileen) Fortune (Constance Hugh) (Halecat, Witherslack, Grange-over-Sands, Cumbria LA11 6RU), elder da of late Owen Hugh Smith, of Old Hall, Langham, Oakham, Rutland (yr brother of 1st Baron Bicester):—
Oliver Hugh, *b* 1952; *ed* Eton and — Coll Camb (MA, MD): *m* 1982, Bernadette, da of John McMullen, of Middlesbrough, and has issue living, John Michael, *b* 1982, — Aidan, *b* 1986, — Naomi Isabel, *b* 1989. —— Nicholas Charles, *b* 1954; *ed* Eton: *m* 1986, Sarah Louise Gilroy, only da of George Henry Gilroy Williams, of Warwick Rd, Maperley Park, Nottingham, and has issue living, Thomas Michael Henry, *b* 1990, — Jack William Oliver, *b* 1993.

Issue of late Rt Hon Oliver Frederick George Stanley, MC, MP, 2nd son of 17th Earl, *b* 1896, *d* 1950: *m* 1920, Lady Maureen Helena Vane-Tempest-Stewart, who *d* 1942, da of 7th Marquess of Londonderry:—
Kathryn Edith Helen (*Lady Dugdale*), DCVO, *b* 1923; JP for Shropshire; a Woman of the Bedchamber (temporary) to HM the Queen 1955-60, Extra Woman of the Bedchamber 1960-72, Woman of the Bedchamber 1972-85; Cdr of Royal Order of North Star of Sweden 1956; 1939-45 in WRNS; CVO 1973; DCVO 1984: *m* 1956, Sir John Robert Stratford Dugdale, KCVO (*see* Dugdale, Bt, *cr* 1936). *Residence* - Tickwood Hall, Much Wenlock, Shropshire.

Grandchildren of late Brig-Gen Hon Ferdinand Charles Stanley, CMG, DSO (infra):—
Issue of late Col Frederick Arthur Stanley, OBE, TD, Cameron Highlanders (TA), *b* 1905, *d* 1978, Ann Jane (Bramshott Lodge, Liphook, Hants), only da of late Col Williams Fellowes Collins, DSO (D Roxburghe):—
Peter Henry Arthur (Cundall Hall, Helperby, York; White's Club), late 2nd Lt Gren Gds, *b* 1933; *ed* Eton: *m* 1st, 1965 (*m diss* 1985), Countess Gunilla Margaretha Antonia Sophie Douglas, da of Count Wilhelm Douglas, of Schloss Langenstein, Baden, Germany; 2ndly, 1990 (*m diss* 1992), Mrs Lucy Barnett Campbell, da of James A. Barnett, of Bel Air, Calif, USA, and formerly wife of (i) Clifford Smith, Jr, and (ii) Colin Guy Napier Campbell (*see* Campbell, Bt, *cr* 1815, colls), and has issue living (by 1st *m*), Robin James Axel, *b* 1968, — Louisa Charlotte Ann, *b* 1966. — Sarah, *b* 1935: *m* 1962, Simon Hawkshaw Creswell, of Markers, Cattistock, Dorset, and has issue living, Alexander John Peter, *b* 1965, — Miranda Ann Louise, *b* 1963: *m* 1994, Rory D. A. Carnegie, of 269A Portobello Rd, W11, and has issue living, Cloudy Ann Hardy *b* 1993, — Sophia Alice Chrystal, *b* 1969.

Issue of late Brig-Gen Hon Ferdinand Charles Stanley, CMG, DSO, 5th son of 16th Earl, *b* 1871, *d* 1935: *m* 1904, Hon Alexandra Frances Anne Fellows, who *d* 1955, el da of 2nd Baron De Ramsey:—
Henry Ferdinand, MC, *b* 1911; *ed* Wellington Coll; late Maj Gren Gds; 1939-45 War (MC): *m* 1949, Grizel Sophie, da of late Air Vice-Marshal Sir Norman Duckworth Kerr MacEwen, CB, CMG, DSO, and formerly wife of late Maj Humphrey Hugh Sykes. *Residence* - Binfield Priory, Bracknall, Berks. *Clubs* - Brooks's, Cavalry and Guards', Royal Automobile.

Issue of late Col Hon Algernon Francis Stanley, DSO, 7th son of 16th Earl, *b* 1874, *d* 1962: *m* 1918, Lady Mary Cavendish Grosvenor, who *d* 1959, da of 1st Duke of Westminster, and widow of Viscount Crichton, MVO, DSO (E Erne):—
Constance Mary, *b* 1919: *m* 1946, Malcolm Weaver, Lieut US Army, and has issue living, Mark Marion, *b* 1960, — Mary Constance, *b* 1954: *m* 1978, Thomas Milton Crain, and has issue living, Allison Mary *b* 1982. *Residence* - Center, Texas, USA.

Issue of late Lt-Col Hon (Frederick) William Stanley, DSO, 8th son of 16th Earl, b 1878, d 1942: m 1905, Lady Alexandra Louise Elizabeth Acheson, who d 1958, el da of 4th Earl of Gosford:—
David William, b 1906; ed Wellington Coll, and Trin Coll, Camb; European War 1939-45 in Middle East, N Africa and Italy as Major REME: m 1937, Marjorie, only da of late Douglas K. Homan, and has issue living, William Douglas (PO Box 318, Hilton 3245, S Africa), b 1938: m 1963, Sally, da of late S. H. Read, of Johannesburg, and has issue living, David Andrew b 1964, Clare Alexandra b 1967, Nicola Avory b 1969, Fiona Anne b 1972, — Patrick (Belstone Cottage, Badgworth, Som), b 1943: m 1968, Jane, el da of D. Evers, of Four Winds, Wolverley, Kidderminster, and has issue living, Andrew b 1969, Deborah b 1971, Clare Rebecca, b 1973, — Caroline Alexandra, b 1940: m 1968, Nigel N. Proddow, of 27 Hertford Av, SW14 8EF, and has issue living, Charles William Nigel b 1969, Guy Edward Stanley b 1971. Residence – Himeville, Natal, S Africa.

Grandchildren of late Charles Henry Stanley, DSM, elder son of Capt Charles Geoffrey Stanley, 2nd son of Hon Henry Thomas Stanley, MP, 2nd son of 13th Earl:—
Issue of late Very Rev Charles Geoffrey Nason Stanley, b 1884, d 1977: m 1st, 1914, Eileen Chapman, who d 1928; 2ndy, 1931, Violet Claire Baldwin (Glendonagh House, Dungourney, Midleton, co Cork):—
(By 1st m) Rev Eric William (Cuanbeg, Ballycotton, co Cork), b 1922; ed Trin Coll, Dublin (MA): m 1949, Phoebe Elizabeth Mary Pollard, and has issue living, Joy, b 1950, — Katherine, b 1953. —— (By 2nd m) Rev Arthur Patrick (Route 1, Box 212, Stanton, Iowa 51573, USA), b 1932; ed Trin Coll, Dublin (MA); late Chap to the Forces: m 1st, 1958, Kathleen Marjorie Ethel, who d 1981, da of Harold Victor Earl, of Waterford; 2ndly, 1983, Jessie Ernestine Fisher, née Tombleson, and has issue living (by 1st m), Stephen Patrick, b 1961, — Belinda Susan, b 1959. —— Sylvia Penelope, b 1936: m 1956, Rev William George Stanley Spence, MSc, of RR2, Box 20, 2494 Parker Rd, Nanoose Bay, BC V0R 2R0, Canada, and has issue living, Peter Edward, b 1959, — Janet, b 1962. —— Hazel Claire, b 1940: m 1963, Richard John Armstrong (Dr Phil), of Nedre Markveg 1, Tromso, Norway, and has issue living, Geoffrey James, b 1966, — Charles Ivan, b 1969, — Niall John, b 1974, — Claire Winifred, b 1964.
Issue of late Frederick George Stanley, b 1888, d 1979: m 1931, Grace Evelyn Thrower, who d 1988:—
Helen Audrey, b 1936: m 1966, George Watts, of 12 Greenways, Abbots Langley, Watford.
Issue of late Henry William Stanley, b 1903, d 1977: m 1930, Kathleen May Hardwick, who d 1981:—
Leslie Hugh (18 Heather Av, Bearsden, Glasgow), b 1931: m 1956, Marjorie Green, and has issue living, Christopher John, b 1958: m 1991, Sally Ann Morrison of Birnie Acre, Balmore by Glasgow, — Geoffrey Hugh, b 1962; BSc: m 1989, Catherine Anne Sheehan, BSc, of Knock Managh co Cork, — Lissa Rachel, b 1963: m 1984, Mark Stephen Ferguson, and has issue living, Geoffrey Christopher b 1990. —— Norman Edward (Carraghan, Church St, Alcombe, Minehead, Som), b 1937: m 1961, Maxine Wyness, and has issue living, Adam, b 1969; BA (Camb), — Dominique, b 1965, — Mia, b 1966; BA (Edinburgh Coll of Art).

Grandson of late Lt-Col Charles Edward Henry Stanley, son of late Col Hon Charles James Fox Stanley, 3rd son of 13th Earl:—
Issue of late Charles Douglas Stanley, b 1878, d 1975: m 1909, Adela Grace, who d 1950, da of F. A. Walker-Jones, JP, formerly of Beddgelert, Gwynedd:—
Charles John Geoffrey (5 Shoreham Place, Shoreham, Sevenoaks, Kent TN14 7RX), b 1918; ed Eton, and St John's Coll, Camb (BA); formerly Capt RAC; France 1940, NW Europe 1944-45: m 1942, Marjorie Laura Awdry, da of J. F. Awdry Ball, and has issue living, Christopher Geoffrey Awdry (The Sheafhouse, Bayton, Kidderminster, Worcs DY14 9LW), b 1949; ed Radley, and London Univ; BSc(Econ): m 1974, Anita Jane Keogh, and has issue living, Thomas Edward Christopher b 1983, Ruth Mary Frances b 1987, — Martin John Llewelyn (Ruard, Neb Lane, Oxted, Surrey), b 1952; ed Radley, and St John's Coll, Oxford; m 1979, Philippa Alison Beauvais, yst da of late W. Beric Southwell, of Ide Hill, Sevenoaks, and has issue living, Charles Douglas Llewelyn b 1982, Max Wilfred Southwell b 1988, Isobel Beauvais b 1984.

Grandsons of late Edward James Stanley, 5th in descent from Peter Stanley, yr son of Sir Thomas Stanley, 2nd Bt, and great-uncle of 11th Earl:—
Issue of late Capt Edward Arthur Vesey Stanley, b 1879, d 1941: m 1st, 1919 (m diss 1932), Sybil, who d 1972, da of late Maj Heathfield Butler Dodgson, DSO (B Vivian, colls); 2ndly, 1936, Marjorie Beatrice (8 Ash Court, Stanway Close, Taunton, Som) (who m 2ndly, 1942, Charles Langford Sidey, who d 1993), da of late A. R. Booth:—
(By 1st m) Peter Vivian (Pinemead, Shefford, Beds), b 1921; ed Eton: m 1960 (m diss 1974), Kay, da of R. S. Wybrow, of Chobham, Surrey. —— (By 2nd m) John Alexander, b 1938; ed Repton: m 1983, Susan, da of Dennis Brown, and has issue living, Thomas Charles Edward, b 1984.

Descendants of the late Sir Thomas Stanley (el son of Sir Thomas Stanley 5th in descent from the Hon Sir John Stanley, 3rd son of 1st Baron Stanley), who was cr a Baronet 1660 (see B Stanley of Alderley).

(In remainder to the Barony of Stanley (cr 1456) only) (see Cs Loudoun.)

PREDECESSORS – (1) Sir THOMAS Stanley, KG; successively Lord Dep and Lord-Lt of Ireland, and Knight of the Shire of Lancashire 1447-51 and 1453-4; summoned to Parliament of England as Baron Stanley 1456; d 1458-9; s by his son (2) THOMAS, KG, 2nd Baron; Justice of Chester 1463-85, Steward of the Household 1474, and Constable of England for life; for the services he rendered at Bosworth Field, where he placed the crown of Richard III on the head of the victorious Richmond (Henry VII), was cr Earl of Derby (peerage of England) 1485; d 1504; s by his grandson (3) THOMAS, 2nd Earl, who in 1488 had s as 2nd Baron Strange, his father having been summoned to Parliament in right of his wife as Baron Strange of Knockyn 1482-97; d 1522; s by his son (4) EDWARD, KG, 3rd Earl; Lord High Steward at coronation of Queen Mary; celebrated for his magnificence and liberality; d 1593; s by his son (5) HENRY, KG; one of the peers who sat upon the trial of Mary, Queen of Scots: m 1555, Margaret, who d 1596, da of Henry Clifford, 2nd Earl of Cumberland, by his wife Eleanor, yr da of Charles Brandon, Duke of Suffolk (niece of King Henry VIII); d 1593; s by his el son (6) FERDINANDO, 5th Earl; is supposed to have been poisoned by certain conspirators who had suggested he should assume the title of king in right of his grandmother, a proposal he had indignantly rejected; d 1594, when the Baronies of Stanley and Strange fell into abeyance among his das, and the earldom devolved upon his brother (7) WILLIAM, KG, 6th Earl; purchased from his nieces their claims on the Isle of Man; d 1642; s by his son (8) JAMES, KG, 7th Earl, who in 1628 had been summoned to Parliament as Baron Strange under the impression that such a barony was enjoyed by his father; the summons cr a new peerage (see B Strange): during the Civil Wars when attached to the royal cause, and his wife Charlotte, da of Claude de la Trémouille, Duke of Thouars, is famed for her defence of Latham House when besieged by the Parliamentarians 1644, and for her energetic protection of the Isle of Man 1651; falling into the hands of the enemy after the battle of Worcester was decapitated at Bolton 1651; s by his son (9) CHARLES, 8th Earl; d 1672; s by his son (10) WILLIAM GEORGE RICHARD, 9th Earl; d 1702; s by his brother (11) JAMES, 10th Earl; dsp 1736 when the Isle of Man and the Barony of Strange, cr 1627, devolved upon the 2nd Duke of Atholl, the other baronies became abeyant between the co-heirs of the 5th Earl, and the earldom reverted to his kinsman (12) Sir EDWARD Stanley, 11th Earl and 5th Bt (see note *infra); d 1776, s by his grandson (13) EDWARD, 12th Earl; Lord-Lt Lancashire; d 1834; s by his son (14) EDWARD SMITH, KG, 13th Earl; Lord-Lt Lancashire; cr Baron Stanley, of Bickerstaffe (peerage of United Kingdom) 1832; d 1851; s by his son (15) EDWARD GEOFFREY, KG, GCMG, PC, DCL, 14th Earl; b 1799; an eminent orator, scholar and statesman; MP for Stockbridge (C) 1820-6, for Preston 1826-30, for Windsor 1830-2, and for N Lancashire 1832-46; Ch Sec for Ireland 1830-3, Sec of State for Colonies and for War 1833-4 and 1841-5, First Lord of the Treasury 1852, 1858-9 and 1866-8, Chancellor of Univ of Oxford, &c; called to House of Lords in his father's Barony of Stanley 1846: m 1825, Hon Emma Caroline Wilbraham, who d 1876, da of 1st Baron Skelmersdale;

d 28 Oct 1869; *s* by his son **(16)** EDWARD HENRY, KG, PC, 15th Earl; *b* 1826; MP for Lynn Regis (*C*) 1848-69; Under Sec for Foreign Affairs 1852, Sec for Colonies 1858, Pres of Board of Control 1858, Sec of State for India 1858-9, for Foreign Affairs 1866-8 and 1874-8, and Sec of State for the Colonies 1882-5: *m* 1870, Mary Catherine, who *d* 1900, da of 5th Earl De La Warr, and widow of 2nd Marquess of Salisbury; *d* 1893; *s* by his brother **(17)** FREDERICK ARTHUR, KG, GCB, GCVO, PC, 16th Earl; *b* 1841; Lord-Lt Lancashire; a Civil Lord of the Admiralty Aug to Nov 1868, Financial Sec to War Office 1874-7, Sec to Treasury 1877-8, Sec of State for War 1878-80, Sec of State for Colonies 1885-6, Pres of Board of Trade 1886-8, and Gov Gen of Canada and Com-in-Ch of Prince Edward Island 1888-93; MP for Preston (*C*) 1865-8 for N Lancashire 1868-85, and for Blackpool Div of Lancashire N 1885-6; cr *Baron Stanley of Preston* (peerage of United Kingdom) 1886: *m* 1864, Lady Constance Villiers, who *d* 1922, el da of 4th Earl of Clarendon; *d* 1908; *s* by his el son **(18)** EDWARD GEORGE VILLIERS, KG, GCB, GCVO, TD, PC, 17th Earl; *b* 1865; Lord-Lt Lancashire; was a Junior Lord of the Treasury 1895-1900, Financial Sec to War Office 1900-1903, Postmaster-Gen 1903-1905, Under Sec of State for War 1916, Sec of State for War 1916-18, Ambassador Extraor and Plen to France 1918-20, and again Sec of State for War 1922-4; sat as MP for Lancashire (SE) Westhoughton Div 1892-6; *m* 1889, Lady Alice Maud Olivia Montagu, who *d* 1957, da of 7th Duke of Manchester; *d* 1948; *s* by his grandson **(19)** EDWARD JOHN (son of the late Rt Hon Edward Montagu Cavendish, *Lord Stanley*, MC, el son of 17th Earl), 18th Earl and present peer; also Baron Stanley of Bickerstaffe, and Baron Stanley of Preston.

(1) EDWARD, of Bickerstaffe, great-grandson of Hon Sir James Stanley, Knt, brother of 3rd Earl; cr a *Baronet* 1627; *s* by his son **(2) *Sir* THOMAS, 2nd Bt; *d* 1653; *s* by his son **(3)** *Sir* EDWARD, 3rd Bt; *d* 1671; *s* by his son **(4)** *Sir* THOMAS, 4th Bt; *d* 1714; *s* by his son **(5)** EDWARD, 11th Earl of Derby and 5th Bt (*see ante*).

DE ROS, BARON (Maxwell) (Baron E 1264)
(Title pronounced "de Roos")

PETER TREVOR MAXWELL, 28th Baron (Premier Baron of England); 23 Dec 1958; *s* 1983; *ed* Headfort Sch, Kells, Stowe, and Down High Sch, Downpatrick: *m* 1987, Angela Siân, da of late Peter Campbell Ross, and has issue.

𝕬rms – Quarterly, 1st and 4th, Argent a saltire gules, *Fitzgerald*, 2nd and 3rd, gules, three water bougets argent *de Ros*. 𝕾upporters – Two falcons wings expanded and inverted proper.
Residence – Old Court, Strangford, co Down.

SON LIVING

Hon FINBAR JAMES, *b* 14 Nov 1988.

DAUGHTERS LIVING

Hon Katharine Georgiana, *b* 1990.
Hon Jessye Maeve, *b* 1992.

SISTER LIVING

Hon Diana Elizabeth MAXWELL, *b* 1957; has resumed her maiden name: *m* 1st, 1976 (*m diss* 1978), Jonathan Watkins; 2ndly, 1978 (*m diss* 1981), Don Richard Bell; 3rdly, 1987 (*m diss* 1992), Eric Ford, and has issue living (by 3rd *m*), Nisha, *b* 1988.

AUNT LIVING (*Sister of* GEORGIANA ANGELA, BARONESS DE ROS)

Rosemary ROSS, *b* 1937: *m* 1973, Beresford George Edward Osborne, MIPA, and has issue living, Joanna Elizabeth, *b* 1975.

GRANDMOTHER LIVING

Hon Angela Ierne Evelyn Dixon, da of 1st Baron Glentoran: *m* 1st, 1929, Lt-Cdr Peter Ross, RN, who was *ka* 1940, el son of Una Mary, Baroness de Ros; 2ndly, 1943, Lt-Col Trevor Langdale Horn, MC, 16th/5th Lancers, who *d* 1966, and has issue living (by 2nd *m*), June Victoria Langdale, *b* 1946. *Residence* – Luckington Court, Chippenham, Wilts.

FATHER LIVING

Cdr (John) David Maxwell, RN; High Sheriff co Down 1981; DL: *m* 1st, 1954, Georgiana Angela, Baroness de Ros in her own right, who *d* 1983; 2ndly, 1984, Mrs Patricia Carolyn Coveney (*née* Ash). *Residence* – Old Court, Strangford, co Down.

COLLATERAL BRANCHES LIVING (*all in remainder*)

Issue of late Hon Charles Dudley Anthony Ross, yr son of Una Mary, Baroness de Ros, *b* 1907, *d* 1976: *m* 1st, 1940 (*m diss* 1949), Lady Elizabeth (ANNESLEY), who *d* 1982, da of 8th Earl of Roden; 2ndly, 1953, Mary Margaret, who *d* 1994, da of late Thomas Graham, of Monaghan:—
(By 1st *m*) Anthony Arthur (Casa Zabora, Brendon Av, Morningside Manor, Sandton, S Africa), *b* 1941; *ed* Winchester; FCA, CASA: *m* 1969, Joan, da of Herbert Cahn, of Highlands N, Johannesburg, and has issue living, Zara Gail, *b* 1971: *m* 1994, Stephen Mark Sanders, of 25 Lone Meadow, Lonehill, Sandton, S Africa, — Deborah Kim, 1972.

Issue of late Lady Eleanor Charlotte Augusta Dawson, yr sister of Una Mary, Baroness de Ros, *b* 1885, *d* 1974: *m* 1st, 1906 (*m diss* 1920), Capt Aubrey Nugent Wade-Palmer; 2ndly, 1920, János Orsolya Kiss, of Hungary, who *d* 1932; 3rdly, 1934, Frigyes Szántó (Dr of Politics), who *d* 1947; 4thly, 1951, Syed Waris Ameer Ali, CIE, ICS, who *d* 1975:—
(By 1st *m*) †Barbara Madeline WADE-PALMER (Myrtle, Quickly Lane, Chorleywood, Herts), *b* 1907: *m* 1923 (*m diss* 1936), Col Béla Domjan de Domjanszeg, of Hungary, and *d* 1992, leaving issue, Robert (Dene Hill, Beechenlea Lane, Swanley Village, Kent BR8 7PR), *b* 1924: *m* 1956, Countess Heilwig Freda Anna Helene Christa Hildegard, da of Count Gerhart von Büdingen, and has issue living, Nicholas Charles Robert *b* 1960; *ed* Dulwich. —— Ismé Ruth (21 Northumberland Court, 62-64 Marine Parade, Brighton), *b* 1908: *m* 1934 (*m diss* 1941), Capt Christian Satzger de Bálványos.

PREDECESSORS – **(1)** ROBERT de Ros took an active part against Henry III and was one of the principal barons summoned to Parliament of England in the king's name 1264; was also again summoned as *Baron de Ros* 1285; *d* 1285; *s* by his son **(2)** WILLIAM, 2nd Baron; unsuccessfully competed for the crown of Scotland 1292 and 1296; *d* 1316; *s* by his son **(3)** WILLIAM, 3rd Baron; *d* 1343; *s* by his son **(4)** WILLIAM, 4th Baron; led a division of the English Army at Crecy; *d* in Palestine 1352; *s* by his brother **(5)** THOMAS, 5th Baron; *d* 1384; *s* by his son **(6)** JOHN, 6th Baron; *d* 1394; *s* by his brother **(7)** WILLIAM, KG, 7th Baron; Lord High Treasurer of England 1403; *d* 1414; *s* by his son **(8)** JOHN, 8th Baron; killed at battle of Baugé 1421; *s* by his brother **(9)** THOMAS, 9th Baron; *d* 1431; *s* by his son **(10)** THOMAS, 10th Baron; summoned to Parliament 1449-60; was attainted 1461 and his honours forfeited; *s* by his son **(11)** EDMUND, 11th Baron; obtained a reversal of attainder 1485, but was not summoned to Parliament; *d* 1508, when the title became abeyant between his two sisters; the abeyance was terminated 15— in favour of **(12)** GEORGE MANNERS (son of Eleanor, the el sister by Sir Robert Manners, Knt), 12th Baron; was not summoned to Parliament; *d* 1513; *s* by his son **(13)** THOMAS , KG, 13th Baron; summoned to Parliament 1515, and *cr Earl of Rutland* (peerage of England) 1525; *d* 1543; *s* by his son **(14)** HENRY, KG, 2nd Earl; *d* 1563; *s* by his son **(15)** EDWARD, 15th Baron; *d* 1587, when the earldom reverted to his brother (*see* D Rutland), and the barony devolved upon his da **(16)** ELIZABETH, wife of William Cecil, afterwards 2nd Earl of Exeter; *d* 1591; *s* by her son **(17)** WILLIAM CECIL, 17th Baron; *dsp* before his father 1618; *s* by his cousin **(18)** FRANCIS Manners, 18th Baron and 6th Earl of Rutland; *cr Baron Ros*, of Hamlake 1616; *d* 1632 without male issue, when the Barony of Ros, of Hamlake, expired, the earldom reverted to his brother, and the old barony devolved upon his da **(19)** KATHERINE: *m* 1st, 1620, 1st Duke of Buckingham, who was assassinated 1628; 2ndly, 1635, 1st Marquess of Antrim; *d* 1666; *s* by her son **(20)** GEORGE, KG, 20th Baron and 2nd Duke; noted for his profligacy and his wit; *d* 1687, when the dukedom expired, and the Barony of de Ros went into abeyance between the descendants of Bridget and Frances, das of John, 4th Earl of Rutland, and remained so until 1806, when it was terminated in favour of **(21)** CHARLOTTE (a descendant of Frances (ante), and da of Hon Robert Boyle-Walsingham, 5th son of 1st Earl of Shannon): *m* 1791, Lord Henry FitzGerald, son of 1st Duke of Leinster; assumed by Roy licence 1806 the additional surname of de Ros; *d* 1831; *s* by her son **(22)** HENRY WILLIAM, 22nd Baron; *d* 1839; *s* by his brother **(23)** WILLIAM LENNOX LASCELLES, PC, 23rd Baron, *b* 1797; a Gen in the Army, Capt Yeomen of the Guard 1852 and 1858-9, and Lieut-Gov of the Tower of London 1852-74, &c: *m* 1824, Georgiana, who *d* 1891, da of 4th Duke of Richmond; *d* 1874; *s* by his son **(24)** DUDLEY CHARLES, KP, KCVO, 24th Baron, *b* 1827; Equerry to the Prince Consort 1853-61, and Queen Victoria 1861-74, and a Lord in Waiting 1874-80, 1885-6, and 1886-92: *m* 1st, 1853, Lady Elizabeth Egerton, who *d* 1892, el da of 2nd Earl of Wilton, GCH; 2ndly, 1896, Mary Geraldine, who *d* 1921, da of Rev Sir William Vesey Ross Mahon, 4th Bt; *d* 1907; *s* by his only da **(25)** MARY FRANCES, *b* 1854: *m* 1878, 3rd Earl of Dartrey (who *d* 1933); she *d* 1939, when the Barony again fell into abeyance between her three daughters and so remained until 1943, when it was terminated in favour of the **(26)** UNA MARY ROSS, *b* 1879: *m* 1904, Arthur John Ross, who was *ka* 1917; *d* 1956, when the Barony again fell into abeyance between her two granddaughters, and so remained until 1958, when it was terminated in favour of the el **(27)** GEORGIANA ANGELA (da of late Lieut-Com Peter Ross RN, el son of Una Mary, Baroness de Ros),_ *b* 1933: *m* 1954, Cdr (John) David Maxwell, RN; *d* 1983; *s* by her only son **(28)** PETER TREVOR, 28th Baron and present peer.

DERWENT, BARON (Vanden-Bempde-Johnstone) (Baron UK 1881, Bt GB 1795)
(Title pronounced "Darwent")

ROBIN EVELYN LEO VANDEN-BEMPDE-JOHNSTONE, LVO, 5th Baron and 7th Baronet, *b* 30 Oct 1930; *s* 1986; *ed* Winchester, and Clare Coll, Camb; DL N Yorks 1991; late 2nd Lieut KRRC, and Lieut Queen Victoria's Rifles (TA Reserve); 3rd Sec Foreign Office 1954-55, and at Paris (Private Sec to British Ambassador) 1955-58, 2nd Sec 1958, at Foreign Office 1958-61, at Mexico City 1961-65, 1st Sec 1962, Washington 1965-68, and Foreign Office 1968-69; Dir N. M. Rothschild and Sons Ltd 1969-85, Man Dir Hutchison Whampoa (Europe) Ltd since 1985, Dir Foreign & Colonial (Pacific) Investment Trust, Cluff Resources plc, Scarborough Building Soc; Chm London and Provincial Antique Dealers' Assocn, and Member Fine Arts and Antiques Export Cttee; Chev of Legion of Honour (France) 1957; LVO 1957; Officier de l'Ordre Nationale du Merite (France) 1978: *m* 1957, Sybille Marie Louise Marcelle, da of late Vicomte de Simard de Pitray, and has issue.

Arms – Quarterly: 1st and 4th argent, a saltire sable, in base a human heart ensigned with a regal crown or, on a chief gules, three woolpacks of the third; 2nd and 3rd per fesse, the 1st or, and the last per pale gules and vert, a demi-eagle with two heads displayed, issuing in chief sable, the dexter base charged with a tower, the sinister with five towers in saltire of the first, the gate and portcullis of each proper. **Crests** – 1st, a winged spur erect or, straps gules, buckles argent; 2nd, out of the battlements a tower argent, issuant therefrom a demi-eagle with two heads displayed sable. **Supporters** – *Dexter*, a lion ermine, crowned or, and charged on the breast with an escutcheon or, thereon a winged spur gules; *sinister*, A horse ermine, bridled and saddled gules, and charged on the shoulder as the dexter.
Residences – Hackness Hall, Scarborough, N. Yorks; 30 Kelso Pl, W8 5QG.

SON LIVING

Hon FRANCIS PATRICK HARCOURT, *b* 23 Sept 1965; *ed* Eton, and Edinburgh Univ: *m* 1990, Cressida E., only da of Christopher Bourke, of 61 Kingsmead Rd, SW2.

DAUGHTERS LIVING

Hon Emmeline Veronica Louise, *b* 1958: *m* 1982, James John Winterbotham, son of Richard Winterbotham, of The Hall, Wittersham, Tenterden, Kent, and has issue living, Alexander William Harcourt, *b* 1988, — Frederick Charles Leo, *b* 1990, — Héloïse Sophie Laura, *b* (twin) 1990. *Residence* – 48 Oakley Rd, N1.

Hon Joanna Louise Claudia, *b* 1962: *m* 1991, Timothy Matthews, yr son of Rev Canon John Matthews, of Walberswick, Suffolk and has issue living, Leopold Kai Maximilian, *b* 1993. *Residence* – 108 Munster Rd, SW6.

Hon Isabelle Catherine Sophie, *b* 1968.

COLLATERAL BRANCHES LIVING

Grandchildren of late Hon Louis Vanden-Bempde-Johnstone, 5th son of 1st Baron:—
Issue of late Lt-Col Granville Henry Vanden-Bempde-Johnstone, DSO, RA, *b* 1891, *d* 1969: *m* 1923, Margarita Ruby, who *d* 1972, da of late Arthur Vernon O'Connell, of Buenos Aires:—

John Louis, *b* 1928; *ed* Eastbourne Coll; late Capt RA: *m* 1964, Eltis, da of W. Robinson, and has issue living, Louise Dorothy Ann, *b* 1967. —— Elizabeth Mary, *b* 1924: *m* 1945, Lt-Col Richard McCaig, MC, RA (ret), of 15 Gorselands, Andover Rd, Newbury, and has had issue, David John *b* 1949; *ed* Wellington Coll; *d* 1977, — Mark Richard, *b* 1959, — Susan Mary, *b* 1951: *m* 1974, Maj Jeremy Turner, RIR, of 1 Holly Villas, Salisbury Rd, Shipton Bellinger, Hants.

Granddaughters of late Hon Gilbert Vanden-Bempde-Johnstone, yst son of 1st Baron:—
Issue of late Lt-Col Mark Vanden-Bempde-Johnstone, *b* 1900, *d* 1956: *m* (Jan) 1928, Susan, who *d* 1993 da of late Geoffrey Head, OBE (Pauncefort-Duncombe, Bt) (and sister of 1st Viscount Head):—

Virginia Susan (127 Cranmer Court, Whiteheads Grove, SW3 3HE), *b* (Oct) 1928.
Issue of late Cdr Felix Gilbert Vanden-Bempde-Johnstone, RN, *b* 1904, *d* 1964: *m* 1st, 1938, Mrs June Estcourt, da of late H. W. Looker; 2ndly, 1945, Frances Elizabeth (Cricket Green House, Hartley Wintney, Hants), da of late Charles McIntyre Brown:—

(By 1st *m*) Sarah June, *b* 1939: *m* 1961, Peter George Glossop, of Penlan Hall, Fordham, Colchester, and has issue living, Nicholas George, *b* 1971, — Georgemma Sarah, *b* 1963: *m* 1990, Richard Morgans, — Lucy Maria, *b* 1966: *m* 1992, James Patrick Atherton, only son of Brig Maurice Alan Atherton, CBE, of Digges Place, Barham, Kent, — Camilla June, *b* 1969.

(In remainder to the Baronetcy only)

Grandchildren of late Capt Charles Johnstone-Scott (infra):—
Issue of late Ronald Johnstone-Scott, *b* 1911, *d* 1967: *m* 1937, Winifred Joan Peck, of 19 Boleyn Drive, Eastcote, Ruislip, Middx:—

Richard Anthony (124 Miladi Farm, Longueville, St Saviours, Jersey, CI), *b* 1946: *m* 1968, Jennifer Le Lerre, and has issue living, Iain Richard, *b* 1972, — Giles Edward, *b* 1978, — Emma Louise, *b* 1970: *m* 1990, Robert John Paul Thomas, of 5 De Quetteville Court, Ann St, St Helier, Jersey, CI, and has issue living, Oliver Robert *b* 1991. —— Bruce Roger (97 Mount Park Rd, Old Eastcote, Pinner, Middx), *b* 1956. —— Gillian Fenton, *b* 1938: *m* 1960, David Godfrey Kimsey, Detective Chief Supt, Met Police, of Squirrels Leap, 94 Broadwood Av, Ruislip, Middx HA4 7XT, and has issue living, Stephen David (70 Collins Drive, Eastcote, Middx), *b* 1962: *m* 1985, Sharon Ivy Elaine Crick, and has issue living, Alyse Louis *b* 1991, — Mark Fenton (12 Elliott Avenue, Ruislip HA4 9LY), *b* 1967; Barrister at Law (LLB): *m* 1994, Emma Jane Sykes, — Deborah Gillian, *b* 1964: *m* 1987, Michael Jon Hennessey, of 46 Hatherleigh Rd, Ruislip, Middx and has issue living, Callum Michael Charles *b* 1992, Emily Kate *b* 1989, — Sarah Cressida, *b* 1972; ALCM. —— Sandra Elizabeth Louise, *b* 1952: *m* 1974, Ivor Owen Tomrley, of Dellside, Dibden Hill, Chalfont St Giles, Bucks, and has issue living, Hannah Jane, *b* 1977, — Charlotte Louise, *b* 1979.

Descendants of late Col John Johnstone, 2nd son of 2nd baronet of Westerhall (*cr* 1700):—

Grandchildren of late Henry Richard Johnstone-Scott, 2nd son of 2nd baronet of Hackness (*cr* 1795), who assumed the additional surname of Scott by R licence 1860:—
Issue of late Capt Charles Johnstone-Scott, *b* 1870, *d* 1948: *m* 1907, Elizabeth Irvine Matheson-Warrack, who *d* 1956:—

Charles Hugh (Malaga, Spain), *b* 1913. —— Aline, *b* 1908: *m* 1934, Errol Chapman Houston, who *d* 1977, and has issue living, Anthony Charles (225 Bree St, Vryheid, Natal), *b* 1935; *ed* Cape Town Univ (BCom, CA): *m* 1960, Ryvés Dawn, only child of Joseph Geber, of 208 San Francisco, Park Lane, Parktown, Johannesburg, and has issue living, Murray James *b* 1964; *ed* Cape Town Univ (BCom), Andrea Leigh *b* 1961: *m* 1984, Bruce John Murray-Reinders, of 12 Seminol, Kingsway Crescent, Riverclub, Johannesburg (and has issue living, Scott Charles *b* 1986), Nicola Brigid *b* 1967, — Sally Patricia, *b* 1942; *m* 1965, Edward Carl William Meyer, of 9 Wood Rd, Rondesbosch, Cape Town, S Africa, and has issue living, Graham Carl *b* 1966, Craig Carl Anthony *b* 1973, Susan Belinda *b* 1968. —— Margaret Cressida, *b* 1915: *m* 1947, Richard Melville Brooker, of Waverley, Lauriston Rd, Gatehouse of Fleet, Castle Douglas, Kirkcudbrightshire, and has issue living, Robin Nicholas, *b* 1948: *m* 1971, Roberta Cope, and has issue living, Caroline *b* 1972, — Richard David (31 Oldaker Rd, Newick, E Sussex BN8 4LN), *b* 1949: *m* 19—, Vivienne Smith, and has issue living, Julian Charles *b* 1981, Jonathan *b* 1984.

Granddaughter of late Charles Julius Johnstone, son of late Rev Vanden Bempde Johnstone, son of late Charles Philipps Johnstone, 2nd son of Charles John Johnstone, brother of 1st baronet:—
Issue of late Cmdr Richard Noel Johnstone, RN, *b* 1896, *d* 1989: *m* 1933, Mary Edmée, da of late Charles William Campbell, CMG:—

Susan Mary (*Lady Rowe*), *b* 1935: *m* 1957, Sir Jeremy Rowe, CBE, of Woodside, Peasmarsh, Rye, Sussex, and has issue living, Lucinda Mary, *b* 1958, — Josephine Alice, *b* 1960, — Nicola Susan, *b* 1963, — Harriet Sarah, *b* 1966.

Descendants, if any, of late Charles Frederick Dale Johnstone (*b* 1858) and late Richard James Annandale Johnstone (*b* 1865), sons of late Edmund John Johnstone, 3rd son of late Richard James Johnstone, 5th son of late Charles John Johnstone, brother of 1st baronet.

PREDECESSORS – (1) RICHARD Johnstone (son of late Col John Johnstone, 2nd son of Sir William Johnstone, 2nd Bt, of Westerhall), MP for Weymouth 1790-96; assumed by Act of Parliament 1793, the surnames of Vanden-Bempde, and in 1795 was authorized by Roy licence to resume the name of Johnstone: *m* 1st, 1756, Catherine, who *d* 1790, da of James Agnew, of Bishop Auckland; 2ndly, 1795, Margaret, who *d* 1853, da of John Scott, of London; *cr a Baronet* 1795, under the name of Bempde-Johnstone, with remainder to the male issue of his brother Charles John; *d* 1807; *s* by his son (2) *Sir* JOHN, successively MP for Yorkshire and Scarborough; *b* 1799: *m* 1825, Louisa Augusta Venables-Vernon, da of the Most Rev Edward Harcourt, Archbishop of York (B Vernon), *d* 1869; *s* by his son (3) *Sir* HARCOURT, 3rd Bt; *b* 1829; MP for Scarborough (*L*) 1869-80; *cr Baron Derwent, of Hackness, co York (peerage of United Kingdom) 1881: m 1850, Charlotte Mills, who d 1903, sister of 1st Baron Hillingdon; d 1916; s by his son* (4) FRANCIS, 2nd Baron; *b* 1851: *m* 1880, Ethel, who *d* 1891, da of Henry Strickland-Constable; *d* 1929; *s* by his nephew (5) GEORGE HARCOURT (son of late Hon Edward Henry Vanden-Bempde-Johnstone, 2nd son of 1st Baron), 3rd Baron, *b* 1899; Hon Attaché at Warsaw 1923, at Brussels 1927, at Madrid 1928, and at Berne 1939: *m* 1929, Comtesse Sabine Ozaykowska, who *d* 1941, da of Gen D. Iliesco (formerly Ch of Gen

Staff, Rumanian Army), of 12 Rue Alexandre Lahovary, Bucharest, Rumania; *d* 1949; *s* by his brother (6) PATRICK ROBIN GILBERT, CBE, 4th Baron; Chm British Road Fedn 1954-62, Min of State, Board of Trade 1962-63, and Min of State, Home Office 1963-64; Dep Speaker House of Lords 1970-85: *m* 1929, Marie-Louise Henriette, who *d* 1985, formerly wife of late Brig Phillip Stafford Myburgh, CBE, DSO and bar, MC, and da of late Albert Picard, of Paris; *d* 1986; *s* by his only son (7) ROBIN EVELYN LEO, 5th Baron and present peer.

DESAI, BARON (Desai) (Life Baron 1991)

MEGHNAD JAGDISHCHANDRA DESAI, son of late Jagdishchandra Chandulal Desai, of Baroda, India; *b* 10 July 1940; *ed* Bombay Univ (BA, MA), and Pennsylvania Univ (PhD 1964); Lecturer LSE 1965-77, Sr Lecturer 1977-80, Reader 1980-83, since when Prof of Economics; Head of Devpt Studies since 1990; Dir Centre for the Study of Global Governance, LSE; Council Member Royal Economic Soc, Exec Cttee Fabian Soc 1990-92, Chm Islington South and Finsbury Constituency Labour Party 1986-92; Pres Assocn of Univ Teachers in Economics 1987-90; author; *cr Baron Desai*, of St Clement Danes in the City of Westminster (Life Baron) 1991: *m* 1970, Gail Graham, da of late George Ambler Wilson, CBE, of Brandon House, North End Av, NW3, and has issue.
Residences – 51 Ellington St, N7 8PN; 5 rue de la Pie, Montaigu de Quercy, 82150 France.

SON LIVING

Hon Sven, *b* 1975.

DAUGHTERS LIVING

Hon Tanvi, *b* 1972.
Hon Nuala, *b* 1974.

DE SAUMAREZ, BARON (Saumarez) (Baron UK 1831, Bt UK 1801)
(Name and Title pronounced "Sommerez")

I hope in God

ERIC DOUGLAS SAUMAREZ, 7th Baron, and 7th Baronet (Premier Baronet of UK creation); *b* 13 Aug 1956; *s* 1991; *ed* Milton Abbey, Nottingham Univ, and RAC Cirencester: *m* 1982 (*m diss* 1990), Christine Elizabeth, yr da of Bernard Neil Halliday, OBE, of Woodford Green, Essex; 2ndly, 1991, Susan, da of late Joseph Hearn, and has issue by 1st *m*.

Arms – Argent, on a chevron gules, between three leopards' faces sable, as many castles triple-towered or. **Crest** – A falcon, displayed proper. **Supporters** – *Dexter*, an unicorn, tail between the legs argent, navally gorged azure, charged on the shoulder with a castle triple-towered or; *sinister*, a greyhound argent, collared gules, rimmed or, charged on the shoulder with a wreath of laurel vert, encircling an anchor sable.
Residence – Shrubland Park, Coddenham, Ipswich, Suffolk.

DAUGHTERS LIVING (By 1st marriage)

Hon Claire, *b* 1984.
Hon Emily, *b* 1985.

BROTHER LIVING

Hon VICTOR THOMAS, *b* (twin) 13 Aug 1956; *ed* Milton Abbey, and Exeter Univ (BA); MBA.

SISTER DECEASED

Hon Louisa, *b* 1955: *m* 1982 (*m diss* 1989), Duncan W. MacGregor, of Tregaer Mill, Monmouth, and *d* 1994, having resumed her maiden name.

AUNTS LIVING (Daughters of 5th Baron)

Hon Veronica, *b* 1915; European War, Red Cross VAD 1940-43 attached RAF Hosps, 1943-5 with ATS: *m* 1945, Brigadier Anthony William Allen Llewellen Palmer, DSO, MC, King's Dragoon Guards, who *d* 1990 (M Lincolnshire ext). *Residence* – Clos du Menage, Sark, CI.
Hon Christine (*Hon Lady Llewellyn*), *b* 1916: 1943-45 War with WRNS: *m* 1944, Lt-Col Sir Henry (Harry) Morton Llewellyn, 7th Bt, CBE, DL, Warwickshire Yeo, of Ty'r Nant, Llanarth, nr Raglan, Gwent NP5 2AR.

WIDOW LIVING OF SIXTH BARON

JOAN BERYL (JULIA) (*Dowager Baroness de Saumarez*), da of Douglas Raymond Charlton, of Windlesham, Surrey: *m* 1953, the 6th Baron, who *d* 1991. *Residence* – Shrubland Park, Coddenham, Ipswich, Suffolk.

PREDECESSORS – (1) Sir JAMES Saumarez, GCB, 3rd son of late Matthew Saumarez; b 1757; Adm of the Red, Gen of the Marine Forces, and a most distinguished naval commander; 2nd in command at the battle of Nile; cr a Baronet 1801, and Baron de Saumarez, of Saumarez, Guernsey (peerage of United Kingdom) 1831: m 1788, Martha, who d 1849, da of Thomas Le Marchant, of Guernsey; d 1836; s by his son **(2)** Rev JAMES, 2nd Baron, b 1789; Rector of Huggate, co York: m 1814, Mary, who d 1849, da of Vice-Adm Lechmere, of Steeple Aston, Oxon; dsp 1863; s by his brother **(3)** JOHN ST VINCENT, 3rd Baron, b 1806: m 1st, 1838, Caroline Esther, who d 1846, el da of William Rhodes, of Kirskill and Bramhope Halls, York: m 2ndly, 1850, Margaret Antoinette, da of William Richard Hopkyns Northey, of Oving House, Bucks; d 1891; s by his el son **(4)** JAMES ST VINCENT, 4th Baron, b 1843: m 1882, Jane Anne, OBE, who d 1933, da of late Capt Charles Acton Vere-Broke, RE; d 1937; s by his son **(5)** JAMES ST VINCENT BROKE, 5th Baron; b 1889; Capt Scots Guards; Founded Rhodesia Fairbridge Coll 1946: m 1914, Gunhild, who d 1985, da of late Maj-Gen Viktor Gustaf Balck, KCMG, of Stockholm; d 1969; s by his son **(6)** JAMES VICTOR BROKE, 6th Baron, b 1924; 1939-45 War with Life Guards; Dir Shrubland Health Clinic: m 1953, Joan Beryl (Julia), da of Douglas Raymond Charlton, of Windlesham; d 1991; s by his elder (twin) son **(7)** ERIC DOUGLAS, 7th Baron and present peer.

Desmond, Earl of; see Earl of Denbigh and Desmond.

DE VESCI, VISCOUNT (Vesey) (Viscount I 1776, Baron I 1750, Bt I 1698)
(Name pronounced 'Veezy')

SUB HOC SIGNO VINCES

Under this sign thou shalt conquer

THOMAS EUSTACE VESEY, 7th Viscount, 9th Baronet; b 8 Oct 1955; s 1983; ed Eton, and Univ Coll, Oxford: m 1987, Sita-Maria Arabella, da of late Brian de Breffny, of Castletown Cox, co Kilkenny, and of Maharaj Kumari Jyotsna Dutt, da of Maharajadhiraja Bahadur Sir Uday Chand Mahtab of Burdwan, KCIE, and has issue.

Arms – Or, on a cross sable, a patriarchal cross of the field. **Crest –** A dexter hand erect in armour holding a laurel branch proper. **Supporters –** Two figures of Hercules, each clad in a lion's skin, and holding a club over the exterior shoulder proper.
Seat – Abbey Leix, co Leix.

SONS LIVING

Hon Damian Brian John, b 1985.
Hon OLIVER IVO, b 16 July 1991.

DAUGHTER LIVING

Hon Cosima Frances, b 1988.

SISTERS LIVING

Hon Emma Frances, b 1951: m 1986, Norman Zalkind, of 186 Highland Av, Newtonville, Mass 02160, USA, and has issue living, Susan, b 1987.
Hon Catherine Anne, b 1953: m 1984, Bruno Cretton, of Le Plot, 74570 Groisy, France, and has issue living, Matthew John, b 1985, — Alexis Pierre, b 1988, — Cecily Anne, b 1986, — Madeleine, b 1991.

AUNTS LIVING (Sisters of 6th Viscount)

Margaret Constance, b 1912: m 1946, Herbert William Quinton, of 6 Forest Field, Horsham, Sussex, and has issue living, Thomas William, b 1947: m 1975, Beverley Eileen, da of H. Lestor Price, — Christopher John, b 1969, Carol, da of Clifford H. Green, and has issue living, William Alan John b 1972, Thomas Henry Alexander b 1973, Michael Patrick James b 1979, Catherine Sarah b 1969, — Peter Valentine, b 1953: m 1979, Deborah Helen, da of Bernard Boucher, — Caroline Mary, b 1950: m 1976, John Grinsted, and has issue, Mathew John b 1981, Sarah Margaret b 1979,
Bridget Georgina (Lady Airey), b 1915: m 1947, Lieut-Gen Sir Terence Sydney Airey, KCMG, CB, CBE, who d 1983. Residence – The White Cottage, Hempnall, Norwich NR15 2NG.

COLLATERAL BRANCHES LIVING

Issue of late Lieut-Col Hon Sir Osbert Eustace Vesey, KCVO, CMG, CBE, brother of 5th Viscount, b 1884, d 1957: m 1910, Dorothy, who d 1961, da of late William Morison Strachan, of Strood Park, Horsham:—
Anne, b 1914; m 1937 (m diss 1949), Maj Lord Roderic Armyne Gordon, MBE, TA (TA) (see M Huntly). Residence – 1 Beechfield, Northiam, Rye, Sussex.

Granddaughter of late Maj-Gen George Henry Vesey, 5th son of Rev Hon Arthur Vesey, 2nd son of 1st Viscount:—
Issue of late Lieut-Col Charles Edward Gore Vesey, b 1871, d 1958: m 1920, Mary Dorothea, who d 1966, da of Arthur Henry Loring:—
Claudine Mary Rosalind, b 1925; MRCS England and LRCP London 1950, DCH England 1954: m 1959, William Anthony Barry Brown, of Red Wing, South Park, Sevenoaks, Kent, and has had issue, Martin Thomas Vesey, b 1960, — James Benedict, b 1961; d 1990, — Adrian Walter, b 1963, — Susan Mary Loring, b 1965: m 1993, Nicholas Stephen Wiltshire, and has issue living, Martha Constance b 1992.

Grandsons of late Gen Sir Ivo Lucius Beresford Vesey, KCB, KBE, CMG, DSO, yst son of Maj-Gen George Henry Vesey (ante):—

Issue of late Major Christopher Thomas Vesey, MC, RHA, *b* 1916, *d* 1956: *m* 1952, Helen Cynthia Mary (who *m* 2ndly, 1969, Brig Ferdinand Shaw Eiloart, OBE, who *d* 1993, of Vinesse Farm, Little Horkesley, Colchester, Essex), da of late Brig Wilfrid Algernon Ebsworth, CB, CBE:—
Nicholas Ivo (c/o Programmes Ltd, Queen's Studio, 121 Salusbury Rd, NW6 6RG), *b* 1954. —— Thomas Wilfrid, *b* 1956: *m* 1981, Marie-Christine Josiane Renée, yst da of late Roger Landon, of Pamiers, France, and has issue living, Alexander Thomas Ferdinand, *b* 1981, — Olivia Denise Helen, *b* 1984.

PREDECESSORS – (1) *Right Rev* THOMAS Vesey; successively Bishop of Killaloe and Ossory; *cr* a *Baronet* 1698; *d* 1730; *s* by his son (2) *Sir* JOHN DENNY, 2nd Bt, MP for Newtown, co Down, and Custos Rotulorum of Queen's Co; *cr Baron Knapton (peerage of Ireland) 1750; d 1761; s by hs son* (3) THOMAS, 2nd Baron: *cr Viscount de Vesci* of Abbeyleix, Queen's Co (peerage of Ireland) 1776; *d* 1804; *s* by his son (4) JOHN, 2nd Viscount: Lord-Lieut of Queen's Co and a Representative Peer; *d* 1855; *s* by his son (5) THOMAS, 3rd Viscount; *b* 1803; MP for Queen's Co (*C*) 1835-7; a Representative Peer: *m* 1839, Lady Emma Herbert, da of 11th Earl of Pembroke; *d* 1875; *s* by his son (6) JOHN ROBERT WILLIAM, 4th Viscount, *cr Baron de Vesci, of* Abbey Leix, Queen's Co (peerage of United Kingdom) 1884; *b* 1844: *m* 1872, Lady Evelyn Charteris, who *d* 1939, da of 8th Earl of Wemyss and March; *d* 1903, when the Barony became Ext and he was *s* in the Irish dignities by his nephew (7) IVO RICHARD (son of late Capt Hon Eustace Vesey, 2nd son of 3rd Viscount), 5th Viscount; *b* 1881; Major Irish Guards; an Irish Representative Peer: *m* 1st, 1906 (*m diss* 1919), Georgina Victoria, who *d* 1930, da of late Gerald Edward Wellesley (E Cowley, colls); 2ndly, 1920, Frances Lois, who *d* 1984, da of Sir Cecil Edmund Lister-Kaye, 4th Bt, and widow of 5th Earl of Rosse; *d* 1958; *s* by his nephew (8) JOHN EUSTACE (son of late Col the Hon Thomas Eustace Vesey, brother of 5th Viscount), 6th Viscount, *b* 1919; FRICS; Lieut IG (Supplementary Reserve), 1939-45 War in Norway, N Africa and Italy (wounded, prisoner): *m* 1950, Susan Anne, who *d* 1986, da of late Ronald Owen Lloyd Armstrong-Jones, MBE, QC; *d* 1983; *s* by his only son (9) THOMAS EUSTACE, 7th Viscount and present peer; also Baron Knapton.

DE VILLIERS, BARON (de Villiers) (Baron UK 1910)

ARTHUR PERCY DE VILLIERS, 3rd Baron; *b* 17 Dec 1911; *s* 1934; *ed* Magdalen Coll, Oxford (BA 1936); Bar Inner Temple 1938: *m* 1939 (*m diss* 1958), Edna Alexis Lovett, el da of late Rev Dr A. D. MacKinnon, of Peachland, British Columbia, and has issue.

Arms – Azure, a bend enhanced argent, on a mount in base a Paschal Lamb proper. Crest – Issuant from a circlet of gold embellished with nine pearls raised upon points, a dexter arm in armour embowed grasping in the hand a seax argent. Supporters – On either side a springbok proper, gorged with a circlet of gold, embellished with nine pearls raised upon points.
Address – PO Box 66, Kumeu, Auckland, NZ.

The hand to the work

SON LIVING

Hon ALEXANDER CHARLES, *b* 29 Dec 1940: *m* 1966.

DAUGHTERS LIVING

Hon Celia Yvonne Lovett, *b* 1942: *m* 1st, 1968 (*m diss* 1978), Robin Hastings Sancroft Beck; 2ndly, 1979, Alan McCallum, and has issue living (by 1st *m*), Donovan Henry, *b* 1969, — Robert Arthur, *b* 1974, — Honor Alexa Catherine, *b* 1970, — (by 2nd *m*) Georgina Kay Lovett, *b* 1983.
Hon Rosemary Aletta, *b* 1946: *m* 1st, 1967 (*m diss* 1979), Robin Anderson Elliott, TD; 2ndly, 1979 (*m diss* 1981), Craig Benthin, of Sangar Hill Farm, Magaliesburg, Transvaal, and has issue living, Robert Alexander Blyth, *b* 1970, — Hector de Villiers James, *b* 1973, — Conrad Lovat Johnston, *b* 1974.

SISTER LIVING

Hon Yvonne Aletta, *b* 1913; *ed* Lady Margaret Hall, Oxford: *m* 1939, James Kenneth Hill, and has issue living, Antony James de Villiers, *b* 1940, — Richard Lansley, *b* 1946, — Hamish Robert, *b* 1949, — Susan Felicity, *b* 1942. *Residence* – 2/7 Tyndall St, Surrey Hills, Vic 3127, Australia.

WIDOW LIVING OF SON OF SECOND BARON

Christine Mary, da of A. C. Buller, of Dwarsriviershoek, Stellenbosch, S Africa: *m* 1946, Hon John Maurice de Villiers, who *d* 1988, and has issue (see colls infra). *Residence* – 61 Berg'n See, Hermanus 7200, Cape, S Africa.

COLLATERAL BRANCH LIVING

Issue of late Hon John Maurice de Villiers, yr son of 2nd Baron, *b* 1915, *d* 1988; *m* 1946, Christine Mary (ante), da of late A. C. Buller, of Dwarsriviershoek, Stellenbosch, S Africa:—
Jeanne Clair, *b* 1947: *m* 1st, 1968, Peter Puttick; 2ndly, 1972, Patrick Grierson, of 228 Erskine Av, Toronto, Canada M4P 1Z4. —— Michèle Jacqueline (1867 Rising Glen Rd, Los Angeles, Calif 90069, USA), *b* 1950.

PREDECESSORS – (1) *Rt Hon Sir* JOHN HENRY de Villiers, KCMG, son of Charles Christian de Villiers, of Paarl, Cape of Good Hope; *b* 1842; Attorney-Gen of Cape Colony 1872-4, and Ch Justice of Cape of Good Hope 1874-1910, and first Ch Justice of Union of South Africa 1910-14; *cr Baron de Villiers,* of Wynberg, Province of Cape of Good Hope and Union of South Africa (peerage of United Kingdom) 1910: *m* 1871, Aletta Johanna, who *d* 1922, da of Jan Pieter Jordaan, of Worcester, Cape of Good Hope; *d* 1914; *s* by his son (2) CHARLES PERCY, 2nd Baron, *b* 1871: *m* (Jan) 1911, Adelheid Helene Selma, who *d* 1968, da of Henri Christian Koch, formerly an Assist Judge, Supreme Court, Natal, of Pietermaritzburg, Natal; *d* 1934; *s* by his el son (3) ARTHUR PERCY, 3rd Baron and present peer.

DEVLIN, BARONY OF (Devlin) (Extinct 1992)

SONS LIVING OF LIFE BARON

Hon Gilpatrick (6 Millfield Lane, N6 6JD), *b* 1938; *ed* Winchester: *m* (Feb) 1967, Glenna, da of John Parry-Evans, MRCS, of Colwyn Bay, and has issue living, Benedict, *b* (Nov) 1967.
Hon Dominick, *b* 1942; *ed* Winchester, and Univ Coll, London (LLB): *m* 1967, Carla, da of Lamberto Fulloni, of Rome, and has issue living, Daniel, *b* 1968, — Christopher, *b* 1972, — Maddalena, *b* 1969.
Hon Timothy, *b* 1944; *ed* Winchester, and Univ Coll, Oxford: *m* 1967, Angela, elder da of A. J. G. Laramy, and has issue living, Sebastian, *b* 1973, — Fabian, *b* 1975, — Miranda, *b* 1969: *m* 1991, Neil McPherson and has issue living, one da, — Esmeralda, *b* 1971.
Hon Matthew (Ruffway, Platt Common, St Mary's Platt, Sevenoaks, Kent), *b* 1946; *ed* Winchester, and New Coll, Oxford: *m* 1969, Rosemary Joan Boutcher, da of Lt-Col E. C. Van der Kiste, of The Old Rectory, Durrington, Wilts, and has issue living, William, *b* 1972, — Edward *b* 1975, — Beatrice, *b* 1970, — Mary, *b* 1977.

DAUGHTERS LIVING OF LIFE BARON

Hon Clare, *b* 1940: *m* 1961 (*m* annulled 1984), Julian Reginald Desgrand Jermy Gwyn, Prof in History, Univ of Ottawa, and has issue living, Christopher, *b* 1965, — Matthew, *b* 1978, — Frances, *b* 1962: *m* 19—, Robert Thorpe, and has issue living, one son and two das, — Anya, *b* 1963: *m* 19—, Jerry Knol, and has issue living, one da, — Elin, *b* 1964: *m* 19—, Robert Vallé, and has issue living, two sons.
Hon Virginia (*Hon Lady Kennedy*), *b* (twin) 1940: *m* 1965, Rt Hon Sir Paul Kennedy, a Lord Justice of Appeal, and has issue living, Christopher, *b* 1966: *m* 1992, Rebecca McCarthy, — John, *b* 1969, — Joanna, *b* 1968, — Brigid, *b* 1971.

WIDOW LIVING OF LIFE BARON

Madeleine Hilda (*Baroness Devlin*), JP, da of Sir Bernard Oppenheimer, 1st Bt: *m* 1932, Baron Devlin, PC (Life Baron), who *d* 1992. *Residence* – West Wick House, Pewsey, Wilts.

DEVON, EARL OF (Courtenay) (Earl E 1553, Bt I 1644)

Where have I fallen, what have I done?

Charles Christopher Courtenay, 17th Earl, and 13th Baronet; *b* 13 July 1916; *s* 1935; *ed* Winchester, and RMC Sandhurst; is patron of four livings; is Capt Coldstream Guards (Regular Army Reserve): European War 1939-45 (wounded, despatches): *m* 1939, Sybil Venetia, da of late Capt John Vickris Taylor (formerly Welsh Guards), of North Aston Manor, Oxford, and formerly wife of 6th Earl of Cottenham, and has issue.

Arms – Quarterly: 1st and 4th or, three torteaux, *Courtenay*; 2nd and 3rd or, a lion rampant azure, *Redvers, Earl of Devon*. **Crests** – 1st, out of a ducal coronet or, a plume of seven ostrich feathers four and three argent; 2nd, a dolphin embowed proper. **Supporters** – Two boars argent, tusked, crined, and unguled or.
Seat – Powderham Castle, near Exeter.

SON LIVING

Hugh Rupert (*Lord Courtenay*) (Powderham Castle, Exeter), *b* 5 May 1942; *ed* Winchester, and Magdalene Coll, Camb: *m* 1967, Dianna Frances, el da of Jack Watherston, of Menslaws, Jedburgh, Roxburghshire, and has issue:—
    Son Living— *Hon* Charles Peregrine, *b* 14 Aug 1975.
    Daughters Living— *Hon* Rebecca Eildon, *b* 1969, — *Hon* Eleonora Venetia, *b* 1971, — *Hon* Camilla Mary, *b* 1974.

DAUGHTER LIVING

Lady Katherine Felicity, *b* 1940: *m* 1966, Antony Stephen Pope Watney, who *d* 1986, and has issue living, Michael Hugh Sanders, *b* 1966. *Residence* – 1 Playhatch Cottages, Playhatch, nr Reading, RG4 9QX.

SISTERS LIVING

Lady Mary Elizabeth, *b* 1910; is a State Registered Nurse. *Residence* – The Briary, Exton, Exeter.
Lady (Marguerite) Kathleen, *b* 1911: *m* 1933, Col Eugene St John Birnie, OBE, Indian Army (ret), who *d* 1976, and has issue living, Marguerite Susan, *b* 1934: *m* 1958, Jasper Meadows Clutterbuck, of Mottisfont House, nr Romsey, Hants, and has issue living, Hugh Meadows *b* 1959, Nichola Marguerite *b* 1961, — Angela Patricia Jane, *b* 1936: *m* 1956, Michael Edmond Joly de Lotbiniére, of Rougham House, Bury St Edmunds (B Hylton, 1990 Edn), and has issue living, Christopher David *b* 1957: *m* 1991, Victoria C., da of Graham Harvey Evers, of Domaine de la Rose, Opio, France AM, Giles Antony *b* 1959: *m* 1990, Veronica J., elder da of John Egerton Levett-Scrivener, of Sibton Abbey, Peasenhall, Suffolk, Tessa Jane *b* 1962: *m* 1984, Nigel N. V. Raywood. *Residence* – The Cottage, Longparish, Hants.
Lady Camilla Gabrielle, *b* 1913. *Residence* – The Briary, Exton, Exeter.
Lady Angela Leslie, *b* 1918: *m* 1947, Harold Cecil Moreton Horsley, MBE, Malayan Civil Ser (ret), who *d* 1969, and has issue living, Richard Geoffrey Courtenay (Elliotts Farmhouse, Adstone, Towcester, Northants NN12 8DY), *b* 1947: *m* 1983, Susan Philippa, only da of E. A. Trotman, of Lower Twinhoe Cottage, Midford, Bath, and has issue living, Moreton William Edward *b* 1985, Anna Gabrielle Susan *b* 1987, — William Frederick Moreton (Jaegerweg 1, D5300, Bonn 2, Germany), *b* 1949: *m* 1979, Noriko, elder da of Tetsuo Makuuchi, of 5-8-10 Ogikubo, Suginami-ku, Tokyo, Japan. *Residence* – Marwood House, Offwell, Honiton, Devon EX14 9RW.

PREDECESSORS – (1) *Sir* Hugh de Courtenay, Knt, 6th feudal Baron of Okehampton, summoned as a Baron to all the Parliaments of Edward II, and to the Parliaments of Edward III 1327-35; was in 1335 summoned as *Earl of Devonshire*; *d* 1340; *s* by his son (2) Hugh, 2nd Earl; *d* 1377; *s* by his grandson (3) Edward, 3rd Earl; Earl Marshal; *d* 1419; *s* by his son

(4) HUGH, 4th Earl; *d* 1422; *s* by his son (5) THOMAS, 5th Earl; a faithfull adherent to the "Red Rose"; *d* 1458; *s* by his son (6) THOMAS, 6th Earl, a strenuous upholder of the Lancastrian cause fell into the hands of the Yorkists at Towton Field, and was beheaded April 1462, his honours being attainted; *s* by his brother (7) HUGH; was restored to a part of his ancestral estates, but subsequently engaged in the Lancastrian quarrel, was attainted and beheaded 1466. (The greater part of the Courtenay estates having been conferred upon Humphry Stafford, Baron Stafford, of Southwicke, he was *cr Earl of Devon* 1469, and in the same year was beheaded as a traitor, when the earldom expired). Hugh (ante), was *s* by his brother (8) JOHN, 8th Earl, who was restored to his honours by the Parliament that replaced the crown upon the head of Henry VI; the subsequent defeat of the Earl of Warwick, at Barnet Field, 14 April 1471, again jeopardised his fortunes, and joining Margaret of Anjou he fell at Tewkesbury, 14 May, following, and his honours were attainted. The representation of the family then devolved upon (9) Sir EDWARD, Knt, grandson of Sir Hugh, next brother of 3rd Earl; participated in the victory of Bosworth and was *cr Earl of Devon* 1485, and obtained regrants of the greater part of the estates of Thomas, 6th Earl; *d* 1509; *s* by his son (10) Sir WILLIAM, *b* ca 1475: *m* 1495, Katherine, 6th da of King Edward IV; was attainted 1504 and doomed to incarceration during the reign of Henry VII; he was released by Henry VIII, but *d* before being formally restored to earldom; his son (11) HENRY, 2nd Earl (*cr* 1485), was restored in blood and honours, and *cr Marquess of Exeter* 1525; was subsequently committed to the Tower for conspiring to place Reginald Pole, Dean of Exeter, upon the throne, and was beheaded 9 Jan 1539, his titles being attainted and his estates annexed to the Duchy of Cornwall; *s* by his son (12) EDWARD; was committed to the Tower 1539 when twelve years of age, and remained there until 1553, when he was released by Queen Mary, and though restored in blood not any of the attainders were reversed; *cr Earl of Devon* 1553; was subsequently imprisoned in the Tower and in Fotheringay Castle for an alleged connection with Wyatt's rebellion, but was released on the marriage of the Queen with Philip of Spain; *d* unmarried at Padua 1556, when, in consequence of the limitations of the patent not being known, the honours became dormant, and remained so until 1831, when it was revived in favour of (13) WILLIAM, 3rd *Viscount Courtenay* (see note*infra), who became 9th Earl (of *cr* 1553); *d* unmarried 1835, when the viscountcy became extinct and his baronetcy and earldom devolved upon his cousin (14) WILLIAM, 10th Earl, son of the Right Rev Henry Reginald, Bishop of Exeter, who was son of Henry Reginald Courtenay, MP, 2nd son of 2nd Bt (see note*infra); *b* 1777: *m* 1st, 1804, Lady Harriet Leslie, da of Sir Lucas Pepys, Bt, and Jane Elizabeth, Countess of Rothes; 2ndly, 1849, Elizabeth Ruth, who *d* 1914, da of late Rev John Middleton Scott; *d* 1859; *s* by his son (15) WILLIAM REGINALD, PC, 11th Earl, *b* 1807; was MP for S Devon (C) 1842-48: *m* 1830, Lady Elizabeth Fortescue, who *d* 1867, da of 1st Earl Fortescue; *d* 1888; *s* by his son (16) EDWARD BALDWIN, 12th Earl, *b* 1836; MP for Exeter (C) 1864-68, and for Devonshire E 1868-70; *d* 1891; *s* by his uncle (17) Rev HENRY HUGH, 13th Earl, *b* 1811; R of Powderham: *m* 1835, Lady Anna Maria Leslie, who *d* 1897, da of late Henrietta Anne, Countess of Rothes; *d* 1904; *s* by his grandson (18) CHARLES PEPYS (son of late Henry Reginald, Lord Courtenay, el son of 13th Earl, by Lady Evelyn Pepys, da of 1st Earl of Cottenham), 14th Earl; *b* 1870; an Inspector in Board of Agriculture 1895-1904; *d* 1927; *s* by his brother (19) Rev HENRY HUGH, 15th Earl, *b* 1872; was R of Powderham 1904-27; *d* (Feb) 1935; *s* by his brother (20) Rev FREDERICK LESLIE, 16th Earl, *b* 1875; was R of Honiton: *m* 1907, Marguerite, who *d* 1950, da of late John Silva, of Itchen Abbas, Hants; *d* (June) 1935; *s* by his son (21) CHARLES CHRISTOPHER, 17th Earl and present peer.

*(1) Sir PHILIP Courtenay, Knt, 6th son of 2nd Earl of Devon of the original *cr*, Lord-Lieut of Ireland 1383-92; *s* by his son (2) RICHARD; Lord Bishop of Norwich; one of the Ambassadors sent by Henry V to the King of France to demand the crown of that kingdom; *d* 1415; *s* by his nephew (3) Sir PHILIP, Knt; *s* by his son (4) Sir WILLIAM, Knt; High Sheriff of Devon 1483; *d* 1485; *s* by his son (5) Sir WILLIAM, Knt; *d* 1512; *s* by his son (6) Sir WILLIAM, Knt; styled "The Great"; *d* 1535; *s* by his grandson (7) Sir WILLIAM, Knt, *de jure* 2nd Earl; killed at storming of St Quintin 1557; *s* by his son (8) Sir WILLIAM, Knt, *de jure* 3rd Earl; one of the undertakers to send over settlers for the better planting of Ireland; *d* 1630; *s* by his son (9) FRANCIS, *de jure* 4th Earl, *d* 1638; *s* by his son (10) WILLIAM, *de jure* 5th Earl; *cr* a *Baronet* 1644 (disdaining the title did not assume it, but was always styled "Sir" in commissions sent by the king); *d* 1702; *s* by his son (11) Sir WILLIAM, 2nd Bt *de jure* 6th Earl; MP for Devon; *d* 1736; *s* by his son (12) Sir WILLIAM, *de jure* 7th Earl; *cr Viscount Courtenay*, of Powderham Castle, co Devon (peerage of Great Britain, 1762); *d* 1762; *s* by his son (13) WILLIAM, 2nd Viscount, and *de jure* 8th Earl; *d* 1788; *s* by his son (14) WILLIAM, 3rd Viscount, who established his right to the Earldom of Devon (see ante).

DEVONPORT, VISCOUNT (Kearley) (Viscount UK 1917, Bt UK 1908)

TERENCE KEARLEY, 3rd Viscount, and 3rd Baronet; *b* 29 Aug 1944; *s* 1973; *ed* Aiglon Coll, Switzerland, and Selwyn Coll, Camb (MA); Dip Arch RIBA; BPhil (Newcastle); ALI; Landscape Architect, Architect-Developer, Farmer and Forester: *m* 1968 (*m diss* 1979), Elizabeth Rosemary, 2nd da of late John Gordon Hopton, Solicitor, of Chute Manor, Andover, and has issue.

Arms – Azure, in chief two mitres argent garnished or, and in base a square tower of the second. Crest – An ancient ship or, the mainsail azure charged with a sea lion gold. Supporters – On either side a sea lion argent, crined, finned, and tufted or, each gorged with a collar gules charged with three roses gold, and each supporting a spear erect proper.
Residence – Ray Demesne, Kirkwhelpington, Northumberland NE19 2RG. *Clubs* – Northern Counties (Newcastle), Beefsteak, RAC, Farmers, MCC and Royal Over-Seas League.

DAUGHTERS LIVING

Hon Velvet Jane, *b* 1975.
Hon Idonia Clare, *b* 1977.

SISTER LIVING

Hon Marilyn Whitson, *b* 1939.

WIDOW LIVING OF SECOND VISCOUNT

The way is made through strength

SHEILA ISABEL (*Viscountess Devonport*) (The Old Vicarage, Peasmarsh, Rye, E Sussex, TN31 6XB), el da of late Col Charles Hope-Murray, of Morishill, Beith, Ayrshire: *m* 1938, the 2nd Viscount, who *d* 1973.

COLLATERAL BRANCH LIVING

Issue of late Hon Mark Hudson Kearley, yr son of 1st Viscount; *b* 1895, *d* 1977: *m* 1928, Mabel Florence, who *d* 1967, da of late John Francis Dagley:—
CHESTER DAGLEY HUGH, *b* 29 April 1932: *m* 1974, Josefa Mesquida. *Residence* – S Patos 466, Denia, Alicante, Spain. —— Patrick Richard Hudson, *b* 1935: *m* 1962, Susanna Brigitta, da of Carl Erik Ringberg, of Stockholm, and has issue living, Selina Anna-Karin, *b* 1967, — Cecilia Laura Anthea, *b* 1974. *Residence* – 9 Chemin Tavarnay, 1218 Geneva, Switzerland. —— Anthea, *b* 1929: *m* 1959, Luigi Triossi, of 141 Via del Babuino, Rome, Italy, and has issue living, Amanda Consuelo Fiorenza, *b* 1963.

PREDECESSORS – (1) *Rt Hon* HUDSON EWBANKE Kearley, son of George Ewbanke Kearley, of Uxbridge; *b* 1856; Parl Sec to Board of Trade 1905-09, Chm of Roy Commn on Sugar Supply 1917, Food Controller 1916-17, and First Chm of Port of London Authority 1909-25; sat as MP for Devonport (*L*) July 1892 to Jan 1910; *cr* a *Baronet* 1908, PC 1909, and *Baron Devonport*, of Wittington, co Buckingham (peerage of United Kingdom) 1910, and *Viscount Devonport*, of Wittington, co Bucks (peerage of United Kingdom) 1917: *m* 1888, Selina, who *d* 1931, da of Edward Chester, of Blisworth, Northampton; *d* 1934; *s* by his el son (2) GERALD CHESTER, 2nd Viscount, *b* 1890: *m* 1938, Sheila Isabel, da of late Col Charles Hope Murray, of Morishill, Beith, Ayrshire; *d* 1973; *s* by his son (3) TERENCE, 3rd Viscount and present peer; also Baron Devonport.

DEVONSHIRE, DUKE OF (Cavendish) (Duke E 1694)

ANDREW ROBERT BUXTON CAVENDISH, MC, PC, 11th Duke; *b* 2 Jan 1920; *s* 1950; *ed* Eton, and Trin Coll, Camb; Hon LLD, Sheffield 1963; Vice-Lieut for Derbyshire 1957-87, and a KStJ; Parliamentary Under-Sec of State for Commonwealth Relations 1960-62, and Min of State, Commonwealth Relations Office 1962-64; Chancellor of Manchester Univ 1965-86; 1939-45 War as Capt Coldstream Guards in Italy (MC); PC 1964: *m* 1941, Hon Deborah Vivien Freeman-Mitford, da of 2nd Baron Redesdale, and has issue.

Arms – Sable, three bucks' heads cabossed argent. **Crest** – A serpent nowed proper. **Supporters** – Two bucks proper, each wreathed round the neck with a chaplet of roses, alternately argent and azure.
Seats – Chatsworth, Bakewell, Derbyshire; Bolton Abbey, Yorks; Lismore Castle, co Waterford. *Residence* – 4 Chesterfield St, W1.

Secure by caution

SON LIVING

PEREGRINE ANDREW MORNY (*Marquess of Hartington*) (Beamsley Hall, Skipton, N Yorks), *b* 27 April 1944; *ed* Eton, and Exeter Coll, Oxford; Sr Steward The Jockey Club: *m* 1967, Amanda Carmen, only da of late Cdr Edward Heywood-Lonsdale, RN, and has issue:—
SON LIVING — William (*Earl of Burlington*), *b* 6 June 1969.

DAUGHTERS LIVING—*Lady* Celina Imogen, *b* 1971, — *Lady* Jasmine Nancy, *b* 1973.

DAUGHTERS LIVING

Lady Emma, *b* 1943: *m* 1963, Hon Tobias William Tennant, of Shaws, Newcastleton, Roxburghshire (*see* B Glenconner).
Lady Sophia Louise Sydney, *b* 1957: *m* 1st, 1979 (*m diss* 1987), Anthony (Gurth) William Lindsay Murphy, elder son of Christopher Murphy; 2ndly, 1988, Alastair John Morrison (*see* B Margadale). *Residence* – The Quadrangle, Tisbury, Wilts.

SISTERS LIVING

Lady Elizabeth Georgiana Alice, LVO, *b* 1926; is a JP; appointed an Extra Lady-in-Waiting to HRH The Princess Margaret 1960; LVO 1976. *Residences* – 19 Radnor Walk, SW3; Moor View, Edensor, Bakewell, Derbyshire.
Lady Anne Evelyn Beatrice, *b* 1927: *m* 1949, Michael Lambert Tree, of 29 Radnor Walk, SW3, and has two adopted das, Isabella Elizabeth Nancy, *b* 1964: *m* 1993, Charles Raymond Burrell, eldest son of Sir (John) Raymond Burrell, 9th Bt, — Esther Anne Mary, *b* 1966: *m* 1992, James Michael Beale Cayzer-Colvin (*see* B Cayzer).

COLLATERAL BRANCHES LIVING

Grandchildren of late Col Rt Hon Lord Richard Frederick Cavendish, CB, CMG (infra):—
Issue of late Capt Richard Edward Osborne Cavendish, JP, DL, *b* 1917, *d* 1972: *m* 1937, Pamela (The Dower House, Holker Hall, Cark-in-Cartmel, Cumbria), da of late Hugh Lloyd Thomas, CMG, CVO (*see* B Bellew, 1976 Edn):—
(Richard) Hugh, *b* 1941; *cr* Baron Cavendish of Furness (Life Baron) 1990 (see that title). —— Edward Osborne (Butley Priory, nr Woodbridge, Suffolk IP12 3NR), *b* 1955: *m* 1st, 1977 (*m diss* 1980), Kirsten, eldest da of Dr Ronald T. St Blaize-Molony, of Fordwich, Kent; 2ndly, 1983, (Anna) Frances, yr da of Spencer Shelley, of Mayhill Lodge, Mayhill, Glos (*see* Shelley, Bt, colls), and has issue living (by 2nd *m*), Elizabeth Angelica, *b* 1985, — Georgiana Rose, *b* 1988. —— Georgiana Elizabeth, *b* 1939: *m* 1968, Capt Andrew Henry Clowes, late Scots Gds, of 52 Bowerdean St, SW6, and has issue (*see* M Lothian, colls). —— Harriet Moyra Aline, *b* 1944: *m* 1972, Capt Anthony Peter Coote Sykes (*see* D Wellington, colls, 1955 Edn), late R Scots Greys, of 27 Fawcett St, SW10, and has issue living, Eyre William, *b* 1975, — Nina Aline, *b* 1973, — Evelyn Harriet, *b* 1980. —— Susan Anne CREWE, *b* 1949; Social Ed *Harpers & Queen* 1991-92, Ed *House & Garden* since 1993: *m* 1st, 1970 (*m diss* 1983), Quentin Hugh Crewe (*see* M Crewe, ext, 1948 Edn); 2ndly, 1984, (Christopher) Nigel John Ryan, CBE, eldest son of late Brig Charles Edmond Ryan, MC, of Uckfield, Sussex, and has issue living (by 1st *m*), Nathaniel Richard, *b* 1971, — Charity *b* 1972.

Granddaughters of late Rt Hon Lord Edward Cavendish, MP, 3rd son of 7th Duke:—
Issue of late Col Rt Hon Lord Richard Frederick Cavendish, CB, CMG, *b* 1871 (raised to rank of a Duke's son 1908), *d* 1946: *m* 1895, Lady Moyra de Vere Beauclerk, who *d* 1942, da of 10th Duke of St Albans:—

Mary Katherine (*Mary, Countess of Crawford and Balcarres*), *b* 1903: *m* 1925, 28th Earl of Crawford and 11th Earl of Balcarres, who *d* 1975. *Residence* – Balcarres, Colinburgh, Fife. —— Sybil, *b* 1915: *m* 1941, Rev Lawrence Gregson Fell Dykes, who *d* 1993, and has issue living, Michael, *b* 1942, — Rose, *b* 1946, — Catherine Mary, *b* 1948. *Residence* – The Garden House, Holker Hall, Cark-in-Cartmel, Cumbria.

Grandchildren of late Maj Cecil Charles Cavendish, yst son of Lt-Col William Henry Frederick Cavendish, el son of Gen Hon Henry Frederick Compton Cavendish, MP (infra):—
Issue of late Maj Frederick George Cavendish, DSO, MC, *b* 1891, *d* 1936: *m* 1919, Milla Jean, who *d* 1976, da of late W. St Clair Grant, of Bhagalpur, Bengal:—
Anne, *b* 1920. —— Jean Caroline, *b* 1932: *ed* Lady Margaret Hall, Oxford: *m* 1st, 1954 (*m diss* 1959), Anthony Richard Champion de Crespigny; 2ndly, 1974, George Charles Denis Lassalle, of 117 Irinis, Limassol, Cyprus, and has issue living (by 1st *m*), Camilla Georgiana, *b* 1955.
Issue of late Brig Ronald Valentine Cecil Cavendish, OBE, MC, *b* 1896, *ka* in Burma 1943: *m* 1923, Violet Helen, who *d* 1974, el da of late Arthur Sackville Boucher, of Sharpcliffe Hall, Staffordshire:—
Peter Boucher, CB, OBE (The Rock Cottage, Middleton, Bakewell, Derbys) *b* 1925; *ed* Winchester; Maj-Gen late 14th/20th King's Hus; Chm NATO Mil Agency for Standardisation; OBE (Mil) 1969; CB (Mil) 1981; MBIM: *m* 1952, Marion Loudon, da of late Robert Alfred Constantine, TD, JP, of Tanton Grange, Stokesley, Yorks, and has issue living, (Ronald) Simon Constantine (191 Annie St, New Farm, Brisbane, Qld 4005, Australia); *b* 1954; *ed* Wellington Coll: *m* 1990, Rosemary Alexandra, yr da of P. G. F. Lancaster, of Aston Flamville, Leics, and has issue living, Nicholas Peter Lancaster *b* 1993, — Mark Francis, *b* 1955; *ed* Wellington Coll, — Rupert William, *b* 1962: *m* 1986, Lesley, el da of late J.K. Buckle, of Harlow, Essex, and has issue living, Sarah Frances *b* 1991. —— †Robin Francis, MBE, *b* 1930; *ed* Winchester; is late Capt King's Roy Rifle Corps; MBE (Civil) 1975: *m* 1957, Diana Mary, yr da of late Lt-Col Latham Valentine Stewart Blacker, OBE (E Peel), and *d* 1994, leaving issue, Jonathan Stewart, *b* 1959: *ed* Eton, and Oxford Univ: *m* 1992, Lesley A., da of Eric Rogers. *Residence* – Furlongs, Drayton St Leonard, Oxford.
Issue of the late (Charles) Vernon Balfour Cavendish, *b* 1902; *d* 1981: *m* 1st, 1938 (*m diss* 1950), Nancy Cranswick Neal, who *d* 1986, da of Ernest William Redstone; 2ndly, 1963, Eve, who *d* 1986, widow of Athelston Douglas Dempster Bonnor:—
(By 1st *m*) Rosalind, *b* 1945: *m* 1971, Alan Hugh Davidson, of 16A Clarendon Rd, Colliers Wood, SW19 2DU.

Grandchildren of late Capt Godfrey Lionel John Cavendish, 2nd (but eldest surv) son of late Reginald Richard Frederick Cavendish, eldest son of late Francis William Henry Cavendish (infra):—
Issue of late Capt Godfrey Herbert Richard Cavendish, *b* 1912, *d* 1958: *m* 1950, Angela Margaret Jervis (9 Oakhill Place, SW15 2QN), da of late Lt-Col William Gerald Officer, late Duke of Wellington's Regt, of 37 Lowndes St, SW1:—
Diana Grace Angela, *b* 1954: *m* 1975, (Frederick) John Reeves, of Kilmichael House, Kilmichael Glassary, by Lochgilphead, Argyll PA31 8QA, and has issue living, Henry Frederick Godfrey, *b* 1981, — Georgina Caroline Angela, *b* 1984, — Olivia Clare Lucy, *b* 1989. —— Caroline Elizabeth Clare (*Hon Mrs Philip Remnant*), *b* 1956: *m* 1977, Hon Philip John Remnant, of 36 Stevenage Rd, SW6 6ET, el son of 3rd Baron Remnant, and has issue (*see* B Remnant).
Issue of late (Hubert) Gordon Compton Cavendish, *b* 1913, *d* 1993: *m* 1942, Beaujolois Inez (Bosvathick, Constantine, Falmouth, Cornwall TR11 5RD), da of late Capt Philip George Wodehouse, DSO, RN (*see* E Kimberley, colls):—
Richard Gordon John (10 Basil Close, Earley, Reading, Berks), *b* 1949; *ed* Sherborne; Capt British Airways: *m* 1st, 1973 (*m diss* 1980), Jill Dare, da of Frank D. Baker, of Sunbury on Thames; 2ndly, 1981, Mrs Susan Denton, da of John Glyndwr Thomas, and has issue living (by 1st *m*), Charles William Gordon, *b* 1975, — Susanna Lucy, *b* 1974, — (by 2nd *m*) Theresa Louise, *b* 1983. —— (Beaujolois) Katharine, *b* 1947: *m* 1978, Stephen Charles Smyth-Tyrrell, of Bosvathick, Constantine, Falmouth, Cornwall TR11 5RD, and has issue living, Philip, *b* 1981, — Eleanor, *b* 1979, — Josephine, *b* 1983.

Grandson of late Ernest Lionel Francis Cavendish, 3rd son of late Francis William Henry Cavendish, 2nd son of Gen Hon Henry Frederick Compton Cavendish, MP, 3rd son of 1st Earl of Burlington, who was uncle of 7th Duke:—
Issue of late Maj Alwyn Lionel Compton Cavendish, *b* 1890, *d* 1928: *m* 1917, Muriel Cecil Harriotte, who *d* 1975, having *m* 3rdly, 1946, 2nd Baron Forteviot, who *d* 1947, da of late Lt-Col Sir Charles Henry Brabazon Heaton-Ellis, CBE, of Wyddiall Hall, Herts, and widow of Richard Charles Graves-Sawle, Lt Coldm Gds (Graves-Sawle, Bt (ext)):—
Charles Francis Alwyn Compton (Cider Cottage, Hemyock, Cullompton, Devon), *b* 1919; *ed* Eton, and at Fettes; is Lieut King's Own Scottish Borderers; formerly 2nd Lt 8th Hussars and Intelligence Corps; 1939-45 War in Middle East and NW Europe (wounded): *m* 1st, 1943 (*m diss* 1946), Margaret Savage (Section Officer, WAAF), who *d* 1961, da of Capt Philip Clayton Alcock, DL, JP, late Gloucester Regt, of Overton Lodge, Ludlow, Salop; 2ndly, 1947, Esther Marion, only da of Col Chichester de Windt Crookshank, of Johnstounburn, Humbie, East Lothian, and has issue living, (by 2nd *m*) William Alwyn Charles Chichester (Pippin Cottage, 3 Gastons Rd, Malmesbury, Wilts), *b* 1956: *m* 1985, Margaret Josephine, da of Joseph Benedict MacDonald, of Antigonish, Nova Scotia, and has issue living, Myles Joseph Charles *b* 1991, Monica Josephine Patricia *b* 1988, — Mark Andrew Lionel Compton, *b* 1958: *m* 1988, Sarah Jane, elder da of Richard Formby, of Chartley Hall, Stafford, and has issue living, George Andrew Francis Stuart *b* 1989, Katharine Mary Louise *b* 1991. *Club* – Turf.

Grandson of late William Henry Alexander George Delmar Cavendish (infra):—
Issue of the late Charles Alfred William Delmar Cavendish, *b* 1878, *d* 1939: *m* 1st, 1914 (*m diss* 1926), Ruth Madeline, yst da of late Henry William Smith, of Sydney, NSW; 2ndly, 1926, Marguerite Florence, who *d* 1943, eldest da of Henri Moreau, of Paris, and Sydney, NSW:—
(By 1st *m*) Richard Blake Delmar, *b* 1916.

Grandson of late William Henry George Cavendish (infra):—
Issue of the late Capt Edwin Pearson Delmar Cavendish, *b* 1908, *d* 1970: *m* 1943, Daphne Joan (Banchory Cottage, Hinton St George, Som), da of the late Maj William John Van de Weyer, MVO (V Powerscourt), and widow of Sqdn Ldr Charles Richard John Pink, RAF:—
Adrian Delmar (The Dairy House, 611 Merrimac Dr, Lexington, Kentucky, USA), *b* 1947; late LG: *m* 1982, Louise Russell, da of Thomas Allison Ray, Snr, of Ramona, California, USA, and has issue living, John Spencer, *b* 1987.

Grandson of late William Henry Alexander George Delmar Cavendish, only child of Capt George Henry Cavendish, 5th son of Gen Hon Henry Frederick Compton Cavendish, MP (ante):—
Issue of late William Henry George Cavendish, *b* 1886, *d* 1964: *m* 1907, Beatrice, who *d* 1914, da of Edwin P. Pearson, or Toronto:—
William Delmar (Via Gramsci 36, 00197 Rome; Public Schools Club), *b* 1911; *ed* Bedford Sch; 1939-45 War, as Capt Middx Regt in Middle East, and NW Europe (twice wounded); Pres, John Cabot Internat Coll, Rome: *m* 1943, Luisa, da of Antonio Fusco, of Catania, Sicily, and has issue living, William Anthony (Via Privata Maria Teresa 8, Milan); *d* 1952; *ed* San Leone Magno Sch, and Columbia Univ, New York; Kt of Order of SS Mauritius and Lazarus: *m* 1979, Liliana Delabarbara, of New York, and has issue living, Edward William Henry Delmar *b* 1987, Georgiana Beatrice *b* 1985, — Jessica Luisa, *b* 1946.

Descendants of late Hon Charles Compton Cavendish (4th son of 1st Earl of Burlington), who was *cr Baron Chesham* 1858 (see that title).

PREDECESSORS – **(1)** *Sir* WILLIAM Cavendish, KB; *cr Baron Cavendish*, of Hardwicke (peerage of England) 1605, and *Earl of Devonshire* (peerage of England) 1618; *d* 1625; *s* by his son **(2)** WILLIAM, 2nd Earl; *d* 1628; *s* by his son **(3)** WILLIAM, 3rd Earl; *d* 1684; *s* by his son **(4)** WILLIAM, KG, PC, 4th Earl; MP for co Derby, Lord-Lieut of Derbyshire and Lord Steward of the Household; *cr Marquess of Hartington*, and *Duke of Devonshire* (peerage of England) 1694; *d* 1707; *s* by his son **(5)** WILLIAM, KG, 2nd Duke; *s* by his son **(6)** WILLIAM, KG, 3rd Duke; Lord Steward of the Household 1729, Lord-Lieut of Ireland 1737-44; *d* 1755; *s* by his son **(7)** WILLIAM, KG, 4th Duke; summoned to House of Lords in his father's Barony of Cavendish 1751; Lord-Lieut of Ireland 1755, First Lord of the Treasury 1756-7, Master of the Horse, Lord Chamberlain 1757, &c: *m* Charlotte Elizabeth, *Baroness Clifford*, da of Richard, 4th Earl of Cork, whose claim to the Barony of Clifford, of Lanesborough (peerage of England, *cr* 1628), had been allowed; his 3rd son, George Augustus Henry, was *cr Earl of Burlington* and *Baron Cavendish*, of Keighley (peerage of United Kingdom) 1831; *d* 1764; *s* by his el son **(8)** WILLIAM, KG, 5th Duke, who in 1754 had *s* his mother as Baron Clifford; *d* 1811; *s* by his son **(9)** WILLIAM SPENCER, KG, PC, 6th Duke, Lord-Lieut of co Derby *d* unmarried 1858, when the Barony of Clifford became abeyant between his two sisters, and the other honours devolved upon **(10)** WILLIAM, KG, 7th Duke, who had in 1834 *s* his grandfather as 2nd Earl of Burlington (el son of the Hon William Cavendish, MP, el son of 1st Earl of Burlington (ante), by Louisa, el da of 1st Baron Lismore), *b* 1808; Chancellor of London Univ 1836-56, and of Camb Univ 1862-91, and Lord-Lieut of Lancashire 1855-8, and of Derbyshire 1858-91; MP for Camb Univ (*L*) 1829-31, for Molton 1831, and for N Derbyshire 1831-4: *m* 1829, Lady Blanche Georgiana Howard, who *d* 1840, da of 6th Earl of Carlisle, KG; *d* 1891; *s* by his el son **(11)** SPENCER COMPTON, KG, GCVO, PC, DCL, LLD, 8th Duke, *b* 1833; attached to Earl Granville's Special Embassy to Russia 1856, and went to St Petersburg to attend the Coronation of Alexander II 1857; a Lord of the Admiralty 1863, Under-Sec for War 1863-6, Sec of State for War 1866, Postmaster-Gen 1868-70, Ch Sec for Ireland 1870-74, Lord Rector of Glasgow Univ 1877-80, Sec of State for India 1880-82 and for War 1882-5, Pres of Board of Education 1900-1902, and Lord Pres of the Council and Pres of Council of National Defence 1895-1903; Lord-Lieut of Derbyshire and High Steward of Derby; MP for N Lancashire 1857-68, for New Radnor (*L*) 1869-80, for Lancashire, NE 1880-85, and for Rossendale Div of NE Lancashire 1885-91 (LU): *m* 1892, Louise Frederica Augusta, who *d* 1911, da of the late Charles, Count von Alten, of Hanover, and widow of 7th Duke of Manchester, *d* 1908; *s* by his nephew **(12)** VICTOR CHRISTIAN WILLIAM, KG, GCMG, GCVO, TD, PC (el son of late Lord Edward Cavendish, MP, 3rd son of the 7th Duke), 9th Duke; *b* 1868; was Treasurer of HM's Household 1900-1903, Financial Sec to the Treasury 1903-5, a Civil Lord of the Admiralty 1915, Gov-Gen and Com-in-Ch, Dominion of Canada 1916-21, Sec of State for the Colonies 1922-4, and Chm of Executive Council of British Empire Exhibition 1924 and 1925; sat as MP for Derbyshire, W Div (LU) 1891-1908; bore Queen Consort's Crown at Coronation of King George V: *m* 1892, Lady Evelyn Emily Mary Fitzmaurice, GCVO, who *d* 1960, da of 5th Marquess of Lansdowne; *d* 1938; *s* by his el son **(13)** EDWARD WILLIAM SPENCER, KG, MBE, TD, 10th Duke; *b* 1895; Train Bearer at Coronation of King George V 1911; was Parliamentary Under-Sec of State for Dominion Affairs 1936-40, for India and Burma 1940-42, and for the Colonies 1942-45; sat as MP for W Div of Derbyshire (*U*) 1923-38: *m* 1917, Lady Mary Alice Gascoyne-Cecil, GCVO, CBE, who *d* 1988, da of 4th Marquess of Salisbury; *d* 1950; *s* by his only surviving son **(14)** ANDREW ROBERT BUXTON, 11th Duke and present peer; also Marquess of Hartington, Earl of Devonshire, Earl of Burlington, Baron Cavendish of Hardwicke, and Baron Cavendish of Keighley.

DIAMOND, BARON (Diamond) (Life Baron 1970)

JOHN DIAMOND, PC, son of late Rev Solomon Diamond, of Leeds; *b* 30 April 1907; *ed* Leeds Gram Sch; LLD (hc); FCA; PPS to Min of Works 1947, and Chm of Finance Cttee, Gen Nursing Council 1947-53; Hon Treas of Fabian Soc 1950-64, Dir Sadler's Wells Trust 1957-64; Hon Treas Labour Cttee for Europe 1961-64; Ch Sec to Treasury (and Member of Cabinet 1968-70) 1964-70; Dep Chm of Cttees, House of Lords 1974; Chm Roy Commn on Distribution of Income and Wealth 1974-79 and of Industry and Parliament Trust 1976-81; MP for Blackley, Manchester (*Lab*) 1945-51, and for Gloucester 1957-70; *cr* PC 1965, and *Baron Diamond* in City of Gloucester (Life Baron) 1970: *m* 1st, 1932 (*m diss* 1947)—; 2ndly, 1948, Julie —, and has issue by 1st and 2nd *m*.

Residence – Aynhoe, Doggetts Wood Lane, Chalford-St-Giles, Bucks HP8 4TH.

SONS LIVING *(By 1st marriage)*

Hon Derek, *b* 1933.
Hon Martin, *b* 1935.

DAUGHTERS LIVING *(By 1st marriage)*

Hon Ruth (3 Hillbrow Close, Wood Street Village, Guildford, Surrey, GU3 3DF), *b* 1937.

(By 2nd marriage)

Hon Joan, *b* 1949.

DICKINSON, BARON (Dickinson) (Baron UK 1930)

RICHARD CLAVERING HYETT DICKINSON, 2nd Baron; *b* 2 March 1926; *s* 1943; *ed* Eton, and Trin Coll, Oxford; late Capt Coldstream Guards: *m* 1st, 1957 (*m diss* 19—), (Margaret) Ann, el da of late Brigadier Gilbert Reader McMeekan, CBE, DSO; 2ndly, 1980, Mrs Rita Doreen Moir, and has issue by 1st *m*.

𝔄rms – Or, a bend cottised between two lions passant gules. 𝔠rest – Issuant from clouds a dexter cubit arm erect the hand holding an olive branch fructed all proper. 𝔖upporters – *Dexter*, a falcon proper, collared and lined or; *sinister*, a dove holding in the beak an olive branch fructed both proper.
Residence – Painswick House, Stroud, Gloucestershire.

SONS LIVING (By 1st marriage)

Hon MARTIN HYETT, *b* 30 Jan 1961.
Hon Andrew, *b* 1963.

BROTHERS LIVING (Raised to the rank of a Baron's sons 1944)

Hon Peter Malcolm de Brissac, *b* 1927; *ed* Eton, and at King's Coll, Camb: *m* 1st, 1953, Mary Rose, who *d* 1988, el da of late Vice-Adm Sir Geoffrey Barnard, KCB, CBE, DSO; 2ndly, 1992, Jennifer Carolyn Robin McKinley, of Blue Hill, Maine, USA, and has issue living (by 1st *m*), John Geoffrey Hyett, *b* 1962: *m* 1992, Philippa Ann, da of Michael Thomson, and has issue living, Rosemary Clare *b* 1994, — James Christopher Meade, *b* 1963: *m* 1988, Sarah Ann, da of John Reid, and has issue living, Samuel George Lambourne *b* 1992, Andrew Francis Southey *b* 1994, — Philippa Lucy Ann, *b* 1955: *m* 1983, Stephen West, son of Reginald West, and has issue living, Nicholas Oliver *b* 1988, — Polly, *b* 1956; assumed the name of Polly in lieu of her baptismal names of Dorothy Louise; has issue by former *m*, David ADELMAN *b* 1988. *Residence* – Bramdean Lodge, nr Alresford, Hants.
Very Rev Hon Hugh Geoffrey (The Deanery, 7 The Close, Salisbury, Wilts SP1 2EF), *b* 1929; *ed* Westminster Sch, and Trin and Cuddesdon Colls, Oxford; Chap, Trin Coll, Camb 1958-63, and Winchester Coll 1963-69, Bishop's Adviser for Adult Education Coventry Diocese 1969-77, V of St Michael's, St Albans 1977-86, since when Dean of Salisbury: *m* 1963, Jean Marjorie, only da of Arthur Storey, of 25 Woodbourne Av, Leeds, 17, and has issue living, Benjamin Mark, *b* 1966, — Teresa, *b* 1964.
Hon David Christopher (Nanneys Bridge, Church Minshull, Nantwich, Ches), *b* 1935; *ed* Eton and Trin Coll, Oxford: *m* 1970, Caroline Mary, da of late Arthur Denton Toosey, and formerly wife of late Peter Yeoward.

MOTHER LIVING

May Southey, da of Charles Lovemore, of Melsetter, Cape Province, S Africa; is a JP: *m* 1924, Hon Richard Sebastian Willoughby Dickinson, DSO, who *d* 1935, only son of 1st Baron. *Residence* – The Poultry Court, Painswick, Gloucestershire.

PREDECESSOR – **(1)** *Rt Hon* WILLOUGHBY HYETT Dickinson, KBE, only son of late Sebastian Stewart Dickinson (MP for Stroud), of Brown's Hill, Stroud; *b* 1859; Chm of London County Council 1900; sat as MP for N Div of St Pancras (*L*) 1906-18; *cr Baron Dickinson*, of Painswick, co Gloucester (peerage of United Kingdom) 1930: *m* 1891, Minnie Elizabeth, who *d* 1967, da of late Gen Sir Richard John Meade, KCSI, CIE; *d* 1943; *s* by his grandson **(2)** RICHARD CLAVERING HYETT (el son of late Hon Richard Sebastian Willoughby Dickinson, DSO, only son of 1st Baron), 2nd Baron and present peer.

DIGBY, BARON (Digby) (Baron I 1620, and GB 1765)

From God not Fortune

EDWARD HENRY KENELM DIGBY, 12th Baron, *b* 24 July 1924; *s* 1964; *ed* Eton, and Trin Coll, Oxford; Hon Fellow of Roy Agric Soc of the Commonwealth 1977; Capt late Coldm Gds; Hon Col 4th Bn Devonshire and Dorset Regt; Lord Lieut Dorset 1984; JP 1960; Pres Wessex Branch Inst of Directors, and Council of St John, Dorset; Patron Dorset Red Cross; Pres Royal Bath and West Soc 1976; Dep Chm SW Economic Planning Council 1972-79; Vice-Chm Dorset County Council 1974-81; Capt Lords and Commons Ski Club 1982-85; Dir Beazer plc, Gifford-Hill Inc, and Paccar (UK) Ltd; ADC to C-in-C Far East Forces 1950-51, and to C-in-C, BAOR 1951-52; 1939-45 War; Malaya 1948-50; KStJ 1985: *m* 1952, Dione Marian, DBE, DL Dorset, da of Rear-Adm Robert St Vincent Sherbrooke, VC, CB, DSO, and has issue.

Arms – Azure, a fleur-de-lis argent. **Crest** – An ostrich with a horse-shoe in its beak, all proper. **Supporters** – Two monkeys proper, environed round the loins and lined or.
Residence – Minterne, Dorchester, Dorset DT2 7AU. *Club* – Pratt's.

SONS LIVING

Hon HENRY NOEL KENELM, *b* 6 Jan 1954; *ed* Eton; ACA; Dir Jardine Fleming Investment Management Ltd: *m* 1980, Susan E., el da of Peter Watts, of 6 Albert Terr Mews, NW1, and has issue living, Edward St Vincent Kenelm, *b* 5 Sept 1985, — Alexandra Jane Kira, *b* 1987.
Hon Rupert Simon, *b* 1956; *ed* Eton, and Southampton Univ: *m* 1986, Charlotte Fleury, yr da of late Robert Hirst, of Durford Mill, nr Petersfield, and has issue living, Arabella Dione, *b* 1989, — Olivia, *b* 1991. *Residence* – Rookwood Farmhouse, Stockcross, nr Newbury, Berks RG16 8JX.

DAUGHTER LIVING

Hon Zara Jane (82 Horder Road, SW6 5EE), *b* 1958; dress designer: *m* 1993, as his 2nd wife, James Edward Caulfeild Percy (*see* D Northumberland, colls).

SISTERS LIVING

Hon Pamela Beryl, *b* 1920; US Amb to Paris since 1993: *m* 1st, 1939 (*m diss* 1946), Maj Hon Randolph Frederick Edward Spencer Churchill, MBE (*see* D Marlborough, colls), who *d* 1968; 2ndly, 1960, Leland Hayward, agent and theatrical prod, who *d* 1971; 3rdly, 1971, (William) Averell Harriman, who *d* 1986. *Residences* – American Embassy, 2 Avenue Gabriel, 75382 Paris; Willow Oaks, Middleburg, Virginia 22317, USA.
Hon Constance Sheila, *b* 1921; in ATS 1939-40, and with British Security Co-ordination 1943-45, *m* 1945, Charles Arthur Moore, who *d* 1989. *Residences* – Bearforest, Mallow, co Cork; 5310 Chemin de Vie, Atlanta, Georgia 30342, USA.
Hon Jaquetta Mary Theresa, *b* 1928; a Member of Mid-Sussex Hosp Cttee 1960-68, and of Dorset Area Health Authority 1974-81; Chm, Hamilton Lodge Sch for Deaf Children, Brighton 1962-80: *m* 1950, David Pelham James, MBE, DSC, MP, who *d* 1986, having assumed the addl surname of Guthrie before his patronymic 1979, el son of Wing-Com Sir Archibald William Henry James, KBE, MC, and has issue living, Peter Edward, *b* 1951; *ed* Downside, — Michael David Ashworth, *b* 1955; *ed* Downside, — Christopher Leslie Donan (Torosay Castle, Isle of Mull, Argyllshire PA65 6AY), *b* 1957; *ed* Downside, and Edinburgh Univ, — Kenelm Henry Thomas, *b* 1962; *ed* Downside, — Patricia Bridget Edwina, *b* 1952; *ed* Mayfield, and York Univ: *m* 1989, Ian Maxwell, of 5 St Marks Place, Edinburgh, and has issue living, Rowan *b* 1992, Anna *b* 1989, — Diana Mary GUTHRIE JAMES (104 High St, Grantown on Spey, Morayshire), *b* 1953: has resumed her maiden name: *m* 1972 (*m diss* 1980), Alan Fry, and has issue living, Daniel James *b* 1972, Adam James *b* 1975, Susannah James *b* 1974; and has further issue, Mairina James *b* 1991. *Residence* – Torosay Castle, Isle of Mull, Argyllshire PA65 6AY.

COLLATERAL BRANCHES LIVING

Granddaughters of late Hon Robert Henry Digby (*infra*):—
Issue of late Henry Berkeley Digby, *b* 1933, *d* 1992: *m* 1st, 1960 (*m diss* 1983), Jacqueline Winifred, elder da of Charles A. Hussey, of Barking, Essex; 2ndly, 1983, Mrs Rosalie McLaren (5 Carlton House Terrace, W1; San Pedro de Alcantara, Prov Malaga, Spain), eldest da of Maj Richard Atkinson-Turner, of Worlington, Suffolk, and formerly wife of Andrew McLaren, of Coughton, Warwicks:—
(By 1st *m*) Jane Diana, *b* 1962: *m* 1987, Christoph D. Auer, eldest son of Ernst Auer, of Grunwald, Munich, Germany, and has issue living, Charles Felix Ernst, *b* 1991. —— (Charlotte) Sophia, *b* 1964.
Issue of late Hon Robert Henry Digby, 2nd son of 10th Baron, *b* 1903; *d* 1959: *m* 1928, Diana Mary, who *d* 1969, da of Sir Berkeley Digby George Sheffield, 6th Bt:—
Caroline Theresa, *b* 1943: *m* 1963, Charles Dermot Fitzroy Musker (*see* V Daventry, 1985 Edn), and has issue living, Dermot Henry, *b* 1964, — Rupert Anthony, *b* 1975, — Emily Mary, *b* 1972, — Chloé Diana Leopoldine, *b* 1979. *Residence* – Bridgham Manor Farm, Norwich, Norfolk.

Grandson of late Sir Kenelm Edward Digby, GCB, KC, el son of late Rev Hon Kenelm Henry Digby (*infra*):—
Issue of late Com Edward Aylmer Digby, KC, *b* 1883, *d* 1935: *m* 1911, Winifred Digby, who *d* 1967, da of Arthur George Watson, DCL, JP:—
Kenelm Hubert (3 Mount St, Wellington, NZ), *b* 1912: *m* 1946, Mutal Agnes Helen, only da of Bertram E. Fielder, of Glebe Farm, Sherfield English, Romsey, and has issue living, Noel Kenelm, *b* 1946, — Geoffrey Aylmer, *b* 1957, — Rosalind Clare, *b* 1948.

Grandson of late Rev Hon Kenelm Henry Digby, brother of 9th Baron:—
Issue of late Algernon Digby, *b* 1849, *d* 1936: *m* 1888, Richenda Catherine, who *d* 1940, da of late Capt Philip Hamond, 34th Regt:—
Thomas Hankinson, *b* 1892; *ed* Marlborough; European War 1914-19 as Capt (despatches); late Live Stock Officer for E Suffolk, Min of Agriculture and Fisheries: *m* (Jan) 1938, Diana Broughton, only da of Capt Guy Knight, and has issue living, Simon Kenelm (12 Busby House, Aldrington Rd, SW16 1TZ), *b* (Dec) 1938: *m* 1st, 1961 (*m diss* 1965), Ann Stallard, da of

Rev Geoffrey Walton; 2ndly, 1965 (*m diss* 1978), Sylvia Josephine, da of John Cheers, and has issue living (by 2nd *m*), Oliver Francis *b* 1966, Roland Anthony *b* 1969, — Patrick Timothy (Bryngwyn, Llandissilio, Clunderwen, Dyfed SA66 7UR), *b* 1941: *m* 1973, Lyneth Anne, da of David Clee, and has issue living, Huw Timothy *b* 1975, Catrin Elizabeth *b* 1978, — Robin Paul (22 Westfield, Ashtead, Surrey), *b* 1944: *m* 1966, Marja Birgitta, da of Helmer Hägglöf, of Njurunda, Sweden, and has issue living, Christina Ruth *b* 1967, Joanna Isabel *b* 1971. *Residence* – Hill Drop Cottage, Wiveton, nr Holt, Norfolk.

PREDECESSORS – (**1**) ROBERT Digby, Gov of King's Co; *cr Baron Digby*, of Geashill, King's Co (peerage of Ireland) 1620; *d* 1642; *s* by his son (**2**) KILDARE, 2nd Baron; *s* by his son (**3**) ROBERT, 3rd Baron; *s* by his brother (**4**) SIMON, 4th Baron; *d* 1686; *s* by his brother (**5**) WILLIAM, 5th Baron; *d* 1752; *s* by his grandson (**6**) EDWARD, 6th Baron; *d* unmarried 1757; *s* by his brother (**7**) HENRY, 7th Baron; *cr Baron Digby*, of Sherborne (peerage of Great Britain) 1765, with remainder to the issue male of his father, and *Viscount Coleshill* and *Earl Digby* (peerage of Great Britain) 1790; *d* 1793; *s* by his son (**8**) EDWARD, 2nd Earl; Lord-Lieut of Dorset; *d* unmarried 1856, when the viscountcy and earldom became extinct, and the baronies devolved upon his kinsman (**9**) EDWARD ST VINCENT, 9th Baron, *b* 1809: *m* 1837, Lady Theresa Anne Maria Fox-Srangways, who *d* 1874, el da of 3rd Earl of Ilchester; *d* 1889; *s* by his el son (**10**) EDWARD HENRY TRAFALGAR, 10th Baron, *b* 1846; sat as MP for Dorsetshire (C) 1876-85; *m* 1893, Emily Beryl Sissy, who *d* 1928, da of Hon Albert Hood; *d* 1920; *s* by his el son (**11**) EDWARD KENELM, KG, DSO, MC, TD, 11th Baron, *b* 1894; Col late Coldstream Guards, Lord-Lieut of Dorset 1952-64, and Chm of Dorset Co Council 1955-64: *m* 1919, Hon Constance Pamela Alice Bruce, OBE, JP, who *d* 1978, da of 2nd Baron Aberdare; *d* 1964; *s* by his only son (**11**) EDWARD HENRY KENELM, 12th Baron and present peer.

DILHORNE, VISCOUNT (Manningham-Buller) (Viscount UK 1964, Bt UK 1866)

The eagle does not catch flies

JOHN MERVYN MANNINGHAM-BULLER, 2nd Viscount, and 5th Baronet; *b* 28 Feb 1932; *s* 1980; *ed* Eton; formerly Lt Coldstream Gds; Barrister at Law (1979); a Fellow of Inst of Taxation and a Member of Wilts Co Council 1967-70: *m* 1st, 1955 (*m diss* 1973), Gillian Evelyn, JP, da of Col George Cochrane Stockwell; 2ndly, 1981, Mrs Susannah Jane Gilchrist, formerly wife of Colin Gilchrist, and da of Cmdr W. C. Eykyn, RN, and has issue living by 1st *m*.

Arms – Quarterly: 1st and 4th, sable, on a cross argent quarterly pierced of the field, four eagles displayed of the first, *Buller*; 2nd and 3rd, sable, a fesse ermine in chief three griffins' heads erased or, *Manningham*. **Crest** – 1st a Saracen's head affrontée couped proper; 2nd, out of a ducal coronet gules, a talbot's head or, collared gules, line terminating in a knot sable. **Supporters** – *Dexter*, An Eagle wings elevated and addorsed ermine beaked and legged or gorged with a ducal coronet gules therefrom a line reflexed over the back and terminating in a knot sable; *sinister*, a Pegasus azure winged crined unguled and queued argent both charged on the shoulder with a Portcullis chained gold. *Residence* – 164 Ebury St, SW1. *Clubs* – Buck's, Pratt's, MCC, Beefsteak, Savage.

SONS LIVING (By 1st marriage)

Hon JAMES EDWARD, *b* 20 Aug 1956; formerly Capt WG: *m* 1985, Nicola Marion, el da of late Sven Mackie, of Ballydugan House, Downpatrick, co Down, and has issue living, Edward John, *b* 25 Jan 1990, — Camilla Mary, *b* 1992. *Residence* – Ballymote House, Downpatrick, co Down.
Hon Mervyn Reginald, *b* 1962: *m* 1989, Lucy Meriel, da of George Thurstan. *Residence* – 126 Hurlingham Rd, SW6 3NF.

DAUGHTER LIVING (By 1st marriage)

Hon Mary Louise, *b* 1970: *m* 1992, Capt James M. Cowan, The Black Watch (Royal Highland Regt), eldest son of Col Edward Cowan, of Marnhull, Dorset.

SISTERS LIVING

Hon Marian Cynthia, *b* 1934: *m* 1955, Edmund Crispin Stephen James George Brudenell (*see* M Ailesbury, colls). *Residences* – Deene Park, Corby, Northants; 18 Laxford House, Ebury St, SW1.
Hon Elizabeth Lydia, *b* 1948.
Hon Anne Constance, *b* 1951: *m* 1982, John Christopher Parsons (*see* E Rosse, colls).

AUNTS LIVING (Daughters of Lt-Col Sir Mervyn E. Manningham-Buller, 3rd Bt)

Myra, *b* 1909: *m* 1940, Lt-Col Percy Cyril Snatt, R Sigs, who *d* 1961. —— Pamela Lilah (Ravenscar, Meadfoot Lane, Torquay), *b* 1919; CC Devon 1973-85: *m* 1951, Norman Wilkinson-Cox, who *d* 1969, and has issue living, Gavia Lilah, *b* 1952.

WIDOW LIVING OF FIRST VISCOUNT

Lady MARY LINDSAY (*Dowager Viscountess Dilhorne*) (6 King's Bench Walk, Temple, EC4), 4th da of 27th Earl of Crawford and Balcarres: *m* 1930, Sir Reginald Edward Manningham-Buller, 4th Bt (*cr* Viscount Dilhorne 1964), PC, who *d* 1980.

PREDECESSORS – (**1**) EDWARD Manningham-Buller, of Dilhorne Hall, Staffs, 3rd son of Sir Francis Buller, 2nd Bt (*cr* 1790) and brother of 1st Baron Churston; *b* 1800; assumed by Roy Licence 1866 the additional surname of Manningham; MP for N Staffs 1833-42, 1867 and 1874, and for Stafford 1842-47; *cr* a Baronet 1866: *m* 1st, 1824, Mary Anne, who *d* 1860, da and heir of Maj-Gen Coote Manningham; 2ndly, 1863, Georgina Charlotte, who *d* 1875, da and heir of Adm of the Fleet Sir Charles Edmund Nugent, GCM, and widow of the Rt Hon George Bankes MP; *d* 1882; *s* by his son (**2**) *Sir* MORTON EDWARD, 2nd Bt, *b* 1825: *m* 1865, Mary, who *d* 1923, da of William Davenport, of Maer Hall, Staffs; *d* 1910; *s* by his nephew (**3**) *Sir* MERVYN EDWARD (only son of Maj-Gen Edmund Manningham-Buller), 3rd Bt; Lt-Col Rifle Bde, and MP for Kettering 1924-29, and Northampton 1931-40: *m* 1903, Hon Lilah Constance Cavendish, OBE, who *d* 1944, da of 3rd Baron Chesham; *d* 1956; *s* by his only son (**4**) *Sir* REGINALD EDWARD, 4th Bt, *b* 1905; Solicitor-Gen 1951-54, Attorney-Gen 1954-62, Lord High

Chancellor 1962-64 and Dep Leader of Opposition, House of Lords 1964-66; a Lord of Appeal in Ordinary 1969-80; MP for Daventry Div of Northants (C) 1943-50, and for S Div of Northants 1950-62; *cr* Knt 1951, PC 1954, *Baron Dilhorne*, of Towcester, co Northampton (peerage of UK) 1962, and *Viscount Dilhorne*, of Greens Norton, co Northampton (peerage of UK) 1964: *m* 1930, Lady Mary Lilian Lindsay, 4th da of 27th Earl of Crawford and Balcarres; *d* 1980; *s* by his only son (5) Sir JOHN MERVYN, 5th Bt, and present peer; also Baron Dilhorne.

DILLON, VISCOUNT (Dillon) (Viscount I 1622)

DUM · SPIRO · SPERO

While I breathe I hope

HENRY (HARRY) BENEDICT CHARLES DILLON, 22nd Viscount; *b* 6 Jan 1973; *s* 1982; is *Count Dillon* in France (*cr* 1711).

Arms – Quarterly: 1st and 4th argent, a lion passant, between three crescents gules, *Dillon*; 2nd and 3rd argent, a fesse between three crescents sable, *Lee*. Crest – A demi-lion gules, holding in its paws an estoile argent. Supporters – Two angels proper, vested argent, winged and crined or, each holding in the exterior hand a branch of palm proper, and having a riband over the shoulder of the second.
Residence – 28 Canning Cross, SE5 8BH.

SISTER LIVING

Hon Beatrice Inès Renée, *b* 1978.

UNCLES LIVING (*Sons of 20th Viscount*)

Hon RICHARD ARTHUR LOUIS (Brook House, Sudborough, nr Kettering, Northants NN14 3BX) *b* 23 Oct 1948; *ed* Downside, and RAC Cirencester; FSVA: *m* 1975, Hon Priscilla Frances Hazlerigg, da of 2nd Baron Hazlerigg, and has issue living, Thomas Arthur Lee, *b* 1 Oct 1983, — Charlotte Frances, *b* 1978.
Hon Patrick Dominic (14 St Mary's Cottages, Drogheda, co Louth), *b* 1956; *ed* Downside, and Trin Coll, Dublin.
Hon Michael Edmond (8 Keslake Rd, NW6 6DL), *b* 1957; *ed* Glenstal, and Hampshire Coll of Agric; painter: *m* 1983, Henrietta Catherine, yr da of Charles Elwell, of Bottrells Close, Chalfont St Giles, Bucks, and has issue living, Charles Augustus Henry, *b* 1985, — Emily Madeleine, *b* 1987, — Catherine Elizabeth, *b* 1989, — Henrietta Sophie, *b* 1993.

AUNTS LIVING AND DECEASED (*Daughters of 20th Viscount*)

Hon Isabel Anne Marie Henrietta, *b* 1942: *m* 1970, Richard Alexander Charles Cobbe, of The Manor House, Yattendon, Newbury, Berks RG16 0UH, and has issue living, Thomas Alexander Michael, *b* 1973, — Henry Frederick Hugh, *b* 1975, — Frances Henrietta, *b* 1971, — Rose Eleanor (twin), *b* 1973.
Hon Inès Marie Jeanne, *b* 1952.
Hon Rosaleen Marie Carmel, *b* 1953; *d* as a result of an accident 1960.
Hon Madeleine Marie (twin) (66 Westbourne Terrace, W2 3UJ), *b* 1957; Assist Private Sec to HRH The Princess Royal since 1988: *m* 1989, Leonard Constantine Louloudis, only son of Constantine Louloudis, and has issue living, Constantine Michael, *b* 1991, — Theodora Catherine Lily, *b* 1993.

WIDOW LIVING OF TWENTIETH VISCOUNT

IRENE MARIE FRANCE (*Irène Viscountess Dillon*) (14 St Mary's Cottages, Drogheda, co Louth), da of René Merandon du Plessis, of Whitehall, Mauritius: *m* 1939, the 20th Viscount, who *d* 1979.

WIDOW LIVING OF TWENTY-FIRST VISCOUNT

(MARY) JANE (*Viscountess Dillon*) (28 Canning Cross, SE5 8BH), da of John Young, of Castle Hill House, Birtle, Lancs; designer: *m* 1972, the 21st Viscount, who *d* 1982.

COLLATERAL BRANCHES LIVING

Grandchildren of late Francis Noel Dillon, only son of late Philip Gerald Dillon, 2nd son of late Hon Constantine Augustus Dillon, 4th son of 13th Viscount:—
Issue of late Patrick Philip Lee Dillon, *b* 1912, *d* 1993: *m* 1937, Joan Elfie (Leefield, Blenheim, NZ), da of G. C. Williams, of Masterton, NZ:—
Patrick Francis (Waikirikiri, RD3, Leeston, Canterbury, NZ), *b* 1946: *m* 1974, Susan Lee, da of Dr Peter Thodey, of Timaru, NZ, and has issue living, Jonathan Patrick Lee, *b* 1977, — Mark Peter Lee, *b* 1981, — Lisa Francis, *b* 1975, — Brigid Louise Lee, *b* 1982. —— Rachel Anne, *b* 1939: *m* 1966, Robert Lionel Savory, of Bengeo Hall, Hereford, and has issue living, Charlotte Katharine Anne, *b* 1968, — Victoria Lucy Lee, *b* 1970. — Josephine Elizabeth, *b* 1972. —— Joanna Lee, *b* 1941: *m* 1963, David Cameron, of Waituma, Waikari, N Canterbury, NZ, and has issue living, Timothy Charles, *b* 1967, — Andrew Lee, *b* 1970, — Nicola Jane, *b* 1965: *m* 1994, Andrew Robert Davie, of Wellington, NZ.
Issue of late Fl-Lt Michael Lee Dillon, RNZAF, *b* 1913, *d* 1968: *m* 1939, Gwendoline Reay (The Tummil, Blenheim, NZ), da of J. W. Trolove, of The Shades, Blenheim, NZ:—
Richard Lee (The Tummil, Blenheim, NZ), *b* 1941: *m* 1965, Elizabeth Campbell, da of J. B. Hay, of Pigeon Bay, Bank's Peninsular, NZ, and has issue living, Nicolas Lee, *b* 1966, — Samuel Hay, *b* 1967, — Sarah Elizabeth, *b* 1971. —— James Michael Lee (Tummil Flat, Blenheim, NZ), *b* 1947; *ed* Christ's Coll, Christchurch: *m* 1974, Maling Eve, da of Michael Joseph Nathan, of Wellington, NZ, and has issue living, Olivia Michal, *b* 1976, — Amber Maling, *b* 1978, — Honor Louisa, *b* 1982. —— Sarah Christine, *b* 1942: *m* 1965, Peter Wallace Coy, of Salt Creek, Woorndoo, Vic, Aust, and has issue living, Edward Francis Dillon, *b* 1974, — Rosa Susan, *b* 1966, — Sally Amanda, *b* 1968, — Georgina Anne, *b* 1971. —— Rosa Lee, *b* 1949: *m* 1975, Michael John Hawdon Davison, of Kaiwara, Culverden, NZ, and has issue living, Frederick Michael Dillon, *b* 1980, — Antonia Frames Alice, *b* 1979, — Georgina Constance Lee, *b* 1982.

Issue of late Maj Gerald Francis Lee Dillon, NZ Forces, b 1917, d 1983: m 1946, Mary Ritson (Spelsbury, Blenheim, RD1, Marlborough, NZ), da of Cdr T. S. Critchley, RN, of Tirohunga, Blenheim, NZ:—
David Sandford Lee (The Throne, Blenheim, NZ), b 1946; late Lieut NZ Army; a farmer: m 1973, Susan Hamilton, da of late P. D. Reid, of Blenheim, NZ, and has issue living, Henry Gerald Lee, b 1976, — Thomas Patrick Lee, b 1979, — Hannah Frances, b 1982. —— Susan Ann Lee, b 1948: m 1974, Richard John Macfarlane, of Winterholme, Kekerengu, Marlborough, NZ, and has issue living, Sandford Samuel, b 1975, — Winston William, b 1977, — Clive Charles, b 1978, — Alexandra Augusta, b 1981.

Granddaughters of late Augustus Henry Fitz-Gibbon, 2nd son of late Hon Gerald Normanby Fitz-Gibbon, 6th son of 13th Viscount:—
Issue of late Capt Gerald Ernest George Fitz-Gibbon, MC, b 1884, d 1929: m 1st, 1908 (m diss 1912), Mary Monica, who d 1930, da of Lt-Col Hugh Marshall Hole, CMG, of 2 London Wall Buildings, EC2; 2ndly, 1914, Hélène, who d 1969, da of Etienne Niel, of Rouen, France and widow of Strentham Ford, of Cape Town:—
(By 1st m) Elizabeth Rosemary, b 1912: m 1934, Henry Bockholst Livingston, CBE, who d 1968, and has issue living, Nicholas Henry (Valfond, Chemin du Moulin Vieux, 84210 St Didier, Vaucluse, France), b 1942; ed King's Sch, Canterbury, and King's Coll, Camb (Foundation Scholar); Foreign Office 1964: m 1968, Ana Maria, da of late Dr Idilio Oneto, and has issue living, Barnaby b 1973, Emma Sophie b 1976. Residence – 15 rue Marignac, 1206 Geneva, Switzerland. —— (By 2nd m) Diana Clare, b 1924: m 1952, Derek Harry Johnson, who d 1977, of Boden Hall, Scholar Green, Cheshire, and d 1993, leaving issue, Gerald Harry (Whiteway House, Chudleigh, Newton Abbot, Devon; PO Box 232, Lamu, Kenya), b 1952; ed Harrow, and St Columba's Coll, Dublin: m 1st, 1980 (m diss 1985), Jasmine Violet, da of late Victor Wild, of Shenley Hill, Shenley, Herts; 2ndly, 1987, Claire, da of Francis Rooney, of 2 Columbia Terr, Rock Rd, St Peter Port, Guernsey, CI, and has issue living (by 2nd m), Harry Francis FitzGibbon b 1989, — Mary Clare Hélène, b 1958: m 1st, 1985 (m diss 1989), Robin Bailey Hamilton Vetch; 2ndly, 1990, Robert Edward Hunter Rodwell, of Lamyatt Lodge, nr Shepton Mallet, Som, and has issue living (by 1st m), Annabel Susannah Clare b 1987.

Descendants, if any, of late Clare Valentine Fitz-Gibbon (b 1859), who was last heard of in Canada, 4th son of late Hon Gerald Normanby Fitz-Gibbon (infra).

Grandchildren of late Lt-Cdr Robert Francis Lee-Dillon, RN (Count Robert F. Lee-Dillon in France) (infra):—
Issue of late (Robert Louis) Constantine FITZ-GIBBON, the author, b 1919, d 1983: m 1st, 1939 (m diss 1944), Margaret Aye Moung; 2ndly, 1944 (m diss 1960), Theodora Rosling, cookery writer, who d 1991 (having m 2ndly, 19—, George Morrison, film archivist); 3rdly, 1960 (m diss 19—), Marion Gutmann; 4thly, 1967, Marjorie, formerly wife of (i) Huntington Hartford, and (ii) Dudley Sutton, actor, and da of Harold Wright Steele, of Cal, USA:—
(By 3rd m) Francis George Herbert Dillon, b 1961: m 1986, Camilla G. Beresford, and has issue living, Lily Theodora, b 1987. Residence – 46 Brondesbury Rd, NW6. —— (By 4th m) Oonagh Louise Dillon, b 1968.

Grandson of late Louis Theobald FITZ-GIBBON, 5th and yst son of late Hon Gerald Normanby FITZ-GIBBON, 6th son of 13th Viscount:—
Issue of late Lt-Cdr Robert Francis LEE-DILLON, RN (Count Robert F. Lee-Dillon in France), b 1884, d 1954; having resumed in 1925 the surname of Lee-Dillon: m 1st, (Feb) 1908 (m diss 1923), Georgette (who d 1972), da of George Winthrop Folsom, of Lenox, Mass, USA; 2ndly, 1924, Kathleen Clare, who d 1950, da of late James Aitchison, CE, of Belfast, and Cardigan, Lavender Bay, Sydney, NSW, and widow of Hon Henry Lee Stanton Lee-Dillon (only son of 17th Viscount Dillon) (see V Dillon, colls, 1985 Edn):—
(By 2nd m) Louis Theobald DILLON FitzGibbon (Flat 2, 8 Portland Place, Brighton, Sussex BN2 1DG), b 1925; assumed by deed poll 1962, the surnames of Dillon FitzGibbon in lieu of Lee-Dillon; Lt RN (ret); Area Pres of St John Ambulance Bde; a Knt of Sovereign Mil Order of Malta; Kt Cdr of Order of Restitution of Poland; Polish Gold Cross of Merit; Cross of Merit (1st Class) of Germany: m 1st, 1950 (m diss 1962), Mrs Josephine McDonald, who d 1979, da of J. H. Webb; 2ndly, 1962, Madeleine Sally Hayward-Surry, who d 1980; 3rdly, 1980, Mrs Joan Elizabeth Jevons, and has issue living (by 2nd m), James Augustus b 1963, — Simone Frances, b 1962, — Michèle Clare, b 1965.

Grandchildren of late John Monro Dillon, 3rd son of late Rev Martin Dillon, 6th in descent from Hon Thomas Dillon, 4th son of 1st Viscount:—
Issue of late Capt Arnold Michael Dillon, b 1892, d 1955: m 1915, Esther Dorothy, da of William Currie Allen, of London, Ontario:—
Arnold Charles, b 1920: m 1947, Donalda Ruth, da of Arthur J. Cowie, of Caledonia, Ontario, Canada, and has issue living, John Michael b 1956, — Dorothy Nina, b 1954. —— Mary Louie Margarette, b 1917: m 1944, Dennis Bishop, late Flying Officer, RAF Vol Reserve, and has issue living, Dennis John, b 1945, — Caroline Mary Beverley Anne, b 1952. Residence –

Grandchildren of late Maurice Ashurst Dillon, 4th son of late Rev Martin Dillon (ante):—
Issue of late Brig Marmaduke Murray Dillon, MC, ED, b 1894, d 1976: m 1st, 1919, Muriel, da of the late Rev Canon Richard Hicks; 2ndly, 1956, Mildred Whitley (842 Wellington St, London, Ont, Canada), widow of Col Charles W. Jeffers, US Army:—
(By 1st m) Richard Maurice, MC, ED, b 1920; BA; Lt-Col (ret) Canadian Mil, Dean of Faculty of Eng Science, W Ont Univ; 1939-45 War in Sicily and Italy (MC); Coronation medal (1953): m 1945, Mary Elizabeth, da of Harry H. Dempsey, of Stratford, Ont, and has issue living, Kelly Elizabeth, b 1949, — Ann Dempsey, b 1952, — Katherine Talbot, b 1955. —— Michael Talbot, CD (Unit 73, 2 Cadeau Terrace, London, Ont N6K 4K7), b 1926; BA, MD; Lt-Col (ret) late RCAMC (M): m 1959, Margaret, da of Roy Kirk Hamilton, of Arthur, Ont, and has issue living, Timothy Arthur, b 1960, — Kirk Fitzgerald, b 1961: m 1989, Julie Anne, da of Charles Duncan, of London, Ont, and has issue living, Rebecca Anne b 1990, Kate Elizabeth Margaret b 1992, — David Morgan, b 1963; has issue living (by Lisa Westulaken), Morgan Jane b 1986. —— Shelagh Muriel, b 1924: m 1945, Neil Archibald Watters, MD, FRCS (Canada), of 172 Rosedale Heights Drive, Toronto, and has issue living, Douglas Bruce, b 1948, — James Murray, b 1952, — Michael Grant, b 1955, — Louise Shelagh, b 1959. —— Diana Mary Morgan, b 1926; BA, MD, FRCP: m 1956, Rev Gerald Cecil Johnson, BA, BTh, of 246 Main St, Ildeston, Ont, NOM 2AO, and has issue living, Patrick Bruce, b 1965, — Kevin Sean (twin), b 1965, — Michele Ann Jean, b 1958, — Margaret Rebecca Morgan, b 1962.

Grandson of late Luke Gerald Dillon, OBE, MD, eldest son of Charles Blake Dillon, son of late Luke Dillon, 5th in descent from Hon Thomas Dillon (ante):—
Issue of late Gerald Dormer Fitzgerald Dillon, b 1901, d 1979: m 1940, Maureen (406A Wimbledon Park Rd, SW19), da of Thomas Stewart, formerly of Cowdenbeath, Fife:—
Martin Luke Gerald (The Red House, Much Hadham, Herts), b 1942; ed Downside, and Queen's Coll, Oxford (BA): m 1965, Diana Mary, da of late Rev Arthur Robert Botting, BA, and has issue living, Anthony Hugh Patrick Martin, b 1965, — Clare Elizabeth Teresa, b 1968: m 1988, Robert James Ashcroft, and has issue living, Thomas Alexander b 1989, Matthew Robert b 1991, William James b 1994.

PREDECESSORS – (1) Sir THEOBALD Dillon, Knt; Lord Pres of Connaught; cr Viscount Dillon, of Costello-Gallen (peerage of Ireland) 1622; d 1624; s by his grandson (2) LUCAS, 2nd Viscount; d 1629; s by his son (3) THEOBALD, 3rd Viscount; d an infant 1630; s by his uncle (4) THOMAS, 4th Viscount, b 1615; Joint Commr of Mayo Nov 1641, and Joint Pres of Connaught and Gov of Fort Athlone 1645-62; exempted from pardon for life by Cromwell 1652 (restored 1660); Custos Rotulorum of co Meath 1662; d 1673; s by his son (5) THOMAS, 5th Viscount; d 1674; s by his kinsman (6) LUCAS, 6th Viscount, el son of Sir

Theobald, 3rd son of Sir Christopher el son of 1st Viscount; *dsp* 1682; *s* by his kinsman **(7)** THEOBALD, 7th Viscount, grandson of Sir Lucas, 2nd son of 1st Viscount; attached himself to the falling fortunes of James II, and was outlawed 1690; *s* by his son **(8)** HENRY, 8th Viscount, in whose favour the outlawry was reversed; *d* 1713; *s* by his son **(9)** RICHARD, 9th Viscount; *d* 1737; *s* by his cousin **(10)** CHARLES, 10th Viscount, el son of Hon Arthur Dillon (2nd son of 7th Viscount), who was *cr* Count Dillon by Louis XIV 1711, Earl Dillon by the Old Pretender 1721 and KT 1722; *dsp* 1741; *s* by his brother **(11)** HENRY, 11th Viscount; a Col in the French army; *d* 1787; *s* by his son **(12)** CHARLES, KP, 12th Viscount; conformed to the Established Church, and his claim to be 12th Viscount was allowed by the House of Lords in 1788 in the names of Dillon-Lee, which he had assumed in 1776 in accordance with the will of his maternal uncle, the 3rd Earl of Litchfield; *d* 1813; *s* by his son **(13)** HENRY AUGUSTUS, 13th Viscount; *b* 1777: *m* 1807, Henrietta, da of Dominick Geoffrey Browne, MP; *d* 1832; *s* by his el son **(14)** CHARLES HENRY, 14th Viscount; *d* 1865; *s* by his brother **(15)** THEOBALD DOMINICK GEOFFREY, 15th Viscount; *d* 1879; *s* by his brother **(16)** ARTHUR EDMUND DENIS, 16th Viscount, *b* 1812: *m* 1843, Ellen, da of James Adderly; *d* 1892; *s* by his el son **(17)** HAROLD ARTHUR, CH, 17th Viscount, *b* 1844; Pres of So of Antiquaries 1897-1904, Curator of the Tower Armouries 1895-1913, and a Trustee of British Museum 1897-1932; Senior Trustee of the National Portrait Gallery, Antiquary of Roy Acad and an Original Fellow of British Acad: *m* 1st, 1870, Julia (Order of Mercy), who *d* 1925, el da of late Isaac Brock Stanton, of the Canadian Civil Ser; 2ndly, 1926, his cousin, Margaret Louisa Everard, who *d* 1954, da of late Rev Henry Edward ffolkes, and widow of Rev John Erasmus Philipps; *d* 1932; *s* by his nephew **(18)** ARTHUR HENRY (el son of Hon Conrad Adderly Dillon, 2nd son of 16th Viscount), 18th Viscount, *b* 1875: *m* 1907, Hilda, who *d* 1966, da of Rt Hon Sir John Tomlinson Brunner, 1st Bt, PC, and widow of Charles Harold Broadbent, JP; *d* 1934; *s* by his brother **(19)** ERIC FITZGERALD, CMG, DSO, 19th Viscount, *b* 1881; Brig (ret) Roy Munster Fusiliers; S Africa 1900-01, 1914-18 War (DSO, CMG), 1939-45 War: *m* 1907, Norah Juanita Muriel, who *d* 1962, only child of late Brig-Gen Charles Edward Beckett, CB; *d* 1946; *s* by his son **(20)** MICHAEL ERIC, 20th Viscount; *b* 1911; Lt-Col RHG, sometime Lt-Col 15/19th The King's Royal Hussars, an Officer of Order of Orange Nassau of the Netherlands with Swords, and a Vice-Pres of Roy Stuart Soc: *m* 1939, Irène Marie France, da of René Merandon du Plessis, of Whitehall, Mauritius; *d* 1979; *s* by his son **(21)** CHARLES HENRY ROBERT, 21st Viscount; *b* 1945: *m* 1972, Mary Jane, da of John Young, of Castle Hill House, Birtle, Lancs; *d* 1982; *s* by his only son **(22)** HENRY BENEDICT CHARLES, 22nd Viscount and present peer.

Dinevor, Baron, see Dynevor.

Dingwall, Lord, see Baron Lucas of Crudwell and Dingwall.

DIXON-SMITH, BARON (Dixon-Smith) (Life Baron 1993)

ROBERT WILLIAM DIXON-SMITH, 2nd son of Dixon Smith, of Lascelles, Braintree, Essex; *b* 30 Sept 1934; *ed* Oundle, and Writtle Agric Coll; 2nd Lieut King's Dragoon Gds 1955-57; DL Essex 1986; Farmer; Chm Essex CC 1986-89 (Councillor since 1965), Chm Assocn of CCs 1992-93 (Vice-Chm 1989-92), Chm of Govs Anglia Poly 1991-93; Freeman Farmers' Co 1988; *cr Baron Dixon-Smith*, of Bocking, co Essex (Life Baron) 1993: *m* 1960, Georgina Janet, da of George Cook, of Halstead, Essex, and has issue.
Residence – Lyons Hall, Braintree, Essex CM7 6SH.

SON LIVING

Hon Adam William George, *b* 1962: *m* 19—, Anna Hogg, and has issue living, Guy, *b* 1994, — Kit, *b* (twin) 1994.

DAUGHTER LIVING

Hon Sarah Jane, *b* 1960: *m* 1986, Christopher Henry St John (Toby) Hoare, son of J. Michael Hoare, and has issue living, Oscar, *b* 1988, — Giles, *b* 1990. *Residence* – 130 Kensington Park Rd, W11 2EP.

DONALDSON OF KINGSBRIDGE, BARON (Donaldson) (Life Baron 1967)

Either peace or war

JOHN GEORGE STUART DONALDSON, OBE, son of late Rev Stuart Alexander Donaldson, Master of Magdalene Coll, Camb, by his wife Lady Albinia Hobart-Hampden, sister of 7th Earl of Buckinghamshire, *b* 9 Oct 1907; *ed* Eton, and Trin Coll, Camb (MA); a Farmer; Member Labour Party 1930-80; a Dir of Roy Opera House, Covent Garden 1959-74, of Sadlers Wells 1962-74, and of British Sugar Corpn 1966-74; Chm Board of Visitors, HM Prison, Grendon, Bucks, 1962-72, Nat Assocn for the Care and Resettlement of Offenders 1966-74, Nat Exec Cttee of Family Service Units 1968-74, Consumer Council 1968-71, Fedn of Zoos 1971-73, and Hotels and Catering NEDO 1972; Pres Nat Assocn for the Care and Resettlement of Offenders since 1974; Pres RSPB 1975-80; Parl Under-Sec of State N Ireland Office 1974-76, Min of State Depart of Education and Science (Min for the Arts) 1976-79; joined SDP 1981, Democrats 1988; 1939-45 War as Lt-Col RE; *cr* OBE (Mil) 1944, and *Baron Donaldson of Kingsbridge*, of Kingsbridge, co Buckingham (Life Baron) 1967: *m* 1935, Frances Annesley, who *d* 1994, da of late Frederick Lonsdale, the playwright, and has issue.

Arms – Or a double headed eagle displayed azure beaked and membered gules, surmounted of a lymphad with two masts sails furled sable flagged on the fore main mast with the Banner of Scotland proper (azure a saltire argent) and on the sinister chief point a sinister hand couped of the third, and on the sinister chief point a book expanded proper, all within a bordure also of the third. **Crest** – A dexter hand holding a sword proper.
Residence – 17 Edna St, SW11 3DP. *Club* – Brooks's.

SON LIVING

Hon Thomas Hay, *b* 1936, *ed* Eton, and Univ of Cincinnati and Trin Coll Camb (BA) *m* 1962, Natalie, da of Basil Wadkovsky, of Miami Beach, Florida, USA, and has issue. *Residence* – The Old Lodge, Mayertorne, Wendover Dean, Wendover, nr Aylesbury, Bucks HP22 6QA.

DAUGHTER LIVING

Hon Rose Albinia, *b* 1937: *m* 1961, Nicholas Deakin, of 126 Leighton Rd, NW5, son of Sir William Deakin, and has issue.
Hon Catherine Frances, *b* 1945: *m* 1973, G. Mark Jennings, of 57 Winsham Grove, SW11, and has issue.

DONALDSON OF LYMINGTON, BARON (Donaldson) (Life Baron 1988)

JOHN FRANCIS DONALDSON, PC, son of late Malcolm Donaldson, FRCS, FRCOG, of Woodstock Rd, Oxford; *b* 6 Oct 1920: *ed* Charterhouse, and Trin Coll, Camb (Hon Fellow 1983), MA Cantab 1948, MA Oxon 1982, Hon DUniv Essex 1983, Hon LLD Sheffield 1984, Hon LLD Nottingham Trent 1992; served 1939-45 War in Roy Signals in NW Europe and Guards Armoured Divnl Signals (Hon Lt-Col 1946); Bar Middle Temple 1946, QC 1961, Dep Chm Hants Quarter Sessions 1961-66, Bencher 1966, Judge of High Court of Justice (Queen's Bench Div) 1966-79, Pres Nat Industrial Relations Court 1971-74, a Lord Justice of Appeal 1979-82, Master of the Rolls 1982-92; Pres Council of Inns of Court 1987-90, Carthusian Soc 1978-82, British Maritime Law Assocn since 1979 (Vice-Pres 1969-78), British Insurance Law Assocn 1979-81 (Dep-Pres 1978-79), British Records Assocn 1982-92; Chm Advisory Council on Public Records 1982-92, Magna Carta Trust 1982-92; FCIArb 1980 (Pres 1980-83), Financial Law Panel since 1993; Gov Sutton's Hosp in Charterhouse 1981-84; Visitor: Nuffield Coll, Oxford 1982-92, UCL 1982-92 and London Business Sch 1986-92; Hon Freeman Worshipful Co of Drapers 1984; *cr* Kt 1966, PC 1979, and *Baron Donaldson of Lymington*, of Lymington, co Hants (Life Baron) 1988: *m* 1945, (Dorothy) Mary, GBE, da of late Reginald George Gale Warwick, of Wickham, Hants, and has issue.

Arms – Sable, two bars or, in chief three petasi argent winged gold. **Crest** – A sealion erect sable, scales, fins and tail or, holding a lymphad also or, the mainsail displaying the arms, viz sable, two bars or, in chief three petasi argent winged gold, each mast ensigned by a cross formy gules.
Address – Royal Courts of Justice, Strand, WC2. *Clubs* – Royal Cruising, Bar Yacht, Royal Lymington Yacht.

SON LIVING

Hon Michael John Francis, *b* 1950; *ed* Stanbridge Earls: *m* 1972, Judith Margaret, da of Edgar William Somerville, FRCS, of Stone House, Garsington, Oxford, and has issue living, William Michael Somerville, *b* 1977, — James John Francis, *b* (twin) 1977. *Residence* – The Old Coach House, Westwood Rd, Windlesham, Surrey GU20 6LT.

DAUGHTERS LIVING

Hon Margaret-Ann Michelle, *b* 1946; *ed* St Paul's Girls' Sch, London Sch of Occupational Therapy (Dip OT), and Univ of Saskatchewan (MCEd and PhD): *m* 1969, Conal Tompson, and has issue living, Douglas Conal, *b* 1974, — Caroline Margaret, *b* 1975. *Residence* – 736 University Drive, Saskatoon, Saskatchewan S7N 0J4, Canada.
Hon Jennifer Mary, *b* 1948: *m* 1970, Michael Lodwig Williams, and has issue three sons.

DONEGALL, MARQUESS OF (Chichester) Sits as BARON FISHERWICK (GB 1790) (Marquess I 1791)

DERMOT RICHARD CLAUD CHICHESTER, LVO, 7th Marquess; *b* 18 April 1916; *s* as 5th Baron Templemore 1953, and as 7th Marquess of Donegall 1975; *ed* Harrow and RMC; Maj (ret) late 7th Queen's Own Hussars; Standard Bearer of HM Body Guard of Hon Corps of Gentlemen at Arms 1984-86; Hereditary Lord High Admiral of Lough Neagh and Gov of Carrickfergus Castle; 1939-45 War in Middle East and Italy (prisoner); LVO 1986: *m* 1946, Lady Josceline Gabrielle Legge, da of 7th Earl of Dartmouth, and has issue.

Arms – Quarterly: 1st and 4th checky, or and gules, a chief vaire, *Chichester*; 2nd and 3rd azure, fretty argent, *Etchingham.* **Crest** – A stork, with an eel in its bill proper. **Supporters** – Two wolves gules, ducally collared and chained or.
Seat – Dunbrody Park, Arthurstown, co Wexford. *Clubs* – Cavalry, Kildare St (Dublin).

Honour follows, though unsought for

SON LIVING

ARTHUR PATRICK (*Earl of Belfast*), *b* 9 May 1952; *ed* Harrow; Lt Coldm Gds: *m* 1989, Caroline Mary, elder da of Maj Christopher Roland Philipson, late Life Guards, of Lofts Hall, Saffron Walden, Essex (*see* By Woolavington, 1985 Edn), and has issue:
    SON LIVING — James (*Viscount Chichester*), *b* 19 Nov 1990.
    DAUGHTER LIVING — *Lady* Catherine Gabrielle, *b* 1992.

DAUGHTERS LIVING

Lady Jennifer Evelyn, *b* 1949: *m* 1971, John Robert Henry Fowler, of Rahinston, Enfield, co Meath, and has issue living, Robert Henry, *b* 1975, — Charles James, *b* 1977.
Lady Juliet Clare, *b* 1954: *m* 1983, Andrew David Frazer, of Hillmount, Cullybackey, co Antrim, and has issue living, William John Andrew, *b* 1985, — Mary Emma, *b* 1985 (twin).

BROTHER LIVING (*Son of 4th Baron Templemore*)

(*Raised to the rank of a Marquess's son, 1977*)

Lord Desmond Clive, MC, *b* 1920; *ed* Harrow, and Ch Ch, Oxford (BA 1944, MA 1945); Maj Coldm Gds (ret); was ADC to Gov-Gen of Canada 1948-50; 1939-45 War in N Africa and Italy (despatches MC); Dir Colne Valley Water Co since 1956 (Chm 1983): *m* 1st, 1946, Lorna Althea, who *d* 1948, da of Capt Montagu Hamer Ravenhill (Colleton, Bt), and widow of (i) Geoffrey Christopher Appleby Holt, Pilot Officer RAF, and (ii) Capt Richard Cecil Twining, Welsh Gds; 2ndly, 1951, Felicity Stella, da of late Maj John Fenwick Harrison (*see* B Burnham, 1969 Edn), and has issue living (by 1st *m*), (Desmond) Shane Spencer (Cygnet House, Martyr Worthy, nr Winchester, Hants SO21 1DZ), *b* 1948: *m* 1976, (Isabel) Jane, da of Michael George Thomas Webster, of The Vale, Windsor Forest, Berks (*see* M Conyngham, 1941 Edn), and has issue living, Patrick Michael Desmond *b* 1980, Henry Richard *b* 1981, Louisa Clare *b* 1978, — (by 2nd *m*) Dermot Michael Claud (Shaw House, Coulter, by Biggar, Lanarkshire), *b* 1953: *m* 1st, 1975 (*m diss* 1980), Frances Jane Berners, da of Michael Edward Ranulph Allsopp (*see* B Hindlip, colls); 2ndly, 1982, Shan, da of Alastair Ros McIndoe, of Heythrop Cottage, Wyck Rissington, Glos, and has issue living (by 2nd *m*), Rory Alastair St Clair *b* 1985, Ottilie *b* 1988, Sapphira *b* 1990. *Residence* – Preston Hill, Preston, Hitchin, Herts. *Club* – White's.

WIDOW LIVING OF SIXTH MARQUESS

MAUREEN (*Maureen, Marchioness of Donegall*) (5 Lakeview Court, SW19), el da of late Maj Geoffrey C. Scholfield, MC, of Birkdale, Lancs, and formerly wife of Douglas McKenzie: *m* 1968, as his 2nd wife, the 6th Marquess, who *d* 1975.

COLLATERAL BRANCHES LIVING

Descendants of late Arthur Chichester (el son of late Lord Spencer Stanley Chichester, 3rd son of 1st Marquess), who was *cr Baron Templemore* 1831:—

    Granddaughter of late Hon Frederick Arthur Henry Chichester, 3rd son of 1st Baron Templemore, el son of Lord Spencer Stanley Chichester, of Dunbrody Park, co Wexford, 3rd son of 1st Marquess:—
Issue of late Maj Spencer Frederick Chichester, *b* 1854, *d* 1931: *m* 1892, Helen, who *d* 1948, da of Archibald Coats, of Woodside, Paisley:—
Verena Frances Elizabeth, *b* 1906: *m* 1931, Cdr Derek Howard Secker, LVO, RN, who *d* 1988, and has issue living, Malcolm Chichester (Flat 9, 10 Porchester Terr, W2) *b* 1934; *ed* Eton. *Residence* – Les Chomettes, Ave Font-de-Veyre, 06150 Cannes, La Bocca, France AM.

    Grandsons of Hon Francis Algernon James Chichester, 5th son of 1st Baron Templemore:—

Issue of late Shane Randolph Chichester, OBE, *b* 1883, *d* 1969: *m* 1914, Madeline Herschel, who *d* 1977, da of Henry Arthur Whately:—

(Oscar) Richard Herschel (Wiscombe Park, Southleigh, Colyton, Devon EX13 6JE; *Clubs* – Pratt's, Army and Navy), *b* 1915; *ed* Wellington Coll, and Trin Coll, Camb (BA); Maj (ret) Rifle Bde (Prince Consort's Own); ADC to High Commr for Palestine 1946-48; Palestine 1936 (medal), 1939-45 War (African Star): *m* 1951, Margaret Edmondson, da of Charles Edgar Farr, JP, of Weston Bury, Weston, nr Hitchin, Herts, and has issue living, Timothy Arthur Shane, *b* 1956: *m* 1983, Mary Frances, yr da of Frank Sebastian Cooksey, CBE, MD, FRCP, of Aldeburgh, Suffolk, and has issue living, John Francis Shane *b* 1985, — Jane Caroline Sheelah, *b* 1952: *m* 1980 (*m diss* 19—), Richard Philip Palmer, son of Reginald H. Palmer, of Dawlish, and has issue living, Daniel *b* 1981, Thomas *b* 1983, — Sara Kathleen Arabella, *b* 1958: *m* 1988, Michael Constant John Raynor, elder son of R. D. Raynor, of Belford House, Four Marks, Hants, and has issue living, Madeline Jacqueline Kathleen *b* 1989. —— Desmond Shane (Holway House, Whatcombe, Blandford, Dorset; *Club* – MCC), *b* 1919; *ed* Wellington Coll, and Trin Coll, Camb (MA); Agent to the Earl of Radnor (ret); FRICS Capt (ret), 80th Heavy Anti-Aircraft Regt RA and N Irish Horse; 1939-45 War in N Africa and Italy: *m* 1951, Patricia, who *d* 1987, yr da of late Lt-Col Henry George Moreton Pleydell-Railston, DSO (Mansel, Bt, colls), and has issue living, Piers Desmond Herschel (Kingston Farmhouse, Winterborne Kingston, Blandford, Dorset), *b* 1954; *ed* Wellington Coll, and RAC Cirencester; FRICS, FAAV: *m* 1989, Charlotte Anne, only da of Lt-Col Peter Richard Heaton-Ellis, OBE, of The Coach House, Chitterne, Warminster, Wilts, and has issue living, Harry Pleydell Whately *b* 1992, Sophia Patricia *b* 1990, — Jonathan Morton (twin) (46 Redway Drive, Whitton, Twickenham, Middx), *b* 1954; *ed* Wellington Coll: *m* 1982, Caroline Margaret, da of Peter Douglas Bird, of W Kirby, Wirral, and has issue living, Peter Shane *b* 1983, Benjamin Charles *b* 1986, Eleanor Madeline Patricia *b* 1987, — (Adrian) George (The Mount, Chieveley, Newbury, Berks), *b* 1955; *ed* Wellington Coll, and Keble Coll, Oxford (MA): FRICS, FAAV: *m* 1988, Caroline Ann, only da of Dr John Richard Storer, of Westfield House, Blewbury, Oxon, and has issue living, Hugh Edmund *b* 1991, Tessa Ann *b* 1989, Camilla Emily *b* 1993, — Morna Rosemary *b* 1952; *ed* Westonbirt Sch, and Lady Margaret Hall, Oxford (MA): *m* 1982, Andrew David Wood Partridge, of 6 Beavers Rd, Farnham, Surrey, son of late Simon Harry Wood Partridge, OBE, of Kilndown, Kent, and has issue living, Katharine Mary Emily *b* 1986, Verena Frances Herschel *b* 1987.

In remainder to the Earldom of Donegall, Viscountcy of Chichester, and Barony of Chichester of Belfast only

Descendants of late Rev William Chichester, el son of late Rev Edward Chichester, who was *cr Baron O'Neill* 1868, great-great-grandson of John Chichester, brother of 2nd Earl (*see* O'Neill, B).

Granddaughters of late Rev Edward Arthur Chichester, son of Rev George Vaughan Chichester, son of late Rev Edward Chichester (ante):—

Issue of late Lt-Col Arthur O'Neill Cubitt Chichester, OBE, MC, *b* 1889, *d* 1972: *m* 1924, Hilda Grace, who *d* 1980, da of late Rt Hon William Robert Young (Macnaghten, Bt):—

Rosemary Hilda (*Rosemary, Viscountess Brookeborough*) (Colebrooke, co Fermanagh, and Ashbrooke, Brookeborough, co Fermanagh), *b* 1926: *m* 1949, 2nd Viscount Brookeborough, who *d* 1987. —— Finola Margaret, *b* 1932: *m* 1st, 1959, William McWilliams, who *d* 1963; 2ndly, 1964, D. Herbison, of Ardvernis Farm, Cullybackey, Ballymena, co Antrim and has issue living (by 1st *m*) Grace Mildred, *b* 1960, — Tracey Margaret Emily, *b* 1961, — (by 2nd *m*), John Patrick Arthur, *b* 1972, — Virginia Maria, *b* 1966, — Cathleen Laura, *b* 1968.

PREDECESSORS – Sir Arthur Chichester, Knt, PC, 2nd son Sir John Chichester, of Raleigh, Pilton Devon, and yr brother of Sir John, grandfather of 1st Bt (*see* Chichester, Bt); 1563; Lord Dep of Ireland 1605-15, Lord Treas of Ireland 1616-1625, and Ambassador to Palestine 1622; *cr Baron Chichester of Belfast* (peerage of Ireland) 1613: *m* 1605, Lettice, who *d* 1620, da of Sir John Perrott, of Haroldson, Pembrokeshire, Lord Dep of Ireland, and widow of (i) John Laugharne, and (ii) Walter Vaughan, of Golden Grove, Carmarthenshire; *d* 1625, when his peerage became ext, but was *s* in estates by his next brother **(1)** Sir Edward, Knt, PC, *b* circa 1568; Gov of Carrickfergus; Joint Commr of the Treasury, Ireland 1632; *cr Viscount Chichester of Carrickfergus*, and *Baron Chichester of Belfast*, both in co Antrim 1625-48: *m* 1st, 1605, Anne, who *d* 1616, da and heir of John Coplestone of Eggesford, Devon; 2ndly, 16—, Mary, who *d* 1637, da of — Denham, of Wortham, Devon, and widow of Otwell Hill; *d* 1648; *s* by his el son **(2)** Arthur, PC, *b* 1606; Gov of Carrickfergus 1660-1675; MP for co Antrim 1634 and 1640-47; being distinguished in Irish Rebellion, was *cr Earl of Donegall*, 1647, with remainder to heirs male of his father's body: *m* 1st, Dorcas, who *d* 1630, da of John Hill of Honiley, Warwicks; 2ndly, before 1638, Lady Mary Digby, who *d* 1648, da of 1st Earl of Bristol; 3rdly, 1651, Letitia (who *m* 2ndly Sir William Franklin, and *d* 1691), da of Sir William Hicks, 1st Bt; *d* 1675; *s* by his eldest son **(3)** Arthur, PC, 2nd Earl, el son of Lt-Col John Chichester, of Dungannon, co Tyrone, 2nd son of 1st Viscount, *b* 18—; MP of Dungannon 1661-66, joint Clerk of the Pipe Roll 1668-78, and Gov of Carrickfergus 1675-78: *m* 1st, 1660/1, Jane, da and heir of John Etchingham, of Dunbrody, co Wexford, who *d* 1712, having *m* 2ndly, Richard Booth of Epsom; *d* 1678; *s* by his el son **(4)** Arthur, 3rd Earl; *b* 1666; Col 35th Regt Foot; Maj Gen of Spanish Forces 1704: *m* 1st before 1676, Lady Barbara Boyle, who *d* 1682, da of 1st Earl of Orrery; 2ndly, 1685, Lady Catherine Forbes, who *d* 1743, da of 1st Earl of Granard; killed at Fort Monjuich 1706; *s* by his son **(5)** Arthur, 4th Earl; *b* 1965; *m* 1716, Lady Lucy Ridgeway, who *d* 1732, da of 4th Earl of Londonderry; *d* 1757; *s* by his nephew **(6)** Arthur, 5th Earl, son of Hon John, MP, 2nd son of 3rd Earl; *b* 1739; *cr Baron Fisherwick*, of Fisherwick, co Stafford (peerage of Great Britain) 1790, *Marquess of Donegall*, and *Earl of Belfast* (peerage of Ireland) 1791: *m* 1st, 1761, Lady Anne, who *d* 1780, da of 5th Duke of Hamilton; 2ndly, 1788, Charlotte, who *d* 1789, da and co-heir of Conway Spencer, of Tremary, co Down, and widow of Thomas Moore; 3rdly, 1790, Barbara, who *d* 1829, da of Rev Luke Godfrey, DD, R of Midleton, York, *d* 1799; *s* by his son **(7)** George Augustus, KP, 2nd Marquess; *b* 1769; Lieut of co Donegal: *m* 1795, Anna, da of Sir Edward May, Bt; *d* 1844; *s* by his son **(8)** George Hamilton, KP, GCH, PC, FRS, 3rd Marquess; *b* 1797; MP for Carrickfergus 1818-20, for Belfast 1820-30, and for Antrim (L) 1830-7; Vice-Chamberlain of the Household 1831-4, Capt of Yeomen of the Guard 1848-52, and Lord-Lieut of co Antrim; *cr Baron Ennishowen* and *Carrickfergus* (peerage of United Kingdom) 1841: *m* 1st, 1822, Harriet Anne who *d* 1860, da of 1st Earl of Glengall (ext); 2ndly, 1862, Harriet, da of Sir Bellingham Reginald Graham, 7th Bt, and widow of Lieut-Gen Sir Frederick Ashworth, KCB; *d* 1883, when the barony of *Ennishowen and Carrickfergus* became extinct; *s* in the other honours by his brother **(9)** Edward, 4th Marquess, *b* 1799; Dean of Raphoe 1832-73; *m* 1821, Amelia Spread Deane, da of Henry Deane Grady; *d* 1889; *s* by his el son **(6)** George Augustus Hamilton, 5th Marquess, *b* 1822; was Clerk of the Peace for co Antrim: *m* 1st, 1859 (*m diss* 1863), Lucy Elizabeth Virginia, da of Henry Holt Oliver, of Weston Priory, Somerset; 2ndly; 1865, Mary Ann Williams, who *d* 1901, da of late Edward Cobb, of Wright's Lane, Kensington, and of Arnold, Kent; 3rdly, 1902, Violet Gertrude, who *d* 1952, only da of late Henry St George Twining, of Halifax, Canada; *d* 1904; *s* by his son **(7)** Edward Arthur Donald St. George Hamilton, 6th Marquess, *b* 1903: Lt-Col Army Cadet Force; Journalist; War Correspondent 1939-45: *m* 1st, 1943 (*m diss* 1968), (Gladys) Jean, who *d* 1991, yr da of late Capt Christian Combe (M Conyngham); 2ndly, 1968, Maureen, el da of late Maj Geoffrey C. Scholfield, MC, of Birkdale, Lancs, and formerly wife of Douglas McKenzie; *d* 1975; *s* by his kinsman (see *infra*), Dermot Richard Claud, 5th Baron Templemore (5th in descent from Lord Spencer Stanley Chichester, 2nd son of 1st Marquess), 7th Marquess and present peer; also Earl of Donegall, Earl of Belfast, Viscount Chichester, Baron Colchester of Belfast, and Baron Fisherwick.

*(1) Arthur Chichester, MP, of Durbrody Park, co Wexford (el son of Lord Spencer Stanley Chichester, 2nd son of 1st Marquess of Donegall); *b* 1797; MP for co Wexford; Lt-Col, a Lord of the Bedchamber to William IV, and a Lord-in-Waiting to HM Queen Victoria; *cr Baron Templemore*, of Templemore, co Donegal (peerage of United Kingdom) 1831: *m* 1820, Lady Augusta Paget, who *d* 1872, da of 1st Marquess of Anglesey; *d* 1837; *s* by his son **(2)** Henry Spencer, 2nd Baron; *b* 1821; *m* 1st, 1842, Laura Caroline Jane, who *d* 1871, 3rd da of late Right Hon Sir Arthur Paget, GCB; 2ndly, 1873, Lady Victoria Elizabeth Ashley, who *d* 1927, da of 7th Earl of Shaftesbury; *d* 1906; *s* by his son **(3)** Arthur Henry, 3rd Baron, *b* 1854: High Sheriff of co Wexford 1890: *m* 1st, 1879, Evelyn, who *d* 1883, da of Rev William James Stracey (*see* Stacey Bt, colls); 2ndly, 1885, Alice Elizabeth, who *d* 1954, da of late Clinton George Augustus Dawkins; *d* 1924; *s* by his son **(4)** Arthur Claud Spencer, KCVO, DSO, OBE, PC, *b* 1880; Col (ret) TA (formerly Comdg 5/7th Batn Hampshire Regt); formerly Major

Irish Guards, and Capt Roy Fusiliers (City of London Regt); S Africa 1902, with Tibet Mission 1904, present at action of Gyantse and march to Lhassa, European War 1915-18; was Private Sec to Under-Sec of State for War 1927-28, and to Paymaster-Gen 1928-29, a Lord-in-Waiting to HM 1929, and 1931-34, and Capt of Yeomen of the Guard 1934-45; Ch Whip in House of Lords 1940-45: *m* 1911, Hon Clare Meriel Wingfield, who *d* 1969, da of 6th Viscount Powerscourt; *d* 1953; *s* by his son **(5)** DERMOT RICHARD CLAUD, 5th Baron, who *s* as 7th Marquess of Donegall (see ante).

DONERAILE, VISCOUNT (St Leger) (Viscount I 1785)
(Title pronounced "Dunnaral" Name Pronounced "Sentleger")

HAUT · ET · BON

Great and good

RICHARD ALLEN ST. LEGER, 10th Viscount (has not yet established his right to the Peerages); *b* 17 Aug 1946; *s* 1983; *ed* Orange Coast Coll, Cal; Air Traffic Control Specialist, Mississippi Univ: *m* 1970, Kathleen Mary, el da of Nathaniel Simcox, of Mallow, co Cork, and has issue.

Arms – Argent, fretty argent, a chief or **Crest** – A griffin passant or. **Supporters** – Two griffins or, wings elevated azure, fretty argent.
Residence – 1020 Skyline Drive, Laguna Beach, CA 92651, USA.

SON LIVING

Hon NATHANIEL WARHAM ROBERT ST JOHN, *b* 13 Sept 1971.

DAUGHTER LIVING

Hon Maeve Isobel Melva, *b* 1974.

BROTHERS LIVING

Hon David Hugh, *b* 1950; *ed* Calif State Univ, Long Beach.
Hon Edward Hayes, *b* 1960; *ed* Univ of Calif, Riverside.

SISTERS LIVING

Hon Elizabeth Adele, *b* 1953. *Residence* –
Hon Karen Jean, *b* 1955: *m* 1977 (*m diss* 1981), Richard Lehman, and has issue living, Corey R., *b* 1980.

WIDOW LIVING OF NINTH VISCOUNT

MELVA JEAN (*Melva, Viscountess Doneraile*), da of George W. Clifton, of St Louis, Mo: *m* 1945, the 9th Viscount, who *d* 1983.

PREDECESSORS – **(1)** ST. LEGER Aldworth, MP, for Doneraile 1761-76, succeeded in 1767 to the estates of his maternal uncle, Hayes St Leger, 4th and last Baron Kilmadon, and Viscount Doneraile (*cr* 1703), and assumed the surname of St Leger in lieu of his patronymic; *cr Baron Doneraile* of Doneraile (peerage of Ireland) 1776, and *Viscount Doneraile* (peerage of Ireland) 1785; *d* 1797; *s* by his son **(2)** HAYES, 2nd Viscount; *d* 1819; *s* by his son **(3)** HAYES, 3rd Viscount; *b* 1786; a Representative Peer: *m* 1816, Lady Charlotte Esther Bernard, da of 1st Earl of Bandon; *d* 1854; *s* by his son **(4)** HAYES, 4th Viscount; *b* 1818; a Representative Peer: *m* 1851, Mary Anne Grace Louisa, who *d* 1907, da of late George Lenox-Conyngham; *d* 1887; *s* by his cousin **(5)** RICHARD ARTHUR, 5th Viscount, son of Rev Richard Thomas Arthur St Leger, and grandson of Hon Richard St Leger MP, 2nd son of 1st Viscount, *b* 1825; *d* 1891; *s* by his nephew **(6)** EDWARD (son of the Rev Edward Frederick St Leger, and great-grandson of Hon Richard St Leger, 2nd son of 1st Viscount), 6th Viscount, *b* 1886; Mayor of City of Westminster 1919-20, and Chm of Metropolitan Asylums Board 1928-30; *d* 1941; *s* by his brother **(7)** HUGH, 7th Viscount; *b* 1869; admitted a Solicitor 1893: *m* 1920, Mary Isobel, who *d* 1976, da of Francis Morice, JP, of Whakapunake, Poverty Bay, NZ; *d* 1956; *s* by his kinsman, **(8)** ALGERNON EDWARD (son of late Richard William St Leger, grandson of late Hon Richard St. Leger, MP, 2nd son of 1st Viscount), 8th Viscount; *b* 1878: *m* 1919, Sylvia Stephenson, who *d* 19—, da of Alexander Mitchell; *d* 1957; *s* by his only son **(9)** RICHARD ST JOHN, 9th Viscount, *b* 1923: *m* 1945, Melva Joan, da of George W. Clifton, of St Louis, Mo; *d* 1983; *s* by his el son **(10)** RICHARD ALLEN, 10th Viscount and present peer; also Baron Doneraile.

DONNET OF BALGAY, BARONY OF (Donnet) (Extinct 1985)

SONS LIVING OF LIFE BARON

Hon Gavin Alexander (9 Scotscraig Place, Broughty Ferry, Dundee DD5 3SU), *b* 1950; *ed* Hyndland Sec Sch, Glasgow: *m* 1976, Margaret Louise Scott, and has issue living, Jane, *b* 19—, — Fiona, *b* 19—.
Hon Stephen Christopher (9 Hollymount, Bearsden, Glasgow G61), *b* 1960, *ed* Jordanhill Coll Sch, and Strathclyde Univ: *m* 1989, Deborah Rae, da of Edward James Campbell, and has issue living, Alexander Edward, *b* 1992.

DAUGHTER LIVING OF LIFE BARON

Hon (Sandra) Lillias, *b* 1947: *m* 1971, Dr Nigel Duguid, of 8 Sackville St, St John's, Newfoundland, A1A 4R3, Canada, and has issue.

WIDOW LIVING OF LIFE BARON

MARY (*Baroness Donnet of Balgay*), da of Gavin Mitchell Black: *m* 1945, Baron Donnet of Balgay (Life Baron), who *d* 1985.

DONOUGHMORE, EARL OF (Hely-Hutchinson) Sits as VISCOUNT HUTCHINSON (UK 1821) (Earl I 1800)
(Title pronounced "Dunomore")

FORTITER GERIT CRUCEM

He bravely bears the cross

RICHARD MICHAEL JOHN HELY-HUTCHINSON, 8th Earl; *b* 8 Aug 1927; *s* 1981; *ed* Winchester, Groton, USA, and New Coll, Oxford (MA, BM and BCh); Capt RAMC; Chm Hodder Headline plc since 1986; *m* 1951, Sheila, da of late Frank Frederick Parsons, and has issue.

Arms – Quarterly: 1st and 4th per pale gules and azure, a lion rampant, between eight cross-crosslets argent, *Hutchinson*; 2nd azure, a fesse between three bucks' heads erased in chief argent, and in base a demi-lion rampant or, *Hely*; 3rd azure, a garb or, between three wolves' heads erased argent, *Nickson*. **Crest** – Out of a ducal coronet a demi cockatrice, wings elevated azure. **Supporters** – Two cockatrices, wings elevated or, collared sable, combs and wattles gules, and charged on the breast with a wreath of laurel vert
Residence – The Manor House, Bampton, Oxon OX8 2LQ. *Club* – Jockey (Paris).

SONS LIVING

JOHN MICHAEL JAMES (*Viscount Suirdale*) (38 Thornton Avenue, W4 1QG), *b* 7 Aug 1952; *ed* Harrow; Man Dir Hodder Headline plc since 19—: *m* 1977, Marie-Claire, da of Gerard van den Driessche, and has issue:—

SON LIVING— *Hon* Richard Gregory, *b* 3 July 1980.

DAUGHTERS LIVING— *Hon* Marie-Pierre Joanna, *b* 1978, — *Hon* Tatiana Louise, *b* 1985.

Hon Timothy Mark, *b* 1953; *ed* Eton.
Hon Nicholas David, *b* 1955; *ed* Harrow: *m* 1982, Fiona Margaret MacIntyre, yr da of the late Maj W. R. Watson, and has issue living, Seamus David, *b* 1987, — Flora Clare, *b* 1984.
Hon Ralph Charles, *b* 1961; *ed* Eton.

BROTHER LIVING

Hon Mark, *b* 1934; *ed* Eton, at Magdalen Coll, Oxford (BSc, MA), and Mass Inst of Technology, USA (SM); late 2nd Lt Irish Guards: *m* 1962, Margaret, yr da of late Dr Robert Rowan Woods of 3 Fitzwilliam Place, Dublin, 2, and has issue living, Henry Peter, *b* 1963, — Walter James, *b* 1966, — Anna Doreen, *b* 1969. *Residence* – Larch Hill, Coolock Lane, Dublin 17.

SISTER LIVING

Lady Sarah Elena, *b* 1930: *m* 1951, William Collins, and has issue living, William Noel, *b* 1952: *m* 1979, Lucinda Rosemary, eldest da of Michael Harper Gow (*see* Greenwell, Bt), and has issue living, Emily Lucinda Julian *b* 1981, Melissa Daisy *b* 1984, — Jane Margarita, *b* 1954, — Tiffany Anne, *b* 1964, — Bryony Mary Pierre, *b* 1974. *Residence* – House of Craigie, by Kilmarnock, Ayrshire.

WIDOW LIVING OF SON OF SIXTH EARL

Barbara Mary, 3rd da of Maj Hugh James Wyld, of Essendon Close, Hatfield, Herts: *m* 1934, Lt-Col Hon David Edward Hely-Hutchinson, who *d* 1984, and has issue (see colls infra). *Residences* – Orchard House, Biddestone, nr Chippenham, Wilts; Cranston, North Berwick, E Lothian.

WIDOW LIVING OF SEVENTH EARL

DOROTHY JEAN, MBE (*Dowager Countess of Donoughmore*); MBE (Civil) 1947; da of late John Beaumont Hotham (*see* B Hotham, colls): *m* 1925, the 7th Earl, who *d* 1981. *Residence* – High Coodham, Symington, Ayrshire.

COLLATERAL BRANCHES LIVING

Issue of late Lt-Col Hon David Edward Hely-Hutchinson, yr son of 6th Earl, *b* 1911, *d* 1984: *m* 1934, Barbara Mary (ante), 3rd da of Maj Hugh James Wyld, of Essendon Close, Hatfield, Herts:—

Rose Mary, *b* 1935: *m* 1959, William Mackinnon Fernie, of Manor Farm, Tellisford, Bath, Avon BA3 6RL, and has issue living, James Mackinnon, *b* 1962: *m* 1987, Fiona Elizabeth Swann, — Barbara Alison, *b* 1960: *m* 1988, Colin Francis Smith, — Juliet Rose, *b* 1967, — Deborah Mary, *b* 1971. ——— Jean Elena, *b* 1939: *m* 1972, Bernard B. D. Kain, of Poplar Farm, Atworth, Melksham, Wilts. ——— Pollyann Elise, *b* 1942: *m* 1970, Capt Hamish J. Lochore, R Scots Greys (ret) (*see* Brooke, Bt, *cr* 1919), of Burgie House, Forres, Moray, and has issue living, Alexander David, *b* 1971, — Hugh Mark, *b* 1974, — Clare Hermione, *b* 1977. ——— Kathryn Gabriel, *b* 1944: *m* 1973, Maj Christopher Brian Amery, Blues and Royals (ret), of Flash Farm, Antrobus, Northwich, Cheshire, and has issue living, Edward Mark Richard, *b* 1975, — Nicholas John David, *b* 1979. ——— Deborah Jane, *b* 1949: *m* 1971, William Backhouse, of Layer Marney Wick, Colchester, Essex, CO5 9UT, and has issue (*see* Backhouse, Bt, colls).

Grandchildren of late Rt Hon Sir Walter Francis Hely-Hutchinson, GCMG, 2nd son of 4th Earl:—
Issue of late Christopher Douglas Hely-Hutchinson, MC, b 1885, d 1958: m 1914, Gladys, who d 1974, da of William
Beachy Head, of Johannesburg:—
Frances Anne (*Lady Stevens*), b 1917; Devon Rep of Nat Art Collections Fund 1977-88: m 1940, Sir John Melior Stevens,
KCMG, DSO, OBE, who d 1973, and has issue living, John Christopher Courtenay, MEP, b 1955; MEP Thames Valley since
1989, — Jane Frances, b 1945; MD, — Mary Anne Victoria, b 1947; MA (London); Art Historian: m 1980, John Myerscough,
of 39 Campden St, W8, and has issue living, John Claude b 1982, Catherine Anne b 1986. *Residence* – East Worlington
House, Crediton, Devon.
Issue of late Maurice Robert Hely-Hutchinson, MC, b 1887, d 1961: m 1920, Melita Agnes Mary, who d 1987, da of
late Adm Sir Colin Richard Keppel, GCVO, KCIE, CB, DSO (*see* E Albemarle, colls, 1985 Edn):—
Henry Aymar, b 1925; ed Eton; late Lieut Coldstream Guards: m 1957, Maria Anna, da of late Charles de Erney, of Budapest,
Hungary, and has issue living, Nicholas Charles, b 1958: m 1986, Kate Johanna, elder da of Timothy Connolly, of Knockholt,
Kent, and has issue living, Harry Thomas b 1992, Rose Mollie b 1990, — Colin Henry (19 Jennings Court, Westport,
Connecticut 06880, USA), b 1959: m 1983, Emma (Pipi), el da of T. Hugh T. Morton, of London and New York, and has
issue living, James Alexander b 1986, Nicholas Henry b 1991, Victoria Sarah b 1984, Alexandra Melita b 1990, — Melita
Louise, b 1962: m 1992, Stephen Blair Glaister, of 8 Frere St, SW11 2JA, son of Thomas Glaister, of Cartmel, Cumbria, and
has issue living, Henry Augustus b 1994, Jessica b 1993. *Residence* – 22 Kylestrome House, Cundy St, SW1W 9JT.
— Colin Christopher (twin) (c/o 22 Kylestrome House, Cundy St, SW1W 9JT), b 1925; ed Eton; late Lt Irish Gds.
— Marie Elizabeth, b 1921. *Residence* – 35, Richmond Court, 200 Sloane St, SW1 9QU. — Diana Margaret, b 1928: m
1960, Walter von Halle, of 7 Condray Place, Battersea Church Rd, SW11 3PE. — Patricia May b 1929, DL, JP: m 1950,
Maj George Burrell MacKean, DL, JP, who d 1983, and has issue living, William Muir b 1954: m 1988, Charlotte, yr da of
Paddy Davies, of Slinfold, Sussex, and has issue living, George Louis b 1992, Emily Rose b 1990, — Shane Charles Robert, b
1958: m 1983, Elizabeth A. Paul, of Maryland, USA, and has issue living, William Muir b 1987, Cassian Donald Burrell b
1988, Milo David Feargus b 1992, India May Frances b 1990, — Kirsten (Curzon) Henrietta, b 1951: m 1st, 1972 (m diss
1986), Sir (Robert) Nicholas Oliver Couper, 6th Bt; 2ndly, 1987, Michael J. Tussaud, elder son of late Angelo Tussaud, —
Claudia Margaret Diana, b 1953; d 1957, — Georgia Isabella, b 1961: m 1983, Maj Michael B. Stubington. *Residence* –
Loughanmore, 51 Loughermore Rd, Antrim BT41 2HN.
Issue of late (Christian) Victor (Noel Hope) Hely-Hutchinson, DMus, b 1901, d 1947; m 1925, Marjorie Anna, who d
1988, da of Dr Dirk de Vos Hugo, of Cape Town, S Africa:—
John Richard (Moolmanshof, 217 Voortrek Str, Swellendam 6740, S Africa), b 1929; MSc, MIEE: m 1957, Allison Joyce, only
da of Ernest Simpson, of Paarl, S Africa, and has two adopted children, John Andrew, b 1960, — Teresa Mary, b 1963.
— Christopher Adrian, b 1931; Lt-Cdr RN (ret): m 1963, Beatrice Mary, yr da of late Stephen Harris, of Barbon, Westmorland, and has issue living, Adam Hugo, b 1968, — Henrietta Lucy, b 1973. *Residence* – The Garden House, Brand Lane,
Ludlow, Shropshire.

Grandchildren of late John Hely-Hutchinson, son of late Capt Hon Coote Hely-Hutchinson, RN, brother of
3rd Earl:—
Issue of late Lieut-Col Coote Robert Hely-Hutchinson, OBE, b 1870, d 1930: m 1914, Julia, who d 1948, da of late
William Browne-Clayton, of Browne's Hill, Carlow:—
Michael (Croft Cottage, New Marton, St Martins, Oswestry, Shropshire), b 1916; Maj (ret) Roy Norfolk Regt: m 1951, Ruth
Somerled, da of late Kenneth Mackenzie, MD, FRCS, of Auckland, New Zealand, and has issue living, Caroline Anne, b 1954:
m 1979, Timothy Neal Harlow, MB, ChB, of Whitley House, Bradninch, Exeter, Devon EX5 4LA, and has issue living,
Alastair Michael b 1984, Jennifer Fiona b 1985. — David Coote, b 1918: m 1948, Geraldine Mary, da of late Donough
Richard O'Brien (*see* B Inchiquin, colls), and has issue living, Fiona Kathryn O'Brien, b 1965. *Residence* – Parteenalax,
Limerick. — Mary Caroline, b (twin) 1914. — Julia Louisa, b 1921.

PREDECESSORS – (1) CHRISTIANA, da of Abraham Nickson and wife of the Rt Hon John Hely-Hutchinson, an eminent
lawyer and statesman of Ireland, was cr Baroness Donoughmore, of Knocklofty, co Tipperary (peerage of Ireland) 1783; d
1788; s by her son (2) RICHARD HELY, 2nd Baron; a Gen in the Army; cr Viscount Donoughmore of Knocklofty (peerage of Ireland) 1797, and Earl of Donoughmore (peerage of Ireland) 1801, with remainder to the heirs male of his mother, and while a
Representative Peer was cr Viscount Hutchinson (peerage of United Kingdom) 1821, with limitation as in peerage of 1801; d
unmarried, when all the honours devolved upon his brother (3) JOHN, GCB (2nd Earl, who in 1801 had been cr Baron
Hutchinson, of Alexandria and Knocklofty peerage of UK); d 1832, when the Barony of Hutchinson became ext and the other
honours, devolved upon his nephew (4) JOHN HELY, 3rd Earl, son of Hon Francis Hely, MP, 3rd son of Baroness
Donoughmore; d 1851; s by his son (5) RICHARD JOHN, PC, 4th Earl; b 1823; Pres of Board of Trade: m 1847, Thomasine
Jocelyn, da of Walter Steele, of Moynalty, co Monaghan; d 1866; s by his son (6) JOHN LUKE GEORGE, KCMG, 5th Earl, b
1848: m 1874, Frances Isabella, who d 1925, da of late Gen Stephens, HEICS; d 1900; s by his son (7) RICHARD WALTER JOHN,
KP, PC, 6th Earl; b 1875; Under-Sec of State for War 1903-1904; Civil Member of the Army Council 1904-1905, and Chm of
Committees and Dep Speaker in House of Lords 1911-31; a Member of Senate of S Ireland 1921; m 1901, Elena Maria, who
d 1944, da of late M. P. Grace, of New York, USA; d 1948: s by his son (8) JOHN MICHAEL HENRY, 7th Earl, b 1902; Col RAC;
MP for Peterborough (C) 1943-45: m 1925, Dorothy Jean, MBE, da of late John Beaumont Hotham (*see* B Hotham, colls); d
1981; s by his el son (9) RICHARD MICHAEL JOHN, 8th Earl and present peer; also Viscount Donoughmore, Viscount
Hutchinson, and Baron Donoughmore.

DONOUGHUE, BARON (Donoughue) (Life Baron 1985)

BERNARD DONOUGHUE, b 8 Sept 1934, son of late Thomas Joseph Donoughue, by his late wife, Maud Violet
Andrews; ed Secondary Modern Sch, Gram Sch, Northampton, and Lincoln Coll and Nuffield Coll, Oxford
(MA, DPhil); FRHistS; Sr Policy Advisor to PM 1974-79, Development Dir Economist Intelligence Unit
1979-81, Assist Ed The Times 1981-82, Head of Investment Policy and Research Grievson Grant & Co
1982-86, Head of Investment Policy and International Research 1986-88, since when Exec Vice Chairman
London, Bishopsgate International plc; author; cr Baron Donoughue, of Ashton, co Northants (Life Baron)
1985: m 1959, Carol Ruth, da of late Abraham Goodman, and has issue.
Residence – 7 Brookfield Park, NW5. *Address* – 1 Sloane Sq, SW1.

SONS LIVING

Hon Paul Michael David, b 1969; ed William Ellis Sch.
Hon Stephen Joel, b 1969; ed William Ellis Sch.

DAUGHTERS LIVING

Hon Rachel Anne, *b* 1965.
Hon Kate Miriam, *b* 1967.

DONOVAN, BARONY OF (Donovan) (Extinct 1971)

SONS LIVING OF LIFE BARON

Hon Hugh Desmond (40 Felden St, SW6), *b* 1934; *ed* Harrow, and New Coll, Oxford: *m* 1968, Margaret Mary, el da of late Hugh Forbes Arbuthnott, of Winterfold House, Chaddesley Corbett, Worcs (*see* V Arbuthnott, colls), and has issue living, Charles Edward Horatius, *b* 1974.

Hon John (Great Rissington Farm, Great Rissington, Glos), *b* 1938; *ed* Harrow, and Univ Coll, Oxford: *m* 1973, Pauline Nicole Christine, yst da of H. A. Klene, of Wittenburgerwerg 4, Wasennaar, The Hague, and has issue living, Florence, *b* 1977, — Miranda, *b* 1979.

DAUGHTER LIVING OF LIFE BARON

Hon Susan Elizabeth, *b* 1936: *m* 1960 (*m diss* 1984), Gerard Francis Horton, of 27 Weemala Rd, Northbridge, NSW, and has issue.

DORCHESTER, BARONY OF (Carleton) (Extinct 1963)

DAUGHTER LIVING OF SECOND BARON

Hon Lorraine Charmian Gabrielle, *b* 1919; formerly Dist Commr Girl Guides, Chelsea, and Hon Sec Chelsea Soc; formerly Chm West Dean Parish Meeting, and Editor FANY Gazette; Cllr Cuckmere Valley Parish Council 1990: *m* 1947, James Metcalfe Knowles, FRIBA, FRICS, MRTP, who *d* 1993, and has issue living Thomas James Metcalfe, *b* 1952: *m* 1993, Colleen M. G., only da of Patrick Sullivan, of New York, — Elizabeth Charmian Carleton, *b* 1949: *m* 1976, Christopher J. A. Coleman. *Residence* – Sheep Pen Cottage, Friston Forest, Westdean, Seaford, E Sussex.

DORMAND OF EASINGTON, BARON (Dormand) (Life Baron 1987)

JOHN DONKIN DORMAND, son of Bernard Dormand, of Haswell, co Durham; *b* 27 Aug 1919; *ed* Bede Coll, Durham, Loughborough Coll, St Peter's Coll, Oxford and Harvard; Hon Fell St Peter's Coll, Oxford; teacher 1940-48; educn adviser 1948-52 and 1957-63, District Educn Offr Easington RDC 1963-70; Dep Chm Teesside Devel Corpn; Assist Govt Whip 1974, a Lord Commr of HM Treasury 1974-79, Chm Parl Labour Party 1981-87, MP (*Lab*) Easington 1970-87; *cr Baron Dormand of Easington*, of Easington, co Durham (Life Baron) 1987: *m* 1963, Doris, da of Thomas Robinson, of Houghton-le-Spring, co Durham. *Address* – c/o House of Lords, London SW1

DORMER, BARON (Dormer) (Baron E 1615, Bt E 1615)

CIO CHE DIO VUOLE IO VOGLIO

What God wills I will

JOSEPH SPENCER PHILIP DORMER, 16th Baron, and 16th Baronet; *b* 4 Sept 1914; *s* 1975; *ed* Ampleforth, and Ch Ch, Oxford; late Capt Scots Gds.

Arms – Azure, ten billets, four, three, two, and one, or; on a chief of the second, a demi-lion issuant sable. **Crest** – A falcon, wings displayed and inverted argent, beaked, membered, and belled or, standing on a falconer's right-hand glove fesseways argent. **Supporters** – Two falcons, wings displayed and inverted argent, beaked, membered, and belled or.
Residence – Grove Park, Warwick CV35 8RF.

SISTER LIVING

Hon Rosamund Jane, *b* 1911. *Residence* – School House, Spetchley, Worcester.

DAUGHTERS LIVING OF FIFTEENTH BARON

Hon Jane Maureen Thérèse, *b* 1945: *m* 1st, 1966, H. A. Samuel Sandbach; 2ndly, 1980, Sqdn-Ldr Geoffrey E. Meek, RAF, who *d* 1984; 3rdly, 1988, Lt-Cmdr R. N. F. Glennie, RN (ret), and has issue living (by 1st *m*), James Peter Charles, *b* 1969, — Emma Pauline Jane, *b* 1967: *m* 1993, Graham Defries, son of Nicholas Defries, of Merstham, Surrey. *Residences* – 44 Homefield Rd, W4 2LW; Church Farm Cottage, East Wittering, Chichester, W Sussex PO20 8PT.

Hon Catherine Mary, *b* 1950: *m* 1st, 1972 (*m diss* 1989), Christopher John Godfrey Bird (*see* Vavasour, Bt); 2ndly, 1992, Dr Michael Simon Stone, and has issue living (by 2nd *m*), Raphael Charles, *b* 1992. *Residence* – 81 Lakeside Rd, N13.

WIDOW LIVING OF FIFTEENTH BARON

Lady MAUREEN THERESE JOSEPHINE NOEL, only da of 4th Earl of Gainsborough: *m* 1st, 1944, the 15th Baron, who *d* 1975; 2ndly, 1982, as his 2nd wife, Peregrine Edward Launcelot Fellowes, of The Court, Chipping Campden, Glos GL55 6JQ.

COLLATERAL BRANCHES LIVING

Grandchildren of late Hon Hubert Francis Dormer, 3rd son of 11th Baron, *b* 1837, *d* 1913: *m* 1865, Mary, who *d* 1938, da of Kenelm Digby:—
    Issue of late Edward Henry Dormer, *b* 1870, *d* 1943: *m* 1903, Hon Vanessa, Margaret, who *d* 1962, da of 1st Baron Borwick:—
GEOFFREY HENRY, *b* 13 May 1920; *ed* Eton, and Trin Coll, Camb; Lt-Cdr RNR; 1939-45 War as Lt RNVR: *m* 1947 (*m diss* 1957), Janet, da of James F. A. Readman, of 16 Lennox Street, Edinburgh; 2ndly, 1958, Pamela, da of late Wallace Levick Simpson, and has issue living, (by 1st *m*) Carol Susan, *b* 1949: *m* 1974, Patrick Howard Lynn, of Hockerwood Park, Southwell, Notts NG25 0PZ, and has issue living, Iain Patrick *b* 1978, Joshua Alexander *b* 1980, Sarah Amy Janet *b* 1986, — Sally Ann Vanessa, *b* 1951: *m* 1973, Roger Arthur Skinner, of Rushwick, Worcester, and has issue living, Timothy Roger *b* 1977, Clare Vanessa *b* 1975, — (by 2nd *m*) William Robert, *b* 1960: *m* 1985, Paula Sharon, da of Peter Robinson, of Heaton Mersey, Cheshire, — Hugh Richard Cecil, *b* 1964. *Residence* – Yew Tree Cottage, Dittisham, Devon TQ7 0EX. *Club* – Naval and Military.
    Issue of late John Hubert Aloysius Dormer, *b* 1874, *d* 1946: *m* 1900, Virginia Sinclair, who *d* 1956, da of late Charles Tankerville Chamberlaine Bey, of Paris:—
Charles Hubert Aloysius (PO Box 423, Hudson, Quebec J0P 1HO, Canada), *b* 1906: *m* 1st, 1930 (*m diss* 1946), Mary Johnson, of Ottawa, Canada; 2ndly, 1946 (*m diss* 1948), Jane Loutitt Ellis; 3rdly, 1948 (*m diss* 1991), Mary Johnson, his 1st wife, and has issue living, (by 2nd *m*) Anthony Fredrick Charles, *b* 1946: *m* 1966, Anita Lusick, of Melbourne, Australia, and has issue living, Aaron *b* 1972, Justine *b* 1974, — Lynn Elizabeth Jane, *b* 1944, — Susan Ann Sturrock, *b* 1948: *m* 1973, Peter James McNevern, of Queensland, Australia. —— Richard Joseph Thaddeus, DSC (Flat 6, The Manor Park Lands Gdns, Inner Park Rd, Wimbledon, SW19), *b* 1913; late RNVR. —— Hélène Venetia Anne, *b* 1907: *m* 1937, Frank R. Kelley, who *d* 1985, of 7 Ridgewood Lane, Westport, Conn 06880, USA, and has had issue, Christopher Francis Valentine (11818 Grey Birch Place, Reston, Virginia 22091-4223, USA), *b* 1939: *m* 1st, 1963 (*m diss* 1976), Ruth Jordan, of Bethesda, Maryland, USA; 2ndly, 1978, Elizabeth Ann Bowser, of Norfolk, Virginia, USA, and has issue living (by 1st *m*), Kevin Francis Dormer *b* 1966, Laura Anne *b* 1964, (by 2nd *m*) Patrick David Christopher *b* 1978, Matthew John Martin *b* 1980, — Peter John Dormer (10 Cranbrook Drive, Centerport, NY 11721, USA), *b* 1943: *m* 1967, Patricia F. Ruehle, of Chicago, USA, and has issue living, Peter John *b* 1983, Elizabeth Louise Estelle *b* 1978, Margaret Evelyn Venetia *b* 1981, — David Richard Paul, *b* 1946; *d* 1972. —— Pia Magdalen Virginia, *b* 1920: *m* 1945, Col Henry Thomas Bernard Bellingham Rooke, MBE, Indian Army (ret) (Somerville, Bt, colls), and has issue living, Henry John Patrick Dormer (c/o Yew Tree Cottage, Higher Holton, Wincanton, Som BA9 8AP), *b* 1946; *ed* Ampleforth; Maj Queen's Own R Irish Hussars: *m* 1969, Helen Elizabeth, da of William McLaren Howard, QC. *Residence* – Pigeons' Piece, Wootton, Woodstock, Oxford. —— Louise Cecilia Mary, *b* 1922 (*m diss* 1954), Capt Peter Bailward, RA; 2ndly, 1954, Maj William Goulding Petrie-Hay, RA, and has issue living (by 1st *m*), David John Aucher Michael (Vancouver, BC, Canada), *b* 1941; *ed* Ampleforth: *m* 1969, Charlotte Martha Petra, da of Herbert Frohberg, of Ottawa, and has issue living, Alan *b* 1975, — Sarah Jane Mary (Sally), *b* 1944: *m* 1965, Lt-Col Richard Grahame Dugard Showell, TD, of The Old School House, Bishampton, Pershore, Worcs WR10 2LX, and has had issue, Jeremy Peter Dugard *b* 1965; *d* 1974, Alexander Geoffrey Dugard *b* 1971; *ed* Belmont Abbey, Claire Louise Dugard *b* 1966, — (by 2nd *m*) Rufus William, *b* 1955. *Address* – Lower Bouts Farm, Inkberrow, Worcs.
    Issue of late Kenelm Everard Dormer, *b* 1879, *d* 1935: *m* 1910, Josephine, who *d* 1965, da of late Hon John T. Toohey, of Sydney:—
John Kenelm (Flat E, 36 Courtfield Gdns, SW5), *b* 1915; *ed* Downside; 1939-45 War as Capt KOYLI: *m* 1984, Kathleen, da of Frederick Rhys Michael, of Cairns, Australia.
    Issue of late Capt Robert Stanhope Dormer, *b* 1880, *d* 1960: *m* 1927, Ebba, who *d* 1961, da of late Charles Cecil Beresford Whyte, of Hatley Manor and Newton Manor, co Leitrim, and widow of Sir Everard Alexander Hambro, KCVO:—
Michael Henry Stanhope, *b* 1930; is a Knight of Sovereign Order of Malta, and a Kt of Justice of the Constantinian Order of St George: *m* 1959, Daphne Margaret, el da of the late Capt O. J. Battine, and has issue living, Merlin Robert Colum Charles, *b* 1963, — Leanda Xenia Sophia Stanhope, *b* 1959: *m* 1984, Peter Andrew Paul March Phillipps de Lisle, of Osbaston

Hall, Osbaston, Leics, 2nd son of Gerard Arnaud Amaury March Phillipps de Lisle, of Quenby Hall, Hungarton, Leics, and has issue living, Rupert Gerard Xavier *b* 1986, Christian Michael Frederick *b* 1988, Dominic Robert Peter *b* 1990, — Athena Cecilia Stanhope, *b* 1961. *Residence* – Bowdown House, Greenham, Newbury.

PREDECESSORS – (1) *Sir* ROBERT DORMER, Knt; *cr* a *Baronet* 10 June, 1615, and *Baron Dormer*, of Wenge (peerage of England) June 20th, 1615; *d* 1616; *s* by his grandson (2) ROBERT, 2nd Baron; a Gen of Horse; *cr Viscount Ascot and Earl of Carnarvon* (peerage of England) 1628; killed at first battle of Newbury 1643; *s* by his son (3) CHARLES, 2nd Earl; *d* 1709, when the ealdom and viscountcy expired, and the barony reverted to his kinsman (4) ROWLAND, 4th Baron, grandson of Hon Anthony, 2nd son of 1st Baron; *d* 1712; *s* by his cousin (5) CHARLES, 5th Baron, grandson of the Hon Robert, 3rd son of 1st Baron; *d* 1728; *s* by his son (6) *Rev* CHARLES, 6th Baron, a Priest of the Church of Rome; did not assume the title; *d* 1761; *s* by his brother (7) JOHN, 7th Baron; *d* 1785; *s* by his el son (8) CHARLES, 8th Baron; *d* 1894; *s* by his son (9) CHARLES, 9th Baron; *d* unmarried 1819; *s* by his half-brother (10) JOHN EVELYN PIERREPONT, 10th Baron; having conformed to the Church of England took his seat in the House of Lords; *d* 1826; *s* by his kinsman (11) JOSEPH THADDEUS, 11th Baron, son of John, 2nd son of 7th Baron; *b* 1790: *m* 1829, Elizabeth Anne, who *d* 1883, da of Sir Henry Joseph Tichborne, 8th Bt; at one time an officer of rank in the Austrian service: *d* 1871; *s* by his son (12) JOHN BAPTIST JOSEPH, 12th Baron, *b* 1830: *m* 1st, 1866, Louisa, who *d* 1868, da of late Col Edward King Tenison, of Kilronan Castle, Roscommon; 2ndly, 1871, Leonie, who *d* 1883, da of Mons Fortamps, a Senator of Belgium, and widow of Count Alfred de Beuren; 3rdly, 1885, Emily Constance Campbell, who *d* 1919, da of John Bald, of Monzie Castle, Perth; *s* by his nephew (13) ROLAND JOHN, 13th Baron, *b* 1862; sometime Sub-Director, Secretariat, Egyptian Ministry of Finance: *m* 1897, Marie Hanem, who *d* 1964, el da of late F. Eywaz, of Cairo; *d* 1920; *s* by his brother (14) CHARLES JOSEPH THADDEUS, CBE, 14th Baron; *b* 1864; Capt RN; a Gentleman Usher to HM King George V 1919-22: *m* 1903, Caroline Mary, who *d* 1951, da of late Sir Robert Cavendish Spencer Clifford, 3rd Bt (ext): *d* 1922: *s* by his el son (15) CHARLES WALTER JAMES, 15th Baron; *b* 1903; ADC to Gov-Gen of NZ 1939-41 *m* 1944, Lady Maureen Thérèse Josephine Noel (who *m* 2ndly, 1982, as his 2nd wife, Peregrine Edward Launcelot Fellowes), only da of 4th Earl of Gainsborough; *d* 1975; *s* by his brother (16) JOSEPH SPENCER PHILIP, 16th Baron and present peer.

Douglas and Clydesdale, Marquess of; son of Duke of Hamilton and Brandon.

DOUGLAS OF BARLOCH, BARONY OF (Douglas) (Extinct 1980)

DAUGHTER LIVING OF FIRST BARON (*By 1st m*)

Hon Frances Margaret, MB and BS London 1943; Fellow of Royal College of Anaethetists 1957: *m* 1943, Kenneth Ulyatt, PhD, MSc, and has issue living, Charles Kenneth, *b* 1945, — James Francis, *b* 1950, — Mary Stella Miranda, *b* 1958. *Residence* – 8 Cambridge Rd, Battersea Park, SW11.

DOUGLAS OF KIRTLESIDE, BARONY OF (Douglas) (Extinct 1969)

DAUGHTER LIVING OF FIRST BARON

Hon Katharine Ann, *b* 1957: *m* 1984, Geoffrey Andrews.

WIDOW LIVING OF FIRST BARON

HAZEL (*Baroness Douglas of Kirtleside*), da of late George Eric Maas Walker, of Mill Hill, NW, and widow of Capt W. E. R. Walker: *m* 1955, as his 3rd wife, the 1st Baron, who *d* 1969, when the title became ext.

DOUGLASS OF CLEVELAND, BARONY OF (Douglass) (Extinct 1978)

DAUGHTER LIVING OF LIFE BARON

Hon Jean, *b* 1928: *m* 1952, Garry Long, FCIS, of Malt House, Farm Lower Rd, Stoke Mandeville, Bucks.

WIDOW LIVING OF LIFE BARON

EDITH (*Baroness Douglass of Cleveland*) (5 The Chase, Stanmore, Middx), da of Charles Amer: *m* 1926, Baron Douglass of Cleveland (Life Baron), who *d* 1978.

Doune, Lord; son of Earl of Moray.

Douro, Marquess of; son of Duke of Wellington.

DOWDING, BARON (Dowding) (Baron UK 1943)

PIERS HUGH TREMENHEERE DOWDING, 3rd Baron; *b* 18 Feb 1948; *s* 1992; *ed* Fettes, and Amherst Coll, Mass, USA (BA); Asso Prof of English at Okayama Shoka Univ, Japan since 1977: *m* 1973, Noriko Shiho, of Japan, and has issue.

Arms – Argent, three bars gemel sable, over all a fleur-de-lys azure, on a chief of the second, three Doric columns of the first. **Crest** – Upon a catherine wheel azure, a falcon rising or, belled and hooded gules.

DAUGHTERS LIVING

Hon Rosemary June, *b* 1975.
Hon Yuki Elizabeth, *b* 1989.

BROTHER LIVING

Hon MARK DENIS JAMES, *b* 11 July 1949; *ed* Wymondham Coll, Norfolk: *m* 1982, Heather, da of Stanley Arter, of S Africa, and has issue living, Alexander, *b* 1983.

MOTHER LIVING

LABORARE · ORARE · EST

To work is to pray

Alison Margaret, da of James Bannerman, LRCP, LRCS, of 158 Newmarket Rd, Norwich, and widow of Maj R. W. H. Peebles: *m* 2ndly, 1947 (*m diss* 1960), Wing-Cdr Hon Derek Hugh Tremenheere Dowding, RAF (later 2nd Baron Dowding), who *d* 1992; 3rdly 1963, David Hartnell-Beavis. *Residence* – The Manor, Norwich Rd, Aylsham, Norfolk NR11 6BN.

WIDOW LIVING OF SECOND BARON

ODETTE LUCIE MARIE SOPHIE (*Odette, Baroness Dowding*), da of late Louis Joseph Houles, of Toulouse, France, and formerly wife of Brian Hughes: *m* 1961, as his 3rd wife, Wing-Cdr the 2nd Baron, RAF, who *d* 1992. *Residence* – 501 Gilbert House, Barbican, EC2Y 8BD.

PREDECESSORS – **(1)** *Air Ch Marshal Sir* HUGH CASWELL TREMENHEERE DOWDING, GCB, GCVO, CMG, son of Arthur John Caswall Dowding; *b* 1882; 1914-18 War (despatches); Dir of Training Air Min 1926-29, AOC Fighting Area, Air Defence of Gt Britain 1929-30, a Member of Air Council (Research and Development) 1930-36, and AOC-in-C Fighter Command 1936-40 *cr Baron Dowding*, of Bentley Priory, co Middlesex (peerage of UK) 1943: *m* 1st, 1913, Clarice Maud, who *d* 1920, da of Capt John Williams; 2ndly, 1951, Muriel, who *d* 1993, da of late John Albino, of Richmond, Surrey, and widow of Jack Maxwell Whiting, P/O RAFVR (*ka* 1944); *d* 1970; *s* by his son **(2)** DEREK HUGH TREMENHEERE, 2nd Baron; *b* 1919; Wing-Cdr RAF, 1939-45 War: *m* 1st, 1940 (*m diss* 1947), Joan Myrle, da of Donald James Stuart, of Nairn; 2ndly, 1947 (*m diss* 1960), Alison Margaret, da of James Bannerman, LRCP, LRCS, of 158 Newmarket Rd, Norwich, and widow of Maj R. W. H. Peebles; 3rdly, 1961, Mrs Odette Lucie Marie Sophie Hughes, da of late Louis Joseph Houles, of Toulouse, France, and formerly wife of Brian Hughes; *d* 1992; *s* by his elder son **(3)** PIERS HUGH TREMENHEERE, 3rd Baron and present peer.

DOWNE, VISCOUNT (Dawnay) Sits as BARON DAWNAY (UK 1897). (Viscount I 1681)

JOHN CHRISTIAN GEORGE DAWNAY, 11th Viscount; *b* 18 Jan 1935; *s* 1965; *ed* Eton and Ch Ch, Oxford; DL N Yorks: *m* 1965, Alison Diana, da of Ian Francis Henry Sconce, OBE, TD, of Brasted, Kent, and has issue.

Arms – Argent, on a bend cottised sable, three annulets of the field. **Crest** – A demi-Saracen in armour couped at the thighs, wreathed about the temples proper, holding in the dexter hand a ring or, stoned azure, and in the sinister a lions' jamb erased gold, armed gules. **Supporters** – Two lions or, ducally crowned argent, each gorged with a collar cottised sable, charged with three annulets of the second. *Seat* – Wykeham Abbey, Scarborough, Yorkshire. *Town Residence* – 5 Douro Place, W8.

SON LIVING

Hon RICHARD HENRY, 9 April 1967.

DAUGHTER LIVING

Hon Sarah Frances, *b* 1970.

WIDOW LIVING OF SON OF TENTH VISCOUNT

TIMET · PUDOREM

He fears shame

Gillian, yst da of late Maj James Cyril Aubrey George Dance, MP, of Moreton House, Moreton Morrell, Warwicks, and formerly wife of Capt Simon George Melville Portal (*see* Portal, Bt, colls): *m* 1976, Hon James Richard Dawnay, who *d* 1991, and has issue (*see* colls, infra).

COLLATERAL BRANCHES LIVING

Issue of late Hon James Richard Dawnay, yr son of 10th Viscount, b 1937, d 1991: m 1976, Gillian (ante), yst da of late Maj James Cyril Aubrey George Dance, MP, of Moreton House, Moreton Morrell, Warwicks, and formerly wife of Capt Simon George Melville Portal (see Portal, Bt, colls):—
Thomas Payan, b 1978.

Issue of late Maj Hon George William ffolkes Dawnay, MC, yr son of 9th Viscount, b 1909, d 1990: m 1945, Rosemary Helen, who d 1969, da of late Lord Edward Grosvenor (see D Westminster, 1969 Edn):—
Valentine George, b 1948; ed Eton. —— Edward William, b 1950; ed Eton. —— Elizabeth Rose, b 1946. —— (Mary) Isabel Dorothy, b 1955: m 1976, Victor Anthony Cazalet, and has issue (see Mainwaring, Bt, ext).

Grandchildren of late Maj Hon Hugh Dawnay, DSO, 2nd son of 8th Viscount:—
Issue of late Maj-Gen Sir David Dawnay, KCVO, CB, DSO, b 1903, d 1971: m 1926, Lady Katharine Nora de la Poer Beresford, who d 1991, da of 6th Marquess of Waterford:—
Hugh (Whitfield Court, Waterford), b 1932; ed Eton; Maj The Royal Hussars (ret): m 1971, Maria Ines, da of Dr D. Cermesoni, of Salta, Argentina, and has issue living, David Danton, b 1972, — Sebastian Hugo, b 1975. —— Peter (99 Camberwell Grove, SE5), b (twin) 1932; ed Eton, and Ch Ch, Oxford (MA): m 1980, Caroline Mary, 2nd da of Gp Capt Nicolas Henry Joseph Tindal, RAF, of Terrybaun, Bofeenaun, Ballina, Mayo, and has issue living, Giles William, b 1981. —— Blanche, b 1928; k in a motor accident in Copenhagen, 1953. —— Rachel, b 1929; d 1983.
Issue of late Vice Adm Sir Peter Dawnay, KCVO, CB, DSC, b 1904, d 1989: m 1936, Lady Angela Christine Rose Montagu Douglas Scott (The Old Post Cottage, Wield, Alresford, Hants), da of 7th Duke of Buccleuch:—
Charles John, b 1938; ed Eton; Lt-Col Welsh Guards: m 1968, Adrian Louise, da of Maj-Gen Godfrey John Hamilton, CBE, DSO (see Colthurst, Bt, 1973-74 Edn), and has issue living, Henry Marcus, b 1969, — George Edward, b 1970, — Nicholas St John, b 1978, — Sophia Penelope, b 1981. —— Moyra Jane, b 1946: m 1969, Timothy Rupert de Zoete, of 33 Pembridge Villas, W11, and has issue living, Alexandra Margot, b 1973.
Issue of late Lt-Col Ronald Dawnay, b 1908, d 1990: m 1st, 1932, Lady Elizabeth Katherine Grey, who d 1941, yr da of 5th Earl Grey; 2ndly, 1949, Sibell Margaret (The Glen, Ballingary, co Limerick), elder da of late Ronald Collet-Norman (see Collet, Bt, ext, 1950 Edn), and formerly wife of Maj Hon Archibald Edward Cubitt (see B Ashcombe):—
(By 1st m) Andrew Charles, b 1934; ed Eton, and Ch Ch, Oxford; late 2nd Lieut Coldstream Guards. —— John Alexander George, b 1938; d 1961. —— Ann Josephine, b 1933; ed Somerville Coll, Oxford. —— Mary (Lady Carew Pole), LVO, JP, b 1936; a Lady-in-Waiting to HRH The Princess Royal since 1970; LVO 1983: m 1974, as his 2nd wife, Sir (John) Richard Walter Reginald Carew Pole, 13th Bt, of Antony House, Torpoint, Cornwall, and has issue.
Issue of late Wing-Cdr Michael Dawnay, RAF, b 1912, d 1946: m 1938, Julian Mary, who d 1979, adopted da of 1st Baron Brassey of Apethorpe:—
Patrick Julian (The Tower House, Sible Hedingham, Essex), b 1939; ed Eton: m 1966, Julie Katharine, da of Lt-Col William Herbert Olivier, TD, DL, RA (see Jones, Bt, cr 1919), and has issue living, Michael William, b 1969, — Katharine Julian, b 1968, — Evelyn Mary, b 1974. —— Romayne Julian, b 1940: m 1972, Peter Rowland Timms, of 70 Prichard St, Fitchburg, Mass 01420, USA, and has issue living, Matthew Rowland Julian, b 1974, — Christopher Rowland Julian, b 1978, — Zoë Virginia Julian, b 1975.

(In remainder to Viscountcy only)

Grandchildren of late Maj-Gen Guy Payan Dawnay, CB, CMG, DSO, MVO (infra):—
Issue of late Lt-Col Christopher Payan Dawnay, CBE, MVO, b 1909, d 1989: m 1939, Patricia, who d 1989, da of late Maj-Gen Sir Hereward Wake, 13th Bt, CB, CMG, DSO:—
Rupert Payan (The Mill House, Longparish, Andover, Hants SP11 6QH), b 1940; ed Eton: m 1982, Carolyn, da of Chapman Marshall, of 7440 SW 117th St, Miami, Florida, USA, and has issue living, Nicholas Marshall, b 1986, — Lewis Payan, b 1986 (twin), — Thomas Payan, b 1988. —— Guy Payan (16 Callcott St, W8), b 1944; ed Eton, and Lausanne Univ: m 1975 (m diss 1990), Charmian Rose, da of Lt-Col Alastair Neilson, of Dene House, Callaly, Northumberland, and has issue living, Christopher Payne, b 1977, — Mark Payne, b 1979. —— Gillian, b 1942: m 1966, Christopher Butler, of 18 Staverton Rd, Oxford, and has issue living, Sophie Rosalind, b 1968, — Josephine Laura, b 1970. —— Sarah, b 1947: m 1970, Jollyon Coombs, Welsh Guards, of Firgo Farm, Whitchurch, Hants, and has issue living, Charles T. Hardy, b 1976, — Arabella Sarah, b 1971, — Victoria Margaret Daisy, b 1974.
Issue of late Capt Oliver Payan Dawnay, CVO, b 1920, d 1988: m 1st, 1944 (m diss 1962), Lady Margaret Dorothea Boyle, da of 8th Earl of Glasgow; 2ndly, 1963, Hon Iris Irene Adele Peake, LVO (Wexcombe House, Marlborough, Wilts; Flat 5, 32 Onslow Sq, SW7), da of 1st Viscount Ingleby:—
(By 1st m) (Charles) James Payan, b 1946; ed Eton: m 1978, Sarah, elder da of (Edgar) David Stogdon, of Witchampton, Dorset (see Fergusson, Bt, 1971, Edn), and has issue living, David Frederick Payan, b 1985, — Alice Britannia, b 1979, — Olivia Margaret, b 1981, — Fenella Christian, b 1988. Residence – Symington House, nr Biggar, Lanarkshire. Clubs – Brooks's, Pratt's. —— Ivo Nicholas Payan, b 1952; ed Eton: m 1st, 1980 (m diss 1986), Chantal Mary Beatrice, da of Michael Rigby Bishop, of Combe House, Beckley, nr Rye, Sussex; 2ndly, 1992, Rachel S., da of Stanley Patrick Johnson, of W Nethercote, Winsford, Som, and has issue living (by 2nd m), Ludovic James Payan, b 1993, Charlotte Millicent b 1994. —— Caroline Margaret, b 1950; Literary Agent; has issue living, Hugo Ronald Alexander MacPherson, b 1980. —— (By 2nd m) Emma Jane Clarissa, b 1964.

Granddaughter of late Lieut-Col Hon Lewis Payan Dawnay 2nd son of 7th Viscount:—
Issue of late Maj-Gen Guy Payan Dawnay, CB, CMG, DSO, MVO, b 1878, d 1952: m 1906, Cecil, who d 1972, yst da of late Frances William Buxton (Buxton, Bt, colls):—
Elizabeth Lavender, b 1914: m 1938, Peter Noel Loxley, Diplo Ser, who d 1945, and has issue living. David Noel, b 1941, — Elizabeth Patricia (Lady Bingham), b 1939: m 1963, Sir Thomas (Hon Mr Justice) Bingham, Master of the Rolls, and has issue living Thomas Henry b 1967, Christopher Toby b 1969, Catherine Elizabeth b 1965. Residence – Heath Cottage, Little Heath Lane, Berkhamsted, Herts.

Granddaughters of late Hon Eustace Henry Dawnay, 5th son of 7th Viscount:—
Issue of late Lt-Col Cuthbert Henry Dawnay, MC, b 1891, d 1964: m 1921, Marjorie Kathleen, who d 1986, da of late Maj Reginald Bernard Loder (see Loder, Bt, colls, 1985 Edn):—
Eve Margaret, b 1926. —— Delia Mary (Lady Millar), b 1931: m 1954, Sir Oliver Nicholas Millar, GCVO, FBA, FSA, Surveyor Emeritus of The Queen's Pictures, of The Cottage, Rays Lane, Penn, Bucks, and has issue living, Charles James, b 1965: m 1990, Alice Katherine, da of John W. P. Martin, of E Molesey, Surrey, — Cynthia Mary, b 1956, — Lucy Anne, b 1958: m 1st, 1977 (m diss 1982), John E. L. Porter; 2ndly, 1983, Barnaby John Dickens, and has issue living (by 1st m), Roland Oliver b 1979, Max John b 1981, (by 2nd m) Archie b 1994, Marianna b 1985, — Beatrix Jane, b 1961: m 1987, Peter Andrew Flory, yr son of G. John Flory, of Saltdean, Sussex, and has issue living, Oliver William b 1991, Nicc Piers b 1993. —— Verena Joan, b 1936: m 1958, John Antony de la Cour Elliott, of 12 Cathcart Rd, SW10, and has issue living, Davina May, b 1962, — Bridget Victoria, b 1964: m 1988, Charles Holme Benthall, of Rectory Farm, W Heslerton, Malton, N Yorks, son of James Holme Benthall, of Benthall Hall, Broseley, Shropshire (2nd son of Sir (Arthur) Paul Benthall, KBE), — Felicity Jane, b 1966: m 1990 Ronald Bourlet, and has issue, Michael b 1990, Rebecca b 1993.

Grandchildren of late Nigel William Dawnay (infra):—

Issue of the late Frederick Cecil Dawnay, *b* 1905, *d* 1983: *m* 1st, 1929 (*m diss* 1955), Margaret Jean, who *d* 1989, da of the late William Coats Hutton, of Lexden Grange, Colchester; 2ndly, 1956, Betty Thora (2 Spring Grove, Sunningdale, Berks), da of the late Samuel Henry Darling, of Wentworth, Surrey:—

(By 1st *m*) Richard William, OBE (Courtside, Richmond Rd, Bath, Avon BA1 5PU), *b* 1930; *ed* Sherborne; Brig The Parachute Regt; OBE (Mil) 1970: *m* 1962, Penelope Anne, da of late Col Norman West Finlinson, DSO, and has issue living, Rupert Charles Richard, *b* 1964, — Philippa Ruth, *b* 1963: *m* 1990, Peter Shepherd, yr son of J. A. Shepherd, of Wimborne, Dorset, and has issue living, Samuel Elliot *b* 1992, Jessica Kate *b* 1991, — Deborah Kate, *b* 1966. —— Christopher Ronald (19 Asher Drive, Mill Ride, Ascot, Berks SL5 8LJ), *b* 1933; *ed* Sherborne; late Capt 10th Hussars.

Issue of late William Richard Dawnay, *b* 1910, *d* 1977: *m* 1st, 1940 (*m diss* 1961), Olive Margaret, da of late Arthur James Barratt, of The Mile House, Oswestry (infra); 2ndly 1963, Pamela (Crouch Farm, Whatfield, Ipswich, Suffolk), da of late Charles Lester, of Piper's Croft, Harpenden, Herts:—

(By 1st *m*) Diana Margaret, *b* 1947.

Grandson of late Hon William Frederick Dawnay, 6th son of 7th Viscount:—

Issue of late Nigel William Dawnay, *b* 1878: *m* 1st, 1903, Daisy Rosalie, who *d* 1940, only da of late Harry Norman Dunnett, of The Kennels, Stratford St. Mary, Suffolk; 2ndly, 1941, Violet Mary Harrison, who *d* 1964:—

(By 1st *m*) Eric Christopher, TD *b* 1913; *ed* Radley; Capt 104th (Essex Yeo) Regt RHA (TA); 1939-45 War (prisoner): *m* 1945, Vera Winifred, da of late Arthur James Barratt, of Mile House, Oswestry (ante), and has issue living, David Nigel (Llyndir, Dolgellau, Gwynedd), *b* 1946: *m* 1975 (*m diss* 1990), Hilary Jane, da of James W. Robins, MC, of Spinners, Lackford, Suffolk, — Michael William, *b* 1950; *ed* Radley, and London Univ (BA). *Residence* – Llyndir, Dolgellau, Gwynedd.

Granddaughter of late Capt Hon Geoffrey Nicolas Dawnay, 7th son of 7th Viscount:—

Issue of late Capt Eric Geoffrey Dawnay, *b* 1890; *d* 1970: *m* 1930, Daisy, who *d* 1967, da of late Lt-Col Lewis Butler, of The Wilderness, Earley, Reading:—

Diana Buttercup, *b* 1931: *m* 1957, Hugh Rowland Murray Barran, of Hildenley, Malton, Yorks (*see* Barran, Bt, colls).

PREDECESSORS – **(1)** CHRISTOPHER DAWNAY; *cr* a *Baronet* 1642; *d* 1644; *s* by his son **(2)** *Sir* THOMAS, 2nd Bt; *d* 1644, aged 12. His uncle **(3)** *Sir* JOHN (MP for Yorkshire 1660, and for Pontefract 1661-88) was *cr Viscount Downe* (peerage of Ireland) 1681, and sat in James's Irish Parliament 1689; *d* 1695; *s* by his son **(4)** HENRY, 2nd Viscount, MP for Yorkshire in several parliaments; *d* 1741; *s* by his grandson **(5)** HENRY PLEYDELL, 3rd Viscount; MP for Yorkshire 1749-51; *dsp* 1760, from wounds received at battle of Campen, near Wesen, when in command of 25th Foot; *s* by his brother **(6)** JOHN, 4th Viscount; *d* 1780; *s* by his son **(7)** JOHN CHRISTOPHER BURTON, 5th Viscount; *cr Baron Dawnay*, of Cowick, co York (peerage of Great Britain) 1796; *d* 1832, when the barony expired; *s* by his brother **(8)** *Rev* WILLIAM HENRY, 6th Viscount; Rector of Sessay and Thormanby; *d* 1846; *s* by his son **(9)** WILLIAM HENRY, 7th Viscount; *b* 1812: *m* 1843, Mary Isabel, da of Rt Rev Hon Richard Bagot, Lord Bishop of Bath and Wells; *d* 1857: *s* by his son **(10)** HUGH RICHARD, KCVO, CB, CIE, 8th Viscount; *b* 1844: Hon Maj-Gen in the Army; Zulu Campaign 1879 (medal with clasp), and S Africa 1900, as ADC to FM Lord Roberts, and in charge of Foreign Mil Attachés (despatches twice, medal with seven clasps, CB), and 1901-2, in charge of Remount Depart; *cr Baron Dawnay*, of Danby, N Riding of York (peerage of United Kingdom) 1897: *m* 1st, 1869, Lady Cecilia Maria Charlotte Molyneux, VA (sometime Lady of the Bedchamber to HM Queen Victoria), who *d* 1910, da of 3rd Earl of Sefton; 2ndly, 1911, Florence Faith, who *d* 1958, (having *m* 2ndly, 1931, Rev Arthur Maxwell Bury, V, of Loose, who *d* 1937), da of late Rev Thomas Henry Dening, formerly V of Holy Trinity, Kilburn, NW, *d* 1924; *s* by his son **(11)** JOHN, CMG, DSO, 9th Viscount, *b* 1872; ADC to FM Lord French 1915-18, and Mil Sec to him in Ireland 1918-19: *m* 1902, Dorothy, who *d* 1957, only da of Sir William Hovell Browne ffolkes, 3rd Bt; *d* 1931 *s* by his el son **(12)** RICHARD, OBE, 10th Viscount; *b* 1903; Col and Hon Brig 5th Bn Green Howards; Comdg 69th Inf Bde and Assist A-G W Africa Command 1939-45 War: *m* 1928, Margaret Christine, who *d* 1967, da of Christian Bahnson, of Passiac, NJ, USA; *d* 1965; *s* by his el son **(13)** JOHN CHRISTIAN GEORGE, 11th Viscount and present peer; also Baron Dawnay.

Downpatrick, Baron; grandson of Duke of Kent.

DOWNSHIRE, MARQUESS OF (Hill) Sits as EARL OF HILLSBOROUGH (GB 1772) (Marquess I 1789)

(ARTHUR) ROBIN IAN HILL, 8th Marquess; *b* 10 May 1929; *s* 1989; *ed* Eton; Hereditary Constable of Hillsborough Fort, and patron of one living: *m* 1st, 1957, Hon Juliet Mary Weld-Forester, who *d* 1986, da of 7th Baron Forester; 2ndly, 1989, Mrs Diana Marion Hibbert, 2nd da of late Rt Hon Sir Ronald Hibbert Cross, 1st Bt, KCMG, KCVO, and has issue by 1st *m*.

Arms – Quarterly: 1st sable, on a fesse argent between three leopards passant guardant or, spotted of the field, as many escallops gules, *Hill*; 2nd per bend sinister ermine and ermines, a lion rampant or, *Trevor*; 3rd gules, a quatrefoil or, *Rowe*; 4th argent, a chevron azure, between three trefoils slipped, per pale, gules and vert, *Rowe*. **Crest** – A reindeer's head couped gules, attired and plain collared or. **Supporters** – *Dexter*, a leopard or, spotted sable, ducally collared and chained gules; *sinister*, a reindeer gules, attired, unguled, and plain collared or. *Seat* – Clifton Castle, Ripon, N Yorks HG4 4AB.

By God and my sword I have obtained

SONS LIVING *(By 1st marriage)*

ARTHUR FRANCIS NICHOLAS WILLS (*Earl of Hillsborough*) (73 Holland Park, W11 3SL), *b* 4 Feb 1959: *m* 1990, Diana Jane, only da of Gerald Leeson Bunting, of Otterington House, Northallerton, Yorks, and has issue:—

DAUGHTERS LIVING—*Lady* Isabella Diana Juliet, *b* 1991, — *Lady* Beatrice Hannah Georgina, *b* 1994.

Lord Anthony Ian, *b* 1961: *m* 1992, Annabel Priscilla Angela, yr da of Hon David Lawrence Robert Nall-Cain (*see* B Brocket), and has issue living, Marcus Robert Francis, *b* 1994.

DAUGHTER LIVING *(By 1st marriage)*

Lady Georgina Mary, *b* 1964.

SISTERS LIVING

Venice Marigold (Rosie), *b* 1930: *m* 1954 (*m diss* 1989), 3rd Baron Kindersley. *Residence* – Ramhurst Manor, Tonbridge, Kent.

Lady Caroline Sylvia, *b* 1938; raised to the rank of a Marquess's daughter 1992: *m* 1976, Dr Alan Charles Nelson Borg, CBE, Dir Gen Imperial War Museum, and has issue living, Leonora Ishbel, *b* 1980, — Helen Olivia, *b* 1982. *Residence* – Telegraph House, 36 West Sq, SE11 45P.

COLLATERAL BRANCHES LIVING

Descendants of late Lord Arthur Edwin Hill-Trevor, 3rd son of 3rd Marquess, who was *cr Baron Trevor* 1880 (see that title).

Descendants of late Lord George Augustus Hill, MP, 5th son of 2nd Marquess, and in remainder to his mother's *Barony of Sandys* (see that title).

PREDECESSORS – (1) TREVOR HILL, PC; successively MP for Aylesbury, Malmesbury and Downshire, and Lord-Lieut of co Down; *cr Baron Hill*, of Kilwarlin, and *Viscount Hillsborough* (peerage of Ireland) 1717, with remainder to the heirs male of his father; *d* 1742; *s* by his son (2) WILLS, PC, 2nd Viscount; MP for Huntingdon, and for Warwick 1742-56, Comptroller of Household to George II, Joint Postmaster-Gen, Sec of State for the Colonies 1768-72 and 1779-82, and Registrar of High Court of Chancery, Ireland; *cr Viscount Kilwarlin* and *Earl of Hillsborough* (peerage of Ireland) 1751, with remainder to his uncle Arthur (later Viscount Dungannon), *Baron Harwich*, of Harwich, co Essex (peerage of great Britain, 1756), *Viscount Fairford and Earl of Hillsborough* (peerage of Great Britain) 1772, and Marquess of Downshire (peerage of Ireland) 1789; *d* 1793; *s* by his son (3) ARTHUR, 2nd Marquess; his wife Mary, da of Hon Martyn Sandys, having succeeded to the estates of Edwin, 2nd and last Baron Sandys (*cr* 1743), was *cr Baroness Sandys*, of Ombersley (peerage of United Kingdom) 1802, with remainder to 2nd and younger sons successively; she *d* 1836, and was *s* by her 2nd son (*see* B Sandys): the Marquess *d* 1801; *s* by his son (4) ARTHUR BLUNDELL SANDYS TRUMBULL, KP, DCL, 3rd Marquess; Lord-Lieut of co Down; *d* 1845; *s* by his son (5) ARTHUR WILLS BLUNDELL SANDYS TRUMBULL WINDSOR, KP, 4th Marquess; *d* 1868; *s* by his son (6) ARTHUR WILLS BLUNDELL, 5th Marquess; *b* 1844; *m* 1870, Georgina Elizabeth, who *d* 1919, da of John Balfour, of Balbirnie, co Fife; *d* 1874; *s* by his son (7) ARTHUR WILLS JOHN WELLINGTON BLUNDELL TRUMBULL, 6th Marquess; *b* 1871: *m* 1st, 1893 (*m diss* 1902), Katherine Mary, who *d* 1959, da of Hon Hugh Henry Hare; 2ndly, 1907, Evelyn Grace May, who *d* 1942, da of Edmund Benson Foster; *d* 1918; *s* by his el son (8) ARTHUR WILLS PERCY WELLINGTON BLUNDELL TRUMBULL SANDYS, 7th Marquess; *b* 1894; Lieut Berks Yeo, attached to British Red Cross in France during European War: *m* 1953, Mrs Noreen Gray-Miller, who *d* 1983, only da of late William Barraclough; *d* 1989; *s* by his nephew (9) (ARTHUR) ROBIN IAN (only son of late Capt Lord (Arthur) Francis Henry Hill, The Greys (Reserve), yr son of 6th Marquess), 8th Marquess, and present peer; also Earl of Hillsborough, Viscount Hillsborough, Viscount Fairford, Viscount Kilwarlin, Baron Harwich, and Baron Hill.

DROGHEDA, EARL OF (Moore) (Earl I 1661, Baron UK 1954) Sits as BARON MOORE (UK 1954)

(Title pronounced "Droyeda")

A brave man may fall but cannot yield

HENRY DERMOT PONSONBY MOORE, 12th Earl; *b* 14 Jan 1937; *s* 1990; *ed* Eton, and Trin Coll, Camb; late 2nd Lieut Life Guards; photographer; Dir Derry Moore (Photography) Ltd: *m* 1st, 1968 (*m diss* 1972), Eliza, da of Stacy Barcroft Lloyd, Jr, of Philadelphia, and St Croix, Virgin Is; 2ndly, 1978, Alexandra, da of Sir Nicholas Henderson, GCMG, KCVO, and has issue by 2nd *m*.

𝔄rms – Azure, on a chief indented or, three mullets pierced gules. 𝔠rest – Out of a ducal coronet or, a Moor's head in profile proper, wreathed round the temples argent and azure. 𝔖upporters – Two greyhounds argent.
Residence – 40 Ledbury Rd, W11. *Club* – Brooks's.

SONS LIVING (By 2nd marriage)

BENJAMIN GARRETT HENDERSON (*Viscount Moore*), *b* 21 March 1983.
Hon Garrett Alexander, *b* 1986.

DAUGHTER LIVING (By 2nd marriage)

Lady Marina Alice, *b* 1988.

COLLATERAL BRANCH LIVING

Granddaughter of late Col Francis Moore, gt grandson of John Moore of Drumbanagher, co Armagh (*d* 1809), grandson of Hon Arthur Moore, 5th son of 1st Viscount:—
Issue of late Col Francis Moore, DSO, OBE, *b* 1879, *d* 1938: *m* 1916, Anne Early, who *d* 1964, da of William Van Wyck, of New York:—
Kathleen Clifford, *b* 1918: *m* 1942, Lieut-Col Stephen Murfin Rose, OBE, R Fusiliers, of Bradford House, Bradford Rd, Sherborne, Dorset, and has issue living, Margaret Anne, *b* 1947: *m* 1975, Col O. Mark Roberts, OBE, R Regt of Wales, of Daisyfield Cottage, Rowledge, Farnham, Surrey, and has issue living, Camilla Margaret Rose *b* 1977, Katharine Frances Rose *b* 1980, — Mary Elizabeth, *b* 1951: *m* 1979, Cdr Jeremy G. Hurlbatt, OBE, RN, of The Grange, Ash, Martock, Somerset, and has issue living, Charles Henry *b* 1984, Claire Alice Rose *b* 1982.

PREDECESSORS – (1) Sir GARRETT MOORE, Knt, MP, *cr Baron Moore*, of Mellefont, co Louth (peerage of Ireland) 1616, and *Viscount Moore*, of Drogheda (peerage of Ireland) 1621; *d* 1627, *s* by his son (2) HENRY, 2nd Viscount; killed at Portlester in service of Charles I 1643; *s* by his son (3) HENRY, 3rd Viscount; *cr Earl of Drogheda* (peerage of Ireland) 1661; *s* by his son (4) CHARLES, 2nd Earl; *d* 1679; *s* by his brother (5) HENRY, 3rd Earl; assumed the name of Hamilton on succeeding to the estates of his brother-in-law Henry, 2nd and last Earl of Clanbrassill; *d* 1714; *s* by his grandson (6) HENRY, 4th Earl; inherited the Monasterevin estates of Arthur, 3rd and last Viscount Loftus, of Elye; *dsp* 1727; *s* by his brother (7) EDWARD, 5th Earl; drowned in passage from England to Dublin 1758; *s* by his son (8) CHARLES, KP; *cr Marquess of Drogheda* (peerage of Ireland) 1791, and *Baron Moore*, of Moore Place, co Kent (peerage of United Kingdom) 1801; *d* 1821; *s* by his son (9) CHARLES, 2nd Marquess; *d* unmarried 1837; *s* by his nephew (10) HENRY FRANCIS SEYMOUR, 3rd Marquess (son of late Lord Henry Seymour Moore, 2nd son of 1st Marquess), *b* 1825; Vice-Adm of Leinster, and Lieut of Kildare: *m* 1847, Hon Mary Caroline Stuart-Wortley, who *d* 1896, da of 2nd Baron Wharncliffe; *d* 1892, when the Marquessate of Drogheda (*cr* 1791) and Barony of Moore (*cr* 1801) became extinct, and the peerages of 1616, 1621 and 1661 devolved upon his cousin (11) PONSONBY WILLIAM (son of late Ponsonby Arthur Moore, great grandson of 5th Earl), 9th Earl, *b* 1846; a Representative Peer for Ireland: *m* 1879, Anne Tower, who *d* 1924, da of late George Moir, LLD, Sheriff of Stirlingshire; *d* 1908; *s* by his son (12) HENRY CHARLES PONSONBY, KCMG, PC, 10th Earl, *b* 1884; was Lieut of Co Kildare 1918-21, a Representative Peer for Ireland 1913-57, Director-Gen of Min of Economic Warfare 1942-5, and Chm of Committees and Dep Speaker of House of Lords 1946-57; *cr Baron Moore*, of Cobham, co Surrey (peerage of UK) 1954: *m* 1st, 1909 (*m diss* 1922), Kathleen, CBE, who *d* 1965, da of late Charles Maitland Pelham Burn, of Grange Park, Edinburgh; 2ndly, 1922, Olive Mary (formerly Lady Victor William Paget), who *d* 1947, da of George Meatyard; *d* 1957; *s* by his only son (13) CHARLES GARRETT PONSONBY, KG, KBE, 11th Earl, *b* 1910, Dir Economist Newspaper Ltd, and of Earls Court and Olympia Ltd, Chm Financial Times Ltd 1971-74 (Man Dir 1946-71), of Newspaper Publishers Assocn 1968-70, and of Royal Opera House, Covent Garden, Ltd 1958-74: *m* 1935, Joan Eleanor, who *d* (16 Dec) 1989, da of late William Henry Carr; *d* (24 Dec) 1989; *s* by his only son (14) HENRY DERMOT PONSONBY, 12th Earl and present peer: also Viscount Moore, and Baron Moore (peerage of Ireland 1616, and of UK 1954).

DRUMALBYN, BARONY (Macpherson) (Extinct 1987)

DAUGHTERS LIVING OF FIRST AND LAST BARON (By 1st marriage)

Hon Jean Stewart (*Hon Lady Weatherall*), *b* 1938: *m* 1962, Vice Adm Sir James L. Weatherall, KBE, of Craig House, Bishop's Waltham, Hants, and has issue living, Ian James Stewart, *b* 1976, — Annie Norah, *b* 1974, — Elizabeth Alwynne (twin), *b* 1976. Adm and the Hon Lady Weatherall also have two adopted children, Niall Anthony Stewart, *b* 1967, — Sarah Margaret, *b* 1968.
Hon Mary Stewart MACPHERSON, *b* 1942; has resumed her maiden name: *m* 1967 (*m diss* 1991), Philip D. Wilson. *Residence* – 87 Sussex Way, N7 6RU.

WIDOW LIVING OF FIRST AND LAST BARON

RITA (*Baroness Drumalbyn*), widow of Harry Edmiston: *m* 1985, as his 2nd wife, 1st Baron Drumalbyn, KBE, PC, who *d* 1987. *Residence* – 108 Montagu Mansions, W1H 1LE.

DUCIE, EARL OF (Moreton) (Earl UK 1837)

By persevering

DAVID LESLIE MORETON, 7th Earl; *b* 20 Sept 1951; *s* 1991; *ed* Cheltenham, London Univ, and Wye Coll (BSc Agric): *m* 1975, Helen, da of M. L. Duchesne, of Langford, Bristol, and has issue.

𝕬rms – Quarterly: 1st and 4th argent, a chevron gules, between three square buckles sable, *Moreton*; 2nd and 3rd or, two lions passant gules, *Ducie*. 𝕮rest – A moorcock's head or, combed and wattled gules, between two wings displayed azure. 𝕾upporters – Two unicorns argent, armed, unguled, maned, and tufted or, each gorged with a ducal coronet per pale gold and gules.
Seat – Tortworth, Wotton-under-Edge, Glos.

SON LIVING

JAMES BERKELEY (*Lord Moreton*), *b* 6 May 1981.

DAUGHTER LIVING

Lady Claire Alison *b* 1984.

BROTHERS LIVING

Hon Douglas Howard, *b* 1958; *ed* Bredon Sch. *Residence* – Tortworth, Wotton-under-Edge, Glos.
Hon Robert Matthew, *b* 1964; *ed* Malvern, and RAC Cirencester: *m* 1988, Heather Elizabeth, only da of Colin Lynton-Jenkins, of Alveston, Avon, and has issue living, Olivia Alexandra Rose, *b* 1991. *Residence* – North Nibley, Dursley, Glos.

SISTER LIVING

Lady (Alison) Jeannette, *b* 1954: *m* 1986, Mark Allan Stewart, of Ottawa, Ontario, Canada, and has issue living, Derek Allan, *b* 1987, — Laura Jessica, *b* 1989. *Residence* – 1159 St Jerome Crescent, Orleans, Ontario, Canada K1C 2A7.

AUNT LIVING (*sister of 6th Earl*)

May Reynolds, *b* 1919.

WIDOW LIVING OF SIXTH EARL

ALISON MAY (*Alison, Countess of Ducie*), da of Leslie Aitken Bates, of Pialba, Queensland: *m* 1950, the 6th Earl, who *d* 1991. *Residence* – Tortworth, Wotton-under-Edge, Glos.

COLLATERAL BRANCHES LIVING

Grandchildren of late Henry John Moreton, 2nd son of late Capt Hon Reynolds Moreton, RN, 5th son of 2nd Earl:—
Issue of late Theodore Reynolds Moreton, *b* 1890, *d* 1970: *m* 1921, Marie Ann Josephine, who *d* 1965, da of David O. Anderson, of Duluth, Minnesota, USA:—
David Oral (PO Box 32, Jackson, NH 03846-0032, USA), *b* 1922: *m* 1948, Barbara Colby, da of late L. Graham Harris, of New York, and has had issue, Henry Packard (7331 Skyline Blvd, Oakland, Calif 94611, USA), *b* 1958, — Theodora, *b* 1954, *d* 1969.
Issue of late Hugh Berkeley Moreton, *b* 1891, *d* 1935: *m* 1923, Phyllis Mott, who *d* 1928:—
Henry John (The Pas, Manitoba, Canada), *b* 1926: *m* 1951, Patricia, da of William A. Russell, and has issue living, John Russell Berkeley, *b* 1956, — Richard Steven, *b* 1963, — Brenda Leigh, *b* 1952: *m* 1973, Dennis Boiteau, and has issue living, Mark Steven *b* 1976, Dereck Troy *b* 1979, Mathew Scott *b* 1982, — Patricia Ann, *b* 1954: *m* 1983, Colin Chopp. —— Carrie Ann, *b* 1924: *m* 1950, Charles William Schmidt, of 509 Washington Ave, Glencoe, Ill 60022, USA, and has issue living, Charles William, *b* 1951, — Stephen Berkeley, *b* 1957, — Susan Moreton, *b* 1953, — Karin Marie, *b* 1955.

Grandchildren of late Reginald Moreton, 4th son of late Capt Hon Reynolds Moreton, RN (ante):—
Issue of late Richard Beresford Reynolds Moreton, *b* 1909, *d* 1984: *m* 1929, Irene Beatrice, who *d* 1986, da of Maj M. Donnithorne, of Torquay:—
David Buckland REYNOLDS-MORETON (Cobb Cottage, 23 Fore St, Bovey Tracey, Devon), *b* 1931: *m* 1965, Cecilie Margaret Elswood, da of Lilian Elswood, of 91 Woodlands Gdns, Isleworth, Middx. —— Anthony REYNOLDS-MORETON (20 St George's Rd, W Harnham, Salisbury, Wilts), *b* 1938. —— Jennifer Anne, *b* 1941: *m* 1969, John Wrigley, of Manor Cottage, E Grimstead, Salisbury, Wilts.

Grandson of late Charles Macdonald-Moreton, el son of late Hon Augustus Henry Macdonald-Moreton, MP, 2nd son of 1st Earl:—
Issue of late John Ronald Moreton-Macdonald, *b* 1873, *d* 1921: *m* 1906, Daisy Maud, who *d* 1966, da of late Brig-Gen Eyre Macdonnell Stewart Crabbe, CB, Grenadier Guards, of Glen Eyre, Southampton:—
John MAXWELL MACDONALD, *b* 1908: *ed* Winchester, and at Magdalen Coll, Oxford (BA 1929), *m* 1930, Anne, da and heir of tailzie of Sir John Maxwell Stirling-Maxwell, 10th Bt, KT, and assumed the surname of Maxwell Macdonald in lieu of his patronymic 1930, and has issue living, John Ronald *b* 1936; is eventual heir to the Baronetcy of Stirling-Maxwell (see that title), — Donald (55 Park Walk, SW10 0AZ), *b* 1938; *ed* Winchester, and Ch Ch, Oxford: *m* 1st, 1962 (*m diss* 1976), Caromy, da of late Robert Jenkins, of The Manor House, Hooton Roberts, Yorks; 2ndly, 1977, Margaret Anne, da of late Alfred King-

erley, and has issue living (by 1st *m*), James Donald *b* 1965, Harriet Caromy Anne *b* 1967. *Residence* – Largie, Tayinloan, Argyllshire. *Clubs* – Travellers', New (Edinburgh), Leander.

Grandchildren of late John Ronald Moreton-Macdonald (ante)—
Issue of late Maj Simon Foster Macdonald Lockhart of The Lee, Lovat Scouts; assumed the surname of Macdonald Lockhart of The Lee 1946; *b* 1916, *d* 1991: *m* 1942, Caitriona (Dunsyre House, Dunsyre, Lanark), elder da of late Seton Gordon, CBD, FZS, of Upper Duntullin, Isle of Skye:—
Angus Hew MACDONALD LOCKHART OF THE LEE (Newholm, Dunsyre, Lanark ML11 8NQ), *b* 1946; *ed* Rannoch, and Aberdeen Agric Coll: *m* 1970, Susan Elizabeth, da of late Hon William Normand (*see* B Normand, 1967 Edn), and has issue living, Ranald William Angus, *b* 1975, — Fiona, *b* 1972. —— Simon James (Crosshill House, Auchterader, Perthshire), *b* 1949; *ed* Winchester: *m* 1973, Lavinia, da of late Col Peter William Marsham, MBE (*see* E Romney, colls), and has issue living, James Seton Alexander, *b* 1976, — Andrew Peter Robert, *b* 1978, — Davina, *b* 1981. —— Norman Philip, *b* 1954. —— Mairi Susan, *b* 1943: *m* 1st, 1962 (*m diss* 1965), Leslie Swan; 2ndly, 1965, Ian Hamilton Finlay, of Stonypath, Dunsyre, Lanark, and has issue living (by 2nd *m*), Alexander, *b* 1966, — Aileen, *b* 1967.

Grandchildren of late Robert Moreton, 2nd surv son of Hon Percy Moreton, 3rd son of 1st Earl:—
Issue of late Maurice Fitzhardinge Reynolds Moreton, *b* 1884, *d* 1976: *m* 1917, Anna Margaretta, who *d* 1971, da of late Rev Edward Brown Charlton, R of Tatenhill:—
Berkeley John Reynolds (Wason House, Castle Cary, Somerset), *b* 1918: *m* 1945, Lois, yr da of late Louis Hardaker, of Ackworth, Yorks, and has issue living, Stephen Maurice, *b* 1950: *m* 1972, Lynn, da of Thomas Milford, of Swansea, — John Evelyn (Treetops, Leckhampton Hill, Cheltenham, Glos), *b* 1952: *m* 1981, Jennifer, yr da of David Davis, of Cheltenham, and has issue living, Robert Berkeley Reynolds *b* 1983, — Jane Mary Margaretta, *b* 1956. —— Evelyn Emily Margaretta, *b* 1921.

PREDECESSORS – (1) MATTHEW DUCIE Moreton; *cr Lord Ducie, Baron of Moreton*, co Stafford (peerage of Great Britain) 1720; *d* 1735; *s* by his son (2) MATTHEW, 2nd Baron; *cr Baron Ducie* of Tortworth, co Gloucester (peerage of Great Britain) 1763, with remainder to the sons of his sister Hon Elizabeth Reynolds; *d* 1770, when the Barony of Moreton expired, and the Barony of Ducie devolved upon his nephew (3) THOMAS Reynolds, 2nd Baron; assumed the surname of Moreton by Act of Parliament 1771; *dsp* 1785; *s* by his brother (4) FRANCIS Reynolds, 3rd Baron; assumed the surname of Moreton by Act of Parliament 1786; *d* 1808; *s* by his son (5) THOMAS REYNOLDS, 4th Baron; *cr Baron Moreton*, of Tortworth, and *Earl of Ducie* (peerage of United Kingdom) 1837; *d* 1840; *s* by his son (6) HENRY GEORGE FRANCIS, 2nd Earl; *b* 1802; *m* 1826, Hon Elizabeth Dutton, da of 2nd Baron Sherborne; *d* 1853; *s* by his son (7) HENRY JOHN, GCVO, FRS, 3rd Earl; *b* 1827; MP for Stroud (*L*) 1852-53; Lord-Lieut of Gloucestershire 1857-1911, and Lord Warden of the Stanneries and a Member of Council of Prince of Wales 1888-1908: *m* 1849, Julia, who *d* 1895, da of late James Haughton Langston, MP, of Sarsden, Chipping Norton; *d* 1921; *s* by his brother (8) BERKELEY BASIL, 4th Earl; *b* 1831; many years engaged in sheep and cattle farming in Queensland; Postmaster-Gen of Queensland 1885 Min of Public Instruction, Queensland 1885-86, and Colonial Sec and Min of Public Instruction 1886-88: *m* 1862, Emily Eleanor, who *d* 1921, da of John Kent, Commr of Crown Lands, Queensland; *d* 1924; *s* by his el son (9) CAPEL HENRY BERKELEY, 5th Earl; *b* 1875; many years engaged in dairy and fruit farming in Australia: *m* 1903 (Maria) Emma, who *d* 1958, da of Frederick Bryant, of Maryborough, Queensland; *d* 1952; *s* by his nephew (10) BASIL HOWARD (son of late Hon Algernon Howard Moreton, 2nd son of 4th Earl), 6th Earl; *b* 1917: *m* 1950, Alison May, da of Leslie Aitken Bates, of Pialba, Qld; *d* 1991; *s* by his eldest son (11) DAVID LESLIE, 7th Earl and present peer; also Baron Ducie, and Baron Moreton.

DUDLEY, BARONESS (Hamilton) (Baron E 1439)

BARBARA AMY FELICITY HAMILTON, *Baroness Dudley; b* 23 April, 1907; *s* 1972: *m* 1st, 1929, Guy Raymond Hill Wallace, who *d* 1967; 2ndly, 1980, Charles Anthony Crosse Hamilton, and has issue by 1st *m*.

ᴀrms – Azure two bars nebuly argent, each charged with as many crescents sable, a chief or, issuant therefrom a demi lion sable. Supporters – On either side, a lion double-queued vert armed and langued gules, gorged with a ducal coronet, attached thereto a cordon passing between the forelegs and reflexed over the back or.
Residence – Hill House, Napleton, Kempsey, Worcs.

SONS LIVING (By 1st marriage)

Hon JIM ANTHONY HILL (Little Grange, Napleton, Kempsey, Worcs), *b* 9 Nov 1930; *ed* Lancing: *m* 1962, Nicola Jane, da of Philip William Edward Leslie Dunsterville, and has issue living, Jeremy William Guilford, *b* 1964, — Nicholas John Hill, *b* 1967.
Hon Robin Guy Hill (Pond House, Ham Hill, Powick, Worcs WR2 4RD), *b* 1936; *ed* Malvern: *m* 1959, Jill Alexandra, da of late Herbert Williams, and has issue living, Simon Alexander Hill, *b* 1962, — Andrew George Hill, *b* 1964.
Hon William John Sutton (Beechmount House, Hallow, Worcs), *b* 1938; *ed* Malvern: *m* 1962, Jean Carol Ann, da of late Albert Edward Shipton, and has issue living, Guy Edward John Sutton, *b* 1963, — Piers William Somery, *b* 1965.

DAUGHTER LIVING (By 1st marriage)

Hon Felicity Lilla, *b* 1944: *m* 1967, Philip Neil Faram, of Heath Hill, Queen Hill, Upton-on-Severn, Worcs, and has issue living, David Stephen, *b* 1968, — Michael Guy, *b* 1970, — Philip John, *b* 1976.

PREDECESSORS – (1) Sir JOHN Sutton de Dudley, KG, son of Sir John Sutton; *b* 1400; summoned to Parliament 1439-40; *d* 1487; *s* by his grandson (2) EDWARD (son of Sir Edmund Dudley), 2nd Baron; *b* 1459; knighted 1487; summoned to Parliament 1492-1529: *m* Cicely, da of Sir William Willoughby; *d* 1531; *s* by his son (3) JOHN, 3rd Baron; *d* 1553; *s* by his son (4) EDWARD, 4th Baron; summoned to Parliament 1584-86; Lieut of Hampnes Castle: *m* 1st, 1555, Katherine, da of 1st Baron Chandos of Sudeley; 2ndly, Jane, da of 3rd Earl of Derby; 3rdly, Mary, da of 1st Baron Howard of Effingham; *d* 1586; *s* by his son (by his 2nd *m*) (5) EDWARD, 5th Baron; *b* 1567; *dsp* 1643; *s* by his granddaughter (6) FRANCES (only da of Sir Ferdinando Sutton, by his wife Honora, only da of Edward Seymour, Lord Beauchamp, and grandda of Lady Katherine Grey, niece of King Henry VIII); *b* 1611; *m* 1628, Sir Humble Ward, who *d* 1670, having been *cr Baron Ward*, of Birmingham, co Warwick 1643, with remainder to the heirs-male of his body, by his wife, Frances; *d* 1697; *s* by her son (7) EDWARD Ward, 7th Lord Dudley and 2nd Baron Ward: *m* Frances, da of Sir William Gretton, 2nd Bt; *d* 1701; *s* by his grandson (8) EDWARD (son of William Ward), 8th Baron Dudley and 3rd Baron Ward; *b* 1683: *m* 1703, Diana, da of Sir Thomas Howard, of Ashtead, Surrey; *d* 1704; *s* by his son (9) EDWARD, 9th Baron Dudley and 4th Baron Ward; *b* (posthumous) 1704; *d* 1731; *s* by his uncle **(10)** WILLIAM, 10th Baron Dudley and 5th Baron Ward (yr brother of the 8th Baron); *b* 168-; *d* 1740, when the Barony of Ward devolved upon the heir-male, and that of Dudley on the heir-general, his nephew **(11)** FERDINANDO DUDLEY Lea, 11th Baron (son of William Lea, of Halesowen Grange, by Frances, sister of the 10th Baron); *b* 1710; *d* 1757, when the Barony of Dudley fell into abeyance between his sisters and co-heirs, and so remained until 1916, when the abeyance was determined in favour of the senior co-heir **(12)** FERDINANDO DUDLEY WILLIAM LEA SMITH (el and only surviving son of late Ferdinando Dudley Lea Smith), 12th Baron: *m* 1904, Sybil Augusta, who *d* 1958, da of late Rev Henry William Coventry (E Coventry, colls); *d* 1936; *s* by his only son **(13)** FERDINANDO DUDLEY LEA, 13th Baron, *b* 1910: *m* 1941 (*m diss* 1965), Kirsten Laura Hedvig, da of Lars Anton Albrechtson, of Vibsig, Denmark; *d* 1972; *s* by his sister **(14)** BARBARA AMY FELICITY, Baroness Dudley and present peeress.

DUDLEY, EARL OF (Ward) (Earl UK 1860)

As I was

WILLIAM HUMBLE DAVID WARD, 4th Earl; *b* 5 Jan 1920; *s* 1969; *ed* Eton, and Ch Ch, Oxford; late Lt and temp Capt 10th R Hussars; 1939-45 War in Italy (wounded): *m* 1st, 1946 (*m diss* 1961), Stella, el da of late Dr Don Miguel Angel Carcano, KCMG, KBE, sometime Argentine Ambassador in London; 2ndly, 1961, Maureen, da of James Swanson, and has issue by 1st and 2nd *m*.

Arms – Checky, or and azure, a bend ermine. **Crest** – Out of a ducal coronet or, a lion's head azure. **Supporters** – Two angels proper, hair and wings or, under robe sanguine, upper robe azure.
Residence – 6 Cottesmore Gdns, W8. *Club* – White's, Pratt's, and Royal Yacht Squadron.

SONS LIVING (By 1st marriage)

WILLIAM HUMBLE DAVID JEREMY (*Viscount Ednam*) (Villa Montanet, Les Garrigues, 84220 Goult-Gordes, France), *b* 27 March 1947; *ed* Eton, and Ch Ch, Oxford: *m* 1st, 1972 (*m diss* 1976), Sarah Mary, da of Sir Alastair Francis Stuart Coats, 4th Bt; 2ndly, 1976 (*m diss* 1980), Debra Louise, da of George Robert Pinney, and has issue (by 2nd *m*):—

DAUGHTER LIVING— (*By 2nd marriage*)— Hon Bethany Rowena, *b* 1977.

(*By 2nd marriage*)

Hon Leander Grenville Dudley, *b* 1971; *ed* Eton, and Univ of S California.

DAUGHTERS LIVING (By 1st marriage)

Lady Rosemary Millicent, *b* 1955: *m* 1980, Castor Cañedo, eldest son of late Castor Cañedo Pidal, and of Sra Maria del Carmen Angoso, of Madrid, and has issue living, Gabriela, *b* 1982. *Residence* – Jorge Juan 37, 28001 Madrid, Spain.
Lady Anne-Marie Ines (twin), *b* 1955: *m* 1978, Laureano Perez-Andujar Gimena, son of Don Laureano Perez de Andujar y Andujar, and of Sra Dona Caridad Gimena de Manas, of Madrid. *Residence* – Marques de Valdecilla 6, 28002 Madrid, Spain.

(*By 2nd marriage*)

Lady Susanna Louise, *b* 1963.
Lady Melissa Patricia Eileen, *b* 1964: *m* 1991, Dr Simon P. Puxley, and has issue living, India Ward, *b* 1991. *Residence* – The Mansard, Vention, Putsborough, nr Georgeham, N Devon EX33 1LD.
Lady Victoria Cecilia Larissa, *b* 1966.
Lady Amelia Maureen Erica, *b* 1967.
Lady Emma Sophia Cressida, *b* 1970.

BROTHER LIVING

Hon Peter Alistair, *b* 1926; *ed* Eton, Univ of British Columbia, and Ch Ch, Oxford; Chm of Baggeridge Brick plc; 1943-45 War with Roy Canadian Air Force, and Fleet Air Arm: *m* 1st, 1956 (*m diss* 1974), Claire Leonora, da of Amyas Evelyn Giles Baring (*see* B Ashburton, colls); 2ndly, 1974, Elizabeth Rose, da of Richard Victor Charles Westmacott, of Ascona, Switzerland (*see* B St Oswald, 1966 Edn), and has issue living (by 1st *m*), Alexander Evelyn Giles, *b* 1961: *m* 1988, Lucy Rose, eldest da of Rupert Lycett Green (*see* Green, Bt, colls), and has issue living, Archibald Rupert William *b* 1993, Jasmine Carrie *b* 1990, — Rachel Claire, *b* 1957; actress: *m* 1983, Bryan Brown, actor, of Sydney, Australia, and has issue living, Rosie *b* 1985, Matilda *b* 1987, — Tracy Louise (*Marchioness of Worcester*), *b* 1958: *m* 1987, Henry John Fitzroy, Marquess of Worcester, eldest son of 11th Duke of Beaufort, — (by 2nd *m*), Jeremy Christopher, *b* 1975, — Benjamin Robin, *b* 1978. *Residences* – 7 Elm Park Lane, SW3; Cornwell Manor, Chipping Norton, Oxon. *Clubs* – White's, Pratt's, and Royal Yacht Squadron.

WIDOW LIVING OF SON OF SECOND EARL

Hon Alethea Gwendoline Alys Mary Fitzalan-Howard, da of 2nd Viscount FitzAlan of Derwent: *m* 1953, as his 2nd wife, Group Capt Hon Edward Frederick Ward, RAF, who *d* 1987. *Residence* – 21b Ave du Temple, Lausanne, Switzerland.

WIDOW LIVING OF THIRD EARL

GRACE MARIA (*Grace, Countess of Dudley*), da of Dr Michel Kolin, of St Jacob, Dubrovnik, and formerly wife of Prince Stanislas Radziwill: *m* 1961, as his 3rd wife, the 3rd Earl, who *d* 1969.

COLLATERAL BRANCHES LIVING

Issue of late Lieut-Col Hon Roderick John Ward, 2nd son of 2nd Earl, b 1902, d 1952: m 1st, 1928 (m diss 1936), Eileen Patricia, da of Lieut-Col Marcus Michael Hartigan, CMG, DSO; 2ndly, 1940 (m diss 1947), Valerie Maud, who d 1989, da of late Robert Jeremiah Skelton, of Nairobi, Kenya Colony; 3rdly, 1947, Charlotte Anne Park, who d 1971, da of late Capt Charles Frederick Osborne, RD, RNR, of Broadstone, Dorset:—

(By 2nd m) Robert John Christopher BARWICK-WARD (Langthorpe Manor, Langthorpe, nr Boroughbridge, N Yorkshire YO5 9BZ); b 1942; ed Millfield, and Grenoble Univ; assumed by deed poll 1952, the additional surname of Barwick: m 1st, 1968 (m diss 1974), Frances Pauline, who d 1975, el da of Sqdn-Ldr Mathieu Donald Einhorn, JP, RCAF, of Cragg Hill House, Killinghall, Yorks; 2ndly, 1976 (m diss 1985), Laura Madeleine, da of late Henry J. Sutcliffe, of Havercroft, Kearby, nr Wetherby, W Yorks, and has issue living (by 1st m), Annabel Jane, b 1970, — (by 2nd m) Lucinda Marie Clare, b 1980. —— (By 3rd m) Rupert Michael, b 1947: m 1970, Frances Margaret Mary, el da of late J. C. Barry, of Adelaide House, Bruff, co Limerick, and has issue living, Eric Roderick Humble, b 1973.

Issue of late Rt Hon George Reginald Ward (Viscount Ward of Witley), PC, yst son of 2nd Earl, b 1907, d 1988; cr Viscount Ward of Witley 1960: m 1st, 1940 (m diss 1951), Ann Diana France Ayesha, da of late Capt Arthur Edward Capel, CBE (see By of Ribblesdale, 1980 Edn); 2ndly, 1962, Barbara Mary Colonsay, who d 1980, da of late Capt Ronald Frank Rous NcNeill, Irish Guards, and formerly wife of late Hon Michael Langhorne Astor (see V Astor):—

(By 1st m) †Hon Anthony Giles Humble, b 1943; ed Eton; d 1983. —— Hon Georgina Anne, b 1941; resumed her maiden name by deed poll 1971: m 1st, 1966 (m diss 1971), Alastair Cameron Forbes; 2ndly, 1978, Patrick Claude Henry Tritton. Residence – Quintana 23, Gustavo A Madero, Mexico DF ZP14.

Grandson of late Major Hon Sir John Hubert Ward, KCVO, 2nd son of 1st Earl:—
Issue of late Col Edward John Sutton Ward, LVO, MC, b 1909, d 1990: m 1st, 1934, Susan, who d 1981, eldest da of late Geoffrey Robert Josceline Corbett, DSO, of Rossferry, Enniskillen, co Fermanagh; 2ndly, 1986, Marion Elizabeth Jesse (Chilton, Hungerford, Berks), da of late Charles M. Clover, formerly wife of Geoffrey Adams, and widow of (i) Capt Lionel Cecil (see M Salisbury, colls, 1963 Edn), and (ii) 4th Baron Romilly:—

(By 1st m) Gerald John, CBE, b 1938; ed Eton, RMA Sandhurst, and RMC Cirencester: m 1st, 1967 (m diss 1984), Rosalind Elizabeth, yr da of late Hon Richard Edward Lygon (see E Beauchamp, colls); 2ndly, 1984, Mrs Amanda Mildred Dinan, only da of late Sir Lacey Eric Vincent, 2nd Bt, and has issue living (by 1st m), Sarah Patricia, b 1968: m 1993, Adrian Richard Scrope (see Sykes, Bt, cr 1783, colls, 1990 Edn), — Margaret Lucy, b 1970. Residence – Chilton Park Farm, Hungerford, Berks.

Granddaughters of late Hon Robert Arthur Ward, OBE, 3rd son of 1st Earl:—
Issue of late Maj Julian Humble Dudley Ward, b 1908, d 1971: m 1st, 1946 (m diss 1954), Ann Elisabeth, only da of late Capt John Walter Wilson Bridges; 2ndly, 1962, Mary Rebecca Jane, da of Albert Edward Morris-Hadwell, of Kidderminster, Worcs, and Ballarat, Vic, Aust, and widow of Col Harry Latham, RHA:—
(By 1st m) Patricia Anne, b 1947. —— Georgina Mary, b 1950. Residence – Millambri, Canowindra, NSW, Australia.

Granddaughter of late Capt William Humble Dudley Ward, 14th Hus, Herts Yeo Cav, only son of Hon Humble Dudley Ward, 2nd son of 10th Baron:—
Issue of late Rt Hon William Dudley Ward, b 1877, d 1946: m 1913 (m diss 1931), Winifred May (who m 2ndly, 1937, Wing-Com Marquis de Casa Maury (Spain), and d 1983), da of late Col Charles Wilfrid Birkin (see Birkin, Bt, 1980 Edn):—
Angela Clare Louise (Lady Laycock), b 1916; a DStJ, JP and Co Councillor for Notts: m 1935, Maj-Gen Sir Robert Edward Laycock, KCMG, CB, DSO, Roy Horse Guards, who d 1968 (E Listowel, colls), and has had issue, †Joseph William Peter, b 1938; ed Eton: m 1971, (Eve) Lucinda (actress as Lucy Fleming) (who m 2ndly, 1986, as his 2nd wife, Simon Williams, actor), yr da of late Lt-Col Peter Fleming, OBE, of Merrimoles House, Nettlebed, Oxon, by his late wife Dame Celia Johnson, DBE, actress, and was accidentally drowned 1980, leaving issue, Robert b 1973, Diggory b 1975, Flora b 1972, drowned with her father 1980, — Benjamin Richard (Lower Raslie, Slockavullin, Kilmartin-by-Lochgilphead, Argyll), b 1947: m 1971, Rose Cuninghame, and has issue, Samuel Edward b 1983, Bonny Mary b 1972, Josephine Clare b 1973, — Edwina Ottilie Jane (217 E 61st St, New York City, USA), b 1936: m 1st, 1955 (m diss 1963), Lt (Richard) Mark Walter Agnew, RN (see Agnew, Bt, cr 1895, colls); 2ndly, 1963, Sidney Davis, who d 1988, — Emma Rose, b 1943: m 1964, Richard Temple, of 6 Clarendon Cross, W11, el son of Sir Richard Antony Purbeck Temple, MC, 4th Bt, — Katherine Martha, b 1949: m 1969, David A Mlinaric, of 61 Glebe Place, SW3, and has issue living, Nicholas Maximilian b 1977, Jessica Rose b 1970, Frances Josepha Octavia b 1972. Residence – La Canada Real, Soto Grande, Cadiz, Spain.

PREDECESSORS – (1) JOHN de Sutton; d 1359; s by his son (2) JOHN; d 1376; s by his son (3) JOHN; d 1407; s by his son (4) JOHN, KG; summoned to Parliament as Baron Dudley, or Sutton of Dudley 1439-87; d 1487; s by his grandson (5) EDWARD, KG, 2nd Baron; summoned to Parliaments 1492-29; d 1531; s by his son (6) JOHN, 3rd Baron; never summoned to Parliament; having suffered great pecuniary losses by the machinations of usurers he eventually lost Dudley Castle, and for many years subsisted upon the charity of friends, being styled "Lord Quondam"; d 1553; s by his son (7) EDWARD, KB, 4th Baron; summoned to Parliaments 1554-86; Queen Mary restored to him by patent Dudley Castle and other lands of great value, which had vested in the crown on the attainder of John Dudley, Duke of Northumberland; d 1586; s by his son (8) EDWARD, 5th Baron, summoned to Parliament 1593-1639; having lavished a large portion of his patrimony in profligacy, gave his grand-da and heir in marriage to Humble Ward, son of an opulent goldsmith and jeweller to Charles I; he d 1643, and was succeeded in the Barony by his grand-da (ante) (9) FRANCES WARD, whose husband, Humble Ward, having been knighted was in 1644 cr Baron Ward, of Birmingham (peerage of England); he d 1670; s by his son (10) EDWARD, 2nd Baron Ward, who also became on the death of his mother in 1697 7th Baron Dudley, and was styled Baron Dudley and Ward; d 1701; s by his grandson (11) EDWARD, 8th Baron Dudley and 3rd Baron Ward; d 1704; s by his son (12) EDWARD, 9th Baron Dudley and 4th Baron Ward; d unmarried 1731; s by his uncle (13) WILLIAM, 10th Baron Dudley and 5th Baron Ward; d unmarried 1740, when the Barony of Dudley passed to Ferdinando Dudley, son of his sister Frances, by her marriage with William Lea, and at his death, in 1757, that title fell into abeyance between his sisters (see B Dudley); s in Barony of Ward by his kinsman (14) JOHN, 6th Baron Ward, grandson of Hon Wiliam Ward, 2nd son of 1st Baron Ward; cr Viscount Dudley and Ward (peerage of Great Britain) 1763; d 1774; s by his son (15) JOHN, LLD, 2nd Viscount; dsp 1788; s by his half-brother (16) WILLIAM, 3rd Viscount; d 1823; s by his son (17) JOHN WILLIAM, 4th Viscount; cr Viscount Ednam and Earl Dudley (peerage of United Kingdom) 1827; d unmarried 1833, when the Viscountcies and Earldom became extinct, and the Barony of Ward passed to his kinsman (18) Rev WILLIAM HUMBLE, 10th Baron Ward; b 1781: m 1816, Amelia, da of William Gooch Pillans, of Bracondale, Norwich; d 1835; s by his son (19) WILLIAM, 11th Baron; b 1817: m 1st, 1851, Selina Constance, who d 1851, da of Hubert de Burgh, of West Drayton Manor, Middlesex; 2ndly, 1865, Georgina Elizabeth, who d 1929, da of Sir Thomas Moncreiffe, 7th Bt; cr Viscount Ednam and Earl of Dudley (peerage of United Kingdom) 1860: d 7 May 1885; s by his son (20) WILLIAM HUMBLE, 2nd Earl, GCB, GCMG, GCVO, PC, b 1867; Parliamentary Sec to Board of Trade 1895-1902; Lord-Lieut of Ireland 1902-5, and Gov-Gen of Commonwealth of Australia 1908-1911: m 1st, 1891, Rachel, CBE, RRC, who d 1920, da of late Charles Gurney; 2ndly, 1924, Gertrude, who d 1952, da of John Millar, widow of Lionel Monckton; d 1932; s by his eld son (21) WILLIAM HUMBLE ERIC MC, TD, 3rd Earl, b 1894; PPS to Under-Sec of State for India 1922-24; High Sheriff of Worcs 1930; MP for Hornsey (C) 1921-24, and for Wednesbury 1931-32; m 1st, 1919, Lady Rosemary Millicent Sutherland-Leveson-Gower, RRC, who d 1930, da of 4th Duke of Sutherland; 2ndly, 1943 (m diss 1954), Frances

Laura, who *d* 1990, da of Hon Guy Lawrence Charteris (*see* E Wemyss); 3rdly, 1961, Grace Maria, da of late Dr Michel Kolin, of Dubrovnik, and formerly wife of Prince Stanislas Radziwill; *d* 1969; *s* by his el son **(22)** WILLIAM HUMBLE DAVID, 4th Earl and present peer: also Viscount Ednam, and Baron Ward.

DUFFERIN AND AVA, MARQUESSATE OF (Hamilton-Temple-Blackwood) (Extinct 1988)

SISTERS LIVING OF FIFTH MARQUESS

Lady Caroline Maureen (80 Redcliffe Sq, SW10), *b* 1931; novelist, as Caroline Blackwood: *m* 1st, 1953 (*m diss* at Juarez, Mexico 1957), Lucian Michael Freud, artist; 2ndly (in New York), 1959 (*m diss* 19—), as his 2nd wife, Israel Citkovitz, composer, who *d* 1974; *m* 3rdly, 1972, as his 3rd wife, Robert Lowell, playwright and poet, who *d* 1977, and has had issue (by 2nd husband), Natalya, *b* 1962; *d* 1978, — Evgenia, *b* 1964: *m* 1990, Julian Sands, actor, son of late William Sands, — Ivana, *b* 1966, — (by 3rd husband) Sheridan, *b* 1971.
Lady Perdita Maureen, *b* 1934; racehorse breeder. *Residence* – Cavallo Farm, Crawfordsburn Rd, Newtownards, co Down.

WIDOW LIVING OF FOURTH MARQUESS

MAUREEN CONSTANCE (*Maureen, Marchioness of Dufferin and Ava*), da of late Hon Arthur Ernest Guinness (*see* E Iveagh, colls): *m* 1st, 1930, the 4th Marquess, who was *ka* in Burma 1945; 2ndly, 1948 (*m diss* 1954), Major Harry Alexander Desmond Buchanan, MC; 3rdly, 1955, His Honour Judge John Cyril Maude, QC (*see* V Hawarden, colls), who *d* 1986. *Residences* – The Owl House, Lamberhurst, Kent; 4 Hans Crescent, SW1.

WIDOW LIVING OF FIFTH MARQUESS

SERENA BELINDA ROSEMARY (LINDY) (*Marchioness of Dufferin and Ava*), only da of late G/Capt (Thomas) Loel Evelyn Bulkeley Guinness, CBE, Auxiliary Air Force (Reserve) (*see* D Rutland): *m* 1964, the 5th Marquess, who *d* 1988, when the title became ext. *Residences* – Clandeboye, co Down; 4 Holland Villas Rd, W14.

COLLATERAL BRANCHES LIVING

Granddaughter of late Maj Price Frederick Blackwood, yst son of late Rev Hon William Stear Blackwood, 4th son of 2nd Baron Dufferin:—
    Issue of late Lieut-Col Albemarle Price Blackwood, DSO (Border Regt), *b* 1881, *d* 1921: *m* 1920, Kyra, who *d* 1937, elder da of late Albert Llewelyn Hughes, and widow of Serge de Boursac:—
Kyra Henrietta, *b* 1921: late Sergeant WAAF: *m* 1st, 1945, Samuel Junior Marshall, US Army Air Force, who *d* 1948; 2ndly, 1951, Iain Gregor Finton Robertson, and has issue living (by 2nd *m*), James Paul (St Helier, 2 Harrowden Rd, Inverness), *b* 1952: *m* 1982, Judith Ellen Bull, and has issue living, Iain David *b* 1989, Kyra Frances *b* 1992. *Residence* – Green Bank Cottage, 9 Langside, E Linton, E Lothian EH40 3AN.

Descendants of late Vice Adm Hon Sir Henry Blackwood, KCB, 7th and yst son of Baroness Dufferin and Clandeboye, who was *cr* a *Baronet* 1814:—
See B Dufferin and Clandeboye.

DUFFERIN AND CLANDEBOYE, BARON (Blackwood) (Baron I 1800, Bt I 1763 and UK 1814)

JOHN FRANCIS BLACKWOOD, 11th Baron, 12th Baronet of Ballyleidy and 8th Baronet of UK; *b* 18 Oct 1944; *s* his father 1991 (although the claim to the peerage has not yet been established); *ed* Barker Coll, Hornsby, and Univ of NSW (B Arch); ARAIA, architect in private practice: *m* 1971, Annette Kay, da of Harold Greenhill, artist, of Seaforth, Sydney, NSW, and has issue.

Arms – Azure a fess or in chief a crescent argent between two mullets of the second and in base a mascle of the third. **Crest** – On a cap of maintenance gules turned up ermine a crescent argent. **Supporters** – *Dexter*, a lion gules gorged with a tressure flory counterflory or; *sinister*, an heraldic tiger ermine gorged with a like tressure gules. **Motto** – Per Vias Rectas.
Residence – 169 Anson St, Orange, NSW 2800, Australia.

· PER · VIAS · RECTAS ·

SON LIVING

Hon FRANCIS SENDEN, *b* 6 Jan 1979.

DAUGHTER LIVING

Hon Freya Jodie, *b* 1975.

BROTHER LIVING

Hon Peter Maurice, *b* 1950; *ed* Knox Gram Sch, Wahroonga, and Macquarie Univ (BA); anthropologist: *m* 1979, Kay Lynette, da of William Maurice Winkle of Brisbane, Qld, and has issue living, Alexander Francis Winkle, *b* 1986, — Alice Kathleen Winkle, *b* 1982. *Residence* – 2 Hawkins Court, Alice Springs, NT 0870, Australia.

SISTER LIVING

Hon Angela Margaret, *b* 1942; *ed* Sydney Univ (BSc), and Charles Sturt Univ (Dip Ed): *m* 1965, Clifton Elliott Barker, BSc, of 141 Campbell Drive, Wahroonga, NSW 2076, Australia, and has issue living, Stephen Michael, *b* 1969: *m* 1993, Sally Ann, da of Douglas Alan Farrington, — Zoë Frances, *b* 1971, — Lucinda Alice, *b* 1975, — Karina Emily, *b* 1980.

George, OBE, DSC (c/o National Westminster Bank, Chichester, Sussex), b 1920; Cdr RN; OBE (Mil) 1970: m 1950, Diana, da of late Lt-Col A. L. A. Flint, and has issue living, Robert George Temple, b 1953, — Michael Francis, b 1959, — Clare Mary, b 1956.

Henry (37 The Crescent, Vaucluse, NSW 2030, Australia), b 1922; ed Knox Gram Sch, Wahroonga; late Lieut RANR(S); Capt Merchant Marine: m 1948, Kathryn, da of D. T. Rankin, of Westwood, W Wyalong, NSW, and has issue living, Maurice Henry (Ebony Hall, Moreton Park Rd, Douglas Park, NSW, Australia), b 1954; ed Sydney C of E Gram Sch, NSW Univ, and Sydney Tech Coll (Assoc Dip Metallurgy); Co Dir: m 1982, Anne Edith, da of M. H. L. Macarthur, of Katoomba, NSW, and has issue living, James Maurice Henry b 1988, Jennifer Anne Halley b 1986.

Mary, b 1917: m 1st, 1940, John Frankcomb, who was ka as P/O RAAF 1942; 2ndly, 1945, Edward Lister Ifould, DSO, DFC and Bar, who d 1981, of 317 Peninsula Gdns, Bayview, NSW, Australia, and has issue living (by 1st m), Dorothy Pamela, b 1942, — (by 2nd m) William Edward, b 1947; ed Sydney C of E Gram Sch, — Marian, b 1946, — Frances Gay Lister, b 1953.

LILIAN MARGARET (Lilian, Lady Blackwood), da of late Fulton J. MacGougan, of Vancouver: m 1921, Sir Francis Elliot Temple Blackwood, 6th Bt, who d 1979. Address – c/o Riversdale Convalescent Hospital, 1090 Rio Lane, Sacramento, Calif, USA.

MARGARET (Dowager Baroness Dufferin and Clandeboye), da of Hector Kirkpatrick, of Lindfield, NSW: m 1941, the 10th Baron, who d 1991. Residence – The Cotswolds, 79/28 Curagul Rd, N Turramurra, NSW 2074, Australia.

COLLATERAL BRANCH LIVING

Issue of late Neville Foster Blackwood, 4th son of 4th baronet, b 1884, d 1964: m 1919, Kathleen Nelly, who d 1959, da of late Henry Sidney Mosenthal:—
Robin Henry (5 Gurney Close, Caversham, Reading, Berks), b 1926.

PREDECESSORS – (1) ROBERT BLACKWOOD, el son of late John Blackwood, of Ballyleidy, co Down: m 1st, 1721, Joyce, da of late Joseph Leeson; 2ndly, 1729, Grace, who d 1788, da of Isaac Macartney, cr a Baronet 1763; d 1774; s by his son (2) Sir JOHN, 2nd Bt; MP in five Parliaments 1761-90; d 1799; in 1800 his widow DORCAS was cr Baroness Dufferin and Clandeboye (peerage of Ireland); she d 1808; s by her son (3) JAMES, 2nd Baron, who had in 1799 s his father as 3rd Bt; MP for Killyleagh in three Parliaments and a Representative Peer, dsp 1836; s by his brother (4) HANS, 3rd Baron; d 1839; s by his son (5) PRICE, 4th Baron; b 1794; Capt RN; m 1825, Helen Selina, da of late Thomas Sheridan; d 1841; s by his son (6) FREDERICK TEMPLE, KP, GCB, GCMG, GCIE, PC, DCL, LLD, FRS, 5th Baron, b 1826; a Lord-in-Waiting to HM Queen Victoria 1848-52, and 1854-8, Under-Sec for India 1864-6, and for War 1866, Chancellor of Duchy of Lancaster and Paymaster-Gen 1868-72, Gov-Gen and Com-in-Ch of Canada 1872-8 Ambassador Extraor and Min Plen at St Petersburg 1879-81, and at Constantinople 1881-4 Viceroy of India 1884-8, Ambassador Extraor and Plen at Rome 1888-91, and Ambassador at Paris 1891-6; assumed by Roy licenses 1862 the additional surname of Hamilton and 1872 that of Temple; cr Baron Clandeboye 1850, and Viscount Clandeboye and Earl of Dufferin (peerage of UK) 1871, and Earl of Ava and Marquess of Dufferin and Ava, of co Down and of Burmah (peerage of UK) 1888; m 1862, Dame Hariot Georgina, VA, CI, DBE, who d 1936, el da of late Archibald Rowan Hamilton, of Killyleagh Castle, co Down; d 1902; s by his son (7) TERENCE TEMPLE, 2nd Marquess; b 1866; a Clerk in Foreign Office 1906-18: m 1893, Florence (Flora), who d 1925, da of John H. Davis, of 24 Washington Sq, New York; d 1918; s by his brother (8) FREDERICK TEMPLE, DSO, PC, 3rd Marquess, b 1875; S Africa 1900 (wounded, despatches twice. Queen's medal with nine clasps DSO), European War 1914-17 as Staff-Capt Household Cav and with a Guards Div (twice wounded, 1914-15 star, two medals); Mil Sec to Gov-Gen of Commonwealth of Australia 1914, Speaker of Senate of N Ireland June 1921 and 1925-30, and Vice-Adm of Province of Ulster 1923-30: m 1908, Brenda, who d 1946, only da of late Robert Woodhouse, formerly of Orford House, Ugley, Bishop's Stortford; d 1930; s by his son (9) BASIL SHERIDAN, 4th Marquess, b 1909; Capt Roy Horse Guards; a Lord-in-Waiting to HM 1936-7, the Under-Sec of State for Colonies 1937-40: m 1930, Maureen Constance, da of Hon Arthur Ernest Guinness; ka in Burma 1945; s by his son (10) SHERIDAN FREDERICK TERENCE, 5th Marquess, b 1938; Trustee of Nat Gallery (London) and the Wallace Collection: m 1964, Serena Belinda Rosemary (Lindy), only da of late G/Capt (Thomas) Loel Evelyn Bulkeley Guinness, CBE, Auxiliary Air Force (Reserve) (see D Rutland); d 1988, when the Marquessate of Dufferin and Ava, the Earldoms of Dufferin and Ava and the Viscountcy and Barony of Clandeboye became extinct; he was s in the Barony of Dufferin and Clandeboye and the Baronetcy of Blackwood of Ballyleidy by his kinsman (11) FRANCIS GEORGE (infra), 10th Baron Dufferin and Clandeboye, b 1916; FIEAust, ARACI, Chemical and Consulting Engr: m 1941, Margaret, da of Hector Kirkpatrick, of Lindfield, NSW; d 1991; s by his elder son (12) JOHN FRANCIS, 11th Baron and present peer.

*The 1st baronet Hon Sir Henry Blackwood, KCB, 7th and yst son of Sir John Blackwood, 2nd Bt (ante), was a Vice Adm of the Blue, and the bearer of despatches announcing the victory of Trafalger; cr a baronet 1814. The 4th baronet, Sir Francis, was Capt RN, and served in the Crimea. His grandson was Sir Francis George, 7th Bt (ante), son of Capt Maurice Baldwin Raymond Blackwood, DSO, RN, who d on active service 1941.

DULVERTON, BARON (Wills) (Baron UK 1929, Bt UK 1897)

(GILBERT) MICHAEL HAMILTON WILLS, 3rd Baron, and 4th Baronet; *b* 2 May 1944; *s* 1992; *ed* Gordonstoun: *m* 1980, Rosalind Johnny Maria, only da of J. van der Velde, of Rozenburg, Holland, and of Mrs R. D. Oliver, of Lochside, Kelso, Roxburgh, and has issue.

Arms – Gules, three estoiles flammant fessewise between two griffins passant wings expanded and inverted all or. **Crest** – Issuant from an annulet or, a demi-griffin gules, charged with an estoile as in the arms, and holding in the dexter claw a battle-axe also or. **Supporters** – *Dexter*, a trumpeter of the Royal North Devon Yeomanry; *sinister*, a huntsman of the Dulverton hunt; both proper. *Seat* – Batsford Park, Moreton-in-Marsh, Gloucestershire.

Wherever the light leads

SON LIVING

Hon ROBERT ANTHONY HAMILTON, *b* 20 Oct 1983.

DAUGHTER LIVING

Hon Charlotte Alexandra Hamilton, *b* 1981.

BROTHER LIVING

Hon (Robert) Ian Hamilton, *b* 1948; *ed* Harrow, and Warwick Univ (BA): *m* 1979, Elizabeth Jane, eldest da of Michael Taylor Downes, of The Old Parsonage, Lower Slaughter, Glos, and has issue living, James Douglas Hamilton, *b* 1984, — Emma Elizabeth Hamilton, *b* 1982. *Residence* – Soundborough Farm, Andoversford, Cheltenham, Glos.

SISTER LIVING

Hon Sarah May Hamilton, *b* 1942. *Residence* – 8 Montrose Court, Prince's Gate, SW7.

UNCLES LIVING (*sons of 1st Baron*)

Hon (Edward) Robert Hamilton, *b* 1918; *ed* Eton; Maj late Gren Gds, European War 1935-45 (wounded); Chm The Farmington Trust. *Residence* – Farmington Lodge, Northleach, Glos.
Hon (Victor) Patrick Hamilton, *b* 1926; *ed* Eton, and Coll of Estate Management; Lieut Gren Gds and Parachute Regt (ret); FLAS 1957; DL Hants 1975, Co Councillor 1965-73; Chm Hants Playing Fields Assocn 1969-79, Trustee Dulverton Trust 1949-81, Gov Internat Students' Trust 1965 (Vice-Pres 1979, Chm 1984), Vice-Chm Trident Trust 1972 (Chm 1978-80), Chm Atlantic Salmon Conservation Trust (Scotland) 1985-91: *m* 1st, 1948 (*m diss* 1962), Felicity Betty, da of late Maj Aubrey Thomas Jonsson, Royal Irish Rifles; 2ndly, 1963, Mrs Jean Felicity Strutt, who *d* 1984, yr da of late Hon Francis Walter Erskine (E Mar and Kellie); 3rdly, 1988 (*m diss* 1993), Mrs Elizabeth Gilmor Shaw, and has issue living (by 1st *m*), Christopher Aubrey Hamilton (Litchfield Down, Whitchurch, Hants), *b* 1953; *ed* Eton; Lieut Gren Gds (ret); a Trustee Dulverton Trust 1979: *m* 1987, Lady Katharine Anne Meade, 5th da of 6th Earl of Clanwilliam, and has issue living, Thomas Robert Hamilton *b* 1991, George Edmund Hamilton *b* 1993, — Jeremy Robert Hamilton (Bevis Farm, Charlbury, Oxon), *b* 1955; *ed* Eton; Capt Gren Gds (despatches 1984): *m* 1982, Alison Mary, da of David Malkin, of Winnington Grange, Market Drayton, Shropshire, and has issue living, Nicholas Patrick Hamilton *b* 1986, Benjamin James Hamilton *b* 1988, — Penelope Margaret Hamilton, *b* 1950: *m* 1976 (*m diss* 1986), David J. Enthoven, and has issue living, James John *b* 1980, Belinda Margaret *b* 1977. *Residence* – Litchfield Manor, Whitchurch, Hants.

WIDOW LIVING OF SECOND BARON

RUTH VIOLET MARY (*Ruth, Baroness Dulverton*), only da of Sir Walter Randolph Fitzroy Farquhar, 5th Bt, and formerly wife of late Maj Richard Gennys Fanshawe, 16th/5th Lancers: *m* 1962, as his 2nd wife, the 2nd Baron, CBE, TD, who *d* 1992. *Residence* – Barnbrook Cottage, Milton Lilbourne, Pewsey, Wilts SN9 5LQ.

COLLATERAL BRANCHES LIVING (*In remainder to the Baronetcy only*)

Grandsons of late Frederick Noel Hamilton Wills (*infra*):—
Issue of late Capt Michael Desmond Hamilton Wills, MC, Coldstream Guards; *b* 1915, *ka* in Middle East 1943: *m* 1939, Mary Margaret (*Lady Gibbs*) (who *m* 2ndly, 1947, Col Sir Martin St John Valentine Gibbs, KCVO, CB, DSO, who *d* 1992, of The Manor House, Ewen, Cirencester, Glos), da of Lt-Col Philip Mitford (*see* Fowler, Bt, ext, 1966 Edn):—
(Michael) Thomas Noel Hamilton (Miserden Park, Miserden, Stroud, Glos), *b* 1940; *ed* Eton; Maj late Coldm Gds (ret); High Sheriff Glos 1985, DL Glos 1991; Exon HM Body Guard of Yeomen of the Guard 1993: *m* 1982, Penelope A., el da of Ben Howard-Baker, of Glascoed Hall, Llansilin, Shropshire, and has issue living, Nicholas James Noel Hamilton, *b* 1983, — Camilla Jane Hamilton, *b* 1985. —— Frederick Hugh Philip Hamilton (twin) (The Old House, Rendcomb, Cirencester, Glos; Coulin Lodge, Kinlochewe, Ross-shire), *b* 1940; *ed* Eton; Capt 11th Hussars (ret): *m* 1969, Priscilla Annabelle, da of late Capt Alec Francis, of The Grange, Malmesbury (*see* L Kinloss, colls), and has issue living, Michael James Hamilton, *b* 1972, — Edward Hamilton, *b* 1974, — Clare Alexandra (twin), *b* 1974. —— (Peter) John Hamilton, *b* 1941; *ed* Eton, and Magdalen Coll, Oxford: *m* 1970, Elizabeth Jean, da of Maj J. J. Mann, of Oxleaze Farm, Filkins, Lechlade, Glos, and has issue living, Richard Henry, *b* 1974, — Grania Sarah, *b* 1972, — Emily Jane, *b* 1975.

Issue of late Frederick Noel Hamilton Wills, 3rd son of 1st baronet, *b* 1887, *d* 1927: *m* 1912, Margery Hamilton (who *m* 2ndly, 1942, Wing-Com Huntly Macdonald Sinclair, RCAF, of Miserden Park, Stroud), el da of late Hon Sir Hugh Fraser, JP, a Judge of High Court of Justice, of Stromeferry House, Ross-shire:—
Sir (Hugh) David Alastair Hamilton, CBE, TD, *b* 1917; late Maj Queen's Own Cameron Highlanders; a DL of Oxford (High Sheriff 1961); 1939-45 War, MBE (Mil) 1946, CBE (Civil) 1971; *cr* Knt 1979: *m* 1949, Eva Helen McMorrough, da of late Maj Arthur Thomas McMorrough Kavanagh, MC (Buxton, Bt, colls), and has had issue, †Martin David Hamilton *b* 1952; *d* 1992, — Catherine Mary Hamilton, *b* 1950. *Residences* – Sandford Park, Sandford St Martin, Oxon; Knockando House, Morayshire. *Club* – Boodle's. —— Rosemary Theodora Hamilton (*Lady MacLeod*), *b* 1913: *m* 1938, Sir John MacLeod, TD, late Capt Queen's Own Cameron Highlanders, who *d* 1984, and *d* 1994, leaving issue, David John Noel, *b* 1939: *m* 1972, Wendy Joy, only da of Edwin Cookson, of Minshull Hall, Nantwich, and has issue living, Fiona Carolyn *b* 1976, Kirsty Davina *b* 1978, Alison Wendy *b* 1980, — Martin Michael Alan, *b* 1949, — Carolyn Margery Hamilton (twin), *b* 1939: *m* 1961, Hugh Petre Barclay (Box 7006, Nakuru, Kenya) (B Petre, colls), and has issue living, Edward Hugh *b* 1963, Jonti Peter *b* 1967, Karen

Theodora *b* 1962, Camilla Patricia *b* 1966, — Jocelyn Ishabel Ann, *b* 1946; a Lady-in-Waiting to HRH The Duchess of York since 1986: *m* 1st, 1967, David Algernon Fleming, who *d* 1975 (Borthwick, Bt, colls); 2ndly, 1978, John Edmund Kincaid Floyd (*see* Floyd, Bt), and has issue living (by 1st *m*), Lara Kate *b* (Jan) 1968, Annabel Theodora *b* (Dec) 1968, Katrina Jane *b* 1971, — Patricia Mary-Rose, *b* 1951: *m* 1979, Nicholas Gaston Ives Bosanquet, of Lee Place Farm, nr Pulborough, W Sussex, and has issue living, Emma Claire *b* 1980, Hermione Lucinda *b* 1981, Davina Jayne *b* (twin) 1981. *Residence* – Bunkers Hill, Farmington, nr Northleach, Glos. —— Margery Angela Hamilton, *b* 1922: *m* 1st, 1948 (*m diss* 1971), Anthony Andrew Francis Tabor, late Capt Herts Yeo; 2ndly, 1972, Thomas Anthony Stainton, who *d* 1988; 3rdly, 1994, as his 2nd wife, Col Rodney Francis Maurice Windsor, CBE, DL, and has issue living (by 1st *m*), (Adrian Andrew) Hamish *b* 1960: *m* 1986, Carolina Giovanna, da of Conte Massimiliano Magnaghi, of Le Martinet, Lausanne, Switzerland, and of Mme Philippe Saint-Armand, of Auxerre, France, and has issue living, Francesca Giovana Angela *b* 1989, Julia Aloisa Allegra *b* 1992, — Marilyn Margery Hamilton, *b* 1949, — Nicola Mary Hamilton, *b* 1952: *m* 1974, Hugh Sherbrooke (*see* Bs Herries, colls). *Residences* – Mains of Warthill, Meikle Wartle, Aberdeenshire; Coruanan Lodge, Fort William, Inverness-shire. —— Audrey Mackenzie Hamilton, *b* 1925: *m* 1946, Capt Peter Houldsworth Gibbs, Scots Gds, and has issue living, (Peter) Noel (Houldsworth) (Combend Manor, Elkstone, Cheltenham, Glos), *b* 1948; *ed* Eton, and Magdalen Coll, Oxford: *m* 1st, 1976 (*m diss* 1989), Clare, da of Nigel Viney; 2ndly, 1991, Katharine Constance, yst da of late Col Richard Lumley Hurst (*see* E Crawford), and widow of Donald M. Corbett, and has issue living (by 1st *m*), Hugo Houldsworth *b* 1984, Chlöe Lucy *b* 1982, Amelia Emma (twin) *b* 1982, — Linda Hamilton, *b* 1951: *m* 1st, 1973, Robert Bruce John Dunipace; 2ndly, 1991, Lt-Col Anthony Singer, KRH, and has issue living (by 1st *m*), Aulden Malcolm Bruce *b* 1975, Fergus Roland Fraser *b* 1981, Imogen Larissa *b* 1976, Flavia Iona Churchill *b* 1983. *Residence* – Hall's Grove, Elkstone, Glos.

PREDECESSORS – **(1)** FREDERICK Wills, son of late Henry Overton Wills, JP, of Bristol, and brother of Sir Edward Payson Wills, KCB, 1st Bt (*cr* 1904), *b* 1838; a Director of Imperial Tobacco Co (Limited); sat as MP for Bristol, N Div (LU) 1900-1906; *cr* a Baronet 1897: *m* 1867, Annie, who *d* 1910, el da of the Rev James Hamilton, DD, of Longridge, Stonehouse; *d* 1909; *s* by his son **(2)** GILBERT ALAN HAMILTON, OBE, 2nd Bt; *b* 1880; Pres of Imperial Tobacco Co (Limited), Parliamentary Private Sec to Postmaster-Gen 1921, High Sheriff of Gloucestershire 1928, MP for Taunton (C) 1912-18, and for Weston-super-Mare Div of Somerset 1918-22; *cr Baron Dulverton*, of Batsford (peerage of United Kingdom), 1929: *m* 1914, Victoria May, OBE, who *d* 1968, da of Rear-Adm Sir Edward Chichester, CB, CMG, 9th Bt; *d* 1956; *s* by his el son **(3)** (FREDERICK) ANTHONY HAMILTON, 2nd Baron, CBE, TD, *b* 1915; Maj Lovat Scouts; Pres Timber Growers' Assocn, and British Deer Soc; Chm Dulverton Trust, and Forestry Cttee of GB, Member Red Deer Commn, and Scottish Advisory Cttee Nature Conservancy; Waynflete Fell Magdalen Coll, Oxford; DL Glos: *m* 1st, 1939 (*m diss* 1960), Judith Betty, who *d* 1983, da of late Lt-Col Hon Ian Leslie Melville, TD (*see* E Leven and Melville); 2ndly, 1962, Mrs Ruth Violet Fanshawe, only da of Sir Walter Randolph Fitzroy Farquhar, 5th Bt; *d* 1992; *s* by his elder son **(4)** GILBERT MICHAEL HAMILTON, 3rd Baron and present peer.

Dumfries, Earl of; see Marquess of Bute.

DUNALLEY, BARON (Prittie) (Baron I 1800)

(HENRY) FRANCIS CORNELIUS PRITTIE, 7th Baron; *b* 30 May 1948; *s* 1992; *ed* Gordonstoun, and Trin Coll, Dublin (BA): *m* 1978, Sally Louise, el da of late Ronald Vere, of Heaton Chapel, Cheshire, and has issue.

Arms – Per pale argent and gules three wolves' heads erased or. **Crest** – A wolf's head erased or. **Supporters** – *Dexter*, a man in armour proper, holding a tilting spear in the right hand; *sinister*, a stag proper, attired, unguled, ducally collared and chained, or.
Residence – 25 Stephen Rd, Oxford OX3 9AY.

Prepared for all things

IN·OMNIA·PARATUS·

SON LIVING

Hon JOEL HENRY, *b* 29 April 1981.

DAUGHTERS LIVING

Hon Rebecca Louise, *b* 1979.
Hon Hannah Beatrice, *b* 1983.
Hon Rachel Sarah, *b* 1987.

BROTHER LIVING

Hon Michael Philip St John, *b* 1961; *ed* Stowe. *Residence* – 36 Kite Hill Road, Santa Cruz, Calif 95060, USA.

SISTER LIVING

Hon Mary Rose Madeline, *b* 1953; has issue living, Flora Tamsine JOYCE, *b* 1981, — Pollyanna Felicity Rose JOYCE, *b* 1990, — Lily Philippa JOYCE, *b* 1992. *Residence* – Athry, Recess, co Galway.

WIDOW OF SIXTH BARON

(MARY) PHILIPPA (*Dowager Baroness Dunalley*), only child of late Hon Philip Plantagenet Cary (*see* V Falkland, colls): *m* 1947, Lt-Col the 6th Baron, who *d* 1992. *Residence* – Church End House, Swerford, Oxford OX7 4AX.

COLLATERAL BRANCH LIVING

Issue of late Hon Terence Cornelius Farmer Prittie, MBE, yr son of 5th Baron, *b* 1913, *d* 1985: *m* 1946, Laura, who *d* 1988, only child of late G. Dreyfus Dundas, of Columbia:—
Oliver Alan Graham (9 Blithfield St, W8), *b* 1948; *ed* Eton: *m* 1st, 1973 (*m diss* 1983), Alison Victoria, da of Arnold Bertram Kingsley Tillie, of Harley Gdns, SW10; 2ndly, 1986, Krystyna Emilia, da of Michael Wasiukiewicz, of 18 Shelley Rd,

Stratford-upon-Avon, Warwicks, and has issue living (by 1st *m*), Jemma Victoria, *b* 1975, — Kinvara Louise, *b* 1978, — (by 2nd *m*) Dominic Terence, *b* 1987, — Laura Zoe, *b* 1989. —— (James) Hugo Cameron (Le Breuilh, St-Meard-de-Dronne, 24600 Riberac, France), *b* 1950; *ed* Eton: *m* 1983, Mrs Helga Isolda Lachnitt, eldest da of late Robert Werthenbach, of Siegen, W Germany.

PREDECESSORS – (1) Henry Prittie, *b* 1743; MP for Banagher 1767-8, for Gowran 1769-76, and for co Tipperary 1776-90; *cr Baron Dunalley*, of Kilboy, co Tipperary (peerage of Ireland) 1800; *d* 1801; *s* by his el son (2) Henry Sadleir, FSA, 2nd Baron, *b* 1775; MP for Carlow 1798-1801, and for Okehampton 1819-24; a Representative Peer; *d* 1854; *s* by his nephew (3) Henry, 3rd Baron, *b* 1807: *m* 1841, Hon Anne Maria Louisa O'Callaghan, who *d* 1867, da of 1st Viscount Lismore; *d* 10 Sept, 1885; *s* by his son (4) Henry O'Callaghan, 4th Baron; *b* 1851; a Representative Peer for Ireland, and Lieut and Custos Rotulorum of co Tipperary: *m* 1876, Mary Frances, MBE, who *d* 1929, da of late Maj-Gen Reginald Onslow Farmer, RA, of Grove House, Aspley Guise; *d* 1927; *s* by his son (5) Henry Cornelius O'Callaghan, DSO, 5th Baron; *b* 1877; Major late Rifle Brigade; S African War; 1914-18 War (DSO): *m* 1911, Beatrix Evelyn, who *d* 1967, da of late James Noble Graham, JP DL, of Carfin, and Stonebyres, Lanarkshire; *d* 1948; *s* by his son (6) Henry Desmond Graham, 6th Baron; *b* 1912; Lt-Col Rifle Bde, served with King's African Rifles 1937-40, 1939-45 War in E Africa, Middle East, Italy and Far East: *m* 1947, Mary Philippa, only child of late Maj Hon Philip Plantagenet Cary (*see* V Falkland colls); *d* 1992; *s* by his elder son (7) Henry Francis Cornelius, 7th Baron and present peer.

DUNBOYNE, BARON (Butler) (Baron I 1324 and 1541)

TIMOR·DOMINI·FONS·VITÆ

The fear of the Lord is the fountain of life

Patrick Theobald Tower Butler, 28th Baron (18th by patent); (*His Honour The Lord Dunboyne, VRD*); *b* 27 Jan 1917; *s* 1945; *ed* Winchester, and Trin Coll, Camb (Pres of Union; MA); Bar Middle Temple (Harmsworth Scholar) 1949, of Inner Temple 1962, and King's Inns, Dublin 1966, a JP; Foreign Office 1945-46; Dep Chm Middlesex Sessions 1963-65; Commissary Gen of Canterbury Diocese 1959-71; Recorder of Hastings 1961-71; Dep Chm Kent Sessions 1963-71, and Inner London Sessions 1971; a Circuit Judge 1972-86; Pres Wireless Telegraphy Appeal Tribunal for England and Wales 1967-70; Home Sec's Commr for ward-boundaries 1960-70; Fellow Irish Genealogical Research Soc (Pres 1971-91); founder-Sec Bar Lawn Tennis Soc 1950-62 (Vice-Pres since 1963), and of Irish Peers Assocn 1963-71 (Pres 1988-91); Lt late Irish Guards (SR); served European War 1939-44 (prisoner, repatriated); Lieut RNVR 1951-58, RNR 1958-60, VRD 1987: *m* 1950, Anne Marie, da of Sir Victor Alexander Louis Mallet, GCMG, CVO, and has issue.

Arms – Or, a chief indented azure, and three escallops in bend counterchanged. Crest – Out of a ducal coronet or, a plume of five ostrich feathers, and issuant therefrom a demi-falcon rising argent. Supporters – *Dexter*, a lion guardant argent; *sinister*, a horse sable, mane, tail and hoofs or. Residences – 36 Ormonde Gate SW3 4HA; The Flat, West Ilkerton Farm, Lynton, Devon EX35 6QA. Clubs – Irish, Pitt (Cambridge), Union (Cambridge), All England Lawn Tennis and Croquet (Wimbledon), International Lawn Tennis of Great Britain (Dep-Pres 1970-73, Pres 1973-83), and 45 Club (Pres 1974-91).

SON LIVING

Hon John Fitzwalter (Argos Hill House, Rotherfield, E Sussex TN6 3QG), *b* 31 July, 1951; *ed* Winchester, and Trin Coll, Camb (MA); Sloan Fellow of London Business Sch: *m* 1975, (Diana) Caroline, da of late Sir Michael Sanigear Williams, KCMG, and has issue living, Richard Pierce Theobald, *b* 5 July 1983, — Genevieve Synolda, *b* 1977, — Imogen Katharine, *b* 1979, — Cleone Isolde, *b* 1986.

DAUGHTERS LIVING

Hon Mary Synolda, *b* 1954; *ed* Benenden, and Girton Coll, Camb (BA 1975, MA 1980); Solicitor 1980: *m* 1984, Alastair Henry Walton, only son of late Sir Raymond Henry Walton, and has issue living, Alexandra Mary, *b* 1985, — Christina Frances, *b* 1986, — Stephanie Katharine, *b* 1988, — Florence Lucy, *b* 1992. *Residence* – 26 Paradise Walk, SW3 4LJ.
Hon Betty Quenelda, *b* 1956; *ed* Benenden, and Girton Coll, Camb (BA 1978, MA 1983); PGCE Cantab: *m* 1985, Edward Roland Haslewood Perks, yr son of His Honour Clifford Perks, MC, TD, FSA, and has issue living, Lawrence Patrick Haslewood, *b* 1989, — Candida Anne Quenelda, *b* 1986. *Residence* – 4 Broomwood Road, SW11 6HT.
Hon Victoria Morina, *b* 1959; *ed* Benenden, St Andrew's Univ (BSc 1982), and Wye Agric Coll, Univ of London (MSc 1983): *m* 1986, Christopher J. P. Eveleigh, eldest son of John Eveleigh, of Croyde, N Devon, and has issue living, George Jethro, *b* 1987, — Sarah, *b* 1990. *Residence* – West Ilkerton Farm, Lynton, Devon EX35 6QA.

SISTERS LIVING

Hon (Doreen) Synolda Tower, *b* 1918: *m* 1945, Major Atholl Duncan, MC, RA, who *d* 1983, and has issue living, (Walter) Alastair, *b* 1947, — Patrick Atholl, *b* 1957; Maj RHA: *m* 1987, Margrit Victoria, da of Franz Frefel, of Frampton, Dorchester, Dorset, and has issue living, Christopher Patrick *b* 1991, Alexander Edward *b* 1993, Charlotte Isabel *b* 1989, — Zara Synolda, *b* 1950: *m* 1979, David Firmin, FRIBA, of 24 Ursula St, SW11 3DW, son of E. H. Firmin, of Aldwick Bay Estate, Bognor Regis, W Sussex, and has issue living, Philip Duncan *b* 1981, Robert Charles *b* 1985, Zoe Charlotte *b* 1980, — Lorna Romayne, *b* 1956: *m* 1987, Lt-Col Bryan M. Elliott, MBE, LI, of 22 Pennard Road, W12 8D5, son of late Cdr Charles Elliott, RN. *Residence* – 9 Marland House, 28 Sloane Street, SW1X 9NE.
Hon Maureen Maude Tower, *b* 1919: *m* 1946, Lieut-Col Robert Caradoc Rose Price, DSO, OBE, late Welsh Guards, who *d* 1988, and has issue (*see* Price, Bt, *cr* 1815, colls). *Residence* – 98 Old Church Street, SW3 6EP.

Hon (Isolde) Sheila Tower, *b* 1925: *m* 1949, Com Penryn Victor Monck, RNVR (E Peel), who *d* 1987, and has issue living,
Rory Penryn (Roughwood, Red Copse Lane, Boars Hill, Oxford), *b* 1951, — Tasha Penryn, *b* 1950: *m* 1st, 1976, Martin P. A.
Travers; 2ndly, 1984, Rev William Donald, of 82 Forest View Rd, Tuffley, Gloucester GL4 0BY, and has issue living (by 1st
m), Isabel Eileen *b* 1977, (by 2nd *m*) Jesse Michael Penryn *b* 1985, — Fiona Penryn, *b* 1957: *m* 1981, Andrew Pettinger, 2nd
son of Eric J. C. Pettinger, of Watsons, Belsford, Harberton, Totnes, Devon TQ9 7SP.

COLLATERAL BRANCHES LIVING

Grandsons of late Brig-Gen Hon Lesley James Probyn Butler, CMG, DSO, 2nd son of 26th Baron:—
Issue of late Lt-Col James Dighton Butler, *b* 1911, *d* 1987: *m* 1943, Pamela, who *d* 1987, da of late William Alfred
Pickwoad, OBE, and widow of Lt-Col A. J. F. Sugden, RA:—
(Michael) James (Morgans Bradley, Templeton, Tiverton, Devon EX16 8BJ), *b* 1944; *ed* Eastbourne Coll, RMA Sandhurst,
and RAC Cirencester (Dip Rural Estate Mgmnt); FRICS; Fellow Western Counties Assocn of Agric Valuers; late 15th/19th
King's Royal Hus: *m* 1981, Jennifer, da of late Percy Williams, of Dundee, and has issue living, Elizabeth Mary, *b* 1985.
—— Robert Patrick, *b* 1947; *ed* Milton Abbey; late Queen's Royal Irish Hus: *m* 1972, Nicola Jane, da of P. W. R. Pope, of W
Stafford, Dorchester, Dorset, and has issue living, Alexander Philip Dighton, *b* 1975, — Edward Patrick, *b* 1978.

Grandchildren of late St John Henry ARCEDECKNE-BUTLER, grandson of late Hon St John Butler, 6th (but
2nd surviving) son of 23rd Baron:—
Issue of late Maj-Gen St John Desmond Arcedeckne-Butler, CBE, *b* 1896, *d* 1959: *m* 1929, Ethel Helen Nesbitt, who
d 1953, da of late Col Reginald Selby Walker, DSO, RE:—
St John Patrick (Parker's Pound, Walton Lane, Old Bosham, W Sussex, PO18 8QB), *b* 1930; Maj (ret), R Signals: *m* 1st,
1956, Jane (Frances Elizabeth Mary), who *d* 1983, da of late Lt-Col F. E. Massie, MC, of W Ayton, Scarborough; 2ndly, 1991,
(Jacqueline) Jean, da of late H. C. Morris, of Dorchester, Dorset, and has issue living (by 1st *m*), St John Terence, *b* 1956,
— Christopher Michael, *b* 1959, — John Patrick, *b* 1969, — Mark Piers, *b* 1972. —— †Michael Francis Peel, RN, *b* 1933;
Lt-Cdr (ret): *m* 1961, Jacqueline, da of late Col George Leonard Carpenter-Garnier, OBE, of Wickham, Hants, and *d* 1993,
leaving issue, Timothy Garnier, *b* 1962, — Nicola Catherine, *b* 1964. *Residence* – Cutlers, Wickham, Hants PO15 5AN.
—— Christal Synolda, *b* 1938: *m* 1961, Geoffrey William Medcalf, of Malt Square House, 15 High St, S Witham, Grantham,
Lincs, and has issue living, Richard William Desmond, *b* 1966, — David Geoffrey, *b* 1969, — Sallie Jane, *b* 1962, — Helen
Sheevaum Christal, *b* 1963, — Patricia Ann, *b* 1964, — Rosemary Janet Slaney, *b* 1970.

Grandchildren of late Edward Arthur Butler, 3rd son of Hon Charles Lennox Butler, 7th son of 23rd
Baron:—
Issue of late Charles Edward Butler, *b* 1874, *d* 1960: *m* 1919, Alice Elizabeth, who *d* 1984, da of late T. J. Worship,
of North Walsham:—
Clarence Francis (West Winds, Baldhoon Rd, Laxey, IoM IM4 7QH), *b* 1920; 1939-45 War as Flight-Lieut RAF (despatches):
m 1944, Pamela Constance, who *d* 1991, da of late F. J. Drakard, of Ingham House, Martlesham, Suffolk, and has issue
living, Julia Rosemary, *b* 1945: *m* 1967, Dennis Curran, of Bishop's Stortford, Herts, — Denise Angela *b* 1947: *m* 1988,
Christopher Bannister Simpson, of Baldhoon, Laxey, I of Man. —— †Brian Charles *b* 1924: *m* 1952, Joyce Caroline (Little
Leigh, Holcombe, Dawlish, Devon), da of G. Hitchcock, of Kenton, Devon, and *d* 1992, leaving issue, Rosena Marie, *b* 1959.
—— Rosalinda Maria, *b* 1921: *m* 1946, Douglas Kyrle Redgrave, of Pantiles, Woodland Av, Teignmouth, Devon TQ14 8UU,
and has issue living, Michael Kyrle, *b* 1950, — Diana Lynne, *b* 1952.
Issue of late Henry Francis Butler, *b* 1877, *d* 1969: *m* 1908, Ethel Isabel Marion, da of late Allix Edward Pardoe, of
Dawlish, Devon:—
Sheila Francis, *b* 1914: *m* 1940, Andrew McKenzie Stevens, of Sandspit Rd, RD 2, Warkworth, Auckland, NZ, and has issue
living, Mary Louise (Mulberry Grove School House, RD1 Tryphena, Great Barrier Island, NZ), *b* 1945: *m* 1966 (*m diss* 1979),
Johnny Bindner, of Copenhagen, and has an adopted son, Daniel *b* 1975.

Grandchildren of late Lieut-Col Charles James BUTLER-KEARNEY, DL, JP, son of William Butler, great-
grandson of Theobald Butler, el son of Richard Butler (*b* 1701), grandson of James Butler, el son of Hon
Theobald Butler, 8th son of 12th Baron:—
Issue of late Theobald William Butler-Kearney, *b* 1876, *d* 1936: *m* 1914, Hester Louise, who *d* 1972, da of late Carew
Davies Gilbert:—
James Davies Theobald (Jordans, Old Odiham Rd, Alton, Hants GU34 4BW), *b* 1916: *m* 1951 (*m diss* 1954), Gillian Mary
Soltau, el da of late Maj W. H. Anketell; 2ndly, 1970, Juliet Mary, da of late Rev Andrew Hunt. —— Catherine Mary, *b*
1918. *Residence* – Spring Cottage, Durcott Rd, Camerton, Bath.
Issue of late Capt Trench Frank Butler-Kearney, *b* 1877, *d* 1954: *m* 1920, Shirley, who *d* 1971, da of late John Bailey
Sequeira:—
Jean *b* 1920. —— Norma, *b* 1924. *Residence* – 15 The Green, Burgh Heath, Surrey KT20 5NP.

Grandchildren of late Charles Herbert Jackson Butler (*b* 1870), 6th son of William Butler (*b* 1814), son of
James Butler (*b* 1785), grandson of James Butler, of Park, co Tipperary, 3rd son of Richard Butler (*b* 1701)
(ante):—
Issue of late George Herbert Butler, *b* 1901, *d* 1955: *m* 1929, Irene Rose, da of late Edward Sparnon:—
†John Charles Edward, *b* 1935; *d* 1993. —— June Rose Margaret (31 Ellis Park Drive, Durban North 4051, S Africa), *b*
1930: *m* 1961, Philip Clement Brown, who *d* 1984, and has issue living, Timothy Philip, *b* 1964; *ed* Natal Univ: *m* 1993, Paula
Claire, da of John Raftesath, of Natal, — Rosalind June, *b* 1962: *m* 1984, Dr Bruce Gummow, and has issue living, Ian
Andrew *b* 1994. —— (Patricia) Colleen (1103 Kensington, 311 North Ridge Rd, Durban 4001, S Africa), *b* 1938.
Issue of late Frederick William Webb Butler, *b* 1903, *d* 1946: *m* 1934, Nancy Anne O'Mahony:—
Patrick Barry Webb, *b* 1941. —— Michael Terence Webb, *b* 1943.

Grandchildren (by 1st *m*) of late Henry John Butler-Lloyd (*b* 1874) (infra):—
Issue of late William Francis Butler-Lloyd, *b* 1899, *d* 1956: *m* 1930, Mary Margaret, da of Thomas FitzGerald:—
Thomas Henry John BUTLER-LLOYD (Richmond, Templemore, co Tipperary), *b* 1932: *m* 1966, Veronica, da of Patrick Harney,
of Manna, Templemore, co Tipperary, and has issue living, William Francis, *b* 1969, — Audrey Veronica, *b* 1972.
Issue of late Henry John Butler-Lloyd, *b* 1910, *b* 19—: *m* 1947, Kathleen (Castleleiny Cottage, Templemore, co
Tipperary), da of — Leacky, of —:—
Henry John BUTLER-LLOYD (57 Maundeby Walk, NW10 2TG), *b* 1948: *m* 19—, Florence, da of Douglas Henry Lewis, of Burnt
Oak, Edgeware, Middx, and has issue living, Jason James, *b* 1977, — Katherine Geraldine, *b* 1973, — Jacqueline Caroline *b*
1975. —— Mary, *b* 19—. —— Maggie-Jo, *b* 19—. —— Caroline, *b* 19—. —— Carmel, *b* 19—. —— Geraldine, *b* 19—.

Grandchildren of late William Butler (*b* 1814) (ante):—
Issue of late Henry John Butler-Lloyd, *b* 1874, *d* 1946: assumed the additional surname of Lloyd 1896: *m* 1st, 1897,
Catherine, who *d* 1907, da of late James Davoran; 2ndly, 1908, Jane, who *d* 1956, da of late Capt W. Headech, 20th
Regt:—
(By 2nd *m*) Charles BUTLER-LLOYD, *b* 1913. —— Anne (Tyn y Rhos Hall, Weston Rhyn, Oswetry), *b* 1908: *m* 1930, Walter
Thompson, and has issue living, Mervyn THOMPSON-BUTLER-LLOYD (Brother Demetrius, AP, Eastern Orthodox Church) (Tyn
y Rhos Hall, Weston Rhyn, Oswestry), *b* 1939; assumed by deed poll 1963 the additional surnames of Butler-Lloyd, —

Kenneth, *b* 1946; *ed* Salford Univ (BA): *m* 1969, Carol, only da of Sidney Shipton, of Liverpool, — Ivor, *b* 1947; RN: *m* 1969, Catherine, da of William Hunter Gardner Russell, of Bo'ness, W Lothian, and has issue living, Carol Anne *b* 1970.

Granddaughters of late Richard John Butler, 2nd son of Whitwell Butler (*b* 1798), 4th son of Rev Richard Butler, DD (infra):—
Issue of late George Whitwell Butler, *b* 1888, *d* 1960: *m* 1918, Ada Isabel Dering, who *d* 1961, da of Arthur Lucius Cary, of Swords, co Dublin:—
Mary Isabel, *b* 1919: *m* 1943, Carass Frederick Bladon Topham, of 25 Selwyn Cres, Radley, Abingdon, Oxon OX14 3HL, and has issue living, Ronald Bladon *b* 1945, — John Carass (114 Mid St, S Nutfield, Surrey), *b* 1951: *m* 1981, Christine Allen, and has issue living, Laurence James Carass *b* 1982, Ralph Lewis Bladon *b* 1984, Phillip George Graham *b* 1987, — Pamela Mary (twin), *b* 1951. —— Eileen Synolda, *b* 1926. *Residence* – 7 Fordhook Av, Ealing Common, W5.

Granddaughter of late Rev Edward Butler, son of Rev Richard Butler, DD, el son of James Butler, of Pries-town, co Meath, el son of Capt Theobald Butler, 2nd son of Pierce Butler, 2nd son of Hon Theobald Butler (ante):—
Issue of late Edward Butler, *b* 1851, *d* 1928: *m* 1887, Emily Frances, who *d* 1951, da of Arthur Battiscombe:—
Judith Eileen, MBE, *b* 1895; MBE (Civil) 1966.

Granddaughter of late George Butler (infra):—
Issue of late Hubert Marshal Butler, *b* 1900, *d* 1991: *m* 1930, Susan Margaret (Maiden Hall, Bennettsbridge, co Kilkenny), da of late Dr Thomas Clement Guthrie, of Annaghmakerrig, co Monaghan (and sister of late Sir Tyrone Guthrie):—
Julia Mary Synolda, *b* 1935: *m* 1959, Dr Richard Savington Crampton, of 1106 Rugby Rd, Charlottesville, Va 22903, USA, and has issue living, Thomas William Butler, *b* 1967, — Anne Cordelia, *b* 1960: *m* 1988, James Vaughan Gelly, of 41 Village Drive, Convent Station, NJ 07960, USA, and has issue living, Piers George Crampton *b* 1991, Bennett Butler Vaughan *b* 1993, — Suzanna Louise, *b* 1963, — Katherine Synolda, *b* 1966.

Grandson of late John Butler, 6th son of late Rev Richard Butler, DD (ante):—
Issue of late George Butler, *b* 1859, *d* 1941: *m* 1898, Harriet Neville, who *d* 1939, da of Marshal Neville Clarke, of Graiguenoe Park, co Tipperary:—
George Gilbert, *b* 1910: *m* 1940, Norah Helen Pomeroy, da of late George Pomeroy Arthur Colley, of Corkagh House, Clondalkin co Dublin (*see* V Harberton, colls), and has issue living, James George, *b* 1942: *m* 1972, Diana Gillian, da of late John Hedges Becher, of Bagenalstown House, co Carlow, and has issue living, Thomas George *b* 1973, John James *b* 1974, — Jessica Harriet (*Baroness Rathdonnell*), *b* 1940: *m* 1965, 5th Baron Rathdonnell. *Residence* – Scatorish, Bennettsbridge, co Kilkenny.

Grandchildren of late James Edward Butler, son of late James Butler (*b* 1820), grandson of Whitwell Butler (*b* 1736), 2nd son of Capt Theobald Butler (ante):—
Issue of late Maj James Whitwell Butler, *b* 1897, *d* 1971: *m* 1927, Hilda Winifred, who *d* 1978, da of Charles Nason Haines:—
James Charles, MC (Belgrove, Cobh, co Cork), *b* 1928; late Lt King's R Irish Hussars; Korea 1951 (MC): *m* 1959, Margaret Perry, da of Harold Perry Goodbody, of The Glen, Cobh, co Cork, and has issue living, James Perry George, *b* 1960, — Corinna Margaret, *b* 1962. —— †Edward Theobald *b* 1929: *m* 1952, Judith (Tullow, Fethard, co Tipperary), da of Edward Webb, of Borris-in-Ossory, co Leix, and *d* 1992, leaving issue, Jennifer Mary, *b* 1954, — Diana Elizabeth, *b* 1956: *m* 1975, John Aloysius Taylor, of Boyertown, Pennsylvania, USA, and has issue living, Kerry Ann *b* 1978, — Caroline Eve, *b* 1960: *m* 1984, Hugh Christopher Stanhope Morshead, elder son of Christopher William Trelawny Morshead, MC, TD, of Bellewstown House, co Meath, and has issue living, Christopher Edward *b* 1986, James Stanhope *b* 1989. —— Hilda Elizabeth, *b* 1932: *m* 1956, Julius Pridden Jameson, of Shell Cove House, Teignmouth Rd, Dawlish, Devon, and has issue living, Robert Julius Whitwell, *b* 1957, — James Leander, *b* 1964, — Linda Rose, 1959.

Descendants of late Hon Peter (or Pierce) Butler, 2nd son of 10th Baron:—

Issue of late Theobald Blake Butler, el son of Theobald Fitzwalter Butler, JP, DL (infra), *b* 1888, *d* 1965: *m* 1st, 1921 (*m diss* 1930), Mary Gammell Stewart, da of William Smytton Davidson; 2ndly, 1933 (*m diss* 1942), Catherine Dorothy, da of Arthur Ashworth; 3rdly, 1962, Elsie, who *d* 1970, da of late Albert Edward Keen:—
(By 1st *m*) James Roland Blake Fox ANDREWS, QC (20 Cheyne Gdns, SW3), *b* 1922; *ed* Stowe, and Camb Univ (BA); Bar Gray's Inn 1949, QC 1968, an ad eundem Member of Middle Temple 1972, and Bencher, Gray's Inn 1974; Recorder of Winchester 1971, since when Hon Recorder; Dep Chm of Devon Quarter Sessions 1970-71; a Recorder of Crown Court 1972-85; Leader of Western Circuit 1982-84, Circuit Judge assigned to Official Referee business 1985; assumed the surname of Fox-Andrews in lieu of his patronymic 1939: *m* 1950, Angela Bridget, who *d* 1991, da of Brig Charles Copley Swift, OBE, MC, and has issue living, (Jonathan) Mark (Piers), *b* 1952; *ed* Eton, and Trin Hall, Camb (BA): *m* 1984, Rosemary, da of Dennis Jenks, and has issue living, Maximillian George *b* 1987, Alfred James *b* 1993, Florence Ruth *b* 1989, Constance Augusta *b* 1992, — Piers Norman James, *b* 1954; *ed* Eton, and Bristol Univ: *m* 1985, Elizabeth Keith, da of Terence Allan, and has issue living, Charles Adam *b* 1986, Guy James *b* 1992, Emma Mary *b* 1988.

Grandson of late Theobald Blake Butler (ante):—
Issue of late John Stuart Blake Butler, *b* 1923, *d* 1957: *m* 1947, Stephanie Elizabeth (who *d* 1970, having *m* 2ndly, 1963, Guy Green), da of Thomas Swann, of The Old Vicarage, Thriplow, Cambs:—
Samuel Thomas Blake, *b* 1949.

Issue of late Fitzwalter Butler, *b* 1889, *d* 1979, 2nd son of Theobald Fitzwalter Butler, JP, DL, 6th and yst son of James Blake Butler, JP, great-grandson of James Butler (*d* 1746), el son of James Butler, of Doone, co Clare, great- great-grandson of late James Butler, el son of Hon Peter (or Piers) Butler (ante):—
Theobald Fitzwalter (Little Croft, 7 Spooner Vale, Windermere, Cumbria LA23 1AU), *b* 1921: *m* 1951, Patricia Penelope, da of Richard Lowe, of Donaghadee, co Down, and has issue living, Simon Blake Fitzwalter, *b* 1958; *ed* Univ of Wales, Lampeter (BA) and Sheffield Univ (MA 1985, PhD 1992), — Judith Margaret, *b* 1953; *ed* Univ Coll, Cardiff (LLB), and Wolverhampton TTC (Cert Ed): *m* 1977, Paul Llewelyn Evans, BSc, of 20 Histons Dr, Codsall, Wolverhampton WV8 2ET, and has issue living, Ian Llewelyn *b* 1981, Richard Theobald *b* 1984, Edward Pierce *b* 1988.

Grandchildren of late Lieut-Col Walter Blake BUTLER-CREAGH (infra):—
Issue of late Richard BUTLER-CREAGH, *b* 1890, *d* 1955: *m* 1919, Ada Murray, who *d* 1949:—
Richard (PO Box 8951, Nairobi, Kenya), *b* 1922: *m* 1957, Therése Agnes Spoorenberg, and has issue living, Michelle Edith, *b* 1957, — Simone Antoinette, *b* 1960. —— Vincent, *b* 19—. —— Walter, *b* 19—. —— Mary, *b* 19—: *m* 19—, William Witham. —— Sheila, *b* 19—: *m* 19—, Michael Baines, solicitor, and has issue living. —— Maureen, *b* 19—: *m* 19—, — Whittingham. —— Clara, *b* 1929: *m* 1953, William Craig, and has issue living, Albert, *b* 1954, — William Richard, *b* 1956, — Robert, *b* 1958. —— Ethanna, *b* 19—: *m* 1957, William Henry Harris. —— Joan, *b* 19—: *m* 19—, — Finn and has issue living, Anthony Richard, *b* 19—, — David *b* 1956, — Linda, *b* 19—, — Bernadette Marie, *b* 1952.

Granddaughter of late Nicholas Butler, son of late Walter Butler, el son of late William Butler, of Bunnahow, co Clare (*b* 1759), son of late Peter Butler, younger son of late James Butler, of Doon, co Clare (ante):—

Issue of late Lieut-Col Walter Blake BUTLER-CREAGH, King's Own Yorkshire LI, *b* 1859, *d* 1943 (having assumed 1889 by R Licence the additional surname and arms of Creagh after his patronymic): *m* 1888, Clara, who *d* 1928, da and co-heir of Cornelius Creagh, of Dangan, co Clare:—

Mary Gertrude, *b* 1892. *Residence* – 2 Waterloo Road, Dublin.

PREDECESSORS – (1) *Sir* Thomas Butler, 3rd son of Theobald Butler or Botiller, 4th hereditary Chief Butler of Ireland (whose 2nd son Edmund was father of 1st Earl of Ormonde (*see* Ormonde, M), was summoned as *Baron of Dunboyne* to Parliament of Ireland 1324: *m* 1320, Synolda, Lady of Dunboyne, da and heiress of William le Petit, 6th Baron of Dunboyne (by tenure), who was summoned to parliament as *Baron of Dunboyne* 1274: *s* by his son (2) PETER, 2nd Baron: *m* before 1353, Katherine, da and heiress of John de Bermingham, Lord of Kiltenian; *d* 1370; *s* by his son (3) WILLIAM, 3rd Baron: *m* Elizabeth, da of Nicholas le Poer, of Kilmeaden, co Waterford; *d* 1405; *s* by his son (4) PETER, 4th Baron, *b* before 1398; *d* unm 1415; *s* by his brother (5) EDMUND, 5th Baron; *d* unm 1419; *s* by his brother (6) JAMES (3rd son of 3rd Baron) 6th Baron: *m* Morina Brien, of Thomond, who *d* 1476; *d* 1445; *s* by his son (7) WILLIAM, 7th Baron; attainted 1455; *d* circa 1459; *s* by his brother (8) EDMOND FITZ-JAMES, 8th Baron; his dignity and estates were restored by Act of Parliament 1471/2, and he received large grants from the Crown for his great services in the Irish Wars: *m* before 1468/9, Catherine, da of Richard Butler MacRichard, of Buolick, co Tipperary; *d* 1498/9; *s* by his son (9) JAMES, 9th Baron: *m* 1st, Elinor, da of Sir Laurence Taafe; 2ndly, Catherine, da of Fineen McCarthy Reagh, Chief of Carberry; *d* 1508; *s* by his son (10) JAMES, 10th Baron: *m* Lady Joan Butler, da of 1st Earl of Ossory and 8th Earl of Ormonde; *d* 1533; *s* by his son (11) EDMUND, KB, 11th Baron, *b* 1517; *cr* by patent *Baron Dunboyne*, of co Meath (peerage of Ireland) 1541: *m* before 1551, Cecilia (who *m* 2ndly, 1568, as his 3rd wife, Richard Bourke, 2nd Baron of Clanricarde), da of Cormac Oge Macarty, of Muskerry; *d* 1566; *s* by his son (12) JAMES, 12th Baron; summoned to Parliament 1569-71 and 1614: *m* 1st, about 1580, Margaret FitzPatrick, da and heiress of 2nd Baron of Upper Ossory; 2ndly, about 1591, Lady Margaret O'Brien, da of 3rd Earl of Thomond; *d* 1624; *s* by his grandson (13) EDMOND (son of late John Butler, son of 9th Baron), 13th Baron: *m* 1st 1625, Margaret Butler, who *d* 1632, da and heiress of 2nd Baron Caher; 2ndly, about 1637, Lady Ellen FitzGerald, who *d* 1660, da of 15th Earl of Desmond, and widow of (1) Sir Donough O'Connor, and (2) Sir Robert Cressy; *d* 1640; *s* by his son (14) JAMES, 14th Baron; twice outlawed in 1642 for his share in the Irish Rebellion 1641 (but the Solicitor-Gen reported in 1827 that as there were serious errors in the drawing up of writs of outlawry, he considered them invalid): *m* Ellen Butler, da of 1st Viscount Ikerrin; *d* 1662; *s* by his cousin (15) PIERCE (only son of late Edmund Butler, el son of late Piers Butler, 2nd son of 11th Baron), 15th Baron; ostensibly outlawed posthumously 1691 for rebelling against William and Mary's government (which the Lord Chancellor stated in 1859 was illegal, as such an outlawry could only have been made by the Lord Ch Justice acting as Coroner, and in this instance the outlawry was in the wrong Christian name, and Pierce, Baron Dunboyne, was not involved in this rebellion): *m* Catherine, da of Sir Thomas Hurley, 1st Bt; *d* 1690; *s* by his son (16) JAMES, *de jure* 16th Baron: *m* 1686, Elizabeth, da of Sir Redmond Everard, Bt; *d* 1701; *s* by his el son (17) PIERCE, *de jure* 17th Baron: *m* Anna, da and heir of Robert Cadell, of Dublin; *d* 1718; *s* by his brother (18) EDMOND, *de jure* 18th Baron: *m* Anne, da of Oliver Grace, of Shanganagh, co Tipperary, Ch Remembrancer of the Exchequer, Ireland, and widow of Richard Nagle; *d* 1732; *s* by his el son (19) JAMES; *de jure* 19th Baron; *dsp* 1768; *s* by his brother (20) PIERCE, *de jure* 20th Baron, *m* 1773, Maria (who *m* 2ndly, 1775, David Walsh), da of George Macnamara, of Cong, co Mayo; *d* 1773; *s* by his son (21) PIERCE EDMOND CREAGH, *de jure* 21st Baron; *d* unm 1785; *s* by his uncle (22) *Right Rev* JOHN, DD (3rd son of 8th Baron), *de jure* 22nd Baron, Roman Catholic Bishop of Cork 1763-86; he resigned his See after succession to the title and requested from the Pope a dispensation to marry, this being refused, he became a Protestant: *m* 1787, Maria (who *m* 2ndly, 1801, John Hubert Moore, of Shannon Grove, King's Co, Bar-at-law, and *d* 1860), da of Theobald Butler, of Wilford, co Tipperary; *dsp* 1800; *s* by his kinsman (23) JAMES (son of late James Butler, grandson of late Edward Butler, grandson of late Hon Edward Butler, 6th son of 11th Baron), *de jure* 23rd Baron; the outlawries of James, 14th Baron and Pierce, 15th Baron, were reversed by Royal Warrant, on the grounds of "the errors therein" 1827, and he was confirmed in the peerage: *m* 1st, 1799, Eleanor, who *d* 1817, da of David O'Connell, of Cork, 2ndly, 1843, Mary Anne Vincent Vaughan, who *d* 1847; *d* 1850; *s* by his son (24) THEOBALD FITZ-WALTER, 24th Baron; *b* 1806; his right to Barony of Dunboyne was confirmed by Committee for Privileges of House of Lords 1860; a Representative Peer: *m* 1832, Julia Celestina Maria, da of late William Brander, of Morden Hall, Surrey; *d* 1881; *s* by his son (25) JAMES FITZ-WALTER CLIFFORD, 25th Baron, *b* 1839: *m* 1860, Marion, who *d* 1919, da of Col Henry Morgan Clifford, of Llantilio Crossenny, Monmouthshire, whose surname he assumed in addition to that of Butler; *d* 1899; *s* by his brother (26) ROBERT ST JOHN FITZ-WALTER, 26th Baron, *b* 1844; a Representative Peer; sometime Senior Master of Supreme Court, and King's Remembrancer: *m* 1869, Caroline Maude Blanche, who *d* 1927, da of late Capt George Probyn (and sister of Gen Rt Hon Sir Dighton Probyn, VC, GCB, GCSI, GCVO, ISO); *d* 1913; *s* by his el son (27) FITZ-WALTER GEORGE PROBYN, 27th Baron, *b* 1874; Capt (ret) RN: *m* 1915, Dora Isolde Butler, who *d* 1977, da of late Tom Francis Fitzpatrick Tower, OBE, late RNVR; *d* 1945; *s* by his son (28) PATRICK THEOBALD TOWER, 28th Baron (and 18th by patent) and present peer.

DUNCAN-SANDYS, BARONY OF (Duncan-Sandys) (Extinct 1987)

SON LIVING OF LIFE BARON (*By 1st marriage*)

Julian George Winston SANDYS, QC (does not use courtesy title) (Charnwood, Shackleford, Godalming, Surrey) *b* 1936; Bar Inner Temple 1959 and Grays Inn 1970; QC (1983): *m* 1970, Elizabeth Jane, only da of John Besley Martin, CBE, of Kenton, and has issue living, Duncan John Winston, *b* 1973, — Jonathan Martin Edwin, *b* 1975, — Roderick Julian Frederick, *b* 1977, — Lucy Diana, *b* 1971.

DAUGHTERS LIVING OF LIFE BARON (*By 1st marriage*)

Hon Edwina, MBE (131 E 66th St, New York, NY 10021, USA) *b* 1938; sculptress: *m* 1st, 1960 (*m diss* 1973), Piers (Pierson John Shirley) Dixon, MP, son of late Sir Pierson John Dixon, GCMG, CB; 2ndly, 1985, Richard D. Kaplan, and has issue living (by 1st *m*), Mark Pierson, *b* 1962; photographer, and co dir, — Hugo Duncan, *b* 1963; journalist.

Hon Celia Mary (4 Bedwyn Common, Gt Bedwyn, Wilts), *b* 1943: *m* 1st, 1965 (*m diss* 1970), Michael Kennedy; 2ndly, 1970 (*m diss* 1979), Dennis Walters, MBE, MP (later Sir Dennis Walters); 3rdly, 1985, Maj-Gen Kenneth Perkins, CB, MBE, DFC, and has issue living (by 1st *m*), Justin, *b* 1967, — (by 2nd *m*) Dominic, *b* 1971, — (by 3rd *m*), Alexander Winston Duncan, *b* 1986, — Sophie Rachel, *b* 1988.

(by 2nd marriage)

Hon Laura Jane, *b* 1964. *Residence* – 30 Hesper Mews, SW5 0HH.

WIDOW LIVING OF LIFE BARON

MARIE-CLAIRE (*Baroness Duncan-Sandys*), da of Adrien Schmitt, of Paris, and formerly wife of 2nd Viscount Hudson: *m* 1962, as his 2nd wife, Baron Duncan-Sandys, CH, PC (Life Baron), who *d* 1987. *Residence* – Flat T, 12 Warwick Sq, SW1V 2AA.

Duncannon, Viscount; son of Earl of Bessborough.

DUNDEE, EARL OF (Scrymgeour) (Earl S 1660)

Disperse

ALEXANDER HENRY SCRYMGEOUR OF DUNDEE, 12th Earl; *b* 5 June 1949; *s* 1983; *ed* Eton, and St Andrew's Univ; Hereditary Standard Bearer for Scotland; contested Hamilton by-election 1978 (*C*); a Lord in Waiting to HM 1986-89: *m* 1979, Siobhan Mary, da of David Llewellyn, and has issue.

Arms – Gules, a lion rampant or armed and langued azure holding in his dexter forepaw a crooked sword or scimitar argent and behind the shield in saltire two representations of the Royal Banner of Scotland viz a lion rampant gules armed and langued azure within a double tressure flory counter flory gules, ropes and tassels of the last (*as Bearer for the Sovereign of the Royal Banner of Scotland*). **Crest** – a lion's paw erased in bend or holding a crooked sword or scimitar argent. **Supporters** – two greyhounds argent collared gules.
Seat – Birkhill, Cupar, Fife. *Clubs* – White's, New (Edinburgh).

SON LIVING

HENRY DAVID (*Lord Scrymgeour*), *b* 20 June 1982.

DAUGHTERS LIVING

Lady Marina Patricia, *b* 1980.
Lady Flora Hermione Vera, *b* 1985.
Lady Lavinia Rebecca Elizabeth, *b* 1986.

WIDOW LIVING OF ELEVENTH EARL

PATRICIA KATHARINE (*Patricia, Countess of Dundee*), da of late Lt-Col Herbert Andrew Montagu Douglas Scott, CMG, DSO (*see* D Buccleuch, colls), and widow of (i) Lt-Col Walter Douglas Faulkner, MC, Irish Guards, and (ii) Lt-Col (Hon) David Scrymgeour-Wedderburn, DSO, Scots Guards (see colls infra): *m* 1946, the 11th Earl, who *d* 1983. *Residence* – Coultra Farm House, Newport-on-Tay, Fife.

COLLATERAL BRANCHES LIVING

Issue of late Lieut-Col (Hon) David Scrymgeour Wedderburn, DSO, Scots Guards, younger son of the *de jure* 10th Earl, *b* 1912, *d* of wounds received in action 1944: *m* 1940, Patricia Katharine (*Patricia, Countess of Dundee*) (ante) (who *m* 3rdly, 1946, 11th Earl of Dundee (infra), who *d* 1983), da of late Lieut-Col Lord Herbert Andrew Montagu Douglas Scott, CMG, DSO (*see* D Buccleuch, colls), and widow of Lieut-Col Walter Douglas Faulkner, MC, Irish Guards:—
Janet Mary, *b* 1941: *m* 1962, Capt (Edward Arthur) Mervyn Fox-Pitt, Welsh Guards, of Grange Scrymgeour, Cupar, Fife, and has issue living, David William, *b* 1964, — Leonie Patricia, *b* 1962: *m* 1982, Aidan Joseph Merry Gibbs (*see* E Erne, colls), — Miranda Mary (*Hon Mrs Peregrine Moncreiffe of Moncreiffe*), *b* 1968: *m* 1988, Hon Peregrine David Euan Malcolm Moncreiffe of Moncreiffe (*see* E Erroll). —— Elizabeth (*Baroness Teynham*) *b* 1943: *m* 1964, 20th Baron Teynham, of Pylewell Park, Lymington, Hants, and The Walton Canonry, Cathedral Close, Salisbury, Wilts.

Issue of late (Hon) Frederick Lewis Scrymgeour-Wedderburn, 2nd son of the *de jure* 9th Earl, *b* 1874, *d* 1936: *m* 1913, Zaida Grace, who *d* 1943, only da of Sir Ffolliott William Erskine, 3rd Bt (*cr* 1821):—
William Alexander, DFC, *b* 1919; European War 1939-45 as Flight-Lieut RAF (DFC and bar): *m* 1st, 1940, Mabel Kathleen, da of F. W. Rowe, of Torquay, S Devon; 2ndly, 1951, Margaret Emily, who *d* 1988, da of William Henry Innes, of Largo, Fife, and has issue living (by 2nd *m*), John Frederick (The West Lodge, Craigtoun, St Andrews, Fife), *b* 1955; PhD: *m* 1984, Sabine, yr da of Hubert Schauten, of Essen, Germany, — Caroline Sarah *b* 1954, — Grace Marion, *b* 1959: *m* 1980, Jonathan W. Humphrey, elder son of D. W. Humphrey, of Cross Farm, Styal, Cheshire. *Residence* – Myrtle Cottage, Orton, nr Fochabers, Moray. —— Cecily Grace, *b* 1915; is a Sister of Bethany. —— Marion, *b* 1917. *Residence* – 8 Feldt St, Flying Fish Point, Innisfail, N Queensland.

Issue of late (Hon) Charles Kenneth Scrymgeour-Wedderburn, 3rd son of *de jure* 9th Earl, *b* 1887, *d* 1963: *m* 1915, Gertrude Louisa Marie, who *d* 1957, only da of late James Carnegie Wemyss, younger, of Wemyss Hall:—
Rosemary (Strowan, by Crieff, Perthshire), *b* 1916: *m* 1st, 1937 (*m diss* 1947), Lt-Col Christian Landale Melville, DSO, who *d* 1984; 2ndly, 1949, Brig William Noel Roper-Caldbeck, DSO, who *d* 1965, and has issue living, (by 1st *m*), Robin Kenneth Christian, WS (Woodborough Manor, nr Pewsey, Wilts), *b* 1938: *m* 1st, 1961 (*m diss* 1984), Elizabeth Mary Melville, da of late Capt Melville Stewart Jameson; 2ndly, 1985, Loraine Sylvia Alice, widow of Benjamin Mark Weston Wells, and has issue living (by 1st *m*), James Landale *b* 1963; Capt Royal Scots Dragoon Gds: *m* 1991, Sophie E., yr da of Brig Peter Marsh, of Camberley, Surrey, Christian Kenneth Bowring *b* 1965; Capt Royal Scots Dragoon Gds, — Edward Charles, WS (Holydean, Melrose, Roxburghshire), *b* 1940: *m* 1966, Alison Sinclair, da of Thomas Sinclair Fraser, and has issue living, Peter Charles Fraser *b* 1970, Rachel Anne Rosemary *b* 1972, — Anthony (7 Hagbourne Close, Woodcote, S Oxon RG8 0RZ), *b* 1942: *m* 1981, — Michael Landale (Strowan, Crieff, Perthshire), *b* 1943; Maj The Black Watch: *m* 1971, Susan Louise Margaret, da of Maj Edmund Robert Cox, TD, JP, and has issue living, Neil Edmund Landale *b* 1976, Sarah Anne Louise *b* 1974, Julia Rosemary Susan *b* 1983. —— Lorna Mabel, *b* 1918: *m* 1966, Ian Miskelly, DSC, JP, who *d* 1993, of Glenara, Methven, Perthshire. —— Aimèe Elspeth, *b* 1920: *m* 1945, James Ferrier Macfarlane, who *d* 1986, of Apt 507, 3495, Mountain St,

Montreal, Quebec, Canada H3G 2A5, and has issue living, Charles Ferrier, *b* 1946: *m* 1970, Kathryn Anne Oppé, and has issue living, James Andrew *b* 1973, — Ian Fraser Oppé *b* 1975, — Jennifer Elspeth, *b* 1948: *m* 1975, William Lorne Lindsay, and has issue living, Christopher Lorne Ferrier *b* 1977, Gillian Aimée *b* 1980.

Issue of late Capt (Hon) William Ogilvy Scrymgeour-Wedderburn, DSC, RN, yst son of *de jure* 9th Earl, *b* 1894, *d* 1958: *m* 1921, Joyce, who *d* 1990, only da of late Col Robert Henry Jennings, CSI, RE:—
Ian Alexander, *b* 1923; Cdr RN (ret); FRIN: *m* 1947, Desirée, da of late Col Richard White, of Church Farm House, Smarden, Kent, and has issue living, James Ian (87 Howards Lane, SW15 6NZ), *b* 1951; *ed* Sherborne, and Hertford Coll, Oxford (MA): *m* 1981, Sarah M. A., da of Col Michael Seys-Phillips, of The Malt House, Mereworth, Kent, and has issue living, Charles Richard *b* 1986, Alexander James *b* 1988, Catherine Juliet *b* 1984. *Residence* – Dunlichty Lodge, Farr, Inverness-shire IV1 2AN. *Club* – Army and Navy. —— Fiona Marigold Joyce, *b* 1925: *m* 1951, Rev James Ainsworth Yates, and has issue living, Katherine Fiona, *b* 1958, — Veronica Margaret (twin), *b* 1958, — and an adopted da, Susannah Elizabeth, *b* 1956. *Residence* – 97 Grove Road, Hitchin, Herts SG5 1SQ.

PREDECESSORS – (1) JOHN Scrymgeour, Hereditary Standard Bearer of Scotland and Constable of Dundee: *cr Viscount Dudhope* and *Lord Scrymgeour* (peerage of Scotland) 1641, with remainder to his heirs male whatsoever: *m* 1596, Margaret, da of George Seton, of Parbroath; *d* 1643; *s* by his el son (2) JAMES, 2nd Viscount, *b* 1597; commanded a Regt of Scottish Inf under the Earl of Leven: *m* 1618, Lady Isobel Kerr, 3rd da of 3rd Earl of Roxburghe; *d* (from wounds received at Battle of Marston Moor) 1644; *s* by his el son (3) *Rt Hon* JOHN, 3rd Viscount, *b* 1622; Col of Horse under Duke of Hamilton 1468 in attempt to rescue Charles I; accompanied Charles II at Battle of Worcester 1650, and was taken prisoner by the English; fought in Middleton's Campaign of 1654; *cr Earl of Dundee*, and *Lord Inverkeithing* (peerage of Scotland) 1660, with remainder to heirs male whatsoever: *m* 1644, Lady Anne Ramsay, da of 1st Earl of Dalhousie; *d* 1668, whereupon all the honours became dormant; *s* (as Viscount Dudhope according to the decision of the Committee for Privileges of House of Lords 1952, and as Earl of Dundee according to the decision of the Committee for Privileges of House of Lords 1953) by his kinsman and heir male, and of line (4) JOHN (son of John Scrymgeour of Kirkton, grandson of John Scrymgeour of Kirkton) (*d* 1629), great-grandson of James Scrymgeour of Kirkton (*d* 1513), grandson of David Scrymgeour, younger son of Sir James Scrymgeour of Dudhope, and brother of Sir John Scrymgeour of Dudhope, and a brother of Sir John Scrymgeour of Dudhope, great-grandfather of John Scrymgeour (*d* 1562), great-grandfather of 1st Viscount Dudhope, *de jure* 2nd Earl; *b* 1628; deprived of the Scrymgeour family estates by the influence of the Duke of Lauderdale with Charles II: *m* 1659, Magdalene, da of Alexander Wedderburn of Kingennie; *d* 1698; *s* by his son (5) JAMES, *de jure* 3rd Earl, *b* 1664; *d* 1699; *s* by his brother (6) ALEXANDER, *de jure* 4th Earl, *b* 1669, Lay Professor of Humanity, Philosophy and Theology, St Andrews Univ: *m* 1697, Janet, only da of David Falconer, Professor of Divinity, St Andrews Univ; 1739; *s* by his son (7) DAVID, *de jure* 5th Earl, *b* 1702; Advocate and Sheriff Depute of Inverness: *m* 1739, Katherine, da of Sir Alexander Wedderburn, 4th Bt of Blackness; *d* 1772; *s* by his son (8) ALEXANDER Scrymgeour-Wedderburn, *de jure* 6th Earl, *b* 1742; *s* to estates, name and arms of Wedderburn of Wedderburn 1778: *m* 1771, Elizabeth Ferguson, da of Lord Pitfour; *d* 1811; *s* by his brother (9) HENRY Scrymgeour-Wedderburn, *de jure* 7th Earl, *b* 1755; attended King George IV, as Hereditary Standard Bearer of Scotland at Holyrood 1822: *m* 1793, Mary Turner, el da of Capt Hon Frederick Lewis Maitland RN, 6th son of Earl of Lauderdale; *d* 1841; *s* by his only son (10) FREDERICK LEWIS, *de jure* 8th Earl, *b* 1808; a JP and DL for Fifeshire: *m* 1st, 1839, Hon Helen Arbuthnott, who *d* 1840, 5th da of 8th Viscount Arbuthnott; 2ndly, 1852, Selina Mary, who *d* 1902; da of Capt Thomas Garth, RN, of Haines Hill, Berks; *d* 1874; *s* by his el son (11) HENRY SCRYMGEOUR, *de jure* 9th Earl; *b* 1840; a JP and DL for Fifeshire and Capt 17th Regt, his right to the hereditary office of Roy Standard Bearer for Scotland was admitted by the Court of Claims at Coronation of Edward VII, when he bore the Standard of Scotland, and confirmed by the House of Lords 1910: *m* 1869, Juliana, who *d* 1921, yst da of Thomas Braddell, of Coolmelagh, co Wexford; *d* 1914; *s* by his son (12) HENRY, *de jure* 10th Earl; *b* 1872; Lieut-Col late TA Reserve and Capt Gordon Highlanders; bore Standard of Scotland at Coronation of George V in place of his father: *m* 1901, Edith, who *d* 1968, only da of John Moffat; *d* 1924; *s* by his son (13) HENRY JAMES Scrymgeour of Dundee (formerly Scrymgeour Wedderburn of Wedderburn), PC, 11th Earl; *b* 1902; claim to Viscountcy of Dudhope admitted by Committee for Privileges of House of Lords 1952, and *s* to Earldom of Dundee 1953; JP and DL for Fifeshire; Parl Under Sec of State for Scotland 1936-39, served with 7th Bn Black Watch 1939-41, and Joint Parl Under-Sec of State for Scotland 1941-42, Min without Portfolio 1958-61, and Min of State, Foreign Office, 1961-63, Dep Leader of House of Lords 1962-64; bore Roy Standard of Scotland at Coronations of King George VI 1937, and of Queen Elizabeth II 1953; MP for W Div of Renfrew 1931-45; *cr Baron Glassary* or Glassary, co Argyll (peerage of UK) 1954: *m* 1946, Patricia Katharine, da of late Lt-Col Lord Herbert Andrew Montagu Douglas Scott, CMG, DSO (*see* D Buccleuch, colls), and widow of (1) Lt-Col Walter Douglas Faulkner, MC, Irish Guards, and (2) Lt-Col (Hon) David Scrymgeour-Wedderburn, DSO, Scots Guards (see ante); *d* 1983; *s* by his only son (14) ALEXANDER HENRY Scrymgeour of Dundee, 12th Earl, and present peer, also Viscount Dudhope, Lord Scrymgeour, Lord Inverkeithing, and Baron Glassary.

DUNDONALD, EARL OF (Cochrane) (Earl S 1669)

By courage and labour

(IAIN ALEXANDER) DOUGLAS BLAIR COCHRANE, 15th Earl; *b* 17 Feb 1961; *s* 1986; *ed* Wellington Coll, and RAC Cirencester; Dir Duneth Securities Ltd, and Associated Cos: *m* 1987, M. Beatrice L., da of Adolphus Russo, of Cumberland Rd, Gibraltar, and has issue.

𝕬rms – Argent, a chevron gules, between three boar's heads erased azure. Crest – A horse passant argent. Supporters – Two greyhounds argent collared and lined or.
Seat – Lochnell Castle, Ledaig, Argyll.

SON LIVING

ARCHIE IAIN THOMAS BLAIR (*Lord Cochrane*), *b* 14 March 1991.

DAUGHTER LIVING

Lady Marina Aphra Mariola, *b* 1992.

SISTER LIVING

Lady Tanya Jean Farquhar, *b* 1964; *ed* Benenden: *m* 1992, Anthony J. L. Peake, yr son of Peter Lowsley Peake, of Chantry Dene, Guildford, Surrey, and has issue living, Patrick Ian Lowsley, *b* 1994. *Residence* – Stanton Waters Farm, Hannington, Highworth, Swindon, Wilts SN6 7RY.

AUNT LIVING (sister of 14th Earl; raised to the rank of an Earl's daughter, 1960)

Lady (Winifred) Anne Grizel, *b* 1923: *m* 1967, Alfred Ashford, who *d* 1981, and has issue living, Alexis, *b* 1969.

WIDOW LIVING OF FOURTEENTH EARL

(ANN) MARGARET (*Dowager Countess of Dundonald*), da of late Sir Joseph Welsh Park Harkness, CMG, OBE, MB, ChB, MA, BSc, and formerly wife of C. F. E. Staib, of Las Palmas, Canary Islands: *m* 1978, as his 2nd wife, the 14th Earl, who *d* 1986. *Residence* – Beau Coin, La Haule, Jersey, CI.

COLLATERAL BRANCHES LIVING

Descendants of late Hon Thomas Horatio Arthur Ernest Cochrane (yr son of 11th Earl), who was *cr Baron Cochrane of Cults* 1919 (see that title).
    Grandchildren of late Horace Egerton Cochrane, yst son of Capt Hon Ernest Grey Lambton Cochrane, 4th son of 10th Earl:—
    Issue of late Richard Ernest Horace Cochrane, *b* 1909, *d* 1985: *m* 1939, Alma Josephine (c/o Mrs James Creamer, 3309 Hopewell Rd, Valley, Alabama 36864, USA), da of Albert Helland, of Powell River, BC, Canada:—
David Lambton Grey, *b* 1957; *ed* Camb Univ and Ulster Poly: *m* 1991, Gillian Christine, da of Edwin O'Brien, of Salford, Lancs, and has issue living, Rachel Katherine, *b* 1991. *Residence* – 61 Great Dover St, SE1 4YF. —— Gayle Patricia, *b* 1941: *m* 1977, James Creamer, of 3309 Hopewell Rd, Valley, Alabama 36864, USA. —— Myrna Avice Ruth, *b* 1946: *m* 1971, James Eddison, of 580 Louis Drive, Mississauga, Ontario L5B 2N2, Canada, and has issue living, David James, *b* 1974, — John Richard, *b* 1976.

    Granddaughter of late Capt John Palmer Cochrane, 3rd son of late Col William Marshall Cochrane, only son of late Maj Hon William Erskine Cochrane, 3rd son of 9th Earl:—
    Issue of late Basil William Dundonald Cochrane, *b* 1891, *d* 1954: *m* 1920, Anne, who *d* 1986, 2nd da of late William Robertson, of Edinburgh:—
Elizabeth Anne, *b* 1926: *m* 1951, Peter Dodds, son of late John William Dodds, of Farnborough, Hants, and has had issue, Peter John Cochrane, *b* 1953; *ed* Gresham's Sch, Norfolk; late Merchant Navy, engr with Dowty Engrg: *m* 1991, Gillian Christine, da of John Stubbs, of Harare, Zimbabwe, and *d* 1993, leaving issue, Andrew John Cochrane *b* 1984, Richard David Cochrane *b* 1986, — David Michael Cochrane, *b* 1954; *ed* Gresham's Sch, Norfolk; photographer, — Anthony Palmer Cochrane, *b* 1962; *ed* Falcon Coll, Zimbabwe: *m* 1993, Mary Lucinda, only da of Clive Aggett, of Kifuku Ranch, Rumuruti, Kenya. *Address* – Box 318, Simon's Town 7995, S Africa.

    Grandchildren of late Wing-Cdr John Erichsen Blair Cochrane (infra):—
    Issue of late John Erskine Dundonald Cochrane, *b* 1920, *d* 1987: *m* 1st, 1943 (*m diss* 1958), Elizabeth Mary, da of late Capt Bertram Allgood; 2ndly, 1958, Bela (Lion Cottage, 24 Park Rd, Chislehurst, Kent BR7 5AY), eldest da of William Carlton, of Leeds:—
(By 1st *m*) Ian Michael Dundonald (79 Styles Close, Styles Hill, Frome, Somerset), *b* 1950: *m* 1973, Nicola Robina, da of Eric Wood, of Rowlands, Stour Provost, Dorset, and has issue living, Adam Thomas Dundonald, *b* 1977, — Katrin Emma, *b* 1975, — Lydia Rose, *b* 1983. —— Alastair Charles Dundonald (Nutters Cottage, Nutters Wood, Cleeve Hill, Cheltenham, Glos), *b* 1956: *m* 1978, Julia, da of George Alan Bedwell, MD, MRCP, of Osgrove, Penn Lane, King's Stanley, nr Stroud, Glos, and has issue living, Charles Alexander Dundonald, *b* 1985, — Victoria Louise, *b* 1978, — Rebecca Frances, *b* 1981, — Francesca Emily, *b* 1990. —— Sarah Elizabeth (36 Jessica Rd, Wandsworth, SW18 2QN), *b* 1946: *m* 1971 (*m diss* 1981), Alastair John Milne Home (*see* E Minto, colls, 1970 Edn), and has issue living, Marcus John Hepburn, *b* 1975, — Camilla Marian Isobel, *b* 1973. —— (By 2nd *m*) David John Dundonald, *b* 1959. —— Peter John Dundonald, *b* 1963. —— Anthony Albert Dundonald, *b* 1967.

    Grandchildren of late Capt John Palmer Cochrane (ante):—
    Issue of late Wing-Cdr John Erichsen Blair Cochrane, *b* 1894, *d* 1949: *m* 1916, his cousin, Mary, who *d* 1958, eldest da of late Com Thomas Erskine Cochrane (*see* E Dundonald, colls, 1958 Edn):—
Basil Thomas Dundonald (Corner Cottage, 8 Resthaven Drive, Tokai 7945, Cape, S Africa), *b* 1924; late RAF: *m* 1st, 1955 (*m diss* 1973), Sally, only da of Henry Edmund Hounsell, of Livingstone, Zambia; 2ndly, 1974, Daphne Maureen Joyce, da of late Elliot Esmond Baxter, of Camberley, Surrey.
    Issue of late Douglas Thomas Cochrane, *b* 1900, *d* 1988: *m* 1st, 1926, Ivy, who *d* 1928, eldest da of G. A. Massdorp,

of Queenstown, Cape Province; 2ndly, 1935, Christine Marie Hammond (The Retreat, 4 Harris Rd, PO Highlands, Harare, Zimbabwe):—
(By 1st *m*) Edward Denzil Dundonald (11 Linda Rd, Claremont 7700, Cape Town, S Africa), *b* 1927; MSM, MSc, CEng: *m* 1953, Janet Ainslie, only da of late Robert Allan, OBE, MC, DCM, and has issue living, Michael Allan Dundonald, *b* 1957: *m* 1980, Fiona Jayne, elder da of Norman MacDonald, and has issue living, Daniel Dundonald *b* 1985, Bridget Jayne *b* 1982, — Susan Elizabeth, *b* 1954: *m* 1980, David William Butcher, only son of James Butcher, and has issue living, Joshua David *b* 1988, Sian Catherine *b* 1982, Clare Louise *b* 1985. ―― Blair Douglas Dundonald (PO Box 101, Karoi, Zimbabwe), *b* 1928: *m* 1958, Thea Jean, eldest da of Norman R. Stevenson, and has issue living, Ian Dundonald, *b* 1959, — Robert Douglas Dundonald, *b* 1961, — Jennifer Mary, *b* 1965, — Sarah Alyson Jane, *b* 1972. ―― (By 2nd *m*) John Robert Colley (PO Box 650, Harare, Zimbabwe), *b* 1939: *m* 1960, Rosemary Josephine Anne, da of G. W. R. Caine, of Zimbabwe, and has issue living, Jeremy Robert, *b* 1962, — Samantha Caroline, *b* 1965. ―― William Thomas (PO Box 650, Harare, Zimbabwe), *b* 1943: *m* 1969, Pamela Evelyn, da of Val Setzkorn, of 46 Danpienaar Drive, Amanzimtoti, Natal, and has issue living, Richard William, *b* 1974, — Ingrid Margaret, *b* 1971, — Lucille Pamela, *b* 1976. ―― Richard Bruce (9 Plymouth Rd, Sandton, Johannesburg, S Africa), *b* 1948: *m* 1975, Pamela Brown, and has issue living, Douglas, *b* 1981, — Alexander Richard, *b* 1984, — Jennifer Leigh, *b* 1983. ―― Steven David (33 Court Rd, Greendale North, Harare, Zimbabwe), *b* 1951; BSc (Agric): *m* 1st, 1973 (*m diss* 1987), Penelope Jane Lutley, eldest da of Denzil Awdry Randles; 2ndly, 1991, Evelyn Judy, da of John Rau, of Harare, and has issue living (by 1st *m*), William James Dundonald, *b* 1975, — Graham Douglas *b* 1977, — James Denzil, *b* 1980, — Abigail Elizabeth *b* 1982, — (by 2nd *m*) Michelle Cecily, *b* 1993. ―― Cecily Mary Elizabeth, *b* 1935: *m* 1959, Kenneth Saywood, of PO Box 177, Karoi, Zimbabwe, and has issue living, Neil Frank, *b* 1960, — David, *b* 1961, — Peter John, *b* 1966, — Michael Anthony, *b* 1970. ―― Una Patricia Louwina COCHRANE (8 Rue Colt Mouchotte, 75014 Paris, France), *b* 1937; has resumed her maiden name: *m* 1958 (*m diss* 1975), Kenneth Davies, and has issue living, Patricia Clare Cochrane, *b* 1959: *m* 1981, Roy Alexander Brooks, and has issue living, William Sebastien *b* 1981, Lawrence Thomas *b* 1983, — Andrea Jane Cochrane, *b* 1962.

Grandsons of late Arthur Henry Douglas Cochrane, 4th and yst son of late Col William Marshall Cochrane (ante):—
    Issue of late Arthur Blair Dundonald Cochrane, *b* 1888, *d* 1936: *m* 1918, Nancy, who *d* 1985, da of late Robert Barber, Bar-at-Law:—
Hugh Benjamin (Hope Cottage, 88 Newland, Sherborne, Dorset DT9 3DT), *b* 1925; late Lt RE: *m* 1953, Anne Deirdre, el da of late William Schoener Scott. ―― Nicholas Baillie (Old Oak Farm, Easthampstead Park, Wokingham, Berks RG11 3DL) *b* 1929; late Capt King's African Rifles: *m* 1958, Diana Isabel, da of late Norman Balfour Craig, and has issue living, Amanda Elizabeth, *b* 1959: *m* 19—, Capt Jeremy Robert Shafto (Army Air Corps), and has issue living, Hamish Alexander Cochrane *b* 1993, — Susan Mary, *b* 1962.

Granddaughters of late Vice-Adm Basil Edward Cochrane, el son of late Basil Edward Arthur Cochrane, 2nd son of late Capt Hon Archibald Cochrane, RN, 4th son of 9th Earl:—
    Issue of late Rear-Adm Archibald Cochrane, CMG, *b* 1874, *d* 1952: *m* 1904, Maye Amelie Lucile, who *d* 1954, da of late Col Alured de Vere Brooke, RE (Brooke, Bt, *cr* 1662, colls):—
Monica Frances Mary, *b* 1908: *m* 1950, George Worcester, who *d* 1969. *Residence* – Penny Cottage, Windlesham, Surrey. ―― Dorothea Stella, *b* 1913: *m* 1951, John Errington Rothwell Harrison, and has issue living, James Anthony Rothwell, *b* 1952: *m* 1975, Louise Marie, da of Louis Matarazzo, of Thunder Bay, Ont, Canada, and has issue living, Neil Owen *b* 1981, Thomas Louis *b* 1984, Laura Catherine *b* 1990, — Anne Lucile Rothwell, *b* 1953: *m* 1988, Robert Wallace Sargalis.

Granddaughter of Rear-Adm Sir Edward Owen Cochrane, KBE (infra):—
    Issue of late Maj James Owen Cochrane, MC, RA, *b* 1914, *ka* 1943: *m* 1941, Margaret Angela Clare (who *m* 2ndly, 1950, Desmond Pertwee, of Rookery House, Great Horkesley, nr Colchester, Essex), da of Vice-Adm Charles Wolfram Round-Turner, CB, CMG:—
Janet Owen, *b* 1942: *m* 1965, Paul Moore, of 14 Freeland Place, Clifton, Bristol 2, and has issue living, Thomas Owen, *b* 1966, — Amy Clare, *b* 1969.

Granddaughter of late Vice-Adm Basil Edward Cochrane (ante):—
    Issue of late Rear Adm Sir Edward Owen Cochrane, KBE, *b* 1881, *d* 1972: *m* 1908, Mary Lucy (Molly), who *d* 1955, da of S. K. George, of The Brackens, Ascot:—
Susanne Gloria, *b* 1918: *m* 1957, David Logan Howell, of 3/5 St George's Sq, SW1.

Grandchildren of late William Edward Cochrane, 4th son of Basil Edward Arthur Cochrane (ante):—
    Issue of late Cdr Arthur FitzGerald Cochrane, RN, *b* 1888, *d* 1967: *m* 1913, Beryl Irma, who *d* 1954, da of Gen Charles Frederick Thomas, of Excliffe, Exmouth, and widow of Percy Hugh Druce:—
Peter William FitzGerald (761 London Rd, Sarnia, Ontario N7T 4X7, Canada), *b* 1916; *ed* Ampleforth, and at McGill Univ; 1939-45 War with Atlantic Ferry Command and as Flying Officer RCAF with Bomber Command: *m* 1944, Margaret Eunice, only da of Wesley William Rowley, of London, Ontario, Canada, and has issue living, Richard Arthur Wesley Rowley, *b* 1948: *m* 1986, Andrina Maria, yst child of Peter Rull, of Hong Kong and New York, and has issue living, Marie Margaret *b* 1987, — Stephen Bryce Rowley *b* 1952: *m* 1980, Tracey, da of R. Gordon Henderson, of BC, Canada, and has issue living, Sydney Margaret *b* 19—. ―― Evelyn Jean FitzGerald, *b* 1914. ―― Shelia Fitzgerald, *b* 1917: *m* 1942, Lt Cdr John Aarvold Loughlin Stubbs, RNVR, of 10 Dorset Close, Harrogate, and has issue living, Penelope Ann, *b* 1945; BSc: *m* 1966, Maj Patrick Joseph David Herberts, MD, of Brigend of Kildarroch, Borgue, Kirkcudbright, and has issue living, Andrew John David *b* 1970, Alison Philippa *b* 1967, Catherine Elizabeth *b* 1972, — Gillian Mary *b* 1947. ―― Cecilia Florence Fitzgerald, *b* 1924: *m* 1955, John Gray Robertson, of Sunlaws, Parkhead, Dumfries, and has issue living, Peter Arthur Cochrane (9 Holmhills Gdns, Cambuslang, Lanarks), *b* 1956; BSc Glasgow: *m* 1982, Shirley Margaret Bradford, and has issue living, Andrew George Cochrane *b* 1987, David John Cochrane *b* 1991, — Philip John Cochrane, *b* 1962: *m* 1984, Rhonda Eleanor Kelly.

Granddaughter (by 2nd wife) of late Thomas Belhaven Henry Cochrane, MVO (infra):—
    Issue of late Lt-Cdr John Cochrane, RN, *b* 1909, *ka* 1941: *m* 1937, Jocelyn Mary (who *d* 1988, having *m* 2ndly, 1946, Col Brian Leslie Sundius-Smith, who *d* 1965), da of late Capt John Francis Robins, RN:—
Vivien Mary Grisell, *b* 1939: *m* 1962, Anthony Cortlandt Richard Chappell, and has issue living, Richard John Anthony, *b* 1967; *ed* Oundle, and Bristol Univ. — Andrew Thomas Robert, *b* 1969; *ed* Oundle, and Leicester Univ, — Caroline Margaret Joan, *b* 1966. *Residence* - Croxton House, Fulmodeston, Fakenham, Norfolk NR21 0NJ.
    Grandson of late Adm of the Fleet Sir Thomas John Cochrane, GCB, MP, eldest son of late Adm Hon Sir Alexander Forester Inglis Cochrane, GCB, MP, 6th son of 8th Earl:—
    Issue of late Thomas Belhaven Henry Cochrane, MVO, Lieut RN, *b* 1856, *d* 1925: *m* 1st, 1887, Lady Adela Charlotte Rous, who *d* 1911, sister of 3rd Earl of Stradbroke; 2ndly, 1911, Beatrice, who *d* 1977, da of late William Henry Knight:—
(By 2nd *m*) Thomas Dundonald Hugh (157 Temelec Circle, Sonoma, Calif 95476, USA), *b* 1912; *ed* Oundle; Lieut RNVR 1940-46: *m* 1937, Margery, da of late Norman Rowe, and has issue living, Norman Thomas (12398 Copenhagen Court, Reston, VA 22091, USA), *b* 1938: *m* 1965, Sarah Wills, and has issue living, Thomas Alexander *b* 1970, Ann Lee *b* 1972, — Sandra Ann, *b* 1946: *m* 1982, Graham Baker, of 7417 Continental Trail, N Richland Hills, Texas 76180, USA.

PREDECESSORS – (1) *Sir* WILLIAM Cochrane (of the family of Cochrane, which had been settled on the Barony of Cochrane in W of Scotland for many centuries), PC, KB, MP for Ayrshire, and Col of Royalist Militia, who assisted in sending the Scots Army into England, was *cr* Lord Cochrane, *of Dundonald* (Peerage of Scotland) 1647, with remainder to the heirs male of his body, and *Earl of Dundonald* and *Lord Cochrane of Paisley and Ochiltree* (peerage of Scotland) 1669, with remainder to his heirs male, whom failing to his heirs female without division who should bear or assume the name of Cochrane, and in failure to his heirs-gen; *d* 1686; *s* by his grandson (2) JOHN, PC, 2nd Earl; *d* 1690; *s* by his el son (3) WILLIAM, 3rd Earl; *d* unmarried 1705; *s* by his brother (4) JOHN, 4th Earl; a Representative Peer; commanded Scottish Horse Guards 1715; *d* 1720; *s* by his son (5) WILLIAM, 5th Earl; *d* unmarried 1725; *s* by his cousin (6) THOMAS , 6th Earl, grandson of William, Lord Cochrane of Dundonald, el son of 1st Earl; *d* 1737; *s* by his son (7) WILLIAM, 7th Earl; killed at Siege of Louisburg 1758; *s* by his cousin (8) THOMAS, 8th Earl (grandson of Col the Hon Sir John Cochrane, 2nd son of 1st Earl), *b* 1691: sat as MP for Renfrewshire 1722-7; *d* 1778; *s* by his son (9) ARCHIBALD, 9th Earl; *b* 1748; served in RN; an eminent Scientist, and inventor; made many beneficial discoveries connected with Chemistry; *s* by his son (10) THOMAS, GCB, 10th Earl; *b* 1775; a distinguished Adm, and one of the greatest Naval Commanders of any age; conducted attack on French Fleet in Basque Roads, with fire and explosion ships, 1809, and was also renowned for many daring exploits in the RN; commanded the Chilian and Peruvian Navy (destroying Spanish Naval power in Pacific), the Brazilian Navy against Portugal (completely successful), and the Greek Fleet, in the Wars of independence of those countries; sat as MP for Westminster, and was an advanced Reformer, and an eminent scientist and inventor; *cr Marquess of Maranham*, in Brazil, 1824; *d* 1860 (buried in Westminster Abbey); *s* by his son (11) THOMAS BARNES, 11th Earl; *b* 1814; was a Representative Peer, and QMG to Forces in Chinese War: *m* 1847, Louisa Harriet, who *d* 1902, da of late William Alexander-Mackinnon, MP, of Mackinnon; *d* 1885; *s* by his son (12) DOUGLAS MACKINNON BAILLIE HAMILTON, KCB, KCVO, 12th Earl; *b* 1852; Lieut-Gen (retired); Nile Expedition 1884-5, S Africa 1899-1901 at Relief of Ladysmith (promoted Maj-Gen for distinguished ser in the field); sometime a Representative Peer for Scotland: *m* 1878, Winifred, who *d* 1924, only child of late Robert Bamford Hesketh, of Gwrych Castle, Abergele, N Wales; *d* 1935, *s* by his son (13) THOMAS HESKETH DOUGLAS BLAIR, 13th Earl; *b* 1886; was a Representative Peer for Scotland 1941-55; *d* 1958; *s* by his nephew (14) IAN DOUGLAS LEONARD (son of late Hon Douglas Robert Hesketh Roger Cochrane, 2nd son of 12th Earl) 14th Earl, *b* 1918; a Representative Peer for Scotland 1959-63, Maj Black Watch, Chm Anglo-Chilean Soc 1958-65: *m* 1st, 1960, Aphra Farquhar, who *d* 1972, da of late Cdr George Fetherstonhaugh, RNR, of The Beacon, Benenden, Kent; 2ndly, 1978, (Ann) Margaret, da of late Sir Joseph Welsh Park Harkness, CMG, OBE, MB, and formerly wife of C.F.E. Staib; *d* 1986; *s* by his only son (15) IAIN ALEXANDER DOUGLAS BLAIR, 15th Earl and present peer; also Lord Cochrane of Dundonald, and Lord Cochrane of Pailsley and Ochiltree.

DUNLEATH, BARON (Mulholland) (Baron UK 1892, Bt UK 1945)

MICHAEL HENRY MULHOLLAND, 5th Baron, and 2nd Baronet; *b* 15 Oct 1915; *s* to baronetcy 1971, and to barony 1993; *ed* Eton, and Pembroke Coll, Camb (BA); late Maj Oxford and Bucks LI; Burma 1942-45: *m* 1st, 1942 (*m diss* 1948), Rosemary, only da of late Maj David Alfred William Ker, OBE (*see* Barrington, Bt, 1947 Edn); 2ndly, 1949, Elizabeth M., who *d* 1989, twin da of late Laurence B. Hyde, of Bexhill-on-Sea, and has issue by 2nd *m*.

Arms – Azure, a stag's head erased argent between three escallops or. **Crest** – An escallop gules, **Supporters** – On either side an elk proper, charged on the shoulder with an escallop or, and holding in the mouth a trefoil slipped vert. *Seat* – Ballywalter Park, Newtownards, co Down. *Residence* – Storbrooke, 31 Massey Av, Belfast 4.

Always girt

SON LIVING *(By 2nd marriage)*

Hon BRIAN HENRY, *b* 25 Sept 1950; *ed* Eton: *m* 1976, Mary Joan, yst da of Maj Robert John Fuller Whistler, of Achaeon, Middleton Rd, Camberley, Surrey, and has issue living, Andrew Henry, *b* 15 Dec 1981, — William Alexander, *b* 1986, — Tara Miranda, *b* 1980. *Residence* – Belle Isle, Lisbellaw, Enniskillen, BT94 5HF.

WIDOW LIVING OF FOURTH BARON

DORINDA MARGERY (*Baroness Dunleath*), da of late Lt-Gen Arthur Ernest Percival, CB, DSO, OBE, MC, of Bullards, Widford, Ware, Herts: *m* 1959, Lt-Col the 4th Baron, TD, who *d* 1993. *Residence* – Ballywalter Park, Newtownards, co Down BT22 2PP.

COLLATERAL BRANCHES LIVING

Issue of late Hon (Godfrey) John Arthur Murray Lyle Mulholland, MC, 4th son of 2nd Baron, *b* 1892; *d* 1948: *m* 1923, Hon Olivia Vernon Harcourt, DCVO, who *d* 1984, da of 1st Viscount Harcourt:—
Martin Edward Harcourt, *b* 1927; formerly Lieut Irish Guards; High Sheriff co Antrim 1961: *m* 1953, Lilian Diana Tindall, only da of Maj John de Blaquiere Tindall Lucas, MC, and has issue living, John Martin (Cautley Cottage, Slaley, Hexham, Northumberland), *b* 1953; late Capt 5th R Inniskilling Drag Gds: *m* 1981, Diana Margaret Sara, da of Geoffrey Walter Wilson, of Garden Lodge, Ballygarvey, Ballymena, co Antrim, and has issue living, Charles John *b* 1984, Sara Juliet *b* 1987, — Simon Edward, *b* 1955; a Page of Honour to HM Queen Elizabeth, The Queen Mother 1969-71: *m* 1991, Catriona M., yst da of J. B. C. Darroch, of Sevenoaks, Kent, — Giles Alexander, *b* 1959. *Residence* – North Hall, E Chiltington, Lewes.
—— Mary Norah, *b* 1924; in WRNS 1943-45: *m* 1944, John William Owen Elliot, late Capt Scots Guards (*see* E Minto, colls).

Grandsons of late Hon Alfred John Mulholland (infra):—
Issue of late John Llewellyn Mulholland, *b* 1908, *d* 1989 (in Brazil): *m* 1st, 1928 (*m diss* June 1930, in Hungary), Helen, da of Vladimir Moss; 2ndly, 1930 (in Hungary) (*m diss* 1937), Olga, da of Nicholas Kuznetzov; 3rdly, 1937 (in France) (*m diss* 1938), Colette, da of Georges Mounier; 4thly, 1944 (in Brazil), Lucia, da of Antonio Izaquirre:—
(By 1st *m*) John Peter Patrick (Chesterfield, Somerford Rd, Cirencester, Glos), *b* 1929; *ed* Berkhamstead, RMA Sandhurst, Trin Coll, Dublin, and Sch of Slavonic Studies (BA); Bar Middle Temple 1969; formerly Brazilian Organiser BBC; MRAC, ACIArb: *m* 1st, 1962 (*m diss* 1970), Suelly, da of Olympio Jose do Lindo; 2ndly, 1973, Rosemary Kathleen Vaughan, only da of late Charles Hawkins, MC, BDS, and has issue living (by 2nd *m*), John Charles, *b* 1975, — James Patrick, *b* 1977.
—— (By 2nd *m*) Alexander Anatol (Rua Senador Vergueiro 237/501, 2230 Rio de Janeiro, Brazil), *b* 1931 (in Hungary); *ed* Colegio S Jose, Rio de Janeiro, Solihull Sch, and Trin Coll, Dublin (BA): *m* 1959, Judith, da of Domicio Francisco de Azevedo, and has issue living, Ines, *b* 1961.

Granddaughters (by 3rd *m*) of late John Llewellyn Mulholland (ante):—
Issue of late Christian Mulholland, *b* 1938 (in France), *d* 1968: *m* 1964, Danielle Andrée (who *m* 2ndly, 19—, R. A. Turner, of 17 Stoke Rd, Leighton Buzzard, Leics), da of late André Emile Bombail, of Relizane, Algeria:—
Valentine Marie Danielle, *b* 1964; BA. —— Hélène Marie Christine, *b* 1965.

Issue of late Hon Alfred John Mulholland, 3rd son of 1st Baron, *b* 1856, *d* 1938: *m* 1889, Mabel Charlotte, who *d* 1934, eldest da of late Llewellyn Traherne Basset Saunderson (*see* E Clonmell, 1911 Edn):—
Alfred Ivo (22 Avon Close, S Brent, Devon TQ10 9PR), *b* 1913; late Maj Bedfordshire and Herts Regt: *m* 1946, Monica Mary, da of late William Lowry Craig Knight, CMG, and has issue living, Mary Rose Emma (Lantern Lodge, Aish, S Brent, Devon TQ10 9JQ), *b* 1951.

PREDECESSORS – (1) JOHN Mulholland, LLD, son of late Andrew Mulholland, JP, DL, of Ballywalter Park; *b* 1819; MP for Downpatrick (*C*) 1874-85; *cr Baron Dunleath,* of Ballywalter, co Down (peerage of United Kingdom) 1892: *m* 1851, Frances Louisa, who *d* 1909, da of Hugh Lyle, of Knocktarna, co Londonderry; *d* 1895; *s* by his second son (2) HENRY LYLE, 2nd Baron, *b* 1854; MP for Londonderry co, N Derry Div (*C*) 1885-95: *m* 1881 Norah Louisa Fanny, OBE, who *d* 1935, da of late Capt Hon Somerset Richard Hamilton Augusta Ward; *d* 1931; *s* by his son (3) CHARLES HENRY GEORGE, CBE, DSO, 3rd Baron, *b* 1886; Capt 11th Hussars; Mil Sec to Lord-Lieut of Ireland 1919-21, and Gov-Gen of Australia 1923-5: *m* 1st, 1920, Sylvia Henrietta, who *d* 1921, da of Sir Arthur Douglas Brooke, 4th Bt; 2ndly, 1932, Henrietta Grace, who *d* 1969, da of late Most Rev Charles Frederick D'Arcy (B Darcy de Knayth, colls); *d* 1956; *s* by his only son (4) CHARLES EDWARD HENRY JOHN, TD, 4th Baron; *b* 1933; Lt-Col cmdg N Irish Horse (T), Hon Col 'D' (N Irish Horse) Squadron Royal Yeomanry Regt, DL co Down, Nat Gov for N Ireland BBC, etc: *m* 1959, Dorinda Margery, only da of late Lt-Gen Arthur Ernest Percival, CB, CMG, DSO, MC; *d* 1993; *s* by his cousin (5) MICHAEL HENRY (son of late Rt Hon Sir Henry George Hill Mulholland, 1st Bt, 3rd son of 2nd Baron), 5th Baron and present peer.

Dunluce, Viscount, see Earl of Antrim.

DUNMORE, EARL OF (Murray) (Earl S 1686)

KENNETH RANDOLPH MURRAY, 11th Earl, *b* 6 June 1913; *s* 1981; late Sergeant 12th/50th Btn Australian Inf, JP: *m* 1938, Margaret Joy, who *d* 1976, da of P. D. Cousins, of Burnie, Tasmania, and has issue.

Arms – Quarterly of six in three ranks, first (in dexter chief) azure, three mullets argent within a double tressure flowered and counterflowered of fleurs de lys or (*Murray of Atholl*); second (in sinister chief) or, a fess chequy azure and argent (*Stewart*); third (in dexter fess) paly of six or and sable (*Atholl*); fourth (in sinister fess) argent, on a bend azure, three bucks' heads cabossed or (*Stanley, Earl of Derby*); fifth (in dexter base) gules, three legs in armour proper garnished and spurred or, flexed and conjoined in triangle at the upper part of the thigh (*Man*); sixth (in sinister base) gules, two lions passant in pale argent armed and langued azure (*Strange*); overall at the honour point a crescent sable. **Crest** – a demi wild man wreathed about the loins and temples with laurel charged on the breast of a crescent sable, holding in his dexter hand a sword proper hilted and pommelled sable and in his sinister hand a key also sable. **Supporters** – dexter, a savage proper wreathed about the loins charged on the breast of a crescent sable; *sinister*, a lion rampant gules, armed and langued azure gorged of a collar argent charged with three crescents sable. **Motto** – Furthward Fortune.
Address – c/o Viscount Fincastle, PO Box 100E, East Devonport, Tasmania 7310, Australia.

SONS LIVING

MALCOLM KENNETH (*Viscount Fincastle*) (PO Box 100 E, East Devonport, Tasmania 7310), *b* 17 Sept 1946: *m* 1970, Joy Anne, da of A. Partridge, of Launceston, Tasmania, and has two adopted children, Leigh Kenneth, *b* 1978, — Elisa Anne, *b* 1981.
Hon Geoffrey Charles (12 Wilson St, Launceston, Tasmania 7250), *b* 1949: *m* 1974, Margaret Irene, da of H. Bulloch, of Blackwall, Tasmania.

BROTHER LIVING

Alexander Edward (Flat 9, 27 Windermere Beach Rd, Claremont, Hobart, Tasmania 7011), *b* 1917; 1939-45 War as Able Seaman RAN: *m* 1st 1943 (*m diss* 1968), June Caroline Lucy, el da of B. Rabinovitch; 2ndly, 1970, Irene Maud Barwick, of Hobart Tas, and has issue living (by 1st *m*), Stephen Alexander (36 Newlands St, Riverside, Launceston, Tasmania 7250), *b* 1953: *m* 1979, Marilyn Ann Rose, and has issue living, Mathew James *b* 1982, Anthony Victor *b* 1989, — Marilyn Joy (11 Leamington St, Reservoir, Vic 3073), *b* 1947: *m* 1st, 1964 (*m diss* 1971), Michael John Hankin; 2ndly, 1979, Brian Carson, and has issue living (by 1st *m*), Brett Michael *b* 1967, Tania Maree *b* 1965, Sharon Louise *b* 1971, — Wendy Lorraine, *b* 1951: *m* 1969, Maxwell Kevin Upton, of 122, Brent St, Glenorchy, Hobart, Tasmania, and has issue living, Jason Boaz *b* 1971, Natasha Ruby Maree *b* 1976.

SISTERS LIVING

Lorraine Edith (62 Talbot Rd, S Launceston, Tasmania 7250), *b* 1914: *m* 1st, 1940, Hector Roy Bird, who *d* 1963; 2ndly, 1966, Stanley Millwood Farquhar, and has issue living (by 1st *m*), Grace Lucinda, *b* 1950: *m* 1969, Haydn Peter Borella, of 35 Hawthorn St, Norwood, Tasmania 7250, and has issue living, Paul Andrew *b* 1973, Angela Jayne *b* 1971.
Constance Margaret, *b* 1922: *m* 1946, John Mallinson, of 12 Munford St, Kings Meadows, Launceston, Tasmania, and has issue living, Edward Arthur John, *b* 1955: *m* 1979, Janice Maree Shipp, and has issue living, Damian Edward *b* 1980, Erin Elizabeth *b* 1983, — David Andrew, *b* 1957.

DAUGHTERS LIVING OF TENTH EARL

Lady Susan, *b* 1949: *m* 1980, Graham Price, of 15 Wandoo Rd, Duncraig, W Australia 6023.
Lady Elizabeth Mary, *b* 1951: *m* 1973, John Michael Parkinson, of 882 Cambridge Rd, Cambridge, Tasmania 7170, and has issue living, James Murray, *b* 1976, — Anna Louise, *b* 1978.

DAUGHTERS LIVING OF NINTH EARL

Lady Kate Rodel, *b* 1969.
Lady Rebecca Moulin, *b* 1970.

DAUGHTERS LIVING OF EIGHTH EARL

Lady Marjorie Hilda, *b* 1904; has Order of Mercy: *m* 1926, Duncan Alexander Stirling, late Capt Coldstream Guards, who *d* 1990, and has issue living, Alexander Murray (Hunterswood House, Chipperfield, Herts), *b* 1927; *ed* Eton, and New Coll, Oxford; late Lieut Coldstream Guards; late Partner Thos R. Miller & Son: *m* 1951, Mary da of late Maj Neville Wakefield, DSO, and has issue living, Robert Alexander *b* 1959: *m* 1988, Susan Mary, yr da of late Rear Adm James Humphrey Walwyn, CB, OBE (and has issue living, Alexander Humphrey *b* 1994, Rory James *b* (twin) 1994), Oliver John *b* 1961: *m* 1991, Susan Caroline Foster (and has issue living, Rufus Alexander Algernon *b* 1993), Annabel Mary Charlotte *b* 1963, — Sir Angus Duncan Æneas (25 Ladbroke Grove, W11), *b* 1933; *ed* Eton, and Trin Coll, Camb; Chm Royal Opera House, Covent Garden, since 1991; Dir-Gen National Trust since 1983; Ktd 1994: *m* 1959, Armyne Morar Helen, da of late William George Broadbent Schofield (*see* B Hastings, colls), and has issue living, Duncan William Angus *b* 1963, Emma Elisabeth *b* 1960: *m* 1988, Andrew Harold Wentworth Sutcliffe, and has issue (*see* V Chetwynd, colls), Candida Helen *b* 1966. *Residence* – 20 Kingston House South, Ennismore Gdns, SW7.
Lady (Mary) Elisabeth, *b* 1918: *m* 1937, Major Peter Carlton Oldfield, OBE, Warwickshire Yeo, and has issue living, Sara Elizabeth (West Manor Stables, Standen, Hungerford, Berks RG17 0RB), *b* 1939: *m* 1961 (*m diss* 1983), William Thomson, late Scots Guards, and has issue living, Lucinda *b* 1965. *Residence* – Ham Cottage, Sydmonton, Newbury, Berks.

WIDOW LIVING OF NINTH EARL

ANNE AUGUSTA (*Countess of Dunmore*) (14 Regent Terr, Edinburgh EH7 5BN), da of Thomas Clouston Wallace, of Holodyke, Dounby, Orkney: *m* 1967, the 9th Earl, who *d* 1980.

WIDOW LIVING OF TENTH EARL

PATRICIA MARY (Kooringal, 27 Beach Rd, Gravelly Beach, 7276, W Tamar, Tasmania), da of Frank Edwin Coles, of Robigana, W Tamar, Tasmania: *m* 1st, 1948, the 10th Earl, who *d* 1981; 2ndly, 1984, Geoffrey Howard Fitze.

COLLATERAL BRANCHES LIVING

Granddaughter of late Charles James Murray, son of late Rt Hon Sir Charles Augustus Murray, KCB, son of 5th Earl:—
Issue of late Charles Wadsworth Murray, *b* 1894, *d* 1945: *m* 1924, Elizabeth, who *d* 1993, da of Frank Grant, of Knockie, Inverness:—
Helen Rosemary, *b* 1928: *m* 1966, Hubert Zipperlen.

Grandchildren of late Reginald Augustus Frederick Murray, eldest son of Capt Virginius Murray, 2nd son of Lt-Col Hon Alexander Murray, 2nd son of 4th Earl:—
Issue of late Virginius Henry Randolph Murray, *b* 1872, *d* 1937: *m* 1910, Alice, who *d* 1966, da of William Clarke, MD, of Banff:—
Patricia Aimee, *b* 1916: *m* 1960, Peter Bayard Horne, of 42 Musgrave St, Mosman 2088, NSW, Australia. —— Judith Dunmore, *b* 1918: *m* 1944, Ian Monk, MB BS, MS, FRACS, FRCS, and has issue living, Virginia Ann, *b* 1949: *m* 1977, Neil Hersfield, of Vancouver, Canada, and has issue living, Zach Dunmore *b* 1983, Gabriel Ian *b* 1988, — Victoria Jane, *b* 1952: *m* 1975 (*m diss* 19—), Tan Choo Lim, economist, — Serena Dunmore, *b* 1954: *m* 1983, Christian Dubois, of Aigle, Switzerland, and has issue living, Oriane Dunmore *b* 1985, Tamara Judith *b* 1988. *Residence* – 35A Raglan St, Mosman 2088, NSW, Australia.
Issue of late Malcolm Fincastle Murray, *b* 1885, *d* 1935: *m* 1915, Rhoda Dorothy, who *d* 1970, da of Richard Davies Hanson, of Adelaide, S Australia:—
Judith Hanson Fincastle, *b* 1923: *m* 1945, Donald Munro Walker, Australian Trade Commr Service, of 3/5 Quondong St, Mooloolaba, Queensland, Australia, and has issue living, Malcolm John Munro, *b* 1946: *m* 1973, Margot Jill Chalmers, da of J. Chalmers, of Wagga Wagga, NSW, and has issue living, Andrew John *b* 1977, Rebecca Lee *b* 1975, — Pamela Murray, *b* 1952.
Issue of late Reginald Herbert Earn Murray, *b* 1893, *d* 1980: *m* 1928, Nina Clarendon, who *d* 1975, da of Clarendon James Seager:—
John Dunmore (Coonawarra, 2 Twin St, Stirling, S Australia 5152), *b* 1929; *ed* Adelaide Univ (B Eng); MIE Aust: *m* 1962, Geraldine Marjorie, da of late Col Rupert Edward Fanning, of S Yarra, Victoria, and has issue living, Catriona Dunmore Stewart, *b* 1965: *m* 1992, Michael David Mills, of 138 Mount Pleasant, Cockfosters, EN4 9HG, son of David Mills, of 9 Coppice Walk, Totteridge, N20 8BZ, — Bridget Dunmore Stewart, *b* 1967, — Vanessa Dunmore Stewart, *b* 1969, — Kirsten Dunmore Stewart, *b* 1971.

Grandchildren of late Capt Virginius Murray, son of late Lieut-Col Hon Alexander Murray (infra):—
Issue of late George Earn Murray, *b* 1850, *d* 1902: *m* 1889, Julia Mary McLeod, who *d* 1933, second da of late Gen C. B. Fuller, RHA (Col Comdt):—
Dudley Stewart, *b* 1892. —— Gladys, *b* 1890.

Grandchildren of late Henry Alexander Murray, 6th and yst son of Capt Virginius Murray (ante):—
Issue of late Lt-Col Henry Alexander Murray, MD, *b* 1893, *d* 1988: *m* 1st, 1916, Josephine Lee, who *d* 1962, da of Neal Rantoul, of Boston, Mass, USA; 2ndly, 1969, Caroline (22 Francis Av, Cambridge, Mass, USA), da of Alfred Chandler, of Wilmington, Delaware, USA:—
(By 1st *m*) Josephine, *b* 1921; MA (1954), MD New York Univ (1961). *Residence* – 41 Concord Av, Cambridge, Mass 02138, USA.
Issue of late Cecil Dunmore Murray, *b* 1897, *d* 1935: *m* 1921, Veronica, who *d* 1988, da of Kenneth Frazier, of Garrison, New York:—
Rev Michael Hunt (301 Indian Springs Rd, Williamsburg, Va 23185, USA), *b* 1922; late Lt USA Naval Air Force: *m* 1st, 1943, Gloria Caruso; 2ndly, 1955, Eliane, da of Eugene Cadilhac, of Paris, France, and has issue living, (by 1st *m*) Eric Dunmore, *b* 1945, — Colin Duncan Alexander, *b* 1949. —— Julia Fannie, *b* 1924: *m* 1953, Robert Linfield Mackintosh, and has issue living, Amy Rogers, *b* 1954, — Louisa Linfield, *b* 1956, — Susan Frazier, *b* 1958. *Residence* – Manchester, Mass, USA.

Grandchildren of late Charles Stewart Murray, CIE, 2nd son of Brig-Gen Alexander Henry Murray, yst son of Lt Col Hon Alexander Murray, 2nd son of 4th Earl:—

Issue of late Cdr Archie Alastair Stewart, RN, *b* 1892, *d* 1964: *m* 1925, Marie Louise Ravend de Martainville, who *d* 1990, da of late Alfred Taylor Pattison, of New Orleans, USA:—

Hugh Archie Stewart (Quinta Arca de Noé, Ferragudo, Algarve, Portugal), *b* 1927; *ed* Stowe, and Trin Coll Oxford (MA); late Lt Welsh Guards: *m* 1st, 1955 (*m diss* 1963), Kathleen Mary, only da of late Clive Raymond Hargreaves; 2ndly, 1967, Eileen Jane Alexandra, da of late Charles Clement Lockhart Ross.

Issue of late Maj Alastair Donald Stewart Murray, MC, *b* 1898, *d* 1966: *m* 1st 1922, Joan Ethel, da of late Robert Moore McMahon, of Holly Mount, Carlow; 2ndly, 1933 (*m diss* 1948), Marjory, who *d* 1959, da of late Capt Anthony Standidge Thomson, CB, CBE, and formerly wife of Capt Herbert Caryl Uniacke, RA; 3rdly, 1951, Oonah Tighe, only da of Thomas Tait, of Gatehouse-of-Fleet, Kirkcudbrightshire, and formerly wife of — McKellar:—

(By 3rd *m*) Alastair Stewart (31 Chater Hall, G/F, 1 Conduit Rd, Mid-Levels, Hong Kong), *b* 1952; Ch Inspector Royal Hong Kong Police; MIExpE, MIABTI: *m* 1973, Sheila, da of — Garvie, and has issue living, Struan Alastair Stewart, *b* 1977, — Ian Nairn, *b* 1980.

Issue of late Charles Stewart Murray, *b* 1900, *d* 1950: *m* 1926 (*m diss* 1933), Beryta, only da of Roland Allport, of Sydney, NS Wales:—

Diana Stewart *b* 1930: *m* 1st, 1948 (*m diss* 1960), Richard de Graaff Hunter; 2ndly, 1969, Arthur Eustace Farmiloe, of 41 Cumberland St, SW1, and has issue living, (by 1st *m*) Sarah Stewart, *b* 1949.

Granddaughter of late Lieut-Col Cyril Francis Tyrrell Murray, CB, MVO, 3rd son of late Brig-Gen Alexander Henry Murray (ante):—

Issue of late Brigadier Cyril Alexander George Octavius Murray, DSO, *b* 1887, *d* 1960: *m* 1922, Marjorie Lilias, who *d* 1965, da of late W. Jennings Milles, MD, FRCS of Shanghai:—

Anne Elizabeth (2 Mansfield Place, Moffat, Dumfriesshire DG10 9DS), *b* 1937.

Granddaughters of late Lt-Col Sir Malcolm Donald Murray, GCVO, CB, CIE, 4th son of late Brig-Gen Alexander Henry Murray (ante):—

Issue of late Lt-Col Iain Arthur Murray, DSO, *b* 1904, *d* 1986: *m* 1st, 1932 (*m diss* 1946), Angela Houssemayne, da of late Lt-Col Arthur Houssemayne du Boulay, DSO; 2ndly, 1947 (*m diss* 1957), Anne, who *d* 1985, da of late Vice-Adm Hon Edmund Rupert Drummond, CB, MVO (*see* E Perth, colls):—

(By 1st *m*) Virginia Anne (45 Castle Rd, Isleworth, Middx), *b* 1936: *m* 1st, 1955 (*m diss* 1963), Anthony Gordon Reid; 2ndly, 1964 (*m diss* 1977), D. Ricardo Saenz de Heredia, and has issue living (by 1st *m*), Iain Malcolm Gordon, *b* 1956: *m* 1980, Susan McLeod, and has issue living, Philippa Susanna *b* 1986, Serena Madeleine *b* 1994, — (by 2nd *m*) Ricardo, *b* 1968, — Roberto, *b* 1969, — Pedro, *b* 1970. ——— Serena Jane, *b* 1939: *m* 1963, Konradin Geotte Vidigal, of Avenida do Brazil, 130 2E Lisbon 5, Portugal.

PREDECESSORS – (1) *Rt Hon Lord* Charles Murray, 2nd son of 1st Marquess of Athole; Master of the Horse to Queen Mary II of England; *cr Lord Murray of Blair, Moulin and Tillimet (Tullimet), Viscount Fincastle* and *Earl of Dunmore* (peerage of Scotland) 1686; *d* 1710; *s* by his el son (2) JOHN, 2nd Earl; a Gen in the Army, and a Representative Peer; *d* 1752; *s* by his brother (3) WILLIAM, 3rd Earl; having taken part in the rebellion of 1745, was in 1746 tried for high treason and pleaded guilty, but obtained the King's pardon; *s* by his son (4) JOHN, 4th Earl; a Representative Peer 1761-84, Gov of New York 1769-70, Virginia 1770-76, and Bahamas 1787-96; *d* 1809; *s* by his son (5) GEORGE, 5th Earl; *cr Baron Dunmore*, of Dunmore (peerage of United Kingdom) 1831; *d* 1836; *s* by his son (6) ALEXANDER EDWARD, 6th Earl: *b* 1804: *m* 1836, Catherine who *d* 1886, da of 11th Earl of Pembroke; *d* 1845; *s* by his son (7) CHARLES ADOLPHUS, 7th Earl; *b* 1841; a Lord-in-Waiting to Queen Victoria 1874-80, and Lord-Lt of co Stirling 1875-85: *m* 1866, Lady Gertrude Coke, who *d* 1943, da of 2nd Earl of Leicester; *d* 1907; *s* by his son (8) ALEXANDER EDWARD, VC, DSO, MVO, 8th Earl; *b* 1871; Maj 16th Lancers; served with Soudan Field Force 1896, and Malakand Field Force 1897-98 (VC); S Africa 1899-1900; Comdg 31st Batn Imperial Yeo 1902; 1915-17 War (twice wounded, DSO); Capt Hon Corps of Gentlemen-at-Arms 1924, and a Lord-in-Waiting to HM 1930-36: *m* 1904, Lucinda Dorothea, who *d* 1966, el da of late Col Horace William Kemble, of Toravaig, Skye (Mackenzie, Bt, *cr* 1702, colls): *d* 1962; *s* by his grandson (9) JOHN ALEXANDER (son of late Capt Edward David, Viscount Fincastle, who *d* 1940), only son of 8th Earl) 9th Earl, *b* 1939; Lt Queen's Own Cameron Highlanders: *m* 1967, Anne Augusta, da of Thomas Clouston Wallace, of Holodyke, Dounby, Orkney; *d* 1980; *s* by his kinsman (10) REGINALD ARTHUR (great great grandson of Lt-Col Hon Alexander Murray, 2nd son of 4th Earl) 10th Earl, *b* 1911: *m* 1948, Patricia Mary (who *m* 2ndly, 1984, Geoffrey Fitze), da of Frank Coles, of Robigana, W Tamar, Tasmania; *d* 1981; *s* by his brother (11) KENNETH RANDOLPH 11th Earl and present peer, also Viscount Fincastle, Lord Murray of Blair, Moulin and Tillimet (Tullimet), and Baron Dunmore.

DUNN, BARONESS (Dunn) (Life Baroness 1990)

LYDIA SELINA DUNN, DBE, da of late Yenchuen Yeh Dunn; *b* 29 Feb 1940; *ed* St Paul's Convent Sch, Hong Kong, and Univ of Calif at Berkeley (BS); Hon LLD Chinese Univ of Hong Kong 1984, Univ of Hong Kong 1991, and Univ of BC 1991; JP; Chm Swire & Maclaine Ltd since 1982, Exec Dir Swire Pacific Ltd since 1982; Chm Hong Kong Trade Devpt Council 1983-91; Dir Cathay Pacific Airways Ltd since 1985, Volvo 1991-93 (Memb Internat Advisory Board 1985-91), and Hong Kong Seibu Enterprise Co Ltd since 1989; Dep-Chm Hongkong & Shanghai Banking Corpn since 1992 (Dir 1981-92), and HSBC Holdings plc (formerly Hong Kong and Shanghai Banking Corpn Holdings (London)) since 1992 (Dir 1990-92); Chm Lord Wilson Heritage Trust since 1993, Hong King/Japan Business Co-operation Cttee since 1988 (Member since 1983); Memb Legislative Council 1976-88 (Sr Memb 1985-88), Hong Kong/US Econ Co-op Cttee 1984-93; Prime Minister of Japan's Trade Award 1987; Sr Member Exec Council Hong Kong since 1988; has retained her maiden name; *cr* OBE (Civil) 1978, CBE (Civil) 1983, DBE 1989, and *Baroness Dunn*, of Hong Kong Island in Hong Kong and of Knightsbridge in the Royal Borough of Kensington and Chelsea (Life Baroness) 1990: *m* 1988, Michael David Thomas, CMG, QC.

Address – John Swire & Sons (HK) Ltd, 5th Floor, Swire House, 9 Connaught Rd, Central Hong Kong.
Clubs – Hong Kong, and Royal Hong Kong Jockey.

DUNRAVEN and MOUNT-EARL, EARL OF (Wyndham-Quin) (Earl I 1822 Bt GB 1781)

THADY WINDHAM THOMAS WYNDHAM-QUIN, 7th Earl, and 7th Baronet; *b* Oct 27th, 1939; *s* 1965; *ed* Le Rosey: *m* 1969, Geraldine, da of Air Commodore Gerard Ward McAleer, CBE, of Wokingham, Berks, and has issue.

Arms – Quarterly, 1st and 4th gules, a hand couped below the wrist grasping a sword all proper between in base two serpents erect and respecting each other, tails nowed or, in chief two crescents argent, *O'Quin of Munster*; 2nd and 3rd azure, a chevron between three lions' heads erased or, a mullet for difference, *Wyndham*. **Crest** – 1st, wolf's head, erased argent, *Quin*; 2nd, a lion's head erased within a fetter-lock and chain or, *Wyndham*. **Supporters** – Two ravens with wings elevated proper, collared and chained or.
Residence – Kilcurly House, Adare, co Limerick. *Club* – Kildare Street.

Head of the serpent for ever

DAUGHTER LIVING

Lady Ana, *b* 1972.

SISTERS LIVING

Lady Melissa Eva Caroline, *b* 1935: *m* 1959, Major Sir George Cecil Francis Brooke, 3rd Bt, MBE, of Glenbevan, Croom, co Limerick, who *d* 1982.
Lady Caroline Olein Geraldine (*Marchioness of Waterford*), *b* 1936: *m* 1957, 8th Marquess of Waterford, of Curraghmore, Portlaw, co Waterford, and Glenbride Lodge, Valleymount, co Wicklow.

COLLATERAL BRANCH LIVING

Issue of late Capt Hon Valentine Maurice Wyndham-Quin, RN, yr son of 5th Earl, *b* 1890, *d* 1983: *m* 1919, Marjorie Elizabeth, who *d* 1969, da of late Rt Hon Ernest George Pretyman (E Bradford):—
Marjorie Olein (*Marchioness of Salisbury*), *b* 1922: *m* 1945, 6th Marquess of Salisbury. —— Pamela (*Dowager Baroness Egremont*), *b* 1925: *m* 1947, 6th Baron Leconfield and 1st Baron Egremont, who *d* 1972. *Residences* – Cockermouth Castle, Cockermouth, Cumbria; 62 Chester Sq, SW1.

PREDECESSORS – **(1)** VALENTINE RICHARD Quin; *cr a Baronet* 1781, *Baron Adare* (peerage of Ireland) 1800, *Viscount Mount-Earl* (peerage of Ireland) 1816, and *Viscount Adare* and *Earl of Dunraven and Mount-Earl* (peerage of Ireland) 1822; *d* 1824; *s* by his son **(2)** WINDHAM HENRY, 2nd Earl; assumed the additional surname of Wyndham by Roy licence 1815; a Representative Peer; *d* 1850; *s* by his son **(3)** EDWIN RICHARD WINDHAM, KP, 3rd Earl; *b* 1812; MP for Glamorganshire (C) 1836-50; Lieut of co Limerick; *cr Baron Kenry*, of co Limerick (peerage of United Kingdom) 1866: *m* 1st 1836, Augusta, who *d* 1866, da of Thomas Goold, a Master in Changery; 2ndly 1870, Anne, who *d* 1917, da of Henry Lambert of Carnagh co Wexford; *d* Oct 6th, 1871; *s* by his son **(4)** *Rt Hon* WINDHAM THOMAS, KP, 4th Earl *b* 1841; Parliamentary Under-Sec of State for the Colonies 1885-86, and HM Lieut for co Limerick 1894-1926; a Senator of Irish Free State 1922-6: *m* 1869, Florence, who *d* 1916, da of late Lord Charles Lennox Kerr; *d* 1926, when the Barony of Kenry became ext, while the Irish titles and the Baronetcy devolved upon his cousin **(5)** WINDHAM HENRY, CB, DSO (el son of late Capt the Hon Windham Henry Wyndham-Quin, 2nd son of 2nd Earl), 5th Earl, *b* 1857; Major 16th Lancers, Capt and Hon Major Gloucestershire Yeo Cav, and Lieut-Col Comdg and Hon Col Glamorganshire Yeo; Transvaal Campaign 1881, S Africa 1900-01 with Imperial Yeo (despatches, DSO); was ADC and Mil Sec to Gov of Madras 1886-89, and High Sheriff for co Limerick 1914; sat as MP for Glamorganshire, S Div (C) 1895-1906: *m* 1885, Lady Eva Constance Aline, who *d* 1940, da of 6th Earl of Mayo; *d* 1952; *s* by his son **(6)** RICHARD SOUTHWELL WINDHAM ROBERT, CB, CBE, MC, 6th Earl, *b* 1887; Master of the Horse and Mil Sec to Lords Lieut of Ireland 1918-21: *m* 1st, 1915 (*m diss* 1932), Helen, who *d* 1962, da of late John Swire, of Hillingdon House, Harlow; 2ndly, 1934, Nancy, who *d* 1994, da of Thomas Burks Yuille, of Halifax Co, Virginia; *d* 1965; *s* by his only son **(7)** THADY WINDHAM THOMAS, 7th Earl and present peer; also Viscount Mount-Earl, Viscount Adare, and Baron Adare.

DUNROSSIL, VISCOUNT (Morrison) (Viscount UK 1959)

JOHN WILLIAM MORRISON, 2nd Viscount, CMG; *b* 22 May 1926; *s* 1961; *ed* Fettes, and Oriel Coll, Oxford (BA 1950, MA 1952); DL Western Isles 1990, Lord Lieut of the Islands Area of the Western Isles 1993; formerly Flight-Lieut RAF, entered Commonwealth Relations Office 1951; was Assist Private Sec to Sec of State 1952-4, 2nd Sec, Canberra 1954-56, and 1st Sec and acting Dep High Commr, Dacca, E Pakistan 1958-60; 1st Sec, Pretoria and Capetown 1961-64, and FO 1964-68, and on loan to Intergovernmental Maritime Consultative Organisation 1968-70, and Counsellor and Head of Chancery, Ottawa, 1975-78, Brit High Commr to Fiji (and non-resident in Nauru and Tuvalu) 1978-82, Brit High Commr to Barbados (and non-resident to Antigua and Barbuda, and to St Lucia, Dominica, Grenada, St Vincent and the Grenadines, and St Kitts and Nevis) 1982-83, Gov and C-in-C of Bermuda 1983-88 (ret); CMG (1981); KSt J (1983): *m* 1st, 1951 (*m diss* 1969), Mavis Dawn, da of A. Llewellyn Spencer-Payne, LRCP, MRCS, LDS; 2ndly 1969, Diana Mary Cunliffe, da of C. M. Vise, and has issue by 1st and 2nd

m.

Arms – Per bend sinister gules and argent a demi-lion rampant issuant or armed and langued azure holding in his paws a battleaxe the shaft curved of the third and the axehead of the fourth in chief, and in base, issuant from the sea undy vert and or, a tower sable windows and port or, over all a bend sinister embattled azure charged with an open crown or jewelled gules between two fleurs-de-lys argent; within a bordure vert for difference. **Crest** – Issuant from waves of the sea azure crested argent, a mount vert, thereon an ambattled wall azure masoned argent, charged with a portcullis or, and issuant therefrom a cubit arm naked proper, the hand grasping a dagger azure hilted or. **Supporters** – Two lions regardant or armed and langued gules collared vert supporting between their exterior forepaws and interior hind paws battleaxes azure, the shafts embowed.

Residence – Dunrossil, by Lochmaddy, N Uist, Outer Hebrides.

SONS LIVING *(By 1st marriage)*

Hon ANDREW WILLIAM REGINALD, *b* 15 Dec 1953; *ed* Eton, and Univ Coll, Oxford: *m* 19—, and has issue living, two das.

Hon Ranald John, *b* 1956; *ed* Westminster, and Univ Coll, London (BSc): *m* 1979, Henrietta Frances, da of late J. H. Wilson, of Addison Rd, W8, and of Mrs Carey-Wilson, of Halewell, Withington, Glos, and has issue living, Richard Donald, *b* 1983, — Alexander Thomas, *b* 1988, — Allison Catherine, *b* 1984, — Rebecca Louise, *b* 1987. *Residence* – 37 Brigstocke Rd, St Paul's, Bristol.

Hon Alasdair Godfrey, *b* 1962: *m* 1987, Tania M., only da of J. A. Redman, of Minehead, Som. *Residence* – 90 St Stephen's Av, W12.

DAUGHTERS LIVING *(By 1st marriage)*

Hon Catriona Mary, *b* 1952: *m* 1973, John James Galt, and has issue living, Iain Robert, *b* 1978, — Malcolm David, *b* 1982, — Sarah Christine, *b* 1976.

(By 2nd marriage)

Hon Joanna Catherine, *b* 1971.
Hon Mary Allison, *b* 1972.

BROTHER LIVING

Hon Alasdair Andrew Orr, *b* 1929; *ed* Fettes, and Balliol Coll, Oxford (MA); PhD, Chicago; High Sheriff of Glos 1983: *m* 1958, Frances Mary, da of Wilfrid Rippon Snow, of Adelaide, S Australia, and has issue living, William Alasdair Ewing, *b* 1960, — Alexandra Mary, *b* 1962: *m* 1989, David T. M. Young, son of late B. R. Young, of Shiplake, Oxfordshire, — Joanna Allison, *b* 1964. *Residence* – Maisemore Lodge, Gloucester.

WIDOW LIVING OF SON OF FIRST VISCOUNT

Sheila Mary, MB BS Lond 1953, MRCS Eng, LRCP Lond 1953, da of Alexander Forbes, of 12 Denmark Rd, Gloucester: *m* 1959, Rev Hon Nial Ranald Morrison, who *d* 1991, following a road accident, and has issue (see colls infra). *Residence* – 24 Fox Close, Stroud, Glos.

COLLATERAL BRANCH LIVING

Issue of late Rev Hon Nial Ranald Morrison, 3rd son of 1st Viscount, *b* 1932, *d* 1991, following a road accident: *m* 1959, Sheila Mary, MB BS, MRCS, LRCP (ante), da of Alexander Forbes, of 12 Denmark Rd, Gloucester:—

Neil William Alexander, *b* 1961: *m* 1992, Clare E., da of John Molloy, of Haslemere, Surrey. —— John Forbes, *b* 1963. —— Hugh Robert Shepherd, *b* 1965. —— (Alison) Mary, *b* 1960: *m* 1992, Paul A. Broad, son of Richard Broad, of Dunkeswell, Devon. —— (Elizabeth) Iona, *b* 1969: *m* 1992, Dr Mark W. James, son of Kenneth James, of Birdwood, Glos.

PREDECESSOR – **(1)** *Rt Hon* WILLIAM SHEPHERD Morrison, GCMG, MC, PC, QC, son of late John Morrison, of Torinturk, Argyll; *b* 1893; Recorder of Walsall Feb to Nov 1935; Private Sec to Solicitor-Gen 1922-23 and 1924-27, and to Attorney-Gen 1927-28; again Parliamentary Private Sec to Attorney-Gen 1931-5, Financial Sec to Treasury 1935-6, Min of Agriculture and Fisheries 1936, Chancellor of Duchy of Lancaster and Min of Food 1939-40, and Postmaster-Gen 1940-43; Min for Town and County Planning 1943-45, Speaker of House of Commons 1951-9, and Gov-Gen and Com-in-Ch of Commonwealth of Australia 1960-61; European War 1914-19 as Capt RFA (Special Reserve) in France (wounded, despatches thrice, MC); sat as MP for Cirencester and Tewkesbury Div of Gloucestershire 1929-59; *cr* Viscount Dunrossil, of Vallaquie, Isle of North Uist, co Inverness (peerage of United Kingdom) 1959: *m* 1924, (Catherine) Allison (a C St J), who *d* 1983, da of late Rev William Swan, DD, Min of South Leith Parish; *d* 1961; *s* by his el son **(2)** JOHN WILLIAM, 2nd Viscount and present peer.

DUNSANY, BARON OF (Plunkett) (Baron I 1439)
(Title pronounced "Dunsayny")

FESTINA LENTE

Quick, without impetuosity

RANDAL ARTHUR HENRY PLUNKETT, 19th Baron; *b* 25 Aug 1906; *s* 1957; *ed* Eton; Lieut-Col (retired) Indian Cav (Guides); N-W Frontier of India 1930 (medal with clasp): *m* 1st, 1938 (*m diss* 1947), Vera, who *d* 1986, formerly wife of late John Felix Charles (Ivar) Bryce, and da of Col Genesio de Sà Sottomaior, of San Paulo, Brazil; 2ndly, 1947, Sheila Victoria Katrin, da of Capt Sir Henry Erasmus Edward Philipps, 2nd Bt (*see* Foley-Philipps, Bt (ext)), and widow of Major John Frederick Foley, Baron de Rutzen, Welsh Guards, and has issue by 1st and 2nd *m*.

Arms – Sable, a bend, and in the sinister chief a tower argent. **Crest** – A horse passant argent. **Supporters** – *Dexter*, a pegasus per fesse or and argent; *sinister*, an antelope argent, armed, unguled, plain collared and chained, or.
Seat – Dunsany Castle, co Meath. *Clubs* – Beefsteak, Bath, Cavalry, Kildare Street.

SON LIVING (By 1st marriage)

Hon EDWARD JOHN CARLOS, *b* 10 Sept 1939; *ed* Eton, Slade Sch of Fine Art, and Ecole des Beaux Arts, Paris: *m* 1982, Maria Alice Villela de Carvalho, and has issue living, Randal, *b* 1983, — Oliver, *b* 1985. *Residences* – 45 East 89th St, New York, NY 10028, USA; 38 East 57th St, New York, NY 10022, USA.

DAUGHTER LIVING (By 2nd marriage)

Hon Beatrice Mary, *b* 1948.

COLLATERAL BRANCH LIVING

Issue of late Adm the Hon Sir Reginald Aylmer Ranfurly PLUNKETT- ERNLE-ERLE-DRAX, KCB, DSO (who assumed by Royal licence for himself and issue 1916, the additional surnames and arms of Ernle, Erle and Drax, after that of Plunkett), 2nd son of 17th Baron, *b* 1880, *d* 1967: *m* 1916, Kathleen, who *d* 1980, da of Quintin Chalmers, MD, JP:—

(Henry) Walter (Charborough Park, Wareham, Dorset), *b* 1928; Lt-Cdr RN (ret); a JP and DL of Dorset, High Sheriff 1988: *m* 1957, Hon Pamela Rose Weeks, da of 1st Baron Weeks, and has issue living, Richard Grosvenor, *b* 1958; late Coldstream Gds: *m* 1985, Zara Victoria, yr da of William Nigel Henry Legge-Bourke (*see* E Dartmouth, colls), and has issue living, Toby Henry *b* 1989, Tamara Katherine *b* 1987, Natasha Shan *b* 1993, — Jeremy Ryton, *b* 1960, — Charles Ranfurly (High Fogrigg, Bardon Mill, Hexham, Northumberland), *b* 1962: *m* 1990, Camilla Mary, only da of Christopher Robin St Quintin Wall, of The Apple Orchard, Bradenham, High Wycombe, Bucks (*see* E Crawford and Balcarres), — Mark Wyndham, *b* 1967, — Edward Quintin, *b* 1971. —— Patricia Doreen, *b* 1919: *m* 1953, Col Neil Stanley Eustace Maude, RM (ret), who *d* 1987, of Priory Farmhouse, Wheathill, Somerton, Som, and has issue living, Nicholas John Eustace, *b* 1953; *ed* Winchester: *m* 1993, Alison, da of Donald Sword, of Yarnhams, Upper Froyle, Hants, — Julia Jane, *b* 1954: *m* 1st, 1986 (*m diss* 1988), Charles Miller, son of late Wladek Miller, of London; 2ndly, 1994, Thomas Walter Bullard King, of 102 Iffley Rd, W6 0PF, son of Peter King, of Bylaugh, Norfolk, — Sarah Anne, *b* 1956: *m* 1981, Richard William James Parry, of 72 Ritherdon Rd, SW17 8QG, and has issue living, William *b* 1989, Sophie *b* 1983, Emily *b* 1985. —— Joan Elizabeth, *b* 1923. —— Mary (*Baroness Robert Rothschild*), *b* 1925: *m* 1st, 1948, Robert Gustaf Percy Hollond; 2ndly, 19—, Baron Robert Rothschild (43 Ranelagh Grove, SW1), and has issue living (by 1st *m*), Thomas Robert, *b* 1950, — John Ernle, *b* 1953, — James Nicholas, *b* 1959: *m* 1985, Beatrice Hannah Millicent, da of Brian Entwhistle Hare, of Chartley, Fleet, Hants, and has issue living, Phoebe Natasha Lara *b* 1989, Lara Blaise *b* 1991, — Eliza Jane, *b* 1965.

PREDECESSORS – **(1)** Sir CHRISTOPHER Plunkett, uncle of 1st Baron Kileen (E Fingall); *cr Baron of Dunsany* by writ (peerage of Ireland) 1439, and by patent 1461; *s* by his son **(2)** RICHARD, 2nd Baron; *s* by his son **(3)** JOHN, KG, 3rd Baron; *s* by his son **(4)** EDWARD, 4th Baron; *d* 1521; *s* by his son **(5)** ROBERT, 5th Baron; one of the Peers of Parliament held at Dublin 1541; *s* by his son **(6)** CHRISTOPHER, 6th Baron; *s* by his son **(7)** PATRICK, 7th Baron; *s* by his son **(8)** CHRISTOPHER, 8th Baron; *s* by his son **(9)** PATRICK, 9th Baron; summoned to Parliament 1625 and 1660-6; *s* by his grandson **(10)** CHRISTOPHER, 10th Baron; *d* unmarried; *s* by his brother **(11)** RANDAL, 11th Baron; for his adherence to James II, was outlawed, but by the treaty of Limerick his estates were restored, but neglecting the forms necessary to re-establish himself in the privileges of the peerage he had not a seat in Parliament; *d* 1735; *s* by his son **(12)** EDWARD, 12th Baron, conformed to the Established Church but took no step to confirm his right to a seat in Parliament; *d* 1781; *s* by his son **(13)** RANDAL, 13th Baron; claimed and was allowed his seat in Parliament 1791; *d* 1821; *s* by his son **(14)** EDWARD WADDING, 14th Baron; *b* 1773: *m* 1st, 1803, Hon Charlotte Louisa Lawless, who *d* 1819, da of 1st Baron Cloncurry; 2ndly, 1823, Hon Eliza, da of 7th Baron Kinnaird; *d* 1848; *s* by his el son **(15)** RANDAL EDWARD, 15th Baron, *dsp* 1852; *s* by his brother **(16)** EDWARD, 16th Baron, *b* 1808; an Adm and a Representative Peer: *m* 1846, Hon Anne Constance Dutton, who *d* 1858, da of 2nd Baron Sherborne; *d* 1889; *s* by his son **(17)** JOHN WILLIAM, 17th Baron; *b* 1853; a Representative Peer for Ireland; MP for Gloucestershire, S, or Thornbury, Div (C) 1886-92: *m* 1877, Ernle Elizabeth Louisa Maria Grosvenor, who *d* 1916 (having assumed by Roy licence 1906 the surnames of Plunkett-Ernle-Drax), only child of late Col Francis Augustus Plunkett Burton, Coldstream Guards; *d* 1899; *s* by his el son **(18)** EDWARD JOHN MORETON DRAX, 18th Baron; *b* 1878; a Poet, Playwright and Author; Byron Professor, Athens Univ 1941, Pres of Authors' Club 1953-57: *m* 1904, Lady Beatrice Child-Villiers, who *d* 1970, da of 7th Earl of Jersey; *d* 1957; *s* by his only son **(19)** RANDAL ARTHUR HENRY, 19th Baron and present peer.

Dunwich, Viscount; son of Earl of Stradbroke.

DU PARCQ, BARONY OF (du Parcq) (Extinct 1949)

SON LIVING OF LIFE BARON

Hon John Renouf (10 Anchor Quay, Norwich, Norfolk NR3 3PR), *b* 1917; *ed* Rugby, and Exeter Coll, Oxford (MA); MIEE: *m* 1940, Elizabeth Anne, da of late Evan Skull Poole, and has issue.

DAUGHTER LIVING OF LIFE BARON

Hon Catherine Simonne: *m* 1939, Leslie Twelvetrees, who *d* 19—. *Residence* – 115 Dover House, Dover Street, Leicester LE1 6PP, and has issue.

Dupplin, Viscount; son of Earl of Kinnoull.

DURHAM, EARLDOM OF (Lambton) (Earl UK 1833, disclaimed 1970)

LE JOUR VIENDRA

The day will come

ANTONY CLAUD FREDERICK LAMBTON; *b* 10 July 1922; *s* as 6th Earl of Durham, 4 Feb 1970; disclaimed his peerages for life 23 Feb, 1970, but was allowed by Mr Speaker Lloyd to sit in the House of Commons as 'Lord Lambton' and later was so designated for three years while holding an office of profit under the Crown; patron of two livings; PPS to Min of Supply 1954, and to Foreign Sec 1955-57; an Under-Sec, Min of Defence 1970-73; MP for Berwick-upon-Tweed (*C*) 1951-73: *m* 1942, Belinda Bridget, da of late Capt Douglas Holden Blew-Jones, and has issue.

𝕬rms – Quarterly: 1st sable, a fesse between three lambs passant argent, *Lambton*; 2nd argent, a fesse gules, between three popinjays vert, collared gules, *Lumley*; 3rd argent, an escutcheon sable, within an orle of eight cinquefoils gules, *Hedworth*; 4th argent, three cinquefoils gules, *D'Arcy*. 𝕮rest – A ram's head cabossed argent, horns sable. 𝕾upporters – (borne by Earls of Durham). Two lions, the *dexter* gules, the *sinister* azure, each ducally gorged or, and supporting a flagstaff or, therefrom flowing a banner azure, the dexter charged with a cross patonce and the sinister with a lion passant guardant or.
Seats – Lambton Castle, Fence Houses, co Durham; Fenton, Wooler, Northumberland. *Residences* – Biddick Hall, Lambton Park, Chester-le-Street, co Durham; Villa Cetinale, Sovicille, Siena, Italy.

SON LIVING

Hon EDWARD RICHARD (styled *Baron Durham*), *b* 19 Oct 1961: *m* 1983, Christabel Mary, yst da of late Roderick (Rory) McEwen, of Bardrochat, Colmonell, Ayrshire (*see* McEwen, Bt, colls), and has issue living, Frederick, *b* 23 Feb 1985.

DAUGHTERS LIVING

Lady Lucinda, *b* 1943; writer, photographer, and television broadcaster as Lucinda Lambton: *m* 1st, 1965 (*m diss* 19—), Henry Mark Harrod, el son of Sir (Henry) Roy Forbes Harrod (*see* Ffolkes, Bt colls, 1976 Edn); 2ndly, 1986 (*m diss* 19—), as his 2nd wife, Sir Edmund John William Hugh Ramsay-Fairfax-Lucy, 6th Bt; 3rdly, 1991, as his 2nd wife, Sir Peregrine Gerard Worsthorne (*see* E Lindsey and Abingdon, colls), and has issue living (by 1st *m*), Henry Barnaby *b* 1965, — Huckleberry Nathaniel *b* 1967. *Residence* – The Old Rectory, Hedgerley, Bucks.
Lady Beatrix Mary, *b* 1949: *m* 1st, 1971, George William Bowdrey, son of Henry George Bowdrey; 2ndly, 1982, Guy Rupert Gerard Nevill (*see* M Abergavenny), who *d* 1993, and has issue living (by 1st *m*), Rose Violet, *b* 1973. *Residence* – The Garden House, Eridge Park, Tunbridge Wells, Kent.
Lady Rose Diana, *b* 1952: *m* 1979 (*m diss* 1989), (Herbert) Oliver FitzRoy Musker (*see* V Daventry, 1985 Edn), and has issue living, Claud, *b* 1977, — Sam, *b* 1982, — Lily, *b* 1981. *Residence* – Malcolm House, Batsford, Moreton-in-Marsh, Glos.
Lady Mary Gabrielle Ann, *b* 1954; actress (as Anne Lambton).
Lady Isabella, *b* 1958: *m* 1980, Sir Philip Vyvian Naylor-Leyland, 4th Bt, and has issue. *Residences* – Nantclwyd Hall, Ruthin, N Wales; The Ferry House, Milton Park, Peterborough, Cambs.

HALF-BROTHER LIVING

Hon John George, *b* 1932. *Residence* – 39 Hill St, W1.

COLLATERAL BRANCHES LIVING

Issue of late Capt Hon Claud Lambton, DSO, yst son of 4th Earl; *b* 1888; *d* 1976: *m* 1916, Olive Isabel Eleanor, who *d* 1955, da of late William Robert Percival Lockwood (V Combermere, colls):—
Barbara Anne (Westnewton, Wooler, Northumberland), *b* 1917.

Issue of late Brig-Gen Hon Charles Lambton, DSO, 4th son of 2nd Earl *b* 1857, *d* 1949: *m* 1912, Lavinia Marion, who *d* 1976, da of late William Henry Garforth, of The Brow, Malton, Yorks (B Middleton):—
Charles William, *b* 1921; *ed* Eton; Major (retired) Coldstream Guards: *m* 1950, Lady Elizabeth Mary Fitzmaurice, da of 6th Marquess of Lansdowne, and has issue living, William Henry Charles, *b* 1951: *m* 1st, 1975, Elizabeth Susan Kingdom; 2ndly, 1989, Sorrel M. G., da of Michael Pym, and has issue living (by 1st *m*), Lucy Marion *b* 1980, Sarah Isabella *b* 1982 (by 2nd *m*), a son *b* 1990, — Julian Edward (Pennybridge House, Pennybridge, Ulverston, Cumbria), *b* 1955: *m* 1986, Vanda Jane, yr da of late Lt-Col Charles David Agnew, of Bilborough, York (*see* Agnew, Bt, colls, *cr* 1895), and has issue living, Patrick David Charles *b* 1992, Georgina Marion *b* 1990, — Christopher John (39 Bellevue Place, Edinburgh EH7 4BS), *b* 1960: *m* 1991, Julie, elder da of Dr James Kenneth Watt Morrice, of Aberdeen, and has issue living, Alexander Maurice *b* 1993, —

Anne Elizabeth, *b* 1952: *m* 1979, Patrick J. Wintour, of Weavers House, Sandridge Lane, Bromham, Chippenham, Wilts, yr son of late Capt E. R. Wintour, and has issue living, Adam Richard *b* 1988, Laura Katherine *b* 1981, Mary Rose Cecilia *b* 1982. *Residence* – The Old Rectory, Calstone, Calne, Wilts SN11 8PZ.

Grandsons of late Hon George Lambton (infra):—
Issue of late John Lambton, Flying Officer RAF, *b* 1909, *ka* 1941: *m* 1934, Ethel Ruth (who *m* 2ndly, 19—, E. Ballard, of USA), only da of late Capt William Henry Nicholson, RN:—
Peter John George, *b* 1935.
Issue of late Capt Edward George Lambton, RHG, *b* 1918, *d* 1983: *m* 1st, 1949 (*m diss* 1959), Anne, only da of late Col Lawrence Lees, of Cheswardine, Salop, and formerly wife of David Rawnsley; 2ndly, 1959, Pauline (Mensil Warren, Newmarket, Suffolk), da of late Herbert Coxon Bolton, and formerly wife of Victor Frederick Cochrane Hervey, Earl Jermyn (afterwards 6th Marquess of Bristol):—
(By 2nd *m*) George, *b* 1962.

Issue of late Hon George Lambton, 5th son of 2nd Earl, *b* 1860, *d* 1945: *m* 1980, Cecily, who *d* 1972, da of late Sir John (Francis Fortescue) Horner, KCVO:—
Ann Katharine Swynford, OBE (Gregory, Kirknewton, Wooler, Northumberland NE71 6XE), *b* 1912; BA, PhD, D Lit, FBA; Prof Emeritus London Univ; Press Attaché, British Embassy, Teheran 1939-46; OBE (Civil) 1943; Reader Emeritus in Diocese of Newcastle.

Grandchildren of Hon Claud Lambton, 7th son of 2nd Earl:—
Issue of late Cdr Hedworth Lambton, DSC, RN, *b* 1904, *d* 1983: *m* 1st, 1935 (*m diss* 1963), Iris Wynnfred Violet, formerly wife of Charles Caulfield Hewitt, and da of William Law Halpin, mining engr; 2ndly, 1963, Olivia, who *d* 1986, widow of Col Denys Redwood Vachell, MC, and da of Reginald Monckton:—
(By 1st *m*) Rosemary Ann, *b* 1936.
Issue of late D'Arcy Lambton, *b* 1908, *d* 1938: *m* 1933, Hon Monica Dorothy Brand (Saxon House, Shottisham, Woodbridge, Suffolk), da of 3rd Viscount Hampden:—
Michael Charles (6 Rosenau Cres, SW11), *b* 1934; *ed* Eton, and Newcastle Univ: *m* 1969, Nancy, da of John Gillespie, and has issue living, D'Arcy, *b* 1970. —— Lorna Katherine, *b* 1938.

PREDECESSORS – (1) *Rt Hon Sir* JOHN GEORGE Lambton, GCB; MP for co Durham 1813-28, Ambassador to Court of Russia, Lord Privy Seal 1830-33, and Gov-Gen of British N America, &c; *cr Baron Durham* (peerage of United Kingdom) 1828, and *Viscount Lambton* and *Earl of Durham* 1833; *d* 1840; *s* by his son (2) GEORGE FREDERICK D'ARCY, 2nd Earl; *b* 1828; Lord-Lieut of co Durham; *m* 1854, Lady Beatrix Frances Hamilton, da of 1st Duke of Abercorn; *d* 1879; *s* by his son (3) *Rt Hon* JOHN GEORGE, KG, GCVO, 3rd Earl, *b* 1855; bore Queens Consort's Ivory Rod with Dove at Coronation of King George V 1911; was Lord High Stewart to HM during visit to India 1911-12: *m* 1882, Ethel Elizabeth Louisa, who *d* 1931, da of late Henry Beilby William Milner; *d* 1928; *s* by his twin brother (4) FREDERICK WILLIAM, 4th Earl, *b* 1855; sat as MP for Durham, S (*L*) 1880-85, and for Durham co S-E Div (LU) 1900-1910: *m* 1879, Beatrix, who *d* 1937, da of John Bulteel, of Pamflete, Ivybridge; *d* 1929; *s* by his el son (5) JOHN FREDERICK, 5th Earl, *b* 1884: *m* 1st, 1919, Diana Mary, who *d* 1924, da of late Granville Frederick Farquhar (Farquhar, Bt); 2ndly, 1931, Hermione, who *d* 1990, da of Sir George Bullough, 1st Bt; *d* 1970; *s* by his son (6) ANTONY CLAUD FREDERICK, 6th Earl, and Viscount Lambton and Baron Durham until he disclaimed his peerages 1970.

DYNEVOR, BARON (Rhys) (Baron GB 1780)

Secret and bold

RICHARD CHARLES URYAN RHYS, 9th Baron; *b* 19 June 1935; *s* 1962; *ed* Eton, and Magdalene Coll, Camb: *m* 1959 (*m diss* 1978), Lucy Catherine King, only da of late Sir John Knewstub Maurice Rothenstein, CBE, and has issue.

Arms – Argent, a chevron between three ravens sable. **Crest** – A raven sable. **Supporters** – *Dexter*, a griffin per fesse or and argent, wings addorsed and inverted, tail between the legs; *sinister*, a talbot argent, collared flory counterflory gules, ears ermine, and charged on the shoulder with a trefoil slipped vert.

SON LIVING

Hon HUGO GRIFFITH URYAN, *b* 19 Nov 1966.

DAUGHTERS LIVING

Hon Miranda Jane Caroline, *b* 1960: *m* 1986, David Rule, 2nd son of Ronald William Pritchard Rule, of Deal, Kent and has issue living, James Gareth, *b* 1986, — Rhiannon, *b* 1987.
Hon Sarah Sophia Rhiannon, *b* 1963: *m* 1987, Dyfrug Williams, eldest son of Daniel Thomas Williams, of Carmarthen, and has issue living, Stefan Orlando, *b* 1988, — Sophie Adeline, *b* 1993.
Hon Susannah Mair Elizabeth, *b* 1964: *m* 1993, Barnaby Stone, 3rd son of Ralph Neville Stone, of Oxford.

AUNT LIVING (*Daughter of 7th Baron*)

Hon Imogen Alice (*Imogen, Viscountess Hampden*) (Trevor House, Glynde, Lewes), *b* 1903: *m* 1936, 5th Viscount Hampden, who *d* 1975.

WIDOWS LIVING OF SONS OF SEVENTH BARON

Diana Sloane, da of Maj Roger Cyril Hans Sloane Stanley: *m* 1931, Capt Hon Elwyn Villiers Rhys, who *d* 1966, and has issue living (see colls, infra). *Residence* – Forest Home, Beechwood Lane, Burley, Hants.
Sheila Mary, formerly wife of Christopher d'Ambrumenil, and only da of late Douglas J. Phillips, of Popley Fields,

Basingstoke: *m* 1963, as his 2nd wife, Capt Hon David Reginald Rhys, who *d* 1991, and has issue (see colls infra). *Residence* – Southwick Court Chapel, Southwick, Trowbridge, Wilts BA14 9QB.

COLLATERAL BRANCHES LIVING

Issue of late Capt Hon Elwyn Villiers Rhys, 2nd son of 7th Baron, *b* 1900, *d* 1966: *m* 1931, Diana Sloane (ante), da of Maj Roger Cyril Hans Sloane Stanley:—
Daphne Margaret, *b* 1933: *m* 1956, Maurice Brain, of Tower Farm, Whiteparish, Salisbury, and has issue living, Graham Stephen Maurice, *b* 1957. — Patrick John Elwyn, *b* 1959.

Issue of late Capt Hon David Reginald Rhys, yst son of 7th Baron, *b* 1907, *d* 1991: *m* 1st, 1933 (*m diss* 1963), Lady Anne Maud Wellesley, only da of 5th Duke of Wellington; 2ndly, 1963, Sheila Mary (ante), formerly wife of Christopher d'Ambrumenil, and only da of late Douglas J. Phillips, of Popley Fields, Basingstoke:—
(By 1st *m*) Llewelyn Arthur, *b* 1935; *ed* Eton: *m* 1961, Rosemary Martha Ann, elder da of late Rev Canon Robert Victor Sellers, of Burnham-on-Sea, Somerset, and has issue living, Robert David Arthur, *b* 1963, — Julian Nicholas James, *b* 1966, — Fiona Martha Alison, *b* 1962: *m* 1986, Capt R. D. C. James, and has issue living, Charles Richard Arthur *b* 1993, Olivia Martha Alison *b* 1987, Lucinda Sophie Rose *b* 1989. —— Elizabeth Maud, *b* 1937: *m* 1966, Peter Matthew Doran, of 7 Killock, Martello Park, Canford Cliffs, Poole, Dorset BH13 7BA. —— (By 2nd *m*) George Dafydd, *b* 1965; *ed* Milton Abbey, and Caen Univ.

Grandchildren of late Rev Hon William Talbot Rice, 3rd son of 5th Baron:—
Issue of late Mervyn Gurney Talbot Rice, *b* 1899, *d* 1979: *m* 1st, 1929, Eleanor Butler Adair, who *d* 1965, da of Andrew Williamson; 2ndly, 1969, Esther Lynette Sutherland, who *d* 1990, da of Maj James Reay Sutherland Mackay, of Doune, Perthshire, and widow of Ronald David Stewart-Brown, QC:—
(By 1st *m*) Andrew Gurney Talbot (33 Cornwall Gdns, SW7 4AP), *b* 1930; *ed* Eton, and Worcester coll, Oxford: *m* 1957, Helen Lalage (Gay), only da of late Charles Buchanan, of Chesterhill, Newport-on-Tay, Fife, and has issue living, Richard Bruce, *b* 1957, — Jonathan William Gurney, *b* 1961, — Julia Margaret, *b* 1959: *m* 1990, Nicholas W. A. Bannister, eldest son of Michael Bannister, of Coniston Hall, Skipton, N Yorks, — Catherine Helen, *b* 1964: *m* 1991, William H. M. Gibson, son of Colin Gibson, of Mare Hill House, Pulborough, W Sussex, and has issue living, Dominic John Mulholland *b* 1993. —— David Mervyn Talbot (43A Elizabeth St, SW1), *b* 1935; *ed* Charterhouse, and Worcester Coll, Oxford. —— Nigel Talbot (Summer Fields, Oxford) *b* 1938; *ed* Charterhouse, and Ch Ch, Oxford (MA, Dip Ed): *m* 1968, Joanna, da of late Air Commodore Frederick John Manning, CB, CBE, and has issue living, Samuel Peter Gurney, *b* 1982, — Sarah Kate, *b* 1969, — Caroline Emma, *b* 1971, — Rebecca Mary, *b* 1973, — Helena Rachel, *b* 1977. —— Margaret Adair Talbot, *b* 1932: *m* 1956, Rev Edward George Humphrey Saunders, of The Hensol, Shires Lane, Chorleywood, Herts WD3 5NH, and has issue living, Hilary Margaret, *b* 1959.

Grandchildren of late Capt Henry Charles Talbot Rice, yr son of late Rev Hon Henry Rice, brother of 5th Baron:—
Issue of late Major Harry Talbot Rice, late Welsh Guards, *b* 1889, *d* 1948: *m* 1927, Hon Blanche Marion Devereux, who *d* 1976, da of 17th Viscount Hereford:—
(David) Arthur Talbot, *b* 1931; *ed* Eton, and Ch Ch, Oxford: *m* 1st, 1957 (*m diss* 1961), Annabella Frances Serena, da of late Major Cyril Augustus Drummond (see E Perth, colls); 2ndly, 1961, Sylvia Dorothea, da of P. B. Metaxas of 71 Eaton Place, SW1, and has issue living (by 2nd *m*), Robert Harry Talbot, *b* 1963; *ed* Eton, and Durham Univ; Capt WG: *m* 1991, (Alice) Elspeth Middleton, yr da of David Middleton Lindsley, of Springfield House, Fremington, Richmond, N Yorks, — Alexander Thomas Talbot, *b* 1969, — Victoria Penelope Helen Talbot, *b* 1961. *Residence* – Barnfield House, Cowfold, Sussex RH13 8AT. *Club* – Cavalry and Guards.
Issue of late Lt-Col Prof David Talbot Rice, CBE, TD, FSA, *b* 1903, *d* 1972: *m* 1927, Tamara, author and art historian, who *d* 1993, adopted da of Boris Abelson, of Paris:—
Nicholas Charles Talbot (Pigeon House, Coln Rogers, Glos, GL54 3LB; Boodle's and Pratt's Clubs), *b* 1944; *ed* Eton, and Ch Ch Oxford: *m* 1973, Jocelyn Mary, da of Maj Robert Higgens, and has issue living, David Henry Talbot, *b* 1975. — Sophia Elizabeth Talbot, *b* 1974. —— Elizabeth Roussoudana Talbot, *b* 1931; *ed* Edinburgh Univ (MA). —— Nina Violet Tamara Talbot, *b* 1941: *m* 1966, Hugh Bredin, and has issue living, Cosmo James, *b* 1970, — Zoë, *b* 1972.

PREDECESSORS – (1) WILLIAM Talbot, 1st *Earl Talbot* (see E Shrewsbury); *cr, Baron Dinevor*, of Dinevor (usually spelt Dynevor) (peerage of Great Britain) 1780, with remainder to his only da and the heirs male of her body; *d* 1782; *s* by his da (2) *Lady* CECIL, wife of the Rt Hon George Rice, PC, MP (10th descent from Sir Rhys ap Thomas, KG, who joined the Earl of Richmond, late Henry VII, after his landing and assisted him at Bosworth); assumed the surname of de Cardonnell only by Roy licence 1787; *d* 1793; *s* by her son (3) GEORGE TALBOT, 3rd Baron; assumed the surname of de Cardonnell by Roy licence 1793, and resumed the name of Rice by Roy licence 1817; Lord-Lieut of Carmarthenshire; *d* 1852; *s* by his son (4) GEORGE RICE, 4th Baron; assumed the additional surname of Trevor by Roy licence 1824; *d* 1869; *s* by his kinsman (5) FRANCIS WILLIAM, 5th Baron, 2nd son of Very Rev Hon Edward Rice, 2nd son of Baroness Dynevor; *b* 1804; V of Fairford; *d* 1878; *s* by his son (6) ARTHUR DE CARDONNEL, 6th Baron, *b* 1836: *m* 1869, Selina, who *d* 1889, da of late Hon Arthur Lascelles; *d* 1911; *s* by his son (7) WALTER FITZ-URYAN, 7th Baron, *b* 1873; was Assist Sec to Sec of State for India 1899-1903, an Assist Private Sec to First Lord of the Admiralty 1903-5, MP for Brighton (*C*) 1910-11, a Co Councillor for Carmarthenshire 1919-35, and Lord Lieut for Carmarthenshire 1928-49; re-assumed by Roy licence 1916 for himself and his issue the surname of Rhys in lieu of Rice: *m* 1898, Lady Margaret Child-Villiers, who *d* 1959, el da of 7th Earl of Jersey; *d* 1956; *s* by his el son (8) CHARLES ARTHUR URYAN, CBE, MC, 8th Baron; *b* 1899; Capt Gren Guards ; MP for Romford (*C*) 1923-29, and Guildford 1931-35; PPS to Financial Sec to War Office 1924-26, to Under-Sec of State for the Colonies 1926-27, and to Prime Min 1927-29; 1939-45 War; Pres of Univ Coll of S Wales and Monmouth 1960-62: *m* 1934, Hope Mary Woodbine, who *d* 1980, formerly wife of Capt Arthur Granville Soames, OBE, and da of late Charles Woodbine Parish, *d* 1962; *s* by his only son (9) RICHARD CHARLES URYAN, 9th Baron, and present peer.

DYSART, COUNTESS OF (Greaves) (Earl S 1643)

ROSAMUND AGNES GREAVES, *Countess of Dysart*, *b* 15 Feb 1914; *s* 1975.

Arms – Azure, and Imperial Crown proper between three mullets argent within a double tressure flory counterflory of. **Supporters** – Two lions gules collared azure, each collar charged with three mullets argent.
Residence – Bryn Garth Farm, Grosmont, Abergavenny, Gwent.

SISTER LIVING

Lady KATHERINE, *b* 1 June 1918: *m* 1941, Lieut-Col John Peter Grant of Rothiemurchus, MBE, Lovat Scouts, who *d* 1987, and has issue living, John Peter, *b* 1946; *ed* Gordonstoun: *m* 1971, (Wendy) Philippa, da of late John Wybergh Chance, of Llanvapley Court, Mon, and has issue living, James Patrick *b* 1977, Louisa Katherine *b* 1975, Alexandra Elizabeth Rose *b* 1985, — Jane Margery, *b* 1943: *m* 1965, Andrew Robert Fowell Buxton, of Bentley Park, Ipswich (*see* Buxton Bt, colls). *Residence* – Rothiemurchus, Aviemore, Invernessshire.

COLLATERAL BRANCHES LIVING

Descendants in the male line of William Tollemache Lord Huntingtower, who was cr a Bt 1793, are also in remainder to this Baronetcy.

Issue of late Lady Mary Greaves, yst da of late Wenefryde Agatha, Countess of Dysart, *b* 1921, *d* 1955: *m* 1942, Capt Bernard Albert Blanger, Sec French Legation, Lisbon, who *d* 1950:—
Brigitte, *b* 1943: *m* 1st, 1964 (*m diss* 1967), John Fotheringham; 2ndly, 1969 (*m diss* 1976), Pavlos Athanasacopoulos. —— Beatrice Wenefryde, *b* 1945: *m* 1977, Robin Evans, and has issue living, Schuyler Benjamin L., *b* 1978.

Grandchildren of late Lady Agatha Manners Tollemache (sister of 9th Earl), who *d* 1941, having *m* 1882, 3rd Lord Westbury, who *d* 1930:—
See that title.

Grandchildren of late Sir Lyonel Felix Carteret Eugene Tollemache, 4th Bt, eldest son of late Caroline Tollemache (only da of late Felix Thomas Tollemache, 2nd son of William, Lord Huntingtower, el son of Louisa, Countess of Dysart), who *d* 1867, having *m* 1853, as his 1st wife, Rev Ralph William Lionel Tollemache-Tollemache (infra):—
Issue of late Sir Humphry Thomas Tollemache, 6th Bt, CB, CBE, *b* 1897, *d* (30 March) 1990: *m* 1926, Nora Priscilla, who *d* (24 Oct) 1990, da of John Taylor, of Broomhill, Eastbourne:—
See BARONETAGE.
Issue of late Cynthia Joan Caroline Tollemache, *b* 1890, *d* 1988: *m* 1918, Harry Scott Judd, who *d* 1948:—
Anthony Hubert Scott JUDD (94 Christchurch Av, NW6 7PE), *b* 1919; FRAM: *m* 1956, Gloria Michele, da of late Harry Solloway, of Los Angeles, Calif, USA, and has had issue, †Terence Dominic, *b* 1957; pianist; *d* 1979, — Diana Caroline, *b* 1963; LRAM. —— Barbara Hersilia, *b* 1926.

Grandchildren of late Cynthia Joan Caroline Tollemache (Mrs Judd) (ante):—
Issue of late John Harry Manners Judd, *b* 1924, *d* 1958: *m* 1954, Sarah (Shooters Hatch, Bishops Green, Barnston, Essex CM6 1NF) (who *m* 2ndly, 1959, H. W. J. Cohen, who *d* 1991), yr da of Gerald Arthur Millar, of Tewes, Little Sampford, Essex:—
Christopher John Harry JUDD, *b* 1957: *m* 1980, Emma Mary Powell, da of late Paul Francis Powell Williams, and has issue living, Thomas Jack Francis, *b* 1984, — Harry Mark Christopher, *b* 1985, — Katherine Mary, *b* 1981. *Residence* – Tendrings, Debden, Saffron Walden, Essex CB11 3LT. —— Isabella Sarah Veronica, *b* 1955.

Grandson of late Emily Katherine Tollemache (Mrs George Fitz Roy Cole), da of late Arthur Lionel Tollemache, son of late Hon Arthur Caesar Tollemache, 3rd son of William, Lord Huntingtower (ante):—
Issue of late Derek Arthur Stephen Fitz Roy COLE, MC, *b* 1895, *d* 1971: *m* 1918, Joan Shirley, who *d* 1971, da of Walter Octavius Hudson:—
John Derek COLE, *b* 1920: *m* 1st 1942 (*m diss* 1959), Beryl Portia Black; 2ndly, 1960, Penelope Ann Hyde-Hartley, and has issue living (by 1st *m*), Nigel John, *b* 1943, — Clive Derek, *b* 1944, — Nicholas Peter, *b* 1949, — (by 2nd *m*) Jeremy Fitz Roy, *b* 1961, — Alicia Jane, *b* 1962. *Residence* – Knapp Cottage, Charlton Hawthorne, nr Sherborne, Dorset.

Descendants, if any, of late Melanie Sophia Tollemache, 2nd da of late Hon Arthur Caesar Tollemache (ante), *b* 1823, *d* 1894, having *m* 1849, Raymond Louis Abrial.
Descendants of late Laura Tollemache, 4th da of late Hon Arthur Caesar Tollemache (ante), *b* 1830, *d* 1908, having *m* 1859, Albert, Comte de Lastic St Jal, who *d* 1865:—
Grandchildren late Henri, Comte de Lastic St Jal, elder son of late Laura Tollemache, Comtesse de Lastic St Jal (ante):—
Issue of late Jehan, Comte de Lastic St Jal, *b* 1897, *d* 1979: *m* 1926, Henriette, da of Baron de Scorbiac:—
Henri Bruno Joseph Hughes (*Comte de Lastic St Jal*), *b* 1927: *m* 1975, Anne, da of François Queinnec. *Residences* – 41 Rue Boursault, Paris 17; Château de Cas, nr St-Antonin, Tarn-et-Garonne, France. —— *Comte* Jean-Claude Lionel Pie Marie Roch, *b* 1933: *m* 1957, Anne-Marie, da of Vicomte Marc de Lesquen du Plessis-Casso, and has issue living, François, *b* 1958; naval officer: *m* 1985, Beatrice Thery, and has issue living, Pierre *b* 1988, Philippe *b* 1989, Victoire *b* 1991, — Thierry, *b* 1963, — Christophe, *b* 1964: *m* 1993, Agnes-Paule Poirot, — Jean-Marc, *b* 1976, — Perrine, *b* 1959: *m* 1990, Dominique Fougeron de Chaumontel, and has issue living, Amelie *b* 1991, Charlotte *b* 1993. *Residence* – 8 Allée des Bergers, 27930 Guichainville, France. —— *Comte* Lyonel Pierre Marie Arthur, *b* 1936: *m* 1960, Jeanne Marie Madeleine, da of René Triniac, and has issue living, Jehan-Philippe, *b* 1961: *m* 1984, Roselyne du Sartel, and has issue living, Jehan *b* 1986, Adelaide *b* 1985, Sauvina *b* 1991, — Hughes-Henri, *b* 1970, — Charlotte-Hélène, *b* 1964: *m* 1986, Comte Laurent de Sayve, and has issue living, Andrien *b* 1987, Palmyre *b* 1989, — Anne-Laure, *b* 1967: *m* 1993, Thomas Bourguignon, and has issue living, Marie *b* 1994. *Residences* – Château de Crabilhè, 46150 Montgesty, Catus, France; 43 Rue du Parc de Clagny, 78000 Versailles, France.

Issue of late Jacques, Comte de Lastic St Jal, *b* 1906, *d* 19—: *m* 1932, Marguerite, da of Gaspard de Lasteyrie, Marquis du Saillant:—
Comte Gérard, *b* 1937: *m* 1967, Marie-Pierre, da of Gen Barberon, and has issue living, Raphaël, *b* 1968, — Grégoire, *b* 1972, — Agathe, *b* 1969. *Residence* – 19 rue St Pierre, 78000 St Germain en Laye, France. —— *Comte* Xavier, *b* 1946: *m* 1981, Marie-Anne de Louvent à St Jean de Luz, and has issue living, Xavier, *b* 1982, — Gonzague, *b* 1984, — Martial, *b* 1990, — Blanche, *b* 1984. *Residence* – 41 rue J. Ibert, 923000 Levallois, France. —— *Comte* Réginald, *b* 1948: *m* 1976, Dominique

Meyssene, and has issue living, Charles Hubert, *b* 1984, — Astrid, *b* 1978, — Ségolène, *b* 1979. *Residence* – 84 av J. Babtiste Clément, 92100 Boulogne sur Seine, France. —— *Comte* Emmanuel, *b* 1950: *m* 1978, Martine, da of Maurice Constans, and has issue living, Caroline, *b* 1979. *Residence* – 3 rue Renée Aspe, 3100 Toulouse, France. —— Béatrice, *b* 1936. *Residence* – 34 rue Jules Guesde, 92300 Levallois, France. —— Marie-France, *b* 1942: *m* 1968, Baron Guy de Flaujac, of 1 rue de Bretagne, 76240 Rouen, France.

Granddaughter of late Laura Tollemache, Comtesse de Lastic St Jal (ante):—
    Issue of late Comte Albéric Jean de Lastic St Jal, *b* (*posthumous*) 1866, *d* 1910: *m* 1907, Laure Bardon, who *d* 1968:—
Jacqueline Laure, *b* 1909: *m* 1930, Pierre-Alain Forveille, and has issue living, Serge Pierre Jean, *b* 1931: *m* 1961, Annick Trarieux, and has issue living, Eric *b* 1962, Gilles *b* 1972, — †Danielle Viviane, *b* 1937; *d* 1985. *Residence* – 18 rue de l'Assomption, 75016 Paris.

Grandchildren of late Sir Lyonel Felix Carteret Eugene Tollemache, 4th Bt, eldest son of late Rev Ralph William Lionel Tollemache-Tollemache, eldest son of Rev Hon Hugh Francis Tollemache, 4th son of William, Lord Huntingtower (ante):—
    Issue of Sir Humphry Thomas Tollemache, 6th Bt, CB, CBE, *b* 1897, *d* (30 March) 1990: *m* 1926, Nora Priscilla, who *d* (24 Oct) 1990, da of John Taylor, of Broomhill, Eastbourne:—
See BARONETAGE, and ante.

Grandchildren of late Lyulph Ydwallo Odin Nestor Egbert Lyonel Toedmag Hugh Erchenwyne Saxon Esa Cromwell Orma Neville Dysart Plantagenet Tollemache-Tollemache, 4th son of late Rev Ralph William Lionel Tollemache-Tollemache (ante):—
    Issue of late Lyulph Thomas Tollemache, *b* 1899, *d* 1977: *m* 1st, 1924 (*m diss* 1943), Mavis, da of late Rev Charles Tuke, of Ellerslie, NZ; 2ndly, 1946, his cousin, Phyllis Agnes Barham (Atkinson Rd, Titirangi, Auckland, NZ), da of late Maj Frederick Pitcairn Nunneley, OBE, MD:—
(By 1st *m*) Lyulph Hugh Tuke (4 Roland Hill, Glen Eden, Auckland 7, NZ), *b* 1933; *ed* at Wanganui Collegiate Sch; MSCP, London: *m* 1960, Nadja, OBE, el da of late U. Victor Benziger (*see* Ctss Dysart, colls, 1990 Edn), and has issue living, Ralph Victor Hugh Thomas, *b* 1968, — Damon Leo, *b* 1969, — Nigel Robert Bentley, *b* 1972, — Rachel Eva, *b* 1961: *m* 1980 (*m diss* 19—), Andrew Thompson, — Amanda Beatrice, *b* 1963, — Melanie Ruth, *b* 1964, — Vanessa Mavis (twin), *b* 1964, — Althea Phyllis Jessica, *b* 1967. —— Diana Rosemary, *b* 1928; *ed* NZ Univ (BA); a JP Croydon: *m* 1949, Saiyad Zarbaft Shah, of Shalimar, 24 Oakfield Rd, West Croydon, Surrey, and has had issue, †Saiyad Mubarak, *b* 1959; Bar Inner Temple 1983: *m* 1988, Cheryl, da of late Paul Scroope, of NSW, Australia, and *d* 1992, leaving issue, Kitab Paul *b* 1989, — Layla Irene Zarbaft, *b* 1949; *ed* Univ of Newcastle upon Tyne; RIBA: *m* 1969, Terry Dawson, MICE, — Shireen Haseena, *b* 1952; *ed* Manchester Univ (BA): *m* 1980, Michael Drew, of 2 Vyvyan Terrace, Clifton, Bristol, and has issue living, Laurence Finn *b* 1983, Rory Capstan *b* 1988, Jay Latimer *b* 1990.
    Issue of late Adrian Francis Tollemache, *b* 1903, *d* 1992: *m* 1938, Una Frances (Peggy) (11/59 Brighton Rd, Scarborough 6019, W Australia), da of late Lionel Edward MacKenzie, of Perth, W Australia:—
John Jeffrey (146 Calais Rd, Wembley Downs, W Australia), *b* 1941: *m* 1969, Mary Monica Kerin, of Kent, England, and has issue living, Luke Jonathan, *b* 1971. —— Peter Clive, *b* 1948: *m* 1978, Nicola Jill Boyd, of Auckland, NZ, and has issue living, Jonathan Robert, *b* 1980, — Christina Kate, *b* 1983. —— Joan, *b* 1944; BEd: *m* 1st, 1966 (*m diss* 1973), Michael Harvey Blewitt; 2ndly, 1977, Ivan Pummer, BA (Hons), DipEd, of 24 Elphin St, Floreat, W Australia 6014, and has issue living (by 1st *m*), Amanda Jacqueline (9 Bramble Terr, Redhill, Qld 4059), *b* 1966; BA.
    Issue of late Saxon George Tollemache, *b* 1904, *d* 1974: *m* 1933, Ruth Bell, who *d* 1975, da of late Frederick George Wayne, of Parawai, Thames, NZ:—
John Saxon Manners (Dysart Lane, Kumeu, NZ), *b* 1943: *m* 1971, Catherine Mary, da of Seymour Jack, and has issue living, Mark Seymour Manners, *b* 1975. —— Elizabeth Mary, *b* 1936: *m* 1966, Maurice John Arthur Fuller, MSc, of 113 Sunrise Av, Mairangi Bay, Auckland, NZ, and has issue living, Michael Arthur, *b* 1968, — Katherine Ruth, *b* 1969, — Louisa Elizabeth, *b* 1974. —— Suzannah Jane, *b* 1940: *m* 1962, John Brian Miller, PhD, ME, of 11 Chaucer Court, Ewelme, Oxford, and has issue living, Hugh Benjamin Tollemache, *b* 1965, — Jane Elizabeth, *b* 1963.
    Issue of late Lyonel Dysart Tollemache, *b* 1908, *d* 1990: *m* 1942, Rita Janet Isabel Rowley, of Auckland, NZ:—
Roland Lionel, *b* 1948: *m* 1970, Sarah Norris, of Auckland, NZ, and has issue living, Peter Michael Dysart, *b* 1973, — Christopher Edwin, *b* 1976. —— Pamela Rita (10 Bryant Place, St Heliers Bay, Auckland, NZ), *b* 1952: *m* 1st, 1976 (*m diss* 1988), Alan John Pickering, LLB; 2ndly, 1994, Dennis Ian Crisp, and has issue living (by 1st *m*), Vanessa Jasmine, *b* 1981.
    Issue of late Winifred Dora Tollemache, *b* 1898, *d* 1981: *m* 1926, Laurence Galwey Walker:—
See 1990 Edn.
    Issue of late Celia Kathrine Mabel Tollemache, *b* 1901, *d* 1990: *m* 1935, Charles Tennant Smith, who *d* 1971:—
See 1990 Edn.

Grandchildren of late Rev Ralph William Lionel Tollemache-Tollemache (ante):—
    Issue of late Lyulph Ydwallo Odin Nestor Egbert Lyonel Toedmag Hugh Erchenwyne Saxon Esa Cromwell Orma Nevill Dysart Plantagenet Tollemache-Tollemache *b* 1876, *d* 1961: *m* 1st, 1897, Winifred Frances, who *d* 1955, da of late Thomas Goldsborough Anderson, of Tauranga, New Zealand; 2ndly, 1957, Kathleen, who *d* 1981, da of Michael Hinge, of Northolt, Middlesex, and widow of Robert William Alexander Geoffrey Gordon, of Huia, New Zealand:—
(By 1st *m*), Archibald Douglas (104 Landscape Rd, Mt Eden, Auckland, NZ), *b* 1910: *m* 1935, Edna, da of late F. C. Willis, of Napier, NZ, and has issue living, Janet Winifred, *b* 1936: *m* 1957, William Winston Lewins, of 75 Belfast St, Hillsborough, Auckland, NZ, and has issue living, Robyn Ann *b* 1963, Denise Gay, *b* 1965, — Yvonne Dorothy, *b* 1938: *m* 1961, John Walker Robinson, c/o 75 Belfast St, Hillsborough, Auckland, NZ, and has issue living, Tania Anne *b* 1962: *m* 1st, 1982, Steven James Cleary who *d* 1989; 2ndly, 1990, Scott Donald Harrison, of 31 Tole St, Ponsonby, Auckland (and has issue living (by 1st *m*), Natalie Yvonne *b* 1985, Rachael Mary *b* (twin) 1985, (by 2nd *m*) Curtis Scott *b* 1991) Vicki Jan *b* 1964: *m* 1986, Jonathan Charles Poole, of 17 Wingrove Av, Epping 2121, Sydney, NSW, Australia, Angela Patricia *b* 1967: *m* 1994, Brett Keith Wilson, of Auckland. —— Vivian Rosamund, *b* 1913: *m* 1934, Rev Harold Graham Titterton, of 15 Te Watu St, Maungatapu, Tauranga, NZ, and has issue living, Graham Richard (Gow's Rd, Opotiki, NZ) *b* 1947: *m* 1974, Gaylene, da of James Cooper, of Kati Kati, NZ, and has issue living, Richard Graham *b* 1979, Sandy James *b* 1985, Gretchen Richa *b* 1975, — Jennifer Graham, *b* 1937: *m* 1964, John Yeeles, of 820 Idylwood Drive SW, Issaquah, Wash, 98027, USA, and has issue living, Christopher John *b* 1964, Peter Graham *b* 1967, Andrew Scott *b* 1971. —— Ruth Lorraine *b* 1915: *m* 1944, Ivan Edward Salter Bartlett, and has issue living, Timothy John (Hahei, NZ), *b* 1951; has issue (by Maxine Kauali), Sarah *b* 1979, Anna *b* 1981, — Jacqueline Jane, *b* 1949: *m* 1971, John Michael Cochrane Piper, of 50 Hamilton Rd, Herne Bay, Auckland, NZ, and has issue living, Michael David *b* 1980, Emma *b* 1983.

Grandchildren of late Rev Ralph William Lionel Tollemache-Tollemache (ante):—
    Issue of late Capt Leo (Quintus Tollemache-Tollemache) de Orellana (Plantagenet) Tollemache, *b* 1879, *ka* 1914 (names in brackets were renounced by deed poll 1908): *m* 1906, Jessie Winifred, who *d* 1967, da of late Charles Bryant, of Highbury New Park, N:—
Rev Robert, TD, *b* 1914; *ed* St Edmund's Coll, Ware, Herts; is in Holy Orders of Church of Rome, and Parish Priest of St Augustine's Hoddesdon; 1939-45 War in Iceland, and as Senior Catholic Chap in Scotland. *Residence* – 18 Market Lane, Linton, Cambridge CB1 6HU. —— †Eva, *b* 1908: *m* 1935, U. Victor Benziger, who *d* 1962, and *d* 1992, leaving issue (*see* 1990 Edn).

Grandchildren of late Capt Leonè Sextus Denys Oswolf Fraudati Filius Tollemache-Tollemache de Orellana Plantagenet Tollemache, Leicestershire Regt, 6th son of late Rev Ralph William Lionel Tollemache-Tollemache (ante):—

Issue of late Denys Herbert George Tollemache, b 1915, d 1991: m 1st, 1939 (m diss 1948), Eileen Frances Mary, who d 1976, da of late Owen Phelim O'Conor, The O'Conor Don; 2ndly, 1972, Elizabeth Sheila (76 The Mint, Rye, Sussex), da of Cecil Hughes:—

(By 1st m) Peter Denys, b 1940. —— Stephen Patrick, b 1946. —— Susan Frances (Lough Urlaur, 13 Willbrook Grove, Rathfarnham, Dublin 14), b 1939. —— Linda Mary, b 1945: m 1975, William Mostyn Llewellyn, of 32 Cambridge Rd, Bexhill-on-Sea, E Sussex, and has issue living, Peter Mostyn Tollemache, b 1982, — Ursula Sarah Tollemache, b 1978.

Grandchildren of late Rev Ralph William Lionel Tollemache-Tollemache (ante):—

Issue of late Maj Lyonulph Cospatrick Bruce Berkeley Jermyn Tullibardine Petersham de Orellaña Dysart Plantagenet Tollemache-Tollemache, b 1892, d 1966: m 1916, Lilian May, who d 1969, da of late Ernest T. W. Pearse, Govt Agent, Kamloops, BC, Canada:—

Miles de Orellaña, b 1918; Lt RNVR: m 1st, 1942, Diana Muriel, da of late Clarence Charles Hatry, publisher; 2ndly, 1944, Margaret E. K., el da of late Henry Williams, of Llwyn Gern, Pontardulais; 3rdly, 1949, Joan Doreen, da of late G. Saxon, Civil Ser, and has issue living, (by 3rd m) Timothy Miles Saxon, b 1950, — Bruce Robert Saxon, b 1951, — Alistair Murray Saxon, b 1953, — Iain Stuart William Saxon (87 Oxford Rd, Cumnor, Oxford OX2 9PD), b 1960; BA: m 1991, Janet Ruth Eva, only da of late Ivor Michael Allen, of Oxford, and has issue living, Nicholas James de Orellaña b 1992, — Elspeth Mary Joan, b 1956: m 1983, Mark Black.

Issue of late Lyona Decima Veronica Esyth Undine Cyssa Hylda Rowena Viola Adele Thyra Ursula Ysabel Blanche Lelias Dysart Plantagenet Tollemache, b 1878, d 1962: m 1909, Major Charles Cecil Stone, late Berks Yeo, who d 1951:—

Lyonel Francis Tollemache STONE (5700 St Charles Av, New Orleans, La 70115, USA. Club – Brooks's), b 1909; Capt late Coldm Gds: m 1st, 1943 (m diss 1951), Mathilde, da of late G. Henry A. Thomas of New Orleans, USA; 2ndly, 1952 (m diss 1966), Marie Lod (MONTELEONE), da of late Frank Marion Attaway, of New Orleans, USA; 3rdly, 1972, Mrs Christiane Claire McRoberts, da of late Petrus Marthoud, of Lyons, France and has issue living (by 1st m), Michael Tollemache (1 Cherokee Lane, Covington, LA, USA), b 1949: m 19—, — , and has issue living, Barton McIntyre b 1975, Andrew Deslonde b (twin) 1975, Michael Tollemache b 1981, — Mathilde Thomas, b 1945: m 1967, Prieur James Leary, of 18 Audubon Place, New Orleans, La, USA, 70118, and has issue living, Prieur James b 1968, Ashley Baldwin b 1973, Mathilde Deslonde b 1971.

Issue of late Lyonella Fredegunda Cuthberga Ethelswytha Ideth Ysabel Grace Monica de Orellana Plantagenet Tollemache-Tollemache, b 1882, d 1952: m 1906, Major Frederick Pitcairn Nunneley, OBE, MD (Oxon), who d 1922, formerly Army Med Ser:—

Lyonella Joan Tollemache, b 1907: m 1935, Ernest Robin Vladimir Kindersley, who d 1986, of Old Cottage Mayfield, Sussex, and has issue living, Patricia Dora Mary (Pond Cottage, Wallcrouch, Wadhurst, E Sussex TN5 7JN), b 1935: m 1966, John Pearman Spencer-Wood, who d 1982, and has issue living, Alexandra Carolina b 1967: m 1988, Richard Neeves, of The Cottage, Lower Platts, Flimwell Rd, Ticehurst, E Sussex TN5 7BZ (and has issue living, Thomas Joshua b 1992, Laura Bryony b 1987, Francesca Sophie b 1991), Sophie Maria b 1970. —— Phyllis Agnes Barham, b 1909: m 1946, as his 2nd wife, her cousin, Lyulph Thomas Tollemache, who d 1977 (ante).

Issue of late Lyonetta Edith Regina Valentine Myra Polwarth Avelina Philippa Violantha de Orellana Plantagenet Tollemache, b 1887, d 1951: m 1909, Adolph Paul Oppé, CB, who d 1957:—

Armide Lyonesse Tollemache (Bartholomews, Corfe Castle, Wareham, Dorset), b 1910.

Grandchildren of late Lyonetta Edith Regina Valentine Myra Polwarth Avelina Philippa Violantha de Orellana Plantagenet Tollemache (Mrs Oppé) (ante):—

Issue of late Maj Denys Lyonel Tollemache Oppé, MBE, b 1913, d 1992: m 1949, Jean Mary (Manor Farm, Newnham, Basingstoke), da of late Charles Struthers White Ogilvie, of Delvine, Murthly, Perthshire:—

John Simon Tollemache OPPÉ, b 1951; ed Ampleforth. —— Lucy Valentine Mary, b 1950. —— Charlotte Mary Clare, b 1954. —— Mary Josephine, b 1956: m 1991, Alexander D. D. Calf, of Chiswick, W4.

Granddaughter of late Hugh Ernest Tollemache, el son of late Rev Ernest Celestine Tollemache, 3rd son of late Rev Hon Hugh Francis Tollemache, brother of 8th Earl:—

Issue of late Maj John Ernest Tollemache, b 1898, d 1969: m 1921, Violet Edith Gertrude, who d 1985, da of late W. Rae Sands:—

Lyona Violet Anne Tollemache, b 1929: m 1950, Lt-Cdr Richard Milford Power Carne, RN, of Tresahor Vean, Constantine, Cornwall and Nairobi, Kenya, and has issue living, William Lyonel Power, b 1957, — Caroline Julia Tollemache, b 1951: m 1970 (m diss 1973), D. A. Godley, — Karenza Lyona Tollemache, b 1953: m 1973, Gordon Taylor (c/o PO Box 2374, Randburg 2125, S Africa).

Grandchildren of late Henry Gilbert Tollemache, 2nd son of late Rev Ernest Celestine Tollemache (ante):—

Issue of late Com Douglas Hugh Tollemache, RN, b 1898, d on active service 1941: m 1931, Alys Kynaston (who d 1992, having m 2ndly, 1943, Com Richard Tolson, DSC, RN, who d 1992), da of late Rev John Henry Bebbington, R of Slinfold, Sussex, and Canon of Chichester:—

Ian Henry Douglas (265 King's Rd, SW3), b 1936; ed Lancing: m 1st, 1973 (m diss 19—), Priscilla A. Coker; 2ndly, 1989, Joanna Wilson. —— (Sheila) Rosemary Edith, b 1939: m 1963, T. Barry Nightingale, FCA, of 5 Spinney View, Great Glen, Leics LE8 0EP, and has issue living, Lucy Frances, b 1964, — Kate Elizabeth, b 1965, — Anna Ruth, b 1967.

Issue of late Dorothy Clare Tollemache, b 1895, d 1949: m 1921, Arthur Edward Durling:—

John Alfred Osborne DURLING (5 Stapylton St, Holder, Canberra, ACT, Aust), b 1929: m 1960, Enid Joan Coling, and has issue living, Paul Edward Porttor b 1962, — Richard John, b 1965, — Julian Clare, b 1969.

Granddaughters of late Dorothy Clare Tollemache (Mrs Durling) (ante):—

Issue of late Pauline Mary Tollemache Durling, b 1924, d 1972: m 1954, John Ingham Brooke, of Brewery House, Southstoke, Bath (see Hewett, Bt):—

Penelope Anne (5 The Cliff, Puddingmoor, Beccles, Suffolk), b 1955. —— Susan Miranda, b 1957: 1986, Alexander Marek Andrew Jan Gregor, of 3 Fairfield Rd, Bristol BS6 5JN, and has issue living, Andrzej Maximilian, b 1986.

Grandson of late Gwendoline Anna Tollemache (Mrs Gilbert Henderson Philips), only da of late Rev Ernest Celestine Tollemache (ante):—

Issue of late Constance Gwendoline Joyce, b 1908, d 1987: m 1934, Rev John William Harper Faulkner, who d 1982:—

Alan Henderson FAULKNER, b 1938: m 1964, Anita Diane, da of Harwood Arthur Bence, of Bedford, and has issue living, Lynn Deborah, b 1966, — Tracey Jane, b 1968. Residence – 43 Oaks Drive, Colchester, Essex CO3 3PS.

Grandson of late Capt Anastasius Eugene Tollemache son of late Rev Hon Hugh Francis Tollemache (ante):—

Issue of late Louisa Ethelgiva Rowena, b 1878, d 1962: m 1910, as his 2nd wife, Lieut-Col Walter Francis Courtenay Chicheley Plowden, who d 1918:—

Cursham Chicheley PLOWDEN, *b* 1911; Capt (ret): *m* 1937, Joan Brown, and has issue living, Robert Henry Bowland Chicheley, *b* 1947. *Residence* – The Sun House, Kentsford Rd, Grand-over-Sands, Cumbria.

> Grandchildren of late Louisa Harrington Tollemache, *b* 1833 (who *d* 1928, having *m* 1862, Col Rt Hon Thomas Edward Taylor, MP, who *d* 1883), 2nd da of late Rev Hon Hugh Francis Tollemache (ante):—

See M Headfort, colls.

> Descendants of late Ada Maria Katherine Tollemache, *b* 1848 (who *d* 1928, having *m* 1868, the 4th Baron Sudeley), younger da of late Hon Frederick James Tollemache, MP, 5th son of William, Lord Huntingtower (ante):—

See B Sudeley.

> Descendants of late Louisa Maria Burke, who *d* 1863 (having *m* 1849, Rev John Montagu Mason), el da of late Hon Louisa Grace Tollemache (who *d* 1830, having *m* 1816, Sir Joseph Burke, 11th Bt (ext)), el da of William, Lord Huntingtower (ante).

> Descendants of late Hon Lady Catherine Camilla Tollemache, *b* 1792, (who *d* 1863, having *m* 1816, Sir George Sinclair, 2nd Bt), 2nd dau of William, Lord Huntingtower (ante).

See V Thurso.

> Descendants, if any, of Algernon Montriou Tollemache (*b* 1884), Lieut Lancashire Hussars Yeo (ret 1919), only son of late Maj Algernon Seymour Tollemache, only son of William Tollemache, 5th son of Hon Charles Tollemache, 3rd son of Louisa, Countess of Dysart (in her own right).

> Granddaughters of late Matilda Jane Tollemache (da of William Tollemache (ante)), who *d* 1918, having *m* 1873, Capt Marcus Augustus Stanley Hare, RN, who *d* 1878:—

Issue of late Ethel Lucy Hare, *b* 1875, *d* 1940: *m* 1901, Sir Herbert Charles Perrott, 6th Bt, CH, CB, who *d* 1922, when the title became ext:—

See Perrott, Bt (ext).

> Descendants of late Lady Catherine Sophia Tollemache, *b* 1769, who *d* 1825 (having *m* 1793, Sir Gilbert Heathcote, 4th Bt), el da of Louisa (in her own right), Countess of Dysart (ante):—

See Heathcote, Bt (of London).

> Descendants of late John Jervis Tollemache, MP (el son of late Adm John Richard Delap Tollemache, who assumed by Roy Licence in 1821 that surname and Arms in lieu of Halliday, el son of late Lady Jane Halliday, youngest da and co-heir of 4th Earl) who was *cr Baron Tollemache* 1876 (see that title, and 1968 and earlier edns).

PREDECESSORS – **(1)** WILLIAM Murray, son of Rev William Murray, Min of Dysart co Fife (grandson of Anthony Murray, of Dollerie, Perthshire, whose elder brother Patrick was ancester of the Murray baronets of Ochtertyre); MP for Fowrey 1626, and for E Looe 1628-9; *cr* by patent *Lord Huntingtower* and *Earl of Dysart* (peerage of Scotland) 1643: *m* 16—, Catherine, da of Col Norman Bruce, of Clackmannan; *d* 1654; *s* by his el da **(2)** ELIZABETH, *Countess of Dysart*, 16—; who in 1670 resigned the peerage and received a new grant thereof by patent with precedency of her father, and with remainder to her heirs of the body, failing which to her heirs whatsoever: *m* 1st, 1647, Sir Lionel Tollemache, 3rd Bt (*cr* 1611), who *d* 1669; 2ndly, 1672, John Maitland, 1st Duke of Lauderdale, by whom she did not have issue; the Duchess *d* 1698; *s* by her el son **(3)** LIONEL, 3rd Earl *b* 1648; *s* his father as 4th Bt in 1669; MP for Orford 1678-85 and for Suffolk 1698-1700; declined an English barony upon accession of Queen Anne: *m* 1680, Grace, who *d* 1740, da of Sir Thomas Wilbraham, 3rd Bt; *d* 1727; *s* by his grandson **(4)** LIONEL, KT, 4th Earl (only son of Lionel, Lord Huntingtower), *b* 1708: *m* 1729, Hon Grace Carteret, who *d* 1755, da of 2nd Earl Granville; *d* 1770; *s* by his son **(5)** LIONEL, 5th Earl, *b* 1734: *m* 1st, 1760, Charlotte, who *d* 1789, natural da of Hon Sir Edward Walpole, KB; 2ndly 1791, Magdalene, who *d* 1823, da of David Lewis, of Malvern Hall, Warwickshire; *dsp* 1799; *s* by his brother **(6)** WILLIAM, 6th Earl, *b* 1739: *m* 1773, Anna Maria, who *d* 1804, da of David Lewis (ante); *d* 1821, when the Baronetcy (*cr* 1611) became ext; *s* in Earldom and Lordship by his sister **(7)** LOUISA; *b* 1745; assumed by Roy licence 1821 (the surname and Arms of Talmash in lieu of Manners): *m* 1765, John Manners, MP, of Grantham Grange, co Lincoln, who *d* 1792: *d* 1840; *s* by her grandson **(8)** LIONEL WILLIAM JOHN, 8th Earl (el son of William, Lord Huntingtower, who in 1793 was *cr* a Baronet, and in 1821 assumed by Roy licence the surname and Arms of Talmash only), *b* 1794; *s* by his father's Baronetcy 1833: *m* 1819, Maria Elizabeth, who *d* 1852, da of Sweeney Toone, of Keston Lodge, Kent: *d* 1878: *s* by his grandson **(9)** WILLIAM JOHN MANNERS, 9th Earl (only son of William Lionel Felix, Lord Huntingtower), *b* 1859: *m* 1885, Cecilia Florence, who *d* 1917, da of late George Onslow Newton, of Croxton Park, St Neots; *d* 1935; *s* in the Baronetcy by his kinsman, Lyonel Felix Carteret Eugene Tollemache, and in the Earldom and Lordship by his niece **(10)** WENEFRYDE AGATHA Greaves (da of late Charles Norman Lindsay Tollemache Scott, by Lady Agnes Mary Manners, who *d* 1912, da of William Lionel Felix, Lord Huntingtower), Countess of Dysart, *b* 1889: *m* 1913, Maj Owain Edward Whitehead Greaves, DL, RHG Machine Gun Regt, who *d* 1941, *d* 1975, *s* by her el da **(11)** ROSAMUND AGNES, Countess of Dysart, and present peeress; also Lady Huntingtower.

EATWELL, BARON (Eatwell) (Life Baron 1992)

JOHN LEONARD EATWELL, son of Harold Jack Eatwell, of Swindon, Wilts; *b* 2 Feb 1945; *ed* Headlands Gram Sch, Swindon, Queens' Coll, Camb (BA, MA), and Harvard Univ (AM, PhD), Teaching Fellow Harvard Univ 1968-69; Research Fellow Queens' Coll, Camb 1969-70, since when Fellow and Dir of Studies in Economics, Trin Coll, Camb; Assist Lecturer in Economics Camb Univ 1975-77, since when Lecturer; Visiting Prof of Economics, New Sch for Social Research, NY since 1980, and Economics Advisor to Rt Hon Neil Kinnock 1985-92; Chm Crusaid since 1993; Member Cambridge Constituency Labour Party, Royal Economics Soc, and American Economics Assocn; Economist; *cr Baron Eatwell*, of Stratton St Margaret, co Wilts (Life Baron) 1992: *m* 1970, Hélène, da of Georges Seppain, of Marly-le-Roi, France, and has issue. *Residence* – Trinity College, Cambridge CB2 1TQ.

SONS LIVING

Hon Nikolai, *b* 1971.
Hon Vladimir, *b* 1973.

DAUGHTER LIVING

Hon Tatyana, *b* 1978.

EBBISHAM, BARONY OF (Blades) (Extinct 1991)

DAUGHTERS LIVING OF SECOND BARON

Hon Susan Mary, *b* 1951: *m* 1980, Peter D. Stevenson, of The White House, Whitehouse Loan, Edinburgh EH9 2EY, son of late Alexander Stevenson, of Westfield House, W Calder, Midlothian, and has issue living, George Dennistoun, *b* 1987, — Mary Flavia, *b* 1984.
Hon Emma Caroline, *b* 1954: *m* 1977, Franklin Brooke-Hitching, of Osmington House, Kintbury, Newbury, Berks, son of Desmond Brooke-Hitching, of 12 Porchester Terrace, W2 and has issue living, Edward Robert, *b* 1982, — Matthew Thomas, *b* 1985, — William Franklin, *b* 1987, — Georgia Emma, *b* 1992.
Hon Catherine Anne, *b* 1955: *m* 1981, Charles J. Spencer, of Search Farm, Stourton, Warminster, Wilts, son of Kenneth Spencer, of St Martin's Farm, Zeals, Wilts, and has issue living, Thomas James, *b* 1985, — Henry Charles Blades, *b* 1990, — Flora Antonia Blades, *b* 1987.

DAUGHTERS LIVING OF FIRST BARON

Hon Margaret Agnes, *b* 1908: *m* 1933, Brig Richard John Penfold Wyatt, MC, TD, DL, JP, late Roy Sussex Regt (TA), who *d* 1954, and has issue living, Hugh Rowland (Cissbury, Findon, W Sussex), *b* 1933; *ed* Winchester: *m* 1959, Jane Ann Elizabeth, da of late Lt-Col Robert Laurence Eden, OBE, TD, of Ashley Close, St Saviour, Jersey, and has issue living, Hugh Geoffrey Robert *b* 1961, Anne Elizabeth *b* 1963, Susan Jane *b* 1965, — John Geoffrey (Canbury School, Kingston Hill, Kingston-on-Thames, Surrey), *b* 1937; *ed* Winchester, and at Ch Ch, Oxford. *Residence* – Hillbarn Cottage, Findon, nr Worthing, Sussex.
Hon (Helen) Elizabeth (*Hon Lady Russell*) (twin), *b* 1908: *m* 1939, Adm Hon Sir Guy Herbrand Edward Russell, GBE, KCB, DSO, who *d* 1977 (*see* B Ampthill). *Residence* – Flat 8, 89 Onslow Sq, SW7 3LT.
Hon Janet Mary, *b* 1916: *m* 1952, Rear-Adm John Edwin Home McBeath, CB, DSO, DSC, DL, who *d* 1982, and has issue living, John Rowland Blades, *b* 1954, — Rosemary Diana Jane, *b* 1957. *Residence* – Woodbury, 9 Annandale Drive, Lower Bourne, Farnham, Surrey GU10 3JD.

WIDOW LIVING OF SECOND BARON

FLAVIA MARY (*Baroness Ebbisham*), yst da of late Charles Francis Meade (*see* E Clanwilliam, colls): *m* 1949, the 2nd Baron Ebbisham, TD, who *d* 1991. *Residence* – St Ann's, Church St, Mere, Wilts BA12 6DS.

EBURY, BARON (Grosvenor) (Baron UK 1857)

VIRTUS · NON · STEMMA

Virtue, not ancestry

FRANCIS EGERTON GROSVENOR, 6th Baron; *b* 8 Feb 1934; *s* 1957; *ed* Eton; is *hp* to Earldom of Wilton: *m* 1st, 1957 (*m diss* 1962), Gillian Elfrida (Elfin), da of Martin Soames (*see* E Perth, colls, 1980 Edn); 2ndly, 1963 (*m diss* 1973), Kyra, da of late L. L. Aslin; 3rdly, 1974, Suzanne Jean, da of Graham Suckling, of Tai Tapu, NZ, and has issue by 1st and 3rd wives.

Arms – Azure, a garb or, a mullet for difference. Crest – A talbot statant or. Supporters – On either side a talbot reguardant or, collared azure, charged on the shoulder with a mullet of the second.
Residence – 8B Branksome Tower, 3 Tregunter Path, Hong Kong. *Clubs* – Melbourne, and Melbourne Savage.

SON LIVING (*by 1st wife*)

Hon JULIAN FRANCIS MARTIN, *b* 8 June 1959; *ed* Gordonstoun: *m* 1987, Danielle, 6th da of Theo Rossi, of Sydney, Australia. *Residence* – 25/16 Leichharot St, Glebe Point, Sydney 2037, NSW.

DAUGHTER LIVING (*by 3rd wife*)

Hon Georgina Lucy, *b* 1973.

HALF-BROTHERS LIVING

Hon William Wellesley, *b* 1942; *ed* Eton, and Trin Coll, Oxford: *m* 1966, Ellen da of late Dr Gunter Seeliger, of Harlaching, Munich, and has issue living, Alexander Egerton, *b* 1968, — Petra Antonia Primrose, *b* 1970. *Residence* – Sheep Lane House, Potsgrove, Woburn, Beds.
Hon Richard Alexander, *b* 1946; *ed* Milton Abbey, and Univs of Perugia, Montpelier, Lyons, Tours and Munich: *m* 1st, 1970 (*m diss* 1986), Gabriella, da of Dr Xavier Speckert; 2ndly, 1989, Frances Ann, da of David Samuel Williams, of Newport, Gwent, and has issue living (by 1st *m*), Bendor Robert Gerard, *b* 1977, — (by 2nd *m*) Letisah Emma, *b* 1989.

HALF-SISTERS LIVING

Hon (Laura Georgina) Kiloran (twin), *b* 1946; resumed the surname of Grosvenor by deed poll 1983: *m* 1st, 1969 (*m diss* 1979), G. R. Mark Cross; 2ndly, 1993, Brian Murrell. *Residence* – 30 Bedford St, Woburn, Beds MK17 9QB.
Hon Linda Denise, *b* 1948: *m* 1973, Christopher D. Vane Percy, and has issue living, Maximilian Egerton, *b* 1979, — Grace Dorothy Denise, *b* 1981, — Tryce Mary Susanne, *b* 1991. *Residence* – Island Hall, Godmanchester, Cambs.

UNCLE LIVING (*Son of 4th Baron*)

Hon Hugh Richard, *b* 1919; *ed* Radley Coll, and RMA Sandhurst; European War 1939-45 as Capt King's Shropshire LL: *m* 1st, 1939 (*m diss* 1952), Margaret, da of James L. Jacobs, of Neilsen, Pednolver Terr, St Ives, Cornwall; 2ndly, 1955, Victoria, only da of H. Wright, of Newport, Salop, and has issue living (by 1st *m*) Margaret Elizabeth, *b* 1947, — (by 2nd *m*) William Peter Wellesley, *b* 1959, — Rebecca Victoria, *b* 1975. *Residence* – River Ridge, Courtlands Park, Carmarthen.

AUNT LIVING (*Daughter of 4th Baron*)

Hon Maud Elizabeth, *b* 1909: *m* 1st, 1931 (*m diss* 1942), 2nd Viscount Harcourt, who *d* 1978; 2ndly, 1942, Lieut-Col Edward O'Shaughnessy, and has issue living, (by 1st *m*) (*see* V Harcourt), — (by 2nd *m*) Elizabeth Mary, *b* 1947, — Caroline Margaret (twin), *b* 1947. *Residence* – Bethavon, Duke St, Northam 6401, Western Australia.

WIDOW LIVING OF SON OF FIFTH BARON

Caroline, only da of late Ronald Harry Higham (*see* V Hampden): *m* 1959, Hon (Robert) Victor Grosvenor, who *d* 1993, and has issue (see colls infra). *Residence* – Bennets, Grafton, Oxon OX18 2RY.

WIDOW LIVING OF FIFTH BARON

SHEILA WINIFRED (ANKER) (*Dowager Baroness Ebury*), yr da of Arthur Edward Dashfield, of Oxford: *m* 1954, as his 3rd wife, the 5th Baron, who *d* 1957. *Residence* – 37 Linkside Av, Oxford OX2 8JE.

COLLATERAL BRANCH LIVING

Issue of late Hon (Robert) Victor Grosvenor, 2nd son (by 1st *m*) of 5th Baron, *b* 1936, *d* 1993: *m* 1959, Caroline (ante), only da of late Ronald Harry Higham (*see* V Hampden):—
Rachel Egerton, *b* 1963: *m* 1986, Tobias S. Buckler, son of Humphrey Buckler, of Bledington, Oxon, and has issue living, Peregrine Humphrey, *b* 1988, — Valentine Robert, *b* 1993, — Kiloran Dorothea Anne, *b* 1989. *Residence* – Llwyn-on, Llanthony, Monmouthshire NP7 7NW. ——— Virginia, *b* 1965: *m* 1988, Mark Quinton Graham, son of late John Graham, of Newcastle-upon-Tyne, and has issue living, Emily Charlotte, *b* 1990. *Residence* – 12 Macfarlane Rd, Bearsden, Glasgow G61.

PREDECESSORS – (1) *Rt Hon* ROBERT Grosvenor, 3rd son of 1st Marquess of Westminster, *b* 1801; MP for Shaftesbury 1822-6, for Chester 1826-47, and for Middlesex (*L*) 1847-57; Comptroller of HM's Household 1830-34, Treasurer thereof 1846-7, and Groom of the Stole to the Prince Consort; was *cr Baron Ebury* (peerage of United Kingdom) 1857: *m* 1831, Hon Charlotte Arbuthnott Wellesley, who *d* 1891, sister of 1st Earl Cowley; *d* 1893; *s* by his el son (2) ROBERT WELLESLEY, 2nd Baron, *b* 1834; Capt 1st Life Guards; MP for Westminster (*L*) 1865-74: *m* 1867, Hon Emilie Beaujolois White, who *d* 1923, da of 1st Baron Annaly; *d* 1918; *s* by his el son (3) ROBERT VICTOR, 3rd Baron, *b* 1868: *m* 1903, Florence, who *d* 1927, da of late Edward M. Padelford, of Savannah, USA; *d* 1921; *s* by his brother (4) FRANCIS EGERTON, DSO, MC, 4th Baron, *b* 1883; Chm Army and Navy Co-operative So, a Director of Union Bank of Australia, and of Roy Exchange Assurance Co (West End Branch), and Major Canadian Forces (Reserve of Officers); European War 1914-18 (wounded, despatches four times, MC with Bar, DSO with Bar, French Croix de Guerre with Palm): *m* 1902, Mary Adela, who *d* 1960, da of late G. Glasson: *d*

1932; *s* by his son **(5)** ROBERT EGERTON, DSO, 5th Baron; *b* 1914; Major Berkshire Yeo; was a Lord of Waiting to HM 1939-40: *m* 1st, 1933 (*m diss* 1941), Anne, who *d* 1982, da of late Major Herbert Walter Acland-Troyte, MC (*see* Acland, Bt, *cr* 1678, colls); 2ndly, 1941 (*m diss* 1954), Hon Denise Margaret Yarde-Buller, da of 3rd Baron Churston; 3rdly, 1954, Mrs Sheila Winifred (ANKER), yr da of Arthur Edward Dashfield, of Oxford; *d* 1957; *s* by his el son **(6)** FRANCIS EGERTON, 6th Baron and present peer.

ECCLES, VISCOUNT (Eccles) (Viscount UK 1964)

DAVID MCADAM ECCLES, CH, KCVO, PC, 1st Viscount, son of late Lt-Col W.C. McAdam Eccles, FRCS; *b* 18 Sept 1904; *ed* Winchester, and at New Coll, Oxford; Hon FRIBA; a Trustee of British Museum 1963-70 (Chm of Trustees 1968-70), Chm Anglo-Hellenic League 1967-70; in Min of Economic Warfare 1939-40; Economic Adviser to British Ambassadors at Lisbon and Madrid 1940-42; in Min of Production 1942-3; Min of Works 1951, Min of Education 1954, Pres of Board of Trade 1957, and again Min of Education 1959-62; MP for Chippenham Div of Wilts (*C*) 1943-62; Paymaster Gen and Min for The Arts 1970-73, since when Chm of British Library Board, and Pres of World Craft Council; *cr* PC 1951, KCVO 1953, *Baron Eccles*, of Chute, co Wilts (peerage of UK) 1962, and *Viscount Eccles*, of Chute, co Wilts (peerage of UK) 1964, CH 1984: *m* 1st, 1928, Hon Sybil Frances Dawson, who *d* 1977, da of 1st Viscount Dawson of Penn; 2ndly, 1984, Mary, widow of Donald Hyde, of Four Oaks Farm, 350 Burnt Mill Rd, Somerville, New Jersey, USA, and has issue by 1st *m*.

Arms – Chevronny argent and sable per pale counterchanged two torches erect or enflamed proper. **Crest** – A three masted ship sails furled pennons and flags flying or, between two wings addorsed sable. **Supporters** – On either side a wolf sable armed and langued gules gorged with a plain collar attached thereto a chain reflexed over the back and resting the interior hind paw on a portcullis chained or. *Residences* – Dean Farm, Upper Chute, Wilts; 6 Barton St, SW1. *Clubs* – Brooks's, Roxburghe, Grolier, Knickerbocker (New York).

SONS LIVING *(By 1st marriage)*

Hon JOHN DAWSON, CBE, *b* 20 April 1931; *ed* Winchester, and at Magdalen Coll, Oxford; CBE (Civil) 1985: *m* 1955, Diana Catherine (*Baroness Eccles of Moulton*), da of late Raymond Sturge, of Lords Mead, Ashmore, Salisbury, and has issue (*see* Bs Eccles of Moulton). *Residences* – Moulton Hall, Moulton, Richmond, Yorks; 6 Barton St, SW1.

Hon Simon Dawson, *b* 1934; *ed* Repton: *m* 1961 (*m diss* 1986), Sheelin, da of late Henry E. Ryan, of Long Meadow, Goring on Thames, Oxon, and has issue living, Anthony James, *b* 1967, — Annabelle Charlotte, *b* 1964: *m* 1988, Leo Zinovieff, and has issue (*see* D Northumberland, colls). *Residence* – 27 Chestnut St, Boston, Mass 02108, USA.

DAUGHTER LIVING *(By 1st marriage)*

Hon (Selina) Polly Dawson (*Polly, Marchioness of Lansdowne*), *b* 1937; *ed* Sherborne Sch for Girls and London Univ: *m* 1st, 1962 (*m diss* 1968), Robin Andrew Duthac Carnegie, late Capt Queen's Dragoon Gds; 2ndly, 1969 (*m diss* 1978), 8th Marquess of Lansdowne, and has issue living (by 1st *m*) Andrew James Duthac, *b* 1963. *Residence* – 29 Maunsel St, SW1.

ECCLES OF MOULTON, BARONESS (Eccles) (Life Baroness 1990)

DIANA CATHERINE ECCLES, 2nd da of late Raymond Wilson Sturge, of Lords Mead, Ashmore, Salisbury, Wilts; *b* 4 Oct 1933; *ed* St James's Sch, W Malvern, and Open Univ (BA), Chm Ealing, Hammersmith & Hounslow Health Authority: *m* 1955, Hon John Dawson Eccles, CBE, son of 1st Viscount Eccles, CH, KCVO, PC, and has issue.
Residences – Moulton Hall, Moulton, Richmond, Yorks; 6 Barton St, SW1.

SON LIVING

Hon William David, *b* 1960; *ed* Winchester, and St John's Coll, Oxford: *m* 1984, Claire Margaret Alison, da of Brian Seddon, of 77 Lawn Rd, Hampstead, NW3, and has issue living, Peter David, *b* 1987, — Thomas Edward, *b* 1988, — Catherine Lucy, *b* 1991. *Residence* – 68 Haldon Rd, SW18.

DAUGHTERS LIVING

Hon Alice Belinda, *b* 1958: *m* 1981, Rev Robert Charles Irwin Ward, eldest son of late John Ward, of The Old Vicarage, Salehurst, Robertsbridge, Sussex, and has issue living, Samuel John, *b* 1982, — James Nicholas, *b* 1984, — David Christopher, *b* 1994, — Susanna Mary, *b* 1988. *Residence* – 1 Hawthorn Villas, The Green, Wallsend-on-Tyne.
Hon Catherine Sara, *b* 1963: *m* 1990, Joseph Brendan Gannon, son of Patrick Gannon, of Dublin, and has issue living, Sorcha Margaret, *b* 1993. *Residence* – 87 Kilravock St, W10.
Hon Emily Frances, *b* 1970.

Eddisbury, Baron, see Baron Sheffield.

EDEN OF WINTON, BARON (Eden) (Life Baron 1983, Bt (E) 1672 and (GB) 1776)

✠ SI · SIT · PRUDENTIA ✠

JOHN BENEDICT EDEN, PC, Life Baron, 9th *Baronet* of 1st creation, and 7th *Baronet* of 2nd creation; *b* 15 Sept 1925; *s* his father, *Sir* TIMOTHY CALVERT, in his baronetcies, 1963; *ed* Eton, and at St Paul's Sch, USA; a Member of House of Commons Estimates Cttee 1960-64, Delegate to Council of Europe and W European Union 1960-62, and to NATO Parliamentarians Conference 1962-66; Min of State for Technology June to Oct 1970, Min for Industry 1970-72, and Min of Posts and Telecommunications 1972-74; Pres Wessex Area Conservatives 1974-77, Pres Wessex Area Young Conservatives 1978-80; a Member of House of Commons Expenditure Cttee 1974-76; Chm Select Cttee on EEC Legislation etc 1976-79; Chm Select Cttee on Home Affairs 1980-83; Chm British Lebanese Assocn since 1990; Vice-Pres Internat Tree Foundation; Chm R Armouries Museum since 1986; Member Timken Co Internat Advisory Board; Chm Lady Eden's Schs Ltd, and Wonder World plc; 1939-45 War as Lt Rifle Bde; 2nd KEO Gurkha Rifles and the Gilgit Scouts; MP for W Div of Bournemouth (*C*) 1954-83; *cr* PC 1972, and *Baron Eden of Winton*, of Rushyford, co Durham (Life Baron) 1983: *m* 1st, 1958 (*m diss* 1974), Belinda Jane, only da of late Sir (Frederick) John Pascoe; 2ndly, 1977, Margaret Ann, da of late Robin Gordon, and formerly wife of John Eric, Viscount Strathallan, son of 17th Earl of Perth, and has issue by 1st *m*.

Arms – Gules, on a chevron argent between three garbs or, branded vert, as many escallops sable. **Crest** – A dexter arm embowed in armour, couped at the shoulder proper and grasping a garb fessewise as in the arms, banded vert. **Supporters** – Two lions rampant guardant gules about the mane of each a chain pendant therefrom a portcullis or that on the dexter side holding by the interior paw a cross patonce also or and that on the sinister side holding by the interior paw a rose branch proper having three double roses argent on gules barbed and seeded proper the compartment comprising a mount rising in the centre and growing therefrom fir trees and beech trees in the foreground a bay with cliffs proper and a rivulet wavy azure running across a sandy beach also proper into the sea barry wavy of four azure and argent.
Residence – 41 Victoria Rd, W8. *Clubs* – Boodle's, Pratt's.

SONS LIVING *(By 1st marriage)*

Hon ROBERT FREDERICK CALVERT, *b* 30 April 1964.
Hon John (Jack) Edward Morton, *b* 1966: *m* 1991, Joanna J., eldest da of Barrie D. Spears, of Hong Kong, and has issue living, Madelaine Alexandra, *b* 1992.

DAUGHTERS LIVING *(By 1st marriage)*

Hon Emily Rose, *b* 1959: *m* 1984, Ronald Etienne Brown, yr son of James Brown, and has issue living, Nicholas James, *b* 1986, — Charlotte Lucy, *b* 1985. *Residences* – 15-2 Sarugaku-Cho, Shibuya-Ku, Tokyo 150, Japan; Combebelle le Haut, Villespassans, St Chinian 34360, Herault, France.
Hon (Arabella) Charlotte, *b* 1960: *m* 1983, Hon Mungo Alexander Cansh McGowan, yst son of 2nd Baron McGowan, and has issue (*see* B McGowan). *Residence* – Bragborough Farm Braunston, Daventry, Northants.

SISTERS LIVING

Ann Caroline, *b* 1923: *m* 1951, Peter Noel Negretti, and has had issue, Alexandra Mary, *b* 1953: *m* 1981, David C. C. Maule, and has issue living, Robert Alexander Carteret *b* 1985, Oliver Raymond Carteret *b* 1990, Emma Charlotte *b* 1983, — Emma Frances, *b* 1954, *d* 1977, — Cristina Gabrielle, *b* 1956: *m* 1982, W. Guy R. Fearon, and has issue living, Christopher Nicholas William *b* 1991, Camilla Frances *b* 1989, — Sarah Ann *b* 1959: *m* 1984, Jonathan Paul Asquith, of 8 Colinette Rd, SW15 6QQ, and has issue (*see* E Oxford and Asquith, colls). *Residence* – Upper Farringdon House, nr Alton, Hants. —— (Meriall) Rose, *b* 1927: *m* 1959, James Dalton Murray, CMG, who *d* 1984, and has issue living, William Andrew Eden, *b* 1960, — and an adopted son, Hugo Felix Dalton, *b* 1963: *m* 1989, Kaye Melanie Underhill, of Bridgewater, Som, and has issue living, Matthew James *b* 1993. *Residence* – 66500 Mosset, Prades, Pyrénées-Orientales, France. —— Amelia Mary, *b* 1933: *m* 1958, Giovanni Borrelli, of Chapel Lane Cottage, Fritham, Lyndhurst, Hants, and has issue living, Timothy Raffaele, *b* 1962, — Matteo Francesco Antonio, *b* 1965, — Chiara Maria Concetta, *b* 1959. —— Elfrida Charlotte *b* 1940: *m* 1963, Richard Gordon Fallowfield, of 78 West Side, Clapham Common, SW4, and has issue living, Timothy Gordon, *b* 1965, — Nicholas John, *b* 1967, — Laura Louise, *b* 1974.

COLLATERAL BRANCHES LIVING

Grandchildren of late Rowland Frederick Eden, 3rd son of late Frederick Morton Eden, eldest son of Rt Rev Robert Eden, DD, Primus of Scotland, and Bishop of Moray and Ross, 3rd son of 2nd baronet of Maryland:—
Issue of late Lt-Cdr Frederick Augustus Morton Eden, RN (Emergency List), *b* 1904, *d* 1985: *m* 1929, Everil Mary, who *d* 1993, eldest da of late John Stephen Lang Whiteaway, of Tankerville, Kingston Hill, Surrey:—
David Frederick Edward, MBE, *b* 1934; *ed* Ampleforth; W/Cdr RAF (ret); MBE (Mil) 1981: *m* 1957, Audrey Joan Wilson, and has issue living, Audrey Mary Caroline, *b* 1958. *Residence* – 31 Howard Court, Rutland Drive, Harrogate, N Yorks HG1 2PB. —— John Graham Walter, *b* 1948. *Residence* – 16 East MacKenzie Park, Inverness IV2 3SR. —— Mary Alexandra Morton, *b* 1945: *m* 1983, Robert S. Cameron, and has issue living, Neil Robert David, *b* 1987. *Residence* – Gallowa' View, Dockhead, Dumfries DG1 2RX.

Descendants of Sir Robert Eden, 1st baronet of Maryland, who was 2nd son of 3rd baronet of West Auckland:—

Grandson of late Charles Calvert Eden, son of late Lieut-Gen George Morton Eden, 4th son of 2nd baronet of Maryland:—
Issue of late Morton Frederic Eden, MBE, *b* 1865, *d* 1948: *m* 1909, Marie Therése MacMahon, who *d* 1962:—
Robert Charles Frederick, MBE, *b* 1916; *ed* Zuoz Coll, Switzerland and at Camb Univ (BA 1940); European War 1939-45 as Capt Intelligence Corps; MBE (Mil) 1948: *m* 1958, Barbara, 2nd da of late George Reginald Benson, and has issue living, Michael Anthony, *b* 1960. *Residence* – Märchligen, 3112 Allmendingen, Berne, Switzerland. *Club* – Alpine.

Descendants of late Rt Hon William Eden (3rd son of 3rd baronet of West Auckland), who was *cr Baron Auckland* 1789 (*see* that title).
Grandchildren of late Lt-Col John Henry Eden, Chief Constable of Durham 1892-1902, eldest son of Rev John Patrick Eden, son of Thomas Eden (*b* 1787), eldest son of Thomas Eden, 4th son of 3rd baronet of West Auckland:—
Issue of late Brig George Wilfrid Eden, CBE, *b* 1903, *d* 1986: *m* 1946, Katharine Margaret Dorothy, MBE (Norchard Farm, Stanton St Gabriel, Morcombelake, Bridport, Dorset), da of late Rev Edward Henry Good, Chap RN:—
John Patrick Edward (c/o Williams & Glyn's Bank, Holt's Whitehall Branch, SW1), *b* 1950; *ed* Charterhouse. ——— Philippa Catherine, *b* 1948: *m* 1976, Stephen Lawrence McDonnell, of 49 St Catherine's Rd, Winchester, Hants, and has issue living, Catherine Claire, *b* 1981.

Grandchildren of late Sqdn Ldr Gerald Balfour Eden (infra):—
Issue of late John Hamilton Rodney Eden, RAF, *b* 1939, *d* 1992: *m* 1964, Sandra Anne (St Judes, Haynes Rd, Westbury, Wilts BA13 3HA), da of Dennis Rowland Toms:—
Anthony Winston Richard (22 Westbury Leigh, Westbury, Wilts), *b* 1965: *m* 1993, Catherine Mary, da of B. O'Connell, and has issue living, John Anthony Bernhard, *b* 1994. ——— Jeremy Rodney Hugh, *b* 1967. ——— Françoise Geraldine, *b* 1968: *m* 1993, James McLaren Eden-Hamilton (formerly Hamilton) (c/o Milton of Ruthven, Blairgowrie, Perthshire), and has issue living, John Alexander, *b* 1993.

Granddaughter of late Right Rev George Rodney Eden, DD (Lord Bishop of Wakefield 1897-1928), 3rd son of Rev John Patrick Eden:—
Issue of late Sqdn Ldr Gerald Balfour Eden, *b* 1896, *d* 1970: *m* 1929, Anne, who *d* 1977, da of late Maj T Macey, late Indian Army:—
Margaret Anne, *b* 1929: *m* 1955, John William Howard Kirkbride, of 66 Swansfield Park Rd, Alnwick, Northumberland NE66 1AR, and has issue living, Nicholas George, *b* 1959: *m* 1989, Philipa Jane, da of Julian Ross Smith, and has issue living, Olivia Clare *b* 1990. — Amanda, *b* 1957: *m* 1980, Adrian Hardwick, of 7 Laverdene Av, Sheffield, Yorks, and has issue living, Mark Andrew *b* 1986. — Katherine, *b* 1961: *m* 1985, Nicholas Graham Clemo, of 28 St Mark's Cres, Maidenhead, Bucks.

Grandson of late Charles Hamilton Eden, OBE, 4th son of late Rev John Patrick Eden (ante):—
Issue of late Brig Henry Charles Hamilton Eden, CBE, MC, *b* 1889, *d* 1963: *m* 1st, 1916, Violet Alice, who *d* 1956, da of Capt Henry Percy Pulleine, of Sandford House, Richmond, Yorks; 2ndly, 1957, Penelope Glynne (Pine Close, Carroll Av, Ferndown, Dorset), da of H. W. Sitwell, of Leamington Hastings, and widow of Lt-Col R. Temple, RA:—
(By 1st *m*) Robert John Pulleine (Badlake Farm, West Anstay, S Molton, Devon), *b* 1920; Capt TA: *m* 1st, 1947 (*m diss* 1969), Hon Rosemary Winifred Vivian, who *d* 1981, da of 3rd Baron Swansea; 2ndly, 1969, Mrs Elizabeth Stanley Cleverly, da of Alan Crowe Rawlinson, and has issue living, (by 1st *m*) Sarah, *b* 1948: *m* 1982, Robin Fasola, — (by 2nd *m*) Catherine, *b* 1969, — Emily Rose, *b* 1972.

Grandson of late Brig Henry Charles Hamilton Eden, CBE, MC (ante):—
Issue of late Michael Charles Eden, *b* 1921, Lieut RE; *ka* at Arnhem 1944: *m* 1944, Patricia (who *m* 2ndly, 1946, Robert Everett, of Roeburn Scar, Roeburndale, Lancaster), da of late Col Reginald James Brook, CBE, DSO, ED:—
Peter Michael (*posthumous*) (Quinta dos Penedos, Elvas, Portugal), *b* 1944: *m* 1965, Rosemary Frances, da of Kenneth Charles Bishop, MBE, TD, Evans House, Sedbergh School, Yorks, and has issue living, Rupert Michael, *b* 1972, — Caroline Rose, *b* 1967, — Claire Louise, *b* 1969: *m* 1992, António Freire Dias da Costa, of Valverde, Evora, Portugal, and has issue living, Sophie Alexandra *b* 1993, — Lucy Catherine, *b* 1985.

Grandsons of Guy Ernest Morton Eden, son of Charles Henry Eden, son of Robert Eden, son of Thomas Eden, 4th son of 3rd baronet:—
Issue of late Charles Egerton Eden, *b* 1908, *d* 1957: *m* 1936, Eileen Antoinette, da of late H. H. Menzies, of Taplow:—
David Guy Egerton, *b* 1937. *Residence* – Essex.
Issue of late Rev Adrian Arthur Eden, *b* 1911, *d* 1980: *m* 1939, Margaret Anne, who *d* 1973, da of H. Edgar Bushell, of Golborne Manor, Tattenhall, Cheshire:—
Robin Guy (3 Othello Court, 50 Shakespeare Rd, Bedford MK40 2ED), *b* 1943; *ed* King's Sch, Canterbury; LTCL; schoolmaster. ——— John Kenneth (Little Wootton, Church Rd, Scaynes Hill, Haywards Heath, Sussex RH17 7NH), *b* 1949; *ed* King's Sch Canterbury, and Dundee Univ (MA); stockbroker: *m* 1st, 1977 (*m diss* 1983), Margaret Elizabeth, da of William Alfred Noy, of 12 Hyacinth Rd, Strood, Rochester, Kent; 2ndly, 1992, Sophie Jane, da of Timothy John Green, of Kaines Orchard, Shugwash Lane, Scaynes Hill, Sussex, and has issue living (by 1st *m*), Christopher Guy Eden, *b* 1978, — Kathleen Anne Elizabeth, *b* 1980.

Descendants of late Morton Eden (5th son of 3rd baronet of West Auckland), who was *cr Baron Henley* 1799 (see that title).
PREDECESSORS – Sir Robert Eden, 1st Bt of W Auckland, co Durham, was son of Col John Eden, who raised a Regt for Charles I. Sir Robert Eden, Gov of Maryland 1776, the 2nd son of the 3rd baronet of West Auckland was created a baronet of Maryland, and the 3rd and 5th sons were respectively created Baron Auckland and Baron Henley. The 5th baronet of West Auckland assumed the additional surname of Johnson. On his death without issue in 1844, he was *s* by Sir William, 4th Bt, of Maryland, the two baronetcies thus becoming merged. Sir Timothy Calvert Eden, 8th Bt, *d* 1963, having *m* 1923, Patricia Edith, who *d* 1990, founder of Lady Eden's Schs, da of late Arthur Prendergast.

EDINBURGH, DUKE OF, see Royal Family.

EDMUND-DAVIES, BARONY OF (Edmund-Davies) (Extinct 1992)

DAUGHTERS LIVING OF LIFE BARON

Hon Ann, *b* 1936; JP 1979: *m* 1959, Frederick Cecil Worlock, MB, BChir, MRCS, LRCP, of Brooklands, Fladbury, Pershore, Worcs WR10 2QB, and has issue, one son and one da.

Hon Elisabeth, *b* 1939: *m* 1st, 1965 (*m diss* 1975), Richard Owen Roberts; 2ndly, 1987, Alan Large, of 7 Swaledale Av, Reedley, Burnley, Lancs BB10 2LJ.

Hon Shân, *b* 1940: *m* 1964, Prof Wolfram Schüffel, MD, of 3550 Marburg/Lahn, Kaffweg 17A, W Germany.

Ednam, Viscount; son of Earl of Dudley.

EFFINGHAM, EARL OF (Howard) (Earl UK 1837)

Virtue is worth a thousand shields

MOWBRAY HENRY GORDON HOWARD, 6th Earl, *b* 29 Nov 1905; *s* July 1946; *ed* Lancing; 1939-45 war with RA and 3rd Maritime Regts: *m* 1st, 1938 (*m diss* 1946), Maria Melvin Gertler; 2ndly, 1952 (*m diss* 1971), Gladys Irene, da of late Capt William Freeman, Merchant Navy, and formerly wife of Frederick Charles Kerry; 3rdly, 1972, (Mabel) Suzanne Mingay, da of late Maurice Jules-Marie Le Pen, of Paris, and widow of Wing-Cdr Francis Talbot Cragg.

Arms – Quarterly: 1st gules, on a bend between six cross-crosslets fitchée argent an escutcheon or, charged with a demi-lion rampant pierced through the mouth with an arrow gules, within the Royal tressure of Scotland. *Howard*; 2nd England, with a label of three points for difference. *Thomas of Brotherton*; 3rd checky or and azure. *Warren*; 4th gules, a lion rampant argent. *Mowbray*; the whole charged with a mullet for difference. Crest – On a cheapan gules, turned up ermine, a lion statant guardant or, tail extended, ducally gorged argent, charged with a mullet sable. Supporters – Two lions argent, each charged on the shoulder with a mullet for difference.
Address – House of Lords, SW1.

WIDOW LIVING OF SON OF FIFTH EARL

Naida Frances, da of Henry Morden Guest, and formerly wife of Hugh Boucher: *m* 2ndly, 1946, as his 2nd wife, Hon John Algernon Frederick Charles Howard, who *d* 1971; 3rdly, 1972, Geoffrey Gaskell Royal, who *d* 1984, and has issue (see colls infra).

COLLATERAL BRANCH LIVING

Issue of late Hon John Algernon Frederick Charles Howard, yr son of 5th Earl, *b* 1907, *d* 1971: *m* 1st, 1938 (*m diss* 1942), Suzanne Patricia, da of late Edgar Macassey; 2ndly, 1946, Naida Frances (ante), (who *m* 3rdly, 1972, Geoffrey Gaskell Royal, who *d* 1984), da of Henry Morden Guest, and formerly wife of Hugh Boucher:—

(By 1st *m*) DAVID MOWBRAY ALGERNON (Readings Farmhouse, Blackmore End, Essex CM7 4DH), *b* 29 April 1939; *ed* Fettes; Cdr RN (ret): *m* 1st, 1964 (*m diss* 1975), Anne Mary, da of late Harrison Sayer, of Saffron Walden; 2ndly, 1992, Mrs Elizabeth Jane Turner, of Gt Saling, Essex, and has issue living (by 1st *m*), Edward Mowbray Nicholas, *b* 1971. —— (By 2nd *m*) Charles Anthony Frederick (5 Wingate Rd, W6 0UR): *b* 1951; *ed* St John's Coll, Camb (MA); Bar Inner Temple 1975: *m* 1978, Geraldine Margaret Theresa, da of Dr Thomas Dorman, of Holly Farm, Morley, Derbys, and has issue living, Alexander Charles Frederick, *b* 1981, — Francesca Clare, *b* 1982.

PREDECESSORS – (1) *Lord* WILLIAM Howard, KG, el son of his 2nd marriage of Thomas 2nd Duke of Norfolk; in 1542 found guilty of misprision of treason for concealing the misconduct of his niece Catherine, Queen of Henry VIII, and condemned with his wife to perpetual imprisonment (pardoned 1544); Lord Dep of Calais 1552-3, Lord High Adm 1553-7, Lord Chamberlain of the Household 1558-72, and Lord Privy Seal 1572; *cr Baron Howard of Effingham* (peerage of England) 1554, *d* 1572; *s* by his son (2) CHARLES, KG, 2nd Baron; was Com-in-Ch of the fleet that destroyed the Spanish Armada 1588; *cr Earl of Nottingham* (peerage of England) 1596; *d* 1624; *s* by his son (3) CHARLES, 2nd Earl; *dsp* 1642; *s* by his half-brother (4) CHARLES, KB, 3rd Earl; *d* 1681, when the earldom expired and the barony reverted to (5) FRANCIS, 5th Baron; *d* 1694; *s* by his son (6) THOMAS, 6th Baron; *dsp* 1725; *s* by his brother (7) FRANCIS, 7th Baron; a distinguished military officer; *cr Earl of Effingham* (peerage of Great Britain) 1731; *d* 1743; *s* by his son (8) THOMAS, 2nd Earl; Dep Earl Marshal; *d* 1763; *s* by his el son (9) THOMAS, 3rd Earl; Dep Earl Marshal; *dsp* 1791; *s* by his brother (10) RICHARD, 4th Earl; *d* 1816, when the earldom became extinct, and the barony devolved upon his kinsman (11) KENNETH ALEXANDER, GCB, 11th Baron; *b* 1767; a Gen in the Army; *cr Earl of Effingham* (peerage of United Kingdom) 1837: *m* 1800, Lady Charlotte Primrose, da of 3rd Earl of Rosebery; *d* 1845; *s* by his son (12) HENRY, 2nd Earl, *b* 1806; sat as MP for Shaftesbury (*L*) 1841-5: *m* 1832, Eliza, da of late Gen Sir Gordon Drummond, GCB; *d* 1889; *s* by his el son (13) HENRY, 3rd Earl, *b* 1837: *m* 1865, Victoria Francisca, who *d* 1899, el da of A. Boyer, of Paris; *d* 1898; *s* by his son (14) HENRY ALEXANDER GORDON, 4th Earl, *b* 1866; *d* 1927; *s* by his cousin (15) GORDON FREDERICK HENRY CHARLES (son of late Capt Hon Frederick Charles Howard, 2nd son of 2nd Earl), 5th Earl, *b* 1873: *m* 1st, 1904 (*m diss* 1914), Rosamond Margaret, who *d* 1957, da of late Edward H. Hudson, of Scarborough; 2ndly, 1924, Madeleine (Mrs Keleher), who *d* 1958, da of William D. Foshay, of USA; *d* 1946; *s* by his son (16) MOWBRAY HENRY GORDON, 6th Earl and present peer; also Baron Howard of Effingham.

EGLINTON and WINTON, EARL OF (Montgomerie) (Earl S 1507, and UK 1859)
(Name pronounced "Muntgummery")

Take good care

ARCHIBALD GEORGE MONTGOMERIE, 18th Earl; *b* 27 Aug 1939; *s* 1966; *ed* Eton; Hereditary Sheriff of Renfrew: *m* 1964, Marion Carolina, only da of John Henry Dunn-Yarker, of Le Château, 1814 La Tour de Peilz, Vaud, Switzerland, and has issue.

Arms – Quarterly, 1st and 4th grand quarters counter quartered, 1st and 4th azure, three fleurs-de-lys or, *Montgomerie*; 2nd and 3rd gules, three annulets or, stoned azure, *Eglinton*, all within a bordure or charged with a double tressure flory counterflory gules; 2nd and 3rd grand quarters counterquartered, 1st and 4th or, three crescents within a double tressure flory counterflory gules, *Seton*; 2nd and 3rd azure, three garbs or, *Buchan*; over all an escutcheon parted per pale gules and azure, the dexter charged with a sword in pale proper, pommelled and hilted or, supporting an imperial crown, the sinister charged with a star of twelve points argent, all within a double tressure flory counterflory gold. **Crest** – 1st, a lady dressed in ancient apparel azure, holding in her dexter hand an anchor or, and in her sinister the head of a savage couped suspended by the hair all proper; 2nd, a ducal coronet or, issuing therefrom a wyvern vomiting fire, his wings elevated proper. **Supporters** – Two wyverns vert, vomiting fire proper.
Residence – The Dutch House, West Green, Hartley Wintney, Hants.

SONS LIVING

HUGH ARCHIBALD WILLIAM (*Lord Montgomerie*), *b* 24 July 1966; RN (ret 1993): *m* 1991, S. Alexandra, eldest da of Niel Redpath, of Fulham, SW6.
Hon William John, *b* 1968.
Hon James David, *b* 1972.
Hon Robert Seton, *b* 1975.

SISTERS LIVING

Lady Susanna, *b* 1941: *m* 1963, Capt David Dundas Euing Crawford, and has issue living, Alexander William Euing, *b* 1967, — Daniel Dundas Euing (twin), *b* 1967, — Arabella Sara, *b* 1965. *Residence* – Rankeilour House, Cupar, Fife.
Lady Elizabeth Beatrice, *b* 1945: *m* 1976, Maj Christopher Miles Barne, The Blues and Royals, of Culeaze, Wareham, Dorset, and has issue living, Charles Miles, *b* 1978.

HALF-UNCLE LIVING (*Son of 16th Earl*) (*by 2nd marriage*)

Hon Roger Hugh, DFC, *b* 1923; *ed* Eton, and at New Coll, Oxford (MA); formerly Flight-Lt RAF; 1939-45 War (DFC).
Residence – Lanehead, Dunscore, Dumfries.

AUNTS LIVING (*Daughters of 16th Earl*)

Lady Janet Egidia, *b* 1911: *m* 1934, Capt Lord Robert Crichton-Stuart, Scots Gds, who *d* 1976 (*see* M Bute). *Residence* – Wards Cottage, Gartocharn, Dunbartonshire.
Lady Betty Mary Seton, *b* 1912: *m* 1933, Capt George Vane Hay-Drummond, Scots Guards (Reserve) (*see* E Kinnoull, colls), who *d* 1984. *Residence* – Vane House, 1 The Glebe, Dunning, Perthshire.

COLLATERAL BRANCHES LIVING

Grandchildren of late Alexander Montgomerie (*b* 1865), eldest son of late Capt Alexander Montgomerie (*b* 1824) (infra):—
Issue of late Alexander James Montgomerie, *b* 1892, *d* 1945: *m* 1919, Winifred Jane, who *d* 1993, aged 99, da of late George Gifford, of Bulls, Rangitikei, New Zealand:—
Alexander Kelvin (35 Washington Av, St Heliers, Auckland, NZ), *b* 1922; 1939-45 War with NZ Scottish Regt and RNZN: *m* 1958, Doreen Evelyn, da of Capt G. F. Price, 51 Woodfield Av, Farlington, Portsmouth, and has issue living, Alexander Andrew (Jurastrasse 16, 5406 Baden-Rutihof, Switzerland), *b* 1962; *ed* Auckland Univ (BTP): *m* 1990, Sandra, only da of Edwin Baumann, of Burglen, Thurgau, Switzerland, and has issue living, Kristina Katherine *b* 1992, Stefanie Kim *b* 1994, — Stuart Hugh, *b* 1966; *ed* Auckland Univ (BA). —— Seton Eglinton, *b* 1924: *m* 1960, Joan, da of late Harry Bladen, and has issue living, Seton Bladen *b* 1962, — Elsa Jane *b* 1964: *m* 1985, Philip Keith Belton, of Te Huia, RD2, Ngutuwera, Waverley, NZ, yst son of John Keith Belton, and has issue living, Christopher Reece *b* 1986, Sarah Jane *b* 1988, Emma Louise *b* 1993. *Residence* – 18 Tongariro St, Castlecliff, Wanganui, NZ. —— Zona Winifred, *b* 1920: *m* 1943, Norman Claude Nicholson, RNZAF, and has issue living, John Montgomerie (BB Beryl Grove, Birchvale, Upper Hutt, NZ), *b* 1947: *m* 1977, Deborah Mary, da of W. J. Evenson, of 91 Pasadena Crescent, Upper Hutt, NZ, and has issue living, Jonathan Montgomerie *b* 1980, Victoria Rose *b* 1983, — Murray James (132 Oberon Rd, Chittaway Bay, Wyong, NSW 2259, Australia), *b* 1950: *m* 1971, Joy Louise, da of V. Frampton, of 1 Mundoora Av, Yattalunga, Gosford, NSW, and has issue living, Mathew James *b* 1974, Jodie Louise *b* 1972, Lisa Eileen *b* 1975, — Claudia Michele, *b* 1945: *m* 1966, Peter William Fitzsimmons, OBE (6 Marigold Place, Mairangi Bay, Auckland, NZ), and has issue living, Timothy Peter *b* 1974, Megan Clare *b* 1977. *Residence* – Woodleigh, Jocelyn Cres, Pinehaven, Silverstream, Wellington, NZ. —— Rana Maude, *b* 1929: *m* 1951, Jack Rogers William Elder, RNZAF, and has issue living David Lawson James (RD2 Matamata, NZ), *b* 1959: *m* 1989, Helen Margaret, da of R. A. Pond, of RD2, Matamata, NZ, and has issue living, Kevin Robert James *b* 1992, — Raèwyne Janice, *b* 1955: *m* 1980, Stephen Hugh Allen, of 2 Greerton Rd, Tauranga, NZ, and has issue living, Matthew Stephen *b* 1983, Kimberley Jane *b* 1981. *Residence* – Broadview, 279 Bellevue Heights, Tauranga, NZ.
Issue of late Archibald William Montgomerie, *b* 1894, *d* 1969: *m* 1942, Barbara Mary (36 Brookvale Rd, Havelock North, NZ), da of Samuel Scott Linton:—
David William, *b* 1944; *ed* McGill Univ, Montreal (PhD). —— Roger Linton (5 Thomas Av, Roseville, NSW 2069, Australia), *b* 1946; *ed* Massey Univ, NZ (B Tech, Dip BIA): *m* 1977, Judith Lorraine, da of R. A. R. Holland, of Sydney, Aust, and has issue living, Simon Holland, *b* 1980, — Andrew Scott, *b* 1987, — Kate Louise, *b* 1982. —— Barbara Mary, *b* 1942: *m* 1973 (*m diss* 1982), Bernard Antoine Vollon, of Paris. —— Jeanne Elizabeth, *b* 1945: *m* 1969 (*m diss* 1982), Griffith Powell

Richards, and has issue living, Nicholas Powell, *b* 1971, — Philip Powell, *b* 1972, — Michael Powell, *b* 1975, — Anna
Elizabeth, *b* 1977. —— Barbara Hylda, *b* 1950.
     Issue of late John Eglinton Montgomerie, *b* 1899, *d* 1971: *m* 1921, Irene Agnes, da of Thomas Ross Cameron, of
New Plymouth, NZ:—
Archibald William, *b* 1931: *m* 1962, Geraldine Anne, da of Gerald Cecil Davy, of Turanga, and has issue living, Michael
William, *b* 1966, — Donna Marie, *b* 1962. —— Robert Patrick (24 Ihaia St, Waitara, Taranki, NZ), *b* 1934: *m* 1960, Myhre
Laughton, da of A. H. Collins, and has issue living, Leighton, *b* 1966, — Wilson Bruce, *b* 1968, — Patricia Ann, *b* 1961: *m*
19—, Charles Patrick McAlister, and has issue living, Charles Luke *b* 1983, Kayla Marie *b* 1988, — Kerrie Lyn, *b* 1963, —
Jillian Beth, *b* 1964. —— Ian James (22 Hursthouse Rd, Inglewood, NZ), *b* 1935: *m* 1961, Diana Long, and has issue living,
Paul Ian, *b* 1963, — Tracy Diana, *b* 1965, — Lisa Alayne, *b* 1967. —— Anita Mary, *b* 1921: *m* 1944, David Gordon Harrison,
of 15 Whiteley St, New Plymouth, NZ, and has had issue, Errol John, *b* 1945: *m* 1970, Shirley Doreen Elwin, and *d* 1993,
leaving, Sheree Ann *b* 1975, Melanie Jane *b* 1977, — Ira James (59B Manu Crescent, New Plymouth, NZ), *b* 1948, — Peter
David (17A Divon St, Oakuru, NZ), *b* 1950: *m* 1970, Susan Wilson, who *d* 1993, and has issue living, Jason David *b* 1970,
Kim Sheree *b* 1973, — Patrick Vivian (399 Main South Rd, Omata, Taranaki, NZ), *b* 1959: *m* 1986, Kay Walter, and has issue
living, Greer Sam Walter *b* 1993, — Carrol Ann, *b* 1946: *m* 1967, Terry Arthur Jordan, of 28 Joseph Banks Drive, Whitby,
Wellington, NZ, and has issue living, Rhys Craig *b* 1968, Carla Ann *b* 1970, — Shirley Mary, *b* 1953: *m* 1977, Marco Grand-
acci, of Camerino, Italy, and *d* 1986, leaving issue, Marco *b* 1977, Natalie Anita *b* 1978, — Yvonne Joan, *b* 1956: *m* 19—,
Ronald Lance Wood, of 35 Matairo St, Titahi Bay, Wellington, NZ, and has issue living, Bianca Jay *b* 1978, Amber *b* 1980,
Candice Skye *b* 1987. —— Nola, *b* 1923: *m* 1941, Eric William Hopson, of RD3, Matamata, NZ, and has had issue, Kevin
Eric (RD Mangakino, NZ), *b* 1943: *m* 1966, Shirley Anne Montague, and has issue living, Trevor John *b* 1968, Warrick David
b 1972, Gareth Andrew *b* 1981, Janelle Marie *b* 1970, — Denis Michael (RD3, Matamata, NZ), *b* 1946: *m* 1980, Elizabeth
Margaret Baker, and has issue living, Teresa Elizabeth *b* 1980, Catherine Anne *b* 1982, Bridget Alice *b* 1984, Rebecca Clare *b*
1985, — Graeme Patrick (RD1, Walton, NZ), *b* 1950: *m* 1972, Diane Elizabeth Hicks, and has issue living, Craig Patrick *b*
1975, Susan Marie *b* 1973, — Murray John, *b* 1953: *m* 1981, Sandra Daphne Brooks, and has issue living, Brendan Murray *b*
1989, Christine Sandra *b* 1983, Andrea Jane *b* 1985, — Allan David, *b* 1956: *m* 1978, Gillian Joy Christopher, and has issue
living, Tanya Kirstin *b* 1978, Renee Jade *b* 1981, — Joan Frances, *b* 1941: *m* 1962, Peter Bruce Donnison, of RD3, Matamata,
NZ, and has issue living, Bruce Stephen *b* 1962: *m* 1987, Adele Wilcockson (and has issue living, Rhys Francis *b* 1991,
Hayley Petria *b* 1993), Paul David *b* 1963: *m* 1990, Kathryn Cuddihy (and has issue living, Callum Michael *b* 1992, Caitlin
Joelle *b* 1993), Gregory James *b* 1965: *m* 1992, Kristin Evans, Martyn John *b* 1966: *m* 1993, Helen Conlon (and has issue
living, Cam John McGrail *b* 1990, Hayley Francesca *b* 1994), Cameron Peter *b* 1975, Matthew Leighton *b* 1978, Regan
Michael *b* 1981, Mylene Joanne *b* 1969, — Maureen Anne, *b* 1948: *m* 1966, Robin Bruce Lindsay, and has issue living, Gene
Bruce *b* 1966: *m* 1994, Sherry Gillard (and has issue living, Troy Bruce *b* 1992), Shane Michael *b* 1970, Sharron Lee *b* 1968:
m 1989, Kenneth Watkinson, Tracey Sharleen *b* 1972: *m* 1993, Gregory James (and has issue living, Hayden Charles *b* 1994),
Kylie Maree *b* 1983, — Karen Irene, *b* 1960: *m* 1982, Warren Crawford, and has issue living, Holly Diane *b* 1991, — Diane
Marie, *b* (twin) 1960: *m* 1982, Paul Moroney, and *d* 1982. —— Peggy Agnes, *b* 1924: *m* 1945, Aubrey Edgar Hopson, of 170
Tukapo St, New Plymouth, NZ, and has issue living, Wayne Leighton, *b* 1946: *m* 1973, Heather Henderson, and has issue
living, Candy Leighton *b* 1977, — Brian James, *b* 1948: *m* 1972, Elizabeth Lawson, and has issue living, Gareth Brian *b* 1982,
Bryce James *b* 1985, Kieran Paul *b* 1989, — Valerie Margaret, *b* 1952: *m* 1975, Graeme McEldowney, and has issue living,
Steven Craig *b* 1977, Dale Andrew *b* 1979, Aaron John *b* 1980, — Barbara Irene, *b* 1953: *m* 1973, Lindsay Gault, and has
issue living, Shane David *b* 1978, Karen Maree *b* 1974, Julie Heather *b* 1976. —— Barbara Winifred (70 Dundebar Rd,
Wanneroo, Perth, W Australia 6065), *b* 1933: *m* 1954 (*m diss* 1978), David Walter Gosling, and has issue living, Ronald David
(25 Celestine Rd, Wanneroo, Perth, W Australia 6065), *b* 1955: *m* 1978, Julie Dawn Bailey, and has issue living, Vicky Rachel
b 1983, Donna Colette *b* 1987, — Ian Peter (70 Dundebar Rd, Wanneroo, Perth, W Australia 6065), *b* 1957: *m* 1980, Clare
Lucy Knights, and has issue living, Thomas Iain *b* 1980, Matt Luke *b* 1981, James Patrick *b* 1985, Daniel Shane *b* 1986,
Jessica Barbara *b* 1983, Rebecca Clare *b* 1989, — Claire Annette, *b* 1963: *m* 1st, 1980 (*m diss* 1983), Michael Currer; 2ndly,
1984 (*m diss* 1990), George Lubert, of Arkansas, USA; 3rdly 1993, Dale Jenkins, of 300 South Hospital Drive, Apt 805,
Jacksonville, Arkansas, USA, and has issue living (by 2nd *m*), Gary Paul *b* 1980, Melissa Dawn *b* 1986, Tiffany Nicole *b* 1987.
     Issue of late George Arnulph Montgomerie, *b* 1901, *d* 1980: *m* 1945, Peggy Patricia Greener, who *d* 1991, formerly
of Wanganui, NZ:—
Wayne Arnold (Box 149, Trent St, Rongotea, NZ), *b* 1947: *m* 1971, Christina Mary, da of late Bernard Colin Williams, and
has issue living, Darien Mary, *b* 1975, — Loren Patricia, *b* 1978. —— Peter John (3 Brudenell Drive, Jerrabomberra, NSW
2619, Australia), *b* 1951: *m* 1977, Jennifer Joan, da of Hugh Carter Milroy, of 290 Great Western Highway, Warrimoo, NSW
2774, and has issue living, Shane Peter, *b* 1983, — Fiona Jenny, *b* 1982.

          Granddaughter of late Capt Alexander Montgomerie (*b* 1824), el son of William Eglinton Montgomerie, el
          son of Alexander Montgomerie, brother of 12th Earl:—
     Issue of late Roger Arnulph Montgomerie, *b* 1866, *d* 1936: *m* 1893, Annie, who *d* 1958, da of late Archibald Mason,
of Tauangatutu, Wanganui, New Zealand:—
Sybil Alexandra, MBE, *b* 1902; MBE (Civil) 1977: *m* 1925, David Rayney Jackson, of Waverley, NZ who *d* 1968, and has
issue living, David Rayney Montgomerie, *b* 1929: *m* 1959, Diana Georgina, yr da of late Frank Galbraith Hyde, of Tarras,
Otago, New Zealand, and has issue living, Edward Hyde Rayney *b* 1963, Sarah Jane Rayney *b* 1960, Belinda Elizabeth *b* 1962.
Residence – 5 Tulloch St, St John's Hill, Wanganui, NZ.

          Grandchildren of late Roger Arnulph Montgomerie (ante):—
     Issue of late Roger Oswald Montgomerie, *b* 1896, *d* 1965: *m* 1940, Beryl Victoria, QSM (13 Laurence St, Tauranga,
NZ), da of late Guy Carlton Clark, of Melbourne:—
John Clark (11 Gardiner Place, Havelock North, NZ) *b* 1943; *ed* Wanganui Collegiate, and Massey Univ: *m* 1972, Glenis
Erina, only da of late Norman Cameron, of Masterton, NZ, and has issue living, Richard John, *b* 1974, — Meredith Jane, *b*
1977. —— Roger Clark (36 Aiken Rd, Wanganui, NZ), *b* 1945; *ed* Wanganui Collegiate: *m* 1971, Patricia Clare, only da of
late Vincent Patrick Donnelly, of Paeroa, NZ, and has issue living, Hayden James *b* 1979. —— Beverley Joan, *b* 1941: *m*
1963, Edward William Gudopp, of 31 Graham Place, Tauranga, NZ, and has issue living, David Charles, *b* 1967, — Deborah
Jane, *b* 1965: *m* 1990, Brent William Lincoln, of 9 Flinders Place, Tauranga, NZ, and has issue living, Daniel William *b* 1993,
Samantha Victoria *b* 1991. —— Helen Victoria, *b* 1959.
     Issue of late Hew Seton Montgomerie, *b* 1898, *d* 1969: *m* 1938, Violet Muriel, who *d* 1976, da of late Donald Harry
Rait, MRCVS, of Palmerston N, NZ:—
Susanna Seton, *b* 1940: *m* 1976, Michael Hensleigh Norris, of Tredudwell, Wiroa Rd, RD3, Kerikeri, NZ, and has issue living,
Hew Seton Hensleigh, *b* 1977. —— Egidia Seton *b* 1942: *m* 1980, Jerome Robert DesRoches, of PO Box 24, Mangonui,
Northland, Kerikeri, NZ.

          Grandchildren of Hew Winton Montgomerie (infra):—
     Issue of late Ian Hew de Greenlaw Montgomerie, *b* 1913, *d* 1981: *m* 1st, 1940 (*m diss* 1948), Elizabeth Isobella
Gregg Stratford; 2ndly, 1948, Marjorie Thelma, who *d* 1975, da of Albert Eugene Brookes, of Auckland, New
Zealand; 3rdly, 1977, his 1st wife, Elizabeth Isobella Gregg Stratford (51 Rawhiti Rd, Onehunga, Auckland, NZ):—
(By 1st *m*) Hew Winton Rowland (51 Rawhiti Rd, Onehunga, NZ), *b* 1941: *m* 1st, 1967 (*m diss* 1978), Carol Leonie, yst da of
Stanley Rollington Cromwell, Headmaster of Whangarei, NZ; 2ndly, 1984, Joana Tinisivo, da of Autiko Quna, of Fiji, and has
issue living (by 1st *m*), Stuart Seton, *b* 1974, — Rachael Leonie, *b* 1970, — (by 2nd *m*) Ian Hew Mocewai, *b* 1992. —— (By
2nd *m*) Lynetta Eugene, *b* 1952: *m* 1971, Albert John Bainbridge, and has issue living, Brent Albert, *b* 1976, — Tanya Lyn, *b*
1973, — Sacha Lee, *b* 1975.

Granddaughters of late Capt Alexander Montgomerie (*b* 1824) (ante):—
Issue of late Hew Winton Montgomerie, *b* 1872, *d* 1920: *m* 1906, Mary Laura, da of Charles J. G. de Greenlaw, of
Syndey, NS Wales:—
Barbara de Greenlaw, *b* 1915: *m* 1942, Ernest Clement Dawson, of 72 Frank St, Papanui, Christchurch 8005, NZ, and has
issue living, Ernest John Linnaeus (19 Kimberley St, Christchurch, NZ), *b* 1945: *m* 1971, Lois Adrienne, da of Norman Farr,
of Christchurch, NZ, and has issue living, Stephanie Justine *b* 1976, Julia Clare *b* 1978, — Bernard Stanley Winton (8
Kamahai Pl, Rotorua, NZ), *b* 1953; *ed* Univ of Canterbury, NZ (PhD Chemistry): *m* 1980, Sharon-May, da of Tan Hock Siang,
of Singapore, and has issue living, Vivian Bernard *b* 1984, — Ann Michelle de Greenlaw, *b* 1943: *m* 1971, Lt-Cdr Edward
Nigel Parry, RN, of Lowford House, School Rd, Bursledon, Hants SO3 8BU, — Linda Egidia Montgomerie, *b* 1949: *m* 1971,
Miguel Zuniga, Chief Petty Offr, US Navy, of 955 N Gracia St, Camarillo, California 93010, USA, and has issue living,
Dominick Miguel *b* 1972, Cheyenne Barbara *b* 1976.
Issue of late Archibald William Eglinton Montgomerie, *b* 1874, *d* 1951: *m* 1901, Elizabeth Grace, who *d* 1956, da of
late Duncan Blair, of Wanganui, New Zealand:—
Nancy Edith, *b* 1903. *Residence* – 54 Durie St, Durie Hill, Wanganui, New Zealand.
Issue (by 1st *m*) of late John Eglinton Montgomerie, *b* 1878, *d* 1930: *m* 1st, 1910, Edith Lillia, who *d* 1921, da of
late Hon George Young, MLC, of Melbourne, Australia; 2ndly, 1928, Sarah (who *m* 2ndly, 19—, George Crowe, of
Arbroath, Angus), da of — Mitchell, of Arbroath, Scotland:—
Sheila Elizabeth, *b* 1911: *m* 1940, Francis Churtain Triggs, who *d* 1977, and has issue living, Michael Francis (Orangewood
Rd, Kerikeri, NZ), *b* 1942: *m* 1972, Susan Marlene, da of late James Lincoln Todd, of Auckland, and has issue living,
Matthew James *b* 1975, Simon Michael *b* 1976, Joanna Elizabeth *b* 1980, — Mary Seton *b* 1946: *m* 1964, Stafford John Reed,
of 35 Springs Rd, Parakai, Auckland, NZ, and has issue living, Darren Stafford *b* 1965: *m* 1987, Lisa Maree Tipping (and has
issue living, Layne Ashley *b* 1988, Brandon Leslie *b* 1992), Mark *b* 1967, Eugene *b* 1971, Rosanna Sheila *b* 1982. *Residence* –
5-89a Royal Rd, Massey, Auckland, NZ. ——— Bettie Winton, *b* 1916: *m* 1940, Thomas Charles Howden, and has issue living,
Ann Montgomerie, *b* 1952, — Janet, *b* 1955. *Residence* – 2/119 Lumsden Rd, Hastings, New Zealand.

PREDECESSORS – **(1)** Sir ALEXANDER Montgomerie, Knt; *cr* Lord Montgomerie (peerage of Scotland) 1449; *d* 1451; *s* by his
grandson **(2)** ALEXANDER, 2nd Lord; *s* by his son **(3)** HUGH, 3rd Lord; nominated after the fall of James IV at Flodden one of
the Queen-Dowager's Councillors, and was afterwards Justice Gen of N parts of Scotland; *cr* Earl of Eglinton (peerage of
Scotland) 1508; *d* 1545; *s* by his grandson **(4)** HUGH, 2nd Earl; *d* 1546; *s* by his son **(5)** HUGH, 3rd Earl; *d* 1585; *s* by his son
(6) HUGH, 4th Earl; assassinated 1586; *s* by his son **(7)** HUGH, 5th Earl; obtained a charter settling the earldom upon his
cousins, Alexander, Thomas and John, sons of his aunt Margaret, by Robert Seton, 1st Earl of Winton; *d* 1611; *s* by his
cousin (ante) **(7)** ALEXANDER Seton, 6th Earl (3rd son of 1st Earl of Winton and 6th Lord Seton); took an active part against
the crown, *temp* Charles I, fought on the Parliament side at Marston Moor; subsequently attached himself to Charles II, and
falling into the hands of the enemy was imprisoned at Berwick 1651-60; *d* 1661; *s* by his son **(8)** HUGH, 7th Earl; espoused
the royal cause during the civil wars and was opposed to his father at Marston Moor; *d* 1669; *s* by his son **(9)** ALEXANDER,
8th Earl; *d* 1701; *s* by his el son **(10)** ALEXANDER, PC, 9th Earl; a Representative Peer; *d* 1729; *s* by his son **(11)** ALEXANDER,
10th Earl; killed during a dispute 1769 by Mungo Campbell, whom the Earl had ordered off his lands and insisted upon the
trespasser delivering up his gun; *s* by his brother **(12)** ARCHIBALD, 11th Earl; a Gen in the Army, MP for Ayrshire 1761, Dep
Ranger of Hyde and St James's Parks, and a Representative Peer 1776-96; *d* 1796; *s* by his kinsman **(13)** HUGH, KT, 12th
Earl, great grandson of the Hon James Seton, 4th son of 6th Earl; MP for Ayrshire 1780-9 and 1796, and a Representative
Peer 1798-1806; *cr* Baron Ardrossan (peerage of United Kingdom) 1806; *d* 1819; *s* by his grandson **(14)** ARCHIBALD WILLIAM,
13th Earl, KT, PC, DCL, LLD; *b* 1812; in 1840 served heir male of George, 4th Earl of Winton (*cr* 1600), and 9th Lord Seton
(*cr* 1448) (peerage of Scotland); *cr* Earl of Winton, and Baron Seton and Tranent (peerage of United Kingdom) 1859; Viceroy
of Ireland 1852 and 1858-9, and Lord-Lieut of Ayrshire; inaugurated and carried out a celebrated tournament at Eglinton
Castle 1839: *m* 1st, 1841, Theresa, who *d* 1853, widow of Com Richard Howe Cockerell, RN; 2ndly, 1858, Lady Adela Capel,
who *d* 1860, da of 6th Earl of Essex; *d* 1861; *s* by his son **(15)** ARCHIBALD WILLIAM, 14th Earl, *b* 1841: *m* 1862, Lady Sophia
Adelaide Theodosia Anderson-Pelham, who *d* 1886, da of 2nd Earl of Yarborough; *d* 1892; *s* by his brother **(16)** GEORGE
ARNULPH, 15th Earl, *b* 1848; Lord-Lieut of Ayrshire: *m* 1873, Dame Janet Lucretia, DBE, LLD, who *d* 1923, da of Boyd
Cunninghame, RN, of Craigends, co Renfrew; *d* 1919; *s* by his son **(17)** ARCHIBALD SETON, 16th Earl, *b* 1880: *m* 1st, 1908 (*m*
diss 1922), Lady Beatrice Susan Dalrymple, who *d* 1962, da of 11th Earl of Stair; 2ndly, 1922, Marjorie, da of Thomas Walker
McIntyre, and widow of Guy Fitzpatrick Vernon; *d* 1945; *s* by his son **(18)** ARCHIBALD WILLIAM ALEXANDER, 17th Earl, *b* 1914:
m 1938, Ursula Joan, who *d* 1987, da of Hon Ronald Bannatyne Watson (*see* B Watson, ext, 1966 Edn); *d* 1966; *s* by his son
(19) ARCHIBALD GEORGE, 18th Earl and present peer; also Earl of Winton, Lord Montgomerie, Baron Seton and Tranent, and
Baron Ardrossan.

EGMONT, EARL OF (Perceval) Sits as BARON LOVEL AND HOLLAND (GB 1762) (Earl I 1733, Bt I 1661)

Under the white cross

FREDERICK GEORGE MOORE PERCEVAL, 11th Earl, and 15th
Baronet; *b* 14 April 1914; established his claim to the Earldom 1939: *m* 1932, Ann Geraldine, da of D. G. Moodie, and
has issue.

Arms – Quarterly; 1st and 4th argent, on a chief indented gules, three
crosses patée of the field, *Perceval*; 2nd and 3rd barry nebulée of six,
or and gules, *Lovel*. **Crest** – A thistle proper. **Supporters** – *Dexter*, an
antelope argent, armed, unguled, ducally collared and chained or,
holding in the mouth a thistle slipped proper; *sinister*, a stag sable,
attired, unguled, ducally collared and chained or, holding in the mouth
a thistle slipped proper.
Residence – Two-Dot Ranch, Nanton, Alberta, Canada.

SON LIVING

THOMAS FREDERICK GERALD (*Viscount Perceval*), *b* 17 Aug 1934.

DAUGHTER LIVING

Lady Geraldine Elizabeth Ursula, *b* 1939.

COLLATERAL BRANCH LIVING

Grandchildren of late Charles Spencer Perceval, LLD, son of late Dudley Montagu Perceval, son of 4th son of 2nd Earl:—

Issue of late Dudley Perceval, b 1874, d 1956: m 1914, Hon Mary Elizabeth Massey, who d 1960, da of 5th Baron Clarina:—

Philip Edward, MD, b 1915; ed St John's Coll, Camb (BA 1936, MA 1940, MB and BCh 1940, MD 1950): m 1945, Joan Margaret, who d 1993, da of Lieut-Col Alfred Hacking, DSO, MC, of Dalmorton, Selsey, Sussex, and has issue living, Elizabeth Margaret, b 1947. *Residence* – 11 Condover Park, Condover, Shropshire SY5 7DU. —— Mary Leonora, b 1916. *Residence* – Armadale, Aston St, Aston Tirrold, Didcot, Oxon OX11 9DJ.

PREDECESSORS – (1) *Rt Hon Sir* JOHN PERCEVAL; *cr* a *Baronet* 1661 with the exceptional privilege of allowing the el son or grandson when twenty-one years of age (and after notice given as provided) to receive the Order of Knighthood and have the rank and precedence of a Bt concurrently with the father or grandfather; d 1665; s by his el son (2) Sir PHILIP, 2nd Bt; d unmarried 1680; s by his brother (3) Sir JOHN, 3rd Bt; d 1686; s by his son (4) Sir EDWARD, 4th Bt; d a minor 1691; s by his brother (5) *Rt Hon Sir* JOHN, 5th Bt; successively MP for co Cork and Harwick, and 1st Pres of Georgia; *cr Baron Perceval*, of Burton, co Cork (peerage of Ireland) 1715, with remainder to the heirs male of his father, *Viscount Perceval* (peerage of Ireland) 1722, and *Earl of Egmont* (peerage of Ireland) 1733; d 1748; s by his son (6) *Rt Hon* JOHN, 2nd Earl; MP 1731-62, Lord High Adm and Postmaster-Gen; summoned to Parliament of Great Britain as *Lord Lovel and Holland*, of Enmore, co Somerst 1762: m 1st, 1737, Catherine, who d 1752, da of 5th Earl of Salisbury; 2ndly, 1756, Catherine, da of Hon Charles Compton (*see* M Northampton); she was *cr Baroness Arden*, of Lohort Castle, co Cork (peerage of Ireland) 1770; he d 1772; s by his son (7) JOHN JAMES, 3rd Earl; d 1822; s by his son (8) JOHN, 4th Earl; d 1835; s by his son (9) HENRY FREDERICK JOHN, 5th Earl; d 1841; s by his cousin (10) GEORGE JAMES, 6th Earl (2nd Baron Arden, of Arden), whose father CHARLES GEORGE (Baron Arden, of Lohort), el son of Catherine, Baroness Arden, of Lohort, had been *cr Baron Arden*, of Arden, co Warwick (peerage of United Kingdom) 1802; *dsp* 1874; s by his nephew (11) CHARLES GEORGE (son of late Rev Hon Charles George Perceval, 4th son of 2nd Baron Arden, of Lohort), 7th Earl, b 1845; MP for Midhurst (C) 1874: m 1869, Lucy, who d 1932, da of late Henry King; d 1897; s by his cousin (12) AUGUSTUS ARTHUR (son of late Charles John Perceval, grandson of 2nd Baron Arden, of Lohort), 8th Earl, b 1856: m 1881, Kate, who d 1926, da of late Warwick Howell, of S Carolina, USA; d 1910; s by his brother (13) CHARLES JOHN, 9th Earl, b 1858: m 1890, Florence, who d 1954, yst da of late George Gibson, MD; d 1929, when the title was claimed by (14) FREDERICK JOSEPH TREVELYAN (a descendant of late Rt Hon Spencer Perceval, MP, 7th son of 2nd Earl), b 1873: m 1911, Cecilia, who d 1916, da of James Burns Moore, of Montreal, Canada; d 1932, without having established his claim to the Earldom; his only son (15) FREDERICK GEORGE MOORE, b 1914; established his claim as 11th Earl 1939; also Baron and Viscount Perceval, Baron Arden, and Baron Lovel and Holland.

EGREMONT, BARON LECONFIELD AND (Wyndham) (Baron UK 1859 and 1963)

To the just, right

(JOHN) MAX HENRY SCAWEN WYNDHAM (*Baron Egremont*), 7th Baron Leconfield, and 2nd Baron Egremont; b 21 April 1948; s 1972; ed Eton, and Ch Ch, Oxford; Member Royal Commn on Historical Manuscripts since 1989; Chm The Friends of the National Libraries since 1985, Trustee Wallace Collection since 1988, and British Museum since 1990, Pres Action With Rural Communities since 1993; author (as Max Egremont), *The Cousins* 1977, *Balfour* 1980, *The Ladies' Man* 1983, *Dear Shadows* 1986, *Painted Lives* 1989, and *Second Spring* 1993: m 1978, (Audrey) Caroline, elder da of Alexander Ronan Nelson, of Muckain, Taynuilt, Argyll (*see* Queenborough, By, 1990 Edn).

Arms – Azure, a chevron between three lions, heads erased or, within a bordure wavy of the last. **Crest** – A lion's head erased or, within a fetterlock, the lock gold, and the bow componée or an azure; the head charged with a saltire wavy gules. **Supporters** – *Dexter*, a winged lion azure, wings, inverted and plain collared or; *sinister*, a griffin argent, gutté de sang, plain collared, gules.
Residences – Petworth House, W Sussex GU28 0AE; Cockermouth Castle, Cumberland.

SON LIVING

Hon GEORGE RONAN VALENTINE, b 31 July, 1983.

DAUGHTERS LIVING

Hon Jessica Mary, b 1979.
Hon Constance Rose, b 1980.
Hon Mary Christian, b 1985.

BROTHER LIVING

Hon Harry Hugh Patrick, b 1957: m 1985, Susan Fiona McLean, eldest da of Bruce Woodall, of 7 Sheffield Terr, W8, and has issue living, Alexander, b 1986, — Richard, b 1990.

SISTER LIVING

Hon Caroline Elizabeth, b 1951: m 1976, Colin Chisholm, son of Archibald Hugh Tennent Chisholm, CBE, and has issue living, Hugh Archibald John, b 1976, — Mark Colin, b 1980, — Laura Carlyn, b 1978.

UNCLE LIVING (Son of 5th Baron Leconfield)

Hon Mark Hugh, OBE, MC (Newmans Cottage, Froxfield Green, Petersfield, Hants), *b* 1921: late Capt 12th R Lancers; Chm of C of E Children's Soc 1967-82; 1939-45 War in Middle East and Italy (twice wounded, MC): *m* 1st, 1947, Anne, da of late *Hon* Reginald Henry Winn (*see* B St Oswald); 2ndly, 1986, Patricia, formerly wife of Maj Henry Claude Lyon Garnett, CBE, and yr da of late Lt-Col Esmond Charles Baring, OBE (*see* B Ashburton, colls), and has issue living (by 1st *m*), Henry Mark (The Old Rectory, Southease, Lewes, E Sussex; *Clubs* – White's, MCC, Pratt's), *b* 1953; *ed* Eton, and Sorbonne, Paris; Christie's 1974-87, Art Dealer 1987-93; Chm Sotheby's UK since 1994; Cttee Member Patrons of British Art, Tate Gallery, since 1993; Gov Thomas Coram Foundation; Member Development Cttee National Gallery: *m* 1978, Rachel Sarah, yst da of late Lt-Col Leslie Francis Gordon Pritchard (*see* Wheler, Bt), and has issue living, Ned Francis Reginald *b* 1983, Leo David *b* 1985, William Henry *b* 1988, — Elizabeth Jane (*Lady Charles Spencer-Churchill*) (81 Pimlico Rd, SW1), *b* 1948: *m* 1970, Lord Charles George William Colin Spencer-Churchill (*see* D Marlborough), — Melissa Anne, *b* 1949.

AUNT LIVING (*Daughter of 5th Baron Leconfield*)

Hon Ursula Constance (Honeyway House, Petworth, Sussex), *b* 1913.

WIDOW LIVING OF SIXTH BARON LECONFIELD AND FIRST BARON EGREMONT

Pamela (*Dowager Baroness Egremont*) (Cockermouth Castle, Cockermouth, Cumbria), da of late Capt the Hon Valentine Maurice Wyndham Quin, RN (*see* E Dunraven): *m* 1947, the 6th Baron Leconfield and 1st Baron Egremont, who *d* 1972.

COLLATERAL BRANCHES LIVING

Issue of late Col Hon Everard Humphrey Wyndham, MC, yst son of 2nd Baron Leconfield, *b* 1888, *d* 1970: *m* 1920, Ruth Constance, who *d* 1984, da of late Hubert Delaval Astley, of Brinsop Court, Herefordshire (*see* B Hastings, colls):—
Michael Patrick (Quarry House, Ampney Crucis, Cirencester, Glos; *Clubs* – White's (Chm), MCC), *b* 1929; late Capt Life Guards: *m* 1st, 1957, Mrs Shelagh Anne Barker, who *d* 1967, da of late Dr Sydenham Frederick Moore, OBE, of Cairo; 2ndly, 1967, Mrs Laura Prudence Rosamund Murray, who *d* 1983, da of late Mervyn Stutchbury, of Gayles, Friston, E Sussex, and formerly wife of Christopher Mark Henry Murray (*see* Jerningham, Bt, ext 1935, 1955 Edn); 3rdly, 1985, Mrs Alison Dean, eldest da of Sir (Anthony) Reay Mackay Geddes, KBE, of 49 Eaton Place, SW1, and widow of Capt (Edward) Martin Dean, of Glen Usk, Gwent, and has issue living, (by 1st *m*) Samantha Madeline, *b* 1962, — Georgina Maria, *b* 1963: *m* 1990, Jimmy G. Penfold, son of late Graham Penfold. ——— Mary Constance (*Baroness Peyton of Yeovil*), *b* 1921: *m* 1st, 1945 (*m diss* 1966), Ralph Hamilton Cobbold, who *d* 1987; 2ndly, 1966, Baron Peyton of Yeovil (Life Baron), and has issue living (by 1st *m*), David Anthony (13 Blvd des Frères Voisin, Paris 75015), *b* 1946: *m* 1972 (*m diss* 1982), Christine Elisabeth Pearcey, and has issue living, Melissa Eve *b* 1975, — Charlotte Ruth, *b* 1949: *m* 1st, 1979 (*m diss* 1984), George Michael Maguire; 2ndly, 1993, David Thomas Williams, of 9 Ashley Rd, Montpelier, Bristol, and has issue living (by 1st *m*), Leo George *b* 1981, (by 2nd *m*) Rafe Thomas *b* 1993.

Granddaughters of late Col Guy Percy Wyndham, CB, MVO (infra):—
Issue of late Maj Guy Richard Charles Wyndham, MC, *b* 1896, *d* 1948: *m* 1st, 1920 (*m diss* 1925), Iris Winifred Youell, da of Andrew Percy Bennett, CMG, Envoy Extraor and Min Plen to Panama; 2ndly, 1930 (*m diss* 1941), Margeretha Wulfsberg:—
(By 1st *m*) Joan Olivia, *b* 1921: *m* 1st, 1947 (*m diss* 1952), Maurice Rowdon; 2ndly, 1952, Alexander Shivarg, of 429 Fulham Rd, SW10, and has issue living, (by 1st *m*) Clare Viola, *b* 1947: *m* 19—, J. Soares, — (by 2nd *m*) Camilla Gabrielle (34 Edith Grove, SW10), *b* 1953. ——— (By 2nd *m*) Ingrid Olivia Georgia, *b* 1931: *m* 1st 1951 (*m diss* 1963), Hon Jonathan Bryan Guinness (later 3rd Baron Moyne); 2ndly, 1963, Rt Hon (Henry) Paul Guinness Channon MP (*see* E Iveagh, 1976 Edn), of 96 Cheyne Walk, SW10, and Kelvedon Hall, Brentwood, Essex, and has had issue, (by 2nd *m*), Henry, *b* 1970, — Olivia Gwendolen Violet, *b* 1964, *d* 1986, — Georgia Honor Margarethe, *b* 1966.

Grandsons of late Capt Hon Percy Scawen Wyndham, 3rd son of 1st Baron Leconfield:—
Issue of late Col Guy Percy Wyndham, CB, MVO, *b* 1865, *d* 1941: *m* 1st, 1892, Edwina Virginia Joanna, who *d* 1919, da of Rev Frederick Fitzpatrick, and widow of John Monck Brooks (*see* M Headfort); 2ndly, 1923, Violet Lutetia, who *d* 1979, da of late Ernest Leverson:—
(By 2nd *m*) Francis Guy Percy (19 Lonsdale Rd, W11) *b* 1924; *ed* Eton, and at Ch Ch, Oxford. ——— Hugh Guy Osbert (64 Osborne St, Swindon), *b* 1926; *ed* Eton, and at Corpus Christi Coll, Oxford, Capt late Coldstream Guards: *m* 1961 (*m diss* 1966), Edith Elizabeth Creswick, el da of late John Watson, FRIBA, of Old Mains, Giffnock, Glasgow and has issue living, Rachel Olivia Violet, *b* 1963; ARCM.

PREDECESSORS – The 7th Duke of Somerset, who inherited the Percy estates, including the lands of Egremont, Cumberland, from his mother Elizabeth, da and heir of the 11th Earl of Northumberland, was *cr Earl of Egremont* 1749, with special remainder to his maternal nephew Sir Charles Wyndham, 4th baronet of Orchard Wyndham, Som. The Egremont estates passed to the 1st Earl of Northumberland (*cr* 1377) on his 2nd *m* to Maud (who *dsp*), sister and heir of Anthony, Lord Lucy. These, and the Sussex estates of the Percys, were devised to the 2nd Earl of Egremont. (1) *Col* GEORGE Wyndham, natural son and adopted heir of George O'Brien, 3rd Earl of Egremont: *b* 1787; a Col in the Army; *cr Baron Leconfield*, of Leconfield, E Riding of York (peerage of United Kingdom) 1859: *m* 1815, Mary Fanny, who *d* 1863, da of Rev William Blunt, of Crabbett, Sussex; *d* 1869; *s* by his son (2) HENRY, 2nd Baron, *b* 1830; MP for W Sussex (C) 1854-69: *m* 1867, Lady Constance Evelyn Primrose, who *d* 1939, having been raised to the rank of an Earl's da 1886, 2nd da of late Lord Dalmeny; *d* 1901; *s* by his el surviving son (3) CHARLES HENRY, GCVO, 3rd Baron; *b* 1872; Co Comdt Roy Sussex Vol 1917-18, and Lord-Lt of Sussex 1917-49: *m* 1911, Beatrice Violet, who *d* 1956, da of late Col Richard Hamilton Rawson, MP; *d* 1952; *s* by his brother (4) HUGH ARCHIBALD, 4th Baron, *b* 1877: *m* 1908, Hon Maud Mary Lyttleton, who *d* 1953, da of 8th Viscount Cobham; *d* 1963; *s* by his brother, (5) EDWARD SCAWEN, DSO, 5th Baron, *b* 1883: *m* 1907, Gladys Mary, who *d* 1971, da of late Fitzroy James Wilberforce Farquhar (*see* Farquhar, Bt, colls), *d* 1967; *s* by his son (6) JOHN EDWARD REGINALD, MBE (who was *cr Baron Egremont*, of Petworth, co Sussex, 1963), 6th Baron, *b* 1920; Private Sec to PM 1957-63; a Trustee of Wallace Collection 1953-72; *m* 1947, Pamela, da of Capt Hon Valentine Maurice Wyndham Quin, RN (E Dunraven), *d* 1972; *s* by his el son (7) JOHN MAX HENRY SCAWEN, 7th Baron Leconfield, 2nd Baron Egremont, and present peer.

ELDON, EARL OF (Scott) (Earl UK 1821)

JOHN JOSEPH NICHOLAS SCOTT, 5th Earl; *b* 24 April 1937; *s* 1976; *ed* Ampleforth Coll, and Trin Coll, Oxford; Lt Scots Gds Army Emergency Reserve: *m* 1961, Countess Claudine, yst da of Count Franz von Montjoye-Vaufrey and de la Roche, of 45 Hasenauerstrasse, Vienna 18, and has issue.

Arms – Argent, an anchor erect sable, between three lions' heads erased gules; on a chief wavy azure, a portcullis with chains or. **Crest** – A lion's head erased gules, gorged with a chain, and pendant therefrom a portcullis or. **Supporters** – Two lions guardant proper, each gorged with a double chain and a portcullis attached thereto gold, pendent from the portcullis a shield argent, charged with a civic wreath vert.

Let honour be without stain

SON LIVING

JOHN FRANCIS THOMAS MARIE JOSEPH COLUMBA FIDELIS (*Viscount Encombe*), *b* 9 July 1962.

DAUGHTERS LIVING

Lady Tatiana Maria Laura Rose Columba Fidelis, *b* 1967: *m* 1989, Anthony C. Wilson, eldest son of Jeffery Graham Wilson, of 1 Grove Rd, Northwood, Middx.
Lady Victoria Laura Maria Magdalene, *b* 1968.

BROTHER LIVING

Hon Simon Peter (Frogden, Kelso, Roxburghshire TD5 8AB), *b* 1939; was a Page of Honour to HM 1953-56; *ed* Ampleforth Coll, Salamanca and Madrid Univs, and Sorbonne (Paris); Lt Scots Guards Army Emergency Reserve: *m* 1966, Mary Isabel, da of late Andrew Ramon Dalzell de Bertodano (*see* E Mexborough, 1948 Edn), and has issue living, Sebastian Andrew, *b* 1967, — Benedict Simon, *b* 1971, — James Joseph Michael, *b* 1974, — Maria Sylvia Rose, *b* 1968.

COLLATERAL BRANCHES LIVING

Grandchildren of late Hon Michael Simon Scott (*infra*):—
Issue of late Michael Richard Scott, *b* 1937, *d* 1981: *m* 1964, Pamela Hanford (Long Lane, Far Hills, NJ 07931, USA) (who *m* 2ndly, 19—, Marshall Jeanes), da of Wellington Vandeveer:—
Michael Simon, *b* 1966. —— Andrew Fraser, *b* 1973. —— Wendy Vendeveer, *b* 1967. —— Katherine Brady, *b* 1970.

Granddaughter of late John, Viscount Encombe, el son of 3rd Earl:—
Issue of late Hon Michael Simon Scott, *b* 1900, *d* 1938: *m* 1928, Ruth (who *d* 1972, having *m* 2ndly, 1944, Lieut-Com Adams Batcheller, who *d* 1950), da of late James Cox Brady:—
Sheila Maria (Box 176, Far Hills, NJ 07931, USA), *b* 1932: *m* 1952, Philip Webster Smith, Jr, and has issue living, Philip Webster (III) (Box 944, Far Hills, NJ 07931, USA), *b* 1955: *m* 1983, Hillary, da of Vincent R. Bailey, and has issue living, Philip Webster (IV) *b* 1988, Courtney Converse *b* 1986, — Michael Simon (Box 56, Far Hills, NJ 07931, USA), *b* 1959: *m* 1987, Anne Marie, da of Cornelius Murray, and has issue living, Katherine Fraser *b* 1989, Elizabeth Clark *b* 1992, — Elizabeth Brady, *b* 1954: *m* 1979, Wayne Barry Lawrence, of 144 Larch Row, Wenham, Mass 01984, USA, and has issue living, Andrew Brady *b* 1986, Alexandra Webster *b* 1984.

Issue of late Hon Sir Ernest Stowell Scott, KCMG, MVO, 2nd son of 3rd Earl, *b* 1872, *d* 1953: *m* 1941, Winifred Kathleen Brodrick, who *d* 1990:—
Margaret Rachel (19 Lambourn Rd, SW4), *b* 1943: *m* 1964 (*m diss* 1973), David Edward Wyndham Tennant (*see* B Glenconner, colls).

Issue of late Hon Osmund Scott, 3rd son of 3rd Earl; *b* 1876, *d* 1948: *m* 1906, Mary Cecilia, who *d* 1941, da of late Com Dudley Charles Stuart, RN (M Bute, colls):—
Harold Eldon, *b* 1907; *ed* Winchester; Lieut-Col (ret) Queen's Own Royal W Kent Regt: *m* 1938, Daphne Josephine, who *d* 1985, da of Col Fitzhardinge Hancock, of Congham Hall, King's Lynn, and has issue living, David Eldon (Encombe House, Corfe Castle, Dorset), *b* 1939: *m* 1966, Clover Noakes, and has issue living, Rupert Eldon *b* 1967, Henry Eldon *b* 1969, — Verena Mary, *b* 1942: *m* 1963, Simon Norman Philips (*see* E Ducie, colls, 1956 Edn), of Huerta Alajate, Manilva, Malaga, Spain, and has issue living, Lucy Jane *b* 1964, Sophie Ann *b* 1966, — Angela Lindsay, *b* 1949: *m* 1st, 1978 (*m diss* 1987), Daniel Sicardi; 2ndly, 1987, Count Christopher Levin Orssich, of Mayfield, W Grafton, Marlborough, Wilts (*see* B Faringdon, colls, 1985 Edn), and has issue living (by 1st *m*), Rebecca Tania *b* 1983, (by 2nd *m*) Nicholas Robert *b* 1988, — Suzanne, *b* 1952: *m* 1977, Peter Woloszynski, of Fortnight Farm, Combe Hay, Bath, Avon, and has issue living, Harry Maximilian Andrew *b* 1982, Emily *b* 1980. *Residence* - East Wing, Encombe House, Corfe Castle, Dorset. —— †Alan Dudley, *b* 1910; late Capt RE; ARIBA, AA Dip: *m* 1936, Dorothy Dulany (Thea) (who *d* 1988, having *m* 2ndly, 1953, Maj Alexander Soldatenkov, who *d* 1954), only da of late Lt-Col Sefton Dulany Brancker, of The Croft, Crowborough, Sussex, and *d* 1951, leaving issue, Dudley John Eldon (Patrijsstraat 49, 6971 VP Brummen, Holland), *b* 1939: *m* 1st, 1961, Irene Florence, only da of Frederick James Smith, of 30 Old Lane, Chobham, Surrey; 2ndly, 1982, Annelies, da of late Jacobus Leonardus Arnoldus Hotz, and has issue living (by 1st *m*), Alan James *b* 1964, Maria Lynn *b* 1963, — Caroline Edith Mary, *b* 1946: *m* 1st, 1969 (*m diss* 1984), Michael John Theobald; 2ndly, 1992, Anthony Terrence Garrett, of 4 Castilian Mews, Ramleaze Drive, Shaw, Swindon, Wilts SN5 9PR, and has issue living (by 1st *m*), Emma Caroline Mary *b* 1975, Amelia Margaret Jennifer *b* 1978, — Jennifer Dorothy Dulany, *b* 1948. —— Eric Surtees, MBE, *b* 1912; *ed* Bradfield, and RMC Sandhurst; Lt-Col (ret) The Buffs (Royal E Kent Regt); N-W Europe 1944-45 (MBE Mil 1945): *m* 1938, Rose Anne, only da of late Lt-Col Charles Edward Stewart, RA, and has issue living, Michael Ian Eldon, CBE, DSO (c/o Royal Bank of Scotland, Whitehall, SW1), *b* 1941; *ed* Bradfield, and RMA Sandhurst; Maj-Gen late Scots Gds; Equerry to HRH The Duke of Gloucester 1965-66; served S Atlantic Campaign 1982 (DSO 1982): *m* 1968, Veronica Mary, yr da of late Capt J. H. Daniell, and of Mrs J. A. Hilton, of 106 Cranmer Court, SW3, and has issue living, Charles Daniell Eldon *b* 1970, Louisa Claire *b* 1971, — Veronica Susan (Wadmill Farm, Stour Row, Shaftesbury, Dorset), *b* 1944: *m* 1965, Michael Conway Phayre-Mudge, who *d* 1983, and has issue living, Marcus Andrew *b* 1968, Zoë Catherine *b* 1970. *Residence* - Pound House, Wareham, Dorset. —— †Kenneth Bertram, MC, *b* 1915; served 1939-45 War (MC) as Maj Royal W Kent Regt: *m* 1939, Denise Primrose Garnet (Kim) (who *d* 1968, having *m* 2ndly, 1952, Alan Blackwell, of Laurel Farm, Little Barningham, Aldborough, Norwich), 2nd da of Garnet Leslie Clark, of The Red House, Tadworth, Surrey, and was *ka* in Sicily 1943, leaving issue, John Kenneth Eldon, *b* 1940; *ed* privately, and at Ruskin Sch of Art, Oxford.

Issue of late Capt Hon Denys Scott, 4th son of 3rd Earl, *b* 1877, *d* 1962: *m* 1907, Lillis Amy, who *d* 1970, da of late Com Dudley Charles Stuart, RN (M Bute, colls):—
John Ernest Dudley (Ridgeway, Eastacombe, nr Barnstaple, N Devon EX31 3NT), *b* 1908; AFRAeS; formerly Sqdn-Ldr RAFO: *m* 1st, 1934 (*m diss* 1937), Joan Gwendolen, da of R. Clayton-Cooper; 2ndly, 1937, Ethel Daphne Smith, who *d* 1956; 3rdly, 1957, Margaret Lila Monro, MRCS, LRCP, who *d* 1973, da of Bertram John Monro, of Rydal Mount, Hendon; 4thly, 1975, Barbara Anne Veit, who *d* 1990, and has had issue (by 1st *m*), Peter Denys John, QC (4 Eldon Rd, W8 5PU; Fountain Court, Temple, EC4), *b* 1935; *ed* Monroe High Sch, Rochester, NY, and Balliol Coll, Oxford (MA); late Lieut RHA; Bar Middle Temple 1960, QC 1978, Chm Bar Council 1987 (Vice-Chm 1985-86), — (by 2nd *m*) Roger John Stuart (Barn Owl, Holmacott, Instow, Bideford, N Devon EX39 4LR), *b* 1939; *ed* Uppingham, and RAF Tech Coll, Henlow; Sqdn-Ldr RAF: *m* 1st, 1967 (*m diss* 1991), Mary Alexandra, eldest da of late Alexander Lynch, of Limerick; 2ndly, 1991, Sally Constance, da of late Donald Golege-Steel, of Hurley Cottage, Hurley, Berks, and has issue living (by 1st *m*), Alexander John Stuart *b* 1968, Louise Katherine *b* 1973, — (Daphne) Charmian, *b* 1942: *m* 1964, Jeremy David Pickett-Heaps, and was *k* in a flying accidcent in Colorado, USA, 1971, leaving issue, David Angus *b* 1967, Rebecca *b* 1969, — Georgina Rosemary, *b* 1944. —— Frederick Denys (Burrough House, Northiam, Bideford, N Devon), *b* 1909; late Lieut DCLI (SR). —— Eustace Ian (Lower Uppacott Farm, Upper Tawstock, Barnstaple, N Devon), *b* 1911; *ed* Harrow; late Capt RA, served 1939-45 War: *m* 1950, Daphne Ann, yst da of late Lt-Col Arthur O'Brien ffrench Blake, of Giles Lane, Canterbury, Kent.

PREDECESSORS – (1) *Rt Hon Sir* JOHN SCOTT, KB, one of the most distinguished lawyers of England, was son of a merchant at Newcastle, and yr brother of Baron Stowell (*cr* 1821, extinct 1836); was Solicitor-Gen 1788, Attorney-Gen 1793, Lord Chief Justice of the Common Pleas 1799-1801, and Lord High Chancellor 1801-6 and 1807-27; *cr Baron Eldon*, of Eldon, co Durham (peerage of Great Britain) 1799, and *Viscount Encombe* and *Earl of Eldon* (peerage of United Kingdom) 1821; *d* 1838; *s* by his grandson (2) JOHN, DCL, 2nd Earl, *b* 1805; MP for Truro 1828-31: *m* 1831, Hon Louisa Duncombe, da of 1st Baron Feversham; *d* 1854; *s* by his son (3) JOHN, 3rd Earl; *b* 1845: *m* 1869, Henrietta Minna, who *d* 1921, da of Capt Henry Martin Turnor; *d* 1926; *s* by his grandson (4) JOHN, GCVO (son of late John, Viscount Encombe, el son of 3rd Earl), 4th Earl; *b* 1899; a Lord-in-Waiting to HM 1937-68: *m* 1934, Hon Magdalen Mary Charlotte Fraser, OBE, who *d* 1969, da of 14th Lord Lovat; *d* 1976; *s* by his el son (5) JOHN JOSEPH NICHOLAS, 5th Earl and present peer; also Viscount Encombe, and Baron Eldon.

ELGIN AND KINCARDINE, EARL OF (Bruce) (Earl S 1633)

We have been

ANDREW DOUGLAS ALEXANDER THOMAS BRUCE, KT, 11th Earl of Elgin and 15th Earl of Kincardine; *b* 17 Feb 1924; *s* 1968; *ed* Eton, and Balliol Coll, Oxford (MA); Hon LLD Dundee and Glasgow, Hon D Litt St Mary's, Nova Scotia; JP and DL of co Fife, Lord Lieut since 1987; HM Lt-Col; Comdt Fife Bn, Army Cadet Force 1951-65; Grand Master Mason of Scotland 1961-65; Lord High Commr to General Assembly of Church of Scotland 1980-81; Ensign Queen's Body Guard for Scotland (Royal Co of Archers), and Bde Pres, Boys' Bde 1963-85; a Dir Scottish Amicable Life Assurance Soc; Chm Nat Savings Cttee for Scotland 1972-78; Hon Col The Elgin Regt (Canada); Hon Col 153(H) Regt RCT(V) TAVR 1980-87; 1939-45 War as Lt Scots Guards (wounded); KT (1981): *m* 1959, Victoria Mary, only da of Maj Dudley George Usher, MBE, TD, Scottish Horse (Hunter Blair, Bt, colls), and has issue.

Arms – Or, a saltire and chief gules, on a canton argent, a lion rampant azure, armed and langued of the second. **Crest** – A lion statant, tail extended azure, armed and langued gules. **Supporters** – Two wild men, proper, wreathed round the temples and loins with laurel vert.
Residence – Broomhall, Dunfermline, Fife KY11 3DU.

SONS LIVING

CHARLES EDWARD (*Lord Bruce*), *b* 19 Oct 1961; *ed* Eton, and St Andrew's Univ (MA); a Page of Honour to HM Queen Elizabeth The Queen Mother 1975-77: *m* 1990, Amanda Leigh, yr da of James Movius, of Fairbanks, Alaska, and has issue:—
    SONS LIVING - Hon James Andrew Charles Robert (*Master of Bruce*), *b* 16 Nov 1991, — *Hon* George Benjamin Thomas, *b* 1993.
    DAUGHTER LIVING - *Hon* Antonia Jean, *b* 1990.
Residence – Blackhall Farm, Grange Rd, Dunfermline KY11 3DY. *Club* – Brooks's.
Hon Adam Robert, *b* 1968; *ed* Glenalmond, Balliol Coll, Oxford (BA) (Pres Oxford Union 1989), and Edinburgh Univ (LLB).
Residence – 8 Montgomery St, Edinburgh EH7 5JS.
Hon Alexander Victor, *b* 1971; *ed* Glenalmond.

DAUGHTERS LIVING

Lady Georgiana Mary, *b* 1960.
Lady Antonia Katherine, *b* 1964: *m* 1989, Marcel Ballot, son of Jacques-Henri Ballot, of Paris.

BROTHERS LIVING

Hon James Michael Edward, CBE, *b* 1927; *ed* Eton; late Lt Scots Guards; a JP of Perthshire; FRSA, FInstD; a Member Home Grown Timber Advisory Cttee; Chm SWOAC Holdings Ltd 1967-93; Hon Fellow Scottish Council for Development & Industry 1993, Hon Fellow Game Conservancy 1993; CBE 1992: *m* 1st, 1950 (*m diss* 1974), Hon (Margaret) Jean Dagbjørt Coats, da of 2nd Baron Glentanar (ext); 2ndly, 1975, Morven-Anne, da of Alistair Macdonald, of Dalguise, Perthshire, and has had issue (by 1st *m*), Robert James Thomas, *b* 1953; *ed* Eton: *d* 1979, — John Edward (Balmanno Castle, Perth PH2 9HG), *b* 1958, — Michael Andrew (Glen Tanar House, Aboyne, Aberdeenshire AB34 5EU), *b* 1961: *m* 1988, Claire M., eldest da of James Mattocks, of Brussels, Belgium, and has issue living, Alasdair James Thomas *b* 1991, Eleanor Marie Jean *b* 1993, — (Janet) Clare, *b* 1954: *m* 1979, John Seton Burrell Carson, of Congalton, N Berwick, E Lothian EH39 5JL, elder son of Alan Carson, of Drumbain, Dunure, Ayrshire, and has issue living, David *b* 1986, Iona Jane *b* 1981, Rachel Anne *b* 1983,

Alice Mary *b* 1989, Rosanna Jean *b* (triplet) 1989, Sophie Katherine *b* (triplet) 1989, — (by 2nd *m*) Alexander James, *b* 1977, — Simon Alistair, *b* 1979, — Katherine Ann, *b* 1980, — Emma Victoria, *b* 1987. *Residence* – Dron House, Balmanno, by Perth. *Clubs* – New (Edinburgh), Pratt's.

Hon Edward David, *b* 1936; *ed* Eton, and Balliol Coll, Oxford (BA 1960); late Lieut Intelligence Corps; Chm Bruce Stevenson Ltd; Chm Youth Clubs Scotland: *m* 1960, Sara Elisabeth Wallop, yr da of late Capt Newton James Wallop William-Powlett, DSC, JP, RN (*see* E Portsmouth, colls) and has issue living, Newton Edward John, *b* 1964, — Anna Catherine *b* 1962: *m* 1988, Edward H. Hocknell, of 5 Dundas St, Edinburgh, elder son of Peter Hocknell, of Willaston, Cheshire, and has issue living, Henrietta Jean Wallop *b* 1992. *Residence* – Blairhill, Rumbling Bridge, Kinross.

SISTERS LIVING

Lady Martha Veronica, OBE, TD, *b* 1921: Gov HM Prison, Greenock 1970-75, Gov HM Institution, Cornton Vale, Stirling 1975-83, and a JP for co Fife; Lady-in-Waiting to HRH late Princess Royal Jan to March 1965; OBE (Mil) 1958. *Residence* – Gardener's Cottage, The Old Orchard, Limekilns, Dunfermline KY11 3HS.

Lady Jean Christian, *b* 1923; formerly in WAAF; DL Perth 1988: *m* 1945, Capt David Wemyss of Wemyss, late Roy Corps of Signals (*see* E Wemyss, colls). *Residence* – Invermay, Fortcviot, Perthshire.

WIDOW LIVING OF SON OF NINTH EARL

Mary Patricia, da of late Maj Donald Ramsay Macdonald, DSO, MC, of Hollymount, co Carlow, and formerly wife of Gerald Francis Annesley, of Castlewellan, co Down: *m* 1976, as his 3rd wife, Maj Hon Bernard Bruce, MC, who *d* 1983. *Residence* – Culross Abbey House, Culross, Dunfermline, Fife KY12 8JB.

COLLATERAL BRANCHES LIVING

Issue of late Major Hon Robert Bruce, CBE, 2nd son of 9th Earl, *b* 1882, *d* 1959: *m* 1910, Mary Katherine, who *d* 1982, da of late Maj-Gen Hon John Edward Lindley (*see* B Lindley):—
Veronica Mary (Finlarig House, Rafford, Morayshire), *b* 1911; Director of Cygnet Ballet Sch, Forres. —— Isobel Ursula, *b* 1920; sometime in WRNS. *Residence* – 114 Watchfield Court, Sutton Court Rd, Chiswick, W4 4ND.

Issue of late Col Hon David Bruce, 4th son of 9th Earl, *b* 1888, *d* 1964: *m* 1919, Jennet, OBE, who *d* 1982, da of late Rt Rev Atherton Gwillym Rawstorne, DD, Suffragan Bishop of Whalley:—
Rachel Mary, *b* 1922; HM Coastguard Ser 1940-45: *m* 1967, as his 2nd wife, Rear-Adm Bryan Cecil Durant, CB, DSO, DSC, who *d* 1983, of The Old House, Bighton, nr Alresford, Hants.

Issue of late Capt Hon John Bernard Bruce, RN, 5th son of 9th Earl, *b* 1892, *d* 1971: *m* 1923, Helen Rachel, who *d* 1983, 3rd da of late Henry Feilden Rawstorne, of Roche Court, Fareham, Hants:—
Henry Victor BRUCE OF SALLOCH (Barley Down House, Ovington Down, Alresford, Hants; Farmers' Club, and MCC), *b* 1924; *ed* Eton and Roy Agric Coll, Cirencester: Lt-Cdr RN (ret), and a Farmer; recognised in the name of Bruce of Salloch by Lord Lyon 1985; JP and DL Hants 1984; Councillor of Winchester, Itchen Stoke and Ovington with Northington 1963-74; Chm of Hants Co Scout Council 1964-75, since when a Vice-Pres; a Gen Commr of Income Tax since 1966: *m* 1951, Helen Vernon Wallop, da of late Vice-Adm Sir Peveril Barton Reibey Wallop William-Powlett, KCB, KCMG, CBE, DSO (*see* E Portsmouth, colls), and has issue living, Peveril John (Hampage House, Ovington, nr Alresford, Hants), *b* 1953; *ed* Eton; ACA 1976, FCA 1981; Farmer: *m* 1986, Rosamond Cornelia McLay (Minna), yr da of Neil McLay Mills (*see* B Hazlerigg, 1990 Edn), and has issue living, Otto Feilden *b* 1989, Finn Cardigan *b* 1992, — Alastair Andrew Bernard Reibey BRUCE OF CRIONAICH (9 Churton Pl, SW1), *b* 1960; *ed* Milton Abbey, and RMA Sandhurst; late Lt Scots Guards, served S Atlantic Campaign 1982; Capt SG (TA); recognised in the name of Bruce of Crionaich by Lord Lyon 1984; OStJ; Assist Vice-Pres Merrill Lynch 1983-89, since when a TV documentary maker and commentator; Gov Milton Abbey, — Robina Helen *b* 1952; SRN 1974; Member Nightingale Fund Council 1982: *m* 1977, Nigel Edward Charles Talbot-Ponsonby, and has issue (*see* E Shrewsbury, colls), — Lucinda Jane, *b* 1956: *m* 1981, Laurence Keith Scott, of Roe Green, Martyr Worthy, Hants, and has issue living, Henry Edward Osborne *b* 1982, Toby Alexander Peveril *b* 1984, Oliver Charles Somerville *b* 1987, Barnaby Richard Laurence *b* 1989, Harvey Michael Lucknam *b* 1991. —— *Rev* Francis Bernard (Bibury Vicarage, Cirencester, Glos; and Westcott House, Cambridge), *b* 1930; *ed* Eton, and Trin Coll, Oxford (MA); Assist Curate of Bury 1954-58, and Sherborne Abbey, and Curate in charge of St Paul's, Sherborne 1958-61, R of St Michael and All Angels, Croston 1961-86, since when V of Bibury with Winson and R of Barnsley, Glos: *m* 1957, Fiona Jane Beryl, da of Capt John Robert Sutherland Haines, CBE, RN, and has issue living, Simon Jock *b* 1959: *m* 1988, Emma Félise, only da of Sir Martin Wakefield Jacomb (*see* Heathcoat-Amory, Bt, colls), and has issue living, Patrick Francis Martin *b* 1991, Dominic Simon Mark *b* 1993, — Jonathan Francis, *b* 1967, — Emma Cecilia Rachel, *b* 1960. —— Victor Robert (Brook House, Henley Rd, Marlow, Bucks), *b* 1932: *ed* Eton; MB, BS London 1956; DRCOG 1958; Surg-Lt RN (ret): *m* 1956, Dorothy May, da of late Rev Arthur E. Pavey, and has issue living, Angus Robert John, *b* 1960: *m* 1985, Jill Moughlin, and has issue living, Hamish Charles Victor, *b* 1962. —— Alexander Rawstorne (9 Av de Foestraets, 1180 Brussels), *b* 1936; *ed* Eton: *m* 1962, Beatrice Germaine, da of Jacques-Etienne Rossièr, of Champbabaud, Veytaux, Vaud, Switzerland. —— The late Capt Hon John B. Bruce, RN, and Mrs Bruce, also adopted a son, Timothy Robertson (The Old Rectory, Combs, Stowmarket, Suffolk IP14 2JS), *b* 1942; *ed* Radley: *m* 1st, 1972 (*m diss* 1983), (Diana) Olivia, da of late George Raymond Tibbitt (*see* Agnew, Bt, *cr* 1895, colls, 1970 Edn); 2ndly, 1988, Mrs Susan Mary Nicholson, da of John Fraser Carnegie, MVO (*see* D Fife, colls), and has issue living (by 1st *m*), Tania Romayne, *b* 1973, — Diana Iona, *b* 1975. —— Constance Madeline, *b* 1927: *m* 1949, Lt-Cdr Godfrey Joseph Hines, RN (ret), of Crossways, Droxford, Hants, and has issue living, Catherine Angela, *b* 1950, — Fiona Madeleine, *b* 1952. —— Mabel Cecilia Helen (Celia), *b* 1939: *m* 1963, Lt-Cdr Lachlan Ronald Duncan, The Mackintosh of Mackintosh, OBE, JP, FSA (Scot), RN (ret), Lord Lieut of Inverness, Cllr Highland Regional Council since 1974, of Moy Hall, Tomatin, Inverness IV13 7YQ, and has issue living, John Lachlan, *b* 1969, — Louisa Celia, *b* 1962: *m* 1987, Stuart Robert Cross, of 2 Drylaw Green, Edinburgh EH4 2AZ, — Bridget Margaret, *b* 1966: *m* 1993, Paul W. Dickson, of 28 Pentland Drive, Comiston, Edinburgh EH10 6PX, and has issue living, Heather Mackintosh *b* 1994.

Grandsons of late Hon Frederick John Bruce (*infra*):—
Issue of late Lewis Bruce, *b* 1880, *d* 1961: *m* 1911, Anne Margaret Macdonald, who *d* 1961, da of late Robert Burt Ranken, WS, of Edinburgh:—
John Frederick Lambton, *b* 1912: *m* 1941, his cousin, Marjory Katherine Fernie, da of Charles Bruce (*infra*), and has issue living, Penelope Margaret, *b* 1943, — Juliet Louisa, *b* 1950, — Janet Marion, *b* 1956. *Residence* – Lambda Cottage, Wick Hill, Finchampstead, Berks. —— Robert Richard Fernie, DFC (1 Orchard Close, Hardwicke, Gloucester GL2 6SZ), *b* 1915; BMus 1938; 1939-45 War as Fl-Lt RAF Vol Reserve (DFC and Bar): *m* 1941, Beatrice, da of late A. Tombolini, of 55 Wainfelin Av, Pontypool, and has issue living, Richard Stephen Witherington (347 Crawford Rd, Inglewood, W Australia 6052), *b* 1942, MB, BS London: FRCA, FANZCA, MRACMA: *m* 1st, 1965 (*m diss* 1969), Frances Mary, da of K. G. Morgan, MRCVS, of Lyttleton, Welsh St, Chepstow; 2ndly, 1969 (*m diss* 1984), Katherine Jane, da of late Mrs J. A. Hunter, of W. Australia, and has issue living (by 1st *m*) Katherine Blanche Mary *b* 1966, — Anthony James Lewis (12 Darwin St, Castle, Northwich, Cheshire), *b* 1948; BSc: *m* 1st, 1972 (*m diss* 1991), Glenys Vaughan, da of late J. Jones, of Caernarvon; 2ndly, 1994, Veronica Ellen, da of late A. B. Seccombe, of Mansfield, and has issue living (by 1st *m*), Elgan Lewis *b* 1977, Lowri Ann *b* 1975, Catrin Ellen *b* 1981, — Katharine Anne Russell, *b* 1945; MCSP: *m* 1968, John Mervyn Henry Clements, MA, ACA (Casal de Granja, Quinta dos Lagos, Várzea de Sintra, Portugal), and has issue living, Timothy Robert Henry *b* 1968, Charles Richard

Edward *b* 1971, Victoria Penelope Louise *b* 1972. —— †James Alexander, *b* 1919: *m* 1952, Joan Beryl Marion Elizabeth, da of Granville Alexander Silby, and widow of Group Capt Walter Donald Butler, RAF, and *d* 1989, leaving issue, Nigel Charles, *b* 1954, — Miranda Veronica, *b* 1953. —— Katharine Anne Doughty (1 Palace Gate, High St, Odiham, Hants RG25 1JZ), *b* 1921; ARCM: *m* 1971, Sidney John Doe, who *d* 1993.

Grandchildren of late Capt Charles Bruce (infra):—
Issue of late Lieut David Charles Richard Bruce, RN, *b* 1928; *d* 1957: *m* 1950, Georgina (PO Box 242, Paphos Post Office, Paphos, Greece) (who *m* 2ndly, 1968, Peter Joseph Bruce-Souster), da of G. E. Keay, of 5 Erith Rd, Bexleyheath, Kent:—
Roland Christopher, *b* 1956. —— Clarissa Jane Fernie, *b* 1952. —— Fiona Geraldine, *b* 1953. —— Miranda Jacqueline, *b* 1955.

Granddaughters of late Hon Frederick John Bruce, yst son of 8th Earl:—
Issue of late Capt Charles Bruce, *b* 1883, *d* 1958: *m* 1918, Joan (Rubec Cottage, Wick Hill, Finchampstead, Berks), da of Isaac Newton Woodiwiss, of Trusthope Hall, Lincolnshire:—
Marjory Katherine Fernie, *b* 1919: *m* 1941, her cousin, John Frederick Lambton Bruce (ante). *Residence* – Lambda Cottage, Wick Hill, Finchampstead, Berks. —— Isobel Seaton, *b* 1921: *m* 1956, Joseph Henry Clift, who *d* 1986, and has issue living, Michael Charles David, *b* 1957, — Simon Paul, *b* 1963. *Residence* – 5 Lemin Parc, Reawla Lane, Gwinear, Hayle, Cornwall TR27 5HJ. —— Jill Rosalind Dodsworth (The Old Rectory, E Bridgford, Nottingham), *b* 1927; BA, Oxford: *m* 1st, 1949 (*m diss* 1968), James Mayo Alastair Gunn; 2ndly, 1977, Bryan L. C. Dodsworth, and has issue living (by 1st *m*), Henry Alastair Bruce, *b* 1951, — David James Paul, *b* 1956, — Nicola Fernie, *b* 1952, — Ann Veronica, *b* 1954.

Granddaughter of Robert Charles Bruce, MC (infra):—
Issue of late David Bruce, *b* 1920, *d* 1978: *m* 1949 (*m diss* 1958), Elizabeth Joan, da of late Maj-Gen Philip Saxon George Gregson-Ellis, CB, OBE (*see* Lloyd, Bt (ext) 1975 Edn):—
(Cynthia) Penelope Helen, *b* 1951: *m* 1981, Charles Walter Bartholomew Pumphrey (*see* Riddell, Bt), of 23 Trinity Crescent, SW17 7AG, and has issue living, Oliver James, *b* 1986, — David Laurence, *b* 1989, — Katharine Elizabeth, *b* 1983.

Granddaughter of late Charles Thomas Bruce, el son of late Hon Thomas Charles Bruce, 5th son of 7th Earl:—
Issue of late Robert Charles Bruce, MC, *b* 1898, *d* 1953: *m* 1919, Hon Kate Mary Maugham, who *d* 1961, da of 1st Viscount Maugham:—
Katherine Mary (Garth House, Llangammarch Wells, Breconshire), *b* 1928: *m* 1st, 1948 (*m diss* 1960), John Scott; 2ndly, 1968, Francis Amcotts Wilson (*see* Wilson, Bt, *cr* 1874), and has issue living, (by 1st *m*) Caroline Judith, *b* 1950: *m* 1st, 1970 (*m diss* 1984), Michael David Sykes; 2ndly, 1990, Adrian Charles de Vries Owen-Smith, and has issue living (by 1st *m*), Jeremy James *b* 1974, Wiliam Oliver *b* 1978, (by 2nd *m*) Emily Florence *b* 1990, — Katherine Dinah (twin) *b* 1950: *m* 1971, John Hunter Pemberton, and has issue living, Michael Hunter *b* 1975, Susan Clare *b* 1973, — and has an adopted son and da (by 2nd *m*) (*see* Wilson, Bt, *cr* 1874).

PREDECESSORS – (1) Thomas BRUCE, of Clackmannan: *m* Marjorie Charteris; *d* 1359; *s* by their son (2) Robert, who had a Charter of King DAVID II of castle, lands and barony of Clackmannan 9 Dec 1359; *s* 1403 by his son (3) Robert; *s* 1405 by his son (4) David; *s* by his son (5) John; *s* by his son (6) Sir David, who made his second son (7) David, heir to Barony of Clackmannan 1481; *s* by his son (8) Sir David, who *m* Jean Blaccader of Tulliallan, and had 6 sons and 4 daughters, of whom 3rd son, (9) Edward Bruce was *m* to Alison Reid, and had 4 sons. Their second son was (10) *Sir* EDWARD Bruce, Knt, PC, a Lord of Session 1597-1603, accompanied King James to England on his accession 1603, was naturalized that year, and appointed Master of the Rolls for life; *cr Lord Kinloss* (peerage of Scotland) 1602, with remainder to his heirs and assigns whatsoever, and *Lord Bruce of Kinloss* (peerage of Scotland) 1604 with remainder to his heirs male; *d* 1611; *s* by his el son (11) EDWARD, KB, 2nd Lord; *k* in a duel 1613; *s* by his brother (12) THOMAS, 3rd Lord; *cr Earl of Elgin* (peerage of Scotland) 1633 with remainder to heirs male whatever bearing the name and arms of Bruce, and *Baron Bruce*, of Whorlton, co York (peerage of England) 1640; *d* 1663; *s* by his son (13) ROBERT, 2nd Earl; *cr Baron Bruce*, of Skelton, co York, *Viscount Bruce*, of Ampthill, Beds, and *Earl of Ailesbury*, co Bucks (peerage of England) 1663; Lord Chamberlain 1685; *d* 1685; *s* by his son (14) THOMAS, 3rd Earl of Elgin and 2nd Earl of Ailesbury; *d* 1741; *s* by his son (15) CHARLES, 4th Earl of Elgin and 3rd Earl of Ailesbury; *cr Baron Bruce*, of Tottenham (peerage of Great Britain) 1746, with remainder to his nephew Hon Thomas-Brudenell, 4th son of 3rd Earl of Cardigan; *d* 1746, when the Lordship of Kinloss became abeyant (*see* Ly Kinloss), the Lordship of Bruce of Kinloss reverted to his nephew (ante) (*see* M Ailesbury), and the Earldom of Elgin devolved upon his kinsman and heir male (16) CHARLES BRUCE, 5th Earl, who in 1740 had *s* as 9th Earl of Kincardine (see note *), assumed the joint title of Earl of Elgin and Kincardine; *d* 1771; *s* by his el son (17) WILLIAM ROBERT, 6th Earl of Elgin and 10th Earl of Kincardine; *d* 1771; *s* by his brother (18) THOMAS, KC, PC, 7th Earl of Elgin and 11th Earl of Kincardine; a Gen in the Army, a Representative Peer 1790-1840, and successively Ambassador to Brussels, Berlin, and Constantinople; the "Elgin Marbles" deposited in the British Museum were collected by him during his residence in Turkey; *d* 1841; *s* by his son (19) JAMES, KT, GCB, KSI, 8th Earl of Elgin and 12th Earl of Kincardine, *b* 1811; MP for Southampton 1841-2, Gov-Gen of Jamaica 1842-6, and of Canada 1846, Ambassador on special missions to China 1859 and 1860, Postmaster-Gen 1859, and Gov-Gen of India 1860-3; *cr Baron Elgin*, of Elgin (peerage of United Kingdom) 1849: *m* 1st, 1841, Elizabeth Mary, who *d* 1843, da of Charles Lennox Cumming-Bruce, MP, of Dunphail, Morayshire; 2ndly, 1846, Lady Mary Louisa Lambton, CI, da of 1st Earl of Durham; *d* 1863; *s* by his son (20) VICTOR ALEXANDER, KG, GCSI, GCIE, PC, 9th Earl of Elgin and 13th Earl of Kincardine, *b* 1849; Treasurer of the Household and Commr of Works and Buildings 1886, Viceroy of India 1894-9, and Sec of State for Colonies Dec 1905 to April 1908; Lord-Lieut of Fife 1886-1917: *m* 1st, 1876, Lady Constance Mary Carnegie, CI, who *d* 1909, da of 9th Earl of Southesk, KT; 2ndly, 1913, Gertrude Lilian, who *d* 1971, da of late Com William Sherbrooke, RN, and widow of Capt Frederick Charles Ashley Ogilvy, RN; *d* 1917; *s* by his el son (21) EDWARD JAMES, KT, CMG, TD, CD, 10th Earl of Elgin and 14th Earl of Kincardine, *b* 1881; Lord High Commr to Gen Assembly of Ch of Scotland 1925-26, Pres and Chm of Scottish Development Council 1931-46; and Lord-Lieut of Fife 1935-65: *m* 1921, Hon Dame Katherine Elizabeth Cochrane, DBE, who *d* 1989, el da of 1st Baron Cochrane of Cults; *d* 1968; *s* by his son (22) ANDREW DOUGLAS ALEXANDER THOMAS, 11th Earl of Elgin, and 15th Earl of Kincardine, and present peer; also Lord Bruce of Kinloss, Lord Bruce of Torry, and Baron Elgin.

*(1) *Sir* EDWARD Bruce, Knt; *cr Lord Bruce of Torry*, and *Earl of Kincardine* (peerage of Scotland) 1647, with remainder to heirs general; *dsp*; *s* by his brother (2) ALEXANDER, PC, 2nd Earl; after the Restoration the Govt of Scotland was placed in his hands, and he was appointed an Extraordinary Lord of Session; *d* 1680; *b* by his son (3) ALEXANDER, 3rd Earl; *d* unmarried 1705, when the honours were claimed by his sister Lady Mary Cochrane, and also by his kinsman only son of Robert Bruce, uncle of 1st Earl; the competition terminated in favour of the latter (4) ALEXANDER, 4th Earl; *s* by his el son (5) ROBERT, 5th Earl; *dsp*; *s* by his brother (6) ALEXANDER, 6th Earl, *dsp*; *s* by his brother (7) THOMAS, 7th Earl; *s* by his el son (8) WILLIAM, 8th Earl; *s* by his son (9) CHARLES, 9th Earl, who *s* as 5th Earl of Elgin.

ELIBANK, LORD (Erskine-Murray) (Lord S 1643, Bt S 1628)
(Title pronounced "Ellibank")

ALAN D'ARDIS ERSKINE-MURRAY, 14th Lord and 14th Baronet; *b* 31 Dec 1923; *s* 1973; *ed* Bedford Sch and Peterhouse, Camb (MA); Bar Middle Temple 1949: *m* 1962, Valerie Sylvia, da of late Herbert William Dennis, of St Margarets, Middx, and has issue.

Arms – Quarterly; 1st and 4th or, a fetterlock azure, on a chief of the 2nd 3 stars argent, *Murray of Blackbarony*; 2nd and 3rd, azure, 3 stars within a double tressure counter-flowered argent and in the centre a martlet or. **Crest** – A lion rampant gules holding a battleaxe proper. **Supporters** – Two horses argent, bridled gules.
Residence – The Coach House, Charters Rd, Sunningdale, Berks.

SONS LIVING

Hon ROBERT FRANCIS ALAN (*Master of Elibank*), *b* 10 Oct 1964; *ed* Harrow, and Reading Univ.
Hon Timothy Alexander Elibank, *b* 1967.

BROTHER LIVING

Patrick Elibank (3 Park View, Bakewell, Derbys), *b* 1927; *ed* Bedford Sch and Pembroke Coll, Camb (MA); FICE: *m* 1957, Jenny Mary Margaret, da of late John Brown, of Bowbank, Middleton-in-Teesdale, co Durham, and has had issue, Vivien Mary, *b* 1958: *m* 1992, John David Jarvis, — Clare Ruth, *b* 1960, — Hilary Margaret, *b* 1965, *d* 1976.

SISTER LIVING

Helen Veronica, *b* 1931, MB, BS London: *m* 1958, Neil MacDonald, FRCS, of 22 Old Broadway, Manchester M20 3DF, and has issue living, Sally, *b* 1959, — Fiona *b* 1961, — Juliet, *b* 1964.

COLLATERAL BRANCHES LIVING

Grandson of late Alexander Erskine ERSKINE-MURRAY, son of late Hon James Murray, 4th son of 7th Lord:—
Issue of late Lieut-Col Arthur Erskine-Murray, CBE, DSO (uncle of 13th Lord), *b* 1877, *d* 1948: *m* 1906, Ena Nelson, who *d* 1942, da of late Henry Ernest Trestrail, FRCS, MRCP, of Mount Pleasant House, Longton, Staffordshire:—
Arthur Sydney Elibank, *b* 1909; *ed* Bedford Sch, and at Birmingham Univ BSc (Civil Eng); MICE; a Dir of Erskine, Murray & Co: *m* 1940, Florence Duncan, da of late William Duncan Robertson, and has issue living, Ann, *b* 1942; MA: *m* 1965, Anthony Peter Bartleet, of Bucklers Farm, Coggeshall, Essex CO6 1SB, and has issue living, James Murray *b* 1967, Thomas Anthony *b* 1969, William Arthur *b* 1971, — Susan, *b* 1945: *m* 1975, Godfrey Stuart Shocket, of 7 Genoa Av, Putney, SW15. *Residence* – Myrtle Bank, Gt Amwell, Ware, Herts SG12 9SN.

Grandchildren of late William Harry Elibank Murray, 2nd son of late Capt James Pulteney Murray (infra):—
Issue of late Douglas Elibank Murray, Australian Light Horse, *b* 1898, *d* 1989: *m* 1st, 1935 (*m diss* 1946), Rewa, da of Joseph Patrick O'Hara, of Fiji; 2ndly, 1947, Ngaio Milva Barnott, who *d* 1976:—
(By 1st *m*) William Eoin Elibank (Lot 8 Burraga Rd, Rockley, NSW 2795), *b* 1938: *m* 1970, Sheila Marion, da of Walter Robert Pont, of E Maitland, NSW, and has issue living, James Douglas Elibank, *b* 1970, — Alexandra Naomi, *b* 1974. —— Pamela Anna Elibank, *b* 1940: *m* 1967, C. T. McKenna, of 78 Fairfield Rd, Hamilton, NZ. —— Rita Gai Elibank, *b* 1942: *m* 1974, Graham John Horrigan Burns, of PO Box 213, Lindfield, NSW.

Granddaughter of late Capt James Pulteney Murray, son of Lieut James Edward Ferguson Murray, RN, el son of Maj-Gen James Patrick Murray, CB, MP, el son of late Gen the Hon James Murray, 5th son of 4th Lord:—
Issue of late Brig-Gen Edward Rushworth Blakiston Murray, *b* 1868, *d* as a result of enemy action 1942: *m* 1905, Hilda Dorothea, el da of late Reginald Paul, formerly of Woodgate, Loughborough:—
Elizabeth (2 Grange Terr, Edinburgh EH9 2LD), *b* 1911.

Grandsons of late Brig-Gen Edward Rushworth Blakiston Murray (ante):—
Issue of late James Patrick Murray, CMG, *b* 1906, *d* 1993: *m* 1934, (Margaret) Ruth (Trewen, Shaftesbury Rd, Woking, Surrey GU22 7DU), da of late Rev Alfred Edward Buchanan, formerly R of Pedmore, Worcs:—
James Alexander Gideon (Selhurst, Selhurst Common, Bramley, nr Guildford, Surrey), *b* 1936; *ed* Trin Coll, Glenalmond; FCA; Vice Chm Standard Commercial Corporation, NC: *m* 1965, Gillian Mary, da of late H. Gordon Adcock, of St Albans, Herts, and has issue living, James Richard, *b* 1967, — Andrew Thomas, *b* 1968. —— Patrick Edward (1 Chelsea Drive, Durban 4051, Natal), *b* 1939; *ed* Trin Coll, Glenalmond: *m* 1963, Marie-Danielle, da of Henri C. Du Cladier de Curac, of Durban, and has issue living, Charles Patrick, *b* 1971, — Danielle Jeanne, *b* 1964, — Diana Ruth, *b* 1965. —— Thomas Walter (The White House, Pembroke Rd, Woking, Surrey GU22 7EB), *b* 1942; Solicitor; *ed* Trin Coll, Glenalmond: *m* 1975, Annette Timms, da of Clifford Tapper, of Solihull, Warwicks, and has issue living, David Thomas, *b* 1976.

PREDECESSORS – (1) PATRICK Murray, el son of Sir Gideon Murray of Elibank, Lord of Session (3rd son of Andrew Murray of Blackbarony, and uncle of 1st Bt, *cr* 1628); *cr* a *Baronet* 1628, and *Lord Elibank*, of Ettrick Forest, co Selkirk (peerage of Scotland) 1643, with remainder to his heirs male whatsoever; one of the six peers who opposed the delivering up of Charles I to the Parliament of England; *d* 1649; *s* by his son (2) PATRICK, 2nd Lord; *d* 1661; *s* by his son (3) PATRICK, 3rd Lord; *d* 1687; *s* by his son (4) ALEXANDER, 4th Lord; *d* 1736; *s* by his el son (5) PATRICK, 5th Lord; *dsp* 1778; *s* by his brother (6) GEORGE, 6th Lord; an Adm; *d* 1785; *s* by his nephew (7) ALEXANDER, 7th Lord, son of Rev Hon Gideon, DD, 3rd son of 4th Lord; Lord-Lieut of co Peebles; *d* 1820; *s* by his son (8) ALEXANDER, 8th Lord; *d* 1830; *s* by his son (9) ALEXANDER OLIPHANT, 9th Lord; *b* 1804; *m* 1838, Emily Maria, da of Archibald Montgomery; *d* 1871; *s* by his son (10) MONTOLIEU FOX OLIPHANT, 10th Lord; *b* 1840; was Lord-Lieut of Peeblesshire 1896-1908; *cr Viscount Elibank*, of Elibank, co Selkirk (peerage of United Kingdom) 1911; *m* 1868, Blanche Alice, who *d* 1936, da of late Edward John Scott, of Portland Lodge, Southsea; *d* 1927; *s* by his son (11) (CHARLES) GIDEON, 2nd Viscount; *b* 1877; was Private Sec to Commr for Native Affairs in S Africa 1901-2, Assist Private Sec to Permanent Under-Sec of State for the Colonies 1907-9, Administrator of St Vincent 1909-14, and of St Lucia 1914-17, and Lord-Lieut for Peeblesshire 1935-45; sat as MP for S Rollox Div of Glasgow (*U*) 1918-22; *m* 1908, Ermine Mary Katherine, JP, who *d* 1955, da of late Henry Robarts Madocks, of Glanywen, Denbigh, and widow of Lieut-Col James Henry Aspinwall; *d* 1951; *s* by his brother (12) ARTHUR CECIL, CMG, DSO, 3rd Viscount, *b* 1879; Capt King's Own

Scottish Borderers and Lt-Col Special Reserve Cav; MP for Kincardineshire (L) 1908-23; PPS to Parliamentary Sec to Board of Trade 1909, to Under-Sec of State for India 1909-10, and to Sec of State for Foreign Affairs (Rt Hon Sir Edward Grey, Bt, MP) 1910-14, and Assist Mil Attaché at Washington 1917-18: *m* 1931, Faith Celli, who *d* 1942 (the dream da in Barrie's "Dear Brutus" 1916 and 1922), da of late Francis H. Standing; *d* 1962, when the UK Viscountcy became ext; *s* in the Lordship by his kinsman **(13)** JAMES ALASTAIR FREDERICK CAMPBELL Erskine-Murray (son of late Sqdn Leader James Robert Erskine-Murray, DSc, el son of late Alexander Erskine Erskine-Murray, el son of late Hon James Murray, 4th son of 7th Lord), 13th Lord; *b* 1902; Maj HLI, *d* 1973, *s* by his cousin, **(14)** ALAN D'ARDIS (son of Maj Robert Alan Erskine-Murray, OBE, uncle of 13th Lord), 14th Lord and present peer.

Eliot, Lord; son of Earl of St Germans.

ELLENBOROUGH, BARON (Law) (Baron UK 1802)

RICHARD EDWARD CECIL LAW, 8th Baron; *b* 14 Jan 1926; *s* 1945; *ed* Eton, and at Magdalene Coll, Camb; Pres, National Union of Ratepayers' Assos; Dir Towry Law plc: *m* 1st, 1953, Rachel Mary, who *d* 1986, only da of late Major Ivor Hedley, 17th Lancers; 2ndly, 1994, Mrs Frances Kimberley, and has issue by 1st *m*.

Arms – Ermine, on a bend engrained, between two cocks gules, three mullets pierced or. **Crest** – A cock gules, charged on the breast with a mitre pendant from a chain round the neck or. **Supporters** – Two eagles, wings elevated sable, each gorged with a chain or, and pendant there from on the breast of the *dexter* supporter a mitre, and on the *sinister* a covered cup gold.
Residence – Withypool House, Observatory Close, Church Rd, Crowborough, Sussex. *Clubs* – Gresham, Turf.

SONS LIVING (By 1st marriage)

Hon RUPERT EDWARD HENRY, *b* 28 March, 1955; Maj Coldm Gds (ret); Coutts & Co since 1988: *m* 1981, Hon Grania Janet Grey, only da of Baron Boardman (Life Baron), and has issue living, James Rupert Thomas, *b* 8 March 1983, — Frederick George Towry Gray, *b* 1990, — Georgina Poppy, *b* 1984.

Hon Edmund Ivor Cecil, *b* 1956; *ed* Peterhouse, Camb (MA): *m* 1982, Susan Claire, el da of Derek Baker, of 5 Jermyn Close, Cambridge, and has issue living, David Christopher, *b* 1984, — John Christian, *b* 1986.

Law and equity combined

Hon Charles Adrian Christian Towry, *b* 1960; *ed* York Univ (BA).

BROTHER LIVING

Hon Cecil Towry Henry, *b* 1931; *ed* Eton; late Lieut King's Dragoon Guards (Reserve) and Chm of Towry Law plc, and all associated cos in Towry Law Group: *m* 1957, Daphne Mary Jean, 2nd da of late Hon Laurence Paul Methuen-Campbell (*see* B Methuen, colls), and has issue living, Edward Henry Towry, *b* 1971; *ed* Eton, and Exeter Univ (BA), — Cecilia Diana, *b* 1958: *m* 1985, James E. Chamberlain, son of E. J. R. Chamberlain, of Box, Glos and has issue living, Jasper Edward *b* 1992, Natasha Diana *b* 1990, — Marianne Jean, *b* 1960; *ed* St Hilda's Coll, Oxford (MA): *m* 1986, George Alexander Wheeler-Carmichael, and has issue (*see* Gibson-Craig-Carmichael, Bt, colls), — Catherine Rose, *b* 1962; *ed* Edinburgh Univ (MA): *m* 1985, Dr Anthony Charles Murray Ayles, 2nd son of Dr William Ayles, of Moray Pl, Edinburgh, and has issue living, William Anthony Carrington *b* 1992, Charlotte Catherine Mary *b* 1988, Emily Flora Isobel *b* 1990. *Residence* – 6 Sussex Sq, W2. *Club* – Cavalry.

WIDOW LIVING OF SEVENTH BARON

(HELEN) DOROTHY (*Dowager Baroness Ellenborough*), da of late H. W. Lovatt, formerly of Tiraun, Newcastle, co Down; a DStJ: *m* 1923, the 7th Baron, who *d* 1945. *Residence* – Shockerwick House, Shockerwick, Bath BA1 7LL

COLLATERAL BRANCHES LIVING

Grandsons of late Thomas Graves Law, LLD, 3rd son of Hon William Towry Law, 5th son of 1st Baron:—
Issue of late Henry Duncan Graves Law, CIE, *b* 1883, *d* 1964: *m* 1st, 1909, Jean, who *d* 1956, da of late Peter Graham, RA, of Westoun, St Andrews; 2ndly, 1958, Nancy Olive Legge, who *d* 1977, da of late Sir Henry Frederick Oswald Norbury:—
(By 1st *m*) Richard Graham (High Trees, Ramsay Wood, Gatehouse-of-Fleet DG7 2HJ), *b* 1918; *ed* Tonbridge, and at Peterhouse, Camb (BA 1940, MA 1947); MB 1947, MD 1952, FRCOG 1961: *m* 1944, Barbara, MB, BS, DPH, da of Horace Wright, and has issue living, Nigel Graham, *b* 1949, — David Jocelyn Wright, *b* 1951, — Penelope Jane, *b* 1955.
—— Christopher (Appleyard, Little Chart, Ashford, Kent), *b* 1921; *ed* Tonbridge, and at Peterhouse Camb; ARIBA: *m* 1954, Alison Mitchell, and has issue living, Jonathan, *b* 1958: *m* 1987, Diane Joyce French, — Ian Graham, *b* 1961; ARICS: *m* 1990, Fiona Mary McIntyre, and has issue living, Duncan Graham *b* 1989, Thomas Henry *b* 1993, Katrina Mary *b* 1988, — Fiona Jean, *b* 1955. —— Michael Haldane (90A Upper Tollington Park, N4 4NB), *b* 1925; *ed* Tonbridge, and at Peterhouse, Camb: *m* 1954, Dorothea von Schön-Kreuzenau, and has issue living, Richard Anthony *b* 1955, — Peter Andrew, *b* 1958, — John Martin, *b* 1961, — Stephen Francis, *b* 1966.

Grandchildren of late Capt William Victor Law (infra):—
Issue of late Frederick Henry Law, *b* 1912, *d* 1986: *m* 1937, Ruth, da of George H. Dill, of Toronto:—

Stephen Frederick (1657 Truscott Dr, Mississauga, Ont, Canada L5J 1Z5), b 1943: m 1966, Julika Fietius, and has issue living, Adrian Crawford, b 1979, — Alexandra Juliane Erika, b 1977. —— Sharron Constance, b 1937: m 1955, James Wilfred Brazier, of 106 Hawthorne Av, Stouffville, Ont, Canada L4A 7Z8, and has issue living, Frederick James, b 1955: m 1980, Mary Maresa, da of Gio Batta Garlatti, and has issue living, Ryan Garlatti b 1982, Jeremy Frederick b 1984, Nadine Constance b 1988, — Danny Allen (316 Lori Av, Stouffville, Ont, Canada L4A 6C2), b 1957: m 19—, Deborah Jane, da of Frank Clifford Carr, — Timothy Stewart, b 1960.

Grandchildren of late Cdr Frederick Charles Law, 4th son of Hon William Towry Law (ante):—
Issue of late John Crawford Law, b 1876, d 1919: m 1917, Eleanor Agnes Letitia, da of Rupert E. Kingsford, of Toronto:—
Margaret Augusta Eleanor, b 1918: m 1st, 1940, Capt Denys Symons, Roy Tank Regt; 2ndly, 1966, Oliver Bosshardt Bennett, CBE, who d 1983, of 14 Graham Terr, SW1, and has issue living, (by 1st m) Ivor James, b 1944, — Dianna Venetia, b 1940.
Issue of late Capt William Victor Law, b 1880, d 1967: m 1912, Helen Violet who d 1971, da of late Henry Morris Watson, Assist Gen Manager of Bank of Hamilton:—
Mary Charlotte Violet (44 Valerie Drive, St Catherines, Ont, Canada L2T 3G5), b 1917: m 1st, 1939, Capt W. Marshal Cleland, Gov-Gen's, Horse Guards, Canadian Army, who d 1958; 2ndly, 1960, John Franklin Horne, who d 1974, and has issue living, (by 1st m), William Marshal (30 Wellington St E, Toronto, Ont, Canada M5E 1S3), b 1944: m 1st, 1967, Sheila, da of Jack M. Reid, of Kingston, Ont; 2ndly, 1979, Lois, da of Robert Charles Pettigrew, — Donald Law (RRI Vittoria, Ont, Canada), b 1947: m 1974, Kathryn, da of Ward E. Kitchen, of RRI, Vittoria, Ont, and has issue living, Eric William b 1978, Kimberley Dawn b 1982, — Calder Bruce (685 Sarah St, Gravenhurst, Ont, Canada), b 1949: m 1st, 1969, Sandra, da of Louis Melnyke, of Brantford, Ont; 2ndly, 1978, Wendy, da of Henry Collens, of Port Carling, Ontario, and has issue living (by 2nd m), Jeremy Marshal b 1978, Calder Daniel b 1981, — Peter Andrew (88 Oakwood Av, Simcoe, Ont, Canada), b 1957: m 1981, Vicky, da of Stephen Kochany, of Simcoe, Ont, and has issue living, Kristin Michele b 1984, Amanda b 1987.
Issue of late Maj Adrian Aloysius Sherwood Law, b 1885, d 1945: m 1914, Maud, who d 1960, da of late Hon Louis Arthur Audette, a Puisne Judge of Exchequer Court, Canada:—
Charles Anthony Francis, DSC, CD, b 1916; Hon D Litt St Mary's Univ, Halifax 1981; Cdr RCN (ret); landscape and seascape painter; artist-in-residence St Mary's Univ, Halifax, Nova Scotia 1967-80; Member Board of Govs Nova Scotia Coll of Art and Design; 1939-45 War (despatches twice, DSC): m 1942, Jane Brumm, da of late Milton Maurice Shaw. Residence – 8 Halls Rd, Halifax, Nova Scotia, Canada, B3P 1P3.

Granddaughter of late Maj Adrian Aloysius Sherwood Law (ante):—
Issue of late Adrian Augustus Stuart Law, b 1918, d 1968: m 1st, 1942 (m diss 1951), Wilhelmina Noble Angus; 2ndly, 1952, Muriel Beverley (2582 MacDonald Drive, Victoria, BC, Canada), da of late Brooke Vaio:—
(By 1st m) Moira Jean (1 Luton Court, Broadstairs, Kent CT10 2DE), b 1943; SRN.

PREDECESSORS – (1) Sir EDWARD LAW, KB, PC, and eminent lawyer, was Attorney-Gen 1801-2, and Lord Ch Justice of England 1802-18; cr Baron Ellenborough, of Ellenborough, co Cumberland (peerage of United Kingdom) 1802; d 1818; s by his son (2) EDWARD, 2nd Baron, PC, GCB; Lord Privy Seal 1828-9, Pres of Board of Control 1829-30, 1834-5, 1841 and 1858, Gov-Gen of India 1841-4, and First Lord of the Admiralty 1846; cr Viscount Southam and Earl of Ellenborough (peerage of United Kingdom) 1844; d 1871, when the viscountcy and earldom became extinct and the barony devolved upon his nephew (3) CHARLES EDMUND TOWRY, 3rd Baron (son of late Hon Charles Ewan, 2nd son of 1st Baron, by Elizabeth Sophia, da of Sir Edward Nightingale, 6th Bt), b 1820; assumed in 1885 by Roy licence the additional surname of Towry: m 1st 1840, Lady Eleanor Cecil Howard, who d 1852, da of 4th Earl of Wicklow; 2ndly, 1855, Anna Elizabeth, who d 1860, da of Rev John Fitzgerald-Day of Beaufort House, Killarney; 3rdly, 1863, Isabella, who d 1874, da of Alexander Ogilby, of Pelipar, Londonderry; 4thly, 1874, Beatrice Joanna, who d 1932, da of Sir Norton Joseph Knatchbull, 10th Bt; d 1890; s by his son (4) CHARLES TOWRY HAMILTON, 4th Baron, b 1856; dsp 1902; s by his cousin (5) EDWARD DOWNES, 5th Baron, b 1841; Com RN; served in Baltic during Russian War 1855, in China Expedition 1859-61, and during Ashantee War 1870-74: m 1906, Hermione Octavia Courtenay, who d 1942, da of E. W. H. Schenley (Rifle Brig), of Little Warsash, S Hants; d 1915; s by his brother (6) CECIL HENRY, CB, 6th Baron, b 1849; entered 54th Regt 1869, and retired as Brevet Col 1906; Afghan Campaign 1878-80, S African War 1900-2: m 1884, Alice Caroline, who d 1916, da of late John Harvey Astell, of Woodbury Hall, Sandy, Beds; d 1931; s by his son (7) HENRY ASTELL, MC, 7th Baron, b 1889; Major (ret) King's Own Yorkshire LI; European War 1914-18 (MC): m 1923, Helen Dorothy, da of H. W. Lovatt, formerly of Tiraun, Newcastle, co Down; d 1945; s by his el son (8) RICHARD EDWARD CECIL, 8th Baron and present peer.

ELLES, BARONESS (Elles) (Life Baroness 1972)

DIANA LOUIE ELLES, da of late Col Stewart Francis Newcombe, DSO; b 19 July 1921; ed London Univ (BA); Bar Lincoln's Inn 1956 (Hon Bencher 1993); 1939-45 War as Flight Officer WAAF (Intelligence, Air Ministry); Member of Outside Organization Sub-Cttee, Conservative Women's Nat Advisory Cttee 1960-72, and of Women's Nat Advisory Cttee 1961-62, and since 1969 (Chm Sub-Cttee on One Parent Families 1970); author of The Housewife and the Common Market 1971; Care Cttee Worker, Kennington SE 1956-72; UK Delegate to UN Gen Assembly 1972; a Member of UN Sub Commn on Prevention of Discrimination and Protection of Minorities 1973 and 74; Chm of Conservative Party International Office 1973-78; International Chm, European Union of Women 1973-79; a Member of UK Delegation to European Parl 1973-75; Opposition Spokesman, Foreign Affairs, House of Lords 1975-79; MEP for Thames Valley 1979-89; Vice-Pres European Parl 1982-87; Chm Legal Affairs Cttee European Parl since 1987; cr Baroness Elles, of City of Westminster (Life Baroness) 1972: m 1945. Neil Moncrieff Elles, barrister, and has issue.

Arms – Not exemplified at time of going to press.
Residences – 75 Ashley Gdns, SW1; Villa Fontana, Ponte del Giglio, Lucca, Italy.

SON LIVING

Hon James Edmund Moncrieff (14 Avenue Maurice, 1050 Brussels, Belgium), b 1949 ed Eton, and Edinburgh Univ: m 1977, Françoise, da of François Le Bail, and has issue, Nicholas, b 1982, — Victoria, b 1980.

DAUGHTER LIVING

Hon (Elizabeth) Rosamund, b 1947; ed St Andrews Univ (MA) and Courtauld Inst, London Univ (MA): m 1971 (m diss 1992), Christopher John Lockhart-Mummery, QC, son of late Sir Hugh Evelyn Lockhart-Mummery, KCVO, and has issue (see V Hampden, colls). Residence – 52 Argyll Rd, W8.

Ellesmere, Earl of, see Duke of Sutherland.

ELLIOTT OF MORPETH, BARON (Elliott) (Life Baron 1985)

·IMPRIMIS·HONOR·

(ROBERT) WILLIAM ELLIOTT, son of Richard Elliott, of Morpeth, Northumberland, by his wife, Mary Elizabeth, da of William Fulthorpe, of Morpeth; *b* 11 Dec 1920; *ed* Morpeth Gram Sch; farmer since 1939; MP (*C*) Newcastle upon Tyne North 1957-83; PPS to joint Parliamentary Secs, Min of Transport & Civil Aviation 1958-59, to Under-Sec Home Office 1959-60, to Min of State Home Office 1960-61, to Sec for Technical Co-operation 1961-63, Assist Govt Whip 1963-64, Opposition Whip 1964-70; Comptroller of the Household June-Sept 1970; Vice-Chm Conservative Party 1970-74; Chm Select Cttee on Agriculture, Fisheries and Food 1980-83; *cr* Kt 1974, and *Baron Elliott of Morpeth*, of Morpeth, in the County of Northumberland and of the City of Newcastle upon Tyne (Life Baron) 1985: *m* 1956, Jane, da of John Burton Morpeth, of Newcastle upon Tyne, and has issue.

Arms – Gules on a bend or cotised dancetty argent bendwise in chief a triple-towered castle gules masoned argent the portal azure with portcullis down gold. **Crest** – Upon a mount vert in front of an oak tree proper fructed or a fountain ensigned by a crown flory azure. **Supporters** – *Dexter*, a stag proper attired and unguled gold; *sinister*, a seahorse erect argent scaled gold, the compartment comprising three grassy mounts proper with between that in the centre and those on either side water barry wavy of four argent and azure.
Residence – Lipwood Hall, Haydon Bridge, Northumberland.

SON LIVING

Hon Richard John, *b* 1959; *ed* Sedburgh Sch, Edinburgh Univ (BA), and RMA Sandhurst: *m* 1988, Susu, yr da of Lionel Robertson, of Abbey Lodge, Park Rd, London, and has issue living, Romy, *b* 1990, — Laura, *b* 1992.

DAUGHTERS LIVING

Hon Alison Mary, *b* 1957; *ed* Oxenford Castle Sch: *m* 1985, Hugh A. Campbell Adamson, yr son of Lt-Col William John Campbell Adamson, TD, JP, of Careston Castle, Brechin, Angus, and has issue living, James William, *b* 1989, — Rosemary Jane, *b* 1987, — Catherine Grace, *b* 1991.
Hon Catherine Victoria, *b* 1962; *ed* St Mary's Convent, Berwick-upon-Tweed, and Durham Univ (BA): *m* 1988, Alexander Julian Taylor, eldest son of J. A. Taylor, of Rumer Hall, Welford-on-Avon, Warwicks, and has issue living, Alexander William John, *b* 1990, — George Arthur James, *b* 1992.
Hon Sarah Ann, *b* 1962 (twin); *ed* New Hall Sch, Essex, and Edinburgh Univ (BA): *m* 1986, George Evelyn Atkinson-Clark, and has issue (*see* B Suffield, colls).
Hon Louise Jane, *b* 1967; *ed* St Anne's, Windermere, and Durham Univ (BA).

ELPHINSTONE, LORD (Elphinstone) (Lord S 1509, and Baron UK 1885)

JAMES ALEXANDER ELPHINSTONE, 18th Lord; *b* 22 April, 1953; *s* 1975; *ed* Eton, and Roy Agric Coll, Cirencester: *m* 1978, Willa Mary Gabriel, yr da of Maj (George) David Chetwode, MBE, Coldm Gds (*see* B Chetwode, colls), and has issue.

Arms – Quarterly: 1st grand quarter argent, a chevron sable, between three boars' heads erased gules, armed of the field, and langued azure, *Elphinstone*; 2nd, grand quarter, counterquartered; 1st, gules, a chevron, within a double tressure, flory counterflory, argent, *Fleming*; 2nd, azure, three frases argent, *Fraser*; 3rd, argent, on a chief gules, three pallets or, *Keith*; 4th, or, three bars wavy gules, *Drummond*; 3rd grand quarter, argent, a chevron, between three otters' heads erased gules, within a bordure of the last, *Fullerton*; 4th grand quarter, sable, on a cross argent, square pierced of the field, four eagles, displayed of the first, in the dexter canton an arm embowed proper, issuing out of a naval crown, the hand holding a trident or, *Buller*. **Crest** – A lady, from the waist upwards, richly habited in red, her arms extended, the right hand supporting a tower, and the left holding a branch of laurel, all proper. **Supporters** – Two wild men, wreathed about the temples and loins with laurel, and holding on their exterior shoulders clubs proper.
Residence – Drumkilbo, Meigle, Blairgowrie, Perthshire.

SONS LIVING

Hon ALEXANDER MOUNTSTUART (*Master of Elphinstone*), *b* 15 April 1980.
Hon Angus John, *b* 1982.

Hon Fergus David, *b* 1985.

DAUGHTER LIVING

Hon Clementina Rose, *b* 1989.

SISTER LIVING

Rosemary Elizabeth, *b* 1947: *m* 1967, James Pigé Leschallas (*see* E Romney, colls), of Maryland, Worplesdon, Guildford, Surrey, and has issue living, Andrew James, *b* 1970, — Alexander Charles, *b* 1978, — Sophie Elizabeth, *b* 1968: *m* 1993, James D. A. Gaselee, LG, son of Nicholas Auriol Digby Charles Gaselee, of Saxon Cottage, Lambourn, Berks.

AUNTS LIVING (*Daughters of 16th Lord*)

Hon Jean Constance, MVO, *b* 1915, Extra Lady-in-Waiting to HRH The Princess Margaret, 1970; MVO (1983): *m* 1936, Maj John Lycett Wills, Life Guards (ret) (*see* Wills, Bt, *cr* 1904, colls). *Residence* – Allanbay Park, Binfield, Berks.
Hon Margaret, *b* 1925; Extra Lady-in-Waiting to HM Queen Elizabeth the Queen Mother since 1991: *m* 1950, Denys Gravenor Rhodes (*see* B Plunket, 1968 Edn), who *d* 1981, and has issue living, Simon John Gravenor, *b* 1957: a Page of Honour to HM 1971-73: *m* 1983, Susan, eldest da of Eden Simon, of Tara Farm, Bindura, Zimbabwe, — Michael Andrew Gravenor, *b* 1960, — Annabel Margaret, *b* 1952: *m* 1st, 1978, Christopher J. D. Strickland-Skailes, twin son of Frank Strickland-Skailes, of Lea Hall, Hatfield Heath, Essex; 2ndly, 1986, G. V. (Charles) Cope, 2nd son of late Herbert Vallack Cope, of Rose Hill, Bideford, Devon, and has issue living (by 1st *m*), Andrew James Downing *b* 1980, — Victoria Ann, *b* 1953: *m* 1974, Nicholas Deans, who *d* 1991. *Residence* – The Garden House, Windsor Great Park, Windsor, Berks.

MOTHER LIVING

Jean Frances, CVO, da of late Capt Angus Valdimar Hambro, MP, and widow of Capt Hon Vicary Paul Gibbs, Gren Gds (*see* B Aldenham and Hunsdon of Hunsdon): *m* 2ndly, 1946, Rev Hon Andrew Charles Victor Elphinstone, who *d* 1975; 3rdly, 1980, Lt-Col John William Richard Woodroffe, of Arnbarrow, Laurencekirk, Kincardineshire (*see* E Ducie, colls, 1968 Edn), and has issue living, (by 1st *m*) (*see* B Aldenham and Hunsdon of Hunsdon, colls), (by 2nd *m*) (ante).

PREDECESSORS – (1) ALEXANDER Elphinstone, son of Sir John Elphinstone, grandson of Sir Henry Elphinstone, of Pittendreich; *cr Lord Elphinstone*, of Elphinstone, co Stirling (peerage of Scotland) 1509; fell at Flodden Field 1513; *s* by his son (2) ALEXANDER, 2nd Lord; slain at Pinkie 1547; *s* by his son (3) ROBERT, 3rd Lord; *s* by his son (4) ALEXANDER, 4th Lord; Lord Treasurer of Scotland; *d* 1638; *s* by his son (5) ALEXANDER, 5th Lord; *d* 1648; *s* by his newphew (6) ALEXANDER, 6th Lord; *d* 1654; *s* by his el son (7) ALEXANDER, 7th Lord; *dsp* 1669; *s* by his brother (8) JOHN, 8th Lord; *d* 1720; *s* by his son (9) CHARLES, 9th Lord; *d* 1757; *s* by his son (10) CHARLES, 10th Lord; *d* 1781; *s* by his son (11) JOHN, 11th Lord; a Representative Peer 1784-94; *d* 1794; *s* by his son (12) JOHN, 12th Lord; a Lt-Gen in the Army, Lord-Lieut of Dunbartonshire, and a Representative Peer 1803-13; *d* 1813; *s* by his son (13) JOHN, GCB, GCH, PC, 13th Lord; a Representative Peer; was Gov of Bombay and of Madras during the Mutiny 1857; *cr Baron Elphinstone*, of Elphinstone, co Stirling (peerage of United Kingdom) 1859; *d* 1860, when the barony of 1859 became extinct, and the Scottish Lordship devolved upon his cousin (14) JOHN (el son of Adm Hon Charles Elphinstone-Fleeming, 2nd son of 11th Lord), 14th Lord; *d* unmarried 1861; *s* by his kinsman (15) WILLIAM (son of Lt-Col James Drummond Buller-Fullerton Elphinstone, 4th son of Hon William Elphinstone, 3rd son of 10th Lord), 15th Lord, *b* 1828; a Representative Peer for Scotland 1867-85, and a Lord-in-Waiting to HM Queen Victoria 1874-80, 1885-6, and 1886-9; *cr Baron Elphinstone*, of Elphinstone co Haddington (peerage of United Kingdom) 1885: *m* 1864, Lady Constance Euphemia Woronzow Murray, who *d* 1922, da of 6th Earl of Dunmore; *d* 1893; *s* by his el surviving son (16) SIDNEY HERBERT, KT, 16th Lord, *b* 1869; Lord High Commr to Gen Assembly of Church of Scotland 1923-4, Capt-Gen of Queen's Body Guard for Scotland (Roy Co of Archers) 1935-52, Clerk Register of Scotland and Keeper of the Signet 1944-55, and Chancellor of Order of the Thistle 1949-55: *m* 1910, Lady Mary Frances Bowes-Lyon, DCVO, who *d* 1961, da of 14th Earl of Strathmore; *d* 1955; *s* by his el son (17) JOHN ALEXANDER, 17th Lord; *b* 1914; Capt Queen's Body Guard for Scotland (Roy Co of Archers); *d* 1975; *s* by his nephew (18) JAMES ALEXANDER, 18th Lord and present peer.

Elphinstone, Master of; son of Lord Elphinstone.

ELTON, BARON (Elton) (Baron UK 1934)

RODNEY ELTON, TD, 2nd Baron; *b* 2 March 1930; *s* 1973; *ed* Eton and New, Coll, Oxford (BA); late Capt Warwicks Yeo, and late Maj Leics and Derbys Yeo; Publisher of Yendor Books; Assist Master Loughborough Gram Sch 1962-67, Fairham Comprehensive Sch for Boys, Nottingham 1967-69, Lecturer Bishop Lonsdale Coll 1969-72; Conservative Whip House of Lords 1974-76; Spokesman for Opposition 1976-79; Under Sec of State, N Ireland Office, 1979-81, Parliamentary Under Sec for Health and Social Security 1981-82, at Home Office 1982-84, Min of State at Home Office 1984-85, and at Dept of Environment 1985-86, Member Exec Cttee Assocn of Conservative Peers 1986-93 and since 1994 (Dep Chm 1990-93); Chm Financial Intermediaries, Managers and Brokers Regulatory Assocn 1989-90, Vice-Chm Andry Montgomery Ltd since 1987, Member Panel on Takeovers and Mergers 1989-90, and Chm Enquiry into Discipline in Schs in England and Wales 1988-89 (Report 1989); Chm Intermediate Treatment Fund 1990-93, since when Chm The Divert Trust: *m* 1st, 1958 (*m diss* 1979), Anne Francis, el da of Brig Robert Adolphus George Tilney, CBE, DSO, TD, DL (*see* Paget, Bt, *cr* 1897 (ext) 1959 Edn); 2ndly, 1979, (Susan) Richenda, a Lady-in-Waiting to HM since 1987, yst da of late Sir Hugh Gurney, KCMG, MVO (*see* E Southesk, colls, 1980 Edn), and has issue by 1st *m*.

Arms – Paly or and gules a bend and on a chief sable three pierced mullets or. **Crest** – Between two pierced mullets and out of a wreath of laurel fructed or a dexter arm embowed in mail proper, tied about the elbow a cord or, the gauntlet grasping a scimitar proper hilt and pommel or. **Supporters** – *Dexter*, a knight in mail and white surcoat supporting with the exterior hand a sword point downwards proper hilt and pommerl or; *sinister*, a Viking habited proper mantled azure supporting with the exterior hand a battleaxe head downwards and outwards proper.
Address – House of Lords, SW1. *Clubs* – Cavalry, Beefsteak, Pratt's.

SON LIVING *(By 1st marriage)*

Hon EDWARD PAGET, *b* 28 May 1966.

DAUGHTERS LIVING *(By 1st marriage)*

Hon Annabel, *b* 1960: *m* 1986, Donald M. Peebles, eldest son of Dr Robert Anthony Peebles, of Hampton Court, Surrey, and has issue living, Emma Richenda, *b* 1988, — Rosalie, *b* 1990.
Hon Jane, *b* 1962: *m* 1989, James A. J. Cronin, son of Vincent Cronin, of Hyde Park Sq, W2, and Le Manoir de Brion, Normandy.
Hon Lucy, *b* 1963: *m* 1993, Hon Andrew Godfrey Diarmid Stuart Campbell-Gray, Master of Gray, son of 22nd Lord Gray.

SISTERS LIVING

Hon Audrey (Hill House, Enford, Pewsey, Wilts) *b* 1922: *m* 1948, the Rev Brian William Frere Goodrich, who *d* 1977, formerly Assist Commr, Singapore Police, and has issue living, John, *b* 1952, — Peter, *b* 1954, — Simon, *b* 1957, — Justin, *b* 1962, — Alexander, *b* 1968, — Sarah, *b* 1949.
Hon Rosemary, *b* 1925: *m* 1st, 1946 (*m diss* 1955), William Yates; 2ndly, 1955, David Charles Attlee, and has issue living, (by 1st *m*) Elizabeth Anne, *b* 1948: *m* 1975, Oliver Raymond Greene, of Holton Hall, Holton St Mary, Colchester, Essex, and has had issue, William Charles Raymond *b* 1979, Nicholas Graham Raymond *b* 1981, Charlotte Eleanor *b* and *d* 1983, Annabel Lucy Raymond *b* 1985, — Angela Faith, *b* 1950: *m* 1st, 1972 (*m diss* 1980), Denis Delahunt; 2ndly, 1983, G. Stafford, and has issue living (by 1st *m*), Christopher William *b* 1974, Thomas James *b* 1977, (by 2nd *m*), David Charles *b* 1986, — (by 2nd *m*) James Tristram, *b* 1956: *m* 1986, Charlotte de Courcy, and has issue living, Joseph *b* 1990, Grace 1988, — Helena Rosemary, *b* 1958: *m* 1986, Alexander Ronald Dalhousie Ramsay, FRGS, of Bryncalled, Bucknell, Craven Arms, Shropshire, elder son of Patrick George Alexander Ramsay, FRSA, of Abcott Manor, Abcott, Clungunford, nr Ludlow, Shropshire. *Residence* – Brockley House, Leintwardine, Craven Arms, Shropshire.

PREDECESSOR – (1) GODFREY Elton, el son of late Edward Fiennes Elton, of Ovington Park, Hants, and Burleigh Court, Glos; *b* 1892; Fellow of Queen's Coll, Oxford and Lecturer in Modern History 1919-39, Dean 1921-23; Hon Political Sec Nat Labour Cttee 1932, and Sec to Rhodes Trust 1939-59; author of "Life of James Ramsay MacDonald 1866-1919", 1939, and other works, *cr Baron Elton*, of Headington, co Oxford (peerage of UK) 1934: *m* 1921, Dedi, who *d* 1977, da of Gustav Hartmann, of Oslo, *d* 1973, *s* by his only son (2) RODNEY, TD, 2nd Baron and present peer.

ELWORTHY, BARONY OF (Elworthy) (Extinct 1993)

SONS LIVING OF LIFE BARON

Hon Timothy Charles, CBE (c/o The Queen's Flight, RAF Benson, Oxon OX10 6AA) *b* 1938: Air Cdre RAF (ret 1993); Capt The Queen's Flight since 1989; Extra Equerry to HM since 1991: *m* 1st, 1961 (*m diss* 1969), Victoria Ann, eldest da of Lt-Col H. C. W. Bowring; 2ndly, 1971, Anabel, da of late Reginald Ernest Harding, OBE, and formerly wife of Nicholas Block, and has issue living, (by 1st *m*) Katharine Emma Victoria, *b* 1963: *m* 1991, Christopher David Cooke, of 23 Lindrop St, SW6, elder son of David Cooke, — Lucinda Rose, *b* 1965, — (by 2nd *m*) Edward Charles, *b* 1974.
Hon Anthony Arthur (Box 782404, Sandton 2146, S Africa), *b* 1940: *m* 1967, Penelope, who *d* 1988, da of E. J. W. Hendry, MBE, and has issue living, Alexander Julius, *b* 1973, — Tracy Lara, *b* 1971.
Hon Christopher Ashton (Gordon's Valley Station, RD2, Timaru, NZ); *b* 1946: *m* 1968, Anne, da of late Harry Bell Lewis Johnstone, and has issue living, Caroline Helen, *b* 1968, — Amanda Victoria, *b* 1970.

DAUGHTER LIVING OF LIFE BARON

Hon Clare Louise Katharine, *b* 1950: *m* 1975, Anthony Joyce Cary, of The Old Vicarage, Knatchbull Rd, SE5 9QU, son of late Sir (Arthur Lucius) Michael Cary, GCB, and has issue living, Sam Michael, *b* 1978, — Thomas Joyce, *b* 1980, — Arthur Lucius, *b* 1983, — Harriet Maude, *b* 1985.

ELWYN-JONES, BARONY OF (Jones) (Extinct 1989)

SON LIVING OF LIFE BARON

Hon Daniel ELWYN-JONES (196 Cable St, E1), *b* 1940; Head of Campaigns, Amnesty Internat: *m* 19—, Denise Turner, and has issue living, Davey Elwyn, *b* 19—, — Sam, *b* 19—, — Polly Elizabeth, *b* 19—.

DAUGHTER LIVING

Hon Josephine, *b* 19—: *m* 1972, James Francis Gladstone (*see* Gladstone, Bt).

ELY, MARQUESS OF (Tottenham) Sits as BARON LOFTUS (UK 1801) (Marquess I 1801, Bt I 1780)

CHARLES JOHN TOTTENHAM, 8th Marquess, and 9th Baronet; *b* 30 May 1913; *s* 1969; *ed* Queen's Univ, Kingston, Ontario (BA); formerly Headmaster, Boulden House, Trin Coll Sch, Port Hope, Ontario: *m* 1st, 1938, Katherine Elizabeth, who *d* 1975, da of Lt-Col W. H. Craig, of Kingston, Ontario; 2ndly, 1978, Elspeth Ann, only da of late P. T. Hay, of Highgate and has issue by 1st *m*.

𝕬rms – Not yet confirmed at the College of Arms for the line of the present Marquess.
Residences – 20 Arundel Court, Jubilee Place, SW3; Trinity College School, Port Hope, Ontario, Canada.

SONS LIVING (By 1st marriage)

CHARLES JOHN (*Viscount Loftus*), *b* 2 Feb 1943; *ed* Trin Coll, Toronto Univ (MA): *m* 1969, Judith Marvelle, da of Dr J. J. Porter, of Calgary, Alberta, and has two adopted children, Andrew, *b* 1973, — Jennifer, *b* 1975.
Lord Timothy Craig, *b* 1948; *ed* Ottawa Teachers' Coll: *m* 1973, Elizabeth Jane, da of Grant McAllister, of Ottawa, Ont, and has issue living, Scott Craig, *b* 1977, — John Douglas, *b* 1981.
Lord Richard Ivor (819 Grace St, Newmarket, Ontario L3Y 2L6, Canada); *b* 1954; *ed* Univ of Western Ont (BA): *m* 1978, Virginia Murney, da of late William Murney Morris of Toronto, Ont, Canada and has issue living, Elizabeth Murney, *b* 1983, — Katherine Ann, *b* 1985.

DAUGHTER LIVING (By 1st marriage)

Rev Lady Ann Elizabeth, *b* 1940; *ed* Trin Coll, Toronto Univ (BA STB), and Union Seminary, New York (MTB); Headmistress, Bishop Strachan Sch, Toronto, Ontario.

SISTER LIVING (Raised to the rank of a Marquess's daughter 1973)

Lady Dora Elizabeth (24 The Gateways, SW3), *b* 1919; *ed* Queen's Univ, Kingston, Ont (BA); 1939-45 War, as Lt WRCNS: a JP for London: *m* 1st, 1946, Lt (E) Bernard Edgar Hall, RN, who *d* 1947; 2ndly, 1950, Sir Ivor Thomas Montague Pink, KCMG, who *d* 1966, and has issue living, (by 2nd *m*) Celia Elizabeth, *b* 1952.

WIDOW LIVING OF BROTHER OF EIGHTH MARQUESS

Jane Elizabeth (Trullwell, Box, nr Stroud, Glos, GL6 9HD), da of Arthur Martin: *m* 1944, Lord George Tottenham, who *d* 1975, and has issue (see colls infra).

WIDOW LIVING OF SEVENTH MARQUESS

THEA MARGARET GORDON (*Thea, Marchioness of Ely*), da of late Lars G. Gronvold, of 36 Wilbury Rd, Hove: *m* 1928, the 7th Marquess, who *d* 1969.

COLLATERAL BRANCHES LIVING

Granddaughter of George Leonard Tottenham, grandson of Charles John Tottenham, el son of late Rt Rev Lord Robert Ponsonby Tottenham, Bishop of Clogher, 2nd son of 1st Marquess:—
Issue of late Cdr Lord George Robert Tottenham, RCN, who was raised to the rank of a Marquess's son 1973, *b* 1914, *d* 1975: *m* 1944, Jane Elizabeth (ante), da of Arthur Martin:—
Jane Elizabeth, *b* 1945: *m* 1971, Capt Mark Graham Robinson, late RA, of Trullwell, Box, nr Stroud, Glos GL6 9HD, and has issue living, Nano Sophie Tottenham, *b* 1973.

Grandchildren of late Very Rev George Tottenham, 10th son of late Rt Rev Lord Robert Ponsonby Tottenham, Bishop of Clogher (ante):—
Issue of late Edward Loftus Tottenham, *b* 1867, *d* 1949: *m* 1899, Jessie Hilda, who *d* 1938, da of late John Honey Trace:—
George William Loftus, *b* 1911: *m* 1949, Margaret Mary Hamilton, da of late Thomas Valentine Powell, and has issue living, (Robert) Ashley Christopher, *b* 1953: *m* 1st, 1978, Philippa Jane, who *d* 1978, el da of Maj P. F. Stevens, of Cornmongers, Runwick, Farnham, Surrey; 2ndly, 1983, Gabriele Maria, da of Anton Schüle, of Rötenbach, Wolfegg, W. Germany, and has issue living (by 1st *m*), Joe *b* 1980, — Alison Margaret, *b* 1951: *m* 1976, Roger Jones, and has issue living. *Residence* – Blaney, Enniskillen, co Fermanagh. ———— Emily Frances: *m* 1931, Henry Gordon Sansom and has issue living. *Residence* – 15 Old Rossopy Park, Enniskillen, co Fermanagh.

PREDECESSORS – (1) JOHN Tottenham, MP for New Ross, etc; *cr* a *Baronet* 1780; *d* 1786; *s* by his son (2) CHARLES, KP, PC (2nd Bt), who had in 1783 *s* to the estates of his uncle Henry Loftus (which surname he assumed), KP, 1st and last Earl of Ely (*cr* 1771), and in 1785 had been *cr Baron Loftus*, of Loftus (peerage of Ireland); was Postmaster-Gen 1789; *cr Viscount Loftus* (peerage of Ireland) 1789, *Earl of Ely* (peerage of Ireland) 1794, *Marquess of Ely* (peerage of Ireland) 1801, and *Baron Loftus*, of Long Loftus, co York (peerage of United Kingdom) 1801; *d* 1806; *s* by his son (3) JOHN, KP, 2nd Marquess; *d* 1845; *s* by his son (4) JOHN HENRY, 3rd Marquess; *b* 1814: *m* 1844, Jane, VA, da of James Hope-Vere, of Craigie and Blackwood, NB; *d* 1857; *s* by his son (5) JOHN HENRY WELLINGTON GRAHAM, 4th Marquess, *b* 1849: *m* 1875, Caroline Anne, who *d* 1917, da of late George Caithness; *d* 1889; *s* by his cousin (6) JOHN HENRY (el son of the Rev Lord Adam Loftus, 3rd son of 2nd Marquess), 5th Marquess, *b* 1851: *m* 1895, Margaret Emma, who *d* 1931, da of F. Aldridge Clark, of Lynton Court, Hove, Sussex, and Gracefield, Prince, Risborough, Bucks; *d* 1925; *s* by his brother (6) GEORGE HERBERT, 6th Marquess, *b* 1854: *m* 1st, 1884, Emily Harriet, who *d* 1886, da of Major Arthur Vandeleur, RA; 2ndly, 1902, Ethel Beatrice Lemprière, who *d* 1927, da of late Nigel Gresley, JP, of Hobart, Tasmania; *d* 1935; *s* by his son (7) GEORGE HENRY WELLINGTON, 7th Marquess, *b* 1903: *m* 1928, Thea Margaret Gordon, da of late Lars G. Gronvold, of Hove; *d* 1969; *s* by his kinsman (8) Charles John (el son of George Leonard Tottenham, grandson of Charles John Tottenham (*b* 1808), el son of the Rt Rev Lord Robert Ponsonby Tottenham, Bishop of Clogher (who resumed the name and arms of Tottenham), 2nd son of 1st Marquess), 8th Marquess and present peer; also Earl of Ely, Viscount Loftus, and Baron Loftus.

ELYSTAN-MORGAN, BARON (Morgan) (Life Baron 1981)

(DAFYDD) ELYSTAN MORGAN, son of late Dewi Morgan; *b* 7 Dec 1932; *ed* Ardwyn Gram Sch, Aberystwyth, Univ Coll of Wales, Aberystwyth; admitted a solicitor 1957; Chm Welsh Parly Party 1967-68; Parly under Sec of State Home Office 1968-70; Barrister at Law Grays Inn 1971; front bench spokesman on Welsh Affairs 1972-74; a Circuit Judge, Wales and Chester circuit since 1987; MP (Lab) Cardiganshire 1966-74; a Recorder (1983); *cr Baron Elystan-Morgan*, of Aberteifi, co Dyfed (Life Baron) 1981: *m* 1959, Alwen, da of William E. Roberts, and has issue.
Residence – Careg Afon, Dolau, Bow Street, Dyfed.

SON LIVING

Hon Owain, *b* 1962.

DAUGHTER LIVING

Hon Eleri, *b* 1960; LLB: *m* 1989, Peter Gerard Hurt, 2nd son of Rudolph Hurt, of Hathern, Loughborough, Leics.

EMMET OF AMBERLEY, BARONY OF (Emmet) (Extinct 1980)

SONS LIVING OF LIFE BARONESS

Hon Christopher Anthony Robert (Seabeach House, Selhurst Park, Halnaker, Chichester, Sussex), *b* 1925; *ed* Ampleforth, and Balliol Coll, Oxford (MA); a JP for W Sussex; a Co Councillor for W Sussex 1952-62: *m* 1947, Lady Miranda Mary Fitzalan Howard, sister of 17th Duke of Norfolk, and has issue living, Robert Anthony Bernard, *b* 1958: *m* 1987, Francesca Lavinia Elizabeth, eldest da of Sebastian Snow, and of Mrs Anthony Longland, of The Old Vicarage, Stinsford, Dorset, and has issue living, Jules Anthony Christopher *b* 1990, Marcus Guy *b* 1992, — Teresa Miriam, *b* 1949: *m* 1969, Anthony Andrew Myers, of 8a Sterne St, W12, and has issue living, Adrian Anthony Geoffrey *b* 1972, Nicholas Andrew Robert *b* 1973, — Catriona Mary, *b* 1951: *m* 1st, 1978 (*m diss* 1983), Paul Striberry; 2ndly, 1984, Christopher John Russell-Pavier, who *d* 1994, of 16 Selby Rd, W5, and has issue living (by 2nd *m*), Charles Adey *b* 1992, Anna Louise *b* 1985, — Rowena Mary Gabriel, *b* 1954: *m* 1st, 1975 (*m diss* 1981), Michael F. Hallinan; 2ndly, 1982, Jonathan Malcolm Green, of Frenchland House, Ashington, Pulborough, W Sussex, and has issue living, (by 2nd *m*) Thomas Oliver *b* 1984, James Edward *b* (twin) 1984, Iona Alice *b* 1989.
Hon David Alastair Rennell (Casilla de Correo 55174, San Carlos, Maldonado, Uruguay), *b* 1928; *ed* Ampleforth, and Worcester Coll, Oxford; a Member of British Community Council, Argentina 1964-68: FRGS: *m* 1967, Sylvia Delia, da of late Willis Knowles, of Buenos Aires, and has issue living, Thomas Ian David, *b* 1970, — Caroline Ann Gloria *b* 1968.

DAUGHTERS LIVING OF LIFE BARONESS

Hon Gloria Lavinia Eileen, *b* 1924: *m* 1950, Maj Mark Winton Slane Fleming, 10th R Hussars (PWO), (ret) of Ardath, Shamley Green, nr Guildford, Surrey GU5 0SY, and has issue living, Andrew Gerard James, *b* 1956; FBHI: *m* 1985, Kathryn Claire, only child of late John William Warner, DSC, and has issue living, Giles William Slane *b* 1989, Jack Francis Edmund *b* 1992, Lucinda Marion Kate *b* 1987, — Mary Georgina, *b* 1951: *m* 1972, Michael David Hardinge, and has issue living, Elizabeth Selene *b* 1972, — Sarah Elizabeth Sophia, *b* 1953: *m* 1979, Jonathan Francis Bruce Ward, and has issue (*see* Bruce, Bt, *cr* 1628, colls), — Charlotte Ann, *b* 1955.
Hon Penelope Ann Clare (Flat 4, 43 Onslow Sq, SW7), *b* 1932: *m* 1951 (*m diss* 1965), Hon Hugo Nevill Money-Coutts (later 8th Baron Latymer).

EMSLIE, BARON (Emslie) (Life Baron 1979)

GEORGE CARLYLE EMSLIE, MBE, PC, son of Alexander Emslie; *b* 6 Dec 1919; *ed* The High Sch of Glasgow, and Glasgow Univ (MA, LLB, Hon LLD); FRSE, 1939-45 War in N Africa, Italy, Greece and Austria (despatches); Bde Maj 1944-46; Advocate Scotland 1948; QC 1957; Advocate Depute to Sheriff Courts 1955-57; Junior Assessor to City of Edinburgh 1955-57; a Member of Scottish Cttee of Council on Tribunals 1962-70; Chm of Scottish Agricultural Wages Board 1968; Sheriff of Perth and Angus 1963-66; Dean of Faculty of Advocates 1965-70, and Senior Assessor to City of Edinburgh 1965-70; Senator of the College of Justice; a Lord of Session with the title of *Lord Emslie* 1970; Lord Justice Gen of Scotland and Lord Pres of the Court of Session 1972; Hon Bencher Inner Temple 1974; *cr* PC 1972, and *Baron Emslie*, of Potterton, in the District of Gordon (Life Baron) 1979: *m* 1942, Lilias Ann Mailer, da of Robert Hannington, of Glasgow, and has issue.

ᚨrms – not exemplified at the time of going to press.
Residence – 47 Heriot Row, Edinburgh EH3 6EX. *Clubs* – New (Edinburgh); Caledonian (London).

SONS LIVING

Hon (George) Nigel Hannington (20 Inverleith Place, Edinburgh EH3 5QB), BA (Cantab), LLB (Edin), QC (Scot) 1986, *b* 1947; *ed* Edinburgh Acad, Trinity Coll, Glenalmond, and Gonville and Caius Coll Camb and Edinburgh Univ; QC: *m* 1973, Heather Ann, da of Arthur Frank Davis, of Bristol, and has issue.
Hon Derek Robert Alexander (35 Ann St, Edinburgh EH4 1PL), BA (Cantab) LLB (Edin), QC (Scot) 1987, *b* 1949; *ed* Edinburgh Acad, Trinity Coll, Glenalmond, Gonville and Caius Coll Camb, and Edinburgh Univ; QC 1987: *m* 1974, Elizabeth Jane Cameron, da of Andrew McLaren Carstairs of Newport-on-Tay, and has issue.
Hon Richard Hannington, *b* 1957, *ed* Edinburgh Acad, Trinity Coll, Glenalmond, and Gonville and Caius Coll Camb (MA).

Encombe, Viscount; son of Earl of Eldon.

ENERGLYN, BARONY OF (Evans) (Extinct 1985)

WIDOW LIVING OF LIFE BARON

JEAN THOMPSON (*Baroness Energlyn*), da of John Miller, of St Andrews Cres, Cardiff: *m* 1942, Baron Energlyn (Life Baron), who *d* 1985. *Residence* – 7 The Dentons, Denton Rd, Eastbourne, East Sussex BN20 7SW.

Enfield, Viscount; son of Earl of Strafford.

ENNALS, BARON (Ennals) (Life Baron 1983)

DAVID HEDLEY ENNALS, PC, son of late Capt Arthur Ford Ennals, MC (*d* 1977); *b* 19 Aug 1922; *ed* Queen Mary's Gram Sch, Walsall, and Loomis Inst, Windsor, Conn, USA; Sec Council for Educn in World Citizenship 1947-52, and of UN Assocn 1952-55, and Overseas Sec, Labour Party 1958-64; Parl Under-Sec of State MOD 1966-67, Parl Sec Home Office 1967-68, and Min of State, Dept of Health & Social Security 1968-70; Min of State, Foreign & Commonwealth Office 1974-76; Sec of State for Social Sers 1976-79; Campaign Dir Nat Assocn for Mental Health 1970-73; Member of Council of Counsel and Care for the Elderly since 1990; MP for Dover (*Lab*) 1964-70, and for Norwich (North) 1974-83; 1939-45 War as Capt Recce Corps (RAC) in France; *cr* PC 1970, and *Baron Ennals*, of Norwich, co Norfolk (Life Baron) 1983: *m* 1st, 1950 (*m diss* 1977), Eleanor Maud, da of late Reginald Victor Caddick; 2ndly, 1977, Mrs Katherine Tranoy, and has issue by 1st *m*.
Residence – 47 Brookfield, Highgate West Hill, N6 6AT.

SONS LIVING (By 1st marriage)

Prof Hon John Richard, *b* 1951; *ed* King's Coll Sch, Wimbledon, Phillip's Academy, Andover, USA, King's Coll, Camb, and London Univ Inst of Educn; Prof Kingston Business Sch since 1990: *m* 1975, Roberta Mary, da of Norman Robert Reedman, of Barnet, Herts, and has issue living, Robert Jonathan, *b* 1979, — Christopher Paul, *b* 1981. *Residence* – 19 Belgrade Rd, Hampton, Middx TW12 2AZ.

Hon Paul Martin, *b* 1957.

Hon Simon David, *b* 1959.

DAUGHTER LIVING (By 1st marriage)

Hon Susan, *b* 1953.

ENNISKILLEN, EARL OF (Cole) Sits as BARON GRINSTEAD (UK 1815) (Earl I 1789)

Worship God; honour the King

ANDREW JOHN GALBRAITH COLE, 7th Earl, *b* 28 April 1942; *s* 1989; *ed* Eton; late Capt Irish Guards: *m* 1964, Sarah Frances Caroline, only da of Maj-Gen John Keith-Edwards, CBE, DSO, MC, of Nairobi, and has issue.

Arms – Argent, a bull passant sable, armed and hoofed or, within a bordure of the second, charged with eight bezants; on a canton sinister per pale gules and azure, a harp of the third, stringed argent. **Crest** – A demi-dragon wings elevated vert, holding a dart in the dexter paw and resting the sinister on an antique buckler, charged as the canton. **Supporters** – Two dragons reguardant vert, each holding in the inner fore paw a dart.
Seat – Florence Court, Enniskillen, co Fermanagh. *Address* – c/o Royal Bank of Scotland, 9 Pall Mall, SW1.

DAUGHTERS LIVING

Lady Amanda Mary, *b* 1966.
Lady Emma Frances, *b* 1969.
Lady Lucy Caroline, *b* 1970.

SISTER LIVING

Lady Linda Mary, *b* 1944: *m* 1975, Sir Richard James Kay Muir, 4th Bt, of Park House, Blair Drummond, Stirling, Perths, and has issue.

UNCLE LIVING (*brother of 6th Earl*)

ARTHUR GERALD, *b* 15 Nov 1920; *ed* Eton; late Capt Irish Guards: *m* 1949, Prudence Tobina, da of late Algernon Richard Aubrey Cartwright (*see* Buxton, Bt, colls), and has issue living, Berkeley Arthur (151 Battersea Rise, SW11 1HP), *b* 1949; *ed* Milton Abbey: *m* 1978, Hon Cecilia Anne Ridley, eldest da of 4th Viscount Ridley, TD, and has issue living, Joshua Berkeley *b* 1986, Richard David *b* 1991, — Hugh Galbraith, *b* 1954; *ed* Milton Abbey, — Richard Lowry (1 Avon View, Upper Seagry, Chippenham, Wilts), *b* 1956; *ed* Eton: *m* 1st, 1977 (*m diss* 1988), Susan Elizabeth, da of David Allen, of Nairobi, Kenya; 2ndly, 1988 (*m diss* 19—), Karen, da of Ernest Robert Victor Ingram, of Chippenham, Wilts, and has issue living (by 1st *m*), Arthur Berkeley David *b* 1983, — Marian Rose, *b* 1951: *m* 1979, Bruce Hobson, of Rosslyn Estate, Box 34247, Nairobi, Kenya, and has issue living, Amelia Rose *b* 1986. *Residence* – 2 Orchard Brae, Edinburgh EH4 1NY.

DAUGHTER LIVING OF FIFTH EARL

Lady Frances Jane, *b* 1914; late Junior Com ATS: *m* 1954, as his 2nd wife, Group Capt Henry Ivan Hanmer, DFC, RAF, who *d* 1984 (*see* Hanmer, Bt, colls). *Residence* – 1 Church Way, Grendon, Northampton.

WIDOW LIVING OF SIXTH EARL

NANCY HENDERSON (*Dowager Countess of Enniskillen*), da of late Dr John Alexander MacLennan, of 105 Brooklawn Place, Bridgeport, Conn, USA; former Washington and United Nations correspondent, *New York Times*; former assistant attaché and vice consul US Foreign Ser; author of *Florence Court, My Irish Home* (1972), and *Amulree and it's Church* (1990): *m* 1955, as his 2nd wife, the 6th Earl, who *d* 1989. *Residence* – Kinloch House, Amulree, Dunkeld, Perthshire PH8 0EB.

COLLATERAL BRANCHES LIVING

Grandchildren of late Hon Arthur Edward Casamaijor Cole, 3rd son of 3rd Earl:—
Issue of late Lowry Arthur Casamaijor Cole, MBE, *b* 1878, *d* 1955: *m* 1910, Adelaide Grizel, who *d* 1965 da of late Frederick Pratt-Barlow (*see* M Anglesey, colls, 1940 Edn):—
Rev Arthur Lowry Frederick (c/o Royal Bank of Scotland, 49 Charing Cross, SW1), *b* 1911; *ed* Eton; was V of Wroxham 1954-59, Assist Priest at St Paul's Knightsbridge, SW1, 1959-60, and Bishop's Chap for Youth, Diocese of Coventry 1960-64; formerly a Chap to Forces. —— Elizabeth Joan, *b* 1919.

Grandchildren of late Claud CHALONER (who assumed the surname of Chaloner under the will of his uncle Richard Chaloner) son of Arthur Willoughby Cole-Hamilton, grandson of late Hon ARthur Cole-Hamilton, MP, 2nd son of 1st Baron Mountflorence:—
Issue of late Maj Claudius Willoughby CHALONER, *b* 1882, *d* 1963: *m* 1918, Winifred Adelaide, who *d* 1969 da of late Col Alexander Sinclair Grove, DSO, MSC:—
Desmond Willoughby Richard (High Bank, Chearsley, Aylesbury), *b* 1920; *ed* Shrewsbury, and at Trin Coll, Dublin (MA); 1939-45 War as Lt King's African Rifles. —— Nancy Winifred (Rathmore House, Rathmore, Naas, co Kildare), *b* 1921: *m* 1st, 1945, Francis G. Cornwall, who *d* 1949; 2ndly, 1959, Prof John Seton Michael Pringle, FRCS, who *d* 1975, and has issue living (by 1st *m*), Francis David Willoughby, *b* 1947, — Ann Patricia (*posthumous*), *b* 1950: *m* 1973, Robert Tristram Rowan Woods, of Beechmount, Orwell Rd, Dublin 14, and has issue living, Robert Seton Rowan *b* 1986, John Francis Cornwall *b* (twin) 1986, Nicola Clare *b* 1982, Lucinda Ann *b* 1983.
Issue of late John Cole CHALONER, *b* 1889, *d* 1940: *m* 1922, Monica Katharine, who *d* 1975, da of late Rev William Ralph Westropp Roberts, DD:—
Charity Patricia *b* 1923: *m* 1949 (*m diss* 1973), Henry FitzGibbon, MD, who *d* 1989, and has issue living, John (638 Monterey Ave, Victoria, BC, Canada), *b* 1951: *m* 1976, Paula Gammell, and has issue living, Fletcher *b* 1987, Gamelle (a da) *b* 1984, — Thomas, *b* 1952, — Frances, *b* 1954: *m* 1993, — Pamela Anne, *b* 1959. —— Mary Frances Jonet, *b* 1925: *m* 1950, Richard John Shackleton, and has issue living, Richard Chaloner, *b* 1953: *m* 1988, Sarah Caroline Benton, and has issue living, Christopher Mark *b* 1989, James Richard *b* 1991, Deborah Mary *b* 1993, — Michael Beattie, *b* 1959, — Christine Mary, *b* 1951: *m* 1988, Samir Habouch, — Jonet Rhoda, *b* 1956: *m* 1984, Thomas Mary Egan, of White Lodge, Kennedy Rd, Dunboyne, co Meath, and has issue living, Eoin Shackleton *b* 1987. *Residence* – Anna Liffey House, Lucan, co Dublin. —— Henrietta Sophia, *b* 1930: *m* 1959, Robert Frederick Twigg, and has issue living, Robert Chaloner (Amber Hill, Kilmeaden, co Waterford), *b* 1960: *m* 1985, Janet Beck, and has issue living, Nathan Robert *b* 1988, Katie Beck *b* 1986, Lucy Astrid *b* 1989, — Nicola *b* 1962: *m* 1993, Christopher Woods, — Fiona, *b* 1963: *m* 1987, Frank O'Reilly, of Granite Lodge, Enniskerry, co Wicklow, and has issue living, Stephen Peter *b* 1988, Alan Robert *b* 1990, Karen Sophie Anne *b* 1993, — Sarah *b* 1970. *Residence* – Newtownmountkennedy, co Wicklow.

Granddaughters of late Rev Arthur Henry Cole-Hamilton, son of late Arthur Willoughby Cole-Hamilton (ante):—

Issue of late George William Cole-Hamilton, *b* 1875, *d* 1946: *m* 1908, Katharine Edith, who *d* 1960, da of late William Clinton-Baker, of Bayfordbury, Herts:—

Katharine Letitia *b* 1909: *m* 1930, Bernard Alleyne Murray, MC, TD, RA, who *d* 1984, and has issue living, Katharine Elizabeth, *b* 1932: *m* 1962, Robert Hugh Shirley, of 7805 Cunliffe Rd, Vernon, BC, Canada, and has issue living, Michael Bruce *b* 1964, Katharine Judith *b* 1966, — Mary Bridget (27 Church Vale, N2), *b* 1935; BM, BCh, FRCP, DCH: *m* 1st, (*m diss* 1974), Randall Clive Smith; 2ndly, 1975, John Robin Edwards. *Residence* – 32 Ormond Av, Hampton, Middx. —— Anne (3 Lower Hacketts, Brickendon, Hertford), *b* 1910: *m* 1st, 1938, Lt David Edmund Cole-Hamilton, DSC, RN (infra), who was *ka* 1942; 2ndly, 1959, Oswald Graham Noel Turnbull, MC, who *d* 1970. —— Mary, TD, *b* 1913; formerly Ch Comm ATS: *m* 1st, 1936 (*m diss* 1952), John Carew Jones; 2ndly, 1952, Col John Locke Lovibond, TD, MD, FRCP, RAMC (TA), who *d* 1954; 3rdly, 1956, Col Donald Barry Girling, MC, TD, RA (TA), who *d* 1986. *Residence* – Highworth Farm, Charlwood, Surrey. —— Elizabeth Peace, *b* 1918: *m* 1st, 1939, Lt-Com Rodney Athelstan Price, RN, who was *ka* 1943; 2ndly, 1945, Col Geoffrey Russell Armstrong, DSO, MC, TD, Hon Artillery Co, and has issue living, (by 1st *m*) David George (Woodcock, Thirsk, Yorks), *b* 1940; MA, Camb: *m* 1970, Diana Catherine Symington, da of late Alastair Symington Davie, of Grangehill, Beith, Ayrshire, and has issue living, Toby Charles Rodney *b* 1972, Simon James Edward *b* 1974, — (by 2nd *m*) Johny (Woodlands House, Colgate, Sussex), *b* 1946: MA Camb: *m* 1976, Elsie Borodale, da of Frederick S. Peters, of New Jersey, USA, and has issue living, Geoffrey Read *b* 1980, Graham Whitney *b* 1983, — Ruth Margaret, *b* 1949: *m* 1976, Henry Clifton Calvert (*see* Brown, Bt, colls), of Holmbush, Faygate, Sussex, and has issue living, Piers Henry *b* 1977, Henrietta Amelia *b* 1980. *Residence* – Axmas Cottage, Rusper, Sussex.

Grandsons of late Ven Richard Mervyn Cole-Hamilton (infra):—

Issue of late Maj Richard Arthur Cole-Hamilton, *b* 1912, *d* 1992: *m* 1947, (Ruth Kathleen) Betty (Hawthorn Villa, 386 Ferry Rd, Edinburgh EH5 3QG), da of Sir William Lorenzo Parker, 3rd Bt, OBE:—

Robin (39 Fawnbrake Av, SE24 OBE), *b* 1948; *ed* Trin Coll, Glenalmond: *m* 1982, Helen, da of late Rev Canon Gerald Archer Luckett, of Meonstoke, Hants, and has issue living, Jonathan Archer, *b* 1986, — Katharine Faith, *b* 1983. —— Richard Simon (Elm Cottage, 54 Culcabock Av, Inverness IV2 3RQ), *b* 1951; *ed* Trin Coll, Glenalmond; CA: *m* 1982, Anni, da of J. G. M. Watt, of Edinburgh, and has issue living, Joanna Ruth, *b* 1983, — Sarah Constance, *b* 1985. —— William Mervyn John (Lethenty Cottage, Fyvie, Aberdeenshire), *b* 1954; *ed* Trin Coll, Glenalmond: *m* 1978, Jill, yst da of Dr K. C. Johnston, and has issue living, Richard James, *b* 1983, — Emma Judith, *b* 1985.

Issue of late Lieut David Edmund Cole-Hamilton, DSC, RN, *b* 1914; *k* on active service in the Mediterranean 1942: *m* 1938, Anne (who *m* 2ndly, 1959, Oswald Graham Noel Turnbull, MC, who *d* 1970), da of late George William Cole-Hamilton (ante):—

Michael Anthony (355 Park Av, Newmarket, Ont L3Y 1V4, Canada; The Ridge, RR2 Lyndhurst, Ont K0E 1N0, Canada), *b* 1940; *ed* Bradfield; late Lieut RN: *m* 1963, Jane Elizabeth Mary, elder da of Arthur Maurice Stewart-Wallace, MD, FRCP, of The Moot House, Ditchling, Sussex, and has issue living, William Michael David, *b* 1967, — Elen Susannah, *b* 1965: *m* 1993, Graham Lunt, elder son of Ronald Lunt, of Boscheok Farm, Duiwelskloof, S Africa, — Alexandra Jane, *b* 1971.

Grandson of late Rev Arthur Henry Cole-Hamilton (ante):—

Issue of late Ven Richard Mervyn Cole-Hamilton, *b* 1877, *d* 1959: *m* 1st, 1911, Margaret, JP, who *d* 1954, da of late Edmund Grove Bennett, of The Close, Salisbury; 2ndly, 1955, Elsie Irén (WARNER), who *d* 1975, da of W. H. Pendlebury, of Shrewsbury:—

(By 1st *m*) Anthony Mervyn, *b* 1919; Lt-Cdr RN (ret); 1939-45 War (despatches): *m* 1st, 1944, Monica Mary (3rd Officer WRNS), who *d* 1954, da of late Lt-Col John Rogers Cartwright, DSO; 2ndly, 1956 (*m diss* 1983), Angela Elizabeth, who *d* 1988, da of J. I. Baeza, FRCS, DPH, of Barbados, and formerly wife of M. A. G. Hanschell and has issue living (by 1st *m*), David John, *b* 1948; Irvine Prof of Chemistry, St Andrews Univ: *m* 1973, Elizabeth Ann, da of Bruce Lloyd Brown, of Vic, BC, Canada, and has issue living, Alexander Geoffrey *b* 1977, Nicholas Anthony Michael *b* 1986, Rose Monica Elizabeth *b* 1979, Sian Fiona Non *b* 1986, — Susan Joan (Reno, Nevada, USA), *b* 1945: *m* 1st, 1969 (*m diss* 1978), Andrew Wallace; 2ndly, 1978, Gerard Garra, — Isobel Margaret, *b* 1950, — Patricia Anne, *b* 1952: *m* 1982, F. Tomlin, and has issue living, Lucy Sarah Patricia *b* 1980, Alison Kirsty *b* 1982. *Residence* – Marine Cottage, Alleyn's Rd, Stevenage, Herts.

Granddaughter of late John Isaac Cole-Hamilton, yst son of late Arthur Willoughby Cole-Hamilton (ante):—

Issue of late Air Vice-Marshal John Beresford Cole-Hamilton, CB, CBE, *b* 1894, *d* 1945: *m* 1928, Hilda Violet Leslie, who *d* 1945, da of late Charles Leslie Fox, of Rumwell Hall, Taunton:—

Diana Patricia Selina, *b* 1932: *m* 1957 (*m diss* 1968), Stephen Wilbraham Ford, and has issue living, Jonathan Hugo, *b* 1960, — Joanna Margaret Randle, *b* 1958. *Residence* - The Old Vicarage, Greywell, Basingstoke.

Granddaughters of late Col Arthur Richard Cole-Hamilton, son of late Capt William Claude Cole-Hamilton, brother of late Claud Chaloner (ante):—

Issue of late Capt William Moore Cole-Hamilton, late RASC, *b* 1883, *d* 1948: *m* 1903, Ada Beatrice, yst da of late William Peter Huddle, of Dover:—

Nora Kathleen, *b* 1904: *m* 1st, 1926 (*m diss* 1944), Carl Rudolf Baltzar von Braun, MRCS, late Capt RAMC; 2ndly, 1944, John Mathew Shufflebotham, of San Agustin, 105 el Tosalet, Denia (Alicante), Spain.

PREDECESSORS – (1) JOHN COLE, MP for Enniskillen, 4th in descent from Sir William Cole, who settled in Co Fermanagh *temp* James I, was *cr Baron Mountflorence*, of Florence Court, co Fermanagh (peerage of Ireland) 1760; *d* 1767; *s* by his son (2) WILLIAM WILLOUGHBY, 2nd Baron; *cr Viscount Enniskillen* (peerage of Ireland), 1776, and *Earl of Enniskillen* (peerage of Ireland) 1789; *d* 1803; *s* by his son (3) JOHN WILLOUGHBY, 2nd Earl; *b* 1768; Lord-Lieut of co Fermanagh; *cr Baron Grinstead*, of Grinstead, Wilts (peerage of United Kingdom) 1815; *d* 1840; *s* by his son (4) WILLIAM WILLOUGHBY, DCL, LLD, FRS; *b* 1807; sat as MP for Fermanagh (C) 1831-40: *m* 1st, 1844, Jane, who *d* 1855, el da of late James Archibald Casamaijor; 2ndly, 1865, Hon Mary Emma Brodrick, who *d* 1896, da of 6th Viscount Middleton; *d* Nov 1886; *s* by his el son (5) LOWRY EGERTON, KP, 4th Earl, *b* 1845, MP for Enniskillen (C) 1880-5: *m* 1869, Charlotte Marion, who *d* 1937, da of late Douglas Baird, of Closeburn, NB; *d* 1924; *s* by his son (6) JOHN HENRY MICHAEL, CMG, 5th Earl, *b* 1876; Lt 7th Hussars, and Lt-Col N Irish Horse, and Chm N Ireland Transport Board: *m* 1st, 1907 (*m diss* 1931), Irene Frances, who *d* 1937, da of Alfred Edward Miller Mundy; 2ndly, 1932, Mary Cecily, da of late Hugh Nevill, and widow of Maj Thomas Syers, RA; *d* 1963; *s* by his nephew (7) DAVID LOWRY, MBE (son of late Hon Galbraith Lowry Egerton Cole, 3rd son of 4th Earl), 6th Earl, *b* 1918; 1939-45 War as Capt Irish Guards; Elected Member Kenya Leg Council (Mt Kenya Constituency) 1961-63, DL, JP co Fermanagh: *m* 1st, 1940 (*m diss* 1955), Sonia, who *d* 1982, da of late Maj Thomas Syers, RA (by his wife Mary Cicely Nevill, who *d* 1963, having *m* 2ndly, 1932, the 5th Earl of Enniskillen); 2ndly, 1955, Nancy Henderson, da of late Dr John Alexander MacLennan, of Bridgeport, Conn, USA; *d* 1989; *s* by his only son (8) ANDREW JOHN GALBRAITH, 7th Earl and present peer; also Viscount Enniskillen, Baron Mountflorence, and Baron Grinstead.

Ennismore, Viscount; son of Earl of Listowel.

Erleigh, Viscount; son of Marquess of Reading.

ERNE, EARL OF (Crichton) Sits as BARON FERMANAGH (UK 1876) (Earl I 1789)
(Name pronounced "Cryton")

HENRY GEORGE VICTOR JOHN CRICHTON, 6th Earl; *b* 9 July 1937; *s* 1940; *ed* Eton; was a Page of Honour to HM 1952-54; late Lieut N. Irish Horse; a JP and Lord Lieut co Fermanagh: *m* 1st, 1958 (*m diss* 1980), Camilla Marguerite, el da of late Wing Com Owen George Endicott Roberts; 2ndly, 1980, Mrs Anna Carin Hitchcock, *née* Bjorck, and has issue by 1st *m*.

Arms – Argent, a lion rampant azure. **Crest** – A wyvern's head couped at the neck vert emitting flames proper from the mouth and ears. **Supporters** – Two lions azure, on the head of each an earl's coronet proper. *Seat* – Crom Castle, Newtown Butler, co Fermanagh. *Clubs* – White's, Lough Erne Yacht Club.

GOD · SEND · GRACE

SON LIVING *(By 1st marriage)*

JOHN HENRY MICHAEL NINIAN (*Viscount Crichton*), *b* 19 June 1971.

DAUGHTERS LIVING *(By 1st marriage)*

Lady Cleone Lucinda, *b* 1959: *m* 1989, Richard F. Versen, and has issue living, Frederick James, *b* 1992. *Residence* – Rosewood Cottage, Ascot, Berks.
Lady Davina Jane, *b* 1961: *m* 1990, Nicholas J. R. Scarr, elder son of late Peter R. R. Scarr, and has issue living, Oliver Peter Renforth, *b* 1992, — Sabrina Katherine Renforth *b* 1993. *Residence* – Lee Park Lodge, Lee, nr Romsey, Hants SO51 9ZD.
Lady Katherine Patricia, *b* 1962: *m* 1989, Jonathan C. Townsend-Rose, son of Colin Townsend-Rose, of W Printonan, Berwicks, and has issue living, Rory Dixon Crichton, *b* 1993, — Alexandra Lucy Flora, *b* 1992. *Residence* – Maxton Westend, Maxton, St Boswells, Roxburghshire TD6 0RL.
Lady Tara Guinevere, *b* 1967: *m* 1993, James William Loyd, yr son of Christopher Lewis Loyd, MC, of Lockinge, Wantage, Berks, and of Mrs Simon Burne, of Charlton, Malmesbury.

SISTERS LIVING

Lady Rosanagh Mary, *b* 1932: *m* 1956, Baron Michael Paul Raben-Levetzau, who *d* 1990, and has issue living, (Siegfried) Matthew (John) (35 Fontenoy Rd, SW12 9LX; *Club* – White's), *b* 1962: *m* 1987, Sarah Jane L., da of Vernon Gordon-Lennox Stratton, of St Helen's Station, IoW, and has issue living, Frederick Michael James *b* 1990, Sophie Eleanor Rose *b* 1993, — Alexander Peter Vincent, *b* 1964, — Christopher Victor Patrick, *b* 1968, — Seamus Julian Henry, *b* 1971. *Residence* – 23 Stack House, Cundy St, SW1.
Lady Antonia Pamela Mary, *b* 1934: *m* 1st, 1953, Timothy William Wardell (*see* Crossley, Bt, 1985 Edn); 2ndly, 1981, Charles William Beckwith, and has issue living (by 1st *m*), Michael John William (13 Verity St, Richmond, Vic 3121, Australia), *b* 1956; *ed* Eton, and Australian Nat Univ: *m* 1980 (*m diss* 1991), Elizabeth O'Neil, and has issue living, Francesca Mary Louise *b* 1984, Sophia Helen Mary *b* 1986, — Antony Henry Constantine, *b* 1959: *m* 1989, Nichola M. L., da of Thomas Wright, of Maudlin Farmhouse, Steyning, Sussex, and has issue living, Thomas William *b* 1993, a da *b* 1991, — David Stewart Timothy, *b* 1963, — Sabrina Mary Louise, *b* 1954: *m* 1974, Michael L. F. Smith, — Henrietta Pamela Mary, *b* 1967. *Residence* – The Dower House, Kirklington, nr Bedale, N Yorks DL8 2LX.

WIDOW LIVING OF FIFTH EARL

Lady DAVIDEMA KATHERINE CYNTHIA MARY MILLICENT BULWER-LYTTON, da of 2nd Earl of Lytton: *m* 1st, 1931, the 5th Earl, who *d* of wounds received in action 1940; 2ndly, 1945, Col Hon Christopher Montague Woodhouse, DSO, OBE, MP (see B Terrington). *Residence* – Willow Cottage, Latimer, Chesham, Bucks.

COLLATERAL BRANCHES LIVING

Issue of late Col Hon Sir George Arthur Charles Crichton, GCVO, Coldstream Guards, 2nd son of 4th Earl, *b* 1874, *d* 1952: *m* 1913, Lady Mary Augusta Dawson, JP, who *d* 1961, da of 2nd Earl of Dartrey:—
David George, LVO, *b* 1914; *ed* Eton; late HM Diplo Ser; LVO 1968; 1939-45 War as Maj Derbys Yeo (TA) (despatches): *m* 1st, 1941, Joan Fenella, who *d* 1992, in a road accident, da of late Lt-Col Douglas Whyte Cleaver, DSO, of Park Palace, Monte Carlo; 2ndly, 1994, Betty, da of late Col M. G. Lee, of Christchurch, NZ, and widow of Andrew George Hughes-Onslow (*see* E Onslow, colls), and has issue living (by 1st *m*), Charles David Blayney, *b* 1953; *ed* Eton: *m* 1st, 1977, Nicola Sian, da of Wing-Cdr Peter Berry, DFC, of Little Bookham, Surrey; 2ndly, 1988, Harriet E., yr da of Martin Monier-Williams, of Burrell House, Chiddingfold, Surrey, and has issue living (by 2nd *m*), Jessica Eloise *b* 1991, Flora Susie *b* 1993, — Fenella Jane, *b* 1948: *m* 1st, 1969 (*m diss* 1974), Hon Anthony Henry Amherst Cecil (*see* B Amherst of Hackney); 2ndly, 1978, John Ernest, and has issue living (by 2nd *m*), Charlotte Matilda *b* 1986. *Residence* – 29B Thorney Crescent, Morgan's Walk, SW11 3TT. *Club* – Boodle's. —— Richard John Vesey, CVO, MC, *b* 1916; *ed* Eton; is Col late Coldstream Guards; Memb HM's Bodyguard of Hon Corps of Gentlemen-at-Arms 1966-86, Lieut since 1981; 1939-45 War (twice wounded, despatches, MC), CVO 1986: *m* 1948, Yvonne (OLIVER), da of late Dr H. E. Worthington, and has issue living, Vesey George (79 Cornwall Gardens, SW7 4AZ), *b* 1949; *ed* Eton, and E Anglia Univ, — Adrian David (2 Kersley St, SW11), *b* 1952; *ed* Eton, Bristol Univ, and INSEAD: *m* 1974, Janie, yr da of Duncan Wauchope, of Pinns Farm, Wellow, Romsey, Hants, and has issue living, Sophie *b* 1981, Henrietta *b* 1983, Laura *b* 1985, — Simon Patrick (Shute End Farm House, Alderbury, Salisbury, Wilts), *b* 1956; *ed* Eton; JP: *m* 1983, Fiona Jane, da of late Colin Midwood, JP, of Grange Cottage, Funtington, W Sussex, and has issue living, Edward William Richard *b* 1989, Charles Patrick Vesey *b* 1992, Georgina Caroline Nicola *b* 1986. *Club* –

Cavalry and Guards'. —— Patrick Henry Douglas, OBE, b 1919; ed Eton, and at Oxford Univ; is Maj Berks Yeo (TA); was a Page of Honour to HM 1932-36; 1939-45 War (despatches); OBE (1991): m 1948, Gillian Moyra, da of late Rt Hon Sir Alexander George Montagu Cadogan, OM, GCMG, KCB (see E Cadogan, colls), and has issue living, Hugh Patrick George, b 1949: m 1984, Kerry, elder da of L. M. Kyle-Little, of Brisbane, Australia, and has issue living, Georgina Jane b 1988, Laura Juliette b 1988 (twin), — Desmond Cadogan (6 Rumbold Rd, SW6 2JA), b 1953; ed Eton: m 1990, Emma Jane, elder da of Maj (Walter Brian) Julian Crawshay, of Tasburgh Grange, Norwich, and has issue living, a son b 1992, a da b 1994, — Jane Elizabeth (twin), b 1949: m 1977, Bevil Charles Fitz Ives Granville, of Ibworth, Basingstoke, Hants, yst son of late Maj Richard St Leger Granville, and has issue living, Harry Court Crichton b 1979, Camilla Jane b 1982. Residence – West Field Cottage, Upton Grey, Basingstoke, Hants RG25 1LG. Club – Boodle's. —— Mary Bridget Anne, b 1927: m 1951, Maj John William Burke Cole, Coldstream Guards (ret) (E Longford, colls), and has issue living, James William John (The Malt House, W Woodhay, Newbury, Berks RG15 0BJ), b 1952; ed Eton: m 1989, Yvonne, da of R. Hawkins, of Hitchin, Herts, and has issue living, Robert William James b 1990, Annabel Charlotte Mary b 1992, Emma Sophie Elizabeth b 1994, — Michael George, b 1955; ed Radley, — Elizabeth Anne, b 1961: m 1984, Simon Leigh Hayes, of The Barn, W Woodhay, Newbury, Berks, elder son of Roger Hayes, of Seaford, Sussex. Residence – The Little Barn, W Woodhay, Newbury, Berks.

Issue of late Hon Arthur Owen Crichton, yst son of 4th Earl, b 1876, d 1970: m 1906, Katherine Helen
Elizabeth, who d 1964, da of late Col Hon Walter Rodolph Trefusis, CB (B Clinton, colls):—
Jean Trefusis (Clover Farm, Shalden, Alton, Hants), b 1912: m 1933, Lt-Col Eion James Henry Merry, MC, R Horse Gds (see V Chetwynd, 1950 Edn), who d 1966; 2ndly, 1969, Capt Montagu William Lowry-Corry, who d 1977 (see E Belmore, colls), and has had issue (by 1st m), Davina Jean (Lady Gibbs) b 1934: m 1955, Field Marshal Sir Roland Christopher Gibbs, GCB, CBE, DSO, MC, late 60th Rifles, of Patney Rectory, Devizes, Wiltshire SN10 3QZ, and has issue living, Aidan Joseph Merry (Phoineas House, by Beauly, Inverness IV4 7BA) b 1957: m 1982, Leonie, el da of Capt (Edward Arthur) Mervyn Fox-Pitt (see E Dundee, colls) (and has issue living, Eion Roland Merry b 1992, Hermione Davina Janet b 1988), James Roland Melvil b 1958, Melissa Margaret Jean b 1966, — Diana, b 1937; d 1980.

Granddaughter of Lieut-Col Hon Charles Frederick Crichton, 2nd son of 3rd Earl:—
Issue of late Major Hubert Francis Crichton, b 1874, ka 1914: m 1903, Esther Eliza (who m 2ndly, 1920, Maj-Gen
Spencer Edmund Hollond, CB, CMG, DSO, who d 1950), da of late Llewellyn Traherne Bassett Saunderson, JP (see
E Clonmell):—
Doris Madeline, b 1904: m 1925, Philip Ivan Pease, who d 1964, and d 1993, leaving issue, Nigel Crichton (Sledwich, Barnard Castle, co Durham DL12 8UU), b 1934; ed Eton: m 1963, Ailsa Smith-Maxwell, and has issue living, Karen b 1970, — Simon Philip (Underley Grange, Kirby Lonsdale, Lancs), b 1945; ed Eton: m 1979, Mrs Clementine Hebeler, and has issue living, Philip John Simon b 1981, — Bridget, b 1926: m 1951, (Geoffrey) David Wentworth-Stanley, of Great Munden House, nr Ware, Herts, and has issue living, (David) Michael b 1952; ed Eton: m 1975, Jane, eldest da of Lt-Col Thomas Armitage Hall, OBE, of Chiselhampton House, Stadhampton, Oxon (see M Dufferin and Ava, 1971 Edn) (and has issue living, Laura Clare b 1978, Emma Jane b 1981, Harriet Sarah b 1985), Nicholas Philip b 1954; ed Eton: m 1985, Clare H., yst da of late Anthony N. Steel, of Rock House Farm, Lower Froyle, Hants (and has issue living, James Nicholas b 1985, Harry David b 1989, Louisa Clare b 1993), Christopher James b 1962; ed Eton, Adrian Charles b 1965; ed Eton: m 1992, Ann N., da of late Capt M. L. Moorberg, USAF, and of Mrs Robert DeBord, of Branford, Conn, USA, — Alison Beatrix, b 1928: m 1954, Christopher Nicholas Weatherby, of Whaddon House, Whaddon, Bucks, and has issue living, Andrew Christopher b 1955, Jonathan Roger b 1959: m 1993, Sophie, da of Roger Cliffe-Jones, Roger Nicholas b 1962, Clare Alison (Hon Mrs Peter Greenall) b 1957: m 1982, Hon Peter Gilbert Greenall, and has issue (see B Daresbury), — Carol Esther, b 1932: m 1959, William E. A. Fox, of Rudham House, East Rudham, King's Lynn, Norfolk, and has issue living, William Philip b 1960, Robert James Ayscough b 1970, Annabel Carol b 1962, Jane Cordelia b 1965. Residence – Cleatlam Hall, Winston, Darlington.

Grandchildren of late Hon Sir Henry George Louis Crichton, KCB, 3rd son of 3rd Earl:—
Issue of late Col Charles William Harry Crichton, DSO, b 1872, d 1958: m 1912, Dorothy Maud, who d 1959, da of
late Hon Eustace Henry Dawnay (see V Downe, colls):—
Ronald Henry, b 1913; ed Radley, and Ch Ch, Oxford; late Capt Rifle Brig. Residence – Flat 2, Clarence House, 8 Granville Rd, Eastbourne, Sussex. —— Brian John, OBE, b 1918; ed Radley, and at Trin Coll, Camb; OBE (Civil) 1977: m 1953, Anne Radclyffe, DL Gwynedd 1989, yr da of late Lt-Col Thomas Hassard Montgomery, DSO, of Cadogan House, Shrewsbury, and has had issue, Susan Jane, b 1955: m 1977, Michael Patrick York, of Boulder, Colorado, Col 80301, USA, and d 1991, leaving issue, Adam Patrick Crichton b 1980, Nicholas Brian b 1990, — Diana Mary, b 1957: m 1984, Richard John Charlton MacMullen, of The Verderers, Bradenham, Norfolk, 2nd son of James MacMullen, MC, of Laxey, I of Man, and has issue living, Patrick James Montgomery b 1989, — Judith Anne CRICHTON (2 Bryn Robert Cottages, Old Llandegfan, Anglesey), b 1959; has resumed her maiden name: m 1983, Anthony Wall, who d 1989, of Ghorst Farm, Leysters, Herefordshire, eldest son of Lt-Col E. Wall, RE. Residence – Plas Trefor, Llansadwrn, Anglesey.
Issue of late Capt Reginald Louis Crichton, RN, b 1874, d 1949: m 1902, Hester Beatrix, who d 1961, da of late Rev
Richard Allen White, R of Wing, Rutland:—
(Francis) Michael, b 1909; is Cdr (ret) RN, and a Fellow of Roy Commonwealth So; 1939-45 War in Atlantic, Mediterranean, Burma, and the Pacific; Roy Sailing Master 1948-50. Residence – Commanders, Lisbellaw, Enniskillen, co Fermanagh. Clubs – Royal Cruising, RN Sailing, Royal Norfolk and Suffolk, Island Sailing (Cowes), Lough Erne Yacht. —— Elisabeth Hester, b 1914: m 1939, Francis Alfred Lepper, FSA, Fellow (now Emeritus) of Corpus Christi Coll, Oxford, of Trewollack House, St Wenn, Bodmin, Cornwall, and has issue living, Patrick Francis Dalway (Falkland House, 21 King's Rd, Berkhamsted, Herts), b 1941: m 1966, Anthea, el da of late W. Douglas C. Scott, of 1 Holly Pl, NW3, and has issue living, Edward Patrick Robert b 1971, Francesca Eugénie b 1967, — Jane Helen Veronica, b 1942: m 1970, Roger James Willoughby, of 35 Defoe Av, Kew, Richmond, Surrey TW9 4DS. —— (Patricia) Jane (Lady Mount), b 1920: m 1st, 1946, John Herbert Mount, who d 1973; 2ndly, 1975, Sir James William Spencer Mount, CBE, of Woolton Farm, Bekesbourne, Canterbury, and has issue living (by 1st m), John Richard Herbert Crichton, b 1953; ed Gordonstoun: m 1977, Martha, only da of Prof Emeteus, of Cambridge, — Mark Donald Crichton b 1957; ed King's Sch, Canterbury, — Virginia Jane, b 1947: m 1968, Richard Henry Ringrose Latham, of Stowting Hill House, Ashford, Kent (see E Jellicoe), — (Selina) Clare, b 1950: m 1st, 1974 (m diss 1978), Alexander Brunton Badenoc; 2ndly, 1978, Andrew Pirie Stuart Robinson.

Granddaughters of late Capt Reginald Louis Crichton, RN (ante):—
Issue of late Cdr Marcus Henry Reginald Crichton, RN, b 1904, d 1985: m 1935, Elizabeth Frances, who d 1993, da
of late Col Francis Holland Dorling, DSO, of The Crouch, Seaford, Sussex:—
Catherine Elizabeth, b 1937: m 1969, Christopher Bates, PhD, of 10 Station Rd, Harston, Cambridge, and has issue living, Gemma Clare Irene, b 1974. —— Frances Margaret, b 1942: m 1962, Maj Patrick Lloyd Ker Thompson, and has issue living, James Marcus Crichton, b 1966, — Bridget Clare, b 1964. —— Madelaine Louise, b 1944: m 1967, Peter George Ridley Dodds, of Meadow Ridge, Stockton, NJ 08559, USA, and has issue living, George Alexander Crichton, b 1970, — Lucy, b 1972.

PREDECESSORS – (1) ABRAHAM Creighton; cr Baron Erne, of Crom Castle, co Fermanagh (peerage of Ireland) 1768; d 1772; s by his son (2) JOHN, 2nd Baron; b 1738 (about); cr Viscount Erne (peerage of Ireland) 1781, and Earl Erne (peerage of Ireland) 1789: m 1761, Catherine, da of Rt Rev Robert Howard, Lord Bishop of Elphin, and sister of 1st Viscount Wicklow; d 1828; s by his son (3) ABRAHAM, 2nd Earl; d unmarried 1842; s by his nephew (4) JOHN, KP, 3rd Earl; b 1802; changed spelling of name to Crichton; was Lord-Lieut of co Fermanagh and a Representative Peer for Ireland; cr Baron Fermanagh, of Lisnaskea (peerage of United Kingdom) 1872: m 1837, Selina Griselda, who d 1884, da of late Rev Charles Cobbe

Beresford; *d* 2 Oct 1885; *s* by his son **(5)** JOHN HENRY, KP, PC, 4th Earl; Lieut of co Fermanagh; MP for Enniskillen (*C*) 1868-80, and for co Fermanagh 1880-83; a Lord of the Treasury 1876-80: *m* 1870, Lady Florence Mary Cole, who *d* 1924, da of 3rd Earl of Enniskillen; *d* 2 Dec 1914; *s* by his grandson **(6)** JOHN HENRY GEORGE (only son of late Major (Henry William) Viscount Crichton, MVO, DSO, Roy Horse Guards (el son of 4th Earl), who was *ka* during European War 31 Oct 1914), 5th Earl; *b* 1907; Major N Irish Horse, and Lieut Roy Horse Guards (Reserve); was a Page of Honour to HM 1921-4, and a Lord-in-Waiting to HM 1936-9: *m* 1931, Lady Davidema Katharine Cynthia Mary Millicent Lytton, da of 2nd Earl of Lytton; *d* of wounds received in action during European War 1940; *s* by his son **(7)** HENRY GEORGE VICTOR JOHN, 6th Earl and present peer; also Viscount Erne, Baron Erne, and Baron Fermanagh.

Errington, Viscount; son of Earl of Cromer.

ERROLL, EARL OF (Hay) (Earl S 1452)

·SERVA · JUGUM·

MERLIN SERELD VICTOR GILBERT HAY, 24th Earl; *b* 20 April 1948; *s* 1978; 28th Hereditary Lord High Constable of Scotland; *s* his father, *Sir* (Rupert) Iain Kay Moncreiffe of that Ilk, CVO, QC, as 12th holder of the Baronetcy, cr (NS) 1685, 1985; *ed* Eton, and Trin Coll, Camb, OStJ; Lt Atholl Highlanders; Member of Queen's Body Guard of Scotland (Royal Company of Archers): *m* 1982, Isabelle Jacqueline Laline, only child of Thomas Sidney Astell Hohler, MC, of Wolverton Park, Basingstoke (*see* V Gort, 1958 Edn), and has issue.
[The LORD HIGH CONSTABLE has precedence in Scotland before Dukes and every other hereditary honour after the Blood Royal. He also maintains his own Officer of Arms, Slains Pursuivant, who first appears on record in 1404.]

Arms – Argent, three inescutcheons gules; above the shield, which is suspended from an ox yoke proper, bows gules, and behind which are set in saltire two batons argent tipped or, is placed His Lordship's coronet, thereon an helmet befitting his degree with a mantling gules doubled ermine. **Crest** – Issuing out of a coronet a falcon volant proper, armed, jessed and belled or. **Supporters** – Two savages wreathed about the middle with laurel, each bearing on his shoulders an ox yoke proper bows gules.
Residence – Wolverton Farm, Basingstoke, Hants RG26 5SX. *Clubs* – White's, Pratt's, Puffin's (Edinburgh).

SONS LIVING

HARRY THOMAS WILLIAM (*Lord Hay*), *b* 8 Aug 1984.
Hon Richard Merlin Iain, *b* 1990.

DAUGHTERS LIVING

Lady Amelia Diana Jacqueline, *b* 1986.
Lady Laline Lucy Clementine, *b* 1987.

BROTHER LIVING

Hon Peregrine David Euan Malcolm MONCREIFFE OF MONCREIFFE; feudal Baron of Easter Moncreiffe and fiar of the feudal Barony of Moncreiffe, *b* 1951; *ed* Eton, and Ch Ch, Oxford; Chm Scottish Ballet; *m* 1988, Miranda Mary, yr da of Capt (Edward Arthur) Mervyn Fox-Pitt, WG (*see* E Dundee, colls), and has issue living, Ossian Peregrine T. G., *b* 1991, — Idina May, *b* 1992. *Residence* – Easter Moncreiffe, Perthshire PH2 8QA. *Clubs* – Turf, White's, Pratt's, New (Edinburgh), Puffin's (Edinburgh), Royal and Ancient Golf (St Andrews), Leander (Henley), and Brook (New York).

HALF-BROTHER LIVING

Hon Jocelyn Jacek Alexander Bannerman CARNEGIE (Crimonmogate, Lonmay, Aberdeenshire), *b* 1966; *ed* Glenalmond: *m* 1990, Susie Mhairi, da of Thomas Mitchell Hastie Butler, of Eastmillhill, Crimond, and has had issue (*see* D Fife, colls).

SISTER LIVING

Lady Alexandra Victoria Caroline Anne, *b* 1955: *m* 1989, Jolyon Christopher Neill Connell, eldest son of late James Christopher Ferrier Connell, of Pitlochry, Perthshire; has issue living, Ivar Francis Grey de Miremont WIGAN, *b* 1979, — Flora Diana Katharine Cecilia, *b* 1990. *Residence* – 65 Sterndale Rd, W14 0HU.

COLLATERAL BRANCHES LIVING

Issue of late Gilbert Allan Rowland Boyd (who *s* as 6th *Baron Kilmarnock* 1941), yr son of 21st Earl, *b* 1903, *d* 1975:—
(see that title)

Issue of late Lady Rosemary Constance Ferelith, da of 21st Earl, *b* 1904, *d* 1944: *m* 1st, 1924 (*m diss* 1935), Lieut-Col Rupert Sumner Ryan, CMG, DSO, who *d* 1952; 2ndly, 1935, Major James Frank Gresham, DSO, Welsh Guards, who *d* 1983:—
(By 1st *m*) †Patrick Victor Charles, *b* 1925: *m* 1949, Rosemary Elizabeth, el da of Francis Rupert Chesterman, of Orford, Tasmania, and *d* 1989, leaving issue, Dominic Rupert Charles (43 Otter St, Collingwood, Vic 3066), *b* 1956, — Siobhan

Ferelith, *b* 1959: *m* 1994, Mark Douglass, of 356 Glen Eira Rd, Elsternwick, Vic 3185, and has issue living, Hunter, *b* 1990. *Residence* – 76 Park St, S Yarra, Vic 3141, Australia.

Issue of late Capt Hon Ivan Josslyn Lumley Hay, MBE, 3rd son of 20th Earl, *b* 1884, *d* 1936: *m* 1921, Pamela, who *d* 1977, da of Francis George Burroughes (B Suffield and E Mayo, colls):—
Elizabeth Anne, *b* 1925; formerly in WRNS: *m* 1945 (*m diss* 1970), Jeremy Christopher Gurney, Lt RN, and has issue living, Michael Jeremy, *b* 1946; *ed* Eton. — William Ivan, *b* 1948; *ed* Eton. *Residence* – 22 Lennox Gdns, SW1. —— Penelope Constance, *b* 1930: *m* 1957, George Harold Armine Dare (*see* Morris, Bt, *cr* 1806, 1972-73 Edn), of 9 Launceston Pl, W8, and has issue living, Henry James, *b* 1959; *ed* Stowe, and Keele Univ, — Amelia Alexandra Elizabeth *b* 1961.

PREDECESSORS – William de la Haye, Butler of Scotland, was granted a charter of feudal Barony of Erroll c 1178-82; Sir Gilbert de la Haye, 3rd feudal Baron of Erroll, co-Regent of Scotland 1255: *m* Lady Idoine, da of William Comyn, Earl of Buchan, and sister of the Constable of Scotland. Their grandson, Sir Gilbert, was for his long adherence to Bruce *cr* by charter hereditary *Great Constable of Scotland* 1314 on the forfeiture of his Comyn cousins (his great-grandson, *Sir Thomas*, 3rd Constable: *m* Elizabeth, da of Robert II, King of Scots); his descendant in the 7th generation was **(1)** *Sir* WILLIAM Hay, 5th Great Constable of Scotland; *cr Lord Hay* (peerage of Scotland) 1449, and *Earl of Erroll* and *Lord Slains* (peerage of Scotland) 1452: *m* Beatrix, da of James, 7th Earl of Douglas; *d* 1463; *s* by his el son **(2)** NICHOLAS, 2nd Earl; *dsp* 1470; *s* by his brother **(3)** WILLIAM, 3rd Earl; *d* 1506; *s* by his son **(4)** WILLIAM, 4th Earl; (*ka* 1513); *s* by his son **(5)** WILLIAM, 5th Earl; *d* 1522; *s* by his son **(6)** WILLIAM, Earl; *d* 1541; *s* by his cousin **(7)** GEORGE (son of Thomas, 2nd son of 3rd Earl), 7th Earl; Lord Lieut of all Central Scotland from the Earn to the Spey 1559; *d* 1573; *s* by his son **(8)** ANDREW, 8th Earl; *d* 1585; *s* by his son **(9)** FRANCIS, 9th Earl; exiled for leading a Catholic rebellion 1594, but subsequently pardoned; *d* 1631; *s* by his son **(10)** WILLIAM, 10th Earl; *d* 1636; *s* by his son **(11)** GILBERT, 11th Earl; *dsp* 1674; *s* by his kinsman **(12)** JOHN (grandson of Sir George, 4th son of 8th Earl), 12th Earl; *d* 1704; *s* by his son **(13)** CHARLES, 13th Earl; *d* unmarried 1717; *s* by his sister **(14)** MARY, wife of Alexander Falconer (brother of 5th Lord Falconer), who assumed the name of Hay of Delgaty; *dsp* 1758; *s* by her grand-nephew **(15)** JAMES (son of William, 4th Earl of Kilmarnock, by Lady Anne Livingtone, da of Lady Margaret Hay (wife of James, 5th Earl of Linlithgow), sister of Mary, Countess of Erroll), 15th Earl; was Lord of Police 1767; *d* 1778; *s* by his el son **(16)** GEORGE, 16th Earl; having let drop a secret of Mr Pitt, committed suicide 1798; *s* by his brother **(17)** WILLIAM, 17th Earl; was Knight-Marischal of Scotland 1805, and Lord High Commr to Ch of Scotland; *d* 1819; *s* by his son **(18)** WILLIAM GEORGE, KT, PC, GCH, 18th Earl, *b* 1801; was Lord Steward of the Household, Master of the Buckhounds, and Lord-Lieut of Aberdeenshire; *cr Baron Kilmarnock*, of Kilmarnock, co Ayr (peerage of United Kingdom) 1831: *m* 1820, Lady Elizabeth Fitzclarence, who *d* 1856, sister of 1st Earl of Munster; *d* 1846; *s* by his son **(19)** WILLIAM HENRY, 19th Earl, *b* 1823; Major (ret) Rifle Brig; Crimea 1854-5 (wounded): *m* 1848, Eliza Amelia, VA, who *d* 1916 da of late Gen the Hon Sir Charles Gore, GCB; *d* 1891; *s* by his son **(20)** CHARLES GORE, KT, CB, LLD, 20th Earl, *b* 1852; Hon Maj-Gen in the Army; sometime Lieut-Col Comdg Roy Horse Guards; a Lord-in-Waiting to King Edward VII 1903-5: *m* 1875, Mary Caroline, who *d* 1934, da of late Edmund L'Estrange, of Tynte Lodge, co Leitrim; *d* 1927; *s* by his son **(21)** VICTOR ALEXANDER SERELD, KCMG, 21st Earl, *b* 1876; acted as Chargé d'Affaires at Berlin 1919-21; was British High Commr of Rhineland Commn 1921-28: *m* 1900, Mary Lucy Victoria, who *d* 1957, only da of Sir Allan Russell Mackenzie, 2nd Bt (*cr* 1890); *d* 1928; *s* by his son **(22)** JOSSLYN VICTOR, 22nd Earl, *b* 1901: *m* 1st, 1923 (*m diss* 1930), Lady (Myra) Idina (GORDON), who *d* 1955, da of 8th Earl De La Warr; 2ndly, 1930, Edith Mildred Mary (RAMSAY-HILL), who *d* 1939, da of late R. W. Maude, of Cleveland, Yorkshire; *d* 1941; *s* in the Barony of Kilmarnock by his brother the Hon Gilbert Allan Rowland Hay, and in the Earldom, and Lordships of Hay and Slains by his only child **(23)** DIANA DENYSE, Countess of Erroll, *b* 1926; retained her maiden name of Hay under Scots Law: *m* 1st, 1946 (*m diss* 1964), Capt Sir (Rupert) Iain Kay Moncreiffe of that Ilk, 11th Bt, who *d* 1985; 2ndly, 1964, Maj Raymond Alexander Carnegie (*see* D Fife); *d* 1978; *s* by her el son **(24)** MERLIN SERELD VICTOR GILBERT, 24th Earl and present peer; also Lord Hay and Lord Slains.

ERROLL OF HALE, BARON (Erroll) (Baron UK 1964)

FREDERICK JAMES ERROLL, TD, PC, 1st Baron, son of George Murison Erroll, of Glasgow, and London; *b* 27 May 1914; *ed* Oundle, and Trin Coll, Camb; Parl Sec to Min of Supply 1955-56, and to Board of Trade 1956-58, Economic Sec to HM Treasury 1958-59, Min of State, Board of Trade, 1959-61, Pres of Board of Trade 1961-63, and Min of Power 1963-64, a Member of National Economic Development Council 1962-63, and Pres of London Chamber of Commerce 1966-69; Dep Chm Decimal Currency Board 1966-71; Chm of Home Office Liquor Licensing Cttee, 1970-72, Pres Electrical Research Assocn since 1971, and Chm of Whessoe, Ltd, Darlington since 1970, Bowater Corpn since 1973, Automobile Assocn since 1974, and Consolidated Gold Fields Ltd since 1976; a Dir of other cos; MP for Altrincham and Sale (*C*) 1945-64; *cr* PC 1960, and *Baron Erroll of Hale*, of Kilmun, co Argyll (Peerage of UK) 1964: *m* 1950, Elizabeth, da of Richard Sowton Barrow, of Exmouth, Devon.

Arms – Per bend azure and gules, on a bend embellished of six electric flashes or a fleur-de-lys and two lozenges sable. **Crest** – A chevronel round embattled sable. **Supporters** – *Dexter*, an elephant Guardant sable; *sinister*, a bear reguardant argent, muzzled azure, and from the muzzle cord sable, ringed or and reflexed over the back.
Address – House of Lords, SW1.

Erskine, Baron; see Earl of Buchan.

ERSKINE OF RERRICK, BARON (Erskine) (Baron UK 1964, Bt UK 1961)

IAIN MAXWELL ERSKINE, 2nd Baron and 2nd Baronet; *b* 22 Jan 1926; *s* 1980; *ed* Harrow; Maj (ret) Gren Gds; a Chevalier of Legion of Honour, and an OStJ; a qualified pilot, a Member of Inst of Directors; MInstM; MIPR; Comptroller to Gov-Gen of NZ 1960-61, PRO Household Div in London Dist HQ 1964-66; sometime professional photographer, promotion consultant; Co Dir; Member of Cttee and Dir of De Havilland Museum, Salisbury Hall, and Chm of Guards' Flying Club: *m* 1st, 1955 (*m diss* 1964), Marie Elisabeth, da of late Maj Richard Burton Allen, 3rd Drag Gds; 2ndly, 1974 (*m diss* 1989), Marie Josephine, da of Dr Josef Klupt; 3rdly, 1993, Debra, da of late Gordon Owen Knight, of Northants, and has issue by 2nd *m*.

Arms – Quarterly: 1st and 4th, argent, a pale sable between two lions rampant azure armeu and langued gules, *Erskine*; 2ndly, argent, a saltire sable, in centre chief a label of three points in centre base a mullet gules, *Maxwell of Nether Rerrick*; 3rd, argent, three hurcheons sable, *Herries*. **Crest** – A cubit arm attired in a manche party sable and azure the hand naked and grasping a partisan bendwyas all proper. **Supporters** – Two griffins per fesse gules and sable powdered with ten bezants and armed and beaked, argent.
Residence – 10 Chesham Place, SW1.

DAUGHTERS LIVING *(By 2nd marriage)*

Hon Henrietta Cora, *b* 1975.
Hon Griselda Maxwell, *b* 1979.
Hon Cora McLeave, *b* 1981.

SISTER LIVING

Hon Elizabeth Olson, *b* 1923; 1939-45 War as Subaltern ATS: *m* 1944, Gilbert Butler of Gatehouse, 8B Churchfields Av, Weybridge, Surrey KT13 9YA, and has issue living, David John Lister, *b* 1949; BA; Solicitor: *m* 1978, Celia Elizabeth, yst da of Prof Stephen D. Elek, of Lausanne, Switzerland, — Brian Robert Erskine (George), *b* 1960; Capt R Scots Drag Gds: *m* 1989, Nicola Mary, da of Col Keith S. Robson, of Babcary, Somerset, — Elizabeth Mary, *b* 1946: *m* 1978, Michael John Dickinson.

WIDOW LIVING OF FIRST BARON

HENRIETTA (*Henrietta, Baroness Erskine of Rerrick*) CStJ (Gatehouse, 8B Churchfields Av, Weybridge, Surrey KT13 9YA), da of late William Dunnett, of E. Canisbay, Caithness: *m* 1922, the 1st Baron, GBE, who *d* 1980.

PREDECESSOR – (1) *Sir* JOHN MAXWELL ERSKINE, GBE, son of John Erskine, of Kirkcudbright, *b* 1893; Pres of Inst of Bankers in Scotland 1937-40; Gov of N Ireland 1964-68; *cr* a *Baronet* 1961, and *Baron Erskine of Rerrick*, of Rerrick, Kirkcudbright (peerage of UK) 1964: *m* 1922, Henrietta, da of late William Dunnett of E. Canisbay, Caithness; *d* 1980; *s* by his only son (2) IAIN MAXWELL 2nd Baron and present peer.

ESHER, VISCOUNT (Brett) (Viscount UK 1897)

We have conquered

LIONEL GORDON BALIOL BRETT, CBE, 4th Viscount; *b* 18
July 1913; *s* 1963; *ed* Eton, and at New Coll, Oxford
(MA); Hon DLitt Strathclyde; Hon D Univ of York; Hon
DSc Edinburgh; Hon Fellow American Inst of Architects;
Pres of RIBA 1965-67; a Member of Roy Fine Art
Commn 1951-69, and of the Arts Council of GB 1972-77;
Rector and Vice-Provost, Roy Coll of Art 1971-78; 1939-45
War as Maj RA (despatches); CBE (Civil) 1970: *m* 1935,
Helena Christian Olive, da of late Col Ebenezer John
Lecky Pike, CBE, MC, and has issue.

Arms – Quarterly: 1st and 4th or, a lion rampant gules holding in
the dexter paw a fasces erect proper, within an orle of crosses
bottonée fitchée of the second; 2nd, per pale or and gules three
leopards' faces counterchanged; 3rd, azure three bears' heads
couped argent, muzzled gules. **Crest** – A lion passant gules,
charged on the shoulder with a cross bottonée fitchée or, and
holding in the dexter paw a fasces proper. **Supporters** – *Dexter*, a
boar sable; *sinister*, a lion sable; each charged on the shoulder
with a cross bottonée fitchée or, and supporting a fasces proper.
Residence – Snowball Hill, Russell's Water, Henley-on-Thames,
Oxford. *Club* – Arts.

SONS LIVING

Hon CHRISTOPHER LIONEL BALIOL (Watlington Park, Oxon), *b* 23 Dec
1936; *ed* Eton, and Magdalen Coll, Oxford: *m* 1st, 1962 (*m diss*
1970), Camilla Charlotte, da of Sir (Horace) Anthony Claud
Rumbold, 10th Bt, KCMG, CB; 2ndly, 1971, Valerie, da of Maxwell
Maurice Harrington, and has issue living, (by 1st *m*) Matthew
Christopher Anthony (12 Dorville Crescent, W6 0HJ), *b* 1963: *m*
1992, Hon Emma Charlotte Denison-Pender, elder da of 3rd Baron
Pender, — Miranda Jane, *b* 1964: *m* 1990, Martin Nicholas Caleb
Thomas, yr son of Prof (Antony) Charles Thomas, CBE, DL, of Lambessow, St Clement, Truro, Cornwall, and has issue
living, Joseph Achilles Caleb *b* 1990, Frederick Jacob Theseus *b* 1992, — Rebecca Catherine, *b* 1966, — (by 2nd *m*), Oliver
Maxwell, *b* 1972, — William Falkland, *b* 1982, — Clare Christian (twin), *b* 1973.
Hon Michael Jeremy Baliol, *b* 1939; *ed* Eton; ARIBA: *m* 1971, Sarah Calloway, of Shelbyville, Kentucky, USA.
Hon Guy Anthony Baliol, *b* 1942; *ed* Eton: *m* 1975, Alexandra Altamirano, of Santiago, Chile, and has issue living, Luciana, *b*
1976.
Hon (Maurice) Sebastian Baliol, *b* 1944; *ed* Eton, and at Trin Coll, Oxford: *m* 1st, 1968 (*m diss* 1971), Pauline R., da of Lt-
Cdr Paul Murray-Jones, RN (ret), of Cordwainers, Titchfield, Hants; 2ndly, 1971 (*m diss* 1980), Mary Maddox; 3rdly, 1980,
Leticia Garrido, and has issue living (by 2nd *m*), Judd, *b* 1972, — (by 3rd *m*) Claudia, *b* 1985.
Hon Stephen Patrick Baliol, *b* 1952; *ed* Bryanston.

DAUGHTER LIVING

Hon Olivia Clare Teresa, *b* 1947: *m* 1970 (*m diss* 1985), Anthony Grey Gascoigne (*see* Wigan, Bt, colls), and has issue living,
Fenn *b* 1977, — May, *b* 1979.

SISTERS LIVING

Hon Nancy Mildred Gladys (*Hon Lady Shuckburgh*), *b* 1918: *m* 1937 Sir (Charles Arthur) Evelyn Shuckburgh, GCMG, CB,
Diplo Ser, el son of Sir John Evelyn Shuckburgh, KCMG, CB, and has issue living, Julian (22 Ellingham Rd, W12 9PR), *b*
1940: *m* 1st, 1963 (*m diss* 1970), Faith Beatrice, da of Sir Paul Hervé Giraud Wright; 2ndly, 1975 (*m diss* 1992), Sarah
Elizabeth, da of Sir David (Valentine) Willcocks, CBE, MC, and has issue living (by 1st *m*), Benjamin Evelyn (13 Bassett Rd,
W10) *b* 1966: *m* 1991, Emma M., yr da of Sir Bernard Albert Ashley, Matilda Ann *b* 1964: *m* 1st, 1983 (*m diss* 1988), Scott
Ziegler, son of Douglas Ziegler, of Hermosa Beach, Calif, USA; 2ndly, 1993, Lyle McCormick, son of Thomas J. McCormick,
of Petaluma, Calif, USA (and has issue living (by 1st *m*), Emma Dorothy *b* 1985), (by 2nd *m*) Alexander William *b* 1982,
Amy Catherine Lorna *b* 1977, Hannah Jane Elizabeth *b* 1979, — Robin Anthony (Holton Place House, Holton, Oxford), *b*
1948: *m* 1972, Philippa Mary, da of Nicholas Spargo, of Maidengrove, Henley-on-Thames, and has issue living, Jacob
Nicholas Anthony *b* 1978, Laura Mary *b* 1983, — Catherine SHUCKBURGH, *b* 1939; has resumed her maiden name: *m* 1961 (*m
diss* 1970), (John) David Caute, author and playwright, and has issue living, Edward Peter *b* 1963, Daniel Alexander *b* 1965.
Residence – High Wood, Watlington, Oxon.
Hon Priscilla Léonie Helen (*Hon Lady Beckett*), *b* 1921: *m* 1941, Capt Sir Martyn Gervase Beckett, 2nd Bt, MC, Welsh
Guards. *Residences* – 3 St Alban's Grove, W8; Kirkdale Farm, Nawton, Yorks.

COLLATERAL BRANCH LIVING

Grandchildren of late Lt-Col Hon Maurice Vyner Baliol Brett, OBE, MVO (*infra*):—
Issue of late Maj Antony Reginald Forbes Baliol Brett, MBE, *b* 1913, *d* 1981: *m* 1939, Bay Helen, who *d* 1989, da of
late Charles Neville Brownell, of Birkenhead:—
Simon Baliol (12 Blowhorn St, Marlborough, Wilts SN8 1BT), *b* 1943; *ed* Ampleforth, and St Martin's Sch of Art: *m* 1974,
Mrs Juliet Shirley-Smith, da of Paul Wood, and has issue living, Emily Agnes, *b* 1977. —— Vanessa Baliol, *b* 1947: *m* 1977,
William Northrop Parker, and has issue living, Guy Hugo, *b* 1987, — Rebecca Brett, *b* 1980.

Issue of late Lieut-Col Hon Maurice Vyner Baliol Brett, OBE, MVO, 2nd son of 2nd Viscount, *b* 1882, *d*
1934: *m* (Jan) 1911, Florence Hariette Zena (the actress, Zena Dare), who *d* 1975, da of late Arthur Albert
Dones:—
Angela Mariel Baliol, *b* (Oct) 1911: *m* 1934, Maj Kenneth Marcus Thornton, and has issue living, Timothy Kenneth
(Juthware Hall, Halstock, nr Yeovil, Som), *b* 1935; *ed* Eton: *m* 1966, Mrs Jacqueline Green, da of David Hillman, and
formerly wife of John Green, of Malmesbury, Wilts, and has issue living, Daniel Timothy *b* 1968; *ed* Eton, Katharine Zena *b*
1970. — Brian Maurice (Priors Mesne, Aylburton, Lydney, Glos), *b* 1937; *ed* Eton: *m* 1959, Verity, da of late Guy Gordon
Lawrence, of Little Easton Manor, Dunmow, and has issue living, Guy Dominic *b* 1960; *ed* Gordonstoun: *m* 1983, Hon Diana

Cara Broughton, elder da of 3rd Baron Fairhaven (and has issue living, Thomas George Cranbrook *b* 1986), Benjamin Douglas *b* 1965; *ed* Eton, and Edinburgh Univ (BSc), Giles Marcus *b* 1966; *ed* Gordonstoun, Jolyon Kenneth *b* 1970; *ed* Harrow, Sam Fergus *b* 1976, Kim Marie *b* 1961: *m* 1986, Geoffrey Stuart Wheating (and has issue living, Tara Nel *b* 1988). *Residence* – Woodside Cottage, Windsor Forest, Berks. —— Marie Louise, *b* 1916: *m* 1938, Cdr Archibald Rider Cheyne, RN, who *d* 1950, and has issue living, Mark Rider (38d Whistlers Avenue, SW11 3TS), *b* 1941; *ed* Rugby, FCA, — Angela Zena, *b* 1947. *Residence* – Spring Hill, Burleigh Rd, Ascot, Berks.

PREDECESSORS – **(1)** *Rt Hon Sir* WILLIAM BALIOL Brett, son of late Rev Joseph George Brett, of Ranelagh, Chelsea, SW; *b* 1815; MP for Helston (C) 1866-8; Solicitor-Gen 1868, a Justice of the Common Pleas 1868-75, a Judge of the High Court of Justice (Common Pleas Div) 1875-6, a Lord Justice of Appeal 1876-83, and Master of the Rolls 1883-97; *cr Baron Esher*, of Esher, co Surrey (peerage of United Kingdom) 1885, and *Viscount Esher*, of Esher, co Surrey (peerage of United Kingdom) 1897: *m* 1850, Eugenie, who *d* 1904, da of Louis Mäyer; *d* 1899; *s* by his eldest son **(2)** REGINALD BALIOL, GCB, GCVO, PC, 2nd Viscount, *b* 1852; Private Sec to Marquess of Hartington 1878-85, MP for Penryn and Falmouth (*L*) 1880-85 Sec to Office of Works and Public Buildings 1895-1902, Dep Constable and Lieut-Gov of Windsor Castle 1901-28, and Constable thereof 1928-30: *m* 1879, Eleanor, RRC, who *d* 1940, da of Sylvain Van de Weyer, of New Windsor, late Belgian Min at the Court of St James's; *d* 1930; *s* by his son **(3)** OLIVER SYLVAIN BALIOL, GBE, 3rd Viscount, *b* 1881; Private Sec to Sec of State for India 1905-10: *m* 1911, Antoinette, who *d* 1965, da of late August Heckscher of New York; *d* 1963; *s* by his only son **(4)** LIONEL GORDON BALIOL, CBE, 4th Viscount and present peer; also Baron Esher.

ESSEX, EARL OF (Capell) (Earl E 1661)

By fidelity and fortitude

ROBERT EDWARD DE VERE CAPELL, 10th Earl; *b* 13 Jan 1920; *s* 1981 (claim admitted by Cttee of Privileges of House of Lords, and writ of summons issued 1989); 1939-45 War as Fl Sgt RAF: *m* 1942, Doris Margaret, da of George Frederick Tomlinson, of Morecambe, Lancs, and has issue.

Arms – Gules, a lion rampant between three cross-crosslets fitchée or. **Crest** – A demi-lion rampant holding in the dexter paw a cross-crosslet fitchée gules. **Supporters** – Two lions or, ducally crowned, gules.
Residence – 2 Novak Place, Torrisholme, Morecambe, Lancs.

SON LIVING

FREDERICK PAUL DE VERE (*Viscount Malden*), ACP, LLCM (TD) FRSA, *b* 29 May 1944; *ed* Lancaster Royal Gram Sch, Didsbury Coll of Educn, and Northern School of Music.

SISTER LIVING

Elsie Elfreda (Flat 28, Raglan Lodge, 23 North Lodge Rd, Parkstone, Dorset), *b* 1921: *m* 1943, Ernest Walls, who *d* 1968, and has issue living, Derek Arthur, *b* 1950, — Jennifer Dawn, *b* 1948.

WIDOW LIVING OF NINTH EARL

NONA ISOBEL (*Nona, Countess of Essex*) (Capell, 3 Leybourne Close, Ledburn, nr Leighton Buzzard, Beds), da of David Wilson Miller, of Christchurch, NZ, and widow of Francis Sydney Smythe, of Yew Tree Cottage, Colgate, Sussex: *m* 1957, as his 2nd wife, the 9th Earl, who *d* 1981.

COLLATERAL BRANCHES LIVING

Granddaughter of late Hon Adolphus Frederick Charles Molyneux Capell, brother of 6th Earl:—
Issue of late Rev Horatio Bladen Capell, *b* 1839, *d* 1933: *m* 1st, 1866, Ada Augusta, who *d* 1916, da of Theophilus Hawkins, formerly of Newton Abbot; 2ndly, 1916, Violet Annie, who *d* 1960, da of Robert Frost, formerly of Snape, Suffolk:—
(By 2nd *m*) Beatrix Violet de Vere, *b* 1919: *m* 1st, 1939 (*m diss* 1950), Raymond Smith; 2ndly, 1950, Edward Reginald Tranter, and has had issue, (by 1st *m*) Anthony Capel, *b* 1940: *m* 1968 (*m diss* 1980), Evelyn Hamilton Bentink Martin, adopted da of Charles Penryn Ackers, and formerly wife of Michael Charles Butler Johnson, and *d* 1993, leaving issue, Matilda Amelia *b* 1967, Emily Jane *b* 1969. *Residence* – Essex House, Great Easton, Dunmow, Essex.

Grandchildren of late Bladen Ozro Capell (infra):—
Issue of late Bladen Horace Capell, *b* 1922, *d* 1978: *m* 1945, Mae Elizabeth, da of late William J. Walley:—
William Jennings, *b* 1952: *m* 1971, Sandra Elaine, da of Chester M. Matson, and has issue living, Jennifer Elaine, *b* 1974. —— Dorita Mae, *b* 1948: *m* 1971, Robert Cooper, and has issue living, Michael Keith, *b* 1974, — Bobby Ryan, *b* 1977. —— Raylene Dee, *b* 1958: *m* 1976, Theodore Schwartz.

Grandchildren of late Horace Charles George Arthur Capell (infra):—
Issue of late Bladen Ozro Capell, *b* 1897, *d* 1959: *m* 1st, 1920 (*m diss* 1929), Marjora Crawford, of Utah, USA, who *d* 1956; 2ndly, 19—, Hazel Kruse:—
(By 1st *m*) Ada *b* 1924: *m* 1941, Kay Boren, and has issue living, Dennis Kay, *b* 1941, — Larry Dean, *b* 1943, — Jeffrey Lee, *b* 1956, — Toni Carol, *b* 1946. *Residence* – North 4904, Elm St, Spokane, Wash, USA. —— Helen Lucille, *b* 1926: *m* 1945, Leonard A. Simpson, and has issue living, David Andrew, *b* 1947, — Danny Jay, *b* 1957, — Barbara Jean, *b* 1956.

Granddaughter of late Rev Horatio Bladen Capell (ante):—
Issue of late Horace Charles George Arthur Capell, *b* 1868, *d* 1953: *m* 1896, Clara Isabel, da of Ozro Jackson, of Dakin, Nebraska, USA:—
Ada Lorena *b* 1901: *m* 1923, Arthur Foster Dagnall.

Grandsons of late Algernon Arthur Capell (infra):—

Issue of late Colin Algernon Andrew Essex Capell, b 1935, d on active service in Rhodesia 1977: m 1957, Cecily Ann (79 Garcia Pl, Brighton Beach, Durban 4052, S Africa), da of late Arend Smith, of Marlborough, Rhodesia:—
Clint Andrew Devereux, b 1960: m 1981, Jeanne, da of Robert Bolton, of Sinoia, Zimbabwe, and has issue living, Joanne Victoria, b 1981. —— Craig Robert Lawrence, b 1962: m 1986, Janet, da of —, and has issue living, Dylan, b 198-.

Grandchildren of late Lt-Col Algernon Essex Capell, CBE, DSO, 2nd son of the Rev Horatio Bladen Capell (ante):—
Issue of late Algernon Arthur Capell, b 1903, d 1950: m 1933, Violet Mary, who d 1988, da of late Andrew Boyd, of Dumfries:—
Robert Devereux Boyd (961 Montcalm Dr, Kelowna, BC, Canada V1Y 3M8), b 1942: m 1967, Elin Rosemary, da of late Alan L. Earle, of Bulawayo, Rhodesia, and has issue living, Jennifer Rosemary, b 1975. —— Rosemary Susan Lois, b 1934: m 1958, Cyril Bryan Hughes, and has issue living, Barry William Vaughan, b 1961, — Kevin Bryan Vaughan, b 1962, — Ross Anthony Vaughan, b 1967, — Susan Anne Vaughan, b 1969.
Address - PO Box 33, Plumtree, Zimbabwe.

Grandson of late Rev Horatio Bladen Capell (ante):—
Issue of late Henry Addison Devereux Capell, b 1873, d 1925: m 1901, Olive Mary, who d 1937, da of late William Richardson-Bunbury (see Richardson-Bunbury Bt, colls):—
Robert, b 1903.

Grandson of late Col Arthur William Capell, Bengal Cav, el son of Lt-Col Edward Samuel Capell, Bengal Army, yst son of Rev Hon William Robert Capell, yst son of 4th Earl:—
Issue of late Capt Terence Capell, RFC, b 1891, d 1962: m 1919, Florence Penelope, who d 1963, da of William Whitham:—
William Terence (Cavalry Club), b 1921; late Capt 11th Hussars: m 1963, Petronella, da of late Maj Peter Beale Lewis, MC, late R Ulster Rifles, and has issue living, Georgina Penelope, b 1964, — Rosalind Elizabeth Maud, b 1968.

PREDECESSORS – (1) ARTHUR Capell; MP for co Hertford in the Long Parliament; cr Baron Capell of Hadham 1641; for his loyalty to the King he was beheaded 1649; s by his son (2) ARTHUR, 2nd Baron, cr Viscount Malden and Earl of the co of Essex (peerage of England, 1661); Viceroy of Ireland 1672-7, and sometime First commr of the Treasury; being accused with Lord Russell of connection with "The Fanatic Plot" was committed to the Tower, where he was found with his throat cut 1683; s by his son (3) ALGERNON, 2nd Earl; a Lt-Gen in the Army and Constable of the Tower of London; d 1709; s by his son (4) WILLIAM, 3rd Earl; d 1743; s by his son (5) WILLIAM ANNE, 4th Earl; d 1799; s by his son (6) GEORGE, DCL, 5th Earl; assumed the surname of Coningsby; d 1839; s by his nephew (7) ARTHUR ALGERNON (son of Hon John Thomas, 2nd son of 4th Earl), 6th Earl, b 1803; assumed in 1880, by Royal licence, for himself and issue the surname of Capell in lieu of Capel; d 1892: m 1st, 1825, Lady Caroline Jeannetta Beauclerk, who d 1876, sister of 9th Earl of Cork; 2ndly, 1863, Lady Louisa Caroline Elizabeth Boyle, who d 1876, sister of 9th Earl of Cork; 3rdly, 1881, Louisa, who d 1914, da of late Charles Fieschi Heneage, and widow of Lord George Augustus Frederick Paget, KCB; s by his grandson (8) GEORGE DEVEREUX DE VERE (el son of Viscount Malden, el son of 6th Earl), 7th Earl, b 1857: m 1st, 1882, Ellenor Harriet Maria, who d 1885, da of late William Henry Harford, JP, of Oldown House, Almondsbury, Gloucestershire; 2ndly, 1893, Adele, who d 1922, el da of late Beach Grant, of New York; d 1916: s by his son, (9) ALGERNON GEORGE DE VERE, 8th Earl, b 1884: m 1st, 1905 (m diss 1926), (Mary) Eveline Stewart, who d 1955, el da of late William Russell Stewart Freeman, JP, DL, of The Old Manor House, Wingrave, Bucks; 2ndly, 1926 (m diss 1950), Alys Montgomery, who d 1977, da of Robert Hayes Falkiner, and formerly wife of Ernest Scott Brown; 3rdly, 1950 (m diss 1956), Zara Mildred Carson, of Los Angeles, Cal, USA; 4thly, 1957, Christine Mary Davis, who d 1985; d 1966: s by his son (10) Reginald George de Vere, TD 9th Earl, b 1906: m 1st, 1937 (m diss 1957), Mary Reeve, da of F. Gibson Ward, of Rosemount, Bermuda, and widow of Col George Ashton Strutt, of Brailsford, Derbys; 2ndly, 1957, Nona Isobel, da of David Wilson Miller, of Christchurch, NZ, and widow of Francis Sydney Smythe, of Yew Tree Cottage, Colgate, Sussex; d 1981; s by his kinsman (11) ROBERT EDWARD DE VERE, gt gt gt grandson of 4th Earl, 10th Earl and present peer; also Viscount Malden and Baron Capell.

Ettrick, Baron, see Lord Napier and Ettrick.

Euston, Earl of; son of Duke of Grafton.

EVANS, BARONY OF (Evans) (Extinct 1963)

DAUGHTER LIVING OF FIRST BARON

Hon Jean Rosemary, b 1934: m (Jan) 1966, Eric Anthony Hathorn, of 51 Netherhall Gdns, NW3, and has issue living, James Horace Vans, b (Dec) 1966, — Charles Thomas Vans, b 1972, — Helen Angela, b 1970.

EVANS OF CLAUGHTON, BARONY OF (Evans) (Extinct 1992)

SON LIVING OF LIFE BARON

Hon David Robert Cynlais, b 1964; ed Birkenhead Sch, and UCL (LLB); Solicitor.

DAUGHTERS LIVING OF LIFE BARON

Hon Elizabeth Ann Cynlais, b 1957: m 1989, Ian F. Johnson, only son of A. F. Johnson, of Oswestry, Shropshire.
Hon Sarah Louise Cynlais, b 1966; ed Liverpool Univ (BA), and Coll of St Paul and St Mary, Cheltenham (PGCE).

Hon Jane Lucy Cynlais, *b* 1968; *ed* Nottingham Univ (BA).

WIDOW LIVING OF LIFE BARON

MOIRA ELIZABETH (*Baroness Evans of Claughton*), da of late James Rankin: *m* 1956, Baron Evans of Claughton (Life Baron), who *d* 1992. *Residence* – Sunridge, 69 Bidston Rd, Claughton, Birkenhead, Merseyside L43 6TR.

EVANS OF HUNGERSHALL, BARONY OF (Evans) (Extinct 1982)

DAUGHTER LIVING OF LIFE BARON

Hon Hilary Ann (Duck Cottage, Puncknowle, Dorchester DT2 9BW), *b* 1931: *m* 1954 (*m diss* 1963), William John Barrow, and has issue.

EWART-BIGGS, BARONY OF (O'Sullivan) (Extinct 1992)

SON LIVING OF LIFE BARONESS (*by 1st marriage*)

Hon Robin Thomas Fitzherbert EWART-BIGGS, *b* 1963: *m* 1993, Katherine Bonner.

DAUGHTERS LIVING OF LIFE BARONESS (*by 1st marriage*)

Hon Henrietta EWART-BIGGS, *b* 1961.
Hon Kate EWART-BIGGS, *b* 1967.

WIDOWER LIVING OF LIFE BARONESS

Kevin O'Sullivan: *m* (18 Sept) 1992, as her 2nd husband, (Felicity) Jane, Baroness Ewart-Biggs (Life Baroness), who *d* (8 Oct) 1992. *Residence* – 63A Abingdon Villas, W8 6XA.

EWING OF KIRKFORD, BARON (Ewing) (Life Baron 1992)

HARRY EWING, son of late William Ewing, of Cowdenbeath, Dunfermline; *b* 20 Jan 1931; *ed* Beath High Sch, Cowdenbeath; held various appointments Union of Post Office Workers 1962-71; Sec Scottish Lab Group 1972-74, Parly Under-Sec of State Scottish Office 1974-79, Sr Vice-Chm Trade Union Group of Lab MPs since 1979, Member Council of Europe and Western European Union since 1987; MP Stirling and Falkirk (*Lab*) 1971-74, Stirling, Falkirk and Grangemouth 1974-83, and Falkirk E 1983-92; *cr Baron Ewing of Kirkford*, of Cowdenbeath, District of Dunfermline (Life Baron) 1992: *m* 1954, Margaret, da of John Greenhill, of Leven, Fife, and has issue.
Residence – Gowanbank, 45 Glenlyon Rd, Leven, Fife KY8 4AA.

SON LIVING

Hon Alan William John, *b* 1961: *m* 1986, June, da of William Adamson, of Kirkcaldy, and has issue living, one son and one da.

DAUGHTER LIVING

Hon Alison Margaret, *b* 1966: *m* 1991, Ian Binnie, son of Sydney Binnie, of Arbroath.

Orr-Ewing, Baron, see Orr.

EXETER, MARQUESS OF (Cecil) (Marquess UK 1801)
(Name pronounced "Cissel")

CORUNUMVIAUNA

One heart, one way

(WILLIAM) MICHAEL ANTHONY CECIL, 8th Marquess; *b* 1 Sept 1935; *s* 1988; Hereditary Grand Almoner, Lord Paramount of the Soke of Peterborough: *ed* Eton: *m* 1967 (*m diss* 1993), Nancy Rose, da of late Lloyd Arthur Meeker, of Loveland, Colorado, USA, and has issue.

ᴁrms – Barry of ten argent and azure, six escutcheons, three, two, and one, sable each charged with a lion rampant argent. ℭrest – On a chapeau gules, turned up with ermine, a garb or, supported by two lions rampant, the *dexter* argent, the *sinister* azure. ᴥupporters – Two lions ermine.
Residence – 100 Mile House, PO Box 8, BC VOK 2EO, Canada.

SON LIVING

ANTHONY JOHN (*Lord Burghley*), *b* 9 Aug 1970; *ed* Eton, and Oxford Univ.

DAUGHTER LIVING

Lady Angela Kathleen, *b* 1975.

HALF-SISTER LIVING

Lady Marina June, *b* 1956: *m* 1980, Peter Jules Workman Castonguay, son of Nelson Castonguay, of Ottawa, Canada, and has issue living, Dylan Martin Nelson, *b* 1984, — Majessa Lillian, *b* 1983. *Residence* – 100 Mile House, PO Box 7, BC VOK 2EO, Canada.

DAUGHTERS LIVING OF SIXTH MARQUESS (*By 1st marriage*)

Lady Davina Mary (*Lady Davina Barnard*), *b* 1931; DStJ: *m* 1952 (*m diss* 1992), 11th Baron Barnard. *Residence* – The Yews, Barningham, Richmond, N Yorks DL11 7DU.
Lady Gillian Moyra Katherine, *b* 1935: *m* 1st, 1954 (*m diss* 1978), Sir Giles Henry Charles Floyd, 7th Bt; 2ndly, 1979, George Michael Kertesz, of 57 Peel St, W8, and Holly House, Northchapel, nr Petworth, West Sussex.
Lady Angela Mary Rose, LVO, *b* 1938; an Extra Woman of the Bedchamber to HM Queen Elizabeth The Queen Mother 1981-82, since when a Woman of the Bedchamber; LVO 1993: *m* 1958, (William Richard) Michael Oswald, CVO, MA, The King's Own Royal Regt, Capt RF, Manager of the Royal Studs, and has issue living, William Alexander Michael, *b* 1962; appointed a Page of Honour to HM 1976; Capt The Life Guards: *m* 1994, Arabella V., da of Nicholas Sydney Cobbold, — Katharine Davina Mary, *b* 1959: *m* 1983, Maj Alexander Fergus Matheson, yr of Matheson, Coldm Gds, and has issue (*see* Matheson, Bt). *Residence* – Flitcham Hall, King's Lynn, Norfolk.

(*By 2nd marriage*)

Lady Victoria Diana, *b* 1947; DL Cambs 1993: *m* 1967, Simon Patrick Leatham (*see* By Buckland, 1976 Edn), and has issue living, Richard David, *b* 1971, — Miranda Rosemary, *b* 1969. *Residences* – Burghley House, Stamford, Lincs PE9 3JY; Flat 18, Chelsea House, 24 Lowndes St, SW1.

AUNT LIVING (*daughter of 5th Marquess*)

Lady Romayne Elizabeth Algitha, OBE, ARRC, *b* 1915; late VAD (attached RN); European War 1939-44 (ARRC); OBE 1986: *m* 1944, Lieut-Col Hon Peter Esmé Brassey, Northants Yeo (*see* B Brassey of Apethorpe). *Residence* – Pond House, Barnack, Stamford, Lincs PE9 3DN.

WIDOW LIVING OF SEVENTH MARQUESS

LILLIAN JANE (*Dowager Marchioness of Exeter*), eldest da of late Roy Peter Kopf Johnson, of Milwaukee, USA: *m* 1954, as his 2nd wife, the 7th Marquess, who *d* 1988. *Residence* – 100 Mile House, PO Box 2054, BC VOK 2EO, Canada.

COLLATERAL BRANCHES LIVING

Granddaughter of late Richard William Francis Cecil, son of late Lieut Lord Francis Horace Pierrepont Cecil, RN, 2nd son of 3rd Marquess:—
Issue of late Lieut Richard Francis Bain Cecil, RN, *b* 1902, *d* 1929: *m* 1926, Marjorie Joan (who *m* 2ndly, 1939, B. Grosvenor Harris, of Monxton Manor, Andover Hants), da of late William Lloyd Evans, of Postlip Hall, Gloucestershire:—
Jean Frances, *b* (*posthumous*) 1929: *m* 1952, Com Henry Walton Jennings, RN, and has issue living, Dirmuid Brian Cecil (Studley Cottage, Haw Lane, Bledlow Ridge, Bucks), *b* 1957; late RN: *m* 1983, Angela, el da of W. Wilson, of Aughton, Lancs, — Stephen Francis, *b* 1960. *Address* – Eastwell, Upper Lansdown Mews, Bath, Avon.

Descendants of late Col Lord William Cecil, CVO, 3rd son of 3rd Marquess, *b* 1854, *d* 1943, who *m* 1st, 1885, Mary Rothes Margaret, who *d* 1919 (*Baroness Amherst of Hackney* in her own right) (see that title).
Grandchildren of late Col Lord John Pakenham JOICEY-CECIL (who assumed by Royal licence 1898 the additional surname of Joicey), 4th son of 3rd Marquess:—
Issue of late Edward Wilfrid George Joicey-Cecil, *b* 1912, *d* 1985: *m* 1945, Rosemary Lusia, who *d* 1989, da of late Capt Hon Fergus Bowes-Lyon, Black Watch (*see* E Strathmore, colls):—
James David Edward (49 Clapham Common South Side, SW4 9BX), *b* 1946; *ed* Eton: *m* 1975, Jane Susanna Brydon, da of late Capt P. W. B. Adeley, of Delcombe Manor, Milton Abbas, Dorset, and has issue living, Katherine Mary, *b* 1978, — Susanna Maud, *b* 1981. —— (Elizabeth) Anne, *b* 1950: *m* 1971, Alastair Richard Malcolm, of Hart Hill Farm, Woodfalls, Salisbury, Wilts, and has issue living, Colin Andrew Fergus, *b* 1973; *ed* Eton, — William James Ronald, *b* 1975; *ed* Eton.

(In remainder to Barony of Burghley only)

Descendants of late Rt Hon Sir Robert Cecil, KG, (yr son of 1st Baron Burghley), who was *cr Earl of Salisbury* 1605 (see M Salisbury).

PREDECESSORS – **(1)** *Sir* WILLIAM Cecil, KG, KB, PC, a lawyer and eminent statesman was Sec of State 1549, 1551, and 1558, Chancellor of Camb Univ 1558-98, Master of the Ward, 1561, and Lord High Treasurer 1572-98; *cr Baron of Burghley* (peerage of England) 1571; *d* 1598; *s* by his son **(2)** THOMAS, KG, KB; MP in five Parliaments; distinguished himself in the wars in the Low Countries; *cr Earl of Exeter* (peerage of England) 1605; *d* 1622; *s* by his son **(3)** WILLIAM, KG, KB, 2nd Earl; *d* 1640; *s* by his nephew **(4)** DAVID, 3rd Earl, son of Sir Richard, MP, 2nd son of 1st Earl; *d* 1643; *s* by his son **(5)** JOHN, 4th Earl; *d* 1678; *s* by his son **(6)** JOHN, 5th Earl; *d* 1700; *s* by his son **(7)** JOHN, 6th Earl; *d* 1721, *s* by his el son **(8)** JOHN, 7th Earl; *d* 1722; *s* by his brother **(9)** BROWNLOW, 8th Earl; *d* 1754; *s* by his son **(10)** BROWNLOW, 9th Earl; *dsp* 1793; *s* by his nephew **(11)** HENRY, 10th Earl, son of the Hon Thomas Chambers, 2nd son of 8th Earl; *cr Marquess of Exeter* (peerage of United Kingdom) 1801; *d* 1804; *s* by his son **(12)** BROWNLOW, KG, 2nd Marquess; *b* 1795; Lord Lieut of cos Northampton and Rutland, Groom of the Stole to Prince Albert 1841-6, Lord Chamberlain 1852, and Lord Steward of the Household 1858-9: *m* 1824, Isabella, da of William Stephen Poyntz, of Cowdray House, Sussex; *d* 1867; *s* by his son **(13)** WILLIAM ALLEYNE, PC, 3rd Marquess, *b* 1825; MP for S Lincolnshire 1847-57, and for N Northamptonshire 1857-67; was Treasurer of HM Queen Victoria's Household 1866-7, and Capt of Hon Corps of Gentleman-at-Arms 1867-8 and 1874-5: *m* 1848, Lady Georgiana Sophia Pakenham, who *d* 1909, da of 2nd Earl of Longford; *d* 1895; *s* by his el son **(14)** BROWNLOW HENRY GEORGE, PC, 4th Marquess, *b* 1849; MP for Northamptonshire N (C) 1877-85 and for Northamptonshire, N Div 1885-95; Vice-Chamberlain of HM Queen Victoria's Household 1891-2: *m* 1875, Isabella, who *d* 1917, da of Sir Thomas Whichcote, 7th Bt; *d* 1898; *s* by his son **(15)** BROWNLOW THOMAS BROWNLOW, KG, CMG, TD, 5th Marquess; *b* 1876; Col RFA (TA); Chm of Govs of Stamford Endowed Schs 1899-1955, Mayor of Stamford 1909-10, Chm of Soke of Peterborough County council 1910-49, Lord Lieut of Northants 1922-52, an Additional ADC to HM 1922-32, and Pres of County Councils Asso 1943 and 1945: *m* 1901, the Hon Myra Rowena Sibell Orde-Powlett, who *d* 1973, only da of 4th Baron Bolton, *d* 1956, *s* by his el son **(16)** DAVID GEORGE BROWNLOW, KCMG, 6th Marquess, *b* 1905, Lt Col Gren Gds, Pres and Chm of Internat Amateur Athletic Fedn, of Amateur Athletic Asso, and of British Olympic Assocn (won an Olympic gold medal in 400 metre hurdles 1928), and Doyen Internat Amateur Athletic Cttee; Pres Burghley Horse Trials, British Empire Chambers of Commerce, and of Radio Industry Council 1952-54, and Vice-Pres of Internat Olympic Cttee 1954-66; Pres British Travel Assocn 1966-69; Assist Dir of Tank Supply 1941-42, Controller of Repair and Overseas Supplies of Aircraft 1942-43, and Gov and C-in-C of Bermuda 1943-45; R of St Andrews Univ 1949-52; Leader of UK Industrial Mission to Pakistan 1950 and to Burma 1954; Mayor of Stamford 1961-62; MP for Peterborough Div of Northants (C) 1931-43: *m* 1st, 1929 (*m diss* 1946), Lady Mary Theresa Montagu Douglas Scott, who *d* 1984, da of 7th Duke of Buccleuch; 2ndly, 1946, Diana Mary, who *d* 1982, da of late Hon Arnold Henderson (*see* B Faringdon, colls), and widow of Lt-Col David Walter William Forbes, MC, Coldstream Guards (*see* B Hotham, colls); *d* 1981; *s* by his brother **(17)** WILLIAM MARTIN ALLEYNE, 7th Marquess, *b* 1909; prominent Canadian cattleman, and leader of spiritual movement Emissaries of Divine Light: *m* 1st, 1934, Edith Lilian, who *d* 1954, only da of late Aurel Csanady de Telegd, of Budapest, Hungary; 2ndly, 1954, Lillian Jane, eldest da of late Roy P. K. Johnson, of Milwaukee, USA; *d* 1988; *s* by his only son **(18)** (WILLIAM) MICHAEL ANTHONY, 8th Marquess and present peer: also Earl of Exeter, and Baron of Burghley.

EXMOUTH, VISCOUNT (Pellew) (Viscount UK 1816, Bt GB 1796)

God being my helper

PAUL EDWARD PELLEW, 10th Viscount, and 10th Baronet; *b* 8 Oct 1940; *s* 1970; *ed* Downside; patron of one living: *m* 1st, 1964 (*m diss* 1974), Maria Krystina de Garay, da of late Don Recaredo de Garay y Garay, of Madrid; 2ndly, 1975, Rosemary Frances, only da of Francis Harold Scoones, MRCS, LRCP, JP, of 83 Abbotsbury Rd, W14, and formerly wife of Murray de Vere, Earl of Burford (later 14th Duke of St Albans), and has issue by 1st and 2nd *m*.

Arms – Gules, a lion passant guardant, in chief two civic wreaths or, on a chief of augmentation wavy argent, a representation of Algiers, and on the dexter side a man-of-war bearing the flag of an admiral of the blue, all proper. **Crest** – Upon waves of the sea the stern of a wrecked ship, inscribed "Dutton" (East Indiaman), upon a rocky shore off Plymouth garrison (*ie* in the background a hill, upon the top of which a tower with a flag hoisted), all proper. **Supporters** – *Dexter*, a lion guardant or, navally crowned azure, his sinister hind paw resting on an increscent argent; *sinister*, a human figure intended to represent a Christian slave, naked from the waist upwards, a cloth round the loins, and thighs and legs habited in blue and white striped trousers, holding in the right hand a cross or, and in his left fetters broken proper.
Residence – Canonteign, near Exeter, Devon.

SONS LIVING *(By 2nd marriage)*

Hon EDWARD FRANCIS, *b* 30 October 1978.
Hon Alexander Paul, *b* 1978 (twin).

DAUGHTER LIVING *(By 1st marriage)*

Hon Patricia Sofia, *b* 1966. *Residence* – Paseo de Rosales 3Z, Madrid, Spain.

BROTHER LIVING

Hon Peter Irving, *b* 1942; *ed* Downside.

SISTERS LIVING

Hon Mary Rose, *b* 1938: *m* 1974, Don Roman Llanso, of Urb Los Pinos, 28220 Majadahonda, Madrid.

Hon Mary Elizabeth Josephine, *b* 1947: *m* 1969, Robin Gerard d'Erlanger, ACA, of Manor Farm House, Compton Valence, Dorchester, Dorset, son of late Sir Gerard John Regis Leo d'Erlanger, CBE, and has issue living, Gerard Pownoll, *b* 1970, — Hugh Robin, *b* 1976, — Josephine Louise, *b* 1972, — Marietta Elizabeth, *b* 1974, — Emilia Mary Florence, *b* 1982.

WIDOW LIVING OF NINTH VISCOUNT

MARIA LUISA (*Maria Luisa, Viscountess Exmouth*), (Marquesa de Olias in Spain *cr* 1652; *s* 1940), da of late Luis de Urquijo, Marques de Amurrio, of Madrid, and widow of Gonzalo Alvarez-Builla: *m* 1938, the 9th Viscount, who *d* 1970. *Residence* – Canonteign Manor, Lower Ashton, Exeter.

COLLATERAL BRANCHES LIVING

Grandchildren of late Fleetwood Hugo Pellew, son of Rev Hon Edward Pellew, 4th son of 1st Viscount:—
Issue of late Major Fleetwood Hugo Pellew, *b* 1871, *d* 1961: *m* 1909, Violet, who *d* 1964, da of late James Du Pre, of Wilton Park, Bucks:—
Fleetwood Hugo, *b* 1910; *ed* Malvern, and RMA Woolwich; Lieut-Col (ret) Roy Signals: *m* 1939, Geraldine Mildred, da of Major William Gerald Hole, of Parke, Bovey Tracey, S Devon, and has issue living, Pamela Geraldine, *b* 1946: *m* 1979, Brian E. Jones, and has issue. *Residence* – Waye Farm, Lustleigh, Devon. —— †Anthony Pownoll, *b* 1911; Cdr (ret) RN: *m* 1st, 1941 (*m diss* 1953), Margaret Julia, da of Clive Cookson, of Nether Warden, Hexham; 2ndly, 1957, Hilary Frances, da of Capt Alfred Garbett Pape, of 20 Northumberland St, Edinburgh, and *d* 1992, leaving issue (by 1st *m*), Mark Edward, LVO (4/51 St George's Sq, SW1), *b* 1942; *ed* Winchester, and Trin Coll, Oxford; HM Diplomatic Ser since 1965; LVO 1980: *m* 1965, Jill Hosford, da of Prof Frank Thistlethwaite, CBE, of St John's Coll, Cambridge, and has issue living, Adam Lee *b* 1966, Dominic Stephen *b* 1968, — Robert (Robin) Anthony (2 Luard Rd, Cambridge CB2 2PJ), *b* 1945; *ed* Marlborough, and Edin Univ; Dir World Wildlife Fund: *m* 1975, Pamela, da of Dr P. D. MacLellan, and has issue living, Toby James Pownoll, *b* 1982, Sophie Harriet *b* 1979. — Phoebe Sarah, *b* 1947: *m* 1974, Faisal Hamzah Ghoth, of Medina, Saudi Arabia, and has issue living, Arabi Faisal *b* 1974, Ibrahim *b* 1976, — (by 2nd *m*) Nicholas Charles (Burnham, Bucks), *b* 1959; *ed* Wellington, Exeter Univ, and Camb Univ: *m* 1989, Doone Philippa, da of Robert Selbie, of Hurstbourne Priors, Hants, and has issue living, Christopher Anthony Lloyd *b* 1992, — Philip Esmond, *b* 1962. *Residence* – 3 Glencairn House, 70 Ridgway, Wimbledon, SW19. —— Myles Addington, *b* 1919; *ed* Malvern: *m* 1957, Jill Primrose Twentyman, yst da of late Capt Alfred Maurice Davis, OBE, of 124 Walton St, SW3, and has issue living, Simon Du Pre, *b* 1959, — Alexandra Twentyman, *b* 1961: *m* 1987, Jeffrey G. Fowler, son of J. T. G. Fowler, of Lambeth, London, — Miranda Frances, *b* 1964. *Residence* – 2 Little Chesters, Beech Lane, Walton-on-the-Hill, Surrey. —— Timothy Winthrop, *b* 1921; *ed* Camb Univ (MA): *m* 1950, Margaret Richmond, da of late Edmund George Hamilton Mewburn, of 20 Norfolk House, Courtlands, Richmond, Surrey, and has issue living, Fleetwood Timothy, *b* 1952, — Adrian Harold, *b* 1954: *m* 1991, Leanne Eileen, da of late Edmund C. Randell, of Mississauga, Ont, Canada, and has issue living, Mallory Anne *b* 1993, — Owen Simon, *b* 1958, — Colin David, *b* 1961, — Mabel Audrey, *b* 1955: *m* 1983, Milenko Milicev, of Toronto. *Residence* – 31 Churchill Av, Willowdale, Ont, Canada. —— Anne, *b* 1915: *m* 1st, 1941, Capt John Pearce Gould, RASC; 2ndly, 1947, Denis Owen Burns, of Clumps End, Lower Bourne, Farnham, Surrey.

PREDECESSORS – (1) *Sir* EDWARD Pellew, GCB: a celebrated Adm; *cr* a *Baronet* 1796, *Baron Exmouth*, of Canonteign, co Devon (peerage of United Kingdom) 1814, and *Viscount Exmouth* (peerage of United Kingdom) 1816; *d* 1833; *s* by his son (2) POWNOLL BASTARD, 2nd Viscount; *d* 1833; *s* by his son (3) EDWARD, 3rd Viscount; *d* 1876; *s* by his nephew (4) EDWARD FLEETWOOD JOHN, 4th Viscount (son of Hon Fleetwood John, 4th son of 2nd Viscount); *b* 1861: *m* 1884, Edith, who *d* 1914, da of late Thomas Hargreaves, of Arborfield Hall, Reading; *d* 1899; *s* by his son (5) EDWARD ADDINGTON HARGREAVES, 5th Viscount, *b* 1890; *d* 1922; *s* by his cousin (6) HENRY EDWARD (only son of late Very Rev the Hon George Pellew, DD, Dean of Norwich, 3rd son of 1st Viscount, by the Hon Frances Addington, da of 1st Viscount Sidmouth), 6th Viscount; *b* 1828; a naturalized American: *m* 1st, 1858, Eliza, who *d* 1869, da of late Hon William Jay, of Bedford, New York, a Judge in New York; 2ndly, 1873, Augusta, who *d* 1917, da of late Hon William Jay (ante); *d* 1923; *s* by his son (7) CHARLES ERNEST, 7th Viscount; *b* 1863: *m* 1st 1886, Margaret, who *d* 1922, da of late Professor C. F. Chandler, of New York; 2ndly 1923, Mabel, who *d* 1949, da of late Richard Gray, of San Francisco; *d* 1945; *s* by his kinsman (8) EDWARD IRVING POWNOLL, OBE, MRCS, LRCP (son of late Capt Pownoll William Pellew, RN, son of Rev Hon Edward Pellew, 4th son of 1st Viscount), 8th Viscount; *b* 1868: *m* 1902, Frances, who *d* 1963, da of Alfred Wells Edwards; *d* 1951; *s* by his son (9) POWNOLL IRVING EDWARD, 9th Viscount; *b* 1908: *m* 1938, Maria Luisa (Marquesa de Olias in Spain; *cr* 1652; *s* 1940), da of late Luis de Urquijo, Marques de Amurrio, of Madrid, and widow of Gonzalo Alvarez-Builla; *d* 1970; *s* by his son (10) PAUL EDWARD, 10th Viscount and present peer; also Baron Exmouth.

EZRA, BARON (Ezra) (Life Baron 1983)

DEREK EZRA, MBE, son of late David Ezra; *b* 23 Feb 1919; *ed* Monmouth Sch, and Magdalene Coll, Camb (MA, Hon Fell 1977); joined Nat Coal Board 1947, Regional Sales Manager 1958-60, Dir-Gen Marketing 1960-65, Board Member 1965-67, Dep-Chm 1967-71, Chm 1971-82; Vice-Pres Brit Inst of Management since 1978 (Chm 1976-78); Chm Assoc Heat Services plc since 1966; Dir of other Cos in Energy Sector; served in Army 1939-47; MBE (Mil) 1945; *cr* Kt 1974, and *Baron Ezra*, of Horsham, co W Sussex (Life Baron) 1983: *m* 1950, Julia Elizabeth, da of Thomas Wilkins, of Portsmouth, Hants.
Address – House of Lords, Westminster, SW1A 0PW.

FAIRFAX OF CAMERON, LORD (Fairfax) (Baron S 1627)

NICHOLAS JOHN ALBERT FAIRFAX, 14th Lord; *b* 4 Jan 1956; *s* 1964: *m* 1982, Annabel Ruth, el da of late Henry Lester Louis Morriss (*see* Jackson, Bt, *cr* 1869), and has issue.

𝔄rms – Or, three bars gemelles gules, surmounted by a lion rampant sable. 𝔆rest – A lion passant guardant sable. 𝔖upporters – *Dexter*, a lion guardant sable; *sinister*, a bay horse proper. *Residence* – 10 Orlando Rd, SW4 0LF.

SONS LIVING

Hon EDWARD NICHOLAS THOMAS, *b* 20 Sept 1984.
Hon John Frederick Anthony, *b* 1986.
Hon Rory Henry Francis, *b* 1991.

BROTHERS LIVING

Hon Hugh Nigel Thomas (4 Routh Rd, SW18. *Club* – Boodle's), *b* 1958; *ed* Eton: *m* 1984, Victoria Janet, elder da of Digby Sheffield Neave (*see* Neave, Bt), and has issue living, Alexander Thomas Digby, *b* 1986, — Laura Jane Ulla, *b* 1987, — Marina, *b* 1989.
Hon Rupert Alexander James, *b* 1961; addl assist Private Sec to HRH The Prince of Wales 1986-88.

Speak and act

SISTER LIVING

Hon Serena Frances, *b* 1952: *m* 1976, William Robert Geoffrey Bell, elder son of William Archibald Ottley Juxon Bell, of Cottisford House, Brackley, Northants (*see* By Wenlock, 1969 Edn), and has issue living, William Thomas D., *b* 1986, — Francesca Rose, *b* 1982.

UNCLE LIVING (*Son of 12th Lord*)

Hon Peregrine John Wishart, *b* 1925; *ed* Eton, and Trin Coll, Camb; late Lt 12th R Lancers; Northumberland Hussars 1955-61; High Sheriff of Northumberland 1971: *m* 1965, Virginia Alexandra de L'Etang, da of Hon Philip Leyland Kindersley (*see* B Kindersley), and has issue living, Thomas Philip, *b* 1966, — Doune Alexandra Wishart, *b* 1968. *Residence* – Mindrum, Northumberland. *Clubs* – Northern Counties (Newcastle), Whites.

WIDOW LIVING OF THIRTEENTH LORD

SONIA HELEN (*Sonia, Lady Fairfax of Cameron*), da of late Capt Cecil Bernard Gunston, MC (*see* M Dufferin and Ava, 1980 Edn); a JP of Berks; a temporary Lady of the Bedchamber to HM 1967-71: *m* 1951, the 13th Lord, who *d* 1964.

COLLATERAL BRANCHES LIVING

Grandchildren of late Raymond Fairfax, son of late Hon Henry Fairfax, 2nd son of 9th Lord:—
Issue of late Henry Reginald Fairfax, MD, *b* 1875, *d* 1955: *m* 1907, Nellie Virginia who *d* 1957, da of M. O. Randolph, of Williamson, West Virginia, USA:—
Reginald Randolph, *b* 1908: *m* 1934, Genevieve, da of J. W. McKee, of Brookhaven, Mississippi, USA. —— Ronald Cary, *b* 1915: *m* 1954, Judith Victoria, da of Jonathan Breckenridge Stovall, of Amherst co Virginia, USA. —— Marion Avery, *b* 1918: *m* 1943, Collin Freeman Baker, MD (Junior), and has issue living, Colin Freeman, *b* 1947, — Carey Leigh, *b* 1952, — Ann Fairfax, *b* 1949.

Grandchildren of Frederick Griffith Fairfax (infra):—
Issue of late Edmund Wharton Fairfax, *b* 1914, *d* 1966: *m* 1943, Nancy (Hague, Virginia, USA), da of James L. King, of Pittsburg, USA:—
Edmund Wharton, *b* 1944. —— Bryan Griffith, *b* 1959. —— Jean Ann, *b* 1951. —— Barbara Jane, *b* 1953.

Grandchildren of late William Henry Fairfax, MD, son of late Ferdinand Fairfax, MD, 3rd son of Hon Ferdinando Fairfax, 2nd son of 8th Lord:—
Issue of late Frederick Griffith Fairfax, *b* 1867, *d* 1948: *m* 1903, his cousin, Mary Fernando, who *d* 1961, da of Capt Edmund Wharton:—
Frederick Griffith, *b* 1916: *m* 1st, 1946 (*m diss* 1956) Dorothy Brooke; 2ndly, 1957, Annette Aiken, of Atlanta, Georgia, and has issue living (by 1st *m*), Frederick Griffith (RR1, Hague, Virginia 22469, USA), *b* 1947, — William Henry (RR1, Box 4, Hague, Virginia 22469, USA), *b* 1950, — (Dorothy) Eleanor, *b* 1946: *m* 19—, — Demastus, — Ada Carter, *b* 1949: *m* 19—, — Wright, — Grace Kate FAIRFAX, *b* 1952; has retained her maiden name: *m* 19—, — —(by 2nd *m*) Mary Lynette, *b* 1960: *m* 19—, — Roane. *Address* – RR1, Box 4, Hague, Virginia 22469, USA. —— Edith Wharton (97 Ridge Dr, Naples, Florida 33940, USA), *b* 1905: *m* 1933, Harold Benjamin Lang, who *d* 1962, and has issue living, Ann Fairfax, *b* 1936: *m* 1958, Virgil A. Ponzoli, MD, and has issue living, Linda Marie *b* 1960, Patricia Ann *b* 1961, Susanne Joan *b* 1963, Amy Carolyn *b* 1968. —— Fernado (da), *b* 1908. *Residence* – RR1, Hague, Virginia 22469, USA. —— Annie Staunton, *b* 1911: *m* 1933, Edward Greco, and has issue living, Edward Fairfax (Rt 1, Box 431, Front Royal, Va 22630, USA) *b* 1935: *m* 1966, Barbara Ruth Gomez, of Rio Vista, Cal, USA, and has issue living, Michelle Anne *b* 1968, William Edward Fairfax *b* 1972, — Frederick Dominic (6618 Ivy Hill Drive, McLean, Va 22101, USA) *b* 1937: *m* 1962, Carole Ann Drake, of Falling Waters, W Va, and has issue living, William Scott *b* 1969, Michael Drake *b* 1972. *Residence* – 2314 Grove Av, Falls Church, Virginia, USA. —— Katherine Rambsey (The Hague, Va, USA) *b* 1919.

Granddaughters of late Lt-Col John Carlyle Fairfax, US Army, elder son of late Archibald Carlyle Fairfax, 3rd son of late Cmdr Archibald Blair Fairfax, 4th son of Hon Ferdinando Fairfax (ante):—
Issue of late John Pollock Fairfax, *b* 1911, *d* 1983: *m* 1935, Dorothy Elsa, da of late Reginald Charles Steeple, of San Mateo, Calif, USA:—
(Dorothy) Anne, *b* 1936: *m* 1st, 1956 (*m diss* 1961), Frederick W. Timby; 2ndly, 1961 (*m diss* 1973), Henry Mohr Hermann; 3rdly, 1974, Jack Margolis, of 1520 Middlefield, Rd, Palo Alto, Calif 94301, USA, and has issue living (by 1st *m*), Jeffrey William Fairfax, *b* 1957, — Christopher Corey, *b* 1959, — (by 2nd *m*), Susan Mohr, *b* 1963. —— Jain Pollock, *b* 1937: *m* 1st, 1960 (*m diss* 1968), John Phillip de Angeles; 2ndly, 1968 (*m diss* 19—), Terry Ernest Jamison; 3rdly, 1983, Michael Langston,

of 2790 South Reed St, Denver, Colorado 80227, USA, and has issue living (by 1st *m*), Melissa Jain, *b* 1962, — Jenna Lynne, *b* 1963.

PREDECESSORS – (1) *Sir* THOMAS Fairfax, Knt; *cr Lord Fairfax of Cameron* (peerage of Scotland) 1627; *s* by his son (2) FERDINANDO, KB, 2nd Lord; successively MP for Boroughbridge and Yorkshire; as Parliamentary Gen of the Northern Forces became eminently distinguished, and had a chief command at the Battle of Marston Moor, where he defeated the Royal Army; was subsequently Gov of York; *d* 1647; *s* by his son (3) THOMAS, KB, 3rd Lord, a distinguished Republican military leader; commanded a Cavalry wing at Marston Moor; appointed Gen in Ch of the Parliaments' Army 1645, and in that year gained the celebrated victory at Naseby; he afterwards defeated the Royalists in a series of engagements, but did not participate in the execution of the king; in 1650 resigned the command of the army to Cromwell, and in 1659 zealously assisted to restore the monarchy; was Constable of the Tower 1647, and Lord of the Isle of Man 1650, and sat as MP for Yorkshire 1660; *d* 1671; *s* by his cousin (4) HENRY, 4th Lord, son of Rev Hon Henry, 2nd son of 1st Lord; *d* 1685; *s* by his son (5) THOMAS, 5th Lord, MP for co York 1688-1707, when the Act of Union he became ineligible; took an active part in promoting the revolution; *d* 1710; *s* by his el son (6) Thomas, 6th Lord; inherited from his mother estates in England which he gave to his brother, and also inherited about 5,700,000 acres of land in Virginia, upon which he erected two mansions, where he resided in baronial splendour; *d* 1781; *s* by his brother (7) ROBERT, 7th Lord; *d* 1793; *s* by his kinsman (8) BRYAN, 8th Lord, grandson of Rev Hon Hnery, 2nd son of 4th Lord (title confirmed by House of Lords 1800); *d* 1802; *s* by his son (9) THOMAS, 9th Lord; *d* 1846; *s* by his grandson (10) CHARLES SNOWDEN, 10th Lord, son of Hon Albert el son of 9th Lord, by Caroline, da of Richard Snowden, of Oakland, Maryland; Speaker of House of Delegates of State of California 1854-7, and Clerk of Supreme Court of California 1857-62; *d* 1869; *s* by his brother (11) JOHN CONTEE, MD, 11th Lord; *b* 1830: *m* 1857, Mary, who *d* 1912, da of Col Edmund Kirkby, of USA: *d* 1900: *s* by his el son (12) ALBERT KIRBY, 12th Lord (confirmed by Committee for Privileges of the House of Lords 1908); *b* 1870; a Representative Peer for Scotland: *m* 1922, Maude Wishart (who *d* 1973, have *m* 2ndly, 1947, Maj Cecil Rookherst Wigan, MC, who *d* 1958; 3rdly, 1962, Brig Felix Alexander Vincent Copland-Griffiths, DSO, MC), da of James McKelvie, of Ducklys Park, East Grinsted, *d* 1939, *s* by his el son (13) THOMAS BRIAN MCKELVIE, 13th Lord; *b* 1923; Lt Grenadier Guards; a Representative Peer for Scotland 1945-63; Assist Conservative Whip, House of Lords 1947-48, PPS to Lord Pres of the Council 1951-53, and to Min of Materials 1953-54, and a Lord-in-Waiting to HM 1954-57: *m* 1951, Sonia Helen, da of late Capt Cecil Bernard Gunston, MC (*see* M Dufferin and Ava, 1980 Edn); *d* 1964; *s* by his el son (14) NICHOLAS JOHN ALBERT, 14th Lord and present peer.

If I can

FAIRHAVEN, BARON (Broughton) (Baron UK 1961)

AILWYN HENRY GEORGE BROUGHTON, 3rd Baron; *b* 16 Nov 1936; *s* 1973; *ed* Eton, and RMA; Maj Blues and Royals; Vice Lord-Lieut of Cambs 1977-84: JP and DL for Cambs: *m* 1960, Kathleen Patricia, el da of Col James Henry Magill, OBE, of Queen's House, Ousden, Suffolk, and has issue.

Arms – Argent, two bars and in the dexter chief point a saltire gules. **Crest** – In front of a bull's head erased sable, armed and collared and chained or, three fleur-de-lis gold. **Supporters** – On either side a winged bull sable, each armed and gorged with a chain or, pendant therefrom an escutcheon charged with the Arms of Broughton.
Residence – Anglesey Abbey, Cambridge. *Club* – Turf.

SONS LIVING

Hon JAMES HENRY AILWYN, *b* 25 May 1963; *ed* Harrow; late Maj The Blues and Royals: *m* 1990, Sarah Olivia, da of Harold Digby Fitzgerald Creighton, of Upper Brook St, W1, and has issue living, Sophie Rose, *b* 1992.
Hon Huttleston Rupert, *b* 1970.
Hon Charles Leander, *b* 1973.
Hon Henry Robert, *b* 1978.

DAUGHTERS LIVING

Hon Diana Cara, *b* 1961: *m* 1st, 1983, Guy Dominic Thornton (*see* V Esher, colls); 2ndly, 1991, as his 3rd wife, Alan Brodie Henderson, and has issue (by 1st *m*) (*see* V Esher, colls).
Hon Melanie Frances, *b* 1966: *m* 1989 (*m diss* 1992), Matthew Eric Smith, and has issue (*see* Hill-Wood, Bt, colls).

PREDECESSORS – (1) URBAN HUTTLESTON ROGERS Broughton, son of Urban Hanlon Broughton, of Park Close, Englefield Green, Surrey (*b* 1857, *d* 1929, before his intended elevation to the Peerage, and who gave Ashridge to Conservative Party), by Cara Leland (who, with her two sons presented Runnymede to the nation 1929, and who was granted by Roy Warrant 1929 the style and title as if her husband had received the barony of Fairhaven), da of Henry Huttleston Rogers, of New York; *cr Baron Fairhaven*, of Lode, co Camb (Peerage of UK 1929) with remainder to heirs male of the body, and *Baron Fairhaven*, of Anglesey Abbey, co Camb (Peerage of UK) 1961, with remainder to his yr brother, and the heirs male of his body; *d* 1966, when the Barony *cr* 1929 became ext; *s* in the Barony *cr* 1961, by his brother (2) HENRY ROGERS, 2nd Baron, *b* 1900: *m* 1st, 1932, Hon Diana Rosamond, who *d* 1937, da of late Capt Hon Coulson Churchill Fellowes (B de Ramsey); 2ndly, 1953, Joyce Irene (who *d* 1989, having *m* 3rdly, 1982, Vice-Adm Sir Geoffrey Thistleton-Smith, KBE, CB, GM, DL), da of Edward Arthur Miller, and widow of Lt Gerald Henry Charles Dickens, RN; *d* 1973; *s* by his only son (3) AILWYN HENRY GEORGE, 3rd Baron, and present Peer.

FAITHFULL, BARONESS (Faithfull) (Life Baroness 1975)

LUCY FAITHFULL, OBE, da of late Sydney Leigh Faithfull, RE; *b* 26 Dec 1910; *ed* Bournemouth High Sch (now Talbot Heath Sch), and Birmingham Univ (Dip in Social Science, and Certificate in Child Care); Hon DLitt Warwick, Hon MA Oxford; Sub-Warden Birmingham Settlement 1933-35, Care Cttee Organiser LCC 1935-40, Regional Welfare Office (Evacuees) Min of Health 1940-48, Inspector, Children's Dept Home

Office 1948-58, Children's Officer Oxford City 1958-70, and Dir of Social Sers Oxford City 1970-74; *cr* OBE (Civil) 1972, and *Baroness Faithfull*, of Wolvercote, co of Oxfordshire (Life Baroness) 1975. *Residence* – 303 Woodstock Rd, Oxford OX2 7NY.

FALCONER OF HALKERTON, LORDSHIP OF (Falconer) (Dormant 1966)

The Lordship of Falconer of Halkerton became dormant on the death of the 10th Earl of Kintore and 12th Lord Falconer of Halkerton in 1966. Owing to the Earls of Kintore not having taken any steps to vote as Lords Falconer for over forty years, the dignity was removed, by mistake, from the Union Roll after the death of the 7th Earl and 9th Lord in 1844. It will be necessary for the next male heir to the Lordship of Falconer of Halkerton to have this peerage restored to the Union Roll by resolution of the House of Lords.

COLLATERAL BRANCHES LIVING
Descendants of late George Falconer (who changed the spelling of his surname to Falconar), brother of 4th Lord:—

Granddaughter of late George Mercer FALCONAR-STEWART (who assumed the additional surname of Stewart after his patronymic), son of late George FALCONAR of Carlowrie, great-grandson of late George Falconer (ante):—
Issue of late Maj Cyril Falconar-Stewart, MC, *b* 1884, *d* 1962: *m* 1915, Nita, who *d* 1968, da of Bryce Allan, of Wemyss Bay, Renfrewshire:—
Grizel Anne, *b* 1917: *m* 1944, Wladyslaw Chlebowski, of 26 Greenhill Gdns, Edinburgh, EH10 4BP, and has issue living, Jan Ronald Stewart, *b* 1945, — Victor Tadeusz Stewart, *b* 1953: *m* 1988, Jean MacLellan, and has issue living, Amy Louisa *b* 1990, Isla Rose *b* 1992, — Alexandra Ewa Stewart, *b* 1948; *m* 1975, Dr William David Smith, of 4 St Margaret's Rd, Edinburgh, and has issue living, Robin Paul Stewart *b* 1977, Tamsin Louise Stewart *b* 1981.

Grandchildren of late John Egerton Falconer, son of Randle Wilbraham Falconer, MD, FRCP, DCL, 6th in descent from Patrick Falconer of Newton, uncle of 1st Lord:—
Issue of late Thomas Falconer, FRIBA, *b* 1879, *d* 1934: *m* 1912, Florence Edith, who *d* 1944, da of late Henry Campbell Serrell, of Brooke House, Hants:—
PETER SERRELL (*presumed heir to the Lordship of Falconer of Halkerton*), *b* 7 March, 1916; *ed* Bloxham; FRIBA: *m* 1941, Mary, da of late Rev C. B. Hodson, and has issue living, Thomas Serrell (Daisy Cottage, Fairseat, Kent), *b* 1946; RIBA: *m* 1981, Philippa Mary, da of J. R. C. Sheldon, of Court House, Fairseat, Kent, and has issue living, Alexander Peter *b* 1989, Olivia Siena *b* 1983, Katharine Daisy *b* 1986, — Richard Alaric (St Davids, Kemps Lane, Painswick, Glos), *b* 1949; RIBA: *m* 1982, Virginia Suzanne Rowell, only da of Richard Francis Jarrett, FRCP, MA, MB, BCh, of Hamfield, Painswick, Glos, and has issue living, Holly Frances *b* 1984, Rosanna Frances *b* 1985, Venetia Frances *b* 1989, — William John (103 Princess Victoria St, Clifton, Bristol), *b* 1952; BA Dip Arch: *m* 1983, Susan Mary, da of Arthur Leslie Bill, of Roslyn, St John's Hill, Wimborne, Dorset, and has issue living, Phoebe Margaret *b* 1993, — Caroline Elisabeth, *b* 1942: *m* 1973, Maj Paul Beresford Weller, late Som LI, of Morcombe Farm House, Caudle Green, Cheltenham, Glos GL53 9PR, and has issue living, Victoria Mary Henrietta *b* 1976, Atalanta Catherine *b* 1978, Pandora May *b* 1983. *Residence* – St Francis, Minchinhampton, Gloucestershire.
——— Peggie Florentia, *b* 1918: *m* 1941, Douglas Guest, CVO, MA, MusD, Emeritus Organist and Master of Choristers, Westminster Abbey, and has issue living, Susan Jennifer *b* 1943: *m* 1966, Martin Hayward Garrett-Cox, of Shrubhill, Hill of Row, by Dunblane, Perthshire FK15 9PA, and has issue living, Jeremy Hayward *b* 1968, Robin Guy *b* 1970, Sacha Clare *b* 1973, — Penelope Anne, *b* 1946: *m* 1970, Prof Simon de Lange, MB BS, PhD, FRCA, of Diepstraat 48, 6245 BL Eijsden, Netherlands, and has issue living, Cara Michelle *b* 1974, Claire Louise *b* 1976. *Residence* – The Gables, Minchinhampton, Glos GL6 9JE.
Issue of late William Wilbraham Phillips Falconer, *b* 1883, *d* 1952: *m* 1912, Gladys, who *d* 1969, da of late David Howard Jones, of Carmarthen:—
John Dalmahoy, *b* 1914; actor: *m* 1956, Edna Johanna, da of Alfred Foulsham Brooks, of Cheam, Surrey. ——— Joan Egerton, MBE, *b* 1920; MBE (Civil) 1991: *m* 1st, 1940 (*m diss* 1944), Maj Gerrit Geel, Netherlands Army; 2ndly, 1945, Col James Bouverie-Brine, and has issue living (by 1st *m*), Marie Ann Falconer, *b* 1943: *m* 1st, 1963 (*m diss* 1986), Edward Alexander Caudwell; 2ndly, 1988, Wing Cdr A. Webb, AFC, RAF, and has issue living (by 1st *m*), Edward James *b* 1966: *m* 1993, Lucinda, da of Brig J. Alexander, of Andover, Hants, Alexandra Jane Marie *b* 1969, — (by 2nd *m*), Christopher James Falconer, *b* 1946: *m* 1968, Ellen Agnes Maria, da of Henk Verkroost, of Utrecht, Holland, — Michael Pusey, *b* 1959: *m* 1984, Claire Andrée, da of Frederick G. Henley, of Swindon, Wilts, and has issue living, George James *b* 1993, Lucy Anne *b* 1992, — Kathleen Joan, *b* 1948: *m* 1968 (*m diss* 1994), Fl Lt Alexander Frederick Paul Rhodes, RAF, and has issue living, Paul William *b* 1969, Helen Kathleen (twin) *b* 1969, — Amelia Pusey, *b* 1953: *m* 1st, 1974 (*m diss* 1981), Edward Alfred Funnell; 2ndly, 1982, Lt-Cmdr Stephen Patrick Lacey, RN, and has issue living (by 1st *m*), Simon Edward *b* 1975, Louise Amelia *b* 1979, (by 2nd *m*) James Patrick *b* 1986, — Elizabeth, *b* 1956: *m* 1st, 1978 (*m diss* 1985), Dudley James Cox, of Nailsea, Avon; 2ndly, 1986, Michael McGaughrin. *Residence* – 9 St Mary's Close, Bradenstoke, Chippenham, Wilts SN15 4ET.
Issue of late John Philip Egerton Falconer (twin), *b* 1883, *d* 1970: *m* 1931, Florence Eleanor, who *d* 1957, da of late Alfred Attwood, of Yeovil, Som:—
David Dunbar (Iris Bank, 47 Cockhill, Trowbridge, Wilts BA14 9BG), *b* 1934; BA: *m* 1959, Gillian Mary, only da of late Wing-Cdr William Richard Owen, MBE, RAF, and has issue living, Jonathan Randle, *b* 1961; BA: *m* 1992, Tracy Anne Gronow, — Patrick Markham, *b* 1964; BA: *m* 1989, Deborah Anne Helena, da of T. C. Close, of Bristol, and has issue living, Georgina Louise *b* 1991, Philippa Jane *b* 1993, — Henrietta Frances, *b* 1970; BA.

PREDECESSORS – (1) Sir ALEXANDER
Falconer of Halkerton, Kincardineshire, whose family descended from Ranulphus Falconer to William the Lion, from which office he assumed the surname of Falconer, was a Lord of Session 1639, MP for co Kincardine 1643, and a Commr of the Treasury 1645; *cr Lord Falconer of Halkerton* (peerage of Scotland) 1646, with remainder to his heirs male whatsoever: *m* 1619, Anne Lindsay, only da and heiress of John, 8th Lord Lindsay of the Byres, co Haddington; *d* 1671; *s* by his son (2) ALEXANDER, 2nd Lord: *m* 16—, Lady Margaret Ogilvy, da of James, 2nd Earl of Airlie; *d* 1684; *s* by his son (3) DAVID, 3rd Lord; *d* unmarried 1724; *s* by his kinsman (4) DAVID (son of Sir David Falconer of Newton, Lord Newton, Lord Pres of Court of Session *m* 1678, Mary, da of George Norvell of Boghall, co Linlithgow), 2nd son of Sir David Falconer, brother of 1st Lord), 4th Lord: *m* 1703, Lady Catherine Margaret Keith, el da of William, 2nd Earl of Kintore, *d* 1751; *s* by his son (5) ALEXANDER, 5th Lord, *b* 1707: *m* 1757, Frances, da of Herbert Mackworth; *d* 1762; *s* by his brother (6) WILLIAM, 6th Lord; Col in Dutch Ser: *m* 1735, Rembertina-Maria van Iddekinge; *d* 1776; *s* by his son (7) ANTHONY ADRIAN, 7th Lord, who *s* as 5th Earl of Kintore 1778 (see that title). On the death of ARTHUR GEORGE, 10th Earl and 12th Lord Falconer of Halkerton 1966, the latter peerage became dormant.

FALKENDER, BARONESS (Falkender) (Life Baroness 1974)

MARCIA MATILDA FALKENDER, CBE, da of Harry Field; *b* 1932; *ed* Queen Mary Coll, London Univ (BA); Sec to Mr Morgan Phillips, Gen Sec Labour Party 1955-56; Private Sec to Rt Hon Sir Harold Wilson, OBE, FRS, MP; Political Columnist, *The Mail on Sunday* 1982-88, since when Lay Gov Queen Mary Coll; Pres UNIFEM UK, United Nations Development Fund for Women UK Cttee; Dir Peckham Building Soc since 1986, S London Investment & Mortgage Corpn since 1987; assumed by deed poll, 1974 the surname of Falkender in lieu of Williams; *cr* CBE (Civil) 1970, and *Baroness Falkender*, of West Haddon, co Northants (Life Baroness) 1974: *m* 1955 (*m diss* 1960), George Edmund Charles Williams; has issue two sons.
Residence – 3 Wyndham Mews, Upper Montagu Street, W1.

FALKLAND, VISCOUNT OF (Cary) (Viscount S 1620)

Faithful in both

LUCIUS EDWARD WILLIAM PLANTAGENET CARY, 15th Viscount, *b* 8 May 1935; *s* 1984; *ed* Wellington Coll; late 2nd Lieut 8th Hus; formerly Ch Exec C. T. Bowring Trading (Holdings) Ltd; export marketing consultant; Deputy Whip SLD, House of Lords since 1988: *m* 1962 (*m diss* 1990), Caroline Anne, only da of late Lt-Cdr Gerald Butler, DSC, RN; 2ndly, 1990, Nicole, da of late Milburn Mackey, and has issue by 1st and 2nd *m*.

Arms – Quarterly: 1st and 4th argent, on a bend sable, three roses of the field, barbed and seeded proper, *Cary*; 2nd sable, two bars nebulée ermine, *Spencer of Spencercombe*; 3rd, France and England quarterly, within a bordure componée argent and azure, *Beaufort*, Duke of Somerset. **Crest** – A swan, wings elevated proper. **Supporters** – *Dexter*, an unicorn argent, armed, crined, tufted and unguled or; *sinister*, a lion guardant proper, ducally crowned, and gorged with a plain collar or. *Address* – House of Lords, SW1.

SONS LIVING (By 1st marriage)

Hon (LUCIUS) ALEXANDER PLANTAGENET (*Master of Falkland*), *b* 1 Feb 1963; *ed* Westminster, Loretto, and RMA Sandhurst; late Capt Scots Guards: *m* 1993, Linda, da of Raymond Purl, of Colorado City, USA.

(By 2nd marriage)

Hon Charles Byron Milburn, *b* 1992.

DAUGHTERS LIVING AND DECEASED (by 1st marriage)

Camilla Anne, *b* 1965; *d* 1972.
Hon Samantha Anne, *b* 1973.
Hon Lucinda Mary, *b* 1974.

HALF-SISTERS LIVING (Daughters of 14th Viscount by 1st m)

Hon Elizabeth Ann Bevil (*Hon Lady Nelson*), *b* 1927: *m* 1945, Sir William Vernon Hope Nelson, 3rd Bt, OBE, who *d* 1991. *Residence* – The Old Post House, Chiselborough, Som.
Hon Jean Rosemary Vera, *b* 1928; artist: *m* 1950, Capt Henry Herman Evelyn Montagu Winch, late High Sheriff of Merioneth, who *d* 1987. *Residence* – Castle Barn, Minffordd, Gwynedd.

UNCLE LIVING (son of 13th Viscount)

Hon Richard Lorenzo Plantagenet, *b* 1915; *ed* Repton, and Downing Coll, Camb: *m* 1959, Dorothy Denise Lloyd.

WIDOW LIVING OF SON OF THIRTEENTH VISCOUNT

Daphne Helen, da of late Capt Edward Westcott King, RA: *m* 1932, Hon Byron Godfrey Plantagenet Cary, who *d* 1971, and has issue (see colls infra). *Residence* – The Cottage, 26 Dorset Rd South, Bexhill-on-Sea, Sussex.

MOTHER LIVING

Constance Mary, da of late Capt Edward Berry: *m* 1933 (*m diss* 1958), as his 2nd wife, Lucius Henry Charles Plantagenet Cary (later 14th Viscount), who *d* 1984. *Residence* – 69 Mount Pleasant Rd, Brixham, Devon.

COLLATERAL BRANCHES LIVING

Issue of late Hon Byron Godfrey Plantagenet Cary, 2nd son of 13th Viscount, *b* 1908, *d* 1971: *m* 1932, Daphne Helen (ante), da of late Capt Edward Westcott King, RA:—
Robert Byron, *b* 1944; *ed* Repton. —— Rosemary Sally (118 High St, Wivenhoe, Essex), *b* 1935: *m* 1980, Neil Pugh. —— Susan Jane, *b* 1938: *m* 1960, Ronald Frederick Featherstone, of 20 Clinton Rd, Lower Buckland, Lymington, Hants, and has issue living, Angus Frederick, *b* 1962, — Penelope Helen, *b* 1961: *m* 1985, Mark Williams, — Louise, *b* 1964: *m* 1987, Mark Snodgrass, — Greta Jane, *b* 1965, — Katy Ann Lorraine, *b* 1967, — Ingrid Laura, *b* 1980.

Issue of late Hon Philip Plantagenet Cary, yst son of 12th Viscount, b 1895, d 1968: m 1920, Esther Mildred, who d 1972, da of Sir George Edward Leon, 2nd Bt:—

(Mary) Philippa (*Dowager Baroness Dunalley*) (Church End House, Swerford, Oxford OX7 4AX), b 1922: 1939-45 War, as 3rd Officer, WRNS: m 1947, Lt-Col 6th Baron Dunalley, who d 1992.

PREDECESSORS – **(1)** Rt Hon Sir HENRY Cary, PC, Comptroller of the Household 1617; MP for Hertfordshire 1620-1, and Lord Dep for Ireland 1622-9; cr *Viscount Falkland* and *Lord Cary* (peerage of Scotland) 1620; d 1633; s by his son **(2)** LUCIUS, 2nd Viscount; MP for Newport, and Sec of State to Charles I; k at first battle of Newbury 1643; s by his el son **(3)** LUCIUS, 3rd Viscount; d 1649; s by his brother **(4)** HENRY, 4th Viscount; MP for Arundell and Lord-Lieut of co Oxford; d 1663; s by his son **(5)** ANTHONY, PC, 5th Viscount; Treasurer of the Navy 1681-89, Commr of the Admiralty to William and Mary, and First Lord of the Admiralty 1693 until his death; committed to the Tower in 1693 by the House of Commons, of which he was a member, for begging and receiving £2,000 from HM, contrary to the ordinary method of issuing and bestowing the King's money; s by his cousin **(6)** LUCIUS HENRY CARY, 6th Viscount, grandson of Hon Patrick Cary, 5th son of 1st Viscount; d 1730; s by his son **(7)** LUCIUS CHARLES, 7th Viscount; d 1785; s by his grandson **(8)** HENRY THOMAS, 8th Viscount, son of Hon Lucius Ferdinand, el son of 7th Viscount; d unmarried 1796; s by his brother **(9)** CHARLES JOHN, 9th Viscount; b 1768; Capt RN; killed in a duel 1809; s by his son **(10)** LUCIUS BENTINCK, GCH, PC, 10th Viscount; b 1803; was a Lord of the Bed-chamber to William IV 1830, a Representative Peer for Scotland 1831-32, Gov of Nova Scotia 1840-46, Capt of Yeomen of the Guard 1846-48, and Gov of Bombay 1848-53; cr *Baron Hunsdon of Scutterskelfe*, co York (peerage of United Kingdom) 1832; d 1884, when the Barony of Hunsdon became extinct; s by his brother **(11)** PLANTAGENET PIERREPONT, 11th Viscount; was an Adm; d 31 Jan 1886; s by his nephew **(12)** BYRON PLANTAGENET (el son of Capt Hon Byron Charles Ferdinand Plantagenet Cary, 3rd son of 9th Viscount), 12th Viscount, b 1845; a Representative Peer: m 1879, Mary (a Lady of Grace of Order of St John of Jerusalem in England), who d 1920, da of late Robert Reade, of New York; d 1922; s by his el son **(13)** LUCIUS PLANTAGENET, OBE, 13th Viscount, b 1880; Capt and Brevet Major Grenadier Guards; Dep Gov of Wandsworth Prison 1910-14; European War 1914-19 (OBE); a Representative Peer for Scotland 1922-31; m 1904, Ella Louise, who d 1954, da of late Edward Walter Catford; d 1961; s by his el son **(14)** LUCIUS HENRY CHARLES PLANTAGENET, 14th Viscount, b 1905: m 1st, 1926 (*m diss* 1933), Joan Sylvia, da of Charles Bonham Southey; 2ndly, 1933 (*m diss* 1958), Constance Mary, da of late Capt Edward Berry; 3rdly, 1958 (*m diss* 1974), Charlotte Anne, elder da of late Bevil Granville, of Chadley, Wellesbourne, Warwicks (*see* Halsey, Bt, 1952 Edn); d 1984; s by his only son **(15)** LUCIUS EDWARD WILLIAM PLANTAGENET CARY, 15th Viscount and present peer; also Lord Cary.

FALMOUTH, VISCOUNT (Boscawen) (Viscount GB 1720)

(Name pronounced "Boscowen")

GEORGE HUGH BOSCAWEN, 9th Viscount; b 31 Oct 1919; s 1962; ed Eton, and at Trin Coll, Camb (MA); Capt Cold-stream Guards, and patron of five livings; Lord Lieut of Cornwall since 1977; 1939-45 War in Italy (wounded, despatches); m 1953, Elizabeth, el da of A. H. Browne, and has issue.

Patience surpasses knowledge

Arms – Ermine, a rose gules, barbed and seeded proper. **Crest** – A falcon close proper. **Supporters** – Two sea lions erect on their tails argent, gutte de larmes. **Motto** – Patience Passe Science.
Seat – Tregothnan, Truro. *Clubs* – Athenaeum, Army and Navy.

SONS LIVING

Hon EVELYN ARTHUR HUGH, b 13 May 1955, ed Eton, and Royal Agric Coll, Cirencester: m 1977, Lucia Caroline, el da of Ralph William Vivian-Neal, of Poundisford Park, Som, and has issue living, (Evelyn George) William, b 1 Oct 1979, — Laura Frances, b 1982.

Hon Nicholas John (Peckham Place, Peckham Bush, Tonbridge, Kent TN12 5NA), b 1957; ed Eton, and RAC Cirencester: m 1985, Virginia Mary Rose, yr da of Robin Beare, MB BS, FRCS, of Scraggs Farm, Cowden, Kent, and has issue living, Louisa Emily Chiara, b 1990, — Georgia Olivia Catharine, b 1992.

Hon Charles Richard (Dennington Lodge, Dennington, nr Framlingham, Suffolk), b 1958; ed Eton, and Trin Coll, Camb (MA): m 1985, Frances Diana, yst da of late Maj Hon George Nathaniel Rous, of Dennington Hall, Woodbridge, Suffolk (*see* E Stradbroke, colls), and has issue living, Arthur George, b 1991, — John Charles, b 1993, — Rosanna Frances, b 1989.

Hon Vere George (4 Kerrison Rd, SW11), b 1964: m 1991, Catharine Mary, da of Christopher Halliday, of Whitton Hall, Westbury, Shropshire, and has issue living, Harry Christopher, b 1992.

BROTHERS LIVING

Hon (Henry) Edward, b 1921; ed Eton, and Peterhouse, Camb; is Lieut RE; European War 1940-45 in Italy and NW Europe; High Sheriff W Sussex 1979-80: m 1951, Anne Philippa, el da of Col Sir Edward Courtenay Thomas Warner, 2nd Bt, DSO, MC, and has issue living, Thomas Edward, b 1964, — Sarah Kathleen, b 1958: m 1986, Jeremy M. Bray, yr son of Christopher Bray, of Southwold, Suffolk, and has issue living, Alice Frances b 1988, Emily Sarah b 1991, Susannah Nesta b 1993, — Jessica Frances, b 1960: m 1990, Hubert Alastair Speare-Cole, son of Cdr M. B. Speare-Cole, of Fulham SW, and has issue living, Antonia Margaret b 1991, Rebecca Anne b 1993. *Residence* – The Garden House, High Beeches Lane, Hand-cross, Sussex.

Rt Hon Robert Thomas, MC, b 1923; ed Eton, and Trin Coll, Camb; late Lt Coldstream Guards; MP for Wells (*C*) 1970-83, and for Somerton and Frome 1983-92; a Lord Commr of HM Treasury 1980-83; Vice Chamberlain HM Household 1983-86, Comptroller HM Household 1986-88; Govt Whip 1979-88; served 1941-45 War in NW Europe (wounded, MC 1944); PC 1992: m 1949, Mary Alice, JP, el da of late Col Sir Geoffrey Ronald Codrington, KCVO, CB, CMG, DSO, OBE, TD (*see* Codrington, Bt, cr 1721), and has issue living, Hugh Geoffrey Robert, b 1954; ed Eton, and Bristol Univ (BA); Lt-Col Coldm

Gds, served Gulf War 1991: *m* 1981, Alexandra Marie-Monique, el da of Anthony Eden, of Torberry House, W Harting, Sussex, and has issue living, Veryan John Hugh *b* 1987, Aldwyn George Hugh *b* 1989, — Dozmary Carolyn Claire, *b* 1951: *m* 1984, David B. Keller, son of late Col Blanton S. Keller, and has issue living, Nicholas Francis David *b* 1988, — Karenza Pamela Mary, *b* 1961. *Residence* – 14 Tite St, SW3. *Clubs* – Pratt's, and Royal Yacht Squadron.

SISTER LIVING

Hon Mary Kathleen, *b* 1926; is a JP for Cornwall; European War 1944-45 in WRNS: *m* 1948, Lieut-Com David Verney (*see* Verney, Bt *cr* 1946), who *d* 1992. *Residence* – Trevella, St Erme, Truro, Cornwall.

AUNT LIVING

Hon Kathleen Pamela Mary Corona, *b* 1902: *m* 1937, Maj Henry Sherek, Rifle Bde, who *d* 1967. *Residence* – 89A Route de Florissant, 1206 Geneva, Switzerland.

COLLATERAL BRANCHES LIVING

(In remainder to the Viscountcy only)

Grandchildren of late Lt-Col John Hugh Boscawen (infra):—
Issue of late Capt Spencer Boscawen, *b* 1887, *d* 1957: *m* 1919, Sydney Iris Kelly, who *d* 1982:—
John Roger, *b* 1922; late Flight Lieut Roy New Zealand Territorial Air Force; formerly with Seaport Operations Ltd; Auckland, New Zealand; SW Pacific 1943-5 (1939-45 star, Pacific star, two medals). *Residence* – Whitford Park Rd, Manurewa RD2, Auckland, NZ. —— Owen Tremayne, *b* 1925; *ed* Otahuhu Coll, and NZ Univ (BSc, BA, DipEd); Prin of Otahuhu Coll; 1939-45 War as LAC, RNZAF: *m* 1st, 1954 (*m diss* 1981), Beverley Rose Wheeler, of Papatoetoe, Auckland, NZ; 2ndly, 1982, Mrs Mary Joan Hilford, and has had issue (by 1st *m*), John Spencer, *b* 1956, — Leanne Kay, *b* 1960, *d* 1980. *Residence* – 232 Whitford Park Rd, Whitford, Auckland, NZ. —— Diana Margaret, *b* 1926: *m* 1950, Alan Frederick Arlington, of PO Box 9, Whitford, Auckland, NZ. —— Sydney Joy, *b* 1931: *m* 1959, Walter Flatz, of 104 Redoubt Rd, Manukau City, Auckland, NZ, and has issue. —— Vanda Vivian, *b* 1935: *m* 1958, Clement Henry Harris, of 172 Whitford Park Rd, Manurewa RD, Auckland, NZ.

Grandchildren of late Rev Hon John Townshend Boscawen, brother of 6th Viscount Falmouth:—
Issue of late Lieut-Col John Hugh Boscawen, *b* 1851, *d* 1937: *m* 1st, 1876, Katharine Isabel, who *d* 1884, da of late Rev John Williams Conway-Hughes, MA of Nydd Vicarage, near Leeds; 2ndly, 1886, Ellen, who *d* 1895, da of late Henry Parker, of Louth; 3rdly, 1896, Teresa Catherine, BA, who *d* 1949, da of C. Gerkens, of Lauder House Lauderdale Estate, Central Otago, New Zealand:—
(By 3rd wife) Edward Aroha, *b* 1895; European War 1916-18 in Palestine, as Lieut New Zealand Mounted Rifles and Camel Corps.

Issue of late Rev Arthur Townshend Boscawen, *b* 1862, *d* 1939: *m* 1902, Christian, who *d* 1940, el da of late Chapell Hodge, of Pounds, Plymouth:—
Violet Mary, *b* 1903: *m* 1st, 1929, Lieut-Com David Cameron Williams RN, who *d* 1931 (*see* Williams, Bt, *cr* 1866, colls); 2ndly, 1946, Humphrey Douglas Tyringham, who *d* 1986, and has issue (by 1st *m*) (*see* Williams, Bt, *cr* 1866, colls).

Granddaughters of late Maj John Perceval Townshend Boscawen , MBE (infra):—
Issue of late James Townshend Boscawen, *b* 1932, *d* 1992: *m* 1955, Deirdre Elsie Elizabeth (Boltachan House, Aberfeldy, Perthshire), yr da of late Frederick Henry (Derek) Curtis-Bennett, QC:—
Caroline Elizabeth, *b* 1959: *m* 1982, Angus G. Fleming, elder son Maj Richard Fleming, of Braemar Farm, Harare, Zimbabwe, and has issue living, James, *b* 1991, — George, *b* 1994, — Lucy, *b* 1984. —— Diana Mary, *b* 1962: *m* 1991, Nigel R. Fielder, son of Geoffrey Fielder, of Wells, Som, and has issue living, Edward Townsend Farrar, *b* 1994, — Georgina Louise, *b* 1992.

Grandson of late Townshend Evelyn Boscawen, 4th son of late Rev Hon John Townshend Boscawen (ante):—
Issue of late Maj John Perceval Townshend Boscawen, MBE, *b* 1906, *d* 1972: *m* 1931, Lady Mary Helen Alma Graham (who *m* 2ndly, 1975, Brig Leslie Colville Dunn, TD, DL, who *d* 1990) (8 Wheatfield Rd, Ayr), elder da of 6th Duke of Montrose:—
Simon John Evelyn (Jackson's Cottage, Rudgwick, Sussex), *b* 1936; *ed* Eton: *m* 1961, Judith Perdita Rosemary, only da of Arthur Gregory George Marshall, of Horseheath Lodge, Linton, Cambs, and has issue living, Alistair John Evelyn (18 Graham Rd, Wimbledon, SW19), *b* 1963: *m* 1990, Victoria A. M., da of late William Porter, of Queen Alexandra's Court, SW19, — David Simon Townshend, *b* 1965: *m* 1993, Clare Victoria, eldest da of John Edmund Kincaid Floyd (*see* Floyd, Bt), — John Michael Arthur, *b* 1969.

(In remainder to the Barony of Le Despencer only)

Descendants of late Rev Hon Miles John Stapleton, 3rd son of 22nd Baron Le Despencer (infra).
Descendants of late Rev Hon Francis Jarvis Stapleton (4th son of Sir Thomas Stapleton, 6th Bt and 22nd Baron Despencer), who *s* his father in the Baronetcy 1831.
See Stapleton, Bt.

PREDECESSORS – (1) HUGH Boscawen, PC, MP for Cornwall, Truro, and Penryn, Groom of the Bedchamber to Prince George, Comptroller of the Household, Warden of the Stanneries, and Vice-Treasurer of Ireland; *cr Baron Boscawen-Rose* and *Viscount Falmouth* (peerage of Great Britain) 1720; *d* 1734; *s* by his son (2) HUGH, 2nd Viscount, a Gen in the Army and Capt of the Yeomen of the Guard; *dsp* 1782; *s* by his nephew (3) GEORGE EVELYN, 3rd Viscount, son of Adm Hon Edward, 2nd son of 1st Viscount; Capt of Band of Gentlemen-at-Arms; *d* 1808; *s* by his son (4) EDWARD, 4th Viscount; *cr Earl of Falmouth* 1821; *d* 1841; *s* by his son (5) GEORGE HENRY, 2nd Earl; *d* 1852, when the earldom became extinct, and the viscountcy devolved upon his cousin (6) EVELYN, 6th Viscount, son of Rev Hon John Evelyn, 2nd son of 3rd Viscount, *b* 1819: *m* 1845, Mary Frances Elizabeth, in her own right Baroness Le Despencer; *d* 1889; *s* by his el son (7) EVELYN EDWARD THOMAS, KCVO, CB, 7th Viscount, *b* 1847; Maj-Gen in the Army; *s* as 24th Baron Le Despencer 1891 (*see* *infra*): *m* 1886, Hon Kathleen Douglas-Pennant, who *d* 1953, da of 2nd Baron Penrhyn; *d* 1918; *s* by his el son (8) EVELYN HUGH JOHN, 8th Viscount; *b* 1887; Alderman of London Co Council 1931-7: *m* 1915, Mary Margaret Desirée, CBE, who *d* 1985, da of late Hon Frederick George Lindley Meynell; *d* 1962; *s* by his 2nd son (9) GEORGE HUGH, 9th Viscount and present peer; also Baron Boscawen-Rose, and Baron Le Despencer.

*(1) HUGH Le Despencer, summoned to Parliament of England 1264 and constituted Justiciary of England; *k* at battle of Evesham 1265; *s* by his son (2) HUGH, 2nd Baron; summoned to Parliament 1283-1326; *cr Earl of Winchester* 1322; was banished the realm 1321; and being subsequently recalled was beheaded Oct 1326 without the formality of a trial; *s* by his son (3) HUGH, Knt, 3rd Baron; summoned to Parliament 1314-25, and *cr Earl of Gloucester*, was Lord Chamberlain to Edward II, and Warden of Forest of Dean; in Nov 1326 he was beheaded, and his honours forfeited; his el son (4) HUGH, commonly called Lord Glamorgan, was summoned to Parliament 1338-49; *dsp* 1349; *s* by his nephew (5) EDWARD, KG, 5th Baron; summoned to Parliament 1357-72; *d* 1375; *s* by his son (6) THOMAS, 6th Baron; summoned to Parliament 1396 and *cr Earl of*

Gloucester 1397; declared a traitor and beheaded 1400 when his honours were forfeited; his sister, **(7)** ISABEL, *m* 1st, Richard Beauchamp, Earl of Worcester and Baron Bergavenny, and 2ndly, Richard, 5th Earl of Warwick; by her 1st *m* she had **(8)** ELIZABETH, who having obtained a reversal of the attainder became Baroness Le Despencer: *m* Sir Edward Neville, KG, 6th son of Ralph, 1st Earl of Westmorland, who was summoned to Parliament, in right of his wife, as Baron Bergavenny 1450-72; on the death of **(9-11)** HENRY, 4th Baron Bergavenny, that barony passed to the heir male and the Barony of Le Despencer reverted to his da **(12)** MARY, wife of Sir Thomas Fane, knt, and in 1604 the barony was confirmed to her by letters patent; *d* 1626; *s* by her el son **(13-20)** FRANCIS, 12th Baron; *cr Baron Burghersh* and *Earl of Westmorland* (peerage of England) 1624; the Barony of Le Despencer was merged in the earldom until 1762 when it became abeyant between the sisters of the 7th Earl; in 1763 the abeyance was terminated in favour of **(21)** FRANCIS Dashwood, 21st Baron, who had in 1724, *s* by his father as 2nd Bt; was Lord-Lieut of Bucks and Groom of the Stole to HRH the Prince of Wales; *dsp* 1781, when the barony again became abeyant, and continued so until 1788 when it was terminated in favour of **(22)** THOMAS Stapleton, 22nd Baron, who had in 1781 *s* his father as 6th Bt; *d* 1831; when the baronetcy reverted to his 4th son, and the barony descended to his granddaughter **(23)** MARY FRANCES ELIZABETH (only child of Hon Thomas, el son of 22nd Baron, by Maria Wynne, da of Henry Bankes, of Kingston Hall, Dorset), *b* 1822: *m* 1845, the 6th Viscount Falmouth, who *d* 1889; *d* 1891; *s* by her el son **(24)** EVELYN EDWARD THOMAS, KCVO, CB, 7th Viscount Falmouth (ante).

FANSHAWE OF RICHMOND, BARON (Royle) (Life Baron 1983)

ANTHONY HENRY FANSHAWE ROYLE, KCMG, el son of late Sir Lancelot Carrington Royle, KBE; *b* 27 March 1927; *ed* Harrow, and RMA Sandhurst; PPS to Under-Sec of State for the Colonies 1960, to Sec of State for Air 1960-62, and to Min of Aviation 1962-64; Conservative Whip 1967-70; Parly Under-Sec of State for Foreign and Commonwealth Affairs 1970-74; Vice-Chm Conservative Parliamentary Organisation and Chm Conservative Internat Offices since 1979; Member Assembly of Council of Europe and WEU 1965-67; late Capt Life Guards, served in Germany, Egypt, Palestine and Transjordan 1945-48, and with 21st SAS (TA) 1948-51; MP for Richmond, Surrey (C) 1959-83; has Most Esteemed Family Order of the State of Brunei (1st class); *cr* KCMG 1974, and *Baron Fanshawe of Richmond*, of South Cerney, co Glos (Life Baron) 1983: *m* 1957, Shirley, da of late John Ramsay Worthington, and has issue.

Arms – Quarterly, 1st and 4th, per pale or and sable on a chevron per pale sable and or between three fleurs-de-lys as many leopards' heads counterchanged, *Royle*; 2nd, or a chevron between three fleurs-de-lys sable, *Fanshawe*; 3rd, checky azure and argent overall a cross gules, *Fanshawe augmentation* 1649. Crest – on a chapeau sable turned up erminois, a dragon's head erased or, breathing flames of fire proper. Supporters – Two dragons or, winged sable each breathing flames of fire proper and gorged with a collar checky argent and azure rimmed gules. Motto – Dux Vitae Ratio in Cruce Victoria (Leadership in Life Depends on Victory in the Cross).
Residences – 47 Cadogan Place, SW1; The Chapter Manor, South Cerney, Glos.
Clubs – White's, Pratt's, Brooks's.

DAUGHTERS LIVING

Hon Susannah Caroline Fanshawe, *b* 1960: *m* 1992, Guy C. Lester, yr son of Gerald Lester, of Rowledge, Hants.

Hon Lucinda Katherine Fanshawe, *b* 1962.

FARINGDON, BARON (Henderson) (Baron UK 1916, UK 1902)

Virtue alone ennobles

Sola · virtus · nobilitat

CHARLES MICHAEL HENDERSON, 3rd Baron, and 3rd Baronet; *b* 3 July 1937; *s* 1977; *ed* Eton, and Trin Coll Camb (BA): *m* 1959, Sarah Caroline, da of Maj John Marjoribanks Askew, Gren Gds (*see* D Sutherland), and has issue.

Arms – Or, three piles issuant from the sinister vert, on a chief ermine three torteaux. **Crest** – A hand holding a torteau charged with a mullet of six points argent. **Supporters** – *Dexter*, a chevalier armed at all points, holding in his dexter hand a lance with his lordship's pennon, bearing the motto "Sursum corda," all proper; *sinister*, a centaur drawing his bow proper.
Seat – Buscot Park, Faringdon, Oxon. *Residences* – Barnsley Park, Cirencester, Glos; 3A Clarendon Rd, W11.

SONS LIVING

Hon JAMES HAROLD, *b* 14 July 1961: *m* 1986, Lucinda Maria, yst da of late Desmond Hanson, of Knipton, nr Grantham, Lincs, and has issue living, George Alexander *b* 18 May 1992, — Annabel Rose, *b* 1989. *Residence* – 25 Edge St, W8 7PN.
Hon Thomas Alexander Gavin, *b* 1966.
Hon Angus George, *b* 1969.

DAUGHTER LIVING

Hon Susannah Jane, *b* 1963: *m* 1986, Aidan James Maitland-Robinson, only son of Joseph W. C. Maitland-Robinson, of Les Arbres, St Lawrence, Jersey, CI, and has issue living, Joseph Charles, *b* 1989, — Joanna Alice, *b* 1987, — Sarah Florence, *b* 1990, — a da, *b* 1992.

UNCLE LIVING (*Raised to the rank of a Baron's son* 1935)

Hon Roderic Harold Dalzell, *b* 1909; *ed* Eton, and Camb Univ (BA); Hon Attaché Diplo Ser 1933-39, Cypher Officer, Montevideo 1939-42, and Private Sec to HM's Ambassador, Buenos Aires 1943-45, Rome 1946, Stockholm 1947. *Residence* – Apt 103, 3800 Washington Rd, West Palm Beach, FL 33405, USA.

COLLATERAL BRANCHES LIVING

Grandchildren of late Hon Alec Puleston Henderson (infra):—
Issue of late Capt Ian Alexander Henderson, *b* 1918, *d* 1968: *m* 1st, (*m diss* 1955), Patience, da of late Lt-Col John Charles Brand, DSO, MC (*see* V Hampden, colls); 2ndly 1955, Sarah Veronica (Westmeads, Butlers Marston, Warwickshire), da of late Cosmo Stafford Crawley (Crawley-Boevey, Bt, colls):—
(By 1st *m*) Veronica, *b* 1946: *m* 1967, Oliver Alexander Guy Baring (*see* B Ashburton, colls). —— (By 2nd *m*) Shamus Alec, *b* 1958: *m* 1986, Camilla Carolyn, da of Robert Ashton Adams, of 139 Prospect Terr, North Hill, N6, and has issue living, James Archie, *b* 1988, — Laura Natasha, *b* 1990.
Issue of late Adrian Donald Henderson, *b* 1922, *d* 1994: *m* 1st, 1944 (*m diss* 1958), Marieluz, da of late Capt Robert Peel Dennistoun-Webster, DSC, RN, of Hurst Grange, nr Twyford; 2ndly, 1959, Mrs Angela Mary Oriana Harrington Pollen, who *d* 1990, eldest da of Maj Felix John Russi, MC, 5th Royal Inniskilling Dragoons:—
(By 1st wife) †Gavin Adrian Alexander, *b* 1944; *ed* Eton: *m* 1984, Juliet Victoria, yr da of late Maj Sir Mark Baring, KCVO (*see* E Cromer, colls), and *d* 1991, leaving issue, Violet Gweneth, *b* 1985. —— Mark Alistair, *b* 1946; *ed* The Oratory Sch, Reading. —— (By 2nd wife) Alexander Jonathan, *b* 1962: *m* 1987, Fiona Mary, yr da of David McLeod, of Park House, Old Hunstanton, Norfolk. —— Victoria Angela, *b* 1956: *m* 1979, John Jeremy Campbell Underwood, of 39 Herondale Av, SW18 3JN, and has issue living, James Michael Campbell, *b* 1981, — Toby George Campbell, *b* 1984. —— Fiona Mary, *b* (twin) 1962: *m* 1988, Antony William Dodd-Noble (*see* E Cork, 1980 Edn).

Issue (by 2nd *m*) of late Hon Alec Puleston Henderson, 2nd son of 1st Baron, *b* 1876, *d* 1931: *m* 1st, 1905, Henrietta Emily Cecil, who *d* 1913, da of late Capt Frederick Arthur Bertie (E Abingdon, colls); 2ndly, 1915, Gladys Rhoda, who *d* 1953, having *m* 2ndly, 1934, as his 2nd wife, Sir Murrough John Wilson, KBE, of Cliffe Hall, Darlington (B Inchiquin, colls), only child of late Major Donald Maclean:—
Susan Violet, *b* 1915: *m* 1st, 1936, Capt Mark Leslie Pilkington, MC, Life Guards, who was *ka* 1942; 2ndly, 1943, Fl Lt Charles Pretzlik, RAFVR, and has issue living (by 1st *m*), Simon Mark (Chalmer's Lodge, 29 Ballantrae Drive, Ayr KA7 2RG), *b* 1938: *m* 1963, Angela Mary Monica, da of late Lord Patrick Crichton-Stuart (*see* M Bute, colls), and has issue living, Rupert Charles *b* 1964, Mark Patrick *b* 1965, Jane Susan *b* 1966, Kate Sophie *b* 1970, — (by 2nd *m*) Nicholas Charles (44 Hornton St W8), *b* 1945: *m* 1970, Ursula Scheuring, and has issue living, Charles Oliver *b* 1971, Luke Nicholas *b* 1972, — Jacqueline Susan, *b* 1944: *m* 1970, Peter Raine, of 57 Chesilton Rd, SW6, and has issue living, Simon Patrick Wallace *b* 1973, Nancy Susan Wallace *b* 1971. *Residence* – Millers House, Isington, Hants.

Grandsons of late Lt-Col Hon Philip Henderson (infra):—
Issue of late David Hope Henderson, *b* 1912, *d* 1977: *m* 1st, 1935 (*m diss* 1938), Alice Reed Rawle, da of Antony Geyelin, of Philadelphia, USA; 2ndly, 1945, Eleanora Anderson (Achie Farm, New Galloway, Kirkcudbrightshire), da of Maj David Anderson Spence, VD, Black Watch, of Dunninald Mains, Montrose:—
(By 2nd *m*) Philip David Hope (21 Bowerdean St, SW6), *b* 1947; *ed* Eton, and RAC Cirencester; FRICS. —— Ian Ramsay Hope (20 Westbourne Park Rd, W2), *b* 1949; *ed* Eton, and Edinburgh Univ (MA, LLB); FCA: *m* 1978, Virginia Phyllis Theresa, yr da of Lt-Col John Edward Broke Freeman (*see* D Norfolk), and has issue living, Alexander Storm David Hope, *b* 1982, — Charles John Bernard Hope, *b* 1984, — George Ian Henry Hope, *b* 1987.

Issue of late Lieut-Col Hon Philip Henderson, 4th son of 1st Baron, *b* 1881, *d* 1939: *m* 1908, Rachel Magdaleine Mary, who *d* 1953, da of late James Charles Hope-Vere (M Linlithgow, colls):—
Ralph Alexander, *b* 1923; *ed* Eton, and Trin Coll, Camb; was 3rd Sec at British Embassy Lisbon 1945-46: *m* 1950, Myriam, who *d* 1987, da of late Adm A. de Souza e Silva, Brazilian Navy, of Rio de Janeiro, and has issue living, Ralph Peter, *b* 1951: *m* 1977, Maria Elisa, da of Luiz Pessoa de Luna, of Rio de Janeiro, — Charles James (twin), *b* 1951: *m* 1983 (*m diss* 1989), Alice, da of Herly Sampaio Vitor, — Lavinia Magdaleine Marie, *b* 1954: *m* 1975, Pedro Rabello Cotrim, and has issue living Nelson *b* 1977, Cecilia *b* 1978. *Residence* – Rua Santa Clara 47, Apt 1201, Copacabana, Rio de Janeiro, Brazil. *Club* – Boodle's.

Grandchildren of late Hon Arnold Henderson, OBE, 5th son of 1st Baron:—
Issue of late Flight-Lieut Roger Arnold Henderson, RAF Vol Reserve, *b* 1909, *d* on active ser 1941: *m* 1934, Judith Violet Christine (who *d* 1966, having *m* 2ndly, 1946, Robert Edward Manifold, of Wiridgil, Camperdown, Victoria, Australia), da of Edmund Thornley, of Gnotuk, Camperdown, Australia:—
David Arnold Thornley (Koorrnong, Tarcutta, NS Wales 2652), *b* 1937: *m* 1962, Sophie Jacqueline Fern Welsh, and has issue living, Roger David, *b* 1963, — Nicholas John Welsh, *b* 1964, — Anna Jacqueline Judith, *b* 1966. —— Davina Christina, *b* 1935: *m* 1st, 1961 (*m diss* 1974), Dr Peter Kaye Bryan; 2ndly, 1974, Richard Lawrence Baillieu, of Clondrisse, Flinders, Vic 3929, Aust, and has issue living (by 1st *m*), Roger Jon, *b* 1961, — Christopher Peter, *b* 1968, — Rebecca Alexandra, *b* 1963: *m* 1990, Nigel Richard Drake Trinca, of 341 Auburn Rd, Hawthorn, Vic 3122, 3rd son of Dr Geoffrey Francis Trinca, and has issue living, Lucy Elizabeth Davina *b* 1993.

Grandchildren of late Hon Eric Brand Butler-Henderson (infra):—
Issue of late Major Lionel Butler-Henderson, *b* 1911, *d* 1961: *m* 1936, Una, who *d* 1992, da of late Guy Fenwick:—
Guy (Beckfield House, Sandon, Buntingford, Herts), *b* 1948: *m* 1st, 1968 (*m diss* 1975), Glynis, da of Kenneth Bladon; 2ndly, 1977, Valerie, elder da of late Thomas Taylor, of Cheshire, and formerly wife of John Arthur Handforth, and has issue living (by 1st *m*) Timothy, *b* 1971, — Gemma, *b* 1975, — (by 2nd *m*) Charles Guy, *b* 1978. —— Jane, *b* 1938: *m* 1st, 1957 (*m diss* 1967), John Guy Mercer; 2ndly, 1968 (*m diss* 19—), George Frederick Hewitt; 3rdly, 1979, Albert George Etheridge, of Wheelers Stud, Peasenhall, Suffolk, and has issue living (by 1st *m*), Christopher John, *b* 1960, — Belinda, *b* 1958, — (by 2nd *m*) Antony George, *b* 1970, — (by 3rd *m*) Susan, *b* 1980.
Issue of late Patrick Butler-Henderson, RAFVR, *b* 1913, *d* 1979: *m* 1st, 1943 (*m diss* 1963), Kathleen Rebe Curtis (Section Officer late WAAF), da of late Lt-Col Herman Curtis Clarke, CBE, DSO; 2ndly, 1968, Mrs Pamela L. Godrich (Apple Tree Cottage, Quenington, Glos GL7 5BW):—
(By 1st *m*) Eric Alexander (The Old Thatch, Stanway, Cheltenham, Glos), *b* 1946: *m* 1st, 1970, Leslie Hallingan; 2ndly, 1993, Pauline Ann Lowe, and has issue living (by 1st *m*), Chad Stuart, *b* 1976, — Kerryn, *b* 1975. —— Christine, *b* 1944: *m* 1st, 1971, Maj Neil James Cameron Sutherland, Queen's Own Highlanders; 2ndly, 1981, Julian Russell Sturgis (*see* Borthwick, Bt, colls), and has issue living (by 1st *m*), Alasdair Patrick Cameron, *b* 1972, — Rachel Bridget, *b* 1974, — (by 2nd *m*) (*see* Borthwick, Bt, colls). —— Amalia Zoe, *b* 1945: *m* 1970, Capt Simon Brian Taylor, of Ardgilzean House, Elgin, Morayshire IV30 3XT (*see* Smith-Dodsworth, Bt).
Issue of late Hon Eric Brand BUTLER-HENDERSON, yst son of 1st Baron, *b* 1884, *d* 1953, having assumed by deed poll 1910 the additional surname of Butler: *m* 1910, Hon Sophia Isabelle (Zoe) Butler-Massey, who *d* 1977, da of 5th Baron Clarina:—
Edward, *b* 1916; *ed* Eton; late Lt-Col 99th (Royal Bucks Yeo) Field Regt, RA (TA): *m* 1939, Elizabeth Marjorie Dacres, who *d* 1988, only da of late Henry George Dacres Dixon (*see* E Yarborough, colls), 1985 Edn), and has issue living, Alan (The Ridings, Lot 1772 DD 221, Sha Ha Rd, Sai Kung, Hong Kong), *b* 1943: *m* 1st, 1964 (*m diss* 1975), Maria Cassy Ugena; 2ndly, 1975, Jacqueline Wright, and has issue living (by 1st *m*), David James *b* 1967, Elizabeth Cassy *b* 1965, (by 2nd *m*) Benjamin *b* 1976, Jason *b* 1982, — Penelope, *b* 1940: *m* 1962, Ian Alan Douglas Pilkington, of Warennes Wood, Mortimer, Berks, and has issue living, Rory Ian Douglas *b* 1968, Camilla Douglas *b* 1966: *m* 1990, Angus Charles Gordon Lennox, and has issue (*see* D Richmond and Gordon, colls), Sarah Douglas *b* 1973. *Residence* – 3 West Halkin St, SW1X 8JJ. —— Kenneth (11 Egerton Place, SW3 2EF), *b* 1929; *ed* Eton: *m* 1952, Phyllis Daphne, da of late Lt-Col Alfred Edward Cartmel, CIE, MM, of 29 Fanshawe St, Hertford, and has issue living, Julian, *b* 1956: *m* 1st, 1980 (*m diss* 1988), Bridget Anne, da of James Robert Patrick Sullivan, of Wyndrush, Stoke Orchard, nr Cheltenham, Glos; 2ndly, 1990, Adina, da of late Peter Smallwood, of Witney, Oxon, and has issue living (by 1st *m*), Oliver Stephen *b* 1982, — Serina, *b* 1953: *m* 1990, Arthur Eugene Burland, late Queen's Royal Irish Hus, and has issue living, Heloise Alice *b* 1991, — Clare, *b* 1954. —— Mary (Netherton Farmhouse, nr Andover, Hants), *b* 1915: *m* 1939, Algernon Desmond Wigan, MC, TD, who *d* 1989, late Maj 23rd Hussars, and has issue living, Desmond (Waresley Cottage, Waresley, Sandy, Beds), *b* 1941: *m* 1969, Anne Louise, da of Prof A. N. Black, and has issue living, Desmond Patrick Neil *b* 1970, Zoe Margaret *b* 1972, — Peter (Witches Cottage, Fletching, Uckfield, E Sussex TN22 3YD), *b* 1943: *m* 1973, Victoria Mary Riddle, and has issue living, Patrick Claude *b* 1974, Jane Lucy *b* 1976, — Christopher (42 Halsey St, SW3 2PT), *b* 1947: *m* 1st, 1970 (*m diss* 1986), Hon Caroline Kinnaird, da of 13th Lord Kinnaird; 2ndly, 1988, Christina Mary Yates, and has issue living, (by 1st *m*) George Rowan *b* 1977, Leila Willow *b* 1974, — Susan (Girt Cottage, Combe Martin, N Devon), *b* 1945: *m* 1985, David Lyons, and has issue living, Ellie *b* 1980. —— Doreen, *b* 1920: *m* 1st, 1939 (*m diss* 1961), John Gordon Wordsworth, OBE, late Lt-Col Suffolk Regt; 2ndly, 1962, Gp Capt William Digby Blackwood, OBE, DFC, RAF, who *d* 1993, of Garsdon House, Garsdon, Malmesbury, Wilts, and has issue living, (by 1st *m*) Antony Christopher Curwen (Little Brockholds Farm, Radwinter, Saffron Walden, Essex CB10 2TF), *b* 1940: *m* 1962, Rosamond Anne, eldest da of Maj John David Summers, and has issue living, Mark Edward Curwen (20 Redan St, W14 0AB) *b* 1965: *m* 1991, Eleanor Margaret, only da of late Ian Mapherson, of Broughton, Hants, (Katherine) Lucy *b* 1968: *m* 1993, Nicholas A. K. Brown, elder son of Michael Brown, of Edinburgh and Hong Kong, Evelyn Mary *b* 1972, — Michael (Marsh Court, Eldersfield, nr Gloucester GL19 4PN), *b* 1942: *m* 1966, Christine Stella Lear, and has issue living, Giles Patrick John *b* 1969, Zara Caroline *b* 1972, — Charles William, *b* 1946: *m* 1968, Maria Reyes Garcia Contillo, and has issue living Alexander Carlos *b* 1978, Cristina *b* 1970, Veronica *b* 1975, — Peter John (19 Thornhill Cres, N1), *b* 1949: *m* 1979, Joan, da of T. W. Hannigan, of Newcastle-upon-Tyne, and has issue living, Caroline Louise *b* 1980, Emma Harriet *b* 1984.

PREDECESSORS – (1) ALEXANDER Henderson, CH, son of late George Henderson, of Langholm, Dumfries; *b* 1850; MP for W Div of Staffordshire (LU) 1898-1906, and for St George, Hanover Square 1913-15; *cr* a *Baronet* 1902, and *Baron Faringdon*, of Buscot Park, co Berks (peerage of United Kingdom) 1916: *m* 1874, Jane Ellen, who *d* 1920, da of late Edward William Davis, *d* 1934; *s* by his grandson (2) ALEXANDER GAVIN (son of late Lieut-Col Hon Harold Greenwood Henderson, CVO, el son of 1st Baron, and late Lady Violet Charlotte Dalzell, da of 12th Earl of Carnwath (ext)), 2nd Baron, *b* 1902; a Member of LCC 1958-61 and an Alderman 1961-65: *m* 1927 (*m annulled* 1931), Hon Honor Chedworth Philipps, who *d* 1961, da of 1st Baron Kylsant (ext); *d* 1977; *s* by his nephew (3) CHARLES MICHAEL (son of late Lt-Col Hon Michael Thomas Henderson, 16th/5th Lancers, 2nd son of 1st Baron), 3rd Baron, and present peer.

FARNHAM BARON (Maxwell) (Baron I 1756, Bt NS 1627)

I am ready

BARRY OWEN SOMERSET MAXWELL, 12th Baron and 14th Baronet; *b* 7 July 1931; *s* 1957; *ed* Eton, and at Harvard Univ; late Lieut Roy Horse Guards; Chm of Brown, Shipley & Co, Merchant Bankers, EC2 1984-91 (Dir 1959-91); Chm Brown Shipley Holdings 1976-91; Chm Avon Rubber plc since 1978 (Dir since 1966); Chm Provident Mutual Life Assurance Assocn since 1989 (Dir since 1967); Pro Grand Master United Grand Lodge of England since 1991; Pres Tree Council since 1992: *m* 1959, Diana Marion, a Lady of the Bedchamber to HM since 1987, a JP, el da of late Nigel Eric Murray Gunnis, of Branden, Sissinghurst, Kent (*see* B Trevor, 1962 Edn), and has two adopted das.

Arms – Quarterly: 1st and 4th, argent, a saltire sable, on a chief of the first three pallets of the second, *Maxwell*, 2nd and 3rd, barry of six argent and gules, *Barry*. **Crest** – A buck's head erased proper. **Supporters** – Two bucks proper. *Residences* – Farnham, co Cavan; 11 Earls Court Gdns, SW5 0TD. *Clubs* – Boodle's, Kildare St, and University (Dublin).

ADOPTED DAUGHTERS LIVING

Harriet Virginia, *b* 1964: *m* 1990, James D. H. Naylor, eldest son of David Naylor, of Oakridge Lynch, Glos, and has issue living, Araminta Sheelin Huntly, *b* 1993.
Sophia Mary, *b* 1967.

BROTHER LIVING (*Raised to the rank of a Baron's son* 1959)

Hon SIMON KENLIS, *b* 12 Dec 1933; *ed* Eton; late Lieut 10th Roy Hussars: *m* 1964, Karol Anne, da of late Maj-Gen George Erroll Prior-Palmer, CB, DSO, and has issue living, Robin Somerset, *b* 1965: *m* 1993, Tessa M., da of David Shepherd, of Stansted, Essex, — Mark Erroll, *b* 1968, — Lorna Suzanna Katherine (twin) *b* 1968. *Residence* – The Dower House, Westcote, Kingham, Oxon.

SISTER LIVING (*Raised to the rank of a Baron's daughter* 1959)

Hon Sheelin Virginia (*Viscountess Knollys*), *b* 1937: *m* 1959, 3rd Viscount Knollys. *Residence* – The Bailiff's House, Bramerton Hall Farm, Norwich NR14 7DN.

AUNT LIVING (*Daughter of 11th Baron*)

Hon Verena Aileen (*Hon Lady Milbank*), *b* 1907: *m* 1st, 1934, Charles Lambart Crawley, who *d* 1935; 2ndly, 1938, as his 2nd wife, Maj Sir Mark Vane Milbank, 4th Bt, KCVO, MC, who *d* 1984. *Residence* – Barningham Park, Richmond, N Yorks.

COLLATERAL BRANCH LIVING

Issue of late Vice-Adm Hon Sir Denis Crichton Maxwell, KCB, CBE, yst son of 10th Baron, *b* 1892, *d* 1970: *m* 1923, Theodora Mary, who *d* 1986, da of Arthur Hickling, of Wing Old Hall, Rutland:—
Elizabeth Crichton, *b* 1926: *m* 1953 (*m diss* 19—), Ivor Mabberley, of Wanborough, Wilts.

PREDECESSORS – (1) JOHN MAXWELL, MP for co Cavan 1727-56; *cr Baron Farnham*, of Farnham, co Cavan (peerage of Ireland) 1756; *d* 1759; *s* by his el son (2) ROBERT, 2nd Baron; *cr Viscount Farnham* (peerage of Ireland) 1761, and *Earl of Farnham* (peerage of Ireland) 1763; *dsp* when the Viscountcy and Earldom expired, and the Barony reverted to his brother (3) BARRY, 3rd Baron; *cr Viscount Farnham* (peerage of Ireland) 1781, and *Earl of Farnham* (peerage of Ireland) 1785; *d* 1800; *s* by his son (4) JOHN JAMES, 2nd Earl; *dsp* 1823, when the Viscountcy and Earldom expired, and the Barony devolved upon his kinsman (5) JOHN MAXWELL BARRY, 5th Baron el son of the Most Rev Hon Henry, DD, PC, Lord Bishop of Meath, 3rd son of 1st Baron; *dsp* 1838; *s* by his brother (6) *Rev* HENRY, 6th Baron: *m* 1798, Lady Ann Butler, da of 2nd Earl of Carrick; *d* 1838; *s* by his el son (7) HENRY, KP, 7th Baron; successively MP for Cavan, and a Representative Peer; killed with his wife in a dreadful accident on NW Railway at Abergele, 20 Aug 1868; *s* by his brother (8) SOMERSET RICHARD, 8th Baron; *b* 1803; was MP for Cavan (C) 1838-40; *dsp* 1884; *s* by his brother (9) JAMES PIERCE, 9th Baron, *b* 1813; MP for Cavan 1843-65; *s* by his kinsman as 11th *Baronet* (*cr* 1627) of Calderwood 1885; *dsp* 1896; *s* by his nephew (10) SOMERSET HENRY (son of late Hon Richard Maxwell, 7th son of 6th Baron), 10th Baron; *b* 1849; Lieut of co Cavan, and a Representative Peer for Ireland: *m* 1875, Lady Florence Jane Taylour, who *d* 1907, da of 3rd Marquess of Headfort: *d* 1900; *s* by his son (11) ARTHUR KENLIS, DSO, 11th Baron; *b* 1879; Lieut-Col (ret) late N Irish Horse, and a Representative Peer: *m* 1903, Aileen Selina, who *d* 1964, da of late Charles Purdon Coote (*see* Coote, Bt, colls); *d* 1957; *s* by his grandson (12) BARRY OWEN SOMERSET (el son of late Lieut-Col Hon Somerset Arthur Maxwell, MP), 12th Baron and present peer.

FARRER, BARONY OF (Farrer) (Extinct 1964)

WIDOW LIVING OF FOURTH BARON

Hon KATHARINE (*Hon Lady Lyell*), da of 1st Viscount Runciman of Doxford: *m* 1st, 1931, the 4th Baron, who *d* 1954; 2ndly, 1955, Hon Mr Justice (Sir Maurice Legat) Lyell, who *d* 1975. *Residence* – Puddephat's Farm, Markyate, Herts.

FAUCONBERG AND CONYERS, BARONIES OF (Pelham) (Baron E 1283 and 1509) (Abeyant 1948)

SACKVILLE GEORGE PELHAM, 5th Earl of Yarborough, 8th Baron Fauconberg, and 14th Baron Conyers; *d* 1948, when the Baronies fell into abeyance (see infra).

DAUGHTERS LIVING OF EIGHTH BARON FAUCONBERG AND FOURTEENTH BARON CONYERS (FIFTH EARL OF YARBOROUGH) (*Co-heiresses to the Baronies*)

Lady DIANA MARY (c/o Zimbank, Box 2270, Harare, Zimbabwe), *b* 5 July 1920; SRN: *m* 1952, Robert Miller, who *d* as the result of a motor accident in Harare 1990, and has issue living, Marcia Anne LYCETT, *b* 1954; adopted by Maj Michael H. L. Lycett (infra) (and renamed Anthea Theresa), whose surname she assumed, but retains right of succession to the Baronies, — Beatrix Diana, *b* 1955: *m* 1991, Simon William Jones Armstrong (Box 49, Gilgil, Kenya), only son of late Christopher Wyborne Armstrong, OBE, of Kwetu Farm, Gilgil, Kenya.

Lady (JUNE) WENDY, *b* 6 June 1922; late 3rd Officer WRNS; Joint Master Tynedale Hunt 1974-77: *m* 1959, Maj Michael Hildesley Lycett Lycett, CBE, late Royal Scots Greys, Joint Master Tynedale Hunt 1975-77. *Residence* – West Grange, Scots Gap, Morpeth, Northumberland NE69 4EQ.

COLLATERAL BRANCHES LIVING

Grandchildren of late Charlotte Katherine Marcia Weld-Blundell, daughter of late Hon Charles Pierrepont D'Arcy Lane-Fox, brother of 15th Baron Darcy de Knayth and great-grandson of Amelia, Baroness Conyers and *de jure* Baroness Darcy de Knayth:—

Issue of late Richard Shireburn Weld-Blundell, *b* 1887, *d* 1916: *m* 1915, Mary Angela (who *d* 1976; she *m* 2ndly, 1927, Alfred Noyes, CBE, who *d* 1958), da of late Capt Jasper Graham Mayne, CBE, Ch Constable of E Suffolk;—

Agnes Mary (*Lady Grey*), *b* 1915: *m* 1936, Sir Paul Francis Grey, KCMG (*see* E Grey, colls). *Residence* – Hill House, Farley, Westerham, Kent.

Issue of late Alice Mary, *b* 1890, *d* 1947: *m* 1923, John Joseph Humphrey Weld, of Birkdale, Lancs, who *d* 1960, having assumed by Royal licence 1923, the additional surname of Blundell:—

Charles Joseph Ignatius WELD-BLUNDELL (Pinehurst, Tongland, Kirkcudbright DG6 4NA), *b* 1928; *ed* Stonyhurst; High Sheriff Lancs 1989: *m* 1951, Veronica Mary, da of late Alfred Noyes, CBE (ante), and has issue living, John Joseph Thomas, *b* 1955; *ed* Stonyhurst, — Peter Alfred, *b* 1956; *ed* Stonyhurst, — George Edric (Loud Mythom, Little Bowland Rd, Chipping, nr Preston, Lancs PR3 2TS), *b* 1960; *ed* Ampleforth, and Liverpool Univ (BSc): *m* 1985, Buddug L., da of G. Selwyn-Lloyd, of Grasmere, Linden Drive, Prestatyn, and has issue living, Joseph Charles *b* 1993, Laura Sian *b* 1987, Philippa Kate *b* 1989, — Mary Alice, *b* 1952, — Lucy Ann, *b* 1953, — Diana Celia, *b* 1958: *m* 1990, Charles E. Hothersall, 2nd son of H. E. Hothersall, of 7 Marlborough Drive, Fulwood, Preston, — Fiona Ann, *b* 1962: *m* 1991, Robert Armstrong, of 20 Balmoral Court, 43-45 Clarence Parade, Southsea, Hants, son of Warwick Armstrong, of Southsea, — Elizabeth, *b* 1969. —— Theresa Mary Katharine (10 Archery Steps, St George's Fields, W2 2YF), *b* 1926; Dame of Honour and Devotion, Sovereign Mil Order of Malta. —— Mary Geraldine, *b* 1929: *m* 1957, Antony St John Davies, of Primrose Cottage, 31 Fife Rd, E Sheen, SW14, and has issue living, Benedict Antony John Whitcliffe, *b* 1960, — Simon, *b* 1963, — Hermione Anne, *b* 1958. —— Anne Mary, *b* 1933: *m* 1960, Thomas Frederick de Pentheny-O'Kelly, of Place, Ashburton, Devon, and has issue living, Edmund Thomas, *b* 1962, — Maureen Louise, *b* 1961, — Carmel Anne, *b* 1964, — Mary Clare, *b* 1967.

PREDECESSORS – (1) Walter de Fauconberg, son of Walter de Fauconberg of Ryse; summoned to Parliament by various writs, the earliest being in 1283, signed the famous letter of the Barons to the Pope in 1301; *d* 1304; *s* by his son (2) WALTER; summoned to Parliament 1303-1318; *d* 1318; *s* by his son (3) JOHN; *d* 1349; *s* by his son (4) WALTER; *d* 1362; *s* by his son (5) THOMAS; *d* leaving an only da and heiress (6) JOAN, *suo jure* Baroness Fauconberg: *m* Sir William Nevill, yr son of the Earl of Westmorland, who was summoned to Parliament and sat therein as *Lord Fauconberg* in right of his wife; distinguished himself greatly in the French Wars and at the siege of Orleans; KG and Adm of England; *cr Earl of Kent* 1461; *d* without male issue in 1463, when the Earldom became extinct; at the death of his wife (1491) the Barony of Fauconberg fell into abeyance between his da and co-heirs, and so remained until 1903, when it was determined by Letters Patent in favour of (7) MARCIA AMELIA MARY, OBE, Countess of Yarborough, she and her sister the Countess of Powis (in whose favour the Barony of Darcy de Knayth was at the same time determined) being the sole heirs of Alice, yr da and co-heiress of Joan, Lady Fauconberg and Countess of Kent, which Alice *m* Sir John Conyers of Hornby, and had issue William, 1st Baron Conyers (see *infra); *b* 1863: *m* 1886, 4th Earl of Yarborough; *d* 1926; *s* by her yr son (8) SACKVILLE GEORGE, 8th Baron Fauconberg, 14th Baron Conyers, and 5th Earl of Yarborough; *b* 1888; Lieut-Col Comdg Notts Yeo (Sherwood Rangers); European War 1914-19 (MC), European War 1939-45; *m* 1919, Nancye, da of late Alfred Brocklehurst; *d* 1948, when he was *s* in the Earldom by his brother and the Baronies of Fauconberg and Conyers fell into abeyance between his two das (see ante).

*(1) Sir WILLIAM Conyers; served at Flodden Field; summoned to the Parliament of England as *Baron Conyers* 1509; *d* 1524; *s* by his son (2) CHRISTOPHER, 2nd Baron; *d* 1538; *s* by his son (3) JOHN, 3rd Baron; *d* without male issue, when the title went into abeyance between his three daughters; the 2nd da, Elizabeth, *m* Thomas, 2nd son of Sir Arthur D'Arcy, 2nd son of Thomas, Baron D'Arcy, who was attainted and beheaded 1538, and had with other issue (4) CONYERS, 4th Baron, in whose favour the abeyance in the Baronies of Darcy de Knayth (*see* Bs Darcy de Knayth) and Conyers were determined by letters patent 1641; *d* 1653; *s* by his son (5) CONYERS, 5th Baron; *cr* 1682 *Earl of Holderness*; *d* 1689; *s* by his son (6) CONYERS, 2nd Earl; *d* 1692; *s* by his grandson (7) ROBERT, 3rd Earl; *d* 1722; *s* by his son (8) ROBERT, 4th Earl; *d* 1778, when the Earldom became extinct, and the Barony of Conyers reverted to his daughter (9) AMELIA, wife of 5th Duke of Leeds; *d* 1784; *s* by her son (10) GEORGE WILLIAM FREDERICK, 10th Baron Conyers and 6th Duke of Leeds; *d* 1838; *s* by his son (11) FRANCIS GODOLPHIN, 11th Baron and 7th Duke; *d* 1859; *s* by his nephew (12) SACKVILLE GEORGE, 12th Baron (son of Sackville Walter Lane-Fox, MP), *b* 1827: *m* 1860, Mary, who *d* 1921, el da of Reginald Curteis, of Windmill Hill, Sussex; *d* 1888, when the title remained in abeyance between his two das, until in 1892 the abeyance was terminated in favour of his el da (13) MARCIA AMELIA MARY, OBE, Countess of Yarborough (ante).

FAULKNER OF DOWNPATRICK, BARONY OF (Faulkner) (Extinct 1977)

SONS LIVING OF LIFE BARON

Hon (Brian) David Alexander, *b* 1951: *m* 1982, Belinda Gail, el da of James Elliott Wilson, OBE, DL, of White Lodge, Boardmills, co Down, and has issue, two sons, one da.

Hon (James) Michael Sewell, *b* 1956; *ed* Glenalmond, and Aberdeen Univ (LLB): *m* 1990, Lynn, da of John McGregor, of Anstruther, Fife.

DAUGHTER LIVING OF LIFE BARON

Hon Lucy Claire, *b* 1954.

FEATHER, BARONY OF (Feather) (Extinct 1976)

SON LIVING OF LIFE BARON

Hon Harry Alexander (The Mill, Sudborough, Northants), *b* 1938; Master Mariner: *m* 1972, Patricia Lesley, JP, da of Gilbert Victor Green.

DAUGHTER LIVING OF LIFE BARON

Hon Patricia Margaret (24 Wheathampstead Rd, Harpenden, Herts), *b* 1934: *m* 1957, Stanley Lawrence Palmer.

Feilding, Viscount; son of Earl of Denbigh and Desmond.

Fermanagh, Baron, title of Earl Erne on Roll of HL.

FERMOY, BARON (Roche) (Baron I 1856)

MON·DIEU·EST·MA·ROCHE

My God is my rock

(PATRICK) MAURICE BURKE ROCHE, 6th Baron; *b* 11 Oct 1967; *s* 1984; *ed* Eton; a Page of Honour to HM Queen Elizabeth The Queen Mother 1982-84; Blues and Royals 1987.

Arms – Gules, three roach naiant in pale argent, a canton of the last. **Crest** – Standing on a rock proper, an osprey, or sea eagle, with wings displayed argent, collared gemelle azure, membered or, holding a roach in its claw. **Supporters** – *Dexter*, a lion erminois, gorged with a collar sable, therefrom pendent an escutcheon gules, charged with three roach naiant in pale argent; *sinister*, a greyhound pean, gorged with a collar or, therefrom pendent an escutcheon per pale of the second and gules, charged with three lions passant guardant in pale counterchanged.
Residences – Axford House, nr Marlborough, Wilts; 21 Paultons House, Paultons Square, SW3.

BROTHER LIVING

Hon (EDMUND) HUGH BURKE, *b* 5 Feb 1972.

SISTER LIVING

Hon Frances Caroline Burke, *b* 1965: *m* 1990, Peter Hugh Charles Stanley (*see* E Derby, colls). *Residence* – New England Stud, Newmarket, Suffolk.

AUNTS LIVING (*Daughters of 4th Baron*)

Hon Mary Cynthia Burke ROCHE, *b* 1934; resumed her maiden surname 1987: *m* 1st, 1954 (*m diss* 1966), Hon Anthony George Berry (later Hon Sir Anthony Berry), who *d* 1984 (*see* V Kemsley); 2ndly, 1973 (*m diss* 1980), Denis Roche Geoghegan; 3rdly, 1981 (*m diss* 1989), Michael Robert Fearon Gunningham. *Residence* – 12M Warwick Sq, SW1V 2AA.
Hon Frances Ruth Burke, *b* 1936: *m* 1st, 1954 (*m diss* 1969), Edward John, Viscount Althorp, LVO (later 8th Earl Spencer), who *d* 1992; 2ndly, 1969 (*m diss* 1990), Peter Shand Kydd. *Residence* – Ardencaple, Isle of Seil, by Oban, Argyll.

WIDOW LIVING OF FIFTH BARON

LAVINIA FRANCES ELIZABETH (*Baroness Fermoy*), only da of late Capt John Pitman, of Foxley House, Malmesbury: *m* 1964, the 5th Baron, who *d* 1984. *Residence* – Axford House, nr Marlborough, Wilts.

COLLATERAL BRANCHES LIVING

Grandson of late Hon Alexis Charles Burke Roche, 3rd son of 1st Baron:—
Issue of late Capt George Denis Burke Roche, MC, *b* 1893, *d* 1954: *m* 1921, Aletta S, who *d* 1982, da of M. M. Venter, of Comodoro, Rivadavia, Argentine, and Cape Province:—
Alexis Martin Burke, *b* 1922; Capt RE: *m* 1st, 1945 (*m diss* 1974), Leonora Alice Hudson, who *d* 1985; 2ndly, 1974, Vera Haydee, da of Luis Uffenheimer, and has issue living (by 1st *m*), Rosalie Anne Burke, *b* 1945, — Caroline Jean Burke, *b* 1950, — Christine Lorna Burke, *b* 1956, — (by 2nd *m*) Peter Martin Burke, *b* 1974, — Vanessa Caroline Burke, *b* 1976. *Residence* – Rosales 2571, Olivos, Buenos Aires, Argentina.

Granddaughter of late Col Hon Ulick De Rupé Burke Roche, CB, 4th son of 1st Baron:—
Issue of late Maj Ulick Edmund Burke Roche, S Wales Borderers (24th/41st Foot), *b* 1906, *d* 1990: *m* 1949, Primrose Eda (Ynysfor, Penrhyndeudraeth, Merionethshire), da of Sir John Karslake Thomas Buchan-Hepburn, 5th Bt:—
Rosemary Evelyn Sybil Burke, *b* 1951: *m* 1982 (*m diss* 1989), Michael Menelaou, and has issue living, Alexander Demitri Burke, *b* 1983, — Nicholas Edmund Burke, *b* 1986.

PREDECESSORS – (1) Edmund Burke Roche, *b* 1815; MP for co Cork (*L*) 1837-55, and for Marylebone 1859-65, and Lord Lieut for co Cork; *cr Baron Fermoy* (peerage of Ireland) 1856: *m* 1848, Elizabeth Caroline, who *d* 1897, da of James B. Boothby, Esq, of Twyford Abbey, near Acton; *d* 1874; *s* by his son (2) Edward Fitz Edmund Burke, 2nd Baron, *b* 1850; *m* 1877, Hon Cecilia O'Grady, who *d* 1919, da of 3rd Viscount Guillamore; *d* 1920; *s* by his brother (3) James Boothby Burke, 3rd Baron, *b* 1852: *m* 1880 (*m diss* 1891, on her petition to Superior Court, Wilmington, Delaware, USA) Frances, who *d* 1947, da of Frank Work, of New York; *d* 1920; *s* by his el son (4) Edmund Maurice, 4th Baron; *b* 1885; sat as MP for King's Lynn Div of Norfolk (*U*) 1924-35, and 1943-5, and was Mayor of King's Lynn 1931-32: *m* 1931, Ruth Sylvia, DCVO, OBE, who *d* 1993, da of late Col William Smith Gill, CB, VD, of Dalhebity, Bieldside, Aberdeenshire; *d* 1955; *s* by his only son (5) Edmund James Burke, 5th Baron; *b* 1939; Capt Royal Horse Guards; Dist Councillor (Hungerford), Newbury Dist Council 1975-79, and Mayor of Hungerford 1982-83: *m* 1964, Lavinia Frances Elizabeth, only da of late Capt John Pitman, of Foxley House, Malmesbury; *d* 1984; *s* by his elder son (6) (Patrick) Maurice Burke, 6th Baron and present peer.

Ferrard, Viscount, see Viscount Massereene and Ferrard.

FERRERS, EARL (Shirley) (Earl GB 1711, Bt E 1611)

Honour is the reward of virtue

Robert Washington Shirley, PC, 13th Earl, and 19th Baronet; *b* 8 June 1929; *s* 1954: *ed* Winchester, and Magdalene Coll, Camb (MA Agriculture); late Lieut Coldstream Guards; Malaya 1950; a Lord-in-Waiting to HM 1962-64, and again 1971-74; DL Norfolk 1983; Parl Sec Min of Agric, Fisheries and Food Jan to March 1974; Joint Dep Leader of Opposition, House of Lords 1976-79 and since 1988, Min of State, Min of Agric, Fisheries and Food 1979-83; Dep Leader of House of Lords 1979-83, and since 1988; Min of State, Home Office since 1988; Member of Armitage Cttee on Political Activity of Civil Servants 1976; Trustee of Trustee Savings Bank of Eastern England 1975-79 (Chm 1977-79); a Dir of Central Trustee Savings Bank Ltd 1978-79; Dir of Norwich Union Insurance Group 1975-79 and 1983-88; a Member of Council, Hurstpierpoint Coll 1959-68; Dir Chatham Dockyard Historic Trust 1984-88; Chm R Commn on Historical Monuments (England) 1984-88; *cr* PC 1982: *m* 1951, Annabel Mary, da of late Brig William Greenwood Carr, CVO, DSO, of Ditchingham Hall, Suffolk, and has issue.

Arms – Paly of six or and azure, a quarter ermine. **Crest** – A Saracen's head in profile, couped at the neck, proper, wreathed round the temples or and azure. **Supporters** – *Dexter*, a talbot ermine, the ears gules, and ducally gorged or; *sinister*, a reindeer gules, attired and ducally gorged or, billettée and charged on the shoulder with a horse-shoe argent.
Seat – Shirley, Brailsford, Derbyshire. *Residence* – Ditchingham Hall, Bungay, Suffolk.
Club – Beefsteak.

SONS LIVING

Robert William Saswalo (*Viscount Tamworth*) (The Old Vicarage, Shirley, Ashbourne, Derbys DE6 3AZ; *Club* – Boodles), *b* 29 Dec 1952; *ed* Ampleforth; FCA; Chartered Accountant 1982-86, Group Auditor and Senior Treasury Analyst with BICC plc 1986-88, Financial Controller Viking Property Group Ltd 1987-92 (Dir 1987), Dir Norseman Holdings Ltd and assoc Cos 1987-92: *m* 1980, Susannah Mary, yst da of late Charles Edward William Sheepshanks, of Arthington Hall, Otley, W Yorks, and has issue:

> Sons Living: *Hon* William Robert Charles, *b* 10 Dec 1984.
> *Hon* Frederick James Walter, *b* 1990.
> Daughter Living: *Hon* Hermione Mary Annabel, *b* 1982.

Hon Andrew John Carr Sewallis (Collycroft House, Clifton, Ashbourne, Derbys DE6 2GN), *b* 1965; *ed* Ampleforth; ARICS: *m* 1992, Tamara R., da of Donald Halfpenny, of Sutton in Ashfield, Notts.

DAUGHTERS LIVING

Lady Angela Mary, *b* 1954: *m* 1975, Jonathan Felix Hugh Ellis, FCA (*see* By Hirst), of The Old Rectory, Thurning, Dereham, Norfolk NR20 5QX, and has issue living, Charles William Donald, *b* 1979, — Louise Mary, *b* 1977, — Georgina Hermione, *b* 1981.
Lady Sallyanne Margaret, *b* 1957.
Lady Selina Clare, *b* 1958: *m* 1989, Antoine Bertrand Robert Chenevière, of 13 Cottesmore Gdns, W8 5PR, yr son of Bertrand Chenevière, of Geneva, and has issue living, Francesca Mary, *b* 1990, — Tatiana Annabel Haritina, *b* 1992.

SISTERS LIVING

Lady Elizabeth Hermione, *b* 1923; formerly with WRNS: *m* 1959, John Fownes Luttrell, of Waterwynch, Itchen Abbas, nr Winchester (Ogilvy-Wedderburn, Bt), who *d* 1985, and has issue living, Robert Hugh Courtenay, *b* 1961: *m* 1991, Pauline Margaret Cecilia, da of John Roddy, of Sydney, Australia, and has issue living, Madeleine Louise Fownes *b* 1992.
Lady Jane Penelope Justice, *b* 1925: *m* 1944, Rev Canon John Maurice Robson, TD, Canon Emeritus of Derby Cathedral (Hon Canon Derby Cathedral 1975), who *d* 1989, of Bristow's Close, Southrop, Lechlade, Glos, and has issue living, David Edward Shirley (Slip of Wood, Cranleigh, Surrey GU6 7BE), *b* 1947: *m* 1st, 1973 (*m diss* 1976), Carol Diana, yr da of late

Wilfrid Durose; 2ndly, 1980, Josephine Ann Charlotte, da of Richard Manwaring-White, and has issue living (by 2nd *m*), Oliver Charles Richard *b* 1986, Jonathan Hugo David *b* 1990, — Julia Phillida Shirley, *b* 1953: *m* 1972, James Douglas Jermain, of 7 Park Rd, Winchester, Hants SO22 6AA.

COLLATERAL BRANCHES LIVING

Grandchildren of late Sewallis Evelyn Shirley, son of Evelyn Philip Shirley, son of Evelyn John Shirley, MP, DCL, son of Evelyn Shirley (infra):—
Issue of late Lieut-Col Evelyn Charles Shirley, *b* 1889, *d* 1956: *m* 1921, Kathleen Mary Phillis, who *d* 1977, da of late Lieut-Col George Ambrose Cardew, CMG, DSO—
John Evelyn, *b* 1922; *ed* Eton; Major (ret) King's Roy Rifle Corps; 1939-45 War: *m* 1952, Judith Margaret, yr da of Sir William Francis Stratford Dugdale, 1st Bt (*cr* 1936), and has issue living, Philip Evelyn, *b* 1955: *m* 1989, Augusta M. R., elder da of Hugo Southern, of Yew Trees, Bratton, Wilts, and has issue living, Evelyn Robert *b* 1990, Horatio John *b* 1993, — Hugh Sewallis, *b* 1961, — Emily Margaret (*Hon Mrs Robin Grimston*), *b* 1957: *m* 1984, Hon Robert John Sylvester Grimston, elder son of 2nd Baron Grimston of Westbury.
Seats – Ettington Park, Stratford-on-Avon; Lough Fea, Carrickmacross, co Monaghan. *Residence* – Ormly Hall, Ramsey, Isle of Man. —— Mary Louisa Phyllis, *b* 1931.

Granddaughter of late Rev William Shirley, son of late Rev Arthur George Sewallis Shirley, son of late Evelyn Shirley, son of late Hon George Shirley, 5th surviving son of 1st Earl:—
Issue of late Col Sewallis Robert Shirley, MC, *b* 1885, *d* 1969: *m* 1st, 1917, Hilda Grace, da of Harry Gavin Young, formerly Indian Army; 2ndly, 1940, Edna Blodwen (7 Minster House, Abbey Park Rd, Beckenham, Kent), da of Albert William Laking:—
(By 1st *m*) Eileen Diana, *b* 1922: *m* 1946, Malcolm Young, of Whyr Farm, Winterbourne Bassett, Swindon, Wilts, and has issue living, Peter Malcolm Gavin (22 Belmont Rd, Mosman, NSW 2088, Australia), *b* 1947: *m* 1989, Anne Elizabeth Sadleir, — Richard William Shirley (6 Nassau Rd, Barnes, SW13), *b* 1949: *m* 1973, Deborah Anne Greene French, and has issue living, James Malcolm Sewallis *b* 1985, Juliet Anne Verity *b* 1978, Stefanie Clare Elizabeth *b* 1980.

PREDECESSORS – (1) George Shirley; *cr* a *Baronet* 1611; *d* 1622; *s* by his son (2) Sir Henry, 2nd Bt: *m* Lady Dorothy, da of Robert Devereux, 2nd Earl of Essex (*cr* 1572), who became on the death of her brother, Robert, 3rd and last Earl, yst co-heir to the Baronies of Ferrers of Chartley, and Bourchier; *d* 1632; *s* by his el son (3) Sir Charles, 3rd Bt; *d* unmarried 1646; *s* by his brother (4) Sir Robert, 4th Bt; *d* a prisoner in the Tower, where he had been committed by Cromwell; *s* by his el son (5) Sir Seymour, 5th Bt; *s* at birth by his posthumous son (6) Robert, 6th Bt; *d* an infant; *s* by his uncle (7) Sir Robert, 7th Bt, in whose favour, in 1677, Charles II terminated the abeyance of one of the peerages of which his grandmother was co-heir (see ante), he thus became *Baron Ferrers of Chartley* (peerage of England) 1299 (see infra *), while his right to the Barony of Bourchier, *cr* 1342, was overlooked; *cr* *Viscount Tamworth*, and *Earl Ferrers* (peerage of Great Britain) 1711; *d* 1717, when the Barony of Ferrers of Chartley, reverted to his granddau (see infra *), and the viscountcy and earldom passed to his 2nd son (8) Washington, 2nd Earl; Lord-Lieut of Staffordshire; *dsp*; *s* by his brother (9) Henry, 3rd Earl; *d* unmarried 1745; *s* by his nephew (10) Laurence, 4th Earl, son of Hon Laurence, 3rd surviving son of 1st Earl; having in a paroxysm of rage killed Mr Johnson, his land-steward, was tried and condemned for murder, and executed at Tyburn 5 May 1760; *s* by his brother (11) Washington, 5th Earl; Vice-Adm; *dsp* 1778; *s* by his brother (12) Robert, 6th Earl; *d* 1787; *s* by his son (13) Robert, 7th Earl; *dsp* 1827; *s* by his brother (14) Washington, 8th Earl; *d* 1842: *s* by his grandson (15) Washington Sewallis, 9th Earl, son of Robert William, Viscount Tamworth, el son of 8th Earl: *m* 1844, Lady Augusta Annabella Chichester, who *d* 1914, da of the 4th Marquess of Donegall; *d* 1859; *s* by his son (16) Sewallis Edward, 10th Earl, *b* 1847: *m* 1885, Lady Ina Maude White, who *d* 1907, da of 3rd Earl of Bantry (*ext*); *d* 1912; *s* by his kinsman (17) Walter Knight (great-great grandson of Rev Hon Walter Shirley, brother of 4th, 5th and 6th Earls), 11th Earl, *b* 1864: *m* 1890, Mary Jane, who *d* 1944, da of late Robert Moon, Bar-at-law, of 10 Prince's Gardens, SW; *d* 1937; *s* by his son (18) Robert Walter, 12th Earl; *b* 1894: *m* 1922, Hermione Justice, who *d* 1969, da of late A. Noel Morley; *d* 1954: *s* by his only son (19) Robert Washington, 13th Earl and present peer; also Viscount Tamworth.
*(1) John de Ferrers, only son of Robert de Ferrers, 8th and last Earl of Derby (*cr* 1138) whose title was forfeited was summoned to Parliament as *Baron Ferrers of Chartley* 1299; *d* 1312; *s* by his son (2) Robert, 2nd Baron; summoned to Parliament 1342; *s* by his son (3) John, 3rd Baron; never summoned to Parliament; *d* 1367; *s* by his son (4) Robert, 4th Baron; never summoned to Parliament; *d* 1413; *s* by his son (5) Edmund, 5th Baron; never summoned to Parliament; *d* 1435; *s* by his son (6) William, 6th Baron; *d* 1450; his da Anne *m* (7) Sir Walter Devereux, who was summoned to Parliament in the dignity of his deceased father-in-law 1461; he *d* at Bosworth Field 1485, and was *s* by his son (8) John, 8th Baron; summoned to Parliament 1488-95; *d* 1499; *s* by his son (9) Walter, 9th Baron; *cr* *Viscount Hereford*(see V Hereford) in whose family it remained until 1646, when it became abeyant, and remained so until it was terminated in favour of (13) Sir Robert Shirley, 7th Bt (ante); *d* 1717; *s* by his granddau (14) Elizabeth, wife of 5th Earl of Northampton (*see* M Northampton).

FERRIER, BARONY OF (Noel-Paton) (Extinct 1992)

SON LIVING OF LIFE BARON

Hon Frederick Ranald (Easter Dunbarnie, Bridge of Earn, Perthshire), *b* 1938; *ed* Rugby, Haverford Coll, Pa, USA, and McGill Univ: *m* 1973, Patricia, da of late Gen Sir William Gurdon Stirling, GCB, CBE, DSO, of Saxham Hall, Bury St Edmunds, and has issue.

DAUGHTERS LIVING OF LIFE BARON

Hon Amanda Mary (*Hon Lady Fergusson*), *b* 1933: *m* 1961, Sir Charles Fergusson of Kilkerran, 9th Bt, of Kilkerran, Maybole, Ayrshire, and has issue.
Hon Caroline (Kirsty), *b* 1934: *m* 1957, Michael Laird, OBE, FSIA, FRIAS, RIBA, of 22 Moray Place, Edinburgh, 3, and has issue.
Hon Fiona Margaret, *b* 1943: *m* 1967, Hon Leslie Bruce Hacking, of Burchetts, Lower Moushill Lane, Milford, Surrey (*see* B Hacking).

FEVERSHAM, BARON (Duncombe) (Baron UK 1826)
(Title pronounced "Fevversham")

(CHARLES ANTONY) PETER DUNCOMBE, 6th Baron; *b* 3 Jan 1945; *s* 1963; *ed* Eton; Chm of Yorks Arts Assocn 1969-1980 and Pres since 1987; Chm Standing Conference of Regional Arts Assocns 1969-76; Chm Trustees of Yorkshire Sculpture Park since 1981; Pres Yorkshire Local Councils Assoc since 1986, and Pres National Assocn of Local Councils since 1992; author of *A Wolf in Tooth* 1967 and *Great Yachts* 1970: *m* 1st, 1966, Shannon, who *d* 1976, da of late Sir Thomas Arthur Wyness Foy, CSI, CIE; 2ndly, 1979, Pauline M., da of John Aldridge, of Newark, Notts, and has issue by 1st and 2nd *m*.

Arms – Quarterly, 1st and 4th, per chevron engrailed gules and argent three talbots heads counterchanged for *Duncombe*; 2nd and 3rd, argent a chevron sable between three crosses flory of the second for *Anderson*. **Crests** – For *Duncombe*, out of a ducal coronet or, a horse's hind leg sable, hoof upwards and shod argent. For *Anderson*, a water spaniel passant or. **Supporters** – *Dexter*, a horse of dark iron grey, guttee and ducally gorged or: *Sinister*, a lion argent semme of fleurs-de-lis sable, his head adorned with a plume of six ostrich feathers argent and azure alternately, issuant from a ducal coronet or.
Seat – Duncombe Park, Helmsley, York.

For God, my king and my country

SONS LIVING *(By 1st marriage)*

Hon JASPER ORLANDO SLINGSBY, *b* 14 March 1968.
Hon Jake Barnaby, *b* 1972.

(By 2nd marriage)

Hon Patrick Charles Kildare, *b* 1981.

DAUGHTER LIVING *(By 1st marriage)*

Hon Melissa Rose, *b* 1973.

SISTER LIVING

Juliet Priscilla Mary, *b* 1937: *m* 1960, Wilfred Trevor Woodley, pianist, and has issue living, Karin Lee, *b* 1961.

DAUGHTER LIVING OF THIRD EARL

Lady Clarissa, *b* 1938: *m* 1966, Nicholas Collin, of Whytherstone House, Pockley, York YO6 5TE, and has issue living, Frederick Slingsby, *b* 1967, — Laura Anne, *b* 1969.

WIDOW LIVING OF THIRD EARL OF FEVERSHAM

Lady ANNE DOROTHY, OBE (*Countess of Feversham*), da of 1st Earl of Halifax; MBE (Civil) 1950, OBE (Civil) 1979: *m* 1936, the 3rd Earl of Feversham, who *d* 1963, when the Earldom became ext. *Residence* – Bransdale Lodge, Fadmoor, Kirkbymoorside, York.

COLLATERAL BRANCHES LIVING

Grandchildren of late William Arthur Duncombe-Anderson, OBE, JP, yr son of Capt Frederick William Duncombe, 3rd son of Adm Hon Arthur Duncombe, 4th son of 1st Baron Feversham:—
Issue of late Maj Roland Frederick DUNCOMBE-ANDERSON, *b* 1908, *ka* 1940: *m* 1935, Elizabeth Frances (who *m* 2ndly, 1952, Brig Howard Greene, CBE, DSO, MC (*d* 1985), of Glebe Cottage, Bishopstrow, Warminster, Wilts), da of late Algernon Mawson:—
Alastair Guy, *b* 1938; *ed* Sherborne: *m* 1961, Judith Anne, da of late F. E. Abbott, and has issue living, Alastair Mark, *b* 1962, — Nicholas, *b* 1963, — Timothy Guy, *b* 1965, — Rebecca Elizabeth, *b* 1966, — Justine Anne, *b* 1971.
Issue of late Wilfred George DUNCOMBE-ANDERSON, *b* 1911, *d* 1982: *m* 1st, 1942, Valerie, who *d* 1969, da of Capt S. M. Pemberton, of Byring, Washington, Sussex; 2ndly, 19—, Mrs Enid Mary Gabrielle Nicholl:—
(By 1st *m*) David Martin (Brookside, Milton Mills, Milton Abbas, Blandford, Dorset DT11 0BQ), *b* 1944; *ed* Sherborne: *m* 1st, 1967, Marlene Kathleen, da of late Herbert Edward Peet, and widow of Lt-Cmdr Earle Peter Weavind; 2ndly, 1991, Brenda Janet Goddard, and has issue living (by 1st *m*), Rachel Katherine Louise, *b* 1972. —— Jane Louise Valerie, *b* 1946: *m* 1969 (*m diss* 19—), Charles Tatton Sykes; 2ndly, 1989, Peter Clementson, FRICS, of Rose Cottage, Acre St, W Wittering, Chichester, W Sussex, and has issue living (by 1st *m*), Oliver Tatton, *b* 1974, — Nicholas Tatton, *b* 1977.

PREDECESSORS – (1) CHARLES DUNCOMBE, *cr Baron Feversham* (peerage of United Kingdom) 1826; *d* 1841; *s* by his son (2) WILLIAM, 2nd Baron, *b* 1798; sat as MP for Yorkshire 1826-30, and for N Riding of York (*C*) 1832-41: *m* 1823, Lady Louisa Stewart, da of 5th Earl of Galloway; *d* 1867; *s* by his son (3) WILLIAM, 3rd Baron, *b* 1829; MP for E Retford (*C*) 1852-7, and for N Riding of York 1859-67; *cr Viscount Helmsley* and *Earl of Feversham* (peerage of United Kingdom) 1868: *m* 1851, Mabel Violet, who *d* 1915, da of the Rt Hon Sir James Graham, 2nd Bt, GCB, PC, of Netherby; *d* 1915; *s* by his grandson (4) CHARLES WILLIAM REGINALD (son of late William Reginald, Viscount Helmsley, el son of 1st Earl), 2nd Earl, *b* 1879; Lieut-Col King's Roy Rifle Corps; MP for Yorkshire, W Riding, Thirsk and Malton Div (*C*) 1906-15: *m* 1904, Lady Marjorie Blanche Eva Greville, da of 5th Earl of Warwick; *ka* 1916; *s* by his el son (5) CHARLES WILLIAM SLINGSBY, 3rd Earl; *b* 1906; Lt-Col 13th/18th Hussars and Hon Col Queen's Own Yorkshire Yeo 1962-3; a Lord-in-Waiting to HM 1934-6, Parl Sec Min of Agriculture and Dep Min of Fisheries 1936-9: *m* 1936, Lady Anne Dorothy Wood, MBE, da of 1st Earl of Halifax; *d* 1963 when the Earldom of Feversham and Viscountcy of Helmsley became ext, and the Barony devolved upon (6) (CHARLES ANTONY) PETER (only son of late Lt-Col Antony John Duncombe-Anderson, TD, eldest son of William Arthur Duncombe-Anderson, OBE, JP, yr son of late Capt Frederick William Duncombe, 3rd son of Hon Arthur Duncombe, 4th son of 1st Baron), 6th Baron and present peer.

FFRENCH, BARON (ffrench) (Baron I 1798, Bt I 1779)

I had rather die than be dishonoured

ROBUCK JOHN PETER CHARLES MARIO FFRENCH, 8th Baron, and 9th Baronet: *b* 14 March 1956; *s* 1986; *ed* Ampleforth, and Blackrock, co Dublin: *m* 1987, Dörthe Marie-Louise, da of Capt Wilhelm Schauer, of Zurich, Switzerland, and has issue.

Arms – Ermine, a chevron sable. **Crest** – A dolphin embowed proper. **Supporters** – *Dexter*, a falcon gules, armed, membered, belled, and wings inverted or; *sinister*, an unicorn gules, armed, unguled, crined, and tufted or, and in its mouth a rose branch thereon, two red roses proper.
Seat – Castle ffrench, Ballinasloe, co Galway.

DAUGHTER LIVING

Hon Tara Elise Sofia Eleonora, *b* 1993.

SISTERS LIVING

Hon Rose Sophia Iris Mary, *b* 1957: *m* 1989, Dr Albert Alois Fuchs, only son of late Albert Alois Fuchs, of Pocking, Bavaria, and has issue living, Julia Katherina Sonia Mariele, *b* 1992.
Hon Clare Katherine Grace Mary, *b* 1958: *m* 1989, Alexander Timothy Joynson, yr son of William, R. H. Joynson, of Hyam, Malmesbury, Wilts, and has issue living, Peter William, *b* 1994.

UNCLE LIVING (*Brother of 7th Baron*)

John Charles Mary Joseph Francis (Stockbridge, Mass, USA), *b* 1928: *m* 1963, Sara-Primm, da of James A. Turner, of Stockbridge, Mass, USA, and has issue living, Johanna Felicitas, *b* 1964, — Teodora Crispina, *b* 1965, — Dorcas Sofia, *b* 1967.

AUNTS LIVING (*Sisters of 7th Baron*)

Freida Dora Katherine Mary Josephine, *b* 1916: *m* 1946, Hans Vajda, and has issue living. *Residence* – 16 Wakefield Rd, Tottenham, N15.
Katherine Mary Margaret Frances Josephine, *b* 1917: *m* 1935, Lieut Christopher Valerio Edward Paul Banon, RN, and has had issue, Christopher Benedict Edward Patrick Fitzsimon (Carrig, Mount William Rd, Lancefield 3435, Victoria, Australia), *b* 1943, — Susan Anne Katherine, *b* 1940, *d* 1980, — Camilla Mary Rose (25 Pakenham St, Blackburn, Victoria, Australia), *b* 1947, — Clemency Mary Katherine, *b* 1957. *Residence* – Carrig, Mount William Rd, Lancefield 3435, Victoria, Australia.
Ellen Frances Anna Maria Josephine, *b* 1918: *m* 1946, Thomas Anderson Courtenay Agnew. *Residence* – Cregmore, Ardrahan, co Galway.

WIDOW LIVING OF SEVENTH BARON

KATHERINE SONIA (*Sonia, Baroness ffrench*), da of late Maj Digby Coddington Cayley, late King's Own Borderers (*see* Cayley, Bt, colls): *m* 1954, the 7th Baron, who *d* 1986. *Residence* – Gordon, Berwickshire.

PREDECESSORS – (1) CHARLES ffrench; *cr* a Baronet 1779; *d* 1784; his widow, Rose, was in 1798 *cr* by patent *Baroness ffrench*, of Castle ffrench, co Galway (peerage of Ireland), with remainder to the heirs male of her body, by her husband Sir Charles ffrench, Bt; she *d* 1805; *s* by her son (2) THOMAS, 2nd Baron, who had in 1784 *s* his father as 2nd Bt; *d* 1814; *s* by his son (3) CHARLES AUSTIN, 3rd Baron, *b* 1786: *m* 1809, Maria, el da of John Browne, of Moyne, co Galway; *d* 1860; *s* by his son (4) THOMAS, 4th Baron, *b* 1810: *m* 1851, Mary Anne, who *d* 1906, da and heiress of Richard Thompson, of Stansty Hall, Wrexham; *d* 1892; *s* by his brother (5) MARTIN JOSEPH, 5th Baron, *b* 1813; Resident Magistrate for co Tipperary 1846-82: *m* 1862, Catherine Mary Anne, who *d* 1908, only da of John O'Shaughnessy, of Birchgrove, co Roscommon; *d* 1893; *s* by his el son (6) CHARLES AUSTIN THOMAS ROBERT JOHN JOSEPH, 6th Baron; *b* 1868: *m* 1st, 1892, Mary Margaret, who *d* 1944, el da of Matthew J. Corbally, JP, DL, of Rathbeal Hall, near Swords, co Dublin; 2ndly, 1951, Catherine Elizabeth, who *d* 1960, yst da of Rt Hon Sir Christopher John Nixon, MD, LLD, 1st Bt; *d* 1955; *s* by his nephew (7) PETER MARTIN JOSEPH CHARLES JOHN (el son of late Capt Hon John Martin Valentine ffrench, yr son of 5th Baron) 7th Baron, *b* 1926: *m* 1954, Katherine Sonia, da of late Maj Digby Coddington Cayley, late King's Own Scottish Borderers (*see* Cayley, Bt, colls); *d* 1986; *s* by his only son (8) ROBUCK JOHN PETER CHARLES MARIO, 8th Baron and present peer.

FIELDHOUSE, BARONY OF (Fieldhouse) (Extinct 1992)

SON LIVING OF LIFE BARON

Hon Mark Elliott James, *b* 1955.

DAUGHTERS LIVING OF LIFE BARON

Hon Amanda Elaine, *b* 1959: *m* 1990, Robert John Chalmers, son of John Chalmers, of Remuera, Auckland, NZ. *Residence* – 335 Bank St, S Melbourne, Victoria 3205, Australia.
Hon Sarah Lucinda, *b* 1962: *m* 1987, Christopher le Maitre, son of Anthony J. le Maitre, of 4 Starle Close, Canterbury, Kent. *Residence* – 1 Lightlands Cottages, Down Lane, Frant, E Sussex.

WIDOW LIVING OF LIFE BARON

MARGARET ELLEN (*Baroness Fieldhouse*), da of late David Dorrington Cull: *m* 1953, Adm of the Fleet Baron Fieldhouse, GCB, GBE (Life Baron), who *d* 1992.

FIFE, DUKE OF (Carnegie) (Duke UK 1900)

JAMES GEORGE ALEXANDER BANNERMAN CARNEGIE, 3rd Duke; *b* 23 Sept 1929; *s* his aunt as Duke of Fife 1959, and his father as 12th Earl of Southesk and 9th Baronet 1992; *ed* Gordonstoun, and RAC Cirencester; Nat Service, Scots Gds (Malayan Campaign) 1948-50; a Liveryman of Clothworkers' Co, and Freeman of City of London; Pres ABA 1959-73, Vice-Patron 1973-94, Vice-Patron of Braemar Royal Highland Soc, and Vice-Pres of British Olympic Assoc; Ship's Pres HMS *Fife* 1967-87: *m* 11 Sept 1956 (*m diss* 1966), Hon Caroline Cecily Dewar, elder da of 3rd Baron Forteviot, and has issue.

Arms – Quarterly, 1st grand quarter, or, a lion rampant gules, armed and langued azure, *Dukedom of Fife*; 2nd grand quarter, counter quartered, 1st and 4th gules, three lions passant guardant in pale or, *England*, 2nd, or, a lion rampant within a double tressure flory counter-flory gules. *Scotland*, 3rd, azure a harp or, stringed argent, *Ireland*; differenced by a label of five points argent, the points charged with two thistles between three crosses of St George gules, *Princess Royal, Duchess of Fife, el da of King Edward VII*; 3rd grand quarter, counter-quartered, 1st and 4th, vert, a fess dancettée ermine between a hart's head cabossed in chief and two escallops in base or, *Duff of Braco*; 2nd and 3rd, gules, three skeans paleways argent hafted and pommelled or, surmounted of as many wolves' heads couped of the third, *Skene of that Ilk*; 4th grand quarter, gules, a banner displayed argent charged with a canton azure, a saltire of the second *Bannerman of Elsick*; over all an inescutcheon ensigned of an Earl's coronet, argent, an eagle displayed azure, armed, beaked, and membered gules, on its breast an antique covered cup or, *Carnegie*. **Crest** – Centre, a thunderbolt proper, winged or, *Carnegie*; dexter, a knight denoting the ancient MacDuff armed at all points on a horse in full speed, in his dexter hand a sword erected all proper, his jupon argent, on his sinister arm a shield or charged with a lion rampant gules, the visor of his helmet shut, over which, on a wreath of his liveries with a long mantling flowing therefrom behind him and ending in a tassel of the fourth, the doubling of the third is set a lion rampant issuing out of the wreath of the third and fourth, the caparisons of the horse gules, fimbriated or and thereon six shields of the last, each charged with a lion rampant of the fourth, *Dukedom of Fife*; sinister, a man in armour issuing from the loins and wearing a tabard emblazoned of the arms, argent on a fess between three boars' heads erased gules three mascles or, sustaining with his dexter hand a banner developed argent having a canton azure charged with a saltire of the first, *Ethel, Countess of Southesk*. **Supporters** – Dexter, a lion rampant guardant gules, langued azure, charged with a label of five points argent, the points charged with two thistles between three crosses of St George gules; *Sinister*, a talbot argent collared gules, the collar charged with a label of three points argent.

Seat – Kinnaird Castle, Brechin, Angus DD9 6TZ.*Residence* – Elsick House, Stonehaven, Kincardineshire AB3 2NT. *Club* – Turf.

SON LIVING

DAVID CHARLES (styled *Earl of Macduff* 1961-92, since when *Earl of Southesk*), *b* 3 March 1961; *ed* Eton, Pembroke Coll, Camb (MA 1988), RAC Cirencester, and Edinburgh Univ (MBA 1990); Clothworkers' Co, and Freeman City of London 1987: *m* 16 July 1987, Caroline Ann, only da of Martin Bunting, and has issue:—
    SONS LIVING — Charles Duff (*Lord Carnegie*), *b* 1 July 1989, — Hon George William, *b* 23 March 1991, — *Hon* Hugh Alexander, *b* 10 June 1993.
Seat – Kinnaird Castle, Brechin, Angus DD9 6TZ.

DAUGHTER LIVING

Lady Alexandra Clare, *b* 20 June 1959; *ed* Heathfield; Member Royal Geographical Soc.

UNCLE LIVING (*son of 10th Earl of Southesk*)

Hon (James) Duthac, TD, *b* 1910; *ed* Eton, and Trin Coll, Camb (BA 1932); late Major 4th/5th Btn Black Watch (TA): *m* 1935, Claudia Katharine Angela, da of late Hon Lord Blackburin (*see* E Strathmore, 1951 Edn), and has issue living, Robin Andrew Duthac (31 Hasker St, SW3 2LE), *b* 1937; *ed* Eton; late Capt Queen's Dragoon Gds: *m* 1st, 1962 (*m diss* 1969), Hon (Selina) Polly Dawson Eccles, da of 1st Viscount Eccles, KCVO, PC; 2ndly, 1970 (*m diss* 1979), Mrs Jennifer Puxley, yr da of George H. Robins, MBE, of Devonshire, Bermuda; 3rdly, 1980, Avice Rosemary, da of Dr Richard Montagu Littledale, of Luckhurst, Pluckley, Ashford, Kent, and has issue living (by 1st *m*), Andrew James *b* 1963, (by 2nd *m*) Simon Duthac *b* 1971, Tessa *b* 1972. *Residence* – Balloch, Alyth, Perthshire. *Club* – Cavalry and Guards'.

AUNT LIVING (*daughter of 10th Earl of Southesk*)

Lady Mary Elisabeth, *b* 1899: *m* 1932, Vice-Adm Sir (Edward Michael) Conolly Abel Smith, GCVO, CB, who *d* 1985, and has issue living, Michael James Abel (The Old Rectory, Daylesford, Moreton-in-Marsh, Glos), *b* 1939; *ed* Eton, and Trin Coll, Camb: *m* 1972, Karen Moireach Aileen, yr da of late Ian Donald Malcolmson, TD, of Icomb Place, Stow-on-the-Wold, Glos (*see* B Belper, 1956 Edn), and has issue living, Jessica Karen Abel *b* 1977, — Rosemary Jane, *b* 1936: *m* 1956, Capt Robert Wolrige Gordon of Esslemont, late Gren Gds, of Esslemont, Ellon, Aberdeenshire AB41 8PA, and has had issue, Charles Iain Robert *b* 1961: *m* 1988, Angela Clare, twin da of Simon Rollo Frisby, of Bramley Grange, Bramley, Hants (*see* M Bristol, 1955 Edn) (and has issue living, Henry Conolly Robert *b* 1990, a son *b* 1994, Flora Louisa *b* 1991), Henrietta Anne *b* 1959, *d* 1983. *Residence* – Forebank, Brechin, Angus.

WIDOW LIVING OF SON OF TENTH EARL OF SOUTHESK

Cynthia Averil, eldest da of late Brig Harold Vincent Spencer Charrington, DSO, MC, and formerly wife of Capt Alexander Hugh Gurney, TD: *m* 1969, as his 2nd wife, Cmdr Hon Alexander Bannerman Carnegie, RN, who *d* 1989. *Residence* – West Court, Crondall, Farnham, Surrey.

COLLATERAL BRANCHES LIVING (*Male line in remainder to the Earldom of Southesk*)

Issue of late Cmdr Hon Alexander Bannerman Carnegie, RN, 2nd son of 10th Earl of Southesk, *b* 1894, *d* 1989: *m* 1st, 1919, Susan Ottilia, who *d* 1968, da of late Maj Ernest Rodakowski (*see* E Southesk, 1952 Edn); 2ndly, 1969, Mrs Cynthia Averil Gurney (ante), eldest da of late Brig Harold Vincent Spencer Charrington, DSO, MC, and formerly wife of Capt Alexander Hugh Gurney, TD:—

(By 1st *m*) Raymond Alexander, *b* 1920; *ed* Eton; late Maj Scots Gds, 1939-45 War (thrice wounded, despatches); writer: *m* 1st, 1943 (*m diss* 1953), Patricia Elinor Trevor, yst da of Cmdr Sir Hugh Trevor Dawson, 2nd Bt, RN; 2ndly, 1964, Diana Denyse Hay, Countess of Erroll (*in her own right*), who *d* 1978; 3rdly, 1989, Maria Congreve, da of Maj Ian Stafford Alexander (*see* Congreve, Bt, ext), and has issue living (by 1st *m*), Alexandra Susan Anne, *b* 1944: *m* 1969, John Sherman, of 97 Barkston Gdns, SW5 0EU, and has issue living, Charles Alexander Hoyt *b* 1970, Ian Andrew Henry *b* 1972, Peter Anthony Carnegie *b* 1978, — Susan Katharine Maud, *b* 1946: *m* 1st, 1968 (*m diss* 1973), Dudley Gordon de Chair, 5th Royal Inniskilling Dragoon Gds; 2ndly, 1974, Rupert Edward Harding-Newman, 4/7th Royal Dragoon Gds, and has issue living (by 1st *m*), Oliver Dudley Raikes *b* 1970, Natasha Alexandra *b* 1971, (by 2nd *m*) Rupert Alexander *b* 1976, Sophia Katharine Louise *b* 1979, — (by 2nd *m*) Hon Jocelyn Jacek Alexander Bannerman, *b* 1966; *ed* Glenalmond: *m* 1990, Susie Mhairi, only da of Thomas Mitchell Hastie Butler, of Eastmillhill, Crimond, and has had issue, Merlin Thomas Alexander Bannerman *b* 1991, Cecilia Diana Catriona Pearl *b* 1993, *d* 1994. *Residence* – Crimonmogate, Lonmay, Aberdeenshire.

Granddaughters of late Rt Hon Sir Lancelot Douglas Carnegie, GCVO, KCMG, 2nd son of *de jure* 9th Earl:—

Issue of late James Murray Carnegie, Capt RA, *b* 1909, *d* 1985: *m* 1939, Diana Winifred Mary (Polefields, Cowden, Kent), da of late Henry Arthur Renshaw (*see* E Leitrim, 1965 Edn):—

Susan Diana, *b* 1943: *m* 1982, James Alexander McKenzie, of 6 Corfe Mews, Caversham Park Village, Reading. —— Charlotte Marion, *b* 1954: *m* 1983, Richard Kenneth Purkis, of Chiswell House, Marsh Green, Edenbridge, Kent, and has issue living, Annabel Diana, *b* 1986, — Rosalind Marion, *b* 1988. —— Sophie Winifred, *b* (twin) 1954.

Grandsons of late Maj Hon Robert Francis Carnegie (*infra*):—

Issue of late Robert Murray Carnegie, *b* 1917, *d* 1954, from injuries received in an aeroplane accident: *m* 1949, Pauline Frances, who *d* 1954, da of Capt Francis H. Farmer, of Fairseat, Kent:—

Ian Francis, *b* 1949; *ed* Wellington Coll. —— Alastair Robert, *b* 1951; *ed* Wellington Coll: *m* 1976, Joanna D., da of Gerry Enderby-Smith, and has issue living, Helena Mary, *b* 1982. —— †Keith Hamilton Peter, *b* 1954; *d* 1961, as the result of a motor accident.

Issue of late Major Hon Robert Francis Carnegie, 3rd son of *de jure* 9th Earl, *b* 1869, *d* 1947: *m* 1913, Violet Mabel, who *d* 1980, da of late Philip Affleck Fraser, of Reelig, Inverness-shire:—

John Fraser, DFC (O Cabeco, Estrada da Serra, 7300 Portalegre, Portugal), *b* 1922; *ed* Prince of Wales Sch, Nairobi; late Flight-Lieut RAF; European War 1941-45 (DFC): *m* 1955, Gunhild Aline Avalon, da of Cmdr Arthur Avalon Mackinnon, OBE, RN (ret), 36th Chief of Clan Fingon, and has had issue, †James Robert *b* 1956; *ed* Trin Coll, Glenalmond; *d* 1976, — Susan Mary, *b* 1957: *m* 1st, 1980 (*m diss* 1987), Mark Julian Lloyd Nicholson, son of late George Raymond Tibbitt, and of Mrs Hugo Romer Nicholson, of Topps Farm, Braemore, Hants (*see* Agnew, Bt, *cr* 1895, colls, 1970 Edn); 2ndly, 1988, as his 2nd wife, Timothy Robertson Bruce, of The Old Rectory, Combs, Stowmarket, Suffolk, adopted son of late Capt Hon John Bernard Bruce, RN (*see* E Elgin, colls), and has issue living (by 1st *m*), Rosalie Sheonagh *b* 1983.

Grandson of late George David Howard Fullerton-Carnegie (*infra*):—

Issue of late Maj George Travers Fullerton-Carnegie, *b* 1921, *d* 1975: *m* 1945, Frances May, who *d* 1974, da of late Lt-Col Alexander Sydney Duggan, MBE:—

(George) Christopher Howard FULLERTON-CARNEGIE, *b* 1946; *ed* La Clerière, Switzerland, and Lausanne Univ: *m* 1988, Cynthia, eldest da of Donald Hildreth, and of Mrs Josefina Amado.

Grandson of late Edward Hugo Wakefield Fullerton-Carnegie, OBE, yst son of late Maj-Gen George Fullerton-Carnegie, elder son of George Fullerton-Carnegie, eldest son of John Carnegie (who assumed the additional surname of Fullerton upon his *m* 1796 to Mary Strachan Fullerton), son of George Carnegie, brother of 3rd Bt and *de jure* 6th Earl:—

Issue of late George David Howard Fullerton-Carnegie, MC, *b* 1894, *d* 1937: *m* 1920, Marian Margery (who *d* 1980, having *m* 2ndly, 1946, Staffan John Söderblom, sometime Swedish Amb to China), da of late Rev R. L. Lacey, of Castlepark House, Exmouth:—

David Howard FULLERTON-CARNEGIE, *b* 1926. *Residence* – Orchard Hill House, Upper Clatford, Andover, Hants SP11 7HA.

PREDECESSORS – (1) WILLIAM Duff, MP for Banffshire 1727-34; *cr* Baron Braco, of Kilbryde, co Cavan (peerage of Ireland) 1735, and *Viscount Macduff*, and *Earl Fife* (peerage of Ireland) 1759; *d* 1763; *s* by his el son (2) JAMES, 2nd Earl; *cr Baron Fife* (peerage of Great Britain) 1790; *d* 1809, when the Barony of Fife expired, and the Irish honours devolved upon his brother (3) ALEXANDER, 3rd Earl; *d* 1811; *s* by his son (4) JAMES, KT, GCH, 4th Earl; a Maj-Gen in the Spanish Army during the Peninsular War, MP 1818-26, Lord Lieut of co Banff, and a Lord of the Bedchamber; *cr Baron Fife* (peerage of United Kingdom) 1827; *d* 1857, when the Barony of Fife expired, and the Irish honours reverted to his nephew (5) JAMES, KT, 5th Earl, son of Gen Hon Sir Alexander, 2nd son of 3rd Earl; *b* 1814; MP for Banffshire (*L*) 1837-57, Lord-Lieut of co Banff 1856-7; *cr Baron Skene* (peerage of United Kingdom) 1857; *d* 1879; *s* by his son (6) ALEXANDER WILLIAM GEORGE, KG, KT, GCVO, PC, 6th Earl; *b* 1849; *cr Earl of Fife* (peerage of United Kingdom) 1885, *Duke of Fife and Marquess of Macduff*, of co Banff (peerage of United Kingdom) 29 July 1889, and *Earl of Macduff*, of co Banff, and *Duke of Fife* (peerage of United Kingdom) 1900, with remainder to the heirs male of his body by his marriage with HRH Princess Louise, and in default of such issue (1) to their el da (*Princess* Alexandra) and her heirs male, (2) in default of such issue to their yr da (*Princess* Maud) and her heirs male, and (3) in default of such issue to each of the after-born daus by HRH Princess Louise and the heirs male of the body and respective bodies of such daus severally and successively, one after another, as they shall be in seniority of age and priority of birth; Lord-Lieut and Custos Rotulorum of co London; Lord-Lieut of Elginshire 1871-1901; MP for Elgin and Nairn (*L*) 1874-9; Capt and Gold Stick of Corps of Gentlemen-at-Arms 1880-81; acted as Lord High Constable at Coronations of King Edward VII and King George V; had Royal Victorian Chain: *m* 27 July 1889, HRH Princess Louise Victoria Alexandra Dagmar (*the Princess Royal*), who *d* 1931, el da of King Edward VII (*see* ROYAL FAMILY); *d* 1912, when the Irish Honours (Barony of Braco, *cr* 1735, and Viscountcy of Macduff and Earldom of Fife, *cr* 1759) became dormant or ext, and the Barony of Skene 1857, Earldom of Fife, *cr* 1885, and Dukedom of Fife and Marquessate of Macduff, *cr* 1889, became ext, while the peerages *cr* 1900 devolved under the special remainder upon his el da (7) HH Princess ALEXANDRA VICTORIA ALBERTA EDWINA LOUISE, RRC; *b* 1891; a GCStJ; appointed Col-in-Ch RAPC 1939; acted as a Counsellor of State during HM's absence abroad 1939, 1943, and 1944: *m* 1913, Maj-Gen HRH Prince Arthur Frederick Patrick Albert of Connaught, KG, PC, KT, GCMG, GCVO, who *d* 1938, only son of HRH the 1st Duke of Connaught and Strathearn; *d* 1959; *s* by her nephew (8) JAMES GEORGE ALEXANDER BANNERMAN Carnegie (*Lord Carnegie*) (only son of 11th Earl of Southesk and HH late Princess Maud Alexandra Victoria Georgina Bertha, yr da of 1st Duke), 3rd Duke, and present peer; also Earl of Macduff, Earl of Southesk, Lord Carnegie of Kinnaird and Leuchars, and Baron Balinhard.

*(1) *Rt Hon Sir* DAVID Carnegie, an Extraordinary Lord of Session of High Sheriff of co Forfar, was *cr Lord Carnegie of Kinnaird* (peerage of Scotland) 1616, and *Earl of Southesk* and *Lord Carnegie of Kinnaird and Leuchars* (peerage of Scotland) 1633, with remainder to heirs male; *d* 1658; *s* by his son (2) JAMES, 2nd Earl; High Sheriff of co Fafar; one of the Commrs

chosen to sit in the Parliament of England 1652; *d* 1669; *s* by his son **(3)** ROBERT, 3rd Earl; High Sheriff of co Forfar; *d* 1688; *s* by his son **(4)** CHARLES, 4th Earl; High Sheriff of co Forfar; did not go to Court or Parliament after the Revolution; *d* 1699; *s* by his son **(5)** JAMES, 5th Earl; engaged in the Rebellion of 1715 (honours attainted by Act of Parliament and estates forfeited); *d* 1729; *s* in representation of family by **(6)** *Sir* JAMES Carnegie, MP, 3rd Bt (see** infra); *s* by his son **(7)** *Sir* DAVID, MP, 4th Bt; *d* 1805; *s* by his son **(8)** *Sir* JAMES, MP, 5th Bt; *b* 1799: *m* 1825, Charlotte, da of Rev Daniel Lysons, of Hempsted Court, Gloucester, *d* 1849; *s* by his son **(9)** *Sir* JAMES, 6th Bt; *b* 1827; confirmed in Earldom as 9th Earl (together with the minor honours) and attainder reversed 1855, and *cr Baron Balinhard*, of Farnell, co Forfar (peerage of United Kingdom) 1860; Lord-Lieut of Kincardineshire 1849-56: *m* 1st, 1849, Lady Catherine Hamilton Noel, who *d* 1855, da of 1st Earl of Gainsborough; 2ndly, 1860, Lady Susan Catherine Mary Murray, who *d* 1915, el da of 6th Earl of Dunmore; *d* 1905; *s* by his el son **(10)** CHARLES NOEL, 10th Earl; *b* 1854: *m* 1891, Ethel Mary Elizabeth, who *d* 1947, only da of Sir Alexander Bannerman, 9th Bt; *d* 1941; *s* by his el son **(11)** CHARLES ALEXANDER, KCVO, *b* 1893; Major Scots Gds, DL Kincardineshire and Angus: *m* 1st, 12 Nov 1923, HH Princess Maud Alexandra Victoria Georgina Bertha Maud (acted as Councellor of State 1943), who *d* 14 Dec 1945, yr da of HRH late Princess Louise (*The Princess Royal*), and 1st Duke of Fife (*see* ROYAL FAMILY and ante); 2ndly, 1952, Evelyn Julia, who *d* (30 Aug) 1992, elder da of late Lt-Col Arthur Peere Williams-Freeman, DSO, OBE, and widow of Maj Ion Edward FitzGerald Campbell, Duke of Cornwall's LI (*see* Campbell, Bt, *cr* 1815); *d* (16 Feb) 1992; *s* by his only son **(12)** JAMES GEORGE ALEXANDER BANNERMAN, 3rd Duke of Fife and 12th Earl of Southesk (ante).

(1) *Hon* ALEXANDER Carnegie, 4th son of 1st Earl of Southesk, *s* by his son **(2)** DAVID, *cr* a *Baronet* 1663; *s* by his son **(3)** JOHN, 2nd Bt; *d* 1729; *s* by his son **(4)** *Sir* JAMES, 3rd Bt, who *s* the 5th Earl as head of the family (see ante).

Fincastle, Viscount; son of Earl of Dunmore.

FINGALL, EARLDOM OF (Plunkett) (Extinct 1984)

WIDOW LIVING OF TWELFTH EARL

CLAIR HILDA (*Countess of Fingall*), da of late Henry Robert Salmon, of Ballarat, Victoria, Australia, and widow of Frank Richardson, of Geelong, Victoria: *m* 1966, as his 2nd wife, the 12th Earl, MC, who *d* 1984, when the title became ext. *Residence* – The Common, Dunsany, co Meath.

FINLAY, VISCOUNTCY OF (Finlay) (Extinct 1945)

DAUGHTER LIVING OF SECOND VISCOUNT

Hon Rosalind Mary (*Hon Lady Hayes*), *b* 1914: *m* 1939, Vice-Adm Sir John Osler Chattock Hayes, KCB, OBE, and issue living, Colin John Finlay (Durhams Farmhouse, Butchers Hill, Ickleton, Saffron Walden, Essex CB10 1SR), *b* 1943: *m* 1969, Rosemary Lucie, da of late Rev Canon Herbert Naunton Bates, of Blaxhall, Woodbridge, Suffolk, and has issue living, Alexander Finlay *b* 1971, Oliver Naunton John *b* 1984, Philippa Lucie *b* 1977, — Malcolm Lionel FitzRoy, *b* 1951, — Griselda Mary, *b* 1954. *Residence* – Wemyss House, Nigg, by Tain, Ross and Cromarty IV19 1QW.

FINSBERG, BARON (Finsberg) (Life Baron 1992)

GEOFFREY FINSBERG, MBE, only son of late Montefiore Finsberg, MC; *b* 13 June 1926; *ed* City of London Sch; JP Inner London since 1962; Member Hampstead Borough Council 1949-65, and Camden Borough Council 1964-74; Member Exec Cttee Nat Union of Conservative and Unionist Assocs 1953-79 (Pres Greater London Area 1986-89), Nat Chm Young Conservatives 1954-57, Chm Greater London Conservative Local Govt Cttee 1972-75, Parly Under-Sec of State Dept of the Environment 1979-81, and Dept of Health and Social Security 1981-83, since when Member Parly Assembly of the Council of Europe, and Western European Union Delegation Leader since 1987; Pres Council of Europe 1991-92; Dep Chm of Commn for the New Towns since 1992; Dir London and SE TSB 1963-75 (Dep Chm SE Regional Board 1986-89), and Industrial Relations Advisor to Great Universal Stores 1968-79 and since 1983; Council Member CBI 1968-79, and Member Post Office Users' Nat Council 1970-77; Freeman City of London; Order of Merit 1st Class Austria, Order of Great Golden Cross Austria, Encomienda de la Expresada Order of Isabel the Catholic of Spain; MP Hampstead (*C*) 1970-83, and Hampstead and Highgate 1983-92; MBE (Civil) 1959, Kt Bach 1984, and *Baron Finsberg*, of Hampstead in the London Borough of Camden (Life Baron) 1992: *m* 1st, 1969, Pamela Benbow, who *d* 1989, da of late Roland Benbow Hill, of Hastings; 2ndly, 1990, Mrs (Yvonne) Elizabeth Sarch, da of late Albert Wright, of Strabane, co Donegal, and formerly wife of Michael Sarch.

𝕬rms – Azure, on a cross quarterly argent and gules between twelve mullets in circle, three, three, three and three or, a sword erect in pale point upwards also or and four fleurs-de-lys gold. 𝕮rest – In a circlet or fretty gules a demi-stag argent, attired and unguled or, gorged with a chaplet of holly proper and holding between the forelegs a miner's lamp gold. 𝕾upporters – *Dexter*, a black cat; *sinister*, a dalmation dog, the compartment comprising a grassy mount extending on each side into a hillock all proper.
Address – c/o House of Lords, SW1. *Club* – Royal Over-Seas League.

FISHER, BARON (Fisher) (Baron UK 1909)

JOHN VAVASSEUR FISHER, DSC, 3rd Baron; *b* 24 July 1921; *s* 1955; *ed* Stowe, and Trin Coll, Camb (BA); sometime Lieut RNVR; 1941-45 War (DSC); JP and DL of Norfolk; *m* 1st, 1949 (*m diss* 1969), Elizabeth Ann Penelope, da of late Maj Herbert Holt, MC, of Nassau, Bahamas; 2ndly, 1970, Hon Rosamund Ann Clifford, da of 12th Baron Clifford of Chudleigh, and formerly wife of late Geoffrey Forrester Fairbairn, and has issue by 1st *m*.

𝕬rms – Argent, in chief two demi-lions rampant erased gules, and in base the stern of an ancient battleship showing three lanterns proper. 𝕮rest – A dexter hand in mail armour couped at the wrist grasping the head of a trident erect all proper. 𝕾upporters – On either side a sailor of the Royal Navy supporting in the exterior hand an anchor cabled, that to the dexter in bend sinister and that to the sinister in bend dexter, all proper.
Residence – Marklye, Rushlake Green, Heathfield, Sussex.

SONS LIVING (By 1st marriage)

Hon PATRICK VAVASSEUR (Highwaymans Vineyard, Heath Barn Farm, Risby, Bury St Edmunds, Suffolk), *b* 14 June 1953: *m* 1977, Lady Karen Jean Carnegie, el da of 13th Earl of Northesk, and has issue living, John Carnegie Vavasseur, *b* 1979, — Benjamin Carnegie Vavasseur, *b* 1986, — Juliet Elizabeth, *b* 1978, — Penelope Mary-Jean, *b* 1981, — Suzannah Jane, *b* 1984.
Hon Benjamin Vavasseur (Overway House, Nowton, Bury St Edmunds, Suffolk), *b* 1958: *m* 1985, Pamela Margaret, only da of A. Cooper, of Tolcarne, Rough Close, Staffordshire, and has issue living, Peter Vavasseur, *b* 1986, — Rose Kathleen, *b* 1988.

DAUGHTERS LIVING (By 1st marriage)

Hon Frances Alice, *b* 1951: *m* 1981, Angus J. White, of Cooks Farm, Nuthurst, nr Horsham, Sussex son of Dr R. A. White, of Mile Ash, Tower Hill, Horsham, Sussex, and has issue living, Thomas Holt, *b* 1983, — Sally, *b* 1985.
Hon Bridget Ann, *b* 1956: *m* 1982, Dr Bruce Stuart Irlam Montgomery, son of Dr S. R. Montgomery, of Telegraph Cottage, Blackdown, nr Haslemere, Surrey, and has issue living, Patrick Christopherson Ross, *b* 1987, — Caroline Jane, *b* 1984, — Katherine Frances, *b* 1985. *Residence* – 31 Newton Rd, W2 5JR.

SISTERS LIVING

Hon Katharine (*Katharine, Baroness Clifford of Chudleigh*), *b* 1919: *m* 1945, 13th Baron Clifford of Chudleigh, who *d* 1988. *Residence* – Flat 3, The Care House, Les Blancs Bois, Rue Cohu, Guernsey, CI.
Hon Barbara, *b* 1925: *m* 1961, Leslie Charles Croft Buswell, and has issue living, Gerald John Croft, *b* 1965, — Pamela Gwendolyn, *b* 1968. *Residences* – Le Petit Feugerel, St John, Jersey, CI; Normandie Farm, Firgrove, Cape 7110, S Africa.

PREDECESSORS – (1) Adm of the Fleet Sir JOHN ARBUTHNOT Fisher, GCB, OM, GCVO, LLD, son of Capt William Fisher, 78th Highlanders; *b* 1841; Adm of the Fleet; Director of Naval Ordnance 1887-91, Adm Sup of Portsmouth Dockyard 1891-2, a Lord of the Admiralty and Controller of the Navy 1892-7, Com-in-Ch on N American and W Indies Station 1897-9, and of Mediterranean Fleet 1899-1902, Second Lord of the Admiralty 1902-3, Com-in-Ch at Portsmouth 1903-4, Principal Naval ADC to HM 1904-11, First Sea Lord of the Admiralty 1904-10, and again First Sea Lord of the Admiralty 1914-15; *cr Baron Fisher*, of Kilverstone, co Norfolk (peerage of United Kingdom) 1909: *m* 1866, Frances Katharine Josepha, who *d* 1918, only da of late Rev Thomas Delves-Broughton; *d* 1920; *s* by his only son (2) CECIL, 2nd Baron; *b* 1868; assumed by Roy licence 1909 the additional name of Vavasseur: *m* 1910, Jane, who *d* 1955, da of Randal Morgan, of Chestnut Hill, Philadelphia, USA, *d* 1955; *s* by his only son (3) JOHN VAVASSEUR, 3rd Baron and present peer.

FISHER OF CAMDEN, BARONY OF (Fisher) (Extinct 1979)

DAUGHTER LIVING OF LIFE BARON

Hon Marilyn Ruth, *b* 1940; BA: *m* 1960, Mervyn Taylor, solicitor, of 4 Springfield Rd, Templeogue, Dublin.

WIDOW LIVING OF LIFE BARON

MILLIE (*Baroness Fisher of Camden*) (48 Viceroy Court, Prince Albert Rd, NW8), da of Isaac Gluckstein, of London: *m* 1930, Baron Fisher of Camden, FCIS (Life Baron), who *d* 1979.

FISHER OF LAMBETH, BARONY OF (Fisher) (Extinct 1972)

SONS LIVING OF LIFE BARON

Hon Sir Henry Arthur Pears, *b* 1918; *ed* Marlborough and Ch Ch, Oxford (MA); is Fellow of All Souls Coll, Oxford; Bar Inner Temple 1947, and a QC 1960; Recorder of Canterbury (1962-67); Chm of Bar Council 1966-68; a Judge of High Court of Justice (Queen's Bench Div) 1968-70; late Pres of Wolfson Coll, Oxford; a dir Thomas Tilling Ltd, and Equity and Law Life Assurance Soc Ltd; formerly Lt-Col R Leics Regt; Burma 1944-45 (despatches); Knt 1968: *m* 1948, Felicity, da of late Eric Sutton, of 15 Cheyne Pl, SW3, and has issue. *Residence* – Garden End, Marlborough, Wilts.

Hon Humphrey Richmond, *b* 1923; *ed* Repton; formerly Lieut RA; a Film Technician and Producer 1946-54, Exec Producer BBC Television 1954-64, Representative in Aust and NZ 1964-67, and Head of Science and Features, BBC Television 1967-69, late Dir of Television Features Aust Broadcasting Commn: *m* 1959, Diana Beresford, da of C. Beresford Davis. *Residence* – 14 Spicer St, Woollahra, NSW 2025, Australia.

Hon Geoffrey Robert Chevallier, *b* 1926; *ed* Repton, and at Emmanuel Coll, Camb (BA 1947, MB and BChir 1949); D (Obst) RCOG 1952; Surg Lieut RN: *m* 1961, Jill Audrey, el da of J. H. Cooper, and has issue. *Residence* – 3 Wendover Drive, New Malden, Surrey KT3 6RN.

Hon Richard Temple, *b* 1930; *ed* St Edward's Sch, Oxford, and King's Coll, Camb (Choral Scholar, MA); Hon Maj TA Gen List, late 16th/5th Queen's R Lancers; Assist Master and Housemaster at Repton 1953-69, Headmaster of Bilton Grange Prep Sch 1969-92; Chm Inc Assoc of Preparatory Schs 1987: *m* 1969, Clare Margaret, el da of J. Lewen Le Fanu, of Newton House, Repton, and has issue. *Residence* – Crossways, 73 Overslade Lane, Rugby, Warwicks CV22 6EE.

WIDOW LIVING OF SON OF LIFE BARON

Ann Gilmour (139 Kermode St, North Adelaide 5006, Australia), da of late Ian Scott Hammond, of Chidikamwadzi, Umvukwes, Zimbabwe: *m* 1st, 1952, Hon Charles Douglas Fisher, who *d* 1978; 2ndly, 1983, Prof Basil S. Hetzel, Chief of Division of Human Nutrition, CSIRO, Adelaide, S Australia.

FISHER OF REDNAL, BARONESS (Fisher) (Life Baroness 1974)

DORIS MARY GERTRUDE FISHER, da of late Frederick James Satchwell, BEM; *b* 13 Sept 1919; *ed* Tinker's Farm Girls' Sch, Fircroft Coll, and Bournville Day Continuation Coll; a JP for Birmingham; a City Councillor, Birmingham 1952-74; Nat Pres of Co-operative Guild 1961-62; Crown Representative of Gen Med Council since 1975; a Member of Warrington New Town Development Corpn since 1975, and of New Towns Staff Commn since 1976; Pres Birmingham Royal Inst for the Blind since 1987, and British Fluoridation Soc since 1994; Guardian Birmingham Assay Office 1982-89; Member Hallmarking Council since 1989; MP for Ladywood Div of Birmingham (*Lab*) 1970-74; Member of European Parl, Strasbourg 1975-81; *cr Baroness Fisher of Rednal*, of Rednal in City of Birmingham (Life Baroness) 1974: *m* 1939, Joseph Fisher, and has issue.
Residence – 60 Jacoby Place, Priory Rd, Birmingham B5 7UW.

DAUGHTERS LIVING

Hon Pauline Mary, *b* 1940: *m* 1961, Michael James Platt, of Little Acre, Ridings Way, Cublington, Leighton Buzzard, Beds.
Hon Veronica Mary, *b* 1945: *m* 1968, John Adrian Pickering, 8 Marlborough Av, Bromsgrove, Worcs, and has issue.

Fisherwick, Baron, title of Marquess of Donegall on Roll of HL.

FISKE, BARONY OF (Fiske) (Extinct 1974)

SON LIVING OF LIFE BARON (*By 1st marriage*)

Hon Giles Geoffrey, *b* 1935.

DAUGHTER LIVING OF LIFE BARON (*By 1st marriage*)

Hon Rosemary *b* 1931: *m* 19—, A. Holbrow, of Worcester.

WIDOW LIVING OF LIFE BARON

JOSEPHINE (*Baroness Fiske*), da of Alan Coppin, JP, of Hong Kong: *m* 1955, as his 2nd wife, Baron Fiske (Life Baron), who *d* 1975.

FITT, BARON (Fitt) (Life Baron 1983)

GERARD FITT, son of George Patrick Fitt; *b* 9 April 1926; *ed* Christian Brothers' Sch, Belfast; Merchant Navy 1941-53; Councillor Belfast Corpn 1958-81 (Alderman); Member (SDLP) N Belfast, N Ireland Assembly 1973-75, and NI Constitutional Convention 1975-76; Dep Ch Exec, NI Exec, 1974; co-founder and

Leader, Social Democratic and Labour Party, 1970-79; MP for W Div Belfast (*Lab*) 1966-83 (Independent Socialist 1979-83); *cr Baron Fitt*, of Bell's Hill, co Down (Life Baron) 1983: *m* 1947, Susan Gertrude, da of — Doherty, and has issue.
Address – c/o House of Lords, SW1.

FITZALAN OF DERWENT, VISCOUNTCY OF (Fitzalan-Howard) (Extinct 1962)

DAUGHTERS LIVING OF SECOND VISCOUNT

Hon Alathea Gwendolen Alys Mary, *b* 1923; Dame of Honour and Devotion, Sovereign Mil Order of Malta: *m* 1953, as his 2nd wife, Hon Edward Frederick Ward, of 21b Ave du Temple, Lausanne, Switzerland (*see* E Dudley, 1985 Edn), who *d* 1987.
Hon Elizabeth Anne Marie Gabrielle (*Hon Lady Hastings*) *b* 1934; High Sheriff Cambs 1993, DL 1994: *m* 1st, 1952 (*m diss* 1960), Sir Vivyan Edward Naylor-Leyland, 3rd Bt, who *d* 1987; 2ndly, 1975, Sir Stephen Lewis Edmonstone Hastings, MC. *Residences* – Milton Hall, Peterborough; 12A Ennismore Gdns, SW7.

FitzHarris, Viscount; son of Earl of Malmesbury.

FITZWALTER, BARON (Plumptre) (Baron E 1295)

I will guard

FITZWALTER BROOK PLUMPTRE, 21st Baron; 15 Jan 1914; *s* (on termination of abeyance) 1953; *ed* Diocesan Coll, Cape Town, and Jesus Coll, Camb; Capt The Buffs (Reserve), a JP for Kent, and a Gov of King's Sch, Canterbury; European War 1939-45 in NW Europe and India; *m* 1951, Margaret Melesina, yr da of Herbert William Deedes, JP (B Ashtown, colls), and has issue.

Arms – Argent, a chevron between two mullets pierced in chief, and an annulet in base sable, a crescent sable for difference. **Crest** – A phoenix or, out of flames proper. **Badge** – An estoile or.
Seat – Goodnestone Park, Canterbury.

SONS LIVING

Hon JULIAN BROOK, *b* 18 Oct 1952; *ed* Radley, and Wye Coll, London Univ: *m* 1988, (Alison) Sally, only da of late I. M. T. Quiney, and has issue living, Edward Brook, *b* 26 April 1989, — Tom Alexander, *b* 1991, — Max Ian, *b* 1993.
Hon Henry Bridges (229 Birrell St, Bondi, Sydney, NSW, Australia), *b* 1954 *m* 1981, Susie, only da of F. T. Payne, of Waverley Station, Scone, NSW, Australia, and has issue living, Sam Anthony Bridges, *b* 1982, — Camilla, *b* 1984.
Hon (Wyndham) George, *b* 1956; *ed* Radley, and Jesus Coll, Camb: *m* 1984, Alexandra Elizabeth, da of Prince Michael Cantacuzene, Count Speransky, and has issue living, Wyndham James Alexander, *b* 1986, — Piers Harry Constantine, *b* 1987, — Hermione Amy Katherina, *b* 1991. *Residence* – Rowling House, Goodnestone, Canterbury, Kent CT3 1QB.
Hon William Edward, *b* 1959; *ed* Milton Abbey: *m* 1991, Joanna, yr da of William Dargue, of Los Gigantes, Tenerife, and has issue living, Jeremy William, *b* 1992.
Hon Francis Charles, *b* 1963; *ed* St Edmund's Sch, Canterbury.

BROTHER LIVING

Peter Bridges, MBE, *b* 1916; *ed* Diocesan Coll, Cape Town, and The King's Sch, Canterbury; Major (ret) The Buffs; European War 1939-45 (MBE); MBE (Mil) 1944: *m* 1944, Maude Helen May, da of late Geoffrey Henry Baird, of Goodnestone, Kent, and has issue living, Timothy George, *b* 1945: *m* 1975, Christine Hamilton, and has issue living, Peter Hamilton *b* 1980, Tamsin Mary *b* 1978, — Jeremy Peter, *b* 1947: *m* 1985, Carmen Nozal Gonzalez, — Michael John, *b* 1955, — Rosalin Helen, *b* 1952: *m* 1970, David Alan Bowler, and has issue living, Nathan Plumptre *b* 1972, Lucy Plumptre *b* 1971. *Residence* – Beechwood, Heathfield, Tavistock, S Devon.

SISTERS LIVING

Judith Patricia (Flat 1, The Old Mitre, Lower Acreman St, Sherborne, Dorset DT9 3EX), *b* 1910.
Elizabeth Mary, *b* 1912: *m* 1941, Rev Philip Vivian Rogers Pennant, TD, MA; formerly Capt RWF, of 2 Manor Close, Bradford Abbas, Sherborne, Dorset DT9 6RN, and has issue living, Thomas George Edmund, *b* 1947; *ed* Wrekin, and Trin Coll, Camb: *m* 1979, Eva Gertrud Elisabeth, elder da of Dr Heinz Esser, of D5093 Burscheid Am Jungholzkamp, W Germany, and has issue living, Christina Agnes Katharina *b* 1981, — Philip Pearson, *b* 1952, — Stephen Owen Falconer (19 Fossil Rd, Lewisham SE13 7DE), *b* 1956: *m* 1985, Jean Madeleine, da of Rev Rene Tassell, of 12 Gardens Walk, Upton-upon-Severn, Worcs WR8 0LL, and has issue living, Douglas Hunter *b* 1987, Elizabeth Madeleine *b* 1985, Florence Maria *b* 1991, — Philippa Berain Elizabeth Plumptre, *b* 1942: *m* 1962, Bryan Henry Farr, of Worksop Manor, Worksop, Notts S80 3DG, and has issue living, Henry John Philip *b* 1966, Rosalinde Mary *b* 1963, Susannah Margaret *b* 1965, — Sarah Fariana Mary Agnes, *b* 1944: *m* 1st, 1966 (*m diss* 1984), Robert Iain Bescoby Jenkins; 2ndly, 1984, Maj Michael Owen Girdlestone, RA, of The Wharf House, Cropredy, Banbury, Oxon OX17 1PQ, and has issue living (by 1st *m*), Robert Brook Pennant *b* 1970, Philip David Alexander *b* 1971, Katie Serena Margaret *b* 1977, — Helen Michèle, *b* 1949: *m* 1986, Jay Hilton Brewer, of Pedlars Cottage, Worthing Rd, Rustington, W Sussex BN16 3PS, son of Joseph Brewer, and has issue living, Rosie Margaretta *b* 1988.
Frederica Anne, *b* 1919: *m* 1942, Anthony Durnford Gaymer, FRIBA, who *d* 1985, late Major RA, of 14 Blofields Loke, Aylsham, Norfolk NR11 6ES, and has issue living, Nigel Anthony Plumptre (Windrush, Flimwell, Sussex), *b* 1944; FCA: *m*

1969, Kathryn Helen Adams, and has issue living, Adam Timothy *b* 1973, Kirstin Anne *b* 1976, — Felicity Anne Plumptre, *b* 1950: *m* 1972, John Edward Parker, of 4590 Sumner Place, Victoria, BC, Canada, and has issue living, Geoffrey James *b* 1973, Anthony William *b* 1974, Jonathan George *b* 1982, Olivia Esther Plumptre *b* 1976, Victoria Rose *b* 1980.

COLLATERAL BRANCHES LIVING

Grandchildren of late Margaretta Agnes Wright, eldest sister of 20th Baron:—
Issue of late Edward Fitzwalter Wright, *b* 1902, *d* 1957: *m* 1927, Jane Fairie Wilson, who *d* 1989, da of late Thomas Chalmers McGuffie:—

John Leslie Fitzwalter WRIGHT, *b* 1934: *ed* Winchester, and at Ch Ch, Oxford; late 2nd Lieut Sherwood Foresters: *m* 1974, Susan Annette, da of Maj-Gen Allan Elton Younger, DSO, OBE, of The Manor House, Twyford, Winchester, and has issue living, Francis Gideon Fitzwalter, *b* 1975, — David Nathanael Beresford, *b* 1979, — James Emanuel Shakespeare, *b* 1981, — John Joseph Camplyon, *b* 1981, — Jemimah Alianore, *b* 1977. *Residence* – Kirby House, Kirby Bedon, Norwich NR14 7DZ.
—— †Jennifer Marion, *b* 1930: *m* 1952, Lt-Cdr Sir John Muir Drinkwater, RN (ret), QC, and *d* 1990, leaving issue, Jonathan Dominick St Clair, *b* 1956: *m* 1984, Philippa Anne, da of Anthony van Beugen Bik, of Busbridge Farmhouse, Godalming, Surrey, and has issue living, Charles Alexander John *b* 1991, Harriet Frances Jessanda *b* 1989, — Jane Fairrie, *b* 1954: *m* 1977, Timothy John Comyn, of Hardington Mandeville, Somerset, and has issue living, James Edward Daniel *b* 1982, Edward John Fitzwalter *b* 1989, Cressida Rose Katharine *b* 1985, — Joanna Elizabeth, *b* 1958, — Juliet Caroline Leslie, *b* 1961: *m* 1992, Jeffrey George Puckett, — Jessanda Katherine Jemima, *b* 1964: *m* 1991, Richard Granville Farrant, of Rose Cottage Farm, Leigh Rd, Norwood Hill, Horley, Surrey. *Residence* – Meysey Hampton Manor, Cirencester. —— Caroline Leslie, *b* 1932. *Residence* – Rowan Cottage, Tadmarton, Banbury.

Grandsons of Edward Fitzwalter Wright (ante):—
Issue of late Margaretta Jane LANGLANDS, *b* 1928, *d* 1984; assumed surname of Langlands 1977: *m* 1949 (*m diss* 1965), Cdr Robert Ian Langlands Pearse, RN:—

Robert Simon Hugh LANGLANDS (4B Orihau Terr, Eastbourne, Wellington, NZ), *b* 1950: *m* 1975, Jane Isobel, da of Raymond Timothy Porter, of Te Awamutu, NZ, and has issue living, Timothy George, *b* 1977, — Rupert Hugh Chalmers, *b* 1988, — Joanna Jane Margaretta, *b* 1980. —— Adam Philip, *b* 1955. —— Dominic Walter, *b* 1959: *m* 1986, France Symons, who *d* 1989.

Grandchildren of late Margaretta Agnes Wright (ante):—
Issue of late Marion Wright, who *d* 1974, having *m* 1920, 7th Viscount Hawarden, who *d* 1958:—
See V Hawarden.
Issue of late Margaretta Wright, who *d* 1977, having *m* 1918, Arthur Philip Coote, who *d* 1954:—
See Coote, Bt, colls.

Issue of late Selina Fanny Plumptre, 2nd sister of 20th Baron, who *d* 1949, having *m* 1897, Lionel Sherbrooke Osmaston, who *d* 1969:—

Robert Lionel OSMASTON, MB, BCh, *b* 1903: *ed* Camb Univ (BA 1924, MB, BCh 1932); MRCS England and LRCP London 1927: *m* 1945, Dorothy, da of Albert Edward Ward, and has issue living, Margaret Elizabeth, *b* 1946: *m* 1st, 1968 (*m diss* 1985), John Richard Bradley, BDS, LDS, RCS; 2ndly, 1987, William Birkmyre Sutherland McIvor, of 42 Belsay, Toothill, Swindon, Wilts SN5 8HB, and has issue living, (by 1st *m*) Robert John *b* 1979, Nicholas James *b* 1982, — Dorothy June, *b* 1947. *Residence* – 11 Lower Stoke, Limpley Stoke, nr Bath, Avon BA3 6HB. —— Marion Margaretta, *b* 1915: *m* 1st, 1941, Capt David Harold Archer, MC, Roy W Kent Regt, who was *ka* in Tunisia 1943; 2ndly, 1973, Lt Cdr Frank Williams, RN, of Ballalhen Cottage, Kirk Andreas, I of Man, and has issue living (by 2nd *m*), Sally Elizabeth, *b* 1954.

Grandson of late Selina Fanny Osmaston (ante):—
Issue of late Gwendolen Selina, *b* 1905, *d* 1989: *m* 1935, Thomas Gerald Elwin Nash, who *d* 1963:—
Stephen Thomas NASH, *b* 1942. *Residence* – Forge Cottage, Goodnestone, nr Canterbury, Kent.

Issue of late Elisabeth Eleanor Plumptre, yst sister of 20th Baron, who *d* 1953, having *m* 1902, Maurice Beresford Wright, OBE, MD, who *d* 1951:—

Marjorie Prunella, *b* 1912: *m* 1939, Charlie Stuart Grunsell, CBE, FRCVS, and has issue living, Robin Nigel Stuart (17 Lowman Rd, N7), *b* 1946: *m* 1968, Angela Boulton, and has issue living, Jonah Charles *b* 1977, Leila *b* 1973, — Elspeth Ann Grant, *b* 1940: *m* 1965, Edward Godfrey Cantrell, MB, MRCP, of Waterside Cottage, South Baddesley Rd, Lymington, Hants SO4 8SD, and has issue living, Matthew Ross *b* 1968, Tamsin *b* 1970: *m* 1992, Danny Byrne, of 152 Efford Way, Pennington, Lymington, Hants, and has issue living, Emily May *b* 1992, — Susanna, *b* 1943. *Residence* – Greenleaves, Mead Lane, Sandford, nr Bristol BS19 5RG.

Grandchildren of late Elisabeth Eleanor Wright (ante):—
Issue of late Nigel Wright, *b* 1908, *d* 1989: *m* 1948, Patricia Kidd (16 Heatherwood, Petersfield Rd, Midhurst, Sussex):—

Andrew Firman WRIGHT (Ashleigh, 14 Ashfield Drive, Macclesfield, Cheshire SK10 3DQ), *b* 1953: MIBiol, PhD: *m* 1977, Susan Bowlas, and has issue living, Alan Nigel, *b* 1986, — Joanna, *b* 1983. —— Susan Jane, *b* 1951: *m* 1974, Robert Andrew Allison, of Redhaven, Melton Drive, Storrington, W Sussex, and has issue living, Elizabeth Sarah, *b* 1980, — Caroline Jane, *b* 1983.

PREDECESSORS – (1) Sir ROBERT FITZWALTER, *b* 1247; Constable of Bere Castle, co Merioneth and of Hadleigh Castle, Essex; Capt and Keeper of the Peace in Essex; summoned to Parliament 1295-1325: *m* 1st, Doverguille, who *d* 1284, da and co-heir of Sir John de Burgh; 2ndly, 1289, Alianore, da of Robert de Ferrers, 6th Earl of Derby (*cr* 1138); 3rdly, 1308, Alice, widow of Sir Warren de l'Isle; *d* 1325; *s* by his son by his 2nd *m* (2) ROBERT, 2nd Baron: *m* Joan da of Thomas Lord Multon; *d* 1328; *s* by his son (3) JOHN, 3rd Baron; summoned to Parliament 1340-60: *m* Alianore, da of Henry, Lord Percy; *d* 1361; *s* by his son (4) WALTER, 4th Baron, *b* 1345; Adm of the Fleet; summoned to Parliament 1369-85: *m* 1st, Alianore, da of Thomas, Lord Dagworth; 2ndly, 1385, Philippa, who *d* 1431, da of John, Lord Mohun; *d* 1386; *s* by his son by his 1st *m* (5) WALTER, 5th Baron, *b* 1368; summoned to Parliament 1390-1404: *m* Joan, da of John, Lord Devereux, of Dinton, Bucks; *d* 1406; *s* by his el son (6) HUMPHREY, 6th Baron, *b* 1398; *d* 1415; *s* by his brother (7) WALTER, 7th Baron, *b* 1400; Master of the King's Hart Hounds and Capt of Vire; summoned to Parliament 1429-30: *m* Elizabeth, da of Sir John Chideock, and widow of William Massy; *d* 1431; *s* by his only child (8) ELIZABETH, Baroness FitzWalter: *m* 1st, of John Radcliffe; 2ndly, 1466, John, Lord Dinham; *d* 1485; *s* by her son (9) JOHN Radcliffe, 9th Baron, *b* 1451; Steward of the King's Household; summoned to Parliament in his mother's Barony 1485-95; attainted of high treason 1495: *m* 1st, Anne, sister of Richard Whetehill, of Calais; 2ndly, Margaret; beheaded 1496; *s* by his son by his 2nd *m* (10) ROBERT, KG, 10th Baron; obtained reversal of attainder by Act of Parliament 1509; summoned to Parliament 1511-23; *cr Viscount FitzWalter* 1525, and *Earl of Sussex* 1529: *m* 1st, Elizabeth, da of Henry Stafford, 2nd Duke of Buckingham; 2ndly, Margaret, da of Thomas Stanley, 2nd Earl of Derby; 3rdly, 1536, Mary, da of Sir John Arundell, of Lanherne, Cornwall; *d* 1542; *s* by his son (11) HENRY, KG, 2nd Earl, *b* 1506: *m* 1st, 1524, Elizabeth, da of 3537, da of Thomas, 2nd Duke of Norfolk; 2ndly, 1539, Anne (whom he divorced), da of Sir Philip Calthorpe; *d* 1556; *s* by his el son (12) THOMAS, KG, 3rd Earl, *b* 1525; summoned in his father's Barony 1553: *m* 1st, 1553, Elizabeth, who *d* 1554, da of 1st Earl of Southampton; 2ndly, 1555, Frances, da of Sir William Sydney; *d* 1583; *s* by his brother (13) HENRY, KG, 4th Earl, *b* 1530: *m* 1549, Honora, da of Anthony Pound; *d* 1593; *s* by his only child (14) ROBERT KG, 5th Earl, *b* 1560; Earl Marshal Oct to Dec 1597 and Oct to Dec 1601: *m* 1st, 1599, Bridget, who *d* 1622, da of Sir Charles Morrison; 2ndly, 1623, Frances, da of Hercules Mentas, and widow of Edward Shute; *dsp* legitimate 1629, when the Viscountcy of FitzWalter and Earldom of Sussex (both of which titles became extinct in 1643) passed to his cousin and heir-male Edward Radcliffe, while the Barony of FitzWalter devolved upon the heir-general (15) Sir HENRY Mildmay (descendant of Lady Frances Mildmay, only da of 2nd Earl of Sussex), *de jure* 15th Baron, *b* 1585; claimed Barony 1641 and 1645 (no order made to the petition): *m* Elizabeth, da of Thomas Darcy; *d* 1654; *s* by his grandson (16) HNERY, *de jure* 16th Baron; claimed the Barony 1660; *d* 1661; *s* by his brother (17) BENJAMIN, 17th Baron, *b* 1646; petitioned for the Barony 1667, and was summoned to House of Lords 1669-70: *m* 1669, Catherine, da of William, 3rd Viscount Fairfax of Emiley; *d* 1679; *s* by his son (18) CHARLES, 18th Baron, *b* 1670: *m* 1693, Elizabeth da of Hon Charles Bertie; *d* 1727; *s* by his brother (19) BENJAMIN, 19th Baron, *b* 1672; Commr of Essex 1720-28; *cr Viscount Harwich*, co Essex, and *Earl FitzWalter* 1735; Treasurer of the Household 1737-55, and Lord-Lieut of Essex 1741-56: *m* 1724, Frederica, da of the 3rd Duke of Schomberg and Duke of Leinster, and widow of Robert Darcy, Earl of Holderness; *d* 1756, when the Earldom and Viscountcy became ext, while the Barony fell into abeyance among the das of Mary, only sister of the 16th and 17th barons (ante) and so remained until 1924 when (after petition to the House of Lords) the abeyance was determined in favour of (20) HENRY FITZWALTER Plumptre, 20th Baron (son of late John Bridges Plumptre, and grandson of Eleanor, wife of Rev Henry Western Plumptre, and da of Sir Brook William Bridges, 4th Bt) (a descendant of Mary, only sister of 16th and 17th Barons), whose el son, Sir Brook William Bridges, 5th Bt, having claimed the Barony of FitzWalter in 1842 as a co-heir, was *cr* Baron FitzWalter by letters patent 1868, but *dsp* 1875, *b* 1860: *m* 1st, 1892, Maude Dora Gertrude, who *d* 1893, da of late Capt Thomas Carpendale Baird (Dorset Regt), of Flatfield, co Ayr; 2ndly, 1908, Emily Harriet Jemima, who *d* 1951, el da of late Capt Thomas Carpendale Baird (ante); *dsp* 1932, when the Barony again fell into abeyance and so remained until 1953, when the abeyance was terminated (after petition to HM the Queen) in favour of (21) FITZWALTER BROOK Plumptre (son of late George Beresford Pumptre, yr brother of 20th Baron), 21st Baron and present peer.

FITZWILLIAM, EARLDOM (Wentworth Fitzwilliam) (Extinct 1979)

DAUGHTER LIVING OF EIGHTH EARL

Lady (Anne) Juliet Dorothea Maud, *b* 1935; *ed* St Hilda's Coll, Oxford (MA); a Co Director, and a former Co Councillor of W Suffolk: *m* 1st, 1960 (*m diss* 1972), as his 2nd wife, 6th Marquess of Bristol, who *d* 1985; 2ndly, 1974, Capt Somerset Struben de Chair, late RHG, of St Osyth Priory, St Osyth, Essex, son of late Admiral Sir Dudley Rawson Stratford de Chair, KCB, KCMG, MVO, and has issue living (by 1st *m*: *see* M Bristol), — (by 2nd *m*) Helena Anne Beatrix Wentworth Fitzwilliam, *b* 1977.

SISTER LIVING OF EIGHTH EARL

Lady (Marjorie) Joan Mary, *b* 1900: *m* 1st, 1925 (*m diss* 1949), Major Grismond Picton Philipps, CVO (Knt 1953), late Gren Gds, who *d* 1967; 2ndly, 1949, Lt-Col William Wallace Smith Cuninghame of Caprington, DSO, JP, DL, late Life Gds, who *d* 1959, and has issue living, (by 1st *m*) Griffith William Grismond (Cwmgwili, Bronwydd Arms, Carmarthen), *b* 1935; *ed* Eton; High Sheriff Carmarthenshire 1972: *m* 1964, Ingrid Götilda, da of Med Dr G. von Sydow, of Gothenburg, Sweden, and has issue living, John George Grismond *b* 1965, Marianne Sioned *b* 1967, Charlotte Ingrid *b* 1969, Ebba Serena *b* 1971, Eva Götilda Joan *b* 1979. *Club* – English-Speaking Union.

WIDOW LIVING OF TENTH EARL

JOYCE ELIZABETH (*Countess Fitzwilliam*) (Milton, Peterborough), da of late Lt-Col Philip Joseph Langdale, OBE (*see* B Mowbray, colls), and formerly wife of 2nd Viscount Fitz Alan of Derwent: *m* 1956, the 10th Earl, who *d* 1979.

FLATHER, BARONESS (Flather) (Life Baroness 1990)

SHREELA FLATHER, da of late Rai Bahadur Aftab Rai, of New Delhi; *b* 19—; *ed* Univ Coll, London (LLB); Bar Inner Temple 1962; JP Berks 1971; infant teacher ILEA 1965-67, teacher of English as a second language 1968-78; Member Cttee of Inquiry into Education of Children from Ethnic Minority Groups (Swann Cttee) 1979-85, Commn for Racial Equality 1980-86, Police Complaints Bd 1982-85, Lord Chancellor's Legal Aid Cttee 1985-88; UK Delegate to Economic and Social Cttee, European Community, 1987-90; Pres Cambs Chilterns and Thames Rent Assessment Panel since 1983, The League of Friends of Broadmoor Hosp since 1991, and Community Council for Berks since 1991; Vice-Pres The Assocn of District Councils since 1990, and Commonwealth Countries League since 1990; Vice-Chm The Refugee Council (Chm UK Policy Group) since 1991; Dir Meridian Broadcasting (MAI) since 1991, and The Thames Valley Enterprise (TEC) since 1990; Trustee The Hillingdon Hosp Trust since 1990; Member LWT Programme Advisory Bd since 1990, Servite Houses Cttee of Management since 1987, and The Carnegie Inquiry into the Third Age since 1991; past member of many national and local social and ethnic cttees; Councillor Royal Borough of Windsor and Maidenhead 1976-91 (first ethnic minority woman councillor in UK), Dep-Mayor 1985-86, Mayor 1986-87 (first Asian woman to hold this office); *cr Baroness Flather*, of Windsor and Maidenhead, co Berks (Life Baroness) 1990: *m* 19—, Gary Denis Flather, QC, and has issue.
Address – House of Lords, SW1A 0PW. *Club* – Oriental.

SONS LIVING

Hon Paul, *b* 1954.
Hon Marcus, *b* 1957.

FLETCHER, BARONY OF (Fletcher) (Extinct 1990)

SONS LIVING OF LIFE BARON

Rev Hon David Clare Molyneux, *b* 1932; *ed* Repton, and Worcester Coll, Oxford; ordained deacon 1958, priest 1959; Scripture Union staff worker 1962-86; Rector of St Ebbe's Oxford since 1986: *m* 1970, Susan Charlotte, da of late Alan Stockdale Langford. *Residence* – St Ebbe's Rectory, 2 Roger Bacon Lane, Oxford OX1 1QE.

Rev Hon Jonathan James Molyneux (Emmanuel Parsonage, 8 Sheep Walk Mews, SW19 4QL), *b* 1942: *ed* Repton, and Hertford Coll, Oxford; incumbent of Emmanuel, Wimbledon SW19, since 1982.

DAUGHTER LIVING OF LIFE BARON

Hon Elizabeth Jane Molyneux, *b* 1938: *m* 1962, David Blair Wilkinson, of Charnwood Lodge, Repton, Derbys DE65 6FN, and has issue.

WIDOW LIVING OF LIFE BARON

BESSIE WINIFRED (*Baroness Fletcher*), da of late James Butt, of Enfield: *m* 1929, Baron Fletcher, PC (Life Baron), who *d* 1990.

FLOREY, BARONY OF (Florey) (Extinct 1968)

SON LIVING OF LIFE BARON

Hon Charles du Vé (Ninewells Hospital and Medical Sch, Dundee, DD1 9SY), *b* 1934; *ed* Camb Univ (BA, MD, BChir); MPH, Yale Univ, USA, FFCM, FRCPEd; Prof Dept of Community Medicine, Ninewells Hospital, Dundee: *m* 1966, Susan Hopkins, and has issue.

DAUGHTER LIVING OF LIFE BARON

Hon Paquita Mary Joanna, *b* 1929: *m* 1955, John McMichael, of 12 Craigleith Gdns, Edinburgh, EH4 3JW, and has had issue.

WIDOW LIVING OF LIFE BARON

Hon MARGARET AUGUSTA Fremantle, DM (*Baroness Florey*) (4 Elsfield Rd, Old Marston, Oxford), da of 3rd Baron Cottesloe, and formerly wife of Denys Arthur Jennings, BM, BCh: *m* 1967, as his 2nd wife, Baron Florey, OM, FRS (Life Baron), who *d* 1968.

FLOWERS, BARON (Flowers) (Life Baron 1979)

BRIAN HILTON FLOWERS, FRS, only son of late Rev Harold J. Flowers, of Swansea; *b* 13 Sept 1924; *ed* Bishop Gore Gram Sch, Gonville and Caius Coll, Camb (MA; Hon Fell) and Birmingham Univ (DSc); Hon DSc Sussex, Wales, Manchester, Leicester, Liverpool and Bristol, Hon DEng Nova Scotia, MA Oxon, Hon DSc Oxon, Hon ScD Dublin; Rutherford Medal and Prize IPPS (1963), Chalmers Medal, Chalmers Univ of Technol, Sweden (1980); Physicist, Head of Theoretical Physics Div at Atomic Energy Research Establishment, Harwell, 1952-58, Prof of Theoretical Physics Manchester Univ 1958-61, Langworthy Prof of Physics 1961-72; Chm Science Research Council 1967-73, Pres Inst of Physics 1972-74, Roy Commn on Environmental Pollution 1973-76, and Standing Commn on Energy and Environment 1978-81; Rector Imp Coll of Science & Technology 1973-85; Pres of European Science Foundation 1974-80; Chm of London Univ Working Party on Future of Medical and Dental Teaching Resources 1979-80; Man Trustee Nuffield Fndn since 1982 and Chm since 1987, Chm Cttee of Vice Chancellors and Principals 1983-85; Vice-Chancellor of London Univ since 1985, Founding Member Exec Council of Academia Europaea 1988; FInstP, Hon FCGI, Hon MRIA, Hon FIEE, Officier de la Légion d'Honneur, Senior Fell Roy Coll of Art; *cr* Kt 1969, and *Baron Flowers*, of Queen's Gate, in the City of Westminster (Life Baron) 1979: *m* 1951, Mary Frances, el da of late Sir Leonard Frederick Behrens, CBE.

Address – c/o The House of Lords, SW1A 0PW.

FOLEY, BARON (Foley) (Baron GB 1776)

ADRIAN GERALD FOLEY, 8th Baron; *b* 9 Aug 1923; *s* 1927; is a composer and pianist: *m* 1st, 1958 (*m diss* 1971), Patricia (DE MEEK), da of Joseph Zoellner III, of Pasadena, California, USA; 2ndly, 1972, Ghislaine, only da of Cornelius Dresselhuys, of The Hague, Holland, formerly wife of (i) Maj Denis James Alexander, Irish Guards (later 6th Earl of Caledon), and (ii) 4th Baron Ashcombe, and has issue by 1st *m*.

Arms – Argent, a fesse engrailed, between three cinquefoils, and the whole within a bordure sable. **Crest** – A lion rampant argent, supporting between the fore paws a shield of the arms of *Foley*. **Supporters** – Two lions argent, semée of cinquefoils sable.
Residence – c/o Marbella Club, Marbella, Malaga, Spain. *Club* – White's.

SON LIVING *(By 1st marriage)*

Hon THOMAS HENRY, *b* 1 April 1961.

DAUGHTER LIVING *(By 1st marriage)*

Hon Alexandra Mary FOLEY, *b* 1960; resumed her maiden name 1989, and again 1994: *m* 1st, 1987 (*m diss* 1989), (Somerset) Carlo de Chair, 3rd surv son of Somerset Struben de Chair, of St Osyth Priory, Essex; 2ndly, 1991 (*m diss* 1994), Janos Klamar. *Residence* – Apt 19C 357 East 57th St, New York, NY 10022, USA.

That I may do good

COLLATERAL BRANCH LIVING

Grandchildren of late Paul Henry Foley, only son of Henry John Wentworth Hodgetts-Foley, great-grandson of 1st Baron:—
Issue of late Henry Thomas Hamilton Foley, MBE, *b* 1905, *d* 1959: *m* 1936, Helen Constance Margaret, who *d* 1985, CStJ, el da of Sir Robert Barclay Pearson:—
Andrew Thomas (Stoke Edith Park, Hereford; *Club* – Boodle's) *b* 1937; *ed* Eton; late Capt Rifle Bde: *m* 1968, Gillian, da of William Carleton Brown, of Over Alderley, Ches, and has issue living, Rupert Thomas, *b* 1970, — Ian Richard *b* 1973. —— John Paul, CB, OBE, MC (*Club* - Boodle's), *b* 1939; *ed* Bradfield; Maj-Gen Rifle Bde; MC 1976, OBE 1979, CB 1991: *m* 1972, Ann Rosamund, only da of John William Humphries, of Coval Court, Sunningdale, Berks, and has issue living, Annabel Frances Helen, *b* 1973, — Joanna Beatrice, *b* 1976. —— Anne Victoria Helen, *b* 1943: *m* 1980, Hugh Nigel Henshaw, of 3 Fernshaw Close, SW10, son of late Harold Henshaw, of Rottingdean, Sussex, and has issue living, Thomas Spencer Edward, *b* 1983, — Katharine Louise Emily, *b* 1981.

PREDECESSORS – Thomas Foley, 2nd and last Baron Foley; *cr* 1712; *d* 1766, and his estates passed to his cousin (1) THOMAS Foley; *cr Baron Foley*, of Kidderminster (peerage of Great Britain) 1776; *d* 1777; *s* by his son (2) THOMAS, 2nd Baron; *d* 1793; *s* by his son (3) THOMAS, 3rd Baron; Lord-Lieut of Worcestershire; *d* 1833; *s* by his son (4) THOMAS HENRY, PC, *b* 1808; MP for Worcestershire W (*L*) 1830-3; Capt of Corps of Gentlemen at Arms: *m* 1849, Lady Mary Charlotte Howard, who *d* 1897, da of 13th Duke of Norfolk; *d* 1869; *s* by his son (5) HENRY THOMAS, 5th Baron, *b* 1850: *m* 1889, Evelyn Vaughan, who *d* 1968, da of Arthur Radford, JP, of Smalley, Derbyshire, and Bradfield Hall, Berks; *d* 1905; *s* by his brother (6) FITZALAN CHARLES JOHN, 6th Baron; *b* 1852; *d* 1918; *s* by his cousin (7) GERALD HENRY (son of late Henry St George Foley, grandson of 3rd son of 3rd Baron), 7th Baron; *b* 1898: *m* 1922, Minoru, who *d* 1968, da of late Harry Greenstone, mine-owner, of Johannesburg, S Africa; *d* 1927; *s* by his son (8) ADRIAN GERALD, 8th Baron and present peer.

Folkestone, Viscount; son of Earl of Radnor.

FOOT, BARON (Foot) (Life Baron 1967)

JOHN MACKINTOSH FOOT, son of late Rt Hon Isaac Foot; *b* 17 Feb 1909; *ed* Bembridge Sch, and Balliol Coll, Oxford (BA); Solicitor 1934; 1939-45 War as Maj RASC (GSO 111, 43rd Div and GSO 11 12th Corps, despatches); *cr Baron Foot*, of Buckland Monachorum, co Devon (Life Baron) 1967: *m* 1936, Anne Bailey, da of Clifford Bailey Farr, MD, of Bryn Mawr, Pa, USA, and has issue.

Arms – Or, on a chevron engrailed sable between three lions' gambs erect and erased gules, three wheels or. **Crest** – Perching on a tower sable, supported by two lions' gambs erect gules, a Cornish chough proper. **Supporters** – *Dexter*, a buck, and *sinister* a Dartmoor pony, each gorged with a wreath of yew proper, and supporting between the legs a sword erect sheathed or, the whole upon a compartment of rock, in the middle thereof a pit proper.
Residence – Yew Tree, Crapstone, Yelverton, Devon.

SON LIVING

For law and liberty

Hon John Winslow, *b* 1939; *ed* Sidcot Sch, and Philadelphia Coll of Art, USA. *Residence* – Knaven Hill Farm, Alderminster, Stratford upon Avon, Warwicks Glos CV37 8PQ.

DAUGHTER LIVING

Hon Katherine Elliott (36 Albert Park Place, Montpelier, Bristol), *b* 1937: *m* 1st, 1955, David Stavely Gordon; 2ndly, 19—, David Illingworth, who *d* 1976, and has issue by 1st and 2nd *m*.

Forbes, Viscount; son of Earl of Granard.

FORBES, LORD (Forbes) (Lord S 1445)

NIGEL IVAN FORBES, KBE, 22nd Lord and Premier Lord of Scotland; *b* 19 Feb 1918; *s* 1953; *ed* Harrow, and RMC; a Representative Peer for Scotland 1955-63; Maj Gren Gds (Reserve); Board Member Aberdeen and Dist Milk Marketing Board 1962-72, Member of Board Sports Council for Scotland 1966-71; Chm of River Don Dist Board, 1960-73; Dep Chm of Tennent Caledonian Breweries, Ltd, 1964-74; Chm of Nat Playing Fields Assocn (Scottish Branch) 1965-80, Chm Rowlawn Ltd since 1975, Pres Scottish Scout Council 1970-88; JP and DL for Aberdeenshire; Adj Gen Guards 1941-43, Staff Coll, a Dist Councillor for Alford 1955-58, a Member of Inter-Parl Union Delegation to Denmark 1956, to Hungary 1965 and to Ethiopia 1971, Pres Roy Highland and Agric Soc of Scotland 1958-59, and a Member Commonwealth Parl Asscn Delegation to Canada 1961 and of Parl Deleg to Pakistan 1962, Mil Assist to High Commr for Palestine 1947-48, Min of State, Scottish Office 1958-59, and a Board Member Scottish Cttee Nature, Conservancy 1962-65; 1939-45 War (wounded): KBE (Civil) 1960: *m* 1942, Hon Rosemary Katharine Hamilton-Russell, only da of 9th Viscount Boyne, and has issue.

Arms – Azure, three bears' heads couped argent, muzzled gules. **Crest** – A stag's head attired with ten tynes proper. **Supporters** – Two bloodhounds argent, collared gules.
Seat – Castle Forbes, Alford, Aberdeenshire. *Residence* – Balforbes, Alford, Aberdeenshire AB3 8DR.
Club – Army and Navy.

SONS LIVING

Hon MALCOLM NIGEL (*Master of Forbes*) (Castle Forbes, Alford, Aberdeenshire AB33 8BL), *b* 6 May 1946: *ed* Eton, and Aberdeen Univ: *m* 1st, 1969 (*m diss* 1982), Carole Jennifer Andrée, da of late Norman Stanley Whitehead, of Aberdeen; 2ndly, 1988, Mrs Jennifer Mary Gribbon, da of Ian Peter Whittington, of Tunbridge Wells, and has issue living (by 1st *m*), Neil Malcolm Ross, *b* 10 March 1970, — Joanne Carole, *b* 1972.
Hon Jonathan Andrew (East Cevidley, Alford, Aberdeenshire AB33 8BH), *b* 1947; *ed* Eton; Capt Grenadier Guards: *m* 1981, Hon Nichola Frances Hawke, da of 10th Baron Hawke, and has issue living, James Frederick Nicholas, *b* 1987, — Camilla Rose, *b* 1983, — Annabella Jane, *b* 1985.

DAUGHTER LIVING

Hon Gillian Rosemary, *b* 1949: *m* 1969, Alexander Neil Foster (*see* E Perth, colls, 1985 Edn), of Church Farmhouse, Blakesley, Towcester, Northants, and has issue living, Michael Alexander, *b* 1973, — Lucia Katharine, *b* 1970.

COLLATERAL BRANCHES LIVING

Granddaughter of late Capt Hon Walter Robert Drummond Forbes, 7th son of 18th Lord:—
Issue of late Sir (Victor) Courtenay Walter Forbes, KCMG, *b* 1889, *d* 1958: *m* 1st, 1916 (*m diss* 1949), Luia, da of late Hon Sir Henry Herbert Juta; 2ndly, 1950, Mary, who *d* 1972, da of Francis George Olivieri, and widow of Walter Carter Bizley:—
(By 1st *m*) Sara Elizabeth Ninita, *b* 1917: *m* 1938, Hugh Gyle-Thompson, who *d* 1972, and has issue living, David Courtenay Gladstone, *b* 1943; *ed* Charterhouse, and Ch Ch Oxford: *m* 1970, Penelope Fearnley, and has issue living, Camilla Kate *b* 1974, — Elizabeth Helen Donita, *b* 1939: *m* 1965, George Oliver Papps, of USA, and has issue living, Gillian Sara *b* 1967, Luia Elizabeth *b* 1970, — Sara Anne Robina, *b* 1941: *m* 1969, Christopher Watson, and has issue living, Timothy Hugh James *b* 1970, Angus Christopher Hugo *b* 1972.

Grandsons of late Hon Montagu Ormond Forbes, 8th son of 18th Lord:—
Issue of late Col Courtenay Fergus Ochoncar Grey Forbes, late Coldm Gds, *b* 1898, *d* 1971: *m* 1st, 1924 (*m diss* 1928), Gundrede Mary, da of late Capt Graham Owen Robert Wyne (B Killanin); 2ndly, 1929, Mary Shelagh, who *d* 1932, da of late Col Arthur Llewellyn, Som LI; 3rdly, 1933 (*m diss* 1954), Dorothea, da of His Honour late Henry Staveley Staveley-Hill, TD, 4thly, 1954, Emilie de Kosenko, who *d* 1981, da of late Mrs Edward Brooks of New York, and widow of 5th Baron Monteagle of Brandon:—
(By 1st *m*) (Fergus) Patrick (Remenham Piece, Henley-on-Thames, Oxon), *b* 1925: *m* 1st, 1950, (Margaret) Elizabeth, da of John Percy Wayte; 2ndly, 1967, Jeanette Fendryck, of Baltimore, and has issue living (by 1st *m*) Christopher Michael Fergus, *b* 1955, — Grania Elizabeth, *b* 1950: *m* (Moira) Isobel *b* 1957: *m* 19—, William M. Underhill, son of late His Honour Judge (Michael) Underhill, and of Mrs William Beaumont, of Richmond, Surrey, and has issue living, a da *b* 1992, a da *b* 1994, — (by 2nd *m*) a son, *b* 1974. —— (By 3rd *m*) John Alistair Ponsonby (All Saints House, nr Axminster, Devonshire EX13 7LR; Boodle's Club), *b* 1937; late Capt Coldm Gds: *m* 1965, Mary Dorothea, da of Sir William Macnamara Goodenough, 1st Bt, and has issue living, James William Courtenay, *b* 1970, — Sophie Louisa Dorothea, *b* 1968.

Granddaughter of late Col Robert Ochoncar Hawkins Forbes, el son of Hon Robert Forbes, 6th son of 17th Lord:—
Issue of late Robert Ochoncar Forbes, *b* 1859, *d* 1913: *m* 1898, Juliana Olga, who *d* 1954, da of Major John Nevinson, formerly 4th Hussars:—
Rosalie Jessie Olga (Flat 1, 20 Lansdowne Rd, W11 3LL), *b* 1904: *m* 1938, Thomas Percival Durant Beighton, who *d* 1971.

Granddaughter of late Rev Malcolm Forbes (infra):—
Issue of late Maj Malcolm Hay Ochoncar Forbes, *b* 1891, *d* 1973: *m* 1st, 1921, Edith Maud, who *d* 1962, only da of G. A. MacMillan; 2ndly, 1966, Mrs Helen Roslyn Dickson, who *d* 1970, da of A. C. Graham:—
(By 1st *m*) Helen Mary Hay, *b* 1922: *m* 1945, Fl-Lt Terence Dudley Thompson, RAAF, and has issue living, Ian Forbes, *b* 1951, — Pamela Forbes, *b* 1947, — Jane Forbes, *b* 1948, — Georgina Helen Forbes, *b* 1968.

Grandchildren of late Robert Inglis Forbes, el son of Col Henry Twisden Forbes, 3rd son of Hon Robert Forbes (ante):—
Issue of late William Robert Townsend Forbes, *b* 1893, *d* 1967: *m* 1925, Evelyn, who *d* 1989, da of late Very Rev Preb H. Erskine-Hill, DD, of Much Dewchurch, Hereford:—
Ian Robert Patrick (93 Steyne Rd, Southborne, Hants), *b* 1926: *m* 1953 (*m diss* 1971), Patricia Heginbotham, of Brighton. —— William Michael (21 Rosenau Cres, SW11), *b* 1934: Cdr RN: *m* 1957 (*m diss* 19—), Wendy Ann Birch of Southsea, and has issue living, David Charles, *b* 1959, — Simon Robert, *b* 1964, — Jeremy Andrew, *b* 1966, — Anne Lesley, *b* 1960; *ed* Bristol Univ (MD). —— *Rev* Patrick (14 East St, Lilley, nr Luton, Beds LU2 8LP), *b* 1938; Broadcasting Officer, Church of England: *m* 1962, Annette Margaret Miller, of Upper Norwood, SE, and has issue living, Stephen Robert, *b* 1967.
Issue of late Kenneth Herbert Forbes, *b* 1899, *d* 1981: *m* 1st, 1929 (*m diss* 1938), Zara Muriel, da of late Walter Currie; 2ndly, 1947, (Dorothy) Joan (Orchard Cottage, Coopers Hill Lane, Englefield Green, Surrey), da of late Alfred Percival Folkard:—
(By 2nd *m*) Colin Kenneth, *b* 1956. *Residence* – 46 Addison Gdns, W14. —— (By 1st *m*) Susan, *b* 1933: *m* 1958, Iain Stuart Bain, FSA, of New Cottage, Newnham, Baldock, Herts, and has issue living, Christina Mary, *b* 1961: *m* 1993, Alasdair Anderson, — Catriona Frances, *b* 1964.

Issue of late Herbert Russell Forbes, *b* 1863, 2nd son of Col Henry Twisden Forbes (ante), *d* 1920: *m* 1896, Amy Ella, who *d* 1935, da of late William Duncan Scott, of Graylands, Chiswick:—
Marjorie Alice, *b* 1900: *m* 1920, John Taylor Porritt, who *d* 1976, of Great Green House, Cockfield, Bury St Edmunds, Suffolk, and has issue living, Joan April, *b* 1921: *m* 19—, — Yates, — Gillian, *b* 1927: *m* 19—, — Lindsey-Renton (PO Box 747, Olifantsfontein 1665, S Africa), and has issue, two das.

Granddaughters of late Charles Twisden Forbes, 3rd son of late Col Henry Twisden Forbes (ante):—
Issue of late Archibald Herbert D'Esterre Forbes, MC, *b* 1899, *d* 1956: *m* 1924, Emily Flora, who *d* 1991, da of late S. K. Keyes, of The Dene, Dartford:—
Isla Hamiton, *b* 1926: *m* 1948, Rev Philip Paul Stanley Brownless, of The Hornpipe, Oak Meadow, Birdham, Chichester, W Sussex, and has issue living, Benjamin Stanley, *b* 1956, — Alison Kilworth, *b* 1950; *ed* Bristol Univ: *m* 1973, Alan Geoffrey Browne, MICE, and has issue living, Radley Alan Forbes *b* 1978, Carola Jody Merchant *b* 1981. — Rona Kilworth, *b* 1928: *m* 1952, Raymond Frank Abraham Hunter, MC, of RR1 Lawrencetown, Nova Scotia, Canada B0S 1MO, and has issue living, Charles William Forbes, *b* 1955: *m* 1979, Christine Mary Parker, and has issue living, Robyn *b* 1981, Chantal *b* 1984, — Jolyon Nigel Forbes, *b* 1958: *m* 1983, Maura Cameron, and has issue living, Matthew *b* 1988, (Raymond) Alexander *b* 1991, Sarah *b* 1986, Emily Jean *b* 1993, — Mark Raymond Forbes, *b* 1960: *m* 1985, Pauline Irvin, and has issue living, Abby *b* 1990, — William John Forbes, *b* 1965: *m* 1988, Rebecca Houtsma, and has issue living, Tegan Anneke *b* 1992, (Rona) Katherine *b* 1994. *Residence* – Hunters, Laurencetown, Nova Scotia.

Granddaughter of late Francis Sutherland Courtenay Forbes, 2nd son of late Col Walter Ernest Forbes, 4th son of Hon Robert Forbes (ante):—
Issue of late Lt-Cdr Haydon Marriott Sutherland Forbes, DSC, RN, *b* 1897, *d* 1927: *m* 19—, Cecily, da of Capt — Armitage, RN:—
Pamela Patricia, *b* 1925.

Granddaughters of late Ernest Colebroke Forbes, yst son of late Col Walter Ernest Forbes (ante):—
Issue of late Atholl Courtenay Forbes, *b* 1892, *d* 1952: *m* 1926, Veronica Elizabeth (who *d* 1966, having *m* 2ndly, 1939, L. A. C. Houston, of 79 Southbourne Gdns, Eastcote, Middlesex), da of Arthur Willis, of Gisbourne, NZ:—

Pamela Jane, *b* 1929; formerly a Sister Tutor, QARNNS: *m* 1958, Richard Bostock, and has issue living, John Edward, *b* 1960: *m* 1986, Katherine Helen Dandy, — David Forbes, *b* 1962: *m* 1990, Yujin Chung, and has issue living, Richard Daejin *b* 1990, — Julia Elizabeth, *b* 1965: *m* 1993, Kevin David Kinsella.
  Issue of late Ernest Twisden Forbes, *b* 1902, *d* 1966: *m* 1932, Mavis Amy, who *d* 1973, da of Edward Ingham of Melbourne:—
Barbara Beatrice, *b* 1934: *m* 1963, Hubert Andrew Thebo, BS (9116 Quintana Drive, Bethesda, Maryland 20034, USA), and has issue living, Christine Forbes, *b* 1967.

          Grandchildren of late Arthur St Quintin Forbes, yst son of late Hon Robert Forbes (ante):—
      Issue of late Bertie St John Ochoncar Forbes, *b* 1882, *d* 1953: *m* 1902, Margaret Smith, who *d* 1946:—
Bertie St John Ochoncar, *b* 1918; 1939-45 War as Maj Indian Army and Roy Scots: *m* 1942, Anne Moore Crozer, and has issue living, Graham Richard, *b* 1946: *m* 1971, Anne Catherine Haigh, of Edinburgh, and has issue living, Callum Richard *b* 1972, — Gillian Margaret *b* 1951. —— Alice Margaret Whitelaw, *b* 1906: *m* 1929, Robert Gray Pottinger, who *d* 1933, and has issue living, Ronald Forbes, *b* 1933; MB and ChB Edinburgh 1959: *m* 1960, Marija Ozanic, and has issue living, David Forbes, *b* 1964.

          Descendants of William Forbes (4th in descent from Hon Duncan Forbes, 2nd son of 2nd Lord), who was *cr* a *Baronet* 1626:
See Stuart-Forbes, Bt.

          Descendants of William Forbes (5th in descent from Hon Sir Patrick Forbes, 3rd son of 2nd Lord), who was *cr* a *Baronet* 1630:
See L Sempill and Forbes, Bt, *cr* 1630.

PREDECESSORS – (1) *Sir* ALEXANDER de Forbes, of that Ilk, feudal baron of Forbes; *cr Lord Forbes* (peerage of Scotland) about 1445; *d* 1448; *s* by his son (2) JAMES, 2nd Lord; *d* 1460; *s* by his son (3) WILLIAM, 3rd Lord; *s* by his el son (4) ALEXANDER, 4th Lord; *s* by his brother (5) ARTHUR, 5th Lord; *d* 1493; *s* by his brother (6) JOHN, 6th Lord; *d* 1547; *s* by his son (7) WILLIAM, 7th Lord; *d* 1593; *s* by his son (8) JOHN, 8th Lord; *d* (June) 1606; *s* by his son (by 2nd *m*) (9) ARTHUR, 9th Lord; *d* 1641; *s* by his son (10) ALEXANDER, 10th Lord; *d* 1672; *s* by his son (11) WILLIAM, 11th Lord; *d* 1691; *s* by his son (12) WILLIAM, PC, 12th Lord; *d* 1716; *s* by his el son (13) WILLIAM, 13th Lord; *d* 1730; *s* by his son (14) FRANCIS, 14th Lord; *d* a minor 1734; *s* by his uncle (15) JAMES, 15th Lord; *d* 1761; *s* by his son (16) JAMES 16th Lord, *d* 1804; *s* by his son (17) JAMES OCHONCAR, 17th Lord; Gen in the Army, Repres Peer, and High Commr to Gen Assembly, Ch of Scotland; *d* 1843; *s* by his son (18) WALTER, 18th Lord, *b* 1798; served at Waterloo: *m* 1st 1825, Horatia, who *d* 1862, da of Sir John Gregory Shaw, Bt; 2ndly 1864, Louisa, who *d* 1921, da of late James Ormond; *d* 1868; *s* by his son (19) HORACE COURTENAY, 19th Lord, *b* 1829; Repres Peer 1874-1906; *d* 1914; *s* by his brother (20) ATHOLL MONSON, 20th Lord; *b* 1841: *m* 1876, Margaret Alice, who *d* 1943, da of Sir William Hammer Dick-Cunnygham, 8th Bt; *d* 1916; *s* by his son (21) ATHOLL LAURENCE CUNYNGHAM, 21st Lord; *b* 1882; Maj Gren Gds; Repres Peer 1917-24: *m* 1914, Lady Mabel Anson, who *d* 1972, da of the 3rd Earl of Lichfield; *d* 1953; *s* by his son (22) NIGEL IVAN, 22nd Lord, and present peer.

*FORESTER, BARON (Weld-Forester) (Baron UK 1821)

(GEORGE CECIL) BROOKE WELD-FORESTER, 8th Baron; *b* 20 Feb 1938; *s* 1977; *ed* Eton, and Roy Agric Coll, Cirencester; patron of three livings; Dir Linley Farms since 1974, and Sipolilo Estates since 1977; formerly Chm Shropshire CLA, Shropshire Tree Council, and Regional Advisory Cttee of the Forestry Commn; Pres The Greenwood Trust since 1990, and Shropshire FWAG since 1991; Member W Midland Council for Sport and Recreation since 1991, Member Exec Cttee CLA, CLA Council, and Minerals Working Party CLA: *m* 1967, Hon (Elizabeth) Catherine Lyttelton, da of 10th Viscount Cobham, and has issue.

Always the same

Arms – Quarterly: 1st and 4th quarterly, per fesse indented argent and sable, in the 1st and 4th quarters, a bugle horn of the 2nd, *Forester*; 2nd and 3rd azure, a fesse nebulée between three crescents ermine, and in the centre chief point across crosslet fitchée or, *Weld*. **Crests** – 1st, a talbot passant argent, collared sable, and line reflexed or; 2nd, a wyvern sable, guttée, collared, and lined and wings elevated or, on the wing an escallop of the first. **Supporters** – Two talbots argent, collared sable, lined or, and pendant from the collar a bugle horn of the second.
Residences – Willey Park, Broseley, Shropshire; Bassett, Banket, Zimbabwe.

SON LIVING

Hon CHARLES RICHARD GEORGE, *b* 8 July 1975.

DAUGHTERS LIVING

Hon Selina Lucy, *b* 1968.
Hon Alice Sophie, *b* 1969.
Hon Alexandra Elizabeth, *b* 1973.

SISTERS LIVING

Hon Christine Helena, *b* 1932: *m* 1st, 1951 (*m diss* 1981), 7th Baron Bolton; 2ndly, 1985, Philip David Miles, of Hinton Hall, Lea Cross, Shrewsbury SY5 8JA, son of late Maj Walter Harold Miles, MBE (*see* Greenwell, Bt), and has issue (by 1st *m*) (*see* B Bolton).
Hon (Mary Angela) Fiona (*Hon Lady Barttelot*) *b* 1944; OStJ 1992: *m* 1969, Col Sir Brian Walter de Stopham Barttelot, 5th Bt, OBE, DL, and has issue. *Residence* – Stopham Park, Pulborough, W Sussex RH20 1EB.

COLLATERAL BRANCHES LIVING

Grandchildren of late Hon Charles Cecil Orlando Weld-Forester, 2nd son of 5th Baron:—
Issue of late Lieut-Com Wolstan Beaumont Charles Weld-Forester, CBE, RN, *b* 1899, *d* 1961: *m* 1932, Anne Grace Christian, who *d* 1987, da of late Capt William Augustus Stirling-Home-Drummond-Moray (B Kensington):—
Wolstan William, *b* 1941. —— Beatrice Nicola Grace, *b* 1933: *m* 1955 (*m diss* 1977), 6th Marquess of Bute, who *d* 1993.
Residence – Tylers Barn, Wood Norton Rd, Stibbard, Norfolk NR21 0EX.

Grandchildren of late Maj Hon Edric Alfred Cecil Weld-Forester, CVO (infra):—
Issue of late Charles Robert Cecil Weld-Forester, Capt Rifle Bde, *b* 1919, *d* 1988: *m* 1st, 1940 (*m diss* 1947), Lady Moyra Rosamond Butler, who *d* 1959, da of 4th Marquess of Ormonde; 2ndly, 1948 (*m diss* 1962), Venetia Dawn, el da of Lt-Col Sir (Ernest) Edward de Winton Wills, 4th Bt (*cr* 1904); 3rdly, 1963, Delia, who *d* 1992, formerly wife of late Robin Alan Keith, and yr da of late Lt-Col Guy Andrew Heinekey Buxton:—
(By 2nd *m*) Anthony Edward (Old Manse, Gartmore, By Stirling FK8 3RP), *b* 1954; *ed* Harrow: *m* 1979, Joanna Mary, yst da of late Eric Cyprian Perry Whiteley, TD, and has issue living, Henry James, *b* 1981, — Alfred Charles, *b* 1983, — Jocelyn Victoria, *b* 1986, — Clementine Ruth Katey, *b* 1989. —— Mary Sylvia, *b* 1957: *m* 1986, Bradley Steven Boyd, of 449 NW State St, Bend, Oregon 97701, USA, son of Robert Boyd, of Woodside, Calif, USA, and has issue living, Alexandra Marisa, *b* 1987, — Jennifer Louise, *b* 1991.

Issue of late Maj Hon Edric Alfred Cecil Weld-Forester, CVO, 6th son of 5th Baron, *b* 1880, *d* 1963: *m* 1916, Lady Victoria Alexandrina, who *d* 1966, da of 1st Marquess of Lincolnshire, and widow of Nigel Walter Henry Legge-Bourke (*see* E Dartmouth):—
Mary Cecilia Georgina (*Hon Mrs W. Nicholas S. L. H. Villiers*), *b* 1917: *m* 1939, Major Hon (William) Nicholas Somers Laurence Hyde Villiers, Grenadier Guards (*see* E Clarendon). —— Elizabeth Rosalind, *b* 1923: *m* 1942, Major Francis Holdsworth Hunt, ERD, late Coldm Gds (Inholmes Holt, Woodlands, St Mary, Newbury, Berks RG16 7SX), and has issue living, Charles Edric Holdsworth (Haworth House, Kintbury, nr Newbury, Berks RG15 0TP), *b* 1943; Capt Coldm Gds: *m* 1968, Sarah Mary, da of Maj Anthony Peter Howarth Greenly (*see* Gibson, Bt, *cr* 1926), and has issue living, Guy Edric Holdsworth *b* 1970, Edward Charles Holdsworth *b* 1972, Sacha Victoria Holdsworth *b* 1975, — Elizabeth, *b* 1947: *m* 1st, 1969 (*m diss* 1980), Maj Conway John Edward Seymour, Gren Gds (*see* M Hertford, colls); 2ndly, 1980, Maj A. F. Gradidge, late 17/21st Lancers.

Issue of late Rev Hon Orlando St Maur Weld-Forester, 2nd son of 4th Baron, *b* 1877, *d* 1944: *m* 1913, Dorothy Salome Wynne, who *d* 1963, da of late Rev William Wynne Willson:—
John Orlando (25 Toms Close, Chard, Som TA20 2HD), *b* 1913; Lieut (ret) 2nd N Rhodesia Regt; entered Colonial Education Ser 1938; Assist Director of African Education, N Rhodesia 1959-61, and Assist Sec 1961-4: *m* 1938, Lydia Gertrude, yr da of late Rev Stephen Harold Wingfield Digby, Canon of Salisbury, Wilts, and of Mombasa, Kenya, and has issue living, Priscilla Mary, *b* 1939: *m* 1974, Neville Henry Prendergast Vereker, of Inglewood, 6 Curzon Av, Beaconsfield, Bucks (*see* V Gort, colls), — Elizabeth *b* 1941: *m* 1962, John Jeremy Inskip Hawkins, of 79 The Park, St Albans, Herts AL1 4RX, and has issue living, Rev John Edward Inskip (St Nicholas Church Vicarage, Dee St, Poplar E14 0DT) *b* 1963: *m* 1986, Rev Emma Woodhead, who *d* 1990, Bruce James Orlando *b* 1965: *m* 1993, Fabienne Tamborini (and has issue living, Jade Marie *b* 1994), Veronica Caroline *b* 1967, Sarah Elizabeth *b* 1969: *m* 1991, Jonathan Mark Levesley, of 67 Walsingham Close, Hatfield, Herts, — (Dorothy) Katharine, *b* 1944: *m* 1967, John Wyndham Simson, of The Old Rectory, Mottistone, Newport, I of Wight, and has issue living, Christopher Adhémar *b* 1969, Henrietta Katharine *b* 1971, Penelope Anne *b* 1974, Philippa Lydia Rosamond *b* 1977, — Caroline Lydia, *b* 1948: *m* 1970, Frank John Montague Wakefield, of Rothley, Kingsgate Rd, Winchester, Hants, and has issue living, Nicholas John Alexander *b* 1978, Anna Charlotte *b* 1972, Holly Christina *b* 1974, — Rosamund Eleanor, *b* 1950: *m* 1971 (*m diss* 1978), Raymond James Edmonds.

PREDECESSORS – (1) CECIL Weld-Forester, *b* 1767; assumed by Roy licence 1811, the additional surname of Weld; *cr Baron Forester*, of Willey Park, co Salop (peerage of United Kingdom) 1821: *m* 1800, Lady Katherine Mary Manners, da of 4th Duke of Rutland; *d* 1828; *s* by his el son (2) JOHN GEORGE WELD, PC, 2nd Baron; MP or Wenlock 1826-8, and Capt of Corps of Gentlemen at Arms 1841-6; *d* 1874; *s* by his brother (3) GEORGE CECIL WELD, PC, 3rd Baron; was Comptroller of HM Queen Victoria's Household 1852 and 1858-9; sat as MP for Wenlock (C) 1828-74; *d* 14 Feb 1886; *s* by his brother (4) *Rev* ORLANDO WATKIN WELD, 4th Baron, *b* 1813; Canon Residentiary and Preb of York: *m* 1st, 1840, Sophia Elizabeth, who *d* 1872, da of Richard Norman; 2ndly, 1875, Emma Maria, who *d* 1898, el da of late William Tollemache; *d* 1894; *s* by his el son (5) CECIL THEODORE WELD, 5th Baron, *b* 1842; MP for Wenlock (C) 1874-85: *m* 1866, Emma Georgina who *d* 1922, da of Sir Willoughby Wolstan Dixie, 8th Bt; *d* 1917; *s* by his el son (6) GEORGE CECIL BEAUMONT WELD, 6th Baron, *b* 1867; Capt Roy Horse Guards; Mayor of Wenlock 1920-21 and 1921-22: *m* 1896, Christine Isabel, who *d* 1948, da of late Lieut-Col Duncan Henry Caithness Reay Davidson: *d* 1932; *s* by his son (7) CECIL GEORGE WILFRED, 7th Baron; *b* 1899; ADC to Gov Gen of Union of S Africa 1924-27, and Mayor of Wenlock 1936, and 1916; *m* 1931, Marie Louise Priscilla (DStJ), who *d* 1988, da of Sir Herbert Charles Perrott, 6th Bt, CH, CB (ext); *d* 1977, *s* by his only son (8) (GEORGE CECIL) BROOKE, 8th Baron and present peer.
*This nobleman has in his possession a licence of the time of Henry VIII, giving to John Forester of Watling St, co Salop, the privilege of wearing his hat in the Royal presence.

Formartine, V; grandson of Marquess of Aberdeen.

FORRES, BARON (Williamson) (Baron UK 1922, Bt UK 1909)

Little is made larger by little

Modice · augetur · modicum

ALASTAIR STEPHEN GRANT WILLIAMSON, 4th Baron, and 4th Baronet; *b* 16 May 1946; *s* 1978; *ed* Eton; Chm Agriscot Ppty Ltd, Dir Jaga Trading Ppty Ltd; Australian Rep for Tattersalls Ltd, Newmarket: *m* 1969, Margaret Ann, da of late George John Mallam, of Mullumbimby, NSW, and has issue.

Arms – Argent, a saltire wavy between a mullet in chief and another in base and as many boars' heads couped in the flanks sable. **Crest** – A garb or. **Supporters** – (as recorded at Lyon Office), — On either side a condor proper. *Address* – c/o Messrs Clark, Oliver, Dewar and Webster, Brothockbank House, Arbroath, Angus. *Residence* – Kenso Park, Orange, NSW, Australia. *Clubs* – Brooks's; Australian Jockey; Tattersalls (Sydney); Sydney Turf.

SONS LIVING

Hon GEORGE ARCHIBALD, *b* 16 Aug 1972.
Hon Guthrie John, *b* 1975.

SISTERS LIVING

Hon Juliet Anne, *b* 1949: *m* 1972, Nigel John Eldon Bankes, of Home Farm House, Williamscot, Banbury, Oxon, and has issue living, William Nigel Wynne, *b* 1974, — Louisa Juliet, *b* 1977, — Fiona Gillian, *b* 1981.
Hon Astrid Signe, *b* 1951: *m* 1976, Peter Karl Dobree Bell, of 15/3rd St, Abbotsford, Johannesburg, S Africa, and has issue living, Hugh John, *b* 1982, — Lucy Claire, *b* 1984.

AUNT LIVING (*daughter of 2nd Baron*)

Hon Jean Mary, *b* 1919: *m* 1941, Wing-Com William James Maitland Longmore, CBE (Maitland, Bt, colls), who *d* 1988, and has issue living, Virginia Marjorie, *b* 1945: *m* 1973, Henry D. N. B. Candy, of Kingstone Warren, Wantage, Berks, and has issue living, Emma Juliet *b* 1974, Sophie Bridget *b* 1978, — Carolyn Mary, *b* 1946: *m* 1st, 1966 (*m diss* 1976), Michael E. Denison; 2ndly, 1981, Michael Desmond Poland, MFH (*see* B Stafford, colls), of Lower Preshaw House, Upham, Southampton, and has issue living (by 1st *m*), James Edward *b* 1968, Lucinda Mary *b* 1971, — Jennifer Maitland, *b* 1953: *m* 1975, Maj Patrick J. R. Snowball, 4/7th R Dragoon Gds, of Ash House, Shalden, Alton, Hants GU34 4EB, and has issue living, Robert Joseph Arthur *b* 1981, Thomas Edward James *b* 1984, Edward William George *b* 1990. *Residence* – Cross Lane Cottage, Bishops Waltham, Hants SO3 1FL.

MOTHER LIVING

Gillian Anne Maclean, el da of late Maj John MacLean Grant, RA: *m* 1st, 1945 (*m diss* 1967), the 3rd Baron, who *d* 1978; 2ndly, 1968, Miles Herman de Zoete, who *d* 1987, of Easter Blinkbonny, Haddington, E Lothian.

COLLATERAL BRANCHES LIVING

Issue of late Capt Hon Gerald Hayne Guthrie Williamson, yr son of 1st Baron, *b* 1893, *d* 1966: *m* 1917, Christian Alicia Hersey, who *d* 1958, da of late Edmund Batten Forbes (Stuart-Forbes, Bt, colls):—
Hersey Caroline Ann (Barr, Minard, by Inveraray, Argyll PA32 8YB), *b* 1920; Jun Cdr ATS, served Middle East 1942-44 (despatches), and Italy 1944-45 (despatches): *m* 1st, 1943, Oliver Breakwell, who was *ka* in N Africa 1943; 2ndly, 1945 (*m diss* 1973), Maj Donald Struan Robertson, SG, who *d* 1991, only surviving son of Rt Hon Sir Malcolm Arnold Robertson, GCMG, KBE, and has had issue (by 2nd *m*), Melville Alexander Struan, *b* 1946; *ed* Eton; *dunm* 1969, — Christian Sarah Hersey, *b* 1948: *m* 1984, Pierre Henri René Daviron, of 16 Lyons Place, Larchmont, NY 10538, USA, and has issue living, Olivier Melville Raoul *b* 1985, Juliette Isabelle Christian *b* 1987, — Alexandra Charlotte, *b* 1952: *m* 1980, James Chandos Blair, and has issue living, Hamish Chandos *b* 1982, Charlotte Rose *b* 1985, — Lucinda Margaret Ann, *b* 1960: *m* 1983, Stephen Dominic Patrick Mahony, of Broadclose House, Babcary, Som TA11 7ED, and has issue living, Dermot Edward Struan *b* 1988, Caroline Mary Hersey *b* 1987. —— Jane Christian Forbes, *b* 1931.

Grandchildren of late Capt Hon Gerald Hayne Guthrie Williamson (ante):—
Issue of late Alexander Fergus Forbes Williamson, *b* 1919, *d* 1987: *m* 1943, Sabina Ann (Tigh-na-Coille, Kincraig, by Kingussie, Inverness-shire), only da of late Col Sir Dermot McMorrough Kavanagh, GCVO:—
James David Alexander (Alvie, Kincraig, by Kingussie, Inverness-shire), *b* 1947; *ed* Gordonstoun, Univ of New Brunswick, and Aberdeen Univ; BSc, PhD: *m* 1976, Lynette Robyn, only da of James Stewart, of Feilding, NZ, and has issue living, Ruaraidh James Stewart, *b* 1976, — Joanna Mary, *b* 1980, — Catherine Ngaire, *b* 1985. —— Dermot Fergus, *b* 1950; *ed* Eton, and Dundee Univ: *m* 1987, Yu Yu Su, of Beijing, China, and has issue living, Paula Jiao-Jiao, *b* 1988, Emma Tian-Tian *b* 1989. —— Caroline Ann, *b* 1945: *m* 1968, Capt Colin MacGregor, RN, of The Dairy House, Corton Denham, nr Sherborne, and has issue living, James Patrick, *b* 1972, — Katherine Helen, *b* 1970. —— Rolline Charlotte, *b* 1956: *m* 1989, Jonathan Briscoe Moreton Frewen, of Park Hall, Healaugh, Richmond, N Yorks, and has issue (*see* V Selby).
Issue of late David Archibald Forbes Williamson, MC *b* 1922, *d* 1980: *m* 1953, Elizabeth Wilbur (33 Fifth Av, San Francisco, Calif, USA), da of Roy Case, of Seattle, USA:—
(David) Stephen Charles, *b* 1958: *m* 19—, Susan, da of —. —— Alexander Fergus Case, *b* 1960. —— Charlotte Mary, *b* 1955.

PREDECESSORS – (1) *Rt Hon* ARCHIBALD WILLIAMSON, PC, el son of late Stephen Williamson (MP for St Andrews Dist 1880-85, and Kilmarnock Dist 1886-85), of Copley, Thornton Hough, Cheshire, and Glenogil, Forfar; *b* 1860; a partner in Balfour, Williamson & Co, and Chm of Lobitos Oilfields, and of Central Argentine Railway, and other cos; Parliamentary Financial Sec to War Office 1919-21; MP for Elginshire and Nairnshire (*l*) Jan 1906 to Nov 1918 and for Moray and Nairn Dec 1918 to June 1922; *cr a Baronet* 1909, PC 1918, and *Baron Forres*, of Glenogil, co Forfar (peerage of United Kingdom) 1922: *m* 1st, 1887, Caroline Maria, who *d* 1911, da of late James Charles Hayne; 2ndly, 1912, Hon Agnes Freda, OBE, who *d* 1942, da of 1st Baron Herschell; *d* 1931; *s* by his el son (2) STEPHEN KENNETH GUTHRIE, *b* 1888; Chm of Lobitos Oilfields, and Anglo-Ecuadorian Oilfields; Director of Office Machinery, Board of Trade 1942-45: *m* 1918, Jessica, who *d* 1972, da of late William Alfred Harford, JP, of Petty France, Badminton, Gloucestershire; *d* 1954; *s* by his el son (3) JOHN ARCHIBALD HARFORD, 3rd Baron, *b* 1922; Pres Roy Forest Agric Assocn, Windsor 1963-64; 1939-45 War in Middle East, Sicily, Italy and Normandy (despatches); ADC to Cdr 6th (British) Armoured Div 1944-45: *m* 1st, 1945 (*m diss* 1967), Gillian Ann Maclean, da of Maj John Maclean Grant, RA; 2ndly, 1969 (*m diss* 1974), (Cecily) Josephine, da of Maj Sir Alexander Penrose

Gordon-Cumming, 5th Bt, MC, and widow of the 2nd Earl of Woolton; *d* 1978; *s* by his only son (4) ALASTAIR STEPHEN GRANT, 4th Baron and present peer.

FORSTER OF HARRABY, BARONY OF (Forster) (Extinct 1972)

DAUGHTER LIVING OF FIRST BARON

Hon Pamela FORSTER, *b* 1921; resumed her maiden surname of Forster: *m* 1948 (*m diss* 1951), Peter Hitcham Palmer. *Residence* – 84 Albemarle Rd, Beckenham, Kent.

FORTE, BARON (Forte) (Life Baron 1982)

CHARLES FORTE, son of Rocco (Giovanni) Forte, of Casalattico, Italy; *b* 26 Nov 1908; *ed* Alloa Academy, Dumfries Coll, and Mamiani, Rome; Hon DUniv Strathclyde 1992; Fellow and Member Exec Cttee, Catering Inst since 1949; Member Small Consultative Advisory Cttee to Min of Food since 1946; Member of Council of Brit Tourist Authority and of Lond Tourist Bd; Hon Consul Gen for Republic of San Marino; FBIM; *cr Baron Forte*, of Ripley, co Surrey (Life Baron) 1982: *m* 1943, Irene Mary, da of Giovanni Chierico, of Venice, and has issue.

Arms – Argent four pallets gules over all a bend argent fimbriated azure and on a chief azure three mullets of six points gyronny of twelve or and argent. **Crest** – Out of the battlements of a tower azure a bunch of grapes between two ears of corn proper. **Supporters** – *Dexter*, A pheasant proper. *Sinister*, A salmon proper. **Motto** – Fortis ut jus.
Address – 166 High Holborn, WC1V 6TT. *Clubs* – Carlton, Caledonian and Royal Thames Yacht.

SON LIVING

Hon Rocco John Vincent, *b* 1945; *ed* Downside, and Pembroke Coll, Oxford (MA); Chief Executive Trusthouse Forte plc; FMICA, ACA: *m* 1986, Aliai, yr da of Prof Giovanni Ricci, of Rome, and has issue living, Charles, *b* 1991, — Lydia Irene, *b* 1987, — Irene, *b* 1988. *Address* – 166 High Holborn, WC1V 6TT. *Clubs* – Garrick, Turf.

DAUGHTERS LIVING

Hon Olga, CBE, *b* 1947; CBE (Civil) 1990: *m* 1st, 1966, Marchese Alessandro Polizzi di Sorrentino, who was *k* in a motor accident; 2ndly, 1993, as his 3rd wife, Hon William Hartley Hume Shawcross, elder son of Baron Shawcross, GBE, PC (Life Baron), and has issue living (by 1st *m*), Alexandra, *b* 1971, — Charlotte, *b* 1974. *Residence* – 3 Clarendon Close, W2.

Hon Marie Louise, *b* 1950: *m* 1975, Robert Alexander Burness, and has issue living, Georgina Gerda, *b* 1976, — Julia Irene, *b* 1978. *Residence* – 4 Clarendon Close, W2.

Hon Irene, *b* 1956: *m* 1977, John J. Danilovich, and has issue living, John Charles Amadeus, *b* 1981, — Alexander Gregory, *b* 1993, — Alice Irene Angelica, *b* 1985. *Residence* – 37 Carlyle Sq, SW3.

Hon Giancarla, *b* 1959: *m* 1981, Michael Ulic Anthony Alen-Buckley, and has issue living, Luke Charles Ulic Locke, *b* 1987, — Portia, *b* 1991. *Residence* – 4 Lansdowne Rd, W11.

Hon Portia, *b* 1964.

FORTESCUE, EARL (Fortescue) (Earl GB 1789)

A strong shield is the salvation of leaders

CHARLES HUGH RICHARD FORTESCUE, 8th Earl; *b* 10 May 1951; *s* 1993; *ed* Eton: *m* 1974, Julia, eldest da of Air Commodore John Adam Sowrey, and has issue.

Arms – Azure, a bend engrailed argent, plain cottised or. **Crest** – An heraldic tiger statant argent, armed, maned, and tufted or. **Supporters** – Two greyhounds argent, ducally gorged and lined gules. *Address* – House of Lords, SW1.

DAUGHTERS LIVING

Lady Alice Penelope, *b* 1978.
Lady Kate Eleanor, *b* 1979.
Lady Lucy Beatrice, *b* 1983.

SISTER LIVING

Lady Celia Anne, *b* 1957: *m* 1988, David Alastair Adams, yst son of Dr Michael Shirley Adams, of Alton House, Seaview, I of Wight, and has issue living, Charles Michael Richard, *b* 1992, — Georgina Penelope Anne, *b* 1990. *Residence* – Spilsbury Farm, Tisbury, Wilts SP3 6RU.

HALF-SISTERS LIVING

Lady Laura Margaret, *b* 1962.
Lady Sarah Jane, *b* 1963.

UNCLE LIVING (*Son of 6th Earl by 1st m*)

Hon MARTIN DENZIL, *b* 5 Jan 1924; *ed* Eton; Lieut RN (Emergency List): *m* 1954, Prudence Louisa, who *d* 1992, da of Sir Charles Samuel Rowley, 6th Bt, TD (*cr* 1786), and has issue living, John Andrew Francis (12 Ursula St, SW11), *b* 1955; *ed* Eton: *m* 1990, Phoebe Anne Cecilia, da of late Rev John Eustace Burridge, of Ham Vicarage, Surrey, and has issue living, Thomas Edmund Horatio *b* 1993, — Anthony William (Ryall's Lodge, Gussage St Michael, Wimborne, Dorset), *b* 1962; *ed* Eton: *m* 1992, Emma Davinia, da of Peter Lambert, of Holly Tree Farm, Fearby, nr Masham, N Yorks, — Katharine, *b* 1956, — Georgina Elizabeth, *b* 1958: *m* 1982, Nicholas Hilary Stuart Armour, HM Diplo Ser, son of late Brig William Stanley Gibson Armour, of Brandsby, York, and has issue living, Emily Frances *b* 1985, Sophie Elizabeth *b* 1987. *Residence* – Wincombe Park, Shaftesbury, Dorset.

HALF-UNCLE LIVING (*Son of 6th Earl by 2nd m*)

Hon Seymour Henry (22 Clarendon St, SW1V 4RF), *b* 1942; *ed* Eton, Trin Coll, Camb (MA), and London Graduate Sch of Business Studies (MSc); Finance and Fund-Raising Dir Imperial Cancer Research Fund since 1991: *m* 1st, 1966 (*m diss* 1990), Julia, da of late Sir John Arthur Pilcher, GCMG; 2ndly, 1990, Jennifer Ann, da of Frank Simon, of Wrexham, and has issue living (by 1st *m*), James Adrian, *b* 1978; *ed* Stowe, — Marissa Clare, *b* 1973; *ed* Westminster, and Worcester Coll, Oxford, — (by 2nd *m*) Alexandra Kate, *b* 1991.

AUNT LIVING (*daughter of 6th Earl of 1st m*)

Lady Bridget Ellinor, *b* 1927: *m* 1952, Wing-Com Gordon Leonard Sinclair, DFC, and has issue living, Alan Gordon William (The White House, Adstock, nr Buckingham), *b* 1956; *ed* Eton: Capt Coldstream Gds: *m* 1983, Fiona B., el da of Maj A. M. MacEwan, of Urless Farm, Corscombe, Dorset, and has issue living, Thomas *b* 1985, Archie *b* 1988, Geordie *b* 1993, — Robert Alistair, *b* 1965; *ed* Eton, — (Caroline) Fiona, *b* 1958: *m* 1982, Julian Raymond Eric Smith, of Balcombe House, W Sussex RH17 6PB, and has issue (*see* Burrell, Bt), — Joanna Rosalind, *b* 1963: *m* 1992, Mark P. R. Rimell, of 11 Louvaine Rd, SW11 2AQ, elder son of Philip Rimell, of SW1, and has issue living, Benjamin Charles Philip *b* 1994. *Residence* – Fairwood House, Great Durnford, Salisbury, Wilts SP4 6BD.

DAUGHTERS LIVING OF FIFTH EARL

Lady Margaret FORTESCUE, *b* 1923; resumed 1966 the surname of Fortescue: *m* 1948 (*m diss* 1968), Bernard van Cutsem, who *d* 1975, and has issue living, Eleanor (*Countess of Arran*), *b* 1949: *m* 1974, 9th Earl of Arran, — Rosamund Isabelle, *b* 1952: *m* 1975, Thomas William Fellowes, son of Sir William Albemarle Fellowes, KCVO (*see* V Hampden, colls). *Residence* – The Garden House, Filleigh, Barnstaple, N Devon.

Lady Elizabeth Joan, *b* 1926: *m* 1946, Major William Lloyd (John) Baxendale, Coldstream Guards, DL, JP, who *d* 1982, and has issue living, David Hugh, *b* 1952: *m* 1977, Jacqueline Loveday, da of late John William Hext, of Trelaske, Lewannick, Cornwall, and has issue living, Guy Jonathan *b* 1980, Thomas Lloyd *b* 1983, — Peter Anthony, *b* 1955, — Lucinda Margaret, *b* 1958: *m* 1st, 1980 (*m diss* 1986), Jonathan Edward McCalmont Harington (*see* Harington, Bt, colls); 2ndly, 1992, Nicolas James Goland Crosthwaite, yr son of Major Ivor Crosthwaite, DSO, and of Mrs John Vincent Sheffield, and has issue living (by 2nd *m*), Rose Elizabeth France *b* 1992. *Residence* – Hailwell House, Framfield, Uckfield, E Sussex.

WIDOW LIVING OF SEVENTH EARL

CAROLYN MARY (*Carolyn, Countess Fortescue*), da of Maj Clement Walter Rowland Hill (*see* V Hill, colls), and formerly wife of Edward Lockwood: *m* 1989, as his 3rd wife, the 7th Earl, who *d* 1993. *Residence* – The Old Rectory, Bradoc, Lostwithiel, Cornwall PL22 0RN.

COLLATERAL BRANCHES LIVING

Grandchildren of late Capt Hon Arthur Grenville Fortescue, 4th son of 3rd Earl:—
Issue of late Capt Grenville Fortescue, Rifle Brig (Prince Consort's Own), *b* 1887, *ka* 1915: *m* 1912, Adelaide (who *d* 1977, having *m* 2ndly, 1930, Brigadier Robin Leslie Hutchins, MC, who *d* 1973), el da of late Henry Jephson, of 4 Cornwall Gardens, SW (Crampton, Bt):—
Arthur Henry Grenville, MBE, MC (Walnut Tree Cottage, Skirmett, Henley, Oxon), *b* 1913; *ed* Winchester, and Ch Ch, Oxford; Brig late Coldstream Guards; 1939-45 War (wounded, despatches, MC, MBE); MBE (Mil) 1946: *m* 1946, Rosita Anne, da of late Maj-Gen John Charles Campbell, VC, DSO, MC, and has issue living, Nicholas Cecil John (80 Langthorne

St, SW6), *b* 1953: *m* 1985, Tessa Jane, yr da of Sir (Thomas) David Ainsworth, 4th Bt, and has issue living, Rosie Olivia *b* 1990, Lily Sarah *b* (twin) 1990. —— Diana FORTESCUE, *b* 1915; resumed her maiden name 1947: *m* 1945 (*m diss* 1947), Lieut-Col Charles Murray Floyd, OBE, RE, who *d* 1971 (*see* Floyd, Bt, colls). *Residence* – Mill Meadow, Burley, Ringwood, Hants.

            Granddaughters of Brig Arthur Henry Grenville Fortescue, MBE, MC (ante):—
        Issue of late Mark Charles Grenville Fortescue, *b* 1947; *d* 1982: *m* 1971, Virginia Rose (Church House, Steeple Ashton, nr Trowbridge, Wilts), formerly wife of Richard Wilfrid Beavoir Berens, and yst da of late Anthony William Fabio Caccia-Birch, MC:—
Sabina Therèse, *b* 1973. —— Clarissa Rose Frances, *b* 1975.

            Grandchildren of late John Bevill Fortescue, yst son of late Hon George Matthew Fortescue, MP, 2nd son of 1st Earl:—
        Issue of late Lt Col John Grenville Fortescue, *b* 1896; *d* 1969: *m* 1917, Daphne Marjorie, who *d* 1962, da of late Hon Algernon Henry Bourke (E Mayo, colls):—
John Desmond Grenville (The Stewardry, Boconnoc, Lostwithiel, Cornwall), *b* 1919; *ed* Eton; Coldstream Guards; a DL and JP; High Sheriff of Cornwall 1966-67; 1939-45 War: *m* 1st, 1942, Nina, who *d* 1976, da of late E. Kendall-Lane of Sask, Canada; 2ndly, 1988, Angela Dorothy, widow of T. C. Keigwin, and has issue living (by 1st *m*), Anthony Desmond Grenville (The White House, Queenwood, Broughton, Stockbridge, Hants SO20 8DF), *b* 1946; *ed* Eton: *m* 1977, Elizabeth Ann Evered, da of late Maj Campbell Evered Poole, and has issue living, Clare Elizabeth *b* 1981, Sarah Alexandra *b* 1984, — Anne Desnia, *b* 1948: *m* 1970, Capt Iain Anthony Mackie, 15/19 Hus, and has issue living, Hamish Anthony *b* 1973, Alastair Desmond *b* 1977, Archibald Iain *b* 1979. —— Rosemary Sylvia, *b* 1920: *m* 1944, Douglas Frederick Thomas White, of The Manor, Berwick Bassett, Swindon, Wilts, and has issue living, John Frederick Fortescue (Overtown Manor, Wroughton, Swindon, Wilts), *b* 1946: *m* 1972, Rosemary Kathleen, da of Maj Edward Palmer, of Fernvale, Northam, N Devon, and has issue living, Douglas John *b* 1985, Nancy Ruth *b* 1976, Jessica Rosemary *b* 1979, — David Grenville (The Old Farm House, Berwick Bassett, Swindon, Wilts), *b* 1948: *m* 1970, Diana Penelope, da of Peter Werden Wilson, of The Manor, Clyffe Pypard, Wilts, and has issue living, Edward John Grenville *b* 1973, Lucia Genevieve Rosemary *b* 1977, Anastasia Sophie *b* 1985, — April Rosemary, *b* 1950: *m* 1971, Robert Edward Simpson, of 4 Belgrave Cres, Edinburgh EH4 3AQ, and has issue living, Charles Robert *b* 1980, Nichola Rosemary *b* 1971, Rachel Elizabeth *b* 1974, Emma Louise *b* 1976. —— June Diana, *b* 1924: *m* 1952, Derek Alistair Bigham, of Chalkstone House, Broad Hinton, Swindon, Wilts, and has issue living, Diana Susan, *b* 1954: *m* 1988, William Brandon Grundy, and has issue living, David Matthew *b* 1988, — Julia Rosemary, *b* 1959: *m* 1988, Anthony Peregrine Dudley Berendt (*see* E Harrowby).

            (In remainder to Barony of Fortescue only)

            Grandchildren of late William Archer IRVINE-FORTESCUE, son of late Archer Irvine-Fortescue, son of Rev William Fortescue, LLB, 2nd son of Capt Hon Matthew Fortescue, 2nd son of 2nd Baron:—
        Issue of late Col Archer Irvine-Fortescue, DSO, *b* 1880; *d* 1959: *m* 1916, Ruth Olive, who *d* 1971, da of late Henry Boddington, JP of Pownall Hall, Wilmslow, Cheshire;—
James William, *b* 1917; *ed* Edinburgh Acad, and Aberdeen Univ (MA honours 1937); CA 1948; 1939-45 War as Maj and Staff Paymaster RAPC; a member of Kincardine Co Council 1952-8 and 1964-73, a JP and DL for Kincardineshire; FSA Scot 1981: *m* 1953, Margaret Guise, da of late Lt-Col G. D. Yates, of Todhillwood, Canonbie, Dumfriesshire, and has issue living, Grenville Archer, *b* 1954; *ed* Fettes; Maj Gordon Highlanders: *m* 1985, Virginia, da of Patrick William Townsend, of The Dower House, Gisburn, nr Clitheroe, Lancs, and has issue living, Alexander Thomas *b* 1987, Simon Archer *b* 1988, Juliet *b* 1991, — Henry Boswell (13 Roseneath Terrace, Edinburgh EH9 1JS), *b* 1958; *ed* St Andrew's Univ (MA 1982): *m* 1989, Hazel J., 2nd da of Ernest Wood, — James Robert (Äsliveien 3A, 1320 Stabekk, Norway), *b* 1960; *ed* Aberdeen and Imperial Coll London (BSc): *m* 1990, Wendy Jayne, da of S. A. W. Milne, of King's Gate, Aberdeen, — Rachel Sarah, *b* 1956. *Residence* – Kingcausie, Maryculter, Aberdeen AB1 0AR. —— Agnes Virginia FORTESCUE (Village au Brun, N Dame de Cenilly, 50210 France), *b* 1922; Mus Bac, Cape Town; LRAM: *m* 1st, 1944, Donald Spencer Nuttall, Lieut RA, who was *ka* in Burma 1945; 2ndly, 1949 (*m diss* 1964), Jerzy Wladislaw Jaholkowski; 3rdly, 1973 (*m diss* 1986), Eric Lee Attwell.
        Issue of late Rev John Faithful Irvine-Fortescue, *b* 1883, *d* 1957: *m* 1917, Anne, who *d* 1976, da of late J. Brockhurst Souter, of Newhaven:—
Hugh William (12 Alameda Rd, Ampthill, Beds), *b* 1930; *ed* Glasgow Acad, and Glasgow Univ (BSc); MIEE: *m* 1967, Patricia Anne Elizabeth, da of late F. J. Dudgeon, of Kingsknowe, Edinburgh, and has issue living, John Hugh, *b* 1968, — Caroline Anne Patricia, *b* 1971, — Katherine Helen Isobel, *b* 1974. —— Edith Caroline, *b* 1921; *ed* Glasgow Univ (MA honours 1942). *Residence* – 5 Seton Place, Edinburgh 9.
        Issue of late Lt-Col William Grenville Irvine-Fortescue, MC (and bar), RE, *b* 1897, *d* 1980: *m* 1st, 1921 (*m diss* 1929), Joan Evelyn Mary, da of Henry Sydney Powell, of Pocklington, Yorkshire; 2ndly, 1941, Sheila, who *d* 1985, da of Dr W. Bennett Jones, of Liverpool:—
(By 1st *m*) Henry (Xalet Henri, Auvinia, S Julia de Loria, Andorra), *b* 1922; *ed* Cheltenham; Maj (ret) R Tank Regt; European War 1941-45, Korea 1953, Malaya 1955, Cyprus 1957: *m* 1st, 1951, Bridget Unity, who *d* 1981, da of late Col Edmund Portman Awdry, MC, TD, DL, of Chippenham, Wilts; 2ndly, 1983 (*m diss* 1987), Anne van Gruisen, and has issue living (by 1st *m*), Alexander Ramsay (Chernocke House, St Cross Rd, Winchestr SO23 9QP), *b* 1952; *ed* Wellington, King's Coll, London (BSc Eng), and Univ of Cape Town (MBA): *m* 1980, Kathryn, da of late Paul Randles, of Natal, S Africa, and has issue living, Mark Paul *b* 1980, Nicholas Alexander *b* 1983, James Ramsay *b* 1987, — Ian Henry (176 6th Road, Erand AH, Midrand, S Africa), *b* 1954; *ed* Wellington Coll, and Keele Univ (BSc): *m* 1986, Vanessa Louise Mary Marion Lloyd, da of John Grey Haswell, of Johannesburg, and has had issue, Logan McWatt *b* 1988; *d* 1990, Drummond McLeod *b* 1990, Brittany Avalon *b* 1991, Romney Foy *b* 1993, — Victoria Awdry, *b* 1957: *m* 1982, Graham Herbert Tibbot, of 7 Delph Lane, Delph, Saddleworth, nr Oldham OL3 5HX, and has issue living, Graham Henry *b* 1985, Bridget Elizabeth *b* 1986, Sarah Hannah *b* 1990, Martha Victoria *b* 1993. —— (By 2nd *m*) William Archer (Wingham House, Canterbury Rd, Wingham, Canterbury, Kent CT3 1BH), *b* 1945; *ed* Wellington Coll, and Wadham Coll, Oxford (MA): *m* 1979, Clare, da of Bernard Ungerson, CBE. —— (By 1st *m*) Valerie Faith (54c Ashgrove Rd, Aberdeen AB2 5AD), *b* 1925. —— (By 2nd *m*), Margaret Ann, *b* 1944; *ed* Aberdeen Univ (MA): *m* 1979, Richard John Jacob, of 2 Christchurch Rd, Norwich NR2 2AD, and has issue living, Mark Robert, *b* 1980, — Peter Richard, *b* 1984.

PREDECESSORS – (1) Sir HUGH Fortescue; summoned to Parliament 1721 in right of his maternal grandmother, as 14th *Baron Clinton* (peerage of England), and *cr Baron Fortescue* of Castle Hill, co Devon, with remainder to his half-brother Matthew, and *Earl of Clinton* (peerage of Great Britain) 1746; was a Lord of the Bedchamber; *dsp* 1751, when the earldom expired, the Barony of Clinton fell into abeyance, and the Barony of Fortescue passed to his half-brother (2) MATTHEW, 2nd Baron; *b* 1719; *d* 1785; *s* by his son (3) HUGH, DCL, 3rd Baron; *cr Viscount Ebrington* and *Earl Fortescue* (peerage of Great Britain) 1789; *d* 1841; *s* by his son (4) HUGH, KG, 2nd Earl, *b* 1783; summoned to House of Lords in his father's Barony of Fortescue 1839, Lord-Lieut of Ireland 1839-41: *m* 1st, 1817, Lady Susan Ryder, who *d* 1827, da of 1st Earl of Harrowby; 2ndly, 1841, Elizabeth, da of Piers Geale, and widow of Sir Marcus Somerville, 4th Bt, MP; *d* 1861; *s* by his son (5) HUGH, 3rd Earl, *b* 1818; summoned to House of Peers in his father's Barony of Fortescue 1859; sat as MP for Plymouth (L) 1841-52, and for Marylebone 1854-9; a Lord of the Treasury, 1846-7, and Sec to Poor Law Board 1847-51; *m* 1847, Georgiana August Charlotte Caroline, who *d* 1866, el da of late Right Hon George Lionel Dawson-Damer; *d* 1905; *s* by his son (6) HUGH, KCB, 4th Earl, *b* 1854; Lord-Lieut of Devonshire 1904-28; MP for Tiverton (L) 1881-5, and for W, or Tavistock, Div of Devonshire 1885-92: *m* 1886, Hon Emily Ormsby-Gore, CBE, who *d* 1929 (an Extra Lady of the Bedchamber to Queen Mary), da of 2nd Baron Harlech; *d* 1932; *s* by his son (7) HUGH WILLIAM, KG, CB, OBE, MC, PC, 5th Earl; *b* 1888; was Col

Comdt Hon Artillery Co 1935-41, Capt of the Hon Corps of Gentlemen-at-Arms April to July 1945, and 1951-8, Lord-in-Waiting to HM 1936-45, and Ch Opposition Whip in House of Lords 1945-51: *m* 1917, Hon Margaret Helen Beaumont, CBE, who *d* 1958, da of 1st Viscount Allendale; *d* 1958, *s* by his brother **(8)** DENZIL GEORGE, MC, TD, 6th Earl; *b* 1893; Lt-Col 96th (R Devon Yeo) Regt 1935-41 and 1st Heavy Regt RA 1942-44: *m* 1st, 1920 (*m diss* 1941), Marjorie Ellinor, OBE, who *d* 1964, da of late Col Charles William Trotter, CB (B Hamilton of Dalzell); 2ndly 1941, Hon Sybil Mary Hardinge, who *d* 1985, da of 3rd Viscount Hardinge; *d* 1977; *s* by his el son **(9)** RICHARD ARCHIBALD, 7th Earl, *b* 1922; Capt Coldstream Guards: *m* 1st, 1949, Penelope Jane, who *d* 1959, yr da of late Robert Evelyn Henderson (*see* Clerke, Bt, 1980 Edn); 2ndly, 1961 (*m diss* 1987), Margaret Anne, da of Charles Michael Stratton, of Hall Farm, Evenley, Northants (*see* E Perth, colls, 1985 Edn); 3rdly, 1989, Mrs Carolyn Mary Lockwood, da of Maj Clement Walter Rowland Hill (*see* V Hill, colls); *d* 1993; *s* by his only son **(10)** CHARLES HUGH RICHARD, 8th Earl and present peer; also Viscount Ebrington, and Baron Fortescue.

FORTEVIOT, BARON (Dewar) (Baron UK 1917, Bt UK 1907)

JOHN JAMES EVELYN DEWAR, 4th Baron, and 4th Baronet; *b* 5 April 1938; *s* 1993; *ed* Eton: *m* 1963, Lady Elisabeth Jeronima Waldegrave, 3rd da of 12th Earl Waldegrave, and has issue.

Arms – Or, on a pale vert the crozier of St Fillan proper, on a chief engrailed gules a holy lamb passant reguardant, staff and cross argent with the banner of St Andrew proper, between two stalks of barley slipped also proper. **Crest** – A cock proper. **Supporters** – (as recorded at Lyon Office), – *Dexter*, the figure of St Fillan holding in his exterior hand his crozier proper; *sinister*, an eagle, wings erected proper.
Seat – Dupplin Castle, Perth. *Residence* – Aberdalgie House, nr Perth. *Clubs* – Boodle's, The Royal Perth Golfing Soc, County & City.

SON LIVING

Hon ALEXANDER JOHN EDWARD, *b* 4 March 1971; *ed* Eton, and Newcastle Univ.

DAUGHTERS LIVING

Hon Mary Emma Jeronima, *b* 1965: *m* 1988, Hon Adam Humphrey Drummond, eldest son of Baroness Strange, and has issue.
Hon Miranda Phoebe, *b* 1968.
Hon Henrietta Cynthia, *b* 1970.

BROTHER LIVING

Hon Simon Thomas (Terling Park, Moree, NSW 2400, Australia), *b* 1941: *m* 1st, 1970, (*m diss* 1973), Helen Elizabeth, da of W. N. Bassett, of Karoola Park, Roma, Qld; 2ndly, 1979, Jennifer Alexandra, da of late John Edward St J. Hedge, of Avoca Beach, NSW, and has issue living (by 2nd *m*), Fiona Mary, *b* 1980. — Alexandra Jean, *b* 1982, — Mary Caroline, *b* 1984.

SISTERS LIVING

Hon Caroline Cecily (*Hon Lady Worsley*), *b* 1934: *m* 1st, 1956 (*m diss* 1966), 3rd Duke of Fife; 2ndly, 1980, as his 2nd wife, Gen Sir Richard Edward Worsley, GCB, OBE, and has issue (by 1st *m*) (*see* D Fife).
Hon Penelope Cynthia, *b* 1935: *m* 1959 (*m diss* 1978), Norman Frank Paul Butler, and has had issue, Paul, *b* 1960, *d* 1988, — Sean, *b* 1963, — Tracey Penelope, *b* 1961. *Residence* – 73 Duchess Drive, Newmarket, Suffolk.

PREDECESSORS – **(1)** JOHN ALEXANDER Dewar, son of late John Dewar, distiller, of Perth; *b* 1856; Chm of John Dewar and Sons (Limited); a Director of Buchanan-Dewar (Limited), and of Distillers Co (Limited); twice Lord Provost of Perth; MP for Inverness-shire (*L*) 1900-1916; *cr* a *Baronet* 1907, and *Baron Forteviot*, of Dupplin, Perthshire (peerage of United Kingdom) 1917: *m* 1st, 1884, Johann, who *d* 1899, da of William Tod, of Gospetry, Kinross-shire; 2ndly, 1905, Margaret Elizabeth, who *d* 1940, el da of late Henry Holland; *d* 1929; *s* by his el son **(2)** JOHN, 2nd Baron, *b* 1885; Lieut-Col and Brevet Col late 6th/7th Batn Black Watch (TA) Chm of Distillers Co Ltd, and Brigadier Roy Co of Archers (King's Body Guard for Scotland); Lord Provost of Perth, 1922-5; European War 1914-19 (MC): *m* 1st, 1919, Marjory Winton Isobel, ARRC, who *d* 1945, 2nd da of late Lieut-Col Sir Charles Henry Brabazon Heaton-Ellis, CBE, of Wyddiall Hall, Herts; 2ndly, 1946, Muriel Cecil Harriotte, who *d* 1975, da of late Lt-Col Sir Charles Henry Brabazon Heaton-Ellis, CBE, and widow of (i) Richard Charles Graves-Sawle (Graves-Sawle, Bt), and (ii) Major Alwyn Lionel Compton Cavendish (D Devonshire, colls); *d* 1947; *s* by his half-brother **(3)** (HENRY) EVELYN ALEXANDER, MBE, *b* 1906, 3rd Baron; *b* 1906; Chm John Dewar & Sons Ltd; JP and DL Perthshire; 1939-45 War as Maj The Black Watch: *m* 1933, Cynthia Monica, who *d* 1986, el da of late Piers Cecil Le Gendre Starkie (*see* de Hoghton, Bt, 1972-73 Edn); *d* 1993; *s* by his elder son **(4)** JOHN JAMES EVELYN, 4th Baron and present peer.

Foxford, Baron, title of Earl of Limerick on Roll of HL.

FRANCIS-WILLIAMS, BARONY OF (Williams) (Extinct 1970)

SON LIVING OF LIFE BARON

Hon John Melville, QC, *b* 1931; *ed* St Christopher Sch, Letchworth, and St John's Coll, Camb, Bar Inner Temple 1955, QC 1977: *m* 1955, Jean Margaret, da of Harold Lucas, of Huddersfield, and has issue. *Residence* – Deers Hill, Abinger Hammer, Dorking, Surrey. *Chambers* – 15 Old Square, Lincoln's Inn, WC2.

DAUGHTER LIVING OF LIFE BARON

Elizabeth Frances (does not use courtesy title), *b* 19—: *m* 1963, George Alexander Thomson, of 27 Haverfield Gdns, Kew, Richmond, Surrey, and has issue.

FRANKS, BARONY OF (Franks) (Extinct 1992)

DAUGHTERS LIVING OF LIFE BARON

Hon Caroline Lesley, *b* 1939: *m* 1962, Prof John Rowland Dinwiddy, of Blackhall Farm, Garford Rd, Oxford, and has issue. He *d* 1990.
Hon Alison Elizabeth, *b* 1945: *m* 1973, Stanley Harris Wright, of 6 Holly Place, Holly Walk, Hampstead, NW3.

FRASER OF ALLANDER, BARONY OF (Fraser) (Disclaimed 1966, Extinct 1987)

DAUGHTERS LIVING OF (DISCLAIMED) SECOND BARON (*By 1st marriage*)

Hon Patricia Lydia, *b* 1963.
Hon Belinda Ann, *b* 1964.
Hon Caroline Emily, *b* 1966.

DAUGHTER LIVING OF FIRST BARON

Hon Ann Lewis, *b* 1932.

WIDOW LIVING OF FIRST BARON

KATIE HUTCHEON (*Baroness Fraser of Allander*) (Allander Lodge, Milngavie, Dunbartonshire), da of late Sir Andrew Jopp Williams Lewis, LLD: *m* 1931, the 1st Baron, who *d* 1966.

FRASER OF CARMYLLIE, BARON (Fraser) (Life Baron 1989)

PETER LOVAT FRASER, PC, son of Rev George Robson Fraser, of Corrennie, Edinburgh; *b* 29 May 1945; *ed* Loretto, Gonville and Caius Coll, Camb, and Edinburgh Univ; QC 1982, Hon Bencher Lincoln's Inn 1989; Advocate since 1969, Visiting Prof of Law, Dundee Univ, since 1985, Standing Junior Counsel (Scotland) to FCO 1979, PPS to Rt Hon George Younger, Sec of State for Scotland, 1981-82, Solicitor-Gen for Scotland 1982-89, since when Lord Advocate, Min of State Scottish Office since 1992; MP Angus South (*C*) 1979-83, and Angus East (*C*) 1983-87; PC 1989; *cr Baron Fraser of Carmyllie*, of Carmyllie in the District Angus (Life Baron) 1989: *m* 1969, Fiona, da of Hugh Murray Mair, of Lanark, and has issue.
Residence – Slade House, Carmyllie, by Arbroath, Angus.

SON LIVING

Hon James Murray, *b* 1974.

DAUGHTERS LIVING

Hon Jane Helen Anne, *b* 1972.
Hon Catriona Elizabeth, *b* 1981.

FRASER OF KILMORACK, BARON (Fraser) (Life Baron 1974)

(RICHARD) MICHAEL FRASER, CBE, yr son of late Dr Thomas Fraser, CBE, DSO, TD, DL, LLD, of 16 Albyn Place, Aberdeen, by his wife Maria-Theresia Kayser, of Hanover; *b* 28 Oct 1915; *ed* Fettes Coll, and King's Coll, Camb (MA); entered Conservative Research Dept 1946 (Head of Home Affairs Section 1950-51, Dir 1951-64, and Chm 1970-74); Sec to the Conservative Party's Advisory Cttee on Policy 1951-64, and Dep Chm 1970-75; Sec to Conservative Leader's Consultative Cttee 1964-70, and 1974-75; Dep Chm Conservative Party Orgn 1964-75; 1939-45 War as Lt-Col RA (MBE); Dir Glaxo Holdings plc and Glaxo Group Ltd 1975-85; Glaxo Enterprises Inc (USA) 1983-86; Whiteaway Laidlaw Bank Ltd since 1981; *cr* MBE (Mil) 1945, CBE (Civil) 1955, Knt 1962, *Baron Fraser of Kilmorack*, of Rubislaw, in Co of City of Aberdeen (Life Baron) 1974: *m* 1944, Elizabeth Chloe, el da of late Brig Cyril Alexander Fraser Drummond, OBE, of Little Knoll, Portishead, Somerset, and has issue.

Arms – Quarterly, 1st and 4th, azure, three cinquefoils argent all within a bordure counter company of the first and second: 2nd and 3rd, argent, three antique crowns gules. **Crest** – A buck's head couped argent collared azure and attired or. **Supporters** – Two pine martens proper.
Residence – 18 Drayton Court, SW10 9RH. *Clubs* – Carlton, St Stephen's-Constitutional (Hon), Coningsby (Pres).

SON LIVING

Hon Angus Simon James (Applecote, Pilgrims Way, Boughton Aluph, Ashford, Kent TN25 4EX), *b* 1945; *ed* Fettes Coll, Selwyn Coll Camb (MA), and INSEAD (MBA); Dir Chloride Group plc and Man Dir Imperial Coll of Science, Technology and Medicine: *m* 1970, Jennifer Ann, da of Colin McKean Craig, FRCS, and has issue.

FRASER OF LONSDALE, BARONY OF (Fraser) (Extinct 1974)

DAUGHTER LIVING OF LIFE BARON

Hon Margaret Joan, *b* 1920: *m* 1939, Arthur Edward McDonald, and has issue.

FRASER OF TULLYBELTON, BARONY OF (Fraser) (Extinct 1989)

SON LIVING OF LIFE BARON

Hon (Alexander) Andrew Macdonell, *b* 1946: *m* 1982 (*m diss* 19—), Sarah J., da of Henry Jones, of Kitsbury Orchard, Oddington, Moreton-in-Marsh, Glos, and has issue living, Bertie *b* 1984.

WIDOW LIVING OF LIFE BARON

MARY URSULA CYNTHIA GWENDOLEN (*Baroness Fraser of Tullybelton*), da of Col Ian Harrison Macdonell, DSO, late Highland LI: *m* 1943, Baron Fraser of Tullybelton, PC (Life Baron), who was *k* in a motor accident 1989. *Residence* – Le Clauzel, 24620 Marquay, France.

FREYBERG, BARON (Freyberg) (Baron UK 1951)
(Name pronounced Fryburg)

VALERIAN BERNARD FREYBERG, 3rd Baron; *b* 15 Dec 1970; *s* 1993.

Arms – Or, on a chief sable four mullets of the field. **Crest** – A demi lion gules holding between the paws an eagle displayed sable. **Supporters** – On either side a salamander proper.
Residence – Munstead House, Godalming, Surrey GU8 4AR.

SISTERS LIVING

Hon Annabel Pauline, *b* 1961.
Hon Venetia Rose, *b* 1963: *m* 1991, Robert Phillips, son of late John Phillips. *Residence* – 61 Myddelton Sq, EC1R 1XX.
Hon Christina Marie-Gabriel, *b* 1967.

WIDOW LIVING OF SECOND BARON

IVRY PERRONELLE KATHARINE (*Baroness Freyberg*), only da of late Cyril Harrower Guild, of Aspall Hall, nr Debenham, Suffolk: *m* 1960, Col the 2nd Baron, OBE, MC, who *d* 1993. *Residence* – Munstead House, Godalming, Surrey GU8 4AR.

PREDECESSORS – **(1)** *Sir* BERNARD CYRIL Freyberg, VC, GCMG, KCB, KBE, DSO, son of J. Freyberg, of Wellington, New Zealand; *b* 1889; Lt-Gen late Grenadier Guards and Manchester Regt; GOC, New Zealand Expeditionary Force 1939-45, and Gov-Gen and C-in-C of New Zealand 1946-52, and Dep Constable and Lt-Gov of Windsor Castle 1953-63; *cr Baron Freyberg*, of Wellington, New Zealand, and of Munstead, co Surrey (peerage of UK) 1951: *m* 1922, Dame Barbara, GBE, who *d* 1973, da of Sir Herbert Jekyll, KCMG, and widow of Hon Francis Walter Stafford MacLaren, MP (B Aberconway); *d* 1963; *s* by his only son **(2)** PAUL RICHARD, OBE, MC, 2nd Baron, *b* 1923; Col late Gren Guards, served Greece and W Desert 1940-42, N Africa and Italy 1942-45, Palestine 1947-48, Cyprus 1956-58, and Cameroons 1961, AAG HQ London Dist 1962-65, Col Gen Staff to Dir Territorials, Volunteers & Cadets 1971-75; author of *Bernard Freyberg, VC: Soldier of Two Nations* 1991: *m* 1960, Ivry Perronelle Katharine, only da of late Cyril Harrower Guild, of Aspall Hall, nr Debenham, Suffolk; *d* 1993; *s* by his only son **(3)** VALERIAN BERNARD, 3rd Baron and present peer.

FULTON, BARONY OF (Fulton) (Extinct 1986)

SONS LIVING OF LIFE BARON

Hon (Kenneth Angus) Oliver, *b* 1941; *ed* Eton, Balliol Coll, Oxford (BA) and Univ of California.
Hon Alan Scott, *b* 1946; *ed* Eton and Balliol Coll, Oxford: *m* 1983, (Herminie) Jane, da of Geoffrey J. Bulman, of Pool House, Harpenden, and has issue.
Hon Duncan John Rowntree, *b* 1949; *ed* Eton and Balliol Coll, Oxford.

DAUGHTER LIVING OF LIFE BARON

Hon Charity Marion Annie, *b* 1951.

WIDOW LIVING OF LIFE BARON

JACQUELINE (*Baroness Fulton*) (Brook House, Thornton-le-Dale, N Yorks), da of Kenneth Edward Towler Wilkinson, of York: *m* 1939, Baron Fulton (Life Baron), who *d* 1986.

FURNESS, VISCOUNT (Furness) (Viscount UK 1918)

WILLIAM ANTHONY FURNESS, 2nd Viscount; *b* 31 March 1929; *s* 1940; *ed* Downside, and in USA; Regent, British Sub-Priory of Bl Adrian Fortescue, Sovereign Mil Order of Malta since 1982; formerly Gdsm Welsh Guards (invalided); Knt of Justice (Solemn Vows 1982) and Grand Cross of Merit, Sovereign Mil Order of Malta, Grand Officer Order of Merit of Italy, Knt Cer, with Star, Order of St Gregory the Great; Grand Cross of Grace, Constantinian Order of St George; KStJ; Delegate to 42nd, 43rd, 44th, 48th, 50th and 52nd Inter-Parl Union Conferences, Washington 1953, Vienna 1954 Helsinki 1955, Warsaw 1959, Brussels 1961 and Belgrade 1963; Founder Chm of Anglo-Mongolian Soc 1963-67; Vice-Pres of London Univ Catholic Chaplaincy Assocn 1952-78 and Sec-Gen of British Assocn of Sovereign Mil Order of Malta 1965-78 (Sec 1956-65, a Member of Sovereign Council 1960-62, Member, Board of Auditors 1979-80); Chm of Council of Soc of St Augustine of Canterbury 1964-73, a Member of Council of Hansard Soc for Parl Govt 1955-67; Vice-Pres, Catholic Stage Guild.

𝖆rms – Or, a talbot sejant sable, in chief three fountains proper. 𝕮rest – Issuant from a chaplet of cinquefoils vert a bear's paw erect argent grasping a javelin in bend sinister sable, pendant therefrom by the straps two spurs or. 𝖘upporters – On either side a sea dog reguardant proper gutte d'eau.

Address – c/o Midland Bank Ltd, 69 Pall Mall, SW1. *Clubs* – Boodle's, Carlton, Travellers' (Paris).

PREDECESSOR – (1) CHRISTOPHER Furness, seventh son of late John Furness, of West Hartlepool, by Averill, da of John Wilson, of Naisbet Hall, co Durham; *b* 1852; a Shipowner, Shipbuilder, and Engine-builder, and founder of the "Furness Line" of Steamships; MP for Hartlepool (*L*) Jan 1891 to June 1895 and Oct 1900 to May 1910; *cr Baron Furness*, of Grantley, W Riding of co York (peerage of United Kingdom) 1910: *m* 1876, Jane Annette, who *d* 1930, da of late Henry Suggitt, of Brierton, co Durham; *d* 1912; *s* by his only son (2) MARMADUKE, 2nd Baron; 1883; a Shipbuilder and an Iron and Steel Works and Colliery Proprietor; *cr Viscount Furness*, of Grantley, W Riding of co York (peerage of United Kingdom) 1918: *m* 1st, 1904, Daisy, who *d* 1921, da of G. J. H. Hogg, of Seaton Carew, co Durham; 2ndly, 1926 (*m diss* 1933), Mrs Thelma CONVERSE, who *d* 1970, da of late Harry Hays Morgan, US Consul-Gen at Buenos Aires; 3rdly, 1933, Enid Maud (who *d* 1973, having *m* 4thly, as his 2nd wife, 6th Earl of Kenmare), da of Charles Lindeman, of Sydney, and widow of (1) Roderick Cameron, of New York, and (2) Brig-Gen Frederick William Lawrence Sheppard Hart Cavendish, CMG, DSO (*see* B Waterpark, colls); *d* 1940; *s* by his only surviving son (3) WILLIAM ANTHONY, 2nd Viscount and present peer; also Baron Furness.

FURNIVALL, BARONY OF (Dent) (Baron E 1295) (Abeyant 1968)

MARY FRANCES KATHERINE DENT, BARONESS FURNIVALL, *d* 1968, when the Barony fell into abeyance between her two daughters.

DAUGHTERS LIVING OF MARY FRANCES KATHERINE DENT, BARONESS FURNIVALL (19th holder of Barony)
(*Co-heiresses to the Barony*)

Hon ROSAMOND MARY (Sister Ancilla, OSB, of St Mildred's Abbey, Minster, Ramsgate), *b* 3 June 1933.

Hon PATRICIA MARY (Trotwood, 11 Gresham Rd, Limpsfield, Oxted, Surrey), *b* 4 April 1935: *m* 1st, 1956 (*m diss* 1963), Capt Thomas Hornsby, late Durham LI, who *d* 1967; 2ndly, 1970, Roger Thomas John Bence, and has issue living, (by 1st *m*), Francis Walton Petre, *b* 1958, — Clare Mary Petre, *b* 1957: *m* 1984, Robert Ralph Harbord, of 22 Winsham Grove, SW11 6ND, and has issue (*see* B Suffield, colls), — (by 2nd *m*) Richard William Petre, *b* 1976, — Katharine Rosamond Petre, *b* 1971.

GAGE, VISCOUNT (Gage) (Sits as Baron GB 1790) (Viscount I 1720, Bt E 1622)

Courage without fear

(HENRY) NICOLAS GAGE, 8th Viscount, and 15th Baronet; *b* 9 April 1934; *s* 1993; *ed* Eton, and Ch Ch, Oxford; 2nd Lieut late Coldstream Gds: *m* 1974, Lady Diana Adrienne Beatty, da of 2nd Earl Beatty, and has issue.

𝕬rms – Quarterly: 1st and 4th, per saltire argent and azure, a saltire gules, *Gage*; 2nd and 3rd azure, a sun in splendour or, *St Clere*. 𝕮rest – A ram statant argent, armed and unguled or. 𝕾upporters – Two greyhounds of a light brown colour, proper, gorged with plain collars, adorned on their upper edges with fleurs-de-lis or.
Seat – Firle Place, Lewes, E Sussex. *Residence* – The Cottage, Charwelton, Daventry, Northants.

SONS LIVING

Hon HENRY WILLIAM, *b* — 1975.
Hon David Benedict, *b* 1977.

SISTER LIVING

Hon Camilla Jane (*Hon Lady Cazalet*), *b* 1937; Dir Lumley Cazalet Ltd since 1967, Trustee Glyndebourne Arts Trust since 1978, and Member Royal National Theatre Board since 1991: *m* 1965, Sir Edward Stephen Cazalet, DL (Hon Mr Justice Cazalet), and has issue living, David Benedict, *b* 1967, — Henry Pelham, *b* 1969, — Lara Imogen Leonora, *b* 1973. *Residences* – 58 Seymour Walk, SW10 9NF; Shaw Farm, Plumpton Green, nr Lewes, E Sussex BN7 3DG.

WIDOW LIVING OF SEVENTH VISCOUNT

DEIRDRE MELINA JANE (*Deirdre, Viscountess Gage*), da of late Thomas James Simmons: *m* 1990, as his 2nd wife, the 7th Viscount, who *d* 1993. *Residence* – Firle Place, Lewes, E Sussex.

COLLATERAL BRANCHES LIVING

Grandchildren (by 2nd *m*) of late John Fitzhardinge Berkeley Gage (*infra*):—
Issue of late John Grenville Berkeley Gage, *b* 1933, *d* 1983: *m* 1961, Pauline (45 Kew Rd, Richmond, Surrey), da of Antony Paul Pape:—
Ælla Rupert Fitzhardinge Berkeley, *b* 1966. —— Cassandra Griselda Louise, *b* 1961; *d* 1992. —— Emma Leonora Falaise, *b* 1963.

Grandchildren of late Lt-Col Ælla Molyneux Berkeley Gage, son of late Lt-Gen Hon Edward Thomas Gage, CB (*infra*):—
Issue of late John Fitzhardinge Berkeley Gage, *b* 1901, *d* 1967: *m* 1st, 1923 (*m diss* 1927), Beth Olivia, who *d* 1948, adopted da of late Brig-Gen Ronald Maclachlan, Rifle Bde; 2ndly, 1931 (*m diss* 1937), Griselda Margaret, who *d* 1992, yr da of late Rear-Adm Sir Godfrey Marshall Paine, KCB, MVO; 3rdly, 19—, Jenny Elvira (15 Rodger's Rd, Gibraltar), da of —:—
(By 2nd *m*) Thomas Ælla Godfrey (Ashwick, Dulverton, Somerset) *b* 1935; *ed* Eton: *m* 1st, 1960 (*m diss* 1982), Dorothy Isobel Margaret, da of John Baxter Wylie; 2ndly, 1983, Ina Merete, da of Johan Frederik Utke Meincke, of Denmark, and has issue living (by 1st *m*), Andrew Thomas Berkeley, *b* 1961, — John Duncan Godfrey, *b* 1962, — Caroline Margaret, *b* 1966, — Amber Camilla, *b* 1969. —— Malcolm Edward Fitzhardinge (c/o Barclays Bank, 1 Cockspur St, SW1), *b* 1936; late RHG; *ed* Eton: *m* 1971, Vanessa Smith, who *d* 1984. —— Dawn Falaise, *b* 1932: *m* 1st, 1952 (*m diss* 1963), John Kershaw Sanders; 2ndly, 1963, Capt John Pym Loughnan, RN, of Creek Cottage, Saltern's Lane, Hayling Island, Hants, and has issue living, (by 1st *m*) John James Godfrey, *b* 1953, — Guy Dominic Robson, *b* 1955, — Hugo Thomas Kershaw, *b* 1957.

Grandsons of late Sir Berkeley Everard Foley Gage, KCMG (*infra*):—
Issue of late Anthony St Clere Berkeley Gage, *b* 1931, *d* 1984: *m* 1965, Virginia Mary, da of Denis H. Ferens, of Bilver, Ipplepen, S Devon:—
Benjamin Francis, *b* 1969. —— Gregory Bernard, *b* 1971. —— Oliver, *b* 1973.

Grandson of late Brig-Gen Moreton Foley Gage, DSO (*infra*):—
Issue of late Sir Berkeley Everard Foley Gage, KCMG, sometime HM Amb to Thailand, *b* 1904, *d* 1994: *m* 1st, 1931 (*m diss* 1954), Hedwig Maria Gertrud Eva, da of Carl von Chappuis, of Liegnitz, Silesia; 2ndly, 1954, Mrs Lillian Riggs Miller (*Lady Gage*) (24 Ovington Gdns, SW3), da of Vladimir Vukmirovich:—
(By 1st *m*) Ulick Charles Christopher, *b* 1938; *ed* Eton, and St John's Coll, Camb (BA); late 2nd Lieut 12th Lancers; ARIBA, ARIAA: *m* 1964, Helen Mary Janet, da of Air Vice-Marshal Evelyn Michael Thomas Howell, CBE, and has issue living, Marius Berkeley, *b* 1966, — Ulicia Mary, *b* 1965. *Residence* – 19 Bruce St, Stanmore, NSW 2048, Australia.

Grandchildren of late Lieut-Gen Hon Edward Thomas Gage, CB, 3rd son of 4th Viscount:—
Issue of late Brig-Gen Moreton Foley Gage, DSO, late 5th Dragoon Guards, *b* 1873, *d* 1953: *m* 1st 1902, Anne Massie, who *d* 1915, el da of William Everard Strong, of New York City, USA; 2ndly, 1916, Frances, who *d* 1955, da of Senator Henry P. Lippitt, of Providence, Rhode Island, USA:—
(By 1st *m*) Edward Fitzhardinge Peyton, *b* 1906; *ed* Eton, and Ch Ch, Oxford (BA); formerly Maj Coldm Gds; High Sheriff Shropshire 1963: *m* 1931, Thailia Westcott, da of Stephen Caldwell Millett, and has issue living, Robert Westcott Moreton (50 Pimlico Rd, SW1W 8LP), *b* 1934; *ed* Eton, and Ch Ch, Oxford; late Lt Life Gds: *m* 1st, 1964 (*m diss* 1978), Maria Teresa Francisca, da of late Don Emilio Maria Diaz-Caneja; 2ndly, 1990, Elisabeth Nicola Maria, da of Benjamin Hubert Dowson, and has issue living (by 1st *m*), Henry St Clere Rokewood *b* 1966, Dolores Isabella *b* 1965, — Anne Caroline Thalia (*Hon Mrs Robin A. Baring*), *b* 1931; *ed* St Hilda's Coll, Oxford (MA): *m* 1960, Hon Robin Alexander Baring (*see* B Ashburton), — Elizabeth Estling (20 Albemarle St, W1), *b* 1937: *m* 1st, 1957 (*m diss* 1965), David Vernon Russell; 2ndly, 1970, David Bruce Douglas Lowe; 3rdly, 1974, Richard Perkins. *Residence* – Château de Combecave, 82190 Bourg de Visa, Tarn et Garonne, France. —— (By 2nd *m*) Quentin Henry Moreton, *b* 1920; *ed* Eton, and Ch Ch, Oxford; formerly Maj Gren Gds; 1939-45 War (wounded): *m* 1949, Hazel Swinton, da of Col George Archibald Swinton Home, DSO, OBE, late 5th Dragoon Gds, and has issue living, Jonathan Moreton, *b* 1954, — Deborah Pamela, *b* 1950. *Residence* – Pelham Cottage, Church Lane, Hellingly, E Sussex BN27 4HA. —— Dorothy Louise, *b* 1917: *m* 1941, Maj Anthony George Akers-Douglas, late 13th/18th Hussars (*see* V Chilston, colls), who *d* 1991. *Residence* – 23 Mytten Close, Cuckfield, W Sussex RH17 5LN.

PREDECESSORS – (1) THOMAS Gage: *cr a Baronet* 1622; *d* 1633; *s* by his son **(2)** *Sir* THOMAS, 2nd Bt; *d* 1655; *s* by his el son **(3)** *Sir* THOMAS, 3rd Bt; *d* unmarried 1660; *s* by his brother **(4)** *Sir* JOHN, 4th Bt; *s* by his el son **(5)** *Sir* JOHN, 5th Bt; *d* 1700; *s* by his brother **(6)** *Sir* THOMAS, 6th Bt; *d* 1713; *s* by his brother **(7)** *Sir* WILLIAM, KCB, 7th Bt, MP for Seaford; *d* unmarried 1744; *s* by his cousin **(8)** THOMAS, 8th Bt el son of Joseph, 4th son of 2nd Bt; MP for Tewkesbury, Verderer of the Forest of Dean and Steward of the Household to Frederick, Prince of Wales; *cr* prior to his succession to the baronetcy *Baron Gage*, of Castlebar, and *Viscount Gage* (peerage of Ireland) 1720; *d* 1754; *s* by his son **(9)** WILLIAM HALL, 2nd Viscount; *cr Baron Gage*, of Firle, co Sussex (peerage of Great Britain) 1780, and *Baron Gage*, of High Meadow, co Gloucester (peerage of Great Britain) 1790, and with remainder to his nephew, heir presumptive to the peerage of 1720 and to the baronetcy; *d* 1791, when the Barony of Gage, of Firle became extinct, and the peerages of 1720 and 1790 devolved upon his nephew **(10)** HENRY, 3rd Viscount, el son of Gen Hon Thomas, 2nd son of 1st Viscount; a Major-Gen in the Army; *d* 1808, *s* by his son **(11)** HENRY HALL, 4th Viscount; *d* 1877; *s* by his grandson **(12)** HENRY CHARLES (son of Hon Henry Edward Hall Gage (el son of 4th Viscount), and Sophia Selina, who *d* 1886, da of Sir Charles Knightley, 2nd Bt), 5th Viscount, *b* 1854: *m* 1894, Leila Georgina, who *d* 1916, da of Rev Frederick Peel; *d* 1912; *s* by his only son **(13)** HENRY RAINALD, KCVO, 6th Viscount, *b* 1895; Vice-Lieut for Sussex 1957-70; Chm and Patron Nat Federation of Housing Socs; a Lord-in-Waiting to HM 1924-29 and 1931-39: *m* 1st, 1931, Hon Alexandra Imogen Clair Grenfell, who *d* 1969, da of 1st Baron Desborough (ext) (*see* Bs Lucas of Crudwell); 2ndly, 1971, Diana, who *d* 1992, da of late Col Rt Hon Lord Richard Frederick Cavendish, CB, CMG (*see* D Devonshire, colls), formerly wife of Robert John Graham Boothby (afterwards Baron Boothby), and widow of Lt-Col Hon Ian Douglas-Campbell-Gray (*see* L Gray); *d* 1982; *s* by his el son **(14)** GEORGE JOHN ST CLERE, 7th Viscount; *b* 1932: *m* 1st, 1971 (*m diss* 1975), Valerie Ann, da of Joseph E. Dutch, of Horam, Sussex; 2ndly, 1990, Deirdre Melina Jane, da of late Thomas James Simmons; *d* 1993; *s* by his brother **(15)** HENRY NICOLAS, 8th Viscount and present peer; also Baron Gage.

GAINFORD, BARON (Pease) (Baron UK 1917)

Peace and hope

JOSEPH EDWARD PEASE, 3rd Baron; *b* 25 Dec 1921; *s* 1971; *ed* Eton, and Gordonstoun; FRGS; MSST; 1939-45 War as Sgt RAF: *m* 1953 Margaret Theophila Radcliffe, da of late Henry Edmund Guise Tyndale, of Winchester Coll, and has issue.

Arms – Per fesse azure and gules, a fesse nebuly ermine between two lambs passant in chief argent, and in base upon a mount proper a dove rising argent, holding in the beak a pea stalk, the blossom and pods proper. **Crest** – Upon the capital of an Ionic column a dove rising, holding in the beak a pea stalk as in the arms. **Supporters** – On either side a Barbary wild sheep ram guardant or. *Residence* – 1 Dedmere Court, Marlow, Bucks SL7 1PL.

DAUGHTERS LIVING

Hon Joanna Ruth Miriam, *b* 1959.
Hon Virginia Claire Margaret, *b* 1960.

BROTHERS LIVING

Hon GEORGE, *b* 20 April 1926; *ed* Eton; ARIBA; MRTPI; ARIAS; 1939-45 War in RNVR: *m* 1958, Flora Daphne, da of late Dr N. A. Dyce-Sharp, and has issue living, Adrian Christopher, *b* 1960, — Matthew Edward, *b* 1962: *m* 1991, Barbara, yr da of E. R. John Griffiths, of Aachen, Germany, and has issue living, Felix George *b* 1992, — Olivia Daphne, *b* 1958: *m* 1984, Stephen Langford, elder son of Roy Langford, of St Peter Port. Guernsey, and has issue living, Rachel Veronica *b* 1988, Esther Rebecca *b* 1992, — Samantha Rachel, *b* 1965. *Residence* – Naemoor Gardens, Rumbling Bridge, Kinross KY13 7PY.
Hon John Michael (The Old Croft House, Roy Bridge, Inverness-shire PH31 4AH), *b* 1930; *ed* Gordonstoun: *m* 1962, Catherine Margaret, da of Duncan F. Shaw, and has issue living, David Michael, *b* 1964, — Andrew Joseph, *b* 1967, — Daniel John *b* 1973.

WIDOW LIVING OF SECOND BARON

VERONICA MARGARET (*Veronica, Baroness Gainford*), (Taigh na Seanamhair, Tayvallich, Lochgilphead, Argyll PA31 8PN), da of Sir George John William Noble, 2nd Bt (*cr* 1902): *m* 1921, the 2nd Baron, who *d* 1971.

PREDECESSORS – (1) *Rt Hon* JOSEPH ALBERT Pease, second son of Sir Joseph Whitwell Pease, 1st Bt (*cr* 1882); *b* 1860; appointed Junior Liberal Whip 1897, a Junior Lord of the Treasury Dec 1905, Parliamentary (Patronage) Sec to the Treasury and Ch Liberal Whip May 1908, Chancellor of Duchy of Lancaster (with a seat in the Cabinet) Feb 1910, Pres of Board of Education Oct 1911, and a Member of Committee of Science Council 1915; was Postmaster-Gen Jan to Dec 1916, Chm of British Broadcasting Co 1922-6, and Dep Chm 1926-31; MP for Northumberland, Tyneside Div (*L*) 1892-1900, for Essex, N, or Saffron Walden, Div May 1901 to Jan 1910, and for Rotherham Div of S Part of W Riding of Yorkshire March 1910 to Dec 1916; *cr Baron Gainford*, of Headlam, co Durham (peerage of United Kingdom) 1917: *m* 1886, Ethel, who *d* 1941, only da of Lieut-Gen Sir Henry Marshman Havelock-Allan, 1st Bt, GCB, VC, MP; *d* 1943; *s* by his son **(2)** JOSEPH, TD, 2nd Baron, *b* 1889: *m* 1921, Veronica Margaret, da of Sir George John William Noble, 2nd Bt (*cr* 1902); *d* 1971; *s* by his el son **(3)** Joseph Edward, 3rd Baron and present peer.

GAINSBOROUGH, EARL OF (Noel) (Earl UK 1841, Bt GB 1781)

ANTHONY GERARD EDWARD NOEL, 5th Earl, and 7th Baronet; *b* 24 Oct 1923; *s* 1927; *ed* Worth, Sussex, and Georgetown, Maryland, USA; is patron of two livings (but being a Roman Catholic cannot present), a JP for Leics, a Bailiff Grand Cross of Sovereign Order of Malta (Pres of British Assocn 1968-74) and KStJ; Chm of Rutland co Council 1970-73: *m* 1947, Mary, da of Hon John Joseph Stourton, TD (*see* B Mowbray), and has issue.

Arms – Or, fretty gules, and a canton ermine. *Crest* – A buck at gaze argent, attired or. *Supporters* – On either side a bull argent, armed and unguled proper, gorged with a naval crown azure, therefrom a chain reflexed over the back gold, pendent from the crown an escutcheon, also azure, charged with an anchor erect, encircled by a wreath of laurel or.
Residence – Horn House, Exton, Oakham, Leics LE15 7QU. *Clubs* – Boodle's, Brooks's, Bembridge Sailing, Royal Yacht Sqdn.

All well, or nothing

SONS LIVING

ANTHONY BAPTIST (*Viscount Campden*) *b* 16 Jan 1950; *ed* Ampleforth, and RAC, Cirencester: *m* 1972, Sarah Rose, el da of Col Thomas Foley Churchill Winnington, MBE (*see* Winnington, Bt) and has issue:—
       SON LIVING— *Hon* Henry Robert Anthony, *b* 1 July 1977.
Seat – Exton Park, Oakham, Leics; 105 Earls Court Rd, W8.
Hon Gerard Edward Joseph (The Manor House, Withington, nr Cheltenham, Glos), *b* 1955; *ed* Ampleforth, and London Univ: *m* 1985, Charlotte, yr (twin) da of Sir William Stratford Dugdale, 2nd Bt, CBE, MC, and has issue living, Reginald, *b* 1987, — Belinda Mary, *b* 1986, — Lettice, *b* 1989.
Hon Thomas (24 Lennox Gdns, SW1), *b* 1958; *ed* Ampleforth, and RAC, Cirencester.
Hon Edward Andrew (25 Slaidburn St, SW10 0JP), *b* 1960; *ed* Ampleforth, and British Inst, Paris: *m* 1990, Lavinia Jane, only da of late Cmdr George Edward Bingham, of Grenville House, Droxford, Hants.

DAUGHTERS LIVING

Lady Juliana Mary Alice (*Countess of Liverpool*) (15 The Green, Exton, Oakham, Leics), *b* 1949: *m* 1970, 5th Earl of Liverpool.
Lady Maria, *b* 1951: *m* 1971, Robert Pridden, of Fort Henry House, Exton, Oakham, Leics, and has issue living, Benedict John Anthony, *b* 1973, — Lucy, *b* 1976.
Lady Celestria Magdalen Mary (8 Peel St, W8), *b* 1954; *ed* St Mary's Convent, Ascot, and St Hilda's Coll, Oxford; Social Ed *Harpers & Queen* since 1992: *m* 1990, Timothy M. Hales, son of late S. W. M. Hales, MC, and of late Mrs C. G. des Salles d'Epinoix, and has issue living, Catherine Rose Mary, *b* 1990.

BROTHER LIVING

Hon Gerard Eyre Wriothesley, *b* 1926; *ed* Georgetown, Maryland, USA and Exeter Coll, Oxford; Bar Inner Temple 1952; Editor of *Catholic Herald* 1971-76, and since 1981: *m* 1958, Adèle Julie Patricia, only da of Maj Bonville Were, of Carrington House, Hertford St, W1, and has issue living, Philip Arthur Nicholas, *b* 1959, — Robert John Baptist, *b* 1962; Bluemantle Pursuivant, Coll of Arms since 1993, — Elizabeth Mary Alice, *b* 1967. *Residence* – Westington Mill, Chipping Campden, Glos.

SISTER LIVING

Lady Maureen Thérèse Josephine, *b* 1917: *m* 1st, 1944, the 15th Baron Dormer, who *d* 1975; 2ndly, 1982, as his 2nd wife, Peregrine Edward Launcelot Fellowes. *Residence* – The Court, Chipping Campden, Glos.

COLLATERAL BRANCHES LIVING

       Issue of late Col Hon Charles Hubert Francis Noel, OBE, son of 3rd Earl, *b* 1885; *d* 1947: *m* 1912, May, who *d* 1964, el da of late Brig-Gen Archibald Campbell Douglas Dick, CB, CMG, of Pitkerro, Angus:—
Archibald Charles William, MC (10 Felden St, SW6), *b* 1914; *ed* Oratory Sch; is Col late Welsh Guards; 1939-45 War in France (MC, prisoner); first Mil Adviser to Rep of S Africa, and Mil Adviser to High Commr: *m* 1st, 1945, Bridget Mary, who *d* 1976, only da of late Brig William Albany Fetherstonhaugh, CB, CBE, DSO (*see* Cayley, Bt, colls, 1955 Edn); 2ndly, 1977, Andrée Marie, el da of Pierre Duchen, of Bayonne, and has issue living (by 1st *m*), Charles William (93 St Dunstan's Rd, W6), *b* 1948: *ed* Ampleforth, and Trin Coll, Camb: *m* 1985, Diane Margaret, only da of Gerald A. de Freitas, of 63 Onslow Gdns, SW7, and has issue living, Alexander Charles Fitzwilliam *b* 1989, Elizabeth Bridget Maggie *b* 1986, — Edward Albany (26 King's Court, Hamlet Gdns, W6), *b* 1956; *ed* Stanbridge Earls Sch. ——— Douglas Robert George (25 Broomhouse Rd, SW6 3QU), *b* 1924; *ed* Oratory Sch; Maj Cold Gds (ret); Italy 1943-45: *m* 1949, Eleanor Susan Jane, da of late Brig George Edward Younghusband, CBE, and has issue living, James Douglas George (74 Kingston Rd, Oxford), *b* 1950; *ed* Downside, and London and Oxford Univs; BA Cert Ed, — William Edward Douglas (Ipsden House, Ipsden, Wallingford, Oxon OX10 6AJ), *b* 1953; *ed* Downside: *m* 1st, 1975 (*m diss* 1982 and annulled 1984), his 4th cousin, Victoria Mary, da of George Oswald Younghusband, of Bessborough House, Nenagh, Ballymacky, co Tipperary; 2ndly, 1993, Mrs Juliet Catherine Hayward, eldest da of Col Arthur Harold Newmarch Reade, LVO, Queens Own Hussars (ret), of Old Post House, Ipsden, Wallingford, Oxon, and formerly wife of Capt Henry Tristram Hayward, The Blues and Royals, and has issue living (by 1st *m*), Arthur Douglas *b* 1977; *ed* Downside, Teresa Sybil *b* 1976; *ed* St Mary's Shaftesbury, and d'Overbroeck's Coll, Oxford, — Caroline Mary Jane, *b* 1956; *ed* St Mary's Convent, Ascot, and Bristol Univ: *m* 1987, Charles Anthony Wentzel, of 81 Balham Park Rd, SW12 8EB, son of John Brunette Wentzel, of Johannesburg, and has issue living, Philippa Mary *b* 1991.

       Grandchildren of late Lt-Col Edward William Charles Noel, CIE, DSO, eldest son of late Lt-Col Hon Edward Noel (*infra*):—
       Issue of late Denys Edward Noel, *b* 1925, *d* 1978: *m* 1947, Petronelle Moore (Weavers Cottage, Coombe St, Lyme Regis, Dorset), only da of C. Austin Bostock, of the Hermitage, Newnham, Cambridge:—
Julian Roden Bostock (9 Wigton Place, SE11 4AN), *b* 1949: *m* 1982, Susanna Elisabeth, da of Benjamin Bentley Dodd, of Eel Pie Island, Twickenham, Middx. ——— Laura Frances, *b* 1951: *m* 1979, Peter Clement Coe, of 33 Courthope Rd, NW3, and has issue living, Toby Richard, *b* 1983, — Lucy Josephine, *b* 1985, — Jennifer Mary, *b* 1988.

Granddaughter of late Lt-Col Hon Edward Noel, 2nd son of 2nd Earl:—
Issue of late Capt John Baptist Lucius Noel, *b* 1890, *d* 1989; Official Photographer on Mount Everest Expeditions 1922 and 1924; assumed addl forename of John by deed poll 1908: *m* 1st, 1915, Sybil, who *d* 1939, da of J. Graham; 2ndly, 1941, Mary Sullivan, who *d* 1984:—
(By 2nd *m*) Sandra Ruth Catherine, *b* 1943. *Residence* – 6 Barrow Hill Place, Ashford, Kent TN23 1NE.

Grandchildren of late Major Gerard Thomas Noel, eldest son of Hon Henry Lewis Noel (infra):—
Issue of late William Henry Middleton Noel, *b* 1898, *d* 1954: *m* 1934, Jacqueline Naomi, who *d* 1984, yr da of R. Bendall, of Ofcolaco, N Transvaal:—
Gerard Roland, *b* 1936: *m* 1975, Lina, da of E. Micayabas, of Malaybalay, Philippines, and has issue living, John William Bakun, *b* 1981. —— Michael John, *b* 1944: *m* 1973, Amanda Jane, only da of late Wing-Cdr A. B. Corfe, RAF, and has issue living, William Gerard, *b* 1975, — Richard Roland, *b* 1979, — Andrew Corfe, *b* 1982. —— Christopher William (Wild Hawk Farm, Ofcolaco, NE Transvaal, S Africa), *b* 1947: *m* 1971, Rhoda, only da of H. Allen, of Trichardt, E Transvaal, and has issue living, Gillian Frances, *b* 1973, — Catherine Elizabeth, *b* 1976. —— Wilfrid Byron (Wild Hawk Farm, Ofcolaco, NE Transvaal, S Africa), *b* 1949: *m* 1975, Patricia Maud, 2nd da of W. D. J. Van Niekerk, of Johannesburg, and has issue living, Colin Byron, *b* 1980, — Gerard Vernon, *b* 1985, — Penelope Jacqueline, *b* 1976, — Susan Liane, *b* 1977. —— Margaret Celestria, *b* 1939: *m* 1963, Hugh Boswell Brown, of Crake Valley Farm, PO Box 3025, Mutare, Zimbabwe, and has issue living, Robert Jason, *b* 1969, — Catherine Ann, *b* 1964, — Joan Cécile, *b* 1965, — Nicola Noel, *b* 1971.

Grandchildren of late Hon Henry Lewis Noel, 3rd son of 1st Earl:—
Issue of late Hugh Middleton Noel, *b* 1862, *d* 1956: *m* 1901, Helen Winnefred, who *d* 1956, da of Robert Gibbs, of 32 St Augustine's Road, Bedford:—
Leland Hugh Wriothesley, *b* 1906; is a Landscape Artist: *m* 1941, Barbara Jean, el da of A. H. Meier, of Chico, Calif, USA, and has issue living, William Hugh (1414 Monroe St, Santa Rosa, Calif, USA), *b* 1950, — Pamela Le NOEL-MacMATH (1724 Terrace Way, Santa Rosa, Calif 95404, USA), *b* 1948: *m* 1984 (*m diss* 1993), Lucas MacMath, and has issue living, Bryce Wolcott *b* 1990, Eston Meier *b* 1987. *Residence* – 1421, McDonald Av, Santa Rosa, Calif, USA. —— Diana Catharine (1526, Shoreline Drive, Santa Barbara, Calif, USA), *b* 1914: *m* 1942, Hollis H. Parker, Sgt AA Artillery, who *d* 1948, and has issue living, Geoffrey Hollis, *b* 1944; USA Coast Guard: *m* 1965, Patricia Edwards, and has issue living, Geoffrey Hollis jr *b* 1967, Matthew Donovan *b* 1976, Michelle Diana *b* 1969, — Stephen Hugh Anderson, *b* 1946; *ed* Hawaii Univ, and Cal State Coll, Long Beach.

Grandchildren of late Henry Hamlyn Noel, 3rd son of Hon Henry Lewis Noel (ante):—
Issue of late Major Edward Francis Hamlyn Noel, MRCVS, Indian Army, *b* 1899, *d* 1953: *m* 1926, Doris Marie, who *d* 1983, da of Albert Claude Verrières, CIE:—
Gerard John Hamlyn (Squirrels Hall, Stratford St Mary, Suffolk), *b* 1930; *ed* Wellington Coll; Capt (ret) RE: *m* 1963, Gillian Ralphia, only da of late W. T. B. Head, of Frinton-on-Sea, Essex, and has issue living, Richard Gerard Hamlyn, *b* 1965, — Victoria Gillian Emilia, *b* 1969. —— Penelope Noel, BD, *b* 1934: *m* 1962, Rev Colin Scott Jee, of Ludgershall Rectory, Aylesbury, Bucks, and has issue living, Rev Jonathan Noel (7 Rosemary Way, Hinckley, Leics), *b* 1963: *m* 1989, Juliet Elizabeth, eldest da of Rev John Dudley Morris, of Rudgwick Vicarage, Horsham, W Sussex, and has issue living, Thomas Peter *b* 1991, Daniel James *b* 1993, Rachel Clare *b* (twin) 1993, — Mary Penelope, *b* 1965: *m* 1989, Rev Andrew Malcolm Rimmer, of Church House, George's Hill, Widmer End, High Wycombe, Bucks, and has issue living, James Edward *b* 1993, Rebecca Mary *b* 1991. —— Lyn Noel (83 Loom Lane, Radlett, Herts), *b* 1947: *m* 1968 (*m diss* 1991), Ian Thomas Kennedy, and has issue living, Gordon Noel, *b* 1971, — James Edward, *b* 1972, — Emilia Jayne, *b* 1980.

Granddaughter of late Hon Roden Berkeley Wriothesley Noel, 4th son of 1st Earl:—
Issue of late Rev Conrad le Despencer Roden Noel, *b* 1869, *d* 1942: *m* 1895, Miriam, who *d* 1961, da of James Greenwood:—
Barbara, *b* 1897: *m* 1921, Rev John Cyril Putterill, of 43 West Rd, Saffron Walden, Essex, and has issue living, Sylvia, *b* 1922: *m* 1952, Desmond Butterworth Heath, of 60 Esmond Road, Bedford Park, Chiswick, W4, and has issue living, Martin Christopher *b* 1955, Jenny Clare *b* 1953, Sally Christine *b* 1959, — Cecilia Rosemary, *b* 1929: *m* 1952, Vernon John Curtis, of East Grove, Marsham Way, Gerrard's Cross, Bucks, and has issue living, Matthew John Stephen *b* 1964, Victoria Jane *b* 1954, Katherine Anne *b* 1965.

(In remainder to Barony of Barham, and to the Baronetcy)

Descendants of late Sir Gerard Noel Noel, 2nd Bt (father of 1st Earl of Gainsborough), by his wife Diana, in her own right, Baroness Barham:—
Granddaughters of late Adm of the Fleet Sir Gerard Henry Uctred Noel, GCB, KCMG, son of late Rev Augustus William Noel, son of late Capt Hon Frederic Noel, RN, 6th son of Diana Baroness Barham:—
Issue of late Francis Arthur Gerard Noel, OBE, *b* 1880, *d* 1955: *m* 1913, Evelyn, who *d* 1988, da of late Benjamin Bond Cabbell, of Cromer Hall, Norfolk:—
Evelyn Diana (*Baroness Nugent*), *b* 1914: *m* 1st, 1936, Major John Vivian Bailey, Roy Scots Fusiliers, who was *ka* 1943; 2ndly, 1946, Capt Sir Hector Wroth Lethbridge, 6th Bt, who *d* 1978; 3rdly, as his 3rd wife, David James Douglas Nugent, Baron Nugent, who *d* 1988, of Gresham Hall Cottage, Gresham Hall, nr Norwich, Norfolk NR11 8RW (*see* E Westmeath, colls), and has issue living (by 1st *m*), Lucy, *b* 1938: *m* 1962, Thomas Harry Farthing, and has issue living, Harry Vivian Stuart *b* 1964, Isabella Jane *b* 1968, — (by 2nd *m*) (*see* Lethbridge, Bt). —— Susan Rachel, *b* 1918.

Granddaughters of late Lt-Col Maurice Waldegrave Noel, AFC (infra):—
Issue of late Peter Maurice William Noel, *b* 1922, *d* 1984: *m* 1946 (*m diss* 19—), Patricia Margaret, yst da of A. C. W. Hill, of Mosman, Sydney, NSW, Australia:—
Diana Margaret NOEL (22 Wudgong St, Mosman, Sydney, NSW 2088, Australia), *b* 1947: *m* 1980, Baron François Maurice Seymour Faverôt de Kerbrech, and has issue living, Chloë Elizabeth Noel, *b* 1980. —— Susan Elizabeth Gay, *b* 1951.

Grandson of late Col William Frederick Noel Noel, el son of Col Edward Andrew Noel, el son of Rev Francis James Noel, 7th son of Sir Gerard Noel Noel, 2nd Bt and Diana Baroness Barham:—
Issue of late Lieut-Col Maurice Waldegrave Noel, AFC, The King's (Liverpool) Regt, *b* 1888, *d* 1958: *m* 1920, Elisabeth Christine Edith, who *d* 1981, el da of late Charles Gairdner, Rangoon, and Tower of Lethendy, Perthshire:—
Robert Gerard Charles (68 Grove End Gdns, NW8 9LN), *b* 1928; *ed* Malvern: late Lt RM (invalided); Stockbroker; FIPR, MSI, OLJ: *m* 1961 (*m diss* 1988), Gillian Margaret Halse.

Grandchildren of late Adm Francis Charles Methuen Noel, 3rd son of Col Edward Andrew Noel (ante):—
Issue of late Com Montague Wriothesley Noel, *b* 1892, *ka* 1941: *m* 1926, Christabel Florence Arthur, who *d* 1965, da of late Rev Henry Startin, V of Horrabridge, Devon:—
Henry Methuen Noel (Rosemount, Stoke Gabriel, Totnes Devon TQ9 6SJ), *b* 1927; *ed* Marlborough Coll, and New Coll, Oxford (MA); FCIS; Capt Queen Victoria's Rifles (TA Reserve) (ret): *m* 1963, Helen Elizabeth Anne, who *d* 1992, da of late Sir William Oliphant Hutchinson, of Cholmondeley Lodge, Richmond, Surrey and has issue living, Robert Montague, *b* 1964;

BSc, ARICS: *m* 1992, Sophie M. J., da of Jean-Marie Bourdaire, of Paris, — William Gerard, *b* 1965; PhD, MA (Cantab), — Emma Margery, *b* 1969. ——— Gerard Lionel Gordon (twin) (The Manor, Rockbeare, Exeter, Devon), *b* 1927; *ed* Marlborough Coll, and Trin Hall, Camb (MA); late RE; FRICS: *m* 1965, Caroline Patricia, da of Brig Eric Llewellyn Griffith Griffith-Williams, CBE, DSO, MC, DL, of Rockbeare Manor, Exeter, Devon, and has issue living, Andrew Francis Methuen, *b* 1966, — Thomas Charles Eric, *b* 1970, — Delia Christabel Mary, *b* 1967, — Matilda Theresa Caroline, *b* 1972, — Amy Margaret, *b* 1979. *Club* – Royal Ocean Racing. ——— Montague Geoffrey Bickersteth (Monastery House, Little Crawley, Newport Pagnell, Bucks), *b* 1931; *ed* Marlborough Coll, and Trin Hall, Camb (BA), MRCS, LRCP, FFARCS; late Lt R Signals: *m* (Jan) 1958, Audrey Mavis, da of Allen Metcalf, of Wingerworth, Chesterfield, Derbys, and has issue living, David Charles, *b* 1963, — Peter, *b* 1966, — Michael (twin), *b* 1966, — Jennifer Anne, *b* (Dec) 1958. ——— Celestria Wilmot Rosalie, *b* 1935: *m* (Jan) 1960, David Jeffrey Bell, of 6 Meadow Close, Tring, Herts, and has issue living, Charles Montague Jeffrey, *b* 1974, — Caroline Barbara Penelope, *b* (Dec) 1960: *m* 1987, Jeremy Wilfred Duncombe, and has issue living, Jeffrey Charles William *b* 1988, Elizabeth Alice Rachael *b* 1989, — Joanna Elizabeth Glencairn *b* 1962; has issue living, Alec Henry *b* 1994, — Alice Christabel Ann, *b* 1967: *m* 19—, Stavros Stangos, of Athens, and has issue living, Asteris *b* 1993, — Christina Mary Noel, *b* 1968.

Grandchildren of late Capt Robert Lascelles Gambier Noel, RN, 4th son of Col Edward Andrew Noel (ante):—
Issue of late Gambier Baptist Edward Noel, *b* 1888, *d* 1957: *m* 1st, 1914 (*m diss* 1922), Beatrice Eva Tytler, who *d* 1966, da of late Rear-Adm John Clarke Byng (V Torrington, colls); 2ndly, 1924 (*m diss* 1931), Rosalie Sibyl, da of Major S. S. Flower, late Northumberland Fusiliers, and formerly wife of Capt W. L. Aplin Harrison, MC:—
(By 1st *m*) Gambier John Byng, CB, *b* 1914; Rear-Adm (ret) 1939-45 War (despatches twice): *m* 1936, Joan, da of late Percy Herbert Stevens, and has issue living, Caroline Byng, *b* 1936: *m* 1st, 1973, Ivor Eagling, who *d* 1979; 2ndly, 1982, William Cairns, MBE, — Penelope Byng, *b* 1939: *m* 1st, 1960 (*m diss* 1967), Anthony Henry John Rawlinson (now 5th Bt); 2ndly, 1967 (*m diss* 1984), Count Axel Du Monceau de Bergendal, — Virginia Byng, *b* 1943: *m* 1967, Prof Michael Stanley Tite, and has issue living, Sarah *b* 1970, Alice *b* 1972, — Vanessa Jane (twin) (24 The Meadows, Guildford, Surrey GU2 5DT), *b* 1943: *m* 1970 (*m diss* 1986), Tom McClure. *Residence* – Woodpeckers, Haslemere, Surrey. ——— Beatrice Louisa Frances, *b* 1915; formerly Section Officer WAAF: *m* 1943, William Falcon Skelton, only son of Engineer Vice-Adm Sir Reginald William Skelton, KCB, CBE, DSO, and has issue living, Peter, *b* 1950; D Phil, — Sally, *b* 1944: *m* 1969, Marcel Wagner, and has issue living, Dameon *b* 1972, Cosima *b* 1970, — Judy, *b* 1946; MA, BLitt (Oxon). *Residence* – Boughton Cottage, Green Lane, Henley-on-Thames, Oxon RE9 LLR.

Grandchildren of late Capt John Andrew Vernatti Noel, 3rd son of late Capt Robert Lascelles Gambier Noel, RN (ante):—
Issue of late Prof Anthony Robert Alistair Noel, *b* 1927, *d* 1984: *m* 1958, Marthina Cornelia Rousseau (4 The Park, Gardens, Cape Town 8001, S Africa), of Roodepoort, Transvaal:—
Darwin John Robert, *b* 1958.
Issue of late John Edward Barham Noel, *b* 1929; *d* 1954: *m* 1952, Grace Vera (who *m* 2ndly, 1966, Anthony Maurice Thomas, of The Cabin, 31 Castle St, IoW PO32 6RD), yst da of A. Paul, of Herne Hill, SE:—
Jacqueline Susan (73 Andromeda Rd, Lordshill, Southampton), *b* 1953: *m* 1972 (*m diss* 1983), Victor Clive Hayton, and has had issue, Thor David Fewlass, *b* 1974, — Jodi William, *b* 1976, *d* 1985.

Granddaughter of late Eugene Frederic Noel, yst son of late Rev Hon Baptist Wriothesley Noel, 10th son of Diana, Baroness Barham:—
Issue of late Evan Baillie Noel, *b* 1879, *d* 1928: *m* 1906, Marjorie, who *d* 1955, da of late R. Deane Sweeting, MD, Bar-at-law, Senior Med Inspector HM Local Govt Board:—
Susan Diana Barham, *b* 1912: *m* 1940, Prof Geoffrey Frederic Powell, DSO, Solicitor and late Sq-Ldr RAFVR, who *d* 1982. *Residence* – 9 Barons Keep, Gliddon Rd, W14 9AT.

PREDECESSORS – (1) *Rt Hon Sir* CHARLES Middleton, PC, Adm of the Red, MP for Rochester and First Lord of the Admiralty, etc; *cr a Baronet* 1781 with remainder to his son-in-law, Gerard Noel Edwards (who in 1798 assumed the surname of Noel), nephew of Henry Noel, 6th Earl of Gainsborough (*cr* 1682), 9th Viscount Campden (*cr* 1628), and 8th Baron Noel (*cr* 1617); *cr Baron Barham* (peerage of United Kingdom) 1805, with remainder to his da Diana, wife of Gerard Noel Noel, Esq (ante); *d* 1813; *s* in baronetcy by his son-in-law (ante), and in barony by his da. (2) DIANA; *d* 1823; *s* by her el son (3) CHARLES, 3rd Baron; *s* to his father's baronetcy 1838, and *cr Baron Noel, Viscount Campden,* and *Earl of Gainsborough* (peerage of United Kingdom) 1841; *d* 1866; *s* by his el son (4) CHARLES GEORGE, 2nd Earl, *b* 1818; Lord-Lieut of Rutland: *m* 1841, Lady Ida Harriet Augusta, who *d* 1867, da of 16th Earl of Erroll; *d* 1881; *s* by his son (5) CHARLES WILLIAM FRANCIS, 3rd Earl, *b* 1850: *m* 1st, 1876, Augusta Mary Catherine, who *d* 1877, da of late Robert Berkeley, of Spetchley Park, Worcester; 2ndly, 1880, Mary Elizabeth, who *d* 1937, da of late James Arthur Dease, of Turbotston, co Westmeath; *d* 1926; *s* by his son (6) ARTHUR EDWARD JOSEPH, OBE, 4th Earl, *b* 1884; Private Chamberlain to Pope Benedict XV and Pope Pius XI; an Hon Attache in Norway and Sweden 1908-12, and at Washington, USA 1913-14: *m* 1915, Alice Mary, who *d* 1970, da of Edward Eyre, of Gloucester House, Park Lane, W1; *d* 1927; *s* by his son (7) ANTHONY GERARD EDWARD, 5th Earl and present peer; also Viscount Campden, Baron Barham, and Baron Noel.

GAITSKELL, BARONY OF (Gaitskell) (Extinct 1989)

SON LIVING OF LIFE BARONESS (*By 1st marriage*)

Hon Raymond FROST, *b* 1924; *ed* Oundle, and Worcester Coll, Oxford, Dir, Econ Development Inst at World Bank: *m* 1958, June Virginia Johnston, da of late Ing Eduardo Gonzalez Rodriquez del Rey, and has issue, one son and one da.

DAUGHTERS LIVING OF LIFE BARONESS (*By 2nd marriage*)

Hon Julia, *b* 1939; *ed* Somerville Coll, Oxford: *m* 1969, George Peter McNeal, of 35 Newstead Rd, SE12 03Y, and has issue.
Hon Cressida (18 Frognal Gdns, Hampstead, NW3), *b* 1942; *ed* Somerville Coll, Oxford (MA), and LSE (MSc): *m* 1964, Gordon Joshua Wasserman, Assist Undersecretary of State, Home Office, and has issue, two das.

GALLACHER, BARON (Gallacher) (Life Baron 1982)

JOHN GALLACHER, son of late William Gallacher, of Alexandria, Dumbartonshire; *b* 7 May 1920; *ed* St Patrick's, Dumbarton, and the Co-operative Coll, Loughborough (Chartered Sec); Pres Enfield Highway Co-operative Soc 1954-68, Parly Sec to Co-operative Union and a Dir Retail Consortium Ltd 1974-83, sometime Pres Inst of Meat; Corporal RAF, served in Coastal Cmd and 2nd Tactical Air Force in UK and W Europe; *cr Baron Gallacher*, of Enfield, in Greater London (Life Baron) 1982: *m* 1947, Freda Vivian, da of late Alfred Chittenden, of Maidstone, Kent, and has issue.
Residence – 27 Whitecliffs, The Leas, Folkestone, Kent CT20 2DT.

SON LIVING

Hon Robert John, *b* 1955; *ed* Broxbourne Sch, Herts.

GALLOWAY, EARL OF (Stewart) (Earl S 1623, Bt S 1627 and 1687)

Valour strengthens from a wound

RANDOLPH KEITH REGINALD STEWART, 13th Earl, and 12th Baronet of Corsewell, and 10th of Burray; *b* 14 Oct 1928; *s* 1978; *ed* Harrow: *m* 1975, Lily May, yst da of late Andrew Miller, of Duns, Berwickshire, and formerly wife of — Budge.

Arms – Or, a fesse checky argent and azure, surmounted of a bend engrailed gules, within a double tressure flory counterflory of the last. **Crest** – A pelican in nest, vulning herself argent, winged or. **Supporters** – *Dexter*, a savage man, wreathed about the head and middle with laurel, and holding in the right hand a club resting on the shoulder, all proper; *sinister*, a lion gules.
Residence – Senwick House, Brighouse Bay, Borgue, Kirkcudbrightshire DG6 4TP.

SISTER LIVING

Lady Antonia Marian Amy Isabel, *b* 1925: *m* 1946, Sir (Charles) Mark Dalrymple, 3rd Bt, who *d* 1971, when the title became ext. *Residence* – Newhailes, Musselburgh, Midlothian.

COLLATERAL BRANCHES LIVING

Grandchildren of late Lt-Col Walter Robert Stewart, DSO, MC, only surv son of late Maj-Gen Hon Alexander Stewart, 3rd son of 9th Earl:—
Issue of late Maj Alexander David Stewart, MBE, TD, *b* 1914, *d* 1985: *m* 1948, Daphne Marion (North Green, Kelsale, Saxmundham, Suffolk), widow of Clyde Euan Miles Graham, Flying Officer, RAF (*see* Peel, E, colls, 1956 Edn), and only da of Sir Reginald Bonsor, 2nd Bt:—
ANDREW CLYDE (9 Lennox Gdns Mews, SW1), *b* 13 March 1949; *ed* Eton: *m* 1977, Sara, only da of Brig Patrick Pollock, and has issue living, Alexander Patrick, *b* 1980, — Tania Jane, *b* 1979, — Zoe Inez, *b* 1983. —— (David) Mark (The Old Hall, Reedham, Norwich, Norfolk NR13 3TZ), *b* 1960: *m* 1987, Victoria Georgina, 2nd da of late Brig Thomas Geoffrey Henry Jackson (*see* Jackson, Bt, *cr* 1869, colls), and has issue living, Samuel Mark, *b* 1990, — Harry Alexander, *b* 1992, — Chloe Rose, *b* 1994. —— (Rosemary) Zara, *b* 1952: *m* 1977, G. Ian Fleming, and has issue living, Alistair James, *b* 1982.
Issue of late Capt Ian Michael Stewart, *b* 1917, *d* 1973: *m* 1941 (*m diss* 1952), Peggy Spencer, who *d* 1957, twin da of Spencer Thornton:—
Alastair Grenfell (Highfield House, Nunnington, York), *b* 1944: *m* 1973, Sarah Monica Scott, and has issue living, James Henry, *b* 1975, — Victoria Rose, *b* 1977. —— Carolyn Mary, *b* 1942: *m* 1963, Alec Charles Hinchcliff Bond, of Stud Farmhouse, Thenford, Banbury, Oxon, and has issue living, William David Hinchcliff, *b* 1970.

Granddaughters of late Rev James Stewart, 2nd son of Hon Montgomery Granville John Stewart, MP, 6th son of 7th Earl:—
Issue of late Horatio George Willoughby Stewart, *b* 1877, *d* 1943: *m* 1929, Beatrice Maud, who *d* 1984, da of late James Bedson:—
Flora Margaret, *b* 1930: *m* 1951, Richard Arthur Revell, who *d* 1986, of 16 Bellencroft Gdns, Merry Hill, Wolverhampton, and has issue living, Nicholas Stewart (10 Kynnersley Lane, Leighton, nr Shrewsbury SY5 6RS), *b* 1952: *m* 1981, Rosemary Jean, yst da of George Stephen Bradley, and has issue living, Matthew James *b* 1983, Stewart George *b* 1985, Melanie Louise *b* 1987, — Clare Victoria, *b* 1956: *m* 1982, Stephen John Brown, and has issue living, Benjamin Jack *b* 1993, — Jennifer Mary, *b* 1968. —— Daphne Isabel, *b* 1932: *m* 1956, Neville Tasker, of 85 Rickard Rd, Warrimoo, NSW 2775, Aust, and has issue living, Sheryl Ann, *b* 1959, — Melanie Jane, *b* 1963.

Granddaughter of late Col Charles Edward Stewart, CB, CMG, CIE, son of late Algernon Stewart, yr son of late Hon Edward Richard Stewart, 7th son of 7th Earl:—
Issue of late Lieut-Col Algernon Bingham Anstruther Stewart, DSO, *b* 1869, *ka* 1916: *m* 1911, Edith Evelyn (who *m* 2ndly, 1922, Henry de Grey Lennox (D Richmond, colls), and *d* 1932), da of late Sir Arthur Pendarves Vivian, KCB (B Swansea, colls):—
Barbara Jean (twin) *b* 1915: *m* 1939, Maj George De Pree, King's Roy Rifle Corps, who *d* 1992, and has issue living, Andrew Hugo Stewart, *b* 1946: *m* 1972, Victoria, only da of David Neilson, of Catton Hall, Burton-on-Trent, and has issue living, Emma *b* 1975, Alice *b* 1978, Olivia *b* 1984, — Jane Mary, *b* 1940: *m* 1961, Giles William Pitman, of Heath House, Patmore Heath, Albury, Ware, Herts, and has issue living, George Eustace *b* 1963, John Struan *b* 1969: *m* 1993, Laura Louise Vintcent, Kate Jane *b* 1965: *m* 1992 Mark Christopher Dalton, — Rachel Anne, *b* 1950: *m* 1970, James Edward Cory Liddell, of Cottonworth House, Fullerton, Andover, Hants (*see* B Ravensworth, colls). *Residence* – 2 Fullerton Manor, Andover, Hants SP11 7LA.

Grandson of late Charles Patrick Stewart, son of late Lt-Col Hon James Henry Keith Stewart, CB, MP, 8th son of 7th Earl:—
Issue of late Charles Nigel Stewart, *b* 1864, *d* 1915: *m* 1895, Edith Mabel, da of late Julius Miller, MD, MRCS:—
Herbert Nigel, *b* 1896; believed to have emigrated to USA.

Grandchildren of late Lt-Col John Stewart, DSO, only son of late John Leveson Douglas Stewart (*b* 1842), grandson of late Leveson Douglas Stewart (*b* 1786), 2nd son of Adm Hon Keith Stewart, 3rd son of 6th Earl:—
Issue of late Lt-Col Keith Ian Douglas Stewart, OBE, *b* 1904, *d* 1990: *m* 1st, 1930, Helena Lucie, who was *k* by enemy action 1940, da of Edward Ashton St Hill, of 7 Queensborough Terr, W2; 2ndly, 1940, Philippa North, who *d* 1966, eldest da of late Robert Nairn, FRCS, of Hastings, NZ; 3rdly, 1967, Frances Auckland Louise Bogue, who *d* 1974, da of late Francis Joseph Hieronymous-Jones; 4thly, 1977, Joan Mary (The Old Rectory, Shepton Beauchamp, Ilminster, Som TA19 0LL), da of late Alban J. H. Francis, of St Peter's, Weston-super-Mare, and widow of Maj Philip Clarke, MC, Royal Worcs Regt:—
(By 1st *m*) John Edward Hamish Keith, *b* 1935; *ed* Lodge Sch, Barbados. —— Jennifer Mary Hamilton, *b* 1931: *m* 1st, 1952 (*m diss* 1962), John Innes Wood; 2ndly, 1963 (*m diss* 1976), Ian Bishop, FRCS; 3rdly, 1977, Dennis Hart, who *d* 1982; 4thly, 1984, David Livingstone, CBE, of 4 Miller's Court, Chiswick Mall, W4 2PF, and has issue living (by 1st *m*), James Keith, *b* 1956, —— Jonathan Charles, *b* 1959, —— Susan Deborah, *b* 1955: *m* 1980, Richard Wade, —— (by 2nd *m*) Louise, *b* 1964.

Grandchildren of late Leveson Douglas Stewart (*b* 1844), eldest son of late George Stewart (*b* 1814), 2nd son of late Leveson Douglas Stewart (*b* 1786) (ante):—
Issue of late Keith Stewart, Canadian Expeditionary Force, *b* 1877, *d* 1947: *m* 1919, Margaret, da of late Nicholas Fox, of Dublin:—
Allan Galloway (1712 Kingslake Blvd, Naples, Florida 33962, USA), *b* 1928: *m* 1st, 1949 (*m diss* 1968), Vivian Waldon; 2ndly, 1969, Marie Marcelle Denise Morand, and has issue living (by 1st *m*), Brian Keith (Toronto, Ontario, Canada), *b* 1952, —— Gail Janice, *b* 1951: *m* 1st, 1970 (*m diss* 1976), André Lafreniere; 2ndly, 1976, Kerry Hillier, and has issue living (by 1st *m*), Michael *b* 1970, (by 2nd *m*) David *b* 1978, Sean *b* 1980, Amanda *b* 1982.
Issue of late Randolph Douglas Stewart, late 7th King's Liverpool Regt, *b* 1884, *d* 1961: *m* 1916, Emily Ellen Fullagher, who *d* 1976:—
Randolph Douglas (3 Forest Lawn, Liverpool L12 5JA), *b* 1920: *m* 1947, Mabel Thompson, and has issue living, Ann, *b* 1947: *m* 1969, Michael Victor Guinney, and has issue living, Mark Stewart *b* 1971, Carl Stewart *b* 1975, —— Eileen, *b* 1950: *m* 1974, Peter D. Lawrence, of 1 Gateacre Park Drive, Liverpool L25 1PA, and has issue living, Adam Harvey *b* 1979, Sara Elizabeth *b* 1976. —— †Alexander M., *b* 1924: *m* 1950 (*m diss* 1963), Marion G. Baker, and *d* 1994, leaving issue, Charles Anthony (9 Chess St, Salisbury 5109, S Australia), *b* 1952: *m* 1973 (*m diss* 1984), Nonda Anne Route, and has issue living, Michelle Katrina *b* 1974, Kathrine Jane *b* 1975, and further issue (by Johnann Christine), Stephanie Melissa *b* 1987. —— Catherine Emily, *b* 1917: *m* 1939, Albert Marrion, of 74 Caesars Close, Castlefields, Runcorn, Cheshire, and has issue living, Norma, *b* 1940: *m* 1959, Gordon Colin Tinsley, of 11 Eskdale Close, Beechwood West, Runcorn, Cheshire WA7 2QX, and has issue living, Mark Stewart *b* 1968, —— Pauline, *b* 1946: *m* 1967, Anthony Joseph Wakefield, of 21 Eskdale Close, Runcorn, Cheshire WA7 2QX, and has issue living, Andrew Anthony *b* 1967, Stewart Joseph *b* 1971. —— Lily, *b* 1919: *m* 1943, Richard E. Williamson, of 28 Townfield View, Windmill Hill, Runcorn, Cheshire WA7 6QD. —— Joan, *b* 1926: *m* 1946, Charles Wright, and *d* 1989, leaving issue, two sons and one da. —— Jean, *b* 1934: *m* 1954, Stanley R. Davies, of 104 Barons Hey, Cantrill Farm, Liverpool L28 0QE, and has issue living, Julie *b* 1959: *m* 1981, John Wishman, of 4 Springfield Way, W Derby, Liverpool 12, and has issue living, Michael John *b* 1984, James David *b* 1988, Sarah Jean *b* 1985.

Grandchildren of late Thomas Corrie Stewart, coffee planter in Natal, 2nd son of late George Stewart (*b* 1814) (ante):—
Issue of late George Henry Stewart, *b* 1873, *d* 1931: *m* 19—, Agnes Robina Jessie, who *d* 1949, da of late Lewis Storm, of Scotland:—
Keith (Flat 105, Glendower Place, 99 Linksfield Rd, Edenvale 1610, S Africa), *b* 1915: *m* 1st, 19—, Kathleen Kruger, who *d* 1975; 2ndly, 1977, Mrs Elsie Smith, da of late Enos Ashworth, and widow of Leslie George Smith, and has issue living (by 1st *m*), Malcolm Keith (15 Cole St, Kensington 2094, S Africa), *b* 1948: *m* 1971 (*m diss* 1980), Joan Carrick, and has issue living, Craig *b* 1972, Neville Keith *b* 1977, Jacqueline *b* 1974, —— Audrey, *b* 1951: *m* 1972, Ernest Arthur Atkins, of 7 Beaumont Rd, King Williamstown 5600, S Africa, and has issue living, Chad *b* 1976, Natalie *b* 1973.
Issue of late Leveson Douglas Stewart, *b* 1880, *d* 1946: *m* 19—, Margaret Walker Wilson, who *d* 1975:—
George Bruce (PO Box 716, Hillcrest 3650, Natal), *b* 1923: *m* 1st, 1950, Catherine Aspinall, who *d* 1985; 2ndly, 1986, Shelagh Irene, da of late Albert Sydney Croft, and has two adopted children, John Keith, *b* 1950, —— Marie Lynne, *b* 1952.
Issue of late Cecil Francis Stewart, *b* 18—, *d* 1940: *m* 19—, Ethel Alexandria Marshall:—
William Thomas, *b* 19—. —— Vera Alexandria, *b* 19—. —— Joan, *b* 19—. —— Dorothy, *b* 1923.

PREDECESSORS – (1) Sir Alexander Stewart, KB, PC (descended from Sir William Stewart, of Jedworth — second son of Sir Alexander Stewart of Darnley and one of the leading men of Scotland during the reigns of his kinsmen, the two first Stewart Kings — whose son Sir John Stewart, *m* Marion, da of Sir Walter Stewart, of Dalswinton); *cr Lord Garlies* (peerage of Scotland) 1607, with remainder to the heirs male of his body succeeding to the estates of Garlies, and *Earl of Galloway* (peerage of Scotland) 1623, with remainder to his heirs male bearing the name and arms of Stewart; *d* 1649; *s* by his son (2) James, 2nd Earl, who in 1627 had been *cr a Baronet* (of Corsewell); for his loyalty to the Royal cause in 1654 was fined £4,000 by Cromwell; *d* 1671; *s* by his el son (3) Alexander, 3rd Earl; *s* by his brother (4) Alexander, 4th Earl; *d* unmarried 1694; *s* by his brother (5) James, PC, 5th Earl; an able statesman *temp* Queen Anne; *d* 1746; *s* by his son (6) Alexander, 6th Earl; a Lord of Police; served heir male as 4th Bt to Sir Archibald Stewart, 2nd Bt (*cr* 1687, of Burray, with remainder to heirs male whatsoever); *d* 1773; *s* by his el son (7) John, KT, 7th Earl; MP for Morpeth, etc, a Lord of the Bedchamber to George III and a Representative Peer 1774-96; *cr Baron Stewart of Garlies* (peerage of Great Britain) 1796; *d* 1806; by his son (8) George, KT, 8th Earl; an Adm, MP for Cockermouth, etc, and a Lord of the Admiralty; *d* 1834; *s* by his son (9) Randolph, 9th Earl, *b* 1800; MP for Cockermouth 1826-31; Lord-Lieut of co Kirkcudbright 1828-45 and of co Wigtown 1828-51: *m* 1833, Lady Harriet Blanche, who *d* 1885, da of 6th Duke of Beaufort; *d* 1873; *s* by his son (10) Alan Plantagenet, KT, 10th Earl: *b* 1835; MP for Wigtownshire 1868-78; Lord High Commr to Gen Assembly for Ch of Scotland 1876-7: *m* 1872, Lady Mary Arabella Arthur, who *d* 1903, da of 2nd Marquess of Salisbury; *d* 1901; *s* by his brother (11) Randolph Henry, 11th Earl; *b* 1836; Crimean Campaign 1855, and Indian Mutiny Campaign 1857-9: *m* 1891, Amy Mary Pauline, who *d* 1942, da of late Anthony John Cliffe, of Belle Vue, co Wexford; *d* 1920; *s* by his son (12) Randolph Algernon Ronald, 12th Earl, *b* 1892; Lt Col and Hon Col KOSB; JP and Lord-Lieut, Stewartry of Kirkcudbright 1932-75; 1914-18 War; Grand Master Mason of Scotland 1945-49: *m* 1924, Philippa Fendall, who *d* 1974, yr da of late Jacob Wendell, of New York; *d* 1978; *s* by his son (13) Randolph Keith Reginald, 13th Earl and present peer; also Lord Garlies, and Baron Stewart of Garlies.

GALPERN, BARONY OF (Galpern) (Extinct 1993)

SON LIVING OF LIFE BARON

Hon Maurice Lionel, *b* 1945: *m* 1971, Karen Ellen, el da of Jay Honickman, of Hyfan Court, Downsview, Ontario, Canada.

DAUGHTER LIVING OF LIFE BARON

Hon Virginia, *b* 1941: *m* 1968 (*m diss* 19—), Alan John Stewart.

WIDOW LIVING OF LIFE BARON

ALICE CAMPBELL, JP (*Baroness Galpern*), da of late Thomas Stewart: *m* 1940, Baron Galpern (Life Baron), who *d* 1993. *Residence* – 42 Kelvin Court, Glasgow.

GALWAY, VISCOUNT (Monckton-Arundell) (Viscount I 1727)—
(Title pronounced "Gaulway")(Name pronounced "Munkton-Arundell")

To extend my fame by deeds

GEORGE RUPERT MONCKTON-ARUNDELL, CD, 12th Viscount, *b* 13 Oct 1922; *s* 1980; Lt-Cdr RCN (ret): *m* 1944, Fiona Margaret, da of late Capt Percival Walter de Putron Taylor, of Sooke, BC, Canada, and has issue.

𝕬rms – Quarterly: 1st and 4th sable, six swallows, three, two, and one, argent, *Arundell*; 2nd and 3rd sable, on a chevron between three martlets or, as many mullets of the field, *Monckton*. 𝕮rest – 1st, on a chapeau azure, turned up ermine, a swallow argent; 2nd, a martlet or. 𝕾upporters – Two unicorns ermine, crined, armed and unguled, and each gorged with an Eastern coronet or. *Residence* – 787 Berkshire Drive, London, Ontario N6J 3S5, Canada.

SON LIVING

Hon (JOHN) PHILIP (1-1237 Avenue Rd, Toronto, Ontario, Canada M5N 2G5), *b* 8 April 1952, *ed* Univ of W Ontario (MA): *m* 1980 (*m diss* 1992), Deborah Kathleen, da of A. Bruce Holmes, of Ottawa, Canada.

DAUGHTERS LIVING

Hon Sheelagh Margaret, *b* 1945: *m* 1967, William Arthur Herd, of 726 Galloway Cres, London, Ontario, Canada N6J 2Y7, and has issue living, John David Fyfe Monckton, *b* 1981, — Meghan Alexandra Monckton, *b* 1977.
Hon (Fiona) Marilyn, *b* 1947: *m* 1974, Robert Wilford Shank, BS, CPA, MSc in Taxation, of 9770 SW Buckskin Terr, Beaverton, Oregon 97005, USA, and has issue living, Kevin William, *b* 1976, — Adriane Leigh, *b* 1978.
Hon Rachel Jean MONCKTON, *b* 1957; has resumed her maiden name: *m* 1978 (*m diss* 1989), Ronald John Pressey, and has issue living, Michael John, *b* 1980, — Christopher Ellis, *b* 1981. *Residence* – 44A Byron Av East, London, Ontario N6C 1C5, Canada.

SISTER LIVING

Sylvia Margaret, *b* 1921: *m* 1947, Thomas Bruce Wilson, late Lt-Cdr, RCN, of 1815, W 30th Av, Vancouver, BC, Canada, and has issue living, Patrick John, *b* 1957, — Kathleen Elizabeth, *b* 1948: *m* 1st, 1969 (*m diss* 1979), Roland R. Stéphan; 2ndly, 1985, Henry Nichols Ervin (II), — Rosemary Jean, *b* 1949: *m* 1971 (*m diss* 1979), Niels Bols; 2ndly; 1984, Edgar A. Hendee.

DAUGHTER LIVING OF ELEVENTH VISCOUNT

Hon Rose Wynsome, *b* 1937; occupational therapist.

DAUGHTER LIVING OF NINTH VISCOUNT

Hon Charlotte Anne, *b* 1955: *m* 1983 (*m diss* 1987), Guy Martin James Morrison, only son of M. J. F. Morrison, of West Tytherley, Wilts, and has issue living, Simon George Strangways, *b* 1984. *Residence* – Melbury House, Dorchester, Dorset DT2 0LF.

DAUGHTERS LIVING OF EIGHTH VISCOUNT

Hon Mary Victoria, *b* 1924: *m* 1st 1947 (*m diss* 1972), David Henry Fetherstonhaugh, Coldm Gds, who *d* 1994; 2ndly, 1974, Maj Robert Patricius Chaworth-Musters, who *d* 1992, of Felley Priory, Jacksdale, Notts, and has issue living (by 1st *m*), Hugh Simon (Faenol Bach, Bodelwyddan, Abergele, Clwyd), *b* 1949; *ed* Eton: *m* 1971, Louise, adopted da of Hon (Richard) Hanning Philipps (B Milford), and has issue living, Edward Dickon Hanning *b* 1981, Fergus Hugh *b* 1990, Sophie Lucia *b* 1973, Alice Maria *b* 1975, — Henry George (Plas Llewellyn, Dolwen, Abergele, Clwyd), *b* 1954; *ed* Eton: *m* 1978, Nicola, only child of late Lt-Col Peter Payne-Gallwey, DSO (*see* Frankland-Payne-Gallwey, colls), and has issue living, Jack David James *b* 1987, Hector Albert Timothy *b* 1990, — Victoria Bronwen, *b* 1951.
Hon Celia Ella Vere (*Hon Lady Rowley*), *b* 1925; JP Suffolk; Extra Lady in Waiting to HRH Princess Alexandra, Hon Lady Ogilvy, since 1970: *m* 1959, Sir Joshua Francis Rowley, 7th Bt, of Holbecks, Hadleigh, Suffolk.
Hon Isabel Cynthia (*Baroness King of Wartnaby*), *b* 1926: *m* 1970, Baron King of Wartnaby (Life Baron), of Wartnaby, Melton Mowbray, Leics.

COLLATERAL BRANCHES LIVING

Grandchildren of late Francis Monckton, el son of late Gen Henry Monckton (*infra*):—
Issue of late Maj Reginald Francis Percy Monckton, TD, *b* 1896, *d* 1975: *m* 1931, Sheila, JP (The White House, Stretton, Stafford), da of late Henry Gervas Stobart, of Thornton-le-Dale, Pickering:—

Alan Stobart (Stretton Hall, Stafford ST19 9LQ), *b* 1934; FRICS; High Sheriff of Staffs 1975, and a DL 1988; a Bridge Life Master, a Dir of Penk, Ltd, Penk Holdings, Ltd, and Savills (Agric and Residential) Ltd; Fellow Woodard Corpn: *m* 1961, Joanna Mary, el da of late George Carlos Bird, of Appleton, Abingdon, Berks, and has had issue, Piers Alastair Carlos, *b* 1962: *m* 1988, Georgiana Margaret Elizabeth, only da of Julian Michael Edmund Byng (*see* E Strafford, 1985 Edn), and has had issue, Oliver George Carlos *b* 1993, Isobel Mary Elizabeth *b* 1989 *d* 1991, Emily Louise *b* 1991, — Simon Francis Carlos, *b* 1967, *d* 1969, — Toby Philip Carlos, *b* 1970, — Davina Claire, *b* 1964: *m* 1987, Gerard John Mytton Downes, of Herrington House, Whiteparish, Salisbury SP5 2RD, and has issue living, Rupert John Mytton *b* 1989, Hugh William Charles *b* 1991, — Sophie Louise (twin), *b* 1967. —— Daphne Alice Cavil, *b* 1937: *m* 1958, Nigel John Lincoln Estlick, Maj RM, of Kent House, Amesbury, Wilts, and has issue living, Robin Monckton, *b* 1968, — Caroline Rosemary, *b* 1962, — Marian Heather, *b* 1965.

Grandchildren of late Lieut-Col Edward Philip Monckton, el son of Edward Henry Cradock Monckton, el son of Philip Monckton, 5th son of Hon Edward Monckton, 5th son of 1st Viscount:—
Issue of late George Edward Monckton, *b* 1868, *d* 1936: *m* 1896, Marguerite Edith Evelyn Eleanor, da of late James Marigold, of Park House, Edgbaston:—
Cavil Grace Mary, *b* 1903: *m* 1925, Sydney Lipscombe Elborne, MBE, JP, Bar-at-Law, who *d* 1986, of Water Newton, Peterborough, and has issue living, Robert Edward Monckton (Seaton Old Rectory, Oakham, Rutland LE15 9HU; 17 Bettridge Rd, SW6 3QH), *b* 1926; *ed* Eton, and Trin Coll, Camb; Bar Inner Temple 1950; Solicitor 1958, formerly Lt Life Guards, and Inns of Court Regt (TA): *m* 1953, Vivienne, yr da of Lt-Gen Sir Ernest Wood, KBE, CB, CIE, MC, and has issue living, Mark Edward Monckton (Exeter House, Barrowden, Oakham, Rutland LE15 8EB) *b* 1958; *ed* Eton and Exeter Univ: *m* 1982, Lucinda Alison, stepda of Michael James Eyles Graham Bower, of 38 Charterfield Av, SW18 (and has issue living, Simon Henry Monckton *b* 1985, Philip Timothy William *b* 1986, Timothy Oliver Rupert *b* 1988, Freddie George Monckton *b* 1992, Amelia Lucy Caroline *b* 1983), William Henry Alexander *b* 1966, *ed* Eton, Charlotte Julia Mary *b* 1956: *m* 1978, (Anthony) Julian Lyell Beare (and has issue living, James Oliver Lyell *b* 1982, Charles Henry Lyell *b* 1984, Rosanna Sarah Cecil *b* 1988), — Margaret *b* 1934: *m* 1st, 1955 (*m diss* 1966), Maj John Richard Montgomery Laird, RA, who *d* 19—; 2ndly, 1967, Edward William Ingram, who *d* 1991, and has issue living, (by 1st *m*) Duncan John Alexander *b* 1958, Caroline Margaret Ann *b* 1956, (by 2nd *m*) Claire Constance Cavil *b* 1968.
Issue of late Philip Tunnard Monckton, *b* 1870, *d* 1928: *m* 1901, Agnes Carr, who *d* 1956, da of Maxwell Smith, of Darjeeling, India:—
Philip Anthony (PO Box EH62, Emerald Hill, Harare, Zimbabwe), *b* 1913; *ed* Sherborne; formerly Pilot Officer RAF Vol Reserve. —— Sybil Carr, *b* 1902; *m* 1st, 1927, Ronald Charles Keith Smith; 2ndly, 1955, Capt George Lardner-Clarke, late King's Regt. —— Mary Philippa *b* 1912: *m* 1st, 1934, William Michael Gambier Sandwith, Sup of Police, Kenya; 2ndly, 1948, Walter John Smail, and has issue living, (by 1st *m*) Caroline Ann, *b* 1938: *m* 1960, Alan Pickering (c/o Barclays Bank, DCO, Box 88, Mombasa, Kenya), and has issue living, Robert Alan *b* 1964, Tania Mary *b* 1962. *Residence* –

Grandson of late Lt-Col William Parry Monckton, 3rd son of Edward Henry Cradock Monckton (*ante*):—
Issue of late Ivor Parry Monckton, *b* 1892, *d* 1978: *m* 1921, Olive, da of William Bassett:—
Dennahouse Parry (10 Daniells Walk, Lymington, Hants SO41 9PN), *b* 1930; *ed* Sherborne; Maj RCT: *m* 1966, Mary Elizabeth Doreen, da of James Carson.

Grandchildren of late Hugh Monckton, yst son of late Edward Henry Cradock Monckton (*ante*):—
Issue of late Hugh Claud Monckton, *b* 1881, *d* 1970: *m* 1st 1910, Emily Sophia Ray (Dapsie), who *d* 1945, da of E. C. Gibson; 2ndly, 1946, Helen Atherton, who *d* 1974, da of late P. A. Morris, of Sydney, NSW:—
(By 1st *m*) Basil Robert (11 Meadowview Drive, Palm Meadows, Gold Coast, Qld 4211, Australia), *b* 1917; *ed* NZ Univ (BE); ME Adelaide: MIC; MIEAust; Civil Engineer, formerly Overseas Property Bureau Dept of Foreign Affairs, Canberra: *m* 1943, Audrey Constance, da of Arthur Charles Tribe, of Auckland, NZ, and has issue living, Robert Parry (Somerville, RMD Emu Creek, Sedgwick, Bendigo, Victoria, Australia 3551), *b* 1948; *ed* Flinders Univ, Adelaide (BSc), Aust National Univ (BSc Hons, PhD), Snr Research Scientist, Regional Veterinary Laboratory, Bendigo: *m* 1975, Joy Mary, da of late Frank Whitelam of Leicester, and has issue living, Christopher Parry *b* 1977, Timothy Alan *b* 1980, — David Christopher (23 Woodrow Drive, Coorparoo, Brisbane, Qld 4151, Australia), *b* 1951; *ed* Canberra Coll of Advanced Education (Bach of Applied Science), and Australian Nat Univ (BEc): *m* 1986, Katrina Angela, da of Mario Basile, of 52 Tonks St, Moorooka, Brisbane, Qld, and has issue living, Georgina Elizabeth *b* 1987, Harriette Susan *b* 1994, — Peter Charles (77 Wood St, Manly, NSW 2095), *b* 1955; *ed* Canberra Coll of Advanced Educn, and Sydney Univ (B Arch Hons 1982): *m* 1983, Diana (BA Des), da of George Marsh, of Sydney. —— †Hugh Noel Campbell *b* 1923: *ed* NZ Univ (BE); MICE, MNZIE, MRCI, ANZIA; Architect and Engineer: *m* 1950, Elizabeth Rubi Young (46 Woods Av, Matua, Tauranga, NZ), da of Arthur Boswell, of Takapuna, NZ, and *d* 1991, leaving issue, Hugh Geoffrey *b* 1954; BE; B Arch, ANZIA: *m* 1977, Helen Eileen, da of Leslie Dassler, and has issue living, Catherine Jane *b* 1990, — Roger John *b* 1958; BE, — Elizabeth Anne *b* 1953; BA. —— Sybil Dorothy (Unit 11/252 Mainroad, Regents Landing, Maroochydore, Qld 4558, Australia), *b* 1916; resumed the surname of Canard 1962: *m* 1st 1940, Ernest Herbert Canard, P/O RAF, *k* on active service in S Africa 1942; 2ndly, 1957 (*m diss* 1962), Nils A. A. H. Gyllenberg; 3rdly, 1966, Frederick Alma Gearing, who *d* 1991, and has issue living (by 1st *m*), Hugh Jason Paul (Ocean River Adventure Co, Marahau Beach, RD2, Motueka, NZ), *b* 1942; *ed* Rutherford Coll of Tech (IHVE), Newcastle upon Tyne: *m* 1968, Elizabeth Frances Wildridge, and has issue living, Jamie Duncan *b* 1971, Dougal Stephen *b* 1972.
Issue of late Eric Parry Monckton, *b* 1883, *d* 1953: *m* 1917, Wilhelmina (Minna), who *d* 1979, da of late H. W. Erhard, of Sydney, NS Wales:—
James Hugh (121 Jenkins Rd, Carlingsford, NSW 2118, Australia), *b* 1921: *m* 1981, Edith Joan, da of Albert Ernest Wearne, of Bingara, NSW. —— Joan Harriette (14 Jackson St, Balgowlah, NSW, Australia), *b* 1918: *m* 1940, Jack Anderson Stackpool, who *d* 1971, and has issue living, Michael John (7 Oyama Av, Manly, NSW 2095, Australia), *b* 1946; ACIV, QRV, AREI: *m* 1980, Lyndall Rosemary, da of Ian George Hudson, of Dural, and has issue living, Miles Ian *b* 1983, Hugh Jack Monckton *b* 1987, Isobel Claire *b* 1985, — Susan Jane (73 Wyndora Av, Harbord, NSW 2096), *b* 1947: *m* 1969 (*m diss* 1985), Stephen Charles Bowden, and has issue living, Peter Karl *b* 1974: *m* 1993, Candice Pippa Lawson, Timothy Robert *b* 1977.

Grandsons of Henry Grant Monckton, son of Henry Monckton, son of William Monckton, 8th son of Hon Edward Monckton (*ante*):—
Issue of Maj Frederick Hardy Monckton, *b* 1892, *d* 1981: *m* 1941, Frances, who *d* 1967, da of Paul Ryan, of Dublin:—
Henry William (19 Queens Gate Drive, Birstall, Leicester), *b* 1945; BA Camb; MICE: *m* 1976, Angela Mary, da of Thomas Spencer, of 33 Bath St, Leek, Staffs. —— Michael Frederick (30 Sedgebrook, Liden, Swindon, Wilts SN3 6EY), *b* 1947; *ed* Manchester Univ (BSc); MICE.

Granddaughters of late Rev James Frederick Monckton, eldest son of late Frederick Edward Monckton, son of late William Monckton, 8th son of Hon Edward Monckton (*ante*):—
Issue of late James Frederick Edward Monckton, *b* 1892, *d* 1985: *m* 1917, Dorothy Verrinder, who *d* 1975, 2nd da of late George Willson, of Upper Sydenham, SE:—
Georgiana Elspeth, *b* 1917: *m* 1st, 1938, Capt Peter Wilkinson Swift, Green Howards, who was *ka* 1942; 2ndly, 1946, Godfrey Walter Thrift, Green Howards, of Penn House, The Way, Reigate, Surrey RH2 0LB, and has issue living (by 1st *m*), Patricia Elspeth *b* 1940: ARCM: *m* 1962, Robin William Langford Gritton, ARCM, ARCO, of Penn House, The Way, Reigate, Surrey RH2 0LB, and has issue living, Peter William *b* 1963; *ed* Clare Coll, Camb (MA); LRAM, Susan Mary *b* 1965; *ed* St Hilda's Coll, Oxford (MA), Lucy Belinda *b* 1970, — (by 2nd *m*) Peter Walter Monckton, *b* 1949; Lloyds Underwriter. —— Patricia Penn, *b* 1920: *m* 1942, Richard James Ellis, late RAN, of Sinnington, 10 Cynthia Cres, Armidale, NSW 2350, and has issue

living, Peter Francis Monckton, *b* 1947; BSc Forestry, Dip Ed: *m* 1978, Rosalie Turner, and has issue living, Martyn Giles *b* 1979, Jacinta Frances *b* 1982, — Michael Richard Penn, *b* 1952; BSc Forestry, Dip Ed: *m* 1982, Elizabeth Giles, and has issue living, Lucy *b* 1982, Emma *b* 1984, — Timothy Willson, *b* 1961: *m* 1984, Rebecca Newland, and has issue living, Michael *b* 1985, — Susan Patricia, *b* 1943: *m* 1970, Geoffrey John Lawson, school master, and has issue living, Patrick Geoffrey *b* 1980, Josephine Emily *b* 1972, — Jennifer Ann, *b* 1949: *m* 1978, Richard Roderick Donaldson, farmer, of Whitewood, Fosters Rd, Armidale, NSW 2350, and has issue living, Warwick John *b* 1979, Christopher Richard *b* 1980, Rachel Patricia *b* 1982, — Winifred Jill, *b* 1958: *m* 1979, Laimonis Kavalieris, MA, PhD (Nat Univ of Canberra, ACT), of Dunedin, NZ. —— Jean Mary, *b* 1927: *m* 1948, Edward Richard Taylor, AM, BE, FIE Aust, of 18A Morella Av, Mosman, NSW, and has issue living, James Edward Monckton (5 Robert Av, N Manly, NSW, Australia), *b* 1949; BE, MIE Aust: *m* 1973, Anne Alison, da of Prof D. G. Stalley, of Manly, NSW, and has issue living, Daniel James Monckton *b* 1977, Peter Edward Richard *b* 1982, Philippa Alice *b* 1980, — Richard John, *b* 1955: *m* 1982, Yasmin, da of Steven Nagy, — David Matthew (twin), *b* 1955, — Catherine Elizabeth Monckton, *b* 1949 (*m diss* 1983), Donald Ross Kennedy, BSc, and has issue living, Rebecca Jean *b* 1974, Catriona Anne *b* 1977.

Issue of late Lt-Col Gordon Cecil Monckton, *b* 1902, *d* 1989: *m* 1st, 1928 (*m diss* 1948), Mary Catherine, da of late Hugh McCaffrey, of Clones, co Monaghan; 2ndly, 1948, Thérèse (47 Old Wokingham Rd, Crowthorne, Berks RG11 6SS), da of Stephen Minarovic, of Loimersdorf, Marchfield, Austria:—
(By 1st *m*) Elizabeth Ann, *b* 1930: *m* 1962, Martin Rosoff, PhD, of 15 Wellesley Av, Yonkers, NY 10705, USA, and has issue living, David Brian, *b* 1965. —— (By 2nd *m*) James Edward (Poynings, Cookoo Corner, Urchfont, nr Devizes, Wilts SN10 4RA), *b* 1951; *ed* Trin Coll of Music (LTCL): *m* 1971, Jacqueline Ann, only da of N. Conner, and has issue living, Timothy Norman, *b* 1975, — Matthew Gordon, *b* 1976, — Jenna Florence Theresia, *b* 1979. —— Evelyn Stephanie, *b* 1948: *m* 1972, David John Penman, of 24 Bladen Valley, Briantspuddle, Dorchester, Dorset DT2 7HP, and has issue living, Philip David Spencer, *b* 1977, — Emma Charlotte, *b* 1980. —— Valentine Penn, *b* 1950: *m* 1976, Robert James Leach, of PO Box 196, Hornsby, NSW 2077, Australia, and has issue living, Benjamin James, *b* 1983, — Emily Alice Penn, *b* 1986. —— Helen Marina, *b* 1953: *m* 1985, Peter Engzler, of Lot 11 Bulgar Rd, Wallaby Joe Flats, via Wingham, NSW 2429, Australia, and has issue living, Rebeka Freda, *b* 1986, — Sarah Thérèse, *b* 1987.

Grandchildren of late Walter Hilary Monckton, 2nd son of late Frederick Edward Monckton (ante):—
Issue of late Hilary James Monckton, *b* 1889, *d* 1969: *m* 1915, Ruby Rose, who *d* 1982, da of late John Crisp, of Cooma, NSW:—
Walter John Bruce (1 Cromwell St, Cooma, NSW 2630), *b* 1918: *m* 1st, 1942, Betty Allen, who *d* 1974, da of late C. W. Keele, of Bellevue Hill, Sydney, NSW: 2ndly, 1975, Susan Jane, da of Ian Antony Litchfield, of Matong, Cooma, NSW, and has issue living (by 1st *m*) Robin Anne *b* 1944: *m* 1969, Martin Pitt, of 14 Kent Rd, Rose Bay, and has issue living, Angus Andrew *b* 1972, Lucinda *b* 1971, — Rosemary Joan, *b* 1946: *m* 1971, Geoffrey William James Stevens, of Woollahra, NSW, who *d* 1984, and has issue living, James Walter Monckton *b* 1979, Alexandra *b* 1975, Sophie *b* 1977, Jessica Clare *b* 1981, — Frances Anne, *b* 1951: *m* 1980, Nigel Geoffrey Howard Pilcher, of Edgecliff, NSW, and has issue living, James Howard Monckton *b* 1983, Henry Nigel Monckton *b* 1985. —— Jean Winifred (The Kopje, 2 Cromwell St, Cooma, NSW), *b* 1916: *m* 1940, Maj Charles Cuthbert Wolfe, R Aust Engineers who *d* 1969, and has issue living, Edwin Charles Monckton, *b* 1941: *m* 1969, Sally Elaine, da of W. G. Cowley, of Armidale, and has issue living, Matthew Charles *b* 1974, Benjamin James *b* 1976, Samuel Luke *b* 1978, Sarah Jane *b* 1972, — Peter Hilary, *b* 1943, — Elizabeth Jean, *b* 1955: *m* 1978, Charles Ian Anthony Litchfield, of Muniong, Cooma, NSW, and has issue living, Stephen Charles Owen *b* 1979, Eleanor Jean *b* 1981.
Issue of late Basil Bruce Monckton, *b* 1894, *d* 1976: *m* 1st, 1929 (*m diss* 1948), Edna, da of E. N. R. McMillan, of Rockdale, NSW; 2ndly, 1949, Violet Lillian (8/822 Military Rd, Mosman, NSW), da of P. S. O'Donnell, of Mosman, NSW:—
(By 1st *m*), Margaret Heather, *b* 1930: *m* 1952, Keith Willoughby Payne, architect, of 18c Kirkoswald Av, Mosman, NSW, and has issue living, Geoffrey William, *b* 1953: *m* 1990, Margaret Mary, da of Geoffrey Hough, of Blakehurst, NSW, — David Bruce, *b* 1956: *m* 1987, Clare Patricia, da of Prof J.E. Morton, of Auckland, NZ, and has issue living, Matthew John *b* 1989, Samuel David *b* 1991, — Robyn Louise, *b* 1959: *m* 1984, Peter Randolph Smith, of 60 Nathan Terr, Yeerongpilly, Qld, and has issue living, Timothy Ian *b* 1990, Karen Rose *b* 1988, Sheila Margaret *b* 1993.

Grandsons of late Frederick Edward Monckton (ante):—
Issue of late Cecil Charles Fisk Monckton, *b* 1867, *d* 1954: *m* 1902, Dorothy Tatham, who *d* 1976, yr da of late Walter Tatham Hughes ISO, of 12 Somerset Place, Bath:—
Edward Walter, OBE, RN, *b* 1903; is Lieut-Com and acting Com; OBE (Mil) 1944: *m* 1932, Margaret Frances, da of late Brig-Gen Frederick Walter Radcliffe, CMG, CIE, CBE, of Whitecroft, Buxton Road, Weymouth, and has issue living, Christopher John Edward (Craigower Lodge, Newtonmore, Inverness-shire), *b* 1942; *ed* Gordonstoun: *m* 1st, 1965 (*m diss* 1976), Judith Benson, of Bournemouth; 2ndly, 19—, Anne Ide, of Guildford, Surrey, and has issue living (by 1st *m*), Oliver Edward Walter *b* 1974, Emily Joanna *b* 1966, Heather Mary *b* 1970, (by 2nd *m*) Lawrence Christopher Darwin *b* 1977, — Hugh Francis (Tillytoghills House, Fettercairn, Kincardineshire), *b* 1948; *ed* Gordonstoun; Master Mariner; MNI, MRIN: *m* 1948, Nila Elizabeth, da of John Snazell, of Taunton, and has issue living, Helen Margaret *b* 1985. *Residence* – 42, Ottoline Drive, Troon, Ayrshire. —— Charles Tatham (Portelet Cottage, Jersey), *b* 1913; late Capt 4th/7th R Dragoon Gds: *m* 1946, Ruth Elizabeth Blandy, and has issue living, Timothy James (Flat 7, John Forbes House, Pitbille Crescent, Cheltenham, Glos GL52 2ZJ), *b* 1947; MRAC, GInstM: *m* 1971, Mary, da of late John Mcleod, of Blackburn, MIEE, and has issue living, Daniel James *b* 1975, John Henry *b* 1979, Antonia Mary *b* 1981, — Richard Charles, *b* 1960: — Felicity Ruth, *b* 1949: *m* 1981, Robert Bastiaan Beydals, of Gouden Regenhof 25, 3434 T J Nieuwegein, The Netherlands, and has issue living, Alexander Herman *b* 1986, Sebastiaan Charles *b* 1988.

PREDECESSORS – (1) JOHN Monckton, MP for Clitheroe 1722-33, and for Pontefract 1734-51, A Commr of Revenue in Ireland 1734-47, and Surveyor Gen of Woods and Forests in England and Wales 1748-51; *cr Baron Killard*, of co Clare, and *Viscount Galway* (peerage of Ireland) 1727; *d* 1751; *s* by his son (2) WILLIAM, 2nd Viscount; MP for Pontefract and Thirsk, and Receiver of Crown Rents, etc; assumed by Roy licence 1769 the additional surname of Arundell; *d* 1772; *s* by his el son (3) HENRY WILLIAM, 3rd Viscount; sat as MP for Pontefract; *d* 1774; *s* by his brother (4) ROBERT MONCKTON ARUNDELL, PC, KB; MP for York, Pontefract, and Thirsk in several Parliaments; *d* 1810; *s* by his son (5) WILLIAM GEORGE, 5th Viscount; discontinued the surname of Arundell by Roy licence 1826, and obtained permission for each successive holders of the title and his el son to use the surnames of Monckton-Arundell, while the younger branches of the family should use the surname of Monckton only; *d* 1834; *s* by his son (6) GEORGE EDWARD ARUNDELL, 6th Viscount, *b* 1805; MP for E Retford (*C*) 1847-76, and a Lord-in-Waiting to HM Queen Victoria 1852: *m* 1838, Henrietta Eliza, da of Robert Pemberton Milnes, Esq, and sister of 1st Baron Houghton; *d* 1876: *s* by his son (7) GEORGE EDMUND MILNES, CB 7th Viscount, *b* 1844; was ADC to Queen Victoria 1897-1901, to King Edward VII. 1901-10 and to King George V 1910-20, and was Lord High Steward of Retford; sat as MP for Nottinghamshire North (*C*) 1872-85; *cr Baron Monckton*, of Serlby, co Nottingham (peerage of United Kingdom) 1887: *m* 1879, Vere, who *d* 1921, only da of late Ellis Gosling, of Busbridge Hall, Godalming; *d* 1931; *s* by his son (8) VERE ARUNDELL, GCMG, DSO, OBE, DL, 8th Viscount, *b* 1882; Lieut-Col late Life Guards; was Gov-Gen and Com-in-Ch of New Zealand 1935-41: European War 1914-19 (DSO, OBE): *m* 1922, Hon Lucia Emily Margaret White, who *d* 1983, da of 3rd Baron Annaly; *d* 1943; *s* by his only son (9) SIMON GEORGE ROBERT 9th Viscount, *b* 1929: *m* 1953, Lady Teresa Jane Fox-Strangways (who *d* 1989, having *m* 2ndly, 1972, Mark Agnew), da of 7th Earl of Ilchester; *d* 1971, when the UK Barony of Monckton (*cr* 1887) became ext; *s* in his other peerages by his kinsman (10) WILLIAM ARUNDELL, who adopted the additional surname of Arundell by Roy Licence on succession for himself and for all successive holders of the title (el son of William Henry Monckton, el son of Hon Edmund Gambier Monckton, 4th son of 5th Viscount), 10th Viscount; *b* 1894; Lt 2nd Bn, R Jersey LI (Militia): *m* 1939, Joan, who *d* 1973, only child of Maj G. A. Williams, S Staffs Regt, of Purbrook, Hants; *d* 1977; *s* by hs brother (11) EDMUND SAVILE, 11th Viscount, *b* 1900; Solicitor: *m* 1927, Kathleen Joyce, who *d* 1975, da of James Musgrave (Musgrave, Bt, *cr* 1782); *d* 1980; *s* by his kinsman **(12)** GEORGE RUPERT (only surv son (his elder brother, John Philip Monckton, F/O, RCAF, *b* 1919, served in World War II, and was *ka* 1943) of Philip Marmaduke Monckton, only son of Marmaduke John Monckton, 3rd son of Hon Edmund Gambier Monckton, 4th son of 5th Viscount), 12th Viscount, and present peer; also Baron Killard.

GARDINER, BARONY OF (Gardiner) (Extinct 1990)

DAUGHTER LIVING OF LIFE BARON (*By 1st marriage*)

Hon Carol (Flat 1F, Montagu Mews N, Crawford St, W1), *b* 1929.

GARDNER, BARONY OF (Gardner) (Dormant 1883)

COLLATERAL BRANCHES LIVING

Grandchildren of late Alan Legge Gardner (styled 5th Baron Gardner), only son of late Alan Hyde Gardner (styled 4th Baron Gardner), son of late Stewart William Gardner, son of Rear-Adm Hon Francis ffarington Gardner, 2nd son of 1st Baron:—
Issue of late Alan William Gardner (styled 6th Baron Gardner), *b* 1908, *d* 1975: *m* 1938, Ethel Lydia, who *d* 1972, da of late James Valentine Gardner, Zamindar of Village Fatehpore, Dist Etah, UP:—
JULIAN JAMES (*claims the title*) (Village Fatehpur, PO Soron, Dist: Etah, Uttar Pradesh, India), *b* 2 June 1942: *m* 1966, Ella, da of Philip Samuel, and has issue living, Ashley Rodney (St Peter's Sch, Mazegaon Rd, Bombay 400010), *b* 10 Nov 1968, — Christabel Berryl, *b* 1967: *m* 1989, David Andrew Luke, and has issue living, Rowan Robin *b* 1992, — Iona Valerie, *b* 1971. —— †Archibald Horace, *b* 1945: *m* 1976, Ena Hendricks, and *d* 1993, leaving issue, Adrian Arnold, *b* 1978, — Ainsley, Edmond, *b* 1981. —— Dennis Stuart (Swedish Alliance Mission, Nandurbar, Dist Dhule, MS, India), *b* 1947: *m* 1984, Kiran, da of Narindernath Khunghar, and has issue living, Denise Ethel, *b* 1985, — Karin Jane, *b* 1986. —— Basil Connel (St Peter's Sch, Mazegaon Rd, Bombay 400010), *b* 1957: *m* 1991, Lynda, da of Royston Henderson, and has issue living, Alan Stewart, *b* 19—. —— Barbara Christiana, *b* 1939: *m* 1982, Charles Leopold Gardner, and has issue living, Dawn Eileen, *b* 1983. —— Norma Mary, *b* 1959: *m* 1979, Lincoln Solomon, and has issue living, Kevin, *b* 1989.

Grandchildren of late Charles van Straubenzee Gardner (*infra*):—
Issue of late Henry Gardner, *b* 1911, *d* 1964: *m* 1941, Emma, who *d* 19—, da of Harry Gardner:—
David Francis, *b* 1945: *m* 19—, — and has issue living, a son, *b ca* 1978. —— Charles Straubenzee, *b* 1951. —— Baldwin, *b* 1955. —— Evelyn, *b* 1948.

Grandchildren of late Edward Gardner, 2nd son of late Stewart William Gardner (*ante*):—
Issue of late Charles van Straubenzee Gardner, *b* 1883, *d* 1951: *m* 1900, his cousin Ellen, who *d* 1952, da of late William Rickards Gardner (*ante*):—
Edward Kingston (c/o Abdul Wahid, Building No 4442, Nasirabad, Rajasthan, India), *b* 1917: *m* 1946, Mary Cicelia, da of G.A. De Silva, and has issue living, Frederick Anthony, *b* 1946, — Terrance Lewis, *b* 1952: *m* 1980, Maryander, da of James Singh, and has issue living, Dorothy *b* 1980, Elvina Cicelia *b* 1981, Agnes Gloria *b* 1984, — Jennet Cicelia, *b* 1949: *m* 1972, Abdul Wahid, and has issue living, Aniz *b* 1974, Hilda *b* 1976, Shelly Ann *b* 1978, Mary Rose *b* 1980. —— Francis Robert, *b* 1920: *m* 1953, Irene Martin, and has issue living, George Washington, *b* 1954. —— Cherry Martha, *b* 1913: *m* 1935, Alfred Samuel Tupper, who *d* 1953, and has issue living, Albert Jasbir Samuel, *b* 1936, — Arthur Alexander, *b* 1942, — Ezekiel Habib, *b* 1948, — Rexey, *b* 1951, — Margaret Shirin, *b* 1938, — Maybelle Iris, *b* 1940. —— Ruby Maggie *b* 1915: *m* 1943, James Gideon, and has issue living, a son, *b* 1944, — a son, *b* 19—, — a da, *b* 19—, — a da, *b* 19—, — a da, *b* 19—, — a da, *b* 19—. —— Marjory Julia, *b* 1925: *m* 1947, Kenneth Charles Johnson. *Residence* -
Issue of late Benjamin Gardner, *b* 1889, *d* 1937: *m* 1914, Sophia Shikó, who *d* 1936:—
Daniel, *b* 1919: *m* 1946, Irene Coal, and has had issue, Noel, *b* 1946; *dunm* 19—, — Ivan, *b* 1949: *m* 1976, Millicent Joseph, and has issue living, Brian *b* 1979, Jennifer *b* 1980, Sherril *b* 1983. —— Lionel Benjamin, *b* 1934: *m* 1960, Celestina Singh, and has issue living, Malcolm, *b* 1962: *m* 1988, Sangeeta Singh, and has issue living, Alice, *b* 1990, — Bobby, *b* 1963: *m* 1987, Venceta James, and has issue living, Rocky *b* 1988, Rubeena *b* 1990, Sandra *b* 1991, — Joyce, *b* 1964. —— Caroline, *b* 1915: *m* 1940, Rene David, and has issue living, three sons and three das. —— Margaret Ruby, *b* 1917: *m* 1936, Linnaeus Arrance Alfred Gardner, son of Alfred Gardner, and has had issue, Albert, *b* 1938: *m* 1st, 19—, Lynda Wright; 2ndly, 19—, Yvonne, da of William Gardner, of Kanpur, and has issue living, (by 1st *m*) Ian *b* 19—, (by 2nd *m*) two sons, — Melvyn Wilfred, *b* 1941: *m* 19—, Quintella, da of William Gardner, — David (Mickey), *b* 1945; *dunm* 19—, — Princeton, *b* 1947: *m* 19—, an Iranian lady, and has issue living, a da *b* 19—, — Elizabeth Faith, *b* 1938: *m* 1960, Francis —, and has issue living, Sandra *b* 19—, — Marian, *b* 1941: *m* 19—, Hubert Star, and has issue living, three sons. —— Queenie, *b* 1921: *m* 1941, Augustine Paul, and has issue living, Noel, *b* 1943, — George, *b* 1945, — Eugene, *b* 1947, — Joyce, *b* 1949. —— Hazel, *b* 1926: *m* 19—, — Mendes, and has issue living, Alvina, *b* 19—: *m* 19—, Robert Gardner (*see* B Gardner, colls, 1985 Edn), and has issue living, Ashley *b* 19—, Desiree *b* 19—. —— Ouida (Vida) Shirley, *b* 1936: *m* 1952, Leslie Clifford Gardner (*infra*).

Grandchildren of late George Gardner, only son of late Tandy Gardner, 3rd son of late Stewart William Gardner (*ante*):—
Issue of late Stewart Gardner, *b* 1897, *d* 1965: *m* 19—, Elizabeth Scott:—
Donald, *b* 19—. —— Norman, *b* 19—. —— Florence (Naini Tal, India), *b* 1926: *m* 19—, — Mackie Hoffland, and has issue living, Robert, *b* 19—: *m* 19—, Sarah Pant, and has issue living, David *b* 19—, Malcolm *b* 19—, — Glenda, *b* 19—: *m* 19—, — Leblond.
Issue of late John Gardner, *b* 1898, *d* 1955: *m* 1918, Clara Callow:—
John (Cloverdale, W Australia), *b* 1926; Lt-Col: *m* 1951, Valerie Jeffroy, and has issue living, John (Attadale, W Australia), *b* 1956: *m* 1980, Eleanor Snowdon, and has issue living, Joshua *b* 1987, Natasha *b* 1981, Alicia *b* 1983, — Deborah, *b* 1953: *m* 19—, Dino Elpitelli, of Bull Creek, W Australia, and has issue living, Daniel *b* 1982, Melissa *b* 1979. —— Phyllis (Nilgiri Hills, India), *b* 1920: *m* 19—, Charles T. O. A. Wright, and has issue living, Dierdre (Bangalore, India), *b* 1953: *m* 1981, P. Khanna, and has issue living, Harshini *b* 1984, Tejangini *b* 1987. —— Jean, *b* 1923: *m* 1947, Terence Healey, and has issue living, Shirley (Balcatta, W Australia), *b* 1951: *m* 1978, Tony Lizza, and has issue living, Oriano *b* 1984, Jean *b* 1982, — Eleanor (Auckland, NZ), *b* 1956: *m* 1980, Glen Boyce, and has issue living, John *b* 1985, Greer *b* 1987.
Issue of late Leopold Gardner, *b* 1899, *d* 1970: *m* 19—, Charlotte Gardner:—

Rockwell (Darjeeling, India), *b* 1931: *m* 19—, Adelaide Edwards, and has issue living, Neville, *b* 19—: *m* 19—, Vivian Edwards, and has issue living, Kieron *b* 19—, Ramona *b* 19—, — Andrew, *b* 19—: *m* 19—, Anuradha Sharma, and has issue living, Anushka *b* 19—, — Roxanne, *b* 19—: *m* 19—, Phillip Chen, and has issue living, Daniel *b* 19—, — Charlotte, *b* 19—: *m* 19—, Pravin Mukhia (20 Chowrasta, The Mall, Darjeeling 734101, WB, India), and has issue living, Alana *b* 19—, Nihar *b* 19—, — Ann, *b* 19—: *m* 19—, Suresh Vaidya, — Ida, *b* 19—: *m* 19—, Pradeep Bhandari, and has issue living, Vinay *b* 19—, Vineeta *b* 19—, Sarita *b* 19—. —— Nelson (Kardinya, W Australia), *b* 1932: *m* 19—, Dorothy Blewitt, and has issue living, Lynette, *b* 1959: *m* 1987, Laurence Rea, — Claudette, *b* 1962: *m* 1985, Steve Lyndon, and has issue living, Kelly *b* 1987. —— Jefferson (Darjeeling, India), *b* 1937: *m* 19—, Ruth Downes, and has issue living, Glen, *b* 19—, — April, *b* 19—. —— Noreen Mabel, *b* 1934: *m* 1st, 19—, — Mitchell; 2ndly, 19—, — Phillips, and has issue living (by 1st *m*), Brian, *b* 19—, — Kevin, *b* 19—, — Jenny, *b* 19—, — (by 2nd *m*), Wendy, *b* 19—. —— Ida, *b* 1945.
    Issue of late Cyril Gardner, *b* 1902, *d* 1988: *m* 1st, 19—, Mavis — —; 2ndly, 19—, Dolly—:—
(By 1st *m*) Ivan (Sydney, NSW, Australia), *b* 1926: *m* 19—, Joan Gawke. —— Reginald, *b* 1928. —— Gertrude, *b* 19—: *m* 19—, — Hernandez, and has issue living, Marcel, *b* 19—, — Max, *b* 19—. —— Dagma (Delhi, India), *b* 1937.
    Issue of late (Louis) Gerald Gardner, *b* 1904, *d* 1943: *m* 1st, 1930, Muriel Gladys Jahans, who *d* 1932; 2ndly, 1935, Myrtle Sheppard (who *m* 2ndly, 1944, Joseph Simpson):—
(By 1st *m*) Maureen, *b* 1930: *m* 19—, Mervyn Raphael, and has issue living, Stephen, *b* 19—: *m* 19—, and has issue living, Christine *b* 19—, Pauline *b* 19—. —— (By 2nd *m*) Gerald, *b* 1936. —— Yvonne, *b* 1937.

    Grandchildren of late Wellington Gardner (infra):—
    Issue of late Richard Gardner, *b* 1919, *d* 1984: *m* 1945, Daisy Margaret, who *d* 1991, da of late Benjamin Gardner (ante):—
Kendrick Navil, *b* 1946: *m* 1973, Enit, da of — Scott, of Kanpur, UP, and has issue living, George Washington, *b* 1974, — Christina, *b* 1975. —— Reginald Wellington, *b* 1950: *m* 1975, Joyce, da of David Shakuntala, of Delhi, and has issue living, Anish, *b* 1976, — Allan Hyde *b* 1979. —— Edgar Terance (Rosary Church School, Raidio Colony, Nirankari Colony, Delhi 9), *b* 1953: *m* 1981, Vinorika, da of Arthur Ruskin, of Fategarh, UP, and has issue living, Basil Richard, *b* 1984, — Adie Navil, *b* 1990. —— Samson, *b* 19—. —— Beryl Dorothy, *b* 1955: *m* 19—, Morris James, of Gaziabad, UP. —— Elsa Linit, *b* 19—: *m* 19—, King Suberoi, of Delhi.

    Grandson of late William Rickards Gardner 4th, son of Stewart William Gardner (ante):—
    Issue of late Wellington Gardner, *b* 1881, *d* 19—: *m* 1916, Dorothy, da of Edward Gardner (ante):—
Leslie Clifford, *b* 1926: *m* 1952, Ouida (Vida) Shirley, da of late Benjamin Gardner (ante), and has issue living, Derek *b* 1960, — Dulcie Vida, *b* 1953: *m* 19—, Hector Solomon, of Bareilly, UP, — Ordi Flosy, *b* 1955, — Philomena *b* 1957.

    Grandchildren of Major Charles Phillips Gardner (infra):—
    Issue of late Lt-Cmdr David William Hyde Gardner, RN, *b* 1913, *d* 1975: *m* 1st, 1936 (*m diss* 1957), Edith Margaret, da of William Henry Wroth; 2ndly, 1958, Susanne Willeter (Lilac Cottage, Waldley, nr Doveridge, Derby), da of John L. Bagshaw, of The Manor House, Uttoxeter, Staffs:—
(By 1st *m*) Alan David Hyde (Bucks, Hyde Lane, Danbury, Essex), *b* 1939: *m* 1973, Penelope Nelson, and has issue living, Edward, *b* 1974, — Nicholas, *b* 1977, — Jane, *b* (twin with Nicholas) 19—. —— John Henry Wroth (Au Bourg, St Astier, Duras, Dordogne, France), *b* 1946: *m* 1973, Tessa Alexandra, da of Capt D. Mallinson, OBE, RN (ret), and has issue living, Thomas Edward Wroth, *b* 1974, — Daniel John Wroth, *b* 1975, — William Henry Wroth, *b* 1978. —— Gillian Margaret, *b* 1941: *m* 1962, John Seager Green, of 2 Herbert Mansions, 35 Sloane St, SW1X 9LP, and has issue living. —— (By 2nd *m*) Wiliam Patrick Hyde, *b* 1960. —— James Francis ffarington, *b* 1962.

    Grandchildren of late Capt Alan Hyde Gardner, RN, yst son of Rear-Adm Francis ffarington Gardner (ante):—
    Issue of late Major Charles Phillips Gardner, *b* 1883, *d* 1932: *m* 1st, 1910, Dorothy Margaret, who *d* 1921, 2nd da of William Mullock, formerly of Llantarnam, Monmouth; 2ndly, 1924, Constance Eileen, who *d* 1975, da of late Major Charles Hay Cox, W Yorkshire Regt:—
(By 1st *m*) Rosamund Dorothy (PO Box 592, Ranchos de Taos, New Mexico 87557, USA), *b* 1915. —— (By 2nd *m*) Susannah Caroline Hyde (*Viscountess Hawarden*), *b* 1928: *m* 1957, 8th Viscount Hawarden, who *d* 1991. *Residence* – Wingham Court, nr Canterbury, Kent.

    Grandchildren of late Capt Herbert Calthorpe Gardner, son of late Gen Hon William Henry Gardner, 3rd son of 1st Baron:—
    Issue of late Herbert Prescott Gardner, *b* 1854, *d* 1938: *m* 1906, Ethel Mary, who *d* 1954, da of late Henry Crouch:—
Alan Henry, *b* 1914: *m* 1942, Gemma Elizabeth, da of late E. K. McCord, of Coonambula, Eidsvold, Queensland, and has issue living, Alan Peter Prescott (Sunnybank, Surat, Queensland), *b* 1944: *m* 1972, Page, da of John M. Neill, of St Lucia, Brisbane, and has issue living, Alice Adrienne *b* 1974, Susan Patricia *b* 1977, — Shane McCord, (Green Ridges, Kangaroo Valley, NSW, Australia), *b* 1946: *m* 1976, Judith da of T. B. Adams of Rainworth, Brisbane, and has issue living, Jacob Adams *b* 1978, Patrick Alan *b* 1982, Sarah Louise *b* 1980, Jessie *b* 1986, — Mark McCord, *b* 1954: *m* 1976, Cathryn Louise, da of Dr Graham Anderson, of Ascot, Brisbane, and has issue living, Gemma Joan *b* 1979, Mardi Cathryn *b* 1982, Tilly Anderson *b* 1984. *Residence* – No 7 Drem St, Toogoolawah, Queensland 4313. —— Olivera Graham, *b* 1911: *m* 1939, Jack Christian Richards, who was *k* in a motor accident 1969, and has issue living, Roger Gardner, *b* 1940: *m* 1966, Annabel Gee, of Launceston, Tasmania, and has issue living, Josephine *b* 1968, Frances *b* 1969, Nikki *b* 1976, — Alan Gardner, *b* 1941: *m* 1969, Sylvia Rasdell, and has issue living, Timothy *b* 1971, Stephan *b* 1973, Jennifer *b* 1975, — Hew Gardner, *b* 1946: *m* 1969, Diana Dennis, and has issue living, James Christian *b* 1971, Matthew Charles *b* 1978, Rosemary *b* 1974, — Susanna, *b* 1944: *m* 1969, Jean-Michel Allaz, of Geneva, and has issue living, Natalie Claire *b* 1970, Catherine Helen *b* 1972. —— Helen Prescott, *b* 1912: *m* 1939, Lt-Col James Peile Love, and has issue living, Antony James (48 Miles St, Wooloowin, Brisbane, Qld), *b* 1946: *m* 1971, Margot Elizabeth, da of J. G. Moore, of Aspley, Brisbane, Qld, and has issue living, Nicholas James *b* 1973, Christopher James *b* 1977, — Judith Prescott, *b* 1940: *m* 1962, Dr John Noble, of High View Court, Prince Henry Heights, Toowoomba, Qld 4350, and has issue living, Andrew James *b* 1963, Cameron Charles *b* 1968, Louise Annabelle *b* 1965, — Rosalind Prescott, *b* 1943: *m* 1970 (*m diss* 1983), Michael Ian Minchin, of 103 Waterworks Rd, Dynnyrne, Hobart, Tasmania, and has issue living, Anna Prescott *b* 1971. *Residence* – 109 Virginia Av, Hawthorne, Brisbane, Qld.

PREDECESSORS – (1) ALAN Gardner, Adm of the Blue, and Maj-Gen Marine Forces; successively MP for Plymouth and Westminster; was *cr* a *Baronet* 1794, *Baron Gardner*, of Uttoxeter (peerage of Ireland) 1800; and *Baron Gardner*, of Uttoxeter, co Stafford (peerage of United Kingdom) 1806; *d* 1809; *s* by his son (2) ALAN HYDE, KCB, 2nd Baron; was an Adm; gazetted a Viscount 30 Sept 1815, and *d* 27 Dec following, before the patent had passed the Great Seal; *s* by his son (3) ALAN LEGGE, 3rd Baron; was a Lord-in-Waiting 1832-41; *d* 1883, since when the title has remained dormant.

GARDNER OF PARKES (Gardner) (Life Baroness 1981)

KEEP · GOING

(RACHEL) TRIXIE ANNE GARDNER, JP, da of late John Joseph Gregory McGirr; *b* 17 July 1927; *ed* Monte Sant Angelo Coll, and Sydney Univ; Dental Surgeon; Member Westminster City Council 1968-78 and GLC, Havering 1970-73, and Enfield Southgate 1977-86; JP (N Westminster, Inner London 1971); British Chm European Union of Women 1978-82; Nat Women's Vice-Chm Conservative Party 1978-82; Gov Nat Heart Hospital 1974-90, UK Rep on UN Status of Women Commn 1982-88; Dir London Electricity Board 1984-89, and Woolwich Building Soc 1988-93; Vice-Chm NE Thames Regional Health Authority 1990-94; Chm PLAN Int (UK) since 1990, and Chm Royal Free Hampstead NHS Trust since 1994; *cr Baroness Gardner of Parkes*, of Southgate, Greater London, and of Parkes in the State of New South Wales and Commonwealth of Australia (Life Baroness) 1981: *m* 1956, Kevin Anthony Gardner, Lord Mayor of City of Westminster 1987-88, son of George Gardner, of Sydney, and has issue.

Arms – Per fess azure and vert in chief a representation of the constellation of the Southern Cross argent issuing in base a sun in splendour or all within a bordure indented gold. **Supporters** – : dexter, a kangaroo or gorged with a crown palisado vert grasping in the sinister forepaw a branch of Tudor roses slipped and leaved proper; sinister, a lion or gorged with a crown palisado vert grasping in the dexter forepaw a branch of wattle slipped and leaved proper, the compartment comprising a grassy mount growing therefrom two waratah flowers slipped and leaved proper.
Address – House of Lords, SW1.

DAUGHTERS LIVING

Hon Sarah Louise, *b* 1960: *m* 1991, Timothy M. Joiner, eldest son of Hugh Joiner, of Gustard Wood, Wheathampstead, Herts.
Hon Rachel Trixie, *b* 1961; MB BS London 1984: *m* 1988, Dr Alvan John Pope, son of Kenneth Pope, of the Old Rectory, Chastleton, Oxon, and has issue living, Christopher, *b* 1991, — Victoria, *b* 1993. *Residence* – 20 Bark Place, W2 4AR.
Hon Joanna Mary, *b* 1964.

Garmoyle, Viscount; son of Earl Cairns.

GARNER, BARONY OF (Garner) (Extinct 1983)

SONS LIVING OF LIFE BARON

Hon Christopher John Saville, *b* 1939: *m* 1962, Janet, only da of Maj Harold Vaughan Rees, of Winnersh, Wokingham, Berks, and has issue.
Hon Joseph Jonathan (44 Holmewood Rd, SW2), *b* 1940: *m* 1969, Brigitte, da of Louis Pittet, of Sens, France, and has issue.

DAUGHTER LIVING OF LIFE BARON

Hon Helena Geneva, *b* 1947: *m* 1981, Iain Morrison.

WIDOW LIVING OF LIFE BARON

MARGARET (*Baroness Garner*), da of late Herman Beckman, of Cedar Lake, Indiana, USA: *m* 1938, Baron Garner, GCMG (Life Baron), who *d* 1983. *Residence* –

Garnock, Viscount; son of Earl of Lindsay.

GARNSWORTHY, BARONY OF (Garnsworthy) (Extinct 1974)

SON LIVING OF LIFE BARON (*by 2nd marriage*)

Hon Charles Edyvean, *b* 1974.

WIDOW LIVING OF LIFE BARON

SUE (*Baroness Garnsworthy*), da of Harold Taylor, and formerly wife of Michael Farley: *m* 1973, as his 2nd wife, Baron Garnsworthy, OBE (Life Baron), who *d* 1974.

GARVAGH, BARON (Canning) (Baron I 1818)

(ALEXANDER LEOPOLD IVOR) GEORGE CANNING, 5th Baron; *b* 6 Oct 1920; *s* 1956; *ed* Eton, and Ch Ch Oxford; MBIM; formerly Member of Court of Painter Stainers; Fellow of Inst of Dirs, a Member Inst of Exports; formerly Chm and Managing Dir of The Lord Garvagh and Assos, Ltd, Consultants, London, and Indep Chartering, Ltd, of Camco Machinery, Ltd, of Intersal Commodities, Ltd, and Anglo Brazilian Investments, Ltd, a Dir of AODC (UK), Ltd, Campden Research & Sales, Ltd, The Lord Garvagh & Partners, Ltd, Stonehaven Tankers, Ltd, and Seaways (London), Ltd, Conslt Ptnr Schtumel Towning WI & Ptnrs; Accredited Rep Trade Industry, The Cayman Is 1981; 1939-45 War, Guides Cav, and Capt Indian Army in Burma (despatches): *m* 1st, 1947 (*m diss* 1973), Edith Christine, da of late Jack Cooper, of Little Bridley, Worplesdon; 2ndly, 1974, Cynthia, da of late Eric Ernest Falk Pretty, CMG, and has issue by 1st *m*.

Arms – Quarterly of six: 1st and 6th argent, three Moors' heads, couped in profile, proper, wreathed round the temples, argent and azure, *Canning*: 2nd gules, three spears' heads palewise in fesse argent, *Salmon*; 3rd gules, a goat salient or *Marshall*; 4th argent, three bendlets azure, within a bordure gules. *Newburg*; 5th, per pale argent and sable, a fesse nebulée, between three griffins' heads erased, all counterchanged, and within a bordure engrailed also counterchanged, of the field, *Spencer*. **Crest** – 1st a demi-lion rampant argent, charged with three trefoils vert, holding in the dexter paw an arrow, pheoned and flighted proper, shaft or: 2nd a demi-lion rampant, holding in the dexter paw a battle-axe; 3rd a demi-griffin segreant. **Supporters** – *Dexter*, a griffin reguardant, wings elevated and expanded azure, guttée d'or; *sinister*, an eagle reguardant, wings elevated and expanded sable.

Yield not to misfortunes, but oppose them

NE CEDE MALIS   SED CONTRA

Residence – Alicante, Spain; *postal address* Apartado 289, 03724 Moraira, Alicante.

SON LIVING (By 1st marriage)

Hon SPENCER GEORGE STRATFORD DE REDCLIFFE, *b* 12 Feb 1953: *m* 1979, Julia Margery Morison, elder da of Col F.C.E. Bye, of Twickenham, Middx, and has issue living, Stratford George Edward de Redcliffe, *b* 7 Feb 1990, — Cordelia Louise Morison, *b* 1985, — Florence, *b* 1988. *Residence* – 1 Church Lane, Little Bedwyn, Marlborough, Wilts.

DAUGHTERS LIVING (By 1st marriage)

Hon (Christine) Alexandra, *b* 1949: *m* 1971 (*m diss* 1987), Louis David Lawrence, and has issue living, Stafford, *b* 1973, — Lucas, *b* 1976.
Hon Louise Eleanor Alice, *b* 1951: *m* 1975, Mark Lawrence, of Croft House, All Cannings, Devizes, Wilts, and has issue living, Jack Canning, *b* 1982, — Rufus Powell, *b* 1986.

SISTERS LIVING

Hon (Dora) Valerie Patricia, *b* 1919: *m* 1st, 1942, Philip Anthony Wellesley Colley, Lieut RA, who was *ka* 1944; 2ndly, 1950, Peter Sutcliffe, who *d* 1991, and has issue living, (by 1st *m*) Angela, *b* 1942: *m* 1973, David Campbell Anderson, of 14 Lauriston Rd, Wimbledon SW19, and has issue living, James *b* 1978, — Elizabeth Jane (*posthumous*), *b* 1945: *m* 1966, Peter John Wilson, of Brook House, Charing, Kent, and has issue living, Camilla Jane *b* 1969, Sarah Louise *b* 1970, Henrietta Mary *b* 1973, Claire Alexandra *b* 1977, — (by 2nd *m*) James (Hemingby House, Hemingby, Lincs LN9 5QF), *b* 1953; *ed* Stowe: *m* 1st, 1980 (*m diss* 1984), Carol Leslie, only da of late Capt C. P. Pratt, of West End, Hants, and of Nigeria; 2ndly, 1988, Susan Diana, da of John Beaumont, of The Manor House, Mill Lane, Legbourne, Louth, Lincs, and formerly wife of Geoffrey Sharp, and has issue living (by 1st *m*), Hannah *b* 1983, (by 2nd *m*) William *b* 1989. *Residence* – 14 Lauriston Rd, SW19 4TQ
Hon Daphne Rose, *b* 1922: *m* 1950, Bancroft Svenningson, and has issue living, Victor Stratford de Redcliffe, *b* 1954, — Jennifer, *b* 1955, — Andrea, *b* 1960. *Residence* – Cavan Valley Farm, Bewdley RR#2, Ontario K0L 1E0, Canada.

PREDECESSORS – (1) GEORGE Canning, FRS, Lord-Lieut of co Londonderry; *cr Baron Garvagh*, of Garvagh, co Londonderry (peerage of Ireland) 1818; *d* 1840; *s* by his son (2) CHARLES HENRY SPENCER GEORGE, 2nd Baron, *b* 1826; Capt 10th Hussars: *m* 1851, Cecilia Susannah, who *d* 1898, da of John Ruggles-Brise, of Spains Hall, Brentwood; *d* 1871; *s* by his son (3) CHARLES JOHN SPENCER GEORGE, 3rd Baron; *b* 1852: *m* 1877, Florence Alice, MBE, who *d* 1926, da of Baron Joseph de Bretton, of Copenhagen; *d* 1915; *s* by his son (4) LEOPOLD ERNEST STRATFORD GEORGE, 4th Baron; *b* 1878: *m* 1st 1906 (*m diss* 1909), Caroline Grace Elizabeth, only da of Charles Ernest Rube; 2ndly, 1919, Gladys Dora May, who *d* 1982, da of Bayley Parker, of Edgbaston, and widow of Lieut-Col D. M. Dimmer, VC, *d* 1956; *s* by his son (5) (ALEXANDER LEOPOLD IVOR) GEORGE, 5th Baron and present peer.

GEDDES, BARON (Geddes) (Baron UK 1942)

Strive to hold fast to the greater things

EUAN MICHAEL ROSS GEDDES, 3rd Baron; *b* 3 Sept 1937; *s* 1975; *ed* Rugby, Gonville and Caius Coll, Camb (MA), and Harvard Business Sch; Lt-Cdr RNR (ret): *m* 1966, Gillian, da of William Arthur Butler, of Henley-on-Thames, Oxon, and has issue.

Arms – Azure three geds naiant or, on a chief engrailed of the last as many boars' heads couped sable, armed argent, langued gules. **Crest** – A demi-pike hauriant environed of the circlet of a Lord Baron's coronet all proper. **Supporters** – On a compartment semée of seapinks, two geds proper. *Residence* – Manor House, Long Sutton, Basingstoke, Hants, RG25 1ST. *Clubs* – Brooks's, The Hong Kong.

SON LIVING

Hon JAMES GEORGE NEIL, *b* 10 Sept 1969.

DAUGHTER LIVING

Hon Margaret Clair, *b* 1967.

SISTER LIVING

Hon Margaret Ross, *b* 1934; *ed* Benenden; is a Member of Asso of Occupational Therapists: *m* 1961, Ralph Emilius Quintus van Koetsveld, and has issue living, Michael William, *b* 1963, — Antony Guy Hans, *b* 1964, — Christopher Dirk, *b* 1969. *Residence* – Northacre, Shackleford, Godalming, Surrey GU8 6AX.

UNCLE LIVING (*Son of 1st Baron*)

Hon David Campbell, TD, *b* 1917; *ed* Stowe, and Gonville and Caius Coll, Camb (MA); PhD (London); late Capt Roy Hong Kong Defence Force, and Maj RA: *m* 1948, Gerda da of late Gerdt Meyer Brunn, of Bergen, Norway, and has issue living, Jane *b* 1950; *ed* Camb Univ (BA), and London Univ (PhD): *m* 1979, Peter Watt, of Kirkland of Coull, Coull, Aboyne, Aberdeenshire AB3 4TS, and has issue living, Henry George *b* 1980, David Peter *b* 1983, — Harriet, *b* 1953; *ed* Camb Univ (BA): *m* 1st, 1976 (*m diss* 1977), Jonathan Allen; 2ndly, 1982, Hugh Devlin, of 20 Windmill Rd, Saintfield, co Down BT24 7DX, and has issue living (by 2nd *m*), Thomas Halcro *b* 1984, James Alexander *b* 1985, Patrick David *b* 1988. *Residence* – Clayfield, Etchingham, E Sussex. *Club* – Army and Navy.

AUNT LIVING (*Daughter of 1st Baron*)

Hon Margaret Campbell (*HRH the Princess of Hesse and the Rhine*), *b* 1913: *m* 1937, HRH Prince Ludwig Hermann Alexander Chlodwig of Hesse and the Rhine, who *d* 1968. *Residence* – Wolfsgarten, 63207 Langen, Hessen, Germany.

WIDOWS LIVING OF SONS OF FIRST BARON

HSH Altgräfin Marie-Anne Helena Emanuela (Berlin-Dahlem, Berlin 33, Max Eyth Str 26, Germany; 55 Chelsea Sq, SW3 6LH), da of HSH the 6th Prince (Franz Joseph) zu Salm-Reifferscheidt, Krautheim und Dyck: *m* 1964, as his 2nd wife, Col Hon Alexander Campbell Geddes, OBE, MC, TD, who *d* 1972; 2ndly, 1978, Prof Dr Otto Georg von Simson, of Berlin, who *d* 1993, and has issue (by 1st *m*) (see colls infra).
Diana Elizabeth (Carrickeens, Moyard, co Galway), da of Brig Charles Copley Swift, OBE, MC: *m* 1944, Hon John Reay Campbell Geddes, TD, who *d* 1978, and has issue (see colls infra).

WIDOW LIVING OF SECOND BARON

ENID MARY (*Enid, Baroness Geddes*) (Ludshott Manor, Bramshott, nr Liphook, Hants GU30 7RD), da of Clarence Howell Butler, of Tenterden, Kent, and formerly of Shanghai, China: *m* 1931, the 2nd Baron, who *d* 1975.

COLLATERAL BRANCHES LIVING

Issue of late Col Hon Alexander Campbell Geddes, OBE, MC, TD, 2nd son of 1st Baron, *b* 1910, *d* 1972: *m* 1st 1934 (*m diss* 1964), Margaret Kathleen, da of late Sir Charles (Stewart) Addis, KCMG; 2ndly, 1964, HSH Altgräfin Marie-Anne Helena Emanuela (who *m* 2ndly, 1978, Prof Dr Otto Georg von Simson, who *d* 1993) (ante), da of HSH the 6th Prince (Franz Joseph) zu Salm-Reifferscheidt, Krautheim und Dyck:—
(By 1st *m*) Andrew Campbell (*His Honour Judge Geddes*) (The Old Vicarage, Minster Lovell, Oxon), *b* 1943; Bar Inner Temple 1972, Circuit Judge, Midland and Oxford Circuit 1994: *m* 1st, 1974 (*m diss* 1983), Jacqueline, 2nd da of Emil Tan-Bunzel; 2ndly, 1985, Bridget Charlotte Helen, formerly wife of John Warren-Swettenham, and da of Lt-Col Christopher White Bowring, of Whelprigg, Casterton, Carnforth, Cumbria, and has issue living (by 1st wife), Nicholas Campbell, *b* 1975, — Dominic Oliver Campbell, *b* 1978, — (by 2nd wife), Leo Patrick, *b* 1981, — Katharine Arabella Campbell, *b* 1986. —— Alexander James Campbell (29 Hugo Rd, N19), *b* 1948: *m* 1971, Vivien, only da of F. H. Salter, of 55 Danycoed Rd, Cyncoed, Cardiff, and has issue living, Christopher Edward Frederick *b* 1983, Emily Claire Kateryna *b* 1984. —— Margaret Campbell, *b* 1937: *m* 1960, Peter Gross, and has four sons and two das, James Jonathan Geddes, *b* 1964, — Michael Carl, *b* 1968, — Daniel Paul Geddes, *b* 1970, — Adam John Geddes, *b* 1972, — Sarah Anne, *b* 1967, — Carla Elizabeth, *b* 1969. —— Christina Helen Campbell *b* 1939; MB, ChB, FFRadT: *m* 1965, Roy Kenneth Horrell, of 14 Linkoping Rd, Rondebosch 7700, Cape, S Africa, and has issue living, Jasper Mark Geddes, *b* 1968, — Hamish Harry Geddes, *b* 1970, — Eliza-Jane Geddes, *b* 1966, — Emma Clare Geddes, *b* 1972. —— Jean Campbell, *b* 1940: *m* 1963, Christopher Lubbock Verity, of Boundary House, Brimpton Common, Berks, and has issue living Richard Christopher Geddes, *b* 1965, — Jonathan William Geddes, *b* 1967. —— Caroline Anne Campbell, *b* 1947: *m* 1970, David Kelly, of 8 Crooms Hill, Greenwich, SE10, and has issue living, Nathaniel David, *b* 1982, — (by 2nd *m*), Leo Patrick, *b* 1981, — Katharine Arabella Campbell, *b* 1986. —— Alexandra Mary, *b* 1972, Tabitha May, *b* 1976, — Lucy Anna Margaret, *b* 1979, — Jemima Joanna, *b* 1985. —— Diana Elizabeth Campbell (twin), *b* 1947. —— (By 2nd *m*) Stephen George (55 Chelsea Sq, SW3 6LH), *b* 1969. —— Camilla Joanna Isabella (55 Chelsea Sq, SW3 6LH), *b* 1966.

Issue of late Maj Hon John Reay Campbell Geddes, TD, 3rd son of 1st Baron, *b* 1915, *d* 1978: *m* 1944, Diana Elizabeth (ante), da of Brig Charles Copley Swift, OBE, MC, RE:—
Hugh John Reay (20 Gatcombe Rd, N19), *b* 1945: *m* 1972, Harriet Diana Christabel, da of late Sqdn Ldr Hon John Francis

McLaren, RAF (*see* B Aberconway, colls), and has issue living, Luke John McLaren, *b* 1974, — Sam Duncan McLaren, *b* 1975.

PREDECESSORS – (1) *Rt Hon Sir* AUCKLAND CAMPBELL GEDDES, GCMG, KCB, TD, MD, second son of late Acland Campbell Geddes, of Edinburgh: *b* 1879; sometime Professor of Anatomy at Roy Coll of Surgs, Ireland, and at McGill Univ, Montreal: S African War 1901-2, European War 1914-18 on Staff at Gen Headquarters, France (Brevet Lieut-Col, Hon Brig Gen); was Director of Recruiting, War Office 1916-17 (with rank of Brig-Gen), Min of National Ser 1917-18, Pres of Local Govt Board 1918-19, Min of Reconstruction Jan to May 1919, Pres Board of Trade 1919-20 (with a seat in the Cabinet), Ambassador Extraor, and Plen to Washington 1920-24, and Commr for Civil Defence for S-E Region 1939-41, and for N-W Region 1941-2; sat as MP for N, of Basingstoke, Div of Hampshire (*U*) 1917-18, and for Basingstoke Div thereof 1918-20; *cr Baron Geddes*, of Rolvenden, co Kent, (peerage of UK) 1942: *m* 1906, Isabella Gamble, who *d* 1962, da of late William A. Ross, of Staten Island, New York; *d* 1954; *s* by his el son **(2)** ROSS CAMPBELL, KBE, 2nd Baron, *b* 1907; Pres of Chamber of Shipping of UK 1968: *m* 1931, Enid Mary, da of Clarence Howell Butler; *d* 1975; *s* by his yr son **(3)** EUAN MICHAEL ROSS, 3rd Baron and present peer.

GEDDES OF EPSOM, BARONY OF (Geddes) (Extinct 1983)

DAUGHTER LIVING OF LIFE BARON

Hon Pamela Margaret GEDDES TAYLOR (The Heathers, Bridge Close, Horam, E Sussex TN21 0HJ), *b* 1925: *m* 1957 (*m diss* 1966), Louis Patrick Taylor.

GEORGE-BROWN, BARONY OF (George-Brown) (Extinct 1985)

DAUGHTERS LIVING OF LIFE BARON

Hon Frieda Mary, *b* 1938: *m* 1964, Brian Warman.
Hon Patricia Janet, *b* 1942: *m* 1967, Derek Knowles.

George, see Earl Lloyd George of Dwyfor.

GERAINT, BARON (Howells) (Life Baron 1992)

GERAINT WYN HOWELLS, son of late David John Howells, of Brynglas, Ponterwyd, Cardiganshire; *b* 15 April 1925; *ed* Ardwyn Gram Sch, Aberystwyth; Farmer; CC Cardiganshire 1952-74; Chm Welsh Liberal Party 1972-74, Pres 1974-78; Vice-Chm British Wool Marketing Board 1971-83, Chm Wool Producers of Wales Ltd 1977-87; Liberal Spokesman on Wales 1985-87, Alliance Spokesman on Welsh Affairs 1987, Liberal Spokesman on Agric 1987-89, Liberal Democrat Spokesman on Agric 1989-92; Member Select Cttee House of Commons Sers; Sec Ponterwyd Eisteddfod; MP (*L* 1974-88, *Lib Dem* 1988-92) Cardigan 1974-83, and Ceredigion and Pembroke N 1983-92; *cr Baron Geraint*, of Ponterwyd, co Dyfed (Life Baron) 1992: *m* 1957, Mary Olwen Hughes, da of Margaret Ann Griffiths, of Tregaron, Dyfed, and has issue.
Residence – Glennydd, Ponterwyd, Ceredigion, Dyfed.

DAUGHTERS LIVING

Hon Gaenor Wyn, *b* 1960.
Hon Mari Wyn, *b* 1964.

GERARD, BARON (Gerard) (Baron UK 1876, Bt E 1611)

ANTHONY ROBERT HUGO GERARD, 5th Baron, and 17th Baronet; *b* 3 Dec 1949; *s* 1992; *ed* Harvard: *m* 1976, Kathleen, eldest da of Dr Bernard Ryan, of New York, and has issue.

Arms – Argent, a saltire gules. **Crest** – 1st, a monkey statant proper, environed round the loins and chained argent; 2nd, a lion rampant ermine, ducally crowned or and charged on the shoulder with a saltire couped gules. **Supporters** – On either side a lion ermine, ducally crowned or, with a collar gemell, and supporting a tilting spear proper.
Residence – 120 E 79th St, New York, NY 10021, USA.

In God is my hope

SONS LIVING

Hon RUPERT BERNARD CHARLES, *b* 17 Dec 1981.
Hon John Frederick William, *b* 1986.

BROTHER LIVING

Peter Charles Rupert, *b* 1951: *m* 1973, Sophie Christine, eldest da of Irénée Du Pont May, of Delaware, USA. *Residence* – 1824 Circle Rd, Baltimore, Maryland 21204, USA.

SISTER LIVING OF FOURTH BARON

Hon Heloise Katherine Marie, *b* 1911; is a nun.

MOTHER LIVING

Huguette Reiss-Brian, da of late Hugo Reiss, of Brazil, and of Mme Guy Brian, of 39 Ave Charles-Floquet, Paris: *m* 1948 (*m diss* 1969), Maj Rupert Charles Frederick Gerard, MBE, who *d* 1978.

COLLATERAL BRANCH LIVING

Grandchildren of late Lt-Col Charles Robert Tolver Michael Gerard, DSO, OBE, only son of Capt Hon Robert Joseph Gerard-Dicconson (who assumed the additional surname and arms of Dicconson by Roy Licence 1896), 2nd son of 1st Baron:—
Issue of late (Robert) Guy Standish Gerard, *b* 1921, *d* 1980: *m* 1st, 1948 (*m diss* 1964), Barbara, da of Leonard J. Stone, of Merivale, Constant Spring, Jamaica; 2ndly, 1964, Ursula, who *d* 1993, da of late Andrew Mackenzie, of Vancouver, and formerly wife of John Cogswell, of Panama:—
(By 1st *m*) Susan Roberta Caroline, *b* 1951: *m* 1st, 1971 (*m diss* 1984), Andrew Nigel Wendover Beeson; 2ndly, 1984, Lucien Lee Bowman, jr, of Ellman House, Glynde, nr Lewes, Sussex, and has issue living (by 1st *m*), James Gerard, *b* 1976, — Susanna Caroline, *b* 1973, — (by 2nd *m*) (Richard) Frederick Gerard *b* 1988, Lisa Ashley Annabel Helena *b* 1985. —— Diana Sarah, *b* 1952: *m* 1991, Michael Macfarlane Irwin, of 2620 Monte Vista Av, El Cerrito, Calif 94530, USA.

PREDECESSORS – (1) *Sir* THOMAS Gerard, Knt; *cr* a *Baronet* 1611; the £1,000 he paid for the dignity was returned to him in consideration of the sufferings of his father in the cause of Mary, Queen of Scots; *s* by his son (2) *Sir* THOMAS, 2nd Bt; *s* by his son (3) *Sir* WILLIAM, 3rd Bt, a zealous royalist who expended a large estate in the cause of Charles I; *s* by his son (4) *Sir* WILLIAM, 4th Bt; *s* by hs el son (5) *Sir* WILLIAM, 5th Bt; *d* 1721; *s* by his el son (6) *Sir* WILLIAM, 6th Bt; *d* 1732; *s* by his brother (7) *Sir* WILLIAM, 7th Bt; *d* a minor 1740; *s* by his brother (8) *Sir* THOMAS, 8th Bt; *d* 1780; *s* by his brother (9) *Sir* ROBERT, 9th Bt; *d* 1784; *s* by his el son (10) *Sir* ROBERT, 10th Bt; *d* a minor 1791; *s* by his brother (11) *Sir* WILLIAM, 11th Bt; *d* 1826; *s* by his nephew (12) JOHN, 12th Bt, el son of John, 3rd son of 9th Bt, by Elizabeth, da of Edward Ferrers, of Baddesley Clinton, co Warwick; *dsp* 1854; *s* by his brother (13) ROBERT TOLVER, 13th; *cr Baron Gerard* (peerage of United Kingdom) 1876: *m* 1849, Harriet, who *d* 1888, da of late Edward Clifton, of Lytham Hall, Lancashire; *d* 1887; *s* by his son (14) WILLIAM CANSFIELD, DSO, 2nd Baron; *b* 1851: *m* 1877, Mary Emmeline Laura, who *d* 1918, da of late Henry Beilby Milner, of West Retford; *d* 1902; *s* by his son (15) FREDERIC JOHN, MC, 3rd Baron; *b* 1883; European War 1914-17 as Capt Roy Horse Guards (twice wounded, MC): *m* 1906, his cousin, Mary Frances Emma, who *d* 1954, da of late Sir Martin Le Marchant Hadsley Gosselin, GCVO, KCMG, CB; *d* 1953; *s* by his only son (16) ROBERT WILLIAM FREDERICK ALWYN, 4th Baron; *b* 1918; *dunm* 1992; *s* by his kinsman (17) ANTHONY ROBERT HUGO (elder son of late Maj Rupert Charles Frederick Gerard, MBE, grandson of late Capt Hon Robert Joseph Gerard-Dicconson, 2nd son of 1st Baron), 5th Baron and present peer.

GIBSON, BARON (Gibson) (Life Baron 1975)

(RICHARD) PATRICK TALLENTYRE GIBSON, son of Thornely Carbutt Gibson; *b* 5 Feb 1916; *ed* Eton, and Magdalen Coll, Oxford (MA, Hon Fellow 1977); 1939-45 War as Maj, with Middx Yeo; N Africa 1940-41, POW 1941-43, Special Ops Exec 1943-45, Political Intelligence FO 1945-46; Chm, S Pearson & Son Ltd 1978-83, and of Pearson Longman Ltd 1967-78; Chm of Advisory Council of Victoria and Albert Museum 1970-74, of Arts Council of Gt Britain 1972-77, and of Financial Times Ltd 1975-78; Vice-Chm Westminster Press 1953-78; Chm National Trust 1977-87, Pres S of England Agric Soc for 1987; Member board Roy Opera House 1977-87, and Trustee of Glyndebourne Festival Opera 1965-72 and 1977-86; *cr Baron Gibson*, of Penn's Rocks, co E Sussex (Life Baron) 1975: *m* 1945, (Elizabeth) Dione, da of late Hon (Bernard) Clive Pearson (*see* V Cowdray, colls), and has issue.

Arms – Per pale azure and argent, three acorns slipped and leaved in fesse between as many storks rising all countercharged. **Crest** – a stork rising argent between two acorns slipped and leaved and holding in the beak an acorn slipped all proper. **Supporters** – two nightingales, each holding in the beak a scroll of music proper.
Residences – Penn's Rocks, Groombridge, Sussex; 4 Swan Walk, SW3 4JJ. *Clubs* – Garrick, Brooks's.

SONS LIVING

Hon Hugh Marcus Thornely (The Fold, Parwich, Ashbourne, Derbys DE6 1QL; Reform Club), *b* 1946; *ed* Eton, and Magdalen Coll, Oxford (BA); DL Derbys 19—: *m* 1967, Hon Frances Towneley Strachey, da of late Hon (Thomas) Anthony Edward Towneley Strachey (*see* B O'Hagan), and has issue living, Jasper Tallentyre, *b* 1975, — Effie Dione, *b* 1970, — Amelia Mary, *b* 1973.
Hon Clive Patrick (27 St James's Place, SW1A 1NR; Brooks's Club), *b* 1948; *ed* Eton, and Magdalen Coll Oxford (BA): *m* 1974, Anne Marie Jeanne, da of late Comte Jacques de Chauvigny de Blot, and has issue living, Patrick Clive, *b* 1975, — Beatrice Dione Elizabeth, *b* 1978.
Hon William Knatchbull (46 Victoria Rd, W8 5RO; Garrick Club), *b* 1951; *ed* Eton, and Magdalen Oxford (BA): *m* 1988, Lori Frances, only da of Herbert Mintz, of Miami, Fla, USA, and has issue living, Matthew Charles, *b* 1990, — Sarah Claire, *b* 1992.
Hon Piers Nathaniel (25 Sumner Place, SW7 3NT), *b* 1956; *ed* Eton, and Magdalen Coll, Oxford (BA): *m* 1981, Melanie Jane Stella, el da of Jack Walters, OBE, of 53 Le Donatello, 13 Avenue des Papalins, Fontvielle 9800, Monaco, and has issue living, Harry Maximilian, *b* 1988, — Theodore Charles, *b* 1991, — Lucy Lavinia, *b* 1986.

GIBSON-WATT, BARON (Gibson-Watt) (Life Baron 1979)

JAMES DAVID GIBSON-WATT, MC, PC, el son of late Maj James Miller Gibson-Watt, JP, DL, of Doldowlod, Llandrindod Wells; *b* 1918; *ed* Eton, and Trin Coll, Camb (BA); 1939-45 War, as Maj Welsh Gds in N Africa, and Italy (MC and bar (twice)); a JP and a DL for Radnorshire; PPS to Parl Under-Sec of State, War Office 1957, and to Chancellor of the Exchequer 1962-64, Assist Govt Whip 1957-59, a Lord Commr of the Treasury 1959-61, Chm of Livestock Export Council 1962-74, and Min of State Welsh Office 1970-74; a Forestry Commr 1976-85, and Chm Timber Growers UK since 1987; Chm of Council on Tribunals 1980-86; FRAgS; MP for Hereford (*C*) 1956-74; *cr* PC 1974, and *Baron Gibson-Watt*, of The Wye, in the District of Radnor (Life Baron) 1979: *m* 1942, Diana, da of late Sir Charles Hambro, KBE, MC, and has issue.
Residence – Doldowlod, Llandrindod Wells, Powys. *Clubs* – Boodle's and Pratt's.

SONS LIVING

Hon David Julian, *b* 1946; *ed* Eton, and Trin Coll, Camb *m* 1st 1970 (*m diss* 1978), Patricia Hope, el da of Sir Lenox Hewitt, OBE, of Red Hill, Canberra, Australia; 2ndly, 1983, Marie-Thérèse, widow of Anton Wallich-Clifford, and da of Michael McQuade, of Newarthill, Lanarkshire.
Hon Robin (Gelli-Garn, Llanyre, Landrindod Wells, Powys), *b* 1949; *ed* Eton; High Sheriff co Powys (1981): *m* 1971, Marcia Susan, el da of Sir Roger Hugh Cary, 2nd Bt, and has issue living, Anthony David, *b* 1975, — Edward Ricardo, *b* 1978, — Guy Charles, *b* 1982, — Phoebe Charlotte, *b* 1980.

DAUGHTERS LIVING

Hon Claerwen, *b* 1952: *m* 1st, 1970 (*m diss* 1979), Enrique Rene Ulvert, son of Marcel J. Ulvert-Portocarrero, sometime Nicaraguan Ambassador in London; 2ndly, 1980, (John) James Randal Green (*see* B Bicester) and has issue living (by 1st *m*), Marcel David Joaquin, *b* 1971, — Charles Nicholas, *b* 1972, — (by 2nd *m*) (*see* B Bicester). *Residence* – Foxboro' Hall, Melton, nr Woodbridge, Suffolk IP12 1ND.
Hon Sian Diana (*Baroness Biddulph*), *b* 1962: *m* 1993, 5th Baron Biddulph, of Makerstoun, Kelso, Roxburghshire.

GIFFORD, BARON (Gifford) (Baron UK 1824)
(Name and Title pronounced "Jifford")

ANTHONY MAURICE GIFFORD, 6th Baron; *b* 1 May 1940; *s* 1961; *ed* Winchester, and King's Coll, Camb; Bar Middle Temple 1962, QC 1982; Senior Partner Gifford, Haughton & Thompson, Attorneys-at-Law since 1991: *m* 1st, 1965 (*m diss* 1988), Katherine Anne, da of Dr Max Mundy, of 75 Bedford Gdns, W8; 2ndly, 1988, Elean Roslyn, da of Bishop David Thomas, of Kingston, Jamaica, and has issue by 1st and 2nd *m*.

Arms – Azure, a chevron between three stirrups, with leathers or, within a bordure engrailed argent, pelletée. **Crest** – A panther's head couped at the neck and affrontée, between two branches of oak proper. **Supporters** – *Dexter*, a bay horse proper charged on the shoulder with a portcullis or; *sinister*, a greyhound, argent, charged on the body with three ermine spots.
Residences – 67 Lancaster Rd, N4; 71 Duke St, Kingston, Jamaica.

NON·SINE·NUMINE

Not without God's assistance

SON LIVING (By 1st marriage)

Hon THOMAS ADAM, *b* 1 Dec 1967.

DAUGHTERS LIVING (By 1st marriage)

Hon Polly Anna, *b* 1969.

(By 2nd marriage)

Hon Sheba Chanel, *b* 1992.

DAUGHTER LIVING OF FOURTH BARON

Hon Serena Mary, *b* 1919: *m* 1st, 1940 (*m diss* 1945), Patrick de Gruchy Vignoles Crawshay Warren; 2ndly, 1951, Arthur Reginald Danks, MBE, TD, and has issue living, (by 1st *m*) Edgar Jeremy, *b* 1941, — (by 2nd *m*) John Francis Reginald, *b* 1954, — Fenella Christian Mary (*Hon Mrs John Best*), *b* 1952: *m* 1981, Hon John Philip Robert Best, only son of 8th Baron Wynford, MBE. *Residence* – Loscombe, Sydling St Nicholas, Dorchester, Dorset DT2 9PD.

PREDECESSORS – (1) *Rt Hon Sir* ROBERT Gifford, PC; appointed Solicitor-Gen 1817, Attorney-Gen 1819, and Lord Ch Justice of Common Pleas Jan 1824; *cr Baron Gifford*, of St Leonard's Devon (peerage of United Kingdom) 1824, and was afterward Master of the Rolls and Dep Speaker of the House of Lords; *d* 1826; *s* by his son (2) ROBERT FRANCIS, 2nd Baron, *b* 1817: *m* 1845, Frederica Charlotte, who *d* 1920, el da of 1st Baron Fitz-Hardinge; *d* 1872; *s* by his son (3) EDRIC FREDERICK, VC, 3rd Baron, *b* 1849; served with Ashanti Expedition, 1873-4 (medal with clasp, VC), and in Zulu War 1879 (medal with clasp): on Staff of Sir Garnet Wolseley, Gov of Natal 1874 and 1879-80; Colonial Sec for W Australia, and MLC 1880-3, and Colonial Sec at Gibraltar 1883-8: *m* 1880, Sophie Catherine, who *d* 1947, da of late Gen John Alfred Street, CB: *d* 1911; *s* by his brother (4) EDGAR BERKELEY, 4th Baron, *b* 1857: *m* 1st, 1879, Mary, who *d* 1913, da of John Osborne, QC, and widow of Thomas Booth, of West Ashby Manor, Horncastle; 2ndly, 1918, Anne Maud, who *d* 1956, da of late Col Aitchison, Scots Fusilier Guards, of Drummore, Musselburgh; *d* 1937; *s* by his nephew (5) CHARLES MAURICE ELTON (son of late Hon Maurice Raymond Gifford, CMG, 4th son of 2nd Baron), 5th Baron; *b* 1899; Chm of Challis & Benson, Ltd; late Com RN and Flight Lieut RAF; ADC to Gov of NS Wales 1930-35: *m* 1939, (Ellice) Margaret, who *d* 1990, da of late Arthur Wigram Allen, of Merioola, Woollahra, Sydney, NS Wales; *d* 1961; *s* by his only son (6) ANTHONY MAURICE, 6th Baron and present peer.

Gillford, Lord; son of Earl of Clanwilliam.

GILMOUR OF CRAIGMILLAR, BARON (Gilmour) (Life Baron 1992, Bt UK 1926)

Not the pen, but custom

IAN HEDWORTH JOHN LITTLE GILMOUR, PC, *Life Baron*, and 3rd *Baronet*; *b* 8 July 1926; *s* to Baronetcy 1977; *ed* Eton, and Balliol Coll, Oxford; Bar Inner Temple 1952; late Lieut Gren Gds; Editor *The Spectator* 1954-59; an Under-Sec Min of Defence 1970-71, Min of State for Defence Procurement Min of Defence 1971-72, Min of State for Defence 1972-74, and Sec of State for Defence 1974; Chm Conservative Research Dept 1974-75; Lord Privy Seal 1979-81; author of *The Body Politic, Inside Right: A Study of Conservatism, Britain Can Work, Riot, Risings and Revolution*, and *Dancing with Dogma*; MP Central Norfolk (*C*) 1962-74, and Chesham and Amersham 1974-92; *cr* PC 1973, and *Baron Gilmour of Craigmillar*, of Craigmillar in the District of the City of Edinburgh (Life Baron) 1992: *m* 1951, Lady Caroline Margaret Montagu Douglas Scott, da of 8th Duke of Buccleuch and Queensberry, and has issue.

Arms – Quarterly, 1st and 4th, azure, three writing pens argent, *Gilmour*, 2nd and 3rd, sable, on a saltire argent a crescent gules, *Little*. **Crest** – A dexter hand holding a scroll of paper within a garland of laurel proper. *Residence* – The Ferry House, Old Isleworth, Middx TW7 6BD. *Clubs* – White's, Pratt's.

SONS LIVING (*in remainder to baronetcy only*)

Hon DAVID ROBERT, *b* 14 Nov 1952; *ed* Eton, and Balliol Coll, Oxford; author of *Lebanon: The Fractured Country; The Transformation of Spain from Franco to the Constitutional Monarchy, The Hungry Generations, Cities of Spain* and *The Last Leopard: A Life of Giuseppe di Lampedusa*, etc: *m* 1975, Sarah Anne, da of Michael Hilary George Bradstock (*see* V Hawarden, colls), and has issue living, Alexander Ian Michael, *b* 19 Feb 1980, — Rachel Anne Caroline, *b* 1977, — Katharine Victoria Mary, *b* 1984, — Laura Elizabeth Rose, *b* 1985. *Residence* – 21 Moray Place, Edinburgh.
Hon Oliver John, *b* 1953; *ed* Eton, Hertford Coll, Oxford, and Akademie Für Musik, Vienna: *m* 1981 (*m diss* 1985), Hon Kathrine (Katya) Grenfell, 2nd da of 2nd Baron St Just, and has issue living, Natalia Clare, *b* 1981. *Residence* –
Hon Christopher Simon, *b* 1956; *ed* Eton, and Univ of E Anglia: *m* 1992, Mardi C., only da of J. L. Haynes, of Louisa Beach, Queensland, Australia, and has issue living, Leonora Rose Bonnie, *b* 1993. *Residence* – 194 Queen's Gate, SW7.
Hon Andrew James, *b* 1964; *ed* Eton, and Balliol Coll, Oxford: *m* 1991, Emma B., only da of Christopher Williams, of Alrewas Hayes, Staffs, and has issue living, Archie John Ludo, *b* 1993. *Residence* – 55 Pembridge Villas, W11.

DAUGHTER LIVING

Hon Jane Victoria, *b* 1959; *ed* St Paul's, and St Hugh's Coll, Oxford: *m* 1986, Hon Peter John Pleydell-Bouverie, yr son of 8th Earl of Radnor, and has issue. *Residences* – 38 Queensdale Rd, W11 4SA; New Court Farmhouse, Downton, nr Salisbury, Wilts.

HALF-BROTHER LIVING

Alexander Clement, CVO, *b* 1931; *ed* Eton; CVO 1990: *m* 1st, 1954 (*m diss* 1983), Barbara Marie-Louise, el da of late Hon Denis Gomer Berry, TD (*see* V Kemsley); 2ndly, 1983, Susan Janet, el da of late Capt Voltelin James Howard Van der Byl, DSC, RN (ret), and formerly wife of (i) Alwyn Richard Dudley Smith, and (ii) 2nd Baron Chetwode, and has issue living (by 1st *m*), Rory Calvyn, *b* 1958, — Christian Alexander, *b* 1970: *m* 1992, Alexandra Ruth, yst da of Rev C. R. Wolsey, of Frimley, Surrey, — Lucinda Roberte, *b* 1956: *m* 1st, 1981 (*m diss* 1989), Robert Crofts Williams Llewellyn; 2ndly, 1989, Adrian G. Burns, and has issue (by 1st *m*) (*see* Llewellyn, Bt, *cr* 1922), (by 2nd *m*) Jamie *b* 1991. *Residence* – 1 Christopher Mews, Penzance St, W11 4QZ. *Club* – White's.

PREDECESSORS – The 1st baronet, Sir Robert Gordon Gilmour, CB, CVO, DSO (son of Henry Wolrige-Gordon, of Esslemont and Hallhead, Aberdeenshire), assumed the surname of Gilmour on succession to the estates of his great uncle, Walter James Little Gilmour. He was a Brig-Gen Capt of King's Body Guard for Scotland (Royal Company of Archers), and Gentleman Usher of the Green Rod (Order of the Thistle). He *d* 1939, and was *s* by his son, Sir John Little Gilmour, 2nd Bt, *b* 1899; a Stockbroker: *m* 1st, 1922 (*m diss* 1929), Hon Victoria Laura Cadogan, OBE, TD, who *d* 1991, da of late Henry Arthur, Viscount Chelsea; 2ndly, 1930, Lady Mary Cecilia Rhodesia Hamilton, who *d* 1984, da of 3rd Duke of Abercorn; *d* 1977; *s* by his elder son, Sir Ian Hedworth John Little Gilmour, PC (*Baron Gilmour of Craigmillar*), 3rd and present baronet.

GISBOROUGH, BARON (Chaloner) (Baron UK 1917)

THOMAS RICHARD JOHN LONG CHALONER, 3rd Baron; *b* 1 July 1927; *s* 1951; *ed* Eton; late Lt 16th/15th Lancers and Capt Northumberland Hussars; Lt-Col Green Howards Territorials 1967-69; Hon Col Cleveland Cadet Force 1982-92; Co Councillor for N Riding of Yorks 1964-74, and of Cleveland 1974-77, Lord-Lieut since 1981; JP; KStJ: *m* 1960, Shane, el da of late Sidney A. Newton (*see* Newton, Bt, colls, *cr* 1924), and has issue.

Arms – Sable, a chevron between three cherubims or. **Crest** – A demi sea-wolf or. **Supporters** – On either side a kneeling angel, wings elevated, inverted and endorsed, each ensigned on the head with a cross, all or.
Residences – Gisborough House, Guisborough, Cleveland TS14 6PT; 37 Bury Walk, SW3. *Club* – White's.

Frugality is the left hand of fortune,

and diligence the right

SONS LIVING

Hon (THOMAS) PEREGRINE LONG, *b* 17 Jan 1961: *m* 1992, Karen E., only da of Alan Thomas, and of Mrs Wendy Ogiela, of Cape Town, S Africa. *Address* – Falcons Nest, PO 1274, Stellenbosch 7599, S Africa.
Hon (Robert) Toby Long, *b* 1966.

SISTER LIVING

Hon (Angela) Mary (Geranium Cottage, Ditchling, Sussex), *b* 1925: *m* 1946 (*m diss* 1973), Roderick Edward Faure Walker, late Maj Coldstream Guards, and has had issue, Rupert Roderick (Woodhill, Danbury, Essex CM3 4AN), *b* 1947; *ed* Eton and Bristol Univ (BSc): *m* 1975, Sally Anne Vivienne, MB, B Chir, da of Lt-Cmdr Francis John Sidebotham, RN, of List House, Long Melford, Suffolk, and has issue living, Nicholas Alexander *b* 1978, Julia Frances *b* 1980, Joanna Phoebe *b* 1984, — James Edward Bruce (88 Greenwood Rd, Hackney, E8 1NE) *b* 1948; *ed* Eton: *m* 1st 1973 (*m diss* 1979), Caryn Lois, da of Dr Robert Becker, of 1701, York Av, New York, USA; 2ndly, 1981, Vivien Margaret, da of Donald Frank Knight, of 122 Southam Rd, Hall Green, Birmingham, — Camilla Mary, *b* 1953: *m* 1973, Timothy J. P. Coghlan, of Weedon Lodge Cottage, Everdon, nr Daventry, Northants NN11 6B2, son of late A. F. Coghlan, of Ludwell Grange, Horsted Keynes, Sussex, and *d* 1981, leaving issue, Christopher Austin *b* 1980, Alice Mary *b* 1979.

AUNT LIVING (*Daughter of 1st Baron*)

Hon Honora Elizabeth Dundas; JP Shropshire; has Kaisar-i-Hind Silver medal: *m* 1929, Col Frank Drummond Shuttleworth Field, OBE, MC, Indian Army, who *d* 1958. *Residence* – Meadow Vale, Monkhopton, Bridgnorth, Shropshire TF13 6ZH.

COLLATERAL BRANCH LIVING

Issue of late Capt Richard Godolphin Hume Chaloner, Wilshire Regt, el son of 1st Baron, *b* 1883, *k* abroad during European War 1917: *m* 1914, Evelyn Maud, JP, who *d* 1973 (she *m* 2ndly, 1918, Lieut-Col John Clement Wolstan Francis, 15/19th Hussars (ret), yr da of A. Benyon, of Ashe, Windsor:—
Diana Margaret Bruce (Biggin Abbey House, Fenditton, Cambs): *m* 1948, Ian Melville Wright, who *d* 1971.

PREDECESSORS – (1) RICHARD GODOLPHIN WALMESLEY Chaloner, second son of late Richard Penruddocke Long, MP, of Rood Ashton, Wilts: *b* 1856; assumed by Roy licence 1888 the surname of Chaloner in lieu of his patronymic (under the will of his material grand-uncle, Adm Thomas Chaloner, CB, who inherited the Gisborough Estates through his mother, who was a descendant, through her grandmother, Margaret Bruce of Kennet, of Robert de Brus, Lord of Skelton, who founded Gisborough Priory 1119); Afghan War 1879-80, S Africa 1900; MP for W or Westbury Div of Wilts (C) 1895-1900, and for Abercromby Div of Liverpool 1910-17; *cr Baron Gisborough*, of Cleveland, Yorkshire (peerage of UK) 1917: *m* 1882, Margaret Brocklesby, who *d* 1941, el da of late Rev Weston Brocklesby Davis, V of Ramsbury, Wilts; *d* 1938; *s* by his second but only surving son (2) THOMAS WESTON PEEL LONG, TD, 2nd Baron, *b* 1889; Maj (ret) Green Howards (TA) and Fl-Lt (Hon Capt) RAF; 1914-18 War in RFC and RAF; 1939-45 War as Fl-Lt RAFVR: *m* 1923, Esther Isabella Madeleine, who *d* 1970, da of late Charles Oswin Hall, of Eddlethorpe Hall, Malton, Yorks; *d* 1951; *s* by his son (3) THOMAS RICHARD JOHN LONG, 3rd Baron, and present peer.

GLADWYN, BARON (Jebb) (Baron UK 1960)

By hope and work

(HUBERT MILES) GLADWYN JEBB, GCMG, GCVO, CB, 1st Baron, son of late Sydney Jebb, of Firbeck Hall, Rotherham, Yorkshire; *b* 25 April 1900; *ed* Eton and Magdalen Coll, Oxford (Hon Fellow 1954); Hon DCL Oxford; Hon Dr Essex and Syracuse; entered Diplo Ser 1924; served at Teheran 1924-7, in Foreign Office 1927-31, at Rome 1931-5, and again in Foreign Office 1935-40 (Private Sec to Parliamentary Under Sec of State 1929-31 and to Permanent Under-Sec of State 1937-40); appointed Foreign Policy Adviser to Min of Economic Warfare with temporary rank of Assist Under-Sec of State 1940, Head of Economic and Reconstruction Depart, Foreign Office 1942, Executive Sec of Preparatory Commn of UN 1945, acting Sec-Gen of UN 1946, Dep to Sec of State on Council of Foreign Mins March 1946, Assist Under-Sec of State and UN Adviser May 1946, UK Representative on Permanent Commn of Brussels Treaty with rank of Ambassador March 1948, Dep Under-Sec of State Dec 1948, Permanent Representative of UK to UN 1950-54, and Ambassador to France 1954-60; ret 1960; Liberal Spokesman in House of Lords on Foreign Affairs and Defence 1965-87; a Member of European Parl 1973-75; Pres of Campaign for Europe, Vice-Pres of European Movement, of Atlantic Treaty Assocn, of Atlantic Inst, and of UN Assocn; Dep Liberal Leader in House of Lords 1967-87; author of *The European Idea*, *Half-Way to 1984*, *De Gaulle's Europe or Why the General Says No*, *Europe after De Gaulle*, and *The Memoirs of Lord Gladwyn*; Grand Cross of Legion of Honour; CMG 1942, CB (Civil) 1947, KCMG 1949, GCMG 1954, GCVO 1957, and *Baron Gladwyn*, of Bramfield, co Suffolk (peerage of UK) 1960: *m* 1929, Cynthia, who *d* 1990, da of Sir Saxton William Armstrong Noble, 3rd Bt (*cr* 1902), and has issue.

Arms – Quarterly vert and or, in the first quarter a falcon argent with bells of the second, and in the last quarter a lure of the third. **Crest** – A lure fessewise argent, and thereon a falcon rising proper with bells or. **Supporters** – *Dexter*, a brown bear proper; *sinister*, a unicorn argent, charged on the shoulder with a patriarchal cross bottony gules.
Residences – Bramfield Hall, Halesworth, Suffolk; 62 Whitehall Court, SW1. *Club* – Garrick.

SON LIVING

Hon MILES ALVERY GLADWYN, *b* 3 March 1930; *ed* Eton, and Magdalen Coll, Oxford (MA); Senior Management with British Airways until 1983; author of *The Thames Valley Heritage Walk* 1980, *A Guide to the South Downs Way* 1984, *Walkers* 1986, *A Guide to the Thames Path* 1988, *East Anglia* 1990, *A Guide to the Colleges of Oxford* 1992, and *Suffolk* 1995. *Residence* – E1, Albany, Piccadilly, W1. *Clubs* – Brooks's; Beefsteak.

DAUGHTERS LIVING

Hon Vanessa Mary (*Baroness Thomas of Swynnerton*), *b* 1931; *ed* St Hugh's Coll, Oxford (MA): *m* 1962, Baron Thomas of Swynnerton (Life Baron), of 29 Ladbroke Grove, W11, and has issue.
Hon Stella Candida, *b* 1933: *m* 1959, Baron Joël de Rosnay, Dir Cité des Sciences, Paris, and scientific writer and lecturer, and has issue living, Alexis Marc Louis Joël, *b* 1967, — (Vanessa) Tatiana Louise, *b* 1961, — Cecilia Fiona Louise, *b* 1963. *Residence* – 146 rue de l'Université, Paris VII, France.

Glamis, Lord; son of Earl of Strathmore and Kinghorne.

Glamorgan, Earl of; grandson of Duke of Beaufort.

Glandine, Viscount; son of Earl of Norbury.

GLANUSK, BARON (Bailey) (Baron UK 1899, Bt UK 1852)

Liberty

DAVID RUSSELL BAILEY, 4th Baron, and 5th Baronet: *b* 19 Nov 1917; *s* 1948; *ed* Eton; Lt Cdr (ret) RN; Managing Dir of Wandel & Goltermann (UK) Ltd, 1966-82; Chm W & G Instruments Ltd 1982-87: *m* 1941, Lorna Dorothy, only da of late Capt E. C. H. N. Andrews, MBE, RA, and has issue.

Arms – Argent, between two bars, three annulets in fesse gules between as many martlets of the last. **Crest** – A griffin sejant argent, semée of annulets gules. **Supporters** – *Dexter*, a collier proper; *sinister*, a smith proper. *Residence* – Apartado 62, 07460 Pollensa, Mallorca, Spain. *Club* – Army and Navy.

SON LIVING

Hon CHRISTOPHER RUSSELL, TD (51 Chertsey Rd, Chobham, Surrey), *b* 18 March 1942; *ed* Eton, and Clare Coll, Camb (BA): *m* 1974, Frances Elizabeth, MA, da of Air Ch Marshal Sir Douglas Charles Lowe, GCB, DFC, AFC, and has issue living, Charles Henry, *b* 12 Aug 1976; *ed* Eton, — Rosemary Elizabeth, *b* 1979.

DAUGHTER LIVING

Hon Susan Mary, *b* 1944: *m* 1970, Peter Mansel Lloyd James, MB BS, FRCS, of 104 Pottergate, Norwich, Norfolk, and has issue living, David Lloyd, *b* 1971, — Richard Lloyd, *b* 1976, — Caspar Lloyd, *b* 1980, — Victoria Mary, *b* 1974.

SISTERS LIVING (*Raised to the rank of a Baron's daughters* 1948)

Hon Shirley Joan (27 Headbourne Worthy House, Winchester, Hants SO23 7JG), *b* 1912: *m* 1946, George Dupin Drayson, who *d* 1969, and has issue living, Charles Dupin, *b* 1947: *m* 1974, Rosemary Ann, da of late Capt D. P. Evans, RN, and has issue living, Timothy William Dupin *b* 1983, Louise Claire *b* 1978, Caroline Gail *b* 1980.
Hon Elspeth Lorraine (*Hon Lady Musson*), *b* 1915: *m* 1939, Gen Sir Geoffrey Randolph Dixon Musson, GCB, CBE, DSO, late KSLI (ret), and has had issue, Peter Geoffrey Dixon, *b* 1946; *ed* Wellington Coll, — Penelope Anne *b* 1941: *m* 1962, Capt William Richard Dudgeon, late The Black Watch, of Old Thatch, Bamber's Green, Takeley, Bishop's Stortford, Herts, and *d* 1981, leaving issue, Angus Geoffrey Peter (The Old Carpenters Arms, Littlebury, nr Saffron Walden, Essex), *b* 1963: *m* 1988, Juliet Ann, da of George Anthony Turnbull (and has issue living, Charles William George *b* 1992, Kitty Penelope Ann *b* 1991), Deborah Elspeth *b* 1968. *Residence* – Barn Cottage, Hurstbourne Tarrant, Andover, Hants.

DAUGHTER LIVING OF THIRD BARON

Hon Elizabeth Shân Josephine, LVO, *b* 1943; Lady-in-Waiting to HRH The Princess Royal since 1978; High Sheriff Powys 1992; LVO 1988: *m* 1964, Capt William Nigel Henry Legge-Bourke, of Penmyarth, Glanusk Park, Crickhowell, Powys NP8 1LP, and has issue (*see* E Dartmouth, colls).

WIDOW LIVING OF THIRD BARON

MARGARET ELDRYDD (*Dowager Viscountess De L'Isle*), da of late Maj-Gen Thomas Herbert Shoubridge, CB, CMG, DSO; High Sheriff Powys 1977: *m* 1st, 1942, as his 2nd wife, the 3rd Baron, who *d* 1948; 2ndly, 1966, as his 2nd wife, 1st Viscount De L'Isle, VC, KG, GCMG, GCVO, PC, who *d* 1991. *Residence* – Glanusk Park, Crickhowell, Powys.

COLLATERAL BRANCHES LIVING

Issue of late Capt Hon Arthur Bailey, 3rd son of 1st Baron, *b* 1868, *d* 1929: *m* 1924, Ethel Sophia, who *d* 1959, da of late James Ledger Hill, JP, of Bulford Manor, Wilts, and Combe Grove, Bath:—
Carola Mary, *b* 1925: *m* 1949, Capt Hugh Denman Way, MC, RHA, who *d* 1971, and has issue living, Nigel Arthur Denman, *b* 1958, — Anthony Hugh Verelst, *b* 1961: *m* 1988, Andrea Elizabeth Dawson-Shephard. *Residence* – Fittleton House, Netheravon, Wilts.

Grandchildren of Capt Hon John Lancelot Bailey (*infra*):—
Issue of late Joseph Ferdinand Carey Bailey, *b* 1907, *d* 1984: *m* 1st, 1935 (*m diss* 1946), Alice Cecilia Anne, da of Oswald Magniac, DL, of Nursling, Hants; 2ndly, 1948, Evelyn Marie, da of Robert P. B. Blauveldt, LLB, of Yarmouth, Nova Scotia:—
(By 1st *m*) Lancelot Oswald, *b* 1936: *m* 1959, Armelle Françoise, da of Jean François Le Roux, of Candé, Maine-et-Loire, France, and has issue living, Antoine Lancelot Gwenaél, *b* 1965. —— Vernon Joseph Russell (43 Prospect St, Montreal, Quebec, Canada H3Z 1W5), *b* 1937: *m* 1968, Melanie Frances Moore, and has issue living, Julian Joseph Russell, *b* 1977, — Sebastian Philip de Magniac, *b* 1979, — Rachel Marjorie, *b* 1969, — Priscilla Anne, *b* 1971. —— Cynthia Mary, *b* 1940: *m* 1963, Patrick Joseph Moran, and has issue living, Malachi Joseph, *b* 1965, — Roisin, *b* 1968, — Garett, *b* 1969, — Fiona Mary, *b* 1964. —— (By 2nd *m*) Herbert Van Courtlandt, *b* 1952: *m* 1989, Kirsteen Susan, da of Alexander Keith Boyle (*see* Kennaway, Bt), and has issue living, Luke Alexander, *b* 1991, — Charlotte Evelyn, *b* 1990. —— Josephine Blauveldt, *b* 1949: *m* 1977, Teddy Dyer, and has issue living, Christopher Teddy, *b* 1979, — Patrick Nicholas Blauveldt, *b* 1982. —— Deborah Evelyn, *b* 1950: *m* 1980, Michael Collison, and has issue living, Andrew, *b* 1981, — Matthew, *b* 1983, — Daniel, *b* 1987, — Jessica, *b* 1992.

Issue of late Capt Hon John Lancelot Bailey, 5th son of 1st Baron, *b* 1878, *d* 1918: *m* 1903, Vivien Dora, who *d* 1938, da of late Ferdinand G. Carey, of Guernsey, and Frogmore, Ceylon:—
Marjorie Vivienne, *b* 1910: *m* 1930, Oliver Fowell Lancaster (*see* Buxton, Bt, colls, 1940 Edn). *Residence* – Daniel Zorrilla 5276, Colon, Montevideo, Uruguay.

Granddaughter of late Richard Crawshay Bailey, son of late Joseph Bailey, el son of 1st baronet:—
Issue of late Rev Canon Charles Henry Bailey, MC, *b* 1882, *d* 1971: *m* 1915, Ethel, who *d* 1962, da of late George Millward:—
Mabel Anna, *b* 1920: *m* 1947, Maj Ronald Patrick Ward, MC, The Border Regt, of Ivall's Farm Cottage, Bentworth, Alton, Hants, and has issue living, Charles Patrick, *b* 1949: *m* 1983, Linda Brown, and has issue living, Rebecca Anne *b* 1983, Henrietta Elizabeth *b* 1985, Charlotte Deborah *b* 1986, — Susan, *b* 1948: *m* 1970, John Grosvenor Phillips, and has issue living, Charles Edward *b* 1973, George William *b* 1976, — Deborah Rose, *b* 1957.

Granddaughters of late John Arthur Crawshay Bailey, only son of late Capt John Crawshay Bailey, RN, 3rd son of 1st baronet:—

Issue of late John Henry Bailey, b 1889, d 1966: m 1913, Ruby, who d 1972, da of Edward Giles:—

Margaret Elizabeth (RR1 Fairview Crescent, Oliver, BC V0H 1TO, Canada), b 1915: m 1939, Derrick Thomas Ashworth Douglas, who d 1975, and has issue living, Derrick John (18, 3221 119th St, Edmonton, Alberta, Canada T6J 2C1), b 1947: m 1st, 1969, Penelope Elizabeth, da of Rudi Krause, of Elmira, Ont; 2ndly, 1978, Marilyn —, and has issue living (by 1st m), Lee Christian b 1971, Todd Matthew b 1973, — David Henry (twin), (6 Kersey Bay, Winnipeg, Manitoba, Canada), b 1947; Sergeant RCMP: m 1970, Charlotte, da of late Stefan Johannson, of Gimli, Manitoba, and has issue living, Stefan Nathan b 1971, Brendan Wyatt b 1981, Jill Elizabeth b 1974, — Judy Ann, b 1941: m 1971, Herbert Flax (115 Ranchlands Court, NW Calgary, Alberta, Canada T3G 1N8), and has issue living, Timothy Aaron b 1974, Joanna Susan b 1972. —— Barbara, b 1927: m 1945, Capt Ernest Ronald Matthewson, of Sa Fontansa, Bagur (Gerona), Spain, and has issue living, Michael Derek (18 Haynes Mead, Berkhamsted, Herts), b 1946: m 1970, Barbara Mary Saunders, and has issue living, Toby b 1974, Kirsty b 1976.

PREDECESSORS – (1) JOSEPH Bailey, yr son of John Bailey, of Wakefield; sat successively as MP for Worcester City and Breconshire; cr a Baronet 1852: m 1st, 1810, Maria, who d 1827, da of Joseph Latham; 2ndly, 1830, Mary Anne, who d 1874, da of late John Thomas Hendry Hopper, of Witton Castle, co Durham; d 1858; s by his grandson (2) JOSEPH RUSSELL (son of late Joseph Bailey, MP, el son of 1st Bt), 2nd Bt, b 1840; cr Baron Glanusk, of Glanusk Park, co Brecknock (peerage of United Kingdom) 1899; MP for Herefordshire (C) 1865-85, and for Hereford, 1886-92; was Lord-Lieut of Breconshire: m 1861, Mary Ann Jane, who d 1935, da of Henry Lucas, MD, of Glan-yr-Afon; d 1906; s by his son (3) JOSEPH HENRY RUSSELL, CB, CBE, DSO, 2nd Baron, b 1864; Lord-Lieut of Breconshire 1905-28: m 1890, Editha Elma, CBE, who d 1938, da of late Major Warden Sergison; d 1928; s by his son (4) WILFRED RUSSELL, DSO, 3rd Baron; b 1891, Lord-Lieut of Breconshire; late Lieut-Col Welsh Guards; European War 1914-19 (DSO): m 1st, 1919 (m diss 1931), Victoria Mary Enid Anne, da of late Lieut-Col Frank Dugdale, CVO; 2ndly, 1942, Margaret Eldrydd (who m 2ndly, 1966, 1st Viscount De L'Isle, VC, KG, GCMG, GCVO, PC, who d 1991), da of late Maj-Gen Thomas Herbert Shoubridge, CB, CMG, DSO; d 1948; s by his cousin (5) DAVID RUSSELL (son of late Hon Herbert Crawshay Bailey, 4th son of 1st Baron), 4th Baron and present peer.

GLASGOW, EARL OF (Boyle) (Earl S 1703)

PATRICK ROBIN ARCHIBALD BOYLE, 10th Earl; b 30 July 1939; s 1984; ed Eton, and Sorbonne; Sub-Lt RNR; sometime Television Documentary Producer and Dir: m 1975, Isabel Mary, adopted da of late George Douglas James, and has issue.

Arms – Quarterly: 1st and 4th or, an eagle with two heads displayed gules, armed and beaked azure; a coat of augmentation for the earldom of Glasgow; 2nd and 3rd per bend embattled argent and gules, Boyle: over all an escutcheon or, charged with three stags' horns gules, for the paternal coat of Boyle of Kelburn. **Crest** – An eagle with two heads displayed per pale embattled gules and argent. **Supporters** – Dexter, a savage, wreathed round the temples and loins, and holding in the dexter hand a branch of laurel all proper: sinister, a lion per pale embattled argent and gules.
Seat – Kelburn, Fairlie, Ayrshire.

SON LIVING

Hon DAVID MICHAEL DOUGLAS (does not use courtesy title of Viscount of Kelburn), b 15 Oct 1978.

DAUGHTER LIVING

Lady Alice Dorothy, b 1981.

SISTERS LIVING

Lady Sarah Dorothea, b 1941: m 1962, John Edward Baily, of 27 Park Walk, SW10 (see E Haddington colls, 1980 Edn), and has issue, Michael, b 1963, d 1985, — Peter, b 1967, — Tanya Jane, b 1965, — Polly Anne, b 1972.
Lady Nichola Jane Eleanora (Minervina), b 1946: m 1976, Thomas G. Carter, and has issue living, Matthew, b 1978, — Ella Frances Lyle, b 1986.

The Lord will provide

DOMINUS · PROVIDEBIT

AUNT LIVING (Daughter of 8th Earl)

Lady Margaret Dorothea, b 1920: m 1st, 1944 (m diss 1962), Capt Oliver Payan Dawnay, CVO, Coldstream Gds, who d 1988 (see V Downe, colls); 2ndly, 1973, Peter Douglas Miller Stirling-Aird of Kippendavie, TD, of Kippendavie Lodge, Dunblane, Perthshire, and 9 Lansdowne Rd, W11.

WIDOW LIVING OF SON OF SEVENTH EARL

Marie (Cushat Wood, Portpatrick, Stranraer, Wigtownshire, DG9 8TH); a JP and Co Councillor for Wigtownshire; da of John Gibb, of Chillesford, Orford, Suffolk, and formerly wife of George Chettle: m 1934, as his 2nd wife, Air Commodore Hon John David Boyle, CBE, DSO, who d 1974.

MOTHER LIVING

Dorothea, only da of Col Sir Archibald Moir Park Lyle, 2nd Bt, MC: m 1937 (m diss 1962), Rear-Adm David William Maurice, Viscount Kelburn, CB, DSC, later 9th Earl of Glasgow, who d 1984. Residences – Marwell House, Owslebury, nr Winchester, Hants; Albany, Piccadilly, W1.

COLLATERAL BRANCHES LIVING

Grandsons of late Capt Hon James Boyle (infra):—
Issue of late Lieut-Col Patrick John Salvin Boyle, Roy Scots Fusiliers, *b* 1910, *ka* 1944: *m* 1938, Mary Elizabeth, OBE, JP, DL (Broughton House, Broughton Gifford, Melksham, Wilts) (who *m* 2ndly, 1948, Lieut-Col Charles Murray Floyd, OBE, who *d* 1971 (*see* Floyd, B, colls)), only child of Robert Fleetwood Fuller, of Great Chalfield, Melksham:—
Andrew Robert James (Hatt House, Box, Wilts), *b* 1939; *ed* Eton: *m* 1971, Julia, da of N. W. Gardener of Boxted Farm, Hemel Hempstead, Herts, and has issue living, James William, *b* 1973. — Olivia Mary, *b* 1975. —— Simon Hugh Patrick (Penpergwm Lodge, Abergavenny, Gwent), *b* 1941; *ed* Eton; High Sheriff Gwent 1993: *m* 1970, Catriona, da of W. G. Gordon, DFC, of Lude, Blair Atholl, Perths, and has issue living, Alice Catriona Jane, *b* 1972, — Mary Helen Fenella, *b* 1974, — Susannah Elizabeth, *b* 1977, — Christian Laura Frances, *b* 1982. —— David Thomas Alan (Fairstead Hall, Terling, Chelmsford, Essex), *b* 1943; *ed* Eton, and Trin Coll, Camb; JP Essex: *m* 1969, Angela Rose, da of George Frederick Pinney, CBE (*see* Lacy, Bt, 1980 Edn), and has issue living, Robert John, *b* 1970; *ed* Eton — Edward George, *b* 1972; *ed* Eton, — Patrick Thomas, *b* 1974, — Katherine Griselda Eveline, *b* 1982.

Issue of late Capt Hon James Boyle, 3rd son of 7th Earl, *b* 1880; *ka* 1914: *m* 1908, Katherine Isabel Salvin, who *d* 1960 (having *m* 2ndly, 1920, 1st Viscount Trenchard, who *d* 1956), da of late Edward Salvin Bowlby, of Gilston Park, Herts, and Knoydart, Inverness-shire:—
Belinda Margaret Graeme, OBE, *b* 1913; is Ch Com ATS; Middle East 1941-4; OBE (Mil) 1944: *m* 1947, Simon Fowell Buxton, who *d* 1974 (Buxton, Bt, colls). *Residence* – Dyer Cottage, Wylye, Wilts.

Issue of late Hon Alan Reginald Boyle, AFC, 5th son of 7th Earl, *b* 1886, *d* 1958: *m* 1916, Isabel Julia, who *d* 1971, da of late Edmund Charles Pendleton Hull, JP, of Park Gate House, Ham Common, Richmond, Surrey:—
Jean Isabel, *b* 1919: *m* 1st, 1941 (*m diss* 1976), Bartholomew Guy Ellison; 2ndly, 1980, Iain Robert Cullen Baillie, and has issue living (by 1st *m*), Caroline Anne, *b* 1942: *m* 1967, John Antony Hobbs, of May Cottage, Alice Bright Lane, Crowborough, Sussex, TN6 3SQ, and has issue living, Jonathan Noel Alan *b* 1970, Francesca Agnes *b* 1968: *m* 1992, Adrian Youings, Rosanna Natasha *b* 1972, — Joanna Fenella, *b* 1945.

(In remainder to Scottish peerages only)

Granddaughters of late Col Patrick David Boyle, el son of late Vice-Adm Alexander Boyle, 2nd son of late Rt Hon David Boyle, Lord Justice-Gen of Scotland, 4th son of late Rev Hon Patrick Boyle, 4th son of 2nd Earl:—
Issue of late Col Cecil Alexander Boyle, CIE, DSO, *b* 1888, *d* 1941: *m* 1923, Gladys (Dulcie), who *d* 1976, da of late Lt-Col Robert Arthur Edward Benn, CIE:—
Mary Grizel, *b* 1924; 1939-45 War with WAAF: *m* 1947, Lt-Col James Berkeley Sackville Hamilton, RE (ret), of The Old Rectory, Acklam, Malton, Yorks, YO17 9RG, and has issue (*see* V Boyne, colls). — Patricia (Le Moulin de Quatre Carres, 47150 Monflanquin, France), *b* 1929: a State Registered Nurse: *m* 1955 (*m diss* 1980), Lt-Col Jonathan Robert Alford, RE, who *d* 1986, and has issue living, Michael Robert Patrick, *b* 1958, — Caroline Jane, *b* 1956, — Melissa Anne, *b* 1960, — Victoria Susan, *b* 1963.

Granddaughters of late Alexander Boyle, yst son of Vice-Adm Alexander Boyle (ante):—
Issue of late Alister Patrick Boyle, *b* 1905, *d* 1973: *m* 1st 1932, Rosa Howard, who *d* 1933, da of Howard Tripp, of S Canterbury, NZ; 2ndly, 1936, Lois Morton (48 Cox St, Christchurch 8001, NZ), da of late C. M. Ollivier:—
(By 1st *m*) Jennifer Frances, *b* 1933: *m* 1965 (*m diss* 1989), Ian Coutts, and has issue living, Hester Frances, *b* 1967, — Rosa Emily, *b* 1969. —— (By 2nd *m*) Mary Montgomerie (9 Andover St, Christchurch 1, NZ), *b* 1937: *m* 1964, Laurence George Holder, who *d* 1974, and has issue living, Patrick George, *b* 1966, — Bridget Mary, *b* 1967, — Alexandra Browning, *b* 1969, — Sara Annabel, *b* 1972. ——Alexandra Montgomerie (Canal House, 120 Lisson Grove, NW8 8LB), *b* 1943: *m* 1988, Douglas Cruden Stephen, who *d* 1991.

Grandsons of late Henry David Boyle, el son of John Boyle, 3rd son of Rt Hon David Boyle (ante):—
Issue of late David Hugh Montgomerie Boyle, CMG, *b* 1883, *d* 1970: *m* 1916, Laura Grant, who *d* 1971, da of late James Tennant, of Fairlieburne, Fairlie:—
Alasdair David Forbes (33 Scotts St, Largs, Ayrshire KA30 9NT), *b* 1919; *ed* Wellington Coll, and RMC; Maj (ret) Argyll and Sutherland Highlanders; MBIM; Sec of Scottish Business Sch; 1939-45 War (wounded, despatches): *m* 1st, 1945 (*m diss* 1958), Elizabeth Winifred, da of late Cdr H. R. Kelway-Bamber, RN; 2ndly, 1958, Mrs Doris Louise Clayton, da of Victor Eaton Usherwood, of Tunbridge Wells, and has issue living, (by 1st *m*) Roderick David Alasdair (Firs Cottage, College Grove, Malvern, Worcs WR14 3HP), *b* 1951: *m* 1977, Althea Victoria, yr da of late Maj Derek Leslie Lloyd, MC (*see* V Chetwynd, colls), and has issue living, Jamie Edward Rory *b* 1978, Harriet Elizabeth Victoria *b* 1980, — Henrietta Elizabeth Flora (*Hon Mrs James M. Rollo*), *b* 1948: *m* 1968, Hon James Malcolm Rollo, of Corwar House, Barrhill, Girvan, Ayrshire (*see* L Rollo), — (and a da from 2nd *m*) Camilla Josephine Brenda Louise, *b* 1964. —— Ranald Hugh Montgomerie, DSC (Downcraig Ferry, Millport, I of Cumbrae; The Wooden House, Fairlie, Ayrshire; 906 Beatty House, Dolphin Sq, SW1), *b* 1921; *ed* Wellington Coll, and Exeter Coll, Oxford; late Sudan Govt Ser, HMOCS Kenya; HM Dip Ser; Hambros Bank; a Member of Queen's Body Guard for Scotland (Royal Co of Archers); 1939-45 War as Lt RNVR (wounded, DSC): *m* 1957, Norma, yst da of late Alexander Gray and has issue living, Fergus David, *b* 1958, — Alexander Ranald, *b* 1959, — Patrick Mungo, *b* 1961, — John Quentin, *b* 1964, — Hamish William, *b* 1970, — Laura Grizel, *b* 1963: *m* 1993, Deane C. B. Pennick, elder son of Lt-Col Peter Pennick, and has issue living, Anastasia Laura *b* 1994, — Beatrice Elizabeth, *b* 1966.

Granddaughter of late William Henry David Boyle, son of late Col William Boyle, CB, 4th son of late Rt Hon David Boyle (ante):—
Issue of late George Frederic Boyle, *b* 1893, *d* 1929: *m* 1920 (*m diss* 1929), Mary Jeffrey (who *d* 1954, having *m* 2ndly, 1929, Douglas Charles Beaumont, MD, MRCP, of Claywood Sway, Hants), da of Sir Peter Jeffrey Mackie, 1st Bt:—
Eleanor Mary, *b* 1921: *m* 1st, 1945 (*m diss* 1962), Capt Hon Arthur Cameron Corbett, Ayrshire Yeo (later 3rd Baron Rowallan), who *d* 1993; 2ndly, 1963, Col (Richard) Derek Cardiff, late Scots Gds, and has issue living (by 1st *m*) (*see* B Rowallan), — (by 2nd *m*) David Richard George, *b* 1964. *Residence* – Flat 1, 13 Embankment Gds, SW3 4LW.

Issue, if any, of Robert Fremoult Boyle (*b* 1887), son of late Charles Fremoult Boyle, of Winnipeg, Manitoba, Canada, NW Mounted Police 1876-80, eldest son of late Capt Robert Boyle, RA (infra).
Granddaughter of late Cdr Edward Louis Dalrymple Boyle, CMG, RN; 3rd son of Capt Robert Boyle, RA, 7th son of Rt Hon David Boyle (ante):—
Issue of late Lt-Col Edward Patrick Ogilvie Boyle, MVO, Royal Scots Fus, *b* 1893, *d* 1966: *m* 1934, Audrey (6 Stack House, Cundy St, SW1) (who *m* 2ndly, 1970, Maj Clarence J. Henry, who *d* 1973), da of late Lt-Col Audley Willis:—
Jennifer Mary, *b* 1934.

PREDECESSORS – **(1)** DAVID BOYLE, MP for Buteshire 1689-99; *cr Lord Boyle*, of Kelburn, Stewartown, Cumbrae, Largs and Dalry (peerage of Scotland) 1699, and *Lord Boyle, Viscount of Kelburn* and *Earl of Glasgow* (peerage of Scotland) 1703, with remainder to his heirs male whatsoever; Lord High Commr to Gen Assembly for Ch of Scotland 1706-10, a Representative Peer 1707-08, and Lord Registrar of Scotland 1708-14; *d* 1733; *s* by his son **(2)** JOHN, 2nd Earl; *d* 1740; *s* by his son **(3)** JOHN, 3rd Earl; was Lord High Commr to Ch of Scotland 1764-72; *d* 1775; *s* by his son **(4)** GEORGE, 4th Earl, *b* 1766; Lord-Lieut of Renfrewshire, and a Representative Peer; *cr Baron Ross*, of Hawkhead, co Renfrew (peerage of United Kingdom) 1815: *m* 1st, 1788, Lady Augusta Hay, da of 14th Earl of Erroll; 2ndly, 1824, Julia, da of the Rt Hon Sir John Sinclair, 1st Bt; *d* 1843; *s* by his 2nd son **(5)** JAMES, 5th Earl; a Capt RN, and Lord Lieut and Sheriff of Renfrewshire; assumed, 1822, by Roy licence the additional surname of Car; *d* 1869; *s* by his half-brother **(6)** GEORGE FREDERICK, 6th Earl, *b* 1825; MP for Buteshire (*C*) 1865, and subsequently Lord Clerk Register of Scotland: *m* 1856, Montagu, who *d* 1931, da of 3rd Baron Abercromby; *d* 1890, when the Barony of Ross became extinct, and the Scottish Peerages devolved upon his cousin **(7)** DAVID, GCMG (son of Patrick Boyle, of Shewalton, co Ayr, and el great-grandson of Hon Patrick Boyle, 3rd son of 2nd Earl), 7th Earl, *b* 1833; Capt RN; served in White Sea during Russian War 1854, and in China 1857; was Gov of New Zealand 1892-7; *cr Baron Fairlie*, of Fairlie, co Ayr (peerage of United Kingdom) 1897: *m* 1873, Dorothea Elizabeth Thomasina, who *d* 1923, da of Sir Edward Hunter-Blair, 4th Bt; *d* 1915; *s* by his el son **(8)** PATRICK JAMES, DSO, 8th Earl, *b* 1874; Capt RN; Convener of Ayr Co Council 1947-58: *m* 1906, Hyacinthe Mary, who *d* 1977, da of late William A. Bell, of Pendell Court, Bletchingley; *d* 1963; *s* by his el son **(9)** DAVID WILLIAM MAURICE, CB, DSC, 9th Earl; *b* 1910; Rear-Adm; Capt of the Fleet, Home Fleet 1957-59; Commodore RN Barracks, Portsmouth 1959-61; Flag-Offr, Malta 1961-63; 1939-45 war in Atlantic, Arctic, and Far East; present at destruction of *Bismarck*; Mem Royal Co of Archers (Queen's Body Guard for Scotland): *m* 1st, 1937 (*m diss* 1962), Dorothea, only da of Col Sir Archibald Moir Park Lyle, 2nd Bt, MC; 2ndly, 1962, Hon Ursula Vanda Maud, who *d* 1984, da of 4th Baron Vivian, and formerly wife of Maj Sir William Fane Wrixon Beecher, 5th Bt, MC; *d* 1984; *s* by his only son **(10)** PATRICK ROBIN ARCHIBALD, 10th Earl, and present peer; also Viscount of Kelburn, Lord Boyle and Baron Fairlie.

GLENAMARA, BARON (Short) (Life Baron 1977)

EDWARD WATSON SHORT, CH, PC, son of Charles Short, of Warcop, Westmorland; *b* 17 Dec 1912; *ed* Bede Coll, Durham Univ (LLB); 1939-45 War as Capt DLI; Opposition Assist Whip 1955-61, Dep Ch Opposition Whip 1962-64, Parl Sec to Treasury and Govt Ch Whip 1964-66, Postmaster Gen 1966-68, Sec of State for Education and Science 1968-70, Dep Leader of Labour Party 1972-76, and Lord Pres of the Council and Leader of House of Commons 1974-76; MP for Central Newcastle upon Tyne (*L*) 1951-76; Chm of Cable and Wireless Ltd, since 1976; author of *The Infantry Instructor, The Story of Durham Light Infantry, Education in a Changing World, Birth to Five; I Knew My Place* and *Whip to Wilson*; *cr* PC 1964, CH 1976, and *Baron Glenamara*, of Glenridding in co Cumbria (Life Baron) 1977: *m* 1941, Jennie, da of Thomas Sewell, of Newcastle upon Tyne, and has issue.
Residences – 21 Priory Gdns, Corbridge, Northumberland; Glenridding, Cumbria.

SON LIVING

Hon Michael Christian (Holly House, Whickham, Tyne and Wear), *b* 1943: *m* 1968, Ann, da of Joseph Gibbon, of Whickham, Tyne and Wear.

DAUGHTER LIVING

Hon Jane Bronwen, *b* 1945: *m* 1970, James Weir Fraser, and has issue. *Residence* – 62 Martis Av, Ramsey, NJ 07446, USA.

Glenapp, Viscount; son of Earl of Inchcape.

GLENARTHUR, BARON (Arthur) (Baron UK 1918, Bt UK 1903)

Do and hope

FAC ET SPERA

SIMON MARK ARTHUR, 4th Baron, and 4th Baronet; *b* 7 Oct 1944; *s* 1976; *ed* Eton; commn'd 10th R Hussars (PWO) 1963, ret as Maj 1975; joined R Hussars TA 1976-80; DL Aberdeenshire 1988; Brig Queen's Body Guard for Scotland (Royal Company of Archers), Capt British Airways Helicopters Ltd 1976-82; a Lord in Waiting (Gvt Whip) to HM 1982-83; Parly Under-Sec of State, Dept of Health & Social Security 1983-85, Home Office 1985-86, Min of State Scottish Office 1986-87, Min of State, Foreign & Commonwealth Affairs 1987-89; Dir Aberdeen & Texas Corporate Finance Ltd 1977-82, and Hanson plc since 1989, Chm St Mary's NHS Trust since 1991, and British Helicopter Advisory Board since 1992, Dir Lewis Group plc since 1993, Dep Chm Hanson Pacific Ltd since 1993; MCIT 1979, FRAeS 1992; Pres National Council for Civil Protection since 1991; *m* 1969, Susan, da of late Cdr Hubert Wyndham Barry, RN (ret) (*see* Barry, Bt, colls), and has issue.

Arms – Sable, an escarbuncle or, within an orle of besants. **Crest** – On a rock a pelican in her piety proper. **Supporters** – (as recorded at Lyon Office), — *Dexter*, a bay horse proper; *sinister*, a lion rampant gules. *Address* – c/o House of Lords, SW1. *Clubs* – Cavalry and Guards, Pratt's, White's.

SON LIVING

Hon EDWARD ALEXANDER, *b* 9 April 1973; *ed* Eton.

DAUGHTER LIVING

Hon Emily Victoria, *b* 1975.

BROTHER LIVING

Hon Matthew Richard (Bingfield East Quarter, Hallington, Newcastle upon Tyne), *b* 1948; *ed* Eton, and RAC Cirencester: *m* 1974, Veronica Rosemary, yr da of Capt Michael Hall, Royal Scots Greys, of the Bridge, Kilternan, co Dublin (*see* B Basing, 1980 Edn), and has issue living, Matthew Frederick Michael, *b* 1981, — Jessica Mary, *b* 1979.

SISTER LIVING

Hon Victoria, *b* 1946: *m* 1976, Hugh Richard Mervyn Vernon, of Pierhill, Annbank, Ayrshire (*see* B Lyveden, colls).

PREDECESSORS – (1) *Sir* MATTHEW Arthur, LLD, el son of late James Arthur, of Carlung, Ayrshire, and Barshaw, Renfrewshire, by Jane, da of Thomas Glen, of Thornhill, Renfrewshire; *b* 1852; Chm of Arthur and Co (Limited), of Glasgow, and of Lochgelly Iron and Coal Co (Limited), and a Member of Roy Co of Archers (King's Body Guard for Scotland); Chm of Glasgow and S-W Railway Co 1920-22; *cr* a Baronet 1903, and *Baron Glenarthur*, of Carlung, Ayrshire (peerage of United Kingdom) 1918: *m* 1876, Janet Stevenson Bennett, OBE, who *d* 1946, yr da of late Alexander Bennett McGrigor, LLD of Cairnoch, Stirlingshire; *d* 1928; *s* by his son (2) (JAMES) CECIL, 2nd Baron; *b* 1883: *m* 1907, Evelyn, who *d* 1959, el da of late Henry March-Phillipps, of Tiverton, N Devon; *d* 1942; *s* by his son (3) MATTHEW, OBE, 3rd Baron *b* 1909: *m* 1st, 1931 (*m diss* 1939), Audrey da of late George Crompton Lees Milne (B Glanusk, colls); 2ndly, 1939, Margaret Risk, who *d* 1993, only da of late Capt Henry James Howie, of Stairaird, Mauchline; *d* 1976; *s* by his el son (4) SIMON MARK, 4th Baron and present peer.

GLENAVY, BARONY OF (Campbell) (Extinct 1984)

DAUGHTER LIVING OF THIRD BARON

Hon Brigid Margaret, *b* 1948: *m* 19—, — Reilly, of 2535 Panorama Dr, N Vancouver, BC, Canada.

GLENCAIRN, EARLDOM OF (Cunningham) (Earl S 1488 Dormant 1796)

COLLATERAL BRANCH LIVING

Descendants of Andrew Cuninghame 1st of Corsehill, 2nd son of 4th Earl:—
See Cuninghame Bt (NS 1672) of Corsehill.

GLENCONNER, BARON (Tennant) (Baron UK 1911, Bt UK 1885)

God will fill the sails

COLIN CHRISTOPHER PAGET TENNANT, 3rd Baron and 4th Baronet; *b* 1 Dec 1926; *s* 1983; *ed* Eton, and New Coll, Oxford; formerly Lieut IG: *m* 1956, Lady Anne Veronica Coke, LVO, da of 5th Earl of Leicester, and has had issue.

Arms – Argent, two crescents in fesse sable, on a chief gules a boar's head couped of the first; a bordure company of the second and first. **Crest** – A mast with a sail hoisted proper. **Supporters** – *Dexter*, a stag proper, gorged with a mural crown or; *sinister*, a tiger also proper, gorged with a crown palissado also or; each charged on the shoulder with a thistle, leaved and slipped, gold.
Residence – Beau Estate, Soufriere, St Lucia, W Indies.

SONS LIVING

Hon CHARLES EDWARD PEVENSEY (30 Fountainhall Rd, Edinburgh EH9 2LW), *b* 15 Feb 1957: *m* 1993, Shelagh, da of Matthew Raymond Scott, of Peebles, and has issue living, a son, *b* 2 Feb 1994.
Hon Christopher Cary, *b* 1967; *ed* Stanbridge Earls.

GRANDSON LIVING

Issue of late Hon Henry Lovell Tennant, 2nd son of 3rd Baron, *b* 1960, *d* 1990: *m* 1983, Teresa Mary (infra), yst da of John McRae Cormack, AFC (*see* B Davies):—
Euan Lovell, *b* 1983.

DAUGHTERS LIVING

Hon (Flora) May Pamela, *b* 1970.
Hon Amy Jasmine Elizabeth (twin), *b* 1970.

HALF-BROTHER LIVING

Hon Tobias William (Shaws, Newcastleton, Roxburghshire), *b* 1941: *m* 1963, Lady Emma Cavendish, el da of 11th Duke of Devonshire, and has issue living, Edward Tobias, *b* 1967, — Isabel, *b* 1964, — Stella, *b* 1970.

HALF-SISTERS LIVING

Hon Emma Christina TENNANT, *b* 1937: *ed* St Paul's Girls' Sch; FRSL; the novelist Emma Tennant, author of *The Bad Sister*, *Wild Nights* and *Woman Beware Woman*, etc; founder editor of *Bananas*, Literary Newspaper; *m* 1st 1957 (*m diss* 1962), Sebastian Yorke (*see* E Hardwicke, colls); 2ndly, 1963 (*m diss* 19—), Christopher John Penrice Booker, author and journalist; 3rdly, 1968 (*m diss* 1973), Alexander Claud Cockburn (*see* Arbuthnot, Bt, colls, *cr* 1829, 1990 Edn), and has issue living, (by 1st *m*) (*see* E Hardwicke, colls), — (by 3rd *m*) Daisy Alice, *b* 1969, — (by late Michael Dempsey) Rose Hippolyta, *b* 1973. *Address* – c/o A. D. Peters & Co, 10 Buckingham St, WC2.
Hon Catherine Elizabeth (*Hon Lady Palmer*), *b* 1947: *m* 1976, Sir (Charles) Mark Palmer, 5th Bt (*cr* 1886), of Mill Hill Farm, Sherborne, Northleach, Glos.

GREAT AUNT LIVING (*Daughter of 1st baronet by 2nd marriage*)

Dame Margaret, DBE (*Margaret, Baroness Wakehurst*), *b* 1899; Hon LLD Belfast; a GCStJ; DBE (Civil) 1965: *m* 1920, 2nd Baron Wakehurst, who *d* 1970. *Residence* – 31 Lennox Gdns, SW1.

WIDOW LIVING OF SON OF FIRST BARON

Shelagh Anne, da of Maj Sean Rainey, and of Mrs Marion Wrottesley: *m* 1963, as his 3rd wife, Hon David Pax Tennant, who *d* 1968.

WIDOW LIVING OF SON OF SECOND BARON

Elizabeth Marya, da of James Dales, of W Vancouver, BC, Canada, and formerly wife of Ian Romer, of Hawkley, Hants: *m* 2ndly, 1962, as his 2nd wife, Hon James Grey Herbert Tennant, who *d* 1992; 3rdly, 1994, Philip Edwards. *Residence* – 37 Cadogan Place, SW1.

WIDOW LIVING OF SON OF THIRD BARON

Teresa Mary, yst da of John McRae Cormack, AFC (*see* B Davies): *m* 1983, Hon Henry Lovell Tennant, who *d* 1990. *Residence* – The Glen, Innerleithen, Peeblesshire.

WIDOW LIVING OF SECOND BARON

ELIZABETH (*Elizabeth, Baroness Glenconner*), da of late Lt-Col Evelyn George Harcourt Powell, Gren Gds, of 31 Hillgate Place, W8: *m* 1935, as his 2nd wife, the 2nd Baron, who *d* 1983. *Residence* – Rovinia, Liapades, Corfu, Greece.

COLLATERAL BRANCHES LIVING

Issue of late Hon James Grey Herbert Tennant, 2nd son of 2nd Baron, *b* 1929, *d* 1992: *m* 1st, 1955 (*m diss* 1962), Emily Fawaz, da of George Licos; 2ndly, 1962, Elizabeth Marya (ante) (who *m* 3rdly, 1994, Philip Edwards), da of James Dales, of W Vancouver, BC, Canada, and formerly wife of Ian Romer, of Hawkley, Hants:—
(By 1st *m*) Alexander David Gabriel, *b* 1957.

Issue of late Hon David Pax Tennant, 2nd son of 1st Baron, *b* 1902, *d* 1968: *m* 1st, 1928 (*m diss* 1937), Hermione Youlanda Ruby Clinton (Hermione Baddeley the actress), who *d* 1986, da of William Herman Clinton Baddeley; 2ndly, 1938 (*m diss* 1953), Virginia Penelope, da of late Alan Parsons, of The Baas, Broxbourne, Herts; 3rdly, 1963, Shelagh Anne (ante), da of Maj Sean Rainey:—

(By 1st *m*) David Edward Wyndham (Pyt Cottage, Tisbury, Wilts SP3 6NY. *Clubs* – White's and Brooks's), *b* 1930; *ed* Eton: *m* 1964 (*m diss* 1973), Margaret Rachel, da of late Hon Sir Ernest Stowell Scott, KCMG, MVO(*see* E Eldon, colls), and has issue living, Aubone Christopher, *b* 1969; *ed* Eton, and Durham Univ, — Ivan, *b* 1970; *ed* Stowe, — Laura Hermione, *b* 1967; *ed* St Paul's Girls' Sch, and Jesus Coll, Camb. —— Pauline Laetitia (*Pauline, Lady Rumbold*), *b* 1929: *m* 1st, 1946 (*m diss* 1953), Capt Julian Alfred Lane-Fox Pitt-Rivers, late R Dragoons (*see* By Forster, 1980 Edn); 2ndly, 1954 (*m diss* 1970), Euan Douglas Graham (*see* D Montrose, colls); 3rdly, 1974, Sir (Horace) Anthony (Claude) Rumbold, 10th Bt, KCMG, KCVO, CB, who *d* 1983, of Hatch Cottage, Cokers Frome, Dorchester, Dorset. —— (By 2nd *m*) Annabel Georgiana Skye (Georgia) (Job's Mill, Warminster, Wilts), *b* 1941; has issue (by Paul Stephen McNaney), Ella May, *b* 1984. —— Sabrina Viola (Josie TENNANT), *b* 1943 (relinquished the forenames of Sabrina Viola and assumed that of Josie by deed poll; has reverted to her maiden surname): *m* 1963 (*m diss* 1977), Jonathan Gathorne-Hardy, and has issue (*see* E Cranbrook, colls).

(In remainder to Baronetcy only)

Grandchildren of late Francis John Tennant, 5th son of 1st baronet:—
Issue of late Group Capt John Edward Tennant, DSO, MC, RAF Vol Reserve, *b* 1890, *d* on active ser 1941: *m* 1st, 1918 (*m diss* 1925), Georgina Helen, da of Gen Sir George Macaulay Kirkpatrick, KCB, KCSI; 2ndly, 1926, Victoria Maud Veronica, MBE, who *d* 1967, da of Sir Robert (Robin) George Vivian Duff, 2nd Bt (*cr* 1911):—
(By 1st *m*) Sir Iain Mark, KT, *b* 1919; *ed* Eton, and Magdalene Coll, Camb; late Capt Scots Guards; a JP (1961) DL (1954) and Lord Lieut Morayshire (now Grampian Region) 1963-94; Chm Gordonstoun Schools Ltd 1956-72, and Grampian TV 1967-89; Crown Estate Commr 1970-90; Dir of the Clydesdale Bank 1968-89 and the Abbey Nat Bldg Soc 1981-89; Lord High Commr to Gen Assembly of Church of Scotland 1987 and 1988; a Member of Queen's Body Guard for Scotland (Roy Co of Archers); 1939-45 War; KT 1986: *m* 1946, Lady Margaret Helen Isla Marion Ogilvy, da of 12th Earl of Airlie, and has issue living, Mark Edward (Innes House, Elgin, Moray), *b* 1947; late Scots Gds; Man Dir (Scotland) Chase Manhattan Bank, Dir Quality Street Ltd: *m* 1971, Hermione Rosamond, da of Lt Col Maurice W. Howe, OBE, and has issue living, Edward Iain *b* 1983, Miranda Hermione Rosamond *b* 1974, Clementine Margaret Georgina *b* 1977, — Christopher John, *b* 1950; a Page of Honour to HM The Queen 1964-66: *m* 1994, Mrs Andrea Lewis, yst da of Donald Payne, — Emma Margaret *b* 1954: *m* 1979, Angus Geoffrey Bruce Ismay Cheape, late Scots Guards, of Middleton Fossoway, Kinross, 2nd son of (Hugh) Bruce Ismay Cheape, TD, of South Lodge, Craignure, Isle of Mull, and has issue living, Henry Bruce Iain Ismay *b* 1980. *Residence* – Lochnabo House, Elgin, Morayshire. —— (By 2nd *m*) Andrew Duff (Muiresk House, Turriff, Aberdeenshire; White's and St James' Clubs), *b* 1928; late Scots Gds: *m* 1953 (*m diss* 1967), Lucinda Evelyn, only da of Arthur Walter James (*see* B Northbourne, colls), and has issue living, Ann Charlotte, *b* 1956. —— Hugh Rinnes Duff (4 Lecky St, SW7), *b* 1932; *ed* Eton; formerly Lt Scots Gds.

Grandchildren of late Rt Hon Harold John Tennant (*infra*):—
Issue of late Maj John Tennant, TD, *b* 1899, *d* 1967: *m* 1st, 1929 (*m diss* 1939), Hon Antonia Mary Roby Benson, who *d* 1982, da of 1st Baron Charnwood; 2ndly, 1948, Rosemary Irene, da of Sir Alfred Theodore Hennessy, KBE:—
(By 1st *m*) Sir Anthony John (Britwell Priors, Longparish, Hants SP11 6QR), *b* 1930; *ed* Eton, and Trin Coll, Camb (BA); late Lt Scots Guards; Chm Guinness plc 1989-92, Chm Christie's since 1993; *cr* Knt Bach 1992: *m* 1954, Rosemary Violet, el da of Lt-Col Henry Charles Minshull Stockdale (*see* B Faringdon, 1976 Edn), and has issue living, Christopher Sebastian (11 Lawrence St, SW3 5NB), *b* 1955; *ed* Eton and St Andrew's Univ (MA): *m* 1987, Sally Jennifer, 3rd da of Jack Berner, of 80 Church Rd, Wimbledon, and has issue living, Francesca Rose Antonia *b* 1992, Harriet Daisy *b* 1993, — Patrick Charles (Hayward Holt, Hungerford, Berks RG17 0QB), *b* 1958; *ed* Eton, Trin Coll, Camb (MA), and Univ of Pennsylvania (MBA, MA): *m* 1986, Meredith Maye, el da of Jerome Shively, of Churt, Surrey, and has issue living, Jemima Jennifer *b* 1990. —— Mark Iain (Royal Courts of Justice, Strand, WC2A 2LL; 30 Abbey Gdns, NW8 9AT; Balfluig Castle, by Alford, Aberdeenshire; Brooks's Club), *b* 1932; *ed* Eton, and New Coll, Oxford (MA); Bar Inner Temple 1958, Master of the Bench 1982, Master of Supreme Court, Queen's Bench Div 1988; Chm Royal Orchestral Soc for Amateur Musicians 1989; Baron of Balfluig: *m* 1965, Lady Harriot Pleydell-Bouverie, da of 7th Earl of Radnor, and has issue living, Lysander Philip Roby, *b* 1968; *ed* Eton (Musical Exhibitioner 1982), and New Coll, Oxford, — Sophia Roby, *b* 1967; *ed* Magdalen Coll, Oxford. —— (By 2nd *m*) Ivo Simon (70 Waterford Rd, SW6), *b* 1955; *ed* Harrow: *m* 1985, Carole V., da of Maj C.P. Martel, of Richmond, N Yorks, and has issue living, Thomas Simon Alfred, *b* 1991, — Camilla Rose, *b* 1987. —— Aurea Maryrose (38 Franche Court Rd, SW17), *b* 1949.

Issue of late Archibald Tennant, *b* 1907, *d* 1955: *m* 1947, Diana Primrose (GIBBS) (12 Victoria Sq, SW1), da of late Percy Cuthbert Quilter (*see* Quilter, Bt, colls):—
Veronica Clare, *b* 1950: *m* 1981, Julius von Mengershausen Lister, of 365 Wimbledon Park Rd, SW19, and has issue living, Marina Helen Clare von Mengershausen, *b* 1982. —— Pamela Mary Diana, *b* 1953: *m* 1979, Charles Adam Laurie Sebag-Montefiore of 21 Hazlewell Rd, SW15, and has issue living (*see* Magnus-Allcroft, Bt).

Issue of late Rt Hon Harold John Tennant, 6th son of 1st baronet, *b* 1865, *d* 1935: *m* 1st, 1889, Helen Elizabeth, who *d* 1892, da of Major Gordon Duff, of Drummuir, Banffshire; 2ndly, 1896, May Edith, CH, JP, who *d* 1946, da of late George Whitley Abraham, of Rathgar, co Dublin:—
(By 2nd *m*) Peter, *b* 1913; *ed* Eton, and Trin Coll, Camb (BA 1934, MA 1951): *m* 1938, Valerie, da of late John S. Nettlefold, of The Manor House, Bampton, Oxfordshire, and has issue living, Alison Valerie, *b* 1939: *m* 1962, Roger Leon Burnley, of 23 Marchmont Crescent, Edinburgh EH9 1HQ, and has issue living, Julian Lee *b* 1969, Andrea Adwoa *b* 1968, — Fiona, *b* 1940: *m* 1964, Neil Graham Douglas Snow, of Moor End, Invertrossachs, Callander, Perthshire, and has issue living, Justin Douglas Tennant *b* 1965, Jonathan Peter *b* 1968, Catriona Louisa *b* 1967, Kirsten Fiona *b* 1970, — Sheila, *b* 1946: *m* 1970, Edward Findlay Burnett, of Rhynaclach, Port of Menteith, Kippen, Perthshire, and has issue living, Joseph Andrew *b* 1976, Helen Sheila *b* 1978. *Residence* – 28 Stroan Rd, Armoy, Ballymoney, co Antrim BT53 8RY.

PREDECESSORS – (1) CHARLES Tennant, son of John Tennant, DL, JP, of St Rollox. Lanark, a descendant of John Tennant of Blairston, Ayrshire (temp 1635-1728), by his wife Jean McTaggart (temp 1669-1723); *b* 1823; MP for Glasgow (*L*) 1879-80, and for Peebles and Selkirkshire 1880-86; *cr* a *Baronet* 1885: *m* 1st, 1849, Emma, who *d* 1895, da of Richard Winsloe; 2ndly, 1898, Marguerite Agaranthe, who *d* 1943, having *m* 2ndly, 1907, Major Geoffrey Lubbock, who *d* 1932, da of late Col Charles Miles, of Burtonhill, Malmesbury; *d* 1906; *s* by his fourth son (2) EDWARD PRIAULX, 2nd Bt, *b* 1859; Lord-Lieut of Peebleshire; MP for Salisbury (*L*) Jan 1906 to Jan 1910; Lord High Commr to Gen Assembly for Church of Scotland 1911, 1912, 1913, and 1914: *cr Baron Glenconner*, of Glen, co Peebles (peerage of United Kingdom) 1911: *m* 1895, Pamela Geneviève Adelaide (who *d* 1928, having *m* 2ndly, 1922, the 1st Viscount Grey of Fallodon), da of late Hon Percy Scawen Wyndham; *d* 1920; *s* by his second son (3) CHRISTOPHER GREY, 2nd Baron, *b* 1899: *m* 1st, 1925 (*m diss* 1935), Pamela Winifred, who *d* 1989, da of Sir Richard Arthur Surtees Paget, 2nd Bt (*cr* 1886); 2ndly, 1935, Elizabeth, da of late Lt-Col Evelyn George Harcourt Powell, of 31 Hillgate Place, W8; *d* 1983; *s* by his eldest son (4) COLIN CHRISTOPHER PAGET, 3rd Baron and present peer.

GLENDEVON, BARON (Hope) (Baron UK 1964)

JOHN ADRIAN HOPE, PC, 1st Baron, 2nd (twin) son of the 2nd Marquess of Linlithgow; *b* 7 April 1912; *ed* Eton, and Ch Ch, Oxford (MA); Capt and temporary Maj Scots Guards (Reserve); Joint Parl Under-Sec of State for Foreign Affairs 1954-56, Parl Under-Sec of State for Commonwealth Relations 1956-57, Joint Parl Under-Sec for Scotland 1957-59, and Min of Works 1959-62; 1939-45 War in Norway and Italy (despatches); ERD (1988): MP for N Div of Midlothian and Peebles (*C*) 1945-50, and for Pentlands Div of Edinburgh 1950-64; *cr* PC 1959, and *Baron Glendevon*, of Midhope, co Linlithgow (peerage of UK) 1964: *m* 1948, Elizabeth, da of late William Somerset Maugham, CH, and formerly wife of Vincent Paravicini, and has issue.

My hope is not broken

Arms – Azure, on a chevron or between three bezants as many bay-leaves pale-ways vert. **Crest** – A broken sphere surmounted of a rainbow proper issuant from two bay-leaves slipped vert on either side of the sphere. **Supporters** – Two female figures denoting Hope, their hair dressed sable and braided vert, garnished or, richly vested Argent garnished of vert, and sustaining bendways in their exterior hands light lifeboat anchors with long shafts azure garnished with chains or, and over their exterior shoulders garlands of white lilies proper.
Residence – Mount Lodge, Mount Row, St Peter Port, Guernsey, C1.

SONS LIVING

Hon JULIAN JOHN SOMERSET, *b* 6 March 1950; *ed* Eton, and Ch Ch, Oxford; operatic producer.
Hon Jonathan Charles, *b* 1952; *ed* Eton.

GLENDYNE, BARON (Nivison) (Baron UK 1922, Bt UK 1914)

ROBERT NIVISON, 3rd Baron, and 3rd Baronet; *b* 27 Oct 1926; *s* 1967; *ed* Harrow; late Lt Grenadier Guards; 1939-45 War: *m* 1953, Elizabeth, yr da of late Sir Stephen Cecil Armitage, CBE, of Hawksworth Manor, Notts, and has issue.

Arms – Per chevron or and azure, in chief two eagles displayed of the second and in base an eagle rising of the first. **Crest** – Upon the battlements of a tower a wolf passsant sable, gorged with a collar and with line reflexed over the back or. **Supporters** – On either side a wolf sable, gorged with a collar with line reflexed over the back or, and charged on the shoulder with a saltire couped argent.
Residence – Craigeassie, by Forfar, Angus DD8 3SE. *Club* – City of London.

SON LIVING

Hon JOHN, *b* 18 Aug, 1960.

DAUGHTERS LIVING

Hon Linda, *b* 1954: *m* 1976, Dr Nikolaus Graf Hartig, of Heuberggasse 9, A-1170 Vienna, Austria, and has issue living, a son, *b* 1982, — a da, *b* 1980.
Hon Sarah Jane Moira, *b* 1957: *m* 1979, Ian Dreverman, of 2A Water St, Wahroonga, NSW 2076, Australia, and has issue living, a son, *b* 1984, — a son, *b* 1988, — Stephen, *b* 1990, — a da, *b* 1982.

The end proves actions

SISTER LIVING

Hon Gillian Wightman, *b* 1931: *m* 1953, Maj-Gen Peter Raymond Leuchars, CBE, late Welsh Guards, and has issue living, Christopher John Raymond, *b* 1956. *Residence* – 5 Chelsea Sq, SW3.

PREDECESSORS – (1) ROBERT Nivison, son of John Nivison, of Sanquhar, Dumfriesshire; *b* 1849; senior partner of R. Nivison and Co; *cr* a *Baronet* 1914, and *Baron Glendyne*, of Sanquhar, co Dumfries (peerage of United Kingdom) 1922: *m* 1877, Jane, who *d* 1918, da of John Wightman, of Sanquhar, Dumfriesshire; *d* 1930; *s* by his son (2) JOHN, 2nd Baron, *b* 1878; senior partner of R. Nivison & Co: *m* 1920, Ivy May, who *d* 1971, da of late J. Rose, of Bournemouth; *d* 1967; *s* by his son (3) ROBERT, 3rd Baron, and present peer.

GLENKINGLAS, BARONY OF (Noble) (Extinct 1984)

DAUGHTERS LIVING OF LIFE BARON

Hon Catharine Gina Amita, *b* 1943: *m* 1st, 1964, Peter Conrad Hamilton Vey; 2ndly, 1989, Denzil Robert Onslow How (*see* E Onslow, colls), and has issue (by 1st *m*).
Hon Marya Anne, *b* 1944: *m* 1969, Peter Egerton-Warburton, of Mulberry House, Bentworth, Hants, and has issue (*see* Grey-Egerton, Bt, colls).

Hon Anastasia Diana, *b* 1948: *m* 1967, Jonathan Sinclair Delap, of Little Armsworth, Alresford, Hants, and has issue living, James Robert Onslow, *b* 1969, — Michael Jonathan Sinclair, *b* 1972.
Hon Rebecca Juliet, *b* 1950: *m* 1973, John Richard Boyle, Lt Cdr RN, of Lickford House, Petworth, Sussex, and has issue (*see* E Cork and Orrery).

WIDOW LIVING OF LIFE BARON

ANNE (*Baroness Glenkinglas*) (Strone, Cairndow, Argyll; 7 Egerton Gdns, SW3), da of Sir Neville Arthur Pearson, 2nd Bt (cr 1916): *m* 1940, Baron Glenkinglas, PC (Life Baron), who *d* 1984.

Glenlivet, see Lord Strathavon and Glenlivet.

GLENTANAR, BARONY OF (Coats) (Extinct 1971)

DAUGHTER LIVING OF SECOND BARON

Hon (Margaret) Jean Dagbjørt, *b* 1928: *m* 1950 (*m diss* 1974), Hon James Michael Edward Bruce (*see* E Elgin and Kincardine). *Residences* – Juniper, 9 Golf Place, Aboyne, Aberdeenshire AB34 5GA; Flat 15, 35 Bryanston Sq, W1.

GLENTORAN, BARON (Dixon) (Baron UK 1939, Bt UK 1903)

By fidelity and constancy

DANIEL STEWART THOMAS BINGHAM DIXON, KBE, 2nd Baron and 4th Baronet; *b* 19 Jan 1912; *s* 1950; *ed* Eton and RMC; Lt-Col (ret) Gren Gds, and Hon Col 6th Bn RUR (TA) 1957-62; Lieut City of Belfast 1950-75, since when Lord-Lieut; 1939-45 War (despatches); CStJ; Member of House of Commons, NI (*U*) 1950-61; Parl Sec, Min of Commerce, NI, 1952-53, and Min of Commerce 1953-61; Min in Senate 1961-64 (Speaker of Senate 1964-72); PC (NI) 1953, KBE (Civil) 1973: *m* 1933, Lady Diana Wellesley, who *d* 1984, da of 3rd Earl Cowley, and has issue.

Arms – Or, on a chevron vair three billets of the first, on a chief crenellé gules a tower proper between two fleurs-de-lis or. **Crest** – A demi-lion rampant azure, charged on the shoulder with a cross patonce surrounded by a civic crown or. **Supporters** – Two war horses argent, unguled or, caparisoned proper, the shabraque sable, broidered of the second.
Residence – Drumadarragh House, Ballyclare, co Antrim. *Club* – Ulster.

SONS LIVING

Hon (THOMAS) ROBIN VALERIAN, CBE (Drumadarragh House, Ballyclare, co Antrim), *b* 21 April 1935; *ed* Eton; Maj Grenadier Guards; DL co Antrim; MBE (Civil) 1969, CBE (Civil) 1992: *m* 1st 1959 (*m diss* 1975), Rona Alice Gabrielle, da of Capt George Cecil Colville, CBE, RN (*see* V Colville of Culross, colls); 2ndly, 1979, Alwyn, da of Hubert A. Mason, of Grove Lodge, Donaghadee, co Down; 3rdly, 1990, Mrs Margaret Rainey, and has issue living (by 1st *m*), Daniel George (1 Deane House Cottage, Deane, nr Basingstoke, Hants RG25 3AR), *b* 1959: *m* 1983, Leslie Hope, da of Julian Hope Brooke, and has issue living, Anthony Thomas *b* 1987, Marcus Hope *b* 1989, — Andrew Wynne Valerian, *b* 1961; commn'd Gren Gds 1980: *m* 1991, Karen Elizabeth, only da of late Hugh Charles Straker, of Gaucin, Spain, — Patrick Anthony (26 Tildarg Rd, Ballyclare, co Antrim), *b* 1963: *m* 1988, Catharine M., yr da of Theo Willy, of S Petherton, Som.
Hon Peter Herbert (The Old Rectory, Yattendon, Newbury, Berks), *b* 1948: *m* 1975, Jane Blanch, da of Eric S. Cutler, of St Martins, Yattendon, Newbury, Berks, and has issue living, Louise Vyvyan Mary, *b* 1977, — Rose Erika Clare, *b* 1980.

DAUGHTER LIVING

Hon Clare Rosalind, *b* 1937: *m* 1965 (*m diss* 1980), Rudolph Ion Joseph Agnew (*see* Campbell, Bt, colls, cr 1815). *Residence* – 35 St Peter's Sq, W6.

SISTERS LIVING

Hon Angela Ierne Evelyn, *b* 1907: *m* 1st, 1929, Lieut-Com (E) Peter Ross, RN, who was *ka* 1940 (*see* B de Ros); 2ndly, 1943, Lieut-Col Trevor L. Horn, 16th/5th Lancers, who *d* 1966, and has issue living (by 1st *m*) (*see* B de Ros), — (by 2nd *m*) June Victoria Langdale, *b* 1946. *Residence* – Luckington Court, Chippenham, Wilts.
Hon Patricia Clare, *b* 1919: *m* 1940, Lieut-Com Adam McLeod Mackinnon, RN, Fleet Air Arm, and has issue living, Michael Bingham, *b* 1941; *ed* Wellington Coll, — Ian Dixon, *b* 1944; *ed* Wellington Coll, — Diana Patricia, *b* 1950: *m* 1978, Richard A. B. Lynes, of Penn House, Bannerleigh Rd, Bristol, — Teresa Claire, *b* 1955: *m* 1993, Raymond Crossen, son of J. Crossen, — Zara Lavinia, *b* 1959: *m* 19—, William Brogden. *Residence* – 7c Chisbury Close, Forest Park, Bracknell, Berks.

PREDECESSORS – (1) *Rt Hon* DANIEL Dixon, MP, son of late Thomas Dixon, of Larne, co Antrim, *b* 1844; was High Sheriff of co Down 1896, MP for N Belfast (*C*) 1905-07, Mayor of Belfast 1892, and Lord Mayor 1893, 1901-3, 1905-6, and 1906-7; *cr* a *Baronet* 1903: *m* 1st, 1867, Lizzie, who *d* 1868, da of late James Agnew, of Belfast; 2ndly, 1870, Annie, who *d*

1918 da of James Shaw, of Belfast; *d* 1907, *s* by his el son **(2)** *Sir* Thomas James, 2nd Bt, *b* 1868; High Sheriff co Antrim 1912, and of co Down 1913, HM's Lieut for Co of City of Blefast, and a Member of Senate of N Ireland 1924-50: *m* 1906, *Dame* Edith Stewart, DBE, da of late Stewart Clark, of Dundas Castle, Linlithgowshire; *d* (May) 1950; *s* by his brother **(3)** *Rt Hon* Herbert, PC, OBE, 3rd Bt; *b* 1880; High Sheriff of co Kildare 1916; Capt 6th Inniskilling Dragoons; S Africa 1899-1902, European War 1914-19 with Remounts; Ch Whip of Unionist Party in Parliament of N Ireland, and Parliamentary Sec to Min of Finance 1921-42, and Min of Agriculture 1942-3; sat as MP for Pottinger Div of Belfast (*U*) 1918 to 1922, and for Belfast, E Div 1922 to 1930; also elected for Belfast, E Div in Parliament of N Ireland 1921 and 1925, and for Bloomfield Div of Belfast 1929, 1945 and 1949; *cr Baron Glentoran*, of Ballyalloly, co Down (peerage of United Kingdom) 1939: *m* 1905, Hon Emily Ina Florence Bingham, who *d* 1957, da of 5th Baron Clanmorris, *d* (July) 1950; *s* by his son **(4)** Daniel Stewart Thomas Bingham, KBE, 2nd Baron and present peer; also 4th baronet.

Glentworth, Viscount; son of Earl of Limerick.

GLOUCESTER, DUKE OF, see Royal Family.

GODBER, BARONY OF (Godber) (Extinct 1976)

DAUGHTERS LIVING OF FIRST BARON

Hon Joyce Violet, *b* 1917: *m* 1938, Andrew Agnew, and has issue living, Heather Elizabeth, *b* 1940: *m* 1966, Dr Charles John Roderick Lewis, of Old Rectory, Bodiam, Robertsbridge, Sussex, and has issue living, Henry Roderick Andrew *b* 1968, Richard John *b* 1972, — Susan Joyce, *b* 1942: *m* 1966, David Gwynder Lewis, of 57 Victoria Rd, W8 5RH, and has issue living, George David Gwynder *b* 1972, Alexandra Joy Gwynder *b* 1969, — Sally Caroline, *b* 1949: *m* 1983, Tom William Mahony Jaine, of Allaleigh House, Blackawton, S. Devon, and has issue living, Matilda Aileen *b* 1985, Frances Belle Violet *b* 1987. *Residence* – Sweethaws Farm, Crowborough, Sussex.
Hon Daphne Joan, *b* 1923: *m* 1942, Archibald Ian Scott Debenham, DFC, and has issue living, Michael George Scott (Homefield, Tandridge Lane, Lingfield, Surrey), *b* 1943: *m* 1st, 1966 (*m diss* 1980), Janine Elizabeth, da of Anthony L. Davies, of Crockham Hill, Edenbridge, Kent; 2ndly, 1981, Roberta, da of Luigi Courir, of Genova, Italy, and has issue living (by 1st *m*), Sarah Elizabeth *b* 1968, Anna Caroline *b* 1970, Tessa Kate *b* 1974, — Peter Frederick Scott (30 Ladbroke Grove, W8 11BQ), *b* 1957: *m* 1983, Sarah, da of A. J. Webster, of Claverley, Shropshire, and has issue living, Hannah Rose *b* 1989, Letitia Jane *b* 1991, — Jane Scott (Briars Orchard, Limpsfield Chart, Oxted, Surrey), *b* 1945: *m* 1st, 1966 (*m diss* 1979), Hamish John Benson Skinner; 2ndly, 1979, Geoffrey Dove, and has issue living (by 1st *m*), Paul Andrew *b* 1968, Hugh Antony *b* 1972, Lucy Jane *b* 1969, — Marye Scott, *b* 1954: *m* 1986, David Warren, of 40 Pursers Cross Rd, SW6. *Residence* – Bowerland Farm, Bowerland Lane, Lingfield, Surrey, RH7 6DF.

GODBER OF WILLINGTON, BARONY OF (Godber) (Extinct 1980)

SONS LIVING OF LIFE BARON

Hon Richard Thomas (Hall Farm, Little Linford, Bucks), *b* 1938; DL Bucks 1993: *m* 1962, Candida, da of late Albert Edward Parrish, and has issue.
Hon Andrew Robin (Folly Barn, Folly Lane, Claxton, Norwich NR14 7AX), *b* 1943: *m* 1969, Genevieve, da of late Kenneth Parrish, and has issue.

WIDOW LIVING OF LIFE BARON

Miriam (*Baroness Godber of Willington*) (Manor Cottage, Willington, nr Bedford), da of Haydon Sanders, of Lowestoft; *m* 1936, Baron Godber of Willington, PC (Life Baron), who *d* 1980, when the title became ext.

GODDARD, BARONY OF (Goddard) (Extinct 1971)

DAUGHTER LIVING OF LIFE BARON

Hon (Janet) Margaret (*Hon Lady Sachs*), *b* 1909: *m* 1934, Rt Hon Sir Eric Sachs, MBE, who *d* 1979, and has issue living, Richard Edwin Goddard, *b* 1935; *ed* Shrewsbury, and Ch Ch Oxford (MA), — Katharine Frances Goddard (*Lady Harman*), *b* 1939: *m* 1st, 1965, George Pulay, who *d* 1981; 2ndly, 1987, as his 2nd wife, Hon Mr Justice (Sir Jeremiah LeRoy) Harman, and has issue living (by 1st *m*), Jessica Mary *b* 1966, Laura Katharine *b* 1968. *Residence* – Antioch House West, Rotten Row, Lewes, E Sussex BN7 1TN.

GOFF OF CHIEVELEY, BARON (Goff) (Life Baron 1986)

Robert Lionel Archibald Goff, PC, DCL, son of late Lt-Col Lionel Trevor Goff, RA, of Queen's House, Monk Sherborne, Basingstoke; *b* 12 Nov 1926; *ed* Eton, and New Coll, Oxford (MA 1953, DCL 1971), Hon

DLitt City 1977, Reading 1990, Hon LLD Buckingham 1990, and London 1990; served in Scots Guards 1945-48; Bar Inner Temple 1951, Bencher 1975, QC 1967; Fellow and Tutor, Lincoln Coll, Oxford 1951-55; High Steward Oxford Univ since 1990, Hon Fell Lincoln Coll and New Coll, Oxford; FBA 1987; practiced at bar 1956-75, a Recorder 1974-75, Judge of High Court of Justice (Queen's Bench Div) 1975-82, a Lord Justice of Appeal 1982-85, a Lord Justice of Appeal in Ordinary since 1986; Chm Council of Legal Educn 1976-82, Board of Studies 1970-76, Common Professional Examination Bd 1976-78; Hon Prof of Legal Ethics, Univ of Birmingham, 1980-81; Maccabean Lectr, British Acad, 1983; Chm British Inst of Internat and Comparative Law since 1986, Chm Court of London Univ 1986-91, Pres Chartered Inst of Arbitrators 1986-91; Member Gen Council of the Bar 1971-74, Senate of Inns of Court and Bar 1974-82 (Chm Law Reform and Procedure Cttee 1974-76); *cr* Kt 1975, PC 1982, and *Baron Goff of Chieveley*, of Chieveley, co Berks (Life Baron) 1986: *m* 1953, Sarah, elder da of Capt Gerald Roger Cousins, DSC, RN, of Child Okeford, Dorset, and has issue (with one son dec'd).

𝔄rms – Az a chevron between two fleurs-de-lis in chief and a lion rampant in base or. Crest – A squirrel sejant proper. Motto – fier sans tache.
Address – House of Lords, SW1.

SON LIVING

Hon Robert Thomas Alexander, *b* 1966.

DAUGHTERS LIVING

Hon Katharine Isobel, *b* 1959.
Hon Juliet Mary Constance, *b* 1961: *m* 1990, Seán D. Jackson, only son of David Jackson, of Armscote House, Stratford-upon-Avon, Warwicks, and has issue living, Anna Katharine, *b* 1992.

GOODMAN, BARON (Goodman) (Life Baron 1965)

To understand all is to pardon all

ARNOLD ABRAHAM GOODMAN, CH, son of Joseph Goodman, *b* 21 Aug 1913; *ed* Cambridge Univ (MA, LLB); Fellow of Univ Coll, London; Solicitor 1936; Founder and Consultant Messrs Goodman, Derrick & Co, 90 Fetter Lane, EC4; Chm of Arts Council of Gt Britain 1965-72; Chm of Council of Newspaper Publishers Assocn 1970-76; Master of Univ Coll, Oxford 1976-86; Chm Housing Corpn and National Building Agency 1973-77, Vice-Chm British Council 1976-91; 1939-45 War as Maj; *cr Baron Goodman*, of City of Westminster (Life Baron) 1965, and CH 1972.

𝔄rms – Azure a chevron wavy argent between in chief two lyres and in base a torch or enflamed proper. Crest – On a cap of maintenance gules turned up ermine two hands couped at the wrists and clasped proper. Supporters – *Dexter*, a carrier pigeon, and *sinister* a seagull proper, about the neck of each a chain suspended therefrom a lyre or.
Address – 90 Fetter Lane, London EC4A 1EQ.

GOOLD, BARON (Goold) (Life Baron 1987)

JAMES DUNCAN GOOLD, son of late John Goold, by his wife Janet Agnes, da of William Kirkland, of New Zealand; *b* 28 May 1934; *ed* Belmont House, and Glasow Acad; D Univ Strathclyde 1994; DL Renfrewshire 1985, Hon FCIOB 1979, Hon FFB 1983; CA 1958, Dir Mactaggart & Mickel Ltd since 1965 (and Chm since 1994), Gibson & Goold Ltd since 1978, American Trust plc since 1984, and Edinburgh Oil and Gas plc since 1986; Pres Scottish Building Contractors Assoc 1971, and Scottish Building Employers Fedn 1977; Chm CBI Scotland 1981-83; Hon Treas Scottish Conservative Party 1981-83 (Chm 1983-89), Hon Pres Eastwood Conservative Assocn since 1978; Gov Belmont House Sch 1972-84, Glasgow Acad 1982-89, Hon Gov since 1994, and Paisley Coll of Technology 1981-87; Chm of Court Strathclyde Univ since 1993; *cr* Kt 1983, and *Baron Goold*, of Waterfoot, in the District of Eastwood (Life Baron) 1987: *m* 1959, Sheena, who *d* 1992, da of late Alexander David Paton, OBE, of Troon, Ayrshire, and has issue.

𝔄rms – per chevron argent and chequy azure and of the first, on a chevron embattled gules between two trefoils vert in chief and a hurt charged of a crescent of the first in base, two silver fern leaves also of the first. Crest – a demi lion rampant argent charged on the shoulder of a trefoil vert. Motto –
Build for the right.
Residence – Sandyknowe, Waterfoot, Clarkston, Glasgow G76 8RN.

SONS LIVING

Hon Michael Kirkland, *b* 1966: *m* 1994, Giannina P., yst da of Teobaldo Moy, of Selsidro, Lima, Peru.
Hon James David, *b* 1968.

DAUGHTER LIVING

Hon Anna Jane, *b* 1972.

Gordon, Duke of, see Duke of Richmond and Gordon.

GORDON-WALKER, BARONY OF (Gordon Walker) (Extinct 1980)

SONS LIVING OF LIFE BARON

Hon Alan Rudolf, *b* 1946; *ed* Wellington Coll and Ch Ch, Oxford (MA); Man Dir Pan Books Ltd: *m* 1976, Louise Frances Amy, el da of Gen Sir Charles Henry Pepys Harington, GCB, CBE, DSO, MC, and has issue. *Residence* – 2 Umbria St, SW15 5DP.
Hon Robin Chrestien, (twin), *b* 1946; *ed* Wellington Coll and E Anglia Univ (BA); Publicity Exec, Dept of Employment: *m* 1st, 1974 (*m diss* 1985), June Patricia, da of Patrick Barr, of Eversholt, Beds; 2ndly, 1987, Magally, da of Gilberto Flores, of Valencia, Venezuela, and has issue by 1st and 2nd *m*. *Residence* – 16 Hexham Rd, SE27 9ED.

DAUGHTERS LIVING BY LIFE BARON

Hon Judith Margaret, *b* 1936; *ed* N London Collegiate Sch, Lady Margaret Hall, Oxford (MA), and Univ Coll, London, (BA, PhD); Lecturer in Psychology, Birkbeck Coll, Univ of London, 1966-76, since when Prof of Psychology, Open Univ: *m* 1st, 1957 (*m diss* 1975), Graham Carleton Greene, CBE, son of late Sir (Hugh) Carleton Green, KCMG, OBE; 2ndly 1981, Prof Norman William Dawson Gowar. *Residence* – 3 Canonbury Lane, N1.
Hon Caroline, *b* 1937: *ed* Cheltenham Ladies' Coll, and Lady Margaret Hall, Oxford (MA); Head of Food and Sciences Unit, Nat Economic Development Office: *m* 1960, David Brierley, of Old Farm, Harthall Lane, King's Langley, Herts, and has issue. *Residence* – La Veille Ferme, St Germain des Belves, Belves, Dordogne 24170, France.
Hon Ann Marguerite GORDON-WALKER (1230 University Bay Drive, Madison, Wisconsin 53705, USA), *b* 1944; *ed* N London Collegiate Sch, Queen's Coll, Dundee, Univ of St Andrews (BSc), and Oxford Univ (D Phil); Administrator, Biophysics Laboratory, Univ of Wisconsin-Madison, USA; has resumed maiden name: *m* 1968 (*m diss* 1983), Laurence Andrew Ball, and has issue.

WIDOW LIVING OF LIFE BARON

AUDREY MURIEL (*Baroness Gordon-Walker*) (Flat 105 Frobisher House, Dolphin Sq, SW1V 3LL), da of Norman Andrew Rudolf, of Hopewell, Jamaica: *m* 1934, Rt Hon Lord Gordon-Walker, CH (Life Baron), who *d* 1980.

GORE-BOOTH, BARONY OF (Gore-Booth) (Extinct 1984)

For widow, sons, and daughters of late Baron Gore-Booth (Life Baron) *see* Gore-Booth, Bt, colls.

GORELL, BARON (Barnes) (Baron UK 1909)

TIMOTHY JOHN RADCLIFFE BARNES, 4th Baron; *b* 2 Aug 1927; *s* 1963; *ed* Eton, and New Coll, Oxford, Bar Inner Temple 1951, formerly Lieut Rifle Bde; an Exec, Royal Dutch and Shell Group 1959-84: *m* 1954, Joan Marion, yr da of late John Edmund Collins, MC, of Sway, Hants, and has two adopted das.

Arms – Azure, two lions passant guardant ermine each holding in the dexter paw a sprig of oak slipped or, between three annulets in pale argent. **Crest** – In front of a cubit arm in armour, the hand grasping a broken sword all proper, the wrist encircled by a wreath of oak or, five annulets interlaced and fesseways argent. **Supporters** – On either side, a ram proper charged on the shoulder with two annulets interlaced azure.
Residence – 4 Roehampton Gate, SW15.

You may break, you shall not bend me

ADOPTED DAUGHTERS LIVING

Susan Elizabeth Gorell, *b* 1958: *m* 1985, Robin H. A. Clark, elder son of J. A. Clark, and has issue living, Kyle Hendrik Gorell, *b* 1988. *Residence* – 39 Purley Oaks Rd, Croydon, Surrey CR2 0NW.
Jennifer Gorell, *b* 1960: *m* 1986, David James Michael Dally, elder son of B. J. M. Dally, and has issue living, Thomas, *b* 1992, — Samuel, *b* 1992 (triplet), — Megan Elizabeth, *b* 1991, — Kate, *b* 1992 (triplet). *Residence* – 72 Grove Av, Hanwell, W7 3SE.

BROTHER LIVING

Hon RONALD ALEXANDER HENRY, *b* 28 June 1931; *ed* Harrow, and New Coll, Oxford; formerly Lieut Roy Fusiliers, seconded King's African Rifles Capt Roy Northumberland Fus (TA); former Public Relations Officer P & O—Orient Lines; formerly Senior Partner of Stockton & Barnes, Estate Agents: *m* 1957, Gillian Picton, yst da of late Picton Hughes-Jones, of Henstridge, Somerset, and has issue living, John Picton Gorell, *b* 1959, — Elizabeth Gail, *b* 1961. *Residence* – Fernbank, Mingoose, Mount Hawke, nr Truro, Cornwall.

PREDECESSORS – (1) *Rt Hon Sir* JOHN GORELL Barnes, PC (Knt), el son of late Henry Barnes, of Liverpool; *b* 1848; a Judge of the Probate, Divorce, and Admiralty Div of the High Court of Justice 1892-1905, and Pres thereof 1905-9; *cr Baron Gorell*, of Brampton, co Derby (peerage of United Kingdom) 1909: *m* 1881, Mary Humpston, who *d* 1918, da of late Thomas Mitchell, of West Arthurlie; *d* 1913; *s* by his el son (2) HENRY GORELL, DSO, 2nd Baron, *b* 1882; Major RFA (F); *ka* 1917; *s* by his brother (3) RONALD GORELL, CBE, MC, 3rd Baron; *b* 1884; Under-Sec of State for Air and Vice-Pres of Air Council 1921-2, Editor of *Cornhill Magazine* 1933-9; Chm of Prime Min's Cttees on Carlton House Terr 1933-40, and on Regents Park Terr 1946-7; Founder Royal Army Educn Corps: *m* 1922, Maud Elizabeth Furse, who *d* 1954, da of late Alexander Nelson Radcliffe, of 45 Kensington Sq, W8; *d* 1963; *s* by his el son (4) TIMOTHY JOHN RADCLIFFE, 4th Baron and present peer.

Gormanston, Baron, title of Viscount Gormanston on Roll of HL.

GORMANSTON, VISCOUNT (Preston) (Viscount I 1478, Baron I 1365-70) Sits as Baron (UK 1868)

JENICO NICHOLAS DUDLEY PRESTON, 17th Viscount, and Premier Viscount of Ireland; *b* 19 Nov 1939; *s* 1940: *m* 1974, Eva Landzianowski, who *d* 1984, and has issue.

Arms – Or, on a chief sable, three crescents of the first. **Crest** – On a chapeau gules turned up ermine, a fox passant proper. **Supporters** – *Dexter*, a fox proper; *sinister* a lion rampant proper, armed and langued gules.
Residence – Dalmeny House, 9 Thurloe Place, SW7 2RY.

Without stain

SONS LIVING

Hon JENICO FRANCIS TARA, *b* 30 April 1974.
Hon William Luke, *b* 1976.

COLLATERAL BRANCHES LIVING

Issue of late Hon Robert Francis Hubert Preston, 2nd son of 15th Viscount, *b* 1915, *d* (7 Jan) 1992; assumed by deed poll 1947 the additional surname of Shaw which he subsequently relinquished: *m* 1st, 1941 (*m diss* 1955), Jean Helen, only child of late Capt Charles Henry Shaw, 15th Hus, of Bourton Hall, Rugby, Warwicks; 2ndly, 1970, Mrs Daphne Helen Anne Bradish-Ellames, who *d* (9 Dec) 1992, only da of late Col Robert Hanbury Brudenell-Bruce, DSO (*see* M Ailesbury, colls):—
(By 1st *m*) Jennifer Anne SHAW PRESTON, *b* 1946: *m* 1977, István Siklóssy von Pernesz, and has issue living, Georgina Isabella Maria, *b* 1977, — Stephanie Victoria Maria, *b* 1980. *Residence* – 390 Ave de Tervuren, B-1150, Brussels.

Grandchildren of late Lt-Col Hon Richard Martin Peter Preston, DSO (infra):—

Issue of late Lt-Cmdr Christopher Edward Martin Preston, OBE, DSC, RN, *b* 1918, *d* 1992: *m* 1949, Joy Celeste Agatha, who *d* 1989, da of late Maj Hugh Davidson, IA:—
Philip Martin Jenico (Washbrook House, Aston-le-Walls, Daventry, Northants), *b* 1950; *ed* Downside: *m* 1983, Anita Cayas-Peña, and has issue living, Edmund Philip Jenico, *b* 1984. ——— Stephen Richard Hugh, *b* 1952; *ed* Downside. ——— †Matthew Christopher Edward, *b* 1955; *d* 1993. ——— Anthony Thomas Patrick, *b* 1964. ——— Camilla Mary Lucy, *b* 1959.

Issue of late Lt-Col Hon Richard Martin Peter Preston, DSO, 2nd son of 14th Viscount, *b* 1884, *d* 1965: *m* 1st, 1908, Belle, who *d* 1936, da of late Frederick Harcourt Hamblin; 2ndly, 1943, Edith Sheilah, who *d* 1951, da of late Reginald de Crecy Steel, of Walton-on-Thames, and widow of Lt-Cer John Hay Forbes, DSO, RN (*see* Stuart-Forbes, Bt colls):—
(By 1st *m*) Ismay Elizabeth, *b* 1912: *m* 1942, Denzil Robert Clarke, of Puffins, who *d* 1986, 8 South Drive, Wokingham, Berks, and has issue living, Michael Richard Neil, *b* 1946: *m* 1973, Francine Van Schepdael, and has issue living, Geraldine Anne Danielle *b* 1973, Muriel Louise Elizabeth *b* 1978, — Jennifer Robérta Anne, *b* 1944: *m* 1968, Simon Anthony Aldridge, of Gt Bowsers, Little Walden, Saffron Walden, and has issue living, Victoria Helmore Elizabeth *b* 1969, — Francesca Elizabeth Anne, *b* 1951: *m* 1976, David Anselm Bull, of 33 Alwyne Rd, SW19 7AB, and has issue living, Edward Anselm Anthony *b* 1981, James Frederick Simon *b* 1983, Alice Elizabeth *b* 1978, Georgina Victoria *b* 1988, Elizabeth Mary *b* 1990. ——— Diana Mary Bruce (Old Sun House, Riseley, Berks), *b* 1914: *m* 1939, John Francis Colledge, who *d* 1954, and has issue living, Simon John (The Well Cottage, Mattingley, Basingstoke), *b* 1940: *m* 1966, Robina Elizabeth Anne, da of late H. L. Light, of Whitewater Cottage, Mattingley, Basingstoke, and has issue living, Thomas Andrew John *b* 1967, Patrick Richard *b* 1968, Henry Charles Valentine *b* 1972, Anna Elizabeth *b* 1980, — Robert Patrick Francis, *b* 1950: *m* 1974, Dena, da of late D. Jones, of Southport, Lancs, and has issue living, James Edward Daniel *b* 1978, Matthew William John *b* 1981, Kate Elizabeth Jane *b* 1976, — Sarah Virginia Mary, *b* 1942, — Judith Cecilia Anne, *b* 1953: *m* 1974, James Calderbank, and has issue living, William Michael *b* 1975, Rachel Claire Joanna *b* 1978. ——— Ursula Anne Marie, *b* 1923: *m* 1952, Cdr Charles Sheridan Moseley, RN, who *d* 1993, of Kilmaloda House, Timoleague, co Cork, and has issue living, Dominic Richard Sheridan, *b* 1955: *m* 1987, Kathryn Fiona, da of late John McLean, and has issue living, James William Sheridan *b* 1988, Edward John Wallace *b* 1990, Charlotte Elizabeth Anne *b* 1992, — Christopher John Wallace, *b* 1957: *m* 1989, Loretta Genevieve, da of Alexander Millar-Brown, of Norwich, — Justin Robert Patrick, *b* 1962, — Virginia Clare Diana, *b* 1954: *m* 1987, Anthony Cyril McGough, son of late John McGough, of Manchester, and has issue living, John Sheridan *b* 1991, Lucy Margaret Anne *b* 1988, Francesca Mary *b* 1989, — Lucy Elizabeth Anne, *b* 1960; Sister Teresa of the Holy Child, Carmelite Convent, Notting Hill, W8.

Issue of late Capt Hon Hubert Anthony John Preston, MC, 3rd son of 14th Viscount, *b* 1885, *d* 1940: *m* (Jan) 1917, Mary, who *d* 1971, da of late Rt Hon William Kenny, a Judge of High Court in Ireland, and widow of R. S. Pringle, Queen's Regt:—
Georgina Ismay Mary, *b* 1919: *m* 1948, Alfred Stanley Head. *Residence* – Hardimans Cottage, High Street, Queen Camel, Yeovil, Somerset BA22 7NE.

Grandchildren of late Capt Hon Charles Preston, 5th son of 12th Viscount:—
Issue of late Charles Arthur Preston, *b* 1857, *d* 1924: *m* 1889, Miriam, who *d* 1936, da of late Hon Charles Alleyne, formerly MP for Quebec, and a ME:—
Arthur, *b* 1902: *m* 1928, Marion Blair, da of late John Dean, and has issue living, Richard Dean, *b* 1929. ——— Hubert Philip, *b* 1905: *m* 1938, Marie Hester, da of Michale Joseph Aberne, QC, and has issue living, Anthony Ernest Michael, *b* 1938, — Ronald Thomas Edward, *b* 1940, — Andrea Margaret, *b* 1941, — Michelle Joan Adrienne, *b* 1944, — Ruth Jocelyn Vickie, — *b* 1945, — Louise Marie Isabel, *b* 1946. ——— Oswald, *b* 1907.

PREDECESSORS – (1) *Sir* Robert de Preston (knighted in the field by Lionel, Duke of Clarence, 1361), Lord of Preston in Lancashire, and sometime Lord High Chancellor of Ireland: *m* Margaret, only da of Walter de Bermingham, of Kells; *cr Lord Gormanston* (peerage of Ireland) about 1365-70; *s* by his son (2) CHRISTOPHER; *s* by his son (3) CHRISTOPHER; *s* by his son (4) *Sir* ROBERT Preston, *Knt*, Dep to Sir John Dynham, Lord Chancellor of Ireland, and during his minority to Richard, Duke of York, Dep of Ireland; *cr Viscount Gormanston* (peerage of Ireland) 1478; sat in the Parliaments of 1490 and 1493; *s* by his son (5) WILLIAM, 2nd Viscount; Dep to Lord Treasurer of Ireland 1493, and Lord Justice of Ireland 1525; *s* by his son (6) JENICO, 3rd Viscount; sat in Parliament 1559; *d* 1560; *s* by his son (7) CHRISTOPHER, 4th Viscount; sat in Parliament 1580; *d* 1599; *s* by his son (8) JENICO, 5th Viscount; sat in Parliament 1613; *s* by his son (9) NICHOLAS, 6th Viscount; *s* by his el son (10) JENICO, 7th Viscount; for his adherence to James II was indicted for high treason and outlawed 1691; *s* by his brother (11) JENICO, 8th Viscount *de jure*; *s* by his brother (12) ANTHONY, 9th Viscount *de jure*; *s* by his son (13) JENICO, 12th Viscount; having successfully instituted proceedings for the removal of the outlawry of Jenico, 7th Viscount, was summoned to take his seat in the Irish House of Peers 1800; *d* 1860; *s* by his son (16) EDWARD ANTHONY JOHN, 13th Viscount, *b* 1796; High Sheriff of Dublin 1845; *cr Baron Gormanston* (peerage of United Kingdom) 1868: *m* 1836, Lucretia, da of late William Charles Jerningham, next brother of 8th Baron Stafford, *d* 1876; *s* by his son (17) JENICO WILLIAM JOSEPH, GCMG 14th Viscount, *b* 1837; Chamberlain to Lord-Lieut of Ireland (Duke of Abercorn, KG) 1866-8, Gov and Com-in-Ch of Leeward Islands 1885-7, of British Guiana 1887-93, and Gov of Tasmania 1893-1900: *m* 1st, 1861, Hon Ismay Louisa Ursula Bellew, who *d* 1875, da of 1st Baron Bellew; 2ndly, 1878, Georgina, who *d* 1932, da of late Peter Connellan, of Coolmore, Kilkenny; *d* 1907; *s* by his el son (18) JENICO EDWARD JOSEPH, 15th Viscount, *b* 1879: *m* 1911, Eileen (who *d* 1964, having *m* 2ndly, 1934, John Black Atkins), da of late Lt-Gen Rt Hon Sir William Francis Butler, GCB; *d* 1925; *s* by his son (19) JENICO WILLIAM RICHARD, 16th Viscount, *b* 1914; acting Capt KOYLI: *m* 1939, Pamela (who *d* 1975, having *m* 2ndly, 1943, Maurice Bernard O'Connor, who *d* 1961), da of late Capt Edward Dudley Hanly (*see* E Denbigh, 1973-74 Edn); *ka* 1940; *s* by his son (20) JENICO NICHOLAS DUDLEY, 17th Viscount and present peer; also Baron Gormanston (peerage of Ireland 1365-70, and of UK 1868).

GORMLEY, BARONY OF (Gormley) (Extinct 1993)

SON LIVING OF LIFE BARON

Hon Francis Edward, *b* 1938: *m* 1961, Barbara, da of John Garner.

DAUGHTER LIVING

Hon Winifred, *b* 1940: *m* 1960, Arthur Evans.

WIDOW LIVING OF LIFE BARON

SARAH ELLEN (*Baroness Gormley*), da of Levi Mather, of Ashton-in-Makerfield: *m* 1937, Baron Gormley, OBE (Life Baron), who *d* 1993.

GORONWY-ROBERTS, BARONY OF (Roberts) (Ext 1981)

SON LIVING OF LIFE BARON

Hon Owen Dafydd, *b* 1946: *m* 1st, 1979, Milana Majka Bartonova, el da of Dr M. M. Jelinek, of London; 2ndly, 1987, Sharon Jennifer, da of Terence Taylor, of Duncan, BC, Canada.

DAUGHTER LIVING OF LIFE BARON

Hon Ann Elisabeth, *b* 1947. *Residence* – Plas Newydd, Pwllheli, Gwynedd.

WIDOW LIVING OF LIFE BARON

MARIAN ANN (*Baroness Goronwy-Roberts*) (Plas Newydd, Pwllheli, Gwynedd), yr da of David Evans, of Tresalem, Aberdare: *m* 1942, Baron Goronwy-Roberts, PC (Life Baron), who *d* 1981.

GORT, VISCOUNT (Vereker) (Viscount I 1816)

Truth conquers

COLIN LEOPOLD PRENDERGAST VEREKER, 8th Viscount, *b* 21 June 1916; *s* 1975; *ed* Sevenoaks; Lt Cdr RNVR; JP of Castletown, Isle of Man 1962; Member of House of Keyes Isle of Man Govt 1966-71; Dir Royal Skandia, IoM, Invesco Fund Managers, IoM, Euronav, IoM, and Eurofish, IoM; 1939-45 War (despatches): *m* 1946, Bettine Mary Mackenzie, da of late Godfrey Green, of Douglas, and formerly wife of Arthur Henry Jarand, and has issue.

Arms – Quarterly: 1st and 4th azure, on a chevron or, a chaplet vert, *Vereker*; 2nd and 3rd gules, a saltire vairy or and azure, *Prendergast*. **Crest** – Out of mural crown gules, a stag's head proper. **Supporters** – *Dexter*, a lion proper; *sinister*, an heraldic antelope proper, each gorged with a plain collar gules, rimmed and chained or, chain reflexed over the back.
Residence – Westwood, The Crofts, Castletown, Isle of Man.

SONS LIVING

Hon FOLEY ROBERT STANDISH PRENDERGAST, *b* 24 Oct 1951; *ed* Harrow: *m* 1st, 1979 (*m diss* 1987), Julie Denise, only da of D. W. Jones, of Ballasalla, Isle of Man; 2ndly, 1991, Sharon Lyn, da of Arnold Quayle.
Hon Nicholas Leopold Prendergast, *b* 1954, *ed* Harrow: *m* 1985, Nicola F., yst da of Michael W. Pitt, of Lias Cottage, Compton Dundon, Somerton, Somerset TA11 6PF.

DAUGHTER LIVING

Hon Elizabeth Jane VEREKER (Fruit Lawn House, Abbeyleix, co Laois; Green Hurst, Grove Mount, Ramsey, IoM), *b* 1948: *m* 1988, Michael L. Marshall, son of late A. E. Marshall, of Baldrine, Isle of Man; has issue living, Jason Colin VEREKER, *b* 1974, — Sarah Jayne VEREKER, *b* 1976.

COLLATERAL BRANCHES LIVING

Grandchildren of late Capt Hon Foley Charles Prendergast Vereker RN, 2nd son of 4th Viscount:—
Issue of late Standish Henry Prendergast Vereker, DCM, *b* 1878, *d* 1953: *m* 1908, Eleanor Elizabeth, who *d* 1957, el da of late Henry Bott, OBE, MRCS, of Washenden Manor, Biddenden, Kent:—
Daphne Eleanor, *b* 1910: *m* 1933, Com Sydney Arthur Moorhouse Else, OBE, RN (ret), who *d* 1979, and has issue living, Patrick Arthur Henry (39 Graemsdyke Rd, East Sheen, SW14), *b* 1934: *m* 1965, Jane Ann Ickringill, and has issue living, Henry Patrick Arthur *b* 1979, Sarah-Jane *b* 1966, Sophia Frances *b* 1969, — Nigel Christopher John (17 The Avenue, Hambrook, Chichester, Sussex ME9 8LB), *b* 1939: *m* 1972, Sandra Whittaker, and has issue living, Lisa Catherine *b* 1975, Fiona Jane *b* 1976, — Oliver Francis (The Hollies, Oad St, Borden, Sittingbourne, Kent ME9 8LB), *b* 1948: MB, BS: *m* 1972, Elizabeth Holman, and has issue living, Timothy Stephen *b* 1974, Christopher John *b* 1976, — Marion Elizabeth, *b* 1940: *m* 1963, Lt-Cdr Peter Russell Gordon-Smith, RN (ret) of Lower Farm, Up Marden, nr Chichester, W Sussex PO18 9LA, and has issue living, Russell Guy Morris (Waters Edge, The Gardens, W Ashling, nr Chichester, W Sussex) *b* 1964: *m* 1989, Fiona Rutland, David Mark *b* 1968, Louise Ann *b* 1965: *m* 1992, Michael Craig Duffy, of 1 More Place Cottages, Wonham Lane, Betchworth, Surrey RH13 7AD (and has issue living, Matthew Peter Michael *b* 1993). *Residence* – 139 Brook Gdns, Emsworth, Hants PO10 7LL.
Issue of late Maurice Charles Prendergast Vereker, MC, *b* 1884, *d* 1963: *m* 1928, Winifred Joan, who *d* 1982, da of late Alberic Arthur Twisleton-Wykeham-Fiennes (*see* B Saye and Sele, colls):—
Charles John Prendergast (Lynn Cottage, Birdingbury, Rugby), *b* 1935: Lt RA (TA); MIPM, MBIM; a JP and Co Councillor of Warwicks, DL Warwicks 1993; Chm Warwicks County Council 1982-84: *m* 1975, Jennifer Lesley Ellaby, and has issue living, Richard John Prendergast, *b* 1978, — Nicholas Charles Prendergast, *b* 1982, — Elizabeth Margaret, *b* 1976. — Jeffrey Maurice Prendergast (The Post House, Bridge St, Fenny Compton, Leamington Spa, Warwicks), *b* 1940: FRICS: *m* 1972, Denzil Farnsworth, SRN, and has issue living, Edward Foley Prendergast, *b* 1973, — Charlotte Louise, *b* 1974. — Margaret Joan, *b* 1929. — Brenda Rosemary, *b* 1931; SRN: *m* 1965, Harold James Mills, Capt RA, of Glebe House, Bentworth, Alton, Hants, and has issue living, Catherine Joanna, *b* 1967; BSc; ACA.

Granddaughter of late Lt-Col John Cayzer Medlicott Vereker, MC (infra):—
Issue of late Lieut John Herbert Radcliffe Medlicott Vereker, RN, *b* 1914, *k* on active ser 1941: *m* 1939, Betty Eleanor Grace (who *m* 2ndly, 1945, Capt Maurice Milton Jones, US Air Force, of Jackson, Mississippi, USA), only child of Charles Edward Shepherd, of Trerice Manor, St Newlyn East, Cornwall:—

Joscelyn, *b* 1940: *m* 1963, Ralph Lancelot Johnston, of Thorpes Gardens, St James, Barbados, W Indies, son of Stanley Everton Lancelot Johnston, and has issue living, Amanda Louise, *b* 1964, — Tracy Kristina, *b* 1967.

Grandchildren of late Major John Medlicott Vereker (infra):—

Issue of late Lt-Col John Cayzer Medlicott Vereker, MC, *b* 1895, who *d* 1962: *m* 1914, Dulce Flores Elder, who *d* 1973, only child of Alexander Randle Skene Radcliffe, formerly of Dilston, Kentville, Nova Scotia:—

Dulciebella Joy BUSWELL (Aldersnapp Cottage, Petersfield, Hants), *b* 1917; assumed surname of Buswell by deed poll 19—: *m* 1st, 1935 (*m diss* 1946), Capt Hender Charles Molesworth St Aubyn (*see* Molesworth-St Aubyn, Bt), who *d* 1986; 2ndly, 1948, Wing-Cdr Harold Frederick Gurney Fry, RAF, who *d* 1978, and has issue living, (by 1st *m*) (*see* Molesworth-St Aubyn, Bt), — (by 2nd *m*) Elizabeth Gurney, *b* 1950: *m* 1st, 1969 (*m diss* 1974), Colin Maurice Sampson; 2ndly, 1975, Colin Roy Wooltorton, and has issue living (by 2nd *m*), George Peter Christopher *b* 1975. —— Shelagh-Maureen (Barton Cottage, Rosebery Rd, W Runton, Cromer), *b* 1925; late WRNAS; *m* 1947 (*m diss* 1971), Hugh Bellasis Martin, MBE, and has issue living, Clive Patrick, *b* 1955; *ed* Harrow, and Wadham Coll, Oxford (BA): *m* 1986, Caroline Anne Freedman, and has issue living, Thomas Christopher *b* 1987, Luke Nicholas *b* 1990, — Corinna Frances Avril *b* 1948; *ed* St Margaret's Sch, Bushey, Homerton Coll, and Newnham Coll Camb: (BEd): *m* 19—, Philip Charles Creasy, MA, of The Head's House, Heath School, Colchester, and has issue living, Mathew Henry *b* 1974, Stella Judith *b* 1977.

Issue of late Capt Stanley Lloyd Medlicott Vereker, OBE, RN, *b* 1899, *d* 1967: *m* 1925, Elaine Irene, who *d* 1982, da of late John Henry Edwards, of 54 Portland Place, W1:—

(John) Stanley Herbert Medlicott (Mallam Waters, Fairfield, Glos; 118 Coleherne Court, SW5), *b* 1927; *ed* Rugby, and Trin Hall, Camb: *m* 1st, 1954 (*m diss* 1976), Valerie Ann Virginia, da of William James Threlfall, CIE, of Skoons, Bembridge, I of W; 2ndly, 1980, Mary St Joan Howard, yr da of Bertram Eric Edmonds (*see* E Carlisle, colls, 1980 Edn), widow of James Ewing Kennaway, and formerly wife of Brian C. Kennaway Cummins, and has issue living (by 1st *m*), Simon Lloyd William Medlicott, *b* 1955, — Rupert David Peregrine Medlicott, *b* 1957: *m* 1986, Philippa J., da of J.C. Geoffrey Stocks, of W Bagborough, Som, and has issue living, Freddie *b* 1990, Jack *b* 1992, — Hugo Dominic Charles Medlicott, *b* 1961: *m* 1983 (*m diss* 1990), Atalanta, da of late John Cowan. —— David William Leslie Edwards (Holton House, Burwash, Sussex), *b* 1930; *ed* Eton, and Trin Hall, Camb (MA): *m* 1965, Jane Elizabeth, da of Alan Campbell Gairdner, FRCS, of Branscombe, Whimple, Devon, and has issue living, William David Lloyd Medlicott, *b* 1966, — Henry Alan Charles Medlicott, *b* 1969.

Issue of late Denis Medlicott Vereker, *b* 1906, *d* 1976: *m* 1927 (*m diss* 1942), Marjory Mary, da of Julius A. Fryer, formerly of Port Elizabeth, S Africa:—

Moyra Maureen, *b* 1928: *m* 1st, 1962 (*m diss* 1971), Rodney Graham Smit, CA (S Africa), ACIS; 2ndly, 1976, Roy William Digby, MB, ChB, of Traralgon, Vic, Aust.

Grandchildren of late Hon John Prendergast Vereker, 3rd son of 3rd Viscount:—

Issue of late Major John Medlicott Vereker, *b* 1863, *d* 1940: *m* 1892 (*m diss* 1913), Mary Agnes, who *d* 1930, el da of Sir Charles William Cayzer, 1st Bt, of Gartmore, Perthshire:—

Charles William Medlicott (Bell Cottage, Wylye, Wilts), *b* 1903; is Cdr (ret) RN; FICS; 1939-45 War and Far East; HM's Vice-consul, Kristiansand, S Norway 1948-51; an Assist, Ship's Manager 1951-55; Legal Executive (Admiralty Court) 1957-78: *m* 1937, Marjorie Hughes, who *d* 1984, da of William Hughes Whatley, and has issue living, Peter William Medlicott (c/o FCO, King Charles St, SW1): *b* 1939; *ed* Marlborough, Trin Coll, Camb (MA), and Harvard Univ (Henry Fellow); HM Diplomatic Service, Dep Permanent Rep UK Mission at Geneva: *m* 1967, Susan Elizabeth, da of Maj-Gen Antony John Dyball, CBE, MC, and has issue living, Connel Charles Medlicott *b* 1971, Toby John Medlicott *b* 1973, Rory James Medlicott *b* 1981, — John Michael Medlicott, CB, *b* 1944; *ed* Marlborough, and Keele Univ; with Min of Overseas Development 1967, World Bank 1970-72, Private Sec to Min for Overseas Development 1976-78, Prime Minister's office 1980-83, Prin Finance Offr Overseas Development Administration 1983-88, Dep Sec Dept of Educn and Science 1988-94, since when Permanent Sec Overseas Development Admin; CB 1992: *m* 1971, Judith Rowen, of Washington, DC, and has issue living, Andrew Shane Medlicott *b* 1975, Jennifer Gail *b* 1973, — Corinna Mary, *b* 1938: *m* 1961, Col John Tadman, R Anglian Regt, of West End Mill, Donhead St Andrew, Shaftesbury, Dorset, and has issue living, Miles William Vereker *b* 1966, Carey Joanna *b* 1962, Fenella Jane *b* 1964. —— Kathleen Sybil (76 Woodside Av, Cowie's Hill, Durban, S Africa), *b* 1904: *m* 1931, Cdr Michael George Marriott, RN, who *d* 1978, and has issue living, Jeremy Edward Alan (Carnamah, W Aust), *b* 1937; Lt RN: *m* 1963, Teresa Katherine, da of Malcolm Francis Ogilvie-Forbes, of Boyndlie, Aberdeenshire, and has issue living, Benedict Michael Andrew *b* 1963, Peter Malcolm *b* 1966, Felicity Anne *b* 1969, — Bridget Mary, *b* 1934: *m* 1956, Julius Horowitz, of 8 Kernick Av, Melrose North, Johannesburg, S Africa, and has issue living, Adam Mark *b* 1957, Ivan Brandon *b* 1961, Seth William (twin) *b* 1961, Ben Robert *b* 1964, Robyn Ester *b* 1956, Yael Tayce *b* 1959.

Grandchildren of late Hon Henry Prendergast Vereker, LLD, 4th son of 3rd Viscount:—

Issue of late Lieut-Col Charles Granville Vereker, *b* 1869, *d* 1947: *m* 1st, 1895, Adeline Eleanor, who *d* 1930, da of late Maj-Gen Thomas Porter Berthon, RA; 2ndly, 1931, Leila Frances Helena (who *d* 1993, having *m* 2ndly, 1973, Robert Hugh Pardoe, of Bridge House, Bibury, Cirencester), da of late Florian Gustavus Bosanquet:—

(By 2nd *m*) Neville Henry Prendergast (Inglewood, 6 Curzon Av, Beaconsfield, Bucks), *b* 1934; FRICS: *m* 1974, Priscilla Mary, el da of John Orlando Weld-Forester (*see* B Forester, colls), and has issue living, John Charles Prendergast, *b* 1975, — Richard Neville Forester, *b* 1977. —— Louise Katherine (Flat N, 78/80 Holland Rd, W14), *b* 1953 (*m diss* 1963), Geoffrey Whitaker Gotch, and has issue living, Peter Charles Thomas, *b* 1955; *ed* Birmingham Univ (BSc), and Aston Univ, Birmingham (DipSH); HM Inspector of Factories, Health & Safety Executive 1979-91, since when Group Health & Safety Adviser Babtie Group: *m* 1982, Deborah Jane Ward, and has issue living, Liam Paul *b* 1984, Gemma Jane *b* 1982.

Issue of late Cdr Henry Gosset Vereker, RN, *b* 1871, *d* 1916: *m* 1903, Kate Beatrice, who *d* 1915, el da of late Frank Herbert:—

Charles Henry, *b* 1913; *ed* Lincoln Coll, Oxford (MA, DPhil); Prof of Political Theory and Insts, Durham Univ 1966, Emeritus Prof since 1973; Patron Buckingham Univ 1984; Hon D Litt 1985: *m* 1942, Patricia, JP, da of late S. G. K. Kastelian, MD, and has issue living, Julian Charles Prendergast (Tythe House, Odstock, Salisbury), *b* 1945: *m* 1968, Elizabeth Glascott Wise, and has issue living, Annabel Louise *b* 1974, — Katherine Elizabeth, *b* 1949: *m* 1972, Edward John Watson Gieve, of 211 Highbury Quadrant, N5, and has issue living, Daniel Vereker *b* 1980, Matthew Vereker *b* 1982, — Deirdre Patricia, *b* 1954.

PREDECESSORS – (1) Sir THOMAS Prendergast, a Brig-Gen in the Army, and MP for Monaghan 1703; *cr* a *Baronet* 1699; killed at Malplaquet 1709; *s* by his son (2) Sir THOMAS PC, 2nd Bt; was MP for Chichester and Clonmel, and Postmaster-Gen of Ireland; *dsp* 1760 before the patent creating him Viscount Clonmel had been completed; the baronetcy having expired the estates passed to his nephew (3) JOHN Smyth, 2nd son of Elizabeth (2nd da of 1st Bt), by Charles Smyth, MP for Limerick 1731-76; successively MP for Carlow and Limerick; assumed the surname of Prendergast in lieu of Smyth 1760, and the additional surname of Smyth 1785; *cr Baron Kiltarton* (peerage of Ireland) 1810 with remainder to his nephew Charles, son of his sister Juliana, by her marriage with Thomas Vereker, and *Viscount Gort* (peerage of Ireland) 1816, with similar limitation; *d* 1817; *s* by his nephew (ante) (4) CHARLES Vereker, PC, 2nd Viscount; MP for Limerick 1790-1817, and afterwards a Representative Peer; *d* 1842; *s* by his son (5) JOHN PRENDERGAST, 3rd Viscount, *b* 1790; successively MP for Limerick and a Representative Peer: *m* 1st, 1814, Hon Maria O'Grady, who *d* 1854, da of 1st Viscount Guillamore; 2ndly, 1861, Elizabeth Mary, who *d* 1880, da of John Jones, and widow of George Tudor, MP for Barnstaple; *d* 1865; *s* by his son (6) STANDISH PRENDERGAST, 4th Viscount, *b* 1819: *m* 1847, Hon Caroline Harriet Gage, who *d* 1888, da of 4th Viscount Gage, *d* 1900; *s* by his el son (7) JOHN GAGE PRENDERGAST, 5th Viscount, *b* 1849: *m* 1885, Eleanor, who *d* 1933, da of late R. Surtees, of Hamsterley Hall, co Durham; *d* 1902; *s* by his el son (8) JOHN STANDISH SURTEES PRENDERGAST, VC, GCB, CBE, DSO, MVO, MC, 6th Viscount *b* 1886; Field Marshal; CIGS 1937-9; European War 1914-18 (four times wounded, MC, DSO with two bars, VC), European War 1939-40 as Com-in-Ch, British Expeditionary Force in France (GCB, Grand Cross of Legion of

Honour); Inspector-Gen to Forces for Training 1940-41, Gov and Com-in-Ch, Gibraltar 1941-2, and Malta 1942-4, and High Commr and Com-in-Ch Palestine, and High Commr for Transjordan 1944-5: *cr Viscount Gort*, of Hamsterley, co Durham (peerage of United Kingdom) 1946: *m* 1911 (*m diss* 1925), his cousin, Corinna Katherine, who *d* 1940, da of late Capt George Medlicott Vereker; *d* 1946, when the United Kingdom Viscountcy became ext and the Irish Viscountcy and Barony passed to his brother **(9)** STANDISH ROBERT GAGE PRENDERGAST, MC, 7th Viscount; *b* 1888; 1914-18 war as Lt RHA; High Sheriff of Co Durham 1934: *m* 1921, Bessy, who *d* 1972, da of late Aubone Alfred Surtees, of Dinsdale Manor, Co Durham; *d* 1975; *s* by his kinsman **(10)** COLIN LEOPOLD PRENDERGAST (only son of Cdr Leopold George Prendergast Vereker, 2nd son of Capt Hon Foley Charles Prendergast Vereker, 2nd son of 4th Viscount), 8th Viscount and present peer also Baron Kiltarton.

GOSCHEN, VISCOUNT (Goschen) (Viscount UK 1900)

GILES JOHN HARRY GOSCHEN, 4th Viscount; *b* 16 Nov 1965; *s* 1977; a Lord in Waiting to HM since 1992: *m* 1991, Sarah, yr da of late A. G. Horsnail, of Westbury-on-Trym, Bristol.

Arms – Argent, a heart fired and transfixed with an arrow bendwise point upwards gules, in chief two anchors erect sable. **Crest** – On an arrow fessewise, a dove wings endorsed all proper. **Supporters** – *Dexter*, a sailor; *sinister*, a private of the Royal Marines, both proper, each holding in the exterior hand a flagstaff of the last, therefrom flowing a banner argent, charged with a pale gules thereon an anchor cabled and erect or. *Residence* – Hilton House, Crowthorne, Berks.

SISTER LIVING

Hon Caroline Elizabeth, *b* 1963: *m* 1991, William E. J. Grant, elder son of Sir (Matthew) Alistair Grant, of Campden Hill Sq, W8, and has issue living, John Alexander, *b* 1992.

WIDOW LIVING OF THIRD VISCOUNT

ALVIN (*Alvin, Viscountess Goschen*) (Hilton House, Crowthorne, Berks RG11 6AH), yr of da of late H. England, of Durban, Natal: *m* 1955, as his 2nd wife, the 3rd Viscount, who *d* 1977.

PREDECESSORS – **(1)** *Rt Hon* GEORGE JOACHIM Goschen, son of late William Henry Goschen, of Austin Friars, EC, and Templeton House, Roehampton; *b* 1831; sometime a partner in firm of Fruhling and Goschen, of Austin Friars, a Director of the Bank of England, and Chm of Lloyd's; Vice-Press of Board of Trade 1865-6, Chancellor of Duchy of Lancaster (with a seat in the Cabinet) 1866, Pres of Poor Law Board 1868-71, First Lord of the Admirality 1871-4, Envoy Extraor and Min Plen to Constantinople on a Special Mission 1880-81, and Ecclesiastical Commr for England 1882-5, Chancellor of the Exchequer Jan 1887 to Aug 1892, and again First Lord of the Admirality 1895-1900: MP for City of London (*L*) 1863-80, for Ripon 1880-85, for E Div of Edinburgh Borough 1885-6, and for St George Hanover Square (*C*) Feb 1887 to Nov 1900; *cr* PC 1865, and *Viscount Goschen*, of Hawkhurst, co Kent (peerage of United Kingdom) 1900: *m* 1857, Lucy, who *d* 1898, da of late John Dalley; *d* 1907; *s* by his son **(2)** *Rt Hon* GEORGE JOACHIM, GCSI, GCIE, CBE, VD, 2nd Viscount, *b* 1866; Private Sec to Gov of NS Wales (Earl of Jersey) 1890-92; sometime a partner in the firm of Goschens and Cunliffe, of 12 Austin Friars, EC and Chm of Med Research Council; Lieut-Col and Hon Col (Lieut-Col Cmdg 1914-18) a Batn Buffs (E Kent Regt); sat as MP for N, or E Grinstead Div of Sussex (*C*) 1895-1906; appointed a Member of Roy Chmmn on King's Bench 1912, and Joint Parliamentary Sec (unpaid) Board of Agriculture 1918; was Controller Labour Div, Food Production Depart 1918-19; Gov of Madras 1924-29 (acted as Viceroy and Gov-Gen of India June to Oct 1929): *m* 1893, Lady Margaret Evelyn Gathorne-Hardy, CI, who *d* 1943, da of 1st Earl of Cranbrook; *d* 1952; *s* by his nephew, **(3)** JOHN ALEXANDER, KBE (son of late Hon Sir William Henry Goschen, KBE, 2nd son of 1st Viscount), 3rd Viscount; *b* 1906; Col Gren Gds: British Mil Mission to Greece 1945-47; Assist Ch Whip, House of Lords 1962-64; Capt Yeomen of the Guard and Dep Ch Whip 1970-71: *m* 1st, 1934 (*m diss* 1949), Hilda Violet Ursula, da of late Col Hon St Leger Henry Jervis, DSO (V St Vincent, colls); 2ndly, 1955, Alvin, yr da of H. England, of Durban, Natal; *d* 1977; *s* by his son **(4)** GILES JOHN HARRY, 4th Viscount and present peer.

GOSFORD, EARL OF (Acheson) Sits as BARON WORLINGHAM (UK 1835) (Earl I 1806, Bt NS 1628)

To the watchful

CHARLES DAVID NICHOLAS ALEXANDER JOHN SPARROW ACHESON, 7th Earl and 13th Baronet; *b* 13 July 1942; *s* 1966; *ed* Harrow, at Byam Shaw Sch of Drawing and Painting, and Roy Acad Schs: *m* 1983, Lynnette Redmond, of Sydney, Australia.

Arms – Argent, an eagle with two heads displayed sable, beaked and membered or; on a chief vert two mullets of the third. **Crest** – A cock gules, standing on a trumpet or. **Supporters** – Two leopards proper, collared and chained or, the sinister reguardant.
Seat – Gosford Castle, Markethill, co Armagh. *Address* – c/o House of Lords, SW1.

SISTERS LIVING AND DECEASED

Lady (Francesca Georgina) Caroline, *b* 1940: *m* 1967, David Wallace Fleming, who *d* (Dec) 1991, and *d* (Aug) 1991, leaving issue, Alexander Montagu Acheson (1045 Fifth Av, New York, NY 10028, USA), *b* 1968.
Isabella Augusta (does not use courtesy title), *b* 1950: *m* 1979, Tevita T. Maka, and has issue living, Charles Nicholas, *b* 1980, — Toby Manu, *b* 1985, — James Alipate, *b* 1989. *Address* – PO Box 1234, Nuku A'Lofa, Tonga, S Pacific.

UNCLE LIVING (*Son of 5th Earl*)

Hon PATRICK BERNARD VICTOR MONTAGU, *b* 4 Feb 1915; *ed* Harrow, Trin Coll, Camb (BA 1937), and Harvard Univ (MBA 1939): *m* 1946, Judith, da of Earle P. Gillette, of Minneapolis, Minnesota, USA, and of Mrs F. B. Bate, of Waterford, Virginia, USA, and has issue living, Nicholas Hope Carter, *b* 1947: *m* 1983, Patricia, da of James Beckford, of Jacksonville Beach, Florida, USA, and has issue living, Eric James Patrick *b* 1988, Kelly Lauren *b* 1987, — Christopher, *b* 1950: *m* 1977, Sheryl, da of Carl Benson, of Columbus, Georgia, USA, and has issue living, Kendall Bate (a son) *b* 1984, Karen Erica *b* 1982, — John Alexander Simon, *b* 1957: *m* 1st, 1982 (*m diss* 1985), Cara, da of Ernest Kulik, of Purcellville, Virginia, USA; 2ndly, 1988, Lisa Kimberly Bickerstaff, da of Carl Benson, of Columbus, Georgia, USA, and has issue living (by 2nd *m*), Katherine Genevieve *b* 1988, Emma Mary Camilla *b* 1991, — Alexandra Sarah Camilla, *b* 1962, — Caroline Mary Patricia (twin), *b* 1962. *Residence* – Box 71, Waterford, Va 22190, USA.

AUNT LIVING (*Daughter of 5th Earl*)

Lady Mary Virginia Shirley, *b* 1919: *m* 1941, Fernando Corcuera, who *d* 1978, and has had issue, Juan Fernando Pedro, *b* 1948: *m* 1971, Paloma Gonzalez, and has issue living, Fernando *b* 1971, Carmen *b* 1974, Camila *b* 1979, — Jaime Marcos Pedro, *b* 1955: *m* 1983, HI & RH Archduchess Myriam Adelhaid Hugoline Omnes Sancti Marcus d'Aviano Melchiora of Austria, 3rd da of HI & RH Archduke Felix of Austria, and has issue living, Karl Sebastian *b* 1984, Pedro Johannes *b* 1985, Felipe *b* 1987, Andres *b* 1988, — Fernanda Mary, *b* 1942: *m* 1967 (*m diss* 1973), Manuel Valles, and *d* 1992, leaving issue, Fernanda *b* 1967, — Monica Ana, *b* 1944: *m* 1970, Harry Troop, and has issue living, Ana Monica *b* 1971, Isabel Gabriela *b* 1972, Maria *b* 1976, — Marisol Manuela, *b* 1946: *m* 1977 (*m diss* 1983), Luis Padilla, and has issue living, Jimena *b* 1977, Natalia *b* 1979. *Residence* – Hidalgo 14, San Angel, Mexico DF 01000, Mexico.

MOTHER LIVING

FRANCESCA AUGUSTA MARIA (47 Quick Rd, Chiswick, W4), da of Francesco Cagiati, of Rome: *m* 1935 (*m diss* 1960), as his 1st wife, the 6th Earl, who *d* 1966.

WIDOW LIVING OF SIXTH EARL

CYNTHIA MARGARET (*Dowager Countess of Gosford*) (Pine Cottage, Camberley, Surrey GU15 2DE), da of late Capt Henry Cave West, MC, RHA, and widow of Maj James Pringle Delius, 13th/18th R Hussars: *m* 1960, as his 2nd wife, the 6th Earl, who *d* 1966.

COLLATERAL BRANCH LIVING

Issue of late Capt Hon Patrick George Edward Cavendish Acheson, DSO, MVO, RN, yr son of 4th Earl, *b* 1883, *d* 1957: *m* 1915, Norah, who *d* 1970, da of Alfred Jones, formerly of Halifax, Nova Scotia;—
Blanche Theodosia (twin), *b* 1923: *m* 1950, Com Oliver Russell Moore, RN (ret), and has issue living, Susan Theodosia, *b* 1952: *m* 1990, Christopher Aston Maltin, and has issue living, Arthur Patrick Aston *b* 1991, Alice Mary Theodosia *b* 1992, — Victoria Caroline, *b* 1954: *m* 1989, Francis William Orlando Bridgeman-Sutton, and has issue living, Katharine Althea Acheson *b* 1992, — Patricia Alexandra, *b* 1956: *m* 1985, David Dowling Styles, and has issue living, Oliver Michael *b* 1987, Henry Dowling *b* 1989. *Residence* – Dash Hayes, Kington Magna, Gillingham, Dorset.

PREDECESSORS – (1) *Sir* ARCHIBALD Acheson of Edinburgh, later of Market Hill, Clonekearney, co Armagh, successively Solicitor-Gen for Scotland, a Senator of Justice (with title of Lord Glencairnie), an Extraor Lord Session, and Sec of State for Scotland; *cr* a *Baronet* (of Nova Scotia) 1628 with remainder to his heirs male whatsoever: *m* 1st, c 1610, Agnes Verno-; 2ndly, 1622, Margaret, da and heir of Hon Sir John Hamilton (D Abercorn); *d* 1634; *s* by his el son (2) *Sir* PATRICK, 2nd Bt (son of 1st *m*): *m* 1634, Martha, da and heir of William Moore: *d* 1638; *s* by his half-brother (3) *Sir* GEORGE, 3rd Bt; *b* 1629: *m* 1st, 1654, Nichola, da of co-heir of Sir Robert Hannay, 1st Bt; 2ndly, 1659, Hon Margaret Caulfeild, da of 2nd Baron Charlemont; *d* 1685; *s* by his son (4) *Sir* NICHOLAS, 4th Bt (son of 1st *m*); MP for co Armagh 1695: *m* 1686, Anne, da of Thomas Taylor, of Kells; *d* 1701; *s* by his son (5) *Sir* ARTHUR, 5th Bt; *b* 1688: *m* 1715, Anne, da and heir of Rt Hon Philip Savage; *d* 1749; *s* by his son (6) *Sir* ARCHIBALD, PC; *b* 1718; successively MP for Dublin Univ, and Enniskillen; *cr Baron*

Gosford, of Market Hill, co Armagh (peerage of Ireland) 1776, and *Viscount Gosford* (peerage of Ireland) 1785: *m* 1740, Mary da of John Richardson, of Rich Hill, co Armagh; *d* 1790: *s* by his son **(7)** ARTHUR, 2nd Viscount; *b* c 1742, MP for Old Leighlin 1783-90; *cr Earl of Gosford* (peerage of Ireland) 1806: *m* 1774, Millicent, da of Lt-Gen Edward Pole, *d* 1807; *s* by his son **(8)** ARCHIBALD, GCB, 2nd Earl; *b* 1776; Gov of Canada; *cr Baron Worlingham* (peerage of UK) 1835; *m* 1805, Mary, da of Robert Sparrow of Worlingham Hall, Suffolk; *d* 1849; *s* by his **(9)** ARCHIBALD, KP, 3rd Earl; *b* 1806; who in 1847 had been *cr Baron Acheson of Clancairny*, co Armagh (peerage of UK): *m* 1832, Lady Theodosia Brabazon, who *d* 1876, da of 10th Earl of Meath; *d* 1864; *s* by his son **(10)** ARCHIBALD BRABAZON SPARROW, KP, 4th Earl; *b* 1841; Lord of the Bedchamber to HRH the Prince of Wales 1886-1901, and Vice-Chamberlain of the Household to HM Queen Alexandra 1901-22; bore Queen Consort's Ivory Rod at Coronation of King Edward VII 1902: *m* 1876, Lady Louisa Augusta Beatrice Montagu, DBE, who *d* 1944, 2nd da of 7th Duke of Manchester, KP; *d* 1922; *s* by his son **(11)** ARCHIBALD CHARLES MONTAGU BRABAZON, MC, 5th Earl; *b* 1877; Col Coldstream Gds; S Africa 1899-1902, 1914-18 War (MC): *m* 1st, 1910 (*m diss* 1928), Mildred, who *d* 1965, da of John Ridgely Carter, of Balt, USA, American Min to the Balkans; 2ndly, 1928, Beatrice Claflin, who *d* 1967, formerly wife of Robert P. Breese, of New York; *d* 1954; *s* by his el son **(12)** ARCHIBALD ALEXANDER JOHN STANLEY, OBE, 6th Earl, *b* 1911; a Lord in Waiting to HM 1957-58: *m* 1st, 1935 (*m diss* 1960), Francesca Augusta Maria, da of Francesco Cagiati, of Rome; 2ndly, 1960, Cynthia Margaret, da of Capt Henry Cave West, MC, RHA, and widow of Maj James Pringle Delius; *d* 1966; *s* by his only son **(13)** CHARLES DAVID NICHOLAS ALEXANDER JOHN SPARROW, 7th Earl and present peer; also Viscount and Baron Gosford, Baron Worlingham and Baron Acheson of Clancairny.

GOUGH, VISCOUNT (Gough) (Viscount UK 1849, Bt UK 1842)

(Name and Title pronounced "Goff")

SHANE HUGH MARYON GOUGH, 5th Viscount and 5th Baronet; *b* 26 Aug 1941; *s* 1951; *ed* Winchester; late Lt Irish Gds; Member Queen's Body Guard for Scotland (Royal Company of Archers); Mem Exec Cttee, Standing Council of the Baronetage; local Dir Central London Bd Roy Insurance (UK) Ltd; Trustee Gardner's Trust for the Blind, and Schizophrenia Research; Member Exec Council RNIB, and Scottish Lifeboat Council RNLI; FRGS.

Arms – Quarterly; 1st and 4th gules, on a mount vert a lion passant guardant or, supporting with his dexter paw the Union flag flowing to the sinister proper, over the same, in chief, the words "China," "India," in letters of gold; 2nd and 3rd azure, on a fesse argent, between three boars' heads, couped or, a lion passant gules; in the centre chief point, pendent from a riband argent, fimbriated azure, a representation of the badge of the Spanish order of Charles III proper, and on a chief, a representation of the east wall of the fortress of Tarifa, with a breach between two turrets, the dexter turret surmounted by the British flag flying, all proper. **Crests** – 1st, a boar's head couped or, motto over "Goojerat" (of augmentation); 2nd, on a mural crown argent, a lion passant guardant or, holding in the dexter paw two flag staves in bend sinister proper, the one being the Union flag of Great Britain and Ireland surmounting the other, the staff thereof broken, with a triangular banner flowing therefrom to represent a Chinese flag, having thereon a dragon, and in an escroll above the word "China"; 3rd a dexter arm embowed, in facings of 87th Regiment (gules, faced vert), the hand grasping the colour of the said Regiment displayed, and a representation of a French eagle reversed and depressed, the staff broken proper, in an escroll above the word "Barossa." **Supporters** – *Dexter*, a lion reguardant or, gorged with an Eastern crown gules, the rim inscribed with the world "Punjab" in letters of gold, with chain reflexed over the back, also gold; *sinister*, a Chinese dragon or, gorged with a mural crown sable, enscribed with the word "China," and chained gold.
Residences – Keppoch House, Strathpeffer, Ross-shire IV14 9AD; 17 Stanhope Gdns, SW7 5RQ. *Clubs* – Pratt's, White's.

PREDECESSORS – **(1)** Field-Marshal Rt Hon Sir HUGH Gough, KP, GCB, GCSI, PC; *b* 1779; an eminent Mil Com who achieved brilliant victories in India, and subjugated and annexed the Punjab to the British Dominions: *cr* a *Baronet* 1842, *Baron Gough*, of Chinkangfoo, in China and of Maharajpore and the Sutlej, in the East Indies (peerage of United Kingdom) 1846, and *Viscount Gough of Goojerat*, in the Punjaub, and of the City of Limerick (peerage of United Kingdom) 1849 (title later abbreviated to *Viscount Gough*); thrice thanked by Parliament and awarded a pension of £2,000 a-year for three lives: *m* 1807, Frances Maria, da of Gen Edward Stephens, RA; *d* 1869; *s* by his son **(2)** GEORGE STEPHENS, 2nd Viscount, *b* 1815; Capt Grenadier Guards: *m* 1st, 1840, Sarah Elizabeth, who *d* 1841, da of late Wray Palliser, of Comragh, Waterford; 2ndly, 1846, Jane, who *d* 1892. da of late George Arbuthnot, of Elderslie, Surrey; *d* 1895; *s* by his el son **(3)** HUGH, KCVO, 3rd Viscount; *b* 1849; Min Resident at Dresden and Coburg, and Chargé d'Affaires at Court of Waldeck 1901-07: *m* 1889, Lady Georgiana Frances Henrietta Pakenham, who *d* 1943, da of 4th Earl of Longford; *d* 1919; *s* by his son **(4)** HUGH WILLIAM, MC, 4th Viscount; *b* 1892; Lieut Col Irish Guards; European War 1914-18 (MC): *m* 1935, Margaretta Elizabeth, who *d* 1977, da of Sir Spencer Pocklington Maryon Maryon-Wilson, 11th Bt; *d* 1951; *s* by his son **(5)** SHANE HUGH MARYON, 5th Viscount, and present peer; also Baron Gough.

GOULD OF POTTERNEWTON, BARONESS (Gould) (Life Baroness 1993)

JOYCE BRENDA GOULD, da of Solomon Joseph Manson; *b* 29 Oct 1932; *ed* Roundhay High Sch for Girls, and Bradford Technical Coll; Dispensing Chemist 1952-65, Assist Regional Organiser and Women's Officer Yorks Labour Party 1969-75, Assist National Agent and Ch Women's Officer 1975-85, Dir of Organisation 1985-93; Exec Member Women's National Commn, Sec National Joint Cttee of Working Women's Organisations, Sec Yorks National Council of Civil Liberties, Cttee Member Campaign Against Racial Discrimination, Exec Member Joint Cttee Against Racism, Member Home Office Cttee on Electoral Matters; Vice-Pres Socialist Internat Women, etc; author of numerous pamphlets on feminism, socialism and sexism, etc; *cr Baroness Gould of Potternewton*, of Leeds, co W Yorks (Life Baroness) 1993: *m* 1953, Kevin Gould, and has issue.
Address – 1/5 Foulser Rd, SW17 8UE.

DAUGHTER LIVING

Hon Jeannette, *b* 1953.

GOWRIE, EARL OF (Ruthven) (Earl UK 1945) (Name pronounced "Rivven")

ALEXANDER PATRICK GREYSTEIL RUTHVEN, PC, 2nd Earl; *b* 26 Nov 1939; *s* to Earldom of Gowrie 1955, and to Barony of Ruthven of Gowrie 1956; in remainder to Lordship of Ruthven of Freeland (*see* E Carlisle); *ed* Eton, at Balliol Coll, Oxford, and Harvard Univ, USA; officially recognised in the name of Ruthven by Warrant of Lord Lyon King of Arms 1957; a Lord-in-Waiting to HM 1972-74; formerly lecturer at State Univ of New York, Univ Coll, London, and Harvard Univ; Conservative Whip 1971-72 and a Lord in Waiting 1972-74; Oppn Spokesman Economic Affrs 1974-79; a Min of State, Dept of Employment 1979-81, N Ireland Office 1981-83; Min for the Arts 1983-85, since when Provost Royal Coll of Art; Chm Sotheby's UK 1987-93; Chm Arts Council since 1994; PC 1983: *m* 1st, 1962 (*m diss* 1974), Xandra, yr da of Col Robert Albert Glanville Bingley, CVO, DSO, OBE; 2ndly, 1974, Countess Adelheid, yst da of late Fritz-Dietlof, Graf von der Schulenburg, and has issue by 1st *m*.

Arms – Paly of six, argent and gules **Crest** – A ram's head couped sable armd or. **Supporters** – Two goats sable, armed, unguled and ducally gorged or, with chains also or reflexed over the back. **Residence** – 34 King St, Covent Gdn, WC2.

SON LIVING *(By 1st marriage)*

PATRICK LEO BRER (*Viscount Ruthven of Canberra*), *b* 4 Feb 1964: *m* 1990, Julie Goldsmith, and has issue living, *Hon* Heathcote Patrick Cornelius Hore, *b* 28 May 1990.

BROTHER LIVING

Malise Walter Maitland Knox Hore RUTHVEN (c/o Chatto & Windus, 30 Bedford Sq, WC2), *b* 1942; *ed* Eton, and Trin Coll, Camb; author of *Islam in the World* (1984), *The Divine Supermarket* (1989), etc: *m* 1967, Ianthe, da of Cmdr (Robert) Hugh Hodgkinson, and has issue living, Chloe, *b* 1969, — Oonagh Orlanda, *b* 1970.

MOTHER LIVING

Pamela Margaret, da of the Rev A. H. Fletcher, of 87, Cadogan Gdns, SW1; was an Extra Woman of the Bedchamber of HM the Queen 1948-51; in 1945 was granted rank and precedence of wife of the el son of an Earl during her widowhood: *m* 1st, 1938, Major Hon (Alexander Harding) Patrick Hore Ruthven, only son of 1st Earl, who *d* of wounds received in action in Libya 1942; 2ndly, 1952, as his 2nd wife, Major (George) Derek Cooper, OBE, MC, The Life Guards.

WIDOW LIVING OF SECOND BARON RUTHVEN OF GOWRIE

JUDITH GORDON (Denbigh, Foreland Rd, Bembridge, Isle of Wight), yr da of late Bertie E. Bell, of Guernsey: *m* 1st, 1953, as his 2nd wife, the 2nd Baron Ruthven of Gowrie (and 10th Lord Ruthven of Freeland), who *d* 1956; 2ndly, 1965, Maj Digby Robert Peel, MC, RA, who *d* 1971.

PREDECESSORS – (1) *Brig-Gen Rt Hon Sir* ALEXANDER GORE ARKWRIGHT Hore Ruthven, VC, PC, GCMG, CB, DSO, 2nd son of 8th Lord Ruthven of Freeland; *b* 1872; Col and Hon Brig-Gen Welsh Guards; Sudan 1898 (despatches, VC), White Nile 1900 (despatches thrice), Somaliland 1903-04, European War 1914-19 in Gallipoli and France (severely wounded, despatches five times, DSO with Bar, French and Belgian Croix de Guerre, CMG, CB); Gov of S Australia 1928-34, Gov of N S Wales 1935-6, and Gov-Gen and Com-in-Ch of Commonwealth of Australia 1936-44; Lieut-Gov and Dep Constable of Windsor Castle 1945-53; *cr Baron Gowrie*, of Canberra in the Commonwealth of Australia, and of Dirleton, co E Lothian (peerage of United Kingdom) 1935, and *Viscount Ruthven of Canberra*, of Dirleton, co E Lothian and *Earl of Gowrie* (peerage of United Kingdom) 1945: *m* 1908, Zara Eileen, who *d* 1965, da of late John Pollok (B Clanmorris); *d* 1955; *s* by his grandson (2) ALEXANDER PATRICK GREYSTEIL (el son of late Maj Hon (Alexander Harding) Patrick Hore Ruthven, only son of 1st Earl), 2nd Earl and present peer; also Viscount Ruthven of Canberra, Baron Gowrie, and Baron Ruthven of Gowrie (*see infra*).
(1) WALTER JAMES RUTHVEN, 9th Lord Ruthven of Freeland (peerage of Scotland) *cr* 1651 (*see* E Carlisle), was *cr Baron Ruthven of Gowrie* (peerage of United Kingdom) 1919: *m* 1869, Lady Caroline Annesley Gore, who *d* 1914, da of 4th Earl of Arran; *d* 1921; *s* by his el son (2) WALTER PATRICK, CB, CMG, DSO, 2nd Baron, *b* 1870; Maj-Gen late Scots Guards; commanded Bangalore Brig 1920-24, and London Dist 1924-8, and was Lieut-Gov of Guernsey 1929-34: *m* 1st, 1895, Jean Leslie, who *d* 1952, da of late Norman George Lampson (Lampson Bt, colls); 2ndly, 1953, Judith Gordon (who *m* 2ndly, 1965, Maj Digby Robert Peel, MC, RA, who *d* 1971), da of late Bertie E. Bell, of Guernsey; *d* 1956; *s* in the Barony of Ruthven of Gowrie (peerage of United Kingdom) by his great-nephew, ALEXANDER PATRICK GREYSTEIL, 3rd Baron, and 2nd Earl of Gowrie (*ante*).

GRADE, BARON (Grade) (Life Baron 1976)

LEW GRADE, son of late Isaac Winogradsky; *b* 25 Dec 1906; *ed* Rochelle St Sch, EC2; 1939-45 War with RA; Fellow BAFTA 1979; Pres of Associated Television Network Ltd; Chm of Stoll Theatres Corpn and Moss Empires since 1973; Chm Bentray Investments Ltd; Chm and Ch Exec of Associated Television Corpn (Internat) Ltd 1973-1982; Chm and Man Dir of ITC Entertainment Ltd 1958-82; Chm and Chief Exec Embassy Communications Internat Ltd 1982-85, since when Chm The Grade Co; Gov Royal Shakespeare Theatre; OStJ, KCSS; *cr* Knt 1969, and *Baron Grade*, of Elstree, co Herts (Life Baron), 1976: *m* 1942, Kathleen Sheila, da of John Moody.

Arms – Per chevron grady vert and or, in chief two pierced mullets or, and in base a bear's jamb erased sable armed gules. **Crest** – A sinister cubit arm erect, vested vert, cuffed argent, charged with a mask of comedy or, the hand proper holding a balalaika or sound box to the dexter. **Supporters** – *Dexter*, upon a lightning flash or, a lion proper gorged with a cord, pendent therefrom a representation of itself, all or: *sinister*, upon a lightning flash or, a horse sable, gorged with a cord, pendent therefrom a representation of itself, all or.
Address – Embassy House, 3 Audley Square, W1Y 5DR.

What I promise I carry out

ADOPTED SON LIVING

Paul Nicholas, *b* 1952: *m* 1st, 19— (*m diss* 19—), Lisa Pearce; 2ndly, 1986, Beverly Hill, and has issue living (by 1st *m*), Daniel, *b* 1978, — Georgina Elizabeth Frances, *b* 1980.

GRAFTON, DUKE OF (FitzRoy) (Duke E 1675)

HUGH DENIS CHARLES FITZROY, KG, 11th Duke; *b* 3 April 1919; *s* 1970; *ed* Eton and Magdalene Coll, Camb; Hon DCL Univ of E Anglia 1990, Hon FRIBA, FSA; late Capt Gren Gds; Hon Air Cdr 2623 (E Anglian) RAAF Regt Sqdn since 1982; ADC to Viceroy of India 1943-47; patron of four livings, and Hereditary Ranger of Whittlebury Forest; DL Suffolk 1973; Member Historic Buildings Council for England 1953-84, Historic Buildings Advisory Cttee and Churches and Cathedrals Cttee English Heritage since 1984; National Trust: Member Exec Cttee, Chm E Anglia Regional Cttee 1966-81, and Member Properties Cttee since 1981; Member Royal Fine Art Commn since 1971; Chm Cathedrals Advisory Commn 1981-91, and Architectural Heritage Fund since 1976, Chm of Trustees Historic Chruches Preservation Trust since 1980, and Sir John Soane's Museum since 1975; Vice Chm of Trustees National Portrait Gallery 1967-92, Trustee Tradescant Trust, Buildings at Risk, Pres Soc for the Protection of Ancient Buildings since 1989, International Students House since 1972, British Soc of Master Glass Painters, E Anglia Tourist Board 1973-93, Suffolk Preservation Soc since 1957, Chm of Trustees Suffolk Historic Churches Trust since 1973; KG 1976: *m* 1946, (Ann) Fortune, GCVO (Mistress of the Robes to HM The Queen), only da of late Capt (Evan Cadogan) Eric Smith, and has issue.

The ornament and recompense of virtue

Arms – The royal arms of Charles II, viz Quarterly: 1st and 4th, France and England quarterly; 2nd, Scotland; 3rd, Ireland: the whole debruised by a baton sinister-compony of six pieces, argent and azure. **Crest** – On a chapeau gules, turned up ermine, a lion statant guardant or, ducally crowned azure, and gorged with a collar counter-compony argent and of the 4th. **Supporters** – *Dexter*, a lion guardant or, ducally crowned azure; *sinister*, a greyhound argent; each gorged with a collar counter-compony argent and azure.
Seat – Euston Hall, Thetford, Norfolk, IP24 2QW. *Club* – Boodle's.

SONS LIVING

JAMES OLIVER CHARLES (*Earl of Euston*) (6 Vicarage Gdns, W8; The Racing Stables, Euston, Thetford, Norfolk), *b* 13 Dec 1947; *ed* Eton, and Magdalene Coll, Camb (MA); FCA; a Page of Honour to HM 1962-63; Assist Dir J. Henry Schroder Wagg & Co 1973-82, Exec Dir Enskilda Securities 1982-87, Dir Jamestown Investments Ltd 1987, Dir Central Capital Holdings 1988, and Capel-Cure Myers Capital Management 1988: *m* 1972, Lady Clare Amabel Margaret Kerr, 3rd da of 12th Marquess of Lothian, and has issue:—

SON LIVING— HENRY OLIVER CHARLES (*Viscount Ipswich*), *b* 6 April 1978.

DAUGHTERS LIVING—*Lady* Louise Helen Mary, *b* 1973, — *Lady* Emily Clare, *b* 1974, — *Lady* Charlotte Rose, *b* 1983, — *Lady* Isobel Anne, *b* 1985.

Lord Charles Patrick Hugh, *b* 1957; *ed* Eton, and Magdalene Coll, Camb (BA); Dir Fine Art Courses Ltd; author of *Italy, a Grand Tour for the Modern Traveller* (1991), etc: *m* 1988, Diana M., da of Hubert Miller-Stirling, of Cape Town, S Africa, and has issue living, Nicholas Augustus Charles, *b* 1991, — George, *b* 1993.

DAUGHTERS LIVING

Lady Henrietta Fortune Doreen, *b* 1949: *m* 1979, Edward G. P. St George, and has issue living, Henry Edward Hugh, *b* 1983, — Katherine Helen Cecilia, *b* 1984. *Residence* – 1 Chester Sq, SW1; *Address* – PO Box F2666, Freeport, Grand Bahama Is, Bahamas.
Lady Virginia Mary Elizabeth, *b* 1954: *m* 1980 (*m diss* 1987), Lord Ralph William Francis Joseph Kerr, yr son of 12th Marquess of Lothian.
Lady Olivia Rose Mildred, *b* 1963.

HALF-BROTHER LIVING

Lord Edward Anthony Charles, *b* 1928; *ed* Eton; late Capt Coldm Gds; a DL Norfolk 1986; High Sheriff 1987; Dir Ross Breeders Ltd, Nat Poultry Breeders (S Africa) Ltd, Ross Poultry New Zealand Ltd, Dep Chm Bd of Management of Eastern Region of TSB; Dir Trustcard Ltd, Chm Caledonian Cartridge Co Ltd, Chm Norfolk Playing Fields Assoc, and on Council, Norfolk Naturalists Trust, Member of Council Royal Norfolk Agric Assocn: *m* 1956, Veronica Mary, da of Maj R. F. Ruttledge, of Cloonee, Ballinrobe, co Mayo, and has issue living, Michael Robert Charles, *b* 1958: *m* 1987, Cornelia A., yr da of Peter Garnett, of Quakers' Orchard, Peaslake, Surrey, and has issue living, Edwin *b* 1992, Olivia Lucy *b* 1989, — Joanna Lucy, *b* 1957: *m* 1982, Martin John Kershaw, and has issue (*see* E Lindsey and Abingdon, colls), — Shauna Anne, *b* 1963: *m* 1989, Adam L. J. Seccombe, yr son of J. A. (Alec) Seccombe, of Pique House, Stockcross, Newbury, Berks, and has issue living, Freddie *b* 1992, Dominick Jasper *b* 1994. *Residences* – Norton House, Norwich, NR14 6RY; 40 Eland Rd, SW11. *Club* – Pratt's.

SISTER LIVING

Lady Anne Mildred Ismay, *b* 1920: *m* 1947, Maj Colin Dalziel Mackenzie, MBE, MC, DL, late Seaforth Highlanders, Vice Lord Lieut of Lochaber, Inverness, and Badenoch and Strathspey since 1986, and has issue living, Philip Austin George (Glenkyllachy, Tomatin, Inverness-shire IV13 7YA), *b* 1949; *ed* Eton, and Magdalen Coll, Oxford (BA); FCA, MICFor: *m* 1976, (Katherine) Emma, da of Anthony Binny (*see* Muir Bt, colls), and has issue living, Lucy *b* 1976, Sabrina *b* 1978, Doune *b* 1980, Isla *b* 1986, Bettine *b* 1991, — Caroline Doreen, *b* 1952: — Laura Patience Kathleen, *b* 1954: BA (Oxon); ALI: *m* 1980, (Ian) Michael Osborne, 2nd son of Maj Gerald Michael Osborne, MC, TD, of Balmadies, Guthrie, Angus, and has issue living, Julian *b* 1982, Oliver *b* 1985, — Harriet Anne, *b* 1958: *m* 1989, Thomas St Andrew Warde-Aldam, yr son of Maj David Julian Warde-Aldam, of Healey Hall, Northumberland, and has issue living, a da *b* 1992. *Residences* – Farr, Inverness-shire; Bergh Apton Manor, Norwich. *Clubs* – Turf, Pratt's, New (Edinburgh).

SISTERS LIVING OF NINTH DUKE (*Raised to the rank of a Duke's daughters* 1961)

(Co-heiresses to the Barony of Arlington, cr 1664, and the Earldom of Arlington cr 1672)

Lady (Margaret) Jane, *b* 1916: *m* 1936, Maj Gen Sir (Eustace) John Blois Nelson, KCVO, CB, DSO, OBE, MC, late Grenadier Guards, who *d* 1993 (Blois, Bt), and has issue living, Jennifer Jane, *b* 1939: *m* 1964, Rodney Simon Dudley Forwood, Capt IG, (ret) of Slade Bottom House, Stoke, Hants, and has issue living, Patrick John Dudley *b* 1967, James Roland Nelson *b* 1969, — Juliet Auriol Sally (*Lady Cholmeley*), *b* 1940: *m* 1960, Capt Sir Montague John Cholmeley, 6th Bt. *Residence* – Tigh Bhaan, Appin, Argyll.
Lady Mary Rose (*posthumous*), *b* 1918: *m* 1945 (*m diss* 1951), Francis Trelawny Williams, late Lieut KRRC, who *d* 1977 (Salusbury-Trelawny, Bt), and has issue living, Linda Jane Auriol, *b* 1947. *Residence* – The Green, Oddington, Moreton-in-Marsh, Glos.

COLLATERAL BRANCHES LIVING

Issue of late Lord John Percy Samuel FitzRoy, brother of 10th Duke, *b* 1899, *d* 1945: *m* 1929, Kathleen Ruthar Mary (who *m* 2ndly, 1946, Leonard Thomas Carr, and *d* 1967), da of late Rev Arthur Willoughby Rokeby, of Clifton Manor, Shefford, Bedfordshire:—
Ismay Diana, *b* 1933. *Residence* – Moat Cottage, Burnham Rd, Althorne, Southminster, Essex.

Grandson of late Harold Charles Cavendish FitzRoy, only son of late Maj Cavendish Charles FitzRoy, elder son of late Lt-Col Rt Hon Lord Charles FitzRoy, MP, 2nd son of 4th Duke:—
Issue of late Charles Cavendish FitzRoy, *b* 1900, *d* 1960: *m* 1st, 1926, Simone Andrée, who *d* 1957, da of Jules Hennebert; 2ndly, 1957, Nora Bardsley, of 57 Harrow View, Harrow, Middlesex:—
(By 1st *m*) Kenneth Cavendish, *b* 1928: *m* 1st, 1952 (*m diss* 1970), Pamela Mary, da of Leslie Dodson; 2ndly, 1980, Patricia Juliet, who *d* 1989, da of Hugo de Schanschieff; 3rdly, 1992, Sally Anne, da of Malcolm Fullerton Laing, and has issue living (by 1st *m*), Ian Charles Cavendish (Scarletts, Furnace Lane, Cowden, Kent), *b* 1954, — Susan Pamela (42 Limes Av, Horley, Surrey RH6 9DG), *b* 1955, — Rosemary Alison (9 Tree View Court, Wray Common Rd, Reigate, Surrey), *b* 1964. *Residence* – Oaken Gates, Tompsets Bank, Forest Row, E Sussex RH18 5BG.

Granddaughter of late Sir Almeric William FitzRoy, KCB, KCVO, el son of Francis Horatio FitzRoy (infra):—
Issue of late Nigel Horatio Trevor FitzRoy, *b* 1889, *d* 1953: *m* 1st, 1917 (*m diss* 1928), Constance who *d* 1974, only da of late Capt Robert Henry Paul, RN, of The Highlands, Banbury; 2ndly, 1936, Diana Frances FitzRoy-Yates, who *m* 2ndly, 1958, William Edward Yates, who *d* 1964, el da of late Brig-Arthur Francis Gore Pery-Knox-Gore, DSO (*see* E Limerick, colls):—
(By 2nd *m*) Susanna Diana Georgina (Colquite, Washaway, Bodmin, Cornwall), *b* 1937: *m* 1st, 1964 (*m diss* 1966), William Anthony Coleridge; 2ndly, 1967, George Henry Peter-Hoblyn (*see* Philipson-Stow, Bt, 1985 Edn), and has issue living (by 2nd *m*), John FitzRoy, *b* 1968: *m* 19—, Isabel —, and has issue living, Harry George FitzRoy *b* 1994, — Emma Frances, *b* 1970.

Grandson of late Francis Horatio FitzRoy, son of late Adm Lord William FitzRoy, KCB, 5th son of 3rd Duke:—
Issue of late Cyril Duncombe FitzRoy, *b* 1861, *d* 1939: *m* 1st, 1903, Leila Margaret, who *d* 1904, da of late Robert Smith, of Goldings, Hertford; 2ndly, 1908, Margaret Cuninghame, who *d* 1948, da of late Rev James Samuel William Durham, DD, R of Ladbroke, Warwickshire:—
(By 2nd *m*) †Charles Francis Mark, *b* 1909: *m* 1936, Baroness Irmgard, el da of late Baron Rudolf von Dincklage, of Hanover, and *d* 1994, leaving issue, Felix Rudolf (26 Cairnhill Gdns, St Andrews, Fife KY16 8QX), *b* 1938; MSc, PhD (Heidelberg): *m* 1976, Renate Brüninghaus, and has issue living, James Francis Stuart *b* 1986, Olga Henrietta *b* 1982, —

Christina Margaret, *b* 1944; BSc: *m* 1974, Ali Kemâl Caba, of Izmir, Turkey. *Residence* – North Lodge, Crimonmogate, Lonmay, Aberdeenshire.

Descendants of late Lieut-Gen Charles FitzRoy (2nd son of Lord Augustus FitzRoy, 2nd son of 2nd Duke), who was *cr Baron Southampton* 1780 (see that title).

(In special remainder to Earldom of Arlington only)

Descendants of late Sir John Bennet, KB (el brother of 1st Earl of Arlington), who was *cr Baron Ossulston* 1682 (*see* E Tankerville).

PREDECESSORS – (1) HENRY CHARLES FitzRoy, KG, 2nd natural son of King Charles II, by Barbara Villiers, Duchess of Cleveland; *cr Baron of Sudbury, Viscount Ipswich*, and *Earl of Euston (peerage of England) 1672, and Duke of Grafton* (peerage of England) 1675: *m* 1682, Isabella, in her own right Countess of Arlington, who in 1673 had *s* by special remainder her father, Henry Bennet, who had been *cr Baron Arlington* of Arlington, Middlesex (peerage of England) 1664, with special remainder, failing issue male to the heirs of his body, and *Baron Arlington*, of Arlington, Middlesex, *Viscount Thetford*, and *Earl of Arlington* (peerage of England) 1672 with like special remainder, and in default of heirs of his body; was Lord High Constable at Coronation of James II, and in 1685 commanded part of HM's forces at the landing of the Duke of Monmouth; was afterwards one of the first to desert his royal master for the Prince of Orange, in which cause he was wounded in storming the City of Cork, and *d* within a fortnight afterwards, 9th Oct 1690; *s* by his son (2) CHARLES, KG, 2nd Duke, who in 1723 *s* to his mother's peerages (ante): *m* 1713, Henrietta, sister of 2nd Duke of Beaufort; *d* 1757; *s* by his grandson (3) AUGUSTUS HENRY, KG, 3rd Duke; a Sec of State 1765, 1st Lord of the Treasury 1766, and Lord Privy Seal 1771: *m* 1st, 1756 (*m diss* 1769), Hon Anne Liddell, da of Henry, Baron Ravensworth (ext 1784); 2ndly, 1769, Elizabeth, da of Very Rev Sir Richard Wrottesley, 7th Bt; *d* 1811; *s* by his el son (4) GEORGE HENRY, KG, 4th Duke; Lord-Lieut of Suffolk: *m* 1784, Lady Charlotte Maria, da of 2nd Earl Waldegrave; *d* 1844; *s* by his son (5) HENRY, 5th Duke; sometime MP for Thetford: *m* 1812, Mary Caroline, da of late Adm Hon Sir George Berkeley, GCB (E Berkeley); *d* 1863; *s* by his el son (6) WILLIAM HENRY, 6th Duke; *b* 1819; MP for Thetford (*L*) 1847-63: *m* 1858, Hon Marie Louisa Anne, who *d* 1928, da of 3rd Baron Ashburton; *dsp* 21 May 1882; *s* by his brother (7) AUGUSTUS CHARLES LENNOX, KG, CB, 7th Duke, *b* 1821; a Gen in the Army; Crimean Campaign 1854 (medal with three clasps, Sardinian and Turkish medals, and 5th class Medjidie); an Equerry to Queen Victoria 1849-82, and an Hon Equerry to Queen Victoria 1882-1901, to King Edward VII 1901-10, and to King George V 1910-18: *m* 1847, Anna, who *d* 1857, da of James Balfour, of Whittinghame Hall, Berwick; *d* 1918; *s* by his son (8) ALFRED WILLIAM MAITLAND, 8th Duke; *b* 1850: *m* 1st, 1875, Margaret Rose, who *d* 1913, da of Eric Carrington Smith, of Ashfold, Sussex; 2ndly, 1916, Susanna Mary, who *d* 1961, da of Sir Mark John MacTaggart-Stewart, 1st Bt, and widow of 17th Baron Borthwick; *d* 1930; *s* by his grandson (9) JOHN CHARLES WILLIAM (son of William Henry Alfred, Viscount Ipswich), 9th Duke: *d* 1936, when the Barony of Arlington (*cr* 1664), and the Viscountcy of Thetford and the Earldom of Arlington (*cr* 1672) fell into abeyance between the sisters of the 9th Duke; *s* in the Dukedom by his kinsman (10) CHARLES ALFRED EUSTON (son of late Rev Lord Charles Edward Fitz-Roy, 4th son of 7th Duke), 10th Duke, *b* 1892: *m* 1st, 1918, Lady Doreen Maria Josepha Sydney Buxton, who *d* 1923, da of 1st Earl Buxton; 2ndly, 1924, Lucy Eleanor, who *d* 1943, da of Sir George Stapylton Barnes, KCB, KCSI (Buxton, By *cr* 1840, colls); 3rdly, 1944, Rita Emily, who *d* 1970, da of late John Ralph Stockley Carr-Ellison, and widow of Lt-Cdr John Thurburn Currie, RN; *d* 1970; *s* by his el son (11) HUGH DENIS CHARLES, 11th Duke, and present peer; also Earl of Euston, Viscount Ipswich, and Baron Sudbury.

Graham, Marquess of; son of Duke of Montrose.

GRAHAM OF EDMONTON, BARON (Graham) (Life Baron 1983)

(THOMAS) EDWARD GRAHAM, son of Thomas Edward Graham, of Newcastle-upon-Tyne; *b* 26 March 1925; *ed* elementary sch, Workers' Educational Assocn Co-operative Coll, and Open Univ (BA); Member and Leader Enfield Council 1961-68; Nat Sec Co-operative Party 1967-74; PPS to Min of State, Dept of Prices and Consumer Protection 1974-76; a Lord Commr of HM Treasury 1976-79; Opposition Spokesman on Environment 1980-83; MP for Enfield, Edmonton (*Lab*) 1974-83; *cr Baron Graham of Edmonton*, of Edmonton, in Greater London (Life Baron) 1983: *m* 1950, Margaret, da of Frederick Golding, of Dagenham, Essex, and has issue.
Residence – 2 Clerks Pierce, Loughton, Essex 1G10 1NR.

SONS LIVING

Hon Martin Nicholas, *b* 1957.
Hon Ian Stuart, *b* 1959.

Granard, Baron, title of Earl of Granard on Roll of HL.

GRANARD, EARL OF (Forbes) Sits as BARON (UK 1806) (Earl I 1684; Bt S 1628)

PETER ARTHUR EDWARD HASTINGS FORBES, 10th Earl, and 11th Baronet; *b* 15 March 1957; *s* 1992; *ed* Eton: *m* 1980, Nora Ann (Noreen), da of Robert Mitchell, of Upper Main St, Portarlington, co Leix, and has issue.

Arms – Azure, three bears' heads couped at the neck argent, muzzled gules. *Crest* – A bear statant argent, guttée de sang, and muzzled gules. *Supporters* – *Dexter*, an unicorn erminois, armed, maned, tufted, and unguled or; *sinister*, a dragon wings elevated ermine.
Seat – Castle Forbes, Newtown Forbes, co Longford. *Residence* – Strathallan Cliff, Strathallan Rd, Onchan, Isle of Man.

The incitement to glory is the firebrand of the mind

SONS LIVING

JONATHAN PETER HASTINGS (*Viscount Forbes*), *b* 24 Dec 1981.
Hon David Robert Hastings, *b* 1984.

Hon Edward Hastings, *b* 1989.

DAUGHTER LIVING

Lady Lisa Ann, *b* 1986.

SISTERS LIVING

Susan, *b* 1948.
Patricia Moira, *b* 1950.
Caroline Mary, *b* 1954: *m* 1st, 1975 (*m diss* 19—), Dominick Charles Hamilton, yr son of Capt Hubert Charles Paulet (Paul) Hamilton, of Moyne, Durrow, co Leix; 2ndly, 1983, Robert John George Dillon-Mahon, and has issue (by 2nd *m*) (*see* Mahon, Bt). *Residence* – Sainte Helene, Quartier Meaulx, 83830 Claviers, Callas, Var, France.

DAUGHTERS LIVING OF NINTH EARL

Lady Moira Beatrice, *b* 1951: *m* 1st, 1971 (*m diss* 1975), HH Prince Charles Antoine Marie Lamoral de Ligne de la Trémoïlle; 2ndly, 1978, José Guerrico, and has issue living (by 2nd *m*), Killian Arthur, *b* 1987, — Shannon Moira Kiara Beatrice, *b* 1983. *Residence* – 5 Avenue Princesse Alice, Monte Carlo.
Lady Georgina Anne, *b* 1952. *Residences* – 11 rue Louis de Savoie, Morges, Switzerland; Castle Forbes, Newtown Forbes, co Longford.

DAUGHTER LIVING OF EIGHTH EARL

Lady Moira Mary, *b* 1910: *m* 1st, 1934 (*m diss* under French civil law 1936), Count Louis de Brantes; 2ndly, 1942 (*m diss* 19—), Count Rossi di Montelera. *Residence* – 16 Chemin des Mouettes, 1007 Lausanne, Switzerland.

MOTHER LIVING

Joan, 3rd da of A. Edward Smith, of Sherlockstown House, Sallins, co Kildare: *m* 1947, Hon John Forbes, yr son of 8th Earl, who *d* 1982. *Residence* – Perigord II, 6 rue des Lacets St Leon, Monte Carlo, Monaco.

COLLATERAL BRANCHES LIVING

Issue of late Col Hon Donald Alexander Forbes, DSO, MVO, 4th son of 7th Earl, *b* 1880, *d* 1938: *m* 1918, Mary Doreen, who *d* 1987, da of late Andrew Sherlock Lawson (*see* V Mountgarret, 1943 Edn):—
Penelope (*Lady Sitwell*), *b* 1923: *m* 1952, Sir Sacheverell Reresby Sitwell, 7th Bt. *Residences* – 4 Southwick Place, W2 2TN; Renishaw Hall, Derbyshire.

Grandchildren of late Lt-Col George Francis Reginald Forbes, eldest son of late Col Hon William Francis Forbes, yr brother of 7th Earl:—
Issue of late Lt-Col Walter Arthur Hastings Forbes, *b* 1905, *d* 1987: *m* 1946, Joan Margaret (Brookfield, Silk Mill Lane, Winchcombe, Cheltenham, Glos GL54 5HZ), formerly wife of late Maj Robert Malise Keith Murray (*see* Murray of Ochtertyre, 1970 Edn), and elder da of late Maj Hugh Kettles-Roy, of Nairobi, Kenya:—
Peter Patrick Spencer, *b* 1949; *ed* Milton Abby, RMA Sandhurst, and Manchester Univ: *m* 1981, Victoria Anne, da of Harry Tudor Bigge, of Lower Lease, Saunton, Braunton, N Devon, and has issue living, Arthur Edward Patrick, *b* 1987, — George Harry Hastings, *b* (twin) 1987, — Katherine Anne, *b* 1983, — Serena Victoria, *b* 1985. *Residence* – Garston House, Sixpenny Handley, Salisbury, Wilts SP5 5PB. —— Rolleen Anne, *b* 1947: *m* 1974, James Christopher Barclay, and has issue living, Robert James, *b* 1977, — Georgina Anne, *b* 1978. *Residence* – Rivers Hall, Waldringfield, Woodbridge, Suffolk.

PREDECESSORS – (1) *Sir* ARTHUR Forbes, Knt, great-great-grandson of the Hon Patrick, 3rd son of 2nd Lord Forbes; *cr* a *Baronet* 1628; obtained grants of land in co Longford; killed in a duel 1632; *s* by his son (2) *Rt Hon Sir* ARTHUR, PC, 2nd Bt; Lt-Gen in the Army; MP for Mullingar 1661; having served under Montrose for the Royal Cause in Scotland, was after the Restoration appointed Marshal of the Army in Ireland, and constituted one of the Lords Justices 1671 and 1673; raised in 1684 the 18th Royal Irish Regt; *cr Baron Clanehugh* and *Viscount Granard* (peerage of Ireland) 1675, and *Earl of Granard* (peerage of Ireland) 1684; *d* 1696; *s* by his son (3) ARTHUR, 2nd Earl; was deprived of his command of the 18th Royal Irish Regt and imprisoned in the Tower; *d* 1734; *s* by his son (4) GEORGE, 3rd Earl; an eminent Adm; Ambassador to Court of Muscovy; called to House of Peers as Lord Forbes in lifetime of his father; *d* 1765; *s* by his son (5) GEORGE, 4th Earl; a Lt-Gen in the Army; *d* 1769; *s* by his son (6) GEORGE, 5th Earl; *d* 1780; *s* by his son (7) GEORGE, 6th Earl; a Gen in the Army, and Clerk of the Crown and Hanaper in Ireland; *cr Baron Granard*, of Castle Donington, co Leicester (peerage of United Kingdom) 1806; *d* 1837; *s* by his grandson (8) GEORGE ARTHUR HASTINGS, KP, 7th Earl (son of Major-Gen George, Viscount Forbes, el son of 6th Earl, by Frances Mary, VA, da of late William Territt, Esq, LLD, of Chilton Hall, Suffolk), *b* 1836; was Lord-Lieut of co Leitrim 1856-72: *m* 1st, 1858, Jane Colclough, who *d* 1872, da of Hamilton Knox Grogan-Morgan, Esq, of Johnstown Castle, Wexford; 2ndly, 1873, Hon Frances Mary, who *d* 1920, da of 12th Baron Petre; *d* 1889; *s* by his el son (9) BERNARD ARTHUR WILLIAM PATRICK HASTINGS, PC, KP, GCVO, 8th Earl; *b* 1874; Lieut-Col 8th Batn City of London Regt, Lieut-Col Reserve of Officers (Scots Guards), Vice-Adm of Province of Connaught, and a Dep Speaker of House of Lords; a Lord-in-Waiting to King Edward VII 1905, Master of the Horse to King Edward VII 1905-10, and to King George V 1910-15; Assist Postmaster-Gen 1906-9, and again Master of the horse 1924-36; a Member of Senate, S Ireland June 1921, and of Irish Free

State Dec 1922 to Dec 1934; HM's Comptroller at Ascot 1936-45: *m* 1909, Beatrice, OBE, who *d* 1972, da of late Ogden Mills, of East 69th Street, New York, and Staatsburg, Dutchess Co, New York; *d* 1948; *s* by his el son **(10)** ARTHUR PATRICK HASTINGS, AFC, 9th Earl; *b* 1915; Air Commodore RAF Vol Reserve, European War 1939-45 (despatches, AFC, Cdr of Legion of Honour, Officer of American Legion of Merit, 4th Class Order of George I of Greece, French Croix de Guerre, Polish Cross of Valour): *m* 1949, Marie Madeleine Eugène, who *d* 1990, yst da of late Jean Maurel, of Millau, Aveyron, and formerly wife of late Prince Humbert de Faucigny Lucinge; *d* 1992; *s* by his nephew **(11)** PETER ARTHUR EDWARD HASTINGS (only son of late Hon John Forbes, yr son of 8th Earl), 10th Earl and present peer; also Viscount Granard, Baron Clanehugh, and Baron Granard.

Granby, Marquess of; son of Duke of Rutland.

GRANTCHESTER, BARON (Suenson-Taylor) (Baron UK 1953)

KENNETH BENT SUENSON-TAYLOR, CBE, QC, 2nd Baron; *b* 18 Aug 1921; *s* 1976; *ed* Westminster and Christ's Coll, Camb (MA, LLM); Bar Middle Temple 1946, ad eundem Lincoln's Inn; QC 1971; Pres of the Value Added Tax Tribunals 1972-87, Chm 1988-92; a Recorder of the Crown Courts 1975-92, Chm of Licensed Dealers' Tribunal 1976-88; Pres of Aircraft and Shipping Industs Arbitration Tribunal 1980-83; Chm Dairy Produce Quota Tribunal since 1984; Chm Financial Services Tribunal 1987-91; Dep Chm in House of Lords since 1988; 1940-45 War as Lt RA; CBE (1985): *m* 1947, Betty, elder da of late Sir John Moores, CBE, and has issue.

Arms – Quarterly, 1st and 4th sable, on a fesse engrailed between in chief a fleur-de-lys between two annulets or, and in base as many like annulets a lion passant of the field, *Taylor*, 2nd and 3rd gules, in chief two swans rousant proper each crowned with an antique crown or, and in base barry wavy of six argent and azure, *Suenson*. **Crests** – 1st, issuant from a crown palisado or an unicorn's head sable and armed and charged on the neck with an annulet of gold and holding in the mouth an acorn leaved and slipped proper, *Taylor*, 2nd, issuant from a coronet composed of eight roses gules seeded argent set upon a rim or, a swan rousant proper crowned with an antique crown gold, *Suenson*. **Supporters** – *Dexter*, an unicorn sable armed, and crined or, gorged with a collar argent, thereon a fesse wavy azure; *sinister*, a lion or, gorged with a collar of four hearts gules.
Address – House of Lords, SW1. *Club* – Buck's.

SONS LIVING

Hon CHRISTOPHER JOHN (Lower House Farm, Back Coole Lane, Audlem, Crewe, Ches), *b* 8 April 1951; *ed* Winchester, and London School of Economics (MA); dairy farmer and cattle breeder: *m* 1973, Jacqueline, da of Dr Leo Jaffe, and has issue living, Jesse David, *b* 1977, — Adam Joel, *b* 1987, — Holly Rachel, *b* 1975, — Hannah Robin, *b* 1984.
Hon Jeremy Kenneth (twin) *b* 1951; *ed* Winchester: *m* 19—, Lindsay Anne Kirby, and has issue living, Daniel, *b* 1983, — Rowan, *b* 1974, — Laurel, *b* 1979, — Zoë, *b* 1982.
Hon James Gunnar (Mole House, 63 Pelhams Walk, Esher, Surrey), *b* 1955; *ed* Eton, and Kingston Univ (BA); Co Dir: *m* 1981, Gillian Susan, yr da of Peter Ayling, of Worcester Park, Surrey, and has issue living, Andrew James, *b* 1985, — Jonathan Gunnar, *b* 1991, — Katherine Joyce, *b* 1988.

DAUGHTERS LIVING

Hon Janet Elizabeth Gudrun, *b* 1949; *ed* Cheltenham Ladies Coll, and St Hilda's Coll, Oxford (MA); Conservator of paintings: *m* 1973, Gerald Edgar Grimstone, of 103 Home Park Rd, SW19, and has issue living, Toby Stephen Gunnar, *b* 1975, — Jenny Elizabeth May, *b* 1979, — Anna Rose Yvonne, *b* 1982.
Hon Deborah Katherine Louise, *b* 1957; *ed* Cheltenham Ladies Coll: *m* 1977, Michael Paul Jones, of The Old Rectory, Earnley, nr Chichester, and has issue living, Christopher Michael, *b* 1987, — Elizabeth Lily, *b* 1992.
Hon Kirsten Victoria Mary, *b* 1961; *ed* Cheltenham Ladies Coll, Godolphin and Latymer, Liverpool Univ (BA), and London Univ (MA): *m* 1988, Keith Lorban.

SISTER LIVING

Hon Monica Esmé Ebba, *b* 1926; *ed* Queen's Coll, London and Newnham Coll, Camb (MA): *m* 1951 (*m diss* 1965), Graeme Spotswood Parish, and has had issue, Andrew Graeme Spotswood, *b* 1954; *ed* Westminster; *d* in an accident 1973, — Alexandra Francesca Spotswood, *b* 1953: *m* 1987, Nicholas Burnell, and has issue living, Joss Elliott Crystal (a son) *b* 1987, Brittany Leah *b* 1991.

PREDECESSOR – **(1)** *Sir* ALFRED JESSE Suenson-Taylor, OBE, son of late Alfred George Taylor, of Stowford, Sutton, Surrey; *b* 1893; Chm of London and Manchester Assurance Co 1953-61; Past Pres of London Liberal Party and joint Hon Treas of Liberal Party Organisation; initiated unofficial meetings of EFTA Parliamentarians at Strasbourg; Delegate to Assemblies Council of Europe and W European Union 1957-66; *cr Baron Grantchester*, of Knightsbridge, in City of Westminster (peerage of UK) 1953: *m* 1920, Mara Henrietta (Mamie), who *d* 1976, da of late Albert Suenson, of Copenhagen; *d* 1976; *s* by his son **(2)** KENNETH BENT, QC, 2nd Baron, and present peer.

GRANTLEY, BARON (Norton) (Baron GB 1782)

I follow a long line of ancestry

JOHN RICHARD BRINSLEY NORTON, MC, 7th Baron; *b* 30 July 1923; *s* 1954; *ed* Eton, and New Coll, Oxford; a Member of Lloyd's; 1939-45 War in Italy as Capt Grenadier Guards (MC): *m* 1955, Lady Deirdre Freda Mary Hare, da of 5th Earl of Listowel, and has issue.

𝔄rms – Azure, a maunch ermine, surmounted by a bend gules. 𝔠rest – A Moor's head affrontée, couped at the shoulders proper, wreathed round the temples with laurel, and round the neck a torse, argent and azure. 𝔖upporters – *Dexter*, a lion, and *sinister*, a griffin, both argent and ducally gorged or, and pendent from the coronets, by a red ribbon, a shield of the arms of *Norton.*
Residences – Markenfield Hall, Ripon; 53 Lower Belgrave St, SW1.
Clubs – White's, Pratt's.

SONS LIVING

Hon RICHARD WILLIAM BRINSLEY (8 Halsey Street, SW3; *Clubs* – White's, Pratt's), *b* 30 Jan 1956; *ed* Ampleforth, and New Coll, Oxford; Pres of Oxford Union 1976; Knt of Honour and Devotion of Sov Mil Order of Malta; a Councillor, R Borough of Kensington and Chelsea 1982-86; merchant banker.
Hon Francis John Hilary, *b* 1960.

SISTER LIVING

Hon Sarah Katherine Elinor (42 Melton Court, Old Brompton Rd, SW7 3JH), *b* 1920: *m* 1st, 1945 (*m diss* 1953), 3rd Viscount Astor, who *d* 1966; 2ndly, 1953 (*m diss* 1965), Maj Thomas Michael Baring, Derbyshire Yeo (*see* B Northbrook, colls).

PREDECESSORS – (1) *Sir* FLETCHER Norton, KB, PC; MP for Appleby 1754-61, and for Wigan 1761-82, Solicitor-Gen 1761, Attorney-Gen 1763 and Speaker of the House of Commons 1769-82; *cr Lord Grantley, Baron of Markenfield*, co York (peerage of United Kingdom) 1782: *d* 1789; *s* by his son (2) WILLIAM, 2nd Baron; *d* 1822; *s* by his nephew (3) FLETCHER, 3rd Baron, son of Hon Fletcher, 2nd son of 1st Baron; present at Quatre Bras and Waterloo; *dsp* 1875; *s* by his nephew (4) THOMAS BRINSLEY, 4th Baron, 2nd son of Hon George Chapple Norton, brother of 3rd Baron; *b* 1831: *m* 1854, Maria Chiara Eliza, who *d* 1892, da of Signor Federigo; *d* 1877; *s* by his son (5) JOHN RICHARD BRINSLEY, 5th Baron; *b* 1855: *m* 1st, 1879, Katharine, who *d* 1897, da of late William Henry McVickar, of USA; 2ndly, 1899, Alice, who *d* 1942, natural da of 7th Viscount Ranelagh; *d* 1943; *s* by his son (6) RICHARD HENRY BRINSLEY, 6th Baron; *b* 1892; *m* 1919, Jean Mary, who *d* 1945, da of Sir David Alexander Kinloch, CB, MVO, 11th Bt; *d* 1954; *s* by his only son (7) JOHN RICHARD BRINSLEY, 7th Baron and present peer.

GRANVILLE, EARL (Leveson-Gower) (Earl UK 1833)
(Name pronounced "Looson-Gore")

You may break, but you will not bend me

GRANVILLE JAMES LEVESON-GOWER, MC, 5th Earl; *b* 6 Dec 1918; *s* 1953; *ed* Eton; Maj Coldm Gds (Supplementary Reserve); a DL for Inverness-shire; Pres of Navy League 1953-66; Lord Lieut Islands Area, Western Isles since 1983; 1939-45 War in Tunisia and Italy (twice wounded, despatches, MC): *m* 1958, Doon Aileen, da of late Flight-Lieut Hon Brinsley Sheridan Bushe Plunket, RAF Vol Reserve (*see* B Plunket), and has issue.

𝔄rms – Quarterly: 1st and 4th, barry of eight, argent and gules, a cross flory sable, *Gower*; 2nd azure, three laurel leaves or, *Leveson*; 3rd gules, three clarions or, *Granville*; in the centre a crescent for difference. 𝔠rest – A wolf passant argent, collared and lined or. 𝔖upporters – Two wolves argent, plain collared, and line reflexed over the back gold, and charged on the shoulder with an escutcheon gules thereon a clarion or.
Residence – Callernish, Lochmaddy, Isle of N Uist, Western Isles.

SONS LIVING

GRANVILLE GEORGE FERGUS (*Lord Leveson*), *b* 10 Sept 1959; appointed a Page of Honour to HM The Queen 1973.
Hon Niall James, *b* 1963.

DAUGHTER LIVING

Lady Marcia Rose Aileen, *b* 1961: *m* 1986, Jonathan Charles Bulmer, yst son of late Edward Charles Bulmer, and has issue living, James Alexander Howard, *b* 1992, — Hector Charles Marcus, *b* 1993, — Hesper Rose Constance, *b* 1990. *Residence* – 26 Chester St, SW1.

SISTER LIVING

Lady Mary Cecilia, *b* 1917: *m* 1958, Samuel Wittewronge Clayton, son of late Brig-Gen Sir Gilbert Falkington Clayton, KCMG, KBE, CB, and has issue living, Gilbert Falkingham, *b* 1958; a Page of Honour to HM Queen Elizabeth The Queen Mother 1973-74, — Rose Cecilia, *b* 1960: *m* 1993, William W. Stancer, son of J. A. Stancer, of Old Rectory, Wick Rissington, Glos.

PREDECESSORS – (1) *Lord* GRANVILLE Leveson-Gower, GCB, PC, yst son of 1st Marquess of Stafford (*see* D Sutherland); *b* 1773; was sometime Sec at War, and successively Ambassador to Russia, Holland and France, *cr Viscount Granville* (peerage of United Kingdom) 1815, and *Baron Leveson*, of Stone, co Stafford, and *Earl Granville* (peerage of United Kingdom) 1833: *m* 1809, Lady Henrietta Elizabeth Cavendish, who *d* 1862, da of 5th Duke of Devonshire; *d* 1846; *s* by his son **(2)** GRANVILLE GEORGE, KG, PC, 2nd Earl, *b* 1815; MP for Morpeth (*L*) 1837-40, and for Lichfield 1841-6; was Under-Sec for Foreign Affairs 1840-41, Vice-Pres of Board of Trade 1848-51, Sec of State for Foreign Affairs 1851-2, 1870-74, and 1880-85, Lord Pres of Council 1852-4, 1855-8, and 1859-66, Chancellor of Duchy of Lancaster 1854-5, Ambassador Extraor to Russia at coronation of Alexander II, 1856, and Sec of State for the Colonies 1868-70 and 1886; sometime Constable of Dover Castle, and Lord Warden of the Cinque Ports: *m* 1st, 1840, Marie Louise Pelline, who *d* 1860, da of Emeric Joseph, Duc de Dalberg, and widow of Sir Ferdinand Richard Edward Acton, 7th Bt; 2ndly, 1865, Castalia Rosalind, who *d* 1938, da of Walter Campbell, of Islay; *d* 1891; *s* by his el son **(3)** GRANVILLE GEORGE, GCMG, GCVO, PC, 3rd Earl, *b* 1872; a Lord-in-Waiting to Queen Victoria 1895-1905, to King Edward VII, 1905-10, and to King George V 1910-15, Envoy Extraor and Min Plen to Greece 1917-21, to Denmark 1921-6, and to the Netherlands 1926-8, and Ambassador Extraor and Plen to Belgium and Luxembourg 1928-33: *m* 1900, Nina Ayesha, who *d* 1955, da of late Walter Baring; *d* 1939; *s* by his brother **(4)** WILLIAM SPENCER, KG, KCVO, CB, DSO, 4th Earl; *b* 1880; Vice-Adm; Ch of Staff and Maintenance Capt the Nore 1924-27, and Rear-Adm Comdg Coast of Scotland 1931-33; Lieut-Gov of Isle of Man 1937-45, and Gov of N Ireland 1945-52; 1914-18 War (DSO): *m* 1916, Lady Rose Constance Bowes-Lyon, GCVO, LLD, who *d* 1967, da of 14th Earl of Strathmore; *d* 1953; *s* by his son **(5)** GRANVILLE JAMES, 5th Earl and present peer; also Viscount Granville, and Baron Leveson.

GRANVILLE OF EYE, BARON (Granville) (Life Baron 1967)

EDGAR LOUIS GRANVILLE, son of Reginald Granville, of Brighton; *b* 12 Feb 1899; *ed* High Wycombe and Melbourne, Australia; Managing Dir of E. L. Granville & Co Ltd; PPS to Sec of State, Sir Herbert Samuel, first Nat Govt 1931, and to Foreign Sec, Sir John Simon, National Govt 1931-36; MP for Eye Div of Suffolk (*L*) 1929-51; Independent 1951; 1914-18 War with AIF, Gallipoli, Egypt and France; 1939-45, helped to raise 119th Suffolk Battery RA, as acting Capt; *cr Baron Granville of Eye*, of Eye, co Suffolk (Life Baron) 1967: *m* 1943, Elizabeth, da of late Rev William Cecil Hunter, British Mission Sch, India and has issue.

Arms – Tierced in pairle vert purpure and azure, in chief two sea gulls volant proper, and in base a sun in splendour charged with an eye, and a bordure or eight beech leaves proper in aestival and autumnal tints alternately. **Crest** – In front of a mount vert, thereon a beech tree proper, a chaplet of roses argent barbed and seeded proper. **Supporters** – *Dexter*, a bay horse, *sinister*, a kangaroo proper.
Residence – 112 Charlton Lane, Cheltenham.

DAUGHTER LIVING

Hon Linda Elizabeth Mary, *b* 1949.

GRANVILLE-WEST, BARONY OF (West) (Extinct 1984)

SON LIVING OF LIFE BARON

Hon Gerald Hugh Granville, *b* 1942: *m* 1969, Barbara, da of Arthur Strath, of Ellwood Dene, Kilndown, Cranbrook, Kent, and has issue.

DAUGHTER LIVING OF LIFE BARON

Hon Vera Lesley Meryl, *b* 1937: *m* 1959, William Smith, of Hollycroft, Sunnybank Rd, Griffthstown Mon, and has issue.

WIDOW LIVING OF LIFE BARON

VERA (*Baroness Granville-West*), JP (Brynderwen, Abersychan, Pontypool, Gwent), da of J. Hopkins, of Pontypool: *m* 1937, Baron Granville-West (Life Baron), who *d* 1984.

GRAVES, BARON (Graves) (Baron I 1794)

The eagle does not catch flies

EVELYN PAGET GRAVES, 9th Baron; *b* 17 May 1926; *s* 1994: *m* 1957, Marjorie Ann, da of late Dr Sidney Ernest Holder, of Wallingford, Berks, and has issue.

Arms – Gules, an eagle, displayed or ducally crowned argent, on a canton of the last an anchor proper. **Crest** – A demi-eagle, displayed and erased or, encircled round the body and below the wings by a ducal coronet argent. **Supporters** – Two royal vultures, wings close proper.
Residence – Woodlands, RSD 846, Deloraine, 7304 Tasmania.

SONS LIVING

Hon TIMOTHY EVELYN, *b* 27 March 1960.
Hon Simon Paget, *b* 1963.

DAUGHTERS LIVING

Hon Wendy Susan, *b* 1958.
Hon Philippa Ann, *b* 1962.

SISTER LIVING

Diana Wellesley, *b* 1934: *m* 1st, 1956 (*m diss* 1974), Edgar Mark Wolfhagen; 2ndly, 1974, Guy Paul Emile Peltzer, of Ravensworth, Langford, 7301 Tasmania, and has issue living (by 1st *m*), Julian Mark, *b* 1957, — Martin Charles, *b* 1959, — Philip Gerret Wellesley, *b* 1963, — Quentin Evelyn, *b* 1969.

DAUGHTER LIVING OF SIXTH BARON

Hon Rosemary Audrey Alys, *b* 1910: *m* 1938, Major Herbert Edward Osborne, MC, who *d* 1951. *Residence* – 30A Rose Bush Court, 34/41 Parkhill Rd, NW3 24E.

COLLATERAL BRANCHES LIVING

Granddaughters of late Capt Hon Adolphus Edward Paget Graves (brother of 5th Baron), 5th son of Hon Henry Richard Graves, 3rd son of 2nd Baron:—
Issue of late Lt-Cmdr Vernon North Graves, DSC, RN *b* 1911, *d* 1960: *m* 1947, Elizabeth Constance (90 Stockton Lane, York Y03 0BS), da of late Capt Robert Francis Uniacke Penrose FitzGerald, RN:—
Janice Iona Penrose (18 Market Place, Kirkbymoorside, York Y06 6DA), *b* 1947: *m* 1st, 1968 (*m diss* 1974), Stephen Van Simons; 2ndly, 1980, Christopher Bernard Rose, and has issue living (by 1st *m*), Isobel Jane, *b* 1972, — (by 2nd *m*) Thomas George, *b* 1981. — Sarah Frances Paget (90 Stockton Lane, York Y03 0BS), *b* 1950: *m* 1979, Iannis Tamvakis, and has issue living, Ewan Ferenc GRAVES-TAMVAKIS, *b* 1975, — Charlotte Elizabeth GRAVES-TAMVAKIS, *b* (twin) 1975.

Granddaughter of late Capt Hon Adolphus Edward Paget Graves (ante):—
Issue of late Cyril Edward Cuthbert Hare Graves, *b* 1860, *d* 1946: *m* 1916, Constance Katherine, who *d* 1951, da of late François Chrysostom Mouflet, of Leamington:—
Mary Caroline Margot, *b* 1919: *m* 1942: *m* 1942 (*m diss* 1964), Albert Arthur Puddick, who *d* 1994, and has issue living, Robert Arthur Graves, *b* 1944; *ed* Cranley: *m* 1st, 1967 (*m diss* 1990), Jane Margaret Ferrand; 2ndly, 1991, Melanie Anne, da of Richard Alastair Stuart-Hunt, and has issue living (by 1st *m*), Simon Nicholas Graves *b* 1969, Julian Urling Graves *b* 1970, (by 2nd *m*) Charles Oscar Graves *b* 1993, — David Stewart Graves, *b* 1946; *ed* Cranley: *m* 1972, Sarah Elizabeth, da of Antony Lamb, and has issue living, Michael Antony Graves *b* 1974, Annabell Sarah *b* 1977, — Christopher Nicholas Graves, *b* 1992; *ed* Cranley: *m* 1992, Selena Ann, da of John Thomas Hobbs.

PREDECESSORS – **(1)** THOMAS GRAVES, 2nd son of late Rear-Adm Thomas Graves, of Thanckes, Cornwall; *b* 1725; Adm of the White; was second in command under Lord Howe at great Naval Victory of June 1st, 1794 (*cr* Baron and granted pension of £1,000 per annum): *m* 1771, Elizabeth, who *d* 1827, da of late William Peere Williams, of Cadhay, Devon; *cr Lord Graves, Baron of Gravesend*, co Londonderry (peerage of Ireland) 1794: *d* 1802; *s* by his son **(2)** THOMAS NORTH, 2nd Baron; MP; a Lord of the Bedchamber and Comptroller of the Household to HRH the Duke of Cumberland: *m* 1803, Lady Mary Paget, who *d* 1835, yst da of 1st Earl of Uxbridge, and sister of 1st Marquess of Anglesey, KG, *d* 1830, *s* by his son **(3)** WILLIAM THOMAS, 3rd Baron, *b* 1804: *m* 1st, 1829, Sophie Therese, who *d* 1833, da of Gen Berthier, and widow of Gen Count Bruyere; 2ndly, Louise Adèle Malene, who *d* 1877; *d* 1870; *s* by his son **(4)** CLARENCE EDWARD, *b* 1847: *m* 1870, Katherine Frederica, who *d* 1926, da of Sir Thomas Wilham Clinton Murdoch, KCMG; *d* 1904; *s* by his cousin **(5)** HENRY CYRIL PERCY (son of late Hon Henry Richard Graves, 3rd son of 2nd Baron), 5th Baron, *b* 1847: *m* 1870, Elizabeth Ellen, who *d* 1914, yst da of late Henry Craven, of Wickham Hall, Kent; *d* 1914; *s* by his cousin **(6)** CLARENCE PERCY RIVERS, 6th Baron, *b* 1871: *m* 1903, his cousin, Mary Ada Isabel, who *d* 1962, da of late Edward Corbett Parker; *d* 1937; *s* by his cousin **(7)** HENRY ALGERNON CLAUDE (son of late Claude Thomas Graves, son of late Hon Henry Richard Graves, 3rd son of 2nd Baron), 7th Baron *b* 1877: *m* 1909 (*m diss* 1922), Vera Blanche Neville, who *d* 1953, da of late Alfred Neville Shepp: *d* 1963: *s* by his son **(8)** PETER GEORGE WELLESLEY, 8th Baron, *b* 1911: Actor: *m* 1960, Winifred Ruby (actress as Vanessa Lee), who *d* 1992, da of Alfred Moule, and widow of Warde Morgan; *d* 1994; *s* by his kinsman **(9)** EVELYN PAGET (only son of late Alwyn Montague Graves, 2nd son of Capt Hon Adolphus Edward Paget Graves (brother of 5th Baron), 5th son of Hon Henry Richard Graves, 3rd son of 2nd Baron), 9th Baron and present peer.

GRAY, LORD (Campbell-Gray) (Lord S 1445)

ANGUS DIARMID IAN CAMPBELL-GRAY, 22nd Lord; *b* 3 July 1931; *s* 1946; *ed* Eton: *m* 1st 1959, Patricia Margaret, who *d* 1987, only da of late Capt Philip Sylvester Alexander, 8th Hussars (*see* E Caledon, colls); 2ndly, 1994, Cilla, widow of Paul Williams, and has issue.

Arms – Gules a lion rampant within a bordure engrailed argent, over all a label of two points or, each point charged gyronny of eight or and sable. **Crest** – An anchor in pole or. **Supporters** – Two lions guardant gules charged with a label as in the arms.
Residence – Airds Bay House, Taynuilt, Argyll. *Clubs* – Carlton, MCC.

SON LIVING *(By 1st marriage)*

Hon ANDREW GODFREY DIARMID STUART (*Master of Gray*), *b* 3 Sept 1964: *m* 1993, Hon Lucy Elton, yst da of 2nd Baron Elton.

DAUGHTERS LIVING *(By 1st marriage)*

Hon Lucinda Margaret, *b* 1961.
Hon Iona Doreen, *b* 1962.
Hon (Cethlyn) Isobell, *b* 1969.

BROTHER LIVING *(Raised to the rank of a Baron's son 1950)*

Hon Cailain Douglas (Fanamor, Taynuilt, Argyll PA35 1HR), *b* 1934; *ed* Eton: *m* 1963, Wendy Helen Katharine, yr da of late W. H. Dunlop, of Doonside, Ayrshire, and has issue living, James Douglas, *b* 1966, — Charlotte Anne, *b* 1968.

COLLATERAL BRANCHES LIVING

Issue of late Hon Fiona Faith Campbell-Gray, sister of 22nd Lord, *b* 1933, *d* 1991: *m* 1955, Maj (Ronald Hugh) Desmond Fabling, 14 PWO The Scinde Horse (IA), and 1st Royal Dragoons (ret), who *d* 1974:—
Victoria Theresa, *b* 1958: *m* 1993, Nicolas A. Shugar, elder son of Alan Shugar, of Manor Park, Bristol. *Residence* – 41 Wandle Bank, SW19 1DW. —— Fenella Mary, *b* 1963.

Issue of late Christine Anne Campbell-Gray, sister of 22nd Lord, *b* 1938, *d* 1987: *m* 1960, Lt-Col Brian Joseph Lockhart, Blues and Royals, of Maugersbury, Glos:—
Crispin Alexander, *b* 1967. —— Edward Angus (adopted son), *b* 1966. —— Serena Emily (*Lady Gillford*) (adopted da), *b* 1965: *m* 1989, Patrick James, Lord Gillford, only son of 7th Earl of Clanwilliam, and has issue.

Issue of late Hon Thora Zelma Grace Gray, da of Eveleen, Lady Gray, *b* 1875: *d* 1966: *m* 1911, Edward Lorne Frederic Clough-Taylor (D Argyll), who *d* 1947:—
Cara Prunella (19 Sherbrooke Rd, SW6), *b* 1919.

Descendants of late Hon Archibald Stuart, 2nd son of late Hon Jean Gray (el da of 11th Lord), who *m* 1763, the 9th Earl of Moray (see that title).

PREDECESSORS – (1) ANDREW, son of Sir Andrew Gray; successively Ambassador to England, Master of the Household to King James II, and a Warden of the Marches; *cr Lord Gray* (peerage of Scotland), 1444-5, according to Exchequer Rolls; *s* by his grandson (2) ANDREW, 2nd Lord; a Justiciary of Scotland; *s* by his son (3) PATRICK, 3rd Lord; *d* 1541; *s* by his nephew (4) PATRICK (son of Gilbert Gray, 2nd son of 2nd Lord); *d* 1584; *s* by his son (5) PATRICK, 5th Lord, *b* 1538; a Lord of Session; *d* 1609; *s* by his son (6) PATRICK, 6th Lord, *b* 1584; *d* 1611; *s* by his son (7) ANDREW, 7th Lord; obtained a new patent with remainder to William Gray, husband of his only da Anne, and his heirs male, and failing which to Sir William Gray, of Pittendrum, father of William Gray (ante), and his heirs male whatsoever; *s* by his grandson (8) PATRICK, 8th Lord, son of Anne and William Gray (ante); resigned his honours Feb 1707, and in the same month obtained a new patent with the former precedency with remainder to John Gray, of Crichie, husband of his da Marjory, and the heirs of their bodies, and failing which to the el heir female without division; in virtue of this patent (9) JOHN GRAY (ante) became 9th Lord, even during the lifetime of Patrick, 8th Lord; John *d* 1724; *s* by his son (10) JOHN, 10th Lord; *d* 1738; *s* by his son (11) JOHN, 11th Lord; *d* 1782; *s* by his third son (12) CHARLES, 12th Lord; was Capt 1st Dragoon Guards; *d* unmarried 1786; *s* by his brother (13) WILLIAM JOHN, 13th Lord; *d* unmarried 1807; *s* by his brother (14) FRANCIS, 14th Lord; was Postmaster Gen of Scotland; *d* 1842; *s* by his son (15) JOHN, 15th Lord; a Representative Peer; *dsp* 1867; *s* by his sister (16) MADELINA; *d* unmarried 1869; *s* by her niece (17) MARGARET, da of Hon Margaret, 2nd da of 14th Lord, and wife of Hon David Henry Murray, son of 3rd Earl of Mansfield; *d* 1878; *s* by her cousin (18) GEORGE PHILIP, 14th Earl of Moray (heir male of Hon Jean el da of 11th Lord Gray ante); *d* 1816; *d* 1895; when the Earldom of Moray and the Baronies of Doune, St Colme, and Stuart passed to his cousin, Edmund Archibald (*see* E Moray), and the Lordship of Gray was adjudged by the Committee for Privileges of the House of Lords to (19) EVELEEN, da of late Lady Jane Pounden, da of 10th Earl of Moray, *b* 1841: *m* 1863, James Maclaren Smith, who *d* 1900, having received Roy licence 1897 to assume for himself and wife the additional surname and arms of Gray, and for his issue to assume the surname of Gray in lieu of their patronymic with the arms of Gray only; *d* 1918; *s* by her son (20) JAMES MACLAREN STUART, 20th Lord, *d* 1919; *s* by his sister (21) ETHEL EVELEEN, *b* 1866: *m* 1888, Henry Tufnell Campbell, who *d* 1945, having assumed by Roy licence 1920, the additional surname of Gray, son of John Thomas Campbell and Lady Anne Katherine, da of 8th Earl of Lindsay; *d* 1946; *s* by her grandson (22) ANGUS DIARMID IAN (son of late Major Hon Lindsay Stuart Campbell-Gray, MC (*Master of Gray*) el son of Ethel Eveleen, Lady Gray), 22nd Lord and present peer.

GRAY OF CONTIN, BARON (Gray) (Life Baron 1983)

HAMISH JAMES HECTOR NORTHEY GRAY, PC, son of late James Northey Gray, of Inverness, who *d* 1979; *b* 28 June 1927; *ed* Inverness R Acad; Assist Gvt Whip 1971-73; a Lord Commr HM Treasury 1973-74; an Opposition Whip 1974-75, Opposition Spokesman on Energy 1975-79, Min of State, Dept of Energy 1979-83;

Min of State for Scotland 1983-86; MP for Ross and Cromarty (*C*) 1970-83; DL Inverness-shire 1989; served in Queen's Own Cameron Highlanders 1945-48; Dir Family and other Cos 1950-70; *cr* PC 1982, and *Baron Gray of Contin*, of Contin, in the District of Ross and Cromarty (Life Baron) 1983: *m* 1953, Judith Waite, da of Noel M. Brydon, MBE, MICE, and has issue.
Residence – Achneim House, Flichity, Inverness-shire IV1 2XE.

SONS LIVING

Hon (James Northey) David, *b* 1955; *ed* Fettes, and Bristol Univ; Head Master Pocklington Sch since 1992: *m* 1978, Lynda Jane Harlow, and has issue living, James Stuart, *b* 1991, — Fiona Sally, *b* 1984, — Julie Harlow, *b* (twin) 1984. *Residence* – Pocklington School, West Green, Pocklington, York.
Hon Peter L., *b* 1959; *ed* Fettes, and Bristol Univ (LLB); Bar and Advocate at Scottish Bar: *m* 1985, Bridget Mary Willcox, and has issue living, Ishbel Mary, *b* 1989, — Madelene Elisabeth, *b* 1992.

DAUGHTER LIVING

Hon Sally Brydon, *b* 1957: *m* 1984, James S. Brown, FRCS, yst son of Stephen W. R. Brown, of Blantyre, Malawi, and has issue living, Angus, *b* 1986, — Duncan James, *b* 1987, — Hamish Stephen, *b* 1989.

GREENE OF HARROW WEALD, BARON (Greene) (Life Baron 1974)

SIDNEY FRANCIS GREENE, CBE, son of Frank James Greene, of London; *b* 12 Feb 1910; Gen Sec NUR 1957-74; Chm of TUC 1969-70; a Dir of Bank of England since 1970; *cr* CBE (Civil) 1966, Knt 1970, and *Baron Greene of Harrow Weald*, of Harrow, Greater London, (Life Baron) 1947: *m* 1936, Masel Elizabeth Carter, and has issue, 3 das.
Residence – 26 Kynaston Wood, Boxtree Rd, Harrow Weald, Middx.

GREENHILL, BARON (Greenhill) (Baron UK 1950)

MALCOLM GREENHILL, 3rd Baron; *b* 5 May 1924; *s* 1989; *ed* Kelvinside Acad, Glasgow, and Glasgow Univ (BSc); a Chartered Patent Agent; a Member of UK Scientific Mission to Washington, USA, 1950-51, with UK Atomic Energy Authority 1954-73, and with Min of Defence 1973-89.

DAUGHTERS LIVING OF SECOND BARON

Hon Catherine Elizabeth, *b* 1948: *m* 1978, Kenneth Youngren, of 4118 Russell Court, N Vancouver, BC, Canada V7G 2C5.
Hon Sheila Anne, *b* 1951: *m* 1979, Robert Davidson, of 10336 Villa Av, Edmonton, Alberta, Canada T5N 3T9.

WIDOW LIVING OF SECOND BARON

MARGARET JEAN (*Baroness Greenhill*), da of Thomas Newlands, of Hamilton, Ontario, Canada: *m* 1946, the 2nd Baron, MD, DPH, who *d* 1989. *Residence* – 10223 137th St, Edmonton, Alberta, Canada T5N 2G8.

PREDECESSORS – (1) ERNEST Greenhill, OBE, LLD, son of late Maurice Greenhill; *b* 1887; Councillor, Glasgow Corpn 1932; *cr Baron Greenhill*, of Townhead in the City of Glasgow (peerage of UK) 1950: *m* 1914, Ida, who *d* 1985, da of late Mark Goodman; *d* 1967; *s* by his el son (2) STANLEY, MD, DPH, 2nd Baron, *b* 1917, FRSM, FRCP (C), Lecturer in Medicine Alberta Univ, Prof Emeritus 1984: *m* 1946, Margaret Jean, da of Thomas Newlands, of Hamilton, Ontario, Canada; *d* 1989; *s* by his brother (3) MALCOLM, 3rd Baron and present peer.

GREENHILL OF HARROW, BARON (Greenhill) (Life Baron 1974)

DENIS ARTHUR GREENHILL, GCMG, OBE, son of late James Greenhill, of Ashfields, Loughton, Essex; *b* 7 Nov 1913; *ed* Bishop's Stortford Coll, and Ch Ch Oxford (MA) (Hon Student 1977); apprentice London NE Railway 1935-39; entered FO 1946, 1st Sec Sofia 1947-49, and at Washington, DC 1949-52, FO 1952-53, Counsellor to UK Delegation to NATO, Paris 1955-56, and to Office of Commr-Gen for SE Asia, Singapore 1956-58, FO 1958-59, Counsellor Washington 1959-62, and Min there 1962-64, Assist Under-Sec FO 1964-66, Dep Under-Sec 1966-69, and Permanent Under-Sec of State FCO, and Head of Diplo Ser 1969-73; Pres of Roy Soc for Asian Affairs and of Anglo-Finnish Soc; Chm of Governing Body of Sch of Oriental and African Studies since 1978, of Kings Coll Hosp Med Sch Council 1978-83; Dep Chm of BUPA since 1978; Dir of Clerical, Medical and General Life Assurance 1973, of Hawker Siddeley Group 1974, of S. G. Warburg and Co Ltd 1974, and The Wellcome Foundation Ltd 1974; Member of Security Commission 1974-82, Trustee of Rayne Foundation; 1939-45 War as Col RE in Middle East, N Africa, Italy, India and SE Asia (despatches twice, OBE); *cr* OBE (Mil) 1941, CMG 1960, KCMG 1967, GCMG 1972, and *Baron Greenhill of Harrow*, of Roy Borough of Kensington and Chelsea (Life Baron) 1974: *m* 1941, Angela, da of late William Leitch McCulloch, and has had issue.

𝕬rms – Vert, two barrulets ermine, in chief a lion passant or, a bordure argent. 𝕮rest – a demi-griffin gules, semée of mullets gold, holding between the claws a mullet also gold. 𝕾upporters – On either side a Griffin gules semy of mullets or, langued and armed azure.
Residence – 25 Hamilton House, Vicarage Gate, W8. *Club* – Travellers'.

SONS LIVING AND DECEASED

(*Hon*) Nigel Denis St George (does not use courtesy title), *b* 1942.
Hon Robin James, *b* 1945: *m* 1970 (*m diss* 1975), Elizabeth, da of Sir Eric Roll (later Baron Roll of Ipsden) (Life Baron), KCMG, CB, and *d* 1986.

Greenock, Lord; son of Earl Cathcart.

GREENWAY, BARON (Greenway) (Baron UK 1927, Bt 1919)

Industry and honour

AMBROSE CHARLES DREXEL GREENWAY, 4th Baron, and 4th Baronet; *b* 21 May 1941; *s* 1975; *ed* Winchester; marine photographer and author: *m* 1985, Mrs Rosalynne Schenk, of Bickleigh, Tiverton, Devon, da of Lt-Col Peter Geoffrey Fradgley, of Upcott Manor, Rackenford, N Devon.

𝕬rms – Per pale ermine and ermines, on a chief azure a crescent between two covered cups or. 𝕮rest – A griffin's head, or, erased gules, holding in the beak an anchor sable. 𝕾upporters – On either side a griffin sable, beak and claws or, holding in the beak an anchor and charged on the shoulder with a covered cupgold.
Address – c/o House of Lords, SW1. *Club* – House of Lords Yacht.

BROTHERS LIVING

Hon MERVYN STEPHEN KELVYNGE (605 Howard House, Dolphin Sq, SW1V 3PG; *Clubs* – MCC, Turf), *b* 19 Aug 1942; *ed* Winchester; FCA, Freeman of City of Lond, Liveryman Vintners Co; Stockbroker with Capel Cure Myers; has issue living, Philippa Mary, *b* 1980.
Hon Nigel Paul, *b* 1944; *ed* Winchester: *m* 1979, Gabrielle, el da of late Walter Jean Duchardt, of Obenheim, Alsace, and has issue living, Nicholas Walter Paul, *b* 1988, — Philippe, *b* 1991.

WIDOW LIVING OF THIRD BARON

CORDELIA MARY (*Cordelia, Baroness Greenway*) (703 Collingwood House, Dolphin, Sq, SW1), da of late Maj Humphrey Campbell Stephen, JP, of High Mead, Dormansland, Surrey; Freeman City of London 1978, Liveryman Glovers' Co: *m* 1939, the 3rd Baron, who *d* 1975.

COLLATERAL BRANCH LIVING

Issue of late Hon Atheling Kelvynge Brooking Greenway, yr son of 2nd Baron, *b* 1921, *d* 1970: *m* 1944 (*m diss* 1962), Stella Alice, da of William Joseph Jennings, of Salisbury, Rhodesia (now Harare, Zimbabwe):—
Neil Kelvynge Brooking (PO Box 374, Harare, Zimbabwe), *b* 1945: *m* 1970, Flora, da of Lindsay Glegg, of Harare,

Zimbabwe, and has issue living, Timothy Kelvynge, *b* 1976, — Ashleigh Stella, *b* 1973, — Teresa Gay, *b* 1974, — Joanne Cordelia, *b* 1977.

PREDECESSORS – (1) CHARLES Greenway, son of John David Greenway, of Taunton, Somerset; *b* 1857: a merchant and banker; snr partner in firm of Shaw Wallace & Co, India and Ceylon, and R. G. Shaw & Co, London; Pres and one of the founders of Anglo-Persian Oil Co Ltd; *cr* a *Baronet* 1919, and *Baron Greenway*, of Stanbridge Earls, co Southampton (peerage of United Kingdom) 1927: *m* 1883, Mabel, who *d* 1940, da of Edwin Augustine Tower; *d* 1934; *s* by his son (2) CHARLES KELVYNGE, 2nd Baron, *b* 1888; Capt Indian Army: *m* 1916, Eileen Constance, who *d* 1963, da of late Maj-Gen Sir Harry Triscott Brooking, KCB, KCSI, KCMG; *d* 1963; *s* by his el son (3) CHARLES PAUL, 3rd Baron; *b* 1917; Maj Parachute Regt: *m* 1939, Cordelia Mary, da of late Maj Humfrey Campbell Stephen, JP, of High Mead, Dormansland, Surrey; *d* 1975; *s* by his el son (4) AMBROSE CHARLES DREXEL, 4th Baron, and present peer.

GREENWOOD, VISCOUNT (Greenwood) (Viscount UK 1937, Bt UK 1915)

DAVID HENRY HAMAR GREENWOOD, 2nd Viscount, and 2nd Baronet; *b* 30 Oct 1914; *s* 1948.

Arms – Gules, on a chevron ermine between three saltires as many portcullises or. **Crest** – A demi-lion per fesse gules and sable resting the sinister paw on a portcullis or. **Supporters** – On either side a lion rampant per fesse gules and sable supporting a staff or, flowing therefrom a banner argent, that on the dexter charged with a rose gules, barbed and seeded proper, and that on the sinister charged with a maple leaf also proper.
Address – c/o 63 Portsea Hall, Portsea Pl, W2 2BY.

BROTHER LIVING

Hon MICHAEL GEORGE HAMAR (63 Portsea Hall, Portsea Pl, W2 2BY), *b* 5th May 1923; *ed* Eton, and Ch Ch, Oxford; late Roy Signals; actor.

SISTER LIVING

Hon Angela Margo Hamar, *b* 1912: *m* 1937, Edward Dudley Delevingne, who *d* 1974, and has had issue, Edward Hamar (Lime Tree Cottage, Dorking, Surrey), *b* 1939: *m* 1982, Fiona, da of Donald Cameron, and has issue living, Katherine *b* 1985, — Charles Hamar (Paddock House, Spencer Park, SW18), *b* 1949: *m* 1983, Pandora Anne, el da of Jocelyn Edward Greville Stevens (*see* Sheffield, Bt), and has issue living, Chloe Jane *b* 1984, Poppy Angela *b* 1986, Cara Jocelyn *b* 1992, — Anne Venetia, *b* 1938: *m* 1985, Edward Lavender, and *d* 1987, — (Elizabeth) Caroline Felicia, *b* 1953: *m* 1978, Thomas G. Elek, of 44 Scarsdale Villas, W8, son of late Dr Imre Elek, of Millom, Cumbria, and has issue living, Charles Thomas Hamar *b* 1986, George Theodore Dudley *b* 1990, Edwina Mary Angela *b* 1980, Flora Tamsin Elizabeth *b* 1982. *Residence* – 22 Ovington St, SW3.

PREDECESSOR – (1) (THOMAS) HAMAR Greenwood, PC, KC, BA, son of John Hamar Greenwood, Bar-at-law, Grays Inn; *b* 1870; Under-Sec of State for Home Depart Jan 1919, an Additional Under-Sec of State for Foreign Depart, Additional Parliamentary Sec to Board of Trade, and Sec to Depart of Overseas Trade July 1919; was last Ch Sec for Ireland (with a seat in the Cabinet) and Chancellor of the Order of St Patrick April 1920 to Oct 1922; sat as MP for York (*L*) 1906-10 for Sunderland 1910-22, and for E Div of Walthamstow (*C*) 1929-4; *cr* a *Baronet* 1915, *Baron Greenwood*, of Llanbister, co Radnor (*peerage of United Kingdom) 1929, and Viscount Greenwood*, of Holbourne, co London (peerage of United Kingdom) 1937: *m* 1911, *Dame* Margery, DBE, who *d* 1968, da of late Rev Walter Spencer, of Fownhope Court, Herefordshire; *d* 1948; *s* by his el son (2) DAVID HENRY HAMAR, 2nd Viscount and present peer also Baron Greenwood.

GREENWOOD OF ROSSENDALE, BARONY OF (Greenwood) (Extinct 1982)

DAUGHTERS LIVING OF LIFE BARON

Hon Susanna Catherine Crawshay GREENWOOD, *b* 1943; has resumed her maiden name: *m* 1970 (*m diss* 1991), Christopher Gardiner, and has issue living, Thomas Keir, *b* 1982, — Anna Kathryn, *b* 1980.
Hon Dinah Karen Crawshay (42 Cheverton Rd, N19), *b* 1946; PhD: *m* 1970, David Murray, and has issue living, Bruno *b* 1974, — Leo, *b* 1976, — Fergus, *b* 1978.

WIDOW LIVING OF LIFE BARON

GILLIAN (*Baroness Greenwood of Rossendale*), da of Leslie Crawshay-Williams, of Bridgend (B Monkswell, colls): *m* 1940, Baron Greenwood of Rossendale, PC (Life Baron), who *d* 1982.

GREGSON, BARON, (Gregson) (Life Baron 1975)

JOHN GREGSON, son of John Gregson; *b* 29 Jan 1924; Engineer; AMCT; CBIM; Non-Exec Dir Fairey Group plc, and a Part Time Member of British Steel Board since 1976; Pres of Defence Manufacturers Assocn; Member Nat Rivers Authority since 1992; DL Greater Manchester 1979; *cr Baron Gregson*, of Stockport in Greater Manchester (Life Baron) 1975.
Address – c/o Fairey Group plc, Cranford Lane, Heston, Middx TW5 9NQ.

GRENFELL, BARON (Grenfell) (Baron UK 1902)

JULIAN PASCOE FRANCIS ST LEGER GRENFELL, 3rd Baron; *b* 23 May 1935; *s* 1976; *ed* Eton, and King's Coll, Camb (BA); Capt Queen's Westminsters (KRRC) (TA); Ch of Information and Public Affairs for World Bank in Europe 1970, Dep Dir European Office, World Bank, 1973, Special Representative of World Bank to United Nations 1974-81, Sr Adviser External Affairs 1983-90, since when Head of External Affairs in Europe: *m* 1st, 1961, Loretta Maria Olga Hildegarde, da of Alfredo Reali, of Il Cupolino, Florence, Italy; 2ndly, 1970, Gabrielle, only da of Dr Ernst Raab, of Berlin; 3rdly, 1987, Mrs Elizabeth Porter, da of Buford Scott, of Richmond, Va, USA; 4thly, 1993, Mrs Dagmar Langbehn Debreil, da of late Dr Carl Langbehn, of Berlin, and has issue by 1st and 2nd *m*.

𝕬rms – Gules, on a fesse between three organ rests or, a mural crown of the first. 𝕮rest – On the battlements of a tower gules, a griffin passant or, holding in the beak a sprig of laurel. 𝕾upporters – *Dexter*, An Egyptian cavalryman; *sinister*, an Egyptian infantryman. *Residence* – 18 rue de Bourgogne, 75007 Paris, France.

Honest duty

DAUGHTERS LIVING *(By 1st marriage)*

Hon Isabella Sarah Frances, *b* 1966.

(By 2nd marriage)

Hon Katharina Elizabeth Anne, *b* 1973.
Hon Vanessa Julia Claire, *b* 1976.

SISTER LIVING

Hon Caroline Sarah Aline, *b* 1933: *m* 1965, Zbyszek Leon Mieczkowski, of Rose Cottage, Henley Park, Henley-on-Thames, and has issue living, Stefan Pascoe St Leger, *b* 1967, — Helena Elizabeth Caroline, *b* 1970.

HALF-SISTER LIVING

Hon Aline Mary, *b* 1950.

WIDOW LIVING OF SON OF FIRST BARON

Eleanor Dorothy Alice, only da of Sir (John) Francis William James, of Tamar Bank, Saltash, Cornwall: *m* 1st, 1933, Major Hon Arthur Bernard John Grenfell, who was *ka* 1942; 2ndly, 1944, Capt Brian Herbert Malyon, 10th Hussars, and has issue living (by 1st *m*) (see colls, infra). *Residences* – Chapmansford, Hurstbourne Priors, Whitchurch, Hants GR28 7RR; Middle Combe, Huntsham, Tiverton, Devon.

MOTHER LIVING

Elizabeth Sarah Polk (1 Durham House, Durham Place, SW3 4ET), da of late Capt Hon Alfred Thomas Shaughnessy (*see* B Shaughnessy, colls): resumed the surname of Stafford 1976 until re-marriage: *m* 1st, 1932 (*m diss* 1946), the 2nd Baron, who *d* 1976; 2ndly, 1946, Maj Berkeley Buckingham Howard Stafford, KRRC, who *d* 1966; 3rdly, 1969 (*m diss* 1976), Trevor Walton King; 4thly, 1983, Com (Arnold) Derek Arthur Lawson, of Passenham Manor, Stony Stratford, Bucks, who *d* 1984.

COLLATERAL BRANCH LIVING

Issue of late Major Hon Arthur Bernard John Grenfell, 2nd son of 1st Baron, *b* 1908, *ka* 1942: *m* 1933, Eleanor Dorothy Alice (ante) (who *m* 2ndly, 1944, Capt Brian Herbert Malyon, 10th Hussars), only da of Sir (John) Francis William James, of Tamar Bank, Saltash, Cornwall:—
FRANCIS PASCOE JOHN (Lenton House, Lenton, Grantham, Lincs), *b* 28 Feb 1938; *ed* Eton, and Ch Ch, Oxford: *m* 1977, Elizabeth Katharine, da of Hugh Kenyon (*see* Thompson Bt (*cr* 1890)). ——John St Leger (Cwm Merwydd, Horeb, Llandyssul, Dyfed SA44 4J2), *b* 1940: *m* 1965, Pauline Mary Walton, and has issue living, Richard Arthur St Leger, *b* 1966, — Julian Francis John, *b* 1971, — Sarah Marion, *b* 1968, — Sophie Elizabeth, *b* 1975. —— Margaret, *b* 1935: *m* 1960, Capt Simon Trevor Smail, 11th Hussars of Melcombe Newton Farm, Melcombe Bingham, Dorchester, Dorset (*see* Heathcoat-Amory, Bt, colls).

PREDECESSORS – (1) *Field Marshal Rt Hon Sir* FRANCIS WALLACE GRENFELL, GCB, GCMG, PC, son of late P. St L. Grenfell, of Maesteg, Glamorgan; *b* 1841; entered 60th Rifles 1859, and became Field-Marshal 1908; raised 1st Brig Egyptian Army 1883; served in Expedition to Griqualand W 1875, in Kaffir Campaign 1878, in Zulu Campaign 1879 (several times mentioned in despatches, medal with clasp), in Egyptian Expedition 1882, present at battle of Tel-el-Kebir, as AAG, Head Quarters (medal with clasp), in Nile Expedition 1884 (3rd class Medjidie, bronze star), and in command of Frontier Field Force, Egypt 1885, a Div at action of Ginnis 1886, of Anglo-Egyptian Expedition at action of Gamaiza, Suakin 1888, and of Anglo-Egyptian Div at action of Toski 1889; an ADC to HM Queen Victoria 1882-9, Sirdar of Egyptian Army 1885-92, DAG for Auxiliary Forces at Headquarters 1892-4, Inspector-Gen of Auxiliary Forces and of Recruiting 1894-7, in command of Army of Occupation in Egypt 1897-8 (specially thanked by both Houses of Parliament), and Gov of Malta, and in command of Troops there 1898-1902, in command of 4th Army Corps 1902-4, and Gen Officer Cmdg-in-Ch the Forces in Ireland 1904-8; *cr Baron Grenfell*, of Kilvey, co Glamorgan (peerage of United Kingdom) 1902: *m* 1st, 1887, Evelyn, who *d* 1899, da of late Gen R. Blucher Wood, CB; 2ndly, 1903, Hon Margaret Aline who *d* 1911, only da of late Lewis Ashurst Majendie, MP (E Crawford); *d* 1925; *s* by his el son (2) PASCOE CHRISTIAN VICTOR FRANCIS, CBE, TD, 2nd Baron; *b* 1905; Dep Speaker, House of Lords and Chm of Cttees 1963-76: *m* 1st, 1932 (*m diss* 1946), Elizabeth Sarah Polk, da of late Capt Hon Alfred Thomas Shaughnessy (B Shaughnessy, colls); 2ndly, 1946, Irene Lilian, who *d* 1993, da of Harry Augustus George Cartwright, of Buenos Aires, Argentina; *d* 1976; *s* by his only son (3) JULIAN PASCOE FRANCIS ST LEGER, 3rd Baron and present peer.

GRETTON, BARON (Gretton) (Baron UK 1944)

JOHN LYSANDER GRETTON, 4th Baron; *b* 17 April 1975; *s* 1989; *ed* Shrewsbury.

Arms – Quarterly, per fesse indented or and gules, in the second quarter an anchor in bend sinister of the first, in the third an antique lamp also, or, fired proper. **Crest** – An arm embowed proper. vested above the elbow argent, holding in the hand a torch erect fired, a sickel in bend sinister both also proper. **Supporters** – *Dexter*, a bull sable; *sinister*, a chestnut horse proper, each gorged with a chain pendent therefrom an anchor or.
Residence – Stapleford Farms, Holygate Farm, Stapleford, Melton Mowbray, Leics LE14 2XQ.

SISTER LIVING

Hon Sarah Margaret, *b* 1971.

AUNTS LIVING (*daughters of 2nd Baron*)

Hon Mary Ann Maud Sigrid (Manor House, Stapleford, Melton Mowbray, Leics), *b* 1939; breeder and internat judge of Arabian horses: *m* 1986, Thomas Henry Wragg, son of T. L. Wragg, of Hinckley, Leics.
Hon Elizabeth Margaret, *b* 1945: *m* 1968, Christopher Mark Meynell, of Bergh Apton Hall, Norwich, Norfolk (*see* E Halifax, colls).

WIDOW LIVING OF SECOND BARON

ANNA HELENA MARGARET (*Margaret, Baroness Gretton*), el da of late Capt Henrik Loeffler, of 51 Grosvenor Sq, W1: *m* 1930, the 2nd Baron, OBE, who *d* 1982. *Residence* – The Old Rectory, Ufford, Stamford.

WIDOW LIVING OF THIRD BARON

JENNIFER ANN (*Baroness Gretton*), only da of late Edmund Sandford Moore, of York (*see* B Grey of Codnor, colls): *m* 1970, the 3rd Baron, who *d* 1989. *Residence* – Stapleford Farms, Holygate Farm, Stapleford, Melton Mowbray, Leics LE14 2XQ.

PREDECESSORS – (1) *Rt Hon* JOHN Gretton, PC, CBE, VD, TD, son of late John Gretton, of Bladon, Burton-on-Trent; *b* 1867; Chm of Bass, Ratcliff & Gretton, Ltd, brewers, of Burton-on-Trent 1908-45; Lieut-Col and Hon Col 6th Batn Prince of Wales's (N Staffs Regt); sat as MP for S Derbyshire (C) 1895-1906, for Rutland 1907-18, and for Burton Div of Staffordshire 1918-43: *cr Baron Gretton* of Stapleford, co Leicester (peerage of United Kingdom) 1944; *m* 1900, Hon Maud Helen Eveleigh-de-Moleyns, who *d* 1934, da of 4th Baron Ventry; *d* 1947; *s* by his son (2) JOHN FREDERIC; OBE, 2nd Baron, MP for Staffordshire, Burton Div (C) 1943-45: *m* 1930, (Anna Helena) Margaret, el da of late Capt Henrik Loeffler, of 51 Grosvenor Sq, W1; *d* 1982; *s* by his elder son (3) JOHN HENRICK, 3rd Baron; *b* 1941; DL Leics: *m* 1970, Jennifer, only da of late Edmund Sandford Moore, of York (*see* B Grey of Codnor, colls); *d* 1989; *s* by his only son (4) JOHN LYSANDER, 4th Baron and present peer.

GREY, EARL (Grey) (Earl UK 1806, Bt GB 1746)

VOULOIR SERVIR

DE BON　　　　LE ROY

To serve the king with good will

RICHARD FLEMING GEORGE CHARLES GREY, 6th Earl, and 7th Baronet; *b* 5 March 1939; *s* 1963; *ed* Hounslow Coll and Hammersmith Coll of Building; Pres of Cost and Exec Accountants Assoc since 1978; Chm Roper Catering Events Ltd, London Cremation Co plc, Academy Beverage Co Ltd; Dir The Countess Grey Collection Ltd; Pres The Cremation Soc of GB, and Lonsdale Internat Sporting Club: *m* 1st, 1966 (*m diss* 1974), Margaret Ann, el da of Henry Bradford, of Ashburton, Devon; 2ndly, 1974, Stephanie Caroline, only da of Donald Gaskell-Brown, of Newton Ferrers, Plymouth, and formerly wife of Surg-Cdr Neil Leicester Denham, RN.

Arms – Gules, a lion rampant, within a bordure engrailed, argent, in dexter chief point a mullet of the last. **Crest** – A scaling ladder or, hooked and pointed sable. **Supporters** – *Dexter*, a lion guardant purpure, ducally crowned or; *sinister*, a tiger guardant, proper. *Address* – c/o House of Lords, SW1.

BROTHER LIVING

PHILIP KENT, *b* 11 May 1940; Master Mariner, licensed Trin House Sea Pilot (Corpn of Hull, Trin House); Officer RFA Ser: *m* 1968, Ann Catherine, yst da of Cecil Applegate, of Shute Farm, South Milton, Kingsbridge, Devon, and has issue living, Alexander Edward, *b* 1968, — Vanessa Catherine, *b* 1975.

HALF UNCLE LIVING

Rodney York DE CHARMOY GREY, *b* 1921; *ed* Queen's Univ, Kingston, Ontario (BA), and Toronto (MA), and London (PhD) Univs; added the name of de Charmoy before Grey 1970; Assistant Dep Min Depart of Finance, Ottawa, Canada; 1939-45 War with RCAF: *m* 1st, 1945 (*m diss* 1952), Margaret Eileen, da of Colin Hawley, of Bristol; 2ndly, 1952 (*m diss* 1970), Roslyn, da of Max Marcus, of Rothesay, New Brunswick, Canada; 3rdly, 1970, Cozette, da of Louis Roger Guy d'Emmerez de Charmoy, and has issue living, (by 1st *m*) Christopher John, *b* 1946, — David York, *b* 1947, — (by 2nd *m*) Simon Alexander, *b* 1958, — Marcus Edward, *b* 1960.

AUNT LIVING

Diana Sybil, *b* 1906: *m* 1957, Lawrence Frederick Burford, who *d* 1979. *Residence* – Room 105, Bradford House, Island Lodge, Porter's Island, Ottawa, Canada K1N 5M2.

DAUGHTER LIVING OF FIFTH EARL

Lady Mary Cecil (*Lady Mary Howick*), *b* 1907: *m* 1935, 1st Baron Howick of Glendale, who *d* 1973. *Residence* – Howick, Alnwick, Northumberland.

COLLATERAL BRANCHES LIVING

Descendants of late Capt Hon Sir George Grey, KCB, RN (3rd son of 1st Earl), who was *cr* a *Baronet* 1814:—
See Grey, Bt, *cr* 1814.

Grandchildren of late Frederick William Grey, eldest son of late Col Leopold John Herbert Grey, CSI, only son of late Leopold James Henry Grey, 3rd son of late Rt Rev Hon Edward Grey, Bishop of Hereford, 5th son of 1st Earl:—
Issue of late Frederick Arthur Herbert Grey, *b* 1895, *d* 1973: *m* 1919, Adelaide Suchan, who *d* 1949:—
Frederick (1826 Peninsula Verde Drive, Lomita, CA 90717, USA), *b* 1921. —— Beverly, *b* 1924: *m* 19—, Lou Kennedy, of 8100 Bleriot St, Los Angeles, CA 90045, USA.

Grandchildren of late Col Leopold John Herbert Grey, CSI (ante):—
Issue of late Frederick William Grey, *b* 1873, *d* 1950: *m* 1st, 1892 (*m diss* 1917), Agnes Annie, who *d* 1938, da of Peter Gow, MP, and Sheriff of Wellington Co, Ontario, Canada; 2ndly, 1919, Mary Harriet, elder da of Edward Moissant, of Santa Amelia, San Salvador:—
(By 1st *m*) Robert Maxwell, *b* 1903: *m* 1928, May Dawn, da of Joseph George Washington Brand, and has issue living, Barbara Anne, *b* 1934: *m* 1951 (*m diss* 1963), Truman Derwood Anderson, and has issue living, Truman Derwood (Jr) *b* 1951, Elizabeth Ann *b* 1953, Rebecca Anne *b* 1956, — Jane Ellen, *b* 1940: *m* 1959, Harold Caleb Whitney, Jr, of 609 South 12th St, Nederland, Texas, USA, and has issue living, Robert Maxwell *b* 1962, Katherine Marie *b* 1961, — Joyce Elaine, *b* (twin) 1940: *m* 1962, Charles Frederick Theriot, USAF, and has issue living, Angelique Elaine *b* 1963. —— †Leopold John, *b* 1905: *m* 1929, Ruth Aleen (137 Camino San Clemente, San Clemente, CA 92672, USA), da of Charles Christian Elmiger, and *d* 1968, leaving issue, Ronald John (23652 Lagarto St, Mission Viejo, CA 92691, USA), *b* 1930: served with US Army in Korean War 1951-53: *m* 1953, Nell Hope, only da of John Fletcher Adams, of Port Charlotte, Florida, USA, and has issue living, Kenneth Alan *b* 1962, Julia Lynn *b* 1959: *m* 1983, Douglas Harlow, of Austin, Texas, — Joel Edward (100 Rockrose Way, Novato, CA 94947, USA), *b* 1944: late US Army Res Med Corps: *m* 1968, Kathryn Lee, da of late Paul Fralic, of Van Nuys, Calif, and has issue living, Adam Brady *b* 1973, Lauren Emily *b* 1977. —— Henry James, *b* 1906: *m* 1930, Alice Mary, da of Alphonse Joseph Samson, and has issue living, Doris Arlene, *b* 1932: *m* 1952, Louis Frederick Repucci, and has issue living, Louis Frederick *b* 1953, Arlene Doris *b* 1954, — Harriet Alice, *b* 1940: *m* 1957, John Ford, and has issue living, Kenneth John *b* 1957, Laurence Robert *b* 1959, Jill Elaine *b* 1960, Janice Carole *b* 19—. —— (By 2nd *m*) Mary Catherine, *b* 1923: *m* 1943, Capt Archibald Bauer MacDonald, USNR (ret), and has issue living, Bruce Grey, *b* 1946, — James Douglas, *b* 1948, — John Mark, *b* 1950, — Craig William, *b* 1962, — Ellen Mary, *b* 1952.
Issue of late Lt-Col Arthur James Herbert Grey, *b* 1880, *d* 1960: *m* 1st, 1911 (*m diss* 1924), Cecile Ruth, da of late François Pogeceniq, Lt Italian Army; 2ndly, 1925, Anna (125, 8403-142 St, Edmonton, Alberta, Canada) (who *m* 4thly, 1963, Cyril Denzil Branch, Bar-at-law, who *d* 1976; *m* 5thly, (Jan) 1978, Clarence V. Frayn, of Edmonton, who

d (Aug) 1978), da of Axel Vennersten, Grand Marshal to Court of Sweden, and formerly wife of (1) Gosta Otto Rudolf Axelson von Schoultz, and (2) Per Hugo Huitfeldt:—
(By 2nd *m*) *Rev* Axel Robert Henry (Canadian Bible Society, Vancouver, BC, Canada), *b* 1933, *ed* Wellington Coll, St Andrew's Coll, S Africa, and St Paul's Theological Coll, S Africa (LTh 1958): *m* 1954, Zenith Catherine, da of James Gallagher, and has issue living, Paul, *b* 1958: *m* 1978, Bernadine Veronica, da of Ralph George Seewalt.

Grandson of late William Francis Hungerford Grey, 2nd son of late Sir William Grey, KCSI, 4th son of late Rt Rev Hon Edward Grey, Bishop of Hereford (ante):—
Issue of late Capt William Archibald Swinton Grey, *b* 1883, *d* 1942: *m* 1919, Kathleen Elsie, who *d* 1949, da of W. Paulson, of Mountsorrel, Leicestershire:—
William Ronald (Salisbury Cottage, 13 Robinson Rd, Kenilworth, Cape Town, S Africa), *b* 1920: *m* 1945, Florence Margaret, da of John Martin, and has issue living, David Swinton (6 Cyprian Court, Sophia St, Orangezicht, Cape Town), *b* 1946: *m* 1975, Joy Bowen, and has issue living, Alistair James Egbert *b* 1978, — Margaret Anne, *b* 1949: *m* 19—, Alan Stewart, of 122 Ladies Mile Rd, Bergvliet 7800, RSA, — Jennifer Frances, *b* 1951: *m* 19— (*m diss* 19—), Simon Sutton, and has issue living, Warrick *b* 19—.

Grandchildren of late Dr Francis Temple Grey (infra):—
Issue of late Egerton Francis Grey, Capt Queen's Own Cameron Highlanders, *b* 1930, *d* 1993: *m* 1961, Elizabeth Mary (Garry Gualach, Invergarry, Inverness-shire), da of late Peter Blackburn, of Roshven, Lochail:—
Simon Temple, *b* 1962. ——— John Egerton, *b* 1966: *m* 1990, Joanne Mary, da of William McAskill, of 3 Broom Drive, Inverness, and has issue living, Angus John, *b* 1992, — Jennifer Ishbel, *b* 1993. ——— Frances Mary, *b* 1963. ——— Jane Elizabeth Catherine, *b* 1965: *m* 1988, Peter Gregory Isaacson, and has issue living, John Alexander, *b* 1992, — Sophie Claire, *b* 1990.

Grandchildren of late Col Arthur Grey, CIE, eldest son of late Lt-Col Francis Douglas Grey, 7th son of late Rt Rev Hon Edward Grey, Bishop of Hereford (ante):—
Issue of late Francis Temple Grey, MB, ChM, MRCP, Bar-at-law, *b* 1886, *d* 1941: *m* 1928, Eglantine Ellice, who *d* 1989, da of late Major Edward Charles Ellice, DSO:—
Robin Douglas, QC (Dun Cottage, The Marsh, Hungerford, Berks), *b* 1931; *ed* Eastbourne Coll, and King's Coll, London (LLB); Bar Gray's Inn 1957; Recorder 1979, QC 1979: *m* 1st, 1968 (*m diss* 1972), Gillian, da of late Maj Esme Austin Reeves Porch; 2ndly, 1972, Mrs Berenice Anna Adams, da of Denis Wheatley, of 9 Nightingale Cres, W. Horsley; 3rdly, 1993, Mrs Annick Regnault, da of late Henri Kerbiriou, and of Lady Winskill, of Angmering, Sussex, and has issue living (by 2nd *m*), Louise Katherine, *b* 1973. ——— John Edward (Ballachulish House, Argyll), *b* 1932; *ed* Epsom Coll: *m* 1965, Elizabeth Anne, only da of late Lt-Col Francis Patrick St Maur Sheil, DSO, and has had issue, †Patrick John, *b* 1966; *ed* Keil Sch, and Stirling Univ (BSc); *k* in a climbing accident on Ben Nevis 1993, — Seumas Edward, *b* 1971, — Ian Michael, *b* 1974, — Claire Alexandra, *b* 1967. ——— Alan Arthur (12 Hough St, Deane, Bolton, Lancs BL3 4LX), *b* 1934; *ed* Epsom Coll, and Univ of Newcastle upon Tyne (BSc): *m* 1966 (*m diss* 1985), Jocelyn Elizabeth, da of John Anthony Cooper, of The Old Croft of Tighphuirst, Glencoe, Argyll (Eden, Bt, colls), and has issue living, Melanie Jane, *b* 1967, — Rebecca Frances, *b* 1968, — Iona Marau, *b* 1972, — Lorna Johane, *b* 1978. ——— Harry George (1 Lantana St, Warrego, nr Tennant Creek, Northern Territory 5760, Australia), *b* 1937; *ed* Allhallows Sch. ——— †Alexander *b* 1939; *ed* Eastbourne Coll, and Oxford Univ, (MA): *m* 1966 (*m diss* 1992), Eleanor, da of Leonard White, *d* 1993, leaving issue, Thomas (75 Elms Crescent, SW4 8QF), *b* 1972, — Anna, *b* 1967, — Lucy, *b* 1969. ——— Elisabeth Adair (22 Ingrams St, Forest Hill Garden, New York, NY 11375, USA), *b* 1929; *ed* Bryn Mawr Coll, Pennsylvania (BA 1950). ——— Joane Eglantine (78 Sandford Walk, Exeter EX1 2ET), *b* 1935; *ed* Edinburgh Unv (MA 1961): *m* 1956, Michael Mervyn Whitmore, BSc, MRCVS, who *d* 1959, and has issue living, James Temple, *b* 1958, — William Rupert, *b* 1959: *m* 1984, Kim Milward, and has issue living, Thomas *b* 1985, Jerry (a da) *b* 1990.
Issue of late Sir Paul Francis Grey, KCMG, *b* 1908, *d* 1990: *m* 1936, Agnes Mary (*Lady Grey*) (Holmwood House, Elstead, Godalming, Surrey), da of late Richard Shireburn Weld-Blundell (*see* By Fauconberg and Conyers, colls):—
Nicholas Richard (Ryehurst Farm, Binfield, Bracknell, Berks), *b* 1937; *ed* Ampleforth, and Ch Ch Oxford: *m* 1964, Mary Cecilia, da of Frederick Hugh Hughes, of 30 Netherby Drive, Fenham, Newcastle-upon-Tyne, and has issue living, Stephen Hugh Francis, *b* 1968, — Benedict Justin, *b* 1971, — Clare Philomena, *b* 1965, — Eleanor Mary Grace, *b* 1966. ——— Richard Charles Edward (The Old Farmhouse, Elstead, Godalming, Surrey), *b* 1939; *ed* Ampleforth, and Ch Ch Oxford: *m* 1964, Hilary Marguerite Térèse, 4th da of Sq/Ldr Malcolm Ogilvie Forbes, of Esseborne Manor, Hurstbourne Tarrant, Andover, Hants, and has issue living, Demitri Malcolm Paul, *b* 1965, — Malcolm Dominic Antony, *b* 1967, — Eloise Teresa Mary, *b* 1968, — Annabel Lucy, *b* 1971, — Saskia Bernadette, *b* 1973. ——— Timothy, *b* 1943; *ed* Ampleforth.
Issue of late Arthur Christopher Grey, BM, BCh, *b* 1911, *d* 1982: *m* 1st, 1941, Diana Marjorie, who *d* 1971, da of Rupert Sackville Gwynne, JP, MP (*see* V Ridley); 2ndly, 1973, Diana, JP, High Sheriff of Isle of Wight (1984) (The White House, Bembridge, Isle of Wight) (who *m* 3rdly, 1984, as his third wife, Rt Rev Edward James Keymer Roberts, formerly Bishop of Ely), da of Ewen Cameron Bruce, DSO, MC, and widow of Anthony Seymour Bellville:—
(By 1st *m*) Rupert Christopher (Hampshire Farm Cottage, S Harting, Petersfield, Hants), *b* 1946; *ed* Wellington Coll, and Univ Coll, London (LLB); solicitor 1976; Roy Humane Soc Vellum Award 1963: *m* 1977, Audrey Janet, da of Donald Vaughan Sinclair, MRCVS, of Southwood Hall, Thirsk, Yorks, and has issue living, Katherine Diana, *b* 1981, — Carmody Theresa Sinclair, *b* 1983, — Rosemary Audrey Sinclair, *b* 1986. ——— Jonathan (Fyning Copse, Rogate, Petersfield, Hants GU31 5GH), *b* 1951; *ed* Wellington Coll, and Architectural Assocn (AA Dip 1977): *m* 1978, Rebecca Hall, da of Libby Turner, of Australia, and has issue living, Harry *b* 1984, — Felix, *b* 1987, — Augusta, *b* 1990. ——— Stephen (7 Cunningham St, Maraville, NSW, Australia), *b* 1954; *ed* Wellington Coll, and Brunel Univ (BA). ——— Edward Christopher (Love Cottage, 20 Chapel St, Petersfield, Hants GU32 3DZ), *b* 1956; *ed* Wellington Coll, and Imperial Coll, London (BSc): *m* 19—, Sonhilde, da of Chauncey Kelley-Patterson, and has issue living, Rowan Tagore, *b* 1992. ——— Diana Christabel, *b* 1952; *dunm* 1990.
Issue of late Maj Martin Grey, *b* 1913, *d* 1975: *m* 1943, Wendy Ursula (East End House, Ditchling, Sussex), da of Charles Creasy Wray:—
David Anthony (East End Cottage, Ditchling, Sussex), *b* 1946; *ed* Allhallows Sch; Chartered Architect; Dip Arch: *m* 1975, Pamela Joan, da of John George Baxter, and has issue living, Thomas Charles, *b* 1979; *ed* Ardingly Coll, — Charles Edward, *b* 1981. ——— Priscilla Jane, *b* 1949: *m* 1974, David John Dyer Lewis.

Grandchildren of late Egerton Spenser Grey, CB, son of Lt-Col Francis Douglas Grey (ante):—
Issue of late Nigel Francis Egerton Grey, *b* 1891, *d* 1974: *m* 1st, 1921 (*m diss* 1949), Eileen Sybil Lyttleton, who *d* 1960, da of late Francis Ludlow Holt; 2ndly, 1949, Mary Rose (THESIGER), who *d* 1962, da of late Hon Guy Laurence Charteris (E Wemyss and March); 3rdly, 1970, Marion, who *d* 1971, da of late Cdr Robert Tennant-Park, OBE, RNR, and widow of Anthony Alfred Harmsworth Marlowe, QC:—
(By 1st *m*) Ann (Pale Green Cottage, Helions Bumpstead, nr Haverhill, Suffolk), *b* 1922: *m* 1955, Pierre Staheyeff, who *d* 1987, and has issue living, Nicholas Peter, *b* 1957: *m* 1st, 1988 (*m diss* 1990), Antoinette Fionna Stagnetto; 2ndly, 1993, Christine Elisabeth, da of William Reiter, of Geneva, Switzerland, — Michael Peter, *b* 1961: *m* 1989, Rosemary, da of Hugh Stafford, OBE, of Wells, Som. ——— (By 2nd *m*) Francis John, *b* 1951: *m* 1979, Frances-Jane Cutler, da of Cdr George Wayne Harper, Jr, USN (ret), of The Old Farm, Upper St Jacques, St Peter Port, Guernsey, CI, and has issue living, Telesfora, *b* 1983, — Mary Rose, *b* 1986. *Residence* – Pounds Cottage, Cowley, Cheltenham, Glos GL53 9NJ.
Issue of late Lt-Cdr Aubrey Arthur Douglas Grey, RN (ret), *b* 1894, *d* 1979: *m* 1928, Joan Fabian, who *d* 1975, da of C. H. Dickinson:—

Aubrey Jeremy Spenser (The Coach House, 4 Beech Av, Worcester), *b* 1929; late R Hampshire Regt and 2nd Bn The Parachute Regt; ret as Capt; late Maj Lancs Fus (TA): *m* 1958, Jennifer M., da of V. J. Keyte, of Lime Cottage, Beaudesert Park, Minchinhampton, Glos, and has issue living, Charles Spenser (92 Tantallon Rd, Balham, SW12), *b* 1959: *m* 1988, Berit, da of Ivar Stokke, of Oslo, Norway, and has issue living, James Axel *b* 1990, Edward Ivar *b* (twin) 1990, — James Aubrey, *b* 1961, — Annabel Clare, *b* 1963: *m* 1993, James R. Chester Walsh, only son of Richard James Chester Walsh, of Letchworth, Herts. —— †Timothy Bryan Richard, *b* 1931: *m* 1st, 1955 (*m diss* 1959), Pamela Anne, da of Col Denys Fitzgerald Murphy, MC; 2ndly, 1960, Gillian A. (The Courtyard, Kirkby Lonsdale, Cumbria), da of E. R. Hillman, of 14 Marshallswick Lane, St Albans, and *d* 1992, leaving issue (by 2nd *m*), Richard Nicholas Aubrey, *b* 1961, — Susannah Emma Jane, *b* 1963: *m* 1993, Capt Martin J. Price, RM. —— Michael Francis Adair (Somerset West, CP, S Africa), *b* 1940: *m* 19—, Elizabeth, who *d* 1987, da of late Ivor Lean, QC, of Isle of Man.

Issue of late John Grey, *b* 1899, *d* 1979: *m* 1926, Nancy Augusta, who *d* 1984, da of Vivian Nickalls, of The High House, Newbury, Berks:—

John Egerton, CB (51 St Peter's Rd, W Mersea, Colchester, Essex CO5 8LL), *b* 1929; Bar Inner Temple 1954; Clerk Assistant, House of Lords 1974-88; CB 1981: *m* 1961, his cousin, Patricia, da of late Col Walter Francis Hanna, MC, RE (E Grey, colls, 1976 Edn.)

PREDECESSORS – **(1)** *Rt Hon Sir* CHARLES Grey, KB, 4th son of Sir Henry Grey, 1st Bt (infra), *b* 1729; Gen, wounded at Minden 1759; C-in-C W Indies 1793, reducing Martinique, St Lucia and Quadeloupe; Gov of Guernsey 1797-1807; *cr Baron Grey of Howick*, Northumberland (peerage of UK 1801), and *Viscount Howick* and *Earl Grey* (peerage of UK) 1806: *m* 1762, Elizabeth, who *d* 1822, da of George Grey, of Southwick, co Durham; *d* 1807; *s* by his 2nd son **(2)** CHARLES *KG*, 2nd Earl; *b* 1764; *s* his uncle *Sir* Henry Grey as 3rd Bt 1808 (see *infra); First Lord of the Admiralty 1806, Foreign Sec 1806-7, and First Lord of the Treasury 1830-4: *m* 1794, Hon Mary Elizabeth Ponsonby, who *d* 1861, da of 1st Baron Ponsonby; *d* 1845; *s* by his son **(3)** *Rt Hon* HENRY GEORGE, KG, GCMG, 3rd Earl, *b* 1802; MP for Winchilsea (*L*) 1826-30, for Higham Ferrers 1831, for Northumberland 1831-3, for N Northumberland 1833-41, and for Sunderland 1841-5; Lord-Lieut of Northumberland 1847-77; Under-Sec for Colonies 1830-33, for Home Depart 1834, and Sec of state for War 1835-9, and for Colonies 1846-52: *m* 1832, Maria, who *d* 1879, da of Sir Joseph Copley, 3rd Bt; *d* 1894; *s* by his nephew **(4)** *Rt Hon* ALBERT HENRY GEORGE, GCB, GCMG, GCVO (son of late Gen Hon Charles Grey, MP, 2nd son of 2nd Earl), 4th Earl; *b* 1851; Administrator of Rhodesia 1894-7; Lord-Lieut of Northumberland 1899-1904, and Chancellor of Order of St Michael and St George 1916-17; MP for Northumberland S 1880-85, and for Tyneside Div of Northumberland 1885-6; Gov-Gen of Canada 1904-11: *m* 1877, Alice, who *d* 1944, da of late Robert Stayner Holford; *d* 1917; *s* by his son **(5)** CHARLES ROBERT, 5th Earl, *b* 1879; Lt 1st Life Guards, Maj in the Army, and Hon Col Comdt, Northumberland Vol Regt: *m* 1906, Lady Mabel Laura Georgiana Palmer, CBE, who *d* 1958, da of 2nd Earl of Selborne; *d* 1963; *s* by his kinsman **(6)** RICHARD FLEMING GEORGE CHARLES (el son of late Albert Harry George Campbell Grey, el son of late George Archibald Grey, only son of late Francis William Grey, 5th son of late Adm Hon George Grey, 4th son of 2nd Earl), 6th Earl and present peer; also Viscount Howick, and Baron Grey of Howick.
***(1)** Sir* HENRY Grey, of Howick, Northumberland, descendant of an ancient family in that Co, 8th in descent from Sir Thomas Grey of Heton, el brother of Sir John Grey, KG, who received the Anglo-Norman Earldom of Tankerville 1419, and 5th in descent from Sir Edward Grey, of Howick, uncle of 1st Baron Grey of Warke (*cr* 1623, ext on death of 4th Baron 1706), *cr* a Baronet 1746: *m* 1720, Hannah, who *d* 1764, da of Thomas Wood, of Falloden; *d* 1749; *s* by his el son **(2)** *Sir* HENRY, 2nd Bt, *b* 1727; MP for Northumberland 1754-68; *d* unm 1808; *s* by his nephew **(3)** CHARLES, 2nd Earl Grey (ante).

GREY DE RUTHYN, BARONY OF (Baron E 1324) (Abeyant 1963)

JOHN LANCELOT WYKEHAM BUTLER-BOWDON, BARON GREY DE RUTHYN, *d* 1963, when the Barony fell into abeyance between the descendants of his four great aunts.

COLLATERAL BRANCHES LIVING (*Representatives of the daughters of Barbara, Baroness Grey de Ruthyn, wife of 2nd Marquess of Hastings, are co-heirs of this Barony*)

Descendants of late Lady Edith Maud Rawdon-Hastings (eldest da of Barbara, Baroness Grey de Ruthyn, by her 1st husband, 2nd Marquess of Hastings), who *s* her brother as *Countess of Loudoun* (see that title).

Descendants of late May Evelyn Bertha Emily (elder da of Lady Victoria Mary Louisa KIRWAN, 3rd da of Barbara, Baroness Grey de Ruthyn, by her 1st husband, 2nd Marquess of Hastings): *m* 1895, Count Louis Lubienski Bodenham, JP, DL, of Rotherwas, Hereford, and Bullingham Manor, Hereford:—

Grandchildren of late Count Stanislas Lubienski Bodenham, yr son of late Count Louis Lubienski Bodenham (ante):—

Issue of late Count Charles Henry Lubienski Bodenham, *b* 1935, *d* 1987: *m* 1964, Lia (79 Mortlake Rd, Kew, Richmond, Surrey TW9 4AA), da of late Giuseppe Zappala, of Via R. Zandonai 85, Rome:—

Count Paul, *b* 1965; co-heir to Barony of Grey de Ruthyn. —— Countess Elizabeth, *b* 1972. —— Countess Monica, *b* (twin) 1972.

Descendants of late Lady Frances Augusta Constance Rawdon-Hastings (4th da of Barbara, Baroness Grey de Ruthyn, by her 1st husband, 2nd Marquess of Hastings): *m* 1863, 4th Earl of Romney, who *d* 1905 (see that title).

Descendants of late Hon Barbara Yelverton (only da of Barbara, Baroness Grey de Ruthyn, by her 2nd husband, Adm Sir Hastings Reginald Henry Yelverton, GCB); *m* 1872, 2nd Baron Churston, who *d* 1910 (see that title).

GREY OF CODNOR, BARON (Cornwall-Legh) (Baron E 1397)

CHARLES LEGH SHULDHAM CORNWALL-LEGH, CBE, 5th Baron; *b* 10 Feb 1903; *s* (on termination of abeyance) 1989; *ed* King's Sch, Bruton, and Hertford Coll, Oxford; assumed the surname of Cornwall-Legh in lieu of Walker by deed poll (upon the *s* of his father to the High Legh estates), enrolled at the College of Arms, 1926; senior rep in the illegitimate line of Richard, King of the Romans, Earl of Cornwall, and Provence, and Count of Poitou, 2nd son of John, King of England; served 1939-45 War with AAF and RAF; JP Cheshire 1938-74, High Sheriff 1939, DL 1949, CC 1949-77, Chm New Cheshire CC 1974-76, and Cheshire Police Authority 1957-74; OBE (Civil) 1971, CBE (Civil) 1977, AE 1946: *m* 1930, Dorothy Catherine Whitson, who *d* 1993, elder da of late John Whitson Scott, of Seal, Sevenoaks, Kent, and has issue.

Arms – Quarterly; 1st argent a lion rampant gules, *Legh*; 2nd ermine a lion rampant gules crowned or a bordure engrailed sable bezanty, *Cornwall*; 3rd per pale azure and vert on a fesse dancetté between three mural crowns or a crescent gules between two torteaux, *Walker*; 4th barry of six argent and azure, *Grey*. **Crest** – A demi-lion rampant gules collared or and charged for distinction on the shoulder with an ermine spot or. **Supporters** – On either side a demi-lion rampant gules crowned charged on the shoulder with an ermine spot and conjoined with the wings and tail of a wyvern erect or.
Seat – High Legh, nr Knutsford, Cheshire. *Residence* – High Legh House, nr Knutsford, Cheshire WA16 0QR.

SON LIVING

Hon RICHARD HENRY, *b* 14 May 1936; *ed* Stowe; High Sheriff Cheshire 1993; late RN (Gen Serv Medal); British Ski Team 1959-61, Capt 1960-61: *m* 1974, Joanna Storm, 7th and yst da of Maj Sir Kenelm Henry Ernest Cayley, 10th Bt, and has issue living, Richard Stephen Cayley, *b* 1976, — Kenelm Michael, *b* 1978, — George Henry, *b* 1982, — Caroline Philadelphia, *b* 1983. *Residence* – Dairy Farm, High Legh, Knutsford, Cheshire WA16 0QS.

DAUGHTERS LIVING

Hon Rosemary, *b* 1932: *m* 1959, Maj Hugh Charles Desmond Laing, late Scots Guards, only son of late Capt Hugh Desmond Bertram Laing, of 16A Prince's Gate Mews, SW7, and has an adopted da, Camilla Catherine Harvey, *b* 1964. *Residence* – 5 Ditchfield Lane, High Legh, Knutsford, Cheshire WA16 0QN.
Hon Julia Margaret, *b* 1939: *m* 1978, Max Prola, DPhil (Psych), of New York, only child of late Joseph Prola, formerly of Aglie, Italy. *Residence* – The Croft, High Legh, Knutsford, Cheshire WA16 0NQ.

COLLATERAL BRANCHES LIVING   *(all in remainder)*

Issue of late Evelyn Henry Shuldham Cornwall-Legh, yr brother of 5th Baron, *b* 1905, *d* 1975; assumed by deed poll 1926 the surname of Cornwall-Legh in lieu of Walker: *m* 1946, Olga Frieda (Mill House, High Legh, Knutsford, Cheshire WA16 6LS), elder da of Heinrich Bodmer, of Zurich, Switzerland:—
Barbara Katharine, *b* 1947: *m* 1st, 1969 (*m diss* 1973), John James Stewart Farmer; 2ndly, 1978, Giles Heathcote Whittome, and has issue living (by 1st *m*), Katharine Frederica, *b* 1971. *Residence* – Legh House, Denston, Suffolk CB8 8PW.

Grandson of late Charles Walker, by his wife Gertrude Mary Cornwall, eldest da of late Rev Henry Cornwall Legh, Rector of Welsh Hampton, Shropshire, great-grandson of late George Legh, of High Legh, Cheshire (who *m* Anna Maria, only da and heiress of Francis Cornwall, 16th and last Baron of Burford, through whom the family inherited the representation of the Barony of Grey of Codnor):—
Issue of late Rev Arthur Edmund Legh Walker, *b* 1878, *d* 1962: *m* 1911, Evelyn Constance, who *d* 1929, 2nd da of late Edward Hosking, ICS:—
Rev Edward Charles Cornwall WALKER, *b* 1918; *ed* Denstone Coll, Selwyn Coll, Camb (BA 1939, MA 1943), and Cuddesdon Coll, Oxford; V of Great Amwell, Herts, 1948-81, since when of Great Amwell with St Margaret's: *m* 1946, Jean Drummond, only da of late Rev Andrew Drummond Harcus, OBE, DD, of Crediton Hill, NW6, and has had issue, Charles Legh Cornwall (Barters Farmhouse, Chapmanslade, Westbury, Wilts), *b* 1947; *ed* Denstone Coll, and Oaklands Coll, St Albans: *m* 1979, Diana, da of Rev Philip Reginald Wilton Tidmarsh, of Presteign, Powys, and has issue living, Andrew Philip *b* 1982, Anna Clair *b* 1985, — Drummond Harcus, *b* and *d* 1952, — Drummond Alban Cornwall (Zypressenstrasse 26, 33699 Bielefeld, Germany), *b* 1959; *ed* Haileybury, and Trin Coll of Music, London: *m* 1987, Diana Carol, da of Nelson Amos, of Michigan, USA, and has issue living, Catherine Carol Cornwall *b* 1991, — Clair Cornwall, *b* 1950: *m* 1971, Maj Nigel Craig Fairley, R Signals, of Clark's Cottage, 61 The Green, Christian Malford, Wilts, son of late Maj John Craig Fairley, and has issue living, Duncan Craig *b* 1973; *ed* Haileybury, and City Univ, Alastair Murray *b* 1975; *ed* Haileybury, — Mary Cornwall, *b* 1961: *m* 1987, Richard David Eliot Haines, of 40 Alexandra Rd, Ash, Aldershot, Hants, 3rd son of Harry Haines, of Churt, Surrey, and has issue living, George Arthur *b* 1989, Holly Nicola *b* 1988. *Residence* – Great Amwell Vicarage, Ware, Herts.

Descendants of late Frances Elinor Cornwall, 3rd da of late Rev Henry Cornwall Legh (ante): *m* 1869, as his 2nd wife, Henry Brooks, of Doctors' Commons, London, and of Windsor:—

Grandsons of late Edmund Hatfield Leslie Cornwall Brooks (infra):—
Issue of late John Edmund Hatfield Brooks, *b* 1909, *d* 1966: *m* 1945, Honoria (71 Tennyson Way, Melton Mowbray, Leics LE13 1LJ), da of late Aloysius O'Donnell, of co Limerick:—
(John) Nicholas Hatfield BROOKS, *b* 1946. —— †Edmund Hugh Cornwall BROOKS, *b* 1949: *m* 1st, 1980 (*m diss* 1987), Barbara, da of Peter Freckingham, of Ab Kettleby, Leics; 2ndly, 1988, Sally Ann (4 All Saints Close, Asfordby, nr Melton Mowbray, Leics), da of John Taylor, of Leicester, and was *k* in a motor accident 1990, leaving issue, John Edmund Cornwall, *b* (*posthumous*) 1990.

Granddaughter of late Mrs Frances Elinor Cornwall Brooks (ante):—
Issue of late Edmund Hatfield Leslie Cornwall Brooks, *b* 1874, *d* 1934: *m* 1907, Constance Sara, who *d* 1948, da of late Thomas Cook, of Wellingborough, Northants:—
Constance Theodora (Rose Villa, High St, Foulsham, Dereham, Norfolk NR20 5RJ), *b* 1911: *m* 1932, Edward Stanley Corner, who *d* 1984, and has issue living, Greta Madeline, *b* 1933: *m* 1961, John Allen, of Manor Farm, Barnham Broom, Norwich, and has issue living, Andrew William *b* 1963, David Edward *b* 1965, — Catherine Jill, *b* 1937: *m* 1964, Nigel Armstrong, of 3

Squires Court, Main St, Bretforton, Evesham, Worcs WR11 5QD, and has issue living, Iain *b* 1965, Timothy *b* 1969, Amanda *b* 1966.

Grandchildren of late Edmund Hatfield Leslie Cornwall Brooks (ante):—

Issue of late Katharine Madeline Brooks, *b* 1917, *d* 1989: *m* 1942, John Cloutte, who *d* 1982:—
Colin David CLOUTTE (93 Wetherill St, Goole, Humberside DN14 6EE), *b* 1944. —— Penelope Jane (40a Huddleston Rd, Tufnell Park, N7 0AG), *b* 1946; has issue living, Dora Sara, *b* 1983. —— Hilary Juliet, *b* 1950: *m* 1968, Nigel Forde, poet and radio presenter, of The Gate House, Burnby Lane, Pocklington, York YO4 2UL, and has issue living, Victoria Louise, *b* 1968, — Sarah Tamsin, *b* 1973.

Grandchildren of late Cecil Thomas Edgar Brooks, 3rd and yst son of late Mrs Frances Elinor Cornwall Brooks (ante):—

Issue of late Cecil Geoffrey Theodore Brooks, *b* 1907, *d* 1980: *m* 1st, 1932 (*m diss* 1945), Jeanne, da of Higham Phillipson, of Yorks; 2ndly, 1946 (*m diss* 1967), Winifred Mary (Anne), da of late Frederick Augustin Coupe, of Banwell, Som, and formerly of Preston, Lancs; 3rdly, 1977, Mrs Eileen Bell, who *d* 1982:—
(By 1st *m*) Michaela Theodora Diane, *b* 1934: *m* 1954, Richard Edridge, of The Thatched House, 267 Hillbury Rd, Warlingham, Surrey CT3 9TL, and has issue living, Richard Tilden Hurley, *b* 1960, — Annalisa, *b* 1963: *m* 1985, Martin Parrott, of Caterham, Surrey, and has issue living, Kira *b* 1987, — Katarina, *b* 1969. —— Wendy Angela Suzanne BROOKS (205 52 Aspland St, Nambour, Qld 4560, Australia), *b* 1936; has resumed her maiden name: *m* 1960 (*m diss* 19—), Stanley Eduard Hoffman, and has issue living, Dahl Wendell Eduard, *b* 1961, — Bradney Stan Theodore, *b* 1964, — Kyla Jeanell Alicia, *b* 1963: *m* 1988, Mark Douglas Summers. —— (By 2nd *m*) Angela Valerie Alicia, *b* 1945: *m* 1963, Ronald Carl Frank, of 383 St Vincent Rd, Nudgee, Qld 4014, Australia, and has issue living, Karl Geoffrey, *b* 1968, — Bethany Anne, *b* 1973. —— Jennifer Anne Christine, *b* 1949: *m* 1974, Francis Martin Balkwill, and has issue living, Michael Peter, *b* 1976, — Sarah Louise, *b* 1977.

Issue of late Desborough Sutherland George Brooks, *b* 1913, *d* 1990: *m* 1st, 1937, Molly, who *d* 1969, da of late Thomas Edwin Morgan, surveyor, of Lincoln's Inn Fields, and of 80 Bridge Lane, NW11; 2ndly, 1970, Mrs Patricia Dulcie Morgan (*née* Spicer) (21 Northway, NW11 6PB), widow of Donald Morgan, son of late Thomas Edwin Morgan (ante):—
(By 1st *m*) Christopher Desborough Colin BROOKS (83 Lake Geneva Place, Calgary SE, Alberta, Canada T2J 2S3), *b* 1938; *ed* Univ Coll Sch, Emmanuel Coll, Camb (MA), and St Thomas's Hosp (MB, BChir), LRCP, MRCS: *m* 1979 (*m diss* 1990), Mrs Linda Foster, of Chattanooga, Tenn, USA, and has issue living, Amanda, *b* 1981. —— Jonathan Henry (21 Northway, NW11), *b* 1948; *ed* Univ Coll Sch, Emmanuel Coll, Camb, and St Thomas's Hosp; FRCS, MRCOG: *m* 1974, Janet Ruth, da of Walter Leggott, of Burtoft, Lincs, and has issue living, George Morgan, *b* 1980, — Jack Christopher, *b* 1987, — Tabitha Molly, *b* 1983, — Henrietta Jane, *b* 1985.

Grandchildren of late Angela Mary Eveline Brooks, only da of late Mrs Frances Elinor Cornwall Brooks (ante): *m* 1895, Sandford Ffolliott Pierpoint Moore:—

Issue of late Edmund Sandford Moore, *b* 1905, *d* 1980: *m* 1931, Emily Joan, da of Francis Cherucca Wheeler, of St Ives, Cornwall:—
Jennifer Ann (*Baroness Gretton*), *b* 1943: *m* 1970, 3rd Baron Gretton, who *d* 1989, and has issue. *Residence* – Stapleford Farms, Holygate Farm, Stapleford, Melton Mowbray, Leics LE14 2XQ.

Issue of late Joyce Mary Theodora Moore, *b* 1907, *d* 1981: *m* 1939, John Guise Malpas:—
Felicity, *b* 1939: *m* 1963, David Isaac. *Residence* – 8 Durnsford Way, Cranleigh, Surrey GU6 7LN.

Grandchildren of late Sir Philip Henry Grey-Egerton, 12th Bt, grandson of late Sir Philip de Malpas Grey-Egerton, 10th Bt, FRS, by his wife Anna Elizabeth, sister of late Rev Henry Cornwall Legh (ante):—

Issue of late Cecely Alice Grey, MBE, *b* 1893, *d* 1981: *m* 1918, Lt-Col Denys Edward Prideaux-Brune, DSO, who *d* 1952:—
Philip Egerton Edmund PRIDEAUX-BRUNE (Plumber Farmhouse, Sturminster Newton, Dorset), *b* 1921; *ed* Harrow; late Warrant Officer RAF: *m* 1944, Pamela Maud, yr da of late Capt George Norman Ferrers-Guy, Worcs Regt (*see* B Avebury, 1965 Edn), and has issue living, Richard John Ferrers, *b* 1946; *ed* Harrow, — Denys Edmund Charles, *b* 1947; *ed* Harrow, — George Brian Philip, *b* 1948, — Timothy Rowland Edward, *b* 1953, — Philippa Anne Madeleine, *b* 1961: *m* 1985, Mark Railing, of 73 Winchendon Rd, SW6 5DH, and has issue living, Maximilian John Prideaux *b* 1987, Philip James *b* 1989, Alexander Peter *b* 1990. —— Rowland Denys Charles (500 Dorchester Rd, San Matao, Calif, USA), *b* 1925; *ed* Eton, Calif Inst of Technology, and Magdalene Coll, Camb (MA); Capt The Rifle Bde 1943-47: *m* 1957, Genevieve Poett, da of late Richard Ashe McLaren, of San Mateo, Calif, and has issue living, Cynthia Mary Dean, *b* 1958, — Diana Evelyn, *b* 1960. —— Cynthia Mary Denise, *b* 1919; JP: *m* 1941, Brian Alexis Fenwick Stephens, MRCS, LRCP, of Tollgate House, Wing, Bucks, and has issue living, Nicholas Edward Egerton (Grafton Lodge, Montford Bridge, Shropshire), *b* 1946; *ed* Charterhouse: *m* 1970, Avril Rose, yr da of Lt-Col Morgan Henry Birch-Reynardson, of Le Carriers, St Mary, Jersey, CI, and has issue living, Samantha *b* 1974, Clare *b* 1976, — Hugo Offley Prideaux, *b* 1956; *ed* Charterhouse, — Cecely Isobel Rich, *b* 1958.

Descendants of late Harriot Cornwall Legh, yr sister of late Rev Henry Cornwall Legh (ante): *m* 1838, Capt Herbert Taylor, 85th LI.

PREDECESSORS – HENRY de Grey, of Codnor, co Derby, Grays Thurrock, Essex, and Aylesford and Hoo, Kent, of the Great House of Grey (*see* GEC's Complete Peerage vol VII), was twice summoned for mil serv in the reign of King Edward I, served in Gascony 1295 and 1297, and was summoned to Parliament 1299-1308 by writs directed *Henrico de Grey*, *d* 1308; *s* by his son RICHARD, *b ca* 1281-2, summoned to Parliament 1309-35, pardoned for any part taken against the Despencers 1321, Steward of Gascony 1324, Constable of Nottingham Castle 1325-30, granted the custody of the manor of Overstone, co Northants: *m* Joan, da of Robert, Lord FitzPayn; *d* 1335; *s* by his son, JOHN, summoned to Parliament 1335-92, a distinguished soldier, served in Scotland, Flanders and France, with King Edward III at Crécy, the siege of Calais, etc, Keeper of Rochester Castle, excused from attendance at parliaments, councils, etc, in consideration of his long mil serv 1371: *m* 1st, Eleanor; 2ndly, Alice, da of Sir Warin de Lisle, of Kingston Lisle; *d* 1392; *s* by his grandson (1) *RICHARD, KG, 1st Baron (son of Sir Henry de Grey by his wife, Joan, da of Thomas, Lord Berkeley), *ca* 1371, summoned to Parliament 1393-1416, served King Richard II in France, Adm of the Fleet from the mouth of the Thames to the North 1401, granted lands in Wales and recommended by Parliament for reward for services against the Welsh rebels 1406, Constable of Nottingham Castle and Master Forester of Sherwood 1407, constantly employed upon confidential missions to the courts of France and Scotland: *m* before 1378, Elizabeth, yr da and co-heiress of Ralph, Lord Bassett of Sapcote; *d* 1418; *s* by his son (2) JOHN, 2nd Baron, *b* in or before 1396; summoned to Parliament 1420-29, Lieut in Ireland 1427 until his death *sp* 1430; *s* by his brother (3) HENRY, 3rd Baron, summoned to Parliament 1430-41: *m* before 1434, Margaret (who *m* 2ndly, Sir Richard Vere, yr son of 12th Earl of Oxford, and *d* 1464), da of Sir Henry Percy, of Atholl; *d* 1444; *s* by his son (4) HENRY, 4th Baron, *b ca* 1435; summoned to Parliament 1459-95, served Queen Margaret at Battle of St Albans 1460, obtained from King Edward IV a licence to practise the transmutation of metals, being answerable to the King for any profit made, given a 40 year grant of lands in Ireland, attended the Coronation of King Richard III, who granted him various manors or lordships in Rutland and Suffolk; *dspl* 1496, when the barony fell into abeyance between his three aunts, the issue of the 1st Baron: (i) Lucy, wife of Sir Roland Lenthall, (ii) Eleanor, wife of Sir Thomas Newport, and (iii) Elizabeth, wife of Sir John Zouche, and so continued until 1989, when the abeyance was terminated (after petition to HM King George V), in favour of (5) CHARLES LEGH SHULDHAM Cornwall-Legh, senior representative of Lady Lenthall, 5th Baron and present peer.

*The Committee for Privileges found that the existence of a barony by writ "can only be established by proof of a Royal Writ summoning some ancestor of the claimant to attend a Parliament followed by an actual sitting of such ancestor in the Parliament to which he was summoned." The first three holders of the title, as enumrated in GEC's Complete Peerage, are therefore not shown as such in the above article.

GREY OF NAUNTON, BARON (Grey) (Life Baron 1968)

RALPH FRANCIS ALNWICK GREY, GCMG, GCVO, OBE, son of late Francis Arthur Grey; *b* 15 April 1910; *ed* Wellington Coll, NZ, Auckland Univ Coll (LLB), and Pembroke Coll, Camb; Hon LLD, Belfast and Nat Univ of Ireland; Hon D Litt, and Hon DSc, New Univ of Ulster; Bar and Solicitor NZ 1932; a GCStJ (Kt Cdr of the Commandery of Ards 1968-77, Bailiff of Egle 1975-87, Chancellor 1987-88), Lord Prior of Order of St John 1988-91; entered Admin Ser, Nigeria 1937; Assist Financial Sec 1948-52, Development Sec 1952-53, Sec to Gov-Gen and Council of Mins 1954, Ch Sec of Federation 1955-57; and Dep Gov-Gen 1957-59; Gov and C-in-C British Guiana 1959-64, Gov of Bahamas 1964-68, of Turks and Caicos Islands 1965-68, and Gov of N Ireland 1968-73, Dep Chm of Commonwealth Development Corpn 1973-79, Chm 1979-80; Grand Pres, Royal Over Seas League since 1993 (Chm 1976-81, Pres 1981-93); Britain-Nigeria Assoc 1983-89; Overseas Service Pensioners' Assoc since 1983; Chancellor of The New Univ of Ulster 1980-84; Chancellor of The Univ of Ulster since 1984; Hon Bencher Inn of Court, N Ireland; Hon Freeman of Belfast, Lisburn and London; *cr* OBE (Civil) 1951, CMG 1955, KCVO 1956, KCMG 1959, GCMG 1964, *Baron Grey of Naunton*, of Naunton, co Gloucester (Life Baron) 1968, and GCVO 1973: *m* 1944, Esme Mae (CStJ), da of late Albert Victor Kerry Burcher, of Remuera, Auckland, NZ, and widow of PO Kenneth Kirkcaldie, RAFVR, and has issue.

Arms – Bendy argent and azure two lions' faces in pale, issuing from either flank of the shield a cross formy flory dimidiated gules. **Crest** – A sheathed sword erect gules garnished hilt and pommel or, each quillon ending in a kiwi's head erased gold the scabbard supported by two lions' gambs erased gules winged azure semy of bees volant or. **Supporters** – *Dexter*, a lion or, *sinister*, a crested crane proper, each gorged with an ancient crown flowing therefrom a mantle gules lined vair.
Residence – Overbrook, Naunton, Glos, GL4 5AX. *Club* – Travellers'.

SONS LIVING

Hon Jolyon Kenneth Alnwick (Upper Swell Farm, Stow on the Wold, Cheltenham, Glos GL54 1EW), *b* 1946; *ed* Marlborough, and Pembroke Coll, Camb (MA); Bar Inner Temple, 1968: *m* 1971, Sarah Jane, da of late Lt-Col Samuel Brian Digby Hood, TD (*see* V Hood, colls), and has issue living, Tobias Alnwick, *b* 1973, — Matthew Samuel, *b* 1976.
Hon Jeremy Francis Alnwick, *b* 1949; *ed* Marlborough, and Roy Agric Coll, Cirencester; Lt-Col King's Royal Hussars (ret); Bursar Rendcomb Coll: *m* 1973, Susan Elizabeth Louise, da of Duncan Richard Fraser, CBE, of Nairobi, Kenya, and has issue living, Barnaby Nicholas Alnwick, *b* 1976, — Sebastian Jonathan Alnwick, *b* 1979.

DAUGHTER LIVING

Hon Amanda Mary Alnwick, *b* 1951; *ed* St Mary's Sch, Calne, and Bedford Coll, Univ. of London (BA (Hons)): *m* 1975, José das Neves. *Residence* – 199 Wakehurst Rd, SW11.

GRIDLEY, BARON (Gridley) (Baron UK 1955)

ARNOLD HUDSON GRIDLEY, 2nd Baron; *b* 26 May 1906; *s* 1965; *ed* Oundle; entered Colonial Ser, Malaya 1928; interned by Japanese in Changi Gaol, Malaya 1941-45; Acting Dep Comptroller, Fedn of Malaya 1956-57; a Member of Council of HM Overseas Ser Pensions Assocn 1966, and of Somerset Co Council Local Valuation Panel 1966; Chm of Centralised Audio Systems Ltd 1971, and of Board of Govs of Hall Sch, Bratten Seymour, Somerset 1974; a Dir of Lawdon Ltd 1968; a Govt Trustee of Far East (POW & Internee) Fund 1973; Knt 1957: *m* 1948, (Edna) Lesley, el da of late Leslie Richard Wheen, of Shanghai, and has issue.

Arms – Gules three bendlets enhanced and in base a portcullis chained or. **Crest** – A wyvern azure semee of lozenges or, resting the dexter claw on a grid iron gules. **Supporters** – *Dexter*, a wyvern azure semee of lozenges or: *sinister*, a lion gules semee of grid irons gold.
Residence – Coneygore, Stoke Trister, Wincanton, Somerset. *Club* – Royal Overseas League.

SON LIVING

Hon RICHARD DAVID ARNOLD, *b* 22 Aug 1956; *ed* Monckton Combe, and Portsmouth Poly: *m* 1st, 1979 (*m diss*), Amanda J., da of late Ian Mackenzie, of Felixstowe, formerly of Ceylon; 2ndly, 198-, Suzanne Elizabeth Ripper, and has issue living (by 2nd *m*), Carl Richard, *b* 5 Feb 1981, — Danielle Lauren, *b* 1983. *Residence* – 79 Purbrook Gdns, Purbrook, Hants.

DAUGHTERS LIVING

Hon Susan Lesley, *b* 1950: *m* 1st, 1975 (*m diss* 1982), John Philip Bruce Scott; 2ndly, 1983, Andrew Kinderbee Woods, of 7 West Way, Old Greenwich, Conn 06870, USA, and has issue living (by 1st *m*), Edward Harry Gridley, *b* 1977, — Carrie Elizabeth Anne, *b* 1979.
Hon Alison Elizabeth Vivienne, *b* 1953: *m* 1975 (*m diss* 1978), Michael John Hall.
Hon Vivienne Nicola, *b* 1955: *m* 1978, John Calvert Harvey, of 78 Impasse de l'Eglise, 60480 Froissy, France, and has issue living, William Marc Gridley, *b* 1986, — Hannah Louise, *b* 1983.

SISTER LIVING

Hon Geraldine, *b* 1918: *m* 1939, Lt-Col Norman John Lascelles Field, OBE, Roy Fusiliers, and has issue living, Richard Clive (Windover House, Birch Close, Lewes Rd, Haywards Heath, W Sussex), *b* 1947: *m* 1976, Susan Rosemary Hunter, 2nd da of Peter Hunter Pearson, of E Sussex, and has issue living, James Peter *b* 1978, Christopher Guy *b* 1981, — Anne Jacqueline, *b* 1942: *m* 1967, Anthony E. Vicars-Miles and has issue living, Sarah Elizabeth *b* 1969, Katherine Juliet *b* 1972. *Residence* – Fair Acres, White Hill, Bilting, nr Ashford, Kent.

COLLATERAL BRANCH LIVING

Issue of late Eric Howard Gridley, yr son of late Sir Arnold Babb Gridley, KBE (later 1st Baron Gridley), *b* 1911, *dvp* 1946: *m* 1936, Florence Sybil, who *d* 1979, da of Charles Darnell Bacon, of Loftus, N Yorks:—
Peter Arnold Charles, *b* 1940; *ed* Nautical Coll, Pangbourne: *m* 1966, Padmani Marie, da of late Maj P. D. Pelpola, MBE, of Gampola, Sri Lanka. *Residence* – Bigmore Cottage, Bigmore Lane, Stokenchurch, Bucks HP14 3UP. —— Howard Eric, *b* 1945; *ed* Fettes, Glasgow Univ (BSc), and Selwyn Coll, Camb (Dip Agric Sci).

PREDECESSOR – (1) *Sir* ARNOLD BABB Gridley, KBE, son of Edward Gridley of Abbey Dore, Herefordshire; *b* 1878; a consulting Engineer; MP for Stockport (*C*) 1935-50, and Stockport S 1950-55; *cr Baron Gridley* of Stockport, co Palatine of Chester (peerage of UK) 1955: *m* 1905, Mabel, who *d* 1955, da of Oliver Hudson, of Fakenham, *d* 1965; *s* by his el son (2) ARNOLD HUDSON, 2nd Baron and present peer.

GRIFFITHS, BARON (Griffiths) (Life Baron 1985)

(WILLIAM) HUGH GRIFFITHS, MC, PC, *b* 26 Sept 1923, only son of late Sir Hugh Ernest Griffiths, CBE (*d* 1961), by his wife, Doris Eirene, da of W. H. James; *ed* Charterhouse, and St John's Coll, Camb (MA); Pres MCC; Bar Inner Temple 1949, QC 1964, a Judge of High Court of Justice (Queen's Bench Div) 1970-80, and National Industrial Relations Court 1973-74; Member Advisory Council on Penal Reform 1967-70, Chm Tribunal of Inquiry on Ronan Point 1968, Vice-Chm Parole Bd 1976-77, Member Chancellor's Law Reform Cttee since 1976, Pres Senate of Inns of Court and the Bar 1982; a Lord Justice of Appeal 1980-85, a Lord of Appeal in Ordinary 1985-93; Chm Security Comm 1985-92; 1939-45 War as Capt Welsh Gds; MC 1944, *cr* Kt 1971, PC 1980, and *Baron Griffiths*, of Govilon, co Gwent (Life Baron) 1985: *m* 1949, Evelyn, da of Col K. A. Krefting, and has issue.
Address – c/o House of Lords, SW1. *Clubs* – Garrick, MCC, Royal & Ancient, St Andrews, Sunningdale Golf.

SON LIVING

Hon David Hugh, *b* 1958; *ed* Eton, and Magdalene Coll, Camb: *m* 1983, Henrietta, da of David Hall, and of Mrs Julian Wellesley, and has issue living, Thomas, *b* 1984, — Eloise, *b* 1986, — Jessica, *b* 1988.

DAUGHTERS LIVING

Hon Anne Serena, *b* 1951: *m* 1976, Peter William Urquhart, son of late Maj-Gen Ronald Walton Urquhart, CB, DSO, DL, and has issue living, James, *b* 1980, — Katherine, *b* 1978, — Flora, *b* 1981, — Serena, *b* 1984.

Hon Carolyn Jane, *b* 1952: *m* 1st, 1974 (*m diss* 1984), Justin Bygott-Webb; 2ndly, 1986, Douglas Christopher Patrick McDougall, son of late Patrick McDougall, and has issue living (by 1st *m*), Mark William, *b* 1976, — Samuel John, *b* 1978, — (by 2nd *m*) Fiona Maria, *b* 1987, — Mary Helen, *b* 1990.

Hon Emma Elizabeth, *b* 1964: *m* 1991, Duncan H. R. Matthews, son of M. Matthews, and of Mrs N. J. Hunter, and has issue living, George, *b* 1994.

GRIFFITHS OF FFORESTFACH, BARON (Griffiths) (Life Baron 1991)

BRIAN GRIFFITHS, son of Ivor Winston Griffiths; *b* 27 Dec 1941; *ed* Dynevor Gram Sch, and London Sch of Economics (BSc, MSc); Assist Lecturer in Economics, LSE, 1965-68, Lecturer in Economics 1968-76, Prof of Banking and Internat Finance, City Univ, 1977-85, Dir Centre for Banking and Internat Finance 1977-82, Dean Business Sch, City Univ, 1982-85, Visiting Prof Rochester Univ, USA, 1972-73, Prof of Ethics, Gresham Coll, 1984-87; Head of Prime Minister's Policy Unit (Rt Hon Margaret Thatcher) 1985-90; Dir Bank of England 1984-86; author; *cr Baron Griffiths of Fforestfach*, of Fforestfach, co W Glamorgan (Life Baron) 1991: *m* 1965, Rachel Jane, da of Howard Jones, and has issue.
Address – House of Lords, SW1. *Club* – Garrick.

SON LIVING

Hon James Brian, *b* 1970.

DAUGHTERS LIVING

Hon Aeronwen Jane, *b* 1968.
Hon Owenna Mary Ruth, *b* 1973.

GRIMOND, BARONY OF (Grimond) (Extinct 1993)

SONS LIVING OF LIFE BARON

Hon John Jasper, *b* 1946; *ed* Eton, Balliol Coll, Oxford, and Harvard Univ (Nieman Fell); Foreign Ed *The Economist*: *m* 1973, Kate, el da of late Lt-Col Peter Fleming, OBE, of Nettlebed, Henley-on-Thames, Oxon, and has issue living, Mary Jessie, *b* 1976, — Rose Clementine, *b* 1979, — Georgia Celia, *b* 1983.

Hon (Thomas) Magnus, *b* 1959; *ed* Stromness Acad, and Edinburgh Univ: *m* 1991, Laura Veldes, da of Rt Hon Sir Timothy Hugh Francis Raison, MP (*see* Cunard, Bt, 1976 Edn), and has issue living, Lucy Clare Laura, *b* 1994.

DAUGHTER LIVING OF LIFE BARON

Hon Grizelda Jane, *b* 1942; *ed* St Paul's Girls' Sch, and St Hugh's Coll, Oxford.

Grimston, Viscount; son of Earl of Verulam.

GRIMSTON OF WESTBURY, BARON (Grimston) (Baron UK 1964, Bt UK 1952)

Moderate things are stable

ROBERT WALTER SIGISMUND GRIMSTON, 2nd Baron, and 2nd Baronet; *b* 14 June 1925; *s* 1979; *ed* Eton; formerly Lt Scots Gds, NW Europe 1944-45; Liveryman of Gold and Silver Wyre Drawers' Co; Chm Grays Inn Underwriting Agency Ltd 1970-88; Dir of Hinton Hill and Coles 1962-83; Dir Stewart & Grays Inn Underwriting Agency Ltd 1970-90: *m* 1949, Hon June Mary Ponsonby, da of 5th Baron de Mauley, and has issue.

Arms – Quarterly: 1st and 4th argent, on a fesse sable, three rowels of six points or pierced gules; in the dexter chief an ermine spot sable, *Grimston*; 2nd sable, a fesse dancettée between two leopards' faces or, *Luckyn*; 3rd argent, three bugle horns sable, stringed gules, *Forrester*. **Crest** – A stag's head erased proper, attired or. **Supporters** – *Dexter*, a stag reguardant proper attired or; *sinister*, a horse reguardant argent.
Address – The Old Rectory, Westwell, nr Burford, Oxon. *Clubs* – Boodle's, and City of London.

SONS LIVING

Hon ROBERT JOHN SYLVESTER, *b* 30 April 1951; *ed* Eton, and Reading Univ (BSc); CA 1984; late Capt R Hus (PWO): *m* 1984, Emily Margaret, da of Maj John Evelyn Shirley, of Isle of Man (*see* E Ferrers, colls), and has issue living, Charlotte Elgiva, *b* 1991.
Hon (Gerald) Charles Walter (c/o Midland Bank, 69 Pall Mall, SW1; *Clubs* – Boodle's, and City of London), *b* 1953; *ed* Eton, and Exeter Univ (BA); late Maj Scots Gds (served N Ireland and S Atlantic Campaign 1982); Dir Grimston Holdings and Subsidiary Cos, J O Hambro Conning Grimston Ltd, and Woodcote Grove Estates Ltd: *m* 1980, Katherine Evelyn, da of Maj Rupert Berkeley Kettle, DL, of Piper's Hill, Bishop's Itchington, Leamington Spa, Warwicks, and has issue living, Edward Charles Luckyn, *b* 1985, — Alexander Rupert Ponsonby, *b* 1989, — Lucy Katherine Elgiva, *b* 1982.

DAUGHTER LIVING

Hon Georgiana Mary, *b* 1961: *m* 1992, Robin Pike, yst son of late Thomas Pike, and has issue living, Jack Augustus Thomas, *b* 1994.

BROTHERS LIVING

Hon Cecil Antony Sylvester (Wellingham Vane, nr Lewes, Sussex, BN8 5SN; Naval and Military Club, MCC), *b* 1927; *ed* Eton, and Camb Univ (MA): FRICS, FRSA; late Coldm Gds: *m* 1958, Dawn Monica Ann, da of Guy Janson, of Fair Hall, Southover, Lewes, and has issue living, Guy Antony Edward, *b* 1963, — John Lionel Charles, *b* 1968.
Hon Michael John Harbottle (3 Trevethan Rd, Falmouth, Cornwall), *b* 1932; *ed* Eton; *m* 1st, 1957 (*m diss* 1978), Julia Mary, da of Sir George Albu, 2nd Bt; 2ndly, 1982, Denise Angove, and has issue living (by 1st *m*), Simon Harbottle, *b* 1960, — Giles Villiers, *b* 1961, — Katherine Flavia, *b* 1962, — Sybilla Jane, *b* 1966.

SISTERS LIVING

Hon Rosemary Sybella Violet, *b* 1929: *m* 1st, 1953 (*m diss* 1964), (Charles) Edward Underdown, who *d* 1989; 2ndly, 1984, Antony Herbert David Rowse, son of late Herbert James Rowse. *Residence* – 75B Flood St, SW3.
Hon Ella Zia, *b* 1937: *m* 1972, Humphrey K. Humphreys, who *d* 1984, and has issue living, Catherine Sybella, *b* 1977. *Residence* – Ferne Park Cottage, Berwick St John, Shaftesbury, Dorset.

PREDECESSOR – (1) *Sir* ROBERT VILLIERS Grimston, el son of Rev Canon Hon Robert Grimston (*see* E Verulam, colls), *b* 1897, Treas of HM Household 1939-42, Assist Postmaster-Gen 1942-45, Parl Sec to Min of Supply May-July 1945, Member of UK Delegation to Gen Assembly of UN 1960, Dep Chm of Ways and Means, House of Commons 1962-64, Pres of Urban Dist Councils Assocn 1949-71; MP for Westbury Div of Wilts (C) 1931-64; *cr a Baronet* 1952, and *Baron Grimston of Westbury*, of Westbury, co Wilts (peerage of UK) 1964: *m* 1923, Sibyl Rose, who *d* 1977, da of Sir Sigmund Neumann, 1st Bt, *d* 1979; *s* by his el son (2) ROBERT WALTER SIGISMUND, 2nd Baron and present peer; also 2nd Baronet.

GRIMTHORPE, BARON (Beckett) (Baron UK 1886, Bt UK 1813)

To benefit the State

CHRISTOPHER JOHN BECKETT, OBE, 4th Baron and 8th Baronet; *b* 16 Sept 1915; *s* 1963; *ed* Eton; patron of two livings; Brig (ret) late 9th Queen's R Lancers; Col Comdg 9th Queen's R Lancers 1955-58; Col 9th/12th Lancers (PWO) since 1973; Brig R Armoured Corps, HQ, Western Command 1961-64, and Dep-Cdr Malta and Libya 1964-67; ADC to HM 1964-68; DL N Yorks; OBE (Mil) 1958: *m* 1954, Lady Elizabeth Lumley, CVO; a Lady of the Bedchamber to HM Queen Elizabeth The Queen Mother 1973; da of 11th Earl of Scarbrough, and has issue.

Arms – Gules, a fesse between three boars' head couped erminois. **Crest** – A boar's head couped of pierced by a cross patée fitchée erect gules. **Supporters** – Two sangliers erminois, each gorged with a collar and pendant therefrom an escutcheon gules charged with a cross patée fitchée or.
Seat – Westow Hall, York. *Club* – Cavalry.

SONS LIVING

Hon EDWARD JOHN, *b* 20 Nov 1954: *m* 1992, Mrs Carey Elizabeth McEwen, yr da of Robin Graham, and has issue living, a son, *b* 28 April 1993.
Hon Ralph Daniel, *b* 1957: *m* 1987, Susanna W., elder da of Colin Townsend-Rose, and has issue living, a son, *b* 1990, — a son, *b* 1992.

DAUGHTER LIVING

Hon Harriet Lucy, *b* 1961: *m* 1985, Capt (Richard) Mark Smyly, 16th/5th Queen's R Lancers (*see* By Buckland, 1980 Edn), and has issue living, Hugo Richard Seymour, *b* 1990, — George William Dennis, *b* 1992. *Residence* – The Old Glebe House, Sparsholt, Wantage, Oxon.

BROTHER LIVING

Hon Oliver Ralph (55 Carlisle Av, St Albans, Herts AL3 5LX), *b* 1918; *ed* Eton; FRSA: *m* 1944, Hélène Agnes, formerly wife of Richard Tasker-Evans, da of late Constantine Fessas, and has issue living, Sarah Christine, *b* 1946; artist: *m* 1966 (*m diss* 1977), Jonathan Crook, and has issue living, John Henry *b* 1967, Tara Leonie *b* 1968, Sarah Aline (twin) *b* 1968, — Juliet Mary, *b* 1949.

HALF-BROTHER LIVING

Hon William Ernest (The Estate House, Serlby Park, nr Bawtry, S Yorks), *b* 1945; *ed* Eton; 2nd Lt 9th/12th R Lancers: *m* 1968, Virginia Helen, only da of late Michael Clark Hutchison, of Wellcroft End, Bucklebury, Berks, and has issue living, Ralph Michael, *b* 1971, — Serena Angela Anne, *b* 1974.

SISTER LIVING

Hon Lucy Clare, *b* 1926: *m* 1957, Wilson Peregrine Nicholas Crewdson (*see* Bacon, Bt), and has issue living, Giles Wilson Mervyn, *b* 1959; Lieut 9th/12th R Lancers: *m* 1990 (*m diss* 1993), Hon Aurelia Margaret Amherst Cecil, only da of 4th Baron Amherst of Hackney, — Diana Constance Mary (twin), *b* 1959: *m* 1980, Christopher J. M. Langley, yr son of Lt-Col James Langley, of The Old Rectory, Alderton, Woodbridge, Suffolk, and has issue living, Venetia Margaret Clare *b* 1983, Edwina Chantal Elizabeth *b* 1985, Rose Katharine Lucy *b* 1988, — Virginia Clare, *b* 1964: *m* 1991, Giles J. G. Appleton, only son of late G/Capt James Appleton. *Residence* – Oak House, Otley, nr Ipswich, Suffolk.

COLLATERAL BRANCH LIVING (*In special remainder*)

Issue of late Hon (William) Gervase Beckett (2nd son of late William, Beckett-Denison, and brother of 2nd Baron), who was *cr* a *Baronet* 1921:—
See Beckett, Bt, cr 1921.

PREDECESSORS – **(1)** *Sir* JOHN Beckett, of Leeds and Somerby Park, Lincs, *b* 1743; *cr* a *Baronet* 1813: *m* 1774, Mary, who *d* 1833, da of Christopher Wilson, Bishop of London; *d* 1826; *s* by his el son **(2)** JOHN, PC, MP, FRS, 2nd Bt; *b* 1775; MP for Cockermouth (*C*) 1820-21, Haslemere 1826-32, and Leeds 1835-7; Judge-Advocate-Gen: *m* 1817, Lady Anne Lowther, who *d* 1871, da of 1st Earl of Lonsdale; *dsp* 1847; *s* by his brother **(3)** THOMAS, 3rd Bt; *b* 1779; *m* 1829, his cousin Caroline, who *d* 1878, da of Joseph Beckett, of Barnsley: *d* 1872; *s* by his brother **(4)** EDMUND, 4th Bt; *b* 1787; MP for W Riding of York (*C*) 1841-59; assumed the name and arms of Denison by Roy licence 1816, and resumed his patronymic on succeeding to the Baronetcy: *m* 1814, Maria, who *d* 1874, da of William Beverley, and great-niece and heir of Anne Smithson, wife of Sir Thomas Denison, Justice of King's Bench 1742; *d* 1874; *s* by his el son **(5)** EDMUND, LLD, KC, 5th Bt; *b* 1816; resumed surname of Beckett in lieu of Denison 1874; Vicar-Gen and Chancellor of York; *cr Baron Grimthorpe*, of Grimthorpe, co York (peerage of UK) 1886, with remainder to the issue male of his father: *m* 1845, Fanny Catharine, who *d* 1901, da of late Right Rev John Lonsdale, DD, Lord Bishop of Lichfield; *d* 1905; *s* under special remainder by his nephew **(6)** ERNEST WILLIAM 2nd Baron (son of late William Beckett, MP, brother of 1st Baron), *b* 1856; MP for Whitby Div of NR of York (*C*) 1885-1905; partner in banking firm of Beckett & Co, of Leeds: *m* 1883, Lucy Tracy, who *d* 1891, da of late William P. Lee, of New York; *d* 1917; *s* by his son **(7)** RALPH WILLIAM ERNEST, TD, 3rd Baron; *b* 1891; Lt-Col (Cmdg 1936-40) Yorkshire Hussars TA, and partner in banking firm of Beckett & Co, of Leeds; PPS to Under Sec of State for War 1919-21: *m* 1st, 1914 (*m diss* 1945), Mary Alice, who *d* 1962, da of Col Mervyn Henry Archdale, 12th Lancers; 2ndly, 1945, Angela, who *d* 1992, da of late Edward Hubert Courage, of Kirkby Fleetham Hall, Bedale, Yorks, and formerly wife of late Cdr David Cecil Lycett Green, RN (*see* Green, Bt, colls); *d* 1963; *s* by his el son **(8)** CHRISTOPHER JOHN, 4th Baron and present peer.

Grinstead, Baron, title of Earl of Enniskillen on Roll of HL.

Grosvenor, Earl; son of Duke of Westminster.

Guernsey, Baron; son of Earl of Aylesford.

GUEST, BARONY OF (Guest) (Extinct 1984)

SONS LIVING OF LIFE BARON (*By 1st marriage*)

Hon (Christopher) John Graham (19 Cheyne Row, SW3 5HW), *b* 1929; *ed* Eton, and Clare Coll, Camb: *m* 1960, Myrna, da of late I. Dukes, of Chicago, USA, and has issue living, Christopher, *b* 1967, — Amanda, *b* 1964. *Club* – Chelsea Arts.

(*By 2nd marriage*)

Hon David William Graham, *b* 1943; *ed* Charterhouse and Clare Coll, Camb (BA; CA): *m* 1992, Dr Jane L. Polglase, da of late E. B. J. Polglase.
Hon Simon Edward Graham, WS (40 Hope Terrace, Edinburgh, EH9 2AR; New and Hon Co of Edinburgh Golfers), *b* 1949; *ed* Charterhouse and Dundee Univ (LLB); Solicitor and WS Edinburgh: *m* 1977, Fiona, da of late Robert Wilson Taylor Lamont, of Kilmarnock, and issue living, Michael Simon Lamont, *b* 1980, — Joanna Katie, *b* 1978.
Hon Andrew Beaumont Graham (Shirgarton House, Kippen, Stirling FK8 3EA), *b* 1951; *ed* Charterhouse, St Andrew's Univ (MA), and Edinburgh Univ: *m* 1980, Elizabeth, only da of late Alan Cuthbert, and has issue living, David John, *b* 1981, — Catherine Charlotte, *b* 1983.

DAUGHTER LIVING OF LIFE BARON (*By 2nd marriage*)

Hon Elizabeth Jane Graham, *b* 1945; *ed* Univ of Delaware, USA (BS, MS): *m* 1968, George Willing Pepper, of 128 Springton Lake Rd, Media, Pa 19063, USA. *Club* – Union League, Philadelphia.

WIDOW LIVING OF LIFE BARON

CATHARINE GERALDINE (*Baroness Guest*) (22 Lennox St, Edinburgh, EH4 1QA), da of late John Beaumont Hotham (*see* Hotham, B, colls): *m* 1941, as his 2nd wife, Baron Guest, PC (Life Baron), who *d* 1984.

Guest, see Baron Haden Guest.

GUILFORD, EARL OF (North) (Earl GB 1752)

With courage and fidelity

EDWARD FRANCIS NORTH, 9th Earl; *b* 22 Sept 1933; *s* 1949; *ed* Eton; DL for Kent 1976; is patron of two livings: *m* 1956, (Osyth) Vere Napier, who *d* 1992, da of Cyril Napier Leeston, of Trottiscliffe, West Malling, Kent, and has issue.

Arms – Azure, a lion passant or, between three fleurs-de-lis argent. **Crest** – A dragon's head erased sable, ducally gorged and chained or. **Supporters** – Two mastiffs proper.
Residence – Waldershare Park, Dover.

SON LIVING

PIERS EDWARD BROWNLOW (*Lord North*), *b* 9 March 1971: *m* 1994, Michèle C., da of late Gilbert Desvaux de Marigny, of Curepipe, Mauritius, and of Mrs Eric Story, of Durban, S Africa.

SISTERS LIVING (*Raised to the rank of an Earl's daughters* 1950)

Lady Barbara Joan, *b* 1928; is an OStJ: *m* 1951, Maj Hon Sir Clive Bossom, 2nd Bt. *Residence* – 97 Cadogan Lane, SW1X 9DU.
Lady Angela Mary, *b* 1931: *m* 1955, Peter John Henry Whiteley, of 10 Henning St, SW11 3DR, and has issue living, Simon William Alastair, *b* 1958: *m* 1988, Winifred, yst da of Alex Wu, CBE, of Hong-Kong, — Justin Henry Francis, *b* 1964: *m* 1988, Juliette Margaret, only da of Philip Howard (*see* Houldsworth, Bt), and has issue living, Harry Thomas Edward *b* 1989, Charlie Hamish Reginald *b* 1992, — Emma Louise, *b* 1959: *m* 1993, Henry Campbell Bellingham, MP (*see* Bellingham, Bt, colls).

UNCLE LIVING (*Son of 8th Earl*)

Hon Charles Evelyn, *b* 1918; *ed* Eton, and London Univ (BSc 1939); European War, 1939-45 as Flight-Lieut RAF: *m* 1st, 1942 (*m diss* 1957), Maureen O'Callaghan, da of Major F. C. B. Baldwin, of Malmo, Park Avenue, Gillingham; 2ndly, 1959, Joan Aston, da of Major F. B. Booker, and has issue living, (by 1st *m*) Peter David, *b* 1943; *ed* Dover Coll, — Susan Caroline, *b* 1947. *Residence* – Park End House, Eythorne, near Dover.

WIDOW LIVING OF SON OF EIGHTH EARL

Wendy Alexandra, yst da of Francis Robert Peters: *m* 1961, as his 4th wife, Hon John Montagu William North, 2nd son of 8th Earl, who *d* 1987. *Residence* – 2 La Brecque Phillippe, Alderney, CI.

COLLATERAL BRANCHES LIVING

Issue of late Hon John Montagu William North, 2nd son of 8th Earl, *b* 1905, *d* 1987: *m* 1st, 1927 (*m diss* 1939), Muriel Norton, who *d* 1989, yr da of Sir William Norton Hicking, 1st Bt (*see* North, Bt); 2ndly, 1939 (*m diss* 1949), Marion Dyer, who *d* 1992, yst da of Frank Erving Chase, of Boston, Mass, USA; 3rdly, 1951 (*m diss* 1960), Polly, da of Dick Peabody, of USA; 4thly, 1961, Wendy Alexandra (ante), yst da of Francis Robert Peters:—

(By 1st *m*) *Sir* (William) Jonathan Frederick, 2nd Bt, *b* 1931; *s* his maternal grandfather 1947 (*see* Baronetage).
—— Georgiana Mary, *b* 1928: *m* 1960, Esmond Unwin Butler, CM, CVO, Sec to Gov-Gen of Canada, who *d* 1989, and has issue living, Mark William, *b* 1961, — Clare Martine, *b* 1963. *Residence* – 149 Rideau Terrace, Ottawa, Ontario, Canada.
—— (By 3rd *m*) Serena Laura Penelope, *b* 1952: *m* 1976, Charles Meredith Hastings Colchester, son of Rev Capt Halsey Sparrowe, Colchester, CMG, OBE, and has issue living, Alexander North Peabody, *b* 1981, — Benjamin Medhurst Pawson, *b* 1983, — Zachary Wheatland Maynard, *b* 1988, — Tamara Sarah Sparrowe, *b* 1985, — Chloë Talitha Jacob, *b* 1991. *Residence* – 53 Romney St, SW1P 3RF.

Issue of late Hon Morton William North, brother of 7th Earl, *b* 1852, *d* 1895: *m* 1879, Hylda Hylton, who *d* 1902, da of late Capt Hylton Jolliffe (B Hylton, colls):—
Roger, *b* 1888: *m* 1912, Alice Amy Le Gros. *Residence* –

Granddaughters of late Frederic Dudley North, CMG, elder son of late Charles Augustus North, elder son of late Brownlow North, only son of late Rev Charles Augustus North, brother of 6th Earl:—
Issue of late (Hon) Charles Frederic John North, *b* 1887, *d* 1979; Member Legislative Assembly for Claremont (Speaker 1947-53): *m* 1916, Bessie, da of William Saddington, of Cheshire:—
Muriel Elvia Joan, *b* 1917: *m* 1942, Roy Wilson Parr. —— Mary Rachael June, *b* 1930: *m* 1st, 1955 (*m diss* 1966), Gareth Murray Denny; 2ndly, 1967, Thomas Nolan Cassidy, and has issue living (by 1st *m*), David North Murray, *b* 1958, — Julie Elizabeth, *b* 1961.
Issue of late George Eustace Dudley North, *b* 1893, *d* 1960: *m* 1920, Florence Ethel Yeo, of Mount Street, Perth, W Australia:—
Mary Elizabeth, *b* 1925; former concert pianist: *m* 1948, Geoffrey Norris Russell, who *d* 19—, and has issue living, John Norris Grant, *b* 1951; *ed* Harrow, and Trin Coll, Dublin, — Francis Guilford, *b* 1953; *ed* Harrow; musician: *m* 1980, Manon Regina, el da of late James Mackay Henry Millington-Drake (*see* E Inchcape, 1980 Edn), — Philip Brownlow, *b* 1959. *Residence* – Dunkathel, Glanmire, co Cork.

Descendants, if any, of late Brownlow John Frederic North (*b* 1883), elder son of late Brownlow Hamilton North (*b* 1854) (infra).
Grandchildren of late Brownlow Hamilton North (*b* 1854), of The Knoll Estate, Coonoor, Nilgiri Hills, S India, only son of late Brownlow John Jarvis North (*b* 1831), 2nd son of late Brownlow North (ante):—
Issue of late George Guilford Dudley North, *b* 1884, *d* (April) 1937: *m* 1st, 19—, — , who *d* 19—; 2ndly, 1921, Jane Berkeley (who *d* 1977, having *m* 2ndly, (Oct) 1937, Austin Benedict Caston, of Garakhpur, UP, India), da of Charles Nathaniel Gregg:—
(By 2nd *m*) †Dudley Charles Guilford, *b* 1923; accidentally drowned 1944, in India, *unm.* —— Patricia Grace Eileen, *b* 1922: *m* 1944, Jackson Samuel Askey, of 7710 Fitzpatrick Drive, Liverpool, NY 13088, USA, and has issue. —— Jean Dorothy, *b* 1928: *m* 1948, Daniel Vegard, who *d* 1978, and *d* 1968, leaving issue, James Dudley, *b* 1948: *m* 1971, Jennie Abrunzo, — Deborah Ann, *b* 1951, — Victoria Jane, *b* 1954: *m* 1993, Frederick Herbert Ahrens, and has issue living, James Frederick *b* 1993. —— Barbara Violet, *b* 1931: *m* 1957, James Edward Semple, of 8201 Golden Bear Loop, Port Richey, Florida 34668, USA, and has issue living, Cathy Barbara, *b* 1958: *m* 1982, Stephen Andrew Dock, and has issue living, James Matthew *b* 1987, Melissa Jean *b* 1985, Carolyn Jane *b* 1991, — Jane Alice, *b* 1962: *m* 1988, Delano Bookings Trott.

PREDECESSORS – (1) *Sir* EDWARD North, an eminent lawyer, MP for Cambridgeshire 1541-2, Lord-Lieut of Cambridgeshire, and one of the executors of Henry VIII; summoned to Parliament as *Baron North*, of Kirtling, co Cambridge (peerage of England) 1554; *d* 1564; *s* by his son (2) *Rt Hon* ROGER, KB, 2nd Baron, Ambassador to France and Treasurer of Queen Elizabeth's Household; *d* 1600; *s* by his grandson (3) DUDLEY, 3rd Baron; *d* 1666; *s* by his son (4) DUDLEY, KB, 4th Baron; *d* 1677; *s* by his son (5) CHARLES, 5th Baron; summoned to Parliament during his father's lifetime as *Baron Grey*, of Rolleston, co Stafford (peerage of England) 1673; *d* 1690; *s* by his son (6) WILLIAM, 6th Baron North and 2nd Baron Grey; *dsp* 1734, when the Barony of Grey expired and the Barony of North devolved upon his cousin (7) FRANCIS, 7th Baron North, who had in 1729 *s* as 3rd *Baron Guilford*, of Guildford, co Surrey (peerage of England), a peerage that had been conferred upon Hon Sir Francis, Lord Ch Justice of the Common Pleas, 2nd son of 4th Baron North; *cr Earl of Guilford* (peerage of Great Britain) 1752; *d* 1790; *s* by his el son (8) *Rt Hon* FREDERICK, KG, 2nd Earl; an eminent statesman who (when Lord North) held high official positions 1759-83, and was Prime Minister 1778-81; *d* 1792; *s* by his son (9) GEORGE AUGUSTUS, 3rd Earl; *d* 1802, when the Barony of North became abeyant (*see* B North), and the earldom devolved upon his brother (10) FRANCIS, 4th Earl; *dsp* 1817; *s* by his brother (11) FREDERICK, 5th Earl; *dsp* 1827; *s* by his cousin (12) *Rev* Francis, 6th Earl; *d* 1861; *s* by his grandson (13) DUDLEYFRANCIS (el son of late Dudley, Lord North, el son of 6th Earl), 7th Earl, *b* 1851: *m* 1874, Georgiana, who *d* 1931, da of Sir George Chetwynd, 3rd Bt; *d* 1885; *s* by his son (14) FREDERICK GEORGE, TD, 8th Earl, 1876; Lieut-Col Roy E Kent Yeo: *m* 1901, Mary Violet, who *d* 1947, el da of late William Hargrave Pawson; *d* 1949; *s* by his grandson (5) EDWARD FRANCIS (only son of late Francis George, Lord North, el son of 8th Earl), 9th Earl and present peer; also Baron Guilford.

GUILLAMORE, VISCOUNTCY OF (O'Grady) (Extinct 1955)

DAUGHTER LIVING OF SIXTH VISCOUNT

Hon Kathleen Gertrude, *b* 1914; late Junior Com ATS: *m* 1945, Capt Geoffrey Hearn, Somersetshire LI, and has issue living, Timothy Charles, *b* 1947. *Residence* – Badgers Mount, Bottle Sq Lane, Radnage, Bucks.

Gwynedd, Viscount, son of Earl Lloyd George of Dwyfor.

HACKING, BARON (Hacking) (Baron UK 1945, Bt UK 1938)

DOUGLAS DAVID HACKING, 3rd Baron, and 3rd Baronet; *b* 17 April 1938; *s* 1971; *ed* Charterhouse, and Clare Coll, Camb (MA); Bar Middle Temple 1963-76; Bar State of New York, USA 1975; with Simpson, Thatcher & Bartlett, New York City 1975-76; Solicitor of Supreme Court of England and Wales 1977; with Lovell, White & King, London and New York City 1976-79, with Richards Butler since 1981; Pres of Assocn of Lancastrians in London 1971-72; Freeman Merchant Taylors' Co, and City of London; Lt RNR (ret): *m* 1st, 1965, Rosemary Anne, el da of late Frank Penrose Forrest, FRCSE, of Lytchett Matravers, Dorset; 2ndly, 1982, Tessa Margaret, MB, MRCP, FRCA, da of Roland Hunt, CMG, of Whitchurch Hill, Reading, and has issue by 1st and 2nd *m*.

Arms – Argent, on a chevron azure between three roses gules barbed and seeded proper, two birds bolts of the field, feathered or. **Crest** – In front of an oak tree eradicated, two axes in saltire all proper. **Supporters** – On either side a griffin gules, on the shoulder an escutcheon argent charged with a blue-bottle (Cyanus), stalked and leaved proper.
Residence – 21 West Square, SE11 4SN.

SONS LIVING *(By 1st marriage)*

Hon DOUGLAS FRANCIS, *b* 8 Aug 1968.
Hon Daniel Robert, *b* 1972.

(By 2nd marriage)

Hon Alexander Roland Harry, *b* 1984.
Hon (Maxwell David) Leo, *b* 1987.
Hon Christian Eric George, *b* 1989.

DAUGHTER LIVING *(By 1st marriage)*

Hon Belinda Anne, *b* 1966.

BROTHER LIVING

Hon (Leslie) Bruce (Burchetts, Moushill Common, Milford, Surrey), *b* 1940; *ed* Eton; Member of Court of Assistants, Haberdashers' Co, and City of London: *m* 1967, Hon Fiona Margaret Noel-Paton, yst da of Baron Ferrier (Life Baron), and has issue living, Matthew Bruce, *b* 1969, — Joanna, *b* 1972.

SISTERS LIVING

Hon Sandra Daphne, *b* 1950: *m* 1972, Damon Patrick de Laszlo, of 42 Albany, Piccadilly, W1, and Pelham Place, Newton Valence, nr Alton, Hants GU34 3NQ (*see* V Greenwood, 1980 Edn), and has issue living, Robert Damon, *b* 1977, — William Patrick, *b* 1979, — Lucy Deborah, *b* 1975.
Hon Carina Gillian, *b* 1956: *m* 1981, Jean Jacobus du Preez, of 8 Winters Wynd, Newlands 7700, Cape Province, S Africa.

UNCLE LIVING *(Son of 1st Baron)*

Hon Edgar Bolton, MBE, TD, *b* 1912; *ed* Charterhouse, and Clare Coll, Camb (BA 1932, MA 1937, MB and BCh 1937); MRCS England and LRCP London 1936: Diploma in Anæsthesia Roy Coll of Physicians and Roy Coll of Surgs 1946; a Member of Faculty of Anæsthetists, Roy Coll of Surgs 1949, a Fellow of Asso of Anæsthetists 1951 and a Fellow of Faculty of Anæsthetists, Roy Coll of Surgs 1954, formerly Senior Assist Anæsthetist, Groote Schnur Hospital, Cape Town; European War 1939-45 as Major RAMC (MBE); MBE (Mil) 1943: *m* 1st, 1943 (*m diss* 1950), Winifred Mary, da of John Christie Kelly, of S Africa; 2ndly, 1950, Evangeline Grace, da of Percy Burtsal Shearing, of S Africa, and has issue living, (by 1st *m*) Elizabeth Anne, *b* 1944, — Susan Margaret, *b* 1946, — (by 2nd *m*) Douglas Percival Bolton, *b* 1955: *m* 1984, Mary, yr da of late Cyril Puttergill, of Indwe, CP, S Africa, — Geoffrey Edgar Bolton, *b* 1958: *m* 1983, Elizabeth, only da of late Edward Hiles, of Somerset West, CP, S Africa, — Margery Ethel, *b* 1952: *m* 1973, George du Plessis, son of late V. du Plessis, of Cape Town, S Africa. *Residence* – Leeming, Alice Rd, Claremont, Cape, S Africa.

AUNT LIVING *(Daughter of 1st Baron)*

Hon Elizabeth Margery (*Hon Lady Waller*), *b* 1916; is a JP (Hants); *m* 1936, Rt Hon Lord Justice (Sir George Stanley) Waller, OBE, and has issue living, *Sir* (George) Mark (*Hon Mr Justice Waller*), *b* 1940, LLB; Bar Gray's Inn, 1964; QC 1979, Recorder 1986, Judge of High Court of Justice, Queen's Bench Div 1989; *cr* Kt 1989: *m* 1967, Rachel Elizabeth, da of Judge Christopher Beaumont, MBE, of Minskip Lodge, Boroughbridge, N Yorks, and has issue living, Charles James *b* 1968, Richard *b* 1969, Philip *b* 1973, — James Irvin (136 Brighton Av, Ottawa, Ont, Canada K1S OT4), *b* 1944; Prof of Criminology, Ottawa Univ: *m* 1st, 1966, Myriam, da of Prof Pierre de Bie, of 2 Chaussée de Namur, Blanden, Belgium; 2ndly, 1983, Susan Gwen, da of Byron Chester Tanner, of 11309 University Av, Edmonton, Alberta, and has issue living, (by 1st *m*) Ann-Virginie *b* 1968, Marie-Katherine *b* 1970, (by 2nd *m*), James Byron Tanner *b* 1984, Mark Patrick Byron Tanner *b* 1986, — Elizabeth Tessa (Prof), *b* 1937: *m* 1959, Prof John Hedley-Whyte, of 355 Fairhaven Rd, Concord, Mass 01742 4404, USA. *Residence* – Hatchway, Hatch Lane, Kingsley Green, Haslemere, Surrey.

WIDOW LIVING OF SECOND BARON

DAPHNE VIOLET (*Daphne, Baroness Hacking*), el da of late Robert Leslie Finnis, of Kensington, W: *m* 1936, the 2nd Baron, who *d* 1971.

PREDECESSORS – **(1)** DOUGLAS HEWITT Hacking, OBE, PC, son of Joshua Hacking, JP, of Clayton-le-Moors, Lancs, *b* 1884; Financial Sec to War Office and a Member of Army Council 1934-35, and Under-Sec of State for Dominions 1935-36; founded Travel Assoc of Great Britain and Ireland 1928; Chm of Conservative Party 1936-42; MP for Chorley (*U*) 1918 to 1945; *cr a Baronet* 1938, and *Baron Hacking*, of Chorley, co Lancaster (peerage of UK) 1945: *m* 1909, Margery Allen, who *d* 1984, aged 97, el da of H. H. Bolton, JP, of Newchurch-in-Rossendale; *d* 1950; *s* by his el son **(2)** DOUGLAS ERIC, 2nd Baron, *b* 1910; Chm of Council Trust Houses 1965-70 and Trust Houses Forte Hotel and Catering Group 1970-71; 1939-45 War as Maj RA: *m* 1936, Daphne Violet, el da of late Robert Leslie Finnis, of Kensington, W, *d* 1971; *s* by his el son **(3)** DOUGLAS DAVID, 3rd Baron and present peer; also 3rd baronet.

HADDINGTON, EARL OF (Baillie-Hamilton) (Earl S 1619)

I undertake and persevere

Virtue is greater than splendour

JOHN GEORGE BAILLIE-HAMILTON, 13th Earl; *b* 21 Dec 1941; *s* 1986; *ed* Ampleforth: *m* 1st, 1975 (*m diss* 1981), Prudence Elizabeth, da of Andrew Rutherford Hayles, of Bowerchalke, Wilts; 2ndly, 1984, Jane, da of John Heyworth, of Bradwell Grove, Burford, Oxon (*see By Tweedmouth*), and has issue by 2nd *m*.

Arms – Quarterly: 1st and 4th grand quarters, 1st and 4th gules, on a chevron between three cinquefoils argent, a buckle azure, between two ermine spots, all within a bordure or, charged with eight thistles vert, *Hamilton of Byres*; 2nd and 3rd argent, a fesse wavy between three roses gules barbed and seeded proper, *Melrose*; 2nd and 3rd grand quarters sable, the sun in his glory betwixt nine stars, three, two, three, and one, argent, *Baillie of Jerviswoode*. **Crests** – 1st, two dexter hands issuing out of clouds, conjoined fessewise and holding betwixt them a branch of laurel erect, all proper; 2nd, a crescent or. **Supporters** – Two talbots argent, plain collared gules.
Seat – Mellerstain, Gordon, Berwicks TD3 6LG.

SON LIVING (By 2nd marriage)

Hon GEORGE EDMUND BALDRED (*Lord Binning*), *b* 27 Dec 1985.

DAUGHTERS LIVING (By 2nd marriage)

Lady Susan Moyra, *b* 1988.
Lady Isobel Joan, *b* 1990.

SISTER LIVING

Lady Mary, *b* 1934: *m* 1st, 1954 (*m diss* 1965), (John) Adrian Bailey, elder son of late Ronald Graham Bailey, of 7 Lansdowne Crescent, W11; 2ndly, 1965, David Russell, son of Brig Hugh Edward Russell, DSO, and has issue living (by 1st *m*), (William) Anthony, *b* 1957: *m* 1993, Anne C., yr da of Mark Ueland, of Philadelphia, Penn, USA, — Philip Graham, *b* 1959: *m* 1990, Georgina A., da of G. M. C. White, and of Mrs Barbara Makins, — Arabella Sarah Lucy (*Viscountess Chandos*), *b* 1955: *m* 1985, 3rd Viscount Chandos, — (by 2nd *m*) Jason Dominic, *b* 1966, — Mariana, *b* 1968. *Residence* – Combe Manor, Newbury, Berks.

WIDOW LIVING OF TWELFTH EARL

SARAH (*Sarah, Countess of Haddington*), da of late George William Cook, of Westmount, Montreal, Canada: *m* 1923, the 12th Earl, who *d* 1986. *Residence* – Tyninghame, E Linton, E Lothian.

COLLATERAL BRANCHES LIVING

Grandchildren of late Rev Thomas George Baillie, son of Rev Hon John Baillie, brother of 10th Earl:—
Issue of late Richard George HAMILTON-BAILLIE, *b* 1869, *d* 1945: *m* 1915, Maud Gertrude, who *d* 1952, only da of late Edward Hadley, Bar-at-Law:—
John Robert Edward, MC, *b* 1919; *ed* Camb Univ (MA); Brig (ret) late RE, MICE; 1939-45 War (MC): *m* 1947, Lettice Mary, da of late C. E. Pumphrey, of Belsay, Northumberland, and has issue living, Thomas Richard (Cavalry and Guards' Club), *b* 1948; *ed* Winchester, London Univ (BA), and Oxford Univ; Lt-Col R Green Jackets: *m* 1975, Marina J. A. S., da of late General Dr Ferdinand von Senger und Etterlin, of Riedern Am Wald, Uhlingen-Birkendorf, Germany, and has issue living, Isobel Ebba *b* 1979, Daisy Ernestine *b* 1982, Cecily Marina *b* 1985, — Benjamin Robert, *b* 1955: *m* 1988, Jennifer A., da of late Leslie Hill, of Pinner, Middx, and has issue living, Laurence Benjamin *b* 1990, Agnes Laetitia *b* 1992, — Griselda Mary, *b* 1950; Trustee Royal Academy since 1990: *m* 1985, William Walter Raleigh Kerr, eldest son of Lord John Andrew Christopher Kerr, and has issue (*see M Lothian*), — Katherine Maud, *b* 1957. *Residence* – Rectory House, Stanford-in-the-Vale, Faringdon, Oxon.
Issue of late Charles Jarviswoode Baillie, *b* 1882, *d* 1973: *m* 1915, Dora Lizzie Dunn-Smith, who *d* 1973:—
Barbara, *b* 1915: *m* 1945, Maurice W. Brown, and has issue living, Laurence Charles, *b* 1955, — Robin Alison, *b* 1947: *m* 1968, Kenneth le Drew, and has issue living, Christopher *b* 1969, — Priscilla Ann, *b* 1952: *m* 1973, Allan P. Roe, and has issue living, Corey Christopher *b* 1977, Jess Patrice *b* 1974, Gillian Martha *b* 1975. *Residence* – RR2 Albers Rd, Lumby, BC, Canada V0E 2G0.

Grandchildren of late Charles Jarviswoode Baillie (*ante*):—
Issue of late Robert Alastair Baillie, *b* 1919, *d* 1984: *m* 1945, Elizabeth Amy (Suite 15, 980 Gilford St, Esher Court, Vancouver, BC, Canada V6G 2N7), da of Alexi Chernoff, of Tiflis, Russia, and of Kelowna, BC:—
Dexter Robert, *b* 1958: *m* 19—, Kristin Grace, da of Ross Bradford, of Warwick, Australia. *Address* – Box 945, Whistler, BC, Canada V0N 1B0. —— Eve Sylvia, *b* 1946: *m* 1968, John Edward Sample, and has issue living, Barton Kirby, *b* 1976, — Sarah Nicole, *b* 1971. *Residence* – 5815 Gilpin St, Burnaby, BC, Canada V5G 2J1. —— Angeline Cecelia, *b* 1950: *m* 1974, Roy Albert Derrick, only son of Rex Raphael Derrick, of Penticton, BC, and has issue living, Kyle Edward, *b* 1987, — Shannon Hillary, *b* 1980, — Colleen Elizabeth, *b* 1984. *Residence* – 3623 Selinger Crescent, Regina, Saskatchewan, Canada S4V 2H7.

Granddaughter of Rev Hon John Baillie, brother of 10th Earl (*ante*):—
Issue of late Rev Thomas George Baillie, *b* 1842, *d* 1917: *m* 1st, 1867, Ellen Isabella, who *d* 1909, da of Richard Gregson, of Sydney, NSW; 2ndly, 1911, Violet Amy Kate, who *d* 1961, da of F. W. Dunn:—

(By 2nd *m*) Violet Georgina Eila, *b* 1912: *m* 1931, Albert Ranney Chewett, who *d* 1965. *Residence* – Reveley Lodge, 88 Elstree Rd, Bushey Heath, Herts WD2 3QY.

Granddaughter (by 1st *m*) of late George Leslie Baillie-Hamilton, sometime Capt 13th Bn Royal Scots (Lothian Regt) (infra):—
Issue of late George Leslie Baillie-Hamilton, *b* 1909, *d* 1968: *m* 1947, Mrs Millicent Margaret Lambert, who *d* 1989, da of late Edmund Sopp, and formerly wife of George Ernest Lambert:—
Ann, *b* 1947: *m* 1966, James William Maxwell Sheridan, of 995 Forest Rd, E17 4BP, and has issue living, Paul Maxwell, *b* 1966; has issue living (by Deborah Suzanne Budd), Jarrod James *b* 1990, Kylie Jade *b* 1988, — Trevor William, *b* 1967, — Gavin Robert, *b* 1976, — Samantha Ann, *b* 1969.

Grandchildren of late Rev George James Baillie-Hamilton, only son of late Capt Peregrine Charles Baillie-Hamilton, elder son of late Charles John Baillie-Hamilton, MP, 2nd son of late Ven Charles Baillie-Hamilton, 2nd son of Hon George Baillie, brother of 7th Earl:—
Issue of late George Leslie Baillie-Hamilton, sometime Capt 13th Bn Royal Scots (Lothian Regt), *b* 1877, *d* 1931: *m* 1st, 1906, Florence Maud Robinson, who *d* 1912; 2ndly, 1919, Katherine Ida Sopp (otherwise Pennicard), who *d* 1943:—
(By 2nd *m*) David Lincoln, *b* 1922: *m* 1956, Mrs Maud Mary Philipps, da of late Samuel George Augustus Schwenke, and widow of Ralph Philipps. — Ella Faith, *b* 1919: *m* 1939, Harry Dan Thomas Turner, and has had issue, two sons and one da. — Jean Elizabeth, *b* 1920: *m* 1943, Reginald H. Walker, and has issue living, two sons and two das.
Issue of late Arthur Vivian Baillie-Hamilton, *b* 1881, *d* 19—: *m* 1906, Ida Maud Harrison:—
Melrose, *b* 1918: *m* 1st, 1940 (*m diss* 1958), Hugh Sproston, of Chicago, Ill, USA; 2ndly, 1973, Jack McCracken, and *d* 1980, leaving issue (by 1st *m*), Ronald (8a George St, Hamilton, NZ), *b* 1944: *m* 1st, 1970 (*m diss* 19—), Jocelyn —; 2ndly, 1984, Estelle Charles, and has issue living (by 1st *m*), Ronnie (Jr) *b* 1975, Heather *b* 1971, — Russell (1569 West 61st St, Vancouver, BC, Canada V6P 2B9), *b* 1946: *m* 1972, Stephanie Haase, and has issue living, Scott *b* 1984, Megan *b* 1973, Robyn *b* 1976, Kelly *b* 1977, Lorie *b* (twin) 1984, — Jerilyn, *b* 1948: *m* 1st, 1969 (*m diss* 19—), Tom Gamet; 2ndly, 19—, Robert deLollis, of Calif, USA, and has issue living (by 1st *m*), Joshua *b* 1972, Michelle *b* 1974, — Frances, *b* 1952: *m* 1st, 1971 (*m diss* 1977), Kelly Morrow; 2ndly, 1979, Ari Alblas, of 9500 Ferndale Rd, Richmond, BC, Canada V6Y 1X3, and has issue (by 1st *m*) Christopher *b* 1972, (by 2nd *m*) Adrian *b* 1980, Andrew *b* 1983, Arlun *b* 1990, Amber-Aileen *b* 1981, Alisha *b* 1984, Alaine *b* 1987, Ariana *b* 1988.

Grandchildren of late Capt Peregrine Charles Baillie-Hamilton (ante):—
Issue of late Rev George James Baillie-Hamilton, V of Woverton, Cheshire, *b* 1851, *d* 1904: *m* 1875, Eliza, who *d* 1931, da of late Rev Lucius Fry:—
†Lucius Hugh Noel, *b* 1886; *d* 1952. — †Patrick Stephen, *b* 1890: *m* 1st, 1924, Elizabeth A. Nation, who *d* 1944; 2ndly, 1945, Elizabeth (Mary) Burden, who *d* 1980, and *dsp* 1973. — Edith Mary, *b* 1876: *m* 1919, James Herbert Crompton, who *d* 1944, and *dsp* 1962. — Aline Melrose, *b* 1879; *dunm* 1975. — Nora Constance, *b* 1883: *m* 1909, Norman Bennett-Powell, MRCS, who *d* 1913, and *dsp* 1927. — Ethel Gordon, *b* 1885: *m* 1914, Lionel Walter Kennedy Scargill, MA, MD, BC, who *d* (20 May) 1944, and *d* (5 Nov) 1944, leaving issue, two sons and one da. — Madeline Violet, *b* 1888: *m* 1913, Arthur Hammond Jones, and *d* 1978, having had issue, one son and one da.

Grandsons of late John BUCHANAN-BAILLIE-HAMILTON, 6th son of Ven Charles Baillie-Hamilton (ante):—
Issue of late John Edmondstone BUCHANAN-BAILLIE-HAMILTON, *b* 1874, *d* 1957: *m* 1925, Bridget Everett, who *d* 1971, da of John E. Baker, formerly of Cambridge:—
John Neil, *b* 1926; *ed* Winchester; Capt (ret) late Black Watch: *m* 1st, 1955, Hon Caroline Barbara Coupar Barrie, who *d* 1978, da of 1st Baron Abertay; 2ndly, 1981, Mrs Gillian M. Macdonald, formerly wife of Roderick Macdonald, of Turvey, Beds, and has issue living (by 1st *m*), John Michael, *b* 1958; *ed* Oxford Univ (MA), — Alexander Neil *b* 1963; Capt The Black Watch; Equerry to HRH The Duke of York 1990-92. *Residence* – Cambusmore, Callander, Perthshire. — James Angus, *b* 1927; late Lt RN; High Sheriff of Glos (1984); is a farmer: *m* 1954, Prudence, only da of Cdr Wenman Humfry Wykeham-Musgrave, RN (ret) (E Grey, colls), of Wheelwrights, Barnsley, Cirencester, Gloucestershire, and has issue living, Charles Wenman, *b* 1957, — Simon James, *b* 1963, — Jane, *b* 1955; MB BS: *m* 1979, Alastair James Dickson, of West Kennacott, Newton Tracey, Barnstaple, N Devon, and has issue living, James *b* 1982, Claire Louise *b* 1984, — Sally, *b* 1961: *m* 1987, James Hippisley Kidner, son of Dr Patrick Gerald Kidner, of Manaton, Devon. *Residence* – South Farm, Shipton Oliffe, nr Cheltenham, Gloucestershire. — Alexander, *b* 1932; *ed* Glenalmond, and Aberdeen Univ (MB and ChB); Diploma of Industrial Medicine, London 1959: *m* 1964, Mrs Lilia Julia Mary Eaton, da of late Alan Peter, of St Lucia, W Indies, and has issue living, Fiona Mary, *b* 1966, — Alexandra Helen, *b* 1969. *Residence* – Knowle Croft, Shoppenhangers, Maidenhead, Berks.

PREDECESSORS – (1) Sir THOMAS Hamilton, successively a Lord of Session (as Lord Drumcairn), a Commr to treat of a Union with England, Lord Clerk Register of Scotland, Sec of State, Pres of Court of Session, and Keeper of the Privy Seal; *cr* Lord Binning (peerage of Scotland) 1613, *Earl of Melrose*, and *Lord Byres and Binning* (peerage of Scotland) 1619; the title of Melrose was changed in 1627, and he was *cr Earl of Haddington* (peerage of Scotland) with precedence of 1619 and limitation to his heirs male bearing the name of Hamilton; *d* 1637, leaving one of the largest fortunes of his time; *s* by his son (2) THOMAS, 2nd Earl, a zealous Covenanter; was killed by an explosion at the Castle of Dunglas, of which he was Gov, 1640; *s* by his el son (3) THOMAS, 3rd Earl; *dsp* 1645; *s* by his brother (4) JOHN, 4th Earl; *d* 1669; *s* by his son (5) CHARLES, 5th Earl; *m* 1674, Lady Margaret Leslie, da of 1st Duke of Rothes, who on the death of her father became in her own right by charter Countess of Rothes; in 1689 was granted a patent confirming the terms of the *m* contract, by which the Earldom of Rothes was to descent to the el son, and the Earldom of Haddington and Lordship of Binning were to revert to the 2nd son; the Countess *d* 1702, and was *s* by her el son (*see* Rothes); the Earl *d* 1681, and was *s* by his 2nd son (6) THOMAS, 6th Earl; obtained a charter of the Earldom, and appointed Hereditary Keeper of Holyrood Palace; a Representative Peer; *d* 1735; *s* by his grandson (7) THOMAS, 7th Earl; el son of Charles, Lord Binning; *d* 1794; *s* by his son (8) CHARLES, 8th Earl; a Representative Peer, and Lord-Lieut of Haddingtonshire; *d* 1828; *s* by his son (9) THOMAS, KT, PC, 9th Earl; Lord-Lieut of Ireland 1833-4; *cr Baron Melrose*, of Tyninghame (peerage of United Kingdom) 1827; in 1843 resigned the office of Hereditary Keeper of Holyrood Palace for the consideration of £40,000; *d* 1858, when the Barony of Melrose became extinct, and the Scottish honours devolved upon his cousin (10) GEORGE, 10th Earl, son of George Baillie, nephew of 7th Earl; *b* 1802; was a Lord-in-Waiting to HM 1867-8, a Representative Peer, and High Commr to Gen Assembly of Ch of Scotland; assumed by Roy licence 1859 the additional surname of Hamilton to that of Baillie, which had been assumed in lieu of Hamilton by his grandfather: *m* 1824, Georgina, da of the Ven Robert Markham, Archdeacon of York; *d* 1870; *s* by his son (11) GEORGE, KT, 11th Earl; *b* 1827; Vice-Lieut of co Berwick 1873-1917, and Lord-Lieut of co Haddington 1896-1917; assumed by Roy licence, 1858, the additional surname of Arden after that of Baillie-Hamilton: *m* 1854, Helen Catherine, da of 1889, da of Sir John Warrender, 5th Bt; *d* 1917; *s* by his grandson (12) GEORGE, KT, MC, TD (son of late Brig-Gen George, Lord Binning, CB, MVO, el son of 11th Earl), 12th Earl, *b* 1894, a Representative Peer for Scotland 1922-63, Capt Scots Greys (Res), Maj 19th (Lothians and Border Horse) Armoured Car Co (TA) and Res of Officers, Lt Queen's Body Guard for Scotland (Royal Company of Archers), Lord Lieut of Berwickshire 1952-69; 1914-18 War in France and Belgium (wounded, MC), 1939-45 War, W/Cdr RAFVR 1941-45; bore the Queen's Ivory Rod at Coronation of King George VI: *m* 1923, Sarah, yst da of late George William Cook, of Westmount, Montreal; *d* 1986; *s* by his only son (13) JOHN GEORGE, 13th Earl and present peer; also Lord Binning, and Lord Byres and Binning.

HADEN-GUEST, BARON (Haden-Guest) (Baron UK 1950)

PETER HADEN HADEN-GUEST, 4th Baron; *b* 29 Aug 1913; *s* 1987; *ed* City of London Sch, and New Coll, Oxford (MA); Dancer (as Peter Michael) 1935-41, with Markova-Dolin Ballet, Ballet Divertissement, Ballet Theatre, Ballet Jooss, and Repertory Dance Theatre; United Nations Official 1946-72 (Ch of Editorial Control UNHQ, NY, Ch Editor Office of the Dir-Gen, UN, Geneva, and Ch of Repertory Editing Group UNHQ, NY); 1939-45 War as Lieut RCNVR (SB): *m* 1st, 1939 (*m diss* 1945), Mrs Elizabeth Louise Ruth Coker, eldest da of late Paul Wolpert, of Konnigsberg; 2ndly, 1945, Jean Pauline, formerly Vice-Pres CBS for Casting and Talent, da of late Dr Albert George Hindes, of 190 Waverly Place, New York City, and has issue by 1st and 2nd wives.

Arms – Sable, two flaunches or, three Welsh triple harps in fess counter-changed. **Crest** – A caladrius displayed sable, beaked, legged and charged on the breast with a sun in splendour gold. **Supporters** – *Dexter*, a leopard sable semy of roundels and grasping in the interior paw a quill gold; *sinister*, a leopard or semy of roundels and grasping in the interior paw a quill sable. *Residence* – 198 Old Stone Highway, East Hampton, NY 11937, USA.

SONS LIVING (*by 1st wife*)

Hon Anthony, *b* 1937; *ed* Gordonstoun, and St John's Coll, Camb; journalist. *Residence* – Garden Apt, 67 East 80th St, New York, NY 10021, USA.

(*by 2nd wife*)

Hon CHRISTOPHER, *b* 5 Feb 1948; actor and singer: *m* 1984, Jamie Lee Curtis, actress, da of Tony Curtis, actor, and has an adopted da, Anne, *b* 1986. *Addresses* – 253A 26th St, Suite 300, Santa Monica, Calif 90402, USA; HC-64 Box 8018, Ketchum, Idaho 83340, USA.

Hon Nicholas, *b* 1951; *ed* New Sch for Social Research (BA), American Coll, Paris, Stella Adler Inst, and Herbert Berghof Studio; actor: *m* 1st, 1980 (*m diss* 1989), Jill Ellen, da of Harry Demby, USAF, of S Orange, NJ; 2ndly, 1989, Mrs Pamela Ann Rack, da of late Lieut Joseph G. Seamon, US Navy, of Akron, Ohio, and formerly wife of Thomas John Rack, and has issue living (by 1st *m*), Julia Demby, *b* 1988, — (by 2nd *m*) Elizabeth Ann, *b* 1990. *Residence* – 10831 Acama St, N Holly-wood, Calif 91602, USA.

DAUGHTER LIVING (*by 2nd wife*)

Hon Elissa, *b* 1953: *m* 1981, Nicholas Carey Smith, son of Corlies Morgan Smith, and has issue living, Nathanael Haden, *b* 1988, — Gena Haden, *b* 1984. *Residence* – 29, 16th Ave, San Francisco, Calif 94118, USA.

DAUGHTER LIVING OF SECOND BARON

Hon Hadley (49 West 16 St, New York, NY 10011, USA), *b* 1949; *ed* City Univ of New York (BA 1977).

WIDOW LIVING OF SECOND BARON

DOROTHY (*Dorothy, Baroness Haden-Guest*) (105 Bayard Lane, Princeton, New Jersey 08540, USA), da of Thomas Roseberry Good; late of Princeton, New Jersey: *m* 1968, as his second wife, the 2nd Baron, who *d* 1974.

WIDOW LIVING OF THIRD BARON

MARJORIE DOUGLAS (*Marjorie, Baroness Haden-Guest*), da of late Dr Douglas Kennard: *m* 1951, as his 3rd wife, the 3rd Baron, who *d* 1987. *Residence* – 3 Chemin des Crêts-de-Champel, 1206 Geneva, Switzerland.

PREDECESSORS – **(1)** LESLIE HADEN Haden-Guest, MC, MRCS, LRCP, son of late Alexander Haden-Guest, Surg and Physician of Manchester; *b* 1877; a Lord-in-Waiting to HM Feb to Oct 1951; sat as MP for N Div of Southwark (*Lab*) 1923-7, and for N Div of Islington 1937-50; *cr Baron Haden-Guest*, of Saling, co Essex (peerage of United Kingdom) 1950: *m* 1st, 1898 (*m diss* 1909), Edith, who *d* 1944, da of Max Low, of London; 2ndly, 1910, Muriel Carmel, who *d* 1943, da of late Col Albert Edward Williamson Goldsmid, MVO; 3rdly 1944, Edith Edgar, who *d* 1977, da of late George Macqueen, of Montrose; *d* 1960; *s* by his el son **(2)** STEPHEN HADEN, 2nd Baron *b* 1902; editor and translator: *m* 1st, 1948 (*m diss* 1954), Barbara Ann, da of James Harvey Pinson, of W Virginia, USA; 2ndly, 1968, Dorothy, da of Thomas Roseberry Good, late of Princeton, New Jersey; *d* 1974; *s* by his brother **(3)** RICHARD HADEN, 3rd Baron, *b* 1904: *m* 1st, 1926 (*m diss* 1934), Hilda, da of late Dr Thomas Russell-Cruise; 2ndly, 1934, Olive Maria, da of late Anders Gotfrid Nilsson; 3rdly, 1951, Marjorie Douglas, da of late Dr Douglas Kennard; *d* 1987; *s* by his half-brother **(4)** PETER HADEN, 4th Baron and present peer.

HAIG, EARL (Haig) (Earl UK 1919)

GEORGE ALEXANDER EUGENE DOUGLAS HAIG, OBE, 2nd Earl (*30th Laird of Bemersyde*); *b* 15 March 1918: *s* 1928; *ed* Stowe, and Ch Ch Oxford (MA); Capt Roy Scots Greys; Hon Maj on disbandment of HG 1958; is a Member of Queen's Body Guard for Scotland (Roy Co of Archers), a DL for Roxburghshire (Vice-Lt Berwicks 1967-70); Assoc Royal Scottish Academy 1988; Pres Scottish Craft Centre 1950-75, Chm SE Scotland Disablement Advisory Cttee 1960-73, a Mem of Scottish Arts Council 1969-75, and Pres of Earl Haig Fund (Scotland) 1980-86, Pres of Officers' Assocn (Scottish Cttee) since 1987 (Chm 1977-87), Chm Bd of Trustees of Scottish National War Memorial since 1983; a Trustee of National Galleries of Scotland 1962-72; FRSA; KStJ; Chm of R British Legion, Scotland 1962-65, and Pres 1980-86; 1939-45 War (prisoner); was a Train Bearer at Coronation of King George VI; OBE (Civil) 1966: *m* 1st, 1956 (*m diss* 1981), Adrienne Thérèse, da of Derrick Morley, of Quaives, Wickhambreaux, Kent; 2ndly, 1981, Donna Gerolama Lopez y Royo, and has issue by 1st *m*.

Arms – Azure, a saltire between a mullet in chief and another in base, a decrescent and an increscent in the flanks argent. **Crest** – A rock proper. **Supporters** – *Dexter*, a bay horse caparisoned thereon mounted a Private of the 7th (Queen's Own) Hussars, habited, armed and accoutred; *sinister* a bay horse, caparisoned, thereon mounted a Lancer of the 17th (Duke of Cambridge's Own) Lancers habited, armed and accoutred all proper.
Seat – Bemersyde, Melrose, Roxburghshire. *Clubs* – Cavalry, New.

SON LIVING *(By 1st marriage)*

ALEXANDER DOUGLAS DERRICK (*Viscount Dawick*), *b* 30 June 1961; *ed* Stowe.

DAUGHTERS LIVING *(By 1st marriage)*

Lady (Adrienne) Rainà, *b* 1958.
Lady (Elizabeth) Vivienne Thérèse, *b* 1959.

SISTERS LIVING

Lady Alexandra Henrietta Louisa (*Baroness Dacre of Glanton*), *b* 1907; Patron Camb Univ Opera, Gov Music Therapy Charity: *m* 1st, 1941 (*m diss* 1954), Rear Adm Clarence Dinsmore Howard-Johnston, CB, DSO, DSC; 2ndly, 1954, Baron Dacre of Glanton (Life Baron), and has issue living (by 1st *m*), James Douglas, *b* 1942; *ed* Eton, and Ch Ch Oxford; university lect in Byzantine history: *m* 1978, Angela Maureen, el da of late Harold Huth, and formerly wife of Quentin Crewe, writer and journalist, and has issue living, Eugenie *b* 1981, — Philip Peter Dawyck (4 Craiglockhart Av, Edinburgh EH14 1DG), *b* 1950: *m* 1990, Mrs Jaqueline J. Mathieson, yr da of late Dr James Robert Kyles, of Lundin Links, Fife, and has issue living, Jessica Emily *b* 1993, — Xenia Violet (92 Vassall Rd, SW9 6JA), *b* 1944: *m* 1977, Rev Lyle Dennen, of Beverly Hills, California, and has issue living, Richard Sergei John *b* 1980, John Dawyck Alexei *b* 1982. *Residence* – The Old Rectory, Didcot, Oxon OX11 7EB.
Lady Irene Violet Freesia Janet Augusta (*Irene, Baroness Astor of Hever*), *b* 1919; CStJ; an hon Life Member Commonwealth Press Union (1985): *m* 1945, 2nd Baron Astor of Hever, who *d* 1984. *Residences* – 11 Lyall St, SW1X 8DH; Holly Tree House, French St, Westerham, Kent TN16 1PW.

PREDECESSOR – (1) *Field Marshal Sir* DOUGLAS HAIG, KT, GCB, OM, GCVO, KCIE, son of late John Haig, of Cameronbridge, Fife, *b* 1861; Nile Expedition 1898, present at battles of Atbara and Khartoum (despatches, Egyptian medal with two clasps, Brevet Major), in S Africa 1899-1902 on the Staff, present at battles of Elandslaagte, operations around Colesberg, relief of Kimberley, and battles of Paardeberg and Belfast, and in command of Mounted Columns with rank of Col (despatches twice, Brevet Lieut-Col and Col, CB), European War 1914-18, first in command of 1st Army Corps, secondly of 1st Army, and thirdly of British Expeditionary Force in France and Flanders (despatches thrice, promoted Gen, Grand Officer Legion of Honour, GCB, GCVO, Field-Marshal, KT, Obilitch medal, Croix de Guerre, Italian Order of St Maurice and St Lazarus, 4th class of Russian Order of St George, and of Michael the Brave of Roumania, Serbian Order of Karageorge with Swords, Order of Tower and Sword of Portugal, Medaille, American Cross of Honour, Grand Cordon of Japanese Order of the Rising Sun with Paulowina, and 1st class Order of Chia Ho of China, Gold Medal of La Solidaridad of Panama, American DSM, thanked by Parliament, *cr* Earl, granted £100,000, presented by people of British Empire with house and fishings of Bemersyde); attached to Egyptian Army 1897-8; appointed an Extra ADC to HM 1902, Inspector-Gen of Cav in India 1903, Director of Mil Training at Head Quarters 1906, Director of Staff Duties there 1907 Ch of Staff in India and a Member of Council of Gov-Gen of India 1909, an ADC Gen to HM 1914, Gen Officer Comdg-in-Ch, Aldershot 1912, and Gen Officer Comdg-in-Ch, Great Britain 1919; *cr Earl Haig, Viscount Dawick*, and *Baron Haig*, of Bemersyde, co Berwick (peerage of United Kingdom) 1919: *m* 1905, Hon Dorothy Maud Vivian (a DGStJ), who *d* 1939, da of 3rd Baron Vivian; *d* 1928; *s* by his son (2) GEORGE ALEXANDER EUGENE DOUGLAS, 2nd Earl and present peer; also Viscount Dawick, and Baron Haig.

Hailsham, Viscountcy of, see Baron Hailsham of St Marylebone.

HAILSHAM OF ST MARYLEBONE, BARON (Hogg) (Viscount UK 1929, disclaimed 1963, Life Baron 1970)

QUINTIN MCGAREL HOGG, KG, CH, PC, FRS; *b* 9 Oct 1907; *s* as 2nd Viscount Hailsham 16 Aug 1950; *ed* Eton, and Ch Ch Oxford (MA, Hon Student); Hon DCL Oxford; FRS; Fellow of All Souls Coll, Oxford 1931-38, and since 1962; Bar Lincoln's Inn 1932, QC 1953, and Bencher 1956; Hon LLD Camb; 1939-45 War as Maj Rifle Bde (TA) (wounded); Joint Under-Sec of State for Air April to July 1945, First Lord of the Admiralty 1956-57, Min of Educ Jan to Sept 1957, Dep Leader of House of Lords 1957-60, Lord Pres of the Council 1957-59, and again 1960-64, Lord Privy Seal 1959-60, Leader of House of Lords 1960-63, Min & Sec of State for Education and Science 1959-64, Lord High Chancellor 1970-74, and 1979-87; elected R of Glasgow Univ 1959, Chancellor Buckingham Univ 1983-91; MP for Oxford City (*C*) 1938-58, and for St Marylebone 1963-70; PC 1956; disclaimed his peerage for life 20 Nov 1963; *cr Baron Hailsham of St Marylebone*, of Herstmonceux, co Sussex (Life Baron) 1970, CH 1974, and KG 1988: *m* 1st, 1931 (*m diss* 1943), Natalie Antoinette, who *d* 1987, da of late Alan Sullivan, of Sheerland House, Pluckley, Kent; 2ndly, 1944, Mary Evelyn, who *d* 1978, only child of Richard Martin, of 46 Wynnstay Gdns, W8; 3rdly, 1986, Deirdre, elder da of late Capt Peter Shannon, and of Mrs Margaret Briscoe,

and has issue by 2nd *m*.

Arms – Argent, three boars' heads erased azure, langued gules, between two flaunches azure each charged with a crescent of the field. **Crest** – Out of an eastern crown argent, an oak-tree fructed proper, and pendent therefrom an escutcheon azure, charged with a dexter arm embowed in armour, the hand grasping an arrow in bend sinister, the point downwards, also proper. **Supporters** – On either side a ram argent armed and unguled or, gorged with a baron's coronet, the *dexter* supporting a representation of the Lord High Chancellor's mace, and the *sinister*, a representation of the Lord High Chancellor's purse, with the initials of Her Majesty Queen Elizabeth II, proper.

SONS LIVING *(By 2nd marriage)*

Rt Hon DOUGLAS MARTIN, MP, *b* 5 Feb 1945; *ha* to Viscountcy of Hailsham; *ed* Eton, and Ch Ch, Oxford; Bar Lincoln's Inn 1968; MP for Grantham (*C*) since 1979; assist Govt Whip 1983-84, Parliamentary Under-Sec Home Office 1986-89, Min of State, Home Office 1986-90, since when Min of State, Dept of Foreign and Commonwealth Affairs; PC 1992: *m* 1968, Hon Sarah Elizabeth Mary, yr da of Baron Boyd-Carpenter (Life Baron), and has issue living, Quintin John Neil Martin, *b* 1973, — Charlotte Mary, *b* 1970.
Hon James Richard Martin, *b* 1951; *ed* Eton; Capt Gren Gds: *m* 1987, D. Clare, yr da of Maurice Raffael, of Wimbledon.

DAUGHTERS LIVING *(By 2nd marriage)*

Hon Mary Claire, *b* 1947; *ed* St Paul's Girls' Sch; Bar Lincoln's Inn 1968, QC 1989, Assist Recorder 1986-90, since when Recorder: *m* 1987, Eric Koops, eldest son of Leendart Koops, of Hellingly, Sussex, and has issue living, William Quintin Eric, *b* 1991, — Katharine Mary, *b* 1989.
Hon Frances Evelyn, *b* 1949; *ed* St Paul's Girls' Sch, and Homerton Coll, Cumbridge; JP: *m* 1970, Richard Quintin Hoare, son of late Quintin Vincent Hoare, and has issue living, Alexander Richard Quintin, *b* 1973, — Charles Martin Richard, *b* 1976, — Elizabeth Mary, *b* 1978. *Residence* – Tangier House, Wootton St Lawrence, Basingstoke, Hants RG23 8PH.
Hon Katharine Amelia, *b* 1962; *ed* Roedean, and St Peter's Coll, Oxford: *m* 1993, Richard A. Collins, son of C. A. Collins, of Penarth, S Glam.

BROTHER LIVING

Hon William Neil McGarel, *b* 1910; *ed* Eton; HM's Diplo Ser (ret).

PREDECESSOR – (1) *Rt Hon Sir* DOUGLAS MCGAREL HOGG, PC, son of Quintin Hogg (*see* Hogg Bt, *cr* 1846, *colls*); *b* 1872; Bar Lincoln's Inn, 1902, a KC 1917, and a Bencher 1920; Attorney-Gen to HRH the Prince of Wales and a Member of Council of Duchy of Cornwall 1920-22, Attorney-Gen (with a seat in the Cabinet) 1924-28, Lord High Chancellor 1928-29 (acted as Prime Min 1928), and Leader of Opposition in House of Lords June to Aug 1931; appointed Sec of State for War (National Govt) and Leader of the House of Lords 1931, and again Lord High Chancellor 1935; Lord President of the Council March to Oct 1938; Recorder of Kingston-upon-Thames 1924-28; sat as MP for St Marylebone (*U*) 1922-28; *cr Baron Hailsham*, of Hailsham, co Sussex (peerage of United Kingdom) 1928, and *Viscount Hailsham*, of Hailsham, co Sussex (peerage of United Kingdom) 1929: *m* 1st, 1905, Elizabeth, who *d* 1925, da of late Judge James Trimble Brown, of Nashville, Tennesee, USA, and widow of Hon Archibald John Majoribanks; 2ndly, 1929, Mildred Margaret, who *d* 1964, da of late Rev Edward Parker Dew, R and Patron of Breamore, Hants, and widow of Hon Alfred Clive Lawrence (B Trevethin & Oaksey); *d* 1950; *s* by his el son (2) QUINTIN MCGAREL, 2nd Viscount, until he disclaimed his peerages 1963; *cr Baron Hailsham of St Marylebone* (Life Baron) 1970.

HAIRE OF WHITEABBEY, BARONY OF (Haire) (Extinct 1966)

SONS LIVING OF LIFE BARON

Hon Michael John Kemeny, *b* 1945; *ed* St Paul's Sch, Univ Coll, London, and Pennsylvania Univ.
Hon Christopher Peter, *b* 1951; *ed* Holland Park Sch.

WIDOW LIVING OF LIFE BARON

SUZANNE ELIZABETH (*Baroness Haire of Whiteabbey*); da of Dr Eugene Kemeny, of Hatvan: *m* 1939, Baron Haire of Whiteabbey (Life Baron), who *d* 1966.

HALE, BARONY OF (Hale) (Extinct 1985)

SON LIVING OF LIFE BARON

Hon Ian William Percy, *b* 1930. *Residence* – The Grove, Swannington, Leics. LE67 8QN.

DAUGHTER LIVING OF LIFE BARON

Hon Dorothy Lesley, *b* 1927. *Residence* – The Grove, Swannington, Leics. LE67 8QN.

HALIFAX, EARL OF (Wood) (Viscount UK 1866, Baron UK 1925, Earl UK 1944, Bt GB 1784)

CHARLES EDWARD PETER NEIL WOOD, 3rd Earl and 7th Baronet, *b* 14 March 1944; *s* 1980; *ed* Eton, and Ch Ch, Oxford; a DL for co Humberside since 1983, High Steward York Minster since 1988; OStJ: *m* 1976, Camilla, da of Charles Younger, of Gledswood, Melrose, Roxburghshire, and formerly wife of Richard Eustace Parker Bowles (*see* E Macclesfield, colls), and has issue.

Arms – 1st and 4th azure, three naked savages ambulant in fesse proper, in the dexter hand of each a shield argent, charged with a cross gules, and in the sinister a club resting on the shoulder also proper, on a canton ermine three lozenges conjoined in fesse sable; 2nd and 3rd palybendy or and azure, a canton ermine. **Crest** – A savage as in the arms, the shield sable charged with a griffin's head erased argent. **Supporters** – On either side a griffin sable, gorged with a collar and pendant therefrom a portcullis or.
Seat – Garrowby, York YO4 1QD. *Clubs* – Pratt's, White's.

SON LIVING

JAMES CHARLES (*Lord Irwin*), *b* 24 Aug 1977.

DAUGHTER LIVING

Lady Joanna Victoria, *b* 1980.

SISTERS LIVING

Lady Caroline Victoria, *b* 1937: *m* 1st, 1958 (*m diss* 1970), Randle Joseph Feilden, son of Maj-Gen Sir Randle Guy Feilden, KCVO, CB, CBE (*see* V Hampden, colls); 2ndly, 1970, John Gosling, of The Claw, Brushford, Dulverton, Somerset.
Lady Susan Diana, *b* 1938: *m* 1959, Brigadier Ian Darsie Watson, CBE, TD, and has issue living, David Charles Darsie, *b* 1960, — Richard Ian, *b* 1962: *m* 1990, Henrietta, only da of Anthony Butterwick, of Pinckneys Green, Berks. *Residence* – Bossall Hall, Bossall, York, YO6 7NT.

UNCLE LIVING (*Son of 1st Earl*)

Rt Hon Richard Frederick, PC (*Baron Holderness*), *b* 1920; *cr* Baron Holderness 1979 (see that title).

AUNT LIVING (*Daughter of 1st Earl*)

Lady Anne Dorothy, OBE (twin) (*Countess of Feversham*), *b* 1910; MBE (Civil) 1950; OBE (Civil) 1979: *m* 1936, 3rd Earl of Feversham, who *d* 1963. *Residence* – Bransdale Lodge, Fadmoor, Kirkbymoorside, York.

COLLATERAL BRANCHES LIVING (*In remainder to Viscountcy and Baronetcy only*)

Grandsons of late Col Hugo MEYNELL, MC (infra):—
Issue of late Nicholas Edward Hugo Meynell, *b* 1937, *d* 1988: *m* 1966 (*m diss* 1987), Hon Alexandra Rachel Mary Catherine Lampson, da of 2nd Baron Killearn:—
Hugo Graham Nicholas, *b* 1970. —— Alexander Frederick Miles, *b* 1972.

Grandchildren of late Lieut-Col Francis Hugo Lindley MEYNELL (infra):—
Issue of late Col Hugo MEYNELL, MC, *b* 1909, *d* 1960: *m* 1936, Dorothy Jean, who *d* 1993, da of Sir Edward Henry Goschen, 2nd Bt—
David Christian Francis (Hollybush Park, Newborough, Burton-on-Trent), *b* 1940: *m* 1962, Susan Lesley, da of George Garfield-Jones, of The Mount, Shrewsbury, and has issue living, Charles Christian George, *b* 1964; Capt The Life Guards: *m* 1992, Elizabeth Zoe, yst da Dr Patrick Lawrence, of The Mill House, Iffley, Oxford, — Edward David Lindley, *b* 1971, — Melissa Alexandra Elizabeth Susanna, *b* 1968. —— Frederick James (Oaklands Cottage, E Tytherley, nr Salisbury, Wilts), *b* 1944: *m* 1st, 1969 (*m diss* 1973), Charmian Joy, da of Maj Harcourt Michael Scudamore Gold, MC (*see* By of Trent); 2ndly, 1975, Mary Anne, da of Trevor Leslie Harris, of The Frenches Farm, The Frenches, Romsey, Hants, and has issue living (by 2nd *m*) Sophie Louise, *b* 1980, — Lucinda Mary, *b* 1983. —— (Karen) Elizabeth Mary (*Hon Mrs George C. D. Jeffreys*), *b* 1947: *m* 1967, Capt Hon George Christian Darell Jeffreys, of Cotswold House, Condicote, Stow-on-the-Wold, Glos GL54 1ES (*see* B Jeffreys). —— Alexandra Dorothy Jean (*Baroness Tollemache*), *b* 1949: *m* 1970, 5th Baron Tollemache, of Helmingham Hall, Stowmarket, Suffolk.

Grandchildren of late Hon Frederick George Lindley MEYNELL (who assumed by R Licence for himself and his issue the surname and arms of Meynell in lieu of his patronymic), 4th son of 1st Viscount:—

Issue of late Lieut-Col Francis Hugo Lindley Meynell, DSO, *b* 1880, *d* 1941: *m* 1907, Lady Dorothy Legge, OBE, who *d* 1974, da of 6th Earl of Dartmouth:—

Rev Canon Mark (2 Double St, Framlingham, Suffolk), *b* 1914; *ed* Eton, and Ch Ch, Oxford; Canon Theologian Emeritus of Coventry: *m* 1940, Diana Mary, da of Col Sir Charles Edward Ponsonby, TD, 1st Bt, and has issue living, Christopher Mark (Bergh Apton Hall, Norwich, Norfolk), *b* 1941: *m* 1968, Hon Elizabeth Margaret Gretton, twin da of 2nd Baron Gretton, and has issue living, Mark John Henryk *b* 1970, Guy Francis *b* 1973, — *Rev* Andrew Francis (The Vicarage, 34 Dobbins Lane, Wendover, Bucks) *b* 1943: *m* 1971, Caroline Anne, da of late Rt Hon Sir John Gardiner Sumner Hobson, OBE, TD, QC, MP, and has issue living, Aidan Jonathan Charles *b* 1974, Francesca Clare *b* 1976, — Peter John, *b* 1947: *m* 1973, Judith, da of late Rt Hon Sir (Harry) Neil Marten, of Swalcliffe House, nr Banbury, Oxon, and has issue living, Marten Charles *b* 1977, Anna Louise *b* 1979, Clea Diana *b* 1982, — Anna Mary Barbara, *b* 1960: *m* 1986, Louis Thomas de Soissons, of Ivy Farm, Witton, nr North Walsham, Norfolk NR28 9TT, eldest son of Brian de Soissons, of Swafield Hall, Norwich, Norfolk, and has issue living, Alexander Thomas *b* 1988, Hugo Charles *b* 1991. —— Rachel, *b* 1917: *m* 1941, John Kift Winter, and has issue living, Mark John (Via San Pio Quinto 20, Turin, Italy), *b* 1948: *m* 1985, Angelisa, da of Vittorio Gualco, of Giusolana, S Agatha Fossili, Alexandria, Italy, and has issue living, Julia Anna *b* 1987, Margherita *b* 1989, — Giles Meynell (The Old Rectory, Wood Norton, Dereham, Norfolk), *b* 1950: *m* 1976, Joanna Tilney, da of Lt-Col John Cooper, of Glan Dwr, Glyn Garth, Menai Bridge, Anglesey, and has issue living, Edward John Cochran *b* 1985, Flora Rachel *b* 1978, Emily Margaret *b* 1979, Poppy Lucinda *b* 1982, — Julia, *b* 1944: *m* 1st, 1975 (*m diss* 1976), Ali Demir Akel, of Instanbul; 2ndly, 1983, her cousin, Anthony Charles Meynell, and has issue living (by 2nd *m*) (infra). *Residence* – 42 Friars Quay, Norwich, Norfolk NR3 1ES.

Issue of late Sir Everard Charles Lindley MEYNELL, OBE, MC, *b* 1885, *d* 1956: *m* 1914, Rose, who *d* 1975, da of late Lionel Bulteel, of Yewden Manor, Henley-on-Thames, Oxon:—

Francis Everard, MBE, *b* 1917; *ed* Eton; Lt-Cdr RN (ret); MBE (Mil) 1962: *m* 1956, Janet Penelope, da of late Engineer-Rear-Adm Albert Kingsley Dibley, CB, and has issue living, Rosemary Janet, *b* 1960: *m* 1984, George Walter Bishop, eldest son of Frank Bishop, of Sunningdale Farm, Nottingham Rd, Natal 3280, and has issue living, Charles Andrew Meynell *b* 1986, Sarah Rose *b* 1989, Mary Janet *b* 1992, — Elizabeth Anne, *b* 1961: *m* 1984, Dr Derek Montague Brink, son of late Dr Johannes Brink and has issue living, Nicholas Francis Meynell *b* 1990, Jonathan James Meynell *b* 1992, — Anne Penelope, *b* 1964: *m* 1987, Capt Anthony David Blumer, Royal Australian Regt, yr son of Dr John Blumer, of Sydney, Australia, and has issue living, Natasha Anne *b* 1993. *Residence* – Valbona, 13 Spilhaus Av, Hohenort, Constantia, Cape Province 7800, S Africa. —— Clare, *b* 1932: *m* 1956, John Marsham Hallward, of 3150, Trafalgar Av, Montreal, Quebec H37 1H7, Canada (*see* By Atholstan, 1976 Edn), and has issue living, Peter Marsham, *b* 1968, — Christopher Graham, *b* 1973, — Jennifer Rose, *b* 1963, — Julia Anne, *b* 1966, — Mary Clare, *b* 1966, — Katherine Rosemary, *b* 1972. —— Mary, *b* 1935: *m* 1974, Robert Leonard Clother, of Martlets, Rodmell, Lewes, Sussex BN7 3HF.

Issue of late Capt Charles Wilfrid Lindley MEYNELL, RN, *b* 1890, *d* 1976: *m* 1917, Ida Beatrice, who *d* 1977, da of late Rt Hon Ernest George Pretyman, MP (E Bradford):—

Richard Walter (Berry Hall, Honingham, Norfolk, NR9 5AX), *b* 1923; FCA; 1939-45 War: *m* 1950, Countess Ilse Teresa, da of Lt-Gen Count Theodor von Sponeck, and has issue living, Anthony Charles (Old Hall Farm Cottages, North Tuddenham, Norfolk), *b* 1952; *ed* Eton: *m* 1983, his cousin, Mrs Julia Akel, da of John Kift Winter (ante), and has issue living, Wilfrid *b* 1986, Rachel *b* 1984, — Charles Humphrey, *b* 1954; *ed* Eton, — Stephen Francis, *b* 1960: *m* 1986, Sharad Jain, of 1002 Asbury Av, Evanston, Illinois 60202, USA, son of Prof S. P. Jain, of Anandlok, New Delhi. —— Beatrice Mary (12A Long St, Devizes, Wilts), *b* 1918: *m* 1945, Maj John Whitcombe, RA, who *d* 1985, and has issue living, Sarah Rose, *b* 1946: *m* 1973, Rev Barry Thorley, and has issue living, Thomas Edward *b* 1984, — Clarissa Beatrice, *b* 1949: *m* 1969, Robert Anthony Gosling, of Pulham Cottage, Wetherden, Stowmarket (*see* B Ampthill, colls).

PREDECESSORS – **(1)** FRANCIS Wood, 2nd son of late Francis Wood, JP, DL, of Barnsley; *b* 1728; *cr a Baronet* 1784, with remainder to his el brother, the Rev Henry, DD, V of Halifax, and failing him to the sons of his younger brother, Charles, of Bowling Hall; *m* 1779, Elizabeth, who *d* 1796, da and heiress of Anthony Ewer, of The Lea, and Bushey Hall, Herts; *d* 1795; *s* by his nephew **(2)** *Sir* FRANCIS LINDLEY, 2nd Bt (son of Charles (ante)); *b* 1771; High Sheriff of Yorkshire 1814-15: *m* 1798, Anne, who *d* 1841, da of Samuel Buck, Recorder of Leeds; *d* 1846; *s* by his son **(3)** CHARLES, GCB, PC, 3rd Bt; *b* 1800; was Chancellor of the Exchequer 1846-52, Pres of Board of Control 1852-5, First Lord of the Admiralty 1855-8, Sec of State for India 1859-66, and Lord Privy Seal 1870-74; sat as MP for Grimsby (*L*) 1826-31, for Wareham 1831-2, for Halifax 1832-65, and for Ripon 1865-6: *cr Viscount Halifax*, of Monk Bretton, co York (peerage of United Kingdom) 1866: *m* 1829, Lady Mary Grey, CI, who *d* 1884, da of 2nd Earl Grey: *d* 1885; *s* by his el son **(4)** CHARLES LINDLEY, *b* 1839; Pres of English Church Union 1869-1919 and 1931-33: *m* 1869, Lady Agnes Elizabeth Courtenay, who *d* 1919, only da of 11th Earl of Devon; *d* 1934; *s* by his only surviving son **(5)** EDWARD FREDERICK LINDLEY, KG, OM, GCSI, GCMG, GCIE, TD, PC, 1st Earl, *b* 1881; formerly Lieut-Col Yorkshire Dragoons Yeo (Hon Col 1935-60); sometime Chm Med Research Council; was Assist Sec Min of National Ser 1917-18, and a British Delegate of League of Nations Assembly 1923; appointed Under-Sec of State for the Colonies 1921; Pres of Board of Education 1922-4, Min of Agriculture and Fisheries 1924-5, Pres of Board of Education (in National Govt) 1932-5, Sec of State for War June to Nov 1935, Lord Privy Seal 1935-7, Leader of the House of Lords 1935-8, Lord Pres of the Council 1937-8, Sec of State for Foreign Affairs 1938 to 1940 (also again Leader of the House of Lords Oct to Dec 1940), and Ambassador Extraor and Plen at Washington 1941-6; a Vice-Pres E India Asso 1931; was Viceroy and Gov-Gen of India 1926-31; elected Chancellor of Oxford Univ 1933, and of Sheffield Univ 1947; appointed Chancellor of Order of the Garter 1943, Chm of Gen Advisory Council of British Broadcasting Corporation 1947 and Grand Master of Order of St Michael and St George 1957; became High Steward of Westminster 1947; bore St Edward's Staff at Coronation of King George VI; sat as MP for Yorkshire, W Riding, E Part, Ripon Div (*C*) 1910-18, and for Ripon Div of W Riding of Yorkshire 1918-25; *cr Baron Irwin*, of Kirby Underdale, co York (peerage of United Kingdom) 1925, and *Earl of Halifax* (peerage of United Kingdom) 1944: *m* 1909, Lady Dorothy Evelyn Augusta Onslow, CI, DCVO, LLD, who *d* 1976, yr da of 4th Earl of Onslow; *d* 1959; *s* by his el son **(6)** CHARLES INGRAM COURTENAY 2nd Earl, *b* 1912; Lord-Lt for E Riding of Yorks, 1968-74, and for Humberside 1974-80; Chm of E Riding of Yorks Co Council 1968-80; High Steward of York Minster 1970-80; Jt Master Middleton Foxhounds 1946-80, Senior Steward Jockey Club 1950-51 and 1958-59; MP for York (*C*) 1937-45: *m* 1936, Ruth Alice Hannah Mary, who *d* 1989, da of late Capt Rt Hon Neil James Archibald Primrose, MC, MP (*see* E Rosebery, colls); *d* 1980; *s* by his only son **(7)** CHARLES EDWARD PETER NEIL, 3rd Earl and present peer, also Viscount Halifax and Baron Irwin.

HALL, VISCOUNTCY OF (Hall) (Extinct 1985)

DAUGHTERS LIVING OF SECOND VISCOUNT (*By 1st marriage*)

Hon Lena Margaret, *b* 1950: *m* 1985, Frederick Neagle, eldest son of late William Neagle.
Hon Georgina Anne, *b* 1953.

WIDOW LIVING OF SECOND VISCOUNT

MARIE-COLETTE *(Viscountess Hall)*, da of late Col Henri Bach: *m* 1974, as his 3rd wife, the 2nd Viscount, who *d* 1985. *Residences* – Belgrave Cottage, Upper Belgrave St, SW1X 8AA; Solvain, 41210 St Viatre, Loir et Cher, France.

Hall, see Barony of King-Hall.

HALSBURY, EARL OF (Giffard) (Earl UK 1898)
(Title pronounced "Haulsbury")

Form no vile wish

JOHN ANTHONY HARDINGE GIFFARD, 3rd Earl; *b* 4 June 1908; *s* 1943; *ed* Eton; BSc, DTech, FIEE, FICE, FEng, FRS; first Chancellor of Brunel Univ 1966: *m* 1st, 1930 (*m diss* 1936), Ismay Catherine, who *d* 1989, da of late Lt-Col Lord Ninian Edward Crichton-Stuart (*see* M Bute, colls, 1985 Edn); 2ndly, 1936, Elizabeth Adeline Faith, who *d* 1983, da of late Maj Harry Crewe Godley, DSO (E Annesley, colls), and has issue by 1st and 2nd *m*.

Arms – Sable, three lozenges conjoined in fesse ermine. **Supporters** – Two swans ermine, beaked and legged gules, each having pendant from the neck by a ribbon of the last a shield charged as the arms.
Residence – 4 Campden House, 29 Sheffield Terr, W8 7NE.

SON LIVING *(By 1st marriage)*

ADAM EDWARD (does not use courtesy title), *b* 3 June 1934; *ed* Stowe, and at Jesus Coll, Camb; late 2nd Lt Seaforth Highlanders: *m* 1st, 1963, Mrs Ellen Huxley, da of late Brynjolf Hovde; 2ndly, 1976, Joanna Elizabeth, da of Frederick Harry Cole, and has issue living (by 2nd *m*), Sarah Cole, *b* 1976, — Emma Cole, *b* 1978. *Address* – New Mills, Snapper, Barnstaple, N Devon EX32 7JZ.

DAUGHTERS LIVING *(By 2nd marriage)*

Lady (Elizabeth) Caroline (Elinor Evelyn), *b* 1939: *m* 1968 (*m diss* 1992), Rodney John Derek Blois, of Cockfield Hall, Yoxford, Saxmundham, Suffolk (*see* Blois, Bt). *Residence* – 22 Conduit Mews, W2 3RE.
Lady Clare Rohais Antonia Elizabeth, *b* 1944: *m* 1964, Col Oliver John Martin Lindsay, CBE, FRHistS, MICFM, Gren Gds, of Brookwood House, Brookwood, nr Woking, Surrey GU23 0NX (*see* Lindsay, Bt).

SISTER LIVING

Lady Flavia Joan Lucy (13 Carlton Terrace, Edinburgh 7), *b* 1910: *m* 1933, James Alasdair Anderson of Tullichewan, who *d* 1982, and has issue living, Douglas Hardinge (56036 Palaia, Prov di Pisa, Italy), *b* 1934: *m* 1st, 1962 (*m diss* 1969), Mary Elizabeth Siani, da of John Jenkins, 2ndly, 1974, Veronica Margaret, da of late John Edward Markes, of Recess House, Recess, co Galway, and has issue living (by 1st *m*), James Henry Wallace *b* 1964: *m* 1992, Beatrice Isabella, da of Adriano Versolato, Lucy Elizabeth *b* 1962: *m* 1985, Bevil Charles Symondson (and has issue) (*see* Innes, Bt, *cr* 1628, colls), (by 2nd *m*) Sophia Esme *b* 1977, — Margaret Minette Rohais (*Lady Campbell of Succoth*), *b* 1937: *m* 1961, Sir Ilay Mark Campbell of Succoth, 7th Bt (*cr* 1808), of Crarae Lodge, by Inveraray, Argyll PA32 8YA.

PREDECESSORS – (1) *Rt Hon Sir* HARDINGE STANLEY Giffard PC, son of late Stanley Lees Giffard, LLD; *b* 1823; was Solicitor-Gen 1875-80, and Lord High Chancellor of England June 1885 to Jan 1886, July 1886 to Aug 1892, and June 1895 to Dec 1905; MP for Launceston (C) 1877-85, Constable of Launceston Castle 1883-1919; *cr* Knt 1875, PC 1885, *Baron Halsbury*, of Halsbury, co Devon (peerage of United Kingdom) 1885, and *Viscount Tiverton*, of Tiverton, co Devon and *Earl of Halsbury*, in co Devon (peerage of United Kingdom) 1898: *m* 1st, 1852, Caroline, who *d* 1873, da of W. C. Humphreys, of Wood Green, Middlesex; 2ndly, 1874, Wilhelmina, who *d* 1927, da of late Henry Woodfall; *d* 1921; *s* by his son (2) HARDINGE GOULBURN, KC, 2nd Earl, *b* 1880; was Recorder of Carmarthen 1923-35: *m* 1907, Esmé, who *d* 1973, da of late James Stewart Wallace; *d* 1943; *s* by his son (3) JOHN ANTHONY HARDINGE, 3rd Earl and present peer; also Viscount Tiverton, and Baron Halsbury.

HAMBLEDEN, VISCOUNT (Smith) (Viscount UK 1891)

DEO NON FORTUNA FRETUS

Relying on God, not on fortune

WILLIAM HERBERT SMITH, 4th Viscount; *b* 2 April 1930; *s* 1948; *ed* Eton: *m* 1st, 1955 (*m diss* 1988), Maria Carmela Attolico di Adelfia, da of late Count Bernardo Attolico, of 15 Via Porta Latina, Rome, Italy; 2ndly, 1988, Mrs Lesley Watson, and has issue by 1st *m*.

Arms – Argent, on a chevron azure between three oak leaves vert, each charged with an acorn or as many leopards' faces jessant-de-lis of the field. **Crest** – A cubit arm erect habited azure, cuffed and charged with three mascles in chevron argent holding in the hand proper three branches of oak vert, fructed or. **Supporters** – *Dexter*, a sea-lion vert langued gules semée of escallops and gorged with a collar or, pendant therefrom by a gold chain a portcullis of the third; *sinister*, a wyvern gules, langued azure, semée of mullets or, and gorged with a gold chain, therefrom pendant a portcullis of the third.
Address – The Estate Office, Hambleden, Henley-on-Thames, Oxon.

SONS LIVING (By 1st marriage)

Hon (WILLIAM) HENRY BERNARD (The Manor House, Hambleden, Henley-on-Thames, Oxon; 109 Eccleston Mews, SW1), *b* 18 Nov 1955: *m* 1983, Sara Suzanne, da of Joseph F. Anlauf, of Palos Verdes Estates, Calif, USA, and has issue living, Sara Marie Celeste, *b* 1986, — Alexandra Patricia, *b* 1989.
Hon Bernardo James, *b* 1957.
Hon Alexander David, *b* 1959.
Hon Nicolas Robin Bartolemeo, *b* 1960.
Hon Lorenzo Patrick Harold, *b* 1962.

BROTHERS LIVING

Hon Richard Edward, *b* 1937: *m* 1973, Christine Hickey, and has issue living, Christopher Richard, *b* 1975.
Hon Philip Reginald, *b* 1945, *ed* Eton; Maj (ret) R Green Jackets (despatches); High Sheriff Glos 1992: *m* 1973, Mary, yst da of late John Roberts, of Bottom Farm, Checkendon, Oxon, and has issue living, Thomas William, *b* 1976, — James Edmund Philip, *b* 1983, — Clare Elizabeth, *b* 1974, — Emily, *b* 1980. *Residence* – Campden House, Chipping Campden, Glos.

SISTERS LIVING

Hon Laura Caroline Beatrice, *b* 1931: *m* 1953, Michael Charles Brand, Lieut Coldstream Guards (*see* V Hampden, colls). *Residence* – 6 Howley Place, W2.
Hon Katherine Patricia, *b* 1933: *m* 1st, 1961, Ivan Moffat; 2ndly, 1973, Peter Robert Gascoigne Townend, and has issue living (by 1st *m*), Jonathan David, *b* 1964: *m* 1986, Carmel J. B., 2nd da of L. M. Sawle, of Perth, W Australia, — Patrick Nicholas, *b* 1968. *Residence* – 122 Hurlingham Rd, SW6.

WIDOW LIVING OF SON OF SECOND VISCOUNT.

Lady Helen Pleydell-Bouverie, OBE (King's Copse House, Bucklebury, Berks); OBE (Civil) 1946; DL R County of Berks; da of 6th Earl of Radnor: *m* 1931, Maj Hon David John Smith, CBE, who *d* 1976, and has issue (see colls infra).

COLLATERAL BRANCH LIVING

Issue of late Maj Hon David John Smith, CBE, yst son of 2nd Viscount, *b* 1907, *d* 1976: *m* 1931, Lady Helen Pleydell-Bouverie, OBE (ante), da of 6th Earl of Radnor:—
Julian David (6 The Hermitage, Barnes SW13), *b* 1932: *m* 1966, Eleanor, da of late John Eustace Blyth, MBE, of Ham Common, Surrey, and has issue living, Dickon Julian Henry, *b* 1972, — Alexandra Esther Helen, *b* 1969. —— Antony Frederick (Bouverie, PO Box 155, Mount Barker, W Australia), *b* 1937; *ed* Eton: *m* 1962, Alison Priscilla, da of late Lt-Col John Clark Pyper, OBE, IMS (ret) of Westbury, Tasmania, and has issue living, James Antony David, *b* 1962, — Philip John, *b* 1964, — Harriet Frances, *b* 1967, — Helen Sarah, *b* 1969. —— Peter Henry (Leighton House, Goodmanham, York YO4 3HX), *b* 1939: *m* 1967, Scilla Ann, el da of Peter Bennett, of Dene House, Little Dene, nr Glynde, Sussex, and has issue living, Charles Henry, *b* 1968, — Clare Scilla, *b* 1971, — Catherine Ann, *b* 1975. —— David Michael (21 Wallingford Rd, Cholsey, nr Wallingford, Oxon), *b* 1947: *m* 1st, 1970 (*m diss* 1992), Caroline, da of R. H. Ardill, of Casa la Briana, Barattano, San Terenziano PG, Italy; 2ndly, 1992, Dr Clare Stephenson, and has issue living (by 1st *m*), Jack Robert, *b* 1977, — Rachel Charlotte, *b* 1973. —— Esther Joanna, *b* 1934; *dunm* 1992.

PREDECESSORS – (1) EMILY Smith, el da of late Frederick Dawes Danvers, of the Duchy of Lancaster; *b* 1828; *cr Viscountess Hambleden*, of Hambleden, Bucks (peerage of United Kingdom) 1891, with remainder to the heirs male of her body by the 2nd *m*: *m* 1st, 1854, Benjamin Auber Leach, who *d* 1855; 2ndly, 1858, Rt Hon William Henry Smith, PC (MP for Westminster (C) 1868-85, and for Strand 1885-91), who *d* 1891, First Lord of the Admiralty, First Lord of the Treasury, Lord Warden of the Cinque Ports, and Leader of the House of Commons; *d* 1913; *s* by her son (2) WILLIAM FREDERICK DANVERS, 2nd Viscount, *b* 1868; senior partner in the firm of W. H. Smith and Son, of Strand House, Portugal Street, WC; European War 1914-17 (despatches); sat as MP for Strand (C) Oct 1891 to Jan 1910: *m* 1894, Lady Esther Caroline Georgiana Gore, who *d* 1955, da of 5th Earl of Arran; *d* 1928; *s* by his son (3) WILLIAM HENRY, 3rd Viscount; *b* 1903; Chm of W. H. Smith & Son, Ltd, of Strand House, Portugal Street, WC: *m* 1928, Lady Patricia Herbert, DCVO, who *d* 1994, da of 15th Earl of Pembroke; *d* 1948; *s* by his son (4) WILLIAM HERBERT, 4th Viscount and present peer.

Hamilton, Marquess of; son of Duke of Abercorn.

HAMILTON AND BRANDON, DUKE OF (Douglas-Hamilton) (Duke S 1643 and GB 1711)

Never behind

ANGUS ALAN DOUGLAS DOUGLAS-HAMILTON, 15th Duke of Hamilton, 12th Duke of Brandon, and Premier Peer of Scotland; *b* 13 Sept 1938; *s* 1973; *ed* Eton, and Balliol Coll, Oxford (MA); is Hereditary Keeper of Palace of Holyrood House; Fl Lt RAF (ret); test pilot Scottish Aviation 1971-72; KStJ and Prior for Scotland of Order of St John 1975-83; Member of The Queen's Body Guard for Scotland (Roy Co of Archers); Hon Air Commodore No 2 MHU RAAF: *m* 1st, 1972 (*m diss* 1987), Sarah Jane, who *d* 1994, da of Sir Walter Scott, 4th Bt (*cr* 1907); 2ndly, 1988, Jillian (*née* Robertson), formerly wife of (i) Martin Page, and (ii) Edward Hulton, son of late Sir Edward Hulton, and has issue by 1st *m*.

Arms – Quarterly: 1st and 4th grand quarter counter-quartered, 1st and 4th gules, three cinque foils ermine, *Hamilton*; 2nd and 3rd argent, a lymphad with the sails furled proper; flagged gules, *Arran*; 2nd and 3rd, grand quarters, argent, a man's heart gules, ensigned with an imperial crown proper, on a chief azure, three mullets of the first, *Douglas*. **Crests** – 1st, on a ducal coronet an oak tree, fructed and penetrated transversely in the main stem by a frame saw proper, the frame or, *Hamilton*; 2nd, on a chapeau gules turned up ermine, a salamander in flames proper, *Douglas*. **Supporters** – Two antelopes argent, armed, unguled, ducally gorged and chained or.
Seat – Lennoxlove, Haddington, E Lothian.

SONS LIVING (By 1st marriage)

ALEXANDER DOUGLAS (*Marquess of Douglas and Clydesdale*), *b* 31 March 1978.
Lord John William, *b* 1979.

DAUGHTERS LIVING (By 1st marriage)

Lady Eleanor, *b* 1973.
Lady Anne, *b* 1976.

BROTHERS LIVING

Lord James Alexander, MP, *b* 1942; *ed* Eton, Balliol Coll, Oxford (MA), and Edinburgh Univ (LLB); Capt Cameronians (RARO); Member Queen's Body Guard for Scotland (Royal Company of Archers); Advocate 1968; Pres of Oxford Union 1964; Town Cllr for Edinburgh 1972-74; a Lord Commr of HM Treasury 1979-81; PPS to Min of State, FCO, 1983-87, Under Sec of State for Home Affairs and the Environment, Scottish Office 1987-92, since when Under-Sec of State for Education and Housing Scottish Office; Hon Pres Scottish Amateur Boxing Assoc; Pres Roy Commonwealth Soc in Scotland; Pres Scottish Council of UNA; MP for Edinburgh W (*C*) since 1974; author: *m* 1974, Hon (Priscilla) Susan Buchan, da of the 2nd Baron Tweedsmuir, and has issue living, John Andrew, *b* 1978, — Charles Douglas, *b* 1979, — James Robert *b* 1981, — Harry Alexander (twin), *b* 1981.
Lord Hugh Malcolm, *b* 1946; *ed* Eton: *m* 1971 (*m diss* and annulled 1991), June Mary Curtis, and has issue living, Brendan Thomas, *b* 1974, — Catherine Bride, *b* 1976. *Residence* – Begbie Farmhouse, Haddington, E Lothian.
Lord Patrick George, *b* 1950: *m* 1989, Cecilia F. M., elder da of Capt T. G. Usher, of Crossford, Fife, and has issue living, Isabel Rose, *b* 1991. *Residence* – Westfield House, Haddington, E Lothian EH41 4HQ.
Lord David Stephen, *b* 1952; *ed* Eton.

UNCLE LIVING (Son of 13th Duke)

Lord (George) Nigel (*Earl of Selkirk*), KT, GCMG, GBE, AFC, QC, *b* 1906; *s* as 10th *Earl of Selkirk* 1940 (see that title).

WIDOWS LIVING OF SONS OF THIRTEENTH DUKE

Natalie, CBE (Apart 10, 174 East 74th St, New York, USA), da of Maj Nathaniel Brackett Wales, of New York, and Boston, USA, and widow of Edward Bragg Paine, of New York, USA: *m* 1953, as his 2nd wife, Lord Malcolm Avondale Douglas-Hamilton, OBE, DFC, who *d* 1964 (see colls, infra).
Ann Prunella, da of late Capt Edward Hugh Bagot Stack, Indian Army: *m* 1st, 1938, Squadron-Leader Lord David Douglas-Hamilton, RAF Vol Reserve, who was *k* on flying operations 1944; 2ndly, 1950, Alfred G Albers, who *d* 1951; 3rdly, 1964, Brian St Quentin Power, and has issue living, (by 1st *m*) (see colls, infra). *Residence* – 14 Gertrude St, SW10.

WIDOW LIVING OF FOURTEENTH DUKE

Lady ELIZABETH IVY PERCY (*Dowager Duchess of Hamilton and Brandon*), OBE, DL (North Port, Lennoxlove, Haddington, E Lothian EH41 4HH), da of 8th Duke of Northumberland, KG, CBE, MVO, LLD: *m* 1937, Douglas, 14th Duke, KT, PC, GCVO, AFC, who *d* 1973.

COLLATERAL BRANCHES LIVING

Issue of late Lord Malcolm Avondale Douglas-Hamilton, OBE, DFC, 3rd son of 13th Duke, *b* 1909, *d* 1964: *m* 1st, 1931 (*m diss* 1952), (Clodagh) Pamela, only child of late Lt-Col Hon Malcolm Bowes-Lyon, CBE (*see* E Strathmore, colls); 2ndly, 1953, Natalie, CBE (ante), da of Maj Nathaniel Brackett Wales, of New York, and Boston, USA, and widow of Edward Bragg Paine, of New York:—
(By 1st *m*) Alasdair Malcolm (Lessudden, St Boswells, Roxburghshire), *b* 1939; *ed* Gordonstoun, and Edinburgh Univ: *m* 1965, Angela Kathleen, 2nd da of James Molony Longley, of W Knoyle, Wilts, and has issue living, Angus Gavin, *b* 1968, — Geordie Fergus, *b* 1969, — Fenella Mairi, *b* 1966, — Tessa Catherine, *b* 1980. —— Diana Mairi (Friarshawmuir, Midlem, nr Selkirk), *b* 1933: *m* 1955 (*m diss* 1982), Gavin William Younger, and has issue living, Douglas Henry, *b* 1956: *m* 1979, Alison Susan, 2nd da of Guy Urwick Goodbody, and has issue living, Harry Neil *b* 1981, Samuel Guy *b* 1984, — Hugh Patrick, *b* 1958, — Malcolm James, *b* 1959, — Robert William, *b* 1964, — Alexandra Anna, *b* 1963. —— Fiona Margaret, *b* 1935: *m* 1973, Jeremy Blackstone Wise, of 3 Croom's Hill Grove, Greenwich, SE10.

Issue of late Squadron-Leader Lord David Douglas-Hamilton, RAF Vol Reserve, 4th son of 13th Duke, *b* 1912, *k* on flying operations 1944: *m* 1938, Ann Prunella (ante) (who *m* 2ndly, 1950, Alfred G. Albers, who *d* 1951; 3rdly, 1964, Brian St Quentin Power), da of late Capt Edward Hugh Bagot Stack, Indian Army:—
Diarmaid Hugh (729 Cabot St, Beverly, Mass 01915, USA), *b* 1940; *ed* Gordonstoun, Balliol Coll, Oxford, and Harvard Univ: *m* 1st, 1967 (*m diss* 1982), Margaret Barlow, only da of Dr William Matthew Hambrecht, of Lakeville, Conn, USA; 2ndly, 1983, Margaret Murray, el da of Duncan McGlashan Spencer, of New York, and Dublin, New Hampshire. —— Iain, OBE (Lake Naivasha, Kenya), *b* 1942; *ed* Gordonstoun and Oriel Coll, Oxford; OBE (Civil) 1993: *m* 1971, Oria, 2nd da of Lt-Col Mario Rocco, of Dominio di Doriano, Naivasha, Kenya, and has issue living, Saba Iassa, *b* 1970; *ed* St Andrews Univ, —— Dudu Mara, *b* 1971; *ed* Cape Town Univ.

Grandchildren of late Algernon Percy Douglas-Hamilton, 2nd son of Col Francis Seymour Douglas-Hamilton, RA, uncle of 13th Duke:—
Issue of late Percy Seymour Douglas-Hamilton, *b* 1875, *d* 1940: *m* 1st, 1901, Edith Annie Hamilton, who *d* 1927, el da of Sir Frederick Wills, 1st Bt; 2ndly, 1929, Barbara Margherita (who *d* 1975 having *m* 2ndly, 1946, David George Arbuthnot (Arbuthnot, Bt, colls)), da of Francis Chiappini, JP, of Wynberg, Cape Province, S Africa:—
(By 2nd *m*) John Percy, *b* 1930: *m* 1st, 1955 (*m diss* 1980), June Mary Clifton Michler, of Rondesbosch, Cape Province, S Africa; 2ndly, 1980, Delia Rose Davies, *neé* Bilbrough, and has issue living (by 1st *m*), John Gavin, *b* 1957, —— Tessa Jeanne, *b* 1958, —— Debra Anne, *b* 1959, —— Diane Barbara (twin), *b* 1959. *Residence* – Hillcrest, Forest Av, Bishopscourt, Cape, S Africa. —— Diana Barbara, *b* 1932: *m* 1954, Ian Emslie Austin, of Klein Constantia, Constantia, Cape Prov, S Africa, who *d* 1973, and has issue living, Christopher James, *b* 1955, —— Philip Ian, *b* 1959 —— David Douglas, *b* 1961, —— Gillian Barbara, *b* 1957.

Grandchildren of late Aubrey Reginald Douglas-Hamilton, 3rd son of late Algernon Percy Douglas Hamilton (ante):—
Issue of late Herbert Eustace Seymour Douglas Hamilton, *b* 1886, *d* 1963: *m* 1912, Ruth, who *d* 1974, da of late Cuthbert Harrison:—
Cecil Seymour (Apt 304, 2020 Bellwood Ave, Burnaby, BC, Canada V5B 4P8), *b* 1916; Fl Lt RCAF (ret): *m* 1943, Ada Louise, da of late Orie Donily, and has an adopted da, Catherine Gail, *b* 1941: *m* 1960 (*m diss* 1978), Norman James Felton, and has issue living, Susan Darlene *b* 1961, Marilyn Jean *b* 1962: *m* 1982, Tony Macdonald (and has issue living, Ryan James *b* 1986, Rachel Catherine *b* 1988).
Issue of late Claud Archibald Aubrey Douglas-Hamilton, MBE, *b* 1889, *d* 1961: *m* 1915, Evelyn Addison, who *d* 1975, only da of late Thomas Addison Chater, of 51 Addison Avenue, Kensington, W, and Chesham Bois, Bucks:—
Evelyn Daphne, *b* 1916: *m* 1st, 1940, Rev Jack Rawlins, Chap to the Forces, who *d* 1946; 2ndly, 1956, Hedley Boardman, MB, ChB, DPH, of 49 Chatsworth Court, Pembroke Rd, W8 6DH, and has issue living (by 1st *m*), Prof Michael David (29 The Grove, Gosforth, Newcastle upon Tyne; Shoreston House, Shoreston, nr Seahouses, Northumberland), *b* 1941; BSc London; MD, BS, FRCP, FRCPE: *m* 1963, Elizabeth Cadbury, only da of Edmund Henry Hambly, MB, BS, FRCS, and has issue living, Victoria Jane *b* 1964: *m* 1988, Andrew George Franks, of West House, Winston, Darlington, co Durham (and has issue living, Laura Elizabeth Sarah *b* 1992, Annabel Jean *b* 1994), Lucy Sarah *b* 1965: *m* 1989, Paul Robert Holmes, of 109 Elstree Rd, Bushy Heath, Herts WD2 3AN (and has issue living, Emily Anna Elizabeth *b* 1993), Susannah Clara *b* 1972, —— Christopher John (24 Glen Hill Rd, Wilton, Connecticut 06897, USA; Windfall Cottage, E Prawle, nr Kingsbridge, Devon), *b* 1945; BSc London; MIM; LRSC; Vice-Pres and Publisher Appleton & Lange Inc: *m* 1969, Mary Joan, only da of Donovan William Goodchild, and has issue living, Jeremy Mark *b* 1974, Sarah Elizabeth *b* 1972; *ed* Coventry Univ (BA), Penelope Jane *b* 1977.

PREDECESSORS – (**1**) JAMES, KG, PC, 3rd Marquess of Hamilton, and 2nd Earl of Cambridge, Gentleman of the Bedchamber, Master of the Horse, etc, *cr Lord Aven and Innerdale, Earl of Arran and Cambridge, Marquess of Clydesdale*, and *Duke of Hamilton* (peerage of Scotland) 1643, with remainder to the heirs male of his body, 2nd in default to his brother William, Earl of Lanark, and his male issue, and in default thereof to his own el da, Anne, and her issue male: appointed Hereditary Keeper of the Palace of Holyrood; commanded the Army raised in Scotland for the relief of Charles I, and being defeated at Preston he surrendered and was beheaded on 9 March 1649; *s* by his brother (**2**) WILLIAM, 2nd Duke, who had in 1639 been *cr Lord Machansire and Polmont*, and *Earl of Lanark* (peerage of Scotland); killed at the battle of Worcester 1651, when his own honours expired and the Dukedom descended to his niece (**3**) ANNE, wife of William, KG, 1st Earl of Selkirk (ante), who in 1660 was *cr Duke of Hamilton* for life: the Duchess surrendered her honours in favour of her el son (**4**) JAMES, KG, KT, 4th Duke, who in 1698 received a novodamus of the titles of Lord *Aven, Polmont, Machansire, and Innerdale, Earl of Arran, Lanark*, and *Cambridge, Marquess of Clydesdale* and *Duke of Hamilton* (peerage of Scotland) with precedence of 1643, and in 1711 was *cr Baron Dutton* and *Duke of Brandon* (peerage of GB): upon applying for his seat in the House of Peers, the House decided that after the union no peer for Scotland could be *cr* a peer of England: killed in a duel 1712; *s* by his son (**5**) JAMES, KT, 5th Duke of Hamilton and 2nd of Brandon; a Lord of the Bedchamber; *d* 1743; *s* by his el son (**6**) JAMES, KT, 6th Duke of Hamilton and 3rd of Brandon; *d* 1758; *s* by his son (**7**) JAMES GEORGE, 7th Duke of Hamilton and 4th of Brandon, *s* to the Marquessate of Douglas and Earldom of Angus (see infra *) 1761; *d* unmarried 1769; *s* by his brother (**8**) DOUGLAS, 8th Duke of Hamilton and 5th of Brandon; was summoned to House of Lords as Duke of Brandon; *dsp* 1799; *s* by his uncle (**9**) ARCHIBALD, 9th Duke of Hamilton and 6th of Brandon; MP for Lancashire 1768-72; *d* 1819; *s* by his son (**10**) ALEXANDER, KG, PC, 10th Duke of Hamilton and 7th of Brandon; Ambassador to St Petersburg; MP for Lancashire 1802; summoned to House of Lords in his father's Barony of Dutton 1806; Lord-Lieut of Lanarkshire; *d* 1852; *s* by his son (**11**) WILLIAM ALEXANDER ARCHIBALD, 11th Duke of Hamilton and 8th of Brandon; *b* 1811; was Lord-Lieut of Lanarkshire: *m* 1843, Princess Mary of Baden, da of Charles Louis Frederick, late reigning Grand Duke of Baden, and cousin to HIM Napoleon III; *d* 1863, *s* by his son (**12**) WILLIAM ALEXANDER LOUIS STEPHEN, KT, 12th Duke of Hamilton and 9th Duke of Brandon; *b* 1845; granted Dukedom of Chatellerault by Imperial decree Napoleon III, dated 20 April 1864 (*see* D Abercorn), and *s* to the Earldom of Selkirk under special remainder 1886: *m* 1873, Lady Mary Louise Elizabeth Montagu, OBE, who *d* 1934, da of 7th Duke of Manchester; *d* 1895; *s* by his cousin (**13**) ALFRED DOUGLAS (great-grandson of Adm Charles Powell Douglas-Hamilton, 2nd son of Lord Anne Douglas-Hamilton, 3rd son of 4th Duke), 13th Duke, *b* 1862: *m* 1901, Nina Mary Benita, who *d* 1951, da of late Major Robert Poore; *d* 1940; when he was *s* in the Earldom of Selkirk (under the terms of special destination) by his second son Lord (George) Nigel Douglas-Hamilton, and in the Dukedom and other peerages by his el son (**14**) DOUGLAS, KT, GCVO, AFC, PC, 14th Duke, *b* 1903; Ch Pilot Mount Everest Flight Expedition 1933; Lord High Commr to Gen Assembly of Church of Scotland, 1953-55 and 1958; Lord Steward of the Household 1940-64; Chancellor of St Andrews Univ 1948-73: MP for E Renfrewshire (C) 1930-40: *m* 1937, Lady Elizabeth Ivy Percy, da of 8th Duke of Northumberland: *d* 1973; *s* by his el son (**15**) ANGUS ALAN DOUGLAS, 15th Duke and present peer: also Duke of Brandon, Marquess of Douglas, Marquess of Clydesdale, Earl of Angus, Earl of Arran, Lanark, and Cambridge, Lord Abernethy and Jedburgh Forest, Lord Aven and Innerdale, Lord Machansire and Polmont, and Baron Dutton.

*William Douglas, *cr* Earl of Douglas (peerage of Scotland) 1358 (title attainted 1455): *m* 3rdly, Lady Margaret Stewart (da of Thomas, 2nd Earl of Angus, and on the decease of her brother the 3rd Earl), Countess of Angus in her own right, and had issue (**1**) GEORGE, who in 1389 obtained a grant of his mother's earldom and became *Earl of Angus* (peerage of Scotland): *m* Princess Mary, da of Robert III, by whom he was granted charters of considerable lands; *d* 1402; *s* by his son (**2**) WILLIAM, 2nd Earl; *d* 1437; *s* by his son (**3**) JAMES, 3rd Earl; betrothed to Princess Jean, 3rd da of James I (of Scotland), but *d* 1446, before the marriage took place; *s* by his uncle (**4**) GEORGE, 4th Earl, 2nd son of 1st Earl; received a grant of the forfeited Lordship of Douglas 1457; when Henry VI took refuge in Scotland, the Earl offered the King substantial aid and was promised an English dukedom; *s* by his son (**5**) ARCHIBALD, 5th Earl; styled the "Great Earl" and "Bell the Cat;" a powerful noble who was High Chancellor of Scotland 1493-8; *d* 1514; *s* by his grandson (**6**) ARCHIBALD, 6th Earl: *m* Princess Margaret of England, Queen Dowager of James IV of Scotland; *d* before Jan 22nd, 1557; *s* by his nephew (**7**) DAVID, 7th Earl; *d* June 1557; *s* by his son (**8**) ARCHIBALD, 8th Earl, who in 1585 *s* his uncle as 5th Earl of Morton (peerage of Scotland, *cr* 1458); *d* 1588; when the Earldom of Morton devolved on Sir William Douglas, of Lochleven, though there were other representatives in a more direct line; *s* in Earldom of Angus by his kinsman **(9)** WILLIAM, KB, 9th Earl, descendant of Sir William, 2nd son of 5th Earl; obtained in 1591 from James VI a charter confirming to himself and his heirs male the ancient privileges of the Douglas family, viz "The first vote in Parliament or Council; to be the king's Hereditary Lieutenant; to have the leading of the van of the army in the day of battle; and to carry the crown of coronations"; *d* 1591: *s* by his son **(10)** WILLIAM, 10th Earl; obtained a charter in 1602 under the great seal confirming the charter granted to his father (ante); *d* 1611; *s* by his son **(11)** WILLIAM, 11th Earl; *cr Lord Abernethy and Jedburgh Forest* and *Marquess of Douglas* (peerage of Scotland) 1633; *m* 1st, Margaret Hamilton, da of 1st Baron Paisley and sister to 1st Earl of Abercorn; 2ndly, Lady Mary Gordon, da of 1st Marquess of Huntly; had with other issue by 1st *m* Archibald, *cr* 1651 *Lord Bothwell and Hartside*, and *Earl of Ormond*, with remainder to the heirs male of his 2nd *m*; William, *cr Lord Daer and Shortcleuch*, and *Earl of Selkirk* (peerage of Scotland) 1646, which peerages he resigned into the King's hands, who in 1688 re-conferred them with precedency of 1646 on his 3rd and yr sons primogeniturely provided that, if any of their representatives succeeded to the Dukedom of Hamilton, *cr* 1648, the Earldom should pass to the then Duke's next brother, and with further remainder to his Grace's other heirs male; he *m* Anne, in her own right, Duchess of Hamilton (see ante), and was himself created *Duke of Hamilton* for life; *d* 1660; *s* by his grandson **(12)** JAMES, 2nd Marquess, who had in 1655 *s* his father (ante) as 2nd Earl of Ormond; *d* 1700; *s* by his son **(13)** ARCHIBALD, 3rd Marquess; *cr Lord Douglas of Bonkill, Viscount of Jedburgh Forest, Marquess of Angus and Abernethy*, and *Duke of Douglas* (peerage of Scotland) 1703, all of which honours expired at his death in 1761, and the Marquessate of Douglas devolved upon James George, 7th Duke of Hamilton (see ante), and the Duke of Douglas's nephew, Archibald Stewart, was returned heir of line to the Duke of Douglas. The Duke of Hamilton disputed the return on the ground of Mr Stewart's birth being surreptitious, the Scottish Courts decided in favour of the Duke, but in 1769 the House of Lords reversed the Scottish judgement and awarded the estates to Mr Stewart, who assumed the name of Douglas. He was *cr Lord Douglas*, of Douglas Castle (peerage of Scotland) 1790 (ext 1857) (*see* E Home).

HAMILTON OF DALZELL, BARON (Hamilton) (Baron UK 1886)
(Title pronounced "Hamilton of Dee-el")

JAMES LESLIE HAMILTON, 4th Baron; *b* 11 Feb 1938; *s* 1990; *ed* Eton; DL Surrey 1993; late Coldstream Guards; Member London Stock Exchange 1967-80; Dir Rowton Hotels plc 1978-84; Gov Queen Elizabeth's Foundation for the Disabled (Chm since 1989); DL Surrey 1993: *m* 1967, (Ann Anastasia) Corinna (Helena), yr da of late Sir Pierson John Dixon, GCMG, CB, and has issue.

Arms – Gules, an annulet or between three cinquefoils pierced ermine. **Crest** – An antelope proper, attired and hoofed or. **Supporters** – *Dexter*, an antelope proper, ducally gorged and chained, the chain reflexed over the back or; *sinister*, a wild man proper, wreathed about the temples and loins with laurel, and holding over the sinister shoulder a club or.
Residences – Stockton House, Norton Shifnal, Shropshire; Betchworth House, Betchworth, Surrey RH3 7RE.

Who will oppose

SONS LIVING

Hon GAVIN GOULBURN, *b* 8 Oct 1968; *ed* Eton, and Buckingham Univ (BSc).
Hon Robert Pierson, *b* 1971; *ed* Eton.
Hon John Duff, *b* (twin) 1971; *ed* Eton.
Hon Benjamin James, *b* 1974; a Page of Honour to HM 1986-88.

BROTHER LIVING

Rt Hon Sir Archibald Gavin, MP (House of Commons, SW1), *b* 1941; *ed* Eton; late Coldm Gds; Cllr R Borough of Kensington and Chelsea 1968-71; contested Dagenham (*C*) Feb and Oct 1974, MP for Epsom and Ewell (*C*) since 1978; Assist Govt Whip 1982-84, Lord Commr to HM Treasury 1984-86, Parliamentary Under-Sec for Defence Procurement 1986-87, PPS to Rt Hon Margaret Thatcher, PM, 1987-88, Min of State for the Armed Forces 1988-93 since when Gov of Westminster Foundation for Democracy; PC 1991; Ktd 1994: *m* 1968, Anne Catharine, da of late Com Trevylyan Napier, DSC, RN, and has issue living, Laura Katharine, *b* 1969, — Iona Janet, *b* 1971, — Alice Rose Alethea, *b* 1974.

SISTER LIVING

Hon Janet, *b* 1936: *m* 1960, Richard Sackville Lane Fox (By Bingley), and has issue living, Andrew Ward Jackson, *b* 1969, — Harriot, *b* 1966. *Residences* – 17 Princedale Rd, W11 4NW; Kingsley Mill, Black Torrington, Beaworthy, Devon.

PREDECESSORS – **(1)** JOHN GLENCAIRN CARTER Hamilton, son of late A. J. Hamilton of Dalzell; *b* 1829; a Lord-in-Waiting to HM Queen Victoria 1892-4; MP for Falkirk Burgh (*L*) 1857-9, for S Lanarkshire 1868-74 and 1880-85 and for Lanarkshire, S Div 1885-6; *cr Baron Hamilton of Dalzell* co Lanark (peerage of United Kingdom) 1886: *m* 1864, Lady Emily Eleanor, who *d* 1882, 4th da of 10th Earl of Leven and Melville; *d* 1900; *s* by his el surviving son **(2)** GAVIN GEORGE, KT, CVO, MC, 2nd Baron; *b* 1872: Major (ret) Scots Guards; Lord-in-Waiting to HM King Edward VII 1905-10, and to HM King George V 1910-11: *m* 1912, Sybil Mary, who *d* 1933, da of late Lieut-Gen Sir Frederick Marshall, KCMG; *d* 1952; *s* by his nephew **(3)** JOHN D'HENIN, GCVO, MC (son of late Major Hon Leslie d'Henin Hamilton, MVO, Coldstream Guards, 3rd son of 1st Baron), 3rd Baron; *b* 1911; Lord Lieut Surrey 1973-86, Chm Surrey Co Agricultural Exec Cttee 1957-68, a Lord-in-Waiting to HM Queewn Elizabeth II 1968-81: *m* 1935, Rosemary Olive, who *d* 1993, da of late Maj Hon Sir John Spencer Coke, KCVO (*see* E Leicester, colls); *d* 1990; *s* by his elder son **(4)** JAMES LESLIE, 4th Baron and present peer.

HAMNETT, BARONY OF (Hamnett) (Extinct 1980)

DAUGHTER LIVING OF LIFE BARON

Hon Sheila, *b* 1933: *m* 1962, Eric Layland, of 31 Sevenoaks Av, Heaton Moor, Stockport, Ches.

HAMPDEN, VISCOUNT (Brand) (Viscount UK 1884)
(Title pronounced "Hamden")

ANTHONY DAVID BRAND, 6th Viscount; *b* 7 May 1937; *s* 1975; *ed* Eton; DL E Sussex 1986: *m* 1st, 1969 (*m diss* 1988), Caroline Fiona, da of late Capt Claud Proby (*see* Proby, Bt, colls); 2ndly, 1993, Mrs Sally Snow, and has issue by 1st *m*.

Arms – Azure, two swords in saltire points, upwards argent, pommels and hilts or, between three escallops of the last. **Crest** – Out of a crown vallory or, a leopard's head argent, semée of escallops and gorged with a gemel gules.
Residence – Glynde Place, Glynde, Lewes, Sussex.

SONS LIVING *(By 1st marriage)*

Hon FRANCIS ANTHONY, *b* 17 Sept 1970.
Hon Jonathan Claud David Humphrey, *b* 1975.

DAUGHTER LIVING *(By 1st marriage)*

Hon Saracha Mary, *b* 1973.

SISTERS LIVING

Hon Jean Margaret, *b* 1938: *m* 1976, Robert John Hodgson (*see* Lacon, Bt, colls). *Residence* – 2 St Hilda's Rd, SW13 9JQ.
Hon Philippa Mary Imogen (*Hon Mrs Chetwode*), *b* 1942: *m* 1961, Hon Christopher Roger Chetwode, of Hill House, Cheriton, Alresford, Hants (*see* B Chetwode)

AUNTS LIVING *(Daughters of 3rd Viscount)*

Hon Joan Louisa (*Hon Lady Hill-Wood*) (Knipton Lodge, Grantham, Lincs), *b* 1904: *m* 1925, Sir Basil Samuel Hill-Wood, 2nd Bt, who *d* 1954.
Hon Barbara Constance, *b* 1907: *m* 1934, Ronald Harry Higham, who *d* 1966, and has issue living, Robin David, *b* 1939: *m* 1978, Janet Emily, yst da of late Michael Edward Gibb, of Forge House, Taynton, Oxon, and has issue living, Jessica Barbara *b* 1982, Edwina *b* 1987, — Caroline (*Hon Mrs Victor Grosvenor*), *b* 1936: *m* 1959, Hon Robert Victor Grosvenor, who *d* 1993, of Bennets Grafton, Oxon (*see* B Ebury). *Residence* – 6, 212 Old Brompton Rd, SW5.
Hon Elizabeth Margaret, *b* 1911: *m* 1935, Cecil Chadwick Lomax, formerly Major 9th Lancers, who *d* 1988, and has issue living, Fiona Valerie, *b* 1936: *m* 1957, Simon Hildebrand Melville Bradley, and has issue living, David Charles *b* 1960, Mark William *b* 1964: *m* 1993, Emily, da of Anthony Skinner, of Devon, Sarah Elizabeth (*Hon Mrs Paul Chetwynd-Talbot*) *b* 1961: *m* 1982, Hon Paul Alexander Anthony Bueno Chetwynd-Talbot, yr son of 21st Earl of Shrewsbury and Waterford, — Dinah Patricia, *b* 1946: *m* 1977, Pascal Voisin, of 12 Ave du Cap de Nice, 06300 Nice, France, and has issue living, Thomas Gregoire *b* 1979, Blaise Noël *b* 1982, Camille Aimée *b* 1977, — Camilla Elizabeth, *b* 1948. *Residence* – Codicote Mill, Hitchin, Herts.
Hon Monica Dorothy, *b* 1914: *m* 1933, D'Arcy Lambton, who *d* 1938 (*see* E Durham, colls). *Residence* – Saxon House, Shottisham, Woodbridge, Suffolk.

DAUGHTERS LIVING OF FOURTH VISCOUNT

See Bs Dacre.

WIDOW LIVING OF FOURTH VISCOUNT

LEILA EMILY (*Leila, Viscountess Hampden*) (Mill Court, Alton, Hants), da of late Lt-Col Frank Evelyn Seely (*see* Seely Bt, colls): *m* 1923, the 4th Viscount, who *d* 1965, and has issue (*see* Bs Dacre).

WIDOW LIVING OF FIFTH VISCOUNT

Hon IMOGEN ALICE RHYS (*Imogen, Viscountess Hampden*) (Trevor House, Glynde, Lewes, Sussex), da of 7th Baron Dynevor: *m* 1936, the 5th Viscount, who *d* 1975.

COLLATERAL BRANCHES LIVING

Issue of late Hon Robert Henry Brand (4th son of 2nd Viscount), who was *cr Baron Brand* 1946 (extinct 1963) (see that title).

(In remainder to Barony of Dacre only)

Issue of late Adm Hon Sir Hubert George Brand, GCB, KCMG, KCVO, 2nd son of 2nd Viscount, *b* 1870, *d* 1955: *m* 1914, Norah Conyngham, who *d* 1924, da of late Rt Hon Sir (William) Conyngham Greene, KCB, Ambassador Extraor and Min Plen to Japan:—
Elizabeth Norah, *b* 1915: *m* 1940, Major John Edward Seymour, Gren Gds, who *d* 1972 (*see* M Hertford, colls). *Residence* – Edgedell Cottage, Martyr Worthy, Winchester.

Issue of late Brig-Gen Hon Roger Brand, CMG, DSO, 5th son of 2nd Viscount, *b* 1880; *d* 1945: *m* 1913, Muriel Hectorina Lilian, who *d* 1988, da of Henry Boyle Montgomery:—

Patricia Helen Winifred, *b* 1926: *m* 1st, 1950 (*m diss* 1957), John Ralph Lubbock (*see* B Avebury, colls); 2ndly, 1957, Pierre Micheletto.

Grandchildren of late Hon Margaret Brand, Mrs Algernon Francis Holford Ferguson, eldest da of 2nd Viscount:—
Issue of late Col Andrew Henry FERGUSON, Life Guards, *b* 1899, *d* 1966: *m* 1927, Marian Louise (*Lady Elmhirst*) (No 2 Bungalow, Dummer Down Farm, Dummer, Basingstoke) (who *m* 2ndly, 1968, Air Marshal Sir Thomas Walker Elmhirst, KBE, CB, AFC, who *d* 1982), da of late Lt-Col Lord Herbert Andrew Montagu Douglas Scott, CMG, DSO (*see* D Buccleuch, colls):—
Ronald Ivor FERGUSON (Dummer Down House, Dummer, Basingstoke), *b* 1931; *ed* Eton; Maj Life Guards: *m* 1st, 1956 (*m diss* 1974), Susan Mary (who *m* 2ndly, 1975, Hector Barrantes, who *d* 1990, of Argentina), da of late FitzHerbert Wright (*see* V Powerscourt, 1990 Edn); 2ndly, 1976, Susan Rosemary, da of Frederick Deptford, and has issue living (by 1st *m*), Jane Louise, *b* 1957: *m* 1st, 1976 (*m diss* 1991), William (Alex) Makim, of Australia; 2ndly, 1994, Rainer Hans Luedecke, and has issue living (by 1st *m*), Seamus *b* 1981, Ayesha *b* 1986, — Sarah Margaret (*HRH the Duchess of York*), *b* 15 Oct 1959: *m* 23 July 1986, HRH The Prince Andrew Albert Christian Edward, Duke of York, CVO, ADC, 2nd son of HM Queen Elizabeth II, and has issue (*see* ROYAL FAMILY), — (by 2nd *m*) Andrew Frederick John, *b* 1978, — Alice Victoria, *b* 1980, — Eliza, *b* 1986.
Issue of late Margaret Susan Ferguson, *b* 1906, *d* 1939: *m* 1931, as his 1st wife, Lt-Col Frederick Edwin Barton Wignall, Life Guards, who *d* 1956 (*see* Tate, Bt, colls, 1956 Edn):—
Ann Margaret, *b* 1932: *m* 1968, as his 3rd wife, James William Hay Verner, and has issue living, two sons. *Residence* – The Dormers, Stembridge, Martock, Somerset TA12 6BL.
Issue of late Jane Charlotte Ferguson, *b* 1912, *d* (26 Feb) 1986: *m* 1934, Capt Sir William Albemarle Fellowes, KCVO, who *d* (6 April) 1986:—
Rt Hon Sir Robert FELLOWES, KCB, KCVO, *b* 1941; Assist Private Sec to HM 1977-85, Dep Private Sec 1985-90, since when Private Sec; LVO 1982, CB 1987, KCVO 1989, PC 1990, KCB 1991; *ed* Eton: *m* 1st, 1958 (*m diss* 1970), Lady Caroline Victoria Wood, el da of 2nd Earl of Halifax; 2ndly, 19—, Mary Francesca, formerly wife of John Valentine Gosling, and eldest da of late G/Capt Henry William Pearson-Rogers, CBE, JP, of Tostock, Suffolk, and has had issue (by 1st *m*), Randle Charles Roderick, *b* 1961, — †Virginia Mary, *b* 1959; *d* 1994, following a ski-ing accident in France, — Fiona Caroline, *b* 1965: *m* 1991, James D. E. Bryant, son of J. M. Bryant, of Whaplode, Lincs, and has issue living, Sarah Elizabeth *b* 1993.
—— Andrew James (The Old Manor House, Minster Lovell, Oxon), *b* 1941; *ed* Eton: *m* 1977, Rowena Jane, LVO, da of Hon Peter Esmé Brassey (*see* B Brassey of Apethorpe), and has issue living, James William Guy, *b* 1980, — Emma Jane, *b* 1979.
Issue of late Maj Cecil Henry Feilden, *b* 1907, *d* 1983: *m* 1st, 1941, Olivia Constance Leonora, who *d* 1975, da of late Lt-Col Hon Guy Victor Baring (B Ashburton, colls); 2ndly, 1976, Tessa Eirene (Bramdean House, Alresford, Hants), da of late Denis Griffiths, of Orlingbury Hall, Northants:—
(By 1st *m*) Victoria Rose, *b* 1942: *m* 1971, Gerald Hugo Cropper Wakefield, and has issue (*see* Wakefield, Bt). —— Mary Henrietta (10 Gertrude St, SW10 0JN), *b* 1944.
Issue of late Dorothy Priscilla Feilden, *b* 1909, *d* 1983: *m* 1941, Lt-Col John Wilson Seton Galbraith, 11th Hussars:—
Jonathan Charles GALBRAITH (Hetland Hill, Carrutherstown, Dumfriesshire), *b* 1947. —— (Arthur) Guy (Newbold Revel, Haddington, E Lothian EH41 4HE), *b* 1947: *m* 1975, Sarah Jane, da of late Maj Robert Philip Henry Elwes, MBE, MC, of Congham House, King's Lynn, Norfolk (*see* E Annandale and Hartfell), and has issue living, Rowena Mary, *b* 1978, — Alice Katherine, *b* 1980. —— Joanna Katherine, *b* 1943: *m* 1967, Capt John William Nelson Mitchell, of Foxwood, Parkgate, Dumfries, and has issue living, Mark Alastair Nelson, *b* 1969, — Katrina Mary, *b* 1972, — Miranda Janet, *b* 1973.

(Male line in remainder to Viscountcy)

Grandsons of late Rear Adm Hon Thomas Seymour Brand, 2nd son of 1st Viscount:—
Issue of late Phoebe Brand, *b* 1893 *d* (17 Aug) 1972: *m* 1914, Lt-Col Edward Anthony Fielden, MC, 10th Hussars, who *d* (26 Aug) 1972:—
David Edward FIELDEN (PO Kilifi, via Mombasa, Kenya), *b* 1915; *ed* Eton; 1939-45 War with E African Forces: *m* 1942, Kathleen, da of Thomas Grant, of Silverbridge, co Down, and widow of Robert Sturge Ball, and has issue living, Joshua Anthony (283 Bowen Terrace, New Farm, Brisbane, Qld 4005, Australia), *b* 1944; *ed* Queens' Coll, Camb (BA), — Sarah Brand, *b* 1947: *m* 1971, as his 2nd wife, Antony Martin Donald Seth-Smith, late Kenya Regt, of Half-a-Hill, PO Box 24818, Nairobi, Kenya, and has issue living, Tana *b* 1977. —— Philip Brand, MC (Manor Farm House, Adlestrop, Moreton-in-Marsh, Glos GL56 0YW), *b* 1919; *ed* Eton, and Magdalen Coll, Oxford; Lt-Col Royal Dragoons (ret); 1939-45 War (MC): *m* 1955, Caroline Mary, yr da of late Sir John Henry Burder, of Swinbrook Manor, Burford, Oxon, and has issue living, Mark Philip (182 Holland Rd, W14 8AH), *b* 1956, — Nicola, *b* 1957: *m* 1986, Terence Edward Stratton, of Lower Farm, Gt Wolford, Shipston-on-Stour, Warwicks, and has issue living, Edward Albert *b* 1988, George Frederick *b* 1991. —— John Anthony (Court of Hill, Ludlow, Shropshire), *b* 1921; *ed* Eton; 1939-45 War as Lieut RNVR: *m* 1953, Helen Mary, 2nd da of late Charles Wakefield Christie-Miller, of Swyncombe House, Henley-on-Thames, and has issue living, Samuel John, *b* 1956, — Lucy Anne, *b* 1954: *m* 1993, David William Aspin, of 65 Eaton Sq, SW1, son of G. C. Aspin, of Hythe, Kent.

Grandchildren of late Maj Hon Charles Brand, 4th son of 1st Viscount:—
Issue of late Lieut-Col John Charles Brand, DSO, MC, *b* 1885, *d* 1929: *m* 1916, Lady Rosabelle Millicent, who *d* 1956, da of 5th Earl of Rosslyn, and widow of David Cecil Bingham (*see* E Lucan, colls):—
Michael Charles BRAND, *b* 1925; European War 1943-5 as Lieut Coldstream Guards (wounded): *m* 1953, Hon Laura Caroline Beatrice Smith, da of 3rd Viscount Hambleden, and has issue living, Charles David William, *b* 1954: *m* 1st, 1985, Kirsten Margaret, da of late John Baillie Hamilton Leckie, of Gerrards Cross, Bucks; 2ndly, 1992, Hon Virginia Leslie Bonham Carter, 2nd da of Baron Bonham-Carter (Life Baron), and has issue living (by 1st *m*), Violet Laura *b* 1992, — Charlotte Katharine *b* 1961, — Rosabelle Patricia, *b* 1965. *Residence* – 6 Howley Place, W2. —— Patience, *b* 1922: *m* 1945 (*m diss* 1955), Capt Ian Alexander Henderson, late R Horse Guards, who *d* 1968 (*see* B Faringdon, colls). *Residence* – Oxleaze Farm, Uffington, Berks.
Issue of late Ruth Brand, *b* 1882, *d* 1967: *m* 1911, 2nd Baron Monk Bretton, who *d* 1933 (see that title).

Grandchildren of late Evelyn Brand (*m* 1916, Sir James Crerar, KCSI, CIE, ICS), yst da of late Maj Hon Charles Brand (ante):—

Issue of late David James Crerar, late Fl Lieut RAFVR, *b* 1922, *d* 1974: *m* 1949, Eileen Ismay, who *d* 1974, eldest da of Henry Francis Chester Walsh, OBE, of Williamstown House, Castlebellingham, co Louth:—

Peter John CRERAR (Rathdaniel, Cellon, co Louth), *b* 1955: *m* 1982, Patricia Anne, da of John Alexander Kennedy, of 33 The Peninsula, Yamba, NSW, Australia, and has issue living, James Henry Alexander, *b* 1988, — Marnie Eileen, *b* 1984, — Eileen, *b* 1991. —— Rory James (21 Springfield Rd, Templeogue, Dublin), *b* 1958: *m* 1983, Margaret Mary, da of late Thomas Paul Marsh, of Glebe House, Stackallen, Navan, co Meath, and has issue living, David James, *b* 1987, — Carla Catherine, *b* 1988. —— Jonathan David, *b* 1963. —— Catherine, *b* 1953: *m* 1978, Edward Anthony Boland, of 33 Grantchester Rd, Cambridge CB3 9ED.

Issue of late Elizabeth Jean Crerar, *b* 1918, *d* 1981: *m* 1946, Sir Hugh Evelyn Lockhart-Mummery, KCVO, who *d* 1988:—

Christopher John LOCKHART-MUMMERY (78 Lansdowne Rd, W11 2SL), *b* 1947; *ed* Stowe, and Trin Coll, Camb (BA); Bar Inner Temple 1971, QC 1986, Recorder of the Crown Court, Bencher Inner Temple: *m* 1st, 1971 (*m diss* 1992), Hon (Elizabeth) Rosamund Elles, da of Neil Moncrieff Elles, by his wife Baroness Elles; 2ndly, 1993, Mrs (Mary) Lou Putley, and has issue living (by 1st *m*), Edward, *b* 1975, — Clare, *b* 1973, — Alice, *b* 1980.

PREDECESSORS – (1) *Hon* HENRY BOUVERIE WILLIAM BRAND, GCB, PC, 2nd son of 21st Baron Dacre, *b* 1814; Speaker of House of Commons 1872-84; *cr Viscount Hampden*, of Glynde, co Sussex 1884 (peerage of UK); *s* his elder brother as 23rd Baron Dacre 1890: *m* 1838, Eliza, da of Gen Robert Ellice; *d* 1892; *s* by his el son (2) HENRY ROBERT, GCMG, 2nd Viscount, *b* 1841; Gov of NSW 1895-99: *m* 1st, 1864, Victoria, who *d* 1865, da of M Jean Sylvain Van de Weyer; 2ndly, 1868, Susan Henrietta, who *d* 1909, da of late Lord George Henry Cavendish, MP (D Devonshire); *d* 1906; *s* by his el son (3) THOMAS WALTER, GCVO, KCB, CMG, 3rd Viscount; *b* 1869; a Lord in Waiting to HM 1924-36: *m* 1899, Lady Katharine Mary Montagu-Douglas-Scott, who *d* 1951, da of 6th Duke of Buccleuch; *d* 1958; *s* by his el son (4) THOMAS HENRY, CMG, 4th Viscount, *b* 1900: *m* 1923, Leila Emily, da of late Lt-Col Frank Evelyn Seely (Seely, Bt Colls), *d* 1965, when the Barony of Dacre fell into abeyance (*see* Bs Dacre); *s* in the Viscountcy by his brother (5) DAVID FRANCIS, 5th Viscount; *b* 1902: *m* 1936, Hon Imogen Alice Rhys, da of 7th Baron Dynevor; *d* 1975; *s* by his son (6) ANTHONY DAVID, 6th Viscount and present peer.

HAMPTON, BARON (Pakington) (Baron UK 1874, Bt UK 1846)
(Name pronounced "Packington")

Valour equals strength

RICHARD HUMPHREY RUSSELL PAKINGTON, 6th Baron, and 6th Baronet; *b* 25 May 1925; *s* 1974; *ed* Eton, and Balliol Coll, Oxford; served RNVR 1944-47: *m* 1958, Jane Elizabeth Farquharson, da of late Thomas Frank Arnott, OBE, TD, MB, ChB, and has issue.

Arms – Per chevron sable and argent, in chief three mullets pierced or, in base as many garbs gules. **Crest** – A demi-hare azure charged on the shoulder with a quatrefoil argent. **Supporters** – *Dexter*, an elephant or, charged on the shoulder with a mullet pierced sable; *sinister*, a talbot argent, charged as the dexter.

SON LIVING

Hon JOHN HUMPHREY ARNOTT, *b* 24 Dec 1964; *ed* Shrewsbury, and Exeter Coll of Art and Design (BA).

DAUGHTERS LIVING

Hon Catharine Mary Grace, *b* 1960; *ed* Bristol Univ.
Hon Sarah Jane Auriol, *b* 1961; *ed* Bedford Coll, London (BA).

SISTERS LIVING

Hon Hilary Evelyn Spicer, *b* 1914: *m* 1938, David John Vaughan Bevan, TD, BA, who *d* 1986, of Kingsland, Bledington, Oxford, OX7 6UX, and has issue living, Timothy David Vaughan (c/o Lloyds Bank, 36 Cheriton High St, Folkestone, Kent CT19 4EH), *b* 1939; Brig LI: *m* 1st, 1964 (*m diss* 1988), Jill, el da of Leslie Murrell, of Harpford, nr Sidmouth, Devon; 2ndly, 1988, Penelope Edyth, da of Douglas Lavers, of Kohimarama, Auckland, NZ, and has issue living (by 1st *m*), Simon David Vaughan *b* 1970, Charlotte Hilary Vaughan *b* 1968, — Nicholas Vaughan, *b* 1942; Headmaster Shiplake Coll, Henley-on-Thames, Oxon: *m* 1st, 1967 (*m diss* 1977), Penelope Jane, da of Col D. H. Tildesley, of Tettenhall Court, Tettenhall, Staffs; 2ndly, 1978, Ann Marie, el da of John Timothy O'Connor, of Leongatha, Vic, Aust, and has issue living, (by 1st *m*) Edward Duder Vaughan *b* 1971, Katherine Jane Vaughan *b* 1969, (by 2nd *m*) Oliver David *b* 1979, Emily Grace *b* 1982, — Richard Vaughan (1145 17th Av E, Seattle, USA), *b* 1943: *m* 1st, 1972 (*m diss* 1980), Christine, el da of late B. G. Harte, of Bromley Kent; 2ndly, 1991, Lesley Burvill-Holmes, and has issue living (by 2nd *m*), Nicholas *b* 1992, — Jennifer Jill Vaughan, *b* 1946: *m* 1975, Gerald Leslie Hayward, and has issue living, James Fulton *b* 1979, Thomas Seaborne *b* 1980, — Margaret Hilary Vaughan, *b* 1953: *m* 1987, Aidan John Kelly, and has issue living, David John *b* 1988, Peter Richard *b* 1990.
Hon Anne, *b* 1919; *ed* Somerville Coll, Oxford.
Hon Auriol Mary Grace, *b* 1922; SRN, SCM.

PREDECESSORS – (1) JOHN SOMERSET Russell, GCB, PC, son of late William Russell, of Powick, by Elizabeth, el da of Sir Herbert Perrott Pakington, 7th Bt; *b* 1799; *s* in 1830 to the estates of his uncle Sir John Pakington, 8th and last Bt, and assumed the surname of Pakington in lieu of his patronymic; sat as MP for Droitwich (*C*) 1837-74; Sec of State for Colonies 1852, First Lord of the Admiralty 1858-9 and 1866-7, Sec of State for War 1867-8, and First Civil Ser Commr 1876-80; *cr a Baronet* 1846, and *Baron Hampton*, of Hampton Lovett and of Westwood, co Worcester (peerage of United Kingdom) 1874: *m* 1st, 1822, Mary, who *d* 1843, da of Moreton Aglionby Slaney; 2ndly, 1844, Augusta Anne, who *d* 1848, da of late Rt Rev George Murray, DD, Bishop of Rochester; 3rdly, 1851, Augusta, da of Thomas Champion de Crespigny, and widow of Col Henry Davies, MP of Elmley Park, Worcester; *d* April 1880; *s* by his son (2) JOHN SLANEY, 2nd Baron, *b* 1826: *m* 1849, Lady Diana Boyle, who *d* 1877, da of 4th Earl of Glasgow; *d* 1893; *s* by his half-brother (3) HERBERT PERROTT MURRAY, 3rd Baron, *b* 1848: *m* 1877, Evelyn Nina Frances, who *d* 1904, da of Sir George Baker, 3rd Bt; *d* 1906; *s* by his son (4) HERBERT STUART CBE, DSO, 4th Baron, *b* 1883; Maj Worcestershire Yeo, *d* 1962; *s* by his brother (5) HUMPHREY ARTHUR, OBE, FRIBA, 5th Baron, *b* 1888; Cdr RN: *m* 1913, Grace Dykes, who *d* 1959, da of Rt Hon Sir Albert Spicer, 1st Bt; *d* 1974; *s* by his son (6) RICHARD HUMPHREY RUSSELL, 6th Baron and present peer.

HAMWEE, BARONESS (Hamwee) (Life Baroness 1991)

SALLY RACHEL HAMWEE, da of late Alec Hamwee, by his wife Dorothy (*née* Saunders); *b* 12 Jan 1947; *ed* Manchester High Sch for Girls, and Girton Coll, Camb (MA); Solicitor; Councillor London Borough of Richmond upon Thames, Chm London Planning Advisory Cttee, and Vice-Chm ALDC (Liberal Democrat Councillors' Assocn); *cr Baroness Hamwee*, of Richmond upon Thames, in the London Borough of Richmond upon Thames (Life Baroness) 1991.
Residence – 101a Mortlake High St, SW14 8HQ.

HANKEY, BARON (Hankey) (Baron UK 1939)

ROBERT MAURICE ALERS HANKEY, KCMG, KCVO, 2nd Baron; *b* 4 July 1905; *s* 1963; *ed* Rugby, and New Coll, Oxford (BA 1926); HM's Chargé d'Affaires in Spain 1949-51, Min to Hungary 1951-53, and Ambassador to Sweden 1954-60, UK Delegate to Organization for European Econimic Co-operation, Paris, 1960, and to Organization for Economic Co-operation and Development 1961-65; Vice-Pres of European Inst of Business Admin, Fontainebleau 1962-80; a Member of Internat Council of United World Colls, and of Council of Internat Baccalaureati Orgn, Geneva 1966-78; a Dir of Alliance Building Soc 1970-83; Pres of Anglo Swedish Soc 1970-78; Grand Cross of Order of the North Star of Sweden; CMG 1947; KCMG 1955, KCVO 1956: *m* 1st, 1930, Frances Bevyl, who *d* 1957, da of late Walter Erskine Stuart-Menteth (Stuart-Menteth, Bt, colls); 2ndly, 1962, Joanna Riddall, who *d* 1991, da of late Rev James Johnstone Wright; 3rdly, 1992, Mrs Stephanie S. Langley, da of late Brig Percy Paulet King, and of Mrs Kenneth Ford, of W Wittering, and has issue by 1st *m*.

Arms – Per pale azure and gules, a wolf salient erminos vulned on the shoulder of the second, a bordure wavy of the third. **Crest** – A wolf's head erased at the neck erminois, gorged with a collar wavy azure.
Residence – Hethe House, Cowden, Edenbridge, Kent TN8 7DZ. *Club* – Royal Commonwealth Society.

SONS LIVING (By 1st marriage)

Hon DONALD ROBIN ALERS (53 Woodfield Av, SW16), *b* 12 June 1938; *ed* Rugby, and Univ Coll, London (Dip Arch), RIBA: *m* 1st, 1963 (*m diss* 1974), Margaretha, yr da of Cand Jur H. Thorndahl of Copenhagen; 2ndly, 1974, Eileen Désirée, yr da of late Maj-Gen Stuart Hedley Molesworth Battye, CB, Fensacre House, Ascot, Berks, and has issue living (by 2nd *m*), Fiona Bevyl, *b* 1975, — Beatrice Eileen, *b* 1978.
Hon Alexander Maurice Alers (5 Rowan Lane, Woodley Park, Skelmersdale, Lancs), *b* 1947; *ed* Rugby, Trin Coll, Camb, and Mass Inst of Tech (PhD): *m* 1970, Deborah, da of late Myron Benson, of 141 Greenwood St, Newton, Mass, USA.

DAUGHTERS LIVING (By 1st marriage)

Hon Juliet Alers, *b* 1931: *m* 1957, Peter John Wrensted Alchin, of Parkstone, Clenches Farm Rd, Sevenoaks, and has issue living, Gordon David, *b* 1961, — Vanessa Frances, *b* 1962, — Chloe Sylvia, *b* 1965.
Hon Adele Bevyl Alers, *b* 1933: *m* 1964 (*m diss* 1987), Dr Erik Emil Anggård, of Linnégatan 96, Stockholm, Sweden, and has issue living, Jon Mikael, *b* 1967, — Eola Anni, *b* 1965, — Irene Malin Adele, *b* 1970. *Residence* – Banergatan 77, 115 53 Stockholm, Sweden.

BROTHERS LIVING

Hon Christopher Alers, OBE (New Cottage, French Street, nr Westerham, Kent), *b* 1911; *ed* Rugby, Oxford (BA honours in History 1932, MA 1947), and London (BSc Eng honours 1939) Univs; Prin Min of Overseas Development 1964-72; 1939-45 War s Major RM; OBE (Civil) 1958: *m* 1st, 1945 (*m diss* 1957), Prudence May, da of Keith Brodribb, of Frodsley, Tasmania; 2ndly, 1958, Helen Christine, yr da of late A. J. Cassavetti, of Puckshott, Oxted Surrey, and has issue living, (by 2nd *m*) Rupert Christopher Alers, *b* 1960: *m* 1984, Jane Elizabeth, eldest da of late Ian Bruce and of Mrs Alan Pote, of The Priory, Rothwell, Northants, — (by 1st *m*) Felicity Laura Alers, *b* 1947: *m* 1969, Henry R. C. Edgell, of Dennistoun, Bothwell, Tasmania 7030, son of Geoffrey Edgell, CBE, and has issue living, Thomas *b* 1971, Edward *b* 1981, Chloe *b* 1975.
Hon Henry Arthur Alers, CMG, CVO (Hosey Croft, Westerham, Kent; United Univ Club), *b* 1914; *ed* Rugby, and New Coll, Oxford; Ambassador to Panama 1966-69; Under Sec, FCO 1969-74; CVO 1959, CMG 1960: *m* 1941, Vronwy, only da of late Rev T. F. Fisher, and has issue living, Christopher Ceri Alers (Route du Gros Chene, Argonay, 74000 France), *b* 1944: *m* 1st, 1970, Eleanor, only da of C. J. C. Beckett, of Danemore House, S Godstone, Surrey; 2ndly, 1980, Annick, only da of Robert Perrucon, of Annecy, and has issue living (by 2nd *m*), Jonathan Ceri Alers *b* 1980, Jason Henry Alers *b* 1989, Deborah Marie Alers *b* 1982, — Maurice Peregrine Alers (The Green, Northmoor, Oxon), *b* 1945: *m* 1970, Juliet, da of Antony Ross Moore, CMG, and has issue living, Antony Thomas *b* 1977, David Henry *b* 1988, Rose Vronwy *b* 1975, — Peter John Alers (39 Chemin des Creux de Leurres, 74600 Quintal, Seynod, France), *b* 1951: *m* 1981, Margaret Catharine, only da of John D. Walker, of 9 Wilbraham Pl, SW1, and has issue living, Robert *b* 198-, William Walker Alers *b* 1991, Katharine Claire Alers *b* 1987, — Veronica Vronwy Alers, *b* 1957: *m* 1980, Sqdn Ldr (ret) Timothy C. M. Newman, RAF, of Wester Golford, Moyness, Nairn, elder son of late W/Cdr A. T. Newman, of Honeycritch Cottage, Froxfield, Hants, and has issue living, Thomas Robert Minôt *b* 1990, Elena Vronwy Mararet *b* 1987.

SISTER LIVING

Hon Ursula Helen Alers (*Hon Lady Benn*), *b* 1909: *m* 1929, Sir John Andrews Benn, 3rd Bt, Surrey, who *d* 1984. *Residence* – 15 The Waldrons, Oast Rd, Hurst Green, Oxted, Surrey RH8 9DY.

PREDECESSOR – (1) *Sir* MAURICE PASCAL ALERS Hankey, GCB, GCMG, GCVO, PC, FRS, LLD son of late Robert Alers Hankey of Warcowie, S Australia and Brighton (whose grandfather, William Alers, of City of London, was authorized to assume the surname of Hankey in addition to Alers and to bear the arms of Hankey only with difference by Roy Licence 1815); *b* 1877; Col RMA; Sec, War Cabinet 1916-7, and Imperial War Cabinet 1917-18, British Sec to Peace Conference 1919, Sec to Cabinet 1920-38, Sec to Imperial Conferences 1921, 1923, 1926, 1930, and 1937, Sec-Gen Hague Conference 1929-30, London Naval Conference 1930, and Lausanne Reparation Conference 1932, Clerk to PC 1923-38; Min without Portfolio in War Cabinet 1939-40; Chancellor of Duchy of Lancaster 1940-41, Paymaster-Gen 1941-2, and Chm of Technical Personnel Cttee 1941-52; *cr Baron Hankey*, of The Chart, Surrey (peerage of UK), and a PC 1939: *m* 1903, Adeline, who *d* 1979, da of late Abraham de Smidt, Surveyor-Gen of Cape Colony; *d* 1963; *s* by his el son (2) ROBERT MAURICE ALERS, 2nd Baron and present peer.

HANSON, BARON (Hanson) (Life Baron 1983)

JAMES EDWARD HANSON, son of late Robert Hanson, CBE, of Huddersfield, Yorks, by his wife Louisa Anne (Cis) *née* Rodgers; *b* 20 Jan 1922; Hon LLD Leeds; Hon DBA Huddersfield; FRSA; CI Mgt; War Service 1939-46; Chm Hanson plc since 1965; Hanson Transport Group Ltd since 1965; Freeman of City of London 1964; Liveryman Worshipful Co of Saddlers 1964; Member of Court of Patrons, Royal Coll of Surgeons of England 1991;Trustee Hanson Fellowship of Surgery, Oxford Univ; Fell Cancer Research Campaign; *cr* Kt 1976, and *Baron Hanson*, of Edgerton, co West Yorkshire (Life Baron) 1983: *m* 1959, Geraldine Kaelin, and has issue.

Arms – Vert in fess point a rose Argent barbed and seeded proper between six like roses three and three in pale. **Crest** – On a wreath Or and Vert A demi Chestnut horse proper charged on the shoulder with a rose Argent barbed seeded slipped and leaved proper. **Supporters** – *Dexter*, a bulldog in trian aspect with a Viking helmet of the seventh century gilded and verde antico on his head proper, and *sinister*, an American Bald Eagle also proper. **Motto** – Prima Peto.
Residence – 1 Grosvenor Pl, SW1X 7JH. *Club* – Brooks's, Huddersfield Borough, The Brook (NY), Toronto.

SONS LIVING

Hon Robert William (White's Club), *b* 1960; *ed* Eton, and St Peter's Coll, Oxford.
Hon (John) Brook (does not use courtesy title) (Brooks's Club), *b* 1964; *ed* Pangbourne.

HANWORTH, VISCOUNT (Pollock) (Viscount UK 1936, Bt UK 1922)

DAVID BERTRAM POLLOCK, 2nd Viscount, and 2nd Baronet; *b* 1st Aug 1916; *s* 1936; *ed* Wellington Coll, and Trin Coll, Camb (BA 1939); Bar Inner Temple 1958; Lt-Col (ret) RE; CEng; MIMechE; FIEE, FIQA, FRPS, and author of books on colour photography: *m* 1940, Isolda Rosamond, da of late Geoffrey Parker (*see* E Macclesfield, colls), and has issue.

Arms – Azure, three fleurs-de-lis within a bordure engrailed or, on a chief ermine two portcullises of the second. **Crest** – A boar passant quarterly or and vert, pierced through the sinister shoulder with an arrow proper. **Supporters** – (hereditary), — On either side a bear or, muzzled, collared, and chain sable.
Residence – Quoin Cottage, Shamley Green, Guildford, Surrey GU5 0UJ.

Boldly and strenuously

SONS LIVING

Hon DAVID STEPHEN GEOFFREY, *b* 16 Feb 1946; *ed* Wellington Coll, Guildford Tech Coll, and Sussex Univ; Lecturer, Econometrics, London Univ: *m* 1968, Elizabeth, da of Lawrence Vambe, of Harare, Zimbabwe, and has issue living, Cecile Abigail Shona, *b* 1971, — Charlotte Anne Catherine, *b* 1973.
Hon Richard Charles Standish, *b* 1951; *ed* Wellington Coll, and Trin Coll, Camb; Maj R Yeo T & AVR; TD (1986): *m* 1982, Annette Louise, da of Peter Lockhart, of Daisy Cottage, Studham, Common Lane, nr Dunstable, Beds, and has issue living, Harold William Charles, *b* 1988, — Frederick Thomas Charles, *b* (twin) 1988. *Residence* – 135 Thorleigh Rd, SW12 8JX.

DAUGHTER LIVING

Hon Gillian Isolda Josephine, *b* 1944: *m* 1963, Timothy von Weber Sarson, of 8 Gatcombe Rd, N19 4PT, and has issue living, Cosmo Harold Antony, *b* 1971, — Alexander, *b* 1977, — Emma Isolda, *b* 1964: *m* 1984, Hugh Davies, only son of Lt-Col R.

M. W. Davies, MC, of Tyn Rhos, Golan, Garn Dolbenmaen, Caernarvonshire, and has issue living, Bryn *b* 19—, Holly *b* 19—, — Hester, *b* 1975.

PREDECESSOR – (1) *Rt Hon Sir* ERNEST MURRAY Pollock, KBE, PC, son of late George Frederick Pollock (Pollock, Bt colls): *b* 1861; was Solicitor-Gen 1919-22, and Master of the Rolls 1923-35; MP for Warwick and Leamington (C) 1910-18, and for Warwick and Leamington Div of Warwickshire 1918-23; *cr a* Baronet 1922, *Baron Hanworth* of Hanworth, co Middlesex (peerage of United Kingdom) 1926, and *Viscount Hanworth*, of Hanworth, co Middlesex (peerage of United Kingdom) 1936: *m* 1887, Laura Helen, who *d* 1954, el da of Sir Thomas Salt, 1st Bt (*cr* 1899); *d* 1936; *s* by his grandson (2) DAVID BERTRAM (only son of late Capt Charles Thomas Anderdon Pollock) (only son of 1st Viscount), *ka* 1918, 2nd Viscount and present peer, also Baron Hanworth.

HARBERTON, VISCOUNT (Pomeroy) (Viscount I 1791)

Fortune is the companion of valour

THOMAS DE VAUTORT POMEROY, 10th Viscount; *b* 19 Oct 1910; *s* 1980; *ed* Eton; Lt-Col (ret) RAOC; formerly Lieut Welsh Guards: *m* 1st, 1939 (*m diss* 1946), Nancy Ellen, only da of late C. A. Penoyer, of San Francisco; 2ndly, 1950, Pauline Stafford, who *d* 1971, da of late Wilfred Sydney Baker, of Stoke, Plymouth; 3rdly, 1978, Wilhelmine (Vilma), da of Heinrich Wahl, and widow of Sir Alfred Butt, 1st Bt.

𝔄rms – Or, a lion rampant gules, armed and langued azure, holding between the fore paws an apple proper. 𝔠rest – A lion rampant as in the arms. 𝔖upporters – Two wolves, the *dexter* proper, the *sinister* argent; both collared and chained or.
Club - Cavalry and Guards'.

BROTHER LIVING

Hon ROBERT WILLIAM, *b* 29 Feb 1916; *ed* Eton; Maj (ret) Welsh Guards: *m* 1953, Winifred Anne, 2nd da of late Sir Arthur Colegate, MP (Worsley, Bt), and has issue living, Henry Robert (42 Stowe Rd, W12), *b* 1958: *m* 1990, Caroline Mary, da of Jeremy Grindle, of Viking Cottage, Bosham, W Sussex, — Richard Arthur, *b* 1960: *m* 1987, Helena Claire, yr da of Andrew Watt Drysdale, of Pitcombe Farm House, Bruton, Somerset (*see* Newman, Bt, *cr* 1836, 1980 Edn), and has issue living, Tallulah *b* 1992. *Residence* - Rockfield House, Nunney, nr Frome, Somerset. *Club* – Bembridge Sailing.

SISTER LIVING

Hon Rosamond Mary (The Cottage in Swains Lane, Bembridge, Isle of Wight; Bembridge Sailing Club) (twin), *b* 1916; 1944-45 War in France and Germany with ATS.

COLLATERAL BRANCHES LIVING

Grandchildren of late John Arthur Pomeroy, el son of Rev Hon Arthur William Pomeroy, 2nd son of 4th Viscount:—
   Issue of late Major Francis Knox Pomeroy, *b* 1876, *d* 1962: *m* 1906, Helen, who *d* 1955, da of Arthur Cinnamond, formerly of St Helens, Belfast:—
Arthur John Cinnamond, VRD (Butternut Farm, River Rd, Cantley, P.Q., Canada; Naval and Military Club), *b* 1907; *ed* Rugby; Com (ret) RNVR; despatches thrice: *m* 1962, Rowena Mary Vesey, da of late Vice-Adm Reginald Vesey Holt, CB, DSO, MVO, and has had issue, Hugh Reginald Arthur, *b* 1963, *d* as the result of an accident 1986, — John Francis Vesey, *b* 1965.
—— Helen Mary Ursula (St George's Nursing Home, Cobham, Surrey), *b* 1909; late Junior Com ATS: *m* 1943, Archibald Richard Sanford Hodgson, DSC, late Lt-Cdr RNVR, who *d* 1990, and has issue living, Nicholas Pomeroy Sanford (The Cottage, Compton, Guildford), *b* 1945; *ed* Eton: *m* 1974, Melissa, yr da of Donald B. Prouty, of 32 Foster St, Littleton, Mass, USA, and has issue living, Christopher Prouty Sanford *b* 1980, Geoffrey Peter Sanford *b* 1986, Alexandra Louise Pomeroy *b* 1978, Olivia Cinnamond *b* 1983, — Helen Rose Sanford, *b* 1947: *m* 1979, Capt Ian Cameron de Sales La Terrière, of Dunalastair, Perthshire, and has issue living, Hugh William *b* 1982, Robert Duncan *b* 1984, — Ursula Virginia Sanford, *b* 1952.

   Grandchildren of late Maj Francis Knox Pomeroy (ante):—
   Issue of late (Jocelyn Francis) Brian Pomeroy, *b* 1912, *d* 1991: *m* 1940, Lucy Margaret, who *d* 1993, da of Robert Hayne, of Osmington, Weymouth:—
Thomas (Avon House, Hartley Wintney, Hants), *b* 1941; *ed* Eton, and Trin Coll, Camb (MA): *m* 1967, Belinda Jane, da of late Maj-Gen John Sheffield, CB, CBE, of 11 Pitt St, W8, and has issue living, Helen Emily Jane, *b* 1971, — Rosalind Lucy, *b* 1973, — Laura Patience, *b* (twin) 1973. —— Simon Robert Valentine (The Old Vicarage, Winscombe, Avon), *b* 1943; *ed* Eton, and Keble Coll, Oxford (BA); FCA: *m* 1972, Ursula Jean, yr da of late John Stephen Barclay, and has issue living, Patricia Margaret (Daisy), *b* 1974, — Elizabeth Frances Mary, *b* 1976, — Catherine Harriet, *b* 1981. —— (Frances) Louise (*Lady Heathcoat-Amory*), *b* 1947: *m* 1972, Sir Ian Heathcoat-Amory, 6th Bt, of Calverleigh Court, Tiverton, Devon, and has issue.

   Grandsons of late George Pomeroy Arthur COLLEY (infra):—
   Issue of late George Dudley Pomeroy COLLEY, *b* 1911, *d* 1959: *m* 1947, Ann Patricia (The Mill House, Kilmatead, Clondalkin, co Dublin), da of late William Burns:—
Finlay FitzGeorge, *b* 1948. —— Anthony William Pomeroy (64 Pembroke Rd, Dublin 4), *b* 1951: *m* 1973, Mary, da of Hugh Kelly, and has issue living, Dudley Hugh Pomeroy, *b* 1975, — Jeffrey Andrew Pomeroy, *b* 1978, — Amy Alexandra Pomeroy, *b* 1984.

   Granddaughters of late Henry FitzGeorge COLLEY, son of late Hon George Francis COLLEY (who assumed the name of Colley in lieu of his patronymic 1830), 3rd son of 4th Viscount:—

Issue of late George Pomeroy Arthur COLLEY, *b* 1866, *d* 1933: *m* 1909, Edith Maude Olivia, who *d* 1975, el da of late Col Henry Thomas Finlay, DL (V Bangor, colls):—
Norah Helen Pomeroy, *b* 1910: *m* 1940, George Gilbert Butler (*see* B Dunboyne, colls). *Residence* – Scatorish, Bennets Bridge, co Kilkenny. —— Veronica Maud Pomeroy (40 Newberry Rd, Weymouth, Dorset), *b* 1913: *m* 1st, 1935 (*m diss* 1968), Maj Jeffry Arden Patrick Lefroy, MBE, Yorkshire Dragoons, who *d* 1985; 2ndly, 1972, Lt-Col Derrick Arthur Hall-Dare, OBE, who *d* 1985, and has issue living, (by 1st *m*) Jeffry George (Carrigglas Manor, Longford, Ireland), *b* 1936; Maj (ret) late R Irish Rangers: *m* 1964, Teresa Margaret, da of Henry Alwyn White, DL, of Orange Hill, Tanderagee, co Armagh, and has issue living, Jeffry Peter Langlois *b* 1965, Edward Christian Perceval *b* 1967, — Laetitia Mary (40 Ailesbury Lawn, Dundrum, Dublin, 14), *b* 1937. —— Valerie Edith Pomeroy, *b* 1915: *m* 1947, William Patrick Hone, MC, and has issue living, Christopher Patrick George, *b* 1949: *m* 1981, Mary Josephine, da of Raymond Jennings, of Riversdale House, Craughwell, co Galway. *Residence* – Kilmatead, Clondalkin, co Dublin. —— Rosemary Pomeroy *b* 1916: *m* 1947, Henry Nicholas Crocker, who *d* 1982, and has issue living, Henry Alistair Nicholas (22 Freeland Place, Bristol), *b* 1949: *m* 1975, Christina, da of William McMillan, of 70 Eckford St, Glasgow, and has issue living, Ursula Margaret Rosemary *b* 1985, Roberta Harriet *b* 1988, — Roderic John (138 Marlborough Av, Hull), *b* 1954: *m* 1980, Irena, da of Dr Jerzy Kuroski, of Hull, and has issue living, Alexandra Ruth *b* 1982, — Virginia Helen, *b* 1948: *m* 1971, Sqdn Ldr James Edward Malcolm Mustard, DFC, RAF (ret), of The Butts, Middle Woodford, Wilts, and has issue living, James Edmond Alexander *b* 1974, Eleanor Clare *b* 1981. *Residence* – 3 Redcliffe Close, Redcliffe Bay, Portishead, Bristol.

Issue of late Rev William Wingfield Colley, *b* 1868, *d* 1947: *m* 1915, Helen Isabel who *d* 1974, da of late Rev Duncan John Brownlow:—
Esmé Florence Helen, *b* 1920. *Residence* – Carbery, 12 Albany Court, Ballybrack, co Dublin.

PREDECESSORS – **(1)** ARTHUR Pomeroy, son of late Rev John Pomeroy; *b* 1723; was MP for co Kildare 1761-83; *cr Baron Harberton* of Carbery (peerage of Ireland) 1783, and *Viscount Harberton* (peerage of Ireland) 1791: *m* 1747, Mary, da of Henry Colley, of Castle Carbery, co Kildare; *d* 1798; *s* by his el son **(2)** HENRY, 2nd Viscount; *b* 1749: *m* 1778, Mary, who *d* 1823, da of Nicholas Grady, of Grange, co Limerick; *d* 1829; *s* by his brother **(3)** ARTHUR JAMES, 3rd Viscount; *b* 1753: *m* 1800, Elizabeth, who *d* 1862, da of Thomas Kinsley; *d* 1832; *s* by his brother **(4)** *Rev* JOHN, 4th Viscount; *b* 1758; Preb of St Patrick's Cathedral, Dublin 1783-1822: *m* 1785, Esther, who *d* 1840, da of James Spencer; *d* 1833; *s* by his son **(5)** JOHN JAMES, 5th Viscount; *b* 1790: *m* 1822, Caroline, who *d* 1886, da of Rev Sir John Robinson, 1st Bt (*cr* 1819); *d* 1862; *s* by his son **(6)** JAMES SPENCER, 6th Viscount; *b* 1836: *m* 1861, Florence Wallace, who *d* 1911, da of William Wallace Legge, DL, of Malone House, co Antrim; *d* 1912; *s* by his el son **(7)** ERNEST ARTHUR GEORGE, 7th Viscount; *b* 1867; sometime Lieut 20th Hussars and Capt Roy Dublin Fusiliers; S Africa 1900 (Queen's medal): *m* 1932, Fairlie, who *d* 1945, da of late Col Charles D'Oyly Harmar, of Ramridge, Andover; *d* 1944; *s* by his brother **(8)** RALPH LEGGE, OBE, 8th Viscount; *b* 1869; Major Reserve of Officers (Dragoon Guards); S African War 1899-1902 (severely wounded) 1914-18 War: *m* 1907, Mary Katherine, who *d* 1971, da of Arthur Leatham, formerly of Smallfield Place, Surrey; *d* 1956; *s* by his son **(9)** HENRY RALPH MARTYN, 9th Viscount, *d* 1980; *s* by his brother **(10)** THOMAS DE VAUTORT, 10th Viscount and present peer; also Baron Harberton.

HARCOURT, VISCOUNTCY OF (Harcourt) (Extinct 1979)

DAUGHTERS LIVING OF SECOND VISCOUNT

Hon (Elizabeth) Ann, *b* 1932: *m* 1954, Crispin Gascoigne (The Manor House, Stanton Harcourt, Oxon), only son of late Maj-Gen Sir Julian Alvery Gascoigne, KCMG, KCVO, CB, DSO (*see* Newman Bt; *cr* 1836, 1980 Edn), and has issue living, William Harcourt Crisp, *b* 1955: *m* 1980, Susan Alexandra, da of Aubrey Greville Williams, of Maypole Farmhouse, E Grimstead, Salisbury, Wilts, and has issue living, Julian Aubrey Harcourt *b* 1984, Frederick William *b* 1986, Ralph Edward *b* 1989, — Elizabeth Laura, *b* 1958: *m* 1986, Peter Nicholas Offord, eldest son of late L. R. Offord, of Winchmore Hill, N21, and has issue living, Nicholas Alvery Harcourt *b* 1990, Venetia Vernon *b* 1988, Cecily Katherine *b* 1992, — Mary Ann, *b* 1961: *m* 1986, Matthew Charles Louis Crosby, only son of Dr Jack Lionel Crosby, of Stanhope, co Durham, and has issue living, Miles William Southe *b* 1989, George Crispin Ivo *b* 1992.
Hon Penelope Mary, *b* 1933: *m* 1954, Capt Anthony David Motion, late 9th Queen's Roy Lancers, of Buckland, Irishtown, Northam, W Australia 6401, and has issue living, Stephen Anthony, *b* 1967, — and an adopted da, Georgina, *bapt* 1965.

HARDING OF PETHERTON, BARON (Harding) (Baron UK 1958)

JOHN CHARLES HARDING, 2nd Baron; *b* 12 Feb 1928; *s* 1989; *ed* Marlborough, and Worcester Coll, Oxford; Maj (ret) 11th Hussars; *m* 1966, Harriet, da of late Maj-Gen James Francis Hare, CB, DSO, and has issue.

Arms – Argent on a bend azure between two lions passant guardant gules as many kukris in saltire proper between two martlets or. **Crest** – Out of a mural crown gules a cubit arm in armour the hand gauntleted grasping a Field Marshal's baton in bend sinister proper. **Supporters** – *Dexter*, a Private of 1st Life Guards of early nineteenth century; *sinister*, a Somerset Light Infantryman of the late eighteenth century; both habited and accoutred proper.
Residence – Barrymore Farm House, Pict's Hill, Langport, Somerset TA10 9EZ.

SONS LIVING

Hon WILLIAM ALLAN JOHN, *b* 5 July 1969.
Hon David Richard John, *b* 1978.

DAUGHTER LIVING

Hon Diana Mary, *b* 1967.

PREDECESSOR – (1) *Field Marshal* ALLAN FRANCIS (JOHN) Harding, GCB, CBE, DSO, MC, son of late Francis E. Harding, of Compton Way, S Petherton, Som, *b* 1896; Field Marshal late Somerset LI, ADC Gen to HM King George VI 1950, and HM The Queen 1952-53; Hon Col N Somerset Yeo, Col 6th Queen Elizabeth's Own Gurkha Rifles 1951-61, Somerset LI 1953-59, SCLI 1959-60, and Life Guards 1957-64; GOC-in-C S Cmnd 1947-49, C-in-C Far East Land Forces 1949-51, and BAOR 1951-52, CIGS 1952-55, Gov and C-in-C of Cyprus 1955-57, Gold Stick to HM 1957-64; *cr Baron Harding of Petherton*, of Nether Compton, co Dorset (peerage of UK) 1958: *m* 1927, Mary Gertrude Mabel, who *d* 1983, da of late Joseph Wilson Rooke, JP, of Knutsford, Cheshire; *d* 1989; *s* by his only son **(2)** JOHN CHARLES, 2nd Baron, and present peer.

HARDING-DAVIES, BARONESS (Harding-Davies)

WIDOW LIVING OF RT HON JOHN EMERSON HARDING HARDING-DAVIES, MBE, WHO WAS NOMINATED A LIFE BARON, BUT WHO DIED BEFORE THE PEERAGE WAS CREATED.

VERA GEORGINA (*Baroness Harding-Davies*), da of late George William Bates; raised to the rank of a Baron's widow 27 Feb 1980: *m* 1943, Rt Hon John Emerson Harding Harding-Davies, MBE, who assumed by deed poll 1979, the additional surname of Harding, and who was nominated a Life Baron on 16 June 1979, but *d* 4 July 1979, before the Peerage was *cr*.

SON LIVING (*Raised to the rank of a Baron's son* 1980)

Hon Francis William Harding DAVIES (PO Box 615, Don Mills, Ontario M3C 2T6, Canada), *b* 1946; *ed* Windlesham House Sch, Nautical Coll Pangbourne, and Strasbourg Univ; Pres ATV Music Gp, Canada, 1982-85, Pres TMP (The Music Publisher) since 1986: *m* 1972, Lynda Margaret Mae Squires, and has issue.

DAUGHTER LIVING (*Raised to the rank of a Baron's daughter* 1980)

Hon Rosamond Ann, *b* 1943: *m* 1968, Charles Marten Metherell.

HARDINGE, VISCOUNT (Hardinge) (Viscount UK 1846, Bt UK 1801)
(Name and Title pronounced "Harding")

CHARLES HENRY NICHOLAS HARDINGE, 6th Viscount and 8th Baronet; *b* 25 Aug 1956; *s* 1984; *ed* Upper Canada Coll, Trin Coll Sch, and McGill Univ; *s* his kinsman, Sir Robert Arnold Hardinge, 7th Bt, in his baronetcy, 1986: *m* 1985, Mrs Julie Therese Sillett, eldest da of Keith Sillett, of Sydney, Australia, and has issue.

Arms – Gules, on a chevron argent, fimbriated or, three escallops sable. **Crest** – A mitre gules, charged with a chevron, as in the arms. **Supporters** – On either side a lion proper, that on the dexter murally crowned, supporting a flag flowing to the dexter or, and that on the sinister crowned with an Eastern crown, supporting a flag flowing to the sinister or.
Residence – 12 Streathbourne Rd, SW17.

MENS ÆQUA REBUS IN ARDUIS
An equal mind in difficulties

DAUGHTERS LIVING

Hon Emilie Charlotte, *b* 1986. —— *Hon* Olivia Margaux, *b* 1989.

BROTHERS LIVING

Hon ANDREW HARTLAND, *b* 7 Jan 1960; *ed* The Gow Sch, and Trin Coll Sch: *m* 1990, Sophia Mary, only da of Capt (William) David (Armstrong) Bagnell, of East Worldham House, Alton, Hants (*see* E Wilton, 1953 Edn), and has issue living, Thomas Henry de Montarville, *b* 19 June 1993. *Residence* – The Garden Flat, 59 Redcliffe Gdns, SW10 9JJ.
Hon Maximillian Evelyn, *b* 1969.

HALF-SISTER LIVING

Hon Georgia Victoria, *b* 1984.

AUNTS LIVING (*Daughters of 4th Viscount*)

Hon Carolyn Mary Wynyard, *b* 1932: *m* 1954, John Arthington Worsley (RR2, Uxbridge, Ont, Canada) (*see* Worsley, Bt).
Hon Gay, *b* 1938: *m* 1963, Pierre Raymond, of Stage Coach Rd, Brome, Prov Quebec, Canada, and has issue living, a son, *b* 1965.

MOTHER LIVING

Zoe Ann, da of Hartland de Montarville Molson, OBE, of Montreal, Senator of Canada: *m* 1st, 1955 (*m diss* 1982), as his 1st wife, the 5th Viscount, who *d* 1984; 2ndly, 1983, Christopher Mark Henry Murray, of La Glinette, St Aubin, Jersey, CI (*see* Jerningham, Bt (ext), 1955 Edn).

WIDOW LIVING OF FIFTH VISCOUNT

Baroness FLORENCE ELISABETH VON OPPENHEIM, da of late Baron Harold von Oppenheim, of Cologne: *m* 1st, 1982, as his 2nd wife, the 5th Viscount, who *d* 1984; 2ndly, 1993, Martin Graham Shelley, son of late John Shelley, of St Boswells, Roxburghshire. *Residence* – 24 Stafford Terrace, W8 7BH.

COLLATERAL BRANCHES LIVING

Issue of late Rt Hon Charles Hardinge, KG, GCB, GCSI, GCMG, GCIE, GCVO, ISO, 2nd son of 2nd Viscount, who was *cr Baron Hardinge of Penshurst* 1910 (see that title).
Granddaughter of late Gen Hon Sir Arthur Edward Hardinge, KCB, CIE, son of 1st Viscount:—
Issue of late Rt Hon Sir Arthur Henry Hardinge, GCMG, KCB, *b* 1859, *d* 1933: *m* 1899, Alexandra Mina, who *d* 1949, da of late Maj-Gen Sir Arthur Edward Augustus Ellis, GCVO, CSI (B Howard de Walden, colls):—
Mary Pamela, *b* 1907; Bar Inner Temple 1940.
(*In remainder to baronetcy only*)
Grandchildren of late Bradford Hardinge, son of late Maj-Gen Richard Hardinge, brother of 2nd baronet:—
Issue of late George Nicholas Hardinge, *b* 1865, *d* 1943: *m* 1923, Lady Lilian Frances Graham-Toler, who *d* 1974, sister of 5th Earl of Norbury:—
Nicholas William (Lock Cottage, Bear St, Nayland, Essex), *b* 1928; *ed* Radley: *m* 1973, Mrs Anne Curtis, da of late Lt-Col Walter Thomas Delamain. —— Phyllis Lilian (Rose Cottage, Bramdean Common, Alresford, Hants), *b* 1925.

PREDECESSORS – (1) *Field Marshal Rt Hon Sir* HENRY Hardinge, GCB, PC, son of Rev Henry Hardinge, R of Stanhope, whose heirs male are in special remainder to the Baronetcy (*cr* 1801); *b* 1785; entered the Army at an early age and was present at all engagements throughout the Peninsular War; became Field-Marshal 1855; sat as MP for Launceston (C) 1826-41; was Clerk of the Ordnance 1823, Sec at War 1828, Ch Sec of Ireland 1830 and 1834, again Sec at War 1841, Gov-Gen of India 1844-8, Master-Gen of the Ordnance 1852, and Gen Com in Ch 1852-6; *cr Viscount Hardinge* (peerage of United Kingdom) 1846; twice thanked by Parliament for his military and civil services, and awarded a pension of £3,000 a year for three lives: *m* 1821, Lady Emily Jane Stewart, who *d* 1865, da of 1st Marquess of Londonderry, KG, and widow of John James; *d* 1856; *s* by his son (2) CHARLES STEWART, 2nd Viscount, *b* 1822; MP for Downpatrick 1851-6: *m* 1856, Lady Lavinia Bingham, who *d* 1864, da of 3rd Earl of Lucan; *d* 1894; *s* by his el son (3) HENRY CHARLES, CB, 3rd Viscount; *b* 1857; Capt Rifle Brig: *m* 1891, Mary Frances (who *d* 1954, having *m* 2ndly, 1928, as his 3rd wife, the 3rd Marquess of Abergavenny), da of late Hon Ralph Pelham Nevill; *d* 1924; *s* by his son (4) CARYL NICHOLAS CHARLES, 4th Viscount, *b* 1905; Maj 7th Hus, an ADC to Gov-Gen of Canada 1926-28, and Mil Assist to AG to Forces 1941-45; MBE (Mil) 1946: *m* 1928, Margaret Elizabeth Arnot, who *d* 1993, da of late Hugh Fleming, of Wynyards, Rockcliffe, Ottawa; *d* 1979; *s* by his only son (5) HENRY NICHOLAS PAUL, 5th Viscount, *b* 1929; Lieut 7th Hus; Snr Vice-Pres World Corporate Banking, R Bank of Canada: *m* 1st, 1955 (*m diss* 1982), Zoe Ann, da of Hartland de Montarville Molson, OBE, of Montreal, Senator of Canada; 2ndly, 1982, Baroness Florence Elisabeth (who *m* 2ndly, 1993, Martin Graham Shelley), da of late Baron Harold von Oppenheim, of Cologne; *d* 1984; *s* by his eldest son (6) CHARLES HENRY NICHOLAS, 6th Viscount and present peer.

HARDINGE OF PENSHURST, BARON (Hardinge) (Baron UK 1910)
(Name and Title pronounced "Harding")

For King and Country

GEORGE EDWARD CHARLES HARDINGE, 3rd Baron; *b* 31 Oct 1921; *s* 1960; *ed* Eton; Lieut-Com (ret) RN; was a Page of Honour to HM 1933-38; a Train Bearer at Coronation of King George VI: *m* 1st 1944 (*m diss* 1962), Janet Christine Goschen, who *d* 1970, da of late Lt-Col Francis Cecil Campbell Balfour, CIE, CBE, MC (E Balfour, colls); 2ndly, 1966, Mrs Margaret Trezise, da of William Thomas Jerrum, and has issue by 1st and 2nd *m*.

Arms – Gules, on a chevron argent fimbriated or three escallops sable; a chief wavy argent, thereon the representation of a French frigate wholly dismasted, towed towards the dexter by an English frigate in a shattered state. Crest – 1st, a dexter hand couped in naval uniform grasping a sword, surmounting a Dutch and French flag in saltire, on the former inscribed "Atalanta," on the latter "Piedmontaise," the sword passing through a wreath of laurel near the point and a little below through one of cypress, all proper; 2nd, a mitre gules, thereon a chevron argent fimbriated or charged with three escallops sable. Supporters – *Dexter*, a bear proper; *sinister*, a Bengal tiger proper.
Residence – Bracken Hill, 10 Penland Rd, Bexhill-on-Sea, Sussex TN40 2JG. *Club* – Brooks's.

SONS LIVING *(By 1st marriage)*

Hon JULIAN ALEXANDER, *b* 23 Aug 1945; *ed* Eton, and Trin Coll, Camb; a Page of Honour to HM The Queen 1959-62.
Hon Hugh Francis (Albion Villa, Church End, Ouer, Cambridge CB4 5NH), *b* 1948; *ed* Eton.
Hon Edward Frederick, *b* 1958: *ed* Gordonstoun.

(By 2nd marriage)

Hon Charles Alexander, *b* 1967; *ed* Eastbourne Coll, and Bradford Univ (BEng).

SISTERS LIVING

Hon Winifred Mary (*Hon Lady Murray*), *b* 1923; late WRNS: *m* 1943, Major Sir John Antony Jerningham Murray, CBE, late Grenadier Guards (Jerningham, Bt (ext)), and has issue living, (George) Alexander John, *b* 1947; City Ed, Sunday Telegraph: *m* 1975, Caroline, da of John Miller. *Residence* – Woodmancote Manor Cottage, Cirencester, Gloucestershire.
Hon Elizabeth Rosemary (*Hon Lady Johnston*), *b* 1927; late WRNS; JP for Berks: *m* 1949, Lt-Col Sir John Frederick Dame Johnston, GCVO, MC, late Gren Gds, a Member of HM Household since 1964, and has issue living, Christopher Michael, *b* 1951, — Joanna Elizabeth, *b* 1953. *Residence* – Studio Cottage, Windsor Great Park, Berks; Stone Hill, Newport, Pembrokeshire.

PREDECESSORS – (1) *Rt Hon* CHARLES HARDINGE, KG, GCB, GCSI, GCMG, GCIE, GCVO, ISO, 2nd son of 2nd Viscount Hardinge, *b* 1858; was an Assist Under-Sec of State for Foreign Affairs 1903-4, Ambassador at St Petersburg 1904-6, Permanent Under-Sec of State for Foreign Affairs 1906-10, Viceroy of India 1910-16, again Permanent Under-Sec of State for Foreign Affairs 1916-20, and Ambassador Extraor and Plen in Paris 1920-23; *cr Baron Hardinge of Penshurst*, co Kent (peerage of United Kingdom) 1910: *m* 1890, Hon Winifred Sturt, CI, who *d* 1914, da of 1st Baron Alington; *d* 1944; *s* by his second and only surviving son (2) ALEXANDER HENRY LOUIS, GCB, GCVO, MC, PC, 2nd Baron, *b* 1894; Major Grenadier Guards (ret); was an ADC to Viceroy and Gov-Gen of India 1915-16; an Equerry in Ord and an Assist Private Sec to HM 1920-36 (Assist Keeper of HM's Privy Purse 1935-6), and an Extra Equerry to HM 1936-60, Private Sec to King Edward VIII 1936, and to King George VI 1936-43; European War 1914-18 (wounded, MC); a Gov of St Bartholomew's Hospital, and King's Sch, Canterbury: *m* 1921, Helen Mary, who *d* 1979, da of late Lord Edward Herbert Gascoyne-Cecil, KCMG, DSO (M Salisbury, colls); *d* 1960; *s* by his only son (3) GEORGE EDWARD CHARLES, 3rd Baron and present peer.

HARDWICKE, EARL OF (Yorke) (Earl GB 1754)

Neither covet nor fear

JOSEPH PHILIP SEBASTIAN YORKE, 10th Earl; *b* 3 Feb 1971; *s* 1974.
Residence – 12 Lansdowne Rd, W11 3LW.

Arms – Argent, a saltire azure charged with a bezant. **Crest** – A lion's head erased proper, gorged with a plain collar gules, charged on the collar with a bezant. **Supporters** – *Dexter*, a lion guardant or, gorged with a plain collar gules, the collar charged with a bezant; *sinister*, a stag proper, attired or, and collared as the lion.

SISTER LIVING (*Raised to the rank of an Earl's daughter 1977*)

Lady Jemima Rose, *b* 1969.

AUNTS LIVING (*Daughters of 9th Earl*)

Lady Amabel Mary Maud, *b* 1935: *m* 1955, Hon Patrick Lindsay, of 12 Lansdowne Rd, W11, who *d* 1986, and has issue (*see* E Crawford).
Lady Victoria Mary Verenia Braganza, *b* 1947: *m* 1976, Nigel Waymouth, of 36 Elms Rd, SW4, and has issue living, Louis Alexander Philip, *b* 1978, — Adam Django Joseph, *b* 1981.
Lady Rose Mary Sydney *b* 1951: *m* 1st, 19- (*m diss* 19-), Kenneth Delbray; 2ndly, 1981 (*m diss* 1985), Herbert Richard Vaughan, who *d* 1987; 3rdly, 1990, Tony Turner; has issue living (by David Thompson), Katharine Sarah Tahlita Valour THOMPSON, *b* 1985.

WIDOW LIVING OF NINTH EARL

ENID MUNNICK (*Countess of Hardwicke*), da of Pieter Grunwald, of S Africa, formerly wife of Roy Boulting: *m* 1970, as his 2nd wife, the 9th Earl, who *d* 1974.

COLLATERAL BRANCHES LIVING

Issue of late Hon Claud John Yorke, 3rd son of 7th Earl, *b* 1872, *d* 1940: *m* 1914, Fay, who *d* 1928, da of John Michael Zarifi, of 6 Norfolk Street, Park Lane, W:—
DAVID JOHN NAPIER EDWARD, *b* 17 Oct 1919; *ed* Eton and Jesus Coll, Camb; Bar Middle Temple 1949; a JP W Sussex; an Underwriting Member of Lloyd's: *m* 1st, 1950, Anne Margaret, who *d* 1984, da of Denis George Mackail (*see* Burne-Jones, Bt (ext), 1953 Edn); 2ndly, 1990, June Rose Charlotte Rachel, only da of late Daniel Walter Thomas Gurney, MC (*see* Troubridge, Bt, 1976 Edn), and widow of Robert Duncan Fyfe, and has issue living (by 1st *m*), Charles Edward (Flat 4, 3 Vicarage Gate, W8 4HH), *b* 1951; *ed* Eton, and Ruskin Sch of Drawing & Fine Art, Oxford; caricaturist, — James Alexander (64 Peterborough Rd, SW6 3EB), *b* 1954; *ed* Eton, Balliol Coll, Oxford (BA 1977), and Birkbeck Coll, Univ of London (BA 1983): *m* 1986, Primrose Alexandra Mary, only da of Brig Harold Kitson, CBE, of Morcombelake, W Dorset, and has issue living, Philip Prospero Alexander *b* 1987, Henry Cosimo Frederick *b* 1991. *Residence* – Gatewick, Steyning, Sussex.

Grandsons of late Vincent Wodehouse Yorke, 2nd son of late John Reginald Yorke, son of late Joseph Yorke, el bro of late Capt James Charles Yorke (*b* 1816) (infra):—
Issue of late Maj Gerald Joseph Yorke, *b* 1901 *d* 1983: *m* 1937, Angela Vivien, who *d* 1988, el da of late Maj-Gen Sir John Duncan, KCB, CMG, CVO, DSO:—
John Sarne (Forthampton Court, Glos), *b* 1938; *ed* Eton, and Trin Coll, Camb; ACA (1965): *m* 1st, 1967, Jean Victoria, who *d* 1989, yr da of Anthony Reynolds, of Sintra, Portugal; 2ndly, 1992, C. Julia, da of late Herbert M. Allen, and has issue living (by 1st *m*), Anabel, *b* 1971, — Sara, *b* 1974. —— Vincent James (The Stalls, Bushley, Glos), *b* 1942; *ed* Eton, and Slade Sch of Art, Univ Coll, Lond: *m* 1970, Francine Caroline, da of late F. W. Barker, of Hythe, and has issue living, Griselda Rose, *b* 1973, — Hester Mary, *b* 1974, — Sophie Catherine, *b* 1977. —— Michael Piers (31 Downside Crescent, NW3), *b* 1944; *ed* Eton, Edin Univ, and London Univ: *m* 1972, Valerie Margaret, da of H. Peter B. Cox, of Chislehurst, Kent, and has issue living, Marcus *b* 1983, — Jessica *b* 1980.
Issue of late Henry Vincent Yorke, *b* 1905, *d* 1973: *m* 1929, Hon Adelaide Mary Biddulph, who *d* 1985, da of 2nd Baron Biddulph:—
Sebastian, *b* 1934: *m* 1957 (*m diss* 1962), Hon Emma Christina Tennant, da of 2nd Baron Glenconner, and has issue living, Matthew Henry, *b* 1958.

Grandchildren of late Capt James Hamilton Langdon Yorke, MC (infra):—
Issue of late James John Simon Yorke, DSC, RN *b* 1912, *d* 1963: *m* 1938, Bridget Essex (Constant, Nevern, Newport, Pembrokeshire), da of Adm Sir Alban Thomas Buckley Curteis, KCB:—
James Hamilton Simon, MBE (2831 S Columbus St, Arlington, Virginia 22206, USA), *b* 1939; *ed* Wellington Coll; Lt-Cdr RN (ret); MBE (Mil) 1990: *m* 1st 1966, (*m diss* 1984), Elizabeth Ann, da of Col John Leeper Anketell Macafee, CBE, of Grove House, Bredhurst, Kent; 2ndly, 1989, Jean Anne, da of C. Richard Louis, of Trenton, Michigan, USA, and has issue living (by 1st *m*), Simon Anketell Hamilton, *b* 1967, — Patrick James Langdon, *b* 1968, — Rebecca Mary Amabel, *b* 1970, — Amabel Lucy Elizabeth, *b* 1972. —— Nicholas Roger (Lower Fishguard, Dyfed) *b* 1944; *ed* Wellington Coll; agric engineer: *m* 1st, 1969 (*m diss* 1976), Kathleen Prentice, da of Kent Sanger; 2ndly, 1977 (*m diss* 1989), Carole Crossman, yst da of late Eldon F. le Poer Power, of Ashfield, Beauparc, co Meath, and has issue living (by 2nd *m*), Philip David Emerson, *b* 1983, — Louisa Harriet, *b* 1979. —— Philippa Mary Essex, *b* 1947: *m* 1968, Roger Morrall, of Lower Boddington, Daventry, Northants, and has issue living, Thomas Simon Neil, *b* 1978, — Bridget Essex, *b* 1973.

Granddaughter of late James Charles Yorke (*b* 1847), eldest son of late Capt James Charles Yorke (*b* 1816), yr son of late Joseph Yorke, elder son of late Rt Rev Hon James Yorke, Bishop of Ely, 5th son of 1st Earl:—
Issue of late Capt James Hamilton Langdon Yorke, MC, *b* 1884, *ka* 1917: *m* 1910, Violet Mary, who *d* 1963, da of late James Edmund Vincent, Chancellor of Diocese of Bangor:—
Susannah Mary, *b* 1915: *m* 1st, 1934, Major Gerald Hartas FitzGerald, IMS, who *d* 1937; 2ndly, 1938, Allan Forbes Malcolmson, and has issue living (by 1st *m*), Anne Sara, *b* 1935: *m* 1959, Richard Michael Johnstone Eastham, of Dolau Dwrbach, Scleddau, Fishguard, Pembrokeshire, and has issue living, Cedric Gerald *b* 1960, Jane Francesca *b* 1962, — (by 2nd *m*) Jean Sheila, *b* 1942: *m* 1971, Peter Robjant, of 32 Hilperdon Rd, Trowbridge, Wilts, and has issue living, David Allan *b* 1973, Mary Anna Susan *b* 1975. *Residence* – 331 The Street, Holt, Trowbridge, Wilts BA14 6QH.

Grandchildren of late Hon Mr Justice (Robert Langdon) Yorke, 2nd son of late James Charles Yorke (*b* 1847) (ante):—

Issue of late Maj Patrick Langdon Yorke, Royal Corps of Signals, *b* 1916, *d* of wounds received in action in NW Europe 1945: *m* 1939, Pamela Mary (who *m* 2ndly, 1950, Robert Michael Clive, of The Spinney, Spinney Drive, Gt Shelford, Cambridge), da of late Lt-Col Harold Rudgard, OBE, of 22 Orchard Drive, Watford:—

Robert Anthony (Silver Birches, Bashurst Hill, Itchingfield, W Sussex), *b* 1944; *ed* Marlborough, and Clare Coll, Camb (MA): *m* 1975, Morag, da of late John S. McD. Dow, of Helensburgh, and has issue living, Andrew Patrick, *b* 1982, — Sarah Catherine, *b* 1978. —— Caroline Ann, *b* 1941: *m* 1969, Peter Roy Chamberlain, of 60 Rock Rd, Cambridge, and has issue living, Juliet Catherine, *b* 1970, — Rachel Claire, *b* 1972.

Grandchildren of late James Charles Yorke (*b* 1847) (ante):—

Issue of late Cdr Joseph Hugh Langdon Yorke, RN, *b* 1888, *d* 1936: *m* 1916, Ursula Mary Vere, who *d* 1959, da of late Col Robert Oliver Lloyd, CB (formerly RE), of Treffgarne Hall, Pembrokeshire:—

Josephine Mary, *b* 1917: *m* 1st, 1945, Maurice Newton, who *d* 1949; 2ndly, 1959, Luis Nicolin y Martinez Del Campo. *Address* – Bolivar 8, 402 Mexico City 1 DF, Mexico. —— April Ursula, *b* 1919; is a Carmelite Nun.

Issue of late Worthington Langdon Yorke, *b* 1901, *d* 1983: *m* 1934, Irene Rebecca (352-12720-111th Av, Edmonton, Alberta, Canada T6H 4K8), da of George O. Britney, of Manyberries, Alberta, Canada:—

Frederick Alton, *b* 1935. —— Katherine Anne, *b* 1937: *m* 1959, Walter William Yakimets, of 4803 Landsdowne Drive, Edmonton, Alberta, Canada T6H 4K8, and has issue living, Walter John, *b* 1961, — Stephen George, *b* 1963: *m* 1986, Marilyn Joan Mitchell, — Neil Edward, *b* 1969, — Dawn-Marie Rebecca, *b* 1967. —— Dianne Marie, *b* 1945: *m* 1965, Walter Herman Henry Petersen, of Box 1462, Stony Plain, Alberta, Canada T0E 2G0, and has issue living, Kevin John, *b* 1966, — Gary Michael, *b* 1968, — Brian Langdon Benjamin, *b* 1971.

Issue of late Capt Philip Cecil Langdon Yorke, OBE, RN, *b* 1903, *d* 1970: *m* 1st, 1936, Elsie Margaret, who *d* 1945, da of late F. Davis, of Barnwood, Glos; 2ndly, 1946 (*m diss* 1960), Violet Helen, da of C. Ormonde Trew, of Little Rough, Hindhead; 3rdly, 1961, Rose, who *d* 1966, da of A. Rubinstein, of London:—

(By 2nd *m*) Clare Amabel, *b* 1948: *m* 1969, Jonathan Robert Barclay, of The Old Vicarage, Stoke Holy Cross, Norwich NR14 8AB (*see* Barclay, Bt).

Grandchildren of late Reginald Somers Yorke, 2nd son of Capt James Charles Yorke (*b* 1816) (ante):—

Issue of late Reginald Henry Crofton Yorke, *b* 1897, *d* (accidentally drowned) 1947: *m* 1927, Gwendolen Maude, da of late Frank Watkinson:—

John Reginald (9 Mornington Rd, Chingford, E4), *b* 1928; *ed* Bradfield, and King's Coll, Camb: *m* 1959, Catherine Stewart, da of late Frank William Borthwick, of West Ham, and has issue living, Margaret Helen, *b* 1967, — Jennifer Frances, *b* 1970. —— Elizabeth Mary, *b* 1930.

Grandchildren of late Algernon Joseph Yorke, yst son of Capt James Charles Yorke (ante):—

Issue of late Lt-Col Simon Algernon Yorke, *b* 1889, *d* 1977: *m* 1920, Annie Paton, da of late J. P. Fyfe, JP, of Craigielea, Greenock:—

Joseph Algernon, *b* 1922: *m* 1945, Mary Robertson, da of Alexander Brown, of Dunshelt, Fife, and has issue living, Marianne Alexandra, *b* 1946, — Josephine Mary Bunty, *b* 1948. Resides in Canada.

Issue of late Harold Branson Yorke, *b* 1890, *d* 1949: *m* 1920, Stella Catherine, who *d* 1968, da of late Rear-Adm Henry Compton Aitchison, of Shrubs Hill, Lyndhurst:—

Thérése, *b* 1925: *m* 1963, as his 2nd wife, Michael Charles Stirling Halford. *Residence* – 6 Old Farm Rd, Nether Stowey, Bridgwater, Som. —— Joan Felicity, *b* 1933: *m* 1957, Count Mario Bizzarri, and has issue living, Flaminia Stella Giovanna Maria, *b* 1958: *m* 1990, Mario di Pilla, of Via Babini 28, Rome, — Alessandra Luisa Teresa Cristina Maria, *b* 1959: *m* 1993, Ben Heijmen, of Groenehilledijk 404A, Rotterdam, Holland, — Paola Maria Augusta Audreina Giovanna, *b* 1960, — Giovanna, *b* 1963, — Carla, *b* 1966. *Residence* – Via Galla e Sidami 49, Rome 00199. —— Christine Anne, *b* 1935: *m* 1958, Alan Neville White, and has issue living, Richard Neville, *b* 1964, — Margaret Lesley, *b* 1959: *m* 1991, Peter Bowden, — Helen Mary, *b* 1960: *m* 1990, Dr David Halpin. *Residence* – Primrose Lodge, Duddleswell, Uckfield, E Sussex.

Grandson of Lt-Col Philip Charles Yorke, el son of Rev Charles Issac Yorke, 2nd son of Rev Philip Yorke, 2nd son of the Rt Rev Hon James Yorke, 5th son of 1st Earl:—

Issue of late Major Henry Reginald Yorke, MC, *b* 1874, *d* 1944: *m* 1903, Beatrix Victoire, who *d* 1960, da of Capt Lynch-Staunton, formerly 14th Hussars:—

Philip (3 Crowsbury Close, Emsworth, Hants, PO10 7TS) *b* 1905; *ed* Harrow: *m* 1945, Elsie May Heasman.

Grandchildren of late Brig Philip Gerard Yorke, DSO (infra):—

Issue of late Lt-Col Arthur Philip Denys Yorke, MC, *b* 1915, *d* 1971: *m* 1957, Mary Elizabeth (who *m* 2ndly, 1983, Jeffrey Michelmore, of Forder Farm, South Brent, Devon), da of John Henry Glasbrook, of Childe Okeford Manor, Blandford:—

Michael Philip, *b* 1959. —— Nicholas Simon, *b* 1961: *m* 1991, Esther Victoria, only da of late Barry Desmond Watkins, of Prince of Wales Mansions, SW11, and has issue living, Robert Maximilian Philip, *b* 1991. —— Delia Mary, *b* 1964.

Granddaughter of Lt-Col Philip Charles Yorke (ante):—

Issue of late Brig Philip Gerard Yorke, DSO, *b* 1882, *d* 1968: *m* 1914, Beryl Emelia, who *d* 1982, da of late Brig-Gen Arthur Henry Croker Phillpotts, formerly RHA (Brady, Bt):—

Amabel Marion, *b* 1924: *m* 1963, Brig Robert Michael Carr, MBE, DFC, formerly RA, of Nethercote, Church Lane, Mottisfont, Romsey, Hants SO51 0LL, and has an adopted son and da, Peter Robert, *b* 1965, — Philippa Amabel, *b* 1966.

PREDECESSORS – **(1)** Sir PHILIP Yorke, having been Solicitor-Gen and Attorney-Gen, was in 1733 appointed Lord Ch Justice of the King's Bench and *cr Baron Hardwicke*, of Hardwicke, co Gloucester (peerage of Great Britain); one of the Lords Justices for Administering the Govt during the King's absences; promoted to be Lord High Chancellor 1737, and *cr Viscount Royston* and *Earl of Hardwicke* (peerage of Great Britain) 1754; resigned the Great Seal 1756; *d* 1764; *s* by his son **(2)** PHILIP, 2nd Earl: *m* 1740, Lady Jemima Campbell (only da of 3rd Earl of Breadalbane), and afterwards in her own right Baroness Lucas of Crudwell (*cr* 1663), and Marchioness de Grey (*cr* 1740, extinct); the Marchioness *d* 1779 when the Marquessate expired, and the Barony of Lucas of Crudwell devolved upon her da Amabel; the Earl *d* 1796 without male issue; *s* by his nephew **(3)** PHILIP, KG, 3rd Earl, el son of Hon Charles, 2nd son of 1st Earl, who had been appointed Lord High Chancellor, and *d* 1770 before the patent conferring upon him the title of Baron Morden was completed; was Viceroy of Ireland 1801-6; *d* without surviving male issue 1834; *s* by his nephew **(4)** CHARLES PHILIP, PC, 4th Earl, son of Vice-Adm Sir Joseph Sydney, KCB, MP, 3rd son of Hon Charles (ante); *b* 1779; was a Vice-Adm; sat as MP for Reigate (*C*) 1831, and for Cambridgeshire 1831-4; Lord-Lieut of Cambridgeshire, Postmaster-Gen 1852, Lord Privy Seal 1858-9, and sometime a Lord-in-Waiting to HM Queen Victoria: *m* 1833, Hon Susan, who *d* 1886, da of 1st Baron Ravensworth; *d* 1873; *s* by his son **(5)** CHARLES PHILIP, 5th Earl, *b* 1836; Comptroller of the Household 1866-8, and Master of the Buckhounds 1874-8; MP for Cambridgeshire (*C*) 1865-73: *m* 1863, Lady Sophie Georgiana Robertine, who *d* 1923, da of 1st Earl Cowley; *d* 1897; *s* by his son **(6)** ALBERT EDWARD PHILIP HENRY, 6th Earl; *b* 1867; Under Sec of State for India 1900-1902, Under Sec of State for War 1902-3, and again Under Sec of State for India 1903-4; *d* 1904; *s* by his uncle **(7)** JOHN MANNERS, 7th Earl; *b* 1840; Capt RN: *m* 1869, Edith, who *d* 1930, da of late Alexander Oswald, of Auchencruive, Scotland; *d* 1909; *s* by his el son **(8)** CHARLES ALEXANDER, 8th Earl; *b* 1869: *m* 1st, 1911 (*m diss* 1927), Ellen, CBE, who *d* 1968, da of late James Russell, of Auckland, NZ;

2ndly, 1930, Mary Radley, who *d* 1938 (having *m* 2ndly, 1938, W. E. L. Jennings, Dist Officer of Dedza, Nyasaland), da of Edward Robert Twist, of Liverpool; *d* 1936; *s* by his nephew **(9)** PHILIP GRANTHAM (son of late Hon Alfred Ernest Frederick Yorke, 2nd son of 7th Earl), 9th Earl; *b* 1906; late Lt LG; 1939-45 War with City of London Yeo, and as Maj SAS: *m* 1st, 1934, Sarah Katharine, who *d* 1965, da of the Rt Hon Sir Francis Oswald Lindley, GCMG, CB, CBE; 2ndly, 1970, Enid Munnick, of S Africa, formerly wife of Roy Boulting; *d* 1974; *s* by his grandson, JOSEPH PHILIP SEBASTIAN (only son of late Philip Simon Prospero Rupert Lindley, Viscount Royston, only son of 9th Earl: *m* 1968, Virginia Anne, who *d* 1988, da of Geoffrey Lyon, of Hambledon, Surrey), 10th Earl and present peer; also Viscount Royston, and Baron Hardwicke.

HAREWOOD, EARL OF (Lascelles) (Earl UK 1812)
(Title pronounced "Harwood")

Salvation in God alone

GEORGE HENRY HUBERT LASCELLES, KBE, 7th Earl; *b* 7 Feb 1923; *s* 1947; *ed* Eton, and King's Coll, Camb (BA); Hon LLD Leeds 1959, Aberdeen 1966, and Bradford 1983; Hon Dr Music, Hull 1962, D Univ York 1982, Hon RAM 1983, Janáček Medal 1978; Capt late Grenadier Guards; was Editor of magazine *Opera* 1950-53, a Dir of R Opera House, Covent Garden 1951-53, and 1969-72, Admin Executive thereof 1953-60, Artistic Dir of Edinburgh Festival 1961-65, Chancellor of York Univ 1963-67; Dir of Leeds Festival 1958-74; and Artistic Adviser of New Philharmonia Orchestra 1966-76; Man Dir of Sadler's Wells Opera (now English Nat Opera) 1972-85 (Chm since 1986); Pres British Board of Film Classification (formerly Censors) since 1985; Artistic Dir Adelaide Festival 1988; Artistic Adviser Buxton Festival 1993; Pres English Football Assn 1963-72; Pres of Leeds United AFC; a Train Bearer at Coronation of King George VI; an ADC to Gov-Gen of Canada 1945-46; acted as a Counsellor of State during HM King George VI's absence abroad 1947, and during HM Queen Elizabeth II's absence abroad 1953-54 and 1956; 1939-45 War in Italy (wounded, prisoner); KBE (1986): *m* 1st, 1949 (*m diss* 1967), Maria Donata Nanetta Paulina Gustava Erwina Wilhelmina (Marion), former concert pianist, da of late Erwin Stein, of Melbury Rd, W14 and formerly of Vienna; 2ndly, 1967, Patricia Elizabeth, former violinist, only da of Charles Tuckwell, of Sydney, Aust, and formerly wife of late Athol Shmith, and has issue by 1st and 2nd *m*.

Arms – Sable, a cross patonce within a bordure or. **Crest** – A bear's head couped at the neck ermine, muzzled gules, buckled or, and gorged with a collar of the second, rimmed and studded gold. **Supporters** – Two bears ermine; each muzzled gules, buckled or, gorged with a collar of the second, rimmed and studded, and with a chain reflexed over the back gold; pendant from the collar an estucheon sable, charged with a cross patonce or.
Seat – Harewood House, Leeds, LS17 9LG.

SONS LIVING (By 1st wife)

DAVID HENRY GEORGE (*Viscount Lascelles*), *b* 21 Oct 1950; *ed* Westminster; Pres Leeds Young Musicians: *m* 1st, 12 Feb 1979 (*m diss* 1989), Margaret Rosalind, da of Edgar Frank Messenger; 2ndly, 11 March 1990, Diane Jane, da of John Prince Howse, and has issue:—

    SONS LIVING (by 1st wife)— *Hon* Benjamin George, *b* 19 Sept 1978, — *Hon* ALEXANDER EDGAR, *b* 13 May 1980, — *Hon* Edward David, *b* 19 Nov 1982.
    DAUGHTER LIVING (by 1st wife)— *Hon* Emily Tsering, *b* 23 Nov 1975.

Hon James Edward, *b* 5 Oct 1953; *ed* Westminster: *m* 1st, 4 April 1973 (*m diss* 1985), Fredericka Ann, da of Prof Alfred Duhrrson, of Deya, Majorca; 2ndly, 4 May 1985, Lori (Shadow), da of John Robert Lee, of Seligman, Arizona, USA, and formerly wife of John Porter, and has issue living, (by 1st *m*) Rowan Nash, *b* 6 Nov 1977, — Sophie Amber, *b* 1 Oct 1973, — (by 2nd *m*) Tewa Ziyan Robert George (a son), *b* 8 June 1985, — Tanit (a da), *b* 1 July 1981.

(*Hon*) (Robert) Jeremy Hugh (does not use courtesy title), *b* 14 Feb 1955; *ed* Westminster: *m* 4 July 1981, Julie, da of Robert Baylis, of Mildenham Mill, Claines, nr Worcester, and has issue living, Thomas Robert, *b* 7 Sept 1982, — Ellen Mary, *b* 17 Dec 1984, — Amy Rose, *b* 26 June 1986.

(By 2nd wife)

Hon Mark Hubert, *b* 5 July 1964; *ed* Bryanston: *m* 1992, Andrea Kershaw.

BROTHER LIVING

Hon Gerald David, *b* 21 Aug 1924; *ed* Eton; late Capt Rifle Bde, 1944-46; Pres Inst of Motor Industry 1969-73, 1975-78; Pres of British Racing Drivers' Club since 1964: *m* 1st, 15 July 1952 (*m diss* 1978), Angela, da of late Charles Stanley Dowding; 2ndly 17 Nov 1978, Elizabeth Evelyn, only da of Brig Sydney Collingwood, CMG, CBE, MC, of The Croft, Dedham, Essex, and has issue living (by 1st wife), Henry Ulick, *b* 19 May 1953: *m* 25 Aug 1979, Alexandra Clare Ruth, da of Peter Morton, and has issue living, Maximillian John Gerald *b* 19 Dec 1991, — (by 2nd wife), Martin David, *b* 9 Feb 1962. *Residence* – Les Croux, Monbazillac, 24240 Sigoules, France.

COLLATERAL BRANCHES LIVING

Granddaughters of late Com Hon Frederick Canning Lascelles, 2nd son of 4th Earl:—
　　Issue of late Rt Hon Sir Alan Frederick Lascelles GCB, GCVO, CMG, MC, *b* 1887; *d* 1981: *m* 1920, Hon Joan
　　Frances Vere Thesiger, who *d* 1971, da of 1st Viscount Chelmsford.
Lavinia Joan, *b* 1923: *m* 1st, 1946 (*m diss* 1960), Maj Edward Westland Renton, The Black Watch; 2ndly, 1962 (*m diss* 1964),
Gavin Maxwell, author, who *d* 1969 (Maxwell, Bt, *cr* 1681); 3rdly, 1969, David Hankinson, RN, of 12A Barkiston Gdns, SW5,
and has issue living (by 1st *m*), Nicholas John (23 Crescent Lane, SW4), *b* 1946: *m* 1975, Caroline Mary, da of Kennedy
Mayo Harrow, of 23 Epsom Av, Auckland, NZ, and has issue living, Alan Edward Mayo *b* 1976, Zoë Eleanor *b* 1979, —
Simon Anthony (33 Church St, Barnes, SW13), *b* 1948: *m* 1977, Amanda Jane, da of David Schrire, of Cape Town, S Africa,
and has issue living, Julia Esther *b* 1979, Claudia Jessamine *b* 1981. —— Caroline Mary (*Hon Mrs David H. Erskine*), *b*
1928: *m* 1st, 1949, 2nd Viscount Chandos, who *d* 1980; 2ndly, 1985, as his 2nd wife, Hon David Hervey Erskine, of Felsham
House, Felsham, Bury St Edmunds, Suffolk, brother of 13th Earl of Mar and Kellie.

　　　　Issue of late Hon William Horace Lascelles, 8th son of 4th Earl, *b* 1868, *d* 1949: *m* 1899, Madeline, who *d*
　　1950, da of late Rev Gerard Barton, of Fundenhall, Norfolk:—
Mary Madge, *b* 1900; *ed* Lady Margaret Hall, Oxford (BA 1922, BLitt, 1927, MA 1931); Fellow of Somerville Coll, Oxford
1932 (Hon Fell since 1967); FBA 1962. —— Susan Olivia, *b* 1907. *Residence* – Cley-next-Sea, Holt, Norfolk.

　　　　Granddaughters of late Hon George Edwin Lascelles, 3rd son of 3rd Earl:—
　　Issue of late Hon Sir Alfred (George) Lascelles, *b* 1857, *d* 1952: *m* 1911, Isabel Carteret, who *d* 1965, da of late
　　Francis John Thynne (M Bath, colls):—
Ursula, *b* 1914: *m* 1946, Alan George Ross Ormiston, and has issue living, James Christopher Ross, *b* 1949; *ed* Eton, and
Worcester Coll, Oxford, — Lavinia Anne Ross (*Baroness Rathcreedan*), *b* 1952: *m* 1978, 3rd Baron Rathcreedan. *Residence* –
Coln Orchard, Arlington, Bibury, Glos. —— Kathleen Louisa Isabel, *b* 1916: *m* 1940 (*m diss* 1953), Brigadier Robert Hugh
Bellamy, CBE, DSO, late DCLI, who *d* 1972, and has issue living, Martin Hugh, *b* 1946; *ed* Stowe: *m* 1979, Elizabeth Burton
(and has issue), — Vivien Patricia, *b* 1943: *m* 1967, Anthony John Wyndham Owston, who *d* 1992 (*see* Bromley, Bt, colls),
and has issue living, Gavin Anthony *b* 1970, Vanessa Rosemary *b* 1968. *Residence* – Manor Cottage, Coln St, Aldwyns,
Cirencester.

　　　　Grandchildren of late Evelyn Herbert Lascelles (infra):—
　　Issue of late John Edward Lascelles, *b* 1923, *d* 1975: *m* 1946, Isabelle Christine Graham Maxwell, of Gordonvale, N
　　Qld:—
David John, *b* 1948: *m* 1986 (*m diss* 1989). —— Peter James (The Counthouse, Wheal Kitty, St Agnes, Cornwall), *b* 1952: *m*
1981, Mary Louise O'Donovan, of Bega, NSW, Australia, and has issue living, Sean Henry, *b* 1981, — Brennan James
Maxwell, *b* 1985, — Marcus Peter, *b* 1990. —— Stephen Charles (11 Tipuana Drive, Capalaba, Qld 4157, Australia), *b* 1954:
m 1991, Theresa Louise Waller, of Brisbane. —— Isabelle Diana, *b* 1957: *m* 19—, Rodney Phillip Spillane, of Brisbane.

　　　　Grandson of late Edward George Lascelles, son of Hon George Edwin Lascelles (ante):—
　　Issue of late Evelyn Herbert Lascelles, *b* 1893, *d* 1982: *m* 1923, Colleen Una, who *d* 1986, da of John Taylor, of
　　Rockwood Station, Qld:—
Geoffrey George (164 Esplanade, Pt Vernon, Hervey Bay, Qld 4655 Australia), *b* 1927; 1939-45 in RAN: *m* 1951, Gwen
Martin, of Yandina, Qld, and has issue living, Scott (60 Battye Av, Beverley Park, Sydney, NSW, Australia), *b* 1952: *m* 1981,
Lynne Jennifer Boultwood, of Earlwood, Sydney, NSW, and has issue living, Robert Scott *b* 1986, Elinor *b* 1983, — Kent, *b*
1954: Lt Cdr RAN: *m* 1st, 1975 (*m diss* 1980), Ann Marie Ludwigsen, of Bellevue Park, Southport; 2ndly, 1985, Vicki Ann
Harris, of Wagga Wagga, NSW, and has issue living, (by 1st *m*) Tamara *b* 1975, (by 2nd *m*) Ashleigh Mary *b* 1988, — Fiona
Jane, *b* 1962: *m* 1991, Paul Longworth, of Farnworth, Bolton, Lancs, and has issue living, Jack Lascelles *b* 1993.

　　　　Grandchildren of late Lieut-Col Henry Arthur Lascelles, MVO, 4th son of Rt Hon William Saunders Seb-
　　right Lascelles MP, 3rd son of 2nd Earl:—
　　Issue of late Edward Charles Ponsonby Lascelles, OBE, *b* 1884, *d* 1956: *m* 1911, Leila Winifred Leonor (a DGStJ),
　　who *d* 1979, da of late Sir Vincent Kennett-Barrington:—
(Henry) Anthony, CB, CBE, DSO, *b* 1912; *ed* Winchester, and Oriel Coll, Oxford (BA); Maj-Gen (ret) late RTR; Maj-Gen,
Gen Staff, HQ Far East Land Forces 1964-66; Dir-Gen of Winston Churchill Trust 1967-80; Pres Brit Water Ski Federation
since 1980; 1939-45 War in Middle East and Italy (despatches twice, DSO, OBE); DSO and OBE (Mil) 1945, CBE (Mil)
1962, CB (Mil) 1967: *m* 1941, Ethne Hyde Ussher, da of late Norman Charles. *Residence* – Manor Farm Cottage, Hedgerley
Green, Bucks. —— Alice Leila *b* 1914; *ed* London Univ (BSc Economics 1936). *Residence* – The Plough, Redford, Midhurst,
Sussex.
　　Issue of late Henry Francis Lascelles, *b* 1886, *d* 1937: *m* 1918, Rose Caroline Georgiana, who *d* 1976, da of late Col
　　Frederick Arthur Aylmer (B Aylmer, colls):—
Oliver, MBE, DSC, *b* 1921, Cdr RN; 1939-45 War (DSC); MBE (Mil) 1950: *m* 1963, Pamela Margaret Enid, da of late Robert
Whillis, and has issue living, Harriet Caroline, *b* 1964: *m* 1989, Anthony William Vaughan Fairbank (*see* V Chetwynd, colls),
— Nicola Jane, *b* 1966. *Residence* – Folly House, Bampton, Oxon.
　　Issue of late Sir Francis William Lascelles, KCB, MC, *b* 1890, *d* 1979: *m* 1924, Esmée Marion, da of late Charles
　　Arthur Bury, of Downings, Salins, co Kildare:—
(Charles) Brian (Bank House, Glenfarg, Perthshire), *b* 1926: *m* 1st, 1953, Elizabeth Mary, who *d* 1978, only da of late Lt-Cdr
Geoffrey Seymour Grenfell, RN; 2ndly, 1986, Margaret Anne, yst da of late Alec Maskell Mitchell, of Ferry Reach, Bermuda
(*see* B Kinross, 1990 Edn), and formerly wife of Ronald Patrick Thorburn, FRICS, and has issue living (by 1st *m*), Charles
Riversdale, *b* 1954: — James Dominic (6 Merthyr Terr, Barnes, SW13), *b* 1956: *m* 1984, Diana Elizabeth, da of late James
Okolo, of Lagos, Nigeria, and has issue living, James Theodore Grenfell *b* 1988, Lucy Elizabeth *b* 1985, — Tobias Francis, *b*
1965. —— (Henry) Giles Francis (119 Halliath Rd, SW4), *b* 1931: *m* 1957, Caroline Venetia, da of late Esmond Charles
Baring, OBE (*see* B Ashburton, colls), and has issue living, Hugo Giles, *b* 1958: *m* 1986, Joanna Catherine, yr da of Maj
Christopher Roland Philipson, of Lofts Hall, Essex (*see* By Woolavington, 1985 Edn), and has issue living, Rose *b* 1988,
Camilla *b* 1991, — Peregrine Simon, *b* 1962, — Sophie Caroline (*Lady Bruce Dundas*), *b* 1958 (twin): *m* 1983, Lord (Richard)
Bruce Dundas, yst son of 3rd Marquess of Zetland.

　　　　Grandson of late Lieut-Col George Reginald Lascelles, CVO, OBE, 2nd son of late Col Walter Richard
　　Lascelles (infra):—
　　Issue of late Lieut-Col John Norman Pulteney Lascelles, *b* 1898, *d* on active ser 1939: *m* 1932, Elizabeth Katharine
　　Joan, who *d* 1986, da of late Lieut-Col Lord Robert William Orlando Manners, CMG, DSO (*see* D Rutland, colls):—
Rupert John Orlando, *b* 1935: *m* 1st, 1963 (*m diss* 1988), Jeanne Gordon, da of Norman Gordon Farquharson, of
Farquharson, of Bryanston, Johannesburg; 2ndly, 1990, Hon Mrs Susan Geraldine Uniacke, only da of 20th Baron
Willoughby de Broke, and has issue living (by 1st *m*), Robert Norman, *b* 1965, — Frances Sarah Elizabeth, *b* 1970.

　　　　Granddaughter of late Col Walter Richard Lascelles, eldest son of late Hon Arthur Lascelles, 5th son of
　　2nd Earl:—
　　Issue of late Lieut-Col Ernest Lascelles, OBE, Rifle Brig, *b* 1870, *d* 1948: *m* 1895, Flora Evelyn, who *d* 1956, da of
　　late John Bulteel, of Pamfleet, Ivybridge, Devon:—

Faith Evelyn, *b* 1903.

PREDECESSORS – **(1)** EDWARD Lascelles, heir at law of Edwin Lascelles, 1st and last Baron Harewood, of Harewood Castle, co York, having sat as MP for Northallerton in several Parliaments was *cr Baron Harewood*, of Harewood, co York (peerage of Great Britain) 1796, and *Viscount Lascelles* and *Earl of Harewood* (peerage of United Kingdom) 1812; *d* 1820; *s* by his son **(2)** HENRY, 2nd Earl; Lord-Lieut of W Riding of York; *d* 1841; *s* by his son **(3)** HENRY, 3rd Earl; *b* 1797; Lord-Lieut of W Riding of York: *m* 1823, Lady Louisa Thynne, da of 2nd Marquess of Bath; *d* 1857; *s* by his son **(4)** HENRY THYNNE, 4th Earl, *b* 1824: *m* 1st, 1845, Lady Elizabeth Joan De Burgh, who *d* 1854, da of 1st Marquess of Clanricarde; 2ndly, 1858, Diana Elizabeth Matilda, who *d* 1904, da of John George Smythe, of Heath Hall, Wakefield; *d* 1892; *s* by his el son **(5)** HENY ULICK, GCVO, 5th Earl, *b* 1846; Lord, Lieut of W Riding of Yorkshire 1904-27; sometime an ADC to King George V: *m* 1881, Lady Florence Katherine Bridgeman, who *d* 1943, da of 3rd Earl of Bradford; *d* 1929; *s* by his el son **(6)** HENRY GEORGE CHARLES, KG, GCVO, DSO, TD, 6th Earl, *b* 1882; a Personal ADC to HM; Lord-Lieut of W Riding of Yorkshire 1927-47; Chancellor of Sheffield Univ 1944; European War 1914-19 with Grenadier Guards (DSO): *m* 28 Feb 1922, HRH Princess (Victoria Alexandra Alice) Mary (*The Princess Royal*), CI, GCVO, GBE, RRC, TD, CD, who *d* 28 March 1965, only da of HM King George V (*see* ROYAL FAMILY); *d* 1947; *s* by his son **(7)** GEORGE HENRY HUBERT, 7th Earl and present peer; also Viscount Lascelles, and Baron Harewood.

HARLECH, BARON (Ormsby Gore) (Baron UK 1876)

Under this sign thou shalt conquer

FRANCIS DAVID ORMSBY GORE, 6th Baron; *b* 13 March 1954; *s* 1985: *m* 1986, Amanda Jane, da of Alan Thomas Grieve, of Stoke Lodge, Ludlow, Shropshire, and has issue.

Arms – Quarterly: 1st and 4th gules, a fesse between three cross-crosslets fitchée or, *Gore*; 2nd and 3rd gules, a bend between six cross-crosslets or, *Ormsby*. **Crest** – 1st, an heraldic tiger rampant argent; 2nd, a dexter arm embowed in armour proper, holding in the hand a man's leg also in armour, couped at the thigh. **Supporters** – *Dexter*, an heraldic tiger argent, maned and tufted sable, ducally gorged or; *sinister*, a lion or.
Residence – The Mount, Oswestry, Shropshire.

SON LIVING

Hon JASSET DAVID CODY, *b* 1 July 1986.

DAUGHTER LIVING

Hon Tallulah Sylvia, *b* 1988.

SISTERS LIVING

Hon Jane Teresa Denyse, *b* 1942: *m* 1966 (*m diss* 1984), Michael Sean O'Dare Rainey, son of Maj Sean Rainey, and Mrs Marion Wrottesley, and has issue living, Saffron (son), *b* 1967, — Gawaine O'Dare, *b* 1971, — Rose Soley, *b* 1969, — Ramona Alba, *b* 1973. *Residence* – Brogyntyn Home Farm, Oswestry, Salop.
Hon Victoria Mary, *b* 1946: *m* 1972, Julian Richard Leslie Lloyd, son of Maj Derek Leslie Lloyd, MC, and has issue (*see* Chetwynd, V, colls). *Residence* – The Glebe, Leixlip, co Kildare.
Hon Alice Magdalen Sarah, *b* 1952. *Residence* – 14 Ladbroke Rd, W11.

HALF-SISTER LIVING

Hon Pandora Beatrice, *b* 1972.

UNCLE LIVING (*Son of 4th Baron*)

Hon John Julian, *b* 1925; *ed* Eton, and New Coll, Oxford; late Capt Coldstream Guards.

AUNTS LIVING (*Daughters of 4th Baron*)

Hon Mary Hermione (*Hon Lady Mayall*), *b* 1914: *m* 1st, 1936 (*m diss* 1946), Capt Robin Francis Campbell, CBE, DSO, who *d* 1985, only son of late Rt Hon Sir Ronald Hugh Campbell, GCMG; 2ndly, 1947, Sir (Alexander) Lees Mayall, KCVO, CMG, who *d* 1992, and has issue living, (by 1st *m*) Gerard Francis (491 Fulham Rd, SW6), *b* 1937: *m* 1964, Theodora Elizabeth, da of Col Sir Roderick (Napoleon) Brinckman, 5th Bt, and has issue living, Tarquin *b* 1966, Caspar *b* 1967, — Charles, *b* 1939: *m* 1963, Philippa, da of J. C. H. Le B. Croke, and has issue living, Phineas *b* 1965, Orlando *b* 1967, — (by 2nd *m*) Robert George Lees (13 St Mark's Place, W10), *b* 1954; *ed* Eton, — Cordelia Isobel, *b* 1948: *m* 1969 (*m diss* 19—), John Nelson Summerscale, son of Sir John Percival Summerscale, KBE, and has issue living, Aaron Piers *b* 1969, Gideon *b* 1970, — Alexandra Beatrice, *b* 1949: *m* 1st, 1971 (*m diss* 1978), John Culme-Seymour; 2ndly, 1992, Dominic Paul Morland, 2nd son of late Sir Oscar Charles Morland, GBE, KCMG. *Residence* – Sturford Mead, Warminster, Wilts.
Hon Dame Katharine Margaret Alice (*Viscountess Macmillan of Ovenden*), DBE, *b* 1921; DBE (Civil) 1974: *m* 1942, Maurice Victor, Viscount Macmillan of Ovenden, who *d* 1984, only son of 1st Earl of Stockton, and has issue (*see* E Stockton). *Residence* – 9 Warwick Sq, SW1.
Hon Elizabeth Jane, *b* 1929: *m* 1962, Hon William Simon Pease (*see* B Wardington). *Residences* – 29 Upper Addison Gdns, W14 8AJ; Lepe House, Exbury, Southampton.

WIDOW LIVING OF FIFTH BARON

PAMELA (*Pamela, Baroness Harlech*), only da of late Ralph Frederick Colin, of New York City: *m* 1969, as his 2nd wife, the 5th Baron, who *d* as the result of a motor accident 1985. *Residence* – 14 Ladbroke Rd, W11 3NJ.

PREDECESSORS – William Gore (*see* E Arran, colls); MP for Leitrim, for Carnarvon Borough, and for N Shropshire: *m* 1815, Mary Jane, da and heiress of Owen Ormsby, whose name he assumed; *d* 1860 leaving issue **(1)** JOHN RALPH Ormsby-Gore, MP for Carnarvonshire (C) 1837-41, and for N Salop 1859-75; a Groom-in-Waiting to HM 1841-59; *cr Baron Harlech*, of Harlech, co Merioneth (peerage of United Kingdom) 1876, with remainder to his brother: *m* 1844, Sarah, who *d* 1898, da and co-heir of Sir John Tyssen Tyrell, 2nd Bt; *d* 1876; *s* by his brother **(2)** WILLIAM RICHARD, 2nd Baron, *b* 1819; Lieut of co Leitrim; MP for Sligo (*C*) 1841-52, and for co Leitrim 1858-76: *m* 1850, Lady Emily Charlotte, who *d* 1892, da of late Adm Sir George Francis Seymour, GCB; *d* 1904; *s* by his el surviving son **(3)** RALPH CHARLES, 3rd Baron, *b* 1855; appointed Lieut of co Leitrim 1904, and Lord-Lieut of Merionethshire and Constable of Harlech Castle 1927; MP for Shropshire W, or Oswestry Div (*C*) 1901-4: *m* 1881, Lady Margaret Ethel Gordon, who *d* 1950, da of 10th Marquess of Huntly; *d* 1938; *s* by his son **(4)** WILLIAM GEORGE ARTHUR, KG, GCMG, PC, 4th Baron; *b* 1885; MP for Denbigh Dist (*C*) 1910-18, and Stafford 1918-38; Under-Sec of State for Colonies 1922-24, Postmaster-Gen Sept to Nov 1931, First Commr of Works 1931-36, and Sec of State for the Colonies 1936-38, High Commr for Bechuanaland, Basutoland and Swaziland, and High Commr in Union of S Africa 1941-44, Lord Lt of Merionethshire 1938-57, Constable of Harlech Castle 1938-64, and Caernarvon Castle 1945-63, Pro-Chancellor of Univ of Wales 1945-56: *m* 1913, Lady Beatrice Edith Mildred Gascoyne-Cecil, DCVO, da of 4th Marquess of Salisbury; *d* 1964; *s* by his yr son **(5)** WILLIAM DAVID, KCMG, PC, 5th Baron, *b* 1918; Maj RA (TA); DL for Salop; Min of State for Foreign Affairs 1957-61; Ambassador to USA 1961-65, and Dep Leader of Opposition House of Lords 1966-67; Chm Harlech TV 1967-85; Pres British Board of Film Censors; MP for Oswestry Div of Salop (*U*) 1950-61; PC 1957, KCMG 1961: *m* 1st, 1940, Sylvia, who was *k* in a motor accident 1967, da of late Hugh Lloyd Thomas, CMG, CVO (*see* Bellew, B, colls, 1967 Edn); 2ndly, 1969, Pamela, only da of Ralph F. Colin, of New York City, and *d* as the result of a motor accident 1985, when he was *s* by his only surv son **(6)** FRANCIS DAVID, 6th Baron and present peer.

HARMAR-NICHOLLS, BARON (Harmar-Nicholls) (Life Baron 1974, Bt UK 1960)

HARMAR HARMAR-NICHOLLS, *Life Baron*, and 1st *Baronet*, son of Charles Edward Craddock Nicholls, of Walsall, Staffs; *b* 1 Nov 1912; assumed by deed poll the surname of Harmar-Nicholls in lieu of his patronymic; *ed* Queen Mary's Gram Sch, Walsall; 1939-45 War as Lt RE in India and Burma; a Dir of J & H Nicholls (Paints) Ltd, of Nicholls and Hennessy Group Ltd, of Radio Luxembourg (London) Ltd, of Cannon Insurance, Ltd, Chm Malvern Festival Theatre Trust; an Underwriter of Lloyd's and a JP for Staffs; PPS to Assist Postmaster-Gen 1951-55, Parl Sec Min of Agric Fisheries and Food 1955-57, and to Min of Works 1957-60; MP for Peterborough Div of Northants (*C*) 1950-74; elected rep to European Assembly 1979; *cr* a Baronet, of Darlaston, co Stafford (UK) 1960 and *Baron Harmar-Nicholls*, of Peterborough, Cambridgeshire: *m* 1940, Dorothy Elsie, el da of James Edwards, of Tipton, Staffs, and has issue.

Arms – Per pale and per chevron gules and sable, two arrows with broad heads pilewise, the shafts argent, the feathers and heads or overall a chevron engrailed gold. **Crest** – Gules and sable two keys in saltire wards upwards argent supporting a Davey lamp proper, all tied about with a Stafford knot, the strands gules and sable, the tassels also gules.
Residence – Abbeylands, Weston, Stafford. *Clubs* – Constitutional, St Stephen's, Unionist City and Counties (Peterborough).

DAUGHTERS LIVING

Hon Judith Ann, *b* 1941: *m* 1973, Alan Aspden.
Hon Susan Frances Nicholls, *b* 1943; actress (as Susan Nicholls): *m* 1993, Mark Eden, actor.

HARMSWORTH, BARON (Harmsworth) (Baron UK 1939)

He does well who works diligently

THOMAS HAROLD RAYMOND HARMSWORTH, 3rd Baron; *b* 20 July 1939; *s* 1990; *ed* Eton, and Ch Ch, Oxford; 2nd Lieut RHG: *m* 1971, Patricia Palmer, da of late Michael Palmer Horsley, of Waltham House, Brough, N Humberside, and has issue.

Arms – Azure, two rolls of paper in saltire or, banded in the centre gules, between two bees volant in pale and as many trefoils in fesse of the second. **Crest** – A cubit arm erect, the hand holding a roll of paper fessewise proper between two ostrich feathers or. **Supporters** – On either side a deep sea fisherman proper.
Residence – The Old Rectory, Stoke Abbott, Beaminster, Dorset DT8 3JT.

SONS LIVING

Hon DOMINIC MICHAEL ERIC, *b* 18 Sept 1973; *ed* Eton.
Hon Timothy Thomas John, *b* 1979.

DAUGHTERS LIVING

Hon Philomena Hélène Olivia, *b* 1975.
Hon Abigail Patricia Thérèse, *b* 1977.
Hon Pollyanna Mary Clare, *b* 1981.

SISTER LIVING

Madeleine Thérèse Margaret, *b* 1941; *ed* Poles Convent, and Somerville Coll, Oxford; journalist. *Residence* – 15 Sudeley St, Islington, N1.

DAUGHTER LIVING OF SECOND BARON

Hon Margaret Askew Alexander, *b* 1928; painter and sculptor: *m* 1st, 1949, Wendell Holmes McCulloch, son of late Wendell McCulloch, of Bowling Green, Kentucky, USA; 2ndly, 1960, Frank Gibson Phillips, son of late Henry Gibson Phillips, of Windmill Hill, Alton, Hants, and has issue living (by 1st *m*), Kevin Desmond Harmsworth (Lime Lodge, Egham, Surrey), *b* 1950; *ed* Harrow, — (by Fredi Re'em), Dan Eric Harmsworth McCULLOCH (369 Montezuma Av, Suite No.110, Santa Fé, NM 87501, USA), *b* 1951; *ed* Bedales; interior designer, photographer, and fine art print publisher: *m* 1st, 1978 (*m diss* 1983), Donna Maria Santoro; 2ndly, 1992, Yana Halouzka, and has issue living (by 1st *m*), Francesca Prembindu *b* 1978, (by 2nd *m*) Angelo Halouzka *b* 1993. *Residences* – 15 Square de Chantillon, Paris 75014, France; Lime Lodge, Egham, Surrey.

STEPMOTHER LIVING

Helen Gordon, da of late Maj-Gen Granville George Loch, CB, CMG, DSO, and formerly wife of late Lt-Col Charles Arthur Norman Hudson, The Black Watch: *m* 1964, as his 2nd wife, Hon Eric Beauchamp Northcliffe Harmsworth, who *d* 1988. *Residence* – 27 Hartington Rd, Chiswick, W4 3TL.

PREDECESSORS – **(1)** CECIL BISSHOPP Harmsworth, 3rd son of late Alfred Harmsworth, Bar-at-Law (see also V Northcliffe (ext) and V Rothermere); *b* 1869; was Parliamentary Private Sec (unpaid) to Pres of Board of Agriculture and Fisheries (Rt Hon W Runciman, MP) 1911-15; Parliamentary Under-Sec of State, Home Depart 1915-19, and for Foreign Affairs 1919-22; in Prime Min's Secretariat 1917-19; sat as MP for Worcestershire Mid, of Droitwich Div (*L*) 1906-10, for S, or Luton Div of Bedfordshire 1911-18, and for Luton Div thereof 1918-22; *cr Baron Harmsworth*, of Egham, co Surrey (peerage of UK) 1939: *m* 1897, Emilie Alberta, who *d* 1942, da of William Hamilton Maffett, Bar-at-Law, formerly of St Helena, Finglas, co Dublin; *d* 1948; *s* by his el son **(2)** CECIL DESMOND BERNARD, 2nd Baron, *b* 1903; painter; Chm Dr Johnson's House Trust: *m* 1926, Dorothy Alexander, who *d* 1990, da of late Hon Joseph Charles Phelps Heinlein (sometime a State Senator), of Bridgeport, Ohio, USA; *d* 1990; *s* by his nephew **(3)** THOMAS HAROLD RAYMOND (son of late Hon Eric Beauchamp Northcliffe Harmsworth, yst son of 1st Baron, by his 1st wife, Hélène Marie, who *d* 1962, elder da of Col Jules-Raymond Dehove, of Paris), 3rd Baron and present peer.

HARRINGTON, EARL OF (Stanhope) (Earl GB 1742)

From God and the king

WILLIAM HENRY LEICESTER STANHOPE, 11th Earl; *b* 24 Aug 1922; *s* 1929 to the Earldom of Harrington, Viscountcy of Petersham and Barony of Harrington; and 1967 to Viscountcy of Stanhope of Mahon and Barony of Stanhope of Elvaston; *ed* Eton; Capt 15th/19th King's R Hussars: *m* 1st, 1942 (*m diss* 1946), Eileen, only da of Sir John Foley Grey, 8th Bt (*see* Lambert, Bt); 2ndly, 1947 (*m diss* 1962), Anne Theodora, only da of late Maj Richard Arenbourg Blennerhassett Chute; 3rdly, 1964, Priscilla Margarete da of late Hon Archibald Edward Cubitt (*see* B Ashcombe, colls), and has had issue by 1st, 2nd and 3rd *m*.

Arms – Quarterly; ermine and gules. **Crest** – A tower azure, a demi-lion rampant issuant from the battlements or, in the paws a bomb fired proper. **Supporters** – *Dexter*, a talbot guardant argent, guttée de poix; *sinister*, a wolf erminois; each gorged with a chaplet of oak proper.
Seat – Greenmount, Patrickswell, co Limerick.

SONS LIVING (By 1st marriage)

CHARLES HENRY LEICESTER (*Viscount Petersham*) (Baynton House, Coulston, West-bury, Wilts), *b* 20 July 1945; *ed* Aysgarth, and Eton: *m* 1st, 1966, Virginia Alleyne Freeman, da of late Capt Harry Freeman Jackson, of Cool-na-Grena, co Cork; 2ndly, 1984, Anita Robsahm, formerly wife of 21st Earl of Suffolk, and da of late Robin Robsahm Fuglesang, of Laycock, Wilts, and has issue:—

SON LIVING (By 1st *m*)— *Hon* William Henry Leicester, *b* 14 Oct 1967; *ed* Aysgarth, and Aiglon Coll.

DAUGHTER LIVING (By 1st *m*)— *Hon* Serena Alleyne (*Viscountess Linley*), *b* 1970: *m* 1993, David Albert Charles, Viscount Linley, only son of 1st Earl of Snowdon, and of HRH The Princess Margaret, Countess of Snowdon.

(By 2nd marriage)

Hon Steven Francis Lincoln (Dooneen Stud, Patrickswell, co Limerick), *b* 1951: *m* 1978, Maureen Elizabeth Irvine, da of Maj Harold William Cole, of Poundbury, Dorchester, Dorset, and has issue living, Ben, *b* 1978, — Tara, *b* 1979.

(By 3rd marriage)

Hon John Fitzroy, *b* 1965.

DAUGHTERS LIVING AND DECEASED (By 1st marriage)

Lady Jane, *b* 1942: *m* 1965, Anthony Cameron, of Dowth Hall, Drogheda, co Meath, son of Clifford Cameron, of Dowth Hall, and was *k* in a motor accident 1974, leaving issue, James William, *b* 1967, — Henrietta Jane, *b* 1970.
Lady Avena Margaret Clare, *b* 1944: *m* 1969, Adrian James Maxwell, of South Lodge, Carrick-on-Suir, co Tipperary, only son

of Maj James Kennedy Maxwell, MC, of Buckby Folly House, E Haddon, Northants, and has issue living, Sacha Jane, *b* 1974, — Kerry Alice, *b* 1978.

(By 2nd marriage)

Lady Trina Maria, *b* 1947.
Lady Sarah Sue (twin), *b* 1951: *m* 1970, Robert John Barry, of Mellon Stud, Kildimo, co Limerick, and has issue living, Mark James, *b* 1972, — Tristan James, *b* 1975, — Guy William (twin), *b* 1975.

(By 3rd marriage)

Lady Isabella Rachel, *b* 1966.

COLLATERAL BRANCHES LIVING

Grandchildren of late Russell Charles Stanhope (*b* 1866) (infra):—
Issue of late Aubrey Charles Stanhope, *b* 1895, *d* 1953: *m* 1st, 1919, Paulette Bordier du Raincy, of France, who *d* 1922; 2ndly, 19—, An American Lady; 3rdly, 1931, Evelyn Wadsworth, who *d* 1981:—
(By 1st *m*) Aubrey Charles, DFC (PO Box 37, Bristol, Maine 04539, USA), *b* 1920; Lt-Col USAF (ret); 1939-45 War, DFC (USA): *m* 1941, Muriel Grace, da of late William Anderson Lauther, of Truro, Nova Scotia, and has issue living, Paulette Beatrice, *b* 1946: *m* 1968, her first cousin once removed, Gilbert Mark Rollo (*see* L Rollo, colls). —— Marie Annick (1606 Golf View Drive, Urbana, Illinois, USA), *b* 1921: *m* 1953, Lt-Col Richard Davis, USAF, who *d* 1977. —— (By 2nd *m*), Jonathan, *b* 19—. —— Christian (a da), *b* 19—. —— (By 3rd *m*) Noel (West Winfield Farm, West Winfield, New York, USA), *b* 1946.
Issue of late Leicester de Maclot Stanhope, *b* 1901, *d* 1978: *m* 1930, Rose Mary Farnham, of New York:—
Leicester (3633 Tangier Terr, Sarasota, Florida, USA) *b* 1932: *m* 1955, Priscilla Carrington Young, of Conn, USA, and has issue living, Leicester de Maclot, *b* 1957, — Russell Charles, *b* 1958, — Margot, *b* 1960, — Jennifer, *b* 1961. —— Philip (Hidden Harbor Rd, Sarasota, Florida, 33578, USA), *b* 1939: *m* 19—, Bonnie —, and has issue living, Philip, *b* 1973, — Sean, *b* 1980, — Justin, *b* 1982. —— Nina (Delray Beach, Florida 33444, USA), *b* 1931: *m* 19—.

Grandchildren of late Russell Charles Stanhope, son of late Hon Sir Francis Charles Stanhope, KCH, 5th son of 3rd Earl:—
Issue of late Russell Charles Stanhope, *b* 1866, *d* 1945: *m* 1894, Augustine Madeleine Thompson, of USA, who *d* 1916:—
Russell Charles (575 Hollow Tree Ridge Rd, Darien, Conn, 06820, USA), *b* 1899: *m* 1934, Jean Kennedy, of New York, and has issue living, Michelle, *b* 1945: *m* 1976, Dr Frank Converse Sparks, and has issue living, Kristin *b* 1978, Ashley *b* 1980, Nicole *b* 1983, — Celeste, *b* 1947: *m* 1964, John Nicholas Pierce, and has issue living, Michela Stanhope *b* 1965, Elizabeth *b* 1971. —— Violet Augustina *b* 1912: *m* 1936, Major Robert Duncan Rollo, Suffolk Regt (*see* L Rollo, colls), who *d* 1986. *Residence* – The Close, Boscombe Village, Salisbury.

PREDECESSORS – (1) *Rt Hon* WILLIAM Stanhope (son of John Stanhope of Elvaston, Derbys); grandson of Sir John Stanhope of Elvaston, yr half-brother of 1st Earl of Chesterfield, (infra) *b* about 1683; Ambassador to Spain 1721-27 and 1729-30, Prin Sec of State 1738-42, Lord Pres of Council 1742-45 and Lord Lt of Ireland 1746-50; in consideration of his services for negotiating Treaty of Seville, *cr* Baron *Harrington*, of Harrington, co Northampton (peerage of GB) 1730, and *Viscount Petersham* and *Earl of Harrington* (peerage of GB) 1742: *m* 1718, Anne, who *d* 1719, da and heir of Col Edward Griffith; *d* 1756; *s* by his son (2) WILLIAM, 2nd Earl; *b* 1719; Gen: *m* 1746, Lady Caroline FitzRoy, who *d* 1784, da of 2nd Duke of Grafton; *d* 1799; *s* by his son (3) CHARLES, GCH, 3rd Earl; *b* 1753; Gen and Col 1st Life Guards; Gov and Constable of Windsor Castle 1812-29: *m* 1779, Jane, who *d* 1824, da and co-heir of Sir John Fleming, 1st Bt of Brompton Park, Middlesex; *d* 1829; *s* by his el son (4) CHARLES, 4th Earl; *b* 1780; Col: *m* 1831, Maria (actress), who *d* 1867, da of Samuel Foote; *d* 1851; *s* by his brother (5) LEICESTER FITZGERALD CHARLES, CB, 5th Earl; *b* 1784; Col: *m* 1831, Elizabeth Williams, who *d* 1898, da and heir of William Green, of Trelawney, Jamaica; *d* 1862; *s* by his son (6) SEYMOUR SYDNEY HYDE, 6th Earl; *b* 1845; *d* 1866; *s* by his cousin (7) CHARLES WYNDHAM, 7th Earl; son of Very Rev Hon FitzRoy Henry Richard, 4th son of 3rd Earl; *b* 1809: *m* 1839, Elizabeth Still, who *d* 1912, da of Robert Lucas de Pearsall; *d* 1881; *s* by his son (8) CHARLES AUGUSTUS, 8th Earl, *b* 1844: *m* 1869, Hon Eva Elizabeth Carington, who *d* 1919, da of 2nd Baron Carrington; *d* 1917; *s* by his brother (9) DUDLEY HENRY EDEN, 9th Earl; *b* 1859: *m* 1883, Kathleen, who *d* 1948, da of J. Carter Wood, of Weybourne Hall, Weybourne, Norfolk; *d* 1928; *s* by his son (10) CHARLES JOSEPH LEICESTER, MC, 10th Earl, *b* 1887; Bt Maj 15th Hussars: *m* 1919, Margaret Trelawney (Susan), who *d* 1952 (having *m* 2ndly, 1934, Luke Theodore Lillingston of Ulverscroft, Leics, and 3rdly, 1949, Maj Stephen C Johnston), da of Maj H. H. D. Seaton, formerly Remount Ser, *d* 1929; *s* by his son (11) WILLIAM HENRY LEICESTER, 11th Earl, and present peer; also Viscount Stanhope of Mahon, Viscount Petersham, Baron Stanhope of Elvaston (see infra*) and Baron Harrington.
*(1) JAMES Stanhope, el son of Hon Alexander Stanhope, yst son of 1st Earl of Chesterfield; *b* 1673; Lt Gen; C-in-C of British Forces in Spain 1708-10 (effected capture of port of Mahon, Minorca 1708 and gained victories of Almenara and Saragossa 1710); Sec of State 1714-17 and 1718-21, 1st Lord of the Treasury and Chancellor of the Exchequer 1717-18; *cr Baron Stanhope of Elvaston*, co Derby, and *Viscount Stanhope of Mahon*, in island of Minorca (peerage of GB) 1717, with remainder to the descendants in the male line of his kinsman, John Stanhope of Elvaston (ante), (whose son William was *cr* Earl of Harrington); *cr Earl Stanhope* 1718*d* (peerage of GB) with remainder to heirs male of his body: *m* 1713, Lucy, who *d* 1723, da of Thomas Pitt of Blandford; *d* 1721; *s* by his el son (2) PHILIP, 2nd Earl; *b* 1714; FRS: *m* 1745, Grisel, who *d* 1811, da of Charles Hamilton, Lord Binning, el son of 6th Earl of Haddington; *d* 1786; *s* by his 2nd son (3) CHARLES, 3rd Earl; *b* 1753; FRS; perfected process of stereotyping and experimented with fire-proof buildings, steam vessels and calculating machines: *m* 1st, 1774, Lady Hester Pitt, who *d* 1780, da of 1st Earl of Chatham; 2ndly, 1781, Louisa, who *d* 1829, da and heir of Hon Henry Grenville (E Temple); *d* 1816; *s* by his el son (4) PHILIP HENRY, 4th Earl; *b* 1782; FRS; Keeper of the Records, Bermingham Tower, Dublin Castle 1805-55: *m* 1803, Hon Catherine Lucy Smith, who *d* 1843, da of 1st Baron Carrington; *d* 1855; *s* by his el son (5) PHILIP HENRY, 5th Earl; *b* 1805; FRS; Under Sec for Foreign Affairs 1834-35; historian; founder and 1st Chm of National Portrait Gallery: *m* 1834, Emily Harriet, who *d* 1874, da of Gen Sir Edward Kerrison, GCH, KCB, 1st Bt; *d* 1875; *s* by his el son (6) ARTHUR PHILIP, 6th Earl; *b* 1838; a Lord of the Treasury 1874-75: *m* 1869, Evelyn Henrietta, who *d* 1923, only da of Richard Pennefather, of Knockeevan, co Tipperary; *d* 1905; *s* by his el son (7) JAMES RICHARD, KG, DSO, MC, PC, 7th Earl; *b* 1880; Civil Lord of the Admiralty 1924-29, Parl and Financial Sec to the Admiralty and Civil Lord 1931, Parl Under Sec of State for War and Vice-Pres of Army Council 1931-34, Parl Under Sec of State for Foreign Affairs 1934-36, 1st Commr of Works 1936-37, Pres of Board of Education 1937-38, 1st Lord of Admiralty 1938-39, and Lord Pres of Council 1939-40; *s* his kinsman, Edward Henry Scudamore-Stanhope, as 13th Earl of Chesterfield and 13th Baron Stanhope of Shelford 1952 (but did not apply for writ of summons): *m* 1921, Lady Eileen Agatha Browne, who *d* 1940, da of 6th Marquess of Sligo; *d* 1967, when the Earldoms of Chesterfield and Stanhope, and the Barony of Stanhope of Shelford became ext, and the Viscountcy of Stanhope of Mahon and the Barony of Stanhope of Elvaston devolved upon the 11th Earl of Harrington (ante), who thereupon became the representative of the Stanhope family.

HARRIS, BARON (Harris) (Baron UK 1815)

GEORGE ROBERT JOHN HARRIS, 6th Baron; *b* 17 April 1920; *s* 1984; *ed* Eton, and Ch Ch, Oxford; Capt RA (ret).

Arms – Vert, on a chevron embattled erminois, between three hedgehogs or, as many bombs sable, fired proper; on a chief of augmentation, a representation of the gates and fortress of Seringapatam, the drawbridge let down, and the Union flag of Great Britain and Ireland hoisted above the standard of Tippoo Sahib, all proper. **Crest** – On a mural crown or, a royal tiger passant guardant vert, striped or, spotted of the first, pierced in the breast with an arrow of the last, vulned gules, and charged on the forehead with the Persian character implying "Hyder", and crowned with an Eastern coronet both of the first. **Supporters** – *Dexter,* a grenadier in uniform of 73rd Foot, supporting with the exterior hand a flag staff, thereon hoisted the Union Flag of Great Britain and Ireland flying towards the dexter over the standard of Tippoo Sultan; and below the same tricoloured flag of the French Republic depressed and furled all proper; *sinister,* a Sepoy of the Madras Establishment of the East India Company, supporting with the exterior hand a flag staff thereon hoisted the flag of the said Company, flying over that of Tippoo Sultan towards the sinister; and below same the tricoloured flag of the French Republic as in the dexter.
Seat – Belmont Park, Faversham, Kent. *Residence* – Huntingfield, Eastling, nr Faversham, Kent.

COLLATERAL BRANCHES LIVING

Grandson of late Lieut-Col Thomas Harris, eldest son of Thomas Inglis Parish Harris, eldest son of late Hon Michael Thomas Harris, 2nd son of 1st Baron:—
Issue of late Maj Thomas Guy Marriott Harris, OBE, *b* 1882, *d* 1955: *m* 1912, Beryl, who *d* 1960, da of Col Frederick Alexander Wilson, formerly Indian Army:—
DEREK MARSHALL, *b* 23 July 1916; Maj Duke of Wellington's Regt (ret): *m* 1st, 1938 (*m diss* 1968), Laura Cecilia, da of late Maj Edward Thomas William McCausland, Indian Army; 2ndly, 1987, Mrs Pauline Elisabeth Skinner (*née* Giles), and has issue living (by 1st *m*), Anthony (1 Linkenholt Mansions, Stamford Brook Av, W6), *b* 1942: *m* 1966, Anstice, da of Alfred Winter, and has issue living, Isabel *b* 1973, Laura *b* 1976, — Amanda (21 Sandhill Place, N19), *b* 1953: *m* 1974 (*m diss* 1984) Jeremy Mainwaring, 2nd son of Maj Mainwaring, and has issue living, Guy *b* 1975, Rosie *b* 1980. *Residence* – The Orchard, Loders, Bridport, Dorset.

Grandchildren of late George Lucian Taylor Harris, eldest son of late George Anstruther Harris (infra):—
Issue of late George Temple James Harris, *b* 1876, *d* 1929: *m* 1910, Eva, who *d* 1942, having *m* 2ndly, 1933, Randle North Kenyon, who *d* 1968 (B Kenyon, colls), da of late Lt-Col Henry Green Wilkinson (B Bateman):—
Ronald George Temple (9 Dunning Court, Dowell St, Honiton, Devon EX14 8FQ), *b* 1911; formerly Capt Air Transport Auxiliary: *m* 1st, 1936 (*m diss* 1958), Simone Hogbin, of Folkestone; 2ndly, 1958, Beryl, el da of George Brown, of 8 Holt Rd, Fakenham. —— Antony John Temple, OBE, *b* 1915; Cdr RN; OBE (Mil) 1963: *m* 1940, Doris, only child of late F. D. Drake, of Winter Park, Florida, USA, and has issue living, Michael George Temple (c/o Naval Sec, Victory Building, HM Naval Base, Portsmouth, Hants PO1 3LS), *b* 1941; Rear Adm RN: *m* 1970, Caroline Sandra Pietre Katrina, da of late Gp Capt Patrick George Chichester, OBE (*see* Chichester, Bt, colls), and has issue living, Tamsin Caroline Temple *b* 1971, Rebecca Eva Temple *b* 1974, Emily Vesta Temple *b* 1979, — John Frank Temple (24 Manor Close, Wickham, Fareham, Hants PO17 5BZ), *b* 1944: *m* 1972, Sandra Dobson, da of C. Stones, of Bishop Auckland. *Residence* – Hawthorns, Wickham, Hants.
—— June Rosemary Temple (4 Dale Av, Hassocks, W Sussex BN6 8LW), *b* 1928.

Granddaughter of late Col Charles John Birch Harris, 3rd son of late George Anstruther Harris (infra):—
Issue of late Hugh Anstruther Harris, *b* 1882, *d* 1951: *m* 1922, Ada Miller, who *d* 1966:—
Nina Denise, *b* 1924: *m* 1946, Donald R. Miller, and has issue living, Michael Jeffrey, *b* 1947, — Gary Lee, *b* 1949, — Jeffrey Hugh, *b* 1952, — Wendy Louise, *b* 1954, — Julie Diane *b* 1962.

Grandchildren of late George Anstruther Harris, 2nd son of Hon Michael Thomas Harris (ante):—
Issue of late Hermann Gundert Harris, *b* 1859, *d* 1950: *m* 1895, Alice Uniacke, who *d* 1927, da of late William Uniacke Townsend, of Ardbrae, Bray (Coote, Bt, *cr* 1621, colls):—
Eric Townsend (1550 Hayworth St, Hollywood, Cal, USA), *b* 1902; 1914-18 War with Canadian Expeditionary Force: *m* 1st, 1920 (*m diss* 1927), Marjorie Peggy, da of late Charles Vokes, of Winnipeg; 2ndly, 1946, Helen, da of late Howard Francis Bidwell, of Boston, Mass, USA, and has issue living, (by 1st *m*) Joan Patricia, *b* 1922, — Elizabeth Anne, *b* 1926, — (by 2nd *m*), Patricia Anne, *b* 1950. —— Doris Emma (Apt 307, 409 Ash St, New Westminster, BC, Canada V3M 3NI), *b* 1900: *m* 1918, Albert O. Snook, who *d* 1966, and has issue living, Glen Townsend (c/o Island Trust Council, Denman Island, BC, Canada), *b* 1924; 1939-45 War with RCN: *m* 1950, Mae Miller, da of Charles Pihan, of Langley, BC, and has issue living, Lloyd Glen *b* 1951, Brian *b* 1954, Deborah Ann *b* 1957.

Grandchildren of Hermann Gundert Harris (ante):—
Issue of late George Rutherford Harris, *b* 1903, *d* 1983: *m* 1927, Olive Hall (5338 Patterson Av S, Burnaby 1, BC, Canada):—
Gerald Rutherford, *b* 1928: *m* 1955, Vernette Harris, and has issue living, Scott, *b* 1960, — Shelley Ann, *b* 1957. —— Alfred James, *b* 1942; RCM Police: *m* 1965, Alexandra Konopelka, and has issue living, Dwayne Stephen, *b* 1966, — Suzanne Marie, *b* 1967. —— Lucille Olive Iona, *b* 1930: *m* 1951, William A. Spaidal, of 1044 Charland St, Coquitlam, BC, Canada, and has issue living, Richard Arnold, *b* 1952, — William Randall, *b* 1957, — Robert Matthew, *b* 1968, — Linda Lucille, *b* 1963. —— Violet Joyce, *b* 1935: *m* 1959, Donald Watkins, of 612 Vermouth Av, Cooksville, Ontario, Canada, and has issue living, Norman Douglas, *b* 1963, — Steven Patrick, *b* 1964.

Grandsons of late George Anstruther Harris (ante):—
Issue of late Alfred Herschell Harris, *b* 1863, *d* 1894, Amèlie, who *d* 1955, da of late E. B. Anstie:—
Robert Louis Anstruther, *b* 1900; *ed* Sherborne, and New Coll, Oxford; was an Actor. *Club* – Garrick. —— Christopher Money, *b* 1907; *ed* Trin Coll, Oxford (MA); JP; Founder Chm Assocn of Prof Foresters; FRSA; 1939-45 War with RAFO: *m* 1935, Ruth Cunliffe, da of late George Harwood, MP, of Bolton, and has issue living, Robert Julian Brownlow, *b* 1943: *m* 1971 (*m diss* 1976), Lady Camilla Dorothy Godolphin Osborne, da of 11th Duke of Leeds, and has issue living, Emily Kate

Godolphin *b* 1972, — Phoebe Georgina, *b* 1950: *m* 1970, Guy Rudolph Bentinck, of Erth Barton, Saltash, Cornwall, and has issue living, Caspar *b* 1973, Chloe *b* 1978. *Club* – Travellers'.

PREDECESSORS – (**1**) *Sir* GEORGE Harris, GCB, a Gen in the Army and Col 73rd Regt was Com in Ch at siege and capture of Seringapatam and conquest of Mysore 1799; *cr Baron Harris*, of Seringapatam and Mysore, E Indies, and of Belmont, co Kent (peerage of United Kingdom) 1815; *d* 1829; *s* by his son (**2**) WILLIAM GEORGE, KCH, CB, 2nd Baron, a Lt-Gen in the Army and Col 73rd Foot; *d* 1845; *s* by his son (**3**) GEORGE FRANCIS ROBERT, GCSI, 3rd Baron; *b* 1810; was Gov of Trinidad 1846-54, and of Madras 1854-9, a Lord in Waiting to HM Queen Victoria 1860-3, and Chamberlain to Princess of Wales 1863-71; *m* 1850, Sarah, who *d* 1853, da of Ven George Cummins, Archdeacon of Trinidad; *d* 1872; *s* by his son (**4**) GEORGE ROBERT CANNING, GCSI, GCIE, CB, 4th Baron, *b* 1852; Under-Sec for India 1885-6, Under-Sec for War 1886-9, Gov of Bombay 1890-95, a Lord-in-Waiting to Queen Victoria 1895-1900, Vice-Lieut of Kent 1914-15; bore Queen Consort's Sceptre with Dove at Coronation of King Edward VII: *m* 1874, Hon Lucy Ada Jervis, CI, who *d* 1930, da of 3rd Viscount St Vincent, *d* 1932; *s* by his son (**5**) GEORGE ST VINCENT, CBE, MC, 5th Baron, *b* 1889; Capt Yeo; served World War I (wounded, despatches); Chm Kent Police Authority; JP, Vice-Lieut (1944-72) and Co Commr for Kent; a Gov King's Sch, Canterbury; St John's Ambulance Brig 1940-45: *m* 1918, Dorothy Mary, who *d* 1981, da of Rev John William Crookes, formerly V of Borden, Sittingbourne; *d* 1984; *s* by his only son (**6**) GEORGE ROBERT JOHN, 6th Baron and present peer.

HARRIS OF GREENWICH, BARON (Harris) (Life Baron 1974)

JOHN HENRY HARRIS, son of Alfred George Harris; *b* 5 April 1930; *ed* Pinner Gram Sch, Middx; Personal Assist to Leader of the Opposition 1959-62; Dir of Publicity, Labour Party 1962-64, Special Assist to Foreign Sec 1964-66, to Home Sec 1966-67, and to Chancellor of the Exchequer 1967-70, and a Min of State, Home Office 1974-79; Chm Parole Board for England and Wales 1979-82; a Political Correspondent with *The Economist* 1970-74; *cr Baron Harris of Greenwich*, of Greenwich in Greater London (Life Baron) 1974: *m* 1st, 1952 (*m diss* 1982), Patricia Margaret, da of George Neuby Alstrom; 2ndly, 1983, Angela Smith, and has issue by 1st *m*.
Address – c/o House of Lords, SW1. *Clubs* – Reform, MCC.

SON LIVING *(By 1st marriage)*

Hon Francis Oliver Alstrom, *b* 1961.

DAUGHTER LIVING *(By 1st marriage)*

Hon Deborah Jane Alstrom, *b* 1958.

HARRIS OF HIGH CROSS, BARON (Harris) (Life Baron 1979)

RALPH HARRIS, *b* 10 Dec 1924; *ed* Tottenham Grammar Sch, and Queens' Coll, Camb (MA); Lecturer in Polit Economy St Andrews Univ 1949-56; Leader-writer *Glasgow Herald* 1956; Gen Dir Inst of Economic Affairs 1957-87, Chm 1987-89, and Founder Pres since 1992; Chm FOREST since 1987; Independent Nat Dir Times Newspaper Holdings since 1991; *cr Baron Harris of High Cross*, of Tottenham, Greater London (Life Baron) 1979: *m* 1949, Jose Pauline, da of late Roger Frederick Jeffery, and has had issue.
Residence – 4 Walmar Close, Beech Hill, Hadley Wood, Barnet, Herts EN4 0LA.

SON DECEASED

Hon Julian Paul, *b* 1956; *d* 1992.

DAUGHTER LIVING

Hon Angela Caroline, *b* 1951: *m* 1977, Roland Triponel, of 15 rue Jean-Louis Delaporte, 1000 Troyes, France, and has issue.

HARROWBY, EARL OF (Ryder) (Earl UK 1809)

The promise made to the ashes of my forefathers has been kept

DUDLEY DANVERS GRANVILLE COUTTS RYDER, TD, 7th Earl; *b* 20 Dec 1922; *s* 1987; *ed* Eton; served 1939-45 War 59 Inf Div (wounded), 5 Para Bde in N-W Europe, India and Java (political officer) 56 Armoured Div, 1941-45, Lt-Col RA OC 254 (City of London) Field Regt RA (TA) 1962-65; a Dep Chm National Westminster Bank plc 1971-87 (Dir 1968), Chm International Westminster Bank 1977-87 and Chm National Westminster Investment Bank 1986-87; Dep Chm Coutts & Co 1970-89 (Man Dir 1949); Chm Dowty Gp plc 1986-91; Powell Duffryn Group 1976-86 (Chm 1981-86); Trustee of Psychiatry Research Trust since 1982, etc; Hon Fell Roy Coll of Psychiatrists 1983; Hon Treas Staffordshire Soc 1947-51 (Pres 1957-59), Exec Ctte of London Area Conservative Assocn 1949-50, Kensington Borough Council 1950-65, Family Welfare Assocn 1951-65, and S Kensington Conservative Assocn 1953-56; Manager of Fulham and Kensington Hospital Gp 1953-56, etc; Bd of Govs Roy and Maudsley (Postgraduate Teaching) Hospitals 1955-73 (Chm 1965-73), also Univ of Keele 1956-68; Lord Chancellor's Advisory Investment Ctte for Court of Protection 1965-77, etc: *m* 1949, Jeanette Rosalthé, da of late Capt Peter Johnston-Saint, and has issue.

Arms – Azure, three crescents or, each charged with an ermine spot sable. **Crest** – Out of a mural coronet a dragon's head argent, charged on the neck with an ermine spot sable. **Supporters** – Two griffins, wings elevated, argent, each charged on the shoulder with an ermine spot sable, gorged with a plain collar azure, thereon three crescents or, and affixed thereto a chain reflexed over the back, of the last.
Seats – Sandon Hall, Stafford; Burnt Norton, Chipping Campden, Glos. *Town Residence* – 5 Tregunter Rd, SW10 9LS.

SON LIVING

DUDLEY ADRIAN CONROY (*Viscount Sandon*), *b* 18 March 1951; *ed* Eton, Univ of Newcastle-upon-Tyne, and Magdalene Coll, Camb (MA); Executive Dir Compton Street Securities Ltd since 1988; Governor John Archer Sch, Wandsworth 1968-88; FRICS; *m* 1977, Sarah Nichola Hobhouse, only da of Capt Anthony Denys Phillpotts Payne, of Carraway Barn, Carraway Lane, Marnhull, Dorset, and has issue. *Address* – c/o Sandon Estate Office, Sandon, Stafford ST18 0DA.

   SONS LIVING— *Hon* Dudley Anthony Hugo Coventry, *b* 5 Sept 1981, — *Hon* Frederick Whitmore Dudley, *b* 1984, — *Hon* Henry Mansell Dudley, *b* 1985.
   DAUGHTER LIVING — *Hon* Emily Georgina Hobhouse, *b* 1992.

DAUGHTER LIVING

Lady Rosalthé Frances, *b* 1954: *m* 1976, Francis Richard Seton Rundall, yr son of Frank Lionel Montagu Rundall, of Stoneleigh House, Longborough, Glos, and has issue living, (Francis) Thomas Mansell, *b* 1981, — Mark Dudley Ridgway, *b* 1982, — John William Nathaniel, *b* 1987. *Residence* – Greater Aston Farmhouse, Aston Subedge, Chipping Campden, Glos.

BROTHER LIVING

Hon John Stuart Terrick Dudley, *b* 1924; *ed* Eton; formerly Warrant Officer Pilot, RAF, European War 1942-45 (wounded): *m* 1946, Dorothy Ethel, da of J. T. Swallow, of Mansfield, and has issue living, John Robert, *b* 1947: *m* 1970, Rosemary Rita Tester, and has issue living, Claire Jane *b* 1970, Sara Helena Louise *b* 1973, — David Anthony, *b* 1951: *m* 1973, Judith Jean Sinclair, of Sydney, NSW, and has issue living, John David Dudley *b* 1979, Jessica Judith Jean *b* 1983. *Residence* – Horley, Surrey.

SISTER LIVING

Lady Frances Virginia Susan, *b* 1926; *ed* St Hugh's Coll, Oxford: *m* 1949, Frank Ernest Berendt, and has issue living, Anthony Peregrine Dudley (56 Lancaster Rd, W11), *b* 1957; *ed* Ampleforth: *m* 1988, Julia Rosemary, only da of Derek Alistair Bigham (*see* E Fortescue, colls), — Susan Venetia, *b* 1952: *m* 1977, Paul Joseph Williams, of Walnut Tree House, 20A Lower Teddington Rd, Hampton Wick, Middlesex, and has issue living, Christopher James Dudley *b* 1980, Gavin Dominic *b* 1986, Paul Gerard Quentin *b* 1988, Hew Anthony John *b* 1990, Emma Louise *b* 1977, Joanna Frances *b* 1981, Helena Lucy *b* 1983. *Residence* – 34 The Marlows, Boundary Rd, NW8.

COLLATERAL BRANCHES LIVING

   Grandchildren of late Hon Archibald Dudley Ryder (infra):—
   Issue of late Richard Dudley Ryder, OBE, *b* 1904, *d* 1987: *m* 1945, Pamela Gerturde, who *d* 1982, da of late Aubrey Hammick Ford, of Wortham, Crowborough, Sussex:—
Victoria, *b* 1948: *m* 1976, Simon J. C. Connell, of Riverside Cottage, Beaminster, Dorset.
   Issue of late Douglas Dudley Ryder, JP, *b* 1905, *d* 1984: *m* 1931, Sheilah Moore (16 St John Garden, Cassia Drive, Port Elizabeth, S Africa), da of S. H. Gillesie, of Carrick Cradock, S Africa:—
Hugh Donald Dudley (44 Princes Rd, Claremont, Cape Town, S Africa), *b* 1936: *m* 1st, 1963 (*m diss* 1969), Pamela Joan, da of S. O. Butow, of East London, Cape Province; 2ndly, 1969, Maria, da of Max Pitterman, of Bielefeld, W Germany, and has issue living (by 2nd *m*), Axel Dudley, *b* 1970, — Douglas Dudley, *b* 1971. —— Atholl Graham Dudley (50 Stella Londt Drive, Port Elizabeth, Cape, S Africa), *b* 1938: *m* 1964, Irène, da of J. J. van Duuren, of Port Elizabeth, and has issue living, Gary Dudley, *b* 1966, — Peter Dudley, *b* 1968, — Jennifer Rosemary, *b* 1979.

   Issue of late Hon Archibald Dudley Ryder, 2nd son of 4th Earl, *b* 1867, *d* 1950; *m* 1898, Eleanor Frederica, who *d* 1958, el da of Edward R. Fisher-Rowe (E Ravensworth):—
Atholl Dudley (502-95 Fiddler's Green Rd, London, Ontario, Canada N6H 4TI), *b* 1909: *m* 1940, Kathleen, yst da of late Robert Pearson, of London, Ontario, and has issue living, Lawrence Dudley (Box 209, 421 Green St, Port Elgin, Ontario, Canada N0H 2CO) (adopted son), *b* 1949: *m* 1st, 1973 (*m diss* 1981), —; 2ndly, 1984, Kathryn Elspeth, da of late Warren Shular, of Southampton, Ont, and has issue living (by 1st *m*), Leigh Janice *b* 1977, — Peter Douglas Dudley (10 Matthew Dr, Guelph, Ont, Canada N1H 7L7), *b* 1952: *m* 1976, Michelle, da of Derek Foreman, of London, Ont, and has issue living, Andrew Douglas Dudley *b* 1985, James Richard Dudley (twin) *b* 1985, Sarah Michelle *b* 1982, Jennifer Elizabeth *b* 1984. —— †Peter Hugh Dudley, MBE (Ardmore, 21 Riverbank Rd, Ramsey, Isle of Man), *b* 1913; Hon Lt-Col late R Armoured Corps; sometime in Political Intell Dept, Foreign Office; MBE (Civil) 1944: *m* 1940, Susannah Sarah, da of late Geoffrey

Francis Bowes-Lyon (*see* E Strathmore, colls), and *d* 1993, leaving issue, Adrian Dudley (Bracken, Blackheath, nr Guildford), *b* 1941; BA (Econ): *m* 1976, Katrina Olga, da of Dr Socrates Christie, PhD, and has issue living, Peter Socrates Dudley *b* 1984, Lara Erasmia *b* 1982, Tanya Serena *b* 1989, — Bruce Dudley (Crix, Hatfield Peverel, Chelmsford, Essex CM3 2EU), *b* 1942: *m* 1969, Charlotte Olivia, da of Mark Frederick Strutt, MC, TD (*see* B Rayleigh, colls), and has issue living, Mark Reedham Dudley *b* 1970, Oliver Hugh Dudley *b* 1974, Leonora Mary Charlotte *b* 1978, — Sandra Anne, *b* 1954: *m* 1978, Dimitris Pepelasis, of Palaion Patron Germanou, Davaki, Philothei, Athens, and has issue living, Diamandis *b* 1979, Alexander *b* 1984

Grandchildren of late Maj Henry Dudley Ryder, MC (infra):—
Issue of late Edward Dorrien Dudley Ryder, *b* 1924, *d* 1984: *m* 1948, Valerie Nina (Yew Tree, Coleman's Hatch, Sussex), only da of late James Beecroft Soames, of Kenya:—
Nicholas Henry Dudley, *b* 1960. —— Jennifer Davina, *b* 1949: *m* 1st, 1971, Charles Berkeley Johnston Dingwall (*see* V Galway, colls, 1985 Edn); 2ndly, 1990, George William Pilkington, of 22 St Mary Abbots Terrace, W14 8NX, and has issue living (by 1st *m*), Sophie, *b* 1972, — Anthea Lucy, *b* 1977, — Amelia Sarah, *b* 1978. —— Vanessa, *b* 1951: *m* 1976, Paul F. Irvine Cole, of Whatcombe, Wantage, Oxon OX12 9NW, and has issue living, Alexander James, *b* 1977, — Oliver Nicholas, *b* 1980, — Mark Edward, *b* 1986.

Grandchildren of late Hon Edward Alan Dudley Ryder, 3rd son of 4th Earl:—
Issue of late Major Henry Dudley Ryder, MC, *b* 1894; *d* 1958: *m* 1918, Dorothy Marion, da of Sidney Streatfeild:—
Maud Marion, *b* 1919. *Residence* – Dean Cottage, Horsted Lane, Sharpthorne, Sussex. —— Dorothy Joan, *b* 1921: *m* 1951, Alan Williams Horton, and has issue living, James McAfee *b* 1954: *m* 1976, Nancy, da of Roger Eastman, of Hanover, NH, USA, and has issue living, Oliver McAfee *b* 1989, Jenna Beth *b* 1985, — Edward Alan Douglas, *b* 1957: *m* 1991, Zoë Jane, el da of Ian Wilkinson, of Esher, Surrey, and has issue living, Lily Azella *b* 1992, — Carol Ryder, *b* 1952. *Address* – RR1, Box 1424, Randolph, New Hampshire 03570, USA.

Issue of late Major Hon Robert Nathaniel Dudley Ryder, 4th son of 4th Earl, *b* 1882, *ka* 1917: *m* 1908, Beryl (who *d* 1970, having *m* 2ndly, 1945, Lt-Col William Baring Du Pre, DL, JP, who *d* 1946), da of Charles Angas, of Lindsay Park, Angaston, S Australia:—
Rosemary Beryl (*Lady Loehnis*), *b* (twin) 1909: *m* 1929, Com Sir Clive Loehnis, KCMG, KN (ret), who *d* 1992, and has issue living, Anthony David, CMG (11 Cranleigh, 139 Ladbroke Rd, W11 3PX), *b* 1936; CMG 1988: *m* 1965, Jennifer Forsyth, da of late Sir Donald Forsyth Anderson (*see* Llewellyn Bt, *cr* 1922), and has issue living, Dominic Anthony *b* 1967, Alexander Garrett *b* 1969, Barnaby David *b* 1971, — Serena Jane (*Baroness Remnant*) (Bear Ash, Hare Hatch, Reading, Berks, RG10 9XR), *b* 1932: *m* 1953, 3rd Baron Remnant. *Residence* – 12 Eaton Place, SW1.

Grandchildren of late Capt Cyril John Ryder, 2nd son of late Dudley Henry Ryder, son of late Hon Granville Dudley Ryder, MP, 2nd son of 1st Earl:—
Issue of late Maj Dudley Claud Douglas Ryder, JP, *b* 1901, *d* 1986: *m* 1st, 1927 (*m diss* 1938), Nancy Edith, who *d* 1985, da of E. M. Baker, late Federated Malay States Civil Ser; 2ndly, 1938, Vera Mary, who *d* 1980, da of Sir Herbert Frederick Cook, 3rd Bt, and formerly wife of George Mervyn Anstey Hamilton-Fletcher:—
(By 1st *m*) James Calcraft Dudley (Rempstone Hall, Corfe Castle, Dorset), *b* 1934; *ed* Sherborne, and RAC Cirencester; late 2nd Lt King's Own Regt: *m* 1st, 1966 (*m diss* 1979), Sarah Victoria, only da of late Michael Guy Bircham, of Reepham, Norfolk; 2ndly, 1984, Georgina Susan, only da of Edward George Adrian Farnham, of Quorn House, Quorn, Leics, and formerly wife of Charles Howard Cole, and has issue living (by 1st *m*), Lara Caroline Dudley, *b* 1968, — Melanie Isobel, *b* 1970, — Emma Katherine, *b* 1974. —— Benjamin Guy Dudley (twin) (The Old Farmhouse, Rempstone, Corfe Castle, Dorset), *b* 1934; *ed* Sherborne: *m* 1960, Philippa Mary, da of Alan Maitland Cunningham, of Compton House, Wareham, Dorset, and has issue living, Douglas Alan Dudley, *b* 1963: *m* 1988, Rosemary Victoria Clara Rhys-Davies, — Guy, *b* 1968, — Vanessa Frances, *b* 1965. —— Gabriel Nancy (*Lady Coghill*), *b* 1928: *m* 1958, Sir Egerton James Nevill Tobias (Toby) Coghill, 8th Bt. —— Jenifer Cherry, *b* 1929: *m* 1953, Jeremy Charles Browne, of Higher Houghton, Blandford, Dorset, and has issue living, Simon Jeremy *b* 1957, — Katherine Richenda, *b* 1956, — Sarah Caroline, *b* 1960, — Emily Charlotte, *b* 1965. —— Jacqueline Iris *b* 1930: *m* 1957 (*m diss* 1969), Thomas Ralph Winser, and has had issue, Hugh James, *b* 1958; *d* 1992, — Polly Joan, *b* 1959, — Tamsin Jacqueline, *b* 1962. —— (By 2nd *m*) Richard Hood Jack Dudley, *b* 1940; *ed* Sherborne, Pembroke Coll, Camb (MA, PhD), Columbia Univ, New York, and Edin Univ (Dip Clinical Psych 1967); Chm Soc for Prevention of Cruelty to Animals 1977-79: *m* 1974, Audrey Jane, da of Frank Rae Arthur Smith, of Chesham Bois, Bucks, and has issue living, Henry Arthur Woden Calcraft Dudley, *b* 1981, — Emily Nancy Charlotte, *b* 1978.

Grandson of late William Henry Ryder, 3rd son of late Dudley Henry Ryder (ante):—
Issue of late Cdr Frederick Granville Dudley Ryder, RNVR, *b* 1905, *d* 1970: *m* 1st, 1929 (*m diss* 1934), Gillian Eleanor, da of C. H. B. Quennell; 2ndly, 1939, Muriel Eleanor, who *d* 1975, da of William S. Corby, of Wash, USA:—
(By 1st *m*) Richard Peter Guy Dudley (Hardway House, 3411 Poinciana Av, Miami, Florida, USA), *b* (Dec) 1929: *m* 1955, Angela Jiovanna, da of Morris M. Melotti, of Johnstown, Pa, USA, and has issue living, Christopher Frederick Dudley, *b* 1959, — Mark Campbell Dudley, *b* 1963.

Granddaughters of late Rev Algernon Charles Dudley Ryder (infra):—
Issue of late Major Algernon Frederick Roland Dudley Ryder, MC, *b* 1891, *d* 1957: *m* 1921, Olive, who *d* 1973, da of John Baillie, of Montreal:—
Dione Frances, *b* 1924: *m* 1954, (Claud Andrew) James Graham-Watson, and has issue living, Frederick Paul, *b* 1957: *m* 1987, Catherine I., elder da of Reginald Rimington Wilson, of Sussex and of W Riding of Yorks, and has issue living, Rory William *b* 1990, Angus James *b* 1991, Thomas *b* 1993, — Iona Mary, *b* 1955, — Sanda Susan, *b* 1959: *m* 1986, James Irvine Hinchcliffe Friend, of Winnington Grange, Market Drayton, Shropshire TF9 4DW, son of Irvine Friend, of Mucklestone Old Rectory, Market Drayton, Shropshire, and has had issue, Harry James Hinchcliffe *b* and *d* 1988, Alexander James Hinchcliffe *b* 1989, Georgina Mary Flavia *b* 1991. *Residence* – Falconers, Shipley, Horsham, Sussex. —— Xanthe Veronica, *b* 1926: *m* 1949, Michael Dalglish, who *d* 1976, and has issue living, James Thomas, *b* 1950: *m* 1974, Avril Elizabeth Smith, and has issue living, Lucas Timothy Frederick *b* 1984, Dominic Benet *b* 1986, — Charles Baillie, *b* 1953: *m* 1976, Miranda Lehmann, and has issue living, Kenneth Michael *b* 1981, Rachel Sarah *b* 1985, Rowan Diana *b* 1986, — Clare, *b* 1956: *m* 1986, William Kenneth Jest, and has issue living, Julian Ryder *b* 1991, Douglas Michael *b* 1994. *Residence* – 142 Priory Lane, Roehampton, SW15. —— Charis Elizabeth, *b* 1930.

Granddaughter of late Rev Algernon Charles Dudley Ryder, 4th son of Hon Frederick Dudley Ryder, 3rd son of 1st Earl:—
Issue of late Lt-Col Hugh Granville Leveson Dudley Ryder, TD, *b* 1900, *d* 1983: *m* 1st, 1926, Diana Vivian, who *d* 1951, el da of Sir Paul Augustine Makins, 2nd Bt; 2ndly, 1955, Patricia Geraldine (66 Whitelands House, Cheltenham Terrace, SW3), da of late Gerald Macleay Browne, OBE, and widow of Maj (Basil Arthur) John Peto, King's Drag Gds (*see* Peto, Bt, colls, *cr* 1927):—
(By 1st *m*) Jane Christine (Haylands, Martyr Worthy, Winchester), *b* 1927: *m* 1955, Denzil Walter Hugh Ffennell, who *d* 1977, and has issue living, Simon, *b* 1956: *m* 1986, Lucinda, elder da of Lt Cdr Christopher John Ringrose-Voase, MBE, RN, of Alnaby House, Upham, Southampton, and has issue living, Jessica *b* 1989, Georgina *b* 1992, — Diana Elizabeth, *b* 1963.

Granddaughters of late Lieut-Col Spencer Charles Dudley Ryder, BSC, son of late Rt Rev Hon Henry Ryder, Bishop of Lichfield and Coventry, 3rd son of 1st Baron Harrowby:—
Issue of late Lieut-Col Wilfred Ironside Ryder, *b* 1866, *d* 1948: *m* 1901, Tempé Rosa Ridehalgh, who *d* 1942, da of late Maj-Gen James Edmund Bacon Parsons, of The Gables, Southbourne-on-Sea, Hants:—
Joan Tempé, *b* 1902: *m* 1945, Francis Edward Maitland, who *d* 1963. *Residence* – Pullens End Cottage, Pullens Lane, Headington, Oxford. —— Margery Julia, *b* 1904: *m* 1934 (*m diss* 1948), Capt Charles Oliver Meeres, late RA. *Residence* – Boult's Lodge, Boult's Lane, Marston, Oxford.

Grandchildren of late Col Charles Henry Dudley Ryder, CB, CIE, DSO (infra):—
Issue of late Major Lisle Charles Dudley Ryder, Roy Norfolk Regt, *b* 1902, *ka* France 1940: *m* 1938, Enid Helen Constance, who *d* 1977, only child of late Maj Robert Ralston-Patrick, of Trearne, Ayrshire:—
Ralston Patrick Dudley, *b* 1939; *ed* Harrow. *Residence* – 7518 Knickerbocker Rd, Ontario, NY 14519, USA.
Issue of late Major Ernle Terrick Dudley Ryder, Indian Army, *b* 1906, *ka* off Sumatra 1942: *m* 1936, Daphne Joan Pillans, only child of late John Greig, of Rosewood, Ascot, Berks:—
Elizabeth Jean *b* 1938: *m* 1959, James John Vernon, MA, of Briarwood, East End, Lymington, Hants, and has issue living, James Michael, *b* 1960: *m* 1994, Mhairi Patricia, eldest da of Maj John Nisbet, of South Lodge, Blackadder, nr Duns, Berwickshire, — Peter John, *b* 1963: *m* 1988, Patricia Jean, da of J. C. N. Nicol, and has issue living, Kate Elizabeth *b* 1992, — William Ernle Hardy, *b* 1965: *m* 1988, Emma Mary, yst da of Sir John Barry Salusbury-Trelawny, 13th Bt, — Julia Elizabeth, *b* 1961: *m* 1992, Jonathan Denton, elder son of late John Denton. —— Anthea Daphne, *b* 1940: *m* 1968 (*m diss* 1974), Donald Leroy Brown, and has issue living, Andrew Kevin, *b* 1972. *Residence* – 357 Boston Rd, Ontario, NY 14519, USA.

Issue of late Capt Robert Edward Dudley Ryder, VC, RN, cmd'd Naval Forces in attack on St Nazaire 1942, *b* 1908, *d* 1986: *m* 1941, (Constance) Hilaré Myfanwy, who *d* 1982, da of Rev Lumley Cecil Green-Wilkinson (*see* Edwards, Bt, *cr* 1907, 1949 Edn):—
Rev Canon Lisle Robert Dudley (1 Holywell Hill, Henwick Rd, Worcester), *b* 1943; *ed* Selwyn Coll, Camb (MA); Diploma in Pastoral Studies, Univ of Birmingham; Hon Canon Worcester Cathedral 1989: *m* 1977, Olivia Elvira, da of Col Roland Stephen Langton, MVO, MC, of Dial House, Peppard Common, Oxon, and has issue living, Philip Robert Dudley, *b* 1982, — Harriet Elvira, *b* 1980. —— Susan Myfanwy Prudence, *b* 1944: *m* 1965, Martin Graves Bates, of 17 Queen's Gate Place, SW7, and has issue (*see* Bates, Bt, *cr* 1880, colls).

Granddaughter of late Lieut-Col Spencer Charles Dudley Ryder, BSC (ante):—
Issue of late Col Charles Henry Dudley Ryder, CB, CIE, DSO, *b* 1868, *d* 1945: *m* 1892, Ida Josephine, who *d* 1948, el da of late Lieut-Col Edward Evans Grigg, ISC, of Orchard Court, Stevenage, Herts:—
Violet Constance, *b* 1898: *m* 1931, Lt-Col Geoffrey Walter Lawson, formerly Somerset LI, and has issue living, Julian Richard, *b* 1933: *m* 1977, Beverley Ann, da of C. T. Coleman, of Isca, Brecon, Powys. *Residence* – Brendon Care Home, Froxfield, Marlborough, Wilts.

PREDECESSORS – Sir Dudley Ryder, Knt (great grandson of Robert Ryder, of Wisbech) Lord Ch Justice of the King's Bench 1754-6, was offered a peerage by the King on 24 May 1756, but *d* the following day, before the patent was completed; *s* by his son **(1)** NATHANIEL, MP for Tiverton; *cr Baron Harrowby*, of Harrowby, co Lincoln (peerage of Great Britain) 1776; *d* 1803; *s* by his son **(2)** DUDLEY, PC, 2nd Baron; *b* 1762; *cr Viscount Sandon* and *Earl of Harrowby* (peerage of United Kingdom) 1809; was successively Sec of State for Foreign Affairs and Lord Pres of the Council; *d* 1847; *s* by his son **(3)** DUDLEY, KG, DCL, 2nd Earl; *b* 1798; sat as MP for Tiverton (C) 1819-31, and for Liverpool 1831-47, was Chancellor of Duchy of Lancaster 1854-5, and Lord Privy Seal 1855-7: *m* 1823, Lady Frances Stuart, da of 1st Marquess of Bute; *d* 1882; *s* by his son **(4)** DUDLEY FRANCIS STUART, PC, 3rd Earl, *b* 1831; MP for Lichfield (C) 1856-9, and for Liverpool 1868-82; was Vice-Pres of Committee of Council on Education 1874-8, Pres of Board of Trade 1878-80, and Lord Privy Seal 1885-6: *m* 1861, Lady Mary Frances Cecil, who *d* 1917, da of 2nd Marquess of Exeter; *d* 1900; *s* by his brother **(5)** HENRY DUDLEY, 4th Earl, *b* 1836: *m* 1859, Susan Juliana Maria Hamilton, who *d* 1913, da of late Villiers Dent, of Barton Court, Lymington; *d* 1900; *s* by his el son **(6)** JOHN HERBERT DUDLEY, 5th Earl; *b* 1864; Lord High Steward of Newcastle under Lyme; Lord-Lieut of Staffordshire 1927-48; MP for Gravesend (C) 1898-1900: *m* 1887, Hon Dame Mabel Smith, DBE, who *d* 1956, da of Emily, Viscountess Hambleden; *d* 1956; *s* by his son **(7)** DUDLEY, 6th Earl, *b* 1892; author of *Geography of Everyday Things*, and *England at Worship*; PPS to Sec of State for Air 1922-23, a Memb of Commn on Historical Manuscripts 1935-66; MP for Salop, Shrewsbury Div (C) 1922-23 and 1924-29: *m* 1922, Lady Helena Blanche Coventry, who *d* 1974, da of late George William, Viscount Deerhurst (*see* E Coventry, 1973-74 Edn); *d* 1987; *s* by his el son **(8)** DUDLEY DANVERS GRANVILLE COUTTS, 7th Earl and present peer; also Viscount Sandon and Baron Harrowby.

HART OF SOUTH LANARK, BARONY OF (Hart) (Extinct 1991)

SONS LIVING OF LIFE BARONESS

Hon Richard Oliver, *b* 1949; *ed* Tiffin's Sch, and King's Coll, Camb: *m* 1985, Dr Ailsa Jane, da of John Allan Auchnie, of Hong Kong, and has issue living, June Judith Auchnie, *b* 1993.
Hon Stephen Cobbett, *b* 1952; *ed* Tiffin's Sch, and King's Coll Camb: *m* 19—, —, and has issue living, Daniel Hart MAYER *b* 1984, — Anna MAYER, *b* 1986.

Hartington, Marquess of; son of Duke of Devonshire.

Hartismere, Baron, title of Baron Henniker on Roll of HL.

HARTWELL, BARON (Berry) (Life Baron 1968)

(WILLIAM) MICHAEL BERRY, MBE, TD, 2nd son of 1st Viscount Camrose; *b* 18 May 1911; *hp* to Viscountcy of Camrose; *ed* Eton, and Ch Ch Oxford (MA); Editor *Sunday Mail*, Glasgow 1934-35, Managing Editor *Financial Times* 1937-39, Chm Amalgamated Press Ltd 1954-59; Chm and Editor-in-Ch of *The Daily Telegraph* and *Sunday Telegraph* (ret 1987); 2nd Lt 11th (City of London Yeo) Light Anti-Aircraft Regt RA (TA) 1938, Maj 1940, Lt-Col Gen Staff 1944; 1939-45 War (despatches twice, MBE); *cr* MBE (Mil) 1945, and *Baron Hartwell*, of Peterborough Court, City of London (Life Baron) 1968: *m* 1936, Lady Pamela Margaret Elizabeth Smith, who *d* 1982, yr da of 1st Earl of Birkenhead, and has issue.

𝕬rms – Argent, three bars gules, over all a pile ermine. 𝕮rest – A griffin sejant reguardant sable, collared or. 𝕾upporters – *Dexter*, a stag and *Sinister* a wolf proper, both collared or, and standing on a compartment with a well between paving to the dexter and grass to the sinister proper.
Residences – Oving House, Whitchurch, nr Aylesbury; 18 Cowley St, SW1. *Clubs* – White's, Beefsteak, Royal Yacht Squadron.

SONS LIVING

Hon Adrian Michael (11 Cottesmore Gdns, W8), *b* 1937; *ed* Eton, and Ch Ch, Oxford: *m* 1967, Marina Beatrice, da of Cyrus Sulzberger, of 2 ter Avenue de Ségur, Paris, and has issue living, Jonathan William, *b* 1970, — Jessica Margaret, *b* 1968.
Hon Nicholas William (22 Rutland Gate, SW7), *b* 1942; *ed* Eton, and Ch Ch, Oxford: *m* 1977, Evelyn, da of late Jacques Prouvost, and has issue living, William Alexander, *b* 1978, — Alexander, *b* 1981.

DAUGHTERS LIVING

Hon Harriet Mary Margaret, *b* 1944: *m* 1981, Martin Cullen, of 117 Cheyne Walk, SW10, and has issue living, Miguel *b* 1982, — Domingo *b* 1983.
Hon Eleanor Agnes, *b* 1950.

HARVEY OF PRESTBURY, BARONY OF (Harvey) (Extinct 1994)

SONS LIVING OF LIFE BARON (By 1st marriage)

Hon Philip William Vere, *b* 1942; *ed* Eton, and Geneva Univ.
Hon Guy Alan Vere, *b* 1947: *m* 1977, Margaret C. B., da of Lewis Robertson, of The Blair, Blairlogie, Stirling.

ADOPTED DAUGHTERS LIVING OF LIFE BARON

Charmaine, *b* 1966: *m* 1991, Paul Gilbert Cox, eldest son of Gilbert Cox, of Canada.
Rowena, *b* 1968.
Petra, *b* 1973.

WIDOW LIVING OF LIFE BARON

CAROL (*Baroness Harvey of Prestbury*), da of late Austin Cassar-Torreggiani: *m* 1978, as his 3rd wife, Baron Harvey of Prestbury, CBE, who *d* 1994. *Residence* – Rocklands, Les Vardes, St Peter Port, Guernsey, CI.

HARVEY OF TASBURGH, BARON (Harvey) (Baron UK 1954, Bt UK 1868)

PETER CHARLES OLIVER HARVEY, 2nd Baron and 5th Baronet; *b* 28 Jan 1921; *s* 1968; *ed* Eton and Trin Coll, Camb; 1939-45 War with RA in N Africa and Italy: *m* 1957, Penelope Anne, yr da of late Lt-Col Sir William Vivian Makins, 3rd Bt, and has issue.

𝕬rms – Erminois, on a chief indented gules between two crescents argent, a representation of the gold medal presented to Sir Robert John Harvey, by command of HRH the Prince Regent, for his services at the battle of Orthes, pendent from a riband gules, fimbriated azure, beneath it the word *Orthes*; a canton ermine charged with a representation of the insignia of a Knight of the Royal Portuguese order of the Tower and Sword, pendent from a riband azure. 𝕮rest – Out of a mural crown or, above a dexter cubit arm erect, proper, a crescent argent between two branches of laurel also proper. 𝕾upporters – *Dexter*, a lion or; *sinister*, a cock or.
Residence – Crownick Woods, Restronguet, Mylor, Falmouth, Cornwall.
Club – Brooks's.

DAUGHTERS LIVING

Hon Juliet Annora Christine, *b* 1958.
Hon Miranda Jean, *b* 1960: *m* 1987, Timothy H. Smithies, 2nd son of R. W. Smithies, of Harrow-on-the-Hill, Middx.

COLLATERAL BRANCH LIVING

Issue of late Hon John Wynn Harvey, yr son of 1st Baron, *b* 1923, *d* 1989: *m* 1950, Elena Maria-Teresa (Coed-y-Maen, Meifod, Powys; 7(a) Frieze Green House, Chelsea Manor St, SW3), yr da of late Giambattista, Marchese Curtopassi:—
CHARLES JOHN GIUSEPPE, *b* 4 Feb 1951; *ed* Eton: *m* 1979, Margaret (Maggie), da of Cecil Walter Brown, and has issue living, John, *b* 1993, — Elena, *b* 1982, — Nina, *b* 1985, — Stephanie, *b* 1989. *Residence* – 162 East Dulwich Grove, SE22. —— Robert Lambart, *b* 1953; *ed* Eton: *m* 1981, Jane Louisa, eldest da of E. Alan Roper, of The Manor, S Brent, Devon, and has issue living, Oliver John Edward Giuseppe, *b* 1988. —— Antonella Sophia Gabrielle Maria, *b* 1957: *m* 1988, Al-Sharif Abdullah bin Al-Hussein, and has issue living, a son, *b* 1992, — Badia (a da), *b* 1990.

PREDECESSORS – (1) ROBERT JOHN Harvey, el son of late Gen Sir Robert John Harvey, KCB, of Mousehold House, Norwich; *b* 1817; MP for Thetford 1865-8; *cr* a *Baronet* 1868: *m* 1845, Lady Henrietta Augusta Lambart, who *d* 1874, sister of 8th Earl of Cavan; *d* 1870; *s* by his son (2) CHARLES, 2nd Bt; *b* 1849; Col 4th Batn Norfolk Regt and a JP: *m* 1st, 1870, Jane Ann, who *d* 1891, da of Benjamin Green, of Newcastle; 2ndly, 1893, Mary Anne Edith, who *d* 1929, da of G. F. Cooke, of Holmewood, Norwich; *d* 1928; *s* by his son (3) CHARLES ROBERT LAMBART EDWARD, 3rd Bt; *b* 1871: *m* 1st, 1891, Jessie, who *d* 1913, da of late E. Turnball, of Smedley, Lancashire; 2ndly, 1921, Lydia, who *d* 19—, da of Alexis Konshine, of Petrograd, Russia; *d* 1954; *s* by his half-brother (4) OLIVER CHARLES, GCMG, GCVO, CB, 4th Bt, *b* 1893; *cr Baron Harvey of Tasburgh*, of Tasburgh, co Norfolk (peerage of UK) 1954; Dep Under-Sec of State, Foreign Office 1946-48; Ambassador to France 1948-54: *m* 1920, Maud Annora, who *d* 1970, da of late Arthur Watkin Williams-Wynn (Williams-Wynn, Bt, colls); *d* 1968; *s* by his son (5) PETER CHARLES OLIVER, 2nd Baron and present peer.

HARVINGTON, BARON (Grant-Ferris) (Life Baron 1974)

ROBERT GRANT GRANT-FERRIS, PC, son of late Robert Francis Ferris, MB, ChB; *b* 30 Dec 1907; *ed* Douai Sch; Bar Inner Temple 1937; Pres of Southdown Sheep Soc of England 1950-52, 1959-60 and 1973; Pres National Sheep Breeders' Assocn 1956-58, and Smithfield Club 1970 (Vice-Pres 1964); a Member of Speaker's Panel of Chm 1962-70, and Chm of Ways and Means, and Dep Speaker of House of Commons 1970-74; 1939-45 War as Wing Cdr R Aux AF in Europe, Malta, Egypt and India (Air Effic Award 1942); KStJ; Kt Sovereign Mil Order of Malta; Cdr Order of Leopold II of Belgium; MP for N St Pancras (C) 1937-45, and for Nantwich 1955-74; *cr* Knt 1969, PC 1971, and *Baron Harvington*, of Nantwich, Cheshire (Life Baron) 1974: *m* 1930, Florence, da of late Maj William Brennan De Vine, MC, of St John's Angmering-on-Sea, Sussex, and has issue.

𝕬rms – Gules, three antique crowns or, within an orle of eight horseshoes, argent. 𝕮rest – A comb fessewise argent between two hazel branches fruited proper. 𝕾upporters – *Dexter*, a Knight Grand Cross of Magistral Grace of the Sovereign and Military Order of Malta in choir dress proper; *Sinister*, a representation of a pilot of the Royal Air Force in service dress circa 1942, also proper, about his kneck a scarf gules spotted argent.
Residence – Apartment 6, Batisse de la Mielle, St Aubin, Jersey. *Clubs* – Carlton, Royal Thames Yacht; Royal Yacht Sqdn, Royal & Ancient Golf, MCC, RAF.

SON LIVING

Rev Hon (Henry Michael) Piers, OSB (St Joseph's Brindle, Chapel Fold, Hoghton, Preston, Lancs PR5 0DE), *b* 1933; *ed* Ampleforth; late Irish Guards; Monk of St Benedict at Ampleforth Abbey; Assist Priest Workington 1977-89, Leyland 1989-93, since when of Hoghton.

DAUGHTER LIVING

Hon Greta Sheira Bernadette (*Hon Lady Brinckman*), *b* 1937: *m* 1st, 1956, John Frederick Edward Trehearne; 2ndly, 1970, Christopher Mark Henry Murray; 3rdly, 1983, as his 2nd wife, Sir (Theodore George) Roderick Brinckman, 6th Bt, and has issue (by 1st *m*) Edward Scarlett, *b* 1963, — Lucinda Elizabeth Scarlett, *b* 1957: *m* 1st, 1984 (*m diss* 1986), 3rd Baron Banbury of Southam; 2ndly, 1990, (John) Patrick Wrigley, of Delbury Hall, Craven Arms, Shropshire, and has issue living (by 2nd *m*), Jack *b* 1991, a da *b* 1992, — (Petrina) Jane, *b* 1959: *m* 1990, Roderick Arthur Scott, and has issue (*see* B Colgrain, colls). *Residence* – Hazleton Manor, Cirencester, Glos.

HASLAM, BARON (Haslam) (Life Baron 1990)

ROBERT HASLAM, son of late Percy Haslam; *b* 4 Feb 1923; *ed* Bolton Sch, and Birmingham Univ (BSc); Hon DTech Brunel Univ 1987, Hon DEng Birmingham Univ 1987; Dep-Chm ICI plc 1980-83, Chm Tate and Lyle plc 1983-86, British Steel Corpn 1983-86, British Coal 1986-90, Bechtel Ltd since 1991, and Wasserstein Perella & Co Internat Ltd since 1991; Dir Bank of England 1985-93; Advisory Dir Unilever plc 1985-93; Hon FIMinE; *cr* Knt 1985, and *Baron Haslam*, of Bolton, Greater Manchester (Life Baron) 1990: *m* 1947, Joyce, da of late Frederick Quinn, and has issue.
Address – House of Lords, SW1A 0PW. *Office* - Wasserstein Perella & Co Internat Ltd, 10-11 Park Place, SW1A 1LP.

SONS LIVING

Hon Roger J., *b* 1948; *ed* Westminster, and Dundee Univ (BSc): *m* 1972, Astrid, da of Kristian Rognøy, of Omsheim, 5470 Rosendal, Norway, and has issue living, Sara Caroline Rognøy, *b* 1974, — Roberta Louise Rognøy, *b* 1980.
Hon Nigel R., *b* 1952; *ed* Westminster, and Birmingham Univ (BA): *m* 1988, Alison Vanessa, da of Alec Raymond Gourd Knight, of Chy Meor, Newquay, Cornwall, and has issue living, James Robert Alexander, *b* 1990, — Sophie Antonia, *b* 1988. *Residence* – 17 Blithfield St, W8 6RH.

HASTINGS, BARON (Astley) (Baron E 1290, Bt E 1660)

Tenacious of justice

EDWARD DELAVAL HENRY ASTLEY, 22nd Baron, and 12th Baronet; *b* 14 April 1912; *s* 1956; *ed* Eton; is Major Coldstream Guards (Reserve), and patron of seven livings; a Lord-in-Waiting to HM 1961-62, and Joint Parl Sec to Min of Housing and Local Government 1962-64; Grand Officer of Order of Merit of Italy: *m* 1954, Catherine (Cecilia) Rosaline Ratcliffe (COATS), yr da of late Capt Harold Virgo Hinton, and has issue.

Arms – Quarterly: 1st azure, a cinquefoil pierced ermine, within a bordure engrailed or, *Astley*; 2nd argent, a lion rampant gules, ducally crowned or, *Constable of Melton*; 3rd gules, two lions passant argent, *Le Strange*; 4th or, a maunch gules, *Hastings*. **Crest** – Out of a ducal coronet or, a plume of five feathers argent. **Supporters** – On either side a lion gules, ducally crowned, and gorged with a plain collar or, pendant therefrom an escutcheon of the arms of *Hastings*.
Seat – Seaton Delaval Hall, Whitley Bay, Northumberland NE26 4QR.
Clubs – Brooks's, Army and Navy, Northern Counties, and Norfolk.

SONS LIVING

Hon DELAVAL THOMAS HAROLD, *b* 25 April 1960; *ed* Radley and Hatfield Coll, Durham: *m* 1987, Veronica M., elder da of Richard A. Smart, of Elizabeth Crescent, Queen's Park, Chester, and has issue living, Jacob Addison, *b* 5 Sept 1991, — Molly, *b* 1993. *Residence* – 39 Colville Gdns, W11.

Hon Justin Edward, *b* 1968. *Residence* – Thornage Hall, Holt, Norfolk.

DAUGHTER LIVING

Hon Harriet Marguerite, *b* 1958. *Residence* – Mill Farmhouse, Thornage, Holt, Norfolk.

SISTERS LIVING

Hon Helen Elizabeth Delaval, *b* 1907: *m* 1st, 1930 (*m diss* 1940), Ian Bulloch; 2ndly, 1941, George Field, who *d* 1941; 3rdly, 1948, John David Haw, who *d* 1982, and has issue living (by 1st *m*), Donald Ian (11 Montclair Av, Woodvale, Perth, W Australia 6026), *b* 1931: *m* 1956, Joyce Illman, and has issue living, Nevill (Harare, Zimbabwe) *b* 1959: *m* 1987, Daria Garizio, Donald *b* 1961, Elinor (Constantia, Cape Prov, S Africa) *b* 1957: *m* 1983 (*m diss* 1993), Andrejz Misiewicz, — James Angus, *b* 1935: *m* 1st, 1956 (*m diss* 1960), Penelope Burrows; 2ndly, 1961, Margaret Conley, of NSW, and has issue living (by 1st *m*), Anthea *b* 1957: *m* 19—, Rohan Vos (PO Box 511, Constantia, Cape Prov 7848, S Africa) (and has issue living, Shaun *b* 1976, Brenda *b* 1978, Bianca *b* 1984, Tiffany 1986), Janet *b* 1958: *m* 1984, Alan Wale (and has issue living, Craig *b* 1987, Keith *b* 1988), (by 2nd *m*) Simon *b* 1961: *m* 1986, Sonia Linkston (and has issue living, Melissa *b* 1989), Keith *b* 1964, — Alasdair George (60 Corbet St, Shelley, Perth, W Australia 6155), *b* 1938: *m* 19—, Marion Mill, and has issue living, Samantha *b* 1966, Pepita *b* 1969, Jaye *b* 1971. *Residence* – Windermere Estate, 158 Bibra Drive, Bibra Lake, W Australia 6163.
Hon Jean, *b* 1917; formerly in WRNS: *m* 1945, Lieut-Com Mark Napier, RN, who *d* 1962, and has issue (*see* L Napier and Ettrick, colls). *Residence* – 12 Grassmere Close, Felpham, Bognor Regis, Sussex.

WIDOW LIVING OF SON OF TWENTY-FIRST BARON

Lady Joan Patricia Quirk, da of 1st Earl Wavell: *m* 1st, 1943, Maj Hon Simon Nevill Astley who *d* 1946; 2ndly, 1948, Harry Alastair Gordon, who *d* 1965; 3rdly, 1973, Maj Donald Struan Robertson, SG, who *d* 1993, of Winkfield Plain Farm, Winkfield, Windsor, Berks, SL4 4QU, son of late Rt Hon Sir Malcolm Arnold Robertson, GCMG, KBE, and has issue living (by 1st *m*) (see colls, infra).

COLLATERAL BRANCHES LIVING   *(All of whom are in remainder to the Barony of Hastings.)*

Issue of late Maj Hon Simon Nevill Astley, 2nd son of 21st Baron, *b* 1919, *d* 1946: *m* 1943, Lady Joan Patricia Quirk (ante) (she *m* 2ndly, 1948, Maj Harry Alastair Gordon, Gordon Highlanders, who *d* 1965, and 3rdly, 1973, Maj Donald Struan Robertson, SG, who *d* 1993, of Winkfield Plain Farm, Winkfield, Windsor, Berks, son of late Rt Hon Sir Malcolm Arnold Robertson, GCMG, KBE), da of 1st Earl Wavell:—
Diana Jane, *b* 1943: *m* 1975, Robert I. W. Kellie, of The King's, Oxlynch, Stonehouse, Glos GL10 3DE, and has issue living, Rupert Simon Chamier, *b* 1977, — Toby Alastair Struan, *b* 1984, — Tara Margaret Joan, *b* 1980.

Issue of late Hon Armyne Margaret Astley, 2nd da of 21st Baron, *b* 1909, *d* 1979: *m* 1933, William George Broadbent Schofield, who *d* 1987:—
Armyne Morar Helen (*Lady Stirling*), *b* 1924: *m* 1959, Sir Angus Duncan Aeneas Stirling, of 25 Ladbroke Grove, W11, and has issue (*see* E Dunmore). —— Ann Blackstone, *b* 1935: *m* 1959, Kinnaird St Clair Cunningham, of Hallmanor, Peebles, and has adopted children, Hugh William Kinnaird, *b* 1962, — Mark Schofield, *b* 1968, — Louise Margaret, *b* 1966. —— Marigold Elizabeth, *b* 1937: *m* 1962, Capt John Anthony Cromek Warrington, The Green Howards, of Low Burton Hall, Masham, N Yorks HG4 4DQ, and has issue living, George Simon Cromek, *b* 1964, — Patrick William Cromek, *b* 1966: *m* 1990, Jane Alice Patience, da of Joseph Andrew Christopher Hoare, of Hartridge Manor Farm, Cranbrook, Kent (*see* E Antrim, 1990 Edn), and has issue living, Flora Lucy Christina *b* 1991, Eleanor *b* 1993, — Olivia Sarah, *b* 1963. —— Cicely Rose, *b* 1941: *m* 1972, Harold Irvin Golden, of 12311 Marine St, Los Angeles, Calif, USA.

Grandchildren of late Capt Hon (Charles) Melton Astley, yst son of 20th Baron:—
Issue of late Maj George Delaval Astley, Royal Fus, *b* 1915, *d* 1993: *m* 1st, 1942 (*m diss* 1946), Hope Shuttleworth, yr da of late Lt-Col Francis Holden Shuttleworth Rendall, DSO, Duke of Cornwall's LI; 2ndly, 1949, Diana Christian (Woodhayne, Beechwood Lane, Burley, Ringwood, Hants BH24 4AR), only da of late Brig-Gen Robert Hugh Hare, CB, CMG, DSO, MVO:—
(By 2nd *m*) (Delaval) Hugh (170 Arundel Av, Toronto, Canada M4K A3D), *b* 1950; *ed* Aiglon Coll, Switzerland: *m* 1976, Penelope, da of Charles Henry Underwood, and has issue living, Christopher Delaval, *b* 1976, — Caroline Zoë, *b* 1975. —— (Caroline) Susan, *b* 1951; resumed her maiden name until remarriage: *m* 1st, 1974 (*m diss* 1984), Charles Philip Barrington Woollett; 2ndly, 1992, James Stymeist, of Youbou, Vancouver Island, Canada, and has issue living (by 2nd *m*), Alexandra Diana, *b* 1992.

Issue of late Hon Hester Winifred Astley, da of 20th Baron, *b* 1899, *d* 1980: *m* 1923, Alan Houghton Brodrick, who *d* 1973:—
John Alan St John BRODRICK, *b* 1924. *Residence* – 33 Chesil Court, Chelsea Manor St, SW3.

Grandson of late Hubert Delaval Astley, son of Lt-Col Francis L'Estrange Astley, brother of 16th Baron:—
Issue of late Col Philip Reginald Astley, CBE, MC, *b* 1896, *d* 1958: *m* 1st, 1931 (*m diss* 1940), Edith Madeleine (the actress Madeleine Carroll), who *d* 1987, da of late John Carroll; 2ndly, 1949, Penelope Joan McKerrow, OBE (15/161 Fulham Rd, SW3 6SN), da of late Trevor Bright of Freshford, Bath:—
(By 2nd *m*) Richard Jacob (20 Staverton Rd, Oxford OX2 6XJ), *b* 1950; *ed* Eton; BA, London: *m* 1974, Rosanna, el da of late Sir (John) Anthony Quayle, CBE, the actor, and has issue living, Thomas Jacob, *b* 1975, — Harry Richard, *b* 1977, — Jenny Miranda, *b* 1980.

PREDECESSORS – This ancient family descends from Sir Thomas Astley, who fell at the battle of Evesham 1265 with Simon de Montfort, Earl of Leicester, *temp* Henry III. *Sir* Isaac Astley, *cr* a Bt 1641 (nephew of Jacob, 1st Baron Astley of Reading, Commander of King Charles I's Infantry at the battle of Naseby, *cr* 1644, ext 1668); *d* without issue 1659, when the Baronetcy expired, and his estates passed to his nephew (1) *Sir* JACOB Astley (son of Edward Astley, by his wife (and cousin), Elizabeth, da of Jacob, 1st Baron Astley of Reading), 40 years MP for Norfolk; *cr* a *Baronet* 1660; *d* 1729; *s* by his son (2) *Sir* PHILIP, 2nd Bt; *d* 1739; *s* by his son (3) *Sir* JACOB, 3rd Bt; *d* 1760; *s* by his son (4) *Sir* EDWARD, 4th Bt; 24 years MP for Norfolk; *d* 1802; *s* by his son (5) *Sir* JACOB HENRY, 5th Bt; 20 years MP for Norfolk; *d* 1817; *s* by his son (6) *Sir* JACOB, 6th Bt; summoned to Parliament by writ and became 16th Baron Hastings 1841, the abeyance (see *infra) having been terminated in his favour; *d* 1859; *s* by his el son (7) JACOB HENRY DELAVAL, 17th Baron; *d* 1871; *s* by his brother (8) *Rev* DELAVAL LOFTUS, 18th Baron; *b* 1825: *m* 1848, Hon Frances Diana Manners Sutton, da of 1st Viscount Canterbury; *d* 1872; *s* by his el son (9) BERNARD EDWARD DELAVAL, 19th Baron; *b* 1855; *d* 1875; *s* by his brother (10) GEORGE MANNERS, 20th Baron; *b* 1857: *m* 1880, Hon Elizabeth Evelyn Harbord, who *d* 1957, da of 5th Baron Suffield; *d* 1904; *s* by his son (11) ALBERT EDWARD DELAVAL, 21st Baron; *b* 1882; Lieut-Col late 7th Hussars; High Steward of Norwich Cathedral; bore one of the Golden Spurs at Coronations of King George VI and Queen Elizabeth II: *m* 1907, Lady Marguerite Helen Nevill, who *d* 1975, da of 3rd Marquess of Abergavenny; *d* 1956; *s* by his son (12) EDWARD DELAVAL HENRY, 22nd Baron and present peer.

*(1) *Sir* JOHN Hastings, who in right of his mother and by tenure of the Castle of Bergavenny was Baron Bergavenny, was summoned to Parliament as *Baron Hastings* 1290-1313; assisted in the Scottish Wars of Edward I, and received in 1273 from the King a grant of the whole co of Menteth, with the Isles and also all the manors and lands of Alan; 6th Earl of Menteth, then declared a rebel; was seneschal of Aquitaine, and in 1290 a competitor for the Crown of Scotland: *m* 1st, 1275, Isabel de Valence, *d* 1305, da of William, Earl of Pembroke; 2ndly, 13-, Isabella Despencer, da of 1st Earl of Winchester; *d* 1313; *s* by his son (2) JOHN, 2nd Baron; summoned to Parliament 1313-25; served in the Scottish Wars of Edward II, and was sometime Gov of Kenilworth Castle: *m* 13-, Juliana (who *m* 2ndly, 1326, Sir Thomas Blount, and 3rdly, 1327, William, Lord Clinton, and *d* 1367), da of Sir Thomas Leybourne; *d* 1325; *s* by his son (3) LAURENCE, 3rd Baron; *b* 1320; *cr Earl of Pembroke* (peerage of England) 1339; served with valour in the French Wars of Edward III: *m* 1328, Agnes Mortimer (who *m* 2ndly, 13-, John Hakelut, and *d* 1368), da of 1st Earl of March; *d* 1348; *s* by his son (4) JOHN, KG, 2nd Earl; *d* 1347; was sent as Lieut into Aquitaine with a fleet of ships, but no sooner had he got his vessels within the harbour of La Rochelle than he was suddenly attacked by the Spanish fleet, and having suffered a signal defeat was taken prisoner and detained four years in capitivity: *m* 1st, 1359, Margaret, who *d* 1361, da of Edward III; 2ndly, 1363, Anne, who *d* 1384, da of Walter, 1st Lord Manny; *d* 1375; *s* by his son (5) JOHN, 3rd Earl; *b* 1372: *m* 1st, 1380 (*m diss* 1383), Elizabeth, da of John of Gaunt, Duke of Lancaster; 2ndly, -, Philippa Mortimer (who *m* 2ndly, 13-, Richard FitzAlan, 15th Earl of Arundel, and 3rdly, 1399, Thomas Poynings, 5th Lord St John of Basing, and *d* 1401), da of the 3rd Earl of March; *d* 1389, when 17 years of age, from a wound received in tilting, from the lance of Sir John St John, when the earldom became ext and he was *s* in the barony (according to the decision of the House of Lords 1841) by his kinsman (6) *Sir* JOHN, *de jure* 6th Baron (el son of Sir Hugh Hastings, son of 1st Baron), *b* 1328, *d* 1393; *s* by his great-nephew (7) *Sir* HUGH (son of Sir Hugh Hastings, of Elsing, Norfolk, and of Fenwick, co York, and grandson of Sir Hugh Hastings, brother of 6th Baron, *b* 1376): *m* 13- Constance (who *m* 2ndly, 14-, Sir John Sutton, of Dudley, Staffs), da of Walter Blount, of Barton Blount, Derbyshire; *d* 1396; *s* by his brother (8) *Sir* EDWARD, *de jure* 8th Baron, *b* 1382; unsuccessfully claimed to carry the Second Sword before the King at Henry IV's Coronation, and to carry Great Gilt Spurs, and to perform the office of Ch Napperer: *m* 1st, 14-, Muriel,

da of Sir John de Dinham, of Hartland, Devon: 2ndly, 14-, Margery (who *m* 2ndly, 14-, John Wyndham, of Felbridge, Norfolk, and *d* 1456), da of Sir Robert Clifton, of Bokenham, Norfolk; *d* 1438; *s* by his son **(9)** JOHN, *de jure* 9th Baron, *b* 1412; Constable of Norwich Castle and Gaol 1441: *m* 1434, Anne, who *d* 1471, da of Thomas Morley, Lord Morley; *d* 1477; *s* by his son **(10)** Sir HUGH, *de jure* 10th Baron, *b* 1447; Sheriff of Yorkshire 1479-80: *m* 1455, Anne, da of Sir William Gascoigne, of Gawthorpe, Yorkshire; *d* 1488; *s* by his son **(11)** Sir JOHN, *de jure* 11th Baron, *b* 1466: *m* 1st, 14-, Isabel, who *d* 1495, da and heir of Sir Ralph Babthorpe, of Babthorpe, Yorkshire; 2ndly, 14-, Katherine, da of Sir John Aske, of Aughton Yorkshire; *d* 1504; *s* by his brother **(12)** Sir GEORGE, *de jure* 12th Baron; *b* 1474: *m* 1493, Joan, da and co-heir of Roger Brabazon, of Eastwell, Leicestershire; *d* 1511; *s* by his son **(13)** JOHN, *de jure* 13th Baron, *b* 1498; *d* 1514; *s* by his brother **(14)** Sir HUGH, *de jure* 14th Baron, *b* 1505: *m* 1523, Katherine (who *m* 2ndly, 1554, Thomas Gawdy, Serjeant-at-Law, and *d* 1558), da of Robert L'Estrange, of Winfarthing, Norfolk; *d* 1540; *s* by his son **(15)** JOHN *de jure* 15th Baron, *b* 1530; *d* unmarried 1542, when the Barony fell into abeyance between his sisters (i) Anne, wife of William Browne, of Elsing, Norfolk, and (ii) Elizabeth, wife of Hamon L'Estrange of Hunstanton, Norfolk, and so remained until 1841, when the House of Lords reported that the co-heirs were Frances Berney, widow of the Rev Richard Browne, Henry L'Estrange Styleman le Strange, of Hunstanton, co Norfolk, and Sir Jacob Astley, 6th Bt, whereupon the abeyance was terminated in favour of the last-named, who was 9th in descent from Elizabeth L'Estrange (ante).

HATCH OF LUSBY, BARONY OF (Hatch) (Extinct 1992)

SONS LIVING OF LIFE BARON (by 1st marriage)

Hon Barrie, *b* 19—: *m* and has issue.
Hon Stewart, *b* 19—: *m* and has issue.

WIDOW LIVING OF LIFE BARON

EVA (*Baroness Hatch of Lusby*), da of —: *m* 19—, as his 2nd wife, Baron Hatch of Lusby (Life Baron), who *d* 1992. *Residence* – 28 The Vale, Swainsthorpe, Norwich, Norfolk NR14 8PL.

HATHERTON, BARON (Littleton) (Baron UK 1835)

One God, and one king

EDWARD CHARLES LITTLETON, 8th Baron, *b* 24 May 1950; *s* 1985; Agronomist: *m* 1974, Hilda María, da of Rodolfo Robert, of San José, Costa Rica, and has issue.

Arms – Argent, a chevron between three escallops sable. **Crest** – A stag's head cabossed sable, attired or; between the attires a bugle horn of the first, garnished and pendant from two annulets conjoined gold. **Supporters** – *Dexter*, a stag proper, plain collared or, and suspended therefrom an escutcheon argent, charged with a bugle stringed sable; *sinister*, a lion gules, ducally gorged, and suspended from the coronet an escutcheon, charged as in the dexter.
Address – PO Box 3358, San José, Costa Rica.

SON LIVING

Hon THOMAS EDWARD, *b* 7 March 1977.

DAUGHTERS LIVING

Hon Melissa Anne, *b* 1975.
Hon Valerie Anne, *b* 1981.

SISTERS LIVING

Aileen Pamela Hyacinthe, *b* 1941: *m* 1963, Roberto Padilla Odor, of PO Box 2280, San Pedro Sula, Honduros, and has issue living, Roberto, *b* 1964, — Andreas, *b* 1968, — Mervyn, *b* 1971, — Luciana, *b* 1964.
Cynthia Ann, *b* 1943: *m* 1964, Giovanni Sosto Peralta, of PO Box 1138, San Jose, Costa Rica, and has issue living, Giovanni, *b* 1967, — Eugenio, *b* 1971, — Carlo, *b* 1972, — Alexandra Eugenia, *b* 1968.

DAUGHTER LIVING OF SEVENTH BARON

Hon Hyacinthe Ann, *b* 1934; LLB Newcastle; Solicitor 1978: *m* 1954, Patrick Peterken, of Claypool Farm, Hutton Henry, Castle Eden, co Durham, and has issue living, Patrick James Littleton, *b* 1957, — Nicholas John Littleton, *b* 1960, — Frances Josephine, *b* 1962.

SONS LIVING OF SIXTH BARON (by 2nd wife)

Hon Richard Brownlow (Foresters Lodge, Nether Alderley, Macclesfield, Cheshire), *b* 1949: *m* 1st, 1975 (*m diss* 19—), Shirley Margaret Adamson; 2ndly, 1992, Linda Hoyland, and has issue living (by 1st *m*), Ian Brownlow, *b* 1981, — Kirsty Emma, *b* 1985.
Hon Jonathan Lloyd (Cornish Arms Cottage, The Square, W Looe, Cornwall), *b* (twin) 1949: *m* 1970, Maxine Elizabeth, da of Alistair Brough Mills, of Mynderley, High Park, All Stretton, Salop, and has issue living, Alexander John Walhouse, *b* 1970, — Rosalind Elizabeth, *b* 1972, — Melissa Mary, *b* 1975.

DAUGHTERS LIVING OF SIXTH BARON

(by 1st wife)

Hon Moonyeen Meriel (c/o Interserve, 325 Kennington Rd, SE11 4QH), *b* 1933.

(by 2nd wife)

Hon Modwena Louise, *b* 1947: *m* 1st, 1968 (*m diss* 1974), Edward Willison; 2ndly, 1978, Peter Fleming Orchard, of Copper Beeches, 9A Hartland Rd, Epping, Essex, and has issue living (by 1st *m*), Trecia, *b* 1969, — Rachel, *b* 1971.

DAUGHTERS LIVING OF FIFTH BARON

Hon Joanna Ida Louisa, *b* 1926: *m* 1948, Robert Westby Perceval, of Pillaton Old Hall, Penkridge, Stafford, and has issue living, Antony Robin Walhouse Westby LITTLETON (Old Walls, Hannington, Basingstoke, Hants), *b* 1950; *ed* Eton; adopted by Roy Licence 1971 the surname of Littleton: *m* 1980, Hon Aileen Mary Fitzherbert, eldest da of 14th Baron Stafford, and has issue living, Thomas Alastair Westby *b* 1986, Katrina Mary *b* 1983, Rosanna Sophie *b* 1989, — Sara Jane Modwena, *b* 1954: *m* 1981, Richard Burnaby Kennedy Dyott, FRICS, of Freeford Manor, Lichfield, Staffs, only son of late William Boyd Kennedy Shaw, OBE, by his wife Eleanor, yr da of late Richard Archibald Dyott, of Freeford Manor (*see* M Anglesey, colls, 1960 Edn), and has issue living, William Richard Perceval *b* 1987, Caroline Eleanor Frances *b* 1985, — Diana Mary, *b* 1959: *m* 1980, Peter Henry Burden, of Gwynfe House, Sutton St Nicholas, Hereford, son of Paul Burden, of Burnham, Bucks, and has issue living, Edward Hugh *b* 1986, Archibald Robert *b* 1990, Alice Titania *b* 1988.
Hon Jane Anne Caroline, *b* 1929: *m* 1967, Rev Charles Piachaud Wright, of Meadowsweet Lodge, Uppingham, Rutland, Leics.

DAUGHTERS LIVING OF FOURTH BARON

Hon Norah Hyacinthe, *b* 1899: *m* 1923, Samuel Ranulph Allsopp, CBE, who *d* 1975 (*see* B Hindlip, colls). *Residence* – Alsa Lodge, Stansted, Essex.
Hon Hester Mary Modwena (Pitt Manor Cottage, Winchester), *b* 1912; 1939-45 with WTS/FANY.

MOTHER LIVING

Margaret Ann (PO Box 3358, San José, Costa Rica), da of Frank Sheehy, of Canada: *m* 1940, Mervyn Cecil Littleton, only son of late Lt-Col Hon Charles Christopher Josceline Littleton, DSO, who *d* 1970.

WIDOW LIVING OF SIXTH BARON

MARY ALICE (*Mary, Baroness Hatherton*), Capt (ret) QAIMNS; da of John Roberts, of Ruthin, Denbighshire: *m* 1955, as his 2nd wife, the 6th Baron, who *d* 1973.

COLLATERAL BRANCHES LIVING

Granddaughters of late Maj Hon William Hugh Littleton (infra):—
Issue of late John William Littleton, *b* 1924, *d* 1992: *m* 1956, Hilda Ruth (The Bridges, 92 King's Av, Christchurch, Hants), only da of J. Pardy, of Christchurch, Hants:—
Deborah Jayne, *b* 1960: *m* 1981 (*m diss* 1993), Thomas Collins, only son of Thomas Collins, of Grimsby, Humberside, and has issue living, Steven Andrew, *b* 1981. —— Susan Jennifer, *b* 1965.

Issue of late Major Hon William Hugh Littleton, 4th son of 3rd Baron, *b* 1882, *d* 1956: *m* 1920, Lilian, who *d* 1954, da of Charles E. Davis, of Clifton, Bristol:—
Margaret Hyacinthe, *b* 1921; 1939-45 War in VAD: *m* 1948, Edward Roderick Dew, CBE. *Residence* – Highdown, Bridge Reeve, Chulmleigh, N Devon.

Grandchildren of late Rear-Adm Hon Algernon Charles Littleton, 2nd son of 2nd Baron:—
Issue of late Capt Algernon Edward Percy Littleton, *b* 1881, *d* 1943: *m* 1912, Violet Agnes Lætitia, who *d* 1973, da of Sir John William Salusbury-Trelawny, 11th Bt:—
Leonard Vere Algernon, *b* 1913; *ed* Malvern; European War 1939-45 as Capt RA: *m* 1941, Sheila Miriam, who *d* 1984, da of late Stanley Couldrey, of Tunbridge Wells. *Residence* – 23 Chancellor House, Mount Ephraim, Tunbridge Wells, Kent. —— Robert Jocelyn Henry, DFC, *b* 1915; *ed* Malvern; Flight-Lt RAF; 1939-45 War (DFC): *m* 1946, Wendy, da of late S. Stevens, and has issue living, Susan Elaine, *b* 1952, — Zoë Annette, *b* 1955. *Residence* – 3 Springfield, Nye Timber, Bognor Regis, W Sussex.
Issue of late Lt-Col Josceline William Littleton, MC, ED, *b* 1886, *d* 1969: *m* 1920, Annie McKerrell, who *d* 1961, da of Lt-Col Arthur George Wolley-Dod:—
Margaret Anne (1345, W Tulare Av, Visalia, Cal 93277), *b* 1921: *m* 1st, 1943 (*m diss* 1948), Fl-Lt Alfred John Smitz, DFC, RAF; 2ndly, 1948 (*m diss* 1963), Robert Leech; 3rdly, 1967 (*m diss* 1974), Arthur Dale Harder, and has issue living (by 1st *m*) Peter Gerard Littleton (96 Hollyburn Rd, Calgary, Alberta, Canada T2V 3HJ), *b* 1944; a Constable, Royal Canadian Mounted Police: *m* 1965, Carol Thew, of Richmond Hill, Ont, and has issue living, Stephen Douglas *b* 1975, Leigh-Ann Kimberly *b* 1971, — (by 2nd *m*) Robert Timothy, *b* 1961, — Marta Anne, *b* 1951: *m* 1969, Kerry Wayne King, of 130 East Cedar, Exeter, Calif 93221, USA, — Josceline Henrietta, *b* 1952: *m* 1st, 1971 (*m diss* 1976), Mark S. Wingo; 2ndly, 1979, Philip Lon Bower, who *d* 1981; 3rdly, 1984, John Douglas Koopman, and has issue living (by 1st *m*), Jason Marcus *b* 1973, (by —) Aisha Christine Gaut *b* 1977, (by 2nd *m*) Delaney Brie *b* 1981.
Issue of late Com Richard Charles Arthur Littleton, RN (ret), *b* 1888, *d* 1945: *m* 1934, Lucy Veronica, who *d* 1979, da of Rev Robert Cecil Salmon, R of Chiddingstone, Kent:—
Joanna Veronica, *b* 1935: *m* 1976, Brian Scarlin Bashall, of Pondtail, Foxhill, Petworth, W Sussex. —— Marilyn Eve (Chibbett, Exford, Minehead, Som), *b* 1937.
Issue of late Capt Cecil Francis Henry Littleton, *b* 1890, *d* of wounds received during European War 1917: *m* 1913, Brenda (who *d* 1972, having *m* 2ndly, 1919, Arthur Alexander Baillie, and 3rdly, 1922 (*m diss* 1934), Alwyne R. M. Scrase-Dickins, who *d* 1983), da of late George Southby Hewitt, of 26A North Audley St, W1:—
Diana, *b* 1915: *m* 19-, — Earley, of 27 Parkside, Cuddesdon, Oxford OX44 9EZ.

PREDECESSORS – *Sir* Edward Littleton, 4th and last Bt, of Pillaton, *cr* 1627, devised his estates to his grand-nephew **(1)** EDWARD JOHN Walhouse, PC (MP for Staffordshire 1812-35), who thereupon assumed the surname of Littleton in lieu of his patronymic; *b* 1791; was Ch Sec for Ireland 1834, and Lord-Lieut of Staffordshire 1854-62; *cr Baron Hatherton*, of Hatherton, co Stafford, 1835: *m* 1st, 1812, Hyacinthe Mary, natural da of 1st Marquess Wellesley; 2ndly, 1852, Caroline Anne, who *d* 1897, da of Richard Hurt, of Worksworth, and widow of Edward Davies Davonport, of Capesthorne, Cheshire; *d* 1863; *s* by his son **(2)** EDWARD RICHARD, CB, 2nd Baron, *b* 1815; sat as MP for Walsall (*L*) 1847-52, and for S Staffordshire 1853-7: *m* 1841, Lady Margaret Percy, who *d* 1897, da of 5th Duke of Northumberland; *d* 1888; *s* by his el son **(3)** EDWARD GEORGE

PERCY, CMG, 3rd Baron, *b* 1842; was Sec and Mil Sec to Earl of Dufferin (Gov-Gen of Canada) 1875-8, Mil Sec to Marquess of Lorne 1878-9, and an Hon Commr in Lunacy 1890-98: *m* 1867, Charlotte Louisa, who *d* 1923, da of Sir Charles Robert Rowley, 4th Bt; *d* 1930; *s* by his el son (4) EDWARD CHARLES ROWLEY, 4th Baron; *b* 1868; formerly Lieut 3rd Batn N Staffordshire Regt; in Ser of Raja of Sarawak 1890-96: *m* 1897, Hester Edith, who *d* 1947, da of late Thomas Tarrant Hoskins, MD, JP, of Tasmania; *d* 1944; *s* by his el son (5) EDWARD THOMAS WALHOUSE, 5th Baron, *b* 1900; Lt Cdr RN: *m* 1st, 1925 (*m diss* 1951), Ida Guendolen, who *d* 1969, da of Robin Legge; 2ndly, Kathleen May, who *d* 1983, da of Clarence Ernest Orlando Whitechurch, and formerly wife of Maj Oscar Westendarp; *d* 1969; *s* by his brother, (6) JOHN WALTER STUART, 6th Baron; *b* 1906: *m* 1st, 1932, Nora Evelyn, who *d* 1955, da of R. C. Smith, of Edgbaston; 2ndly, 1955, Mary Alice, Capt (ret) QUAIMNS, da of John Roberts, of Ruthin, Denbighshire; *d* 1973; *s* by his brother (7) THOMAS CHARLES TASMAN, TD, 7th Baron, *b* 1907: Capt RA (TA): *m* 1933, Ann Scott, who *d* 1994, only da of late Lt-Cdr Thomas MacLeod, RN; *d* 1985; *s* by his kinsman (8) EDWARD CHARLES (only son of late Mervyn Cecil Littleton, only son (by 1st *m*) of Lt-Col Hon Charles Christopher Josceline Littleton, DSO, 3rd son of 3rd Baron), 8th Baron and present peer.

HAVERS, BARONY OF (Havers) (Extinct 1992)

SONS LIVING OF LIFE BARON

Hon Philip, *b* 1950; *ed* Eton, and Corpus Christi Coll, Camb; barrister-at-law, Junior Counsel to the Crown, Common Law: *m* 1976, Patricia Frances, da of Sidney Alexander Searle, of Tideways, Old Bosham, Chichester, and has issue living, Daniel Alexander, *b* 1981, — Holly Linnell, *b* 1978. *Residence* – 75 Cadogan Place, SW1. *Club* – Garrick.

Hon Nigel, *b* 1951; actor: *m* 1st, 1974 (*m diss* 1989), Carolyn Gillian, da of Vincent Cox; 2ndly, 1989, Mrs Polly Bloomfield, da of late Hugh Williams, and has issue living (by 1st *m*), Katharine, *b* 1977. *Residence* – 125 Gloucester Rd, SW7.

WIDOW LIVING OF LIFE BARON

CAROL ELIZABETH, da of Stuart Lay, of London: *m* 1st, 1949, Baron Havers, PC, QC (Life Baron), who *d* 1992; 2ndly, 1993, Charles Frederick Hughesdon, AFC, of Leckhampstead House, Leckhampstead, nr Reading, Berks RG16 8QH.

HAWARDEN, VISCOUNT (Maude) (Viscount I 1793, Bt I 1705)
(Name pronounced ("Haywarden")

(ROBERT) CONNAN WYNDHAM LESLIE MAUDE, 9th Viscount, and 11th Baronet; *b* 23 May 1961; *s* 1991; *ed* St Edmund's Sch, Canterbury, and RAC Cirencester.

Arms – Quarterly: 1st and 4th azure, a lion rampant argent, *Maude*; 2nd and 3rd argent, three bars gemelles sable, over all a lion rampant gules, charged on the shoulder with a cross-crosslet fitchée or. **Crest** – A lion's jamb erased erect proper, grasping a sprig of oak leaves slipped vert. **Supporters** – Two lions gules, each charged on the shoulder with a cross-crosslet fitchée or.
Seat – Wingham Court, nr Canterbury. *Residence* – Great Bossington Farm House, Adisham, Canterbury, Kent.

VIRTVTE SIC SECVRVS

Safe by manliness

BROTHER LIVING

Hon THOMAS PATRICK CORNWALLIS, *b* 1 Oct 1964; *ed* Rudolph Steiner Sch, nr Canterbury, and Hadlow Agric Coll. *Residence* – Cedar Lodge, Wingham Court, nr Canterbury, Kent.

SISTER LIVING

Hon Sophia-Rose Eileen, *b* 1959: *m* 1982, Timothy Michael Steel, only son of Anthony Steel, of Rock House Farm, Lower Froyle, Alton, Hants, and has issue living, Anthony Nicholas Robert, *b* 1988, — Isabella Ann Augusta, *b* 1984, — Emily Susannah Letitia, *b* 1992. *Residence* – 83 Eaton Terrace, SW1.

UNCLE LIVING (*son of 7th Viscount*)

Hon Henry Cornwallis, *b* 1928; *ed* Marlborough, and Worcester Coll, Oxford (BA 1953, MA 1957); co-patron of five livings; High Sheriff Kent 1989; 1939-45 War with Queen's R Regt, and as Sergeant Educational Corps: *m* 1964, Elizabeth Georgina, only da of David McNaught Lockie, of Grasse, France, and has issue living, Francis Hugh Cornwallis, *b* 1966; *ed* Eton, and Clare Coll, Camb (BA 1988), — Anthony Eustace David, *b* 1972; *ed* Winchester, — Elizabeth Arabella Marion, *b* 1967; *ed* Benenden, — Diana Caroline Alice, *b* 1971; *ed* West Heath. *Residence* – Wingham Well House, Wingham, Canterbury, Kent.

AUNT LIVING (*daughter of 7th Viscount*)

Hon Helen Margaretta, *b* 1921: *m* 1947 (Walter) Peter Baxter, who *d* 1977, and has issue living, Charles Peter, *b* 1950; *ed* Marlborough: *m* 1974, Nicola Caroline, 2nd da of late Maj N. S. John, of Warminster, Wilts, — Joanna Rosamond, *b* 1948: *m* 1970, Michael George Patrick Falkiner, of Downclose Stud, N Perrott, Crewkerne, Som (see Falkiner, Bt), — Margaretta Helena, *b* 1954: *m* 1983, John Giles Mansfield, of Broadmoor Drive, Little Rock, Arkansas, USA, son of Cyril Peter Mansfield, of Kiambu, Kenya, — Victoria Marion, *b* 1956: *m* 1st, 1977 (*m diss* 1985), Brian John Blundy; 2ndly, 1986, William Stephen Cadman, of Woodhouse Cross, Gillingham, Dorset. *Residence* – Stourbridge House, Milton-on-Stour, Gillingham, Dorset.

WIDOW LIVING OF EIGHTH VISCOUNT

SUSANNAH CAROLINE HYDE (*Viscountess Hawarden*), da of late Maj Charles Phillips Gardner (*see* By Gardner, colls): *m* 1957, the 8th Viscount, who *d* 1991. *Residence* – Wingham Court, nr Canterbury, Kent.

COLLATERAL BRANCHES LIVING

Grandchildren of late Cdr Eustace Downman Maude, RN, 2nd son of late Lt-Col Sir George Ashley Maude, KCB, 2nd son of late Rev Hon John Charles Maude, 5th son of 1st Viscount:—
Issue of late George Ashley Maude, *b* 1889, *d* 1973: *m* 1921, Ruth, who *d* 1984, da of Cdr M Updegraff, US Navy:—
George Ashley (10137, W Saanich Rd, Sidney, BC, Canada), *b* 1925: *m* 1952, Nancy Mary, da of John Ingvard Reitan, and has issue living, Anthony John Ashley, *b* 1954: *m* 1st, 1978 (*m diss* 1980), Gale Victoria, da of Lt-Cdr Sydney Dalton Bryant, RCN; 2ndly, 1982, Saryl, da of William Edward Rusk, — Christopher George, *b* 1957: *m* 1982, Pamela Mary, da of Leonard Lang, and has issue living, Curtiss John Ashley *b* 1984, Glenn Douglas George *b* 1989, — David Philip, *b* 1964. —— Alison Beauclerk, *b* 1923.

Granddaughters of late Lt-Col Aubrey Maurice Maude, 4th son of late Lt-Col Sir George Ashley Maude, KCB (ante):—
Issue of late Brig Christian George Maude, DSO, OBE, MC, *b* 1884, *d* 1971: *m* 1st, 1920 (*m diss* 1930), Hon Patience Kemp, who *d* 1935, da of 1st Baron Rochdale; 2ndly, 1931, Hester Joan, who *d* 1993, da of late Charles Augustus Egerton, of Mountfield Court, Robertsbridge, Sussex:—
(By 2nd *m*) Gillian Mabelle Beauclerk, *b* 1932: *m* 1st, 1960, Maj Estcourt Richard Cresswell, MC, MA 15th/19th King's R Hussars, who *d* 1983; 2ndly, 1984, John Anthony David Lord, son of late Lt-Col John Arthur Lord, of Saintbury Close, Broadway, Worcs. *Residence* – Four Wells, Lower Slaughter, Cheltenham, Glos. —— Priscilla Douglas, *b* 1934: *m* 1962, Michael Frederick Tremain Maude (infra). —— Elizabeth Joan, *b* 1940: *m* 1st, 1967, Capt Christopher Evelyn Twiston-Davies, late 4th/7th R Dragoon Gds, who *d* 1980, son of late Sir Leonard Twiston-Davies, KBE, of Rockfield Park, Monmouth; 2ndly, (June) 1992, Malcolm Allinson Anson, who *d* (Aug) 1992, son of late Sir (George) Wilfrid Anson, MBE, MC, of West Hay, Wrington, Bristol, and has issue living (by 1st *m*), William Ashley Christopher, *b* 1969, — Benjamin James, *b* 1971. *Residence* – Drax House, Tilshead, Salisbury, Wilts.

Granddaughter of late Brig Christian George Maude, DSO, OBE, MC (ante):—
Issue of late Capt Peter George Egerton Maude, *b* 1926, *k* in the Manchester air accident 1957: *m* 1952, Olivia Elizabeth (who *m* 2ndly, 1961, Brig Hugh Marlborough Hale Ley, CBE, DL, of The Dower House, Burrow, via Carnforth, Lancs, LA6 2RJ), el da of Lt-Col Hugh O. Wright, of Melling, Carnforth, Lancs:—
Sarah Patience, *b* 1954.

Grandchildren of late Maurice Ceely Maude, 3rd son of Rev Hon John Charles Maude, 5th son of 1st Viscount:—
Issue of late Christopher Hugh Maude, *b* 1867, *d* 1942: *m* 1924, Mary Elizabeth Christiana, who *d* 1952, da of Rt Rev James Macmanaway, DD, 91st Bishop of Clogher:—
Maurice Christopher, *b* 1925; late Capt KRRC: *m* 1st, 1954 (*m diss* 1963), Venetia, da of William Patterson Doyle, of Kuwait; 2ndly, 1967, Susan Frances, da of George Lepper, of Blacknest, Alton, Hants, and has issue living (by 2nd *m*), Christopher George, *b* 1969.
Issue of late Ceely Maude, *b* 1870, *d* 1929: *m* 1901, Jane Marion, who *d* 1949, da of late C W O'Hara, JP, DL, of Annaghmore, and Coopers Hill, co Sligo:—
Venetia Marion Ceely, *b* 1905. *Residence* – 142A, Ashley Gdns, SW1.

Grandchildren of late Lt-Gen Sir Frederick Stanley Maude, KCB, CMG, DSO, son of Gen Sir Frederick Francis Maude, VC, GCB, 4th son of Rev Hon John Charles Maude (ante):—
Issue of late Brig Edward Frederick Maude, OBE, *b* 1897, *d* 1984: *m* 1929, Sylvia, who *d* 1987, da of Robert Brewster, of New York, USA:—
Michael Frederick Tremain (Etchilhampton House, Devizes, Wiltshire, SN10 3JH), *b* 1935: *m* 1962, Priscilla Douglas, da of late Brig Christian George Maude, DSO, OBE, MC (ante), and has issue living, Rupert Frederick, *b* 1965, — Andrew Tremain, *b* 1967, — Alexandra, *b* 1963: *m* 1993, Maj James Nicholas John Gray, 1st Queen's Dragoon Gds, son of Col Nicholas Gray, RA, of Yalding, Kent, — Victoria, *b* 1970. —— Eileen FOSTER (621 Pleasant St, Boulder, Colorado 80302, USA), *b* 1931; assumed by deed poll the surname of Foster 1959 for herself and her issue: *m* 1954, Lloyd George, who *d* 1974, and has issue living, Lloyd Edward, *b* 1955, — Robert Douglas, *b* 1957: *m* 1981, Virginia Huffman, and has issue living, Robert David *b* 1981, Jennifer *b* 1985, — Ronald Wayne, *b* 1957: *m* 1987, Audrey Poage, and has issue living, Richard *b* 1986, Renée *b* 1987, — Michael Daniel, *b* 1959: *m* 1984, Christine Oberholzer, and has issue living, Daniel George *b* 1987, Laura Elizabeth *b* 1986, — Laura Ellen, *b* 1956: *m* 1982, John Grace, and has issue living, Matthew Eric *b* 1984, Jeremy Colin *b* 1986. —— Barbara (11 Southwell Gdns, SW7 4SB), *b* 1932: *m* 1958 (*m diss* 1988), William Clarkson Marshall, and has issue living, Thomas Alan, *b* 1963, — Cynthia, *b* 1959.

Granddaughter of late Cyril Francis Maude, actor-manager, eldest son of Capt Charles Henry Maude, 2nd son of Capt Hon Francis Maude, RN, 6th son of 1st Viscount:—
Issue of late His Honour Judge John Cyril Maude, QC, *b* 1901, *d* 1986: *m* 1st, 1927 (*m diss* 1954), Rosamund Willing, da of Dr T. Morris Murray, of 21 Marlborough St, Boston, USA; 2ndly, 1955, Maureen Constance (BUCHANAN) (*Maureen, Marchioness of Dufferin and Ava*) (4 Hans Crescent, SW1; The Owl House, Lamberhurst, Kent), da of late Hon Arthur Ernest Guinness (*see* E Iveagh, colls), and widow of 4th Marquess of Dufferin and Ava:—
(By 1st *m*) Anne Murray, *b* 1929: *m* 1950, Michael Hilary George Bradstock, of Whitefold, Clunas, Nairn IV12 5UT, and has issue living, James Michael Murray, *b* 1951, — Rupert John (Lower Farm, Combe, Newbury, Berks), *b* 1958: *m* 1987, Anna L., yr da of Maj John Riley, of Trinity Manor, Jersey, CI, and has issue living, James Rupert *b* 1993, — Alastair George, *b* 1961, — Sarah Anne (*Hon Mrs David R. Gilmour*), *b* 1954: *m* 1975, Hon David Robert Gilmour, of 21 Moray Place, Edinburgh, eldest son of Baron Gilmour of Craigmillar, PC (Life Baron).

Grandchildren of late Alwyn Julian Maude, 4th son of late Capt Charles Henry Maude (ante):—
Issue of late Dr Dudley Jack Maude, *b* 1897, *d* 1988: *m* 1925, Marcia, da of late John Williamson, solicitor, of Sydney, NSW:—
John Alwyn (Lynton, 618 Argyle St, Moss Vale, NSW 2577, Australia), *b* 1930: *m* 1955, Susan Theresa Gidley, da of George Gidley King, of Sydney, NSW, and has issue living, John Philip Cornwallis, *b* 1959: *m* 1986 (*m diss* 1991), Helen Tatt, and has issue living, Angela *b* 1989, — Lisa Margaret, *b* 1960: *m* 1984, Martin James Bryant, and has issue living, Maximillian Quentin Hugh *b* 1985, Oscar Charles Rowsell *b* 1987, Leopold George Roy *b* 1989, — Jessica Mary, *b* 1970. —— Jacqueline Mary, *b* 1927: *m* 1956, Llewellyn Daniel Wheeler, Surg, of 124 Ruthven St, Bondi Junction, NSW 2022, and has issue living, Andrew John, *b* 1957: *m* 1st, 1982 (*m diss* 1989), Louise Elna, da of Denis V. Hansen, of Caringbah, NSW; 2ndly, 1991, Anne Margaret, da of John Verschuer, and has issue living (by 2nd *m*), Georgiana Rhiannon *b* 1992, — Daniel Julian, *b* 1959: *m* 1982, Michele Anne, da of L. Bruce Harper, of Pacific Hill, Dubbo, NSW, and has issue living, Rachel Ellen *b* 1989, Fallon Elizabeth *b* 1990, — Frances Llewellyn Maude, *b* 1961: *m* 1988, Andrew Philip Dudman.

Grandchildren of late Capt Charles Henry Maude (ante):—

Issue of late Maurice Douglas Maude, b 1868, d 1953: m 1906, Zima Irene Lily, who d 1952, da of John Godfrey Koch, FSL, formerly Assit Sup of Surveys, Perak, Malaya:—

Valerie Blanche, b 1908: m 1939, John Chichester Longhurst, who d 1957. ——Cicely, b 1918: m 1948, Roland Cumberbatch, MB, of Middle Farm House, Sutton, Ditcheat, Shepton-Mallet, Somerset, and has issue living, Toby John, b 1949, — Judith Mary, 1952, — Hyacinth Anne, b 1954.

Issue of late Major Ralph Walter Maude, DSO, b 1873, d 1922: m 1905 (m diss 1915), Alice, only da of Noël Hereford Thomson, of Dinan, France:—

Rev Ralph Henry Evelyn, b 1909; ed St Peter's Hall, Oxford (MA): m 1933, Marjorie Cecilia Emily, da of late Rev Philip Harold Rogers, and has issue living, Roger Philip (School Cottage, School Lane, Ockham, nr Ripley, Surrey), b 1937: m 1972, Penelope Joy, da of late Christopher Rowe, Solicitor, and has issue living, Peter Timothy Daniel b 1975, Polly Emma Frances b 1978, — Rachel Anne, b 1934: m 1964, John Donald Cullum, of 20 Gorang Rd, Westleigh, NSW 2120, Australia, and has issue living, Simon Richard b 1967, Joanna Margaret b 1969. Residence - 4 Manor Court, Pewsey, Wilts.

Granddaughter of late Raymond William de Latham Maude, son of late Capt Hon Francis Maude, RN (ante):—

Issue of late Lieut-Col Charles Raymond Maude, OBE, MC, b 1882, d 1943: m 1907, Lillian Nancy Bache, CBE, who d 1970, da of late William Henry Price, of Rockmount, Kinver, Stourbridge:—

Joan Nancy, b 1908: m 1st, 1933, Frank Henry Waters, who d 1954; 2ndly, 1956, Oliver Frederick John Bradley Woods, MC, who d 1972, and has issue living, (by 1st m) Sarah Jenny, b 1938: m 1963 (m diss 1973), Maj James Alexander Dunsmure, SG, and has issue living, Rupert Alexander Frank b 1969, Miranda Louise b 1967. Residence - 8 East St, Lewes.

PREDECESSORS – (1) ROBERT Maude, MP for Gowran 1703, St Canice 1715, and Bangor 1729, was cr a Baronet 1705; d 1750; s by his el son (2) Sir THOMAS, 2nd Bt, MP for co Tipperary 1761; cr Baron de Montalt, of Hawarden, co Tipperary (peerage of Ireland) 1776; d 1777, when the barony expired and the baronetcy devolved upon his brother (3) Sir CORNWALLIS, 3rd Bt, MP for Roscommon; cr Baron de Montalt, of Hawarden, co Tipperary (peerage of Ireland) 1785, and Viscount Hawarden (peerage of Ireland) 1793; d 1808; s by his el son (4) THOMAS RALPH, 2nd Viscount; d 1807, without issue; s by his half-brother (5) CORNWALLIS, 3rd Viscount; b 1780; m 1811, Jane, who d 1852, da of Patrick Crawford Bruce, of Taplow Lodge, Bucks; d 1856; s by his son (6) CORNWALLIS, 4th Viscount; b 1817; a Lord-in-Waiting to Queen Victoria 1866-8 and 1874-80; cr Earl de Montalt, of Dundrum, co Tipperary (peerage of United Kingdom) 1886: m 1845, Clementina, who d 1865, el da and co-heir of late Adm Hon Charles Elphinstone-Fleeming; d 1905, when the Earldom of De Montalt became ext, and he was s in the other honours by his cousin (7) ROBERT HENRY, son of late Very Rev Hon Robert William Henry Maude, Dean of Clogher, 2nd son of 1st Viscount), 5th Viscount, b 1842: m 1881, Caroline, who d 1930, da of late Major Arthur Ogle; d 1908; s by his son (8) ROBERT CORNWALLIS, 6th Viscount, b 1890; Lieut Coldstream Guards; ka 1914; s by his cousin (9) EUSTACE WYNDHAM (son of late Ludlow Eustace Maude, son of late Very Rev Hon Robert William Henry Maude, 2nd son of 1st Viscount), 7th Viscount; b 1877; Major (ret) Queen's Roy Regt: m 1920, Marion, who d 1974, da of late Albert Leslie Wright (B Fitzwalter); d 1958; s by his el son (10) ROBERT LESLIE EUSTACE, 8th Viscount, b 1926; European War 1945 in Coldstream Guards (invalided): m 1957, Susannah Caroline Hyde, da of late Maj Charles Phillips Gardner (see By Gardner, colls); d 1991; s by his elder son (11) (ROBERT) CONNAN WYNDHAM LESLIE, 9th Viscount and present peer; also Baron de Montalt.

HAWKE, BARON (Hawke) (Baron GB 1776)

EDWARD GEORGE HAWKE, TD, 11th Baron; b 25 Jan 1950; s 1992; ed Eton; 1st Bn Coldstream Gds 1970-73, The Queen's Own Yeo 1973-93; FRICS: m 1993, Bronwen M., da of William T. James, BVMS, MRCVS.

Arms – Argent, a chevron erminois, between three pilgrims' staves purpure. Crest – A hawk rising ermine, belled, and charged on the breast with a fleur-de-lis or. Supporters – Dexter, a figure of Neptune, his mantle vert, edged argent, crowned with an eastern crown or, his dexter arm erect and holding in the act of striking, a trident sable, point downwards silver, and resting his left foot on a dolphin proper; sinister, a sea horse or, holding between the fore fins a banner argent, the staff broken sable.

SISTERS LIVING

Hon Nichola Frances, b 1949: m 1981, Hon Jonathan Andrew Forbes, and has issue (see L Forbes). Residence - East Cevidley, Alford, Aberdeenshire AB33 8BH.

Hon Vanessa Nathalie Mary, b 1957: m 1985, (Peter) Adam William Brodie, yst son of late Maj-Gen Thomas Brodie, CB, CBE, DSO, of Green Ball, Crawley Ridge, Camberley, Surrey, and has issue living, Nathalie Jane, b 1986, — Elizabeth Sarah, b 1989. Residence - Brook Farm, Eglwys Cross, Whitchurch, Shropshire SY13 2JT.

Hon Julia Georgette, b 1960.

HALF-SISTERS LIVING

Hon Sarah Elizabeth Jane, b 1935: m 1957, John Norris Fennell, elder son of late Col Harold Percival Fennell, and has issue living, Adrian Martin Alexander (70 Broxash Rd, Clapham, SW11 6AB), b 1963: m 1990, Anna Meriel, da of William John Gowing, of Buxton, Norfolk, and has issue living, Alexander Theo Felix b 1993, — Olivia Louise (Hon Mrs Martin Hunt), b 1961: m 1993, Hon Martin John Hunt, yr son of Baron Hunt of Tanworth, GCB (Life Baron). Residence - 31 Summers St, Lostwithiel, Cornwall PL22 0DH.

Hon Catherine Mary, b 1940: m 1963, Charles Groves Darville Brook, MD, FRCP, yst son of late Air Vice-Marshal William Arthur Darville Brook, CB, CBE, and has issue living, Charlotte Griselda Mary, b 1965, — Henrietta Diana Darville, b 1968. Residence - 7 The Hermitage, Richmond, Surrey.

DAUGHTERS LIVING OF NINTH BARON

Hon Caroline Ina Maud, *b* 1937; Bar Middle Temple 1959: *m* 1960, John Francis Easton, Bar-at-law, and has issue living, Nicholas John, *b* 1961, — Ina Frances, *b* 1964: *m* 1988, Vincent L. Nelson, son of S. A. Nelson of Black River, Mandeville, Jamaica, and has issue living, Oliver John *b* 1989, Saffron *b* 1992. *Residence* – The Old Hall, Barley, nr Royston, Herts.

Hon Annabel, *b* 1940: *m* 1961, Nicholas Adam Ridley, and has issue living, Caspar Hawke Michael, *b* 1967, — Celia Kirstin, *b* 1964: *m* 1991, Nicholas John Willis, yr son of Dr Peter Willis, of Stillington, Yorks, — Harriet Clare, *b* 1970. *Residence* – 29 Richmond Hill, Richmond, Surrey.

Hon Cecilia Anne, *b* 1943: *m* 1st, 1963 (*m diss* 1971), Peter Hannay Bailey Tapsell, MP (later Sir Peter Tapsell); 2ndly, 1979, Rt Hon Nicholas Paul Scott, MBE, JP, MP, and has had issue (by 1st *m*) James Hawke, *b* 1966, *d* 1985, — (by 2nd *m*) Patrick Martin Iain, *b* 1982, — Amber Teresa, *b* 1987.

Hon Lavinia Mary, *b* 1945: *m* 1965, Maj Nicholas Maclean Verity Bristol, OBE, KOSB, of Breacachadh Castle, Isle of Coll, Argyll, and has issue living, Charles Bladen Maclean, *b* 1967, — Alexander Stanhope Maclean, *b* 1970, — Lauchlan Neil Maclean, *b* 1974.

Hon Rowena Margaret, *b* 1948; a Lady in Waiting to HRH Princess Michael of Kent: *m* 1st, 1971, Philip William Leatham (*see* By Buckland, 1976, Edn); 2ndly, 1990, William T. Sanders, of Hankerton Priory, nr Malmesbury, Wilts SN16 9JZ, and has issue living (by 1st *m*), Patrick Hawke, *b* 1974, — Frederick Bladen, *b* 1981, — Arabella Rose, *b* 1976.

Hon Prunella Jane Alice *b* 1951: *m* 1976, Albert Hendrik Servatius, of Van Alkemadelaan 354, 2597 As Den Haag, Netherlands, and has issue living, Timothy, *b* 1979, — Julian, *b* 1982.

Hon Olivia Mary, *b* 1955: *m* 1983, Timothy John Pethybridge, of 64 Hendham Rd, SW17 7DQ, only son of J. H. Pethybridge, of Barn Park, Bodmin, Cornwall, and has issue living, Henry John Hawke, *b* 1989, — Mary-Rose Olivia, *b* 1985, — Flora Louise, *b* 1987.

AUNT LIVING (*daughter of 8th Baron*)

Hon Veronica Margery, *b* 1915: *m* 1940, Jack Briscoe Masefield, who *d* 1993 and has had issue, Jacqueline Rosemary, *b* 1942; *dunm* 1966, — Delphinia Frances Annie, *b* 1947: *m* 1969, Richard James Fairfax Hall, of Weston Farmhouse, Weston, Petersfield, Hants, and has issue living, Leander Arthur Caspar *b* 1973, Hereward Ambrose Bertram *b* 1974, Innogen Penelope Veronica *b* 1977, — Camilla Margery, *b* 1942; *d* 1973. *Residence* – Down Lodge, East Harting, Petersfield, Hants.

WIDOW LIVING OF NINTH BARON

INA MARY FAURE (*Dowager Baroness Hawke*), da of late Henry Faure Walker, of Highley Manor, Balcombe, Sussex: *m* 1934, the 9th Baron, who *d* 1985. *Residence* – Faygate Place, Faygate, Sussex.

WIDOW LIVING OF TENTH BARON

GEORGETTE MARGARET (*Georgette, Baroness Hawke*), da of late George S. Davidson, of 73 Eaton Sq, SW1: *m* 1947, as his 2nd wife, the 10th Baron, who *d* 1992. *Residence* – Old Mill House, Cuddington, Northwich, Cheshire CW8 2TA.

PREDECESSORS – (1) *Adm Sir* EDWARD HAWKE, KCB, son of late Edward Hawke, Bar-at-law, of Lincoln's Inn; *b* 1710; a celebrated Naval commander; signally defeated the French off Bellisle 1759 (thanked by Parliament, rewarded with a pension of 2,000 a year); was First Lord of the Admiralty 1766-71; *cr Baron Hawke*, of Towton, co York (peerage of Great Britain), 1776: *d* 1781; *s* by his son (2) MARTIN BLADEN, LLD, 2nd Baron; *d* 1805; *s* by his son (3) EDWARD, 3rd Baron; assumed the additional surname of Harvey; *d* 1824; *s* by his el son (4) EDWARD WILLIAM, 4th Baron; *d* 1867; *s* by his brother (5) STANHOPE, 5th Baron; *d* unmarried 1870; *s* by his cousin (6) *Rev* EDWARD HENRY JULIUS, 6th Baron, son of late Hon Martin Bladen Edward, 2nd son of 2nd Baron, by Hannah, da of Thomas Nisbet, of Mersington, *b* 1815; *m* 1857, Jane, who *d* 1915, da of late Henry Dowker, of Laysthorpe, York; *d* 1887; *s* by his son (7) MARTIN BLADEN, 7th Baron, *b* 1860: *m* 1916, Maude, who *d* 1936, da of late William Peacock Edwards, JP, and widow of Arthur Graham Cross; *d* 1938; *s* by his brother (8) EDWARD JULIAN, 8th Baron; *b* 1873: *m* 1900, Frances Alice, who *d* 1959, da of late Col John Randal Wilmer, Indian Army; *d* 1939; *s* by his son (9) BLADEN WILMER, 9th Baron, *b* 1901; a Lord-in-Waiting to HM 1953-57 and a Church Commr 1958-74: *m* 1934, Ina Mary Faure, da of late Henry Faure Walker, of Highley Manor, Balcombe, Sussex; *d* 1985; *s* by his brother (10) (JULIAN STANHOPE) THEODORE, 10th Baron; *b* 1904; S/Ldr Auxiliary Air Force: *m* 1st, 1933 (*m diss* 1946), Angela Margaret Griselda, who *d* 1984, da of late Capt Edmund William Bury; 2ndly, 1947, Georgette Margaret, da of late George S. Davidson, of 73 Eaton Sq, SW1; *d* 1992; *s* by his only son (11) EDWARD GEORGE, 11th Baron and present peer.

Hawkesbury, Viscount; son of Earl of Liverpool.

HAYHOE, BARON (Hayhoe) (Life Baron 1992)

BERNARD JOHN (BARNEY) HAYHOE, PC, son of late Frank Stanley Hayhoe; *b* 8 Aug 1925; *ed* Borough Poly; Conservative Research Dept (Head of Research Section) 1965-70, PPS to Lord Pres and Leader of House of Commons 1972-74, Opposition Spokesman on Employment 1974-79, Parly Under Sec of State for Defence (Army) 1979-81; Min of State for Civil Service 1981, Treasury 1981-85, and Health 1985-86; Gov Birkbeck Coll 1976-79; Chm The Hansard Soc since 1990; MP Heston and Isleworth (*C*) 1970-74, Hounslow, Brentford and Isleworth 1974-92; *cr* PC 1985, Kt Bach 1987, and *Baron Hayhoe*, of Isleworth in the London Borough of Hounslow (Life Baron) 1992: *m* 1962, Ann Gascoigne, da of late Bernard W. Thornton, and has issue.
Residence – 20 Wool Rd, SW20 0HW. *Club* – Garrick.

SONS LIVING

Hon Crispin Bernard Gascoigne, *b* 1963.
Hon Dominic Adam Scott, *b* 1965.

DAUGHTER LIVING

Hon Sarah Anne Sherwood, *b* 1967.

HAYTER, BARON (Chubb) (Baron UK 1927, Bt UK 1900)

Safe by being cautious

GEORGE CHARLES HAYTER CHUBB, KCVO, CBE, 3rd Baron, and 3rd Baronet; *b* 25 April 1911; *s* 1967; *ed* Leys Sch, and Trin Coll, Camb (MA); Chm of Chubb & Son's Lock & Safe Co Ltd; CBE (Civil) 1976, KCVO 1977: *m* 1940, Elizabeth Anne, MBE, only da of late Thomas Arthur Rumbold (*see* Rumbold, Bt, colls), and has issue.

Arms – Quarterly: 1st and 4th azure, a cross erminois between in first and fourth quarters a bezant and in second and third quarters a rose or, *Chubb*, 2nd and 3rd azure, a chevron between two bulls' heads couped in chief, and in base an escallop all or, *Hayter*. **Crest** – In front of a demi lion rampant azure supporting between the paws a bezant charged with a rose gules, a key fesswise wards upwards or. **Supporters** – On either side a lion azure, holding in the mouth a rose gules, barbed seeded, leaved and slipped proper, and charged on the shoulder with a key pale-wise wards downwards and to the dexter or.
Residence – Ashtead House, Ashtead, Surrey.

SONS LIVING

Hon GEORGE WILLIAM MICHAEL (Mapledurwell House, Mapeldurwell, nr Basingstoke, Hants), *b* 9 Oct 1943; *ed* Marlborough and Nottingham Univ (BSc): *m* 1983, Waltraud, yr da of J. Flackl, of Sydney, Australia, and has issue living, Thomas Frederik Flackl, *b* 23 July 1986.
Hon John Andrew (Manor Farm House, Warborough, Oxon), *b* 1946; *ed* Marlborough and Southampton Univ; FCA: *m* 1975, Sandra, only da of late Alfred E. Brereton, of London, and has issue living, Alfred, *b* 1977, — Georgia, *b* 1978.
Hon Charles Henry Thomas (Tower Hill, 101 High St, Kidlington, Oxford OX5 2DS), *b* 1949; *ed* Marlborough, and King's Coll, Camb (MA 1974); MB BS (Barts 1978), MRCGP: *m* 1979, (Ann) Nicola, da of late Charles William Stewart French Manning, FRCS, of Moor Lane House, Sarratt, Herts, and has issue living, (Mark) Henry, *b* 1980, — Jack Charles, *b* 1985, — Josephine Anne, *b* 1983, — Alice Christine, *b* 1989.

DAUGHTER LIVING

Hon Sarah, *b* 1941: *m* 1963, Rev David Humphrey Clark, of St Peter's Rectory, 1 Leicester Rd, Oadby, Leicester LE2 5BD, and has issue living, Andrew David, *b* 1964, — Alison Tamsen, *b* 1967, — and two adopted children, Simon William, *b* 1968, — Katherine Mary, *b* 1970.

WIDOW LIVING OF SON OF SECOND BARON

Veronica, da of William Clifton, of Shanghai: *m* 1939, Cmdr Hon David William Early Chubb, RN, who *d* 1993, and has issue (see colls infra). *Residence* – St Mary's Cottage, Broughton, Hants.

COLLATERAL BRANCH LIVING

Issue of late Cmdr Hon David William Early Chubb, RN, yr son of 2nd Baron, *b* 1914, *d* 1993: *m* 1939, Veronica (ante), da of William Clifton, of Shanghai:—
Jeremy David Knyvett, *b* 1941; *ed* Sherborne: *m* 1978, Mrs Valerie Anne Evans, yst da of H. J. Wightman, and has issue living, Patrick David, *b* 1980, — Andrew Harry, *b* 1982.

PREDECESSORS – GEORGE HAYTER Chubb, 2nd son of late John Chubb; *b* 1848; a lock and safe manufacturer: *m* 1870, Sarah Vanner, who *d* 1940, da of late Charles Early, JP, of Witney, Oxon: *cr* a Baronet 1900, and *Baron Hayter*, of Chislehurst, co Kent (peerage of United Kingdom) 1927; *d* 1946; *s* by his son **(2)** CHARLES ARCHIBALD, 2nd Baron, *b* 1871; Managing Dir of Chubb & Sons Lock & Safe Co Ltd: *m* 1st, 1898, Mary, who *d* 1948, el da of John F. Haworth, JP, of Manchester; 2ndly, 1949, Margaret Alison, who *d* 1986, da of J. G. Pickard, of Leicester; *d* 1967; *s* by his el son **(3)** GEORGE CHARLES HAYTER, 3rd Baron and present peer.

HAZLERIGG, BARON (Hazlerigg) (Baron UK 1945, Bt E 1622)

ARTHUR GREY HAZLERIGG, MC, 2nd Baron, and 14th Baronet; *b* 24 Feb 1910; *s* 1949; *ed* Eton, and Trin Coll, Camb (BA 1932); is a Major RA (TA), and a JP and DL; European War 1939-45 (MC): *m* 1945, Patricia, who *d* 1972, da of late John Pullar of Durban, Natal and has issue.

Arms – Argent, a chevron sable between three hazel leaves vert. **Crest** – Issuant from a cap of maintenance gules turned up ermine a Scot's head and shoulders couped proper. **Supporters** – *Dexter*, a Cromwellian Soldier holding in his exterior hand a sword point downwards; *sinister*, a Coldstream Guardsman of the seventeenth century supporting with his exterior hand by the muzzle a musket all proper.
Seat – Noseley Hall, Billesdon, Leicester LE7 9EH. *Clubs* – Army and Navy, MCC.

PRO ARIS ET FOCIS

For our altars and our hearths

SON LIVING

Hon ARTHUR GREY, *b* 5 May 1951: *m* 1986, Laura, eldest da of Sir William Stratford Dugdale, 2nd Bt, CBE, MC, and has issue living, Arthur William Grey, *b* 13 May 1987, — Eliza Patricia, *b* 1989, — Amelia Frances, *b* (twin) 1989, — Viola Camilla Alice, *b* 1993. *Residence* – Noseley Hall, Billesdon, Leics LE7 9EH.

DAUGHTERS LIVING

Hon Angela Christine, *b* 1946: *m* 1969, Timothy Effingham MacDowel, Capt (TA) 15th/19th The King's Roy Hussars, of 22 Murrayfield Gdns, Edinburgh EH12 6DF, and has issue living, Benjamin St George, *b* 1970, — Richard Arthur *b* 1973.
Hon Priscilla Frances, *b* 1952: *m* 1975, Hon Richard Arthur Louis Dillon, and has issue (*see* V Dillon).

BROTHERS LIVING

Hon Thomas Heron (Caflida, Klosters, Switzerland; *Club* – White's), *b* 1914; *ed* Eton, and Trin Coll, Camb (BA); late Maj Leicestershire Yeo; formerly Flying-Officer RAF Reserve: *m* 1st, 1942 (*m diss* 1956), Audrey Cecil, who *d* in a motor accident 1994, da of late Maj Cecil Robert Bates DSO, MC (*see* Bates, Bt, *cr* 1880); 2ndly, 1957 (*m diss* 1974), Doussa (CAYZER), da of Fahmy Bey Wissa, of Remleh, Egypt; 3rdly, 1979, Anne Frances Roden, el da of late Capt Roden Henry Victor Buxton, CBE, RN (*see* Buxton, Bt, colls), and formerly wife of Henry Winterstein Gillespie, MD, and has issue living (by 1st *m*), Rupert Heron (94 Elms Rd, SW4), *b* 1943; *ed* Eton: *m* 1979, Caroline, el da of John Burkinshaw Fitzwilliams, and formerly wife of John Hugh Chetwynd (*see* V Chetwynd, colls), and has issue living, Cecilia *b* 1980, Alexandra *b* 1983, — Simon Martival (20 Stamford Brook Av, W6 0YD), *b* 1945; *ed* Eton; Maj (TA) 15th/19th The King's Roy Hussars: *m* 1984, Caroline Margaret Mary, yr da of Edward Ahlberg, and has issue living, Antonia *b* 1985, Alice *b* 1987.
Hon Robert Maynard, *b* 1916; *ed* Eton, and Trin Coll, Camb (BA 1938); Maj RA (TA); European War 1939-45: *m* 1942, Rose, da of Charles Cox, and has issue living, Rosemary, *b* 1942: *m* 1965, Malcolm Connell, of 18 Kenilworth Av, Wimbledon, SW19 7LW, and has issue living, Emma *b* 1972, — Gillian, *b* 1946: *m* 1974, Maurice Bradley, of 9 Church St, Northboro, Peterborough, and has issue living, Robert William *b* 1987, Jessica Mary *b* 1988. *Residence* – Cottons Field Farm, Noseley, Billesdon, Leicester LE7 9EB.

COLLATERAL BRANCHES LIVING (*In remainder to Baronetcy only*)

Grandson of late Lt-Col Thomas Hazlerigg, DSO, 2nd (but elder surv) son of late Maj-Gen Thomas Maynard Hazlerigg (infra):—
Issue of late Lt-Col Arthur William Hazlerigg, *b* 1904, *d* 1987: *m* 1st, 1935 (*m diss* 1946), Marjorie Dorothea, da of late Col George Frederick Brown Turner, DSO, of Blackheath, SE3; 2ndly, 1947, Jane, who *d* 1977, da of late David Wilson, OBE:—
(By 1st *m*) Arthur Robert, *b* 1936; *ed* Leys Sch, and Coll of Estate Management (BSc), FRICS, FRVA: Capt RHA (ret): *m* 1963, Janet Christine Hermione, only da of late Edward Simpson Anderson, MBE, of Elgin, and has issue living, Catrina Louise, *b* 1964: *m* 1992, Lars Jaeger, son of Mrs L. Ager-Harris, of Easingwold, Yorks. *Residence* – Paddock Lodge, Whitchurch-on-Thames, Pangbourne, Reading, Berks RG8 7EX.

Grandchildren of late Capt Greville Hazlerigg, yst son of late Maj-Gen Thomas Maynard Hazlerigg, 2nd son of 12th Bt:—
Issue of late Capt Arthur Greville Maynard Hazlerigg, *b* 1910, *d* 1990: *m* 1941, Nancy (Downside, North St, Mere, Wilts BA12 6AZ), da of late Capt John Alexander Ingles, RN:—
(Arthur) Patrick (30 West St, Bere Regis, Dorset), *b* 1943; *ed* Milton Abbey; Maj RA (ret 1994): *m* 1973, Susan Elizabeth, da of Lt-Cmdr Patrick Kenneth Truckle, RN, and has issue living, Arthur Philip Greville, *b* 1978, — Harriet Jane, *b* 1976. —— Diana Elizabeth, *b* 1947: *m* 1971, Col Anthony Michael Thomas Moody, Royal Irish Rangers, of West Hayes, South St, S Petherton, Som TA13 5AD, elder son of late Maj Thomas Moody, of Omagh, co Tyrone, and has issue living, Victoria Natalie, *b* 1973, — Alexandria Jane, *b* 1976. —— Sheelagh Marion, *b* 1951: *m* 1985, Cmdr Andrew D. Bell, RN, of Firenze, Chetcombe Rd, Mere, Wilts BA12 6AZ, son of C. D. T. Bell, of Westerham, Kent, and has issue living, Georgina Hazlerigg, *b* 1986, — Natasha Hazlerigg, *b* 1988.

Granddaughter of late Rev William Greville Hazlerigg, 4th son of 12th Bt:—
Issue of late Roger Greville Hazlerigg, *b* 1877, *d* 1952: *m* 1919, Esther Rosamond, who *d* 1976, da of Lacey Nussey Everett, of Rushmere Lodge, Pool, nr Leeds:—
Jean Mary, *b* 1921: *m* 1947, Major Kenneth Leonard Perrin. *Residence* – The Old Rectory, Great Comberton, nr Pershore, Worcestershire.

Grandson of late Allen Martival Hazlerigg, yst son of 12th Baronet:—
Issue of late Martival Grey Hazlerigg, *b* 1884, *d* 1971: *m* 1925, Marian (Flat 1, Craddock Court, Forest Green Nailsworth, Glos), da of late Michael Ray:—
Martival Spencer Woolf (33 Belvedere Mews, St Mary's, Chalford, Stroud, Glos GL6 8PF), *b* 1927: *m* 1947, Kitty, da of late William Johnson Bowhill, of Carhampton, Som, and has issue living, Marilyn Kay, *b* 1952; BScEng: *m* 1976, Roger Huckerby, BScEng, of 31 Bowes Rd, Walton-on-Thames KT12 3HT, — Martine Grey (21 Bowbridge Lock, Stroud, Glos GL5 2JZ), *b* 1957: *m* 1977 (*m diss* 1991), Raymond Anthony Dawson, MScEng.

Grandchildren (by 1st *m*) of late Grey Hazlerigg, OBE (infra):—

Issue of late Herbert William Grey Hazlerigg, *b* 1910, *d* 1991: *m* 1937, Gladys Margaret (37 Barrhill Av, Brighton BN1 8UE), da of David Alan Knighton, of Ealing:—

Alexander David Grey, *b* 1939; BSc, PhD: *m* 1961, Rosemary, el da of Leslie Clarence Ottewill, and has issue living, David Grey, *b* 1967; *ed* Camb Univ (BSc, PhD), — Andrew Alexander, *b* 1969; BA. *Residence* – Glanclywedog, Staylittle, Llanbrynmair, Powys SY19 7BU. —— Alan Peter Maynard, *b* 1941; BSc. —— Arthur Richard Thomas, *b* 1945; Lt-Col Royal Logistic Corps: *m* 1st, 1967 (*m diss* 1979), Lesley —; 2ndly, 1980, Elaine Elizabeth, da of John Machey Reed, and has issue living (by 1st *m*), Nichola Michelle, *b* 1973, — (by 2nd *m*) Charles Rupert Edward, *b* 1984, — Antonia Rebecca Alexandrina, *b* 1983, — Alexandra Machey Elizabeth, *b* 1986. —— Margaret Julia, *b* 1946: *m* 1967, John David Gilbert, BSc, PhD, and has issue living, Christopher Peter, *b* 1973, — Susan Ruth, *b* 1971; RGN.

Grandchildren of late Rev Grey Hazlerigg, 3rd son of 11th baronet:—

Issue of late Grey Hazlerigg, OBE, *b* 1879, *d* 1948: *m* 1st, 1908 (*m diss* 1924), Sarah Dorothy, who *d* 1965, da of late Herbert Bakewell Whetstone, JP, formerly of Ilketshall Hall, Bungay, Suffolk; 2ndly, 1933, Fannie, who *d* 1949, widow of Frederick Hardy, late of Staunton Hall, Notts:—

(By 1st *m*) Alexander Maynard, *b* 1914; *ed* Lewes County Sch; entered Colonial Civil Ser 1935; appointed Sub-Inspector of Constabulary, Trinidad 1937. —— Dorothy Mary Louise, *b* 1912.

Granddaughter of late Arthur Hesilrige, Lieut 59th Regt, son of late Rev Charles Maynard Hesilrige, brother of 11th baronet:—

Issue of late Arthur George Maynard Hesilrige, Editor of *Debrett* 1887-1935, *b* (*posthumous*) 1863, *d* 1953: *m* 1889, Amy Florence, who *d* 1947, da of late M. S. Myers, of Thorney Hedge, High Road Chiswick, W4:—

Violet Maynard, *b* 1900: *m* 1943, Maj George Reginald Jackson, RASC, late Reserve of Officers, who *d* 1954. *Residence* – 6 Sunstar Lane, Polegate, Sussex.

Grandchildren of late Thomas Greville Hesilrige, son of late Rev Charles Maynard Hesilrige (ante):—

Issue of late Thomas Greville Hesilrige, *b* 1878, *d* 1955: *m* 1st, 1901, Florence Elizabeth, who *d* 1919, da of Edwin Henry Griffiths, formerly of Mount Pleasant, Shrewsbury; 2ndly, 1921, Gertrude May, who *d* 1985, da of William Downs, formerly of Uplands, Coventry:—

(By 2nd *m*) Roger Greville, *b* 1932: *m* 1957 (*m diss* 1976), Barbara Shirley, da of Henry Edward Daniel, of 80 Manor Estate, Wolston, nr Coventry, and has issue living, Charles Greville, *b* 1958: *m* 1985, Elizabeth June Davies, and has issue living, Rebecca Lynne *b* 1987. *Residence* – 168 Rugby Rd, Binley Woods, Coventry.

Issue of late Robert Maynard Hesilrige, *b* 1884, *d* 1951: *m* 1914, Dora, who *d* 1969, da of Thomas Cope, of The Lount Farm, Osbaston:—

Isabel Maynard, *b* 1916: *m* 1938, Reginald Gerald Watts, and has issue living, Richard Maynard *b* 1941. *Residence* – Hillcrest, 89 Pioneer Avenue, Desborough, Kettering.

PREDECESSORS – (1) Thomas Hesilrige, son of late Thomas Hesilrige, of Noseley Hall, Leicestershie; *b* 1564; MP for Leicestershire 1614 and 1624-5 (Sheriff 1612-13; *cr* a *Baronet*, 1622: *m* 16—, Frances, who *d* 1638, da of late Sir William Gorges, of Alderton; *d* 1629; *s* by his son (2) Arthur, 2nd Bt; *b* 16—; MP for Leicestersire 1640-45 and for Leicester 1654-9; sometime Gov of Newcastle, during Civil War, in which he rendered signal Sers, was Col in Parliamentary Army Comdg a Regt of Cuirassiers (known as the Lobsters): *m* 1st 1625, Frances, who *d* 1632, da of late Thomas Elmes; 2ndly, 16—, Dorothy, who *d* 1650, da of late Fulke Greville, and sister of 2nd Baron Brooke (*cr* 1620); *d* (whilst a prisoner in Tower of London) 1660; *s* by his el son (3) Thomas, 3rd Bt; *b* 1625: *m* 1664, Elizabeth, who *d* 1673, da of late George Fenwick, of Brunton Hall, Northumberland; *d* 1680; *s* by his only son (4) Thomas, 4th Bt; *b* 1664; MP for Leicestershire 1690-95 (Sheriff 1686-7); *d* 1700; *s* by his uncle (5) Robert (only surviving son of 2nd Bt), 5th Bt; *b* 1640: *m* 1664, Bridget, who *d* 1697, da of late Sir Samuel Rolle, of Heanton, Devon; *d* 1713; *s* by his son (6) Robert, 6th Baronet; *b* 1668; Sheriff of Leicestersire 1715-16: *m* 1696, Hon Dorothy Maynard, who *d* 1748, da of 3rd Baron Maynard (*cr* 1721); *s* by his only son (7) Arthur, 7th Bt; *b* 17—: *m* 1725, Hannah Sturges, who *d* 1765; *d* 1763; *s* by his son (8) Robert, 8th Bt; *b* 17—: *m* 17—, Sarah, who *d* 17—, da of late Nathaniel Waller, of Roxburgh, New England, USA; *d* 17—; *s* by his son (9) Arthur, 9th Bt; *b* 17—; sometime in HEICS; *m* 1st, 17—, Elizabeth Charnaud, of Smyrna, who *d* 1797; 2ndly, 17—, Charlotte Elizabeth, who *d* 1817 (having *m* 2ndly, 1805, Capt Henry William Wilkinson), da of Capt F. E. S. Grey; *d* 1805; *s* by his uncle (10) Thomas Maynard (3rd son of 7th Bt), 10th Bt; *b* 17—: *m* 1st, 1805, Mary, who *d* 1809, da of late Edmund Tyrrell, of Gipping Hall, Suffolk; 2ndly, 1811, Hon Letitia Wodehouse, who *d* 1864 (having *m* 2ndly, 1842, Frederick Fielding, Bar-at-Law), da of 1st Baron Wodehouse; *d* 1817; *s* by his nephew (11) Arthur Grey (el son of Col Grey Hesilrige, 5th son of 7th Bt), 11th Bt, *b* 17—; assumed by Roy licence 1818 the surname of Hazlerigg in lieu of his patronymic: *m* 1811, Henrietta Anne, who *d* 1868, da of late John Bourne, of Stanch Hall, Hants; *d* 1819; *s* by his el son (12) Arthur Grey, 12th Bt; *b* 1812; Sheriff of Leicestershire 1837: *m* 1835, Henrietta, who *d* 1883, da of late Charles Allen Phillips, of St Bride's Hill, Pembrokeshire; *d* 1890; *s* by his grandson (13) Arthur Grey (only son of Lieut-Col Arthur Grey Hazlerigg, el son of 12th Bt), 13th Bt; *b* 1878; was Lord Lieut and Custos Rotulorum for Leicestershire (High Sheriff 1909); *cr Baron Hazlerigg*, of Noseley, co Leicester (peerage of United Kingdom) 1945: *m* 1903, Dorothy Rachel, who *d* 1972, el da of late John Henry Buxton, JP, DL, of Easneye, Ware; *d* 1949; *s* by his son (14) Arthur Grey, 2nd Baron and present peer.

HEAD, VISCOUNT (Head) (Viscount UK 1960)

RICHARD ANTONY HEAD, 2nd Viscount; *b* 27 Feb 1937; *s* 1983; *ed* Eton, and RMA Sandhurst; late Capt Life Gds; racehorse trainer 1968-83; farmer: *m* 1974, Alicia Brigid, el da of Julian John William Salmond, of The Old Manor House, Didmarton, Badminton, Avon (*see* B Lucas of Crudwell, colls), and has issue.

Arms – Sable a chevron argent between two unicorns' heads couped in chief, and in base as many arrows in saltire and filed by a ducal crown or. **Crest** – A unicorn's head couped sable armed and crined or, between two arrows erect, points downward of the last. **Supporters** – On either side a Staffordshire terrier sable gorged with a dog collar or.
Residence – Throope Manor, Bishopstone, Salisbury. *Clubs* – White's, Cavalry and Guards'.

SONS LIVING

Hon HENRY JULIAN, *b* 30 March 1980.
Hon George Richard, *b* 1982.

DAUGHTER LIVING

Hon Sarah Georgiana, *b* 1984.

BROTHER LIVING

Hon Simon Andrew, *b* 1944; *ed* Eton, Ch Ch, Oxford, and Berkeley Univ, Cal, USA; assist ed *Far East Economic Review*, Hong Kong, 1966-67, correspondent *Financial Times*, SE Asia, 1970-72, New York correspondent, *New Statesman*, 1970-76, a contributor on foreign affairs to New York *Review of Books* since 1973; contested S Dorset Div for SDP-Liberal Alliance, 1983. *Residence* – 155 Cranmer Court, Sloane Av, SW3.

SISTER LIVING

Hon Teresa Mary, *b* 1938: *m* 1972 (*m diss* 1983), Richard Deacon Haddon, and has had issue, Edward Antony Deacon, *b* 1973, — Joseph Richard, *b* 1974 *d* 1994, in an accident, — Alice Mary, *b* (twin) 1974. *Residence* – The Granary, Fawler, Oxford OX7 3AH.

PREDECESSORS – ANTONY HENRY Head, GCMG, CBE, MC, PC, son of Geoffrey Head, of 51 South St, W1; *b* 1906; Brig Life Gds, Assist Sec Cttee of Imperial Defence 1940-41, GSO2, Guards Armoured Div 1942, Ch Mil Planner (Combined Operations) 1942-43, and Representative (Brig) with Directors of Plans for Amphibious Operations 1943-46; Sec of State for War Oct 1951-Oct 1956, Min of Defence Oct 1956-Jan 1957; High Commr for UK in Fed of Nigeria 1960-63, High Commr for UK in Fed of Malaysia 1963-66; MP for Carshalton Div of Surrey (C) 1945-60; *cr Viscount Head*, of Throope, co Wilts (peerage of UK) 1960: *m* 1935, Lady Dorothea Louise Ashley-Cooper, who *d* 1987, da of 9th Earl of Shaftesbury; *d* 1983; *s* by his el son (2) RICHARD ANTONY, 2nd Viscount and present peer.

HEADFORT, MARQUESS OF (Taylour) Sits as BARON KENLIS (UK 1831) (Marquess I 1800, Bt I 1704)

(Name pronounced 'Taylor')

THOMAS GEOFFREY CHARLES MICHAEL TAYLOUR, 6th Marquess, and 9th Baronet; *b* 20 Jan 1932; *s* 1960; *ed* Stowe, and Christ's Coll, Camb (MA); FRICS, FIArb; holds Commercial Pilots' Licence; Freeman of Guild of Air Pilots and Air Navigators; late 2nd Lt Life Guards, and acting PO RAFVR: *m* 1st, 1958 (*m diss* 1969), Hon Elizabeth Angela Veronica Rose Nall-Cain, da of 2nd Baron Brocket; 2ndly, 1972, Virginia, da of late Mr Justice Nable, of Manila, and has issue by 1st *m*.

Arms – Quarterly: 1st and 4th ermine, on a chief gules a fleur-de-lys between two boars' heads couped and erect or: 2nd vert, a Pegasus courant, wings endorsed ermine, a chief or a crescent for difference, *Quin*; 3rd argent, two bendlets gules, on a chief azure a lion passant of the first. **Crest** – A naked arm couped at the shoulder embowed, holding an arrow proper. **Supporters** – *Dexter*, a lion guardant or; *sinister*, a leopard guardant proper, both collared and chained argent.
Residence – 1558 Carissa St, Das Marinas Village, Makati, MM, Philippines; Ellerslie, Crosby, IoM. *Clubs* – Cavalry and Guards', Kildare Street and University, RAF Reserve, Lansdowne, Manila Yacht, Manila Polo, House of Lord's Yacht, Aberdeen Boat, Hong Kong Club, Foreign Correspondents', Royal Hong Kong Jockey, Hong Kong Aviation, Little Ship Club.

He attains whatever he seeks

SON LIVING *(By 1st marriage)*

THOMAS MICHAEL RONALD CHRISTOPHER *(Earl of Bective)*, *b* 10 Feb 1959: *m* 1987, Susan Jane, elder da of late C. Anthony Vandervell, of Horseshoe Hill House, Burnham, Bucks, and has issue. *Residence* – 8 Milner St, SW3 2PU.

SONS LIVING—THOMAS RUPERT CHARLES CHRISTOPHER *(Baron Kenlis)*, *b* 18 June 1989.
Hon Henry, *b* 1991.

DAUGHTERS LIVING *(By 1st marriage)*

Lady Rosanagh Elizabeth Angela Mary, *b* 1961: *m* 1983, Andrew Congreve Dent, of Newbarn Farm, Ditchley Park, Chipping Norton, Oxon, eldest son of Robin Dent, of Olivers, Painswick, Glos, and has issue living, Michael, *b* 1989, — Iona Katherine, *b* 1991.
Lady Olivia Sheelin Davina Anne, *b* 1963: *m* 1986, David Charles Henry Waddy, of Milburn, Cheviot, Canterbury 2RD, NZ, elder son of 495 Durham St, Christchurch 1, NZ, and has issue living, Veronica, *b* 1993.

SISTER LIVING

Lady Olivia Elsie June, *b* 1929: *m* 1955, Victor Echevarri Waldron, and has issue living, Sarah Rose Echevarri, *b* 1956: *m* 1983, Peter Allen Sweeny, of 364 President St, Brooklyn, NY 11231, USA, and has issue living, Miles Taylour *b* 1991, Petrea Rose Echevarri *b* 1989, — Virginia Elizabeth Echevarri, *b* 1957: *m* 1st, 1979 *(m diss* 1989), Anil Kumar Varma, who *d* 1990, only son of Devki Varma; 2ndly, 1991, Mark D. R. Clifford-Holmes, of PO Box 113, Constantia, Cape Town 7848, S Africa, yr son of Hugo Holmes, of Totnes, Devon, and has issue living (by 1st *m*), Jai Kumar (a son) *b* 1986, Lauren Devika Olivia *b* 1985. *Residences* – Idleigh Cottage, nr Meopham, Kent; 516 74th St, Holmes Beach, Florida 34217, USA.

COLLATERAL BRANCHES LIVING *(in remainder to Earldom of Bective only)*

Descendants of late Hon Clotworthy TAYLOR (4th son of 1st Earl of 1st Earl of Bective), who was *cr* Baron Langford 1800 (see that title).

Grandson of late Capt Basil Reginald Hamilton TAYLOUR, RN, yr son of Col The Rt Hon Thomas Edward Taylor (infra):—
Issue of late Basil Richard Henry Osgood TAYLOUR, *b* 1904, *d* 1969: *m* 1935, Gwendoline Edith Marion, who *d* 1975, da of His Honour late William Evans:—
(Douglas) Terence William Lenthall TAYLOUR (Drumman House, Milltownpass, co Westmeath), *b* 1939: *m* 1964, Marjorie Rosalind, da of Rev Robert Bowie Thompson, and has issue living, Edward Terence, *b* 1966, — Kenlis Jean, *b* 1965: *m* 1988, Holger Sircoulomb, son of Adi Sircoulomb, of SW Africa, — Gwendoline May, *b* 1983.

PREDECESSORS – (1) *Rt Hon* THOMAS Taylor, son of late Thomas Taylor, of Kells, co Meath; *b* 1662; sometime MP for Kells; *cr* a *Baronet* 1704: *m* 1682, Anne, who *d* 1710, da of Sir Robert Cotton, 1st Bt; *d* 1736; *s* by his son (2) *Sir* THOMAS, PC, 2nd Bt, *b* 1686; MP for Kells 1711; *s* by his son (3) *Sir* THOMAS, KP, PC, 3rd Bt, *b* 1724; MP for Kells 1747; *cr* Baron *Headfort*, of Headfort, co Meath (peerage of Ireland) 1760, *Viscount Headfort* (peerage of Ireland) 1762, and *Earl of Bective* (peerage of Ireland) 1766; *d* 1795; *s* by his son (4) THOMAS, KP, 2nd Earl, *b* 1757; a Lord of the Bedchamber; assumed the surname of Taylour in lieu of his patronymic; *cr Marquess of Headfort* (peerage of Ireland) 1800; *d* 1829; *s* by his son (5) THOMAS, KP, PC, 2nd Marquess; *b* 1787; was a Lord-in-Waiting to HM Queen Victoria 1837-41, and Lord-Lieut of Cavan; *cr* Baron *Kenlis*, of Kenlis, co Meath (peerage of United Kingdom), 1831: *m* 1st, 1822, Olivia, who *d* 1834, el da of Sir John Stevenson; *d* 1870; *s* by his son (6) THOMAS, KP, PC, 3rd Marquess, *b* 1822; MP for Westmorland (C) 1854-70; Lord-Lieut of Co Meath: *m* 1st, 1842, Amelia, who *d* 1864, only da of late W. Thompson, MP, of Underley Hall, Westmoreland; 2ndly, 1875, Emily Constantia, who *d* 1926, da of late Rev Lord John Thynne, DD, and widow of Capt Eustace John Wilson-Patten; *d* 1894; *s* by his yr son (7) GEOFFREY THOMAS, 4th Marquess, *b* 1878; a Senator of Irish Free State 1928-8: *m* 1901, Rose, who *d* 1958, da of Charles Boote; *d* 1943; *s* by his el son (8) TERENCE GEOFFREY THOMAS, TD, 5th Marquess: *b* 1902; Capt Warwick Yeo (TA); was ADC to Gov of S Australia 1939-40: *m* 1928, Elsie Florence, who *d* 1972, da of James Partridge Tucker, of Devon, and widow of Sir Rupert Turner Havelock Clarke, 2nd Bt (*cr* 1882); *d* 1960; *s* by his only son (9) THOMAS GEOFFREY CHARLES MICHAEL, 6th Marquess and present peer; also Earl of Bective, Viscount Headfort, Baron Headfort, and Baron Kenlis.

HEADLEY, BARONY OF (Allanson-Winn) (Extinct 1994)

DAUGHTERS LIVING OF SEVENTH AND LAST BARON

Hon Pamela Jean, *b* 1928: *m* 1948, Ivan Beshoff, and has issue living, David Rowland, *b* 1950.
Hon Janet Diana, *b* 1932: *m* 1st, 1955 *(m diss* 1969), Antony John Vlassopulos, Bar-at-Law; 2ndly, 1975, David Walter Webb, of Springs, Rookery Drive, Westcott, Surrey, and has issue living (by 1st *m*), Christopher John Antony, *b* 1958, — Mark Charles Antony, *b* 1959.
Hon Susan Ethel, *b* 1936.

WIDOW LIVING OF SON OF FIFTH BARON

Ruth, da of late Cecil Orpin, of Strand House, Youghal, co Cork, and formerly wife of Harry Stuart Pearson: *m* 1938, Hon Owain Gwynedd Allanson-Winn, who *d* 1993. *Residence* – PO Box 4340, George East, S Africa.

HEALEY, BARON (Healey) (Life Baron 1992)

DENIS WINSTON HEALEY, CH, MBE, PC, son of late William Healey, of Keighley, Yorks; *b* 30 Aug 1917; *ed* Bradford Gram Sch, and Balliol Coll, Oxford (MA); Hon Fellow Balliol Coll 1980, Hon DLitt Bradford 1983, Hon LLD Sussex 1989; 1939-45 War as Maj RE in N Africa and Italy (despatches, MBE); Sec Internat Dept Labour Party 1945-52, Member Parl Cttee Labour Party 1959-64 and 1970-74, Sec of State for Defence 1964-70, Chancellor of the Exchequer 1974-79, Dep-Leader Labour Party 1981-83; Freeman City of Leeds 1991; Grand Cross Order (W Germany) 1979; author; MP SE Div of Leeds *(Lab)* 1952-55, and E Div of

Leeds 1955-92; MBE (Mil) 1945, PC 1964, CH 1979, and *Baron Healey*, of Riddlesden, co W Yorks (Life Baron) 1992: *m* 1945, Edna May, da of Edward Edmunds, of Coleford, Glos, and has issue.
Residence – Pingles Place, Alfriston, E Sussex.

SON LIVING

Hon Timothy Blair, *b* 1949; *ed* Highgate, and Balliol Coll, Oxford: *m* 1972, Joanna Margerison, da of Ralph Broehl, of Neville Terrace, SW7, and has issue living, Charles Edward, *b* 1984, — Susanna Jade, *b* 1979.

DAUGHTERS LIVING

Hon Jenifer Clare, *b* 1948; *ed* Camden Sch for Girls: *m* 1971, Derek Copsey, and has issue living, Thomas, *b* 1975, — Kate, *b* 1978.
Hon Cressida, *b* 1954; *ed* Camden Sch for Girls.

HELSBY, BARONY OF (Helsby) (Extinct 1978)

SON LIVING OF LIFE BARON

Hon Nigel Charles (Abbots Wood, The Street, Salcott-cum-Virley, Maldon, Essex, CM9 8HW), *b* 1941: *m* 1969, Sylvia Rosena, da of Ronald Brown, of Burnham-on-Crouch, and has issue.

DAUGHTER LIVING OF LIFE BARON

Hon Margaret Wilmett, *b* 1939: *m* 1st, 1960, (John Frederick) Keith St Pier, of Chadhurst Farm, Coldharbour Lane, Dorking, Surrey; 2ndly, 1976, Brian Davey of 7 Brook Rd, Thornton Heath, Surrey CR7 7RD.

WIDOW LIVING OF LIFE BARON

WILMETT MARY (Logmore Farm, Dorking, Surrey), da of late W. G. Maddison, of Durham: *m* 1st, 1938, Baron Helsby, GCB, KBE (Life Baron), who *d* 1978; 2ndly, 1983, R. K. Hines.

HEMINGFORD, BARON (Herbert) (Baron UK 1943)

DENNIS NICHOLAS HERBERT, 3rd Baron; *b* 25 July 1934; *s* 1982; *ed* Oundle, and Clare Coll, Camb (MA); known professionally as Nicholas Herbert; with Reuters 1956-61; assistant Washington correspondent, The Times 1961-65; Middle East correspondent 1966-68; Dep Features Editor 1968-70; Editor, Cambridge Evening News 1970-74; Editorial Director, Westminster Press 1974-92, since when Dep Chief Executive; Pres Guild of British Newspaper Editors 1980-81; Pres Media Soc 1982; Member British Exec, Internat Press Inst, Hon Sec Assocn of British Editors since 1985, Member E Anglian Regional Cttee Nat Trust since 1983 (Chm since 1990), Gov Bell Educational Trust 1986-90; Pres Huntingdonshire Family History Soc since 1985; Fell of Royal Soc for the Encouragement of Arts, Manufactures and Commerce (RSA) since 1989: *m* 1958, Jennifer Mary Toresen, da of late Frederick William Bailey, of 42 Kent Rd, Harrogate, and has issue.
Residence – The Old Rectory, Hemingford Abbots, Huntingdon, Cambs. *Clubs* – City Livery, Commonwealth Trust.

SON LIVING

Hon CHRISTOPHER DENNIS CHARLES, *b* 4 July 1973; *ed* Oundle, and Victoria Univ, Manchester.

DAUGHTERS LIVING

Hon Elizabeth Frances Toresen, *b* 1963; *ed* Durham Univ (BA): *m* 1994, John Nigel Evered Witt.
Hon Caroline Mary Louise, *b* 1964; *ed* Liverpool Poly (BEd).
Hon Alice Christine Emma, *b* 1968: *m* 1992, Christopher McManus, son of Ira McManus, of Florham Park, NJ, USA.

SISTERS LIVING

Hon Celia McClare (*Hon Lady Goodhart*), *b* 1939; *ed* St Hilda's Coll, Oxford (MA): *m* 1966, Sir William Howard Goodhart, QC, of 43 Campden Hill Sq, W8, and has issue living, Benjamin Herbert, *b* 1972, — Annabel Frances, *b* 1967, — Laura Christabel, *b* 1970.
Hon Catherine Grevile, *b* 1942: *m* 1962, Harry Traherne Moggridge, OBE, and has issue living, Geoffrey Dillwyn, *b* 1967, — Lawrence Weston, *b* 1970, — Harriet Fearne, *b* 1965: *m* 1992, Dr Nicholas John Lawrence, and has issue living, Joseph Lawrence Moggridge *b* 1993.

UNCLE LIVING (*Son of 1st Baron*)

Hon Oliver Hayley Dennis *b* 1919; *ed* Oundle, and Wadham Coll, Oxford; formerly Major Queen's Roy Regt, attached Indian Army: *m* 1976 (*m* annulled 19—), Rosemary Muriel, da of Rev Canon Roland Bate.

COLLATERAL BRANCH LIVING

Issue of late Lt-Col Hon Valentine Henry Okes Herbert, RA, 2nd son of 1st Baron; *b* 1905; *d* 1983: *m* 1st, 1931, Winifred Mabel, who *d* 1955, da of late Sir Herbert Grayhurst Pearson; 2ndly, 1956, Janet, who *d* 1982, da of late Rev Gerrard Edmund Wigram (*see* Wigram, Bt colls):—

(By 1st *m*) Timothy William Okes, *b* 1936; *ed* Oundle; Maj RWF: *m* 1977, Erica Anne Jackson, *née* Odell. ——— Rosemary Ann, *b* 1932: *m* 1957, William George Rhyll Turner, Duke of Edinburgh's Roy Regt, and has issue living, Valerie Jane, *b* 1958, — Penelope May, *b* 1960, — Susan Diana, *b* 1964. ——— Sylvia Valentine, *b* 1948: *m* 1st, 1978, P. Jeremy B. Sayce, who *d* 1980; 2ndly, 1983, J. Robin K. Peile, and has issue living (by 1st *m*), Emily Valentine, *b* 1978, — (by 2nd *m*) Maxwell Herbert, *b* 1984.

PREDECESSORS – (1) *Rt Hon Sir* DENNIS HENRY Herbert, KBE, el son of late Rev Henry Herbert, R of Hemingford Abbots, Huntingdon; *b* 1869; was Dep Chm of Ways and Means in House of Commons 1928-9 and Chm of Ways and Means and Dep Speaker 1931-43; sat as MP for Watford Div of Herts (*U*) 1918-43; *cr Baron Hemingford,* of Watford, co Hertford (peerage of United Kingdom) 1943: *m* 1903, Mary Graeme, who *d* 1966, da of late Valentine Graeme Bell, CMG; *d* 1947; *s* by his son (2) DENNIS GEORGE RUDDOCK, 2nd Baron, *b* 1904; Lord Lieut of Huntingdon and Peterborough 1968-74, Lieut for Cambs 1974-5; Head Master of King's Coll, Budo, Uganda 1939-47, Rector of Achimota Training Coll, Gold Coast 1948-51, Chm of Africa Bureau 1952-63: *m* 1932, Elizabeth McClare, who *d* 1979, da of late Col John McClare Clark, TD, of Haltwhistle, Northumberland; *d* 1982; *s* by his son (3) DENNIS NICHOLAS, 3rd Baron and present peer.

HEMPHILL, BARON (Martyn-Hemphill) (Baron UK 1906)

CONSTANTER·AC NON·TIMIDE

Steadily and fearlessly

PETER PATRICK FITZROY MARTYN MARTYN-HEMPHILL, 5th Baron; *b* 5 Sept 1928; *s* 1957; *ed* Downside, and Brasenose Coll, Oxford (MA); assumed by deed poll 1959 the additional surname of Martyn: *m* 1952, Olivia Anne, el da of Major Robert Francis Ruttledge, MC, of Cloonee, Ballinrobe, co Mayo, and has issue.

Arms – Or, on a fesse gules between two chevronels and three stars, as many trefoils slipped of the field. Crest – A Boar passant gules charged with a chevron and a portcullis or. Supporters – On either side an Irish wolfhound gorged with a plain collar or.
Residence – Raford, Kiltulla, co Galway. *Clubs* – Royal Irish Yacht, Irish Cruising, White's, Royal Irish Automobile, County (Galway).

SON LIVING

Hon CHARLES ANDREW MARTYN, *b* 8 Oct 1954; *ed* Downside, and St Benet's Hall, Oxford (BA); Dir Morgan Grenfell Asset Management: *m* 1985, Sarah J. F., eldest da of Richard Lumley, of Roundwood, Windlesham, Surrey, and has issue living, Richard Patrick Lumley, *b* 17 May 1990, — Clarissa Mary, *b* 1986, — Amelia Rose, *b* 1988, — Marina Olivia Astrid, *b* 1992. *Residence* – 78 Streathbourne Rd, SW17 8QY. *Club* – White's.

DAUGHTERS LIVING

Hon Angela Mary Martyn, *b* 1953: *m* 1982, Robert Edwin Cookson (*see* V Falmouth, colls, 1990 Edn), and has issue living, Edward Peter, *b* 1988, — Serena Louise, *b* 1986. *Residence* – Manor Farm, Upper Slaughter, Cheltenham, Glos.
Hon Mary Anne, *b* 1958.

PREDECESSORS – (1) CHARLES HARE Hemphill, PC, son of late John Hemphill, of Cashel, and Rathkenny, co Tipperary; *b* 1821; MP for N Div of Tyrone co (*L*)1895-1965; Solicitor-Gen, for Ireland 1892-5; *cr Baron Hemphill,* of Rathkenny and of Cashel, co Tipperary (peerage of United Kingdom) 1906: *m* 1849, Augusta Mary, who *d* 1899, da of late Major Hon Sir Francis Charles Stanhope, KCH; *d* 1908; *s* by his el son (2) STANHOPE CHARLES JOHN, 2nd Baron, *b* 1853: sometime Crown Prosecutor for co Wicklow: *m* 1913, Hon May Clarke Mary Nisbet Hamilton, who *d* 1970, da of Lord Belhaven and Stenton; *d* 1919; *s* by his brother (3) FITZROY, 3rd Baron, *b* 1860; Dep Chm of London Co Council 1907-8, Mary, who *d* 1958, da of late Andrew Martyn, of Spiddal, co Galway; *d* 1930; *s* by his son (4) MARTYN CHARLES ANDREWS, 4th Baron; *b* 1901; Bar King's Inns, Dublin and Middle Temple: *m* 1927 (*m diss* in Reno, USA 1945), Emily, who *d* 1990, da of F. Irving Sears, of Webster, Massachusetts, USA; *d* 1957; *s* by his only son (5) PETER PATRICK FITZROY MARTYN, 5th Baron and present peer.

HENDERSON OF BROMPTON, BARON (Henderson) (Life Baron 1983)

PETER GORDON HENDERSON, KCB, son of James Alexander Leo Henderson, of London; *b* 16 Sept 1922; *ed* Stowe, and Magdalen Coll, Oxford; served with Scots Guards 1942-44; Clerk, House of Lords 1954-60; seconded to HM Treasury as Sec to Leader and Chief Whip, House of Lords 1960-63; Reading Clerk and Clerk of Public Bills 1964-74; Clerk Assistant 1974; Clerk of the Parliaments 1974-83; Member Cttee on Preparation of Legislation 1973-74; *cr* KCB 1975, and *Baron Henderson of Brompton,* of Brompton in the Royal Borough of Kensington and Chelsea and of Brough, co Cumbria (Life Baron) 1983: *m* 1950, Susan Mary, da of Richard Charles Gordon Dartford, of Swallowfield Park, Berks, and has issue.
Residences – 16 Pelham Street, SW7 2NG; Helbeck Cottage, Brough, Kirkby Stephen, Cumbria CA17 4DD.

SONS LIVING

Hon Launcelot Dinadan James (17 Carlisle Rd, NW6 6TL), *b* 1951; *ed* Westminster, and Balliol Coll, Oxford: *m* 1989, Elaine Elizabeth, elder da of Kenneth Frank Webb, of Dringhouses, York, and has issue living, Peter George Galahad, *b* 1990, — Arthur Frank Gabriel, *b* 1994, — Matilda Jane, *b* 1992.
Rev Canon the Hon Richard Crosbie Aitken, *b* 1957; *ed* Westminster, and Magdalen Coll, Oxford: *m* 1985, Anita Julia, da of Antony Gerald Stroud Whiting. *Residence* – The Rectory, Skibereen, co Cork.

DAUGHTERS LIVING

Hon Lucy Jess, *b* 1954: *m* 1980, Paul Benedict Askew.
Hon Mary Sophia, *b* 1965: *m* 1994, Robert Cumming.

HENLEY, BARON (Eden) Sits as BARON NORTHINGTON (UK 1885) (Baron I 1799)

OLIVER MICHAEL ROBERT EDEN, 8th Baron; *b* 22 Nov 1953; *s* 1977; *ed* Clifton, and Durham Univ; bar Middle Temple, 1977; a Lord in Waiting 1989; Pres Cumbria Assocn of Local Councils 1981-89, Chm Penrith & Border Conservative Assocn 1987-89, Cumbria County Council 1986-89; Under Sec of State, Dept of Social Security 1989-93, since when Parly Under Sec of State, Dept of Employment: *m* 1984, Caroline Patricia, JP, da of A. G. Sharp, of Mackney, Oxon, and has issue.

Arms – Quarterly: 1st and 4th gules, on a chevron argent, between three garbs or, banded vert, as many escallops sable, *Eden*; 2nd and 3rd azure, a lion rampant argent, ducally crowned or, within a bordure of the second, charged with eight torteaux, *Henley*. **Crest** – A dexter arm in armour couped at the shoulder proper, and grasping a garb or. **Supporters** – *Dexter*, a lion argent, semée of torteaux, ducally crowned or having a plain collar or the last rimmed azure, on the collar three escallops sable, and pendent therefrom a shield gold, charged with an eagle displayed with two heads sable; *sinister*, a stag argent, semée of torteaux, attired or, and gorged with a plain collar of the last rimmed azure, and charged with three escallops sable, pendent therefrom an escutcheon also or, charged with an eagle displayed with one head also sable.
Residence – Scaleby Castle, Carlisle. *Clubs* – Brooks's, Pratt's.

SI SIT PRVDENTIA

If there be prudence

SONS LIVING

Hon JOHN MICHAEL OLIVER, *b* 30 June 1988.
Hon Patrick Francis, *b* 1993.

DAUGHTER LIVING

Hon Elizabeth Caroline, *b* 1991.

BROTHER LIVING

Hon Andrew Francis (Watford Fields House, Watford, Northampton NN6 7UR), *b* 1955.

HALF-SISTER LIVING

Hon Victoria Catherine Elizabeth, *b* 1944: *m* 1965, Hon John Hedworth Jolliffe, son of 4th Baron Hylton.

SISTERS LIVING

Hon Ursula Nancy, *b* 1950: *m* 1978, William Thomas, and has issue, Philip Stephen William, *b* 1982, — Jessica Nadine, *b* 1978.
Hon Ingaret Barbara (37 Fairholme Rd, W14), *b* 1951.
Hon Rose Griselda, *b* 1957: *m* 1st, 1976 (*m diss* 1978), Stuart Ballin; 2ndly, 1984 (*m diss* 1991), Hon Christopher James Bellew, yr son of 7th Baron Bellew; 3rdly, 1993, Lawrence Emerson Foulds, yr son of Emerson Foulds, of Guildford, Surrey.

UNCLE LIVING (*Son of 6th Baron*)

Hon Roger Quentin Eden, *b* 1922; *ed* Rugby; MRAeS; formerly F/O RAFVR: *m* 1st, 1946, Carys Wynne, who *d* 1990, da of late I. H. D. Davies, of Camwy, Penrhyndeudraeth, Gwynedd; 2ndly, 1994, Barbara Daphne, da of late J. F. W. Singleton, of Glasgow and Calcutta, and has issue living (by 1st *m*), Morton Roger (59 Grove Close, Thulston, Derbys), *b* 1949; *ed* Rugby, and St Cuthbert's Soc, Durham: *m* 1975, Sally L., da of late W. H. Brittain, of Redcar, Cleveland, and has issue living, William Morton *b* 1985, — Elvyn Alexander (7 Radcliffe Rd, N21), *b* 1954; *ed* Shiplake Coll: *m* 1982, Claudia Marli, da of late Sid Colin, of 52 Church Path, W4, and has issue living, Dorcas Claudia *b* 1983, Emma Alexandra *b* 1983 (twin), Gudrun Dorothy *b* 1989, — Carol Rosamund, *b* 1947, — Jane Rebecca, *b* 1956: *m* 1983, William Nicholas Russell Kellock, of 432 Upper Richmond Rd, SW15, and has issue living, Howard Nicholas *b* 1985, Christopher Charles *b* 1989, Siân Louise *b* 1987, Clara Carys *b* 1992. *Residence* – 29A, Hamilton Terrace, NW8 9RE.

AUNTS LIVING (*Daughters of 6th Baron*)

Hon Barbara Dorothy, *b* 1915: *m* 1938, Peter Calvocoressi, formerly Wing-Com RAF Vol Reserve, and has issue living, Paul Peter, *b* 1939; *ed* Eton, — David Sebastian (11a Bathwick St, Bath, Avon BA2 6NX), *b* 1941; *ed* Eton: *m* 1971 (*m diss* 1992), Dzagbe Cudjoe, of Accra, Ghana, and has issue living, Nuku Vanonyi *b* 1974, Nuname Ankaret *b* 1976, Nujoji Peter *b* 1977. *Residence* – 1 Queen's Parade, Bath, Avon BA1 2NJ.
Hon Griselda Rosalind, *b* 1917: *m* 1939 (*m diss* 1964), John Buckman, late Squdn Ldr RAFVR, and has issue living, Christopher Simon, *b* 1940: *m* 1970, Gwendola, da of Comte de Kersaintgilly of Poizay les Ormes, France, and has issue living, Andrew Pierre *b* 1972, Sophie Rosalind *b* 1978, — Jennifer Susan, *b* 1944: *m* 1963, John Jellis Ashby, of The Limes, Watford, Rugby, and has issue living, Jeremy Robert *b* 1964, Sarah Charlotte *b* 1966. *Residence* – 8 High St, W Haddon, Northampton.
Hon Nancy Clare, *b* 1918: *m* 1941, Edmund Ernest Wynne, Lt Reconnaissance Corps, and has issue living, Robert Edmund, *b* 1956, — Rosalind Clare, *b* 1942: *m* 1965, David Gow, of Eagle Heights, Madison, USA, and has issue living, Donovan Fergus *b* 1970, Caitlin Fiona *b* 1972, — Deborah Dorothy, *b* 1944: *m* 1968, Michael Stagonakis, of 67 Mikras Asias, Athens Greece,

— Clare Catherine, *b* 1946: *m* 1969, Colin Smith, and has issue living, Christian *b* 1971, Eleanor Charlotte *b* 1975, — Marilyn Anne, *b* 1947: *m* 1967, Stephen Padgett, of 13 Priory Gate, Blackpool, and has issue living, Christopher Stephen *b* 1969, Richard Anthony *b* 1970, — Alexandra Mary, *b* 1953.

MOTHER LIVING

Nancy Mary (10 Abbey St, Cerne Abbas, Dorchester, Dorset DT2 7JQ), only da of Stanley Walton of The Hill, Gilsland, Carlisle: *m* 1949 (*m diss* 1975), as his 2nd wife, 7th Baron Henley, who *d* 1977.

COLLATERAL BRANCHES LIVING

Issue of late Brig-Gen Hon Anthony Morton HENLEY, CMG, DSO, 3rd son of 3rd Baron, *b* 1873, *d* 1925: *m* 1906, Hon Sylvia Laura Stanley, OBE, who *d* 1980, da of 4th Baron Sheffield (*see* B Stanley of Alderley):—
Juliet Olive, *b* 1917: *m* 1944 (*m diss* 1965), John Stuart Daniel, QC, Bar-at-law, who *d* 1977, and has issue living, Laura, *b* 1947. *Residence* – 20 Fitzroy Gdns, SE19.

Grandsons of late Capt Charles Beauclerk HENLEY, Royal Indian Navy (infra):—
Issue of late Cdr Robert Stephen HENLEY, OBE, DSC, RN, *b* 1917, *d* 1991: *m* 1940, Noreen (Eden Lodge, Liss, Hants GU33 6JQ), only da of late Eric Hudson:—
(Robert Anthony) Nigel (5 Orchard Rise, Richmond, Surrey), *b* 1942: *m* 1st, 1968 (*m diss* 1986), Celia, only da of Leslie Ford; 2ndly, 1988, Anne, only da of James Beadle, of Great Missenden, Bucks, and has issue living, (by 1st *m*) Robert Alexander, *b* 1973, — Deborah Lucie *b* 1971, — Victoria Elizabeth, *b* 1978, — (by 2nd *m*) Richard James, *b* 1989, — Joanna Katharine, *b* 1992. —— Timothy David (48 Arthur Rd, Wimbledon SW19 7DS), *b* 1945: *m* 1972, Jane Hughes, da of late John Fisher, of Chiswick Staithe, W4, and has issue living, Sarah Margaret, *b* 1975, — Rachel Katherine, *b* 1978. —— (Christopher) Basil Patrick (42 St Maur Rd, SW6), *b* 1953. —— Jonathan Paul Sebastian (Finches Cottage, Langley, nr Liss, Hants GU33 7JL), *b* 1956: *m* 1st, 1980 (*m diss* 1986), Caroline Fiona, yr da of D.D.A. Beattie, of Aston Mead, Windsor, Berks; 2ndly, 1987, Rowena Jane, da of Lionel David Cowan, of Cobham, Surrey, and has issue living (by 2nd *m*), James William, *b* 1989, — Clare Olivia *b* 1991, — Katherine Alexandra, *b* 1993.

Grandchildren of late Rev Hon Robert HENLEY, 2nd son of 2nd Baron:—
Issue of late Capt Charles Beauclerk HENLEY, Royal Indian Navy, *b* 1869, *d* 1945: *m* 1910, Nellie Barbara, who *d* 1961, da of late E. F. Stranack:—
David Beauclerk (Alpina, 36 Bruce Av, Worthing, BN11 5JU), *b* 1923: *m* 1951, Eileen Fuller. —— Elizabeth Barbara, *b* 1911. *Residence* – 9 Wynne's Park Cottages, Brookhouse Rd, Denbigh, Clwyd LL16 4YB. —— Violet Hope (22 Highgate Heights, 77 Shepherd's Hill, N6 5RF), *b* 1914: *m* 1937, Owen Austen Davis, who *d* 1992, and has issue living, Nicholas Austen (1 Meadway Gate, NW11 7LA), *b* 1940: *m* 1965, Mieke Jongebreur, and has issue living, Austen Peter *b* 1966, Ann Christa *b* 1968, — Simon Antony (220 Douglas Drive, Toronto M4W 2C1, Canada), *b* 1942: *m* 1967, Carol Ann Neibert, and has issue living, Christopher Antony *b* 1968, Amy Katharine *b* 1970, Maggie Alison *b* 1974.

Grandchildren of late Lt William Gaven Eden, RN, el son of late Rev Arthur Eden, only surv son of late Rev William Eden (infra):—
Issue of late Cecil Eden, *b* 1876, *d* 1963: *m* 1914, Inez Gilmour (Estancia Santa Inez, 2609- Maríe Teresa, Argentina), da of William Orr:—
Cecil Gilmour Orr (Estancia Santa Inez, 2609- Maria Teresa, Prov Santa Fé, Argentina), *b* 1921: *m* 1953, Anne Mabel, da of George Bridger, and has issue living, Robert Gilmour, *b* 1954, — David Arthur, *b* 1961, — Joanna Inez. *b* 1957, — Margaret Alice (twin), *b* 1961. —— Constance Edna, *b* 1924: *m* 1956, Geoffrey Arthur Lees, of St George's College Preparatory Sch, 1978- Quilmes, Argentina, and has issue living, John Arthur, *b* 1960, — Elizabeth Inez, *b* 1958.

Grandchildren of late Robert Charles Eden, yst son of late Rev Hon William Eden, 2nd son of 1st Baron:—
Issue of late Morton Edward Eden, *b* 1867, *d* 1914: *m* 1894, Marie Elizabeth, who *d* 1900, da of late James Stewart, of Dansville, New York, USA:—
Robert Henley Stuart, *b* 1896.

Issue of late Reginald Yelverton Eden, *b* 1871, *d* 1949: *m* 18—, Sophie, da of T. Hart, USA:—
Anne Louise: *m* 19—, Lurelle Van Arsdale Guild, and has issue living, Cynthia Eden, *b* 1938. —— Beatrice Elizabeth, *b* 1902.

PREDECESSORS – (1) MORTON Eden, 8th son of Sir Robert Eden, 3rd Bt (*see* Eden of Winton, B); Min at Vienna and Madrid; *cr Baron Henley*, of Chardstock (peerage of Ireland) 1799; *d* 1830: *m* 1783, Lady Elizabeth Henley, who *d* 1821, yst da of 1st Earl of Northington, Lord Chancellor, and sister and co-heir of the 2nd Earl; *s* by his son (2) ROBERT Henley, 2nd Baron; *b* 1789; was a Master in Chancery; assumed by Roy licence 1831 the surname of Henley in lieu of his patronymic: *m* 1823, Harriet, who *d* 1869, da of Sir Robert Peel, 1st Bt; *d* 1841; *s* by his son (3) ANTHONY HENLEY, 3rd Baron, *b* 1825; MP for Northampton (*L*) 1859-74; *cr Baron Northington*, of Watford, co Northampton (peerage of UK) 1885: *m* 1st, 1846, Julia Emily Augusta, who *d* 1862, da of late Very Rev John Peel, DDD, Dean of Worcester; 2ndly, 1870, Clara Campbell Lucy, who *d* 1922, da of late Joseph H. S. Jekyll; *d* 1898; *s* by his el son (4) FREDERIC, 4th Baron, *b* 1849: *m* 1900, Augusta Frederica, who *d* 1905, da of late Herbert Langham; *d* 1923; *s* by his brother (5) ANTHONY ERNEST, 5th Baron, *b* 1858: *m* 1st, 1882, Georgina Caroline Mary, who *d* 1888, da of late Lieut-Col Richard Michael Williams; 2ndly, 1889, Emmeline Stuart, who *d* 1933, da of late George (Gammie) Maitland, of Shotover Park, Oxon; *d* 1925; *s* by his half-brother (6) FRANCIS ROBERT, 6th Baron, *b* 1877; Chm of Northants Co Council 1945-9; assumed by deed poll (enrolled at College of Arms) 1925, the surname of Eden in lieu of Henley: *m* 1913, Lady Dorothy Georgiana Howard, who *d* 1968, da of 9th Earl of Carlisle; *d* 1962; *s* by his son (7) MICHAEL FRANCIS, 7th Baron, *b* 1914; Member of Council of Country Landowners Association; Chm of Council for Protection of Rural England: *m* 1st, 1943 (*m diss* 1947), Elizabeth, da of Sir Arthur Lawrence Hobhouse (*see* Jackson, Bt, *cr* 1869, colls, 1965 Edn); 2ndly, 1949 (*m diss* 1975), Nancy Mary, only da of Stanley Walton, of The Hill, Gilsland, Carlisle; *d* 1977; *s* by his el son (8) OLIVER MICHAEL ROBERT, 8th Baron and present peer; also Baron Northington.

HENNIKER, BARON (Henniker-Major) Sits as BARON HARTISMERE. (UK 1866) (Baron I 1800, Bt GB 1765)

God the greater support

JOHN PATRICK EDWARD CHANDOS HENNIKER-MAJOR, KCMG, CVO, MC, 8th Baron and 9th Baronet; *b* 19 Feb 1916; *s* 1980; *ed* Stowe, and Trin Coll, Camb (MA); a DL of Suffolk 1988; Maj (ret) Rifle Bde; Head of FO Personnel Dept 1953-60; Ambassador to Jordan 1960-62, and Denmark 1962-66; Dir-Gen of British Council 1968-72, Dir of Wates Foundation 1972-78; 1939-45 War (wounded, MC); CMG 1956, CVO 1960, KCMG 1965: *m* 1st 1946, Margaret Osla, who *d* 1974, da of late James William Benning, of Montreal; 2ndly 1976, Mrs Julia Marshall Poland, el da of George M. Mason, of Kew, and has issue, by 1st *m* .

Arms – Quarterly: 1st and 4th azure, three Corinthian columns, two and one palewise, or each having on the capital a golden ball, *Major*; 2nd and 3rd or, on a chevron gules, between two crescents in chief and an escallop in base azure, three estoiles argent, *Henniker*. **Crests** – 1st a dexter arm embowed, habited azure, cuffed argent, and charged on the elbow with a plate; the hand proper, holding a baton or; 2nd, and escallop, or, charged with an estoile gules. **Supporters** – *Dexter*, a stag argent, attired and unguled or, gorged with a chaplet of oak proper, fructed gold, and pendent therefrom an escutcheon azure, charged with the crest of Henniker; *sinister*, an otter argent, gorged with a ducal coronet or, and pendent therefrom an escutcheon of the arms of Major. *Residence* – The Red House, Thornham Magna, Eye, Suffolk. *Club* – Special Forces.

SONS LIVING (By 1st marriage)

Hon MARK IAN PHILIP CHANDOS (Thornham Hall, Thornham Magna, Eye, Suffolk), *b* 29 Sept 1947; *ed* Eton, and Trin Coll, Camb (MA); LLM (London); FCI Arb; MRAeS; Solicitor: *m* 1973, Mrs Lesley Antoinette Masterton-Smith, da of Wing Cdr G. W. Foskett, of Fernvale, Qld, Australia, and has issue living, Frederick John Chandos, *b* 31 March 1983, — Edward George Major, *b* 1985, — Jessica Sarah, *b* 1977, — Josephine Helen, *b* 1979, — Harriet Laura, *b* 1981.

Hon Charles John Giles, *b* 1949; *ed* Stowe: *m* 1980, Mrs Sally D. M. Kemp, el da of Donald Newby, of Halesworth, Suffolk, and has issue living, Thomas Charles John, *b* 1982, — Osla Mary, *b* 1981, — Ruth Felicity, *b* 1985. *Residence* – Great Chilton Farm, nr Ferry Hill, co Durham DL17 0JY.

DAUGHTER LIVING (By 1st marriage)

Hon Jane Elizabeth, *b* 1954: *m* 1979 (*m diss* 1993), Richard John Grenville Spring, son of late Herbert Spring, of 2 Regency Park, Kenilworth, Cape Town, and has issue living, Frederick John Otway, *b* 1987, — Sophia Romilly Alexandra, *b* 1983. *Residence* – 124 Cambridge St, SW1V 4QF.

BROTHER LIVING

Hon Richard Arthur Otway (13 Market Cross Place, Aldeburgh, Suffolk), *b* 1917; *ed* Stowe and Magdalene Coll, Camb (BA); admitted a Solicitor 1948; Lieut (ret) RA; 1939-45 War (prisoner): *m* 1946, Nancy Pauline, da of late Sir John Armitage Stainton, KCB, KBE, QC (B Forteviot), and has issue living, David Richard (Westbourne House, 37 Northside, Hutton Rudby, nr Yarm, Cleveland), *b* 1949: *m* 1973, Valerie Ann, el da of Francis Martin Lanigen-O'Keeffe, MD, of 10 Priory Rd, Kenilworth, Warwicks, and has issue living, Anna Natalie *b* 1976, Fiona Louise *b* 1978, — John Alexander (Harewell House, Stourton, nr Shipston-on-Stour, Warwicks CV36 5HG), *b* 1952: *m* 1976, Mary Mathiesen, and has issue living, George Richard *b* 1985, Charlotte Alice *b* 1979, Rose Clementine *b* 1982, — Susan Rose, *b* 1947: *m* 1976, Peter John Croft.

COLLATERAL BRANCHES LIVING

Grandsons of late Capt Frederick Henniker, yst son of Rear-Adm Hon Maj Jacob Henniker, brothr of 3rd Baron:—
Issue of Charles Henry Henniker, *b* 1880, *d* 1966: *m* 1914, Dorothy Albinia Cecil, who *d* 1959, da of late Rev Cecil Locke:—
Charles John Chandos (16 Clos de Verrières, 91 Verrières le Buisson, France), *b* 1916; *ed* Univ of BC (BApSc), and Washington (PhD) Univs: *m* 1954, Magdeleine Adèle, da of Albert Caton, chartered accountant, of Marseilles, France, and has issue living, Hélène Dorothy, *b* 1957: *m* 1983, Baron Pierre de Prittwitz, and has issue living, Gregory Charles *b* 1983, Igor Antoine *b* 1993, Fiona Natacha *b* 1988, — Eve Alice, *b* 1962.
Issue of late Capt Augustus Major Henniker, *b* 1884, *d* 1957: *m* 1910, Dorothy Roche, who *d* 1956, da of Lieut-Col Roche Rahilly, formerly RAMC:—
Anthony Trecothic Major, *b* 1912; European War 1939-40 in France as Pilot Officer RAF: *m* 1950, Ann Elizabeth Gwinnell, who *d* 1993, el da of Lt-Col G. C. G. Grey, OBE, late RA, and has issue living, Christopher Anthony Major (29 Rusthall Av, Bedford Park, W4), *b* 1952; *ed* Bedford Sch, and Manchester Univ (LLB); Sol 1978: *m* 1979, Bernadette, da of F. J. Ball, of Wallington, Surrey, and has issue living, Charles Edwin Major *b* 1984, James Christopher Major *b* 1986, Rosanna Josephine Major *b* 1989. *Residence* – 7 Evans Av, Allestree, Derby.

Descendants of late Lieut-Gen Hon Sir Brydges Trecothic Henniker (yst son of 1st Baron) who was *cr* a Baronet 1813:—
See Henniker, Bt.

PREDECESSORS – (1) JOHN MAJOR, MP for Scarborough 1761, and senior Elder Brother of the Trinity House 1741-81, was *cr* a *Baronet* 1765, with remainder to John Henniker, husband of his da Anne; *d* 1781; *s* by his son-in-law (2) JOHN HENNIKER, 2nd Bt, successively MP for Sudbury and Dover; *cr Baron Henniker*, of Stratford-upon-Slaney, co Wicklow (peerage of Ireland) 1800; *d* 1803; *s* by his son (3) JOHN, 2nd Baron; MP 1777-1802; assumed the surname of Major by Roy licence 1792; *dsp* 1821; *s* by his nephew (4) JOHN MINET, 3rd Baron, son of Hon Major Henniker, 2nd son of 1st Baron; assumed the additional surname of Major by Roy licence 1822; *d* 1832; *s* by his son (5) JOHN, 4th Baron; sat as MP for E. Suffolk 1832-47 and 1856-66; *cr Baron Hartismere*, of Hartismere, co Suffolk (peerage of United Kingdom) 1866: *m* 1837, Anna, who *d* 1889, da of Lieut-Gen Sir Edward Kerrison, GCH, KCB, 1st Bt (*ext*); *d* 1870; *s* by his son (6) JOHN MAJOR, 5th Baron; *b* 1842; MP for E Suffolk (C) 1866-70; a Lord-in-Waiting to Queen Victoria 1877-80, 1885-6, 1886-92, and July to Nov 1895, and Lieut-Gov of Isle of Man 1895-1902: *m* 1864, Lady Alice Mary, who *d* 1892, da of 3rd Earl of Desart; *d* 1902; *s* by his el surviving son (7) CHARLES HENRY CHANDOS, 6th Baron; *b* 1872; Col Rifle Brig; *d* 1956; *s* by his brother (8) JOHN ERNEST DE GREY, 7th Baron, *b* 1883; Page of Honour to Queen Victoria 1895-99; European War as Staff-Lieut, and in RAF (Croix de Guerre); *m* 1914, Molly, who *d* 1953, da of late Sir Robert William Burnet, KCVO, MD; *d* 1980; *s* by his el son **(9)** JOHN PATRICK EDWARD CHANDOS, 8th Baron and present peer; also Baron Hartismere.

Herbert, Lord; son of Earl of Pembroke and Montgomery.

HEREFORD, VISCOUNT (Devereux) (Viscount E. 1550, Bt E1611)
(Name pronounced 'Deverooks')

Envy is the attendant of virtue

ROBERT MILO LEICESTER DEVEREUX, 18th Viscount, Premier Viscount of England, and 15th Baronet; *b* 4 Nov 1932; *s* 1952; *ed* Eton; OStJ: *m* 1969 (*m diss* 1982), Susan Mary, only child of Maj Maurice Godley, of Ide Hill, Sevenoaks, Kent and has issue.

Arms – Argent, a fesse gules, in chief three torteaux. **Crest** – Out of a ducal coronet or, a talbot's head argent, eared gules. **Supporters** – *Dexter*, a talbot argent, eared gules, ducally gorged of the last; *sinister*, a reindeer gules, attired, gorged with a ducal coronet, and lined or. **Second Motto** – *Basis virtutum constantia* (Firmness the basis of virtue).
Residence – Lyford Cay Club, PO Box N 7776, Nassau, Bahamas.

SONS LIVING

Hon CHARLES ROBIN DE BOHUN, *b* 11 Aug 1975.
Hon Edward Mark de Breteuil *b* 1977.

SISTER LIVING

(Raised to rank of a Viscount's daughter 1953)

Hon Diana Bridget, *b* 1931: *m* 1967, Col Samuel Charles Casamajor Gaussen, Welsh Guards, of 60 Alder Lodge, Stevenage Road, SW7, and Nutbeam, Duntisbourne Leer, Cirencester, Glos, and has issue living, Robert Casamajor, *b* 1968, — Mariana Diana, *b* 1971.

COLLATERAL BRANCHES LIVING

Grandchildren of late Humphrey Bourchier Devereux, eldest son of late Hon Henry de Bohun Devereux (infra):—
Issue of late Rupert Montague Devereux, *b* 1907, *d* 1974: *m* 1940, Joan Ursula, who *d* 1983, da of D. W. Thomas:—
(Blanche) Rosemary, *b* 1943: *m* 1966, Harvey Nausbaum, of 4 James Cook Esplanade, Qld 4216, Australia, and has issue living, Aaron, *b* 1972, — Sarah Rosemary, *b* 1974. —— Susan Ursula, *b* 1947: *m* 1967, Terrence Adrian Currie, of 125 Koutu Rd, Rotorua, NZ, and has issue living, Simon Zane, *b* 1967, — Bridget Susan, *b* 1971.
Issue of late George Makgill de Bohun Devereux, *b* 1909, *d* 1976: *m* 1937, Olga Christian (3 Mays Rd, Onehunga, Auckland, SE5, NZ), da of late Karl S. Larsen, of Auckland, NZ:—
Colin de Bohun, *b* 1941: *m* 1st, 1964, (*m diss* 1976), Helen Ann, da of K. Buchanan, of Takanini, NZ; 2ndly, 1976, Carole Ann, da of J. Parkes, of Dannevirke, NZ, and has issue living (by 2nd *m*), Justin de Bohun, *b* 1976. —— Dorothy Wyn, *b* 1938: *m* 1958, Graham Leaning, of 3 Mays Rd, Onehunga Auckland, SE5, NZ, and has issue living, Karl Stuart, *b* 1964, — Christine Ann, *b* 1961. —— Marilyn Joan, *b* 1948: *m* 1971, Robert Leslie Hessey, of 28 Littlejohn St, Hillsborough, Auckland, NZ, and has issue living, Steven James, *b* 1977, — Rachel Ann, *b* 1975.

Grandchildren of late Hon Henry de Bohun Devereux, 2nd son of 15th Viscount:—
Issue of late Godfrey Vaughan Devereux, *b* 1893, *d* 1976: *m* 1925, Ellen, who *d* 1986, da of late John Black, of Keri Keri, Bay of Islands, NZ:—
Robin Geoffrey (76 Colman Av, Upper Riccarton, Christchurch, NZ), *b* 1927: Capt RNZAC: *m* 1953, Glennis Fyfe, da of T. F. Kerr, and has issue living, Susan Lee, *b* 1956: *m* 1981, R. Noel Strez, of 49 Sayers Cres, Christchurch, NZ, and has issue living, Simon Geoffrey *b* 1986, Kirsten Anna *b* 1983, — Vicki Anne, *b* 1959: *m* 1982, James Bennie, of 46 Woodard Terrace, Christchurch, NZ. —— David de Bohun (432 Fraser St, Tauranga, NZ), *b* 1928: *m* 1951, Roberta Barbara, da of late F. G. R. Souness, and has issue living, Malcolm Fergus (8 Rowenwood Close, Christchurch 3, NZ), *b* 1952; F/Lt RNZAF: *m* 1975, Barbara, da of R. Irwin, of Pukekohe, NZ, and has issue living, Mark Robert *b* 1978, Ross Timothy *b* 1980, — Wendy Anne, *b* 1956: *m* 1st, 1978 (*m diss* 1989), John Roy Donaldson; 2ndly, 1990, Ashley Richard Philip, of 3 Endeavour Ave, Tauranga, NZ, and has issue living (by 1st *m*), Matthew James *b* 1988, Melissa Joy *b* 1983, Sarah Marie *b* 1985. —— Francis Richard (Tangowahine, RD2, Dargaville, NZ), *b* 1937: *m* 1978 (*m diss* 1984), Linda Jane, da of John Wright of Dargaville, NZ, and has issue living, Richard John, *b* 1982. —— Jennifer Mary, *b* 1933: *m* 1959, Lt-Col George Scott Finlayson, RNZ Corps of Sigs, and has issue living, George Robert, *b* 1960: *m* 1991, Michelle Judith, da of A. R. McLennan, — James Scott, *b* 1963, — Helen Mary, *b* 1966, — Judith Anne, *b* 1970.

Grandchildren of late Walter de Laci Devereux, only son of late Rear-Adm Hon Walter Bourchier Devereux, 3rd son of 14th Viscount:—
Issue of late Lt-Col Robert de Bohun Devereux, MBE, *b* 1897; *d* 1981: *m* 1925, Enid Marion, who *d* 1976, da of late Gen Sir Henry Bulkley Burlton Watkis, KCB:—

Robert Humphrey Bourchier (Woolbeding Cottage, Bepton, nr Midhurst, W Sussex), *b* 1930; *ed* Marlborough, and Exeter Coll, Oxford: *m* 1954, Barbara, who *d* 1989, only da of Norman Heywood, of Ealing, W5, and has issue living, Robert Harold Ferrers (5 Ladbroke Terrace, W11), *b* 1955; *ed* Marlborough, and Downing Coll, Camb: *m* 1983, Vanessa, da of Edward James Branson, of Tanyard Farm, Shamley Green, Guildford, Surrey, and has issue living, Noah Edward de Bohun *b* 1987, Louis Robert de Laci *b* 1991, Florence Barbara Clare *b* 1989, — Godfrey Edmund de Bohun, *b* 1956; *ed* Marlborough: *m* 1982, Barbara, da of late William Accousti, of Connecticut, USA, and has issue living, Arum *b* 1983, — Henrietta Marion Clare, *b* 1960. —— Marion Blanche, *b* 1927: *m* 1958, Rev Timothy Knowles Hollis, and has issue living, Timothy John Walter, *b* 1968: *m* 1991, Michaela Francis, and has issue living, Ryan Arthur *b* 1991, Rebecca Anne *b* 1993, — Jennifer Marion, *b* 1961, — Lucy Anne, *b* 1962.

PREDECESSORS – **(1)** WALTER Devereux, KG; in 1500 *s* his father as 10th *Baron Ferrers*, of Chartley (peerage of England, *cr* 1299, see E Ferrers); *cr Viscount Hereford* (peerage of England) 1550; distinguished himself in the French Wars of Henry VIII; was Justice of S Wales 1524; *d* 1558; *s* by his grandson **(2)** WALTER, KG, 2nd Viscount, son of Sir Richard, 2nd son of 1st Viscount; *s* 1570, in right of his gt-grandmother, as 8th *Baron Bourchier* (peerage of England, *cr* 1342, see * infra); *cr Earl of Essex* (peerage of England) 1572; was Field-Marshal of the Forces sent to suppress the Rebellion of the Earls of Northumberland and Westmorland; was also Earl Marshal of Ireland; *d* 1576; *s* by his son **(3)** ROBERT, KG, 2nd Earl; was Lord Lieut of Ireland and Earl Marshal of England; well known in history as the unfortunate favourite of Queen Elizabeth; was Master of the Horse, Earl Marshal of England, Lord Dep of Ireland, and Chancellor of Cambridge Univ; having conspired against the Queen he made a fruitless effort at insurrection, was taken prisoner, convicted of high treason, and beheaded on Tower Hill 25 Feb 1601; *s* by his son **(4)** ROBERT, KG, who in 1603 was restored in blood and became 3rd Earl; was attached to the Royal cause until 1642, when he accepted a commission in the Parliament army and afterwards distinguished himself as a Parliamentary Generalissimo; *d* 1646; interred with national obsequies in Westminster Abbey, the two Houses of Parliament attending the funeral; at his death the Earldom of Essex expired, the Barony of Ferrers became abeyant (abeyance terminated 1677, see E Ferrers), the Barony of Bourchier became abeyant (and still remains so), and the Viscountcy of Hereford devolved upon his kinsman **(5)** WALTER, 5th Viscount, son of Sir Edward Devereux (*cr Baronet* 1611 and *d* 1622), who was 4th son of 1st Viscount; *s* by his son **(6)** LEICESTER, 6th Viscount; *d* 1676; *s* by his el son **(7)** LEICESTER, 7th Viscount, *d* aged 9 years 1683; *s* by his brother **(8)** EDWARD, 8th Viscount; *dsp* 1700; *s* by his kinsman **(9)** PRICE, 9th Viscount, great-grandson of Sir George, Knt, (ante); *d* 1760; *s* by his el son **(12)** EDWARD, 12th Viscount; *dsp* 1783; *s* by his son **(15)** *Rev* ROBERT, 15th Viscount; *b* 1809; was an Hon Canon of Durham: *m* 1841, Emma Jemima, who *d* 1870 (having *m* 2ndly, 1857, Lieut-Col John Ireland-Blackburne), da of George Ravenscroft; *d* 1855; *s* by his son **(16)** ROBERT, 16th Viscount; *b* 1843: *m* 1863, Hon Mary Anna Moran, who *d* 1924, da of 1st Baron Tredegar; *d* 1830; *s* by his son **(17)** ROBERT CHARLES, 17th Viscount; *b* 1865; was Capt 1st (Breconshire) Vol Batn S Wales and Borderers, and Chm of Breconshire Quarter Sessions 1907-27: *m* 1892, Ethel Mildred, who *d* 1945, da of late John Shaw, of Welburn Hall, Kirkby Moorside; *d* 1952; *s* by his grandson **(18)** ROBERT MILO LEICESTER (only son of late Hon Robert Godfrey de Bohun Devereux, only son of 17th Viscount), 18th Viscount and present peer.

*(1) ROBERT de Bourchier, sometime Lord Chancellor of England, afterwards distinguished himself at Crecy; summoned to English Parliament as *Baron Bourchier* 1342-9; *d* 1349; *s* by his son **(2)** JOHN, KG, 2nd Baron; summoned to Parliament 1381-99; was engaged for many years in the French Wars of Edward III and Richard II, and was sometime Ch Gov of Flanders; *d* 1400; *s* by his son **(3)** BARTHOLOMEW, 3rd Baron; summoned to Parliament 1400-9; *d* 1409; *s* by his only da **(4)** ELIZABETH; she *m* 1st, Sir Hugh Stafford, KB, and 2ndly, Sir Lewis Robsart, KG, each of whom on his marriage assumed the dignity of Lord Bourchier, but was only summoned to Parliament in his own name; *d* without issue 1432; *s* by her cousin **(5)** HENRY, 5th Baron, grandson of William, 2nd son of 1st Baron, and son of William Bourchier, 1st Count of Eu, in Normandy, by Anne, heiress of Thomas of Woodstock, Duke of Gloucester (yst son of Edward III), and his wife Allianore de Bohun, el co-heir of the last Earl of Hereford, Essex, and Northampton; he previously *s* his father as 2nd Count of Eu, in Normandy title created by Henry V; summoned to Parliament as 'Count of Ewe' 1435, and as Viscount Bourchier 1446, and constituted Lord Treasurer of England 1455; subsequently espoused the interests of the Earls of March and Warwick, and was, on the accession of Edward IV, re-invested with Lord Treasureship, and shared largely in the confiscated estates of the attained Earls of Warwick and Wiltsire and Lord Roos; *cr Earl of Essex* (peerage of England) 1461; *d* 1483; *s* by his grandson **(6)** HENRY, 2nd Earl; had a principal command at the Battle of Blackheath; at the famous tournament held by Henry VIII, on 19-20 May, 1516, he answered all comers; accompanied HM to France, and assisted at the pagentry in the King's interview with Francis I upon the Field of the Cloth of Gold; *d* 1539, when the Earldom of Essex and the Viscountcy of Bourchier expired, and the Barony of Bourchier devolved upon his only da **(7)** ANNE, Lady Parr; *d* 1570, but her issue being illegitimated (by Act of Parliament 5th of Edward VI), the Barony passed to **(8)** WALTER Devereux, 2nd Viscount Hereford (ante).

HERRIES OF TERREGLES, LADY (Cowdrey) (Lordship S 1490)

ANNE ELIZABETH FITZALAN-HOWARD, el da of 16th Duke of Norfolk; *b* 12 June 1938; *s* 1975: *m* 1985, Sir (Michael) Colin Cowdrey, CBE, cricketer.

Arms – Not exemplified at time of going to press.
Seat – Angmering Park, Little Hampton, W Sussex.

SISTERS LIVING

See D Norfolk, of whom *Lady* MARY KATHARINE MUMFORD is *hp*.

COLLATERAL BRANCHES LIVING

Issue of late Hon Angela Mary Constable-Maxwell, yr da of 11th Lord, *b* 1877, *d* 1965: *m* 1904, 16th Earl of Perth, who *d* 1951:—
See E Perth.

Grandchildren of late Hon Joseph CONSTABLE-MAXWELL- SCOTT, 3rd son of 10th Lord:—
Issue of late Maj-Gen Sir Walter Joseph Constable-Maxwell-Scott, Bt, CB, DSO, who was *cr* a *Baronet* 1932:—
See Constable-Maxwell-Scott, Bt (*cr* 1932) (ext).
Issue of late Rear-Adm Malcolm Joseph Raphael Constable-Maxwell-Scott, DSO, RN, *b* 1883, *d* 1943: *m* 1918, Fearga Victoria Mary, who *d* 1969, da of late Rt Hon Sir Nicholas Roderick O'Connor, GCB, GCMG (M Linlithgow colls):—
See Constable-Maxwell-Scott, Bt (*cr* 1642).
Issue of late Herbert Francis Joseph Constable-Maxwell-Scott, *b* 1891, *d* 1962: *m* 1924, Eileen Josephine, who *d* 1974, da of late Henry Smail, of Donhead Lodge, Wimbledon, SW:—
Simon Malcolm (Foss House, Strensall, York), *b* 1939: *m* 1962, Moyna, da of S. Y. Gore, of Calcutta, India, and has issue living, Amanda Mary, *b* 1962: *m* 1987, Charles John Kay, son of Dr John Anthony Kay, of Alne, York, — Fiona Anne, *b* 1964, — Joanna Jane, *b* 1965. —— David Darragh (66 Marryat Rd, Wimbledon, SW19), *b* 1944: *m* 1969, H. Isabel, da of Leonard

Caplan, QC, of 1 Pump Court, Temple, EC4, and has issue living, James Herbert, *b* 1971, — Charles Leonard, *b* 1975. —— Aurea Mary Josephine, *b* 1926: *m* 1947, Peter Humphrey Williams, who *d* 1987, of 66 Valecrest Drive, Islington, Ontario, Canada M9A 4P6, and has had issue, Michael Humphrey (657 Carlaw Av, Toronto, Ontario, Canada M4K 3K6), *b* 1948: *m* 1983, Anne Catherine, da of late Edgar James Thomas, and has issue living, Jake Peter Thomas *b* 1988, — Ian Maxwell (66 Valecrest Drive, Islington, Ontario, Canada M9A 4P6), *b* 1951: *m* 19—, Mary Jo —, and has issue living, Christopher *b* 19—, Trevor *b* 19—, Kathleen *b* 19—, — David Andrew (26 Falling Leaf Court, Aurora, Ontario, Canada L4G 6K6), *b* 1955, — Deborah Mary, *b* 1950; accidentally drowned 1956, — Elizabeth Anne, *b* 1953: *m* 1975, Jan Joseph Rzyzora, of Box 889, Knowlton, Prov Quebec, Canada J0E 1VO, and has issue living, Matthew Scott *b* 1981, Simon Peter *b* 1982, Deborah Katherine *b* 1984, Andrea Jan *b* 1978, — Sheila Mary, *b* 1956: *m* 1985, Andries Johannes Stephanus van der Merwe, of Basteistrasse 28b, 5300 Bonn 2, Germany, and has issue living, Pamela Jo *b* 1987, Stephanie Ann *b* 1990, Megan Elizabeth *b* 1993, — Joanna Susan (848 Goodwin Rd, Mississauga, Ontario, Canada L5G 4JT), *b* 1958. — Pamela Jane, *b* 1961; *d* 1976. —— Susan Mary (2 Westfield House, West Cross, Tanterden, Kent TN30 6JL), *b* 1931. —— Mary Monica (St Mary's House, St George's Retreat, Burgess Hill, Sussex), *b* 1945.

Issue of late Mary Josephine Constable-Maxwell-Scott, *b* 1876, *d* 1922: *m* 1897, Alexander Augustus Dalglish:— James Campbell DALGLISH, *b* 1898, whose grandson is Mr John Dalglish, of Pomeroy, Goulburn, NSW, Australia.

Grandchildren (by 2nd *m*) of late Hon Bernard CONSTABLE MAXWELL, 4th son of 10th Lord (infra):— Issue of late Capt Ian Simon Joseph Constable-Maxwell, *b* 1891, *d* 1975: *m* 1937, Janette Louisa, who *d* 1944, elder da of Lt-Col Wilfrid Ricardo, DSO, of Hook Hall, Surrey:— Jeanette Alice Norah (Flat 9, N°12 Chelsea Embankment, SW3), *b* 1942.

Issue of late Wing Com Gerald Joseph Constable-Maxwell, MC, DFC, AFC, *b* 1895, *d* 1959: *m* 1920, Caroline Burns, who *d* 1984, da of George Alexander Carden, of New York:— Peter George (The Park House, Old Alresford Park, Hants; Cavalry and Guards' Club), *b* 1944; *ed* Ampleforth, and New Coll, Oxford; Lieut Gren Gds; Kt of Sovereign Mil Order of Malta: *m* 1973, Virginia Ann, da of Lt-Col John Ewart, and has issue living, Benedict Gerald John, *b* 1976, — Laura Katherine, *b* 1974, — Eleanor Margaret, *b* 1977, — Elizabeth Marsha, *b* 1983. —— Anne Mary Teresa (*Duchess of Norfolk*), CBE, *b* 1927; Founder and Co-Chm Help the Hospices; CBE (Civil) 1992: *m* 1949, 17th Duke of Norfolk, and has issue. *Residences* – Arundel Castle, Sussex; Carlton Towers, Goole, Humberside; Bacres House, Hambleden, Henley-on-Thames, Oxon. —— (Veronica) Diana Margaret, *b* 1930: *m* 1960, Timothy Lawrie Boyd Wilson, Scots Gds (Reserve), of California, USA, and of Ardelve, Kyle of Lochalsh, Ross-shire, and has issue living, William Lawrie Joseph, *b* 1963, — Lucy Mary Carolyn, *b* 1961, — Magdalen Margaret, *b* 1966. —— Carolyn Mary, *b* 1938: *m* 1960, Maj Count Charles John de Salis, DL, Scots Gds (Reserve), of Yarlington House, Wincanton, Som, and Bondo Promontagno, Grisons, Switzerland, and has issue living, Isobel Oriane Clare, *b* 1961; MB BS: *m* 1992, Dr Hugh J. Herzig, and has issue living, Jessica Angelica Rachel *b* 1993, — Frances Mary Josephine, *b* 1963. — Julia Mary Blanche, *b* 1968, — Theresa Mary Bridget, *b* 1970. —— Rosemary Isabel, *b* 1941: *m* 1965, Antony Craven Chambers, Gren Gds, of The Lake House, Alresford, Hants, and has issue living, Dominic Peter Craven (1 Dorncliffe Rd, SW6), *b* 1966: *m* 1992, Nicola Marina Merry, yst da of Maj Hon Edward Renfric Arundell (*see* B Talbot of Malahide), — Sebastian George Craven (12 Quilter St, Bethnal Green, E2 7BT), *b* 1967: *m* 1989, Maria Mercedes, only da of John Frederick Scrope (*see* Sykes, Bt, *cr* 1783, 1990 Edn), — Edmund Mungo Craven, *b* 1977, — Antonia Mary Craven, *b* 1974, — Alexandra Bridget Craven, *b* 1979.

Issue of late Maj David TURVILLE-CONSTABLE-MAXWELL, TD, RA; assumed the additional surname of Turville before his patronymic 1960, *b* 1904, *d* 1985: *m* 1930, Mary Alethea Elizabeth Evelyn (Penthouse, Bosworth Hall, Husbands Bosworth, Lutterworth, Leics), 2nd da of late Lt-Col Oswald Henry Philip Turville-Petre (*see* B Petre, colls):— Robert John TURVILLE-CONSTABLE-MAXWELL (Bosworth Hall, Husbands Bosworth, Lutterworth, Liecs LE17 6LZ; Cavalry and Guards' and Pratt's Clubs), *b* 1933; *ed* Ampleforth; late Lieut Gren Gds; assumed the additional surname of Turville before his patronymic 1960: *m* 1960, Susan Mary, only da of late Capt Stephen Francis Gaisford-St Lawrence, RN (*see* Mostyn, Bt, colls, 1985 Edn), and has issue living, Anthony Nicholas, *b* 1961; *ed* Ampleforth, — Stephen Bernard, *b* 1963; *ed* Ampleforth: *m* 1992, Louise Anne, only da of Alan Crossland, of Twichells, Wychnor, nr Burton on Trent, Staffs, — Alice Marion, *b* 1969. —— Christopher (Kit) Thomas Bernard TURVILLE-CONSTABLE-MAXWELL (La Silonniere, 37240 Ciran, Indre et Loire, France; Cavalry and Guards' Club), *b* 1940; *ed* Ampleforth; late Lieut Scots Gds; FRGS; assumed the additional surname of Turville before his patronymic 1960: *m* 1963, Lavinia Moira, only da of late Hubert Arthur George Howard (*see* E Carlisle, colls), and has issue living, Simon Hubert, *b* 1965, — Gavin Herries, *b* 1967. —— †Mary Belinda, *b* 1931: *m* 1951 (*m diss* 1976), 9th Earl of Carrick, who *d* 1992, and *d* 1993, leaving issue. —— Jennifer Mary, *b* 1937: *m* 1970, Christopher David Newton, TD, JP, of Rumsey House, Calne, Wilts, and has issue living, James Nicholas Turville, *b* 1971; *ed* Eton, — Lucinda Rosalinde Mary, *b* 1975. —— Marcia Helen (Château de Cheseaux, 1033 Vaud, Switzerland), *b* 1947: *m* 1st, 1968, Capt Sir (Joseph Benedict) Everard Henry Radcliffe, 6th Bt, MC, who *d* 1975; 2ndly, 1988, Howard Montagu Stuart Tanner.

Issue of late Lt-Col Andrew Bernard Constable Maxwell, MBE, MC, Scots Gds (Res), *b* 1906, *d* 1990: *m* 1949, Militza (1181 Vincy, Vaud, Switzerland), da of Mark Kerkes, of USA:— Andreina Philomena, *b* 1950.

Issue of late Hon Bernard CONSTABLE MAXWELL, 4th son of 10th Lord, *b* 1848, *d* 1938: *m* 1st, 1881, Mathilda, who *d* 1882, da of late Alfred D. Jessup, of Philadelphia; 2ndly, 1890, Hon Alice Charlotte Fraser, who *d* 1958, da of 15th Lord Lovat:— (By 2nd *m*) Michael Hugh CONSTABLE MAXWELL, DSO, DFC (Theobalds House, Old Park Ride, Waltham Cross, Herts EN7 5HX; Newton House, Kirkhill, Inverness-shire IV5 7PU; RAF, New (Edinburgh), and White's Clubs), *b* 1917; *ed* Ampleforth, and Hertford Coll, Oxford (BA 1939, MA 1943); Wing-Cdr RAF (ret); a Member of Queen's Body Guard for Scotland (Royal Company of Archers), and Knt of Sovereign Mil Order of Malta; commn'd 4th Bn Queen's Own Cameron Highlanders (TA) 1935, transferred to RAF 1939, Battle of Britain 1940 (DFC 1943, DSO 1944), Netherlands E Indies 1944-45 (despatches): *m* 1962, Susan Joan, da of late W. Trevor Davies, of Glanrhiw, Oakdale, Gwent, and has issue living, Hugh Peter (34 Rumbold Rd, SW6 2HX; White's Club), *b* 1963; *ed* Ampleforth, and Digby Stuart Coll, Roehampton (BSc 1985), — Thomas Bernard (Ash Mount, Husthwaite, York), *b* 1966; *ed* Ampleforth, and Heythrop Coll, Lond Univ: *m* 1992, Alice Ellinor Mary, only da of Jonathan Julian Cotterell (*see* B Camoys), and has issue living, Helena Mary *b* 1993. —— Ursula Marcia Mary, *b* 1911: *m* 1960, Chalmers Davidson, FRCP. *Residence* – Farlie House, Beauly, Inverness-shire.

Grandchildren (by 2nd *m*) of late Hon Bernard Constable Maxwell (ante)— Issue of late Mary Philomena Constable Maxwell, *b* 1893, *d* 1953: *m* 1926, Maj Anthony Buxton, who *d* 1953:— *See* Buxton, Bt, colls.

Issue of late Winifride Mary Ethelreda Constable Maxwell, *b* 1898, *d* 1994: *m* 1923, Capt Ronald Arthur Charteris Foster, late Rifle Bde, who *d* 1977:— David Philip FOSTER, *b* 1924; *ed* Ampleforth, and Trin Coll, Camb (BA); Capt RE (ret); ARIAS: *m* 1969, Margaret Helen, eldest da of late Ian Gordon Lindsay, OBE (*see* B Loch, 1973-74 Edn), and has issue living, Ronald Ian, *b* 1972, — Peter John, *b* 1976, — Elizabeth Mary, *b* 1970; *ed* Aberdeen Univ (BEng). *Residence* – Wyndford Farm, Broxburn, W Lothian EH52 6NW. —— Giles Anthony FOSTER, *b* 1927; *ed* Ampleforth, and RAC Cirencester; late Lt Rifle Bde.

Issue of late Joan Constable Maxwell, *b* 1901, *d* 1991: *m* 1930, Lt-Col Hon Henry George Orlando Bridgeman, DSO, MC, who *d* 1972:— *See* E Bradford, colls.

Grandchildren of late Mary Anne Constable Maxwell, yst da of 10th Lord: *m* 1884, her cousin, Edmund Constable-Maxwell-Stuart (infra).

Granddaughter of late Capt Francis Joseph CONSTABLE-MAXWELL-STUART (infra):—
Issue of late Capt Peter D'Arcy John Joseph Constable-Maxwell-Stuart, IA, *b* 1922, *d* 1990: *m* 1956, Flora (Traquair House, Innerleithen, Peeblesshire), da of Sir Alexander Morris Carr-Saunders, KBE:—
Catherine Margaret Mary, *b* 1964. *Residence* – Traquair House, Innerleithen, Peeblesshire.

Grandchildren of late Edmund CONSTABLE-MAXWELL-STUART, 4th son of late Hon Henry Constable-Maxwell-Stuart, brother of 10th Lord:—
Issue of late Capt Francis Joseph Constable-Maxwell-Stuart, *b* 1886, *d* 1962: *m* 1917, Dorothy Mary, who *d* 1975, da of late J. D'Arcy Hartley, of Billesdon Coplow, Leics:—
Michael Joseph Edmund (Baitlaws, Lamington, Lanarks), *b* 1932: *m* 1970, Kirsty, el da of late Capt H. K. Salvesen, of Inveralmond, Edinburgh, and has issue living, Justin, *b* 1973, — Laura Mary, *b* 1971. —— Madeleine Mary Josephine, *b* 1918: *m* 1946, John Sherbrooke, of Churchen Green, East Morden, Wareham, Dorset, and has issue living, Simon (Bolney, Salisbury Rd, Blandford, Dorset DT11 7SP), *b* 1947: *m* 1977, Miranda, da of Michael McCrea, of Tweedbank, Kelso, Roxburghshire, and has issue living, Archie John *b* 1980, Benedict *b* 1984, Luke *b* 1986, Edmund *b* 1993, Rosanna *b* 1982, — Hugh (Middle Farm, Taston, Oxford OX7 3JL), *b* 1948: *m* 1974, Nicola Mary Hamilton, yr da of Anthony Andrew Francis Tabor (*see* B Dulverton, colls), and has issue living, Charles *b* 1976, Mark *b* 1979, Henry *b* 1985, Georgina *b* 1978. — Alexander, *b* 1957, — Elizabeth, *b* 1959. —— †Joan Margaret Mary, *b* 1920: *m* 1943, Charles Erik Paterson, who *d* 1983, and *d* 1987, leaving issue, David Francis Joseph (15B, 6 Po Shan Rd, Hong Kong; 30 Walpole St, SW3), *b* 1944: *m* 1983, Jayne, da of late T. Y. Tung, of Hong Kong, — Michael Charles Joseph (10 Dalebury Rd, SW17), *b* 1948: *ed* Stonyhurst, and Oriel Coll, Oxford: *m* 1987, Marguerite, da of Vice Adm Sir Iwan Raikes, KCB, CBE, DSC, DL, of Aberyscir Court, Brecon, and has issue living, Hermione *b* 1987, Sophia *b* (twin) 1990, — Caroline Mary Madeleine, *b* 1945: *m* 1975, Edward Pearce Serocold, of 1 Morella Rd, SW12, son of Lt-Col Walter Pearce Serocold, DSO, TD, of Ridge House, Highclere, Berks, and has issue living, Charles *b* 1976, Mark *b* 1979, Henry *b* 1985, Georgina *b* 1978.
Issue of late William Joseph Peter Constable-Maxwell-Stuart, *b* 1895, *d* 1964: *m* 1st, 1932, Ruth Patricia Craven, who *d* 1952, da of late Charles Craven Sykes, of 15 Oval Rd, Regent's Park, NW; 2ndly, 1955, Anne Christine, da of late Peter John Williamson, of 42 East Claremont St, Edinburgh:—
(By 2nd *m*) Joseph Peter, *b* (Jan) 1956: *m* 1988, Deirdre, yr da of John O'Neil, of Struthers Cres, E Kilbride, and has issue living, Laurence, *b* 1990, — Rebecca, *b* 1989. —— Julian Francis, *b* (Dec) 1956.
Issue of late Mary Josephine Constable-Maxwell-Stuart, *b* 1885, *d* 1973: *m* 1918, Capt Hamish Morton Anderson, MB, ChB, formerly RAMC:—
Patricia Maria (*Lady Vallat*), *b* 1919: *m* 1988, Sir Francis Vallat, GBE, KCMG, QC, of 17 Ranelagh Grove, SW1.
Issue of late Marcia Mary Gertrude Constable-Maxwell-Stuart, *b* 1888, *d* 1956: *m* 1920, Douglas Christopher Leng, who *d* 1930:—
Christopher Anthony William LENG, OBE (Juniper Bank, Walkerburn, Peeblesshire), *b* 1922; *ed* Downside, and Hertford Coll, Oxford (BA 1947, MA 1947); European War 1939-45 as Capt 27th Lancers in Middle East, and in Italy (despatches) and Burma; Dep Lord Lieut of Peeblesshire since 1983; OBE (Civil) 1987: *m* 1953, Patricia, da of W. Edmund Lillywhite, of Pilgrims, Chilham, Kent, and has issue living, Malcolm Simon Christopher (West Bold, Walkerburn, Peeblesshire), *b* 1959: *m* 1990, Fiona C., elder da of P. A. M. Murray, of Painswick Lodge, Painswick, Glos, and has issue living, Demelza Fiona *b* 1993, — Rupert William (13 St Steven's Place, Edinburgh), *b* 1961: *m* 1991, Helen R., da of late H. A. Nicholson, of Balnald, Kirkmichael, — Fiona Anne, *b* 1954: *m* 1988, as his 2nd wife, Nicholas Charles Gilmour Marshall, and has issue (*see* Gilmour, Bt, *cr* 1897, colls), — Teresa Madeleine, *b* 1955. —— David Joseph Timothy LENG, *b* 1924; *ed* Downside, and New Coll, Oxford (BA 1948); European War 1940-45, as Capt 4th Batn Gren Gds: *m* 1951, Dorothy Lucie, who *d* 1967, da of late C. Seymour, of Folkstone, and has issue living, Felicity Mary, *b* 1952: *m* 19—, George Whitman (of USA), of 37 Rue de la Bucherie, 75005 Paris, and has issue living, Sylvia *b* 1979, — Leonara Rosemary, *b* 1956.

Granddaughter of late Hon Henry CONSTABLE-MAXWELL-STUART (ante):—
Issue of late Henry Joseph Constable-Maxwell-Stuart, *b* 1861, *d* 1932: *m* 1908, Florence, who *d* 1956, da of William Wickham, of Chestnut Grove, Boston Spa, Yorks:—
Clare Mary, *b* 1914: *m* 1938, S/Ldr James Patrick Cafferkey, RAF (ret), who *d* 1978, and has issue living, Patrick Charles, *b* 1941. *Residence* – 4 Apple Garth, Easingwold, York YO6 3LZ.

PREDECESSORS – (1) HERBERT Herries, was summoned to Parliament of Scotland as *Lord Herries of Terregles* 1490; *s* by his son (2) ANDREW, 2nd Lord; *d* 1513; *s* by his son (3) WILLIAM, 3rd Lord; *s* by his el da (4) AGNES: *m* Sir John Maxwell, 2nd son of 5th Lord Maxwell (*cr* 1440), who became *jure uxoris* Lord Herries of Terregles; *d* 1582; *s* by his son (5) WILLIAM, 5th Lord, *d* 1603; *s* by his son (6) JOHN Maxwell, 6th Lord; *d* 1631; *s* by his son (7) JOHN, 7th Lord: who in 1667 *s* by special remainder his kinsman as 3rd Nithsdale (the 1st Earl, Robert, 9th Baron Maxwell, was *cr* Lord Maxwell, Eskdale and Carlyle, and Earl of Nithsdale, with remainder to his heirs male, and precedence of 1581); *s* by his son (8) ROBERT, 4th Earl; *d* 1685; *s* by his son (9) WILLIAM, 5th Earl; celebrated for effecting his escape from the Tower of London the night before his execution, through the agency of his wife; peerages attainted; *d* 1744, leaving a son WILLIAM (6th Earl but for the attainder); *d* 1776, leaving a da WINIFRED (who but for the attainder would have inherited the Lordship): *m* William Haggerston-Constable (2nd son of Sir Carnaby Haggerston, 3rd Bt); *d* 1801; her son MARMADUKE WILLIAM Constable-Maxwell; *d* 1819; *s* by his son (10) WILLIAM, who became 10th Lord by decision of House of Lords 1858 (the descendants of the 5th Earl of Nithsdale having been restored in blood by Act of Parliament 1848); *b* 1804: *m* 1835, Marcia, who *d* 1883, da of Hon Sir Edward Marmaduke Joseph Vavasour, 1st Bt, *d* 1876; *s* by his son (11) MARMADUKE FRANCIS, 11th Lord; *b* 1837; Lord-Lieut of Kirkcudbrightshire and of E Riding of York; *cr* Baron Herries, of Carlaverock Castle, co Dumfries (peerage of UK) 1884: *m* 1875, Hon Angela Mary Charlotte Fitzalan-Howard, who *d* 1919, da of 1st Baron Howard of Glossop; *d* 1908, when the UK Barony became ext and the Scottish Lordship devolved upon his el da (12) GWENDOLEN MARY, *b* 1904, 15th Duke of Norfolk, who *d* 1917; *d* 1945; *s* by her only son (13) BERNARD MARMADUKE, KG, GCVO, GBE, TD, PC, 13th Lord, who had *s* as 16th Duke of Norfolk 1917; see that title; *b* 1908, *d* 1975, *s* by his el da (14) ANNE ELIZABETH, present peeress.

HERSCHELL, BARON (Herschell) (Baron UK 1886)

ROGNVALD RICHARD FARRER HERSCHELL, 3rd Baron; *b* 13 Sept 1923; *s* 1929; a Page of Honour to HM 1935-40; was a Train Bearer at Coronation of King George VI; Capt Coldstream Guards, served 1942-47; has Coronation medal (1937): *m* 1948, Lady Heather Margaret Mary Legge, da of 8th Earl of Dartmouth, and has issue.

Arms – Per fesse azure and sable, in fesse a fasces proper between three stags' heads couped or. **Crest** – On a mount vert a stag proper, gorged with a collar gemel azure, and supporting with its dexter forefoot a fasces in bend or. **Supporters** – On either side a stag proper, collared azure, standing on a fasces or.
Residence – Westfield House, Ardington, Wantage, Oxon.

Quickly

DAUGHTER LIVING

Hon Arabella Jane, *b* 1955: *m* 1984, Brig John Panton Kiszely, late SG, son of Dr John Kiszely, of Whitefield, Totland Bay, IoW, and has issue living, Alastair, *b* 1986, — Mathew, *b* 1987, — Andrew, *b* 1990.

PREDECESSORS – **(1)** FARRER HERSCHELL, GCB, PC, son of late Rev Ridley Herschell; *b* 1837; Recorder of Carlisle 1873-80, Solicitor-Gen 1880-85, and Lord High Chancellor Feb to July 1886 and Aug 1892 to June 1895; MP for Durham (peerage of United Kingdom) 1886: *m* 1876, Agnes Adela, da of Edward Leigh Kindersley, of Clyffe, Dorset; *d* 1899; *s* by his only son **(2)** RICHARD FARRER, GCVO, 2nd Baron; *b* 1878; Private Sec to Lord-Lieut of Ireland (Earl of Aberdeen) Dec 1905 to Aug 1907, and a Lord-in-Waiting to King Edward VII 1907-10, and to King George V 1910-19, and 1924-29: *m* 1919, Annie Vera Violet, who *d* 1961, da of Sir Arthur Thomas Bennett Nicolson, 10th Bt; *d* 1929; *s* by his son **(3)** ROGNVALD RICHARD FARRER, 3rd Baron, and present peer.

HERTFORD, MARQUESS OF (Seymour) (Marquess GB 1793)
(Title pronounced "Harford" and name "Seamer")

HUGH EDWARD CONWAY SEYMOUR, 8th Marquess; *b* 29 March 1930; *s* 1940; *ed* Eton; Lieut (ret) Grenadier Guards, and patron of three livings: *m* 1956, Countess Pamela Louise de Caraman-Chimay, only da of late Lt-Col Prince Alphonse de Chimay, TD (*see* D Abercorn, colls, 1985 Edn), and has issue.

Arms – Quarterly: 1st and 4th sable, on a bend cotised argent, a rose gules between two annulets of the first, *Conway*; 2nd and 3rd quarterly, 1st and 4th or, a pile gules, charged with three lions of England between six fleurs-de-lis azure; 2nd and 3rd gules, two wings conjoined in lure or, *Seymour*. **Crest** – 1st, the bust of a Moor in profile couped at the shoulders proper and wreathed about the temples argent and azure, *Conway*; 2nd, out of a ducal coronet a demi-phœnix in flames, *Seymour*, **Supporters** – Two Blackamoors proper, wreathed about the temples or and sable, habited in a short garment or, adorned about their waists and shoulders with green and red feathers and buskins gold; each resting his exterior hand on an antique shield azure, adorned gold; that of the *dexter* supporter charged with the sun in splendour, and that of the *sinister* with a crescent.
Seat – Ragley Hall, Alcester, Warwickshire. *Clubs* – Turf, White's and Pratt's.

By faith and love

SON LIVING

HENRY JOCELYN (*Earl of Yarmouth*), *b* 6 July 1958: *m* 1990, Beatriz, da of Jorge Karam, of Copacabana, Rio de Janeiro, Brazil, and has

issue:—

SON LIVING — WILLIAM FRANCIS (*Baron Conway of Ragley*) *b* 2 Nov 1993.
DAUGHTER LIVING — *Lady* Gabriella Helen, *b* 1992.

DAUGHTERS LIVING

Lady Carolyn Mary, *b* 1960.
Lady Diana Helen, *b* 1963: *m* 1992, Timothy Verdon, son of late George Verdon, of Manor Farm Cottage, Minstead, Hants.
Lady Anne Katherine, *b* 1966.

COLLATERAL BRANCHES LIVING

Grandsons of late Com Lord George Frederick Seymour, RN (*infra*):—
Issue of late Squadron Leader Paul de Grey Horatio Seymour, RAF, *b* 1911, *ka* 1942: *m* 1937, Hilary (Town Mill, Marlborough, Wilts) (who *m* 2ndly, 1948, Ian Hamilton Barrett, who *d* 1985), da of late Douglas Crickmay, OBE:—

Andrew Conway Paul, *b* 1939; *ed* Stowe; Air Cdre RAF 1963-93: *m* 1964, June Ann, da of Frederick Gardner, and has issue living, Elizabeth Jane, *b* 1972.
  Issue of late Lieut-Col George Victor Seymour, MC, Roy Scots Fusiliers, *b* 1912, *d* 1953: *m* 1946, Mrs Hilda Elizabeth Kemp, who *d* 1986, da of late Harold Lionel Phillips (*see* Phillips, Bt, *cr* 1912):—
Nicholas George Mark (*posthumous*), *b* 1953: *m* 1978 (*m diss* 1981), Nicola Clare, da of Walter William Burgoyne Chalwin (*see* O'Brien, Bt). *Residence* – 15 Cargill Rd, SW18 3ED.

  Issue of late Com Lord George Frederick Seymour, RN, 4th son of 6th Marquess, *b* 1881, *d* 1940: *m* 1906, Norah, who *d* 1959, da of late Archibald Peyton Skipwith (Skipwith, Bt, colls):—
Edith Patricia Mary SEYMOUR (Coachmans Cottage, West Walks, Dorchester, Dorset DT1 1RE), *b* 1913; reverted to her maiden name by deed poll 1972: *m* 1933 (*m diss* 1972), Rev Emmanuel Casdagli, and has issue living, David Seymour Emmanuel (c/o Midland Bank, Cornhill, Dorchester), *b* 1934: *m* 1965, Christine Ethne, only da of late Brig H. H. Cottier, and has issue living, Carolyn David *b* 1975, — Mrs E. P. M. Seymour also has two adopted das, Susan Margaret, *b* 1946: *m* 1970, Michael Gilligan, of St Anthony's, Rousdon, Lyme Regis, Dorset, and has issue living, Liam Patrick *b* 1978, Dominic Francis *b* 1980, Arran Thomas *b* 1982, — Celia Jane (Coachmans Cottage, West Walks, Dorchester, Dorset DT1 1RE), *b* 1948: *m* 1970 (*m diss* 1977) John de Wageneer.

  Grandchildren of late Col Lord Albert Charles Seymour, 2nd son of 5th Marquess:—
  Issue of late Lieut-Col Charles Hugh Napier Seymour, DSO, *b* 1874, *d* 1933: *m* 1905, Mary Adelaide, who *d* 1977, da of William Morton Philips (E Courtown, colls):—
William Napier (Park House, Shaftesbury, Dorset), *b* 1914; *ed* Eton; Major (ret) Scots Guards; Palestine 1936, Burma 1941-42 (despatches), Palestine 1946, Malaya 1948: *m* 1945, Rachel Mary, da of late Capt Angus V. Hambro, of Milton Abbas, Dorset, and has issue living, Carolyn Sarah, *b* 1946: *m* 1967, Simon Thomas Cecil Hanbury, late Life Gds, of La Mortola, 18030 Ventimigia, Italy, and has issue living, Jonathan Cecil *b* 1977, Serena Mary *b* 1970, Melissa Jane *b* 1971, — Sarah Jane, *b* 1947: *m* 1974, Richard David O'Mahony Page, of Rathcon, co Wicklow, and has issue living, Dermot Michael *b* 1976, Patricia Hannah *b* 1978, Arabella Jennifer *b* 1980, — Arabella Mary, *b* 1952: *m* 1973, Christopher Julian Elwes, of The Old Rectory, Checkendon, Oxon, and has issue living, Rupert William *b* 1975, James Rex *b* 1983, Charlotte Vanda *b* (twin) 1983.

  Grandchildren of late Rev Lord Victor Alexander Seymour (infra):—
  Issue of late Major Conway Hugh Seymour, MC, *b* 1886, *d* 1931: *m* 1916, Kathleen Louisa, who *d* 1950, da of Lieut-Col Francis John Paul Butler, of Wyck Hill, Gloucestershire:—
Adrian John Conway, *b* 1918; *ed* Radley, and Ch Ch, Oxford (MA); Col (ret) Scots Guards; Lt-Col Comdg Scots Guards 1962-64; 1939-45 War (despatches): *m* 1953, Elizabeth Ann, da of Lieut-Gen Sir Edwin Otway Herbert, KBE, CB, DSO, and has had issue, Virginia Kathleen, *b* 1955: *m* 1983, Alexander Theodore Terence Rottenburg, of 14 Sugden Rd, SW11, and has issue living, William Alexander Seymour *b* 1986, Charlotte Elizabeth Virginia *b* 1988, — Angela Mary, *b* 1957; *d* 1979. *Residence* – Wantsley Farm, Broadwindsor, Dorset. —— Francis Hugh, *b* 1922; *ed* Radley: *m* 1951, Helen Elizabeth, who *d* 1986, da of Rev Canon David J. Cornish, of Port Dover, Ont, Canada, and has issue living, William Thomas (1923 Richardson Rd, Nanaimo, BC, Canada V9R 5K1), *b* 1955: *m* 1984, Cindy Linda Marie, da of Christian Murray, of Chicoutimi, Quebec, and has issue living, Gillian Nathalie Elizabeth *b* 1987, Hilary Roseline *b* 1990, — Margaret Louise, *b* 1953: *m* 1986, George William Boldick, of Surrey, BC, Canada. *Residence* – Crescent Road, Qualicum Beach, British Columbia.
  Issue of late Cdr William John Seymour, RN, *b* 1900, *d* 1967: *m* 1930, Wilma, who *d* 1987, da of late W. J. T. Clarke, of Wimmarleigh, Toorak, Vic, Aust:—
Conway William Hugh (43 Officers Parade, Condobolin, NSW 2877, Australia), *b* 1934: *m* 1959, Susan Evizel, da of R. R. McKay, of Coonabarabran, NSW, and has issue living, Conway Ronald Hugh, *b* 1962, — Kristin Susan, *b* 1960, — Jane Evizel, *b* 1965. —— Sarah Gardenia, *b* 1939.

  Issue of late Rev Lord Victor Alexander Seymour, 4th son of 5th Marquess *b* 1859, *d* 1935: *m* 1885, Elizabeth Margaret, who *d* 1958, da of late Albemarle Cator, of Woodbastwick Hall, Norwich:—
Anne Christian, *b* 1896: *m* 1st, 1920, Capt Cajetan Louis Victor Marno, who *d* 1930; 2ndly, 1934, Victor Frederick Engleheart, who *d* 1949, and has had issue (by 1st *m*), John Seymour (Scotts House, Hunton, Kent), *b* 1921; *ed* Felsted; formerly Capt Irish Gds: *m* 1943, Diana Helen, da of late Capt Henry Christian Dunell, RA, of Ryarsh Place, W Malling, Kent, and *d* 1988, leaving issue, Peter Cajetan Seymour *b* 1948; *ed* Lancing: *m* 1981, Felicity Jayne, da of Commodore T. R. Fisher, RAN (ret), of 46 Murdoch St, Cremorne, Sydney, NSW 2090, Australia (and has issue living, Edward Christian Seymour *b* 1983, Alice Jane Thorburn *b* 1986), Julia Mary Christian *b* 1945, — Edward Charles, *b* 1923; late Rifle Bde (invalided): *m* 1947 (*m diss* 1957), Joan Chrysogon, da of late Brig Edward William Drummond Vaughan, CB, DSO, MC, of White Knights, Newick, Sussex, and *d* 1988, leaving issue, Phyllida Jane *b* 1951: *m* 1981, Christopher William John Cornfield, of 55 Temple Sheen Rd, E Sheen, SW14 7QF, — William Victor (Ty Watty, Rhandirmwyn, Llandovery, Dyfed), *b* 1925; late Capt RA: *m* 1st, 1952 (*m diss* 1968), Cressida Doyle Jones; 2ndly, 1969 (*m diss* 1979), Hazel Dorothy Westley; 3rdly, 1983, Clare Linette Mordaunt, and has issue living (by 1st *m*), Nicholas Douglas *b* 1961, Madeleine Sarah *b* 1954, Denise Barbara *b* 1955, Alison Jane *b* 1958, (by 2nd *m*) Lowri *b* 1973. *Residence* – c/o The Mount, Bishops Down Rd, Tunbridge Wells, Kent.

  Grandchildren of Hugh Francis Seymour, MP, 2nd son of Adm Lord Hugh Seymour, 5th son of 1st Marquess:—
  Issue of late Sir Horace James Seymour, GCMG, CVO, *b* 1885, *d* 1978: *m* 1917, Violet Amy, da of Thomas Edward Erskine (*see* E Buchan, colls):—
Hugh Francis (Luccombe Mill, Bratton, Westbury, Wilts), *b* 1926: *m* 1954, Mary Elizabeth, da of T. H. Roberts, of Pucklechurch House, nr Bristol, and has issue living, (Hugh) James (92 Lupus St, SW1), *b* 1956: *m* 1986, Felicity Anne, who *d* 1993, da of P. H. Webber, of Jincox Farm, Oxted, Surrey, and has issue living, Hugo Frederick James *b* 1988, Rupert Alexander Erskine *b* 1992, Octavia Claire Camac *b* 1990, — Julian, *b* 1961, — Francis Benedict, *b* 1966, — Charlotte, *b* 1957, — Sarah Catherine, *b* 1962. —— Virginia (The Old Bakery, Kimpton, Andover, Hants), *b* 1919: *m* 1st, 1945, as his 2nd wife, Sir Ivo Herbert Evelyn Joseph Stourton, CMG, OBE, who *d* 1985, and has issue (*see* B Mowbray, colls); 2ndly, 1986, William Hilary Young, CMG. —— Joan (97 Forbes Rd, Orange, NSW, Australia), *b* 1920: *m* 1945, Flight-Lt Clive Gordon Thompson, DFC, RAAF, who *d* 1969, and has issue living, Anthony Seymour, *b* 1946, — Nicholas Austen, *b* 1948, — Jeremy, *b* 1950.

  Grandchildren of late Frederick Charles William Seymour, 5th son of late Adm Lord Hugh Seymour (ante):—
  Issue of late Horace Alfred Damer Seymour, CB, *b* 1843, *d* 1902 (having been nominated, but not invested, a KCB): *m* 1880, Elizabeth Mary (raised to the rank of a Knight's Widow 1902), who *d* 1950, da of late Col Frederick Romilly:—
Leopold Robert, *b* 1888; sometime in Depart of Pensions and National Health, Canada; 1914-18 War as Pte 31st Bn Canadian Force (wounded): *m* 1914, Mary Elizabeth, who *d* 1955: *m* 1994, Henrietta Margaret Cynthia, da of Gerald Arthur, da of late Thomas Frayer. *Residence* – 1716, 5A Street, SW, Calgary, Alberta, Canada. —— Margaret Lily Winifred, *b* 1891: *m* 1916, Maj Cecil Francis Aleck Walker, MC, Grenadier Guards, who *d* 1925.

  Grandchildren of late Lt-Col Leopold Richard Seymour, 2nd son of the Rt Hon Sir George Hamilton Seymour, GCB, GCH, el son of Lord George Seymour, MP, 7th son of 1st Marquess:—
  Issue of late Richard Sturgis Seymour, MVO, *b* 1875, *d* 1959: *m* 1911, Lady Victoria Alexandrina Mabel, who *d* 1969, da of late Rev Lord Charles Edward FitzRoy (D Grafton):—

Leopold (Leo) Richard, *b* 1912; late Capt Grenadier Guards; High Sheriff of Herts 1964: *m* 1940, Sheila, da of Lt-Col Charles Butler, and has issue living, Hugh Leopold (Home Farm, Stobo, Peebles), *b* 1943: *m* 1st, 1971 (*m diss* 1978), Emma Mary, da of Robert Alistair Henderson (*see* Lowther, Bt, *cr* 1824, colls); 2ndly, 1979, Camilla Madelaine Gerard, yr da of Col William Henry Gerard Leigh (*see* Leslie, Bt, *cr* 1625), and has issue living (by 2nd *m*), Molly Rose *b* 1983, — Charles Richard, *b* 1955: *m* 1994, Henrietta Margaret Cynthia, da of Gerald Arthur Hohler (*see* Stucley, Bt), — Anthea Rosemary (*Hon Mrs David E. H. Bigham*), *b* 1941: *m* 1965, Hon David Edward Hugh Bigham, of Hurston Place, Pulborough, W Sussex (*see* V Mersey). — Sarah Victoria Frances, *b* 1952: *m* 1979, William Jay Ducas, of 194 Village Av, Dedham, Mass, USA, son of late Robert Ducas, and Mrs Jean Weir Ducas, of Quaker Hill, Pawling, NY, and has issue living, Benjamin Colin *b* 1981, Patrick Leopold *b* 1983, William Alexander *b* 1988, — Lavinia Sheila, *b* 1954: *m* 1977, John Norman Gerard Leigh (*see* Leslie, Bt, *cr* 1625). *Residence* – 2 Pembroke Gdns, W8. *Club* – Brooks's. —— †George FitzRoy, *b* 1923; *ed* Winchester; Lord of the Manor of Thrumpton, a JP and DL of Notts (High Sheriff 1966), and patron of one living; 1939-45 War with KRRC (invalided): *m* 1946, Hon Rosemary Nest Scott-Ellis, da of 8th Baron Howard de Walden, and *d* 1994, leaving issue, Thomas Oliver, *b* 1952; *ed* Radley: *m* 1989, Sallie Ward, da of Henry P. Coolidge, of Lincoln, Mass, USA, and has issue living, Edward Alexander *b* 1992, Charlotte Emily *b* 1990, — Miranda (The Garden Flat, 53 Belsize Park Gardens, NW3), *b* 1948: *m* 1st, 1972 (*m diss* 1986), Andrew Annandale Sinclair; 2ndly, 1989, Anthony John Gottlieb, son of Felix Gottlieb, of London, and has issue living (by 1st *m*), Merlin George *b* 1973. *Residences* – Thrumpton Hall, Notts; 38 Molyneux St, W1. *Clubs* – White's, MCC. —— Alexandra Victoria, *b* 1914: *m* 1939, Capt Samuel Edmund Gurney, TD, who *d* 1990, of Heggatt Farm House, Horstead, Norfolk, son of late Sir Eustace Gurney, and has had issue, Timothy Samuel, *b* 1940; *ed* Radley, and Magdalene Coll, Camb; *k* in a motor accident 1962, — Richard Eustace Thomas (Heggatt Hall, Horstead, Norfolk), *b* 1943: *ed* Radley, and RAC Cirencester: *m* 1977, Margaret Elizabeth Diana, da of Stephen William Agnew (*see* Agnew, Bt, *cr* 1895), and has issue living, Henry Robert Timothy *b* 1980, Oliver Samuel *b* 1983, Isabel Margaret *b* 1979, Richenda Victoria Amelia *b* 1986, — Jane Mary Alexandra (White House Farm, Rackheath, Norfolk NR13 6LB), *b* 1948: *m* 1970, Simon Warren Macfarlane, son of late William Keith Macfarlane, of Lymington, Hants, and has issue living, Thomas Edward Hastings *b* 1972, Louisa Alexandra *b* 1974, Alice Victoria *b* 1979.

Grandsons of late Maj Sir Edward Seymour, KCVO, DSO, OBE, 3rd son of late Lt-Col Leopold Richard Seymour (ante):—
Issue of late Maj John Edward Seymour, *b* 1915, *d* 1972: *m* 1940, Elizabeth Norah (Edgedell Cottage, Martyr Worthy, Winchester), only child of late Adm Hon Sir Hubert George Brand, GCB, KCMG, KCVO (*see* V Hampden, colls):—
Conway John Edward, *b* 1941; Lt-Col Gren Gds, ret 1992: *m* 1st, 1969 (*m diss* 1980), Elizabeth, da of Maj Francis Holdsworth Hunt, late Coldm Gds (*see* B Forester, colls); 2ndly, 1981, Diana Elizabeth, da of late Michael Gibb, of Forge House, Taynton, Oxon, and formerly wife of Hon Trevor Garro Trefgarne (*see* Trefgarne, B), and has issue living (by 1st *m*), Harry Edward, *b* 1971, — Arabella Elizabeth, *b* 1974, — (by 2nd *m*), Emily Diana, *b* 1982. —— Richard Hubert (Dell House, Chilland Lane, Martyr Worthy, Winchester, Hants SO21 1EB), *b* 1947: *m* 1982, Amanda Claire, yr da of Ian McAuslan Hardie, of 15 and 16 Admirals Court, Hamble, Hants, and has issue living, James Richard Edward, *b* 1985, — Sarah Kathleen, *b* 1987.

Grandchildren of late Lt-Col Leopold Richard Seymour (ante):—
Issue of late Maj Beauchamp Seymour, *b* 1878, *d* 1965: *m* 1928, Eva Douglas, who *d* 1949, da of late Rev Herbert Brown, R of St Lawrence, Southminster, Essex:—
Julian Conway (Waterdale House, E Knoyle, Salisbury, Wilts), *b* 1934; *ed* Eton: *m* 1st, 1958, Alexandra, only da of Douglas MacLeod, of The Mill House, Stratton, Dorchester; 2ndly, 1971, Lavinia Margaret, el da of Sir William Lawrence, 4th Bt, and has issue living (by 1st *m*), Leopold Conway, *b* 1959; Lieut RN, — Mark Hamilton, *b* 1960; Lieut RN: *m* 1989, Louise C, eldest da of late W. T. Whittingham, — (by 2nd *m*) Harry William, *b* 1974, — Camilla Jane, *b* 1973. —— Jane Mary Naomi (16D Portland Rd, W11 4LA), *b* 1929: *m* 1954 (*m diss* 1976), Maj Desmond Eric Renforth Scarr, 14th/20th King's Hussars, and has issue living, Edward Desmond Renforth, *b* 1958, — Susan Renforth, *b* 1956, — Sarah Anne Renforth, *b* 1960. —— Anne Victoria (twin), *b* 1929: *m* 1951, Maj Henry Robert Mansel Porter, MBE, 60th Rifles, Palestine 1946-48 (MBE, despatches), High Sheriff Worcs 1970, of Brockham, Birlingham, Pershore, Worcs, and has issue living, Henry Christopher Mansel, *b* 1953; editor Illustrated London News 1987-89, — Michael Beauchamp Mansel, *b* 1954: *m* 1989, Elizabeth A. P., da of late Maj George Hadshar, KHS, of Woburn Sands, Beds.

Grandchildren of late Brig-Gen Archibald George Seymour, DSO, MVO, eldest son of late George Evelyn Seymour, 4th son of late Rt Hon George Hamilton Seymour, GCB, GCH (ante):—
Issue of late Lt-Col (Evelyn) Roger Seymour, OBE, TD, RA, *b* 1908, *d* 1987: *m* 1936, Rosemary Evelyn (Sakins, Roydon, Essex), da of late Maj Horace John Flower, DSO, MC, 60th Rifles:—
(Archibald) John (Bingham's Park, Water End, Hemel Hempstead, Herts), *b* 1937; *ed* Eton; served with 10th Hussars 1957-58: *m* 1961, (Lavinia Mary) Louise, 2nd da of Christopher York, DL, of South Park, Long Marston, York, and has issue living, Charlotte Louise, *b* 1963, — Susanna Clare, *b* 1966: *m* 1993, James E. Fletcher, yr son of G. E. Fletcher, of Stourton, Staffs, — Melinda Nell, *b* 1969. —— Julian Roger (37 Surrey Lane, SW11 3PA), *b* 1945; *ed* Eton: *m* 1984, Diana Daniels, and has issue living, Archie Christopher, *b* 1989, — Rose Elizabeth, *b* 1987.
Issue of late Maj Christopher George Seymour, *b* 1913, *d* 1983: *m* 1940, Honor (Pamplins, Bentley, Farnham, Surrey), da of late Capt Cecil Leatham, of Redbourn House, Wentworth:—
(Christopher) Mark, *b* 1942; *ed* Eton, and RNC Dartmouth: *m* 1968, Carol Daphne, yr da of Peter Pitman, of Muirfield Wood, Gullane, E Lothian, and has issue living, Thomas Mark Middleton, *b* 1972, — Peter Christopher James, *b* 1977, — Katherine Louise, *b* 1970. *Residence* – The Mill House, Fintry, Stirlingshire. —— Penelope Jane, *b* 1944: *m* 1st, 1966 (*m diss* 1974), (Robert Alexander) Neon Reynolds; 2ndly, 1979, Neil James Kennedy, and has issue living (by 1st *m*), Alexander Seymour, *b* 1969, — (by 2nd *m*) Patrick, *b* 1978, — Lisa, *b* 1979. *Residence* – 27 Fisher Rd, Bishops Itchington, Leamington Spa, Warwicks CV33 0RE.

Grandchildren of late George Evelyn Seymour, 4th son of late Rt Hon Sir George Hamilton Seymour, GCB, GCH (ante):—
Issue of late Lieut-Col Sir Reginald Henry Seymour, KCVO, *b* 1878; *d* 1938: *m* 1st, 1922, Winifred Boyd-Rochfort, who *d* 1925, da of late John Bathurst Akroyd; 2ndly, 1930, Lady Katharine Hamilton, DCVO, who *d* 1985, da of 3rd Duke of Abercorn:—
(By 1st *m*) George Raymond, CVO, *b* 1923; is Major King's Roy Rifle Corps; High Sheriff Berks 1989, DL 1992; appointed a Page of Honour to HM King George V 1935, an Extra Equerry to HM Queen Elizabeth the Queen Mother 1956, and an Equerry to HM Queen Elizabeth the Queen Mother since 1984; was a Train Bearer at Coronation of King George VI; Assist Private Sec and Equerry to HM Queen Elizabeth the Queen Mother since 1993; LVO 1972, CVO 1990: *m* 1957, Hon Mary Quenelda Ismay, da of 1st Baron Ismay, and widow of Robert Mervyn Fitz Finnis, and has issue living, Katharine Margaret Lucy (*Hon Mrs John Harbord-Hamond*), *b* 1959: *m* 1983, Hon John Edward Richard Harbord-Hamond, 2nd son of 11th Baron Suffield. *Residences* – The Old Vicarage, Bucklebury, Reading, Berks; Appletrees, Swains Rd, Bembridge, Isle of Wight. *Club* – Boodles. —— (By 2nd *m*) Henry Charles (The Dower House, West Wycombe, Bucks) *b* 1936; *ed* Eton; was a Page of Honour to HM King George VI 1949-52, and to HM Queen Elizabeth II 1952-53: *m* 1st, 1960 (*m diss* 1965), Yolande, da of Richard Murray, of Banhoek, Stellenbosch, S Africa; 2ndly, 1966, Alexandra Mary Hilda, da of Maj Sir Victor Basil John Seely, 4th Bt, and has had issue (by 2nd *m*), Conway Seely Reginald, *b* 1968, *d* 1980. —— Mary Virginia, *b* 1932.

PREDECESSORS – **(1)** *Rt Hon* FRANCIS Seymour, PC, 4th son of the Rt Hon Sir Edward Seymour, PC, 4th Bt (*cr* 1611) (*see* D Somerset); *b* 1697; at the death of his el brother, *s* to the estates of his cousin, Edward, 1st and last Earl of Conway; MP for Bramber 1701-02 and Gov of Carrickfergus 1728-32; assumed the additional surname of Conway; *cr Lord Conway, Baron Conway of Ragley*, co Warwick (peerage of England) 1703, and *Baron Conway of Killultagh*, co Antrim (peerage of Ireland) 1712: *m* 1st, 1703, Lady Mary Hyde, who *d* 1708, da of 1st Earl of Rochester; 2ndly, 1716, Charlotte, who *d* 1733, da of John Shorter of Bybrook, Kent; *d* 1732; *s* by his son **(2)** FRANCIS, KG, 2nd Baron, *b* 1718; was successively Lord-Lieut of co Warwick, Viceroy of Ireland, Master of the Horse, and Vice-Chamberlain of the Household; *cr Viscount Beauchamp* and *Earl of Hertford* (peerage of Great Britain) 1750, and *Earl of Yarmouth* and *Marquess of Hertford* (peerage of Great Britain) 1793: *m* 1741, Lady Isabella FitzRoy, who *d* 1782, yst da of 2nd Duke of Grafton; *d* 1794; *s* by his son **(3)** FRANCIS, KG, PC, 2nd Marquess; *b* 1743; was successively Lord Chamberlain of the Household, Lord-Lieut of co Warwick, and Gov of Antrim; assumed by Roy licence the additional surname of Ingram: *m* 1768, Hon Alice Elizabeth Windsor, who *d* 1772, da of 2nd Viscount Windsor; 2ndly, 1776, Hon Isabella Anne Ingram Shepherd, who *d* 1836, da of 9th Viscount Irvine; *d* 1822; *s* by his son **(4)** FRANCIS CHARLES, KG, PC, 3rd Marquess; *b* 1777; Warden of the Stannaries and Ch Steward and Vice-Adm of the Duchy of Cornwall: *m* 1798, Maria Emily Fagniani, who *d* 1856; *d* 1842; *s* by his son **(5)** RICHARD, KG, 4th Marquess; *b* 1800; *d* 1870; MP for co Antrim (*C*) 1822-6; *s* by his cousin **(C)** FRANCIS HUGH GEORGE, GCB, GCH (son of late Adm of the Fleet Sir George Francis Seymour, GCB, GCH, el son of Adm Lord Hugh Seymour, 5th son of 1st Marquess), 5th Marquess; *b* 1812; was a Gen in the Army, and Lord Chamberlain of the Household 1874-9: *m* 1839, Lady Emily Murray, who *d* 1902, da of 3rd Earl of Mansfield; *d* 1884; *s* by his el son **(7)** HUGH DE GREY, CB, PC, 6th Marquess; *b* 1843; Lord-Lieut of Warwickshire; Comptroller of Queen Victoria's Household 1879-80: *m* 1868, Hon Mary Hood, who *d* 1909, da of 1st Viscount Bridport; *d* 1912; *s* by his el son **(8)** GEORGE FRANCIS ALEXANDER, 7th Marquess; *b* 1871: *m* 1903 (*m diss* 1908), Alice Cornelia, da of late William Thaw, of Pittsburg, USA; *d* 1940; *s* by his nephew **(9)** HUGH EDWARD CONWAY (son of late Brig-Gen Lord Henry Charles Seymour, DSO, 2nd son of 6th Marquess), 8th Marquess and present peer; also Earl of Hertford, Earl of Yarmouth, Viscount Beauchamp, Lord Conway, Baron Conway of Ragley, and Baron Conway of Killultagh.

HESKETH, BARON (Fermor-Hesketh) (Baron UK 1935, Bt GB 1761)

Now and always

THOMAS ALEXANDER FERMOR-HESKETH, 3rd Baron, and 10th Baronet; *b* 28 Oct 1950; *s* 1955; *ed* Ampleforth; Lord in Waiting 1986-89, Under Sec at DoE 1989-90, Min of State Dept of Trade and Industry 1990-92, since when Capt, Gentlemen at Arms (Chief Whip): *m* 1977, Hon Claire Georgina Watson, el da of 3rd Baron Manton, and has issue.

Arms – 1st and 4th, argent, on a bend sable three garbs or, *Hesketh*; 2nd and 3rd, argent, a fesse sable between three lions' heads erased gules, *Fermor*. **Crests** – A garb or banded azure; 2nd, out of a ducal coronet or, a cock's head gules, combed and wattled or. **Supporters** – On either side a griffin or, gorged with a collar gules, thereon a fleur-de-lis gold, and charged on the shoulders with a rose also gules barbed and seeded proper.
Seat – Easton Neston, Towcester, Northants.

SON LIVING

Hon FREDERICK HATTON, *b* 13 Oct 1988.

DAUGHTERS LIVING

Hon Flora Mary, *b* 1981.

Hon Sophia Christian, *b* 1984.

BROTHERS LIVING

Hon Robert, *b* 1951; *ed* Ampleforth: *m* 1979, Jeanne, da of Patrick McDowell, of co Clare, and has issue living, Blaise Isambard Robert, *b* 1987.
Hon John, *b* 1953; *ed* Ampleforth: *m* 1st, 1980, Anna, only da of Hamish Wallace, of Old Corrimony, Glen Urquhart, Inverness; 2ndly, 1986, Helena Marian, only da of Robert Hunt, of Petropolis, Brazil, and has issue living (by 2nd *m*), Alice Mary Louisa, *b* 1987. *Residence* – 53 Old Church St, SW3 5BS.

AUNT LIVING (*Daughter of 1st Baron*)

Hon Louise (*Hon Lady Stockdale*), *b* 1911: *m* 1937, Sir Edmund Villiers Minshull Stockdale, 1st Bt. *Residence* – Hoddington House, Upton Grey, Basingstoke.

WIDOW LIVING OF SECOND BARON

CHRISTIAN MARY (*Dowager Baroness Hesketh*), OBE, only da of Sir John Helias Finnie McEwen, 1st Bt, DL, JP; Hon LLD Leicester Univ 1982; DL Northants; High Sheriff 1981; OBE 1984: *m* 1949, the 2nd Baron, who *d* 1955. *Residences* – Pomfret Lodge, Towcester, Northants; 20a Tregunter Rd, SW10.

PREDECESSORS – **(1)** THOMAS Hesketh, el surviving son of late Thomas Hesketh, of Rufford, Lancashire, whose family had been settled in Lancashire since the 13th century (a Robert Hesketh being knighted by Henry VIII, and a Thomas by Queen Elizabeth I); *cr* a *Baronet* 1761, with special remainder, failing heirs male of his body, to his brother, Robert: *m* Harriett, who *d* 1807, da of Ashley Cowper; *d* 1778; *s* (under special remainder) by his brother **(2)** ROBERT, 2nd Bt; *b* 1729; obtained permission 1792, to assume the surname and arms of his maternal great-grandfather, Sir William Juxon, Bt: *m* 1748, Sarah, who *d* 1792, da of late William Plumbe, of Wavertree, Lancashire; *d* 1796; *s* by his grandson **(3)** THOMAS DALRYMPLE, 3rd Bt; *b* 1777: *m* 1798, Sophia, who *d* 1817, da of late Rev Nathaniel Hinde; *d* 1842; *s* by his el son **(4)** THOMAS HENRY, 4th Bt; *b* 1799: *m* 1824, Annette Maria, who *d* 1879, el da of Robert Bomford, of Rabinstown House, Meath; *d* 1843; *s* by his son **(5)** THOMAS GEORGE, 5th Bt; *b* 1825; MP for Preston (*C*); assumed by Roy licence 1867 for himself, and his 2nd son (later 7th Bt) the surname of Fermor before Hesketh and the arms of Fermor and Hesketh quarterly: *m* 1846, Lady Anna Maria Arabella Fermor, who inherited Easton Neston and who *d* 1870, sister and heiress of George 5th and last Earl of Pomfret (ext); *d* 1872; *s* by his el son **(6)** THOMAS HENRY, 6th Bt; *b* 1847; *d* 1876; *s* by his brother **(7)** THOMAS GEORGE, 7th

Bt; *b* 1849: *m* 1880, Florence Emily, who *d* 1924, da of William Sharon; *d* 1924; *s* by his only surviving son **(8)** Thomas, 8th Bt; *b* 1881; MP for Enfield Div of Middlesex (C) 1922-23; *cr Baron Hesketh*, of Hesketh, co Palatine of Lancaster (peerage of United Kingdom) 1935: *m* 1909, Florence Louise, who *d* 1956, da of late John Witherspoon Breckinridge, of San Francisco, USA; *d* 1944; *s* by his el surviving son **(9)** Frederick, 2nd Baron; *b* 1916; Major Scots Guards and DL Northants: *m* 1949, Christian Mary, OBE, only da of Sir John Helias Finnie McEwen, 1st Bt, DL, JP, LLD; *d* 1955; *s* by his el son **(10)** Thomas Alexander, 3rd Baron and present peer.

HEWLETT, BARONY OF (Hewlett) (Extinct 1979)

SONS LIVING OF LIFE BARON

Hon (Thomas) Anthony, *b* 1952; *ed* Oundle, and Magdalene Coll, Camb (MA); Proprietor Portland Gallery since 1985: *m* 1980, Jane Elizabeth, da of Brian A. Dawson, of Aldeburgh, Suffolk, and has issue living, Harry, *b* 1986, — Charles, *b* (twin) 1986, — Emily, *b* 1983, — Georgina, *b* 1984. *Residence* – Kyson House, Woodbridge, Suffolk.
Hon (John) Richard, *b* 1955; *ed* Oundle, and Bath Acad of Art: *m* 1982, Rachel, younger da of late Peter Kay, of Weston-super-Mare, Avon, and has issue living, George Clyde William, *b* 1985, — Polly Elizabeth, *b* 1983. *Residence* – 21 Galveston Rd, SW15.

HEYCOCK, BARONY OF (Heycock) (Extinct 1990)

SON LIVING OF LIFE BARON

Hon Clayton Rees (6 Tanygroes Place, Taibach, Port Talbot, W Glam); *b* 1941; *ed* Univ of Wales (MSc), and Leicester Univ (MA); Sec Welsh Joint Education Cttee: *m* 1964, Lynda Williams, and has issue living, Alyson Sian, *b* 1970, — Rebecca Louise, *b* 1973.

HEYTESBURY, BARON (Holmes à Court) (Baron UK 1828, Bt GB 1795)

GRANDESCUNT · AUCTA · LABORE

Increased by labour, they grow large

Francis William Holmes A Court, 6th Baron, and 7th Baronet; *b* 8 Nov 1931; *s* 1971; *ed* Bryanston, and Pembroke Coll, Camb (BA): *m* 1962, Alison J., el da of Michael Graham Balfour, CBE, of 5B, Prince Arthur Rd, NW3, and has issue.

Arms – Quarterly: 1st and 4th, barry wavy of six, or and azure; on a canton gules, a lion of England, *Holmes*; 2nd and 3rd per fesse or and paly of six erminois and azure, in chief an eagle displayed sable, beaked and membered gules, charged on the body with two chevronels argent, *à Court*. Crests – 1st, out of a naval crown or, an arm embowed in armour, the hand proper, grasping a trident azure, headed or; 2nd, an eagle displayed sable, charged on the body with two chevronels or, and holding in the beak a lily slipped proper. Supporters – Two eagles, wings elevated and displayed sable, beaked and membered gules, each holding in the beak a lily slipped proper.
Residence – Manor House, Tarrant Keyneston, Dorset.

SON LIVING

Hon James William, *b* 30 July 1967.

DAUGHTER LIVING

Hon Sarah Camilla, *b* 1965: *m* 1989, James T. C. Dobell, twin son of Mrs Jenny Dobell, of London EC2, and has issue living, Edward, *b* 1993. *Residence* – 73 Montagu Mansions, W1H 1LG.

COLLATERAL BRANCHES LIVING

Grandchildren of late Peter Worsley Holmes à Court, yr son of late Hon Henry Worsley Holmes à Court, brother of 3rd and 4th Barons:—
Issue of late (Michael) Robert (Hamilton) Holmes à Court, *b* 1937, *d* 1990: *m* 1966, Janet Lee, BSc (22 The Esplanade, Peppermint Grove 6011, W Australia; Heytesbury Stud, Keysbrook 6206, W Australia), da of late F. H. Ranford of Perth, W Australia:—
Peter Michael Hamilton, *b* 1968; *ed* Middlebury Coll, Vermont, USA (BA), and — Coll, Oxford (MA). —— Simon Antony, *b* 1972. —— Paul William, *b* 1973. —— Catherine Elizabeth, *b* 1969; *ed* Univ of W Australia (BA).

Grandchildren of late Hon Charles George Holmes a Court, 4th son of 2nd Baron:—
Issue of late Capt Reginald Ashe Holmes à Court, MC, *b* 1879, *d* 1973: *m* 1911, Gwladys Mary Eyre, who *d* 1971, da of Henry Ralfe, Bar-at-law, of Tasmania:—

Ruth Vaughan Ashe (Colts Close, E Burton, Wool, Wareham, Dorset), *b* 1915; 1939-45 War as Jr Cdr ATS: *m* 1944, Maj-Gen George Peregrine Walsh, CB, CBE, DSO, who *d* 1972, and has issue living, David Peregrine (Claypits Farm, Winfrith New-burgh, Dorchester, Dorset), *b* 1949; *ed* Sherborne, and Fitzwilliam Coll, Camb (MA); commn'd 1st The Queen's Dragoon Gds 1968: *m* 1980, Harriet Glen, of Sydney, NSW, — Jonathan à Court Peregrine, *b* 1950; *ed* Sherborne; commn'd 16th/5th Queen's Royal Lancers 1972: *m* 1977, Diana Susan, da of late William Ernest Jones, and has issue living, Charles Peregrine *b* 1980, Thomas William Peregrine *b* 1983, Rebecca Jane à Court *b* 1979, — Anne à Court Peregrine, *b* 1952: *m* 1976, Maj T. A. Colquhoun, of Higher Norris Mill, Bockhampton, Dorchester, Dorset, and has issue living, Alastair George *b* 1979, Emma Louise *b* 1980.

Issue of late Lieut-Col Alan Worsley Holmes à Court, MD, *b* 1887, *d* 1957, *d* 1957: *m* 1913, Eileen who *d* 1971, da of Arthur Rouse, of Sydney, NS Wales:—
Peter (5 Wolsely Rd, Mosman 2088, NSW, Aust), *b* 1925; *ed* Sydney Univ (BEng); late RAAF: *m* 1950, Margaret Browne, da of Col Eric Campbell, DSO, of Billaboola, Young, NSW, and has issue living, Alan William, *b* 1953; *ed* Sydney Univ (BEng): *m* 1977, Jane Purnell, of Sydney, NSW, and has issue living, Nicholas William *b* 1981, Timothy Charles *b* 1983, — Campbell Worsley, *b* 1958, — Penelope, *b* 1951: *m* 1977, E. A. Notter, and has issue living, Stephanie Juliet *b* 1980, Harriet Andrea *b* 1982, — Juliet Helen, *b* 1955. —— Pamela, *b* 1921: *m* 1945, Mark Russell Glasson, RAAF, and has issue living, David Alan Russell, *b* 1949: *m* 1976, Jane Barton Heap, and has issue living, Jonathan Russell *b* 1979, Sarah Russell *b* 1977, — Anne Russell, *b* 1946: *m* 1968, William Howard Pendrill Charles, of Rockybah, Nimmitabel, NSW, and has issue living, Andrew Mark Pendrill *b* 1973, Sally Pendrill *b* 1971, — Jillian Russell, *b* 1951: *m* 1980, Adam Richard Granger Johnson, Barrister-at-law, of 129 Queen St, Woollahra, NSW, and has issue living, William Mark Granger *b* 1987. *Residence* – Jimenbuan, Dalgety, NSW.

Grandchildren of late Capt William Alexander Russell Holmes à Court (infra):—
Issue of late William Charles Holmes à Court, *b* 1918, *d* 1967: *m* 1st, 1943 (*m diss* 1946), Joan Patricia, only da of J. Lindsay Ellis, of Sutton, Surrey; 2ndly, 1946, Elisabeth Anne (7 920 Croydon Av, Winnipeg, Canada R3M 0Y5), yr da of Eric Tayleur, of Winnipeg, Canada:—
(By 2nd *m*) William Walter (532 Avenue F South, Saskatoon, Canada SFM 1T7), *b* 1948: *m* 1975 (*m diss* 1981), Catherine Anne Bannister. —— Phillip John (Box III, Caronport, Sask, Canada 50H 050), *b* 1960: *m* 1988, Deborah Anne Haachman. —— Eric Robert, *b* 1963, *d* 1985. —— Margaret Anne, *b* 1951: *m* 1973, Ronald Chevrefils, of Box 571, Pine Falls, Manitoba, Canada, and has issue living, Lawrence, *b* 1980, — Kevin, *b* 1983. —— Deborah Mary, *b* 1953: *m* 1976, Francis Richard Nogier, of 134 Forester Rd, Saskatoon, Sask, and has issue living, William Charles Heathcote, *b* 1973, — Margaret Elisabeth, *b* 1978, — Stacy Annette, *b* 1979, — Melissa Lee Anne, *b* 1982. —— Barbara Jane, *b* 1955: *m* 1980, A. Ross Russell, of 4605 Moreuilwood Dr SW, Calgary, Alberta, Canada TST 5NI, and has issue living, Christopher, *b* 1982, — Nicholas, *b* 1984.

Grandchildren of late Hon Arthur Wyndham Holmes à Court, 6th son of 2nd Baron:—
Issue of late Capt William Alexander Russell Holmes à Court, Canadian Mil, *b* 1878, *d* 1942: *m* 1916, Priscilla (who *d* 1955, having *m* 2ndly, 1954, Reginald Victor Miles), da of Charles Grey, of Bosham, Sussex:—
Priscilla Anne, *b* 1917: *m* 1948, Herbert Samuel McCloy, and has issue living, Samuel Boyd (RR1, Prince Albert, Saskatchewan, Canada), *b* 1952: *m* 1976, Elaine Joyce, da of Raymond Smith, of Holbein, Saskatchewan, and has issue living, Jaret Kyle *b* 1983, — Russell Alexander (672 Sylvan Rd, Prince Albert, Saskatchewan, Canada S6V 7R7), *b* 1954: *m* 1st, 1973 (*m diss* 1980), Elaine June, da of Albert Aalbers, of Prince Albert, Saskatchewan; 2ndly, 1987, Janet Muriel Crosland-Shane Alexander, and has issue living (by 1st *m*), Jason Albert *b* 1974, (by 2nd *m*) Bethany Jane *b* 1990, — James Andrew, *b* 1959: *m* 1978, Sherri Dawn, da of Peter Dyck, of Prince Albert, Saskatchewan, and has issue living, Benjamin John *b* 1978, Ryan James *b* 1981, Kristin Dawn *b* (twin) 1981, — Constance Gail, *b* 1961: *m* 1980, Kent Mark Walters, of Box 434, Prince Albert, Saskatchewan, Canada, and has issue living, Matthew Adam *b* 1983, Brock Carl *b* 1987, Amy Monelle *b* 1989. *Address* – RR 1, Prince Albert, Saskatchewan, Canada S6V 5P8.

Issue of late Thomas Edward Holmes à Court, *b* 1879, *d* 1943: *m* 1918, Violet Constance, da of Templeton Black-well, of Poona, India:—
Constance Ann Berkeley, *b* 1924.

Grandchildren of Leonard William Daly Holmes à Court, MBE, 4th and yst son of late Hon Arthur Wyndham Holmes à Court (ante):—
Issue of late Robert Douglas Hardtman Holmes à Court, *b* 1913, *d* 1983: *m* 1941, Sheila Gwendolyn (101 Montana Vista, Aliwal Rd, Kenilworth 7700, S Africa), da of Hugo Hauffman Gibbon, of Trinidad:—
Robert Leonard (104 Forest Lodge, Main Rd, Rondebosch 7700, S Africa), *b* 1946; *ed* Haileybury, and Univ of Cape Town (MSc Elec Eng). —— Sheila Lou, *b* 1942: *m* 1964, Nigel Gordon Armstrong, of The Bungalow, Ellwood Green, Ellwood, nr Coleford, Glos GL16 7NB.

PREDECESSORS – (1) WILLIAM PIERCE ASHE à COURT, MP for Heytesbury 1781-1806, and Col in the Army; *cr a Baronet* 1795; *d* 1817; *s* by his son (2) *Sir* WILLIAM, GCB, PC, 2nd Bt; *b* 1779; MP for Dorchester 1812-14; *cr Baron Heytesbury*, of Heytesbury, co White (peerage of United Kingdom) 1828; was Ambassador to St Petersburg 1828-32, and Viceroy of Ireland 1844-6: *m* 1808, Maria Rebecca, da of Hon William Henry Bouverie (E Radnor), *d* 1860; *s* by his son (3) WILLIAM HENRY ASHE, 2nd Baron, *b* 1809; MP for Isle of Wight (C) 1837-47; assumed the additional surname of Holmes on his marriage, 1833, with Elizabeth, who *d* 1874, da of late Sir Leonard Worsley Holmes, Bt; *d* 1891; *s* by his grandson (4) WILLIAM FREDERICK (son of late Hon William Leonard Holmes à Court Beadon), *b* 1862: *m* 1887, Margaret Anna, who *d* 1920, da of late J. N. Harman, of Tadmarton, Oxford; *d* 1903; *s* by his brother (5) LEONARD, 4th Baron, *b* 1863; Major (ret) Wiltshire Regt, and Col late Special Reserve: *m* 1896, Sybil Mary, who *d* 1937, da of late Capt Frank B. Morris, Bengal Army; *d* 1949; *s* by his son (6) WILLIAM LEONARD FRANK, 5th Baron, *b* 1906: *m* 1926, Beryl, who *d* 1968, yst da of Albert Edward Bredin Crawford, DCL, LLD, of Aston Clinton House, Bucks; *d* 1971; *s* by his son (7) FRANCIS WILLIAM, 6th Baron and present peer.

HILL, VISCOUNT (Clegg-Hill) (Viscount UK 1842, Bt GB 1727)

ANTONY ROWLAND CLEGG-HILL, 8th Viscount, and 10th Baronet; *b* 19
March 1931; *s* 1974; *ed* Kelly Coll and RMA; late Capt RA; has free-
dom of Shrewsbury: *m* 1st, 1963; (*m diss* 1976), Juanita Phyllis, da of
John W Pertwee, of White Gates, Cross Oak Lane, Salfords, Surrey;
2ndly, 1989, Elizabeth Harriett, da of Ronald Offer, of Salisbury,
Wilts.

Arms – Quarterly: 1st and 4th, ermine, a fesse sable, charged with a castle,
triple towered argent, *Hill*; 2nd and 3rd, per pale sable and azure a cross-
crosslet crossed between two acorns in bend dexter, and as many fleurs-de-lys
in bend sinister argent, *Clegg*. **Crest** – 1st, a tower argent, issuant from the
battlements a wreath of laurel, all proper, *Hill*; 2nd, in front of two branches of
oak in saltire, fructed proper, a cross-crosslet crossed or, *Clegg*. **Supporters** –
Dexter, a lion argent, murally crowned or and gorged with a wreath of oak
fructed proper: *sinister*, a horse argent, bridled and saddled, and gorged with a
mural crown gules.
Address – c/o House of Lords, SW1.

Forward

WIDOW LIVING OF SON OF SIXTH VISCOUNT

Alice Dorothy, da of late Rear-Adm Cuthbert Godfrey Chapman, MVO (B New-
borough): *m* 1938, Major Hon Frederick Raymond Clegg-Hill, King's Shropshire
LI, who was *ka* in Germany 1945, and has issue living (see colls, infra).
Residence – The Old Forge, Stone in Oxney, nr Tenterden, Kent.

WIDOW LIVING OF SEVENTH VISCOUNT

CATHERINE MARY (MOLLY) (*Molly, Viscountess Hill*), da of Dr Rowland Venables Lloyd-Williams of Malford, Denbigh: *m* 1942,
as his 2nd wife, the 7th Viscount, who *d* 1974.

COLLATERAL BRANCHES LIVING

Issue of late Major Hon Frederick Raymond Clegg-Hill, King's Shropshire LI, 2nd son of 6th Viscount, *b*
1909, *ka* in Germany 1945: *m* 1938, Alice Dorothy (ante), da of late Rear-Adm Cuthbert Godfrey Chapman,
MVO (B Newborough):—
PETER DAVID RAYMOND CHARLES, *b* 17 Oct 1945 (*posthumous*): *m* 1973, Sharon Ruth Deane, of Kaikohe, NZ, and has issue
living, Paul Andrew Raymond, *b* 4 May 1979, — Michael Charles David, *b* 1988, — Catherine Anne, *b* 1974, — Jennifer
Louise, *b* 1976, — Susan Dorothy, *b* 1980, — Rachel Emma, *b* 1984, — Melissa Jane, *b* 1986.

Issue of late Capt Hon Gerald Spencer Clegg-Hill, JP, 5th son of 3rd Viscount, *b* 1879, *d* 1930: *m* 1907,
Dorothy, who *d* 1978, da of Rev Sir George Boughey, 5th Bt:—
Anne Selina Elizabeth (Aqualate Hall, Newport, Shropshire), *b* 1915: *m* 1st, 1940 (*m diss* 1947), Edward Hanbury Carington
David Lloyd-Davies; 2ndly, 1947, Janusz Maria Stanislaw Eugeniusz Juhre, late 2nd Lt Polish Army, of Lwow, Poland, and
has issue living (by 2nd *m*), Tadeusz Maria Gerald Alexander (Aqualate Hall, Newport, Shropshire), *b* 1951, — Maria
Jadwiga Teresa, *b* 1948: *m* 1973, Andrew Maryniák, of 181 Pitshanger Lane, W5, and has issue living, Richard *b* 1977, Martin
b 1980, Stefan *b* 1982, Joanna *b* 1974, — Jadwiga Maria Teresa Celina, *b* 1949: *m* 1972, Richard Saller, of 92 Grove Av, W7,
and has issue living, Michael *b* 1976, Jan Fryderyk *b* 1983, Teresa *b* 1974, Monika *b* 1990, — Anna
Zofia Maria (18 Parkcroft Rd, Westbridgeford, Nottingham), *b* 1954: *m* 1974 (*m diss* 1991), Dr George Behnke, and has issue
living, Wojciech *b* 1983, Margaret *b* 1980, Katheryn *b* 1981. *Residence* – Aqualate Hall, Newport, Salop.

(In remainder to Barony and Baronetcy)

Grandchildren of late John Hill, son of late Rev John Hill (infra):—
Issue of late John Kenyon Hill, *b* 1869, *d* 1945: *m* 1906, Mary Ruby, da of Frank Watkins, of Parklands, Nairobi,
Kenya:—
Mary Sybil (Box 269 Graskop 1270, E Transvaal, S Africa), *b* 1909: *m* 1935 (*m diss* 1947), Sq-Ldr Colin Alexander
MacKenzie, RAFVR, and has issue living, Ewen Rowland Francis (PO Box 269, Graskop 1270, E Transvaal, S Africa), *b* 1936.
—— Muriel Rachel, *b* 1911: *m* 1934, John Wilson Lichfield Harris, of Tantoni, PO Box 63, Kilifi, Kenya, and has issue living,
Charles John, *b* 1935, — David Lichfield, *b* 1942, — Mary Victoria, *b* 1940.
Issue of late Frederick Rowland Hill, *b* 1870, *d* 1947: *m* 1910, Theodora Ann, who *d* 1961, da of late Rev R. H.
Quick:—
Rev Preb Richard Hebert, *b* 1911; *ed* Wrekin Coll; Preb Emeritus of Hereford Cathedral, and a Freeman of Shrewsbury;
1939-45 War: *m* 1945, Suzanne, da of late Dr Horace Gooch, of Ragleth House, Church Stretton, and has issue living,
Frederick Peter Gooch (Springbank, Well Lane, Little Witley, Worcester WR6 6LN), *b* 1946; *ed* Worksop Coll, and Grey Coll,
Durham; admitted a sol 1972; Freeman of Shrewsbury: *m* 1975, Diana Mary, da of Richard Ekin, and has issue living,
Matthew Anthony *b* 1982, Mary Elizabeth *b* 1976, — Richard Stephen (The Old Vicarage, Cockshutt, Ellesmere, Shropshire
SY12 0JQ), *b* 1949; *ed* Worksop Coll, and Sheffield Poly (BSc); FRICS; Freeman of Shrewsbury: *m* 1976, Susan, da of Ronald
Wren, of NZ, and has issue living, Nicholas Anthony Owen *b* 1979, Jeremy David Rhydian *b* 1981. *Residence* – 4 Old School,
Henley Rd, Ludlow, Shropshire SY8 1RA.

Grandsons of late Frederick Rowland Hill (ante):—
Issue of late Rev Canon Rowland Edward Hill, *b* 1913; *d* 1981: *m* 1939, Elizabeth, who *d* 1981, da of late Roland
Maddison Vaisey, of Tring, Herts:—
David Rowland (9 Mansion House Rd, Edinburgh EH9 1TZ), *b* 1940; *ed* Glenalmond, and Keble Coll, Oxford (MA), Dip Ed,
BA, MSc, Inst for Applied Language Studies, Edinburgh Univ; Freeman of Shrewsbury: *m* 1st, 1969 (*m diss* 1984), Sonya, da
of Stuart McClusky; 2ndly, 1984, Janet Elizabeth, da of Harold John Powell, and has issue living (by 1st *m*), Charlotte Ruth,
b 1973, — (by 2nd *m*) a son, *b* 19—, — Katharine Martha, *b* 1987. —— Nigel John (32 Colebrooke Av, Ealing W13 8JY), *b*
1943; *ed* Trin Coll, Glenalmond, and Univ Coll, Durham (BA); Inspector Met Police; Freeman of Shrewsbury: *m* 1968, Gillian
Mary, yr da of late Ian Heath Stock, MC, and has issue living, Oliver Rowland Vaisey *b* 1972, — Clarissa Mary, *b* 1969, —
Rosanna Seymour, *b* 1978. —— James Geoffrey (The Priory, 11 Friars Lane, Lanark ML11 9EL), *b* 1948; *ed* Trin Coll,
Glenalmond, Univ Coll, Durham (BA), and Birmingham Univ (MB, ChB); Freeman of Shrewsbury: *m* 1974, Eileen Frances
Rachel, da of late Charles Rodney Webster, WS, of Edinburgh, and has issue living, Katriona Helen *b* 1976, — Anna
Elizabeth *b* 1979, — Sara Frances, *b* 1983, — Nicola Margaret, *b* 1985. —— Andrew Vaisey (17 Cockle Crescent, Clovelly,
Cape Province, S Africa), *b* 1950; *ed* Shrewsbury, and Univ Coll, Durham (BA), Freeman of Shrewsbury: *m* 1st, 1974 (*m diss*

19—), Zaria Caroline Annabel, da of late Maj Joseph Theodore Knowles, Wilts Regt; 2ndly, 19—, —, and has issue living (by 1st *m*), Jonathan Rowland Vaisey, *b* 1980, — Rowena Jane Imogen, *b* 1977.

Grandchildren of late Rev John Hill, son of late Col John Hill, father of 2nd Viscount:—
Issue (by 2nd *m*) of late Sir Clement Lloyd Hill, KCB, KCMG, MP, *b* 1845, *d* 1913: *m* 1st, 1889, Charlotte Eliza Mary Jane, who *d* 1900, da of Sir George William Denys, 2nd Bt, and widow of Charles Waring; 2ndly, 1906, Muriel Mary, who *d* 1958, da of late Colin Glencairn Campbell, of 34, Lower Belgrave Street, SW (Macnaghten, Bt):—
Clement Walter Rowland (Croft House, Great Dunmow, Essex CM6 1HR), *b* 1909; *ed* Eton; Freeman of Shrewsbury; Major Queen's Own Cameron Highlanders; 1939-45 War (wounded): *m* 1st, 1935, (*m diss* 1941), Violet, who *d* 1988, el da of Charles Phillimore, of The Old Farm, Swinbrook, Oxford; 2ndly, 1947, Elizabeth Theresa, who *d* 1970, da of late Capt J. J. J. de Knoop, and formerly wife of late John Henry Hambro, CMG; 3rdly, 1971, Kathleen, who *d* 1982, da of Frank Dickie, of Truro, Nova Scotia, and widow of Norman Walduck, and has issue living (by 1st *m*), Carolyn Mary (*Carolyn, Countess Fortescue*), *b* 1937: *m* 1st, 1968 (*m diss* 1983), Edward Lockwood; 2ndly, 1989, as his 3rd wife, 7th Earl Fortescue, who *d* 1993, and has issue living (by 1st *m*), Richard Rowland *b* 1971, Louisa Elizabeth *b* 1969, — Joanna Clementine, *b* 1939: *m* 1965, Charles C. Bastin, of Rutland Lodge, 83 Albert Bridge Rd, SW11 4PH, and Larroque, 47370 Tournon d'Agenais, France, and has issue living, Alexander Charles *b* 1969, Nicholas Rowland *b* 1970.

Grandchildren of late Henry Alan Hill, eldest son of Henry Philip Hill, yr son of Lt-Col Richard Frederick Hill, 3rd son of Col John Hill (ante):—
Issue of late Henry James Hill, *b* 1921, *d* 1985: *m* 1953, Ina Philpott, of El Refugio, 2852 E Carbo, Entre Rios, Argentina:—
Henry John (El Refugio, 2852 E Carbo, Entre Rios, Argentina), *b* 1962. —— Virginia, *b* 1954: *m* 1975, Ronald Joffre Bain, of La Josefina, 9019 Prov Santa Cruz, Bolivia, and has issue living, Joffre Enrique, *b* 1978, — Alan, *b* 1980, — Karen Irene, *b* 1976. —— Margaret Ina, *b* 1956: *m* 1980, Christian Dowgall. —— Christine, *b* 1959.

Grandson of late Henry Philip Hill, yr son of Lt-Col Richard Frederick Hill, 3rd son of Col John Hill (ante):—
Issue of late Rowland Philip Hill, *b* 1888, *d* 1979: *m* 1912, Ruth, who *d* 1976, da of C. H. Stott:—
Brian Henry Rowland (7 Thompson Rd, Napier, NZ), *b* 1917; *ed* Christ's Coll, Christchurch, NZ, and Otago Univ (MB, ChB); DDM Sydney; Middle East 1945 with Roy NZ Med Corps: *m* 1945, Marjorie Virginia, da of Capt Euan Dickson, DSC, DFC, of Auckland, NZ, and has issue living, Heathcote Henry Rowland, *b* 1949, — Simon Philip, *b* 1951, — Angela Francesca, *b* 1946: *m* 1977, Kim Campbell, and has issue living, Benjamin *b* 1980.

(In remainder to Baronetcy)

Grandchildren of Robert Hill, son of Capt Alfred Edward Hill, 2nd son of Sir Robert Chambré Hill, CB, 4th son of 3rd Baronet:—
Issue of late Alfred Brabant Hill, *b* 1896, *d* 1979: *m* 1933, Frances, who *d* 1986, da of Edward Pooley:—
John Richard, *b* 1935; *ed* British Columbia Univ (BSc), and McGill Univ (PhD). —— Peter Robert (1840 Nigel Court, Vienna, Va 22182, USA), *b* 1937; *ed* British Columbia Univ (BA, Sc): *m* 1st, 1968, Mary Lynn, who *d* 1993, da of late Keller Smith; 2ndly, 1994, Mrs Joyce Ann Ralston, da of late Robert E. Prowty, and has issue living (by 1st *m*), Peter Brabant, *b* 1970, — Charles Edward Keller, *b* 1980, — Molly Cochran, *b* 1972.

Grandson of late Henry Daniel Hill, 3rd son of late Robert Greene Hill (*b* 1801), son of late Rev Robert Wilbraham Bromhall Hill, el son of late Rev Robert Hill, 4th son of 1st baronet:—
Issue of late Roger Wilbraham Hill, *b* 1883, *d* 1962: *m* 1912, Mary Ann, who *d* 1971, da of James Sadler, of Acton, Chester:—
Gerald Roger (Hough Gates, Hough, Crewe), *b* 1921; *m* 1953, Jane Elizabeth, JP, da of Frank Haighton, of Elm House, Nantwich, and has issue living, Gerald Robert Wilbraham, *b* 1958, — Elizabeth Mary *b* 1955; PhD.

Grandchildren of late John Francis Hill (infra):—
Issue of late Alaric Bryan Hill, *b* 1921, *d* 1992: *m* 1948, Elizabeth Margaret Allen (49 Crown St, Dubbo, NSW 2830, Australia):—
Dallas John (PO Box 283, Kokstad, E Griqualand, S Africa), *b* 1950: *m* 1975, Bronwyn Lucie Van Der Leeuw, and has issue living, Christopher John, *b* 1975, — Rowland John, *b* 1978, — Dallas Joseph, *b* 1989. —— Carol Elizabeth, *b* 1953: *m* 1974, Gordon Redvers Bell, of 12 Gibson Close, Singleton Heights, NSW 2330, Australia, and Box 278, Singleton, NSW 2330, Australia, and has issue living, Julian Redvers, *b* 1978, — Cherié Elizabeth, *b* 1974.

Granddaughters of late Francis Robert Wilbraham Hill, 5th and yst son of late Robert Greene Hill (*b* 1801) (ante):—
Issue of late John Francis Hill, *b* 1882, *d* 1948: *m* 1916, Natalie Ivy, who *d* 1967, da of Thomas Payne St James (*see* V Hill, colls, 1937 Edn):—
Ellen Maryan, *b* 1920: *m* 1946, Thomas Duncan MacMillan, ACIS, formerly 2nd Transvaal Scottish, and has issue living, Bruce Warwick Hugh (Farmlet Rd, Hastings, NZ), *b* 1951; BSc, Dip Ed: *m* 1973 (*m diss* 1980), Deborah Suzanne Cathey, and has issue living, Fiona Louise *b* 1978, — Brenda Caroline Dale, *b* 1955: *m* 1979, Gary Malcolm Filer, Dip Opt, of 131 Crossfield Rd, Glendowie, Auckland 5, NZ, and has issue living, Natalie Jean Caroline *b* 1983, Claire Bridget Alice *b* 1985. *Residence* – 12A Combes Rd, Remuera, Auckland 1005, NZ. —— Vivette Natalie, *b* 1925: *m* 1949, Johan Heinrich Moll, BSc, FMIMechE, and has issue living, Victor Derek (Box 1309 Oranjemund, Namibia), *b* 1954: *m* 1984, Patricia Du Randt, — Coleen Yvonne MOLL, *b* 1951, BSocSc, B Com; has resumed her maiden name: *m* 1975 (*m diss* 1983), Roger Charles Peplow, MSc, of Durban, Natal, S Africa. *Residence* – 15 Straker Av, Gun Hill, Harare, Zimbabwe.

Grandchildren of late Lt-Gen George Mytton Hill, yr son of late Richard Hill, 5th son of late Rev Robert Hill (ante):—
Issue of late Maj Arthur Rowland Hill, *b* 1880, *ka* 1915: *m* 1908, Kathleen, da of late C. James Todd:—
Christian Mary (*Baroness Riverdale*), *b* 1909: *m* 1933, as his 2nd wife, 2nd Baron Riverdale, of Ropes, Grindleford, via Sheffield. —— Alison Kathleen, *b* 1911: *m* 1934, Henry Seaward Morley, MD, FRCP, who *d* 1961, and has issue living, John Henry (Derwent Lodge, Oldfield Rd, Maidenhead, Berks), *b* 1936; *ed* Wellington Coll, and Downing Coll, Camb (MA): *m* 1963, Felicity Faith Beryl, el da of John Peile, of Grindleford, Sheffield, and has issue living, Rupert Oliver Henry *b* 1965, Benjamin William Mervyn *b* 1969, — Timothy Rowland, *b* 1939; *ed* Wellington Coll, and Downing Coll, Camb (MA); MB, BCh, FRCS, LRCP: *m* 1966, Mary Elspeth Holborn, da of Noel Frederick Adeney, FRCS, of Bournemouth, and has issue living, David Mark Rowland *b* 1969; *ed* London Univ (BA), Nicola Susie Gray *b* 1968; *ed* Leeds Univ (BSc): *m* 1993, Andrew Philip Martello Gray. *Residence* – Fife House, Heath Drive, Walton-on-the-Hill, Tadworth, Surrey KT20 7QQ.
Issue of late Cdr George Mytton Hill, RN, *b* 1883, *d* 1935: *m* 1919, Olive Odell, who *d* 1966, da of W. Millar, of Eskbank:—
Doreen Odell, *b* 1920: *m* 1950, Maj Hector McNeill Tytler Reith, RA (ret), of 78B Granville Rd, Sevenoaks Kent, and has issue living, Douglas McNeill Mytton, *b* 1953, *ed* St George's Sch, Tonbridge, and Webber Douglas Acad of Dramatic Art.
Issue of late Harold Brian Cunningham Hill, FRGS, *b* 1887, *d* 1980: *m* 1920, Elsie, who *d* 1971, da of J. Jeppe, JP, Consul-Gen for Greece and for Roumania, and Senior Roy Danish Consul in S Africa:—

Noel Brian (Balneath Manor Farm, S Chailey, nr Lewes, E Sussex BN8 4AP), b 1926; ed Eastbourne Coll: m 1958, Gladys Rosa, da of late Sidney George West, OBE, and has issue living, Nicola Anne, b 1959; ed Moira House, and Warwick Univ (BA): m 1985, Paul Jonathan Woodley, and has issue living, Christopher Benjamin b 1989, Daisy Anne b 19—, — Philippa Jane, b 1962, — and an adopted da, Jill Adrienne, b 1953; ed Moira House, and Sussex Univ (BA). —— Julian (Huntsland Cottage, Huntsland Lane, Crawley Down, Sussex RH10 4HB; Clubs – Naval & Military and MCC), b 1932; ed Eastbourne Coll; served as Lieut 1st Bn 22nd (Cheshire) Regt in Egypt 1953-54; Man Dir Julian Hill Ltd, and Scanhill Ltd; Freeman of City of London; FBIM; MInstM; FIOD: m 1956, Ruth Monica, yst da of late Paul Sekvens Toll, of 10 Villagatan, Stockholm, and has issue living, Rowland Paul (16 Ashley Mansions, SW1), b 1956; ed Eastbourne Coll; ACA, — Michael Mytton (La Ruelle, 62770 Le Fresnoy, France), b 1960; ed Eastbourne Coll, W Surrey Coll of Art & Design (BA), and Duncan of Jordanstone Coll of Art, Dundee (MA): m 1990, Priscilla, yst da of Frank Morgan, and has issue living, Christopher Robert b 1993, — Anne-Louise (67 Weston Park, Crouch End, N8 9PN), b 1963; ed Moira House, St Claire's Hall, Oxford, and Edinburgh Univ (MA).

Issue of late Reginald Herbert Hill, b 1889, d 1978: m 1st, 1914, Elizabeth Wallace, da of late A. S. Coubrough, JP, of Blanefield, Stirlingshire; 2ndly, 1931, Gertrude, da of J. Perry, of Tavistock, Devon:—
(By 1st m), Kathleen Agnes, b 1916: m 1946, George Elden Burrell, of 2760 Burdick Av, Victoria, BC, Canada, and has issue living, Robin Elden Adair, b 1951: m 1982, Katharine Regina, da of Colin D. McCullough, of Victoria, BC, — Keith Edgar, b 1953: m 1981, Leslie Jean, da of Ian C. Colquhoun, of Vancouver, BC, and has issue living, Scott Thomas b 1983, — Wendy Evelyn, b 1948: m 1969, Bruce Ronald McConnan, of 2481, Central Av, Victoria, BC, and has issue living, Brock Stewart b 1976, Kelly Evelyn b 1973. —— Winifred Evelyn, b 1920: m 1945, Charles M. Humphrys, of 3613 Nico Wynd Drive, Surrey, BC V2A 2W3, Canada, and has issue living, Daphne Mary, b 1947: m 1968, Douglas James Lovick, of Vancouver, BC, and has issue living, Heidi Marie b 1970, Cynthia Evelyn b 1973, Anna Marjory b 1983, — Sheila Elizabeth, b 1947: m 1969, Brian Paul Jagger, and has issue living, Brigham Humphry b 1976, Ryan Selwyn b 1978, Christina Catherine b 1974, Stephanie Elizabeth b 1980, — Brenda Ann, b 1953: m 1974, David William Haskett, of Calgary, Alberta, and has issue living, Kevin b 1983, Kathryn Jane b 1982, Kelly Evelyn b 1988, — Nancy Maureen, b 1958: m 1981, Douglas Alan Leard, of Vancouver, BC, and has issue living, James Douglas b 1984, Kerry Alana b 1986. —— (By 2nd m) (Arthur) Brian Montague (2545 Rolling Hills Court, Alamo, Cal 94507, USA), b 1932: m 1960, Brenda Margaret, da of W. A. Murray of Bebington, Ches, and has an adopted son, George Mytton, b 1969.

PREDECESSORS – Sir Richard Hill, PC, an eminent statesman and diplomatist; d unmarried, and devised his Hawkstone estates to his nephew (1) ROWLAND Hill, who in consideration of his uncle's important sers was cr a Baronet 1727, with remainder to his cousins Samuel Hill, of Shenstone, Thomas Hill, of Tern, whose el son was cr Baron Berwick, and to Rowland Hill, brother of Thomas (ante); sat as MP for Lichfield 1734; d 1783; s by his el son (2) Sir RICHARD, 2nd Bt, MP for co Salop 1780-1802; d unmarried 1809; s by his brother (3) Sir JOHN, 3rd Bt, MP for Shrewsbury 1784-1802; his 2nd son Rowland, GCB, a distinguished Gen and Com in Ch 1828-42, was cr Baron Hill, of Almarez and of Hawkstone, co Salop (peerage of United Kingdom) 1814, and Viscount Hill (peerage of United Kingdom) 1842, with remainder in each instance to the issue of his el brother John; Sir John d 1824, and was s by his grandson (4) ROWLAND, 4th Bt, son of John (ante); in 1842 s his uncle (ante) as 2nd Viscount Hill; b 1800; was MP for Shropshire 1821-32 and for N Shropshire (C) 1832-42, and Lord Lieut of Salop: m 1831, Anne, only child of Joseph Clegg, of Peplow Hall, Salop, and sole heir of Arthur Clegg; d 1875; s by his son (5) ROWLAND CLEGG, 3rd Viscount, b 1833; MP for N Shropshire (C) 1857-65; assumed in 1875 the additional surname of Clegg: m 1st, 1855, Mary, who d 1874, da of William Madax; 2ndly, 1875, Hon Isabella Elizabeth Wynn, who d 1898, da of 3rd Baron Newborough; d 1895; s by his el son (6) ROWLAND RICHARD, 4th Viscount, b 1863; was Master of Spectacle Makers' Co: m 1890, Aunie Edith, who d 1937, da of late William Irwin, of Tandrago, co Sligo; d 1923; s by his brother (7) FRANCIS WILLIAM, 5th Viscount, b 1866: m 1905, Caroline Anna, who d 1941, da of late Capt Frank Corbett, of Greenfield, Presteign, Radnorshire; d 1924; s by his half-brother (8) CHARLES ROWLAND, DSO, 6th Viscount, b 1876; Lieut-Col late Roy Welch Fusiliers: m 1st, 1903, Mildred, who d 1936, da of Thomas Bulteel; 2ndly, 1936, Berthe Maria Emilie, who d 1959, da of late A. Schmidt-Immer, of Strasbourg, Alsace-Lorraine; d 1957; s by his son (9) GERALD ROWLAND, 7th Viscount, b 1904: m 1st, 1930 (m diss 1942), Elisabeth Flora, who d 1967, da of Brig-Gen George Nowell Thomas Smyth-Osbourne, CB, CMG, DSO, DL, of Ash, Iddlesleigh, N Devon; 2ndly, 1942, Catherine Mary (Molly), da of Dr Rowland Venables Lloyd-Williams, of Maiford, Denbigh; d 1974; s by his el son (10) ANTONY ROWLAND, 8th Viscount and present peer; also Baron Hill.

HILL OF LUTON, BARONY OF (Hill) (Extinct 1989)

SONS LIVING OF LIFE BARON

Hon Robert (33 Meadow View, Dunvant, Swansea, W Glamorgan), b 1938; ed Epsom, and Harper Adams Agricultural Coll: m 1960, Ann, da of E. Williamson, of Southampton, and has issue.
Hon John (48 Sheehan St, Pearce, ACT 2607, Australia), b 1945; ed Epsom, and Camb Univ: m 1974, Dawn, da of I. Lance, of Sydney, NSW, Australia and has issue.

DAUGHTERS LIVING OF LIFE BARON

Jennifer (does not use courtesy title), b 1933: m 1st, 1960 (m diss 1973), Robert Duncan Barnaby Leicester, MB; 2ndly, 1975, Thomas Trenerry, of 8/6 Bells Rd, Dundas, NSW 2117, Australia, and has issue (by 1st m).
Hon Elizabeth, b 1935: m 1964, David Maxwell Morris, of 9 St Leonards Rd, Exeter, and has issue.
Hon Susan, b 1936: m 1958, David Ritchie Fairbairn, of 11 Oak Way, West Common, Harpenden, Herts, and has issue.

HILL-NORTON, BARON (Hill-Norton) (Life Baron 1978)

·TRY·HARDER·

PETER JOHN HILL-NORTON, GCB, son of Capt Martin John Norton; *b* 8 Feb 1915; *ed* RN Colls Dartmouth and Greenwich; Adm of the Fleet; Com-in-Ch UK Forces in Far East 1969-70; First Sea Lord 1970-71; Chief of the Defence Staff 1971-74; Chm NATO Military Cttee 1974-77; *cr* CB (Mil) 1964, KCB (Mil) 1967, GCB (Mil) 1970 and *Baron Hill-Norton*, of South Nutfield, co Surrey (Life Baron) 1978: *m* 1936, Margaret Eileen, da of Carl Adolph Linstow, and has issue.

Arms – On a bend gules between in chief a terrestrial sphere proper and in base three cannon balls sable within an annulet azure four anchors or. **Crest** – Out of a naval crown or on a mount vert a springbok trippant proper. **Supporters** – On either side a hippocampus holding in the tail an anchor proper. *Residence* – Cass Cottage, Hyde, Fordingbridge. *Clubs* – Army and Navy, Royal Navy of 1765.

SON LIVING

Hon Sir Nicholas John, KCB, *b* 1939; Vice Adm RN; KCB (Mil) 1991: *m* 1966, (Ann) Jennifer, da of Vice-Adm Dennis Mason, CB, CVO, and has issue living, Simon Nicholas Sebastian, *b* 1967, — Peter Tom, *b* 1975, — Claudia Genevieve Jane, *b* 1969: *m* 1994, Thomas M. Bradby.

DAUGHTER LIVING

Hon Carla Ann, *b* 1943: *m* 1st, 1966, Christopher Thomas Jowett; 2ndly, 1974, Graeme McLintock, of Old Beith House, Mill-and, Liphook, Hants, and has had issue (by 1st *m*), Benjamin, *b* 1967, — James, *b* 1969, *d* 1991.

HILLINGDON, BARONY OF (Mills) (Extinct 1982)

DAUGHTERS LIVING OF FIFTH BARON

Hon Sarah Patricia, *b* 1933: *m* 1955, Maj Jonathan Michael Henry Balcon, TD, Inns of Court and City Yeo, of The Grey House, Seal, Sevenoaks, Kent, and has issue living, Deborah Louisa Kate, *b* 1956: *m* 1978, Timothy Jackson Wilson, and has issue living, Alexander Edward Jackson *b* 1982, Oliver Patrick Henry *b* 1985, — Sarah Clair, *b* 1957: *m* 1987, Julian James Neuburger, only son of Henry Neuburger, of Locrano, Switzerland, and has issue living, James Michael *b* 1991, Lucy *b* 1989, — Henrietta Beatrice Jane, *b* 1960: *m* 1985, Maj Timothy Hugh Breitmeyer, Gren Gds, and has issue (*see* Abertay, By).
Hon Jenefer, *b* 1935: *m* 1962, His Honour Joseph Dean, of The Hall, West Brabourne, Kent, and has issue living, Ptolemy Hugo, *b* 1967, — Antigone Lucy, *b* 1963, — Tacita Charlotte, *b* 1965.

DAUGHTERS LIVING OF FOURTH BARON

Hon Victoria Elizabeth *b* 1948: *m* 1st, 1971 (*m diss* 1979), Anthony Roff; 2ndly, 1981, D. G. R. Cruickshank, of 15 Elder St, E1, and has issue living (by 1st *m*), Nandi Rita, *b* 1972, — Alice Diana, *b* 1974, — (by 2nd *m*) Isabel Mary Rose, *b* 1981.
Hon Jessica Anne, *b* 1957: *m* 1991, Benjamin Henry Gaskell (*see* B Bagot, colls, 1973-74 Edn).
Hon Catherine Gray, *b* 1963.

DAUGHTER LIVING OF THIRD BARON.

Hon Ursula Sibyl (Wakefield Cottage, Wembworthy, nr Chulmleigh, Devon), *b* 1918.

WIDOW LIVING OF FOURTH BARON

PHOEBE MAXWELL (*Baroness Hillingdon*), da of late Capt Mervyn James Hamilton, of Cornacassa, Monaghan (V Bangor, colls), and formerly wife of (i) Lt-Cdr John Sholto Fitzpatrick Cooke, CBE, RNVR, and (ii) John Cooper; *m* 1978, as his 2nd wife, the 4th Baron, who *d* 1978. *Residence* – Shalom Hall, Layer Breton, Colchester, Essex.

Hillsborough, Earl of; son of Marquess of Downshire.

HILTON OF EGGARDON, BARONESS (Hilton) (Life Baroness 1991)

JENNIFER HILTON, da of late John Robert Hilton, CMG, of London; *b* 1936; *ed* Bedales Sch, and Manchester Univ (MA); Police Officer, Metropolitan Police Ser 1956-90 (Cdr 1984-90); *cr Baroness Hilton of Eggardon*, of Eggardon, co Dorset (Life Baroness) 1991.

Arms – Azure, between two bees in fess and volant upwards and outwards proper, growing from a grassy mount in base and protected by palings about its trunk an oak tree also proper and fructed gold. **Supporters** – *Dexter*, on a grassy mount growing therefrom two dog roses proper, a crested newt statant erect vert holding by its inner forefoot a tipstaff proper; *sinister*, on a grassy mount growing therefrom two dog roses proper, a griffin statant erect argent, armed, winged and tail tufted or, grasping in its inner foreclaw a serpent entwined about the foreleg also proper.
Address – c/o Barclays Bank plc, 1 The Causeway, Teddington, Middx.

HINDLIP, BARON (Allsopp) (Baron UK 1886, Bt UK 1880)

Hasten slowly

CHARLES HENRY ALLSOPP, 6th Baron, and 6th Baronet; *b* 5 Aug 1940; *s* 1993; *ed* Eton; late Lieut Coldstream Gds; Dir Christie Manson & Wood 1970, Dep Chm 1985, Chm 1986: *m* 1968, Fiona Victoria Jean Atherley, only child of late Hon William Johnston McGowan (*see* B McGowan, colls), and has issue.

Arms – Sable, three pheons in chevron or, between as many doves rising argent, each holding in the beak a wheat-ear or. **Crest** – A plover, holding in beak a wheat-ear or, standing on a pheon also gold. **Supporters** – Two fox-hounds, each gorged with a pair of couples proper.
Residences – The Cedar House, Inkpen, Berks; 55 Campden Hill Rd, W8. *Clubs* – White's, Pratt's.

SON LIVING

Hon HENRY WILLIAM, *b* 8 June 1973.

DAUGHTERS LIVING

Hon Kirstie Mary, *b* 1971.
Hon Sophia Atherley, *b* 1980.
Hon Natasha Fiona, *b* 1986.

BROTHER LIVING

Hon John Peter, *b* 1942; *ed* Eton: *m* 1976, Daryl, 3rd da of Leonard Shawzin, of Huisinbois, Constantia, CP, South Africa, and has issue living, James Leonard, *b* 1978, — Kathryn Sarah, *b* 1981, — Camilla Rose, *b* 1990.

SISTER LIVING

Hon Sarah Cecily, *b* 1944: *m* 1967, Hugh Robert Myddelton, of 139, Holland Park Av, W11, and has issue (*see* M Lansdowne).

AUNTS LIVING (*Daughters of 3rd Baron*)

Hon Diana Joan (*Hon Lady Hardy*), *b* 1908: *m* 1930, Lieut-Col Sir Rupert John Hardy, 4th Bt, Life Guards (ret), and has issue. *Residence* – Gullivers Lodge, Guilsborough, Northampton.
Hon Nancy Marion, *b* 1910: *m* 1936, Peter Geoffrey Brooke, and has issue living, Michael Peter, *b* 1937; Maj 16th/15th Lancers: *m* 1970, Susan Rhona Martin, yr da of A. W. Peacop, of Blue Hills, Finchampstead, Berks. *Residence* – Dial House, Chilmark, Wilts.

DAUGHTERS LIVING OF FOURTH BARON

Hon Penelope Jane, *b* 1940: *m* 1965, Theodore Demetrius Velissaropoulos. *Residence* – Taxilis 75, Athens 15771, Greece.
Hon Elizabeth Tulla, *b* 1942. *Residence* – 40 Bloomfield Terr, SW1W 8PQ

WIDOW LIVING OF FIFTH BARON

CECILY VALENTINE JANE (*Dowager Baroness Hindlip*), only da of late Lt-Col Malcolm Borwick, DSO, of Haselbech Hill, Northampton: *m* 1939, Maj the 5th Baron, who *d* 1993. *Residence* – Tytherton House, E Tytherton, Chippenham, Wilts.

COLLATERAL BRANCHES LIVING

Grandchildren of late Lt-Col Hon Ranulph Allsopp, 4th son of 1st Baron:—
Issue of late Samuel Ranulph Allsopp, CBE, *b* 1899, *d* 1975: *m* 1923, Hon Norah Hyacinthe Littleton, da of 4th Baron Hatherton:—
Michael Edward Ranulph (Little Coxwell Grove, Faringdon, Oxon; White's and Pratt's Clubs), *b* 1930; *ed* Eton: *m* 1953, Patricia, da of late Geoffrey H. Berners of Little Coxwell Grove, Faringdon, Oxon, and has issue living, Frances Jane Berners, *b* 1955: *m* 1st, 1975 (*m diss* 1980), Dermot Michael Claud Chichester (*see* M Donegall); 2ndly, 1984, Maj David John Basil Woodd, 14th/20th King's Hus, of The Homestead, Little Coxwell, Faringdon, Oxon, elder son of late Col Basil Bethune Neville Woodd, of Kingsgate, Rolvenden, Kent, and has issue living (by 2nd *m*), Matilda Elizabeth *b* 1990, Tabitha Ann *b* 1991, — Carolyn Anne Berners, *b* 1957, — Davina Hyacinthe Berners (*Lady Powell*), *b* 1960: *m* 1987, as his 2nd wife,

Sir Nicholas Folliott Douglas Powell, 4th Bt, and has issue, — Jessica Elizabeth Berners (*Hon Mrs Edward Leigh-Pemberton*), *b* (twin) 1960: *m* 1984, Hon Edward Douglas Leigh-Pemberton, of Longcot House, Longcot, Faringdon, Oxon, 3rd son of Baron Kingsdown, PC (Life Baron), and has issue. ———— David Samuel (37 Cadogan Place, SW1), *b* 1933; *ed* Eton: *m* 1st, 1960 (*m diss* 1966), Tan Doris May, da of Frederick J Arnold, of Turbary Rd, Parkstone, Dorset; 2ndly, 1972, Sally, da of late V. H. Thirkell, of High Tilt Farm, Cranbrook, Kent, and has issue living (by 2nd *m*), James Samuel, *b* 1972, — Melanie Angela, *b* 1977. ———— Juliet Modwena, *b* 1925; formerly WRNS: *m* 1952, Samuel Arthur Scott (*see* Scott, Bt *cr* 1962). ———— Charmian Hyacinthe (Sycamore House, Tissington, Ashbourne, Derby), *b* 1926: *m* 1962, Rev David Henry FitzHerbert, who *d* 1976 (*see* FitzHerbert, Bt).

Issue of late Capt John Ranulph Allsopp, *b* 1908, *ka* in N Africa 1943: *m* 1934, Audrey Carteret Priaulx (who *d* 1960, having *m* 2ndly, 1944, Oliver Van Oss, who *d* 1992), da of late Major E. G. Fellows, of Barberry Cottage, Cheapside, Ascot:—

Mark Ranulph (Coles Oak House, Dedham, Colchester, Essex), *b* 1938; *ed* Eton: *m* 1960, Tania Anna, da of late Capt John Eustace-Smith, of Thrunton, Whittingham, Northumberland, and has issue living, Jonathan Ranulph, *b* 1962, — Richard Mark, *b* 1963: *m* 1990, Alexandra Dominica, da of Maj John Grosch, of Stoke-by-Nayland, Suffolk, and has issue living, a da *b* 1993, — Charles Samuel, *b* 1970; *ed* Eton, and RMA Sandhurst, — Arabella Sarah Georgianna, *b* 1972. ———— Peter William (Mill Barn, Mill Lane, Bramley, Surrey), *b* 1940; *ed* Eton: *m* 1962, Pepita, da of Lt-Cmdr Peter E. Mason, DSC, of Auburn, Bramshott Court, Liphook, Hants, and has issue living, Amanda Caroline, *b* 1964: *m* 1988, John Howard Perry, only son of H. A. Perry, of Bradpole, Bridport, Dorset, — Sophie Victoria, *b* 1967, — Katherine Pepita, *b* 1970: *m* 1993, Timothy Scott Ireland, of Kogarah, NSW, Australia, 2nd son of Donald Ireland, of North Rocks, Sydney, NSW.

PREDECESSORS – (1) *Sir* HENRY Allsopp, 3rd son of late Samuel Allsopp, of Burton-on-Trent *b* 1811; sat as MP for E Worcestershire (*C*) 1874-80; *cr* a *Baronet* 1880, and *Baron Hindlip*, of Hindlip, co Worcester and of Alsop-en-le-Dale, co Derby (peerage of United Kingdom) 1886: *m* 1839, Elizabeth, who *d* 1906, da of William Tongue, of Comberforf Hall, Tamworth; *d* 1887; *s* by his son (2) SAMUEL CHARLES, 2nd Baron; *b* 1842; MP for E Staffordshire (*C*) 1873-80, and for Taunton 188207: *m* 1868, Georgiana Millicent, who *d* 1939, da of late Charles Rowland Palmer-Morewood, of Alfreton, Derbyshire; *d* 1897; *s* by his son (3) CHARLES, OBE, 3rd Baron, *b* 1877; S Africa 1900, European War 1914-18 (despatches, twice, OBE, Legion of Honour); Junior Unionist Whip in House of Lords 1907-14; *m* 1904, Agatha Lillian, who *d* 1963, da of late John Charles Thynne (M Bath, colls), *d* 1931; *s* by his el son (4) CHARLES SAMUEL VICTOR, 4th Baron, *b* 1906: *m* 1st, 1932 (*m diss* 1934), Bridget, da of late Harold Nickols; 2ndly, 1939, Hansina Cecilia Elfrida (Tulla), who *d* 1988, da of late Frederick William Harris; *d* 1966; *s* by his brother (6) HENRY RICHARD, 5th Baron, *b* 1912; Maj Coldstream Gds, American Bronze Star Medal; a JP and DL for Wilts: *m* 1939, Cecily Valentine Jane, da of late Lt-Col Malcolm Borwick, DSO, of Haselbech Hill, Northampton; *d* 1993; *s* by his elder son (7) CHARLES HENRY, 6th Baron and present peer.

HINTON OF BANKSIDE, BARONY OF (Hinton) (Extinct 1983)

DAUGHTER LIVING OF LIFE BARON

Hon Susan Mary, *b* 1932: *m* 1957: Arthur Charles Mole, of 2 Second Av, Charmandean, Worthing, Sussex, BN14 9NX, son of late Sir Charles Johns Mole, KBE, MVO, and has issue, two sons, the elder of whom, Christopher C., *b* 1960: *m* 1986, Carolyn J., elder da of S. E. Deboo, of Telham, Battle, Sussex.

HIRSHFIELD, BARONY OF (Hirshfield) (Extinct 1993)

WIDOW LIVING OF LIFE BARON

BRONIA (*Baroness Hirshfield*), da of Joseph Eisen: *m* 1951, Baron Hirshfield, who *d* 1993. *Residence* – 44 Imperial Court, Prince Albert Rd, NW8 7PT.

HIRST, BARONY OF (Hirst) (Extinct 1943)

GRANDDAUGHTER OF FIRST BARON

Issue of late Harold Hugh Hirst (Lt 21st Manchester Regt, attached RE Signals), son of 1st Baron, *b* 1893, *d* 1919: *m* 1917, Carol Iris, MBE (by whom he had an only son, Hugh Harold Hirst, Pilot Officer RAFVR, *b* 1919, *k* 1941, while on operational duties), da of late Lewis Lindon, of Sussex Sq, W; she *m* 2ndly, 1926, Maurice Theodore Alexander Dreyfus, and *d* 1966:—

Hon Pamela Muriel Dorine, MBE (Peartrees, Dormansland, Surrey RH7 6QY) *b* 1918: late Junior Com ATS; raised to rank of a Baron's daughter 1943; a member of Godstone RDC 1955-74 (Chm 1969-72) and of Tandridge Council 1974-75; Hon Alderman of Tandridge District Council; Chm of Lingfield Parish Council 1957-69; MBE (civil) 1983: *m* 1st, 1940 (*m diss* 1947), Capt Arthur George Bevington Colyer, RA; 2ndly, 1949, Roy Edward Goodale, who *d* 1969, and has issue living (by 2nd *m*), Hugh Roy (H. R. Goodale Ltd, Edenbridge, Kent), *b* 1953: *m* 1985, Colette Mansuy, and has issue living, Hugo *b* 1991, Marianne *b* 1986.

DAUGHTER LIVING OF FIRST BARON

Hon Irene Phyllis, CBE, *b* 1901; Admin WVS 1940-46, Member LCC (N Lewisham) 1952-58, and again 1961-65; Chm Greater Lond Area, Women's Advisory Cttee, and Member Conservative Nat Exec Cttee 1952-65; CBE (Civil) 1961: *m* 1922, Group-Capt Trevor Felix David Rose, RAF Vol Reserve and late Major RFA and RHA, who *d* 1946, and has had issue, Veronica Phyllis, *b* 1924: *m* 1943, Major Timothy Basil Ellis, King's Shropshire LI (ret) of Trinity Hall, Bungay, Suffolk, and has issue living, Jonathan Felix Hugh *b* 1951: *m* 1975, Lady Angela Mary Shirley, da of 13th Earl Ferrers (and has issue, *see* E Ferrers), Jennifer Bryony *b* 1946: *m* 1966, Anthony Gibson, of Newbiggin, Hexham, Northumberland (and has issue living, Benjamin Timothy *b* 1968, Toby *b* 1969, Richard *b* (twin) 1969, Daniel *b* 1975), — Evelyn Felicity, *b* 1927: *m* 1947 (*m diss* 1975), Maj H. D. Bailey, late Welsh Guards, and *d* 1990, leaving issue, Patrick Robin (Hoe Benham Farmhouse, Hoe Benham, Newbury, Berks RG16 8PD) *b* 1953; late Welsh Guards; FRICS: *m* 1982, Laura Larthe (and has issue living, Hugo *b* 1989, Charlotte *b* 1983), Sandra Caroline *b* 1948: *m* 1984, Dr Timothy W. Potter, PhD, of Summerfield, 8 Sydenham Av, SE26 6UH (and has issue living, Simon *b* 1985, Belinda *b* 1988).

HIVES, BARON (Hives) (Baron UK 1950)

JOHN WARWICK HIVES, 2nd Baron; *b* 26 Nov 1913; *s* 1965; *ed* Derby Sch; a farmer (ret): *m* 1st, 1937, Olwen Protheroe Llewellin, who *d* 1972; 2ndly, 1972, Gladys Mary, da of Alfred Seals.

ᴀrms – Or on a chevron sable, three bee hives of the field. Crest – In front of a sun in splendour or, an eagle rising proper. Supporters – *Dexter*, the figure of a mechanic proper overalls azure, holding in the exterior hand a micrometer; *sinister*, the figure of a draughtsman proper coat argent holding under the exterior arm a set square and a T square also proper.
Residence – Lang Dale House, Sutton on the Hill, Derbys.

BROTHERS LIVING

Hon Michael Bruce, *b* 1926;*ed* Repton: *m* 1951, Janet Rosemary, da of late W. E. Gee, of Lynngarth, Duffield, Derby, and has issue living, Robert George (The Meadows, Church Lane, Barrow Upon Trent, Derby), *b* 1953: *m* 1975, Annabelle Vickers, and has issue living, William Duncan *b* 1977, Jeremy Robert *b* 1982, Thomas Francis *b* 1985, Victoria Jane *b* 1980, — Paul Michael, *b* 1963: *m* 1987, Ellen, da of J. M. Kaufman, of 33 Fifth Av, New York City, NY, — Jillian Sarah, *b* 1955: *m* 1988, Kevin Titterton, of 6 Keats Av, Littleover, Derbys. *Residence* – Fairfield, The Pastures, Duffield, Derbys.
Hon David Benjamin, *b* 1931; *ed* Repton; Gp Capt RAF: *m* 1954, Shirley, da of late Harold Walker, of Cumberhill House, Duffield, Derby, and has issue living, Nigel Ian Edward, *b* 1960: *m* 1983, Helen Louise, da of W. N. K. Rowley, of Derby, and has issue living, Lawrence Ernest William *b* 1987, Imogen Jean *b* 1990, — Sally Margaret, *b* 1955: *m* 1978, Malcolm Howard Lambie, and has issue living, Peter Benjamin *b* 1984, William Ian *b* 1985, Hannah Louise *b* 1989, — (Sandra) Dawn, *b* 1958: *m* 1990, Col Jack M. W. Stenhouse, OBE, MVO, The Gordon Highrs, elder son of Lt-Col D. R. Stenhouse, MBE, of East Sheen, SW14, and has issue living, Catriona Rose *b* 1991, Elizabeth Maitland *b* 1993. *Residence* – Cumberhill House, Duffield, Derbys DE56 4HA.

SISTERS LIVING

Hon Joan Mary, *b* 1917: *m* 1939, Adrian Gee, and has issue living, Wendy Elizabeth, *b* 1943: *m* 1963, Thomas Neville, of Beech Tree House, Audlem, Cheshire, and has issue living, Alexander William *b* 1965, Sally Anne *b* 1968, — Jane Anne, *b* 1945: *m* 1967, John Hodgson Berry, of Bunystone Cottage, Bunnison Lane, Colston Bassett, Notts, and has issue living, Duncan Gee *b* 1968, Nicholas Gee *b* 1970. *Residence* – 9 Chestnut Close, Duffield, Derbys DE6 4HD.
Hon Ruth Margaret, *b* 1922: *m* 1941, Joseph Graham Riley, and has issue living, Michael Edward, *b* 1947, — John Andrew (twin), *b* 1947, — David Ernest, *b* 1951. *Residence* – 7 Avenue Rd, Duffield, Derbys.
Hon Philippa Ann, *b* 1928: *m* 1978, His Honour Judge Alexander John Henderson Morrison, of Eastwood Drive, Littleover, Derby.

WIDOW LIVING OF SON OF FIRST BARON

Dinah (Harmer Garry, Harmer Green Lane, Welwyn, Herts), da of F. Wilson-North, of Walcott, Norfolk: *m* 1956, Hon Peter Anthony Hives, who *d* 1974, and has issue living (see colls, infra).

COLLATERAL BRANCH LIVING

　　　　Issue of late Hon Peter Anthony Hives, Lt RNVR, el son of 1st Baron, *b* 1921, *d* 1974: *m* 1956, Dinah (ante), da of F. Wilson-North, of Walcott, Norfolk:—
MATTHEW PETER, *b* 25 May 1971. —— Julie Laura, *b* 1957: *m* 1st, 1979, Thomas J. Macnab, who *d* 1988, only son of late J. Campbell Macnab, of Troon, Ayrshire; 2ndly, 1990, Dr Anthony Reed, of Mardley Bury Manor, Knebworth, Herts, son of late Dr E. S. Reed, MBE, of Shalford, Surrey, and has issue living (by 1st *m*), Robert Thomas Peter Campbell, *b* 1982, — Camilla Laura, *b* 1984, — (by 2nd *m*) Frederick Anthony Spencer, *b* 1992, — Clementine Florence, *b* 1991. —— Lisa Joanna, *b* 1963; has issue living, Oscar, *b* 1992, — Alice, *b* 1993. —— Sophie Josephine, *b* 1964.

PREDECESSORS – (1) ERNEST WALTER HIVES, CH, MBE, son of John Hives, of Reading; *b* 1886; Chm and Managing Dir of Rolls-Royce Ltd; *cr Baron Hives*, of Duffield, co Derby (peerage of UK) 1950: *m* 1913, Gertrude Ethel, who *d* 1961, da of John Warwick, of Derby; *d* 1965; *s* by his el son (2) JOHN WARWICK, 2nd Baron and present peer.

HOBSON, BARONY OF (Hobson) (Extinct 1966)

DAUGHTER LIVING OF LIFE BARON

Hon Marian Elizabeth, *b* 1941; *ed* Newnham Coll, Camb (MA, PhD): *m* 1968, Michel Jeanneret, MA, Dr ès L, and has issue. *Residence* – 21 Church Lane, Trumpington, Cambridge CB2 2LA.

HOLDEN, BARONY OF (Holden) (Extinct 1951)

DAUGHTER LIVING OF SECOND BARON

Hon Donna Diana, *b* 1916. *Residence* – Hadleigh Court, Stanley Rd, Cary Park, Babbacombe, Torquay TQ1 3JZ.

HOLDERNESS, BARON (Wood) (Life Baron 1979)

RICHARD FREDERICK WOOD, PC, 2nd surv son of 1st Earl of Halifax; *b* 5 Oct 1920; *ed* Eton and New Coll, Oxford; Hon LLD Sheffield 1963; Hon LLD Leeds 1978; Hon LLD Hull 1982; late Lt KRRC; Hon Col Queen's Roy Rifles 1962-67, Hon Col 4th (vol) Bn R Green Jackets, T & AVR 1967-89; Parl Sec to Min of Pensions and Nat Insurance 1955-58, and to Min of Labour 1958-59; Min of Power 1959-63 and Min of Pensions and Nat Insurance 1963-64, and Min of Overseas Development 1970-74; Chm Disablement Services Authority 1987-91; Regional Dir Lloyd's Bank (Yorks and Humberside) 1981-90; 1939-45 War in Middle East (severely wounded); MP for Bridlington Div of E Riding of Yorks (*C*) 1950-79; a DL for E Riding 1967; PC 1959; *cr Baron Holderness*, of Bishop Wilton, co Humberside (Life Baron) 1979; *m* 1947, Diana, only da of late Col Edward Orlando Kellett, DSO, MP, and has issue.

Arms – 1st and 4th azure, three naked savages ambulant in fesse proper in the dexter hand of each a shield argent, charged with a cross gules and in the sinister a club resting on the shoulder also proper, on a canton ermine three lozenges conjoined in fesse sable, *Wood*; 2nd, or, three torteaux gules and differenced with a lable axure, *Courtenay*; 3rd, or, a lion rampant azure. In the centre a mullet gules. **Crest** – A savage as in the arms, the shield sable charged with a griffin's head erased argent. **Supporters** – *Dexter*, an officer of the Kings Royal Rifle Corps circa 1904. *Sinister*, a boar sable armed unguled and bristled or, gorged with a collar argent thereon Cornish cloughs proper and pendant therefrom a cinquefoil argent resting the inner rear leg upon an anchor bendwise gold.

Residence – Flat Top House, Bishop Wilton, York.

SON LIVING

Hon Edward Orlando Charles, *b* 1951: *m* 1st, 1977, Joanna Harriet, elder da of John Pinches, MC, of Parliament Piece, Ramsbury, Wilts; 2ndly, 1993, Katherine M., yst da of Brig Denis Leonard Ormerod, CBE, of Kirkbank House, High Halden, Kent, and has issue living (by 1st *m*), Leonora Sarah Clare, *b* 1982.

DAUGHTER LIVING

Hon Emma Myrtle Mary Anne (*Hon Lady Brooksbank*), *b* 1949: *m* 1970, Capt Sir (Edward) Nicholas Brooksbank, 3rd Bt.

HOLLENDEN, BARON (Hope-Morley) (Baron UK 1912)

GORDON HOPE HOPE-MORLEY, 3rd Baron; *b* 8 Jan 1914; *s* 1977; *ed* Eton; Maj (ret) Black Watch; 1939-45 War; Alderman City of London 1954-58: *m* 1945, Sonja, da of late Thorlf Sundt, of Bergen, Norway, and has issue.

Arms – Argent, a leopard's face jessant-de-lis sable between three griffins heads erased gules. **Crest** – A demi-griffin argent, wings elevated ermine, holding between the claws a leopard's face jessant-de-lis as in the arms. **Supporters** – On either side a stag proper, chained around the neck and suspended therefrom an anchor or.
Seat – Hall Place, Leigh, Tonbridge, Kent.

Tenacious of purpose

SONS LIVING

Hon IAN HAMPDEN, *b* 23 Oct 1946; *ed* Eton: *m* 1st, 1972 (*m diss* 19—), Beatrice Saulnier, da of Baron Pierre d'Anchald, of Paris; 2ndly, 1988, Caroline N., only da of Kim Ash, of Johannesburg, S Africa, and has issue living (by 1st *m*), Edward, *b* 9 April 1981, — Juliette, *b* 1974, — (by 2nd *m*), Alastair Kim, *b* 1990, — Henry Gordon, *b* 1993. *Address* – c/o Hampden Estate Office, Gt Hampden, Gt Missenden, Bucks.
Hon Robin Gordon, *b* 1949; *ed* Brickwall, Northiam. *Residence* – Flat 2, 159 Ebury St, SW1.
Hon Andrew James Sundt, *b* 1952; *ed* Eton.

SISTERS LIVING (Raised to the rank of a Baron's daughters 1979)

Hon Ann Rosemary Hope (*Hon Lady Newman*) (Blackpool House, Dartmouth, S Devon), *b* 1916; 1939-45 War as Junior Comdt ATS: *m* 1946, Sir Ralph Alured Newman, 5th Bt, who *d* 1968.
Hon Stella Hope, *b* 1919; 1939-45 War as 2nd Officer WRNS: *m* 1950, Neville Whiteoak Robinson, of 107 Old Church St, SW3, and has issue living, Anthony David Whiteoak, *b* 1953: *m* 1982, Claire Milligan, and has issue living, Michael Humphrey Whiteoak *b* 1988, — Brian Robert Whiteoak, *b* 1956: *m* 1988, Jayne Connelly, — Julia Mary, *b* 1954.
Hon Lorna Margaret Dorothy (*Hon Lady Hanley*) *b* 1929; JP: *m* 1957, Sir Michael Bowen Hanley, KCB, and has issue living, Peter Michael, *b* 1968, — Sarah Margaret, *b* 1967: *m* 1992, Simon L. H. Ash, yst son of late Michael Ash, of Trowbridge, Wilts.

DAUGHTER LIVING OF SECOND BARON

Hon (Mary) Joan Fenella Hope, *b* 1915: *m* 1st, 1941 (*m diss* 1965), David Babington Smith, who *d* 1989, son of late Sir Henry Babington Smith, GBE, CH, KCB, CSI (E Elgin); 2ndly, 1966, Geoffrey John, of Thornfield Grange, Thropton, Morpeth, Northumberland NE65 7HX, and has issue living (by 1st *m*), Catherine, *b* 1952: *m* 1979, Maj John McMorrough Carr-Ellison, el son of Sir Ralph Harry Carr-Ellison, TD, of Hedgeley Hall, Powburn, Northumberland (Buxton, Bt, colls), and has issue living, Thomas Ralph *b* 1987, a son *b* 1991, Lucy Emma *b* 1986, Hannah Mary *b* 1989.

WIDOW LIVING OF SECOND BARON

VIOLET NORRIS (*Anne, Baroness Hollenden*) (Valley Farm, Duntisbourne Hill, nr Cirencester) da of Alfred Leverton, of Glapthorn, Peterborough, and widow of Dr Frank Dutch Howitt, CVO, MD, FRCP: *m* 2ndly, 1963, as his 3rd wife, the 2nd Baron Hollenden, who *d* 1977.

PREDECESSORS – (1) SAMUEL HOPE Morley, el son of late Samuel Morely, JP, DL (MP for Nottingham 1865-6, and for Bristol 1868-85), by his wife, Rebekah Maria, da of Samuel Hope, of Liverpool; *b* 1845; a partner in the firm of I. and R. Morley, of Wood Street, EC; was a Gov of the Bank of England 1903-5; *cr Baron Hollenden*, of Leigh, Kent (peerage of United Kingdom) 1912: *m* 1884, Laura Marianne, who *d* 1945, da of late Rev G. Royds Birch; *d* 1929; *s* by his son (2) GEOFFREY HOPE Hope-Morley, 2nd Baron, JP for Kent; High Sheriff of co London 1917; Prime Warden of Fishmongers' Co 1938-39; assumed by deed poll (enrolled at College of Arms) 1923 the additional surname of Hope: *m* 1st, 1914 (*m diss* 1928), Hon Mary Sidney Katherine Almina Gardner, who *d* 1982, da of 1st Baron Burghclere; 2ndly, 1929, Muriel Ivy, who *d* 1962, yst da of Sir John Evelyn Gladstone, 4th Bt; 3rdly, 1963, Violet Norris, da of Alfred Leverton, of Glapthorn, Peterborough, and widow of Frank Dutch Howitt, CVO, MD, FRCP; *d* 1977; *s* by his nephew (3) GORDON HOPE HOPE-MORLEY (only son of late Capt Hon Claude Hope Hope-Morley, yr son of 1st Baron), 3rd Baron and present peer.

HOLLICK, BARON (Hollick) (Life Baron 1991)

CLIVE RICHARD HOLLICK, son of Leslie George Hollick, of Southampton; *b* 20 May 1945; *ed* Taunton's Sch, Southampton, and Nottingham Univ (BA); joined Hambros Bank Ltd 1968, Dir since 1973; Chief Exec MAI plc since 1974 (formerly Mills & Allen Internat plc); Chm Shepperton Studios Ltd 1976-84, and Garban Ltd (USA) since 1983; Dir Logica plc since 1987, Avenir Havas Media SA since 1989, and Satellite Information Systems Ltd since 1990; Founding Trustee Inst for Public Policy Research since 1988, Member Nat Bus Co Ltd since 1984; *cr Baron Hollick*, of Notting Hill, Royal Borough of Kensington and Chelsea (Life Baron) 1991: *m* 1977, Susan Mary Woodford, da of HE P. L. U. Cross, of Trinidad and Tobago, and has issue.
Residence – 14 Kensington Park Gdns, W11. *Club* – Royal Automobile.

DAUGHTERS LIVING

Hon Caroline Daniela, *b* 1975.
Hon Georgina Louise, *b* 1979.
Hon Abigail Miranda, *b* 1981.

HOLLIS OF HEIGHAM, BARONESS (Hollis) (Life Baroness 1990)

PATRICIA LESLEY HOLLIS, da of H. L. G. Wells, of Norwich; *b* 24 May 1941: *ed* Plympton Gram Sch, Plymouth, Coll, Camb (BA 1962, MA 1965), Univ of California, Berkeley, Columbia Univ, NY, and Nuffield Coll, Oxford (DPhil 1968); FRHistS; DL Norfolk 1994; Harkness Fellow 1962-64, Nuffield Scholar 1964-67, Reader in Modern History, E Anglia Univ since 1967, Senior Fellow, also Dean of English and American Studies 1988-90; Councillor Norwich City Council 1968-91 (Leader 1983-88), and Norfolk CC 1981-85; Member E Anglia Economic Planning Council 1975-79, Govt Cmmn on Housing 1975-77, Regional Health Authority 1979-83, Press Council 1989-91, BBC Regional Advisory Cttee, Commr English Heritage 1988-91, etc; author of *The Pauper Press* 1970, *Class and Class Conflict 1815-50* 1973, *Pressure from Without* 1974, *Women in Public 1850-1900* 1979, *Ladies Elect: Women in English Local Government 1865-1914* 1987; *cr* Baroness Hollis of Heigham, of Heigham, City of Norwich (Life Baroness) 1990: *m* 1965, (James) Martin Hollis, and has issue.
Residence – 30 Park Lane, Norwich.

SONS LIVING

Hon Simon, *b* 1969.
Hon Matthew, *b* 1971.

HOLM PATRICK, BARON (Hamilton) (Baron UK 1897)

HANS JAMES DAVID HAMILTON, 4th Baron; *b* 15 March 1955; *s* 1991; *ed* Harrow: *m* 1984, Mrs Gill Francesca Anne du Feu, eldest da of late Sqdn Ldr Kenneth James (Toby) Harding, DFC, RAF, of Binisafua, Minorca, and has issue.

Arms – Gules, three cinquefoils ermine, a mullet argent for difference; on a chief or, a heart gules. **Crest** – A demi-antelope argent, hoofed and armed or, holding a heart gules, and charged on the shoulder with a mullet of the last. **Supporters** – *Dexter*, an antelope argent gorged with a collar flory counterflory or, pendent therefrom an escutcheon ermine charged with a heart gules; *sinister*, a lion gules gorged with a collar flory counterflory or, pendent therefrom an escutcheon ermine, charged with a heart of the first.
Residence – 67 Vicarage Rd, St Agnes, Cornwall TR5 0JH.

The same as from the beginning

SON LIVING

Hon James Hans Stephen, *b* 1982.

BROTHERS LIVING

Hon ION HENRY JAMES (The Steward's Lodge, Ballinlough, Clonmellon, co Westmeath), *b* 12 June 1956; *ed* Harrow.
Hon Evelyn William James, *b* 1961; *ed* Rannoch: *m* 1990, Nicola Jane Fullerton, and has issue living, Ross Andrew James, *b* 1990.

AUNT LIVING (*Daughter of 2nd Baron*)

Hon Caroline, *b* 1926: *m* 1951, Maj John Henry Hamilton Bonham, and has issue living, Oliver John Hans (1245 Grand Blvd, Oakville, Ont, Canada), *b* 1954; *ed* St Columba's, Trin Coll, Dublin (BA), and Dalhousie Univ, Halifax, Nova Scotia (MSc): *m* 1979, Ann, da of Michael Proulx, of Gainsborough, Lincs, and has issue living, Michael John *b* 1985, Patricia *b* 1981, Elizabeth *b* 1983, — Francis Richard Hamilton (40 The Fairway, South Ruislip, Middx HA4 0R7), *b* 1956; *ed* St Columba's, and Trin Coll, Dublin (BA, MSc): *m* 1983, Christine, da of George Hunter, of Blackrock, co Dublin, and has issue living, Kate *b* 1990, — John Arthur Norris, *b* 1961; *ed* St Columba's: *m* 1990, Amanda, da of David Potterton, of Dunboyne, co Meath, and has issue living, Richard David *b* 1993. *Residence* – Trumroe, Castlepollard, co Westmeath.

WIDOW LIVING OF THIRD BARON

ANNE LOYS ROCHE (*Anne, Baroness Holm Patrick*), only da of Cdr Ernest Padwick Brass, RN (ret), of Haroldston House, Haverfordwest, Pembrokeshire: *m* 1954, the 3rd Baron, who *d* 1991. *Residence* – The Burlington, Owls Rd, Bournemouth.

PREDECESSORS – (1) ION TRANT Hamilton, PC, son of late James Hans Hamilton, MP for co Dublin 1841-63; *b* 1839; Lord-Lieut and Custos Rotulorum of co Dublin; MP for Dublin co (C) 1863-85; *cr Baron Holm Patrick*, of HolmPatrick, co Dublin (peerage of United Kingdom), 1897: *m* 1877, Lady Victoria Alexandrina Wellesley, who *d* 1933, sister of 3rd and 4th Dukes of Wellington; *d* 1898; *s* by his only son (2) HANS WELLESLEY, DSO, MC, 2nd Baron; *b* 1886; late Capt 16th Lancers and Bde Maj; 1914-18 War (MC, DSO): *m* 1925, Lady Edina Dorothy Hope, who *d* 1964, da of 4th Marquess Conyngham; *d* 1942; *s* by his only son (3) JAMES HANS, 3rd Baron, *b* 1928; late Lieut 16/5th Lancers; Keeper of the Matchbook at the Irish Turf Club, Sec Kenyan Jockey Club: *m* 1954, Anne Loys Roche, only da of Cdr Ernest Padwick Brass, RN (ret), of Haroldston House, Haverfordwest, Pembrokeshire; *d* 1991; *s* by his eldest son (4) HANS JAMES DAVID, 4th Baron and present peer.

HOLME OF CHELTENHAM, BARON (Holme) (Life Baron 1990)

RICHARD GORDON HOLME, CBE, son of late Jack Richard Holme; *b* 27 May 1936; *ed* Royal Masonic Sch, and St John's Coll, Oxford (MA); Chm Constitutional Reform Centre since 1984, Chm Threadneedle

Publishing Group since 1988; Vice-Chm Liberal Party Exec 1966-67, Pres Liberal Party 1980-81, Dir Campaign for Electoral Reform 1976-85, Sec Parly Democracy Trust since 1977; Chm Dod's Publishing and Research since 1988, Black Box Publishing since 1988, and Hollis Directories since 1988; commn'd 10th Gurkha Rifles, Malaya, 1954-56 *cr* CBE (Civil) 1983, and *Baron Holme of Cheltenham*, of Cheltenham, co Glos (Life Baron) 1990: *m* 1958, Kay Mary, da of Vincent Powell, and has issue.
Clubs — Reform, Brooks's.

SONS LIVING

Hon Richard Vincent, *b* 1966: *m* 1992, Caroline Elizabeth, da of Michael Holman, of Hazlemere, Bucks.
Hon John Gordon, *b* (twin) 1966.

DAUGHTERS LIVING

Hon Nicola Ann, *b* 1959.
Hon Penelope Jane, *b* 1962.

Home, Earldom of, see Baron Home of the Hirsel.

HOME OF THE HIRSEL, BARON (Douglas-Home) (Earl S 1605, disclaimed 1963) (Life Baron 1974)
(Name pronounced "Hume")

ALEXANDER FREDERICK DOUGLAS-HOME, KT, PC; *b* 2 July 1903; *s* as 14th Earl of Home 11 July 1951; *ed* Eton; Hon DCL Oxford 1960, and Hon Student of Ch Ch, Oxford 1962; Maj Lanark Yeo (TA Reserve), Brig Roy Co of Archers (Queen's Body Guard for Scotland), and a DL for Lanarkshire, appointed PPS to Parliamentary Sec to Min of Labour 1935-36, to Chancellor of the Exchequer 1936-37 and to Prime Min 1937-40; Joint Under-Sec of State for Foreign Affairs May to July 1945, Min of State, Scottish Office Oct, 1951 to April 1955, Sec of State for Commonwealth Relations April 1955 to July 1960 (also Lord Pres of the Council Jan to Sept 1957-60), Sec of State for Foreign Affairs July 1960 to Oct 1963, Prime Min and First Lord of the Treasury 1963-64, Leader of the Opposition 1964-65; Sec of State for Foreign and Commonwealth Affairs 1970-74; Grand Master of Primrose League and first Chancellor of Heriot-Watt Univ Edinburgh 1966; Pres of the MCC 1966; Pres of NATO Council 1974, Pres of Peace Through NATO 1985; Chancellor of Order of the Thistle 1973-92; Freeman of Selkirk, Edinburgh, Coldstream and Crieff; bore Sword of Scotland at Coronation of Queen Elizabeth II; MP for Lanark Div of Lanarkshire (*C*) 1931-45, and 1950-51, and for Kinross and W Perth Div of Perthshire and Kinross-shire 1963-74; PC 1951, KT 1962; disclaimed his peerages for life 23rd Oct 1963, and *cr Baron Home of the Hirsel*, of Coldstream, co Berwick (Life Baron) 1974: *m* 1936, Elizabeth Hester (first woman to be elected a Fellow of Eton Coll), who *d* 1990, da of late Very Rev Cyril Argentine Alington, DD, Dean of Durham (*see* V Cobham, 1958 Edn), and has issue.

Arms – Quarterly: 1st and 4th grand quarters counter quartered, 1st and 4th grand quartered, 1st and 4th vert, a lion rampant argent, armed and langued gules, *Home*; 2nd and 3rd argent, three popinjays vert, beaked and membered gules, *Pepdie*; over all an escutcheon or, charged with an orle azure, *Landale*; 2nd and 3rd grand quarters counter-quartered, 1st azure, a lion rampant argent, armed and langued gules, crowned with an imperial crown or, *Lordship of Galloway*; 2nd or, a lion rampant gules, armed and langued azure, debruised of a ribbon sable, *Abernethy*; 3rd argent, three piles gules, *Lordship of Brechin*; 4th or, a fesse checky azure and argent, surmounted of a bend sable, charged with three buckles of the field, *Stewart of Bonkhill*; over all on an escutcheon argent, a man's heart, ensigned with an imperial crown proper, and a chief azure, charged with three mullets of the field, *Douglas*. **Crests** – 1st, on a cap of maintenance proper, a lion's head erased argent, *Home*; 2nd, on a cap of maintenance proper, a salamander vert, encircled with flames of fire proper. **Supporters** – Two lions argent, armed and langued gules.
Seat — The Hirsel, Coldstream, Berwickshire; Castlemains, Douglas, Lanarkshire. *Clubs* – Travellers', Carlton, Buck's.

SON LIVING

Hon DAVID ALEXANDER COSPATRICK, CBE (99 Dovehouse Street, SW3; Turf Club), *b* 20 Nov 1943: styled *Lord Dunglass* 1951-63, when he discontinued the use of this courtesy title, and obtained official recognition at Lyon Court in his new name; *ed* Eton, and Ch Ch Oxford; Dir Morgan Grenfell & Co, Ltd; CBE (Civil) 1991: *m* 1972, Jane Margaret, da of Col John Francis Williams-Wynne, CBE, DSO (*see* Williams-Wynn, Bt, colls), and has issue living, Michael David Alexander, *b* 30 Nov 1987, — Iona Katherine, *b* 1980, — Mary Elizabeth, *b* 1982.

DAUGHTERS LIVING

(All of whom discontinued the prefix of *Lady* and obtained official recognition at Lyon Court in their new names 1963).
Hon (Lavinia) Caroline (Dove Cottage, The Hirsel, Coldstream TD12 4LP Berwickshire), *b* 1937; a Woman of the Bedchamber to HM Queen Elizabeth the Queen Mother 1963-65; a Lady in Waiting to HRH the Duchess of Kent 1966-67; Trustee Nat Museum of Antiquities of Scotland 1982-86; FSA Scot; DL for Berwickshire since 1983.
Hon Meriel Kathleen, *b* 1939: *m* 1964, Adrian Marten George Darby, Fellow of Keble Coll, Oxford, of Kemerton Court, Tewkesbury, Glos, and has issue living, Matthew George, *b* 1967, — Catherine Monica, *b* 1964.
Hon Diana Lucy, *b* 1940: *m* 1963 (*m diss* 1976), James Archibald Wolfe Murray (*see* Murray, Bt *cr* 1928, colls).

BROTHER LIVING

Hon Edward Charles, *b* 1920; *ed* Eton; 2nd Lt RA; 1939-45 War (wounded, prisoner); *m* 1946, Nancy Rose, only da of Sir Thomas Dalrymple Straker-Smith, of Carham Hall, Cornhill-on-Tweed, and has issue living, Simon (70 Cloncurry St, SW6), *b* 1947: *m* 1971, Sally Beard, and has issue living, Edward *b* 1980, Joanna *b* 1973, Louisa *b* 1976, — Andrew (The Lees, Coldstream, Berwickshire), *b* 1950: *m* 1980, Jane, da of the late Maurice Oliver Pease, and has had issue, Richard *b* 1983, Nicholas *b* 1985, Freddie *b* 1989 *d* 1990, — Mark (25 India St, Edinburgh), *b* 1951: *m* 1976, Colette O'Reilly, and has issue living, Rory *b* 1981, Rebecca *b* 1978. *Residence* – Westnewton, Kirknewton, Wooler, Northumberland.

SISTER LIVING

Lady Rachel (*Lady William W. Montagu Douglas Scott*), *b* 1910: *m* 1937, Lt-Col Lord William Walter Montagu Douglas Scott, MC, who *d* 1958 (*see* D Buccleuch). *Residence* – Beechwood, Melrose.

WIDOWS LIVING OF SONS OF THIRTEENTH EARL

Felicity Betty, da of late Maj Aubrey Thomas Jonsson, and formerly wife of Hon Victor Patrick Hamilton Wills (*see* B Dulverton): *m* 1966, as his 3rd wife, Maj Hon Henry Montagu Douglas-Home, MBE, who *d* 1980, and has issue (see colls infra). *Residence* – Old Greenlaw, Berwickshire.
Rachel Leila, Baroness Dacre (in her own right): *m* 1951, Hon William Douglas-Home, who *d* 1992, and has issue (*see* Bs Dacre). *Residence* – Derry House, Kilmeston, nr Alresford, Hants.

COLLATERAL BRANCHES LIVING

Grandsons of late Maj Hon Henry Montagu Douglas-Home, MBE (infra):—
Issue of late Capt (Cecil) Robin Douglas-Home, *b* 1932, *d* 1968: *m* 1959 (*m diss* 1965), Sandra Clare (who *m* 2ndly, 1975, Rt Hon Michael Howard, QC, MP, Home Sec since 1993), yr da of late W/Cmdr Saville Paul, MRCS, LRCP, of High Chimneys, Windlesham, Surrey:—
(Alexander) Sholto (20 Redcliffe St, SW10 9DT), *b* 1962: *m* 1992, Alexandra J., yr da of Benjamin Miller, of 42 Pembroke Rd, W8.
Issue of late Charles Cospatrick Douglas-Home, *b* 1937, *d* 1985; editor of *The Times* 1982-85: *m* 1966, Jessica Violet (who *m* 2ndly, 1993, Rodney Leach) (63 Hillgate Place, W8), da of late Maj John Nevile Wake Gwynne, RA (*see* Morrison-Bell, Bt, *cr* 1923, ext):—
Tara John, *b* 1969. —— Luke Cospatrick, *b* 1971.

Issue of late Maj Hon Henry Montagu Douglas-Home, MBE, 2nd son of 13th Earl, *b* 1907, *d* 1980: *m* 1st, 1931 (*m diss* 1947), Lady (Alexandra) Margaret Elizabeth Spencer, da of 6th Earl Spencer; 2ndly, 1947, Vera Bugge, who *d* 1963, da of late Carl Herman Jensen, of Oslo, Norway, and formerly wife of Ivan Johansen; 3rdly, 1966, Felicity Betty (ante) da of late Maj Aubrey Thomas Jonsson, and formerly wife of Hon Victor Patrick Hamilton Wills (*see* B Dulverton):—
(By 1st *m*) Fiona Margaret (*Lady Fraser*), *b* 1936; resumed her maiden name until remarriage: *m* 1st, 1962 (*m diss* 1981), Gregory Martin; 2ndly, 1993, as his 2nd wife, Sir Ian James Fraser, CBE, MC (*see* L Lovat, colls), and has issue living (by 1st *m*), Kezia Alexandra Lilian, *b* 1970, — Lydia Georgiana Bridget, *b* 1975. —— (By 2nd *m*) George Erik Montagu, *b* 1948. —— (By 3rd *m*) Peregrine Montagu, *b* 1967. *Residence* – Old Greenlaw, Berwickshire.

Issue of late Hon William Douglas-Home, playwright, 3rd son of 13th Earl, *b* 1912, *d* 1992: *m* 1951, Rachel Leila, Baroness Dacre (in her own right) (ante):—
See Bs Dacre.

PREDECESSORS – **(1)** Sir ALEXANDER Home, of Home, Berwickshire, Baron of Douglass, (el son of Sir Alexander Home) *k* at Battle of Verneuil 1424: Ambassador to England 1459; *cr Lord Home* (peerage of Scotland) 1473; *m* 1st, before 1424, Marion, da and heir of John Lauder; 2ndly, before 1467, Margaret, da of Alexander Momtgomerie, Master of Montgomerie; *d* 1491; *s* by his grandson **(2)** ALEXANDER, 2nd Lord (son of Alexander Home), and Agnes, da of Sir Adam Hepburn of Hailes: *m* 1st, Isabel Douglas (annulled on grounds of consanguinity 1476); 2ndly, before March 1493, Nichola (who *d* 1527/28 having *m* 2ndly, Sir Alexander Ramsay of Dalhousie), da of George Ker of Samuelston, Haddington; *d* 1506; *s* by his son **(3)** ALEXANDER, 3rd Lord, commanded the van with the 4th Earl of Huntly at Flodden, and was one of the few surviving commanders of that battle; afterwards embraced the English interest in opposition to the Regent Albany; whilst visiting the Court in 1516 was taken prisoner, and after a hasty trial was executed, and his titles and estates declared forfeit; these were restored in 1522 to his brother **(4)** GEORGE, 4th Lord: *m* 1531, Mariot Halyburton, who *d* about 1563, da and co-heir of the 5th Lord Dirletun; killed in a skirmish at Fauside two days before battle of Pinkie 1547; *s* by his son **(5)** ALEXANDER, 5th Lord; supported Mary Queen of Scots; convicted of treason 1573 and his title and estates forfeited: *m* 1st, Margaret, da of Sir Walter Kerr; 2ndly, Agnes (who *m* 3rdly, Sir Thomas Lyon, Master of Glamis), da of 4th Lord Gray, and widow of Sir Robert Logan of Restalrig; *s* by his son (by 2nd wife) **(6)** ALEXANDER, 6th Lord; *b* about 1566; *cr Lord Dunglass* and *Earl of Home* (peerage of Scotland) 1605 with remainder to his heirs male whatsoever: *m* 1st, 1586, Christian, da of 6th Earl of Morton, and a widow of Laurence, Master of Oliphant; 2ndly, before June 1607, Mary Sutton, who *d* 1645, da of 9th Baron Dudley; *d* 1619; *s* by his son (by 2nd wife) **(7)** JAMES, 2nd Earl; *b* about 1607: *m* 1st, 1622, Hon Katherine Cary, da of 1st Viscount Falkland; 2ndly, Lady Grace Fane, da of 1st Earl of Westmorland; *dsp* 1633; *s* by his kinsman **(8)** JAMES, 3rd Earl, only son of Sir James Home of Whitrig (by Lady Anna * el dau and co-heir of George Home, 1st Earl of Dunbar and 1st Lord Home (or Hume) of Berwick), el son of Sir John Home of Cowdenknows, great grandson of Mungo Home, el son of John yr brother of 2nd Lord: *m* 1640, Lady Jean Douglas, who *d* 1694, da of 7th Earl of Morton; *d* 1666; *s* by his el son **(9)** ALEXANDER, 4th Earl: *m* 1671, Lady Anne Sackville, who *d* 1672, da of 5th Earl of Dorset; *d* 1974; *s* by his brother **(10)** JAMES, 5th Earl: *m* Lady Anne Ramsay, da of 2nd Earl of Dalhousie; *d* 1687; *s* by his brother **(11)** CHARLES, 6th Earl: *m* about 1680, Anne, da of Sir William Purves of Purves, Bt; *d* 1706; *s* by his son **(12)** ALEXANDER, 7th Earl; imprisoned in Edinburgh Castle 1715-16 on suspicion of being involved in Jacobite rising: *m* Lady Anne Kerr (who *d* 1727, having *m* 2ndly, Henry Ogle), da of 2nd Marquess of Lothian; *d* 1720; *s* by his el son **(13)** WILLIAM, 8th Earl; Gov of Gibraltar 1757-61: *m* 1742, Elizabeth, who *d* 1784, da and heir of William Gibbons, and widow of James Lawes; *d* 1761; *s* by his brother **(14)** *Rev* ALEXANDER, 9th Earl: *m* 1st, Hon Primrose Elphinstone, who *d* 1759, da of 9th Lord Elphinstone; 2ndly, Marion, who *d* 1765, da of his uncle Hon James Home; 3rdly, 1768, Abigail Browne, who *d* 1814, da and co-heir of John Ramey, of

Yarmouth; *d* 1786; *s* by his son **(15)** ALEXANDER, 10th Earl; *b* 1769; assumed by Royal Licence the addition surname of Ramey 1814: *m* 1798, Lady Elizabeth Scott, who *d* 1837, da of 3rd Duke of Buccleuch; *d* 1841; *s* by his son **(16)** COSPATRICK ALEXANDER, 11th Earl; *b* 1799; Under-Sec for Foreign Affairs 1828-30, a Representative Peer 1842-74, Lt-Gen of Royal Co of Archers, and Keeper of the Great Seal of Scotland; on death of his mother 1877 took the additional surname of Douglas of Douglas under deed of entail of Douglas estates; *cr Baron Douglas*, of Douglas, co Lanark (peerage of United Kingdom), 1875: *m* 1832, Hon Lucy Elizabeth, who *d* 1877, el da of 2nd and last Baron Montagu of Boughton; by Jane Margaret, da of Archibald Douglas (formerly Stewart) 1st Baron Douglas of Douglas (*cr* 1790, ext 1857); *d* 1881; *s* by his son **(17)** CHARLES ALEXANDER, KT, 12th Earl, *b* 1834: *m* 1870, Maria, who *d* 1919, da of late Capt Charles Conrad Grey, RN; *d* 1918; *s* by his son **(18)** CHARLES COSPATRICK ARCHIBALD, KT, TD, 13th Earl; *b* 1873; Brig of King's Body Guard for Scotland (Roy Co of Archers): *m* 1902, Lady Lilian Lambton, who *d* 1966, da of 4th Earl of Durham; *d* 1951; *s* by his son **(19)** ALEXANDER FREDERICK, 14th Earl, and Lord Home, Lord Dunglass, until he disclaimed his peerage 1963.

*The Lordship of Home (or Hume) of Berwick, *cr* by patent 1604 upon George Home, High Treasurer of Scotland (who in 1605 was *cr* Earl of Dunbar), with remainder to his heirs for ever, is held to have descended to the Earls of Home through Lady Anna Home. Whether this was an English Barony, as thought by Dugdale, or a Scottish Lordship, which is thought more likely in view of the remainder, is uncertain.

HOOD, VISCOUNT (Hood) (Viscount GB 1796, Bt GB 1778)

With favourable winds

ALEXANDER LAMBERT HOOD, 7th Viscount, and 7th Baronet; *b* 11 March 1914; *s* 1981; *ed* Trin Coll, Camb (MA), and at Harvard (MBA); Lt-Cdr RNVR; former Dir Continental & Industrial Trust plc, Tanks Investment plc, George Wimpey plc, and of other cos: *m* 1957, Diana Maud, CVO, el da of late Hon George William Lyttelton (*see* V Cobham, colls) and has issue.

Arms – Azure, a frette argent, on a chief or three crescents sable. **Crest** – A Cornish chough sable, in front of an anchor in bend sinister or. **Supporters** – *Dexter*, a merman, holding in the right hand a trident; *sinister*, a mermaid, holding in the left hand a look-glass. *Residences* – Loders Court, Bridport, Dorset; 67 Chelsea Sq, SW3. *Club* – Brooks's.

SONS LIVING

Hon HENRY LYTTELTON ALEXANDER (4 Alexander St, W2 5NT), *b* 16 March 1958: *m* 1991, Flora Susan, yr da of Cdr Michael Bernard Casement, OBE, RN (*see* Greenwell, Bt), and has issue living, Archibald Lyttelton Samuel, *b* 16 May 1993.
Hon John Samuel (72 Thurleigh Rd, SW12), *b* 1959: *m* 1982, Melissa Anne, 2nd da of Kerry D. Bell, of 221 Burns Bay Road, Lane Cove, New South Wales 2066, Australia, and has issue living, Christian Alexander, *b* 1989, — Samuel Francis Wheeler, *b* 1991, — Gemma Kathryn, *b* 1986.

Hon James Francis Touzalin (86 Oxford Gdns, W10 5UW), *b* 1962.

COLLATERAL BRANCHES LIVING

Granddaughters of Lt-Col Hon Neville Albert Hood, CMG, DSO, RGA (infra):—
Issue of late Peter Neville Hood, *b* 1913, *d* 1969: *m* 1936, Nancy Warrington, who *d* 1968, da of late Tristram W. Haward, JP, of Abbey Lands, Alnwick, Northumberland:—
Sally Penelope, *b* 1937: *m* 1959, Edward Martin Amphlett Thompson, of The Bolt Hole, Six Ashes, Bridgnorth, Salop (E Coventry, colls), and has issue living, Stephen Peter, *b* 1960, — Mary Jane, *b* 1963, — Sarah Ann, *b* 1965, — Rosemary Claire, *b* 1969. —— Anna Rosemary (220 Marlborough Rd, Oxford), *b* 1940: *m* 1968 (*m diss* 1974), Peter Christopher Glazebrook, and has issue living, Anthony Peter, *b* 1970, — Daniel George, *b* 1978. —— Eveline Jane Venetia, *b* 1957; has issue living, Katherine, *b* 1992.

Issue of late Lieut-Col Hon Neville Albert Hood, CMG, DSO, RGA, 4th son of 4th Viscount, *b* 1872, *d* 1948: *m* 1908, Eveline Mary, who *d* 1967, da of late Herman Usticke Broad (who subsequently assumed the surname of Pender), of Tresilian, Falmouth:—
Edith Rosemary (4000 Massachusetts Av, NW 924, Washington DC 20016, USA), *b* 1909: *m* 1st, 1931 (*m diss* 1947), Martin Ayerst Ingram, late Lt RNVR; 2ndly, 1947 (*m diss* 1956), Capt Donald Grant Macleod, late Black Watch, and has issue living (by 1st *m*), Margot Faye (628 Penllyn Pike, Penllyn, Pa 19422, USA), *b* 1934: *m* 1959 (*m diss* 1982), John A. H. Shober, and has issue living, John Andrews Harris *b* 1961: *m* 1987 (*m diss* 1991), Dena Louise Smith, Martin Pemberton *b* 1966, Cintra Suzanne *b* 1964: *m* 1992, Joseph Hardcastle, — (by 2nd *m*) Carole Alice Grant, *b* 1948: *m* 1982, Paul Noel Inman, and has issue living, Annabelle May Ruth *b* 1983, Hannah Myfanwy Mary *b* 1986. —— Eveline Suzanne, *b* 1917: *m* 1945, as his 2nd wife, Henry Arthur Frederick Hohler, CMG (V Gort), and has issue living, Katherine Elizabeth, *b* 1948: *m* 1972, Christopher Ernest Nelson Harries, and has issue living, Eleanor Annabel *b* 1972, Emma Susan *b* 1975, — (Edith) Mabel, *b* 1952: *m* 1984, Stephen D. McLeod, elder son of G. R. McLeod, of Bethesda, Maryland, USA, and has issue living, Robert Charles *b* 1986, Franklin Henry *b* 1990, Susan Leighann *b* 1988. *Address* – Budock, RR4 Gloucester, Virginia, USA.

Grandchildren (by 1st *m*) of Mrs Edith Rosemary Macleod (ante):—
Issue of late Annabelle Ingram, *b* 1933, *d* 1967: *m* 1963, Julian Payne Freret (5507 Parkston Rd, Maryland 20016, USA):—
Mary Suzanne, *b* 1964. —— Carole Arthemise, *b* 1965: *m* 1990, Theirry van Bastalaer.

Grandson of late Col Hon Francis George Hood, yst son of 4th Viscount:—
Issue of late Francis Basil Hood, *b* 1905, *d* 1986: *m* 1934, Catherine Anna (302-2427 Amherst St, Sidney, BC, Canada V8L 2HI), da of late Hon Sir Richard McBride, KCMG, KC, Premier of British Columbia 1903-16:—
John Francis Alexander (4533 46B St, Delta, BC, Canada V4K 2N2), *b* 1935: *m* 1963, Barbara Anne, da of late Cyril Turner, of Vic, BC, and has issue living, Valerie Anne, *b* 1966, — Christine Frances, *b* 1971.

Grandchildren of late Hon Albert Hood, 2nd son of 3rd Viscount:—
Issue of late Capt Albert Oscar Hood, Irish Guards, *b* 1870, *d* 1952: *m* 1912, Theresa Emily Margery, who *d* 1970, da of late Col Hon Everard Charles Digby (B Digby colls):—
John Oscar Everard, *b* 1913; *ed* Eton, and Worcester Coll, Oxford; Middle East 1940-45 with Sudan Defence Forces (despatches): *m* 1953, Winifred Mary Milne. *Residence* – Longpré, Gorey, Jersey. —— Georgina Mary, *b* 1915: *m* 1944, Anthony Morley, Lt Life Guards, and has issue living, Andrew Mark, *b* 1945: *m* 1979, Antoinette Barbara Betts, and has issue living, Samuel Anthony *b* 1980, Edward Giles *b* 1982, — Geoffrey John, *b* 1948: *m* 1973, Christian Aline, da of late Sir Hugh Fitzgerald Arbuthnot, 7th Bt, and has issue (*see* Arbuthnot, Bt, *cr* 1823). *Residence* – Shanks House, Wincanton, Somerset.
Issue of late Capt Alexander Frank Hood, *b* 1874, *d* 1923: *m* 1905, Gladys Ursula, who *d* 1968, 3rd da of late Edward C. Youell, of Galatz, Roumania:—
John Michael Alexander (11 Shiremore Hill, Marriott, Somerset TA16 5PH), *b* 1918.
Issue of late Robert Valentine Hood, *b* 1876, *d* 1942: *m* 1917, Mignon, who *d* 1973, da of late John E Cooke:—
Robin Julian Patrick (50 Pont St Mews, SW1), *b* 1919; *ed* Eton.

Grandchildren of late Capt Alexander Frank Hood (ante):—
Issue of late Lt-Col Samuel Brian Digby Hood, TD, *b* 1910, *d* 1988: *m* 1937, Myrtle Baron, who *d* 1982, niece and adopted da of Sir Louis Bernhard Baron, 1st Bt (ext):—
Alexander Robert, *b* 1945; *ed* Eton; late Rifle Bde: *m* 1967, Ann Marie, da of John O'Donovan, of Greenwich, and has issue living, Samuel, *b* 1967, — Padraig, *b* 1971, — Jane, *b* 1969, — Sarah, *b* 1972. *Residence* – Greys Green Farm, Rotherfield Greys, Henley-on-Thames, Oxon RG9 4QG. —— Sarah Jane (twin) (*Hon Mrs Jolyon Grey*), *b* 1945: *m* 1971, Hon Jolyon Kenneth Alnwick Grey (*see* B Grey of Naunton). *Residence* – Upper Swell Farm, Stow-on-the-Wold, Cheltenham, Glos GL54 1EW.

Grandson of late Hon Alexander Frederick GREGORY (who assumed by Roy licence in 1910 the surname of Gregory in lieu of his patronymic, and the arms of Gregory quarterly with his family arms), 3rd son of 3rd Viscount:—
Issue of late Major Charles Hugh GREGORY-HOOD, The Buffs (ret), *b* 1877, *d* 1951 (having assumed by deed poll 1927 (enrolled at College of Arms) the additional surname of Gregory): *m* 1911, Dorothy, who *d* 1983, da of late Hon Marshall Jones Brooks (*see* B Crawshaw, colls):—
Alexander Marshall Horace, OBE, MC, *b* 1915; *ed* Winchester; Col (ret) late Grenadier Guards; MBE (Mil) 1954, OBE (Mil) 1959; European War 1939-45 (despatches, wounded, MC and Bar): *m* 1943 (*m diss* 1949), Diana, who *d* 1987, da of Major Sir John Little Gilmour, 2nd Bt (*see* Gilmour, Bt, *cr* 1929, 1985 Edn), and has issue living, Peter Charles Freeman (73 Cambridge St, SW1) *b* 1943; Diplo Ser: *m* 1966, Camilla, da of Richard Anthony Bethell (*see* E Radnor), and has issue living, Clare *b* 1968, Carolyn Jane *b* 1970, Lucy *b* 1973, — Jane, *b* 1946: *m* 1965, Brian A. FitzGerald, of Sherfield Mill, Sherfield English, Romsey, Hants SO51 6FN, and has issue living, Richard Derek *b* 1967, James Mark *b* 1973, Sarah Jane *b* 1968. *Residence* – Loxley Hall, Warwick.

Descendants of late Hon Samuel Hood (2nd son of 2nd Viscount), and grand-nephew of Sir Alexander Hood, MP (brother of 1st Viscount), who was *cr Baron Bridport* (peerage of Ireland) 1794, *Baron Bridport* (peerage of Great Britain) 1796, and *Viscount Bridport* (peerage of Great Britain) 1800, and whom he *s* (under special remainder) in the Irish Barony (*see* V Bridport).

PREDECESSORS – (1) *Adm Sir* SAMUEL Hood, GCB, a celebrated Naval Com; *cr* a *Baronet* 1778, *Baron Hood*, of Catherington, co Hants (peerage of Ireland) 1782, and *Viscount Hood* (peerage of Great Britain) 1796; his wife Susannah, who *d* 1806, da of Edward Linzee, of Portsmouth, was *cr Baroness Hood*, of Catherington, co Hants (peerage of Great Britain) 1795; *d* 1816; *s* by his son (2) HENRY, 2nd Viscount, who had in 1806 *s* his mother as 2nd Baron Hood (*cr* 1795); *d* 1837; *s* by his grandson (3) SAMUEL, 3rd Viscount; *b* 1808; assumed the additional name of Tibbits by Roy licence 1840: *m* 1837, Mary Isabella, da and heiress of Richard John Tibbits, of Barton Seagrave; *d* 1846; *s* by his son (4) FRANCIS WHEELER, 4th Viscount; *b* 1838: *m* 1865, Edith Lydia Drummond, who *d* 1911, da of Arthur W. Ward, of Calverley, Tunbridge Wells; *d* 1907; *s* by his son (5) GROSVENOR ARTHUR ALEXANDER, OBE, 5th Viscount; *b* 1868; sometime Major Grenadier Guards and Lieut-Col comdg 7th Batn London Regt: *m* 1st, 1911, Jane Primrose, who *d* 1919, da of Col Hon Richard Southwell George Stapleton-Cotton: 2ndly, 1928, his cousin, Marguerite (Margot) Jenny, who *d* 1966, da of Hon Albert Hood; *d* 1933; *s* by his nephew (6) SAMUEL, GCMG (son of late Rear-Adm Hon Horace Lambert Alexander Hood, KCB, MVO, DSO, 3rd son of 4th Viscount), 6th Viscount, *b* 1910; Assist Private Sec to Sec of State for India 1936-39, Private Sec to Min of Information 1939-41; 1st Sec Madrid 1947-48; Counsellor at British Embassy, Paris 1948-51, and Min at British Embassy, Washington, USA 1958-62; Dep Under-Sec Foreign Office 1962-69; *dunm* 1981; *s* by his brother (7) ALEXANDER LAMBERT, 7th Viscount and present peer; also Baron Hood.

HOOPER, BARONESS (Hooper) (Life Baroness 1985)

GLORIA HOOPER, da of Frederick Hooper, *b* 25 May 1939; *ed* Southampton Univ (BA); admitted Solicitor 1973; ptnr Taylor & Humber (now Taylor Joynson Garret) 1974-85; Member European Parliament (*C*) Liverpool 1979-84, Baroness-in-Waiting 1985-87, Under-Sec for Education 1987-88, Under-Sec for Energy 1988-89, Under-Sec for Health 1989-92; *cr Baroness Hooper*, of Liverpool and of St James's in the City of Westminster (Life Baroness) 1985.
Address – c/o House of Lords, SW1A 0PW.

HOOSON, BARON (Hooson) (Life Baron 1979)

(HUGH) EMLYN HOOSON, QC, son of late Hugh Hooson, of Colomendy, Denbigh; *b* 26 March 1925; *ed* Denbigh Gram Sch, and Univ Coll of Wales; Bar Gray's Inn 1949, QC 1960, Bencher 1968; Dep Chm Merioneth Quarter Sessions 1960-67, Chm 1967-71, Dep Chm Flint Quarter Sessions 1960-71; Recorder of Merthyr Tydfil 1971, of Swansea 1971; a Recorder of Crown Court from 1972; Treas Gray's Inn 1986; MP for Montgomeryshire (*L*) 1962-79; Leader Welsh Liberal party 1966-79, a Vice-Pres of Peace through NATO 1985; *cr Baron Hooson*, of Montgomery, co Powys (Life Baron) 1979: *m* 1950, Shirley Margaret Wynne, da of late Sir George Hamer, CBE, of Summerfield, Llanidloes, Powys, and has issue living, two das.
Address – 2 Gray's Inn Sq, Gray's Inn, WC1.

Hopetoun, Earl of; son of Marquess of Linlithgow.

HORDER, BARON (Horder) (Baron UK 1938, Bt UK 1923)

THOMAS MERVYN HORDER, 2nd Baron, and 2nd Baronet; *b* 8 Dec 1910; *s* 1955; *ed* Winchester, and Trin Coll, Camb (BA 1932, MA 1937); Wing-Com RAF Vol Reserve: *m* 1946 (*m diss* 1957), Mary Ross, da of late Dr W. S. McDougall, of Wallington, Surrey.

𝕬rms – Per chevron argent and sable bezantée, in chief a male griffin passant of the second. 𝕮rest – Issuant from a rock proper a demi-male griffin sable. 𝕾upporters – Not recorded at time of going to press.
Address – 4 Hamilton Close, NW8 8QY.

SISTER LIVING

Hon Dorothea Joy, *b* 1905: *m* 1930, Edward Revill Cullinan, CBE, MD, FRCP, who *d* 1965, and has issue living, Edward Horder (62 Camden Mews, NW1), *b* 1931; ARIBA: *m* 1961, Rosalind Sylvia, yst da of late V. M. Yeates, and has issue living, Thomas Edward *b* 1965, Emma *b* 1962, Kate *b* 1963, — Timothy Revill, *b* 1932: *m* 1956, Helen Veronica, yst da of Brig Edmund James Paton-Walsh, and has issue living, Paul *b* 1957, Dominic *b* 1960, Charlotte *b* 1959, Harriet *b* 1962, — Paul Anthony, *b* 1935, — Susan Joy, *b* 1937: *m* 1st, 1959 (*m diss* 1978), John Murray Owen; 2ndly, 1981, Michael Houlihan, and has issue living (by 1st *m*), Clare Joy *b* 1960, Joanna *b* 1961, Philippa *b* 1963, Lucy *b* 1965. *Residence* – 10 Camden Mews, NW1.

PREDECESSOR – (1) *Sir* THOMAS JEEVES Horder, GCVO, MD, son of Albert Horder, *b* 1871; was Physician-in-Ord to HRH the Prince of Wales 1923-36, to King Edward VIII 1936, and to King George VI 1936-49, and Extra Physician to King George VI 1949-52, and to Queen Elizabeth II 1952-55; *cr a Baronet* 1923, and *Baron Horder*, of Ashford, co Southampton (peerage of United Kingdom) 1933: *m* 1902, Geraldine, who *d* 1954, da of late Arthur Doggett: *d* 1955; *s* by his son *b* (2) THOMAS MERVYN, 2nd Baron and present peer.

HOTHAM, BARON (Hotham) (Baron I 1797, Bt E 1622)
(Name pronounced Hutham")

For my country.

HENRY DURAND HOTHAM, 8th Baron, and 18th Baronet; *b* 3 May 1940; *s* 1967; *ed* Eton; late Lt Grenadier Guards; patron of one living; ADC to Gov of Tasmania 1963-66; DL Humberside 1981: *m* 1972, Alexandra Mary, 2nd da of late Maj Andrew Charles Stirling Home Drummond Moray, and has issue.

𝕬rms – Barry of ten argent and azure, on a canton or, a Cornish chough proper. 𝕮rest – Out of waves of the sea a demi-man naked, holding a sword erect proper, and having on the left arm a shield of the arms of Hotham. 𝕾upporters – Two sailors habited proper, and resting their exterior hands on a cutlass point downwards.
Seats – Dalton Hall, Dalton Holme, Beverley, Yorks; Scorborough Hall, Driffield, Yorks.

SONS LIVING

Hon WILLIAM BEAUMONT, *b* 13 Oct 1972
Hon George Andrew, *b* 1974; *ed* Harrow.

DAUGHTER LIVING

Hon Elizabeth Henrietta Alexandra, *b* 1976.

BROTHERS LIVING

Hon Peter William, *b* 1944; *ed* Eton, and Ch Ch, Oxford (BA): *m* 1978, Deborah S., da of late G. Macdonald-Brown, of Rose Cottage, Campsall, Doncaster, and has issue living, Charles Peter, *b* 1982, — Caroline Susan, *b* 1979.
Hon Nicholas Charles Frederick, *b* 1947; *ed* Eton: *m* 1974, Jane Brydon, of Thirley Beck Farm, Harwood Dale, Scarborough, Yorks, and has issue living, David Charles, *b* 1976, — Catherine Frances, *b* 1978.

AUNT LIVING (*sister of 7th Baron*) (*Raised to the rank of a Baron's daughter* 1924)

Hon Catherine Muriel (*Hon Lady Bower*), *b* 1908: *m* 1939, Lieut-Gen Sir Roger Herbert Bower, KCB, KBE, late King's Own Yorkshire LI, who *d* 1990, and has had issue, Jeremy Roger, *b* and *d* 1944, — Anne Catherine, *b* 1940: *m* 1972, Robert Sackville Riseley, and has issue living, Mark James *b* 1974, David Michael *b* 1977. The Hon Lady Bower also has an adopted son, Michael Roger, *b* 1952. *Residence* – The Dower House, Headbourne Worthy, Winchester, Hants.

DAUGHTER LIVING OF SIXTH BARON

Hon Jocelyne Mary Emma, *b* 1908.

WIDOWS LIVING OF BROTHERS OF SEVENTH BARON

Margaret (Plas Newydd, Glascoed, Abergele, N Wales), yr da of Col Sir Robert William Herbert Watkin Williams-Wynn, 9th Bt, KCB, DSO, TD: *m* 1934, Maj Hon Peter Hotham, late KOYLI, who *d* 1991 (having been raised to the rank of a Baron's son 1924), and has issue (see colls, infra).

Aileen (31 Brynmaer Rd, SW11), da of late Capt Harry Coates, Durham LI: *m* 1st, 1939, Lieut-Com Hon John David Hotham, DSC, RN, who *d* 1962 (having been raised to the rank of a Baron's son 1924); 2ndly, 1969, Cdr Colin Hugh Smith, RN, who *d* 1975, and has issue living by 1st *m* (see colls, infra).

COLLATERAL BRANCHES LIVING

Issue of late Maj Hon Peter Hotham, late KOYLI, brother of 7th Baron, *b* 1904, *d* 1991: *m* 1934, Margaret (ante), yr da of Col Sir Robert William Herbert Watkin Williams-Wynn, 9th Bt, KCB, DSO, TD:—
Edward Durand, *b* 1944; *ed* Stowe; late Lieut 15th/19th King's Royal Hussars; *m* 1982, Susan Elisabeth, da of late Noel Tilley, of Stokke, Marlborough, Wilts. —— Caroline Alathea, *b* 1937: *m* 1959, Col Harry Llewellyn Davies, RA, who *d* 1981, and has issue living, Catherine Margaret, *b* 1962, — Thora Lucinda, *b* 1965. —— Mary Elizabeth, *b* 1940: *m* 1964, Lt-Col Peter Harman, 14th/20th King's Hussars, and has issue living, Andrew Charles, *b* 1967, — Nicola Jane, *b* 1969.

Issue of late Lieut-Com Hon John David Hotham, DSC, RN, brother of 7th Baron, *b* 1911, *d* 1962: *m* 1939, Aileen (ante) (she *m* 2ndly, 1969, Cdr Colin Hugh Smith, RN), who *d* 1975, da of late Capt Harry Coates, Durham LI:—
Martin Patrick (The Old Rectory, Drinkstone, Bury St Edmunds, Suffolk), *b* 1941; *ed* Stowe: *m* 1965, Erica Antoinette, twin da of late Lt-Col Brian Maxwell Strange, of Maes Heulyn, Denbigh, and has had issue, Charles Beaumont David, *b* 1969, — Henry Ralph, *b* 1974; *d* 1986, — Sophia Henrietta, *b* 1967, — Amelia Oriana Philadelphia, *b* 1971. —— Henrietta Elizabeth, *b* 1944: *m* 1967, Maj Philip A. J. Wright, late Gren Gds, Dep Assistant Serjeant-at-Arms, House of Commons, son of late Sir Andrew Barkworth Wright, KCMG, CBE, MC, and has issue living, Romayne Louise, *b* 1972, — Melanie Clare, *b* 1974. —— Georgina Rose, *b* 1947: *m* 1971, Lt-Col John V. E. F. O'Connell, Gren Gds (c/o Barclays Bank, 19 Fleet St, EC4), and has issue living, James Alexander, *b* 1973, — Simon David Sebastian, *b* 1974, — Emily Mary Frances, *b* 1976.

Grandchildren of late Adm of Fleet Sir Charles Frederick Hotham, GCB, GCVO, el son of Capt John Hotham, 4th son of Lt-Col George Hotham, el son of Gen George Hotham, brother of 1st Baron:—
Issue of late John Beaumont Hotham, *b* 1874, *d* 1924: *m* 1905, Gladys Mary, who *d* 1972, 2nd da of late Col John Gerald Wilson, CB, of Cliffe Hall, Yorkshire (B Inchiquin, colls):—
John David Durand, *b* 1917; *ed* Eton, and New Coll, Oxford; formerly Lieut Roy Armoured Corps (TA): *m* 1954, Marianne Becker, of Vienna. *Residence* – Milne Graden, Coldstream, Berwickshire. —— Dorothy Jean (*Dowager Countess of Donoughmore*), MBE, *b* 1906; is Vice-Pres, Co London Branch, British Red Cross Soc, and a Serving Sister of Order of St John of Jerusalem; MBE (Civil) 1947: *m* 1925, 7th Earl of Donoughmore, who *d* 1981. *Residence* – High Coodham, Symington, Ayrshire. —— Anne (*Baroness Howard of Penrith*), *b* 1913: *m* 1st, 1934, Anthony Gardner Bazley, who *d* 1937 (*see* Bazley, Bt, colls); 2ndly, 1944, 2nd Baron Howard of Penrith. *Residence* – Dean Farm, Coln St Aldwyns, Gloucestershire. —— Catharine Geraldine (*Baroness Guest*), *b* 1915: *m* 1941, Baron Guest, a Lord of Appeal in Ordinary (Life Baron), who *d* 1984. *Residence* – 22 Lennox St, Edinburgh.

Grandson of late Capt John Hotham (ante):—
Issue of late George Hotham, *b* 1856, *d* 1948: *m* 1896, Louisa Hildegarde Neumeister, who *d* 1958, of Le Mar, Plymouth Co, Iowa, USA:—
George Edward, *b* 1906.

Grandchildren of late Capt William Charles Hotham, son of late Rev Edwin Hotham (infra):—
Issue of late Lieut-Col John Clarence Hotham, *b* 1882, *d* 1959: *m* 1909, Margaret Emily Anne, who *d* 1952, el da of Horace Wilmer, formerly of Church House, Brede, Sussex:—
Diana, *b* 1918: *m* 1948, John Calkin Whately-Smith, and has issue living, David John, *b* 1949: *m* 1982, Penny Stone, and has issue living, Alastair Charles *b* 1986, Jessica Clare *b* 1984, — Jeremy William, *b* 1956: *m* 1988, Kathrin Norah Murray Prior, and has issue living, Jonathan *b* 1990, — Susan Jane, *b* 1950: *m* 1973, Oswald Eberhardt, of Schlosshotel, Rosenegg, Fieberbrunn, Tyrol, Austria, and has issue living, Andreas *b* 1980, Elisabeth *b* 1978, Kathrin *b* (twin) 1978, — Charlotte Anne, *b* 1952: *m* 1978, David Richard Charles Agnew, and has issue (*see* Agnew, Bt, *cr* 1895, colls). *Residence* – Grey Cott, Church Walk, Aldeburgh, Suffolk.
Issue of late Com William Montagu Hotham, Roy Canadian Navy, *b* 1884, *d* 1951: *m* 1905, Margaret Broune:—
Ronald St Vincent Carew, *b* 1911; *ed* St Michael's Sch, Victoria: *m* 1936, Muriel Eva Maria Sheather. —— Alan Geoffrey (1130, Channel Drive, Santa Barbara, California, USA), *b* 1921; *ed* Brentwood Sch, and at British Columbia Univ (BASc); 1939-45 War in Research Branch, RCAF: *m* 1951, Kathleen Cramer-Coxhead, and has issue living, Peter Alan, *b* 1952, — Daryl, *b* 1953, — Lisa, *b* 1955.

Grandsons of late Rev Edwin Hotham, el son of late Adm Sir William Hotham, GCB, 2nd son of late Gen George Hotham (ante):—
Issue of late Montagu Conyers Hotham, *b* 1850, *d* 1931: *m* 1883, Francisca Rosa Pizarro:—
Edwin, *b* 1887. —— George, *b* 1899: *m* 1932, Adriana Maria Franco, and has issue living, Charles Edward, *b* 1934, — Richard Alan, *b* 1936.

PREDECESSORS – **(1)** Sir JOHN Hotham, Knt; Gov of Hull, *temp* Charles I; *cr* a *Baronet* 1622; he and his el son being discovered in correspondence with the Royalists were tried by Court Martial at Guildhall, sentenced to death and beheaded on Tower Hill 1645; *s* by his grandson **(2)** Sir JOHN, 2nd Bt; *d* 1689; *s* by his son **(3)** Sir JOHN, 3rd Bt; *d* 1691; *s* by his cousin **(4)** Sir CHARLES, 4th Bt; MP for Beverley; *s* by his son **(5)** Sir CHARLES, 5th Bt; MP for Beverley, and a Groom of the Bedchamber; *d* 1737; *s* by his son **(6)** Sir CHARLES, 6th Bt; a Groom of the Bedchamber; *d* 1767; *s* by his uncle **(7)** Sir BEAUMONT, 7th Bt; *d* 1771 *s* by his el son **(8)** Sir CHARLES Hotham-Thompson, 8th Bt; assumed the additional surname of Thompson; *d* 1794; *s* by his brother **(9)** Rt Rev Sir JOHN Hotham, 9th Bt, Lord Bishop of Clogher; *d* 1795; *s* by his son **(10)** Sir CHARLES, 10th Bt; *s* by his uncle **(11)** WILLIAM, 11th Bt, 3rd son of 7th Bt; a distinguished Adm; *cr Baron Hotham*, of South Dalton (peerage of Ireland) 1797, with remainder to the heirs male of his father; *d* unmarried 1813; *s* by his brother **(12)** BEAUMONT, KB, 2nd Baron; a Baron of the Court of Exchequer; *d* 1814; *s* by his grandson **(13)** BEAUMONT, 3rd Baron; a Gen in the Army; served at Waterloo; MP for Leominster 1820-41, and for E Riding of York 1841-68; *d* unmarried 1870; *s* by his nephew **(14)** CHARLES, 4th Baron, son of Rear-Adm George Frederick (brother of 3rd Baron), by Lady Susan Maria O'Bryen, el da and co-heir of 2nd Marquess of Thomond; served with 18th Foot in Crimean Campaign 1855 (wounded); *d* unmarried 1872; *s* by his brother **(15)** JOHN, 5th Baron; *b* 1838; *d* unmarried 1907; *s* by his cousin **(16)** FREDERICK WILLIAM, 6th Baron (son of late Rev William Francis Hotham, son of 2nd Baron), *b* 1863: *m* 1902, Benita, who *d*

1954, da of late Thomas Sanders, of Sanders Park, Charleville, co Cork; *d* 1923; *s* by his cousin **(17)** HENRY FREDERICK, CBE, (el son of late Capt Henry Hotham, son of late Rev Frederick Harry Hotham, son of 3rd son of 2nd Baron), 7th Baron, *b* 1899; Maj Grenadier Guards; Hon Col 440th LAA; *m* 1937, Lady Letitia Sibell Winifred Cecil, who *d* 1992, da of 5th Marquess of Exeter; *d* 1967; *s* by his 3rd son **(18)** HENRY DURAND, 8th Baron and present peer.

HOTHFIELD, BARON (Tufton) (Baron UK 1881, Bt UK 1851)

The bird flies to its own

ANTHONY CHARLES SACKVILLE TUFTON, 6th Baron, and 7th Baronet; *b* 21 Oct 1939; *s* 1991; *ed* Eton, and Magdalene Coll, Camb (MA); C Eng, MICE: *m* 1975, Lucinda Marjorie, da of Capt Timothy John Gurney (*see* de Bathe, Bt, ext), and formerly wife of Capt Graham Morison Vere Nicoll (*see* Madden, Bt), and has issue.

Arms – Sable, an eagle displayed ermine, within a bordure wavy or. **Crest** – A sea lion sejant argent, debruised by a bendlet wavy sable. **Supporters** – On either side an eagle ermine, gorged with a collar gules pendent therefrom an escutcheon of the arms of Tufton.
Residence – Drybeck Hall, Appleby-in-Westmorland, Cumbria CA16 4TF.

SON LIVING

Hon WILLIAM SACKVILLE, *b* 14 Nov 1977; *ed* Eton.

DAUGHTER LIVING

Hon Emma, *b* 1976.

BROTHER LIVING

Hon Nicholas William Sackville, *b* 1946; *ed* Eton, and RAC Cirencester: *m* 1978, Meriel, da of Maj William Acworth, and has issue living, Richard Charles, *b* 1980; *ed* Eton, — Henry George, *b* 1983. *Residence* – The Red House, Barkway, nr Royston, Herts.

SISTER LIVING

Hon Jennifer Margaret, *b* 1937: *m* 1965, Edward Robert Raikes, yr son of late Julian Henry Raikes, and has issue living, Jason Alexander, *b* 1966; *ed* Stowe, and Exeter Univ: *m* 1992, Emma, da of Peter Budgen, and has issue living, Thomas William, *b* 1994, — Benedick Arthur, *b* 1969; *ed* Eton, and LSE, — Stella Mary Evelyn, *b* 1972. *Residence* – Parsonage Oasts, Yalding, Kent.

UNCLE LIVING (*brother of 5th Baron*)

Francis Charles Sackville, VRD (Church Farm House, Clothall, nr Baldock, Herts SG7 6RG), *b* 1913; *ed* Eton, and Trin Coll, Oxford (MA); Lt-Cdr (ret) RNVR; a Knight of Order of Dannebrog of Denmark: *m* 1942, Eileen Joyce Clara, who *d* 1985, da of Sir Edward Henry Goschen, 2nd Bt (*cr* 1916), and has issue living, Edward Philip Sackville (70 Perrymead St, SW6), *b* 1948; *ed* Eton, and Magdalene Coll, Camb (MA), — Mary Josephine, *b* 1943: *m* 1979, John Yorkston Paxton, of Church Farm House, Upwood, nr Ramsay, Cambs, and has issue living, John Edward Sackville, *b* 1985, Charles Thomas *b* 1988.

AUNT LIVING (*sister of 5th Baron*)

Susan Stella, *b* 1908: *m* 1936, Col Thomas Alexander Hamilton Coltman, OBE, DL, RA, of Laigh Aldons, Girvan, Ayrshire KA26 0TB, and has issue living, Timothy Charles (Skellingthorpe Hall, nr Lincoln LN6 5UU), *b* 1939; *ed* Eton, and Trin Coll, Camb (BA): *m* 1st, 1964, Joanna Mary, who *d* 1986, only da of John Richard Bergne-Coupland, of Skellingthorpe Hall, nr Lincoln; 2ndly, 1989, Anne C., da of Rt Rev Kenneth Riches, and has issue living (by 1st *m*), Sarah Elizabeth *b* 1966, Mary Jane *b* 1968, — David Alexander (Haystoun House, Peebles PH45 9JG), *b* 1942; *ed* Eton, and Edinburgh Univ: *m* 1972, Hon Mary Cecilia, 3rd da of 1st Viscount Whitelaw, and has issue living, Susannah Mary Lucinda *b* 1987.

COLLATERAL BRANCH LIVING

(In remainder to Baronetcy only)

Grandchildren of late Alfred Charles Tufton, brother of 1st Baron:—
Issue of late Alfred Guy Tufton, *b* 1889, *d* 1968: *m* 1916, Marjorie Neville, who *d* 1979, da of late Frederick Charles Thompson, of 40 Porchester Sq, W2:—
Rev Canon Colin Charles Guy (3 Manor Rd North, Seaford, E Sussex BN25 3RA), *b* 1924; *ed* Oriel Coll, Oxford (MA); late Lt RM; Hon Canon of Canterbury Cathedral 1968; formerly R of St Peter with St Alphege and St Margaret, St Mildred with St Mary de Castro, and Master of Eastbridge Hosp, Canterbury. —— Barbara Marjorie (3 Manor Rd North, Seaford, E Sussex BN25 3RA), *b* 1920.

PREDECESSORS – **(1)** RICHARD Tufton, *b* at Verdun, France, 1813; *s* by devise to the estates of his reputed natural father Henry, 11th and last Earl of Thanet; naturalized, with his family, 1849; *cr* a *Baronet* 1851: *m* 1843, Adelaide Amelie Lacour; *d* 1871; *s* by his son **(2)** Sir HENRY JAMES, 2nd Bt, *b* 1844; *s* as 2nd *Baronet* 1871, and *cr Baron Hothfield*, of Hothfield, co Kent (peerage of United Kingdom) 1881; Lord-Lieut, of Westmorland 1881-1926, Vice-Admiral of Coast of Cumberland and Westmorland 1883-1926, and a Lord-in-Waiting to Queen Victoria 1886: *m* 1872, Alice Harriet Argyll, who *d* 1914, da of late Rev William James Stracey-Clitherow; *d* 1926; *s* by his son **(3)** JOHN SACKVILLE RICHARD, DSO, 2nd Baron, *b* 1873; Lieut 1st Life Guards, and Major Roy Sussex Regt; Mayor of Appleby 1937-44; S Africa 1901-2, European War 1915-18 (DSO): *m* 1st, 1896, Lady Ierne Louisa Arundel Hastings, who *d* 1935, da of 13th Earl of Huntingdon; 2ndly, 1935, Sybil Augusta, who *d* 1950, da of John Sant; *d* 1952; *s* by his son **(4)** HENRY HASTINGS SACKVILLE THANET, 3rd Baron, *b* 1897; Lieut 15th/19th Hussars; appointed Assist Director of Public Relations, Home Forces 1942: *m* 1918, Dorothy, who *d* 1981, el da of late William George Raphael, of 9 Connaught Place, W2; *d* 1961; *s* by his cousin **(5)** THOMAS SACKVILLE (only son of late Hon Sackville Philip Tufton, 2nd son of 1st Baron), 4th Baron, *b* 1916; *dunm* 1986; *s* by his cousin **(6)** GEORGE WILLIAM ANTHONY (elder son of late Hon Charles Henry Tufton, CMG, 3rd son of 1st Baron), 5th Baron, *b* 1904; Lt-Col RA (TA), DL Herts: *m* 1936, Evelyn Margarette, who *d* 1989, eldest da of late Eustace Mordaunt (*see* Mordaunt, Bt, 1990 Edn); *d* 1991; *s* by his elder son **(7)** ANTHONY CHARLES SACKVILLE, 6th Baron and present peer.

HOUGHTON OF SOWERBY, BARON (Houghton) (Life Baron 1974)

ARTHUR LESLIE NOEL DOUGLAS HOUGHTON, CH, PC, son of late John Houghton, of Long Eaton, Derbys; *b* 11 Aug 1898; Sec Inland Revenue Staff Fedn 1922-60; Broadcaster, BBC 1941-64, an Alderman, London Co Council 1947-49, a Member of Gen Council TUC 1952-60, Chm (Staff Side) Civil Ser National Whitley Council 1956-58, and of Public Accounts Cttee 1963-64, Chancellor of Duchy of Lancaster 1964-66, Min without Portfolio 1966-67, and Chm of Parl Labour Party 1967-74; MP for Sowerby Div of W Riding of Yorks (*Lab*) 1949-74; *cr* C 1964, CH 1967, and *Baron Houghton of Sowerby*, of Sowerby in Co of W Yorks (Life Baron) 1974: *m* 1939, Vera, da of John Travis, of Southall, Middx.

Arms – Or, issuant from a barrulet wavy azure a stone bridge of three arches throughout proper, in chief a rose gules barbed, slipped with two sprigs, leaved proper, charged with another rose argent, seeded proper, in base a Barn Owl statant, also proper. **Crest** – On a cap of maintenance gules, turned up ermine, a representation of the ruins of the Church of Saint Thomas of Canterbury, Heptonstall, proper. **Supporters** – On either side a badger proper, gorged with a collar or, charged with a barrulet wavy azure.
Residences – 110 Marsham Court, SW1; Becks Cottage, White Hill lane, Bletchingley, Surrey.

HOWARD DE WALDEN AND SEAFORD, BARON (Scott-Ellis)
(Baron E 1597 and UK 1826)

Light in darkness.

Not by whom, but in what manner

JOHN OSMAEL SCOTT-ELLIS, 9th Baron Howard de Walden, and 5th Baron Seaford; *b* 27 Nov 1912; *s* 1946; *ed* Eton, and Magdalene Coll, Camb (BA 1934); is Major Westminster Dragoons (TA): *m* 1st, 1934, Countess Irene Harrach, who *d* 1975, yst da of Count Hans Albrecht Harrach; 2ndly, 1978, Gillian Magaret, only da of Cyril Francis Stuart Buckley, and formerly wife of 17th Viscount Mountgarret, and has issue by 1st *m*.

Arms – Quarterly: 1st and 4th erminois, a cross sable, charged with five crescents argent, *Ellis*; 2nd and 3rd or, on a bend azure a star betwixt two crescents of the field, in chief a crescent gules, all within a bordure engrailed of the last, *Scott*. **Crests** – 1st, on a mount vert, a goat's head erased argent, *Ellis*; 2nd, a dexter hand issuing out of the wreath holding an annulet or in which is set a carbuncle proper, *Scott*. **Supporters** – Two lions argent, each charged on the neck with three trefoils slipped vert, within a collar gules.
Residences – Avington Manor, Hungerford, Berks RG17 0UL; Flat K, 90 Eaton Sq, SW1W 9AG. **Clubs** – Turf, White's, Jockey.

DAUGHTERS LIVING (*By 1st marriage*) (*Co-heiresses to the Barony of Howard de Walden*)

Hon (MARY) HAZEL CARIDWEN, *b* 12 Aug 1935: *m* 1957, Count Joseph Czernin, and has issue living, Peter John Joseph, *b* 1966, — Charlotte Mary Sidonia, *b* 1958: *m* 1986, Neil A. Girkins, of Kingston House, Kingston, Wareham, Dorset BH20 5LQ, son of Gerard Girkins, of Bordeaux, France, and has issue living, Benedict James Seward *b* 1992, Emily Alexandra Mary *b* 1991, — Henrietta Mary Rosario, *b* 1960: *m* 1985, C. Alistair Currey, eldest son of Charles Currey, of Bosham, Sussex, and has issue living, Camilla Rose Francesca *b* 1986, Alice Catarina Mary *b* 1988, Louisa Henrietta Anne *b* 1990, Rosanna Mariella Claire *b* 1992, — Alexandra Mary Romana, *b* 1961: *m* 1992, David Mark Noël Kelly, and has issue (*see* D Norfolk), — Philippa Mary Loretta, *b* 1963, — Isabelle Mary Benedicta, *b* 1967. *Residences* – 47 Queens Gate Gdns, SW7 5ND; White Oak House, Highclere, Newbury, Berks RG15 9RJ.
Hon (BLANCHE) SUSAN FIONODBHAR, *b* 6 Oct 1937: *m* 1961, Capt David William Sinclair Buchan of Auchmacoy (E Caithness), and has issue living, (John) Charles Augustus David, *b* 1963, — James Alexander Stephen, *b* 1964, — Thomas Richard Sinclair, *b* 1966, — Robert Edward William, *b* 1968, — Sophia Jane Elizabeth, *b* 1962: *m* 1991, David William Hamilton Ruck, son of Dr Colin Ruck, of Crowborough, Sussex, and has issue living, Matilda Rose Athena *b* 1994. *Residences* – Auchmacoy House, Ellon, Aberdeenshire AB41 8RB; 28 The Little Boltons, SW10 9LP.
Hon JESSICA JANE VRONWY, *b* 6 Aug 1941: *m* 1966, Adrian Tancred White (*see* Lawson-Tancred, Bt, colls, 1980 Edn), and has issue living, Nicholas John Sebastian, *b* 1967, — Simon James Alexander, *b* 1968, — Richard Dominic Edward, *b* 1970, — Michael Philip Alistair, *b* 1977. *Residence* – Farnborough Downs Farm, Wantage, Oxon OX12 8NW.
Hon CAMILLA ANNE BRONWEN, *b* 1 April 1947: *m* 1971, Guy Acloque, and has issue living, Alexander John Sebastian, *b* 1978, — Henrietta Mary Rose, *b* 1979, — Laura Isabella Helen, *b* 1979 (twin). *Residence* – Alderley Grange, Wotton-under-Edge, Glos, GL12 7QT.

SISTERS LIVING

Hon Bronwen Mary (twin), *b* 1912: *m* 1933, Hon James Louis Lindsay (*see* E Crawford). *Residence* – Sutton Manor, Sutton Scotney, nr Winchester, Hants SO21 3JX.
Hon Margaret Irène Gaenor, *b* 1919: *m* 1938, Richard Frank Heathcoat-Amory, who *d* 1957 (*see* Heathcoat-Amory, Bt, colls). *Residence* – Hele Manor, Exebridge, Dulverton, Somerset TA22 9RN.
Hon Rosemary Nest, *b* 1922: *m* 1946, George FitzRoy Seymour (*see* M Hertford, colls), who *d* 1994. *Residences* – Thrumpton Hall, Notts; 38 Molyneux St, W1.

COLLATERAL BRANCHES LIVING

Grandchildren of late Henry Guysulf Bertram Ellis (infra):—
Issue of late Maj William Felton Ellis, *b* 1912, *d* 1978: *m* 1940, Edwina, who *d* 1977, da of late Maj R. E. Bond, Indian Army:—
COLIN HUMPHREY FELTON ELLIS (Bush Farm, West Knoyle, Warminster, Wilts BA12 6AE), *b* 19 April 1946; *ed* Sherborne, *hp* to Barony of Seaford: *m* 1st, 1971 (*m diss* 1992) Susan Magill; 2ndly, 1993, Penelope Mary Bastin, and has issue living (by 1st *m*), Benjamin Felton Thomas, *b* 1976, — Humphrey Henry Guysulf, *b* 1983, — Harriet Fay, *b* 1973, — Charlotte Susan, *b* 1975. —— Jill Kathleen, *b* 1944: *m* 1968, Jeremy Dudgeon Anderson, of 6 Scholars Close, Caversham, Reading, Berks RG4 7DN, and has issue living, William Maurice, *b* 1973, — Kathleen Fleur, *b* 1971.

Granddaughters of late Rev Hon William Charles Ellis, 2nd son of 6th Baron:—
Issue of late Henry Guysulf Bertram Ellis, *b* 1875; *d* 1947: *m* 1911, Kathleen Roberta, who *d* 1940, only da of William Charles Mitchell, formerly of Marmount, co Down:—
Henrietta Roberta Elizabeth, *b* 1911: *m* 1943, Thomas Stewart Lewis Russell, and has issue living, David Guysulf, *b* 1944, — Peter Stuart, *b* 1948, — Michael Roland, *b* 1950. *Residence* – 44 Churchside, Vigo Village, Meopham, Kent. —— Catherine Rosemary (Court House, West Milton, Bridport, Dorset DT6 3SH), *b* 1918: *m* 1945, Douglas Alexander Clarke-Smith, who *d* 1959, and has issue living, Humphrey Douglas Bevis (24 Ave Y. Lutens, 1150 Brussels, Belgium), *b* 1948: *m* 1975, Christine Quy, and has issue living, Benedict *b* 1978, Orlando *b* 1980, — Lucinda Mary, *b* 1946: *m* 1977, Nigel Henzell-Thomas, of Town Mill House, Whitchurch, Hants RG28 7LZ, and 8 Streatham Crescent, Johannesburg, S Africa, and has issue living, Lucy *b* 1978, — Susan, *b* 1950: *m* 1973, Joseph Santolini, of The Stables, Milton Court, Alfriston, E Sussex RG26 5RT, and has issue living, Lindsay *b* 1979.

(In remainder to the Barony of Howard de Walden only)

Issue of late Hon Elisabeth Gwendolen Scott-Ellis, 2nd da of 8th Baron, *b* 1914, *d* 1976: *m* 1st, 1935, Lt-Cdr Count Serge Orloff-Davidoff, RNVR, who was *k* in a motor accident 1945; 2ndly, 1959, Bernard Wheeler Robinson, DSc:—
(By 1st *m*) Tatiana, *b* 1936: *m* 1972, William John Whitworth Mallinson, MB, MRCP, and has issue living, Thecla, *b* 1973. Mrs Mallinson also has issue Sophie ORLOFF-DAVIDOFF, *b* 1963. *Residence* – 5 Halsey St, SW3 2QH. —— Marina (*Viscountess Bury*), *b* 1937; ARIBA, AADip: *m* 1964, as his 2nd wife, Derek William Charles, Viscount Bury, who *d* 1968, eldest son of 9th Earl of Albemarle. *Residence* – Piazza di Bellosguardo 10, Florence 50124, Italy.

Issue of late Hon (Essylt) Priscilla Scott-Ellis, 3rd da of 8th Baron, *b* 1916, *d* 1983: *m* 1st, 1945 (*m diss* 1972), Jose Luis de Vilallonga y Cabeza de Vaca, Marques de Castellvell (Grandee of Spain); 2ndly, 19—, Ian Hanson, who *d* 19—:—
(By 1st *m*) Juan Alfonso DE VILALLONGA, *b* 1946: *m* 19—, Michelle, da of —, and has issue living, Atalanta, *b* 1987. —— Susanna Carmen Margarita Beatriz, *b* 1947: *m* 1975, Gregory John Foster, and has issue living, Adam Kevin Salvador, *b* 1978. *Residence* – 11 Paekitawhiti St, Turangi, NZ.

Grandchildren of late Hon Evelyn Henry Ellis, 5th son of 6th Baron:—
Issue of late Mary Ellis, OBE, *b* 1888, *d* 1971: *m* 1916, Maj Denis Granville Coskey Critchley Salmonson, MC, RSF, who *d* 1943:—
John Albert Miles CRITCHLEY SALMONSON (The Manor House, Gt Barton, Bury St Edmunds), *b* 1916; Maj (ret) 12th R Lancers: *m* 1946, Joan da of Col Robert Henry Haseldine, DSO, OBE, and has issue living Denis Patrick Antony (The Glebe House, Dunsyre, Carnwath, Lanarks), *b* 1953; *ed* Downside; Capt Coldm Gds: *m* 1976, Angela Jane, da of Brig Hon (Henry Ernest) Christopher Willoughby (*see* B Middleton), and has issue living, John Henry Guy *b* 1986, Katherine Adini Mary *b* 1979, Isabella Caroline *b* 1981, — Mary Clare, *b* 1947: *m* 1989, Henry John Scrope (*see* E Mexborough, 1972-73 Edn), of Brandsby, York, and has issue living, William John A. *b* 1991, — Antonia Isabella Mary, *b* 1949: *m* 1973, Christopher William Courtenay Tregoning, of The Old Vicarage, Chrishall, Royston, Herts, 3rd son of late Col John L. Tregoning, MBE, and has issue living, Harold John William *b* 1976, Daniel Christopher Leonard *b* 1977, Thomas Anthony Cecil *b* 1982, — Henrietta Margaret Mary, *b* 1959: *m* 1985, Jacques Baudouin, of 431 rue des Auges, Grandfresnoy, France, only son of late Lt-Col Roger Baudouin (Chevalier de la Legion d'Honneur), of 35 rue Vauvenargues, Paris, and has issue living, Alexandre John *b* 1986, Maxime Roger *b* 1987, Luke Jacques *b* 1990, Timothy Joseph *b* 1994. —— Peter Evelyn George CRITCHLEY, OBE (Dormans, Combe St Nicholas, Chard, Somerset), *b* 1919; has adopted the surname of Critchley by deed poll 1954; OBE (Civil) 1975: *m* 1948, Grace, da of Col J. L. Oliver, and has issue living, Michael Shavin, *b* 1952, — Kim Hardinge, *b* 1954, — Peter Kerr, *b* 1957, — Mark Nicholas, *b* 1959. —— Denise Irene Mary, *b* 1918.

PREDECESSORS – (1) Sir THOMAS HOWARD, KG, PC, el son of 4th Duke of Norfolk by his 2nd *m* to Margaret, da and heiress of Thomas KG, 1st and last Baron Audley of Walden summoned to Parliament of England as *Baron Howard of Walden* 1597, and *cr Earl of Suffolk* (peerage of England) 1603 (see E Suffolk); *d* 1626; *s* by his son (2) THEOPHILUS, KG, PC, 2nd Earl; *d* 1640; *s* by his son (3) JAMES, KB 3rd Earl; *d* without male issue, when the earldom devolved upon his brother, and the barony became abeyant between his daus Essex and Elizabeth; in 1784 the abeyance was terminated in favour of the descendant of Essex (4) *Field Marshal Sir* JOHN GRIFFIN Whitwell-Griffin, KB, 4th Baron; *cr Baron Braybrooke* (peerage of Great Britain) 1788; twice *m*, but *dsp* 1797, when the Barony of Braybrooke devolved in terms of the remainder upon his kinsman (see B Braybrooke), and the Barony of Howard of Walden reverted to the heir male of Elizabeth (ante) (5) Right Rev FREDERICK AUGUSTUS Hervey, 4th Earl of Bristol (see M Bristol); *d* 1803; when the earldom passed to his 2nd son, and the Barony of Howard of Walden to his great-grandson (6) CHARLES AUGUSTUS, GCB, 6th Baron, grandson of John Augustus, Lord Hervey, whose da Elizabeth Catherine Caroline *m* Charles Rose Ellis, who *d* 1845 having been *cr Baron Seaford*, of Seaford, co Sussex (peerage of United Kingdom) 1826; *b* 1799; was Min Plen at Stockholm 1832-3, at Lisbon 1833-46, and at Brussels 1846-68: *m* 1828, Lady Lucy Cavendish-Bentinck, da of 4th Duke of Portland; *d* 1868; *s* by his son (7) FREDERICK GEORGE, 7th Baron Howard de Walden, and 3rd Baron Seaford, *b* 1830: *m* 1876 (*m diss* 1893), Blanche, who *d* 1911, having *m* 2ndly 1903, (2nd Baron Ludlow), da of late William Holden, of Palace House, Lancashire; *d* 1899; *s* by his son (8) THOMAS EVELYN, 8th Baron Howard de Walden and 4th Baron Seaford, *b* 1880; Hon Col Westminster Dragoons, and Pres of Queen Charlotte's Hospital; assumed by Roy licence 1917 the additional surname and arms of Scott: *m* 1912, Margherita, CBE, who *d* 1974, da of late Charles Van Raalte, of Brownsea Island, Dorset; *d* 1946; *s* by his son (9) JOHN OSMAEL, 9th Baron and present peer; also Baron Seaford.

HOWARD OF HENDERSKELFE, BARONY OF (Howard) (Extinct 1984)

SONS LIVING OF LIFE BARON (*see* E Carlisle, colls)

Hon Henry Francis Geoffrey, *b* 1950.
Hon Nicholas Paul Geoffrey, *b* 1952.

Hon Simon Bartholomew Geoffrey, *b* 1956.
Hon (Anthony) Michael Geoffrey, *b* 1958.

HOWARD OF PENRITH, BARON (Howard) (Baron UK 1930)

Virtue alone is unconquerable

FRANCIS PHILIP HOWARD, 2nd Baron: *b* 5 Oct 1905; *s* 1939; *ed* Downside, and Trin Coll, Camb (BA); Bar Middle Temple 1931; Capt RA; 1939-43 War: *m* 1944, Anne da of late John Beaumont Hotham (*see* B Hotham, colls), and widow of Anthony Gardner Bazley (*see* Bazley, Bt, colls), and has issue.

Arms – Quarterly, 1st, gules, a bend between six cross-crosslets fitchée argent; on the bend an escutcheon or, charged with a demi-lion rampant, pierced through the mouth with an arrow, within a double tressure flory counterflory all gules, *Howard*; 2nd, gules three lions passant guardant in pale or, and in chief a label of three points argent, *Brotherton*; 3rd, checky or and azure, *Warren*; 4th, gules, a lion rampant or, *Fitzalan*. **Crests** – 1st, issuant from a ducal coronet or, a pair of wings gules, each charged with a bend between six cross-crosslets fitchée argent; 2nd, on a chapeau gules, turned up ermine, a lion statant guardant with tail extended or, ducally gorged argent; 3rd, on a mount vert a horse passant argent, holding in the mouth a slip of oak fructed proper. **Supporters** – *Dexter*, a lion argent: *sinister*, a horse argent, holding in the mouth a sprig of oak fructed proper; each charged on the shoulder with an escutcheon barry of six argent and azure, three chaplets gules.
Residence – Dean Farm, Hatherop, Gloucestershire.

SONS LIVING

Hon PHILIP ESME (45 Erpingham Rd, SW15), *b* 1st May 1945; *ed* Ampleforth, and Ch Ch Oxford: *m* 1969, Sarah, da of late Barclay Walker, and has issue living, Thomas Philip, *b* 1974, — Michael Barclay, *b* 1984, — Natasha Mary, *b* 1970, — Laura Isabella, *b* 1976.
Hon Michael Edmund, *b* 1947; *ed* Ampleforth.
Hon David Francis, *b* 1949; *ed* Ampleforth: *m* 1981, Diana, da of late John S. Radway, and formerly wife of Timothy L. B. Davis, and has issue living, Rachel Anne, *b* 1982, — Alice Isabella, *b* 1983, — Olivia Charlotte, *b* 1986, — Frances Elizabeth, *b* 1988, — Charlotte Grace, *b* 1993. *Residence* – Glebe House, Ulcombe, nr Maidstone, Kent ME16 1DN.
Hon William John, *b* 1953: *m* 1981, Alexandra Josephine, da of Maurice Graham, and has issue living, Miranda Catherine, *b* 1982, — Elizabeth Clara, *b* 1984.

BROTHER LIVING

Hon Edmund Bernard Carlo, CMG, MVO, *b* 1909; *ed* Downside, and New Coll, Oxford (BA); Bar Middle Temple 1934; Capt KRRC 1939-45 War; 2nd Sec (Information) Rome 1947-51, and in Foreign Office 1951-53, 1st Sec Madrid 1953-57, Head of Chancery Bogota 1957-59, Consul-Gen, San Marino and Consul Florence, 1960-61, Counsellor Rome 1961-65, and Consul-Gen Genoa 1965-69, MVO (4th class) 1961, CMG 1969: *m* 1936, Cécile, da of Charles Geoffroy-Dechaume, of Valmondois, France, and has issue living, Esme Francis (57 Westcroft Sq, W6 0TA), *b* 1938, *ed* Downside, and New Coll, Oxford (BA): *m* 1st, 1963 (*m diss* 1973), Tessa Longhurst, da of late Maj Kenneth Evan Meredith, Dorset Regt; 2ndly, 1979, Diane Marie Kačić, of St Louis, Missouri, USA, and has issue living (by 1st *m*), Dominic William *b* 1964: *m* 1993, Belinda Sarah, yr da of Anthony Cassidy, of Albury, Surrey, Stephen Anthony *b* 1966, Elizabeth Anne *b* 1965, (by 2nd *m*) Edmund Philip *b* 1980, Katherine Lelia *b* 1984, — John Edmund (4 Ivy Cross, Shaftesbury, Dorset) *b* 1940; *ed* Downside, and New Coll, Oxford (BA): *m* 1971, Gloria Cano, of Medellin, Colombia, and has issue living, Alejandro *b* 1973, Edmund Francis *b* 1985, Patricia Anita *b* 1972, Caterina *b* 1977, — Anthony Richard (48 Batoum Gdns, W6 7QD), *b* 1947; *ed* Downside, and Guildhall Sch of Music and Drama (GGSM): *m* 1978, Anstice Bridget, 2nd da of Maj Martin Antony Gibbs, of Sheldon Manor, Chippenham, Wilts (*see* Hamilton-Dalrymple, Bt), and has two children, Geoffrey John Bernard *b* 1986, Cecily Mary Margaret *b* 1983, — Katherine Isabella, *b* 1952: *m* 1977, Rev Christopher Woods, of Holy Trinity Vicarage, Traverse St, Parr Mount, St Helen's Merseyside, and has issue living, Francis *b* 1981, Thomas *b* 1983, Isabella *b* 1977, Madeline *b* 1979, Lydia *b* 1989. *Residence* – Jerome Cottage, Marlow Common, Bucks SL7 2QR.

WIDOW LIVING OF SON OF FIRST BARON

Adèle le Bourgeois (Bushby House, Greystoke, Penrith, Cumberland), da of late Reese Denny Alsop, of New York City, USA; *m* 1937, Lt-Col Hon Henry Anthony Camillo Howard CMG, Coldm Gds, who *d* 1977, yst son of 1st Baron, and has issue living (see colls infra).

COLLATERAL BRANCH LIVING

Issue of late Lt-Col Hon Henry Anthony Camillo Howard, CMG, yst son of 1st Baron, *b* 1913, *d* 1977: *m* 1937, Adèle le Bourgeois (ante), da of late Reese Denny Alsop, of New York City, USA:—
Mary Rosalind, *b* 1938, *m* 1961, Ian Harlowe Lowe, of Newton Reigny, Penrith, Cumbria, and has issue living, Esme Charles Harlowe, *b* 1962; *ed* Ampleforth; Coldstream Gds: *m* 1990, Carlotta L. M., elder da of Gian Carlo Guglielmino, of Chester Sq, SW1, and has issue living, Cosima Anne Julia *b* 1992. —— Susan Isabella, *b* 1940; Canoness of St Augustine; *d* 1963. —— Joan Dacre, *b* 1946, *m* 1st, 1966 (*m diss* 1979), William Lacey; 2ndly, 1980, Gordon W. Richards, of Old Rectory, Greystoke, Penrith, Cumbria, and has issue living (by 1st *m*), William John, *b* 1967: *m* 1993, Claire Baker, — Anne Marie, *b* 1972. —— Adèle Cristina Sophia (*Hon Mrs Timothy J. Palmer*), *b* 1952: *m* 1984, Hon Timothy John Palmer, of West Woodyates Manor, Salisbury, Wilts, yr son of late Maj Hon Robert Jocelyn Palmer, MC, by his late wife Anne Rosemary, Baroness Lucas of Crudwell, and Lady Dingwall (both in her own right), and has issue (*see* B Lucas of Crudwell). —— Charlotte Fell, *b* 1953: *m* 1985, Ian Mintrim.

PREDECESSOR – **(1)** ESME WILLIAM Howard, GCB, GCMG, CVO, 4th son of late Henry Howard, MP, of Greystoke, Cumberland (D Norfolk, colls); *b* 1863; was Envoy Extraor and Min Plen to Swiss Confederation 1911-13, and to Sweden 1913-19, and Ambassador Extraor and Plen to Spain 1919-23, and to Washington 1923-30; *cr Baron Howard of Penrith*, of

Gowbarrow, co Cumberland (peerage of United Kingdom) 1930: *m* 1898, Lady Maria Isabella Giovanna Teresa Gioacchina Giustiniani-Bandini, who *d* 1963, da of 8th Earl of Newburgh; *d* 1939; *s* by his 2nd but el surviving son (2) FRANCIS PHILIP, 2nd Baron and present peer.

HOWE, EARL (Curzon) (Earl UK 1821)

FREDERICK RICHARD PENN CURZON, 7th Earl; *b* 29 Jan 1951; *s* 1984; *ed* Rugby, and Ch Ch Oxford (MA); a Lord-in-Waiting to HM 1991-92; Govt Spokesman on Employment and Transport 1991-92, since when Parly Sec, Ministry of Agriculture, Fisheries and Food: *m* 1983, Elizabeth Helen, elder da of Capt Burleigh Edward St Lawrence Stuart (*see* E Castle Stewart, colls), and has issue.

Arms – Quarterly: 1st and 4th or, a fesse between three wolves' heads couped sable, *Howe*; 2nd and 3rd argent, on a bend sable, three popinjays or, collared gules, *Curzon*. **Crests** – 1st, out of a ducal coronet or, a plume of five ostrich feathers azure, *Howe*; 2nd, a popinjay wings displayed and inverted or, collared gules, *Curzon*. **Supporters** – On either side a Cornish chough proper, around the neck a plain gold chain.

Residence – Penn House, Amersham, Bucks HP7 0PS.

DAUGHTERS LIVING

Lady Anna Elizabeth, *b* 1987.
Lady Flora Grace, *b* 1989.
Lady Lucinda Rose, *b* 1991.

SISTER LIVING (*raised to the rank of an Earl's daughter* 1985)

Lady Emma Charlotte, *b* 1953; SRN.

MOTHER LIVING

Jane Victoria, da of late Malcolm Mackenzie Fergusson, of Toronto, Canada: *m* 1950 (*m diss* 1965), as his 2nd wife, Cdr Chambré George William Penn Curzon, RN (ret), who *d* 1976.

DAUGHTERS LIVING OF SIXTH EARL (*By 1st marriage*)

Lady (Priscilla) Mary Rose, *b* 1940: *m* 1962, Charles William Lyle Keen, of The Old Rectory, Duntisbourne Rous, Glos, and has issue living, William Walter Maurice, *b* 1970, — Laura Mary Catherine (*Hon Mrs Nicholas D. Beatty*), *b* 1963: *m* 1990, Hon Nicholas Duncan Beatty, yr son of 2nd Earl Beatty, — Eleanor Margaret, *b* 1965, — Alice Priscilla Lyle, *b* 1966: *m* 1994, Peter C. P. Oswald, eldest son of Peter David Hamilton Oswald, of Fliskmillan, Fife.
Lady Jennifer Jane, *b* 1941: *m* 1962, Alan Joseph Ponté, and has issue living, David Joseph Marcus Blundell, *b* 1964, — Gideon Léo FitzRoy, *b* 1965, — Joshua Albert Coriat *b* 1970, — Luke Antony Archibald, *b* 1974, — Rebecca Kate Priscilla Clara, *b* 1967.

(*By 2nd marriage*)

Lady Mary Gaye Georgiana Lorna CURZON, *b* 1947; has resumed her maiden name: *m* 1st, 1971 (*m diss* 1976), (Kevin) Esmond (Peter) Cooper-Key (*see* V Rothermere), who *d* 1985; 2ndly, 1977 (*m diss* 1987), John Austen Anstruther-Gough-Calthorpe (*see* Anstruther-Gough-Calthorpe, Bt); 3rdly, 1988 (*m diss* 1994), Jeffrey Bonas, son of late Harry Bonas, of Grangewood Hall, Netherseale, Burton-on-Trent, and has issue living (by 1st *m*) (*see* V Rothermere), — (by 2nd *m*) (*see* Anstruther-Gough-Calthorpe, Bt), — (by 3rd *m*) Cressida, *b* 1989. *Residence* – The Old Rectory, Ovington, Alresford, Hants.
Lady Charlotte Elizabeth Anne, *b* 1948: *m* 1988, (John) Barry Dinan, former Capt Irish Guards, and has issue living, Richard Assheton Dermot, *b* 1986. *Residence* – Chalkpit House, Knotty Green, Beaconsfield, Bucks.

DAUGHTERS LIVING OF FIFTH EARL (*By 2nd and 3rd marriages*)

Lady Frances Esmé, *b* 1939: *m* 1st, 1962, Derek Alan Whiting; 2ndly, 1976, Harold Denman (*see* B Denman) and has issue living (by 1st *m*), Alexander, *b* 1967, — Frances, *b* 1965, — (by 2nd *m*) (*see* B Denman).
Lady Sarah Marguerite, *b* 1945: *m* 1st, 1966, Piers Raymond Courage, who *d* 1970; 2ndly, 1972, John Victor Aspinall, of 1 Lyall St, SW1, and has issue living (by 1st *m*) Jason Piers, *b* 1967, — Amos Edward Sebastian, *b* 1969, — (by 2nd *m*) Bassa Wulfhere, *b* 1972.

WIDOW LIVING OF FIFTH EARL

SYBIL BOYTER (Jesters, Kings Legend, Aldeburgh, Suffolk), only child of late Capt Francis Johnson, of Palmeira Sq, Hove, and formerly wife of late Maj Ernest Duncombe Shafto: *m* 2ndly, 1944, as his third wife, the 5th Earl, who *d* 1964; 3rdly, 1972, Graham Goodson, who *d* 1988.

COLLATERAL BRANCHES LIVING

Grandchildren of late Hon Henry Dugdale Curzon, 4th son of 1st Earl:—
Issue of late Henry Curzon, *b* 1865, *d* 1912: *m* (Jan) 1899, Ellen, who *d* 1953, da of Samuel Hibberd:—
†Henry CURZON-HOWE, *b* (Oct) 1899; *ed* Midhurst Gram Sch; served 1939-45 War as Corporal RAF, and Sergeant Royal Marine Police; Schoolmaster; assumed the additional surname of Howe 1949: *m* 1940, Florence Jane (246 Newhaven Rd, Edinburgh EH6 4LH), da of late Charles Stanley Skinner, of Rest Harrow, Trevone, Padstow, Cornwall, and *dsp* 1985. —— Ivy Eleanor, *b* 1902; *dunm* 1973.

Grandchildren of late Charles Ernest Basset Lothian Curzon, only son of Maj Ernest Charles Penn Curzon, eldest son of Col Hon Ernest George Curzon, 6th son of 1st Earl:—
Issue of late Capt James Quintin Penn Curzon, Gordon Highlanders, *b* 1923, *d* 1985: *m* 1st, 1966 (*m diss* 1980), Jennifer Anne, da of late Percy Douglas Harrison, of Southsea; 2ndly, 1980, Mary Ann Vere OGILVY (who *m* 3rdly, 1987, Maj John David Makgill-Crichton-Maitland; *see* E Lauderdale, colls), only da of late Maj Charles Herbert Harberton Eales, MC (*see* Ogilvy, Bt, colls), and formerly wife of Charles Pepler Norton:—
(By 1st *m*) (CHARLES) MARK PENN, *b* 12 Nov 1967. —— Camilla Mary, *b* 1969.

Granddaughter of late Major Ernest Charles Penn Curzon, son of late Col Hon Ernest George Curzon (ante):—
Issue of late Charles Ernest Basset Lothian Curzon, *b* 1885, *d* 1952: *m* 1917, Geraldine Fosbery, who *d* 1962, da of Sir James Mills, KCMG:—
Mary Eleanora Basset, *b* 1920: *m* 1941, Maj James Malcolm Hay of Seaton, Gordon Highlanders (*see* M Tweeddale, colls), who *d* 1987. *Residence* – Edinglassie, Huntly, Aberdeenshire.

Grandchildren of late Adm Hon Sir Assheton Gore Curzon-Howe, GCVO, KCB, CMG (infra):—
Issue of late Capt Leicester Charles Assheton St John CURZON-HOWE, MVO, RN, *b* 1894, *d* on active ser 1941: *m* 1923, Marguerite Graham, who *d* 1977, da of A. Allan Mackenzie of Montreal:—
Anne Rita, *b* 1923; late WRNS: *m* 1st, 1955, as his 2nd wife, 19th Baron Teynham, who *d* 1972; 2ndly, 1975, Dr Ian Edwards, who *d* 1988. *Residence* – Inwood House, Holly Hill Lane, Sarisbury Green, Southampton SO3 6AH.
Issue of late Lieut-Col Assheton Penn CURZON-HOWE-HERRICK, RA, *b* 1898, *d* 1959, having assumed by Roy licence 1946, the additional surname and arms of Herrick: *m* 1930, Joan Henrietta, OBE (The Hermitage, Thornton Watlass, Ripon N Yorks), da of late James Windsor Lewis, of 67 Cadogan Place, SW1:—
Assheton Montagu Windsor (Le Chastanet, Collonges, Corrèze, France), *b* 1939. —— Marigold Mary, *b* 1934; SRN: *m* 1982, Patrick Benjamin Walker, and *d* 1983.

Issue of late Adm the Hon Sir Assheton Gore CURZON-HOWE, GCVO, KCB, CMG, 9th son of 1st Earl, *b* 1850, *d* 1911: *m* 1892, Alice Anne, who *d* 1948, da of late Maj-Gen Rt Hon Sir John Clayton Cowell, KCB:—
Joyce Mary, MBE, *b* 1906; MBE (Civil) 1982: *m* 1st, 1934, Lieut-Col Thomas Ethelston Hussey, RA, who was *ka* in France 1944; 2ndly, 1950, Rear-Adm Robert Kirk Dickson, CB, DSO, who *d* 1952. *Residence* – Shadings, Hangersley Hill, Ringwood, Hants.

PREDECESSORS – (1) ASSHETON Curzon, 2nd son of Sir Nathaniel Curzon, 4th Bt (*see* B Scarsdale); MP for Clitheroe 1754-77 and 1790-4; *cr Baron Curzon*, of Penn, co Bucks (peerage of Great Britain) 1794, and *Viscount Curzon* (peerage of United Kingdom) 1802; his only son, Assheton, MP, *d* 1797, having *m* SOPHIA CHARLOTTE, who in 1799 on the death of her father, Richard, KG, 1st and last Earl Howe (*cr* 1788 *Baron Howe*, of Langar, co Notts peerage of Great Britain, with remainder to his das), became Baroness Howe; (2-3) Assheton had by his marriage to the Baroness one son RICHARD WILLIAM PENN, PC, GCH, who in 1820 *s* his grandfather as 2nd Viscount and Baron Curzon, and in 1836 *s* his mother as 3rd Baron Howe; assumed the additional name of Howe by Roy licence 1821; *cr Earl Howe* (peerage of United Kingdom) 1821; was Lord Chamberlain to Queen Adelaide: *m* 1st, 1820, Harriet Georgiana, who *d* 1836, da of 6th Earl of Cardigan; 2ndly, 1845, Anne who *d* 1877, da of late Adm Sir John Gore; *d* 1870; *s* by his son (4) GEORGE AUGUSTUS FREDERICK LOUIS, 2nd Earl; *b* 1821; sat as MP for S Leicestershire (*C*) 1857-70; *d* 1876; *s* by his brother (5) RICHARD WILLIAM PENN, GCVO, CB, 3rd Earl, *b* 1822; a Gen in the Army; Mil Sec to Com-in-Ch in India 1854, and sometime ADC to HRH the Duke of Cambridge: *m* 1858, Isabella Katherine, who *d* 1922, da of late Maj-Gen Hon George Anson; *d* 1900; *s* by his son (6) RICHARD GEORGE PENN, GCVO, 4th Earl, *b* 1861; Treasurer of Queen Victoria's Household 1896-1900, a Lord-in-Waiting to Queen Victoria Oct 1900 to Jan 1901, and to King Edward VII Jan 1901 to Sept 1903, and Lord Chamberlain to late Queen Alexandra Sept 1903 to Nov 1925; MP for S, or Wycombe, Div of Bucks (*C*) 1885-1900; received Roy Victorian Chain 1925: *m* 1st, 1883, Lady Georgiana Elizabeth Spencer Churchill, who *d* 1906, da of 7th Duke of Marlborough; 2ndly, 1919, Florence (Flora), who *d* 1925, da of John H. Davis, of 24 Washington Square, New York, and widow of 2nd Marquess of Dufferin and Ava; 3rdly, 1927, Lorna Katherine, who *d* 1961, da of Major Ernest Charles Penn Curzon, and widow of Capt Quintin Dick, DL; *d* 1929; *s* by his son (7) FRANCIS RICHARD HENRY PENN, CBE, VD, PC, 5th Earl, *b* 1884; Chm of Roy National Life-Boat Instn: *m* 1st, 1907 (*m diss* 1937), his cousin Mary, who *d* 1962, da of Col Hon Montagu Curzon, 8th son of 1st Earl Howe; 2ndly, 1937 (*m diss* 1943), Joyce Mary McLean, da of Charles McLean Jack, of Johannesburg; 3rdly, 1944, Sybil Boyter (who *m* 3rdly 1972 Graham Goodson), da of Capt Francis Johnson, of Edinburgh, and formerly wife of late Maj Ernest Duncombe Shafto; *d* 1964; *s* by his only son (8) EDWARD RICHARD ASSHETON PENN, CBE, 6th Earl *b* 1908; Pres British Automobile Racing Club and Inst of Road Safety Officers: *m* 1st, 1935 (*m diss* 1943), Priscilla Crystal Frances Blundell, only da of Sir (William Ernest George) Archibald Weigall, 1st Bt, KCMG; 2ndly, 1946, Grace Lilian, OStJ, who *d* 1985, da of Stephen Frederick Wakeling, of Durban, S Africa, and formerly wife of Capt A. N. Barker; *d* 1984; *s* by his kinsman (9) FREDERICK RICHARD PENN (only son (by 2nd *m*) of Cdr Chambré George William Penn Curzon, RN (ret), son of Hon Frederick Graham Curzon, 2nd son of 3rd Earl), 7th Earl and present peer; also Viscount Curzon, Baron Curzon, and Baron Howe.

HOWE OF ABERAVON, BARON (Howe) (Life Baron 1992)

(RICHARD EDWARD) GEOFFREY HOWE, PC, elder son of late Benjamin Edward Howe, of Port Talbot, Glam; *b* 20 Dec 1926; *ed* Winchester, and Trin Hall, Camb (MA, LLB, Hon Fellow 1992); Hon LLD Wales 1988; Bar Middle Temple 1952, Member Gen Council of the Bar 1957-61, QC 1965, Bencher 1969, Member Exec Cttee "Justice" 1963-70, Dep-Chm Glamorgan Quarter Sessions 1966-70, Solicitor- Gen 1970-72, Min for Trade and Consumer Affairs 1972-74, Chancellor of the Exchequer and Lord Commr of the Treasury 1979-83, Chm IMF Policy-Making Interim Cttee 1982-83, Sec of State Foreign and Commonwealth Affairs 1983-July 1989, Leader of the Commons and Lord Pres of the Council July 1989-Nov 1990, Dept PM July 1989-Nov 1990; Member of Council Surrey Univ since 1970, Patron Enterprise Europe since 1990, Joint-Pres Wealth of Nations Foundation since 1991, Pres GB-China Centre since 1992, etc; non-exec Dir Glaxo plc and BICC plc, Special Advisor to Jones, Day, Reavis & Pogue, Member Internat Advisory Councils of J. P. Morgan & Co, Inst for Internat Studies Stanford Univ, and Bertelsmann Foundation Bonn; Visitor to Sch of Oriental and African Studies London Univ since 1991; Grand Cross Order of Merit Germany 1992; served 1945-48 as Lieut Royal Signals and E African Signals; MP Bebington (C) 1964-66, Reigate 1970-74, and E Surrey 1974-92; *cr* Kt Bach 1970, PC 1972, and *Baron Howe of Aberavon*, of Tandridge, co Surrey (Life Baron) 1992: *m* 1953, Elspeth Rosamund Morton, JP, da of late Philip Morton Shand, and has issue.
Addresses – c/o House of Lords, SW1; Barclay's Bank, 4 Vere St, W1.

SON LIVING

Hon Alexander Edward Thomson, *b* 1959; *ed* Marlborough, and York Univ.

DAUGHTERS LIVING

Hon Caroline, *b* 1955: *m* 19— (*m diss* 19—), — Thornton, and has issue living, Christopher, *b* 1980.
Hon Amanda, *b* (twin) 1959: *m* 19—, S. F. Glanvill, and has issue living, James, *b* 1989.

HOWELL, BARON (Howell) (Life Baron 1992)

DENIS HERBERT HOWELL, PC, son of Herbert Howell, of Birmingham; *b* 4 Sept 1923; *ed* Gower St Sch, and Handsworth Gram Sch; Member Birmingham City Council 1946-56; Joint Parly Under Sec DES 1964-69, Min for Sport, and Chm Sports Council 1964-70, Min of State Housing and Local Govt 1969-70, and for Recreation and Sport (Dept of the Environment) 1974-79, Min i/c of co-ordinating drought measures 1976; Chm Labour Movement for Europe; Pres Assocn of Professional, Executive, Clerical and Computer Staff (APEX) 1971-83; Member Labour Party Nat Exec Cttee 1982-83; Gov Handsworth Gram Sch; Vice-Pres Warwicks County Cricket Club since 1986, and Birchfield Harriers since 1987; formerly a football league referee; Silver Medal, Olympic Order, 1981; Dir Wembley Stadium Ltd, etc; Hon Freeman City of Birmingham 1990; author; MP All Saints Div, Birmingham (*Lab*) 1955-59, and Small Heath 1961-92; *cr* PC 1976, and *Baron Howell*, of Aston Manor in the City of Birmingham (Life Baron) 1992: *m* 1955, Brenda Marjorie, da of Stephen Willson, and has issue (with one son dec'd).

Arms – Quarterly or and gules, a pale raguly per pale counter-changed, in the first quarter a lion rampant contourny azure armed and langued gules, in the second quarter a bear statant erect or, in the third quarter a like bear also contourny or, in the fourth quarter a lion rampant azure armed and langued gules, overall on a fess ermine a portcullis or between two squirrels respectant each holding a nut proper. **Crest** – A mural crown per pale gules and or, issuing therefrom an arm embowed vested palewise or and gules, the hand grasping a hammer proper.
Residence – 33 Moor Green Lane, Moseley, Birmingham B13 8NE.

SONS LIVING

Hon Andrew, *b* 1957: *m* 1986, Ceridwen, da of—
Hon Michael, *b* 1959: *m* 1992, Elizabeth, da of—

DAUGHTER LIVING

Hon Kathryn, *b* 1962: *m* 1983, Michael Molloy.

HOWICK OF GLENDALE, BARON (Baring) (Baron UK 1960)

CHARLES EVELYN BARING, 2nd Baron; *b* 30 Dec 1937; *s* 1973; *ed* Eton, and New Coll, Oxford; Dir of Baring Brothers & Co Ltd 1969-82; Member of Exec Cttee Nat Art Collections Fund: *m* 1964, Clare Nicolette, yr da of Col Cyril Darby, MC, of Kemerton Court, Tewkesbury, Glos, and has issue.

Arms – Azure, a fesse or, in chief a bear's head proper muzzled and ringed or, differenced by an eastern crown azure. **Crest** – A mullet erminois between two wings argent. **Supporters** – *Dexter*, a tiger guardant proper gorged with an Eastern crown or; *Sinister*, a lion guardant purpure crowned with a ducal coronet or, and gorged with an eastern crown or.
Residence – Howick, Alnwick, Northumberland.

To serve the King with goodwill

SON LIVING

Hon DAVID EVELYN CHARLES, *b* 26 March 1975.

DAUGHTERS LIVING

Hon Rachel Monica, *b* 1967: *m* 1989, Capt (George Charles) Nicholas Lane Fox, The Blues and Royals, son of George Lane Fox, of Bramham Park, Wetherby, W Yorks (*see* B Bingley, ext, 1980 Edn), and has issue living, a da, *b* 1991.
Hon Jessica Mary Clare, *b* 1969.

Hon Alice Olivia, *b* 1971.

SISTERS LIVING

Hon Katherine Mary Alice (*Hon Lady Wakefield*), *b* 1936: *m* 1974, as his 3rd wife, Sir (Edward) Humphry Tyrrell Wakefield, 2nd Bt.
Hon Elizabeth Beatrice, *b* 1940: *m* 1962, Capt Nicholas Albany Gibbs, who *d* 1984, and has issue living, Andrew Lionel John, *b* 1966, — Mary Camilla, *b* 1964, — Eliza Jane, *b* 1968. *Residence –* .

WIDOW LIVING OF FIRST BARON

Lady MARY CECIL GREY (*Lady Mary Howick*), (Howick, Alnwick, Northumberland), da of 5th Earl Grey: *m* 1935, the 1st Baron, who *d* 1973.

PREDECESSOR – (1) *Hon Sir* EVELYN Baring, KG, GCMG, KCVO, yst of 1st Earl of Cromer, *b* 1903; Gov of S Rhodesia 1942-44, UK High Commr in Union of S Africa, and for Basutoland, Bechuanaland and Swaziland 1944-51, and Gov of Kenya 1952-59; *cr Baron Howick of Glendale*, of Howick, co Northumberland 1960: *m* 1935, Lady Mary Cecil Grey, da of 5th Earl Grey; *d* 1973; *s* by his son **(2)** CHARLES EVELYN, 2nd Baron, and present peer.

HOWIE OF TROON, BARON (Howie) (Life Baron 1978)

WILLIAM HOWIE, el son of Peter Howie of Troon; *b* 2 March 1924; *ed* Marr Coll, Troon, and Royal Tech Coll, Glasgow (BSc); Civil Engineer, lecturer, publisher and journalist; FICE; Assistant Whip 1964-66; Lord Commr of the Treasury 1966-67, Comptroller HM Household 1967-68 and a Vice-Chm Parl Labour Party 1968-70: MP for Luton (*Lab*) 1963-70; Member of Council Instn of Civil Engineers 1964-67, and of Gov Body, Imperial Coll of Science and Technology 1965-67, and of Gov Council, City Univ since 1968; Pro-Chancellor City Univ since 1984; Member of Cttee of Inquiry into the Engineering Profession since 1977; *cr Baron Howie of Troon*, of Troon, Kyle and Carrick (Life Baron) 1978: *m* 1951, Mairi Margaret, da of late John Sanderson, of Troon.
Residence – 34 Temple Fortune Lane, NW11 7UL.

SONS LIVING

Hon Angus, *b* 1963.
Hon Alexander Robin, *b* 1965.

DAUGHTERS LIVING

Hon Annabel Martha, *b* 1956: *m* 1979, — Gibb.
Hon Alisoun Mary Kyle, *b* 1959.

Howland, Baron; grandson of Duke of Bedford.

HOY, BARONY OF (Hoy) (Extinct 1976)

SON LIVING OF LIFE BARON

Hon Ian Richard, *b* 1945; *ed* George Heriot's Sch, Edinburgh; Member City of Edinburgh Dist Council since 1988.

HUDSON, VISCOUNTCY OF (Hudson) (Extinct 1963)

DAUGHTER LIVING OF SECOND VISCOUNT

Hon Annabel Jocelyne (8 Moncorvo Close, SW7), *b* 1952: *m* 1970, (Anthony) Juan Garton, and has issue living, Anthony William, *b* 1974, — Angela Maria Annabel, *b* 1972, — Annabel Katherine Madeline Maria, *b* 1982, — Annabel Rose Maria Francesca, *b* 1984.

HUGHES, BARON (Hughes) (Life Baron 1961)

WILLIAM HUGHES, CBE, PC, son of late Joseph Hughes; *b* 22 Jan 1911; *ed* Balfour Street Sch, Dundee, and at Dundee Technical Coll; Hon LLD St Andrews 1960; Chm Roy Commn on Legal Sers in Scotland 1976-80, and E Kilbride Development Corpn 1975-82; Pres Scottish Fedn of Housing Assocns; Delegate to Council of Europe and Western European Union 1976-87; a DL for co of City of Dundee, and a Chevalier of Legion of Honour; formerly a Member of Dundee Town Council (Lord Provost and Lord-Lt of co of City of Dundee 1954-60); Chm of E Regional Hosp Board (Scotland) 1948-60 and a Member of Court of St Andrews Univ 1954-63 and of Council of Queen's Coll, Dundee 1954-63, Chm of Glenrothes Development

Corporation 1960-64, and a Member of N Scotland Hydro-Electric Board 1956-64; a Parl Under-Sec of State, Scottish Office 1964-69, and Min of State, Scottish Office 1969-70, and 1974-75; ARP Controller, Dundee, 1939-43, India, Borneo and Burma 1944-46 as Capt RAOC; *cr* OBE (Civil) 1942, CBE (Civil) 1956, *Baron Hughes*, of Hawkhill, co of City of Dundee (Life Baron) 1961, and PC 1970: *m* 1951, Christian Clacher, da of late James Gordon, and has issue.
Residence – The Stables, Ross, Comrie, Perthshire PH6 2JU.

DAUGHTERS LIVING

Hon Christian Alison, *b* 1952; *ed* Strathclyde Univ (BSc): *m* 1973, Alan Cameron Cassels Henry, of Tigh-an-Lios, Ross, Comrie, Perthshire, and has issue.
Hon Janet Margaret (Alltan, by Tulloes, Forfar), *b* 1956; *ed* Edinburgh Univ (BSc).

Hunsdon of Hunsdon, Baron, see Baron Aldenham.

HUNT, BARON (Hunt) (Life Baron 1966)

(Henry Cecil) John Hunt, KG, CBE, DSO, son of late Capt C. E. Hunt, MC, Indian Army; *b* 22 June 1910; *ed* Marlborough, and RMC; Hon DCL Durham, Hon LLD Aberdeen, London City, and Leeds, Hon DSc Sheffield; Col and Hon Brig late KRRC; Cmd 11th Indian Inf Bde in Europe 1944-46, and GSO at HQ Allied Staff Central European Command 1949-52; Leader of British Expedition to Mount Everest 1952-53; Assist Comdt Staff Coll, Camberley 1953-55, Rector of Aberdeen Univ 1936-66, and Dir of Duke of Edinburgh's Award Scheme 1956-67; Chm of Parole Board for England and Wales 1967-73; Pres of Council for Volunteers Overseas 1968-74; Head of Relief Missions to Nigeria 1968-70; Chm Advisory Cttee on Police in N Ireland 1969; Member of Roy Commn on the Press; Pres Nat Assocn of Probation Officers 1974-80, of Roy Geographical Soc 1977-80, and of Council for National Parks 1980-86; 1939-45 War in Middle East, India, Greece and Italy; *cr* DSO 1944, CBE (Mil) 1945, Knt 1953, KG 1979, and *Baron Hunt*, of Llanfairwaterdine, co Salop (Life Baron) 1966: *m* 1936, Joy, da of late Dr Mowbray-Green, and has issue, four daughters, Sally, Susan, Prudence and Jennifer.

Arms – Argent a Himalayan black bear passant proper, a chief dancetty azure. **Crest** – Upon a wreath argent and azure, on two mountain peaks the first higher than the second, a chamois statant regardant proper. **Supporters** – *Dexter*, On a mount of grass and reedmace proper, issuant from water barry wavy argent and azure, a swan wings elevated and addorsed proper; *sinister*, on a rock a buzzard wings also elevated and addorsed proper.
Residence – Highway Cottage, Aston, Henley-on-Thames.
Clubs – Ski Club of Great Britain, Alpine.

HUNT OF FAWLEY, BARONY OF (Hunt) (Extinct 1987)

SONS LIVING OF LIFE BARON

Dr the Hon Jonathan Philip Henderson, *b* 1947; MA, BM, BCh, Oxford: *m* 1977, Monika, only da of Dr Herbert Kuhlmann, of Schloss Urstein, Salzburg, Austria, and has issue, three das. *Residence* – 29 South Terrace, SW7.
Dr the Hon Christopher Godfrey Evill (twin) *b* 1947; MB, BS London; MRCS Eng; LRCP London; DObst, RCOG: *m* 1979, Carol McDermott, of Toronto, Ontario, Canada, and has issue, two das. *Residence* – 4455 West 2nd Avenue, Vancouver, BC, Canada.

DAUGHTERS LIVING OF LIFE BARON

Hon Rosemary, *b* 1943; *ed* St Andrews Univ (MA): *m* 1974, Dr Clive Malcolm Senior, BA, PhD, of 20 Derby St, Swanbourne, Perth, W Australia, and has issue, one son and one da.
Hon Gillian Mary, *b* 1951: *m* 1972, Paul Andrew Richards, MA, of Arborfield, Wantage, Oxon, and has issue, three sons and one da.

WIDOW LIVING OF LIFE BARON

Elisabeth Ernestine (*Baroness Hunt of Fawley*), da of Norman Evill, FRIBA: *m* 1941, Baron Hunt of Fawley, CBE, FRCP, FRCS, FRCGP (Life Baron), who *d* 1987. *Residence* – Seven Steep, Fawley Green, nr Henley-on-Thames, Oxon.

HUNT OF TANWORTH, BARON (Hunt) (Life Baron 1980)

JOHN JOSEPH BENEDICT HUNT, GCB, son of late Maj Arthur L. Hunt, MC; *b* 23 Oct 1919; *ed* Downside, and Magdalene Coll, Camb (MA); Hon Fellow 1977; Lieut RNVR 1940-45; entered Dominions Office 1946; 2nd Sec UK High Commr's Office, Ceylon 1948-50, 1st Sec UK High Commr's Office, Canada 1953-56; Pte Sec to Sec of Cabinet 1956-58, and to Permanent Sec to Treas and Head of Civil Ser 1957-58; Assist Sec, Commonwealth Relations Office 1958-60, Cabinet Office 1960-62, and HM Treas 1962-65, and Under Sec HM Treas 1965-68; 1st Civil Ser Commr 1968-71, Dep Sec HM Treas 1971-72, and 2nd Permanent Sec, Cabinet Office 1972-73, and Sec of the Cabinet 1973-79; Chm Banque Nationale de Paris plc since 1980; Chm Prudential Corpn plc since 1985, and Dir IBM (UK) Ltd since 1980; Advisory Dir Unilever since 1980; Chm Ditchley Foundation since 1983; *cr* CB (Civil) 1968, KCB (Civil) 1973, GCB (Civil) 1977, and *Baron Hunt of Tanworth*, of Stratford-upon-Avon (Life Baron) 1980: *m* 1st, 1941, Hon Magdalen Mary Robinson, who *d* 1971, da of 1st Baron Robinson (ext); 2ndly, 1973, Madeleine Frances, da of late Sir William Hume, CMG, FRCP, and widow of Sir John Charles, KCB, FRCP, and has issue by 1st *m*. *Residence* – 8 Wool Rd, SW20 0HW.

SONS LIVING *(By 1st marriage)*

Hon Michael Anthony (86 Foxhill, Olney, Bucks MK46 5HF), *b* 1942: *m* 1st, 1963 (*m diss* 19—), Rosemary Ann, only da of late Col Theodore Ernle Longridge, OBE, of Marylands, Lynch Rd, Farnham, Surrey; 2ndly, 19—, Jennee Lynn, da of G. Thomas Baker, of Malibu, Calif, USA, and has issue.
Hon Martin John, *b* 1962; *ed* Worth: *m* 1993, Olivia Louise, only da of John Norris Fennell (*see* B Hawke). *Residence* – 24 Burnthwaite Rd, SW6 5BE.

DAUGHTER LIVING *(By 1st marriage)*

Hon Charlotte Mary Magdalen, *b* 1947: *m* 1976, Dr Herbert Gill, of 22230 Drums Court, Woodland Hills, California 91364, USA, and has issue.

HUNTER OF NEWINGTON, BARONY OF (Hunter) (Extinct 1994)

SONS LIVING OF LIFE BARON

Hon Robert Douglas (2 Lindsay Av, Cheadle Hulme, Cheshire SK8 7BQ), *b* 1945: *m* 1969, Marion Mackenzie.
Hon Alan Marshall (31 Hillcrest Av, Nether Poppleton, York YO2 6L0), *b* 1946: *m* 1971, Elizabeth Goodall.
Hon Ian Thorburn (27 Affleck Gdns, Monikie, by Dundee), *b* 1951: *m* 1974, Angela Hill.

DAUGHTER LIVING OF LIFE BARON

Hon Gillian Margaret, *b* 1948: *m* 1973, Malcolm Greig Edward, of 82 Lordswood Rd, Harborne, Birmingham B17 9BY.

WIDOW LIVING OF LIFE BARON

KATHLEEN MARGARET (*Baroness Hunter of Newington*), da of James Wilkie Douglas: *m* 1940, Baron Hunter of Newington, MBE, FRCP (Life Baron), who *d* 1994. *Residence* – 3 Oakdene Drive, Barnt Green, Birmingham 45 8LQ.

HUNTINGDON, EARL OF (Hastings-Bass) (Earl E 1529)

Victory is in truth

WILLIAM EDWARD ROBIN HOOD HASTINGS-BASS, 16th Earl; *b* 30 Jan 1948; *s* 1990; *ed* Winchester, and Trin Coll, Camb; Trainer to HM at W Ilsley Stables since 1989: *m* 1989, Susan Mary Gavin, da of John Jellicoe Pelham Francis Warner (son of late Sir Pelham Warner, MBE).

Arms – Argent, a maunch sable. **Crest** – A bull's head erased sable, armed and ducally gorged or. **Supporters** – Two man tigers (or lions guardant with human faces) or, the faces proper.
Residence – Hodcott House, W Ilsley, nr Newbury, Berks.

BROTHERS LIVING (*Raised to the rank of an Earl's sons*, 1992)

Hon SIMON AUBREY ROBIN HOOD, *b* 2 May 1950, *ed* Winchester, and Trin Coll, Camb. *Residence* – Coronation House, Newmarket, Suffolk.
Hon John Peter Robin Hood, *b* 1954; *ed* Winchester, and Trin Coll, Camb: *m* 1982, Sophie, only da of Peter Ewald Scarisbrick, of 11 Chester Terr, NW1, and has issue living, Alice Victoria Mary, *b* 1983. — Lily Frances Mary, *b* 1986. *Residence* – Ashmansworth Manor, Newbury, Berks.

SISTER LIVING (*Raised to the rank of an Earl's daughter*, 1992)

Lady Emma Alice Mary, *b* 1949: *m* 1969, Ian Anthony Balding, LVO (Trainer to HM), son of late Gerald Balding, of Weyhill House, Andover, Hants, and has issue living, Andrew Matthews, *b* 1972. — Clare Victoria, *b* 1971. *Residence* – Park House, Kingsclere, Newbury, Berks.

DAUGHTERS LIVING OF FIFTEENTH EARL (*by 1st marriage*)

Lady Moorea, *b* 1928: *m* 1st, 1957 (*m diss* 1966), Woodrow Lyle Wyatt (later Baron Wyatt of Weeford) (Life Baron); 2ndly, 1967, Brinsley Black, and has issue living (by 1st *m*) (*see* B Wyatt of Weeford), — (by 2nd *m*) Octavius Orlando Irvine Casati, *b* 1968. *Residence* – 17 Lansdowne Walk, W11.

(*by 2nd marriage*)

Lady Selina Shirley HASTINGS (c/o Rogers, Coleridge & White, 20 Powis Mews, W11 1JN), *b* 1945; writer.
Lady (Caroline) Harriet, *b* 1946: *m* 1970, Hon Charles Edward Ernest Shackleton, who *d* 1979, only son of Baron Shackleton (Life Baron); has issue living, David Charles, *b* 1986, — Emma Jane Miranda, *b* 1985.

MOTHER LIVING

Priscilla Victoria, da of Capt Sir Malcolm Bullock, 1st Bt, MBE (ext): *m* 1947, Capt Peter Robin Hood Hastings-Bass, who *d* 1964, having assumed by deed poll the additional surname of Bass 1954. *Residence* – Wells Head House, Kingsclere, Newbury, Berks.

COLLATERAL BRANCHES LIVING

Granddaughter of late Capt Hon Osmond William Toone Westenra Hastings, 2nd son of 13th Earl:—
Issue of late Lt-Col Robin Hood William Stewart Hastings, DSO, OBE, MC, *b* 1917, *d* 1990: *m* 1950, Jean Suzanne (The Malt House, Bramdean, Alresford, Hants; 2 Billing Rd, SW10), da of late Henry Palethorpe, of Stone Manor, Chaddesley Corbett, Worcs, and formerly wife of John Ronald Christopher Holbech:—
Lucinda Ileene, *b* 1955: *m* 1983, Michael Thomas Waterhouse (*see* D Marlborough, 1990 Edn), and has issue living, Robin Hood E. T., *b* 1987, — Marcus Charles, *b* 1990. *Residence* – Middleton Hall, Bakewell, Derbys.

Issue of late Hon Aubrey Craven Theophilus Robin Hood Hastings, 3rd son of 13th Earl, *b* 1878, *d* 1929: *m* 1907, Winifred, who *d* 1977, da of T. Forsyth-Forrest, formerly of The Querns, Cirencester:—
Joan, *b* 1917: *m* 1st, 1942, Thomas Frank Bartlett; 2ndly 1948, Kenneth Porter, who *d* 1986, of 347 Wheatley Rd, Old Westbury, Long Island, NY 11568, USA, and has issue living (by 2nd *m*), Steven Kenneth, *b* 1951: *m* 1977, Melinda Smith, and has issue living Whitney Kemp *b* 1979, Steven Lawrence *b* 1981, — Grant Aubrey, *b* (twin) 1951: *m* 1976, Christina French, and has issue living, Christina Chrysler *b* 1982.

Grandson of late Hans Francis Hastings (*infra*):—
Issue of late George Godolphin Hastings, *b* 1905, *d* 1981: *m* 1932, Marjorie Harris:—
Warren Francis (3/8A Mosman St, Mosman 2088, NSW, Australia), *b* 1938: *m* 1st, 1968 (*m diss* 1976), Elaine Adams; 2ndly, 1976, Elisabeth Kay Vine-Hall, and has issue living (by 2nd *m*), Adam Francis, *b* 1977, — Emma Louise, *b* 1979. —— Edyth Leonie, *b* 1933: *m* 1956 (*m diss* 19—), Ross Ekins, and has issue living, David Ross, *b* 19—, — Russell John, *b* 19—, — Linda Margaret, *b* 19—.

Granddaughter of late Vice-Adm Hon George Fowler Hastings, CB, 2nd son of 11th Earl:—
Issue of late Hans Francis Hastings, *b* 1865, *d* 1933: *m* 1900, Edyth Mary, who *d* 1959, da of late George O. Spratt, formerly of Lamorna, Gibraltar:—
Edythe Cecile, *b* 1910: *m* 1930, Col Geoffrey Anderton, RAMC, who *d* 1981, and has issue living, *Rev* Frederic Michael (100 Harvist Rd, NW6 6HL), *b* 1931: *m* 1977, Angela Robin Coulson, and has issue living, Sophia Vera Kathrin *b* 1982, — Richard Hastings (38 Acacia Rd, Hampton, Middx TW12 3DF), *b* 1946: *m* 1974, Susan Challis Bousfield, and has issue living, James Challis *b* 1978, Sarah Hastings *b* 1981, — Cecile Mary Frances, *b* 1933: *m* 1959, Trevor Gerald Townsend, of 18 Virgins Lane, Battle, Sussex TN33 0JH, and has issue living, Michael John *b* 1966, Jane Cecile *b* 1963. *Residence* – Edendale, 5 The Green, St Leonards, E Sussex.

Granddaughters of late Adm Alexander Plantagenet Hastings, CB, 2nd son of late Capt Hon Edward Plantagenet Robin Hood Hastings, 3rd son of 11th Earl:—
Issue of late Capt Edward George Godolphin Hastings, CBE, RN, *b* 1887, *d* 1973: *m* 1922, Hon Grisell Annabella Gem Cochrane-Baillie, who *d* 1985, da of 2nd Baron Lamington:—

(Sheila) Felicity Phoebe, *b* 1925: *m* 1954, John Humphrey Scrimgeour, TD, of Huntick Farm, Lytchett Matravers, Dorset, and has issue living, Alexander John Humphrey, *b* 1957: *m* 1993, Sarah Beatrix, only da of late John Horatio (Rae) Gordon Shephard, — Benjamin Victor Shedden, *b* 1960: *m* 1988, Christian Clare, yst da of Maj Sir Hamish Stewart Forbes, 7th Bt, MBE, MC, and has issue living, India *b* 1993, — Sally Belinda, *b* 1955: *m* 1987, Graham Lewis Mitchell, of Golden Grove Estate, Tobago, only son of Mrs E. W. Hill, of Dukes Kiln, Gerrards Cross, Bucks. —— Bridget Anne, *b* 1928: *m* 1955, Patrick Stephens Leigh, and has issue living, William Patrick, *b* 1956; *ed* Eton, and Ch Ch Oxford: *m* 1987, Nancy Oliveira, da of João Lavinsky, of Bahia, Brazil, and has issue living, Natasha Maria *b* 1988, — Edward Harold, *b* 1960, *ed* Eton: *m* 1988, Blanca Daphne, da of Paul Wansbrough, and has issue living, Benjamin Patricio *b* 1989, Dominic Pablo *b* 1991, — Belinda Grisell, *b* 1958; has issue living, Eppie Irene *b* 1988, — Annabella Hylda, *b* 1968. *Residence* – Ragged Lands, Glynde, nr Lewes, Sussex BN8 6RP.

Grandson of late Henry John Churchill Hastings, yst son of late Rev Hon Richard Godolphin Hastings, 4th son of 11th Earl:—

Issue of late Henry Theophilus James Hastings, *b* 1910, *d* 1977: *m* 1941, Muriel Hyde, who *d* 1977, da of Walter Turner, of Athol Place, Banket, Rhodesia:—

David Walter Theophilus (Robin Hood Estate, Box 54, Shamva, Zimbabwe), *b* 1947: *m* 1971, Margaret Netta Allyson, da of Douglas Andrew Wilkinson, of Umvukwes, Rhodesia, and has issue living, Ian David, *b* 1975, — Kate Rosemary, *b* 1973.

PREDECESSORS – **(1)** *Sir* WILLIAM de Hastings, Knt (descent deduced from Robert de Hastings, Dispensator to William the Conqueror); *cr Baron Hastings*, of Ashby de la Zouch (peerage of England) 1461; as Master of the Mints at London and Calais introduced the "Noble," a gold coinage of the value of 8*s*. 4*d*.; was Ambassador in France and Lord Chamberlain; subsequently fell a victim to the Protector, Gloucester (Richard III), and was beheaded at the Tower 1483; *s* by his son **(2)** EDWARD, KB 2nd Baron, who in 1482 had been summoned to Parliament of England in right of his wife as *Baron Hungerford*, she having obtained the reversal of the attainder of her father and grandfather in the baronies of Hungerford (*cr* 1462), Botreaux (*cr* 1368), and De Moleyns (*cr* 1347); *d* 1507; *s* by his son **(3)** GEORGE, 3rd Baron; attended Henry VIII 1513 at taking of Teruenne and Tournay; *cr Earl of Huntingdon* (peerage of England) 1529; *d* 1544; *s* by his el son **(4)** FRANCIS, KG, PC, 2nd Earl; was Lt-Gen and Com-in-Ch of the Army 1549, Lord-Lieut of Rutland, Leicester, and Warwick, and Master of the Queen's Hart Hounds: *m* 1532, Katherine, who *d* 1576, da and co-heiress of Henry Pole, Lord Montague, and grandda of Margaret, Countess of Salisbury (da and sole heiress of George, Duke of Clarence, brother of King Edward IV); *d* 1560; *s* by his son **(5)** HENRY, KG, 3rd Earl; *d* 1595; *s* by his brother **(6)** GEORGE, 4th Earl; *d* 1605; *s* by his grandson **(7)** HENRY, 5th Earl; *d* 1643; *s* by his son **(8)** FERDINANDO, 6th Earl; *d* 1655; *s* by his son **(9)** THEOPHILUS, 7th Earl; *d* 1701; *s* by his el son **(10)** GEORGE, 8th Earl; carried the sceptre at Coronation of Queen Anne 1702; *d* 1705, *s* by his half-brother **(11)** THEOPHILUS, 9th Earl; carried the Sword of State at Coronation of George II; *d* 1746 *s* by his son **(12)** FRANCIS, 10th Earl; carried the Sword of State at Coronation of George III; *d* 1789, when the Baronies of Hastings, Botreaux, and De Moleyns devolved upon his el sister, Elizabeth, wife of 1st Earl Moira (see E Loudoun), and the Earldom became dormant, although it was assumed by the lineal descendant of the 2nd Earl, Rev Theophilus Henry Hastings, el uncle of **(13)** HANS FRANCIS, *b* 1779, who took his seat as 11th Earl 1819; was Gov of Dominica: *m* 1st, 1803, Frances, who *d* (March) 1820, da of Rev Richard Chaloner, R of Great Marlow, Bucks; 2ndly (Sept) 1820 Eliza Mary, who *d* 1846 (having *m* 2ndly, 1838, Col Sir Thomas Noel Harris, KH), da of Joseph Bettesworth, of Ryde, Isle of Wight, and widow of Alexander Thistelthwayte; *d* 1828; *s* by his son **(14)** FRANCIS THEOPHILUS HENRY, 12th Earl: *m* 1835, Elizabeth Anne, who *d* 1857, da of Richard Power, MP; *d* 1875; *s* by his son **(15)** FRANCIS POWER PLANTAGENET, 13th Earl, *b* 1841: *m* 1867, Mary Anne Wilmot, who *d* 1894, da of Hon John Craven Westenra, MP; *d* 1885; *s* by his son **(16)** WARNER FRANCIS JOHN PLANTAGENET, 14th Earl, *b* 1868: *m* 1892, Maud Margaret, who *d* 1953, da of late Sir Samuel Wilson, of 10 Grosvenor Square, W; *d* 1939; *s* by his son **(17)** FRANCIS JOHN CLARENCE WESTENRA PLANTAGENET, 15th Earl, *b* 1901, an artist (pupil of Diego Rivera, Mexican mural painter), Prof Sch of Arts & Crafts, Camberwell, and Central Sch of Arts and Crafts, London, chm Cttee of Soc of Mural Painters 1951-58, and Pres of Solent Protection Soc 1958-68, Parl Sec to Min of Agriculture and Fisheries 1945-50, author: *m* 1st, 1925 (*m diss* 1943), Maria Cristina, who *d* 1953, da of the Marchese Casati, of Palazzo Barberini, Rome; 2ndly, 1944, Margaret (the writer Margaret Lane), who *d* 1994, only child of late Harry George Lane, of Vernham Dean, Andover, and formerly wife of Bryan Wallace (son of late Edgar Wallace, author); *d* 1990; *s* by his cousin (18) WILLIAM EDWARD ROBIN HOOD, eldest son of late Capt Peter Robin Hood Hastings-Bass (who assumed by deed poll the additional surname of Bass 1954) (only son of late Hon Aubrey Craven Theophilus Robin Hood Hastings, 3rd son of 13th Earl), 16th Earl and present peer.

HUNTINGFIELD, BARON (Vanneck) (Baron I 1796, Bt GB 1751)

Just and loyal

JOSHUA CHARLES VANNECK, 7th Baron, and 9th Baronet; *b* 10 Aug 1954; *s* 1994; *ed* Eton, and Magdalene Coll, Camb (MA); 2nd Lieut Scots Dragoon Gds: *m* 1982, Arabella Mary, eldest da of late Maj Alastair Hugh Joseph Fraser, MC, of Moniack Castle, Kirkhill, Inverness-shire (*see* L Lovat, colls), and has issue.

Arms – Argent, three bugle horns, two and one, gules, stringed or, and in the fesse point a torteau. **Crest** – A bugle horn gules, between two wings elevated argent, tipped or. **Supporters** – Two greyhounds ermine, each gorged with a collar paly of six, gules and or, and chained gold. **Residence** – 1 Clanricarde Mansions, Clanricarde Gdns, W2.

SONS LIVING

Hon GERARD CHARLES ALASTAIR, *b* 12 March 1985.
Hon John Errington, *b* 1988.
Hon Richard Fraser, *b* 1990.
Hon David Guise, *b* (twin) 1990.

DAUGHTER LIVING

Hon Vanessa Clare, *b* 1983.

SISTERS LIVING AND DECEASED

Hon Sara Anne, *b* 1944: *m* 1966 (*m diss* 1976), as his 1st wife, Marcus Hugh Crofton Binney, and *d* 1979.
Hon Christina Louise, *b* 1946: *m* 1967, Anthony Darell-Brown, R Green Jackets, and has issue living, Mark Philip Anthony, *b* 1969, — Henry Robert, *b* 1971, — Juliet Cordelia Diana, *b* 1973. *Residence* – The Old Rectory, Witnesham, Ipswich, Suffolk.
Hon Katharine Grace (twin), *b* 1954; BA: *m* 1976, Nicholas John Bacon, of School Lane Farmhouse, Colston Bassett, Notts NG12 3FD, and has issue living, Sara Elizabeth, *b* 1980, — Frances Louise, *b* 1983, — Charlotte Helena, *b* 1991.

UNCLE LIVING (son of 5th Baron)

Hon Sir Peter Beckford Rutgers, GBE, CB, AFC, AE, *b* 1922; *ed* Geelong Gram Sch, Aust, Stowe, Trin Coll, Camb (MA), and at Harvard Univ, USA; Hon DSc, City Univ TEng (CEI); late Lt (P) RN; 601 Sqdn RAuxAF 1950-57, Hon Air Commodore RAuxAF; OC No 3619 (Suffolk) Fighter Control Unit RAuxAF 1959-61; Inspector, RAuxAF 1962-73; Hon Inspector-Gen RAuxAF 1974-83; Hon Air Commodore No 1 MHU RAuxAF; ADC to HM 1963-73; a Gentleman Usher to HM 1967-79, and Alderman of City of London 1969-79 (a Sheriff 1974-75); Lord Mayor of London 1978-79; elected rep to European Assembly 1979-89; High Sheriff of Suffolk 1974; KJStJ; a DL Gtr London; 1939-45 War in RN; OBE (Mil) 1963, CB (Mil) 1973, GBE (Civil) 1977: *m* 1st, 1943 (*m diss* 1984), Cordelia, da of Capt Reginald Hugh Errington, RN (ret) (*see* E Dartmouth, colls, 1980 Edn); 2ndly, 1984, Elizabeth Lechmere, formerly wife of Spencer Malcolm Edward Forbes (*see* Stuart-Forbes, Bt, colls), and da of late Sandys Stuart Macaskie, of Lustleigh, S Devon, and has issue living (by 1st *m*), Charlotte Susan, *b* 1947: *m* 1972, H. Dennistoun Stevenson, CBE, of 32 Catherine Place, SW1E 6HL, and has issue living, Alexander *b* 1974, John Heneage *b* 1978, Charles Dennistoun *b* 1980, William Beckford James *b* 1984. *Residences* – 2/10 Brompton Square, SW3; Red House, Sudbourne, Woodbridge, Suffolk IP12 2AT. *Clubs* – White's, Pratt's, Royal Yacht Squadron and Royal London Yacht.

AUNTS LIVING (daughters of 5th Baron)

Hon Sara Carola, *b* 1913: *m* 1936, David Arthur Peel, MC, T/Major Irish Guards, who was *ka* in NW Europe 1944 (*see* E Peel, colls). *Residence* – Huntingfield Hall, Halesworth, Suffolk, IP19 0QA.
Hon Anne Margaret Theodosia, *b* 1918: *m* 1940 (*m diss* 1984), Peter Moro, FRIBA, and has issue living, Frances, *b* 1945: *m* 1st, 1966 (*m diss* 1979), John Barnes; 2ndly, 1987, Michael Edward Thomas Molloy, of 61 Annandale Rd, SE10, and has issue living (by 1st *m*), Samuel *b* 1968, Jessie *b* 1972, — Alice, *b* 1948: *m* 1978, Jacek Lech Basista, of 23 Culverden Park, Tunbridge Wells, Kent TN4 9QT, and has issue living, Tom *b* 1984, Rose Zofia *b* 1991, — Dinah, *b* 1960.

WIDOW LIVING OF BROTHER OF FIFTH BARON

Britta Ingeborg Nilsdotter (Sylchester, 2/4 Trahlee Rd, Bellevue Hill, Sydney 2023, Aust) da of Count Nils Gustaf Bonde, of Stockholm: *m* 1939, as his 2nd wife, late Hon Andrew Nicolas Armstrong Vanneck, MC, who was raised to the rank of a Baron's son 1922, and *d* 1965, and has issue living (see colls infra).

WIDOW LIVING OF SIXTH BARON

JANETTA LOIS (*Dowager Baroness Huntingfield*), da of Capt Reginald Hugh Errington, RN (*see* E Dartmouth, colls, 1980 Edn): *m* 1941, the 6th Baron, who *d* 1994. *Residence* – 53 Barron's Way, Comberton, Cambs CB3 7EQ.

COLLATERAL BRANCHES LIVING

Issue of late Hon Andrew Nicolas Armstrong Vanneck, MC, 3rd son of Hon William Arcedeckne Vanneck, 2nd son of 3rd Baron, *b* 1890, *d* 1965: *m* 1st , 1930 (*m diss* 1933), Louise, who *d* 1970, da of Henry Clews, of The Chateau of La Napoule, France, AM; 2ndly, 1939, Britta Ingeborg Nilsdotter (ante), only da of Count Nils Gustaf Bonde, of Stockholm, Sweden:—
(By 2nd *m*) William Bonde (31 Pymble Av, Pymble, NSW 2073, Australia), *b* 1943: *m* 1971, Jane Blanton, and has issue living, Mark Alexander Blanton, *b* 1979, — Nina Sara, *b* 1975. —— Margita, *b* 1940: *m* 1961, David Michael Wheeler, of Broadlands, La Hougue Bie, Grouville, Jersey, CI, and has issue living, Andrew Michael, *b* 1963, — James Nicholas, *b* 1966.

Grandchildren of late John Torrance Vanneck, grandson of late Hon Tompson Vanneck, 3rd son of 1st Baron:—

Issue of late John Vanneck, *b* 1906, *d* 1974: *m* 1930, Barbara (Parsonage Point, Rye, NY, 10580, USA), da of Frank Bailey:—

John Bailey (1100 Park Av, New York, NY 10128, USA), *b* 1938: *m* 1st, 1965 (*m diss* 1981), Isabelle Adele Knipe; 2ndly, 1985, Cynthia Laney, and has issue living (by 1st *m*), F. Bailey, *b* 1970, — Alexandra Knipe, *b* 1965: *m* 1991, Charles Capel Smith, jr, — Cynthia Gordon, *b* 1967. —— William Prentice (521 Riversville Rd, Greenwich, Conn 06831, USA), *b* 1941: *m* 1st, 1962 (*m diss* 1990), Nancy Buck; 2ndly, 1990, Rebecca Heffington, and has issue living (by 1st *m*), John Lanphear, *b* 1963, — Richard Prentice, *b* 1966: *m* 1991, Karen Elizabeth Bugniazet, and has issue living, Lindsay Bailey *b* 1992, — Christine Walker, *b* (twin) 1963: *m* 1992, Robert Thomas Owen, and has issue living, Sarah Ann *b* 1992, — Sandra Brookman, *b* 1967. —— Marion Louise (Plymouth Rd, Rye, NY 10580, USA), *b* 1937: *m* 1959 (*m diss* 1989), Raymond Robert Konopka, and has had issue, Raymond Robert, *b* 1961; *d* 1993, — Lee Bailey, *b* 1963: *m* 1987, Ann Smith, and has issue living, Christopher Walter *b* 1988, Grace Ann *b* 1991, — Steven Bailey, *b* 1966: *m* 1992, Megan Cassidy, — Suzanne Louise, *b* 1959: *m* 1983, Bryan M. Fitzpatrick, and has issue living, Bryan Michael II *b* 1986, Morgan Bailey *b* 1988, Bryce Galvin *b* 1989, Ashley Louise *b* 1985. —— Barbara Anne (Kelleher Rd, Dorset, Vermont, USA), *b* 1946: *m* 1968 (*m diss* 1976), James S. May, and has issue living, Wendy Bailey, *b* 1968, — Tanya Sheridan, *b* 1973.

PREDECESSORS – (**1**) JOSHUA Vanneck, an eminent London banker; *cr* a *Baronet* 1751; *d* 1777; *s* by his el son (**2**) *Sir* Gerard, MP, 2nd Bt; *d* unmarried 1791, *s* by his brother (**3**) *Sir* JOSHUA, 3rd Bt, MP for Dunwich; *cr Baron Huntingfield*, of Heveningham Hall (peerage of Ireland) 1796; *d* 1816; *s* by his el son (**4**) JOSHUA, 2nd Baron; *b* 1778: *m* 1st 1810, Catherine, da of Chaloner Arcedeckne, of Glevering Hall, co Suffolk; 2ndly, 1817, Lucy Anne, who *d* 1889, da of Sir Charles Blois, Bt; *d* 1844: *s* by his son (**5**) CHARLES ANDREW, 3rd Baron, *b* 1818: *m* 1839, Louisa, who *d* 1898, da of late Andrew Arcedeckne, of Glevering Hall, Suffolk; *d* 1897; *s* by his el son (**6**) JOSHUA CHARLES, 4th Baron; *b* 1842; *d* 1915; *s* by his nephew (**7**) WILLIAM CHARLES ARCEDECKNE, KCMG (son of Hon William Arcedeckne Vanneck, 2nd son of 3rd Baron), 5th Baron, 1883; MP for Eye Div, E Suffolk (*C*) 1923-29; Gov of Vic, Aust 1934-39; *m* 1st, 1912, Margaret Eleanor (CStJ), who *d* 1943, only da of late Judge Ernest Crosby, of New York; 2ndly, 1944, Muriel May Georgina, who *d* 1953, da of late Col Jemmet Duke, 17th Lancers, and widow of 1st Baron Eltisley; *d* 1969; *s* by his el son (**8**) GERARD CHARLES ARCEDECKNE, 6th Baron, *b* 1915; UN Secretariat 1946-75; 1939-45 War as Fl Sgt RAFVR: *m* 1941, Janetta Lois, da of Capt Reginald Hugh Errington, RN (*see* E Dartmouth, colls, 1980 Edn); *d* 1994; *s* by his only son (**9**) JOSHUA CHARLES, 7th Baron and present peer.

HUNTLY, MARQUESS OF (Gordon) (Marquess S 1599)

Abiding.

By courage, not by stratagem

GRANVILLE CHARLES GOMER GORDON, 13th Marquess, and Premier Marquess of Scotland; *b* 4 Feb 1944; *s* 1987; *ed* Gordonstoun; Member Council Nat Trust for Scotland 1977-80, Nat Cttee Scottish Georgian Soc 1976-81: *m* 1st, 1972 (*m diss* 1990), Jane Elizabeth Angela, da of late Lt-Col Alistair Monteith Gibb, R Wilts Yeo (*see* V Cowdray, 1980 Edn); 2ndly, 1991, Mrs Catheryn Millbourn, da of Gay Kindersley (*see* B Kindersley), and has issue by 1st and 2nd *m*.

Arms – Quarterly: 1st azure, three boars' heads couped or, *Gordon*; 2nd or, three lions' heads erased gules, langued azure, *Badenoch*; 3rd or, three crescents within a double tressure flory counter-flory gules, *Seton*; 4th azure, three fraises argent, *Frazer*. **Crest** – Issuing from a ducal coronet or, a hart's head and neck affrontée proper, attired with ten tynes of the first. **Supporters** – Two deer-hounds argent, each gorged with a collar gules, the collars charged with three buckles or.
Seat – Aboyne Castle, Aberdeenshire.

SON LIVING (*by 1st marriage*)

ALISTAIR GRANVILLE (*Earl of Aboyne*), *b* 26 July 1973; *ed* Harrow.

DAUGHTERS LIVING (*by 1st marriage*)

Lady Amy Jane, *b* 1975.
Lady Lucy Yoskyl, *b* 1979.

(*By 2nd marriage*)

Lady Rose Marie-Louise, *b* 1993.

SISTER LIVING

Lady (Pamela) Lemina, *b* 1941: *m* 1970, Hon Ian Henry Calthorpe Lawson Johnston, of Tillycairne, Dinnet, Aboyne, Aberdeenshire AB34 5PE (*see* Luke).

UNCLES LIVING (*brothers of 12th Marquess*) (*Raised to the rank of a Marquess's sons, 1937*)

Lord Roderic Armyne, MBE, TD, *b* 1914; *ed* Stowe; Maj 72nd (Hampshire) Anti-Aircraft, Brig RA (TA); N Africa 1943 (MBE); MBE (Mil) 1943: *m* 1st, 1937 (*m diss* 1949), Anne, yr da of late Lt-Col Hon Sir Osbert Eustace Vesey, KCVO, CMG, CBE (*see* V De Vesci, colls); 2ndly, 1949, Baroness Joana Alexandra, formerly wife of (i) Prince Serban Ghica, and (ii) Chevalier de Stuers, and 2nd da of Ion Bujoiu, of Bucharest, Roumania, and has issue living (by 1st *m*), David Esme Douglas, *b* 1937; *ed* Sherborne: *m* 1st, 1959 (*m diss* 1962), Audrey Diana, da of E. Dermot Carey, of Knutsford, Cheshire; 2ndly, 1962, Valerie Elizabeth, da of Henry Charles Guy Owen; 3rdly, 1979, Anne, da of Per Thor Brockdorff-Knutzon, of Copenhagen, and has issue living (by 2nd *m*), Samantha *b* 1962, — Angus Lindsay Eustace, *b* 1941; *ed* Nautical Coll, Pangbourne, and Bloxham Sch: *m* 1966, Diana Mary, formerly wife of Graham Clive Crockford, and da of Robert C. Pawlyn, of Windsmont, Mevagissey, Cornwall. *Residence* – 101 The Davenport, 1011 12th Av SW, Calgary, Alberta, Canada.
Lord Douglas Claude Alexander, DSO, *b* 1916; *ed* Eton; Lt-Col Black Watch, and a Memb of Queen's Body Guard for Scotland (Royal Company of Archers); Italy 1943-45 (DSO); was a Page of Honour to HM 1930-33; DSO 1945: *m* 1st, 1940 (*m diss* 1961), Suzanne, da of late Lt-Col Arthur Houssemayne du Boulay, DSO; 2ndly, 1962, Bridget, formerly wife of Maj Alexander Hutchison, of Fife, and da of late Gerald Bryan Ingham, and has issue living (by 1st *m*), Andrew Granville

Douglas (Elm Lodge, 230 Petersham Rd, Richmond, Surrey TW10 7AL), *b* 1942; *ed* Eton; a Page of Honour to HM 1957-60; *m* 1st, 1963 (*m diss* 1969), Gillian Thorne; 2ndly, 1976, Brigitte, da of Herbert Marx, and has issue living (by 1st *m*), David *b* 1963, Jamie *b* 1965, (by 2nd *m*), Glen *b* 1984, Kitty *b* 1980. — Douglas George (Geordie) Alexander (25 Coleherne Mews, SW10 9DZ; Whitehouse of Dunira, Comrie, Perthshire), *b* 1947; *ed* Gordonstoun; a Memb of Queen's Body Guard for Scotland (Royal Company of Archers): *m* 1975, Celina d'Orey, da of Peter Landsberg, CBE, of Rio de Janeiro, Brazil, and has issue living, Thomas Peter Douglas *b* 1979, James Alexander Douglas *b* 1984, Georgina Violet *b* 1976. — Jane Elizabeth (*Lady Robert Mercer Nairne*), *b* 1950: *m* 1972, Lord Robert Harold Mercer Nairne, of The Old Manse, Kinclaven, by Stanley, Perthshire, and of 10105 SE, 25th Bellevue, Washington 98004, USA, yr son of 8th Marquess of Lansdowne, — (by 2nd *m*), Sarah Alexandra, *b* 1963. *Residence* – The Old Rectory, Stockbridge, Hants. *Club* – Army and Navy.

WIDOW LIVING OF BROTHER OF TWELFTH MARQUESS

Pamela (Hethersett, Littleworth Cross, Seale, Farnham, Surrey), da of Alexander Herriot Bowhill, CBE, of Inchmarlo, Banchory, Kincardineshire: *m* 1947, Maj Lord Adam Granville Gordon, KCVO, MBE, RA, who *d* 1984, and has issue (see colls infra).

MOTHER LIVING

Hon (Mary) Pamela Berry, da of 1st Viscount Kemsley: *m* 1941 (*m diss* 1965), as his 1st wife, the 12th Marquess, who *d* 1987. *Residence* – 80 Old Church St, SW3 6EP.

WIDOW LIVING OF TWELFTH MARQUESS

ELIZABETH HAWORTH (*Dowager Marchioness of Huntly*), da of late Lt-Cdr Frederick Haworth Leigh, RD, RNR: *m* 1977, as his 2nd wife, the 12th Marquess, who *d* 1987. *Residence* – Hollybrook, Ewhurst Rd, Cranleigh, Surrey.

COLLATERAL BRANCHES LIVING

Issue of late Maj Lord Adam Granville Gordon, KCVO, MBE, RA, brother of 12th Marquess (raised to the rank of a Marquess's son 1937), *b* 1909, *d* 1984: *m* 1947, Pamela (ante), da of Alexander Herriot Bowhill, CBE, of Inchmarlo, Banchory, Kincardineshire:—
Adam Alexander (Heatheryleys, by Glenfarg, Perthshire), *b* 1948; *ed* Eton; Member Queen's Body Guard for Scotland (Royal Company of Archers): *m* 1979, Jennifer Susan, el da of Col William George McHardy, CVO, MBE, MC, of Woodend House, Banchory, Kincardineshire, and has issue living, Alexander Charles Adam, *b* 1989, — Joanna Mary, *b* 1986. —— Douglas Herriot, *b* 1951; a Page of Honour to HM 1965-67; Member Queen's Body Guard for Scotland (Royal Company of Archers): *m* 1978, Susan Jennifer, da of Anthony White, of 46 Aubrey Walk, W8, and has issue living, James Adam Anthony *b* 1991, — Alexandra Anne, *b* 1979, — Katherine Louisa, *b* 1981, — Isabella Clare, *b* 1985. *Residence* – 16 Bowerdean St, SW6 3TW.

Granddaughters of late Lieut-Col George Grant Gordon, CVO, CB, son of late Lieut-Col Lord Francis Arthur Gordon, 6th son of 9th Marquess:—
Issue of late Christian Frederic Gordon, *b* 1866, *d* 1934: *m* 1st, 1894 (*m diss* 1901), Margaret, who *d* 1920 (having *m* 2ndly, 1902, Lord Granville Armyne Gordon, 6th son of 10th Marquess of Huntly), widow of Frederick Brooks Close, and da of W. F. Humble; 2ndly, 1909, Kate Elizabeth, who *d* 1969, da of late Henry Frederick Swan, CB:—
(By 1st *m*) Cicely Margot, *b* 1899: *m* 1923, Dr Alix Lefort, of Paris. —— (By 2nd *m*) Kittie Ernestine Muriel, *b* 1911; resumed the surname of Gordon in lieu of Loam 1948: *m* 1st, 1934, — Loam; 2ndly, 1948, Paul Edward Weldon, who *d* 1972, of Hinton House, Hinton St Mary, Sturminster Newton, Dorset, and *d* 1990, leaving issue (by 1st *m*), Nadia O'CONNOR (8 Queens Rd, Thames Ditton, Surrey KT7 0QX), *b* 1939 (legally adopted by her stepfather); resumed the surname of O'Connor 1992: *m* 1st, 1959 (*m diss* 1974), Michael John Brown (who later assumed the surname of Cory Brown); 2ndly, 1975 (*m diss* 1984), Robin O'Connor; 3rdly, 1991 (*m annulled* 1993), Robert Wellings, and has had issue (by 1st *m*), Simon Nicholas *b* 1962; *d* 1990, Paula Elizabeth *b* 1960; *d* 1962, Nichola Kate *b* 1964: *m* 1991, Paul G. O'Connor (and has issue living, Marcus Michael Gerrard *b* 1991, Freya Laura Ellen *b* 1994), — (by 2nd *m*) Paul Frederic Edward (Strouds House, Farrington, Blandford, Dorset DT11 8RA), *b* 1948; *ed* Milton Abbey, and Millfield: *m* 1st, 1976 (*m diss* 1989), Deborah Evelyn, da of Richard Condon, author; 2ndly, 1992, Sally, da of late Anthony Campbell, of Berwick St John, Dorset, and of Argentina, and formerly wife of Charles Muspratt.

PREDECESSORS – Sir Adam Gordon, Knt, of Huntly, being slain at the battle of Homildon 1402, was *s* in his estates by his da.(1) ELIZABETH, wife of Alexander Seton, who in conjunction with her husband obtained in 1408 from Robert, Duke of Albany, a charter of the lands of Gordon, etc, with remainder to their joint heirs; *s* by their son (2) ALEXANDER Seton; *cr Earl of Huntly* (peerage of Scotland) 1445; employed in various negotiations to the Court of England 1451-8; defeated the Earl of Crawford then in rebellion at Brechin 1452; *s* by his son (3) GEORGE, 2nd Earl; *d* 1470; *s* by his son (4) ALEXANDER, PC, 3rd Earl; commanded with Lord Home the left wing of the Scottish Army at Flodden Field; was one of the Council of Regency 1517; *s* by his grandson (5) GEORGE, 4th Earl; constituted Lord Chancellor of Scotland 1546; *ka* 1562; his body was afterwards produced in Parliament and in 1563 an Act of Attainder was passed whereby all his honours became forfeited; *s* by his son (6) GEORGE, 5th Earl; condemned to death for high treason in 1563; was subsequently pardoned, and in 1565 was constituted Lord Chancellor of Scotland; procured a reversal of his father's attainder 1567; *d* 1576; *s* by his son (7) GEORGE, 6th Earl; engaged in a treasonable correspondence with Court of Spain 1588, erected the standard of rebellion in the North 1589, and surrendered to James VI; tried and found guilty of treason, but was released shortly afterwards on the occasion of the King's marriage; in 1593 his honours were forfeited for complicity in the Spanish and Jesuit Conspiracy; in conjunction with the Earl of Errol defeated the Royal Army at Strathaven 1594; in 1597 his honours were restored; *cr Marquess of Huntly, Earl of Enzie, and Lord Gordon of Badenoch* (peerage of Scotland) 1599; *d* 1636; *s* by his son (7) GEORGE, 2nd Marquess, who in 1611 had received a charter of the Lordship of Badenoch and in 1632 had been *cr Viscount Aboyne* with special remainder to his second son; was a zealous adherent of Charles I, and in consequence was beheaded and his honours attainted in 1649; *s* by his son (8) LEWIS, 3rd Marquess; in 1651 was granted by the King remission of the attainder of 1649; *s* by his son (9) GEORGE, 4th Marquess; in 1661 the attainder of 1649 (which had been remitted by the King in 1651) was reversed by Act of Parliament; *cr Duke of Gordon, Marquess of Huntly, Earl of Huntly and Enzie, Viscount of Inverness, Lord Badenoch, Lochaber, Strathavon, Balmore, Auchindoun, Garthie, and Kincardine* (peerage of Scotland) 1684; *d* 1716; *s* by his son (10) ALEXANDER, 2nd Duke; an earnest partisan of the Chevalier St George, 1715; *d* 1728; *s* by his son (11) COSMO GEORGE, KT, 3rd Duke; a Representative Peer; *d* 1752; *s* by his son (12) ALEXANDER, KT, 4th Duke; *cr Baron Gordon of Huntly and Earl of Norwich* (peerage of Great Britain) 1784; inherited (through his grandmother) the Barony of Mordaunt of Turvey (*cr* 1532), and possibly that of Beauchamp of Bletsoe (*cr* 1363); *d* 1827; *s* by his son (13) GEORGE, GCB, 5th Duke; a Gen in the Army, etc; *d* 1836, when the Dukedom of Gordon (and its accompanying titles, *cr* 1684), the Earldom of Norwich, and the Barony of Gordon of Huntly became ext, the Baronies of Mordaunt of Turvey and Beauchamp of Bletsoe became abeyant, and he was *s* in the Marquessate (*cr* 1599) by his kinsman (who also claimed the Earldom of Enzie and the Lordship of Gordon of Badenoch, but whose claim to the Marquessate only was allowed) (14) GEORGE, KT, 9th Marquess (see note * infra); a Representative Peer 1796-1807; *d* 1853; *s* by his son (15) CHARLES, 10th Marquess; *b* 1792; MP for East Grinstead: *m* 1st, 1826, Elizabeth Henrietta, who *d* 1839, da of 1st Marquess of Conyngham; 2ndly, 1844, Maria Antoinette, who *d* 1893, da of the Rev Peter William Pegus, and his wife Susannah Elizabeth, Countess Dowager of Lindsey; *d* 1863; *s* by his son (16) CHARLES, PC, 11th Marquess, *b* 1847; was a Lord-in-Waiting to HM Queen Victoria 1870-

73, and Capt of Hon Corps of Gentlemen-at-Arms 1881: *m* 1st, 1869, Amy, who *d* 1920, da of Sir William Cunliffe Brooks, 1st and last Bt; 2ndly, 1922, Charlotte Isabella, who *d* 1939, da of late John H. Fallon, and widow of James Macdonald, of Cincinatti, Ohio, USA; *d* 1937; *s* by his great-nephew **(17)** DOUGLAS CHARLES LINDSEY, son of late Lieut-Col (Granville Cecil) Douglas Gordon, CVO, DSO (son of late Granville Armyne Gordon, 6th son of 10th Marquess), 12th Marquess, *b* 1908; Lieut Gordon Highlanders: *m* 1st, 1941 (*m diss* 1965), Hon (Mary) Pamela Berry, da of 1st Viscount Kemsley; 2ndly, 1977, Elizabeth Haworth, da of late Lt-Cdr F. H. Leigh, RD, RNR; *d* 1987; *s* by his only son **(18)** GRANVILLE CHARLES GOMER, 13th Marquess and present peer; also Earl of Aboyne, Lord Gordon of Strathavon and Glenlivet, and Baron Meldrum.

(1) Lord CHARLES Gordon, 4th son of 2nd Marquess; *cr Earl of Aboyne*, and Lord Gordon of Strathavon and Glenlivet (peerage of Scotland) 1660; *d* 1681; *s* by his son **(2)** CHARLES, 2nd Earl; *d* 1702; *s* by his son **(3)** JOHN, 3rd Earl; *d* 1732; *s* by his son **(4)** CHARLES, 4th Earl; *d* 1794; *s* by his son **(5)** GEORGE, 5th Earl; *cr Baron Meldrum*, of Morven, co Aberdeen (peerage of United Kingdom) 1815: *s* his kinsman as 9th Marquess of Huntly (ante).

HURD, BARONY OF (Hurd) (Extinct 1966)

SONS LIVING OF LIFE BARON

Right Hon Douglas Richard, CBE, MP, *b* 1930; *ed* Eton, and Trin Coll, Camb; Dip Ser 1952-66, Private Sec to Leader of Opposition 1968-70, Political Sec to Prime Min 1970-74; a Min of State, FCO, 1979-83; Min of State, Home Office 1983-84, Sec of State N Ireland 1984-85, Home Sec 1985-89, since when Foreign Sec; MP (*C*) for Mid Oxon 1974-83, for Witney since 1983; CBE (Civil) 1974; PC 1982: *m* 1st, 1960, Tatiana Elizabeth Michelle, da of late A. C. Benedict Eyre, MBE, of West Burton House, Bury, Sussex; 2ndly, 1982, Judy J., da of Sidney Smart, of Oak Ash, Chaddleworth, Berks, and has issue living (by 1st *m*), Nicholas Richard, *b* 1962: *m* 1988, Kim, elder da of Ray Richards, of Hartley Court, Reading, and has issue living, Maximillian *b* 1991, Gus *b* 1993, — Thomas Robert Benedict, *b* 1964, — Alexander Paul Anthony, *b* 1969, — (by 2nd *m*) Philip Arthur, *b* 1983, — Jessica Stephanie, *b* 1985.

Hon Stephen Anthony, JP (Browns Farm, Marlborough), *b* 1933; *ed* Winchester, and Magdalene Coll, Camb: *m* 1973, Pepita Lilian, yr da of late Lt-Col Walter George Hingston, OBE, of The Old Vicarage, Ramsbury, Marlborough, and has issue living, William Robert, *b* 1976, — Christopher Francis Walter, *b* 1977.

Hutchinson, Viscount, title of Earl of Donoughmore on Roll of HL.

HUTCHINSON OF LULLINGTON, BARON (Hutchinson) (Life Baron 1978)

JEREMY NICOLAS HUTCHINSON, QC, only son of late St John Hutchinson, QC, by his wife Mary, only da of late Sir Hugh Shakespear Barnes, KCSI, KCVO, BCS (*see* Strachey, Bt, 1892 Edn), *b* 28 March 1915; *ed* Stowe, and Magdalen Coll, Oxford; Bar, Middle Temple 1939, Bencher 1963; Recorder of Bath 1962-72, and a Recorder of Crown Court 1972-76; a Member of Cttee on Immigration Appeals 1966-68, and Cttee on Identification Procedures 1974-76; Vice-Chairman, Arts Council of Great Britain since 1977; Chm Trustees, Tate Gallery, since 1979; RNVR 1939-45 War; *cr Baron Hutchinson of Lullington*, of Lullington, co East Sussex (Life Baron) 1978; *m* 1st, 1940 (*m diss* 1966), Dame Peggy (Edith Margaret Emily) S. Ashcroft, DBE, the actress, who *d* 1991, da of late William Worsley Ashcroft, of Croydon, and formerly wife of (i) Rupert (later Sir Rupert) Hart-Davis, and (ii) Theodore Komisarjevsky; 2ndly, 1966, Mrs June Osborn, da of late Capt Arthur Edward Capel, CBE (*see* By Ribblesdale, 1980 Edn), and formerly wife of Franz Osborn, and has issue by 1st *m*.

Arms – Not exemplified at the College of Arms at time of going to press.
Residence – 10 Blenheim Rd, NW8; Queen Elizabeth Building, Temple, EC4. *Club* – MCC.

SON LIVING (By 1st marriage)

Hon Nicholas St John, *b* 1946: *m* 19—, — , and has issue living, March (a da), *b* 19—.

DAUGHTER LIVING (By 1st marriage)

Hon Eliza, *b* 1941: *m* 1974, Pierre Loizeau, of Les Bouleaux, 2 Rue de Gazet, Seine Port, 77 France, and has issue living, Manon, *b* 19—, — Emily, *b* 19—.

Hyde, Lord; son of Earl of Clarendon.

HYLTON, BARON (Jolliffe) (Baron UK 1866, Bt UK 1821)

As much as I can

RAYMOND HERVEY JOLLIFFE, 5th, Baron, and 5th Baronet; *b* 13 June 1932; *s* 1967; *ed* Eton (King's Scholar), and at Trin Coll; Oxford (MA); Lt Coldstream Guards (Reserve); DL Som 1975-90; ARICS; Assist Private Sec to Gov-Gen of Canada 1960-62; Chm Catholic Housing Aid Soc 1972-73, a Trustee of Shelter Housing Aid Centre 1969-76, and Chm Nat Fedn of Housing Assocns 1973-76; Chm Help the Aged Housing Trust, and of Housing Assocns Charitable Trust; Trustee: Acorn Christian Healing Trust, Christian Coll for Adult Educn, and Hugh of Witham Foundation; Pres N Ireland Assocn for Care and Resettlement of Offenders: *m* 1966, Joanna Elizabeth, da of late Andrew de Bertodano (*see* E Mexborough, 1948 Edn), and has issue.

Arms – Quarterly: 1st and 4th argent, on a pile vert, three dexter hands proper, *Jolliffe*; 2nd and 3rd argent, two bars azure, *Hylton*. **Crest** – A cubit arm erect, the hand grasping a scimitar proper, vested vert, cuffed argent, on the sleeve a pile of the last. **Supporters** – Two lions guardant azure, each charged on the shoulder with three annulets, two and one, or.
Residence – Ammerdown, Radstock, Bath.

SONS LIVING

Hon WILLIAM HENRY MARTIN, *b* 1 April 1967 *ed* Ampleforth, and RAC Cirencester.
Hon Andrew Thomas Peter, *b* 1969.
Hon Alexander John Charles Martin, *b* 1973.
Hon John Edward Arthur, *b* 1977.

DAUGHTER LIVING

Hon Emily Sylvia Rose Elizabeth, *b* 1975.

BROTHER LIVING

Hon John Hedworth (Church House, Chesterblade, Shepton Mallet, Som), *b* 1935; *ed* Eton (King's Scholar), and Ch Ch Oxford (BA); High Sheriff Som 1993; a Dir of Bain Dawes plc 1979-89, and of Ukraine Business Agency since 1993; edited *Raymond Asquith, Life and Letters* (1980), author *Clive Pearson* (1992): *m* 1965, Hon Victoria Catherine Elizabeth Eden, el da of 7th Baron Henley, and has issue living, Hugo Conrad William, *b* 1966, — Robert Francis Raymond, *b* 1968, — Benedict Thomas Aldhelm, *b* 1970.

SISTER LIVING

Hon (Mary) Alice, *b* 1937: *m* 1st 1959 (*m diss* 1969), John Paget Chancellor (*see* Paget, Bt, *cr* 1886); 2ndly, 1969, Hon Richard Archer Alan Windsor-Clive, of Combe, Nettlecombe, Taunton (*see* E Plymouth).

WIDOW LIVING OF FOURTH BARON

Lady PERDITA ROSE MARY ASQUITH (*Dowager Baroness Hylton*) (Church House, Chesterblade, Shepton Mallet, Somerset BA4 4QX), sister of 2nd Earl of Oxford and Asquith: *m* 1931, the 4th Baron, who *d* 1967.

COLLATERAL BRANCHES LIVING

Granddaughters of late Maj Berkeley Gerald Jolliffe (infra):—
Issue of late John Neil Hylton Jolliffe, *b* 1923, *d* 1976: *m* 1957, Eileen Mary (Barratts Farm, Corton Denham, Sherborne, Dorset), da of late Col George Harold Absell Ing, CMG, DSO:—
Sarah, *b* 1960: *m* 1981, Dominic William Michael Nelson, 2nd son of Sir William Vernon Hope Nelson, 3rd Bt, OBE.
—— Lucy, *b* 1962: *m* 1992, Samuel Anthony Kellie-Smith, of 59 Cornwall Gdns, SW7 (*see* Chaytor, Bt, colls, 1985 Edn).

Granddaughters of late Capt Hon William Sydney Hylton Jolliffe, 4th son of 1st Baron:—
Issue of late Maj Berkeley Gerald Jolliffe, *b* 1878, *d* 1956: *m* 1919, Mary Viola, who *d* 1984, da of Capt John Douglas Maude Guthrie, of Guthrie Castle, Scotland:—
Cynthia Myra, *b* 1920. —— Eileen Daphne, *b* 1921: *m* 1st, 1946 (*m diss* 1955), Arthur Harold Morse; 2ndly, 1955, Richard Arthur Edwards, and has issue living (by 1st *m*) Simon Arthur Davidson, *b* 1952, — Lavinia May, *b* 1947, — (by 2nd *m*) Chloë Annabel, *b* 1956, — Miranda Bridget, *b* 1961.

PREDECESSORS – (1) WILLIAM GEORGE HYLTON Jolliffe, PC, son of late Rev William John Jolliffe, son of William Jolliffe, MP and his wife Eleanor, da of heir of Sir Richard Hylton Bt of Hayton Castle, Cumberland (by Anne, his wife, sister and co-heir of John Hylton, of Hylton Castle, co Durham); *b* 1800; sat as MP for Petersfield (C) 1830-1 and 1837-66; Under-Sec for Home Depart 1852, and Joint Sec of Treasury 1858-9; *cr* a *Baronet* 1821, and *Baron Hylton*, of Hylton Castle, co Durham, and of Petersfield, co Southampton (peerage of United Kingdom) 1866, being heir representative of Barony of Hylton or Hilton (*cr* 1295): *m* 1st, 1825, Eleanor, who *d* 1862, da of the Hon Berkeley Paget; 2ndly, 1867, Sophia Penelope, who *d* 1882, da of Sir Robert Sheffield, 4th Bt, and widow of 4th Earl of Ilchester; *d* 1876; *s* by his son (2) HEDWORTH HYLTON, *b* 1829; MP for Wells (C) 1855-68; *m* 1st, 1858, Lady Agens Mary Georgiana Byng, who *d* 1878, da of 2nd Earl of Strafford; 2ndly, 1879, Anne, who *d* 1917, da of Henry Lambert, of Carnagh, co Wexford, and widow of 3rd Earl of Dunraven and Mount Earl; *d* 1899; *s* by his el son (3) HYLTON GEORGE HYLTON, 3rd Baron, *b* 1862; in Diplo Ser 1888-95; MP for Wells Div of Somerset (C) 1895-9; was Lord-in-Waiting to HM 1915-18, Joint Ch Govt Whip in House of Lords 1916-22, and Capt of Yeomen of the Guard 1918-24: *m* 1896, Lady Alice Adeliza Hervey, who *d* 1962, da of co-heir of 3rd Marquess of Bristol; *d* 1945: *s* by his son (4) WILLIAM GEORGE HERVEY, 4th Baron, *b* 1898; Lt-Col Coldstream Guards; Lord-Lieut of Somerset 1949-67: *m* 1931, Lady Perdita Rose Mary Asquith, sister of 2nd Earl of Oxford and Asquith; *d* 1967; *s* by his son (5) RAYMOND HERVEY, 5th Baron.

HYLTON-FOSTER, BARONESS (Hylton-Foster) (Life Baroness 1965)

AUDREY PELLEW HYLTON-FOSTER, DBE, da of 1st Viscount Ruffside (ext); *b* 19 May 1908; *ed* St George's Ascot, and at Ivy House, Wimbledon, Pres of Co London Branch British Red Cross Soc 1960-73 (Dir of Chelsea Div 1950-60, Pres and Chm London Branch 1960-85, Patron 1984); a Member of National Council 1966-76, Hon Consultant 1984-86; Pres Prevention of Blindness Research Fund 1965-76; Convenor Cross Bench Peers since 1974; sits as an Independent Peer; *cr* DBE 1990, and *Baroness Hylton-Foster*, of City of Westminster (Life Baroness 1965): *m* 1931, Rt Hon Sir Harry Braustyn Hylton Hylton-Foster, QC, MP, Speaker of House of Commons 1959-65, who *d* 1965.
Residence – The Coach House, Tanhurst, Leith Hill, Holmbury St Mary, Dorking, Surrey, RH5 6LQ.

HYNDLEY, VISCOUNTCY OF (Hindley) (Extinct 1963)

DAUGHTER LIVING OF FIRST VISCOUNT

Hon Elizabeth Cairns (Meads Lodge, Rondle Wood, nr Liphook, Hants) *b* 1912.

IDDESLEIGH, EARL OF (Northcote) (Earl UK 1885, Bt E 1641)
(Title pronounced "Idsly"(Name pronounced "Northcut")

STAFFORD HENRY NORTHCOTE, 4th Earl and 11th Baronet; *b* 14 July 1932; *s* 1970; *ed* Downside; late 2nd Lt Irish Gds; DL Devon 1979; Dir Devon & Exeter Steeplechases Ltd, and Gemini Radio Ltd; Chm South West TSB 1980-83; SW Regional Chm England and Wales TSB 1983-88, Dir TSB Group plc 1987-88, United Dominions Trust Ltd 1983-88, and Television South West plc 1982-92; Knt of Honour and Devotion Sovereign Mil Order of Malta: *m* 1955, Maria Luisa (Mima) Alvarez-Builla y Urquijo (Condesa del Real Agrado in Spain, *cr* 1771), OBE, DL Devon 1987, only da of late Don Gonzalo Alvarez-Builla y Alvera, and of Maria Luisa, Viscountess Exmouth, and has issue.

The Cross of Christ is my Light

Arms – Argent, three cross-crosslets in bend sable. **Crest** – Upon a chapeau gules, turned up ermine a stag trippant argent. **Supporters** – Two stags proper, and pendant from the neck of each by a gold chain an escutcheon ermine, charged with a fir-cone or.
Seat – Pynes, Exeter, EX5 5EF. *Residence* – Shillands House, Upton Pyne, Exeter, Devon, EX5 5EB. *Club* – Army and Navy.

SON LIVING

JOHN STAFFORD (*Viscount St Cyres*) (Hayne Barton, Newton St Cyres, Devon), *b* 15 Feb 1957; *ed* Downside, and Roy Agric Coll, Cirencester: *m* 1983, Fiona Caroline Elizabeth, da of Paul Alan Campbell Wakefield, of Barcelona, Spain, and has issue:—

SON LIVING— *Hon* Thomas Stafford, *b* 5 Aug 1985.
DAUGHTER LIVING— *Hon* Elizabeth Rose Adèle, *b* 1989.

DAUGHTER LIVING

Lady Mary Louise, *b* 1959: *m* 1981, Maj Simon Nicholas Fishwick, late 13th/18th Royal Hus, of Lower Woodrow, Brampford Speke, nr Exeter, Devon EX5 5DY, yr son of Clifford Fishwick, of Salisbury House, Monmouth St, Topsham, Devon, and has had issue, James Nicholas, *b* 1983, — Hugh Simon, *b* 1984, *d* 1987, — Lucy Mary, *b* 1988.

BROTHER LIVING

Hon Edward Frederic, TD, *b* 1934; *ed* Downside, and Trin Coll, Oxford (MA); Maj Intelligence Corps (T & AVR); Cyprus 1957; Assocn of Inst of Cost and Works Accountants; a Prin Officer HM Treasury 1969-71; FSS: *m* 1963 (*m diss* 1980), Vivien Sheena, da of Col Robert John Augustine Hornby, OBE (*see* Bruce, Bt, colls, *cr* 1628), and has issue living, Edward Bede Robert Hornby, *b* 1964; *ed* Wimbledon Coll, — Alexander Benet Paul Hornby, *b* 1971, — Modwenna Vivien Hornby, *b* 1968. *Residence* – Flat 38, Westmore Court, Carlton Drive, SW15 2BU.

SISTERS LIVING

Lady Catherine Cecilia Mary, *b* 1931; is a Religious of the Assumption; teacher and author.
Lady Hilda Susan Mary, *b* 1937; Dame of Honour and Devotion Sovereign Mil Order of Malta: *m* 1957, Sir Conrad Marshall John Fisher Swan, KCVO, PhD, Garter Principal King of Arms at College of Arms since 1992, Kt of Honour and Devotion Sovereign Mil Order of Malta, and has issue living, Andrew Conrad Henry Joseph (Silverleigh House, Church Hill, Burstall, Ipswich, Suffolk), *b* 1964; *ed* Downside, and Liverpool Univ (BSc); ACA; Kt of Honour and Devotion Sovereign Mil Order of Malta: *m* 1989, Fenella Jane, yr da of ACM Sir John Rogers, KCB, CBE, and has issue living, Isabelle Frances Anne *b* 1992, — (Mary) Elizabeth Magdalen, *b* 1959; SRN, RM: *m* 1981, Roger Peter Le Strange Herring, of Saffron House, Old Stowmark-et Rd, Woolpit, Bury St Edmunds, Suffolk, elder son of Col P. W. Le S. Herring, OBE, of Garden House, Shipton Bellinger, Tidworth, Hants, and has issue living, John Roger Le Strange *b* 1987, Thomas Peter Le Strange *b* 1990, Rafe Henry Le Strange *b* 1991, Alice Elizabeth Le Strange *b* 1985, — (Hilda) Juliana Mary, *b* 1961: *m* 1982, Patrick D. T. Galvin, of Long-wood House, Nayland, Suffolk, yr twin son of late Maj T. D. Galvin, of Nayland, Suffolk, and has issue living, Thomas Paul

Conrad b 1984, Edward Andrew Henry b 1985, Nicholas Patrick William b 1986, Alexander James Stafford b 1988, Frederick Mark David b 1990, Elizabeth Anna Mary b 1982, — Catherine Sylveria Mary, b 1962: m 1986, John Jeremy Walters, of The Old Rectory, Monks' Eleigh, Suffolk, son of late Capt Greaves Walters, DSC, RN, of Mill Cottage, Lower Broadbridge, Horsham, W Sussex, and has issue living, Alfred Hugh Charles b 1987, Francis Henry Conrad b 1991, Eleanor Hilda Mary b 1989, — Anastasia Cecilia Mary, b 1966; RN: m 1989, Peter Galbraith Mark Hatvany, of 33 High St, Rode, Bath BA3 6PA, eldest son of Paul Imre Hatvany (Baron Hatvany de Hatvan), of Ardgay, Box, Wilts, and has issue living, Alexander Imre b 1991, Alicia Mary b 1993. *Residence* – Boxford House, Suffolk CO10 5JT.

COLLATERAL BRANCHES LIVING

Grandson of late Rev Hon Arthur Francis Northcote, 4th son of 1st Earl:—
Issue of late Sir Geoffrey Alexander Stafford Northcote, KCMG, b 1881, d 1948: m 1910, Edith Juliet Mary, who d 1958, da of late Rev James Williams Adams, VC (Willshire Bt):—
Maxwell Adams Stafford, b 1911; ed King's Sch, Canterbury, and Balliol Coll, Oxford m 1958, Katharine, yst da of late Charles Campbell Sheild, of Taumarunui, New Zealand. *Address* – PO Box 827, Nairobi, Kenya.

Granddaughter of late Sir Geoffrey Alexander Stafford Northcote, KCMG (ante):—
Issue of late Major Amyas Henry Stafford Northcote, MC, b 1916, ka in Burma 1944: m 1941, Mollie Gordon Buchanan (who m 2ndly, 1947, Antony Smallwood), da of Major Gordon Buchanan Scott, of Zaria, Horsham:—
Sylvia Rosalind Stafford, b 1942: m 1968, Antony Cokayne Doulton, of 41 Hans Place, SW1, and has issue living, Amyas John Stafford, b 1977, — Natasha Ophelia Stafford, b 1971.

Granddaughter of late Hon Hugh Oliver Northcote, 5th son of 1st Earl:—
Issue of late Hugh Hamilton Stafford Northcote, b 1887, d 1929: m 1925, Josephine, who d 1928, da of late Thomas O'Shaughnessy, of Killacolla, Glin, co Limerick:—
Mary Edith (29 Thackeray Court, Elystan Place, SW3 3LB), b 1926.

(In remainder to Baronetcy, cr 1641, only)

Grandchildren of late James Alfred Northcote, MBE, 5th son of late Rev Henry Moubray Northcote, brother of 8th Bt:—
Issue of late Thomas Francis Northcote, b 1894, d 1977: m 1924, Frances Vera (Highfield, Waiau, NZ), da of late Arthur Hope, of Tumanako, Timaru, NZ:—
Peter Stafford, b 1928: m 1957, Geraldine Margaret, who d 1980, da of Gerald Murray, of Glenmore, Lake Tekapo, NZ, and has issue living, Hugh Stafford, b 1960, — Michael John, b 1962, — Margaret Anne, b 1959. ——— George Arthur (Old West Coast Rd, No 1 RD, Christchurch, NZ), b 1929: m 1960, Julia Elvira Morton Watkins, and has issue living, Charles Moubray, b 1961: m 1984, Ynez Powers, — Cynthia Jane, b 1962, — Diana Mary, b 1964. ——— Frances Roma, b 1931: m 1956, John Endell Wanklyn, and has issue living, David Endell, b 1959, — Catherine, b 1957, — Jaquetta, b 1958.

Granddaughters of late Cecil Stafford Northcote (infra):—
Issue of late Lewis Stafford Northcote, b 1907, d 1977: m 1935, Esme Geraldine Seignelay, who d 1979, da of late Capt Arthur Robert Seignelay Lyon-Campbell, of Stockhill, Settle, Yorks:—
Sarah Caroline Stafford, b 1936: m 1962, Capt Patrick Timothy Sheehan, CBE, RN, Sub Treasurer Inner Temple, of St Catherine's, East Hendred, Wantage, Oxon, and has issue living, Timothy Stafford, b 1966, — Clare Anne, b 1963: m 1994, Thomas Richard Glen Downes, — Joanna Mary, b 1965: m 1993, David Charles Carreras, solicitor. ——— Jaqueta Seignelay, b 1937.

Grandchildren of late Capt Lewis Stafford Northcote, only son of late Rev Stafford Charles Northcote, 3rd son of 7th Bt:—
Issue of late Cecil Stafford Northcote, b 1870, d 1912: m 1906, Ida Sybil Mary, who d 1963, da of Capt Joseph Boulderson:—
Cecil Henry, OBE, b (*posthumous*) 1912; ed Douai, and Queen's Coll, Oxford (MA); is Headmaster of St Bede's Sch, Bishton Hall, Staffs, a Co Councillor of Staffs, Chm of Stafford and Stone Conservative Assocn, and of Co Records & Shugborough & Co Museum Cttee, a Gov of King Edward VI Gram Sch Stafford and Church of England Sch, Colwich, Staffs; High Sheriff co Staffs (1981), and a Knight of Honour and Devotion of Sovereign Order of Malta; a Rural Dist Councillor; OBE (Civil) 1982: m 1936, Freda, da of late Frederic Williams and has issue living, Amyas Henry Stafford, b 1937; ed Ampleforth, and Ch Ch, Oxford (MA); a JP of Staffs; a Kt of Honour and Devotion of Sovereign Mil Order of Malta, — Hugh Cecil Camden (Bishton Hall, Staffs), b 1938; ed Ampleforth, and Trin Coll, Camb (MA) a Kt of Honour and Devotion, Sov Mil Order of Malta: m 1974, Hilary Jane, yr da of Col R. J. C. Evans, TD, DL, of Cage Hill, Stowe-by-Chartley, and has issue living, Charles Walter Hugh b 1977, Arabella Lucy Mary b 1975, Beatrice Eleanor Margaret b 1979, Helena Jane Alice b 1980, Katherine Sybil Ruth b 1983, — Julia Marguerite Mary, b 1941; ed Assumption, Bury St Edmunds, and Webber Douglas Sch of Dramatic Art. *Residence* – Bishton Hall, Staffs. ——— Sybil Mary, b 1910: m 1952, George Hudson, who d 1970, and has issue living, Mary Agnes, b 1955. *Residence* – Icknield, East Hendred, Wantage, Oxon.
Issue of late Ernest Alfred Stafford Northcote, b 1875, d 1944: m 1900, Sarah Potwin, who d 1911, da of late Col Gilbert Dwight Munson, Judge and Lawyer, Ohio, USA:—
Oliver Stafford, b 1906; ed Stanford Univ Cal (AB, LLB); Bar Cal, 1933; a member of legal firm of Chandler, Wright, Tyler & Ward, of Los Angeles, USA, and of American, Californian and Los Angeles Bar Assos, and Lt-Cdr USNR; Lt USN 1942-45: m 1933, Dorothy Lucille, da of James A. Ham, and has issue living, Philip Stafford (2192 Racquet Hill, Santa Ana, Calif 92705, USA), b 1937: m 1966, — , da of Henry Reichert, and has issue living, Kent Stafford b 1969, Kristin b 1970, — Geoffrey Stafford (twin) (305 Calle Paisano, San Clemente, Calif 92672, USA) b 1937: m 1964, Sharon Ann, da of Vachel Conn Foree, Jr, and has issue living, Douglas Stafford b 1971, — John Stafford (PO Box 754, Carmel, Calif 93921, USA), b 1940: m 1966, Virginia Lee Camden, da of late William Henry Wright, and has issue living, Stafford Oliver b 1975. *Residence* – 830 W Orange Grove Av, Arcadia, Calif 91006, USA.

Grandchildren of late Stafford Henry Northcote (b 1872), eldest son of late Stafford Charles Northcote (b 1844), eldest son of Stafford Henry Northcote (b 1813), son of Stafford Northcote (b 1783), 2nd son of Henry Northcote, 2nd son of 5th Bt:—
Issue of late Stafford Charles Robert Northcote, b 1909, d 1977: m 1st, 1947, Helen Isabel, who d 1965, da of Herbert Nelson Hawker, of Christchurch, NZ; 2ndly, 1972, Sheila Mary, who d 1986, widow of Dr Paul H. Sandifer:—
(By 1st m) Stafford Robert, b 1948: m 1969, Penelope Anne Tracy, da of (Thomas) Michael Eastham, QC. ——— Helena Ann Stafford (48 Rothsay Rd, Forest Gate, E7), b 1951.
Issue of late Geoffrey Stafford Northcote, b 1912, d 1968: m 1938, Rhoda C. Ruth (who m 2ndly, 1975, Philip Williamson), da of late A. McNeill, of Auckland, NZ:—
Robert Stafford (38 Cooper Place, Beaumont, 5066, S Aust), b 1939; ed Univ of Wellington (MSc), and Univ of Adelaide (PhD); Prof of Computer Studies, SA Inst of Tech, Adelaide: m 1963, Patricia Margaret, da of late Arthur Baillie, of Adelaide, and has issue living, Roger Stafford, b 1966, — Bruce Stephen, b 1969, — Michelle Patricia, b 1972. ——— Alan McNeill (71 James Cook Drive, Welcome Bay, Tauranga, NZ), b 1940; ed Univ of Wellington (BCom), ACANZ, ACIS: m 1963, Mary

Vesey, da of late E. A. Zambra, of Napier, NZ, and has issue living, Peter Bruce, *b* 1964, — Stuart Paul, *b* 1966, — Susan Mary, *b* 1967. —— Geoffrey John (25 Spencer Rd, Mosman, NSW 2088, Australia), *b* 1947; Gen Man. —— Margaret Moralee (101 Grange Rd, Tauranga, NZ), *b* 1950: *m* 1971, (*m diss* 1994), Wallace Donald Thomson, and has issue living, Robert Wallace, *b* 1974, — Kathryn Helen, *b* 1977.

Grandchildren of late Cyril Charles Stafford Northcote, 2nd son of late Stafford Charles Northcote (*b* 1844) (ante):—
Issue of late John Wilfrid Cyril Stafford Northcote, *b* 1904, *d* 1970: *m* 1st, 1933 (*m diss* 1937), Mary Caroline, yr da of late Robert Collier, FRIBA; 2ndly, 1938, Grace Carruthers, da of E. Carruthers Webb, of Mill Hill, Middx; 3rdly, 1952, Janet, el da of Ronald Grose, of Manor Rd, Taunton:—
(By 1st *m*) Jennifer Anne Stafford, *b* 1935: *m* 1955, John Morley, of 18 The Parkway, Leabrook, Adelaide, S Aust, and has issue living, Robert, *b* 1956, — Jasper, *b* 1959, — David John, *b* 1964, — Amanda Caroline, *b* 1966. —— (By 3rd *m*) Martin Charles Stafford (30 Madeley Rd, W5 2LH), *b* 1953: *m* 199-, Lucy Patricia, da of late P. A. Willard, and has issue living, Henry Charles, *b* 1992, — Nadia Mary, *b* (twin) 1992. —— Nigel John Stafford, *b* 1960. —— Andrew Alexander Stafford, *b* 1964. —— Gillian Stafford, *b* 1954.

Grandchildren (by 1st *m*) of late Maj Leonard Augustus Stafford Northcote (infra):—
Issue of late Lt-Col Denis Leonard Stafford Northcote, RA, *b* 1904, *d* 1978: *m* 1st, 1929, Sylvia Mary Manners, da of late Col John Manners Smith, VC, CIE, CVO, IA; 2ndly, 1947, Beatrice Margaret, who *d* 1985, da of late Robert Malcolm, of Rawalpindi, India:—
(By 1st wife) William John, *b* 1939. —— Sylvia Alison, *b* 1930. —— Veronica Phyllis, *b* 1932. —— (By 2nd wife) Jaqueta Stafford, *b* 1941: *m* 1968, Michael Robert Philip, of Bank House, Hatherton, Nantwich, Cheshire CW5 7PQ, and of Bollington Grange, Nether Alderley, Cheshire, and has issue living, Nicholas Alexander Michael, *b* 1973; *ed* Wrekin Coll, — Olivia Kate, *b* 1975; *ed* West Chester Coll of Art, and Aberystwith Univ.

Grandchildren of late Stafford Charles Northcote (ante):—
Issue of late Maj Leonard Augustus Stafford Northcote, *b* 1879, *d* 1942: *m* 1st, 1903 (*m diss* 1914), Lilian Cora, da of late J. van Praagh, formerly of 209 Maida Vale, W; 2ndly, 1916, Ida, who *d* 1978, da of 5th Marquis Testaferrata-Olivier du Puget (Maltese Nobility):—
(By 1st *m*) Iris Blanche Stafford, *b* 1909; formerly Fashion Ed (as Iris Ashley) *Daily Mail* (ret 1964): *m* 1st, 1928 (*m diss* 19—), Maurice Ashley Brown, who *d* 1978; 2ndly, 1939, (Stanley) John Knowles, who *d* 19—; 3rdly, 1964, His Honour Desmond Harvey Weight Vowden, QC, who *d* 1990, and has issue living (by 2nd husband), Penelope Ann (2 Clarendon Place, W2 2NP), *b* 1937: *m* 1962, Michael John Wigram, of Madrid, Spain, and has issue living, Lionel Nicholas Richard *b* 1962: *ed* Eton, and Brasenose Coll, Oxford, Benjamin Peter Desmond *b* 1970; *ed* Emanuel Sch, Sophie Denia *b* 1964; *ed* St Paul's Girls' Sch, and Somerville Coll, Oxford. —— (By 2nd *m*) (Henry) James STAFFORD NORTHCOTE, *b* 1922; *ed* Downside; served 1939-45 War with Oxfordshire and Buckinghamshire LI, and Intelligence Corps in Europe and SEAC; feature film technician: *m* 1949 (*m diss* 1961), Sheila, actress, da of late Capt John Manahan, of Dublin.
Issue of late Major Arthur Frederick Stafford Northcote, DSO, *b* 1881, *d* 1949: *m* 1st, 1905 (*m diss* 1930), Constance Fanny (who *d* 19—), da of late Col William Henry Salmon, Indian Army (ret); 2ndly, 1930, Dora, who *d* 1932, da of Congreve Jackson, OBE; 3rdly, 1938, Beryl, who *d* 1989, da of late Rev W. H. Weekes, of Devizes:—
(By 2nd *m*) Annette Stafford, *b* 1931: *m* 1st 1952 (*m diss* 1970), Harry Alexander Thomas McPhee; 2ndly, 1971, David Crichton Paterson, who *d* 1993, of 365 E Queen's Rd, N Vancouver, BC, Canada V7N 1G7, and has issue living (by 1st *m*), Roderick Jody, *b* 1965, — Beverly Eve, *b* 1956: *m* 1990, John Alexander Dodd, and has issue living, Jordi Michael *b* 1993, Sarah Elizabeth *b* 1991, — Deborah Jane, *b* 1959, — Judith Leah, *b* 1960, — (by 2nd *m*) John Leslie, *b* 1973.

Grandchildren of Leonard Beauchamp Northcote, yst son of late Stafford Henry Northcote (*b* 1813) (ante):—
Issue of late Henry Peter Northcote, *b* 1891, *d* 1971: *m* 1924, Eileen (Coston, Moreland Drive, Gerrards Cross, Bucks), da of Edwin Charles Irish:—
Edwin Charles Stafford (Alwin, The Green, Jordans, Beaconsfield, Bucks), *b* 1926; *ed* Blundell's Sch: *m* 1956 (*m diss* 1974), Angela, da of James Edward Hutton, and has issue living, Ashley James Stafford, *b* 1959, — Belinda Susan, *b* 1965. —— Anne, *b* 1936: *m* 1959 (*m diss* 1972), Ernst Zumbrunn, of Interlaken, Switzerland, and has issue living, Helene Diana, *b* 1963.
Issue of late Frederick Beauchamp Northcote, *b* 1893, *d* 1937: *m* 1923, Jessie Florence, who *d* 1988, da of William James:—
Leon Frederick James (29 Orchard Rd, Longlevens, Gloucester), *b* 1924; *ed* Swansea Grm Sch; European War with RN 1942-46; in first wave of tank landing craft on Juno beach on D Day 1944: *m* 1951, Valerie May, da of Victor Thomas George Bennett, of Gloucester, and has issue, Richard Leon Stafford, *b* 1952: *m* 1976, Jeanette May, da of Thomas Rich, of Upton St Leonards, Gloucester, and has issue living, Christopher Thomas Stafford *b* 1985, Jessica Elizabeth *b* 1981, — Susan Elizabeth, *b* 1954: *m* 1st, 19— (*m diss* 1979), — ; 2ndly, 1981, Peter William Dove, of 5 Wren Close, Saint Bridge, Gloucester, and has issue living, (by 1st *m*) Stewart Richard DOVE *b* 1972; legally adopted by his stepfather, David Graham DOVE *b* 1978; legally adopted by his stepfather, (by 2nd *m*) James Peter *b* 1983.

Grandchildren of late Edward Northcote, son of late Gilbert Charles Northcote, 7th son of late Stafford Northcote (*b* 1783) (ante):—
Issue of late Gilbert Charles Northcote, *b* 1903, *d* 1967: *m* 1930, Marguerite Muriel, who *d* 1984, da of Joseph William Nicholas:—
Mildred Reynell, *b* 1931: *m* 1961, Alexander Walter English, of Redbank, Deniliquin, NSW, and has issue living, Alexander Northcote Charles, *b* 1966, — Jean Constance Northcote, *b* 1962, — Marguerite Louise Northcote, *b* 1964: *m* 1987, Kenneth Maxwell Davis, of Pine View, Corowa, NSW, and has issue living, William James *b* 1990, Kimberley Ann *b* 1989, Georgina Louise *b* 1992. —— Gillian Mary Stafford, *b* 1932: *m* 1954, Mardi Walker, of Rankin Park, PO 142, Holbrook, NSW 2644, and has issue living, Rowena Marius, *b* 1960: *m* 1985, Michael Henry Stubbe, of 2 Poath Rd, Oakleigh, Vic, and has issue living, John Gilbert *b* 1988, Christopher Michael *b* 1990.

Granddaughters of late Horace Northcote (infra):—
Issue of late Ronald Cecil Northcote, OBE, MM, *b* 1895, *d* 1972: *m* 1934, Joan Eileen, who *d* 1992, da of John Everard Grafton Grattan:—
Veronica Stella *b* 1940: *m* 1987, Trevor Claude Long (who *d* 1991, having assumed by deed poll 1988 the surname NORTHCOTE-LONG in lieu of his patronymic). *Residence* – Nimrod, 5 Aspen Close, Woodbridge, Suffolk IP12 1SG.
Issue of late Capt Malcolm Philip Northcote, *b* 1908, *d* 1971: *m* 1st, 1933 (*m diss* 1954), Eileen Natalie Colt (*dec*), da of Edward Walter David Colt Williams, MC, Bar-at-law; 2ndly, 1956, Moya Angela, who *d* 1990, yr da of late William Maidment, of Parrett Lodge, Bridgwater, Som:—
(By 2nd *m*) Amanda Louise, *b* 1958: *m* 1982, Michael Anthony Burling, and has issue living, Philippa Frances, *b* 1986. *Residence* – 16 Abingdon Mansions, Pater St, W8 6AB. —— Vanessa Jane (twin), *b* 1958: *m* 1986, Justin Timothy Donegan, 2nd son of Patrick Terence Nessan Donegan, QC, of Petworth, Sussex, and has issue living, Matthew Justin Philip, *b* 1992, — Chloë Elizabeth, *b* 1989.

Granddaughter of late Ronald Cecil Northcote, OBE, MM (ante):—

Issue of late Geoffrey Malcolm Northcote, b 1942; d 1981: m 1969 (m diss 1974), Diana Maria, da of late Edmund Maria Hellmer, of Vienna:—
Lara Veronica (Schrottstrasse 1, 6033 Arzl, Austria), b 1970.

Granddaughter of late Gilbert Charles Northcote (ante):—
Issue of late Horace Northcote, b 1865, d 1914: m 1890, Stella Louise, who d 1931, da of late Charles James Reynolds:—
Guinevere Olga, b 1900: m 1st, 1927 (m diss 1946), Leslie Ernst Wintersgill, who d 1969; 2ndly, 1952, John Collier, who d 1985, and has issue living, (by 1st m) Temple Robin Ernst NORTHCOTE (51 Granville Place, High Rd, N12), b 1928; assumed the surname of Northcote in lieu of his patronymic by deed poll 1949; FIPM: m 1950, Eira Marion, da of late Leonard Walter Johnson, and has issue living, Ifor Alan Temple (12 Gilmore St, Tarcoola, Geraldton 6530, W Australia), b 1952: m 1st, 1976, Gwendoline Florence, da of late Frederick John Duckfield, and formerly wife of William Charles Cook; 2ndly, 1987, Beverley Ann, da of Peggie Dean (and has issue living, Sarah Victoria b 1986, and has adopted his stepson Andrew Michael b 1979), Kim Norman Austin (119 St George's Av, Sheerness, Isle of Sheppey, Kent) b 1957: m 1979, Alison Hazel, da of Ronald Frank Bridger (and has issue living, Lewis James Austin b 1983, Heather Jane Austin b 1982), — Diana Guinevere, b 1930: m 1952, Brian James Dobbie, of 3 Sene Park, Hythe, Kent, and has issue living, Janet Marion b 1956, Gillian Patricia b 1958, Katherine Ann b 1965. Residence – 3 Lansdowne Rd, Finchley, N3.

PREDECESSORS – (1) JOHN NORTHCOTE, MP for Ashburton 1640-48, for Devon 1654-60, and for Barnstaple 1667-76, cr a Baronet 1641; d 1676; s by his son (2) ARTHUR, 2nd Bt; d 1688; s by his son (3) FRANCIS, 3rd Bt; dsp 1709; s by his brother (4) HENRY, MD, 4th Bt; d 1729; s by his son (5) HENRY, 5th Bt, MP for Exeter 1734-43; d 1743; s by his son (6) STAFFORD, 6th Bt; d 1771; s by his son (7) STAFFORD HENRY, 7th Bt; d 1851; s by his grandson (8) STAFFORD HENRY, GCB, DCL, PC, 8th Bt, son of late Henry Stafford Northcote, Esq (el son of 7th Bt); b 1818; was Pres of Board of Trade 1866-7, Sec of State for India 1867-8, Chancellor of the Exchequer 1874-80, First Lord of the Treasury 1885-6, Sec of State for Foreign Affairs 1886-7, and Lord-Lieut of Devonshire; sat as MP for Dudley (C) 1855-7, for Stamford 1858-66, and for N Devon 1866-85; cr Viscount St Cyres, of Newton St Cyres, co Devon, and Earl of Iddesleigh (peerage of United Kingdom) 1885: m 1843, Cecilia Frances, CI, who d 1910, sister of 1st Baron Farrer, d 12 Jan 1887; s by his el son (9) WALTER STAFFORD, CB, 2nd Earl, b 1845; Private Sec to his father 1867-8, and 1874-7, Commr of Inland Revenue 1877-86, Dep Chm thereof 1886-92, and Chm 1892: m 1868, Elizabeth Lucy, who d 1928, da of Sir Harry Stephen Meysey-Thompson, 1st Bt; d 1927; s by his nephew (10) HENRY STAFFORD (yst son of late Rev Hon John Stafford Northcote, 3rd son of 1st Earl), 3rd Earl, b 1901: m 1930, Elizabeth, JP, who d 1991, da of late Frederic Sawrey Archibald Lowndes, of 9 Barton St, Westminster, SW1; d 1970; s by his son (11) STAFFORD HENRY, 4th Earl and present peer; also Viscount St Cyres.

Ikerrin, Viscount; son of Earl of Carrick.

ILCHESTER, EARL OF (Fox-Strangways) (Earl GB 1756)

MAURICE VIVIAN DE TOUFFREVILLE FOX-STRANGWAYS, 9th Earl; b 1 April 1920; s 1970; ed Kingsbridge Sch; Group Capt RAF (ret); CEng, MRAeS, FINucE (Pres 1982-84), FIMgt, Hon FSE (Pres 1974); Hon Fellow Coll of Preceptors; Co Dir; Pres RAF Assoc (SE Area); Pres Grant-Maintained Schs Foundation; Member House of Lords Select Cttee on Science and Technology 1984-89; Liveryman Guild of Air Pilots and Air Navigators: m 1941, Diana Mary Elizabeth, el da of late George Frederick Simpson, of Cassington, Oxon.

Arms – Quarterly: 1st and 4th sable, two lions passant paly of six argent and gules, Strangways; 2nd and 3rd ermine, on a chevron azure, three foxes' heads erased or, a canton of the 2nd, charged with a fleur-de-lis of the 3rd, Fox. **Crest** – On a chapeau azure, turned up ermine, a fox sejant or. **Supporters** – Dexter, a fox ermine, frette or, collared dovetail azure, and the collar charged with three fleurs-de-lis gold; sinister, a fox proper, collared as the dexter.
Residence – Farley Mill, Westerham, Kent. Club – RAF.

Deeds without words

BROTHER LIVING

Hon RAYMOND GEORGE (Cherry Orchard Yews, Trull, Taunton, Som TA3 7LF), b 11 Nov 1921; ed Exeter Sch, and Seale Hayne Agric Coll; Civil Ser 1949-76 (ret); 1939-45 War in RAF: m 1941, Margaret Vera, da of late James Force, of North Surrey, BC, and has issue living, Robin Maurice (Little Haven, Frankton, nr Rugby, Warwicks CV25 9PL), b 1942; ed Loughborough Coll; in banking: m 1969, Margaret Elizabeth, da of late Geoffrey Miles, of Camberley, Surrey, and has issue living, Simon James b 1972, Charlotte Helen b 1974, — Paul André (Cherry Orchard Yews, Trull, Taunton), b 1950; ed Loughborough Coll, and Sussex Univ (BSc (hons), MA); Univ Lecturer.

SISTER LIVING

Lady Jeanne Doreen (Elisabeth), b 1931; Founder and Principal Lady Elizabeth Livingstone Modelling School 1983: m 1st, 1958 (m diss 1969), Peter Skelton, publisher; 2ndly, 1977, John Livingstone, and has one da (from 1st m), Caroline, b 1962. Residence – 72a Fore St, Bovey Tracey, Newton Abbot, Devon.

DAUGHTER LIVING OF SIXTH EARL

Lady Mabel Edith (Dowager Viscountess Wimborne), b 1918: m 1938, 2nd Viscount Wimborne, who d 1967, and has issue. Residence – Magnolia House, Candie, St Peter Port, Guernsey.

PREDECESSORS – (1) STEPHEN FOX, MP for Shaftesbury 1726-41; cr Lord Ilchester, of Ilchester, co Somerset, Baron of Woodford Strangways, co Dorset (peerage of Great Britain) 1741, Lord Ilchester and Stavordale, Baron of Redlynch, co Somerset (peerage of Great Britain) 1747, with remainder to the issue male of his brother Henry, and Earl of Ilchester (peerage of Great Britain) 1756, with like remainder; assumed the additional surname of Strangways 1758; *d* 1766; *s* by his son (2) HENRY THOMAS, 2nd Earl; *d* 1802; *s* by his son (3) HENRY STEPHEN, DCL, 3rd Earl; Capt of Yeomen of the Guard; *d* without surviving male issue 1858; *s* by his half-brother (4) WILLIAM THOMAS HORNER, 4th Earl; *b* 1795; was Under Sec of State for Foreign Affairs 1835 and Ambassador to German Confederation 1840-9; *dsp* 1865; *s* by his nephew (5) HENRY EDWARD (son of Hon John George Charles, 4th son of 2nd Earl, by Amelia, who *d* 1886, sister of 1st Baron Tweedmouth), 5th Earl; *b* 1847; Capt of HM Queen Victoria's Corps of Gentlemen-at-Arms 1873-4, and Lord-Lieut of Dorsetshire: *m* 1872, Lady Mary Eleanor Anne Dawson, who *d* 1935, only da of 1st Earl of Dartrey; *d* 1905; *s* by his son (6) GILES STEPHEN HOLLAND, GBE, 6th Earl; *b* 1874; Chm of Trustees of National Portrait Gallery, a Trustee of British Museum, Chm of Roy Commn on Historical Documents (England), and a FSA; Pres of Roy Literary Fund 1940-50: *m* 1902, Lady Helen Mary Theresa Vane-Tempest-Stewart, who *d* 1956, da of 6th Marquess of Londonderry; *d* 1959; *s* by his el son (7) EDWARD HENRY CHARLES JAMES, 7th Earl: *b* 1905: *m* 1931, Helen Elizabeth, who *d* 1970, da of late Capt the Hon Cyril Augustus Ward, MVO (E Dudley); *d* 1964; *s* by his kinsman (8) WALTER ANGELO (el son of Maurice Walter Fox-Strangways, CSI, 2nd son of Col Walter Fox-Strangways, great-grandson of Rev Hon Charles Fox-Strangways, 3rd son of 1st Earl), 8th Earl, *b* 1887: *m* 1916, Laure Georgine Emilie, who *d* 1970, da of late Evanghelos Georgios Mazaraki, Treasurer, Suez Canal Co; *d* 1970; *s* by his el son (9) MAURICE VIVIAN DE TOUFFREVILLE, 9th Earl and present peer; also Baron Ilchester, Baron Strangways, and Baron Ilchester and Stavordale.

ILIFFE, BARON (Iliffe) (Baron UK 1933)

EDWARD LANGTON ILIFFE, 2nd Baron; *b* 25 Jan 1908; *s* 1960; *ed* Sherborne, and at Clare Coll, Camb; Vice-Chm *Birmingham Post & Mail, Ltd*, 1957-74; a Dir of *Coventry Evening Telegraph*, and a Trustee of Shakespeare's Birthplace; High Sheriff, Berks 1957; 1939-45 War in RAF Vol Reserve (despatches): *m* 1938, Renée, da of R. Merandon du Plessis, of Mauritius.

Arms – Sable, a lion rampant double-queued between four crosses pattée flory or. **Crest** – In front of a demi-lion rampant double-queued sable, collared or, three crosses as in the arms. **Supporters** – *Dexter*, a scribe holding in the exterior hand an open parchment proper; *sinister*, a printer of the time of Caxton holding in the exterior hand in front of his body a composing stick proper.
Residence – Basildon House, Lower Basildon, nr Reading, Berks RG8 9NR. *Clubs* – Brooks's, Carlton, Royal Yacht Squadron.

Live, that you may live

WIDOW LIVING OF SON OF FIRST BARON

Christine Marie, da of Alfred Eaton Baker, MD, of Hastings, Sussex: *m* 1940, Hon William Henry Richard Iliffe, who *d* 1959, and has issue living (see colls infra). *Residences* – Church Cottage, Aldworth, Reading, Berks; 11 Evelyn Gdns, SW7 3BE.

COLLATERAL BRANCH LIVING

Issue of late Hon William Henry Richard Iliffe, yr son of 1st Baron, *b* 1911, *d* 1959: *m* 1940, Christine Marie (ante), da of Alfred Eaton Baker, MD, of Hastings, Sussex:—

ROBERT PETER RICHARD (Yattendon Park, Yattendon, Berks), *b* 22 Nov 1944; High Sheriff of Warwicks 1983: *m* 1966, Rosemary Anne, twin da of Cdr Arthur Grey Skipwith, RN (*see* Skipwith, Bt, colls), and has issue living, Edward Richard, *b* 1968, — George Langton, *b* 1970, — Thomas Arthur, *b* 1973, — Florence Clare (twin), *b* 1973. —— John David, *b* 1947.

PREDECESSOR – (1) EDWARD MAUGER Iliffe, GBE, son of late William Isaac Iliffe, JP, of Allesley, near Coventry; *b* 1877; Chm of Guildhall Insurance Co, Ltd, a Director of London Assurance, Pres and Principal Proprietor *Birmingham Post* and *Birmingham Mail*, proprietor of *Coventry Evening Telegraph*, and *Cambridge Daily News*, and a Member of Lloyd's; sometime Chm of Kelly's Directories, Ltd, and of Iliffe & Sons, Dep Chm of Allied Newspapers, Ltd, and part owner of *Daily Telegraph*; Controller of Machine Tool Depart, Min of Munitions 1917-18; Pres of Asso of British Chambers of Commerce 1932-3, and of Govs of Shakespeare Memorial Theatre of Stratford-on-Avon 1933-58, Master of Coach Makers' and Coach Harness Makers' Co 1936, of Stationers' and Newspapermakers' Co 1937, and of Clockmakers' Co 1946; Hon Air-Commodore No 916/7 Squadron RAF 1939-44; Chm of Duke of Gloucester's Red Cross and St John Fifty-Seven Million Fund 1939-45; sat as MP for Warwickshire, Tamworth Div (*U*) 1923-9; *cr Baron Iliffe*, of Yattendon, co Berks (peerage of United Kingdom) 1933: *m* 1902, Charlotte, who *d* 1972, da of Henry Gilding, JP, of Gateacre, near Liverpool; *d* 1960; *s* by his el son (2) EDWARD LANGTON, 2nd Baron and present peer.

INCHCAPE, EARL OF (Mackay) (Earl UK 1929)

KENNETH PETER LYLE MACKAY, 4th Earl; *b* 23 Jan 1943; *s* 1994; *ed* Eton; late Lieut 9/12th Royal Lancers; AIB; Chm The Glenapp Estate Co, Dir Inchcape Family Investments Ltd, Duncan MacNeill (Holdings) Ltd, The Assam Co Ltd, and formerly Dir Gray Mackenzie & Co Ltd, and Inchcape UK Ltd; Master Grocers' Co 1993-94, 5th Warden Shipwrights' Co 1994-95; Pres Inchcape Soc since 1994; Member Queen's Body Guard for Scotland (Royal Company of Archers): *m* 1966, Georgina, da of Sydney Cresswell, and has issue.

𝔄rms – Per chevron azure and argent in chief two lymphads of the last, and in base a Bengal tiger proper. 𝔊rest – A cubit arm holding a falcon proper. 𝔖upporters – *Dexter*, a lion rampant gules supporting a pendant argent charged with a saltire also gules; *sinister*, a Bengal tiger proper supporting a like pendant.
Residences – Manor Farm Clyffe Pypard, nr Swindon, Wilts; 63 Pont St, SW1. *Clubs* – White's, City of London, Oriental, New (Edinburgh), Pratt's.

With a strong hand

SON LIVING

FERGUS JAMES KENNETH (*Viscount Glenapp*), *b* 9 July 1979.

DAUGHTERS LIVING

Lady Elspeth Pease, *b* 1972, — *Lady* Ailsa Fiona, *b* 1977.

BROTHER LIVING

Hon James Jonathan Thorn (34A Dorset Sq, NW1), *b* 1947; *ed* Eton, and Trin Coll, Camb (MA), *m* 1970, Mary Caroline, el da of Peter Joyce, of Becklands Farm, Whitchurch Canonicorum, Dorset, and has issue living, Aidan James Turner, *b* 1978, — Sophie, *b* 1974.

HALF-BROTHERS LIVING

Hon Shane Lyle, *b* 1973.
Hon Ivan Cholmeley, *b* 1976.

ADOPTIVE BROTHER LIVING

Anthony Kenneth, *b* 1967.

SISTER LIVING

Lady Lucinda Louise MACKAY, *b* 1941; *ed* Edinburgh Univ (MA); has resumed her maiden name: *m* 1983 (*m diss* 1987), David Bogie; Sheriff of Grampian, Highlands and Islands.

UNCLE LIVING (*son of 2nd Earl*)

Hon Alan John Francis, *b* 1919; *ed* Eton, and at Trin Coll, Camb: *m* 1st, 1945 (*m diss* 1947), Janet Mary (*d* 1978), da of Frederick Wallis, of Elvendon Priory, Goring-on-Thames; 2ndly, 1948 (*m diss* 1953), Sonia Cecilia Helen, da of late Capt James Richard Tylden, of Milsted Manor, Kent; 3rdly, 1955, Countess Lucie Catinka Christiane Julie, only da of Count Curt Ludwig Haugwitz-Hardenberg-Reventlow, of Brahe-Trolleborg, Korinth, Fyn, Denmark, and previously wife of John Boswell, and has issue living, (by 2nd *m*) Siobhan Amanda, *b* 1949: *m* 1973, Christopher O. B. Carver, — Kristina Mary, *b* 1951: *m* 1975, Simon M. F. Lamb. *Residence* – Enterkine, Annbank, Ayrshire KA6 5AL. *Clubs* – Naval and Military, Union (Sydney), Royal Sydney Golf, Eccentric, Lansdowne.

HALF-UNCLE LIVING (*son of 2nd Earl by 2nd marriage*)

Hon Simon Brooke (*Baron Tanlaw*), *b* 1934; *cr* Baron Tanlaw (Life Baron) 1971 (see that title).

HALF-AUNT LIVING (*daughter of 2nd Earl by 2nd marriage*)

Lady Rosemary, *b* 1936: *m* 1957, Francis Martin French, and has had issue, Ewan Alexander Francis, *b* 1959; *d* 198—, — Anna-Louise Rosemary, *b* 1961, — Nicola Catharine, *b* 1967: *m* 1993, Lawrence Charles Reintjes, elder son of Anthony Reintjes, of Preston, Herrs, — Kirsty Elizabeth, *b* 1970. *Residence* – Little Offley, Hitchin, Herts.

MOTHER LIVING

Aline Thorn, da of Sir Richard Arthur Pease, 2nd Bt (*cr* 1920), and widow of Patrick Claude Hannay, FO AAF: *m* 2ndly, 1941 (*m diss* 1954), 3rd Earl of Inchcape, who *d* 1994; 3rdly, 1955 (*m diss* 1968), Thomas Chambers Windsor Roe, who *d* 1988. *Residence* – 23 Rue Pre-du-Marché, Apt 114, Lausanne, Switzerland.

WIDOW LIVING OF SECOND EARL

LEONORA MARGARET, el da of HH the late Rajah (Sir Charles Vyner Brooke) of Sarawak, GCMG (V Esher): *m* 1st, 1933, as his 2nd wife, the 2nd Earl, who *d* 1939; 2ndly, 1946, Col Francis Parker Tompkins, US Army.

WIDOW LIVING OF THIRD EARL

CAROLINE CHOLMELEY (*Dowager Countess of Inchcape*), el da of Cholmeley Harrison, of Emo Court, co Leix: *m* 1965, as his

2nd wife, the 3rd Earl of Inchcape, who *d* 1994. *Residence* – Starvall Farm, Farmington, Northleach, Cheltenham, Glos GL54 3NF.

PREDECESSORS – **(1)** JAMES LYLE Mackay, GCSI, GCMG, KCIE, son of late James Mackay, of Arbroath, Forfarshire, by his wife, Deborah Lyle; *b* 1852; four years Pres of Bengal Chamber of Commerce, and a Member of Council of India 1897-1911; a partner in Mackinnon, Mackenzie and Co, of Calcutta, Bombay, Karachi, Colombo, Hong Kong, and Shanghai, of Gray, Dawes and Co, and of Macdonald, Hamilton and Co of Australia, a Director of National Provincial Bank, Ltd, Chm and Managing Director of British India Steam Navigation Co, and P and O Steam Navigation Co, Chm of P & O Banking Corporation, and Vice-Pres of Suez Canal Co; *cr Baron Inchcape*, of Strathnaver, co Sutherland (peerage of United Kingdom) 1911, *Viscount Inchcape*, of Strathnaver, co Sutherland (peerage of United Kingdom) 1924, *Viscount Glenapp*, of Strathnaver, co Sutherland, and *Earl of Inchcape* (peerage of United Kingdom) 1929: *m* 1883, Jane Paterson, who *d* 1937, el da of late James Shanks, of Rosely, Arbroath, Forfarshire; *d* 1932; *s* by his son **(2)** KENNETH, 2nd Earl; *b* 1887; a partner in Mackinnon, Mackenzie & Co, Pres of P & O Banking Corporation, and a Director of P & O Steam Navigation Co: *m* 1st, 1915 (*m diss* 1931), Frances Caroline Joan (who *d* 1933), da of late Rt Hon John Francis Moriarty, Lord Justice of Appeal; 2ndly, 1933, Leonora Margaret, el da of HH the late Rajah (Sir Charles Vyner Brooke) of Sarawak, GCMG (V Esher); *d* 1939; *s* by his son **(3)** KENNETH JAMES WILLIAM, 3rd Earl, *b* 1917; 1939-45 War with 12th Lancers in France, and Maj 27th Lancers in Central Mediterranean; Life Pres Inchcape plc (Exec Chm 1958-82), Chm Inchcape Family Investments Ltd, sometimes Dir BAII, Burmah Oil Co, British Petroleum, and Standard Chartered Bank plc; Pres Royal Soc for India, Pakistan and Ceylon, and Gen Council of British Shipping: *m* 1st, 1941 (*m diss* 1954), Aline Thorn, da of Sir Richard Arthur Pease, 2nd Bt (*cr* 1920), and widow of Patrick Claude Hannay, FO AAF; 2ndly, 1965, Caroline Cholmeley, el da of Cholmeley Harrison, of Emo Court, co Leix; *d* 1994; *s* by his eldest son **(3)** KENNETH PETER LYLE, 4th Earl and present peer, also Baron Inchcape, Viscount Inchcape, and Viscount Glenapp.

INCHIQUIN, BARON (O'Brien) (Baron I 1543, Bt I 1686)

Strength from above

CONOR MYLES JOHN O'BRIEN, 18th Baron, and 10th Baronet; *b* 17 July 1943; *s* 1982; *ed* Eton; late Capt 14th/20th King's Hussars: *m* 1988, Helen O'Farrell, da of Gerald Fitzgerald O'Farrell, of Curry Lodge, Longford, co Longford, and has issue.

Arms – Quarterly: 1st and 4th, gules, three lions passant guardant in pale; per pale or and argent; 2nd, argent, three piles meeting in point issuing from the chief gules; 3rd, or, a pheon azure. **Crest** – Issuing from a cloud an arm embowed, brandishing a sword argent, pommel and hilt or. **Supporters** – Two lions guardant per fesse or and argent.
Residence – Thomond House, Dromoland, co Clare.

DAUGHTERS LIVING

Hon Slaney Alexandra Anne, *b* 1989.
Hon Lucia Josephine, *b* 1991.

SISTER LIVING

Fiona Jane, *b* 1941: *m* 1965, Romano Louis Obert de Thieusies (2nd son of late Vicomte Alain Martel Marie Joseph Ghislain Obert de Thieusies), of 47 Chiddingstone St, SW6 3TQ, and Chateau de Thoricourt, Thoricourt, Hainaut, Belgium, and has issue living, Patrick Conor Alain, *b* 1968, — Isabelle Stephanie, *b* 1966, — Sophie Patricia, *b* 1972.

DAUGHTERS LIVING OF SIXTEENTH BARON

Hon Deirdre Jane Frances, *b* 1924: *m* 1954, Horace Beecher Chapin, MD, who *d* 1992. *Residence* – Mizzentop No 47, Harbour Rd, Warwick, Bermuda.
Hon Grania Rachel, *b* 1928; was Social Sec to British Ambassador to Peru 1958-60, and to British Ambassador to Japan 1954-57 and Spain 1952: *m* 1973, Hugh William Lindsay Weir, of Ballinakella Lodge, Whitegate, co Clare.

WIDOW LIVING OF SON OF FOURTEENTH BARON

Edith Lawrie (3 Ibris Place, N Berwick, E Lothian), widow of T. M. Steele: *m* 1964, as his 2nd wife, Capt Hon Henry Barnaby O'Brien, who *d* 1969.

MOTHER LIVING

Josephine Reine (1 Dault Rd, SW18 2NH), da of late Joseph Eugene Bembaron, of The Old House, Westcott, Surrey: *m* 1939, Hon Fionn Myles Maryons O'Brien, who *d* 1977, 3rd son of 15th Baron.

WIDOW LIVING OF SEVENTEENTH BARON

VERA MAUD (*Vera, Baroness Inchiquin*) (Hanway Lodge, Richards Castle, Ludlow, Shropshire), da of late Rev Clifton Samuel Winter: *m* 1945, Maj the 17th Baron, who *d* 1982.

COLLATERAL BRANCHES LIVING

Issue of Lieut-Col Hon Murrough O'Brien, DSO, MVO, 2nd son of 14th Baron, *b* 1866, *d* 1934: *m* 1906, Marguerite, who *d* 1958, da of William Lewis, of New York:—
MURROUGH RICHARD, *b* 25 May 1910; *ed* Eton, and at Balliol Coll, Oxford; sometime Major Irish Guards; 1939-45 War: *m* 1st, 1942, Irene Clarice (formerly wife of (i) the 10th Marquess of Queensberry, and (ii) Sir James Hamet Dunn, 1st Bt (*cr* 1921), who *d* 1977), da of H. W. Richards, of Regent's Park, NW1; 2ndly, 1952, Joan, da of Charles Pierre Jenkinson, and

widow of Capt Woolf Barnato, and has issue living, (by 2nd *m*) Conor John Anthony (Midgham Park Farm House, Midgham, Berks), *b* 1952; *ed* Eton: *m* 1982, Vivian, yr da of Col Adrian Rouse, of 17 Alexander Sq, SW3, and has issue living, Fionn Murrough *b* 1987, Slaney Victoria *b* 1989. — Melissa Jane *b* 1956: *m* 1st, 1979, Nicholas Simunek, of New York, USA; 2ndly, 19—, Jorge de Paiva Raposo, of 462 King's Rd, SW3, and has issue living (by 2nd *m*), Alessandra Belinda *b* 1991. *Residences* – Shelleys House, Wick Lane, Englefield Green, Surrey TW20 0XE; 34 Connaught Sq, W2. *Club* – White's. —— Edward Cecil, OBE (The Old Barn, 1 Station Rd, Docking, Norfolk PE31 8LS), *b* 1915; *ed* Eton; sometime Capt Irish Gds, and Maj Parachute Regt; OBE (Civil) 1959: *m* 1st, 1943 (*m diss* 1968), Elizabeth Margaret, da of late Col Sir Henry William Henry Dyke Acland, 3rd Bt (*cr* 1890), MC, AFC, TD; 2ndly, 1991, Phyllis Elsie Margaret, da of Phillip Heber-Jones, and formerly wife of Derek Chudleigh, and has issue living (by 1st *m*), Lucia Jane, *b* 1947: *m* 1973, David Lawrence Gilbert Smith, of 68 Goldington Av, Bedford, and has issue living, Caroline Theresa Slaney *b* 1976, Isabel Helen *b* 1980, — Emily Teresa, *b* 1952: *m* 1978, Stephen Anson, of 67 Courtfield Gdns, SW5, and has issue living, Nicholas Phaedrig Charles *b* 1989.

Granddaughters of late Capt Hon Henry Barnaby O'Brien (infra):—
Issue of late Desmond Barnaby O'Brien, *b* 1926, *d* 1969: *m* 1955, Cherry Angela Mary, who *d* 1992, yr da of late Lt-Col (Frank) James (Wriothesley) Seely (*see* Seely Bt, colls):—
Karen, *b* 1956: *m* 1978, Paul William Cowan, of The Old Farmhouse, Weald, Bampton, Oxon, and has issue living, Jonathan, *b* 1981, — Lara Frances, *b* 1979, — Nina Elizabeth, *b* 1980, — Molly, *b* 1988. —— Sara Jane, *b* 1961: *m* 1986, Simon Cellan-Jones, of 34 Stockwell Park Rd, SW4, and has issue living, Kate *b* 1988.

Issue of late Capt Hon Henry Barnaby O'Brien, 5th son of 14th Baron, *b* 1887, *d* 1969: *m* 1st, 1925, Lady Helen Baillie-Hamilton, OBE, who *d* 1959, sister of 12th Earl of Haddington; 2ndly, 1964, Edith Lawrie (ante), widow of T. M. Steele:—
(By 1st *m*) Michael George, *b* 1928; late Irish Guards: *m* 1955, Susan Mary Matilda, da of late Wing-Cdr Robert Cevil Talbot Speir, OBE, RAF, and has issue living, Peter Thomond, *b* 1961, — John Michael, *b* 1964, — Gillian Ursula Helen, *b* 1956, — Rebecca, *b* 1957.

Grandchildren of late Hon William Henry Ernest Robert Turlough O'Brien, 3rd son of 13th Baron:—
Issue of late Turlough George Henry O'Brien, *b* 1907, *d* 1976: *m* 1939 (*m diss* 1966), Catherine, da of late Dr John Watt Senter, of Edinburgh:—
Patrick Brian (via Marco Aurelio 42, Flat 15, Rome, Italy), *b* 1943. —— Diana, *b* 1941: *m* 1961, Ronald Anthony Ostwald, of 8 Cholmeley Park, Highgate, N6, and has issue living, Christian Mark Sebastian, *b* 1962; has issue (by Joanna Lynn Kelly), Kitty Annabel Kelly *b* 1993, — Cassie Kate Louise, *b* 1978.

Grandchildren of late William Dermod O'Brien (infra):—
Issue of late Brendan Edward O'Brien, MD, FRCPI, *b* 1903, *d* 1984: *m* 1936, Pamela Kathleen Helen, RHA, Pres of Water Colour Soc of Ireland, who *d* 1982, only da of Maj H. G. Wilmer, IA:—
Dermod Wilmer (Glenside, Lee Rd, Carrigohane, co Cork; R Cork Yacht Club), *b* 1941; *ed* Dublin Univ (BA, BAI): *m* 1966, Rosalind, da of Robert G. Service, of Helensburgh, and has issue living, Jeremy William, *b* 1971, — Lucia Jane, *b* 1969, — Charlotte Elizabeth, *b* 1974. —— Anthony Derek, *b* 1947; *ed* Haileybury, and Dublin Univ (BA): *m* 1974, Najma Madhavjee, and has issue living, Cormac Brendan, *b* 1979, — Murrough Idries, *b* 1983, — Zahara Grace, *b* 1976.
Issue of late Maj David Lucius O'Brien, MRCVS, *b* 1904, *d* 1988: *m* 1st, 1929 (*m diss* 1946), Mary Katharine Drummond, who *d* 1987, da of Rt Hon Sir Arthur Drummond Ramsay-Steel-Maitland, 1st Bt (ext); 2ndly, 1954, Shirley (Scottsdale, Tasmania), da of late C. P. Hurford, of Worcester Park, Surrey:—
(By 1st *m*) Michael David, *b* 1930. *Residence* – Addlestead Farm, Headley, Epson, Surrey. —— Lucia Margaret, *b* 1932. *Residence* – 84 Colehill Lane, SW6. —— (By 2nd *m*) Tasman David, *b* 1955: *m* 1986, Brenda Goodwin, and has issue living, Kirby, *b* 1986, — Conor Michael, *b* 1988. *Residence* – 13 Harrison Close, Whitfield Park, Cairns 4870, N Queensland, Australia. —— Donough William, *b* 1956. *Address* – c/o Daylesford, Victoria, Australia.

Grandchildren of late Edward William O'Brien, JP, DL, of Cahirmoyle, co Limerick, eldest son of William Smith O'Brien, MP, (infra):—
Issue of late William Dermod O'Brien, *b* 1865, *d* 1945: *m* 1902, Mabel Emmeline, who *d* 1942, da of late Sir Philip Crampton Smyly, MD (B Plunket):—
(Horace) Donough, AM (30 Queen St, Burnie, Tasmania), *b* 1911; *ed* Dublin Univ (MB and BCh 1934); FRCSI 1939; FRACS 1958; FACRM; Lt-Col (ret) RAMC; AM 1976: *m* 1st, 1941 (*m diss* 1950), Pamela Charlotte, da of Capt Barrington Goodbody; 2ndly, 1950, Lucy Ann Stafford, da of T. E. Stafford O'Brien, and has issue living, (by 2nd *m*) Bartholemew Brendan (28 Wheaton Rd, Stepney, Adelaide 5069, S Australia), *b* 1953; RGN, BN, PhD: *m* 1981, Lauri Therese, da of late James Cadzow, and has issue living, David Nicholas *b* 1990, Alice Louise *b* 1986, — Alexander Kennedy, *b* 1955: *m* 1985 (*m diss* 1992), Lynley Keynes, — (by 1st *m*) Caroline Phyllis Ann, *b* 1942: *m* 1982, Arthur James Cox (14409 Brookmead Drive, German-town, Maryland 20874, USA), son of late J. Cox, of Pulaski, Virgina, USA. —— Mary Elinor, *b* 1907; BA: *m* 1934, Bruce Martin Flegg, ARIBA, late Sqdn-Ldr RAF, and has issue living, Aubrey Martin, *b* 1938; BA, PhD: *m* 1966, Jennifer Condell, MLitt, of Dublin, and his issue living, Nigel Patrick Martin *b* 1970, Eleanor Minta *b* 1967, — Katharine Elinor, *b* 1934; ARCM: *m* 1964, N. Dimitriakopoulos, of Thessaloniki, Greece. *Residence* – St Nicholas House, Rostrevor Rd, Rathgar, co Dublin. —— Rosaleen Brigid, *b* 1909; a Roy Hibernian Academician: *m* 1936, Andrew Ganly, MA, FFD, RCSI, BDentSc, who *d* 1982, and has issue living, Eoghan Timothy, *b* 1938: *m* 1966, Vera Behan, and has issue living, Brian *b* 1967, — Helen Phillida, *b* 1939: *m* 1963, Henry Brian Smith, MB, and has issue living, Conor Melville *b* 1967, Desmond Brian *b* 1978, Kathleen Brigid *b* 1970. *Residence* – 5A Laurel Hill, Glenageary Rd, Dun Laoghaire, co Dublin.

Grandchildren of late Very Rev Lucius Henry O'Brien, son of William Smith O'Brien, MP, brother of 13th Baron:—
Issue of late Donough Richard O'Brien, *b* 1876, *d* 1938: *m* 1914, Cecilia Maud, who *d* 1981, da of Rev Frederick Neville Carus-Wilson, of Glenfield, Bath:—
Patricia Cicely, *b* 1918: *m* 1939, Rev John Godwin Benson, MA, Hon CF, son of Rev R.S. Benson, of Greencastle, co Donegal, and *d* 1991, leaving issue, Donough O'Brien (316 Strickland Av, S Hobart, Tasmania 7000), *b* 1940; has issue living (by Carolyn Hall-Jones), Donough O'Brien *b* 1975, Lucia Patricia *b* 1979, — Murrough John (37 Findlay Av, Roseville, Sydney, NSW 2069, Australia), *b* 1946: *m* 1969, Eileen Joyce Cox, and has issue living, Murrough William George *b* 1985, Patrick John Godwin *b* 1987, — Brian Lucius (15 Murray St, Highton, Geelong, Victoria 3216, Australia), *b* 1950: *m* 1975, Jane Evelyn Martin, and has issue living, Antony Paul *b* 1976, Richard Lucius *b* 1988, Carus Edward *b* 1989, Cicely Jane *b* 1985, Brianna Maud *b* 1991. *Residence* – Kincora, 27 Curdievale Rd, Timboon, Victoria 3268, Australia. —— Geraldine Mary, *b* 1922: *m* 1948, David Coote Hely-Hutchinson, and has issue (*see* E Donoughmore, colls). *Residence* – Parteenalax, Limerick.
Issue of late Charles Murrough O'Brien, *b* 1877, *d* 1939: *m* 1903, Agnes Purdon, who *d* 1970, da of James Wilson, formerly of McLeod, Alberta, Canada:—
†Donough Robert Murrough, *b* 1910: *m* 1940, Rita Denny, da of late Rev William Musson, of Buckingham, and *d* 1991, leaving, Murrough (230 Hector Rd, RR3, Victoria, BC V8X 3X1), *b* 1947: *m* 1968, Patricia Arlene, da of George C. Ellison, of N Vancouver, — Francine Denny O'Brien (1736 Maple Bay Rd, RR5, Duncan, BC V9L 4T6), *b* 1942 has resumed her maiden name, (*m diss* 1991): *m* 1969; Donald Vincent Kissinger, and has issue living, Simon Raven John *b* 1972, Sarah Tsu Emily O'BRIEN (has assumed the surname of O'Brien) *b* 1974. —— Eileen Moira Agnes, *b* 1912: *m* 1939, Dan Stephenson Heelas, who *d* 1985, of 79, 5550 Langley By-Pass, Langley, BC V3A 7Z3, and has issue living, Moira Jessica, *b* 1942: *m* 1963, Henry Stephens, of 7902 Glover Rd, RR6 Langley, BC, V3A 4P9, and has issue living, Sheryl Lynn *b* 1963: *m* 1984, Guy

Anthony Widiner (and has issue living, Brett Stephen *b* 1990, Dylan Daniel *b* 1994), Yvonne Doreen *b* 1967, — Joan Zenda, *b* 1944: *m* 1973, Lynden Sharman, of 3942 Indian River Drive, N Vancouver, BC V7G 2G9, and has issue living, Paul Richard *b* 1977, Keith Stephenson *b* 1980.

Grandchildren of late Charles Murrough O'Brien (*b* 1849), son of late William Smith O'Brien MP (ante):—
   Issue of late Brian O'Brien, MD, *b* 1872, *d* 1915: *m* 1903, Mary Henrietta, who *d* 1968, da of late Maurice Charles Hime, JP, LLD, BL, of Cluain Fóis, Buncrana, co Donegal:—
Charles Murrough, *b* 1903; *ed* Trin Coll, Dublin (MB and BCh 1928): *m* 1930, Elizabeth Joyce, who *d* 1988, da of late Ven Gerald W. Peacocke, Archdeacon of Kildare, and has issue living. Brian Murrough Fergus (20 Manchester St, W1; Reform and Kildare St Clubs), *b* 1931; *ed* Bedford Sch, and at Univ Coll, Oxford (MA); Bar Lincoln's Inn 1955, — David Donough (Hambleton, nr Oakham, Leics), *b* 1933: *m* 1962, Carole June Walters, and has issue living, Nicholas Charles Donough, *b* 1963: *m* 1993, Mrs Kathryn Ann Hutchins (*neé* Randle), and has issue living, Anastasia Grace Ailne *b* 199—, Seamus Timothy Lucius, *b* 1965. *Residence* – 73 Knighton Drive, Leicester. —— Mary Grainne, *b* 1905: *m* 1935, Ian Galbraith Robson, who *d* 1977, and has issue living, Michael William *b* 1948.

Grandchildren of late Brian O'Brien, MD (ante):—
   Issue of late Brian O'Brien, MD, *b* 1908, *d* 1968: *m* 1938, Dorothea, who *d* 1980, da of John F. A. Simms, of Combermore, Lifford:—
Brian Dermod, *b* 1942; *ed* Univ of Alberta, Edmonton, and Queen's Univ, Kingston (BSc, MD, LMCC); FRCPC 1978, served RCAF Medical Branch 1959-89 (ret as Col): *m* 1962, Barbara Eileen, da of W/Cmdr John F. Brennagh, of Ottawa, Ont, and has issue living, Brian David, *b* 1963: *m* 1990, Susan Anne, da of Francis Martin, of Halifax, and has issue living, Christopher Keaton *b* 1989, Eliot Mary Brennagh *b* 1992, — Patrick John, *b* 1965: *m* 1988, Karen Helen, da of John Lyons, of Calgary, Alberta, — Christopher Michael, *b* 1969: *m* 1994, Sheila Isobel, da of Dr Robert Loughrey, of Brockville, Ontario, — Katherine Jennifer Eileen, *b* 1971. *Residence* – 5863 Macleod Drive, Halifax, NS, Canada B3H 1C6. —— George Lucius (95 Empress Ave, North York, Ontario, Canada M2N 3T5), *b* 1944; *ed* Queen's Univ, Kingston (MSc), and Dartmouth Coll, New Hampshire (AM, PhD): *m* 1976, Elizabeth Frances, da of Thomas Sharpless Ely, of Rochester, NY, and has issue living, William Thomas, *b* 1982, — Margaret Clare, *b* 1984, — Katherine Elizabeth, *b* 1987. —— Deirdre O'BRIEN (40 Butler Crescent NW, Calgary, Alberta, Canada T2L 1K3), *b* 1940; *ed* Ottawa Univ (BSc, MHA); Reg N; resumed the surname of O'Brien 19—: *m* 1963 (*m diss* 1975), James Moxley Shearer, BSc, and has issue living, James O'Brien, *b* 1965, — George Brodie, *b* 1969, — Margaret Kathleen, *b* 1967, — Joan Hilary, *b* 1968.

Grandchildren of late Robert Vere O'Brien, yr son of late Hon Robert O'Brien (raised to the rank of a Baron's son by R Licence 1862), brother of 13th Baron:—
   Issue of late Hugh Murrough Vere O'Brien, MC, *b* 1887, *d* 1955: *m* 1915, his 2nd cousin, Margaret Ernestine, who *d* 1968, da of late Edward William O'Brien (ante):—
Murrogh Vere, *b* 1919; *ed* Dublin Univ (BAI 1940), and at Roy Sch of Mines, London (ARSM 1947); BSc London 1947; Dir Geological Survey of Ireland 1952-64; Fell Inst of Mining and Metallurgy 1974, and Hon Fell 1987: *m* 1945, Zsuzsánna Eva Szeréna, da of Károly Károlyi, of Budapest, Hungary, and has had issue, Colm Murrogh Vere; *b* 1947; *ed* Dublin Univ; represented Ireland at fencing in Olympic Games Mexico 1968; *d* 1985, in Miami, Florida, — Hugh Stephen Vere (10 Dungar Terr, Dun Laoghaire, co Dublin), *b* 1948; *ed* Univ Coll, Dublin; architect: *m* 1983, Alison Ann Cooke, and has issue living, Robert Murrogh Vere *b* 1991, Donough Patrick Vere *b* 1992, Catherine Lucy Bebhinn *b* 1987, — Sylvia Caroline Piroska, *b* 1946; *ed* Dublin Univ (BA), and Simon Fraser Univ (MSc); botanist: *m* 1971 Julian Douglas Reynolds, Fell and Sr Lecturer in Biology at TCD, of 115 Weirview Drive, Stillorgan, co Dublin, and has issue living, Conor Charles O'Brien *b* 1976, Owen Ralph Douglas *b* 1981, Elinor Florence Dirny *b* 1978, — Iseult Anne, *b* 1952: *m* 1981, Bryan Fergus Murphy, of Thatch House, Adare, co Limerick, and has issue living, Hugh Patrick Fergus *b* 1982, Slany Elizabeth *b* 1985, — Charlotte Elinor, *b* 1962; *ed* Dublin Univ (BA 1984), and Imperial Coll Lond (MSc 1985). *Residences* – Monare, Foynes, co Limerick; 69 The Elms, Mt Merrion Av, Blackrock, Co Dublin. —— Elinor Vere (62 Carroll House, Lancaster Gate, W2), *b* 1918: *m* 1956, Reginald Wiltshire, who *d* 1968.

Grandchildren of late Edward O'Brien, el son of Rev Hon Henry O'Brien (raised to the rank of a Baron's son by R Licence 1862), yst brother of 13th Baron:—
   Issue of late Major Murrough Charles O'Brien, MD, JP, Canadian Army Med Corps, *b* 1868, *d* 1955: *m* 1901, Margaret Eleanor Barber, who *d* 1958:—
Muriel Oclanis, *b* 1904: *m* 1932, Hamilton Stewart McKee.
   Issue of late Lieut-Col Aubrey John O'Brien, CIE, CBE, *b* 1870, *d* 1930: *m* 1906, Annie Winifred, who *d* 1936, da of late James D'Arcy, of Kew:—
Turlough Aubrey, CBE (11 Kiln Gdns, Hartley Wintney, Hants), *b* 1907; *ed* Charterhouse, and at Ch CH, Oxford (MA); late Maj RA; 1939-45 War as Maj RA; CBE (Civil) 1959: *m* 1945, Phyllis Mary, who *d* 1986, twin da of late Edward Grosvenor Tew (B Hawke), and has issue living, Teige Henry Patrick (10 Fairlawn Grove, W4 5EH); *b* 1949: *m* 1976, Sarah Catherine, da of Henry Wilson, and has issue living, Grania Catherine *b* 1982, Finola Clare *b* 1985, — (Brian Edward) Nicholas (83a Cromwell Rd, SW19 8LF), *b* 1951: *m* 1992, Miranda Penelope Gillian, da of late Maj Jack Warren Pollock, RA (*see* Pollock, Bt, colls), — Corinna Moira (2 Kingswood Rd, SW19), *b* 1955: *m* 1993, Christopher Edge, son of Bruce Edge. *Club* – United University. —— Moira Winifred Oclanis, *b* 1912: *m* 1st, 1932, John Michael Orpen Barstow, who *d* 1976; 2ndly, 1990, Capt George Baillie Barstow, RN, who *d* 1991, and has issue living (by 1st *m*), Elizabeth Catharine Oclanis, *b* 1933: *m* 1959, Charles Richard Cubitt Bevis, of 3 Granville Rd, Barnet, Herts, and has issue living, Elizabeth Margaret Moira *b* 1960: *m* 1982, Julian Bryan Stevens (and has issue living, Frederick *b* 1988, Harriet *b* 1985), Maria Catharine Oclanis *b* 1962, Alexandra Anne Cecilia *b* 1963: *m* 1986, Steven Andrew Carl White, Lucinda Mary Sophia *b* 1965: *m* 1986, Jonathan David Walter Starling (and has issue living, Anna *b* 1986, Sophia *b* 1988), Selena Penelope Beatrice *b* 1969, Xanthe Frances Henrietta *b* 1972, — Anne Moira Olivia (74 Clarence Rd, St Albans, Herts), *b* 1940: *m* 1st, 1965, Derek Landale Christie, who *d* 1974; 2ndly, 1977, Roger Beament, and has issue living, (by 1st *m*) John Michael Landale *b* 1966: *m* 1993, Karen, da of Michael Heaney, Edward Hugh Landale *b* 1968, Annabella Moira Orpen *b* 1969, (by 2nd *m*) Emily Catharine Olivia *b* 1978, — Mary Geraldine Sheila, *b* 1943: *m* 1970, Graham McGregor Finch, of 38 Sion Hill, Bath, Avon, and has issue living, Henrietta Lucy Anne *b* 1975, Cressida Mary Frances *b* 1979, — Henrietta Penelope, *b* 1945: *m* 1968, Nicholas Frank Killeen Rose, of 23 All Saints Villas Rd, Cheltenham, Glos, and has issue living, Thomas Michael Orpen *b* 1978, Beatrice Caroline Ellen *b* 1974, — Brigid Evelyn Cecilia, *b* 1947: *m* 1973, Charles Michael Brett, of St Margaret's, St Michael's Rd, Winchester, Hants, and has issue living, Aubrey Francis Patrick *b* 1974, Caroline Moira Cecilia *b* 1977. *Residence* – Butt House, Painswick, Glos. —— Winifred Mary Sheila, *b* 1918; is Sister Sheila, Community of St John Baptist. *Address* – Convent of St John Baptist, Hatch Lane, Windsor, Berks.

Grandchildren of late Lt-Col Aubrey John O'Brien, CIE, CBE (ante):—
   Issue of late Edward Donough O'Brien, *b* 1909, *d* 1979: *m* 1st, 1936, Sylvia Inchbold, who *d* 1950, da of Court Denny, of 30 Addison Rd, W14; 2ndly, 1952, Leonora Thayne (49 Kenway Rd, SW5), el da of Manning Leonard Railton:—
(By 1st *m*) Donough Antony (66 Clonmel Rd, SW6), *b* 1939: *m* 1st, 1969, Clare, da of Leonard Read; 2ndly, 1980, Philippa, da of Maj-Gen Mervyn Janes, CB, MBE; 3rdly, 1990, Elizabeth, da of Lieut Gen Sir John Guise Cowley, GC, KBE, CB, and has issue living (by 1st *m*) Murrough, *b* 1971, — (by 2nd *m*) Edmond Mahon, *b* 1981. —— Natalie Deirdre Teresa, *b* 1941: *m* 1964, Roger Henry Brough Whittaker, of Cubberley House, Ross-on-Wye, Herefords, son of late Edward Whittaker, of Nairobi, and has two sons and three das, (Edward) Guy, *b* 1974, — Alexander Michael, *b* 1978, — Emily Clare, *b* 1968: *m*

1991, Stewart Malcolm Kennedy, son of late S/Ldr Ewen Kennedy, — Lauren Marie, *b* 1970, — Jessica Jane, *b* 1973. —— Geraldine Moira, *b* 1945: *m* 1968, Rolfe Elholm, of Norway, and *d* 1987, leaving issue, Astri, *b* 1971. —— (By 2nd *m*) Fionn Murrough Manning (Amsterdam), *b* 1953: *m* 1973, Carole Ann, da of William Whitlock, and has issue, Zoe, *b* 1973. —— Lucius Edward (22 Henrick Av, SW12), *b* 1957: *m* 1986, Caroline Veronica Mary, da of Maj Hywel Colwyn Phillips, of Mostyn, Clwyd, and has issue living, Caroline Louisa Maire, *b* 1992, — Olivia Alison Clare, *b* 1993.

Granddaughter of late Lt-Col Henry Eoghan O'Brien, DSO, only son of Murrough John O'Brien, 2nd son of Rev Hon Henry O'Brien (ante):—

Issue of late Lieut-Com Brian Eoghan O'Brien, RN, *b* 1907; *ka* 1940: *m* 1936, Elizabeth (who *m* 2ndly, 1949, P. Dennis, who *d* 1983), da of Stuart Séguin Strahan, MB, BCh, of Hong Kong:—

Olivia Fiona, *b* 1938: *m* 1960, Sebastian Robinson, of 22 Athole Gdns, Glasgow, W2, and has issue living, James Lucius O'Brien, *b* 1962, — Amanda Mary Victoria, *b* 1961: *m* 1983, Martyn D. Smith.

Descendants, if any, of late George O'Brien (*b* 1821), son of late Adm Robert O'Brien, 3rd son of late Sir Lucius Henry O'Brien, 3rd Bt.

PREDECESSORS – Turlogh, King of Munster and principal King of Ireland, had with other issue, Dermot, King of Munster, from whom descended Conor O'Brien, inaugurated King of Thomond 1528; *d* 1540, when his son Donough was set aside, the principality being usurped by his brother **(1)** MURROUGH O'Brien, PC, who surrendered his royalty to Henry VIII, and was *cr* 1543 *Earl of Thomond* (peerage of Ireland), with remainder to his nephew Donough, and *Baron Inchiquin* (peerage of Ireland) to him and the heirs male of his body; *s* in the Barony by his son **(2)** DERMOT, 2nd Baron; *d* 1557; *s* by his son **(3)** MURROUGH, 3rd Baron; *d* 1573; *s* by his son **(4)** MURROUGH, 4th Baron; *d* 1597; *s* by his son **(5)** DERMOT, 5th Baron; *d* 1624; *s* by his son **(6)** MURROUGH, 6th Baron; a military officer of great renown; *cr Earl of Inchiquin* (peerage of Ireland) 1654; *d* 1674; *s* by his son **(7)** WILLIAM, 2nd Earl; Gov of Jamaica; *d* 1691; *s* by his son **(8)** WILLIAM, 3rd Earl; *d* 1719; *s* by his son **(9)** WILLIAM, 4th Earl; *d* 1777; *s* by his nephew and son-in-law **(10)** MURROUGH, KP, 5th Earl son of the Hon James, MP, 3rd son of 3rd Earl; *cr Marquess of Thomond* (peerage of Ireland) 1800; with remainder to the issue male of his brother Edward, and *Baron Thomond*, of Taplow, co Bucks (peerage of United Kingdom) 1801; *d* 1808, when the Barony of Thomond expired and the Marquessate and Barony of Inchiquin devolved upon his nephew **(11)** WILLIAM, KP, 2nd Marquess, 3rd son of Hon Edward, 2nd brother of 2nd Earl; a Representative Peer; *cr Baron Tadcaster*, of Tadcaster, co York (peerage of United Kingdom) 1826; *d* 1846, when the barony of Tadcaster expired and the Irish peerages devolved upon his brother **(12)** JAMES, GCH, 3rd Marquess; an Adm; *d* 1855, when all the titles became extinct except the Barony of Inchiquin, which descended to **(13)** LUCIUS O'Brien, 13th Baron and 5th Bart (see note * infra); *b* 1800; sat as MP for co Clare (C) 1826-30 and 1847-52; a Representative Peer, and Lord-Lieut of Clare: *m* 1st, 1837, Mary, who *d* 1849, el da of William Fitzgerald; 2ndly, 1854, Louisa, da of Major James Finucane, of Ennistymon House, Clare; *d* 1872; *s* by his son **(14)** EDWARD DONOUGH, 14th Baron, KP, *b* 1839; a Representative Peer, and Lieut for co Clare: *m* 1st, 1862, Hon Emily Holmes à Court, who *d* 1868, da of 2nd Baron Heytesbury; 2ndly, 1874, Hon Ellen Harriet White, who *d* 1913, da of 2nd Baron Annaly; *d* 1900; *s* by his son **(15)** LUCIUS WILLIAM, 5th Baron; *b* 1864; a Representative Peer for Ireland: *m* 1896, Ethel Jane, who *d* 1940, el da and co-heiress of late Johnston J. Foster, of Moor Park, Ludlow; *d* 1929; *s* by his el son **(16)** DONOUGH EDWARD FOSTER, 16th Baron; *b* 1897; Capt Rifle Bde: *m* 1921, Hon Anne Molyneux Thesiger, who *d* 1973, da of 1st Viscount Chelmsford; *d* 1968; *s* by his brother **(17)** PHAEDRIG LUCIUS AMBROSE, 17th Baron, *b* 1900, Maj Rifle Bde, Colonial Service Geological Survey, 1939-45 War in Somalia, Abyssinia and Madagascar, attached E African Intelligence Corps (wounded, despatches): *m* 1945, Vera Maud, da of late Rev Clifton Samuel Winter; *d* 1982; *s* by his nephew **(18)**, CONOR MYLES JOHN, only son of late Hon Fionn Myles Maryons O'Brien, yst son of 15th Baron, 18th Baron and present peer.

* **(1)** DONOUGH O'BRIEN, PC and MP for co Clare, was *cr* a Baronet 1686; *d* 1717; *s* by his grandson **(2)** Sir EDWARD, 2nd Bt; was MP for Clare; *d* 1765; *s* by his son **(3)** Sir LUCIUS, PC, 3rd Bt, MP for co Clare; *d* 1795; *s* by his son **(4)** Sir EDWARD, 4th Bt, MP for Ennis and co Clare; *d* 1837; *s* by his son **(5)** Sir LUCIUS, 5th Bt, who *s* as 13th Baron Inchiquin (ante).

INCHYRA, BARON (Millar) (Baron UK 1962)

ROBERT CHARLES RENEKE HOYER MILLAR, 2nd Baron; *b* 4 April 1935; *s* 1989; *ed* Eton, and New Coll, Oxford; Gen British Bankers' Assocn Dir Bankers since 1988; late Scots Guards; Member Queen's Body Guard for Scotland (Royal Company of Archers): *m* 1961, Fiona Mary, da of late Edmund Charles Reginald Sheffield (*see* Sheffield, Bt, colls), and has issue.

𝕬rms – Quarterly: 1st, or, a cross moline azure and base barry undy gules and vert, on a chief of the third a lozenge of the first between two spur-revels also of the first, *Millar*; 2nd, per bend argent and vert a lion passant gules, *Hoyer*; 3rd Azure, a chevron argent between two spur-revels in chief and a demi-moon reversed or, *van Swinderen*; 4th, azure, a cross argent cantoned between four roses or, *de Marees*. 𝕮rest – A cubit arm, the hand erect and in the act of blessing proper. 𝕾upporters – Two blackcock proper.
Residence – Rookley Manor, King's Somborne, Stockbridge, Hants SO20 6QX. *Clubs* – White's and Pratt's.

SON LIVING

Hon CHRISTIAN JAMES CHARLES HOYER, *b* 12 Aug 1962; *ed* Eton, and Edinburgh Univ: *m* 1992, Caroline J., da of late Robin Swan, of Lower Wield, Hants. *Residence* – 20 Milson Rd, W14.

DAUGHTERS LIVING

Hon Henrietta Julia Hoyer, *b* 1964: *m* 1988, Carlos Manuel Villanueva Brandt, son of Manuel Villanueva, of Caracas, Venezuela, and has issue living, a son, *b* 1993. *Residence* – 34 Guildford Rd, SW8 2BX.
Hon Louisa Mary Hoyer, *b* 1968.

BROTHER LIVING

Hon Alastair James Harold Hoyer, *b* 1936; *ed* Eton; late Scots Guards; Sec Pilgrim Trust since 1980: *m* 1974, Virginia Margaret Diana, da of late William Perine Macauley, of Ballyward House, Manor Kilbride, co Wicklow (*see* V Camrose), and has issue living, Mark Christian Frederick, *b* 1975, — Martha Harriet Alice, *b* 1976. *Residence* – 16 Pembridge Villas, W11.

SISTERS LIVING AND DECEASED

Hon Elizabeth Anne Hoyer, *b* 1933: *m* 1965, William Euan Wallace, who *d* 1977 (*see* E Lytton, 1964 Edn), and *d* 1990.
Hon Annabel Alice Hoyer, LVO, *b* 1943; a Lady in Waiting to HRH Princess Margaret, Countess of Snowdon 1971-75, an Extra Lady in Waiting 1975-92, since when a Lady in Waiting; LVO 1986: *m* 1973, Christopher James Bovill Whitehead, of 5 Vicarage Gdns, W8, and has issue living, Robert William Bovill, *b* 1977, — (Christina) Daisy Elizabeth, *b* 1975.

WIDOW LIVING OF FIRST BARON

ELIZABETH (*Dowager Baroness Inchyra*), da of late Jonkheer Reneke de Marees van Swinderen, sometime Netherlands Min in London: *m* 1931, the 1st Baron, GCMG, CVO, who *d* 1989. *Residence* – Inchyra House, Glencarse, Perthshire.

PREDECESSOR – (1) FREDERICK ROBERT HOYER Millar, GCMG, CVO, son of late Robert Hoyer Millar; *b* 1900, entered Diplo Ser 1923, 1st Sec at Washington 1939, Min Washington 1948, High Commr German Federal Republic 1953-55, Ambassador 1955-56, and Permanent Under-Sec for Foreign Affairs 1957-61, *cr Baron Inchyra*, of St Madoes, co Perth (peerage of UK 1962): *m* 1931, Elizabeth, da of late Jonkheer Reneke de Marees van Swinderen, formerly Netherlands Min in London; *d* 1989; *s* by his elder son (2) ROBERT CHARLES RENEKE HOYER, 2nd Baron and present peer.

Ingestre, Viscount; son of Earl of Shrewsbury.

INGLEBY, VISCOUNT (Peake) (Viscount UK 1956)

MARTIN RAYMOND PEAKE, 2nd Viscount; *b* 31 May 1926; *s* 1966; *ed* Eton, and Trin Coll, Oxford; Bar Inner Temple 1955; late Lt Coldstream Guards; a Co Councillor of N Riding of Yorks 1964-67: *m* 1952, Susan, da of Capt Henderson Russell Landale, of Ewell Manor, W Farleigh, Maidstone, and has had issue.

Arms – Sable three crosses pattee argent within an orle of eight fleurs-de-lys and a bordure or. **Crest** – A heart gules between two wings displayed erminois. **Supporters** – On either side a Blackfaced Swaledale ram proper holding in the mouth a rose argent barbed seeded slipped and leaved also proper.
Residences – Snilesworth, Northallerton, N Yorks; Flat 1, 61 Onslow Sq, SW7.

SON DECEASED

Hon Richard Martin Herbert, *b* 7 Aug 1953; *ed* Eton; *d* 19 July 1975.

DAUGHTERS LIVING

Hon Fiona Catherine, *b* 1955: *m* 1977, (Gavin) Tobias Alexander Winterbottom Horton (formerly Winterbottom), of Whorlton Cottage, Swainby, Northallerton, N Yorkshire DL6 3ER, nephew of late Baron Winterbottom (Life Baron), and has issue living, George William Arthur, *b* 1983, — Thomas Henry Ralph, *b* 1985, — Alice Emily Rose,
b 1978, — Violet Constance Lily, *b* 1980.
Hon Sarah Rachel, *b* 1958: *m* 1982, James Felton Somers Hervey-Bathurst, and has issue (*see* Hervey-Bathurst, Bt).
Hon Henrietta Cecilia Imogen, *b* 1961: *m* 1990, James J. P. McNeile, elder son of Rory J. McNeile, of Nonsuch, Bromham, Wilts.
Hon Katherine Emma Charlotte, *b* 1963.

SISTERS LIVING (*Daughters of 1st Viscount*)

Hon Iris Irene Adele, LVO, *b* 1923; Lady-in-Waiting to HRH Princess Margaret 1952-62, and an Extra Lady-in-Waiting 1962-63; LVO 1957: *m* 1963, Capt Oliver Payan Dawnay, CVO, of Flat 5, 32 Onslow Sq, SW7, and Wexcombe House, nr Marlborough, Wilts (*see* V Downe, colls), who *d* 1988.
Hon Sonia Mary, *b* 1924: *m* 1st, 1946 (*m diss* 1958), Lt David George Montagu Hay, GC, RNR (later 12th Marquess of Tweeddale); 2ndly, 1966, Maj Michael William Vernon Hammond-Maude, JP, 5th R Inniskilling Dragoon Gds (ret), of Mitton Cottage, Arncliffe, Skipton, N Yorks, and has issue (by 1st *m*) (*see* M Tweeddale).
Hon Mary Rose, *b* 1940: *m* 1959, Major Everard John Robert March Phillipps de Lisle, DL, Roy Horse Guards (ret), and has issue living, Charles Andrew Everard, *b* 1960; *ed* Eton, and Worcester Coll, Oxford; — Timothy John *b* 1962; *ed* Eton and Worcester Coll, Oxford: *m* 1991, Amanda Helen, 2nd da of Clive Julian Stanley Barford, of Pibworth House, Aldworth, Berks (*see* B Ashfield, 1985 Edn), and has issue living, Daniel Barford *b* 1994, — Mary Rosanna, *b* 1968; *ed* St Hugh's Coll, Oxford.
Residences – Stockerston Hall, Uppingham, Leics LE15 9JD; 4 Hereford Mansions, Hereford Rd, W2 5BA.

UNCLE LIVING (*Not in remainder*)

Edward Charles, *b* 1911; *ed* Eton, and at Trin Coll, Camb; Bar Inner Temple 1939; formerly Flight-Lieut RAF Vol Reserve; unsuccessfully contested Blaydon Div of Durham (C) July 1945, and Cleveland Div of N Riding of Yorkshire Feb 1950: *m* 1935, Baroness Santina Maria, da of Baron Alfred von Henikstein, of Salzburg, Austria, and has had issue, Henry Alfred, *b* 1937; *ed* Ampleforth, and Ch Ch, Oxford; *dunm* 1990, — Robert Alexander (96 Campden Hill Rd, W8 7AP), *b* 1938; *ed* Ampleforth, and Trin Coll, Dublin: *m* 1968, Meriel Elizabeth, da of William Lyon Bowie, of Dublin, and has issue living, James Robert William *b* 1978, Lucy Meriel *b* 1972; *ed* Charterhouse, — Christopher George (34 Bettridge Rd, SW6 3QD), *b* 1951; *ed* Ampleforth, and Queens' Coll, Camb: *m* 1993, Ann Marie, only da of John O'Rourke, of Chelsea, SW3, — Marianna Clotilde, *b* 1939: *m* 1974, Maj Rupert Charles Langham, R Corps of Signals, of 5 Bournside Rd, Cheltenham, Glos GL51 5AL, and has issue living, Jonathan Charles *b* 1975, Caroline Mary *b* 1976, — Christina Maria, *b* 1949: *m* 1974, Dr Peter Francis Leadlay of 17 Clarendon Rd, Cambridge CB2 2BH, and has issue living, Francesca Catherine *b* 1978, Louisa Clare *b* 1980, Serena Imogen Alice *b* 1985. *Residence* – 6 Westberry Court, Grange Rd, Cambridge CB3 9BG. *Clubs* – Brooks's, Travellers'.

COLLATERAL BRANCH LIVING

(Not in remainder)

Issue of late Air-Commodore Sir Harald Peake, brother of 1st Viscount, *b* 1899, *d* 1978: *m* 1st, 1933 (*m diss* 1944), Countess Resy de Baillet-Latour, da of Henri, Count Baillet-Latour, of Brussels; 2ndly, 1952, *Dame* Felicity Hyde, DBE, AE, JP (Court Farm, Tackley, Oxon, OX5 3AQ; Flat 5, 35 Bryanston Sq, W1H 7LP), da of late Col Humphrey Watts, OBE, TD, and widow of John Charles Mackenzie Hanbury, P/O RAF:—
(By 1st *m*) David Alphy Edward Raymond (Sezincote, Moreton-in-Marsh, Glos; 15 Ilchester Place, W14), *b* 1934: *m* 1962, Susanna, da of Lt-Cdr Sir Cyril Hugh Kleinwort, RNVR (*see* Kleinwort, Bt, colls), and has issue living, Edward, *b* 1964, — Katharine Sophie, *b* 1965: *m* 1989, Thomas Assheton, and has issue (*see* B Clitheroe). —— (By 2nd *m*) Andrew Charles, *b* 1956: *m* 1990, Suzette Ray, elder da of Sampson Mitchell, DL, of Woore, Shropshire, and has issue living, Alexander, *b* 1993.

PREDECESSOR – **(1)** OSBERT Peake, PC, son of Maj George Herbert Peake; *b* 1897; Under Sec of State for Home Affairs 1939-44, Financial Sec to Treasury 1944-45, Min of National Insurance 1951-55 (and Pensions 1953-55); MP for N Leeds (*C*) 1929-55, and N-E Leeds May to Dec 1955; *cr Viscount Ingleby*, of Snilesworth, N Riding of York (peerage of UK) 1956: *m* 1922, Lady Joan Rachel de Vere Capell, who *d* 1979, da of 7th Earl of Essex; *d* 1966; *s* by his only son **(2)**, MARTIN RAYMOND, 2nd Viscount and present peer.

INGLEWOOD, BARON (Fletcher-Vane) (Baron UK 1964)

(WILLIAM) RICHARD FLETCHER-VANE, MEP, 2nd Baron; *b* 31 July 1951; *s* 1989; *ed* Eton, Trin Coll, Camb (MA), and Cumbria Coll of Agriculture and Forestry; DL Cumbria 1993; Bar Lincoln's Inn 1975; ARICS; British Conservative Spokesman Cttee on Legal Affairs since 1989; Chief Whip British Conservative Group since 1994; Member Lake District Special Planning Board 1984-89, and NW Water Authority 1987-89; MEP Cumbria and Lancashire North since 1989; ARICS: *m* 1986, Cressida R., photographer, yst da of late Alan Desmond Frederick Pemberton-Pigott, CMG, of Fawe Park, Keswick, and has issue.

Arms – Azure three sinister gauntlets or. **Crest** – A dexter hand in armour couped at the wrist proper, holding a sword argent pommel and hilt or. **Supporters** – On either side a roebuck proper collared and pendent from the collar a pheon argent.
Seat – Hutton-in-the-Forest, Penrith, Cumbria CA11 9TH. *Clubs* – Travellers', Pratt's.

SON LIVING

Hon HENRY WILLIAM FREDERICK, *b* 24 Dec 1990.

DAUGHTERS LIVING

Hon Miranda Mary, *b* 1987.
Hon Rosa Katharine, *b* 1989.

BROTHER LIVING

Hon Christopher John, *b* 1953; *ed* Eton, and Trin Coll, Camb (MA); Bar Inner Temple 1976: *m* 1990, Margaret M., da of late Dr Paul Eisenklam, of London, and has issue living, Francis William Paul, *b* 1992, — Olivia Evelyn Mary, *b* 1991. *Residences* – 41 Larkspur Terrace, Jesmond, Newcastle upon Tyne NE2 2DT; Morton House, Morton, Calthwaite, Penrith, Cumbria CA11 9PZ. *Clubs* – Travellers', Northern Counties (Newcastle upon Tyne).

PREDECESSOR – **(1)** WILLIAM MORGAN Fletcher-Vane, TD, son of late Col Hon William Lyonel Vane (*see* B Barnard colls), *b* 1909, assumed by deed poll 1931 the surname of Fletcher-Vane in lieu of his patronymic, Joint Parl Sec to Min of Pensions and National Insurance 1958-60, and to Min of Agriculture 1960-62, Leader of UK Delegation to World Food Congress (FAO) Washington 1963, MP for Westmorland (*C*) 1945-64, DL Westmorland, *cr Baron Inglewood*, of Hutton in the Forest, co Cumberland (peerage of UK) 1964: *m* 1949, Mary, who *d* 1982, eldest da of late Maj Sir Richard George Proby, 1st Bt, MC; *d* 1989; *s* by his elder son **(2)** WILLIAM RICHARD, 2nd Baron and present peer.

INGROW, BARON (Taylor) (Life Baron 1982)

JOHN AKED TAYLOR, OBE, TD, son of late Percy Taylor, of Knowle Spring House, Keighley, by his wife Gladys Broster (who *m* 2ndly, Sir (John) Donald Horsfall, 2nd Bt); *b* 15 Aug 1917; *ed* Shrewsbury; served in 1939-45 War (Major, Duke of Wellington's Regt and Royal Signals); Member Keighley Town Council 1946-67; Mayor 1956; Vice Lord-Lieut West Yorkshire 1976-85, Lord Lieut 1985-92; JP (1949) Borough of Keighley; DL West Yorkshire 1971; TD 1951; *cr* OBE (Civil) 1960, Knt 1972, and *Baron Ingrow*, of Keighley, co W Yorks (Life Baron) 1982: *m* 1949, Barbara Mary, da of Percy Wright Stirk, of Crestmead, Keighley, and has issue.

Arms – Vert two chevronels between in chief as many garbs of barley and in base a talbot sejant or holding in the mouth an arrow in bend the head downwards proper. **Crest** – A demi talbot or holding in the mouth an arrow in bend the head downwards proper. **Supporters** – *Dexter*, a shire horse arg harnessed and bridled proper; *Sinister*, a lion or head and mane gules gorged with a chaplet of roses arg barbed and seeded proper, the compartment comprising a grassy mount growing therefrom on each side a rose arg barbed, seeded and leaved proper between two sprigs of oak fructed also proper.
Residence – Fieldhead, Keighley, West Yorkshire.

DAUGHTERS LIVING

Hon Anne Elizabeth, *b* 1951: *m* 1975, Charles Jonathan Dent, of Ribston Hall, Wetherby, Yorks, elder son of John Harker Dent.
Hon Diana Mary, *b* 1953: *m* 1979, John Patrick Dent, of Clock Farm, Hunsingore, Yorks, yr son of John Harker Dent.

INMAN, BARONY OF (Inman) (Extinct 1979)

DAUGHTER LIVING OF FIRST BARON

Hon Rosemary, *b* 1933: *m* 1st, 1955 (*m diss* 1982), Nickolas Kollitsis, MD, FRCS; 2ndly, 1982, Dr Raphael Eban, FRCP, FRCR, and has issue living (by 1st *m*), Philip Milton, *b* 1957, — Marina Christallene, *b* 1956, — Alexandra, *b* 1961. *Residence* – Parsonage House, Goosey, Oxon.

WIDOW LIVING OF SON OF FIRST BARON

Judith (c/o Fuengirola Car Hire Ltd, Edificio Mediterraneo, Fuengirola, Malaga, Spain), da of Albert George James Gibbins, of Mount Pleasant, Stocklane, Langford, Bristol: *m* 1st, 1966, as his 3rd wife, Hon Philip John Inman, who *d* 1968, only son of 1st Baron; 2ndly, 1970, Jonathan Fitzuryan Rhys Wingfield (*see* V Powerscourt, colls).

COLLATERAL BRANCH LIVING

Issue of late Hon Philip John Inman, only son of 1st Baron, *b* 1929; *d* 1968: *m* 1st, 1952 (*m diss* 1957), Jennifer, da of George Clark; 2ndly, 1957 (*m diss* 1964), Denise, da of Mme Brisson; 3rdly, 1966, Judith (ante), (who *m* 2ndly, 1970, Jonathan Fitzuryan Rhys Wingfield, *see* V Powerscourt, colls), da of Albert George James Gibbins:—
(By 1st *m*) Althea Rosalind, *b* 1954.

INVERFORTH, BARON (Weir) (Baron UK 1919)

ANDREW PETER WEIR, 4th Baron; *b* 16 Nov 1966; *s* 1982.

Arms – On a fesse azure, between in chief an escutcheon per bend azure and gules, charged with a bend sinister gules and azure a bend argent, and in base an ancient galley, flags flying to the dexter gules, three mullets of the first. **Crest** – A dexter and sinister hand couped at the wrists proper supporting an ancient galley as in the arms. **Supporters** – On either side a sail or of the Mercantile Marine.
Residence – 27 Hyde Park St, W2 2JS.

SISTER LIVING

Hon Clarinda Jane, *b* 1968: *m* 1994, Jonathan S.H.A. Kane, son of Douglas Kane.

UNCLE LIVING (*Son of 2nd Baron*)

Hon (JOHN) VINCENT (85 Whitehall Ct, SW1A 2EL), *b* 8 Feb 1935; *ed* Malvern; late Chm Andrew Weir Group.

WIDOW LIVING OF SECOND BARON

IRIS BERYL (*Iris, Baroness Inverforth*) (24 Clarence Terr, Regents Park, NW1 4RD), da of late Charles Vincent, 4th Bn The Buffs: *m* 1929, the 2nd Baron, who *d* 1975.

Through labour to honour

WIDOW LIVING OF THIRD BARON

JILL ELIZABETH (*Baroness Inverforth*) (27 Hyde Park St, W2), da of late John Ward Thornycroft, CBE, of Steyne, Bembridge, I of W: *m* 1966, the 3rd Baron, who *d* 1982.

PREDECESSORS – **(1)** *Rt Hon* ANDREW WEIR, PC, *b* 1865; senior partner in the firm of Andrew Weir & Co, shipowners and merchants, Surveyor-Gen of Supply, War Office and a Member of Army Council 1917-19, and Min of Munitions 1919-21; *cr Baron Inverforth*, of Southgate, co Middlesex (peerage of United Kingdom) 1919: *m* 1889, Anne, who *d* 1941, yr da of late Thomas Kay Dowie; *d* 1955; *s* by his only son **(2)** ANDREW ALEXANDER MORTON, 2nd Baron; *b* 1897: *m* 1929, Iris Beryl, da of late Charles Vincent, 4th Bn The Buffs; *d* 1975; *s* by his el son **(3)** (ANDREW CHARLES) ROY, 3rd Baron, *b* 1932: *m* 1966, Jill Elizabeth, da of late John Ward Thornycroft, CBE; *d* 1982; *s* by his only son **(4)** ANDREW PETER, 4th Baron and present peer.

Inverurie, Lord; son of Earl of Kintore.

Ipswich, Viscount; grandson of Duke of Grafton.

IRONSIDE, BARON (Ironside) (Baron UK 1941)

EDMUND OSLAC IRONSIDE, 2nd Baron; *b* 21 Sept 1924; *s* 1959; *ed* Tonbridge; Lt (ret) RN; Coronation Medal 1953, Hon FCGI 1987; 1939-45 War: *m* 1950, Audrey Marigold, yst da of late Col Hon Thomas George Breadalbane Morgan-Grenville, DSO, OBE, MC (*see*Ly Kinloss, colls), and has issue.

Arms – Per bend sable and gules, on a bend argent a bendlet wavy azure, in sinister chief a garb or, and in base a lion salient or, and in fess a gauntletted dexter hand grasping a sword paleways argent hilted or. **Crest** – A dexter gauntletted hand grasping a sword paleways argent hilted and pommelled or. **Supporters** – Two bull terriers proper.
Residence – Priory House, Old House Lane, Boxted, Colchester, Essex CO4 5RB.

SON LIVING

Hon CHARLES EDMUND GRENVILLE (46 Mayford Rd, SW12 8SN), *b* 1 July 1956: *m* 1985, Hon Elizabeth Mary Law, eldest da of 2nd Baron Coleraine, and has issue living, Frederick Thomas Grenville, *b* 22 April 1991, — Emily Charlotte Olivia, *b* 1988, — Alice Octavia Louise, *b* 1990.

DAUGHTER LIVING

Hon Fiona Georgina, *b* 1954: *m* 1978, Roland Maclean Jack, of The Old Vicarage, Lyford, Wantage, Oxon, and has issue living, Oliver Edmund Maclean, *b* 1983, — Anthea Audrey Charlotte, *b* 1985.

SISTER LIVING

Hon Elspeth Mariot, *b* 1917: *m* 1941, Capt Andrew Gilbert Hendry, Black Watch (Roy Highland Regt), who *d* 1987, and has issue living, Michael Andrew, *b* 1942, *ed* Stanbridge Earls Sch, Romsey, — John Edmund Gordon (4 Royal Circus, Edinburgh), *b* 1949: *m* 1979, Gillian Margaret, da of David Young, of Sheilds House, Newtonhill, Kincardineshire, and has issue living, Edmund John Ironside *b* 1988, Johanna Katherine *b* 1981, Sophia Elizabeth Hariot *b* 1984, — David Robert Charles, *b* 1955. *Residence* – 4 Easter Ferrygate, Abbotsford Rd, N Berwick, E Lothian EH39 5DD.

PREDECESSOR – (1) *Field Marshal Sir* (WILLIAM) EDMUND Ironside, GCB, CMG, DSO, Hon LLD, son of late Surg-Maj William Ironside, RHA; *b* 1880; S Africa 1899-1902, special serv 1902-04, European War 1914-19, finally as Chief of Staff Comdg-in-Ch Allied Forces at Archangel, N Russia; Ismid 1920; GOC NW Persia 1920-21, European War 1939-40; was Comdt of Staff Coll 1922-6, 2nd Div, Aldershot 1926-8, and Meerut Dist 1928-31, Lieut Gov of Tower of London 1931-3, appointed QMG of Army in India 1933, Gen Officer Comdg-in-Ch, E Command 1936, ADC-Gen to HM 1937-40; Gov and Com-in-Ch, Gibraltar 1938-39, Inspector-Gen of Overseas Forces July 1939, and Ch of Imperial Gen Staff Sept 1939; Com-in-Ch Home Forces, May to July 1940; Col Comdt RA 1932-47; *cr Baron Ironside*, of Archangel, and of Ironside, co Aberdeen (peerage of United Kingdom) 1941: *m* 1915, Mariot Ysabel, who *d* 1984, da of late Charles Cheyne, ISC; *d* 1959; *s* by his only son (2) EDMUND OSLAC, 2nd Baron and present peer.

IRVINE OF LAIRG, BARON (Irvine) (Life Baron 1987)

ALEXANDER ANDREW MACKAY IRVINE, son of Alexander Irvine, by his wife Margaret Christina, da of late Alexander MacMillan; *b* 23 June 1940: *ed* Inverness Acad, Hutchesons' Boys' Gram Sch, Glasgow, Glasgow Univ (MA, LLB), and Christ's Coll, Camb (BA, LLB); Bar Inner Temple 1967, QC 1978, Bencher 1985; Univ Lecturer LSE 1965-69; a Recorder 1985-88; *cr Baron Irvine of Lairg*, of Lairg, District of Sutherland (Life Baron) 1987: *m* 1974, Alison Mary, yst da of Dr James Shaw McNair, MD, and has issue.
Address – 11 King's Bench Walk, Temple, EC4Y 7EQ. *Club* – Garrick.

SONS LIVING

Hon David, *b* 1974.
Hon Alastair, *b* 1976.

IRVING OF DARTFORD, BARONY OF (Irving) (Extinct 1989)

SON LIVING OF LIFE BARON

Hon Stephen John (25 Princes Av, Dartford, Kent DA2 6NF), *b* 1959; *ed* Dartford Gram Sch: *m* 1984, Lesley Anne, yr da of late (Richard) Neil Herbert, of Wilmington, Kent, and has issue living, James Richard, *b* 1994, — Emily Rebecca, *b* 1990.

DAUGHTER LIVING OF LIFE BARON

Hon Susan Anne, *b* 1946: *m* 1966, John House, of 4 The Turnpike, Ely, Cambs CB7 4JJ, only son of late John House, and has issue living, Katharine Anne, *b* 1969, — Victoria Julienne, *b* 1971, — (Alison) Louise, *b* 1973.

WIDOW LIVING OF LIFE BARON

MILDRED (*Baroness Irving of Dartford*), da of Charlton Weedy, of Morpeth, Northumberland: *m* 1942, Baron Irving of Dartford, PC (Life Baron), who *d* 1989. *Residence* – 10 Tynedale Close, Dartford, Kent.

Irwin, Lord; son of Earl of Halifax.

ISMAY, BARONY OF (Ismay) (Extinct 1965)

DAUGHTERS LIVING OF FIRST BARON

Hon Susan Katharine (The Bothy, Wormington Grange, Broadway, Worcs) *b* 1922: *m* 1st, 1942 (*m diss* 1946), Maj Neville Ewart Hyde Chance; 2ndly, 1949, Lieut-Col Michael John Evetts, MC, RHF, son of late Lt-Gen Sir John Fullerton Evetts, CB, CBE, MC, and has issue living, (by 1st *m*) Patricia Kathleen, *b* 1942: *m* 1963, David Henry Smyly (*see* By Buckland, 1980 Edn), and has issue living, Giles Richard Ismay *b* 1966, Susannah Louise *b* 1964, — (by 2nd *m*) John Hastings (Wormington Grange, nr Broadway, Worcs) *b* 1951: *m* 1980, Mrs Caroline Fiona Jane Tropman, da of David Lucius Shakespeare Vardy, of Abbeylands, Stackhouse, Settle, Yorkshire, and has issue living. Matthew John *b* 1987, Lucy Katherine *b* 1989, — James Michael Ismay (Ryefield House, Wormington, Broadway, Worcs). *b* 1953: *m* 1986, Peta Jeanette, only da of Ridley Lamb, of Boville Park, Osmotherley, N Yorks, and has issue living, Thomas Ridley Becher *b* 1989, Camilla Alice *b* 1987.
Hon Sarah Field, *b* 1928: *m* 1948 (*m diss* 198-), 3rd Viscount Allendale. *Residences* – Bywell Hall, Stocksfield-on-Tyne, Northumberland, and Allenheads Hall, Allenheads, Northumberland.
Hon Mary Quenelda, *b* 1929: *m* 1st, 1952, Robert Mervyn Fitz Finnis, who *d* 1955; 2ndly, 1957, Major George Raymond Seymour, CVO (*see* M Hertford, colls), and has issue living (by 1st *m*) Jane Laura, *b* 1953: *m* 1975, Peter Butselaar, of Melbourne, Australia, and has issue living, Nicholas Peter *b* 1981, Emily Kate *b* 1978, Vanessa Mary *b* 1987, — Sarah Lavinia, *b* 1955: *m* 1987, Mark C. G. Menzies, yr son of Michael Menzies, of Oyster Bay, New York, and has issue living,

Angus *b* 1989, Harry *b* 1991, Amelia *b* 1993, — (by 2nd *m*) (*see* M Hertford, colls). *Residence* – The Old Vicarage, Bucklebury, nr Reading, Berks.

IVEAGH, EARL OF (Guinness) (Earl UK 1919, Bt UK 1885)
(Title pronounced "Iver")

SPES MEA IN DEO

My hope is in God

ARTHUR EDWARD RORY GUINNESS, 4th Earl, and 4th Baronet; *b* 10 Aug 1969; *s* 1992.

Arms – Quarterly; 1st and 4th, per saltire gules and azure, a lion rampant, or; on a chief ermine a dexter hand couped at the wrist of the first, *Guinness*; 2nd and 3rd argent, on a fesse between three crescents sable a trefoil slipped or, *Lee*. **Crests** – 1st, a boar passant, quarterly or and gules; 2nd, on a pillar argent, encircled by a ducal coronet or, an eagle preying on a bird's leg erased proper. **Supporters** – Two stags gules, collared gemmel and attired or, each resting a hind hoof upon an escutcheon vert, charged with a lion rampant or.
Address – Iveagh House, 41 Harrington Gdns, SW7 4JU.

BROTHER LIVING

RORY MICHAEL BENJAMIN, *b* 12 Dec 1974.

SISTERS LIVING

Lady Emma Lavinia, *b* 1963; *ed* Lincoln Coll, Oxford.
Lady Louisa Jane, *b* 1967.

AUNTS LIVING AND DECEASED (*sisters of 3rd Earl*) (*raised to the rank of an Earl's daughters* 1969)

Lady Elizabeth Maria, *b* 1939; JP Berks: *m* 1st, 1960 (*m diss* 1990), David Hugh Lavallin Nugent (*see* Nugent, Bt, *cr* 1795); 2ndly, 1992, as his 2nd wife, (Robert) Martin Mays-Smith. *Residence* – Chaddleworth House, Chaddleworth, Newbury, Berks.
Lady Henrietta, *b* 1942: *m* (3 Feb) 1978, Luigi Marinori, of Spoleto, Italy, and *d* (3 May) 1978, leaving issue, Sara, *b* 1977.

GREAT AUNTS LIVING (*daughters of 2nd Earl*)

Lady Patricia Florence Susan (*Patricia, Viscountess Boyd of Merton*), *b* 1918: *m* 1938, 1st Viscount Boyd of Merton, who *d* 1983. *Residences* – 2 Bloomfield Terrace, SW1; Ince Castle, Saltash, Cornwall PL12 4RA.
Lady Brigid Katharine Rachel, *b* 1920: *m* 1st, 30 July 1945, HRH Prince Friedrich Georg Wilhelm Christoph of Prussia, who *d* 1966 (*see* ROYAL FAMILY); 2ndly, 3 July 1967, Maj Anthony Patrick Ness, who *d* 1993. *Residence* – Patmore Hall, Hadham, Herts.

MOTHER LIVING

Miranda Daphne Jane, da of late Maj (Charles) Michael Smiley, of Castle Fraser, Aberdeenshire (*see* Smiley, Bt, colls): *m* 1963 (*m diss* 1984), the 3rd Earl, who *d* 1992. *Residence* – 5 Cottesmore Gdns, W8 5PR.

COLLATERAL BRANCHES LIVING

Issue of late Hon (Arthur) Ernest Guinness, 2nd son of 1st Earl, *b* 1876, *d* 1949: *m* 1903, Marie Clotilde, who *d* 1953, da of Sir George Russell, MP, 4th Bt (*cr* 1812):—
Aileen Sibell Mary PLUNKET, *b* 1904; has resumed the surname of Plunket: *m* 1st, 1927 (*m diss* 1940), Flight-Lieut Hon Brinsley Sheridan Bushe Plunket, RAF Vol Reserve, who *d* on active ser 1941 (*see* B Plunket, colls); 2ndly, 1956 (*m diss* 1965), Valerian Stux-Rybar. *Residence* – Old Mead, Elsenham, nr Bishops Stortford, Herts. ⸺ Maureen Constance (*Maureen, Marchioness of Dufferin and Ava*), *b* 1907: *m* 1st, 1930, 4th Marquess of Dufferin and Ava, who was *ka* in Burma 1945; 2ndly, 1948 (*m diss* 1954), Major (Harry Alexander) Desmond Buchanan, MC; 3rdly, 1955, His Honour Judge John Cyril Maude (*see* V Hawarden, colls), who *d* 1986. *Residences* – 4 Hans Crescent, SW1; The Owl House, Lamberhurst, Kent. ⸺ Oonagh, *b* 1910: *m* 1st, 1929 (*m diss* 1936), Hon Philip Leyland Kindersley (*see* B Kindersley); 2ndly, 1936 (*m diss* 1950), 4th Baron Oranmore and Browne; 3rdly, 1957, Miguel Ferreras. *Residence* – Luggala, Roundwood, co Wicklow.

Descendants of late Rt Hon Walter Edward Guinness, DSO (3rd son of 1st Earl), who was *cr Baron Moyne* 1932 (see that title).

PREDECESSORS – (1) *Sir* EDWARD CECIL Guinness, KP, GCVO, 3rd son of Sir Benjamin Lee Guinness, MP, 1st Bt, by Elizabeth, who *d* 1865, 3rd da of late Edward Guinness, of Dublin; *b* 1847; High Sheriff for Dublin City 1876; *cr* a *Baronet* 1885, *Baron Iveagh*, of Iveagh, co Down (peerage of United Kingdom) 1891, KP 1897, *Viscount Iveagh*, of Iveagh, co Down (peerage of United Kingdom) 1905, GCVO 1910, and *Earl of Iveagh*, and *Viscount Elveden*, of Elveden, co Suffolk (peerage of United Kingdom) 1919: *m* 1873, Adelaide Maria, who *d* 1916, da of late Richard Samuel Guinness, MP for Barnstaple (B Ardilaun, colls); *d* 1927; *s* by his son (2) RUPERT EDWARD CECIL LEE, KG, CB, CMG, 2nd Earl; *b* 1874; Chm of Arthur Guinness, Son & Co 1927-62, Chancellor Dublin Univ 1927-63; MP for Haggerston Div, Shoreditch (*C*) 1908-10, S-E Essex 1912-18, and Southend-on-Sea 1918-27; S Africa 1900 (despatches, medal, CMG): *m* 1903, Lady Gwendolen Florence Mary Onslow, CBE, who *d* 1966, da of 4th Earl of Onslow; *d* 1967; *s* by his grandson (3) ARTHUR FRANCIS BENJAMIN (only son of Maj Arthur Onslow Edward, Viscount Elveden (by his wife, Lady Elizabeth Cecilia Hare, OBE, who *d* 1990, having *m* 2ndly, 1947, (Edward) Rory More O'Ferrall, who *d* 1991, yr da of 4th Earl of Listowel), 2nd son of 2nd Earl), 3rd Earl; *b* 1937; Chm Guinness Group: *m* 1963 (*m diss* 1984), Miranda Daphne Jane, da of late Maj (Charles) Michael Smiley, of Castle Fraser, Aberdeenshire (*see* Smiley, Bt, colls); *d* 1992; *s* by his elder son (4) ARTHUR EDWARD RORY, 4th Earl and present peer; also Viscount Iveagh, Viscount Elveden, and Baron Iveagh.

JACKSON OF BURNLEY, BARONY OF (Jackson) (Extinct 1970)

DAUGHTERS LIVING OF LIFE BARON

Hon Anne Boswall, *b* 1939: *m* 1967, David Garner Freeston, and has issue.
Hon Ruth Lesley, *b* 1945: *m* 1970, David John Moffatt, of 191 Myton Rd, Warwick, and has issue.

WIDOW LIVING OF LIFE BARON

MARY ELIZABETH (*Baroness Jackson of Burnley*), da of Dr Robert Oliphant Boswall: *m* 1938, Baron Jackson of Burnley (Life Baron), who *d* 1970. *Residence* – Flat 6, Ritchie Court, 380 Banbury Rd, Oxford.

JACKSON OF LODSWORTH, BARONY OF (Jackson) (Extinct 1981)

SON LIVING OF LIFE BARONESS

Hon Robert Ward, *b* 1956: *m* 1978, Caroline Benedik, da of late Richardson Peele, of Grey House, Stow-on-the-Wold, Glos.

JACOBSON, BARONY OF (Jacobson) (Extinct 1988)

SONS LIVING OF LIFE BARON

Hon Philip (29 Carmalt Gdns, SW15), *b* 1938; Paris correspondent *The Times*: *m* 1967, Ann, da of late Gilbert Mathison.
Hon Colin (48 Parkway, NW1), *b* 1941: *m* 1972, Josephine, da of John William Gates.

DAUGHTER LIVING OF LIFE BARON

Hon Pamela (Witteys Lane, Thorncombe, nr Chard, Som), *b* 1944.

WIDOW LIVING OF LIFE BARON

PHYLLIS JUNE (*Baroness Jacobson*), da of late Frank S. Buck: *m* 1938, Baron Jacobson, MC (Life Baron), who *d* 1988. *Residence* – 6 Avenue Rd, St Albans, Herts.

JACQUES, BARON (Jacques) (Life Baron 1968)

JOHN HENRY JACQUES, son of Thomas Dobson Jacques, of Ashington, Northumberland; *b* 11 Jan 1905; *ed* Co-op Coll, Manchester, and Victoria Univ, Manchester (BA Com); a JP of Portsmouth; Managing Sec, Moorsley Co-op Soc, co Durham 1925-29, Tutor, Co-op Coll, Manchester 1929-42, accountant Plymouth Co-op Soc 1942-45, and Ch Exec Officer, Portsea Island (Portsmouth) Co-op Soc 1945-65; Pres of Co-op Congress 1961; Mem Retail Consortium Council 1963-70; Chm of Co-op Union 1964-70; Pres Distributive Trades Educational and Training Council 1971-75; a Lord-in-Waiting to HM 1974-77; a Dep Speaker, House of Lords since 1977; *cr Baron Jacques*, of Portsea Island, co Southampton (Life Baron) 1968: *m* 1929, Constance, da of Harry White, of Bournville, Birmingham, and has issue.
Club - Co-operative (Portsmouth).

SONS LIVING

Hon Cecil Philip, *b* 1930; BSc (Hons) London: *m* 1st 1960 (*m diss* 1978), Rita Ann Florence Hurford; 2nd 1983, Carrine Royston, *née* Johnson, and has issue (by 1st *m*), John, *b* 1962, — Neil, *b* 1963.
Hon Paul (Pinestead, 1(b) Twentylands Drive, East Leake, Loughborough, Leics), *b* 1932; MB, ChBEd: *m* 1958, Nina Mollie MacKenzie, and has issue.

DAUGHTER LIVING

Hon Anne, *b* 1941.

JAKOBOVITS, BARON (Jakobovits) (Life Baron 1988)

IMMANUEL JAKOBOVITS, son of Rabbi Julius Jakobovits, of Konigsberg, Germany; *b* 8 Feb 1921; *ed* London Univ, Jews' Coll, London, and Yeshivah Etz Chaim, London; Minister of three London synagogues 1941-49, Chief Rabbi of Ireland 1949-58, Rabbi Fifth Ave Synagogue, New York 1958-67, Chief Rabbi of The United Hebrew Congregations of the British Commonwealth of Nations 1967-91, since when Emeritus Chief Rabbi; author; *cr* Kt 1981, and *Baron Jakobovits*, of Regent's Park in Greater London (Life Baron) 1988: *m* 1949, Amelie, da of Rabbi Elie Munk, of Paris, and has issue.
Address – 44A Albert Rd, NW4 2SJ.

SONS LIVING

Hon Julian, *b* 1950; doctor: *m* 1973, Michelle Tauber, and has issue living, Nechemya, *b* 1974, — David, *b* 1975, — Nathan, *b* 1977, — Elie, *b* 1982, — Jeremy, *b* 1985, — Penina, *b* 1979, — Tzippora, *b* 1981, — Sima, *b* 1988.
Hon Samuel, *b* 1951; Rabbi: *m* 1973, Ester Gitel Kahana, and has issue living, Yaacov, *b* 1979, — Shraga Feitel, *b* 1975, — Zipora, *b* 1977, — Yehudit, *b* 1988.

DAUGHTERS LIVING

Hon Esther, *b* 1953: *m* 1971, Rabbi Chaim Zundel Pearlman, and has issue living, Yehuda, *b* 1972, — Eliezer, *b* 1974, — Ephraim, *b* 1978, — Eliyohu, *b* 1982, — Daniel, *b* 1985, — Zipporah, *b* 1976, — Adina, *b* 1980, — Sarah, *b* 1988.
Hon Jeanette, *b* 1956: *m* 1977, Norman David Turner, and has issue living, Ezriel, *b* 1978, — Yehuda, *b* 1981, — Elie, *b* 1983, — Hadassa, *b* 1979, — Ayala, *b* 1987, — Simcha, *b* 1994.
Hon Aviva, *b* 1958: *m* 1978, Dr Joseph Samuel Adler, and has issue living, Pierre, *b* 1979, — Nathan, *b* 1980, — Abraham, *b* 1989, — Tobi, *b* 1992, — Ann, *b* 1982, — Tzippora, *b* 1983, — Gila, *b* 1985.
Hon Elisheva, *b* 1966: *m* 1985, Sam Eli Homburger, and has issue living, Meir, *b* 1986, — Pinchos Jacob, *b* 1988, — Yehoshua, *b* 1990, — Isaac Aryeh, *b* 1992, — Avigail Esther, *b* 1987.

JAMES OF HOLLAND PARK, BARONESS (White) (Life Baroness 1991)

PHYLLIS DOROTHY JAMES, OBE, da of late Sydney Victor James; *b* 3 Aug 1920; *ed* Cambridge High Sch for Girls; Assoc Fellow Downing Coll, Camb 1986, Hon DLitt Buckingham 1992, and London 1993; FRSL, FRSA; JP Willesden 1979-82, Inner London 1984; Administrator NHS 1949-68; Principal Police and Criminal Policy Dept, Home Office, 1968-79; novelist, author (as P. D. James) of *Cover Her Face* (1962), *A Mind to Murder* (1963), *Unnatural Causes* (1967), *Shroud for a Nightingale* (1971), *The Maul and the Peartree* (with T. A. Critchley, 1971), *An Unsuitable Job for a Woman* (1972), *The Black Tower* (1975), *Death of an Expert Witness* (1977), *Innocent Blood* (1980), *The Skull Beneath the Skin* (1982), *A Taste for Death* (1986), and *Devices and Desires* (1989), *The Children of Men* (1992), *Original Sin* (1994); Member BBC Gen Advisory Council 1987-88, Arts Council 1988-92 (Chm Literature Advisory Panel 1988-92), British Council 1988-93 (Literature Advisory Cttee since 1988); Chm Booker Prize Panel of Judges 1987, and Soc of Authors 1984-86; a Gov BBC 1988-93; Member Detection Club; OBE (Civil) 1983, *cr Baroness James of Holland Park*, of Southwold, co Suffolk (Life Baroness) 1991: *m* 1941, Connor Bantry White, who *d* 1964, and has issue.

Arms – Vert, between two oak trees eradicated or a bend sinister wavy argent, thereon another azure charged with a quill pen argent, the quill or, a chief azure issuant thereon a representation of Southwold Lighthouse proper. **Supporters** – On either side a tabby cat salient guardant proper wearing a collar vert, edged, buckled and studded or, reposing the exterior paw upon an open book, the pages lettered proper edged or and bound gules each upright on a set of two closed books edged or, their spines outward, one bound vert lying on top of the other azure.
Address – c/o Greene & Heaton Ltd, 37 Goldhawk Rd, W12 8QQ.

DAUGHTERS LIVING

Hon Clare Bantry, *b* 1942: *m* 1963, Lyn Flook.
Hon Jane Bantry, *b* 1944: *m* 1972, Peter Duncan McLeod.

JAMES OF RUSHOLME, BARONY OF (James) (Extinct 1992)

SON LIVING OF LIFE BARON

Hon Oliver Francis Wintour (Sleightholmedale, Kirkbymoorside, York), *b* 1943; *ed* Winchester, and Balliol Coll, Oxford (MA, BM, BCh): *m* 1965, Rosanna, el da of late Maj Gordon Bentley Foster, of Sleightholme Dale, Fadmoor, York (*see* B Revelstoke, colls), and has issue living, Patrick Esmond, *b* 1967, — Helen, *b* 1970.

WIDOW LIVING OF LIFE BARON

CORDELIA MARY (*Baroness James of Rusholme*), da of Maj-Gen FitzGerald Wintour, CB, CBE (*see* Foster, Bt (ext), 1980 Edn): *m* 1939, Baron James of Rusholme (Life Baron), who *d* 1992. *Residence* – Penhill Cottage, W Witton, Leyburn, N Yorks.

JANNER, BARONY OF (Janner) (Extinct 1982)

SON LIVING OF LIFE BARON

Hon Greville Ewan, QC, MP (House of Commons, SW1); *b* 1928; *ed* Bishop's Coll Sch Quebec, St Paul's Sch, London, and Trin Hall, Camb (MA) and Harvard Law Sch; Hon PhD Haifa Univ; Bar Middle Temple 1954; Pres Board of Deputies of British Jews 1979-85; Pres Commonwealth Jewish Council; Exec World Jewish Congress; Chm Select Cttee on Employment;

non-Exec Dir Ladbroke plc; FIPM 1976; MP for NW Leicester (*Lab*), 1970 to Feb 1974, since when for Leicester, West: *m* 1955, Myra Louise, da of Emmanuel Sheink, of Melbourne, Vic, and has issue.

DAUGHTER LIVING OF LIFE BARON

Hon Ruth Joan Gertrude Rahle (*Baroness Morris of Kenwood*); *b* 1932; *ed* St Paul's Girls' Sch; Solicitor 1956; Chm Dept of Social Security Appeals Tribunal, Pres Habonim Dror, Trustee Rowan Educn Trust, Dir and Trustee Womankind Worldwide, Exec Memb Steering and Management Cttee Women of the Year Luncheon (Greater London Fund for the Blind): *m* 1958, 2nd Baron Morris of Kenwood. *Residence* – Lawn Cottage, Orchard Rise, Kingston upon Thames, Surrey.

WIDOW LIVING OF LIFE BARON

ELSIE SYBIL (*Baroness Janner*), CBE, JP(45 Morpeth Mansions, Morpeth Terrace, SW1), da of late Joseph Cohen; CBE (Civil) 1968; JP Inner Lon; Freedom of the City of London 1975; Chm Stonham Memorial Trust since 1976, Pres Stonham Housing Assocn, Fellow Inst of Advanced Motorists, etc; former Chm Juvenile Courts Panel; Pres of Brady Clubs and Settlement; Dep Chm Mitchell City of London Trust; Vice-Pres The Magistrates' Assoc; author of *Barnett Janner — a Personal Portrait*: *m* 1927, Baron Janner (Life Baron), who *d* 1982.

JAUNCEY OF TULLICHETTLE, BARON (Jauncey) (Life Baron 1988)

CHARLES ELIOT JAUNCEY, only child of late Capt John Henry Jauncey, DSO, RN, of Tullichettle, Comrie, Perthshire; *b* 8 May 1925; *ed* Radley, Ch Ch Oxford (MA 1953, Hon Student 1990) and Glasgow Univ (LLB 1949); late Sub Lieut RNVR, served European War 1943-46; Advocate Scottish Bar 1949, Standing Jnr Counsel to Admiralty 1954, Kintyre Pursuivant of Arms 1955-71, Hon Sheriff Substitute of Perthshire 1962, QC 1963, Sheriff Principal of Fife and Kinross 1971-74, Judge of the Courts of Appeal of Jersey and Guernsey 1972-79, a Lord of Session in Scotland 1979, a Lord of Appeal in Ordinary since 1988; Member of Royal Co of Archers (The Queen's Body Guard for Scotland) 1951; Memb Historic Buildings Council for Scotland 1971-92; *cr Baron Jauncey of Tullichettle*, of Comrie, in the District of Perth and Kinross 1988: *m* 1st, 1948 (*m diss* 1969), Jean, only da of late Adm Sir Angus Edward Malise Bontine Cunninghame Graham, KBE, CB, of Ardoch, Cardross, Dunbartonshire; 2ndly, 1973 (*m diss* 1977), Elizabeth, widow of Maj John Ballingal, MC, and da of Capt R. H. V. Sivewright, DSC, RN; 3rdly, 1977, (Sarah) Camilla, yst da of late Lt-Col Charles Frederick Cathcart, DSO (*see* E Cathcart, colls), and has issue by 1st and 3rd *m*.

Arms – Or, three chevronels engrailed Gules in chief two lions rampant and respectant of the Second. **Crest** – An arm embowed in armour Argent, holding in the gauntlet Or a battle-axe in fess, also Argent, the forearm environed of a wreath of laurel Vert. **Supporters** – *dexter*, a lion Gules gorged of a collar Or, charged with a chevronel engrailed Gules; *sinister*, a buck Proper, attired, collared and chained Or, the collar charged with a chevronel engrailed Gules. **Motto** – Virtute Majorum.
Seat – Tullichettle, Comrie, Perthshire; 1 Plowden Buildings, Temple, EC4. *Club* – Royal (Perth).

SONS LIVING (*By 1st marriage*)

Hon James Malise Dundas, *b* 1949: *ed* Radley, and Aberdeen Univ (LLB); author of *The Albatross Conspiracy* 1991, and *The Mapmaker* 1994: *m* 1st, 1980 (*m diss* 1986), Caroline Elizabeth, da of Charles Ede, of The Garden House, Hollington, Newbury, Berks; 2ndly, 1988, Sarah Jacqueline, yr da of late Lt-Col (David Ludovic) Peter Lindsay, DSO (*see* E Crawford and Balcarres, colls), and has issue living (by 1st *m*), Sophie Jean Elizabeth, *b* 1980, — Eleanor Fleur, *b* 1983, — (by 2nd *m*) Jake Ludovic Dundas, *b* 1991, — Anna Maria, *b* 1989. *Residence* – Altchroskie, Enochdhu, Kirkmichael, Perthshire PH10 7PB.
Hon Simon Helias, *b* 1953; *ed* Radley, and Bristol Univ (BA): *m* 1979, Aurora, da of Juan de Jesus Castaneda, of Apartado Aereo 33394, Bogota, Colombia, and has issue living, Jeremy Cunninghame, *b* 1984, — Thomas Charles, *b* 1987. *Residence* – Upper Ballunie, Kettins, Coupar Angus, Perthshire.

DAUGHTERS LIVING (*By 1st marriage*)

Hon Arabella Bridget Rachel, *b* 1965: *m* 1989, James H. B. Maudslay, yr son of late Sir (James) Rennie Maudslay, GCVO, MBE, and has issue living, Angus Charles Rennie, *b* 1993. *Residence* – 84 Muncaster Rd, SW11 6NU.

(by 3rd marriage)

Hon Cressida Jane, *b* 1981.

JAY, BARON (Jay) (Life Baron 1987)

DOUGLAS PATRICK THOMAS JAY, PC, son of late Edward Aubrey Hastings Jay, OBE, of Hampstead, NW3; *b* 23 March 1907; *ed* Winchester, and New Coll, Oxford; Fellow All Souls, Oxford 1930-37 and since 1968; on staff of *The Times* 1929-33, and *The Economist* 1933-37, City Editor *Daily Herald* 1937-40; Assist Sec Min of Supply 1940-43, Prin Assist Sec Board of Trade 1943-45, Personal Assist to PM 1945-46, Economic Sec to

Treasury 1947-50, Financial Sec to Treasury 1950-51, and Pres Board of Trade 1964-67; a Member of Board of Courtaulds 1967-70; Chm Common Market Safeguards Campaign 1970-77, and London Motorway Action Group 1968-80; author of *The Socialist Case* (1937), *Who is to Pay for the Peace and the War?* (1941), *After the Common Market* (1968), *Change and Fortune* (1980), and *Sterling* (1985); MP (*Lab*) for Div of Battersea N 1946-74, and Wandsworth, Battersea N 1974-83; *cr* PC 1951, and *Baron Jay*, of Battersea in Greater London (Life Baron) 1987: *m* 1st, 1933 (*m diss* 1972), Margaret Christian, da of James Clerk Maxwell Garnett, CBE; 2ndly, 1972, Mary Lavinia, da of Hugh Lewis Thomas, and has issue by 1st *m*.
Residence – Causeway Cottage, Minster Lovell, Oxford OX8 5RN.

SONS LIVING *(By 1st marriage)*

Hon Peter, *b* 1937; *ed* Winchester, and Ch Ch Oxford (MA); HM Amb to USA 1977-79; writer, broadcaster and publishing exec; *m* 1st, 1961 (*m diss* 1986), Margaret Ann (later Baroness Jay of Paddington, Life Baroness), da of Rt Hon (Leonard) James Callaghan, KG (later Baron Callaghan of Cardiff, Life Baron); 2ndly, 1986, Emma Bettina, da of Peter Kai Thornton, and has issue living (by 1st *m*) (*see* Bs Jay of Paddington), — (by 2nd *m*) Thomas Hastings, *b* 1987, — Samuel Arthur Maxwell, *b* 1988, — James William Hagen Thornton, *b* 1992, — (by Jane Tustian) Nicholas James TUSTIAN, *b* 1980. *Residence* – Hensington Farmhouse, Woodstock, Oxon OX20 1LH. *Club* – Garrick.

Hon Martin, *b* 1939; *ed* Winchester, and New Coll, Oxford (BA); industrialist: *m* 1969, Sandra Williams, and has issue living, Adam, *b* 1976, — Claudia, *b* 1971, — Tabitha, *b* 1972. *Residence* – Bishop's Court, Bishop's Sutton, Alresford, Hants.

DAUGHTERS LIVING *(By 1st marriage)*

Hon Helen, *b* 1945; *ed* North London Collegiate, and Sussex Univ (BA): *m* 1st, 1975 (*m diss* 1982), David Kennard; 2ndly, 1986, Rupert Pennant-Rea, and has issue living (by 1st *m*), Amanda, *b* 1976, — Juliet, *b* 1979, — (by 2nd *m*) Edward, *b* 1986.
Hon Catherine, *b* (twin) 1945; *ed* North London Collegiate, and Sussex Univ (BA): *m* 1970, Stewart Boyd, QC, and has issue living, Matthew, *b* 1976, — Rachel, *b* 1972, — Emily, *b* 1973, — Hannah, *b* 1987. *Residences* – 1 Gayton Cres, Hampstead, NW3; Wraxall Manor, Higher Wraxall, Dorchester, Dorset DT2 0HP.

JAY OF PADDINGTON, BARONESS (Jay) (Life Baroness 1992)

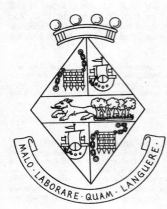

MARGARET ANN JAY, elder da of Baron Callaghan of Cardiff, KG, PC (Life Baron); *b* 18 Nov 1939; *ed* Blackheath High Sch, and Somerville Coll, Oxford (BA); formerly in Current Affairs and Educn depts of BBC TV; Reporter for *Panorama* 1981-86, Reporter and Producer *This Week* 1986-88, since when a Broadcaster and Presenter for Radio and Television, including *Social History of Medicine, Family Matters, Newsnight,* etc; sometime Member Ealing, Hounslow and Hammersmith Area Health Authority, Member Governing Board Queen Charlotte's Maternity Hosp, and Chelsea Hosp for Women, Member Paddington and N Kensington Dist Health Authority (now Parkside Health Authority) since 1984 (Vice-Chm since 1990), Member Central Research and Devpt Cttee for NHS since 1991, Member Min for Health's AIDS Action Group since 1991, Patron ReAction Trust (part of Help the Aged) since 1991, Council Member The London Lighthouse, and Member Management Board of Positively Women; Founder and Dir Nat AIDS Trust since 1988; co-author *Battered- The Story of Child Abuse* (1986); *cr* Baroness Jay of Paddington, of Paddington in the City of Westminster (Life Baroness) 1992: *m* 1961 (*m diss* 1986), Peter Jay (later Hon Peter Jay), son of Rt Hon Douglas Patrick Thomas Jay (later Baron Jay, Life Baron), and has issue.

Arms – Quarterly vert and azure in the former a portcullis or in the latter a lymphad with an anchor at its prow and masted or the sail set argent and pennants flying gules overall a fess or to the sinister thereof a grassy mount with a hurst of oak trees and issuing therefrom passant to the dexter a wolf proper.
Residences – 44 Blomfield Rd, W9 2PF; Elm Bank, Glandore, co Cork.

SON LIVING

Hon Patrick James Peter, *b* 1971; *ed* Winchester, and Sch of Oriental and African Studies, London Univ.

DAUGHTERS LIVING

Hon Tamsin Margaret, *b* 1965; *ed* St Paul's Girls' Sch and Bristol Univ: *m* 1989, Simon Anthony Raikes (*see* Hanson, Bt). *Residence* – 63 St Peter's St, N1 8JR.
Hon Alice Katharine, *b* 1968; *ed* Bedales, and Pembroke Coll, Oxford.

JEFFREYS, BARON (Jeffreys) (Baron UK 1952)

Every gift from God

CHRISTOPHER HENRY MARK JEFFREYS, 3rd Baron; *b* 22 May 1957; *s* 1986; *ed* Eton: *m* 1985, Anne Elisabeth, da of Antoine Denarie, and of Mrs Derek Harry Johnson, of Boden Hall, Scholar Green, Cheshire, and has issue.

𝕬rms – Ermine a lion rampant sable, and a canton sable. 𝕮rest – On a wreath ermine and sable a demi-lion or, grasping with the dexter claw a wreath of laurel vert. 𝕾upporters – On either side a lion regardant sable crowned with an ancient crown or, and charged on the shoulder with two swords in saltire points upwards gold.
Residence – Bottom Farm, Eaton, Grantham, Lincs NG32 1ET. *Club* – White's.

SON LIVING

Hon ARTHUR MARK HENRY, *b* 18 Feb 1989.

DAUGHTER LIVING

Hon Alice Mary, *b* 1986.

BROTHER LIVING

Hon (Alexander) Charles Darell, *b* 1959; *ed* Harrow: *m* 1991, Sonamara M. A., da of Barry Sainsbury, of London.

SISTERS LIVING

Hon Laura, *b* 1961.
Hon Rose Amanda, *b* 1962: *m* 1993, Dominic C. Prince, elder son of late John Prince, of Chipping Warden, Oxon.

HALF-SISTER LIVING (*Daughter of 2nd Baron by 2nd marriage*)

Hon Sophie Louise, *b* 1972.

UNCLE LIVING (*Brother of 2nd Baron*) (*Raised to rank of a Baron's son 1961*)

Hon George Christian Darell, *b* 1939; *ed* Eton; late Capt Grenadier Guards; Dir of Seccombe Marshall and Campion plc 1976: *m* 1967, Karen Elizabeth Mary, elder da of late Col Hugo Meynell, MC, of Hollybush Park, Burton-on-Trent (*see* E Halifax, colls), and has issue living, Christopher George Hugo, *b* 1984. — Zara Serena, *b* 1972, — Susannah Elizabeth, *b* 1975. *Residence* – Cotswold House, Condicote, Stow-on-the-Wold, Glos GL54 1ES. *Club* – Boodle's.

MOTHER LIVING

Sarah Annabella, only da of late Maj Henry Claude Lyon Garnett, of Somerton House, Winkfield, Berks: *m* 1st, 1956 (*m diss* 1967), the 2nd Baron, who *d* 1986; 2ndly, 1968, Alexander Edward Pennant Clarke (*see* Falkiner, Bt, 1963 Edn). *Residence* – Foxhill House, Hawling, Glos.

WIDOW LIVING OF SECOND BARON

SUZANNE, da of James Stead, of Trowswell, Goudhurst, Kent, and formerly wife of — Gilbert: *m* 2ndly, 1981, as his 3rd wife, the 2nd Baron, who *d* 1986; 3rdly, 1990, Geoffrey C. Martin, of Heathfield, Sussex.

PREDECESSORS – (1) *Gen Sir* GEORGE DARELL JEFFREYS, KCB, KCVO, CMG, DL, son of late Rt Hon Arthur Frederick Jeffreys, JP, DL, MP, of Burkham House, Hants; *b* 1878; Col of Grenadier Guards 1952-60; Comdt Guards Depot 1911-14; Nile Expedition 1898, present at battle of Khartoum, S Africa 1900-1902, European War 1914-18 Comdg successively 2nd Batn of his Regt, 58th, 57th, and 1st Guards Brig, and 19th Div; in command of Light Div, Army of the Rhine 1919, and London Dist 1920-24; commanded 43rd (Wessex) Div TA and Wessex Area 1926-30; Gen Officer Comdg-in-Ch S Command, India 1932-36, and ADC Gen to HM 1936-38; Chm of Basingstoke Co Bench 1925-32, and again 1936-52, Hon Col 48th (Hampshire) Anti-Aircraft Regt RA (TA) (now 583rd (Hampshire) Heavy Anti-Aircraft Regt, RA) 1938-48, and Col of Roy Hampshire Regt 1945-48; sat as MP for Petersfield Div od Hampshire (*C*) 1941-51; *cr Baron Jeffreys*, of Burkham, co Southampton (peerage of United Kingdom) 1952; *m* 1905, Dorothy, who *d* 1953, da of John Postle Heseltine, of Walhampton, Lymington, and widow of Viscount Cantelupe, el son of 7th Earl De La Warr; *d* 1960; *s* by his grandson (2) MARK GEORGE CHRISTOPHER (son of late Capt Chrisoper John Darell Jeffreys, MVO, who was *ka* 1940, by his wife, Lady Rosemary Beatrice Agar, who *d* 1984, da of 4th Earl of Normanton, only son of 1st Baron), 2nd Baron, *b* 1932; Maj Gren Gds: *m* 1st, 1956 (*m diss* 1967), Sarah Annabella, only da of late Maj Henry Claude Lyon Garnett, of Somerton House, Winkfield, Berks; 2ndly, 1967 (*m diss* 1981), Anne-Louise, yr da of His Honour Judge Sir (William) Shirley Worthington-Evans, 2nd Bt (ext); 3rdly, 1981, Mrs Suzanne Gilbert (who *m* 3rdly, 1990, Geoffrey C. Martin, of Heathfield, Sussex), da of James Stead, of Goudhurst, Kent; *d* 1986; *s* by his elder son (3) CHRISTOPHER HENRY MARK, 3rd Baron and present peer.

JEGER, BARONESS (Jeger) (Life Baroness 1979)

LENA MAY JEGER, da of Charles Chivers, of Yorkley, Glos *b* 19 Nov 1915; *ed* Southgate County Sch, Middlesex and Birkbeck Coll, London Univ (BA); Civil Ser, Customs and Excise, Minof Information and Foreign Office 1936-49, Manchester Guardian, London Staff 1951-54 and since 1961; Member St Pancras Borough Council 1945-59, and LCC for Holborn and St Pancras South 1952-55; Member Nat Exec Cttee, Labour Party since 1963, and of Chm's Panel, House of Commons since 1971; UK Rep on Status of Women Commn UN 1967, Member Consultative Assembly of Council of Europe and of W European Union 1969-71; Chm Labour Party 1979-80; MP (*Lab*) for Holborn and St Pancras South 1953-59 and 1964-74, and

for Camden, Holborn and St Pancras South 1974-79; *cr Baroness Jeger*, of St Pancras in Greater London (Life Baroness) 1979: *m* 1948, Dr Santo Wayburn Jeger, MP, who *d* 1953.
Residence – 9 Cumberland Terr, Regent's Park, NW1.

JELLICOE, EARL (Jellicoe) (Earl (UK) 1925)

GEORGE PATRICK JOHN RUSHWORTH JELLICOE, KBE, DSO, MC, PC, 2nd Earl; *b* 4 April 1918; *s* 1935; *ed* Winchester, and at Trin Coll, Camb (Exhibitioner); FRS 1990; in Foreign Ser 1947-57; formerly 1st Sec, Washington, DC, and Brussels and Dep Sec-Gen Baghdad Pact; a Lord-in-Waiting to HM Feb to June 1961, Joint Parliamentary Sec, Min of Housing and Local Govt 1961-62, Min of State, Home Office 1962-63, and First Lord of Admiralty 1963-64, and Min of Defence for RN April to Oct 1964; Dep Leader of Opposition, House of Lords 1967-70; Lord Privy Seal, and Leader of House of Lords 1970-73; Chm of Tate & Lyle Ltd, 1978-82; a Dir of S G Warburg & Co Ltd, since 1973, Sotheby Holdings 1973, Smiths Industries 1973 and Morgan Crucible 1974; Chm MRC 1982, and BOTB 1983; Review of Prevention of Terrorism Act 1982-83; Pres Parly and Scientific Cttee 1980-83, London Chamber of Commerce and Industry 1979-82, and Chm Council, King's Coll, London; a Page of Honour at Coronation of King George VI; 1939-45 War in Middle East as Lt-Col Coldm Gds, I SAS Regt and SBS Regt (wounded, despatches thrice, DSO, MC, Legion of Honour, French Croix de Guerre, Greek Mil Cross); DSO 1942; *cr* PC 1963, and KBE 1986: *m* 1st, 1944 (*m diss* 1966), Patricia Christine, only da of Jeremiah O'Kane, of Vancouver, Canada; 2ndly, 1966, Philippa, da of late Philip Dunne, of Gatley Park, Leominster, and has issue by 1st and 2nd *m*.

Arms – Argent, three bars wavy azure, over all a whale hauriant sable. Crest – Out of a crown or, a demi-wolf azure. Supporters – On either side a sea griffin or.
Residences – 97 Onslow Sq, SW7; Tidcombe Manor, Tidcombe, nr Marlborough, Wilts. *Club* – Brooks's.

SONS LIVING *(By 1st marriage)*

PATRICK JOHN BERNARD (*Viscount Brocas*), *b* 29 Aug 1950; *ed* Eton: *m* 1971 (*m diss* 1981), Geraldine Ann FitzGerald Jackson, and has issue:—
        SON LIVING—*Hon* Justin Amadeus, *b* 1970.
Hon Nicholas Charles, *b* 1953; *ed* Eton, and York Univ: *m* 1982, Patricia, da of late Count Arturo Ruiz de Castilla, of Madrid, and Lima, Peru, and has issue living, Zoë Anaya, *b* 1988. *Residence* – 14A Willow Bridge Rd, N1 2LA.

(By 2nd marriage)

Hon John Philip, *b* 1966.

DAUGHTERS LIVING *(By 1st marriage)*

Lady Alexandra Patricia Gwendoline, *b* 1944: *m* 1970, (Edward) Philip Wilson, of 24 Highbury Place, N5 (*see* Wilson, Bt, *cr* 1874, colls).
Lady Zara Lison Josephine JELLICOE, *b* 1948; has resumed her maiden name: *m* 1983 (*m diss* 1987), Bruce Gilliam, son of Alvin Bruce Gilliam, of Houston, Texas. *Residence* – 37c Oliva Drive, Novato, Calif 94947, USA.

(By 2nd marriage)

Lady Emma Rose, *b* 1967.
Lady Daisy, *b* 1970.

SISTERS LIVING *(In special remainder to the Viscountcy only)*

Lady Gwendoline Lucy Constance Rushworth, *b* 1903: *m* 1935, Col Edward Latham, MC, RHA, who *d* 1957, and has issue living, John Edward Jellicoe (Harwood's House, Bledington, Oxon. *Club* – Cavalry), *b* 1936; *ed* Eton; late 2nd Lt RAC: *m* 1967, Catherine Patricia, da of Allan William Forsyth Craig, MB, of Greenways, Darlington Place, Bath, and has issue living, Jasper Nicholas Jellicoe *b* 1970, Gabrielle Jane *b* 1971, Rosalind Vaari (twin) *b* 1971, — Richard Henry Ringrose (Stowting Hill House, Ashford, Kent, TN25 6BE), *b* 1943; *ed* Eton, and Univ of Paris; late Sub-Lt RN; MBA Cranfield Inst of Tech; Lt RNR: *m* 1968, Virginia Jane, el da of John Mount (*see* E Erne, colls), and has issue living, Edward George Ringrose *b* 1970; *ed* Eton, and St Catherine's Coll, Oxford (BA); 2nd Lieut Coldm Gds, Harry John Jellicoe *b* 1972; *ed* Milton Abbey, and Guildhall Sch of Music and Drama, Selina Louise *b* 1976, Emily Rose Jane *b* 1979, — Susan Phyllida, *b* 1938; *ed* Lady Margaret Hall, Oxford (BA), and Birkbeck Coll, London (PhD): *m* 1958, Michael Rose, Solicitor of Heath Winds, Merton Lane, Highgate, N6, and has issue living, David Jacob Edward *b* 1959, Bernard John Max *b* 1960, Philip Thomas Solomon *b* 1963, Dinah Gwen Lison *b* 1965. *Residence* – Oak Knoll, Sunningdale, Ascot, Berks.
Lady Norah Beryl Cayzer, *b* 1910: *m* 1935, Major Edward William Rhys Wingfield, King's Roy Rifle Corps (*see* V Powerscourt, colls), who *d* 1984. *Residence* – Salterbridge, Cappoquin, co Waterford.
Lady Prudence Katharine Patton, *b* 1913; formerly a JP for Co of Kent: *m* 1936, Francis William Hope Loudon, who *d* 1985, and has issue living, James Rushworth Hope (Olantigh, Wye, Ashford, Kent), *b* 1943; *ed* Eton, and Magdalene Coll, Camb (BA): *m* 1975, Jane Gavina Fryett, and has issue living, Hugo John Hope *b* 1978, Alexander Guy Rushworth *b* 1980, Antonia Louise Cameron *b* 1977, — Katharine Louise Frederica (*Lady Wilkinson*), *b* 1937: *m* 1964, Sir William Henry Nairn Wilkinson, of 119 Castlenau, SW13, and has issue living, Matthew Loudon Nairn *b* 1969, Sophia Louise Prudence *b* 1971, Alice Laura Gillian *b* 1974, — Annabella Constance, *b* 1939: *m* 1965, Ian Jonathan Scott, of Lasborough Manor, Tetbury, Glos, and

has issue living, Alexander James Jonathan *b* 1966, Justin William Erskine *b* 1970, Julia Katharine Selina *b* 1969. *Residence –* 92 Bridge St, Wye, nr Ashford, Kent.

COLLATERAL BRANCH LIVING   *(In remainder to Viscountcy only)*

Issue of late Lady Myrtle Grace Brocas Jellicoe. 3rd da of 1st Earl, *b* 1908, *d* 1945: *m* 1932, Lionel Maxwell Joachim Balfour, who *d* 1973.
Christopher John Jellicoe, *b* 1934; *ed* Trin Coll, Camb (BA): *m* 1960, Ann Schuyler Butlin, and has issue living, Maxwell James, *b* 1961, — Juliet Ann, *b* 1963, — Katherine Susan, *b* 1968. *Residence –* 25 Clausentum Rd, St Cross, Winchester SO23 9QE Battledean Rd, N5 1UZ.   —— Karen Myrtle, *b* 1944: *m* 1967, Fabyan Peter Leaf Evans, and has issue living, Nigel Henley Fabyan, *b* 1971, — Alexander Peter Sommerville, *b* 1976, — Jessica Ann, *b* 1973.

PREDECESSORS – **(1)** *Adm of the Fleet Sir* JOHN RUSHWORTH Jellicoe, GCB, OM, GCVO, son of late Capt John Henry Jellicoe, of Northfield, Ryde, Isle of Wight; *b* 1859; Egyptian War 1882 (medal, bronze star), China 1900, Comdg Naval Brig and as Ch of Staff to Vice-Adm Sir E Seymour during attempt to relieve British Legation at Pekin (severely wounded, CB), European War 1914-16 in command of Grant Fleet, and at battle of Jutland (GCB, GCVO, OM, Order of Leopold of Belgium, French and Belgian Croix de Guerre, Grand Cross of Legion of Honour, Grand Cross of Military Order of Savoy, Japanese Order of the Rising Sun with Paulownia, 3rd class of Russian Order of St George, American DSM, Adm of the Fleet, thanked by Parliament, granted £50,000); commander of HMS "Victoria" when lost off Tripoli June 1893; was Director of Naval Ordnance 1905-7, a Lord of the Admiralty and Controller of the Navy 1908-10, in command of Atlantic Fleet 1910-11, and of 2nd Squadron of Home Fleet 1911-12, Second Sea Lord of the Admiralty 1912-14, Com-in-Ch of Grand Fleet 1914-16, and First Sea Lord of the Admiralty (also Ch of Naval Staff) 1916-17; Pres of British Legion 1928-32; Gov-Gen and Com-in-Ch of New Zealand 1920-24; *cr Viscount Jellicoe*, of Scapa, co Orkney (peerage of United Kingdom) 1917, with remainder to heirs male of his body, and in default of such issue with remainder (1) to his el da and to the heirs male of her body, and (2) to every other da successively in order of seniority of age and priority of birth, and heirs male of their bodies, and *Viscount Brocas*, of Southampton, co Southampton, and *Earl Jellicoe* (peerage of UK) 1925: *m* 1902, Florence Gwendoline, who *d* 1964, da of Sir Charles William Cayzer, 1st Bt (*cr* 1904); *d* 1935; *s* by his son **(2)** GEORGE PATRICK JOHN RUSHWORTH, 2nd Earl and present peer; also Viscount Jellicoe, and Viscount Brocas.

JENKIN OF RODING, BARON (Jenkin) (Life Baron 1987)

(CHARLES) PATRICK FLEEMING JENKIN, PC, son of late Charles O. F. Jenkin, of Gerrards Cross, Bucks; *b* 7 Sept 1926; *ed* Clifton, and Jesus Coll, Camb; Queen's Own Cameron Highlanders 1945-48; Bar Middle Temple 1952-57; Distillers Co Ltd 1957-70; Front Bench Spokesman on Treasury, Trade and Finance 1965-70; Joint Vice-Chm Conservative Parl Trade and Power Cttee 1966, Financial Sec to Treasury 1970-72, Chief Sec 1972-74, Minister for Energy Jan-March 1974, Shadow Spokesman on Energy 1974-76, and on Social Services 1976-79, Sec of State for Social Services 1979-81, Industry 1981-83, and DoE 1983-85; Chm Friends Provident Life Office, Forest Healthcare NHS Trust, Target Finland Ltd, and UK-Japan 2000 Group 1986-90, Council Memb UK Centre for Economic and Environmental Development, Chm Taverner Concerts Trust, Westfield Coll Trust, Queen Mary and Westfield Coll Public Policy Research Unit Advisory Board, Visual Handicap Group; Sr Vice-Chm World Congress on Urban Growth and the Environment, Hong Kong 1994; Memb Supervisory Board Avero Centraal Beheer (Holdings) BV, and Internat Advisory Board Marsh & McLennan Group of Cos Inc; Advisor Andersen Consulting Nat Economic Research Assocs Inc, and Sumitomo Trust and Banking Co Ltd, London Branch; Memb of Council of Guide Dogs for the Blind Assocn; MP for Wanstead and Woodford (*C*) 1964-87; *cr* PC 1973, and *Baron Jenkin of Roding*, of Wanstead and Woodford in Greater London (Life Baron) 1987: *m* 1952, Alison Monica, eldest da of late Capt Philip Skelton Graham, RN (*see* Christison, Bt, ext), and has issue.

Arms – Argent a lion rampant reguardant sable armed and langued gules within a bordure also sable. **Crest** – On a mural crown per pale argent and sable a lion rampant reguardant sable armed and langued gules. **Supporters** – *Dexter*, a seal erect on a rock; *Sinister*, a stag erect guardant on a grassy mound all proper.
Residences – Home Farm, Matching Rd, Hatfield Heath, Bishop's Stortford, Herts CM22 7AS; 703 Howard House, Dolphin Sq, SW1V 3LX.

SONS LIVING

Rev Hon Charles Alexander Graham, *b* 1954; *ed* Highgate, Univ Coll, London, and Westcott House, Camb; ordained 1984; Team Rector Melton Mowbray since 1994: *m* 1984, Susan, da of Roy Collins, and has issue living, Alexandra Emily, *b* 1989, — Rebecca Charlotte, *b* 1991. *Residence –* Melton Mowbray Rectory, 67 Dalby Rd, Melton Mowbray, Leics.
Hon Bernard Christison, *b* 1959; *ed* Highgate, William Ellis Sch, and CCC Camb: *m* 1988, Anne Caroline, elder da of late *Hon* Charles Richard Strutt (*see* B Rayleigh), and has issue living, Robert Patrick Christison, *b* 1989, — Peter Andrew Graham, *b* 1991. *Residence –* 116 Kennington Rd, SE11 6RE.

DAUGHTERS LIVING

Hon Nicola Mary, *b* 1956; *ed* N London Collegiate Sch, Royal Coll of Music, and Hochschüle für Müsik, Vienna. *Residence –* Top Flat, 16 Handforth Rd, SW9 0LP.
Hon Flora Margaret, *b* 1962; *ed* Felsted, St John's Coll, Durham, and Trin Coll of Music: *m* 1990, Jacoby Michael Thwaites, yst son of Prof Sir Bryan Thwaites. *Residence –* 11 Heyford Av, SW8 1EA.

JENKINS OF HILLHEAD (Jenkins) (Life Baron 1987)

Roy Harris Jenkins, OM, PC, only son of late Arthur Jenkins, MP, of Greenlands, Pontypool; *b* 11 Nov 1920; *ed* Abersychan Gram Sch, and Balliol Coll, Oxford; Hon DCL Oxford, and honorary degrees from twenty three other Univs; Hon FBA 1993; 1939-45 War with RA; PPS to Sec of State for Commonwealth Relations 1940-50, Min of Aviation 1964-65, Home Sec 1965-67, Chancellor of the Exchequer 1967-70, Dep Leader of Parl Labour Party 1970-72, Home Sec 1974-76; Pres Commn of European Communities 1977-81; Founder Member SDP 1981, Leader SDP 1982-83; Trustee Pilgrim Trust since 1973, Pres Univ of Wales Inst of Science and Technology 1975-81, Chancellor Oxford Univ since 1987, Pres Royal Soc of Literature since 1988; Dir Morgan Grenfell Holdings 1981-82; author of *Mr Attlee, Pursuit of Progress, Mr Balfour's Poodle, Sir Charles Dilke, Asquith, Afternoon on the Potomac, Nine Men of Power, Truman, Baldwin, Twentieth Century Portraits, European Diary 1977-81, A Life at the Centre, Portraits and Miniatures,* etc; MP for Central Div of Southwark (*Lab*) 1948-50, and Stechford Div of Birmingham 1950-76; *cr* PC 1964, OM 1993, and *Baron Jenkins of Hillhead,* of Pontypool, co Gwent (Life Baron) 1987: *m* 1945, Dame (Mary) Jennifer, DBE, da of late Sir Parker Morris, and has issue.
Residences – St Amand's House, E Hendred, Oxon; 2 Kensington Park Gdns, W11 3HB. *Clubs* – Brooks's, Athenaeum, Reform, Pratt's, United Oxford and Cambridge, Beefsteak.

SONS LIVING

Hon Charles Arthur Simon, *b* 1949; *ed* Winchester, and New Coll, Oxford: *m* 1971, Ivana Sertić, and has issue living, Alexandra Dorothea, *b* 1986, — Helena Harriet, *b* 1988. *Residence* – 9 Leppoc Rd, SW4.
Hon Edward Nicholas, *b* 1954; *ed* City of London Sch, and Trin Hall, Camb: *m* 1979, Sally Turner, and has issue living, Fergus Orlando Nicholas, *b* 1986, — Flora Rayne Victoria, *b* 1984. *Residence* – 7 Carthew Villas, W6.

DAUGHTER LIVING

Hon Cynthia Delanie, *b* 1951; *ed* St Paul's Girls' Sch, and St Anne's Coll, Oxford: *m* 1984, John Crosthwait, and has issue living, David Robert Jenkins, *b* 1982, — Hugh Michael Jenkins, *b* 1985, — George Nicholas Jenkins, *b* 1988.

JENKINS OF PUTNEY, BARON (Jenkins) (Life Baron 1981)

Hugh Gater Jenkins, son of Joseph Walter Jenkins; *b* 27 July 1908; *ed* Enfield Gram Sch; Research and Publicity Officer National Union of Bank Employees; Assist Gen Sec British Actors Equity Assocn; London CC 1952-64; Chm Standing Advisory Cttee on Local Authorities and the Theatre 1950-64; Min for the Arts 1974-76; Consultant (formerly Chm) The Theatres Trust; Vice-Pres (formerly Chm) Theatres Advisory Council; Campaign for Nuclear Disarmament (formerly Chm); Fl-Lt Fighter Command UK and SEAC (Burma) 1941-46; MP for Putney (*Lab*) 1964-79; *cr Baron Jenkins of Putney,* of Wandsworth, Greater London (Life Baron) 1981: *m* 1936, Marie Ethel, who *d* 1989, da of Sqdn-Ldr Ernest Christopher Crosbie; 2ndly, 1991, Helena Maria, who *d* 1994, da of Nicholas Paulidis, architect, of Athens.
Address – c/o House of Lords, SW1.

JERSEY, EARL OF (Child Villiers) (Earl E 1697)
(Name pronounced "Villers")

George Francis Child Villiers, 9th Earl; *b* 15 Feb 1910; *s* 1923; *ed* Eton, and Ch Ch, Oxford; formerly Major RA (TA): *m* 1st, 1932 (*m diss* 1937), Patricia Kenneth, da of Kenneth Richards, of Cootamundra NSW, Australia; 2ndly, 1937 (*m diss* 1946), Virginia, da of James Cherrill, of Hollywood, USA, and formerly wife of late Archibald Alexander Leach (film actor as Cary Grant); 3rdly, 1947, Bianca Maria Adriana Luciana, da of late Enrico Mottironi, of Via Goffredo Casalis, Turin, Italy, and has issue by 1st and 3rd *m.*

Arms – Quarterly: 1st and 4th, argent, on a cross gules, five escallops or, *Villiers*; 2nd and 3rd, gules, a chevron engrailed ermine, between three eaglets argent, ducally gorged or, and in the chief point, for distinction, an escallop or, *Child.* **Crests** – 1st, a lion rampant argent, ducally crowned or; 2nd, on a rock proper, an eagle rising argent, ducally gorged or, holding in the beak an adder proper, and charged on the breast, for distinction, with an ermine spot. **Supporters** – Two lions argent, ducally crowned or, and gorged with a plain collar gules, charged with three escallops or.
Residence – Radier Manor, Longueville, Jersey.

The Cross is the test of faith

SONS LIVING (By 3rd marriage)

George Henry (*Viscount Villiers*) (The Flat, Radier Manor, Longueville, Jersey), *b* 29 Aug 1948; late 2nd Lt 11th Hussars and Roy Hussars: *m* 1st, 1969 (*m diss* 1973), Verna, 2nd da of late Kenneth A. Stott, of St Mary, Jersey; 2ndly, 1974 (*m diss* 1988), Sacha Jane Hooper, only da of Peter Hooper Valpy, of Jersey, and formerly wife of K. F. Lauder; 3rdly, 1992, Stephanie Louise, da of John Ian Penman, and has issue:—

> SON LIVING (*By 2nd m*) — *Hon* (George Francis) William, *b* 5 Feb 1976, — (*by 3rd m*) *Hon* Jamie Charles, *b* 1994.
>
> DAUGHTERS LIVING (*By 1st m*) — *Hon* Sophia Georgiana, *b* 1971, — (*by 2nd m*)— *Hon* Helen Katherine Luisa *b* 1978, — *Hon* Luciana Dorothea Sacha, *b* 1981.

GRANDDAUGHTERS LIVING

Issue of late Hon Charles Victor Child Villiers, yr son (by 3rd *m*) of 9th Earl, *b* 1952, *d* 1991: *m* 1975 (*m diss* 1989), Brigitte Elisabeth Germaine, da of Robert Jean Rolland Marchand:—
Eleanor Monica, *b* 1979. ——— Barbara Béatrice, *b* 1981.

DAUGHTERS LIVING (*By 1st marriage*)

Lady Caroline, *b* 1934: *m* 1st, 1952 (*m diss* 1965), Viscount Melgund, MBE (later 6th Earl of Minto); 2ndly, 1969 (*m diss* 1972), Hon John Douglas Stuart, who *d* 1990, son of 1st Viscount Stuart of Findhorn; 3rdly, 1980, Hon James Donald Diarmid Ogilvy, yst son of 12th Earl of Airlie. *Residence* – Sedgebrook Manor, nr Grantham, Lincs.

(*By 3rd marriage*)

Lady Isabella Bianca Rosa, *b* 1950: *m* 1974, Peter Edward Harrison, and has issue living, Matthew Alexander Charles, *b* 1980, — Alexandra Venetia, *b* 1977. *Residence* – Constantia Manor, Isfield, nr Uckfield, E Sussex TN22 5XU.

SISTERS LIVING

Lady Joan, *b* 1911: *m* 1933, Lieut David Richard Colville, RNVR (*see* V Colville, colls), who *d* 1986. *Residence* – Old Vicarage, Dorton, near Aylesbury, Bucks.
Lady Ann, *b* 1916: *m* 1937, Major Alexander Henry Elliot, late RA (*see* E Minto, colls), who *d* 1986. *Residence* – Broadford, Chobham, Surrey.

COLLATERAL BRANCHES LIVING

Issue of late Sqn-Ldr Hon (Edward) Mansel Child-Villiers, yr son of 8th Earl, *b* 1913, *d* 1980: *m* 1st, 1934 (*m diss* 1940), Barbara Mary, who *d* 1991, only da of late Capt William John Goulburn Shipdem Frampton, E Lancs Regt, of Newton Hall, Clitheroe; 2ndly, 1946 (*m diss* 1971), Princess Maria Gloria Pignatelli Aragona Cortez, only da of late Prince Antonio Pignatelli Aragona Cortez, Duke of Terranova, of Rome:—
(By 1st *m*) (Edward) John Mansel Hugh Frampton (Stable House, Mystole, Canterbury, Kent CT4 7DB), *b* 1935; *ed* Harrow: *m* 1958, Celia Elinor Vadyn, only da of late Cyril Hall Green, of Ballyvolane House, Castlelyons, co Cork (*see* Blake, Bt, *cr* 1622, colls), and has issue living, Alexander, *b* 1961: *m* 1988 (*m diss* 1993), Linda-Benedicte, da of Bjørn-Arild Solheim, of Oslo, Norway, and has issue living, Frederick Mansel *b* 1990, — Roderick Anthony (46 Elm Park Gdns, SW10), *b* 1963. ——— (By 2nd *m*) (George Anthony) Robert (4 Kensington Gate, W8), *b* 1947; *ed* The Oratory Sch, Reading: *m* 1973 (*m diss* 1989), Margot Vida Stott; has issue living (by Norah Mary Jennifer Gladwell, *née* Binyon), Miranda Kate, *b* 1986. ——— Mary Ann (Newlands Cottage, Rue Militaire, St Ouen, Jersey, CI), *b* 1951: *m* 1971 (*m diss* 1986), Stephen John Beck, and has issue living, Christian Mark Stephen, *b* 1976, — Honor Marie, *b* 1979. ——— (Maria) Consuelo (Lily) (3 Hazelmere Rd, NW6), *b* 1953; has issue living (by Prince Costantino Filippo Maria Ruspoli di Poggio Suasa), Bartolomeo Sebastian, *b* 1976.

Descendants of late Hon Thomas Villiers (2nd son of 2nd Earl of Jersey) who was *cr Earl of Clarendon* 1776 (see that title).

PREDECESSORS – (1) Sir OLIVER St John; *cr Viscount Grandison of Limerick* (peerage of Ireland) 1620 with remainder to the male heirs of his niece Barbara, wife of Sir Edward Villiers, el half-brother of George, Duke of Buckingham, the celebrated favourite of James I; *d* 1630; *s* by his el grand-nephew (2) WILLIAM Villiers, 2nd Viscount, el son of Barbara (ante); a zealous partisan of Charles I; *d* of wounds received at battle of Bristol 1643; *s* by his brother (3) JOHN, 3rd Viscount; *dsp*; *s* by his brother (4) GEORGE, 4th Viscount; *d* 1699; *s* by his grandson (5) JOHN, 5th Viscount; *cr Earl Grandison* (peerage of Ireland) 1721; *d* 1766, when the Earldom became ext, and he was *s* in the Viscountcy by his kinsman (6) WILLIAM, 3rd Earl of Jersey (see * infra); *d* 1769; *s* by his son (7) GEORGE BUSSY, 4th Earl; successively a Lord of the Admiralty, Lord Chamberlain of the Household and Master of the Buckhounds; *d* 1805; *s* by his son (8) GEORGE, 5th Earl; assumed the additional surname of Child by Roy licence 1819, was twice Lord Chamberlain to William IV, and twice Master of the Horse to Queen Victoria; *d* 1859; *s* by his son (9) GEORGE AUGUSTUS FREDERICK, 6th Earl; *b* 1908; successively MP for Honiton, Weymouth, and Cirencester (C): *m* 1841, Julia, da of the Rt Hon Sir Robert Peel, 2nd Bt; *d* 1859; *s* by his son (10) VICTOR ALBERT GEORGE, GCB, GCMG, PC, 7th Earl, *b* 1845; a partner in the banking firm of Child and Co, Fleet Street, EC; a Lord-in-Waiting to HM Queen Victoria 1875-7; Lord-Lieut for Oxfordshire 1887-1915; Paymaster-Gen 1889-90; Gov and Com-in-Ch of NS Wales 1890-93, and Acting Agent-Gen for New South Wales in London 1904-5: *m* 1872, Hon Margaret Elizabeth Leigh, DBE, who *d* 1945, da of 2nd Baron Leigh; *d* 1915; *s* by his el son (11) GEORGE HENRY ROBERT CHILD, 8th Earl, *b* 1873; a partner in the firm of Child and Co, bankers, of Fleet Street, EC; a Lord-in-Waiting to HM Jan to Aug 1919: *m* 1908, Lady Cynthia Almina Constance Mary, who *d* 1947 (having *m* 2ndly, 1925, Com William Rodney Slessor, RNVR, who *d* on active ser 1945), da of 3rd Earl of Kilmorey; *d* 1923: *s* by his son (12) GEORGE FRANCIS, 9th Earl and present peer; also Viscount Villiers of Dartford, Viscount Grandison of Limerick, and Baron Villiers of Hoo.
*Sir Edward Villiers, 5th son of Barbara St John, niece of 1st Viscount Grandison, had with other issue (1) EDWARD, PC, Knt, *cr Baron Villiers of Hoo*, co Kent, and *Viscount Villiers of Dartford*, co Kent (peerage of England) 1691, and *Earl of the Island of Jersey* (peerage of England) 1697; successively Special Ambassador to the Hague, Ambassador to the States Gen and to France, Lord Justice of Ireland, Sec of State, Master of the Horse, Lord Chamberlain of the Household and Knight Marshal; *d* 1711; *s* by his son (2) WILLIAM, 2nd Earl; *d* 1731; *s* by his son (3) WILLIAM, PC, 3rd Earl, who *s* his kinsman as 6th Viscount Grandison (ante).

JESSEL, BARONY OF (Jessel) (Extinct 1990)

GRANDDAUGHTER LIVING OF SECOND BARON

Issue of late Hon Timothy Edward Jessel, only son of 2nd Baron, *b* 1935, *d* 1969: *m* 1st, 1961 (*m diss* 1965), Janet Calliope, yr da of Maurice Smith, of Bidborough, Kent; 2ndly, 1965, Jill Elizabeth (infra) (who *m* 2ndly, 1977, (Edwin) Donald Gomme), only da of late George Alexander Powell, of Auckland, NZ:—

(By 2nd *m*) Annabel Helen, *b* 1968.

DAUGHTER LIVING OF SECOND BARON (*By 1st marriage*)

Hon Camilla Edith Mairi Elizabeth JESSEL, *b* 1940; has resumed her maiden name: *m* 1960 (*m* annulled 1972), as his 1st wife, Don Juan Carlos del Prado y Ruspoli, Marques de Caicedo, and has issue living, *Don* Miguel Angel, *b* 1961: *m* 1989, Natalia, da of Nicolas Sartorius, of Spain, and has issue living, Claudia Rebeca Leonor *b* 1992, — *Don* Alfonso Segundo, *b* 1966. *Residence* – Calle Lope de Vega 29, Madrid Spain.

WIDOW LIVING OF SON OF SECOND BARON

Jill Elizabeth, da of late George Alexander Powell, of Auckland, NZ: *m* 1st, 1965, as his 2nd wife, Hon Timothy Edward Jessel, who *d* 1969; 2ndly, 1977, (Edwin) Donald Gomme, and has issue (by 1st *m*) (ante). *Residence* – Av Edouard Rod 30, 1007 Lausanne, Switzerland.

WIDOW LIVING OF SECOND BARON

JESSICA MARIAN (*Baroness Jessel*), da of late William de Wet, of Rondesbosch, Cape Town, S Africa: *m* 1960, as his 2nd wife, the 2nd Baron, CBE, who *d* 1990, when the title became extinct. *Residence* – 4 Sloane Terrace Mansions, SW1X 9DG.

Jocelyn, Viscount; son of Earl of Roden.

JOHN-MACKIE, BARON (Mackie) (Life Baron 1981) (Extinct 1994)

JOHN MACKIE, son of late Maitland Mackie, OBE, and brother of Lord Mackie of Benshie (Life Baron); *b* 24 Nov 1909; *ed* Aberdeen Gram Sch and at North of Scotland Coll of Agriculture; Farmer; Parl Sec Min of Agriculture, Fisheries and Food 1964-70; Chm Forestry Commn 1976-79; MP for Enfield East (*Lab*) 1959-74; Oppn Agriculture Spokesman (resigned 1988); *cr Baron John-Mackie*, of Nazeing, co Essex (Life Baron) 1981: *m* 1934, Jeannie, da of Robert Milne, and has issue. Lord John-Mackie *d* 25 May 1994. *Residence* – Harold's Park Farm, Nazeing, Essex. *Club* – Farmers'.

SONS LIVING

Hon James Alexander (Bent, Laurence Kirk, Kincardineshire), *b* 1935: *m* 19—, Irene Fullerton.
Hon John Maitland (52 Lucas Lane, Hitchin, Herts), *b* 1944: *m* 1st, 19—, Marion Halliday; 2ndly, 1984, Janet Ann Hart, and has issue living (by 2nd *m*), Louise, *b* 1985.
Hon George Yull (The Bungalow, Harolds Park Farm, Nazeing, Essex), *b* 1949: *m* 1983, Catherine MacLeod.

DAUGHTERS LIVING

Hon Jean Simpson (31 Arbirlot Rd, Arbroath), *b* 1937: *m* 19—, Alexander Fairweather.
Hon Mary Yull, *b* 1940.

JOHNSTON OF ROCKPORT, BARON (Johnston) (Life Baron 1987)

CHARLES COLLIER JOHNSTON, eldest son of late Capt Charles Moore Johnston, by his late wife Muriel Florence, da of Reuben Mellon; *b* 4 March 1915; *ed* Tonbridge; Maj RA (ret), served in 1939-45 War; TD; Man Dir Standex Internat Ltd (formerly Roehlen-Martin Ltd) 1948-76 (Chm 1951-77), Engravers and Engrs, Chm Standex Holdings since 1986; Chm Macclesfield Constituency Conservative Assocn 1961-65, Hon Treas NW Conservatives and Memb Conservative Bd of Finance 1965-71, Chm NW Area Conservatives 1971-76; a Vice Pres Nat Union of Conservative and Unionist Assocs, Joint Hon Treas Conservative Party 1984-87; *cr* Kt 1973, and *Baron Johnston of Rockport*, of Caversham, co Berks (Life Baron) 1987: *m* 1st, 1939, Audrey Boyes, da of late Edgar Monk; 2ndly, 1981, Mrs Yvonne Shearman, da of late Reginald Marley, and has issue by 1st *m*. *Address* – c/o House of Lords, SW1.

SONS LIVING (*By 1st marriage*)

Hon Michael Charles (Court Hay Cottage, Farrington, Blandford Forum, Dorset), *b* 1942.
Hon Timothy Courtenay (22 Nerida Rd, Kareela, NSW 2232, Australia), *b* 1945.

JOICEY, BARON (Joicey) (Baron UK 1906, Bt UK 1893)

Every land is a native country to a brave man

JAMES MICHAEL JOICEY, 5th Baron, and 5th Baronet; *b* 28 June 1953; *s* 1993; *ed* Eton, and Ch Ch, Oxford: *m* 1984, (Agnes) Harriet Frances Mary, yr da of Rev William Thompson, of Oxnam Manse, Jedburgh, Roxburghshire, and has issue.

Arms – Argent, three lozenges sable within two bendlets invected gules between two miner's picks in bend proper. **Crest** – A demi-man affrontée in armour proper, garnished or, the helmet adorned with three feathers gules, holding in the dexter hand a scimitar of the first, pommel and hilt gold, supporting with the sinister hand an escutcheon argent, charged with three torteaux within two bendlets invected of the second between two fleurs-de-lis sable. **Supporters** – On either side a Shetland pony proper, haltered or.
Seats – Etal Manor, Berwick-on-Tweed, TD15 2PU; Ford Castle, Berwick-on-Tweed. *Residence* – East Flodden Farmhouse, Milfield, Wooler, Northumberland.

SONS LIVING

Hon WILLIAM JAMES, *b* 21 May 1990.
Hon Richard Michael, *b* 1993.

DAUGHTER LIVING

Hon Hannah Elisabeth, *b* 1988.

BROTHER LIVING

Hon Andrew Hugh, *b* 1955; *ed* Eton, and Ch Ch, Oxford. *Residence* – New Etal, Cornhill-on-Tweed, Northumberland TD12 4XL.

SISTER LIVING

Hon Katherine Jane, *b* 1959: *m* 1984, Thomas Crosbie Dawson (*see* Sutton, Bt, 1985 Edn), and has issue living, Robert Hugo, *b* 1992, — Lucy Charlotte, *b* 1987, — Helen Amanda, *b* 1989. *Residence* – Pawston, Mindrum, Northumberland.

DAUGHTER LIVING OF SECOND BARON

Hon Sylvia Alice, *b* 1908: *m* 1934 (*m diss* 1951), Lieut-Col Richard Ian Griffith Taylor, DSO, MC (Waldie-Griffith, Bt), (ext), who *d* 1984, and has issue living, Simon James (Rothbury Park, RD4, Hamilton, NZ), *b* 1936; *ed* Harrow: *m* 1963, Janiece, da of late Stanley Marshall, and has issue living, Jeremy Nicholas *b* 1963, Richard Simon *b* 1967, Fiona Josephine *b* 1965, Susan *b* 1966, Melissa Jane *b* 1969, — (Alexander Thomas), *b* 1941; *ed* Harrow: *m* 1974, Sarah da of Col Richard Martin-Bird, of Stockinwood, Chelford, Cheshire, — Valerie, *b* 1946: *m* 1969, Alan Yuill Walker, of Sheepdrove Park, Lambourn, Berks, and has issue living, Lavinia Mary *b* 1972, Georgina Anne *b* 1974. *Residence* – Field House, Whittingham, Alnwick, Northumberland.

WIDOW LIVING OF FOURTH BARON

ELISABETH MARION (*Elisabeth, Baroness Joicey*), da of late Lt-Col Hon Ian Leslie Melville, TD (*see* E Leven and Melville, colls): *m* 1952, the 4th Baron, who *d* 1993. *Residence* – Etal Manor, Berwick-on-Tweed TD15 2PU.

PREDECESSORS – (1) JAMES Joicey, son of George Joicey, of Newcastle-upon-Tyne; *b* 1846; MP for Durham co, Chester-le-Street Div (L) 1885-1905; *cr* a Baronet 1893, and *Baron Joicey* of Chester-le-Street, co Durham (peerage of United Kingdom) 1906: *m* 1st, 1879, Elizabeth Amy, who *d* 1881, da of late Joseph Robinson, JP, of North Shields; 2ndly, 1884, Marguerite Smyles, who *d* 1911, da of late Col Drever, HEICS; *d* 1936; *s* by his el son (2) JAMES ARTHUR, 2nd Baron, *b* 1880; was High Sheriff of co Durham 1910: *m* 1904, Georgina Wharton, who *d* 1952, da of Major Augustus Edward Burdon, formerly of Hartford Hall, Bedlington, Northumberland; *d* 1940; *s* by his brother (3) HUGH EDWARD, 3rd Baron, *b* 1881; High Sheriff of Northumberland 1933: *m* 1921, Lady Joan Katherine Lambton, who *d* 1967, da of 4th Earl of Durham; *d* 1966; *s* by his yr son (4) MICHAEL EDWARD, 4th Baron, *b* 1925; Capt Coldstream Guards; DL Northumberland 1985: *m* 1952, Elisabeth Marion, da of late Lt-Col Hon Ian Leslie Melville, TD (*see* E Leven and Melville, colls); *d* 1993; *s* by his elder son (5) JAMES MICHAEL, 5th Baron and present peer.

Jones, see Baron Wynne-Jones.

JOSEPH, BARON (Joseph) (Life Baron 1987, Bt (UK) 1943, of Portsoken, City of London)

KEITH SINJOHN, JOSEPH, CH, PC, *Life Baron*, and 2nd *Baronet*; *b* 17 Jan 1918; *s* his father, *Sir* SAMUEL GEORGE, in his baronetcy, 1944; *ed* Harrow, and Magdalen Coll, Oxford; Fellow of All Souls' Coll 1946-60, and since 1972; Bar Middle Temple 1946; Parl Private Sec to Under-Sec of State for Commonwealth Relations 1957-59, Parl Sec, Min of Housing and Local Govt 1959-61, Min of State at Board of Trade 1961-62, Min of Housing and Local Govt, and Min for Welsh Affairs 1962-64, Sec of State for Social Services 1970-74, for Industry 1979-81, and for Educn and Science 1981-86; formerly an Underwriting Member of Lloyd's; Fellow of Inst of Builders, and Liveryman of Vintners' Co; an Alderman of City of London 1946-49; Dir Gilbert-Ash Ltd 1949-59, Bovis Holdings Ltd 1951-59 (Dep Chm 1964-70), and Chm Bovis Ltd 1958-59;

co-founder and first Chm Foundation for Management Educn 1959, founder and first Chm Mulberry Housing Trust 1965-69, Chm Jewish Affairs Research Board 1966-70, founder and Chm of Management Cttee of Centre for Policy Studies Ltd 1974-79; Part-time Consultant: Bovis Ltd 1986-89 (since when Dir), Cable & Wireless plc 1986-91, and Trusthouse Forte 1986-89; 1939-45 War in Italy as Capt RA (wounded, despatches); MP for NE Div of Leeds (*C*) 1956-87; *cr* PC 1962, CH 1986, and *Baron Joseph*, of Portsoken, City of London (Life Baron) 1987: *m* 1st, 1951 (*m diss* 1985), Hellen Louise, yr da of Sigmar Guggenheimer, of New York; 2ndly, 1990, Mrs Yolanda V. Sheriff, of Connecticut, USA, and has issue by 1st *m*.

Arms – Per chevron gules and barry wavy of ten azure and or a fesse embattled of the last masoned sable in chief a sun in splendour gold. **Crest** – In front of an annulet azure encircling a tower gules two sprigs of honesty leaved and slipped saltire-wise proper.
Address – House of Lords, SW1A 0PW.

SON LIVING (*by 1st marriage*)

Hon JAMES SAMUEL, *b* 27 Jan 1955; *ed* Harrow.

DAUGHTERS LIVING (*by 1st marriage*)

Hon Emma Catherine Sarah, *b* 1956.
Hon Julia Rachel, *b* 1959: *m* 1985, Jonathan David Rolnick, only son of Jacob Rolnick, of New York, USA, and has issue living, David Sebastian, *b* 1991.
Hon Anna Jane Rebecca, *b* 1964.

PREDECESSOR – The 1st baronet, Sir Samuel George Joseph, son of Abraham Joseph, was Co-Chm and Man Dir of Bovis Ltd, and Underwriter of Lloyd's, and Hon Col 56th (1st London) Div RE; also Mayor of St Marylebone 1928-30, Sheriff of City of London 1933-34, Alderman thereof 1933, and Lord Mayor 1942-43; served during European War 1914-19 (wounded, despatches).

JOWITT, EARLDOM OF (Jowitt) (Extinct 1957)

DAUGHTER LIVING OF FIRST EARL

Lady Penelope, *b* 1923: *m* 1943, George Wynn-Williams, FRCS, FRCOG, who *d* 1993, and has issue living, William Jowitt Dafydd (26 Bassingham Rd, SW18), *b* 1st, 1975 (*m diss* 1988), Amanda S. B., only da of Col John Childs, of 23 Lennox Gdns, SW3; 2ndly, 1990, Fiona Mary, da of Graham Pilcher, and has issue living (by 1st *m*), William Alexander Taillefer *b* 1978, James Henry Jowitt *b* 1983, — Huw James (Brook House, Philpot Lane, Chobham, Surrey GU24 8HD), *b* 1955; Bar Middle Temple 1977: *m* 1979, Mary L., only da of William Vaughan, of Chobham Farm Cottage, Chobham, Surrey, and has issue living, Harry George *b* 1984, Laura Jane *b* 1982, Lucy Mary *b* 1987, — Lesley-Jane, *b* 1944: *m* 1st, 1965 (*m diss* 1976), William Mortimer Man; 2ndly, 1976 (*m* annulled 1980), John Richard Weguelin; 3rdly, 1981, Peter Charles Nicholson, of Mere House, Hamble, Hants, and has issue living (by 1st *m*), David Mortimer *b* 1969: *m* 1994, Hon Stephanie Jane Moore, only da of Baron Moore of Lower Marsh, PC (Life Baron), Philippa Lesley *b* 1966: *m* 1989 (*m diss* 1991), — (and has issue living, Ben ODGERS *b* 1989), Fiona Lesley *b* 1970. *Residence* – 39 Hurlingham Court, Ranelagh Gdns, SW6 3UW.

JUDD, BARON (Judd) (Life Baron 1991)

FRANK ASHCROFT JUDD, son of late Charles Wilfred Judd, CBE, of 42 The Crescent, Belmont, Sutton, Surrey; *b* 28 March 1935; *ed* City of London Sch, and LSE (BSc); F/O RAF 1957-59; Gen Sec Internat Voluntary Ser 1960-66; PPS to Min of Housing and Local Govt 1967-70, to Leader of Opposition 1970-72, Joint Opposition Defence Spokesman 1972-74, Parly Under Sec of State for Defence RN 1974-76, Min for Overseas Devpt 1976-77, FCO 1977-79; Assoc Dir Internat Defence & Aid Fund for Southern Africa 1979-80, Dir VSO 1980-85, Chm Internat Council of Voluntary Agencies 1985-90, and Dir Oxfam 1985-91; Council Member Overseas Devpt Inst, Member Governing Body Queen Elizabeth House, Oxford Univ, and Gov LSE since 1982; Member Council for Charitable Support since 1991, Member World Health Organisation Task Force on Health and Development Policies since 1994; Gov Westminster Coll, Oxford; Trustee Portsmouth Cathedral Development Trust, plc; Hon Fellow Portsmouth Univ 1978, Hon DLitt Bradford Univ 1987, FRSA 1988; MP Portsmouth W (*Lab*) 1966-74, and Portsmouth N 1974-79; author; *cr Baron Judd*, of Portsea, co Hants (Life Baron) 1991; *m* 1961, Christine Elizabeth Louise, da of late Frederick Ward Willington, of Kent, and has issue.
Residence – Belmont, 21 Mill Lane, Old Marston, Oxford OX3 0PY. *Club* – Commonwealth Trust.

DAUGHTERS LIVING

Hon Elizabeth, *b* 1967.
Hon Philippa, *b* 1969.

KABERRY OF ADEL, BARONY OF (Kaberry) (Extinct 1991)

WIDOW AND SONS LIVING OF LIFE BARON

(see Kaberry, Bt)

KADOORIE, BARONY OF (Kadoorie) (Extinct 1993)

SON LIVING OF LIFE BARON

Hon Michael David *b* 1941; *ed* King George V Sch, Hong Kong, and Le Rosey, Switzerland; Chm The Hong Kong & Shanghai Hotels Ltd, etc: *m* 1984, Betty, da of Juan E. Tamayo, of Coral Gables, Fla, USA, and has issue living, Philip *b* 1992, — Natalie *b* 1986, — Bettina, *b* 1987. *Residence* - 68 Deep Water Bay Rd, Hong Kong.

DAUGHTER LIVING OF LIFE BARON

Hon Rita Laura, *b* 1940: *m* 1965, Ronald James McAulay, and has issue living, Andrew James Kadoorie, *b* 1967, — Deborah Jane Kadoorie, *b* 1969.

WIDOW LIVING OF LIFE BARON

MURIEL (*Baroness Kadoorie*), da of D. S. Gubbay, of Hong Kong: *m* 1938, Baron Kadoorie, CBE (Life Baron), who *d* 1993. *Residence* - 24 Kadoorie Av, Kowloon, Hong Kong.

KAGAN, BARON (Kagan) (Life Baron 1976)

JOSEPH KAGAN, son of Benjamin Kagan (who *d* 1988, aged 109), of Leeds; *b* 6 June 1915; *ed* High Sch, Kaunas, Lithuania, and Leeds Univ (BA, BCom Hons); a Dir of Kagan Textiles; Chm of Gannex Group of Cos (founded 1951); *cr* Knt 1970 (cancelled and annulled 1981), and *Baron Kagan*, of Elland in co of West Yorkshire (Life Baron) 1976: *m* 1943, Margaret, da of George Strom, and has issue.

Arms – Per chevron vert and gules a chevron rompu or fretted with barbed wire sable between in chief two pairs of the text letter K each pair addorsed and in base two triangles interlaced gold on a bordure argent eight martlets gules. **Crest** – Upon a helm with a wreath or, vert and gules issuant from a circlet of barbed wire meshed sable and from flames proper a phoenix or charged on the breast with two triangles interlaced sable. **Supporters** – *Dexter*, an artisan wearing a *Gannex* apron and bib, holding in the exterior hand a shuttle proper. *Sinister*, a Hebrew scholar of circa 1550 habited in a long gown and wearing a skull cap sable, holding in front of him in the exterior hand an open book proper bound gules, edged or, having on the dexter page the Roman numerals XV and III, and on the sinister page the numerals MCDLXI sable. **Motto** – (in Hebrew), Knowledge, Work, Compassion.
Residence – Delamere, Fixby, Huddersfield HD2 2JL, Yorks.

SONS LIVING

Hon Michael George, *b* 1950.
Hon Daniel, *b* 1953.

DAUGHTER LIVING

Hon Anne Eugenia, *b* 1965.

KALDOR, BARONY OF (Kaldor) (Extinct 1986)

DAUGHTERS LIVING OF LIFE BARON

Hon Katharine Margaret, *b* 1937: *m* 1958, Anthony Hungerford Hoskyns, of 25 Hamilton Gdns, NW8 (see Hoskyns, Bt).
Hon Frances Julia, *b* 1940: *m* 1962, Michael John Stewart, of 39 Upper Park Rd, NW3.
Hon Penelope Jane, *b* 1942: *m* 1964, Robert Charles Milsom, of 2 Adams Rd, Cambridge.
Hon Mary Henrietta, *b* 1946; writer.

WIDOW LIVING OF LIFE BARON

CLARISSA ELISABETH (*Baroness Kaldor*), da of Henry Frederick Goldschmidt: *m* 1934, Baron Kaldor, FBA (Life Baron), who *d* 1986. *Residences* - 27 Egerton Gdns, SW3; 2 Adams Rd, Cambridge; 18 rue St Joseph, 83680 La Garde-Freinet, France.

KEARTON, BARONY OF (Kearton) (Extinct 1992)

WIDOW LIVING OF LIFE BARON

AGNES KATHLEEN (*Baroness Kearton*), da of Samuel Pratt Brander: *m* 1936, Baron Kearton, OBE, FRS (Life Baron), who *d* 1992. *Residence* – The Fox, Nethercote, Bourton-on-the-Water, Glos GL54 2DT.

KEITH OF AVONHOLM, BARONY OF (Keith) (Extinct 1964)

SON LIVING OF LIFE BARON

Hon Henry Shanks (*Baron Keith of Kinkel*), *b* 1922; *cr Baron Keith of Kinkel* (Life Baron) 1976 (see that title).

DAUGHTER LIVING OF LIFE BARON

Hon Elizabeth Hamilton, *b* 1916: *m* 1945, Raymond Alan Lolley, who *d* 1980, and has issue.

KEITH OF CASTLEACRE, BARON (Keith) (Life Baron 1979)

Truth conquers

KENNETH ALEXANDER KEITH, son of late Edward Charles Keith, of Swanton Morley House, Dereham, Norfolk, *b* 30 Aug 1916; *ed* Rugby; 1939-45 War as Lt-Col WG in N Africa and NW Europe (despatches, Croix de Guerre with Silver Star); Chm Hill Samuel Gp Ltd 1970-80, and Rolls Royce Ltd 1972-80; Pres Royal Norfolk Agricultural Assocn 1989, Pres British Standards Inst since 1989, Pres RoSPA since 1989; *cr* Knt 1969, and *Baron Keith of Castleacre*, of Swaffham, co Norfolk (Life Baron) 1979: *m* 1st, 1946 (*m diss* 1958), Lady Ariel Olivia Winifred Baird, da of 1st Viscount Stonehaven, by his wife late Countess of Kintore (in her own right); 2ndly, 1962 (*m diss* 1972), Nancy, who *d* 1990, da of Edward B. Gross, of Monterey, Calif, and formerly wife of (i) Howard Hawks (*d* 1977), film dir, and (ii) Leland Hayward (*d* 1971), of Manhasset, New York; 3rdly, 1973, Marieluz, elder da of late Capt Robert Peel Dennistoun-Webster, DSC, RN, of Hurst Grange, nr Twyford, formerly wife of (i) Adrian Donald Henderson (*see* Faringdon, B, colls), and widow of Col James Robert Hanbury, of Burley-on-the-Hill, Oakham, Rutland, and has issue by 1st *m*.

Arms – Paly of six or and gules, on a chief argent three stags heads caboshed proper. **Crest** – A garb or supported by two stags respectant proper. **Supporters** – *Dexter*, A foreman proper, his overall argent charged on the breast pocket with a monogram composed of the letters RR superimposed one above the other, with the word Rolls and beneath the word Royce, all in capital letters gules, the collar azure, holding in his outer hand a worksheet in its folder proper: *Sinister*, a farmer in plus-four suit and cap of brown tweed with heather mixture stockings, and brown boots holding in the crook of his outer arm a shotgun proper.
Residences – 9 Eaton Sq, SW1W 9DB; The Wicken House, Castleacre, Norfolk PE32 2BP. *Clubs* – Pratt's, White's; Links Club (New York).

SON LIVING (By 1st marriage)

Hon Alastair James, *b* 1947; *ed* Eton, and Harvard Univ; *m* 1983, Jayne Will, yr da of late Walter C. Teagle, jr, and has issue living, Alexander Teagle, *b* 1984.

DAUGHTER LIVING (By 1st marriage)

Hon Camilla Margaret (twin) (*Hon Lady Mackeson*) (Apt 36E, 1365 York Av, New York 10021, USA), *b* 1947: *m* 1968 (*m diss* 1972), Sir Rupert Henry Mackeson, 2nd Bt.

KEITH OF KINKEL, BARON (Keith) (Life Baron 1976)

HENRY SHANKS KEITH, PC, son of late Baron Keith of Avonholm (Life Baron); *b* 7 Feb 1922; *ed* Edinburgh Acad, Magdalen Coll, Oxford (MA; Hon Fellow 1977) and Edinburgh Univ (LLB); Bar Gray's Inn 1951; Bencher 1976; Advocate Scotland 1950; QC 1962; Standing Jr Council to Dep of Health for Scotland 1957-62; a Member of Scottish Valuation Advisory Council 1959-70 (Chm 1972-76), of Law Reform Cttee for Scotland 1964-70, of Panel of Arbiters under European Fisheries Convention 1964-71, and under Convention on Settlement of Investment Disputes between States and Nationals of other States 1968-71, and of Cttee on Law of Defamation 1971-75; Dep Chm Parl Boundaries Commn for Scotland 1975; Sheriff-Prin of Roxburgh, Berwick and Selkirk 1970-71; 1939-45 War in Scots Gds (despatches); a Lord of Session

with title of Lord Keith 1971-76, since when Lord of Appeal in Ordinary; Chm Joint Cttee on Consolidation Bills 1978-80; Chm Cttee on Enforcement Powers of the Revenue Depts 1980-84; *cr Baron Keith of Kinkel*, of Strathtummel in District of Perth and Kinross (Life Baron) 1976 and PC 1976: *m* 1955, Alison Hope Alan, JP, yr da of Alan Brown, and has issue.
Residence – Strathtummel, Pitlochry, Perthshire PH16 5RP.

SONS LIVING

Hon James Alan, *b* 1959: *m* 1987, Eleanor Mary, yr da of Col Michael ffolliott Woodhead, OBE, of 56 Chesilton Rd, SW6, and has issue living, Samuel Henry Michael, *b* 1994, — Flavia, *b* 1991.
Hon Thomas Hamilton, *b* 1961; *ed* Magdalen Coll, Oxford; Bar-at-law. *Chambers* – Fountain Court, Temple, EC4Y 9DH.
Hon Hugo George, *b* 1967.
Hon Alexander Lindsay, *b* 1967.

DAUGHTER LIVING

Hon Deborah Jane, *b* 1957; *ed* Magdalen Coll, Oxford (BSc, MSc); Bar-at-Law. *Chambers* – 3 Raymond Buildings, Gray's Inn, WC1R 5BP.

Kelburn, Viscount of; son of Earl of Glasgow.

Kellie, Earl of; Earl of Mar and Kellie.

KEMSLEY, VISCOUNT (Berry) (Viscount UK 1945, Bt UK 1928)

Persevere and conquer

(GEOFFREY) LIONEL BERRY, 2nd Viscount, and 2nd Baronet; *b* 29 June 1909; *s* 1968; *ed* Marlborough, and Magdalen Coll, Oxford; FRSA; a KStJ; a DL for Leics 1972; a Co Councillor for Northants 1964-70; Dep Chm, Kemsley Newspapers, Ltd, 1938-59; Master of Spectacle Makers' Co 1949-51 and 1959-61; Pres of Assocn of Independent Hospitals 1976-83; Chm of St Andrew's Hosp, Northampton 1973-84; a Member of Chapter Gen of OStJ; 1939-45 War as Capt Grenadier Gds (invalided out 1942); MP for Buckingham (*C*) 1943-45; High Sheriff of Leics 1967; *m* 1933, Lady Hélène Candida Hay, DStJ, da of 11th Marquess of Tweeddale, and has issue.

Arms – Gules, three bars or, on a pile ermine as many martlets sable. **Crest** – A griffin sejant sable, collared and chained, the chain reflexed over the back and resting the dexter claw on a catharine wheel or. **Supporters** – On either side a stag guardant or, gorged with a chaplet of mistletoe proper.
Residence – Field House, Thorpe Lubenham, Market Harborough, Leics LE16 9TR. *Clubs* – Royal Overseas, Turf, Pratt's.

DAUGHTERS LIVING

Hon Mary Anne, *b* 1934: *m* 1960, Charles Henry van Raalte, of 7 Meadowcourt Rd, Oadby, Leics, and has issue living, Marcus Lionel, *b* 1961, — Kristina Beryl, *b* 1962: *m* 1984, — Ghislaine Sara, *b* 1964.
Hon Pamela Jane Margaret (*Hon Lady Mobbs*), *b* 1937: *m* 1961, Sir Gerald Nigel Mobbs, of Widmer Lodge, Lacey Green, Aylesbury, Bucks, HP17 0RJ, and has issue living, Christopher William, *b* 1965: *m* 1991, Elizabeth Dora, yr da of late Maj J. F. A. Overton, LI, of Hillesden, Bucks, and has issue living, Lucinda Dora Jane *b* 1992, — Virginia Elizabeth, *b* 1968, — Penelope Helen (twin), *b* 1968.
Hon Caroline Helen, *b* 1942: *m* 1965, John Peter Houison Craufurd of Craufurdland and Braehead, of Craufurdland Castle, Kilmarnock, Ayrshire, and has issue living, John Alexander, *b* 1966, — Simon Douglas, *b* 1972, — Teresa Eleanor, *b* 1967: *m* 1991, Christopher L. Geall, son of John D. Geall, of Bickley Lodge, No Mans Heath, Cheshire.
Hon Catherine Francis Lilian, *b* 1944: *m* 1969, Richard Douglas Fowler Bream, of Manor Farm, Grace Dieu, Whitwick, Leics, and has issue living, Tamerlane Douglas Fowler, *b* 1971, — Atlanta Mary, *b* 1970.

BROTHER LIVING

Hon (William) Neville, *b* 1914; *ed* Harrow, and at Magdalen Coll, Oxford; Capt Gren Gds 1939-46; Man Dir Daily Record and Sunday Mail, Glasgow, 1938-39, and Editor News Guardian (Guards Div) 1945-46; author of *Dunkirk* (1940): *m* 1951, Christobel (NORRIE), only da of late John Wallis More-Molyneux, of Loseley Park, Guildford. *Residence* – Bermuda, 49 Ave Hector Otto, Monaco. *Clubs* – Turf, Pratt's.

SISTER LIVING

Hon (Mary) Pamela (*Pamela, Marchioness of Huntly*), *b* (twin) 1918: *m* 1941 (*m diss* 1965), 12th Marquess of Huntly, who *d* 1987. *Residence* – 80 Old Church St, SW3 6EP.

WIDOW LIVING OF SON OF FIRST VISCOUNT

Sarah Anne (*Hon Lady Berry*) (Fox's Walk, Shurlock Row, Reading, Berks RG10 0PB), da of Raymond Clifford-Turner: *m* 1966, as his 2nd wife, Hon Sir Anthony George Berry, MP, who *d* 1984, and has issue (see colls infra).

COLLATERAL BRANCHES LIVING

Issue of late Maj Hon Denis Gomer Berry, TD, 2nd son of 1st Viscount, *b* 1911, *d* 1983: *m* 1st, 1934 (*m diss* 1942), Rosemary Leonora, elder da of late Lionel Nathan de Rothschild (*see* B Rothschild, colls); 2ndly, 1947, Pamela, who *d* 1987, formerly wife of Lt Charles Robert Archibald Grant, RN, and elder da of late Capt Lord Richard Wellesley (*see* D Wellington, colls):—

(By 1st *m*) Barbara Marie-Louise (Fox House, Little Coxwell, Faringdon, Oxon,), *b* 1935: *m* 1954 (*m diss* 1983), Alexander Clement Gilmour, and has issue (*see* B Gilmour of Craigmillar). —— Susan Lilian Constance, *b* 1938: *m* 1st, 1963 (*m diss* 1978), Christopher George Francis Harding (later Sir Christopher Harding); 2ndly, 1989, Raymond Muir, and *d* 1989, leaving issue (by 1st *m*), Rupert Christopher, *b* 1965, —— Louise Amanda, *b* 1966. —— (By 2nd *m*) RICHARD GOMER (Sandpit House, Toothill, Romsey, Hants SO51 9LN), *b* 17 April 1951; *ed* Eton: *m* 1981 (*m diss* 1988), Tana-Marie, elder da of Clive William Lester, of Beaufre, Beaulieu, Hants. —— (Anne) Denise, *b* 1948: *m* 1970, Brian Peter Harvey Orange, of Fromans House, King's Somborne, Hants, and has issue living, Michael Richard, *b* 1973, —— Simon George, *b* 1974, —— Jonathan Charles, *b* 1976.

Issue of late Hon Sir Anthony George Berry, MP, yst son of 1st Viscount, *b* 1925, *d* (*k* in the bomb explosion at the Grand Hotel, Brighton) 1984: *m* 1st, 1954 (*m diss* 1966), Hon Mary Cynthia Burke Roche, da of 4th Baron Fermoy; 2ndly, 1966, Sarah Anne (ante), da of Raymond Clifford-Turner:—

(By 1st *m*) Edward Anthony Morys (103 Stormont Rd, SW11), *b* 1960: *m* 1989, Joanna Clare, yr da of Anthony George Leschallas (*see* E Romney, colls), and has issue living, William Anthony Edward, *b* 1993, —— Alice Elisabeth, *b* 1990, —— Rose Ophelia, *b* 1992. —— Alexandra Mary, *b* 1955: *m* 1982, Reinhold Bartz. —— Antonia Ruth, *b* 1957: *m* 1990, Mark F. Butterworth, of 3 Lansdowne Crescent, Bath, son of A. K. Butterworth, of Dharamsala, India, and has issue living, Jessica *b* 1990. —— Joanna Cynthia, *b* (twin) 1957. —— (By 2nd *m*) George Raymond Gomer, *b* 1967. —— Sasha Jane, *b* 1969.

PREDECESSOR – (1) (JAMES) GOMER Berry, GBE, son of Alderman John Mathias Berry, JP, of Gwaelodygarth, Merthy Tydfil (V Camrose); *b* 1883; Newspaper proprietor; Chm of Kemsley Newspapers Ltd, and Editor-in-Ch, *Sunday Times*, 1937-59; *cr* a Baronet 1928, *Baron Kemsley*, of Farnham Royal, co Bucks (peerage of UK) 1936, and *Viscount Kemsley*, of Dropmore, co Bucks (peerage of UK) 1945, GBE (Civil) 1959: *m* 1st, 1907, Mary Lilian, who *d* 1928, da of late Horace George Holmes, JP, of 8 Brondesbury Park, NW6; 2ndly, 1931, Edith, who *d* 1976, da of E. N. Merandon du Plessis, of Constance, Flacq, Mauritius, formerly wife of Cornelius Willem Dresselhuys; *d* 1968; *s* by his el son (2) (GEOFFREY) LIONEL, 2nd Viscount and present peer; also Baron Kemsley.

KENILWORTH, BARON (Siddeley) (Baron UK 1937)

(JOHN) RANDLE SIDDELEY, 4th Baron; *b* 16 June 1954; *s* 1981; *ed* Northease Manor, West Dean Coll, and London Coll of Furniture; Lord of Manor of Kenilworth: *m* 1st, 1983 (*m diss* 1990), Kim, only da of Danie Serfontein, of Laybourne Cottage, Jesmond Dene Rd, Newcastle upon Tyne; 2ndly, 1991, Mrs Kiki McDonough (*née* Axford), formerly wife of David McDonough, and has issue by 2nd *m*.

Arms – Per chevron or and azure in chief two goats' heads erased and in base a triangular castle with three towers, on a chief of the second two wings conjoined in fesse all counterchanged. **Crest** – Issuant out of the battlements of a tower a goat's head argent armed or in front of a rising sun also issuant gold. **Supporters** – On either side a goat or gorged with a collar azure pendent therefrom by a chain gold and escutcheon chequy of the first and second a chief ermine.
Address – c/o House of Lords, SW1.

By striding

SONS LIVING (*by 2nd marriage*)

Hon WILLIAM RANDLE, *b* 24 Jan 1992.
Hon Edward Oscar, *b* 1994.

SISTER LIVING

Hon Belinda Jane, *b* 1950: *m* 1st 1971 (*m diss* 1974), Christopher Aston James; *m* 2ndly 1983, David Ian McCarraher, and has issue living (by 2nd *m*), Tara Louise, *b* 1989. *Residence* – Silver Coppers, College Rd, Epsom, Surrey.

WIDOW LIVING OF SON OF FIRST BARON

Pamela (1 Belle Vue Court, Longueville, St Saviour, Jersey), da of late G. A. Williams, of Gorey, Jersey: *m* 1953, as his 2nd wife, Hon Norman Goodier Siddeley, who *d* 1971.

WIDOW LIVING OF THIRD BARON

JACQUELINE PAULETTE (*Jacqueline, Baroness Kenilworth*) (2 Lexham Walk, W8), da of late Robert Gelpi: *m* 1948, the 3rd Baron, who *d* 1981.

COLLATERAL BRANCH LIVING

Issue of late Hon Ernest Hall Siddeley, 2nd son of 1st Baron, *b* 1895, *d* 1985: *m* 1921, Muriel, who *d* 1988, da of late John R. Quick:—

Audrey Joan, *b* 1922; resumed her maiden name by deed poll 1968: *m* 1st, 1951 (*m diss* 1955), John Main; 2ndly, 1971 (*m diss* 1974), Francis Bermingham. *Residence* – Belmont, Barford Rd. Bloxham, Banbury, Oxon OX15 4EZ.

PREDECESSORS – (1) JOHN DAVENPORT Siddeley, CBE, son of late William Siddeley, of Manchester; *b* 1866; a Motor and Aircraft Engineer; was Chm and Managing Director of Armstrong-Siddeley Motors, Ltd, of Parkside, Coventry, and of Sir W. G. Armstrong-Whitworth Aircraft, Ltd; High Sheriff of Warwickshire 1932; *cr Baron Kenilworth*, of Kenilworth, co Warwick (peerage of United Kingdom) 1937: *m* 1893, Sara Mabel, who *d* 1953, da of late James Goodier, of Macclesfield; *d* 1953; *s* by his el son (2) CYRIL DAVENPORT, CBE, TD, 2nd Baron; *b* 1894; *d* 1971: *m* 1919, Marjorie Tennant, who *d* 1977, da of late Harry Firth, of Dewsbury, Yorks; *s* by his son (3) JOHN DAVENPORT, 3rd Baron, *b* 1924: *m* 1948, Jacqueline Paulette, da of Robert Gelpi; *d* 1981; *s* by his only son (4) (JOHN) RANDLE, 4th Baron and present peer.

Kenlis, Baron, grandson of Marquess of Headfort, and title of Marquess of Headfort on Roll of HL.

KENNET, BARON (Young) (Baron UK 1935)

In colle domus.

A house on a hill

WAYLAND HILTON YOUNG, 2nd Baron; *b* 2 Aug 1923; *s* 1960; *ed* Stowe, and at Trin Coll, Camb; Hon FRIBA; Writer; a Member of British Delegation, Assemblies W European Union and Council of Europe 1962-65, and Chm of UK Cttee for International Co-operation Year 1965; Parl Sec, Min of Housing and Local Govt 1966-70; Chm of Advisory Cttee on Oil Pollution of the Sea 1970-74, and of Council for Protection of Rural England 1971-72, and of Internat Parl Conferences on the Environment 1971-80; Dir of Europe Plus Thirty 1974-76; a Member of European Parliament 1978-79; Chm of the Architecture Club 1983-94; Vice-Pres of Parliamentary and Scientific Cttee since 1989; SDP Chief Whip in House of Lords 1981-83 and Spokesman on Foreign Affairs and Defence 1981-90; 1939-45 War as Ordinary Seaman and Sub-Lt RNVR; in Foreign Office 1946-47, and 1949-51: *m* 1948, Elizabeth Ann, da of late Capt Bryan Fullerton Adams, DSO, RN, of Cherry Tree, Hacheston, Suffolk, and has issue.

Arms – Per fesse sable and argent: in chief two lions rampant-guardant, and in base an anchor erect with a cable, all counterchanged. **Crest** – A demi-unicorn couped ermine, armed, maned, and hoofed or, gorged with a naval crown azure supporting an anchor erect sable.
Residence – The Lacket, Lockeridge, Marlborough, Wilts SN8 4EQ.

SON LIVING

Hon (WILLIAM ALDUS) THOBY, *b* 24 May 1957; *ed* Marlborough, and Sussex Univ: *m* 1987, Hon Josephine Mary Keyes, yr da of 2nd Baron Keyes, and has issue living, Archibald Wayland Keyes, *b* 7 June 1992, — Maud Elizabeth Aurora, *b* 1989. *Residence* – 100 Bayswater Rd, W2 3HJ.

DAUGHTERS LIVING

Hon Easter Donatella, *b* 1949; *ed* Keele Univ: *m* 1981, Frank Joffre Russell, and has issue living, Louis Inigo, *b* 1983, — Theo Joffre, *b* 1986, — Alice Ella, *b* 1979.
Hon Emily Tacita, *b* 1951; *ed* Chelsea Sch of Arts, and St Martin Sch of Art; has issue living, Arthur William Phoenix Young Jeffes, *b* 1978.
Hon Mopsa Mary, *b* 1953; *ed* Holland Park Sch: *m* 1981, Richard Douglas English, and has issue living, Joseph Edward, *b* 1987, — Thomas Eliot, *b* 1991, — Lilian Mary, *b* 1989.
Hon (Audrey) Louisa, *b* 1959; *ed* Trinity Coll, Camb: has issue, Isabel Adomakoh YOUNG, *b* 1993.
Hon (Alice Matelda) Zoe, *b* 1969; *ed* Sussex Univ.

PREDECESSOR – (1) EDWARD HILTON Young, GBE, DSO, DSC, PC, yst son of Sir George Young, 3rd Bt (*cr* 1813); *b* 1879; Bar Inner Temple 1904; European War 1914-19 in HMS "Iron Duke" and "Centaur" with British Naval Mission in Serbia, with Naval Guns in Flanders, at Zeebrugge in "Vindictive", and in N Russia in charge of Armoured Train; was Assist Editor *Economist* 1909-10, and City Editor *Morning Post* 1910-14, Parliamentary Private Sec to Pres of Board of Education 1919-21, Financial Sec to the Treasury 1921-22, Ch Liberal Whip 1922-3, Parliamentary Sec to Depart of Overseas Trade (in National Govt) Sept to Nov 1931, and Min of Health 1931-35; a Member of Hague Commn 1922; sat as MP for Norwich (*L*) 1915-22, and 1924-29 (*L*, afterwards *C*), and for Sevenoaks Div of Kent (*C*) 1929-35; *cr Baron Kennet*, of the Dene, co Wilts (peerage of United Kingdom) 1935: *m* 1922, Edith Agnes Kathleen, who *d* 1947, da of late Rev Canon Lloyd Stewart Bruce (Bruce, Bt, *cr* 1804, colls), and widow of Capt Robert Falcon Scott, CVO, RN; *d* 1960; *s* by his only son (2) WAYLAND HILTON, 2nd Baron and present peer.

KENSINGTON, BARON (Edwardes) (Baron I 1776 and UK 1886)

Keep the faith

HUGH IVOR EDWARDES, 8th Baron; *b* 24 Nov 1933; *s* 1981; *ed* Eton: *m* 1961, Juliet Elizabeth Massy, da of late Alexander Massy Anderson, and has issue.

Arms – Quarterly: 1st and 4th ermine, a lion rampant sable, *Edwardes*; 2nd and 3rd gules, a chevron between three crosses bottony or, *Rich*. **Crest** – On a mount vert, a wyvern, wings expanded, argent. **Supporters** – Two reindeer proper, armed and unguled or.
Residence – Friar Tuck, PO Box 549, Mooi River, 3300 Natal, S Africa.

SONS LIVING

Hon William Owen Alexander, *b* 21 July 1964: *m* 1991, Marie Hélène Anne Véronique, eldest da of Jean-Alain Lalouette, of 29 River Walk, Vacoas, Mauritius, and has issue living, William Francis Ivor, *b* 23 March 1993.
Hon Hugh Rupert, *b* 1967.

DAUGHTER LIVING

Hon Amanda Louise Massy, *b* 1962: *m* 1984, Anthony Michael Greene, eldest son of Michael Victor Greene, of Natal, S Africa, and has issue living, James Stuart, *b* 1985, — Stephanie Louise Massy *b* 1987, — Rachel Delia, *b* 1988.

SISTER LIVING (*Raised to the rank of a Baron's daughter* 1982)

Hon Meriel Davina, *b* 1935: *m* (Jan) 1972, David Andrew Long, of Hill House, Filmore Hill, Privett, Alton, Hants GU34 3NX, and has issue living, James Philip, *b* (Dec) 1972, — Harry Simon, *b* 1976.

WIDOW LIVING OF SON OF SIXTH BARON

Elizabeth (Carpenter's Yard, Compton Pauncefoot, Yeovil, Som), yst da of late Robert Alexander Longman Broadley, of Suddon Farm, Wincanton, Som: *m* 1939, Com Hon David Edwardes, DSC, RN, 3rd son of 6th Baron, who *d* 1983, and has issue (see colls infra).

MOTHER LIVING

Angela Dorothea, da of late Lieut-Col Eustace Shearman, 10th Hussars, and widow of George Benson, 15th/19th Hussars: *m* 2ndly, 1932, Capt Hon (Hugh) Owen Edwardes, who *d* 1937; 3rdly, 1951, Lieut-Com John Hamilton, RN (ret). *Residence* – 1 Scaur o'Doon Rd, Doonfoot, Ayr.

COLLATERAL BRANCHES LIVING

Issue of late Com Hon David Edwardes, DSC, RN, 3rd son of 6th Baron, *b* 1907, *d* 1983: *m* 1939, Elizabeth (ante), yst da of late Robert Alexander Longman Broadley, of Suddon Farm, Wincanton, Som:—
Susan, *b* 1945: *m* 1967, Col Hugh Michael Sandars, The Queen's Own Hus (Twin Pillars Cottage, Micheldever, Winchester, Hants), and has issue living, Andrew George, *b* 1969, — Claire Catherine, *b* 1972. —— Mary Ann, *b* 1947: *m* 1968, Brig Hugh William Kellow Pye, 9th/12th R Lancers (Prince of Wales's), of Tuxwell Farm, Spaxton, Bridgwater, Somerset TA5 1DF, and has issue living, Robert Alec Kellow, *b* 1970, — Victoria Ann, *b* 1973. —— Louisa Jane, *b* 1950: *m* 1979 (*m diss* 1994), Christopher L. P. Weedon, and has issue living, George David Martin, *b* 1985, — Simon Edward Peter, *b* 1987.

Issue of late Capt Hon George Henry Edwardes, MC, 4th son of 4th Baron, *b* 1877, *d* 1930: *m* 1903, Olive, who *d* 1968, da of late Charles Wyndham Rudolph Kerr (M Lothian, colls):—
George Llewellyn, *b* 1906.

Granddaughter of late Lt-Col Hon Cuthbert Ellison Edwardes, 2nd son of 3rd Baron:—
Issue of late Capt Richard Edwardes, *b* 1894, *d* 1967: *m* 1929, Ada Mary, who *d* 1979, da of late William R. MacGeorge, of Glasgow:—
Joan Margaret, *b* 1932: *m* 1958, John Spencer Clarke, of The Roos, Whitchurch, Hants, and has issue living, Charles Richard Spencer, *b* 1960: *m* 1986, Jane Caroline Sargeant, — James Alured, *b* 1964, — Sally Aletta, *b* 1959: *m* 1982, Clive Julian Spencer, — Fiona Jane, *b* 1963.

Grandchildren of late Rev Hon Thomas Edwardes, 6th son of 2nd Baron:—
Issue of late Edward Henry Edwardes, OBE, *b* 1875, *d* 1955: *m* 1907, Eleanor Matilda, who *d* 1925, da of late Rev William Nuttall (formerly V of Atherton, Manchester), of 58 Park Road, Southport:—
Barbara, *b* 1909: *m* 1939, August Henry Gernaey, of Oakwood House, Birkacre, Chorley, Lancs, and has issue living, Susan Leonie, *b* 1940, — Joanna, *b* 1942, — Caroline, *b* 1945. —— Eleonora, *b* 1911: *m* 1942, Joseph Hugh Scott Gardner, who *d* 1989, and has issue living, Hugh Martin, *b* 1951, — Sarah, *b* 1944.

Grandsons of late Edward Henry Edwardes, OBE (ante):—
Issue of late William Edwardes, *b* 1908, *d* 1983: *m* 1st, 1937, Dorothy Robertshaw, only da of Aaron Wedgwood, of Worsley, Lancs; 2ndly, 1943, Joan (Spinneys, Church St, Eccleshall, Stafford), only da of Ernest Topping, of Atherton, Lancs:—
(By 2nd *m*) David William (41 Redwood Av, Stone, Staffs), *b* 1944: *m* 1972, Diana June, yst da of William Eden Morton, of London, and has issue living, Rebecca Evelyn, *b* 1983, — Gemma Rachael, *b* 1985.
Issue of late Rev Edward Edwardes, *b* 1912, *d* 1973: *m* 1940, Norah, who *d* 1991, only da of late J. W. Watson, of Corbridge, Newcastle:—
Antony (1 Priory Close, Newport Pagnell, Bucks MK16 9AQ) *b* 1942. —— Nigel Kim, *b* 1948: *m* 1972, Kay Marjorie, el da of late Samuel Barnes, of Pitt Farm, Whitchurch Canonicorum, Dorset, and has issue living, Guy Kristian, *b* 1974. *Residence* – Little Owls, Hound Rd, Netley Abbey, Southampton S03 5FZ.

PREDECESSORS – (1) WILLIAM Edwardes, MP for Haverfordwest; inherited through his mother on the death of his cousin the 7th Earl of Warwick the estates of the Rich family; *cr Baron Kensington* (peerage of Ireland) 1776; *d* 1801; *s* by his son (2) WILLIAM, 2nd Baron; *b* 1777; MP for Haverfordwest 1801-18; *d* 1852; *s* by his son (3) WILLIAM, 3rd Baron Capt RN and Lord-Lieut of co Pembroke; *m* 1833, Laura Jane, da of Cuthbert Ellison, Esq, of Hepburn, Durham; *d* 1872; *s* by his son (4) WILLIAM, PC, 4th Baron, *b* 1835; Lord-Lieut of co Pembroke; MP for Haverfordwest (*L*) 1868-85; a Groom-in-Waiting to HM Queen Victoria 1873-4, Comptroller of HM Queen Victoria's Household 1880-85, a Lord-in-Waiting to HM Queen Victoria

1886, and Capt of Yeomen of the Guard 1892-5; *cr Baron Kensington*, of Kensington, co Middlesex (peerage of United Kingdom) 1886; *m* 1867, Grace Elizabeth, who *d* 1910, da of late Robert Johnstone-Douglas, *d* 1896; *s* by his el son **(5)** WILLIAM, 5th Baron, *b* 1868; Capt 2nd Life Guards; *d* 1900; *s* by his brother **(6)** HUGH, CMG, DSO, TD, 6th Baron, *b* 1873; Col (ret) TA; S Africa 1900-1901 (DSO), European War 1914-19 (CMG): *m* 1903, Mabel Carlisle, who *d* 1934, da of George Pilkington, of Stoneleigh, Woolton, Lancashire; *d* 1938; *s* by his son **(7)** WILLIAM, 7th Baron, Lt-Col IA; ADC to Gov of Punjab 1933-35; *d* 1981; *s* by his nephew, **(8)** HUGH IVOR (s of Hon Capt (Hugh) Owen Edwardes, 2nd son of 6th Baron), 8th Baron and present peer.

KENSWOOD, BARON (Whitfield) (Baron UK 1951)

JOHN MICHAEL HOWARD WHITFIELD, 2nd Baron, *b* 6 April 1930; *s* 1963; *ed* Harrow, at Grenoble Univ, and at Emmanuel Coll, Camb (BA 1952): *m* 1951, Deirdre Anna Louise, da of late Colin Malcolm Methven, and has issue.

Give me wisdom

Arms – Azure an argosy in full sail pennons flying or, a chief argent thereon a lion passant gules holding in the dexter forepaw a thunderbolt proper. **Crest** – between two wings or, a sprig of oak fructed proper. **Supporters** – *Dexter*, a figure representing St Cecilia habited argent cloaked azure with organ-pipes proper in her exterior hand; *sinister*, a figure representing St Gregory the Great habited argent cloaked gules holding with his exterior arm a papal staff or and holding in the hand a book proper bound sable.
Residence – Domaine de la Forêt, 31340 Villemur s/Tarn, France.

SONS LIVING

Hon MICHAEL CHRISTOPHER, *b* 3 July 1955.
Hon Anthony John, *b* 1957.
Hon Steven James, *b* 1958.
Hon Benjamin Matthew, *b* 1961.

DAUGHTER LIVING

Hon Anna Louise, *b* 1964.

SISTER LIVING

Hon Ann Sophia Madeline, *b* 1928: *m* 1st, 1948, Richard Bethuen Buzzard, BM, BCh, who *d* 1980 (B Monkswell, colls); 2ndly, 19—, — Cabot, of USA, and has issue living, Nicholas John, *b* 1952, — Jacqueline Frances, *b* 1950, — Jennifer Ann, *b* 1954, — Angela Caroline, *b* 1956.

PREDECESSOR – **(1)** ERNEST ALBERT Whitfield, son of John Henry Whitfield, of London; *b* 1887; professional violinist; ret from concert platform 1935; a Gov of BBC 1946-50; Pres, National Federation of Blind 1951-4: *m* 1st, 1920, Sophie Madeline, who *d* 1961, da of Ernest Walters Howard; 2ndly, 1962, Mrs Catherine Chilver-Stainer, who *d* 1992, da of Frank Luxton, and widow of Charles A. Chilver-Stainer, RIBA; *cr Baron Kenswood*, of St Marylebone, co London (peerage of UK) 1951; *d* 1963; *s* by his only son **(2)** JOHN MICHAEL HOWARD, 2nd Baron and present peer.

KENT, DUKE OF, see Royal Family.

KENYON, BARON (Tyrell-Kenyon) (Baron GB 1788, Bt GB 1784)

Sustain the Cross with magnanimity

LLOYD TYRELL-KENYON, 6th Baron, and 6th Baronet; *b* 13 July 1947; *s* 1993; *ed* Eton, and Magdalene Coll, Camb (BA); High Sheriff Clwyd 1986; memb Cttee of The Regions since 1993; patron of one living: *m* 1971, Sally Carolyn, eldest da of Jack Frank Page Matthews, of The Firs, Thurston, Bury St Edmunds, and has issue.

Arms – Quarterly: 1st and 4th sable, a chevron engrailed or, between three crosses-flory argent *Kenyon*; 2nd and 3rd argent, two chevronels azure, within a bordure engrailed gules, *Tyrell*. **Crests** – 1st, a lion sejant proper, resting the dexter fore paw on a cross flory argent; 2nd, a boar's head couped and erect argent, and issuing from the mouth a peacock's tail proper. **Supporters** – On either side a tiger reguardant proper, round the neck a chain or pendent therefrom an escutcheon of the arms of *Tyrell*.
Seat – Gredington, nr Whitchurch, Shropshire SY13 3DH.

SONS LIVING

Hon LLOYD NICHOLAS, *b* 9 April 1972; *ed* Eton, and Manchester Univ.
Hon Alexander Simon, *b* 1975; *ed* Eton.

BROTHERS DECEASED

Hon Richard, *b* 1948; *ed* Eton, and Seale Hayne Coll; *d* 1982 (see colls, infra).
Hon Thomas, *b* 1954; *ed* Tabley House; *d* 1993.

SISTER LIVING

Hon Katherine, *b* 1959: *m* 1985, David Nigel Vardon Churton, MBE, elder son of Col Geoffrey Vardon Churton, MBE, MC, TD, of Manley Cottage, Manley, nr Warrington, Cheshire, and has issue living, Oscar Vardon, *b* 1987, — Rollo Crispin, *b* 1989, — Zara Fleur, *b* 1991.

AUNT LIVING (*Daughter of 4th Baron*)

Hon Sarah Myfida Mary, MBE, *b* 1917; formerly in VAD; MBE (Civil) 1952: *m* 1966, Col Desmond Aubrey Robert Bancroft Cooke, late 13/18th Hussars, who *d* 1987.

WIDOW LIVING OF FIFTH BARON

LEILA MARY (*Dowager Baroness Kenyon*), da of late Cmdr John Wyndham Cookson, RN (*see* Colquhoun, Bt, 1963 Edn), and widow of Hugh William Jardine Ethelston Peel, Lieut Welsh Guards (*see* Buchanan-Jardine, Bt, 1945 Edn): *m* 1946, the 5th Baron, CBE, who *d* 1993. *Residence* – Redbridge House, Birch Lane, Ellesmere, Shropshire SY12 9AA.

COLLATERAL BRANCHES LIVING

Issue of late Hon Richard Tyrell-Kenyon, 2nd son of 5th Baron, *b* 1948, *d* 1982: *m* 1st, 1970 (*m diss* 1976), Davina Jane, da of David Charles George Jessel (*see* Jessel, Bt); 2ndly, 1980, Janet LINLEY (née Nelson), stepda of Donald Linley, of Denbigh, Clwyd:—
(By 1st *m*) Vanessa Zoë, *b* 1974.

Grandson of late Rev Hon William Trevor Kenyon, 5th son of 3rd Baron:—
Issue of late Gordon Lloyd Trevor Kenyon, *b* 1873, *d* 1951: *m* 1909, Dorothy Charlotte, who *d* 1961, da of late D. J. Wood, MusD, FRCO, of The Close, Exeter:—
Lloyd Gordon Trevor, *b* 1911: *m* 1939, Joyce Alma, da of late F. J. Parker, and has issue living Roger Lloyd, *b* 1960, — Pamela Joan, *b* 1940: *m* 1963, Barry Thomas Gouldstone, of 9 Mortimer Close, Mudeford, Christchurch, Dorset, and has issue living, Jeremy Thomas *b* 1964; BMus (London Univ), Penelope Joan *b* 1968; *ed* Brighton Univ (BA), — Carol Ann, *b* 1944. *Residence* – 31 Frays Av, W Drayton, Middx.

Granddaughter of late Lt-Col Herbert Edward Kenyon, DSO (infra):—
Issue of late Kenneth Herbert Kenyon, *b* 1908, *d* 1970: *m* 1934, Barbara Joan, who *d* 1979, da of late J. E. M. Urry, of Homedene, Cranley Gdns, N10:—
Anne Judith (7 Hembury Park, Buckfast, Devon TQ11 0ES), *b* 1939.

Grandchildren of late Maj-Gen Edward Ranulph Kenyon, CB, CMG (infra):—
Issue of late Lieut-Col Herbert Edward Kenyon, DSO, *b* 1881, *d* 1958: *m* 1907, Gwendoline Ethel Graham, who *d* 1958, da of late F. G. Ommanney, of Sheen House, Walmer:—
Lloyd Douglas (15 Oxford St, Waimate, S Canterbury, NZ), *b* 1912; *ed* Framlingham Coll, and Waitaki BHS: *m* 1939, Joan, da of late R. Appleby, of Geraldine, New Zealand, and has issue living, Gwendolyn Jane, *b* 1942: *m* 1964, Trevor William Payton, of 274 Pine Hill Rd, Pine Hill, Dunedin, NZ, and has issue living, Grant Michael *b* 1974, Kim Maree *b* 1966: *m* 1991, Miran Kremesec, Jill Michelle *b* 1967, Raeleen Jan *b* 1971, — Sally Mavourneen, *b* 1944: *m* 1966, David George Drayton, of 102 Huntsbury Av, Christchurch 2, NZ, and has issue living, Tania May *b* 1970, Leanne Mavourneen *b* 1971. —— John Frederick, OBE, MC, *b* 1921; *ed* Marlborough; Col (ret) RA and Gen Staff, Mil Asst to C in C Far East Land Forces 1962-64, and Defence, Naval and Mil Attaché, Belgium and Luxembourg 1971-73; County Co Shropshire 1977-85; a Freeman of Shrewsbury (Grand Master) and of the City of London; President of the Freemen of England 1981-91; SE Asia 1943-45 (MC); OBE (Mil) 1970; Officer of Order of Leopold of Belgium 1989: *m* 1st, 1947 (*m diss* 1960), Jean Molyneux, da of late Howard Godfrey, MC; 2ndly, 1960, Mrs Margaret Bowker Franks, da of late Mrs C. C. B. Remington, of Wadham, Horsell, Surrey; 3rdly, 1982, Mrs Janet Mary Jackson (*née* Maddicott), of Dainton Cross, Ipplepen, Devon, and has issue living, (by 1st *m*) John Robert (28 Radyr Court Close, Radyr Court Rd, Llandaff, Cardiff CF5 2QG), *b* 1948; *ed* St Edward's Sch, Oxford, and Southampton Univ (BA); ALA, FSA, FRHistS: *m* 1973, Christine Ann, da of Mrs E. M. Green, of Lightcliffe, Yorks, and has issue living, Philippa Mary *b* 1974, Joanna Louise Charlotte *b* 1978, — Richard Howard Trevor (The Coppice, Tararua Drive, RD8, Masterton, NZ), *b* 1951; *ed* St Edward's Sch, Oxford, and Harper Adams Agric Coll: *m* 1977, Mrs Carol Jackson, da of C. F. May, of Blenheim, NZ, and has issue living, Wendy Jean *b* 1977. *Residence* – Pradoe, Oswestry, Shropshire. *Club* – Farmers. —— Margaret Gwendoline (65 Clark St, Wolcott, Conn, USA 06716) *b* 1918; 1939-45 War with VAD (Defence and War Medals): *m* 1945, Stanley Steven Baranoski, 1st/Sgt (ret) US Marines, who *d* 1979, and has issue living, Robert Steven, *b* 1947; 1st/Sgt US Marines; Okinawa and Viet Nam: *m* 1971, Kyoko Nakama, and has issue living, Stanley Steven *b*

1972, Margaret Gwendoline *b* 1971, — Michael John, *b* 1948; *ed* Massachusetts Coll of Arts (BFA in Architecture): *m* 1978, Diane Lynn Fasciano, — David Stanley, *b* 1953: *m* 1972, Alana Sue Jones, and has issue living, Jeremy David *b* 1973, — Peter Kenyon, *b* 1955, — Richard Lloyd, *b* 1957: *m* 1981, Nereida Otero, — Kenneth Owen, *b* 1963: *m* 1985, Janice Marie Pease, and has issue living, Brittany Marie *b* 1989, — Gwendoline Mary, *b* 1949, — Heather Joy, *b* 1956; *ed* Univ of Connecticut Agric Sch: *m* 1981, Terri Lim. —— Irene Patricia, *b* 1923, late WAAF (War medal): *m* 1953, Keith Louis Kerr, of 6 Ancrum St, Roxburgh, Central Otago, NZ, and has issue living, Graham Keith, *b* 1954; *ed* Waitaki BHS, Oamaru, NZ (BSc), — Patricia Louise, *b* 1956: *m* 1st, 1976 (*m diss* 1988), Ian Leslie Reeves; 2ndly, 1989, Kenneth MacKenzie, of Otapiri, Southland, NZ, and has issue living (by 1st *m*), Joshua Mark *b* 1979, Jamie Matthew *b* 1980, (by 2nd *m*) Jenna Kelland Louise *b* 1992.

Grandchildren of late John Robert Kenyon, QC, DCL (infra):—
Issue of late Maj-Gen Edward Ranulph Kenyon, CB, CMG, *b* 1854; *d* 1937: *m* 1880, Katharine Mary McCrea, who *d* 1908, da of late Maj-Gen John Cromie Blackwood De Butts, RE:—
Winifred Lilian, *b* 1892: *m* 1921, Herbert Stansfield Williamson, ICS (ret), who *d* 1955, and has issue living, Paul Kenyon (Staplegrove House, Taunton, Somerset), *b* 1925; *ed* Rugby, and at Trin Coll, Camb: *m* 1956, Gillian Anderson, da of Lt-Col John Anderson Smith, OBE, RA, of Leamington Spa, and has issue living, Michael Paul *b* 1957, Peter John 1958, Clare Honor *b* 1961, — Mark Herbert, OBE (Dalby Old Rectory, Terrington, York YO6 4PF), *b* 1928; *ed* Rugby, and at Ch Ch, Oxford (MA, D Phil); Prof of Biol Univ of York: *m* 1958, Charlotte, da of late Hugh Macdonald, of Fyfield, Abingdon, and has issue living, Hugh Thomas Saumarez *b* 1961; *ed* St Peter's Sch, York, and Sussex Univ (BA), Emma Charlotte Mary *b* 1963; *ed* Rugby, and New Hall, Camb (MA, BM, BCh, MRCP), Sophia Louisa Harriet *b* 1965; *ed* The Mount Sch, St Peter's Sch, York, and Southampton Univ (BM), — Ann Katharine, *b* 1922; *ed* Lady Margaret Hall, Oxford (MA), and Edinburgh Univ (M Phil): *m* 1948, John Angus Macbeth Mitchell, CB, CVO, MC, of 20 Regent Terr, Edinburgh EH7 5BS, and has issue living, Jonathan James, QC (30 Warriston Crescent, Edinburgh EH3 5LB) *b* 1951; *ed* Marlborough, New Coll, Oxford (BA), and Edinburgh Univ; QC 1992: *m* 1987, Melinda McGarry (and has issue living, Ewan Patrick McGarry *b* 1992, Hannah Catriona *b* 1988), Andrew Macbeth (36 Buckingham Terrace, Edinburgh EH4 3AP) *b* 1958; *ed* Edin Acad, and Reading Univ (BA): *m* 1991, Maureen Wilkie (and has issue living, Donald Macbeth *b* 1993), Isabel Charlotte *b* 1953; *ed* St George's, Edinburgh, and Birmingham Coll of Art & Design: *m* 1st, 1972 (*m diss* 19—), Martin Charles Mooney; 2ndly, 1981, Michael Grimm Foxen, of 72 Trinity Rd, Edinburgh EH5 3JT (and has issue living, Jamie Mischa Ruaridh Macbeth *b* 1986, Haley Catherine *b* 1983), Catherine Olivia *b* 1956; *ed* St George's Edinburgh, and Robt Gordon's Inst of Tech, Aberdeen: *m* 1987, David Cross. *Residence* – Red Lodge, Hope Corner Lane, Taunton TA2 7PB, Som.

Grandsons of late Eustace Alban Kenyon, son of late John Robert Kenyon, QC, DCL (infra):—
Issue of late Lieut-Col William Patrick Kenyon, MC, late RWF, *b* 1898, *d* 1992: *m* 1928, Joan Mary, who *d* 19—, yr da of late Allan Edward Batchelor (*see* Makins, Bt, 1951 Edn):—
Martin Robert (70 Stockwell Park Rd, SW9; *Club* – Travellers'), *b* 1929; *ed* Eton, and Corpus Christi Coll, Oxford; late 2nd Lieut RWF; Exec Sec Overseas Students' Trust since 1962: *m* 1975, Mary Anne, da of Lt-Cdr Patrick Henry James Southby, RN (ret) (*see* Southby, Bt), and has issue living, Eliza Hope, *b* 1976, — Nina Joan, *b* 1977. —— (Eustace Allan) Michael (Manor Farm, Wadenhoe, nr Peterborough), *b* 1931; *ed* St Edward's Sch, Oxford; late Lieut RWF; a Farmer, Manager Nicolton Orchards, Suffolk: *m* 1977, Susanna, da of late Maj Arthur H. Pearson, of Hillside, Bayford Hill, Wincanton. —— Thomas David (Toby), *b* 1932; *ed* Wellington Coll, and RMA Sandhurst; Maj RWF; served Malaya 1954 (wounded), and Cyprus 1958.
Issue of late Rowland Lloyd Kenyon, *b* 1901; *d* 1959: *m* 1936 (*m diss* 1950), Gwendoline Doris Dorman (who *m* 2ndly), 1954 (*m diss* 1969), Maj Leslie Dunn, Coldm Gds and E Surrey Regt (ret):—
Peter Rowland (Lady Whincups, Rendham, Saxmundham, Suffolk), *b* 1937; late RAF; market gardener: *m* 1962, Wilma, da of Ludwig Pranger of Pöttsching (Burgenland), Siedlung, 16, Austria, and has issue living, Rupert Peter, *b* 1968, — Berenice Sofia, *b* 1964, — Rebecca Louise, *b* 1966. —— Robert Nicholas Andrew (2/5 Franks Grove, Kew, Vic 3101, Aust), *b* 1939; formerly in RE.

Granddaughter of late Maj-Gen Lionel Richard Kenyon, CB, son of late John Robert Kenyon, QC, DCL (infra):—
Issue of late Major Harold Anthony Kenyon, MC, *b* 1897, *d* 1934: *m* 1931, Iris Veronica Margaret, (who *m* 2ndly), 1936, as his 2nd wife Maj-Gen Mervyn Savile Wheatley, CB, CBE, who *d* 1979, da of late Lt-Col M. McL. Corbyn, of Little Grange, Woodbridge, Suffolk:—
Elisabeth Veronica, *b* 1931: *m* 1953 (*m diss* 1974), Robert Arthur David Shutes, and has issue living, Anthony David, *b* 1955; *ed* Wellington Coll, and Univ Coll, London (BSc); CEng, MIMM (1982): *m* 1983, Lucille Alison Hunter, and has issue living, Frederick Thomas Kenyon *b* 1991, Phillippa Fern Kenyon *b* 1988, Henrietta Iris Kenyon *b* 1994, — Caroline Ann Veronica, *b* 1954: *m* 1976, John Dalziel Riddell, and has issue living, Oliver John *b* 1978, Benjamin James *b* 1980, Daniel Robert *b* 1981. *Residence* – Ford Cottage, Send, nr Guildford, Surrey.

Granddaughter of late John Robert Kenyon, QC, DCL, son of late Hon Thomas Kenyon, 3rd son of 1st Baron:—
Issue of late Sir Frederic George Kenyon, GBE, KCB, TD, *b* 1863, *d* 1952: *m* 1891, Amy, who *d* 1938, da of late Rowland Hunt, of Boreatton Park, Shropshire:—
Nora Gwendolen Margaret, *b* 1908; *ed* St Paul's Girls' Sch, and at Somerville Coll, Oxford (MA): *m* 1936, John Ritchie, MBE, Master of Supreme Court (Queen's Bench Div), who *d* 1988, and has issue living, Jeremy Kenyon Tod (Rosehill, Erbistock, Wrexham, Clwyd), *b* 1942; *ed* Winchester, and Magdalen Coll, Oxford (MA); JP: *m* 1971, Barbara Ann Blackwell, and has issue living, Simon John *b* 1974, Amy Helen *b* 1977, — Janet Margaret Amy, *b* 1939: *m* 1963, Alan Seward Penson Heath, of The Hollies, Thrussington, Leics, and has issue living, Nicholas Gordon John *b* 1966, Christopher Frederic William *b* 1968, Caroline Margaret Janet *b* 1971, — Elspeth Nora Watson, *b* 1948; *ed* St Hugh's Coll, Oxford (BA): *m* 1972, Giulio Nevio Panichi, and has issue living, Almarica Nina Serena *b* 1980, Tamara Anna Helen *b* 1983. *Residence* – 4 Millwood Rise, Overton-on-Dee, Clwyd LL13 0EL.

Grandchildren (by 1st *m*) of late Maj Robert Orlando Rodolph Kenyon-Slaney (infra):—
Issue of late Robert Ivan Kenyon-Slaney, *b* 1926, *d* 1984: *m* 1964, Meriel Rose (who *m* 2ndly, 1985, Peter Maurice Afia, of 14 Douro Place, W8 5PH, and Hatton Grange, Shifnal, Shropshire TF11 9HS), da of late Capt Joseph Gurney Fowell Buxton (*see* Buxton, Bt, colls):—
Rupert David, *b* 1965; *ed* Eton, and Univ of East Anglia (BA). —— Thomas Alexander, *b* 1966; *ed* Eton, and European Univ, Versailles; late Lieut Gren Gds. —— Natasha Vivien, *b* 1969; *ed* Wycombe Abbey, and Royal Holloway and Bedford New Coll, Univ of London (BA).

Grandchildren of late Col the Rt Hon William Slaney Kenyon-Slaney, MP, el son of Col William Kenyon-Slaney, 5th son of Hon Thomas Kenyon, (ante):—
Issue of late Maj Robert Orlando Rodolph Kenyon-Slaney, *b* 1892, *d* 1965: *m* 1st, 1917 (*m diss* 1930), Lady Mary Cecilia Rhodesia Hamilton, who *d* 1984, da of 3rd Duke of Abercorn; 2ndly, 1931, Nesta, who *d* 1947, da of Sir George Ferdinand Forestier-Walker, 3rd Bt (*cr* 1835):—
(By 1st *m*) Ursula Jane, *b* 1920: *m* 1st, 1940 (*m diss* 1946), Lt-Col David Ludovic Peter Lindsay, DSO, Irish Gds (*see* E Crawford, colls); 2ndly, 1946, as his 2nd wife (*m diss* 1950), Group Capt Hon (John William) Maxwell Aitken, DSO, DFC, later Sir Maxwell Aitken, 2nd Bt, who *d* 1985 (*see* B Beaverbrook); 3rdly, 1951, Robert Edward John Compton (*see* M North-

ampton, colls), of Newby Hall, Ripon, Yorks. ⸻ (By 2nd *m*) William Simon Rodolph (Chyknell, Bridgnorth, Shropshire), *b* 1932; *ed* Eton; late Lt Gren Gds; FRICS; JP; KStJ; County Councillor 1977-85; High Sheriff 1979, DL 1986: *m* 1960, Mary Helena, el da of late Lt-Col Hon Henry George Orlando Bridgeman, DSO, MC (*see* E Bradford, colls), and has issue living, Henry James Rodolph, *b* 1961; *ed* Eton, and Southampton Univ (BSc), — Andrew William Orlando, *b* 1965; *ed* Cranleigh, Shrewsbury, and Reading Univ (BSc), — Francis Alan, *b* 1966; *ed* Eton, and Reading Univ (BSc).

Grandchildren of late Percy Robert Kenyon-Slaney (infra):—
Issue of late Gerald William Kenyon-Slaney, OBE, *b* 1899, *d* 1953: *m* 1928, Barbara Nannette (6 Mount Pleasant, Tenterden, Kent), da of late Rev Granville Gore Skipwith (*see* Skipwith, Bt, colls):—
Orlando Michael Philip, *b* 1929; *ed* Winchester and at Ch Ch, Oxford (BA 1953): *m* 1960, Philippa Margaret, da of Sir Thomas Claude Harris Lea, 3rd Bt, and has issue living, Jeremy Francis Gerald, *b* 1966; *ed* Bethany Sch, — Philip Thomas Christopher, *b* 1969; *ed* Marlborough. *Residence* – Bachelors Cottage, High Halden, Ashford, Kent. ⸻ Gerald Timothy Granville (6 Mount Pleasant, Tenterden, Kent), *b* 1937; *ed* Bradfield Coll; late Grenadier Guards. ⸻ Thomasina Angela Jane, *b* 1933: *m* 1st, 1954 (*m diss* 1968), Maj Thomas David Ogilvy Codner, late Coldstream Guards; 2ndly, 1982, William Albert Tarling of 12 Bettridge Rd, SW6, and has issue living, Vivien Ogilvy, *b* 1957: *m* 1988, Aziz Laghzaoui, of 25 Margaretta Terr, SW3, and has issue living, Otto *b* 1990, Kenza May *b* 1992, — Clare Jane, *b* 1959: *m* 1993, Marcus Emerson.

Granddaughters of late Charles Robert Kenyon, el son of late Rev Charles Orlando Kenyon, 6th son of late Hon Thomas Kenyon (ante):—
Issue of late Charles Orlando Kenyon, *b* 1886, *d* 1973: *m* 1st, 1915, Marguerite Laura, who *d* 1948, da of Alexander Kealman, of Santos, Brazil; 2ndly, 1950, Sarah (Santos, Brazil), da of:—
(By 1st *m*) Dorothy Beatrice, *b* 1917; 1939-45 War with WAAF (Defence Medal): *m* 1946, Donald Stanford Egremont, and has issue living, Christopher Andrew, *b* 1948: *m* 1st, 1975 (*m diss* 1986), Annabel Heather, da of Malcolm Proverbs, and of Mrs James Ward; 2ndly, 1989, Jacqueline Sarah, eldest da of late Capt Peter Bateman, of Cheselbourne, Dorset, and has issue living (by 1st *m*), Christopher William *b* 1983, James Donald *b* 1985, (by 2nd *m*) Thomas Joshua *b* 1993, Lucinda Rebecca *b* 1990, Hannah Mary *b* (twin) 1993, — Donald Alexander, *b* 1955. ⸻ Elizabeth Matilda, *b* 1920: *m* 1st, 1942 (*m diss* 1945); 2ndly, 1947, Robert E. Dennison, of 865 Riomar Dr, Vero Beach, Florida 32963, USA, and has issue living (by 2nd *m*), Robert Kenyon, *b* 1948, — William Alexander (24 West Delaware Av, Pennington, NJ 08534, USA), *b* 1951: *m* 1976, Tara, da of Pamela Brotherton, of Earlswood House, Pitton, Salisbury, Wilts, and has issue living, William Oliver *b* 1984, Edwina Elizabeth Kenyon *b* 1987, — John Keasbey, *b* 1958. ⸻ (By 2nd *m*) Sylvia Elena, *b* 1952.

PREDECESSORS – (1) Sir Lloyd Kenyon, KB; Ch Justice of Chester 1780, Attorney-Gen 1782, Master of the Rolls 1784, and Lord Ch Justice of England 1788; *cr* a Baronet 1784, and *Lord Kenyon, Baron of Gredington*, co Flint (peerage of Great Britain) 1788; *d* 1802; *s* by his son (2) George, 2nd Baron; *d* 1855; *s* by his son (3) Lloyd, 3rd Baron; *b* 1805; *d* 1869; *s* by his grandson (4) Lloyd (son of late Hon Lloyd, el son of 3rd Baron), 4th Baron, *b* 1864; Lord-Lieut of Denbighshire, and Registrar of Priory of Order of St John for Wales; a Lord-in-Waiting to Queen Victoria and King Edward VII 1900-1905, and to King George V 1916-18; assumed by Roy licence 1912 the additional surname of Tyrell: *m* 1916, Gwladys Julia, who *d* 1965, da of late Col Henry Richard Lloyd Howard, CB; *d* 1927; *s* by his only son (5) Lloyd, CBE, 5th Baron; *b* 1917, Capt RA (TA), JP and DL Flintshire, Dir Lloyds Bank 1962-85, Pres Univ Coll, N Wales 1947-82, Ch Commr Boy Scouts for Wales 1948-66, Member Standing Commn on Museums and Art Galleries 1953-60, Gov Welbeck Coll 1952, Trustee Nat Portrait Gallery 1953-87 (Chm 1966), Member Royal Commn on Historical MSS since 1966: *m* 1946, Leila Mary Peel, da of late Cmdr John Wyndham Cookson, RN (*see* Colquhoun, Bt, 1963 Edn), and widow of Hugh William Jardine Ethelston Peel, Lieut Welsh Guards (*see* Buchanan-Jardine, Bt, 1945 Edn); *d* 1993; *s* by his eldest son (6) Lloyd, 6th Baron and present peer.

KERSHAW, BARON (Kershaw) (Baron UK 1947)

Edward John Kershaw, JP, 4th Baron; *b* 12 May 1936; *s* 1962; *ed* Selhurst Gram Sch, Croydon; RAF 1955-57; Chartered Accountant 1964; JP 1982: *m* 1963, Rosalind Lilian, da of late Ian Strachan Rutherford, of 16 Castlegate, Richmond, and has issue.
Residence – 38 High View, Hempsted, Glos.

SON LIVING

Hon John Charles Edward, *b* 23 Dec 1971.

DAUGHTERS LIVING

Hon Victoria Anne, *b* 1964: *m* 1989, Ian C. Harvey-Piper, son of C. D. Harvey-Piper, of Wimbledon, SW19.
Hon Isobel Mary, *b* 1967: *m* 1993, Robert A. Slater, son of J. F. Slater, of Derby.

SISTER LIVING

Hon Patricia Margaret, *b* 1943: *m* 1968, David Anniss Pickett, BSc, BMus, and has issue living, Caroline Mary, *b* 1969, — Rachel Elizabeth, *b* 1972.

UNCLE LIVING (*Son of the 1st Baron*)

Hon Peter John, *b* 1924; *ed* Queen Elizabeth's Sch, Barnet, and at King's Coll, London (BSc, 1948) FEng, FICE; Sub-Lieut RNVR 1945-46: *m* 1948, Brenda Margaret, da of late James Austin Smith, of Brighton, and has issue living, Michael James, *b* 1951. *Residence* – 22 Orchard Rise, Richmond, Surrey, TW10 5BX.

WIDOWS LIVING OF SECOND AND THIRD BARONS

Cissie Burness (*Cissie, Baroness Kershaw*), da of Charles E. Smythe, of Friern Barnet: *m* 1933, the 2nd Baron, who *d* (July) 1961. *Residence* – 29 St Ann's Rd, Newquay, Cornwall.
Katharine Dorothea (*Katharine, Baroness Kershaw*), da of Charles H. Staines, of Clapham, SW: *m* 1935, the 3rd Baron, who *d* 1962. *Residence* – 3 Windmill Court, Northern Crescent, E Wittering, W Sussex PO20 8RJ.

COLLATERAL BRANCH LIVING

Issue of late Hon Donald Arthur Kershaw, 3rd son of 1st Baron, *b* 1915, *d* 1991: *m* 1942, Barbara Edith, who *d* 1986, only child of Lt-Col Cecil Graham Ford, of Richmond:—

Ian Graham Frederick, *b* 1948. *Residence* – 22 Priory Gdns, Old Basing, Hants RG24 7DS. —— Mark Nigel, *b* 1951. *Residence* – 19 Beechnut Lane, Solihull, West Midlands B91 2NN.

PREDECESSORS – (1) FRED KERSHAW, OBE, son of John Joseph Kershaw, of Prestwich, Lancashire; *b* 1881; a Dep Speaker House of Lords, a Gov of Westminster Hospital, Chm of Gordon Hospital, and of Marie Curie Memorial Foundation, a Co Director, Vice-Pres of Workers' Temperance League, and Founder Member of Manor House Hospital; a Lord-in-Waiting to HM King George VI 1949-51; *cr* Baron Kershaw, of Prestwich, co Palatine of Lancaster (peerage of United Kingdom) 1947: *m* 1903, Frances Edith, who *d* 1960, da of James Thomas Wigmore, of Hereford; *d* (Feb) 1961; *s* by his el son (2) HERBERT, 2nd Baron; *b* 1904; European War and Far East 1939-45 as Sub Lieut RNVR: *m* 1933, Cissie Burness, da of Charles E. Smythe, of Friern Barnet; *d* (July) 1961; *s* by his brother (3) EDWARD AUBREY, 3rd Baron; *b* 1906: *m* 1935, Katharine Dorothea, da of Charles H. Staines, of Clapham, SW; *d* 1962; *s* by his son (4) EDWARD JOHN, 4th Baron and present peer.

KEYES, BARON (Keyes) (Baron UK 1943, Bt UK 1919)

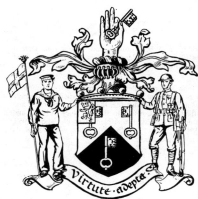

Acquired by virtue

ROGER GEORGE BOWLBY KEYES, 2nd Baron and 2nd Baronet, *b* 14 March 1919; *s* 1945; Lieut RN (ret 1949); European War 1939-45 in N Sea and Mediterranean: *m* 1947, Grizelda Mary, who *d* 1993, da of late Lieut-Col William Vere Packe, DSO, and has issue.

Arms – Per chevron gules and sable, three keys or, the wards of the two in chief facing each other, and of the one in base to the sinister, on a canton argent a lion rampant of the first. **Crest** – An open hand couped at the wrist proper, holding between the forefinger and thumb a key or. **Supporters** – (hereditary), — *Dexter*, a sailor of the Royal Navy in blue working rig proper, supporting in the exterior hand a staff argent ensigned with a naval crown or, and flying the banner of Saint George also proper; *sinister*, a Royal Marine in field service dress, armed and equipped for trench raiding, all proper.
Residence – Farleigh House, East Farleigh, Maidstone, Kent, ME15 0JW. **Clubs** – Anglo-Belgian, House of Lords Yacht.

SONS LIVING

Hon CHARLES WILLIAM PACKE, *b* 8 Dec 1951; *ed* Eton: *m* 1st, 1978, Sadiye Yasmin, da of Mahir Coskun, of Istanbul; 2ndly, 1984, Sally, da of Thomas Jackson, and has issue living (by 2nd *m*), Anna Merula, *b* 1985. *Residence* – 64 Bourne Way, Hayes, Bromley, Kent BR2 7EY.
Hon Leopold Roger John, *b* 1956; *ed* Eton: *m* 1988, Jane Elizabeth, only da of Trevor B. Owen, CBE, of Meadow Cottage, Carswell Marsh, Oxon.

Hon Adrian Christopher Noel, *b* 1962; *ed* Lancing.

DAUGHTERS LIVING

Virginia Mary Clementine (does not use courtesy title), *b* 1950; *ed* Sherborne, and Sheffield Univ: *m* 1972, Rev Roger Martyn Crompton, of The Vicarage, Church St, Golcar, Huddersfield HD7 4PX, and has issue living, Heather Rose Mary, *b* 1976, — Bryony Judith, *b* 1978, — Rowan Elizabeth, *b* 1981, — Holly Susannah, *b* 1983.
Hon Josephine Mary, *b* 1958; *ed* Benenden, and Newnham Coll, Camb: *m* 1987, Hon (William Aldus) Thoby Young, only son of 2nd Baron Kennet, and has issue. *Residence* – 100 Bayswater Rd, W2 3HJ.

SISTER LIVING

Hon Katherine Elizabeth, *b* 1911: *m* 1935, Major Peter de Barton Vernon Wallop William-Powlett, MC, 3rd Hussars (Reserve), who *d* 1988 (*see* E Portsmouth, colls). *Residence* – 22 St Leonard's Terrace, SW3.

PREDECESSOR – (1) *Sir* ROGER JOHN BROWNLOW Keyes, GCB, KCVO, DSO, DCL, LLD, son of late Gen Sir Charles Patton Keyes, GCB; *b* 1872; entered RN 1885, and became Adm of the Fleet 1930; E Africa 1890, China 1900, European War 1914-19 as Commodore Submarines, subsequently as Ch of Staff, E Mediterranean Squadron, Capt and Rear-Adm Grand Fleet, Director of Plans at Admiralty, and Acting Vice-Adm Comdg Dover Patrol (despatches, CMG, DSO, Com Legion of Honour, KCB, KCVO, thanked by War Cabinet, Belgian and French Crois de Guerre Grand Cordon of Order of Leopold of Belgium, Grand Officer Legion of Honour, Com of Order of St Maurice and St Lazarus of Italy, American DSM, thanked by Parliament, *cr* Baronet, granted £10,000 for blocking the sea-ward end of Bruges ship canal, sole exit for ocean-going U-Boats based at Bruges, at Zeebrugge 23 April 1918); a Lord of the Admiralty and Dep-Ch of Naval Staff, Admiralty 1921-5; commanded Mediterranean Fleet 1925-8; Com-in-Ch Portsmouth 1929-31; Hon Col Comdt, Portsmouth Div, RM 1932-42; 1st Ch of Combined Operations 1940-41; Special Liason Officer to King of the Belgians May 1940; sat as MP for N Div of Portsmouth (C) 1934-43; *cr* a Baronet 1919, and Baron Keyes, of Zeebrugge, and of Dover, co Kent 1943: *m* 1906, Eva Mary Salvin, who *d* 1973, da of late Edward Salvin Bowlby, DL, of Gilston Park, Herts, and Knoydart, Inverness-shire (his el son, Lt-Col Geoffrey Charles Tasker, VC, MC, Croix de Guerre, Roy Scots Greys (*b* 1917) was killed leading his (11th) Commando attempt to capture General Rommel at Sidi Rafa, Libya 1941, for which he was awarded a posthumous VC); *d* 1945; *s* by his only surviving son (2) ROGER GEORGE BOWLBY, 2nd Baron and present peer.

KILBRACKEN, BARON (Godley) (Baron UK 1909)

JOHN RAYMOND GODLEY, DSC, 3rd Baron; *b* 17 Oct 1920; *s* 1950; *ed* Eton, and Balliol Coll, Oxford (BA and MA 1948); is an Author and Journalist; European War 1940-45 in RNVR (Air Branch), Lieut-Com (A) 1945 (DSC): *m* 1st, 1943 (*m diss* 1949), Penelope Anne, yst da of late Rear-Adm Sir Cecil Nugent Reyne, KBE; 2ndly, 1981 (*m diss* 1989), Susan Lee, da of late Norman Heazlewood, of Melbourne, Australia, and has issue by 1st and 2nd *m*.

𝕬rms – Argent, three unicorns' heads erased sable, horned gules, two and one, and three trefoils slipped vert, one and two. 𝕮rest – A unicorn's head erased argent, horned gules, charged with three trefoils slipped vert. 𝕾upporters – *Dexter*, a griffin sable charged with four stars argent in cross; *sinister*, a lion argent, charged with four roses gules in cross.
Seat – Killegar, co Leitrim (postal address: Killegar, Cavan).

SONS LIVING (By 1st marriage)

Hon CHRISTOPHER JOHN (Four Firs, Marley Lane, Haslemere, Surrey), *b* 1 Jan 1945; *ed* Rugby, and Reading Univ (BSc Agric 1967); Agriculturalist: *m* 1969, Gillian Christine, da of late Lt-Cdr S. W. Birse, OBE, DSC, RN (ret), of Alverstoke, Hants, and has issue living, James John, *b* 1972, — Louisa Laheen, *b* 1974.

(By 2nd marriage)

Hon Seán Garech, *b* 1981.

BROTHER LIVING

Prof the Hon Wynne Alexander Hugh (16 Eltisley Av, Newnham, Cambridge) *b* 1926; *ed* Rugby, and at New Coll, Oxford (BA 1947); Fellow of King's Coll, Camb and Prof of Applied Economics: *m* 1955, Mrs Kathleen Eleanora (Kitty) Freud, da of late Sir Jacob Epstein, KBE, and formerly wife of Lucian Freud, and has issue living, Eve Katharine, *b* 1967.

PREDECESSORS – (1) *Sir* JOHN ARTHUR Godley, GCB, only son of late John Robert Godley, of Killegar; *b* 1847; Commr of Inland Revenue 1882-3, and Permanent Under-Sec for India 1883-1909; *cr Baron Kilbracken*, of Killegar, co Leitrim (peerage of United Kingdom) 1909: *m* 1871, Hon Sarah James, who *d* 1921, da of 1st Baron Northbourne; *d* 1932; *s* by his elder and only surv son (2) HUGH JOHN, CB, KC, 2nd Baron; *b* 1877; Assist Parliamentary Counsel to the Treasury 1917-22, and Counsel to Chm of Committees, House of Lords 1922-44: *m* 1st, 1919 (*m diss* 1936), Elizabeth Helen Monteith, who *d* 1958, da of Vereker Monteith Hamilton, and widow of W/Cdr N. F. Usborne, RNAS; 2ndly, 1936, Rhoda Leonora, who *d* 1948, da of Percy Taylor; *d* 1950; *s* by his elder son (3) JOHN RAYMOND, 3rd Baron and present peer.

KILBRANDON, BARONY OF (Shaw) (Extinct 1989)

SONS LIVING OF LIFE BARON

Hon Patrick James (Highfield, Taynuilt, Argyll), *b* 1938: *m* 1964, Elisabeth Grace Melfort Gibson, and has issue living, Donald Patrick, *b* 1967, — Shuna Caroline, *b* 1965, — Heather Grace, *b* 1971, — Eilidh Elisabeth, *b* 1973.
Hon Michael Frank (Kilbrandon House, Balvicar, by Oban, Argyll) *b* 1944: *m* 1978, Catherine Ballantine, and has issue living, Torquil James Brandon, *b* 1981, — Tamara Caroline, *b* 1980.

DAUGHTERS LIVING OF LIFE BARON

Hon Teresa Caroline Glencairn (PO Box Rongai, Kenya) *b* 1940: *m* 1969, Christopher D. A. Orme-Smith, and has issue living, Andrew, *b* 1974, — Philippa, *b* 1969: *m* 1990, Robin J. E. Witt, of 7 Church St, Nunney, nr Frome, Som, eldest son of Michael Witt, of Whatley, Som, — Nicola, *b* 1971: *m* 1993, James F. D. Hutchings, eldest son of Maj Edgar Hutchings, of Withypool, Som.
Hon Mary Anna, *b* 1946: *m* 1971, Thomas Horatio Congreve Shephard, and has issue (*see* Congreve, Bt, ext). *Residence* – Claigan Farmhouse, Dunvegan, Isle of Skye.
Hon Elizabeth Cecilia, *b* 1948: *m* 1984, Jean-Marc Peysson, and has issue living, Jean-Christophe, *b* 1986, — Claire Elizabeth, *b* 1991. *Residence* – La Maison Neuve, 03210 Autry Issards, Allier, France.

WIDOW LIVING OF LIFE BARON

RUTH CAROLINE (*Baroness Kilbrandon*), da of Frank Morrison Seafield Grant, of Knockie, Inverness: *m* 1937, Baron Kilbrandon, PC (Life Baron), who *d* 1989. *Residence* – Kilbrandon House, Balvicar, by Oban, Argyll PA34 4RA.

Kildare, Marquess of; son of Duke of Leinster.

KILLANIN, BARON (Morris) (Baron UK 1900, Bt UK 1885)

SI·DEUS·NOBISCUM·QUIS·CONTRA·NOS

Si Deus nobiscum quis contra nos
If God be with us, who is against us?

MICHAEL MORRIS, MBE, TD, 3rd Baron, and 3rd Baronet; *b* 30 July 1914; *s* 1927; *ed* Eton, Sorbonne, Paris, and Magdalene Coll, Camb (MA); Hon LLD, Nat Univ Ireland; Hon DLitt New Univ Ulster; author, late war correspondent for *Daily Mail* 1937-38, and political correspondent for *Sunday Dispatch*, film producer, MRIA, FRSA, hon Life Member Roy Dublin Soc, FRSAI, etc; Pres of Olympic Council of Ireland 1950-73 (Hon Pres 1981); Mem Internat Olympic Cttee 1952 (Pres 1972-80, since when Hon Life Pres); Chm Irish Nat Heritage Council since 1988; a Member Nat Monuments Advisory Council of Ireland (Chm 1960-65), Irish Nat Hunt Steeplechase, and Irish Turf Club (Steward); Chm Dublin Theatre Festival 1960-70; a Dir Gallaher (Dublin) Ltd, Life Assocn Hibernia, Northern Telecom Ltd, and Syntex (Ireland) Ltd, and Chubb Ireland, Ltd; Member of Lloyd's; formerly Chm Ulster Bank, Ulster Investment Bank and Lombard and Ulster Banking; a Trustee of Irish Sailors and Soldiers Land Trust, since 1947, Member Cultural Relations Cttee 1947-72, and of Irish Red Cross Soc 1949-72 (Hon Sec 1952-68), John Huston's Commn on the Film Industry (associated with John Ford on *The Quiet Man*, and subsequently prod *The Rising of The Moon*, *Playboy of the Western World*, etc), Ctte of Management of RNLI since 1959 (Exec Cttee 1970-84, Vice Pres since 1972); Chm Irish Govt Commn on Thoroughbred Horse Breeding 1984-86; Hon Consul-Gen for Monaco in Ireland 1961-84; Pres of Irish Club, London 1947-65; formerly Maj KRRC; NW Europe 1944-45 (MBE); a Knight of Sovereign Order of Malta, Grand Cross of the Order of Civil Merit (Spain) 1976, Yugoslav Flag with Ribbon 1984, Grand Officer of the Order of Merit of Republic of Italy 1973, Grand Officer of the Order of Merit (Tunisia) 1976, Grand Officer of the Order of the Phoenix of Greece 1976, Commander's Order of Merit with Star (Poland) 1979, Commander of the order of Grimaldi (Monaco) 1961, Grand Cross of the German Federal Republic 1972 (Commander), Commander of the Congolese Order of Merit 1975, Star of the Sacred Treasure (Second Class) (Japan) 1972, Commander of the Order of Sports Merit (Ivory Coast) 1977, Commander of the Legion of Honour (France) 1980, Chevalier Order of Duarte Sanchez y Mella (Dominican Republic) 1977, Order of the Madara Rider (Bulgaria), Star of Solidarity, 1st Class (Italy) 1957, Medal Miroslav Tyrs (Czechoslovakia) 1970, Olympic Order of Merit (Gold) 1980, decorations from Colombia, Brazil, Cameroons, China, USSR, etc; MBE (Mil) 1945: *m* 1945, Mary Sheila Cathcart, MBE, da of Rev Canon Douglas Dunlop, of Oughterard, co Galway, and has issue.

Arms – Ermine, a fesse indented sable, in base a lion rampant of the last armed and langued gules. **Crest** – On a fasces fessewise proper, a lion's head erased argent, guttë de sang. **Supporters** – Two lions gules, each gorged with a chain or, pendant therefrom an escutcheon ermine charged with a sword erect proper, pommel and hilt gold and standing on a fasces also proper.
Seat – St Annins, Spiddal, co Galway. *Residence* – 9 Lower Mount Pleasant Av, Dublin 6. *Clubs* – Garrick, Stephen's Green (Dublin), County (Galway), Beefsteak.

SONS LIVING

Hon (GEORGE) REDMOND (FITZPATRICK) (Doughty Cottage, Richmond Hill, Richmond, Surrey TW10 6RN), *b* 26 Jan 1947; *ed* Gonzaga Coll, Dublin, Ampleforth, and Trin Coll, Dublin: *m* 1972, Pauline, only da of Geoffrey Horton, of The Lawns, Cabinteely, co Dublin, and has issue living, Luke Michael Geoffrey, *b* 1975, — Olivia Rose Elizabeth, *b* 1974.
Hon Michael Francis Leo (Everard's Grange, Fethard, co Tipperary), *b* 1951; *ed* St Conleth's Coll, Dublin and Ampleforth: *m* 1979, Susanna Frank, and has issue living, James Michael, *b* 1983, — Christopher Michael, *b* 1985.
Hon John Martin (5 Rus-in-Urbe, Lower Glengeary Rd, Dun Laoghaire, co Dublin), *b* 1951 (twin); *ed* St Conleth's Coll, Dublin, and Ampleforth: *m* 1972, Thelma, da of Mrs Mansfield, of Monkstown, co Dublin, and has issue living, Roderic Michael, *b* 1976, — Michael-John, *b* 1979.

DAUGHTER LIVING

Hon (Monica) Deborah, *b* 1950: *m* 1970, William Campbell Rough Bryden, Associate Dir National Theatre, since 1975, and has issue living, Dillon Michael George, *b* 1972, — Mary Kate, *b* 1975. *Residence* – 3 Orchard Cottage, Clifton Rd, Kingston upon Thames, Surrey.

PREDECESSORS – (1) *Rt Hon* MICHAEL Morris, PC, son of late Martin Morris, JP, of Spiddal, co Galway; *b* 1827; MP for Galway (LC) 1865-7; Recorder of Galway 1857-65; Solicitor-Gen for Ireland 1866, Attorney-Gen 1866-7, Justice of common Pleas for Ireland 1867-76, Lord Ch Justice thereof 1876-87, Lord Ch Justice of Ireland 1887-9, an a Lord of Appeal in Ordinary 1889-1900: *cr* a *Baronet* 1885, *Baron Morris* (life peerage), of Spiddal, co Galway 1889, and *Baron Killanin*, of Galway, co Galway (peerage of United Kingdom) 1900: *m* 1860, Anna, who *d* 1906, da of late Hon H. G. Hughes, a Baron of the Exchequer in Ireland; *d* 1901, when the Barony of Morris, being a Life Peerage, expired, and he was *s* in the Barony of Killanin by his el son (2) MARTIN HENRY FITZPATRICK, PC, 2nd Baron, *b* 1867: Member of Senate of Roy Univ of Ireland 1904-9, Gov of Univ Coll, Galway 1909-22; MP for Galway (*C*) 1900-1; Lieut and Custos Rotulorum for co Galway; *d* 1927; *s* by his nephew (3) MICHAEL (son of late Lieut-Col Hon George Henry Morris, yr son of 1st Baron), 3rd Baron and present peer.

KILLEARN, BARON (Lampson) (Baron UK 1943)

Persevere and conquer

GRAHAM CURTIS LAMPSON, 2nd Baron, and 4th Baronet (of Rowfant, Worth, Sussex); *b* 28 Oct 1919; *s* to Barony, 1964, and to Baronetcy 1971; *ed* Eton, and Magdalen Coll, Oxford (MA); formerly Maj Scots Guards (US Bronze Star): *m* 1946, Nadine Marie Cathryn, only da of late Vice-Adm Cecil Horace Pilcher, DSO, and has issue.

Arms – Per saltire argent and gules, two gryphons' heads in fesse and as many escarbuncles in pale counterchanged. **Crest** – A gryphon's head erased gules, charged with an escarbuncle argent, between two wings paly of four, argent and gules. **Supporters** – *Dexter*, a camel proper with head stall and rope reflexed over the back gules; *sinister*, a Chinese dragon also proper.
Residence – 58 Melton Court, Old Brompton Rd, SW7 3JJ.

DAUGHTERS LIVING

Hon Alexandra Rachel Mary Catherine Angelica (Black Horse House, East Knoyle, Wilts), *b* 1947: *m* 1966 (*m diss* 1987), Nicholas Edward Hugo Meynell (*see* E Halifax, colls), who *d* 1988.
Hon Nadine Marisa (*Hon Lady Bonsor*), *b* 1948; a JP for Beds: *m* 1969, Sir Nicholas Cosmo Bonsor, 4th Bt, MP, of Liscombe Park, Leighton Buzzard, Beds.

HALF-BROTHER LIVING

Hon VICTOR MILES GEORGE ALDOUS (Little Soulbury Manor, Glos), *b* 9 Sept 1941; *ed* Eton; formerly Capt Scots Guards: *m* 1971, Melita Amaryllis Pamela Astrid, 2nd da of Rear Adm Sir Morgan Charles Morgan-Giles, DSO, OBE, GM, DL, and has issue living, Miles Henry Morgan, *b* 1977, — Alexander Victor William, *b* 1984, — Pamela Camilla Roxana, *b* 1973, — Miranda Penelope Amber, *b* 1975.

HALF-SISTERS LIVING

Hon Jacquetta Jean Frederica, *b* 1943: *m* 1964 (*m diss* 1990), 10th Earl of St Germans.
Hon Roxana Rose Catherine Naila, *b* 1945: *m* 1966, Ian Cowper Ross, and has issue living, Atticus Matthew Cowper, *b* 1968, — Milo Joseph Charles, *b* 1970, — Leopold Lincoln Fitzgerald, *b* 1980, — Holly Zahava Josephine, *b* 1971, — Mia Vanilla Catherine, *b* 1973, — Liberty Lettuce Clark, *b* 1978. *Residence* – 16 Kelfield Gdns, W10 6LS.

WIDOW LIVING OF FIRST BARON

JACQUELINE ALDINE LESLIE (*Dowager Baroness Killearn*) (23 Harley St, W1N 1DA; Haremere Hall, Etchingham, Sussex); da of late Marchese Senator Aldo Castellani, KCMG, FRCP, FACP, DSc, MD; a CStJ: *m* 1934, as his 2nd wife, the 1st Baron, who *d* 1964.

DAUGHTER LIVING OF THIRD BARONET

Sophia Curtis (Mill House Farm, Brightling, Sussex), *b* 1935: *m* 1955, Ronald J. Milwidsky, BSc(Eng), AMIEE, who *d* 1966, and has issue living, Peter Julian, *b* 1960, — Caroline Natasha, *b* 1956, — Sarah Janet, *b* 1962.

PREDECESSORS – (1) *Rt Hon Sir* MILES WEDDERBURN Lampson, GCMG, CB, MVO, 2nd son of late Norman George Lampson, yst son of 1st Bt (*infra*), *b* 1880; Min to China 1926-33, High Commr for Egypt and the Sudan 1933-36, Ambassador to Egypt and High Commr for Sudan 1936-46 and Special Commr in S-E Asia 1946-48; *cr Baron Killearn*, of Killearn, co Stirling (peerage of UK) 1943: *m* 1st, 1912, Rachel Mary Hele, who *d* 1930, da of William Wilton Phipps; 2ndly, 1934, Jacqueline Aldine Leslie, da of late Marchese Senator Aldo Castellani, KCMG, FRCP, FACP, DSc, MD; *d* 1964; *s* by his el son (2) GRAHAM CURTIS, 2nd Baron and present peer.
*(1) *Sir* CURTIS MIRANDA Lampson (yst son of William Lampson, of New Haven, Vermont, USA); *b* 1806, naturalized British subject 1848; Dep Chm Atlantic Telegraph Co 1865, which Co laid the first Atlantic telegraph cable, for which sers he was *cr a Baronet* 1866; Founder of C M Lampson & Co: *m* 1827, Jane Walter, who *d* 1891, da of Gibbs Sibley, of Sutton, Mass, USA; *d* 1885; *s* by his el son (2) Sir GEORGE CURTIS, 2nd Bt, *b* 1833: *m* 1887, Sophia, who *d* 1926, yst da of Manuel Van Gelderen; *d* 1899; *s* by his only son (3) *Sir* CURTIS GEORGE, 3rd Bt; *b* 1890; FRGS; explorer in Central and W Africa, author and journalist: *m* 1920, Maud Lawton, who *d* 1960, da of Alfred Wrigley, of Manchester; *d* 1971; *s* by his cousin, 2nd Baron Killearn (*ante*).

KILMAINE, BARON (Browne) (Baron I 1789, Bt NS 1636)

Follow right

Wick, Kingston upon Thames, Surrey.

JOHN DAVID HENRY BROWNE, 7th Baron, and 13th Baronet, *b* 2 April 1948; *s* 1978; *ed* Eton; a Dir of Fusion (Bickenhill) Ltd, and of Whale Tankers Ltd: *m* 1982, Linda, yr da of Dennis Robinson, of East Terrace, Budleigh Salterton, and has issue.

Arms – Sable, in bend three lions passant between two double cotises argent. **Crest** – An eagle displayed vert. **Supporters** – Two lions reguardant argent, ducally crowned, plain collared and chained or.

SON LIVING

Hon JOHN FRANCIS SANDFORD, *b* 4 April 1983.

DAUGHTER LIVING

Hon Alice, *b* 1985.

SISTERS LIVING

Hon Carola, *b* 1932: *m* 1960, John Michael Carlyon Lowry Hudson, and has issue living, John Carlyon, *b* 1961: *m* 1989, Fiona J., yr da of G. F. White, of Dunedin, NZ, and has issue living, Tristrem Carlyon Francis *b* 1993, — Thomas Christopher, *b* 1963, — Phyllida, *b* 1966. *Residence* – Gwavas Station, Tikokino, Hawkes Bay, NZ.

Hon Phyllida, *b* 1935: *m* 1959, John Edward Previté, QC, Circuit Judge, and has issue living, Andrew Capper, *b* 1961: *m* 1992, Antonia Hamilton Davis, yr da of E. W. Davis, of SW3, — Matthew John, *b* 1963: *m* 1992, Elizabeth S., elder da of A. J. Pull, of Headley, Hants, and has issue living, Grace Alexandra *b* 1993. *Residence* – The Wilderness, Hampton

WIDOW LIVING OF SIXTH BARON

WILHELMINA PHYLLIS (*Dowager Baroness Kilmaine*) (The Red Cottage, High Street, Brasted, Kent), only da of late Scott Arnott, of Tanners, Brasted, Kent: *m* 1930, Lt-Col the 6th Baron, CBE, who *d* 1978.

COLLATERAL BRANCHES LIVING

Grandson of late Frederick Howe Browne, yst son of late George Richard Browne, son of late Hon Richard Howe Browne, 5th son of 2nd Baron:—
Issue of late Noel Francis HOWE BROWNE, *b* 1884, *d* 1943: *m* 1919, Jessie Selwyn Tudhope:—
Peter Kilmaine (Morningside Farm, PO Box 692, Rustenburg, Transvaal), *b* 1920; late Capt King's African Rifles: *m* 1948, Grace Dorothy Robson, of Nakuru, Kenya, and has issue living, Margaret Jess, *b* 1950, — Joan Selwyn, *b* 1951.

Grandchildren of Capt Aubrey Caulfeild Browne (infra):—
Issue of late Cecil John Osborne Caulfeild Browne, *b* 1892, *d* 1983: *m* 1st, 1923, Gladys Isobel Mason, who *d* 1962; 2ndly, 1965, Mrs Madeline Constance Ferguson (15 Caroma Av, Kyeemagh, N Brighton, NSW, Australia):—
(By 1st *m*) *Rev* Aubrey Robert Caulfeild (c/o USPG, 15 Tufton St, SW1), *b* 1931; *ed* Newington Coll, Sydney, and Moore Coll, Sydney (ThL); Regional Manager, United Soc for Propagation of the Gospel.
Issue of late Edward James Caulfeild Browne, MBE, *b* 1903, *d* 1984: *m* 1st, 1925 (*m diss* 1941), Eileen, da of Jack O'Hearn, of Ireland; 2ndly, 1942, Mary Winifred, who *d* 1987, da of George Albert Green:—
(By 1st *m*) Reginald M. (30 Inkersall Drive, Mosborough, Sheffield), *b* 1928: *m* 1st, 1954 (*m diss* 19—), Valerie Therese Hogan; 2ndly, 1965, Margaret Kathleen —, and has issue living, (by 1st *m*) Loretta Sandra *b* 1955, — Yolanda Therese, *b* 1956, — (by 2nd *m*) Mark, *b* 1966, — Helen Louise, *b* 1973. —— Noreen, *b* 1926: *m* 19—, — Sharp. —— (By 2nd *m*) Nigel George, *b* 1947: *m* 1st, 1968 (*m diss* 1973), Susan Mary Green; 2ndly, 1974 (*m diss* 1983), Jill Christine Masters; 3rdly, 1984, Jane Elizabeth Skinner, and has issue living, (by 1st *m*) Sharon Ann, *b* 1970, — (by 2nd *m*) James Alexander, *b* 1976, — Sophie Victoria, *b* 1978, — Lucy Alexandra, *b* 1980, — (by 3rd *m*) Matthew John, *b* 1987. —— Robin James, *b* 1949: *m* 1970 (*m diss* 1978), Annette Heavey; 2ndly, 1979, Denise Dodd, and has issue living, (by 1st *m*) Edward Patrick, *b* 1972, — Christopher Robert, *b* 1974, — (by 2nd *m*) Jason Robin, *b* 1987. —— Dawn Rosemary, *b* 1943: *m* 19—, Robert Edward Collins, and has issue living, Mark Robert, *b* 1973, — Amanda Jane, *b* 1972.

Grandchildren of late Rev William James Caulfeild Browne, son of late Rev James Caulfeild Browne, DCL, son of late Hon George Browne, 3rd son of 1st Baron:—
Issue of late Capt Aubrey Caulfeild Browne, *b* 1860, *d* 1953: *m* 1st, 1888, Caroline Mitchell, who *d* 1893; 2ndly, 1894, Ida B. Graham, who *d* 1942:—
(By 2nd *m*) Norah, *b* 1896. —— Kathleen, *b* 1898.
Issue of late James Cecil Caulfeild Browne, *b* 1862, *d* 1917: *m* 1887, Elsie M., who *d* 19—, da of late G. Manning, British Consul at San Salvador:—
Edwin Caulfeild, *b* 1895. —— Cecily Caulfeild, *b* 1891: *m* 1908, Henry Snell.
Issue of late Harold John Caulfeild Browne, *b* 1864, *d* 1953: *m* 1916, Margaret Delamere Booth, who *d* 1971, da of Maj James Booth Clarkson:—
Edith Margaret, *b* 1919: *m* 1955, Thomas Henry Standish Goodlake, who *d* 1989. *Residence* – 1336 W King Edward Av, Vancouver, BC V6H-1Z9, Canada.

(In remainder to Baronetcy only)

Descendants of John Browne, MP, of Westport, co Mayo (grandson of Col John Browne, 2nd son of 1st baronet), who was *cr Earl of Altamont* 1771 (*see* M Sligo).
Descendants of John Browne, only son of Peter Browne, el son of Dominick Browne, 3rd son of 1st baronet:—

Granddaughter of late Dominick Andrew Browne, great-grandson of Dominick Browne, grandson of Dominick Browne (ante):—

Issue of late Major Dominick Sidney Browne, JP, DL, *b* 1866, *d* 1927: *m* 1895, Elizabeth Naomi, who *d* 1965, having *m* 2ndly, 1928, as his 2nd wife, Arthur Melville Hood Walrond (*see* B Waleran, colls), el da of Hon R. R. Dobell, of Beauvoir Manor, Quebec, Canada:—
Moyra Rose, *b* 1903: *m* 1922, Maj Guy Percy Lumsden Drake-Brockman, DSO, MC, who *d* 1952, and has issue living, Guy Dominick, 1925, — Marcia (twin), *b* 1925: *m* 1944, Charles Williams, mechanical engineer, and has issue living, Charles Dominick *b* 1945, Andrew *b* 1949, Christopher Michael *b* 1954. *Residence* – 1/307 Vancouver St, Victoria V8V 3T2, BC, Canada.

Grandchildren of late Maj Dominick Sidney Browne, JP, DL (ante):—
Issue of late Brig Dominick Andrew Sidney Browne, CBE, *b* 1904; *d* 1982: *m* 1930, Iris Kathleen, who *d* 1977, da of late Gerald Henry Deane, of Littleton House, Winchester, Hants:—
Peter Dominick, MBE, *b* 1949; Lt-Col R Green Jackets (ret 1990); MBE (Mil) 1984: *m* 1974, Sally Jane, el da John Eric Marrett, MRCS, LRCP, of Clare House, Howe Green, Sandon, Essex, and has issue living, Henry Dominick, *b* 1989, — Eleanor Jane, *b* 1987. *Residence* – Ludwell Farm, Glympton, Woodstock, Oxon OX20 1AZ. ⸺ Fiona Naomi, *b* 1935: *m* 1956, Cdr Hugh Douglas Younger Faulkner, RN, of Currie Lee, Crichton, nr Pathhead, Midlothian E37 5XD, and has issue living, Christopher Gerald (6 Rosemount Rd, W Ealing, W13 0HJ), *b* 1958: *m* 1987, Ming F., da of late Mark Veevers-Carter, and of Mrs John Blower, of Beau Pré St Martins, Guernsey, CI, and has issue living, Clarence Dominick Hugh *b* 1992, Olivia *b* 1990, — Anthony Dominick Hugh, *b* 1961. ⸺ Anne Patricia, *b* 1944: *m* 1st, 1967, David J. Forcey; 2ndly, 1978, Robin John Hay, of Stoke Cottage, Fullards Av, Taunton, Som TA1 3DE, and has issue living (by 1st *m*), Annabelle Jane, *b* 1971, — (by 2nd *m*) Alexander Robin, *b* 1980.

PREDECESSORS – (1) John Browne, el son of Josias Browne, of The Neale; *cr* a *Baronet* 1636; *d* 1670; *s* by his son (2) Sir George, 2nd Bt; *d* 1698; *s* by his son (3) Sir John, 3rd Bt; *d* 1711; *s* by his el son (4) Sir George, 4th Bt; *dsp* 1737; *s* by his brother (5) Sir John, 5th Bt; *d* 1762; *s* by his el son (6) Sir George, 6th Bt; *d* 1765; *s* by his brother (7) Sir John, MP; 7th Bt; *cr Baron Kilmaine*, of The Neale, co Mayo (peerage of Ireland) 1789; *d* 1794; *s* by his el son (8) James Caulfeild, 2nd Baron; *d* 1825; *s* by his el son (9) John Cavendish, 3rd Baron; *b* 1794; a Representative Peer; *m* 2ndly, 1839, Mary, da of Hon Charles Ewan Law, MP (B Ellenborough); *d* 1873; *s* by his son (10) Francis William, 4th Baron, *b* 1843; a Representative Peer for Ireland: *m* 1877, Alice Emily, who *d* 1925, da of Col Deane Shute; *d* 1907; *s* by his only son (11) John Edward Deane, 5th Baron, *b* 1878; a Representative Peer for Ireland: *m* 1901, Lady Aline Kennedy, who *d* 1957, da of 3rd Marquess of Ailsa; *d* 1946; *s* by his son (12) John Francis Archibald, CBE, 6th Baron; *b* 1902; High Steward of Harwich; 1939-45 War as Lt-Col RASC; Sec to Oxford Soc 1933-40 (Chm 1949-73), to Pilgrim Trust 1945-67, and to Dulverton Trust 1953-66; a Trustee of Historic Churches Preservation Trust: *m* 1930, Wilhelmina Phyllis, only da of Scott Arnott, of Tanners, Brasted, Kent; *d* 1978; *s* by his son (13) John David Henry, 7th Baron and present peer.

KILMANY, BARONY OF (Anstruther-Gray) (Life Baron 1966, Bt UK 1956) (Extinct 1985)

DAUGHTERS LIVING OF LIFE BARON

(*See* Anstruther of that Ilk, Bt, colls).

KILMARNOCK, BARON (Boyd) (Baron UK 1831)

I trust

Alastair Ivor Gilbert Boyd, 7th Baron; *b* 11 May 1927; *s* 1975; *ed* Bradfield, and King's Coll, Camb; Lt late IG; Chief of Clan Boyd; Page to Lord High Constable of Scotland at Coronation of HM King George VI; author of *Sabbatical Year* 1958, *The Road from Ronda* 1969, *The Companion Guide to Madrid and Central Spain* 1974, *The Essence of Catalonia* 1988, *The Sierras of the South* 1992, etc; Palestine 1947-48: *m* 1st, 1954 (*m diss* 1969), Diana Mary Grant, who *d* 1975, only da of D. Grant Gibson; 2ndly, 1977, Hilary Ann, yr da of Leonard Sidney, and formerly wife of Kingsley Amis (later Sir Kingsley Amis, CBE), and has issue by 2nd wife.

Arms – Quarterly: 1st azure a fesse chequy argent and gules, *Boyd*; 2nd argent three inescutcheons gules, *Hay*; 3rd argent three gillyflowers with a double tressure flory counter flory vert, *Livingston*; 4th sable a bend between six billets or, *Callendar*. Crest – A dexter hand erect in pale having the two outer fingers bowed inwards. Supporters – Two squirrels proper.
Residence – 1 Bridge St, Thornborough, Bucks MK18 2DN. *Club* – Pratt's.

SON LIVING (by 2nd wife)

Hon James Charles Edward, *b* 1972.

BROTHER LIVING

Hon Robin Jordan, *b* 6 June 1941; *ed* Eton, and at Keble Coll, Oxford (MA); MB BS, LRCP, MRCS, DCH; Page to Lord High Constable of Scotland at Coronation of HM Queen Elizabeth II 1953. *Residence* –

HALF-BROTHERS LIVING

Hon Jonathan Aubrey Lewis, *b* 1956: *m* 1982, Annette Madeleine, el da of Joseph Constantine, FRICS, of 3 Cottesmore Gdns, W8, and has issue living, a son, *b* 1989. *Residence* – 3 Evelyn Gdns, SW7.

Hon Timothy Ian, *b* 1959: *m* 1988, Lucy Teresa Emily, yr da of Michael Gray, and has issue living, Daisy, *b* 1988. *Residence* – Flat 2, 23 Ladbroke Cres, W11 1PS.

SISTERS LIVING

Hon Laura Alice, *b* 1934: *m* 1962, (Robert) Anthony Hyman, and has issue living, Anthony A., *b* 1962, — Merlin M., *b* 1969, — Francesca M. D., *b* 1963: *m* 1994, Charles Mills, son of Capt K. H. Mills, of Chickerell, Dorset.
Hon Caroline Juliet, *b* 1939: *m* 1969, Alan Bloss.

PREDECESSORS – **(1)** WILLIAM GEORGE HAY, KT, GCH, PC, 18th Earl of Erroll; *b* 1801; was Lord Steward of the Household, Master of the Staghounds, and Lord-Lieut of Aberdeenshire; *cr Baron Kilmarnock* of Kilmarnock, co Ayr (peerage of United Kingdom) 1831: *m* 1820, Lady Elizabeth Fitzclarence, who *d* 1856, nat da of King William IV; *d* 1846; *s* by his son **(2)** WILLIAM HENRY, 19th Earl, *b* 1823; Maj (ret) Rifle Brig; Crimea 1854-55: *m* 1848, Eliza Amelia, VA, who *d* 1916, da of late Gen Hon Sir Charles Gore, GCB; *d* 1891; *s* by his son **(3)** CHARLES GORE, KT, CB, LLD, 20th Earl, *b* 1852; Hon Maj-Gen in the Army; a Lord-in-Waiting to King Edward VII, 1903-5: *m* 1875, Mary Caroline, who *d* 1934, da of late Edmund L'Estrange, of Tynte Lodge, co Leitrim; *d* 1927; *s* by his son **(4)** VICTOR ALEXANDER SERELD, KCMG, 21st Earl, *b* 1876; acted as Chargé d'Affaires at Berlin 1919-21; was British High Commr of Rhineland Commn 1921-28: *m* 1900, Mary Lucy Victoria, who *d* 1957, only da of Sir Allan Russell Mackenzie, 2nd Bt (*cr* 1890); *d* 1928; *s* by his son **(5)** JOSSLYN VICTOR, 22nd Earl; *b* 1901: *m* 1923 (*m diss* 1930), Lady (Myra) Idina (Gordon) Sackville, who *d* 1957, da of 8th Earl De La Warr; 2ndly, 1930, Edith Mildred Mary (RAMSAY-HILL), who *d* 1939, da of late R. W. Maude, of Cleveland, Yorks; *d* 1941, when the Earldom of Erroll devolved upon his only da, and he was *s* in the Barony of Kilmarnock by his brother **(6)** GILBERT ALLAN ROWLAND, MBE, TD, 6th Baron, *b* 1903; deputised for Lord High Constable of Scotland at Coronation of HM Queen Elizabeth II 1953; assumed for himself and issue by Warrant of Lord Lyon King of Arms 1941, the surname of Boyd in lieu of that of Hay: *m* 1st, 1926, (*m diss* 1955), Hon Rosemary Sibell Guest, who *d* 1971, da of 1st Viscount Wimborne; 2ndly, 1955, Denise Aubrey Doreen, who *d* 1989, only da of late Maj Lewis Coker (*see* M Donegall, colls, 1985 Edn); *d* 1975; *s* by his el son **(7)** ALASTAIR IVOR GILBERT, 7th Baron and present peer.

KILMOREY, EARL OF (Needham) (Earl I 1822)
(Title pronounced "Kilmurry")

Now, or never

RICHARD FRANCIS NEEDHAM, PC, MP, 6th Earl (does not use his peerage); *b* 29 Jan 1942; *s* 1977; *ed* Eton; did not use courtesy title of Viscount Newry and Morne 1969-77; Hereditary Abbot of the Exempt Jurisdiction of Newry and Mourne; late co councillor, Som; former Chm RGM Print Holdings Ltd; Personal Assist to Rt Hon James Prior 1974-79, Member Public Accounts Cttee 1982-83, PPS to Rt Hon James Prior 1983-84, and to Rt Hon Patrick Jenkin 1984-85; an Under-Sec of State, N Ireland Office, 1985-92, since when Min of Trade, Dept of Trade and Industry; author of *Honourable Member* (1983); MP for Chippenham (*C*) 1979-83, since when for Wiltshire North (*C*); PC 1994: *m* 1965, Sigrid Juliane Thiessen-Gairdner, only da of late Ernst Thiessen, of Hamburg, and of Mrs John Gairdner, and has issue.

Arms – Argent, a bend azure, between two bucks heads cabossed sable. **Crest** – A demi phœnix proper. **Supporters** – *Dexter*, a bay horse, mane and tail sable *sinister*, a stag proper.
Seat – Mourne Park, Newry, co Down. *Address* – c/o House of Commons, SW1. *Clubs* – Pratt's; Beefsteak.

SONS LIVING

ROBERT FRANCIS JOHN (*Viscount Newry and Morne*), *b* 30 May 1966; *ed* Eton, Lady Margaret Hall, Oxford, and Imperial Coll, London (MBA): *m* 1991, Laura Mary, only da of Michael Tregaskis, of Cosham, Hants.
Hon Andrew Francis, *b* 1969; *ed* Eton, and Edinburgh Univ.

DAUGHTER LIVING

Lady Christina Clare, *b* 1977.

BROTHERS LIVING

Hon Christopher David, *b* 1948; *ed* Milton Abbey: *m* 1974, Marina, el da of Rodi Malvezzi, of Milan, and has issue living, Francis, *b* 1982, — Armyne, *b* 1978. *Residence* – 63 Foro Buonaparte, Milan, Italy.
Hon (Patrick) Jonathan, *b* 1951: *m* 1979 (*m diss* 1993), Jane, 2nd da of Geoffrey Hinbest, of Winterbourne, Bristol. *Residence* – 9 Vale View Terrace, Batheaston, Bath BA1 7RH.

AUNT LIVING (*Raised to the rank of an Earl's daughter* 1962)

Lady Mary Esther Constance, *b* 1918: *m* 1949, Com Anthony Boyce Combe, RN (ret), who *d* 1990, and has issue living, David Boyce, *b* 1952: *m* 19— (*m diss* 1991), Fiona Helen, da of Derek C. Thomson, of Invereighty House, Forfar, and has issue living, James Anthony Derek *b* 1987, Alexander *b* 1988, Annabel *b* 1989, — Peter, *b* 1955, — John (twin), *b* 1955, — Anne Romaine, *b* 1950: *m* 1985, Douglas Jardine, eldest son of Col N. Jardine, of Port Alfred, Cape, S Africa. *Residence* – Grove Cottage, South Creake, Fakenham, Norfolk.

WIDOW LIVING OF BROTHER OF 5TH EARL

Janet Beatrice Winifred (*Hon Mrs Peter Needham*) (The Old Manor House, Helmsley, York), yst da of late Capt George Taylor Ramsden, MP, of Bramham, Yorks: *m* 1951, Maj Hon Arthur Edward Peter Needham, who was raised to the rank of an Earl's son 1962, and *d* 1979.

WIDOW LIVING OF FIFTH EARL

HELEN BRIDGET (*Countess of Kilmorey*), da of Sir Lionel Lawson Faudel Faudel-Phillips, 3rd Bt; resumed her former style 1990: *m* 1st, 1941, the 5th Earl, who *d* 1977; 2ndly, 1978 (*m diss* 1990), Harold William Elliott. *Residence* – 8 The Dormers, Highworth, Swindon, Wilts.

COLLATERAL BRANCHES LIVING

Grandchildren of Maj Hon Francis Edward Needham, MVO, 2nd son of 3rd Earl:—
Issue of late Maj Hon Arthur Edward Peter Needham (raised to the rank of an Earl's son 1962), *b* 1921, *d* 1979: *m* 1951, Janet Beatrice Winifred (ante), yst da of late Capt George Taylor Ramsden, MP, of Bramham, Yorks:—
Robert (Robin) Arthur John, *b* 1953: *m* 1981, Lucy Potter, only da of Capt Howard Bucknell III, USN (ret), of East Hampton, NY, USA, and has issue living, Nathaniel Peter, *b* 1984, — Robert Bucknell, *b* 1985, — Sonali Anna, *b* 1989, — Rupali Sarah, *b* (twin) 1989. *Residence* – The Old Manor House, Helmsley, York. —— Thomas Francis, *b* 1959: has issue living (by Caroline Stockbridge), Finn Barnaby NEEDHAM, *b* 1992. —— Jane Diana, *b* 1955: *m* 1975 (*m diss* 1993), John Bell, of The Hall, Thirsk, N Yorks (*see* M Ailsa, 1969 Edn), and has issue living, Daisy *b* 1984, — Lettice, *b* 1987, — Zillah, *b* 1990.

Granddaughter of late Francis Henry Needham, 3rd son of Hon Francis Henry Needham (infra):—
Issue of late Francis Charles Needham, *b* 1889, *d* 1958: *m* 1922, Violet, who *d* 1963, da of William Kaye Parker:—
Thyra Frances (G6/182 Dornoch Terr, Highgate Hill, Brisbane, Qld, Australia), *b* 1923.

Grandsons of late Alfred Edwin Needham, 3rd son of late Hon Francis Henry Needham, 3rd son of 2nd Earl:—
Issue of late Francis Jack Needham, *b* 1892; *d* 1974: *m* 1926 Mary Clare, who *d* 1979, da of late Patrick Alban O'Sullivan of Brisbane:—
Patrick Francis Jack (93 Haigh Av, Belrose, NSW 2085, Australia), *b* 1927: *m* 1955, Margaret Anne, el da of Hilton John Daley, of Monavale Station, Hughenden, Qld, and has issue living, Robert Francis Jack (57 Stone Parade, Davidson, NSW 2085, Australia), *b* 1956: *m* 1981, Kathleen Anne, only da of John O'Connor, of Dubbo, NSW, and has issue living, Andrew Francis Jack *b* 1983, Christopher Robert *b* 1985, Thomas John *b* 1988, Jack Patrick Dominic *b* 1991, — John Edward (33 Angophora Crescent, Forestville, NSW 2087, Australia), *b* 1963: *m* 1987, Jennifer Gay Doreen, da of Graham Napier, of Bilgola Plateau, NSW, and has issue living, Clare Jennifer *b* 1993, — Patrick Thomas (19 Bowen Close, Cherry Brook, NSW 2126, Australia), *b* (twin) 1963: *m* 1987, Michelle Anne, da of Louis Samuel Harris, of Normanhurst, NSW, and has issue living, Benjamin Edward *b* 1994, — Mary Margaret, *b* 1958: *m* 1980, Anthony Francis Walsh, of 14 Sandy Beach Rd, Korora, NSW 2450, Australia, and has issue living, Michael Francis *b* 1983, Simon Anthony *b* 1985, Daniel Robert *b* 1987, Robert Christopher *b* 1993, — Judith Anne, *b* 1960: *m* 1978, Brian Lindsay Kerr, of 24 Merrilee Crescent, Frenchs Forest, NSW 2086, Australia, and has issue living, Sandra Kate *b* 1978, Danielle Jan *b* 1980, Judith Louise *b* 1987, Jacqueline Margaret *b* 1989, Olivia Anne *b* 1992, — Patricia Clare, *b* 1973. —— Robert Cust (40 Palm Av, Ascot, Brisbane, Qld), *b* 1928: *m* 1958, Annette Mary Beiers, el da of Michael Patrick O'Rourke, of 104 Reeve St, Clayfield, Brisbane, and has issue living, Robert Michael, *b* 1963, — Michael Francis Jack, *b* 1967, — Morna Irene, *b* 1959: *m* 1982, John Henry Allen, of Woodville St, Clayfield, Brisbane, and has issue living, Prudence Anne *b* 1986, Isobelle Susan *b* 1988, — Susan Clare, *b* 1961, — Lucy Ann, *b* 1969. —— Thomas Edwin (Narrien Court, Samford, Qld 4520, Australia), *b* 1931: *m* 1964, Julia Elizabeth, da of William O. Moore, of Shadyside, Longreach, Qld, and has issue living, Deborah Clare, *b* 1970, — Natalie Barbara, *b* 1972. —— Edward Laurence (Christian Brothers, St Mary's Provincial House, 179 Albert Rd, Strathfield, NSW 2135, Australia), *b* 1936; assumed by deed poll 19— the forename of Laurence in lieu of Francis.

Grandchildren of late Frederick William Needham (infra):—
Issue of late Capt James Owen Needham, *b* 1897, *d* 1975: *m* 1929, Marjorie Hylda (13 Voltaire, Kew, Surrey), da of late Charles George Lumley Cator (Blois, Bt):—
Christopher James Blois (Snode Hill House, Beech, Alton, Hants), *b* 1931: *m* 1955, Nicola Anne, only da of late Capt Robert Coles, and has issue living, Henrietta Aeddan, *b* 1957: *m* 1979, Russell Baylis, only son of J. R. Baylis, of Rose Cottage, Great Comberton, Worcs, and has issue living, Camilla Annabelle *b* 1981, Harriet Alicia *b* 1983, Emily Charlotte *b* 1985, Araminta Rose *b* 1988, — Alicia Claire, *b* 1959: *m* 1988, Henry Vane Eden (*see* B Auckland), — (Camilla) Romaine, *b* 1961: *m* 1986, Nicholas R. I. Foot, eldest son of Dennis Foot, of Lyde Mill House, Newnham, Hants, and has issue living, Alexander *b* 1987. —— David John Manners (Pine Lodge, Cokes Lane, Chalfont St Giles, Bucks), *b* 1934: *m* 1965, Evelyn Elizabeth (who assumed by deed poll 1965, for herself and her issue the surname of Palmers-Needham), da of Theodore L. Palmers, Consul Gen for Nicaragua in London, and has issue living, Katherine Elizabeth Theodora, *b* 1970. —— Patricia Deline, *b* 1942: *m* 1st, 1968 (*m diss* 1982), John Michael Singer; 2ndly, 1984, Lt-Cdr William Jonathan Richard Pennefather, RN, of Westmark House, Westmark, Sheet, Petersfield, Hants GU31 5AT, and has issue living (by 1st *m*), Jeremy James, *b* 1974, — Caroline Emma Louise, *b* 1969, — Serena Claire, *b* 1972.

Granddaughter of late Hon Francis Henry Needham (ante):—
Issue of late Frederick William Needham, *b* 1861, *d* 1928: *m* 1886, Geraldine, who *d* 1946, da of Edmund Arthur Paget, of Thorpe Satchville Hall, Melton Mowbray:—
Audrey Deline, *b* 1895: *m* 1918, Capt Adrian Dura Stoop, MC, TA (ret), who *d* 1957, and has issue living, James Richard, *b* 1920; Sqdn-Ldr RAF (ret), — Michael, MC, *b* 1922; *ed* Univ Coll, Oxford; Maj (ret) Gren Gds; 1939-45 War (MC): *m* 1st, 1948 (*m diss* 19—), Micheline, da of Baron de Posson, of 56 Rue Gachard, Brussels; 2ndly, 19— (*m diss* 19—), Mrs Diana Buchanan; 3rdly, 1959, Beverley Ann, da of Herbert Roberts, of Glangwa, Caernarvon, and has issue living, (by 1st *m*) Adrian Gaston *b* 1949, Caroline *b* 1950. *Residence* – Half-Tiles, 5 Meadow Lane, Hartley Wintney, Hants.

PREDECESSORS – (1) Sir ROBERT Needham, KB, one of the Council of the Pres of Wales; *cr Viscount Kilmorey* (peerage of Ireland) 1625; *d* 1625; *s* by his el son (2) ROBERT, 2nd Viscount; *d* 1653; *s* by his son (3) Robert, 3rd Viscount; *dsp* 1657; *s* by his half-brother (4) CHARLES, 4th Viscount; *d* 1660; *s* by his el son (5) ROBERT, 5th Viscount; *b* 1655; *d* 1668; *s* by his brother (6) THOMAS, 6th Viscount; *d* 1687; *s* by his son (7) ROBERT, 7th Viscount; *d* 1710; *s* by his el son (8) ROBERT, 8th Viscount; *d* 1716; *s* by his brother (9) THOMAS, 9th Viscount; *dsp* 1768; *s* by his brother (10) JOHN, 10th Viscount; a Col in the Army; *d* 1791; *s* by his el surviving son (11) ROBERT, 11th Viscount; *d* 1818; *s* by his brother (12) FRANCIS, 12th Viscount; a Gen in the Army; *cr Viscount Newry and Morne* and *Earl of Kilmorey* (peerage of Ireland) 1822; *d* 1832; *s* by his son (13) FRANCIS JACK, 2nd Earl; MP for Newry 1818-26: *m* 1st, 1814, Jane, who *d* 1867, da of George Gun Cuninghame, of Mount Kennedy, co Wicklow; 2ndly, 1867, Martha, who *d* 1907, da of John Foster, of Lenham, Kent; *d* 1880; *s* by his grandson (14) FRANCIS CHARLES, KP (el son of Francis Jack (Viscount Newry and Morne), MP for Newry 1941-51, by Anne Amelia, da of Gen Hon Sir Charles Colville, GCB (B Colville)), 3rd Earl; *b* 1842; a Representative Peer; MP for Newry (*C*) 1871-4: *m* 1881, Ellen Constance, who *d* 1920, da of late Edward Holmes Baldock, MP for Shrewsbury; *d* 1915; *s* by his el son (15) FRANCIS CHARLES ADELBERT HENRY, OBE, VRD, PC, 4th Earl; *b* 1883; Capt 1st Life Guards, Capt Comdg Ulster Div RNVR, Lieut for co Down, and High Sheriff 1913; Vice-Adm of Ulster 1937-61: *m* 1920, Lady Norah Frances Hastings, who *d* 1985, da of 14th Earl of Huntingdon; *d* 1961; *s* by his nephew (16) FRANCIS JACK RICHARD PATRICK (son of late Major Hon

Francis Edward Needham, MVO, 2nd son of 3rd Earl), 5th Earl; *b* 1915; Maj Gren Gds: *m* 1941, Helen Bridget (who *m* 2ndly, 1978, Harold William Elliott), da of Sir Lionel Lawson Faudel Faudel-Phillips, 3rd Bt; *d* 1977; *s* by his el son **(17)** RICHARD FRANCIS, 6th Earl and present peer; also Viscount Kilmorey, and Viscount Newry and Morne, but does not use his peerages.

KILMUIR, EARLDOM OF (Fyfe) (Extinct 1967)

DAUGHTERS LIVING OF FIRST EARL

Lady Pamela Maxwell, *b* 1928; a JP of Inner London: *m* 1st, 1950, Clive Wigram, Bar-at-law, who *d* 1956; 2ndly, 1957, Courtenay Thomas Gardner Blackmore, who *d* 1992, and has issue living, (by 1st *m*) Caroline, *b* 1952: *m* 1983, A. Jonathan D. Pearson, and has issue living, John William *b* 1986, Hannah Jane *b* 1988, — (by 2nd *m*) Thomas David Maxwell Fyfe (C44 Du Cane Court, Balham, SW17 7JG), *b* 1960: *m* 1985, Susan Eleanor, yr da of late Senhouse Martindale Casson, of Bury St Edmunds, Suffolk, — Katharine Fanny, *b* 1958: *m* 1984, J. W. Partridge, of 17 Meadow Rd, SW19, only son of Bryan Partridge, of Hastings, Sussex, — Victoria Jane, *b* 1965. *Residence* – 61 Riverview Gdns, SW13 9QZ.
Lady Miranda Maxwell, *b* 1938: *m* 1960, Michael Ormiston Cormack, who *d* 1993, and has issue living, David Ormiston, *b* 1964: *m* 1984, Helen, yr da of Keith Jarvis, of Sevenoaks, Kent, — Alistair Kilmuir, *b* 1970, — Helen Madeleine, *b* 1963. *Residence* – 31 White Hart Wood, Sevenoaks, Kent.

KIMBALL, BARON (Kimball) (Life Baron 1985)

MARCUS RICHARD KIMBALL, son of late Maj Lawrence Kimball, Leics Yeo, of Alderholt Park, Fordingbridge, Hants, by his 1st wife, late Kathleen Joan, only surv da of Richard Henry Ratcliff, of Stanford Hall, Loughborough, Leics; *b* 18 Oct 1928; *ed* Eton, and Trin Coll, Camb; Lieut Leics Yeo (TA) 1947, Capt 1952, Maj 1955; MP for Gainsborough Div of Lincs (*C*) 1956-83, CC Rutland 1955-62, and a DL Leics since 1984; Privy Council Rep, Council of RCVS, 1969-82 (Hon ARCVS 1982); External Member Council Lloyd's 1982-89; Chm British Field Sports Soc 1966-82; *cr* Knt 1981, and *Baron Kimball*, of Easton, co Leics (Life Baron) 1985: *m* 1956, June Mary, only da of Montagu John Fenwick, JP, of Great Stukeley Hall, Huntingdon (*see* D Manchester, colls, 1942 Edn), and has issue.

Arms – Arg, a pale gu, charged with a lion rampant of the field, on a chief sa a bezant between two crescents or. Crest – In front of two arrows points downwards saltirewise gu, a bull's head erased sa, armed or, ducally crowned also gu, between two branches of laurel fructed ppr. Supporters – On either side a wild turkey proper.
Residence – Great Easton Manor, Market Harborough, Leics LE16 8TB. *Clubs* – White's, Pratt's.

DAUGHTERS LIVING

Hon (Sarah) Marcia, *b* 1958: *m* 1982, David Alexander Somerset Gibbs, 2nd son of Patrick Somerset Gibbs, of Hazeley House, Mortimer, Reading, and has issue living, James Patrick, *b* 1983, — Emily Rose, *b* 1985, — Alexandra Harriet, *b* 1989. *Residence* – Kentmere House, Castor, Peterborough, Cambs PE5 7BU.

Hon Sophie Henrietta, *b* 1960: *m* 1982, Reuben Thomas Coppin Straker, 4th and yst son of late Hugh Charles Straker, of Gaucin, Spain, and has issue living, Edward Marcus Reuben, *b* 1991, — Camilla Sophie, *b* 1985, — Lucy Charlotte, *b* 1988. *Residence* – Stonecroft, Fourstones, Hexham, Northumberland NE47 5AX.

KIMBERLEY, EARL OF (Wodehouse) (Earl UK 1866, Bt E 1611)
(Name pronounced "Woodhouse")

Strike hard

JOHN WODEHOUSE, 4th Earl and 11th Baronet; *b* 12 May 1924; *s* 1941; *ed* Eton and Magdalene Coll, Camb; Lt Gren Gds 1942-45, Guards Armoured Div 1943-45; Vice-Pres of World Council on Alcoholism; Chm of Nat Council on Alcoholism since 1982; former Liberal Spokesman on Aerospace, Defence and Voluntary Community Services; Hon Sec House of Lords All Party Defence Study Group since 1978, Pres since 1992, Chm Foreign Affairs Cttee, Monday Club, 1979-83, Air League Council since 1981, British Maritime League Council since 1977, Member Royal United Services Inst since 1976, Int Inst for Strategic Studies, etc; Associate Royal Aeronautical Soc since 1977; UK Delegate to N Atlantic Assembly 1981-93: *m* 1st, 1945 (*m diss* 1948), Diana Evelyn only da of late Lt-Col Hon Sir Piers Walter Legh, GCVO, CMG, CIE, OBE (*see* B Newton, colls); 2ndly, 1949 (*m diss* 1952), Carmel June, who *d* 1992, formerly wife of Derek Dunnett, and 3rd da of late Michael Joseph Maguire, of Melbourne, Aust; 3rdly, 1953 (*m diss* 1960), Cynthia Abdy, formerly wife of Charles Gustav Westendarp, and yr da of Eric Abdy Collins, FRCS, MRCP, of The Chantrey, Saxmundham, Suffolk; 4thly, 1961 (*m diss* 1965), Margaret, da of Albert Simons; 5thly, 1970 (*m diss* 1982), Gillian, da of Col Norman Ireland-Smith, and formerly wife of John Raw; 6thly, 1982, Sarah Jane Hope, eldest da of Lt-Col Christopher D'Arcy Preston Consett, DSO, MC, and has issue by 2nd, 3rd and 4th *m*.

𝕬rms – Sable, a chevron or, gutté de sang between three cinquefoils ermine. 𝕮rest – A dexter arm couped below the elbow, vested argent, and grasping a club or. 𝕾upporters – Two wild men, wreathed about the loins, and holding in the exterior hand a club, raised in the attitude of striking, sable.
Residence – Hailstone House, Cricklade, Swindon, Wilts SN6 6JP. *Clubs* – White's, MCC, Naval and Military, House of Lords Yacht.

SONS LIVING *(By 2nd marriage)*

JOHN ARMINE (*Lord Wodehouse*) (Glendalough, Innings Rd, Little Frieth, Henley-on-Thames, Oxon RG9 6NU), *b* 15 Jan 1951; *ed* Eton, and Univ of E Anglia (MSc); systems programmer with Glaxo Group Research Ltd from 1979 (joined as research chemist in 1974); Assoc Fellow British Interplanetary Soc since 1981, Fellow 1984; Chm of UK Info Users GP 1981-83; Member British Computer Soc 1988; FRSA: *m* 1973, Hon Carol Lylie Palmer, el da of 3rd Baron Palmer, and has issue:—
    SON LIVING—*Hon* David Simon John, *b* 10 Oct 1978.
    DAUGHTER LIVING—*Hon* Katherine Frances, *b* 1976.

(By 3rd marriage)

Hon Edward Abdy (17 Ada Rd, SE5 7RW), *b* 1954; *ed* Eton: *m* 1st, 1980 (*m diss* 1983), Pandora JEFFREYS, eldest da of Mrs W. J. Germing, of Castlenau, Barnes; 2ndly, 1988, Sarah Katherine, da of Richard Allen, of Ranskill, Retford, Notts, and of Mrs Patrick Dean, of E Mere, Lincoln.
Hon Henry Wyndham, *b* 1956; *ed* Millfield: *m* 1st, 1979 (*m diss* 1988), Sarah M., only da of J. A. Fleming, of Hampton, Middx; 2ndly, 1992, Elizabeth Ellen, da of Edmund Parkin, and has issue living (by 1st *m*), Thomas Henry John, *b* 1981, — Clare Margaret, *b* 1980.

(By 4th marriage)

Hon Charles James, *b* 1963.

COLLATERAL BRANCHES LIVING

(In remainder to Baronetcy only)

Granddaughters of late Rev Philip John Wodehouse, el son of Col Philip Wodehouse, el son of Rev Philip Wodehouse, 2nd son of 5th Bt, and brother of 1st Baron:—
Issue of late Capt Philip George Wodehouse, DSO, RN, *b* 1883, *d* 1973: *m* 1st, 1915 (*m diss* 1928), Beaujolois Theresa Constance, who *d* 1986, only da of late Arthur George Ridout, of Condercum, Benwell, Northumberland; 2ndly, 1928, Alice Margaret (Ebor House, Park Lane, Barnstaple, N Devon), da of late William Rowe:—
(By 1st *m*) Beaujolois Inez, *b* 1919: *m* 1942, Capt Hubert Gordon Compton Cavendish, RASC, who *d* 1993, of Bosvathick, Constantine, Falmouth, Cornwall (*see* D Devonshire, colls). —— Valencia, *b* 1920; served 1939-45 War in ATS. *Residence* – Cliff Cottage, Point, Devoran, Truro, Cornwall TR3 6NQ.

Granddaughter of late Col Charles Wodehouse, CIE, 2nd son of Col Philip Wodehouse (ante):—
Issue of late Lieut-Col Frederic William Wodehouse, CIE, *b* 1867, *d* 1961: *m* 1st, 1893, Mary Helen, who *d* 1920, da of late George Nugent Lambert, Sup Engineer Sind; 2ndly, 1940, Hilary Mary, who *d* 1974, only da of late William Henry Pell, of Holme House, Nottinghamshire:—
(By 1st *m*) Kathleen Doris Laetitia, *b* 1897: *m* 1922, Air Vice-Marshal Stanley James Goble, CBE, DSO, DSC, RAAF, who *d* 1948, and has issue living, John Douglas (308 Coonawarra Rd, Terrey Hills, NSW 2084, Australia), *b* 1923; Commodore RAN (ret): *m* 1953, Annette Margaret, da of Col G. Youl, of Launceston, Tasmania, and has issue living, Margaret Kate *b* 1959, — Alan James (Delamore, Prince's Highway, Stratford, Vic 3862, Australia), *b* 1925; MB and BS; MD Melbourne; FRACP; FRCP London: *m* 1950 (*m diss* 1968), Patricia, da of R. A. Johnston, of Corowa, NSW, and has issue living, David Stanley *b* 1955, Anne Louise *b* 1957, — Ivor Norman, *b* 1929: *m* 1st, 1954, (*m diss* 1969) June, da of A. E. Peart, of Maroona, Vic; 2ndly,

1971, Janis Esther, da of Reed White, of Salem, Oregon, USA, and has issue living (by 1st *m*) Ann Sally *b* 1956, (by 2nd *m*) Scott Michael *b* 1975, Amy Vervaine *b* 1974. *Residence* – Eastern District Private Nursing Home, Maroondah Highway, Croydon, Victoria 3136, Australia.

Grandsons of late Rev Frederic Armine Wodehouse, 3rd son of late Col Philip Wodehouse (ante):—
Issue of late Vice-Adm Norman Atherton Wodehouse, CB, RN, *b* 1887, *ka* 1941: *m* 1923, Theodosia Frances, who *d* 1966, da of late Com Edward Louis Dalrymple Boyle, CMG, RN, and widow of Capt Douglas William Swire, Shropshire Yeo (*see* E Glasgow, colls):—
Rev Armine Boyle (103 Orient Palace, 1 rue de la Republique, 06500 Menton, France), *b* 1924; *ed* Radley; 1939-45 War with Gren Gds: *m* 1952, Diana Helen Arabella, who *d* 1990, only da of late Charles Sidney Bowen Wentworth-Stanley, CBE (*see* Brocklebank, Bt, colls, 1948 Edn), and has issue living, Armine Mark Robin (Villa Concordia, Ave de Lattre de Tassigny, 06360 St Laurent d'Eze, France), *b* 1960; *ed* Radley, and Downing Coll, Camb: *m* 1986, Yoma Irene Mandra, da of J. B. Jackson, of Monte Carlo and has issue living, Sarah Casmen Diane *b* 1989, — Julia Katherine, *b* 1955: *m* 1981, William John Hunt, of 43 Hamilton Terr, NW8 9RG, son of late W. E. Hunt, and has issue living, Oliver William *b* 1988, Miranda Katherine *b* 1984, Arabella Katrina *b* 1985, — Victoria Frances, *b* 1957: *m* 1979, Evan John Thatcher, of Peel Forest, Geraldine, S Canterbury, NZ, and has issue living, Hamish John *b* 1981, David Michael *b* 1983, Benjamin Samuel *b* 1993, Lucinda Katherine *b* 1980. —— Charles Norman Boyle, *b* 1927: *m* 1953, Joyce Marie Williamson, da of late John Dobson, MC, and has issue living, Dominic Charles John, *b* 1968, — Fiona Clare, *b* 1958, — Charlotte Thea Fleur, *b* 1962: *m* 1991, Philip M. Bubb, elder son of M.A.T. Bubb, of Measham, Burton-on-Trent. *Residence* – 23 Altenburg Gdns, SW11 1JH.

Grandchildren of late Henry Ernest Wodehouse, CMG, 5th son of late Col Philip Wodehouse (ante):—
Issue of late Ernest Armine Wodehouse, *b* 1879, *d* 1936: *m* 1919, Helen, da of late Patrick Harnett:—
Patrick Armine, *b* 1920; *ed* Cheltenham, and Imperial Coll of Science and Technology; BSc; ACGI, MIEE; Consultant Eng; Fl-Lt RAuxAF (ret): *m* 1947, Joyce Lilian, da of Charles Champion, and has issue living, Nigel Armine, *b* 1948.
Issue of late Richard Lancelot Deane Wodehouse, *b* 1892, *d* 1940: *m* 1st, 1925, Katherine, who *d* 1932, da of W Wallace Cook, OBE; 2ndly, 1934, Winifred Baker, who *d* 1979, da of Brig-Gen William Baker-Brown, CB, and widow of Robert Arthur Williams:—
(By 1st *m*) Ann Elizabeth, *b* 1930: *m* 1953, Lt-Col Richard Gerald Higgins, RA of 11/12 Red Lion St, Kings Sutton, nr Banbury, Oxon OX17 3RH, and has issue living, Andrew Richard, *b* 1954: *m* 1982, Alison Margaret, da of Col Anthony Gilks, of The Grange, Brunston, Rutland, and has issue living, Peter Anthony *b* 1989, James Patrick *b* 1991, — Michael James, *b* 1956: *m* 1985, Kim Maria Stevens, elder da of Col N. Flower, of 47 York Rd, Camberley, Surrey, — John Deane, *b* 1962: *m* 1988, Rosemary Jane Cecilia, da of F. J. D. Boot, of 57 Woodthorpe Drive, Nottingham. —— Katharine Jane Armine, *b* 1932: *m* 1955, Graeme Roper Wallace, of Little Grondra, Shirenewton, Chepstow, Mon, and has issue living, Ross Matthew Walker, *b* 1956, — Neil Richard Deane, *b* 1958, — Constance Armine Louise,

Granddaughters of late James Hay Wodehouse (*b* 1861), elder son of late Maj James Hay Wodehouse (*b* 1824), 2nd son of late Ven Charles Nourse Wodehouse, 2nd son of late Rev Philip Wodehouse (ante):—
Issue of late James Archibald Hay Wodehouse, *b* 1895, *d* 1973: *m* 1st, 1916, Florence, who *d* 1937, da of Edward Boyd: 2ndly, 1938, Elizabeth K., da of William K. Buchanan:—
(By 1st *m*) Mildred Pauahi Hay, *b* 1916: *m* 1942, Capt Asa Alan Clark III, US Navy, of 46-416 Hulupala Place, Kaneohe, Hawaii 96744, and has issue living, Asa Alan (IV) (134 E 93rd St, 3B, NY, USA), *b* 1944: Col US Army (ret): *m* 1968, Margie Slocum, and has had issue, Matthew Shannon *b* 1968: *d* 1988, Christopher *b* 1972, — Jeffrey Wodehouse (Rt 1, Box 190, Manton, California 96059, USA), *b* 1947, — Bruce Shannon (54-112 Kealalani Place, Hauula, Hawaii 96717), *b* 1953: *m* 1992, Diane Kelly. —— (By 2nd *m*) James Hay, *b* 1946. —— (Florence) Elizabeth Hay, *b* 1939: *m* 1963, George Warren Freeland, of 439 Front St, Lahaina, Maui, Hawaii 96761, and has issue living, George Warren, *b* 1965, — Kimberley Kaiulani, *b* 1967; has issue living, Nohea Edward FREELAND *b* 1993, — Denby Elizabeth Hay, *b* 1971.

Grandchildren of late Guy Armine Wodehouse (*b* 1863), 2nd son of late Maj James Hay Wodehouse (*b* 1824) (ante):—
Issue of late Everard Hay Wodehouse, *b* 1895, *d* 1970: *m* 1st, 1927 (*m* annulled 1934), Dorothy Eileen, da of J. G. Cameron, of Santiago, Chile; 2ndly, 1937, Winifred Mary, who *d* 1978, da of Reginald Ashton, of Lima, Peru:—
(By 2nd *m*) Richard Everard, *b* 1949: *m* 1979, Mary Jean, da of William Warren Johnson, of Elkton, Oregon, and has issue living, Carissa Renée, *b* 1982, — Paloma Carin, *b* 1988. *Residence* – 628 Pacific View Drive, San Diego, California 92108, USA. —— Diana Elaine, *b* 1939: *m* 1964, Donald Ralph Strong, and has issue living, Everard George, *b* 1968, — Miriam Ruth, *b* 1966. *Residence* – 1700 W 106th St, Chicago, Illinois 60643, USA. —— (Marilyn) Joanna, *b* 1943: *m* 1964, Garvin Olaf Muri, and has issue living, Michelle Ingrid, *b* 1967, — Jenelle, *b* 1970. *Residence* – 934 31st St, Bismark, N Dakota 58501, USA.
Issue of late James Millie Wodehouse, *b* 1896, *d* 1971: *m* 1930, Helen Mary Edith, who *d* 1994, elder da of Sir John Murray, 12th Bt (*cr* 1628):—
Lily Ann, *b* 19——. *Residence* – Casilla 7, Vallenar, Chile.

Granddaughter of late Maj James Hay Wodehouse (*b* 1824) (ante):—
Issue of late Guy Armine Wodehouse, *b* 1863, *d* 1926, *m* 1894, Elisa Millie, who *d* 1935, da of David Millie, of Coquimbo, Chile:—
Ivy Maud, *b* 1901: *m* 1937, Edward James Campbell, of Av El Bosque 131, Depto 63, Santiago, Chile.

Grandchildren of late Kenneth Charles Wodehouse, yst son of late Maj James Hay Wodehouse (*b* 1824) (ante):—
Issue of late John Hay Wodehouse, *b* 1917, *d* 1993: *m* 1st, 1941, Maria Francisca Garrido, who *d* 1945; 2ndly, 1947 (*m diss* 1959), Carmen Meza Valdés; 3rdly, 1960, Jeanette Wackenhut (Calle Madre Mazarello 6745, Las Condes, Santiago, Chile):—
(By 1st *m*) Cyprian Gerard (6 Whittier Place, Apt 15H, Boston, Mass 02114, USA), *b* 1941; has issue living, Lisa Sharon, *b* 1982. —— (By 2nd *m*) Kenneth John (1166 Carrollton Av, Metairie, Louisiana 70005, USA; 337 39h St, New Orleans, Louisiana 70124, USA), *b* 1957: *m* 1987, Lisa Marie, da of Paul T. White, and has issue living, Evan John, *b* 1989, — Craig Alen, *b* 1993. —— (By 3rd *m*) Roderick Dhu, *b* 1965. —— Sharon Elizabeth, *b* 1962.

Grandchildren of late Rear-Admiral Capel Wodehouse, yr son of late Rev Nathaniel Francis Wodehouse, son of late Thomas Wodehouse, 3rd son of 5th Bt, and brother of 1st Baron:—
Issue of late Brigadier Edmond Wodehouse, CBE, *b* 1894, *d* 1959: *m* 1935, Persis (who *m* 2ndly, 1980, Lt-Col Robert Michael FitzHugh, of The Brow, Overton, Wrexham, Clwyd), only da of Plumer Rooper, of Min-yr-Afon, Overton Bridge, Wrexham:—
Armine John (c/o Lloyds Bank, 6 Pall Mall, SW1), *b* 1936; *ed* Winchester; Maj Roy Welch Fusiliers: *m* 1965, Louise Kynaston, da of Mark Kynaston Mainwaring (Rankin Bt), of Oteley, Ellesmere, and has issue living, Edmond Armine, *b* 1968, — Rosemary Louise, *b* 1966, — Rowena Carolyn, *b* 1971. —— Hugh Capel, *b* 1945; *ed* Winchester, and Wadham Coll, Oxford: *m* 19——, Mrs Anthea M. Courtauld, da of R. H. Priestley, of Oakley, Hants, and has issue living, Katie Rose, *b* 1983. —— Rachel Mary (Down House, Soberton, Hants), *b* 1938: *m* 1965, Robert Charles Copeman, and has issue living, James Robert, *b* 1966, — Charlotte Anne, *b* 1968. —— Carolyn Persis, *b* 1943: *m* 1968, Michael Cemlyn-Jones, and has issue living, Tara Persis, *b* 1970, — Jessica Melfis, *b* 1973.

PREDECESSORS – (1) *Sir* PHILIP Wodehouse, son of late Sir Roger Wodehouse, MP, *b* 15—; was MP for Castle Rising 1586-7; *cr* a *Baronet* 1611: *m* 1582, Grizell, who *d* 1635, da of William Yelverton, of Rougham, Norfolk, and widow of Hamon L'Estrange, of Hunstanton, Norfolk; *d* 1623; *s* by his son (2) *Sir* THOMAS, 2nd Bt; MP for Thetford 1640-53; *d* 1658; *s* by his son (3) *Sir* PHILIP, 3rd Bt; *b* 1608: MP in Restoration Parliament; *d* 1681; *s* by his grandson (4) *Sir* JOHN, 4th Bt; *b* 1669, MP for Norfolk; *d* 1754; *s* by his son (5) *Sir* ARMINE, 5th Bt; *b* 1714; MP for Norfolk 1737-67; *d* 1777; *s* by his son (6) *Sir* JOHN, 6th Bt; *b* 1741; MP for Norfolk 1784-97; *cr Baron Wodehouse*, of Kimberley, Norfolk (peerage of Great Britain) 1797; *d* 1834; *s* by his son (7) JOHN, 2nd Baron; *b* 1771; MP for Great Bedwyn 1802-6, and Marlborough 1820-26, and Lord-Lieut of Norfolk, *etc*; *d* 1846; *s* by his grandson (8) JOHN, KG, PC (son of Hon Henry, el son of 2nd Baron, by Anne, da of Theophilus Thornhaugh Gurdon, of Letton, Norfolk), 3rd Baron; *b* 1826; Under-Sec for Foreign Affairs 1852-6 and 1859-61, Envoy to Russia 1856-8, Special Envoy to Copenhagen 1863, Under-Sec for India 1864, Lord-Lieut of Ireland 1864-6, Lord Privy Seal 1868-70, Sec of State for Colonies 1870 and 1880-82, Chancellor of Duchy of Lancaster 1882-3, Sec of State for India 1882-5 and Jan to July 1886, Sec of State for India and Lord Pres of the Council Aug 1892 to March 1894, and Sec of State for Foreign Affairs March 1894 to June 1895; *cr Earl of Kimberley* (peerage of United Kingdom) 1866: *m* 1847, Lady Florence FitzGibbon, CI, who *d* 1895, el da of 3rd and last Earl of Clare (*ext*); *d* 1902; *s* by his son (9) JOHN, 2nd Earl, *b* 1848: *m* 1875, Isabel Geraldine, who *d* 1927, da of Sir Henry Josias Stracey, 5th Bt; *d* 1932; *s* by his son (10) JOHN, CBE, MC, 3rd Earl; *b* 1883; MP for Norfolk, Mid Div (L) 1906-10: *m* 1922, Frances Margaret, who *d* 1950, da of late Lieut-Col Leonard Howard Lloyd Irby; *d* as a result of enemy action 1941; *s* by his only son (11) JOHN, 4th Earl and present peer; also Baron Wodehouse.

<h2 style="text-align:center">KINDERSLEY, BARON (Kindersley) (Baron UK 1941)</h2>

ROBERT HUGH MOLESWORTH KINDERSLEY, 3rd Baron, *b* 18 Aug 1929; *s* 1976; *ed* Eton, Trin Coll, Oxford, and Harvard Business Sch, USA; Lt Scots Gds in Malaya 1948-49; Chm Commonwealth Development Corpn 1980-89, a Dir of Lazard Brothers & Co Ltd 1960-90, a Dir of Sun Alliance & London Insurance Gp, and Maersk Co Ltd: *m* 1st, 1954 (*m diss* 1989), Venice Marigold (Rosie), da of late Capt Lord (Arthur) Francis Henry Hill, The Greys (Reserve) (*see* M Downshire); 2ndly, 1989, Patricia Margaret, only da of late Brig Hugh Ronald Norman, DSO, of Lower St Clere, Kemsing, Kent, and formerly wife of Henry Colum Crichton-Stuart (*see* M Bute, colls), and has had issue by 1st *m*.

Arms – Per bend gules and azure, a lion rampant argent, within an orle of cross crosslets and fleurs-de-lis alternately or. **Crest** – In front of a hawthorn tree proper, charged with an escutcheon azure, thereon a lion rampant argent a greyhound sejant also argent. **Supporters** – *Dexter*, a greyhound argent, gorged with a collar azure, charged with three cross crosslets or; *sinister*, a lion argent, gorged with a collar gules, charged as the dexter; each standing on a branch of hawthorn proper.
Residence – West Green Farm, Shipbourne, Kent TN11 9PU.

With God's assistance

<h3 style="text-align:center">SONS LIVING (By 1st marriage)</h3>

Hon RUPERT JOHN MOLESWORTH (22 Sugden Rd, SW11 5EF), *b* 11 March 1955; *ed* Eton: *m* 1975, Sarah Anne, da of late John D. Warde, and has issue living,
Frederick Hugh Molesworth, *b* 9 Jan 1987, — Rebecca, *b* 1985.
Hon Dickon Michael (3 Ingelow Rd, SW8 3PZ), *b* 1962: *m* 1991, Victoria S., eldest da of T. J. Coles, of Saltwood, Brasted Chart, Kent and has issue living, Phoebe, *b* 1993.

<h3 style="text-align:center">GRANDDAUGHTER LIVING</h3>

Issue of late Hon Hugh Francis Kindersley, 2nd son of 3rd Baron, *b* 1956, *d* 1991: *m* 1987 (*m diss* 1990), (Evelyn) Rosamond, eldest da of (Robert Jestyn) Gwent Forestier-Walker (*see* Forestier-Walker, Bt, colls):—
Rosanna, *b* 1987.

<h3 style="text-align:center">DAUGHTER LIVING (By 1st marriage)</h3>

Hon Anna Lucy, *b* 1965.

<h3 style="text-align:center">SISTERS LIVING</h3>

Hon Patricia Nassau (*Hon Lady Crookenden*), *b* 1922: *m* 1948, Lt-Gen Sir Napier Crookenden KCB, DSO, OBE, late Cheshire Regt, and has issue living, James Napier *b* 1949: *m* 1974, Claire Ella Thorne, and has issue living, Benjamin Napier Lane *b* 1978, Lucinda Nan Annaliese *b* 1975, — Charles Stephen Napier, *b* 1957, — Elizabeth Jane, *b* 1950: *m* 1st, 1970 (*m diss* 1980), Sam G. S. Hughes, of Toronto; 2ndly, 1980, Thomas Charles Wilson, of The Old Rectory, Upper Clatford, nr Andover, Hants, and has issue living (by 1st *m*), Geoffrey Samuel *b* 1977, (by 2nd *m*), James Thomas *b* 1984, Tobina Kate *b* 1981, — Catherine Nancy, *b* 1958: *m* 1993, Martin Clive Jamieson, son of W/Cdr H. C. Jamieson, of Farnham, Surrey. *Residence* – Twin Firs, Four Elms, Edenbridge, Kent.
Hon Ginette Molesworth, *b* 1924: *m* 1st, 1945 (*m diss* 1949), Dominick Moore Sarsfield, Irish Gds; 2ndly, 1953, Henry James Buller Kitson (B Stathcona and Mount Royal), and has issue living, (by 1st *m*) Simon Patrick, *b* 1945: *m* 1st, 1967, Sandra, da of Robert Pearce, of Chichester, Sussex; 2ndly, 19—, Rohini, da of Arunasalem Rajasundaram, of Sri Lanka, and has issue living, (by 1st *m*) Andante Mercedes *b* 1969 (by 2nd *m*) Dushianthi *b* 1984, Declan *b* 1986, — Shaun Dominick, *b* 1947. *Residence* – Nine Acres, Wallcrouch, Wadhurst, E Sussex.

<h3 style="text-align:center">UNCLE LIVING (Son of 1st Baron)</h3>

Hon Philip Leyland, *b* 1907; *ed* Eton, and at Oxford Univ; is Capt Coldstream Guards; European War 1939-43 in N Africa (wounded, prisoner): *m* 1st, 1929 (*m diss* 1936), Oonagh, da of Hon (Arthur) Ernest Guinness (*see* E Iveagh); 2ndly, 1936, Violet Valerie, da of late Lt-Col Hon (Edward) Gerald Fleming French, DSO (*see* E Ypres, colls), and has issue living, (by 1st *m*) Gay (Laines, Aldbourne, Marlborough, Wilts), *b* 1930; *ed* Eton: *m* 1st, 1956 (*m diss* 1976), Margaret Diana, da of

Hugh Wakefield; 2ndly, 1976, Philippa Harper, and has issue living (by 1st *m*), Robin *b* 1956, Kim *b* 1960, Catheryn (*Marchioness of Huntly*) *b* 1958: *m* 1st, 1980, Robert Lennon Millbourn, son of late Cecil Millbourn, of 1 Eaton Place, SW1; 2ndly, 1991, as his 2nd wife, 13th Marquess of Huntly, of Aboyne Castle, Aberdeenshire, Tania *b* 1967, (by 2nd *m*) Rory *b* 1977, Oliver *b* 1980, — (by 2nd *m*), Christian Philip (11 St Maur Rd, SW6 4DR; White's Club), *b* 1950: *m* 1st, 1973 (*m diss* 1991), Hilary Luise, da of David Radcliffe Guard, of Ryders Wells House, Lewes, Sussex; 2ndly, 1992, Lara Hepburn, da of Frederick George Pohl, of Constantia, Cape Town, and has issue living (by 1st *m*), Alexander *b* 1982, Vanessa *b* 1980, Davina *b* 1986, — Nicolette Leila, *b* 1939: *m* 1963, Robert Nicholas Philipson-Stow, of Priors Court, Long Green, Gloucester, (*see* Philipson-Stow, Bt, colls), — Virginia Alexandra Alexandra de l'Etang (*Hon Mrs Peregrine J. W. Fairfax*) *b* 1943: *m* 1965, Hon Peregrine John Wishart Fairfax, of Mindrum, Northumberland (*see* L Fairfax of Cameron). *Residence* – Smith's House, The Square, Aldbourne, nr Marlborough, Wilts. *Club* – White's.

AUNT LIVING (*Daughter of 1st Baron*)

Hon Elizabeth Joan, *b* 1911: *m* 1930, Major Hon James Perrott Philipps, TD (*see* B Milford). *Residence* – Dalham Hall, Newmarket, Suffolk.

PREDECESSORS – (1) *Sir* ROBERT MOLESWORTH Kindersley, GBE, son of late Capt Edward Nassau Molesworth Kindersley, of Sherborne, Dorset; *b* 1871; was a Director of Bank of England 1916-46, Pres of National Savings Committee 1920-46 (first Chm 1916-20), High Sheriff of Sussex 1928-9, and Prime Warden of Fishmongers Co 1933-4; *cr Baron Kindersley*, of West Hoathly, co Sussex (peerage of United Kingdom) 1941: *m* 1896, Gladys Margaret, who *d* 1968, da of late Maj-Gen J. P. Beadle, RE, of 6 Queen's Gate Gdns, SW; *d* 1954; *s* by his son (2) HUGH KENYON MOLESWORTH, CBE, MC, 2nd Baron, *b* 1899; Man Dir of Lazard Brothers & Co Ltd 1927-64 (Chm 1953-64); Chm of Rolls-Royce Ltd 1956-68; Gov of the Royal Exchange Assurance 1955-69; 1914-18 War; 1939-45 War as Brig Scots Gds (wounded): *m* 1921, Nancy Farnsworth, who *d* 1977, da of late Dr Geoffrey Boyd, of Toronto, Canada; *d* 1976; *s* by his son (3) ROBERT HUGH MOLESWORTH, 3rd Baron and present peer.

King, see Baron Maybray-King.

KING OF WARTNABY, BARON (King) (Life Baron 1983)

JOHN LEONARD KING, yr son of Albert John King, by his wife Kathleen; *b* Aug 1918; Chm Babcock International plc (formerly Babcock & Wilcox) since 1972; Chm British Airways since 1981-92, since when Pres; Chm other cos; Chm Alexandra Rose Day since 1980; MFH Badsworth Foxhounds 1944-58; MFH Duke of Rutland's Foxhounds (Belvoir) 1958-72; FBIM; Cmdr Royal Order of the Polar Star (Sweden) 1983; *cr* Knt 1979, and *Baron King of Wartnaby*, of Wartnaby, co Leics (Life Baron) 1983: *m* 1st, 1941, Lorna Kathleen, who *d* 1969, da of Arthur Sykes, of Clandon; 2ndly, 1970, Hon Isabel Cynthia Monckton, yst da of 8th Viscount Galway, and has issue by 1st *m*.

Arms – Or five piles two reversed vert each charged with an acorn slipped or. **Crest** – An otter sejant vert holding in the dexter paw a sceptre or. **Supporters** – On either side two horses reguardant sable unguled or in the mouth of each a sprig of oak vert fructed gold.
Residences – Wartnaby, Melton Mowbray, Leics LE14 3HY; 15 Eaton Sq, SW1. *Clubs* – White's, Brook (New York).

SONS LIVING (*By 1st marriage*)

Hon Richard John Rodney, *b* 1943; *ed* Le Rosey: *m* 1985, Monika, da of Erich Boehm, of Boca Raton, Florida, USA, and has issue living, John-Erich *b* 1986. *Residence* – 7612 Covey Chase, Charlotte, NC 28210, USA.
Hon Philip James Stephen, *b* 1950; *ed* Harrow: *m* 1989, Caroline, da of E. G. A. Hillesley, of Gillingham, Kent, and has issue living, Charlotte Kathleen Rachel, *b* 1990. *Residence* – 77 Stanhope Mews East, SW7.
Hon (John) Rupert Charles, *b* 1950 (twin); *ed* Harrow: *m* 1986, Cherry M., only da of R. B. Jessop, OBE, of Ingoldsby, Lincs, and has issue living, Philip James Bateman, *b* 1988. *Residence* – Garden Cottage, Wartnaby, Melton Mowbray, Leics.

DAUGHTER LIVING (*By 1st marriage*)

Hon Rachel Mary Frances, *b* 1945, *m* 1st, 1968 (*m diss* 1974), Michael Gibson; 2ndly 1980 (*m diss* 1985), Guy Henry René Bondonneau, of Paris; 3rdly, 1987, Melvyn Marckus. *Residence* – 25 Waterford Rd, SW6 2DJ.

KING-HALL, BARONY OF (King-Hall) (Extinct 1966)

DAUGHTERS LIVING OF LIFE BARON

Hon Ann (11 North Side, Clapham Common, SW4 0RF), *b* 1920.
Hon (Frances Susan) Adrianna (Old Barn, Northdown Rd, Woldingham, Caterham, Surrey CR3 7BD), *b* 1927.
Hon Jane (SE7 Javea, Alicante, Spain) KING-HALL, *b* 1930; has resumed maiden name: *m* 1951 (*m diss* 19—), Yves Barraud, of Les Saules, Les Cullayes, Vaud, Switzerland.

Kinghorne, Earl of, see Earl of Strathmore and Kinghorne.

KINGSALE, BARON (de Courcy) (Baron I about 1340, precedence 1397)

Truth conquers all things

JOHN DE COURCY, 30th Baron, and Premier Baron of Ireland; *b* 27 Jan 1941; *s* 1969; *ed* Stowe; 2nd Lt IG.

Arms – Argent, three eagles, displayed gules, ducally crowned or. Crest – Out of a ducal coronet or, an eagle displayed with two heads argent. Supporters – Two unicorns azure, armed unguled, crined and tufted, gorged with collars adorned with crosses pattée and fleurs-de-lis, and chained, all gold.
Addresses – 15 Dallimore Mead, Nunney, Frome, Somerset BA11 4NB; 1st Floor Macarthur Chambers, 201 Edward St, Brisbane, Queensland 4000, Australia.
Club – Cavalry and Guards'

SISTER LIVING

Dione May, *b* 1937: *m* 1965 (*m diss* 1976), David Kemp Daffin, and has issue living, Miles Irl de Courcy, *b* 1969, — Thomas Chester de Courcy, *b* 1971.

AUNTS LIVING (*Daughters of 29th Baron*) (*by 1st marriage*)

Hon Bridget Doreen, *b* 1915: *m* 1st, 1938 (*m diss* 1951), Rev George Ian Falconer Thomson, who *d* 1987; 2ndly, 19—, Stephen Watson, and has issue living, (by 1st *m*), Margaret Doreen Rosemary (Emma), *b* 1940, — (by 2nd *m*), a son *b* 19—.
Hon Eleanor Geraldine, *b* 1919: *m* 1940 (*m diss* 1947), John Campbell Clarke, who *d* 1966, and has issue living, Peter, *b* 1945. *Residence* – 48 Fore St, North Tawton, Devon.

(by 2nd marriage)

Hon Diana Ruth, *b* 1951.

COLLATERAL BRANCHES LIVING

Granddaughters of late Hon Robert Charles Sinclair de Courcy, 4th son of 27th Baron:—
Issue of late Group-Capt John Arthur Gerald de Courcy, MC, RAF, *b* 1894, *d* on active service 1940: *m* 1917, Anna Felicia, who *d* 1952, da of late Hon George Wright, a Judge of High Court of Justice, Ireland (Barrington, Bt):—
Fay (42 Grantchester Rd, Cambridge), *b* 1919: resumed the surname of de Courcy 1968: *m* 1947 (*m diss* 1962); re-*m* 1982, Hugh Sykes Davies, Fellow of St John's Coll, Camb, who *d* 1984 and has issue living, Katharine Felicia, *b* 1953. — Suzanne, *b* 1923: *m* 1948, Edward James Bryant, and has issue living, Edward de Courcy (29 Wingate Rd, W6), *b* 1951; *ed* Rugby, and Magdalene Coll, Camb (MA); Bar Middle Temple 1976: *m* 1982, Frances, eldest da of Dr Guy Newton, of Oxford, — David de Courcy, *b* 1954; *ed* Rugby. *Residence* – Marsh Morgen, Stradishall, nr Newmarket.

Grandson of late Col Nevinson Willoughby de Courcy, CB, 2nd son of late Capt Nevinson de Courcy, RN, son of Adm Hon Michael de Courcy, 3rd son of 20th Baron:—
Issue of late Nevinson William de Courcy, *b* 1869, *d* 1919: *m* 1919, Matilda Hetty Grace, who *d* 1967, da of late John B. Russell, of Auckland, NZ:—
NEVINSON RUSSELL, *b* (*posthumous*) 21 July 1920: *m* 1954, Nora Lydia, da of James Arnold Plint, of Great Crosby, Lancs, and has issue living, Nevinson Mark, *b* 1958, — Katherine Grace, *b* 1955: *m* 1979, Gregory Lawrence Smith, and has issue living, Robert Russell Maunganui *b* 1987, Henrietta Lydia de Courcy *b* 1984. *Residence* – 15 Market Rd, Remuera, Auckland 5, NZ.

Granddaughter of late Rupert John Nevinson de Courcy, son of John Sinclair Bremer de Courcy, 3rd son of Capt Nevinson de Courcy, RN (ante):—
Issue of late Nevinson Egerton de Courcy, *b* 1885, *d* 1979: *m* 1923, Dorothy Mary, who *d* 1979, da of John Bernard Carroll:—
Angela Mary, *b* 1927: *m* 1951, Ian McDonald Wright, of The Rosary, Lock Island, Marlow-on-Thames, Bucks SL7 1QE, and has issue living, Teresa Dorothy de Courcy, *b* 1955: *m* 1988, Jeremy Paul Ryall, of The Garden Flat, 9 Acfold Rd, Fulham, SW6, and has issue living, Benjamin Charles *b* 1992, Max Joseph *b* 1993, Poppy Alexandra *b* 1990, — Isobel Eileen, *b* 1958: *m* 1985, Geoffrey Thomas Martin, of Dangleberries, Wash Hill, Wooburn, Bucks, and has issue living, James Peter de Courcy *b* 1990, Alexander Nevinson *b* 1993, Laura de Courcy *b* 1987.

Granddaughter of late Walter Stephen de Courcy (infra):—
Issue of late John Frederick Manuel de Courcy, *b* 1901, *d* 1974: *m* 1941, Norah de Courcy, el da of late Dr R. P. Beatty, of Swindon House, Swindon, Wilts:—
Mary Kathleen, *b* 1947: *m* 1967, David Allen Carse.

Descendants of Hon James de Courcy, 3rd son of 10th Baron (according to pedigree recorded at the Office of the Chief Herald of Ireland):—

Grandson of late Stephen de Courcy, son of Patrick de Courcy, great grandson of David de Courcy, 2nd son of James de Courcy, el son of Hon James de Courcy (ante):—
Issue of late Walter Stephen de Courcy, *b* 1869, *d* 1911: *m* 1899, Wilhelmina Regina, who *d* 1950, da of late Frederick William Schafer:—
Kenneth Hugh (Yeomans, Longborough, Moreton-in-Marsh, Glos; 82 Merrion Sq, Dublin, 2), *b* 1909; formerly Lt Coldm Gds: *m* 1950 (*m diss* 1973), Rosemary Catherine, only da of late Cdr Henry Leslie Spofforth Baker, OBE, RN (ret), of Carrowduff House, Ballymacurly, co Roscommon, and has issue living, Joseph Kenneth Charles (Blacklains Farm, Birdlip, Glos), *b* 1955, *ed* Radley, and Oriel Coll, Oxford: *m* 1987, Jayne P. Potter, of Midhurst, W Sussex, and has issue living, Patrick Miles Hugh *b* 1993, Rachel Frances *b* 1987, Alice Olivia *b* 1990, — Richard Henry Stephen, *b* 1960; *ed* Radley, — Rosemary Minnie Frances, *b* 1951; *ed* Girton Coll, Camb: *m* 1979, Anthony J. V. Cheetham, of Paxford Manor, nr Chipping Campden, Glos, yr son of Sir Nicolas Cheetham, KCMG, and has issue living, Emma Rosemary *b* 1981, Rebecca Sophie *b* 1983, — Catherine Sarah, *b* 1952: *m* 1989, Charles Edward Martin Benson, of Fen Farm, Wavendon, Milton Keynes, Bucks MK17 8AA, elder son of Edward Douglas Benson.

PREDECESSORS – The origin and early descent of this Peerage is obscure. In 1489, when eleven Irish barons were summoned to Greenwich, this Barony ranked after Athenry and before Gormanston. *The Complete Peerage* considers that Miles de Courcy, *b* about 1286, may have become *Lord Courcy of Kinsale* about 1340, but adds a footnote "it is more probable that the family acquired peerage rank 50 years later." In 1397, William de Courcy received a licence, as *Dominus et Baro de Courcy*, to buy a ship in England and sail it to France. Precedence of the Barony in the Peerage of Ireland had been given from this date. A list of Peers present at the Irish Parliament 1490 includes *Dominus de Kinsale*, but until the 17th century, *Lord Courcy, of Ringrone and Kinsale* was the style more usually adopted. Patrick de Courcy, whose parentage is uncertain, but who was most probably a descendant or close relative of Sir John de Courcy, Baron by tenure of Kingsale prior to 1205: *m* a da of Miles de Cogan; *d* before 1261. His son, Miles *d c* 1290. His son John was killed 1291. His el son **(1)** MILES, 1st Baron, *b c* 1286; Sheriff of Cork 1329-32: *m* 13— Joan; *d* before 1344; *s* by his son **(2)** MILES, 2nd Baron, *d* unm 1372; *s* by his kinsman **(3)** JOHN, 3rd Baron, (perhaps son of Edmund de Courcy, whose lineage is uncertain); *d c* 1390; *s* by his son **(4)** WILLIAM, 4th Baron: *m* Margaret Peinnel (who had Robes of the Garter 1399); *d c* 1400; *s* by **(5)** NICHOLAS, 5th Baron, *d* c by **(6)** PATRICK, 6th Baron, *d c* 1499; *s* by his el son **(7)** NICHOLAS, 7th Baron: *m* Mary, da of More O'Mahony; *d c* 1475; *s* by his el son **(8)** JAMES, 8th Baron: *m* Ellena Roche, da of David, Baron of Fermoy; *d* 1499; *s* by his only surviving son **(9)** EDMUND, 9th Baron, *d c* 1505; *s* by his uncle **(10)** DAVID, 10th Baron (2nd son of 7th Baron): *m* Joan, da of Edmund Roche; *d c* 1520; *s* by his el son **(11)** JOHN, 11th Baron: *m* Sarah, da of Donogh MacCarthy, of Dowallagh; *d* 1535; *s* by his only son **(12)** GERALD, 12th Baron; commanded an Irish Regt at siege of Boulogne; knighted on the field 1567: *m* Ellen, da of Cormac MacDonagh McCarthy of Carbery; *d* 1599; *s* by **(13)** JOHN, 13th Baron (son of Edmund Oge de Courcy, grandson of 10th Baron); fought against Spaniards at Siege of Kinsale 1601; was a Gentleman of the Bedchamber to King James I: *m* 1st, Catherine, da of William Cogan; 2ndly, Mary, da of Cormac O'Cruly, of Carbery, co Cork; *d* 1628; *s* by his el son **(14)** GERALD, 14th Baron: *m* 16—, Elene, da of Sir John FitzGerald, of Dromana, co Waterford; *d* 1642; *s* by his brother **(15)** PATRICK, 15th Baron: *m* 16—, Mary, who *d* 1678, da of Sir John Fitzgerald (ante); *dc* 1663; *s* by his son **(16)** JOHN, 16th Baron: *m* 16—, Ellen, da of Charles MacCarthy Reagh; *d* 1667; *s* by his el son **(17)** PATRICK, 17th Baron, *b* 1660; *d* 1669; *s* by his brother **(18)** ALMERICUS, 18th Baron; outlawed 1691 for his adhesion to the fortunes of James II, but which outlawry was removed 1692: *m* 1698, Anne, da of Robert Dring, of Isleworth, Middlesex; *d* 1719; *s* by his cousin **(19)** GERALD, 19th Baron (son of Col Hon Miles de Courcy, 3rd son of 15th Baron), *b* 1700; PC Ireland 1744; *m* 1725, Margaretta, who *d* 1750, da of John Essington, of Grossington Hall, Glos; *d* 1759; *s* by his kinsman **(20)** JOHN, 20th Baron (son of Miles de Courcy, of Newport, Rhode Island, N America, 2nd son of Anthony de Courcy, of Bandon, co Cork, only son of Hon David de Courcy, yst son of 13th Baron); confirmed in the Baronies of Kingsale and Ringrone 1761, and their descent in the male line: *m* 1746, Martha, who *d* 1803, da of Rev William Heron, of Dorchester, Dorset; *d* 1776; *s* by his son **(21)** JOHN, 21st Baron: *m* 1763, Susanna, who *d* 1819, da of Conway Blennerhassett, of Castle Conway, co Kerry; *d* 1822; *s* by his son **(22)** *Rev* THOMAS, 22nd Baron, *b* 1774; *d* 1832; *s* by his nephew **(23)** JOHN STAPLETON, 23rd Baron (son of Capt Hon Michael de Courcy, RN, 3rd son of 21st Baron), *b* 1805: *m* 1825, Sarah, who *d* 1883, da of Joseph Chadder, of Portlemouth, Devon; *d* 1847; *s* by his son **(24)** JOHN CONSTANTINE, 24th Baron, *b* 1827; Capt E Devon Mil: *m* 1855, Adelaide, who *d* 1885, da of Joseph Proctor Brown-Westhead, of Lea Castle, Worcs; *d* 1865; *s* by his brother **(25)** MICHAEL CONRAD, 25th Baron, *b* 1828; *d* 1874; *s* by his cousin **(26)** JOHN FITZROY, 26th Baron (el son of Lieut-Col Hon Gerald de Courcy, 4th son of 21st Baron), *b* 1821; Maj in Turkish Contingent during Crimean War 1854-5, and Col in Federal Army during American Civil War: *m* 1864, Elia Elizabeth, who *d* 1893, da of C. de François de Ponchalon, of Alençon, France, and widow of C. de Bosque de Beaumont, of Airel, Manche; *d* 1890; *s* by his cousin **(27)** MICHAEL WILLIAM, 27th Baron (el son of Rev Michael de Courcy, DD, son of Adm Hon Michael de Courcy, 3rd son of 20th Baron), *b* 1822: *m* 1st, 1852, Esther Eleanor, who *d* 1864, da of Thomas Williams, of Dublin; 2ndly, 1874, Jessie Maud, who *d* 1902, da of Rev Edward Polwhele, sometime R of Fillaton, *d* 1895; *s* by his el son **(28)** MICHAEL CONSTANTINE, 28th Baron, *b* 1855: *m* 1880, Emily Frances Anne, who *d* 1926, da of late William Sinclair de Courcy, brother of 27th Baron Kingsale, *d* 1931; *s* by his son **(29)** MICHAEL WILLIAM ROBERT, DSO, 29th Baron, *b* 1882: *m* 1st, 1906, Constance Mary Rancé, who *d* 1946, da of late Maj-Gen Sir Tom Percy Woodhouse, KCMG, CB; 2ndly, 1947 (*m diss* 1957), Ruth, only child of Herbert Thomas Holmes, OBE; *d* 1969; *s* by his grandson **(30)**, JOHN (only surviving son of Lt-Cdr Hon Michael John Rancé de Courcy, RN, only surviving son of 29th Baron, *b* 1907, *k* on active ser 1940, who *m* 1st, 1929 (*m diss* 1933), Glory Elizabeth, da of Eng-Cdr Alfred Claremont Evans, RN (ret); 2ndly, 1936, Joan, who *d* 1967, da of Robert Reid, JP, of Moor Park, nr Harrogate), *b* (*posthumous*) 1941, 30th Baron and present Peer; also Baron of Ringrone.

Kingsborough, Viscount; son of Earl of Kingston.

KINGSDOWN, BARON (Leigh-Pemberton) (Life Baron 1993)

ROBERT (ROBIN) LEIGH-PEMBERTON, KG, PC, eldest son of late Capt Robert Douglas Leigh-Pemberton, MBE, MC, of Torry Hill, Kent (*see* Frankland-Payne-Gallwey, Bt, 1985 Edn); *b* 5 Jan 1927; *ed* Eton, RMC, and Trin Coll, Oxford (MA 1953, Hon Fellow 1984); late Lieut Gren Guards, Hon Col Kent and Sharpshooters Yeo Sqdn, 265 (KCLY) Signal Sqdn (V), 5 (Vol) Bn The Queen's Regt, Pres SE TAVR Assocn and Kent SSAFA; Bar Inner Temple 1954, London and SE Circuit 1954-60, Hon Bencher 1983; Dir Birmid Qualcast 1966-83 (Dep-Chm 1970, Chm 1975-77), University Life Assurance Soc 1967-78, Redland Ltd 1972-83 and since 1992, and Equitable Life Assurance Soc 1979-83, Chm National Westminster Bank 1977-83 (Dir 1972-83, Dep-Chm 1974), and Cttee of London Clearing Bankers 1982-83, Gov Bank of England 1983-93; Dir Glaxo plc, Hambros plc, and Foreign and Colonial Investment Trust since 1993; JP Kent 1961-75, CC 1961-77, DL 1970, Vice Lord-Lieut 1972-82, since when Lord-Lieut; Trustee Emeritus Royal Academy of Arts Trust, Trustee Kent CCC, Kent County Playing Fields Assocn, Kent County Agric Soc, etc, Chm Canterbury Cathedral Appeal Trust Fund, Seneschal of Canterbury Cathedral, Pres Royal Agric Soc of England 1989-90, Pro-Chancellor Kent Univ 1977-83, Member RSA; FCIB; Hon DCL Kent 1983, Hon DLitt City of London 1988, Loughborough 1989, and City Poly 1990; KStJ; *cr* PC 1987, KG 1994, and *Baron Kingsdown*, of Pemberton, co Lancs (Life Baron) 1993: *m* 1953, Rosemary Davina, only da of late Lt-Col David Walter Arthur William Forbes, MC, Coldstream Guards, of Callendar House, Falkirk (*see* B Faringdon, colls, 1980 Edn), and has had issue.

Arms – Ermine, an estoile or, between three buckets sable, hoops and handles of the 2nd. **Crest** – A dragon's head ermine, erased gules ducally gorged or, and transfixed by an arrow fesswise proper. **Motto** – Ut tibi sic alteri (do to others as you would to yourself).
Residence – Torry Hill, Sittingbourne, Kent. *Club* – Brooks's, Cavalry and Guards'.

SONS LIVING AND DECEASED

Hon John David, *b* 1955; *ed* Eton, and Magdalen Coll, Oxford: *m* 1st, 1980, Rosamond P., 4th da of Oliver Richard Jessel, of Sponden House, Sandhurst, Cranbrook, Kent; 2ndly, 1985, Kathryn Felice, da of Martin Robert Lampard, of Theberton House, Theberton, Suffolk, and has issue. *Residence* – Yokes Court, Frinstead, Sittingbourne, Kent.
Hon James Henry, *b* 1956; *ed* Eton, and ChCh, Oxford: *m* 1985, Catarina Elizabeth, da of John Cowan, of New Coll, Oxford, and of Mrs Karin Stielow, of Hamburg, and has issue living, Sophia Loveday, *b* 1985, — Lucinda Rose, *b* 1987, — Letitia Jane, *b* 1989. *Residence* – The Old Rectory, Milstead, Sittingbourne, Kent ME9 0AS.
Hon Edward Douglas, *b* 1959; *ed* Eton, and RAC Cirencester: *m* 1984, Jessica Elizabeth Berners, yr twin da of Michael Edward Ranulph Allsopp (*see* B Hindlip, colls), and has issue living, David Geoffrey Berners, *b* 1988, — Ranulph Berners, *b* 1989, — Patrick Berners, *b* 1991. *Residence* – Longcote House, Longcote, Faringdon, Oxon SN7 7TF.
†Thomas Robert Arnold, *b* 1961; *ed* Eton, St Edmund Hall, Oxford; *k* in a motor accident in Zimbabwe 1993.
Hon William Francis, *b* 1964; *ed* Eton, and Jesus Coll, Oxford.

KINGS NORTON, BARON (Roxbee Cox) (Life Baron 1965)

HAROLD ROXBEE COX, son of late William John Roxbee Cox; *b* 6 June 1902; *ed* King's Norton Gram Sch, and at Imperial Coll of Science and Technology (BSc, DIC, PhD London, Fellow); Hon DSc Birmingham, Warwick and Cranfield, DTech Brunel; Hon; LLD (CNAA); Chancellor, Ganfield Inst of Technology since 1969; Chm of Air Registration Board 1966-72 Chm and Man Dir of Power Jets (Research and Development) Ltd 1944-46, Dir of Nat Gas Turbine Establishment 1946-48, Pres of Roy Aero Soc 1947-49, Chm of Nat Council for Technological Awards 1960-64 (Vice-Chm 1955-60), of Council for Scientific and Industrial Research 1961-65, and of Metal Box Co Ltd 1961-67, Chm of Council for Nat Academic Awards 1964-71, and of Berger, Jenson & Nicholson Ltd 1967-75, and Pres of Roy Institution of Great Britain 1969-76; American Medal of Freedom with Silver Palm; Freeman City of London, Liveryman Guild of Air Pilots and Air Navigators; *cr* Knt 1953, and *Baron Kings Norton*, of Wotton Underwood, co Bucks (Life Baron) 1965: *m* 1st, 1927, (Doris) Marjorie, who *d* 1980, da of late Ernest Edward Withers, of Northwood, Middx; 2ndly, 1982, Joan Ruth, da of late William George Pack, of Torquay, Devon, and formerly wife of K. A. Pascoe, and has issue by 1st *m*.

Arms – Azure a chevron or between in chief two jet engines palewise, flames downward, and in base a balloon with car proper. **Crest** – A hare sejant erect proper in front of two sceptres in saltire, each terminating in a fleur-de-lys or. **Supporters** – On either side a cock standing on a rock proper.
Residence – Westcote House, Chipping Campden, Glos. *Clubs* – Athenaeum, Turf.

SONS LIVING *(By 1st marriage)*

Hon Christopher Withers (29 Pages Lane, Bexhill-on-Sea, E Sussex TN39 3RD), *b* 1928: *m* 1955, Rosemary, da of late Frederick Day Ardagh, and has issue, two sons.
Hon Jeremy William, *b* 1932: *m* 1962, Anne, da of late Albert Moore Linton, and has issue, one son and one da.

KINGSTON, EARL OF (King-Tenison) (Earl I 1768, Bt I 1682)

Heaven is our highest hope

BARCLAY ROBERT EDWIN KING-TENISON, 11th Earl, and 15th Baronet; *b* 23 Sept 1943; *s* 1948; *ed* Winchester; late Lt R Scots Greys: *m* 1st, 1965 (*m diss* 1974), Patricia Mary, da of late E. C. Killip, of Beoley Lodge, Uttoxeter, Staffs; 2ndly, 1974 (*m diss* 1979), Victoria, only da of D. C. Edmonds of Northwood, Middlesex; 3rdly, 1990, Corleen Jennifer Rathbone, and has issue by 1st *m*.

𝔄rms – Quarterly: 1st and 4th gules, on a bend engrailed or, between two leopards' faces of the last, jessant-de-lis-azure, three crosses-crosslett sable, *Tenison*, 2nd and 3rd gules, two lions rampant combatant; supporting a dexter hand, couped at the wrist and erect all argent, *King*. ℭrests – 1st, a leopard's face as in the arms in front of a crozier and a cross-crosslett fitchée in saltire sable, *Tenison*; 2nd, out of a five-leaved ducal coronet or a dexter hand erect, the third and fourth fingers turned down proper, *King*. 𝔖upporters – Two lions, per fesse argent and gules ducally crowned of the last.
Address –

SON LIVING *(By 1st marriage)*

ROBERT CHARLES HENRY (*Viscount Kingsborough*), *b* 20 March 1969.

DAUGHTER LIVING *(By 1st marriage)*

Lady Maria Lisette, *b* 1970.

SISTER LIVING

Lady Kara Virginia Louisa, *b* 1938: *m* 1964 (*m diss* 1974), Anthony John Conroy Hawks, MB, BS, DCH, and has issue living, Honor Louise, *b* 1966.

COLLATERAL BRANCHES LIVING

Grandson of late Sir Charles Anthony King-Harman, KCMG, yst son of late Hon Lawrence Harman King-Harman, 2nd son of 1st Viscount Lorton, and brother of 6th Earl of Kingston:—
Issue of late Capt Robert Douglas King-Harman, DSO, DSC and bar, RN, *b* 1891, *d* 1978: *m* 1st, 1916 (*m diss* 1926), Lilly, who *d* 1966, da of late Alexander Moffatt, Sheriff-Substitute of Stirlingshire, of Arnotdale, Falkirk; 2ndly, 1927, Bessie Lilian Bull, who *d* 1974, da of late William James Davis, of Junee Reefs, NSW; 3rdly, 1975, Eva Mary, who *d* 1987, da of late Archdale Stuart Palmer:—
(By 1st *m*) Anthony Lawrence, OBE (Ouse Manor, Sharnbrook, Beds, MK44 1PG; Anglo-Belgian Club), *b* 1918; *ed* Wellington Coll; Col late RA; 1939-45 War (despatches); OBE (Civil) 1983; OStJ 1987; DL Beds 1987: *m* 1944, Jeanette Stella Dunkerley, and has issue living, Anthony William (60a Ladbroke Grove, W11 2PB), *b* 1946; *ed* Wellington Coll, and RMAS; Col late RA: *m* 1991, Mrs Judith Serena Buxton, da of John Richard Rumsey, and formerly wife of Robert Hugh Buxton (*see* Buxton, Bt, colls), — Michael Charles, *b* 1947; *ed* Wellington Coll, William and Mary, and Univ of Virginia; Dir of Hunt Deltel and Co, Seychelles; has issue (by Barbara Elizabeth, da of Kenneth Veasey Lightfoot, of 23 Matangi St, Christchurch 4, NZ), Charles *b* 1988, Jasper *b* 1991, Alize *b* (triplet) 1988, Bibett *b* (triplet) 1988.

Granddaughters of late Col John Robert King, 2nd son of Capt John Wingfield King (infra):—
Issue of late Capt Robert Guy Cyril King, Roy Australian Artillery, *b* 1877, *d* 1940: *m* 1st, 1905, Albertina Millicent, da of Philip Steele, of Melbourne; 2ndly, 1919, Mary Catherine, da of John Robert Russell, of Brackly:—
(By 1st *m*) Millicent Francklyn (22 Millicent Av, Toorak, Australia 3142), *b* 1907: *m* 1st, 1928, Archibald Jennings Ironside, who *d* 1941; 2ndly, 1942, William Bethel Thompson, Sqdn Ldr RAAF, who *d* 1945, and has issue living, (by 1st *m*) Margaret Joan Francklyn, *b* 1929, — Philip Norman Jennings, *b* 1931: *m* 1960, Dorothy Rosemary Joy, da of Alan Bell, of Melbourne, and has issue living, Andrew Philip *b* 1962, Alan Francklyn *b* 1964.
Issue of late Lt-Col John Francklyn King, RAOC, *b* 1882, *d* 19—: *m* (Jan) 1914, Mary Elspeth, da of Edwin Hellard:—
Phyllis Mary, *b* (Nov) 1914. *Residence* – 21 Chapman Terrace, Kingscote, S Australia 5223.

Grandchildren of Gerald Fitzgerald King, 5th son of Capt John Wingfield King, eldest son of Lt-Gen Hon Sir Henry King, KCB, 3rd son of 2nd Earl:—
Issue of late Wingfield Charles Gerald King, *b* 1886, *d* 1972: *m* 1st, 1912, Annabel Mae Brown, who *d* 1914; 2ndly, 1915, Lena Mae Stewart, who *d* 1934; 3rdly, Mamie Green Slusser, who *d* 1990, of Augusta, Georgia, USA:—
(By 2nd *m*) (John Charles) Alwyn (Hallowes) (121 South Hanover St, Carlisle, Pennsylvania 17013, USA), *b* 1920; *ed* McGill Univ (BEng), Columbia Univ, New York (MSc), and Stuttgart Technical Univ (DSc); Col US Army (ret); 1939-45 War in Pacific and NW Europe: *m* 1st, 1942, Mary Parker, da of Herbert Daniel Casey, of Ozark, Alabama, USA; 2ndly, 1952, Grace Margaret Stanley, who *d* 1988, and has issue living, (by 1st *m*) Judy Marilyn, *b* 1943, — (by 2nd *m*) Carolyn Joan, *b* 1957. —— Elizabeth Avarina Joan, *b* 1926: *m* 1952, Duane Caldwell, of 827 Pioneer Drive, N Tonawanda, New York, USA and has issue living, Stewart Duane Sandes, *b* 1953: *m* 1982, Johanna Grace Howard, and has issue living, Mary Rebecca Christine *b* 1985, Kathleen Avarina Suzanne *b* 1989, — Deborah Grace, *b* 1955; has issue living, Megan Avarina-Mae CALDWELL, *b* 1978, — Gail Heather, *b* 1963: *m* 1982, David Spencer Barone, jr, and has issue living, David Spencer (III) *b* 1986, Lisa Ann *b* 1985, Christina Marie *b* 1988.
Issue of late John Wingfield King, *b* 1891, *d* 1975: *m* 1916, Alice Mary Prefontaine, who *d* 1974:—
Gerald Rene Wingfield (C-10 Harding Rd, RR1, Powell River, BC, Canada), *b* 1924; Sqdn Ldr RCAF; Maj (ret) Canadian Armed Forces (War Medal 1939-45), two medals; Airways Inspector, Min of Transport (ret): *m* 1st, 1958 (*m diss* 1972), Sonia Lanjin, of Yugoslavia; 2ndly, 1987, Grace Marion Sayce.

Grandchildren of late Capt John Wingfield King (ante):—
Issue of late Percy Wingfield King, *b* 1868, *d* 1930: *m* 18—, Mary Cecelia Foley:—
†James Fitzgerald, *b* 1911: *m* 19—, and *d* 1976, leaving issue, James, *b* 19—, — John, *b* 19—, — Eileen, *b* 19—. ——— Ena, *b* 1901: *m* 19—. ——— Mary, *b* 1903: *m* 19—. ——— Ida, *b* 1907: *m* 19—.

Granddaughters of late Percy Wingfield King (ante):—
Issue of late John Wingfield King, *b* 1899, *d* 1963: *m* 1st, 1922, Margaret Fraser, who *d* 1941, da of late Isaac Van Cleef, of New Jersey, USA, 2ndly, 1944, Alice, who *d* 1989, da of late John Malone, of Philadelphia, Pa, USA:—
(By 1st *m*) Jean Margaret, *b* 1923: *m* 1944, Raymond A. Connelly, of Rt 5 Box 100, Troutville, Va 24175, USA, and has issue living, Robert (26 Longwood Rd, Austin, Texas 78737, USA), *b* 1948: *m* 1st, 1969, Jacqueline Marie Schlickenmaier; 2ndly, 1982, Jane Heffington, and has issue living (by 1st *m*), Shane Jason *b* 1974, Stacy Michael *b* (twin) 1974, Heather Janelle *b* 1972, — Carol, *b* 1945: *m* 1st, 1963, D. R. Robles; 2ndly, 1973, George Michael Belanger, of 6359 Christie Lane, Roanoke, Virginia 24018, USA, and has issue living (by 1st *m*), Kateri Jean Louise *b* 1965: *m* 1988, Michael Joles, of 3666 Sylvan Lane, Virginia Beach, Virginia 23456, USA (and has issue living, Sydney Elaine *b* 1991), (by 2nd *m*) Victoria Elizabeth Caroline *b* 1977. ——— (By 2nd *m*) Patricia Barry, *b* 1950. *Residence* – 35 Plum St, Vincentown, NJ 08088, USA.

Granddaughters of late Col Edward Richard King, son of late Lieut Gen Hon Sir Henry King, KCB (ante):—
Issue (by 2nd *m*) of late Lieut-Col Robert Ambrose Cecil King, *b* 1852, *d* 1897: *m* 1st, 1884, Bessie, who *d* 1892, da of late Rev J. Mecredy, DD, R of Killalan, and widow of Major J. L. Bell, RA; 2ndly, 1893, Lilian Walters, da of Rochfort Davies, formerly ICS:—
Eileen Mary Fridiswede, *b* 1894. ——— Sybil Doreen, *b* 1896.

PREDECESSORS – (1) ROBERT King, PC, MP for co Roscommon; *cr* a *Baronet* 1682; *d* 1708; *s* by his el son (2) *Sir* John, 2nd Bt, MP for co Roscommon; *dsp* 1720; *s* by his brother (3) *Sir* HENRY, PC, 3rd Bt; MP for co Roscommon; *m* 1722, Isabella Wingfield, sister of 1st Viscount Powerscourt; *d* 1740; *s* by his el son (4) *Sir* ROBERT, 4th Bt; *cr Baron Kingsborough* (peerage of Ireland) 1748; *d* unmarried 1755 when the barony expired, and the baronetcy devolved upon his brother (5) *Sir* EDWARD, 5th Bt; *cr Baron Kingston of Rockingham*, co Roscommon (peerage of Ireland) 1764, *Viscount Kingston of Kingsborough*, co Sligo (peerage of Ireland) 1766, and *Earl of Kingston* (peerage of Ireland) 1768; *d* 1797; *s* by his son (6) ROBERT, 2nd Earl; was MP for co Cork; his 2nd son, Robert Edward, a Gen in the Army, and Lord-Lieut of Roscommon, was *cr Baron Erris*, of Boyle, co Roscommon (peerage of Ireland) 1800, and *Viscount Lorton*, of Boyle, co Roscommon (peerage of Ireland) 1806; the Earl *d* 1799; *s* by his son (7) GEORGE, 3rd Earl: *cr Baron Kingston of Mitchelstown*, co Cork (peerage of United Kingdom) 1821; *d* 1838; *s* by his el surviving son (8) ROBERT HENRY, 4th Earl; *d* 1867; *s* by his brother (9) JAMES, 5th Earl: *m* 1860, Anne, da of Matthew Brinkley, of Parsonstown, Meath; *dsp* 1869 when the Barony of Kingston of Mitchelstown expired, and the Irish peerages reverted to his cousin (10) ROBERT, 6th Earl, who had in 1854 *s* his father as 2nd Viscount Lorton; *b* 1804: *m* 18298, Anne, da of Sir Robert Newcomen Gore-Booth, Bt; *d* 1869; *s* by his el son (11) ROBERT EDWARD, 7th Earl; *d* 1871; *s* by his brother (12) HENRY ERNEST NEWCOMEN, 8th Earl, *b* 1848; Lord-Lieut of co Roscommon, and a Representative Peer for Ireland; assumed by Roy licence 1883, the additional surname of Tenisor.: *m* 1872, Florence Margaret Christine, who *d* 1907, da of late Col Edward Tenison, of Kilronan Castle; *d* 1896; *s* by his only son (13) HENRY EDWYN, 9th Earl, *b* 1874; a Representative Peer for Ireland; sometime Capt Irish Guards; S Africa 1900-02, 1914-18 War (wounded): *m* 1897, Ethel Lisette, who *d* 1949, yst da of Sir Andrew Barclay Walker, 1st Bt (*cr* 1886); *d* 1946; *s* by his only son (14) ROBERT HENRY ETHELBERT, 10th Earl, *b* 1897; sometime Lieut Roy Scots Greys: *m* 1st, 1937 (*m diss* 1947), Gwyneth (Joan), who *d* 1987, da of William Howard Evans, of Tenby, Pembrokeshire; 2ndly, 1947, Jean Sinclair, who *d* 1983 (having *m* 2ndly, 1953, Cecil Geoffrey Monson who *d* 1974), da of late James L. Alexander, of Orkney and Aberdeen; *d* 1948; *s* by his only son (15) BARCLAY ROBERT EDWIN, 11th Earl and present peer; also Viscount Kingston of Kingsborough, Viscount Lorton, Baron Kingston of Rockingham, and Baron Erris.

KINLOSS, LADY (Freeman-Grenville) (Lordship S 1602)

For God, country and friends

(BEATRICE) MARY GRENVILLE FREEMAN-GRENVILLE, *b* 1922; *s* 1944; assumption with her husband of the surname of Freeman-Grenville recognised by decree of Lord Lyon King of Arms 1950: *m* 1950, Greville Stewart Parker Freeman, DPhil, MA, BLitt (Oxon), FSA, FRAS, Capt late Roy Berks Regt, Kt of the Holy Sepulchre of Jerusalem, Papal Cross *Pro Ecclesia et Pontifice* (for services on Pope John Paul II's visit to York 1982), and has issue.

Arms – Quarterly, 1st vert, on a cross argent five torteaux, *Grenville*; 2nd, paly of six argent and or, a lion rampant reguardant sable, armed and langued gules, charged with a cross-crosslet of the second, between four quatrefoils of the third, *Morgan*; 3rd, or, a pile gules, *Chandos*; 4th per fess azure and vair-ancient, three fusils in chief, a bordure or for difference, *Freeman*; over all, an escutcheon ensigned with the coronet of a Lord-Baron in the Peerage of Scotland for her Lordship of Kinloss, quarterly 1st and 4th, or, a saltire gules, on a chief of the last three crescents of the first, *Bruce*; 2nd and 3rd, argent, two open crowns in fesse gules and a martlet in base azure, on a chief of the last a mullet of the field, *Kinloss*. **Crest** – On a chapeau gules furred, ermine a lion passant, tail extended gules, armed and langued azure, supporting with his dexter forepaw a shield emblazoned with the arms of Kinloss, vizt, argent, two open crowns in fess gules, and a martlet in base azure, on a chief of the last a mullet of the field. **Supporters** – Two savages wreathed about the middle and temples with laurel, supporting in their exterior hands banners floating inwards, that on the dexter having a staff of these liveries or and azure and surmounted of an abbot's mitre, of the ensigns armorial of the abbot of Kinloss, vizt, azure, semée of fleur-de-lys or, an inescutcheon parted per pale, the dexter bendy of six or and azure within a bordure gules, sinister, argent, two open crowns in fesse gules and a martlet in base azure, on a chief of the last a mullet of the field; that on the sinister with a staff of these liveries gules and or, and ensigned with a Baroness's coronet, of the ensigns armorial of Bruce of Kinloss, vizt, or, a saltire gules, on a chief of the last three crescents of the first.

Residence – North View House, Sheriff Hutton, York. *Club* – Civil Service.

SON LIVING

Hon BEVIL DAVID STEWART CHANDOS (*Master of Kinloss*), *b* 20 June 1953.

DAUGHTERS LIVING

Hon Teresa Mary Nugent, *b* 1957.
Hon Hester Josephine Anne, *b* 1960: *m* 1984, Peter Haworth, yr son of A. F. C. P. Haworth, of Malton, York, and has issue living, Joseph Anthony, *b* 1985, — David Arnold, *b* 1987, — Christopher John, *b* 1989. *Residence* – Newstead Grange, Thirsk Rd, Easingwold, York YO6 3NH.

SISTERS LIVING (*Raised to the rank of a Baron's daughters* 1947)

Hon (Lilian) Anne Grenville, *b* 1924: *m* 1st, 1951, Ernest Frederick Harris, CBE, who *d* 1965; 2ndly, 1965, Maurice Emile Deen, who *d* 1971; 3rdly, 1973, Willem Dirkse-van-Schalkwyk, of 26 Boulevard des Moulins, Monte Carlo, MC 98000, Monaco, formerly S. African Amb to Canada, France and Italy.
Hon Caroline Jane Grenville, *b* 1931: *m* 1958, Gordon Glynne-Walton, FRGS, FRMetSoc, FRAS, FGS, late Duke of Wellington's Regt, and has issue living, Charlotte Elizabeth Sophia Caroline Louise, *b* 1961; MBA (Bradford), BA (Leeds Metropolitan Univ), Diplom Betriebswirt (Bremen), Post Graduate Certificate of Education (Leeds): *m* 1990, Paul Stephen Fox, yst son of J. M. Fox, of Clifton, W Yorkshire. *Residence* – White Lea Grange, Batley, W Yorks.

COLLATERAL BRANCHES LIVING

Grandchildren of late Lt-Col *Hon* Thomas George Breadalbane Morgan-Grenville, DSO, OBE, MC (infra):—
Issue of late Pamela Mary Ruth, *b* 1919, *d* 1989: *m* 1944, Capt Alec David Charles Francis, late WG, of The Grange, Malmesbury, Wilts, who *d* 1993:—
Nigel Charles Audley FRANCIS, *b* 1949: *m* 1990, Julia Anne Grayson. —— Priscilla Annabelle, *b* 1947: *m* 1969, Frederick Hugh Philip Hamilton Wills, Capt late 11th Hus, and has issue (*see* B Dulverton, colls).

Issue of late Lt-Col *Hon* Thomas George Breadalbane MORGAN-GRENVILLE, DSO, OBE, MC, 3rd son of Mary, Lady Kinloss, *b* 1891, *d* 1965: *m* 1916, Georgina May St John, who *d* 1973, da of late Albert St John Murphy, of The Island House, Little Island, co Cork:—
Cynthia Avril, *b* 1921: *m* 1948, Christopher Michael Aliaga-Kelly, of Chancery House, Rakehanger, Hill Brow, Liss, Hants, and has issue living, Peter Edward Grenville, *b* 1956, — Veronica Ann Cynthia, *b* 1950: *m* 1978, John P. V. Bevan, of 2 Harcourt Bldgs, Temple, EC4Y 9DB, and has issue living, Henry Thomas Vaughan *b* 1981, Charlotte Emily Vaughan *b* 1985. —— Audrey Marigold (*Baroness Ironside*), *b* 1931: *m* 1950, 2nd Baron Ironside, of Priory House, Boxted, Colchester, Essex CO4 5RB.

Grandson (by 1st *m*) of late Capt *Hon* Robert William Morgan-Grenville (infra):—
Issue of late Robert Grenville Plantagenet Morgan-Grenville, *b* 1916, *d* 1993: *m* 1944, Mabel, who *d* 1985, da of Charles Osborne Ellis, of Birmingham:—
Richard Harvey MORGAN-GRENVILLE (67 Chartwell Drive, Durban, S Africa), *b* 1947; *ed* Millfield: *m* 1st, 1969 (*m diss* 19—), Diana Jane, da of Ralf Chambler, of 29 Osprey Av, Birdwell, Barnsley, Yorks; 2ndly, 1982, Valerie de Marigny, and has issue living (by 1st *m*), Robert Ralf, *b* 1974, — Richard John, *b* 1977, — Georgina Jane, *b* 1975. —— †Caroline Irene, *b* 1949: *m* 1st, 1972 (*m diss* 1976), Edward James Windham-Bellord (*see* Bowyer-Smyth, Bt, colls); 2ndly, 1977, Robert Denman, and *d* 1979, leaving issue (by 1st *m*) (*see* Bowyer-Smyth, Bt, colls).

Issue of late Capt *Hon* Robert William Morgan-Grenville, 4th son of Mary, Lady Kinloss, *b* 1892, *d* 1988: *m* 1st, 1915, Irene Alice Gertrude, who *d* 1916, da of Sir Robert Grenville Harvey, 2nd Bt; 2ndly, 1922, Elizabeth Hope Bine, who *d* 1969, da of Sir Charles Bine Renshaw, 1st Bt, and widow of Maj Francis William Lindley Gull (Gull, Bt):—
(By 2nd *m*) John Richard Bine MORGAN-GRENVILLE, DL (Upperton House, Petworth, Sussex), *b* 1927; High Sheriff W Sussex 1989: *m* 1955, Joan Margaret, 2nd da of Air Ch Marshal Sir Wilfred Rhodes Freeman, 1st Bt, GCB, DSO, MC, and has issue living, Roger Temple, *b* 1959: *m* 1993, Caroline Mary, da of David Michael Summerhayes, CMG, of Harting, W Sussex, — Joanna Jane, *b* 1957: *m* 1991, Cdr John C. L. Wotton, RN, of Tichborne Cottage, Tichborne, Alresford, Hants SO23 0NA, son of Lt-Col Gordon Wotton, of Old Bursledon, Hants, and has issue living, Laura Elizabeth *b* 1993. —— Gerard Wyndham (Milton Mill, W Milton, Bridport, Dorset), *b* 1931; *ed* Eton; late Capt Rifle Bde: *m* 1st, 1955 (*m diss* 1981), Virginia Anne, eldest da of late Maj (Basil Arthur) John Peto, King's Drag Gds (*see* Peto, Bt, *cr* 1927, colls); 2ndly, 1981 (*m diss* 1989), Mrs Fern Diana Roberts, who *d* 1993, 2nd da of Capt E.R.S. Jackson, RN, and formerly wife of Tim Roberts, and has issue living (by 1st *m*), Hugo Gerard, *b* 1958: *m* 1992, Sophie eldest da of William Andrewes, of Ludlow, Shropshire, — George Septimus, *b* 1964, — Laura Isabel Hester, *b* 1961: *m* 1984, Capt Euan Glen Kelway-Bamber, SG, of Laurel Farmhouse, Heath, nr Chesterfield, Derbys (*see* D Devonshire, colls, 1980 Edn), and has issue living, Rose Olivia *b* 1987, Selina Anne *b* 1989.

Issue of late *Hon* Harry Nugent Morgan-Grenville, OBE, 5th son of Mary, Lady Kinloss, *b* 1896, *d* 1979: *m* 1921, Mary Alice Oliphant, who *d* 1981, da of late Capt *Hon* Edward Oliphant Murray (*see* L Elibank, colls):—
David Bevil MORGAN-GRENVILLE (Tamarack Farm, Sutton, Quebec, Canada), *b* 1928: *m* 1951, Nancy, el da of late Prof Seymour Guy Martin, of Washington, DC, and has issue living, Geoffrey (310 Pine Av, Oakville, Ontario, Canada), *b* 1956: *m* 1981, Julia Louise Newcomb, — Andrew (1243 Laurel St, Apt D, Menlo Park, Calif, USA), *b* 1967: *m* 1992, Jennifer Howard, — Sarah, *b* 1953: *m* 1981, Prof Steven Antler, of 534 Stratford St, Chicago, Illinois, USA. —— Rosalind Mary, *b* 1933: *m* 1st, 1955 (*m diss* 1975), Maj Phillip Ivor Caleb, DFC, AFM, late USAF; 2ndly, 1976, John Frederick Weston, of 336 Grove Court, Elkhart, Ind 46514-3060, USA, and has issue living (by 1st *m*), Caroline Mary, *b* 1956, — Penelope Frances, *b* 1963. —— Elizabeth Caroline (Moor Hill Cottage, Fovant, Salisbury, Wilts), *b* 1944: *m* 1969 (*m diss* 1981), John Kendrick Williams, CEng, MICE, and has issue living, Victoria Caroline Kendrick, *b* 1971, — Rachael Mary Kendrick (twin), *b* 1971.

Grandsons of late Lt-Col Richard Sydney Grenville Close-Smith, OBE (infra):—
Issue of late Robert Richard Close-Smith, *b* 1936, *d* 1992: *m* 1960, Ena Mary (Ashmore Farm, Water Stratford, Buckingham), da of Edwin Rooks, of Quinton:—
Charles Robert CLOSE-SMITH, *b* 1961. —— Christopher Paul, *b* 1962: *m* 1989, Charlotte Nina, da of Dr William Lloyd Brace, of Woodford Green, Essex. —— Henry Richard Christian, *b* 1965.

Grandchildren of late *Hon* Caroline Mary Elizabeth Grenville Close-Smith (infra):—
Issue of late Lt-Col Richard Sydney Grenville Close-Smith, OBE, *b* 1910, *d* 1973: *m* 1st, 1935 (*m diss* 1954), Baroness Florence von Ompteda, da of late Robert, Baron von Ompteda; 2ndly, 1954, (Josephine) Judith (Steart Hill Lodge, Little Horwood, Milton Keynes, Bucks), da of Vincent Wood Mullins, and widow of Michael Bruce Urquhart Dewar, of Stagenhoe Park, Hitchin:—

(By 1st *m*) Venice Mary Grenville, *b* 1938: *m* 1959, John Duncan Maitland Gordon-Colebrooke, of 2 Minshull Close, Moreton Rd, Buckingham, and has issue living, James Richard Maitland, *b* 1961: *m* 1988, Wendy Jane, da of Mrs D. Stokes, of Grenville Rd, Buckingham, — Jeremy Patrick Grenville, *b* 1963, — John Angus Childerstone, *b* 1967.
         Issue of late Charles Nugent Close-Smith, TD, *b* 1911, *d* 1988: *m* 1946, (Elizabeth Emily) Vivien (The Heymersh, Britford, Salisbury, Wilts), da of late Maj William Augustus Cecil Kinsman, DSO, OBE, late Royal Inniskilling Fus (ret):—
Thomas William CLOSE-SMITH, *ed* Eton: *m* 1st, 1973, Lillian Moira Weston, twin da of John Weston Adamson, of Oldstead Hall, Coxwold, York; 2ndly, 1979, Rachel M., yst da of L. B. Earp, of Priory Farmhouse, Wilmington, Sussex, and has issue living (by 2nd *m*), James Grenville, *b* 1982, — Nicola Jane, *b* 1980, — Sophie Mary, *b* 1986. —— Anthony Grenville, *b* 1950; *ed* Eton, and Liverpool Univ: *m* 19—, Sara, eldest da of David Breton, of 12 Thurloe Sq, SW7, and has issue living, a da, *b* 1988. —— Edward Vivian, *b* 1951; *ed* Eton: *m* 1983, Sarah Felicity, eldest da of William Daniel Dane, of 11 Biltmore Estates, Phoenix, Arizona, USA, and has issue living, Charles William, *b* 1987, — Samantha Vivien, *b* 1984, — Caroline, *b* 1985.

                 Grandson of Mary, Lady Kinloss:—
         Issue of late Hon Caroline Mary Elizabeth Grenville Morgan-Grenville, *b* 1886, *d* 1972: *m* 1909, Maj Thomas Close-Smith, who *d* 1946:—
Henry Temple CLOSE-SMITH (The Old Vicarage, Messing, Colchester, Essex), *b* 1918; assumed the additional surname of Close; late Welsh Gds: *m* 1948, Cicely Margaret Wingfield, yr da of late Rev Eustace Hill, and has issue living, Richard Henry, *b* 1951, — Caroline Mary, *b* 1954: *m* 1981, Jonathan Lawrence Compton, of Birch Holt, Layer Marney, Colchester, Essex, 2nd son of A. J. A. Compton, of Bohemia Cottage, Rookley, I of Wight, and has issue living, Emily Glen May *b* 1984, Rosalind Eleanor Caroline *b* 1986.

            Descendants of late Lady Anne Eliza Mary, da of 2nd Duke of Buckingham and Chandos, *b* 1820, *d* 1879: *m* 1846, William Henry Powell Gore-Langton, MP, who *d* 1873 (*see* E Temple of Stowe).

PREDECESSORS – (1) *Rt Hon Sir* EDWARD Bruce, a Lord of Session 1597-1603, accompanied King James to England on his accession 1603, was naturalized that year, and appointed Master of the Rolls for life; received charter of Kinloss with title of *Lord Kinloss* (peerage of Scotland) 1602, with remainder to his heirs and assigns and *cr Lord Bruce of Kinloss* (peerage of Scotland) 1604, with remainder to his heirs male whatsoever, and later (1608) with remainder to heirs male of the body, failing whom to heirs and assigns *d* 1610; *s* by his el son (2) EDWARD, KG 2nd Lord; killed in a duel 1613; *s* by his brother (3) THOMAS, 3rd Lord; *cr Earl of Elgin* (peerage of Scotland) 1633, with remainder to heirs male whatever bearing the name and arms of Bruce, and *Baron Bruce*, of Whorlton, co York (peerage of England) 1640, (4—6) in which title the Lordship of Kinloss was merged until the death of the 6th Earl of Elgin in 1746, when it devolved (in accordance with the subsequent decision of the House of Lords) on (7) JAMES, 3rd Duke of Chandos, as *de jure* 7th Lord Kinloss; at his death his da (8) ANNA ELIZA (Duchess of Buckingham and Chandos) became *de jure* Lady Kinloss, and her son (9) RICHARD PLANTAGENET (Duke of Buckingham and Chandos) *de jure* 9th Lord Kinloss; in 1868 his son (10) RICHARD PLANTAGENET CAMPBELL Temple-Nugent-Brydges-Chandos-Grenville, GCSI, CIE, PC, DCL, 3rd Duke of Buckingham and Chandos (*see* V Cobham), established his right to the title as 10th Lord Kinloss, *b* 1823; Chm of Committees and Dep Speaker in House of Lords: *m* 1st, 1851, Caroline, who *d* 1874, da of Robert Harvey, of Langley Park, Bucks; 2ndly, 1885, Alice Anne, who *d* 1931, el da of Sir Graham Graham-Montgomery, 3rd Bt; *d* 1889; *s* by his el da (11) MARY Morgan, *b* 1852: *m* 1884, Luis Ferdinand Harry Courthope Morgan, of Biddlesden Park, Bucks, who *d* 1896 (having assumed by Roy licence the additional surname and arms of Grenville 1890): *d* 1944; *s* by her granddaughter (12) BEATRICE MARY GRENVILLE, el da of late Rev Hon Luis Chandos Francis Temple Morgan-Grenville (*Master of Kinloss*), 2nd and el surviving son of Mary, Lady Kinloss, present holder of the title.

KINNAIRD, LORD (Kinnaird) (Lord S 1682, and Baron UK 1860)

Wandering lights deceive

GRAHAM CHARLES KINNAIRD, 13th Lord; *b* 15 Sept 1912; *s* 1972; *ed* Eton; F/O RAFVR; late Lt 4/5th Bn Black Watch (TA): *m* 1st, 1938 (*m diss* 1940), Nadia, only child of Harold Augustus Fortington, OBE (*see* Jardine, Bt, *cr* 1919, 1985 Edn); 2ndly, 1940, Diana Margaret Elizabeth, yr da of late Robert Shuckburgh Copeman, of Roydon Hall, Diss, Norfolk, and has had issue by 2nd *m* (of whom his son, Nicholas Charles *b* 1946, *d* 1951).

Arms – Quarterly: 1st and 4th or, a fesse wavy between three mullets gules, *Kirkaldy*; 2nd and 3rd gules, a saltire between four crescents or, *Kinnaird*. **Crest** – A crescent arising from a cloud, having a star issuing from between its horns, all within two branches of palm disposed in orle proper. **Supporters** – Two naked men wreathed about the loins with oak leaves, each holding in his exterior hand a garland of laurel, their interior ankles surrounded by a fetter, and the chain held in the interior hand.
Residences – The Garden House, Rossie Estate, Inchture, Perthshire; Durham House, Durham Place, SW3.

DAUGHTERS LIVING (By 2nd marriage)

Hon Caroline, *b* 1949: *m* 1st, 1970 (*m diss* 1986), Christopher Wigan (*see* B Faringdon, colls); 2ndly, 1986, James Douglas Best, and has issue (by 1st *m*) (*see* B Faringdon, colls), — (by 2nd *m*) Samuel Douglas, *b* 1987, — Arthur Jack, *b* 1989. *Residence* – Castlehill House, Inchture, Perthshire PH14 9SH.
Hon Anna, *b* 1952: *m* 1988, Edward Henry Liddell, and has issue (*see* B Ravensworth, colls). *Residence* – 97 Narbonne Av, SW4.
Hon Susan, *b* 1956: *m* 1987, Francis Rupert Chad Lea (*see* Lea, Bt).

Sure salvation by the cross

Residence – Duxford Mill, nr Cambridge.
Hon Mary Clare, *b* 1960: *m* 1988, Jonn C. Staib, only son of Edward Staib, of Las Palmas, Canary Is, and of the Dowager Countess of Dundonald, and has issue living, James Alexander Christian, *b* 1990, — Annabel Mary, *b* 1992.

ERRANTIA LUMINA FALLUNT

CERTA CRUCE SALUS

SISTER LIVING

Hon Madeline Elisabeth, *b* 1908: *m* 1929, Rt Rev Hugh Rowlands Gough, CMG, OBE, TD, DD, Archbishop of Sydney and Primate of Australia 1959-66, and has issue living, Lucy (*Baroness Swansea*), *b* 1931: *m* 1st, 1959 (*m diss* 1971), Harold Mervyn Temple-Richards (*see* Temple, Bt, colls, 1990 Edn); 2ndly, 1983, as his 2nd wife, 4th Baron Swansea, and has a da (from 1st *m*), Olivia Merielle Lucy *b* 1964: *m* 1991, Timothy C. Heywood, elder son of Christopher Heywood, of Wimbledon, SW20. *Residence* – Forge House, Over Wallop, Stockbridge, Hants.

PREDECESSORS – (1) *Sir* GEORGE PATRICK Kinnaird, KB, PC, MP for Perthshire; was a descendant of Reginald Kinnaird, yr son of Sir Richard Kinnaird of that Ilk, founder of the family, who had had a charter of Kinnaird from William the Lion 1172-1184; *cr Lord Kinnaird*, of Inchture (peerage of Scotland) 1682; *d* 1689: *s* by his son (2) PATRICK, 2nd Lord; *d* 1701; *s* by his son (3) PATRICK, 3rd Lord; *d* 1713; *s* by his son (4) CHARLES, 4th Lord; *d* 1728; *s* by his uncle (5) CHARLES, 5th Lord; *d* 1759; *s* by his kinsman (6) CHARLES, 6th Lord, grandson of Hon George, 6th son of 1st Lord; *d* 1767; *s* by his son (7) GEORGE, 7th Lord; a Representative Peer; *d* 1805; *s* by his son (8) CHARLES, 8th Lord; *b* 1780; MP for Leominster 1802-5; elected a Representative Peer 1806: *m* 1806, Lady Olivia Letitia Catherine FitzGerald, da of 2nd Duke of Leinster, *d* 1826; *s* by his el son (9) GEORGE WILLIAM FOX, KT, 9th Lord; *cr Baron Rossie* (peerage of United Kingdom) 1831, and *Baron Kinnaird*, of Rossie, co Perth (peerage of United Kingdom) 1860, with remainder to his brother Arthur; *d* 1878, when the Barony of Rossie became ext, and the Lordship and Barony of Kinnaird devolved upon his brother (10) ARTHUR WELLESLEY, 10th Lord; *b* 1814; MP for Perth (*L*) 1837-9 and 1852-78; *d* 1887; *s* by his el son (11) ARTHUR FITZ-GERALD, KT, 11th Lord; *b* 1847; a Director of Barclays Bank (Limited); Lord High Commr to Church of Scotland 1907, 1908, and 1909: *m* 1875, Mary Alma Victoria, who *d* 1923, da of Sir Andrew Agnew, 8th Bt (*cr* 1629); *d* 1923; *s* by his son (12) KENNETH FITZ-GERALD, KT, KBE, 12th Lord, *b* 1880; Capt Scottish Horse; Lord High Commr to Church of Scotland 1936 and 1937; Lord-Lieut of Perthshire 1942-60: *m* 1903, Frances Victoria, JP, who *d* 1960, da of late Thomas Henry Clifton (Agnew Bt, *cr* 1629); *d* 1972; *s* by his son (13) GRAHAM CHARLES, 13th Lord and present peer.

KINNOULL, EARL OF (Hay) (Earl S 1633)

Renew your courage

ARTHUR WILLIAM GEORGE PATRICK HAY, 15th Earl; *b* 26 March 1935; *s* 1938; *ed* Eton; FRICS; a Member of Agricultural Valuers' Assocn; a Member, Queen's Body Guard for Scotland (Royal Company of Archers) since 1965; Pres of National Council on Inland Transport 1964-76, Junior Conservative Whip, House of Lords 1966-68; Pres of Scottish Clans Assocn 1970; Vice-Pres of Nat Assocn of Parish Councils 1971-83; a Dir of Property Owners' Building Soc 1972 (Chm 1979); Snr Partner, Langley-Taylor Chartered Surveyors; Mem British Delegation, Council of Europe 1983; Council Mem, R Nat Mission to Deep Sea Fishermen 1978: *m* 1961, Gay Ann, elder da of Sir Denys Colquhoun Flowerdew Lowson, 1st Bt, and has issue.

Arms – Quarterly: 1st and 4th grand quarters counterquartered, 1st and 4th azure, an unicorn salient argent, armed, maned and unguled or, within a bordure of the last, charged with eight half thistles vert, and as many half roses gules joined together per pale as a coat of augmentation, *Kinnoull*; 2nd and 3rd argent, three escutcheons two and one gules, *Hay*; 2nd and 3rd grand quarters counterquartered 1st and 4th or, three bars wavy gules, surmounted of a scimitar in pale argent, *Drummond*; 2nd and 3rd or, a lion's head erased within a double tressure flory counterflory gules, a coat of augmentation, *Strathallan*. **Crest** – A countryman, couped at the knees, vested grey, his waistcoat gules and bonnet azure, bearing on his right shoulder an ox yoke proper. **Supporters** – Two countrymen habited as in the crest, the *dexter* holding over his shoulder the coulter, and the *sinister* the paddle of a plough proper.
Residences – 15 Carlyle Sq, SW3; Pier House, Seaview, Isle of Wight.

Clubs – Lansdowne, Turf, Pratt's, White's, and MCC.

SON LIVING

CHARLES WILLIAM HARLEY (*Viscount Dupplin*), *b* 20 Dec 1962, *ed* Eton, and Ch Ch Oxford; Bar Middle Temple 1990; Atholl Highlander. *Residences* – 59 Scarsdale Villas, W8; Pitkindie House, Abernyte, Perthshire. *Clubs* – White's, Turf, MCC.

DAUGHTERS LIVING

Lady Melissa Ann, *b* 1964.
Lady Iona Charlotte, *b* 1967.
Lady Atalanta Rose, *b* 1974.

SISTERS LIVING

Lady Venetia Constance Kathleen Luz, *b* 1929: *m* 1953, Maj Joseph Trevor Davies, who *d* 1992, and has issue living, Nicola Jane, *b* 1957, — Sally May, *b* 1960: *m* 1992, A. Mark Fairbanks Smith, of 10 Milton Mansions, Queen's Club Gdns, W14 9RP, only son of Esmond Fairbanks Smith, of Warrenhurst, Barns Green, W Sussex. *Residence* – 14 Old School Court, Grimston Gdns, Folkestone, Kent CT20 2UA.
Lady June Anne, *b* 1932: *m* 1955, Sir Cranley Gordon Douglas Onslow, KCMG, MP (*see* E Onslow, colls). *Residence* – Highbuilding, Fernhurst, Sussex.

GREAT-AUNT LIVING (*Daughter of 13th Earl*)

Lady Elizabeth Blanche Mary, *b* 1903: *m* 1st, 1925 (*m diss* 1935), Peter Stanley Chappell; 2ndly, 1935 (*m diss* 1945), Douglas

William Ernest Gordon, who *d* 1951; 3rdly, 1945, William H. S. Dent, MC, and has issue living, (by 1st *m*) Michael Stanley Fitzroy (760 Grover Av, Coquitlam, New Westminster, BC, Canada), *b* 1926: *m* 1952, Eileen Day, of Vancouver, Canada.

COLLATERAL BRANCHES LIVING

Grandchildren of late Col Arthur William Henry Hay-Drummond, son of Lt-Col Hon Charles Rowley Hay-Drummond (son of 11th Earl), who assumed in 1900 the additional surname and arms of Drummond on succeeding his brother Arthur in the Cromlix and Innerpeffray estates:—
Issue of late Capt George Vane HAY-DRUMMOND, Scots Guards, *b* 1910, *d* 1984: *m* 1933, Lady Betty Mary Seton Montgomerie (Vane House, 1 The Glebe, Dunning, Perthshire), da of 16th Earl of Eglinton and Winton:—
Robert Vane HAY-DRUMMOND (Westridge House, Westridge Green, Streatley, Berks), *b* 1936; *ed* Eton; CA (Scot); a Member of Queen's Body Guard for Scotland (Royal Company of Archers): *m* 1959, Auriol Fyler, yr da of Cdr George Martin Pares, RN, of The Old School, Aldworth, Berks. ——— Auriol Vane, *b* 1933: *m* 1st, 1957 (*m diss* 1979), John Anthony Murray; 2ndly, 1984, John Strang Mackenzie Young, of 7 Inkerman Terr, Allen St, W8, and has issue living (by 1st *m*), Andrew Henry William Vane, *b* 1964; *ed* Eton: *m* 1992, Annabel Charlotte Pring, ——— Louise Mary, *b* 1958: *m* 1981, David Hall, and has issue living, Anna Louise *b* 1983, Melissa Sarah *b* 1985.

Descendants of late Capt Edward William Auriol Drummond-Hay, son of late Very Rev Edward Auriol Hay-Drummond, DD, Dean of Bocking, brother of 10th Earl:—
Grandchildren of late Rev Frederic Drummond-Hay, elder son of late Sir Edward Hay Drummond-Hay, elder son of late Capt Edward William Auriol Drummond-Hay (ante):—
Issue of late Robert Drummond-Hay, *b* 1870, *d* 1907: *m* 1895, Gertrude Agatha, who *d* 1924, da of Thomas Forbutt:—
Geoffrey Francis DRUMMOND-HAY (19 Buckmans Rd, Crawley, Sussex), *b* 1898: *m* 1936, Margaret Fenlon, who *d* 1959, and has issue living, Peter (Grange Garden, Flowers Hill, Pangbourne, Berks), *b* 1943: *m* 1st, 1966 (*m diss* 1972), Carolyn Macdonald, of Wichita, Kansas, USA; 2ndly, 1972, Celia Humphris, and has issue living (by 1st *m*), Samantha *b* 1966, (by 2nd *m*) Luke *b* 1974, ——— Alison *b* 1946: *m* 1968, Keith Wills of 26 Worcester Heights, 14 Wiley Rd, Kowloon, Hong Kong, and has issue living, Alexander *b* 1972, Jake *b* 1974. ——— Barbara May Gertrude, *b* 1904: *m* 1938, Peter Drummond-Hay, of New Wing, Nerina Gdns, Recreation Rd, Fish Hoek 7975, CP, S Africa, son of James Chapman Drummond-Hay, and has issue living, Peter James Robert, *b* 1939, ——— Anthony John Blackwood, *b* 1940, ——— Errol David Joseph, *b* 1944, ——— Christopher Ian, *b* 1945, ——— Michael Kevin, *b* 1946, ——— Fiona Mary, *b* 1942. ——— Veronica Florence Muriel Aileen (Flat 16, The Hawthorns, 354 London Rd, Leicester LE2 2PL), *b* 1907: *m* 1926, Alfred Camacho, who *d* 1964, and has issue living, Margaret Mary, *b* 1928, ——— Sheila Mary, *b* 1930.

Grandchildren of late Robert Drummond-Hay (*b* 1870) (ante):—
Issue of late Ernest Patrick Hay, *b* 1900, *d* 1988; discontinued use of surname Drummond: *m* 1930, Elsie May Baldwin, who *d* 1973, formerly of Leytonstone, London:—
Kenneth John HAY, *b* 1932: *m* 1951, Rita Edith, da of late Fred Barton, of Wembley, Middx, and has issue living, Roberta Elaine, *b* 1956: *m* 1978 (*m diss* 1984), Martin William Long, and has issue living, Christopher Ross LONG *b* 1981, and further issue (by John Covill, of Fern Lea, Natland Green, Kendal, Cumbria), Sam COVILL *b* 1988. *Residence* – 18 Esthwaite Av, Heron Hill, Kendal, Cumbria LA9 7NN. ——— Shirley Patricia, *b* 1935: *m* 1954, Peter William Johnson, and has issue living, Garry Daniel, *b* 1955: *m* 1981, Maureen, da of Kevin O'Shea, and has issue living, James Christopher *b* 1982, Sarah Jane *b* 1984, ——— Aileen Denise, *b* 1959. *Residence* – 26 Justin Av, Pacific View Est, Mt Tamborine, Qld 4272, Australia.

Grandchildren of late Sir Robert Hay-Drummond-Hay, CMG, son of late Rt Hon Sir John Hay Drummond-Hay, GCMG, KCB, yr son of late Capt Edward William Auriol Drummond-Hay (ante):—
Issue of late Edward William Hay-Drummond-Hay, *b* 1877, *d* 1941: *m* 1904, Margaret Alice, who *d* 1954, da of late E. W. Meade-Waldo, of Stonewall Park, and Hever Castle, Kent:—
John Waldo Edward HAY-DRUMMOND-HAY, TD, *b* 1906; *ed* Marlborough, and at Trin Coll Camb; Major (ret), Queen's Own Roy W Kent Regt (TA), and attached Indian Army: *m* 1st, 1937, Anne Rachel, who *d* 1975, da of W. T. Prideaux, of Elderslie, Ockley; 2ndly, 1976, Mrs Jennifer Roosen, who *d* 1989, da of Bostock-Wilson, and has issue living (by 1st *m*), Robert Prideaux (Upper Panshill Farm, Murcott, Islip, Oxon), *b* 1941; *ed* Eton: *m* 1965, Sally Catherine, da of Ian Redfern, of Winchester, and has issue living, (Robert) Simon *b* 1967: *m* 1991, Julia E., da of John Roberts, of Cowbridge, S Glamorgan, Katherine Louise *b* 1973, Caroline Sarah *b* 1974, ——— Peter Charles Hay DRUMMOND-HAY (86 Rowayton Av, Rowayton, Connecticut 06853, USA; Le Pestou, Castelsagrat, France), *b* 1948; *ed* Eton, and Trin Coll, Camb; assumed 1975 the surname of Drummond Hay in place of Hay-Drummond-Hay and the christian name of Hay: *m* 1975, Lady Bettina Mary Lindsay, da of the 29th Earl of Crawford, and 12th Earl of Balcarres, and has issue living, Thomas Auriol Leo *b* 1989, Tamsin Rachel *b* 1977, Alice Ruth *b* 1980, Lily Iona *b* 1983, ——— Auriol Marion, *b* 1946: *m* 1968, Donald Alvin Hessemer, of 209 Ramoneda St, Bay St Louis, Mississippi, USA. *Residence* – The Oaks, Swainham Lane, St Leonards-on-Sea, E Sussex TN38 8ED.
Issue of late Cecil Lawrence Hay-Drummond-Hay, *b* 1882, *d* 1952: *m* 1st, 1911 (*m diss* 1924), Jessie, who *d* 1961, yr twin da of late Lawrence Munro; 2ndly 1925, Doris Rachel, who *d* 1971, da of late Dudley Hill, of Christchurch, NZ:—
(By 2nd *m*) Annette Alistair, *b* 1927: *m* 1948 (*m diss* 1977), David Stanford, and has issue living, Matthew Bedell, *b* 1951, ——— Jonathan David, *b* 1953, ——— Giles Timothy, *b* 1961, ——— Anna Bethell, *b* 1949, ——— Charlotte Sylvia *b* 1963.

Grandchildren of Humphry Ringler Drummond-Hay, eldest son of late Charles Drummond-Hay (*b* 1856), eldest son of late Col Thomas Robert Hay Drummond-Hay, 3rd son of late Capt Edward William Auriol Drummond-Hay (ante):—
Issue of late George Thomson Drummond-Hay, *b* 1916, *d* 1983: *m* 1st, 1939 (*m diss* 1949), Elizabeth Barbara Fraser, of Regina; 2ndly, 1949 (*m diss* 1960), Mrs Adrienne Ruth Russell, da of John William Southin, of Vancouver, BC; 3rdly, 1964, Mrs Shirlee Montgomery, da of Harry J. Gibbons, of Sioux City, Iowa, USA:—
(By 1st *m*) Elizabeth Sandra, *b* 1945. *Residence* – —. (By 2nd *m*) Eric Thomson (10 Trumbull Court, Novato, California 94947, USA), *b* 1951: *m* 1981, Mary Elizabeth, da of Sherwin Ray Murry, and has issue living, Charles Thomson, *b* 1987, ——— Anne Elizabeth, *b* 1985. ——— Charles Webster (4616 SE Roethe 78, Milwaukie, Oregon, 97267 USA), *b* 1952. ——— Leslie Katherine (128 N Humboldt 9, San Mateo, California 94401, USA) *b* 1954.

Grandchildren of late Harold Sanford Drummond-Hay (infra):—
Issue of late Charles Robert Drummond-Hay, late Fl-Lt RCAF, *b* 1917, *d* 1966: *m* 1940, Ina Mary (103-4675 Valley Drive, Vancouver, BC, Canada V6J 4B7), da of late George H. Disbrow, of Vancouver:—
Humphrey Blake, *b* 1945. ——— Brian Maxwell, *b* 1947. ——— Lee Sanford, *b* 1950. ——— Jane Macpherson, *b* 1953: *m* 1990, David Alexander Saba, of 3005 West 29th St, Vancouver, BC, Canada V6L 1Y5, son of late Clarence Saba, of Vancouver, BC, Canada.

Granddaughter of late Charles Drummond-Hay (*b* 1856) (ante):—
Issue of late Harold Sanford Drummond-Hay, *b* 1890, *d* 1951: *m* 1915, Effie Caldwell, who *d* 1964, da of late Robert Adamson, of Winnipeg:—
Jeanette (Jean) Audrey (Suite 1202, 1122 Gilford St, Vancouver, BC, Canada W6G 2P5), *b* 1919.

Grandchildren of late Sir Francis Ringler Drummond-Hay, 5th son of late Capt Edward William Auriol Drummond-Hay (ante):—
  Issue of late Francis Edward Drummond-Hay, MVO, *b* 1868, *d* 1943: *m* 1895, Eveline Austey, MBE, who *d* 1963, da of late Rev Edmund Thomas Bennett, formerly R of Littleton, Winchester, of Castle Roe, co Londonderry:—
Claude Francis, *b* 1898; *ed* Cheltenham Coll; 1915-18 War in Salonika and France as Capt Black Watch (R Highlanders): *m* 1st, 1921, (*m diss* 1928), Gladys Grant; 2ndly, 1933, Ellenor, da of late G. Carlin, of Cleadon Meadows, Cleadon, Durham; 3rdly, 1957, Mrs Gladys Beatrice Robinson, of Babbacombe Cliffs, Torquay, and has issue living, (by 2nd *m*) John Francis (44 Inanda Rd, Hillcrest, Natal), *b* 1938: *m* 1961, Beverley Ann, da of Francis Howes, of Hillcrest, Natal, and has issue living, Sean Francis *b* 1962, Deborah Joan *b* 1963, — Jeffrey Derrick Edward, *b* 1943, — Joan, *b* 1935.
  Issue of late Frederick William Drummond-Hay, *b* 1870, *d* 1923: *m* 1st, 1894, Ellen Marion, who *d* 1896, da of late Major Charles Johnson Anthony Deane, Indian Army; 2ndly, 1905, Louise Agnes Burke, who *d* 1920, da of Denis Comerford, of co Tipperary:—
(By 2nd *m*) Rita O'Brien, *b* 1906: *m* 1932 (*m diss* 1954), Arthur Harly Whitcomb, and has issue living, Cheyne, *b* 1933, — Brenda, *b* 1935.

PREDECESSORS – (1) *Sir* GEORGE Hay, KB; was successively a Gentleman of the Bedchamber, and Clerk Register of Scotland, and Lord High Chancellor of Scotland 1622-34; *cr Viscount Dupplin* and *Lord Hay of Kinfauns* (peerage of Scotland) 1627, with remainder to his heirs male of his body, and *Earl of Kinnoull, Viscount Dupplin,* and *Lord Hay of Kinfauns* with remainder to his heirs male (peerage of Scotland) 1633; *d* 1634; *s* by his son (2) GEORGE, PC, 2nd Earl; Capt of Yeomen of the Guard; *d* 1644; *s* by his el son (3) GEORGE, 3rd Earl, of whom "The Scots Peerage," published 1908, says "is not given by the Peerage writers, but there is undoubted evidence for his existence"; *d* about 1650; *s* by his brother (4) WILLIAM, 4th Earl; became in 1660 proprietor of the Island of Barbados, and in 1661 disposed of it to Charles II; during the Civil Wars was taken by the Republicans and committed to Edinburgh Castle whence he escaped 1654, and in Nov of that year was made prisoner by the English; *d* 1677; *s* by his el son (5) GEORGE, 5th Earl; *d* 1687; *s* by his brother (6) WILLIAM, 6th Earl; *d* 1709; after resignation received a re-grant of his honours in 1704, with remainder to his kinsman Thomas, Viscount Dupplin, and heirs male of his body, whom failing to his heirs of tailzie and provision; *s* by the said (7) THOMAS, 7th Earl, great-grandson of Peter Hay, yr brother of 1st Earl; MP for Perthshire 1693-7; had been *cr Viscount Dupplin* (peerage of Scotland) 1697 with remainder to heirs male of his body, whom failing to his heirs of entail; imprisoned in Edinburgh Castle 1715 on breaking out of rebellion; *d* 1719; *s* by his son (8) GEORGE HENRY, 8th Earl, who had in 1711 been *cr Baron Hay,* of Pedwardine, co Hereford (peerage of Great Britain); *d* 1758; *s* by his son (9) THOMAS, 9th Earl; *dsp* 1787; *s* by his nephew (10) ROBERT HAY-DRUMMOND, PC, 10th Earl, son of the Most Rev the Hon Robert Hay-Drummond, Archbishop of York, 2nd son of 8th Earl; assumed for himself the additional surname of Drummond; was Lord Lyon King of Arms; *d* 1804; *s* by his el son (11) THOMAS ROBERT, 11th Earl; *b* 1785; was Lord-Lieut of Perthshire, and Lyon King of Arms: *m* 1824, Louisa Burton, who *d* 1885, da of Adm Sir Charles Rowley, GCB, 1st Bt; *d* 1866; *s* by his el son (12) GEORGE, 12th Earl, *b* 1827: *m* 1848, Lady Emily Blanche Charlotte Somerset, who *d* 1895, da of 7th Duke of Beaufort, KG; *d* 1897; *s* by his el surviving son (13) ARCHIBALD FITZROY GEORGE, 13th Earl; *b* 1855; served with late Baker Pasha, as Ch of his Staff during Campaign on Red Sea: *m* 1st, 1879 (judicially separated 1885), Josephine Maria, who *d* 1900, da of late John Hawke, solicitor, of Burlington Gardens, W; 2ndly, 1903, Florence Mary, who *d* 1941 (having *m* 2ndly, 1919, Major John Joseph Berington, RMA), da of late Edward Tierney Gilchrist Darell; *d* 1916; *s* by his grandson (14) GEORGE HARLEY (only surviving son of late Capt Edmund Alfred Rollo George, Viscount Dupplin, el son of 13th Earl), 14th Earl, *b* 1902: *m* 1st, 1923 (*m diss* 1927), Enid Margaret Hamlyn, only child of Major Ernest Gaddesden Fellows; 2ndly, 1928, Mary Ethel Isobel, who *d* 1938, da of late Ferdinand Richard Holmes Meyrick, MD, of 59 Kensington Court, W8; *d* 1938; *s* by his 3rd but only surviving son (15) ARTHUR WILLIAM GEORGE PATRICK, 15th Earl, and present peer; also Viscount Dupplin, Lord Hay of Kinfauns, and Baron Hay of Pedwardine.

Kinrara, Earl of March and; son of Duke of Richmond.

KINROSS, BARON (Balfour) (Baron UK 1902)

Nothing rashly

CHRISTOPHER PATRICK BALFOUR, 5th Baron, *b* 1 Oct 1949; *s* 1985; *ed* Eton, St Andrew's Univ, and Edinburgh Univ (LLB); WS: *m* 1974, Susan Jane, da of Ian Robert Pitman, WS, and has issue.

𝕬rms – Ermine, on a chevron sable between in chief two torteaux and in base an open book, an otter's head proper. 𝕮rest – On a rock a mermaid holding in the dexter hand an otter's head erased, and in the sinister a swan's head erased, all proper. 𝕾upporters – On either side an otter proper, charged on the shoulder with two swords saltirewise, also proper.
Residence – 11 Belford Pl, Edinburgh.

SONS LIVING

Hon ALAN IAN, *b* 4 April 1978.
Hon Derek Andrew, *b* 1981.

HALF SISTER LIVING (*daughter of 4th Baron by 1st m*)

Hon Ariadne Maria (2 Halesden Rd, Heaton Chapel, Stockport, Cheshire), *b* 1939: *m* 1961 (*m diss* 1990), Richard Elliot Nicholson, yr son of late Robert Watson Nicholson, of Newcastle-upon-Tyne, and has issue living, Robert David, *b* 1964, — Matthew Charles, *b* 1968, — Edward Alan, *b* 1971, — Camilla Jane, *b* 1962.

AUNTS LIVING (*daughters of 2nd Baron*)

Hon Pamela Lilias, *b* 1907: *m* 1933, Humphrey Scott-Plummer, who *d* 1991, and has issue living (Patrick) Joseph (Mainhouse, Kelso, Roxburghshire), *b* 1943: *m* 1st, 1970 (*m diss* 1977), Grizel Elizabeth-Anne (Lulla), only da of Lt-Col Anthony Way, of Kincairney, Dunkeld, Perthshire; 2ndly, 1977, Christine Margaret Hermione, da of late Capt Hon Anthony Gerard Hugh Bampfylde (*see* B Poltimore), and formerly wife of Peter William Denby Roberts (*see* Roberts, Bt, *cr* 1909, colls), and has issue living (by 1st *m*), Charles Humphrey *b* 1972, Annabel Cecilia *b* 1974, (by 2nd *m*) (Anthony) Guy *b* 1978, — Julia Elizabeth *b* 1935: *m* 1958, Rae Lionel Haggard Lyster, of Malting Green House, Layer de la Haye, Essex, and has issue living, Nicholas Charles *b* 1959, Amanda Pamela *b* 1961, Lucy Caroline *b* 1963, — (Olivia) Jane *b* 1946: *m* 1968,

Thomas Yates Benyon, of The Old Rectory, Adstock, Bucks, and has issue living, Thomas Yates *b* 1974, Oliver William Yates *b* 1981, Clare Julia Yates *b* 1969, Camilla Lucinda Joan Yates *b* 1972. *Residence* – Mainhouse Kelso, Roxburghshire.
Hon Ursula Nina, *b* 1914: *m* 1939, Col Christopher James York Dallmeyer, DSO and bar, WS, Lothian and Border Horse Yeo, and has issue living, Gavin Richard James (Craigiewood, N Kessock, by Inverness), *b* 1942: *m* 1970, Araminta Morgan and has issue living, Thomas Charles *b* 1979, Flora Jane *b* 1975, — Andrew Victor (20 Ann St, Edinburgh 4), *b* 1945: *m* 1969, Vivienne Dixon, and has issue living, Tobias *b* 1973, Amy Jane Eleanor *b* 1985, — James (c/o Australian Associated Press, JL Kemang Raya G83, Kemang, Jakarta Selatan, Indonesia), *b* 1948: *m* 1978, Margherita Elizabeth Dimambro, — Rosemary Nina *b* 1940: *m* 1962, Rev Paul Roderick Nicolson, of The Vicarage, Turville, nr Henley-on-Thames, Oxon, and has issue living, Roderick John *b* 1962, Hugo James *b* 1965, Thomas Paul *b* 1966, Claire Katherine *b* 1968, Kristina Belle *b* 1975. *Residence* – Green Corner, Tyninghame, Dunbar, E Lothian.

WIDOW LIVING OF FOURTH BARON

Ruth Beverley (*Dowager Baroness Kinross*), da of late William Henry Mill, SSC, of Edinburgh, and formerly wife of Kenneth William Bruce Middleton, Sheriff of Lothian and Borders at Edinburgh and Haddington: *m* 1972, as his 3rd wife, the 4th Baron, OBE, TD, who *d* 1985. *Residence* – 58 India St, Edinburgh.

COLLATERAL BRANCH LIVING

Issue of late Hon Harry Robert Chichester Balfour, 4th son of 1st Baron, *b* 1882, *d* 1964: *m* 1921, Dorothy Constance, who *d* 1963, da of late Henry Goulburn Willoughby Chetwynd (V Chetwynd, colls):—
Anthony John Chetwynd, CBE (Cymbeline, Ellesborough Rd, Wendover, Bucks; Leander Club), *b* 1926; *ed* Eton, and at King's Coll, Camb (MA, MB, BChir); Consultant in Pathology, RAF Med Branch; FRCPath; Air Commodore (ret) RAF; CBE (Mil) 1987: *m* 1958, Judith Ann Margaret, yr da of Leslie Field Anderson, of Pines Av, Worthing, and has issue living, Peter John Torquil, *b* 1959; BSc, MB, ChB (Birmingham): *m* 1st, 1985 (*m diss* 19—), Nicola Jane, da of David Charles Yarwood, of Mount Sorel, Leics; 2ndly, 1994, Patricia, da of Jerome Dawson, of Orangefield Gdns, Belfast, — Harry Luke Chetwynd, *b* 1963, — Helena Clare, *b* 1961; SRN: *m* 1989, John Trevor Eades, of Wimbledon, and has issue living, Louis John Frederick *b* 1991, Jack Edward Luke *b* 1993. ——— Hilary Joan Gwendolen (1 The Maisonettes, Icknield Rd, Goring-on-Thames, nr Reading, Berks), *b* 1924.

PREDECESSORS – (1) John Blair Balfour, son of Rev P. Balfour, Min of Clackmannan; Solicitor-Gen for Scotland April 1880 to Aug 1881, and Lord-Advocate Aug 1881 to June 1885, Feb to July 1886, and Aug 1892 to June 1895; MP for Clackmannan and Kinross-shire (L) Nov, 1880 to Nov 1899, when he became Lord Justice-General for Scotland (with judicial title of *Lord Blair Balfour*); cr a PC 1883, and *Baron Kinross*, of Glasclune, co Haddington (peerage of United Kingdom) 1902: *m* 1st, 1869, Lilias Oswald, who *d* 1872, da of late Hon Lord Mackenzie, a Lord of Session; 2ndly, 1877, Hon Marianne Eliza, who *d* 1913, da of 1st Baron Moncreiff: *d* 1905; *s* by his el son (2) Patrick, KC, 2nd Baron; *b* 1870; a Brigadier, Roy Co of Archers (King's Body Guard for Scotland); Sheriff of Dumfries and Galloway, 1927-39: *m* 1903, Caroline Elsie, who *d* 1969, da of late Arthur Henry Johnstone-Douglas (M Queensberry): *d* 1939; *s* by his son (3) John Patrick Douglas, 3rd Baron, *b* 1904; Author and Journalist; Sqdn-Ldr RAFVR: *m* 1938 (*m diss* 1942), Angela Mary, da of late Capt George Culme-Seymour (Culme-Seymour, Bt, colls): *d* 1976; *s* by his brother (4) David Andrew, OBE, TD, 4th Baron; *b* 1906; Col RA (TA); a Member of Queen's Body Guard for Scotland (R Co of Archers); Hon Col 27th (Lowland) Field Regt, City of Edinburgh Artillery; a DL for City of Edinburgh; Chm British Legion, Scotland, 1965-68; Vice-Chm RA Council for Scotland; 1939-45 War in UK and Burma: *m* 1st, 1936 (*m diss* 1941), Araminta, da of late Lt-Col Willoughby Ewart Peel, DSO (*see* Hunter-Blair, colls, 1966 Edn); 2ndly, 1948, Helen Anne, who *d* 1969, da of late Alan Welwood Hog, of Edinburgh, and formerly wife of Lt-Col Patrick Cassan Perfect; 3rdly, 1972, Ruth Beverley, da of late William Henry Mill, of Edinburgh; *d* 1985; *s* by his only son (5) Christopher Patrick, 5th Baron and present peer.

KINTORE, EARL OF (Keith) (Earl S 1677)

Michael Canning William John Keith, 13th Earl and 4th Baronet; *b* 22 Feb 1939; *s* 1989; *ed* Eton, and RMA Sandhurst; late Lieut Coldstream Guards: *m* 1972, Mary, only da of late Sqdn Ldr Elisha Gaddis Plum, of Rumson, NJ, USA, and has issue.

Arms – Quarterly; 1st and 4th, argent on a chief, gules three pallets or, *Keith*; 2nd, azure, a falcon displayed between three mullets argent, on his breast a man's heart gules, *Falconer of Halkerton*; 3rd, per pale engrailed gules and or, a boar passant counterchanged, *Baird of Ury*; over all, on an inescutcheon gules, a sceptre and sword in saltire with an Imperial Crown between the upper corners all proper, within an orle of eight thistles slipped near the head or, ensigned with an Earl's coronet (*being the Coat of Augmentation granted to John, 1st Earl of Kintore, for his services in the preservation of the Regalia of Scotland*). **Crests** – Dexter, a noble lady from the middle richly attired, holding in her right hand a garland proper (*Crest of Augmentation for Earldom of Kintore*); Sinister, a roebuck's head proper, attired or, *Keith*. **Supporters** – Two men in complete armour proper, each holding a spear gules banded argent, in posture of sentinels.
Seat – Keith Hall, Inverurie, Aberdeenshire.

SON LIVING

James William Falconer (*Lord Inverurie, Master of Kintore*), *b* 15 April 1976; *ed* Gordonstoun.

DAUGHTER LIVING

Lady Iona Delia Mary Gaddis, *b* 1978.

BROTHER LIVING

Hon Alexander David Baird, *b* 1946; *ed* Tabley House. *Residence* – 3 Osterley Crescent, Isleworth, Middx.

SISTER LIVING

Lady Diana Elizabeth Virginia Sydney, *b* 1937: *m* 1957, John Francis Holman, OBE, of Rickarton House, Stonehaven, Kincardineshire, and 6 St Luke's St, SW3 3RS (*see* By Trent, 1985 Edn), and has issue living, Richard Ian HOLMAN-BAIRD, *b* 1958: *m* 1985, Saragh, who *d* 1987, only da of Maj Robert Wood, of Sycamore House, Glassonby, Penrith, Cumbria, — Edward Alexander, *b* 1960, — Georgina Mary, *b* 1962: *m* 1989, Charles Stirrup, eldest son of John Stirrup, of Johannesburg, S Africa, — Emma Charlotte, *b* 1966: *m* 1990, Ben Charles Cole, elder son of Anthony Brian Cole of Staplecross, Sussex, and has issue living, a son *b* 1994, Sophie Charlotte *b* 1992.

AUNTS LIVING (*daughters of (Ethel) Sydney, Countess of Kintore*)

Lady Ariel Olivia Winifred, CVO, *b* 1916; appointed Lady-in-Waiting to HRH Princess Alice, Countess of Athlone 1940: *m* 1946 (*m diss* 1958), Sir Kenneth Alexander Keith, late Lt-Col WG (later Baron Keith of Castleacre), and has issue (see that title). *Residence* – 16 Melton Court, Old Brompton Rd, SW7 3JQ.
Lady (Hilda) Ava Fiona Nancy, *b* 1919: *m* 1945, Lt-Col Ronald Fulton Lucas Chance, MC, King's Roy Rifle Corps, and has issue living, Nicholas John Lucas (Caulcott House, Caulcott, Oxon OX5 3NE), *b* 1946: *m* 1975, Anne Heather Gard, only da of Maj J. E. V. Rice, of Exhurst Manor, Staplehurst, Kent, and has issue living, Alexander *b* 1978, Hugo *b* 1980, Sophia *b* 1984, — Louise Annette *b* 1950: *m* 1976, Edward Alexander Goschen, son of Maj Sir Edward Christian Goschen, 3rd Bt, DSO, and has issue living (*see* Goschen, Bt). *Residence* – 2 Abbot's Gdns, Malmesbury, Wilts SN16 9HY.

WIDOW LIVING OF SON OF FIRST VISCOUNT STONEHAVEN AND (ETHEL) SYDNEY, COUNTESS OF KINTORE

Dorviegelda Malvina, da of late Alexander Ronald MacGregor (*see* MacGregor of MacGregor, Bt, colls): *m* 1st, 1939, Sqdn-Ldr Hon (Robert Alexander) Greville Baird, RAF, who was *ka* 1943; 2ndly, 1947, Sqdn-Ldr Algernon Ivan Sladen, DSO, who *d* 1976, late RAF (E Dunmore), and has issue living (by 1st *m*) (*see* colls, infra). *Residence* – Stone Lodge, Browning Hill, Baughurst, Basingstoke, Hants.

WIDOW LIVING OF TWELFTH EARL

DELIA (*Delia, Countess of Kintore*), da of late William Lewis Brownlow Loyd, of Upper House, Shamley Green, Guildford (*see* B Brabourne, 1967 Edn): *m* 1935, the 12th Earl, who *d* 1989. *Residence* – 16 Garden Wood, Inchmarlo, Banchory, Kincardineshire AB3 4AW.

COLLATERAL BRANCHES LIVING

Issue of late Sqdn-Ldr Hon (Robert Alexander) Greville BAIRD, RAF, 2nd son of 1st Viscount Stonehaven and (Ethel) Sydney, Countess of Kintore, *b* 1910, *ka* 1943: *m* 1939, Dorviegelda Malvina (ante), who *m* 2ndly, 1947, Sqdn-Ldr Algernon Ivan Sladen, DSO, who *d* 1976, late RAF (E Dunmore), da of Alexander Ronald MacGregor (*see* MacGregor, Bt, *cr* 1795):—
†Alaisdair Aulin John, *b* 1942, lost at sea 1962. —— Ceanan Donald (Arford House, Headly Down, Hants), *b* (*posthumous*) 1943: *m* 1973, Janet Mary, da of Donald R. Scott, and has issue living, Hamish Duncan, *b* 1975, — Amanda Louisa, *b* 1977. —— Rinalda Malvina, *b* 1940: *m* 1963, Col David Henry Sandford Leslie Maitland-Titterton, late 9th/12th R Lancers, of Rimes Gigot, Rhymes Lane, Baughurst, Basingstoke (*see* E Lauderdale, colls, 1985 Edn), and has issue living, Rupert Seymour Aulin Leslie, *b* 1965, — Shán Gelda Jane, *b* 1967.

Granddaughters of late Lady Blanche Catherine Keith-Falconer (who *m* 1883, Col Granville Roland Francis Smith, CVO, CB), da of the 8th Earl of Kintore:—
Issue of late Granville Keith-Falconer Smith, *b* 1886, *d* 1914: *m* 1910, Lady Kathleen Clements, who *d* 1975, having *m* 2ndly, 1919, Cdr Ronald Granville Studd, DSO, RN, who *d* 1956 (Studd, Bt), da of the 4th Earl of Leitrim:—
Rosemary Winifred, *b* 1912. *Residence* – Thatchers, Princes Risborough, Bucks. —— Merial Kathleen, *b* 1914. *Residence* – Postboys, Stoke by Nayland, Colchester, Essex.

Grandchildren of late Rev Roland Audley Smith, 2nd son of late Lady Blanche Catherine Smith (ante):—
Issue of late Granville Roland Smith, *b* 1919, *d* 1984: *m* 1st, 1944, Aimée Rosemary Patricia, who *d* 1963, only da of late George Henry Preston Moore-Browne, of Port Stewart Castle, co Derry, and formerly wife of Dr John Forbes; 2ndly, 1965, Margaret Clare (40 Raynham St, Hertford, Herts), da of Daniel Coonan, of Tenterfield, NSW:—
(By 1st *m*) Rachael Margaret Pleasance ROLAND SMITH, *b* 1944.
Issue of late Samuel Erskine Roland Smith, *b* 1924, *d* 1963: *m* 1948, Margaret Anne, who *d* 1990, el da of Brig John Eric Chippindall, CBE, MC, of 11 The Royal Cres, Bath:—
Amanda Jane ROLAND SMITH, *b* 1951; has retained her maiden name: *m* 1986, Stephen Ireland, of Forest Grove House, 3 Weston Av, Mount Hooton Rd, Nottingham, and has issue living, Emma Jane, *b* 1986. —— Vanessa Anne, *b* 1955: *m* 1980, Frederick Norris, who *d* 1993, of 9 Queen's Acre, Newnham, Glos GL14 1DJ, and has issue living, Samantha Mary, *b* 1978.
Issue of late Marion Blanche Smith, *b* 1915, *d* 1989: *m* 1952, Cdr Michael Peer-Groves, RN, who *d* 1988:—
William Keith PEER-GROVES (1 Rosemary Cottages, Cottered, Buntingford, Herts), *b* 1954. —— Michael Roland PEER-GROVES, *b* 1957: *m* 1991, Linda Wurster, of Long Island, NY, USA.

Granddaughters of late Lady Blanche Catherine Smith (ante):—
Issue of late Lt-Gen Sir Arthur Francis Smith, KCB, KBE, DSO, MC, *b* 1890, *d* 1977: *m* 1918, Hon Monica Victoria Crossley, who *d* 1990, da of 1st Baron Somerleyton:—
Auriol Blanche, *b* 1919: *m* 1944, Maj Michael Warren Ingram, late Gren Gds, of The Manor House, S Cerney, Cirencester (*see* Ingram, Bt). —— Susan Monica, *b* 1921: *m* 1943, Capt Thomas Gillespie Browne, late RE, of 12 Walpole Court, Puddletown, Dorset DT2 8TJ, and has issue living, Jennifer Anne, *b* 1944: *m* 1st, 1965 (*m diss* 1975), John Patrick Michael Hugh Evelyn; 2ndly, 1978, Robert Alexander Neon Reynolds, of Fairleigh Farm, Folly Gate, Okehampton, Devon, and has issue living (by 1st *m*), Peter John *b* 1970, (by 2nd *m*) Susanna Clare *b* 1979, — Hilary Jane, *b* 1945: *m* 1965, Julian Alexander Ludovic James, of St Aubyns School, Rottingdean, Brighton, Sussex, and has issue living, Christopher Mark William *b* 1967, David Hugh Geoffrey *b* 1969, Andrew Michael Richard *b* 1976, — Monica Jean, *b* 1949: *m* 1st, 1970 (*m diss* 1981), David Robin Millais James-Duff; 2ndly, 1986, Michael Anthony Spalding Gould Stewart, of Fernfield, Crinan, Argyllshire, and has issue living (by 1st *m*), Rory Thomas *b* 1978, Fiona Louise *b* 1971, Tania Robin *b* 1973, Nicola Mary *b* 1980.

Grandchildren of late Lt-Gen Sir Arthur Francis Smith, KCB, KBE, DSO, MC (ante):—
Issue of late Hazel Charlotte Smith, *b* 1924, *d* 1981: *m* 1943, Maj Peter Gordon Rowley, RA, who *d* 1987:—
David Gordon ROWLEY, *b* 1946; *ed* Bryanston. —— Wendy Drusilla, *b* 1950. —— Hazel Jane, *b* 1959.

PREDECESSORS – (1) *Hon* Sir JOHN Keith, 3rd son of William, 6th Earl Marischal, *cr Lord Keith of Inverurie and Keith Hall*, and *Earl of Kintore* (peerage of Scotland) 1677 with remainder to the heirs male of his body; in 1694 he resigned his honours and had a regrant of the titles and estates to him and the heirs male of his body, whom failing to the heirs male of his brother George, Earl Marischal, whom failing to the heirs-general of his own body; appointed 1660 hereditary Knight-

Marischal of Scotland in consideration of his loyalty in preserving the regalia of Scotland from the hands of Cromwell; *d* 1714; *s* by his son (2) WILLIAM, 2nd Earl; being engaged in the rebellion of 1715 lost the office of Knight-Marischal; *d* 1718; *s* by his el son (3) JOHN, 3rd Earl; appointed Knight-Marischal; *dsp* 1758; *s* by his brother (4) WILLIAM, 4th Earl; *d* 1761, when the estates devolved upon George, 10th Earl Marischal (title attainted 1715), and the peerage remained dormant until his decease 1778, when it passed to his kinsman (5) ANTHONY ADRIAN Falconer, 5th Earl, who in 1776 *s* as 7th *Lord Falconer of Halkerton* (see that title); *d* 1804; *s* by his son (6) WILLIAM, 6th Earl; *d* 1812; *s* by his son (7) ANTHONY ADRIAN, 7th Earl; *cr Baron Kintore*, of Kintore, co Aberdeen (peerage of United Kingdom) 1838; *d* 1844; *s* by his son (8) FRANCIS ALEXANDER, 8th Earl; *b* 1828; Lord-Lieut of co Kincardine 1856-64, and of co Aberdeen 1864-80: *m* 1851, Louisa Madeleine, who *d* 1916, da of Francis Hawkins, Esq; *d* 1880; *s* by his son (9) ALGERNON HAWKINS THOMOND, KT, GCMG, PC, 9th Earl; *b* 1852; a Lord-in-Waiting to Queen Victoria 1885-6, Capt of the Yeomen of the Guard 1886-9, Gov of S Australia 1889-95, again a Lord-in-Waiting to Queen Victoria 1895-1901, and to King Edward VII 1901-5; a Dep Speaker House of Lords 1915, and a Member of Select Committee on Peerages in abeyance 1925: *m* 1873, Lady Sydney Charlotte Montagu, who *d* 1932, da of 6th Duke of Manchester; *d* 1930; *s* by his son (10) ARTHUR GEORGE, 10th Earl, *b* 1879; officially recognised by the name of Keith by Warrant of Lord Lyon King of Arms 1956: *m* 1937, Helena, who *d* 1971, da of Eugene Zimmerman of Cincinnati, USA, and formerly wife of 9th Duke of Manchester; *d* 1966, when the Barony of Kintore (peerage of UK) became ext, the Lordship of Falconer of Halkerton became dormant (see that title), and the Earldom and the Lordship of Keith of Inverurie and Keith Hall devolved on his sister (11) ETHEL SYDNEY, Countess of Kintore, *b* 1874: *m* 1905, the 1st Viscount Stonehaven, who *d* 1941; *d* 1974, *s* by her el son (12) JAMES IAN, 12th Earl, *b* 1908, changed his name and arms from Baird to Keith by Interlocutor Lyon Court 28 June 1967, Vice-Lieut Kincardineshire, served 1939-45 War as Maj RM: *m* 1935, Delia, da of late William Lewis Brownlow Loyd, of Upper House, Shamley Green, Guildford (*see* Brabourne, 1967 Edn); *d* 1989; *s* by his elder son (13) MICHAEL CANNING WILLIAM JOHN, 13th Earl and present peer; also Viscount Stonehaven, Baron Stonehaven, and Lord Keith of Inverurie and Keith Hall (see infra).

*(1) Sir ALEXANDER Baird, GBE, son of late John Baird, of Urie; Lord-Lieut of Kincardineshire 1889-1918; *cr* a *Baronet* 1897: *m* 1873, Hon Annette Maria, who *d* 1884, da of 1st Baron Haldon; *d* 1920; *s* by his el son (2) *Rt Hon Sir* JOHN LAWRENCE, GCMG, DSO, PC, 2nd Bt, *b* 1874; European War 1914-15 (despatches, DSO); appointed Parliamentary Private Sec to the Leader of the Opposition in the House of Commons (Rt Hon A. Bonar Law, MP) 1911, Parliamentary Representative of Air Board 1916, Parliamentary Under-Sec of State to Air Min 1918, and Joint Parliamentary Sec to Min of Munitions 1919 (but declined); was Parliamentary Under-Sec of State, Home Depart 1919-22, First Commr of Works (also Min of Transport) 1922-4, Gov-Gen and Com-in-Ch of Commonwealth of Australia 1925-30, and Chm of Conservative Party 1931-6; sat as MP for Warwickshire, Rugby Div (C) 1910-22, and for Ayr 1922-5; *cr Baron Stonehaven*, of Ury, co Kincardine (peerage of United Kingdom) 1925, and *Viscount Stonehaven*, of Ury, co Kincardine (peerage of United Kingdom) 1938: *m* 1905, Lady Ethel Sydney Keith-Falconer (who *d* 1974, having *s* as Countess of Kintore 1966) da of 9th Earl of Kintore; *d* 1941, *s* by his el son (3) (JAMES) IAN, 2nd Viscount (see ante).

KIRKHILL, BARON (Smith) (Life Baron 1975)

JOHN FARQUHARSON SMITH, son of Alexander Findlay Smith; *b* 7 May 1930; *ed* Robert Gordon's Colls, Aberdeen; Hon LLD Aberdeen; Lord Provost of Aberdeen 1971-75, Min of State, Scottish Office 1975-79; Delegate to Parliamentary Assembly of COE and WEU since 1981; Chm Cttee on Legal Affairs and Human Rights of the COE since 1991; *cr Baron Kirkhill*, in District of City of Aberdeen (Life Baron) 1975: *m* 1965, Frances Mary Walker Reid.
Residence – 3 Rubislaw Den North, Aberdeen.

KIRKWOOD, BARON (Kirkwood) (Baron UK 1951)

DAVID HARVIE KIRKWOOD, 3rd Baron; *b* 24 Nov 1931; *s* 1970; *ed* Rugby, and Trin Hall, Camb (MA, PhD); CEng: *m* 1965, Judith Rosalie, da of late John Hunt, of Leeds, and has issue.

Arms – Argent, two chevronels round-embattled on their upper edges sable between two oak-sprigs slipped and fructed proper in chief and a cog-wheel azure in base. **Crest** – The bow of a ship afrontée proper. **Supporters** – *Dexter*, an Ayrshire bull; *sinister*, a Clydesdale stallion, both proper, the latter harnessed or.
Residence – 56 Endcliffe Hall Av, Sheffield.

DAUGHTERS LIVING

Hon Ruth Emily, *b* 1966.
Hon Anne Judith, *b* 1969.
Hon Lucy Jennifer, *b* 1972.

BROTHER LIVING

Hon JAMES STUART (The Cearne, Kent Hatch, Crockham Hill, Edenbridge, Kent), *b* 19 June 1937; *ed* Rugby, and at Trin Hall, Camb (MA); FRICS: *m* 1965, Alexandra Mary, da of late Alec Dyson, of Holt, Norfolk, and has issue living, Kate Victoria, *b* 1966, — Georgina Grace, *b* 1969.

WIDOW LIVING OF SECOND BARON

EILEEN GRACE (*Eileen, Baroness Kirkwood*) da of late Thomas Henry Boalch, of Pill, Bristol: *m* 1931, the 2nd Baron, who *d* 1970.

COLLATERAL BRANCHES LIVING

Issue of late John Kirkwood, eldest son of 1st Baron, *b* 1900, *d* 1942: *m* 1932, Ellen Florence, who *d* 1976, da of late Thomas Peter Haggar, of Witham, Essex:—
Jean (288 Warwick Rd, Solihull, W. Midlands), *b* 1935.

Issue of late Robert Smith Kirkwood, 2nd son of 1st Baron, *b* 1901, *d* 1950: *m* 1927, Annie Kerr, who *d* 1963, da of John Marshall, of Shettleston, Glasgow:—
Agnes Young (11 Chesterfield Court, Glasgow, W2), *b* 1930. —— Elizabeth Smith, *b* 1937.

Issue of late Hon James Smith Kirkwood, 4th and yst son of 1st Baron, *b* 1912, *d* 1983: *m* 1944, Mary Helen, who *d* 1970, da of James Marshall, of Elgin:—
David, *b* 1945. —— James Marshall Smith, *b* 1954. —— Elizabeth Joan, *b* 1947, *d* 19—.

PREDECESSORS – (1) *Rt Hon* DAVID Kirkwood, PC, son of late John Kirkwood, of Parkhead, Glasgow; *b* 1872; was Chm of David Kirkwood and Sons, Ltd, of 9 Woodside Place, Glasgow; sat as MP for Dumbarton Burghs (*Lab*) 1922-50, and for E Div of Dunbartonshire 1950-51; *cr Baron Kirkwood*, of Bearsden, co Dunbarton (peerage of United Kingdom) 1951: *m* 1899, Elizabeth, da of Robert Smith, of Parkhead, Glasgow; *d* 1955; *s* by his 3rd (but el surviving) son (2) DAVID, 2nd Baron; *b* 1903: *m* 1931, Eileen Grace, da of late Thomas Henry Boalch, of Pill, Bristol; *d* 1970; *s* by his el son (3) DAVID HARVIE, 3rd Baron and present peer.

KISSIN, BARON (Kissin) (Life Baron 1974)

HARRY KISSIN, son of Israel Kissin; *b* 23 Aug 1912; *ed* Danzig, and Univ of Basle (LLD); Life Pres GPG plc (formerly Guinness Peat Group plc) since 1979, Pres Lewis & Peat Holdings Ltd since 1987; Pres Guinness Mahon Holdings plc since 1988; Chm Lewis & Peat Ltd 1961-73, Guinness Peat Group 1973-79, Lewis & Peat Holdings Ltd 1982-87; Linfood Holdings 1974-81; Esperanza International Services plc 1970-83; Dir Transcontinental Services NV 1982-86; Tycon Spa Venice since 1975; Dir Royal Opera House Covent Garden 1973-84; Trustee: Royal Opera House Trust 1974-87 (Chm 1974-80) Chmn Council Inst of Contemporary Arts 1968-75; Gov Bezalel Academy of Arts & Design 1975-; Hebrew University of Jerusalem 1980-; Cdr Ordem Nacional do Cruzeiro do Sul (Brazil) 1977; Chev Légion d'Honneur (France) 1981; *cr Baron Kissin*, of Camden, in Greater London (Life Baron) 1974: *m* 1935, Ruth Deborah, da of Siegmund Samuel, and has issue.

Arms – Or, between two chevronels, three mullets, six points gules, a chief chequy argent and gules, thereon a pale gules charged with a pair of scales gold. Crest – A lion sejant erect or, winged gules, on the breast the Hebrew letter ‎   gules, reposing the sinister paw upon a cornucopia, head downwards, discharging fruit all gold. Supporters – *Dexter*, a lion rampant guardant or, maned, the tail tufted gules and *sinister*, a bulldog guardant proper; both crowned with a mural crown chequy gules and argent, issuing therefrom a mullet of six points gules.
Address – c/o House of Lords, SW1. *Clubs* – Reform, East India, Sports and Public Schools.

SON LIVING

Hon Robert David (34 Cadogan Place, SW1X 9RX), *b* 1947: *m* 1976, Lesley Chapman, and has issue living, Alexander Jonathan Toby, *b* 1985, — Samantha Rose, *b* 1984.

DAUGHTER LIVING

Hon Evelyn Anne, *b* 1944: *m* 1972, Jack Donald Singer, MD, FAAPaed, of 45 Campden Hill Court, Campden Hill Rd, W8, and has issue, Jeremy, *b* 1974, — Juliet, *b* 1978.

KITCHENER OF KHARTOUM AND OF BROOME, EARL (Kitchener) (Earl UK 1914)

HENRY HERBERT KITCHENER, TD, 3rd Earl; *b* 24 Feb 1919; *s* 1937; *ed* Winchester, and at Trin Coll, Camb; a Page of Honour at Coronation of King George VI; a DL for Cheshire; Maj (ret) R Signals (TA).

Arms – Gules, between three bustards close proper a chevron azure, cotised argent. **Crest** – A stag's head couped, the neck transfixed by an arrow proper between the attires a horseshoe or. **Supporters** – *Dexter*, a camel proper, bridle trappings and line pendent reflexed over the back gules, gored with a collar or suspended therefrom an escutcheon paly bendy azure and ermine, a canton of the last charged with a portcullis gold; *sinister*, a gnu proper gorged with a collar or suspended therefrom an escutcheon ermine charged with a chevron engrailed vert thereon four horseshoes or.
Residence – Westergate Wood, Eastergate, Chichester, W Sussex PO2O 6SB.
Club – Brooks's.

SISTER LIVING (*Raised to the rank of an Earl's daughter* 1938)

Lady Kenya Eleanor, *b* 1923; late 3rd Officer WRNS; BA, MCSP, SRP; Chartered Physiotherapist in private practice since 1971: *m* 1947, as his 2nd wife, John Stewart Tatton-Brown, who *d* 1971, and has issue living, Margaret Caroline, *b* 1950: *m* 1984, A. John Aanonson, son of A. W. Aanonson, of Hornsey, — (Adela) Charlotte, *b* 1951: *m* 1982, Patrick B. Appleby, of Shrubs Hill, Itchen Abbas, Winchester, Hants, yr son of late Kenneth Appleby, and has issue living, Charles *b* 1983, Benjamin *b* 1985, James Michael *b* 1988, — Augusta Kenya, *b* 1955: *m* 1976, James D. P. Saunders, of PO Box 149, Jerramungup, 6337 W Australia, and has issue living, Duncan John *b* 1977, Peter Eden *b* 1979.
Residence – Westergate Wood, nr Chichester, Sussex.

WIDOW LIVING OF BROTHER OF THIRD EARL (*who was raised to the rank of an Earl's son* 1938)

Ursula Hope (Croylands, Old Salisbury Lane, Romsey, Hants), da of late Capt Cyril Montagu Luck, CMG, DSO, Roy Indian Navy: *m* 1959, Hon Charles Eaton Kitchener, who *d* 1982, and has issue (infra).

COLLATERAL BRANCH LIVING

Issue of late Hon Charles Eaton Kitchener, yr son of Capt Henry Franklin Chevallier, *Viscount Broome*, RN, only son of 2nd Earl, *b* 1920; *d* 1982: *m* 1959, Ursula Hope Luck (ante):—
Emma Joy, *b* 1963: *m* 1990, Julian Alexander Fellowes, yst son of Peregrine Edward Launcelot Fellowes, of The Court, Chipping Campden, Glos, and has issue living, Peregrine Charles Morant Kitchener, *b* 1991. *Residence* – 15 Moore St, SW3 2QN.

Granddaughters of Lt-Gen Sir Frederick Walter Kitchener, KCB, yr brother of 1st Earl (*in special remainder*) (infra):—
Issue of late Major Henry Hamilton Kitchener, *b* 1890, *d* 1984: *m* 1st, 1916, Winifred Esther Everest, who *d* 1959, el da of Hon A. W. Bluck; 2ndly, 1961, Mrs Gwynneth Champion, who *d* 1983:—
(By 1st *m*) Winifred Jean, *b* 1917: *m* 1954, Lieut Peter John Hall, RN, of Oakfield House, Spreyton, Crediton, Devon EX17 5AL, and has issue living, Christopher Peter, *b* 1955: *m* 1981, Sarah Jane Downs, and has issue living, James Henry *b* 1985, Robert Hamilton *b* 1987, George Howard *b* 1990. —— Eleanor Elizabeth Madge (86 Waller Cres, Campbell, ACT 2601, Australia), *b* 1920: *m* 1947, Louis Norman Cornhill, who *d* 1971, and has issue living, Peter Robert, *b* 1949, — Robert Louis Henry, *b* 1953.

Issue of late Lieut-Gen Sir Frederick Walter Kitchener, KCB, yr brother of 1st Earl, *b* 1858, *d* 1912: *m* 1884, Caroline, who *d* of Major Fenton, 9th and 53rd Regts:—
Philippa Chevallier, *b* 1895: *m* 1917, Brig Terence Desmond Murray, CBE, DSO, MC, late Roy Tank Corps, who *d* 1961, and has had issue, Molly Patricia, *b* 1919: *m* 19—, and *d* 19—, leaving issue, two das, — Sybil Madge, *b* 1921: *m* 19—, and has issue living, three sons, — Sheila Chevallier, *b* 1926: *m* 19—, Michael Butler, of St Neot, Cornwall. *Address* – c/o Hoare & Co, 37 Fleet St, EC4.

PREDECESSORS – (1) *Field Marshal Rt Hon Sir* HORATIO HERBERT Kitchener, KG, KP, GCB, OM, GCSI, GCMG, GCIE, second son of late Lieut-Col Henry Horatio Kitchener (13th Dragoons), of Cossington, Leicester; *b* 1850; served in Soudan Campaign 1883-5, being DAA and QMG 1884-5 (despatches frequently, medal with clasp, 3rd class Osmanieh), in command of troops at action of Handoub 1888 (severely wounded, 2nd class Medjidie), a Brig of Soudanese troops at action of Gemaizah, Suakin, 1888 (despatches, clasp). Mounted troops at action of Toski on the Nile 1889 (despatches, clasp, CB), Dongola Expedition 1896 (despatches, Grand Cordon Osmanieh, promoted Maj-Gen), Nile Expedition 1897 (despatches) and 1898 (despatches), and Soudan Campaign 1898, present at battle of Omdurman, recapture of Khartoum, and subsequent expedition to Fashoda (Khedive's medal with five clasps, peerage, GCB, specially thanked by both Houses of Parliament, granted £30,000), and in S Africa 1899-1902 first as Ch-of-the-Staff (despatches twice, GCMG), and subsequently as Com-in-Ch (thanked by Parliament, promoted Gen, *cr* Viscount, granted £50,000), and acted as High Commr of S Africa, and Administrator of Transvaal and of Orange River Colony 1901; employed on Palestine Survey 1874-8, and on Cyprus Survey 1878-9 (awarded Livingstone gold medal 1915); Director of Survey, Cyprus 1880-82, Vice-Consul in Anatolia 1879-80, in command of Egyptian Cavalry 1882-4, HM Queen Victoria's Commr for delimitation of territory of Sultan of Zanzibar 1885, Gov of Suakin 1886-8 (2nd class Medjidie), ADC to HM Queen Victoria 1888-96, and AG and 2nd in command of Egyptian Army, as well as Inspector-Gen of Police 1888-92 (2nd class Osmanieh), Sirdar of Egyptian Army 1892-99 (1st class Medjidie and Osmanieh), Gov-Gen of the Soudan 1899, and Com-in-Ch in India and a Member of Viceroy's Council 1902-9, Agent and Consul-Gen in Egypt 1911-14, and Sec of State for War 1914-16 (forming during European War "Kitchener's Army"); *cr Baron Kitchener of Khartoum*, and of Aspall, co Suffolk (peerage of United Kingdom) 1898, and *Viscount Kitchener of Khartoum*, and of the Vaal, Colony of the Transvaal, and of Aspall, co Suffolk (peerage of United Kingdom) 1902, with remainder to the heirs male of his body, and in default of such issue with remainder (i) to his first daughter and the heirs male of her body, (ii) to his other daughters and the heirs male of their bodies (infra), and (iii) in default of such issue, with remainder to his elder brother, Henry Elliott Chevallier Kitchener, and the heirs male of his body, and (iv) with remainder to his yr brother, Frederick Walter Kitchener, and the heirs male of his body, and *Earl Kitchener of Khartoum and of Broome, Viscount Broome*, of Broome, co Kent, and *Baron Denton*, of Denton, co Kent (peerage of United Kingdom) 1914 with similar special remainders to the above-mentioned; *d* on active ser 1916 when the Barony *cr* 1898 became ext and he was *s* (under the special remainder) in the other peerages by his el brother (2) HENRY ELLIOTT CHEVALLIER, 2nd Earl; *b* 1846; Col (ret); formerly Lieut-Col Duke of Cornwall's LI; France 1870 (medal), Burma 1891 (despatches, medal with clasp),

Manipur Expedition 1891 (despatches, clasp), European War 1914-17 (1914 star, two medals, Croix de Guerre); was DAAG, Jamaica 1893-8; sometime Col Comdg W India Regt Depôt: *m* 1877, Eleanor Fanny, who *d* 1897, only child of late Lieut-Col Franklin Lushington, CB; *d* 1937; *s* by his grandson **(3)** Henry Herbert (son of late Capt Henry Franklin Chevallier, Viscount Broome, only son of 2nd Earl), 3rd Earl and present peer; also Viscount Kitchener of Khartoum, Viscount Broome, and Baron Denton.

Knebworth, Viscount; son of Earl of Lytton.

KNIGHTS, BARON (Knights) (Life Baron 1987)

Philip Douglas Knights, CBE, QPM, son of late Thomas James Knights, of Ottershaw, Surrey; *b* 3 Oct 1920; *ed* King's Sch, Grantham, and Police Staff Coll; DL W Midlands 1985; Sergt Lincs Constabulary 1946, Home Office 1946-50, Inspector Lincs Constabulary 1953, Supt 1955, Chief Supt 1957, Assist Chief Constable Birmingham City Police 1959, Home Office and Dep Comdt Police Coll 1962-66, Dep Chief Constable Birmingham City Police 1970, Chief Constable Sheffield and Rotherham Constabulary 1972-74, S Yorks Police 1974-75, and W Midlands Police 1975-85; Pres Assocn of Chief Police Offiers 1978-79, Trustee Police Foundation since 1979, Member Advisory Council Cambridge Inst of Criminology since 1986, Member of Council Aston Univ since 1985; served 1939-45 War in RAF; CBIM, QPM (1964), OBE (1971), CBE (1976), Knt 1980, *cr Baron Knights*, of Edgbaston, co W Midlands (Life Baron) 1987: *m* 1945, Jean, da of late James Henry Burman.
Address – c/o House of Lords, SW1A 0PW.

KNOLLYS, VISCOUNT (Knollys) (Viscount UK 1911)
(Name and Title pronounced "Noles")

IN·UTRUMQUE·PARATUS

In every way prepared

David Francis Dudley Knollys, 3rd Viscount; *b* 12 June 1931; *s* 1966; *ed* Eton; late 2nd Lt Scots Guards: *m* 1959, Hon Sheelin Virginia, da of late Lt-Col Hon Somerset Arthur Maxwell, MP (*see* B Farnham), and has issue.

Arms – Per pale gules and argent a chevron counterchanged and charged with three roses also counterchanged barbed and seeded proper. **Crest** – Between two crosses moline per pale azure and or fimbriated counterchanged an elephant statant argent. **Supporters** – On either side an Heraldic Antelope the dexter argent and sinister or both tufted, horned and unguled sable and charged on the shoulder with a cross as in the Crest.
Residence – The Bailiff's House, Bramerton Hall Farm, Norwich, NR14 7DN, Norfolk. *Club* – White's.

SONS LIVING

Hon Patrick Nicholas Mark, *b* 11 March 1962; *ed* Wymondham Coll, Norfolk, and RMA Sandhurst; commn'd Scots Guards 1982 (ret 1988).
Hon Christopher Edward, *b* 1964; *ed* Exeter Univ (BA); commn'd Scots Guards 1987.
Hon Michael James George, *b* 1968; *ed* Wymondham Coll, Norfolk, and RMA Sandhurst; commn'd Scots Guards 1989.

DAUGHTER LIVING

Hon Clarinda Susan, *b* 1960: *m* 1988, Andrew M. B. Snowball, yr son of late Brig Edward Joseph Dove Snowball, OBE, of Ballochneck, Thornhill, Perthshire, and has issue living, Emma Sheelin, *b* 1992. *Residence* – Mill of Remichie, Dallas, Forres, Moray IV36 0RW.

SISTER LIVING

Hon Ardyne Mary, *b* 1929: *m* 1958, Ronald James Owen, of Paradise Wood, Upper Hartfield, Sussex, and has two das, Sandra Mary, *b* 1953, — Rachel Elizabeth, *b* 1965.

PREDECESSORS – (1) Rt Hon Sir Francis Knollys, GCB, GCVO, KCMG, ISO, second son of late Gen Rt Hon Sir William Thomas Knollys, KCB, PC; *b* 1837; a Gentleman Usher Quarterly Waiter to Queen Victoria 1868-1901, Groom-in-Waiting to the Prince of Wales 1886-1901, and Private Sec to Prince of Wales 1870-1901, and to King Edward VII 1901-10, Joint Private Sec to King George V 1910-13, and a Lord-in-Waiting to Queen Alexandra 1910-24; *cr Baron Knollys*, of Caversham, co Oxford (peerage of UK) 1902, and *Viscount Knollys*, of Caversham, co Oxford (peerage of UK) 1911: *m* 1887, Hon Ardyn, who *d* 1922, who *d* 1987, da of Sir Henry Thomas Tyrwhitt, 3rd Bt; *d* 1924, *s* by his son **(2)** Edward George William Tyrwhitt, GCMG, MBE, DFC, 2nd Viscount, *b* 1895; Gov of Bermuda 1941-43, Chm of BOAC 1943-47, of Vickers Ltd 1956-62, and of Northern and Employers Assurance Co 1954-66: *m* 1928, Margaret Mary Josephine, who *d* 1987, da of Sir Stuart Auchinloss Coats, 2nd Bt; *d* 1966, *s* by his son **(3)** David Francis Dudley, 3rd Viscount, and present peer; also Baron Knollys.

KNUTSFORD, VISCOUNT (Holland-Hibbert) (Viscount UK 1895, Bt UK 1853)

RESPICE ASPICE PROSPICE

Look backwards, look around, look forwards

MICHAEL HOLLAND-HIBBERT, 6th Viscount, and 7th Baronet, *b* 27 Dec 1926: *s* 1986; *ed* Eton, and Trin Coll, Camb; late Capt Welsh Gds; DL Devon 1977, High Sheriff 1977-78; a Dir Barclays Bank, Exeter 1956-86, Member Nat Trust Exec Cttee and Council 1965-86, and Finance Cttee since 1986: *m* 1951, Hon Sheila Constance Portman, da of 5th Viscount Portman, and has issue.

Arms – Quarterly, 1st and 4th ermine, on a bend nebuly sable three crescents argent, in the sinister chief point a cross bottonée fitchée of the second, *Hibbert*; 2nd and 3rd per pale argent and azure, semée-de-lis, a lion rampant guardant all counterchanged, the whole debruised by a bendlet engrailed gules, *Holland*. Crests – 1st, in front of a dexter cubit arm erect proper, vested azure, cuff ermine, holding in the hand a crescent argent a demi catherine wheel also argent, *Hibbert*; 2nd, out of a crown vallery or, a demi-lion guardant per bend argent and azure, debruised by a bendlet engrailed counterchanged, and holding in the dexter paw a fleur-de-lis of the second, *Holland*. Supporters – Two lions guardant argent gutée de larmes, each charged on the body with two fleur-de-lis in fesse between bars-geme engrailed azure.
Residence – Broadclyst House, Exeter, Devon.

SONS LIVING

Hon HENRY THURSTAN, *b* 6 April 1959; *ed* Eton, and RAC Cirencester; Lieut Coldm Gds: *m* 1988, Katherine, da of Sir John Bruce Woollacott Ropner, 2nd Bt (*cr* 1952), and has issue living, Thomas Arthur, *b* 15 Dec 1992, — Rosanna (Rosie) Sarah, *b* 1990. *Residence* – Munden, Watford, Herts WD2 7PZ.

Hon James Edward, *b* 1967; *ed* Eton.

DAUGHTER LIVING

Hon Lucy Katherine, *b* 1956: *m* 1979, Mark Charles Liddell, yr son of late Peter John Liddell, DSC, of Moorhouse Hall, Warwick-on-Eden, Carlisle, and has issue living, James Peter, *b* 1987, — Katherine Alexandra, *b* 1983, — Sophie Charlotte, *b* 1990. *Residence* – Cumrew House, Cumrew, Carlisle.

SISTERS LIVING

Lavinia, *b* 1919; served 1939-45 War as Jun Com ATS: *m* 1953, Maj Peter John Orde, 15th/19th King's Roy Hussars (ret), son of Sir Percy Lancelot Orde, CIE, and has two adopted children, Justin Robert, *b* 1957; *ed* Stowe, and RMA Sandhurst, — Clarissa Mary, *b* 1958: *m* 1989, Andrew Windsor Latchmore, of The Old School House, Weeton, nr Leeds, N Yorks LS17 0AW, son of Arthur John Craig Latchmore, MBE, FRCS, of Linton, Wetherby, Yorks, and has issue living, Max Andrew *b* 1993, Chlöe Roseanna *b* 1991. *Residence* – Newbrough Park, Hexham, Northumberland.

Delia Mary, *b* 1922; served 1939-45 War as 3rd Officer WRNS: *m* 1946, Lt-Col William McGhie Cunningham, LVO, OBE, MC, late 11th Hussars, who *d* 1992, elder son of James Scott Cunningham, of Auchendarroch, Wishaw, Lanarkshire, and has issue living, Jeremy James, *b* 1948; *ed* Eton, and Pembroke Coll, Oxford, — Mark William, *b* 1950; *ed* Eton, and New Coll, Oxford, — Lavinia Mary, *b* 1952. *Residence* – Southfield Farm, Wigginton, Banbury, Oxon.

COLLATERAL BRANCHES LIVING

(In remainder to the Baronetcy only)

Grandchildren of Capt Michael James Holland, MC (*infra*):—
Issue of late Antony Francis Holland, MC, *b* 1913, *d* 1982: *m* 1946, Ann (Lullings, Balcombe, Sussex), da of Henry Faure Walker, of Highley Manor, Sussex:—
Thurstan James, *b* 1948; *ed* Eton, and Nottingham Univ: *m* 1987, Elizabeth Joan Serena, 2nd da of late Alistair Philip Cobbold, of Holbrook Lodge, Ipswich, Suffolk (*see* M Abergavenny, colls, 1958 Edn), and has issue living, Frederick Thurstan Alistair *b* 1991. *Residence* – Old Lullings, Balcombe, Sussex RH17 6QY. —— Anthea, *b* 1947: *m* 1973, John St Andrew Warde, of Squerryes Court, Westerham, Kent, and has issue living, Charles Anthony, *b* 1974, — Henry John, *b* 1976, — Anne Charlotte, *b* 1982. —— Arabella Ann, *b* 1956.

Grandchildren of late Rev Francis James Holland, brother of 1st Viscount:—
Issue of late Capt Michael James Holland, MC, *b* 1870, *d* 1956: *m* 1911, Marion Ada Flora, who *d* 1969, da of late H. J. T. Broadwood, of Lyne, Horsham, Sussex:—
David Cuthbert Lyall, CB, *b* 1915; *ed* Eton, and at Trin Coll, Camb; late Roy Sussex Regt; Librarian, House of Commons 1967-76; CB (Civil) 1976: *m* 1949, Rosemary, da of David Llewellyn Griffiths, OBE, and has had issue, *Rev* Matthew Francis, *b* 1952; *ed* Eton, LSE, and Queen's Coll, Birmingham: *m* 1979, Jayne Emerson, and has issue living, Joseph John *b* 1988, Bridget Mary *b* 1984, Caitlin Frances *b* 1986, — Peter Gwinnell, *b* 1954, *d* 1983, — Lucinda Jane, *b* (twin) 1954: *m* 1977, Paul Carpenter, and has issue living, William James *b* 1978. *Residence* – The Barn, Milton St, Polegate, E Sussex. *Club* – Athenaeum.

PREDECESSORS – (1) HENRY Holland; *b* 1788; Physician in Ordinary to HM Queen Victoria 1850-73, and to HRH the Prince Consort 1840-61, was *cr* a *Baronet* 1853: *m* 1st, 1822, Margaret Emma, who *d* 1830, da of James Caldwell of Linley Wood, co Stafford; 2ndly, 1834, Saba, who *d* 1866, da of Rev Sydney Smith, Canon of St Paul's; *d* 1873; *s* by his el son (2) HENRY THURSTAN, GCMG, PC, 2nd baronet; *b* 1825; Legal Adviser to Colonial Office 1867-70, Assist Under-Sec there 1870-74, Financial Sec to Treasury 1885, Vice-Pres of Committee of Council on Education Sept 1885 to Jan 1886, and July 1886 to Jan 1887, and Sec of State for Colonies Jan 1887 to Aug 1892; MP for Midhurst (*C*) 1874-85, and for Hampstead 1885-8; *cr* PC 1885, GCMG 1886, *Baron Knutsford*, of Knutsford, Cheshire (peerage of United Kingdom) 1888, and *Viscount Knutsford*, of Knutsford, Cheshire (peerage of United Kingdom) 1895: *m* 1st, 1852, Elizabeth Margaret, who *d* 1855, da of Nathaniel

Hibbert, of Munden, Watford, Herts; 2ndly, 1858, Margaret Jean (a Lady of Justice of Order of St John of Jerusalem in England), who *d* 1906, el da of Sir Charles Edward Trevelyan, KCB, 1st Bt; *d* 1914; *s* by his el son (2) SYDNEY GEORGE, 2nd Viscount, *b* 19 March 1855; many years Chm of London Hospital: *m* 1883, Lady Mary Ashburnham, who *d* 1947, da of 4th Earl of Ashburnham; *d* 1931; *s* by his twin brother (3) ARTHUR HENRY Holland-Hibbert, 3rd Viscount, *b* (twin) 19 March 1855; High Sheriff of Herts 1891; assumed by Roy licence 1876, the additional surname and arms of Hibbert: *m* 1884, Ellen, who *d* 1949, el da of Sir Wilfrid Lawson, 2nd Bt (*cr* 1831); *d* 1935; *s* by his el son (4) THURSTAN, 4th Viscount; *b* 1888: *m* 1912, Viola Mary, who *d* 1954, da of late Thomas Meadows Clutterbuck, of Putteridge Bury, Herts, and Micklefield Hall, Rickmansworth, Herts; *d* 1976; *s* by his son (5) JULIAN THURSTAN, CBE, 5th Viscount, *b* 1920; Lt Coldm Gds; JP for Herts; served 1939-45 War (wounded); *d* 1986; *s* by his cousin (6) MICHAEL (son of Hon Wilfrid Holland-Hibbert, 2nd son of 3rd Viscount), 6th Viscount and present peer; also Baron Knutsford.

KYLSANT, BARONY OF (Philipps) (Extinct 1937)

DAUGHTERS LIVING OF FIRST BARON

Hon Nesta Donne, *b* 1903; a DL of Carmarthenshire; 1939-45 War as Ch Com, ATS: *m* 1st, 1921, the 10th Earl of Coventry, who was *ka* 1940; 2ndly, 1953, Maj Terrance Vincent Fisher-Hoch, RA.
Hon Olwen Gwynne, *b* 1905: *m* 1st, 1925 (*m diss* 1937), the 7th Baron Suffield; 2ndly, 1937, Lieut-Col Frank Richard Peter Barker, who *d* 1974, and has issue living, (by 2nd *m*) Timothy Gwynne (Beadles Hall, Chignal Smealey, Chelmsford, Essex), *b* 1940: *m* 1964, Philippa Rachel Mary, da of Brig Mervyn Christopher Thursby-Pelham, of Ridgeland House, Finchampstead, Berks, and has issue living, Christopher Gwynne *b* 1970, Camilla Gwynne *b* 1968. *Residence* – Orchar House, Nawton, York.

LAING OF DUNPHAIL, BARON (Laing) (Life Baron 1991)

HECTOR LAING, son of Hector Laing, of Edinburgh, by his late wife, Margaret Norris, da of Sir Alexander Grant, 1st Bt (ext 1947); *b* 12 May 1923; *ed* Loretto, and Jesus Coll, Camb; Hon DUniv Stirling and Heriot Watt; FRSE 1989; served European War 1939-45 as Capt Scots Guards 1942-47 (American Bronze Star, despatches 1944); joined McVitie & Price 1947 (Chm 1963), Dir United Biscuits 1953 (Man Dir 1964, Chm United Biscuits (Holdings) plc, 1972-90), Chm Food and Drink Industries Council 1977-79, Scottish Business in the Community 1982-90, City and Industrial Liaison Council 1985-94, and Business in the Community 1987-91; Dir Bank of England 1973-91 and Exxon Corpn Inc 1984-94; Gov Wycombe Abbey 1981-94; Pres Project Trident 1992-94; Treas Conservative Party 1988-93, Chm Trustees The Lambeth Fund 1983, and Joint Chm The Per Cent Club 1986-90; Trustee Royal Botanic Gardens, Kew Foundation, 1990; *cr* Knt 1978, and *Baron Laing of Dunphail*, of Dunphail, District of Moray (Life Baron) 1991: *m* 1950, Marian Clare, da of Maj-Gen Sir John Emilius Laurie, 6th Bt, CBE, DSO, and has issue.

𝕬rms – Per pale Or and Gules, a chief counterchanged. 𝕮rest – a dexter cubit arm issuant cuffed as in the Arms grasping a dagger Proper hilted and pommelled Or all paleways. 𝕾upporters – two Pekinese dogs guardant Proper.
Residence – High Meadows, Windsor Rd, Gerrards Cross, Bucks SL9 8ST. *Club* – White's.

SONS LIVING

Hon Mark Hector, *b* 1951; *ed* Eton, and Selwyn Coll, Camb: *m* 1980, Susanna Anson, da of John Anson Crawford, of Chatton Lodge, 108 Hepburn Gdns, St Andrews, Fife, and has issue living, Hector Grant, *b* 1988, — Kathryn Rose, *b* 1983, — Georgina Clare, *b* 1985. *Residence* – The White House, Totley Wells, by Winchburg, W Lothian EH52 6QJ.
Hon Robert John, *b* 1953; *ed* Eton, and Selwyn Coll, Camb: *m* 1992, Mrs Fiona M. Nunneley, da of late Freddy Grant, of Church House, Washington, Sussex. *Residence* – Humbie House, Humbie, E Lothian EH36 5PB.
Hon Anthony Rupert, *b* 1955: *ed* Eton: *m* 1985, Fiona, yr da of John Brooke-Hunt, of Bairnkine Lodge, Jedburgh, Roxburghshire, and has issue living, Rupert Andrew, *b* 1986, — Christopher Hector, *b* 1988, — Rebecca Claire, *b* 1990. *Residence* – 14 Saxe Coburg Place, Edinburgh EH3 5BR.

LAMBERT, VISCOUNT (Lambert) (Viscount UK 1945)

THE GOOD EARTH PROVIDES

MICHAEL JOHN LAMBERT, 3rd Viscount; *b* 29 Sept 1912; *s* 1989: *m* 1939, Florence Dolores, da of late Nicholas Lechmere Cunningham Macaskie, QC, and has issue.

Arms – Azure, a chevron or fretty of the first between, in chief two garbs and in base a fleece of the second. Crest – Issuant from a mount vert an apple tree fructed proper. Supporters – On either side of a Cornish chough proper collared or.
Residence – Casanuova di Barontoli, 53010 S Roccu a Pilli, Siena, Italy.

DAUGHTERS LIVING

Hon Sophia Jane, *b* 1943.
Hon Caelia Anne Georgiana, *b* 1946: *m* 1971 (*m diss* 1985), Emmanuel Irismir Pereira, and has issue living, Joaquim Michael, *b* 1975, — Antonia Catarina, *b* 1972. *Residence* – 60 Bolingbroke Rd, W14.
Hon Flavia Mary, *b* 1949. *Residence* – 9 Alwyne Rd, Canonbury, N1.

DAUGHTER LIVING OF SECOND VISCOUNT

Hon Louise Barbara (*Hon Lady Gibbings*), *b* 1944: *m* 1975, Sir Peter Walter Gibbings, of 10 The Vale, Chelsea, SW3, and has issue living, Dominic George Lambert, *b* 1976.

SISTERS LIVING

Hon Grace Mary, *b* 1905.
Hon Margaret Barbara, CMG, *b* 1906, BA Oxon; PhD London; CMG 1965. *Residence* – 39 Thornhill Rd, N1.

PREDECESSORS – (1) *Rt Hon* GEORGE Lambert, son of late George Lambert; *b* 1866; Capt 3rd Batn Devonshire Regt; Civil Lord of the Admiralty 1905-15; was a County Councillor for Devonshire 1889-1912, and a County Alderman 1912-52; sat as MP for N, or S Molton, Div; of Devonshire (*L*) 1891-1918, and for S Molton Div of Devon 1918-24, and 1929-45; *cr Viscount Lambert*, of South Molton, co Devon (peerage of United Kingdom) 1945: *m* 1904, Barbara, who *d* 1963, da of late George Stavers, of Morpeth; *d* 1958; *s* by his el son (2) GEORGE, TD, 2nd Viscount, *b* 1909, Lt-Col TA, served 1939-45 War, Chm Devon and Exeter Savings Bank 1959-70, Pres National Federation of Young Farmers' Clubs 1968-70, DL Devon 1969, MP for S Molton Div of Devon (*L*) 1945-50 and for Torrington Div of Devon (*Nat L* and *C*) 1950-58: *m* 1939, Patricia Mary, who *d* 1991, da of late Joseph Francis Quinn, of London; *d* 1989 (his only son, Hon George Lambert, *b* 1941, Capt RHG, *d* 1970); *s* by his brother (3) MICHAEL JOHN, 3rd Viscount and present peer.

Lambton, Viscount, see Earldom of Durham.

LAMBURY, BARONY OF (Lord) (Extinct 1967)

DAUGHTERS LIVING OF FIRST BARON

Hon Joan Marquerite, *b* 1927: *m* 1st, 1951 (*m diss* 1965), Miles Lucas Breeden; 2ndly, 1966, Angus James Macdonald, and has issue living, (by 1st *m*) Guy Charles, *b* 1953, — Gail Amanda, *b* 1956.
Hon Patricia Ann, *b* 1929: *m* 1951 (*m diss* 1968), Capt Morfryn James Howard-Smith, RN, and has issue living, Nigel Philip, *b* 1954, — Susan Merilyn, *b* 1952.
Hon Pauline Ruth, *b* 1931: *m* 1954 (*m diss* 1974), John Pither, and has issue living, Steven Edward, *b* 1957: *m* 1988, Fiona, eldest da of Brian Young, of Chalfont St Giles, Bucks, — Gary John, *b* 1959. *Residence* – Appletree Farmhouse, Chorleywood Common, Herts.

LANE, BARON (Lane) (Life Baron 1979)

GEOFFREY DAWSON LANE, PC, AFC, son of late Percy Albert Lane of Lincoln; *b* 17 July 1918; *ed* Shrewsbury, and Trin Coll, Camb; Bar Gray's Inn 1946, and QC 1962; a Judge of High Court of Justice (Queen's Bench Div) 1966-74; a Lord Justice of Appeal 1974-79, a Lord of Appeal in Ordinary 1979-80, Lord Ch Justice of England 1980-92; 1939-45 War Sqdn-Ldr RAF; AFC (1943); *cr* Knt 1966, PC 1974, and *Baron Lane*, of St Ippollitts, co Hertfordshire (Life Baron) 1979: *m* 1944, Jan, da of Donald Macdonald, and has issue.
Address – c/o Messrs Child & Co, 1 Fleet St, EC4.

SON LIVING

Hon Richard, *b* 1948.

LANE OF HORSELL, BARON (Lane) (Life Baron 1990)

PETER STEWART LANE, son of late Leonard George Lane; *b* 29 Jan 1925; *ed* Sherborne; Sub-Lieut RNVR 1943-46; JP Surrey since 1976; FCA, Senior Partner BDO Binder Hamlyn, Chartered Accountants, 1979-92, Chm Brent International since 1985, Attwoods plc since 1994, and Elswick since 1993, Dep Chm More O'Ferrall since 1985; Gov Nuffield Nursing Homes Trust 1985-92, since when Chm; Chm Exec Cttee Nat Union of Conservative Assocns 1986-91; Freeman City of London; cr Knt 1984, and *Baron Lane of Horsell*, of Woking, co Surrey (Life Baron) 1990: *m* 1951, Doris Florence, who *d* 1969, da of late Robert Simpson Botsford, and has issue.

𝕬rms – Per pale and per chevron azure and or counterchanged, on a chevron gules three leopard's heads or langued azure all between as many mullets of six points also counterchanged and pierced of the field. 𝕮rest – A demi-lion azure, head and mane or, charged on the body with pierced mullets each of six points also or and supporting by both forepaws a branch of oak fructed of five acorns gold. 𝕾upporters – *Dexter*, A male griffin regardant argent its head, neck, mane and forelegs or rayed also or beaked argent and holding in the beak a double warded key bow downwards gold; *sinister*- A strawberry roan horse proper maned and hooved or its head elevated and regardant holding in its jaws a double warded key bow downwards gold, the compartment comprising a grassy mount raised on each side and growing therefrom two springs of oak each fructed of an acorn gold.
Address – c/o House of Lords, SW1. *Clubs* – Boodle's, MCC.

DAUGHTERS LIVING

Hon Rosalie (*Baroness Trefgarne*), *b* 1946: *m* 1968, 2nd Baron Trefgarne, and has issue. *Address* – c/o National Westminster Bank, Woking, Surrey.
Hon Alexandra, *b* 1956: *m* 1978, Rev Jeremy Peter Cresswell, and has issue living, Caroline Ruth Anastasia, *b* 1981, — Lucinda Miriam Charlotte, *b* 1983, — Alice Mary Clementine, *b* 1987. *Address* – c/o Lloyds Bank, Woking, Surrey.

LANESBOROUGH, EARL OF (Butler) (Earl I 1756)

DENIS ANTHONY BRIAN BUTLER, TD, 9th Earl; *b* 28 Oct 1918; *s* (Aug) 1950; Maj RA (TA), a JP and DL for Leics: *m* 1939 (*m diss* 1950), Bettyne Ione, only da of late Sir (William) Lindsay Everard, JP, DL, MP (V Hawarden, colls), and has had issue.

𝕬rms – Argent, three covered cups between two bendlets engrailed, sable. 𝕮rest – A demi-cockatrice couped vert, combed, beaked, wattled, and ducally gorged or, wings elevated argent. 𝕾upporters – *Dexter*, a cockatrice vert, wings elevated argent, ducally gorged or, comb, beak, and wattles also gold; *sinister*, a wyvern vert, plain collared and chained or.
Seat – Alton Lodge, Kegworth, Derby.

DAUGHTERS LIVING AND DECEASED

Hon Georgina Ione, *b* 1941; *d* 1947.
(*Lady*) Denyne Gillian Patricia (does not use courtesy title), *b* 1945; Canadian citizen since 1970. *Residence* – 12294 Imperial Drive, Richmond, BC, Canada V7E 6J6.

COLLATERAL BRANCHES LIVING

Granddaughters of late Capt Hon Francis Almeric Butler (infra):—
Issue of late Cdr Terence Brinsley John Danvers Butler, RN, *b* 1913, *d* 1987: *m* 1st, 1937 (*m diss* 1947), Hermione, only child of late Cdr T. C. H. Williams, RN; 2ndly, 1947 (*m diss* 1970), Beryl, da of late George Trotter, and formerly wife of Frederick Kennedy Axten; 3rdly, 1972, Mrs Jacqueline Balmer, da of late Winthrop Greene, of Washington, DC:—
(By 1st *m*) Valentine Gay, *b* 1939: *m* 1st, 1964 (*m diss* 1973), Arthur Clyde Nicholson, of Ponder, Texas, USA; 2ndly, 1975, Desmond Waterstone, of 3 Greenfield Manor, Greenfield Park, Donnybrook, Dublin 4, son of John Waterstone, of Caterham, Surrey, and has issue living (by 1st *m*), Felicity, *b* 1969, — (by 2nd *m*) Simon John, *b* 1975, — Harry Desmond, *b* 1978. —— (By 2nd *m*) (Clemency Anne) Susan (Birstwith House, Birstwith, Harrogate, N Yorks), *b* 1949; MA Oxon, CPA: *m* 1974, John Behrens, son of late Col William Edward Boaz Behrens, of Swinton Grange, Malton, N Yorks, and has issue living, Timothy Edward John, *b* 1978, — Georgina Emily Caroline, *b* 1976. —— Charlotte Gabrielle, *b* 1951: *m* 1983, Marek Skuratowitcz, of Poland, and has issue living, Sophia Lara, *b* 1986. —— Perryn Joanna, *b* 1953: *m* 1984, Robert Hughes, and has issue living, Felix, *b* 1988, — Ramsey, *b* 1989. —— Teresa Jane, *b* 1959; MSc; *d* 1989.

Issue of late Capt Hon Francis Almeric Butler, 3rd son of 6th Earl, *b* 1872, *d* 1925: *m* 1902, Madeline Sarah, who *d* 1961, da of late Richard Birkett Gibbs;—
Maida Daughne Laurel, *b* 1906: *m* 1928, Com Christopher Bryan Stracey Clitherow, DSC, RN, who *d* 1977 (*see* Stracey, Bt, colls). *Residence* – The Mill Cottage, Frogmore, East Meon, Petersfield, Hants.

PREDECESSORS – **(1)** Rt Hon THEOPHILUS Butler, successively MP for co Cavan and for Belturbet; *cr Baron of Newtown Butler*, of co Fermanagh (peerage of Ireland) 1715, with remainder to the heirs male of his father; *dsp* 1723; *s* by his brother **(2)** BRINSLEY, PC, 2nd Baron; successively Gentleman Usher of the Black Rod, Col of the battle-axe Guards, and MP for Kells and Belturbet; *cr Viscount Lanesborough* (peerage of Ireland) 1728; *d* 1735; *s* by his son **(3)** Rt Hon HUMPHREY, 2nd Viscount; was sometime MP for Belturbet, and Dep Speaker of Irish House of commons; *cr Earl of Lanesborough* (peerage of Ireland) 1756; *d* 1768; *s* by his son **(4)** BRINSLEY, 2nd Earl; was Joint Clerk of the Pipe, MP for co Cavan, and Commr for Revenues; *d* 1779; *s* by his son **(5)** ROBERT HERBERT, 3rd Earl; *d* 1806; *s* by his son **(6)** BRINSLEY, 4th Earl; *d* unmarried 1847; *s* by his cousin **(7)** GEORGE JOHN DANVERS, 5th Earl, el son of late Hon Augustus Richard, 2nd son of 2nd Earl; *d* 1866; *s* by his nephew **(8)** JOHN VANSITTART DANVERS (son of Capt Hon Charles Augustus, 6th son of late Hon Augustus Richard (ante), by Letitia Rudyerd Ross, da of late Col John W. Frese), 6th Earl, *b* 1839: *m* 1864, Anne Elizabeth, who *d* 1909, da of late Rev John Dixon Clark, of Belford Hall, Northumberland; *d* 1905; *s* by his el son **(9)** CHARLES JOHN BRINSLEY, MVO, 7th Earl, *b* 1865; a Representative Peer for Ireland; was Assist Mil Sec to Com-in-Ch Mediterranean Forces 1907-9: *m* 1st, 1891, Dorothea Gwladys, who *d* 1920, da of late Maj-Gen Sir Henry Tombs, KCB, VC; 2ndly, 1922, Dorothy Kate, who *d* 1935, da of late James Dean Brand (formerly Mrs Guy Watkins); *d* 1929; *s* by his brother **(10)** HENRY CAVENDISH, 8th Earl, *b* 1868: *m* 1st, 1894, Isabel, who *d* 1905, da of late Ralph Allen Daniell; 2ndly, 1917, Grace Lilian, who *d* 1983, da of Sir Anthony Charles Sykes Abdy, 3rd Bt; *d* 1950; *s* by his el son **(11)** DENIS ANTHONY BRIAN, 9th Earl and present peer; also Viscount Lanesborough, and Baron of Newtown Butler.

LANGFORD, BARON (Rowley-Conwy) (Baron I 1800)

With faith and love

GEOFFREY ALEXANDER ROWLEY-CONWY, OBE, 9th Baron; *b* 8 March 1912; *s* 1953; *ed* Marlborough, and RMA Woolwich; Constable of Rhuddlan Castle, and Lord of the Manor of Rhuddlan; DL of co Clwyd; Freeman City of London; commn'd RA 1932, served 1939-45 War, Singapore (Maj RA, evaded capture) and Burma (Lt-Col Indian Mountain Artillery) 1941-45 (OBE); Staff Coll, Quetta 1945, Berlin Air Lift 1948-49, GSO I 42 Inf Div TA 1949-52 (ret 1957), Hon Col 470 Regt RA TA 1961-67, since when Hon Col; OBE (Mil) 1943: *m* 1st, 1939 (*m diss* 1956), Ruth St John, who *d* 1991, da of late Albert St John Murphy, of the Island House, Little Island, co Cork; 2ndly, 1957, Grete, who *d* 1973, da of late Col E. T. C. von Freiesleben, Danish Army, of Strandvej 104, Snekkersten, Denmark; 3rdly, 1975, Susan, da of C. H. C. Denham, of Wrexham, and has issue by 2nd and 3rd wives.

Arms – Quarterly: 1st and 4th, sable on a bend argent cotised ermine a rose gules barbed and seeded proper between two annulets of the first, *Conwy*, 2nd and 3rd, or on a bend cotised gules three crescents argent, *Rowley*. **Crests** – 1st, a moor's head couped at the shoulders sable wreathed about the temples and tied at the back the ribbons argent and sable, *Conwy*; 2nd, a wolf's head couped at the shoulders sable collared argent, *Rowley*. **Supporters** – *Dexter*, a wolf sable collared and from the collar a chain reflexed over the back argent; *sinister*, a horse argent crined hooved and collared and from the collar a chain reflexed over the back sable.
Residence – Bodrhyddan, Rhuddlan, Clwyd. **Club** – Army and Navy.

SONS LIVING (By 2nd wife)

Hon Peter Alexander (17 St John's Rd, Neville's Cross, Durham), *b* 1951; *ed* Marlborough, and Magdalene Coll, Camb (MA, PhD Archaeology); Lecturer, Durham Univ: *m* 1979, Deborah Jane, only da of Col John H. G. Stevens, late RE, of All Hallows Cottage, Middle St, Brockham, Dorking, and has issue living, Gabrielle Catrin, *b* 1984, — Eleanor, *b* 1986.
Hon John Seymour (66 Fentiman Rd, SW8), *b* 1955; *ed* Marlborough, Magdalene Coll,Camb (BA) and Oriel Coll, Oxford (MSc): *m* 1983, Emma Josephine, da of Maj Peter Brown, of Longworth, Oxon, and has issue living, William Geoffrey Peter, *b* 1988, — Huw Grenville *b* 1993, — Katherine Grete Clare, *b* 1985.
Hon OWAIN GRENVILLE (Aberkinsey, Dyserth, Clwyd), *b* 27 Dec 1958; *ed* Marlborough, and RAC Cirencester: *m* 1986 (*m diss* 1993), Joanna, da of Jack Featherstone, of Cae Siôn, Trefnant, Clwyd, and has issue living, Thomas Alexander, *b* 20 March 1987, — Madeleine Guinevere, *b* 1988.

(By 3rd wife)

Hon Christopher Geoffrey Hugh, *b* 1978.

DAUGHTER LIVING (By 3rd wife)

Hon Charlotte Susan Gabrielle, *b* 1980.

SISTER LIVING (Raised to the rank of a Baron's daughter 1955)

Hon Rose Marian, *b* 1915: *m* 1938, Ralph Becher Skinner, who *d* 1994 and has issue living, David Rafe (28 Natal St, Bellvue East 2198, S Africa), *b* 1939: *m* 1981, Shirley, da of late Francis James Fulton Starrett, — Meriel Ann, *b* 1941: *m* 1963, Jasper M. Garnham, of Harewood Lodge, Bulstrode Way, Gerrards Cross, Bucks, — Rosalind Hope (83 Links Way, Croxley Green, Rickmansworth Herts), *b* 1942. *Residence* – The Fold, Cwm, Dyserth, Clwyd.

PREDECESSORS – **(1)** Hon CLOTWORTHY Taylour, 4th son of 1st Earl of Bective assumed the surname of Rowley, and was *cr Baron Langford*, of Summerhill, co Meath (peerage of Ireland) 1800; *d* 1825; *s* by his son **(2)** HERCULES LANGFORD, 2nd Baron; *d* 1839; *s* by his son **(3)** CLOTWORTHY WELLINGTON WILLIAM ROBERT, 3rd Baron; *b* 1824: *m* 1846, Louisa Augusta, da of late Col Edward Michael Conolly, MP; *d* 1854; *s* by his son **(4)** HERCULES EDWARD ROWLEY, KCVO, 4th Baron, *b* 1848; State Steward to Viceroy of Ireland 1886-92, and Comptroller of the Household to Lord-Lieut of Ireland 1895:1902: *m* 1st, 1889, Georgina Mary, who *d* 1901, da of Sir Richard Sutton, 4th Bt; 2ndly, 1915, Margaret Antonia, who *d* 1976, da of late Rev William Mitchell-Carruthers, of Kingham Hill, Kingham, Oxon; *d* 1919; *s* by his son **(5)** JOHN HERCULES WILLIAM, 5th Baron: *b* 1894; *d* 1922; *s* by his uncle **(6)** WILLIAM CHAMBRE, 6th Baron, *b* 1849: *m* 1889, Hon Mabel Maud Leigh, who *d* 1966, da of

1st Baron Newton; *d* 1931; *s* by his nephew **(7)** CLOTWORTHY WELLINGTON THOMAS EDWARD (son of late Hon Randolfe Thomas Randolfe Thomas Rowley, 3rd son of 3rd Baron), 7th Baron; *b* 1885: *m* 1922, Florence Eileen O'Donovan, who *d* 1989, da of Isaac Shiel, of Dublin; *d* 1952; *s* by his kinsman **(8)** ARTHUR SHOLTO LANGFORD, CMG (son of late Col Hon Hercules Langford Boyle Rowley, 2nd son of 2nd Baron), 8th Baron; *b* 1870; HM's Consul-Gen at Barcelona 1917-23, at Antwerp 1923-30, and Paris 1930-32: *m* 1st, 1908, Margareta Ines, who *d* 1928, da of Hugh R. F. Jameson, of Iquique, Chile; 2ndly, 1929, Maude Alice, who *d* 1958, da of late Henri Lelacheur, of Guernsey; *d* 1953; *s* by his kinsman **(9)** GEOFFREY ALEXANDER (only son of late Maj Geoffrey Seymour Rowley-Conwy (*ka* Gallipoli 1915) (by his wife, Bertha Gabrielle, who *d* 1984, da of Lt Alexander Cochran, RN, of Ashkirk, Selkirkshire), 3rd son of late Capt Conwy Grenville Hercules Rowley-Conwy, only son of late Hon Richard Thomas Rowley, 2nd son of 1st Baron), 9th Baron and present peer.

LANSDOWNE, MARQUESS OF (Mercer Nairne Petty-Fitzmaurice) (Marquess GB 1784)

GEORGE JOHN CHARLES MERCER NAIRNE PETTY-FITZMAURICE, PC, 8th Marquess; *b* 27 Nov 1912; *s* 1944; *ed* Eton, and Ch Ch, Oxford; is a Member of Queen's Body Guard for Scotland (R Company of Archers), a Patron of two livings; a DL for Wilts 1952-73; 1939-45 War as Capt Scots Greys and Maj with French Free Forces (Legion of Honour, Croix de Guerre); appointed Private Sec to HM's Ambassador in Paris 1944; a Lord-in-Waiting to HM 1957-58, Joint Parl Under Sec of State for Foreign Affairs 1958-62, and Min of State for Colonial Affairs 1962-74; assumption of additional surnames of Petty-Fitzmaurice recognized by decree of Lord Lyon 1947; PC 1964: *m* 1st, 1938, Barbara, who *d* 1965, da of Harold Stuart Chase, of Santa Barbara, Calif, USA; 2ndly, 1969 (*m diss* 1978), Hon Selina Polly Dawson Eccles, da of 1st Viscount Eccles, and formerly wife of Robin Andrew Duthac Carnegie (*see* E Southesk); 3rdly, 1978, Gillian Anna, who *d* 1982, da of Alured Morgan, and has issue by 1st *m*.

By courage, not words

Arms – Quarterly: 1st and 4th, ermine, on a bend azure, a magnetic needle pointing to the polar star or, *Petty*; 2nd and 3rd, argent, a saltire gules, and a chief ermine, *Fitzmaurice*. **Crests** – 1st a bee-hive beset with bees, volante, all proper; 2nd, a sagittary passant proper. **Supporters** – On either side a pegasus ermine, winged, and unguled or, each charged on the shoulder with a fleur-de-lis azure.
Residence – Meikleour House, Perthshire. *Clubs* – Turf, New (Edinburgh).

SONS LIVING *(By 1st marriage)*

CHARLES MAURICE (*Earl of Shelburne*), *b* 21 Feb 1941; *ed* Eton; late Kenya Regt, R Wilts Yeo and R Wessex Yeo; DL Wilts 1991; a Page of Honour to HM 1956-57; Pres Wiltshire Playing Fields Assocn 1965-74; Chm Calne and Chippenham RDC 1972-73; Co Councillor of Wilts since 1970-85; Chm N Wilts Dist Council 1973-76, since when Pres Wiltshire Assocn of Boys and Youth Clubs; Member of S-W Economic Planning Council 1972-77; Chm Population and Settlement Cttee (SWEPC) 1972-77; Parly Candidate for Coventry NE 1977-79; Member Historic Buildings and Monuments Commn 1983-89; Pres N Wilts Conservative Assocn 1986-90, and Historic Houses Assocn 1988-93; Member of Council of Duchy of Cornwall since 1990: *m* 1st, 1965 (*m diss* 1987), Lady Frances Helen Mary Eliot, da of 9th Earl of St Germans; 2ndly, 1987, Fiona Mary, da of Donald Merritt, and has issue by 1st *m*:—

> SONS LIVING (*by 1st marriage*) — Simon Henry George (*Viscount Calne and Calstone*), *b* 24 Nov 1970, — Hon William Nicholas Charles, *b* 1973.
> DAUGHTERS LIVING (*by 1st marriage*) — *Lady* Arabella Helen Mary, *b* 1966: *m* 1993, Rupert W. H. Unwin, yr son of Martin I. H. Unwin, of Shipton Moyne, Glos, — *Lady* Rachel Barbara Violet, *b* 1968: *m* 1991, James William Richard Spickernell (*see* E Leicester, colls).

Residence – Bowood House, Calne, Wilts. *Clubs* – Brooks's, Turf.
Lord Robert Harold MERCER NAIRNE (The Old Manse, Kinclaven, by Stanley, Perth), *b* 1947; *ed* Gordonstoun, Univ of Kent (BA), and Univ of Washington Graduate Sch of Business (MBA, PhD); FBIM: *m* 1972, Jane Elizabeth, el da of Lt-Col Lord Douglas Claude Alexander Gordon, DSO (*see* M Huntly), and has issue living, Samuel George, *b* 1976, — Joseph Douglas, *b* 1980, — Emily Jane, *b* 1974.

DAUGHTERS LIVING AND DECEASED *(By 1st marriage)*

Lady Caroline Margaret, *b* 1939; *d* 1956.
Lady Georgina Elizabeth, *b* 1950: *m* 1st, 1974 (*m diss* 1980), Guy Hamilton; 2ndly, 1981, Robert Eric Miller, of 75 Fisher Av, Brookline, Mass 02146, USA; and has issue living (by 1st *m*), Josiah Stirling, *b* 1975, — Emma Carissa, *b* 1977.

SISTER LIVING *(Raised to the rank of a Marquess's daughter 1946)*

Lady Mary Margaret Elizabeth, *b* 1910: *m* 1931, Lt-Col Ririd Myddelton, CVO, Coldstream Gds, who *d* 1988, and has issue living, David Foulk (Caeaugwynion, Chirk, Wrexham), *b* 1932; late Coldstream Gds; High Sheriff of Clwyd 1980: *m* 1st, 1965 (*m diss* 1968), Anne, only da of late Charles Brotherton, of Kirkham Abbey, York; 2ndly, 1970, Christine Serena Cherry, da of Arthur Malcolm Morris, OBE, Depart of External Affairs, Canberra, Aust, and has issue living, (by 1st *m*), Guy Charles *b* 1966, (by 2nd *m*) Mark Ririd *b* 1973, Sian Moyra *b* 1971, — Hugh Robert (139 Holland Park Av, W11), *b* 1938, late Coldstream Gds: *m* 1967, Hon Sarah Cecily Allsopp, da of 5th Baron Hindlip, and has issue living, Alexander Ririd Henry *b* 1969, Claerwen Georgina Margaret *b* 1972, — Fiona Violet (*Lady Aird*), LVO *b* 1934; appointed a Lady-in-Waiting to HRH Princess Margaret 1960, LVO 1980: *m* 1963, Capt Sir Alastair Sturgis Aird, KCVO, Capt 9th Lancers (*see* Aird, Bt, colls). *Residence* – Chirk Castle, nr Wrexham, N Wales.

DAUGHTERS LIVING OF SIXTH MARQUESS

Lady Katherine Evelyn Constance (*Dowager Viscountess Mersey*), *b* 1912; *s* as *Lady Nairne* in her own right 1945 (see that title): *m* 1933, the 3rd Viscount Mersey, who *d* 1979. *Residence* – Bignor Park, Pulborough, Sussex.

Lady Elizabeth Mary, *b* 1927: *m* 1950, Major Charles William Lambton, Coldstream Guards (ret) (*see* E Durham, colls). *Residence* – The Old Rectory, Calstone, Calne, Wilts.

COLLATERAL BRANCH LIVING

Descendants of late Hon Thomas FitzMaurice (son of 1st Earl of Shelburne and brother of 1st Marquess of Lansdowne), who *m* 1777, Mary, *Countess of Orkney* (in her own right) (*see* E Orkney).

PREDECESSORS – **(1)** THOMAS FitzMaurice; *cr Baron of Kerry and Lixnaw* (peerage of Ireland); *d* 1280; *s* by his son **(2)** MAURICE, 2nd Baron; sat in Parliament at Dublin 1295; *d* 1303; *s* by his son **(3)** NICHOLAS, 3rd Baron; *s* by his son **(4)** MAURICE, 4th Baron; having a dispute with Desmond Oge MacCarthy, killed that chief on the bench before the Judge of Assize at Tralee in 1325, for which he was tried and attainted by the Parliament of Dublin, but was not put to death; his lands were, however, forfeited, but restored after his decease in 1339 to his brother and successor **(5)** JOHN, 5th Baron; summoned to Parliament 1375; *s* by his son **(6)** MAURICE, 6th Baron; *d* 1398; *s* by his son **(7)** PATRICK, 7th Baron; *d* 1410; *s* by his son **(8)** EDMUND, 8th Baron; *d* 1469; *s* by his son **(9)** EDMUND, 9th Baron; *d* 1489; *s* by his son **(10)** EDMUND, 10th Baron; resigned his estates to his el son and became a lay brother of the Order of St Francis in the Friary of Ardfert; *d* 1954; *s* by his son **(11)** EDMOND, 11th Baron; *cr Baron Odorney*, of co Kerry, and *Viscount Kilmaule* (peerage of Ireland) 1537; *d* without male issue 1541, when the Baron of Odorney and Viscountcy became extinct, and the Barony of Kerry devolved upon his brother **(12)** PATRICK, 12th Baron; *d* 1547; *s* by his el son **(13)** THOMAS, 13th Baron; *d* a minor 1549; *s* by his brother **(14)** EDMUND, 14th Baron; *d* 1549; *s* by his uncle **(15)** GERALD, 15th Baron; *d* 1550; *s* by his brother **(16)** THOMAS, 16th Baron; served many years in the military service of Emperors of Germany; *d* 1590; *s* by his son **(17)** PATRICK, 17th Baron; brought up at Court of Queen Elizabeth, but was in rebellion against HM after his succession to title; *d* 1600; *s* by his son **(18)** THOMAS, 18th Baron; surrendered his estates to James I, who in 1604 granted him a free pardon, and in 1612, by patent, confirmed his estates to him and his heirs and assigns for ever; *d* 1630; *s* by his el son **(19)** PATRICK, 19th Baron; took his seat in Parliament 1634, and removed to England 1641; *d* 1660; *s* by his el son **(20)** WILLIAM FITZMAURICE, 20th Baron; *d* 1697; *s* by his son **(21)** *Rt Hon* THOMAS, 21st Baron; *cr Viscount Clan Maurice and Earl of Kerry* (peerage of Ireland) 1722; *d* 1741; *s* by his son **(22)** WILLIAM, PC, 2nd Earl; Gov of Ross Castle, Col of Coldstream Guards, and Custos Rotulorum of co Kerry; *d* 1747; *s* by his son **(23)** FRANCIS THOMAS, 3rd Earl; *dsp* 1818; *s* by his cousin **(24)** HENRY Petty-FitzMaurice, KG, PC, 3rd *Marquess of Lansdowne* (see * infra); a distinguished statesman; Lord Lieut of Wilts, MP for Camelford Chancellor of the Exchequer 1806-7, Lord Pres of the Council 1830-4 and 1846-52, and a member of the Cabinet without office 1852-8; *d* 1863; *s* by his son **(25)** HENRY, KG, 4th Marquess; *b* 1816; sat as MP for Calne (*L*) 1847-56; was a Lord of the Treasury 1847, and Under-Sec for Foreign Affairs 1856-8; summoned to Parliament in his father's Barony of Wycombe: *m* 1843, Emily Jane Mercer Elphinstone de Flahault, who *d* 1895, in her own right Lady Nairne (infra): *d* 1866; *s* by his son **(26)** HENRY CHARLES KEITH, KG, GCSI, GCMG, GCIE, who *s* as 9th Lord Nairne 1895, 5th Marquess, *b* 1845; a Commr of Exchequer of Great Britain, and of Treasure of Ireland 1868-72, Under-Sec of State for War 1872-4, Under-Sec for India 1880, Gov-Gen of Canada and Com-in-Ch of Prince Edward Island 1883-8, Viceroy of India 1888-94, Sec of State for War 1895-1900, and Sec of State for Foreign Affairs 1900-1905, and Min (without portfolio) May 1915 to Dec 1916; Lord-Lieut of Wilts 1896-1820; Chancellor or Order of St Michael and St George 1917-20; had Roy Victorian Chain; bore Royal Standard at Coronation of King George V 1911: *m* 1869, Lady Maud Evelyn Hamilton, VA, CI, GBE, CH, who *d* 1932, da of 1st Duke of Abercorn, KB; *d* 1927; *s* by his son **(27)** HENRY WILLIAM EDMOND, DSO, MVO, 6th Marquess, *b* 1872; MP for W Div of Derbyshire (*U*) 1908-18; sometime a Senator of Irish Free State: *m* 1904, Elizabeth Caroline (who *d* 1964, having *m* 2ndly, 1940, Lord Colum Edmund Crichton-Stuart), da of Sir Edward Stanley Hope, KCG; *d* 1936; *s* by his son **(28)** CHARLES HOPE, 7th Marquess *b* 1917; Capt Roy Wilts Yeo (TA); *ka* Italy 20 Aug 1944, when he was *s* in the Lordship of Nairne by his el sister, Lady Katherine Evelyn Constance Bigham, and in all the other peerages by his cousin **(29)** GEORGE JOHN CHARLES MERCER (only son of late Major Lord Charles George Francis MERCER-NAIRNE, MVO, 2nd son of 5th Marquess) 8th Marquess and present peer; also Earl of Wycombe, Viscount Calne and Calstone, Lord Wycombe, Baron of Chipping Wycombe, Earl of Kerry, Earl of Shelburne, Viscount ClanMaurice and FitzMaurice, Baron of Kerry and Lixnaw, and Baron Dunkerron.

*(1) *Hon* JOHN FitzMaurice, PC, 2nd son of 1st Earl of Kerry (ante) inherited the estates of his maternal uncle Henry, 1st and last Earl of Shelburne (*cr* 1719) whose surname of Petty he assumed; was sole Gov of co Kerry, and MP for Chipping Wycombe; *cr Baron Dunkeron* and *Viscount FitzMaurice* (peerage of Ireland) 1751, *Earl of Shelburne* (peerage of Ireland) 1753, and *Baron Wycombe*, of Chipping Wycombe, co Bucks (peerage of Great Britain) 1760; *d* 1761; *s* by his son **(2)** WILLIAM, KG, PC, 2nd Earl; MP for Chipping Wycombe 1763, a Lord of Trade, a Major-Gen in the Army, ADC to HM 1760, a Principal Sec of State 1766, and Prime Minister and First Lord of the Treasury 1782; *cr Viscount Calne and Calstone, Earl of Wycombe*, and *Marquess of Lansdowne* (peerage of Great Britain) 1784; *d* 1805; *s* by his son **(3)** JOHN HENRY, 2nd Marquess; MP for Chipping Wycombe 1786-90; *dsp* 1809; *s* by his half-brother **(4)** HENRY, 3rd Marquess (see ante).

Lascelles, Viscount; son of Earl of Harewood.

LATHAM, BARON (Latham) (Baron UK 1942)

It is good to try

DOMINIC CHARLES LATHAM, 2nd Baron; *b* 20 Sept 1954; *s* 1970; *ed* NSW Univ (BE Civil 1977, Hons I, MEngSc 1981); Civil Engr with Electricity Commn of NSW 1979-88; Structural Engr with Rankine & Hill Consulting Engrs 1988-91; Sr Structural Engr, Gerard Barry Assocs 1992; Social Dancing Teacher since 1993.

Arms – Per fesse gules and chequy or and sable a fesse barry wavy argent and azure in chief a seax fessewise point to the sinister cutting edge upwards proper pomel and hilt of the second ensigned with a Saxon crown also of the second. Crest – Two spurs one in bend the other in bend sinister rowels upwards or straps sable with buckles gold. Supporters – On either side a horse sable charged on the shoulder with a plate and gorged with a mural coronet with chain reflexed over the back or.
Address – PO Box 355, Kensington, NSW 2033, Australia.

BROTHER LIVING

ANTHONY MICHAEL (twin), *b* 20 Sept 1954.

AUNTS LIVING (*Daughters of 1st Baron*)

Hon Barbara Wendy (Maia), *b* 1920; 1942-44 War as 1st class Aircraftwoman WAAF: *m* 1st, 1941 (*m diss* 1945), Capt Denis Charles Wildish, RASC; 2ndly, 1946 (*m diss* 1951), Peter Anthony Charles Kurt Bruckmann, late Capt E Surrey Regt; 3rdly, 1966, Malcolm Blundell Cole-Fontayn, solicitor, and has issue living, (by 2nd *m*) Karin Franchesca, *b* 1948.
Hon Jean Helen *b* 1921; WRNS 1940-45: *m* 1st 1945 (*m diss* 1961), Sqdn-Ldr Ronald Gellatly, RNZAF; 2ndly, 1970, James Oswald Dykes, and has issue living, (by 1st *m*), Paul *b* 1946.
Hon Diana Dorothy, *b* 1925: *m* 19—, Barringer.

PREDECESSOR – (1) CHARLES Latham, son of late George Latham, of Norwich; *b* 1888, Leader of LCC 1940-47, Chm of London Transport Exec 1947-53; Chm of Finance Cttee of Metropolitan Water Board 1957-65; Lord Lieut of Middx 1945-56; *cr Baron Latham*, of Hendon, co Middx (peerage of UK) 1942: *m* 1st, 1913 (*m diss* 1957) Maya Helen, who *d* 1978, da of Louis George Allman, of Hendon; 2ndly, 1957, Sylvia May, who *d* 1985, da of Alexander Newmark, of London, and widow of Alexander Kennard; *d* 1970; *s* by his grandson (2) DOMINIC CHARLES (el twin son of Hon Francis Charles Allman Latham, who *d* 1959, having *m* 1951, as his 3rd wife, Gabrielle Monica, who *d* 1987, da of Dr S. M. O'Riordan), 2nd Baron and present peer.

LATYMER, BARON (Money-Coutts) (Baron E 1431-2)

To be, not to seem

HUGO NEVILL MONEY-COUTTS, 8th Baron; *b* 1 March 1926; *s* 1987; *ed* Eton: *m* 1st, 1951 (*m diss* 1965), Hon Penelope Ann Clare, yr da of late Thomas Addis Emmet, and of Baroness Emmet of Amberley (Life Baroness, ext 1980); 2ndly, 1965, Jinty Ann, 2nd da of late Peter George Calvert (*see* B Ashcombe, 1963 Edn), and has issue by both *m*.

Arms – Quarterly: 1st and 4th, a stag's head erased gules, between the attires a pheon azure, all within a bordure embattled of the last, charged with four buckles or, *Coutts*; 2nd and 3rd or, on a pile azure ten besants, four, three, two, and one, on a chief ermine a lion passant of the second, *Money*. Crests – 1st, a man from the middle upwards, shooting an arrow from a bow, all proper, *Coutts*; 2nd, a besant between two wings azure, each semée-de-lis, or, *Money*. Supporters – On either side a griffin or.
Residence – Vivero Hortus, Santa Maria, Mallorca.

SONS LIVING (By 1st marriage)

Hon CRISPIN JAMES ALAN NEVILL, *b* 8 March 1955; *ed* Eton, and Keble Coll, Oxford: *m* 1978, Hon Lucy Rose Deedes, yst da of Baron Deedes (Life Baron), and has issue living, Drummond William Thomas, *b* 11 May 1986, — Sophia Patience, *b* 1985, — Evelyn Rose, *b* 1988. *Address* – c/o Coutts & Co, 440 Strand, WC2R 0QS.
Hon Giles Thomas Nevill, *b* 1957; *ed* Eton, and Oriel Coll, Oxford.

(by 2nd marriage)

Hon Henry Eugene, *b* 1967; *ed* Eton.

DAUGHTERS LIVING (By 1st marriage)

Hon Clare Louise, *b* 1952; *ed* Cobham Hall: *m* 1979, John Edmunds, son of John Edmunds, of Quinton, Glos. *Residence* – Buscott Farm, Ashcott, Bridgwater, Som.

(by 2nd marriage)

Hon Vera Dulcie Harriet, *b* 1972; *ed* Bryanston.
Hon Fanny Clara Maria, *b* 1973; *ed* Bryanston.

SISTERS LIVING

Hon Joanna Harriet Nevill, *b* 1928: *m* 1951, Pierre Langlais, and has issue living, Eric, *b* 1952, — Nicole, *b* 1953, — Louise, *b* 1954, — Odette, *b* 1961, — Jacqueline, *b* 1962. *Residence* – PO Box 113, N Hartland, Vermont 05052, USA.
Hon Susan Margaret Nevill, *b* 1933: *m* 1st 1956 (*m diss* 1965), Michael John Turner, QC (*cr* Kt Bach 1985) (*see* By Schuster, 1980 Edn); 2ndly, 1965, Ian A. K. Dipple, of Nether Walstead, Lindfield, Sussex, and has issue living (by 1st *m*), Mark Christopher, *b* 1959; *ed* Radley: *m*, — Louise Margaret Ruth, *b* 1960: *m* 1993, Michael H. Crouch, of Stepaside Cottage, Aldingbourne, Chichester, W Sussex PO20 6UB, son of late Henry Crouch, of Walton-on-Thames, Surrey, — (by 2nd *m*) Alexandra Margaret, *b* 1967, — Joanna Shannon, *b* 1968.

COLLATERAL BRANCHES LIVING

Issue of late Lieut-Col Hon Alexander Burdett Money-Coutts, OBE, 2nd son of 6th Baron, *b* 1902, *d* 1994: *m* 1930, Mary Elspeth, who *d* 1990, da of Sir Reginald Arthur Hobhouse, 5th Bt:—
Sir David Burdett, KCVO (Magpie House, Peppard Common, Henley-on-Thames, Oxon RG9 5JG), *b* 1931; *ed* Eton, and New Coll, Oxford; late Capt Royal Gloucestershire Hussars; Chm Coutts & Co 1976-93, Chm M & G Group plc since 1991; KCVO 1991: *m* 1958, Helen Penelope June Utten, da of late Cdr Killingworth Richard Utten Todd, Royal Indian Navy, and has issue living, Benjamin Burdett (43 Holmes Rd, Twickenham, Middx TW1 4RF), *b* 1961: *m* 1987, Patricia Anne, eldest da of Dr Carl Trepagnier, of Houston, Texas, and has issue living, Christopher Burdett *b* 1990, Zachary Alexander *b* 1994, Cecily Anne *b* 1992, — Harriet St Bride, *b* 1959: *m* 1st, 1979 (*m diss* 1985), Charles Spencer Chetwode Ram, yst son of late Maj Henry Stopford Chetwode Ram, RE; 2ndly, 1985, Martin Neil Pottinger, of Mount Pleasant Cottage, Upottery, Honiton, Devon EX14 9PF, yr son of late Peter Henry Jameson Pottinger, of Corstorphine, Edinburgh, and has issue living (by 2nd *m*), William Jameson, *b* 1985, Thomas George *b* 1989, Robin David *b* 1990, Flora St Bride *b* 1987, — Laura Isabella, *b* 1965: *m* 1987, P. Jamie Corrie, of 16 Wayside Green, Woodecote, Reading, Berks RG8 0QJ, elder son of Peter Corrie, of Corner House, Peppard Common, Henley-on-Thames, Oxon, and has issue living, Joshua Richard *b* 1992.

Issue of late Maj Hon Godfrey Burdett Money-Coutts, 3rd son of 6th Baron, *b* 1905, *d* 1979: *m* 1931, Anne Cecilia, who *d* 1969, da of late Hon Wilfred James (B Northbourne, colls):—
Julia Jane *b* 1933; assumed the surname of St John Aubin 1968 until remarriage: *m* 1st, 1951 (*m diss* 1968), Capt Richard John Fisher Turner, RN; 2ndly, 1991, Christopher Thomasson, of Somerton Castle, Boothby Graffoe, Lincoln LN5 0LL, and has issue living (by 1st *m*), Antony Robin Fisher, *b* 1952: *m* 1973, Barbara Maeve, da of Harry Stokes, of Guildford, Surrey, and has issue living, Barnaby Adam Fisher *b* 1978, Adam Benedict Fisher *b* 1982, — Simon John Fisher, *b* 1954, — James Michael Fisher, *b* 1956: *m* 1983, Linda Richardson.

Issue of late Hon Mercy Burdett Money-Coutts, only da of 6th Baron, *b* 1910, *d* 1993: *m* 1947, Michael Seiradhakis, of 19 Odos Seirenon, Byronas, Athens 162 31:—
John Hugh SEIRADHAKIS (Ethnikis Symfiliosis 39, GR 57019, Perea, Greece), *b* 1948: *m* 1978, Benedicta Teppe, and has issue living, Michael, *b* 1981, — Elena, *b* 1979. — Sophia Hester SEIRADHAKI (Photimari, Kea, 830 02 Greece), *b* 1949; has continued to use her maiden name since 1978: *m* 1st, 1974 (*m diss* 1978), George Pinderis; 2ndly, 1985, Charalambos Papoutsakis.

Issue of late Hon Clara Burdett Money-Coutts, el da of 5th Baron, *b* 1877, *d* 1969: *m* 1905, Rev Melville Watson Patterson, Fellow and Sr Tutor, Trin Coll, Oxford, who *d* 1944:—
Rosamund Margaret (Little Garth, Charlton, Banbury, Oxon), *b* 1905: *m* 1934, Selwyn Duruz, who *d* 1976. —— Joan Elisabeth, *b* 1908: *m* 1st, 1931 (*m diss* 1937), Sebastian Max Alexander Myer Clement Salaman, who *d* 1976; 2ndly, 1947, Raymond Coxon, IG, of Little Garth, Charlton, Banbury, Oxon, and has issue living, (by 1st *m*) Clement Francis (40 Bickerton Rd, N19), *b* 1932: *m* 1961, Juliet Nicholson, — Frederick Nicholas Paul (Flat 6, 62 Elm Park Gdns, SW10), *b* 1936; *ed* Radley, and Trin Coll, Oxford: *m* 1st, 1960 (*m diss* 1974), Elisabeth Cecily, da of Francis Sclater, of Bunces Farm, Newick, Uckfield, Sussex; 2ndly, 1983, Lyndsay Margaret, da of James Meiklejohn, of Wise Lane, Mill Hill, and has issue living (by 1st *m*), Sophia *b* 1963, Charlotte *b* 1966, (by 2nd *m*) Rose Clementine *b* 1983, Phoebe Joy *b* 1987. —— Lindsay Marion, *b* 1916: *m* 1939, Humphry Gilbert Bohun Lynch, of 19 Eastfield Court, Church St, Faringdon, Oxon, and has issue living, Francis Nicholas (Hadley, Wootton Rivers, Marlborough, Wilts), *b* 1944; *ed* Merton Coll, Oxford: *m* 1st, 1965 (*m diss* 1974), Amanda Underwood; 2ndly, 1983, Susan, da of Eric Wright, of Hawaii, USA, and has issue living (by 2nd *m*), Hugh Arthur *b* 1991 , — Alison Harriet, *b* 1955.

Grandchildren of late Hon Joan Burdett Nixon (infra):—
Issue of late Arundel James Nixon, *b* 1907, *d* 1949: *m* 1st, 1930 (*m diss* 1940), Edna Duffy; 2ndly, 1941, Paloma Margaret (who *m* 2ndly, 1951, Geoffrey Thomas Luke, of Victoria, Australia, and *d* 1980), da of David Maccreesh, of USA:—
(By 1st *m*) Peter NIXON, *b* 1934. *Residence* – Australia. —— (By 2nd *m*) David Guy NIXON-LUKE, *b* 1945: *m* 1970, Charryce Laleen Yolanna, yst da of Montague Neville Lea, of 188 Rocky Point Rd, Kogarah, NSW, Australia, and has issue living, Guy Jaeger Evans Arundel, *b* 1976, — Jordan Geoffrey Bradshaw, *b* 1982, — Reece David Valmont, *b* 1986. *Residence* – 22 Lambert Rd, Toorak, Victoria 3142, Australia. —— Nikki, *b* 1942: *m* 1961 (*m diss* 1982), Robert William Martin, and has issue living, James Patrick, *b* 1965, — Sarah Jane, *b* 1963. *Residence* – 96 Bendigo St, E Richmond, Victoria, Australia.

Issue of late Hon Joan Burdett Money-Coutts, 3rd da of 5th Baron, *b* 1882, *d* 1968: *m* 1905 (*m diss* 1941), Lt-Col James Arundel Nixon, DSO, formerly King's Own (R Lancaster) Regt, who *d* 1950:—
Guy John NIXON (47 Mount Row, St Peter Port, Guernsey GY1 1NU), *b* 1909; *ed* Eton, and Pembroke Coll, Camb (BA); AIB: *m* 1933, Barbara Helen, who *d* 1991, yr da of late Francis William Whitbourn Morgan; 2ndly, 1992, Mrs Michelle James, da of late James Frederick Carey, of Guernsey, and has issue living (by 1st *m*), Sara, *b* 1933: *m* 1959, John Gordon Mathias, and has issue living, Jeremy *b* 1963, Penelope, *b* 1960.

Granddaughters of Hon Margaret Burdett Still (infra):—
Issue of late Robert Still, *b* 1910, *d* 1971: *m* 1944, Elizabeth Eleanor (Bucklebury Lodge, Bucklebury, Berks), da of S. K. Westman, FRCS, of Harley St, W1:—
Susan, *b* 1945: *m* 1965, R. C. R. Chesters, of Winchester, and has issue living, William, *b* 1971, — Celia, *b* 1973. —— Anthea, *b* 1947: *m* 1974, Michael Dillon, of Oxford, and has issue living, Simon, *b* 1975, — Timothy, *b* 1983, — David, *b* 1985, — Ruth, *b* 1977. —— Katharine, *b* 1949: *m* 1971, Peter Hyde, of Hove, and has issue living, Robert, *b* 1972, — David, *b* 1981, — Jonathan, *b* 1990, — Elizabeth, *b* 1983. —— Claudia, *b* 1954: *m* 1977 (*m diss* 1987), Lucian W. N. Camp, of Hampstead, London.

Issue of late Hon Margaret Burdett Money-Coutts, yst da of 5th Baron, *b* 1886, *d* 1948: *m* 1907, Major Francis Churchill Still, solicitor, of 5 New Sq, Lincoln's Inn, WC2, who *d* 1937:—
Ursula Margaret, *b* 1913: *m* 1935, Archibald Walter Bury. Resides in Australia.

PREDECESSORS – **(1)** Sir GEORGE Nevill, 5th son of 1st Earl of Westmorland; summoned to Parliament by writ as *Baron Latymer* 1431-2: *m* Elizabeth, da of 5th Earl of Warwick; *d* 1469; *s* by his grandson **(2)** RICHARD, *b* 1468 summoned to Parliament 1492-1529: *m* 1490, Anne, da of Sir Humphrey Stafford, of Grafton and Blatherwycke; *d* 1530; *s* by his son **(3)** JOHN, *b* 1493; summoned to Parliament 1533-4 and 1541-2: *m* 1st, 1518, Elizabeth, da of Sir Richard Musgrave, of Hartland; 2ndly, Dorothy, who *d* 1526-27, da of Sir George Vere; 3rdly Katharine (who subsequently *m* King Henry VIII), da of Sir Thoms Parr, of Kendal and widow of Edward, Lord Burgh; *d* 1543; *s* by his only son by 2nd *m* **(4)** JOHN; summoned to Parliament 1543-80: *m* Lucy, da of 2nd Earl of Worcester; *d* 1577, when the Barony fell into abeyance between his four das and co-heirs; in July 1912, the Committee for Privileges of the House of Lords reported (other co-heirs not appearing) that a claim to the Barony had been made out by **(5)** FRANCIS THOMAS Money-Coutts, 5th Baron, only son of late Rev James Drummond Money, by Clara Maria, who *d* 1899 (having assumed by Roy licence 1880, for herself and son, the additional surname of Coutts), 4th da of Sir Francis Burdett, 5th Bt (*cr* 1618-19); *b* 1852; proved his claim to the Barony before the Committee for Privileges of the House of Lords July 1912 (claiming through Frances, el da of Lucy (who *m* Sir William Cornwallis), 3rd da of 4th Baron), and the abeyance was determined in his favour Dec 1912; assumed by Roy licence 1914, the additional surname and arms of Nevill in lieu of that of Money and after that of Coutts: *m* 1875, Edith Ellen, who *d* 1942, da of Charles Churchill, of Weybridge Park, Surrey; *d* 1923; *s* by his son **(6)** HUGH BURDETT Money-Coutts, TD, 6th Baron; *b* 1876; sometime Capt N. Devon Hussars Yeo; European War 1915-17 in Gallipoli and Egypt; *m* 1900, Hester Frances, who *d* 1961, da of late Maj-Gen John Cecil Russell, CVO; *d* 1949; *s* by his son **(7)** THOMAS BURDETT, 7th Baron, *b* 1901; Chm London Cttee of Ottoman Bank and of Investment Trust Corpn Ltd, Dir Coutts and Co and of Nat Prov Bank, Vice-Chm Middlesex Hosp: *m* 1925, Patience Margaret, who *d* 1982, da of late William Courtenay-Thompson; *d* 1987; *s* by his only son **(8)** HUGO NEVILL, 8th Baron and present peer.

LAUDERDALE, EARL OF (Maitland) (Earl S 1624, Bt S 1680)

By wisdom and courage

PATRICK FRANCIS MAITLAND, 17th Earl, and 13th Baronet; *b* 17 March 1911; *s* 1968; *ed* Lancing, and Brasenose Coll, Oxford (BA); Hereditary Bearer of National Flag of Scotland by decrees of Lord Lyon King of Arms 1790 and 1952; recognised by Lord Lyon as Chief of Clan Maitland 1968; Editor of *The Fleet Street Letter Service*, and *The Whitehall Letter* 1945-58; Pres of Church Union 1959-62; MP for Lanark (*C*) 1951-59; a Member of Coll of Guardians of Nat Shrine of Our Lady of Walsingham 1949-65, since when Guardian Emeritus; Founder of Expanding Commonwealth Group of House of Commons (Chm 1955-61); Chm Sub-Cttee F (Energy, Transport Research) of House of Lords Select Cttee on EEC 1974-79: *m* 1936, Stanka, da of Prof Milivoye Losanitch, of Belgrade, and has issue.

Arms – Or, a lion rampant gules couped at all his joints of the field, within the Royal tressure azure, in a dexter canton argent a saltire azure, surmounted of an inescutcheon or, charged with a lion rampant within a double tressure flory counterflory gules, behind the shield on staffs in saltire proper two representations of the Sovereign's National Flag of Scotland (Cross of St Andrew), fringed or, ropes and tassels of the last (Insignia of Office of Bearer for the Sovereign of the Sovereign's National Flag of Scotland). **Crest** – A lion sejant affrontee gules, ducally crowned proper, in his dexter paw a sword of the last, hilted and pommelled or, and in his sinister a fleur-de-lis azure. **Supporters** – Two eagles proper.
Residence – 12 St Vincent St, Edinburgh.

SONS LIVING

IAN (*Viscount Maitland, Master of Lauderdale*) (150 Tachbrook St, SW1V 2NE), *b* 4 Nov 1937; *ed* Radley, and Brasenose Coll, Oxford (MA); Lt RNR: *m* 1963, Ann Paule, da of Geoffrey Clark, of 511 Hood House, Dolphin Sq, SW1, and has issue:—
   SON LIVING—*Hon* John Douglas (*Master of Maitland*), *b* 1965; *ed* Radley, and — Coll, Durham (BSc).
   DAUGHTER LIVING—*Hon* Sarah Caroline MAITLAND PARKS, *b* 1964; *ed* St Paul's Girls' Sch, and Trevelyan Coll, Durham (BA): *m* 1988, Stuart G. Parks, son of late K. Parks, of Wargrave, Berks. *Residence* – 150 Tachbrook St, SW1V 2NE.

Rev the Hon Sydney Milivoye Patrick (14 Kersland St, Glasgow G12 8BL), *b* 1951; *ed* Eton, Edinburgh University (BSc) and Strathclyde University (Dip TP); ordained Priest in Scottish Episcopal Church 1987: *m* 1974, (Dorothy) Eileen, da of A. R. Bedell of The Knowe, Chapleton, Strathaven, Lanarkshire.

DAUGHTERS LIVING

Lady (Helen) Olga, *b* 1944: *m* 1969, Robin William Patrick Hamilton Hay, of 21 Cloudesley St, N1, and has issue living, Alastair Patrick Hamilton, *b* 1972, — Fergus William Hamilton *b* 1981, — Camilla Charlotte Hamilton, *b* 1975.
Lady Caroline Charlotte Militsa (12 St Vincent St, Edinburgh), *b* 1946.

GRANDDAUGHTERS LIVING OF FIFTEENTH EARL (*Raised to the rank of an Earl's daughters* 1953)

Issue of late Ivor Colin James (*Viscount Maitland*) Lieut RAC (TA), only son of 15th Earl, *b* 1915, *ka* 1943: *m* 1936, Helena Ruth (infra), yr da of Sir Herbert Charles Perrott, 6th Bt (ext), CH, CB:—
Lady Mary Helena (*Lady Mary Biddulph*) *b* 1938: *m* 1958, 4th Baron Biddulph, who *d* 1988, of Makerstoun, Kelso, Roxburghshire. — *Lady* Anne Priscilla, *b* 1940: *m* 1968, John Joseph Eyston, of Mapledurham House, Reading (*see* E Mexborough, 1985 Edn), and has issue living, Edward Thomas Ivor, *b* 1969, — Katharine Agnes Mary, *b* 1970, — Mary Amicia Helena, *b* 1972. —— *Lady* Elizabeth Sylvia *b* (*posthumous*) 1943. *Residence* – 11 Boundary Close, Woodstock, Oxon OX20 1LR.

WIDOW LIVING OF SON OF FIFTEENTH EARL

Helena Ruth (*Helena, Viscountess Maitland*), yr da of Sir Herbert Charles Perrott, 6th Bt (ext), CH, CB; is an OStJ: *m* 1936, Ivor Colin James, Viscount Maitland, Lieut RAC (TA), who was *ka* 1943, only son of 15th Earl, and has issue living (ante). *Residences* – Flat E, 34 Cadogan Sq, SW1; Park House, Makerstoun, Kelso, Roxburghshire, TD5 7PA.

WIDOW LIVING OF SIXTEENTH EARL

IRENE ALICE MAY (*Irene, Countess of Lauderdale*), (White Lodge, S Strand, Angmering-on-Sea, W Sussex), da of late Rev C. P. Shipton, of Halsham, Yorks: *m* 1940, as his 2nd wife, the 16th Earl, who *d* 1968.

COLLATERAL BRANCHES LIVING

Descendants of late Gen Hon Sir Alexander Maitland (5th son of 6th Earl), who was *cr* a *Baronet* 1818:—
See Maitland, Bt.

        Descendants of Capt Hon Frederick Lewis Maitland, RN, of Rankeilour, 8th son of 6th Earl, *b* 1730, *d* 1786: *m* 1767, Margaret, who *d* 1825, da of James Dick of Rankeilour (heir of line of Makgill of Rankeilour), son of Rev William Dick, of Cupar, by his wife, Isabel, yr da of David Makgill of Rankeilour, *de jure* 3rd Viscount of Oxfuird, and had issue, Charles Maitland of Rankeilour, sometime 17th Dragoons, *b* 1769, *d* 1820: *m* 1794, Mary, who *d* 1824, da of David Johnston of Lathrisk:—

Granddaughter of Maj Charles Julian Maitland-Makgill-Crichton (*b* 1880) (infra):—
Issue of late Maj Douglas Maitland-Makgill-Crichton, *b* 1909, *d* 1968: *m* 1936, Sybil Frederica Coore, who *d* 1992, da of late Frederick Lechmere Paton, JP (B Ashtown, colls):—
Veronica Ann, *b* 1938: *m* 1978, Ian Joicey Dickinson, of The Manor House, Riding Mill, Northumberland.

Grandson of late Maj Douglas Maitland-Makgill-Crichton (ante):—
Issue of late Charles Maitland Makgill Crichton of that Ilk; recognised by Lord Lyon as Chief of Clan Crichton 1980; *b* 1942, *d* 1992: *m* 1971, Isla Susan (Monzie Castle, Crieff, Perthshire), da of late Matthew Frederick Gloag, of Bonhard, Perthshire:—
David, *b* 1971; heir of line of 1st Viscount Frendraught.

Granddaughters of late David Maitland-Makgill-Crichton (*b* 1854), son of late Charles Julian Maitland-Makgill-Crichton, eldest son of late David Maitland-Makgill-Crichton (*b* 1801) (infra):—
Issue of late Major Charles Julian Maitland-Makgill-Crichton, Gordon Highlanders, *b* 1880, *ka* 1915: *m* 1902, Sybil Twynihoe, who *d* 1984 (aged 105), da of late Twynihoe William Erle, a Master of Supreme Court, of Bramshott Grange, Liphook, Hants:—
Mary Sylvia (33 Thurloe Court, Fulham Rd, SW3), *b* 1905. —— Rosemary Julian (37 Clareville Grove, SW7) *b* 1915: *m* 1940, James Herbert Lonsdale Musker, Fl Lt RAFVR, formerly 7th Hussars, who *d* 1966, and has issue living, Juliet Alexandra Sarah, *b* 1941: *m* 1965, William Edward Barry, of 12 Kensington Park Mews, W11, and has issue (*see* Barry, Bt, colls).
Issue of late Lt-Cdr James Henry Maitland-Makgill-Crichton, RN (ret), *b* 1885, *d* 1948: *m* 1908, Emily Christina, who *d* 1972, yr da of late Hugh Weir-MacColl, of Appin, Argyll, and The Woods, Newlands, Cape Province,S Africa:—
Alice Mary Emily, *b* 1914: *m* 1937, Vernon Charles Chambers, of Iverna Court, Kensington, W8, who *d* 1983, and has issue living, Virginia, *b* 1942: *m* 1968, George Digby MacDougall Dodd, who *d* 1987, and has issue living, Tamsin Serena Georgina *b* 1971, Julian Crichton *b* 1973, — Vanessa, *b* 1946: *m* 1977, James Alan Fleischmann, MB, BCh, MRCP (UK), MRCGP, DCH, DRCOG, of Portland House, Rt 1, 217A, Caledonia, Minnesota 55921, USA, and of Portland House, 45 Dresden Rd, N19 3BG, and has issue living, James Maitland *b* 1985, Diana Maitland *b* 1982. *Residence* – Portland House, Rt 1 217A Caledonia, Minnesota 55921, USA.

Granddaughters of late Cdr Coventry Makgill-Crichton-Maitland, RN, eldest son of late Maj-Gen David Makgill-Crichton-Maitland (*b* 1841) (infra):—
Issue of late Col Henry David Makgill-Crichton-Maitland, OBE, *b* 1904, *d* 1970: *m* 1st, 1930 (*m diss* 1949), Barbara Ellen, da of Brig-Gen Sir George Ayscough Armytage, 7th Bt, CMG, DSO; 2ndly, 1949, Audrey Estelle Ljuflng (who *m* 3rdly, 1982, Maurice J. C. Allom, of Dene Park, Tonbridge, Kent), da of Henry John Hyde-Johnson, and widow of Lt Peter Thorp Eckersley, RNVR, MP:—
(By 1st *m*) Judith Elizabeth, *b* 1933: *m* 1965, Anthony John Houssemayne du Boulay, of Langford Farm, Sydling St Nicholas, Dorchester, Dorset. —— Sarah, *b* 1936: *m* 1st, 1958, Count Alessandro Monneret de Villard; 2ndly, 1984, Francesco Boscu, of Via Monti 11, Varallo, Pombia, Italy, and has issue living (by 1st *m*), Raffaella, *b* 1961, — Xenia, *b* 1965, — Tatiana, *b* 1970.

Grandchildren of late Maj-Gen David Makgill-Crichton-Maitland (*b* 1841), (changed the sequence of his surnames 1884), 2nd son of late David Maitland-Makgill-Crichton (*b* 1801), 2nd son of late Capt Charles Maitland, el son of the Hon Frederick Lewis Maitland RN (ante):—
Issue of late Col Mark Edward Makgill-Crichton-Maitland, CVO, DSO, *b* 1882, *d* 1972: *m* 1924, Patience Irene Fleetwood, who *d* 1974, da of Sir John Michael Fleetwood Fuller, 1st Bt, KCMG:—
John David (Daluaine, Rhynie, Huntly, Aberdeenshire AB54 4HL), *b* 1925; *ed* Eton; Maj (ret) Gren Gds; Lord Lieut of Renfrewshire 1980-94: *m* 1st, 1954, Jean Patricia, who *d* 1985, da of late Maj-Gen Sir Michael O'Moore Creagh, KBE, MC (McGrigor, Bt); 2ndly, 1987, Mary Ann Vere, widow of Capt James Quintin Penn Curzon (*see* E Howe, colls), formerly wife of Charles Pepler Norton, and only da of late Maj Charles Herbert Harberton Eales, MC (*see* Ogilvy, Bt, colls), and has issue living (by 1st *m*), Mark Archibald (44 Cloncurry St, SW6), *b* 1955; *ed* Eton: *m* 1987, Mrs Judith I. G. Mainwaring, elder da of late H. G. Turner, of Mapperly Park, Nottingham, and has issue living, Archie David *b* 1988, Nicholas Hugh *b* 1990, — Mary Elizabeth, *b* 1962: *m* 1993, Roy North, son of K. North, of Horncastle, Lincs. —— Mark Michael (2 Grosvenor Cres, Edinburgh, EH12 5EP), *b* 1928; Maj (ret) Gordon Highlanders. —— Irene Margaret, *b* 1927: *m* 1953 (*m diss* 1986), Maj Michael Christopher Alfred Codrington, late 16th/5th Lancers (*see* Codrington, Bt, *cr* 1721, colls).

Grandchildren of late Andrew Coventry Maitland-Makgill-Crichton, yst son of late David Maitland-Makgill-Crichton (*b* 1801) (ante):—
Issue of late Lieut-Col David Edward Maitland-Makgill-Crichton, Queen's Own Cameron Highlanders, *b* 1879, *d* 1952: *m* 1909, Phyllis, who *d* 1982, da of late Claude Arthur Cuthbert, formerly of Bryn Garth, Much Dewchurch, Herefordshire (Rankin, Bt):—
Sir Andrew James (55 Hans Place, Knightsbridge, SW1; Mill House, Earl Soham, Suffolk), *b* 1910; *ed* Wellington Coll; Col late Indian Army; Chm of Overseas Containers, Ltd; Dir of P & O Steam Navigation Co; Dept Dir of Movements GHQ, New Delhi 1944-45, and Chm Employers' Side, Nat Joint Council for Port Transport Industry and of Nat Assocn of Port Employers 1958-65; an Arbitrator for Police Council of Great Britain since 1966; Vice-Chm Port of London Authority since 1967; *cr* Knt 1963: *m* 1948, Isabel, da of A. J. McGill, of Sydney, NSW, and widow of John Eric Bain. —— Edward, OBE (211 Braid Road, Edinburgh EH10 6HT), *b* 1916; *ed* Bedford Sch and RMC; Maj-Gen late Cameron Highlanders; GOC 51st Highland

Div 1966-68; ret 1968; Middle East 1940-44 (wounded, despatches), NW Europe 1944-45 (MBE); MBE (Mil) 1945, OBE (Mil) 1948: *m* 1951, Sheila Hibbins, and has issue living, David Edward, *b* 1952; *ed* Bedford Sch; Capt Queen's Own Highlanders: *m* 1979, Sheena Anne, da of Alexander Dougal Callander, of Coldon, Stirlingshire, and has issue living, a son *b* 1986, Amanda Claire *b* 1984, — (Andrew) James, *b* 1953; *ed* Bedford Sch, and RMA; Capt The Gordon Highlanders: *m* 1977, Karen Gail, da of Derick Charles Smith, of Copperhill, Sutton Valence, Kent, and has issue living, William Roderick *b* 1979, a son *b* 1982, a son *b* 1986, Eila Victoria *b* 1990, — Charles William, *b* 1961; *ed* Strathallan Sch, and RMA . ——— Katherine Grizel, *b* 1930: *m* 1951, Russell Barton, MRCP, of 2322, Clover St, Rochester, NY 14618, USA, and has issue living, Karen Elizabeth, *b* 1956, — Sarah Muriel, *b* 1958.

Issue of late Brigadier Henry Coventry Maitland-Makgill-Crichton, CB, CMG, DSO, late Roy Scots Fusiliers, *b* 1830, *d* 1953: *m* 1911, Dorothy Margaret, who *d* 1979, da of late Sir Walter Thorburn, of Glenbreck, Peeblesshire:—
Diana Elizabeth Katherine, TD, *b* 1916. *Residence* – Hedge Cottage, Kingston Deverell, Warminster, Wilts.

Issue of late John Denys Maitland-Makgill-Crichton, *b* 1897, *d* 1931: *m* 1930, Denise (who *m* 2ndly, 1932 (*m diss* 1943), Douglas S Fraser, and *d* 1984, having resumed her former name of Maitland-Makgill-Crichton), da of J. H. Crosby:—
Michael John, *b* 1931; *ed* Rhodes Univ (BA 1952), at Witwatersrand (LLB 1954), and Oriel Coll, Oxford: *m* 1958, Euphemia Daphne Joan Hopkins, and has issue living, Anthony John, *b* 1960, — Philippa Anne, *b* 1965. *Address* – Candy Cottage, PO Box 177, Rivonia 2128, Johannesburg, S Africa.

Grandchildren of late Rear-Adm Lewis Maitland, of Lindores, Fife, 5th son of late Charles Maitland of Rankeilour, sometime 17th Light Dragoons (*b* 1769) (ante):—
Issue of late Frederick Lewis Maitland, *b* 1874, *d* 1915: *m* 1896, Constance Zeila, da of late A. Dewar-Durie, MD, of Craigluscar, Fife:—
David Randolph, VRD, *b* 1902; formerly Surg-Lieut-Com RNVR; has Diploma of Med Radiology, Diagnostic; MB, ChB, FRCPE: *m* 1930, Barbara Mary Carnegie, da of late Edward Wemyss, of Kirkton, Fife, and has issue living, David Lewis, *b* 1932: *m* 1st, 1961, Anna Mary Smith, who *d* 1968, ward of J. de R. Kent, of Valewood, Haslemere, Surrey; 2ndly, 1969, Jennifer Mary Davies, and has issue living (by 1st *m*), Lewis Randolph *b* 1962, Niall David (twin) *b* 1962, Angus Charles *b* 1964 (by 2nd *m*) Sarah Mary *b* 1971, — Henry Christopher (Grange of Lindores, Newburgh, Fife) *b* 1935: *m* 1968, Charlotte Mary Ross, da of R. Tod, of 17 South Oswald Rd, Edinburgh, and widow of Lt J. W. Harvey, RN, and has issue living, Christopher Ross *b* 1969, Gavin Edward *b* 1976, Barbara Anne *b* 1972, Mary Flora Muriel (twin) *b* 1976, — Mary *b* 1939: *m* 1962, Peter Lauritz Wang, of Lawhead Loch, W. Calder, Midlothian EH55 8LW, and has issue living, Mark Sigurd Maitland *b* 1963, Patrick David *b* 1965, Robert Magnus *b* 1969. *Residence* – Hatton Hill, Newburgh, Fife.

Issue of late Anna Lewise Maitland, *b* 1872, *d* 1914: *m* 1893, Rev Charles Henry Titterton, BD, who *d* 1958 (*see* 1985 and earlier edns)

Granddaughters of late Andrew Agnew Maitland-Heriot (latterly Heriot-Maitland), el son of late Frederick Maitland-Heriot (*b* 1818), el son of late James Maitland-Heriot of Ramornie, 2nd son of Capt Hon Frederick Lewis Maitland, RN (ante), 8th son of 6th Earl:—
Issue of late Frederick Lewis Heriot-Maitland, *b* 1889, *d* 1953: *m* 1919, Mabel Mary, who *d* 1962, da of late James Keenan, of Rosario, Argentina:—
Pamela Gertrude, *b* 1921: *m* 1940, Major Christopher Evelyn Boothby, RM, who *d* 1991 (*see* Boothby Bt, colls). *Residence* – 26 Cwrt Deri, Heol-y-Felin, Rhiwbina, Cardiff CF4 6JB. ——— Jean Ursula (82 Beaufort Mansions, Beaufort St, SW3 5AF), *b* 1923; 1941-45 with WRNS: *m* 1st, 1944 (*m diss* 1952), Capt Alan Seaforth Cox; 2ndly, 1955, John G. Adams, who *d* 1978, and has issue living, (by 1st *m*) Andrew Frederick Seaforth (8 Morpeth Mansions, Morpeth Terr, SW1), *b* 1945: *m* 1st, 1964 (*m diss* 1976), Carol Ilott; 2ndly, 1978, Tricia Harley, and has issue living (by 1st *m*), Oliver *b* 1967, Emma *b* 1964, Zoe *b* 1969, (by 2nd *m*) Toby *b* 1974, Charlie *b* 1982, — (by 2nd *m*) Sebastian Thomas Maitland, *b* 1961.

Grandchildren of late Frederick Maitland-Heriot, 2nd son of late Frederick Maitland-Heriot (*b* 1818) (ante):—
Issue of late Frank de Courcy Maitland-Heriot, *b* 1882, *d* 1957: *m* 1st (Jan) 1912, Marguerita Mary, who *d* 1935, da of George Logan, MD, of Cressfield, Ecclefechan, Dumfriesshire; 2ndly, 1939, Marion Mercer Moore, of Greystone, Los Cocos, Sierras de Cordoba, Argentina:—
(By 1st *m*) Jean, *b* 1915: *m* 1935, Henry Ranald, Martin, OBE, who *d* 1979, and has issue living, Ian Duncan (PO Box 546, Asunción, Paraguay), *b* 1937: *m* 1961, June Hope Castleton, and has issue living, Angus Ian *b* 1973, Patrick Duncan Ian *b* 1975, Virginia Jean *b* 1963. Anthea Lorraine *b* 1966, Andrea June *b* 1968, — Norman (Estancia Chica, Radial Conchillas, Dept Colonia, Uruguay), *b* 1941: *m* 1965, Jacqueline Ann Booth, and has issue living, Ian Ranald Calvert *b* 1966, Alastair Reginald *b* 1968, Nicholas Andrew *b* 1970, Anthony Norman *b* 1974, — Donald de Courcy (Box 9, Valencia, Venezuela), *b* 1943: *m* 1969, Elizabeth Mary Christie, of Montevideo, and has issue living, Angus Donald *b* 1973, Kenneth James *b* 1976, Veronica Ann *b* 1971, Fiona Jean *b* 1976, — Adrian Ranald, *b* 1953. *Residence* – Guardizabal 1619, Montevideo, Uruguay.
Issue of late (Charles) Adrian Maitland-Heriot, DSC, *b* 1886, *d* 1919: *m* 1919, Dorothy Mary, who *d* 1979, da of A. Egerton-Savory, of Eastbourne:—
Audrey Enid, *b* 1921; 1939-45 War in WAAF: *m* 1972, John Rogerson, of 95 Ridgmount Gdns, WC1E 7AZ.
Issue of late George Vivian Maitland-Heriot, *b* 1891, *d* 1979: *m* 1919, Marjorie Kathleen, who *d* 1983, da of Edward J. Silcock, MICE, of Roundhay, Leeds:—
Torrance (Galvez 1423 D°2, Rosario, Argentina), *b* 1920; *ed* Lancing; 1939-45 War with RAF (wounded): *m* 1947, Elda Carmen, who *d* 1963, da of John Stevenson Pearson, of Adrogue, Argentina, and has issue living, Edward John Stevenson, *b* 1950: *m* 197—, Leonore, da of —. ——— Frederick Euan, *b* 1926; 1939-45 War with Fleet Air Arm: *m* 1954, Vera Margaret, yst da of late Gavin Greig Watson. ——— †Nigel Hugh, *b* 1926; 1939-45 War in Far East with RAC: *m* 1953, Beryl Francis, who *d* 1989, eldest da of John Robert Anderson, and *d* 1991, leaving issue, Christopher John (Rancho Alegre, Yei-Pora, Concordia, Entre Rios, Argentina), *b* 1955: *m* 1980, Maria Elena Cristina Cocco, and has issue living, Leonardo Nicolas *b* 1984, Pablo Alexander *b* 1986, Veronica Natalia *b* 1982, — Elizabeth Vivian, *b* 1959: *m* 1993, Ernesto Bernardo Sarli, of Dr Chabrillon 50, 3200 Concordia, Entre Rios, Argentina. ——— Clare Antoinette, *b* 1922; 1939-45 War with WAAF: *m* 1980, Oscar Cividiño.
Issue of late Ralph Lionel Maitland-Heriot, MC, *b* 1895, *d* 1935: *m* 1927, Moira (who *d* 1985, having *m* 2ndly, 1938, George Scott), da of Harry Hugh Jefferies, of Fisherton, Argentina:—
Ralph Desmond, *b* 1930: *m* 1955, Anneslie Atkinson, and has issue living, Richard Patrick, *b* 1956, — Timothy James, *b* 1958, — Rosalind Elizabeth, *b* 1962. ——— Pamela Avril (9 Grasmere Av, SW15), *b* 1928: *m* 1952, Anthony Benjamin Oliveira, FRCS, who *d* 1983, and has issue living, David Benjamin Graeme (52 London Rd, Harston, Cambridge), *b* 1955; *ed* Stowe, and Camb Univ; MRCP, PhD: *m* 1984, Patricia Margaret, da of G/Capt John Edward Ffrancon Williams, CBE, and has issue living, Benjamin Anthony *b* 1985, Samuel John *b* 1987, Amelia Sophie *b* 1988, — Lynette Moira, *b* 1957: *m* 1992, Fl Lt Jonathan P. Q. Reid, son of Sir John Reid.
Issue of late Lt-Col Gerald Ian Maitland-Heriot, MC, ED, *b* 1898, *d* 1987: *m* 1931, Paula Elsie Barbara (Constantia Hill Farm, Belair Drive, Constantia, CP, S Africa), da of late Cuthbert Henry Gordon, of Bihar, India:—
Celia, *b* 1934: *m* 1961, Robert Edmund Scott Hanbury, of Drumstinchall, Dalbeattie, Kirkcudbrightshire, and has issue living, Roland William Edmund, *b* 1964; *ed* Eton: *m* 1993, Heather Gail, da of Douglas Adams, of Dunmurry, co Antrim, — Melanie Rhona, *b* 1967.

Grandchildren of late Cdr William Maitland Dougall, 2nd son of late James Maitland-Heriot of Ramornie (*b* 1774) (ante):—

Issue of late Col Wilmot Edward Maitland Dougall, DSO, MC, *b* 1890, *d* 1972: *m* 1st, 1930, Mary Louisa, who *d* 1959, da of Capt Arthur Schreiber, of Brook's Hall, Ipswich; 2ndly, 1960, Hilda, widow of Lt-Col J. R. H. Baddeley:— (By 1st *m*) Colin (Dowhill, Kelty, Fife), *b* 1933; Lt-Cdr RN: *m* 1964, Philippa Blackstone, da of Cdr G. H. Wise, RN, of Titchfield, Hants, and has a son, Frederick Andrew, *b* 1973. —— Eve Diana (The Priest's House, Sutton Montis Yeovil, Som), *b* 1936: *m* 1st, 1959 (*m diss* 1977), her 3rd cousin, Maj Arthur John French, R Irish Rangers (*see* E Lauderdale, colls, 1954 edn); 2ndly, 1977 (*m diss* 1993), Desmond Saville Hunter, TD, and has issue living (by 1st *m*), Miles Arthur Maitland (77 rue du Moulin de Saquet, 94800 Villejuif, France), *b* 1961, *ed* Wellington Coll: *m* 1991, Mrs Anne Rosemary Maurice, elder da of Sir Charles Boscawen Frederick, 10th Bt, and has issue living, Raphael Maitland *b* 1994, Naomi Hilda *b* 1992, — Dominick George Maitland, *b* 1970, — Amelia Mary Katherine, *b* 1963.

Grandchildren of late Brig-Gen James Dalgleish Heriot-Maitland, CMG, DSO (infra):—
Issue of late Richard Ogilvy Heriot Maitland, JP, DL, *b* 1913, *d* 1972: *m* 1935, Patricia (Woodlands Lodge, Errol, Pethshire), el da of late Lt-Col Cecil Bevis:—
Lewis Dalgleish, TD (Errol Park, Errol, Perthshire), *b* 1943: *m* 1976, Prudence Jane, da of John Richard Bertram Norris, of Canberra, Aust, and has issue living, James Richard *b* 1978, — Lucia Jane, *b* 1981, — Eliza, *b* 1983, — a da, *b* 1985. —— Patrick Richard (Fossoway Lodge, Kinross), *b* 1947: *m* 1978, Marilyn Lois, da of Russell Grant, of St Petersburg, Florida, USA, and has issue living, Charles, *b* 1980, — Katherine, *b* 1983, — Joanna, *b* 1985, — Alexandra, *b* 1989. —— Mary Lorne, *b* 1945.

Granddaughter of late Maj-Gen Sir James Makgill Heriot-Maitland, KCB, yst son of James Maitland-Heriot Dalgleish, of Ramornie (*b* 1774) (ante):—
Issue of late Brig-Gen James Dalgleish Heriot-Maitland, CMG DSO, *b* 1874, *d* 1958: *m* 1903, (Lady) Mary Turner, who *d* 1937, da of late Henry Scrymgeour-Wedderburn, *de jure* 9th Earl of Dundee (Hereditary Standard Bearer of Scotland), of Birkhill, Fife:—
Joan Margaret (White House of Aros, Isle of Mull), *b* 1909.

Grandson of Lt-Gen John Maitland, yst son of John Maitland, only son of John Maitland, only son of Hon Patrick Maitland, 7th son of 6th Earl:—
Issue of late Patrick Lauderdale Maitland, *b* 1862, *d* 1939: *m* 1904: Julia Elizabeth, who *d* 1953, da of late George May, of Cleveland, Ohio, USA:—
Lawrence Lauderdale, *b* 1905; *ed* Ackworth Sch, and Sheffield Univ; Major (ret) late Gordon Highlanders, and an Engineer. *Residence* – 24 Coopersfield, Debenham, Stowmarket, Suffolk IP14 6QR.

PREDECESSORS – (**1**) Sir JOHN MAITLAND, Knt, Keeper of the Privy Seal 1567, and a Lord of Session 1568-70, when his office was forfeited for his adhesion to the Queen's party; appointed a Lord of Session 1581, constituted a Sec of State for life 1584, and Keeper of the Great Seal of Scotland for life with title of Vice Chancellor 1586; *cr Lord Maitland of Thirlestane* (peerage of Scotland) 1590; *d* 1595; *s* by his son (**2**) JOHN, 2nd Lord; was a Lord of Session or Pres of the Council; *cr Viscount of Lauderdale* (peerage of Scotland) 1616, with remainder to his heirs male and successors in the Lordship of Thirlestane, and *Lord Thirlestane and Boltoun, Viscount Maitland* and *Earl of Lauderdale* (peerage of Scotland), 1624 with remainder to his heirs male bearing the name and arms of Maitland; *d* 1645; *s* by his el son (**3**) JOHN, 2nd Earl, KG, PC, a zealous partizan of Charles II and one of the historic personages of his time; was a Commr appointed by the Church of Scotland to meet the assembly of Divines at Westminster 1643, and was several times employed as a Parliament Commr; taken prisoner as battle of Worcester 1651 and was confined in the Tower until 1660; for his fidelity to the king he was made Sec of State, Pres of the Council, Heritable High Sheriff of co Edinburgh, an Extraordinary Lord of Session, First Commr of the Treasury, Lord High Commr to the Parliament, and Gov of Edinburgh Castle; *cr Marquess of March* and *Duke of Lauderdale* (peerage of Scotland) 1672, and *Baron Petersham* and *Earl of Guilford* (peerage of England) 1682, when all the peerages conferred upon himself became extinct and the other honours reverted to his brother (**4**) CHARLES, 3rd Earl; was Gen of the Mint, and Dep Treasurer and a Judge of the Court of Session; *d* 1691; *s* by his el son (**5**) RICHARD, KB, PC, 4th Earl; was Gen of the Mint, and Lord Justice Gen 1681-4; outlawed 1694 for his adhesion to the cause of James II; *dsp* 1695; *s* by his brother (**6**) JOHN, 5th Earl; *cr* a Baronet of Nova Scotia 1680; MP for co Edinburgh 1685; a Lord of Session with title of Lord Ravelrig 1689-1710; *d* 1710; *s* by his son (**7**) CHARLES, 6th Earl, a Representative Peer, Master of the Mint, and Lord-Lieut of co Edinburgh; *d* 1744; *s* by his son (**8**) JAMES, 8th Earl; *cr Baron Lauderdale*, of Thirlestane, co Berwick (peerage of United Kingdom) 1806; *d* 1839; *s* by his el son (**10**) JAMES, 9th Earl; MP for Appleby 1820-31, and Lord-Lieut of co Berwick; *d* unmarried 1860; *s* by his brother (**11**) ANTHONY, GCB, KCMG, 10th Earl; an Adm of the Red; *d* 1863, when the English barony expired, and the other peerages devolved upon his cousin (**12**) THOMAS, GCB, 11th Earl, son of Gen Hon William Mordaunt Maitland, 3rd son of 7th Earl; a Representative Peer, and Adm of the Fleet, etc; *d* 1878; *s* by his kinsman (**13**) CHARLES, 12th Earl, who *d* Aug 1884; *s* by his kinsman (**14**) FREDERICK HENRY (son of late Gen Frederick Colthurst Maitland, son of late Patrick Maitland, 2nd son of Col Hon Richard Maitland, 4th son of 6th Earl), 13th Earl, *b* 1840; established his claim to the title before Committee for Privileges of the House of Lords, July 1885; Lord-Lieut of Berwickshire 1889-1901; for 31 years a Representative Peer for Scotland; *m* 1st, 1864, Charlotte Sarah, who *d* 1879, da of the late Lieut-Col Sleigh (77th Regt); 2ndly, 1883, Ada Twyford, who *d* 1931, da of late Rev Henry Trail Simpson, R of Adel, York; *d* 1924; *s* by his son (**15**) FREDERICK COLIN, OBE, 14th Earl, *b* 1868; a Representative Peer for Scotland, one of HM's Hon Corps of Gentlemen-of-Arms, and Ensign Roy Co of Archers (King's Body Guard for Scotland): *m* 1890, Gwendoline Lucy, who *d* 1929, da of late Judge R. Vaughan Williams, of Bodlonfa, Flintshire; *d* 1931; *s* by his son (**16**) IAN COLIN, 15th Earl; *b* 1891; a Member of Queen's Body Guard for Scotland (Roy Co of Archers); was ADC to Viceroy of Ireland 1915-16 and 1918: *m* 1912, Ethel Mary, who *d* 1970, da of James Jardine Bell-Irving, of Makerstoun House, Kelso; *d* 1953; *s* by his cousin (**17**) Rev ALFRED SYDNEY FREDERICK (son of late Rev Hon Sydney George William Maitland, 2nd son of 13th Earl), 16th Earl, *b* 1904: *m* 1st, 1938, Norah Mary, who *d* 1938, da of late William Henry La Touche; 2ndly, 1940, Irene Alice May, da of late Rev C. P. Shipton, of Halsham, Yorks; *d* 1968; *s* by his brother (**18**) PATRICK FRANCIS, 17th Earl and present peer; also Viscount of Lauderdale, Viscount Maitland, Lord Maitland of Thirlestane, and Lord Thirlestane and Boltoun.

LAWRENCE, BARON (Lawrence) (Baron UK 1869, Bt UK 1858)

DAVID JOHN DOWNER LAWRENCE, 5th Baron and 5th Baronet; *b* 4 Sept 1937; *s* 1968.

Arms – Ermine, on a cross raguly gules an Eastern crown or; a chief azure, thereon two swords in saltire proper, pommels and hilts gold, between as many leopards' faces argent. **Crest** – Out of an Eastern crown or, a cubit arm entwined by a wreath of laurel and holding a dagger all proper. **Supporters** – *Dexter*, an officer of the Guide Cavalry (Irregulars), of the Pathan tribe, in the province of Peshawar, habited and accoutred proper; *sinister*, an officer of the Sikh Irregular Cavalry, also habited and accoutred proper.
Address – 2 Gray's Inn Sq, WC1.

AUNTS LIVING (*Daughters of 3rd Baron*)

Hon Catherine Dorina Mary, *b* 1910. *Residence* – W Wittering Nursing Home, Sussex.
Hon Nona Georgette, *b* 1922: *m* 1945, W/Cdr Vincent George Byrne, RAF, who *d* 1978, and has issue living, Nicholas John Joseph (Moat House, Chapel Lane, W Wittering, Sussex), *b* 1946: *m* 1968, Catherine Penelope, da of Douglas Smith, and has issue living, Kirstie Mary Kate *b* 1969, Tara Mary Fiona *b* 1971, Fiona Georgina Mary *b* 1976, — James Vincent (Hawkyard House, Chipping Norton, Oxon), *b* 1950; MD, FRCS, FRCR: *m* 1975, Juliet Elizabeth Anson, da of John Bailey, and has issue living, Thomas Vincent Lawrence *b* 1979, George Henry St Clare *b* 1981, Henry Charles Mogeridge *b* 1985, Rowena Catherine Anson *b* 1977, — (Vincent) Patrick (17 Birchland Av, SW12), *b* 1952: *m* 1989, Mary Gabriel, 2nd da of Sir James Napier Finnie McEwen, 2nd Bt, and has issue living, Elliot James *b* 1991, Rosanna Clare *b* 1993, —
Dominic Lawrence, *b* 1959; MD, MRCOG: *m* 1990, Susan Amanda, BSc, MRCOG, da of Capt Richard Bates, RN, of Winchester, and has issue living, Katharine Letitia *b* 1992, — Rory Shaun (30 West Hill Rd, SW18), *b* 1961: *m* 1988, Andrea Carina, da of Peter Riediker, of Zurich, Switzerland, and has issue living, Edward Alexander *b* 1990, Christian Rory *b* 1992, Jessica Katherine *b* 1989, — Teresa Marie, *b* 1947: *m* 1968, Robin Herbert Wickham, of Maynards Farm, Matfield, Tonbridge, Kent, and has issue living, Simon James Wykeham *b* 1969, Patrick David Wykeham *b* 1972, — Clare Mary Anne, *b* 1955: *m* 1981, Tass Whittaker, of 8 Sudbrook Rd, SW12, and has issue living, Lara Nona Jane *b* 1983, Amy Marie Clare *b* 1986, Eleanor Charlotte *b* 1988, — Fiona Rosaleen Mary, *b* 1957: *m* 1983, Robert J. Rolls, of 41 Doneraile St, SW6, and has issue living, Giles Thomas Alexander *b* 1984, Annabel India Sarah *b* 1986, Sophie Amelia Lucy *b* 1988. *Residence* – Blackberry Cottage, W Wittering, W Sussex.

WIDOW LIVING OF FOURTH BARON

JOAN ALICE MILDRED, da of late Col Arthur John Lewer, OBE, of Bonchurch, I of Wight: *m* 1st, 1948, as his 2nd wife, the 4th Baron, who *d* 1968; 2ndly, 1969, John Eddison, who *d* 1989, of White Bays, 21 Bellevue Rd, Ryde, Isle of Wight, PO33 2AR.

PREDECESSORS – (1) *Rt Hon Sir* JOHN LAIRD MAIR LAWRENCE, GCB, BCSI, PC, DCL LLD, 5th son of late Lieut-Col Alexander Lawrence, Gov of Upton Castle, Kent, *b* 1811; entered Bengal Civil Ser 1828, and having held numerous minor positions became Commr of the Jullunder Doab 1846, and was subsequently Member of Board of Administration for the Punjab 1849-52, Chief Commr of the Punjab 1852-8, First Lt-Gov of that province 1858-9, Viceroy of India 1864-8, and chm of London School Board 1870-3; *cr* a *Baronet* 1858, and *Baron Lawrence*, of the Punjab and of Grateley, co Southampton 1869; *m* 1841, Harriette Katherine, CI, who *d* 1917, da of Rev Richard Hamilton; *d* 1879; *s* by his son (2) JOHN HAMILTON, 2nd Baron, *b* 1846; Lord-in-Waiting to Queen Victoria 1895-1901, and to King Edward VII 1901-5: *m* 1872, Mary Caroline Douglas, who *d* 1938, only da of late Richard Campbell of Auchinbreck and Glencarradle, Argyllshire; *d* 1913; *s* by his son (3) ALEXANDER GRAHAM, 3rd Baron, *b* 1878; *m* 1st, 1907, Dorothy Helen, CBE, who *d* 1935, da of late Anthony Pemberton Hobson, many years Inspector-Gen of Police, St Vincent, W Indies; 2ndly, 1935, Jessie, who *d* 1936, da of late Col Byron Gordon Daniels, US Army, and widow of William Frederic Lawrence, of Cowesfield House, Wilts; 3rdly, 1938, Catherine Louisa, who *d* 1965, da of late Charles Fernihough, and widow of William Burnet Craigie; *d* (June) 1947; *s* by his son (4) JOHN ANTHONY EDWARD, 4th Baron, *b* 1908: *m* 1st, 1936 (*m diss* 1947), Margaret Jean, who *d* 1977, da of Arthur Downer, of Rotherfield, Kent; 2ndly, 1948, Joan Alice Mildred (who *m* 2ndly, 1969, John Eddison who *d* 1989), da of Maj Arthur John Lewer, OBE, of Norwood Green, Middx; *d* 1968; *s* by his son (5) DAVIS JOHN DOWNER, 5th Baron and present peer.

LAWSON, BARONY OF (Lawson) (Extinct 1965)

DAUGHTERS LIVING OF FIRST AND LAST BARON

Hon Irene, *b* 1909: *m* 1935, Charles Frederick Campbell Lawson, and has issue living, Ruth Ellison, *b* 1936, — Elizabeth Graham, *b* 1943, — Elaine Campbell, *b* 1944. *Residence* – Dourene, Park Road North, Chester-le-Street, co Durham.
Hon Edna, *b* 1912: *m* 19—, D. Brown, and has issue living, David, *b* 1945. *Residence* –
Hon Alma, *b* 1920.

LAWSON OF BLABY, BARON (Lawson) (Life Baron 1992)

NIGEL LAWSON, PC, only son of late Ralph Lawson; *b* 11 March 1932; *ed* Westminster, and Ch Ch, Oxford (BA 1954); Fellow Nuffield Coll, Oxford 1972-73; editorial staff *Financial Times* 1956-60, City Ed *Sunday Telegraph* 1961-63, Ed *The Spectator* 1966-70; Special Assist to PM (Sir Alec Douglas-Home) 1963-64, and Special Political Adviser Conservative HQ 1973-74; Financial Sec to the Treasury 1979-81, Energy Sec 1981-83, Chancellor of the Exchequer 1983-Oct 1989 (resigned); Dir Barclays Bank since 1990, Dir GPA

Group 1990-93, Chm Central Europe Trust since 1990; Sub-Lieut RNVR 1954-56; MP Blaby (*C*) 1974-92; *cr* PC 1981, and *Baron Lawson of Blaby*, of Newnham, co Northants (Life Baron) 1992; *m* 1st, 1955 (*m diss* 1980), Vanessa Mary Addison, who *d* 1985, 2nd da of late Felix Addison Salmon, of Ham Common Surrey; 2ndly, 1980, Thérèse Mary, da of late Henry Charles Maclear Bate, of Putney, London, and has had issue by 1st and 2nd wives.
Address – c/o House of Lords, SW1. *Clubs* – Garrick, Pratt's.

SONS LIVING (*by 1st wife*)

Hon Dominic Ralph Campden, *b* 1956; *ed* Westminster, and Ch Ch, Oxford; Ed *The Spectator* since 1990; author: *m* 1st, 1982, Jane Fiona, da of David Christopher Wastell Whytehead, of W Dulwich, SE21; 2ndly, 1991, Hon Rosamond Mary Monckton, only da of 2nd Viscount Monckton of Brenchley, CB, OBE, MC, and has issue living (by 2nd *m*), Savannah Vanessa Lucia, *b* 1992. *Clubs* – Academy, MCC.

(*by 2nd wife*)

Hon Thomas Nigel Maclear, *b* 1976; *ed* Eton.

DAUGHTERS LIVING AND DECEASED (*by 1st wife*)

Hon Nigella Lucy, *b* 1960; *ed* Godolphin & Latymer, and Lady Margaret Hall, Oxford; journalist and broadcaster: *m* 1992, John Diamond, and has issue living, Cosima Thomasina, *b* 1993.
Hon Thomasina Posy, *b* 1961: *m* 1985, Ivan Hill, and *d* 1993.
Hon Horatia Holly, *b* 1966.

(*by 2nd wife*)

Hon Emily Hero, *b* 1981.

LAYTON, BARON (Layton) (Baron UK 1947)

GEOFFREY MICHAEL LAYTON, 3rd Baron; *b* 18 July 1947; *s* 1989; *ed* St Paul's Sch, Stanford Univ, and Univ of Southern Calif: *m* 1st, 1969 (*m diss* 1970), Viviane, da of François Cracco, of Louvain, Belgium; 2ndly, 1989, Caroline Jane, da of William Thomas Mason, of Fairford, Glos, and formerly wife of Adm Spyros Soulis, of Athens.

SISTER LIVING

Hon Deanna Christine, *b* 1938: MB, BS, MRCS, LRCP: *m* 1964, Melvin Calverley Jennings, MB, FRCS, Barn Ridge, 18 High Trees Rd, Reigate, Surrey RH2 7EJ, and has issue living, Andrew Melvin, *b* 1965, — Simon, *b* 1967, — Robert, *b* 1970.

UNCLES LIVING (*sons of 1st Baron*)

Hon DAVID, MBE (18 Grove Terrace, Highgate Rd, NW5), *b* 5 July 1914; *ed* Gresham's Sch, Holt, and Trin Coll, Camb; MBE (Mil) 1946: *m* 1st, 1939 (*m diss* 1972), Elizabeth, da of Robert Gray; 2ndly, 1972, Joy Parkinson, and has issue living (by 1st *m*), Jonathan Francis, *b* 1942: *m* 1971, Julia Goodwin, and has issue living, Jeremy *b* 1978, Robert *b* 1982, Jessica *b* 1974, — Mark Oliver, *b* 1944, — Hilary Ruth, *b* 1947.
Hon Christopher Walter, *b* 1929; *ed* Oundle, and King's Coll, Camb: *m* 1st, 1952 (*m diss* 1957) Annaliese Margaret, da of Joachim von Thadden, of Hanover; 2ndly, 1961, Margaret Ann, da of Leslie Moon, of Molesey, Surrey, and has had issue (by 1st *m*), John Stephen, *b* 1955, — Diana, *b* 1953, — (by 2nd *m*) Eleanor Rachel, *b* 1963; *d* 1985, — Sarah Jean *b* 1964, — Lesley Claire, *b* 1971. *Residence* – Grimstone Mews, Jordan Lane, Horrabridge, nr Yelverton, Devon PL20 7QY.

AUNTS LIVING (*daughters of 1st Baron*)

Hon Jean Mary, *b* 1916: *m* 1944, Paul Eisler, who *d* 1966, and has issue living, John, *b* 1946: *m* 1977, Eva Tlustá, of Prague, and has issue living, Martin *b* 1977, Mark *b* 1980, — Ivan, *b* 1948: *m* 1971, Zuzana Tibenska, of Bratislava, Slovakia, and has issue living, Philip *b* 1973, Lucinka *b* 1976. *Residence* – Syskon Cottage, 2 Millfield Lane, N6 6JD.
Hon Olive Shirley, *b* 1918: *m* 1943, Peter Gellhorn, conductor, and has issue living, Martin Oliver, *b* 1945: *m* 1969 (*m diss* 1976), Susanna Elizabeth, da of Thomas Howard Beauchamp Gladstone, MB, BS, of Ilkeston, Derbys, and has issue living, Catherine *b* 1969, — Philip Nicholas, *b* 1951, — Mary Ann, *b* 1959, — Barbara Dorothea, *b* 1960. *Residence* – 33 Leinster Av, SW14 7JW.
Hon Elizabeth Ruth Frances, *b* 1923: *m* 1944 (*m diss* 1965), Bobbie Pegna, and has issue living, Robin, *b* 1945: *m* 1968, Catherine Bridge Gray, da of John Henderson, of Greenwood, Frant, Sussex, and has issue living, Jonathan *b* 1982, Catherine *b* 1973, Alice *b* 1976, — Christopher John, *b* 1956, — Shirley, *b* 1951. *Residence* – 2 Farmington, Cheltenham, Glos GL54 3NQ.

PREDECESSORS – (1) WALTER THOMAS Layton, CH, CBE, son of Alfred John Layton, of Woking, Surrey; *b* 1884; Editor, *The Economist* 1922-38, and Chm 1944-63, Chm News Chronicle Ltd 1930-50, and Star Newspaper Co Ltd 1936-50; Head of Joint War Production Staff and Ch Adviser on Programmes and Planning Min of Production 1942-43, and Vice-Pres of Assembly of Council of Europe 1949-57; *cr Baron Layton*, of Danehill, co Sussex (peerage of UK) 1947: *m* 1910, Eleanor Dorothea, who *d* 1959, da of Francis Beresford Plumtre Osmaston, of Stoneshill, Limpsfield, Surrey: *d* 1966; *s* by his el son (2) MICHAEL JOHN, 2nd Baron, *b* 1912; Dir Wolff Steel Holdings Ltd 1977-83, and *The Economist* Newspaper Ltd 1973-85; Head Internat Relations Dept of British Iron and Steel Fedn 1948-55, etc: *m* 1938, Dorothy, who *d* 1994, da of Albert Luther Cross, of Rugby; *d* 1989; *s* by his only son (3) GEOFFREY MICHAEL, 3rd Baron and present peer.

LEATHERLAND, BARONY OF (Leatherland) (Extinct 1992)

SON LIVING OF LIFE BARON

Hon John Charles (4 Manor Way, Chingford, E4), *b* 1929; *ed* Brentwood; *m* 1954, Esther Stella Steckman, and has issue.

DAUGHTER LIVING OF LIFE BARON

Hon Irene Mary (19 The Greens Close, Loughton, Essex), *b* 1923: *m* 1961 (*m diss* 1977), Douglas Richards, and has issue.

LEATHERS, VISCOUNT (Leathers) (Viscount UK 1954)

While I breathe I serve

FREDERICK ALAN LEATHERS, 2nd Viscount; *b* 4 April 1908; *s* 1965; *ed* Brighton Coll, and Emmanuel Coll, Camb; Chm of Wm Cory & Son, Ltd: *m* 1st, 1940 (*m diss* 1983), Elspeth Graeme, da of late Sir Thomas Alexander Stewart, KCSI, KCIE; 2ndly, 1983, Lorna May, widow of Arthur A. C. Barnett, and da of late A. K. Marshall, and has issue by 1st *m*.

Arms – Azure, a lymphad, sails set or, flags flying to the dexter gules, on a chief of the second three lozenges sable. **Crest** – A lozenge sable in front of two anchors in saltire or. **Supporters** – *Dexter*, a sea-lion; *sinister*, a sea horse argent gorged with a collar of lozenges conjoined sable.
Residence – Park House, Chiddingfold, Surrey GU8 4TS.

SONS LIVING *(By 1st marriage)*

Hon CHRISTOPHER GRAEME (Sunhill, Mold Rd, Bodfari, Denbigh, Clwyd LL16 4DP), *b* 31 Aug 1941; *ed* Rugby; JP: *m* 1964, Maria Philomena, yr da of Michael Merriman, of Charlestown, co Mayo, and has issue living, James Frederick, *b* 1969, — Melissa Maria, *b* 1966.
Hon Jeremy Baxter, *b* 1946: *m* 1969, Fiona Lesley, el da of late G. S. Pitt, of Rowbarns Manor, E Horsley, Surrey, and has issue living, Luke Alexander, *b* 1974, — Tara Charlotte, *b* 1972, — Fern Griselda, *b* 1979.

DAUGHTERS LIVING *(By 1st marriage)*

Hon Anne Catherine, *b* 1944: *m* 1977, Arthur Sydney Centner, of 11 Orchard Rd, Orchards, Johannesburg 2192, South Africa, and has issue living, Lucy Emma, *b* 1977.
Hon Deborah Elspeth, *b* 1947: *m* 1st, 1966, Thomas Richard Chadbon; 2ndly, 1980, Richard William Pitt, of 6 Bassingham Rd, SW18 3AG, yst son of late G. S. Pitt (ante), and has issue living (by 1st *m*), Dominic Thomas, *b* 1966, — Nicholas Richard, *b* 1968, — (by 2nd *m*), Isabelle, *b* 1981.

BROTHER LIVING

Hon Leslie John (Middleton Park, Middleton Stoney, nr Bicester, Oxon OX6 8SQ), *b* 1911; *ed* Brighton Coll; admitted a Solicitor 1935; is Maj late RA: *m* 1937, Elizabeth Stella, only da of Thomas Stanley Nash, of Sidcup, and has issue living, Michael John Nash (Oldhams, Fox Hill, Petworth, W Sussex GU28 9NU), *b* 1938: *m* 1962, Shelley Matthews, da of late Keith Marten, of Gedgrave Hall, Orford, Suffolk, and has issue living, Simon Michael John *b* 1964, Sean Patrick James *b* 1966, Richard Anthony *b* 1968, Benjamin Matthew *b* 1971, Nicholas Paul Tarquin *b* 1974, — David Frederick James (14 Holmead Rd, SW6 2JG), *b* 1942: *m* 1968, Amanda Elizabeth Ann Vyvyan, da of Lt-Col Arthur Vyvyan Denton, of Dial House, Lower Bourne, Farnham (*see* Strickland Constable, Bt, colls), and has issue living, Jonathan James *b* 1974, Andrew Thomas *b* 1975, — Rosemary Elizabeth, *b* 1945: *m* 1972, Winfried F. W. Bischoff, of 28 Bloomfield Terr, SW1W 8PQ, son of Paul Helmut Bischoff, of Johannesburg and Dusseldorf, and has issue living, Christopher William *b* 1973, Charles Francis *b* 1975.

SISTER LIVING

Hon Audrey Mary, *b* 1915: *m* 1938, Edward Noel Evans, who *d* 1964, and has had issue, Richard Edward Craig, *b* 1945: *m* 1973, Jillian Sonia, yr da of late H. W. Reid, of The Manse, Royston, Herts, and has issue living, Charles Noel Edward *b* 1975, Hilary Jane *b* 1977, Melissa Kate *b* 1981, — Peter James, *b* 1946: *m* 1979, Lynne, da of James Irving Cosgrove, and widow of Desmond Hawe, and *d* 1988, leaving issue, Katie Samantha *b* 1982, Jessica Jane *b* 1984, — Jacqueline Mary, *b* 1940: *m* 1st, 1961 (*m diss* 1969), Barrington Hugh Lawes; 2ndly, 1969, Michael Hind, of 66 Erpingham Rd, SW15, and has issue living, (by 1st *m*) Nicholas Hugh *b* 1962: *m* 1987, Julie, da of Sir Noel Edward Vivian Short, MBE, MC, Suzanna Jane *b* 1964, (by 2nd *m*) Sally Louise *b* 1970. *Residence* – 28 Hyde Park Gdns, W2.

PREDECESSOR – (1) FREDERICK JAMES Leathers, CH, PC, son of Robert Leathers, of Stowmarket, Suffolk; *b* 1883; Min of War Transport 1941-45, and Sec of State for Co-ordination of Transport Fuel and Power 1951-53; *cr Baron Leathers* of Purfleet, co Essex (Peerage of UK) 1941, and *Viscount Leathers*, of Purfleet, co Essex (Peerage of UK) 1954: *m* 1907, Emily Ethel, who *d* 1971, da of late Henry Baxter, of Southend; *d* 1965; *s* by his el son (2) FREDERICK ALAN, 2nd Viscount and present peer; also Baron Leathers.

Leconfield, Baron, see Baron Egremont.

LEE OF NEWTON, BARONY OF (Lee) (Extinct 1984)

DAUGHTER LIVING OF LIFE BARON

Hon Pamela Margaret, *b* 1945: *m* 1965, Rodney Flint, of The Willows, Church Drive, Newton-le-Willows, Merseyside, WA12 9SR.

WIDOW LIVING OF LIFE BARON

AMELIA (*Baroness Lee of Newton*) (52 Ashton Rd, Newton-le-Willows, Merseyside EA12 0AE), da of William Shay: *m* 1938, Baron Lee of Newton, PC (Life Peer), who *d* 1984.

LEEDS, DUKEDOM OF (Osborne) (Extinct 1964)

DAUGHTER LIVING OF ELEVENTH DUKE

Lady Camilla Dorothy Godolphin, *b* 1950: *m* 1st, 1971 (*m diss* 1976), Robert Julian Brownlow Harris (*see* B Harris, colls); 2ndly, 1977, Nigel Richard Patton Dempster, and has issue living (by 1st *m* — *see* B Harris, colls), — (by 2nd *m*) Louisa Beatrix, *b* 1979.

WIDOW LIVING OF ELEVENTH DUKE

CAROLINE FLEUR (*Dowager Lady Hobart*) yr da of late Col Henry Monckton Vatcher, MC, of Valeran, St Brelade's Jersey: *m* 1st, 1955, as his 3rd wife, the 11th Duke, who *d* 1963; 2ndly, 1968 (*m diss* 1975), Peter Hendrik Peregrine Hoos (*see* B Brownlow); 3rdly, 1975, as his 2nd wife, Lt-Cdr Sir Robert Hampden Hobart, 3rd Bt, who *d* 1988.

LEICESTER, EARL OF (Coke) (Earl UK 1837)
(Name pronounced "Cook")

EDWARD DOUGLAS COKE, 7th Earl; *b* 6 May 1936; *s* 1994; *ed* St Andrew's Coll, Grahamstown, Cape Province; DL Norfolk: *m* 1st, 1962 (*m diss* 1985), Valeria Phyllis, eldest da of late Leonard A. Potter, of Berkhamsted, Herts; 2ndly, 1986, Mrs Sarah de Chair, da of Noel Henry Boys Forde, of Wells-next-the-Sea, Norfolk, and formerly wife of (i) — Hancock, and (ii) Colin Graham Ramsey de Chair, and has issue by 1st *m*.

𝔄rms – Per line gules and azure, three eagles displayed argent. ℭrest – On a chapeau azure, turned up ermine, an ostrich argent, holding in its mouth a horse-shoe. 𝔖upporters – On either side an ostrich argent, that on the *dexter* gorged with a ducal coronet per pale gules and azure, line reflexed over the back of the first; that on the *sinister* gorged with a like coronet, per pale azure and gules, and line reflexed over the back azure.
Seat – Holkham Hall, Wells, Norfolk. *Club* – Brooks's, White's, Farmers'.

He is prudent who is patient

SONS LIVING (*By 1st marriage*)

THOMAS EDWARD (*Viscount Coke*), *b* 6 July 1965; *ed* Eton, and Manchester Univ (BA); sometime Page of Honour to HM, and Equerry to HRH The Duke of Kent 1991-93.
Hon Rupert Henry John, *b* 1975.

DAUGHTER LIVING (*By 1st marriage*)

Lady Laura-Jane Elizabeth, *b* 1968: *m* 1993, Jonathan Paul, elder son of Alastair Paul, of Edinburgh, and of Mrs Jonathan Woollatt, of Honiton, Devon.

BROTHER LIVING

Hon (Wenman) John (PO Box 784 Rivonia 2128, Johannesburg, S Africa), *b* 1940: *m* 1969, Carolyn Mary, el da of late D. D. Steuart Redler, of Cape Town, S Africa, and has issue living, Anthony Stuart, *b* 1969, — Richard Oliver, *b* 1975, — Rosalind Elizabeth, *b* 1971.

SISTER LIVING

Lady Almary Bridget, *b* 1938: *m* 1963, Peter Ivens-Ferraz, of Splashy Fen, PO Box 186, Underberg, Natal 4590, S Africa, and has issue living, Robyn Ann, *b* 1964, — Bronwen Mary, *b* 1965, — Penelope Kate, *b* 1967, — Caitlin Tessa, *b* 1970.

AUNT LIVING (*sister of 6th Earl*) (*Raised to the rank of an Earl's daughter,* 1977)

Lady Diana Merial (1 Stoke Green Cottages, Slough, Bucks), *b* 1907: *m* 1930 (*m diss* 1938), Trevor Moorhouse, who *d* 1975, and has issue living, Carolyn, *b* 1935: *m* 1961, Emil Landau, of Houston Cove, PO Box 1238, Damariscotta, ME 04543, USA, and has issue living, Alexander James *b* 1969.

DAUGHTERS LIVING OF FIFTH EARL

Lady Anne Veronica (*Baroness Glenconner*), LVO, *b* 1932; Train Bearer to HM The Queen at the Coronation, 1953, an Extra Lady-in-Waiting to HRH The Princess Margaret, Countess of Snowdon, since 1971; Pres Nat Assocn for Maternal and Child Welfare 1985, Pres SOS 1979-83; LVO 1991: *m* 1956, 3rd Baron Glenconner. *Residences* – Flat 2, 19 Holland Park, W11; East End Farm, Burnham Thorpe, King's Lynn, Norfolk PE31 8HW; Beau Estate, Soufriere, St Lucia, WI.
Lady Carey Elizabeth, *b* 1934: *m* 1960, Bryan Ronald Basset, CBE (*see* E Dartmouth). *Residence* – Quarles, Wells-next-Sea, Norfolk NR23 1RY.
Lady Sarah Marion, *b* 1944: *m* 1970, Maj David Finlayson Wylie Hill Walter, late Scots Gds, of Westwood, Balthayock, by Perth, and has issue living, Nicholas Robert, *b* 1972, — James George, *b* 1975.

DAUGHTER LIVING OF FOURTH EARL

Lady Silvia Beatrice (The Manor House, Burnham Thorpe, Kings Lynn), *b* 1909; is a JP: *m* 1932, Capt Simon Harvey Combe, MC, Irish Guards, who *d* 1965, and has issue living, Robin Harvey (Bayfield Hall, Holt, Norfolk), *b* 1934; Lt RN: *m* 1960, Olga, da of R. J. Wise, of Bridgend, Glam, and has issue living, Roger Mark Harvey *b* 1960, Simon James (4 Brandlehow Rd, SW15 2ED) *b* 1962: *m* 1992, Elizabeth A., da of John Knight, of Spratton, Northampton, Carey Romaine *b* 1964, Silvia *b* 1967, — Rowena Marion, *b* 1935: *m* 1963 (*m diss* 1983), Jocelyn Rupert Rowland Geoffrey Feilding (*see* E Denbigh, colls).

WIDOW LIVING OF SIXTH EARL

ELIZABETH HOPE SMITH (*Dowager Countess of Leicester*), da of Clifford Arthur Johnstone, of Kiswani, Addo, CP, S Africa: *m* 1985, as his 3rd wife, the 6th Earl, who *d* 1994. *Residence* – Hillhead, PO Box 544, Plettenberg Bay 6600, CP, S Africa.

COLLATERAL BRANCHES LIVING

Issue of late Maj Hon Richard Coke, Scots Gds, 3rd son of 2nd Earl, *b* 1876, *d* 1964: *m* 1st, 1907 (*m diss* 1927), Hon Doreen O'Brien, who *d* 1960, da of 14th Baron Inchiquin; 2ndly, 1932, Elizabeth Vera Catherine Alice, who *d* 1988, da of late Louis-Leopold M. B. de Beaumont (*see* B O'Hagan, 1973-74 Edn):—
(By 1st *m*) Richard Lovel, DSO, MC, ERD (Weasenham Hall, King's Lynn, Norfolk), *b* 1918; *ed* Stowe, and RAC Cirencester; 1939-45 War as Maj Scots Gds in Italy (MC, DSO); DSO 1945; ERD 1992; DL 1977 and High Sheriff Norfolk 1981: *m* 1951, Molly, yr da of W. T. Fletcher, of Dorchester, and has had issue, Richard Townshend, *b* 1954, — Edward Justin *b* 1961, — Diana Caroline *b* 1953: *m* 1975, 20th Earl of Caithness, and *d* 1994, leaving issue (*see* E Caithness). —— Hersey (Waterloo Cottage, Gayton, King's Lynn, Norfolk), *b* 1915: *m* 1946, Lt-Col Peter William Marsham, MBE, Gren Gds (ret), who *d* 1970 (*see* E Romney, colls). —— Bridget Doreen (*Baroness Rathcavan*), *b* 1924: *m* 1st, 1943 (*m diss* 1952), Capt Thomas Richard Edwards-Moss, who *d* 1974 (*see* Edwards-Moss Bt, colls); 2ndly, 1953, 2nd Baron Rathcaven. —— (By 2nd *m*) Henry Francis (4 Dormy House, Brancaster, King's Lynn, Norfolk), *b* 1938: *m* 1st, 1966 (*m diss* 1971), Marie Christina Rosalind, da of Robert McCrone, of Pitliver, by Dumferline, Fife; 2ndly, 1976 (*m diss* 1993), Margaret Victoria Louise, da of Patrick Brodie, of Horley, Surrey, and has issue living (by 1st *m*), Nicola Katherine, *b* 1967, — Sarah Victoria Dayas, *b* 1971, — (by 2nd *m*) Georgina Sarah Brodie, *b* 1979, — Camilla Anne Brodie, *b* 1980. —— (Mildred Jeanne) Carolyn, *b* 1934: *m* 1966, David Stephen Harms, of 41 Christchurch Hill, Hampstead, NW3 1LA, and has issue living, Hera *b* 1956: *m* 1991, Derek Dale Peterson, eldest son of Dale Gunnar Peterson, of Belleview, Florida, USA, and has issue living, Jacob Gunnar *b* 1994, — Jane Mary, *b* 1968. —— (Elizabeth) Charmian, *b* 1935: *m* 1960, Richard Francis Spickernell (*see* Boothby, Bt, colls, 1970 Edn), (Bincknoll House, Wootton Bassett, Wilts), and has issue living, Godfrey John Wenman, *b* 1962, — James William Richard, *b* 1965: *m* 1991, Lady Rachel Barbara Violet Petty-Fitzmaurice, yr da of Charles Maurice, Earl of Shelburne (*see* M Lansdowne).

Grandchildren of late Maj Hon Sir John Spencer Coke, KCVO (infra):—
Issue of late Lt-Col Gerald Edward Coke, CBE, *b* 1907, *d* 1990: *m* 1939, Patricia (Jenkyn Place, Bently, Hants), da of late Rt Hon Sir Alexander George Montagu Cadogan, GCMG, KCB (*see* E Cadogan, colls):—
John Alexander, *b* 1946; *ed* Eton: *m* 1980 (*m diss* 1987), Karen Johnson. —— †Michael Gerald, *b* 1949; *ed* Eton; *d* 1972. —— David Edward, *b* 1951; *ed* Eton, and Univs of E Anglia and Manchester: *m* 1973, Karen Phillips, and has issue living, Michael Alexander, *b* 1979, — Charis Hester, *b* 1975. — Lavinia Mary, *b* 1944: *m* 1967, Peter Raymond Wilson, of Vale Court, Colerne, Chippenham, Wilts, and has issue living, Nicholas Peter, *b* 1971, — Andrew Michael, *b* 1974, — Miranda Mary, *b* 1969.

Issue of late Major Hon Sir John Spencer Coke, KCVO, Scots Gds, 5th son of 2nd Earl, *b* 1880, *d* 1957: *m* 1907, Hon Dorothy Olive Levy Lawson, who *d* 1937, da of 1st Viscount Burnham:—
Celia Dorothy, *b* 1919: *m* 1942, Stamp Godfrey Brooksbank, Capt Coldm Gds (*see* Brooksbank, Bt). *Residence* – 45 Cedar Lodge, Lythe Hill Park, Haslemere, Surrey.

Issue of late Capt Hon Reginald Coke, DSO, 8th son of 2nd Earl, *b* 1883, *d* 1969: *m* 1924, Katharine, who *d* 1977, da of late Hon Edward Alan Dudley Ryder (*see* E Harrowby, colls, 1976 Edn):—
Mary Margaret (76 Abercrombie St, SW11 2JD) *b* 1925. —— Katharine Vera, *b* 1927: *m* 1951, Peter John Cator, of Paxton House, Blockley, nr Moreton-in-Marsh, Glos (B Mostyn, colls), and has issue living, Charles Henry (35 Faroe Rd, W14 0BL), *b* 1952; *ed* Eton and Bristol Univ; Dir Christie, Manson & Woods Ltd, — Caroline Sarah, *b* 1954: *m* 1985, Piers H. de la Force, of 8 Lindore Rd, SW11 1HJ, yr son of late Martin de la Force, of Montevideo, Uruguay, and late Mrs Falaise de la Force, of 3 Herbert Cres, SW1, and has issue living, James Edward *b* 1987, Alexandra Eloise *b* 1989.

Grandchildren of late Hon Henry John Coke, 3rd son of 1st Earl:—
Issue of late Reginald Grey Coke, *b* 1864, *d* 1930: *m* 1st, 1887 (*m diss* 1888), Elizabeth Wilson; 2ndly, 1892 (*m diss* 1908), Phylis Susan, who *d* 1939, da of late Francis William Bott, of Somersal, Derby; 3rdly, 1909, Galia, who *d* 1947, da of Michael Hambourg, formerly of 2 Clifton Gardens, W.:—
(By 3rd *m*) Henry, *b* 1912: *m* 1934, Joyce, da of Gerald E. Rattigan, and has issue living, Basil, *b* 1935. —— Stella, *b* 1910: *m* 1931, John Michael Ryan, of 43 Westminster Court, St Stephens Hill, St Albans, Herts, and has issue living.

PREDECESSORS – **(1)** THOMAS WILLIAM Coke, son of late Wenman Coke (formerly Roberts); *b* 1754; many years MP for co Norfolk; *cr Viscount Coke* and *Earl of Leicester* (peerage of United Kingdom) 1837: *m* 1st, 1775, Jane, who *d* 1800, da of James Dutton; 2ndly, 1822, Lady Anne Amelia Keppel, who *d* 1884 (having *m* 2ndly, 1843, Rt Hon Edward Ellice, MP), da of 4th Earl of Albemarle; *d* 1842; *s* by his son **(2)** THOMAS WILLIAM, KG, 2nd Earl; *b* 1822; Lord-Lieut of Norfolk 1846-1906; sometime a Member of Council of Duchy of Cornwall and Keeper of the Privy Seal: *m* 1st, 1843, Juliana, who *d* 1870, da of late Samuel Charles Whitbread, of Southill, Beds; 2ndly, 1875, Hon Georgiana Caroline Cavendish, who *d* 1937, el da of 2nd Baron Chesham; *d* 1909; *s* by his el son **(2)** THOMAS WILLIAM, GCVO, CMG, 3rd Earl; *b* 1848; sometime col 2nd Batn Scots Guards; Egypt 1882, Suakin 1885, S Africa 1901-2 (CMG); Lord-Lieut of Norfolk 1906-29: *m* 1879, Hon Dame Alice White, DBE, who *d* 1936, da of 2nd Baron Annaly; *d* 1941; *s* by his el son **(4)** THOMAS WILLIAM, 4th Earl; *b* 1880; Lord-Lieut of Norfolk 1944-49: *m* 1905, Marion Gertrude, who *d* 1955, da of late Col Hon Walter Rodolph Trefusis, CB; *d* 1949; *s* by his son **(5)** THOMAS WILLIAM EDWARD, MVO, 5th Earl; *b* 1908; an Equerry to HRH The Duke of York 1934-36, an Extra Equerry to HM King George VI 1936-52, and to HM Queen Elizabeth II 1952-76: *m* 1931, Lady Elizabeth Mary Yorke, DCVO, who *d*

1985, da of 8th Earl of Hardwicke; *d* 1976; *s* by his cousin **(6)** ANTHONY LOUIS LOVEL (son of late Hon Arthur George Coke, 2nd son of 3rd Earl), 6th Earl, *b* 1909; 1939-45 War in RAF: *m* 1st, 1934 (*m diss* 1947), Moyra Joan, who *d* 1987, da of late Douglas Crossley; 2ndly, 1947, Vera, who *d* 1984, da of Herbert William Haigh, of Durham; 3rdly, 1985, Elizabeth Hope Smith, da of Clifford Arthur Johnstone, of Kiswani, Addo, CP, S Africa, and *d* 1994, in S Africa; *s* by his elder son **(7)** EDWARD DOUGLAS, 7th Earl and present peer; also Viscount Coke.

LEIGH, BARON (Leigh) (Baron UK 1839)

All comes from God

JOHN PIERS LEIGH, 5th Baron; *b* 11 Sept 1935; *s* 1979; *ed* Eton, Oxford, and London Univ: *m* 1st, 1957 (*m diss* 1974), Cecilia Poppy, yst da of late Robert Cecil Jackson, of Redlynch, Wilts; 2ndly, 1976 (*m diss* 1982), Susan, yst da of John Reginald Cleave, of Whitnash, Leamington Spa; 3rdly, 1982, Lea, only da of Col Harry Noël Havelock Wild, and formerly wife of Lt-Col Brian Gustavus Hamilton-Russell (*see* V Boyne), and has issue by 1st and 2nd *m*.

Arms – Gules, a cross engrailed argent and in the first quarter a lozenge argent. **Crest** – An unicorn's head erased, armed and crined or. **Supporters** – On either side an unicorn, armed, maned, tufted and unguled or, gorged with a ducal coronet gules, pendant therefrom an escutcheon charged with the arms of *Brydges*, viz argent, a cross sable, thereon a leopard's face or.
Address – c/o House of Lords, SW1.

SONS LIVING (By 1st marriage)

Hon CHRISTOPHER DUDLEY PIERS, *b* 20 Oct 1960; *ed* Eton, and RAC Cirencester: *m* 1990, Sophy-Ann, da of Richard Burrows, of The Old Hall, Groby, Leics, and has issue living, Rupert Dudley, *b* 21 Feb 1994. *Residence* – Fern Farm, Adlestrop, Moreton-in-Marsh, Glos GL56 0YL.

(by 2nd marriage)

Hon Piers Henry John, *b* 1979.

DAUGHTER LIVING (By 1st marriage)

Hon Camilla Anne, *b* 1962.

BROTHERS LIVING

Hon William Rupert, *b* 1938; *ed* Eton, RMA Sandhurst and RAC Cirencester; late Lt 11th Hussars: *m* 1965, Priscilla Elizabeth, yr da of late Lt-Cdr Edward Francis Patrick Cooper, RN (ret), of Markree Castle, co Sligo (*see* B Castlemaine, colls, 1967 Edn), and has had issue, James Rupert, *b* 1967, — Edward William, *b* 1968, — Richard Thomas, *b* 1974; *d* 1978, — Francis Dudley, *b* 1982. *Residence* – Ranaghan, Collooney, co Sligo.

Hon Benjamin Chandos, *b* 1942; *ed* Eton; late Lt 11th Hussars: *m* 1979, Jennifer Vivian, da of late Capt Peter Winser, and formerly wife of Hon Richard Henry Strutt (*see* B Belper), and has issue living, Samantha Jane Hazel, *b* 1980. *Residence* – Little Rissington House, Little Rissington, Cheltenham, Glos GL54 2NB.

Hon Michael James, *b* 1945; *ed* Eton, and Keble Coll, Oxford: *m* 1972 (*m diss* 1980), Cherry Rosalind, da of late David Long-Price. Resides in Australia.

PREDECESSORS – **(1)** CHANDOS Leigh, son of late James Henry Leigh, *b* 1791; gained favourable reputation as a poet; *cr Baron Leigh*, of Stoneleigh, co Warwick (peerage of United Kingdom) 1839: *m* 1819, Margarette, who *d* 1860, da of late Rev William Shippen Wiles, of Astrop House, Northamptonshire, *d* 1850; *s* by his son **(2)** *Rt Hon* WILLIAM HENRY, LLD, 2nd Baron; *b* 1824; Lord-Lieut and a High Steward of Sutton Coldfield *m* 1848, Lady Caroline Amelia Grosvenor who *d* 1906, da of 2nd Marquess of Westminster; *d* 1905; *s* by his son **(3)** FRANCIS DUDLEY, 3rd Baron; Lord-Lieut of co Warwick: *m* 1st, 1890, Frances Hélène Forbes, who *d* 1909, da of late Hon N. M. Beckwith, of New York; 2ndly, 1923, Marie, who *d* 1949, da of late Alexander Campbell, of New York; *d* 1938; *s* by his nephew **(4)** RUPERT WILLIAM DUDLEY, TD, DL (only son of late Major Hon Rupert Leigh, 3rd son of 2nd Baron), 4th Baron, *b* 1908; High Steward of Sutton Coldfield; Lt-Col 1st Roy Glos Hussars: *m* 1931, Anne, who *d* 1977, da of late Ellis Hicks Beach (*see* E St Aldwyn, colls); *d* 1979; *s* by his el son **(5)** JOHN PIERS, 5th Baron and present peer.

LEIGHTON OF ST MELLONS, BARON (Seager) (Baron UK 1962, Bt UK 1952)

By Courage and Faith

JOHN LEIGHTON SEAGER, 2nd Baron and 2nd Baronet; *b* 11 Jan 1922; *s* 1963; *ed* Leys Sch, Camb: *m* 1953, Elizabeth Rosita, who *d* 1979, only dau of late Henry Hopgood; 2ndly, 1982, Ruth Elizabeth, widow of John Hopwood, and has issue by 1st *m*.

Arms – Azure a cross moline between in bend dexter two lymphads and in bend sinister as many mullets all argent. **Crest** – Between two wings azure each charged with a mullet a cross moline argent. **Supporters** – *Dexter*, a sea-horse (hippocampus) azure; *sinister*, a dragon segreant gules. *Residence* – 346 Caerphilly Rd, Cardiff.

SONS LIVING *(By 1st marriage)*

Hon ROBERT WILLIAM HENRY LEIGHTON, *b* 28 Sept 1955.
Hon Simon John Leighton, *b* 1957.

DAUGHTER LIVING *(By 1st marriage)*

Hon Carole Mary Leighton, *b* 1958.

BROTHER LIVING

Hon Douglas Leighton (Leighton House, 5929 Hudson, Vancouver BC, Canada), *b* 1925: *m* 1960, Gillian Claire, da of Leonard Warwick Greenwood, of Pound Piece, Astley, Stourport, Worcs, and has issue living, Nicola Claire Leighton, *b* 1961, — Wendy Elizabeth Leighton, *b* 1963, — Michelle Leighton, *b* 1967.

SISTERS LIVING

Hon Thelma Margaret Leighton, *b* 1923: *m* 1st, 1951 (*m diss* 1981), Michael Edmonds; 2ndly, 1983, Joseph Evan Lloyd, and has issue living (by 1st *m*), Christopher Leighton, *b* 1958: *m* 1992, Diane, da of William Burnell, — Susan Leighton, *b* 1952: *m* 1971, Timothy Vicary, — Jane Leighton, *b* 1954: *m* 1984, John Nelson.

Hon Zoë Leighton, *b* 1928: *m* 1st, 1955, Malcolm James Peniston, of The Fishermans, King St, Emsworth, Hants, who *d* 1981; 2ndly, 1984, Alan Carnegie Stewart, of Westwood, Hardgate, Castle Douglas, Kirkcudbrightshire DG7 3LD, and has issue living (by 1st *m*), Douglas James *b* 1959: *m* 1990, Lyana, da of Peter Hodgson, of Tiverton, Cheshire, and has issue living, Charlotte Eloise *b* 1991, Arabella Leighton *b* 1993, — Angela Clare, *b* 1956: *m* 1982, Jeremy J. Adams, — Rosemary Leighton, *b* 1964.

PREDECESSOR – **(1)** Sir (GEORGE) LEIGHTON SEAGER, CBE (son of Sir William Henry Seager, of Lynwood, Cardiff, founder of the firm of W. H. Seager & Co, shipowners and managers, and ships' suppliers); *b* 1896; an underwriting member of Lloyd's, Pres of Cardiff Chamber of Commerce 1934-35, and of Council of Shipping 1944; High Sheriff of Monmouthshire 1938-39 and Vice-Lieut 1957-63; *cr* a Knt 1938, a *Baronet* 1952 and *Baron Leighton of St Mellons*, of St Mellons, co Monmouth 1962: *m* 1921, Marjorie, who *d* 1992, da of William Henry Gimson, of Breconshire, *d* 1963; *s* by his son **(2)** JOHN LEIGHTON, 2nd Baron and present peer.

LEINSTER, DUKE OF (FitzGerald) Sits as VISCOUNT (GB 1747) (Duke I 1766)

Crom to Victory

(Title pronounced "Linster")

GERALD FITZGERALD, 8th Duke and Premier Duke, Marquess, and Earl of Ireland; *b* 27 May 1914; *s* 1976; *ed* Eton, and RMC; late Maj 5th R Inniskilling Dragoon Gds; 1939-45 War (wounded): *m* 1st, 1936 (*m diss* 1946), Joane, el da of late Maj Arthur MacMurrough Kavanagh, MC (Buxton, Bt, colls); 2ndly, 1946, Anne, yr da of late Lt-Col Philip Eustace Smith, MC, and has issue by 1st and 2nd *m*.

Arms – Argent, a saltire gules. Crest – A monkey statant proper, environed round the loins and chained or. Supporters – Two monkeys proper environed round the loins and chained or.
Residence – Kilkea House, Wilcote Lane, Ramsden, Oxon OX7 3BA.

SONS LIVING (By 2nd marriage)

MAURICE (*Marquess of Kildare*) (Courtyard House, Oakley Park, Frilford Heath, Oxon OX13 6QW), *b* 7 April 1948; *ed* Millfield: *m* 1972, Fiona Mary Francesca, da of late Harry Hollick, of Long Barn, Sutton Courtenay, Oxon, and has issue:—
    SON LIVING — THOMAS (*Earl of Offaly*), *b* 12 Jan 1974.
    DAUGHTERS LIVING — *Lady* Francesca Emily Purcell, *b* 1976, — *Lady* Pollyanna Louisa Clementine, *b* 1982.

Lord John (Graham Lodge, Newmarket, Suffolk), 1952; *ed* Millfield, and RMA Sandhurst; late Capt 5th R Inniskilling Dragoon Gds: *m* 1982, Barbara, el da of late Andreas Zindel, of St Moritz, Switzerland, and has issue living, Edward, *b* 1988, — Hermione, *b* 1985.

DAUGHTERS LIVING (By 1st marriage)

Lady Rosemary Ann FITZGERALD (Beggars Roost, Lilstock, nr Bridgwater, Som TA5 1SU), *b* 1939; *ed* Lady Margaret Hall, Oxford; has resumed the surname of FitzGerald: *m* 1963 (*m diss* 1967), Mark Killigrew Wait.
Lady Nesta, *b* 1942: *m* 1977, Philip Charles Seppings Tirard, who *d* 1993, of Coolnabrune, Borris, co Carlow, Eire, and has issue living, Siobhan Eleanor, *b* 1978, — Eithne, *b* 1982.

COLLATERAL BRANCHES LIVING

    Grandchildren of late Lord Charles FitzGerald, 5th son of 4th Duke:—
    Issue of late Rupert Augustus FitzGerald, *b* 1900, *d* 1969: *m* 1st, 1924 (*m diss* 1932), Irene, da of J. Jennings, of Melbourne, Vic, Aust; 2ndly, 1936, Ivy, who *d* 1945, da of late J. Simmons, of Melbourne, Aust—
(By 1st *m*) Peter Charles, *b* 1925; 1939-45 War with AMF: *m* 1950, June, da of W. Murray, of East St Kilda, Vic, Aust, and has issue living, Stephen Peter, *b* 1953, — Lynette Pamela, *b* 1951. —— (By 2nd *m*) Elizabeth Mary, *b* 1937: *m* 1958, Ronald Smith, of 24 Ireland Av, Doncaster East, Vic, Aust, and has issue living, Gary Ronald, *b* 1960, — Amanda Elizabeth, *b* 1962.

    Issue of late Lord Henry FitzGerald, 7th son of 4th Duke, *b* 1863, *d* 1955: *m* 1891, Inez, who *d* 1967, da of late Cdr William John Casberd-Boteler, RN, of Eastry, Kent:—
Denis Henry, DSO, OBE, *b* 1911; *ed* Eton; was ADC to Gen Officer Comdg N Ireland Dist 1938-39, and GSO, Headquarters Guards Armoured Div 1941-42, Instructor at Staff Coll, Camberley 1942-43, and GSO at Headquarters 30th Corps 1944, AQMG, War Office 1949-50, and Headquarters, London Dist 1950-51, Col Comdg Irish Guards 1951-52, Brigadier Comdg 4th Guards Brig 1953-55, Imperial Defence Coll 1956, and Director of Plans (War Office) 1957-58; European War 1939-45 in Norway and N-W Europe (DSO), Palestine 1947; DSO, 1945, OBE (Mil) 1951. *Residence* - Glenshelane House, Cappoquin, co Waterford.

PREDECESSORS – (1) GERALD FitzGerald; *cr Baron of Offaly*, co Kildare, before 1203; *d* about 1203; *s* by his son (2) MAURICE, 2nd Baron; Lord Ch Justice of Ireland; introduced into Ireland 1216 the Order of the Franciscans, and in 1229 the Order of the Dominicans, built in 1231 the Franciscan Abbey of Youghal, where he *d* 1257; *s* by his son (3) MAURICE, 3rd Baron; was Ch Gov of Ireland; *d* 1277; *s* by his son (4) GERALD, 4th Baron; founded the Franciscan Order at Clane 1271; *d* 1287; *s* by his cousin (5) MAURICE, 5th Baron; *dsp*; *s* by his cousin (6) JOHN, 6th Baron; a valiant soldier who assisted Edward I in his Scottish campaigns 1296, 1299, and 1301, and afterwards dispersed the rebels in Munster, and opposed Robert Bruce who had entered the N of Ireland with 6,000 men, *cr Earl of Kildare* (peerage of Ireland) 1316; there is a tradition that the Earl while an infant was asleep at Woodstock Castle, near Athy, when an alarm of fire was raised; in the confusion the child was forgotten, and on the servants returning to search for him they found the room in which he had lain to be in ruins; soon after, hearing a strange noise in one of the towers, they looked up and saw an ape, which was usually kept chained, carefully holding the child in his arms; he afterwards in gratitude for his preservation adopted a monkey for his crest; *d* 1316; *s* by his son (7) THOMAS, 2nd Earl; was three times Lord Justice of Ireland; *d* 1328; *s* by his son (8) RICHARD, 3rd Earl; *d* 1329; *s* by his brother (9) MAURICE, KB, 4th Earl; present at siege of Calais; *d* 1390; *s* by his son (10) GERALD, 5th Earl; was Lord Dep to Thomas, Duke of Gloucester, Lord-Lieut of Ireland; *d* 1410; *s* by his brother (11) JOHN, 6th Earl; strengthened and enlarged the Castle of Maynooth; *d* 1427: *s* by his son (12) THOMAS, 7th Earl; was Lord Dep of Ireland 1454-9, and Lord Chancellor of Ireland 1468; being involved with the Earl of Desmond he was attainted, but subsequently pardoned, released, restored in blood by Act of Parliament, and appointed Lord Justice of Ireland 1471; *d* 1477; *s* by his son (13) GERALD, KG, 8th Earl; Lord Dep and Lord Justice of Ireland for thirty-three years, an eminent military commander who invaded Ulster, took numerous castles, and in 1504 obtained a complete victory over the Irish chiefs of Connaught; *d* 1513; *s* by his son (14) GERALD, 9th Earl; Lord Dep of Ireland, was deprived of his high office, and with his five half-brothers was committed to the Tower and sentenced to be executed as a traitor; *d* a prisoner 1534; *s* by his son (15) THOMAS, 10th Earl; having heard that his father was to be beheaded he threw off all allegiance to the English crown; he eventually surrendered on the promise of receiving a full pardon; this promise was violated by Henry VIII, and in 1537 he, together with his five uncles, was hanged, drawn and quartered at Tyburn, and his honours were attainted; *s* by his half-brother (16) GERALD, 11th Earl; was *ed* Rome by his kinsman Cardinal Pole, and subsequently became Master of the Horse to Cosmo de Medici, Duke of Florence, returned to England after the death of Henry VIII and received Knighthood from Edward VI, and a regrant of all the Irish family estates, and Queen Mary restored to him all his ancestral honours; *d* 1585; *s* by his son (17) HENRY, 12th Earl; *d* 1597; *s* by his brother (18) WILLIAM, 13th Earl; lost at sea 1599; *s* by his cousin (19) GERALD, 14th Earl; *d* 1612; *s* by his son (20) GERALD, 15th Earl; *d* 1620; *s* by his cousin (21) GEORGE, 16th Earl; *d*

1655; *s* by his son **(22)** WENTWORTH, 17th Earl; *d* 1664; *s* by his son **(23)** JOHN, 18th Earl; *dsp* 1707; *s* by his cousin **(24)** ROBERT, 19th Earl; an eminent statesman; *d* 1744; *s* by his son **(25)** JAMES, 20th Earl; Master-Gen of the Ordnance in Ireland; *cr Viscount Leinster* (peerage of Great Britain) 1747, *Earl of Offaly* and *Marquess of Kildare* (peerage of Ireland) 1761, and *Duke of Leinster* (peerage of Ireland) 1766; *d* 1733; *s* by his son **(26)** WILLIAM ROBERT, KP, 2nd Duke; *d* 1804; *s* by his son **(27)** AUGUSTUS FREDERICK, PC, 3rd Duke; *b* 1791; HM Lieut of co Kildare: *m* 1818, Charlotte Augusta Stanhope, da of 3rd Earl of Harrington; *d* 1874; *s* by his son **(28)** CHARLES WILLIAM, PC, 4th Duke; *b* 1819; sat as MP for Kildare 1847-52; *cr* (in the lifetime of his father) *Baron Kildare* (peerage of United Kingdom) 1870: *m* 1847, Lady Caroline Sutherland Leveson-Gower, da of 2nd Duke of Sutherland; *d* 1887; *s* by his son **(29)** GERALD, PC, 5th Duke, *b* 1851; HM Lieut of co Kildare: *m* 1884, Lady Hermione Whilhelmina Duncombe, who *d* 1895, da of 1st Earl of Feversham; *d* 1893; *s* by his el son **(30)** MAURICE, 6th Duke, *b* 1887; *d* 1922; *s* by his brother **(31)** EDWARD, 7th Duke; *b* 1892; *m* 1st, 1913 (*m diss* 1930), May (May Etheridge, the stage soubrette), who *d* 1935, da of late Jesse Etheridge; 2ndly, 1932 (*m diss* 1946), Agnes Rafaella, who *d* 1993, da of Robert Davidson Kennedy, and formerly wife of late Clare Van Neck; 3rdly, 1946, Jessie, who *d* 1960, da of late Alfred John Smither, and formerly wife of (1) 3rd Baron Churston and (2) Theodore Wessel; 4thly 1965, Vivien Irene, who *d* 1992, da of late Thomas Albert Felton, of London, and formerly wife of George William Conner; *d* 1976; *s* by his son **(32)** Gerald, 8th Duke and present peer; also Marquess of Kildare, Earl of Kildare, Earl and Baron of Offaly, Viscount Leinster, and Baron Kildare.

Lennox, Duke of, see Duke of Richmond and Gordon.

LEONARD, BARONY OF (Leonard) (Extinct 1983)

SON LIVING OF LIFE BARON

Hon Derek John, *b* 1956; *ed* Harrow, and Aberystwyth Univ (LLB); ptnr Leonard & Kalim, Solicitors. *Address* – 777/9 High Rd, Leytonstone, E11.

DAUGHTER LIVING OF LIFE BARON

Hon Elizabeth Margaret, *b* 1946; *ed* Univ of Wales (LLB): *m* 1963, Michael Harwood of The Hague, Netherlands.

WIDOW LIVING OF LIFE BARON

GLENYS EVELYN (*Baroness Leonard*), da of Ernest Kenny: *m* 1945, Baron Leonard, OBE (Life Baron), who *d* 1983. *Residence* – 19 Queen Anne Sq, Cardiff CF1 3ED.

Le Poer, Baron; grandson of Marquess of Waterford.

LESTER OF HERNE HILL, BARON (Lester) (Life Baron 1993)

ANTHONY PAUL LESTER, QC, son of late Harry Lester, of London; *b* 3 July 1936; *ed* City of London Sch, Trin Coll, Camb (BA), and Harvard Law Sch (LLM); 2nd Lieut RA 1955-57; Bar Lincoln's Inn 1963, QC 1975, Bencher 1985, NI Bar 1984, and Irish Bar 1983, Recorder SE Circuit 1987; Special Advisor to Home Sec 1974-76, and Standing Commn on Human Rights in NI 1975-77; Chm Board of Govs James Allen's Girls' Sch, Interights (Internat Centre for Legal Protection of Human Rights), Trustee Runnymede Trust; Member Court of Govs LSE; Hon Visiting Prof of Law Univ Coll London; ACIArb; author and contributor to learned journals; *cr Baron Lester of Herne Hill*, of Herne Hill, in the London Borough of Southwark (Life Baron) 1993: *m* 1971, Catherine Elizabeth Debora, da of late Michael Morris Wassey, of London, and has issue.

Chambers - 2 Hare Court, Temple, EC4Y 7BH. *Club* – Garrick.

SON LIVING

Hon Gideon, *b* 1972.

DAUGHTER LIVING

Hon Maya, *b* 1974.

LEVEN and MELVILLE, EARL OF (Leslie Melville) (Earl S 1641 and 1690)

For King and country
Heaven at last

ALEXANDER ROBERT LESLIE MELVILLE, 14th Earl of Leven and 13th Earl of Melville; *b* 13 May 1924; *s* 1947; *ed* Eton; Capt (ret) Coldstream Guards, served NW Europe (wounded), ADC to Gov-Gen of NZ 1951-52; a DL for Nairn; Lord Lieut for Nairn since 1969, Chm Nairn CC 1970-74; Chm of Governors Gordonstoun Sch 1971-89; Pres British Ski Federation 1981-85, and Hon Pres Scottish Nat Ski Council: *m* 1953, Susan, da of Lieut-Col Ronald Steuart-Menzies of Menzies, of Arndilly House, Craigellachie, Banffshire, and has issue.

Arms – Quarterly: 1st, azure, a thistle slipped proper, ensigned with an Imperial Crown or, a coat of augmentation to the arms of *Leslie*; 2nd, gules, three crescents within a bordure argent, charged with eight roses of the first, *Melville*; 3rd argent, a fesse gules, *Melville of Raith*; 4th, argent, on a bend azure, three buckles or, *Leslie*. **Crests** – 1st, a demi-chevalier in complete armour, holding in his right hand a dagger point downwards proper, pommel and hilt or, *Leslie*; 2nd, a ratch-hound's head erased proper, collared gules, *Melville*. **Supporters** – *Dexter*, a knight in complete armour, holding in his dexter hand the banner of Scotland, all proper, *Leslie*; *sinister*, a ratchhound proper, collared gules, *Melville*.
Seat – Glenferness, Nairn. **Club** – New (Edinburgh).

SONS LIVING

DAVID ALEXANDER (*Lord Balgonie*), *b* 26 Jan 1954; *ed* Eton: *m* 1981, Julia Clare, yr da of Col Ian Ranald Critchley, OBE, The Black Watch, of Greenden, by Brechin, Angus (*see* V Arthbuthnott, 1980 Edn), and has issue living, Alexander Ian, *b* 29 Nov 1984, — Louisa Clare, *b* 1987. *Residence* – The Old Farmhouse, West St, Burghclere, Newbury, Berks RG15 9LB.
Hon Archibald Ronald, *b* 1957; *ed* Gordonstoun; Lt Queen's Own Highlanders: *m* 1987, Julia Mary Greville, yr da of Basil Fox, of 32 Pembroke Gdns, W8, and has issue living, Alice Catherine, *b* 1990, — Camilla Jane, *b* 1992. *Residence* – Orwell House, Manse Rd, Milnathort, Kinross-shire KY13 7LN.

DAUGHTER LIVING

Lady Jane Catherine, *b* 1956: *m* 1977, Philip Mark Gurney Hudson, of Southcott Lodge, Pewsey, Wilts, and has issue living, Katherine, *b* 1983, — Susanna, *b* 1986.

BROTHERS LIVING

Hon George David (twin), *b* 1924; *ed* Eton, and Trin Coll, Camb (BA); Maj Black Watch (TA Reserve), FRICS, FLAS, FAI; 1942-45 War as Capt Rifle Bde in N-W Europe (wounded): *m* 1955, Diana Mary, da of late Brig Sir Henry Walter Houlds-worth, KBE, DSO, MC, TD (*see* E Morton, colls, 1980 Edn), and has issue living, James Hugh, *b* 1960: *m* 1987, Clare Jean, 2nd da of Lt-Col Robert Henry Heywood-Lonsdale (*see* L Rollo), and has issue living, John (Jack) *b* 1991, George *b* 1993, — Annabel Clare, *b* 1956: *m* 1979, Nigel R. Savory, of Thorpland Hall, Fakenham, Norfolk NR21 0HD, son of John Savory, of Bridge Cottage, Thorpland, Fakenham, Norfolk. *Residence* – Inneshewen, Aboyne, Aberdeenshire AB34 5BH. *Club* – Naval and Military.
Hon Alan Duncan, *b* 1928; *ed* Eton; Capt (ret) Rifle Bde. *Residence* – Fingask, Kirkhill, Inverness.

SISTER LIVING

Lady Jean Elizabeth, *b* 1921. *Residence* – Flat 24, Homesmith House, Evesham, Worcs WR11 4EH.

WIDOW LIVING OF SON OF THIRTEENTH EARL

Ruth, only da of late Dr John Duckworth: *m* 1962, Hon Ronald Joscelyn Leslie Melville, 3rd son of 13th Earl, who *d* 1987, and has issue (see colls infra). *Residence* – Little Deuchar, Fern, Forfar, Angus DD8 3QZ.

COLLATERAL BRANCHES LIVING

Issue of late Hon Ronald Joscelyn Leslie Melville, 3rd son of 13th Earl, *b* 1926, *d* 1987: *m* 1962, Ruth (ante), only da of late Dr John Duckworth:—
Roderick Justice, *b* 1965. —— Robert Jeffrey, *b* 1967. —— Angus Jack, *b* 1968. —— Rosamund Joscelyn, *b* 1962.

Issue of late Hon David William Leslie Melville, MBE, 3rd son of 11th Earl, *b* 1892, *d* 1938: *m* 1st, 1914 (*m diss* 1928), Susanna Elizabeth Johanna, da of Francis Sleigh, of Cape Town, S Africa; 2ndly, 1929, Eleanor Mary, who *d* 1974, having *m* 2ndly, 1939, Capt Arthur Miller, who *d* on active ser 1942, da of Arthur John Abrahall, formerly of Shustoke, near Coleshill, Warwickshire, and has issue living:—
(By 2nd *m*) Gillian Mary (Flat 503 San Jose, 51 Olivia Rd, Berea 2198, Johannesburg, S Africa), *b* 1930: *m* 1st, 1950 (*m diss* 19—), Peter Riley; 2ndly, 19—, Martin Dowling, and has issue living (by 2nd *m*), David, *b* 19—, — Eleanor, *b* 19—.

Issue of late Lt-Col Hon Ian Leslie Melville, TD, yst son of 11th Earl, *b* 1894, *d* 1967: *m* 1915, Charlotte Isabel, who *d* 1968, da of late Maj William Stirling, of Fairburn, Ross-shire:—
Michael Ian, TD (19 Cramond Vale, Edinburgh), *b* 1918; *ed* Eton, and Balliol Coll, Oxford (MA); Maj Lovat Scouts (Reserve), DL for W Lothian 1957-64, and Selkirkshire 1974-89, Hon Sheriff 1983-89, a Member of Queen's Body Guard for Scotland (Royal Company of Archers); FRICS: *m* 1943, Cynthia, who *d* 1986, da of Sir Charles Jocelyn Hambro, KBE, MC, and has issue living, Ian Hamish (Lochluichart, by Garve, Ross-shire; Turf, New (Edinburgh) and Pratt's Clubs), *b* 1944; *ed* Eton, and Ch Ch Oxford (MA); a Member of Queen's Body Guard for Scotland (Royal Company of Archers): *m* 1968, Lady Elizabeth Compton, yr da of 6th Marquess of Northampton, and has issue living, James Ian *b* 1969, Henry Bingham *b* 1975, — Pamela, *b* 1947, — Fiona Evelyn, *b* 1950; ARCM: *m* 1973, James Campbell David Brodie, yr son of late Maj David James Brodie of Lethen, and has issue living, Alexander John *b* 1974, Charlotte Sophia *b* 1976, Anna Louise *b* 1979. —— Elisabeth

Marion (*Elisabeth, Baroness Joicey*), *b* 1928: *m* 1952, 4th Baron Joicey, who *d* 1993. *Residence* – Etal Manor, Berwick-on-Tweed.

Granddaughters of late Galfrid John Leslie Melville, only son of late Capt Hon Norman Leslie Melville, 4th son of 9th Earl:—
Issue of late Norman Victor Leslie Melville, *b* 1896, *d* 1974: *m* 1918, Dorothea, who *d* 1982, da of late Walter Stead:—
Joan Frances Ruth (The Close, Fairford, Glos), *b* 1922: *m* 1st, 1941 (*m diss* 1954), Norman Henry Gibbs, DPh, who *d* 1990; 2ndly, 1955, Richard John Marshall Amphlett, who *d* 1978, and has issue living (by 1st *m*), Kathleen Vanessa, *b* 1942: *m* 1965, Peter John Quarrell, of Vyners Cottage, Long Compton, Shipston-on-Stour, Warwicks, and has issue living, Rachel Emma Louise *b* 1968, Philippa Kathryn *b* 1970, — Judith Rowena, *b* 1946: *m* 1967, William Rupert Brent Pelly, of Linden House, Fairford, Glos (*see* Pelly, Bt, colls). —— Anne, *b* 1929: *m* 1953 (*m diss* 1977), Matthew Joseph McDermott. *Residence* – Kitebrook House, nr Moreton-in-Marsh, Glos.

Granddaughters of late Rev Frederick Abel Leslie Melville, 5th son of late Hon Alexander Leslie Melville, yst son of 7th Earl:—
Issue of late Malcolm Alexander Leslie Melville, *b* 1882, *d* 1946: *m* 1924, Ruth Ellen, who *d* 1982, having *m* 2ndly, 1951, Arthur Ernest Mallett, who *d* 1960, da of James Dowker, of Mount Tolmie, Victoria, BC:—
Eleanor Constance, *b* 1926: *m* 1953, David William Metcalfe, and has issue living, Margaret Rose, *b* 1955: *m* 1979, Albert Lawson Munday, — Sandra Gail, *b* 1957: *m* 1976, Bruce Douglas Crowe, and has issue living, Andrew Jackson, *b* 1989, — Heather May, *b* 1965. *Residence* – 640 Fernhill Rd, Victoria, British Columbia. —— Margaret Wardlaw (1833, West 37th Av, Vancouver V6M 1N3, British Columbia), *b* 1928.

PREDECESSORS – (1) Sir ROBERT Melville, KB, PC, was twice Ambassador to England, Hereditary Keeper of Linlithgow Palace Vice-Chancellor and Treasurer depute, and an Extraordinary Lord of Session with title of Lord Murdocarnie 1594-1601; *cr Lord Melville of Monymaill* (peerage of Scotland), 1616, with remainder to heirs male of his brother John; *d* 1621, *s* by his son (2) ROBERT, PC, KB, 2nd Lord; an Extraordinary Lord of Session as Lord Burntisland 1601-8; in 1628 obtained a new charter of the lordship with remainders to his heirs general bearing the name of Melville; *d* 1635; *s* by his cousin (3) JOHN, 3rd Lord, son of John (ante), brother of 1st Lord; *d* 1643; *s* by his son (4) GEORGE, 4th Lord; being involved in the rebellion of the Duke of Monmouth he was attainted by Act of Parliament 1685; he escaped to Holland, from whence in 1688 he returned to England with the Prince of Orange (William III); in the following year the attainder was rescinded, and in 1690 he was *cr Lord Raith, Monymaill and Balwearie, Viscount Kirkaldie* and *Earl of Melville* (peerage of Scotland) 1690; Sec of State 1690-1, High Commr to Parliament 1690, Keeper of the Privy Seal 1691-6, and Pres of the Council 1696: *m* Lady Catherine Leslie, da of 2nd Earl of Leven; *d* 1707; *s* by his son (5) DAVID, PC, 2nd Earl, who had in 1682 *s* as 3rd of Leven (see note * infra); was Gov of Edinburgh Castle, Gen of the Ordnance, Lieut-Gen and Com in Ch in Scotland, a Commr of the Union, and a Representative Peer; *d* 1728; *s* by his grandson (6) DAVID, 4th Earl of Leven and 3rd Earl of Melville; *d* a minor 1729; *s* by his uncle (7) ALEXANDER, 5th and 4th Earl; was a Lord of Session, a Representtive Peer 1747, and High Commr to Church of Scotland 1741-3; *d* 1745; *s* by his son (8) DAVID, 6th and 5th Earl; High Commr to Gen Assembly 1783-1801; *d* 1802; *s* by his son (9) ALEXANDER, 7th and 6th Earl; *d* 1820; *s* by his el son (10) DAVID, 8th and 7th Earl; a Rear-Adm, Comptroller of the Customs in Scotland, and a Representative Peer; *d* 1860; *s* by his brother (11) JOHN THORNTON, 9th and 8th Earl; *b* 1786; a Representative Peer: *m* 1st, 1812, Harriet, who *d* 1832, da of Samuel Thornton, MP, of Albury park and Clapham; 2ndly, 1834, Sophia, who *d* 1887, da of Henry Thornton, of Battersea, Surrey; *d* 1876; *s* by his son (12) ALEXANDER, 10th and 9th Earl, *d* 1817; a Representative Peer; *d* 1889; *s* by his half-brother (13) RONALD RUTHVEN, PC, KT, 11th and 10th Earl, *b* 1835; a Representative Peer and Lord Keeper of the Privy Seal of Scotland; Lord High Commr to Gen Assembly of Church of Scotland 1898, 1899, 1900, 1901, 1902, 1903, 1904, and 1905: *m* 1885, Hon Emma Selina, who *d* 1941, da of 2nd Viscount Portman; *d* 1906; *s* by his el son (14) JOHN DAVID, 12th and 11th Earl, *b* 1886; a Representative Peer; *d* 1913; *s* by his brother (15) ARCHIBALD ALEXANDER, 13th and 12th Earl, *b* 1890; a Representative Peer, Lieut-Col and Brevet-Col (retired) Lovat Scouts, and Lord Lieut of Nairnshire: *m* 1918, Lady Rosamond Sylvia Diana Mary Foljambe, who *d* 1974, da of 1st Earl of Liverpool (*cr* 1905); *d* 1947; *s* by his son (16) ALEXANDER ROBERT, 14th and 13th Earl and present peer; also Viscount Kirkaldie, Lord Melville of Monymail, Lord Balgonie, and Lord Raith, Monymaill and Balwearie.

*(1) Sir ALEXANDER Leslie, having served with distinction in the Swedish Army, in which service he attained the rank of Field-Marshal in 1638, took command of the Covenanters' Army and defeated the King's troops in various engagements; at the treaty of peace signed at Ripon 1641 the King *cr* him *Lord Balgonie* and *Earl of Leven* (peerage of Scotland) 1641, with remainder to his heirs whatsoever; he subsequently joined the Parliamentary Army with 21,000 men, and defeated the Royalists at Marston Moor 1644, but after the execution of the King he served against the Parliamentarians and joined in the cause of the Restoration; he was in 1651 surprised and taken prisoner by Gen Monk, and incarcerated in the Tower, from whence he was released at the intercession of Christina, Queen of Sweden; *d* 1661; *s* by his grandson (2) ALEXANDER, 2nd Earl; who obtained in 1665 a charter with remainder to (i) the heirs male of his body, (ii) the heirs female of his body, (iii) the 2nd son of John, 6th Earl of Rothes, (iv) the heirs male of George, 4th Lord Melville (ante), (v) the 2nd son of David, 2nd Earl of Wemys, (vi) his own heirsmale whatsoever, and (vii) to his heirs and assignees whatsoever; *d* without male issue 1663; *s* by his el da (3) MARGARET; *dsp* 1674; *s* by her sister (4) KATHERINE; *d* 1682; *s* by her kinsman (5) DAVID, 3rd Earl (see 2nd Earl of Melville (ante)), the three first remainders having failed.

LEVER, BARONY OF (Lever) (Extinct 1977)

SON LIVING OF LIFE BARON

Hon Bernard Lewis (45 Hardman St, Manchester M3 3HA), *b* 1951; *ed* Clifton, and Queen's Coll, Oxon, Bar Middle Temple 1975: *m* 1985, Anne Helen, only da of Patrick Chandler Gordon Ballingall, MBE, of Seaford, E Sussex, and has issue.

DAUGHTER LIVING OF LIFE BARON

Hon June A, *b* 1940: *m* 1962, Emanuel S. Rosen, MD, FRCS, FRPS, of 18A Torkington Rd, Wilmslow, Cheshire SK9 2AE, and has issue.

WIDOW LIVING OF LIFE BARON

RAY ROSALIA (*Baroness Lever*) (9 Plowley Close, Didsbury, Manchester, M20 2DB), only child of Dr Leonard Levene of Leicester; JP for Manchester: *m* 1939, Baron Lever (Life Baron), who *d* 1977.

LEVER OF MANCHESTER, BARON (Lever) (Life Baron 1979)

(NORMAN) HAROLD LEVER, PC, son of late Bernard Lever; *b* 1914; *ed* Manchester Gram Sch, and Manchester Univ (LLB); Bar Middle Temple 1935; Joint Parl Under-Sec of State, Dept of Economic Affairs 1967, Financial Sec HM Treasury 1967-69, and Paymaster Gen 1969-70; Chancellor of Duchy of Lancaster 1974-79; Chm of Public Accounts Cttee 1970-73; MP for Exchange Div of Manchester (*Lab*) 1945-50, for Cheetham Div of Manchester 1950-74, and for Manchester (Central) 1974-79; 1939-45 War as F/O RAF; *cr* PC 1969, and *Baron Lever of Manchester*, of Cheetham, City of Manchester (Life Baron) 1979: *m* 1st, 1939 (*m diss* 19—), Ethel, da of Mendel Samuel, and formerly wife of Harris Sebrinski (otherwise Samuels); 2ndly, 1945, Betty (Billie), who *d* 1948, formerly wife of Monty Featherman, and da of Myer Woolfe; 3rdly, 1962, Mrs Diane Zilkha, da of late Saleh Bashi, of Geneva, and has issue by 2nd and 3rd *m*.
Address – House of Lords, SW1A 0AA.

DAUGHTERS LIVING *(By 2nd marriage)*

Hon Judith, *b* 1947.

(by 3rd marriage)

Hon Annabelle P. F., *b* 1962.
Hon Isabelle A. N., *b* 1964: *m* 1988, Dr Antony Laurent, elder son of late Jacques Condou, and of Mme Jacques Bertheau, of Nanteau-sur-Essonne, France, and has issue living, Lily, *b* 1993.
Hon Donatella Arabelle Yasmine, *b* 1966.

LEVERHULME, VISCOUNT (Lever) (Viscount UK 1922, Bt UK 1911)
(Title pronounced "Leverhume")

I scorn to change or fear

PHILIP WILLIAM BRYCE LEVER, KG, TD, 3rd Viscount, and 3rd Baronet; *b* 1 July 1915; *s* 1949; *ed* Eton, and Trin Coll, Camb; Hon Col (Cheshire Yeo Sqdn) The Queen's Own Yeo, RAC, TAVR since 1972. Advisory Dir of Unilever, Ltd, a JP and a KStJ; Lord-Lieut of Cheshire 1949-90; Steward of Jockey Club 1973-76; Chancellor Liverpool Univ 1980-93, Hon LLD 1967, Hon FRCS 1970, KG 1988: *m* 1937, Margaret Ann, who *d* 1973, only child of John Moon, of Tiverton, Devon, and has issue.

Arms – Quarterly, 1st and 4th, per pale argent and barry of eight or and azure, two bendlets sable, the upper one engrailed; 2nd and 3rd, per chevron or and gules, in chief two chaplets of roses and in base a lion's head all counterchanged. Crest – A trumpet fessewise, thereon a cock proper, charged on the breast with a rose as in the arms. Supporters – On either side an elephant or, the dexter charged on the shoulder with a rose gules and the sinister with a chaplet of roses also gules.
Residences – Thornton Manor, Thornton Hough, Wirral, Cheshire; Badanloch, Kinbrace, Sutherland; Flat 6, Kingston House East, Princes Gate, SW7 1LJ.
Clubs – Boodle's, Jockey.

DAUGHTERS LIVING

Hon Susan Elizabeth Moon *b* 1938: *m* 1957 (*m diss* 1973), (Hercules) Michael Roland Pakenham (*see* E Longford, colls). *Residence* – Dibbinsdale Lodge, Bromborough, Wirral, Cheshire.
Hon Victoria Marion Ann, *b* 1945: *m* 1st, 1966 (*m diss* 1973), John Richard Walter Reginald Carew Pole (later Sir Richard Carew Pole, 13th Bt); 2ndly, 1975, Robert Gordon Lennox Apsion; 3rdly, 1990, Brig Peter Tower, of 8 Mulberry Walk, SW3, and has issue living (by 2nd *m*), Philip Gordon William, *b* 1976, — Robert George Neville, *b* 1978, — Alexandra Victoria, *b* 1983.
Hon Margaret Jane, *b* 1947: *m* 1966, Algernon Eustace Hugh Heber-Percy, of Hodnet Hall, Market Drayton, Shropshire (*see* D Northumberland, colls).

SISTER LIVING

Hon Rosemary Gertrude Alexandra, *b* 1919: *m* 1938, Lieut-Col William Erskine Stobart Whetherly, formerly King's Dragoon Guards, and has issue living, Dennis William Stobart, *b* 1940, — Robin Christopher Philip, *b* 1947; late RHG: *m* 1971, Sally Ann, da of Maj R. C. S. Price, of Birdhurst, Alderbury, Wilts, — Dawn Elizabeth Evelyn, *b* 1946: *m* 1st, 1967 (*m diss* 1981), Andrew James Little; 2ndly, 1987, Kevin S. Perrett, of College Farm, Wyck Rissington, Glos GL54 2PN, and has issue living (by 1st *m*), Mark William Douglas *b* 1969, Emma Louise *b* 1973, Alexandra Rose *b* 1977. *Residence* – Hallam, Ogbourne St George, Marlborough, Wilts.

PREDECESSORS

PREDECESSORS – (1) WILLIAM HESKETH Lever, son of the late James Lever, of Bolton, Lancashire; *b* 1851; founder of Port Sunlight, and Chm of Lever Bros (Limited); High Sheriff of Lancashire 1917-18; MP for Wirral Div of Cheshire (*L*) Jan 1906 to Dec 1909; *cr* a *Baronet* 1911, *Baron Leverhulme*, of Bolton-le-Moors, co Palatine of Lancaster (peerage of United Kingdom) 1917, and *Viscount Leverhulme*, of The Western Isles, in the cos of Inverness and Ross and Cromarty (peerage of United Kingdom) 1922: *m* 1874, Elizabeth Ellen, who *d* 1913, da of Crompton Hulme, of Bolton; *d* 1925; *s* by his son **(2)** WILLIAM HULME, 2nd, Viscount, *b* 1888; Gov of Lever Bros, and of Unilever Ltd; High Sheriff of Cheshire 1923; Pres of London Chamber of Commerce 1931-4, of Institution of Chemical Engineers 1932-4, of Roy Warrant Holders' Asso 1933, and of So of Chemical Industry 1936-8; was Pro-Chancellor Liverpool Univ 1932-6; Charter Mayor of Bebington 1937 (first Hon Freeman

1945): *m* 1st, 1912 (*m diss* 1936), Marion Beatrice, who *d* 1987, having *m* 2ndly, 1937, Wing-Cdr Selden Herbert Lond, DSO, MC (*d* 1952), da of late Bryce Smith, of Whalley and Manchester; 2ndly, 1937, Winifred Agnes (Lee Morris), who *d* 1966, yr da of Lt-Col Lloyd, of Brentwood, Bidston, Cheshire; *d* 1949; *s* by his son **(3)** Philip William Bryce, 3rd Viscount and present peer; also Baron Leverhulme.

Leveson, Lord; son of Earl Granville.

LEWIN, BARON (Lewin) (Life Baron 1982)

Terence Thornton Lewin, KG, GCB, MVO, DSC, son of late E.H. Lewin; *b* 19 Nov 1920; *ed* The Judd Sch; Hon DSc City Univ, Hon DLitt Univ of Greenwich 1993; joined RN 1939; Comd HMS *Corunna* 1955-56, and HM Yacht *Britannia* 1957-58; Capt (F) Dartmouth Trgn Sqdn and HMS *Urchin* and *Tenby* 1961-63; Dir of Naval, Tactical and Weapons Policy Div, MoD 1964-65; Comd HMS *Hermes* 1966-67; Assist Chief of Naval Staff (Policy) 1968-69; Flag Officer, Second-in-Comd, Far East Fleet 1969-70; Vice-Chief of Naval Staff 1971-73; C-in-C Fleet 1973-75; C-in-C Naval Home Comd 1975-77; Chief of Naval Staff and First Sea Lord 1977-79; Flag ADC to HM 1975-77; First and Principal ADC to HM 1977-79; Chief of Defence Staff 1979-82; Elder Brother, Trinity House 1975; Hon Freeman Skinners' Co 1976, and Shipwrights' Co 1978; Hon FNI; Trustee Nat Maritime Museum since 1981 (Chm since 1987), Pres Shipwrecked Fishermen and Mariners' R Benevolent Soc since 1984, British Schs Exploring Soc since 1985, and Soc for Nautical Research since 1989; served in 1939-45 War in Home and Mediterranean Fleets (despatches); DSC 1942; *cr* MVO 1958, KCB (Mil) 1973, GCB (Mil) 1976, *Baron Lewin*, of Greenwich in Greater London (Life Baron) 1982, and KG 1983: *m* 1944, Jane, da of late Rev Charles James Branch Evans, and has issue.

Arms – Quarterly gules and azure three boars heads two and one couped or tusked argent on a chief barry wavy of four bleu celeste and argent a naval gun circa 1800 proper mounted on its carriage gold. **Crest** – Out of a naval crown azure a lion rampant in trian aspect or on its head a baron's coronet and cap of estate proper brandishing in the dexter paw a sword proper hilt knuckle guard and pommel in the form of an eagle's head gold. **Supporters** – *Dexter*, an Able Seaman of Her Majesty's Ship Victory; *sinister*, a Royal Marine, both wearing the South Atlantic Medal, the compartment comprising a grassy mount with outcrops of rock proper and having on each side a sea inlet barry wavy argent and azure. **Motto** – Flexible But Firm of Purpose.
Address – c/o House of Lords, SW1.

SONS LIVING

Hon Timothy Charles Thornton, *b* 1947: *m* 1973, Carolyn Thain.
Hon Jonathan James, *b* 1959: *m* 1990, Madeline Marsh.

DAUGHTER LIVING

Hon Susan, *b* 1949: *m* 1969, Peter Roe, and has issue living, Cosmo, *b* 1972, — Emily, *b* 1975, — Jessica, *b* 1982.

LEWIS OF NEWNHAM, BARON (Lewis) (Life Baron 1989)

JACK LEWIS, son of Robert Lewis of Askham; *b* 13 Feb 1928; *ed* Barrow Gram Sch, London Univ (BSc, DSc), Nottingham Univ (PhD), Manchester Univ (MSc), and Camb Univ (MA, ScD); Hon DUniv Rennes 1980, Open 1982, and Kingston 1993, Hon DSc E Anglia 1983, Nottingham 1983, Keele 1984, Waterloo (Canada) 1988, Birmingham 1988, Leicester 1988, Manchester 1990, Wales 1990, Sheffield 1992, and Cranfield Inst of Technology, Hon Fell UCL 1990, UMIST 1990 and Univ of Central Lancs 1993; FRS, FRIC, FRSA; lecturer and reader UCL 1957-61, Prof of Chemistry Manchester Univ 1961-67, UCL 1967-70, and Camb Univ since 1970; Warden Robinson Coll, Camb since 1975; Chm Royal Commn on Environmental Pollution 1985-92, and Dept of Educn and Science Visiting Cttee to Cranfield Inst 1982-92, Pres Royal Soc of Chemistry 1986-88; member of various Science Research Council Cttees, etc; *cr* Kt 1982, *Baron Lewis of Newnham*, of Newnham, co Cambs (Life Baron) 1989, and Chevalier l'Ordre des Palmes Académiques 1993: *m* 1951, Elfreida Mabel, da of Frank Alfred Lamb, of Manchester, and has issue.
Residence – Warden's Lodge, 4 Sylvester Rd, Cambridge. *Club* – Oxford & Cambridge.

SON LIVING

Hon Ian Peter, *b* 1958; *ed* Leys Sch.

DAUGHTER LIVING

Hon Penelope Jane, *b* 1956: *m* 1982, Howard Allaker Chase, and has issue living, George Howard, *b* 1984, — Charlotte Elizabeth, *b* 1986.

Lewisham, Viscount; son of Earl of Dartmouth.

LICHFIELD, EARL OF (Anson) (Earl UK 1831)

NIL + DESPERANDUM

Despair of nothing

THOMAS PATRICK JOHN ANSON, 5th Earl; *b* 25 April 1939; *s* 1960; *ed* Harrow, and RMA Sandhurst; late Lt Gren Gds; photographer; FBIPP; FRPS: *m* 1975 (*m diss* 1986), Lady Leonora Mary Grosvenor, elder da of 5th Duke of Westminster, and has issue.

Arms – Quarterly: 1st, argent, three bends engrailed and in the sinister chief point a crescent gules, *Anson*; 2nd, ermine, three cats-a-mountain passant guardant, in pale sable, *Adams*; 3rd, azure, three salmon naiant in pale, per pale or and argent, *Sambrooke*; 4th, sable, a bend or, between three spears' heads argent, *Carrier*. **Crest** – 1st, out of a ducal coronet or, a spear head proper; 2nd, a greyhound's head erased ermines, gorged with a collar, double gemelle or. **Supporters** – *Dexter*, a sea-horse; *sinister*, a lion guardant, both proper and each gorged with a collar double gemelle or.
Residences – Shugborough Hall, Stafford; 86 Holland Park, W11. *Studio* — 133 Oxford Gdns, W10 6NE.

SON LIVING

THOMAS WILLIAM ROBERT HUGH (*Viscount Anson*), *b* 19 July 1978.

DAUGHTERS LIVING

Lady Rose Meriel Margaret, *b* 1976.
Lady Eloise Anne Elizabeth, *b* 1981.

SISTER LIVING (*Raised to the rank of an Earl's daughter* 1961)

Lady Elizabeth Georgiana, *b* 1941; founder Party Planners 1960, trading as Lady Elizabeth Anson: *m* 1972, as his 2nd wife, Sir Geoffrey Adam Shakerley, 6th Bt. *Residence* – 56 Ladbroke Grove, W11 2PB.

AUNT LIVING (*Daughter of 4th Earl*)

Lady Betty Marjorie, *b* 1917: *m* 1944, Col Thomas Foley Churchill Winnington, MBE, Grenadier Guards (*see* Winnington, Bt). *Residence* – 182 Rivermead Court, Ranelagh Gdns, SW6 3SG.

COLLATERAL BRANCHES LIVING

Issue of late Capt Hon Rupert Anson, yst son of 3rd Earl, *b* 1889, *d* 1966: *m* 1919, Marion Emma Ruthven, who *d* 1965, da of James Halliday, of Harrow-on-the-Hill:—
Geoffrey Rupert (2000 Jonathan Drive, Martinsburg, W Virginia 25401, USA), *b* 1929: *m* 1957, Verna Grace Hall, and has had issue, George Rupert (The Hillings, Drayton Parslow, Bucks MK17 0JJ), *b* 1960: *m* 1987, Kirsty Jane, da of A. S. D. Day, of Billesdon, Leics, and has issue living, Douglas Rupert *b* 1992, Josceline Elizabeth *b* 1989, — Christopher Leonard, *b* 1963, — †Edward Peter, *b* 1965; *d* 1982, — Jennifer Marion *b* 1961. ⸺ Thomas Peter (Coneygre Farmhouse, Hardwick, Bicester, Oxon OX6 9SU), *b* 1933: Col Queen's R Irish Hussars: *m* 1964, Judith Hilary, da of late Capt John Nicholl Kennard, RN, and has issue living, Henry James (8 Althea St, SW6 2RY), *b* 1967: *m* 1992, Joanna C., da of D. R. Lamb, of W Littleton, Bath, — Patrick John, *b* 1969. ⸺ Anne Rosemary (c/o Coutts & Co, 440 Strand, WC2R 0GS), *b* 1924: *m* 1946 (*m diss* 1974), Capt Paul Coombe, and has issue living, Geoffrey Paul (Dianalaan 7, Amstelveen, Holland), *b* 1951, — Michael Anthony (PO Box 171, Milsons Point, NSW 2061, Australia), *b* 1955: *m* 1st, 1975, Karen Elizabeth O'Hara, who *d* 1990; 2ndly, 1992, Karin Penny South, and has issue living (by 1st wife), Benjamin Michael *b* 1982, (by 2nd wife) Lucy Romy *b* 1992, — Diana Mary, *b* 1947: *m* 1st, 1967 (*m diss* 1986), Timothy Gaines; 2ndly, 1987 (*m diss* 1989), Jess Mount; 3rdly, 1990, Richard Stewart, of PO Box 970, Canyonville, Oregon 97417, USA, and has issue living (by 1st *m*), David Allan *b* 1970, Daniel Anson *b* 1972, Devon Ashley *b* 1974. ⸺ Felicity Marion (Shepherds, Ansty, Dorchester, Dorset), *b* 1927: *m* 1952, John Arbon Woodhouse, who *d* 1986, and has issue living, Mark John Michael (Cherrington Farm Cottage, N Cheriton, Templecombe, Som BA8 0AP), *b* 1955: *m* 1979, Teresa Jane, only da of Michael Kennedy Merriam, of Stowell House, Sherborne, Dorset (*see* M Ailsa, 1985 Edn), — Andrew Harold Rupert, *b* 1957, — Clare Marian, *b* 1965.

Granddaughters of late Lt-Col Hon Sir George Augustus Anson, KCB, CBE, MVO, 2nd son of 2nd Earl:—
Issue of Claud Ronald Anson, *b* 1895, *d* 1965: *m* 1st, 1915, Frederica Heath, who *d* 1941, da of late Frederic James Harrison, of Maer Hall, Staffs; 2ndly, 1944, Mrs Lilian Gallia Meiklejohn, da of late David George Davies, of New York; 3rdly, 1949, Mrs Noreen Stella Cross, da of late H. G. Barlow:—
(By 1st *m*) Mary (Weston Meres, Maer, Newcastle, Staffs, and Lyons Hill, Minterne Magna, Dorchester, Dorset), *b* 1918: *m* 1940 (*m diss* 1960), Lt-Col John Anthony Dene, Duke of Cornwall's LI, and has issue living, John Michael, *b* 1946, — David Frederick, *b* 1948, — Margaret Katharine, *b* 1942: *m* 1st, 1962 (*m diss* 1976), Michael Charles Power; 2ndly, 1977, Patrick Bernard Lucas, of Chalknewton House, Maiden Newton, Dorchester, Dorset, and has issue living (by 1st *m*), Anthony George Bertram *b* 1968, Katharine Mary *b* 1965, Erica Margaret *b* 1967. ⸺ Joan (Enton Wood, Godalming, Surrey), *b* 1919: *m* 1945, Maj J. C. Lee, Roy Netherlands Army, who *d* 1963.

Grandchildren of late Hon Claud Anson, 5th son of 2nd Earl:—
Issue of late Anthony John Anson, *b* 1904, *d* 1981: *m* 1926, Rosalind Désirée, who *d* 1985, only da of Rear-Adm Sir Robert Keith Arbuthnot, 4th Bt, KCB, MVO:—
John Anthony Robert (30 Tibbets Close, SW19), *b* 1927; MRCS, LRCP: *m* 1st, 1962, (Fiona) Brook, MB BS, who *d* 1987, da of late Colin Frederick George Wills; 2ndly, 1989, (Angela) Jane Millican, and has had issue (by 1st *m*), Rupert Anthony Wills, *b* 1963, — Annabel Frances Rosalind, *b* 1967, *d* 1988. ⸺ Colin Shane (18 Ripplevale Grove, N1), *b* 1931; *ed* Stowe. ⸺ Sarah Rose, *b* 1944: *m* 1969, Capt Robin Gifford Kerr, RN, of 3 Lansdown Place East, Bath, and has issue living, Bryony Charlotte, *b* 1972, — Julia Emily, *b* 1974.
Issue of late Maj Hugo Edward Anson, *b* 1908, *d* 1991: *m* 1st, 1935 (*m diss* 1946), Elizabeth, eldest da of late Capt Sir Harold George Campbell, GCVO, DSO, RN (ret) (*see* E Leven and Melville, colls, 1946 Edn); 2ndly, 1946, Duchessa Annina Badoglio, who *d ca* 1991-92, da of Marchese Silj, of Rome, and widow of Duca Paolo Badoglio:—
(By 1st *m*) Michael (Windrush Hill, Hawling, Cheltenham, Glos), *b* 1937; *ed* Stowe, and Edinburgh Univ; a Page of Honour to HM 1950-53: *m* 1963, Claire-Elizabeth Seymour, da of late Lt-Col Frederick Arthur Morris, of St Katherine's, Cradley, Malvern, Worcs, and has issue living, Alexandra Albinia, *b* 1965: *m* 1992, Marcus A. Hodge, of San Bartolomé 10, Palma 07001, Majorca, elder son of Spencer Hodge, of Roquebrune, France, — Josephine Emma, *b* 1968, — Catherine Elizabeth, *b* 1971. ⸺ (By 2nd *m*) Bernard Anthony (Villa Silj, via di Santa Cornelia Kml, 008891 Prima Porta, Rome), *b* 1948; *ed* Harrow, and Trin Coll, Dublin: *m* 1st, 1975 (*m diss* 1984), Anna, da of John Cooper; 2ndly, 1984, Eleanora, da of Carlo Monini. ⸺ Andrea Vittorio (203 Prince St, New York, NY 10012, USA), *b* 1951; *ed* Harrow.

Grandchildren of late Hon Francis Anson, 6th son of 2nd Earl:—
Issue of late Wing-Com Henry Adelbert Anson, RAF, *b* 1895, *d* 1955: *m* 1st, 1927 (*m diss* 1930), Hilda Suzanne, da of S. Carson Allen, of 39 Circus Road, St John's Wood, NW8; 2ndly, 1930, Muriel Irene, da of Edgar C. Smith:—
(By 1st *m*) David Richard, *b* 1929. Resides in Australia. ⸺ (By 2nd *m*) Vanessa Irene (*Lady Hannam*), *b* 1940: *m* 1st, 1962, John Edward Robert Wauchope; 2ndly, 1983, Sir John Gordon Hannam, MP, and has issue living (by 1st *m*) Andrew Charles Anson, *b* 1974, — Arabella Jane, *b* 1963: *m* 1986, G. H. C. P. (Harry) Huddart, of 101 Camberwell Grove, SE5, only son of Edward William Huddart, of Littlecourt, Derriford, Plymouth, and has issue living, Joseph Edward Anson *b* 1988, Georgiana Rose *b* 1986, Augusta Louisa *b* (twin) 1989, Flora Vanessa Elizabeth *b* 1990, — Lucy Anne Margaret, *b* 1965: *m* 1987, James F. D. Rolls, only son of John Rolls, of Las Lomas, Spain, — Alexandra Gladys, *b* 1968. *Residence* – 27 Fentiman Rd, SW8 1LD.

Grandchildren of late Maj William Alfred Anson (*infra*):—
Issue of late Francis Richard Anson, *b* 1926, *d* 1989: *m* 1st, 1948 (*m diss* 1960), Ann, da of Sir John Lionel Armytage, 8th Bt; 2ndly, 1960 (*m diss* 1983), Bridgett Ann, only da of Dudley Gerald Greenhough, of 25 Aldford House, Park Lane, W1; 3rdly, 1984, Elisabeth Gildroy (11 Anley Rd, W14), da of late Edward Philip Shaw, of Commoners, Englefield Green, Surrey, and formerly wife of late Oliver Simon Willis Fleming:—
(By 1st *m*) Anthony Francis (Pigeon House, Pigeon Lane, Hanmer, Whitchurch, Shropshire), *b* 1951; *ed* Harrow: *m* 1985, Sally C., da of Col Geoffrey Vardon Churton, MBE, MC, TD, and has issue living, Caroline Myra, *b* 1990. ⸺ Amanda Jane, *b* 1950: *m* 1982, Jeremy D. P. Pratt, of 63 Colehill Lane, SW6 5EF, son of David Pratt, of The Old Rectory, Shottisham, Woodbridge, Suffolk. ⸺ (By 2nd *m*) Juliet May, *b* 1961. ⸺ Emma Louise, *b* 1963: *m* 1988, Dr Alan Hargreaves, of 994 Augusta Court, Kelowna, BC, Canada V1Y 7I9, son of Eric Hargreaves, of Durban, S Africa.

Grandchildren of late Hon Francis Anson, 6th son of 2nd Earl:—
Issue of late Major William Alfred Anson, *b* 1897, *d* 1952: *m* 1919 Dorothy Helme, who *d* 1988, da of late Richard Mashiter, of 22 Princes Gate, SW, and Hillend, Glamorgan:—
Edward William, *b* 1929; *ed* Harrow. ⸺ Harriet Louise, *b* 1924.

Issue of late Capt Hon William Anson, 7th son of 2nd Earl, *b* 1872, *d* 1926: *m* 1917, Louisa Goddard, who *d* 1952, da of Frederick De Voe Van Wagenen, of Fulton, New York:—
Edith, *b* 1921: *m* 1st, 1943, Capt Alfred Ryland Howard, who was *ka* in Normandy 1944; 2ndly, 1947, Lieut-Col Ford Millspaugh Boulware, and has issue living (by 1st *m*), Alfred Ryland (III) (114 Park Hill, San Antonio, Texas 78212, USA), *b* 1944: *m* 1985, Pamela, only da of Hugh A. Fitzsimons, of San Pedro Ranch, Carrizo Springs, Texas, and of Mrs William

Negley, of San Antonio, Texas, and has issue living, Anson Boulware *b* 1987, Laura Isabel *b* 1989, Louisa Carrigan *b* 1992. *Residence* – 1104 Montecito Dr, San Angelo, Texas 76901, USA.

PREDECESSORS – (1) THOMAS ANSON; MP for Lichfield 1789-1806 (great nephew of Adm George Anson, who circumnavigated the world 1740, and was *cr Lord Anson, Baron of Soberton*, co Southampton 1747); *cr Baron Soberton*, co Southampton, and *Viscount Anson* (peerage of United Kingdom) 1806; *d* 1818; *s* by his son (2) THOMAS WILLIAM, PC, 2nd Viscount; *b* 1795; *cr Earl of Lichfield* (peerage of United Kingdom) 1831; Master of the Buckhounds 1830-34, and Postmaster-Gen 1835-41: *m* 1819, Louisa Barbara Catherine, who *d* 1879, da of Nathaniel Phillips, of Slebech Hall, co Pembroke; *d* 1854; *s* by his son (3) THOMAS GEORGE, 2nd Earl, *b* 1825; MP for Lichfield 1847-54, and Lord-Lieut of Staffordshire 1863-71; *m* 1855, Lady Harriet Georgiana Louisa Hamilton, who *d* 1913, el da of 1st Duke of Abercorn, KG; *d* 1892; *s* by his el son (4) THOMAS FRANCIS, 3rd Earl, *b* 1856: *m* 1878, Lady Mildred Coke, who *d* 1941, da of 2nd Earl of Leicester; *d* 1918; *s* by his son (5) THOMAS EDWARD, 4th Earl; *b* 1883; Capt London Regt; ADC and Acting Master of the Horse to Lord-Lieut of Ireland (Earl of Aberdeen 1906-10); Lord High Steward of Borough of Stafford 1933: *m* 1st, 1911, Evelyn Maud, who *d* 1945, da of late Col Edward George Keppel, MVO; 2ndly, 1949, Violet Margaret (PHILIPS), who *d* 1988, da of late Henry Dawson Dawson-Greene, JP, of Slyne, and Whittington Hall, Lancashire; *d* 1960; *s* by his grandson (6) THOMAS PATRICK JOHN (son of late Lt-Col Thomas William Arnold, Viscount Anson (by his 1st wife, Anne Ferelith Fennella, who *d* 1980, da of Hon John Herbert Bowes-Lyon, 2nd son of 14th Earl of Strathmore and Kinghorne), el son of 4th Earl), 5th Earl and present peer; also Viscount Anson, and Baron Soberton.

LIFFORD, VISCOUNT (Hewitt) (Viscount I 1781)

(EDWARD) JAMES WINGFIELD HEWITT, 9th Viscount; *b* 27 Jan 1949; *s* 1987; Member London Stock Exchange; Dir Cobbold Neilson Ltd, and Winchester Assured Tenancies plc: *m* 1976, Alison Mary, da of Robert Law, of Turnpike House, Withersfield, Suffolk, and has issue.

Arms – Gules, a chevron engrailed, between three owls argent. **Crest** – On a stump of a tree, with one branch growing thereon, an owl proper. **Supporters** – *Dexter*, a vulture, proper, wings inverted, gorged with a plain collar sable, thereon three bezants; *sinister*, a griffin, proper, wings elevated, gorged as the dexter. *Residence* – Field House, Hursley, nr Winchester, Hants. *Clubs* – Boodle's, Hampshire, Pratt's.

SON LIVING

Hon JAMES THOMAS WINGFIELD, *b* 29 Sept 1979.

DAUGHTERS LIVING

Hon Annabel Louise, *b* 1978.
Hon Alice Mary, *b* 1990.

SISTERS LIVING

(*Hon*) Lydia Mary (does not use courtesy title) (Quedley Farm, Flimwell, Wadhurst, E Sussex), *b* 1938: *m* 1965 (*m diss* 1983), Michael Christopher Swann, el son of Sir Anthony Charles Christopher Swann, 3rd Bt, CMG, OBE.
Hon Belinda Anne, *b* 1939: *m* 1963, Rev Piers Eliot de Dutton Warburton, of The Rectory, Hartley Wintney, Hants and has issue living, Piers Richards Grove, *b* 1964, — Elizabeth Jane, *b* 1967.
Hon Flora Elizabeth, *b* 1947: *m* 1965 (*m diss* 1975), Edward Bell Henderson, and has issue living, Samantha Elizabeth, *b* 1967, —

Victoria Amanda, *b* 1971.

WIDOW LIVING OF EIGHTH VISCOUNT

ALISON MARY PATRICIA (*Mary Viscountess Lifford*), 2nd da of late Thomas Wingrave Ashton, of The Cottage, Hursley, nr Winchester: *m* 1935, the 8th Viscount, who *d* 1987. *Residence* – The Barn, Hursley, Winchester, Hants.

COLLATERAL BRANCHES LIVING

Grandsons of late James Francis Katharinus Hewitt, 3rd son of late Rev Hon James John Pratt Hewitt, 2nd son of 2nd Viscount:—
Issue of late John Stanley Hewitt, *b* 1875, *d* 1937: *m* 1909, Avice Alureda, who *d* 1939, da of late Rev Arthur Langdale Langdale-Smith, R of Holton, Wheatley, Oxon:—
Terence John Lifford, *b* 1911; European War 1940-45 as Act Capt Gurkha Rifles, Liaison Offr 2/9 Gurkhas (pow 3½ years, Siam-Burma rlwy): *m* 1946, Rowena Edith Mabel, 2nd da of late Ernest Taylor England, of 26 Field Park, Newbridge, Monmouthshire, and has issue living, Anthea Avice Yvonne, *b* 1947: *m* 1970, Richard Geoffrey Horsford Kemp, of Slaymaker, Holton, Oxon. *Residence* – Holton Cottage, Holton, Oxon. — Theodore Denis, *b* 1918; 1940-45 War as Lt and acting Capt Gurkha Rifles.
Issue of late Cdr Brian Lifford Hewitt, OBE, RN, *b* 1881, *d* 1962: *m* 1914, Roie (11 Ely Av, Remuera, Auckland, NZ), da of late Alfred Nathan, of Wickford, Auckland, New Zealand:—
†Michael James Alfred Lifford, *b* 1916: *m* 1947, Sybil Grace (724 Gladstone Rd, Gisborne, New Zealand), yst da of late William Arthur Izard (E Eglinton and Winton, colls), and *d* 1993, leaving issue, Peter Lifford (3 Kawau St, One Tree Hill, Auckland, NZ), *b* 1948: *m* 1983, Mary, da of J. A. Parkinson, and has issue living, Christopher *b* 1984, Ellen *b* 1986, — Anthony James (26 Martin Way, Woking, Surrey), *b* 1951: *m* 1978, Susan Elizabeth, da of Lt-Col M. J. J. Rolt, of Byfleet, Surrey, and has issue living, Oliver Michael James *b* 1985, Victoria Louise *b* 1980, Emily Kate *b* 1982, — Rosemary Ruth, *b* 1949: *m* 1975, Geoffrey Martin Brodie, of 31 Carlton Mill Rd, Merivale, NZ, and has issue living, Thomas Nathan *b* 1982, Timothy Paul *b* 1984, Caroline *b* 1977, Amy *b* 1979, — Elizabeth Grace *b* 1956: *m* 1990, Kevin Francis Bradley, of 36 Fancourt St, Meadowbank, Auckland, NZ, and has issue living, Hamish Michael Patrick *b* 1992, Olivier Roie *b* 1993.

—— Patrick Francis (31 Dell Av, Remuera, Auckland, NZ), *b* 1921: *m* 1st, 1944 (*m diss* 19—), Mary, da of Trevor N. Holmden, of Remuera, Auckland, NZ; 2ndly, 1954, Judith, da of late John Hellaby, of 5 Ridings Rd, Remuera, Auckland, NZ, and has issue living (by 1st *m*) Brian James Lifford (9 Marrakai St, Hawker, ACT 2614, Australia) *b* 1945; Lt-Col Royal NZ Artillery 1965, served Vietnam 1969-70; memb Commonwealth Monitoring Force in Zimbabwe-Rhodesia 1979-80; joined Australian Army 1989: *m* 1st, 1972 (*m diss* 1984), Erin Margaret, eldest da of Keith Charles Walshe, of Te Anau, NZ; 2ndly, 1984, Julie Margaret-Anne, eldest da of Maurice James Beuth, of Ashburton, NZ, and has issue living, (by 1st *m*) Richard James Lifford *b* 1975, Rebecca Roie Cecilia *b* 1978, (by 2nd *m*) Danielle Margaret *b* 1985, Antonia Julie *b* 1987.

Grandchildren of late John Edward Hewitt, eldest son of late Capt James Dudley Ryder Hewitt, RN (infra):—
Issue of late William Robert Riddiford Hewitt, *b* 1903, *d* 1976: *m* 1930, Nancy Charlotte Ellen, who *d* 1988, el da of Sydney Arthur Robert Mair, of Wharekuru, NZ:—
†Ian Robert *b* 1931: *m* 1955, Jean Hamilton (Camerons Line, RD5, Feilding, NZ), da of Henry Nicholas Johnson, MD, of Invercargill, NZ, and *d* 1992, leaving issue, Robert Johnson (Nokomai, Hanmer Springs, NZ), *b* 1962: *m* 1992, Margot Joan, da of Ian Hanmer Atkinson, of Hanmer Springs, NZ, and has issue living, William Ian Atkinson *b* 1994, — Louise Johnson, *b* 1958: *m* 1983, Malcolm Lawrence Sincock, and has issue living, James Robert *b* 1986, Matthew Thomas *b* 1990, Tara Jane *b* 1985, — Mary-Anne Johnson, *b* 1959: *m* 1984, Christopher William Gates, and has issue living, Rebecca Mary *b* 1989, Stephanie Louise *b* 1991. —— Peter David (Balfour Farm, RD4, Pahiatua, NZ), *b* 1937: *m* 1963, Heather Jean, da of Robert Allen Donald, of Papatahi, NZ, and has issue living, James Donald, *b* 1965: *m* 1991, Susan Jean, da of Snow Petersen, — Peter John, *b* 1967, — Timothy David, *b* 1968, — Teena Anne, *b* 1964: *m* 1994, Stephen Scoular Richards. —— Judith Anne, *b* 1936: *m* 1965, John Henry Armstrong, of 121a Waiwhetu Rd, Lower Hutt, NZ, and has issue living, Jane Margaret, *b* 1966: *m* 1994, Paul Andrew Hanson, — Kate Amanda, *b* 1969, — Nicola Anne, *b* 1972.

Granddaughters of late Capt James Dudley Ryder Hewitt, RN (infra):—
Issue of late Lt-Col Dudley Riddiford Hewitt, CIE, *b* 1877, *d* 1971: *m* 1913, Marjorie Middlemas, who *d* 1954, yr da of late William Fleming Inglis, of Shanghai:—
Dorothy Mary Riddiford, *b* 1914: *m* 1948, Capt William James Lysley, 11th Hussars, who *d* 19—, and has issue living, Rachel Marjorie Sarah Anne, *b* 1949: *m* 1979, Michael Norman Scott Ruddock, and has issue living, Alexander James Scott *b* 1984, Camilla Dorothy Scott *b* 1982. *Residence* – Flint House, Gt Barton, Bury St Edmunds, Suffolk IP31 2SW.
Issue of late Charles Gervais Hewitt, *b* 1885, *d* 1970: *m* 1911, Elsie Mary, who *d* 1974, el da of Herbert Pryce, of Rangitawa, Halcombe, NZ:—
Cushla Mary (Ngakouka, Carterton, Wellington, NZ), *b* 1916. —— Ruth Lifford, *b* 1918.

Grandchildren of James Francis Daniel Hewitt (infra):—
Issue of late Richard Walter Hewitt, *b* 1909, *d* 1974: *m* 1951, Joan Millicent (35 Kitchener St, Masterton, NZ), el da of Thomas Edward Holdgate, of Timaru, NZ:—
Timothy James (Taratanui, Ponatahi, Carterton, Wellington, NZ), *b* 1954: *m* 1978, Judith Clair, da of Trevor Simson, of Waverley, NZ, and has issue living, Richard James, *b* 1979, — Thomas Cameron, *b* 1987, — Catherine Jane, *b* 1981. —— Mary Ellen, *b* 1952: *m* 1975, David Carleton Hadfield, of Lindale, Main Rd, Paraparaumu, Wellington, NZ, eldest son of Barry Hadfield, of Lindale, Paraparaumu, NZ, and has issue living, Richard Henry, *b* 1979, — Samuel Mark, *b* 1984, — Melissa Maisie, *b* 1976.

Granddaughter of late Capt James Dudley Ryder Hewitt, RN, 6th son of Rev Hon James John Pratt Hewitt (ante):—
Issue of late James Francis Daniel Hewitt, *b* 1881, *d* 1963: *m* 1st, 1908, Ellen Westbury, who *d* 1938, da of R. S. Abraham, of Palmerston North, New Zealand; 2ndly, 1942, May Evelyn, da of E. J. Wright, of Kerikeri, New Zealand:—
(By 1st *m*) June Lifford, *b* 1910: *m* 1934, Robert Oswald Young of 14 Matenga St, Waikanae, NZ, and has issue living, Robin Slingsby, *b* 1935, — Simon Vivian Riddiford, *b* 1936, — James Francis, *b* 1940, — Thomas Lifford, *b* 1951, — Ellen Jennifer, *b* 1938.

PREDECESSORS – **(1)** JAMES Hewitt, PC, was a Justice of the King's Bench in England 1766-8, and Lord Chancellor of Ireland 1768-82; *cr Baron Lifford*, of Lifford, co Donegal (peerage of Ireland) 1768, and *Viscount Lifford* (peerage of Ireland) 1781; *d* 1789; *s* by his son **(2)** JAMES, DD, 2nd Viscount; was Dean of Armagh; *d* 1830; *s* by his son **(3)** JAMES, 3rd Viscount; *b* 1783; *m* 1809, Hon Mary Anne Maude, who *d* 1877, da of 1st Viscount Hawarden; *d* 1855; *s* by his son **(4)** JAMES, 4th Viscount, *b* 1811: was a Representative Peer: *m* 1st, 1835, Lady Mary Acheson, who *d* 1850, el da of 2nd Earl of Gosford; 2ndly, 1851, Lydia Lucy, who *d* 1919, el da of Rev John Digby Wingfield Digby, V of Coleshill, and widow of Charles Purdon-Coote; *d* 1887; *s* by his el son **(5)** JAMES WILFRID, 5th Viscount; *b* 1837: *m* 1867, Annie Frances, who *d* 1927, el da of late Sir Arthur Hodgson, KCMG, of Clopton House, Stratford-on-Avon; *d* 1913; *s* by his brother **(6)** ARCHIBALD ROBERT, 6th Viscount, *b* 1844; Capt RN: *m* 1878, Helen Blanche, who *d* 1942, only da of late Charles S. Geach; *d* 1925; *s* by his son **(7)** EVELYN JAMES, DSO, 7th Viscount; *b* 1880; Lieut-Col (ret) Dorsetshire Regt; S Africa 1902, European War 1914-18 (DSO and Bar): *m* 1919, Charlotte Rankine, who *d* 1954, da of late Sir Robert Maule, and widow of Capt Edgar Walker; *d* 1954; *s* by his cousin **(8)** ALAN WILLIAM WINGFIELD (son of late Hon George Wyldbore Hewitt, 7th son of 4th Viscount), 8th Viscount, *b* 1900; Lieut Hants Regt: *m* 1935, Alison Mary Patricia, 2nd da of late Thomas Wingrave Ashton, of The Cottage, Hursley, nr Winchester; *d* 1987; *s* by his only son **(9)** (EDWARD) JAMES WINGFIELD, 9th Viscount and present peer; also Baron Lifford.

LILFORD, BARON (Powys) (Baron GB 1797)
(Name pronounced "Poe-is")

GEORGE VERNON POWYS, 7th Baron; *b* 8 Jan 1931; *s* 1949; *ed* Stonyhurst: *m* 1st, 1954, Mrs Eve Bird; 2ndly, 1957 (*m diss* 1958), Anuta, only da of L. F. Merritt, of Johannesburg, S Africa; 3rdly, 1958 (*m diss* 1961), Norma Yvonne, only da of V. Shell, of Johannesburg, S Africa; 4thly, 1961 (*m diss* 1969), Mrs Muriel Spottiswoode; 5thly, 1969 (*m diss* 1991), Margaret, da of A. Penman, of Roslin, Midlothian, and has issue living by 4th and 5th *m*.

𝕬rms – Or, a bear's jamb erased in bend dexter, between two cross crosslets fitchée in bend sinister, gules. 𝕮rest – A lion's jamb couped and erect gules, holding a staff headed with a fleur-de-lis, also erect or. 𝕾upporters – *Dexter*, a reaper habited in a loose shirt, leather breeches loose at the knees, white stockings, and black hat and shoes; in his hat ears of corn, in his right hand a reaping-hook, and at his feet a garb, all proper; *sinister*, a man in the uniform of the Northamptonshire Yeomanry Cavalry, viz a green long coat, ornamented on the cuffs and button-holes with gold lace, yellow waistcoat and breeches, and black top boots; a black stock; a round hat; adorned with a white feather in front and a green one behind, the sword-belt inscribed with the letter NY and the exterior hand resting on his sword sheathed and point downwards.
Seat – Bank Hall, Bretherton, Preston, Lancs. *Residence* – Le Grand Câtelet, St John, Jersey CI.

To maintain acquired possessions

SON LIVING (By 5th marriage)

Hon MARK VERNON, *b* 16 Nov 1975.

DAUGHTERS LIVING (By 4th marriage)

Hon Clare Lynette, *b* 1962.
Hon Emma-Jane, *b* 1964.

(By 5th marriage)

Hon Sarah Margaret, *b* 1971.
Hon Hannah Victoria, *b* 1974.

SISTERS LIVING

Hilary Betty (4 Braeside Rd, Kenilworth, Cape 7700, S Africa), *b* 1929: *m* 1950, Philip Donald Millar, who *d* 1967, and has issue living, Christopher, *b* 1961: *m* 1989, Tracey Lynn Boddington, and has issue living, Guy Philip *b* 1992, — Philippa Ann, *b* 1958: *m* 1989, Paul Edward Roisen Sater, of 4 Westcroft Mews, W6 0TL.
Beryl Irene, *b* 1932.

COLLATERAL BRANCHES LIVING

Grandson of late Henry Littleton Powys, 4th son of late Robert Horace Powys, 2nd son of 2nd Baron:—
Issue of late Frank Lilford Powys, *b* 1902, *d* 1972: *m* 1929, Gertrude Frances Elizabeth (Erensrust, 3 Hilltop Rd, Hillcrest, Natal), da of G. G. F. Meyer:—
Robert Charles Lilford (PO Box 2138, Port Alfred 6170, Cape, S Africa), *b* 1930: *m* 1st, 1957 (*m diss* 1972),Charlotte Webb; 2ndly, 1973, Janet Wightwick.

Grandchildren of late Wilfred Owen Powys (infra):—
Issue of late Horace Victor Powys, *b* 1907, *d* 1956: *m* 1928, Olive Maude Peets, of Durban, S Africa:—
Michael John (PO Box 661, Link Hills 3652, Natal), *b* 1934: *m* 1957, Lynette Bernice Hodges, of Durban, Natal, and has had issue, Victor Michael (PO Box 710, Link Hills 3652, Natal), *b* 1961: *m* 1986, Yvonne Joan McCort, and has issue living, Victoria Amy *b* 1993, — †Andrew John, *b* 1970; *k* in a motor accident 1985, — †Paul Michael, *b* 1974; *k* in a motor accident 1985, — Susan Lynn (PO Box 432, Link Hills, Natal), *b* 1958: *m* 1978, Peter Gary Bahrs, and has issue living, Justin Peter *b* 1983, Jacqueline Susan *b* 1979, Nicola Susan *b* 1981, Megan Lynn *b* 1986. —— Pamela Ann, *b* 1929: *m* 1st, 1949 (*m diss* 1959), Ian Falconer; 2ndly, 1959, Harry Rowntree, of 24 Meyer Gdns, Umbilo, Durban 4001, Natal, and has issue living, (by 1st *m*) Malcolm, *b* 1950, — Donald, *b* 1952, — Colin, *b* 1955, — Neil, *b* 1956, — (by 2nd *m*) Mark, *b* 1960, — Anne, *b* 1961.

Granddaughter of the late Robert Horace Powys (ante):—
Issue of late Wilfred Owen Powys *b* 1873, *d* 1944: *m* 1905, Constance Mary, who *d* 1948, da of Robert Michael Bradford:—
Marjory Gladys (124 Northway, Durban North 4051, Natal), *b* 1911: *m* 1933, Cecil Wilme Collier, who *d* 1986, and has issue living, Frank Wilme, *b* 1942: *m* 1969, Christine Dewar, of Vryheid, Natal, and has issue living Andrew Blaine *b* 1972, Claire *b* 1974, — David Owen, *b* 1947: *m* 1970, Fay McKenzie, of Richmond, Natal, and has issue living, Vicki *b* 1974, Paula *b* 1976, Kate *b* 1978.

Grandsons of late Richard Atherton Norman Powys, 2nd son of Rev Hon Atherton Legh Powys, 4th son of 2nd Baron:—
Issue of late Atherton Richard Norman Powys, *b* 1888, *d* 1976: *m* 1st, 1915, Elsie Dyus, who *d* 1957, da of late Frederick Robert Mattingly; 2ndly, 1957, Edith, who *d* 1977, da of John Smart, of Edinburgh:—
(By 1st *m*) John Frederick Atherton, *b* 1916. —— Richard Atherton Legh (19 Wyatt Rd, N5), *b* 1923: *m* 1962, Ann Patricia Blanchard, and has issue living, Anthony Richard Atherton, *b* 1963, — David John Atherton, *b* 1965, — Christopher James Atherton, *b* 1967, — Michael Paul Atherton, *b* 1970, — Nicholas, *b* 1971. —— Mary Elizabeth Anne, *b* 1921. —— (By 2nd *m*) Ian Atherton (97 Robin Hood Lane, Kingston Vale, SW15 3QR), *b* 1930; *ed* Haileybury, and RMA Sandhurst: *m* 1955, Beryl Mary, da of late Percy Hirst Lomax, of Bolton, and has issue living, Richard Ian Lomax, *b* 1955, — Andrew John, *b* 1961.

Grandsons of late Thomas Charles Leycester Powys-Keck, el son of late Thomas Bancho Powys-Keck (infra):—
Issue of late Thomas Leycester POWYS-KECK, *b* 1919, *d* 1959: *m* 1949, Joyce (Clarence Drive, Littlehampton, Sussex), da of Albert Hills, of Worthing, Sussex:—

Thomas Charles Leycester, *b* 1951: *m* 1st, 1979 (*m diss* 1983), Judith Harris; 2ndly, 1985, Evelyn K. Dobner, and has issue living (by 1st *m*), Leycester Charles, *b* 1981, — (by 2nd *m*), Christian Rhys, *b* 1992, — Jacqueline Lauren, *b* 1989. —— Piers Anthony Leycester, *b* 1954: *m* 19—, Pauline Ann Short, and has issue living, Thomas Anthony Leycester, *b* 1988, — Emma Leigh, *b* 1983, — Danielle Kelly, *b* 1985.

Granddaughter of late Thomas Bancho Powys-Keck, son of late Maj Hon Henry Littleton Powys-Keck, 5th son of 2nd Baron:—
Issue of late Capt Horatio James POWYS, King's Roy Rifle Corps, *b* 1873, *d* 1952, have resumed in 1930 for himself only the family name of Powys only in lieu of Powys-Keck: *m* 1902, Edith Mary POWYS-KECK, who *d* 1971, da of Alexander Harvey, of St John's, Newfoundland:—
Gwladys Maïta Joan, *b* 1911; has discontinued the use of the christian name of Margarita, and is known as Maïta: *m* 1933 (*m diss* 1959), David Fenwick, who *d* 1982, and has issue living, Anthony Benedict Xavier (Sholebroke, Towcester, Northants), *b* 1934; *ed* Ampleforth: *m* 1958, Susan Deirdre, yr da of Lt-Col Peter Heber-Percy, OBE (*see* D Northumberland, colls), and has issue living, Alexius John Benedict (15 Glazbury Rd, W14), *b* 1959: *m* 1st, 1984 (*m diss* 1988), Briony Gretel, elder da of Bruce Gyngell, of Sydney, Australia; 2ndly, 1990, Lady Sophia Anne Crichton-Stuart, only surv da of 6th Marquess of Bute (and has issue living (by 2nd *m*), Georgia Jessie *b* 1990), Celestria Chantal Arabella *b* 1963: *m* 1987, James B. Alexander-Sinclair, of Blackpitts House, Whittlebury, Northants, elder son of Maj-Gen David Boyd Alexander-Sinclair, CB (and has issue living, Archie Benedict Boyd *b* 1988, Stroma Georgina *b* 1990), — Charles Christopher Sebastian, LVO (Barhams Manor, Higham, Colchester), *b* 1946; *ed* Ampleforth; Maj Gren Gds; Adjt 1973-75; Equerry to HRH The Duke of Edinburgh 1975-77; LVO 1977, — Timothy Dominic Ignatius (Rue du Mont 1, 5650 Biesmes-la-Colonoise, Belgium), *b* 1947 *ed* Ampleforth: *m* 1971, Jeanne Marie Julienne, only da of Joseph Marechal, of Bastogne, Belgium, — Justin Francis Quintus, QC (Geldeston Hall, Geldeston, Norfolk), *b* 1949; *ed* Ampleforth, and Clare Coll, Camb; Maj Gren Gds; Adjt 1977-79; Equerry to HRH The Duke of Edinburgh 1979-81; Bar Inner Temple 1980, QC 1993: *m* 1975, Marcia Mary, el da of late Archibald Dunn, of Overbury Hall, Hadleigh, Suffolk (*see* Astley, Bt), and has issue living, Hubert George Francis *b* 1990, Corisande Mary *b* 1983, Rosamond Xanthe *b* 1985, Madeleine Isobel *b* 1988, — Sebastian Edmund Stephen (Puslynch, Yealmpton, Plymouth, Devon), *b* 1953; *ed* Ampleforth, — Serena Mary (Hope Cottage, Gerrards Cross, Bucks), *b* 1944. *Residence* – Oratory Lodge, Brompton Rd, SW7 2RW.

PREDECESSORS – (1) THOMAS Powys, MP for Northamptonshire 1774-97; *cr Baron Lilford* of Lilford, co Northampton (peerage of Great Britain) 1797; *d* 1800; *s* by his son (2) THOMAS 2nd Baron; *d* 1825; *s* by his son (3) THOMAS ATHERTON, 3rd Baron; was a Lord-in-Waiting to HM Queen Victoria: *m* 1830, Hon Mary Elizabeth Fox, da of 3rd Baron Holland; *d* 1861, *s* by his son (4) THOMAS LITTLETON, 4th Baron, *b* 1833: *m* 1st, 1859, Emma Elizabeth, who *d* 1884, da of Robert William Brandling, of Low Gosforth, Northumberland; 2ndly, 1885, Clementina Georgiana, who *d* 1929, da of late Ker Baillie-Hamilton, CB; *d* 1896; *s* by his el surviving son (5) JOHN, 5th Baron, *b* 1863: *m* 1894, Milly Louisa, who *d* 1940, da of late George William Culme Soltau-Symons, of Chaddlewood, Plympton: *d* 1945; *s* by his brother (6) STEPHEN, 6th Baron, *b* 1869; *d* 1949; *s* by his kinsman (7) GEORGE VERNON (son of late Robert Horace Powys, only son of late Robert Vernon Powys, 2nd son of late Robert Horace Powys, el son of late Hon Robert Vernon Powys, 2nd son of 2nd Baron), 7th Baron and present peer.

LIMERICK, EARL OF (Pery) Sits as BARON FOXFORD (UK 1815) (Earl I 1803)

By courage, not by craft

PATRICK EDMUND PERY, 6th Earl, KBE, *b* 12 April 1930; *s* 1967; *ed* Eton, and New Coll, Oxford (MA); DL W Sussex 1988; late Maj City of London Yeo (TA), Hon Col 71st Yeo Signal Regt (Vol); CA; Dir Kleinwort Benson Ltd 1967-87 (Vice-Chm 1983-85, Dep-Chm 1985-87), Dir Kleinwort Benson Group 1982-90, Parly Under Sec of State for Trade 1972-74, Chm British Overseas Trade Board 1979-83 (Board Memb 1975-91), Chm Cttee for Middle East Trade 1975-79 (Vice-Chm 1968-75), Chm British Invisibles 1984-91 (Board Memb 1983-91); Pres Inst of Export since 1983, Dir Kleinwort Benson Australian Income Fund Inc since 1986, Chm Pirelli UK plc since 1989, Chm AMP Asset Management plc since 1992, Chm of Trustees City Parochial Foundation since 1992 (Trustee since 1971), Chm De La Rue plc since 1993 (Dir since 1983), Pres Canning House since 1994; Chm Court of Govs London Guildhall Univ (formerly City of London Polytechnic) since 1984; Pres S of England Agric Soc since 1993; *cr* KBE (Civil) 1983: *m* 1961, Sylvia Rosalind, CBE, Chm Council of British Red Cross Soc (since 1985), el da of late Brig Maurice Stanley Lush, CB, CBE, MC, and has issue.

Arms – Quarterly: gules and or, on a bend argent three lions passant sable. **Crest** – A fawn's head erased proper. **Supporters** – *Dexter*, a lion ermine; *sinister*, a fawn proper, ducally collared and chained or.
Residences – Chiddinglye, West Hoathly, East Grinstead, W Sussex RH19 4QT; 30 Victoria Rd, W8 5RG.

SONS LIVING

EDMUND CHRISTOPHER (*Viscount Glentworth*), *b* 10 Feb 1963; *ed* Eton, New Coll, Oxford, and Pushkin Inst, Moscow; Bar Middle Temple 1987; HM Diplomatic Ser 1987-92; Freshfields Solicitors since 1993: *m* 1990, Emily K., only da of Michael Gavin Lynam Thomas, of Worcester, and has issue:—
SONS LIVING — *Hon* Felix Edmund, *b* 16 Nov 1991, — *Hon* Ivo Patrick, *b* 1993.
Residence – 61 Monkton St, SE11 4TX.

Hon Adrian Patrick, *b* 1967; *ed* Eton, Reading Univ, and RMA Sandhurst.

DAUGHTER LIVING

Lady Alison Dora, *b* 1964.

BROTHER LIVING

Hon Michael Henry Colquhoun (Ardtur, Appin, Argyll), *b* 1937; *ed* Eton, and New Coll, Oxford (BA 1960); late Lt Inns of Court and City Yeo; formerly Man Dir, Sifam Ltd; Dir London Life Assoc: *m* 1963, Jennifer Mary, el da of J. A. Stuart-Williams, of Causeway House, Braughing, Herts, and has issue living, Marcus Alexander Kemal, *b* 1965, — Fergus Anthony Colquhoun, *b* 1967, — Pervaneh Frances, *b* 1969, — Azelle Fiona, *b* 1971.

SISTER LIVING

Lady Anne Patricia, *b* 1928; *ed* North Foreland Lodge, and St Hugh's Coll, Oxford (MA, DPhil); Sr Research Fellow at Imperial Coll London, author of *Spectrophysics* 1974, 1988, and of many papers published in scientific journals: *m* 1959, Lt-Col Sir Peter Francis Thorne, KCVO, CBE, ERD, former Serjeant at Arms of House of Commons, yst son of late Gen Sir (Augustus Francis) Andrew (Nicol) Thorne, KCB, CMG, DSO, DL, and has issue living, Andrew Henry, *b* 1965, — Bridget Iolanthe, *b* 1961, — Meriel Patricia, *b* 1963, — Janet Melinda, *b* 1968. *Residence* – Chiddinglye Farmhouse, W Hoathly, E Grinstead, Sussex.

COLLATERAL BRANCHES LIVING

Grandchildren of late Hon Edmond Aubrey Templar Pery (Sub-Lt RN), 3rd son of 2nd Earl:—
Issue of late Harry Reddall de Vere Pery, *b* 1877, *d* 1937: *m* 1907, Bertha, who *d* 1936, da of John Edward Fouscha:—
Lyndon de Vere (20 Wyandra Cres, Port Macquarie, NSW 2444, Australia), *b* 1914: *m* 1934, Eileen May, da of Henry Ernest Reid, and has issue living, Barry Lyndon de Vere (9/120 Ramsgate Rd, Ramsgate, NSW 2217, Australia), *b* 1935, — Carol Ann, *b* 1940: *m* 19—, James Fletcher, of 45 Bibby St, Carlton, NSW 2218, Australia. —— Gretta de Vere, *b* 1911: *m* 1944, Daniel John Foster (PO Box 36, Ulladulla, NSW).

Grandchildren of Edmond Arthur Gore PERY-KNOX-GORE, el son of Edmond Henry Cokayne PERY-KNOX-GORE (infra):—
Issue of late Maj Edmond Myles PERY-KNOX-GORE, *b* 1904, *d* 1965: *m* 1st, 1929 (*m diss* 1948), Gundrede Mary, da of late Capt Graham Owen Robert Wynne (B Killanin); 2ndly, 1948, Ingrid Margaret Mary (Coolcronan Cottage, Ballina, co Mayo), da of late Henry MacDermot, KC, of 19 Fitzwilliam Sq, Dublin, and widow of Capt Francis Holdsworth ffrench-Davis, RASC (*see* B Mowbray, colls):—
(By 1st *m*) Simon (12 Eastbrook Rd, SE3), *b* 1927: *m* 1961, Moira, da of Thomas Jariath Egan, of The Rise, Sevenoaks, Kent, and has issue living, Myles, *b* 1970, — Caroline, *b* 1962, — Katherine Lucy, *b* 1964, — Siobhan, *b* 1966: *m* 19—, Steven Way, and has issue living, Edward Seain *b* 1993. —— (By 2nd *m*) Mark (173 Orwell Rd, Rathgar, Dublin 6), *b* 1955: *m* 1986, Ann, da of Patrick Mallon, of Ambrosetown House, Duncormic, co Wexford. —— Sarah, *b* 1950.

Grandchildren of late Edmond Henry Cokayne PERY-KNOX-GORE, el son of Hon Edmond Sexten Pery, 4th son of 1st Earl:—
Issue of late Brigadier Arthur Francis Gore PERY-KNOX-GORE, CB, DSO, late RASC, *b* 1880, *d* 1954: *m* 1909, Evangeline, who *d* 1967, da of late Capt John William St John Hughes (Hughes, Bt, *cr* 1773, colls):—
Diana Frances FITZROY-YATES (The Malt House, W Ilsley, Newbury, Berks), *b* 1914, assumed by deed poll 1965 the surname of FitzRoy-Yates: *m* 1st, 1936, as his 2nd wife, Nigel Horatio Trevor FitzRoy, who *d* 1953 (*see* D Grafton, colls); 2ndly, 1958, William Edward Yates, who *d* 1964. —— Mary Agnes (*Lady Barrowclough*), *b* 1923: *m* 1949, Sir Anthony Richard Barrowclough, QC, and has issue living, Richard Edmond (Pyncombe Farm, Wiveliscombe, Som), *b* 1953: *m* 1978, Laura Selina Madeline, only da of Prof Sir (Albert) Raymond Maillard Carr (*see* Strickland-Constable, Bt, colls), and has issue living, Milo Edmond *b* 1984, Conrad Oliver *b* 1986, a son *b* 1990, Sibell Augusta *b* 1982, — Claire Cecilia, *b* 1956: *m* 1982, Nicholas Welham Paul, of 5 King's Rd, Richmond, Surrey, and has issue living, Flora Valentine *b* 1985, Phoebe Henrietta *b* 1986, Dominica Rose *b* 1989. *Residence* – The Old Vicarage, Winsford, Minehead, Som.
Issue of late Major Edmond Pery-Knox-Gore, OBE, *b* 1883, *d* 1960: *m* 1916, Monica, who *d* 1973, da of Capt John Strachan Bridges (E Courtown):—
Cullen, *b* 1917: *m* 1st, 1942, Barbara, who *d* at sea 1942 as a result of enemy action, only da of G. L. Stuart, of Dalkeith, Bramhall, Cheshire; 2ndly, 1948, Priscilla Wendy, da of J. S. Corr, of Johannesburg, S Africa, and has issue living (by 2nd *m*), Janet Barbara, *b* 1950, — Dianna Wendy, *b* 1951. —— David Edmond Strachan, *b* 1920; is Lt RNVR; 1940-45 War (despatches): *m* 1948, Molly, da of late A. Daly, of Pretoria, S Africa, and widow of Maj Frank Robertson, S African Air Force.

PREDECESSORS – (1) *Right Rev* WILLIAM CECIL Pery (yr brother of Edmond Sexten Pery, *cr Viscount Pery* 1785, ext 1800), successively Bishop of Killala and Limerick; *cr Baron Glentworth*, of Mallow (peerage of Ireland) 1790; *d* 1794; *s* by his son (2) EDMOND HENRY, 2nd Baron; MP for Limerick City 1785-94; *cr Viscount Limerick* (peerage of Ireland), 1800, *Earl of Limerick* (peerage of Ireland) 1803, and *Baron Foxford*, of Stackpole Court, co Limerick (peerage of United Kingdom) 1815; *d* 1844; *s* by his grandson (3) WILLIAM HENRY TENNISON, 2nd Earl; *b* 1812: *m* 1st, 1838, Susannah, da of William Sheaffe, of Cornwall; 2ndly, 1842, Margaret Jane, da of Capt Nicholas Horsley, 96th Regt; *d* 1866; *s* by his son (4) WILLIAM HALE JOHN CHARLES, KP, PC, 3rd Earl; *b* 1840; a Lord-in-Waiting to HM Queen Victoria 1886-9, and Capt of the Yeomen of the Guard 1889-92 and 1895-6: *m* 1st, 1862, Caroline Maria, who *d* 1877, da of late Rev Henry Gray; 2ndly, 1877, Isabella, who *d* 1927, da of late Chevalier James Colquhoun; *d* 1896; *s* by his el son (5) WILLIAM HENRY EDMOND DE VERE SHEAFFE, 4th Earl; *b* 1863: *m* 1890, May Imelda Josephine, CBE, who *d* 1943, da of late Joseph Burke Irwin, formerly Resident Magistrate, of Stelleen House, Drogheda; *d* 1929; *s* by his half-brother (6) EDMUND COLQUHOUN, GBE, CH, KCB, DSO, TD, 5th Earl; *b* 1888; Brevet Col RHA (TA) and Comdg 11th Bde; Pres of Med, Research Council 1952-60, and Council of T & AFA 1954-56: *m* 1926, Angela Olivia, GBE, CH, who *d* 1981, da of Lt-Col Sir Henry Trotter, KCMG, CB, *d* 1967; *s* by his el son (7) PATRICK EDMUND, 6th Earl and present peer; also Viscount Limerick, Baron Glentworth, and Baron Foxford.

LINCOLN, EARL OF (Fiennes-Clinton) (Earl E 1572)

EDWARD HORACE FIENNES-CLINTON, 18th Earl; *b* 23 Feb 1913; *s* 1988 (although he has not yet established his right to the Peerage): *m* 1st, 1940, Leila Ruth, who *d* 1947, da of late John James Millen, of Kalgoorlie, W Australia; 2ndly, 1953, Linda Alice, da of Charles Cred, and widow of James O'Brien, of Kalgoorlie, W Australia, and has issue by 1st *m*.

Arms – Argent six cross crosslets fitchy sable three two and one on a chief azure two mullets or pierced gules. **Crest** – Out of a coronet gules a plume of five ostrich feathers argent banded with a line laid chevronwise and knotted azure. **Supporters** – Two greyhounds argent collared and line gules. **Motto** – Loyaulte n'a Honte.
Residence – Flat 45, Elanora Villas, 37 Hastie St, Bunbury, W Australia 6230.

SON LIVING *(By 1st marriage)*

Hon EDWARD GORDON, *b* 7 Feb 1943: *m* 1970, Julia, da of William Howson, of 10 Waltham Rd, Armadale, Perth, and has issue living, Robert Edward, *b* 1972, — William Roy, *b* 1980, — Marian Dawn, *b* 1973. *Residence* – 6 Jasminum Place, Carcoola Estate, Pinjarra, W Australia 6208.

DAUGHTER LIVING *(By 1st marriage)*

Lady Patricia Ruth, *b* 1941: *m* 1959 (*m diss* 1970), Alexander George Stuart Elrick, who *d* 1979, and has issue living, Nicholas James, *b* 1959: *m* 1st, 1979 (*m diss* 1992), Rosa Audino; 2ndly, 19—, Monique Veronica Gardner (*née* Truman), and has issue living (by 1st *m*), Steven John *b* 1980, Peter James *b* 1981, — David Wayne, *b* 1961, — Warren Stuart, *b* 1962, — Leilani Yvonne, *b* 1974. *Residence* – Lot 27 West Rd, Bullsbrook, W Australia 6084.

COLLATERAL BRANCHES LIVING

Grandsons of late Henry Fiennes-Clinton, only son of late Clement Walter Fiennes-Clinton, 3rd son of Rev Henry Fiennes-Clinton, only son of Clinton James Fynes-Clinton, MP, 2nd son of Rev Charles Fynes-Clinton (infra):—
Issue of late Henry Bernard Fiennes-Clinton, *b* 1929, *d* 1990; *m* 1961 (*m diss* 1980), Carol Priscilla, da of James Greig, of Toronto:—
Gregory Edward (2 Lissom Crescent, North York, Ontario, Canada M2R 2PI), *b* 1970: *m* 1994, Sharon Quammie, of Toronto. — Richard James (27 Pintail Crescent, North York, Ontario, Canada M3A 2Y6), *b* 1972.

Grandchildren of late Rev Osbert Fynes-Clinton, 3rd son of late Rev Charles John Fynes-Clinton, 3rd son of late Rev Charles Fynes-Clinton, lineal representative of late Hon Sir Henry Fynes-Clinton, 3rd son of 2nd Earl of Lincoln:—
Issue of late Rev Charles Edward Fynes-Clinton, *b* 1868, *d* 1955: *m* 1902, Quenilda Mary, who *d* 1917, da of late James Begg Shaw, of Didsbury:—
†Hugh Arthur, *b* 1913; *ed* St John's Coll, Camb (MA); formerly Headmaster of St Chad's Coll, Ladysmith, Natal, and Inspector of African Education, S Rhodesia: *m* 1945, Pauline Ruth Ashton Dold (2 Downash Court, Rosemary Lane, Flimwell, E Sussex), and *d* 1991, leaving issue, Oliver John (Trees, Priory Rd, Forest Row, Sussex), *b* 1948; *ed* Cape Town Univ (BA): *m* 1978, Christine Elisabeth Brittaine, and has issue living, Francis Bernard Peter *b* 1979, Laura Emily *b* 1984, — Rozanne Jean, *b* 1946. — Eleanor Lloyd (12 Pakenham Close, Cambridge), *b* 1907.

Grandsons of late Osbert Henry Fynes-Clinton, 2nd son of late Rev Osbert Fynes-Clinton (ante):—
Issue of late David Osbert Fynes-Clinton, *b* 1909, *d* 1978: *m* 1st 1933 (*m diss* 1947), Laure Léoncie Mathilde Reyne, only da of late Pierre Felix Suquet; 2ndly, 1947 (*m diss* 1958), Betty Annie, who *d* 1989, da of late Arthur C. Lawrence, of Iquique, Chile:—
(By 2nd *m*) Michael Peter (13 Wickwood Court, Woodstock Rd, St Albans, Herts), *b* 1949: *m* 1973 (*m diss* 1978), Paula Valerie Neuss, who *d* 1988.
Issue of late Robert Fynes-Clinton, *b* 1879, *d* 1962: *m* 1907, Margaret Emma, who *d* 1949, yr da of late Rev Stephen Philipps, DD, of Heacham, Norfolk:—
Pelham (1 Gerrard Rd, West Kirby, Wirral), *b* 1910; *ed* Radley: *m* 1937, Joan Elizabeth, who *d* 1984, da of Alfred Chaplin, of West Kirby, and has issue living, Margaret Julia, *b* 1949.

Grandson of late Rev Canon Geoffrey Fynes-Clinton, 6th son of Rev Charles John Fynes-Clinton (ante):—
Issue of late Geoffrey De Berdt Granger Fynes-Clinton, *b* 1878, *d* 1922: *m* 1903, Maybelle, who *d* 1971, da of late John Finamore Edwardes:—
Philip Nevill (James Ommaney Village, 146 Capitol Drive, Jindalee, Queensland 4074), *b* 1908: *m* 1931, Isobel Maud Wilks, and has had issue, Geoffrey William Norreys, *b* 1932; *ed* Queensland Univ (BA, LLB), *m* 1957, Joyce Kathleen Lynch (9 Ormond St, Ascot, Queensland), and *d* 1987, leaving issue, Stephen Philip *b* 1960; *ed* Queensland Univ, Matthew James *b* 1963: *m* 1988, Jane Williams, Timothy Pelham *b* 1965, Emma Mary *b* 1968, — Arthur Nevill (Pantheon St, Jindalee, Queensland 4074), *b* 1934; *ed* Queensland Univ (BA): *m* 1956, Jacqueline Baker, and has issue living, Jamie *b* 1957: *m* 1987, Elizabeth Jean Morgan (and has issue living, Ben Thomas *b* 1988), Alan *b* 1958, Neil *b* 1962.

PREDECESSORS – **(1)** EDWARD, KG, PC, 9th Baron Clinton (*see* B Clinton), successively Lord High Adm, Gov of Boulogne, a Lord of the Bedchamber, Gov of the Tower, and Com in Ch of the fleet and forces sent against France and Scotland; was *cr Earl of Lincoln* (peerage of England) 1572; *d* 1585; *s* by his son **(2)** HENRY, KB, PC, 2nd Earl; *d* 1616; *s* by his son **(3)** THOMAS, 3rd Earl; *d* 1619; *s* by his son **(4)** THEOPHILUS, KB, 4th Earl; was a staunch Royalist, and performed the office of Carver at the Coronation of Charles II; *d* 1667; *s* by his grandson **(5)** EDWARD, 5th Earl; *dsp* 1692, when the Barony of Clinton became abeyant (*see* B Clinton), and the earldom reverted to his cousin **(6)** FRANCIS FIENNES, KB, 6th Earl, grandson of Sir Edward, 2nd son of 2nd Earl; *d* 1693; *s* by his son **(7)** HENRY, KG, 7th Earl, *b* 1684; was unsuccessfully a Gentleman of the Bedchamber to Prince George of Denmark, Master of the Horse to Prince of Wales, Paymaster-Gen, Constable of the Tower, and Cofferer of the Household: *m* 1717, Lucy, who *d* 1736, da of 1st Baron Pelham, and sister of Thomas, 1st Duke of Newcastle; *d* 1728; *s* by his el son **(8)** GEORGE, 8th Earl, *b* 1717; *d* 1730; *s* by his brother **(9)** HENRY FYNES, KG, PC, 9th Earl, *b* 1720; was a Gentleman of the Bedchamber, Lord-Lieut of Cambridge, High Steward of Westminster, and Comptroller of the Customs of Port of London: *m* 1744, his cousin, Catherine, who *d* 1760, da and heiress of Right Hon Henry Pelham, and in 1768, inherited the Dukedom of Newcastle, on the death of his maternal, and the countess's paternal uncle, Thomas Pelham Holles, who in 1756 had been *cr Duke of Newcastle-under-Lyme* (peerage of Great Britain), with special remainder to Henry, 9th Earl of Lincoln; assumed the additional surname of Pelham by Roy licence; *d* 1794; *s* by his son **(10)** THOMAS, 3rd Duke, *b* 1752; Maj-Gen in the Army and Col 17th Light Dragoons: *m* 1782, Lady Anna Maria Stanhope, who *d* 1834 (having *m* 2ndly, 1800, Gen Sir Charles Gregan Craufurd, GCB, who *d* 1821); *d* 1795; *s* by his son **(11)** HENRY PELHAM, KG, 4th Duke, *b* 1785; Lord-Lieut of co Nottingham, *m* 1807, Georgiana Elizabeth, da of Edward Miller Mundy, of Shipley, Derbyshire: *d* 1851; *s* by his son **(12)** HENRY PELHAM, KG, 5th Duke, *b* 1811; was Sec of State for the Colonies 1852-4 and 1859-64, Ch Sec for Ireland, Sec of State for War, Lord Warden of the Stanneries, and successively MP for S Notts, and the Falkirk Burghs: *m* 1832 (*m diss* 1850), Lady Susan Harriet Catherine Hamilton Douglas-Hamilton, who *d* 1889 (having *m* 2ndly, 1860, M. Opdebeck, of Brussels); *d* 1864; *s* by his son **(13)** HENRY PELHAM ALEXANDER, 6th Duke; *b* 1834: *m* 1861, Henrietta Adela, who *d* 1913, da of late Henry Thomas Hope; *d* 1879; *s* by his son **(14)** HENRY PELHAM ARCHIBALD DOUGLAS, 7th Duke, *b* 1864: *m* 1889, Kathleen Florence May, OBE, who *d* 1955, da of late Major Henry Augustus Candy; *d* 1928; *s* by his brother **(15)** HENRY FRANCIS HOPE, 8th Duke; *b* 1866; assumed by Roy licence 1887 the additional surname of Hope: *m* 1894 (*m diss* 1902), Mary Augusta (an actress), who *d* 1938, da of William Yohe; 2ndly, 1904, Olive Muriel, who *d* 1912, da of late George Horatio Thompson, banker, of Melbourne, and formerly wife of Richard Owen; *d* 1941; *s* by his son **(16)** HENRY EDWARD HUGH, OBE, 9th Duke, *b* 1907; Sqdn-Ldr and Acting Wing-Com Auxiliary Air Force: *m* 1st, 1931 (*m diss* 1940), Eugenia Van Voorhees, who *d* 1968, adopted da of David Banks, of Park Av, New York; 2ndly, 1946 (*m diss* 1959), Lady (Mary) Diana Montagu-Stuart-Wortley-Mackenzie, da of 3rd Earl of Wharncliffe; 3rdly, 1959, Mrs Sally Ann Wemyss Hope, formerly wife of Fikret Jemal, and elder da of Brig John Henry Anstice, DSO, of Kyrenia, Cyprus; *d* (4 Nov) 1988; *s* by his kinsman **(17)** EDWARD CHARLES (elder but only surv son of late Capt Guy Edward Pelham-Clinton, MC, yr son of late Henry William Pelham-Clinton, 2nd son of late Lord Charles Pelham-Clinton, 2nd son of 4th Duke), 10th Duke, *b* 1920; lepidopterist, Dep Keeper Royal Scottish Museum, Edinburgh; served 1939-45 War as Capt RA (despatches); *dunm* (25 Dec) 1988, when the Dukedom of Newcastle became ext, and the Earldom of Lincoln passed to his distant kinsman **(18)** EDWARD HORACE (grandson of late Charles Edward Fiennes-Clinton, grandson of late Rev Charles Fynes-Clinton, lineal representative of Hon Sir Henry Fynes-Clinton, 3rd son of 2nd Earl), 18th Earl and present peer.

LINDGREN, BARONY OF (Lindgren) (Extinct 1971)

SON LIVING OF LIFE BARON

Hon Graham Alastair, *b* 1928: *m* 1953, Gwendolyne Mary, who *d* 1991, da of late Arthur Miller. *Residence* – 43 Westly Wood, Welwyn Garden City, Herts AL7 1QN.

LINDSAY, EARL OF (Lindesay-Bethune) (Earl S 1633)
(Name pronounced "Beeton")

I love

JE·AYME

JAMES RANDOLPH LINDESAY-BETHUNE, 16th Earl; *b* 19 Nov 1955; *s* 1989; *ed* Eton, Edinburgh Univ (MA), and California Univ, Davis (BA); Landscape Architect: *m* 1982, Diana Mary, elder da of Maj Nigel Donald Peter Chamberlayne-Macdonald, OBE, LVO (*see* Bosville-Macdonald, Bt), and has issue.

Arms – Quarterly, 1st and 4th gules, fesse checky argent and azure, in chief three mullets of the second; 2nd and 3rd, counter quartered, 1st and 4th azure, a fesse between three lozenges or; 2nd and 3rd argent, on a chevron sable an otter's head erased of the first, all within a bordure embattled gold. **Crest** – A swan with wings expanded proper. **Supporters** – Two griffins gules, armed and beaked or. *Residence* – Lahill, Upper Largo, Fife KY8 6JE. *Club* – New (Edinburgh).

LIVE

DREID

BUT

SONS LIVING

WILLIAM JAMES (*Viscount Garnock*), *b* 30 Dec 1990.
Hon David Nigel, *b* 1993.

DAUGHTERS LIVING

Lady Frances Mary, *b* 1986.
Lady Alexandra Penelope, *b* 1988.
Lady Charlotte Diana, *b* (twin) 1993.

SISTER LIVING

Lady Caroline Janet, *b* 1957: *m* 1981, Sir George Richard Bourchier Wrey, 15th Bt, and has issue. *Residences* – Hollamoor Farm, Tawstock, Barnstaple, N Devon; 60 The Chase, SW4.

UNCLE LIVING (*son of 14th Earl*)

Hon John Martin (Muircambus, Elie, Leven, Fife KY9 1HD), *b* 1929; *ed* Eton, and Trin Hall, Camb; formerly Lieut Scots Gds: *m* 1st, 1953 (*m diss* 1976), Enriqueta Mary Jeanne, only da of Peter Koch de Gooreynd (*see* M Queensberry, colls, 1990 Edn); 2ndly, 1977, Jean Maxwell, da of Brig Eric Brickman, and formerly wife of Stephen John Younger, and has issue living (by 1st *m*), Nicholas John (48 Clifford Av, East Sheen, SW14 7BP), *b* 1956: *m* 1977, Maria Teresa, da of Luis Prats, of 2467 Singalong St, Manila, and has issue living, Andrew Nicholas *b* 1979, Henry William *b* 1983, Dominic Luis *b* 1985, — Jonathan Patrick, *b* 1959, — Simon Charles, *b* 1962: *m* 1990, Melissa Jane, only da of Roderick Webb, of Ditchling, Sussex, — Sally Alexandra Jane, *b* 1954: *m* 1977, Peter Breeden, of Woodside House, Freshford, Bath BA3 6EJ, and has issue living, Alexander Peter *b* 1979, Jamie George *b* 1981, Benjamin Jonathan *b* 1985, Rosie Alexandra Charlotte *b* 1987.

AUNTS LIVING (daughters of 14th Earl)

Lady Elizabeth Marjory Beatrice, *b* 1932: *m* 1960 (*m diss* 1971), Maj David Laurence Greenacre, late Welsh Gds, and has issue living, Philip Laurence, *b* 1961: *m* 1993, Anna Katharine, da of Robin Muschamp Garry Simpson, QC, of Drayton Gdns, SW10, and of Lady Webster, of Bratton, Wilts, — Andrew Lindsay, *b* 1969, — Louise Caroline, *b* 1967. *Residence* – Selby House, Ham Common, Richmond, Surrey.

Lady Mary Bethune, *b* 1935: *m* 1956, Capt Owen Buckingham Varney, late Scots Gds and has issue living, Mark Lindesay Buckingham, *b* 1958; late Scots Gds: *m* 1987, Katie J., yr da of Eric Bean, of Leckhamstead Thicket, Newbury, Berks, and has issue living, Alexander Edward Lindesay *b* 1991, Joscelyn James Buckingham *b* 1993, — Guy Nicholas Buckingham, *b* 1962; Capt late Scots Gds: *m* 1992, Louise D., elder da of Peter Owen, of Whitelands Farm, Ashington, Sussex, — Georgina Mary Bethune, *b* 1960: *m* 1984, Christopher Neil Hunter Gordon, yst son of late Maj Patrick Hunter Gordon, CBE, MC, DL, JP, of Ballindoun House, Beauly, Inverness-shire, and has issue living, Sam William *b* 1988, Ivan Patrick *b* 1989, Ione Mary *b* 1992. *Residence* – Hill House, Dedham, nr Colchester, Essex.

MOTHER LIVING

Hon Mary Clare Douglas Scott Montagu, yst da of 2nd Baron Montagu of Beaulieu: *m* 1st, 1953 (*m diss* 1968), David Bethune, Viscount Garnock (later 15th Earl of Lindsay), who *d* 1989; 2ndly, 1979, Timothy Charles Austin Horn. *Residence* – Chapel House, Builth Wells, Powys.

WIDOW LIVING OF FIFTEENTH EARL

PENELOPE GEORGINA (*Penelope, Countess of Lindsay*), da of late Anthony Crommelin Crossley, MP (*see* Crossley, Bt, colls), and formerly wife of Maj Henry Ronald Burn Callander, MC: *m* 1969, as his 2nd wife, the 15th Earl, who *d* 1989. *Residence* – Steward's Cottage, Combermere Whitchurch, Shropshire SY13 4AJ.

PREDECESSORS – **(1)** *Sir* William Lindsay, a celebrated knight, 4th son of David 6th Lord Crawford, obtained the Barony of the Byres by charter 1366 on the resignation of his elder brother Sir Alexander of Glenesk, from whom descends the present Earl of Crawford and Balcarres: *m* Christian, da of Sir William More, of Abercorn; *s* by his son **(2)** Sir William, 2nd of the Byres (and Lord of Abercorn); *s* by his son **(3)** *Sir* JOHN, Justiciary of Scotland N of the Forth 1457; *cr Lord Lindsay of the Byres* (peerage of Scotland) 1445; *s* by his el son **(4)** DAVID, 2nd Lord; noted in history as having presented the "great grey horse" to James III on the eve of the battle of Sauchieburn 1488; *dsp* 1492; *s* by his brother **(5)** JOHN, 3rd Lord, surnamed "John out with the Sword"; *d* without male issue 1497; *s* by his brother **(6)** PATRICK, 4th Lord; a celebrated advocate; had a grant of the Sheriffdom of Fife to himself, his son and grandson; *d* 1526; *s* by his grandson **(7)** JOHN, 5th Lord; one of the four nobles to whom the charge of the infant Queen Mary was committed in 1542, and whose mediation between the Lords of the Congregation and the Regent, Mary of Guise, led to the pacification of 1559; *d* 1563; *s* by his son **(8)** PATRICK, 6th Lord; an ardent Reformer and Lord of the Congregation; remembered for his share in the murder of Rizzio, the deposition of Queen Mary, and his challenge to Bothwell at Carbery Hill; appointed hereditary bailie of the regality of the Archbishopric of St Andrews; *s* by his son **(9)** JAMES, 7th Lord; *d* 1601; *s* by his el son **(10)** JOHN, 8th Lord; *d* 1609; *s* by his brother **(11)** ROBERT, 9th Lord; *s* by his son **(12)** JOHN, 10th Lord; *cr Lord Parbroath* and *Earl of Lindsay* (peerage of Scotland) 1633, with remainder to his heirs male, and being described in the patent as "one of the most ancient of the Scottish nobility, and the first in the rank of the greater Barons and Lords of Parliament"; Ludovic, 16th Earl of Crawford, having no children resigned in 1642 the Earldom of Crawford into the hands of Charles I for a re-grant in favour of John, Earl of Lindsay, and the heirs male of his body, and failing which with remainder to Earl Ludovic's collateral heirs male; sentence of forfeiture having been passed on Earl Ludovic by Parliament in rebellion 1644 John, 10th Lord Lindsay was during Earl Ludovic's lifetime (he *d* 1652), put in possession of the dignity as 17th *Earl of Crawford* (peerage of Scotland, *cr* 1398), and he and his five next successors each assumed the style of "Earl of Crawford-Lindsay"; he was one of the leading spirits of the Covenant, High Treasurer of Scotland 1644, and President of the Parliament 1645; opposed the surrender of Charles I to the English 1647, and joined the engagement for the King's rescue 1648; taken prisoner by Cromwell 1651, and confined in the Tower and Windsor until the Restoration 1660, when he was reconstituted Treasurer-President of Parliament and Extraordinary Lord of Session; retired into private life 1663; *d* 1676; *s* by his son **(13)** WILLIAM, 18th Earl of Crawford, 2nd Earl of Lindsay, and 11th Lord Lindsay; known as "great and good Earl of Crawford": an ardent Presbyterian; concurred in the Revolution of 1688; was President of the Convention 1689; *d* 1698; *s* by his son **(14)** JOHN, 19th and 3rd Earl and 12th Lord; a Gen in the Army, and a Representative Peer; *d* 1713; *s* by his son **(15)** JOHN, 20th and 4th Earl, and 13th Lord; a celebrated military commander; was the first officer to command the Black Watch (Royal Highlanders, then known as "Lord Crawford-Lindsay's Highlanders"); *d* 1749, from the effects of a wound received at the battle of Krotska in 1738; *s* by his kinsman **(16)** GEORGE, 21st and 5th Earl, and 14th Lord, who had in 1738, *s* as 4th *Viscount Garnock* (see * infra); *d* 1778; *s* by his son **(17)** GEORGE, 22nd Earl of Crawford, 6th Earl of Lindsay, 7th Viscount Garnock, and 15th Lord Lindsay; a Maj-Gen in the Army; *d* 1808, when the Earldom of Crawford devolved upon Alexander, 6th Earl of Balcarres as heir male of Ludovic, 16th Earl of Crawford (*see* E Crawford and Balcarres) and the Earldom of Lindsay and minor honours reverted to his kinsman **(18)** DAVID, *de jure* 7th Earl of Lindsay, 6th Viscount Garnock, and 16th Lord Lindsay (the descendant of David, brother of 5th Lord Lindsay); was a Sergeant in the Perths Militia; several noblemen offered money to enable him to establish his claim to the peerage, and the Duke of York offered him a commission if his claim succeeded; *d* 1809; *s* by his kinsman **(19)** PATRICK, KB, *de jure* 8th Earl, 7th Viscount, and 17th Lord; a distinguished Gen: *dsp* 1839; *s* by his kinsman **(20)** HENRY Lindsay-Bethune, *de jure* 9th Earl, 8th Viscount, and 18th Lord, the heir male of William, 2nd son of 4th Lord Lindsay; *b* 1787; served with remarkable distinction as Commander of the Persian forces against Russian 1804-19, and against the rebel Zulli Sultan 1834-6; *cr* a Bt 1836, at the request of the Shah; assumed the additional surname of Bethune 1816; *m* 1822, Coutts, who *d* 1877, da of John Trotter, of Dyrham Park; *d* 1851; *s* by his son **(21)** JOHN TROTTER, 10th Earl, 9th Viscount, and 19th Lord, *b* 1827; *s* as 2nd Bart 1857, and established his right to the Earldom of Lindsay and minor honours 1878: *m* 1858, Jeanne Eudoxie Marie, who *d* 1897, da of Mons Jacques Victor Duval, of Bordeaux; *d* 1894, when the Baronetcy became extinct, and he was succeeded in the other titles by his cousin **(22)** DAVID CLARK Lindesay (son of late David Aytone Lindesay, a descendant of 4th Lord), 11th Earl, *b* 1832; assumed (without official authority) the surname and arms of Bethune in lieu of those of Lindesay: *m* 1866, Emily Marian, who *d* 1920, da of late Robert Crosse, of Doctors' Commons, and widow of Capt Edmund Charles Barnes (of HM's late St Helena Regt); *d* 1917; *s* by his son **(23)** REGINALD BETHUNE Lindesay-Bethune, 12th Earl, *b* 1867; was a Representative Peer for Scotland 1917-39; matriculated the Arms and additional surname of Lindesay 1918: *m* 1892, Beatrice Mary, who *d* 1944, da of late John Shaw, of Welburn Hall, Kirbymoorside, Yorkshire; *d* 1939; *s* by his brother **(24)** ARCHIBALD LIONEL, 13th Earl, *b* 1872: *m* 1900, Ethel, who *d* 1942, da of W. A. Tucker, of 47 Bay State Road, Boston, USA; *d* 1943; *s* by his son **(25)** WILLIAM TUCKER, 14th Earl, *b* 1901; Maj Scots Gds, Hon Col Fife and Forfar Yeo, Scottish Horse; a Member Queen's Body Guard for Scotland (R Company of Archers); a Representative Peer 1947-59; Pres Shipwrecked and Mariners R Benevolent Soc: *m* 1925, Marjory, who *d* 1988, da of late Arthur Graham Cross; *d* 1985; *s* by his elder son **(26)** DAVID BETHUNE, 15th Earl *b* 1926, Vice-Chm (Canada) British Overseas Trade Bd, N America, Dir Internat Harvester, Carpets Internat plc, Bank of Montreal, Festiniog Railway Co, etc, FRSA: *m* 1st, 1953 (*m diss* 1968), Hon Mary Clare Douglas Scott Montagu, yst da of 2nd Baron Montagu of Beaulieu; 2ndly 1969, Mrs Penelope Georgina CALLANDER, da of late Anthony Crommelin Crossley, MP (*see* Crossley, Bt); *d* 1989; *s* by his only son **(27)** JAMES RANDOLPH, 16th Earl and present peer; also Viscount Garnock, Lord Parbroath, Lord Kilbirnie, Kingsburn and Drumry, and Lord Lindsay of the Byres.

*(1) JOHN Lindsay, son of Patrick, 2nd son of 1st Earl of Lindsay; *cr Lord Kilbirnie, Kingsburn, and Drumry,* and *Viscount*

Garnock (peerage of Scotland) 1703; *d* 1709; *s* by his son **(2)** Patrick, 2nd Viscount; *d* 1735; *s* by his el son **(3)** John, 3rd Viscount; *dsp* 1738; *s* by his brother **(4)** George, 4th Viscount *s* as 21st Earl of Crawford (ante).

LINDSAY OF BIRKER, BARON (Lindsay) (Baron UK 1945)

James Francis Lindsay, 3rd Baron; *b* 29 Jan 1945; *s* 1994; *ed* Geelong Gram Sch and Keele Univ; joined Australian Dept of Foreign Affairs 1972; 1st Sec Australian High Commn, Dhaka: *m* 1966, Mary Rose, da of W. G. Thomas, of Cwmbran, Mon.
Address – Australian Foreign Service, Dept of Foreign Affairs, Canberra, ACT, Australia.

SISTERS LIVING AND DECEASED

Hon Erica Susan, *b* 1942; *d* 1993.
Hon Mary Muriel, *b* 1951: *m* 1976, Kenneth Kyle Abbott, Jr, and has issue living, Thomas Lindsay, *b* 1978, — Michael William, *b* 1985.

UNCLE LIVING (*son of 1st Baron*)

Hon Thomas Martin, MBE, *b* 5 March 1915; *ed* Sidcot Sch, and at Edinburgh Univ; is Major Sherwood Rangers; European War 1939-45 (despatches); MBE (Mil) 1946: *m* 1st, 1939 (*m diss* 1951), Denise Theresa, da of Gerald Albert Vaughan; 2ndly, 1951 (*m diss* 1961), Felicitas, da of Dr Martin Lange; 3rdly, 1961, Erica, da of Maj Eric Thirkell-Cooper, and has issue living (by 1st *m*), Alexander Sebastian, *b* 1940, — Thomas Martin, *b* 1942, — Teresa, *b* 1945, — (by 2nd *m*) Stuart Martin, *b* 1951, — Alexander Gordon, *b* 1952, — (by 3rd *m*) Benjamin Martin *b* 1962, — Robert William, *b* 1967.

AUNT LIVING (*Daughter of 1st Baron*)

Hon (Anna) Drusilla (*Hon Lady Scott*), *b* 1911: *m* 1937, Sir Ian Dixon Scott, KCMG, KCVO, CIE, and has issue living, Peter John Lindsay, *b* 1948: *m* 1976, Susan Dobson, — (Mary) Pauline, *b* 1939: *m* 1971, Samih Sadek, — Rachel Erica, *b* 1940: *m* 1960, David Britton, — Ann Catherine, *b* 1942: *m* 1975, Jack Shepherd, — Monica Margaret, *b* 1947: *m* 1975, Ian Lanman. *Residence* – Ash House, Alde Lane, Aldeburgh, Suffolk IP15 5DZ.

WIDOW LIVING OF SECOND BARON (*By 1st marriage*)

Hsiao Li (*Dowager Baroness Lindsay of Birker*), da of Col Li Wen Chi, Chinese Army, of Lishih, Shansi, China: *m* 1941, the 2nd Baron Lindsay of Birker, who *d* 1994. *Residence* – 6812 Delaware St, Chevy Chase, Maryland 20815, USA.

PREDECESSORS – **(1)** Alexander Dunlop Lindsay, CBE, LLD, son of late Rev T. M. Lindsay, DD, Principal of United Free Church Coll, Glasgow; *b* 1879; Fellow and Classical Tutor, Balliol Coll 1906, Jowett Lecturer in Philosophy 1910, and Professor of Moral Philosophy, Glasgow Univ 1922; Master of Balliol Coll, Oxford 1924-49, Vice-Chancellor of Oxford Univ 1935-38, and Principal of Univ Coll, N Staffs 1949-52; *cr Baron Lindsay of Birker*, of Low Ground, co Cumberland (peerage of United Kingdom) 1945: *m* 1907, Erica Violet, who *d* 1962, da of F. Storr; *d* 1952; *s* by his el son **(2)** Michael Francis Morris, 2nd Baron; *b* 1909; Prof of Far Eastern Studies, American Univ, Washington, DC 1959-74: *m* 1941, Hsiao Li, da of Col Li Wen Chi, Chinese Army; *d* 1994; *s* by his only son **(3)** James Francis, 3rd Baron and present peer.

LINDSEY AND ABINGDON, EARL OF (Bertie) (Earl E 1626 and 1682)
(Name pronounced "Barty")

Valour is stronger than a battering ram

RICHARD HENRY RUPERT BERTIE, 14th Earl of Lindsey and 9th Earl of Abingdon, *b* 28 June 1931; *s* 1963; *ed* Ampleforth; Lt, late Royal Norfolk Regt; High Steward of Abingdon since 1963: *m* 1957, Norah Elizabeth Farquhar-Oliver, 2nd da of late Mark Oliver, OBE (*see* Farquhar, Bt, colls, 1980 Edn), and has issue.

𝕬rms – Argent, three battering rams fessewise in pale proper headed, armed and garnished azure. 𝕮rest – A Saracen's head affrontée, couped at the shoulders proper, ducally crowned or, and charged on the chest with a fret azure. 𝕾upporters – *Dexter*, a friar habited in russet grey, with a crutch and rosary, all proper; *sinister*, a savage proper wreathed about the temples and waist with oak leaves vert; each charged on the breast with a fret azure.
Residences – Gilmilnscroft, Sorn, Mauchline, Ayrshire; 3 Westgate Terrace, SW10. *Clubs* – Pratt's, Turf, White's.

SONS LIVING

HENRY MARK WILLOUGHBY (*Lord Norreys*), *b* 6 June 1958; *ed* Eton, and Edinburgh Univ: *m* 1989, Lucinda Sol, 2nd da of Christopher Stewart Moorsom, and of María del Pilar Sánchez y Betancourt, Mrs Bayard Osborn. *Residence* – Alameda de la Alcaldesa 1, Urb La Virginia, 29600 Marbella (Málaga), Spain. *Clubs* – Pratt's, Puffin's (Edinburgh).
Hon Alexander Michael Richard, *b* 1970; *ed* Eton, and Queen's Coll, Oxford. *Residence* – 226 Ladbroke Grove, W10.

DAUGHTER LIVING

Lady Annabel Frances Rose, *b* 1969; *ed* St Mary's, Ascot, and Edinburgh Univ. *Residence* – 24 Leamington Rd Villas, W11.

STEP MOTHER LIVING

Lilian Isabel, elder da of late Charles Edward Joseph Cary-Elwes, of Staithe House, Beccles, Suffolk, and widow of Lt-Cdr Francis Dayrell Montague Crackanthorpe, RN: *m* 1949, as his 2nd wife, Lt-Col Hon Arthur Michael Bertie, DSO, MC, who *d* 1957.

WIDOW LIVING OF SON OF SEVENTH EARL OF ABINGDON

Lady JEAN CRICHTON-STUART (*Lady Jean Bertie*) (Casa de Piro, Attard, Malta), da of 4th Marquess of Bute; Dame Grand Cross of Honour and Devotion Sovereign Mil Order of Malta: *m* 1928, Lt-Cdr Hon James Willoughby Bertie, RN, 3rd son of 7th Earl of Abingdon, who *d* 1966, and has issue (see colls infra).

COLLATERAL BRANCHES LIVING

Issue of late Lt-Cdr Hon James Willoughby Bertie, RN, 3rd son of 7th Earl of Abingdon, *b* 1901, *d* 1966: *m* 1928, Lady Jean Crichton-Stuart (ante), da of 4th Marquess of Bute:—
His Most Eminent Highness Frà Andrew Willoughby Ninian (Palazzo Malta, via Condotti 68, 00187 Rome, Italy) *b* 1929; Lt Scots Guards (SR), Prince and Grand Master of Sovereign Mil Order of Malta since 1988 (*Arms* - Quarterly: 1st and 4th, gules a cross argent, *Order of Malta*; 2nd and 3rd, argent three battering rams fessewise in pale proper armed and garnished azure, *Bertie*). —— (Charles) Peregrine Albemarle (Frilsham Manor, Hermitage, Newbury, Berks RG16 9UZ), *b* 1932; Capt late Scots Guards, and a Kt of Obedience of Sovereign Mil Order of Malta, Kt Cdr Order of St Gregory, Cdr of Merit with Swords Order of Pro Merito Melitensi; Member Queen's Body Guard for Scotland (Royal Company of Archers); High Sheriff Berks 1986; OstJ: *m* 1960, Susan Griselda Ann Lyon, el da of Maj John Lycett Wills, Life Guards (ret) (*see* Wills, Bt, *cr* 1904), and has issue living, David Montagu Albemarle, *b* 1963: *m* 1994, Catherine Cecily, only da of Anthony Feilden Mason-Hornby, of Dalton Hall, nr Carnforth, Cumbria (*see* Wigan, Bt, colls, 1980 Edn), — Caroline Georgina Rose, *b* 1965: *m* 1991, Andrew L. Carrington, son of Capt Norman Carrington, of Saxonmead, Haywards Heath, Sussex.

(In remainder to Barony of Norreys of Rycote only)

Issue of late Lady Mary Caroline Bertie, da of 7th Earl of Abingdon, *b* 1859, *d* 1938: *m* 1879, 1st Viscount Fitz Alan of Derwent, who *d* 1947 (extinct 1962) (see that title).
Grandsons of late Lady Alice Josephine Bertie (Lady Alice Reynties), da of 7th Earl of Abingdon:—
Issue of late Priscilla Cecilia Maria, CBE, *b* 1899, *d* 1991: *m* 1st, 1921 (*m diss* 1929), Alexander Koch de Gooreynd, who *d* 1985, having assumed by deed poll 1923 the surname of Worsthorne in lieu of de Gooreynd; 2ndly, 1933, 1st Baron Norman, who *d* 1950:—
(By 1st *m*) *Sir* Simon Peter Edmund Cosmo William TOWNELEY, KCVO (Dyneley Hall, Burnley, Lancs), *b* 1921; Lieut KRRC; Lord Lieut and JP Lancs; Member of Council of Duchy of Lancaster, Co Councillor Lancs 1961-64, High Sheriff 1971-72, Trustee British Museum 1988-93; 1939-45 War (prisoner); hon Col Duke of Lancaster's Own Yeo 1979-88; assumed by deed poll 1945 the additional surname of Towneley before his patronymic, and, by Royal Licence 1955, the arms of Towneley, and relinquished by deed poll 1955 the surname of Worsthorne; KStJ, KCSG, KCVO 1994: *m* 1955, Mary, da of late Cuthbert Fitzherbert, and has issue living, Peregrine Henry, *b* 1962, — Alice Mary, *b* 1956: *m* 1984, Michael O'Neill, — Charlotte Mary, *b* 1957: *m* 1986, Arthur Edmund French, and has issue (*see* B de Freyne, colls), — Katharine Mary, *b* 1958: *m* 1985, William Marr Couper Grant, WS, yr son of Douglas Marr Kelso Grant, of Drumellan House, Maybole, Ayrshire, and has issue living, Cosmo Douglas *b* 1991, Clementine Priscilla *b* 1986, Eliza Mary *b* 1989, — Victoria Mary, *b* 1964, — Cosima Cecilia, *b* 1967, — Frances Teresa, *b* 1969. —— *Sir* Peregrine Gerard WORSTHORNE (6 Kempson Rd, SW6), *b* 1923; Lieut Oxford and Bucks LI attached GHQ Liaison Regt (Phantom) 1939-45 War; Knt 1991: *m* 1st, 1950, Mrs Claudia Baynham, who *d* 1990, da of Victor Bertrand de Colasse, of 43 Ave Ernest Rayer, Paris; 2ndly, 1991, Lady Lucinda Lambton, eldest da of Antony Claud Frederick Lambton (6th Earl of Durham until he disclaimed his title 1970), and has issue living (by 1st *m*), Dominique Elizabeth Priscilla, *b* 1952: *m* 1978, Jonathan Busill Maynard Keeling, son of Robert Keeling, of Hembury Knoll, Hook Heath Rd, Woking, Surrey.

Issue of late Lady Gwendeline Theresa Mary Bertie, da of 7th Earl of Abingdon, *b* 1885, *d* 1941: *m* 1908, Maj John Strange Spencer-Churchill, DSO, who *d* 1947 (*see* D Marlborough, colls).

Issue of late Lady Elizabeth Constance Mary (Betty) Bertie, OBE, da of 7th Earl of Abingdon, b 1895, d 1987: m 1st 1914, Maj Sigismund William Joseph Trafford, Rifle Bde (Prince Consort's Own), who d 1953; 2ndly, 1956, Col Henry Antrobus Cartwright, CMG, MC, who d 1957:—
(By 1st m) Edward Willoughby TRAFFORD, b 1924; ed Harrow, and Downside; late Scots Guards; Knight of Honour and Devotion of Sovereign Mil Order of Malta: m 1952, June Imelda, only da of Richard Joseph Anthony Harding, of Echo Valley, Springbook, Queensland, and has issue living, Michael Francis (Valley Farm, Frettenham, Norwich, Norfolk), b 1953; ed Downside, — Bernard Edward (Kingstone Villa, Kingstone, Hereford HR2 9ET), b 1955; ed Downside: m 1980, Corinne Jean, da of Alan Furnell, of Bryn Collen, Llandover, Gwent, and has issue living, Edward Alexander b 1981, Charles Henry b 1983, — Andrew Martin, b 1960, — Amanda Gabrielle Mary, b 1959: m 1984, Mark Edmond Garthwaite, and has issue living, Alice Sophie Elizabeth b 1987. Residence – Broad House, Wroxham, Norfolk. ——— Helen Mary, b 1915: m 1936, Capt Peter Evelyn Fanshawe, CBE, DSC, RN (see E Erne, colls, 1948 Edn), who d 1994, of 12 Lincoln Av, Wimbledon, SW19 5JT, and has issue living, Richard Henry William (Rafters, Waldron, Heathfield, E Sussex TN21 0QY), b 1939; ed Ampleforth, and RNC Dartmouth: m 1966, Hon Maura Clare Evans-Freke, da of 11th Baron Carbery, and has issue living, Louisa Mary Constance b 1987, — Veronica Evelyn, b 1947: m 1977, Maj Charles Napier St Pierre Bunbury, MBE, The Duke of Wellington's Regt (see Bunbury, Bt, colls). ——— Sophie Mary (Baroness Lyell), b 1916: m 1938, 2nd Baron Lyell, VC, who was ka 1943. Residence – Kinnordy, Kirriemuir, Angus. ——— Diana Rosemary, b 1920: m 1st, 1951, John Reford; 2ndly, 1977, Col L. M. Collins, who d 1984. Residence – 15 St Petersburgh Mews, W2.

(In remainder to the Earldoms and Barony)

Grandchildren of late Rev Hon Alberic Edward Bertie, 3rd son of 6th Earl of Abingdon:—
Issue of late Lieut-Com Aubrey Charles Bertie, RN, b 1882, d 1944: m 1916, Jeanne, da of M. A. Vissers:—
Albert Arnaud (Maison du Coin, Route du Coin, St Brelade, Jersey CI), b 1919: m 1950, Joan, da of A. E. Sidery, and has issue living, John Peregrine b 1952: m 1st, 1972 (m diss 1977), Mary, da of Cedric Rosenvinge; 2ndly, 1986, Belinda, da of Timothy Orpe Adkin, and has issue living (by 1st m), Caroline Emma b 1973, (by 2nd m) Georgina Anne b 1990, Harriet Olivia b 1992, Sabrina Dawn b 1993, — Peter Mark, b 1959; ed Pembroke Coll, Camb (MA): m 1993, Karen, da of Raymond Anthony Hewitt. ——— Christine Caroline, b 1917.
Issue of late Schomberg Montagu Bertie, b 1888; d 1937: m 1922, Edith Mary (who m 2ndly, 1941, Harry August Anders, and d 1982), da of John England:—
Caroline Edith (6 Burley Griffin Place, Heidelberg, Melbourne, Australia), b 1923: m 1952, Gordon Ernest Ross, who d 1971, and has issue living, Alan Gordon Schomberg b 1955, — Dagmar Caroline Edith, b 1953, — Hilary, b 1960. ——— Rose Patricia, b 1926; ed Queensland Univ (MSc Agr): m 1951, Harold Edwin Kleinschmidt, of 45 Kersley Rd, Kenmore, Brisbane, Queensland, and has issue living, Christopher Montagu, b 1963: m 1991, Tammy Joan, eldest da of Henry Vincent Neller, — Felicity Rose, b 1965: m 1989, Raymond Andrew Hembrow, and has issue living, Elise Robyn b 1994, — Elise Caroline, b 1970.
Issue of late Capt Alberic Willoughby Bertie, MC, b 1891, d 1969: m 1922, Maria Flore who d 1925, da of Philippe Reinhort:—
Marie Lucette: m 1943, Capt Ronald Frank Kershaw, late 60th Rifles, of Firs House, Ramsdell, Basingstoke, and has issue living, Martin John (Brights Farm, Christian Malford, Chippenham, Wilts SN15 4DA), b 1954: m 1982, Joanna Lucy, el da of Lord Edward Anthony Charles FitzRoy (see D Grafton), and has issue living, Simon Edward b 1985, William Ronald b 1987, David Robert b 1990, Louisa b 1992, — Clarissa Mary, b 1944: m 1970, Capt Peter Malcolm Roe, The Royal Hussars (PWO), of Clench Farm House, nr Marlborough, Wilts, and has issue living, Jeremy Malcolm Ninian b 1973, Christopher John Edward b 1975, Nicholas James Buxton b 1982, — Serena Jane, b 1948: m 1975, James Fergus Surtees Graham, of Kirkandrews Tower, Longtown, Cumbria, and has issue (see Graham Bt, cr 1783), — Gabrielle Lavinia, b 1951: m 1975, Christopher James Hodgson, of Souldern Court, nr Bicester, Oxon, and has issue living, Henry James b 1977, Clare Lucy b 1979, Sarah Rebecca b 1982, Camilla Rose b 1984.
Issue of late Lavinia May Bertie, b 1887, d 1978: m 1921, Theodore Stephen Hubbard, who d 1934:—
Theodore Bernard Peregrine HUBBARD (Thurston Croft, Thurston, Bury St Edmunds, Suffolk), b 1923; Lt-Cdr (ret) RN; 1939-45 War: m 1952, Lady Miriam Fitzalan Howard, sister of 17th Duke of Norfolk, and has issue living, Martin Peregrine Thomas (Flat 6, Weston House, Weston Lane, Bridgetown, Totnes, Devon), b 1954; ed Ampleforth, — Theodore Bernard Peter (143 Studdridge St, SW6 3TI), b 1959; ed —Coll, Camb (MA): m 1985, Penelope D., eldest da of Alan Thomas Street, of Ollerton Hall, Knutsford, Cheshire, and has issue living, Francesca b 1989, Kinvara b 1992, — Mary-Miranda Josephine, b (Jan) 1956: m 1974, Roger John Pratt, of 32 High St, Haddenham, Ely, Cambs, and has issue living, Alexander Roger Martin b 1978, James Malcolm b 1980, Matthew Charles b 1982, — Lucinda Mary Lavinia, b (Dec) 1956; ed Leeds Univ (BSc), and Liverpool Univ (MSc): m 1988, Richard Patrick Blakiston Houston (see Blakiston, Bt, colls). — Vanessa Mary Theresa, b 1958: m 1st, 1980 (m diss 1987), David St Vincent Llewellyn (see Llewellyn, Bt, cr 1922); 2ndly, 1987, as his 2nd wife, John Austen Anstruther-Gough-Calthorpe (see Anstruther-Gough-Calthorpe, Bt). ——— Thomas Francis (15 rue Cler, Paris VII), b 1925; ed Wadham Coll, Oxford (BA 1949); Sub-Lieut (ret) RN; 1939-45 War: m 1954, Melise Marie, eldest da of late Marquis de Merindol, of 34 Gordon Place, W8, and has issue living, John Francis, b 1955, — Mark Fernand, b 1957, — Richard Peter, b 1959.

Granddaughter of late Capt Frederic Arthur Bertie, 5th son of late Rev Hon Frederic Bertie, 4th son of 4th Earl of Abingdon:—
Issue of late Margaret Grace Bertie, b 1883, d 1978: m 1914, Lt-Col Hugh Cleivion Jagger, OBE, RAVC (TA), who d 1931:—
Margaret Rosemary Helen, b 1922; formerly in WRNS: m 1950, Drayton Alfred Wiltshire, and has issue living, Richard Drayton, b 1951, — Robin Cleivion, b 1956: m 1986, Catherine Eva FitzSimon, and has issue living, Rupert Charles b 1993. Residence – Mount Pumps Oast, London Rd, Hurst Green, Etchingham, E Sussex TN19 7QY.

PREDECESSORS – (1) ROBERT Bertie, KG, 12th Baron Willoughby de Eresby (for his predecessor see that family); was Gov of Berwick and Lord High Adm of England; established his claim in right of his mother to the hereditary office of Lord Great Chamberlain of England; cr Earl of Lindsey (peerage of England) 1626; k at battle of Edgehill when in command of a division of the King's army 1642; s by his son (2) MONTAGU, KG, PC, 2nd Earl; surrendered himself a prisoner at Edgehill, in order to attend upon his mortally wounded father; subsequently fought at both battles of Newbury, and at Naseby, etc; was a Lord of the Bedchamber to Charles I, and Lord-Lieut of Oxfordshire; his el son by his 2nd marriage was cr Earl of Abingdon; d 1666; s by his el son (3) ROBERT, 3rd Earl; d 1701; s by his son (4) ROBERT, 4th Earl; summoned to Parliament in his father's lifetime as Baron Willoughby de Eresby; was Lord Lieut of co Lincoln and one of the Lords Justices before the arrival of George I; cr Marquess of Lindsey (peerage of Great Britain) 1706, and Duke of Ancaster and Kesteven (peerage of Great Britain) 1715; d 1723; s by his son (5) PEREGRINE, PC, 2nd Duke; summoned to Parliament in his father's Barony of Willoughby de Eresby; was Lord-Lieut of Lincolnshire and Lord Warden of all HM's parks, chasse, forests, etc, North of the Trent; d 1742; s by his son (6) PEREGRINE, 3rd Duke; was a Gen in the Army, Master of the Horse, and Recorder of Lincoln; officiated as Lord Great Chamberlain at the Coronation of George III; d 1778; s by his son (7) ROBERT, 4th Duke; d unmarried 1779, when the Barony of Willoughby de Eresby became abeyant between his sister, Priscilla (afterwards Baroness Willoughby de Eresby) and Georgiana (Marchioness of Cholmondeley), the Lord Great Chamberlainship devolved jointly upon those ladies, and the dukedom reverted to his uncle (8) BROWNLOW, 5th Duke; d without male issue 1809, when the dukedom and marquessate became extinct, and the earldom devolved upon his kinsman (9) ALBEMARLE, 9th Earl, great-grandson of Hon Charles Bertie, of Uffington, 5th son of 2nd Earl: b 1744; was a Gen in the Army, Col 89th Regt, Gov of Blackness Castle, and sometime MP for Stamford: m 1809, Charlotte Susannah Elizabeth, da of Very Rev Charles P. Layard, Dean of Bristol; d 1818; s by his el son (10) GEORGE AUGUSTUS FREDERICK ALBEMARLE 10th Earl; d unmarried 1877; s by his brother (11) MONTAGU PEREGRINE, 11th Earl b 1815: m 1854, Felicia Elizabeth, who d 1927, da of late Rev John Earle Welby; d 1899; s by his only son (12) MONTAGU PEREGRINE ALBEMARLE, 12th Earl, b 1861: m 1890, Millicent, who d 1931, el da of J. C. Cox, formerly of Craig Cruich, Sydney, NS Wales; d 1938; s by his kinsman (13) MONTAGU HENRY EDMUND CECIL, 13th Earl (who had s as 8th Earl of Abingdon 1928) (see * infra); succession recognized 1951; b 1887; Capt Gren Gds; High Steward of Abingdon: m 1928, Elizabeth Valetta, who d 1978, da of late Maj-Gen Hon Edward James Montagu-Stuart-Wortley, CB, CMG, DSO (E Wharncliffe, colls); d 1963; s by his cousin (14) RICHARD HENRY RUPERT (son of late Lt-Col Hon Arthur Michael Bertie, DSO, MC, 2nd son of 7th Earl of Abingdon), 14th Earl of Lindsey, 9th Earl of Abingdon, and present peer; also Baron Norreys of Rycote.

*(1) Sir HENRY NORRIS, KB, Ambassador to France, was summoned to Parliament 1572-97; d 1600; s by his grandson (2) FRANCIS, 2nd Baron; cr Viscount Thame and Earl of Berkshire (peerage of England) 1620, and d the same year without male issue when the Viscountcy and Earldom became extinct; his only da had issue, one da, who m as his second wife the 2nd Earl of Lindsey, by whom she had (3) JAMES BERTIE, summoned to Parliament of England 1675 as Baron Norreys of Rycote (with Precedence of 1572), and cr Earl of Abingdon (peerage of England) 1682; was Lord-Lieut of Oxfordshire 1674-97; d 1699; s by his son (4) MONTAGU, 2nd Earl; assumed by Roy licence 1687 the additional surname of Venables; d 1743; s by his nephew (5) WILLOUGHBY, 3rd Earl, el son of Hon James, 2nd son of 1st Earl; d 1760; s by his el son (6) WILLOUGHBY, 4th Earl; d 1799; s by his son (7) MONTAGU, DCL, 5th Earl, b 1784; was Lord-Lieut of Berkshire, and officiated as cup-bearer at the coronation of George IV; d 16 Oct 1854; s by his el son (8) MONTAGU, DCL, 6th Earl, b 1808; sat as MP for Oxfordshire 1830 and 1832-52, and for Abingdon (LC) 1852-54; was Lord-Lieut of Berks 1855-81: m 1835, Elizabeth Lavinia, who d 1858, da of late George Granville Vernon-Harcourt, MP, of Nuneham Park, Oxfordshire; d 1884; s by his el son (9) MONTAGU ARTHUR, 7th Earl; b 1836; High Steward of Abingdon: m 1st, 1858, Caroline Theresa, who d 1873, da of late Charles Towneley, of Towneley, Lancs; 2ndly, 1883, Gwendeline Mary, who d 1942, da of late Lt-Gen Hon Sir James Charlemagne Dormer, KCB; d 1928; s by his grandson (10) MONTAGU HENRY EDMUND CECIL (son of late Capt Montagu Charles Francis, Lord Norreys, el son of 7th Earl), who s as 13th Earl of Lindsey 1938 (succession recognised 1951), 8th Earl.

Linley, Viscount; son of Earl of Snowdon.

LINLITHGOW, MARQUESS OF (Hope) (Marquess UK 1902, Bt NS 1698)

But my hope is not broken

AT·SPES·NON·FRACTA

ADRIAN JOHN CHARLES HOPE, 4th Marquess and 12th Baronet; b 1 July 1946; s 1987; ed Eton: m 1st, 1968 (m diss 1978), Anne Pamela, eldest da of Arthur Edmund Leveson, of Hall Place, Ropley, Hants; 2ndly, 1980, Peta Carol, da of Charles Victor Ormonde Binding, of Congresbury, Somerset, and has issue by 1st and 2nd m.

Arms – Azure, on a chevron or, between three bezants, a laurel leaf vert. **Crest** – A broken terrestrial globe, surmounted by a rain-bow proper. **Supporters** – Two female figures representing "Hope" habited in loose garments and with hair dishevelled, each resting the exterior hand on an anchor all proper.
Seat – Hopetoun House, South Queensferry, W Lothian. *Town Residence* – 123 Beaufort St, SW3.

SONS LIVING *(By 1st marriage)*

ANDREW VICTOR ARTHUR CHARLES (*Earl of Hopetoun*), b 22 May 1969; ed Eton, and Exeter Coll, Oxford; a Page of Honour to HM Queen Elizabeth the Queen Mother 1984-86: m 1993, Skye Laurette, elder da of Maj Bristow Charles Bovill, 5th Royal Inniskilling Dragoon Gds, of Shipston-on-Stour, Warwicks (see Leigh, Bt, 1985 Edn).
Lord Alexander John Adrian, b 1971.

(by 2nd marriage)

Lord Robert Charles Robin Adrian, b 1984.

DAUGHTER LIVING *(By 2nd marriage)*

Lady Louisa Vivienne, b 1981.

SISTER LIVING

Lady (Mary) Sarah Jane, b 1940: m 1967 (m diss 1978), Michael Gordon Learoyd, yr son of late Philip Halkett Brooke Learoyd, of Pryonnos, Britwell Salome, Watlington, Oxon, and has issue living, Jeremy Anthony Gordon, b 1971; ed Milton Abbey. *Residence* – East Lodge, Hopetoun, South Queensferry, W Lothian.

UNCLE LIVING *(son of 2nd Marquess)*

Lord John Adrian, PC (*Baron Glendevon*) (twin), b 1912; cr Baron Glendevon 1964 (see that title).

AUNTS LIVING *(Daughters of 2nd Marquess)*

Lady Anne Adeline, b 1914: m 1939, Lt-Com Patrick Henry James Southby, RN (see Southby, Bt). *Address* – Robins Mill, Overbury, Tewkesbury, Glos.
Lady Doreen Hersey Winifred, b 1920: m 1948, Maj-Gen George Erroll Prior-Palmer, CB, DSO, 9th Lancers, who d 1977, and has issue living, Simon Erroll, b 1951: m 1984, Lady Julia Margaret Violet Lloyd George, da of 3rd Earl Lloyd George of Dwyfor, and has issue living, George Erroll Owen b 1988, Arthur Frederick Victor b 1991, Lara Ruth Hope b 1994, — Lucinda Jane, MBE, b 1953, three-day eventer; MBE (Civil) 1978: m 1981, David M. Green, yr son of Barry Green, of Brisbane, Queensland, Australia, and has issue living, Frederick b 1985, Lissa b 1989. *Residence* – The Tree House, Appleshaw, Andover, Hants.

GREAT AUNT LIVING (*Daughter of 1st Marquess*)

Lady Mary Dorothea (*Mary, Countess of Pembroke and Montgomery*), CVO, *b* 1903; is Hon 1st Officer WRNS; a Lady-in-Waiting to HRH the Duchess of Kent 1934-49 and an Extra Lady-in-Waiting 1949-68; CVO 1947: *m* 1936, 16th Earl of Pembroke and Montgomery, who *d* 1969. *Residence* – The Old Rectory, Wilton, Salisbury.

COLLATERAL BRANCHES LIVING (*In remainder to the Earldom of Hopetoun*).

　　　　　Granddaughters of late John George Frederick Hope-Wallace, el son of Lt-Col Hon James Hope-Wallace, MP, 2nd son of 4th Earl of Hopetoun:—
　　　　　Issue of late James Hope-Wallace, Lt Northumberland Fusiliers, *b* 1872, *ka* 1917: *m* 1909, Hon Ursula Mary Addington, who *d* 1962, da of 4th Viscount Sidmouth:—
Ruth, *b* 1911: *m* 1937, Capt Eric Cairns, Roy Northumberland Fusiliers, and has issue living, Jane, *b* 1939: *m* 1965, Peter Butcher, of Crooks Farm, Gilsland, Carlisle, Cumbria, and has issue living, David James Peter *b* 1967, — Clare, *b* 1947: *m* 1985, Michael Jeffery Steinberg, of 1216 Cornell Av, Berkeley, CA 94706, USA. *Residence* – Hallbank Head, Featherstone, Haltwhistle, Northumberland.
　　　　　Issue of late Charles Nugent Hope-Wallace, MBE, *b* 1877; *d* 1953: *m* 1905, Mabel, who *d* 1970, da of late Col Allan Chaplin, formerly Madras Army:—
Nina Mary (*Nina, Lady Hoare*), *b* 1905: *m* 1932, Maj Sir Edward O'Bryen Hoare, 7th Bt, RASC (ret), who *d* 1969. *Residence* – 61 Flask Walk, Hampstead, NW3. —— Dorothy Jacqueline, CBE, *b* 1909; *ed* Lady Margaret Hall, Oxford (BA); Under-Sec, Nat Assistance Board 1958-64, and Min of Housing and Local Govt 1965-69; ret 1969; a Commonwealth Fellow 1952-53; CBE (Civil) 1958. *Residence* – 17 Ashley Court, Morpeth Terrace, SW1P 1EN.

　　　　　Grandchildren of late James Louis Alexander Hope, 2nd son of late Lt-Col Hon James Hope-Wallace, MP (ante):—
　　　　　Issue of late Capt Laurence Nugent Hope, *b* 1890, *d* 1973: *m* 1st, 1919, Hilda Mary, who *d* 1938, only da of late Michael Joseph Hunter, JP, of Stoke Hall, Derbys; 2ndly, 1941, Constance Elizabeth Shell (Whitney Court, Herefordshire):—
(By 1st *m*) John Nugent (The Power House, Whitney-on-Wye, Herefords), *b* 1924; *ed* Eton, and Magdalene Coll, Camb: *m* 1st, 1953, Polly, el da of late Sir Hugh Charles Stockwell, GCB, KBE, DSO; 2ndly, 1986, Mrs Penelope Berengaria Walker, el da of late Lawrence George Durrell, FRSL, the writer, and has issue living (by 1st *m*), Augustine Jason Nugent, *b* 1961: *m* 1991, Maureen Patricia, da of Douglas Hymers, of Seattle, USA, and has issue living, John Gabriel *b* 1992. —— Jocelyn Mary, *b* 1922: *m* 1948, Michael Fortune Cleghorn, of Cape Town, S Africa.

　　　　　Grandson of late Sir Charles Dunbar Hope-Dunbar, 6th Bt (who proved his claim to the Baronetcy of Dunbar of Baldoon 1916); grandson of late Hon Charles Hope, 3rd son of 4th Earl of Hopetoun:—
See Hope-Dunbar, Bt.

　　　　　Granddaughter of late Capt Hon Louis Hope, 7th son of 4th Earl of Hopetoun:—
　　　　　Issue of late Herbert George Hope, MBE, *b* 1875, *d* 1956: *m* 1920, May Winifred, who *d* 1960, da of late Lt-Col F. F. Sheppee, RA, and widow of John Harley:—
Isabel Susan, *b* 1922: *m* 1955, Peter Haviland Hiley, son of late Col Sir (Ernest) Haviland Hiley, KBE, and has issue living, William John Haviland (9 Worfield St, SW11 4RB), *b* 1960; *ed* Eton, and Bristol Univ: *m* 1993, Camilla Jane, elder of Charles Edward Weatherby, of Mixbury Lodge Farm, Brackley, Northants (*see* Ley, Bt). *Residence* – Byways, Steep, Petersfield, Hants, GU32 1AD.

　　　　　Grandchildren of late Capt George Everard Hope of Luffness, MC, only son of late Henry Walter Hope of Luffness, 2nd son of late George William Hope of Luffness, MP, 2nd son of late Gen Hon Sir Alexander Hope, GCB, 4th son of 2nd Earl:—
　　　　　Issue of late Col Archibald John George Hope of Luffness, MBE, RA, *b* 1912, *d* 1987: *m* 1937, Mary Pilar Elizabeth, who *d* 1989, yr da of late Brig-Gen Alister Fraser Gordon, CMG, DSO (*see* B Stafford, colls, 1969 Edn):—
George Archibald Hope of Luffness (Luffness, Aberlady, E Lothian EH32 0QB; Cavalry and Guards, Pratt's and Hong Kong Clubs), *b* 1938; *ed* Eton, and Edinburgh Univ; late Gren Gds and Royal Scots (TA); Memb Queen's Body Guard for Scotland (Royal Company of Archers); Kt of Honour and Devotion, Sov Mil Order of Malta; CA; Fell Hong Kong Soc of Accountants. —— Margaret Mary Lucy, *b* 1940: *m* 1978, Richard Simon Baillie, of Allanbank, Lauder, Berwickshire TD2 6RW, elder son of Capt Alexander Maciej Gucewicz-Baillie, of Hendersyde, Kelso, Roxburghshire, and has issue living, Alexander Simon, *b* 1982, — Edward George, *b* 1985. —— Mary Catherine Elizabeth, *b* 1943: *m* 1989, Bey Yalçin Adar, of Istanbul, Turkey. —— Elizabeth Caroline, *b* 1948: *m* 1984, James Patrick Scott, of 6 Rede Place, W2 4TU, son of Munro Mackenzie Scott, of Cakemuir, Tynehead, Midlothian, and has issue living, James William Hope, *b* 1988, — Catriona Mary, *b* 1984. —— Cecilia Mary, *b* 1952; *ed* St Andrew's Univ (MA): *m* 1987, Christopher Peter Latilla-Campbell, of Lochton, Abernyte, Perthshire PH14 9TA, elder son of Peter Latilla-Campbell, of Bulawayo, and of Mrs Merrick Burrell.

　　　　　Granddaughter of late Maj John Alexander Henry Hope, only son of late Sir Edward Stanley Hope, KCB, 5th son of late George William Hope of Luffness, MP (ante):—
　　　　　Issue of late Maj Edward James Hope, MC, *b* 1911, *d* 1989: *m* 1st, 1937 (*m diss* 1950), Enid, who *d* 1988, da of late Robert Gunther, of Parkwood, Englefield Green; 2ndly, 1952, Winifred Gwendolyne Marie (Ibstock Close, Little Tew, Oxon), el da of late Maj John Byng Paget:—
(By 1st *m*) Sarah Elizabeth (Avendale, 6 Nags Head Lane, Avening, Glos), *b* 1942: *m* 1964 (*m diss* 1987), Benjamin L. C. Wordsworth, and has issue living, Marcia, *b* 1965: *m* 1993, Mark Walton, of Christchurch, NZ, — Lucy, *b* (twin) 1965: *m* 1992, Kostka Garcia Miñaur de la Rica, and has issue living, Lucas Dylan *b* 1992, — Rebecca, *b* 1967: *m* 1989, Julian A. Lloyd, of Stroud, Glos, and has issue living, Oscar Benjamin *b* 1989.

　　　　　Descendants of late Rt Hon James Fitzalan Hope (*Baron Rankeillour*); *cr* Baron Rankeillour 1932, son of James Robert Hope-Scott, QC, 3rd son of Hon Sir Alexander Hope, GCB (ante) (see that title).

　　　　　Grandchildren of late Charles Douglas Hope (infra):—
　　　　　Issue of late Major Adrian Alexander Hope, Transvaal Scottish, *b* 1897; *ka* in Italy 1945: *m* 1926, Eleanor (35 Leisure Gdns, Knysna 6570, S Africa), da of Lieut-Col George Ritchie Thomson, CMG, MB:—
William Adrian (9 Montagu St, Knysna 6570, S Africa), *b* 1927; *ed* Michaelhouse, Natal, at Witwatersrand Univ (BA), and at Trin Coll, Oxford (MA); an Advocate of Johannesburg, S Africa, and of Salisbury, Rhodesia; published *A Digest of Rhodesian Mining Law* 1965; 1939-45 War with S African Artillery in Italy: *m* 1960, Hazel, da of Adelbert Johnstone, of Gwelo, Rhodesia, and has issue living, Adrian Charles, *b* 1962, — James Graham, *b* 1961, — Sarah Jane, *b* 1964. —— Anne Eleanor (407 Thayer Av, Silverspring, Md 20910, USA), *b* 1930, BA Rhodes Univ; Diploma in Education, Oxford.
　　　　　Issue of late James Hope, *b* 1899, *d* 1970: *m* 1937, Doreen (1 Protea Flats, Protea Av, Fish Hoek, Cape 7975, S Africa), da of Prof Armstrong:—
Christopher James (273 Burton Rd, Oakville, Ontario L6K 2K7, Canada), *b* 1938: *m* 19—, Erica —, and has issue living, Thomas, *b* 19—. —— Alastair Frederick (5 Malleson Rd, Mowbray, Cape, S Africa), *b* 1941: *m* 1963, Mary Elizabeth, da of

Arthur Cecil Bilbrough, of Carmunnock, Somerset West, S Africa, and has issue living, Charles Andrew, *b* 1966, — Paul James, *b* 1968, — Bridget Moira, *b* 1964. ——— Angela Ruth Alice, *b* 1939: *m* 19— (*m diss* 19—), Warwick Manning, and has issue living, Joanne, *b* 19—.

Issue of Henry Francis Hope, *b* 1900, *d* 1971: *m* 1930, Aileen Elinor, who *d* 1993, da of late William Falkiner Harnett, CBE;—
Gillian Margaret, *b* 1933: *m* 1955, Neville Price Boyce, of 23 Ashwold Rd, Saxonwold, Johannesburg, and has issue living, Richard Henry Price, *b* 1957, — Diana Mary, *b* 1959, — Margaret Louise, *b* 1961. ——— Rosemary Patricia, *b* 1936: *m* 1963, Guy Everingham Hitchings, of Spring Bank, Speldhurst, Kent, and has issue living, Charles Robin, *b* 1967, — Mark Alexander, *b* 1969, — Andrew Hope, *b* 1971, — Alice Elizabeth, *b* 1965: *m* 1994, Michael Andrew Bennett, of 2 The Ridgway, Wimbledon.

Issue of late Charles Christopher Hope, *b* 1902, *d* 1963: *m* 1937, Una Mainguy, who *d* 1989, da of late W. P. Le Feuvre, MD, of Kenilworth, Cape Town:—
Charles Richard Christopher (8 Blue Grass Drive, RR2 Aurora, Ont L4G 3G8, Canada); Royal Canadian Yacht Club, and Royal Commonwealth Society, *b* 1938; *ed* Downside and Toronto Univ (BA): *m* 1970, Mary Lou da of John Francis Fitzpatrick of 178 King St, Saint John, New Brunswick, and has issue living, Mary Mainguy, *b* 1971, — Tiffany Anne Granton, *b* 1972.

Granddaughters of late Lieut-Col William Hope, VC, el son of late Rt Hon John Hope (Lord Justice Clerk of Scotland) el son of late Rt Hon Charles Hope (Lord Justice-Gen of Scotland), el son of late John Hope (*b* 1739), 2nd son of late Hon Charles Hope-Vere, 2nd son of 1st Earl of Hopetoun:—
Issue of late Charles Douglas Hope, *b* 1867, *d* 1947: *m* 1896, Alice Mary, who *d* 1947, da of Hon A. Wilmot (Papal Count, Papal Chamberlain), MLC, of Cape Colony:—
Alice Margaret Mary (More House, 29 Tite St, SW3) *b* 1906. ——— Patricia Anne (2642 Ottawa Av, W Vancouver, BC, Canada), *b* 1908: *m* 1937, Capt Sebastian F. Newdigate, DSC, RNR, who *d* 1954, and has issue living, Anne Charlotte, *b* 1938: *m* 1960, Humphrey Edward Waldock, of 3638 Osler St, Vancouver 9, BC, Canada, son of late Sir (Claud) Humphrey (Meredith) Waldock, CMG, OBE, QC, and has issue living, Harold Sebastian *b* 1961, Henry Bernard *b* 1962, Thomas Edward *b* 1965: *m* 1988, Jane Little, Mary Beatrice *b* 1969, Alice Patricia *b* 1973, Susan Katherine Margaret *b* 1977, — Lilah Mary Amphelis (Sister Mary Lucy) (Carmelite Monastery, PO Box 6, Kew, Vic 3101, Aust), *b* 1940.

Grandson of late Adm Sir George Price Webley Hope, KCB, KCMG, 2nd son of late Rear Adm Charles Webley Hope (infra):—
Issue of late Brig Maurice Webley Hope, DSO, *b* 1901, *d* 1986: *m* 1943, Pamela (Ivy Bank, Vinegar Hill, Milford-on-Sea, Hants), da of late J. K. Osborne, of NSW:—
David George Osborne, *b* 1944; *ed* Winchester, and Balliol Coll, Oxford: *m* 1970, Jane Lesley, da of Edward Ellis, of Durham, and has issue living, Joseph Cornelius Ellis, *b* 1971.

Grandchildren of late Rear-Adm Charles Webley Hope, only son of Rear-Adm Charles Hope, 2nd son of the Rt Hon Charles Hope (Lord Justice-Gen of Scotland), (ante):—
Issue of late Lt-Col William Henry Webley Hope, CMG, *b* 1871, *d* 1919: *m* 1900, Florence, who *d* 1918, da of late Charles Walter Hill, of Clapham, Sussex:—
James Webley, OBE (60 Kenilworth Gdns, PO Box 267, Bowral, NSW 2576; Australia (Sydney) Club), *b* 1903; Lt-Col (ret) S Wales Borderers; Waziristan 1937 (despatches), Burma 1945 (despatches, OBE); OBE (Mil) 1946: *m* 1st, 1928, Harriet Mary, who *d* 1931, da of late Henry Louis King, DL, JP, of Ballylin, Ferbane, King's co (V Bangor, colls); 2ndly, 1934, Veda Annie, who *d* 1986, da of late Dr Alfred Walter Campbell, of Sydney, Aust, and has issue living, (by 2nd *m*) Gillian Florence, *b* 1935: *m* 1961, Col George Mark Chirnside, late 13th/18th Hus, of Stone Cottage, Beer Hackett, Sherborne, Dorset.
Issue of the late Col Adrian Victor Webley Hope, CIE, *b* 1873, *d* 1960: *m* 1920, Ethel Mary, who *d* 1938, da of late J. S. Middleton, of Cadamaney, Mysore:—
Margaret Isobel, *b* 1921: *m* 1st, 1943 (*m diss* 1949), James Veitch Telfer; 2ndly, 1950, Squadron-Leader James Geoffrey Cutcliffe Hepburn, DFC, and has issue living, (by 1st *m*) Alison, *b* 1944; BA Oxon; PhD London: *m* 1970, Terence Parry Jones, and has issue living, William George Parry *b* 1976, Sally Louise Parry *b* 1974, — Kate, *b* 1947; MA Roy Coll of Art; has issue living, Usha Junge *b* 1978, — (by 2nd *m*) Harriet Rose, *b* 1965; BA Oxon. *Residence* – 68 Parliament Hill, Hampstead, NW3.
Issue of late Adm Herbert Willes Webley Hope, CB, CVO, DSO, RN, *b* 1878, *d* 1968: *m* 1905, Katherine Maria Antoinette, who *d* 1966, da of late Rev Francis Kewley:—
Ellen Katherine Webley, *b* 1907: *m* 1st, 1929 (*m diss* 1937), David William Heneker, formerly Lt-Col RASC, son of late Lt-Gen Sir William Charles Giffard Heneker, KCB, KCMG, DSO; 2ndly, 1941, Lt-Col Charles Vaughan King, OBE, Devonshire Regt, of 8 New Court, Sutton Manor, Sutton Scotney, Winchester, Hants, and has issue living (by 1st *m*), Peter David Grenfell (Parc Helyg, Llechryd, Cardigan, Dyfed SA43 2NJ), *b* 1931; *ed* Wellington Coll, and Brasenose Coll, Oxford: *m* 1954, Josephine Anne, eldest da of Lt-Col James William Lewis-Bowen, of Boncath, Dyfed, and has issue living, David Marius *b* 1958, Sam Gerald William *b* 1961, Nicholas Charles Adrian *b* 1963, Piers Herbert *b* 1964, Simon Thomas *b* 1965, — (by 2nd *m*) Adrian Charles Richard, *b* 1944.

Granddaughters of late Lieut-Col William Henry Webley Hope, CMG, 3rd son of Rear Adm Charles Webley Hope (ante):—
Issue of late Lt-Cdr Charles Webley Hope, RN, *b* 1902; *d* on active ser: *m* 1933, Harriott Barbara, who *d* 1970, da of late Lt-Col R. G. E. Locke, DL, JP, of Hartlip House, Hartlip, Kent:—
Mary, *b* 1934. ——— Janet, *b* 1937: *m* 1960, Richard Wilson Froggatt, of Stonecross Farm, Wadhurst, Sussex, and has issue living, Ian Wilson, *b* 1962, — Peter Webley, *b* 1964: *m* 1990, Michele Hobday, and has issue living, Hayley Louise *b* 1990, — Nigel Thomas, *b* 1966, — Eric Charles (twin), *b* 1966, — Jenny Patricia (twin), *b* 1962: *m* 1987, Simon John Pickhaver, and has issue living, Joanna Ruth *b* 1990, Sarah Elizabeth *b* 1992, — Alison Clare (twin), *b* 1964.

Grandsons of late Adrian James Robert Hope, CIE, only son of late Charles William Hope, eldest son of late James Hope, 3rd son of late Rt Hon Charles Hope (Lord Justice-Gen of Scotland and Lord Pres of the Court of Session) (ante):—
Issue of late Charles Adrian Hope, *b* 1918, *d* 1986: *m* 1951, Susan Elizabeth Rona Kruse (23 Ann St, Edinburgh EH4 1PL):—
Adrian Kruse Anthony (23 Dublin St, Edinburgh EH1 3PG), *b* 1953; *ed* Edinburgh Acad, and Sheffield and Edinburgh Colls of Art; designer and silversmith: *m* 1977, Linda Caroline Lewin, and has issue living, Adam Poyntz, *b* 1981, — Claire Evelyn, *b* 1984. ——— James William Drever (10 Brondesbury Park Mansions, NW6), *b* 1957; *ed* Edinburgh Acad, Bristol Univ and Bristol Old Vic Theatre Sch; actor.

Grandchildren of late James Arthur Hope, WS (infra):—
Issue of late Lt-Col Arthur Henry Cecil Hope, OBE, TD, WS, *b* 1896, *d* 1986: *m* 1937, Muriel Ann Neilson Collie (28B Moray Pl, Edinburgh):—
James Arthur David (*Rt Hon Lord Hope*), PC (34 India St, Edinburgh EH3 6HB), *b* 1938; *ed* Edinburgh Acad, Rugby, St John's Coll, Camb (BA), and Edinburgh Univ (LLB); late Lieut Seaforth Highlanders; Advocate 1965, Advocate-Depute 1978-82, Dean of Faculty of Advocates 1986-89, since when Lord Justice-Gen and Lord Pres of the Court of Session; PC 1989: *m* 1966, Katharine Mary Kerr, and has issue living, William Thomas Arthur, *b* 1969; *ed* Edinburgh Acad, George Watson's Coll,

and Univ of Victoria, BC (BA), — James David Louis, *b* (twin) 1969; *ed* Edinburgh Acad, Christ's Coll, Camb (BA), and Edinburgh Univ (LLB), — Lucy Charlotte Mary, *b* 1971; *ed* St George's Sch for Girls, St Andrew's Univ (BSc), and Edinburgh Univ. —— John William Lewis (28B Moray Place, Edinburgh EH3 6BX), *b* 1940; *ed* Edinburgh Acad, and St Andrew's Univ (MA): *m* 1974, Hazel Goh Mei Ling, da of Goh Siew Hiong, of Kuching, Sarawak, Borneo, and has issue living, Charles Arthur Robertson, *b* 1976, — Thomas John Alexander, *b* 1978, — Geraldine Katherine Ann, *b* 1982. —— Alexander Robertson Boyle (Croftinloan Sch, Pitlochry, Perthshire), *b* 1947; *ed* Edinburgh Acad, Rugby, and Durham Univ (BA). —— Elspeth Mary Neilson (51 Whitehall Rd, Aberdeen), *b* (twin) 1947: *m* 1969 (*m diss* 1994), Dolf Andries Mogendorff, and has issue living, Andrew Michael Alexander, *b* 1972, — Richard Arthur John, *b* 1974, — David Martin James, *b* 1978, — Robin Paul Neilson, *b* 1980. —— Angela Muriel Evelyn, *b* 1948; SRN: *m* 1976, Brian Richard Anscombe, of 12 Linckleas Ave, Victoria, BC, Canada, and has issue living, Philip Hayward, *b* 1979, — Jacqueline Hope, *b* 1981.

Grandson of late David Boyle Hope, 2nd son of late James Hope, WS (ante):—
Issue of late James Arthur Hope, WS, *b* 1865, *d* 1925: *m* 1895, Geraldine Lucy, da of late Rev Charles Hope Robertson, formerly R of Smeeth, Kent:—
James Louis, TD, WS, *b* 1906; *ed* Edinburgh Acad, Rugby, and Edinburgh Univ (MA, LLB); Lt-Col (ret) Roy Scots (TA): *m* 1939, Kathleen Colquhoun Sconce, and has issue living, Charles Louis (Woodside, Ockham Road North, West Horsley, Surrey), *b* 1940; *ed* Edinburgh Acad, Rugby, and Magdalene Coll, Camb (MA); CEng, MIEE: *m* 1963, Susan Jane Elizabeth McDowall, and has issue living, Joanna Mary *b* 1968, Fiona Jane *b* 1972, — Michael Edmund (12 Castle Rd, Sherborne, Dorset), *b* 1943; *ed* Edinburgh Acad, Rugby, Trin Coll, Dublin (BA), and St Andrews Univ (MA). *Residence* – 34a Murrayfield Rd, Edinburgh 12.

Descendants of Vice-Adm Sir William Johnstone-Hope, GCB, 3rd son of John Hope (*d* 1739), 2nd son of Hon Charles Hope-Vere, 2nd son of 1st Earl of Hopetoun:—
See E Annandale and Hartfell.

Grandchildren of late Charles Hope (*b* 1845) yr son of Maj-Gen Frederick Hope, 2nd son of Capt Charles Hope, RN, 4th son of Hon Charles Hope-Vere (ante):—
Issue of late Charles Henry Sawyer Hope, *b* 1880, *d* 1964: *m* 1913, Olive Lois, who *d* 1954, da of late Arthur Francis Godwin, of 16 Hans Place SW1:—
Jaqueline (42 Telegraph Lane East, Norwich), *b* 1914; a State Registered Physiotherapist, Supt Physiotherapist Univ Coll Hosp West Indies 1953-55, Norfolk and Norwich Hospital 1950-53 and 1955-73; MCSP; 1939-45 War with Naval VAD. —— Anne Vere (42 Telegraph Lane East, Norwich), *b* 1918; 1939-45 War with ATS, as architectural draughtswoman.
Issue of late George Leonard Nelson Hope, *b* 1884, *d* 1973: *m* 1908 Honoria Mary Victoria, who *d* 1968, yst da of late John Giffard Riddell, of Swinburne Castle and Felton Park, Northumberland:—
Sir (Charles) Peter, KCMG, TD (Guillard's Oak House, Midhurst, W Sussex; White's Club), *b* 1912; *ed* Oratory Sch and London (BSc), and Camb Univs; 1939-45 War as Lt-Col RA; HM Foreign Ser 1946 as 1st Sec Paris; Assist Head of UN Dept; FO 1950, Counsellor, Bonn 1953, Head of News Dept, FO 1956, HM Min, Madrid 1959, HM Consul-Gen for Texas and New Mexico 1963, Alternate British Repres to UN 1965-68, and Ambassador to Mexico 1968-72; Grand Cross Order of Aztec Eagle of Mexico; TD 1946, KStJ 1984; CMG 1957, KCMG 1972: *m* 1936, Hazel Mary, da of late G. L. Turner, and has issue living, (Charles) Jeremy (Netherhill, Awbridge, Romsey, Hants SO51 0HG), *b* 1937, *ed* Downside; late Gren Gds; Kt of Honour and Devotion, Sov Mil Order of Malta: *m* 1961, Judith Ann, da of late H. T. Pearce, and has issue living, Dominic Mark *b* 1963, Jonathon Paul *b* 1965, — Adrian Philip, *b* 1942; *ed* Downside, and Trin Coll, Camb, — Richard Andrew, *b* 1947; *ed* Downside, and St Thomas Univ, Houston, Texas.

PREDECESSORS – (1)*Sir* CHARLES Hope, KT, grandson of late Sir James Hope, KB, 6th son of Sir Thomas Hope, 1st Bt (*cr* 1628); *cr Lord Hope, Viscount Aithrie* and *Earl of Hopetoun* (peerage of Scotland) 1703, with remainder to heirs male and female of his body; *d* 1742; *s* by his son (2) JOHN, 2nd Earl, in whom the *Baronetcy* (*cr* NS 1698) of Kirkliston; became vested on the death of the 3rd Bt 1783; Lord High Commr to Gen Assembly of Church of Scotland; *d* 1781; *s* by his son (3) JAMES, 3rd Earl; Lord-Lieut of co Linlithgow, and a Representative Peer 1784-94; in 1792 *s* to the estates of his grand-uncle, George, 3rd Marquess of Annandale (title dormant), and assumed the additional surname of Johnstone; *cr Baron Hopetoun*, of Hopetoun (peerage of United Kingdom) 1809, with remainder to the heirs male of his father; *d* 1817; *s* by his half-brother (4) JOHN, GCB, 4th Earl; Col of 42nd Regt, a distinguished Gen in the Peninsula; *cr Baron Niddry*, of Niddry Castle, co Linlithgow (peerage of the United Kingdom) 1814, with remainder to the male issue of his father; *d* 1823; *s* by his son (5) JOHN, 5th Earl; Lord-Lieut of co Linlithgow; *d* 1843; *s* by his son (6) JOHN ALEXANDER, 6th Earl; *b* 1831; Lord-Lieut of co Linlithgow; *m* 1860, Ethelred Anne, who *d* 1884, da of Charles Thomas Samuel Birch-Reynardson, of Holywell Hall, near Stamford; *d* 1873; *s* by his son (7) JOHN ADRIAN LOUIS, KT, GCMG, GCVO, PC, 7th Earl; *b* 1860; a Lord-in-Waiting to Queen Victoria 1885-6 and 1886-9, Lord High Commr of Gen Assembly of Church of Scotland 1887-9, Gov of Victoria 1889-95, Paymaster-Gen 1895-8, Lord Chamberlain of Queen Victoria's Household 1898-1900, first Gov-Gen of the Commonwealth of Australia 1900-1902, and Sec for Scotland and Keeper of the Great Seal of Scotland, with a seat in the Cabinet Feb to Dec 1905; *cr Marquess of Linlithgow*, co Linlithgow or West Lothian (peerage of United Kingdom) 1902: *m* 1886, Hon Hersey Alice Eveleigh-de Moleyns, who *d* 1937, da of 4th Baron Ventry; *d* 1908; *s* by his son (8) *Rt Hon* VICTOR ALEXANDER JOHN, KG, KT, GCSI, GCIE, OBE, TD, 2nd Marquess; *b* 1887; Civil Lord of the Admiralty 1922-24, Viceroy and Gov-Gen of India 1936-43, and Lord High Commr to Gen Assembly of Church of Scotland 1944-45; Chancellor of Edinburgh Univ 1944: Lord-Lieut of W Lothian, Capt King's Body Guard for Scotland (Roy Co of Archers), Chm Midland Bank 1945-52, and a PC, *m* 1911, Doreen Maud, CI, who *d* 1965, yr da of Rt Hon Sir Frederick George Milner, 7th Bt; *d* 1952; *s* by his son (9) CHARLES WILLIAM FREDERICK, TD, MC, 3rd Marquess, *b* 1912 (twin), Capt Lothians and Border Horse, RAC (TA), Lieut Scots Guards (Reserve), Lord Lieut W Lothian, 1939-43 War (prisoner): *m* 1st, 1939, Vivien, who *d* 1963, da of Capt Robert Orlando Rodolph Kenyon-Slaney (B Kenyon, colls); 2ndly, 1965, Judith, who *d* 1991, da of late Stanley Matthew Lawson, of Cincinnati, USA, widow of Lt-Col Esmond Charles Baring, OBE (*see* B Ashburton, colls), and formerly wife of John Symonds Radway; *d* 1987; *s* by his only son (by 1st *m*), (10) ADRIAN JOHN CHARLES, 4th Marquess and present peer; also Earl of Hopetoun, Viscount Aithrie, Lord Hope, Baron Hopetoun, and Baron Niddry.

LISBURNE, EARL OF (Vaughan) (Earl I 1776)

I will not return unavenged

JOHN DAVID MALET VAUGHAN, 8th Earl; *b* 1 Sept 1918; *s* 1965; *ed* Eton, and Magdalen Coll, Oxford (MA); Bar Inner Temple 1948; patron of one living; 1939-45 War as Capt Welsh Guards: *m* 1943, Shelagh, da of late T. A. Macauley, of Montreal, Canada, and has issue.

Arms – Sable, a chevron between three fleurs-de-lis argent. **Crest** – An arm embowed in armour, the hand holding a sword, point to the sinister, all proper. **Supporters** – *Dexter*, a dragon reguardant, armed and langued or, collared sable and chained gold, the collar charged with three fleurs-de-lis argent; *sinister*, a unicorn reguardant argent, the mane, horn and hoofs or, collared and chained as the other. *Residence* – Cruglas, Ystrad Meurig, Dyfed.

SONS LIVING

DAVID JOHN FRANCIS MALET *(Viscount Vaughan)* *b* 15 June 1945; *ed* Ampleforth: *m* 1973, Jennifer Jane, only da of late James Desiré John William Fraser Campbell, of Glengarry, Inverness-shire, and has issue:—

SON LIVING—*Hon* Digby Dylan, *b* 1973.

DAUGHTER LIVING—*Hon* Lucy Bronwyn, *b* 1971.

Hon Michael John Wilmot Malet, *b* 1948; *ed* Ampleforth, and New Coll, Oxford (MA): *m* 1978, Hon Lucinda Mary Louise Baring, da of 7th Baron Ashburton, and has issue living, Emma Rose Nightingale, *b* 1993. *Residence* – 44 Pembroke Sq, W8.

Hon John Edward Malet, *b* 1952; *ed* Ampleforth: *m* 1st, 1977 *(m diss* 1983), Catharine Euphan, only da of J. P. Waterer, of Coombe Bissett, Salisbury; 2ndly, 1989, Sandra Caroline Janet, formerly wife of Michael Charles Craufurd Cooper, and da of Brian Harold Thomson, of Kemback House, by Cupar, Fife, and has issue living (by 2nd *m*), Henry John Augustus, *b* 1990. *Residence* – 19 Bowerdean St, SW6 3TN.

SISTERS LIVING

Lady Gloria Regina Malet, *b* 1916: *m* 1st, 1935 *(m diss* 1952), Maj Nigel Thomas Loveridge Fisher, MC, Welsh Guards (later Sir Nigel Fisher), son of late Cdr Sir Thomas Fisher, KBE, RN; 2ndly, 1952, Ronald Philip Flower, OBE, who *d* 1993, of Manor Farm Cottage, Weston Patrick, nr Basingstoke, and has issue living, (by 1st *m*) Mark Nigel Thomas Vaughan, MP, *b* 1944; MP *(Lab)* Stoke-on-Trent Central since 1983: *m* 1971, Mrs Ingrid Hunt, da of late James Hoyle Geach, — Amanda Gloria Morvyth Vaughan, *b* 1939, — (by 2nd *m*) Philip Ronald, *b* 1953; *ed* Eton: *m* 1991, Kate, only da of Michael Percival, of SW1, and has issue living, Joshua Ronald *b* 1992.

Lady Honor Morvyth Malet, *b* 1919; a JP for Cardiganshire: *m* 1943, Maj William Herbert Rhidian Llewellyn, MC, Welsh Gds, of 4 St Omer Rd, Guildford, Surrey GU1 2DB *(see* Llewellyn, Bt, *cr* 1922).

Lady Auriel Rosemary Malet, *b* 1923. *Residence* – Haute Folie de Breux, par Tillières sur Avre, 27570 Eure, France

COLLATERAL BRANCH LIVING

Grandchildren of late Edmund Mallet Vaughan, son of late Hon William Mallet Vaughan, 4th son of 3rd Earl:—

Issue of late Major Eugène Napoléon Ernest Mallet Vaughan, DSO, *b* 1878, *d* 1934: *m* 1914, Hilda Winifred, who *d* 1972, el da of late Neville Hanbury Mander, of Penn Wolverhampton:—

Edmund Bernard Mallet (The Bath Farm, Codsall Wood, Wolverhampton) *b* 1920; Maj (ret) late Gren Gds: *m* 1950, Jean, only da of late Col John Walton Nelson, of Sevenoaks, Kent, and has issue living, David John, *b* 1953, — Michael Edmund, *b* 1957, — Diana Mary (twin), *b* 1953. —— Mary Christine (Brewood, Stafford), *b* 1916.

PREDECESSORS – **(1)**JOHN Vaughan, MP for Cardiganshire in several Parliaments; *cr Baron Fethard*, of Feathered, co Tipperary, and *Viscount Lisburne* (peerage of Ireland) 1695: *d* 1720; *s* by his el son **(2)** JOHN, 2nd Viscount; *d* 1741; *s* by hs brother **(3)** WILMOT, 3rd Viscount; *d* 1766; *s* by his son **(4)** WILMOT, 4th Viscount; was MP for Cardiganshire 1755-61 and 1768-96, Lord-Lieut of Cardiganshire, a Lord of Trade 1768, and a Lord of the Admiralty 1770-82; *cr Earl of Lisburne* (peerage of Ireland) 1776; *d* 1800; *s* by his el son **(5)** WILMOT, 2nd Earl; *d* 1820; *s* by his half-brother **(6)** JOHN, 3rd Earl; Col in the Army; *d* 1831; *s* by his 2nd son **(7)** ERNEST AUGUSTUS, 4th Earl; *b* 1800: *m* 1st, 1835, Mary, who *d* 1851, da of Sir Lawrence Palk, 2nd Bt; 2ndly, 1853, Hon Elizabeth Augusta Harriett, who *d* 1883 (formerly a Maid of Honour to HM Queen Adelaide), da of Col Hugh Henry Mitchell: *d* 1873; *s* by his son **(8)** ERNEST AUGUSTUS MALLET, 5th Earl, *b* 1836: *m* 1st, 1858, Laura Gertrude, who *d* 1865, da of Edwyn Burnaby, of Baggrave Hall, Leicester; 2ndly, Alice Dalton, who *d* 1933 (having *m* 2ndly, 1889, as his 2nd wife, 3rd Earl Amherst), da of late Edmund Probyn, of Huntley Manor, near Gloucester; *d* 1888; *s* by his son **(9)** ERNEST GEORGE HENRY ARTHUR, 6th Earl; *b* 1862: *m* 1888, Evelyn, who *d* 1931, da of late Edmund Probyn, of Huntley Manor and Longhope, Gloucester; *d* 1899; *s* by his son **(10)** ERNEST EDMUND HENRY MALET, 7th Earl; *b* 1892; Lord-Lieut for Cardiganshire 1923-56 (Sheriff 1923): *m* 1st, 1914, Regina, who *d* 1944, da of late Don Julio Bittencourt, Attaché to Chilean Legation in London; 2ndly, 1961, Audrey Maureen Leslie, who *d* 1978, yst da of late James Meakin, of Westwood Manor, Staffs, and widow of Hon Robert Godfrey de Bohun Devereux (V Hereford); *d* 1965; *s* by his son **(11)** JOHN DAVID MALET, 8th Earl and present peer; also Viscount Lisburne, and Baron Fethard.

NON·REVERTAR·INULTUS

LISLE, BARON (Lysaght) (Baron I 1758)
(Title pronounced "Lyle") (Name pronounced "Lycett")

Wars! horrid wars!

JOHN NICHOLAS HORACE LYSAGHT, 7th Baron, *b* 10 Aug 1903; *s* 1919: *m* 1st, 1928 (*m diss* 1939), Vivienne, who *d* 1948, da of Rev M. Brew; 2ndly, 1939, Marie Helen, da of late A. D. Purgold, of Parkgate, Cheshire.

Arms – Argent, three spears erect gules, on a chief azure, a lion passant guardant or. **Crest** – A dexter arm embowed in armour, the hand holding a sword proper. **Supporters** – Two lions or.
Residence – The Chestnuts, Barge Farm, Taplow, Bucks SL6 0AE.

SISTER LIVING

Alice Amy: *m* 1930, Henry Lysaght, who *d* 1963, 5th son of William Lysaght, JP, of Hazlewood, co Cork, and has issue. *Residence* –

COLLATERAL BRANCHES LIVING

Issue of late (Horace) James William Lysaght, younger brother of 7th Baron (*ante*), *b* 1908, *d* 1977: *m* 1st, 1930 (*m diss* 1951), Joanna Mary, who *d* 1985, da of late Dr J. S. Nolan, of Bedwas, Mon; 2ndly, 1953, Vyrna (The Meadows, Mathern, Chepstow, Mon), da of J. Jones, of Pontypool:—
(By 1st *m*), PATRICK JAMES, *b* 1 May 1931, *ed* Shrewsbury; late Lt Gren Gds: *m* 1957 (*m diss* 19—), Mary Louise, da of late Lt-Col Geoffrey Reginald Devereux Shaw, of Scottow Hall, Norfolk (*see* Durrant, Bt, 1960 Edn), and formerly wife of Euan Guy Shaw-Stewart (later 10th Bt), who *d* 1980, and has issue living, John Nicholas Geoffrey, *b* 1960, — David James, *b* 1963, — Mary-Jane, *b* 1959: *m* 1986, Paul Stephen Roberts, of Manor Farm House, Manor Rd, Wantage, Berks, son of Mrs D. McCarthy, of Bingham, Notts, and has issue living, Lucy *b* 1988. —— Dermot Edward (Crews Court, Upton Bishop, Herefords), *b* 1935; late 2nd Lt, King's R Irish Hussars: *m* 1961, Tessa Susan, da of late Capt Terence Hugh Back, CBE, RN, and has issue living, Cornelius James Terence (16A Dunraven Rd, W12), *b* 1965; *ed* Eton, — Georgina Mary, *b* 1966; *ed* Exeter Univ (BA 1988). —— (By 2nd *m*) Deirdre Elizabeth Jane, *b* 1954. —— Philippa Jane, *b* 1955: *m* 1982, Capt Paul McMahon, RCT, of 5 Mount View, Church Lane West, Aldershot, Hants, son of J. J. McMahon, of Gosport, Hants.

Issue of late George Henry Lysaght, yst brother of 7th Baron (*ante*), *b* 1911, *d* 1985: *m* 1935, Pauline Ann, elder da of Patrick J. Dillon, of The Grove, Girley, Kells, co Meath:—
Horace George (Abbeycourt, Kinsale, co Cork), *b* 1936: *m* 1961, Anne Phyllis, da of late David Daly, of Cork, and has issue living, Stephen Henry, *b* 1963, — John Gareth, *b* 1965, — Susan Anne, *b* 1962, — Jennifer Mary, *b* 1967. —— Lawrence George (Killestry, Killaloe, co Clare), *b* 1937; LRCPI, LRCSI. —— John Patrick George (Vancouver, BC, Canada), *b* 1939. —— Pauline Anne, *b* 1942.

Grandchildren of late Rev Hon Henry Lysaght, 4th son of 5th Baron:—
Issue of late Rev John Arthur Constantine Lysaght, *b* 1876, *d* 1950: *m* 1902, Mary Nicholl, who *d* 1967 da of Adam Fettiplace Blandy, of The Warren, Abingdon:—
†John Charles Fettiplace, *b* 1909; *ed* Clifton Coll: *m* 1939, Phyllis Jean, da of late T. H. Massey, of Newcastle, NS Wales, and *d* 1976, leaving issue, John Daniel Blandy, *b* 1943, — Nicholas Richard Fettiplace, *b* 1946, — Primrose Mary, *b* 1940, — Sarah Louise, *b* 1953. *Address* – Bank of NSW, Port Kembla, NSW. —— Christopher David Blandy, *b* 1919. —— Winifred Joyce, *b* 1903.

Granddaughters of late Rev John Arthur Constantine Lysaght (*ante*):—
Issue of late Rev Nicholas Henry Lyster Lysaght, TD, DL, *b* 1911, *d* 1977: *m* 1950, Gillian Mary (6 Hafod Gdns, Ponthir, Newport, Gwent; Naval and Military Club), da of R. F. Huggett, of Risca, Gwent:—
Mary Susan, *b* 1952: *m* 1988, John Wallace Lanning, son of Maj E. C. Lanning, MBE, FSA, of S Godstone, Surrey, and has issue living, Sophie Alexandra Rose, *b* 1991. —— Philippa Jane, *b* 1954: *m* 1985, Nicholas M. S. Dale-Harris, eldest son of T. I. Dale-Harris, of Milson Rd, W14, and Mrs Allday, of Tretire, Herefordshire, and has issue living, Lucy Annabel, *b* 1986, — Polly Louise, *b* 1988, — Chloe Alexandra, *b* 1989. —— Elizabeth Anne, *b* 1961: *m* 1986, Wayne Vernon Lysaght-Mason (formerly Mason), of Walnut Tree Cottage, 112 Chester Rd, Hazel Grove, Stockport, Cheshire SK7 6HE, 2nd son of late B. A. Mason, of Walsgrave, Coventry, and has issue living, Charlotte Jennifer, *b* 1991, — Abigail Frances, *b* 1992.

Issue of late W/Cdr Philip Michael Vaughan Lysaght, Auxiliary Air Force, *b* 1914; *ka* 1943: *m* 1941, Christine, who *d* 1968, having *m* 2ndly, 1948, Cdr C. G. Procter, RN (ret) (RR9, Wood Lake, Columbus 47201, Indiana, USA), da of late W. Mackenzie Edwards, of Inverness:—
Diana Mary Philippa, *b* 1943: *m* 1962, Graham Edward Frank Snell, of 2B Moor Park Rd, SW6, and has issue living, Matthew Michael Charles, *b* 1965, — Louise Jane, *b* 1969.

PREDECESSORS – (1) JOHN Lysaght, MP for Charleville 1727; *cr Baron Lisle*, of Mount North, co Cork (peerage of Ireland) 1758; *d* 1781; *s* by his son (2) JOHN, 2nd Baron; *d* 1798; *s* by his el son (3) JOHN, 3rd Baron; *dsp* 1834; *s* by his brother (4) GEORGE, 4th Baron, *b* 1783: *m* 1st, 1810, Elizabeth, who *d* 1815, da of Samuel Knight; 2ndly, 1816, Elizabeth Anne, who *d* 1825, da of John Davy Foulkes; 3rdly, Elizabeth, da of John Church; *d* 1868; *s* by his son (5) JOHN ARTHUR, 5th Baron; *b* 1811: *m* 1837, Henrietta Anne, who *d* 1860, da of late John Church; *d* 1898; *s* by his el son (6) GEORGE WILLIAM JAMES, 6th Baron; *b* 1840; served throughout Maori War 1864-5; *m* 1868, Amy Emily, who *d* 1918, da of late Ayliffe Langford, of St Heliers, Jersey, and Ventnor, Isle of Wight; *d* 1919; *s* by hs grandson (7) JOHN NICHOLAS HORACE (son of late Hon Horace George Lysaght, only son of 6th Baron), 7th Baron and present peer.

LISTOWEL, EARL OF (Hare) Sits as BARON HARE (UK 1869) (Earl I 1822)

I hate whatever is profane

WILLIAM FRANCIS HARE, GCMG, PC, 5th Earl; *b* 28 Sept 1906; *s* 1931; *ed* Magdalene Coll, Camb; late 2nd Lt Intelligence Corps; a Co Councillor for London 1937-44, and Lord Chm of Cttees 1965-76, Dep Speaker, House of Lords since 1965; Chief Whip of Labour Party in House of Lords 1940-44, Parl Under-Sec of State for India and Burma 1944-45, Postmaster-Gen 1945-47, Sec of State for India 1947-48 and Minister of State for Colonial Affairs 1948-50, Parl Sec to Min, of Agriculture and Fisheries 1950-51, and Gov-Gen and Com-in-Ch of Ghana 1957-60; PC 1946, GCMG 1957: *m* 1st, 1933 (*m diss* 1945), Judith, da of Raoul de Marffy-Mantuano, of Budapest, Hungary; 2ndly, 1958 (*m diss* 1963), Stephanie Sandra Yvonne, da of Samuel Wise, of Toronto, Canada, and formerly wife of Hugh Currie; 3rdly, 1963, Pamela Mollie, da of late Francis Day, of Croydon, Surrey, and formerly wife of John Alexander Reid, and has issue by 1st, 2nd and 3rd *m*.

Arms – Gules, two bars and a chief indented or. **Crest** – A demi-lion rampant argent, ducally gorged or. **Supporters** – Two dragons, ermine.
Residence – 10 Downshire Hill, NW3.

SONS LIVING (*By 3rd marriage*)

FRANCIS MICHAEL (*Viscount Ennismore*), *b* 28 June 1964.
Hon Timothy Patrick, *b* 1966.

DAUGHTERS LIVING (*By 1st marriage*)

Lady Deirdre Freda Mary (*Baroness Grantley*), *b* 1935; *ed* Lady Margaret Hall, Oxford: *m* 1955, 7th Baron Grantley. *Residences* – Markenfield Hall, Ripon; 53 Lower Belgrave St, SW1.

(*By 2nd marriage*)

Lady Fiona Eve Akua, *b* 1960: *m* 1987, Christopher G. D. Mackintosh, son of Charlach Mackintosh, of Calgary, Alberta, and has issue living, Billy Douglas, *b* 1990, — Emma Frances, *b* 1988, — Zoë Beatrice, *b* 1992. *Address* – 133 Sunnyside Av, Ottawa, Ontario, Canada K15 0R2.

(*By 3rd marriage*)

Lady Diana, *b* 1965: *m* 1990, Timothy J. Voss, yst son of Douglas J. Voss, of Adelaide, Australia.

BROTHER LIVING

Hon Alan Victor, MC, *b* 1919; *ed* Eton, and New Coll, Oxford; formerly Maj Life Gds; was 1st Sec, British Embassy, Athens 1957-60; European War and Far East 1939-45 (MC): *m* 1945, Jill da of Gordon North, and has issue living, (Alan Simon) Mercury (11 Denbigh St, SW1), *b* 1948; *ed* Eton: *m* 1988, Hon (Alexandra) Elizabeth Charmian Amery, yst da of Baron Amery of Lustleigh, PC (Life Baron), and has issue living, Alice *b* 1989, — Marcia Persephone (*Viscountess Blakenham*), *b* 1946: *m* 1965, her cousin, 2nd Viscount Blakenham. *Residence* – 53 Rutland Gate, SW7. *Club* – White's.

SISTER LIVING

Lady (Ethel) Patricia (*Lady Patricia Milnes-Coates*), *b* 1912: *m* 1st, 1936, Lt-Col Charles Thomas Milnes Gaskell, Coldm Gds, who was *k* on active ser 1943 (E Ranfurly); 2ndly, 1945, Lt-Col Sir Robert Edward James Clive Milnes-Coates, 3rd Bt, DSO, Coldm Gds, who *d* 1982, and has issue living, (by 1st *m*) James, *b* 1937; *ed* Eton, and Queens' Coll, Camb: *m* 1982, Celia Elizabeth Voelcker, of Montpelier, Nevis, West Indies, and has issue living, Charles Paul *b* 1983, Anna Elizabeth *b* 1985, — Andrew, *b* 1939; *ed* Eton, and Trin Coll, Dublin, — Tom, *b* 1942; *ed* Eton, and McGill Univ, — (by 2nd *m*) (*see* Milnes-Coates, Bt). *Residence* – Helperby, York.

COLLATERAL BRANCHES LIVING

Issue of late Rt Hon John Hugh Hare, OBE, PC (*Viscount Blakenham*), 3rd son of 4th Earl:—
See Blakenham, V.

Grandchildren of late Rear-Adm Hon Richard Hare, 2nd son of 2nd Earl:—
Issue of late Capt Harry Vivian Hare, *b* 1881, *ka* 1914: *m* 1908, Ellen Louisa Marie, who *d* 1968, da of Sir Edward Hudson Hudson-Kinahan, 1st Bt:—
Richard George Windham, OBE, RN, *b* 1910; is Capt; European War 1939-43 (despatches); OBE (Mil) 1942: *m* 1937, Doreen Chetwode, who *d* 1993, da of late Rev Nixon Chetwode Ram, and has issue living, Rosemary Vivien, *b* 1939: *m* 1961, Roger Philip Laurence Chetwode Clarke, of 26 Gowan Av, SW6 6RF, and has issue living, Dominic Windham *b* 1963, Cleone Rachel Vivien *b* 1964, — Caroline Veronica, *b* 1941: *m* 1968, Richard Baden Bradley, late Capt R Fus, of 14 Moore St, SW3 2QN, and has issue living, Robert Edward Baden *b* 1969, Virginia Clare Baden *b* 1970, Victoria Elizabeth Baden *b* 1973, — Shelagh Virginia (twin), *b* 1941: *m* 1964 (*m diss* 1983), James Alan Edward Morshead, and has issue living, Charmian Juliet *b* 1966, Veronica Anne *b* 1969, Caroline Violet *b* 1971. *Residence* – Temple Grove, Heron's Ghyll, nr Uckfield, Sussex. ⸺ Emily Lavender, *b* 1912: *m* 1935, Tom E. Montgomery, who *d* of wounds received at Arnhem 1944; 2ndly, 1948, Ronald Paul Lancaster Rose, who *d* 1977 (*see* Rose, Bt *cr* 1874, colls), and has issue living (by 1st *m*), Thomas Carey *b* 1937, — Dawn Vivian *b* 1936: *m* 1963, David Connington, of Warden's Lodge, Kingston, Ilminster, Som, and has issue living, Sarah Rose *b* 1964, Lucy Clare *b* 1966.

Granddaughters of late Hon Henry Hare, 4th son of 2nd Earl:—
Issue of late Capt Percy Richard Hare, TD, *b* 1870, *d* 1937: *m* 1903, Matilda Gertrude, who *d* 1972, da of late Henry F. Tiarks, of Foxbury, Chislehurst:—
Victoria Katherine, *b* 1914: *m* 1961, as his 2nd wife, Maj George Seton Wills, Roy Wilts Yeo, who *d* 1979 (*see* Wills Bt, *cr* 1904). *Residence* – Eastridge, Ramsbury, nr Marlborough, Wilts. ⸺ Lilah Mary, *b* 1915: *m* 1st, 1935 (*m diss* 1946), Maj

George Seton Wills, Roy Wilts Yeo, who *d* 1979 (ante); 2ndly, 1946, as his 2nd wife, Col Nigel Victor Stopford Sackville, CBE, TD, who *d* 1972 (*see* E Courtown, colls). *Residence* – The Weirs, Chilton Foliat, Hungerford, Berks.

Grandchildren of late Robert Dillon Hare, son of late Hon Robert Hare, brother of 2nd Earl:—
Issue of late Brig-Gen Robert William Hare, CMG, DSO, late Norfolk Regt, *b* 1872, *d* 1953: *m* 1908, Helen Mary, who *d* 1972, da of late Lt-Col Guy Newcomen Atkinson, JP (E Kingston, colls):—
Robert Gerald Dillon, *b* 1910; Lieut-Col (ret) Roy Norfolk Regt; ADC to Gov and Com-in-Ch, Gibraltar 1937-9; European War 1939-45: *m* 1951, Evelyn Nora, da of late Thomas Pratt, and has issue living, Anthony Gerald, *b* 1956, — Carolyn Elizabeth, *b* 1952. *Residence* – 12 Camberley Rd, Norwich, NR4 6SJ. *Club* – Army and Navy. —— Elizabeth (*Elizabeth, Lady Shakespeare*) *b* 1914; Freeman of City of London 1974; Section Officer WAAF 1940-45 (despatches, Bronze Star of USA): *m* 1952, as his 2nd wife, Rt Hon Sir Geoffrey Hithersay Shakespeare, 1st Bt, who *d* 1980. *Residence* – Flat 6, Great Ash, Lubbock Rd, Chislehurst, Kent, BR7 5JZ. —— Nancy Violet (*Lady Temple*), *b* 1915: *m* 1942, Sir John Meredith Temple, and has issue living, Guy, *b* 1946: *m* 1972, Philomena Henrietta Baynes, of Seal, Sevenoaks, Kent, and has issue living, Christina Philomena Nancy *b* 1973, — Diana, *b* 1943: *m* 1965, Robert McConnell, of The Priests House, Puddington, Wirral L64 5SS, and has issue living, Frederick Bruce *b* 1970, — Anne Helen *b* 1968. *Residence* – Picton Gorse, Chester.

PREDECESSORS – (1) WILLIAM Hare, el son of late Richard Hare; MP for Cork City 1790-7, and for Athy 1798-1800; *cr Baron Ennismore*, co Kerry (peerage of Ireland) 1800, *Viscount Ennismore and Listowel* (peerage Ireland) 1816, and *Earl of Listowel* (peerage of Ireland) 1822: *m* 1st, 1772, Mary, who *d* 1810, only da of late Henry Wrixon, of Ballygiblin, co Cork; 2ndly, 1812, Anne, who *d* 1859, da of late John Latham, of Meldrum, co Tipperary; *d* 1837; *s* by his grandson (2) WILLIAM, KP (son of late Richard, Viscount Ennismore, el son of 1st Earl), 2nd Earl; *b* 1801; was Vice-Adm of Munster: *m* 1831, Maria Augusta, who *d* 1871, da of Vice-Adm William Windham, of Felbrigge Hall, and widow of George Thomas Wyndham, of Cromer Hall, Norfolk: *d* 1856; *s* by his son (3) WILLIAM, KP, 3rd Earl; *b* 1833; *cr Baron Hare* (peerage of United Kingdom) 1869; a Lord-in-Waiting to Queen Victoria in 1880: *m* 1865, Lady Ernestine Mary Brudenell-Bruce, who *d* 1936, da of 3rd Marquess of Ailesbury: *d* 1924; *s* by his el son (4) RICHARD GRANVILLE, 4th Earl, *b* 1866; sometime in Life Guards: *m* 1904, Hon Freda Vanden-Bempde-Johnstone, who *d* 1968, da of 2nd Baron Derwent; *d* 1931; *s* by his el son (5) WILLIAM FRANCIS, 5th Earl, and present peer; also Viscount Ennismore and Listowel, Baron Ennismore, and Baron Hare.

LIVERPOOL, EARL OF (Foljambe) (Earl UK 1905)
(Name pronounced "Fulljum")

Be steadfast

EDWARD PETER BERTRAM SAVILE FOLJAMBE, 5th Earl; *b* 14 Nov 1944; *s* 1969; *ed* Shrewsbury: *m* 1970, Lady Juliana Mary Alice Noel, eldest da of 5th Earl of Gainsborough, and has issue.

Arms – Sable, a bend between six escallops or, and as an honourable augmentation (granted Aug 1906) on the bend in chief, on an escutcheon vert a key surmounted by a baton in saltire or. **Crest** – 1st (of honourable augmentation granted Aug 1906), on a chapeau gules turned up ermine a lion rampant of the first, charged on the shoulder with a besant, thereon an eagle displayed sable, and resting the dexter hind paw on a plate charged with a bend azure, thereon three garbs or, and surmounted by an escutcheon argent charged with an eagle displayed also sable, charged on the breast with a fleur-de-lis also or, the lion crowned gold and supporting with the fore paws a man-of-war's church pennant proper; 2nd, a seaweed rock proper, thereon a sea-lion sejant azure resting the *dexter* paw on an escutcheon per fesse wavy argent and azure, in chief a cormorant sable, beaked and legged gules, holding in the beak a branch of seaweed, called laver, inverted vert (*Liverpool*), and in base a hawk, wings elevated and addorsed argent (*Hawkesbury*); 3rd a man's leg unarmed, couped at the thigh, quarterly or and sable spurred gold. **Supporters** – On either side a griffin, wings elevated or, beaked, membered, ducally gorged, and on the wing three fleurs-de-lis one and two all azure, that on the *dexter* side charged on the breast with a torteau thereon a cross-crosslet fitchée argent (the badge of *Howard*), and that on the *sinister* with a pellet thereon a stag's head cabossed also argent (*Cavendish*).
Residences – 56 Bolingbroke Rd, W14 0AH; Scofton Farm House, Osberton, Nr Worksop, Notts S81 0OE. *Clubs* – Turf, Pratt's.

SONS LIVING

LUKE MARMADUKE PETER SAVILE (*Viscount Hawkesbury*), *b* 25 March 1972.
Hon Ralph Edward Anthony Savile, *b* 1974.

SISTER LIVING (*Raised to the rank of an Earl's daughter* 1970)

Lady Jane Rosamond Mary, *b* 1943; *ed* Durham Univ (BA); SRN 1982. *Residence* – Kilvington Hall, Thirsk, N Yorks.

AUNT LIVING

Ursula Susan Annette Mary, *b* 1916: *m* 1939, Maj Stephen Carrington Smith, TD, of Dawnedge, Aspley Guise, Beds, and has issue living, Maj Nigel Antony Carrington (Redwings, Orchard Close, Brancaster Staithe, Kings Lynn, Norfolk), *b* 1943: *m* 1980, Jane Elizabeth Lee, and has issue living, Guy Savile *b* 1983, Miles Stephen *b* 1985, Sarah Jane *b* 1982, Diana Mary *b* 1989, — Angela Selina Carrington, *b* 1948: *m* 1971, John Bunker, of Woburn Lane, Aspley Guise, Bucks MK17 8JH, and has issue living, Nicholas James *b* 1977, Alice Louise *b* 1974.

PREDECESSORS – (1) *Sir* CHARLES Jenkinson, 7th Bt, el son of Col Charles Jenkinson (who was 2nd in command of the Blues at Dettingen, and commanded them at Fontenoy, 3rd son of Sir Robert Jenkinson, 2nd Bt), *b* 1729, held many high offices of State, and was *cr Baron Hawkesbury*, of co Gloucester (peerage of Great Britain) 1786, and *Earl of Liverpool* 1796; *d* 1808; *s* by his el son (2) ROBERT BANKS, KG, 2nd Earl, *b* 1770; called to the House of Lords 1803, in the lifetime of his father; Prime Min and First Lord of the Treasury 1812-27; *dsp* 1828; *s* by his half-brother (3) CHARLES CECIL COPE, GCB, 3rd Earl, *b* 1784; Lord Steward 1841-6: *m* 1810, Julia Evelyn Medley, who *d* 1814, only child of Sir George Shuckburgh-Evelyn, 6th Bt; *d* 1851, when the peerages became ext and the baronetcy reverted to his cousin; the *Barony of Hawkesbury* was revived 1893, and the *Earldom of Liverpool* 1905 in the person of his grandson and principal heir (4) CECIL GEORGE SAVILE Foljambe, PC, el son of late George Savile Foljambe, of Osberton, Notts, and Aldwarke, Yorks, by his 2nd wife, Selina Charlotte, 2nd da and co heiress (el leaving issue) of 3rd Earl of Liverpool (*cr* 1796, *ext*), and 3rd Baron Hawkesbury (*cr* 1786, *ext*), and widow of William Charles, Viscount Milton; *b* 1846; a Lord-in-Waiting to Queen Victoria 1894-5, and Lord Steward of King Edward VII's Household 1905-7; MP for N Nottinghamshire (*L*) 1880-85, and for Notts, Mansfield Div 1885-92; *cr Baron Hawkesbury*, of Haselbech, co Northampton, and of Ollerton, Sherwood Forest, co Nottingham (peerage of United Kingdom) 1893, and *Viscount Hawkesbury*, of Kirkham, co York, and of Mansfield, co Nottingham, and *Earl of Liverpool* (peerage of United Kingdom) 1905; PC 1906: *m* 1st, 1869, Louisa Blanche, who *d* 1871, el da of late Frederick John Howard, of Compton Place, Sussex (E Carlisle, colls); 2ndly, 1877, Susan Louisa, who *d* 1917, el da of late Lieut-Col William Henry Frederick Cavendish, of West Stoke, Sussex, and 47 Cromwell Houses, SW, 2nd cousin both paternally and maternally of his 1st wife; *d* 1907; *s* by his el son (5) ARTHUR WILLIAM DE BRITO SAVILE, GCB, GCMG, GBE, MVO, PC, 2nd Earl, *b* 1870; was State Steward and Chamberlain to Lord-Lieut of Ireland 1906-8, Comptroller of HM's Household 1909-12, Gov of New Zealand 1912-17, and First Gov-Gen of the Dominion of New Zealand 1917-20: *m* 1897, Hon Annette Louise Monck, GBE, who *d* 1948, only da of 5th Viscount Monck; *d* 1941; *s* by his half-brother (6) GERALD WILLIAM FREDERICK SAVILE, DSO, 3rd Earl *b* 1878; Lieut-Col King's Roy Rifle Corps; S Africa 1899-1902; 1914-18 War as OC 21st Bn: *m* 1909, Constance Isabelle, who *d* 1976, only da of John Holden, of Nuttall Temple, Notts; *d* 1962; *s* by his brother (7) ROBERT ANTHONY EDWARD ST ANDREW SAVILE, 4th Earl; *b* 1887; *d* 1969; *s* by his great-nephew (8) EDWARD PETER BERTRAM SAVILE (grandson of Maj Hon Bertram Marmaduke Osbert Savile Foljambe, MC, 6th son of 1st Earl), 5th Earl and present peer; also Viscount Hawkesbury, and Baron Hawkesbury.

LLEWELYN-DAVIES, BARONY OF (Llewelyn Davies) (Extinct 1981)

DAUGHTERS LIVING OF LIFE BARON

Hon Melissa, *b* 1945; documentary film maker: *m* 1974, Christopher Desmond Curling (*see* Bonham, Bt, 1990 Edn), of 3 Richmond Crescent, N1, and has issue living, Richard William Samuel, *b* 1983, — Allegra Rose Elizabeth, *b* 1979.
Hon Harriet Lydia Rose, *b* 1955.
Hon Rebecca, *b* 1957: *m* 1983, Hon Daniel William Rea, of 4 Queensgate Villas, Victoria Park Rd, E9, 2nd son of 3rd Baron Rae, and has issue living (*see* Rae, B).

WIDOW LIVING OF LIFE BARON

ANNIE PATRICIA, PC (*Baroness Llewelyn-Davies of Hastoe*) (see that title).

LLEWELYN-DAVIES OF HASTOE, BARONESS (Llewelyn-Davies) (Life Baroness 1967)

ANNIE PATRICIA LLEWELYN DAVIES, PC, da of C. P. Parry, of Prenton, Cheshire, *b* 16 July 1915; *ed* Liverpool Coll, Huyton, and Girton Coll, Camb (Hon Fellow 1978); Dir of Africa Educational Trust 1960-69; a Member of Board of Govs of Hosp for Sick Children, Great Ormond St, since 1955 (Chm 1967-69); co-Chm of Women's Nat Commn since 1976; a Baroness in Waiting (Govt Whip) 1960-70; Opposition Ch Whip since 1973 (Dep Ch Whip 1971-72); Ch Whip House of Lords and Capt of the Hon Corps of Gentlemen-at-Arms 1974-79, Principal Dep Chm of Cttees and Chm Select on the European Communities 1982-86; *cr Baroness Llewelyn-Davies of Hastoe*, of Hastoe, co Hertford (Life Baroness) 1967, and PC 1975: *m* 1943, Baron Llewelyn-Davies (Life Baron), who *d* 1981, and has issue (see that title).
Residences – Flat 15, 9-11 Belsize Grove, NW3; Carpenters Yard, Tring, Herts.

LLOYD, BARONY OF (Lloyd) (Extinct 1985)

DAUGHTERS LIVING OF SECOND BARON

Hon Davina Margaret, *b* 1943. *Residence* – 11 Morpeth Mansions, Morpeth Terr, SW1.
Hon Laura Blanche Bridget, *b* 1960. *Residence* – 4 Patience Rd, SW11.

WIDOW LIVING OF SECOND BARON

Lady VICTORIA JEAN MARJORIE MABELL OGILVY (*Baroness Lloyd*) (Clouds Hill, Offley, Hitchin, Herts), da of 12th Earl of Airlie: *m* 1942, the 2nd Baron, MBE, DL, who *d* 1985.

LLOYD GEORGE OF DWYFOR, EARL (Lloyd George) (Earl UK 1945)

OWEN LLOYD GEORGE, 3rd Earl; *b* 28 April 1924; *s* 1968; *ed* Oundle; an underwriting member of Lloyd's; carried the Sword at Investiture of HRH the Prince of Wales, Caernarvon Castle 1969; a Member of Historic Buildings Council for Wales since 1971, and of Court, Nat Museum of Wales, since 1978; 1939-45 War as Capt Welsh Guards; DL Dyfed: *m* 1949 (*m diss* 1982), Ruth Margaret, only da of late Richard Coit, of 18 Thurloe Sq, SW7; 2ndly, 1982, (Cecily) Josephine, el da of Maj Sir Alexander Penrose Gordon Cumming, MC, 5th Bt, widow of 2nd Earl of Woolton, and formerly wife of 3rd Baron Forres, and has issue by 1st *m*.

Arms – Azure over water barry wavy in base a bridge of one arch proper, on a chief argent a portcullis sable between two daffodils stalked and leaved also proper. **Crest** – A demi-dragon gules holding between the claws a portcullis sable. **Supporters** – *Dexter*, a dragon or; *sinister*, an eagle wings addorsed or; each gorged with a collar vert.
Residences – Ffynone, Boncath, Pembrokeshire SA37 0HQ; 47 Burton Court, SW3 4SZ.
Clubs – White's, Pratt's.

SONS LIVING (By 1st marriage)

DAVID RICHARD OWEN (*Viscount Gwynedd*) (Cobblers, The Old Hill, Wherwell, nr Andover, Hants SP11 7JB), *b* 22 Jan 1951; *ed* Eton: *m* 1985, Pamela Alexandra, only da of late Alexander Kleyff, and has issue:—
    SONS LIVING *Hon* William Alexander, *b* 16 May 1986, *Hon* Frederick Owen, *b* 1987.
Hon Robert John Daniel (23 Shek O, Big Wave Bay Rd, Hong Kong), *b* 1952; *ed* Eton (King's Scholar), and Univ Coll, Oxford; Chm Lloyd George Mgmnt Ltd (Hong Kong); author of *A Guide to Asian Stock Markets* (1989), and *The East West Pendulum* (1991): *m* 1st, 1978 (*m diss* 1991), Kim, only da of Carl Fischer, of New York City; 2ndly, 1992, Donna Jean, only da of John Archbold Hufty, of Palm Beach, Florida, and has issue living (by 1st *m*), Richard Joseph, *b* 1983, — Alice Margaret, *b* 1987, — (by 2nd *m*) Alexander Gwilym, *b* 1994, — Julia Frances, *b* 1993.

DAUGHTER LIVING (By 1st marriage)

Lady Julia Margaret Violet, *b* 1958: *m* 1984, Simon Erroll Prior-Palmer, and has issue (*see* Linlithgow, M).

SISTER LIVING

Lady Valerie Davidia, *b* 1918: *m* 1940, Sir Goronwy Hopkin Daniel, KCVO, CB, DPhil, and has issue living, David Llewelyn (31 Westway, Petts Wood, Kent), *b* 1950: *m* 1977, Mary Helen, da of A Kent Maytham, of Glen Druid, Cabinteely, co Dublin, and has issue living, Owen Maytham *b* 1982, Katharine Megan *b* 1984, — Anne Margaret, *b* 1944: *m* 1977, Bernard Thomas Harrison, of 29 St Stephen's Rd, Ealing W13, and has issue living, Florence Ceridwen Dorothy *b* 1977, Eleanor Mary Gwyneth *b* 1979, — Gwyneth Roberta, *b* 1946: *m* 1971, Avi Shlaim, of 8 Chalfont Rd, Oxford, and has issue living, Tamar Megan *b* 1980. *Residence* – Cae Ffynnon, St Michael's Rd, Llandaff, Cardiff.

COLLATERAL BRANCH LIVING

    Issue of late Rt Hon Gwilym Lloyd George, TD (*Viscount Tenby*), yr son of 1st Earl Lloyd George of Dwyfor, *b* 1894, *d* 1971; *cr* Viscount Tenby 1957:—
See that title.

PREDECESSORS – *Rt Hon* DAVID Lloyd George, OM, son of late William George, of Bulford, Pembrokeshire; *b* 1863; Hon DCL Oxford 1908 and Durham 1919, Hon LLD Wales 1908, Glasgow 1917, Edinburgh 1918, Cambridge 1920, and Birmingham 1921, Hon DLitt Sheffield 1919, Hon Fellow Jesus Coll, Oxford 1910; admitted Solicitor 1884; sometime a partner in the legal firm of Lloyd George and George, of Criccieth; a JP, DL, and County Alderman for Caernarvonshire (Chm of Quarter Sessions 1929-38), Prior and Chancellor of the Priory for Wales of Order of St John of Jerusalem, a KGStJ, and a Freeman of many towns; appointed Pres of the Board of Trade Dec 1905, Chancellor of the Exchequer April 1908, Min of Munitions May 1915 (also a Member of Cabinet War Council), and Sec of State for War and Member of Army Council July 1916; was Prime Minister and First Lord of the Treasury Dec 1916 to Oct 1922; elected Lord Rector of Edinburgh Univ 1920; Sessional Chm of Parliamentary Liberal Party 1924-31; appointed Constable of Caernarvon Castle 1908; Ch British Representative at Paris Peace Conference 1919 (1914-15 star, War and Victory medals, Grand Cordon of Legion of Honour, and Italian Order of St Maurice and St Lazarus); sat as MP for Caernarvon Dist (*L*) April 1890 to Dec 1944; *cr Viscount Gwynedd*, of Dwyfor, co Caernarvon, and *Earl Lloyd George of Dwyfor* (peerage of United Kingdom) 1945: *m* 1st, 1888, *Dame* Margaret, GBE, LLD, JP, who *d* 1941, da of Richard Owen, of Mynydd Ednyfed, Criccieth; 2ndly, 1943, Frances Louise, CBE, who *d* 1972, da of John Stevenson, of Wallington, Surrey; *d* 1945; *s* by his el son (2) RICHARD, 2nd Earl, *b* 1889: *m* 1st, 1917 (*m diss* 1933), Roberta Ida Freeman, who *d* 1966, da of Sir Robert McAlpine, 1st Bt; 2ndly, 1935, Winifred Emily, who *d* 1982, da of late Thomas William Peedle, and formerly wife of Henry Michael Calve; *d* 1968; *s* by his son (3) OWEN, 3rd Earl and present peer; also Viscount Gwynedd.

LLOYD OF BERWICK, BARON (Lloyd) (Life Baron 1993)

ANTHONY JOHN LESLIE LLOYD, PC, son of Edward John Boydell Loyd, of Little Bucksteep, Dallington, Sussex; *b* 9 May 1929; *ed* Eton, and Trin Coll, Camb; late Coldstream Gds; DL E Sussex 1983; Bar Inner Temple 1955, QC 1967, Attorney-Gen to HRH The Prince of Wales 1969-77, Judge of High Court of Justice (Queen's Bench Div) 1978-84, Lord Justice of Appeal 1984-93, since when a Lord of Appeal in Ordinary; former Memb Top Salaries Review Body, Memb Criminal Law Revision Cttee since 1981; Chm Civil Ser Security Appeals Panel since 1982, Security Commn since 1992; Memb Parole Board 1983-84; Chm Glyndebourne Arts Trust since 1975; Dir RAM since 1979; *cr* Knt 1978, PC 1984, and *Baron Lloyd of Berwick*, of Ludlay, co E Sussex (Life Baron) 1993: *m* 1960, Jane Helen Violet, High Sheriff of E Sussex 1994, da of Cornelius William Shelford, of Chailey Place, nr Lewes, Sussex.

Arms – Per fess gules and or a pale per fess and a fess per fess, in chief an escallop between two hedgehogs and in base a hedgehog between two escallops all counterchanged. **Crest** – A hedgehog gules spined or holding in its dexter claw an ostrich plume erect proper.
Residences – Ludlay, Berwick, E Sussex; 68 Strand-on-the-Green, Chiswick W4 3PF.
Club – Brooks's.

LLOYD OF HAMPSTEAD, BARONY OF (Lloyd) (Extinct 1992)

DAUGHTERS LIVING OF LIFE BARON

Hon Naomi Katharine, *b* 1946: *m* 1967, Peter Campbell Hodges, of 3 Cleveland Rd, Barnes, SW13, and has issue.
Hon Corinne Deborah (14 Locarno Av, Kallista, Melbourne, Victoria 3791, Australia), *b* 1951; MA: *m* 1st, 1971 (*m diss* 1977), Dr Michael Newman, MB, BCh; 2ndly, 1990, Hugh Henderson, MBA.

WIDOW LIVING OF LIFE BARON

RUTH EMMA CECILIA (*Baroness Lloyd of Hampstead*), da of Carl Tulla: *m* 1940, Baron Lloyd of Hampstead, QC (Life Baron), who *d* 1992. *Residence* – Flat 2, 12 King's Gdns, Hove, E. Sussex BN3 2PF.

LLOYD OF KILGERRAN, BARONY OF (Lloyd) (Extinct 1991)

DAUGHTERS LIVING OF LIFE BARON

Hon Elizabeth Mary Gerran, *b* 1944; JP S London since 1989: *m* 1968, Daniel Gerard Robins, QC, BSc, LLB, who *d* 1989, of 66 Church Road, Wimbledon, SW19, and has issue living, Charlotte Jane Gerran, *b* 1971, — Sophie Elizabeth Gerran, *b* 1974, — Anneli Mary Gerran, *b* 1976.
Hon Catherine Gerran, *b* 1947: *m* 1972, Philip Gwynfryn Edwards, of 2 Woodhill House, Kentish Lane, Essendon, Herts AL9 6JY, and has issue living, Thomas Gerran, *b* 1982, — Rosalind Gerran, *b* 1975, — Bryony Gerran, *b* 1976, — Felicity Gerran, *b* 1980.

WIDOW LIVING OF LIFE BARON

PHYLLIS MARY (*Baroness Lloyd of Kilgerran*), da of late Ronald Shepherd, JP, of Chilworth, Hants: *m* 1940, Baron Lloyd of Kilgerran, CBE, QC (Life Baron), who *d* 1991. *Residence* – 15 Haymeads Drive, Esher, Surrey.

Lloyd, see Baron Geoffrey-Lloyd.

LOCH, BARONY OF (Loch) (Extinct 1991)

DAUGHTER LIVING OF FOURTH BARON (*by 1st marriage*)

Hon Sara Nan, *b* 1949. *Residence* – The Old House, The Close, Blandford, Dorset DT11 7HA.

DAUGHTER LIVING OF THIRD BARON (*by 4th marriage*)

Hon Allegra Helen, *b* 1982.

DAUGHTERS LIVING OF SECOND BARON

Hon Jean Sibyl, *b* 1908: *m* 1930, Guy Arthur Newman, who *d* 1982, and has issue (*see* Newman, Bt, *cr* 1912, colls). *Residence* – Stanners Hill Manor, Chobham, Surrey.

Hon Helen, MBE, *b* 1919; MBE (Civil) 1987; DL Perthshire 1980, JP 1976: *m* 1947, (George) Ronald Service, who *d* 1961, and has issue living, James Ronald, *b* 1948: *m* 1976, Mrs Gabrielle Armitage, da of late Philip Lloyd, of Thornton Hough, Wirral, Cheshire. *Residence* – Kinfauns House, Kinfauns, by Perth.

WIDOW LIVING OF THIRD BARON

SYLVIA BARBARA, da of Alexander Gordon Beauchamp Cameron, of Delmahoy, Midlothian, and formerly wife of Christopher Beauchamp-Wilson; *m* 2ndly, 1975, as his 4th wife, Maj the 3rd Baron Loch, who *d* 1982; 3rdly, 1984, Richard G.P. Hawkins. *Residence* – Cornard Tye House, Sudbury, Suffolk.

WIDOW LIVING OF FOURTH BARON

DAVINA JULIA (*Baroness Loch*), da of late FitzHerbert Wright, of Collihole Farm, Chagford, Devon (*see* V Powerscourt, 1990 Edn), and formerly wife of Sir Richard Boughey, 10th Bt: *m* 1979, as his 2nd wife, Maj the 4th Baron Loch, MC, who *d* 1991, when the title became extinct. *Residence* – Bratton House, Westbury, Wilts; Lochluichart by Garve, Ross-shire.

LOCKWOOD, BARONESS (Hall) (Life Baroness 1977)

BETTY LOCKWOOD, da of Arthur Lockwood; *b* 22nd Jan 1924; *ed* Eastborough Council Sch, Dewsbury, and Ruskin Coll, Oxford; a DL for W Yorks (1987); Ch Woman Officer, Labour Party 1967-75, Chm Equal Opportunities Comm 1975-83; since when Pres Birkbeck Coll, London Univ; Pro-Chancellor of Univ of Bradford since 1987, and Chm of Council since 1992; Member of Council Advertising Standards Authority since 1983, and Leeds Development Corpn since 1988; *cr Baroness Lockwood*, of Dewsbury, co W Yorks (Life Baroness) 1977: *m* 1978, Lt-Col Cedric Hall, who *d* 1988. *Residence* – 6 Sycamore Dr, Addingham, Ilkley, W Yorks LS29 0NY.

Loftus, Viscount; son of Marquess of Ely.

LONDESBOROUGH, BARON (Denison) (Baron UK 1850)

ADVERSA VIRTUTE REPELLO
I repel adversity with courage

RICHARD JOHN DENISON, 9th Baron; *b* 2 July 1959; *s* 1968; *ed* Wellington and Exeter Univ: *m* 1987, Rikki, da of J. E. Morris, of Bayswater, London, and has issue.

𝕬rms – Quarterly: 1st and 4th ermine, a bend azure, cotised sable, between an unicorn's fitchée in base gules, *Denison*; 2nd and 3rd argent, a shake fork between three mullets one and two sable, *Conyngham*. 𝕮rest – 1st, issuant from clouds a dexter arm in bend proper, vested gules, cuffed ermine, and charged with a covered cup or, pointing with the fore finger to an estoile radiated gold, *Denison*; 2nd, an unicorn's head erased argent, armed and maned or, *Conyngham*. 𝕾upporters – *Dexter*, a horse argent, maned, unguled, and charged on the shoulder with an eagle displayed or, with a crescent sable for difference; *sinister*, a stag argent, attired, unguled, and charged on the shoulder with a griffin's head erased or, with a crescent sable for difference.
Residence – Edw Cottage, Aberedw, Powys.

SON LIVING

Hon JAMES (JACK) FREDERICK, *b* 4 June 1990.

DAUGHTER LIVING

Hon Laura Rose, *b* 1992.

DAUGHTER LIVING OF FOURTH EARL

Lady Zinnia Rosemary *b* (*posthumous*), 1937: *m* 1st, 1957 (*m diss* 1961), Peter Comins, oil exec; 2ndly, 1961 (*m diss* 1964), John David Leslie Melville (author of books on wild life, including *Raising Daisy Rothschild*), who *d* 1984 (*see* E Leven and Melville, colls, 1980 Edn); 3rdly, 1964 (*m diss* 1967), Maj Hugh Cantlie, Scots Gds; 4thly, 1968, (Ralph) John Hamilton Pollock, who *d* 1980 (*see* Pollock, Bt, colls); 5thly, 1982, James Hubert Judd (*see* E Erne, colls, 1973-74 Edn), and has issue living, (by 1st *m*) Timothy Hugo POLLOCK, *b* 1958, who assumed surname of Pollock 1968: *m* 1993, Jeanie Anne, elder da of Capt Simon Hugh Walford (*see* B Bellew), — (by 3rd *m*) Charles Edgar, *b* 1965. *Residence* – Stewkley Grange, Leighton Buzzard, Beds.

WIDOW LIVING OF SEVENTH BARON

JOCELYN HELEN (*Jocelyn, Baroness Londesborough*) (Anchor Cottage, Bembridge, Isle of Wight) da of late Lt-Cdr Hugh Duppa Collins, RN: *m* 1952, as his 3rd wife, the 7th Baron, who *d* 1967.

COLLATERAL BRANCH LIVING

Granddaughter of late Hon Henry Charles Denison, 3rd son of 1st Baron:—
Issue of late Commodore Edward Conyngham Denison, MVO, RN, *b* 1888, *d* 1960: *m* 1919, Maira Amy Brabazon (Ilsum House, Tetbury, Glos), da of late Lt-Col Sir Charles Henry Brabazon Heaton-Ellis, CBE, of Wyddiall Hall, Buntingford, Herts:—
Sonia Myrtle, *b* 1921: *m* 1st, 1940, Major Edgard FitzGerald Heathcoat-Amory, Roy Devon Yeo, who was *ka* in Normandy 1944 (*see* Heathcoat-Amory, Bt, colls); 2ndly, 1947, Brigadier Roderick Heathcoat-Amory, MC, The Royals (*see* Heathcoat-Amory, Bt). *Residence* – Allington Grange, Chippenham, Wilts SN14 6LW.

PREDECESSORS – (1) *Lord* ALBERT Conyngham, KCH, FRS, 2nd surviving son of Henry, 1st Marquess Conyngham, by Elizabeth, da of Joseph Denison of Denbies, co Surrey; *b* 1805; was Vice-Adm of Yorkshire; assumed the surname of Denison by Roy licence 1849: *cr Baron Londesborough*, of Londesborough, co York (peerage of United Kingdom) 1850: *m* 1st, 1833, Henrietta Maria, who *d* 1841, da of 1st Baron Forester; 2ndly, 1847, Ursula Lucy Grace (who *d* 1883, having *m* 2ndly, Rt Hon Lord Otho Augustus Fitzgerald, PC, MP, who *d* 1882 (D Leinster)), da of Rear-Adm Hon Charles Bridgeman (E Bradford); *d* 1860; *s* by his son (2) WILLIAM HENRY FORESTER, 2nd Baron, *b* 1834; MP for Beverley (*L*) 1857-9 and for Scarborough 1859-60; *cr Viscount Raincliffe*, of Raincliffe, co York, and *Earl of Londesborough* (peerage of United Kingdom) 1887: *m* 1863, Lady Edith Frances Wilhelmine Somerset, who *d* 1915, da of 7th Duke of Beaufort; *d* 1900: *s* by his son (3) WILLIAM FRANCES HENRY, KCVO, 2nd Earl, *b* 1864: *m* 1887, Lady Grace Augusta Fane, who *d* 1933, da of 12th Earl of Westmorland; *d* 1917; *s* by his son (4) GEORGE FRANCIS WILLIAM HENRY, 3rd Earl, *b* 1892; *d* 1920; *s* by his brother (5) HUGO WILLIAM CECIL, 4th Earl, *b* 1894: *m* 1935, Marigold Rosemary Joyce (who *d* 1976, having *m* 2ndly, 1948 (*m diss* 1954), Zygmund de Lubicz-Bakanowski), da of late Edgar Lubbock, LLB (B Avebury, colls); *d* 1937, when the Earldom and Viscountcy became ext, and the Barony passed to his kinsman (6) ERNEST WILLIAM, MBE (son of late Rear Adm Hon Albert Denison Somerville Denison, 2nd son of 1st Baron), 6th Baron; *b* 1876; Capt RN; MBE (Civil) 1946: *m* 1905, Sybil May, who *d* 1963, da of late Capt H. T. Anley, of The First, Binstead, Isle of Wight; *d* 1963; *s* by his cousin (7) CONYNGHAM CHARLES, DSO, RN (only son of Cdr Hon Conyngham Albert Denison, RN, 4th son of 1st Baron), 7th Baron, *b* 1885; Cdr RN: *m* 1st 1912 (*m diss* 1925), Vera, da of late Francis Hugh Baxendale; 2ndly, 1926, Mabel, who *d* 1951, da of Matthew George Megaw; 3rdly, 1952, Jocelyn Helen, da of late Lt-Cdr Hugh Duppa Collins, RN; *d* 1967; *s* by his cousin (8) JOHN ALBERT LISTER, TD (only son of Hon Harold Albert Denison, 5th son of 1st Baron). 8th Baron; *b* 1901: *m* 1st 1949 (*m diss* 1953), Lesley Maxwell Gordon, OBE, da of late Lt-Col Herbert Forbes Churchill, OBE, and widow of Lt-Col J. H. Wooldridge, Indian Army; 2ndly, 1957, (Elizabeth) Ann, who *d* 1994, da of late Edward Little Sale, ICS, and formerly wife of late Thomas Chambers Windsor Roe; *d* 1968; *s* by his son (9) RICHARD JOHN, 9th Baron and present peer.

LONDONDERRY, MARQUESS OF (Vane-Tempest-Stewart) Sits as EARL VANE (UK 1823)
(Marquess I 1816)

The dragon's crest is to be feared

ALEXANDER CHARLES ROBERT VANE-TEMPEST-STEWART, 9th Marquess; *b* 7 Sept 1937; *s* 1955; *ed* Eton: *m* 1st, 1958 (*m diss* 1971), Nicolette Elaine Katherine, who *d* 1993, only da of late Michael Harrison, of Netherhampton House, Netherhampton, Wilts, and 33 Chesham Place, SW1; 2ndly, 1972, Doreen Wells, and has issue by 1st and 2nd *m*.

Arms – Quarterly: 1st and 4th or, a bend counter compony argent and azure, between two lions rampant, gules, *Stewart*; 2nd argent, a bend engrailed, between six martlets, three and three, sable, *Tempest*; 3rd azure, three sinister gauntlets, *Vane*. **Crest** – 1st, a dragon statant or, *Stewart*; 2nd, a griffin's head erased, per pale argent and sable, beaked gules, *Tempest*; 3rd, a dexter cubit arm in armour, the hand in a gauntlet proper grasping a sword also proper, pommel and hilt or, *Vane*. **Supporters** – *Dexter*, a Moor, wreathed about the temples argent and azure, holding in the exterior hand a shield of the last, garnished or, charged with the sun in splendour gold; *sinister*, a lion or, collared argent, the collar charged with three mullets sable.

SONS LIVING *(By 2nd marriage)*

FREDERICK AUBREY (*Viscount Castlereagh*), *b* 6 Sept 1972.
Lord Reginald Alexander, *b* 1977.

DAUGHTERS LIVING *(By 1st marriage)*

Lady Sophia Frances Anne, *b* 1959: *m* 1987, Jonathan Mark Pilkington, yst son of Ronald Charles Leslie Pilkington, of Hill House, Stanstead Abbots, Herts, and has issue living, Hermione Alice, *b* 1989, — Allegra Rose, *b* 1991.
Lady Cosima Maria Gabriella (*Lady John Somerset*), *b* 1961: *m* 1st, 1982 (*m diss* 1986), Cosmo Joseph Fry, son of Jeremy Fry, of Bath; 2ndly, 1990, Lord John Robert Somerset, yst son of 11th Duke of Beaufort, and has issue (by 2nd *m*) (*see* D Beaufort).

SISTERS LIVING

Lady Jane Antonia Frances (*Baroness Rayne*), *b* 1932: *m* 1965, as his 2nd wife, Baron Rayne (Life Baron), of 33 Robert Adam St, W1M 5AH, and has issue (*see* B Rayne).
Lady Annabel, *b* 1934: *m* 1st, 1954 (*m diss* 1975), Marcus Oswald Hornby Lecky Birley, son of late Sir Oswald Hornby Lecky Birley, MC; 2ndly, 1978, Sir James Michael Goldsmith, and has had issue (by 1st husband), Rupert Oswald Robin, *b* 1955; missing, presumed drowned at sea, Lomé, W Africa, 1986, — Robin Marcus, *b* 1958, — India Jane Romaine, *b* 1961: *m* 1st, 1981 (*m diss* 1988), Jonathan Halsey Luke Colchester, son of Rev Halsey Sparrowe Colchester, CMG, OBE; 2ndly, 1993, Francis Bruce Pike, son of Esmund Francis Victor Wallace Pike, — (by 2nd husband) Zacharias Frank, *b* 1975, — Benjamin James, *b* 1980, — Jemima Marcelle, *b* 1974. *Residences* – Ormeley Lodge, Ham Common, Surrey; Cavenham House, Park Lane, Cranford, Middx.

Lady Mairi Elizabeth (*Lady Mairi Bury*), *b* 1921; is a JP for co Down: *m* 1940 (*m diss* 1958), Lt-Col Derek William Charles, Viscount Bury, late 13th/18th Hussars, who *d* 1968, el son of 9th Earl of Albemarle. *Residence* – Mount Stewart, Newtownards, co Down.

COLLATERAL BRANCHES LIVING

Grandson of late Lord Adolphus Frederick Charles William Vane-Tempest, MP, 3rd son of 3rd Marquess:—
Issue of late Major Francis Adolphus Vane-Tempest, *b* 1863, *d* 1932: *m* 1901, Gertrude Magdalen, who *d* 1925, da of late F. A. Elliot:—
Francis Charles Joseph, *b* 1911; *ed* Downside; 1939-45 War: *m* 1st, 1931 (*m* annulled 1935), Pamela Mary, who *d* 1953, da of Maj Edwin Abel Smith, formerly of Great Kimble House, Princes Risborough, Bucks; 2ndly, 1936 (*m diss* 1952), Penelope Joan, da of Edmund Henry Bevan, JP (*see* B Grantley, 1942 Edn). *Residence* – Anne Boleyn Cottage, New St, Henley-on-Thames.

Grandson of late Charles Henry Vane-Tempest, son of late Lord Ernest M'Donnell Vane-Tempest, 4th son of 3rd Marquess:—
Issue of late Ernest Charles William Vane-Tempest, DSC, *b* 1894, *d* 1957: *m* 1st, 1918 (*m diss* 1933), Aline Mary Loftus, who *d* 1967, da of late Loftus St George (St George, Bt, colls); 2ndly, 1933, Anne Elizabeth, who *d* 1968, da of Capt Evan Humphreys, of Borth-y-gest, Portmadoc, Caernarvonshire:—
(By 1st *m*) Charles Stewart M'Donnell, *b* 1921; *ed* Haileybury; 1939-45 War with RAF: *m* 1st, 1948 (*m diss* 1956), Diana Constance, da of late Maj Kenneth Arthur Seth-Smith; 2ndly, 1957, Maija-Liisa, da of Col Erkki Elias Puomi, and has issue living, (by 1st *m*) (Charles) Stewart Martin St George (Lower House Farm, The Endway, Steeple Bumpstead, Suffolk CB9 7DW), *b* 1950; *ed* Stowe: *m* 1st, 1972 (*m diss* 1976), Pamela Elizabeth, da of M. Jenkin; 2ndly, 1977, Jillian Barbara, da of Dr John Evelyn Bulow, of Bondi, 34 Shirley Av, Cheam, Surrey, and has issue living (by 2nd *m*), Christopher James Stewart *b* 1978, James Alexander Stewart *b* 1981, — Aline Elizabeth Stewart, *b* 1952: *m* 1984, Philip John Lester Nash, son of Lancelot Lester Nash, of Veronica Cottage, Thruxton, Hants, and has issue living, Jonathan Guy Randell *b* 1988, Camilla Judith *b* 1986, — (by 2nd *m*) Charles Erkki William, *b* 1958: *m* 1981, Stina Maria Veronica, da of Per-Erik Tornblom, of Virkby, Finland, — Donald John Ernest, *b* 1961: *m* 1985, Pirkko Maritta, da of Vaino Salminen, of Alastaro, Finland, and has issue living, Thomas Christopher *b* 1986, — Harold Michael St George, *b* 1962: *m* 1987, Merja Anneli, da of Teuvo Karinkanta, of Vantaa, Finland, — Mary-Anne Elizabeth (twin), *b* 1962. *Residence* – Ollaksentie 20, SF-02940 Esbo 94, Finland.

PREDECESSORS – **(1)** ROBERT Stewart, MP for co Down 1770-89; *cr Baron Londonderry* (peerage of Ireland) 1789, *Viscount Castlereagh* (peerage of Ireland) 1795, *Earl of Londonderry* (peerage of Ireland) 1796, and *Marquess of Londonderry* (peerage of Ireland) 1816; *d* 1821; *s* by his el son **(2)** ROBERT, KG, 2nd Marquess; a distinguished statesman; *dsp* 1822; *s* by his half-brother **(3)** CHARLES WILLIAM, KG, GCB, GCH, 3rd Marquess, who had in 1814 been *cr Baron Stewart*, of Stewart's Court and Ballylawn, co Donegal (peerage of United Kingdom); *b* 1778; a distinguished general and diplomatist, Lord-Lieut of co Durham, Custos Rotulorum of cos Londonderry and Down, and Col 2nd Life Guards; *cr Viscount Seaham* and *Earl Vane* (peerage of United Kingdom) 1823, with remainder to the male issue of his 2nd marriage; *d* 1854, when the Viscountcy of Seaham and Earldom of Vane passed to his 2nd son George Henry (infra), and the marquessate and minor honours devolved upon his el son **(4)** FREDERICK WILLIAM, KP, PC, 4th Marquess; MP for co Down 1831-52; *dsp* 1872; *s* by his half-brother **(5)** GEORGE HENRY ROBERT CHARLES WILLIAM, KP, LLD, 5th Marquess who had in 1854 *s* his father as 2nd Earl Vane: assumed in 1851 the additional surname of Tempest; sat as MP for N Durham (*C*) 1847-54; was Lord-Lieut of Durham: *m* 1846, Mary Cornelia, only da of Sir John Edwards, 1st Bt (*ext*); *d* 6 Nov 1884; *s* by his son **(6)** CHARLES STEWART, KG, GCVO, CB, PC, 6th Marquess, *b* 1852; Postmaster-Gen 1900, first Pres of Board of Education 1902, also Lord Pres of the Council 1903, Pres of Committee on Education in Scotland 1905, Lord-Lieut of Ireland 1886-9, and Lord-Lieut of co of City of Belfast 1900-1903; assumed by Roy licence 1885 the additional and principal surname of Stewart: *m* 1875, Lady Theresa Susey Helen, who *d* 1919, el da of 19th Earl of Shrewsbury; *d* 1915; *s* by his son **(7)** CHARLES STEWART HENRY, KG, MVO, TD, PC, 7th Marquess; *b* 1878; Major and Brevet Lieut-Col late Life Guards; Lord-Lieut of co Durham; was Finance Member of Air Council 1919, Under-Sec of State for Air and Vice-Pres of Air Council 1920-21, first Min of Education in Ulster Parliament 1921-6, a Member of Senate of N Ireland 1921-9 (Leader 1921-6), First Commr of Works (England) 1928-9, and (in National Govt) Aug to Nov 1931, Sec of State for Air 1931-5, and Lord Privy Seal and Leader of House of Lords June to Nov 1935; appointed Chancellor of Queen's Univ, Belfast 1923, and of Durham Univ 1930; sat as MP for Maidstone (*C*) 1906-15: *m* 1899, Dame Edith Helen Chaplin, DBE, who *d* 1959, da of 1st Viscount Chaplin; *d* 1949; *s* by his son **(8)** EDWARD CHARLES STEWART ROBERT, 8th Marquess; *b* 1902; Hon Col 12th Batn (Cadet) Durham LI; Hon Attaché, British Embassy, Rome 1924-5; sat as MP for co Down (*C*) 1931-45; *m* 1931, Romaine, who *d* 1951, da of Major Boyce Combe, of Great Holt, Dockenfield, Surrey; *d* 1955; *s* by his son **(9)** ALEXANDER CHARLES ROBERT, 9th Marquess, and present peer; also Earl of Londonderry, Earl Vane, Viscount Castlereagh, Viscount Seaham, Baron Londonderry, and Baron Stewart.

LONG, VISCOUNT (Long) (Viscount UK 1921)

RICHARD GERARD LONG, CBE, 4th Viscount; *b* 30 Jan 1929; *s* 1967; *ed* Harrow; late Wilts Regt; a Lord in Waiting to HM since 1979; Vice-Pres Wilts Roy British Legion, and Bath Light Operatic Club; Pres Bath & Wilts Gliding Club; CBE (Civil) 1993: *m* 1st, 1957 (*m diss* 1984), Margaret Frances, da of late Ninian B. Frazer; 2ndly, 1984 (*m diss* 1990), Mrs Catherine Patricia Elizabeth Mier Woolf, da of Charles Terrence Miles-Ede, of South Africa; 3rdly 1990, Helen Millar Wright Fleming-Gibbons, and has had issue by 1st *m*.

Arms – Sable, within two flaunches and semée of cross-crosslets or, a lion rampant argent. **Crest** – A lion's head argent, erased or, holding in the mouth a dexter hand erased gules. **Supporters** – On either side a lion argent, holding a flag-staff erect proper, flowing therefrom a pennon sable, that on the dexter charged with a portcullis chained and that on the sinister with a fetterlock or. **Residence** – Rose Cottage, Turleigh, Bradford-on-Avon, Wilts.

Pious, though valiant

SON LIVING (By 1st marriage)

Hon JAMES RICHARD, *b* 31 Dec 1960.

DAUGHTERS LIVING AND DECEASED (By 1st marriage)

Hon Sarah Victoria, *b* 1958: *m* 1990, George G. C. Littler, elder son of George Clegg Littler, and of Mrs Frithjof Meidell-Anderson.
Hon Charlotte Helen, *b* 1965; actress; *d* 1984 in a motor accident.

BROTHER LIVING

Hon John Hume, *b* 1930; *ed* Harrow; late Black Watch, BSA Police Rhodesia 1951: *m* 1957 (*m diss* 1969), Averil Juliet, only da of Henry Stobart, of Salisbury, Rhodesia, and has issue living, Bridget Gwendolyn, *b* 1963.

SISTER LIVING

Hon Noreen, *b* 1921: *m* 1947, Capt John Cairns Bartholomew, Roy Wilts Yeo, and has issue living, Charles J. E., *b* 1951: *m* 1979, Rosemary Anne, da of Rev Canon V. H. Julien, of The Rectory, Hamilton, Melbourne, Vic, Australia, — William W., *b* 1956: *m* 1982, Carolyn J. W., el da of Barry Pride, of Knock House, Stone-in-Oxley, Kent, and has issue living, Jack William *b* 1989, Sophie Virginia *b* 1990, — Susan, *b* 1949: *m* 19—, — Bruce. *Residence* – Poulshot Court, Poulshot, Devizes, Wilts.

DAUGHTER LIVING OF SECOND VISCOUNT

Hon (Antoinette) Sara (Frances Sibell), *b* 1934: *m* 1954 (*m diss* 1984), Hon Charles Andrew Morrison, MP (later Hon Sir Charles Morrison) (*see* B Margadale). *Residences* – 45 Westminster Gdns, SW1; Upper Farm, Milton Lilbourne, Pewsey, Wilts.

PREDECESSORS – (1) *Rt Hon* WALTER HUME Long, son of late Richard Penruddock Long, MP; *b* 1854; Parliamentary Sec to Local Govt Board Aug 1886 to June 1892, a Member of Roy Commn on Agricultural Depression 1893, Pres of Board of Agriculture (with a seat in the Cabinet) July 1895 to Nov 1900, Pres of Local Govt Board (with a seat in the Cabinet) Nov 1900 to March 1905, Ch Sec for Ireland (with a seat in the Cabinet) March to Dec 1905 and Lord-Lieut of Wilts 1920-24; appointed again Pres of Local Govt Board May 1915, Sec of State for the Colonies in National Min Dec 1916, and First Lord of the Admiralty Jan 1917 (resigned Feb 1921); MP for N Wilts (C) April 1880 to Nov 1886, for Wilts, E, or Devizes, Div Nov 1885 to June 1892 for Liverpool, W Derby Div Jan 1893 to Sept 1900, for Bristol, S Div Oct 1900 to Jan 1906, for Dublin co, S Dublin Div Jan 1906 to Jan 1910, for Strand 1910-18, and for St George's Div of Westminster 1918 to May 1921; *cr* *Viscount Long*, of Wraxall, co Wilts (peerage of United Kingdom) 1921: *m* 1878, Lady Dorothy Blanche Boyle, who *d* 1938, da of 9th Earl of Cork and Orrery; *d* 1924; *s* by his grandson (2) WALTER FRANCIS DAVID (son of late Brig-Gen Walter Long, CMG, DSO, who was *ka* 1917), 2nd Viscount, *b* 1911; Major Coldstream Guards: *m* 1933 (*m diss* 1943), Frances Laura, who *d* 1990, da of Hon Guy Lawrence Charteris (E Wemyss and March); *ka* 1944; *s* by his uncle (3) (RICHARD) ERIC (ONSLOW), TD (2nd son of 1st Viscount), 3rd Viscount, *b* 1892; a JP for Wilts 1923-67, and a DL 1946-67; MP for Wilts Westbury Div (C) 1927-31: *m* 1916, Gwendolyne Hague, who *d* 1959, da of late Thomas Reginald Hague Cook (Elliot, Bt); *d* 1967; *s* by his el son (4) RICHARD GERARD, 4th Viscount and present peer.

LONGFORD, EARL OF (Pakenham) Sits as BARON PAKENHAM (UK 1945) (Earl I 1785)

Glory is the shadow of virtue

FRANCIS AUNGIER PAKENHAM, KG, PC, *b* 5 Dec 1905; *cr Baron Pakenham*, of Cowley, City of Oxford (peerage of UK) 1945, PC 1948, KG 1971, and *s* as 7th Earl 1961; *ed* Eton, and New Coll, Oxford (BA 1928, MA 1934); was a Lord-in-Waiting to HM Oct 1945 to Oct 1946, Parliamentary Under-Sec of State for War Oct 1946 to April 1947, Chancellor of Duchy of Lancaster April 1947 to May 1948, Min of Civil Aviation May 1948 to May 1951, First Lord of the Admiralty May to Oct 1951 and Lord Privy Seal 1964-65, Sec of State for the Colonies 1965-66, again Lord Privy Seal 1966-68; Chm of Nat Youth Employment Council 1968-71, and of Sidgwick & Jackson 1970-80, author: *m* 1931, Elizabeth, CBE, MA, writer, da of Nathaniel Bishop Harman, FRCS, of 108 Harley St, W1, and has had issue.

Arms – Quarterly: 1st quarterly or and gules, in the first quarter an eagle displayed vert *Pakenham*; 2nd argent, a bend dancette sable, between two plain cottises azure, the bend charged with three fleurs-de-lis argent, each cottise charged with three bezants, *Cuffe*; 3rd ermine, a griffin segreant azure, *Aungier*; 4th per bend embattled argent and gules, *Boyle*. **Crest** – Out of a mural coronet or, a demi-eagle displayed gules. **Supporters** – *Dexter*, a lion azure, charged on the shoulder with a carbuncle or; *sinister*, a griffin azure, wings, elevated ermine, beaked and clawed or.
Residences – Bernhurst, Hurst Green, Sussex; 18 Chesil Court, Chelsea Manor St, SW3.

SONS LIVING

THOMAS FRANK DERMOT (does not use courtesy title) *b* 14 Aug 1933; *ed* Ampleforth, and Magdalen Coll, Oxford; writer, author of *The Scramble for Africa* (1992), etc: *m* 1964, Valerie Susan, yst da of Maj Ronald Guthrie McNair Scott, of Huish House, Old Basing, nr Basingstoke, Hants (*see* V Camrose), and has issue living, Edward Melchior, *b* 1970, — Frederick Augustus, *b* 1971, — Anna Maria, *b* 1965, — Eliza, *b* 1966: *m* 1993, Alexander James Chisholm (*see* B Windlesham). *Residence* – Tullynally, Castlepollard, co Westmeath.
Hon Patrick Maurice *b* 1937; *ed* Ampleforth, and Magdalen Coll, Oxford; Bar Inner Temple 1962: *m* 1968, Mary Elizabeth, el da of Maj H. A. J. Plummer, of Winchester, and has issue living, Richard, *b* 1969, — Guy, *b* 1970, — Harry Michael, *b* 1972. *Residence* – 24 Chesil Court, Chelsea Manor St, SW3.
Hon Michael Aidan, CMG (23 Sutherland Pl, W2; 3052 P St, Washington DC, USA), *b* 1943; *ed* Ampleforth, Trin Coll, Camb, and Rice Univ, Texas, USA; CMG 1993: *m* 1980, Meta (Mimi) Landreth, el da of William Conway Doak, of Philadelphia, USA, and formerly wife of — Lavine, and has issue living, Alexandra Clio, *b* 1981, — Clio Isabelle Blaise, *b* 1985.
Hon Kevin John Toussaint, *b* 1947: *ed* Ampleforth, New Coll, Oxford, and St Antony's, Oxford: *m* 1st, 1972 (*m diss* 1984), Ruth Lesley, da of Leslie Douglas Colbeck Jackson; 2ndly, 19—, Mrs Clare CHATEL, elder da of John Edward Melvill Hoare, of Montague House, Holton St Peter, Halesworth, Suffolk, and has issue living (by 1st wife), Thomas John Chamberlain, *b* 1977, — Catherine Ruth, *b* 1975, — (by 2nd wife), Benjamin John, *b* 1983, — Dominic Balthazar, *b* 1989, — Hermione Clare, *b* 1984.

DAUGHTERS LIVING AND DECEASED

Lady Antonia, *b* 1932; *ed* Oxford Univ (MA 1969), writer: *m* 1st 1956, (*m diss* 1977), Rt Hon Sir Hugh Charles Patrick Joseph Fraser, MBE, MP, who *d* 1984 (*see* L Lovat); 2ndly, 1980, Harold Pinter, CBE, playwright.
Judith Elizabeth (does not use courtesy title) (32 Ladbroke Grove, W11 3BQ), *b* 1940; *ed* Oxford Univ (BA 1961): *m* 1963 (*m diss* 1982), Alexander John Kazantzis, and has issue living, Arthur Constantine, *b* 1967, — Miranda Elizabeth, *b* 1964.
Lady Rachel Mary, *b* 1942; *ed* London Univ (BA); writer: *m* 1967, Kevin Billington, of 30 Addison Av, W11, and The Court House, Poyntington, Dorset, and has issue living, Nathaniel Kevin, *b* 1970, — Caspar Leo, *b* 1979, — Catherine Rose, *b* 1973, — Chloe Margaret, *b* 1976.
Lady Catherine Rose, *b* 1946; *k* in a motor accident 1969.

SISTERS LIVING

Lady (Margaret) Pansy (Felicia), *b* 1904: *m* 1928, Henry Taylor Lamb, MC, RA, who *d* 1960, son of late Sir Horace Lamb, LLD, DSc, and has issue living, Valentine Edward Martin (Stable Block, Castletown House, Celbridge, co Kildare), *b* 1939: *m* 1970, Anne Graecen, and has issue living, Celia Margaret *b* 1971, Stephanie Christine *b* 1972, Fiona *b* 1977, — Henrietta Frances, *b* 1931: *m* 1960, William Anthony Dominic Phipps, of 31 Chepstow Villas, W11 (*see* M Normanby, colls), — (Horatia Mary) Felicia (Low Winsley Farm, Burnt Yates, Harrogate, Yorks), *b* 1933: *m* 1958, William Henry Tugwell Palmer, and has had issue, Rufus Henry *b* 1967, *d* 1986, Primrose Felicia (*Hon Mrs Alastair Campbell*) *b* 1960: *m* 1993, Lt-Col Hon Alastair James Calthrop Campbell, yr son of Baron Campbell of Croy, MC, PC (Life Baron), Harriet Eve *b* 1961. *Residence* – Via di Sto Stefano del Cacco 22, Rome, Italy.
Lady Mary Katharine, *b* 1907: *m* 1939, Major Meysey George Dallas Clive, Grenadier Guards, who was *ka* 1943, and has issue living, George Meysey, *b* 1940; *ed* Eton, and Ch Ch Oxford, — Alice Mary (*Viscountess Boyd of Merton*), *b* 1942: *m* 1962, 2nd Viscount Boyd of Merton, of 9 Warwick Sq, SW1, and Wivelscombe, Saltash, Cornwall. *Residence* – Whitfield, Allensmore, Herefordshire.
Lady Violet Georgiana, *b* 1912: *m* 1934, Anthony Dymoke Powell, CH, CBE, and has issue living, Tristram Roger Dymoke (3 Stockwell Park Cres, SW9 0DQ), *b* 1940: *m* 1968, Virginia Beatrice, da of late Archibald Julian Lucas (B Grenfell), and has issue living, Archibald Thomas Llywelyn *b* 1970, Georgia *b* 1969, — John Marmion Anthony (137 Kennington Park Rd, SE11), *b* 1946. *Residence* – The Chantry, nr Frome, Som.

COLLATERAL BRANCHES LIVING

Grandson of late Col Hercules Arthur Pakenham, CMG (infra):—
Issue of late Major Hercules Dermot Wilfrid Pakenham, *b* 1901, *d* of wounds received in action 1940: *m* 1927, Hetty Margaret (who *m* 2ndly, 1950 (*m diss* 1959), Lieut-Col Richard Walter Byng Pembroke, OBE, late Coldstream Guards (*see* V Torrington, colls, 1969 Edn)), da of late Capt Roland Stuart Hebeler, The Queen's Roy Regt:—

(Hercules) Michael Roland, b 1935: ed Eton: m 1st, 1957 (m diss 1973), Hon Susan Elizabeth Moon Lever, da of 3rd Viscount Leverhulme, KG; 2ndly, 1973 (m diss 1982), Margaret, da of Charles William Fisher, of Wold Cottage, Upham, Hants; 3rdly, 1984, Fiona Jane, da of Gordon Barrie Peters, of Tiphams End, nr Dorking, Surrey, and has issue living (by 2nd m), Rebecca Kate, b 1977, — and two adopted children (by 1st m), Dermot Philip Michael, b 1961: m 1988, Johanna, elder da of Dr Ian Perry, of The Old Farm House, Grateley, Hants, and has issue living, Arthur b 1992, Emma b 1989, Alice b (twin) 1989, Claire Alexandra (Anna) b 1990, — Caroline Susan Margaret, b 1963: m 1990, A. Henry M. Wilson, yst son of late John Wilson, of Ovington Gdns, SW3, and has issue living, Alexander James Kirkland b 1991, Madelaine Rose Kirkland b 1993. Residence – Old Hall, Penley, Wrexham, Clwyd.

Granddaughter of late Lieut-Gen Thomas Henry Pakenham, CB, 3rd son of late Lieut-Gen Hon Sir Hercules Pakenham, KCB, 3rd son of 2nd Baron:—
Issue of late Col Hercules Arthur Pakenham, CMG, b 1863, d 1937: m 1895, Lilian Blanche Georgina, who d 1939, da of late Rt Hon (Anthony) Evelyn Melbourne Ashley (see E Shaftesbury, colls):—
Joan Esther Sybella (Hon Mrs Angus D. Campbell), b 1904; JP Cheshire: m 1926, Hon Angus Dudley Campbell, CBE, JP, who d 1967 (see B Colgrain). Residence – Beech Cottage, 24 Cheerbrook Rd, Willaston, Nantwich, Cheshire.

Granddaughter of late Lieut-Col William Wingfield Verner Pakenham, Indian Army, son of late William Sandford Pakenham (infra):—
Issue of late William Henry Verner Pakenham, b 1885, d 1956: m 1905, Alice, who d 1966, da of Charles Smith, of Fulwood Park, Liverpool:—
Frances Josephine, b 1919: m 1946, Eric Douglas Rowlands, of 2 Acorn Grove, Scholes, Holmfirth, Huddersfield, and has issue living, William Verner Pakenham (5 Highfield Rd, Highburton, Huddersfield, W Yorks HD8 0RQ), b 1947; LIM: m 1974, Ann, only da of late John Tyas, of Skelmanthorpe, Yorks, and has issue living, Richard William b 1976, Victoria Nicola b 1977, — Cynthia Jane Olive, b 1951: m 1974, Andrew Fisher, of 299 Shenley Fields Rd, Selly Oak, Birmingham 29.

Granddaughter of late Frederick Edward Sandford Pakenham, 2nd son of late William Sandford Pakenham (infra):—
Issue of late Michael Ceely Sandford Pakenham, b 1903, d 1978: m 1st, 1933 (m diss 1948), Aline Mary Loftus, who d 1967, da of late Loftus St George (St George, Bt colls), and formerly wife of Ernest Charles William Vane-Tempest, DSC (see M Londonderry, colls); 2ndly, 1948, Patricia, who d 1986, da of late Capt William Harvey Murray, of Mill House, Boyton, Essex:—
(By 1st m) Aline Marguerite Constance Sandford, b 1934: m 1959, Keith William Boyd, of 137 Rouse St, Tenterfield, NSW, Australia, and has issue living, William Michael Sandford, b 1964, — Jane Maria Loftus, b 1960, — Christina Theresa, b 1961.

Grandsons of late William Sandford Pakenham, son of late Very Rev Hon Henry Pakenham, 5th son of 2nd Baron:—
Issue of late Robert Sandford Pakenham, b 1866, d 1959: m 1st, 1910, Edith Carter, who d 1912; 2ndly, 1920, Mildred Alice Armstrong, who d 1940:—
(By 1st m) Robert Wingfield, b 1912; ed Malvern, and Trin Coll, Camb (BA 1934, MA 1938): m 1941, Alice Gwendoline, who d 1982, da of late T. H. James, and has issue living, Clive Sykes (31 Barton Gdns, Sherborne, Dorset), b 1947: m 1973, Jane, yst da of H. J. Antell, of Sherborne, Dorset, and has issue living, Daniel Nicholas b 1973, Adam Geoffrey b 1978. Residence – Longthorns, Priestlands, Sherborne, Dorset DT9 4HN.
Issue of late Hamilton Richard Pakenham, MB, BCh, b 1867, d 1957; Church Missionary Soc, Fukien Prov, S China: m 1900, Emily Willis, who d 1975, da of late Thomas Stringer, of Merrion Hall, Dublin:—
†Richard Hercules Wingfield, CBE, b 1906; ed Monkton Combe Sch, and Trin Coll, Camb (MA); HM Overseas Civil Ser 1929-56 (Senior Commr, Zanzibar 1948-56); Gen Sec Lebanon Evangelical Mission 1956-69; MBE (Civil) 1943, OBE (Civil) 1949, CBE (Civil) 1955, 2nd class Order of Brilliant Star of Zanzibar 1956: m 1947, Eileen Isolde, el da of late Oscar Faber, CBE, DCL, DSc, and d 1993, leaving issue, John Hubert, b 1951: m 1991, Maureen Denise, da of W/Cdr Patrick Woolley, RAF, of Rayleigh, Essex, — and an adopted son, Richard Arthur, b 1949. Residence – 9 Kirkwick Av, Harpenden, Herts. —— Henry Desmond Verner, CBE, b 1911; ed Monkton Combe, and St John's Coll, Oxford (scholar); British Dep High Commr, Sydney, NSW 1968-71; CBE (Civil) 1964: m 1st, 1946 (m diss 1960), Crystal Elizabeth, da of late Lt-Col Edward York Brooksbank (see Brooksbank, Bt); 2ndly, 1963, Venetia, da of William Paterson Doyle, and formerly wife of Maurice Christopher Maude, and has issue living (by 1st m), Anthony Edward, b 1952; ed Eton, and Ch Ch, Oxford, — Pandora Clare, b 1948: m 1969, Matthieu Millet, and has issue living, Alexandre François b 1974, Thomas b 1990, Sophie Emilie b 1976, Catherine b 1981, — (by 2nd m) Mark Edmund, b 1965, — Sarah Catherine, b 1966. Residence – Rose Farm, Brettenham, Suffolk.

Grandchildren of late Gustavus Conolly Pakenham, 2nd son of late Capt George Dent Pakenham (infra):—
Issue of late Thomas Compton Pakenham, MC, b 1893, d 1957: m 1st, 1915 (m diss 1920), Phyllis Mona, da of Col William Price, RE; 2ndly, 1921, Alma Clark; 3rdly, 1925, Sara, who d 1976, da of Charles Manning Furman, of Clemson, S Carolina, USA:—
(By 1st m) Simona Vere, b 1916: m 1st, 1938, Noel Paterson Durnford Iliff, who d 1984; 2ndly, 1984, Kenneth William Bruce Middleton, and has issue living (by 1st m), David Anthony (Green Willows, Station Rd, Woodmancote, Cheltenham, Glos GL52 4HN), b 1939: m 1966, Celia Winifred Foot, and has issue living, Stephanie Brigid Laura b 1968, Alison Deborah Caroline b 1970. Residences – 103 Darwin Court, Gloucester Av, NW1 7BH; Cobbler's Cottage, Ledwell, Chipping Norton, Oxon OX7 7AN. —— (By 2nd m) Compton Christopher (RD2, Box 275, Hickory Lane, Califon, NJ 07830, USA), b 1921: m 1947, Dorothy Rebecca Cullingford, who d 1984, and has issue living, Diane, b 1949: m 1980, — Pennington, of RD 1, Box 35A, Pipersville, PA 18947, USA, — Monica, b 1954, — Jennifer (twin), b 1954: m 1983, Gary Sandy Sawhill, of Mattix Run Equestrian Center & Polo Club, Moss Mill Rd, Towne of Smithville, NJ 08201, USA. —— (By 3rd m) Edward Michael, b 1932; editor New York Daily News. —— Joan Compton, b 1932: m 19—, — Breiter.

Grandsons of late Frederick Edward Pakenham (infra):—
Issue of late Thomas Hume Pakenham b 1907, d 1965: m 1st, 1928 (m diss 1945), Margaret Olwen da of late Capt Thomas Corrance, of Ervin, Wigtownshire; 2ndly, 1946, Isabella Nimmo, da of Archie Cowie, of Airdrie, Lanarkshire:—
(By 1st m) Thomas David Corrance (1100 Normandy Cres, Ottawa, Ont K2C 0L8, Canada), b 1929: m 1951, Edith McDerby, and has issue living, Thomas McDerby (1024 Arrowhead Place, Ottawa, Ont K1C 2S4, Canada), b 1961: m 1987, Maura Ann, da of William Tubridy, of Toronto, and has issue living, Kathryn Tubridy b 1993, — James Arthur, b 1962, — Teresa Christine Pakenham (156F Woodridge Cres, Ottawa, Ont K2B 7S9, Canada), b 1959; has resumed her maiden name: m 1977 (m diss 1984), Michael Sabourin, and has two adopted das, Angela Sarah Christine Pakenham b 1976, Candace Debra Elaine Pakenham b 1984, — Jocelyn Patricia, b 1955: m 1975, Warren Reade, of SS3 Site 9 Comp 87, Prince George, BC V2N 2S7, Canada, and has issue living, Jennifer Alison Ella b 1979, Kathryn Ann Dorothy b 1981, — Edith Lorraine (1388 Chatelaine Ave, Ottawa, Ont K1Z 8A8, Canada), b 1958: m 19—, Donald Bond, and has issue living, Shaun Donald Pakenham b 1980, Daniel Scott b 1983, — Maria Aline, b 1965. —— John Edwin, b 1930: m 1st, 1954 (m diss 1959), Wendy Cox; 2ndly, 1962, Gaylynn Evon, da of Weir Powellson Armstrong, and has issue living, (by 1st m) Cheryl Olwen, b 1955, — (by 2nd m) Sean Thomas, b 1963, — Edward Austin Westmoreland, b 1967, — Naja Chrisanna, b 1968.

Grandchildren of late Capt George Dent Pakenham, only son of late Thomas Pakenham, 2nd son of late Adm Hon Sir Thomas Pakenham, GCB, yst son of 1st Baron Longford and Elizabeth Countess of Longford:—
Issue of late Frederick Edward Pakenham, b 1869, d 1923: m 1906, Nancy Jane, da of Charles Youmans, formerly of Hazleton, British Columbia:—
Arthur Godfrey, b 1910: m 1st, 1938 (m diss 1950), Wanda Hatcher; 2ndly, 1951, Rose Marie, da of Anton Eberle, and has issue living, (by 2nd m) Patricia Eve, b 1956. Residence – 1210 NE 124th Street, Seattle, Washington 98125, USA. ⸺ William Christopher, b 1922: m 1st, 1943 (m diss 1954), Mona May Morris; 2ndly, 1955, Marjorie Jane, da of late Duncan Ried Wilson, of Montrose, Scotland, and has issue living, (by 1st m) Frederick Edward, b 1944, ⸺ (by 2nd m) Ronald Arthur, b 1957. Residence – 845 Kyle Court Apt 206, Brockville, Ont, Canada K6V 6K7. ⸺ Norma Muriel Doreen, b 1913: m 1938, Donald Holmes, and has issue living. Residence – 1333 North 125th St 19, Seattle, Washington 98133, USA.

Grandchildren of late William Law Pakenham, el son of Wellington Montagu Pakenham (infra):—
Issue of Capt the late Rev Thomas Arthur Charles Pakenham, RN, b 1900, d 1981: m 1925, Clara Talbot, who d 1985, da of late William Middleton, of Monks Pond, Lymington:—
William Thomas Talbot (Croft Mews, Botley, Hants), b 1926; Capt RN; 1944-45 War: m 1957, Antonia Mary, da of late Capt Antony Coleby, RN, of Hapton House, Hambledon, Hants, and has issue living, Robin Thomas Cliff, b 1963, ⸺ John Neville, b 1964, ⸺ Katherine Clara, b 1960. ⸺ Rev Stephen Walter (The Malthouse, Frogmore, Kingsbridge, Devon TQ7 2PG), b 1929; ed Cambridge Univ (MA); Lt RN (ret); V of Donnington and Apuldram 1964-75, V of Durrington 1975-81, V of St Mary Bourne and Woodcott 1981-88; 1968 record singlehanded crossing of Atlantic in 21 days, 15 hrs and 7 mins in a 32ft ketch: m 1957, Elizabeth Ann, only da of late Rt Rev Kenneth Edward Norman Lamplugh, Suffragan Bishop of Southampton, and has issue living, Jonathan Hugh Rust, b 1958: m 1985, Nina Diana, da of late Lawrence Woodhouse Mason, of Winchester, and has issue living, George Lawrence b 1987, Timothy James b 1990. ⸺ Marcus Charles, b 1960: m 1991, Lisa A. M., da of Bengt Delaryd, of Repulse Bay, Hong Kong, ⸺ Olivia Judith Clare, b 1963: m 1992, Mark Elton, eldest son of Ronald George Johnson, and has issue living, Bethany Charlotte Pakenham b 1993.

Grandchildren of late Com Arthur McClellan Pakenham, RD, RNR (infra):—
Issue of late Peter Hugh Percy Holwell Pakenham, b 1913; d 1982: m 1st 1939, Nancy, who d 1966, da of Herbert George Alexander, of Woodlands, Westonbirt, Glos; 2ndly, 1973, Ailsa Jean (The Red Cottage, Roode Ashton, Trowbridge, Wilts), widow of Kenneth George Marsh, of Potticks House, Bradford on Avon, Wilts:—
(By 1st m) Jeremy Edwin Montagu (The Old Manor, Rudge, Frome, Somerset), b 1948: m 1974, Caroline, da of late Albert Maurice Redman, of Wonham House, Bampton, Devon, and has issue living, James Edwin Holwell, b 1977, ⸺ Edward Charles Montagu, b 1980, ⸺ Victoria Louise, b 1984. ⸺ Susan Daphne, b 1942: m 1965, Capt George Gerald Blakey, RE, of Farrington House, Farrington, Dorset, and has issue living, Lucinda Jane, b 1967.

Grandson of late Wellington Montagu Pakenham, 2nd son of late Adm John Pakenham, 4th son of late Adm Hon Sir Thomas Pakenham, GCB (ante):—
Issue of late Com Arthur McClellan Pakenham, RD, RNR, b 1876, d 1948: m 1st, 1910, Ethel Louise, who d 1934, da of late R. A. W. Holwell; 2ndly, 1938, Katharine Joan (who m 2ndly 19—), da of Sidney A. Horstman, of Fair Lawn, Bath:—
(By 1st m) Patrick Christopher Montagu Holwell, b 1922; formerly Capt Roy Signals; Burma 1942-45 (despatches twice). Residence – 2 Ave de Bude, Geneva 1202, Switzerland.

Grandchildren of late Maj Charles Pakenham, 4th son of Rev Robert Pakenham, DD, 6th son of Adm Hon Sir Thomas Pakenham, GCB (ante):—
Issue of late Col George de la Poer Beresford Pakenham, CMG, CBE, DSO, b 1875, d 1960: m 1st 1905, Emilie Elsie, who d 1921, da of late William Fowler, of Broadlands, Liverpool; 2ndly, 1923, Marie Marthe Amalie, who d 1968, widow of Capt Jacques Henri Joucia, French Army:—
(By 1st m) Raymond Beresford (RAF Club), b 1907; ed Haileybury; Lt-Col (ret) Border Regt and acting Group Capt RAF: m 1st, 1930 (m diss 1934), Sheila Barbara Kathleen, da of late Joseph Masoon (Price, Bt, cr 1815, colls); 2ndly, 1934 (m diss 1937), Sophie Patricia, da of late Capt R. D. Pollock, of Teign-na-Mara, Bangor, co Down, co Down; 3rdly, 1948, Catherine Lillian Elizabeth, da of late H. Smith, of Salisbury.
Issue of late Capt Hewitt John Havelock Pakenham, b 1880, d 1978: m 1st, 1906, Claire May, who d 1944, only da of late Edmond Berdoe-Wilkinson, of Eashing, Godalming; 2ndly, 1946, Molly, who d 1976, el da of late William Henry Cook, of The Old Cross Houyse, Heretford, and widow of Capt Oswell Jones, Roy West Kent Regt:—
(By 1st m) Arthur John Edmond, b 1907; is Maj Queen's R Regt (W Surrey) TA (Reserve); Burma 1942-45: m 1st 1932 (m diss 1948), Sarah, da of late Capt Rowland Alston, late Coldm Gds, formerly of Odell Castle, Beds; 2ndly, 1952, Heidi, el da of late Emil Wegmann, of Frauenfeld, Switzerland, and has issue living, (by 2nd m) Timothy James Robert, b 1961: m 1989, Kim, da of John Gibson, of Bayston Hill, Shropshire, and has issue living, Sophie b 1993. ⸺ Christine Catherine, b 1953: m 1980 (m diss 1989), Nigel Buckler Cooper, and has issue living, Robert John b 1987. Residence – School House, Tandridge, Oxted, Surrey. ⸺ Cynthia Marion Blanche (The Hollies, 3A Compton Way, Olivers Battery, Winchester, Hants), b 1909: m 1st, 1935 (m diss 1947), Capt Alexander Glazebrook Acton Pierce, RA; 2ndly, 1947, Guy Fothergill Batho, MBE, who d 1992, and has issue living (by 2nd m), William Nicholas Pakenham, b 1948; ed Canford Sch, and RNC Dartmouth; Cmdr RN: m 1973, Jennifer, da of W. R. Best, of Embleton, Northumberland, and has issue living, William Guy Pakenham b 1980, Julia Elizabeth b 1978.

PREDECESSORS – (1) THOMAS Pakenham, MP for Longford Borough; cr Baron Longford (peerage of Ireland) 1756; he d 1776, and his widow was cr Countess of Longford (peerage of Ireland) 1785; she d 1794; he was s by his el son (2) EDWARD MICHAEL, PC, 2nd Baron; MP for co Longford 1765; d 1792; s by his son (3) THOMAS, 3rd Baron, who became in 1794, on the death of his grandmother, 2nd Earl of Longford; cr Baron Silchester, of co Southampton 1821; b 1774: m 1817, Lady Georgiana Emma Charlotte Lygon, da of 1st Earl Beauchamp; d 1835; s by his el son (4) EDWARD MICHAEL, 3rd Earl; was Capt 2nd Life Guards; d unmarried 1860; s by his brother (5) WILLIAM LYGON, GCB, 4th Earl; b 1819; was Col 1st and 2nd Btns Northumberland Fusiliers: m 1862, Hon Selina Rice-Trevor, who d 1918, da of 4th Baron Dinevor; d 1887; s by his son (6) THOMAS, KP, MVO, 5th Earl, 1864; Col Life Guards; Lieut and Custos Rotulorum for co Longford 1887-1915: m 1899, Lady Mary Julia Child Villiers, who d 1933, da of 7th Earl of Jersey; ka at Dardanelles while Brig-Gen 2nd S Midland Mounted Brig, 1915; s by his el son (7) EDWARD ARTHUR HENRY, 6th Earl, b 1902; a Senator of Eire 1946-8: m 1925, Christine Patty, who d 1980, da of late Richard Trew, of Cheddar, Somerset; d 1961; s by his brother (8) FRANCIS AUNGIER, 7th Earl and present peer; also Baron Longford (peerage of Ireland), Baron Silchester, and Baron Pakenham.

LONSDALE, EARL OF (Lowther) (Earl UK 1807, Bt GB 1764)

The office shows the man

JAMES HUGH WILLIAM LOWTHER, 7th Earl and 8th Baronet; *b* 3 Nov 1922; *s* 1953; *ed* Eton; 1939-45 War in RAC and as Capt E Riding Yeo (despatches): *m* 1st, 1945 (*m diss* 1954), Tuppina Cecily, who *d* 1984, da of late Capt Geoffrey Henry Bennet; 2ndly, 1954 (*m diss* 1962), Hon Jennifer Lowther, da of late Maj Hon Christopher William Lowther (*see* V Ullswater); 3rdly, 1963, Nancy Ruth (STEPHENSON), da of late Thomas Cobbs, of Pacific Palisades, Cal, USA; 4thly, 1975, Caroline Sheila, yst da of Sir Gerald Gordon Ley, TD, 3rd Bt, and has issue by 1st, 2nd, 3rd and 4th *m*.

Arms – Or, six annulets, three, two, and one sable. **Crest** – A dragon passant argent. **Supporters** – Two horses argent, gorged with wreaths of laurel vert.
Residences – Askham Hall, Penrith, Cumbria CA10 2PF. *Club* – Brooks's.

SONS LIVING *(By 1st marriage)*

HUGH CLAYTON (*Viscount Lowther*) (Towcett House, Newby, Penrith), *b* 27 May 1949: *m* 1st, 1971, Pamela Colleen Middleton; 2ndly, 1986, Angela Mary, da of Capt Peter Wyatt, of Dartmouth, Devon.

(By 2nd marriage)

Hon William James, *b* 1957.

(By 3rd marriage)

Hon James Nicholas, *b* 1964.

(By 4th marriage)

Hon Charles Alexander James, *b* 1978.

DAUGHTERS LIVING *(By 1st marriage)*

Lady Jane Helen Harbord, *b* 1947: *m* 1st, 1969, Gary Hunter Wooten, of Calif, USA; 2ndly, 1978, Robert Charles Benson, eldest son of late Lt-Cdr Nicholas Robin Benson, of Aycote House, Rendcomb, Cirencester, Glos (*see* D Rutland, 1971 Edn), and has issue living (by 2nd *m*), Laura Jane, *b* 1980, — Sophie Camilla, *b* 1984. *Residence* – Glebe House, Lowther, Penrith, Cumbria.

(By 2nd marriage)

Lady Miranda, *b* 1955; resumed maiden name by deed poll 1983-86: *m* 1st, 1978, Martin Dunne; 2ndly, 1986, Ian Cronshaw; 3rdly, 19—, Michael Glen, and has issue living (by 2nd *m*), Samantha, *b* 1986, — (by 3rd *m*) Sarah, *b* 1992.
Lady Caroline, *b* 1959: *m* 1st, 1978 (*m diss* 19—), Guy P. T. Forrester; 2ndly, 1982, Stephen Christopher Ernest Hunt; 3rdly, 1987, Charles John Patrick Lawson, only son of Col Sir John Charles Arthur Digby Lawson, 3rd Bt (*cr* 1900), DSO, MC, and has issue living (by 2nd *m*), George Stephen, *b* 1982, — (by 3rd *m*) (*see* Lawson, Bt, *cr* 1900). *Residence* – Heckwood, Sampford Spiney, Yelverton, Devon PL20 6LJ.

(By 4th marriage)

Lady Marie-Louisa Kate, *b* 1976.

WIDOW LIVING OF BROTHER OF SEVENTH EARL

Lavinia (Whitbysteads, Askham, Penrith, Cumbria), only child of late Thomas H. Joyce, of San Francisco, Cal, USA: *m* 1958, Capt Hon Anthony George Lowther, MBE, who *d* 1981, and has issue (see colls infra).

WIDOW LIVING OF SON OF SIXTH EARL

Susan Ann FOÀ, da of Capt Leonard Stephen Smallwood, of Jersey: *m* 1977, as his 2nd wife, Hon Timothy Lancelot Edward Lowther, who *d* 1984, and has issue (see colls infra). *Residence* – Ivystone House, Rue De La Croix, St Clements, Jersey, Channel Is JE2 6LQ.

COLLATERAL BRANCHES LIVING

Issue of late Capt Hon Anthony George Lowther, MBE, yr brother of 7th Earl (raised to the rank of an Earl's son 1954), *b* 1925; *d* 1981: *m* 1958, Lavinia (ante), only child of late Thomas H. Joyce, of San Francisco, USA:—
Thomas Scott Anthony, *b* 1966. —— Camilla Ann, *b* 1959. —— Arabella Mary, *b* 1962. —— Sarah Lavinia, *b* 1964: *m* 1990, Steven G. Husband, 2nd son of George William Husband, of Billingham, Cleveland.

Issue of late Hon Timothy Lancelot Edward Lowther, yr son (by 2nd *m*) of 6th Earl, *b* 1925, *d* 1984: *m* 1st, 1966 (*m diss* 1976), Margaret Elizabeth, elder da of late John Herring, MC, of 50 Harley St, W1, and formerly wife of Baron Giovanni Testaferrata-Abela: 2ndly, 1977, Susan Ann FOÀ (ante), da of Capt Leonard Stephen Smallwood, of Jersey:—
(By 2nd *m*) Melinda Clare, *b* 1978.

Descendants of late Rt Hon Sir James William Lowther, GCB (son of late Hon William Lowther, brother of 3rd Earl), who was *cr Viscount Ullswater* 1921 (see that title).

(In remainder to Viscountcy only)

Descendants of late John Lowther, MP (brother of 1st Earl), who was *cr a Baronet* 1824:—
See Lowther, Bt, *cr* 1824.

PREDECESSORS – **(1)** *Sir* JOHN Lowther, MP for Westmorland 1660-75; 30th Knight of the family in almost direct succession; *cr a Baronet* 1640; *d* 1675, and was *s* by his grandson **(2)** *Sir* JOHN, PC, 2nd Bt, MP for Westmorland 1680-96; was Vice-Chamberlain of the Household, First Lord Commr of the Treasury, and Lord-Lieut of Westmorland and Cumberland; *cr Baron Lowther and Viscount Lonsdale* (peerage of England) 1696; *d* 1700; *s* by his el son **(3)** RICHARD, 2nd Viscount; *d* 1713; *s* by his brother **(4)** HENRY, who *dsp* 1750, when the peerages became extinct, and the baronetcy devolved upon **(5)** *Sir* JAMES, MP, 5th Bt, grandson of Richard, 2nd son of 1st Bt; *cr Baron Lowther, Baron Kendal, Baron Burgh, Viscount Lowther,* and *Earl of Lonsdale* (peerage of Great Britain) 1784, and *Baron Lowther* and *Viscount Lowther* (peerage of Great Britain) 1797, with remainder to the heirs male of his cousin, Rev Sir William Lowther, Bt, of Swillington (*cr* 1764); *dsp* 1802; *s* in the honours of 1797 by his kinsman **(6)** *Sir* WILLIAM KG, 2nd Viscount; *cr Earl of Lonsdale* 1807; *d* 1844; *s* by his el son **(7)** WILLIAM, PC, 2nd Earl; *b* 1787; Lord of the Admiralty 1809, a Commr for Indian Affairs 1810-18, a Lord of the Treasury 1813-27, Ch Commr of Woods and Forests 1828-30, Vice Pres of Board of Trade and Treasurer of the Navy 1834-5, and Lord Pres of the Council 1852; *d* 1872; *s* by his nephew **(8)** HENRY, 3rd Earl; *b* 1818; sometime MP for W Cumberland, Capt 1st Life Guards Col Cumberland and Westmorland Yeo Cav, and Lord-Lieut and Custos Rotulorum of Westmorland and Cumberland: *m* 1852, Emily Susan, who *d* 1917, da of St George Francis Caulfeild, of Donamon; *d* 1876; *s* by his el son **(9)** ST. GEORGE HENRY, 4th Earl; *b* 1855; *d* 8 Feb 1882; *s* by his brother **(10)** HUGH CECIL, KG, GCVO, TD, 5th Earl; *b* 1857; Lord-Lieut and Custos Rotulorum of Cumberland, and Chm of Quarter Sessions for Westmorland; Mayor of Whitehaven 1894 and 1895: *m* 1878, Lady Grace Cicelie Gordon, CBE, who *d* 1941, da of 10th Marquess of Huntly; *d* 1944; *s* by his brother **(11)** LANCELOT EDWARD, OBE, 6th Earl, *b* 1867; European War 1914-19 as Capt 3rd Batn Border Regt, and Gen Staff (OBE): *m* 1st, 1889, Sophia Gwendoline Alice, who *d* 1921, el da of Sir Robert Sheffield, 5th Bt; 2ndly, 1923, Sybil Beatrix, who *d* 1966, da of late Maj-Gen Edward Feetham, CB, CMG; *d* 1953; *s* by his grandson **(12)** JAMES HUGH WILLIAM (son of late Anthony Edward, Viscount Lowther, el son of 6th Earl), 7th Earl and present peer; also Viscount Lowther and Baron Lowther.

Lorne, Marquess of; son of Duke of Argyll.

LOTHIAN, MARQUESS OF (Kerr) (Marquess S 1701)
(Name pronounced "Karr")

Late, but in earnest

Sero Sed Serio

PETER FRANCIS WALTER KERR, KCVO, 12th Marquess; *b* 8 Sept 1922; *s* 1940, *ed* Ampleforth Coll, and Ch Ch, Oxford; FRSA; Lt Scots Guards, a Member of Queen's Body Guard for Scotland (Royal Company of Archers), DL Roxburghshire 1962, Comdt, Roxburgh, Selkirk and Berwickshire Special Constabulary, and a Knight of Sovereign Order of Malta; Joint Parl Sec to Min of Health, April to Oct 1964; Lord-in-Waiting to HM 1962-64, and again 1972-73; an Under-Sec, Foreign and Commonwealth Office 1970-72; Lord Warden of the Stannaries and Keeper of the Privy Seal of Duke of Cornwall 1977-83; *cr* KCVO 1983: *m* 1943, Antonella, da of late Maj-Gen Sir Foster Reuss Newland, KCMG, CB, and has issue.

Arms – Quarterly: 1st and 4th azure, a sun in splendour or, *Lothian*; 2nd and 3rd gules, on a chevron argent three mullets of the field, *Kerr*. **Crest** – 1st, a sun in splendour or; 2nd, a stag's head erased proper. **Supporters** – *Dexter*, an angel proper, verted azure, surcoat vert, winged and crined cr; *sinister*, an unicorn argent armed, unguled, manned, and tufted or.
Seats – Melbourne Hall, Derby DE7 1EN; Ferniehirst Castle, Jedburgh, Roxburghshire; *Town Residence* - 54 Upper Cheyne Row, SW3. *Clubs* – Boodle's, Beefsteak, New (Edinburgh).

SONS LIVING

MICHAEL ANDREW FOSTER JUDE (*Earl of Ancram*), MP, *b* 7 July 1945; *ed* Ampleforth, and Ch Ch, Oxford (MA, LLB); Advocate Edinburgh 1970; Member Queen's Body Guard for Scotland (Royal Company of Archers); DL Roxburgh, Ettrick and Lauderdale 1990; Member Select Cttee on Energy 1979-83; Chm Conservative Party in Scotland 1980-83; Under Sec of State, Scottish Office, 1983-87, and N Ireland Office 1993-94, since when Min of State for N Ireland; MP for Berwickshire and E Lothian (C) Feb to Oct 1974, for Edinburgh South 1979-June 1987, and for Devizes since 1992: *m* 1975, Lady (Theresa) Jane Fitzalan-Howard, da of 16th Duke of Norfolk, and has issue:—

DAUGHTERS LIVING — *Lady* Clare Therese, *b* 1979, — *Lady* Mary Cecil, *b* 1981.

Lord Ralph William Francis Joseph (20 Upper Cheyne Row, SW3; Melbourne Hall, Melbourne, Derby DE7 1EN), *b* 1957; *ed* Ampleforth: *m* 1st 1980 (*m diss* 1987), Lady Virginia Mary Elizabeth FitzRoy, 2nd da of 11th Duke of Grafton; 2ndly, 1988, Marie-Claire, yr da of (Michael) Donald Gordon Black, MC, of Edenwood, Cupar, Fife, and has issue living (by 2nd *m*), John Walter Donald Peter, *b* 8 Aug 1988, — Frederic James Michael Ralph, *b* 1989, — Francis Andrew William George, *b* 1991.

DAUGHTERS LIVING

Lady Mary Marianella Anne, *b* 1944; BA (Open Univ): *m* 1970, Charles von Westenholz, of Little Blakesware, Widford, Ware, Herts, and has issue living, Alexander Peter Frederik, *b* 1971, — Mark Henry Cosimo, *b* 1973, — Nicholas Anthony Philip, *b* 1975.
Lady Cecil Nennella Therese *b* 1948; BA (London Univ): *m* 1974, Donald Angus Cameron of Lochiel yr, elder son of Sir Donald Hamish Cameron of Lochiel (*see* D Montrose, 1976 Edn), and has issue (*see* E Cranbrook, colls). *Residences –* Achnacarry, Spean Bridge, Inverness-shire; 26 The Little Boltons, SW10.
Lady Clare Amabel Margaret (*Countess of Euston*), *b* 1951; *ed* London Univ (BA, MA): *m* 1972, James Oliver Charles, Earl of Euston, son of 11th Duke of Grafton. *Residences –* The Racing Stables, Euston, Thetford, Norfolk; 6 Vicarage Gdns, W8.
Lady Elizabeth Marian Frances (*Countess of Dalkeith*), *b* 1954; Chm Scottish Ballet since 1990: *m* 1981, Richard Walter John, Earl of Dalkeith, son of 9th Duke of Buccleuch. *Residences –* Dabton, Thornhill, Dumfriesshire; 6/1 Pembridge Cres, W11.

BROTHER LIVING (*Raised to the rank of a Marquess's son* 1941)

Lord John Andrew Christopher, *b* 1927; *ed* Ampleforth, and Ch Ch, Oxford; late Capt Scots Guards: *m* 1949, Isabel Marion, da of Sir Hugh Gurney, KCMG, MVO (E Southesk, colls), and has issue living, William Walter Raleigh (The Dower House, Melbourne Derby; 11 Micklethwaite Rd, SW6 1QD), *b* 1950: *m* 1985, Griselda Mary, elder da of Brig John Robert Edward Hamilton-Baillie, MC (*see* E Haddington, colls), and has issue living, Robert John Edward *b* 1987, Walter William Raleigh *b* 1992, Cordelia Isabel Marie *b* 1988, — David John, *b* 1952: *m* 1980, Carol Prior, and has issue living, John Andrew David *b* 1981, Andrew Christopher *b* 1984, — Andrew Peter Hugh (29 The Green, Steventon, Oxon), *b* 1955, — Marion Isabel, *b* 1960: *m* 1987, Simon David May, of 7 Granville Rd, SW19, elder son of C. J. May, of 1 The Rushes, Marlow, Bucks, and has issue living, Susannah Isabel Catherine *b* 1990, — Catherine Richenda Margaret, *b* 1965: *m* 1991, Alan McCallie, of 19/9 Nilson Av, Hillsdale, NSW, Australia, yst son of J. McCallie, of 23 Birnham Av, Banana Point, NSW, and has issue living, Beau James *b* 1991, Matthew Ross *b* 1991. *Residence –* Holly Bank, Wootton, Woodstock, Oxford.

COLLATERAL BRANCHES LIVING

Grandchildren of late Francis Ernest Kerr, 3rd and yst son of Rev Lord Henry Francis Charles Kerr, 2nd son of 6th Marquess:—
Issue of late Capt Henry Francis Hobart Kerr, *b* 1878, *d* 1972: *m* 1915, Gertrude Mary, who *d* 1969, da of James Anthony:—
Francis Robert Newsam, OBE, MC, *b* 1916; *ed* Ampleforth; Lt-Col R Scots (TA); DL Berwicks (Vice-Lieut 1971); Palestine 1938-39; 1939-45 War in France, E Africa, and SE Asia (wounded, MC); OBE (Mil) 1961: *m* 1941, Anne Frederica, da of William E. Kitson, of Blanerne House, Edrom, Duns, Berwicks, and has issue living, Henry Mark William (Keveral Gdns, Sea Moss, Seaton, Cornwall), *b* 1946: *m* 1982, Pamela Christine, da of Alfred Edward Noel Delafield, of 59 Howard Rd, Plymstock, Plymouth, Devon, — David Anthony Francis (Blanerne, Edrom, Duns, Berwicks), *b* 1953: *m* 1975, Julia Veronica, da of late William James Bertram, and has issue living, Sarah Anne *b* 1978, Jane Elizabeth *b* 1980, — Susan Mary Kerr, *b* 1952; has retained her maiden name: *m* 1981, Andrew Robert King, of 7 Chelmsford Rd, Mount Lawley, Perth, W Australia 6050, and has issue living, Rory Francis King *b* 1985. *Residence –* Blanerne, Edrom, Duns, Berwicks. —— Monica Mary Cecil, *b* 1917: *m* 1939, Gp Capt William George Devas, CBE, DFC, AFC, RAF (ret), and has issue living, Christopher William Kerr (35 Lurline Gdns, SW11 4DD), *b* 1944; JP 1992: *m* 1970 (*m diss* 1983), Hon Penelope Anne, da of Baron O'Neill of The Maine (Life Baron), and has issue living, William Thomas *b* 1975, — John Robin Ambrose (4 St Martin's Sq, Chichester), *b* 1947; AA Dip, ARIBA: *m* 1970, Rachel Geraldine, da of late Capt Gerald Seymour Tuck, DSO, RN, and has issue living, Frédéric Seymour *b* 1978, Claire Noëlle *b* 1976. *Residence –* 3 Cavendish St, Chichester, W Sussex PO19 3BS. —— Anne Margaret D'Arcy, *b* 1923: *m* 1948, Christopher Scott of Gala (who assumed the surname of Scott in lieu of his patronymic 1940), only son of late Philip Beaumont Frere, MC, and has had issue, John Philip Henry Schomberg, *b* 1952: *m* 1977, Jaqueline Dawn, el da of Colin Rae, of Little Weston House, Little Weston, Som, and has issue living, Alexander Hugh Frere *b* 1982, James Julian Frere *b* 1985, — Dominic Christopher Hugh (Netherbarns Farm House, Netherbarns Farm, by Galashiels), *b* 1955: *m* 1984, Melanie Lydia, elder da of late Craven Nicholas Charrington, of Bures Manor, Reigate, Surrey, and has issue living, Samara Olga Frere *b* 1985, Isabella Zinaida Frere *b* 1986, Anastasia Amelia Frere *b* 1989, Sasha Scarlett Frere *b* 1991, — Julian Sebastian Frere *b* 1956: *m* 1982, Alexandra Hough, and *d* 1984, — Rupert Benjamin Bartle Frere (2 Whitehorse St, W1), *b* 1958, — Sebastian Simon Frere, *b* 1961. *Residences –* Hollybush, Galashiels, and Flat 27, 50 Sloane St, SW1.

Grandchildren of late Charles Wyndham Rodolph Kerr, el son of Lt-Col Lord Charles Lennox Kerr, 4th son (el by 2nd *m*) of 6th Marquess:—
Issue of late Charles Iain Kerr (*Baron Teviot*), DSO, MC, *b* 1874, *d* 1968 (see that title).
Issue of late Major Basil Kerr, DSC, *b* 1879, *d* 1957: *m* (Feb) 1912, Winifred Katharine, who *d* 1974, da of late George Blezard (V Chetwynd):—
Diana Katharine (*Lady Clowes*), MBE, *b* 1916; MBE (Civil) 1977: *m* 1941, Col Sir Henry Nelson Clowes, KCVO, DSO, OBE, late Scots Gds (V Hatherton, colls), who *d* 1993, and has issue living, Andrew Henry (52 Bowerdean St, SW6 3TW), *b* 1942; late Capt Scots Gds; Equerry to HRH the Duke of Gloucester 1966-68: *m* 1968, Georgiana Elisabeth, da of Capt Richard Edward Osborne Cavendish (*see* D Devonshire, colls), and has issue living, Richard (Dickon) William Andrew *b* 1971, Emma Georgiana *b* 1974. *Residence –* 57 Perrymead St, SW6 3TW. —— Elizabeth, *b* 1919: *m* 1946, Lt-Col George Demetriadi, MBE, TD, US Bronze Star, late R Welsh Fus. *Residence –* 9 Wilton St, SW1.

Grandchildren of late Arthur Herbert Kerr, elder son of late Adm Lord Frederic Herbert Kerr (infra):—
Issue of late Com Mark Peregrine Charles Kerr, RN, *b* 1891, *d* 1951: *m* 1918, Mary Catherine, who *d* 1982, da of late Henry Offley Wakeman (*see* Wakeman, Bt, colls):—
Frederic Mark, DFM, *b* 1919; *ed* Canford; 1939-45 War as WO RAFVR (prisoner): *m* 1st, 1947 (*m diss* 1952), Iris Margaret (Urquhart), da of late William Palk Tully; 2ndly, 1952, June, da of Capt Lancelot Gerrard Laurence, and has issue living, (by 2nd *m*) Peregrine Gerrard Mark (Charlton Cottage, Flax Bourton, Bristol), *b* 1955: *m* 1988, Susan Jane, da of Dennis Tucker, of Pound Farm, Cumnor, Oxford, — Christian Anthony Mark, *b* 1960. —— (Mark) David (4/5 Russell Garth Cottage, Eynsford, Dartford, Kent), *b* 1921; *ed* Canford, and Keble Coll, Oxford (BA); late F/O RAFVR; 1939-45 War (despatches): *m* 1959, Diana Law, da of late Arthur Fawcett, of Newmarket. —— John Anthony (East Membury Farm, Membury, E Devon), *b* 1926; *ed* Radley. —— Andrew Philip (Rectory Cottage, Church End, Standlake, Oxon) *b* 1933; *ed* Radley. —— Elizabeth Mary, *b* 1928: *m* 1957, Walter Michael Woodin, of Oak Tree Cottage, Appleton, Abingdon, Oxon, and has issue living, Mark Chandler, *b* 1966, — Elizabeth Mary Anne, *b* 1960: *m* 1982, Robert Patrick Frank Florey, of Rectory Farm, Northmoor, nr Oxford, son of Patrick Florey, of Northmoor, nr Oxford, and has issue living, James Edward Robert *b* 1985, Samuel Michael Thomas *b* 1987.

Granddaughter of late Adm Lord Frederic Herbert Kerr, 6th and yst son of 6th Marquess:—
Issue of late Adm Mark Edward Frederic Kerr, CB, MVO, *b* 1864, *d* 1944: *m* 1906, Rose Margaret, OBE, who *d* 1944, da of late Wilfred Gough, Royal Dragoons:—
Luise Rosemary, *b* 1908. *Residences –* 26 Upper Strand St, Sandwich, Kent; 19 Draycott Av, SW3.

Granddaughters of late Frederic Walter Kerr, DSO, yst son of late Adm Lord Frederic Herbert Kerr (ante):—

Issue of late Ronald William Kerr, *b* 1906, *d* 1972: *m* 1939, Barbara Helen (Barnacarry, Kilninver, Oban, Argyll), da of C. J. Crawford, of Wayside, St Andrews:—
Patricia Margaret, *b* 1940: *m* 1965, Robert James Wakeford, of The Hatch, Staverton, Daventry, Northants, and has issue living, Mark Robert, *b* 1966: *m* 1993, (Julie) Belinda Stannage, — James Richard, *b* 1968, — Ian Frederick, *b* 1974. —— Angela Helen, *b* 1942: *m* 1971, John James Goddard, of 20 Hackthorne Rd, Cashmere, Christchurch, NZ, and has issue living, Nicholas James, *b* 1975, — Penelope Helen, *b* 1978. —— Elizabeth Daphne, *b* 1949: *m* 1975, Charles Colclough Butterworth, who *d* 1988, of Knipochmore, Kilmore, Oban, Argyll, and has issue living, Tom William, *b* 1978, — Janet Helen, *b* 1980.

         Descendants of late Vice-Adm Lord Mark Robert Kerr (3rd son of 5th Marquess), who *m* 1799, Charlotte, *Countess of Antrim* in her own right (see that title).
         Grandsons of late Capt William Walter Raleigh Kerr, grandson of Lt-Col Lord Robert Kerr, 4th son of 5th Marquess:—
         Issue of late Lt-Col Sir (Louis William) Howard Kerr, KCVO, CMG, OBE, late Equerry to HRH the Duke of Gloucester, *b* 1894, *d* 1977: *m* 1928, Christina Stephanie Mary, who *d* 1986, da of late Arthur Ram, of Ramsfort, co Wexford:—
Henry Howard Philip Sackville Casamayor Ram (13 Westbourne Gdns, Hove, Sussex), *b* 1932. —— Andrew Robert Stephen Casamayor (Ninian House, Glasserton, nr Whithorn, Wigtownshire), *b* 1936: *m* 1988, Jacqueline Ellen Andre, da of late Frederick John Bryan, CA, of Vancouver, Canada. —— Julian James Casamayor (53 Belper Rd, Derby), *b* 1941: *m* 1966, Glenys Ann, da of Rev Thomas Hugh Roberts, of Grantham, Lincs, and has issue living, Andrew James, *b* 1967, — Philip Hugh, *b* 1971, — Robert Michael, *b* 1974.

(Not in remainder to the Marquessate)

         Grandchildren of late Col John MacGregor Kerr, son of late Col Alexander Boyd Kerr, grandson of late Patrick Kerr, 6th of Abbotrule, great-grandson of Hon Charles Kerr, 2nd of Abbotrule, yst son of 1st Earl of Lothian:—
         Issue of late Lt-Col Alexander Nairne Kerr, MC, 10th of Abbotrule, *b* 1882; *d* 1964: *m* 1922, Eva Theresa, who *d* 1973, only da of late Francis Herman Milford Wayne, OBE, of Campfield, Battle, Sussex (Kinloch, Bt *cr* 1873):—
†John Kinloch KERR OF ABBOTRULE, *b* 1924; 11th of Abbotrule (matriculated arms at Lyon Court 1975); Capt 17th Dogra Regt, Indian Army; India, Burma and Malaya 1942-45; Cadet Colonial Police Service 1946, served in Singapore, Supt ret 1958: *m* 1951, Jane Barbara, yst da of Montgomery Du Bois Ferguson, OBE, MD, of York, and *d* 1994, leaving issue, James Alexander (153 Leathwaite Rd, SW11 6RW), *b* 1952; yr of Abbotrule; late Capt Coldm Gds: *m* 1984, Alice Rosamond, yr da of Beresford Norman Gibbs, DL, of The Willow Tree, Crudwell, Malmesbury, Wilts, and has issue living, John Montgomery *b* 1989, Henrietta Cecily *b* 1992, — Andrew Nigel (Poplar Gate Lodge, Stanley Downton, Stonehouse, Glos GL10 3QX), *b* 1953; late Capt 17th/21st Lancers, and Royal Gloucestershire Hus: *m* 1979, Frances Columbel, only da of late Maj Robin Leach, of Greengates, Pirbright, Surrey, and has issue living, Alexander Robert *b* 1985, Laura Columbel *b* 1981, Lucy Rose *b* 1982, — Rosemary Ann, *b* 1955: *m* 1980, Roger Edward Wilson, of Parks Farm, Winchcombe, Cheltenham, Glos, GL54 5BX, Glos, 2nd son of Kenneth Wilson, JP, DL, of Sudeley Lodge, Winchcombe, Cheltenham, and has issue living, Charles Kenneth *b* 1982, Henry John *b* 1984, Rupert Thomas Edward *b* 1988, — Georgina Eve, *b* 1960: *m* 1982, Rodney Hill Style, and has issue (*see* Style, Bt, colls), of Green Acre, Steeple Aston, Oxon OX5 3RT. *Residence* – Frocester Lodge, Stonehouse, Glos.
         Issue of late Lt-Col Evan Sinclair Kerr, late The Queen's Own Royal W Kent Regt, *b* 1894, *d* 1990: *m* 1925, Marian Catherine, who *d* 1970, da of late Ven Archdeacon Thomas Karl Sopwith, of Canterbury:—
Janetta Marian, *b* 1927: *m* 1949, Louis Philip Mieville, of Sandhill Farmhouse, Rogate, Petersfield, and has issue living, Marian Susan Julia, *b* 1951: *m* 1977, Guy Wyndham Stocker, and has issue living, Guy Philip William *b* 1981, Louisa Marian *b* 1978, — Sarah Jane, *b* 1955: *m* 1992, William Bruce Woodhead, and has issue living, Anna Jane *b* 1992.

PREDECESSORS – (1) MARK Ker (el son of Mark Ker of Cessford, Commendator or Abbot of Newbottle), an Extraordinary Lord of Session, and Master of Requests, had the Abbey of Newbottle including the Baronies of Newbottle and Prestongrange erected into a barony with title of *Baron* 1587; was *cr Lord Newbottle* (peerage of Scotland) with remainder to his heirs male and assignees 1591; a Commr for holding the Parliament 1597; *cr Earl of Lothian* (peerage of Scotland) with remainder to heirs male of his body 1606; *d* 1609; *s* by his el son (2) ROBERT, 2nd Earl; Master of Requests 1606; not having male issue obtained permission from Crown to transfer titles and estates to el da; *d* 1624, when the earldom was assumed by his next brother William, who, however, was interdicted from using it by the Lords of Council 1632, and the titles were confirmed to his niece (3) ANNE, Countess of Lothian, who *m* Sir William Kerr, Knt, of Ancram branch of the Kerrs of Ferniehurst and a zealous convenanter (engaged in all actions of Scottish Army from commencement of differences between King and Parliament till 1643), el son of Robert Kerr, who in 1633 was *cr Lord Kerr*, of Nisbet, Long-newton and Dolphinstoun, and *Earl of Ancram* (peerage of Scotland), with remainder to the issue male of his 2nd marriage, and in default of those to his heirs male whatsoever; Sir William, was *cr Lord Newbottle*, and *Earl of Lothian* (peerage of Scotland) 1631: *d* 1675; *s* by his el son (4) ROBERT, PC, 4th Earl; received in 1678 a patent of the Earldom with original precedence; *s* by his kinsman Charles, 2nd Earl of Ancram, who *dsp*, in Earldom of Ancram and minor honours; was Justice Gen and in 1692 High Commr to Gen Assembly to Church of Scotland; *cr Lord Ker*, of Newbottle, Oxnam, Jedburgh, Dolphinstoun, and Nisbet, *Viscount of Briene, Earl of Ancram*, and *Marquess of Lothian* (peerage of Scotland) 1701, with remainder to heirs of entail succeeding to his estate in all times to come: *d* 1703; *s* by his son (5) WILLIAM, KT, 2nd Marquess, who had in 1692 *s* by special remainder his kinsman as 4th *Lord Jedburgh* (peerage of Scotland) *cr* 1622; was a Representative Peer, Col 7th Dragoons, and a Lieut-Gen; *d* 1722; *s* by his son (6) WILLIAM, KT, 3rd Marquess; was a Representative Peer 1731-60, Lord Clerk Register 1739-56, and Lord High Commr to Gen Assembly 1732-8; *d* 1767; *s* by his son (7) WILLIAM HENRY, KT, 4th Marquess; a Gen in the Army; sat as MP for Richmond 1747-60, and was afterwards a Representative Peer: *m* 1735, Caroline, who *d* 1778, da of 3rd Earl of Holderness; *d* 1775; *s* by his son (8) WILLIAM JOHN, KT, 5th Marquess; a Gen in the Army, Col 1st Life Guards, and a Representative Peer 1778-84; *d* 1815; *s* by his son (9) WILLIAM, KT, 6th Marquess, *d* 1763; Lord-Lieut of Midlothian and co Roxburgh; *cr Baron Ker*, of Kersheugh, co Roxburgh (peerage of United Kingdom) 1821: *m* 1st, 1793, Henrietta, who *d* 1805, da of 2nd Earl of Buckinghamshire; 2ndly, 1806, Harriet, who *d* 1833, da of 3rd Duke of Buccleuch and Queensberry; *d* 1824; *s* by his el son (10) JOHN WILLIAM ROBERT, 7th Marquess; *b* 1794; Lord-Lieut of co Roxburgh: *m* 1831, Lady Cecil Chetwynd Talbot, da of 2nd Earl Talbot; *d* 1841; *s* by his el son (11) WILLIAM SCHOMBERG ROBERT, 8th Marquess, *b* 1832: *m* 1857, Lady Constance Harriet Mahonesa Talbot, who *d* 1901, da of 18th Earl of Shrewsbury; *dsp* 1870; *s* by his brother (12) SCHOMBERG HENRY, 9th Marquess; *b* 1833; sometime in Diplo Ser; Sec for Scotland, Keeper of Great Seal of Scotland, and Vice-Pres of Scottish Education Depart 1887-92; Capt-Gen of Roy Co of Archers and Gold Stick of Scotland, Lord Keeper of Privy Seal of Scotland, and Pres of So of Antiquaries of Scotland: *m* 1865, Lady Victoria Alexandrina Montagu-Douglas-Scott, who *d* 1938, da of 5th Duke of Buccleuch, KG; *d* 1900; *s* by his only surviving son (13) ROBERT SCHOMBERG, 10th Marquess; *b* 1874; *d* 1930; *s* by his cousin (14) PHILIP HENRY, KT, CH, PC (son of late Maj-Gen Lord Ralph Drury Kerr, KCB, 3rd son of 7th Marquess), 11th Marquess; *b* 1882; Sec to Prime Min 1917-21, and to Rhodes Trust 1925-39, Chancellor of Duchy of Lancaster Aug to Nov 1931, Under-Sec of State for India Nov 1931 to Sept 1932, and Ambassador Extraor, and Plen at Washington 1939-40; *d* 1940; *s* by his kinsman (15) PETER FRANCIS WALTER (son of late Capt Andrew William Kerr, RN, grandson of 7th Marquess), 12th Marquess and present peer; also Earl of Ancram, Earl of Lothian, Viscount of Briene, Lord Newbottle, Lord Jedburgh, Lord Kerr (*cr* 1633), Lord Ker (*cr* 1701), and Baron Ker (*cr* 1821).

LOUDOUN, COUNTESS OF (Abney-Hastings) (Lordship S 1601 and 1633. Earldom S 1633)

BARBARA HUDDLESTON ABNEY-HASTINGS, *Countess of Loudoun*; *b* 3 July 1919; *s* 1960; assumed (with her husband) by deed poll 1955 the surname of Abney-Hastings in lieu of that of Griffiths; Hereditary Gov of Repton Sch, and Etwall Hospital; is a co-heiress (with her sister, nephew and nieces) to the Baronies of Botreaux, Stanley (*cr* 1456) and Hastings (*cr* 1461): *m* 1st, 1939 (*m diss* 1945), Capt Walter Strickland Lord; 2ndly, 1945, Capt Gilbert Frederick Greenwood, who *d* 1951; 3rdly, 1954, Peter Griffiths, who assumed the surname of Abney-Hastings in lieu of his patronymic by deed poll, 1955, and has issue by 1st, 2nd, and 3rd *m*.

Arms – Quarterly; 1st and 4th argent, a maunch sable, *Hastings*; 2nd and 3rd or, on a chief gules, a demi-lion issuant argent, *Abney*. **Supporters** – *Dexter*, a man in armour, plumed on the head with three feathers gules, and holding with the right hand a spear in bend proper; *sinister*, a lady richly apparelled plumed on the head with three feathers argent, and holding in the left hand a letter of challenge.
Residence – Mount Walk, Ashby-de-la-Zouch, Leics.

SONS LIVING *(By 1st marriage)*

MICHAEL EDWARD ABNEY-HASTINGS (*Lord Mauchline*) (74 Coreen St, Jerilderie, NSW 2716, Australia), *b* 22 July 1942; *ed* Ampleforth; assumed by deed poll 1946 the surname of Abney-Hastings in lieu of his patronymic: *m* 1969, Noelene Margaret, da of W. J. McCormick, of Barham, NSW, and has issue:—
   SONS LIVING—*Hon* SIMON MICHAEL, *b* 1974, — *Hon* Marcus William, *b* 1981.
   DAUGHTERS LIVING—*Hon* Amanda Louise, *b* 1969, — *Hon* Lisa Maree, *b* 1971, — *Hon* Rebecca Lee (twin), *b* 1974.

(By 2nd marriage)

Hon Frederick James ABNEY-HASTINGS, *b* 1949.

DAUGHTERS LIVING *(By 2nd marriage)*

Lady Selina Mary, *b* 1946: *m* 1967, William Newman, and has issue living, Christopher James Loudoun, *b* 1972, — Selina Anne, *b* 1968. *Residence* – Old Place, Ansty, W Sussex.

(By 3rd marriage)

Lady Margaret Maude, *b* 1956: *m* 1977, Brian Peter Ludlow, and has issue living, Thomas William, *b* 1983, — Peter Arthur, *b* 1987, — Kathleen Rose, *b* 1981, — Iona Clare (twin), *b* 1981, — Alice Selina, *b* 1985, — Joy Elizabeth, *b* 1990.
Lady Mary Joy, *b* 1957: *m* 1982, David John Flowers, and has issue living, Clare Hannah, *b* 1987.
Lady Clare Louise ABNEY-HASTINGS, *b* 1958.

SISTER LIVING *co-heiress to the Baronies of Botreaux, Stanley (cr 1456) and Hastings (cr 1461)*

Lady Edith Huddleston, *b* 1925: *m* 1947, Major David Kenneth Maclaren, and has issue living Norman Angus, *b* 1948, — Roderic John (Ardvullin, Ardgour, by Fort William, Inverness-shire) *b* 1950: *m* 1st, 1981 (*m diss* 1993), Victoria Helen Elizabeth Glaysher; 2ndly, 1993, Kirsty Rowena Amabel, yr da of Sir Charles Edward McGrigor, 5th Bt, and formerly wife of David Norman G. Barraclough, and has issue living (by 1st *m*), Christopher Rory James *b* 1988, (by 2nd *m*) Catriona Mary Edith *b* 1993. *Residence* – Ard daraich, Ardgour, by Fort William, Inverness-shire.

COLLATERAL BRANCHES LIVING *also in remainder to the Baronies of Botreaux, Stanley (cr 1456), and Hastings (cr 1461)*

Grandchildren of late Edith Maud, Countess of Loudoun, 13th holder of the peerage:—
Issue of late Lady Jean Huddleston Campbell of Loudoun (*s* to the estate by deed of gift from her mother, and assumed the surname of Campbell), *b* 1920, *d* 1981: *m* 1st, 1940 (*m diss* 1949), Edgar Wright Wakefield; 2ndly, 1954 (*m diss* 1964), Capt Arthur Alexander Hubble, Queen's Bays:—
(By 1st *m*) Sheena, *b* 1941; co-heiress to Baronies of Botreaux, Stanley and Hastings: *m* 1968, Donald Russell Williams, of New York City, USA, and has issue living, Amanda Sara Edith, *b* 1970. *Residence* – Loudoun, 7840 North Desert Pass Rd, Tucson, Arizona 85743, USA. —— (By 2nd *m*) Flora Ann Madeleine, *b* 1957; co-heiress to Baronies of Botreaux, Stanley and Hastings: *m* 1975 (*m diss* 1992), John Robert Kerr, and has issue living, John Campbell, *b* 1980, — Britt Jean, *b* 1975, — Emma Jennifer, *b* 1977. *Residence* – Peelhill Farm, Drumclog, Lanarks ML10 6RQ.
Issue of late Lady Fiona Huddleston Abney-Hastings, *b* 1923, *d* 1990: *m* 1940, Capt Robert Conroy-Robertson (Cessnock Castle, Galston, Ayreshire), who assumed by deed poll 1944 the surname of de Fresnes, in lieu of his patronymic, having *s* his maternal grandfather as 12th Baron de Fresnes (*cr* France 1642):—
(Christopher) Ian (Elm Tree House, High Halden, Ashford, Kent), *b* 1942; co-heir to Baronies of Botreaux, Stanley and Hastings; *ed* Ampleforth, and Glasgow Sch of Art: *m* 1st, 1969 (*m diss* 1971), Elvira Maria, da of W/Cdr Marcel Pustelniak; 2ndly, 1973, Angela Margaret, da of Lt-Col Denys Ainsworth Yates, and has issue living (by 1st *m*), Robert Marcel, *b* 1970, — (by 2nd *m*) Rawdon Alexander Denys, *b* 1974, — Nicola Margaret, *b* 1975. —— Nigel Diarmid (8839 Broadway St, Chilliwack, BC, Canada), *b* 1944; *ed* Ampleforth: *m* 1965, Dolores Emelyn, da of Isidore Douglas Grinder, of Clinton, BC, Canada, and has issue living, Robert Aaron Bryan, *b* 1969, — Christel Rose Helen, *b* 1966: *m* 1993, Michael John Fisher, and has issue living, Adrian Isidore Robert *b* 1991, — Iona Elisabeth Louise, *b* 1968. —— Paulyn Armand, *b* 1949; *ed* Ampleforth: *m* 1973 (*m diss* 19—), Kaija, da of Dr Franf, of Finland, and has issue living, Ida Piri Pulikukka Fiona, *b* 1974. —— Vivian Robert James George, *b* 1960; *ed* Merchiston Castle Sch, Edinburgh: *m* 1988, Jill, da of Peter Hendric, of Edinburgh, and has issue living, Peter James *b* 1989, Joseph Robert *b* 1990. —— (Iona Mary) Nicole, *b* 1957: *m* 1982, Timothy John Kerr Kirkwood, of Culfoichmore, Advie, Grantown on Spey, Morayshire, and has issue living, Toby John, *b* 1989, — Arthur George, *b* 1992, — Harriet Mary, *b* 1984, — Matilda Alice, *b* 1986, — Jemima Jane, *b* 1987, — Phoebe Maud, *b* 1990, — Augusta Fiona, *b* 1994.

Issue of late Hon Lelgarde de Clare Elizabeth Rawdon Hastings, only da of 1st Viscount St Davids, by his

2nd wife Elizabeth Frances, Baroness Strange of Knokin, Hungerford and de Moleyns (yr sister of Edith Maud, Countess of Loudoun), *b* 1918, *d* 1984: *m* 1950 (*m diss* 1967), Colin Charles Evans:—
See V St Davids.

Granddaughters of late Gilbert Theophilus Clifton, 3rd Baron Donington, brother of 11th Earl of Loudoun:—
Issue of late Hon Margaret Selina Flora Maud, *b* 1895, *d* 1975: *m* 1917, Sir Edward Orde MacTaggart-Stewart, 2nd Bt, late Capt Gren Gds, who *d* 1948:—
See MacTaggart-Stewart, Bt (ext).
Issue of late Hon Irene Mary Egidia, *b* 1898, *d* 1961: *m* 1927, Lt-Col Richard St Barbe Emmott, MFH, late 6th Gurkha Rifles, who *d* as the result of a hunting accident 1949:—
Patricia Egidia Hastings, *b* 1929: *m* 1950, Lt-Col Stafford Nugent Floyer-Acland, CBE, King's Own Yorkshire LI, who *d* 1994, and has issue (*see* Acland, Bt, *cr* 1678, colls). *Residence* – The Dairy House, W Stafford, Dorchester, Dorset. —— Moira Anne St Barbe, *b* 1931: *m* 1st, 1953 (*m diss* 1965), Capt David Anderson Vetch, Queen's Royal Irish Hus; 2ndly, 1980, Lt-Col Alec Dow, who *d* 1987, of 1 Parkway, Ruishton, Taunton, Som TA3 5JX, and has issue living (by 1st *m*), James William Anderson (47 New North Rd, South Park, Reigate, Surrey RH2 8LZ), *b* 1958: *m* 1978, Patricia Eileen, da of Daniel Haste, of 59 Hatch Gdns, Tadworth, Surrey, and has issue living, Rachel Anne *b* 1980, Amanda Jane *b* 1982, — Belinda Louise, *b* 1956; has issue living (by Ian James McKee, of 41 Charlotte St, Lilyfield, NSW 2040, Australia), Aniella Caitlin Emmott McKee *b* 19—. —— Bridget Griselda Kemble, *b* 1934: *m* 1955, John Anthony Copley, JP, DL, and has issue living, Robert Anthony, *b* 1960: *m* 1986, Diana Mary, yst da of Charles Talbot Rhys Wingfield (*see* V Powerscourt, colls), and has issue living, Jack Anthony Talbot *b* 1989, Alice Florence Hastings *b* 1992, — Jane Belinda, *b* 1957: *m* 1985, John David Beaton, of The Old Rectory, Kinnerley, Shropshire, and has issue living, Camilla Jane Moira *b* 1987, Emily *b* 1989. *Residence* – Winter Field Farm, Melbury Abbas, Dorset.

Descendants of late Lady Victoria Mary Louisa Kirwan, 3rd da of 2nd Marquess of Hastings and 7th Earl of Loudoun (*see* By Grey de Ruthyn).

Descendants of late Lady Frances Augusta Constance Muir, yst da of 2nd Marquess of Hastings and 7th Earl of Loudoun, and wife of 4th Earl of Romney (see that title).

PREDECESSORS – (1) *Sir* HUGH Campbell of Loudoun, co Ayr, PC; *cr Lord Campbell of Loudoun* (peerage of Scotland) 1601; *d* 1622; *s* by his grand-da (2) MARGARET (el da of George, Master of Loudoun): *m* c 1620, Sir John Campbell of Lawers (descended from Campbell of Glenorchy), who was *cr Earl of Loudoun* and *Lord Tarrinzean and Mauchline* (peerage of Scot) 1633, with remainder to his heirs male, but, since he opposed the crown, the patent was superseded until 1641, when it was issued with original precedence; Lord Chancellor of Scotland 1641-1660 and 1st Commr of the Treasury, 1641-44; *d* 1662; *s* by his son (3) JAMES, 2nd Earl: *m* 1666, Lady Margaret Montgomerie, da of 7th Earl of Eglinton; *d* 1684; *s* by his son (4) HUGH, KT, PC, 3rd Earl; resigned his titles 1707, and obtained a new patent with remainder to heirs male of his body, heirs gen of 1st Earl and heirs male whatsoever of 1st Earl; Lord Keeper of Scotland 1708-13: *m* 1700, Lady Margaret Dalrymple who *d* 1779, da of 1st Earl of Stair; *d* 1731; *s* by his son (5) JOHN, 4th Earl; *b* 1705, Gen; *d* unm 1782; *s* by his cousin (6) JAMES, Mure-Campbell, 5th Earl (son of Hon Sir James Campbell, 3rd son of 2nd Earl); Maj-Gen *m* 1777, Flora, who *d* 1780, da of John MacLeod of Raasay; *d* 1786; *s* by his only da (7) FLORA, Countess of Loudoun; *b* 1780: *m* 1804, Francis Rawdon-Hastings, 2nd Earl of Moira,* who was *cr Marquess of Hastings* 1816 and *d* 1826; she *d* 1840, and was *s* by her only surv son (8) GEORGE AUGUSTUS FRANCIS, 7th Earl (and 2nd Marquess of Hastings); *b* 1808: *m* 1831, Barbara, Baroness Grey de Ruthyn, who *d* 1858, (having *m* 2ndly, 1845, Adm Sir Hastings Reginald Yelverton, GCB); *d* 1884; *s* by his el son (9) PAULYN REGINALD SERLOE, 8th Earl (and 3rd Marquess); *b* 1832; *d* unm 1851; *s* by his brother (10) HENRY WEYSFORD CHARLES PLANTAGENET, 9th Earl (and 4th Marquess); *b* 1842; *s* his mother 1858 as *Baron Grey de Ruthyn*: *m* 1864, Lady Florence Cecilia Paget, who *d* 1907 (having *m* 2ndly, 1870, Sir George Chetwynd, 4th Bt); *d* 1868, when the Marquessate of Hastings and subsidiary peerages became ext (except the English Baronies mentioned below), and the Scottish peerages devolved upon his el sister (11) EDITH MAUD; *b* 1833: *m* 1853, Charles Frederick Clifton, who assumed 1859 by Act of Parl the surname of Abney-Hastings, was *cr Baron Donington* 1880, and *d* 1895; she *d* 1874; *s* by her son (12) CHARLES EDWARD HASTINGS, 11th Earl; *b* 1855; assumed 1887 by Roy licence the name of Rawdon-Hastings; bore one of the gold spurs at Coronation 1902 and 1911: *m* 1880, Hon Alice Mary Elizabeth Fitzalan-Howard, who *d* 1915, da of 1st Baron Howard of Glossop; *d* 1920, when the Barony of Donington passed to his 2nd brother, and the Scottish peerages to his niece, (13) EDITH MAUD, Countess of Loudoun (el da of Hon Paulyn Francis Cuthbert Rawdon-Hastings); *b* 1883: *m* 1916 (*m diss* 1947), Capt Reginald Mowbray Chichester Huddleston: they assumed by Roy licence 1918 the surname of Abney-Hastings; *d* 1960; *s* by her el da (14) BARBARA HUDDLESTON, present peeress, also Lady Campbell of Loudoun, and Lady Tarrinzean and Mauchline.

*The 1st Marquess of Hastings, *s* in 1808 to the Baronies of Botreaux (*cr* 1368), Hungerford (*cr* 1426), Moleyns (*cr* 1445), and Hastings (*cr* 1461). They fell into abeyance 1868 between the sisters of the 4th Marquess of Hastings, but were called out in 1871 in favour of Edith Maud Countess of Loudoun (*b* 1833). They again fell into abeyance in 1920 between Edith Maud Countess of Loudoun (*b* 1883) and her sisters. In 1921 the baronies of Botreaux, Stanley (*cr* 1456), and Hastings were called out of abeyance in favour of the Countess of Loudoun, but on her death in 1960 they again fell into abeyance between her daughters, of whom the el is the Countess of Loudoun.

Loughborough, Lord; son of Earl of Rosslyn.

LOUTH, BARON (Plunkett) (Baron I 1541)

Hasten slowly

OTWAY MICHAEL JAMES OLIVER PLUNKETT, 16th Baron; *b* 19 Aug 1929; *s* 1950; *ed* Downside: *m* 1951, Angela Patricia, da of W. Cullinane, of St Helier, Jersey, and has issue.

Arms – Sable, a bend, and in the sinister chief a tower argent. **Crest** – A horse passant argent. **Supporters** – *Dexter*, a pegasus, wings inverted, per fesse, or and argent; *sinister*, an antelope argent, armed, unguled, plain collared and chained or.
Residence – Les Sercles, 8 La Grande Pièce, St Peter, Jersey.

SONS LIVING

Hon JONATHAN OLIVER (Les Sercles, La Grande Pièce, St Peter, Jersey), *b* 4 Nov 1952; *ed* de la Salle Coll, Jersey, Hautlieu Sch, Jersey, and Hull Univ (BSc); AMIEE: *m* 1981, Jennifer, da of Norman Oliver Hodgetts, of Coventry, and has issue living, Matthew Oliver, *b* 22 Dec 1982, — Agatha Elizabeth, *b* 1985.

Hon Otway Jeremy Oliver (36 Midhurst Av, W Croydon, Surrey CR0 3PR), *b* 1954: *m* 1st, 1971 (*m diss* 1982), Ruth Levine; 2ndly, 1983, Alice Veronica Tierney, and has issue living (by 1st *m*), Oliver, *b* 1972, — Benjamin Otway, *b* 1974.

Hon Timothy James Oliver (17 South Riding, Bricket Wood, St Albans, Herts AL2 3NG), *b* 1956; *ed* de la Salle Coll, Jersey: *m* 1984, Julie Anne Cook, and has issue living, Joseph Timothy Oliver, *b* 1989, — Sophie Louise, *b* 1987, — Emma Jane, *b* 1991, — Stephanie Anne, *b* 1993.

DAUGHTERS LIVING

Hon Olivia Jane, *b* 1953: *m* 1974 (*m diss* 1982), Trevor Billingsley, and has issue living, James Michael *b* 1975, — Nicola Jane, *b* 1977.

Hon Stephanie Patricia (Forest Farm, Forest Lane, Hanbury, Worcs B60 4HP), *b* 1963.

WIDOW LIVING OF SON OF FOURTEENTH BARON

Gwendoline Mary, da of E. A. Cowling, of Torquay: *m* (Feb) 1936, Hon Randal Patrick Ralph Oliver Plunkett, who *d* (July) 1936. *Residence* –

COLLATERAL BRANCHES LIVING

Issue (if any) of late Harry Edward Plunkett, el son of late Hon Edward Sydney Plunkett (*infra*), *b* 1848, *d* 1906: *m* 1877, Marianne, da of George Smith, of Dalkey, co Dublin.

Grandchildren of late Charles Seale Plunkett, Lieut 95th Regt, son of late Major Hon Edward Sydney Plunkett, 5th son of 11th Baron:—

Issue of late Sydney Wilmott Plunkett, *b* 1877, *d* 1955: *m* 1904, Elizabeth Josephine, who *d* 1960, da of John Patrick Higgins, of Rathmines, Dublin:—

Charles Seale (180 Perth Street West, Hull), *b* 1908; 1939-45 War (despatches): *m* 1934, Julia Elizabeth, da of Walter Brown, of Hull, and has issue living, Merrick Shawe (51 Woodlands Rd, Willerby, Hull), *b* 1934: *m* 1956, Eileen, da of T. Armstrong, of Leeds, and has issue living, Patrick Allan *b* 1958; *ed* Hull Gram Sch, and Bretton Hall Coll (BEd), Glenn Charles *b* 1966, Angela *b* 1963. —— Norman Dawson (19A Alwyne Rd, Canonbury, N1), *b* 1910; *ed* Bishop Wordsworth's Sch, Salisbury, Muresk Agricultural Coll, W Aust, and Sch of Mines and Metallurgy, W Aust (BA, BSc); Founder of Norden Youth Club: *m* 1932, Caroline, da of R. Bernhales, of Milan, Italy, and has issue living, Terence Norman, *b* 1933: *m* 1957, Lilian Elizabeth, da of John Warren, of London, and has issue living, Michael Terence *b* 1958, Curtis Alan *b* 1962. —— Randal Otway (5 Brompton Close, Bricknell Av, Hull, Yorks), *b* 1914; 1939-45 War: *m* 1935, Sylvia May, da of E. Rutherford, of Hull, and has issue living, Anthony Patrick (29 Davenport Av, Hessle, N Humberside HU13 0RL), *b* 1939; *ed* Hull Gram Sch: *m* 1969, Ann Elisabeth Bennett, and has issue living, Matthew Patrick *b* 1972, Simon James *b* 1975, — Eve, *b* 1935: *m* 1958, Philip John Turner, and has issue living, Mark Stephen *b* 1959: *m* 1994, Francesca, da of K. E. Dodd, of Welwyn, Herts, Nicholas Matthew *b* 1960. —— Oliver Penson *b* 1917: *m* 1947, Jean Elizabeth, da of H. Hewson, of Hull, and has issue living, Sean Patrick (41 Kennington Av, Bishopston, Bristol), *b* 1948; *ed* Hull Gram Sch, and Ealing Tech Coll: *m* 1985, Antonia Susan, da of Florian Brann, of London, and has issue living, Leo Joseph *b* 1988, Caitlin Martha *b* 1986. *Residence* – 4 Hartoft Rd, Hull, Yorks.

Grandchildren of late Matthew Penson Plunkett, 4th son of Merrick Shawe Plunkett, 2nd son of Hon Matthew Plunkett, 2nd son of 10th Baron:—

Issue of late Sydney Penson Plunkett, *b* 1903, *d* 1976: *m* 1928 (*m diss* 1955), Helen Margaret, only da of H. A. Pattullo, MB, of Kelsall, Cheshire:—

Anthony Penson (Rydings Cottage, Mackies Hill, Peaslake, Surrey), *b* 1931: *m* 1956, Anne Malkin White, of Harpenden, Herts, and has issue living, Timothy Penson, *b* 1959: *m* 1982, Carol Anne Parr, of Fetcham, Surrey, — Andrew Christopher, *b* 1961: *m* 1985, Christine Anne Meysner, of Leicester. —— Jean Margaret, *b* 1929: *m* 1955, John Travers Clark, and has issue living, Charles James Travers, *b* 1961: *m* 1988, Maura Teresa Lynch, — Caroline Travers, *b* 1957: *m* 1985, Sqdn Ldr Clive Wood, and has issue living, Benjamin Richard *b* 1987, — Bridget Travers, *b* 1959: *m* 1981, Richard Pilling, and has issue living, Katherine Anne *b* 1987.

PREDECESSORS – (1) *Sir* OLIVER Plunkett, Knt; *cr Baron Louth* (peerage of Ireland) 1541; *s* by his son (2) THOMAS, 2nd Baron; *d* 1571; *s* by his el son (3) PATRICK, 3rd Baron; was slain 1575 in endeavouring to recover cattle that had been stolen from him; *s* by his brother (4) OLIVER, 4th Baron, *d* 1607; *s* by his son (5) MATTHEW, 5th Baron; *d* 1629; *s* by his son (6) OLIVER, 6th Baron; joined the Royalists 1639, and served at the siege of Drogheda; appointed Col-Gen of all the forces to be raised in co Louth; outlawed 1642; *d* 1679; *s* by his son (7) MATTHEW, PC, 7th Baron; was restored to his estates after the Restoration, and appointed Lord Lieut of co Louth; attached himself to the cause of James II, and was exiled 1689; *d* 1689; *s* by his son (8) OLIVER, 8th Baron, who however was not permitted to take his seat in consequence of his father's outlawry not having been reversed; *d* 1707; *s* by his son (9) MATTHEW, 9th Baron; *d* 1754; *s* by his son (10) OLIVER, 10th Baron; *d* 1763; *s* by his son (11) THOMAS OLIVER, 11th Baron; procured a reversal of the outlawry, and was restored to his ancestral honour 1798; *d* 1823; *s* by his son (12) THOMAS OLIVER, 12th Baron; *d* 1809; *d* 1849; *s* by his son (13) RANDAL PERCY OTWAY, 13th Baron, *b* 1832: *m* 1st, 1867, Anna Maria McGeough, who *d* 1868, da of late Walter McGeough Bond, of Drumsill and the Argory, co Armagh; 2ndly, 1877, Elizabeth Lily, who *d* 1916, da of late John Black of Ceylon; *d* 1883; *s* by his son (14) RANDAL PILGRIM RALPH, 14th Baron, *b* 1868: *m* 1st 1890 (*m diss* 1912), Eugénie de Miarritze, who *d* 1952, da of late Capt Edmund Hooke Wilson Bellairs, HM's Vice-Consul at Biarritz, France; 2ndly, 1913, Dorothy Lettice, who *d* 1923, da of late Col Thomas Lewis Hampton-Lewis, of Henllys, Anglesey; 3rdly, 1926, Marie Ethel, who *d* 1941, da of late Charles Read, solicitor, of Hampstead, NW, and widow of Sir John Prichard-Jones, 1st Bt; *d* 1941; *s* by his son (15) OTWAY RANDAL PERCY

OLIVER, 15th Baron, *b* 1892: *m* 1927, Ethel Molly, who *d* 1992, da of Walter John Gallichen, of Jersey: *d* 1950; *s* by his son
(16) OTWAY MICHAEL JAMES OLIVER, 16th Baron and present peer.

LOVAT, LORD (Fraser) (Lord S 1458-64, Baron UK 1837)

(Title pronounced "Luvvut")

I am ready

SIMON CHRISTOPHER JOSEPH FRASER, DSO, MC, TD, 15th (*de facto*) Lord and 17th but for the attainder; *b* 9 July 1911; *s* 1933; *ed* Ampleforth Coll, and Magdalen Coll, Oxford (MA); Hon LLD Nova Scotia 1952, and Simon Fraser Univ 1962, and 1972; 24th Ch of Clan Fraser; a JP of Inverness; Brig Army Commandos, Scots Gds, and Lovat Scouts (TA), and a DL for Inverness; OStJ; Knt of Sovereign Mil Order of Malta; Joint Under-Sec of State for Foreign Affairs May to July 1945; 1939-45 War at operations in Norway, at Dieppe and in Normandy (wounded MC, DSO, Legion of Honour, Croix de Guerre, Order of Suvorov, 3rd class, of USSR, Norwegian Cross); DSO 1942: *m* 1938, Rosamond, only da of Maj Sir Henry John Delves Broughton, 11th Bt, and has had issue.

Arms – Quarterly: 1st and 4th azure, three cinquefoils argent; 2nd and 3rd argent, three antique crowns gules. Crest – A buck's head erased, proper. Supporters – Two bucks, proper.
Seat – Beaufort Castle, Beauly, Inverness-shire. *Residence* – Balblair House, Beauly, Inverness-shire. *Club* – Guards'.

SONS LIVING AND DECEASED

†*Hon* Simon Augustine, Master of Lovat, *b* 28 Aug 1939; *ed* Ampleforth; Lieut Scots Guards: *m* 1972, Virginia, da of David Grose, of 49 Elystan St, SW3, and *d* (26 March) 1994, leaving issue, SIMON (*Master of Lovat*), *b* 13 Feb 1977; *ed* Harrow, — Jack, *b* 1984, — Violet, *b* 1972, — Honor, *b* 1973.
Hon Kim Maurice (Wedhampton Cottage, Devizes, Wilts SN10 3QE), *b* 1946; *ed* Ampleforth; Lt Scots Gds: *m* 1975, Joanna Katherine, da of Maj Geoffrey Edward Ford North, MC (*see* B Walsingham), and has issue living, Thomas Oswald Mungo, *b* 1976, — Joseph Oscar Edward, *b* 1978, — Maximilian Alexander Kim, *b* 1981.
Hon Hugh Alastair Joseph, *b* 1947; *ed* Ampleforth, and Ch Ch, Oxford: *m* 1976, Drusilla Jane, da of J. Alastair Montgomerie, of Gilmilnscroft Mains, Sorn, Ayrshire, and has issue living, Raoul Alastair Joseph, *b* 1980, — Poppy Augusta, *b* 1979, — Eloise Hermione, *b* 1986.
†*Hon* Andrew Roy Matthew, *b* 1952; *ed* Ampleforth, and Magdalen Coll, Oxford: *m* 1979, Lady Charlotte Anne Greville (Calle Betis 63, Seville 41010, Spain), only da of 8th Earl of Warwick, and was *k* in a hunting accident in E Africa (15 March) 1994, leaving issue, Daisy Rosamond, *b* 1985, — Laura Alfreda, *b* 1987.

DAUGHTERS LIVING

Hon Fiona Mary, *b* 1941: *m* 1982, Robin Richard Allen (PO Box 6655, Dubai, United Arab Emirates).
Hon Annabel Térèse, *b* 1942: *m* 1st, 1964 (*m diss* 1978), 14th Lord Reay; 2ndly, 1985, Henry Neville Lindley Keswick, of 28 Arlington House, Arlington St, SW1, eldest son of late Sir William Keswick, of Glenkiln, Shawhead, Dumfries (*see* By Lindley, 1950 Edn), and has issue (by 1st *m*) (*see* L Reay).

SISTER LIVING

Hon Veronica Nell (*Hon Lady Maclean of Dunconnel*), *b* 1920: *m* 1st, 1940, Lieut Alan Phipps, RN, who was *ka* Leros 1943 (*see* M Normanby, colls), 2ndly, 1946, Brigadier Sir Fitzroy Hew Royle Maclean of Dunconnel, 1st Bt (*cr* 1957), KT, CBE, MP, and has issue living, (by 1st *m*) (*see* M Normanby, colls), — (by 2nd *m*) (*see* Maclean, Bt), *cr* 1957. *Residence* – Strachur House, Argyll.

COLLATERAL BRANCHES LIVING

Issue of late Rt Hon Sir Hugh Charles Patrick Joseph Fraser, MBE, MP, yr son of 14th Lord, *b* 1918, *d* 1984: *m* 1956 (*m diss* 1977), Lady Antonia Pakenham, da of 7th Earl of Longford:—
Benjamin Hugh (Eilean Aigas, Hughton, Inverness-shire), *b* 1961: *m* 1991, Hon Lucy Elspeth Roper-Curzon, 3rd da of 20th Baron Teynham, and has issue living, Thomas Roper, *b* 1992, — Eliza Wedderburn, *b* 1993. —— Damian Stafford, *b* 1964: *m* 1992, Paloma Porraz del Amo, da of Don Alfredo Porraz Ortiz de la Huerta, of Mexico City. —— Orlando Gregory, *b* 1967. —— Rebecca Rose, *b* 1957; writer and journalist: *m* 1988, Edward Hamilton Fitzgerald, yr son of late Carroll Fitzgerald, and has issue living, Blanche Catherine, *b* 1990, — Atalanta Rose, *b* 1992. —— Flora Elizabeth, *b* 1958; *ed* St Paul's Girls' Sch, and Wadham Coll, Oxford; writer: *m* 1980 (*m diss* 1992), Robert J. Powell-Jones, barrister, son of John Ernest Powell-Jones, CMG, and has issue living, Stella Elizabeth, *b* 1987. —— Natasha Antonia, *b* 1963.

Grandchildren of late Maj Hon Alastair Thomas Joseph Fraser, DSO (*infra*):—
Issue of late Maj Alastair Hugh Joseph Fraser, MC, Lovat Scouts, *b* 1919, *d* 1986: *m* 1950, Philippa Margaret (Moniack Castle, Kirkhill, Inverness-shire), da of late Sir Anselm William Edward Guise, 6th Bt:—
Alastair James (Petit Moniack, CH-1873 Val d'Uliez, VS, Switzerland), *b* 1951; *ed* Ampleforth: *m* 1981, Elizabeth von Wartburg, and has issue living, Victoria Alexandre, *b* 1982, — and an adopted son, Philip, *b* 1985, — and an adopted da, Anne-Sophie, *b* 1983. —— Roderick Joseph (Berwicks Farm House, Hatfield Peverel, Chelmsford, Essex), *b* 1953; *ed* Ampleforth: *m* 1981, Mary Jean, yr da of late Hon Charles Henry Strutt (*see* B Rayleigh, colls), and has issue living, Charles Alastair, *b* 1982, — Harry Edward, *b* 1984, — Caroline Mary, *b* 1988, — Georgina, *b* 1990. —— Christopher (Kit) James (Moniack Castle, Kirkhill, Inverness-shire), *b* 1954; *ed* Ampleforth: *m* 1983, Sarah Louise, only da of J. H. Gladwin, of

Bishops Stortford, Herts, and has issue living, Sandy John, *b* 1988, — Angelica Ishbel, *b* 1987. —— (Peter) Anselm (Myreside Grange, Gifford, E Lothian), *b* 1957; *ed* Ampleforth: *m* 1981, Antonia Hope, da of Lt-Col Thomas Holroyd Gibbon, OBE, of The Field House, Sutton, W Sussex, and has issue living, James Anselm, *b* 1986, — Thomas Alastair, *b* 1987. —— Arabella Mary (*Baroness Huntingfield*), *b* 1959: *m* 1982, 7th Baron Huntingfield, and has issue. —— Sophia Margaret, *b* 1964: *m* 1992, Robin Yates.

Issue of late Maj Hon Alastair Thomas Joseph Fraser, DSO, Lovat Scouts, yst son of 13th Lord, *b* 1877, *d* 1949: *m* 1915, Lady Sibyl Grimston, who *d* 1968, da of 3rd Earl of Verulam:—
Sir Ian James, CBE, MC (South Haddon, Skilgate, Som), *b* 1923; *ed* Ampleforth, and Magdalen Coll, Oxford; Capt Scots Guards (ret); Chm Rolls-Royce Motors Ltd 1971-80, and Chm Lazard Bros & Co Ltd 1980-85; 1939-45 War (MC); *cr* CBE (Civil) 1972, Kt 1986: *m* 1st, 1958, Anne, who *d* 1984, yr da of late Maj Allaster Edward Grant, late Capt 9th Lancers (*see* E Carnarvon, colls, 1985 Edn); 2ndly, 1993, Mrs Fiona Margaret Douglas-Home, da of late Maj Hon Henry Montagu Douglas-Home, MBE (*see* B Home of the Hirsel, colls), and formerly wife of Gregory Martin, and has issue living (by 1st *m*), Alexander Charles Evelyn, *b* 1962, — James Hector Ian, *b* 1963, — Consuelo Catherine Sibyl, *b* 1959: *m* 1989, Guy William Anthony Barker, only son of Kenneth W. Barker, of Cadogan Gdns, SW, and has issue living, Inigo Julian Clare *b* 1993, Theodora *b* 1990, — Domenica Margaret Anne, *b* 1960: *m* 1989, Philip Martin Dunne, elder son of Thomas Raymond Dunne, of Gatley Park, Leominster, Herefords, and has issue living, Evelyn Anne *b* 1990, Matilda Rose *b* 1992. —— †Roderick Andrew Joseph Fraser, *b* 1927; late Lieut Scots Guards: *m* 1958, Ethel Mary (who *m* 2ndly, 1969, Edward Eyre, of The Field House, Gt Durnford, Salisbury, Wilts (*see* B Acton)), da of late Cdr Charles H. Drage, RN (ret), of 38 Sheffield Terrace, W8, and *d* 1964, leaving issue, Anthony Henry Joseph (Flat 4, Wilmington House, Highbury Crescent, N5), *b* 1959; *ed* Ampleforth, and Downing Coll, Camb; Capt Scots Guards: *m* 1994, Hon Fiona Mary Biddulph, only da of 4th Baron Biddulph, — Archibald Ian Charles, *b* 1960; *ed* Ampleforth, and Magdalen Coll, Oxford, — Thomas William Gerard, *b* 1964: *m* 1989 (*m diss* 1994), Emma Louise, da of Ronald Russell Hobbs, of Harrogate, N Yorks, and Mrs Andrew Wilson, of Canford Park, Poole, Dorset, — Eleanor Clare, *b* 1961: *m* 1993, Count Olivier Tanguy Antoine Marie-Ghislain de Rosmorduc, son of late Count Tanguy de Rosmorduc, of Château de Pencran, F-2 800, Pencran, France. —— Simon Joseph (38 Clarendon Rd, W11), *b* 1929; *ed* Ampleforth, and Magdalen Coll, Oxford: *m* 1956, Elspeth Jane, da of H. S. Mackintosh, of 7 Cheyne Court, SW6, and has issue living, Rupert James (132 Stephendale Rd, SW6), *b* 1958: *m* 1987, Anne Elizabeth, da of J. H. Kingston, of Gresham, Woldingham, Surrey, and has issue living, Simon Peter James *b* 1993, Lucy Miranda Jean *b* 1989, Alice 1991, — Cordelia Jane, *b* 1959: *m* 1986, Arthur I. Trueger, of 50 Laurel St, San Francisco, Calif, USA, and has issue living, Alastair William James *b* 1987, Hugh Robin Charles *b* 1988, Ruari *b* 1990, Ian Julian Joseph *b* 1992, — Katharine Julia, *b* 1961: *m* 1990, Mark D. R. Rowan, of Kerswell Priory, Broadhembury, nr Cullompton, Devon EX15 2EA, yr son of late Sir Thomas Leslie Rowan, KCB, CVO, and has issue living, Thomas Simon Leacroft *b* 1992, Alexander Charles Hugh *b* 1994, — Olivia Mary Juliet, *b* 1965: *m* 1991, William Benedict Hamilton-Dalrymple, yst son of Sir Hew Fleetwood Hamilton-Dalrymple, 10th Bt, KCVO, — Perdita Rachel Josephine, *b* 1967, — Helena Jane, *b* 1972. —— Frances Mary, *b* 1916: *m* 1948, Lt-Col Humphrey Joseph Giles Weld, MC, The Queen's Bays (ret), of Chideock Manor, Dorset, and has issue living, Charles Humphrey Joseph, *b* 1949: *m* 1991, Georgina Helen, 2nd da of Sir Francis John Vernon Hereward Dashwood, 11th Bt (*cr* 1707) and has issue (*see* Dashwood, Bt, *cr* 1707), — Gabrielle Mary Frances, *b* 1950: *m* 1980, Amyas Michael George Martelli, of Wooth Manor, Bridport, Dorset, and has issue living, Frederick Amyas *b* 1984, Bartholomew Michael Augustus *b* 1989, Anna-Rose *b* 1983, — Lucinda Mary Rose, *b* 1952: *m* 1977, Tomas Alastair Christie, of Kellas House, by Elgin, Moray, and has issue living, Alexander Tomas *b* 1980, Robert Sylvester *b* 1981, Ewen Humphrey *b* 1988, Isabella Frances Mary *b* 1984, Georgina Mary Rose *b* 1986, — Candida Mary Sibyl, *b* 1956: *m* 1980, Sebastian Anthony Arbuthnot-Leslie, of Warthill, Aberdeenshire, and has issue living, William Anthony *b* 1982, John Alexander *b* 1989, Sofia Louisa *b* 1984, Rose Eleanor *b* 1987, Portia Elizabeth *b* 1990.

PREDECESSORS – (1) Hugh Fraser, one of the hostages for the ransom of James I 1424 was by that monarch granted the Barony of Kinnell, and is sometimes known as Lord Lovat: *d* 1440; *s* by his son (2) Thomas; *d* 1450; *s* by his son (3) Hugh; *cr* a Lord of Parliament as *Lord Lovat or Lord Fraser of Lovat* 1458-64; *s* by his son (4) Thomas, 2nd Lord; *s* by his son (5) Hugh, 3rd Lord; having resigned his estates, they were incorporated into a Barony, and granted 1539 with remainder to his heirs male whatsoever, failing whom to his heirs whatsoever; *s* by his (6) Alexander, 4th Lord; *d* 1557; *s* by his son (7) Hugh, 5th Lord, *d* 1576; *s* by his son (8) Simon, 6th Lord; *s* by his son (9) Hugh, 7th Lord; *d* 1646; *s* by his grandson (10) Hugh, 8th Lord; *d* 1672; *s* by his son (11) Hugh, 9th Lord; *d* 1696; *s* by his great-uncle (12) Thomas, 10th Lord, 3rd son of 7th Lord; *d* 1696; *s* by his son (13) Simon, 11th Lord; was outlawed in 1701 for having seized the widow of the 9th Lord, getting the marriage ceremony performed, and forcibly consummating the nuptials; returned in 1715 on the breaking out of Rebellion, and supported the Govt, for which his outlawry was reversed; in 1745 joined the Pretender, who appointed him Gen of the Highlands, and *cr* him Duke of Fraser; was arrested 1746, and being found guilty of treason was beheaded on Tower Hill, 9 April 1747, his honours and estates being forfeited; his el son (14) Simon; obtained a full pardon and subsequently distinguished himself as a British Gen; *d* 1782; *s* by his brother (15) Archibald Campbell; Col in the Army; *dsp* 1815; his kinsman (16) Thomas Alexander, heir male of Thomas, 2nd son of 4th Lord; *b* 1802; Lieut and Sheriff Principal of co Inverness; *cr Baron Lovat*, of Lovat, co Inverness (peerage of United Kingdom) 1837; in 1854 obtained the reversal of the 11th Lord's attainder, and in 1857 established his right to be 12th Lord Lovat (peerage of Scotland): *m* 1823, Hon Charlotte Georgina Jerningham, da of 7th Baron Stafford; *d* 1875; *s* by his son (17) Simon, 13th Lord; *b* 1828; Lord-Lieut of Inverness: *m* 1866, Alice, who *d* 1938, da of Thomas Weld Blundell, of Ince Blundell Hall, near Liverpool; *d* 1887; *s* by his son (18) Simon Joseph, KT, GCVO, KCMG, CB, DSO, TD, 14th Lord; *b* 1871; Hon Maj-Gen (ret) TA; S Africa 1900-02, as Capt Lovat Scouts (which he raised), 1914-18 War, Comdg Highland Mounted Bde, and as a Dir of Forestry; Chm Forestry Commn 1919-27, and Under-Sec of State for Dominion Affairs Dec 1926 to Dec 1928: *m* 1910, Hon Laura Lister, who *d* 1965, da of 4th Baron Ribblesdale (ext); *d* 1933; *s* by his son (19) Simon Christopher Joseph, 15th Lord and present peer.

Lovel and Holland, Baron, title of Earl of Egmont on Roll of HL.

LOVELACE EARL OF (King) (Earl UK 1838)

Labour itself is a pleasure

PETER AXEL WILLIAM LOCKE KING, 5th Earl; *b* 26 Nov 1951; *s* 1964; *ed* privately: *m* 1st, 1980 (*m diss* 1989), Kirsteen Oihrig, da of Calum Kennedy, of Leethland House, Leethland, Renfrewshire; 2ndly, 1994, Kathleen Anne Smolders, of Melbourne, Australia.

Arms – Sable, three spear heads argent, imbrued proper, on a chief or as many battleaxes azure. **Crest** – A cubit arm vested azure, charged with three ermine spots in fesse or, cuffed argent, grasping in the hand proper, the broken shaft of a spear in bend sinister sable, the butt argent. **Supporters** – Two mastiffs reguardant of a black colour with white belly and nose, collared gules.
Residence – Torridon House, Torridon, Ross-shire.

PREDECESSORS – (1) *Sir* PETER King, Knt, PC; MP for Beeralston 1700-14; was successively Recorder of London, Ch Justice of the Common Pleas, and 1725-33 Lord High Chancellor; *cr Lord King, Baron of Ockham,* co Surrey, 1725; *d* 1734; *s* by his el son (2) JOHN, 2nd Baron; was Out Ranger of Windsor Forest; *dsp* 1740; *s* by his brother (3) PETER, 3rd Baron; *d* unmarried 1754; *s* by his son (6) PETER, 6th Baron; *d* 1793; *s* by his son (7) PETER, 7th Baron; *b* 1776: *m* 1804, Lady Hester Fortescue, da of 1st Earl Fortescue; *d* 1833; *s* by his son (8) WILLIAM, 8th Baron, *b* 1805; *cr Viscount Ockham* and *Earl of Lovelace* (peerage of United Kingdom) 1838; Lord-Lieut of Surrey; assumed for himself and issue by Roy licence 1860, the additional surname and arms of Noel: *m* 1st, 1835, Augusta Ada, who *d* 1852, only da of 6th Baron Byron (the poet); 2ndly, 1865, Jane Crawford, who *d* 1908, widow of Edward Jenkins, BCS; *d* 1893; *s* by his 2nd son (9) RALPH GORDON NOEL Milbanke, 2nd Earl, *b* 1839; assumed by Roy licence 1861 the surname of Milbanke in lieu of Noel; in 1862; *s* as 13th Baron Wentworth (*see* E Lytton): *m* 1st, 1869, Fannie, who *d* 1878, 3rd da of late Rev George Heriot, of Fellow Hills, Berwick; 2ndly, 1880, Mary Caroline, who *d* 1941, el da of late Rt Hon James Stuart-Wortley; *d* 1906, when the Barony of Wentworth passed to his only child Ada Mary, while in the other honours he was *s* by his half-brother (10) LIONEL FORTESCUE, DSO, 3rd Earl, *b* 1865; European War 1915-19 as Major Northumberland Fusiliers, and Staff-Capt; in 1895 received for himself only, Roy licence to continue to use the additional surname and arms of Noel, but resumed by Roy licence 1908 the surname and arms of King only for himself and issue: *m* 1895, Lady Edith Anson, who *d* 1932, da of 2nd Earl of Lichfield; *d* 1929; *s* by his son (11) PETER MALCOLM, 4th Earl, *b* 1905: *m* 1st, 1939, Doris Evison, who *d* 1940; 2ndly, 1951, Manon Lis, who *d* 1990, da of Axel Sigurd Transo of Copenhagen, Denmark, and widow of Baron Carl Frederick von Blixen Finecke; *d* 1964; *s* by his only son (12) PETER AXEL WILLIAM LOCKE, 5th Earl and present peer; also Viscount Ockham, and Lord King, Baron of Ockham.

LOVELL-DAVIS, BARON (Lovell-Davis) (Life Baron 1974)

PETER LOVELL LOVELL-DAVIS, son of late William Lovell Davis, *b* 8 July 1924; *ed* Christ's Coll, Finchley, King Edward VI Sch, Stratford-on-Avon, and Jesus Coll, Oxford (MA); 1939-45 War as Fl Lt, RAF; Man Dir of Davis & Harrison Ltd 1971-73, and of Central Press Features Ltd 1952-71; a Member of Press Gallery of House of Commons 1951-71; Chm of The Features Syndicate Ltd 1972-74; a Dir of other Printing Publishing and Newspaper Cos; a Lord in Waiting to HM 1974-75; Parl Under-Sec of State for Energy 1975-76; Member of Board Commonwealth Development Corpn 1978-84; Vice-Pres of Youth Hotels Assocn since 1977; Trustee of Academic Centre of Whittington Hosp, Highgate, since 1980; Chm Lee Cooper Licensing Services Ltd 1983-90, and Pettifer Morrow & Assocs Ltd since 1986; Member Islington Health Authority 1982-85; *cr Baron Lovell-Davis,* of Highgate, in Greater London (Life Baron) 1974: *m* 1950, Jean, da of late Peter Foster Graham, and has issue.
Residence – 80 North Rd, Highgate, N6 4AA.

SON LIVING

Hon Stephen Lovell, *b* 1955.

DAUGHTER LIVING

Hon Catherine Ruth, *b* 1958.

LOWRY, BARON (Lowry) (Life Baron 1979)

ROBERT LYND ERSKINE LOWRY, PC, son of late Rt Hon Mr Justice (William) Lowry; *b* 1919; *ed* Roy Belfast Academical Inst, and at Jesus Coll, Camb (MA, Hon Fellow 1977); Bar N Ireland 1947, Bencher 1955; Hon Master of Bench, Middle Temple 1973; Hon Bencher King's Inns, Dublin 1973; a Judge of High Court, N Ireland 1964-71, since when Lord Ch Justice of N Ireland, Lord of Appeal in Ordinary 1988-94; Hon Col 5th Bn R Irish Fus 1967-71, and of 5th (Vol) Bn R Irish T & AVR 1971-76; 1939-45 War as Maj R Irish Fus in Tunisia; *cr* PC (NI) 1971, PC (UK) 1974, Knt 1971, and *Baron Lowry,* of Crossgar, co Down (Life Baron) 1979: *m* 1st, 1945, Mary Audrey, who *d* 1987, da of John Martin, of Belfast; 2ndly, Mrs Barbara Adamson Calvert, QC, da of late Albert Parker, CBE, and has issue by 1st *m*.
Residence – White Hill, Crossgar, co Down. *Clubs* – Army and Navy, MCC and R & A.

Hon Sheila Mary, *b* 1950: *m* 1974, Jonathan Austyn Corrall, of 5 Beaconsfield Rd, St Albans, Herts.
Hon Anne Lynd, *b* 1952: *m* 1980, Neville McCoubrey, QGM, and has issue, one son and two das.
Hon Margaret Ina, *b* 1956.

Lowther, Viscount; son of Earl of Lonsdale.

LUCAN, EARL OF (Bingham) Sits as BARON BINGHAM (UK 1934) (Earl I 1795, Baron UK 1934, Bt S 1634)

RICHARD JOHN BINGHAM, 7th Earl, 3rd Baron (UK), and 13th Baronet; *b* 18 Dec 1934; *s* 1964; *ed* Eton; Lt Coldstream Guards (Reserve); Patron of one living: *m* 1963, Veronica Mary, 3rd da (el by 2nd *m*) of late Maj Charles Moorhouse Duncan, MC, and has issue. (The 7th Earl has been missing since 7 Nov 1974).

Arms – Azure a bend plain cottised between six crosses patee or. **Crest** – On a mount vert a falcon rising proper, armed, membered, and belled or. **Supporters** – Two wolves azure, plain collared and chained or.

SON LIVING

GEORGE CHARLES (*Lord Bingham*), *b* 21 Sept 1967; *ed* Eton, and Trin Hall, Camb.

DAUGHTERS LIVING

Lady Frances, *b* 1964; *ed* St Swithun's, Winchester, and Bristol Univ.
Lady Camilla, *b* 1970; *ed* St Swithun's, Winchester, and Balliol Coll, Oxford.

BROTHER LIVING

Hon Hugh (6 Gledhow Gdns, SW5), *b* 1939; *ed* Charterhouse, and Hertford Coll, Oxford.

Christ is my hope

SISTERS LIVING

Lady Jane, *b* 1932; *ed* Badminton Sch, Bristol; MB and BS London 1957: *m* 1960, James D. Griffin, and has issue living, Nicholas Driscoll, *b* 1962, — John Christopher *b* 1963, — Benjamin Dawson, *b* 1966, — Kaitilin Bingham, *b* 1961.
Residence – 444 East 66th St, New York, NY 10021, USA.
Lady Sarah, *b* 1936; *ed* Badminton Sch, Bristol: *m* 1958, Rev Canon William Gilbert Gibbs, and has issue living, Oliver John, *b* 1961: *m* 1993, Isabelle, da of Lt-Col John Halford, of Paris, — Marcia Kaitilin, *b* 1959: *m* 1986, Capt Charles H. C. Lynch-Staunton, LI, yr son of Maj A. C. Lynch-Staunton, of The Coach House, Nunney, Somerset, and has issue living, George Henry *b* 1988, Nicholas John *b* 1989, Patrick Charles *b* 1993, — Selina Helen, *b* 1964: *m* 1989, Abdullah Akinci, son of late A. O. Akinci, of Umraniye, Istanbul, and has issue living, Mustafa Noah *b* 1990, Lütfiye (a da) *b* 1992 , — Madeleine Susannah, *b* 1965. *Residence* – The Vicarage, Guilsborough, Northampton.

WIDOW LIVING OF SON OF FIFTH EARL

Dorothea, yr da of late Rev John Kyrle Chatfield, BD, LLB: *m* 1942, Maj Hon John Edward Bingham, TD, who *d* 1992, and has issue (*see* colls, infra). *Residence* – Nicholls, Udimore, Rye, E Sussex.

COLLATERAL BRANCHES LIVING

Issue of late Maj Hon John Edward Bingham, TD, yr son of 5th Earl, *b* 1904, *d* 1992: *m* 1942, Dorothea (ante), yr da of late Rev John Kyrle Chatfield, BD, LLB:—
Nicholas Charles (Court Lodge Oast, Udimore, Rye, E Sussex TN31 6BB), *b* 1943; *ed* Eton, and INSEAD (Fontainebleau) (MBA): *m* 1976, Catherine Violet, eldest da of late Maj Nigel Stuart Hunter, and has issue living, Charles Nigel, *b* 1979, — Alexandra Romina, *b* 1977. ——— Peter John (Lambsland Farm, Rolvenden, Kent TN17 4PX), *b* 1945; *ed* Eton, and RNC Dartmouth: *m* 1971, Penella, only da of late Dr E. C. Herten-Greaven, of Buenos Aires, and has issue living, Philip Charles, *b* 1974, — Richard Patrick, *b* 1978. ——— David Julian (31 Crescent Grove, SW4 7AF), *b* 1951; *ed* Eton, and Trin Coll, Camb (MA); ARICS.

Grandson of late Maj-Gen Hon Sir Cecil Edward Bingham, GCVO, KCMG, CB, 2nd son of 4th Earl:—
Issue of late Lt-Col Ralph Charles Bingham, CVO, DSO, *b* 1885, *d* 1977: *m* 1913, Dorothy Louisa, who *d* 1967, da of late Edward Roger Murray Pratt (B Dunleath):—
John Nigel (Stone House, Brimpton, Reading), *b* 1915; *ed* Eton, and Trin Coll, Camb (BA); Capt Coldm Gds (Reserve); 1939-45 War: *m* 1943, Elisabeth Rosamund, da of late Maj Sir Algernon Thomas Peyton, 7th Bt, and has issue living, Lavinia Frances, *b* 1949: *m* 1975, Robert David Barbour, of Baglake Farm, Litton Cheney, Dorchester, Dorset, only son of late Brig David Charles Barbour, OBE, of Shortheath House, Sulhamstead, Reading, and has issue living, Henry George *b* 1979, Alexandra Frances *b* 1981, — Veronica Annabel, *b* 1952: *m* 1988, Raymond John Williams, of Praise Court, Farthingstone, Northants, eldest son of Howard John Williams, of 21 Pilgrims Lane, Bugbrook, Northants, and has issue living, Anna Grace Joan *b* 1994.

PREDECESSORS – (1) HENRY Bingham; *cr* a *Baronet* 1634; *s* by his son (2) *Sir* GEORGE, 2nd Bt; *s* by his el son (3) *Sir* HENRY, 3rd Bt; *dsp*; *s* by his half-brother (4) *Sir* GEORGE, 4th Bt; *s* by his son (5) *Sir* JOHN, 5th Bt, MP for and Gov of co Mayo; *d* 1749; *s* by his el son (6) *Sir* JOHN, 6th Bt, MP for co Mayo; *d* unmarried 1752; *s* by his brother (7)*Sir* CHARLES, 7th Bt, MP for co Mayo; *cr Baron Lucan*, of Castlebar (peerage of Ireland) 1776, and *Earl of Lucan* (peerage of Ireland) 1795; *d*

1799; *s* by his son **(8)** RICHARD, 2nd Earl; *b* 1764; a Representative Peer: *m* 1794, Lady Elizabeth Belasyse, da and co-heir of Henry, 2nd Earl Fauconberg, and the divorced wife of Bernard Edward, 12th Duke of Norfolk; *d* 1839; *s* by his son **(9)** GEORGE CHARLES, GCB, 3rd Earl, *b* 1800; was Field Marshal in the Army: *m* 1829, Lady Anne Brudenell, who *d* 1877, da of 6th Earl of Cardigan; *d* 1888; *s* by his el son **(10)** GEORGE, KP, 4th Earl, *b* 1830; a Representative Peer; bore Sceptre with Dove at Coronation of King Edward VII; sat as MP for Mayo (LC) 1865-74; Lieut and Custos Rotulorum of co Mayo, and Vice-Adm of the Province of Connaught: *m* 1859, Lady Cecilia Catherine Gordon-Lennox, who *d* 1910, da of the 5th Duke of Richmond, KG, *d* 1914; *s* by his el son **(11)** GEORGE CHARLES, GCVO, KBE, CB, TD, PC, 5th Earl, *b* 1860; Hon Brig-Gen, a Lord-in-Waiting to HM 1920-24, and 1924-9, and Capt of Hon Corps of Gentleman-at-Arms 1929 and 1931-40; sat as MP for N-W, or Chertsey, Div of Surrey (C) 1904-06; *cr Baron Bingham*, of Melcombe Bingham, co Dorset (peerage of UK) 1934; *m* 1896, Violet Sylvia Blanche, OBE, who *d* 1972, da of late J. Spender Clay, of Ford Manor, Lingfield; *d* 1949; *s* by his el son **(12)** GEORGE CHARLES PATRICK, MC, 6th Earl, *b* 1898; Col Coldstream Guards (OC, 1st Bn, 1940-42); Capt of Yeomen of Guard 1950-51; Parl Under-Sec of State for Commonwealth Relations June to Oct 1951, and Ch Opposition Whip, House of Lords 1954-64: *m* 1929, Kaitilin Elizabeth Anne, who *d* 1985, da of late Capt Hon Edward Stanley Dawson, RN (E Dartrey, colls); *d* 1964; *s* by his el son **(13)** RICHARD JOHN, 7th Earl and present peer; also Baron Lucan, and Baron Bingham.

LUCAS OF CHILWORTH, BARON (Lucas) (Baron UK 1946)

MICHAEL WILLIAM GEORGE LUCAS, 2nd Baron, *b* 26 April 1926; *s* 1967; *ed* Peter Symond's Sch, Winchester, and Luton Tech Coll; late RTR; TEng (CEI); FIMI, FInst TA; Pres League of Safe Transport Drivers 1976-80, Inst of Transport Admin 1980-83, UK delegate N Atlantic Assembly 1981-83 and since 1988, Member RAC Public Policy Cttee 1981-83 and since 1989, Member House of Lords Select Cttee Science & Technology 1980-83, a Lord in Waiting to HM 1983, Parliamentary Under-Sec of State, Dept of Trade and Industry, 1984-87; Vice Pres RoSPA since 1980, and Institute of the Motor Industry since 1992: *m* 1955 (*m diss* 1990), Anne-Marie, only da of Ronald William Buck, of Southampton, and has issue.

Arms – Per fesse wavy or and azure, in chief between two annulets a rose gules barbed and seeded proper, and in base two bars wavy argent surmounted by a bull's head caboshed sable. **Crest** – A representation of Apollo affronte or. **Supporters** – *Dexter*, a lion or; *sinister*, a Russian bear sable, each resting the interior paw upon an annulet therein a rose gules barbed and seeded proper.
Address – c/o House of Lords, SW1. *Club* – RAC.

SONS LIVING

Hon SIMON WILLIAM, *b* 6 Feb 1957; *ed* Leicester Univ (BSc): *m* 1993, Fiona, yr da of Thomas Mackintosh, of Vancouver, BC, Canada.
Hon Timothy Michael, *b* 1959; *ed* Lancing, and Surrey Univ (BSc).
Residence – 23 Common Lane, Weybridge, Surrey.

DAUGHTER LIVING

Hon Rachel Ann, *b* 1963: *m* 1991, Howard J. Wilder, elder son of John R. Wilder, of Eastleigh, Hants, and has issue living, a da, *b* 1993.

BROTHER LIVING

Hon Ivor Thomas Mark, CMG, *b* 1927; *ed* St Edward's Sch, Oxford, and Trin Coll, Oxford (BA 1951, MA 1956); late RA; Diplo Ser 1951-84; CMG 1980: *m* 1954, Christine Mallorie, el da of late Com Arthur Mallorie Coleman, OBE, DSC, RN (ret), of 44 Dartmouth Row, SE10, and has issue living, Mark Haselden, *b* 1955: *m* 1983, Melinda Jane, yr da of Sir Alastair Frederick Down, OBE, MC, of Brieryhill, by Hawick, Roxburghshire, and has issue living, Nicholas Alastair James *b* 1988, Georgina Sophie *b* 1986, Laura Evelyn *b* 1990, — Crispin Mallorie, *b* 1958: *m* 1993, Heather Patricia, elder da of William Boyd, of Aldeburgh, Suffolk, — Adrian George, *b* 1963. *Residence* – 65 Newstead Way, SW19.

SISTERS LIVING

Hon Nadia, *b* 1923: *m* 1944 (*m diss* 1980), Flight Lieut Hamish Selkirk, DFC, RAF, and has had issue, Christopher Rattray Lucas, *b* 1949; — Alastair Hamish Lawson, *b* (twin) 1949; *d* 1982, — Lindsay Alexandra, 1945: *m* 1st, 1965 (*m diss* 1970), Alan Stuart-Hutcheson; 2ndly, 1979, as his 3rd wife, David Jacobs, radio and television broadcaster, and has issue living (by 1st *m*), Guy James *b* 1966.
Hon Tatiana Sonia, *b* 1933: *m* 1964, Kenneth Bradford, of Nashdom, 13 Woodlands Rd, Surbiton, Surrey, son of Arthur Bradford, of Beckenham, Kent, and has issue living, Adam George, *b* 1966: *m* 1992, Caroline Louise, eldest da of R. John Dorrell, of Surbiton, Surrey, — Justin Nicholas, *b* 1967: *m* 1993, Anne Caroline Younger, da of Mrs S. Horwood, of Claygate, Surrey.

PREDECESSOR – **(1)** GEORGE WILLIAM Lucas, son of Percy William Lucas, of Oxford; *b* 1896; a Lord-in-Waiting to HM 1948-49, Capt of Yeomen of the Guard 1949-50, and Parl Sec to Min of Transport 1950-51; *cr Baron Lucas of Chilworth*, of Chilworth, co, Southampton (peerage of UK) 1946: *m* 1917, Sonia, who *d* 1979, da of Marcus Finkelstein, of Libau, Latvia; *d* 1967; *s* by his el son **(2)** MICHAEL WILLIAM GEORGE, 2nd Baron and present peer.

LUCAS OF CRUDWELL, BARON, AND DINGWALL, LORD (Palmer) (Lordship S 1609 and Barony E 1663)

RALPH MATTHEW PALMER, 11th Baron Lucas of Crudwell and 8th Lord Dingwall; *b* 7 June 1951; *s* 1991; *ed* Eton, and Balliol Coll, Oxford: *m* 1978, Clarissa Marie, da of George Vivian Lockett, TD, of Stratford Hills, Stratford St Mary, Colchester, and has issue.

Arms – Argent, two bars sable, charged with three trefoils slipped of the field; in chief a greyhound courant of the second, collared or. **Crest** – A mount vert, thereon a greyhound sejant sable, collared or, charged on the shoulder with a trefoil slipped argent. **Supporters** – On either side a wyvern with wings erect or. *Residence* – The Old House, Wonston, Winchester, Hants.

SON LIVING

Hon LEWIS EDWARD, *b* 7 Dec 1987.

DAUGHTER LIVING

Hon Hannah Rachel Elise, *b* 1984.

BROTHER LIVING

Hon Timothy John, *b* 1953; *ed* Eton, and Balliol Coll, Oxford: *m* 1984, Adèle Cristina Sophia, 4th da of late Lt-Col Hon Henry Anthony Camillo Howard, CMG (*see* B Howard of Penrith, colls), and has issue living, Henry Jocelyn, *b* 1987, — Robert Dominic, *b* 1993, — Nan Cristina, *b* 1985, — Isabella Spring, *b* 1989. *Residence* – West Woodyates Manor, Salisbury, Wilts.

SISTER LIVING

Hon Anthea Amabel, *b* 1956; assumed by deed poll 1963 the additional christian name of Amabel; *ed* Westfield Coll, London.

COLLATERAL BRANCHES LIVING

(In remainder to Lordship of Dingwall and Baronies of Butler and Lucas of Crudwell)

Issue of late Hon Rachel Cooper, yr da of Nan Ino, Baroness Lucas of Crudwell, *b* 1921, *d* 1976: *m* 1948, Maj Hon Spencer Douglas Loch, MC (later 4th Baron Loch), who *d* 1991:—
Hon Sara Nan, *b* 1949. *Residence* – The Old House, The Close, Blandford, Dorset DT11 7HA.

Grandchildren of late Ethel Anne Priscilla Fane, only da of Hon Julian Henry Charles Fane (4th son of 11th Earl of Westmorland) by his wife Lady Adine Eliza Anne Cowper, sister of 7th Earl Cowper: *m* 1887, 1st Baron Desborough:—
Issue of late Hon Monica Margaret Grenfell, *b* 1893, *d* 1973: *m* 1924, as his 2nd wife, Marshal of the RAF Sir John Maitland Salmond, GCB, CMG, CVO, DSO, who *d* 1968:—
Julian John William SALMOND, *b* 1926: *m* 1950, Brigid Louise, da of late FitzHerbert Wright (*see* V Powerscourt, 1990 Edn), and has issue living, David John Julian, *b* 1969, — Alicia Brigid (*Viscountess Head*), *b* 1951: *m* 1974, 2nd Viscount Head, of Throope Manor, Bishopstone, Salisbury, — Georgiana Monica, *b* 1952: *m* 19—, Roberts, of—, and has issue living, Miran (a son), *b* 19—, — Venetia Anne, *b* 1957: *m* 1984, David John Morrison, of 21 Albert Bridge Rd, SW11 (*see* B Margadale). *Residence* – Old Manor House, Didmarton, Badminton, Avon.

Grandchildren of late Hon Monica Margaret Grenfell (Hon Lady Salmond) (ante):—
Issue of late Hon Rosemary Laura Salmond, *b* 1928, *d* 1991: *m* 1947 (*m diss* 1974), 3rd Baron Ravensdale (see that title).
Grandchildren of late Ethel Anne Priscilla Fane (Baroness Desborough) (ante):—
Issue of late Hon Alexandra Imogen Clare Grenfell, *b* 1905, *d* 1969: *m* 1931, 6th Viscount Gage, who *d* 1982 (see that title).
Descendants of late Lady Amabel Cowper, sister of 7th Earl Cowper: *m* 1873, Adm of the Fleet Lord Walter Talbot Kerr, GCB (*see* M Lothian).

(In remainder to Barony of Lucas of Crudwell only)

Descendants of late Mary Evelyn Compton Vyner (assumed by Royal Licence 1915 the additional surname and arms of Vyner), da of Robert Charles de Grey Vyner, son of Lady Mary Gertrude de Grey, da of 2nd Earl Grey: *m* 1886, Capt Lord Alwyne Frederick Compton, DSO, son of 4th Marquess of Northampton (see that title).
Descendants (by 1st *m*) of late Violet Aline Vyner, yr da of Robert Charles de Grey Vyner (ante): *m* 1st, 1890 (*m diss* 1902), 5th Earl of Rosslyn; 2ndly, 1903, Lt-Col Charles Jarrott, OBE (*see* E Rosslyn).

PREDECESSORS – *LORDSHIP OF DINGWALL — (1) Sir RICHARD Preston, KB; *cr* Lord Dingwall (peerage of Scotland) 1609, with remainder to his heirs whatsoever; *s* by his da **(2)** ELIZABETH, wife of James, 12th Earl of Ormonde, *cr* Duke of Ormonde (*see* M Ormonde) her el son who predeceased his father, was summoned by writ to English Parliament, as *Baron Butler*, of Moore Park, 1666; she *d* 1684; *s* by her grandson **(3)** JAMES, KG, 2nd Duke of Ormonde and 3rd Lord Dingwall, who had in 1680 *s* as 2nd Baron Butler; was attainted of high treason and deprived of all his honours 1715, and the Lordship of Dingwall and the Barony of Butler remained dormant till 1871, when the attainder was removed and the titles reverted to **(4)** FRANCIS THOMAS de Grey, 7th Earl Cowper, as heir of Henrietta, Countess Grantham, 2nd da of 1st Baron Butler, whose 2nd da, Lady Henrietta, *m* 2nd Earl Cowper; *b* 1834; Lord-Lieut of Bedfordshire; Viceroy of Ireland 1880-82: *m* 1870, Lady Katrine Cecilia Compton, who *d* 1913, da of 4th Marquess of Northampton; *d* 1905, when the Barony of Butler fell into abeyance, and the Lordship of Dingwall and Barony Lucas of Crudwell passed to his nephew **(5)** AUBERON THOMAS Herbert (son of late Hon Auberon Edward William Molyneux Herbert, by Lady Florence Amabel, who *d* 1886, el sister of 7th Earl Cowper), 9th Lord Dingwall, and 8th Baron Lucas of Crudwell (right confirmed by Committee for Privileges of House of Lords 1907), *b* 1876; Parliamentary Under-Sec of State for War and a Member of Army Council 1908-11, when he became Under-Sec of State for the Colonies; appointed Parliamentary Sec of Board of Agriculture and Fisheries Oct 1911, and Pres thereof 1914; served during 1914-18 War in RFC; *ka* 1916; *s* by his sister **(6)** NAN INO; *b* 1880; *m* 1917, Col Howard Lister Cooper, late RAF, who *d* 1972; *d* 1958; *s* by her elder da **(7)** ANNE ROSEMARY; *b* 1919: *m* 1950, Maj Hon Robert Jocelyn

Palmer, MC, late Coldstream Guards, who *d* (30 Nov) 1991, 3rd son of 3rd Earl of Selborne; *d* (31 Dec) 1991; *s* by her elder son **(8)** RALPH MATTHEW, 8th and present Lord Dingwall, also 11th Baron Lucas of Crudwell.

BARONY OF LUCAS — **(1)** MARY, only child of Sir John Lucas, Knt (*cr* Baron Lucas of Shenfield), was *cr Baroness Lucas of Crudwell* (peerage of England) 1663, with remainder to her heirs male by Anthony Grey, 11th Earl of Kent, and failing which to her heirs female without division; *d* 1702; *s* by her el son **(2)** HENRY GREY, 2nd Baron Lucas and 12th Earl of Kent; *cr Viscount Goderich, Earl of Harold*, and *Marquess of Kent* (peerage of Great Britain) 1706, *Duke of Kent* (peerage of Great Britain) 1710, and *Marquess Grey* (peerage of Great Britain) 1740, with remainder to his grand-da, Lady Jemima Campbell, da of 3rd Earl of Breadalbane; *d* 1740, when the peerages of 1706 and 1710 became extinct, *s* in the Barony of Lucas and Marquessate of Grey by his grand-da **(3)** JEMIMA (ante): *m* Philip, 2nd Earl of Hardwicke; *d* without male issue 1797; *s* in Barony of Lucas of Crudwell by her da **(4)** AMABEL GREY; *cr Countess de Grey* (peerage of United Kingdom) 1816, with remainder to her sister, Mary Jemima, wife of 2nd Baron Grantham, and her heirs male (M Ripon); *d* 1833; *s* by her nephew **(5)** THOMAS PHILIP, 2nd Earl, 5th Baron Lucas of Crudwell, and 3rd Baron Grantham; *d* 1859, without male issue; *s* in Barony of Lucas of Crudwell by his da **(6)** ANNE FLORENCE: *m* 1833, George Augustus, 6th Earl Cowper; *d* 1880; *s* by her son **(7)** FRANCIS THOMAS DE GREY, 7th Earl Cowper, 7th Baron Lucas of Crudwell, and 4th Lord Dingwall* (ante).

<h2 style="text-align:center">LUKE, BARON (Lawson Johnston) (Baron UK 1929)</h2>

IAN ST JOHN LAWSON JOHNSTON, KCVO, TD, 2nd Baron; *b* 7 June 1905; *s* 1943; *ed* Eton, and Trin Coll, Camb (MA); a DL and JP for Bedfordshire, a Lieut for City of London; a CStJ, Chm of Bovril Ltd 1943-70; past Chm and Life Pres of Electrolux Ltd, past Chm of National Playing Fields Assocn, and of Gateway Building Soc, a Dir of Ashanti Goldfields Corpn, Ltd, former Dir of Lloyds Bank, Ltd, of Lloyds Bank Internat, Ltd, of IBM United Kingdom, Ltd, of IBM United Kingdom Holdings, Ltd, of Aktiebolaget Electrolux, and of Bunhill Holdings, Ltd, and former Pres of Outdoor Advertising Council, and of Inst of Export; a Member of Internat Olympic Cttee 1951-88, since when an Hon Member; Hon Col 5th Bn Bedfordshire and Hertfordshire Regt 1947-62; a Member of Church Assembly (House of Laity) 1935, Chm of Area Cttee for National Fitness in Herts and Bedfordshire 1937-39, of London Hospital Street Collections Central Cttee 1943-45, of Bedfordshire TA Assocn 1943-46, and of Duke of Gloucester's Red Cross and St John Fund 1943-46; a Co Councillor (Chm of Standing Joint Cttee 1943-61) for Bedfordshire 1943-52; Hon Sec of Assocn of British Chambers of Commerce 1944-52; Nat Vice-Pres of Roy British Legion since 1950, Co Chm, Bedfordshire British Legion 1946-59, and a Member of BBC Central Advisory Council 1946-52; Pres of London Chamber of Commerce 1952-55, and of Incorporated Sales Managers' Assocn 1953-56, and of Operation Britain Organization 1957-62; Vice-Pres of National Fedn of Young Farmers' Clubs (Eastern Area) 1948-57, and Chm of Moorfields Eye Hosp 1947-56; a Warden of Drapers' Co 1955 (Master 1962-63); Pres of Advertising Assocn 1955-58; 1939-45 War as Lt-Col Bedfordshire and Herts Regt; KCVO 1976: *m* 1932, Barbara, da of Sir Fitzroy Hamilton Anstruther-Gough-Calthorpe, 1st Bt, and has issue.

Never unprepared

Arms – Argent, on a saltire sable between four daggers points downwards gules, the sun in his splendour or, on a chief of the third three cushions of the fourth. **Crest** – A spur between two wings or. **Supporters** – *Dexter*, a heron; *sinister*, a flamingo; both proper.
Residence – Odell Castle, Odell, Bedfordshire, MK43 7BB. *Club* – Carlton.

<h3 style="text-align:center">SONS LIVING</h3>

Hon ARTHUR CHARLES ST JOHN, *b* 13 Jan 1933; *ed* Eton, and Trin Coll, Camb (BA); a Co Councillor for Beds 1965-70 (Chm of Staffing Cttee 1967-70); High Sheriff of Beds 1969-70; Pres of Nat Assocn of Warehouse-keepers 1962-78; Member of Court of Corpn of Sons of the Clergy; FRSA, KStJ; Cdr of St John Ambulance Bde in Beds since 1985; Warden Drapers' Co 1993: *m* 1st, 1959 (*m diss* 1971), Silvia Mary, yr da of Don Honorio Roigt, former Argentine Ambassador at The Hague; 2ndly, 1971, Sarah Louise, da of Richard Hearne, OBE, and has issue living, (by 1st *m*) Ian James St John, *b* 1963, — Rachel Honoria, *b* 1960: *m* 1984, Antony William Parrack, elder son of late Kenneth Parrack, of Wimbledon, and has issue living, Archie Beach *b* 1990, Felix Honorio Beach *b* 1991, — Sophia Charlotte, *b* 1966, — (by 2nd *m*) Rupert Arthur, *b* 1972. *Residence* – Odell Manor, Beds.
Hon (Ian) Henry Calthorpe (Coldstone House, Logie Coldstone, Aboyne, Aberdeenshire AB34 5NP) *b* 1938: *m* 1970, Lady (Pamela) Lemina Gordon, da of 12th Marquess of Huntly, and has issue living, Percy FitzRoy, *b* 1971, — Henrietta Lemina, *b* 1973.
Hon (George) Andrew (Invernan House, Strathdon, Aberdeenshire), *b* 1944: *m* 1968, Sylvia Josephine Ruth, el da of Michael Richard Lloyd Hayes (*see* Shelley, Bt, *cr* 1611, colls) and has issue living, Justin, *b* 1971, — Giles Spencer, *b* 1974, — Daniel George, *b* 1978, — Tania Georgiana, *b* 1977.
Hon Philip Richard (307 Woodstock Rd, Oxford OX2 7NY), *b* 1950; *ed* Eton: *m* 1977, Saskia Moyne, eldest da of Terence George Andrews, MBE, and has issue living, Harry, *b* 1979, — Edward *b* (twin), 1979, — Samuel, *b* 1982, — Saskia Rose, *b* 1985.

<h3 style="text-align:center">DAUGHTER LIVING</h3>

Hon Caroline Jean, *b* 1935: *m* 1958, James Bristow, and has issue living, Timothy Dominic Ian James (Manor Farm House, Hulcote, Towcester, Northants), *b* 1959: *m* 1984 (*m diss* 1992), Annabel J. D., yr da of David Palmer, of The Old Vicarage, Biddenham, Beds, and has issue living, Arthur Timothy James *b* 1986, Lily Annabel Mary *b* 1989, — George Edward FitzRoy, *b* 1961: *m* 1987, Juliet J., only da of Paul Knocker, of Windsor, Berks, and has issue living, Edward George *b* 1990,

Lucinda Joy *b* 1989, — Barnaby James St John, *b* 1966, — Melissa Caroline, *b* 1963: *m* 1994, Mathew Thurlow Laws, only son of Charles Laws, of Winford, Somerset. *Residence* – Penmorfa, Seaview, Isle of Wight PO34 5HE.

BROTHER LIVING

Hon Hugh de Beauchamp, TD, *b* 1914; *ed* Eton, and Corpus Christi Coll, Camb (MA); *s* Capt 5th Batn Bedfordshire Regt (TA Reserve); with Bovril 1935-71 (Chm 1971), Chm Pitman Ltd 1973-81 and Tribune Investment Trust Ltd; Chm of Cttees United So for Christian Literature 1949-82; High Sheriff of Beds 1961-62, and a DL 1964; author of *Argentina Revisited*: *m* 1946, Audrey Warren, da of late Col Frederick Warren Pearl, of 20 Lowndes Sq, SW1, and has issue living, Primrose Pearl, *b* 1948: *m* 1975, Martin Arthur Hudson, of 7 Grove Park Gds, W4 3RY, and has issue living, Hugh James *b* 1977, Mark Oliver *b* 1978, Ian Alexander *b* 1979, Christopher Martin *b* 1981, — Juliet Amy, *b* 1950: *m* 1975, Simon Crocker, of 62 Battledean Rd, Highbury, N5, and has issue living, Barnaby William de Beauchamp *b* 1976, Amy *b* 1979, — Marguerite Laura, *b* 1952: *m* 1977, Timothy John Clark, of Wappenham Manor, nr Towcester, Northants, and has issue living, Jamie Duncan *b* 1979, Thomas Edward *b* 1986, Anna Camilla *b* 1981, Jessica Roddie *b* 1984. *Residences* – Flat 1, 28 Lennox Gds, SW1 0DJ; Woodleys Farm House, Melchbourne, Beds.

SISTER LIVING

Hon (Laura) Pearl, OBE, *b* 1916; a JP for Beds 1941-84 (Chm 1978-84); County Pres St John Ambulance Brig 1971-90, and a DStJ; DL, High Sheriff Beds 1985, OBE (Civil) 1946. *Residence* – Woodleys Stud House, Melchbourne, Beds MK44 1AO.

PREDECESSOR – (1) George Lawson Johnston, KBE, 2nd son of John Lawson Johnston, of Kingswood, Kent, *b* 1873; a Director of Lloyds Bank, Ltd, and Bovril Ltd, and Lord-Lieut, Co Councillor, and a JP for Bedfordshire (High Sheriff 1924); *cr Baron Luke*, of Pavenham, co Bedford (peerage of United Kingdom) 1929: *m* 1902, Hon Edith Laura St John, who *d* 1941, da of 16th Baron St John of Bletso; *d* 1943; *s* by his el son (2) Ian St John, 2nd Baron and present peer.

Lumley, Viscount; son of Earl of Scarbrough.

LURGAN, BARONY OF (Brownlow) (Extinct 1991)

SISTER LIVING OF FIFTH BARON (*Raised to the rank of a Baron's daughter* 1986)

Hon Daphne Angela, *b* 1917: *m* 1942, Lt-Col (George Edward) Brian Brazier-Creagh, Lt-Col RARO, who *d* 1993. *Residence* –

WIDOW LIVING OF FOURTH BARON

(Florence) May (*Baroness Lurgan*), da of Louis Francis Squire Webster, of Johannesburg, S Africa, and widow of Eric Cooper, of Johannesburg, S Africa: *m* 1979, the 4th Baron, who *d* 1984. *Residence* – 42 The Manor, PO Box 76196, Wendywood 2144, S Africa.

LYELL, BARON (Lyell) (Baron UK 1914, Bt UK 1894)

Forti non ignavo.

To the brave, not to the dastardly

Charles Lyell, 3rd Baron, and 3rd Baronet; *b* 27 March 1939; *s* 1943; *ed* Eton and Ch Ch Oxford; late 2nd Lt Scots Gds; DL Angus; CA; a Lord in Waiting to HM 1979-84, since when an Under Sec of State for N Ireland.

Arms – Or, a cross parted and fretty azure between four crosses patée gules, all within a bordure of the last. **Crest** – Upon a rock a dexter cubit arm erect in armour proper, charged with a cross parted and fretty gules, the hand grasping a sword in bend sinister also proper. **Supporters** – Not yet recorded at College at Arms.
Seat – Kinnordy, Kirriemuir, Angus. *Town Residence* – 20 Petersham Mews, SW7.
Clubs – Turf, Whites.

AUNT LIVING

Margaret Laetitia, *b* 1912; BSc Economics (London); Assist Comm Sec British Embassy, Moscow 1944-45: *m* 1st, 1937, Maj Hon Francis Alan Stewart-Mackenzie of Seaforth, RA (TA), who was *ka* 1943 (*see* E Midleton); 2ndly, 1944, Charles Henry Pearson Gifford, OBE, who *d* 1994, and has issue living, (by 2nd *m*) Patrick Antony Francis (250 Randolph Av, W9) *b* 1945; *ed* Winchester, and Magdalene Coll, Camb (BA): *m* 1969, Mary, da of John Kilgour, and has issue living, Antony Patrick *b* 1971, Michael John *b* 1975, Katharine Laetitia *b* 1970, Frances Mary *b* 1976, — John Vernon (5 Clarence St, Edinburgh), *b* 1946; *ed* Bradfield, and New Coll, Oxford BLitt, — William Lyell (39 Portland St, Leamington Spa), *b* 1950; *ed* Bedales Sch, and Birmingham Univ (BA): *m* 1972, Carolyn, da of Maj B. W. Mortimore, and has issue living, Thomas *b* 1976, Lydia *b* 1979, — Andrew Graham (18 Fentiman Rd, SW8), *b* 1953; *ed* Bedales Sch, and Edinburgh Univ (BA): *m* 1990, Charlotte, da of Michael White, and has issue living, Henry John Montrésor *b* 1992, — Mary Charlotte, *b* 1948; BA, MSc: *m* 1971 (*m diss* 1987), Michael Neumann, of C135 Ulster St, Toronto, Canada, and has issue living, Daniel Franz *b* 1981, Thomas Edward *b* 1986. *Residence* – Wyndham House, Aldeburgh, Suffolk.

WIDOW LIVING OF SECOND BARON

Sophie Mary (*Baroness Lyell*), da of late Major Sigismund William Joseph Trafford (see E Lindsey and Abingdon, colls): *m* 1938, the 2nd Baron, VC, who was *ka* 1943. *Residences* – Kinnordy, Kirriemuir, Angus; 20 Petersham Mews, SW7.

PREDECESSORS – **(1)** LEONARD Lyell, el son of late Lieut-Col Henry Lyell, and nephew and heir of Sir Charles Lyell, 1st Bt (*cr* 1864) (ext); *b* 1850; MP for Orkney and Shetland (*L*) 1885-1900; *cr* a *Baronet* 1894, and *Baron Lyell*, of Kinnordy, co Forfar (peerage of United Kingdom) 1914: *m* 1874, Mary, who *d* 1929, da of late Rev John Mayne Stirling; *d* 1926; *s* by his grandson **(2)** CHARLES ANTONY, VC (son of late Major Hon Charles Henry Lyell, only son of 1st Baron), 2nd Baron; *b* 1913; Capt Scots Guards; European War 1939-43 (VC): *m* 1938, Sophie Mary, da of Major Sigismund William Joseph Trafford; *ka* 1943; *s* by his only son **(3)** CHARLES, 3rd Baron and present peer.

LYLE OF WESTBOURNE, BARONY OF (Lyle) (Extinct 1976)

DAUGHTER LIVING OF FIRST BARON

Hon (Barbara) Suzanne, *b* 1915: *m* 1938 (*m diss* 1953), William Thomas Charles Skyrme, CBE, TD, JP (CB 1966, KCVO 1974), and has issue living, Anthony Lyle (37 South Eaton Place, SW1W 9EL), *b* 1946; *ed* Harrow: *m* 1972, Carole-June, da of W. J. Glover, of Sandown House, Belfast, and has issue living, Sebastian *b* 1976, Samantha *b* 1973, — Carolyn Anne, *b* 1940: *m* 1966, Maj Philip Norman Holbrook, of The Pond House, Well, Long Sutton, nr Basingstoke, Hants RG25 1TL, son of Col Sir Claude Vivian Holbrook, CBE, of Upper Durford, Petersfield, and has issue living, Charles Philip Elstan *b* 1968, Miranda Carolyn *b* 1967, — Diana Suzanne (*Lady Waterlow*), *b* 1943; JP: *m* 1965, Sir (James) Gerard Waterlow, 4th Bt (*cr* 1930). *Residences* – River House, Remenham, Henley-on-Thames, Oxon; 1 Sloane Court East, SW3.

Lymington, Viscount; son of Earl of Portsmouth.

LYONS OF BRIGHTON, BARONY OF (Lyons) (Extinct 1978)

SONS LIVING OF LIFE BARON

Hon Rodney Max (The Studio, Avington Park, Winchester, Hants SO21 1DD), *b* 1941; *ed* St Paul's, and Magdalen Coll, Oxford (BA, post-grad Cert Ed); Principal of Taunton's Coll, Southampton since 1989: *m* 1963, Cory Frances, da of Dr William Owen Hassall, of the Manor House, Wheatley, Oxford, and has issue, one son and one da. *Hon* William (9 Clifton Av, W12 9DR), *b* 1945; Writer, Story Ed, and Storyliner *EastEnders*, etc; Winner Writers' Guild of GB Award for Educational Drama 1977: *m* 1st, 1963 (*m diss* 19—), Petra Deanna, da of William Tibble; 2ndly, 1986, Gillian Mary, da of Alfred Tullett, and has issue living (by 1st *m*), Kevin Oliver, *b* 1964, — Teena Fern, *b* 1967, — (by 2nd *m*) Braham William Ash, *b* 1990, — Natasha Beatrice Holly, *b* 1987.

DAUGHTER LIVING OF LIFE BARON

Hon Deborah, *b* 1965.

LYTTON, EARL OF (Lytton) (Earl UK 1880, BT UK 1838)

JOHN PETER MICHAEL SCAWEN LYTTON, 5th Earl and 6th Baronet; *b* 7 June 1950; *s* 1985; *ed* Downside, and Reading Univ; FRICS; sole proprietor John Lytton & Co, Chartered Surveyors, since 1988; Chm Leasehold Enfranchisement Advisory Service since 1994; Pres Newstead Abbey Byron Society; Chm Horsham Chamber of Trade and Commerce since 1993: *m* 1980, Ursula, da of Anton Komoly, of Vienna, Austria, and has issue.

This is the work of valour

Arms – Quarterly: 1st and 4th, ermine on a chief dancettée azure, two ducal coronets or, a canton argent, charged with a rose gules, *Lytton*; 2nd and 3rd gules, on a chevron argent, between three eaglets reguardant or, as many cinquefoils sable, *Bulwer*. **Crests** – 1st a griffin's head erased ermine, eared and maned or; 2nd, a bittern in flags, all proper; 3rd, an eagle, reguardant argent, holding in the beak a branch of laurel vert. **Supporters** – Two angles proper, each holding an easter crown or.

Address – c/o House of Lords, SW1.

SONS LIVING

PHILIP ANTHONY SCAWEN (*Viscount Knebworth*), *b* 7 March 1989, — *Hon* Wilfrid Thomas Scawen, *b* 1992.

DAUGHTER LIVING

Lady Katrina Mary Noel, *b* 1985.

BROTHER LIVING

Hon (Thomas) Roland Cyril Lawrence, *b* 1954; *ed* Downside. *Residence* – Bratton Court Farm, Minehead, Somerset.

SISTERS LIVING

Lady Caroline Mary Noel, *b* 1947; *ed* Birmingham Univ, and Sir John Cass Sch of Art; silversmith.
Lady Lucy Mary Frances, *b* 1957.
Lady Sarah Teresa Mary, *b* 1959: *m* 1984, P. David Nash Solly, yst son of late Lt-Col R. J. N. Solly, and has issue living, a da, *b* 1992.

HALF-AUNT LIVING *(Daughter of 3rd Earl by 2nd wife)*

Lady Madeleine Elizabeth (4 rue des Hauts-Tillets, 92310 Sèvres, France), *b* 1921; dancer, choreographer and teacher; has issue living, Eleanore LYTTON, *b* 1957; lyricist.

DAUGHTERS LIVING OF SECOND EARL

Lady (Margaret) Hermione (Millicent) (*Lady Hermione Cobbold*), *b* 1905: *m* 1930, 1st Baron Cobbold, who *d* 1987. *Residence* – Lake House, Knebworth, Herts.
Lady Davidema Katharine Cynthia Mary Millicent, *b* 1909: *m* 1st, 1931, 5th Earl Erne, who *d* of wounds received in action 1940; 2ndly, 1945, Col Hon Christopher Montagu Woodhouse, DSO, OBE (*see* B Terrington). *Residence* – Willow Cottage, Latimer, Chesham, Bucks.

WIDOW LIVING OF FOURTH EARL

CLARISSA MARY (*Dowager Countess of Lytton*), da of late Brig-Gen Cyril Eustace Palmer, CB, CMG, DSO (Blakiston, Bt, colls): *m* 1946, the 4th Earl, who *d* 1985. *Residence* – Garden Wing, Newbuildings Place, Shipley, nr Horsham, W Sussex RH13 7JQ.

PREDECESSORS – **(1)** *Rt Hon Sir* EDWARD GEORGE EARLE Bulwer-Lytton, GCMG, PC, DCL, LLD; *b* 1803; a distinguished poet, novelist, orator, and statesman; MP for St Ives 1831, for Lincoln (*L*) 1832-41, and for Hertfordshire 1852-66; was Sec of State for the Colonies 1858-9, and Lord Rector of Glasgow Univ 1856-8; author of numerous popular novels, of well-known poems and dramas, and of essays on general literature and politics; assumed the additional surname of Lytton 1844; *cr* a *Baronet* 1838, and *Baron Lytton*, of Knebworth, co Herts (peerage of United Kingdom) 1866: *m* 1827, Rosina Doyle, who *d* 1822, da of Francis Massey Wheeler; *d* 1873; *s* by his son **(2)** EDWARD ROBERT LYTTON, GCB, GCSI, CIE, PC, 2nd Baron; *b* 1831; a distinguished diplomatist and poet; Minister at Lisbon 1874-6, Viceroy and Gov-Gen of India 1876-80, and Ambassador at Paris 1887-91; Lord Rector of Glasgow Univ 1887-90; *cr Earl of Lytton*, of co Derby, and *Viscount Knebworth*, of co Herts, 1880: *m* 1864, Edith, VA, CI, who *d* 1936, da of late Hon Edward Ernest Villiers; *d* 1891; *s* by his son **(3)** VICTOR ALEXANDER GEORGE ROBERT, KG, GCSI, GCIE, PC, 2nd Earl; *b* 1876; appointed a Civil Lord of the Admiralty 1916, additional Parliamentary Sec to Admiralty 1917, British Commr for Propaganda in France 1918, Dep First Lord of the Admiralty 1918, again Civil Lord of the Admiralty 1919, and Under-Sec of State for India 1920; was Gov of Bengal 1922-7 (acted as Viceroy of India and Gov-Gen April to Aug 1925): *m* 1902, Pamela Frances Audrey, CI, who *d* 1971, da of late Sir Trevor John Chichele Chichele-Plowden, KCSI; *d* 1947; *s* by his brother **(4)** NEVILLE STEPHEN, OBE, 3rd Earl; *b* 1879; a Portrait and Landscape Painter: *m* 1st, 1899 (*m diss* 1923), Judith Anne Dorothea (*Baroness Wentworth* in her own right), who *d* 1957; 2ndly, 1924, Rosa Alexandrine Fortel, who *d* 1980, of St Rambert-en-Burgey, Ain, France; *d* 1951: *s* by his son **(5)** NOEL ANTHONY SCAWEN, 4th Earl; *b* 1900; Lt-Col Rifle Bde; assumed by deed poll 1925 the additional surname of Milbanke after that of Lytton; discontinued by deed poll 1951 the use of this additional surname: *m* 1946, Clarissa Mary, da of late Brig-Gen Cyril Eustace Palmer, CB, CMG, DSO (Blakiston, Bt, colls); *d* 1985; *s* by his son **(6)** JOHN PETER MICHAEL SCAWEN, 5th Earl and present peer; also Viscount Knebworth, Baron Wentworth (see * infra), and Baron Lytton.
*(1) *Rt Hon Sir* THOMAS Wentworth, PC, summoned to English Parliament as *Baron Wentworth*, 1529-48; was Lord Chamberlain of the Household; *d* 1551; *s* by his son **(2)** THOMAS, 2nd Baron; *d* 1584; *s* by his son **(3)** HENRY, 3rd Baron; *d* 1593; *s* by his son **(4)** THOMAS, 4th Baron; *cr Earl of Cleveland*, co York (peerage of England) 1625; *d* 1667; *s* by his son **(5)** THOMAS, 5th Baron; *b* 1613; was summoned in his father's Barony of Wentworth 1640; *dvp* 1665 (*see* **(6)** HENRIETTA; *s* by her aunt **(7)** ANNE, wife of 2nd Baron Lovelace; *d* 1697; *s* by her grandda **(8)** MARTHA, who was confirmed in the Barony 1702: *d* 1745; *s* by her kinsman **(9)** *Sir* EDWARD Noel, 6th Bt, heir of Hon Margaret Noel, da of Anne, Baroness Wentworth (ante), who became 9th Baron; *cr Viscount Wentworth* (peerage of England) 1762; *d* 1774; *s* by his son **(10)** THOMAS, LLD, 2nd Viscount; as a Lord of the Bedchamber; *dsp* 1815, when the viscountcy became extinct, and the barony became abeyant and remained so until 1856, when it was terminated in favour of **(11)** ANNE ISABELLA, widow of George Gordon, 6th Baron Byron, who in 1822 assumed by Roy licence the additional surname of Noel; *d* 1860; *s* by her grandson **(12)** BYRON NOEL King-Noel (Viscount Ockham), el son of Hon Augusta Ada, da of Anne Isabella, Baroness Wentworth and Byron (ante) by her marriage with William, 1st Earl of Lovelace; *d* unmarried 1862; *s* by his brother **(13)** RALPH GORDON, 13th Baron; *b* 1839; assumed by Roy licence 1861 the surname of Milbanke in lieu of Noel in 1893; *s* as 2nd Earl of Lovelace (see that title): *m* 1st, 1869, Fannie, who *d* 1878, 3rd da of late Rev George Heriot, of Fellow Hills, Berwick; 2ndly, 1880, Mary Caroline, el da of late Right Hon James Stuart-Wortley; *d* 1906, when the Earldom of Lovelace, Viscountcy of Ockham, and Barony of King devolved upon his half-brother Lionel Fortescue King-Noel, while he was *s* in the Barony of Wentworth by his ony child **(14)** ADA MARY *b* 1871; *d* 1917; *s* by her aunt **(15)** ANNE ISABELLA (da of 1st Earl of Lovelace), *b* 1837: *m* 1869, Wilfrid Scawen Blunt, who *d* 1922, of Crabbet Park, Crawley, Sussex; *d* 1917; *s* by her da **(16)** JUDITH ANNE DOROTHEA, *b* 1873; assumed by deed poll 1904 the surname of Blunt-Lytton: *m* 1899 (*m diss* 1923), Maj Hon Neville Stephen Bulwer-Lytton, OBE, who *d* 1951, afterwards 3rd Earl of Lytton; *d* 1957; *s* by her son **(17)** NOEL ANTHONY, who *s* as 4th Earl of Lytton 1951 (ante), and 17th Baron Wentworth.

LYVEDEN, BARON (Vernon) (Baron UK 1859)

RONALD CECIL VERNON, 6th Baron; *b* 10 April 1915; *s* 1973: *m* 1938, Queenie Constance, da of Howard Ardern, and has issue.

Arms – Quarterly: 1st and 4th argent, a fret sable, *Vernon*; 2nd and 3rd gules, three bars gemelles argent a chevron ermine, on a chief of the second three blackamoors' heads proper; a canton of the field, charged with a battle axe or, all within a bordure counter compony of the second and azure, *Smith*. **Crests** – *Dexter* (Vernon) 1st, a boar's head erased sable, ducally gorged or; 2nd, *Sinister* (Smith) a cubit arm erect, in armour proper, charged with a battle-axe sable, the hand grasping two wreaths of laurel, pendant on either side, also proper. **Supporters** – *Dexter*, a boar sable, ducally gorged, and suspended therefrom by a chain an escutcheon or, charged with a rose gules slipped proper; *sinister*, a wyvern vert, plain collared, and suspended therefrom by a chain an escutcheon or, charged with a rose, slipped, proper.
Residence – 20 Farmer St, Te Aroha, NZ.

Vernon always flourishes

SONS LIVING

Hon JACK LESLIE (17 Carlton St, Te Aroha, NZ), *b* 10 Nov 1938: *m* 1961, Lynette June, da of William Herbert Lilley, and has issue living, Colin Ronald, *b* 3 Feb 1967, — Wendy Caroline, *b* 1962, — Karen Marie, *b* 1964.
Hon Robert Howard (2175 Avenue Rd Apt 4, Toronto, Ontario, Canada), *b* 1942: *m* 1968, Louise Smith, and has issue living, Russell Sydney *b* 1969.
Hon Grant (40 Emma St, Te Aroha, NZ), *b* 1952: *m* 1992, Karen Teresa Margaret Green, and has issue living, Daniel Grant James, *b* 1993.

SISTERS LIVING

Hon Audrey Joan, *b* 1922: *m* 1940, Russell Parker and has issue living, Robert Barry, *b* 1944: *m* 1965, Helen Wilkinson, and has issue living, Michelle *b* 1965, — Allan Sydney Russell (12 Argus St, Rotorua, NZ), *b* 1946: *m* 1967, Judi Patterson and has issue living, Kerry James *b* 1968, Grant Allen *b* 1970, — Raymond John, *b* 1953, — Barbara Joan, *b* 1942: *m* 1961, John Sydney Barnett, and has issue living, Craig John *b* 1963, Gregory Mark *b* 1965, Tracy Megan *b* 1969.
Hon Maureen Dawn, *b* 1926: *m* 1946, Noel Surrell, of 10 Koha Road, Taupo, NZ, and has issue living, Andrew Gray (21 Hindmarsh Drive, Taupo, NZ), *b* 1952: *m* 1970, Rowena Anne Doel, and has issue living, Jason Carey *b* 1971, Carlene *b* 1974.

COLLATERAL BRANCHES LIVING

Granddaughters of late Cecil Sydney Archibald Vernon, 2nd son of late Hon Greville Richard Vernon (infra):—
Issue of late John Lyveden Vernon, *b* 1895; *d* 1970: *m* 1922, Catherine Mary Draffin, who *d* 1970:—
Bettina Mary Paulinus NAIR (81 Charles St, Westshore, Napier, NZ), *b* 1926: *m* 1950 (*m diss* 1977), Archibald Reid McLeay, and has issue living, Eain Dougald John, *b* 1953: *m* 1977, Jennifer Raye Thomsen, and has issue living, Devin Eain *b* 1983, Holley Jennifer *b* 1981, Casey Leah *b* 1986, — Jane Imelda, *b* 1951 (and has issue living, Amber Lea *b* 1977), — Leah Paule (twin), *b* 1951: *m* 1974, Ralph John Johansson, of Bucklands Beach, Auckland, NZ, — Victoria Catherine Ethel (twin), *b* 1953: *m* 1974 (*m diss* 1977), Lee Nicholas Fatouros, and has issue living, Marley Reid *b* 1980. —— Jillyan Imelda, *b* 1935: *m* 1955, Charles Woolnough Locke, of 55 Pacific Parade, Whangaparaoa Peninsula, Auckland, NZ, and has issue living, Gregory Charles Woolnough, *b* 1957, — Antoinette Marie, *b* 1956: *m* 1977, William Sylvester Stuart, of 12 Cameron St, Sydney, Australia, and has issue living, William Gregory Charles *b* 1978, Kellie Ann Imelda *b* 1979, — Katherine Hélène, *b* 1961: *m* 1987, Olivier Michel Jean Wardecki, of Ferme de Vaufron, Vezelay, France.

Grandson of late Capt Eustace Vernon, 4th son of late Hon Greville Richard Vernon (infra):—
Issue of late Greville Rupert Eustace Vernon, *b* 1899, *d* 1967: *m* 1925, Francisca (1/88 Elphin Rd, Launceston, Tas, Aust), da of John Henry Little:—
Greville Richard Eustace (Unit 21 Paddington Place, 2 Lyon St, Dicky Beach, Queensland 4551, Australia) *b* 1926; BSc TTC: *m* 1953, Nancy Grace Haslam, and has issue living, Jane Suzanne, *b* 1957: *m* 1978, Laurence James Rogers, of 17 Tanner Drive, Legana, Tasmania, and has issue living, Jonathan *b* 1986, Kate Frances *b* 1984.

Grandsons of late Greville Rupert Eustace Vernon (ante):—
Issue of late Robert Harcourt Vernon, *b* 1929, *d* 1987: *m* 1954, Isobel Jennifer Miller (2 Kenyon St, Launceston, Tasmania):—
Robert Courtenay John (44 Richardson Cres, Burnie, Tasmania, Australia), *b* 1955: *m* 1982, Vicki Maree Davis, and has issue living, Robert Andrew, *b* 1983, — Christopher Richard, *b* 1986. —— Hugh Gowran, *b* 1957. —— David Stewart Lyveden, *b* 1958: *m* 1982, Meredith Caroline Reeve, and has issue living, Stephanie Caroline, *b* 1985, — Rebecca Isobel, *b* 1988, — Georgina Amy, *b* 1991.

Grandchildren of late Robert Rupert Charles Vernon (infra):—
Issue of late Maj Mervyn Sydney Bobus Vernon, MVO, late Gren Guards, *b* 1912, *d* 1991: *m* 1937, Lady Violet Mary Baring, who *d* 1978, yr da of 2nd Earl of Cromer:—
Greville Edward Mervyn (Newington House, Kingscote, Glos), *b* 1944; *ed* Eton: *m* 1969, Fiona Dawn Cory, da of Lt-Col William Handley Ferguson, of Ozleworth Park, Wooton-under-Edge, Glos (*see* Cory, Bt, 1985 Edn), and has issue living, James Fitzpatrick Greville, *b* 1971, — Zara Caroline, *b* 1973, — Sasha Elizabeth, *b* 1979. —— (Hugh) Richard Mervyn (Stairaird, Mauchline, Ayrshire), *b* 1947: *ed* Eton: *m* 1976, Hon Victoria Arthur, da of 3rd Baron Glenarthur, and has issue living, Andrew Robert Richard *b* 1979, — Catherine Victoria, *b* 1977, — Emma Mary, *b* 1983. —— Veronica Elizabeth, *b* 1938: *m* 1968, as his 3rd wife, (George) Jonathan Hargreaves (*see* V Goschen, 1990 Edn), who *d* 1991, of Glen Cottage, Luckington, Chippenham, Wilts.

Granddaughter of late Hon Greville Richard Vernon, 4th son of 1st Baron:—
Issue of late Robert Rupert Charles Vernon, DSO, *b* 1872, *d* 1940: *m* 1906, Dorothy Inez Elinor, who *d* 1965, only da of George Benjamin Thorneycroft, of Dunston Hall, Stafford:—
Susan Diana Mary, *b* 1915: *m* 1946, Francis Reitman, MD, who *d* 1955, and has issue living, Robert Vernon Michael (Thiat, Bussière Poitevine 87320, France), *b* 1947; *ed* Radley, — Susan Theresa Maria (45 Hatherley Court, Hatherley Grove, W2), *b* 1950, — Roseanna Mary Blanche (*Countess of Stradbroke*) *b* 1953: *m* 1977, 6th Earl of Stradbroke. *Residence* – The West Wing, Triscombe House, Bishop's Lydeard, Taunton, Som.

PREDECESSORS – **(1)** ROBERT Vernon (son of Robert Percy Smith, of Cheam, Surrey, Judge Advocate Gen in India, MP for City of Lincoln, by his wife, Caroline Maria, 2nd da of Richard Vernon, MP, of Hilton Park, Stafford), PC, MP for Tralee 1829-31 and for Northampton (L) 1831-59; was a Lord of the Treasury 1830-4, Sec of Board of Control 1835-9, Under-Sec for the Colonies 1839-41, Sec of War 1852, and Pres of Board of Control 1855-8; assumed for his children in 1846 by Roy licence the surname of Vernon, and in 1859 assumed for himself the surname of Vernon in lieu of his patronymic Smith; *cr Baron Lyveden*, of Lyveden, co Northampton (peerage of United Kingdom) 1859; *b* 1800: *m* 1823, Emma Mary Fitz Patrick who *d* 1882, sister of 1st Baron Castletown; *d* 1873; *s* by his son **(2)** FITZ-PATRICK HENRY, 2nd Baron, *b* 1824; in Diplo Ser 1846-50: *m* 1st, 1853, Lady Albreda Elizabeth Wentworth-FitzWilliam, who *d* 1891, da of 4th Earl FitzWilliam, KG; 2ndly, 1896, Julia Kate, who *d* 1949, da of Albert Emary, of Harold Road, Clive Vale, Hastings; *d* 1900; *s* by his nephew **(3)** COURTENAY ROBERT PERCY (son of late Rev Hon Courtenay John Vernon, 3rd son of 1st Baron), 3rd Baron; *b* 1857, Capt 3rd Bn, Highland LI; Pres British Cttee for study of foreign municipal insts; Prussian Order of the Crown (2nd class); a Purser in the Mercantile Marine; European War 1914-13 as Lieut-Com RNVR; a Member of the Dramatic Profession: *m* 1st, 1890, Fanny Zelie, who *d* late Maj Charles Hill, of Wollaston Hall, nr Wellingborough; 2ndly, 1925, Mrs Ada SPRINGATE (the actress Lynda Martell), who *d* 19—, da of Arthur Hodgkinson, of Accrington, and formerly wife of Richard Springate; *d* 1926: *s* by his son **(4)** ROBERT FITZ-PATRICK COURTENAY, 4th Baron, *b* 1892: *m* 1949, Doris Violet, who *d* 1985, da of late Henry Francis Coghlan White, previously wife of Cdr J. G. Bower, RN, and widow of Capt Eric Paterson; *d* 1969; *s* by his kinsman **(5)** SYDNEY MUNROE ARCHIBALD (grandson of Hon Greville Richard Vernon, yst son of 1st Baron), 5th Baron, *b* 1888: *m* 1st, 1912, Ruby, who *d* 1932, da of Robert John Shandley; 2ndly, 1957, Gladys, who *d* 1986, widow of John Cassidy; *d* 1973; *s* by his only son **(6)** RONALD CECIL, 6th Baron and present peer.

MABANE, BARONY OF (Mabane) (Extinct 1969)

WIDOW LIVING OF FIRST BARON

STELLA JANE (*Baroness Mabane*), da of late Julian Duggan, of Buenos Aires: *m* 1944, the 1st Baron, who *d* 1969, when the title became extinct. *Residence* –

McALPINE OF MOFFAT, BARONY OF (McAlpine) (Extinct 1990)

SONS AND DAUGHTERS OF LIFE BARON (*see* McAlpine, Bt, and following article)

McALPINE OF WEST GREEN, BARON (McAlpine) (Life Baron 1983)

(ROBERT) ALISTAIR McALPINE, 2nd son of Baron McAlpine of Moffat (Life Baron) (see Baronetage); *b* 14 May 1942; *ed* Stowe; Hon Treasurer 1975-80 (jtly since 1981) and Dep Chm 1979-83, Conservative and Unionist Party; Dir Sir Robert McAlpine Ltd since 1963; Hon Treasurer European Democratic Union since 1978; Member Arts Council of Great Britain 1981-82, Chm Arts Council Touring Cttee; Vice-Pres Ashmolean Museum; *cr Baron McAlpine of West Green*, of West Green, co Hants (Life Baron) 1983: *m* 1st, 1964 (*m diss* 1979), Sarah Alexandra, da of late Paul Hillman Baron, of 72 Bryanston Court, George Street, W1; 2ndly, 1980, Romilly Thompson, only da of Alfred Thompson Hobbs, of Knights Farm House, West Green, Hartley Wintney, Hants, and has issue by 1st and 2nd *m*.

Arms – Per chevron vert and or two chevronels one in chief argent the other in base azure. **Crest** – A cubit arm grasping a chaplet of pine fructed proper. **Supporters** – *Dexter*, an aborigine girt with a body belt pendent therefrom a lonca-lonca armed with a spear and in his sinister hand a boomerang and extending the other to and behind the head of a kangaroo sejant beside him all proper; *sinister*, a gardener in his working clothes wearing an apron of green baize in his exterior hand a spade and having perched upon the wrist and palm of his other hand a parrot proper.
Residence – 31 South Audley St, W1. *Clubs* – Garrick, Carlton.

DAUGHTERS LIVING (*by 1st marriage*)

Hon (Mary) Jane, *b* 1965: *m* 1987, Simon J. E. du B. Taylor, eldest son of Timothy Taylor, of Meadle, Bucks.
Hon Victoria Alice, *b* 1967: *m* 1992, Lionel Digby Sheffield Neave (*see* Neave, Bt, colls), and has issue, Alice Artemis, *b* 1994.

(*By 2nd marriage*)

Hon Skye, *b* 1984.

MacANDREW, BARON (MacAndrew) (Baron UK 1959)

CHRISTOPHER ANTHONY COLIN MacANDREW, 3rd Baron; *b* 16 Feb 1945; *s* 1989; *ed* Malvern: *m* 1975, Sarah Helen, only da of Lt-Col Peter Hendy Brazier, of Nash Court Farmhouse, Marnhull, Dorset, and has issue. *Residence* – Hall Farm, Archdeacon Newton, Darlington, co Durham

SON LIVING

Hon OLIVER CHARLES JULIAN, *b* 3 Sept 1983.

DAUGHTERS LIVING

Hon Diana Sarah, *b* 1978.
Hon Tessa Deborah, *b* 1980.

BROTHER LIVING

Hon Nicholas Rupert (The Old Chapel, Greywell, Odiham, Hants), *b* 1947; *ed* Eton: *m* 1975, Victoria Rose, da of George Patrick Renton, of Isington Close, Alton, Hants, and has issue living, Robin Glen, *b* 1978, — Rose Clare, *b* 1980, — Rachel Emma, *b* 1984.

SISTER LIVING

Hon Deborah Jane *b* 1956: *m* 1979, Lt-Col Mark William Bingham Faulkner, Royal Dragoon Gds, and has issue (*see* de Trafford, Bt, colls). *Residence* – Hollintree House, Newsham, Thirsk, N Yorks YO7 4DH.

AUNT LIVING (*daughter of 1st Baron by 1st marriage*)

Hon Elizabeth Lilian Graham (*Hon Lady Coats*), *b* 1929: *m* 1950, Sir William David Coats, and has issue living, Brian Glen Heywood, *b* 1951; *ed* Eton: *m* 1979, Consuelo, da of Luis Eduardo Marquez, of Carrera 3A, no 18-24, Pereira, Risaralda, Colombia, and has issue living, Andrew William Heywood *b* 1983, Julia Caroline *b* 1981, — Adrian James MacAndrew *b* 1955; *ed* Eton: *m* 1979, Mary Elizabeth, da George Robin Clover, of 3 Wallside, Monkwell Sq, Barbican, EC2, and has issue living, Alistair Thomas Edward *b* 1984, Rachel Olivia Askernish *b* 1982, — Frances Alice *b* 1958: *m* 1982, Michael John Adam Fowle, and has issue living, Jonathan Richard Adam *b* 1986, Alexandra Jane Adam *b* 1985. *Residence* – The Cottage, Symington, Ayrshire.

HALF-AUNT LIVING (*daughter of 1st Baron by 2nd marriage*)

Hon Mary Margaret Hastings, *b* 1942: *m* 1967, Maj-Gen Charles Alexander Ramsay, of Bughtrig, Coldstream, Berwickshire (*see* Ramsay, Bt (*cr* 1806), colls).

PREDECESSORS – (1) CHARLES GLEN MacAndrew, TD, PC, served in European War 1914-19 with Machine Gun Corps, Cmd'd Ayrshire Yeo 1932-36; Dep Speaker and Chm Ways and Means Cttee, House of Commons 1951-59; MP for Kilmarnock Div. of Ayrshire and Bute (C) 1924-29, for Patrick Div of Glasgow 1931-35, and for Bute and N Ayrshire Dir of Ayrshire and Bute 1935-59; *cr Kt* 1935, PC 1952, and *Baron MacAndrew*, of the Firth of Clyde (peerage of United Kingdom) 1959: *m* 1st, 1918 (*m diss* 1938), Lilian Cathleen, who *d* 1978, da of James Prendergast Curran, of St Andrews; 2ndly, 1941, Mona, who *d* 1994, da of James Alexander Ralston Mitchell, of Perceton House, Irvine, Ayrshire; *d* 1979; *s* by his el and only surv son, (2) COLIN NEVIL GLEN, 2nd Baron, *b* 1919, served 1939-45 War with Ayrshire Yeo, sometime Master of Zetland Foxhounds: *m* 1943, Ursula Beatrice, who *d* 1986, yr da of Capt Joseph Steel, of Kirkwood, Lockerbie, Dumfriesshire; *d* 1989; *s* by his elder son (3) CHRISTOPHER ANTHONY COLIN, 3rd Baron and present peer.

McCARTHY, BARON (McCarthy) (Life Baron 1975)

WILLIAM EDWARD JOHN MCCARTHY, son of Edward McCarthy; *b* 30 July 1925; *ed* Holloway County Sch., Ruskin Coll, Merton Coll, and Nuffield Coll, Oxford (MA, DPhil); a Fellow of Nuffield Coll; Univ Lecturer in Industrial Relations, Oxford; *cr Baron McCarthy*, of Headington in City of Oxford (Life Baron) 1975: *m* 1957, Margaret, da of Percival Godfrey.
Residence – 4 William Orchard Close, Old Headington, Oxford. *Club* – Reform.

MACAULAY OF BRAGAR, BARON (Macaulay) (Life Baron 1989)

DONALD MACAULAY, son of late John Macaulay, shipyard labourer, of 627 Glasgow Rd, Clydebank, by his wife, Effie (*née* McLean); *b* 14 Nov 1933; *ed* Clydebank High Sch, and Glasgow Univ (MA, LLB); Faculty of Advocates 1963; QC (Scot) 1975; *cr Baron Macaulay of Bragar*, of Bragar, co Ross and Cromarty (Life Baron) 1989: *m* 1962, Mary, da of Murdo Morrison, of Bragar, and has issue, two das.
Address – c/o House of Lords, SW1.

MACCLESFIELD, EARL OF (Parker) (Earl GB 1721)

Dare to be wise

RICHARD TIMOTHY GEORGE MANSFIELD PARKER, 9th Earl; *b* 31 May 1943; *s* 1992; *ed* Stowe, and Worcester Coll, Oxford (BA 1965): *m* 1st, 1967 (*m diss* 1985), (Tatiana) Cleone Anne, only da of Maj Craig Wheaton Smith, US Army (*see* Craig, Bt, ext); 2ndly, 1986, Mrs Sandra Hope Mead, da of Sylvio Fiore, of Florida, USA, and has issue by 1st *m*.

Arms – Gules, a chevron between three leopards faces or. **Crest** – A leopard's head erased at the neck affrontée, or, ducally gorged gules. **Supporters** – Two leopards reguardant proper, ducally gorged gules.
Seat – Shirburn Castle, Watlington, Oxon OX9 5DL.

DAUGHTERS LIVING *(By 1st marriage)*

Lady Tanya Susan, *b* 1971.

Lady Katharine Ann, *b* 1973.
Lady Marian Jane, *b* (twin) 1973.

BROTHER LIVING

Hon JONATHAN DAVID GEOFFREY, *b* 2 Jan 1945; *ed* Stowe: *m* 1968, Lynne Valerie, yr da of George William Butler, of Middle Barton, Oxon, and has issue living, Timothy George, *b* 23 Aug 1969; *ed* Stowe, — Elizabeth Anne, *b* 1971, — Jessica, *b* 1977. *Residence* – Model Farm, Shirburn, Watlington, Oxford OX9 5DX.

UNCLE LIVING *(son of 7th Earl)*

Hon Jocelyn George Dudley, *b* 1920; *ed* Stowe; European War 1939-45 as Lieut RNVR: *m* 1948, Daphne Irene, 2nd da of late Maj George Cecil Whitaker, of Britwell House, Watlington, Oxon, and has issue living, Robert George, *b* 1955, — Mary Joanna Isabel (Eastfield Farm, Shirburn, Watlington, Oxon), *b* 1951: *m* 1973, Peter Robert Boone, who *d* 1986, son of Maj Ronald Edward Boone, late Parachute Regt. *Residence* – Pyrton Field Farm, Watlington, Oxon.

WIDOW LIVING OF EIGHTH EARL

Hon VALERIE MANSFIELD (*Dowager Countess of Macclesfield*), only da of 4th Baron Sandhurst: *m* 1938, the 8th Earl, who *d* 1992. *Residence* – Shirburn Castle, Watlington, Oxon.

COLLATERAL BRANCHES LIVING

Granddaughters of late Hon Cecil Thomas Parker, 2nd son of 6th Earl:—
Issue of late Geoffrey Parker, *b* 1880, *d* 1954: *m* 1912, Isolda Mabel Cecil, who *d* 1955, da of Sir Charles William Frederick Craufurd, 4th Bt.—
Cecily Mary Caroline, *b* 1913. —— Isolda Rosamond (*Viscountess Hanworth*), *b* 1918: formerly Senior Cdr Auxilliary Territorial Ser; a JP of Surrey (Supplementary List), DL: *m* 1940, 2nd Viscount Hanworth. *Residence* – Quoin Cottage, Shamley Green, Guildford, Surrey.

Grandchildren of late Robert Edward Parker (infra):—
Issue of late Capt Robert Kenyon Parker, *b* 1907, *d* 1968: *m* 1st, 1935, Frances Mary, who *d* 1964, da of Robert William Gawthropp, of Little Somerford, Wilts; 2ndly, 1965, Ealga Hester Balgriffin (Water Meadows, Station New Rd, Brundall, Norwich, NR13 5PQ), eldest da of late Cyril Joseph Kildare Burnell, MA, of co Dublin:—
(By 1st *m*) Nigel Kenyon (3 Hopetoun Terr, Bucksburn, Aberdeen), *b* 1942: *m* 1964, Joey, da of John Jack, and has issue living, Karen Antonia, *b* 1965, — Lisa Anne, *b* 1969. —— Jennifer Elizabeth, *b* 1938.
Issue of late Alexander Patrick Parker, *b* 1910, *d* 1991: *m* 1st, 1949 (*m diss* 1962), Joan Olive, da of Benjamin Sayer, of Saxingham Thorpe, Nethergate, Norwich; 2ndly, 1965, Helen Mary (Algarsthorpe, Marlingford, Norwich), da of late John Owen Bond, of Eaton Hill, Norwich:—
(By 1st *m*) Patrick Edward Benjamin, *b* 1958. —— Tania Lynn, *b* 1950: *m* 1st, 1970 (*m diss* 1975), Stephen William Widdows; 2ndly, 1978, Thomas Patrick Moore, of 22 The Plantation, Aldburgh, Suffolk, and has issue living (by 1st *m*), Matthew Adam, *b* 1973, — (by 2nd *m*) Thomas Edward Alexander, *b* 1982, — Tiphanie Anne, *b* 1980. —— Alexandra Vanessa PARKER-MILNE (Read Mead, Glastonbury, Som), *b* 1952: *m* 1976 (*m diss* 1986), William Andrew Milne, and has issue living, Charlotte Francesca, *b* 1977, — Jessica Emily, *b* 1980. —— Amanda Rose, *b* 1960: *m* 1988, Rodney William Beckwith, of Mill Cottage, Marlingford, Norwich.

Grandchildren of late Rev Hon Algernon Robert Parker, 3rd son of 6th Earl:—
Issue of late Robert Edward Parker, *b* 1878, *d* 1942: *m* 1904, Emily, who *d* 1951, da of late J. J. Dawson Paul, JP, DL:—
Michael Edward (Oriental Club), *b* 1916; *ed* Eton; 1939-45 War as Lt-Col Norfolk Yeo (RA): *m* 1st, 1940 (*m diss* 1956), Florence Margaret Catto, da of James Catto Duffus, OBE, MC; 2ndly, 1958, Estella Mary, da of H. A. Dalby, of York, and widow of George Hall, of Sheriff Hutton, Yorks, and has issue living (by 1st *m*), Timothy Robert Walter, *b* 1944, — Alexander Michael, *b* 1950, — Elizabeth Susan, *b* 1947. —— Elizabeth Mary, *b* 1914: *m* 1940, Frederick Colin George Preston, and has issue living, Frederick Robert (Toad Hall, Mulbarton, Norwich, Norfolk NR14 8JT), *b* 1947, — Anna Susan, *b* 1943: *m* 1979, Dirk Murray Bouwens, of Ivy Green House, Wymondham, Norfolk, and has issue living, Theodore Frederick Thomas *b* 1981. *Residence* – Paddock Farm, Mulbarton, Norwich.
Issue of late Hugh Algernon Parker, *b* 1879, *d* 1954: *m* 1911, Averil Frances, who *d* 1969, da of late Brownlow Richard Christopher Tower (B Brownlow):—
Camilla Mary, *b* 1916: *m* 1st, 1939, Capt Sir Lionel Francis Phillips, 2nd Bt, who was *ka* in Italy 1944; 2ndly, 1950, John G. Pisani, of 21 Chancellor House, 17 Hyde Park Gate, SW7 5DQ, who *d* 1982, and has issue living (by 1st *m*) (*see* Phillips, Bt). —— Juliet Leonora (Swallowfield Park, Reading, Berks), *b* 1920: *m* 1945, John Frederick Cathers McCreery, late RNVR and HM Overseas Civil Ser, who *d* 1993, and has issue living, Crispin Hugh, *b* 1953, — Sean Frederick, *b* 1964.
Issue of late Eustace BOWLES, *b* 1884, *d* 1952, having assumed by R licence 1920, the surname of Bowles in lieu of his patronymic, and the Arms of Bowles quarterly with those of Parker: *m* 1913, Wilma Mary Garnault, who *d* 1938, da of Col Sir Henry Ferryman Bowles, 1st Bt (ext), of Forty Hall, Enfield:—
Daphne Wilma Kenyon (*Daphne Lady Poole*) (38 Pembroke Sq, W8), *b* 1917: *m* 1st, 1939 (*m diss* 1950), Brig Algernon George William Heber-Percy, DSO, who *d* 1961 (*see* D Northumberland, colls); 2ndly, 1952 (*m diss* 1964), as his 2nd wife, 1st Baron Poole, CBE, TD, PC, who *d* 1993.

Grandchildren of late Eustace BOWLES (ante):—

Issue of late Derek Henry PARKER BOWLES, *b* 1915, *d* 1977: *m* 1939, Ann, DCVO, CBE, who *d* 1987, el da of Sir Humphrey Edmund de Trafford, 4th Bt, MC:—

Andrew Henry, OBE, *b* 1939; *ed* Ampleforth, and RMA Sandhurst; Silver Stick in Waiting since 1987, Brig 1991; OBE (Mil) 1983: *m* 1973, Camilla Rosemary, da of Maj Bruce Shand, MC (*see* B Ashcombe), and has issue living, Thomas Henry Charles, *b* 1974, — Laura Rose, *b* 1978. —— Simon Humphrey (17 Scarsdale Villas, W8), *b* 1941; *ed* Eton: *m* 1974, Carolyn, yr da of Sir (William) Ian Potter, of Del Rio, Elizabeth Bay, Sydney, Australia, and has issue living, Luke Derek Ian, *b* 1978, — Sam William Francis, *b* 1981. —— Richard Eustace, *b* 1947; *ed* Ampleforth: *m* 1973 (*m diss* 1976), Camilla, da of Charles Younger, of Garrowby, Yorks, and has issue living, Emma Teresa, *b* 1974. —— Mary Ann (North Lodge Farm, Warfield, Berks), *b* 1945: *m* 1967 (*m diss* 1987), Maj Nicolas Vincent Somerset Paravicini, Life Gds, and has issue living, Charles Vincent Somerset, *b* 1968, — Derek Nicolas Somerset, *b* 1979, — Elizabeth Ann, *b* 1970.

Grandchildren of late Hon Francis Parker, 4th son of 6th Earl:—

Issue of late Capt Oliver Ivan Parker, *b* 1891, *d* 1968: *m* 1921, Margaret Noel, da of Frederick Kerr, formerly of Twynceri, Barry, Glam:—

Timothy Oliver, *b* 1924; formerly Capt Gren Gds: *m* 1952, Rosemary, who *d* 1984, da of Maj John Henry Dent-Brocklehurst, OBE (*see* B Trevor, 1968 Edn), and has issue living, Oliver John (18 Elia St, N1 8DE), *b* 1953: *m* 1990, Amanda Jane, yr da of late Lt-Col W. D. H. McCardie, — Michael Henry (59 Clapham Manor St, SW4), *b* 1955: *m* 1991, Julia Jane Craven, elder da of Nigel Craven Humphreys, of Meadow House, Smannell, Andover, Hants, and has issue living, Thomas Edward *b* 1992, — Emma Mary, *b* 1964: *m* 1991, James M. Garvin, of 30 Trygon Rd, SW8 1NH, son of Stephen Garvin, MBE, of Little Bricklehurst, Stonegate, E Sussex, and has issue living, Eliza Rose Clare *b* 1994.

Issue of late Ivo Murray Parker, *b* 1899, *d* 1957: *m* 1923, Dulcibella, who *d* 1974, da of late Capt Charles William Daubeny, of The Brow, Combe Down, Bath:—

Penelope Joan, *b* 1924: *m* 1946, Arthur John Hughes, MC, TD, DL, who *d* 1984, and has issue living, Max Ivo Arthur (Chaffeymoor House, Bourton, Gillingham, Dorset), *b* 1947; BSc Hons: *m* 1974, Clara Christabel Harries, and has issue living James Ivo Arthur *b* 1976, Emma Penelope *b* 1975, — Jane Philippa, *b* 1948: *m* 1972, Richard I. W. Ware, of The Elms, Little Wymondley, Hitchin, Herts, and has issue living, Christopher Arthur Corry *b* 1972, Samantha *b* 1975, Georgina *b* 1977, Henrietta Daubeny *b* 1979. *Residence* – Vineyards, Welwyn, Herts AL6 9NE.

Grandchildren of late Rev Hon Archibald Parker, 9th son of 6th Earl:—

Issue of late Capt Charles Edward Parker, MC, *b* 1890, *d* 1962: *m* 1915, Hilda Margaret, who *d* 1979, da of Sir John Ralph Starkey, 1st Bt:—

Charles George Archibald (The White House, Nuffield, Oxon), *b* 1924; *ed* Eton, and New Coll, Oxford (MA); 1939-45 War as Capt Rifle Bde; JP and DL Oxon (High Sheriff 1989): *m* 1958, Mrs Shirley Follett Rutland, da of Lt-Col Frank Follett Holt, TD, JP, of Corrybrough, Tomatin, Inverness-shire, and adopted his da, Davina Jane, *b* 1954: *m* 1986, John Walter of 5 Elms Rd, SW4 9ER, only son of late John Walter, of Lugano, Switzerland, and of late Mrs Vladimir Daskaloff, of Palma, Mallorca (*see* E Enniskillen, colls, 1990 Edn), and has issue living, John Charles *b* 1987, Edward William *b* 1990.

Issue of late Frederic Archibald Parker, *b* 1894, *d* 1977: *m* 1927, his cousin, Evereld Adela, who *d* 1980, da of late Capt James Randolph Innes-Hopkins, of London, SW:—

Joan Sylvia, *b* 1931: *m* 1956, Theodore Luke Giffard Landon, of Great Bromley House, nr Colchester, and has issue living, Mark Eustace Palmer, *b* 1958; *ed* Downside: *m* 1st, 1983 (*m diss* 1987), Julia Ruth, elder da of John Luddington, of Mill House, Brancaster, Norfolk; 2ndly, 1987, Veronica Claire, only da of late Harvey Jones, of 10 Palace Rd, Llandaff, Cardiff, and has issue living (by 2nd *m*), Samuel *b* 1994, Bethan Emily *b* 1990, — Philip James Aislabie, *b* 1962; *ed* Downside, and Kent Univ (BA), — Benjamin Edward Giffard, *b* 1967; *ed* Worth, Durham Univ (BA), and Keele Univ (MA), — Coll, Durham (BA), and Keele Univ (MA), — Felicity Juliana Mary, *b* 1960; *ed* New Hall: *m* 1990, Christopher Gerald Payne, and has issue living, Edward Charles Aislabie *b* 1992, — Rohais Elizabeth Jane, *b* 1964; *ed* New Hall, and Warwick Univ (MA): *m* 1992, David Peter Haughton, of Forge View, Lower Rd, Somersham, Ipswich IP8 4PH.

Grandchildren of late Frederic Archibald Parker (ante):—

Issue of late Archibald Henry Parker, *b* 1928, *d* 1984: *m* 1st, 1951 (*m diss* 1979), Una-Mary, da of late Hugh Power Nepean-Gubbins, of Rumbling Bridge Cottage, Dunkeld, Perthshire; 2ndly, 1979, Comtesse Georgeite Contini di Lumezzane da of late William Bryant Backer, of New York:—

(By 1st *m*) Philip Archibald Reginald (Buffy) *b* 1955: *m* 1981, Kathryn Jane Micaela, da of Dr John Frederick Lewis Aldridge, OBE, of East House, Charlton, Chichester, W Sussex, and has issue living, Archie William Charles, *b* 1987, — Lucy Elizabeth Rebecca, *b* 1983, — Charlotte Laura Mary, *b* 1990. *Residence* - Finkley House, Finkley, nr Andover, Hants SP11 6AE. —— Una-Mary Diana, *b* 1953: *m* 1976, Robert Henry Hobart, and has issue (*see* Hobart, Bt). *Residence* - 12 Brunswick Gardens, W8.

Issue of late Hon Henry Parker, 10th son of 6th Earl, *b* 1860, *d* 1952: *m* 1916, Henrietta Judith, who *d* 1946, da of late Rev Robert Lowbridge Baker (E St Aldwyn):—

Peter Henry, *b* 1918; *ed* Eton, and New Coll, Oxford (MA); Maj (ret) KRRC; JP and DL Oxon (High Sheriff 1973); 1939-45 War: *m* 1953, Susan Rosemary, el da of late Maj Mowbray Buller, MC, of Downes, Crediton, Devon (E Portsmouth), and has issue living, Henry Mowbray *b* 1957; *ed* Eton, and Exeter Coll, Oxford: *m* 1991, Susan Jane da of John William Alvin, and of Mrs A. Thomson, of 24 Belvedere Park, Edinburgh, and has issue living, Redvers Charles *b* 1992, — Belinda Rosemary (*Hon Mrs A. Julian Aylmer*), *b* 1955: *m* 1990, Hon (Anthony) Julian Aylmer, only son of 13th Baron Aylmer, and has issue (*see* B Aylmer). *Residence* - The Hays, Chipping Norton, Oxon OX7 3BA.

Grandchildren of late Hon Alexander Edward Parker, OBE, 11th son of 6th Earl:—

Issue of late Sidney Alexander Parker, *b* 1899, *d* 1969: *m* 1st 1937, Adelaide Mary, who *d* 1947, da of late Maj Sidney George Everitt, RWF; 2ndly, 1951, June Rosemary, who *d* 1954, da of late Rev Herbert Arthur Woodman, R of Filleigh, N Devon; 3rdly, 1955, Rosemary Moon (Conygree Farm, Aldsworth, Glos), da of late Capt Henry Errington Moon Ord, and widow of Derek Welton:—

(By 1st *m*) David Alexander (Greghams Farm, Fords Water, Axminster, Devon), *b* 1943; *ed* Wellington: *m* 1971, Frances Marie, da of Francis W. Meehan, and has issue living, Christopher Alexander, *b* 1976, — Charles Edward, *b* 1977, — Sarah Adelaide, *b* 1973. —— Anne Mary, *b* 1940: *m* 1961, Paul Georges Emile Clément, of Mas de Valetière, Le Fontanil, 38120 St Egrève, France, and has had issue, Germaine Anne Marie, *b* 1962, — Dominique Jeanne Alice, *b* 1964, — Adelaide, *b* and *d* 1968, — Marie-Jeanne Paule Andrée, *b* 1969, — Alexandra Paule Emmanuelle, *b* 1970. —— Rosemary Elizabeth, *b* 1945: *m* 1964, Walter John Dawe Taylor, of Cricket St Thomas, Chard, Som, and has issue living, Jeremy John Alexander, *b* 1967, — Celia May Adelaide, *b* 1966, — Olivia Anne Nicola, *b* 1972.

(In special remainder to Earldom)

Descendants of Elizabeth (da of 1st Earl), who *m* 1720, Sir William Heathcote MP, 1st Bt:—
See Heathcote, Bt (of Hursley).

PREDECESSORS – (1) *Sir* THOMAS Parker, Knt; was MP for Derby 1705-8, Ch Justice of Queen's Bench 1710-18, and Lord High Chancellor of Great Britain 1718-25; *cr Lord Parker, Baron of Macclesfield*, co Chester (peerage of Great Britain) 1716, *Viscount Parker* and *Earl of Macclesfield* (peerage of Great Britain) 1721, with remainder (in default male issue) to his da

Elizabeth, wife of Sir William Heathcote, 1st Bt, of Hursley Park, and her issue male; the Earl of 1725 was impeached on charges of corruption, and being convicted at the bar of the House of Lords, was, after a trial of twenty-one days, found guilty and sentenced to pay a fine of £30,000; *d* 1732; *s* by his son **(2)** GEORGE, 2nd Earl; was Pres of R Society; *d* 1764; *s* by his son **(3)** THOMAS, 3rd Earl; *d* 1795; *s* by el son **(4)** GEORGE, 4th Earl: was Lord-Lieut of Oxfordshire; *d* 1842; *s* by his brother **(5)** THOMAS, DCL, 5th Earl; *b* 1763: *m* 1st, 1796, a da of Lewis Edwards, of Talgarth, co Merioneth; 2ndly, 1807, Eliza, who *d* 1862, da of William Breton Wolstenholme, of Hollyhill, Sussex; *d* 1850; *s* by his son **(6)** THOMAS AUGUSTUS WOLSTENHOLME, 6th Earl, *b* 1811; MP for Oxfordshire (*C*) 1837-41; High Steward of Henley and Vice-Lieut of Oxfordshire: *m* 1st, 1839, Henrietta, who *d* 1839, da of Edmund Turnor, of Stoke Rochford, Lincolnshire; 2ndly, 1842, Lady Mary Frances Grosvenor, who *d* 1912, da of 2nd Marquess of Westminster: *d* 1896; *s* by his grandson **(7)** GEORGE LOVEDEN WILLIAM HENRY (son of George Augustus, Viscount Parker, el son of 6th Earl), 7th Earl: *b* 1888; Lord-Lieut of Oxon 1954-63: *m* 1909, Lilian Joanna Vere, who *d* 1974, da of late Maj Charles John Boyle (E Cork, colls); *d* 1975; *s* by his el son **(8)** GEORGE ROGER ALEXANDER THOMAS, 8th Earl; *b* 1914; served European War 1939-45 as Lieut RNVR: *m* 1938, Hon Valerie Mansfield, only da of 4th Baron Sandhurst; *d* 1992; *s* by his elder son **(9)** RICHARD TIMOTHY GEORGE MANSFIELD, 9th Earl and present peer; also Viscount and Baron Parker.

McCLUSKEY, BARON (McCluskey) (Life Baron 1976)

JOHN HERBERT MCCLUSKEY, QC, son of Francis John McCluskey, solicitor; *b* 12 June 1929; *ed* St Bede's Coll, Manchester, Holy Cross Acad, Edinburgh, and Edinburgh Univ (MA, LLB); F/O (Sword of Honour) RAF 1953; Advocate Scotland 1955; QC 1967; Sheriff Prin of Dumfries and Galloway 1973-74, Solicitor-Gen for Scotland 1974-79; *cr Baron McCluskey*, of Churchhill in District of City of Edinburgh (Life Baron) 1976: *m* 1956, Ruth, da of Aaron Friedland, and has issue.
Residence – 5 Lansdowne Cresc, Edinburgh, EH12 5EQ.

SONS LIVING

Hon John Mark, *b* 1960: *m* 1986, Judith Fernie.
Hon David Francis, *b* 1963: *m* 1989, Katherine Elizabeth Marion Douglas.

DAUGHTER LIVING

Hon Catherine Margaret, *b* 1962.

McCOLL OF DULWICH, BARON (McColl) (Life Baron 1989)

IAN MCCOLL, son of late Frederick George McColl, of Dulwich; *b* 6 Jan 1933; *ed* Hutchesons' Gram Sch, Glasgow, St Paul's, London, and London Univ (MB BS 1957); FRCS 1962, FRCSE 1962, MS 1966, FACS 1975; Research Fellow Harvard Med Sch, and Moynihan Fellowship, Assocn of Surgs 1967; Reader in Surgery St Bartholomew's Hosp Med Coll 1967 (Sub Dean 1969); Hon Sec British Soc of Gastroenterology 1970-74, Dir of Surgical Unit, Guy's Hosp, since 1971, Prof of Surgery Univ of London (United Med Schs of Guy's and St Thomas's Hosps) since 1971, Consultant Surg Guy's Hosp since 1971, Dir of Surgery since 1985, and Consultant Surg Edenbridge Dist Memorial Hosp 1978-91, and Lewisham Hosp since 1983; Vice-Chm Special Health Authority for Disablement Servs 1987-91; Hon Consultant in Surgery for the Army since 1982, Chm King's Fund Centre Cttee 1976-86, Medical Advisor to BBC 1976-92, Member of Council of Met Hosp Sunday Fund 1986-89, Gov-at-Large for England, Board of Govs, American Coll of Surgs 1982-88, Chm Govt Working Party on Artificial Limbs, Wheelchairs and Appliance Centres in England 1984-86, Pres Mildmay Mission Hosp since 1985, Member Council of Royal Coll of Surgeons since 1986, Pres Soc of Minimally Invasive Gen Surgery since 1991, Vice-Pres John Groom's Assocn for Disabled People since 1990, and Gov Dulwich Coll Prep Sch since 1978; author of numerous medical articles, etc; *cr Baron McColl of Dulwich*, of Bermondsey, London Borough of Southwark (Life Baron) 1989: *m* 1960, Dr Jean Lennox, 2nd da of late Arthur James McNair, FRCS, FRCOG, of London, and has issue.

Arms – Azure, a cross or between in the first quarter a leg embowed in armour; in the second quarter a dove volant to the sinister; in the third quarter a fleam, and in the fourth quarter a fish haurient, all argent. **Crest** – A demi-lion rampant or, head and mane gules, gorged with three barrulets wavy argent, flanked by oak branches formed chevronwise as an 'M' leaved argent and fructed or, on an escroll proper. **Supporters** – *dexter*, a dachshund rampant proper; *sinister*, an eagle close also proper armed or and crowned with an ancient crown gold.
Address – House of Lords, SW1. *Club* – Royal College of Surgeons.

SON LIVING

Dr the Hon Alastair James, *b* 1961: *m* 1987, Dr Michelle Judd.

DAUGHTERS LIVING

Dr the Hon Caroline Lennox, *b* 1963: *m* 1994, Simon Brook Holmes.
Hon Mary Alison, *b* 1966: *m* 1989, Rory Nicholas Knight.

McCORQUODALE OF NEWTON, BARONY OF (McCorquodale) (Extinct 1971)

DAUGHTER LIVING OF FIRST BARON

Hon Prudence Fiona, *b* 1936: *m* 1962, Carel Maurits Mosselmans, TD, and has issue living, Michael Lodowick Stewart (8 Cedars Rd, SW13), *b* 1962: *m* 1992, Heather E., da of R. Croot, of Gowerton, W Glam, — Julian Frederick Willem, *b* 1964. *Residence* – 15 Chelsea Sq, SW3 6LF.

MacDERMOTT, BARONY OF (MacDermott) (Extinct 1979)

SONS LIVING OF LIFE BARON

Rt Hon Lord Justice John Clarke, *b* 1927; *ed* Campbell Coll, Belfast, at Trin Hall, Camb (BA), and at Queen's Univ, Belfast; Bar Inner Temple and N Ireland 1949: QC, N Ireland 1974; Judge of High Court NI 1973; Lord Justice 1987: *m* 1953, Margaret Helen, da of late Hugh Dales, of Belfast, and has issue living, Helen, *b* 1954, — Anne, *b* 1956, — Janet, *b* 1958, — Gillian, *b* 1959. *Residence* – 6 Tarawood, Holywood, co Down BT18 0HS.
Rev Hon Robert William Johnston (The Manse, 9 Sandymount Green, Dublin 4), *b* 1934: *ed* Campbell Coll, Belfast, Trin Hall, Camb (BA 1955), at New Coll, Edinburgh (BD), at Assembly's Coll, Belfast, and Yale Univ Divinity Sch (STM): *m* 1979, Janet, da of Very Rev Dr T. A. B. Smyth.

DAUGHTERS LIVING OF LIFE BARON

Hon Edith Louise, *b* 1930; MB and BCh 1954: *m* 1955, Samuel Barbour Cunningham, of Ballytrim, Killyleagh, co Down, and has issue.
Hon Lydia Elizabeth Palmer, *b* 1939; *ed* Wycombe Abbey Sch, and at Belfast Coll of Art: *m* 1964, Capt David McKenzie Chalmers, RAF (ret), of Upland House, Upper Harford, Bourton-on-the-Water, Glos GL54 3BY, and has issue.

WIDOW LIVING OF LIFE BARON

Louise Palmer (*Baroness MacDermott*) (Glenburn, 8 Cairnburn Rd, Belfast BT4 2HR), only da of Rev J. C. Johnston, DD: *m* 1926, Baron MacDermott, MC, PC (Life Baron), who *d* 1979.

MACDONALD, BARON (Macdonald of Macdonald) Baron I 1776

By sea and land

FRAOCH EILEAN

The Heathery Isle

GODFREY JAMES MACDONALD OF MACDONALD, 8th Baron; *b* 28 Nov 1947; *s* 1970; *ed* Eton; Chief of the Name and Arms of Macdonald: *m* 1969, Claire, el da of Commodore Thomas Noel Catlow, CBE, RN, of Gabriel Cottage, Tunstall, via Carnforth, Lancs and has issue.

Arms – Quarterly: 1st argent, a lion rampant gules armed and langued azure; 2nd or, a hand in armour fesseways holding a cross-crosslet fitchée gules; 3rd or, a lymphad, sails furled and oars in action sable, flagged gules; 4th vert, a salmon naiant in fesse proper; over all (as Chief of the Name and Arms of Macdonald), on an inescutcheon en surtout or, an eagle displayed gules, surmounted of a lymphad, sails furled. oars in action sable. **Crest** – A hand in armour fesseways couped at the elbow proper, holding a cross-crosslet fitchée gules. **Supporters** – Two leopards proper.
Residence – Kinloch Lodge, Isle of Skye.

SON LIVING

Hon (GODFREY EVAN) HUGO THOMAS, *b* 24 Feb 1982.

DAUGHTERS LIVING

Hon Alexandra Louisa, *b* 1973.
Hon Isabella Claire, *b* 1975.
Hon Meriel Iona, *b* 1978.

BROTHER LIVING

Hon Alexander Donald Archibald, *b* 1953; *ed* Eton.

SISTER LIVING

Hon Janet Anne, *b* 1946.

PREDECESSORS – (1) DONALD MacDonald, of Slate; *cr a Baronet* of Nova Scotia 1625, with a special clause of precedency, placing him second of that order in Scotland; *d* 1643; *s* by his son (2) *Sir* JAMES, 2nd Bt; joined the Marquess of Montrose 1645, and sent some of his men to assist Charles II, when he marched into England in 1651: *d* 1678; *s* by his son (3) *Sir* DONALD, 4th Bt; joined the Rebellion of 1715, and was attainted; *d* 1718; *s* by his son (5) *Sir* DONALD, 5th Bt; *d* unmarried 1720; *s* by his uncle (6) *Sir* JAMES, 6th Bt; *d* 1723; *s* by his son (7) *Sir* ALEXANDER, 7th Bt, for whom as "Alexander Macdonald of Macdonald" the family estates were re-erected into a feudal Barony of Macdonald 1727; *d* 1746; *s* by his el son (8) *Sir* JAMES, 8th Bt; *d* unmarried 1766; *s* by his brother (9) *Sir* ALEXANDER, 9th Bt; *cr Baron Macdonald*, of Slate, co Antrim (peerage of Ireland) 1776; *d* 1795; *s* by his el son (10) ALEXANDER WENTWORTH, 2nd Baron; *d* 1824; *s* by his brother (11) GODFREY, 3rd Baron: a Maj-Gen in the Army; assumed in 1814 by R licence the additional surname of Bosville and discontinued it by Roy licence 1824; *m* (in England) 15 Dec 1803, Louisa Maria La Coast, who *d* 1835, ward of Farley Edsir; *d* 1832, when (according to a decree of the Court of Session in June 1910) the Scottish Baronetcy passed *de jure* to Alexander William Bosville (*b* 12 Sept 1800, before the date of his parents' English marriage, but according to the law of Scotland legitimated by this *m*) (*see* Bosville Macdonald, Bt): *s* in the Irish peerage by his el son (born after the *m*) (12) GODFREY WILLIAM WENTWORTH, 4th Baron; *b* 1809: *m* 1845, Maria Anne, who *d* 1892, da of George Thomas Wyndham, of Cromer Hall, Norfolk; *d* 1863; *s* by his son (13) SOMERLED JAMES BRUDENELL, 5th Baron; *d* 1874; *s* by his brother (14) RONALD ARCHIBALD, 6th Baron, *b* 1853: *m* 1875, Louisa, who *d* 1922, da of Col George William Holmes Ross, of Cromarty; *d* 1947; *s* by his grandson (15) ALEXANDER GODFREY, MBE, TD (son of late Hon Godfrey Evan Hugh Macdonald, who was *ka* 1914, 7th Baron, *b* 1909; Maj Queen's Own Cameron Highlanders); Lord Lieut for Inverness-shire 1952-70: *m* 1945, Anne, who *d* 1988, only da of late Alfred Whitaker; *d* 1970; *s* by his el son (16) GODFREY JAMES, 8th Baron and present peer.

MACDONALD OF GWAENYSGOR, BARON (Macdonald) (Baron UK 1949)

GORDON RAMSAY MACDONALD, 2nd Baron; *b* 16 Oct 1915; *s* 1966; *ed* Upholland Gram Sch, and Manchester Univ (MA); UK Trade Commr in Australia 1947-53, Man Dir Internat Group, Tube Investments Ltd 1953-64, Plessey Ltd 1964-66, and Chm and Ch Exec Hayek Engineering Ltd (UK) 1966-77, since when Economic and Commercial Adviser to various business groups; 1939-45 War in Burma (despatches), Malaya, India and Middle East as Maj RA and a GSO: *m* 1941, Leslie Margaret, da of John Edward Taylor, of Rainford, Lancs, and has issue.

DAUGHTERS LIVING

Hon Susan (73 Swinburne Rd, Putney, SW15), *b* 1947: *m* 1968 (*m diss* 1991), David Hensley Adair Stride, and has had issue, Toby David Macdonald, *b* 1972, — Jessica Charlotte Macdonald, *b* 1970, *d* 1984.
Hon Helen Margaret, *b* 1950: *m* 1974 (*m diss* 19—), James Edward Richard Prisinzano.
Hon Marylyn Jane, *b* 1951: *m* 1977, Peter Jost, and has issue living, Edward Peter, *b* 1980, — Thomas William, *b* 1983.

SISTER LIVING

Hon Glenys, *b* 1923; a JP for Lancs: *m* 1949, Robert Fullard, BSc, and has issue living, Judith Mary, *b* 1952: *m* 1973, Christopher John Norton Ellis, and has issue living, Richard Gordon *b* 1979, Laura Kate *b* 1981, — Cathryn Elisabeth, *b* 1955: *m* 1978, Michael John Morris, and has issue living, Robert James *b* 1982, Rachel Elisabeth *b* 1984. *Residence* – 2 Thornley Lane, Grotton, Oldham.

WIDOW LIVING OF SON OF FIRST BARON

Maureen Margaret, only da of late David Watson-Allan, of Churston Ferrers, Devon: *m* 1952, Hon Kenneth Lewis Macdonald, yr son of 1st Baron, who *d* 1990. *Residence* – Fir Trees, Frog Lane, Balsall Common, West Midlands CV7 7FP.

COLLATERAL BRANCH LIVING

Issue of late Hon Kenneth Lewis Macdonald, yr son of 1st Baron, *b* 1921, *d* 1990: *m* 1952, Maureen Margaret (ante), only da of late David Watson-Allan, of Churston Ferrers, Devon:—
Sarah Margaret, *b* 1954: *m* 1974, David Henry Waldron, of Barn Cottage Farm, Little Shrewley, Warwick, and has issue living, William David MacDonald, *b* 1980, — Charlotte Sarah, *b* 1978. —— Laura Jane, *b* 1966: *m* 1994, James Edward Reeve.

PREDECESSOR – (1) *Sir* GORDON Macdonald, KCMG, PC, son of Thomas Macdonald, of Gwaenysgor, Flintshire; *b* 1888; Member Miners' Fedn of Gt Britain 1920-29; Chm of Cttees, House of Commons 1934-41, Gov and C-in-C of Newfoundland 1946-49, and Chm of Commn of Govt of Newfoundland and Dependencies 1946-49, Paymaster-Gen 1949-51; MP for Ince Div of Lancs (*Lab*) 1929-42 (resigned), Controller Min of Fuel and Power 1942-46, Gov BBC, Chm BBC (Wales) 1952-60, Dir Colonial Development Corpn 1952-59; *cr Baron Macdonald of Gwaenysgor*, of Gwaenysgor, co Flint (peerage of UK) 1949: *m* 1913, Mary who *d* 1967, da of William Lewis, of Blaenau Festiniog; *d* 1966; *s* by his el son (2) GORDON RAMSAY, 2nd Baron and present peer.

McFADZEAN, BARON (McFadzean) (Life Baron 1966)

WILLIAM HUNTER McFADZEAN, KT, son of late Henry McFadzean, of Stranraer; *b* 17 Dec 1903; *ed* Stranraer Acad and High Sch, and Glasgow Univ; a Chartered Accountant, and a Comp IEE; Pres of FBI 1959-61, British Elec Power Convention 1961-62, and British Nuclear Forum 1964-66, Vice-Pres of British-Swedish Chamber of Commerce 1963-74, and Middle East Assocn 1965, and City of London Soc 1965-72, Chm of Industrial Fedn of EFTA 1960-63, Founder Chm of Export Council for Europe 1960-64 (Hon Pres 1964) and of British National Export Council and Commonwealth Export Council 1964-66 (Pres 1966-68), a Member of Council of Inst of Dirs 1954-74, of Min of Labour Advisory Board on Resettlement of Ex-Regulars 1957-60, of Board of Trade Advisory Council on Middle East Trade 1958-60, of Min of Transport's Shipping Advisory Panel 1962-64, of Court of British Shippers Council 1964, of Anglo-Danish Soc (Chm 1969-75, Hon Pres 1975), and of Council Confedn of British Industry 1965, of Advisory Cttee for the Queen's Award to

Endeavour

Industry 1965-67, and of Council Foreign Bondholders 1968; Chm of British Insulated Callender's Construction Co, Ltd, 1952-64, of British Insulated Callender's Cables, Ltd (now BICC plc) Chm 1954-73 (Managing Dir 1954-61) Hon Life Pres 1973, of British Insulated Callender's (Submarine Cables), Ltd, 1954-73; Chm of British Insulated Callender's Cables Finance, NV 1971-73; Dep Chm of RTZ/BICC Aluminium Holdings, Ltd, 1967-73, and of The Canada Life Assurance Co of Great Britain 1971-84; a Dir of Midland Bank, Ltd 1959-77 (Dep Chm 1968-77), of Anglesey Aluminium, Ltd, 1968-73, of Canada Life Assurance Co 1969-79, of Midland Bank Executor & Trustee Co Ltd, 1959-67, of English Electric Co Ltd 1966-68, of The Steel Co of Wales, Ltd 1966-67, and of Canadian Imperial Bank of Commerce 1967-74 (now Dir Emeritus); Pres Coal Trade Benevolent Assocn 1967-68, of Electrical and Electronic Industries Benevolent Assocn 1968-69, and of British Shippers, Council 1968-71; Chm of Review Cttee for The Queen's Award to Industry for 1970, of Standard Broadcasting Corpn (UK) Ltd 1969-79, of Broadcasting Marketing Sers 1974-76, and of Home Oil (UK) Ltd 1972-78, and Scurry Rainbow (UK) Ltd 1974-78; JDipMa; Grand Cdr of Order of Dannebrog, of Denmark; Grand Officer Order of Prince Henry the Navigator of Portugal; *cr* Knt 1960, *Baron McFadzean*, of Woldingham, co Surrey (Life Baron) 1966, and KT 1976: *m* 1933, Eileen, el da of Arthur Gordon, of Blundellsands, Lancs, and has issue.

Arms – Vert a saltire argent between in chief a thistle slipped and leaved, in base a thunderbolt, and in fess two garbs or banded gules. **Crest** – A lion's gamb gules grasping a caduceus or, the serpents vert within an orle of wild flowers proper. **Supporters** – On either side a lion vert supporting a caduceus or the serpents vert.
Residence – 16 Lansdown Crescent, Bath BA1 5EX. *Clubs* – Carlton.

SON LIVING

Hon (Gordon) Barry (17 Yeoman's Row, SW3 2AL), *b* 1937; *ed* Winchester, and Ch Ch, Oxford (MA); FCA: *m* 1st, 1968 (*m diss* 1972), Julia Maxine, da of Max Dillon (now Sir Max Dillon), of Pymble, Sydney, NSW; 2ndly, 1984, Diana Rosemary, yst da of late Sam Waters, of Norfolk, and has issue (by 1st *m*), two das.

DAUGHTER LIVING

Hon Angela Caroline, *b* 1942: *m* 1963, Robin Vyvyan Carter Donald, of Osborne House, Bathampton, Bath, and has issue.

ADOPTED DAUGHTER DECEASED

Daphne Juliet, *b* 1941: *m* 1965, Douglas Riehl, of RRI Hyde Park, Ontario, Canada, and *d* 1993, leaving issue, two sons and two das.

McFADZEAN OF KELVINSIDE, BARONY OF (McFadzean) (Extinct 1992)

DAUGHTER LIVING OF LIFE BARON (*by 1st marriage*)

Hon Felicity Carmen Francesca (*Baroness Marsh*), *b* 1946: *m* 1979, Baron Marsh, PC (Life Baron).

WIDOW LIVING OF LIFE BARON

SONJA LIAN HOA NIO (*née* Khung) (*Baroness McFadzean of Kelvinside*), of Indonesia: *m* 1988, as his 2nd wife, Baron McFadzean of Kelvinside (Life Baron), who *d* 1992. *Address* – c/o Lloyds Bank plc, 56 High St, Marlow, Bucks SL7 1AJ.

MACFARLANE OF BEARSDEN, BARON (Macfarlane) (Life Baron 1991)

NORMAN SOMERVILLE MACFARLANE, son of late Daniel Robertson Macfarlane; *b* 5 March 1926; *ed* Glasgow High Sch; commn'd RA 1945, served Palestine 1945-47; founder N. S. Macfarlane & Co 1949, which became Macfarlane Group (Clansman) plc 1973, since when Chm (Man Dir 1973-90), Chm United

Distillers plc since 1987, United Distillers UK (formerly Arthur Bell Distillers plc) since 1989, American Trust plc since 1980, and The Fine Art Soc plc since 1976; Jt Chm Guinness 1987-89; Dep Chm Guinness plc 1989-92; Dir Clydesdale Bank plc since 1980 (Dep Chm since 1993), Gen Accident, Fire & Life Assurance Corpn plc since 1984, Edinburgh Fund Managers plc since 1980; Dir Glasgow Chamber of Commerce 1976-79, Scottish Nat Orchestra 1977-82, Third Eye Centre 1978-81; Pres Stationers' Assoc of GB and Ireland 1965, and Stationers' Co of Glasgow 1968-70; Member Royal Fine Art Commn for Scotland 1980-82, Pres Royal Glasgow Inst of the Fine Arts 1976-87, Gov Glasgow Sch of Art 1976-87, Board Member Scottish Devpt Agency 1979-87, Member of Court Glasgow Univ 1980-88, Dir Scottish Ballet 1975-83 and Vice Chm Scottish Ballet 1983-87, Scottish Patron The Nat Art Collection Fund since 1978, Lord High Commr to Gen Assembly of Church of Scotland 1992 and 1993, Chm of Govs Glasgow High Sch 1979-92; Chm Glasgow Action 1985-90; Chm Glasgow Development Agency 1990-92; Trustee Nat Heritage Memorial Fund, and Nat Galleries of Scotland; Hon Vice Pres Glasgow Batn Boys' Bde; Underwriting Member of Lloyd's; Hon FRIAS 1984, Hon LLD Strathclyde 1986, Glasgow 1988, Hon D Univ Glasgow Caledonian Univ 1993, Hon RSA 1987, Hon RGI 1987, Hon FRCPS Glasgow 1992, Hon DUniv Stirling 1992, Hon Dr *honoris causa* Edinburgh 1992, Hon Fell Glasgow Sch of Art 1993; *cr* Knt 1983, and *Baron Macfarlane of Bearsden*, of Bearsden in the District of Bearsden and Milngavie (Life Baron) 1991: *m* 1953, Marguerite Mary, da of John Johnstone Campbell, of 17 Norwood Drive, Whitecraigs, and has issue. *Residence* – 50 Manse Rd, Bearsden, Glasgow. *Club* – New (Edinburgh).

SON LIVING

Hon Hamish, *b* 1961: *m* 1990, Laura Pitt.

DAUGHTERS LIVING

Hon Fiona, *b* 1955: *m* 1982, J. S. M. McNaught.
Hon Gail, *b* 1957: *m* 1992, Lt Simon Allbutt, RN.
Hon Marjorie, *b* 1960: *m* 1991, J. B. (Jack) Roberts, son of J. B. Roberts, of Bearsden, Glasgow.
Hon Marguerite, *b* 1966.

McFARLANE OF LLANDAFF, BARONESS (McFarlane) (Life Baroness 1979)

Prof JEAN KENNEDY MCFARLANE, da of James McFarlane; *b* 1926; *ed* Howell's Sch, Llandaff, and Bedford and Birkbeck Colls, Univ of London (MA, BSc (Soc)); Hon DSc (Ulster), Hon DEd (CNAA), FCN (Australia) 1984; SRN, SCM, FRCN 1976; Univ of Manchester; Sen Lecturer in Nursing, Dept of Social and Preventive Medicine 1971-73; Sen Lecturer and Head of Dept of Nursing 1973-74; Prof and Head of Dept of Nursing 1974-1988; Chm English Board for Nursing, Midwifery and Health Visting 1980-83; Member of Commn of Commonwealth War Graves 1983-86 *cr Baroness McFarlane of Llandaff*, of Llandaff, co Glamorgan (Life Baroness) 1979.
Address – Dept of Nursing, Manchester Univ, Stopford Building, Oxford Rd, Manchester M13 9PT.

McGOWAN, BARON (McGowan) (Baron UK 1937)

Union is strength

HARRY DUNCAN CORY MCGOWAN, 3rd Baron; *b* 20 July 1938; *ed* Eton: *m* 1962, Lady Gillian Angela Pepys, da of 7th Earl of Cottenham, and has issue.

Arms – Per saltire argent and azure two lions rampant in pale gules and as many horseshoes in fesse proper. **Crest** – A tower or, between two horseshoes proper. **Supporters** – *Dexter*, a figure representing St Barbara proper, holding in the exterior hand a tower or; *sinister*, a figure representing St Kentigern proper, holding in the exterior hand his crozier or.
Residences – Highway House, Lower Froyle, Alton, Hants; 12 Stanhope Mews East, SW7. *Club* – Boodle's.

SON LIVING

Hon HARRY JOHN CHARLES, *b* 23 June 1971.

DAUGHTERS LIVING

Hon Emma Louise Angela, *b* 1963: *m* 1987, Guy H. C. Hill, eldest son of R. J. C. Hill, of Croxton Kerrial, Leics, and has issue living, Charles, *b* 1988, — Davina, *b* 1991. *Residence* – 30 Westover Rd, SW18.
Hon Annabel Kate Cory, *b* 1965: *m* 1991, Ashley J. Bealby, yr son of J. Bealby, of Barrowby, Lincs.

BROTHERS LIVING

Hon Dominic James Wilson (Bragborough Hall, Daventry, Northants), *b* 1951: *m* 19—, Brigitta, eldest da of late C. Papadimitriou, of Athens.
Hon Mungo Alexander Cansh (Bragborough Farm, Daventry, Northants), *b* 1956: *m* 1983, Hon (Arabella) Charlotte Eden, yr da of Baron Eden of Winton (Life Baron), and has issue living, James Alexander Cory, *b* 1985, — Laura Charlotte Iona, *b* 1987, — Rose, *b* 1991.

SISTERS LIVING

Hon Moana Elizabeth Jean, *b* 1948: *m* 1978, as his 2nd wife, John David Vaughan Seth-Smith, only son of late Cdr David Keith Seth-Smith, and has issue living, Edward David Harry, *b* 1979, — William Jonathan Cory, *b* 1985. *Residence* – The Old School House, Whilton, Daventry, Northants.
Hon Catriona Carmen Harriet, *b* 1953.

WIDOW LIVING OF SECOND BARON

CARMEN (*Dowager Baroness McGowan*) (Bragborough Hall, Daventry, Northants), da of Sir (James) Herbert Cory, 1st Bt: *m* 1937, the 2nd Baron, who *d* 1966.

COLLATERAL BRANCH LIVING

Issue of late William Johnston McGowan, TD, yr son of 1st Baron, *b* 1909, *d* 1977: *m* 1946, Helen Myrtle Dorothy, MBE, JP, who *d* 1976, da of late Arthur Atherley, JP, DL, of Landguard Manor, Isle of Wight, and widow of Col Edward Orlando Kellett, DSO, MP:—
Fiona Victoria Jean Atherley (*Baroness Hindlip*), *b* 1947: *m* 1968, 6th Baron Hindlip. *Residences* – The Cedar House, Inkpen, Berks; 55 Campden Hill Rd, W8.

PREDECESSORS – (1) *Sir* HARRY DUNCAN McGowan, KBE, son of late Henry McGowan, of Glasgow, *b* 1874; Hon Pres (Chm 1930-50) of Imperial Chemical Industries Ltd, Pres of So of Chemical Industry 1931, of Institute of Fuel 1934-5, and of British Standards Institution 1947; *cr Baron McGowan*, of Ardeer, co Ayr (peerage of UK) 1937: *m* 1903, Jean Boyle, who *d* 1952, da of late William Young, of Paisley; *d* 1961; *s* by his el son (2) HARRY WILSON, 2nd Baron, *b* 1906: *m* 1937, Carmen, da of Sir (James) Herbert Cory, 1st Bt, *cr* 1919; *d* 1966; *s* by his el son (3) HARRY DUNCAN CORY, 3rd Baron and present peer.

McGREGOR OF DURRIS, BARON (McGregor) (Life Baron 1978)

Prof OLIVER ROSS MCGREGOR, son of late William McGregor; *b* 25 Aug 1921; *ed* Worksop Coll, Aberdeen Univ, and LSE (Hon Fell 1977), Hon LLD Bristol 1986; temp civil servant, War Office and Min of Agric 1940-44, Assist Lecturer and Lecturer in Economic History, Hull Univ 1945-47, Lecturer, Bedford Coll 1947-60, and Reader in London Univ 1960-64, since when Prof of Social Instns London Univ; joint Dir, Rowntree Legal Research Unit since 1966; Simon Senior Research Fellow, Manchester Univ 1959-60, Fellow of Wolfson Coll, Oxford 1972-75, and Dir, Centre for Socio-Legal Studies, Oxford Univ 1972-75; Chm of R Commn of the Press 1975-77; Member of Legal Aid Advisory Cttee 1964-78, Pres, Nat Council for One Parent Families since 1975, and of Nat Assocn of Citizens Advice Bureaux 1981-87; Chm Advertising Standards Authority since 1980; Trustee of Reuters 1984, Chm Reuters Founders' Share Co since 1987; Member of Countryside Commn 1966-80; *cr Baron McGregor of Durris*, of Hampstead in Greater London (Life Baron) 1978: *m* 1944, Nellie, da of Harold Weate, of Manchester, and has issue.
Residence – Far End, Wyldes Close, NW11 7JB. *Club* – Garrick.

SONS LIVING

Hon William Ross, *b* 1948; *ed* Haberdashers' Aske's Sch: *m* 1981, Ann Holmes, da of Archibald MacGregor, of Fife, and widow of Matthew Johnson, of Edinburgh.
Hon Alistair John, *b* 1950.
Hon Gregor Weate, *b* 1952: *m* 1978, Wendy Elizabeth, da of Sydney Carlisle, of Yorkshire.

McINTOSH OF HARINGEY, BARON (McIntosh) (Life Baron 1982)

ANDREW ROBERT MCINTOSH, son of late Prof Albert William McIntosh, OBE, by his wife Helena Agnes (Jenny) Britton; *b* 30 April 1933; *ed* Haberdashers' Aske's Sch, Royal Gram Sch, High Wycombe, Jesus Coll Oxford (MA), and Ohio State Univ (Fell in Economics 1956-57); Member Hornsey Borough Council 1963-65; Member Haringey Borough Council 1964-68; mem GLC for Tottenham 1973-83 (Leader of the Opposition 1980-81), Dep Leader of the Opposition and Opposition Spokesman on Home Affairs, House of Lords, since 1992; Chm Market Research Society 1972-73; Chm Fabian Soc 1985-86; Dep Chm IFF Research Ltd since 1988 (Man Dir 1965-81, Chm 1981-88); Chm SVP United Kingdom since 1983; *cr Baron McIntosh of Haringey*, of Haringey in Greater London (Life Baron) 1982; *m* 1962, Naomi Ellen Sargant, Pro Vice-Chancellor (Student Affairs), Open Univ 1974-78, Prof of Applied Social Research 1978-81, Senior Commissioning Editor, Channel Four Television Co Ltd 1981-88, da of late Thomas Sargant, OBE, JP, and previously wife of Peter Joseph Kelly, and has issue.
Residence – 27 Hurst Av, N6 5TX.

SONS LIVING

Hon Francis Robert, *b* 1962; *ed* Highgate Wood Sch, and London Coll of Furniture.
Hon Philip Henry Sargant, *b* 1964; *ed* Highgate Wood Sch, and Kingston Polytechnic.

MACKAY OF ARDBRECKNISH, BARON (Mackay) (Life Baron 1991)

JOHN JACKSON MACKAY, son of late Jackson Mackay, of Tayvallich, Argyll; *b* 15 Nov 1938; *ed* Glasgow Univ (BSc, Dip Ed); formerly Head of Maths Dept, Oban High Sch; PPS to Sec of State for Scotland (Rt Hon George Younger) 1982, Parly Under Sec of State Scottish Office 1982-87; Chief Exec Scottish Conservative Central Office 1987-90, Chm Sea Fish Industry Authority 1990-93, Lord-in-Waiting (Govt Whip) Oct 1993-Jan 1994, since when Parly Under Sec of State Dept of Transport (Min for Aviation and Shipping); MP Argyll (*C*) 1979-83 and Argyll and Bute 1983-87; *cr Baron Mackay of Ardbrecknish*, of Tayvallich, District of Argyll and Bute (Life Baron) 1991: *m* 1961, Sheena, da of late James Wagner, of Bishopton, Renfrewshire, and has issue.

Residence – Innishail, 51 Springkell Drive, Glasgow G41 4EZ.

SONS LIVING

Hon David Ferguson, *b* 1967.
Hon Colin James, *b* 1969.

DAUGHTER LIVING

Hon Fiona Jackson, *b* 1964.

MACKAY OF CLASHFERN, BARON (Mackay) (Life Baron 1979)

JAMES PETER HYMERS MACKAY, PC, QC, FRSE, son of James MacKay; *b* 2 July 1927; *ed* George Heriot's Sch, Edinburgh, and Edinburgh Univ (MA); BA Camb 1952; LLB Edinburgh 1955; FRSE (1984); admitted to Faculty of Advocates 1955; Sheriff Prin Renfrew and Argyll 1972-74; Vice-Dean, Faculty of Advocate 1973-76, Dean 1976-79, Lord Advocate 1979-84, since when Senator College of Justice in Scotland 1985, Lord Justice of Appeal in Ordinary 1985, Lord High Chancellor since (Oct) 1987; *cr* PC 1979 and *Baron Mackay of Clashfern*, of Eddrachillis in the District of Sutherland (Life Baron) 1979: *m* 1958, Elizabeth Gunn Hymers, and has issue.

Arms – Azure, on a chevron Argent between two bears' heads couped Argent, muzzled Gules in chief and a fleece Argent in base, a roebuck's head erased between two hands grasping daggers, the points turned towards the buck's head all Proper. **Crest** – a dexter arm, couped at the elbow Proper, the hand grasping a pair of balances Or. Behind the Shield are placed in saltire two great maces ensigned with Imperial Crowns Or and pendent below the Shield by string, nowed, buttoned and tassled, a Purse Gules, embroidered all over with the Royal Arms to denote the Office of Lord High Chancellor. **Supporters** – *Dexter*, a male figure attired in the Robes of the Lord High Chancellor, *Sinister*, a male figure attired in the Robes of one Her Majesty's Counsel learned in the Law in Scotland Proper.

Address – Lord Chancellor's Residence, House of Lords, Westminster, SW1. *Club* – New (Edinburgh).

SON LIVING

Hon James, *b* 1958; *ed* Camb Univ (MA), Edinburgh Univ (MB, ChB); Hon Registrar and Research Fell Dept of Clinical Surg Univ of Edinburgh: *m* 1991, Marion E., da of J. E. McArthur, of Edinburgh, and has issue living, Heather Mairi, *b* 1992.

DAUGHTER LIVING

Hon Elizabeth Janet, *b* 1961: *m* 1982, James Campbell, of Milton of Ness Side, Inverness and has issue living, two sons and one da.
Hon Shona Ruth, *b* 1968.

MACKENZIE-STUART, BARON (Mackenzie Stuart) (Life Baron 1988)

ALEXANDER JOHN MACKENZIE STUART, only son of late Prof Alexander Mackenzie Stuart, KC, of Aberdeen; *b* 18 Nov 1924; *ed* Fettes, Sidney Sussex Coll, Camb (BA), and Edinburgh Univ (LLB); Hon DUniv Stirling 1973, Hon Fell Sidney Sussex Camb 1977, Hon LLD Exeter 1978, Edinburgh 1978, Glasgow 1981, Aberdeen 1983, Camb 1987, and Birmingham 1988; served RE 1942-47; admitted Faculty of Advocates 1951; QC (Scot) 1963, Hon Bencher Middle Temple 1978, and King's Inn, Dublin 1983; Keeper of Advocates Library 1970-72, Standing Junior Counsel, Scottish Home Dept 1956-57, Inland Revenue in Scotland 1957-63, Sheriff-Prin of Aberdeen, Kincardine and Banff 1971-72, Senator of Coll of Justice in Scotland (as Hon Lord Mackenzie Stuart) 1972, Judge of the Court of Justice, European Communities, Luxembourg 1973-84, Pres 1984-88; Gov Fettes Coll 1962-72; Prix Bech for services to Europe 1989; *cr Baron Mackenzie-Stuart*, of Dean in the District of the City of Edinburgh (Life Baron) 1988: *m* 1952, Anne Burtholme, da of late John Sidney Lawrence Millar, WS, of Edinburgh, and has issue.

Residences – 7 Randolph Cliff, Edinburgh EH3 7TZ; Le Garidel, Gravieres, 07140 Les Vans, France.

DAUGHTERS LIVING

Hon Amanda Jane, *b* 1954: *m* 1977, Michael George Hay, son of George Ronald Hay, and has issue living, Daisy Elizabeth, *b* 1981, — Marianna Clare, *b* 1985. *Residence* – 8 Swan St, Osney, Oxford.
Hon Katherine Anne, *b* 1956. *Residence* – 99a Grosvenor Av, Highbury, N1.
Hon Laura Margaret, *b* 1961. *Residence* – 85 Riverview Gdns, W6.
Hon Judith Mary, *b* 1964: *m* 1989, Nicholas David Aspinall, elder son of late Dr Dennis L. Aspinall. *Residence* – 194 Av de Tervuren, 1150 Brussels Belgium.

MACKIE OF BENSHIE, BARON (Mackie) (Life Baron 1974)

GEORGE YULL MACKIE, CBE, DSO, DFC, son of late Maitland Mackie, OBE, and brother of Lord John-Mackie (Life Baron); *b* 10 July 1919; *ed* Aberdeen Gram Sch, and Aberdeen Univ; 1939-45 War with Bomber Command RAF (DSO, DFC); Farmer; Chm of Scottish Liberal Party 1965-70 (Vice-Chm 1960-65); MP for Caithness and Sutherland (*L*) 1964-66; former Chm Caithness Glass Ltd; a Member of National and Local Cttees for Scotland, of NFU, and of Scottish Advisory Cttee of British Council; Rector of Dundee Univ 1981-83; *cr* DSO 1944, CBE (Civil) 1971, and *Baron Mackie of Benshie*, of Kirriemuir, co Angus (Life Baron) 1974: *m* 1st, 1944, Lindsay Lyall, who *d* 1985, da of late Alexander Sharp, Advocate, of Aberdeen; 2ndly, 1988, Jacqueline, da of late Col Marcel Rauch, French Air Force, and widow of Andrew Lane, and has issue by 1st *m*.
Residence – Cortachy House, by Kirriemuir, Angus, DD8 5QG. *Clubs* – Garrick, Farmers', Scottish Liberal (Edinburgh), RAF.

DAUGHTERS LIVING *(By 1st marriage)*

Hon Lindsay Mary, *b* 1945: *m* 1982, Alan Rusbridger.
Hon Diana Lyall, *b* 1946: *m* 1968, John Carlyle Hope, of 3 St Bernard Cres, Edinburgh.
Hon Jeannie Felicia, *b* 1953: *m* 1982, David Leigh.

MACKINTOSH OF HALIFAX, VISCOUNT (Mackintosh) (Viscount UK 1957, Bt UK 1935)

JOHN CLIVE MACKINTOSH, 3rd Viscount and 3rd Baronet, *b* 9 Sept 1958; *s* 1980; *ed* The Leys Sch, and Oriel Coll, Oxford, Chartered Accountant: *m* 1982 (*m diss* 1993), Elizabeth, only da of late D. G. Lakin, and has issue.

𝕬rms – Or, on a chevron between two lions rampant in chief and a lymphad in base sable, a bezant charged with a representation of the head of St John the Baptist proper, between two hearts of the field. 𝕮rest – Upon a rock proper, charged with two roses argent, barbed and seeded, a cat sejant also proper. 𝕾upporters – On either side a squirrel proper. suspended from the neck by a cord a purse or.
Address – House of Lords, Westminster, SW1.

SONS LIVING

Hon THOMAS HAROLD GEORGE, *b* 8 Feb 1985.
Hon George John Frank, *b* 1988.

BROTHER LIVING

Hon Graham Charles, *b* 1964.

HALF-SISTERS LIVING

Hon Diana Mary, *b* 1947.
Hon Elizabeth Constance (*Baroness Astor of Hever*), *b* 1950: *m* 1st, 1972, Timothy Cutting; 2ndly, 1980, Nicolas Chagrin; 3rdly, 1990, as his 2nd wife, 3rd Baron Astor of Hever, and has issue living (by 2nd *m*), Natalya Isabel, *b* 1981, — (by 3rd *m*) (*see* B Astor of Hever).

AUNT LIVING *(Daughter of 1st Viscount)*

Hon Mary, *b* 1927; is a JP for Norfolk: *m* 1949, (Charles) Michael Watt, and has issue living, Charles Jonathan (Narborough House, Stoke Holy Cross, Norwich, Norfolk), *b* 1950: *m* 1974, Catherine Anna Lilley, and has issue living, Charles Henry William *b* 1980, Edward Alastair Donald *b* 1984, Elizabeth Anna *b* 1977, — Henry Donald *b* 1962: *m* 1992, Tania Elizabeth, only da of Charles Ian Strafford, of Chelmsford, Essex, — Susan Mary, *b* 1953: *m* 1980, Ivan Alexander Shenkman, of 34 Royal Crescent, W11, and has issue living, Maximilian Ivan Michael *b* 1982, Alexander Ivan Marcus *b* 1988, Melissa Alexandra Mary *b* 1984. *Residence* – Wychwood House, Hethersett, nr Norwich, Norfolk, NR9 3AT.

WIDOW LIVING OF SECOND VISCOUNT

GWYNNETH CHARLESWORTH (*Viscountess Mackintosh of Halifax*) (The Old Hall, Barford, Norwich NR9 4AY), da of late Charles Henry Gledhill: *m* 1956, as his 2nd wife, 2nd Viscount Mackintosh of Halifax, OBE, BEM, who *d* 1980.

PREDECESSORS – **(1)** Sir HAROLD VINCENT MACKINTOSH, son of John Mackintosh, JP, of Greystones, Halifax; *b* 1891; Chm of John Mackintosh & Sons Ltd, toffee manufacturers, of Halifax; Chm of National Savings Cttee 1943-64, and Pres 1958-64; *cr* a *Baron Mackintosh of Halifax*, of Hethersett, co Norfolk (peerage of UK) 1948, and *Viscount Mackintosh of Halifax*, of Hethersett, co Norfolk (peerage of UK) 1957: *m* 1916, Constance Emily, who *d* 1975, da of Edgar Cooper Stoneham, OBE, of Acton, W3; *d* 1964; *s* by his only son **(2)** JOHN, OBE, BEM, 2nd Viscount, *b* 1921; Dir John Mackintosh & Son Ltd: *m* 1st, 1946 (*m diss* 1956), Bronda, only da of late Louis John Fibiger, of South Shields, co Durham; 2ndly, 1956, Gwynneth Charlesworth, da of Charles Henry Gledhill; *d* 1980; *s* by his el son **(3)** JOHN CLIVE, 3rd Viscount and present peer; also Baron Mackintosh of Halifax.

MACLAY, BARON (Maclay) (Baron UK 1922, Bt UK 1914)

JOSEPH PATON MACLAY, 3rd Baron and 3rd Baronet; *b* 11 April 1942; *s* 1969; *ed* Winchester; Man Dir Denholm Maclay Co, Ltd, and a Dir of Milton Shipping Co, Ltd, North of England Protection & Indemnity Assocn and The British Steamship Short Trades Assocn, Man Dir Milton Timber Services Ltd since 1983: *m* 1976, Elizabeth Anne, only da of G. M. Buchanan, of Delamere, Pokataroo, NSW, and has issue.

Arms – Or, a lion rampant azure, armed and langued gules, resting its sinister paw on an anchor sable, all within an orle of the second. **Crest** – A lymphad sails furled sable, flagged proper. **Supporters** – Two wolves proper, each gorged with a chain, pendant therefrom an escutcheon argent, charged with a salmon on its back holding a ring in its mouth proper.
Residences – Duchal, Kilmacolm, Renfrewshire; Milton, Kilmacolm, Renfrewshire.

SONS LIVING

Hon JOSEPH PATON, *b* 6 March 1977.
Hon Thomas Maxwell, *b* 1981.

DAUGHTER LIVING

Hon Rebecca Delamere, *b* 1979.

BROTHERS LIVING

Hon David Milton (12 Langton St, SW10), *b* 1944; *ed* Winchester: *m* 1968, Valerie, da of late Lt-Cdr J. P. Fyfe, of Kinkell, St Andrews, Fife, and has issue living, Duncan, *b* 1974.
Hon Angus Grenfell (House of Gruinard, Laide, by Achnasheen, Ross-shire), *b* 1945; *ed* Winchester: *m* 1st, 1970, Hon (Elizabeth) Victoria Baillie, who *d* 1986, el da of 3rd Baron Burton; 2ndly, 1990, Jane Elizabeth Angela, da of late Lt-Col Alistair Monteith Gibb, R Wilts Yeo (*see* V Cowdray, 1980 Edn), and formerly wife of 13th Marquess of Huntly, and has issue living (by 1st *m*), Robert Michael, *b* 1972, — Fergus *b* 1981, — Sarah Elizabeth, *b* 1977.

SISTERS LIVING AND DECEASED

Hon Sarah, *b* 1937: *m* 1968, David Richard Hayes, of Factors House, Pityulish, Aviemore, Inverness-shire (*see* Muir, Bt).
Hon Lucy, *b* 1938: *m* 1966, James Ian Alexander Robertson, of Glenside Farm, Plean, Stirlingshire, and *d* 1987, leaving issue, Hugh Sebastian, *b* 1967, — David Ian, *b* 1969, — Dominic James, *b* 1973, — Anna Marcelle, *b* 1971; *d* 1989.

WIDOW LIVING OF SECOND BARON

NANCY MARGARET (*Nancy, Baroness Maclay*) (Milton, Kilmacolm, Renfrewshire), da of Robert Coventry Greig, of Hall of Caldwell, Uplawnmoor, Renfrewshire: *m* 1936, the 2nd Baron, who *d* 1969.

COLLATERAL BRANCHES LIVING

Grandchildren of late Hon Walter Symington Maclay, CB, OBE, MD (infra):—
Issue of late Dr Walter Strang Symington Maclay, *b* 1931, *d* 1987: *m* 1956, Elizabeth Ann (Findings, Hambledon, Surrey GU8 5TS) (who *m* 2ndly, 1991, Thomas Roderick Loxley Waring), eldest da of Willis C. Cooper, of Tintern, Esher Close, Esher, Surrey:—
Andrew Strang, *b* 1958: *m* 1987, Felicity Neal. —— Christopher Willis, *b* 1964: *m* 1988, Louise Nelson. —— Janet Susan, *b* 1960.

Issue of late Hon Walter Symington Maclay, CB, OBE, MD, 4th son of 1st Baron, *b* 1901, *d* 1964: *m* 1928, Dorothy, who *d* 1993, da of late William Lennox, WS:—
John Lennox Sim (40 Kensington Sq, W8) *b* 1937; *ed* Winchester, and St John's Coll, Camb. —— Mark Paton (Sladen Green, Binley, Andover, Hants), *b* 1943; *ed* Winchester, and RAC Cirencester; ARICS: *m* 1967, Elizabeth Ruth, da of Worsfold McClenaghan, of Westfield House, Highclere, Newbury, Berks, and has issue living, James Paton, *b* 1971, — Alasdair Worsfold, *b* 1973, — Caroline Elizabeth, *b* 1976. —— (Shirley) Georgina (Cedar House, Hellidon, Daventry, Northants NN11 6LG), *b* 1933: *m* 1955 (*m diss* 19—), Robert David Ogden, and has issue living, Robert Nicholas, *b* 1958, — Joseph Jeremy (twin), *b* 1958, — Benjamin Patrick, *b* 1966, — Emma Maclay, *b* 1961.

PREDECESSORS – **(1)** *Rt Hon* JOSEPH PATON Maclay, son of late Ebenezer Maclay, of Glasgow; *b* 1857; sometime Chm of Maclay & Macintyre, Ltd, shipowners, of 21 Bothwell Street, Glasgow; Min of Shipping and a Member of War Cabinet 1916-21; *cr* a *Baronet* 1914, and *Baron Maclay*, of Glasgow, co Lanark (peerage of United Kingdom) 1922: *m* 1889, Martha, who *d* 1929, da of William Strang, manufacturer of Glasgow; *d* 1951; *s* by his el surviving son **(2)** JOSEPH PATON, KBE, 2nd Baron, *b* 1899; MP for Paisley (L) 1931-45; *m* 1936, Nancy Margaret, da of Robert Coventry Greig, of Hall of Caldwell, Uplawnmoor, Renfrewshire; *d* 1969; *s* by his el son **(3)** JOSEPH PATON, 3rd Baron and present peer.

MACLEAN, BARONY OF (Maclean) (Extinct 1990)

SON, DAUGHTER AND WIDOW OF LIFE BARON (see Maclean, Bt, cr 1631)

McLEAVY, BARONY OF (McLeavy) (Extinct 1976)

SON LIVING OF LIFE BARON

Hon Frank Waring, *b* 1925: *m* 1954, Verena, da of Emil Lüscher, of Unterkulm, Switzerland, and has issue.

WIDOW LIVING OF SON OF LIFE BARON

Janet Elizabeth (40 Ruskin Drive, Morecambe, Lancs), da of Harry Ogden: *m* 1958, Hon Douglas John McLeavy, who *d* 1969, and has issue, Mark, *b* 1969, — Ruth, *b* 1964.

MACLEHOSE OF BEOCH, BARON (MacLehose) (Life Baron 1981)

CRAWFORD MURRAY MACLEHOSE, KT, GBE, KCMG, KCVO, son of late Hamish A. MacLehose, of Grange, Culroy, Ayrshire; *b* 16 Oct 1917; *ed* Rugby, and Balliol Coll; a DL of Ayr and Arran; Malayan Civil Ser 1939-46, Foreign Ser 1946-82; acting Consul Hankow 1947-48, acting Consul-Gen 1948-49, and 1st Sec 1949-50, 1st Sec and Consul Prague 1951-54, seconded to Wellington, NZ 1954-56, 1st Sec at Paris 1958-59, Counsellor and Political Advisor, Hong Kong 1959-62, Head of Far Eastern Dept, FO 1963-65, Prin Private Sec to Foreign Sec 1965-67, and Ambassador to Vietnam 1967-69, and to Denmark 1969-71, Gov and C-in-C of Hong Kong 1971-82; Dir Nat Westminster Bank 1983-88, Chm Victoria League for Commonwealth Friendship 1983-87, Scottish Trust for the Physically Disabled, and Margaret Blackwood Housing Assocn since 1983; 1939-45 War as Lt RNVR; *cr* MBE (Mil) 1946, CMG 1964, KCMG 1971, KCVO 1975, GBE 1977, KT 1983, and *Baron MacLehose of Beoch*, of Maybole, in the district of Kyle and Carrick, and of Victoria in Hong Kong (Life Baron) 1981: *m* 1947, Margaret Noel, yst da of late Sir (Thomas) Charles Dunlop, TD, of Doonside, Ayrshire, and has issue.

𝖆rms – Argent, on a chevron ensigned at the top with a cross pattée Sable, between two escutcheons Azure each charged of a mullet of the First in chief and a demi double headed eagle displayed Azure beaked Sable in base, a book expanded Argent. 𝕮rest – a dragon's head erased affrontée Or, armed and langued Gules. 𝕾upporters – *dexter*, a Chinese dragon Or and langued Gules gorged of a collar indented Sable; *sinister*, a black faced ram Proper. 𝕸otto – Spe vitae melioris.
Residence – Beoch, Maybole, Ayrshire. *Club* – Athenaeum.

DAUGHTERS LIVING

Hon Elfrida Sandra, *b* 1949: *m* 1971, Martin Amery Wedgwood, of Collalis, Gartocharn, by Alexandria, Dunbartonshire, and has issue.
Hon Sylvia Margaret, *b* (twin) 1949: *m* 1970 Ronald Leighton, Sandeman, of Rosgaradh, West Dhuhill Drive, Helensburgh, Dunbartonshire G84 9AW, and has issue.

MACLEOD OF BORVE, BARONESS (Macleod) (Life Baroness 1971)

EVELYN HESTER MACLEOD, da of late Rev Gervase Vanneck Blois (*see* Blois, Bt, colls), *b* 19 Feb 1915; JP for Middx; a DL of Greater London; first Chm of National Gas Consumers' Council 1972-77; Chm Nat Assocn of Leagues of Hospital Friends 1976-85 (Pres 1985-89), Pres Nat Assocn of Widows since 1976; Member IBA 1972-77, Parole Bd 1978-82; Gov Queenswood Sch 1977-85; Pres Crisis at Christmas since 1970; *cr Baroness Macleod of Borve*, of Borve, Isle of Lewis (Life Baroness) 1971: *m* 1st, 1937, Mervyn Charles Mason, who was *k* by enemy action 1940; 2ndly, 1941, Rt Hon Iain Norman Macleod, MP, who *d* 1970, and has issue by 2nd *m*.
Residence – Luckings Farm, Coleshill, Amersham, Bucks HP7 0LS.

SON LIVING (By 2nd marriage)

Hon Torquil Anthony Ross, *b* 1942; *ed* Harrow: *m* 1967 (*m diss* 1973) (Elizabeth) Meriol, da of late Brig Arthur Pelham Trevor, DSO, and has issue living, Iain Ross, *b* 1970.

DAUGHTER LIVING (By 2nd marriage)

Hon Diana Hester, *b* 1944; *m* 1968 David Heimann, of Hertfordshire House, Coleshill, Bucks, and has three sons, Hugo Iain Philip, *b* 1972, — James Iain Philip, *b* 1974, — Charles Gervase Andrew, *b* 1977.

MacLEOD OF FUINARY, BARONY OF (MacLeod) (Extinct 1991)

SONS AND DAUGHTER OF LIFE BARON (*see* MacLeod, Bt, *cr* 1924)

Macmillan of Ovenden, Viscount; son of Earl of Stockton.

McNAIR, BARON (McNair) (Baron UK 1955)

Danger in delay

DUNCAN JAMES McNAIR, 3rd Baron; *b* 26 June 1947; *s* 1989; *ed* Bryanston: *m* 19—, Kodikaraarachige Perera, of Sri Lanka, and has issue.

Arms – Gules, three barrulets wavy argent surmounted of a lion rampant or, armed and langued azure, between two thistleheads stalked and leved paleways of the third. **Crest** – On a wreath of the liveries an ancient ship under full sail, flagged azure, the sail emblazoned of ensigns armorial as on the escutcheon. **Supporters** – Two Bedlington terriers proper.

SON LIVING

Hon Thomas John, *b* 1972.

DAUGHTERS LIVING

Charlotte, *b* 1968 (adopted da).
Hon Victoria, *b* (twin) 1972.

BROTHER LIVING

Hon WILLIAM SAMUEL ANGUS, *b* 19th May 1958: *m* 1981 (*m diss* 19—), Emma U. Procter, and has issue living, John Samuel, *b* 1984, — Emily Harriet, 1982.

SISTER LIVING

Hon Josephine Margaret, *b* 1949.

AUNTS LIVING (*daughters of 1st Baron*)

Hon Sheila Margaret Ramsay, *b* 1918: *m* 1946, John Harold Barwell, who *d* 1983, and has issue living, Hugh John (c/o 33 Fulbrooke Rd, Cambridge CB3 9EE), *b* 1949: *m* 1973, Glynis Christine Rolfe, and has issue living, Guy Harold *b* 1989, Leigh Ellen *b* 1978, — Alice Marjorie Sheila, *b* 1947; *ed* Somerville Coll, Oxford; DPhil, FRHistS: *m* 1971, Franklyn Kimmel Prochaska, PhD, FRHistS, of 9 Addison Bridge Place, W14 8XP, and has issue living, William Anton Franklin *b* 1982, Elizabeth Harriet *b* 1980, — Lucy Elizabeth (470 Hunting Ridge Rd, Stamford, Connecticut 06903, USA), *b* 1951: *m* 1st, 1973 (*m diss* 1978), Lloyd Herman Bernstein; 2ndly, 1990, Mitch Diamond, — Claire Bridget, *b* 1953; *ed* Somerville Coll, Oxford (BA 1975): *m* 1979, Gil Aufray, of 53c Randolph Av, W9, and has issue living, Oliver Daniel *b* 1988. *Residence* – 33 Fulbrooke Rd, Cambridge CB3 9EE.
Hon Elinor Ruth, *b* 1924: *m* 1955, Raymond Hanscomb, and has issue living, Benjamin Douglas *b* 1956, — and two adopted children, George Sebastian, *b* 1965, — Emma Frances Mary, *b* 1963. *Residence* – Powells End, Kempley, Dymock, Glos.

WIDOW LIVING OF SECOND BARON

VERA (*Vera, Baroness McNair*), da of Theodore James Faithfull, MRCVS, of Birmingham: *m* 1941, the 2nd Baron, who *d* 1989. *Residence* – 1 The Laurels, Eastcombe, Stroud, Glos GL6 7DN.

PREDECESSORS – (1) *Sir* ARNOLD DUNCAN McNAIR, CBE, QC, LLD, FBA, son of late John McNair, of Court Lane, Dulwich Village, SE; *b* 1885; Vice-Chancellor of Liverpool Univ 1937-45; a Judge of Internat Court of Justice 1946-55 (pres. 1952-55); Pres Inst of Internat Law 1959-60; 1st Pres of Court of European Rights at Strasbourg 1959-65; *cr Baron McNair*, of Gleniffer, co Renfrew (peerage UK) 1955: *m* 1912, Marjorie, who *d* 1971, da of late Hon Sir Clement Meacher Bailhache; *d* 1975; *s* by his only son **(2)** (CLEMENT) JOHN, 2nd Baron, *b* 1915: *m* 1941, Vera, da of Theodore James Faithfull, MRCVS, of Birmingham; *d* 1989; *s* by his elder son **(3)** DUNCAN JAMES, 3rd Baron and present peer.

MACPHERSON OF DRUMOCHTER, BARON (Macpherson) (Baron UK 1951)

Touch not this cat but a glove

If there's no ripple at the bow, there's something wrong.

(JAMES) GORDON MACPHERSON, 2nd Baron; *b* 22 Jan 1924; *s* 1965; *ed* Loretto, and Wells House, Malvern; FRES, FRSA, FZS, a JP for Essex 1961 and Chm of Macpherson, Train & Co, Ltd, Food and Produce Importers and Exporters, and subsidiary and Assoc Cos since 1964, and A. J. Macpherson & Co Ltd, Bankers since 1973; Past Chm of W India Cttee 1973-75; Hon Game Warden for the Sudan since 1974; Member 1001 (nature trust); a Member of London Chamber of Commerce 1958-75; Pres of British Importers Confedn 1972; Dep Chm Brentwood Bench 1972-75; a Trustee of Head Injuries Rehabilitation Trust 1970-75; Freeman of City of London, a Member of Butchers' Co since 1969, and a Gov of Brentwood Sch 1970-74; Member Northern Meeting, Highland Soc of London (1975); 1939-45 War with RAF: *m* 1st, 1947, (Dorothy) Ruth, who *d* 1974, da of late Rev Henry Coulter, of Bellahouston, Glasgow; 2ndly, 1975, Catherine Bridget, only da of Dr Desmond MacCarthy, of Queens Rd, Brentwood, and has issue by 1st and 2nd *m*.

Arms – Per fesse or and azure, a lymphad sail furled flags and pennon flying counter-changed between in chief a dexter hand fessewise couped at the wrist grasping a dagger point upwards, and a crosscrosslet fitchée gules, and in base an oak tree eradicated proper fructed or. **Crest** – A wildcat sejant guardant proper holding a crosscrosslet fitchée gules. **Supporters** – *Dexter*, a lion gules, gorged with a collar, pendent therefrom an escutcheon or, charged with a garb azure; *sinister*, a bull gules, armed and unguled azure, gorged with a collar pendent therefrom an escutcheon gold charged with a boar's head couped also azure.

Residence – Kyllachy, Tomatin, Inverness-shire. *Clubs* – Boodle's, E India, Devonshire Sports, Public Schools.

SON LIVING *(By 2nd marriage)*

Hon JAMES ANTHONY, *b* 27 Feb 1979.

DAUGHTERS LIVING *(By 1st marriage)*

Hon Wendy Shona Coulter, *b* 1950: *m* 1st, 1972 (*m diss* 1980), Brian Anthony Fountain; 2ndly, 1987, Derek Everest, and has issue living, (by 1st *m*) Stewart James Coulter, *b* 1978. — Shona Fountain, *b* 1981, — (by 2nd *m*) Douglas, *b* 1988.
Hon Elizabeth Shirley, *b* 1953: *m* 1st, 1978 (*m diss* 1989), Mark William Ransome; 2ndly, 1990, Robert Frederick Shaw, of 3 Olympic Rd, Blairgowrie, Randburg, S Africa, and has issue living (by 1st *m*), James Gordon, *b* 1981, — Sarah Emma Ashley, *b* 1984.

(By 2nd marriage)

Hon Jennifer Margaret, *b* 1976.
Hon Anne Alexandra, *b* 1977.

SISTER LIVING

Hon Shona Catherine Greig, *b* 1929: *m* 1952, Donald le Strange Campbell, MC, and has issue living Donald Bruce le Strange (8 Dewhurst Rd, W14 0ET) *b* 1956: *m* 1982, Kristine, el da of Maj L. H. Nash, of Woodruff, Kingsley Green, Haslemere, Surrey, — Victoria Louise, *b* 1959: *m* 1985, Russell Charles Crockford, of 40 Ashcombe St, SW6 3AN, son of Charles Crockford, of Donnell, Camberley, Surrey, and has issue living, Alexander Charles *b* 1990. *Residence* – Little Dartmouth House, Dartmouth, Devon TQ6 0JP.

PREDECESSOR – (1) THOMAS Macpherson, son of James Macpherson, of Muirhead, Chryston, Lanarkshire; *b* 1888; Chm of Macpherson, Train & Co Ltd, Food and Produce Importers and Exporters; MP for Romford (*Lab*) 1945-50; *cr Baron Macpherson of Drumochter*, of Gt Warley, co Essex (peerage of UK) 1951: *m* 1920, Lucy, who *d* 1984, da of late Arthur Butcher, of Heybridge Basin, Maldon, Essex; *d* 1965; *s* by his only son (2) JAMES GORDON, 2nd Baron and present peer.

MAELOR, BARONY OF (Jones) (Extinct 1984)

SON LIVING OF LIFE BARON

Hon James Glynmore, *b* 1929.

DAUGHTER LIVING OF LIFE BARON

Hon Enid Angharad, *b* 1936: *m* 1961, E. Jurkiewicz, of 16 Snowdon Drive, Wrexham.

Maidstone, Viscount; son of Earl of Winchilsea and Nottingham.

MAIS, BARONY OF (Mais) (Extinct 1993)

SONS LIVING OF LIFE BARON

Hon Richard Jeremy Ian (79 Seal Hollow Road, Sevenoaks, Kent. *Clubs* – AA, and BARC), *b* 1945; *ed* Stowe; MIOB; Man Dir Clarke, Nickolls & Coombs plc, Chm Beacontree Estates Ltd, Exec Chm CNC Properties Ltd, Altbarn Properties Ltd, CNC Developments Ltd, CNC Benfleet Ltd, Pres CNC California Investments Inc: *m* 1972, Janice, el da of Ralph Dean, of 11 The Spinney, Frogmill, Hurley, Berks, and has issue living, Alexander, *b* 1975, — Vanessa, *b* 1977, — Lydia, *b* 1981.
Hon Jonathan Robert Neal (Farthings, 5 Pound Lane, Topsham, Exeter EX3 0NA), *b* 1954; *ed* Hurstpierpoint: *m* 1978, Frances Louise, da of late Robert Mark Barrington Brown, and has issue living, Joel Robert Barrington, *b* 1979, — Duncan Jonathan Christopher, *b* (twin) 1979.

DAUGHTER LIVING OF LIFE BARON

Hon Angela Clare (11100 River Rd, Potomac, Maryland 20854, USA), *b* 1946; *ed* St Margaret's, Bushey, and House of Citizenship: *m* 1976, Robert M Beckman.

WIDOW LIVING OF LIFE BARON

LORNA ALINE (*Baroness Mais*), da of late Stanley Aspinall Boardman, of Addiscombe, Surrey: *m* 1936, Baron Mais, GBE, ERD, TD (Life Baron), who *d* 1993. *Residence* – Griffins, 43A Sundridge Av, Bromley, Kent.

Maitland, Viscount; son of Earl of Lauderdale.

Malden, Viscount; son of Earl of Essex.

MALLALIEU, BARONESS (Mallalieu) (Life Baroness 1991)

ANN MALLALIEU, da of late Sir (Joseph Percival) William Mallalieu, of Village Farm, Boarstall, Aylesbury, Bucks; *b* 27 Nov 1945; *ed* Holton Park Girls' Gram Sch, Wheatley, Oxon, and Newnham Coll, Camb (MA, LLM; first woman pres Camb Union Soc; Hon Fell 1993); Bar Inner Temple 1970, Recorder 1985-93, QC 1988; *cr Baroness Mallalieu*, of Studdridge, co Bucks (Life Baroness) 1991: *m* 1979, as his 2nd wife, Timothy Felix Harold Cassel, eldest son of His Honour Sir Harold Felix Cassel, 3rd Bt, and has issue.

Arms – Azure, on a chevron ermine between three fleurs-de-lys argent four bezants, on a chief ermines a rose of the third barbed and seeded proper. **Supporters** – *Dexter*, a horse argent; *sinister*, a fox-hound proper both gorged with a torse argent and azure and each statant erect on a field of stubble with a hedgerow that on the dexter having a stile and palings and that on the sinister a gate with palings all in perspective proper.
Chambers - 6 King's Bench Walk, Temple, EC4.

DAUGHTERS LIVING

Hon Bathsheba Anna, *b* 1981.
Hon Cosima Ione Harriet, *b* 1984.

MALMESBURY, EARL OF (Harris) (Earl GB 1800)
(Title pronounced Marmsbury")

I will maintain

To remember my country everywhere

WILLIAM JAMES HARRIS, TD, 6th Earl; *b* 18 Nov 1907; *s* 1950; *ed* Eton, and Trin Coll, Camb (MA); Maj late R Hampshire Regt (TA), Hon Col 65th Signal Regt TA 1959-66 and of 2nd Bn Wessex Vols 1971-74; ARICS; Chm Hants & Isle of Wight T & AF Asscn 1960-68, and of E Wessex TA & VR Assocn 1968-70 (Vice-Pres 1973-78, since when Pres); Chm New Forest 9th Centenary Trust 1977-87, since when Pres; Personal Liaison Officer to Min of Agric for W Cos for SE Region 1959-64; Master of Skinners' Co 1952-53; Chm of Hants Agric Exec Cttee 1959-66; Lord Lt for co Southampton 1973-82, and a DL for Hants since 1983; Vice Pres Mary Rose Trust since 1979; Official Verderer of New Forest 1966-74; KStJ; JP; a Gold Staff Officer at Coronation of King George VI; has Coronation Medals (1937 and 1953) and Silver Jubilee Medal 1977; TD (two clasps): *m* 1st, 1932, Hon Diana Claudia Patricia Carleton, who *d* 1990, da of 2nd Baron Dorchester; 2ndly, 1991, Margaret Fleetwood, OBE, widow of Capt Raymond Alexander Baring (*see* Baring, Bt), and yst da of late Col Robert William Pigott Clarke Campbell-Preston, of Ardchattan Priory, Argyllshire, and has issue by 1st *m*.

Arms – Azure, a chevron erminois, between three hedgehogs or, on a chief argent, the black eagle of Prussia, crowned with an imperial crown, holding in the claws a sceptre and mound, charged on the breast with the cipher "FR" and on each wing a trefoil slipped, all gold. **Crest** – A hedgehog or, charged on the body with three arrows, one erect and two in saltire, sable, and over them a key barwise azure. **Supporters** – *Dexter*, an eagle, wings expanded and elevated sable, crowned with an imperial crown and charged on the breast with the cipher "FR" and on each wing with a trefoil slipped, all gold; *sinister*, a reindeer proper, attired and hoofed or.
Residence – The Coach House, Greywell Hill, Greywell, Basingstoke, Hants, RG25 1DB. **Club** – Royal Yacht Squadron (Vice-Commodore 1971-77).

SON LIVING (By 1st marriage)

JAMES CARLETON (*Viscount FitzHarris*) (Greywell Hill, Greywell, Basingstoke, Hants, RG25 1DB), *b* 19 June 1946; *ed* Eton and Queens Coll, Univ of St Andrews: *m* 1969, Sally Ann, yr da of Sir Richard Newton Rycroft, 7th Bt, and has issue:—
     SONS LIVING, — *Hon* James Hugh Carleton, *b* 29 April 1970, — *Hon* Charles Edward, *b* 1972, — *Hon* Guy Richard, *b* 1975.
     DAUGHTERS LIVING, — *Hon* Frances Maria *b* 1979, — *Hon* Daisy Catherine *b* 1981.

DAUGHTERS LIVING (By 1st marriage)

Lady Sylvia Veronica Anthea, *b* 1934; *m* 1956, John Newcombe Maltby, CBE, son of late Air Vice-Marshal Sir Paul Copeland Maltby, KCVO, KBE, CB, DSO, AFC, DL, and has issue living, William John, *b* 1959: *m* 1985, Sarah Catherine, da of Cdr James Ekins, of Old Lime House, Easton, Winchester, Hants, and has issue living, George Christopher William *b* 1989, Alice Diana *b* 1992, Poppy Elizabeth *b* 1994, — Caroline Jane, *b* 1957: *m* 1990, Alexander F. J. Roe, elder son of Frederick Roe, of The Bacchus House, Elsdon, Northumberland, and has issue living, Charlotte *b* 1992, — Sophia Louise, *b* 1963. *Residence* – Broadford House, Stratfield Turgis, Basingstoke, Hants.
Lady Nell Carleton, *b* 1937: *m* 1962, Capt Michael Patrick Radcliffe Boyle, Irish Guards (ret) (*see* E Shannon, colls). *Residence* – The Dower House, Greywell, Basingstoke, Hants.

PREDECESSORS – (1) *Rt Hon Sir* JAMES Harris, GCB, PC, el son of James Harris, MP, Sec and Comptroller to Queen Charlotte (wife of King George III), *b* 1746; an eminent diplomatist; was Ambassador to Spain 1771, to Berlin 1772, to Russia 1776, to the Hague 1783 and 1788, and to France 1796-7, Lieut Gov of Isle of Wight 1807, and Lord-Lieut of Hants; *cr Baron Malmesbury*, of Malmesbury, co Wilts (peerage of Great Britain) 1788, and *Viscount FitzHarris* and *Earl of Malmesbury* (peerage of Great Britain) 1800; *s* by his el son (2) JAMES EDWARD, 2nd Earl, *b* 1778; was MP for Helston 1802, and Gov of the Isle of Wight: *m* 1806, Harriet Susan, who *d* 1815, da of Francis Bateman Dashwood, of Well Vale, Lincolnshire; *d* 1841; *s* by his el son (3) JAMES HOWARD, GCB, PC, 3rd Earl, *b* 1807; sat as MP for Wilton (C) 1841; Sec for Foreign Affairs 1852, and 1858-9, and Lord Privy Seal 1866-8, and 1874-6: *m* 1st, 1830, Lady Corisande Emma Bennet, who *d* 1876, da of 5th Earl of Tankerville; 2ndly, 1880, Susan, who *d* 1935 (having *m* 2ndly, 1884, Maj-Gen Sir John Charles Ardagh, KCMG, KCIE, CB, LLD, RE, who *d* 1907), da of late John Hamilton, of Fyne Court, Somerset; *dsp* 1889; *s* by his nephew (4) EDWARD JAMES, 4th Earl (el son of late Adm Hon Sir Edward Alfred John Harris, KCB, 2nd son of 2nd Earl), *b* 1842; Lieut-Col (ret) 2nd Batn Roy Irish Rifles: *m* 1870, Sylvia Georgina, who *d* 1934, yr da of late Alexander Stewart, of Ballyedmond Castle, Rostrevor, co Down; *d* 1899; *s* by his el son (5) JAMES EDWARD, 5th Earl, *b* 1872; was Assist Private Sec (unpaid) to Under Sec of State for the Colonies 1901, a Co Councillor for London 1904-5, a Lord-in-Waiting to HM 1922-24, and Chm of Hants Co Council 1927-38: *m* 1905, Hon Dorothy Gough Calthorpe, CBE, who *d* 1972, yst da of 6th Baron Calthorpe; *d* 1950; *s* by his only son (6) WILLIAM JAMES, 6th Earl and present peer; also Viscount FitzHarris, and Baron Malmesbury.

Maltravers, Lord; grandson of Duke of Norfolk

MALVERN, VISCOUNT (Huggins) (Viscount UK 1955)

ASHLEY KEVIN GODFREY HUGGINS, 3rd Viscount; *b* 26 Oct 1949; *s* 1978.

Arms – Argent, on a fesse sable between three hearts gules a lion passant guardant or. **Crest** – A lion sejant rampant guardant or the sinister paw resting on a fountain. **Supporters** – *Dexter*, a lion guardant gules grasping in the exterior forepaw a rod of aesculapius proper; *sinister*, a sable antelope guardant proper.
Address – c/o Standard Bank, Cecil Sq, Harare, Zimbabwe.

BROTHER LIVING

Hon Michael Patrick John *b* 1946.

SISTER LIVING

Hon Haoli Elizabeth Jane, *b* 1953.

UNCLE LIVING (Son of 1st Viscount)

Hon (MARTIN) JAMES, *b* 13 Jan 1928; *ed* Hilton Coll, Natal; a farmer.

WIDOW LIVING OF SECOND VISCOUNT

Let us all persevere together

PATRICIA MARJORIE (*Viscountess Malvern*), da of Frank Renwick-Bower, of Durban: *m* (Jan) 1949, the 2nd Viscount, who *d* 1978.

PREDECESSORS – **(1)** *Rt Hon Sir* GODFREY MARTIN Huggins, CH, KCMG, FRCS, son of late Godfrey Huggins; *b* 1883; Prime Min of S Rhodesia 1933-53 and Fedn of Rhodesia and Nyasaland 1953-56; *cr Viscount Malvern*, of Rhodesia and of Bexley, co Kent (peerage of UK) 1955: *m* 1921, Blanche Elizabeth, who *d* 1976, da of late James Slatter, of Pietermaritzburg, Natal; *d* 1971; *s* by his el son **(2)** JOHN GODFREY, 2nd Viscount, *b* 1922; 1939-45 War as Fl/Lt RAF; pilot with a commercial airline in Rhodesia: *m* (Jan) 1949, Patricia Marjorie, da of Frank Renwick-Bower, of Durban; *d* 1978; *s* by his yr son **(3)** ASHLEY KEVIN GODFREY, 3rd Viscount, and present peer.

MANCHESTER, DUKE OF (Montagu) (Duke GB 1719)

ANGUS CHARLES DROGO MONTAGU, 12th Duke; *b* 9 Oct 1938; *s* 1985; *ed* Gordonstoun: *m* 1st, 1961 (*m diss* 1970), Mary Eveleen, da of Walter Gillespie McClure, of Geelong, Australia; 2ndly, 1971 (*m diss* 1985), Diane Pauline, da of Arthur Plimsaul, of 50 Highmoor Rd, Corfe Mullen, Wimborne, Dorset; 3rdly, 1989, Mrs Ann-Louise Bird, da of Dr Alfred Butler Taylor, of Cawthorne, S Yorks, and has issue by 1st *m*.

Arms – Quarterly: 1st and 4th argent, three lozenges conjoined in fesse gules, within a bordure sable, *Montagu*; 2nd and 3rd or, an eagle displayed vert, beaked and membered gules, *Monthermer*. **Crest** – A griffin's head couped at the neck or, gorged with a plain collar argent, charged with three lozenges gules between two wings sable. **Supporters** – *Dexter*, a heraldic antelope, or, armed, unguled, and tufted argent: a *sinister*, griffin, wings elevated or, collared as in the crest.
By disposing of me, not by changing me
Residence – 15 Broad Reach, The Embankment, Bedford MK40 3PB.

SONS LIVING (By 1st marriage)

ALEXANDER CHARLES DAVID DROGO (*Viscount Mandeville*), *b* 11 Dec 1962. —— *Lord* Kimble, *b* 1964.

DAUGHTER LIVING (By 1st marriage)

Lady Emma, *b* 1965.

WIDOW LIVING OF TENTH DUKE

ELIZABETH (*Dowager Duchess of Manchester*) (PO Box 303, Pebble Beach, Cal 93953, USA; Ca Vendramin, 13 Giudecca, 30123 Venice, Italy), da of Samuel Clyde Fullerton, of Miami, USA, and formerly wife of W. W. Crocker: *m* 1969, as his 2nd wife, the 10th Duke, who *d* 1977.

WIDOW LIVING OF ELEVENTH DUKE

ANDREA (*Andrea, Duchess of Manchester*), da of Lt-Col Cecil Alexander Joss, MC, TD, and formerly wife of (i) Maj Stuart Whitehead, AFC, and (ii) G. J. W. Kent: *m* 1978, as his 2nd wife, the 11th Duke, who *d* 1985. *Address* – PO Box 24667, Karen, Nairobi, Kenya.

COLLATERAL BRANCHES LIVING

Issue of late Lord Edward Eugene Fernando Montagu, yr son of 9th Duke, *b* 1906, *d* 1954: *m* 1st, 1929 (*m diss* 1937), Norah Macfarlane, da of Albert Edward Potter, of Ontario, Canada; 2ndly, 1937 (*m diss* 1947), Dorothy Vera Peters; 3rdly 1947, Martha Mathews Hatton Bowen, who *d* 1951; 4thly 1953, Roberta (*dec*), da of Mrs Flora Herald Joughin:—

(By 1st *m*) Roderick Edward Drogo, *b* 1930: *m* 1968, Mary Deas.

Grandchildren of late Lt-Cdr Robert Acheson Cromie Montagu, RN, 2nd son of Rt Hon Lord Robert
Montagu (infra):—
Issue of late John Michael Cromie Montagu, *b* 1881, *d* 1966; *m* 1907, Libia Maria, who *d* 1979, da of late Senor
Martin Montes, of Quilmes, Argentine Republic:—
Robert Alexander (88 Chestnut Rise, Plumstead, SE18 1RL), *b* 1917: *m* 1946, Eileen Teresa, da of John Lamont, and has
issue living, Michael Anthony, *b* 1955, — Eileen Patricia, *b* 1947: *m* 1968, Hugh McGarry, of 3 Antrim Gdns, Portrush, co
Antrim, and has issue living, Stephen Hugh *b* 1968, Michael Edward Drogo *b* 1983, Shirley Ellen *b* 1969, Alicia Patricia
Teresa *b* 1971, Susan Mary Doreen *b* 1975, — Sylvia Valerie Heather, *b* 1949: *m* 1969, Colin Sidney Brooks, of 12 Leckwith
Av, Bexleyheath, Kent, and has issue living, Stuart Robert *b* 1971, Steven Alexander *b* 1982, Cheryl Ann *b* 1973, — Cynthia
Christine Jeanette, *b* 1949 (twin): *m* 1st, 1967 (*m diss* 1979), David Nicholls; 2ndly, 1979, Victor Pawley, of Portsmouth,
Hants, and has issue living (by 1st *m*), Michael David Nicholls *b* 1967 (assumed the surname of PAWLEY by deed poll 1979),
Robert Alexander *b* 1972 (assumed the surname of PAWLEY by deed poll 1979), (by 2nd *m*) Rebecca Jane *b* 1974, Dawn
Michele (twin) *b* 1974, — Helena May, *b* 1951: *m* 1973, Peter George Suckling, of 21 First Av, Bexleyheath, Kent DA7 5SS,
and has issue living, Jayne Ellen *b* 1981, Louise Ann *b* 1984, — Deirdre Veronica, *b* 1959: *m* 1982, Brian Richards, of 132
Sutherland Av, Welling, Kent, and has issue living, Barry Charles Montagu *b* 1984, Alan James Montagu *b* 1986, Michael
Anthony Montagu *b* 1988. ——— Alicia May JOHNSON MONTAGU (30 Canterbury Court, Station Rd, Dorking, Surrey RH4 1HH),
b 1919: assumed by deed poll 1963 the surname of Johnson Montagu: *m* 1st, 1941, Fl-Lt Stuart James Lovell, RAF, who was
ka 1944; 2ndly, 1946 (*m diss* 1963), John Dobney Johnson, PhD, and has issue living, (by 2nd *m*), Adrian Michael Montagu,
b 1947: *m* 1982, Elizabeth Ann, da of late T. J. O'Shea, of Maesteg, S Wales, — Warwick Martin Montagu, *b* 1950: *m* 1970,
Gaye Marina Harding, and has issue living, Robert James *b* 1978, Simon David *b* 1981, Melissa Gaye *b* 1973, Sarah Louise *b*
1975, — Phillip Leicester Montagu (Brook Cottage, Yeovil Marsh, Som), *b* 1951: *m* 1973, Fiona Madeleine Williams, and has
issue living, Rebecca Claire Montagu *b* 1981, — Michèle Veronica Montagu, *b* 1953: *m* 1st, 1973 (*m diss* 1982), Alan Craig
Worrell; 2ndly, 1984, David John Robinson.
Issue of late Austin Robert Montagu, *b* 1885, *d* 1958: *m* 1934, Violet Vera, who *d* 1982, da of late Charles William
Sandles:—
Henry Robert Sanderson (22 Sandpiper St, Florida Lake, Florida 1710, S Africa), *b* 1935: *m* 1963, Margaret Elizabeth, da of
Norman Sinclair Pyper, of Sandpiper St, Florida, and has issue living, Gail, *b* 1968: *m* 1986, John Dugmore, and has issue
living, Lloyd John *b* 1986, — Janet Frances, *b* 1972. ——— Cyril John Sanderson (101 Melville Av, Discovers Park, Florida
1709, S Africa), *b* 1937: *m* 1966, Annette Mary, da of late Castlyn Barnard, and has issue living, Graeme Peter, *b* 1967, —
Christopher John *b* 1968. ——— Gerard Philip Sanderson (34 Boeing Drive, Helderkruin ext 1, Roodeport 1725, S Africa), *b*
1940: *m* 1963, Elizabeth Sinden, da of late John Sinden Jarvis, and has issue living, Matthew Gerard, *b* 1976, — Alison
Elizabeth, *b* 1971.

Grandchildren of late Capt Monthermer Stanley Hume Montagu, MC (infra):—
Issue of late Capt Walter Bernard St John Montagu, TD, *b* 1915, *d* (April) 1992: *m* 1948, Doris Jean, who *d* (Jan)
1992, da of late J. Albany Morton, of Culzean, Busby, Lanarks:—
John Charles Monthermer Albany (c/o Child's Bank, 1 Fleet St, EC4Y 1BZ), *b* 1951; *ed* Gordonstoun, and Hull Univ (LLB);
late Gren Gds and HAC. ——— Elizabeth Anne Kennedy (15 Priory Rd, Cambridge CB5 8HT), *b* 1949: *m* 1971 (*m diss* 1983),
Victor Bayntun Hippisley, and has issue living, Antonia Frances Serena Olivia, *b* 1975.

Grandchildren of late Rt Hon Lord Robert Montagu, MP, 2nd son of 6th Duke:—
Issue of late Capt Monthermer Stanley Hume Montagu, MC, *b* 1868, *d* 1953: *m* 1913, Harriet Jessie, who *d* 1959, da
of late James Keith Forbes, of Valparaiso, and widow of John Stratford Collet, ICS:—
Olivia Millicent Jane, *b* 1914; 1939-45 War with Women's Transport Ser (E Africa): *m* 1943, Edward Rodwell, FRGS. *Address*
- PO Box 82819, Mombasa, Kenya.
Issue of late Capt Henry Bernard Montagu, RN, *b* 1872, *d* 1941: *m* 1922, Rosamond, who *d* 1972, da of late Dudley
Bowditch Fay, of Boston, USA:—
John Drogo, *b* 1923; MRCS England and LRCP London, 1946; late Surg-Lieut RNVR: *m* 1946, Katharine Mary, da of late
Brig-Gen Noble Fleming Jenkins, CMG, CBE, and has issue living, Robert Drogo (7 St Margaret's Close, Barming, Maid-
stone, Kent), *b* 1947: *m* 1st, 1970 (*m diss* 1985), Glenis Diane Littaur; 2ndly, 1985, Lancy Lim, and has issue living (by 1st
m) James Drogo *b* 1975, Rachel Bernard *b* 1974, — Christopher Bernard (c/o National Westminster Bank, Haymarket,
SW1), *b* 1950; W/Cdr RAF: *m* 1975, Christine Elizabeth Peatfield, and has issue living, David William *b* 1976, Thomas
Edward *b* 1979, — Rosamond Anne, *b* 1953: *m* 1984, Jonathan Chapple, of 106 Woodside, Wimbledon, SW19, and has issue
living, Katharine Rose *b* 1984. *Residence* – High Acre, Hunger Hill, East Stour, Gillingham, Dorset SP8 5JR. ——— Katharine
Anne, *b* 1925; *ed* St Andrew's Univ (MSc). *Residence* – 52 Ennerdale Rd, Kew, Surrey.

(Not in remainder to Dukedom)

Descendants of late Hon James Montagu, MP, 3rd son of 1st Earl of Manchester:—

Grandson of late Gen Sir Horace William Montagu, KCB, son of late Rev George Montagu, 2nd son of late
Gerard Montagu, 3rd in descent from late James Montagu, el son of late Hon James Montagu, MP
(ante):—
Issue of late Col Edward Montagu, CBE, *b* 1861, *d* 1941: *m* 1894, Charlotte Eva, who *d* 1952, da of Edward Kemble,
formerly a Judge of Supreme Court, Jamaica:—
Charles Edward, *b* 1900; *ed* Wellington Coll; is Capt (ret) RE: *m* 1928, Rachel Alice, da of late W. H. Martin, of Shrublands,
Swaffham, Norfolk, and has issue living, Michael Drogo, *b* 1929; Maj RA: *m* 1955, Verity Jane, da of late William James
Coode, OBE, of Polgooth, St Austell, Cornwall, and has issue living, Richard Lionel James (Jocks Lodge, Geldeston, Norfolk)
b 1956: *m* 1984, Aileen Amanda, da of Charles Gordon Birchall, of The Close, Norwich (and has issue living, George Charles
Drogo *b* 1993, Lucy Elizabeth *b* 1990), Alan Edward *b* 1958: *m* 1990, Louise Helen, twin da of A. G. H. Gaden of Trull,
Taunton, Som (and has issue living, Madeleine *b* 1993), James Robert *b* 1962, — Ralph Edward (Old Hall Farm, Ringsfield,
Beccles, Suffolk), *b* 1932: *m* 1st, 1963, June Margaret (Lisa), da of late James William Finlayson, of
Vaucluse, Sydney, Australia; 2ndly, 1989, Stephanie Roberta, da of late Patrick Arthur Cattell, of Pallastown, Belgooly, co
Cork, and has issue living (by 1st *m*), David Charles *b* 1965, Caroline Elizabeth *b* 1964, Victoria Jane *b* 1967, Katharine Fiona
b (twin) 1967. *Residence* – Cameron House, Ballygate, Suffolk.

Grandsons of late Maj James Gerard Edgar Drogo Montagu, only son of late Capt Cecil Edgar Montagu,
yr son of late Edgar Montagu, 3rd and yst son of late Gerard Montagu (ante):—
Issue of late Lt-Cdr William Gerard Drogo Montagu, RN, *b* 1921, *d* 1991: *m* 1950, Charlotte Delma (7 Shernfold
Park, Frant, E Sussex TN3 9DL), only child of late Frank Reitmeyer Calburn, of Effingham Manor, Surrey:—
Charles Edward Drogo, *b* 1952; *ed* Tonbridge Sch, and CCC, Oxford: *m* 1986, Marie-Jocelyne, da of Gabriel Dardenne, of
Napier Rd, Tottenham, and has issue living, Edward Harry *b* 1990, — Emily Frances, *b* 1993. ——— Francis Gerard Drogo
(White Lodge, Ropers Lane, Wrington, Avon), *b* (twin) 1952; *ed* Tonbridge Sch, and Pembroke Coll, Camb; Solicitor: *m* 1991,
Olivia Mary, da of Dr Patrick John Hardie, MBE, of Elm Cottage, Shipton Moyne, Tetbury, Glos. ——— James William
Drogo (Culvers, Hartfield, E Sussex), *b* 1954; *ed* Tonbridge Sch: *m* 1979, Charlotte Elizabeth, da of Richard John Goad

Crosfield, of May Hill House, Droxford, Hants, and has issue living, Elizabeth Charlotte Ann, b 1983, — Sarah Caroline, b 1985.

Grandchildren of late Capt George Edward Montagu, el son of late Adm John William Montagu, son of late Adm Sir George Montagu, GCB, son of late Adm John Montagu, MP (infra):—
Issue of late John William Montagu, b 1877, d 1954: m 1913, Violet Irene, who d 1970, da of James Shuter, late of Little Park, Newbury:—
(John) Drogo, b 1916; ed Exeter Sch, and RMC Sandhurst; Lt-Col (ret) Indian Army; Far East 1939-45 (despatches): m 1952, Dorothy Boreham, who d 1990, yr da of C. E. Chuter, of Brisbane, Australia, and has issue living, Michael Charles Drogo, b 1956; Maj 2nd LI: m 1984, Caroline Louise Marie, only da of John George Griffiths, of Algarve, Portugal, and has issue living, James Robert Drogo b 1985, Frederic Charles b 1988, Arthur John b 1992, — Nigel Edward, b 1958; Maj RE, — Richard John, b 1959; Capt LI: m 1986, Jane Emma, da of Bruce Pearson, of Twynholm, Galloway, — Sally Ann, b 1954: m 1988, Lt-Col Harold Crispin Hardy Ellison, MBE, RTR, son of His Honour Judge (John Harold) Ellison, of Egham, Surrey, and has issue living, Harriet Dorothy Montagu b 1992, — Felicity Jane, b 1960: m 1985, Alan Sutherland Nixon, son of Prof George Sutherland Nixon, of St Andrews, and has issue living, Olivia Chuter b 1990. Residence – The Officer's House, Freshwater, I of Wight. ——— James Edward, b 1920; late Capt RA; 1939-45 War: m 19——, Joan, da of late J. McPherson, of Fieldway, Barrow-in-Furness, and has issue living, Philip James, b 1949, — Robin William, b 1953. Residence – 64 Hill Rd, Barrow-in-Furness, Lancashire. ——— Mary Hamilton, b 1914. Residence – Caesars, Freshwater, Isle of Wight.

Grandchildren of late John Francis Vaughan Montagu, (infra):—
Issue of late John Edward Coley Montagu, b 1910, d 1983: m 1st, 1936 (m diss 1955), Flora Elizabeth, who d 1981, da of late Col James Robertson-Cumming, of Langrigg, Strathearn, Scotland; 2ndly, 1958, Anne Alice Harriet (47 Pomona Gdns, Hillcrest, Natal, S Africa), da of late Col Donald Rolfe Hunt, of Natal, S Africa:—
(By 1st m) John Anthony Francis (3 Kelvin Grove, Beacon Bay, E London, S Africa), b 1938: m 1966, Denise Catherine, eldest da of late James Peter Dallas, of E London, S Africa, and has issue living, James Anthony John, b 1976, — Joanne Catherine, b 1969, — Leigh Elizabeth, b 1971. ——— David Vaughan, b 1948: m 1966, Victoria Alice, yr da of Allan Cunningham, of 4 Riverside Av, Newquay, Cornwall, and has issue living, Christopher John Allan, b 1977, — Laura Anne, b 1979. ——— Gillian Denise, b 1940: m 1966, Michael Keyworth Glover, of 35 Esmeralda Cres, Randburg, Transvaal, and has issue living, Mark Keyworth, b 1968, — Marguerite Tracey, b 1967, — Jennifer Lynn, b 1972.

Grandson of late Edward Vaughan Montagu, 2nd son of late John Edward Montagu, eldest son of late John Montagu (b 1797) (infra):—
Issue of late John Francis Vaughan Montagu, b 1877, d 1960: m 1909, Ada Mary, who d 1957, da of late James Dougal Coley, of Claremont, Cape Town, S Africa:—
Denis Vaughan, b 1913: m 1st, 1939, Margarieta, who d 1981, da of Henry Usher Gradwell, of Bloemfontein, S Africa; 2ndly, 1983, Joan Patricia Chambers. Residence – 65 Gold Reef Village, Brakpan, Transvaal, S Africa.

Grandsons of late Frederick George Montagu (infra):—
Issue of late Arthur Drogo Turing Montagu, b 1900, d 1969: m 1934, Dorothy Rittener (Hill Crest, Gourley Rd, Eerste River, 7100, S Africa), el da of Harry Taylor Pitt, of Hill-Top, Woodingdean, Brighton:—
John Drogo, b 1935: m 1980, Margaret, 2nd da of late Lt-Cdr John Richard Windle, RNR, of Broadway House, Broadway, Blyth, Northumberland. ——— William Pitt (13 Windsor Rd, Oosterzee, 7500 S Africa) b 1939: m 1966, Elsa, da of late J. A. Fourie, of Eerste River, Cape, and has issue living, Michelle, b 1969, — Colleen, b 1971, — Wendy (twin) b 1971.

Grandchildren of late Lieut-Gen Alfred Worsley Montagu, yr son of late John Montagu (b 1797), son of late Lt-Col Edward Montagu, 4th son of late Adm John Montagu, great grandson of late Hon James Montagu, MP, (ante):—
Issue of late Alfred Worsley Montagu, b 1860, d 191—: m 1887, Ruth Lily Wallace, of Stawell, Victoria, Australia:—
Herbert Clive, b 1897. ——— Ruth Mabel Josephine, b 1888. ——— Jeffie Ina, b 1891. ——— Vere Faerie, b 1984.

PREDECESSORS – (1) Sir HENRY Montagu, PC; MP for London 1604-16, and Recorder of London; appointed Lord Ch Justice of the King's Bench 1615, Lord Treasurer of England 1620, and Lord Privy Seal 1626; cr Baron Montagu, of Kimbolton, co Huntingdon, and Viscount Mandeville (peerage of England) 1620, and Earl of Manchester (peerage of England) 1626; d 1642; s by his son (2) EDWARD, 2nd Earl, KG, KB, PC, FRS, who had previously been summoned to Parl as Baron Kimbolton; was a distinguished Gen in the Parliamentary army, and gained the celebrated victory at Marston Moor; he refused to sanction the execution of Charles I, and retired from Parliament until 1660, when he voted for the restoration of Charles II, and was deputed by the Lords as their speaker to congratulate the King upon his return to his capital; Lord Chamberlain 1660-71, Chancellor of Camb Univ 1660-71, Lord-Lieut of Hunts and Northants; d 1671; s by his son (3) ROBERT, 3rd Earl; MP for Hunts 1660-71, Lord-Lieut of Hunts d 1682; s by his son (4) CHARLES, PC, 4th Earl; served at the battle of the Boyne; was Ambassador to Venice 1696, to France 1699, and to Vienna 1707, Principal Sec of State 1701, Lord-Lieut of Hunts, and a Lord of the Bedchamber to George I; cr Duke of Manchester (peerage of Great Britain) 1719; d 1722; s by his el son (5) WILLIAM, KB, 2nd Duke; Capt Yeomen of the Guard 1737-39, Lord-Lieut of Hunts, Lord of the Bedchamber to King George I and King George II d 1739; s by his brother (6) ROBERT, 3rd Duke; Capt Yeomen of the Guard, Lord Chamberlain to Queen Charlotte 1761, Lord-Lieut of Hunts, Lord of the Bedchamber to King George II d 1762; s by his son (7) GEORGE, PC, 4th Duke; Master of the Horse 1780; Lord Chamberlain 1782-83; Ambassador to France 1783, Lord-Lieut of Hunts, Lord of the Bedchamber to King George III d 1788; s by his son (8) WILLIAM, 5th Duke; was Gov of Jamaica 1807-27; Postmaster Gen 1827-30; Collector of Customs for Port of London, and Lord-Lieut of Hunts: m 1793, Lady Susan Gordon, who d 1828, da of 4th Duke of Gordon, KT; d 1843; s by his son (9) GEORGE, 6th Duke; a com RN, MP for Hunts (C) 1826-37: m 1st, 1822, Millicent, who d 1848, da of Gen R. B. Sparrow, of Brampton Park, Hunts; 2ndly, 1850, Harriet Sydney, da of Conway Richard Dobbs, of Castle Dobbs, co Antrim; d 1855; s by his son (10) WILLIAM DROGO, 7th Duke, b 1823; sat as MP for Bewdley (C) 1848-52, and for Huntingdonshire 1852-5; Capt Gren Gds, Col Hunts Mil, a Lord of the Bedchamber to the Prince Consort 1852: m 1852, Countess Louise Frederica Augusta, who d 1911 (having m 2ndly, 1892, 8th Duke of Devonshire), da of Count von Alten, of Hanover; d 1890; s by his son (11) GEORGE VICTOR DROGO, 8th Duke, b 1853; Capt R Irish Fus; MP for Hunts 1877-80: m 1876, Consuela Yznaga, who d 1909, da of Senor Antonio Yznaga de Valle, of Louisiana, USA, and Cuba; d 1892; s by his el son (12) WILLIAM ANGUS DROGO, PC, 9th Duke, b 1877; Capt Lancs Fus; Capt of Yeomen of the Guard 1906-7: m 1st, 1900 (m diss 1931), Helena, who d 1971, having m 2ndly, 1937, 10th Earl of Kintore, da of late Eugene Zimmerman, of Cincinnati, USA; 2nd, 1931, Kathleen, who d 1966, da of W. H. Dawes, d 1947; s by his son (13) ALEXANDER GEORGE FRANCIS DROGO, OBE, 10th Duke, b 1902; late RN; Capt RNVR; d 1977; s by his el son (14) SIDNEY ARTHUR ROBIN GEORGE DROGO, 11th Duke, b 1929: m 1st, 1955 (m diss 1978), (Adrienne) Valerie, who d 1988, da of late John Kenneth Christie, of Sedgerfield, Cape Prov, S Africa; 2ndly, 1978, Andrea, da of Cecil Alexander Joss, of Johannesburg, and formerly wife of (i) Maj Stuart Whitehead, and (ii) G. J. W. Kent; d 1985; s by his brother (15) ANGUS CHARLES DROGO, 12th Duke and present peer; also Earl of Manchester, Viscount Mandeville, and Baron Montagu of Kimbolton.

MANCROFT, BARON (Mancroft) (Baron UK 1937, Bt UK 1932)

BENJAMIN LLOYD STORMONT MANCROFT, 3rd Baron; *b* 16 May 1957; *s* 1987; *ed* Eton; MFH; Chm Drug and Alcohol Foundation since 1994: *m* 1990, Emma L., eldest da of Thomas Peart, of Addison Rd, W8, and has issue.

Arms – Gules, a chevron chequy argent and sable, between in chief two portcullises chained and in base a castle (Farnham) triple towered or, on a chief of the last a lion pasant guardant of the third. **Crest** – In front of a castle (Norwich) with three cupolas, issuant from each a staff proper flying therefrom a banner argent, charged with a cross gules, a sword sheathed also gules, garnished or, pomel and hilt of the last, and a mace gold in saltire (ie, a representative of the ancient Crystal Mace and the Sword in the Regalia of the Corporation of the City of Norwich). **Supporters** – On either side a Whiffler of the Corporation of the City of Norwich.
Address – House of Lords, SW1A 0PW.

DAUGHTER LIVING

Hon Georgia Esme, *b* 1993.

SISTERS LIVING

Hon Victoria (*Princess Nicholas von Preussen*), *b* 1952: *m* 1980, HRH Prince (Frederick) Nicholas von Preussen, of Maperton House, Wincanton, Som, and has issue (*see* Royal Family).
Hon Jessica Rosetta, *b* 1954: *m* 1983, as his 2nd wife, Simon Clervaux Dickinson (*see* Chaytor, Bt, 1990 Edn), of Wortley House, Wotton-under-Edge, Glos, and has issue living, Milo Clervaux Mancroft, *b* 1989, — Phoebe Victoria, *b* 1984, — Octavia Jessica, *b* 1986.

AUNT LIVING (*Daughter of 1st Baron*)

Hon Rosetta Mancroft SAMUEL, *b* 1918: *m* 1st, 1947, Alfred John Bostock Hill, late Puisne Judge, Malaya, who *d* 1959; 2ndly, 1966, Dr Cai Christian Holm, who *d* 1983. *Residence* – 12 Eaton Place, SW1.

WIDOW LIVING OF SECOND BARON

DIANA ELIZABETH (*Diana, Baroness Mancroft*), only da of Lt-Col Horace Lloyd, DSO, and formerly wife of Richard St John Quarry: *m* 1951, the 2nd Baron, KBE, TD, who *d* 1987.

PREDECESSORS – (1) ARTHUR MICHAEL SAMUEL, el son of late Benjamin Samuel, of Norwich; *b* 1872; Parliamentary Under-Sec of State for Foreign Affairs, Parliamentary Sec to Board of Trade, and Minister for Depart of Overseas Trade 1924-7, and Financial Sec to the Treasury 1927-9; Chm of Public Accounts Committee of House of Commons 1930 and 1931; was Lord Mayor of Norwich 1912-13, received Hon Freedom of City of Norwich 1928; sat as MP for Farnham Div of Surrey (*U*) 1918-37: *cr* a *Baronet* 1932, and *Baron Mancroft*, of Mancroft, in City of Norwich (peerage of UK) 1937: *m* 1912, Phoebe, who *d* 1969, 2nd da of late Dr (George) Alfred Chune Fletcher, Med Officer to the Charterhouse, London; *d* 1942; *s* by his son (2) STORMONT MANCROFT, KBE, TD, 2nd Baron, *b* 1914, Bar Inner Temple 1938, Pres London Tourist Board 1963-73, and of St Marylebone Conservative Assocn 1961-67, Lord-in-Waiting to HM 1952-54, Chm Horserace Totalisator Board 1972-76; etc; served 1939-45 War as Lt-Col RA (TA) (despatches twice, MBE, Croix de Guerre); assumed by deed poll 1925 the surname of Mancroft: *m* 1951, Diana Elizabeth, only da of Lt-Col Horace Lloyd, DSO, and formerly wife of Richard St John Quarry; *d* 1987; *s* by his only son (3) BENJAMIN LLOYD STORMONT, 3rd Baron and present peer.

Mandeville, Viscount; son of Duke of Manchester

MANNERS, BARON (Manners) (Baron UK 1807)

POUR·Y· PARVENIR

In order to accomplish

JOHN ROBERT CECIL MANNERS, 5th Baron; *b* 13 Feb 1923; *s* 1972; *ed* Eton, and Trin Coll, Oxford; Fl-Lt RAFVR: *m* 1949, Jennifer Selena, da of late Stephen Ian Fairbairn (*see* Arbuthnot, Bt, colls, 1990 Edn), and has issue.

Arms – Or, two bars azure, a chief quarterly, azure and gules, the 1st and 4th quarters charged with two fleurs-de-lis gold, and the 2nd and 3rd with a lion of England. **Crest** – On a chapeau gules, turned up ermine, a peacock in pride proper. **Supporters** – Two unicorns, argent, armed, unguled, crined, and tufted, or, the *dexter* charged on the shoulder with a cross flory, azure; the *sinister* similarly charged with a portcullis, sable.
Residence – Sabines, Avon, Christchurch, Dorset. *Clubs* – Brooks's, Boodles'.

SON LIVING

Hon JOHN HUGH ROBERT, *b* 5 May 1956; *ed* Eton: *m* 1983, Lanya Mary Patricia, da of late Dr H. E. Heitz, and of Mrs Ian Jackson, of 23 Springfield Rd, NW8, and has issue living, Harriet Frances Mary, *b* 1988, — Catherine Mary Patricia, *b* 1992. *Residence* – 14 North Ripley, Avon, nr Christchurch, Dorset BH23 8EP. *Club* – Pratt's.

DAUGHTERS LIVING

Hon Venetia Jane, *b* 1950: *m* 1972, Alasdair John Colborne-Malpas, of Keeper's Cottage, Ramsdell, Hants.
Hon Selena Mary, 1952: *m* 1974, Maj Christopher Jeremy George Langlands, 1st The Queen's Drag Gds, of Hartgrove House, Shaftesbury, Dorset, and has issue living, Andrew Charles, *b* 1981, — George William, *b* 1987, — Lucinda Mary, *b* 1977.

BROTHERS LIVING

Hon Richard Neville, *b* 1924; *ed* Eton: *m* 1945, Juliet Mary, da of late Col Sir Edward Hulton Preston, 5th Bt, DSO, MC, and has issue living, Edward Preston (Askania, Askania Park, Ourimbah, NSW 2258, Australia; *Club* – The Australian), *b* 1948; *ed* Gresham's Sch, Holt: *m* 1973, Catherine, da of late Mr Justice (William) Ash, of Turramurra, NSW, and has issue living, Sarah *b* 1981, — Rupert Francis Henry (Box 788, Armidale, NSW 2350, Australia), *b* 1950; *ed* Gresham's Sch, Holt: *m* 1975, Wynn, da of W. Miller, of Sydney, NSW, and has issue living, Stephen Francis *b* 1978, Philip *b* 1980, — (Thomas) Benjamin CABBELL MANNERS (West Wing, Cromer Hall, Cromer, Norfolk), *b* 1954; *ed* Gresham's Sch, Holt: *m* 1981, Diana (Dido) Dorothy Elizabeth, yr da of Maj Anthony Richard Gurney, of Manor Farm, Northrepps, Cromer, Norfolk, and has issue living, Rupert *b* 1990, Hugh *b* 1993, Jessica *b* (twin) 1990, — Christine Margaret Lavender, *b* 1946: *m* 1970, Timothy John Barry Pallister, of The Old Vicarage, Tunstead, Norfolk, and has issue living, James Francis Timothy *b* 1971, Richard John *b* 1976, Charlotte Henrietta *b* 1972. *Residence* – South Wing, Cromer Hall, Norfolk.
Hon Thomas Jasper, *b* 1929; *ed* Eton: *m* 1955, Sarah, da of late Brigadier Roger Peake, DSO, OBE, and has issue living, Charles Henry, *b* 1957: *m* 1986, Nichola E., da of late Peter Howard Thompson, of Astley Farm, Bridgnorth, Shropshire, and has issue living, Joseph Peter *b* 1991, Zoë *b* 1989, — Arthur Roger, *b* 1959: *m* 1984, Anna C. M., da of Roger Ryland, of 32A Pembroke Sq, W8, and has issue living, a son *b* 1989, Olivia *b* 19—, — Robert Hugh, *b* 1962: *m* 1989, Samantha S., da of Richard Jukes, of Old Rectory, Pattiswick, Braintree, Essex, and has issue living, Archie Thomas *b* 1993. *Residence* – The Old Malt House, Ashford Hill, Newbury, Berks. *Clubs* – White's; Pratt's.

SISTER LIVING

Hon Patricia Anne, *b* 1927: *m* 1946, John Bonham Kidston, late Lt Grenadier Guards, who *d* 1968 (Bonham, Bt), and has issue living, Francis George, *b* 1947, — Jonathan James, *b* 1951: *m* 1981, Joanna R., da of late Col Michael Panton, — Virginia Lilian, *b* 1953.

PREDECESSORS – (1) THOMAS Manners-Sutton, PC, 5th son of Lord George Manners Sutton (3rd son of 3rd Duke of Rutland and father of 1st Viscount Canterbury); was Solicitor Gen of England 1802-5, a Baron of the Exchequer in England 1805-7, and Lord Chancellor of Ireland 1807; *cr Baron Manners*, of Foston, co Lincoln (peerage of United Kingdom) 1807; *d* 1842; *s* by his son (2) JOHN THOMAS, 2nd Baron; *b* 1818: *m* 1848, Lydia Sophia, who *d* 1916, da of Vice-Adm William Bateman Dashwood; *d* 1864; *s* by his el son (3) JOHN THOMAS, 3rd Baron; *b* 1852: *m* 1st, 1885, Constance Edwina, who *d* 1920, da of late Col Henry Edward Hamilyn-Fane; 2ndly, 1922, Zoë Virginie, who *d* 1953, da of late Albert Llewellyn Nugent, and widow of Claude Hume Campbell Guinness; *d* 1927; *s* by his son (4) FRANCIS HENRY, MC, 4th Baron; *b* 1897: *m* 1921, Mary Edith, who *d* 1994, da of late Rt Rev Lord William Rupert Ernest Gascoyne-Cecil, DD, 65th Bishop of Exeter (M Salisbury); *d* 1972; *s* by his el son (5) JOHN ROBERT CECIL, 5th Baron, and present peer.

MANSFIELD AND MANSFIELD, EARL OF (Murray) (Earl GB 1776 and 1792)

I hope for better things

Friendly to virtue alone

WILLIAM DAVID MUNGO JAMES MURRAY, 8th Earl; *b* 7 July 1930; *s* 1971; *ed* Wellesley House, Eton, and Ch Ch Oxford; Bar Inner Temple 1958; Lt Scots Gds (Reserve); Malaya 1949-50; Hereditary Keeper of Bruce's Castle of Lochmaben; Hon Sheriff of Perthshire 1974; a Co Councillor of Perthshire 1971-75, JP 1975, and DL Perth and Kinross since 1980; a Member of Tay Salmon Fishery Board 1971-79, and a Dir of General Accident Fire & Life Assurance Gp 1972-79 and since 1985, and other cos; a Member of British Delegation to European Parl 1973-75, an Opposition Front Bench Spokesman in House of Lords 1975-79; Min of State Scottish Office 1979-83, Min of State N Ireland Office 1983-84; Pres of Scottish Assocn of Boys' Clubs 1974-79, Ordinary Dir of Royal Highland & Agric Soc 1976-79, Pres of Scottish Assocn for the Care and Resettlement of Offenders 1974-79, and Chm of Historic Houses Assocn in Scotland 1976-79; Pres of Saint Andrew Soc (Glasgow) 1972-82, Royal Scottish Country Dance Soc since 1977, and Fedn des Assocns de Chasse de l'Europe 1977-79, Hon Pres Scottish Bee-keepers' Assocn; First Crown Estate Commissioner since 1985: *m* 1955, Pamela Joan, (OStJ 1982), da of late Wilfred Neill Foster, CBE, and has issue.

Arms – Quarterly: 1st and 4th, azure, three mullets argent, within a double tressure flory counter flory or, *Murray;* 2nd and 3rd, gules, three crosses patée argent *Barclay.* **Crest** – A buck's head couped proper, between his attires a cross patée argent **Supporters** – Two lions gules, armed or.
Seat – Scone Palace, Perthshire PH2 6BE. *Town Residence* – 16 Thorburn House, Kinnerton St, SW1X 8EX. *Clubs* – Turf, Pratt's, White's, Beefsteak.

SONS LIVING

ALEXANDER DAVID MUNGO (*Viscount Stormont*), *b* 17 Oct 1956; *ed* Eton: *m* 1985, Sophia Mary Veronica, only da of late Philip Biden Derwent Ashbrooke (*see* B Mowbray, colls), of St John, Jersey, and has issue:—
  SON LIVING - Hon William Philip David Mungo (*Master of Stormont*), *b* 1 Nov 1988.
  DAUGHTERS LIVING - Hon Isabella Mary Alexandra, *b* 1987, — Hon Iona Margaret Sophia, *b* 1992.
Clubs – White's, Turf, Pratt's.
Hon James William, *b* 1969.

DAUGHTER LIVING

Lady Georgina Dorothea Mary, *b* 1967.

SISTERS LIVING

Lady Malvina Dorothea (*Countess of Moray*), *b* 1936: *m* 1964, 20th Earl of Moray, of Doune Park, Doune, Perthshire, and Darnaway Castle, Forres, Morayshire.
Lady Mariota Cecilia, *b* 1945; *m* 1969, Hon (Charles) Malcolm Napier (*see* L Napier and Ettrick), of Bardmony House, Alyth, Perthshire.

COLLATERAL BRANCH LIVING

        Issue of late Major Hon Alexander David Murray, brother of 6th Earl, *b* 1871, *d* 1924: *m* 1908, Christian Maule, who *d* 1964, da of Sir James Thomas Stewart-Richardson, 14th Bt:—
David John, TD, *b* 1919; *ed* Wellington Coll, and at Magdalene Coll, Camb; Maj Seaforth Highlanders; European War 1939-45 in France, Middle East, Italy and Germany: *m* 1961, Joanna, da of late Lt J. G. Lincoln, RN, and has issue living, Alexander David, *b* 1962: *m* 1987, Susan Jayne, da of Brian Savage, and has issue living, Emma Kate *b* 1988, — William John David, *b* 1976. *Residence* – Moy House, Forres, Morayshire. —— Maryot Louisa (Windyridge, Dunphail, Morayshire) *b* 1910. —— Elizabeth Helen (34 Muirfield Gdns, Gullane, E Lothian), *b* 1912: *m* 1937 (*m diss* 1945), Lt-Col Charles Richard Wynn Brewis, MC, Welch Regt, who *d* 1967, and has issue living, Simon David Richard Wynn, MBE, *b* 1941; Lt-Col Parachute Regt. —— Christian Anne, *b* 1913; late 3rd Officer WRNS.

PREDECESSORS – (1) *Sir* DAVID Murray, Knt, Cupbearer and Master of the Horse, and Capt of the Guard to James VI of Scotland; accompanied the King to England, and was *cr Lord Scone* (peerage of Scotland) 1605, and *Viscount Stormont* (peerage of Scotland) 1621, with remainder to Sir Mungo Murray, 4th son of John, 1st Earl of Tullibardine (D Atholl), to John (Earl of Annandale), and to Andrew Murray, who in 1641 was *cr Lord Balvaird* peerage of Scotland &c; *dsp* 1631; *s* by (2) *Sir* MUNGO, 2nd Viscount (ante); *dsp* 1642; *s* by (3) JAMES 3rd Viscount, who had previously *s* as 2nd *Earl of Annandale*; *dsp* 1658, when the Earldom of Annandale became extinct, and the Lordship of Scone and Viscountcy of Stormont devolved upon (4) DAVID, 4th Viscount, who had previously *s* by his father Andrew Murray (ante) as 2nd *Lord Balvaird*; was fined £1,500 by Cromwell's Act of grace and pardon 1654; *d* 1668; *s* by his son (5) DAVID, 5th Viscount; opposed the Union, and was called upon to surrender at the breaking out of the Rebellion 1715; *d* 1731; *s* by his son (6) DAVID, 6th Viscount; *d* 1748; *s* by his son (7) DAVID, KT, PC, 7th Viscount; was Justice Gen of Scotland, Ambassador to Paris and Vienna 1772-8, a Sec of State 1779-82, Pres of the Council, and a Representative Peer 1754-90; *s* his uncle as 2nd *Earl of Mansfield* (see * infra) 1793; *m* 2ndly, 1776, Hon Louisa Cathcart (E Cathcart), who in 1793 *s* her uncle as Countess of Mansfield under patent of 1776, she *d* 1843, and was *s* by her grandson the 4th Earl; *d* 1796; *s* by his son (8) WILLIAM, KT, 3rd Earl; *b* 1777; was Lord-Lieut of Clackmannanshire: *m* 1797, Frederica, da of the Most Rev William Markham, Archbishop of York; *d* 1840; *s* by his son (9) WILLIAM DAVID, KT, 4th Earl; *b* 1806; MP for Aldborough (*C*) 1830, for Woodstock 1831, for Norwich 1832-7, and for Perthshire 1837-40; a Lord of the Treasury 1834-5, and Lord High Commr of Scottish Gen Assembly 1852, 1858, and 1859; Lord-Lieut and Sheriff Principal of Clackmannan; in 1843 *s* his grandmother (ante) in the Earldom of 1776: *m* 1829, Louisa, who *d* 1837, da of Cuthbert Ellison, of Hebburn, Durham; *d* 1898; *s* by his grandson (10) WILLIAM DAVID, PC (son of late William David, Viscount Stormont), 5th Earl; *b* 1860; *d* 1906; *s* by his brother (6) ALAN DAVID, 6th Earl; *b* 1864; Gentle-man Usher of the Green Rod (Order of the Thistle) 1895-1917: *m* 1899, Margaret Helen Mary, who *d* 1933, da of Sir Malcolm MacGregor, 4th Bt: *d* 1935; *s* by his son (7) MUNGO DAVID MALCOLM, 7th Earl; *b* 1900; Gov of Edinburgh and E of

Scotland Coll of Agric 1925-30; Lord High Commr to Gen Assembly of Ch of Scotland 1961-62; Lord Lieut of Perthshire 1960-71; MP for Perthshire and Kinross 1931-35: *m* 1928, Dorothea Helena, who *d* 1985, da of late Rt Hon Sir Lancelot Douglas Carnegie, GCVO, KCMG (E Southesk, colls); *d* 1971; *s* by his son **(8)** WILLIAM DAVID MUNGO JAMES, 8th Earl and present peer; also Viscount Stormont, Lord Scone, and Lord Balvaird.

__(1)__ *Hon* WILLIAM Murray, 3rd son of 5th Viscount Stormont; successively Solicitor-Gen Attorney-Gen, and Lord Ch Justice of England; *cr Baron Mansfield*, co Notts (peerage of Great Britain) 1756, and *Earl of Mansfield*, co Nottingham (peerage of Great Britain) 1776, with remainder to his niece Louisa, wife of his nephew David, 7th Viscount Stormont, and *Earl of Mansfield*, co Middlesex (peerage of Great Britain) 1792, with remainder to his nephew David, 7th Viscount Stormont (ante); *dsp* 1793, when the Barony of Mansfield expired, and the Earldom of 1776 devolved upon LOUISA (ante), and the Earldom of 1792 upon his nephew DAVID, 7th Viscount Stormont (ante).

MANTON, BARON (Watson) (Baron UK 1922)

JOSEPH RUPERT ERIC ROBERT WATSON, 3rd Baron; *b* 22 Jan 1924; *s* 1968; *ed* Eton; late Capt 7th Hussars, and Life Guards; Sr Steward Jockey Club 1982-85 and former Jockey Club Representative on Horserace Betting Levy Bd 1970-75; DL Humberside 1980: *m* 1951, Mary Elizabeth, da of late Maj Thomas Dennehy Hallinan, of Ashbourne, Glounthaune, co Cork, and has issue.

Arms – Argent, on a chevron azure between four martlets, three in chief and one in base sable, a crescent between two roses of the field. **Crest** – A gryphon passant sable in front of an oak tree proper. **Supporters** – On either side a gryphon per fesse azure and argent, charged on the shoulder with a rose also argent.
Residence – Houghton Hall, Sancton, York. *Clubs* – White's, Jockey.

SONS LIVING

Hon MILES RONALD MARCUS, *b* 7 May 1958; *ed* Eton; Maj Life Gds: *m* 1984, Elizabeth Adams, eldest da of Julian Russell Story, of Westcott, Surrey, and has issue living, Thomas Nigel Charles David, *b* 19 April 1985, — Ludovic Waldo Rupert, *b* 1989.
Hon Thomas Philip (triplet), *b* 1958; *ed* Eton, and RAC Cirencester; late Lt Queen's Own Hus, Lt Yorks Yeomanry: *m* 1988, Venetia Margaret Cadogan, da of Paul Spicer, of 22 Ovington Gdns, SW3, and has issue living, Alexander Paul Rupert, *b* 1989, — Tara Cadogan, *b* 1993.

DAUGHTERS LIVING

Hon Claire Georgina (*Baroness Hesketh*), *b* 1952: *m* 1977, 3rd Baron Hesketh, of Easton Neston, Towcester, Northants.
Hon Fiona Caroline Mary, *b* 1953: *m* 1978, Mark Swinfen Cottrell, of Molehill, Paris, Ashton-under-Hill, Evesham, Worcs, son of David Vernon Swynfen Cottrell, of Tewkesbury, Glos, and has issue living, George, *b* 1993, — Laura Marina, *b* 1988.
Hon Victoria Monica (triplet), *b* 1958: *m* 1993, as his 2nd wife, Anthony Henry (Harry) Westropp, of Wootton Downs Farmhouse, Woodstock, Oxon OX20 1AF, yr son of late Col Lionel Henry Mountifort Westropp, of Wye, Kent, and has issue living, a da, *b* 1993.

COLLATERAL BRANCHES LIVING

Issue of late *Hon* Robert Fraser Watson, 2nd son of 1st Baron, *b* 1900, *d* 1975: *m* 1st, 1928, Angela Blanche, who *d* 1959, da of late Lt-Col George Talbot Lake Denniss, R. Wilts Regt; 2ndly, 1961, Enid Agnes Maud, who *d* 1993, da of the late Arthur Levita, and formerly wife of Ewen Donald Cameron:—
(By 1st *m*) Shirley Angela Josephine, *b* 1932: *m* 1st, 1958 (*m diss* 1974), David T Chantler; 2ndly, 1977, John Hines Kennedy, MD (Harvard), of Old Court, Nethergate St, Clare, Suffolk; and 48 Egerton Gdns, SW3, and has issue living (by 1st *m*), Peter David Robert, *b* 1963, — Angela Margaret Jennifer, *b* 1961.

Issue of late *Hon* Alastair Joseph Watson, 3rd son of 1st Baron, *b* 1901, *d* 1955: *m* 1925, Joan, who *d* 1988, da of late Capt Philip Wyndham Cobbold (M Abergavenny, colls):—
Michael Oliver, *b* 1926; *ed* Stowe; late Capt Life Gds; JP: *m* 1950, Virginia, da of late Eustace Benyon Hoare (E Coventry), and has issue living, Alastair James, *b* 1958; *ed* Stowe; late Capt Life Gds: *m* 1991, Camilla Jane, da of Maj Christopher Wordsworth, late The Life Gds, — George William, *b* 1962; *ed* Stowe, and Wye Coll London (MSc); Lt RN, — Amanda Virginia, *b* 1956: *m* 1985, Antony Richardson Finley, and has issue living, Harry George *b* 1987, Thomas Geoffrey *b* 1989. *Residence* – Chillesford Lodge, Sudbourne, Woodbridge, Suffolk. *Club* – Cavalry. —— Andrew Philip, *b* 1930; *ed* Eton, and at Magdalene Coll, Camb (BA 1952, MA 1957): *m* 1957, Annette Mary Helena, da of Gerald Wellington Williams, JP (*see* D Northumberland, colls, 1985 Edn), and has issue living, Simon Mark, *b* 1959, — Nicholas Andrew, *b* 1961, — Jonathan Philip, *b* 1965, — Hugh Gerald, *b* 1968. *Residence* – Faldonside, Melrose, Roxburghshire.

PREDECESSORS – **(1)** JOSEPH Watson, only son of George Watson, of Donisthorpe House, Moor Allerton, Yorkshire; *b* 1873; Chm of Joseph Watson and Sons (Limited), and of Olympia Agricultural Co (Limited), and a Director of London and North-Western Railway; *cr Baron Manton*, of Compton Verney, co Warwick (peerage of United Kingdom) 1922: *m* 1898, Frances Claire, who *d* 1944, da of Harold Nickols, of Sandford House, Kirkstall, near Leeds, and 2 Seamore Place W: *d* 1922; *s* by his el son **(2)** GEORGE MILES, 2nd Baron, *b* 1899: *m* 1st, 1923 (*m diss* 1936), Alethea Alice Mary Pauline, who *d* 1979, da of late Lt-Col Philip Joseph Langdale, OBE, JP, DL (B Mowbray, colls); 2ndly, 1938, Leila Joan (who *m* 3rdly, 1969, as his 3rd wife, 6th Baron Brownlow, and *d* 1983) da of late Maj Philip Guy Reynolds, DSO, and formerly wife of late John Dane Player; *d* 1968; *s* by his only son **(3)** JOSEPH RUPERT ERIC ROBERT, 3rd Baron and present peer.

MANVERS, EARLDOM OF (Pierrepont) (Extinct 1955)

DAUGHTER LIVING OF SIXTH EARL

Lady (Frederica) Rozelle (Ridgway), *b* 1925; 1939-5 War as Leading Wren Stoker WRNS (1943-46); a writer: *m* 1st, 1953 (*m diss* 1961), Maj Alexander Montgomerie Greaves Beattie, Coldstream Gds; 2ndly, 1965, Richard Hollings Raynes, MB, BS, DPH, MFCM. *Residences* – Dolphin's Leap, St Margaret's Bay, Kent CT15 6HP; 88 Narrow St, E14 8BP.

MAR, COUNTESS OF (of Mar) (Earl precedence S 1404)

Think more

MARGARET OF MAR, Countess in her own right (Premier Earldom of Scotland); *b* 19 Sept 1940; *s* 1975; recognised in the surname of "of Mar" by warrant of Lord Lyon 1967, when she abandoned her second christian name of Alison: *m* 1st, 1959 (*m diss* 1976), Edwin Noel Artiss (who was recognised in the surname of "of Mar" by warrant of the Lord Lyon 1969; 1967; 2ndly, 1976 (*m diss* 1981), John Leslie Salton, who was recognised in the surname of "of Mar" by warrant of the Lord Lyon 1976, when he abandoned his christian name of Leslie; 3rdly, 1982, John H. Jenkin, MA, FRCO, LRAM, ARCM, and has issue by 1st *m*.

Arms – Azure, a bend between six cross-crosslets fitchée or. **Crest** – Upon a chapeau gules faced ermine, two wings each of ten pen feathers, erected and addorsed both blazoned as the shield. **Supporters** – On either side a griffin argent, armed, beaked and winged or.
Residence – St Michael's Farm, Great Witley, Worcs WR6 6JB.

DAUGHTER LIVING (By 1st marriage)

Lady SUSAN HELEN (*Mistress of Mar*), *b* 31 May 1963.

SISTER LIVING

Lady Janet Helen OF MAR, *b* 1946; *ed* St Andrews Univ (MA): *m* 1969, Lt-Cdr Laurence Duncan McDiarmid Anderson, MA, RN, who was recognised in the surname of "of Mar" by warrant of Lord Lyon 1969, and has issue living, Elizabeth, *b* 1970, — Catherine Jane, *b* 1971. *Address* – c/o Midland Bank, 26 Biggin St, Dover, Kent CT16 1BJ.

COLLATERAL BRANCHES LIVING

Issue of late Lady Margaret Isabel Lane (raised to the rank of an Earl's daughter 1967), sister of 30th Earl, *b* 1921, *d* 1989: *m* 1943, Maj John Bulley Bray Ayre, TD, RA (ret):—
Michael Desmonde Erskine AYRE (419 Wilverside Way, Calgary SE, Alberta, Canada T2J 1Z6), *b* 1944; *ed* Sir George Williams' Univ, Montreal (BEng): *m* 1971, Jane Erica, da of Cmdr E. G. Lock, RN, and has issue living, Nicholas Robert Erskine, *b* 1973, — Robin Michael, *b* 1975. ——— Rosemary Bray (Apt 507, 95 La Rose Ave, Etobicoke, Ontario, Canada M9P 3T2), *b* 1950; *ed* McGill Univ (BA).

Grandchildren of late Maj Seymour Hamilton Maule Cole, VD, eldest son of late Lady Eliza Philadelphia Erskine Goodeve (who *m* 1862, Rev Edward Maule Cole), sister of 27th Earl:—
Issue of late Maj Douglas Seymour Francis Erskine Maule Cole, *b* 1898, *d* 1985: *m* 1st, 1924 (*m diss* 1934), Iris, who *d* 1972, da of late Col G. S. Broome, IA (ret); 2ndly, 1942, Rosa Florence, who *d* 1983, only da of late Lieut Stanley George Bartley, RN:—
(By 1st *m*) Louis Malcolm Erskine MAULE COLE (20 St Catherine's Rd, Crawley, Sussex), *b* 1931: *m* 1955, Kathleen Jarvis, and has issue living, Julia Erskine, *b* 1961: *m* 1984, Timothy John Barber, of 3 Kenmara Close, Three Bridges, Crawley, W Sussex, and has issue living, Matthew James *b* 1989, Philip John *b* 1993, Rachael Eleanor Alice *b* 1991, — Louise Erskine, *b* 1963; has issue living (by Russell Short, of 15 Trentham Rd, Redhill, Surrey), Eve Erskine MAULE COLE *b* 1989. ——— Iris Erskine, *b* 1929: *m* 1950, Roger Harrison, MPS, of Hippica Internacional, Camino de la Sierra, Churriana, Malaga, Spain, and has issue living, Sally Erskine, *b* 1951: *m* 1st, 1970, Andrew Aitkenhead, who *d* 1971; 2ndly, 1973 (*m diss* 1976), Grenville Stacey; 3rdly, 1978 (*m diss* 1987), Anthony Curtis; 4thly, 1988, Duncan McLaren, of Moonbeam Cottage, 79 High St, Bagshot, Surrey, and has issue living (by 3rd *m*) Candice Samantha *b* 1978, — Victoria Erskine, *b* 1956: *m* 1975, Garry Stephen Doherty, of 1 Lilac Grove, Chadderton, Manchester, and has issue living, Lorraine Ann *b* 1982.

Grandchildren of late Mrs Florence Violet Erskine Clive (infra):—
Issue of late John Ivor Erskine Penn Bowen, *b* 1916, *d* 1967: *m* 1939, Kate Molly Faith, who *d* 1990, da of Capt Bernard Arthur Mildmay, IA:—
Hugh Erskine PENN BOWEN (36 Porter Way, Clacton on Sea, Essex), *b* 1945: *m* 1st, 1963 (*m diss* 1983), Marion May Wells; 2ndly, 1989, Mrs Bernadette Evelyn Grace Widlake (*née* Carlsson), and has issue living (by 1st *m*), Mark James, *b* 1964: *m* 1st, 1987 (*m diss* 1992), Susan Aspridge; 2ndly, 1993, Catherine Ann, da of Brian Paul Taylor, — Jason Ivor, *b* 1970: *m* 1st, 1989 (*m diss* 1992), Shirley M. Szafinski; 2ndly, 1994, Mrs Sarah Jane Parker, da of Dieter Heinz McDonald, and has issue living (by 2nd wife), Holly May *b* 1994. ——— Elizabeth Angelo PENN BOWEN (PO Box 129, Urangan, Queensland 4655, Australia), *b* 1947; has resumed her maiden name: *m* 1966 (*m diss* 19—), (David) Peter D. Gregory, and has issue living, David, *b* 19—, — Samantha Georgette A., *b* 1967, — Phaedra Simone, *b* 1968. Mrs Penn Bowen also has further issue, Liam, *b* 19—, — Jesse, *b* 19—. ——— Halcyon SIMPSON (6 Juno Mews, Colchester, Essex CO2 9PQ), *b* 1949; assumed the surname of Simpson by deed poll 1982: *m* 1st, 1965 (*m diss* 1973), Brian Sidney Mole; 2ndly, 1974 (*m diss* 1981), Andrew David Lee, and has issue living (by 1st *m*), Wendy Lynn, *b* 1965: *m* 1986, Carl Gary Baker, and has issue living James Carl *b* 1988, Holly Sarah *b* 1991.

Grandchildren of late Maj Seymour Hamilton Maule Cole, VD (ante):—
Issue of late Florence Violet Erskine CLIVE, *b* 1893; resumed her former surname of Clive 1948, *d* 1967: *m* 1st, 1911 (*m diss* 1924), Col John Alexander Barclay Penn Bowen, RE (ret); 2ndly, 1925, Maj Henry William Fitzroy Clive, Indian Army, who *d* 1932; 3rdly, 1933 (*m diss* 1944), Frederick James St John Croley:—

(By 1st *m*) Barbara Lilian (503 President Av, Sutherland, NSW 2232, Australia), *b* 1918: *m* 1941, Raleigh Cornwallis Amesbury, who *d* 1986, and has issue living Christopher Raleigh Cornwallis (31 Annesley Av, Stanwell Tops, NSW 2508), *b* 1943: *m* 1966, Wendy Lloyd, and has issue living, Richard Anthony *b* 1971, Michelle Ann *b* 1967, Heather Marie *b* 1969, — Bruce Hamilton (1 Poets Glen, Werrington Downs, NSW 2750), *b* 1944: *m* 1st, 1964 (*m diss* 1971), Maureen Patricia Presswell; 2ndly, 1981, Maria Luz Pritchett, and has issue living (by 1st *m*), Joanne Patricia *b* 1966, (by 2nd *m*) Grant Raleigh Ross *b* 1983, Crystal Luzette *b* 1982, — Gary John (92 Beaconsfield Rd, Revesby, NSW 2212), *b* 1949: *m* 1980, Marilyn Watts, and has issue living, Jason Raleigh *b* 1982, Melanie Rae *b* 1985, — Stephen Anthony (8 Eames Av, Baulkham Hills, NSW 2153), *b* 1953: *m* 1982, Jacquelene, da of D. Hunt, of Blaxland, NSW, and has issue living, Caitlin Maree *b* 1987, — Tina Maria, *b* 1959: *m* 1985, Harry Ernest Ivison, of Lot 33 Hume Drive, Helensburgh, NSW 2508, and has issue living, Danielle Barbara *b* 1987. —— (By 2nd *m*) Henry Robert Somerset CLIVE (1-21 Burke St, Concorde West, NSW 2137, Australia), *b* 1926; *ed* Wellington Coll: *m* 1949, —, da of late Mohintri Passi, of Raniganj, W Bengal, and has had issue, Saluchna, *b* 1950, *d* 1952.

Issue of late Crystal Mary Vera Erskine Cole, *b* 1895, *d* 1972: *m* 1915 (*m diss* 1925), Leonard Charles Simpson, who *d* 1958, late Indian State Railways:—
†Robert Seymour Erskine SIMPSON *b* 1917; *ed* Dulwich, served 1939-45 War as Flt-Lieut RAF, Pilot, Atlantic Star: *m* 1945, Ivy May Jackson (33 Woodley Crescent, Melville Heights, W Australia 6156), and *d* 1994, leaving issue, Robert Neil (48 Riverview Terrace, Mount Pleasant, W Australia 6153), *b* 1952; *ed* Dulwich; Air Traffic Controller, Perth, WA: *m* 1978, Catherine Faull, and has issue living, Alicia Catherine Faull *b* 1986, Hannah Jackson Waddy *b* 1987, — Jean Elizabeth, *b* 1947: *m* 1968, Johan Daniel Stub Ravn, of 49 Barbican St, Shelley, W Australia 6155, and has issue living, Johan Daniel Stub *b* 1970, Kristian Robert *b* 1973, Ingrid Kirsten *b* 1974. —— Yvonne Lilian (7927 Plantation Lakes Drive, Port St Lucie, Florida 34986, USA), *b* 1919: *m* 1941, Frank Dator, who *d* 1985, and has issue living, William Frank (597 Wyckoff Av, Mahwah, NJ 07430, USA), *b* 1943: *m* 1964, Linda O'Lear, and has issue living, William Frank *b* 1971, Lisa Lynn *b* 1965, Rebecca Ann *b* 1969, — Raymond James (12 S Railroad Av, Mahwah, NJ 07430, USA), *b* 1946: *m* 1967 (*m diss* 1978), Barbara Ann Roosa, and has issue living, Michele Lynn 1967, Erin Ashley *b* 1969, — Darryl (14 Snow Drive, Mahwah, NJ 07430, USA), *b* 1947: *m* 1976 (*m diss* 1993), Thomas John Kopplin, and has issue living, Michael Thomas *b* 1985, Katherine Elisabeth *b* 1981. —— Pamela Bernadene (106 Manns Rd, Narara, NSW 2250, Australia), *b* 1921: *m* 1st, 1940 (*m diss* 1948), Thomas Wallace Greenwood; 2ndly, 1948, Lt-Col Reginald John Isaac, OBE, MC, Intelligence Corps, who *d* 1984, and has issue living, (by 1st *m*) Patricia Frances, *b* 1941; HM Diplo Ser 1962-74; JP W Norfolk 1991: *m* 1981, Peter Knights, of The Old Music House, 5 London Rd, King's Lynn, Norfolk PE30 5PY, — (by 2nd *m*) James Robert ISAAC-COLE (106 Manns Rd, Narara, NSW 2250, Australia), *b* 1950; *ed* Millfield: *m* 1973, Suzanne Gay Musgrove, of Sydney, NSW, and has issue living, Russell Jason *b* 1984, — Lionel Seymour John (38 Burke St, Capalaba, Qld 4157, Australia), *b* 1954; *ed* Wells Cathedral Sch, Som, and Loughborough Univ (BSc): *m* 1984, Beth Slater, and has issue living, Alexander *b* 1993, Philadelphia Jane *b* 1987, Natasha *b* 1989.

Issue of late Edna Beryl Mavis Erskine Cole, *b* 1896, *d* 1985: *m* 1919, Constantine Demetriadi, MBE, who *d* 1951:—
Michael Anthony DEMETRIADI, OBE, TD (Office Farm House, Brandeston, Woodbridge, Suffolk IP13 7AR; Army and Navy Club), *b* 1920; *ed* Radley; Col TAVR: served 1939-45 War as Maj RWF (wounded, despatches twice, Burma Star); Member Territorial Assocn of Lowlands of Scotland 1968-75, and E Anglia 1976-85; Vice Chm Suffolk Cttee; ADC to HM 1974-75; MInst PS, MInst AM; a JP for Dunbartonshire 1973-76; Member Sec of State for Scotland's Advisory Cttee to Lord Lieut on appt of JPs; a cotton expert, with J & P Coats Ltd, Glasgow, 1951-75; Dep Sec Diocese of St Edmundsbury & Ipswich 1979-86; KJStJ; Commr St John Ambulance Bde, Suffolk, 1979-85, Dir St John Ambulance Assocn, Suffolk since 1986, and Cmdr since 1982, OBE (Civil) 1993: *m* 1948, Nancy Anna, el da of late Ambrose John Rodocanachi, of Rolletts, Darsham, Saxmundham, Suffolk, and has issue living, Peter Michael (Byron House, The Street, Weeley, Clacton-on-Sea, Essex CO16 9JF; MCC), *b* 1953; *ed* Radley, and Univ Coll, London (BA): *m* 1980, France Marie Anne Nicole, eldest da of Judge Bodson, of Av Commandant Lothaire 58, 1040 Brussels, and has issue living, Guy Peter Michael Erskine *b* 1983, James Paul Christian Erskine *b* 1985, Jennifer Anne Nancy *b* 1982, — Philippa Nancy (No 3 Kleomenous St, Kolonaki, Athens), *b* 1949: *m* 1st, 1975 (*m diss* 1983), Nikos Stamatopoulos; 2ndly, 1986, Jan Doman, and has issue living (by 1st *m*) Lucinda Polixeni *b* 1976, — Antonia Claire (du Cane Court, Balham High Rd, SW17), *b* 1959; *ed* Wycombe Abbey; editor.

Issue of late Lilian Maude Erskine Cole, *b* 1900, *d* 1965: *m* 1st, 1926 (*m diss* 1933), Cyril Ernest Musgrave Ridsdale, BN Railway, who *d* 1957; 2ndly, 1933, William Louis Charles Gerard Cook, OBE (formerly Indian Imperial Police):—
(By 2nd *m*) David William Erskine Gerard COOK, *b* 1936; *ed* Bedford Sch: *m* 1960, Joanne Elizabeth, da of John Fisher, of Sydney, and has issue living, Jonathan David, *b* 1961, — Caroline Louise, *b* 1965. *Residence* – Weyborn, 20 Lansdowne Av, Codsall, Staffs. —— (By 1st *m*) Suzanne June Toy, *b* 1928: *m* 1st, 1951 (*m diss* 1955), David John Lush; 2ndly, 1957, Claude Guy de la Faye d'Entrains Biard, and has issue living, (by 1st *m*) Sarah Jane Judith, *b* 1952: *m* 1st, 1974 (*m diss* 1981), Christopher John Dean; 2ndly, 1982, Andrew Quinton Steggall, of Ormond House, Temple St, Brill, Bucks, and has issue living (by 1st *m*), Matthew Christopher *b* 1975, Adam James *b* 1977 (by 2nd *m*) Edward Dicken *b* 1984. *Residence* – 19 Ansdell Terr, W8.

Grandchildren of late Beatrice Madeline Erskine Ferguson (infra):—
Issue of late George Hamilton Ferguson, KPM, *b* 1896, *d* 1970: *m* 1931 (*m diss* 1948), Dorothy Mary Kate Susie Emily Vaughan, da of the late Sir Robert (Vaughan) Gower, KCVO, OBE, MP:—
Robert Maule Gower FERGUSON, *b* 1932; *ed* Harrow. —— Beatrice Margaret, *b* 1933: *m* 1963, Norman Carey Booth Creek, of 9433 Ardmore Dr, RR2 Sidney, BC, Canada and has issue living, Carey Hamish Ferguson, *b* 1964, — Benjamin Robert, *b* 1965, — Nicola Robin, *b* 1967, — Kanina Susanna Erskine, *b* 1970. —— Sally Pauline June (c/o Royal Bank of Scotland, Oban, Argyll), *b* 1941: *m* 1968, Lt-Cdr Ian Cochrane, RN (ret), who *d* 1988, and has issue living Frances Sarah Nicola, *b* 1960 (adopted by her stepfather 1968), — Harriet Elizabeth Alexandra *b* 1970, — Emma Catherine Anne *b* 1972.

Issue of late Roland Edward Stuart Ferguson, late RNAS, RAF and IA, *b* 1899, *d* 1976: *m* 1941, Veronica Catherine (Tangs, Shipley Bridge, S Brent, S Devon TQ10 9ED), yr da of Henry Gore Hawker, of Strode, Ermington, Devon):—
Andrew Stuart FERGUSON (Penllyn, Cathedine, Bwlch, Powys), *b* 1948; Ionosphericist and sometime Base Cdr with British Antarctic Survey 1971-74; Nature Conservancy Council since 1979: *m* 1975, Helen Alice, only da of Col P. N. Lodge, RA (ret), of The Manor House, Compton Abdale, Glos, and has issue living, Geoffrey Roland, *b* 1976, — Ian Antony, *b* 1980. —— Janet Erskine (Cracklewood, Didworthy, S Brent, S Devon), *b* 1946; WRNS 1964-68: *m* 1st, 19— (*m diss* 1977), John Goodwin Fisk, 8th Hussars; 2ndly, 1978, Lt Cdr Adrian John Bomback, MC, RN, who was *k* while on leave by a tree during the storm of 25 Jan 1990, and has issue living (by 1st *m*), Adrian John Stuart Erskine, *b* 1970, — Peter Maule Erskine, *b* 1973.

Issue of late Helen Evelyn Ferguson, *b* 1886, *d* 1962: *m* 1914, Harold Henry Wyndham Newman, who *d* 1963:—
Durnford Frederick Wyndham NEWMAN (c/o National Westminster Bank, PO Box 320, 5 Station Approach, West Byfleet, Surrey KT14 6YJ), *b* 1917; Diploma of Faraday House; CEng, FIEE; Ch Eng, British Airports Authority, Heathrow Airport, London 1972-77; late Sqdn-Ldr RAF; 1939-45 War as Capt RE: *m* 1948, Joan (Jane) Merriel Hollway, and has issue living, James Richard Wyndham (Studlands, 8 The Knoll, Fairmile Park Rd, Cobham, Surrey), *b* 1950; BSc (Hons): *m* 1st, 1975, Ann Caroline Lawrence, who *d* 1984; 2ndly, 1985, Carole Ann Dove, and has issue living, (by 2nd *m*) Thomas Philip Wyndham *b* 1987, James Frederick Wyndham *b* 1991, — Clare Marian Wyndham, *b* 1953: *m* 1982, Robert Tony Alter, of 11145 NW 1st Place, Coral Springs, Florida 33071, USA, and has issue living, Edward Donald *b* 1989.

Issue of late Mary Beatrice Erskine Ferguson, *b* 1888, *d* 1970: *m* 1st, 1912, Maj Hubert Symons, RFA, who was *ka* 1918; 2ndly, 1937, Graham Parsons Earwaker, who *d* 1971:—
(By 1st *m*) Jean Erskine (Withycombe, Winsford, Minehead, Somerset), *b* 1916: *m* 1940, Maj Richard Andrew Joscelyne, MC, RTR, who *d* 1992, and has issue living, Andrew Michael Hubert, *b* 1946; Col Gren Gds, — Sarah Anne, *b* 1941: *m* 1963, Anthony Owen Blishen, OBE, HM Diplo Ser, of 59 Arragon Rd, Twickenham, Middx, and has issue living, James Peter Anthony *b* 1966, Robert Edward Henry *b* 1970, David Francis Andrew *b* 1972, Catherine Annabelle *b* 1964.

Grandchildren of late Mary Beatrice Erskine Earwaker (ante):—
Issue of late Peter Nicholas Symons, *b* 1917, *d* 1951: *m* 1940, Suzanne Penzer Haynes (*Lady Marshall*) (who *m* 2ndly, 1953, Cdr Sir Douglas Marshall, RNVR, who *d* 1976), of Hatt, Saltash, Cornwall:—
Heugh Sherwood SYMONS (Bicton Farm House, Hatt, Saltash, Cornwall) *b* 1949: *m* 1976, Fiona Ann Mitchell, and has issue living, Genevieve Penn, *b* 1979, — Emily Penn, *b* 1980. — Suzanna Penn, *b* 1984. ——— Nicola Penn, *b* 1942: *m* 1963, John Philip Coverdale, of Bevere Manor, Bevere, Worcester, and has issue living, Peter John, *b* 1970, — Philip Anthony *b* 1978, — Anna Frances Mary, *b* 1966: *m* 1990, Andrew Christopher Kennedy Davis, and has issue living, Oliver John Kennedy *b* 1991, — Sarah Elizabeth, *b* 1968. ——— Celia Mary (Swiftaford Farmhouse, Hatt, Saltash, Cornwall PL12 6PP), *b* 1947: *m* 1973 (*m diss* 1988), Erich Gerhard Rinagl, and has issue living, Marc Gerard Penn, *b* 1979, — Nina Penn, *b* 1983. —— Melanie Anne, *b* (twin) 1947: *m* 1970, Jeremy John Shales, of 70 Princes Rd, Teddington, Middx, and has issue living, Joanna Penn, *b* 1979, — Louise Alexandra Penn, *b* 1980.

Granddaughter of late Lady Eliza Philadelphia Erskine (ante):—
Issue of late Beatrice Madeline Erskine Cole, *b* 1863, *d* 1936: *m* 1884, Henry Tanner Ferguson, MICE, late of Wolleigh, Bovey Tracey, Devon, who *d* 1909:—
Violet Madeline (11 Unsworth Rd, N Ringwood, Victoria 3134, Australia), *b* 1893: *m* 1919 (*m diss* 1926), Philip Eric Bernard, and has issue living, Barbara Nancy (11 Unsworth Rd, N Ringwood, Victoria 3134, Australia), *b* 1920: *m* 1945, Ronald Hyde, MRCS, LRCP, who *d* 1965, and has issue living, Timothy David Erskine *b* 1946; Member Sydney Stock Exchange 1983: *m* 1987, Caroline Noelle Scheidat (and has issue living, Philippa Annabelle Jane *b* 1987), Robin Paul Christopher *b* 1948; a Member of Australian Inst of Export: *m* 1st, 1975 (*m diss* 1979), Margaret Anne Weichelt; 2ndly, 1979, Aoura Sangsingkeo (and has issue living (by 2nd *m*), Andrew Chatvalin *b* 1985, Samantha Darupat *b* 1983), Max Anthony John *b* 1951; *ed* Monash Univ, Victoria (BA): *m* 1983, Carla Lavinia Holding (and has issue living, Rebecca Louise Austen *b* 1984), James Rupert *b* 1955: *m* 1988, Stella Moutos (and has issue living, Jeremy *b* 1989, Stephanie Anne *b* 1987), Lucy Susan Elizabeth (twin) *b* 1955: *m* 1976, Anthony John Lemprière Sheaffe (and has issue living, Jonathan Lemprière *b* 1979, Susan Elizabeth *b* 1980, Alexandra Jane *b* 1984).

Descendants of late Hon Henry David Erskine, 3rd son of 24th Earl (*see* E Mar and Kellie).
Granddaughter of late Mary Margaret Anna ZWILCHENBART-ERSKINE, da of late Rev Hon Thomas Erskine (4th son of 24th Earl), *b* 1829, *d* 1906 (having assumed the additional name of Erskine for herself and son 1884): *m* 1864, as his 2nd wife, Rodolph Zwilchenbart, who *d* 1833:—
Issue of late Gratney Rodolph ZWILCHENBART-ERSKINE, *b* 1871, *d* 1930: *m* 1896, Theodora, who *d* 1958, da of late W. H. Laverton, of Leighton, Westbury, Wilts;—
Helen Mary, *b* 1901: *m* 1928, Brigadier Alec Palmer ffleetwood Churchill, OBE, Indian Army, who *d* 1947, and has issue living, John ffleetwood (111 Albert Bridge Rd, SW11), *b* 1934; *ed* Wellington Coll, and at Trin Hall, Camb: *m* 1970, Stephanie, da of H. van den Bergh, of The Hague, Holland, and has issue living, John Edward ffleetwood *b* 1973, Gratia Mary Anne ffleetwood *b* 1975, Juliet Kathleen ffleetwood *b* 1978, — Charles ffleetwood (Summer Fields, Oxford), *b* 1937; *ed* Wellington Coll, and at Jesus Coll, Camb. *Residence* – Givons Grove, Reading Road North, Fleet, Hants GU13 8HT.

PREDECESSORS – According to Lord Hailes the origin of the Earls of Mar is "lost in antiquity" A Mormaer of Mar served at the battle of Clontarf 1014. **(1)** ROTHRI, Mormaer (or Earl) of Mar witnessed foundation charter of Scone 1114-15, and King David I's charter to Dunfermline Abbey 1124-29; *s* by **(2)** MORGUND, who was *s* by **(3)** GILCHRIST, *s* by **(4)** DUNCAN (son of Morgund), who was *s* by his son **(5)** WILLIAM; *s* by his son **(6)** DONALD, father of **(7)** GRATNEY, who *s* about 1297: *m* Christian (*1st Lady of Garioch*), sister of King Robert I of Scotland; *d* before 1305; *s* by his son **(8)** DONALD, Regent of Scotland, *d* 1332; *s* by his son **(9)** THOMAS, Great Chamberlain of Scotland; Lordship of Garioch confirmed 1357; *dsp* 1373/4; *s* by his sister **(10)** MARGARET, Countess of Mar; *d* 1390; *s* by her da (by her 1st husband William, Earl of Douglas) **(11)** ISABEL, Countess of Mar; *d* 1408, having in 1404 granted a life rent in the Earldom to her husband, **(12)** Sir ALEXANDER Stewart, who *d* 1435; *s* by **(13)** ROBERT, 1st Lord Erskine, son of Sir Thomas Erskine, of Alloa and Dun, by his 2nd wife, Janet; returned heir of line of Isabel (ante), and assumed the Earldom; *d* 1452; *s* by his son **(14)** THOMAS, 2nd Lord Erskine (and *de jure* 14th Earl); in 1457 before an Assize of Error the Earldom was found to have devolved upon the Crown, but this was negatived by Queen Mary's restoration and by the ruling of the Court of Session in 1626: he was *s* by his son **(14)** ALEXANDER (*de jure* 15th Earl), who was *s* by his son **(16)** ROBERT (*de jure* 16th Earl); fell at Flodden 1513; *s* by his son **(17)** JOHN (*de jure* 17th Earl); *d* 1555; *s* by his son **(18)** JOHN, 6th Lord Erskine, who was in 1565 *restored* by Queen Mary to the Earldom of Mar and Lordship of Garioch (through Janet, great-granddaughter of Gratney, 7th Earl of Mar (ante)), and of which his ancestor Thomas, 2nd Lord Erskine was declared to have been unjustly dispossessed, and this restoration was confirmed by an Act of Parliament which expressly recognized Robert, 1st Lord Erskine to have been rightfully Earl of Mar, and in the Decreet of Ranking of 1606 (according to the documents then produced) the Earl of Mar was assigned a position conformable to writs of 1393 and 1404: was Regent of Scotland 1571-72; *d* 1572; *s* by his son **(19)** JOHN, KG, 19th Earl; attainted 1584 and restored 1585; was Lord Treasurer of Scotland 1616-30; *cr Lord Cardross* 1610 (with power of nomination); *d* 1634; *s* in the Lordship of Cardross (according to nomination) (*see* E Buchan), and in the Earldom of Mar by his son, **(20)** JOHN, PC, 20th Earl, an Extraordinary Lord of Session 1620-26 and 1628-30; *d* 1654; *s* by his son **(21)** JOHN, 21st Earl; *d* 1668; *s* by his son, **(22)** CHARLES, PC, 22nd Earl; Col Roy Scots Fusiliers, which Regt he raised; *d* 1689; *s* by his son, **(23)** JOHN, KT, PC, 23rd Earl; Sec of State 1706, Keeper of the Signet, and a Representative Peer; having defended the cause of the Stuarts in 1715 his honours were attainted and his estates forfeited; *d* 1732, and the Alloa property was entailed on his da Lady Frances Erskine, who but for the attainder would have been Countess of Mar; *s* by his grandson **(24)** JOHN FRANCIS Erskine, 24th Earl, to whom the Earldom was restored by Act of Parliament 1824 through his mother, Lady Frances, as "grandson and lineal representative" of the attainted Earl; *d* 1825; *s* by his son **(25)** JOHN THOMAS, 25th Earl; *d* 1828; *s* by his son, **(26)** JOHN FRANCIS MILLER, 26th Earl; served at Waterloo; successfully claimed to be 11th *Earl of Kellie* 1835; *dsp* 1866, when the Earldom of Kellie devolved upon his cousin, while he was *s* in the ancient Earldom of Mar by his nephew (the heir-general) **(27)** JOHN FRANCIS ERSKINE Goodeve-Erskine, 27th Earl (son of Lady Frances Jemina (el sister of 26th Earl), by her marriage with William James Goodeve, of Clifton); *b* 1836; assumed by legal authorization 1866 the additional surname of Erskine; for 36 years a Representative Peer for Scotland: succession to heir-general confirmed with precedence of 1404 by the Declaratory Act of Parliament passed in 1885 (Restitution of Mar Act): *m* 1866, Alice Mary Sinclair, who *d* 1924, da of late John Hamilton, of Hilston Park, Monmouthshire; *d* 1930; *s* by his only son, **(28)** JOHN FRANCIS HAMILTON SINCLAIR CUNLIFFE BROOKS FORBES, 28th Earl: *m* 1903, Sibyl May Dominica, who *d* 1958, da of late Robert Heathcote; *d* 1932; *s* by his cousin **(29)** LIONEL WALTER Young, 29th Earl (grandson of Lady Frances Jemima Erskine Young), el sister of 27th Earl, *b* 1891; assumed the additional name of Erskine (registered in Court of Lord Lyon) 1933; *d* 1965; *s* by his kinsman, **(30)** JAMES CLIFTON, 30th Earl (el son of Charles Macdonald Lane), CSI, el son of Alice, who *m* James Horsburgh Lane, da of Lady Frances Jemima Erskine Young (ante); recognised in the surname of "of Mar" by warrant of Lord Lyon 1959: *m* 1st, 1939 (*m diss* 1958), Millicent Mary, who *d* 1993, da of William Salton; 2ndly, 1960, Marjorie Aileen, who *d* 1975, da of late John Reginald Miller, and widow of Maj C. W. S. Grice, Indian Army; *d* 1975; *s* by his el da **(31)** MARGARET, present peeress, and Lady Garioch.

MAR and KELLIE, EARL OF (Erskine) (Earl of Mar S 1565, Earl of Kellie S 1616)

I think more
He adds honour to that of his ancestors

UNIONE · FORTIOR
Strengthened by unity

JAMES THORNE ERSKINE, 14th Earl of Mar, and 16th Earl of Kellie, Premier Viscount of Scotland; *b* 10 March 1949; *s* 1993; *ed* Eton, Moray House Coll of Educn, Edinburgh (Dip Social Work, Dip Youth & Co Work), and at Inverness Coll (Certificate in Building); Hereditary Keeper of Stirling Castle, DL Clackmannan 1991; Page of Honour to HM 1962-63; Social Worker; P/O RAuxAF 1979-82, F/O 1982-86 (2622 Highland Sqdn), Memb RN Aux Ser 1985-89: *m* 1974, Mrs Mary Irene Mooney, yr da of late Dougal McDougal Kirk, of Edinburgh, and formerly wife of Roderick James Mooney.

Arms – Quarterly: 1st and 4th argent, a pale sable, *Erskine*; 2nd and 3rd azure, a bend between six cross crosslets fitchée or, *Mar*. over all, on an escutcheon gules, the royal crown of Scotland proper, within a double tressure flory counterflory or, ensigned with an earl's coronet, *Kellie*; behind the shield are placed in saltire a key, wards outwards or, and a baton gules, garnished or, and ensigned with a castle of the last (the insignia of the office of Hereditary Keeper of the Castle of Stirling). **Crests** – 1st, on a cap of maintenance gules, turned up ermine a dexter hand, holding a skene in pale argent, hilted and pommelled or, over crest "Je pense plus" (I think more); 2nd, on a cap of maintenance gules, turned up ermine a demi-lion rampant guardant gules, armed argent, over crest "Decori decus addit avito" (He adds honour to the honour of his ancestors). **Supporters** – Two griffins gules, armed, beaked, and winged or.
Residence – Erskine House, Kirk Wynd, Clackmannan, FK10 4JF; *Club* – New (Edinburgh).

BROTHERS LIVING

Hon ALEXANDER DAVID (34 Awaba St, Mosman, NSW 2088, Australia), *b* 26 Oct 1952; *ed* Eton, and Pembroke Coll, Camb (BA): *m* 1977, Katherine Shawford, elder da of late Thomas Clark Capel, of Narrabri, NSW (*see* M Bute, colls), and has issue living, Alexander Capel, *b* 1979, — Isabel Katherine, *b* 1982.
Rev Hon Michael John, *b* 1956; *ed* Eton, and Edinburgh Univ (MA, BD): *m* 1987, Jill, elder da of late Campbell S. Westwood, of 11 Leighton Gdns, Ellon, and has issue living, Euan Stewart, *b* 1992, — Laura Anne, *b* 1990. *Residence* – The Manse, Kilmelfort, Argyllshire.

SISTER LIVING

Lady Fiona, *b* (twin) 1956: *m* 1980, Lt-Col Andrew P. W. Campbell, Argyll and Sutherland Highlanders, yr son of late Wilson Campbell, of Coquet House, Warkworth, Northumberland, and has issue living, Barnabas William Erskine, *b* 1983, — Elizabeth Poppy, *b* 1985, — Rosanna Katherine, *b* 1986.

UNCLES LIVING (*Brothers of 13th Earl of Mar*)

Hon David Hervey, *b* 1924; *ed* Eton, and Trin Coll, Camb (MA); Bar, Inner Temple 1950; late Capt Scots Gds; Co Councillor 1969-85, and a JP and DL for Suffolk; Italy and Palestine 1943-45 (Italy star): *m* 1st, 1953, Jean Violet, who *d* 1983, el da of Lt-Col Archibald Vivian Campbell Douglas, late Scots Gds (*see* de Bunsen, Bt, ext); 2ndly, 1985, Caroline Mary, yr da of late Rt Hon Sir Alan Frederick Lascelles, GCVO, KCB, CMG, MC (*see* E Harewood, colls), and widow of 2nd Viscount Chandos, and has issue living (by 1st *m*), Janet Cicely, *b* 1955: *m* 1980, Gordon Drake Arthur, of Highfields, Smeeton Westerby, Leicester LE8 0LT, elder son of Allan Arthur, MBE, DL, of Mount Maskall, Boreham, Essex, and has issue living, Allan Douglas Erskine *b* 1987, Isobel Jean Douglas *b* 1984, Margaret Frances Ramsay *b* 1989, — Catherine Marjorie, *b* 1958: *m* 1979, Edward Georges Rossdale, son of John Rossdale, of 37 De Vere Gdns, W8, and has issue living, Venetia *b* 1981, Sophie *b* 1982, Caroline *b* 1986, — Mary (Molly) Viola, *b* 1962: *m* 1987, (Edward) Seymour Adams, of 33 Radipole Rd, SW6 5DN, son of Philip Adams, of Havant, Hants, and has issue living, Max Philip Erskine *b* 1992, Ellen Catherine Jean *b* 1990. *Residences* – Felsham House, Felsham, Bury St Edmunds; 17 Clareville Court, Clareville Grove, SW7. *Club* – Brooks's.
Hon Robert William Hervey, *b* 1930; *ed* Eton, and King's Coll, Camb; late 2nd Lieut Scots Gds: *m* 1st, 1955 (*m diss* 1964), Jennifer Shirley, yr da of L. J. Cardew Wood, of Farnham Royal Bucks; 2ndly, 1969 (*m diss* 1975), Annemarie, da of Jean Lattès, of 31 Rue Guinegand, Paris VI; 3rdly, 1977, Belinda Mary Rosalind, da of Raymond Blackburn, of London, and has issue living, (by 2nd *m*) Alistair Robert, *b* 1970, — (by 3rd *m*) Thomas Gerald, *b* 1978, — Felix Benjamin, *b* 1980. *Residence* – 100 Elgin Cres, W11 2JL.

WIDOW LIVING OF THIRTEENTH EARL

PANSY CONSTANCE (*Dowager Countess of Mar and Kellie*), OBE, UK Pres Unicef 1979-84, Chm Youth at Risk Advisory Group 1968-91, JP, CStJ, da of late Gen Sir (Augustus Francis) Andrew Nicol Thorne, KCB, CMG, DSO (*see* B Penrhyn, 1967 Edn): *m* 1948, Maj the 13th Earl, who *d* 1993. *Residence* – Claremont House, Alloa, Clackmannan FK10 2JF.

COLLATERAL BRANCHES LIVING

Issue of late Capt Hon Francis Walter Erskine, yr son of 12th Earl, *b* 1899, *d* 1972: *m* 1925, Phyllis, who *d* 1974, da of late John F. Burstall, of Quebec, Canada:—
Rosemary Susan, *b* 1927: *m* 1st, 1947 (*m diss* 1974), Mark Alastair Coats, late Lt Gren Gds; 2ndly, 1974, David Laidlaw, of Grand Rue, 81170, Cordes, France, and has issue living (by 1st *m*), Nicholas James (8 Kempson Rd, SW6), *b* 1952: *m* 1987, Belinda, da of Gordon McKechnie, and has issue living, James Michael *b* 1987, Rosanna Sarah *b* 1990, — Virginia Jane, *b* 1954: *m* 1977, Andrew Nicholas John Hay, of 10 Favart Rd, SW6, son of Sir (Alan) Philip Hay, KCVO, TD (*see* M Hertford, 1973-74 Edn), and has issue living, Timothy George Nicholas *b* 1980, Christopher James Philip *b* 1984, Olivia Margaret Rose *b* 1990.

Issue of late Rt Hon Sir William Augustus Forbes Erskine, GCMG, MVO, Ambassador to Poland 1928-31, 2nd son of 11th Earl, *b* 1871, *d* 1952: *m* 1908, Georgie Viola Eleanor, who *d* 1972, da of late William Humble Dudley Ward (E Dudley, colls):—

Cynthia Romola, *b* 1910: *m* 1943, Pierre Bressy, former Ambassador, French Diplo Ser, who *d* 1973, and has issue living, Francois Pierre Erskine (18 rue de la Basse Roche, Villebon sur Yvette (Essonne), France), *b* 1946: *m* 1975, Monique Vanwelsenaere, and has issue living, Jean Sebastien *b* 1979, — Catherine Marie Charlotte, *b* 1945: *m* 1972, Vicomte Jean-Marie de Bourgoing, of 54 Boulevard de la Tour-Maubourg, Paris VII, and has issue living, Guillaume Pierre Denis *b* 1976, Philippe Marie François *b* 1978, Marguerite Roseline Romola *b* 1975. *Residence* – Alloa, Bargemon, Var 83, France.
—— Margaret Elsie Viola, *b* 1913: *m* 1950, Major Denys Ernest Glynn Oglander, who *d* 1977, and has had issue, William Auberon Erskine, *b* 1953, — John Peter Erskine (West Lodge, Nunwell, Brading, IoW), *b* 1957: *m* 1987 (*m diss* 1988), Fiona Stuart, da of Ronald Stuart Brisbane, of 105 Down St, Belgrave, Leicester, and has issue living, Susanna Anastasia *b* 1987, — Frances Mary Viola Oglander, *b* 1951: *m* 1977, Michael Solosy, of Hardingshute Farm, Ryde, IoW, and has issue living, Robert John Solosy Oglander *b* 1981, — Mary Theresa Catherine Joan, *b* 1955: *m* 1981, Josef Hubbard, and *d* 1982. *Residence* – Nunwell Park, Brading, Isle of Wight.

Issue of late Rev Hon Alexander Penrose Forbes Erskine, 3rd son of 11th Earl, *b* 1881, *d* 1925: *m* 1916, Irene Annette who *d* 1968, having *m* 2ndly, 1930, Rt Rev Frederic Llewellyn Deane (Bishop of Aberdeen and Orkney 1917-43), who *d* 1952, da of late Rt Rev Archibald Ean Campbell, Bishop of Glasgow and Galloway (E Midleton):—
Archibald Walter Forbes, *b* 1918; *ed* Eton, and New Coll, Oxford (BM and BCh 1942, MA 1946): *m* 1958, J. M. Thérèse, el da of late John Benedict Heppel, of Bromley, Kent, and has issue living, James Alexander, *b* 1959; MB BS, DA, DTM & H: *m* 1993, Debbie de Lacy-Leacey, — Robert John (41 Park Lane, Sutton Bonington, Leics LE12 5NQ), *b* 1960; MB BS, FRCA: *m* 1990, Dr Gillian Margaret Turner, da of Charles Thomas Turner, and has issue living, Lucy Emmeline *b* 1994, — Benjamin David, *b* 1971. *Residence* – 130 Walm Lane, NW2. —— David Alexander John, TD, *b* 1921; *ed* Eton, and New Coll, Oxford (MA); formerly Capt 5th Bn Queen's Own Cameron Highlanders (TA); 1939-45 War: *m* 1st, 1947 (*m diss* 19—), Margaret Eleanor, da of late Rear-Adm Steuart Arnold Pears, CBE; 2ndly, 1970, Mrs Joan Mary Gilmour, da of Brig James Brindley Bettington, DSO, MC, and has issue living, (by 1st *m*) Robin David (East Deanraw, Langley-on-Tyne, Hexham, Northumberland NE47 5LY), *b* 1948; *ed* Eton: *m* 1985, Belinda Ann, formerly wife of David W. Pulford, and 2nd da of Thomas Aydon Bates, of Langley, Northumberland (*see* Musgrave, Bt, *cr* 1782), and has issue living, Caspar James Pears *b* 1986, Imogen Felicia Anne *b* 1989, — Peter Alexander (Packwood Haugh, Ruyton-XI-Towns, Shrewsbury), *b* 1950: *m* 1976, Charlotte, twin da of late Wing-Cdr Sir (Eric) John Hodsoll, CB, and has issue living, Andrew John Hodsoll *b* 1985, Emily Clare *b* 1978, Harriet Alice *b* 1981, — Alistair John (58 Ravenslea Rd, SW12), *b* 1959: *m* 1987, Fiona Sue Awdry, eldest da of Maurice Lovett-Turner, of Windlesham, Surrey, and has issue living, Oliver Stewart *b* 1989, Edmund Alexander *b* 1993. *Residence* – Les Loriers, Rue Beau Repaire, St Peter Port, Guernsey.

Granddaughter of late Augustus Erskine, el son of late Hon James Augustus Erskine (infra):—
Issue of late Capt Bushby Lyons Erskine, *b* 1890, *d* 1919, Lilian, da of Francis William Blenkey, of Beckenham:—
Sheelah Kathleen Erskine, *b* 1921; resumed surname of Erskine 19—: *m* 19—, — Tortonese.

Grandchildren of late Hon James Augustus Erskine, brother of 12th Earl of Kellie:—
Issue of late Evelyn Pierrepont Erskine, *b* 1870, *d* 1953: *m* 1897, Amy Maria, who *d* 1959, da of Joseph Hough, grazier, of Collie River, W Australia:—
Charles Seymour (21 Bellevue Terr, Swanbourne, W Australia 6010), *b* 1905: *m* 1928, Mona Roslynn, da of Henry Murphy, of co Cork. —— Gratney Pierrepont (12 Devon Rd, Swanbourne, W Australia 6010), *b* 1911; 1939-45 War with AIF: *m* 1st, 1931 (*m diss* 1935), Elsie Evelyn, da of late I. Nutall, of W Australia; 2ndly, 1940, Beth Rosemary Kenworthy, and has issue living (by 1st *m*), Yvonne Constance (23 Catesby St, City Beach, W Australia PC 6015), *b* 1932, — (by 2nd *m*) Gratney Evelyn (20 Knight St, Wembley Downs, W Australia), *b* 1941: *m* 1967, Elaine Joy Marchant, of Claremont, W Australia, and has issue living, Gregory Bryce *b* 1972, Janine Gaye *b* 1969. —— Maime Rhoda Wilhelmina (6 Tasman St, Albany, W Australia 6330): *b* 1898: *m* 1926, Lawrence Ridley Field, who *d* 1971, and has issue living, Spencer Erskine, *b* 1927; *m* 1956, Coral, da of F. White, of Albany, W Australia, and has issue living, Murray *b* 1958, Susan *b* 1957, Kay *b* 1961, — Barrie Ridley (5 Crocker Way 6018, Innaloo, W Australia), *b* 1930: *m* 1956, Gwen Murphy, of Victoria Park, W Australia, and has issue living, Stephen *b* 1955, Clinton *b* 1958, Bradley *b* 1959, Marilyn *b* 1954, — Robin Erskine (155 Hare St, Albany, W Australia), *b* 1938: *m* 1960, Lorraine Whitfield, of Albany, W Australia, and has issue living, Alan *b* 1966, Yvonne *b* 1963, Beverly *b* 1965, — Naomi Laurel Erskine, *b* 1928: *m* 1949, John O'Keefe, of 4 Tasman St, Albany, W Australia, and has issue living, Neil *b* 1959, Carol *b* 1950: *m* 19—, Gary Thomas Adams, of Albany, W Australia (and has issue living, Tracy Lana *b* 1966: *m* 1983, Trevor White, of Albany, W Australia, and has issue living, Ryan Trevor *b* 1983, Jade *b* 1986, Michelle Lisa *b* 1968: *m* 1989, Larry Hill, of Osborne Park, WA, and has issue living, Jacinta Bree *b* 1985), Linda *b* 1952: *m* 1st, 1970, Kevin Albert Wallinger, of North Rd, Albany, W Australia; 2ndly, 1984, Wayne Alexander Halliday (and has issue living, Hayley *b* 1972, Brent *b* 1976, Cher Odette *b* 1986), Diane *b* 1954: *m* 1971, Lindsay Horton, of Tasman St, Albany, W Australia, (and has issue living, Wade *b* 1972, Chad *b* 1976), — Derrice, *b* 1933: *m* 1953, John Joseph Jones, of Parkerville, W Australia, and has issue living, Laurence John *b* 1955: *m* 1988 Nadine Alger, Mark *b* 1957, Matthew *b* 1961, Rachel *b* 1963: *m* 1988, Clement Foley.
Issue of late Hugh Bushby Johnson (who assumed by Deed Poll 1952 that surname in lieu of his patronymic for himself only), *b* 1872, *d* 1956: *m* 1897, May, who *d* 1950, da of John Valentine, of Bunbury, W Australia:—
John William Erskine, *b* 1899: *m* 19—, and has issue living, Hugh Walter Bushby, *b* 19—: *m* 19—, — Doris Gwen Crundwell, and has issue living, Christine Maria *b* 1946. —— Esmé Mai Lydia, *b* 1910: *m* 1935, Claude Wentworth Jefferson, late Flt-Lt RAAF, who *d* 1974, and has issue living, Ian David (1/3 Werambri St, Woolwich Sydney, NSW 2110, Australia), *b* 1945: *m* 1968, Kay Leslie, da of John Farren Price, of Sydney, NSW, and has issue living, Kalena Ann *b* 1971, Fiona *b* 1975. *Residence* – 1 Budgree St, Norah Head, NSW 2263, Australia.

Grandchildren of late Hugh Bushby Johnson (ante)
Issue of late Kellie Edmund Erskine, *b* 1902, *d* 1988: *m* 1924, Annie, who *d* 1975, da of Robert Knox:—
Kellie Knox (4 Palermo Place, Allambie Heights, NSW 2100, Australia), *b* 1931: *m* 1959, Pamela Ann, da of late Alfred Edward Leer, and has issue living, Bryan Andrew, *b* 1966, — Robyn Ann, *b* 1963, — Keryn Maree, *b* 1971.
Issue of James Keith Brodie Erskine *b* 1907, *d* 1981: *m* 1949, Mary Douglas (Cobham Av, W Ryde, NSW, Australia), da of Arthur Ernest Savage, of Woolwich, NSW, Australia:—
Lynette Mary, *b* 1950: *m* 1978, Patrick Philip Duncan, son of Patrick Duncan, of Wellington, NZ, and has issue living, Guy Philip, *b* 1980, — Stacey Mary, *b* 1982. —— Catherine Evelyn, *b* 1953. —— Joanne Margaret, *b* 1960.

PREDECESSORS – (1) Sir Robert Erskine of Alloa and Dun by his 2nd wife, Janet, da and heir of Sir Edward Keith, of Synton, and widow of Sir David Barclay, of Brechin, a Commr to treat for the release of James I 1421, and one of the hostages for his ransom 1424, sat as *Lord Erskine* in Scottish Parliament 1426; served heir of Isabel, Countess of Mar 1438; *s* by his son (2) Thomas, 2nd Lord; dispossessed of the Earldom at an Assize of Error 1457; sat in Parliament as Lord Erskine 1467: *m* Janet Douglas; *d* 1493; *s* by his son (3) Alexander, 3rd Lord; guardian of James IV; *d* 1510; *s* by his son (4) Robert, 4th Lord; killed at Flodden 1513; *s* by his son (5) John, 5th Lord, guardian of James V; Ambassador to France 1515 to 1535, and an Extraordinary Lord of Session, &c; *d* 1555; *s* by his son (6) John, PC, 6th Lord; was Regent of Scotland 1571, and guardian of James VI, &c; Mary Queen of Scots restored to him the *Earldom of Mar* by charter 1565, though, according to the decision of the Committee of Privileges of the House of Lords in 1875, a new Earldom was created with remainder to heirs male; *d* 1572; *s* by his son (7) John, KG, PC, 2nd Earl; High Treasurer of Scotland 1615-30; attainted 1584, and restored 1585; Ambassador to England 1603; *cr Lord Cardross* (peerage of Scotland) 1610, with the right to assign the Lordship to whomsoever he might elect, which right was confirmed by charter in favour of his 2nd son Henry 1618; *d* 1634; *s* in Lordship of Cardross by his grandson David (*see* E Buchan), and in Earldom by his son (8) John, PC, KB, 3rd

Earl; an Extraordinary Lord of Session 1620-6 and 1628-30, &c; *d* 1654; *s* by his son **(9)** JOHN, 4th Earl; *d* 1668; *s* by his son **(10)** CHARLES, PC, 5th Earl; was Col Roy Scots Fusiliers 1679-86, which regt he raised; *d* 1689; *s* by his son **(11)** JOHN, KT, PC, 6th Earl; Sec of State 1706, Keeper of the Signet, and a Representative Peer 1707-13; was attainted by Act of Parliament for having raised the insurrection of 1715; his forfeited estates were purchased by his brother Lord Grange (a Lord of Session) and David Erskine, of Dun, and the Alloa property was entailed on the heirs male of his da Lady Frances Erskine, wife of James Erskine, Lord Grange's son; *d* 1732; *s* by his grandson **(12)** JOHN FRANCIS, 7th Earl, who in 1824 was restored to the Earldom by Act of Parliament (but the Lordship of Erskine remains forfeit) as grandson and lineal representative of the attainted Earl; *d* 1825; *s* by his son **(13)** JOHN THOMAS, 8th Earl; *d* 1828; *s* by his son **(14)** JOHN FRANCIS MILLER, 9th Earl, as an officer in the Guards served at Waterloo; in 1835 successfully claimed to be 11th *Earl of Kellie* see * (infra); *dsp* 1866; *s* in Earldom of Kellie, the Viscountcy of Fentoun, and Lordship of Erskine of Dirleton, and of Dirleton by his cousin **(15)** WALTER CONINGSBY, CB, 12th Earl of Kellie, Viscount Fentoun and Lord Erskine of Dirleton, 3rd son of Hon Henry David, 3rd son of 7th Earl of Mar; served in India with distinction, both as a military and a political officer; *d* 1872; *s* by his son **(16)** WALTER HENRY, 13th Earl of Kellie (who in 1875 successfully claimed to be 11th Earl of Mar; *b* 1839; was a Representative Peer for Scotland: *m* 1863, Mary Anne, who *d* 1927, da of the late Wiliam Forbes; *d* 1888; *s* by his el son **(17)** WALTER JOHN FRANCIS, KT, 12th Earl of Mar, and 14th Earl of Kellie; *b* 1865; was Lord-Lieut of Clackmannanshire 1898-1955; appointed Hereditary Keeper of Stirling Castle (with remainder to heirs male) 1923; Lord Clerk Register and Keeper of Signet of Scotland 1936-44, and Chancellor of Order of the Thistle 1933-49: *m* 1892, Lady Susan Violet Ashley, who *d* 1938, da of 8th Earl of Shaftesbury; *d* 1955; *s* by his grandson **(18)** JOHN FRANCIS HERVEY (el son of late John Francis Ashley, Lord Erskine, GCSI, GCIE, el son of 12th Earl), 13th Earl of Mar, and 15th Earl of Kellie; *b* 1921; Maj Scots Gds and Argyll and Sutherland Highlanders (TA), 1939-45 War (despatches), a Representative Peer for Scotland, Lord Lieut and Vice Convenor Clackmannanshire, and an Elder of Church of Scotland: *m* 1948, Pansy Constance, OBE, da of late Gen Sir (Augustus Francis) Andrew Nicol Thorne, KCB, CMG, DSO (*see* B Penrhyn, 1967 Edn); *d* 1993; *s* by his eldest son **(19)** JAMES THORNE, 14th Earl of Mar, and 16th Earl of Kellie, and present peer; also Viscount Fentoun, Lord Erskine of Dirleton, and Lord Dirleton.

***(1)** Sir* THOMAS ERSKINE, KG, 4th Earl of Hon Sir Alexander, 4th son of 5th Lord Erskine; *cr Lord Erskine of Dirleton* (peerage of Scotland) 1604, *Viscount Fentoun* and *Lord Dirleton* (peerage of Scotland) 1606, with remainder to his heirs male whatsoever, and *Earl of Kellie* (peerage of Scotland) 1619, with remainder to his heirs male whatsoever bearing the name of Erskine; *d* 1639; *s* by his grandson **(2)** THOMAS (son of Alexander, Viscount Fentoun), 2nd Earl; *d* unmarried 1643; *s* by his brother **(3)** ALEXANDER, 3rd Earl, whose line failed on the death of **(4-7)** ALEXANDER, 7th Earl; *d* 1797; *s* by his kinsman **(8)** *Sir* CHARLES Erskin, 8th Earl, descendant of Hon Charles, 3rd son of 1st Earl, who in 1666 and been *cr* a *Baronet*; *d* unmarried 1799; *s* by his grandson **(9)** THOMAS, 9th Earl: *m* 1771, Anne, who *d* 1829, da of Adam Gordon, of Ardoch, *d* 1828; *s* by his brother **(10)** METHVEN, 10th Earl: *m* 1781, Joanna, da of Adam Gordon (ante); *d* 1829; *s* by his kinsman **(11)** JOHN FRANCIS MILLER, 11th Earl, who had previously *s* as 9th Earl of Mar (see ante).

March and Kinrara, Earl of (peerage of England); son of Duke of Richmond.

March, Earl of (peerage of Scotland), see Earl of Wemyss and March.

MARCHAMLEY, BARON (Whiteley) (Baron UK 1908)

JOHN WILLIAM TATTERSALL WHITELEY, 3rd Baron; *b* 22 April 1922; *s* 1949; European War 1939-45 as Lieut Roy Armoured Corps, attached Indian Army: *m* 1967, Sonia Kathleen Pedrick, and has issue.

Arms – Per fesse dancettèe sable and gules, in chief a pale or, theron three bars of the second, in base a fleur-de-lis argent. **Crest** – A stag's head couped argent, attired or, holding in the mouth a bell gold. **Supporters** – *Dexter*, a griffin sejant: *sinister*, a hawk; both per fesse gules and sable, armed and membered or, each charged on the fesse line with a fleur-de-lis argent. *Address* – c/o House of Lords, SW1A 0PW.

SON LIVING

Hon WILLIAM FRANCIS, *b* 27 July 1968.

SISTER LIVING

Hon Alice Tattersall, *b* 1917; sometime Junior Com ATS: *m* 1946, Lt-Col Robert Danby Bradford, who *d* 1986, and has issue living, Robert William Danby (8A Maunsel St, SW1P 2QL), *b* 1947; *ed* Fettes: *m* 1972 (*m diss* 1983), Dinah Jane, da of Thomas Gerald Porter, and has issue living, Lydia Jane *b* 1973, Antonia Sarah *b* 1975, Jessica Jennifer *b* 1978, — Andrew Mark Danby (20 Gurney St, Stonehaven, Kincardineshire AB3 2EB), *b* 1949; *ed* Fettes: *m* 1980, Janice, el da of A. E. Diverty, of 43 Barfield Rd, Buckie, Banffshire, and has issue living, Claire Alison *b* 1981, Sarah Gillian *b* 1983. *Residence* – Membland, Haddington, E Lothian, EH41 4JH.

WIDOW LIVING OF SON OF FIRST BARON

Marjorie Gordon (*Lady Dreyer*), da of Ernest Jukes, of Rickmansworth, Herts: *m* 1st, 1939, Maj Hon Ronald George Whiteley, OBE, who *d* 1957; 2ndly, 1959, Adm Sir Desmond Parry Dreyer, GCB, CBE, DSO (ret). *Residence* – Brook Cottage, Cheriton, Alresford, Hants SO24 0QA.

PREDECESSORS – **(1)** GEORGE Whiteley, PC, el son of late George Whiteley, JP, of Woodlands, Blackburn; *b* 1855; Parliamentary (Patronage) Sec to the Treasury and Ch Liberal Whip Dec 1905 to June 1908; MP for Stockport (*L*) Feb 1893 to Sept 1900, and for Pudsey Div of E Part of W Riding of Yorkshire Oct 1900 to June 1908; *cr Baron Marchamley*, of Hawkstone, co Salop (peerage of United Kingdom) 1908: *m* 1881, Alice, who *d* 1913, only child of late William Tattersall, JP, of

Quarry Bank, Blackburn, and St Anthony's Milnthorpe; *d* 1925: *s* by his (2) WILLIAM TATTERSALL, 2nd Baron; *b* 1886; High Sheriff, co Southampton 1921; European War 1915-18 as Lieut-Com RNVR, European War 1939-45 as Flight-Lieut RAF: *m* 1911, Margaret Clara, who *d* 1974, da of Thomas Scott Johnstone, formerly of Glenmark, Waipara, NZ; *d* 1949; *s* by his only son (3) JOHN WILLIAM TATTERSALL, 3rd Baron and present peer.

MARCHWOOD, VISCOUNT (Penny) (Viscount UK 1945, Bt UK 1933)

Always prepared

DAVID GEORGE STAVELEY PENNY, 3rd Viscount, and 3rd Baronet; *b* 22 May 1936; *s* 1979; *ed* Winchester; late 2nd Lieut RHG; Managing Dir of Moët & Chandon (London) Ltd and holds other directorships in Moët-Hennessy Group: *m* 1964, Tessa Jane, 2nd da of Wilfred Francis Norris, of Glebe Park, Lurgashall, nr Midhurst, Sussex, and has issue.

Arms – Gules, six fleurs-de-lis, three, two, and one or, on a chief engrailed of the second, three roses of the first, barbed and seeded proper. **Crest** – Issuant from a circlet or, a demi lion gules, collared sable, charged on the shoulder with a rose, and holding in the dexter paw a fleur-de-lis gold. **Supporters** – *Dexter*, a Malayan tiger proper; *sinister*, a sea lion proper.
Residence – The Filberts, Aston Tirrold, Didcot, Oxon. *Clubs* – White's, MCC.

SONS LIVING

Hon PETER GEORGE WORSLEY, *b* 8 Oct 1965.
Hon Nicholas Mark Staveley, *b* 1967.
Hon Edward James Frederick, *b* 1970.

BROTHER LIVING

Hon Patrick Glyn (33 Wellington Sq, SW3 4NR. *Club* – White's), *b* 1939; *ed* Nautical Coll, Pangbourne; Lieut R. Wilts Yeo 1962-65, late 2nd Lieut RHG: *m* 1st, 1968 (*m diss* 1974), Sue Eleanor Jane, da of late Charles Phipps Brutton, CBE; 2ndly, 1979, Lynn Vanessa Knox, da of John Leslie Wyles, of Wimbledon, and formerly wife of (i) Colin Hart, and (ii) John Birkett Knox, and has issue living (by 1st *m*), Sasha Jane, *b* 1969.

SISTER LIVING

Hon Carol Ann, *b* 1948: *m* 1978, Patrick John Quirk, of 9 Lambourn Rd, SW4 0LX, and has issue living, Tom Michael, *b* 1979, — Toby James, *b* 1983.

PREDECESSORS – (1) (FREDERICK) GEORGE PENNY, KCVO, 2nd son of late Frederick James Penny, of Sydney Cottage, Bitterne, Hants; *b* 1876; a Master Mariner, and Master of Master Mariners' Co 1941-5; Senior Partner of Fraser & Co, Government exchange brokers, of Singapore; was Parliamentary Private Sec to Financial Sec to War Office 1923-4, a Govt Whip 1926-8, a Junior Lord of the Treasury 1928-9 and (in National Govt) Sept to Nov 1931, Vice-Chamberlain of HM's Household 1931-2, Comptroller of HM's Household 1932-5, and Treasurer of HM's Household 1935-7; sat as MP for Kingston-upon-Thames (C) 1922-37; *cr* a *Baronet* 1933, *Baron Marchwood* of Penang and of Marchwood, co Southampton (peerage of United Kingdom) 1937, and *Viscount Marchwood*, of Penang and of Marchwood, co Southampton (peerage of United Kingdom) 1945: *m* 1905, Anne Boyle, who *d* 1957, da of late Sir John Gunn, *JP*, of St Mellons, Cardiff; *d* 1955; *s* by his only son (2) PETER GEORGE, MBE, 2nd Viscount, *b* 1912; Hon Maj RA 1939-45 War; Dir George Wimpey & Co, Contractors 1960-71: *m* 1935, Pamela, who *d* 1979, only child of John Staveley Colton-Fox, JP, of Todwick Grange, nr Sheffield; *d* 1979; *s* by his el son (3) DAVID GEORGE STAVELEY, 3rd Viscount and present peer; also Baron Marchwood.

MARGADALE, BARON (Morrison) (Baron UK 1964)

JOHN GRANVILLE MORRISON, TD, 1st Baron, son of late Hugh Morrison, of Fonthill House, Tisbury, Wilts (*see* E Granville, 1934 Edn); *b* 16 Dec 1906; *ed* Eton, and Magdalene Coll, Camb; KStJ; a JP of Wilts (High Sheriff 1938, DL 1950-69) and Argyll; Lord Lieut of Wilts 1969-81; a DL for Wilts since 1983; MP for Salisbury (*C*) 1942-64; Chm of 1922 Cttee 1945-55; Hon Col R Wilts Yeo 1960-72, and R Yeo 1965-72; Pres British Field Sports Soc since 1980; 1939-45 War with R Wilts Yeo in Middle East; *cr Baron Margadale*, of Islay, co Argyll (peerage of UK) 1964: *m* 1928, Hon Margaret Esther Lucie Smith, who *d* 1980, da of 2nd Viscount Hambleden, and has issue.

Arms – Tierced in pairle azure, sable and gules, in chief a Saracen's head couped affrontée and in base two Saracens' heads addorsed in profile all argent, and at the fess point an inescutcheon parted per pale dexter per bend sinister embattled gules and or, in dexter chief a battle axe paleways argent, and in sinister base, issuant from a base undy azure and argent, a tower sabre, masoned argent, port gules (*Morrison of Islay*) sinister, vert powdered with bezants, a horse rearing on its hind legs argent, langued and hoofed gules (*Lordship of Margadale*). **Crest** – Three Saracens' heads conjoined in one neck one looking to the dexter, one affrontée, and one looking to the sinister all proper. **Supporters** – Two Woodcocks proper.
Residences – Fonthill House, Tisbury, Wilts; Eallabus, Bridgend, Isle of Islay, Argyll. *Clubs* – Turf, White's Jockey.

SONS LIVING

Hon JAMES IAN, TD (Hawking Down, Hindon, Salisbury, Wilts), *b* 17 July 1930; *ed* Eton, and RAC Cirencester; Hon Col R Wilts Yeo 1982-89; formerly 2nd Lt Life Guards; a Co Councillor for Wilts 1955, and 1973-77, since when DL Wilts (Alderman 1969-74 and High Sheriff 1971); Chm of Westbury Conservative Assocn 1967-71, Pres 1972-84; Chm Tattersalls Cttee 1969-80: *m* 1952, Clare, da of Anthony Lister Barclay, of Broad Oak End, Hertford, and has issue living, Alastair John (The Quadrangle, Tisbury, Wilts), *b* 4 April 1958: *m* 1988, Lady Sophia Louise Sydney Murphy, yr da of 11th Duke of Devonshire, PC, and formerly wife of Gurth Murphy, and has issue living, Declan James *b* 11 July 1993, — Hugh, *b* 1960: *m* 1986, Jane, da of Bryan Jenks, of Le Schuylkill, Boulevard de Suisse, Monte Carlo, and has issue living, Geordie Anthony *b* 1989, Amber Belinda *b* 1993, — Fiona Elizabeth (*Viscountess Trenchard*), *b* 1954: *m* 1975, 3rd Viscount Trenchard.

Hon Sir Charles Andrew (Madresfield Court, Malvern, Worcs WR13 5AU), *b* 1932; *ed* Eton; Capt (ret) R Wilts Yeo; late 2nd Lt Life Guards; Chm Nat Cttee for Electoral Reform 1985-91; Chm Game Conservancy since 1987; MP for Devizes Div of Wilts (*C*) 1964-92; Knt 1988: *m* 1st, 1954 (*m diss* 1984), Hon (Antoinette) Sara Frances Sibell Long, da of 2nd Viscount Long; 2ndly, 1984, Mrs Rosalind Elizabeth Ward, da of late Hon Richard Edward Lygon (*see* E Beauchamp), and formerly wife of Gerald John Ward (*see* E Dudley, colls), and has issue living (by 1st *m*), David John (21 Albert Bridge Rd, SW11), *b* 1959: *m* 1984, Venetia Anne, 2nd da of Julian John William Salmond (*see* B Lucas of Crudwell, colls), and has issue living, Ivo Charles D. *b* 1990, Tara Sibyl Caolila *b* 1988, — Anabel Laura Dorothy, *b* 1955: *m* 1st, 1979, Michael Harry Stapleton; 2ndly, 1985, David William Arnold Loyd (*see* E Albemarle, colls), of 17 Larkhall Rise, SW4 6JB, and has issue living (by 1st *m*), Harry Edward John *b* 1982, Scarlett Margaret Laura *b* 1980 (by 2nd *m*) (*see* E Albemarle, colls).

Rt Hon Sir Peter Hugh, MP (81 Cambridge St, SW1V 4PS) *b* 1944: *ed* Eton, and Keble Coll, Oxford; Under Sec of State, Dept of Employment 1981-83; Min of State for Employment 1983-85, for Dept of Trade and Industry 1985-86, and for Dept of Energy 1987-90, PPS to Rt Hon Margaret Thatcher, Prime Minister, 1990, and Dep-Chm Conservative Party 1986-89; a Lord Commissioner of HM Treasury and Govt Whip 1979-81 (oppn Whip 1976-79); MP for Chester (*C*) since 1974; *cr* PC 1988, Knt 1990.

DAUGHTER LIVING

Hon Mary Anne, DCVO, *b* 1937: *ed* Heathfield Sch, Ascot; a Woman of the Bedchamber to HM since 1960; DCVO 1982. *Residences* – Fonthill House, Tisbury, Wilts; Eallabus, Bridgend, Islay, Argyll.

MARGESSON, VISCOUNT (Margesson) (Viscount UK 1942)

LOYAUTÉ ME LIE

Loyalty binds me

FRANCIS VERE HAMPDEN MARGESSON, 2nd Viscount; *b* 17 April 1922; *s* 1965; *ed* Eton and Trin Coll, Oxford; Information Officer, British Consulate-General, New York, 1964-70; 1939-45 War as Lt RNVR: *m* 1958, Helena, da of late Heikki Backstrom, of Oulu, Finland, and has issue.

Arms – Sable, a lion pasant guardant argent, a chief engrailed or, thereon between two pallets azure a pale of the last charged with an ostrich feather erect of the second. **Crest** – Upon a coronet composed of four roses set upon a rim or, a lion passant guardant sable, collared gold, and charged with a rose argent, barbed and seeded proper. **Supporters** – On either side a falcon, wings elevated argent, armed and belled or, and charged with a portcullis chained sable.
Residence – Ridgely Manor, Box 254, Stone Ridge, New York 12484, USA.

SON LIVING

Hon RICHARD FRANCIS DAVID, *b* 25 Dec 1960; Maj Coldm Gds: *m* 1990, Wendy Maree, da of James Hazelton, of Kempsey, NSW, Australia.

DAUGHTERS LIVING

Hon Rhoda France, *b* 1962.
Hon Sarah Helena, 1963.
Hon Jane Henrietta, *b* 1965.

SISTER LIVING (*Daughter of 1st Viscount*)

Hon (Mary) Gay Hobart (*Baroness Charteris of Amisfield*), *b* 1919: *m* 1944, Baron Charteris of Amisfield, GCB, GCVO, OBE, QSO, PC, of 11 Kylestrome House, Cundy St, SW1W 9JT, and Wood Stanway, Cheltenham, Glos GL54 5PG.

PREDECESSOR – (1) HENRY DAVID REGINALD Margesson, MC, PC, el son of Sir Mortimer Reginald Margesson and Lady Isabel Augusta Hobart-Hampden, sister of 7th Earl of Buckinghamshire; *b* 1890; Ch Govt Whip 1931-40, and Sec of State for War 1940-42; MP for Upton Div, W Ham (*C*) 1922-23, and for Rugby 1924-42; *cr Viscount Margesson*, of Rugby, co Warwick (peerage of UK) 1942: *m* 1916 (*m diss* 1940), Frances, who *d* 1977, da of Francis H Leggett, of New York, *d* 1965; *s* by his only son (2) FRANCIS VERE HAMPDEN, 2nd Viscount and present peer.

MARKS OF BROUGHTON, BARON (Marks) (Baron UK 1961)

STRIVE APPLY PROBE

MICHAEL MARKS, 2nd Baron, *b* 27 Aug 1920; *s* 1964; *ed* St Paul's and Corpus Christi Coll, Camb: *m* 1st, 1949 (*m diss* 1958), Ann Catherine, da of Maj Richard James Pinto, MC; 2ndly, 1960 (*m diss* 1965), Helene, da of Gustave Fischer; 3rdly, 1976 (*m diss* 1985), Toshiko Shimura, of Japan and has issue by 1st *m*.

Arms – Pily argent and azure a pair of scales or. **Crest** – A dove wings addorsed argent, beaked and membered gules, gorged with an antique crown, and to the beak a gimmel ring. **Supporters** – On either side a lion or supporting a cornucopia argent the fruit proper, that on the dexter holding aloft with the interior forepaw a red rose slipped and leaved also proper, and that on the sinister two interlaced triangles or.
Residence – Michael House, Baker St, W1A 1DN.

SON LIVING (By 1st marriage)

Hon SIMON RICHARD, *b* 3 May 1950; *ed* Eton, and Balliol Coll, Oxford: *m* 1982, Marion, only da of Peter F. Norton, of the Azores, and has issue living, Michael, *b* 13 May 1989, — Miriam Ann, *b* 1983, — Susannah Elizabeth, *b* 1986.

DAUGHTERS LIVING (By 1st marriage)

Hon Naomi Anne, *b* 1952: *m* 1980, Martin Christian Wölffer, and has issue living, Joanna Claire, *b* 1982, — Georgina Chloe, *b* 1985.
Hon Sarah Elizabeth, *b* 1953: *m* 1979 (*m diss* 1989), Nicholai Radomir, and has issue living, Michael Richard, *b* 1981, — Leo Mark, *b* 1985.

SISTER LIVING

Hon Hannah Olive, *b* 1918: *m* 1st, 1941 (*m diss* 1959), Alec Lerner; 2ndly, 1960, Gerald William Harold Marcow, who *d* 1992, and has issue living (by 1st *m*), Joel David, *b* 1942: *m* 1982, Deborah, da of C. Travers of Woking, — Diana Toby, *b* 1947, — Maureen Ann, *b* 1952: *m* 1983, Terence A. Willson, of 78 Waterford Rd, SW6, stepson of Edward Helliwell. *Residence* – Le Rowcabella, 24 Avenue Princesse Grace, Monte Carlo, 28000 Monaco.

PREDECESSORS – (1) *Sir* SIMON Marks, son of Michael Marks, of Manchester; *b* 1888; Chm and joint Managing Dir of Marks & Spencer Ltd; *cr Baron Marks of Broughton*, of Sunningdale, co Berks (peerage of UK) 1961: *m* 1915, Miriam, who *d* 1971, da of Ephraim Sieff; *d* 1964; *s* by his only son (2) MICHAEL, 2nd Baron and present peer.

MARLBOROUGH, DUKE OF (Spencer-Churchill) (Duke England 1702)
(Name pronounced "Maulbro")

Faithful, though unfortunate

FIEL · PERO · DESDICHADO

JOHN GEORGE VANDERBILT HENRY SPENCER-CHURCHILL, 11th Duke, *b* 13 April 1926; *s* 1972; *ed* Eton; late Capt Life Gds; JP and DL of Oxon: *m* 1st, 1951 (*m diss* 1960), Susan Mary, only da of late Michael Charles St John Hornby (*see* E Dudley, colls, 1985 Edn); 2ndly, 1961 (*m diss* 1971), Athina (Tina), who *d* 1974, da of late Stavros G. Livanos, and formerly wife of late Aristotle Onassis: 3rdly, 1972, (Dagmar) Rosita (Astri Libertas), da of late Count Carl Ludwig Douglas, and has issue by 1st and 3rd *m*.

Arms – Quarterly: 1st and 4th sable, a lion rampant argent; on a canton of the second a cross gules, *Churchill*; 2nd and 3rd quarterly argent and gules; on a bend sable, between two frettes or, three escallops of the first, *Spencer*, over all (as an honourable augmentation), in the centre chief point, on an escutcheon argent, the cross of St George surmounted by another escutcheon azure, charged with three fleurs-de-lis, two and one or. **Crest** – 1st, a lion couchant and guardant argent, supporting a banner gules, charged with a dexter hand couped argent, *Churchill*; 2nd, out of a ducal coronet or, a griffin's head, gorged with a collar gemelle gules, between two wings expanded, argent, *Spencer*. **Supporters** – Two wyverns, wings elevated, gules.
Seat – Blenheim Palace, Woodstock, Oxon. *Residence* – Lee Place, Charlbury, Oxon.

SONS LIVING *(By 1st marriage)*

(CHARLES) JAMES (*Marquess of Blandford*), *b* 24 Nov 1955; *ed* Harrow: *m* 1990, Rebecca Mary, da of Peter Few Brown, and of Mrs John Winnington-Ingram, and has issue:—
SON LIVING- George (*Earl of Sunderland*), *b* 28 July 1992.

(By 3rd marriage)

Lord Edward Albert Charles, *b* 1974.

DAUGHTERS LIVING *(By 1st marriage)*

Lady Henrietta Mary, *b* 1958: *m* 1980 (*m diss* 1989), Nathan Gelber, son of Aba Gelber, and has issue living, David Aba, *b* 1981, — Maximilian Henry, *b* 1985. *Residence* – 60 Radnor Walk, SW3.

(By 3rd marriage)

Lady Alexandra Elizabeth Mary, *b* 1977.

BROTHER LIVING

Lord Charles George William Colin, *b* 1940; *ed* Eton: *m* 1st, 1965 (*m diss* 1968), Gillian, da of Andrew Fuller, of New York City, and Fort Worth, Texas, USA; 2ndly, 1970, Elizabeth Jane, el da of Capt Hon Mark Hugh Wyndham, MC (*see* B Egremont), and has issue living (by 2nd *m*), Rupert John Harold Mark, *b* 1971, — Dominic Albert Charles, *b* 1979, — Alexander David, *b* 1983.

SISTERS LIVING

Lady Sarah Consuelo (9454 Lloyd Crest Drive, Beverly Hills, Los Angeles, California 90210, USA), *b* 1921: *m* 1st, 1943 (*m diss* 1966), Lt Edwin F. Russell, USA Navy; 2ndly, 1966 (*m diss* in Mexico 1967), Guy Burgos, of Santiago, Chile; 3rdly, 1967 (at Philadelphia), Theodorous Roubanis, and has issue living (by 1st *m*), Serena Mary Churchill, *b* 1944: *m* 1st, 1966 (*m diss* in Mexico 1967), R. Stephen Salant; 2ndly, 1968, Neil A. McConnell; 3rdly, 1978, Neil Roxburgh Balfour, of 55 Warwick Sq, SW1V 2AJ, and has issue living (by 2nd *m*), Morgan Alexandra *b* 1973, Lucinda Mary *b* 1975, (by 3rd *m*) Alastair Albert David *b* 1981, Consuelo Lily *b* 1979, — Consuelo Sarah, *b* 1946: *m* 1st, 1968 (*m diss* in Mexico 1969), James Toback; 2ndly 1970, Mark Schulman, of New York City, USA; 3rdly, 19—, B. William Judson, and has issue living (by 3rd *m*), Nicholas *b* 1976, Ian *b* 1978, — Alexandra Brenda, *b* 1949: *m* 1970, Timothy Biech, of Camp Hill, Penn, USA, — Jacqueline, *b* 1958: *m* 19—, Eugene Williams.
Lady Rosemary Mildred, *b* 1929: *m* 1953, Charles Robert Muir, who *d* 1972, and has issue living, Alexander Pepys, *b* 1954, — Simon Huntly (Angel Farm, Monks Alley, Binfield, Berks), *b* 1959: *m* 1990, Sarah-Jane E., only da of Barry Jenkinson, of Chetton Grange, Bridgnorth, Shropshire, and has issue living, Robin Hugo *b* 1993, — Mary Arabella, *b* 1962: *m* 1991, J. Timothy Haynes, of 29 Henning St, SW11 3DR, son of late J. H. Haynes, of Fuente del Rempujo, San Enrique de Guadiaro, Spain, and has issue living, Jack Cresswell *b* 1993. *Residence* – Orange Hill House, Binfield, Bracknell, Berks.

WIDOW LIVING OF SON OF NINTH DUKE

Betty, da of late J. C. Cunningham, of 27 Culross Street, W1: *m* 1947, Lord Ivor Charles Spencer-Churchill, who *d* 1956, and has issue living (see colls infra).

COLLATERAL BRANCHES LIVING

Issue of late Lord Ivor Charles Spencer-Churchill, yr son of 9th Duke, *b* 1898, *d* 1956: *m* 1947, Betty (ante), da of late J. C. Cunningham, of 27 Culross Street, W1:—
Robert William Charles, *b* 1954; *ed* Eton: *m* 1979, Jeanne M., el da of Etienne Maze, of 47 Victoria Rd, W8 (son of late Paul Maze, DCM, the painter), and has issue living, John Robert I—, *b* 1984, — Ivor Charles E—, *b* 1986.

Grandchildren of late Rt Hon Sir Winston Leonard Spencer-Churchill, KG, OM, CH, TD, FRS (infra):—

Issue of late Hon Randolph Frederick Edward Spencer-Churchill, MBE, b 1911, d 1968: m 1st, 1939 (m diss 1946), Hon Pamela Digby, da of 11th Baron Digby; 2ndly, 1948 (m diss 1961), June Hermione, who d 1980, da of Col Rex Hamilton Osborne, DSO:—
(By 1st m) Winston, MP (House of Commons, Westminster, SW1A 0AA), b 1940; ed Eton, and Ch Ch, Oxford; journalist and writer; MP for Stretford (C) 1970-83, since when MP for Manchester Davyhulme (C); Member of Executive 1922 Cttee 1979-88, Member of Select Cttee on Defence since 1983; Conservative Party Defence Spokesman 1976-78 and 1982-84: m 1964, Mary Caroline, da of late John Regis d'Erlanger, CBE, and has issue living, Randolph Leonard, b 1965; Lieut RN (ret): m 1992, Catherine Z., elder da of Antony Lancaster, of Kensington, — John Gerard Averell, b 1975, — Jennie, b 1966: m 1993, James P. Repard, yr son of Hugo Repard, of Westerton, Sussex, — Marina, b 1967. ———— (By 2nd m) Arabella (2 St Edmund's Cottages, Bove Town, Glastonbury, Somerset), b 1949; Dir The Children's World Charity; Gov Avalon Special Sch: m 1st, 1972, James J. Barton; 2ndly, 1988, Ian McLeod (juggler, as Haggis McLeod), son of late Harold Leonard Hodges, and has issue living (by 1st m), Jake Nicholas, b 1973, — (by 2nd m) Jessica Jules, b 1988.

Grandchildren of late Rt Hon Lord Randolph Henry Spencer-Churchill, MP, 3rd son of 7th Duke:—
Issue of late Rt Hon Sir Winston Leonard Spencer-Churchill, KG, OM, CH, TD, Prime Minister 1940-45 and 1951-55, b 1874, d 1965: m 1908, Dame Clementine Ogilvy, GBE (Baroness Spencer-Churchill), who d 1977 (cr a Life Baroness 1965), da of late Col Sir Henry Montagu Hozier, KCB (see E Airlie, 1925 Edn):—
Hon Mary, DBE (Baroness Soames), b 1922; formerly Junior Cdr ATS; author; Hon Fell Churchill Coll, Camb; a Gov of Harrow Sch; Chm Royal Nat Theatre Board since 1989; Chm Winston Churchill Memorial Trust since 1991; MBE (Mil) 1945, DBE (Civil) 1980: m 1947, Baron Soames, GCMG, GCVO, CH, CBE, PC, Life Baron, who d 1987.
Issue of late Major John Strange Spencer-Churchill, DSO, b 1880, d 1947: m 1908, Lady Gwendeline Theresa Mary Bertie, who d 1941, da of 7th Earl of Abingdon:—
Henry Winston (Peregrine), b 1913; ed Harrow, and Camb Univ (BA 1934); is a CE: m 1st, 1954, Patricia Ethel Louisa, who d 1956, da of late Thomas March; 2ndly, 1957, Yvonne Henriette Marie, da of Constant Jéhannin, of Rennes, France. Residence – Fairdown, Vernham Dean, Hants. ———— Clarissa (Countess of Avon), b 1920: m 1952, as his 2nd wife, 1st Earl of Avon, who d 1977. Residence – 32 Bryanston Square, W1H 7LS.

Granddaughter of late Maj John Strange Spencer-Churchill, DSO (ante):—
Issue of late John George Spencer-Churchill, painter, sculptor and composer, b 1909, d 1992: m 1st, 1934 (m diss 1938), Angela Mary, da of late Capt George Culme-Seymour (see Culme-Seymour, Bt, colls); 2ndly, 1941 (m diss 1952), Mary, only da of late Kenneth Cookson, OBE, of Wynberg, CP, S Africa (see Butler, Bt, cr 1628, colls, 1980 Edn); 3rdly, 1953, Mrs Kathlyn Maude Muriel Hall Tandy, who d 1957, only da of late Maj-Gen Walter Samuel Hall Beddall, CB, OBE; 4thly, 1958 (m diss 1972), Anna Gunvor Maria (Lullan), da of Johan Janson, of Kristianstad, Sweden, and widow of Granger Boston:—
(By 1st m) Sarah Cornelia (Baroness Ashburton), b 1935: m 1st, 1957, James Colin Crewe (see M Crewe, 1948 Edn); 2ndly, 1987, 7th Baron Ashburton, KG, KCVO, and has issue living (by 1st m), Peregrine John, b 1959, — Emma, b 1962: m 1993, Nicholas G. S. Vester, — Annabel Sophia, b 1965. Residence – Lake House, Northington, Alresford, Hants.

Descendants of late Lord Francis Almeric Spencer (3rd son of 4th Duke) who was cr Baron Churchill 1815 (see V Churchill).
Grandchildren of late Sir Charles Gordon Spencer, 4th son of late Rev Charles Vere Spencer (infra):—
Issue of late John Gray Churchill SPENCER BERNARD, MA, MD, FRCS (who assumed the additional name of Bernard by deed poll 1955), b 1907, d 1977: m 1933, Elsie Phyllis, MA (Nether Winchendon House, Aylesbury, Bucks), da of Ferrand Corley, of The Christian Coll, Madras, and of Woodside, Witney:—
Charles Francis Churchill (18 rue Barbette, 75003 Paris, France), b 1942; ed Marlborough, and Magdalene Coll, Camb: m 1974, Rosalyn Anne, da of Maj Patrick Plunkett, of Hazelbury Plucknett, Som (see Wheler, Bt, 1985 Edn), and has issue living, Jane Beatrice, b 1979, — Sarah Penelope Katharine, b 1983, — Elizabeth Joanna b 1986. ———— Robert Vere (Nether Winchendon House, Aylesbury, Bucks HP18 0DY), b 1944; ed Marlborough and Trin Coll, Oxford; Bar Inner Temple 1969: m 1975, Katharine Margaret, da of Lt-Col Claud Everard Montagu Douglas Scott, MC (see D Buccleuch and Queensberry, colls). ———— Julia Diana, b 1936: m 1959, John Simon Baskerville Cadwallader Hopton, of Village Farm House, Boarstall, Aylesbury, Bucks, and has issue living, Richard Henry Cadwallader, b 1962, — Edward Charles Adams, b 1964, — Isobel Georgiana, b 1967. ———— Clare Rosemary, b 1938: m 1963, Rio Tyrell Arthur Hohler, of Chevreloup, 27 Route de Perdreauville, 78950 Gambais, France, elder son of Henry Arthur Frederick Hohler, CMG, and has issue living, Rupert John Frederick, b 1972, — Harriet Valentine, b 1967, — Camilla Clare, b 1968, — Amanda Sophie, b 1970.
Issue of late Charles Bernard Spencer, b 1909, d 1963: m 1st, 1936, Nora, who d 1947, da of Frederick Gibbs; 2ndly, 1961, Anne Margaret Helen (who m 2ndly, 1969, Rock Noel Humphreys, of Bark Barn Cottage, 12 West Dean, Salisbury, Wilts), da of late Alan George Marjoribanks:—
(By 2nd m) Piers Bernard, b 1963. Residence – 36 Alma Sq, St John's Wood, NW8 9QD

Granddaughters of late Rev Charles Vere Spencer, son of Rev Frederick Spencer, son of late John Spencer, MP, el son of late Lord Charles Spencer, MP, 2nd son of 3rd Duke:—
Issue of late Rev Frederick Augustus Morland Spencer, DD, b 1878, d 1962: m 1913, Gertrude, Lucie, MA, who d 1970, el da of late George John Burke, MICE, of St Kilda Melbourne:—
Marion Gertrude (9 Sympson Close, Abingdon, Oxon), b 1916: m 1940 (m diss 1971), Kenneth Ninian Hoare, MBE, MA, and has issue living, Gillian Sheila, b 1947: m 1971, Richard James Kenneth Button, of PO Box 22344, Kitwe, Zambia, and has had issue, Daniel Mark b 1983 d 1987, Sarah Nicola b 1971, Teresa Jane b 1974, — Celia Jennifer, b 1952: m 1975, Capt Keith Reading, RN, of Hidcote, 10 Longdown Lane North, Ewell, Epsom, Surrey KT17 3JQ, and has issue living, Kyle Gareth b 1983, Katrina Louise b 1976. ———— Geraldine Mildred (Currony St, Canberra, ACT) b 1920; ed Sydney Univ, NSW (BA).

Descendants of late John Spencer, MP (son of late Hon John Spencer, MP, 3rd son of 3rd Earl of Sunderland), who was cr Earl Spencer 1765 (see that title).

PREDECESSORS – (1) Right Hon Sir JOHN CHURCHILL, KG, PC, el son of Sir Winston Churchill; b 1650; the most distinguished Gen of his time, was cr Lord Churchill, of Eyemouth, co Berwick (peerage of Scotland) 1682, Baron Churchill of Sandridge co Hertford (peerage of England) 1685, Earl of Marlborough (peerage of England) 1689, Marquess of Blandford and Duke of Marlborough (peerage of England) 1702, Prince of the Holy Roman Empire 1704 (and to all descendants male and female), and Prince of Mindelheim in Suabia 1705; was sometime Ambassador to France from James II, he assisted at the victory of Sedgmoor, and in the Convention Parliament voted in favour of the Prince and Princess of Orange filling the throne; commanded the English troops in the Netherlands 1689; having displeased William III, he was confined for a short time in the Tower; appointed upon the accession of Queen Anne, Capt-Gen of all HM's forces in England; in 1702-3 he reduced Venloo, Stevenswaert, Ruremonde, and Liége; in 1704 won the celebrated victory of Blenheim, and afterwards achieved other victories, notably Ramillies 1706, Oudenard 1708, and Malplaquet 1709; for his victories at and before Blenheim he was awarded by Act of Parliament the royal manor of Woodstock, and a splendid palace was erected by HM's orders; in 1706 an Act was passed settling his honours on his posterity and granting him and each successor in the title a pension of £5,000 a year: m 1678, Sarah, who d 1744, da and co-heiress of Richard Jennings, of Sandridge, Herts; he had surviving issue Henrietta, wife of Francis, 2nd Earl of Godolphin, and Anne, 2nd wife of Charles Spencer, KG, 3rd Earl of Sunderland (see infra); d 1722, when the Scottish Barony of Churchill of Eyemouth became ext; s in his other under the special Act of Parliament by his da (2) HENRIETTA (ante); d without surviving male issue 1733; s by her nephew (3) CHARLES,

KG, 3rd Duke, 2nd son of Anne (ante), who had in 1729 *s* his brother as 5th *Earl of Sunderland* (see*infra); was Lord-Lieut of cos Oxford and Buckingham, and a distinguished military commander; *d* 1758; *s* by his son **(4)** GEORGE, KG, 4th Duke; Lord Chamberlain of the Household 1762-3, and Lord Privy Seal 1763-5; *d* 1817; *s* by his son **(5)** GEORGE, 5th Duke; MP for Oxford 1790-96 and for Tregony 1802-6; assumed in 1817 by Roy licence the additional surname of Churchill; called to House of Lords in his father's barony of Spencer 1806; *d* 1840: *s* by his son **(6)** GEORGE, 6th Duke, *b* 1793; was Lord-Lieut of Oxfordshire; *d* 1857; *s* by his son **(7)** JOHN WINSTON, KG, DCL, 7th Duke; sat as MP for Woodstock (C) 1844-5 and 1847-57; was Lord-Lieut of co Oxford, Lord Pres of the Council 1868, and Viceroy of Ireland 1876-80: *m* 1843, Lady Frances Anne Emily Vane, da of 3rd Marquess of Londonderry; *d* 1883; *s* by his son **(8)** GEORGE CHARLES, 8th Duke, *b* 1844: *m* 1st, 1869 (*m diss* 1883), Lady Albertha Frances Anne Hamilton, who *d* 1932, da of 1st Duke of Abercorn, KG; 2ndly, 1888, Lillian Warren (who *m* 3rdly 1895, Lord William de la Poer Beresford, VC, KCIE, and *d* 1909), da of Cdr Cicero Price, of US Navy and widow of Louis Hammersley, of New York; *d* 1892, *s* by his only son **(9)** CHARLES RICHARD JOHN, KG, PC, 9th Duke, *b* 1871; Lord-Lieut of Oxfordshire; Paymaster-Gen 1899-1902; acted as Lord High Steward at Coronation of King Edward VII; Under-Sec of State for Colonies 1903-5, and John Parl Sec (unpaid) to Board of Agriculture 1917-18: *m* 1st, 1895 (*m diss* 1920), Consuelo, who *d* 1964, da of late William Kissam Vanderbilt, of New York; 2ndly, 1921, Gladys Marie, who *d* 1977, da of Edward Parker Deacon, of Boston, USA; *d* 1934; *s* by his el son **(10)** JOHN ALBERT EDWARD WILLIAM, 10th Duke, *b* 1897; Lt-Col Life Gds (Reserve); High Steward of Oxford 1937: *m* 1st, 1920, Hon Alexandra Mary Hilda Cadogan, CBE, JP, who *d* 1961, da of late Henry Arthur, Viscount Chelsea (E Cadogan); 2ndly, 1972, Frances Laura, who *d* 1990, da of late Capt Hon Guy Lawrence Charteris (E Wemyss and March, colls), formerly wife of (i) 2nd Viscount Long and (ii) 3rd Earl of Dudley, and widow of Michael Temple Canfield, *d* 1972; *s* by his el son **(11)** JOHN GEORGE VANDERBILT HENRY, 11th Duke, and present peer; as Duke of Marlborough, Earl of Sunderland, Earl of Marlborough, Baron Spencer, and Baron Churchill of Sandridge, as well as Prince of the Holy Roman Empire, and Prince of Mindelheim in Suabia.

*****(1)** *Sir* ROBERT Spencer, Knt; *cr Baron Spencer*, of Wormleighton, co Northampton (peerage of England) 1603; *d* 1627; *s* by his son **(2)** WILLIAM, 2nd Baron; *d* 1636; *s* by his son **(3)** HENRY, 3rd Baron; *cr Earl of Sunderland* (peerage of England) 1643; killed at Newbury 1643, fighting for the royal cause, *s* by his son **(4)** ROBERT, KG, 2nd Earl; *d* 1702; *s* by his son **(5)** CHARLES, KG, 3rd Earl; was a Principal Sec of State to Queen Anne and George I; *d* 1722; *s* by his son **(6)** ROBERT, 4th Earl; *d* unmarried 1729: *s* by his brother **(7)** CHARLES KG, 5th Earl, who *s* as 3rd Duke of Marlborough (ante).

MARLESFORD, BARON (Schreiber) (Life Baron 1991)

MARK SHULDHAM SCHREIBER, only son of late John Shuldham Schreiber, DL, of Marlesford Hall, Woodbridge, Suffolk (*see* B Faringdon, 1946 Edn); *ed* Eton, and Trin Coll, Camb (MA); late Lieut Coldstream Guards; DL Suffolk 1991; Fisons Ltd 1957-63, Conservative Research Dept 1963-67, Dir Conservative Public Sector Research Unit 1967-70, Special Advisor HM Govt 1970-74, to Leader of the Opposition 1974-75, Editorial Consultant *The Economist* 1974-91 (Parliamentary Lobby Correspondent); Dir Eastern Electricity plc since 1989; and Times Newspaper Holdings since 1991; Member Countryside Commn 1980-92 and Rural Devpt Commn 1985-93; Chm Council for the Protection of Rural England since 1993; Lord of the Manor of Marlesford and patron of the living; *cr Baron Marlesford*, of Marlesford, co Suffolk (Life Baron) 1991: *m* 1969, Gabriella Federica, da of Conte Teodoro Veglio di Castelletto Uzonne, and has issue.

Arms – Ermine, on a roundel sable between three griffin's heads erased vert a cross engrailed or. **Crest** – A dexter arm in armour the upper arm charged with a roundel sable thereon a cross engrailed or the hand grasping a dagger point downwards proper hilt and pomel or. **Supporters** – Two griffins ermine the aquiline parts vert forelegs or both collared with a ring of clouds radiated proper and each segreant on a grassy mount also ppr.

Seat – Marlesford Hall, Woodbridge, Suffolk IP13 0AU. *Town Residence* – 5 Kersley St, SW11 4PR. *Club* – Pratt's.

DAUGHTERS LIVING

Hon Nicola Charlotte, *b* 1971.
Hon Sophie Louisa, *b* 1973.

MARLEY, BARONY OF (Aman) (Extinct 1990)

WIDOW LIVING OF SECOND AND LAST BARON

CATHERINE DOONE (*Baroness Marley*), da of late Frank Angwyn Beal, of L'Eden, Cap d'Ail, France: *m* 1956, as his 2nd wife, 2nd Baron Marley, who *d* 1990. *Residence* – 104 Ebury Mews, SW1.

MARPLES, BARONY OF (Marples) (Extinct 1978)

WIDOW LIVING OF LIFE BARON

RUTH (*Baroness Marples*), da of late F. W. Dobson, JP, FSA, of Nottingham: *m* 1956, as his 2nd wife, Baron Marples, PC (Life Baron), who *d* 1978.

MARSH, BARON (Marsh) (Life Baron 1981)

RICHARD WILLIAM MARSH, PC, son of William Marsh, of Belvedere Kent; *b* 1928; *ed* Jennings Sch, Swindon, Woolwich Poly and Ruskin Coll, Oxford; Parly Sec Min of Labour 1964-5; jt Parly Sec Min of Technology 1965-66, Min of Power 1966-68, Min of Transport 1968-70; Chm British Railways 1970-75, Chm Newspaper Publishing Assoc 1975-90; Chm British Iron and Steel Consumers Council 1977-83 and Lee Cooper plc since 1982; Dep Chm TVAM Ltd 1981 and Chm 1983; Chm Lopex plc, Laurentian Finance Group plc, and China & Eastern Inv Co Ltd; FCIT; MP for Greenwich (*Lab*) 1959-71; *cr* Kt 1977, and *Baron Marsh*, of Mannington, co Wilts (Life Baron) 1981: *m* 1st, 1950 (*m diss* 1973), Evelyn Mary, da of Frederick Andrews, of Southampton; 2ndly, 1973, Caroline Dutton, who *d* 1975; 3rdly, 1979, Hon Felicity Carmen Francesca McFadzean, da of Baron McFadzean of Kelvinside (Life Baron), and has issue living by 1st *m*.

𝕬rms – Argent four pallets wavy azure on a chevron over all gules a leopard's face between two keys wards upwards and outwards or on a chief gules a double warded key wards upwards between two leopards' faces gold. 𝕮rest – Upon a mount vert a bear sejant upon its haunches and erect or holding between its forepaws a mitra preciosa gold pannelled vert garnished and lined gules the infulae vert and fringed at their ends gold. 𝕾upporters – On either side a Japanese crane (Grus japonensis) proper the interior wing and leg of each supporting the shield the whole upon a compartment composed of water barry wavy of four azure and argent between two banks of marshy ground proper sprouting therefrom plants of marsh buckler fern marsh mallow and bulrush all slipped and leaved proper. 𝕸otto – Non Est Vivere Sed Valere Vita.
Address – c/o House of Lords, SW1A 0PW.

SONS LIVING *(By 1st marriage)*

Hon Andrew, *b* 1950.
Hon Christopher, *b* 1960.

MARSHALL OF GORING, BARON (Marshall) (Life Baron 1985)

WALTER CHARLES MARSHALL, CBE, FRS, son of late Frank Marshall by his wife Amy, da of Edgar Pearson, of Wales; *b* 5 March 1932; *ed* Birmingham Univ; Hon DSc Salford (1977), Fellow R Swedish Acad of Engrg Sciences (1977), Hon Fellow St Hugh's Coll, Oxford (1983), Foreign Associate Nat Acad of Engrg, USA; Research Physicist Univ of California 1957-58, Harvard Univ 1958-59; Atomic Energy Research Establishment, Harwell, Group Leader Solid State Theory 1959-60, Head of Theoretical Physics Div 1960-66, Dep Dir 1966-68, Dir 1968-75; Chief Scientist Dept of Energy 1974-77; UK Atomic Energy Authority, Dir Research Group 1969-75, Dep Chm 1975-81, Chm 1981-82; Member Nat Research Development Council 1969-75; Chm Advisory Council on Research & Development for Fuel and Power 1974-77, Offshore Energy Technology Board 1975-77; Chm Central Electricity Generating Board 1982-89; Chm World Association of Nuclear Operators (WANO) 1989-93, since when Amb to same; Adviser to Inst of Nuclear Safety System Inc (founded by Kansai Electric Power Co) since 1992; Adviser to Nuclear Insurance Syndicate, Lloyd's of London since 1991; author of various research papers; FRS (1971); *cr* CBE (Civil) (1973), Kt (1982), and *Baron Marshall of Goring*, of South Stoke, co Oxfordshire (Life Baron) 1985; *m* 1955, Ann Vivienne, da of late Ernest Vivian Sheppard, of Cardiff, and has issue.

𝕬rms – Per pale or and gules two barrulets dancetty between three escutcheons on each a thunderbolt all counterchanged. 𝕮rest – A crown rayonny per pale or and gules issuing therefrom a male griffin segreant gules beaked rayed and the tail tufted or holding between the fore-claws also or a representation of a neutron therefrom three flashes of lightning all gold. 𝕾upporters – Dexter, standing with one foot on a mountain peak the figure of Mercury proper vested argent and mantled azure holding by his dexter hand against his shoulder a caduceus proper; *sinister*, on a grassy mount the figure of Minerva helmetted proper vested azure mantled argent extending her sinister hand and perched on the wrist thereof an owl also proper. 𝕸otto – Sapientia Et Glaritas.
Residence – Bridleway House, Goring-on-Thames, Oxon RG8 0HS.

SON LIVING

Hon Jonathan Charles Walter, *b* 1963; *ed* Abingdon Sch, Oxford, and Univ Coll, London (BSc, MD, MRCP).

DAUGHTER LIVING

Hon Victoria Ann, *b* 1959; *ed* St Helen's Sch, Abingdon, and Birmingham Univ (BSc), and Reading Univ (PhD); *m* 1984, Alan Burrill.

MARSHALL OF LEEDS, BARONY OF (Marshall) (Extinct 1990)

DAUGHTERS LIVING OF LIFE BARON

Hon Angela Hermione (The Home Farm, Sand Hutton, York Y04 1JZ), *b* 1944: *m* 1st, 1966 (*m diss* 1979), Myles Spencer Harrison Hartley; 2ndly, 1986, Maj Geoffrey J. Widdows, 15/19 Royal Hussars, yr son of A/Cdre S. C. Widdows, of St Peter Port, Guernsey, C1, and has issue living (by 1st *m*), Robert, *b* 1974, — Annabelle, *b* 1967, — Alexandra, *b* 1972.
Hon Virginia Mary, *b* 1949: *m* 1971, Nigel James Alexander Learmond, of 52 Marryat Rd, Wimbledon, SW19, and has issue living, Alexander Marshall, *b* 1989, — Marissa Virginia Stuart, *b* 1973.

WIDOW LIVING OF LIFE BARON

Mary (*Baroness Marshall of Leeds*), da of Robert Barr, of Shadwell House, Leeds: *m* 1941, Baron Marshall of Leeds (Life Baron), who *d* 1990. *Residence* – Holtby, York Y01 3UA.

MARTONMERE, BARON (Robinson) (Baron UK 1964)

John Stephen Robinson, 2nd Baron; *b* 10 July 1963; *s* 1989; *ed* Lakefield Coll Sch, and Senaca Univ.

Arms – Argent a three masted merchant ship of early eighteenth century date, the mainsails furled proper, on a chief azure a portcullis chained between two roses or. **Crest** – A lion's head erased or in the mouth a crescent gules. **Supporters** – *Dexter*, a lion or collared flory counterflory gules; *Sinister*, a stag gules attired and unguled collared flory counterflory or.
Residence – 390 Russell Hill Rd, Toronto, Ontario, Canada M4V 2V2.

BROTHER LIVING

David Alan, *b* 15 Sept 1965; *ed* Upper Canada Coll, Neuchatel, Switzerland, and Queen's Univ; BA Weston Univ; MBA.

SISTER LIVING

Carolyn Elizabeth, *b* 1969.

AUNT LIVING (*daughter of 1st Baron*)

Hon Loretta Anne, *b* 1939: *m* 1963, Edward Samuel Rogers, and has issue living, Edward Samuel, *b* 1969, — Lisa Anne, *b* 1967, — Melinda Mary, *b* 1971, — Martha Loretta, *b* 1972. *Residence* – 3 Frybrook Rd, Toronto, Canada M4V 1Y7.

MOTHER LIVING

Wendy Patricia, da of late James Cecil Blagden, of Bapchild Court, nr Sittingbourne, Kent: *m* 1959, Hon Richard Anthony Gasque Robinson, only son of 1st Baron, who *dvp* 1979. *Residence* – 390 Russell Hill Rd, Toronto, Ontario, Canada M4V 2V2.

PREDECESSOR – (1) (John) Roland Robinson, GBE, KCMG, PC, son of late Roland Walkden Robinson, of Blackpool; *b* 1907, Chm Conservative Commonwealth Affairs Cttee, House of Commons, 1954-64, and of Gen Council of Commonwealth Parliamentary Assocn 1960-61, Gov of Bermuda 1964-72, and MP for Widnes Div of Lancs (*C*) 1931-45, and for S Div of Blackpool 1945-64; *cr Baron Martonmere*, of Blackpool, co Palatine of Lancaster 1964: *m* 1930, Maysie, who *d* (Oct) 1989, da of late Clarence Warren Gasque, and *d* (May) 1989; *s* by his grandson (2) John Stephen, elder son of late Hon Richard Anthony Gasque Robinson (only son of 1st Baron), 2nd Baron and present peer.

MASHAM OF ILTON, BARONESS (Cunliffe-Lister) (Life Baroness 1970)

Susan Lilian Primrose Cunliffe-Lister (*Countess of Swinton*), yr da of late Sir Ronald Norman John Charles Udny Sinclair, 8th Bt (*cr* 1704), *b* 14 April, 1935; *ed* Heathfield, and London Polytechnic; Vice-Chm All-Party Drug Misuse Cttee since 1984, Vice-Chm All-Party Aids Cttee; Member All-Party Penal Affairs Group since 1975, All-Party Children's Group and All-Party Disablement Cttee since 1970; President of N Yorks Red Cross 1963-88, Chartered Soc of Physiotherapy 1975-82, and Papworth and Enham Village Settlements 1973-85; President, Vice-President, or Chm of many other associations for the disabled and physically handicapped; Hon Fell of Royal Coll of General Practitioners 1981; Hon MA Open Univ 1981; Hon MA York 1985; Hon Master of Law Leeds 1988; Hon Fell of Bradford and Ilkley Community Coll 1988; Hon DSc Ulster 1990; Hon LLD Univ of Teesside 1993; Hon Freeman of Borough of Harrogate 1989; DL N Yorks 1991; *cr Baroness of Masham of Ilton*, of Masham in N Riding, co York (Life Baroness) 1970: *m* 1959, 2nd Earl of Swinton, and has two adopted children (*see* E Swinton).

Arms – Not exemplified at time of going to press.
Residences – Dykes Hill House, Masham, Ripon, Yorks HG4 4NS; 46 Westminster Gdns, Marsham St, SW1.

MASON OF BARNSLEY, BARON (Mason) (Life Baron 1987)

ROY MASON, PC, son of late Joseph Mason, of Carlton, nr Barnsley; *b* 18 April 1924; *ed* Carlton and Royston Elementary Schs, and LSE; Min of State, Board of Trade 1964-67, Min of Defence for Equipment 1967-68, Postmaster Gen April-June 1968, Min of Power 1968-69, and Pres of Board of Trade 1960-70; Sec of State for Defence 1974-76, Sec of State for N Ireland 1976-79; MP (*Lab*) for Barnsley 1953-83, and for Barnsley Central 1983-87; *cr* PC 1968, and *Baron Mason of Barnsley*, of Barnsley, S Yorks (Life Baron) 1987: *m* 1945, Marjorie, da of Ernest Snowden, of Royston, W Riding, Yorks, and has issue.
Residence – 12 Victoria Av, Barnsley, S Yorks.

DAUGHTERS LIVING

Hon Susan Ann, *b* 1947: *m* 1969, Allen Duke, and has issue living, Steven Allen, *b* 1975, — Caroline Ann, *b* 1978.
Hon Jill Diane, *b* 1955: *m* 1979, Kevin Charles Edward Martin, and has issue living, Andrew Ian, *b* 1986.

MASSEREENE AND FERRARD, VISCOUNT (Skeffington) Sits as BARON ORIEL (UK 1821)
(Viscount I 1660)

Through difficulties to honours

JOHN DAVID CLOTWORTHY WHYTE-MELVILLE FOSTER SKEFFINGTON, 14th Viscount; *b* 3 June 1940; *s* 1992; *ed* Millfield, and Inst Monte Rosa; Gren Gds 1959-61; Stockbroker with Dunbar, Boyle & Kingsley; Patron of one living: *m* 1970, Anne Denise, da of late Norman Rowlandson, and has issue.

Arms – Quarterly: 1st and 4th, argent, three bulls' heads erased sable, armed or, *Skeffington*; 2nd and 3rd azure a chevron between three chaplets, or, *Clotworthy*. **Crest** – A mermaid with comb and mirror, all proper. **Supporters** – Two stags sable, attired and unguled or, each gorged with a chaplet of roses argent.
Seat – Chilham Castle, Canterbury, Kent. *Residence* – Scarisdale House, New Rd, Esher, Surrey. *Clubs* – Turf, Pratt's, House of Lords Yacht.

SONS LIVING

Hon CHARLES JOHN FOSTER CLOTWORTHY WHYTE-MELVILLE, *b* 7 Feb 1973.
Hon Henry William Norman Foster Clotworthy, *b* 1980.

DAUGHTER LIVING

Hon Harriette Denise Margaretta Eileen, *b* 1975.

SISTER LIVING

Hon Oriel Annabelle Diana, *b* 1950: *m* 1st, 1971 (*m diss* 1989), Dominik Luczyc-Wyhowski; 2ndly, 1992, Michael Francis Stratford, and has issue living (by 1st *m*), Sofia Oriel Laura, *b* 1973, — Kassia Annabelle Susan, *b* 1980. *Residence* – Chilham Castle, Canterbury, Kent.

WIDOW LIVING OF THIRTEENTH VISCOUNT

ANNABELLE KATHLEEN (*Dowager Viscountess Massereene and Ferrard*), elder da of late Henry David Lewis, of Combwell Priory, Hawkhurst, Kent: *m* 1939, the 13th Viscount, who *d* 1992. *Residence* – Chilham Castle, Canterbury, Kent.

COLLATERAL BRANCHES LIVING (*In remainder to Viscountcy of Massereene and Barony of Loughneagh only*)

  Grandchildren of late Hon Norah Florence Margaretta, Mrs Charles Johnston, eldest da of 11th Viscount:—
  Issue of late Algernon George Henry Johnston, *b* 1899, *d* 1948: *m* 1926, Eileen Magdalene, da of — Kearney, of Creagh House, Doneraile, co Cork:—
Anthony James Rex JOHNSTON, *b* 1931. —— Rosemary Margaretta Norah, *b* 1929. —— Gabrielle, *b* 1943.
  Issue of late John Edward Arthur Johnston, *b* 1902, *d* 1958: *m* 1933, Grietje, yst da of Jelle Zoethout, of Leeuwarden, Holland:—
†Michael John Anthony, JOHNSTON, *b* 1939: *m* 1965, Myrtle Stevens, of Springs, S Africa, and *d* 1965, leaving issue, Craig Alastair, *b* 1964. —— Peter Charles Anthony, *b* 1945: *m* 1967, Deborah Jane, da of John Wilding, of Forest Town, Johannesburg, and has issue living, Christopher John, *b* 1970, — Katharine Ann, *b* 1973, — Susan Margaret, *b* 1974.

  Grandchildren of late Hon Ethel Mary Catherine, Mrs Richard Atherton d'Anyers Willis, 2nd da of 11th Viscount:—
  Issue of late Maj Charles Rodolph d'Anyers Willis, *b* 1907, *d* 1961: *m* 1936, Ursula (who *m* 2ndly, 1963, Maj E. J. Fitz-Gerald, late Coldstream Guards), only child of late Brig-Gen Sir Robert Harvey Kearsley, KCVO, CMG, DSO (Peto, Bt, *cr* 1855, colls):—

Martin Atherton d'Anyers WILLIS, *b* 1939; *ed* Eton. —— Julian Charles d'Anyers (53 Halford Rd, Durban, S Africa), *b* 1945; *ed* Eton: *m* 1972, Gillian Curtis, el da of Earle Smith, of Pietermaritzburg, and has issue living, Sean d'Anyers, *b* 1974. —— Caroline Ann (2 Sandways Cottage, Bourton, Gillingham, Dorset) *b* 1937: *m* 1st, 1960 (*m diss* 1967), Col Dudley Lancelot Guy Carleton Smith, who *d* 1984; 2ndly, 1967 (*m diss* 1971), Richard Courtenay Thorne, and has issue living (by 2nd *m*), David Courtenay, *b* 1968.

    Issue of late Winifred Alice, *b* 1910, *d* 1977: *m* 1934, Lt-Col Count Peter Francis de Salis, Coldstream Gds, who *d* 1982:—

Richard John DE SALIS (Lucks Farm, Greenwood's Lane, Punnetts Town, Heathfield, E Sussex TN21 9HU), *b* 1935; *ed* Downside, and Trin Coll, Camb (BA); Maj RA: *m* 1959, Susan Elizabeth, da of Cdr G. H. Thompson, RN, and has issue living, Peter John Francis, *b* 1964, — Elizabeth Mary, *b* 1961, — Jane Sarah, *b* 1962, — Anne Frances, *b* 1970. —— Bernard Peter (12 Park Vista, Greenwich, SE10 9LZ), *b* 1936; *ed* Downside, and RNC Dartmouth; Lt-Cdr RN: *m* 1967, Monica Juanita, yst da of Cdr Robert Tatton Bower, RN (*see* Strickland, By), and has issue living, Piers Robert, *b* 1969, — Hugo John, *b* 1971. —— Nicholas George (20 Belmont Hill, SE13), *b* 1938; *ed* Downside: *m* 1964, Norma Christine, da of Maj C. H. Dennis, RAMC, of Ashtead, Surrey, and has issue living, Alexander Edward, *b* 1969, — Christian Henry, *b* 1973. —— James Anthony (Fern Cottage, Milton-under-Wychwood, Oxon), *b* 1949; *ed* Downside: *m* 1987, Helen Margaret Guy. —— Thomas Peter (26 Eastwell Close, Paddock Wood, Kent), *b* 1950; *ed* Downside.

    Issue of late Hon Constance Harriet Georgiana Skeffington, 3rd da of 11th Viscount, *b* 1877, *d* 1965: *m* 1905, Maj Herbert Rushton Sykes, who *d* 1952:—

(Arthur) Patrick SYKES, MBE, *b* 1906; *ed* Eton, and Magdalene Coll, Camb (BA 1928); Lt-Col KRRC (ret); served N Africa 1943 (wounded); MBE (Mil) 1945; JP and DL Shropshire, High Sheriff 1961-62: *m* 1st, 1936 (*m diss* 1967), Prudence Margaret, eldest da of late Maj-Gen Donald Elpinston Robertson, CB, DSO; 2ndly, 1968, Katharine Diana Bartlett, and has issue living (by 1st *m*), William, *b* 1939: *m* 1970, Pamela Strickland Skailes, and has issue living, Camilla *b* 1971, Angela *b* 1973, — (Gillian Diana) Juniper, *b* 1937: *m* 1964, Maj (William) John Martin Greener, OBE, DL, of Langebride House, Long Bredy, Dorset DT2 9HU, and has issue living, James *b* 1967, Juliet *b* 1970. *Residence* – Lydham Manor, Bishops Castle, Shropshire. —— †Humphrey Hugh, *b* 1907; *ed* Rugby; Maj late 9th Lancers: *m* 1st, 1936 (*m diss* 1948), Grizel Sophie, da of late AV-M Sir Norman Duckworth Kerr MacEwen, CB, CMG, DSO; 2ndly, 1958, Muriel, da of late Col John Charles Hooper, DSO, of Harewell, Faversham, Kent, and Hallyards, Peebles, and *d* 1991, leaving issue (by 1st *m*), Richard, *b* 1940, — Alexander, *b* 1942, — Jane, *b* 1938: *m* 1963, John Deen, and has issue living, Emma Sophie Louise *b* 1964, — Annabelle, *b* 1944. —— Robin George, TD, *b* 1917; *ed* Eton, and Ch Ch, Oxford (MA, BM, BCh, DA, FFARCS); Col late RAMC (TA); HM Hon Surg 1964: *m* 1947, Jean, da of H. Cunningham, of Muirlagganmore, Killin, Perthshire, and has issue living, Edward Colin Richard, *b* 1952, — Gillian, *b* 1950. *Residence* – Greenwood, Shotley Bridge, co Durham.

    Grandchildren of late Florence Clementina VERE-LAURIE (infra):—
    Issue of late Lt-Col George Halliburton Foster Peel VERE-LAURIE, *b* 1906, *d* 1981: *m* 1st, 1932 (*m diss* 1968), Caroline Judith, yr da of Edward Francklin, JP, of Gonalston Hall, Notts; 2ndly, 1968 (*m diss* 197-), Bridget Mary, da of F. Arthur Good; 3rdly, 1979, Joyce Mary Letts (The Dower House, Carlton-on-Trent, Newark, Notts):—

(By 1st *m*) George Edward VERE-LAURIE (Carlton Hall, Carlton-on-Trent, Newark, Notts), *b* 1935; *ed* Eton; Lt-Col 9th/12th Lancers; DL Notts 1993: *m* 1st, 1962 (*m diss* 1977), Georgina Nefert, da of Anthony Claud Riall, of Rutland Cottage, Rutland Gdns, SW7; 2ndly, 19—, Barbara Ann Tweed, and has issue living (by 1st *m*), George Anthony, *b* 1963, — Georgina Caroline Sylvia Victoria, *b* 1965: *m* 1990, C. Martin Hale, of The Red House, Church Corner, Raydon, Ipswich, Suffolk IP7 5LW, only son of C. Hale, of Folkestone, Kent, and has issue living, James George *b* 1991, William Edward, *b* 1992. —— (Florence) Mary, *b* 1939; Lord Lieut Hants since 1994: *m* 1960, Capt Christopher Tarleton Feltrim Fagan, late Gren Gds, of Deane Hill House, Deane, Basingstoke, and has had issue, †Christopher Hugh Tarleton Feltrim, *b* 1964; *d* in a motor accident 1987, — James Tarleton Feltrim, *b* 1965.

    Grandchildren of late Hon Sydney William Foster-Skeffington, 3rd son of 10th Viscount Massereene:—
    Issue of late Florence Clementina VERE-LAURIE, *b* 1873, *d* 1978; assumed by deed poll 1915 the additional surname of VERE: *m* 1st, 1905, Lt-Col George Brenton Laurie, R Irish Rifles, who was *ka* 1915; 2ndly, 1940, as his 2nd wife, her cousin, 12th Viscount Massereene and Ferrard (infra), who *d* 1956:—

(By 1st *m*) Sydney John Athelstan VERE-LAURIE (Farholme House, Sutton-on-Trent, Newark, Notts), *b* 1910; Hon Fellow London Coll of Music and a Freeman of City of London. —— Eleanor Blanche Helen Margaretta (PO Box 44, 69 Crescent Av, Hudson Heights, Prov Quebec, Canada), *b* 1907; Freeman of City of London: *m* 1932, Andrew Wauchope Johnstone, who *d* 1980 (*see* Johnstone, Bt, colls).

PREDECESSORS – (1) *Sir* JOHN Clotworthy, *cr Baron Loughneugh* and *Viscount Massereene* (peerage of Ireland) 1660, with remainder to his son-in-law Sir John Skeffington, 5th Bt, of Fisherwick and his issue male, and in default thereof to his heirs-general; *d* 1665; *s* by **(2)** *Sir* JOHN Skeffington (ante) 2nd Viscount; *d* 1695; *s* by his son **(3)** CLOTWORTHY, 3rd Viscount; *d* 1713; *s* by his son **(4)** CLOTWORTHY, 4th Viscount; *d* 1738; *s* by his son **(5)** CLOTWORTHY, 5th Viscount; *cr Earl of Massereene* (peerage of Ireland) 1756; *d* 1757; *s* by his el son **(6)** CLOTWORTHY, 2nd Earl; *dsp* 1800; *s* by his brother **(7)** HENRY, 3rd Earl; *d* unmarried 1811; *s* by his brother **(8)** CHICHESTER, 4th Earl; *d* 1816, when the Baronetcy and Earldom expired, and the Barony of Loughneagh and the Viscountcy of Massereene devolved upon his da **(9)** HARRIET wife of Thomas Henry Foster, 2nd Baron *Oriel* and 2nd *Viscount Ferrard* (see **infra*); *d* 1831; *s* by her son **(10)** JOHN, KP, 10th Viscount; *b* 1812; assumed the surname of Skeffington in addition to that of Foster 1843; *m* 1835, Olivia Deane, da of Henry Deane O'Grady, of Lodge, co Limerick, and Stillorgan Castle, Dublin; *d* 1863; *s* by his son **(11)** CLOTWORTHY JOHN EYRE, 11th Viscount; *b* 1842; Lieut co Louth and co and Town of Drogheda *m* 1870, Florence Elizabeth, who *d* 1929, only child of the late Major George John Whyte-Melville; *d* 1905; *s* by his son **(12)** ALGERNON WILLIAM JOHN CLOTWORTHY, DSO, 12th Viscount; *b* 1873; Major N Irish Horse, and 17th Lancers, and Hon Col 188th (Antrim) Heavy Battery RA (TA); S Africa 1900-2 (wounded, despatches twice, DSO), European War 1914-18 (despatches); Lieut for co Antrim 1916-45; first Parliamentary Sec to Prime Min in Ulster Parliament, and a Member of Senate, N Ireland 1921-9: *m* 1st, 1905, Jean Barbara, who *d* 1937, el da of Sir John Stirling Ainsworth, MP, 1st Bt; 2ndly, 1940, his cousin, Florence Clementina Vere, who *d* 1978, da of late Hon Sydney William Foster Skeffington, and widow of Lt-Col George Brenton Laurie; *d* 1956; *s* by his only son **(13)** JOHN CLOTWORTHY TALBOT FOSTER WHYTE-MELVILLE, 13th Viscount, *b* 1914; Lieut Black Watch (Supp Res) 1933-36 and 1939-40 (invalided), served Small Vessels Pool, RN 1944; Freeman City of London, DL co Antrim 1957, Gold Staff Officer at Coronation of Queen Elizabeth II 1953; Whip, Conservative Peers Cttee (IUP) House of Lords 1958-65, Dep-Chm 1965-70; Chm Scottish Clans Assocn of London 1974-76, etc: *m* 1939, Annabelle Kathleen, elder da of late Henry David Lewis, of Combwell Priory, Hawkhurst, Kent; *d* 1992; *s* by his only son **(14)** JOHN DAVID CLOTWORTHY WHYTE-MELVILLE FOSTER, 14th Viscount and present peer; also Baron of Loughneagh, Baron Oriel, of Collon, and Baron Oriel, of Ferrard.

***(1)** JOHN FOSTER, PC, MP for many years, and sometime Speaker of the Irish Parliament was *cr Baron Oriel*, of Ferrard, co Louth (peerage of United Kingdom) 1821: *m* 1764, Margaret Amelia, *cr Baroness Oriel*, of Collon (peerage of Ireland) 1790, and *Viscountess Ferrard* (peerage of Ireland) 1797, da of Thomas Burgh, of Birt, co Kildare, she *d* 1831; *s* by her son **(2)** THOMAS HENRY, 2nd Viscount Ferrard (see ante), who had in 1828 *s* his father as 2nd Baron Oriel, and in 1817 has assumed by Roy licence the surname of Skeffington in lieu of Foster.

MASSY, BARON (Massy) (Baron I 1776)

HUGH HAMON JOHN SOMERSET MASSY, 9th Baron; *b* 11 June 1921; *s* 1958; *ed* Clongowes Wood Coll, and Clayesmore Sch; European War 1940-45 as Private RAOC: *m* 1943, Margaret Elizabeth, da of late John Flower, of Barry, co Meath, and has issue.

Arms – Argent, on a chevron between three lozenges sable, a lion passant or. **Crest** – Out of a ducal coronet or, a bull's head gules, armed sable. **Supporters** – *Dexter*, a lion; *sinister*, a leopard reguardant; both proper and collared and chained or.
Residence –

For the liberty of my country

SONS LIVING

Hon DAVID HAMON SOMERSET, *b* 4 March 1947; *ed* St George's Coll, Weybridge; serving with Merchant Navy.
Hon John Hugh Somerset, *b* 1950: *m* 1978, Andrea, da of Alan West, of Leicester.
Hon Graham Ingoldsby Somerset, *b* 1952.
Hon Paul Robert, *b* 1953: *m* 1976, Anne Bridget, da of James McGowan, of Leicester, and has issue living, Kevin James Somerset, *b* 1978, — Colin Hugh Somerset, *b* 1979.

DAUGHTER LIVING

Hon Sheelagh Marie Louise, *b* 1958.

AUNT LIVING (*Daughter of 7th Baron*)

Hon Muriel Olive, *b* 1892.

COLLATERAL BRANCHES LIVING

Granddaughter of late Hugh Hamon John Massy, son of late Hon George William Massy, 2nd son of 3rd Baron:—
Issue of late Rollo Dillon Dunham Massy, *b* 1856, *d* 1934: *m* 1884, Emma Augusta, who *d* 1926, da of James Inman, of Lymington:—
Louisa Bythia, *b* 1887.

Grandchildren of late Rev Xavier Peel Massy, 4th son of Edward Taylor Massy, of Cottesmore, co Pembroke, only son of Hon Edward Massy, of Ballynort, co Limerick, 2nd son of 2nd Baron:—
Issue of late Godfrey Massy, *b* 1879, *d* 1953: *m* 1908, Marianne, who *d* 1951, da of late Ezra Gooderidge, of Goold, Yorkshire:—
Lawrence Xavier Peel (Box 165, Savona, nr Kamloops, BC, Canada), *b* 1909: *m* 1934, Hazel, da of Edwin Hartt, of Thelma, Alberta, and has issue living, Marianne Belle, *b* 1938: *m* 19—, Edward Heidinger.
Issue of late Lieut Lawrence Peel Massy, DSC, RNR, *b* 1883, *d* 1932: *m* 1914, Constance Jean Anne, who *d* 1949, el da of late John James Galletly, solicitor, of Inchdrewer, Colinton, Midlothian, and Kinnaird, Pitlochry:—
Doreen Constance Peel, *b* 1919; late WRNS; LRAM: *m* 1st, 1945 (*m diss* 1956), Conrad Laviolette; 2ndly, 1959, John Woolls, of Maipenrai, Sea Dyke Way, Marshchapel, Lincs, and has issue living (by 1st *m*) Derry Keith, *b* 1951; CPO, RN (ret), — Lorna Doreen, *b* 1946; late WRNS: *m* 1967, Percival N. Skedgell, of Bearsden, Glasgow, and has issue living, Elinor Peel *b* 1971, Lindsey Northcott *b* 1976.

Grandsons of late Lieut Lawrence Peel Massy, DSC, RNR (ante):—
Issue of late Maj Arthur Lawrence John Peel Massy, W Yorks Regt, *b* 1916, *d* 1992: *m* 1943, Margaret Alison, who *d* 19—, da of late Rev Ernest Bell Sharpe, of Purulla, India:—
David Lawrence Peel, *b* 1949; Sub Lieut (E) RNR: *m* 1976, Linda, da of Edgar Clarachan, of Malibu, Calif, USA. —— John Eversdon Peel, *b* 1954.

Grandchildren of late Arthur Wellington Massy, 5th son of Edward Taylor Massy (ante):—
Issue of late Lt-Gen Hugh Royds Stokes Massy, CB, DSO, MC, *b* 1884, *d* 1965, *m* 1912, Maud Ina Nest, who *d* 1960, da of late Col Thomas James Roch, JP, DL, of Llether Pembrokeshire:—
Hugh Peter Stokes (Long Acre, Owermoigne, Dorchester, Dorset), *b* 1914; *ed* Bradfield Coll; Lt-Col (ret) Roy Tank Regt 1939-45 War (despatches): *m* 1945, Jean H., who *d* 1993, da of late Sqdn Ldr M. G. Kidston, of Kamiti Downs, Kahawa, Kenya, and has issue living, Diana Rosamund, *b* 1947: *m* 1973, Lt-Col Philip Eric Scott, 16th/5th Lancers, and has issue living, James *b* 1975, — Pauline Lorraine, *b* 1951: *m* 1980, Richard Malcolm Cyril Scott, of 34 Christchurch Rd, Longham, Wimborne, Dorset, and has issue living, Louise Sarah *b* 1984. —— Mary Nest (Fulmar House, Twyford, Fontmell Magna, Shaftesbury, Dorset), *b* 1915: *m* 1940 (*m diss* 1947), Gerald Wilfred Charles Carter, and has issue living, Miles Richard, *b* 1941, — Jandy, *b* 1943: *m* 1975, Acting Cdr David Andrew Hobbs, MBE, son of A. S. Hobbs, and has issue living, Andrew Arthur Duncan *b* 1978.
Issue of late Brig Charles Walter Massy, CBE, DSO, MC, *b* 1887, *d* 1973: *m* 1st, 1920, Muriel Lorna Bell, who *d* 1958, da of J. A. Hallinan, of Glandalane, Fermoy; 2ndly, 1958, Irene Gillbee, who *d* 1990, da of late Richard Gillbee Thorold (*see* Thorold, Bt, colls), and widow of Clifford Hackney, MRCS:—
(By 1st *m*) Hugh Charles (RR No 1, Box 30, South Woodstock, Vermont 05071, USA), *b* 1921: *m* 1970, Janice, da of late Maurice de Kay Thompson, of Boston, Mass, and widow of Grenville Goodwin. —— John Royds, MRCS, LRCP (Hazel Lodge, Hensting Lane, Fishers Pond, Eastleigh, Hants S05 7HH), *b* 1925; MRCS and LRCP 1960: *m* 1957, Eileen, da of F. Evans, of Thornfield, Hobb Lane, Hedge End, Southampton, and has issue living, David Hugh, *b* 1962, — Peter John (19 Netley Firs Rd, Hedge End, Southampton S03 4AY), *b* 1964: *m* 1987, Jennifer Freeman, and has issue living, Helen Clare, *b* 1993, — Anne Sarah, *b* 1959: *m* 1991, Kees de Koning, of Holland, — Clare Muriel, *b* 1960: *m* 1991, Jonathan Brian Evans, of 142 Astonville St, SW18 5AG, son of T. J. Evans, of Radyr, S Glamorgan, and has issue living, Harriet Frances *b* 1994.

Granddaughter of late Rev George Eyre Massy, Rector of Gumfreston, co Pembroke, 6th and yst son of Edward Taylor Massy (ante):—
Issue of late Capt Villiers Wilfred Peel Massy, *b* 1882, *d* 1932: *m* 1915, Beatrice, who *d* 1952, da of late Carlos Vetter, of 6 Neville Street, SW:—

Bridget Ursula Elaine, *b* 1920: *m* 1948, Leonard Arthur Hammond Riddett, and has issue living, John Villiers (Alder Cottage, Lucas Lane, Ashwell, Herts), *b* 1949: *m* 1985, Linda Marie West, of Auckland, NZ, and has issue living, Paul James Massy *b* 1990, Guy Edward West *b* 1992, — Patrick Hammond (Box 76, Takaka, NZ), *b* 1951, — Philip Peel (4 Macquarie Terr, Balmain, NSW, Australia), *b* 1957, — Sara Caroline, *b* 1953: *m* 1981, Dominic Kingsley Eason Scott, of 34 St Andrew's Rd, Henley-on-Thames, Oxon, and has issue living, Martha Jane *b* 1983, Jemima Kate *b* 1986. *Residence* – Half Acre, Witheridge Hill, Henley on Thames, Oxon RG9 7PE.

> Grandsons of late Hugh Hamon George Massy, only son (by 1st *m*) of Lt-Col George Eyre Massy (infra):—
>> Issue of late Hugh Hamon de Moleyns Massy, *b* 1895, *d* 1976: *m* 1923, Helen Violet, da of late Allen Hamilton Morgan, of Hope Vale, Natal:—
Hugh Allen Oliver, *b* 1925. *Address* – PO Box 361, Pietermaritzburg, Natal 3200. — Evan (abandoned Christian names of Eyre Pennefather) (60 Maclean St, Umkomaas, Natal 4170), *b* 1930: *m* 1965, Lynette Marion, da of Arthur Stuart Clark, of Tenby, Hilton, Natal, and has issue living, Jennifer Lynne, *b* 1966, — Helen Louise, *b* 1969.

> Grandchildren of late Capt James Eyre Massy (infra):—
>> Issue of late George Eyre Massy, *b* 1914, *d* 1989: *m* 1950: Marella Margaret Helen (19 Broome St, Nedlands, W Australia), da of late James McQueen:—
Timothy James Hamon, *b* 1953: *m* 1983, Karen Maria, da of Gerard McCrea, of Karratha, W Australia, and has issue living, Lauren Elizabeth, *b* 1984. — Jacqueline Cynthia, *b* 1952. — Nicola Jane, *b* 1954.

> Granddaughter (by 2nd *m*) of Lt-Col George Eyre Massy, eldest son of Hugh Massy, eldest son of Hon George Eyre Massy, 3rd son of 2nd Baron:—
>> Issue of late Capt James Eyre Massy, *b* 1873, *d* 1952: *m* 1903, May Evelyn, who *d* 1980, da of John Carmichael, JP, of Tracton Park, co Cork:—
Cynthia Evelyn, *b* 1916: *m* 1938, Eric Reade, of Conifers, The Close, Brighton Rd, Sway, Hants SO41 6ED, son of late Arthur Reade, DSO, MC, of Monmouth, and has issue living, Michael Wildin, *b* 1948, — Phylida Anne, *b* 1946.

> Grandchildren of late John George Beresford Massy-Beresford, only surv son of late Very Rev John Maunsell Massy-Beresford, 3rd son of late John Massy, 4th son of 2nd Baron:—
>> Issue of late Brig Tristram Hugh Massy-Beresford, DSO, MC, *b* 1896, *d* 1987: *m* 1927, Helen Lindsay, who *d* 1979, da of late Lindsay Crompton Lawford, of Montreal:—
Michael James (11 Charleville Mansions, Charleville Rd, W14), *b* 1935; *ed* Eton, and Jesus Coll, Camb (BA); Maj RGJ (ret). — Christopher Kerry (4 Vaughan Av, Stamford Brook, W6), *b* 1939; *ed* Eton, and Ch Ch, Oxford (MA): *m* 1979, Marjory Snow, and has issue living, Helen Emily, *b* 1980. — Patricia Nell, *b* 1931: *m* 1958, Maj James Otway George Paton, 13th/18th Hus (ret), of Park Corner Farm, Odiham, Hants, and has issue living, Timothy James, *b* 1964, — Nicholas George, *b* (twin) 1968, — Penelope Loveday, *b* 1963: *m* 1992, Matthew Alan Fleet, — Elizabeth Gwendoline, *b* 1967.

> Grandchildren of late Francis Staunton Massy-Dawson, son of late Francis Dennis Massy-Dawson, son of late James Hewitt Massy-Dawson, son of late Hon James Massy-Dawson, 2nd son of 1st Baron:—
>> Issue of late Capt Francis Evelyn Massy-Dawson, DSO, RN, *b* 1872, *d* 1939: *m* 1st, 1922, Emily Banner Clough, who *d* 1928, da of Lieut-Com Somerset James Somerset-Johnstone, RN, and widow of Capt Herbert Algernon Adam, CBE, RN (Johnstone, Bt colls); 2ndly, 1928, Mary Caroline, who *d* 1950, da of Herbert Taylor, of Holmer, Hereford:—
(By 2nd *m*) Francis Patrick, *b* 1934: *m* 1961, Anne Marie, da of W. H. Heritage, and has issue living, Suzanne, *b* 1963, — Nicola Jane, *b* 1965. — Rosemarie Julia, *b* 1933: *m* 1961, John William Halse.

> Grandson of late William Massey, son of late Robert George Massey, eldest son of Hon George Massy (infra):—
>> Issue of late George William Hughes MASSEY, *b* 1864, *d* 1914: *m* 1st, 1889, Edith Margaret, who *d* 1910, da of late John Birrell, of Beechwood, London, Ontario, Canada; 2ndly, 1912, Marion (who *d* 1973, having *m* 2ndly, 1935, Brig Jesse (Jake) Pevensey Duke, DSO, MC, Royal Warwicks Regt), da of late George Bryson Clarke, of Petton Grange, Shropshire:—
(By 2nd *m*) Patrick Godfrey Goolden MASSEY, MC (Arawai House, Liss, Hants), *b* 1913; *ed* Harrow, and RMC Sandhurst; Hodson's Horse IA 1933, served 1939-45 War in India, Iraq, Iran and Burma (despatches, MC 1945), Lt-Col comdg 5/10th Baluch Regt, Comdt HE Gov-Gen's Body Guard 1946, transferred Royal Dragoons, Lt-Col comdg 1947 (ret): *m* 1st, 1941, Bessie Lee, who *d* 1978, da of late William J. Byrne, of Melbourne, Australia; 2ndly, 1978, Aylmer Jean Philippa, da of late Donald Macfarlane, CIE, of Little Hadlow, Sussex, and widow of (i) Capt Brian Eveleigh, 16/5th Lancers (*ka* 1944), and (ii) Maj Philip le Grand Gribble, and has issue living (by 1st *m*), Hamon Patrick Dunham (Pollachar, Isle of S Uist, Outer Hebrides), *b* 1950; *ed* Harrow, and RMA Sandhurst; Lt-Col The Blues and Royals, Comdg Household Cavalry Mounted Regt 1992: *m* 1st, 1973 (*m diss* 1987), Caroline, who *d* 1988, da of Lt-Col George Baker, of Dickhurst, Haslemere, Surrey; 2ndly, 1988, Mrs Cathleen Teresa Poole, da of Neil Campbell, of Benbecula, Outer Hebrides, and has issue living (by 1st *m*), Edward Hamon Russell *b* 1976, Eleanore Joan Diana *b* 1977, (by 2nd *m*) Lee (a da) *b* 1989, Garda (a da) *b* 1990, — Peregrine Tatton Eyre (Prospect Place, Bilsington, Ashford, Kent), *b* 1952; *ed* Harrow, and Magdalene Coll, Camb (MA); Bar Middle Temple 1975: *m* 1977, Deirdre Mary, eldest da of Commodore Spencer Heneage Drummond, DSC, RN (*see* E Perth, colls), and has issue living, Emma Rachel Lee *b* 1981, Alexandra Clare Louise *b* 1983, Laura Helena Ruth *b* 1986, — William Greville Sale (30 Brodrick Rd, SW17; The Barn, Beanacre, Melksham, Wilts), *b* 1953; *ed* Harrow, and Hertford Coll, Oxford (BA); Bar Middle Temple 1977: *m* 1978, Cecilia D'Oyly, 2nd da of Daniel Edmund Awdry, TD, DL, of Old Manor, Beanacre, Melksham, Wilts, and has issue living, Patrick William Edmund *b* 1983, Richard Daniel Hugh *b* 1985, Edmund Greville Robert *b* 1990.

> Grandchildren of late Hugh Massy, yr son of late Hon George Massy, 6th and yst son of 1st Baron:—
>> Issue of late Beresford Massy, *b* 1840, *d* 1878: *m* 1869, Elizabeth Harriet, who *d* 1926, only da of late Rev George Harrison Reade, of Inniskeen Rectory, Dundalk:—
†*Rev* Cecil Hugh, *b* 1870: *ed* Trin Coll, Dublin; Curate of Staplestown, co Carlow; *dunm* 1946. — †Sydney Beresford, *b* 1876; Capt in the Army: *m* 19—, Eileen McMahon, who *d* 1974, da of Canon O'Grady, of Bantry, co Cork, and *d* 1946. — Frances Mary Georgina, *b* 18—; *dunm* 1955. — Eva Constance, *b* 18—: *m* 1916, Frederick Joseph Smissen, Lieut RIR, and *d* 1957.
>> Issue of late George Hugh Massy, *b* 1844, *d* 1912: *m* 1880, Lydia Georgina Robertson, who *d* 1920, da of late George Edgeworth Fenwick, MD, Prof of Surgery at McGill Univ, Montreal:—
†Beresford Fenwick, *b* and *d* 1885. — †Gordon Eyre, *b* 1886: *m* 1958, Irene Powell, and *dsp* 1967. — †Hugh de Hertal, *b* 1893; *ka* 1915 at Ypres. — Mary Charlotte Robertson, *b* 1881: *m* 1914, Charles W. Blackham, who *d* 1961, and *d* 1950, having had issue, one son (*ka* 1939-45 War), and one da. — Ethel Gertrude, *b* 1882; *dunm* 1961. — Kathleen, *b* and *d* 1884. — Constance Emily, *b* (twin) 1885: *m* 1913, Hugh Nehal Gahan, who *d* 1975, and *d* 1970, leaving issue, two sons and two das. — Marion Edgeworth, *b* 1889; *dunm* 1971. — Evelyn de Hertal, *b* 1890: *dunm* 1939. — Georgina Annie Gahan, *b* 1891; *dunm* 1974.

PREDECESSORS – (1) HUGH Massy, MP For co Limerick in several parliaments, was *cr Baron Massy*, of Duntrileague, co Limerick (peerage of Ireland) 1776; *d* 1788; *s* by his son (2) HUGH, 2nd Baron; MP for co Limerick; *d* 1790; *s* by his son (3) HUGH, 3rd Baron; *d* 1812; *s* by his son (4) HUGH HAMON, 4th Baron; *b* 1793; *m* 1826, Matilda, who *d* 1883, da of Luke White Esq, of Woodlands, co Dublin; *d* 1836; *s* by his el son (5) HUGH HAMON INGOLDSBY, 5th Baron: *m* 1855, Isabella, who *d* 1917, da of George MacNisbett; *dsp* 1874; *s* by his brother (6) JOHN THOMAS WILLIAM, 6th Baron, *b* 1835; a Representative Peer: *m* 1863, Lady Lucy Maria Butler, who *d* 1896, da of 3rd Earl of Carrick; *d* 1915; *s* by his son (7) HUGH SOMERSET JOHN, 7th Baron, *b* 1864: *m* 1886, Ellen Ida Constance, who *d* 1922, da of late Charles William Wise, of Rochester, Cahir, co Tipperary; *d* 1926; *s* by his son (8) HUGH HAMON CHARLES GEORGE, 8th Baron, *b* 1894: *m* 1919, Margaret, who *d* 1971 da of late Richard Leonard, of Meadsbrook, Ashbourne, co Limerick, and widow of Dr   Moran, of Tara, co Meath; *d* 1958; *s* by his only son (9) HUGH HAMON JOHN SOMERSET, 9th Baron, and present peer.

MATTHEWS, BARON (Matthews) (Life Baron 1980)

VICTOR COLLIN MATTHEWS, FIOB, FRSA, son of A. Matthews; *b* 5 Dec 1919; *ed* Highbury; served RNVR 1939-45; Dep Chm Trafalgar House Ltd 1973-86 (Group Ch Executive 1977-83, Group Managing Dir 1968-77); Chm and Ch Executive Express Newspapers Ltd 1977-85; Chm The Cunard Steam-Ship Co Ltd 1971-83, Cunard Cruise Ships Ltd 1978-83, and Cunard Line Ltd 1978-83; Chm Trafalgar House Developments Holdings Ltd 1970-83, Trafalgar Offshore Ltd 1975-83, and Trafalgar House Construction Holdings Ltd 1977-83; Chm Fleet Publishing International Holdings Ltd 1978-85, Eastern International Investment Trust Ltd 1974-85 and The Ritz Hotel (London) Ltd 1976-83; *cr Baron Matthews*, of Southgate, in the London Borough of Enfield (Life Baron) 1980: *m* 1942, Joyce Geraldine, da of A. Pilbeam, and has issue.

Arms – Azure a roundel gules fimbriated argent between two roundels also argent and all between four pallets or, a chief also or chapé azure. **Crest** – A horse forcene or against a corinthian column of white marble proper. **Supporters** – *Dexter*, A horse reguardant or, gorged with a wreath of two ribands tenné and grey tied at the rear and the ends flying to the dexter; *sinister*, a stag reguardant azure attired, unguled and gorged with a laurel wreath gold.

Residence – Waverley Farm, Mont Arthur, St Brelades Bay, Jersey, CI. *Clubs* – RAC, MCC, Royal and Ancient.

SON LIVING

Hon Ian V., *b* 1962: *m* 1986, Mrs Helen Christina Cooke, da of Francis Norman Jasper, of Trelyn, 10 Croft Way, Frimley, Camberley, Surrey. *Residence* – Trinity Hall, La Profonde Rue, Trinity, Jersey, CI.

Mauchline, Lord; son of Countess of Loudoun.

Maud, see Baron Redcliffe-Maud.

MAUDE OF STRATFORD-UPON-AVON, BARONY OF (Maude) (Extinct 1993)

SONS LIVING AND DECEASED OF LIFE BARON

†*Hon* Charles John Alan, *b* 1951; *ed* Abingdon Sch, and Corpus Christi Coll, Camb; stage designer; *d* 1993.
Rt Hon Francis Anthony Aylmer, *b* 1953; *ed* Abingdon Sch, and Corpus Christi Coll, Camb; Barrister-at-law; MP (C) Warwickshire N 1983-92; an Under-Sec of State, Dept of Trade & Industry, 1987-89, Min of State, Foreign and Commonwealth Office 1989-90, Financial Sec HM Treasury 1990-92; PC 1992: *m* 1984, Christina Jane, yr da of A. Peter Hadfield, of Copthorne, Shewsbury, and has issue living, Henry Peter Angus, *b* 1990, — Julia Elizabeth Barbara, *b* 1986, — Cecily Mary Anne, *b* 1988.

DAUGHTERS LIVING OF LIFE BARON

Hon Elizabeth Jane, *b* 1946, *m* 1973, Peter Brotherton Spurrier, lately York Herald, of 15 Morella Road, Wandsworth Common, SW12, and has issue living, Benedict John Emlyn, *b* 1979, — Thomas Alan Earnshaw, *b* 1982, — Lucinda, *b* 1985.
Hon Deborah Gervaise, *b* 1948; *ed* Banbury Gram Sch, and Bristol Univ: *m* 1973, Paul David Grenville Hayter, LVO, Chief Clerk House of Lords, of Walnut House, Charlton, Banbury, Oxon, and has issue living, William James Goodenough, *b* 1978, — Giles Angus Danvers, *b* 1981, — Arabella Katherine Maude, *b* 1984.

WIDOW LIVING OF LIFE BARON

BARBARA ELIZABETH EARNSHAW (*Baroness Maude of Stratford-upon-Avon*), only da of late John Earnshaw Sutcliffe, of Bushey, Herts: *m* 1946, Baron Maude of Stratford-upon-Avon, TD, PC (Life Baron), who *d* 1993. *Residence* – Old Farm, South Newington, nr Banbury, Oxon.

MAUGHAM, VISCOUNTCY OF (Maugham) (Extinct 1981)

DAUGHTERS LIVING OF FIRST VISCOUNT

Hon Edith Honor Betty, *b* 1901: *m* 1925, Sebastian Earl, who *d* 1983, and has had issue, Julian Romer, *b* 1927: *m* 1962, Phyllis (70 Randolph Av, W9 1BG), da of late Dr Richard Blum, of New York, and *d* 1990, leaving issue, Sebastian *b* 1965, Austin Richard *b* 1967, Cordelia *b* 1963: *m* 1992, Maxim Eugene Uys, of 35 Wymering Rd, W9 2NB, son of Stanley Uys (and has issue living, Theodore *b* 1992), — (Quentin) Stephen (Church House, Old Headington, Oxford), *b* 1931: *m* 1957, Rosemary, da of Lester Blake-Jolly, Dist Officer of N Rhodesia, and has issue living, Colin Raphael *b* 1958, (Mark) Justin *b* 1959, Tristram Andrew *b* 1962, Jocelyn Malcolm *b* 1968. *Residence* – Flat 6, 6 Onslow Sq, SW7 3NP; Chilland Ford, Martyr Worthy, nr Winchester.

Hon Diana Julia: *m* 1932, Kenneth Marr-Johnson, who *d* 1986, and has issue living, Frederick James Maugham, *b* 1936; Circuit Judge SE Circuit 1991: *m* 1966, Susan, da of late Maj Richard Philip Hastings Eyre, OBE, of Winsford, Som, and has issue living, Thomas Maugham *b* 1966, Helen Rachel *b* 1969, — (Clifford) Simon Romer (8 Bassett Rd, W10), *b* 1938: *m* 1966, Catharine Mary, da of late Cdr John Smyth. OBE, of Llanbedr, Breconshire, and has issue living, Prosper Henry, *b* 1967, Alexander Merlin, *b* 1971, Diana Romilly *b* 1969, — (John) William (62 Rodenhurst Rd, SW4 8AR) *b* 1945: *m* 1986, Marion Elaine Hamilton, only da of Col J. H. Allford, DSO, of Withersdale, Suffolk. *Residence* – Flat 3, 14 Onslow Sq, SW7.

MAY, BARON (May) (Baron UK 1935, Bt UK 1931)

With God's help work prospers

MICHAEL ST JOHN MAY, 3rd Baron and 3rd Baronet; *b* 26 Sept 1931; *s* 1950; *ed* Wycliffe Coll, and Magdalene Coll, Camb; late Lt Roy Signals: *m* 1st, 1958 (*m diss* 1963), Dorothea Catherine Ann, da of Charles McCarthy, of Boston, USA; 2ndly, 1963, Jillian Mary, only da of late Albert Edward Shipton, of Wroxton Mill, Wroxton, Oxon, and has issue by 2nd *m*.

Arms – Gules, on a chevron between in chief three billets or, and in base an eagle argent, three roses of the field, barbed and seeded proper. **Crest** – A demi-leopard proper, holding in the dexter paw a bezant and resting the sinister paw on a terrestrial globe also proper. **Supporters** – *Dexter*, a griffin, and *sinister* a dragon or, each charged on the shoulder with a sprig of mayflower slipped and leaved proper.
Residences – Gautherns Barn, Sibford Gower, Oxon; 9 Palace Mews, SW6.

SON LIVING (By 2nd marriage)

Hon JASPER BERTRAM ST JOHN, *b* 24 Oct 1965; *ed* Harrow.

DAUGHTER LIVING (By 2nd marriage)

Hon Miranda Jane, *b* 1968.

SISTER LIVING

Hon June Lisette, *b* 1929; *ed* St Paul's Sch: *m* 1958, Raymond Charles Lisser, and has issue living, Aidan Charles, *b* 1959. *Residences* – School House, Stanton, Broadway, Worcs; 6H Hyde Park Mansions, NW1.

AUNT LIVING (*Daughter of 1st Baron*)

Hon Elizabeth Frances, *b* 1907: *m* 1955, George Leonard Brunton Henderson, MRCVS, BSc, and has issue living, Christopher Iain, *b* 1959, — Simon Neil, *b* 1960. *Residence* – Oak Lodge, Oak Hill Grove, Surbiton, Surrey, KT6 6DS.

WIDOW LIVING OF SECOND BARON

ELISABETH, da of George Ricardo Thoms: *m* 1st, 1929, as his second wife, the 2nd Baron, who *d* 1950; 2ndly, 19-, W. H. Hallam. *Residence* – 46 Lyndon Rd, Bramham Mead, Yorks.

COLLATERAL BRANCH LIVING

Issue of late Hon Patrick William May, yr son of 1st Baron, *b* 1911, *d* 1956: *m* 1st, 1934 (*m diss* 1948), Dorothy Patience, da of Francis Du Croz, of Weybridge; 2ndly, 1951, (Audrey) Gillian (JACKSON), who *d* 1989, da of Edward Bagot, of Cross Farm, West Coker, Somerset:—
(By 1st *m*) Caroline, *b* 1934: *m* 1954, Edwin Waldman, of 45 Burleigh St, Waterville, Maine, 04901, USA, and has issue living, Joshua Patrick, *b* 1957, — Noah William, *b* 1962, — Victoria Rose, *b* 1959, — Andrea Karen, *b* 1961. —— Valentine Virginia, *b* 1938: *m* 1963, Malcolm Walker MacLeod, of 70 Belden Hill Rd, Wilton, Conn 06897, USA, and has issue living, Sarah Walker, *b* 1965, — Alexandra Louise, *b* 1968. —— (By 2nd *m*) Philippa Jane, *b* 1952: *m* 1987, Anthony Crabtree of Cornwall House, Cross St, Tenbury Wells, Worcs WR15 8EG, and has issue living, Christopher, *b* 1987, — Melanie, *b* 1988, — Alice, *b* 1990. —— (Elisabeth) Patricia (*posthumous*), *b* 1957; has issue living, Tanya, *b* 1980, — Samantha, *b* 1981.

PREDECESSORS – (1) *Sir* GEORGE ERNEST May, KBE, son of William C. May, of Cheshunt, *b* 1871; many years Sec of Prudential Assurance Co; sometime Manager of American Dollar Securities Committee; appointed Chm of Import Duties Advisory Committee 1932; *cr a* Baronet 1931, and *Baron May*, of Weybridge, co Surrey (peerage of United Kingdom) 1935: *m* 1903, Lily Julia, OBE, who *d* 1955, yr da of G. Strauss; *d* 1946; *s* by his el son (2) JOHN LAWRENCE, 2nd Baron; *b* 1904: *m* 1st, 1925, Cicely Beryl, who *d* 1928, only child of late Ernest Fleming, of Raska, Clarendon Road, Watford; 2ndly, 1929, Elisabeth, da of George Ricardo Thoms; *d* 1950; *s* by his only son (3) MICHAEL ST JOHN, 3rd Baron and present peer.

MAYBRAY-KING, BARONY OF (Maybray-King) (Extinct 1986)

DAUGHTER LIVING OF LIFE BARON (By 1st marriage)

Hon Margaret Eleanor, *b* 1926: a JP of Havant: *m* 1945, Roy Wilson, of 26 Blenheim Rd, Westbury Park, Bristol.

WIDOW LIVING OF LIFE BARON

SHEILA CATHERINE (*Baroness Maybray-King*), da of — Atkinson: *m* 1986, as his 4th wife, Baron Maybray-King, PC (Life Baron), who *d* 1986. *Residence* – 37 Manor Farm Rd, Bitterne Park, Southampton S09 3FQ.

MAYHEW, BARON (Mayhew) (Life Baron 1981)

CHRISTOPHER PAGET MAYHEW, son of late Sir Basil Edgar Mayhew, KBE; *b* 12 June 1915; *ed* Haileybury, and Ch Ch, Oxford (MA); Parl Under-Sec of State for Foreign Affairs 1946-50, Min of Defence (RN) 1964-66; Nat Exec Cttee Liberal Party 1980; Liberal Party Spokesman on Defence; Pres Middle East Internat (Publishers) Ltd, Pres The ANAF Foundation, Pres The Parly Assoc for Euro-Arab Co-operation; formerly Chm MIND (Nat Assocn for Mental Health); author of *Men Seeking God, Britain's Role Tomorrow, Party Games, Publish It Not,* and *Time to Explain* (autobiography); joined Surrey Yeo RA 1939, served with BEF 1939-40, British N Africa Force and CMF, British Liberation Army 1944 (despatches); Maj; MP for S Norfolk (*Lab*) 1945-50, for Woolwich (East) (*Lab*) 1951-74, and for Woolwich (East) (*L*) June-July 1974; *cr* Baron Mayhew, of Wimbledon, Greater London (Life Baron) 1981: *m* 1949, Cicely Elizabeth, da of George Ludlam, and has issue.
Residence – 39 Wool Rd, Wimbledon, SW20 OHN. *Club* – National Liberal.

SONS LIVING

Rev the Hon David Francis (The White House, 20 Whickham View, Newcastle-upon-Tyne), *b* 31 July 1951; *ed* St Paul's, and Ch Ch Oxford; MA; ordained deacon 1991, priest 1992: *m* 1979, Elizabeth Helen, da of Lt-Col Pusinelli, of Chinagarth, Thornton-le-Dale, N Yorks, and has issue living, Jessica Elizabeth, *b* 1980, — Nicola Helen, *b* 1981, — Hannah Ruth, *b* 1986.
Hon (Christopher) James (Le Passous, Quettreville sur Seine 50660, France), *b* 1959; *ed* St Paul's, and King's Coll, London (BSc): *m* 1985, Deborah Anne, only da of Mark John Lewis, of Hong Kong, and has issue living, Emily Rose, *b* 1989.

DAUGHTERS LIVING

Hon Teresa Ruth, *b* 1953: *m* 1991, Robert Arthur Wyatt Lyle, only son of late Robert David Lyle Lyle (formerly Wyatt), of Bonython Manor, Helston, Cornwall, and has issue living, Christopher, *b* 1992.
Hon Judith Emily Ann, *b* 1955.

MAYO, EARL OF (Bourke) (Earl I 1785)
(Name pronounced "Burke")

Salvation from the Cross

TERENCE PATRICK BOURKE, 10th Earl; *b* 26 Aug 1929; *s* 1962; Lt RN (ret): *m* 1st, 1952 (*m diss* 1987), (Margaret) Jane (Robinson), who *d* 1992, only da of late Gerald Joseph Cuthbert Harrison, DL, of Wetheral, Cumberland; 2ndly, 1987, Sally Anne, only da of F. G. Matthews, of Bampton, Oxon, and has issue by 1st and 2nd *m*.

Arms – Per fesse or and ermine, a cross gules, in the 1st quarter a lion rampant, and in the 2nd a dexter hand erect couped at the wrist, both sable. **Crest** – A cat-a-mountain sejant guardant proper, collared and chained or. **Supporters** – Two Chevaliers in complete armour, each holding in the exterior hand a pole-axe, proper.
Residence – Château d'Arlens, Couloumé Mondebat, 32160 Plaisance-du-Gers, France *Clubs* – RNVR, Galway County.

SONS LIVING (By 1st marriage)

CHARLES DIARMUIDH JOHN (*Lord Naas*) (Derryinver, Beach Rd, Clifden, co Galway), *b* 11 June 1953; *ed* Portora Royal Sch, and Queen's Univ, Belfast; Works Manager, MAG Briggs Amasco Ltd, Leeds: *m* 1st, 1975 (*m diss* 1979), Marie Antoinette Cronnelly; 2ndly, 1985, Marie Veronica, da of Francis Mannion, of Clifden, co Galway, and has issue by 1st and 2nd *m*:—

SONS LIVING (by 2nd *m*)— *Hon* Richard Thomas, *b* 7 Dec 1985, — *Hon* Eoin Patrick, *b* 1989.
DAUGHTER LIVING (by 1st *m*)— *Hon* Corinne Mary Jane, *b* 1975.

Hon Patrick Antony, *b* 1955.

Hon Harry Richard, *b* 1960.

(*By 2nd marriage*)

Hon James Edward Maurice, *b* 1986.

SISTER LIVING

Sheelagh Wilmot, *b* 1925: *m* 1955, Frank Merton Trier, of Fairlawn, W Horsley, Surrey, and has issue living, Terence Anthony Merton, *b* 1957, — Ysolde Gwynedd, *b* 1956.

AUNT LIVING (*Daughter of 8th Earl*)

Lady Betty Jocelyne, *b* 1917: *m* 1st, 1943, Capt Ronald Banon, late 60th Rifles, who *d* 1943; 2ndly, 1953, Samuel Clarke, who *d* 1980, and has issue living, (by 2nd *m*) Elizabeth Charlotte, *b* 1955, — Jocelyne Margaret, *b* 1957: *m* 1st, 1981 (*m diss* 1988), Michael J. Woodman; 2ndly, 1992, Carl Coert Grobler. *Residence* – 361 Woodstock Rd, Oxford.

STEPMOTHER LIVING

Patricia May, el da of late H. B. Dickinson, MD, FRCS, of Hereford: *m* 1952, as his 2nd wife, Capt Hon Bryan Longley Bourke, RIF, who *d* 1961. *Residence* – Dashells, Dog Village, Broadclyst, Exeter, Devon EX5 3AB.

COLLATERAL BRANCHES LIVING

Grandsons of late Maj Hon Edward Roden Bourke, 6th son of 5th Earl:—
  Issue of late Col Nigel Edward Jocelyn Bourke, *b* 1886, *d* 1970: *m* 1927, Doris, who *d* 1949, da of Allan Wills, of Aberdeen:—
Josslyn Allan Roden, *b* 1930: *m* 1951, Barbara Alison, da of Wilson Braddock, and has issue living, Alice Grania, *b* 1954, — Deborah Madeline, *b* 1958, — Susan Doris, *b* 1960.

Grandson of late Lt Hubert Edward Madden BOURKE-BORROWES, RN, son of Richard Bourke, son of late Rev Hon George Theobald Bourke, 4th son of 3rd Earl:—
  Issue of late Dermot Richard Southwell Bourke-Borrowes, *b* 1884, *d* 1968: *m* 1941, Mrs Elizabeth Burton, da of G. F. Burgess, of Hall Garth, Over Kellett, Lancs:—
Kildare Hubert (The Lower House, North Aston, Oxon OX6 4JA), *b* 1942; *ed* Wellington and Magdalen Coll, Camb; JP: *m* 1st 1971 (*m diss* 1983), Pippa Marguerite, who *d* 1992, yr da of late Lt-Col O. S. Steel, of Meriden Court, Chelsea Manor St, SW3; 2ndly, 1984, Sarah Louise, da of late John Robert McCready, of Naro Moru, Kenya, and has issue living (by 1st *m*), Olivia Helene, *b* 1974, — Catherine Hayley, *b* 1977, — (by 2nd *m*) Hubert Alexander Robert, *b* 1985, — Thea Anne, *b* 1986.

Granddaughter of late Maj-Gen Sir George Deane Bourke, KCMG, CB, son of late Lieut-Col Thomas Joseph Deane Bourke, son of late Rev Hon George Theobald Bourke (ante):—
  Issue of late Group-Capt Ulick John Deane Bourke, CMG, *b* 1884, *d* 1948: *m* 1917 (*m diss* 1932), Irene, da of Lewis Ashhurst, of Norwich:—
Bridget (Sparrows, North Aston, Oxon), *b* 1920; Bar Lincoln's Inn 1956: *m* 1963, Leigh Edward Parker, who *d* 1973.

PREDECESSORS – This family, formerly of Moneycrower, co Mayo, descends from John Bourke, 4th son of Sir Thomas Bourke, 1397 styled "MacWilliam Eighter", head of Mayo or Lower Connaught branch, as distinct from "MacWilliam Oughter" of Galway or Upper Connaught (*see* M Sligo), whose 2nd son Edmund was ancestor of Viscounts Mayo (*cr* 1627, ext or dormant 1767), and was a branch of the Anglo-Norman family of de Burgh **(1)** *Rt Hon* JOHN Bourke, of Moneycrower, MP, First Commr of Revenue, Ireland 1749-80; *cr Baron Naas,* of Naas, co Kildare 1776, and *Viscount Mayo,* of Moneycrower, co Mayo 1781; and *Earl of Mayo* 1785 (all in Peerage of Ireland): *m* 1726, Mary, who *d* 1774, da of Rt Hon Joseph Deane; *d* 1790; *s* by his el son **(2)** JOHN, 2nd Earl, *b* about 1729; MP: *m* 1764, Lady Margaret Leeson, who *d* 1794, da of 1st Earl of Milltown; *d* 1792; *s* by his brother **(3)** *Most Rev* JOSEPH Deane, DD, 3rd Earl; *b* 1736; Bishop of Leighlin 1772-82, and Archbishop of Tuam 1782-94: *m* 1760, Elizabeth Meade, who *d* 1807, sister of 1st Earl of Clanwilliam; *d* 1794; *s* by his son **(4)** JOHN, GCH, PC, 4th Earl; *b* 1766; a Representative Peer 1816-49: *m* 1792, Arabella (Lady of the Bedchamber to Queen Adelaide), who *d* 1843, da of William Mackworth Praed, of Bitton House, Devon; *d* 1849; *s* by his nephew **(5)** ROBERT (only son of Rt Rev Hon Richard Bourke, Bishop of Waterford and Lismore, 2nd son of 3rd Earl), 5th Earl, *b* 1797; a Representative Peer 1852-67: *m* 1820, Anne Charlotte, who *d* 1867, da of Hon John Jocelyn (E Roden); *d* 1867; *s* by his son **(6)** *Rt Hon* RICHARD SOUTHWELL, KP, GCMG, 6th Earl; *b* 1822; MP for Kildare (C) 1847-52, for Coleraine 1852-7, and for Cockermouth 1857-68; Ch Sec for Ireland 1852, 1858, and 1866, and Gov-Gen of India 1868-72, when he was assassinated in the Andaman Islands: *m* 1848, Blanche Julia, CI, VA, who *d* 1918, da of 1st Baron Leconfield; *s* by his el son **(7)** *Rt Hon* DERMOT ROBERT WYNDHAM, KP, 7th Earl; *b* 1851; a Representative Peer for Ireland and Lieut of co Kildare; a Member of Senate of Irish Free State 1922-7: *m* 1885, Geraldine Sarah, who *d* 1944, da of late Hon Gerald Henry Brabazon Ponsonby; *d* 1927; *s* by his cousin **(8)** WALTER LONGLEY (son of late Rev Hon George Wingfield Bourke, 4th son of 5th Earl), 8th Earl; *b* 1859: *m* 1st, 1887, Ethel Kathleen Jane, who *d* 1913, only da of late Capt John Freeman, of Rockfield, Herefordshire; 2ndly, 1916, Margaret Anah, da of late Major John Harvey Scott, Indian Army; *d* 1939; *s* by his son **(9)** ULICK HENRY, 9th Earl; *b* 1890; 2nd Lt, King's Roy Rifle Corps; 1914-18 War as Lt, King's African Rifles: *m* 1937, Nöel Jessie Haliburton, who *d* 1993, aged 102, da of late William James Wilson, of High Park, nr Kendal; *d* 1962; *s* by his nephew **(10)** TERENCE PATRICK (only son of late Hon Bryan Longley Bourke, 3rd son of 8th Earl), 10th Earl and present peer; also Viscount Mayo, and Baron Naas.

MEATH, EARL OF (Brabazon) Sits as BARON CHAWORTH (UK 1831) (Earl I 1627)

My life is devoted

ANTHONY WINDHAM NORMAND BRABAZON, 14th Earl; *b* 3 Nov 1910; *s* 1949; *ed* Eton; European War 1939-45 as Major Grenadier Guards (wounded): *m* 1940, Elizabeth Mary, da of late Capt Geoffrey Vaux Salvin Bowlby (*see* V Valentia, 1985 Edn), and has issue.

Arms – Gules: on a bend or, three martlets sable. **Crest** – On a mount vert, a falcon rising or. **Supporters** – Two wyverns or, collared and chained gules. *Residence* – Killruddery, Bray, co Wicklow.

SONS LIVING

JOHN ANTHONY (*Lord Ardee*) (Ballinacor, Rathdrum, co Wicklow), *b* 11 May 1941; *ed* Harrow; a Page of Honour to HM 1956-58; late Gren Gds: *m* 1973, Xenia, yr da of P. Goudime, of Windlesham Park, Surrey, and has issue:—

SON LIVING— *Hon* Anthony Jacques, *b* 30 Jan 1977.
DAUGHTERS LIVING— *Hon* Corinna Lettice, *b* 1974, — *Hon* Serena Alexandra, *b* 1979.

Hon David Geoffrey Normand (North Wing, Killruddery, Bray, co Wicklow), *b* 1948: *m* 1972, Gay Dorothea, yr da of Cdr William (Jock) Whitworth, DSC, RN, of Trudder, co Wicklow (M Ely), and has issue living, Geoffrey William *b* 1975, — Celia Antonia, *b* 1973, — Diana Elizabeth, *b* 1981.

DAUGHTERS LIVING

Lady Romayne Aileen, *b* 1943: *m* 1968, Capt Robert Eben Neil Pike, late Gren Gds, of Kidborough House, Danehill, Sussex, and has issue living, Harry Eben, *b* 1974, — Tamsin Lucy, *b* 1972.
Lady Lavinia Anne, *b* 1945: *m* 1969, John Ernest Baron Jobson, of Barnacullia, Kilmacanoge, co Wicklow, and has issue living, James Robert, *b* 1977, — Rebecca Catherine, *b* 1971, — Charlotte Naomi Marya, *b* 1973, — Suzannah Elizabeth, *b* 1976.

SISTER LIVING

Lady Meriel Aileen, *b* 1913: *m* 1947, Maj Ernest Gerald Howarth, MBE, who *d* 1967, and has issue living, Sarah Anne, *b* 1950: *m* 1st, 1972 (*m diss* 1982), Robert A. H. Smeddle (*see* Hughes, Bt, *cr* 1773, colls); 2ndly, 1987, Alastair D. M. Ritchie, of 53 Temple Sheen Rd, SW14 7QF, son of Lt-Col C. W. M. Ritchie, of The Grange, Dolphinton, Peeblesshire, and has issue living, Catherin Elizabeth, *b* 1953: *m* 1980, James Keith Forrester, of Copper Beeches, Sikeside, Kirklinton, Carlisle CA6 6DR, and has issue living, Anne-Marie Catherin *b* 1983, Charlotte Antonia *b* 1986, Alice Elizabeth *b* 1988. *Residence* – Robin Hood Cottage, Standford, Borden GU35 8RA. —— Felicity Margaretta, *b* 1917; *ed* London Univ (BA 1939); formerly 1st Officer WRNS: *m* 1948, Gilbert Stanley Hodson, who *d* 1972, and has issue (*see* Hodson, Bt colls). *Residence* – Luska, Puckane, Nenagh, co Tipperary.

COLLATERAL BRANCHES LIVING

Issue of late Lieut-Col Hon Claud Maitland Patrick Brabazon, OBE, 3rd son of 12th Earl, *b* 1874, *d* 1959: *m* 1915, Kathleen, who *d* 1961, da of late Arthur Maitland, of Shudy Camps Park, Cambridgeshire:—
Elizabeth Maitland, *b* 1915: *m* 1942, Lieut-Col Evered Mansfield Poole, RA (ret) (By Ilkeston (ext)), who *d* 1982, and has issue living, Catherin Elizabeth, *b* 1953: *m* 1980, James Keith Forrester, of Copper Beeches, Sikeside, Kirklinton, Carlisle CA6 6DR, and has issue living, Anne-Marie Catherin *b* 1983, Charlotte Antonia *b* 1986, Alice Elizabeth *b* 1988. *Residence* – Robin Hood Cottage, Standford, Borden GU35 8RA. —— Felicity Margaretta, *b* 1917; *ed* London Univ (BA 1939); formerly 1st Officer WRNS: *m* 1948, Gilbert Stanley Hodson, who *d* 1972, and has issue (*see* Hodson, Bt colls). *Residence* – Luska, Puckane, Nenagh, co Tipperary.

(In special remainder to the Earldom)

Descendants of late Hon Sir Anthony Brabazon, 3rd son of 1st Baron Ardee:—
Grandsons of Samuel Levinge Brabazon (*b* 1829), elder son of late Rev James Brabazon, son of late Anthony Brabazon, elder son of late Philip Brabazon (*b* 1733), great grandson of late Capt James Brabazon, son of late Hon Sir Anthony Brabazon (ante):—
Issue of late Gerald Hugh Brabazon, *b* 18—, *d* 19—: *m* 189—, Eleanor Murphy:—
Clarence Levinge, *b* 18—. —— Claude Hugh, *b* 18—. —— Edward Alfred, *b* 18—.

Grandchildren of late Charles James Anthony Brabazon, eldest son of late Anthony Godsell Brabazon (*b* 1841), yr son of late Rev James Brabazon (ante):—
Issue of late Anthony Godsell Brabazon, *b* 1899, *d* 1982: *m* 1925, Margaret Victoria, only da of late J. A. Gibson, of Sydney, NSW:—
Margaret Ann (1 Boorana St, Jindalee, Brisbane, Qld 4074, Australia), *b* 1927; FASA, ACIS, JP: *m* 1974, Rt Rev Ian Wotton Allnutt Shevill, sometime Bishop of Newcastle, NSW, who *d* 1988.
Issue of late Charles Reginald Brabazon, *b* 1904, *d* 1987: *m* 1940, Minnie Isabel (17 Morgan St, Albion Heights, Brisbane, Qld, Australia), da of James Lennox Arthur, of Quambetook, Nelia, N Qld:—
Charles James Lennox (48 Tenth Av, St Lucia, Brisbane, Qld, Australia), *b* 1944; BA, LLM, QC: *m* 1981, Michelle May, QC, and has issue living, Sarah Margaret, *b* 1991, — Lucinda Claire, *b* (triplet) 1991, — Alice Elizabeth, *b* (triplet) 1991. —— Richard Anthony, *b* 1949; *ed* The Southport Sch: *m* 1975, Susan Margaret, da of G. Greentree, and has issue living, Timothy Richard, *b* 1979, — Jennifer Amy, *b* 1981.
Issue of late Rupert William Brabazon, *b* 1908, *d* 1979: *m* 1952, Margaret Cecil Pender, da of late Edward Pender Phillott, of Colane, Winton, Qld:—
Anthony Edward (39 Kingcaid Drive, Highland Park, Qld 4211, Australia), *b* 1953: *m* 1993, Tracy Clarkson. —— †William Robert, *b* 1960; *d* 1982. —— Wendy Pender (19 Edgar St, Newmarket, Brisbane, Qld 4051, Australia), *b* 1955. —— Patricia Rain (3 Reef Court, Mermaid Waters, Qld 4218, Australia), *b* 1957.

Granddaughters of late Rupert Levinge Brabazon (infra):—
Issue of late Rupert Macdonald Brabazon, *b* 1907, *d* 1983: *m* 1934, Moyra Joy, who *d* 1974, da of Edgar Joyce, of The Overflow, Beaudesert, Qld:—

Barbara Joan, *b* 1938: *m* 1963, Kenneth Maddox, of 41 Mabel St, Cunnamulla, Qld 4490, Australia, and has issue living, Kim Anita, *b* 1965; has issue living, Zachary Wayne *b* 1990, — Kerryanne, *b* 1967: *m* 1993, Mark Edward Andrews. —— Patricia Elizabeth, *b* 1940: *m* 1960, Harold Bergman, of 46 Kooringal Drive, Jindalee, Qld 4074, Australia, and has issue living, Anthony, *b* 1965, — Thomas *b* 1966, — Patricia, *b* 1961, — Colleen, *b* 1963, — Rosemary, *b* 1968, — Margaret, *b* 1970, — Jeanette, *b* 1972.

Grandchildren of late Anthony Godsell Brabazon (*b* 1841) (ante):—
Issue of late Charles James Anthony Brabazon, *b* 1869, *d* 1944: *m* 1897, Amy Ruby Victoria, who *d* 1947, da of William McMillan, of Culparoo, Longreach, Qld:—
Kathleen Patricia (6/9 Norwood St, Toowong, Brisbane, Qld 4066, Australia), *b* 1903. —— Eileen Emma, *b* 1907: *m* 1929, Bernard Carr Clark, of 2/121 Maloney St, N Rockhampton, Qld 4701, Australia, and has had issue, †Michael George, *b* 1930; *d* 1991, — Adam Charles (Bimbadeen, Taroom, Qld 4420), *b* 1933: *m* 1954, Dorothy Isabel, da of J. S. B. Milne, of Dalby, Qld, and has issue living, Bruce Robert *b* 1955: *m* 1987, Judy Clare, da of J. Bazley, of Brooklands, Ullenhall, Warwicks (and has issue living, Darryl James Carr *b* 1993, Nicole Hanna Carr *b* 1991), Ian Charles *b* 1956, Owen Mark *b* 1967: *m* 1991, Helen Marian, da of D. Kimber, of Bowen, Qld (and has issue living, Emily Kate *b* 1992, Rachael Louise *b* 1993), Kevin Adam *b* 1969, Wendy Ann *b* 1961: *m* 1981, Rodney Hans Woodrow, of Juandah Plains, Wandoan, Qld 4419 (and has issue living, Rowan Max *b* 1985, Ryan Wayne *b* 1990, Megan Rose *b* 1983, Krystal Lee *b* 1988), — Robert Anthony (Mutation, Clermont, Qld 4721), *b* 1936: *m* 1967, Margot Grant, da of late A. F. G. Cameron, of Brisbane, Qld, and has issue living, Michael Robert *b* 1969, Ann Laura *b* 1970.
Issue of late Rupert Levinge Brabazon, *b* 1871, *d* 1924: *m* 1904, Grace Eva, who *d* 1948, da of late Campbell Living-stone Macdonald, of Bromelton, Beaudesert, Qld:—
Robert Charles, *b* 1912: *m* 1950, Geraldine Hope Gordon, da of Robert John Gordon Burrow, and has issue living, Mark Levinge, *b* 1958; *ed* Brisbane Boys' Coll; BA, LLB.

Granddaughter of late George Philip Augustus Brabazon (infra):—
Issue of late Cecil George Le Normand Brabazon, *b* 1887, *d* 1975: *m* 1927, Gladys May (183 3rd Av, 700 Chula Vista, Cal 92010, USA), da of Nathan Wyman Downs, of Chula Vista, Cal, USA:—
Cora Jane, *b* 1934: *m* 1962, Charles F. Ruhr, of 4750 Washington Av, White Bear Lake, Minnesota 55110, USA, and has issue living, Christopher Patrick, *b* 1968, — Ann Cecilia, *b* 1965.

Granddaughter of late Rev Philip Robert Waller Brabazon, son of late Rev George Brabazon (*b* 1780), yr son of late Philip Brabazon (*b* 1733) (ante):—
Issue of late George Philip Augustus Brabazon, *b* 1845, *d* 1912: *m* 1886, Rhoda Jane, who *d* 1946, da of late Edmond Nugent, MD, FRCSI, of San Diego, California:—
Marian Constance, *b* 1900: *m* 1936, Howard Jonathan Edwards, who *d* 1950. *Residence* – Cloisters Con Centre, 3680 Reynard Way, San Diego, California, USA.

Grandson of late George Philip Augustus Brabazon (ante):—
Issue of late Montague Philip Le Normand Brabazon, *b* 1890, *d* 1967: *m* 1916, Edwina Meston, da of late George T. Smith, of Alpine, San Diego, Cal, USA:—
Keith Elmer (5738 Willows Rd, Alpine, Cal 92001, USA), *b* 1917: *m* 1963, Clara Carolina, da of Rudolph Wenger, of Max, N Dakota, and has issue living, Lee Monte (5670 Willow Rd, Alpine, Calif 92001, USA), *b* 1964: *m* 19—, Kathleen Lorraine, da of Barry Hulahan, of San Diego, Calif.

PREDECESSORS – (1) *Rt Hon Sir* EDWARD Brabazon, KT, PC, MP for co Wicklow 1585, and High Sheriff of Staffordshire 1606; *cr Baron Ardee* (peerage of Ireland) 1616; *d* 1625; *s* by his son (2) WILLIAM, KB, 2nd Baron; *cr Earl of Meath* (peerage of Ireland) 1627, with remainder to his brother Anthony; *d* 1675; *s* by his son (3) EDWARD, 2nd Earl; *d* 1675, *s* by his son (4) WILLIAM, 3rd Earl; *d* 1684; *s* by his el son (5) EDWARD, 4th Earl; was Ranger of the Phoenix Park, Dublin; *dsp* 1707; *s* by his brother (6) CHAMBRE, 5th Earl; *d* 1715; *s* by his el son (7) CHAWORTH, 6th Earl; *dsp* 1758; *s* by his brother (8) EDWARD, 7th Earl; *d* 1772; *s* by his son (9) ANTHONY, 8th Earl; *d* 1790; *s* by his el son (10) WILLIAM, 9th Earl; killed in a duel 1797; *s* by his brother (11) JOHN CHAMBRE, KP, 10th Earl; *b* 1772; Lord-Lieut of co Dublin; *cr Baron Chaworth*, of Eaton Hall, co Hereford (peerage of United Kingdom) 1831: *m* 1801, Lady Melosina Adelaide, who *d* 1866, da of 1st Earl of Clanwilliam; *d* 1851; *s* by his son (12) WILLIAM, 11th Earl; *b* 1803: *m* 1873, Harriot, who *d* 1898, da of Sir Richard Brooke, 6th Bt; *d* 1887; *s* by his son (13) REGINALD, KP, GCVO, GBE, PC, 12th Earl, *b* 1841; Founder and Chm of Metropolitan Public Gardens Asso; Chancellor of Roy Univ of Ireland 1902-6: *m* 1868, Lady Mary Jane Maitland, who *d* 1918, only da of 11th Earl of Lauderdale; *d* 1929; *s* by his son (14) REGINALD LE NORMAND, CB, CBE, 13th Earl; *b* 1869; Brig-Gen (ret) late Grenadier and Irish Guards; S Africa 1900-02, European War 1914-19 (CB, CBE): *m* 1908, Lady Aileen May Wyndham Quin, who *d* 1962, da of 4th Earl of Dunraven; *d* 1949; *s* by his son (15) ANTHONY WINDHAM NORMAND, 14th Earl and present peer; also Baron Ardee, and Baron Chaworth.

Medina, Earl of; son of Marquess of Milford Haven.

Medway, Lord; son of Earl of Cranbrook.

MELCHETT, BARON (Mond) (Baron UK 1928, Bt UK 1910)

PETER ROBERT HENRY MOND, 4th Baron, and 4th Baronet; *b* 24 Feb 1948; *s* 1973; *ed* Eton, Pembroke Coll, Camb, and Keele Univ; a Lord in Waiting to HM 1974-75, and Under-Sec of State, Industry 1975-76; Min of State, N Ireland 1976-79; Pres of Ramblers Assoc 1981-84; Chm of Community Industry 1979-85, and the Working Party on Pop Festivals 1975-76; Member of Friends of Release; Chm Wildlife Link 1981-86; Chm Greenpeace UK 1986-89; Executive Dir Greenpeace UK since 1989.

Arms – Quarterly, 1st and 4th, gules, a demi-lion rampant argent between in chief a decrescent and an increscent, and in base a crescent, all or; on a chief argent an eagle displayed between two mullets sable, *Mond*; 2nd and 3rd, azure, on a pile between three mullets argent, an eagle displayed sable, *Lowenthal.* **Crest** – A demi-bear holding between the paws a fountain, both proper. **Supporters** – *Dexter*, a Doctor of Science of the University of Oxford, holding in the exterior hand a chemical measure glass; *Sinister*, a labourer, holding in the exterior hand a pick resting on the shoulder all proper. *Address* – c/o House of Lords.

SISTERS LIVING

(Hon) Kerena Ann (does not use courtesy title), *b* 1951: *m* 1st, 1980, Richard Moorehead; 2ndly, 1985, Adam Boulton, and has issue living, (by 1st *m*) Lucy, *b* 1981, — (by 2nd *m*) Blaise, *b* 1990, — Hannah, *b* 1987.
Hon Pandora Shelley, *b* 1959: *m* 1991, Nicholas Wesolowski, son of late Michael Joseph Wesolowski, of Pelham St, SW3.

AUNT LIVING (*Daughter of 2nd Baron*)

Hon Karis Valerie Violet, *b* 1927: *m* 1st, 1949 (*m diss* 1956), John Hackman Sumner; 2ndly, 1956, Brian Wallace, and has issue living, (by 1st *m*) Justin Mark, *b* 1953, — (by 2nd *m*) Jessica Karis, *b* 1957, — Arabella Katherine, *b* 1959. *Residence* – Greenways, Lambourn, Berks.

WIDOW LIVING OF SON OF SECOND BARON

Yvonne Victoria, only child of T. Douglas Searle, of Cornerways, The Park, Cheltenham: *m* 1st, 1942, Lt Hon Derek John Henry Mond, RNVR, who was *k* on active ser 1945; 2ndly, 1951, Richard Louis Rowe. *Residence* – 4133 Marlowe Av, Montreal H4A 3M3, Canada.

WIDOW LIVING OF THIRD BARON

SONIA ELIZABETH (16 Tite St, Chelsea, SW3), da of late Col Roland Harris Graham, RAMC (ret), of The Lodge, Bridge, Kent; novelist and travel writer; Council Member Royal Court Theatre since 1983, and The Royal National Theatre 1983-84: *m* 1st, 1947, the 3rd Baron, who *d* 1973; 2ndly, 1984, as his 2nd wife, Dr Andrew Annandale Sinclair, author.

PREDECESSORS – (1) *Rt Hon* ALFRED MORITZ Mond, LLD, DSc, FRS, son of late Ludwig Mond, PhD, FRS, of The Poplars, 20 Avenue Road, St John's Wood, NW, and Winnington Hall, Norwich, by his wife, Frieda, who *d* 1923, da of Adolph Meyer Löwenthal, of Cologne; *b* 1868; first Chm of Imperial Chemical Industries, Ltd, Chm of Mond Nickel Co, and of Amalgamated Anthracite Collieries, Ltd, a Director of Westminster Bank, Ltd, Pres of British Science Guild, Chm of National Federation of Chemical Employers, and of Council of Jewish Agency for Palestine, and Joint Chm of Conference on Industrial Reorganisation and Industrial Relations; was First Commr of Works 1916-21, and Min of Health 1921-2; MP for Chester (*L*) Jan 1906 to Jan 1910, for Swansea, Swansea Town Div (*L*) Jan 1910 to Nov 1918, for W Div thereof (*L*) Dec 1918 to Nov 1923, and for Carmarthenshire, Carmarthen Div (*L*) Aug to Oct 1924, and (*C*) Oct 1924 to June 1928; *cr a Baronet*, of Hartford Hill, Great Budworth, co Chester 1910, and *Baron Melchett*, of Landford, co Southampton (peerage of United Kingdom) 1928: *m* 1894, Violet Florence Mabel, who *d* 1945, DBE, da of late James Henry Goetze; *d* 1930; *s* by his son (2) HENRY LUDWIG, 2nd Baron; *b* 1898; was Vice-Chm of Imperial Chemical Industries Ltd, a Director of International Nickel Co of Canada, Ltd, of Industrial Finance and Investment Corporation, Ltd, and of Palestine Electric Corporation, Ltd, Chm of Palestine Plantations, Ltd, etc, and a Trustee of Ramsay Memorial Fellowship; sat as MP for Isle of Ely (*L*) 1923-4, when he was defeated, and for Liverpool, E Toxteth Div (*C*) 1929-30: *m* 1920, Amy Gwen, who *d* 1982, da of late John Wilson, of Parktown, Johannesburg, S Africa; *d* 1949; *s* by his son (3) JULIAN EDWARD ALFRED, 3rd Baron, *b* 1925; Chm of British Steel Corpn 1967-73, and a Member of NEDC 1969-73: *m* 1947, Sonia Elizabeth, da of late Col Roland Harris Graham, RAMC (ret), of the Lodge, Bridge, Kent; *d* 1973; *s* by his son (4) PETER ROBERT HENRY, 4th Baron and present peer.

Melgund, Viscount; son of Earl of Minto.

MELLISH, BARON (Mellish) (Life Baron 1985)

ROBERT JOSPEH MELLISH, PC, son of John Mellish, of Deptford, SE8; *b* 1913; *ed* St Joseph's RC Sch, Deptford; PPS Admiralty 1948-49 to Min of Supply 1949-51, and to Min of Pensions 1951-64, Parl Sec, Min of Housing and Local Govt 1964-67, and again May to June 1970, Min of Public Buildings and Works 1967-69, and Govt Ch Whip 1969-70, and 1974-76, Ch Labour Whip 1970-74; Dep Chm London Docklands Development Corpn since 1981; served 1939-45 as Capt RE in SE Asia; MP for Rotherhide Div of Bermondsey (*Lab*) 1946-50, Bermondsey 1950-74, and Southwark Bermondsey 1974-82; *cr* PC 1967, and

Baron Mellish, of Bermondsey, Greater London (Life Baron) 1985: *m* 1938, Anne Elizabeth, da of George Warner, of Bermondsey, SE16, and has issue.
Residence – 39 Bromley Rd, Catford, SE6.

SONS LIVING

Hon Robert (20 Shermanbury Rd, Worthing), *b* ca 1942/43: *m* 19—, Erica.
Hon David (47 Little Heath, SE7), *b* 1944: *m* 1967, Mary Josephine, da of John Patrick Leahy, and has issue living, Daniel David, *b* 1969, — Claire Mary, *b* 1968.
Hon Paul, *b* ca 1952/53.
Hon Stephen (45 Lancing Park, Lancing, Sussex), *b* 1955: *m* 1976, Elizabeth Ann, da of John Henry Skinner, and has issue living, Nicholas, *b* 1986.

Melville, see Earl of Leven and Melville.

MELVILLE, VISCOUNT (Dundas) (Viscount UK 1802)

ROBERT DAVID ROSS DUNDAS, 9th Viscount; *b* 28 May 1937; *s* 1971; *ed* Wellington Coll; Capt (Reserve) Scots Gds; Lieut Ayrshire Yeo; Pres Lasswade Civic Soc, CC and District Councillor, Lasswade, Midlothian: *m* 1982, Fiona Margaret, da of late Roger Kirkpatrick Stilgoe, of Derby House, Stogumber, Taunton, Somerset, and has issue.

Arms – Argent, a lion rampant gules, armed and langued azure, within a bordure of the last charged with three boar's heads couped or, armed proper and langued of the second. **Crest** – A lion's head affrontée gules struggling through an oak-bush proper. **Supporters** – *Dexter*, a leopard regardant proper; *sinister*, a stag proper attired argent.
Residences – Solomons Court, Chalford, Stroud, Glos; 3 Roland Way, SW7. *Clubs* – Cavalry and Guards', Turf, Midlothian County.

SONS LIVING

Hon ROBERT HENRY KIRKPATRICK, *b* 23 April 1984.
Hon James David Brouncker, *b* 1986.

COLLATERAL BRANCHES LIVING

Issue of late Hon Cospatrick Philip Brooke Dundas, 2nd son of 6th Viscount, *b* 1879, *d* 1954: *m* 1913, Isabella, who *d* 1969, da of E. A. W. McKenzie:—
Daphne Roseabella Louise, *b* 1923: *m* 1943, Rankin Hodgin, of Lethbridge, Alberta, Canada.

Issue of late Hon Richard Serle Dundas, 3rd son of 6th Viscount, *b* 1880, *d* 1968: *m* 1st, 1907, Lydia Catherine, who *d* 1922, da of E. A. W. R. McKenzie, of Pelly, Saskatchewan, Canada; 2ndly, 1926, Mathilde Mary who *d* 1979, da of Louis Saxon, of York Town, Saskatchewan, Canada:—
(By 1st *m*) Hugh McKenzie (298 Alfred St, Pembroke, Ont, Canada K8A 3A6; *Clubs* – Toronto Royal Canadian Military Institute, and Pembroke Golf and Country), *b* 1910; *ed* Sask Univ (BA); 1939-45 War: *m* 1939, Catherine Sanderson, who *d* 1994, da of late John Wallace, of Edinburgh, and has issue living, Robert Hugh Sanderson (Box 82, Hesperia, CA 92345, USA), *b* 1943; *ed* Sask Univ (BA), Carleton Univ (MA): *m* 1980, Nancy, da of Kenneth Howard Sullivan, of Montreal, — Catherine Marion Wallace (298 Alfred St, Pembroke, Ontario, Canada K8A 3A6), *b* 1948; *ed* Carleton Univ (BA). —— Richard Serle (II) (Box 281, Paradise Hill, Saskatchewan, Canada S0M 2G0), *b* 1911; 1939-45 War: *m* 1942, Marianne Elizabeth, da of late William Hugh Semple, of N Battleford, Sask, Canada, and has issue living, Richard Serle (III) (1300-12th Av, Williams Lake, BC, Canada V2G 3X4), *b* 1948: *m* 1970, Denise Paulette, da of Frank Dechant, of Manning, Alberta, Canada, and has issue living, Richard Serle (IV) *b* 1971, Kelsi Shannon *b* 1974, — Dianne Mary, *b* 1946: *m* 1965, Lyle Merle Winder, of Box 301 Paradise Hill, Saskatchewan, Canada S0M 2G0, and has issue living, Laurie Dianne *b* 1966, — Carolyn Patricia, *b* 1954; *ed* Univ of Regina, Sask (BEd): *m* 1978, Daniel Brian Gervais, of 2302-49th Av, Lloydminster, Sask, Canada S9V 1M1, and has issue living, Aaron Daniel *b* 1983, Danelle Lindsay *b* 1979, Whitney Nicole *b* 1986. —— †Kenneth Brooke, *b* 1913; *ed* Sask Univ (BE Civil); Tech Dir of R & D Domtar Chemicals, Ltd, Montreal: *m* 1942, Dorothy Helen, who *d* 1994, da of late John A. Walters, of Saskatoon, and *d* 1988, leaving issue, Anthony John, *b* 1946; *ed* Queens Univ Ont, (BA), and Duke Univ (MA); *m* 1972, Carol A., da of R. Brunini of Pointe Claire, Quebec, and has issue living, Amy Leana *b* 1978, Kristina *b* 1982, — Peter Melville, *b* 1948; *ed* Univ of Sask (BA): *m* 1973, Mary Ann, da of J. Thorne, of Ottawa, and has issue living, Zachary David *b* 1979, Jennifer Mary *b* 1975, — Christopher Charles, *b* 1950; *ed* Queens Univ (BA) and Univ of California (MBA): *m* 1976, Marie Madeleine Suzanne, da of late Vianney Provencher, of Gentilly, Quebec, and has issue living, Sarah Daisy *b* 1977, Carla *b* 1982, — Dorothy Anne, *b* 1945: *m* 1977 (*m diss* 19—), R. Stephen Becker, of Springfield, Ill, USA. —— †Gerald Alexander, *b* 1916: *m* 1939, Alice Marjorie, da of Richard M. Lister, of Pelly, Saskatchewan, Canada, and *d* 1966, leaving issue, Richard Melville (Apt 8, Bld 531, Pleasantville, St John's Newfoundland), *b* 1940; RCMP: *m* 1965, Dorothy Vivian, da of Alex Bursey, of St John's, Newfoundland, and has issue living, Karen Anne *b* 1965, Katherine Dawn *b* 1969, — Gerald James, *b* 1959: *m* 1982, — Pamela Marion, *b* 1942; SRN: *m* 1965, Anthony Braun, who *d* 1980. —— Robert Montague (5738 Wallace St, Vancouver, BC, Canada), *b* 1920; *ed* BC Univ; Lt-Cdr RCN (ret); 1939-45 War as Lt RCNVR: *m* 1953, Shirley Janet, da of Urwin Finch, of Vancouver, and has had issue, James Urwin, *b* 1954, — †Fr Hugh Montague, *b* 1959; Roman Catholic Priest; *d* 1993, — Janet Glencora, *b* 1952: *m* 1982, Stephen Corbett, of 4640 Duncliffe Rd, Richmond, BC V7E 3N1, Canada, and has issue living, George Miles *b* 1984, Madeline Janet *b* 1987, — Patricia Hope, *b* 1965. —— Grace Edith Marian, *b* 1918; *ed* Sask Univ (BHSc). —— (By 2nd *m*) Oenone Judith, *b* 1927: *ed* BC Univ (BA), London Univ (MA); PhD Wisconsin. —— Iris Ann Alayne (Salt Spring Island, BC, Canada), *b* 1928: *m* 1952, Rt Rev Ronald Francis Shepherd, late Bishop of British Columbia, formerly Dean of Montreal, and R of Christ Church

Cathedral, and has issue living, Jeremy Michael, *b* 1956, — Christopher Patrick, *b* 1958, — Timothy David, *b* 1962, — Peter Andrew Dundas, *b* 1966, — Mary Mathilde, *b* 1954, — Susan Clare, *b* 1960.

Grandson of late Lieut Hon Kenneth Robert Dundas, RNVR, 4th son of 6th Viscount:—
Issue of late Claud Kenneth Melville, *b* 1911, *d* 1993: *m* 1939, Janet (The Haven, Woodlands Drive, Barnston, Cheshire), da of John Donaldson:—
Kenneth Ninian Melville, *b* 1943; *ed* Trin Coll, Glenalmond: *m* 19—, Susan —.

PREDECESSORS – (1) HENRY DUNDAS, PC (4th son of Robert Dundas of Arniston, cadet of Dundas of that Ilk), MP for co Edinburgh 1774-90, and for Edinburgh City 1790-1802; was successively Lord Advocate for Scotland, Sec of State for Home Depart, Pres of India Board of Control, Keeper of Privy Seal of Scotland, Sec of State for War, Treasurer of the Navy, and First Lord of the Admiralty; *cr Baron Dunira*, of co Perth, and *Viscount Melville* (peerage of United Kingdom) 1802; was impeached by the House of Commons in 1805 of malversation whilst treasurer of the Navy, and being tried by his peers was acquitted; *d* 1811; *s* by his son (2) ROBERT, KT, PC, 2nd Viscount; *b* 1771; sat as MP for Hastings and co Edinburgh 1794-1811; was successively Pres of Indian Board of Control, Ch Sec for Ireland, Registrar of Seizins and Lord Privy Seal of Scotland; Gen and Vice-Pres of Royal Co of Archers, an Elder Brother of the Trinity House, etc; assumed for himself the additional surname of Saunders: *m* 1796, Anne, da of Richard Huck Saunders, MD; *d* 1851; *s* by his el son (3) HENRY, GCB, 3rd Viscount; a Gen in the Army, Gov of Edinburgh Castle, Col 60th Rifles, and Vice Pres of Royal Co of Archers; *d* unmarried 1876; *s* by his brother (4) ROBERT, 4th Viscount; *d* unmarried 1886; *s* by his nephew (5) HENRY (son of late Rev Hon Charles Dundas, 4th son of 2nd Viscount, by Louisa Maria, da of Sir William Boothby, 9th Bt), 5th Viscount; *b* 1835: *m* 1891, Hon Violet Marie Louise Cochrane-Baillie, who *d* 1943, da of 1st Baron Lamington; *d* 1904; *s* by his brother (6) CHARLES SAUNDERS, ISO, 6th Viscount, *b* 1843; Consul at Santos 1869-77, for Canary Islands 1877-82, and Stettin 1882-5, and Consul-Gen at Hamburg 1885-97, and at Christiania 1897-1906: *m* 1st, 1872, Grace Selina Marian, who *d* 1890, da of late William Scully, of Rio de Janeiro, and formerly of co Tipperary; 2ndly, 1891, Mary, who *d* 1919, da of late George Hamilton, MD, of Falkirk; 3rdly, 1920, Margaret, who *d* 1961, da of late William James Todd; *d* 1926; *s* by his son (7) HENRY CHARLES CLEMENT, 7th Viscount, *b* 1873; was Vice-Consul at Zanizibar 1897-8, at Dar-es-Salaam 1898-1902, at Galatz 1902-6, and at Algiers 1906-7, and Consul for Boliviaa 1907-8, for Tahiti 1908-9, for Bahia 1909, and for Corsica 1909-21: *m* 1899, Agnes Mary Florence, who *d* 1954, da of late Henry Brouncker, of Boveridge Park, Cranborne, Dorset; *d* 1935; *s* by his son (8) HENRY CHARLES PATRIC BROUNCKER, 8th Viscount, *b* 1909, *d* 1971; *s* by his nephew (9) ROBERT DAVID ROSS (only son of late Hon Robert Maldred St John Melville Dundas, yr son of 7th Viscount), 9th Viscount and present peer; also Baron Dunira.

MENUHIN, BARON (Menuhin) (Life Baron 1993)

YEHUDI MENUHIN, OM, KBE, son of late Moshe Menuhin; *b* 22 April 1916, New York, USA; *ed* privately; adopted British nationality 1985; Hon DMus Oxford, Belfast, Leicester, London and Camb; Hon LLD Liverpool, St Andrews, Sussex and Bath; Hon DLit Warwick; FRCM, Snr Fellow Royal Coll of Art, Hon Fellow and Pres Trin Coll of Music, Hon Fellow St Catharine's Coll, Camb; has received many honorary doctorates from overseas univs; Cobbett Medal Musicians' Co 1959, Gold Medal Royal Philharmonic Soc 1962, Mozart Medal 1965, Gold Medal Canadian Music Council 1975, Albert Medal RSA 1981, Una Vita Nella Musica Italy 1983, Brahms Medal Hamburg 1987, Brahms Orden Hamburg 1988, Gold Medal Cordoba Univ 1990, Glenn Gould Prize Canada 1990, Yehudi Menuhin and Luciano Berio Wolf Prize 1991; Violinist and Conductor; initiated annual Music Festivals at Gstaad 1957, Bath 1959 and Windsor 1969; Founded Yehudi Menuhin Sch of Music, Surrey, 1963, Founder and Pres Internat Menuhin Music Acad at Gstaad 1976, Founder Live Music Now 1977; former Pres UK Internat Music Council of UNESCO, Pres and Associate Conductor Royal Philharmonic Orchestra since 1982 and Hallé Orchestra since 1992, Pres European String Teachers' Assocn, Young Musicians' Symphony Orchestra, and Musicians' Internat Mutual Aid Fund; Principal Guest Conductor English String Orchestra since 1988, Founder and Conductor Asian Youth Orchestra; Jawaharlal Nehru Award for Internat Understanding 1968, Legion of Honour 1986, Cdr de l'Ordre des Arts et des Lettres and Cross of Lorraine (France), Cdr Order of Leopold (Belgium) and Officer of the Crown of Belgium, Kt Cdr and Grand Cross Order of Merit (Germany), Order of Merit of the Republic (Italy), Order of the Phoenix (Greece), and Cdr Order of Orange-Nassau (Netherlands); Freeman Cities of Edinburgh and Bath; Hon Swiss Citizenship 1970; *cr* Hon KBE (Civil) 1965, OM 1987, and *Baron Menuhin*, of Stoke D'Abernon, co Surrey (Life Baron) 1993: *m* 1st, 1938, Nola Ruby, da of late George Nicholas, of Melbourne, Australia; 2ndly, 1947, Diana Rosamond, da of late Gerard L. E. Gould, of Paris and London, and of late Lady Harcourt (Evelyn Suart, the pianist), and has issue by 1st and 2nd *m*.
Address – c/o Sym Music Company, 110 Gloucester Av, NW1 8JA. *Clubs* – Athenaeum, Garrick.

SONS LIVING *(By 1st marriage)*

Hon Krov Nicholas, *b* 1940: *m* 1967, Elizabeth Ann, da of late Herbert Christoffers, and has issue living, Aaron Nicholas, *b* 1982. *Residence* – Mas de la Baleine, 13210 St Remy de Provence, France.

(by 2nd marriage)

Hon Gerard, *b* 1948: *m* 1983 (*m diss* 19—), and has issue living, Maxwell Duncan, *b* 1990. *Address* – PO Box 55, CH-3780, Gstaad, Switzerland.
Hon Jeremy, *b* 1951: *m* 1983 (*m diss* 19—), Hon Brigid Gabriel Forbes-Sempill, yst da of 19th Lord Sempill, and has issue living, Petroc Forbes, *b* 1988, — Nadja Cecilia, *b* 1985.

DAUGHTER LIVING *(By 1st marriage)*

Hon Zamira, *b* 1939: *m* 1st, 1960 (*m diss* 1969), Fou Ts'ong, concert pianist; 2ndly, 1975, Jonathan Charles Mackenzie Benthall, son of late Sir (Arthur) Paul Benthall, KBE, of Benthall Hall, Broseley, Shropshire, and has issue living (by 1st *m*), Lin MENUHIN (a son), *b* 1964, — (by 2nd *m*), Dominic, *b* 1976, — William, *b* 1981. *Residence* – 212 Hammersmith Grove, W6 7HG.

Mereworth, Baron, title of Baron Oranmore and Browne on Roll of HL.

MERLYN-REES, BARON (Merlyn-Rees) (Life Baron 1992)

MERLYN MERLYN-REES, PC, son of Levi Daniel Rees, of Cilfynydd, S Wales; assumed by deed poll 1992 the surname of Merlyn-Rees in lieu of his patronymic; *b* 18 Dec 1920; *ed* Harrow Weald Gram Sch, Goldsmiths' Coll, London, LSE and London Univ Inst of Educn; Hon DLL Wales Univ; RAF 1941-46 as Sqdn-Ldr; Schoolmaster 1949-60, Economics Lecturer 1962-63; PPS to Chancellor of the Exchequer 1964, Parly Under Sec MOD (Army) 1965-66, (RAF) 1966-68, and Home Office 1968-70, NI Sec 1974-76, and Home Sec 1976-79; Member Franks Cttee on Official Secrets Act 1972, and Franks Cttee on Falklands 1982; Chm S Leeds Groundwork Trust 1987; Dir Groundwork Foundation 1989; Pres Video Standards Cncl 1990; Freeman of the City of Leeds 1993; Fell of Goldsmiths' Coll 1984; Hon DL Univ 1992; Chancellor of Glamorgan Univ 1994; author; MP S Leeds (*Lab*) 1963-83, and Morley and Leeds S 1983-92; *cr* PC 1974, and *Baron Merlyn-Rees*, of Morley and S Leeds, co W Yorks, and of Cilfynydd, co Mid Glam (Life Baron) 1992: *m* 1949, Colleen Faith, da of Henry F. Cleveley, of Kenton, Middx, and has issue.
Address – c/o House of Lords, SW1.

SONS LIVING

Hon Patrick Merlyn, *b* 1954; Solicitor: *m*, and has issue, one son and one da.
Hon Gareth David, *b* 1956; Barrister-at-law: *m*, and has issue, one son and two das.
Hon Glyn Robert, *b* 1960: *m*, and has issue, one son and one da.

MERRIMAN, BARONY OF (Merriman) (Extinct 1962)

DAUGHTER LIVING OF FIRST BARON

Hon Violet Grace, OBE (c/o Westminster Bank, 195 Earls Court Rd, SW5), *b* 1911; a British Council Officer; OBE (Civil) 1948.

WIDOW LIVING OF FIRST BARON

JANE LAMB (*Baroness Merriman*), da of late James Stormonth, of Belfast: *m* 1953, as his 3rd wife, the 1st Baron, who *d* 1962, when the title became ext. *Address* – Northern Bank Ltd, 9 Donegall Sq North, Belfast.

MERRIVALE, BARON (Duke) (Baron UK 1925)

JACK HENRY EDMOND DUKE, 3rd Baron; *b* 27 Jan 1917; *s* 1951; *ed* Dulwich, in France, and Ecole des Sciences Politiques, Paris; FRSA; Pres Institute of Traffic Administration, of Railway Development Assocn, and Chm of Anglo-Malgasy Soc; (despatches): *m* 1st, 1939 (*m diss* 1974), Colette, da of John Douglas Wise; 2ndly, 1975, Betty, widow of Paul Baron, and has issue by 1st *m*.

Arms – Argent, an anchor fouled sable between three chaplets, all within a bordure engrailed azure. **Crest** – Issuant from a chaplet fessewise argent a demi-griffin holding between the claws a fasces erect or. **Supporters** – On either side a griffin or, the *dexter* gorged with a chain sable, pendant therefrom an escutcheon argent charged with a saltire between four castles sable, and the *sinister* gorged with a like chain suspended therefrom an escutcheon per pale gules and sable, charged with a triple towered castle or.
Residence – 16 Brompton Lodge, 9-11 Cromwell Road, SW7.

We conquer by degrees

SON LIVING *(By 1st marriage)*

Hon DEREK JOHN PHILIP, *b* 16 March 1948: *m* and has issue, three children.

DAUGHTER LIVING *(By 1st marriage)*

Hon Elizabeth Anne Marie Violet, *b* 1939.

SISTER LIVING

Hon Elizabeth Suzanne, *b* 1921: *m* 1st, 1942 (*m diss* 1953), Capt Jean Pompei, French Air Force; 2ndly, 1955, Jacques Bechmann, banker, who *d* 1985, and has issue living, (by 1st *m*) François (18 rue Ferdinand Duval, 75004 Paris), *b* 1944: *m* 1973 (*m diss* 1992), Elizabeth, da of Christian Dupuy, and has issue living, Antoine *b* 1975, Louis *b* 1977, Philip *b* 1978, Marie *b* 1980, — Nicole (43 Rue de Boulainvilliers, 75016 Paris), *b* 1946: *m* 1968 (*m diss* 1980), Jean Louis Bouchard, and has issue living, Robert *b* 1971, Alexandra *b* 1969: *m* 1991, Laurent Rousseau, of 10 rue Raynouard, 75016 Paris (and has issue living, Marie *b* 1993), — (by 2nd *m*) Pierre, *b* 1957. *Residence* – La Charité, 60500 Chantilly, France.

PREDECESSORS – (1) *Rt Hon Sir* HENRY EDWARD DUKE, son of William Edward Duke, granite merchant, of Merrivale, S Devon; *b* 1855; MP for Plymouth (*C*) 1900-1906, and for Exeter 1910-18, Attorney-Gen and a Member of Council of Duchy of Cornwall 1915, Ch Sec for Ireland 1916-18, a Lord Justice of Appeal 1918-19, and Pres of Probate, Divorce, and Admiralty Div of High Court of Justice 1919-33; *cr Baron Merrivale*, of Walkhampton, co Devon (peerage of United Kingdom) 1925: *m* 1876, Sarah, who *d* 1914, da of late John Shorland; *d* 1939; *s* by his son (2) EDWARD, OBE, 2nd Baron; *b* 1883; Sec to Pres of Probate, Divorce and Admiralty Div of High Court of Justice 1919-33; S Africa 1901 as Lieut, European War 1914-19 as Capt (OBE): *m* 1st, 1912 (*m diss* 1939), Odette, da of Edmond Roger, of Paris; 2ndly, 1939, Meta Therèse, who *d* 1980, da of Hermann Wolczon, of Danzig; *d* 1951; *s* by his son (3) JACK HENRY EDMOND, 3rd Baron and present peer.

MERSEY, VISCOUNT (Bigham) (Viscount UK 1916)

I advance

RICHARD MAURICE CLIVE BIGHAM, 4th Viscount; *b* 8 July, 1934; *s* 1979; *ed* Eton, and Balliol Coll, Oxford; formerly Lieut Irish Guards; a documentary film producer; is *ha* to Lordship of Nairne (see that title): *m* 1961, Joanna Dorothy Corsica Grey, el da of late John Grey Murray, CBE, of Cannon Lodge, Cannon Place, NW3 (Shuttleworth, B), and has issue.

Arms – Per bend dancettée azure and or, a bend invected between three crosses patée in chief and as many horseshoes in base all counterchanged. **Crest** – A horse per pale or and sable, charged on the body with three horseshoes fesseways counterchanged, and resting the dexter foreleg on a cross patée gules. **Supporters** – On either side a mermaid proper crowned with a naval crown gules, that to the *dexter* supporting with the exterior hand an anchor or, that to the *sinister* an oar argent.
Residence – Bignor Park, Pulborough, Sussex.

SON LIVING

Hon EDWARD JOHN HALLAM, *b* 23 May 1966; *ed* Eton, and Balliol Coll, Oxford: *m* 1994, Claire L., da of David Haigh.

BROTHERS LIVING

Hon David Edward Hugh (Hurston Place, Pulborough, Sussex), *b* 1938; *ed* Eton; late Cornet RHG; Dir Tryon Gallery: *m* (Jan) 1965, Anthea Rosemary, el da of Capt Leopold Richard Seymour (*see* M Hertford, colls), and has issue living, Charles Richard Petty, *b* 1967, — Patrick David Hugh, *b* 1969, — James Edward Conway, *b* 1973, — Lucinda Emma, *b* (Nov) 1965.
Hon Andrew Charles (Bignor Park, Pulborough, Sussex; Brooks's Club), *b* 1941; *ed* Eton, and Worcester Coll, Oxford; late 2nd Lt Irish Gds; Schoolmaster, Aysgarth Sch, Bedale, N Yorks 1968-89, since when at Sunningdale Sch, Berks.

WIDOW LIVING OF THIRD VISCOUNT

Lady KATHERINE EVELYN CONSTANCE (*Dowager Viscountess Mersey*) (*Lady Nairne* in her own right) (Bignor Park, Pulborough, Sussex), el da of 6th Marquess of Lansdowne: *m* 1933, the 3rd Viscount, who *d* 1979.

COLLATERAL BRANCH LIVING

Issue of late Hon Sir (Frank) Trevor Roger Bigham, KBE, CB, yst son of 1st Viscount, *b* 1876, *d* 1954: *m* 1st, 1901, Frances Leonora, who *d* 1927, da of late J. L. Tomlin; 2ndly, 1931, Edith Ellen, who *d* 1985, da of Lieut-Col David Drysdale:—
(By 1st *m*) Celia Margaret Hermione, *b* 1909. *Residence* – 4 Harley Gardens, SW10 9SW.

PREDECESSORS – (1) *Rt Hon Sir* JOHN CHARLES Bigham, son of late John Bigham, merchant, of Liverpool, *b* 1840; MP for Liverpool, Exchange Div (LU) 1895-7; a Judge of the High Court of Justice 1897-1909 (also Judge in Bankruptcy 1904-8), and Pres of Probate, Divorce, and Admiralty Div 1909-10; Roy Commr for Revision of Martial Law in S Africa 1902, and Pres of Railway and Canal Commn of United Kingdom 1912, and a Member of Roy Commn of Civil Ser 1915; *cr Baron Mersey*, of Toxteth, co Palatine of Lancaster (peerage of United Kingdom) 1910, and *Viscount Mersey of Toxteth, co Palatine of Lancaster* (peerage of United Kingdom) 1916: *m* 1871, Georgina Sarah, who *d* 1925, da of John Rogers, of Liverpool; *d* 1929; *s* by his el son (2) CHARLES CLIVE, PC, CMG, CBE, 2nd Viscount; *b* 1872; Lieut-Col late Grenadier Guards, Dep Speaker of House of Lords and Dep Chm of Committees, and Chm of Westminster Territorial Committee; was Hon Attaché in Diplo Ser 1896-1900, ADC to Lord-Lieut of Ireland 1901-2, and Ch Liberal Whip in House of Lords 1944-9; China 1900 (CMG), European War 1914-18 (CBE): *m* 1904, Mary Gertrude, JP, who *d* 1973, da of late Horace Alfred Damer Seymour, CB (nominated, but not invested, KCB); *d* 1956; *s* by his el son (3) EDWARD CLIVE, 3rd Viscount, *b* 1906; a DL for W Sussex; 1939-45 War as Capt Irish Gds: *m* 1933, Lady Katherine Evelyn Constance Petty-Fitzmaurice (*Lady Nairne* in her own right), el da of the 6th Marquess of Lansdowne; *d* 1979; *s* by his el son (4) RICHARD MAURICE CLIVE, 4th Viscount and present peer, also Baron Mersey.

MERTHYR, BARON OF (Lewis) (Baron UK 1911, Bt UK 1896, disclaimed 1977)

Perseverance.

Do thy duty come what may

(*Sir*) TREVOR OSWIN LEWIS, CBE, *b* 29 Nov 1935; *s* as 4th Baron Merthyr and 4th Baronet, 5 April 1977; disclaimed his peerage for life 26 April 1977, and does not use his title of baronet; *ed* Eton, Magdalen Coll, Oxford, and Magdalene Coll, Camb; Member, Countryside Commn 1973-83, Dep Chm 1980-83, and Chm of Cttee for Wales 1973-80; JP for Dyfed; CBE (1983): *m* 1964, Susan Jane, da of Arthur John Birt-Llewellin, of Boulston Manor, Haverfordwest, and has issue.

𝕬rms – Sable, a lion rampant argent, over all a fesse or charged with three bees volant proper. 𝕮rest – An eagle displayed azure, charged on the breast with a bee volant or, and holding in the beak a roll of paper argent. 𝕾upporters – (borne by Baron Merthyr) On either side a lion rampant sable, charged on the shoulder with a bezant thereon a bee volant proper.
Seat – Hean Castle, Saundersfoot, Dyfed, SA69 9AL.

SON LIVING

DAVID TREVOR, *b* 21 Feb 1977.

DAUGHTERS LIVING

Lucy Delia, *b* 1967; Lieut RN 1987-94: *m* 1990, Harvey John Bradnam, only son of John Bradnam, of Craigs Farmhouse, Crossford, by Dunfermline, Fife.
Elizabeth Anne, *b* 1970.

Jessamy Jane, *b* 1972.

BROTHERS LIVING

Hon Peter Herbert (The Old Rectory, Chilfrome, Dorchester DT2 0HA), *b* 1937; *ed* Eton; Lt-Col 9th/12th R Lancers (POW): *m* 1974, Caroline Monica, el da of Erik Cadogan, of Wasperton Hill, Barford, Warwick (*see* E Cadogan, colls), and has issue living, Amanda Caroline, *b* 1977.
Hon John Frederick (1 Cedar Hill, Carisbrooke, I of Wight), *b* 1938; *ed* Eton, and St John's Coll, Camb: *m* 1966, Margaret (Gretl), twin da of Lt-Col James William Lewis-Bowen, of Clynfiew, Boncath, Dyfed, and has issue living, Paul William, *b* 1979, — Deborah, *b* 1967, — Sarah, *b* 1968, — Hannah, *b* 1983.
Hon Robin William, OBE (Orchard House, Llanstephan, Carmarthen, Dyfed SA33 5HA), *b* 1941; *ed* Eton, and Magdalen Coll, Oxford; Chm and Man Dir The Magstim Co Ltd; Chm The Nat Trust Cttee for Wales; Chm Gen Advisory Council of IBA 1989-90; High Sheriff Dyfed 1987; OBE 1988: *m* 1967, Judith Ann, da of Vincent Charles Arthur Giardelli, of Llethr, Pendine, Dyfed, and has issue living, Christopher William, *b* 1970, — Katharine Ann, *b* 1972.
Hon Antony Thomas (The Skreen, Erwood, Builth Wells, Powys LD2 3SJ), *b* 1947; *ed* Eton: *m* 1974, Mary Carola Melton, yr da of Rev Humphrey John Paine, of Fressingfield Vicarage, Diss, Norfolk.

WIDOW LIVING OF THIRD BARON

VIOLET (*Baroness Merthyr*) (Churchton, Saundersfoot, Dyfed, SA69 9BB), da of Brig-Gen Sir Frederick Charlton Meyrick, 2nd Bt, CB, CMG: *m* 1932, the 3rd Baron, who *d* 1977.

PREDECESSORS – (1) *Sir* WILLIAM THOMAS LEWIS, GCVO, el son of late Thomas William Lewis, of Abercanaid House, Merthyr Tydfil, by Mary Anne, who *d* 1887, da of Watkin John; *b* 1837; was a large employer of labour in connection with Collieries, Iron and Steel Works, Tinplate Works, and other industries in S Wales, Founder (many years Chm) of Monmouthshire and S Wales Coal Asso, of S Wales Sliding Scale Committee (18 Year Chm), and of S Wales Miner's Provident Fund (30 years Chm); *cr* a *Baronet* 1896, and *Baron Merthyr*, of Senghenydd, co Glamorgan (peerage of United Kingdom) 1911: *m* 1864, Anne, who *d* 1902, el da of William Rees colliery proprietor, of Llettyshenkin, Glamorgan; *d* 1914; *s* by his el son (2) HERBERT CLARK, 2nd Baron, *b* 1866: *m* 1899, Elizabeth Anna, who *d* 1925, el da of late Maj-Gen Richard Short Couchman, formerly MSC, of 117 Victoria St, SW; *d* 1932; *s* by his son (3) WILLIAM BRERETON COUCHMAN, KBE, PC, TD, 3rd Baron; *b* 1901; Lord Chm of Cttees, House of Lords 1957-65, and Dep Speaker, House of Lords 1957-74; a Member of Several Roy Commns; Vice-Pres Nat Marriage Guidance Council (Chm 1951-57), Magistrates Assocn (Chm of Council 1952-70) and Family Planning Assocn; Hon Treas NSPCC 1952-57 and RSPCA 1953-57; Bar-at-law, and Maj Pembroke Heavy Regt RA (TA) (prisoner Hong Kong 1941-45): *m* 1932, Violet, da of Brig-Gen Sir Frederick Charlton Meyrick, 2nd Bt, CB, CMG; *d* 1977; *s* by his el son (4) TREVOR OSWIN, 4th Baron, until he disclaimed his peerage for life.

Merton, Viscount; son of Earl Nelson.

MESTON, BARON (Meston) (Baron UK 1919)

JAMES MESTON, 3rd Baron; *b* 10 Feb 1950; *s* 1984; *ed* Wellington, St Catharine's Coll, Camb, and Leicester Univ; Bar Middle Temple 1973; Jr Counsel to Queen's Proctor since 1992: *m* 1974, Jean Rebecca Anne, yr da of John Carder, of Stud Farm House, Chalvington, Sussex, and has issue living.

Arms – Argent, a palm tree, eradicated proper, on a chief azure, an Eastern crown between two thistles slipped and leaved or. **Crest** – An angel proper, habited argent, holding in the dexter hand an Eastern crown as in the arms. **Supporters** – *Dexter*, a demoiselle crane proper; *sinister*, a stag also proper, charged on the shoulder with a saltire argent.
Chambers - Queen Elizabeth Building, Temple, EC4.

SON LIVING

Hon THOMAS JAMES DOUGALL, *b* 21 Oct 1977; *ed* Eton.

DAUGHTERS LIVING

Hon Laura Anne Rose, *b* 1980.
Hon Elspeth Mary, *b* 1988.

BROTHER LIVING

In God is my trust

Hon William Dougall (11 The Green, Mistley, Manningtree, Essex CO11 1EU), *b* 1953; *ed* Wellington Coll: *m* 1982, Elizabeth Mary Agnes, yst da of late Dr Peter Dawes, of Cavendish Mansions, W1, and Mijas, Spain, and has issue living, Dougall William, *b* 1985, — Felix Peter, *b* 1987.

WIDOW LIVING OF SECOND BARON

DIANA MARY CAME (*Diana, Baroness Meston*), only da of late Capt Otto Sigismund Doll, FRIBA, of 16 Upper Cheyne Row, SW3: *m* 1947, the 2nd Baron, who *d* 1984. *Residence* – Staplehurst, High St, Mistley, Manningtree, Essex CO11 1HD.

PREDECESSORS – (1) Sir JAMES SCORGIE Meston, KCSI, son of late James Meston, of Aberdeen; *b* 1865; Financial Sec to Govt of India 1906-12, and Lieut-Gov of United Provinces of Agra and Oudh 1912-18; Finance Member of Viceroy's Executive Council 1918-19; Chancellor of Aberdeen Univ 1928; *cr Baron Meston*, of Agra and Dunottar (peerage of United Kingdom) 1919: *m* 1891, Jeanie, CBE (a DStJ), who *d* 1946, only da of late James McDonald; *d* 1943; *s* by his son (2) DOUGALL, 2nd Baron, *b* 1894; Bar Lincoln's Inn, SE Circuit: *m* 1947, Diana Mary Came, only da of Capt Otto Sigismund Doll, FRIBA; *d* 1984; *s* by his el son (3) JAMES, 3rd Baron and present peer.

METHUEN, BARON (Methuen) (Baron UK 1838)
(Name and Title pronounced "Méthwen")

ANTHONY JOHN METHUEN, 6th Baron; *b* 26 Oct 1925; *s* 1975; *ed* Winchester and Roy Agric Coll, Cirencester; ARICS; 1943-47 in Scots Gds and R Signals; Land Officer, Air Min 1951-62.

Arms – Argent, three wolves' heads erased, proper, borne on the breast of an imperial eagle. **Supporters** – Two fiery lynxes reguardant proper, collared and lined or.
Seat – Corsham Court, Wilts.

BROTHER LIVING

Hon ROBERT ALEXANDER HOLT (The Cascades, Nether Green, Bonsall, nr Matlock, Derbyshire), *b* 22 July 1931; *ed* Shrewsbury, and Trin Coll, Camb: *m* 1st, 1958, Mary Catharine Jane, da of the Ven Charles German Hooper, Archdeacon of Ipswich; 2ndly, 1994, Margrit Andrea, da of Friedrich Karl Ernst Hadwiger, of Vienna and has issue living (by 1st *m*), Charlotte Mary, *b* 1964, — Henrietta Christian (Kittie), *b* 1965: *m* 1990, Robert Llewelyn Jones, who assumed the surname of METHUEN-JONES, elder son of D. Ll. Jones, of Reigate, Surrey, and has issue living, Teresa Mary *b* 1990, Keziah Lynne *b* 1992.

Virtue is the mark of envy

SISTER LIVING

Hon Elizabeth Penelope, *b* 1928: *m* 1956, Malcolm Henry Alastair Fraser, late RHG, of Southbank House, Lacock Rd, Corsham, Wilts SN13 9HS, and has issue living, Elizabeth Mary Alexandra, *b* 1957: *m* 1982, Mark Geoffrey Sewell, late Gren Gds (*see* Williams-Wynn, Bt, colls, 1990 Edn), and has issue living, Emma Lucy Alexandra *b* 1985, Rosanna Mary Alice *b* 1988, Lucinda Charlotte Anne *b* 1993, — Anne Catriona Hamilton, *b* 1961.

COLLATERAL BRANCHES LIVING

Issue of late Hon Laurence Paul METHUEN, 3rd son of 3rd Baron; *b* 1898; assumed the additional surname of Campbell, which he relinquished by deed poll 1969; *d* 1970: *m* 1st, 1927, Hon Olive Douglas Campbell, who *d* 1949, da of 4th Baron Blythswood (ext); 2ndly, 1950, Lady Maureen Margaret Brabazon, who *d* 1980, da of 13th Earl of Meath:—
(By 1st *m*) Christopher Paul Mansel Campbell METHUEN-CAMPBELL (Penrice Castle, Reynoldston, Gower, Glam), *b* 1928: *m* 1st, 1950 (*m diss* 1973), Oona Cicily, da of John Dalrymple Winn Treherne (*see* M Sligo, colls); 2ndly, 1975, Mrs Judith Anne Bassett (*née* Crowther), formerly wife of David Bassett and has issue living (by 1st *m*), James Paul Archibald, *b* 1952, — Joanna Olive, *b* 1951: *m* 1977, Edward Ashley Martin, — Lucinda Sheelah, *b* 1959, — Catherine Alice Mansel, *b* 1965, — (by 2nd *m*), Thomas Rice Mansel, *b* 1977. —— David Archibald James (45 Redcliffe Rd, SW10), *b* 1929: *m* 1978, Elizabeth Anne, da of James Fletcher Martin of Egdon Cottage, Swanage, Dorset. —— Diana Evelyn (*Lady McNair-Wilson*), *b* 1932: *m* 1953, Capt Sir Patrick McNair-Wilson, MP, of 5 Kelso Pl, W8, and has issue living, Guy Patrick Adam Campbell, *b* 1968, — Jennifer Jean, *b* 1954, — Arabella Jane Campbell, *b* 1959: *m* 1984, David Nicholas (Nick) Ashley, of Flat 8, 50 Cornwall Gdns, SW7, son of late Sir Bernard Albert Ashley, — Patricia Ann Campbell, *b* 1964, — Kate Campbell, *b* 1975. —— Daphne Mary Jean (*Hon Mrs Cecil T. H. Law*), *b* 1935: *m* 1957, Hon Cecil Towry Henry Law (*see* B Ellenborough). —— (By 2nd *m*) Caroline Aileen, *b* 1952; assumed by deed poll 1969 the surname of Methuen in lieu of her patronymic: *m* 1988, Charles Lloyd Fox, of Tredrea, Perranarworthal, Truro, Cornwall TR3 7QE, 2nd son of Philip Hamilton Fox, of Glendurgan, Falmouth, Cornwall, and has issue living, Meriel Sophia, *b* 1990, — Stella Caroline, *b* 1992.

Granddaughters of late Hon St John George Paul Methuen, son of 1st Baron:—
Issue of late Rev St John Frederick Charles Methuen, *b* 1862, *d* 1953: *m* 1st, 1892, Louisa Elizabeth, who *d* 1933, da of late Maj-Gen James Hyde Champion; 2ndly, 1940, Millicent Emma Foskett, who *d* 1970, da of Samuel George Wittey, of Penzance:—
(By 1st *m*), Kathleen Louisa Mildmay (c/o Hurst Lodge, Lyme Rd, Axminster, Devon EX13 5SW) *b* 1896. —— Beatrice Ethel Gertrude (c/o Thornton Dale Care and Retirement Home, Hurrell Lane, Thornton Dale, N Yorks), *b* 1905.

PREDECESSORS – (1) PAUL Methuen, MP for Wiltshire in several parliaments, *cr Baron Methuen* of Corsham, co Wilts (peerage of United Kingdom) 1838; *b* 1779: *m* 1810, Jane Dorothea, da of Sir Henry Paulet St John Mildmay, 3rd Bt; *d* 1849; *s* by his son (2) FREDERICK HENRY PAUL, 2nd Baron, *b* 1818; ADC to HM Queen Victoria; was a Lord-in-Waiting to HM Queen Victoria 1859-66, 1868-74, 1880-85, and 1886: *m* 1844, Anna Horatia Caroline, da of Rev John Stanford, of Nynehead, Somerset; *d* 1891; *s* by his el son (3) PAUL SANFORD, 3rd Baron, GCB, GCMG, GCVO, LLD, *b* 1845; a Field-Marshal; Ashantee War 1873-4, as AA and QMG in Egyptian Campaign 1882, as Press Censor during Tirah Expedition 1897, in S Africa 1899-1902, in command of 1st Inf Div at battles of Belmont, Enslin, Modder River, and Magersfontein; Mil Sec Ireland 1877, Mil Attaché at Berlin 1877-81, AA and QMG Home Dist 1881-4, DAG Cape of Good Hope 1888-90, in command of Home Dist 1892-7, of E Command 1904-8, and of troops in S Africa 1908-12 (Gov of Natal 1910), and Gov and Com-in-Ch, Malta 1914-19; commanded "Methuen's Horse" in Bechuanaland 1885; was Constable of Tower of London 1920-32: *m* 1st, 1878, Evelyn, who *d* 1879, da of Sir Frederick Hutchinson Hervey-Bathurst, 3rd Bt; 2ndly, 1884, Mary Ethel, CBE, who *d* 1941, da of late William Ayshford Sanford, of Nynehead Court, Somerset; *d* 1932; *s* by his son (4) PAUL AYSHFORD, 4th Baron, *b* 1886; FSA, Royal Academician; a Trustee of Nat Gallery, and Tate Gallery 1938-45, and Imperial War Museum 1950-52: *m* 1915, Eleanor Norah, who *d* 1958, da of late William John Hennessy, of Rudgwick, Sussex; *d* 1974; *s* by his brother (5) ANTHONY PAUL, 5th Baron; *b* 1891; Chartered Architect, 1914-18 War as Capt Scots Gds: *m* 1920, Grace Durning, who *d* 1972, da of Sir Richard Durning Holt, 1st Bt (*cr* 1935), *d* 1975; *s* by his 2nd son (6) ANTHONY JOHN, 6th Baron, and present peer.

MEXBOROUGH, EARL OF (Savile) (Earl I 1766)

JOHN CHRISTOPHER GEORGE SAVILE, 8th Earl; *b* 16 May 1931; *s* 1980; *ed* Eton, and Worcester Coll, Oxford; late 2nd Lieut Gren Gds: *m* 1st, 1958 (*m diss* 1972), Lady Elisabeth Hariot Grimston, who *d* 1987, el da of 6th Earl of Verulam; 2ndly, 1972, Catherine Joyce, yst da of James Kenneth Hope, CBE, DL, of West Park, Lanchester, co Durham, and formerly wife of Maj Hon Nicholas Crespigny Laurence Vivian (later 6th Baron Vivian), and has issue by 1st and 2nd *m*.

Arms – Argent, on a bend sable, three owls of the field. **Crest** – An owl argent. **Supporters** – Two lions proper, collared and chained or.
Seat – Arden Hall, Hawnby, York; *Town Residence* – 14 Lennox Gdns Mews, SW1. *Clubs* – All England Lawn Tennis, Air Squadron.

SONS LIVING (By 1st marriage)

JOHN ANDREW BRUCE (*Viscount Pollington*), *b* 30 Nov 1959.

(*By 2nd marriage*)

Hon James Hugh Hope John, *b* 1976.

DAUGHTERS LIVING (By 1st marriage)

Lady Alethea Frances Clare, *b* 1963.

(*By 2nd marriage*)

Lady Lucinda Sarah Catherine, *b* 1973.

BROTHER LIVING

Hon (Charles) Anthony, *b* 1934; *ed* Eton, and Trin Coll, Cambridge; late Lt Grenadier Guards: *m* 1966, Zita Loretta, da of Leslie White, and has issue living, Henry Charles, *b* 1970, — Andrew David, *b* 1973. *Residence* – Youngsbury, Ware, Herts. *Club* – All England Lawn Tennis.

COLLATERAL BRANCH LIVING

Granddaughter of late Rev Hon Philip Yorke Savile, 3rd son of 3rd Earl:—
Issue of late Rev William Hale Savile, *b* 1859, *d* 1925: *m* 1888, Mabel Ann, who *d* 1947, only da of late Maj Count Hippolyt Victor Alexander von Bothmer, a Count of the Holy Roman Empire (naturalized 1857):—
Veronica Yorke Hélène Cecilia, *b* 1902: *m* 1926, Willem Karel Marie de Bruijn van Gouderack, Belgian Consulate Service (ret), who *d* 1984, only son of late Eduard Rudolf Marie de Bruijn. *Residence* – Huis De Werve, Cartier van Disselstraat 64, Breda, Netherlands 4835 KP.

PREDECESSORS – (1) *Sir* JOHN SAVILE, KB, *b* 1719; MP for Hedon, co York 1747-54; *cr Baron Pollington*, Ireland (peerage of Ireland) 1753, and *Viscount Pollington* and *Earl of Mexborough* (peerage of Ireland) 1766; *d* 1778; *s* by his son (2) JOHN, 2nd Earl; *d* 1830; *s* by his son (3) JOHN, 3rd Earl; *b* 1783; MP for Pontefract: *m* 1807, Lady Anne, who *d* 1870, da of 3rd Earl of Hardwicke; *d* 1860; *s* by his son (4) JOHN CHARLES GEORGE, 4th Earl, *b* 1810; MP for Gatton (C) 1831, and for Pontefract 1835-47: *m* 1st, 1842, Lady Katherine Walpole, who *d* 1854, el da of 3rd Earl of Orford; 2ndly, 1861, Agnes Louisa Elizabeth, who *d* 1898, da of John Raphael; *d* 1899: *s* by his el son (5) JOHN HORACE, 5th Earl, *b* 1843; High Sheriff of Yorkshire 1877: *m* 1st, 1867, Venetia Stanley, who *d* 1900, da of Sir Rowland Stanley Errington, 11th Bt; 2ndly, 1906, Donna Sylvia Cecilia Maria, who *d* 1915, da of the Noble Carlo de Ser Antoni, of Lucca and Naples, and widow of Capt Claude Clerke, CIE; 3rdly, 1916, Anne, who *d* 1943 (having *m* 3rdly, 1920 (*m diss* 1926), as his 2nd wife, Alfred Charlemagne Lambart, who *d* 1943), da of late Rev Andrew Holmes Belcher, of Fasque, Kincardineshire, and formerly wife of George Bainbridge Ritchie; *d* 1916; *s* by his half-brother (6) JOHN HENRY, 6th Earl, *b* 1868; Hon Capt in the Army: *m* 1905, Hon Margaret Eva de Burgh Knatchbull-Hugessen, who *d* 1957, el da of 2nd Baron Brabourne; *d* 1945; *s* by his son (7) JOHN RAPHAEL WENTWORTH, 7th Earl, *b* 1906; ADC to Gov of Bihar 1944-45; Pres York Lawn Tennis Club, and English Billiards Assoc: *m* 1930, Josephine Bertha Emily, who *d* 1992, da of late Capt Andrew Mansel Talbot Fletcher (Winnington, Bt); *d* 1980; *s* by his son (8) JOHN CHRISTOPHER GEORGE, 8th Earl and present peer; also Viscount and Baron Pollington.

MICHELHAM, BARONY OF (Stern) (Extinct 1984)

(Title pronounced "Mitch-lam")

WIDOW LIVING OF SECOND BARON

MARIE-JOSE DUPAS (*Baroness Michelham*): *m* 1980, as his 2nd wife, the 2nd Baron, who *d* 1984, when the title became ext. Resides in France.

MIDDLETON, BARON (Willoughby) (Baron GB 1711, Et E 1677)

Truth without fear

(DIGBY) MICHAEL GODFREY JOHN WILLOUGHBY, MC, 12th Baron, and 13th Baronet; *b* 1 May 1921; *s* 1970; *ed* Eton, and Trin Coll, Camb (MA); patron of seven livings; a CC and JP for E Riding and Kingston upon Hull 1964-74, a CC for N Yorks 1974-77, DL of N Yorks; a Member of Yorks & Humberside Economic Planning Council 1968-79; Pres Yorks Agric Soc 1976, and of the Country Landowners Assoc 1981-83; a Member of Nature Conservancy Council 1986-89; a Member of House of Lords Select Cttee on European Communities; Hon Col 2nd Bn Yorks Vol 1976-87; 1939-45 War a Maj Coldm Gds (despatches, MC, Croix de Guerre): *m* 1947, Janet; JP N Yorks; Founding Chm Lloyds External Names Assocn; only da of Gen Sir James Handyside Marshall Cornwall, KCB, CBE, DSO, MC, and has issue.

𝔄rms – Quarterly: 1st and 4th or, fretty azure, *Willoughby of Parham*; 2nd and 3rd or, on two bars gules three water bougets two and one argent, *Willoughby of Middleton*. 𝔈rest – The bust of a man couped at the shoulders and affrontée proper, ducally crowned or. 𝔖upporters – *Dexter*, a pilgrim or grey friar in his habit proper, with his beads, cross, etc, and staff in his right hand, argent; *sinister*, a savage with a club in his exterior hand, wreathed about his temples and middle with laurel all proper; each supporter holding a banner gules fringed, or ensigned with an owl argent, gorged with a ducal coronet collared and chained gold, the owl being the crest of *Willoughby of Middleton*. *Residence* – Birdsall House, Malton, N Yorks. *Club* – Boodle's.

SONS LIVING

Hon MICHAEL CHARLES JAMES (North Grimston House, Malton, N Yorks), *b* 14 July 1948; *ed* Eton; late Lt-Coldm Gds and Queens Own Yeomanry: *m* 1974, Hon Lucy Corinna Agneta Sidney, yst da of 1st Viscount De L'Isle, VC, KG, and has issue living, James William Michael, *b* 8 March 1976; *ed* Eton, — Charles Edward Henry, *b* 1986, — Charlotte Jacqueline Louise, *b* 1978, — Emma Coralie Sarah, *b* 1981, — Rose Arabella Julia, *b* 1984.
Hon (John) Hugh Francis (4 Westmorland Terr, SW1), *b* 1951; *ed* Eton; late Capt Coldm Gds.
Hon (Thomas Henry) Richard *b* 1955; *ed* Harrow, and Manchester Univ (BSc).

BROTHER LIVING

Hon (Henry Ernest) Christopher, *b* 1932; *ed* Eton and RMA Sandhurst; Brig Coldm Gds, and Brig Defence Attache Ankara: *m* 1st, 1955 (*m diss* 1990), Jean Adini, da of Lt-Col John David Hills, MC (*see* E Cromer); 2ndly, 1990, J. Elizabeth, da of late Robert Philip Sidney Bache, OBE, of Himbleton, Worcs, and has issue living (by 1st *m*), Guy Nesbit John (Gilchristland House, Thornhill, Dumfriesshire DG3 5HN), *b* 1960; *ed* Eton; late Coldstream Gds; Director The HALO Trust: *m* 1990, Fiona K., da of Patrick Stewart-Blacker, of Blairgowrie, Perthshire, and has issue living, Louisa Ariana Rose *b* 1992, — Angela Jane, *b* 1956: *m* 1976, Capt Denis Patrick Antony Critchley-Salmonson, Coldm Gds, and has issue (*see* B Howard de Walden, colls), — Caroline Rosemary, *b* 1957. *Residence* – Somerleyton House, White Hart St, E Harling, Norfolk NR16 2NE. *Club* – Army and Navy.

SISTERS LIVING

Hon Angela Hermione Ida, *b* 1924: *m* 1947, Lieut-Com Hon Charles Henry Romer Wynn, RN, and has issue (*see* B Newborough). *Residence* – Bunkersland, Withleigh, Tiverton, Devon.
Hon Jean Elizabeth Mary (*Hon Lady Matheson*), *b* 1928; JP: *m* 1952, Major Sir Fergus John Matheson, 7th Bt, Coldstream Guards, and has issue (*see* Matheson, Bt). *Residence* – Hedenham Old Rectory, Bungay, Norfolk.

COLLATERAL BRANCHES LIVING

Issue of late Col Hon Claude Henry Comaraich Willoughby, CVO, 7th son of 8th Baron, *b* 1862, *d* 1932: *m* 1904, Sibyl Louise, who *d* 1957, da of late Charles James Murray (E Dunmore, colls):—
Mary Bridget (*Lady Howard-Vyse*) (Town Farm Cottage, Langton, Malton, Yorks), *b* 1910: *m* 1940, Lt-Gen Sir Edward Dacre Howard-Vyse, KBE, CB, MC, who *d* 1992, and has issue living, Richard Edward (Town Farm, Langton, Malton, Yorks) *b* 1941; TD, JP: *m* 1965, Sally Rosemary, da of Cdr R. R. Whalley, RN, and has issue living, Thomas Norcliffe *b* 1971, Mary Elizabeth *b* 1975, Alice Joan Lucy *b* 1978, — John Cecil (Old Vicarage, Burneston, Bedale, N Yorks DL8 2HP), *b* 1947; Lt-Col RA: *m* 1972, Jennifer Anne, el da of Maj-Gen Geoffrey de Egglesfield Collin, MC, of Roecliffe, Boroughbridge, and has issue living, James Edward *b* 1977, Georgina *b* 1975, Victoria *b* 1980, — Elizabeth, *b* 1945: *m* 1983, Rev George A. Perera, of St Hilda's Vicarage, 7 Kingsmead Drive, Hunts Cross, Liverpool L25 0NG, elder son of J. K. P. Perera, FRCS, of Blundellsands, Liverpool, and has issue living, Timothy Mark Grant *b* 1985, Christopher John Kenneth *b* 1987, Robert *b* 1989.

Granddaughters of late Capt Hon Alexander Hugh Willoughby, yst son of 8th Baron:—
Issue of late Wing-Com James Alexander Willoughby RAF, *b* 1890, *d* 1955: *m* 1st, 1918 (*m diss* 1926), Dorothea Marion, da of late Richard Hilton Burbrook, of 7 Buxton Gdns, W; 2ndly, 1926, Jill, who *d* 1977, yr da of late David Denton, FRCC, of Newport Pagnell, Bucks:—
(By 1st *m*) Diana Evelyn Mary, *b* 1919: *m* 1941, John Erwin Martens, Flt Capt ATA, who *d* 1984. *Residence* – 1 Tower House, London Rd, Arundel, W Sussex BN18 9BH. —— Susan Clara, *b* 1922: *m* 1963, Robert Bellord, Maj IG, who *d* 1970, and has issue living, Sarah Mary, *b* 1950: *m* 1st, 1969 (*m diss* 1984), Martin Charles Neale Thompson, son of late Lt-Col Sir Edward Hugh Dudley Thompson, MBE, TD, DL, of Culland Hall, Brailsford, Derby; 2ndly, 1986, Richard William Godfrey Astell, of 14 Keswick Rd, SW15, and has issue living (by 1st *m*), Rupert Alexander Robert Neale *b* 1973, Edward Charles Neale *b* 1974, Miranda Mary *b* 1971. *Residences* – 60 Clarewood Court, Crawford St, W1H 5DF; Shaggs Cottage, E Lulworth, Dorset. —— (By 2nd *m*) Griselda Mary Honoria, *b* 1931: *m* 1955, Lt Paul Julian David Gifford, RN, of Holly Lodge, Weathercock Lane, Woburn Sands, Bucks, and has issue living, Mark Richard Alexander, *b* 1960, — Nicola Jane, *b* 1965.
Issue of late Capt Joe Henry Claude Willoughby, RN, *b* 1892, *d* 1966: *m* 1919, Enid Mary, who *d* 1980, da of Harry J. Clements, of Somerville House, Sutton Coldfield:—
Anne Honoria Mary, *b* 1920: *m* 1st, 1940, Sqdn-Ldr P. Campbell Canney, RAF, who was *ka* 1942; 2ndly, 1944 (*m diss* 19——), John Dean; 3rdly, 19——, Wayne Etive, of 3184, Pioneer Rd, Medford, Oregon, USA, and has issue living (by 1st *m*), Josephine, *b* 1942.

Granddaughter of late Maj Charles Stuart Percival Willoughby, son of late Rev Hon Charles James Willoughby (infra):—
Issue of late Maj Geoffrey St Maur Willoughby, Hampshire Regt, *b* 1881, *d* 1954: *m* 1st, 1910, Julia Henrietta Cave, who *d* 1946, da of Rev Edmund Joseph Francis Johnson (formerly R of Sarsden, Oxon); 2ndly, 1947, Gwyneth Preston, who *d* 1981, only da of Arthur Henry Willmore, of Oak Ridge, Chandler's Ford, Hants:—
(By 1st *m*) Julia Hermione, *b* 1913: *m* 1936, Lt-Com (S) Richard William Chamberlen, RNR. *Residences* – Little Pitt, Wonston, Winchester, Hants SO21 3LR; Edificio Portanova 310, Palma Nova, Majorca, Spain.

Grandchildren of late James Frederick Digby Willoughby, OBE (infra):—
Issue of late Cdr Ronald James Edward Willoughby, RN (ret), *b* 1884, *d* 1971: *m* 1930, Constance Louisa, who *d* 1977, da of late Rev Nevile Sherbrooke:—
Christopher Ronald (World Bank, 1818 H St NW, Washington, DC 20433, USA), *b* 1929: *m* 1972, Marie-Anne, el da of late Emile Normand of Chamalières, Clermont-Ferrand, France. —— Josephine Cicely Alice (45 Templar Rd, Oxford OX2 8L5), *b* 1931; SRN. —— Nina Mary, *b* 1933: *m* 1959, Cdr David Lines, OBE, RN, of Ewens Farm, West Chelborough, Dorchester, Dorset DT2 0PY, and has issue living, Charles Willoughby, *b* 1960: *m* 1986, Catherine Campbell, and has issue living, Jonathan Richard *b* 1992, Jessica Mary *b* 1987, — Patrick Simon, *b* 1963, — James Michael, *b* 1965, — Rupert Martin, *b* 1969, — Vanessa Jane, *b* 1961: *m* 1988, Richard Harold Davison, son of late Eric Davison, and has issue living, Edward Henry *b* 1990, Harriet Lucy *b* 1991, Sarah Constance Louisa *b* 1994.
Issue of late Com Archibald Macdonald Willoughby, RN, *b* 1887, *d* on active ser 1943: *m* 1st, 1912 (*m diss* 1935), Mabel Doris, who *d* 1956, el da of Sir William Norton Hicking, 1st Bt (North, Bt); 2ndly, 1935, Elizabeth (who *m* 2ndly, 1951, Capt C. Devaynes Smyth, who *d* 1962), da of late Maj-Gen Sir John Hanbury-Williams, GCVO, KCB, CMG:—
(By 1st *m*) Pamela Mary Norton (Flat 5, 21 Osberton Rd, Oxford), *b* 1916: *m* 1952, Rev Ronald Curnow Parkinson, who *d* 1984. —— Prudence Joan Mabel, *b* 1918: *m* 1949, John Alexander Hannay, and has issue living, Jonathan Howard, *b* 1951, — Philippa Catherine, *b* 1953. *Residence* – Hill Cottage, 11-13 The Hill, Gt Walsingham, Norfolk. —— Sheila Katherine, *b* 1921: *m* 1952, Cdr Edward Astley-Jones, RN, and has issue living, Hugh Edward Arthur, *b* 1953, — Hilary Margaret Doris, *b* 1958. —— Anne Rosemary, *b* 1926: *m* 1956, George Frederick Rothwell, and has issue living, James Peter, *b* 1958, — Gerald Charles, *b* 1963, — Charlotte Jane, *b* 1964. —— Frances Elizabeth, *b* 1966. *Residence* – Little Breach, Moulsford, Oxon OX10 9JN.

Grandson of late Rev Hon Charles James Willoughby, 2nd brother of 8th Baron:—
Issue of late James Frederick Digby Willoughby, OBE, *b* 1856, *d* 1947: *m* 1881, Mary Elizabeth, who *d* 1927, da of Rev Edward John Randolph (Rich, Bt, colls):—
Rev Canon Bernard Digby (Salruck, Renvyle, co Galway), *b* 1896; *ed* Wellington Coll; Canon of Tuam Cathedral 1963-73; late R of Knappagh, co Mayo; formerly Maj Indian Army: *m* 1944, Ruth, da of late W. B. Barber, of Beacon Hill, Hucknall, Notts, and has issue living, Colin James, *b* 1949; *ed* Portora Royal Sch: *m* 1976, Bridget, da of late Brig Philip Henry Cecil Hayward, CBE, of The Old Mill House, Roughton, Norwich, and has issue living, Philip Mark Digby *b* 1993, — Elisabeth Grace, *b* 1945: *m* 1964, Thomas Miller Ormsby, of Milford, Cloghan's Hill, Tuam, co Galway, and has issue living, Thomas

Anthony Bowen Miller *b* 1969: *m* 1993, Amanda Lex Edgley, John Charles *b* 1971, Lucy Anne *b* 1966: *m* 1992, Geoffry Tottenham, of Cloragh, Ashford, co Wicklow, Catherine *b* 1973.

Granddaughter of late Col Herbert Percival Willoughby, RA, eldest son of late Rev Hon Percival George Willoughby (infra):—
Issue of late Capt John Herbert Willoughby, RM, *b* 1896, *d* 1975: *m* 19—, Dorothy Mary, da of —:—
Lois Ann Mary, *b* 19—. Resides in Australia.

Grandchildren of late Rev Nesbit Edward Willoughby, 2nd son of late Rev Hon Percival George Willoughby, 3rd brother of 8th Baron:—
Issue of late Rear Adm Guy Willoughby, CB, *b* 1902, *d* 1987: *m* 1923, Mary, who *d* 1990, da of James George Wilcox Aldridge, AMICE:—
Hugh Nesbit (12 Park Court, Park Rd, Stroud, Glos GL5 2HQ), *b* 1925; *ed* Monckton Combe; ARIBA, AADip of Architectural Assocn; served World War II in RAF, and in RE 1943-47.
Issue of late Surg-Cdr Lawrence Willoughby, RNVR, *b* 1908, *d* 1980: *m* 1st, 1936, Dorothy Hughes, who *d* 1956; 2ndly, 1957, Elizabeth, who *d* 1987, da of late Alexander Sadowski, of Rosko, Poland;—
(By 2nd *m*) Guy Alexander (11823-83rd St, Edmonton, Alberta, Canada), *b* 1958. ——— Veronica Anne, *b* (twin) 1958.

PREDECESSORS – (1) FRANCIS Willoughby; *cr Baronet* 1677, with remainder to his only brother; *d* 1688; *s* by his brother (2) *Sir* THOMAS, 2nd Bt; successively MP for Newark and Nottinghamshire; *cr Baron Middleton*, of Middleton, co Warwick (peerage of Great Britain) 1711; *d* 1729; *s* by his son (3) FRANCIS, 2nd Baron; *d* 1758; *s* by his el son (4) FRANCIS, 3rd Baron; *d* unmarried 1774; *s* by his brother (5) THOMAS, 4th Baron; *d* 1781; *s* by his cousin (6) HENRY, 5th Baron, son Hon Thomas, 2nd son of 1st Baron; *d* 1800; *s* by his son (7) HENRY, 6th Baron; *dsp* 1835; *s* by his cousin (8) DIGBY, 7th Baron, Capt RN, grandson of late Hon Thomas, 2nd son of 1st Baron; *d* unmarried 1856; *s* by his cousin (9) HENRY, 8th Baron, great-grandson of late Hon Thomas, 2nd son of 1st Baron; *b* 1817; *d* 1843, Julia Louisa, da of late Alexander William Bosville, *de jure* 12th Bt, of Thorpe and Gunthwaite, co York; *d* 1877; *s* by his el son (10) DIGBY WENTWORTH BAYARD, 9th Baron, *b* 1844: *m* 1860, Eliza Maria, who *d* 1922, da of Sir Alexander Penrose Gordon Cumming, 3rd Bt; *d* 1922; *s* by his brother (11) GODFREY ERNEST PERCIVAL, 10th Baron, *b* 1847; Midshipman RN; subsequently entered 9th Lancers and retired as Capt; sometime Starter to the Jockey Club: *m* 1881, Ida Eleanora Constance, who *d* 1924, da of late George W. H. Ross, of Cromarty House, Cromarty; *d* 1924; *s* by his 2nd son (12) MICHAEL GUY PERCIVAL, KG, MC, TD, 11th Baron; *b* 1887; Chancellor of Hull Univ 1931-70; Lord-Lt for E Riding 1936-68: *m* 1920, Angela Florence Alfreda, who *d* 1978, da of late Charles Oswin Hall, of Eddlethorpe Hall, Malton; *d* 1970; *s* by his el son (13) (DIGBY) MICHAEL GODFREY JOHN, MC, 12th Baron.

MIDLETON VISCOUNT (Brodrick) (Viscount I 1717, Baron GB 1796)

ALAN HENRY BRODRICK, 12th Viscount: *b* 4 Aug 1949: *s* 1988: *ed* St Edmund's Canterbury: *m* 1978, Julia Helen, da of Michael Pitt, of Lias Cottage, Compton Dundon, Somerton, Som, and has issue.

Arms – Argent, on a chief vert, two spears' heads of the field, erect, and embrued gules. **Crest** – Out of a ducal coronet or, a spear head argent, embrued gules. **Supporters** – Two men in armour, proper, each holding a spear in the exterior hand.
Residence – 2 Burrell's Orchard, Westley, Bury St Edmunds, Suffolk IP33 3TH.

SONS LIVING

Hon ASHLEY RUPERT, *b* 25 Nov 1980.
Hon William Michael, *b* 1982.

DAUGHTER LIVING

Hon Charlotte Helen, *b* 1983.

SISTERS LIVING

Susan Margaret, *b* 1945: *m* 1971, Robert Andrew Swann, of 44 Munster Rd, Teddington, Middx, and has issue living, Benedick Rupert Christopher, *b* 1976, — Tabitha Mary, *b* 1972, — Jessica Araminta May, *b* 1978.
Elizabeth Ann, *b* 1947: *m* 1974, Stephen James Kershaw, of 1 Westbourne Rd, N7 8AR.

WIDOW LIVING OF SON OF FIRST EARL

Margaret Lætitia, only da of late Maj Hon Charles Henry Lyell (*see* B Lyell); was Assist Commercial Sec, British Embassy, Moscow 1944-45: *m* 1st, 1937, Maj Hon Francis Alan STEWART-MACKENZIE OF SEAFORTH, who was *ka* 1943, having assumed by declaration 1935 the surname of Stewart-Mackenzie of Seaforth in lieu of his patronymic; 2ndly, 1944, Charles Henry Pearson Gifford, OBE. *Residence* – 1 Wyndham House, Aldeburgh, Suffolk.

MOTHER LIVING

Alice Elizabeth, da of late George Robertson Roberts, of Maloya, Purley, Surrey: *m* 1941, Alan Rupert Brodrick, who *d* 1972. *Residence* – 104 Fitzjohn's Av, Hampstead, NW3 6NT.

WIDOW LIVING OF ELEVENTH VISCOUNT

SHEILA CAMPBELL (*Sheila, Viscountess Midleton*), da of late Charles Campbell MacLeod, of Cawthorpe House, Bourne, Lincs: *m* 1940, the 11th Viscount, who *d* 1988. *Residence* – Private Nursing and Residential Home, Church Walk, off South St, Bourne, Lincs PE10 9LX.

COLLATERAL BRANCHES LIVING

Issue of late His Honour Norman John Lee Brodrick, brother of 11th Viscount, *b* 1912, *d* 1992: *m* 1940, Ruth Severn (Slade Lane Cottage, Rogate, Petersfield, Hants GU31 5BL), da of late Sir Stanley Unwin, KCMG:—

His Honour Judge Michael John Lee (The Clock House, Swarraton, Alresford, Hants S024 9TQ), *b* 1941; *ed* Charterhouse, and Merton Coll, Oxford (MA); Bar Lincoln's Inn 1965, Western Circuit, elected to Senate of Inns of Court and the Bar 1979, served 1979-82, Recorder 1981-87, Memb Wine Cttee of W Circuit 1982-86, Judicial Memb of Transport Tribunal since 1986, Circuit Judge Western Circuit since 1987, Liaison Judge to SE Hants Magistrates 1989-93, and IoW Magistrates since 1989; Memb Lord Chancellor's Advisory Cttee for Appointment of Magistrates for Portsmouth 1990-93, and for SE Hants 1993; Counsellor to Dean and Chapter of Winchester Cathedral since 1993: *m* 1969, Valerie Lois, da of Gerald Max Stroud, of Pond House, Rogate, Petersfield, Hants, and has issue living, Robert John Lee, *b* 1972; *ed* Charterhouse, and Univ of London, R Holloway Coll, — Tessa Elizabeth, *b* 1975. —— Christopher David (30 Wroxton Terrace, Christchurch, NZ), *b* 1953; *ed* Gordonstoun: *m* 1975, Kirsty Margaret, da of late Hon Sir Ian Macarthur, of Christchurch, NZ, and has issue living, Peter Hannay, *b* 1978, — Katherine Ruth, *b* 1980. —— Peter Matthew (Hillcroft, Midcross Lane, Chalfont St Peter, Bucks SL9 0LF), *b* 1954; *ed* Charterhouse, and Charing Cross Hosp Medical Sch, Univ of London (MB BS), LRCP, MRCS (Royal Colls), FRCA (Royal Coll of Anaesthetists): *m* 1982 (*m diss* 1993), Melanie Jean, da of Lloyd Forbes, of 8 Challacombe Place, Newton, Swansea, and has an adopted son and da, James Christopher, *b* 1988, — Camila, *b* 1989. —— Frances Mary Severn, *b* 1947: *m* 1972, Pedro Prá-Lopez, of 59 Twyford Av, N2, and has issue living, Nicholas Norman Pedro, *b* 1974, — Thomas Severn, *b* 1977.

Issue of late Col Hon Arthur Grenville Brodrick, 3rd son of 8th Viscount, *b* 1868, *d* 1934: *m* 1912, Lesley Venetia, who *d* 1954, da of late Lieut-Col Edward Harrison Clough-Taylor, formerly Roy Welch Fusiliers (D Argyll):—

Elisabeth Venetia Marian, *b* 1914. *Residence* – 89 Chatsworth Court, Pembroke Road, W8.

Granddaughter of late Rev Hon Alan Brodrick, 5th son of 7th Viscount:—

Issue (by 1st *m*) of late Alan Melvill Brodrick, *b* 1868, *d* 1933: *m* 1st, 1898 (*m diss* 1901), Beatrice, da of Henry Ernst Hall, formerly of Unsted Park, Godalming; 2ndly, 1912, Diana, who *d* 1930, widow of Thomas Davey Peacey:—

Beatrice Mary Alleyne, *b* 1899: *m* 1945, Alban Churton Roe, Flying Officer, RAF Vol Reserve. *Residence* –

PREDECESSORS – (1) ALAN Brodrick, Solicitor-Gen for Ireland 1695, Attorney-Gen 1707; MP for Cork 1692-1709, and for Midhurst 1717-22, sometime Speaker of the House of Commons in Ireland, Ch Justice of the King's Bench in Ireland 1709-10, Lord Chancellor of Ireland 1714-28, and a Lord Justice of Ireland 1716-17, 1719, and 1723-4; *cr Baron Brodrick*, of Midleton, co Cork (peerage of Ireland), 1715, and *Viscount Midleton* (peerage of Ireland), 1717; *d* 1728; *s* by his son (2) ALAN, 2nd Viscount; a Commr of English Customs; *d* 1747; *s* by his son (3) GEORGE, 3rd Viscount; MP for Ashburton 1754-61; *d* 1765; *s* by his son (4) GEORGE, 4th Viscount; MP for Whitchurch, Hants 1774-96; *cr Baron Brodrick*, co Surrey (peerage of Great Britain) 1796, with remainder to the issue male of his father; *d* 1836; *s* by his son (5) GEORGE ALAN, 5th Viscount; *dsp* 1848; *s* by his cousin (6) CHARLES, 6th Viscount, el son of Most Rev Hon Charles, Archbishop of Cashel, 4th son of 3rd Viscount; *d* 1863; *s* by his brother (7) WILLIAM JOHN, 7th Viscount; *b* 1798; was Dean of Exeter and Chaplain to HM Queen Victoria: *m* 1st, 1824, Lady Elizabeth Anne Brudenell, da of 6th Earl of Cardigan, and widow of Hon John Perceval (E Egmont); 2ndly, 1829, Hon Harriet Brodrick, 3rd da of 4th Viscount Midleton; *d* 1870; *s* by his son (3) WILLIAM, 8th Viscount; *b* 1830; Lord High Steward of Kingston 1875-93, and Lord-Lieut of co Surrey 1896-1905; MP for Mid Surrey (C) 1868-70: *m* 1853, Hon Augusta Mary, who *d* 1903, da of 1st Baron Cottesloe; *d* 1907; *s* by his el son (9) WILLIAM ST JOHN FREMANTLE, PC, KP, 9th Viscount; *b* 1856; an Alderman of London County Council 1907-13; was Financial Sec to War Office 1886-92; and Under-Sec of State for War 1895-8, Under-Sec of State for Foreign Affairs 1898-1900, Sec of State for War 1900-03, Sec of State for India 1903-5, and a Member of Irish Convention 1917-18; elected a Member of Senate of S Ireland June 1921; sat as MP for W Div of Surrey (C) 1880-85, and for SW or Guildford Div of Surrey 1885-1906; *cr Viscount Dunsford* of Dunsford, co Surrey, and *Earl of Midleton* (peerage of UK) 1920: *m* 1st, 1880, Lady Hilda Charteris, who *d* 1901, da of 9th Earl of Wemyss and March; 2ndly, 1903, Madeleine Cecilia Carlyle, who *d* 1966, da of late Lt-Col Hon John Constantine Stanley; *d* 1942; *s* by his el son (10) GEORGE ST JOHN, MC, 2nd Earl, *b* 1888: *m* 1st 1917 (*m diss* 1925), Margaret, da of J. Rush, of Cromer; 2ndly, 1925 (*m diss* 1975), Jeanne Guinivere, who *d* 1978, da of Alexander Sinclair, of Dublin, widow of George Jay Gould (of the Banking Family of New York); 3rdly, 1975, Irène Lilian Creese (Rène Ray the actress), who *d* 1993, and *d* 1979, when the Earldom of Midleton and the Viscountcy of Dunsford became extinct, and the Viscountcy of Midleton and the other peerages devolved upon his kinsman (11) TREVOR LOWTHER (el son of William John Henry Brodrick, OBE, 2nd son of Rev Hon Alan Brodrick, yst son of 7th Viscount), 11th Viscount, *b* 1903: *m* 1940, Sheila Campbell, da of late Charles Campbell MacLeod, of Cawthorpe House, Bourne, Lincs; *d* 1988; *s* by his nephew (12) ALAN HENRY (only son of late Alan Rupert Brodrick, yr brother of 11th Viscount), 12th Viscount and present peer; also Baron Brodrick, of Midleton, and Baron Brodrick of Peper Harow.

Midlothian, Earl of, see Earl of Rosebery.

MILFORD, BARON (Philipps) (Baron UK 1939, Bt UK 1919)

Patriotism my motive

HUGO JOHN LAURENCE PHILIPPS, 3rd Baron, and 3rd Baronet; *b* 27 Aug 1929; *s* 1993; *ed* Eton, and King's Coll, Camb; a farmer: *m* 1st, 1951 (*m diss* 1958), Margaret, only da of late Capt Ralph Heathcote, DSO, RN, of Gressingham, Lancs; 2ndly, 1959 (*m diss* 1984), Hon Mary Makins, twin da of 1st Baron Sherfield, GCB, GCMG; 3rdly, 1989, Mrs Felicity Leach, da of late Murray Ballantyne, of Montreal, Canada, and has issue by 1st and 2nd *m.*

Arms – Argent, a lion rampant sable ducally gorged and chained or. **Crest** – A lion as in the arms. **Supporters** – On either side a horse, argent charged on the shoulder with three bars wavy azure.
Residence – Llanstephan House, Llanstephan, Brecon, Powys.

SONS LIVING *(By 2nd marriage)*

Hon GUY WOGAN, *b* 25 July 1961; *ed* Eton, and Magdalen Coll, Oxford (BA); Bar Inner Temple 1986: *m* 1988, Rebecca, yr da of Nigel Nicolson, MBE, of Sissinghurst Castle, Cranbrook, Kent (*see* B Carnock, colls). *Residence* – 68 Westbourne Park Rd, W2 5PJ.
Hon Roland Alexander, *b* 1962; *ed* Eton, and Trin Coll, Camb (MA): *m* 1991, Felicity Kate, da of Hilary Harold Rubinstein, of 61 Clarendon Rd, W11. *Residence* – 231 Westbourne Park Rd, W11 IEB.
Hon Ivo Laurence, *b* 1967; *ed* Eton, and Bristol Univ.

DAUGHTERS LIVING *(By 1st marriage)*

Hon Anna Margaret, *b* 1954: *m* 1975, Christopher Richard James Woodhouse, MB BS, FRCS, and has issue (*see* B Terrington). *Residence* – 14 Crescent Grove, SW4.

(by 2nd marriage)

Hon Katherine Nina, *b* 1964.

UNCLE LIVING *(son of 1st Baron)*

Hon Richard Hanning, MBE, *b* 1904; *ed* Eton; Maj Welsh Gds (Reserve), Hon Col Pembroke Yeo, Hon Pres of Schweppes, Ltd, Chm Milford Haven Conservancy Board 1963-75; a Member of Civic Trust for Wales, and a JP; Lord-Lt for Pembrokeshire 1958-74, and for Dyfed 1974-79; Keeper of the Rolls for Dyfed 1974-79; NW Europe 1944-45; MBE (Mil) 1945: *m* 1930, Lady Marion Violet Dalrymple, JP, da of 12th Earl of Stair, and has issue living, Jeremy Hew, *b* 1931; *ed* Eton; a Member of Lloyds, and Chm of Laurence Philipps & Co, Ltd: *m* 1959, Susan, yr da of H. E. B. Gundry, of Grange, Honiton, Devon, and has issue living, Clare Marion *b* 1961, Nicola *b* 1964, — Louise (adopted da), *b* 1946: *m* 1971, Hugh Simon Fetherstonhaugh, and has issue (*see* V Galway). *Residence* – Picton Castle, Haverfordwest, Dyfed. *Club* – Boodle's.

AUNT LIVING *(daughter of 1st Baron)*

Hon Gwenllian, OBE, *b* 1916; formerly Subaltern ATS; is a JP for Radnorshire; a Co Councillor for Radnorshire 1959-64, and High Sheriff 1970-71; OBE (Civil) 1962. *Residence* – The Old Rectory, Boughrood, Llyswen, Brecon.

WIDOWS LIVING OF SONS OF FIRST BARON

Hon Elizabeth Joan Kindersley (Dalham Hall, Newmarket, Suffolk), da of 1st Baron Kindersley: *m* 1930, Maj Hon James Perrott Philipps, TD, who *d* 1984, and has issue (see colls infra).
Lady Jean Meriel McDonnell (Slebech Park, Haverfordwest, Dyfed), da of 7th Earl of Antrim: *m* 1939, Capt Hon William Speke Philipps, CBE, who *d* 1975, and has issue (see colls infra).

WIDOW LIVING OF SECOND BARON

TAMARA (*Dowager Baronnes Milford*), da of — Kravetz, of —, and widow of William Rust: *m* 1954, as his 3rd wife, the 2nd Baron, who *d* 1993. *Residence* – Flat 2, 8 Lyndhurst Rd, Hampstead, NW3 5PX.

COLLATERAL BRANCHES LIVING

Issue of late Maj Hon James Perrott Philipps, TD, 3rd son of 1st Baron, *b* 1905, *d* 1984: *m* 1930, Hon Elizabeth Joan Kindersley (ante), da of 1st Baron Kindersley:—
Peter Anthony (Parsonage Farm, Ugley, nr Bishop's Stortford, Herts), *b* 1933; *ed* Eton, and Trin Coll, Camb; Member of London Stock Exchange: *m* 1957 (*m diss* 1981), Susannah Margaret, el da of S. W. Eaton, and has issue living, Charles Edward Laurence, *b* 1959, — James Anthony Hanning, *b* 1961, — Gavin Piers Alexander, *b* 1963. —— Penelope Doune, *b* 1931: *m* 1950, Capt Anthony Walsham Neville Lake, of Higham's Farm, Wimbish, Saffron Walden, Essex, and *d* 1985, leaving issue (*see* Walsham, Bt, colls). —— Daphne Deirdre (Springfield Maltings, Stogumber, Taunton, Som), *b* 1940: *m* 1963, Robin Hugh Lewes, TD, who *d* 1969, and has issue living, James Hugh, *b* 1967, — Katherine Mary, *b* 1968, — Sarah Jane (twin), *b* 1968.

Issue of late Capt Hon William Speke Philipps, CBE, yst son of 1st Baron, *b* 1908, *d* 1975: *m* 1939, Lady Jean Meriel McDonnell (ante), da of 7th Earl of Antrim:—
Geoffrey Mark (Slebech Park, Haverfordwest, Dyfed), *b* 1948; *ed* Eton: *m* 1984, Georgina Bridget, only da of Rear-Adm John Gervaise Beresford Cooke, CB, DSC, of Downstead House, Morestead, Winchester, and has issue living, Alexander Gervaise, *b* 1985, — Lara Helen, *b* 1986, — Leonora Isabel Jean, *b* 1989. —— David William, *b* 1952: *m* 1971, Stella Katharine Anne, only da of A. W. Fordham, and has issue living, Frederick William, *b* 1973. —— Georgina Rose, *b* 1942: *m* 1967, David Llewellyn Pryse Lloyd, and has had issue, Huw Llewellyn, *b* 1971, — Jonathan, *b* 1973, — Isabel Rose Pryse, *b* 1968; *d* 1989, — Juliet Ann, *b* 1970. —— Theresa Margaret, *b* 1946: *m* 1972, Christopher John Payne, and has issue living, Joseph Vernon William, *b* 1975, — Benjamin Christopher John, *b* 1978, — Harriet Sarah Jean, *b* 1982.

PREDECESSORS – Sir Richard Philipps, 7th Bt (*cr* 1621) (*see* V St Davids); *cr Baron Milford* 1776, which title became ext on his death in 1823, and was revived in favour of (1) LAURENCE RICHARD Philipps, 6th son of Rev Canon Sir James Erasmus Philipps, 12th Bt; *b* 1874; High Sheriff of Hants 1915; a Gov of Univ Coll of Wales and Founder of Paraplegic Hospital in Wales; *cr* a Bt 1919, and *Baron Milford*, of Llanstephan, co Radnor (peerage of UK) 1939: *m* 1901, Ethel Georgina, who *d* 1971, da of late Rev Benjamin Speke, of Jordans, Somerset; *d* 1962; *s* by his el son (2) WOGAN, 2nd Baron; *b* 1902; Memb Internat Brigade, Spanish Civil War; Communist Cllr Cirencester RDC 1946-49; Painter: *m* 1st, 1928 (*m diss* 1944), Rosamond Nina, CBE (the celebrated novelist, Rosamond Lehmann), who *d* 1990, da of late Rudolph Chambers Lehmann, of Fieldhead, Bourne End, Bucks, and formerly wife of Walter Leslie Runciman (later 2nd Viscount Runciman of Doxford); 2ndly, 1944, Maria Cristina, who *d* 1953, da of the Marchese Casati, of Palazzo Barberini, Rome, and formerly wife of 15th Earl of Huntingdon; 3rdly, 1954, Tamara (*née* Kravetz), widow of William Rust, Editor of the *Daily Worker*, *d* 1993; *s* by his only son (3) HUGO JOHN LAURENCE, 3rd Baron and present peer.

MILFORD HAVEN, MARQUESS OF (Mountbatten) (Marquess UK 1917)

GEORGE IVAR LOUIS MOUNTBATTEN, 4th Marquess; *b* 6 June 1961; *s* 1970: *m* 1989, Sarah Georgina, elder da of George Alfred Walker, and has issue.

Arms – Quarterly: 1st and 4th azure, a lion rampant double-queued barry of ten argent and gules, armed and langued of the last, crowned or, within a bordure compony of the second and third; 2nd and 3rd argent, two pallets sable, charged on the honour point with an escutcheon of the arms of the late *Princess Alice* (i.e. the Royal arms differenced with a label of three points argent, the centre point charged with a rose gules barbed vert, and each of the other points with an ermine spot sable. **Crests** – 1st, out of a ducal coronet or two horns barry of ten argent and gules, issuing from each three linden leaves vert, and from the outer side of each horn four branches barwise, having three like leaves pendent therefrom of the last, *Hesse*; 2nd, out of a ducal coronet or a plume of four ostrich feathers alternately argent and sable, *Battenberg*. **Supporters** – On either side a lion double-queued and crowned all or.
Residence – Moyns Park, Birdbrook, Essex.

SON LIVING

HENRY (HARRY) DAVID LOUIS (*Earl of Medina*), *b* 19 Oct 1991.

DAUGHTER LIVING

Lady Tatiana Helen Georgia, *b* 1990.

BROTHER LIVING

Lord Ivar Alexander Michael, *b* 1963: *m* 1994, Penelope A. V., da of Colin Thompson, of Warminster, Wilts, and Mrs Rosemary Walker, of Chippenham, Wilts.

WIDOW LIVING OF THIRD MARQUESS

JANET MERCEDES (*Janet, Marchioness of Milford Haven*), only da of late Maj Francis Bryce, OBE: *m* 1960, as his 2nd wife, the 3rd Marquess, who *d* 1970.

PREDECESSORS – LOUIS ALEXANDER Mountbatten, GCB, GCVO, KCMG, son of HGDH late Prince Alexander of Hesse, GCB, by his morganatic *m* to Julie, Princess of Battenberg; *b* 24 May 1854; naturalized 1868 as Prince Louis of Battenberg; Adm of the Fleet; was Naval Adviser to Inspector-Gen of Fortifications 1893-4, Assist Director of Naval Intelligence 1899-1901, Director thereof 1902-5, in Command of second Cruiser Squadron 1905-7, Second in Command of Mediterranean Fleet 1907-8, Com-in-Ch of Atlantic Fleet 1908-10, in Command of 3rd and 4th Divs Home Fleet 1911, Second Sea Lord of the Admiralty 1911-12, and First Sea Lord 1912-14; appointed Hon ADC to Queen Victoria 1896, and Personal Naval ADC to King Edward VII 1901 and to King George V 1910; *cr Viscount Alderney*, co Southampton, *Earl of Medina*, and *Marquess of Milford Haven* (peerage of United Kingdom) 17 July 1917, having by Roy Warrant, 14 July 1917, at HM's request, discontinued the use, style and title of "Serene Highness" and "Prince," and appellation of "Battenberg," and assumed for himself and descendants the surname of Mountbatten: *m* 1884, Victoria Alberta Elizabeth Mathilde Marie, VA, who *d* 1950, el da of HRH the late Grand Duke Ludwig IV of Hesse, KG, by HRH Princess Alice Maud Mary, VA, 2nd da of HM Queen Victoria; *d* 1921; *s* by his el son (2) GEORGE LOUIS VICTOR HENRY SERGE, GCVO, 2nd Marquess; *b* 1892; Capt (ret) RN; European War 1914-18, present at battle of Heligoland, Dogger Bank, and Jutland: *m* 1916, Countess Nadejda de Torby, VA, who *d* 1963, yr da of HIH the late Grand Duke Michael Michaelovitch of Russia and late Countess de Torby; *d* 1938; *s* by his only son (3) DAVID MICHAEL, OBE, DSC, 3rd Marquess; *b* 1919: *m* 1st, 1950, Romaine Dahlgren (*m diss* 1960), she having obtained a divorce at El Paso, Mexico 1954), only da of late Vinton Ulric Dahlgren Pierce, and formerly wife of William Simpson; 2ndly, 1960, Janet Mercedes, only da of late Maj Francis Bryce, OBE; *d* 1970; *s* by his el son (4) GEORGE IVAR LOUIS, 4th Marquess and present peer; also Earl of Medina, and Viscount Alderney.

MILLER OF HENDON, BARONESS (Miller) (Life Baroness 1993)

DOREEN MILLER, MBE, da of Bernard Henry Feldman; *b* 13 June 1933; *ed* LSE; Co Dir; Chm Barnet Family Health Services Authority since 1990; Crown Agents since 1990; Member Monopolies & Mergers Commn 1992-93; Treasurer Greater London Area Conservative Assocns 1990-93, since when Chm; JP Brent 1970; MBE (Civil) 1989; *cr Baroness Miller of Hendon*, of Gore, in the London Borough of Barnet (Life Baroness) 1993; *m* 1955, Henry Lewis Miller, son of Ben Miller, and has issue.

Address – c/o House of Lords, SW1. *Clubs* – St Stephen's Constitutional, Reform, Carlton.

SONS LIVING

Hon Michael Steven, *b* 1956.
Hon Paul Howard, *b* 1959: *m* 1992, Sharon Hunt.
Hon David Philip, *b* 1962.

MILLS, VISCOUNT (Mills) (Viscount UK 1962, Bt UK 1953)

CHRISTOPHER PHILIP ROGER MILLS, 3rd Viscount; *b* 20 May 1956; *s* 1988; *ed* Oundle Sch, and London Univ: *m* 1980, Lesley Alison, elder da of Alan Bailey, of Lichfield, Staffs.

Arms – Per chevron azure and argent in chief two millrinds of the last and in base a balance sable. **Crest** – A bear's gamb erased or, supporting a flint-lock proper. **Supporters** – On either side a lion or collared and chained azure pendant from the collar an escutcheon of the last charged with a sun in splendour gold.
Residence – Oak Cottage, Larg Buildings, Sawley, nr Clitheroe, Lancs BB7 4LE.

SISTERS LIVING

Hon Felicity Jane, *b* 1947: *m* 1970, Roger B. Pickford, of Heddfan, Ffawyddog, Llangattock, Crickhowell, Powys.
Hon Phillipa Susan, *b* 1950: *m* 1970, Russell Scott Arthurton.

AUNT LIVING (*daughter of 1st Viscount*)

Hon Beatrice Margaret, *b* 1916: *m* 1941, Walter Goodwin Davis, and has issue living, Patrick, *b* 1947, — Andrew, *b* 1950, — Jane, *b* 1957. *Residence* – Chantry House, Sheep St, Stow-on-the-Wold, Glos.

WIDOW LIVING OF SECOND VISCOUNT

JOAN DOROTHY (*Dowager Viscountess Mills*), da of James Shirreff, of London: *m* 1945, Maj the 2nd Viscount, who *d* 1988. *Residence* – Whitecroft, 24 Abbey Rd, Knaresborough, N Yorks HG5 8HY.

PREDECESSORS – (1) *Rt Hon Sir* PERCY HERBERT Mills, KBE, PC, son of D. Mills, of Stockton-on-Tees; *b* 1890; Min of Power 1957-59; Paymaster-Gen 1959-61; Min without Portfolio 1961-62; Controller-Gen of Machine Tools, Min of Supply 1940-44; *cr* a Baronet 1953, *Baron Mills*, of Studley, co Warwick 1957, and *Viscount Mills*, of Kensington, co London 1963: *m* 1915, Winifred Mary, who *d* 1974, da of George Conaty, of Birmingham; *d* 1968; *s* by his only son (2) ROGER CLINTON, 2nd Viscount, *b* 1919; Bar Inner Temple, Colonial Ser Kenya, Maj RA 1939-45 War: *m* 1945, Joan Dorothy, da of James Shirreff, of London; *d* 1988; *s* by his only son (3) CHRISTOPHER PHILIP ROGER, 3rd Viscount, and present peer; also Baron Mills.

MILNE, BARON (Milne) (Baron UK 1933)

Studies make illustrious

GEORGE DOUGLASS MILNE, 2nd Baron; *b* 10 Feb 1909; *s* 1948; *ed* Winchester and New Coll, Oxford; a Member of Inst of Chartered Accountants of Scotland; Master of Grocers' Co 1961-62; a Member of Lambeth Hosp Management Cttee 1947-51; Dep Chm of London and Northern Group 1982-87; TD; 1939-45 War as Maj RA (TA) in Norway and Middle East (despatches, wounded, prisoner): *m* 1940, Cicely, da of late Ronald Leslie, and has issue.

Arms – Or, a cross moline pierced lozengeways of the field between four mullets azure. **Crest** – A dexter hand holding up an open book proper, leaved or. **Supporters** – *Dexter*, an officer of the Royal Horse Artillery; *sinister*, an officer of the Greek Evzone Guard, both in full dress uniform.
Residence – 33 Lonsdale Road, Barnes, SW13.

SONS LIVING

Hon GEORGE ALEXANDER (188 Broom Rd, Teddington, Middx), *b* 1 April 1941; *ed* Winchester; Livery of Grocers' Co 1971.
Hon Iain Charles Luis (96 Romsey Rd, Winchester, Hants), *b* 1949, *ed* Oundle; FCA; Livery of Grocers' Co: *m* 1987, Berta (Ita), da of Enrique Urzua Acevedo, of San Felipe, Chile, and has issue living, Iain Eduardo Alexander, *b* 1990, — Leslie Axel Fernando, *b* 1993.

DAUGHTER LIVING

Hon Ann Geraldine, *b* 1946, Freeman of City of London (1967) and Livery of Grocers' Co 1984: *m* 1969, Ian Frederick Lawrence Straker, of Hever Warren, Hever, Kent, and has issue living, Ross Alexander Lawrence, *b* 1977; *ed* Millfield, — Frances Georgina *b* 1980.

SISTER LIVING

Hon Joan Claire Florence, *b* 1907: *m* 1937, as his 2nd wife, James Hart Rutland, who *d* 1954. *Residence* – Cromwell Cottage, Church St, Alresford, Hants.

PREDECESSOR – **(1)** *FM Sir* GEORGE FRANCIS Milne, GCB, GCMG, DSO, son of late George Milne, of Westwood, Aberdeen; *b* 1866; became Field-Marshal 1928; Nile Expedition 1898, S Africa 1899-1902 (DSO), European War 1914-19 on Staff and as Gen Officer Comdg Salonika Army (KCB, KCMG, GCMG); was Lieut of The Tower 1920-23, Ch of Imperial Gen Staff 1926-33, Master Gunner, St James's Park 1929-46, and Constable of the Tower 1933-8; Grand Pres of British Empire Ser League, Chm Empire Sos War Hospitality Committee, Pres of London Fever Hospital, Chm of Executive Committee of Roy Cancer Hospital, Patron of Salonika Reunion Asso, and Pres of Old Contemptibles' Asso, Army Cadet Asso, Roy Artillery Asso, and Roy Artillery Memorial Asso; bore second sword at Coronation of King George VI; *cr Baron Milne*, of Salonika and of Rubislaw, co Aberdeen (peerage of United Kingdom) 1933: *m* 1905, Claire Marjoribanks, MBE, who *d* 1970, da of Sir John Nisbet Maitland, 5th Bt; *d* 1948; *s* by his son **(2)** GEORGE DOUGLASS, 2nd Baron and present peer.

MILNER OF LEEDS, BARON (Milner) (Baron UK 1951)

(ARTHUR JAMES) MICHAEL MILNER, AE, 2nd Baron; *b* 12 Sept 1923; *s* 1967; *ed* Oundle, and Trin Hall, Camb (MA); Solicitor 1951; consultant in the legal firm of Gregory, Rowcliffe & Milners, of London; Opposition Whip 1971-74; Ft Lt 609 (W Riding) Sqdn RAuxAF 1947-52; 1939-45 War as Fl Lt RAF: *m* 1951, Sheila Margaret, da of late Gerald Hartley, of Leeds, and has had issue.

Arms – Gules on a chevron ermine between in chief two bits or and in base a rose argent barbed and seeded proper a Teazel sable. **Crest** – Perched on a sword with point to the dexter proper and hilt and pomel or an owl also proper, gorged with a collar sable thereon three mullets argent, pendent therefrom a pair of scales and resting on the dexter claw on a portcullis chained or. **Supporters** – On either side an owl proper gorged with a collar sable thereon three mullets argent pendent therefrom a portcullis chained or.
Residence – 2 The Inner Court, Old Church St, SW3 5BY.

SON LIVING

Hon RICHARD JAMES, *b* 16 May 1959; *ed* Charterhouse, and Surrey Univ (BSc): *m* 1988, Margaret Christine, yst da of Gerald Francis Voisin, of Jersey, CI, and has issue living, Charlotte Emma, *b* 1990, — Nicola Louise Christine, *b* 1992.

DAUGHTERS LIVING AND DECEASED

Hon Geraldine Jane, *b* 1954: *m* 1978, Mark Anthony Fenton, of 8 Glebe Terrace, Leeds LS16 5NA, and has issue living, Harry James Oliver, *b* 1982, — Alexander Philip Guy, *b* 1992, — Kate Emma Jane, *b* 1984.
Hon Meredith Ann, *b* 1956, *dunm* 1993.

SISTER LIVING

Hon Shelagh Mary Margaret, *b* 1925: *m* 1948 (*m diss* 1965), Harry Barker Grimshaw, and has issue living, John Sherwood, *b* 1950, — Miranda, *b* 1952. *Residence* – High Barn, Thorner, Yorks.

PREDECESSOR – **(1)** *Rt Hon* JAMES Milner, MC, TD, PC, el son of late James Henry Milner of Leeds; *b* 1889; MP for SE Leeds (Lab) 1929-51; Chm of Ways and Means and Dep Speaker of House of Commons 1943-45, and 1945-51; *cr Baron Milner of Leeds*, of Roundhay, City of Leeds (Peerage of UK) 1951: *m* 1917, Lois Tinsdale, who *d* 1982, da of Thomas Brown, of Roundhay, Leeds; *d* 1967, *s* by his only son **(2)** (ARTHUR JAMES) MICHAEL, 2nd Baron, and present peer.

MILVERTON, BARON (Richards) (Baron UK 1947)

Mind makes the man

Rev FRASER ARTHUR RICHARD RICHARDS, 2nd Baron; *b* 21 July 1930; *s* 1978; *ed* Ridley Coll, Ontario, Clifton Coll, Egerton Agric Coll, Njoro, Kenya, and Bishop's Coll, Cheshunt, Herts; in Roy Signals 1949-50; in Kenya Police 1952-53; made Deacon 1957, ordained Priest 1958, Curate 1957-63, V of Okewood, Surrey 1963-67, Vicar of Christian Malford with Sutton Benger and Tytherton Kellaways 1967-93; Chap to Wilts ACF: *m* 1957, Mary Dorothy, BD, da of late Leslie Fly, of Pulteney St, Bath, and has issue.

𝕬rms – Argent, three lozenges conjoined in fesse gules between two barrulets sable, all within two flaunches of the second, both charged with a spearhead of the field. 𝕮rest – A Malay tiger's head erased proper, gorged with a collar lozengy argent and gules. 𝕾upporters – On either side a Malay tiger proper, gorged with a collar lozengy argent and gules.
Residence – Riverview, Bath Rd, Manton, Marlborough, Wilts SN8 1PS.

DAUGHTERS LIVING

Hon Susan Mary, *b* 1962: *m* 1991, Robert Adam Brisbane Cross, elder son of Diarmid A. Cross, of Tavistock, Devon, and has issue living, Alice Rose, *b* 1993.
Hon Juliet Elizabeth, *b* 1964: *m* 1992, Maurice Charles Steuart-Corry, yr son of William Steuart-Corry, of Helensburgh, Dunbartonshire, and has issue living, Sophie, *b* 1993, — Emma, *b* (twin) 1993.

BROTHER LIVING

Hon MICHAEL HUGH, *b* 1 Aug 1936; *ed* Ridley Coll, Ont, Clifton Coll, and RMA Sandhurst; Capt (ret) Rifle Bde; Malaya 1957 (despatches); attached R Nigerian Army 1962, and a Member of UN Congo Force 1963-65; Man Dir Philip Morris Nigeria Ltd 1972-77; Dir Africa Carreras Rothmans Ltd 1978-82; Man Dir Murray Sons and Co 1982-87; Personnel Dir Rothmans International Tobacco 1987-93; Man Dir Rothmans of Pall Mall (New Zealand) Ltd since 1993: *m* 1960, Edna Leonie B., yst da of Col Leo Stevenie, OBE, MC, IA (ret), and has issue living, Arthur Hugh, *b* 10 Jan 1963. *Club* – Cavalry and Guards'.

SISTER LIVING

Hon Diana Benda, *b* 1928; *ed* Havergal Coll, Toronto, Cheltenham Ladies' Coll, at London Univ, and Sorbonne, Paris: *m* 1960, Sq-Ldr Glyn John Clement, RAF, and has issue living, Paul Nicholas Arthur, *b* 1961, — Caroline Benda, *b* 1966. *Residence* – The Bell House, Kewstoke Rd, Worle, Weston-super-Mare.

WIDOW LIVING OF FIRST BARON

NOELLE BENDA, CStJ (*Noelle, Baroness Milverton*), da of Charles Basil Whitehead, of Torquay: *m* 1927, the 1st Baron, who *d* 1978. *Residence* – Flete, Ermington, Ivy Bridge, S Devon.

PREDECESSOR – **(1)** *Sir* ARTHUR FREDERICK Richards, GCMG, son of late William Richards, of Bristol; *b* 1885; Gov of N Borneo 1930-33, of Gambia 1933-36, and of Fiji (and High Commr of Pacific) 1936-38, Capt-Gen and Gov-in-Ch of Jamaica 1938-43, and Gov of Nigeria 1943-47; *cr* CMG 1933, KCMG 1935, GCMG 1942, and *Baron Milverton*, of Lagos, and of Clifton, in the City of Bristol (Peerage of UK) 1947: *m* 1927, Noelle Benda, CStJ, da of Charles Basil Whitehead, Torquay; *d* 1978; *s* by his el son **(2)** *Rev* FRASER ARTHUR RICHARD, 2nd Baron and present peer.

Minster, Baron, title of Marquess Conyngham on Roll of HL.

MINTO, EARL OF (Elliot-Murray-Kynynmound) (Earl UK 1813, Bt S 1700)

He needs not the bow

Mildly but firmly

GILBERT EDWARD GEORGE LARISTON ELLIOT-MURRAY-KYNYNMOUND, OBE, 6th Earl, and 9th Baronet; *b* 19 June 1928; *s* 1975; *ed* Eton, and RMA Sandhurst; Capt Scots Gds (Reserve); Brig Queen's Body Guard for Scotland (Royal Company of Archers); JP for Roxburghshire; DL Borders Region, Roxburgh, Ettrick and Lauderdale; Chm Scottish Council on Alcoholism; Member of Borders Regional Council (Hermitage Div) 1974-80; Dep Traffic Commr for Scotland 1975-81; Exec Vice-Pres S Scotland Chamber of Commerce 1978-80, Pres 1980-82; Dir Noel Penny Turbinse Ltd since 1971; 2nd Lieut Scots Gds 1948, served in Malaya 1949-51; ADC to CIGS 1953-55, and to Gov of Cyprus 1955; MBE (Mil) 1955, OBE (Civil) 1986: *m* 1st, 1952 (*m diss* 1965), Lady Caroline Child-Villiers, da of 9th Earl of Jersey; 2ndly, 1965, Mary Elizabeth, who *d* 1983, da of late Peter Ballantine, of Stonehouse Farm, Gladstone, NJ, USA; 3rdly, 1991, Mrs Caroline Jane Larlham, da of Stanley Godfrey, of Ruislip, Middlesex, and formerly wife of Christopher Larlham, and has issue by 1st *m*.

Arms – Quarterly: 1st and 4th grand quarters quarterly, 1st and 4th argent, a hunting horn sable, stringed gules, and on a chief azure, three mullets of the field, *Murray*; 2nd and 3rd azure, a chevron argent, between three fleurs-de-lis or, *Kynynmound*; 2nd and 3rd grand quarters gules, within a bordure vair, a bend engrailed or, thereon a baton azure, *Elliot*; above all a chief of augmentation argent, and thereon a Moor's head sable, being the arms of the island of Corsica. **Crest** – A dexter arm embowed issuant from clouds, throwing a dart, all proper. **Supporters** – *Dexter*, an Indian sheep proper; *sinister*, a fawn proper.
Seat – Minto, Hawick, Roxburghshire; *Club* – Puffin's (Edinburgh)

SON LIVING *(By 1st marriage)*

GILBERT TIMOTHY GEORGE LARISTON (*Viscount Melgund*), *b* 1 Dec 1953; *ed* Eton, and NELP (BSc); ARICS; Lt Scots Gds, Member Queen's Body Guard for Scotland (Royal Company of Archers): *m* 1983, Diana Barbara, yr da of Brian S. L. Trafford (*see* B Taylor of Hadfield), of Tismans, Rudgwick, W Sussex, and has had issue. *Residence* – Upper Ham Farm, Thornhill, Wootton Bassett, Wilts. *Club* – White's.

SONS LIVING AND DECEASED — *Hon* GILBERT FRANCIS, *b* 15 Aug 1984, — *Hon* Lorne David, *b* and *d* 1986, — *Hon* Michael Timothy, *b* 1987.
DAUGHTER LIVING — *Hon* Clare Patricia, *b* 1991.

DAUGHTER LIVING *(By 1st marriage)*

Lady Laura, *b* 1956: *m* 1984, John Reginald David Palmer, yr son of William Alexander Palmer, of Bussockwood House, Newbury, Berks, and has issue living, Sam, *b* 1985, — Nicholas, *b* 1987. *Residence* – The New House, Carlton Curlieu, Leics LE8 0PH.

BROTHER LIVING

Hon (George Esmond) Dominic ELLIOT (88 St James's Street, SW1A 1PW; *Clubs* – White's and New (Edinburgh)), *b* 1931; *ed* Eton, and Madrid Univ; formerly Lt Scots Gds: *m* 1st, 1962 (*m diss* 1970), Countess Marianne, da of late Count Thomas Esterhazy; 2ndly, 1983, Jane Caroline, da of Lawrence Reeve, of Sandridge Lodge, Bromham, Wilts, and has had issue (by 1st *m*), Alexander, *b* 1963, *d* 1985, — Esmond, *b* 1965, — (by 2nd *m*) George William Hugh, *b* 1990, — Violet Elizabeth Marion, *b* 1988.

SISTERS LIVING

Lady Bridget, *b* 1921: *m* 1st, 1944, Lt-Col James Averell Clark, Jun, DFC, USAAF, who *d* 1990; 2ndly, 1954 (*m diss* 1963), Major Henry Claude Lyon Garnett, CBE, who *d* 1990; 3rdly, 1966 (*m diss* 1970), Major (Edward) Peter Godfrey Miller Mundy, MC, who *d* 1981, and has issue living (by 1st *m*), Christopher (Crow Hall Farm, Denver, Norfolk PE38 0DG), *b* 1949: *m* 1986, Alice, only da of late Thomas Auckland Hall, of the Old Hall, Rockland St Mary, Norwich, and has issue living, Thomas Averell *b* 1987, James Auckland *b* 1994, Scarlett Alexandra *b* 1989. *Residence* – The Dower House, Crow Hall Farm, Denver, Norfolk.
Lady Willa, *b* 1924: *m* 1946, Major George David Chetwode, MBE, Coldstream Guards, and has issue (*see* B Chetwode, colls). *Residence* – Swiss Farm House, Upper Slaughter, Cheltenham, Glos GL54 2JP.

COLLATERAL BRANCHES LIVING

Grandson of late Hon Arthur Ralph Douglas Elliot, 2nd son of 3rd Earl:—
Issue of late Capt Hubert William Arthur Elliot, *b* 1891, *d* 1967: *m* 1st, 1919, Mary Hester, who *d* 1945, da of late Hon Sir Langer Meade Loftus Owen, CBE, KC, formerly Ch Judge in Divorce, Supreme Court of NSW; 2ndly, 1955, Mrs Pamela Violet Cathcart (Lochlane Smithy, Crieff, Perthshire), da of late Lt-Col Patrick Douglas Stirling, OBE, MC, JP, of Kippendavie:—
(By 1st *m*) John William Owen (Old House Farm, Cockfield, Bury St Edmunds, Suffolk), *b* 1921; *ed* Eton, and Trin Coll, Camb; Capt late Scots Gds: *m* 1944, Mary Norah, da of late Hon (Godfrey) John Arthur Murray Lyle Mulholland, MC (*see* B Dunleath, colls), and has issue living, Hugh John (1361 East St SE, Washington DC, USA), *b* 1946; *ed* Eton, and Gonville and Caius Coll, Camb (MA): *m* 1987, Mary Anna. da of John Portner, of Washington DC, USA, — Timothy David (Green House, Timworth, nr Bury St Edmunds, Suffolk) *b* 1952; *ed* Eton and Bristol Univ: *m* 1975, Helen Margaret, da of Michael Graham Lacey, of Honycombe House, Weare Giffard, Bideford, N Devon, and has issue living, Robert John *b* 1977, Michael David *b* 1982, Rebecca Frances *b* 1979, — Susan Mary *b* 1948: *ed* Goldsmith's Coll, London Univ (DipEd): *m* 1969, Patrick Gilbert Dominick Toriglioni del Cassero-Nisbett, Gren Gds, of Wood Hall, Little Waldingfield, Suffolk, and has issue living, Dominick Gilbert *b* 1972, Hugo Alexander *b* 1977, Edmond Dudley *b* 1982, Olivia Eleanora *b* 1975.

Granddaughter of late Hugh Samuel Roger Elliot, son of late Hon Hugh Frederick Hislop Elliot, 3rd son of 3rd Earl:—
  Issue of late Herbert Hugh Elliot, Pilot Officer RAF, *b* 1909, *k* on active ser 1942: *m* 1939, Kate Marjorie, who *d* 1972, da of late Rev Vernon Iles, of South Marston, Swindon, Wilts:—
Patricia, *b* 1940: *m* 1964, Maj Ieuan Davies, 11th Hussars. *Residence* – Fistral, Southway, Windmill, Padstow, Cornwall PL28 8RZ.

Granddaughter of late Rt Hon Sir Henry George Elliot, GCB, 2nd son of 2nd Earl:—
  Issue of late Sir Francis Edmund Hugh Elliot, GCMG, GCVO, *b* 1851, *d* 1940: *m* 1881, Henrietta Augusta Mary, who *d* 1938, da of late Rt Hon Sir Francis Clare Ford, PC, GCB, GCMG:—
Dorothy, *b* 1888: *m* 1914, Henry Montesquieu Anthony, CBE, who *d* 1949, and has issue living, Lydia Margaret Elliot, *b* 1918. *Residence* – 14 Princes St, S Exeter.

Grandchildren of late Gilbert Compton Elliot (infra):—
  Issue of late Maj Alexander Henry Elliot, RA, *b* 1913, *d* 1986: *m* 1937, Lady Ann Child-Villiers (Broadford, Chobham, Surrey), da of 8th Earl of Jersey:—
Gilbert Francis, *b* 1949. —— Victoria Cynthia, *b* 1938: *m* 1960, John Robert Hunter, RN (ret), of Minto, Mount Rankin, Bathurst, NSW, Australia, and has issue living, David John, *b* 1961, — James Max, *b* 1963, — Michael Alexander, *b* 1965, — Andrew William, *b* 1976. —— Patricia Joan (Selwood Cottage, Odiham, Hants), *b* 1940: *m* 1964 (*m diss* 1986), David John Curry, RAF, and has issue living, Alexander David Ian, *b* 1974, — Georgina Sophie Gay, *b* 1967.

Granddaughter of late Frederick Boileau Elliot, son of late Adm Hon Sir George Elliot, KCB, MP, 2nd son of 1st Earl:—
  Issue of late Gilbert Compton Elliot, *b* 1871, *d* 1931: *m* 1910, Marguerita, who *d* 1955, da of late Henry Barbey, of New York:—
Cynthia Sophie, BEM (c/o Chase Manhatten Bank, Tortola, British Virgin Islands), *b* 1916; whilst herself a prisoner, rendered sers to prisoners in hospitals in Germany during 1939-45 War (BEM): *m* 1st, 1944, 1st Baron Hore-Belisha, who *d* 1957; 2ndly, 1957, Maj Ian Victor Major, DSC, RM (ret), who *d* 1973.

Grandchildren of late Capt Charles Sinclair Elliot, RN, 3rd and yst son of late Capt Amyand Powney Charles Elliot, 3rd son of late Hon John Edmund Elliot, MP, 3rd son of 1st Earl:—
  Issue of late Dudley Sinclair Elliot, *b* 1890, *ka* 1917: *m* 1913, Annie Caroline, da of William Hammett Howard, of Sydney, N S Wales:—
Dudley Charles Howard (PO Box 84, Murwillumbah, NSW 2484), *b* 1918; *ed* Sydney Univ (LLB); 1939-45 War with RAAF: *m* 1943, Rosalie Yvonne, da of late Francis Walter Vizard, of S Aust, and has issue living, Gilbert Dennis (19 Wilga St, Concord West, NSW 2138), *b* 1947; *ed* Univ of NSW (Dip Hosp Admin): *m* 1973, Jane, da of John Guinane, of NSW, and has issue living, Robert Gilbert Sinclair *b* 1979, Gerard Charles Cameron *b* 1982, Lenore Elizabeth *b* 1977, — Victor Roderick, *b* 1950, — Hugh Kent, *b* 1953, — Roslyn Kristin, *b* 1944: *m* 1966, Ronald Charles Newland, and has issue living.
  Issue of late Maj Alban Charles Elliot, MC, AIF, *b* 1892, *d* 1978: *m* 1919, Fanny Compton, who *d* 1974, da of Francis Henry Atherton, of Gympie, Queensland, and of Taunton, Som:—
Charles Atherton (Pathfield, Bells Line of Road, Bilpin, NSW 2758, Australia), *b* 1921; *ed* Sydney Univ (LLB): 1939-45 War with AIF in New Guinea: *m* 1955, Doris May, da of late William Edward Pritchard, RWF, of Denbigh, N Wales, and has issue living, Timothy Charles, *b* 1960, — Owen Francis, *b* 1963. —— Eileen (79 Gordon St, Manly Vale, NSW 2093, Australia), *b* 1924; served in World War II with AWAS in New Guinea: *m* 1947, Alasdair David Thomson, who *d* 1993, and has issue living, Peter David, *b* 1948, — Ian Charles, *b* 1953, — John Elliot, *b* 1958, — Patricia Eileen, *b* 1951. —— Hilary, *b* 1927; served in World War II with AWAS: *m* 1952, Denys Eric Head, of 6 Greenacres, Crooksbury Rd, Runfold, Farnham, Surrey GU10 1QU, and has issue living, Roger Denys, *b* 1957, — Lynette Ann, *b* 1954, — Gillian Margaret, *b* 1955.

Grandchildren of late Ninian Lowis Elliot, 3rd son (by 1st *m*) of Augustus John Elliot (infra):—
  Issue of late Lieut-Com Archibald Guthrie Elliot, RN, *b* 1898, *d* 1931: *m* 1929, Evelyn Agnes, who *d* 1965, da of late Alexander Buchanan:—
John Alexander Ninian (Portman's Bridge, Box 6, Gilgil, Kenya), *b* 1930: *m* 1962, Jean Patricia, da of Arthur Willis Winfield Sale, of Pulborough, Sussex. —— Margaret Dolores, *b* (*posthumous*) 1931: *m* 1953, Timothy Romer Matthews, of 7 Chislehurst Rd, Richmond, Surrey, and has issue living, Sophia Elizabeth *b* 1955: *m* 1982, William Gerald Kelly, of The Mall, Ramelton, co Donegal.

Grandchildren of late Archibald Campbell Elliot, 4th son (by 1st *m*) of Augustus John Elliot (infra):—
  Issue of late Lt-Col Augustus John Elliot, IA, *b* 1901, *d* 1979: *m* 1st, 1930 (*m diss* 1946), Theodora Dorothy, who *d* 1982, da of late Engr-Cdr T. G. R. Harvey, RIM Bombay (ret); 2ndly, 1946, Ilona (who *m* 2ndly, 1980, Arthur Douglas Ingrams, who *d* 1988, of Martins, Furley, Axminster, Devon), da of late Frederic Charles Wilson Bindley, of Eastbourne:—
(By 1st *m*) Archibald Keith (78 Howard Rd, Queens Park, Bournemouth), *b* 1932; RAF (ret): *m* 1957, Pauline Mary, da of late Cecil Edwin Pearman Parker, of Watford, Herts, and has issue living, Ross Ian, *b* 1958, — Clive Graham, *b* 1960: *m* 1993, Helena Mary, da of Denis Martin Prendergast, of co Kerry. —— Angus Ian (Gorse Cottage, 82 Coleshill Rd, Marston Green, Birmingham 37), *b* 1937: *m* 1959, Carol Ann, da of William Henry Evans, and has issue living, Mark Keith, *b* 1960, — Jamie Ian, *b* 1964. —— Betty Anne, *b* 1933: *m* 1956, Capt Jeffrey Edward Power Browning, 8th King's R Irish Hus (ret), of The Grange, Worlingworth, Woodbridge, Suffolk, and has issue living, Charles Richard Power, *b* 1957: *m* 1993, Kate Borwick, — Alastair Jeffrey Power, *b* 1960, — Philippa Anne Campbell, *b* 1963: *m* 1994, Timothy John Inskip, — Joanna Elizabeth Newcombe, *b* 1967.

Grandchildren of late Augustus John Elliot, 4th son of late Hon John Edmund Elliot, MP (ante):—
  Issue of late Gilbert Augustus Elliot, *b* 1873, *d* 1959: *m* 1905, Phyllis Baret, who *d* 1972, da of late Major Edward William Stokes, 4th King's Own Regt, of Ellel Hall Lancaster:—
Gilbert Cecil Ninian (Corner Garth, Old Earswick, York YO3 9SL) *b* 1907: *m* 1942, Esther Rosamond, who *d* 1987, da of late Capt Hugh Alfred Cholmley (*see* V Hill, colls, 1969 Edn), and has issue living, Gilbert Hugh Cholmley (22 Limewood Close, St Johns, Woking, Surrey), *b* 1947; *ed* St Peter's Sch, York: *m* 1979, Beryl Breakspear, and has issue living, Jonathan *b* 1983, Rebecca *b* 1981, — Rowland George Cholmley (2 Old Earswick Village, York), *b* 1949: *m* 1986, Ruth Skovgaard, of Bornholm, Denmark, and has issue living, Samuel Gilbert *b* 1990, Hanna Rosamond *b* 1988, — Jane (Fairfield House, Upavon, nr Pewsey, Wilts), *b* 1943: *m* 1963 (*m diss* 1985), Maj Iain Alastair McKay, Scots Gds, and has issue living, Alastair James Mark *b* 1963, Andrew Simon Charles *b* 1970, Catriona Jane *b* 1966, Arabella Charlotte *b* 1968, — Lorna (Foxhanger Cottage, Priorsfield Rd, Godalming, Surrey GU7 2RG), *b* 1945: *m* 1967 (*m diss* 1991), John Edward Clive, and has issue living, Simon John David *b* 1970, Edward Thomas *b* 1974, Sarah Margarita *b* 1968. —— Daphne Patricia, *b* 1917: *m* 1949, Capt Godfrey Carrington Royle, RA (TA), of Home Farm, Balscote, nr Banbury, Oxon OX15 6JP.

(In remainder to Baronetcy only)

Grandson of late Frederick Augustus Hugh Elliot, CIE, el son of late Edward Francis Elliot, 2nd son of late Rt Hon Hugh Elliot, 2nd son of 3rd baronet:—

Issue of late Lieut-Col Edward Halhed Hugh Elliot, DSO, *b* 1876, *d* as a result of enemy action 1944: *m* 1911, Ethel Winifred, who *d* 19-, da of late John Fair:—
Frederick John Hugh, *b* 1914.

PREDECESSORS – (1) GILBERT Elliot, KT, having been under forfeiture 1685-90 as an accessory to the Rebellion of 1679, received Knighthood; was afterwards Clerk to PC, MP for Roxburghshire 1702-7, and a Lord of Session (as Lord Minto); *cr a Baronet* 1700, with remainder to his heirs male; *d* 1718; *s* by his son **(2)** *Sir* GILBERT, 2nd Bt; MP for Roxburghshire 1722-7; was a Lord of Session (as Lord Minto) 1726-33. a Lord of Justiciary 1733-63, and Lord Justice Clerk 1763-6, *d* 1766; *s* by his son **(3)** *Sir* GILBERT, 3rd Bt, MP for co Selkirk 1753-65, and for Roxburghshire 1765-77; was Lord of the Admiralty 1756, Treasurer of the Chamber 1762, Keeper of the Signes in Scotland 1767, and Treasurer of the Navy 1770; *d* 1777; *s* by his son **(4)** *Sir* GILBERT, 4th Bt; MP for co Roxburgh 1777-84, and for Helston 1790-5; was Viceroy of Corsica 1795-7, Envoy Extraor to Vienna 1799, Pres of Board of Control India 1806, and Gov-Gen of Bengal 1807-13; assumed by Roy licence 1797 the additional surnames of Murray-Kynynmound after that of Elliot; *cr Baron Minto*, of Minto, co Roxburgh (peerage of Great Britain) 1797, and *Viscount Melgund* and *Ecrl of Minto* (peerage of United Kingdom) 1813; *d* 1814; *s* by his son **(5)** GILBERT, 2nd Earl, GCB, PC; *b* 1782; was MP for Roxburghshire 1812-14, Ambassador to Berlin 1833-4, First Lord to the Admiralty 1835-41, and Lord Privy Seal 1846-52: *m* 1806, Mary, who *d* 1853, da of Patrick Brydone, of Lennel House, Berwick; *d* 1859; *s* by his son **(6)** WILLIAM HUGH, KT, 3rd Earl, *b* 1814; MP for Hythe (*L*) 1837-41, for Greenock 1847-52, and for Clackmannanshire 1857-9: *m* 1844, Emma Eleanor Elizabeth, who *d* 1882, heiress of Gen Sir Thomas Hislop, Bt (*ext*); *d* 1891; *s* by his el son **(7)** GILBERT JOHN, KG, GCSI, GCMG, GCIE, PC, 4th Earl; *b* 1845; was Gov-Gen of Canada 1898-1904, and Viceroy and Gov-Gen of India 1905-10: *m* 1883, Mary Caroline, CI, who *d* 1940, da of late Gen Hon Charles Grey; *d* 1914; *s* by his el son **(8)** VICTOR GILBERT LARISTON GARNET, 5th Earl, *b* 1891; Capt Scots Gds: *m* 1921, Marion, OBE, who *d* 1974, da of George William Cook, of Montreal; *d* 1975; *s* by his el son **(9)** GILBERT EDWARD GEORGE LARISTON, 6th Earl and present peer; also Viscount Melgund, and Baron Minto.

MISHCON, BARON (Mishcon) (Life Baron 1978)

VICTOR MISHCON, son of Rabbi Arnold Mishcon; *b* 14 Aug 1915; *ed* City of London Sch; Solicitor 1937; Consultant to Mishcon De Reya, Member of Nat Theatre Board 1965-90, and of South Bank Theatre Board 1977-82; former Chm LCC and various Cttees; former Chm General Purposes Cttee GLC; former Chm Finance Cttee of Lambeth Borough Council; former Member House of Lords European Community Cttee, and of Lords Standing Joint Cttee with Commons on Consolidation of Bills; Vice-Chm Law Society All Parliamentary Gp; Official Opposition Spokesman on Home Affairs and Legal Matters; Member of various Govt Departmental Cttees; Member of Select Cttee of House of Lords on Medical Ethics 1993-94; QC (Hon); Hon LLD Birmingham; Hon Fell of Univ Coll, London; DL for Greater London; Cdr Order of North Star of Sweden and Star of Ethiopia; *cr Baron Mishcon*, of Lambeth, Greater London (Life Baron) 1978: *m* 1976, Joan Estelle, da of Bernard Monty, and has issue by former *m* to Beryl Honor, da of J. E. Posnansky.

Arms – Per pale argent and azure between in chief and in base bar gennel wavy counterchanged a tent per pale azure and argent lined gules. **Crest** – Upon a wreath argent and azure a lion or and a lamb proper rampant and supporting between them a sword erect gules the pommel resting on a book bound azure edged and garnished gold. **Supporters** – *Dexter*, a lamb reguardant proper gorged with a collar gules with flames issuing above and below proper; *sinister*, a lion reguardant or gorged with a Saxon crown azure. **Motto** – Dwell in peace.
Address – House of Lords, Westminster, SW1.

SONS LIVING (*By former m*)

Hon Peter Arnold (89 Elgin Crescent, W11 2JF), *b* 1946: *m* 1967, Penny Green, and has issue living, Oliver, *b* 1968, — Anna, *b* 1972, — Kate, *b* 1973, — Eliza, *b* 1977.
Hon Russell Orde (Wick Lodge, Englefield Green, Surrey TW20 0HJ), *b* 1948; *ed* City of London Sch: *m* 1975, Marcia Regina Leigh, and has issue living, Joel, *b* 1977, — Portia, *b* 1979—Honor Meg, *b* 1991.

DAUGHTER LIVING (*By former m*)

Hon Jane Malca, *b* 1950: *m* 1st, 1971 (*m diss* 1979), Anthony Jay; 2ndly, 1990, Edward Landau, and has issue living (by 1st *m*), Adam, *b* 1972, — Lucy, *b* 1974.

MITCHISON, BARONY OF (Mitchison) (Extinct 1970)

SONS LIVING OF LIFE BARON

Hon Denis Anthony, CMG (14 Marlborough Rd, Richmond, Surrey), *b* 1919; *ed* Abbotsholme Sch, and Trin Coll, Camb (MB, ChB), FRCP London, FRCPath; Emeritus Prof of Bacteriology, London Univ; *m* 1st, 1940, Ruth Sylvia, MB, BCh, da of Hubert Gill; 2ndly, 1993, Honora, da of Christopher Carlin, and has issue (by 1st *m*) two sons and two das.
Hon (John) Murdoch (Great Yew, Ormiston, E Lcthian EH35 5NJ), *b* 1922; FRS, FRSE; *ed* Winchester, and Trin Coll, Camb (MA, ScD); Prof of Zoology, Edinburgh Univ 1963-88; mem of Roy Commission on Environmental Pollution 1974-79 and the Science Board SRC 1976-79: *m* 1947, Rosalind Mary, da of Edward Murray Wrong, of Toronto, and has issue one son and three das.

Hon Nicholas Avrion (14 Belitha Villas, N1), *b* 1928; FRS; Prof of Zoology, London Univ: *m* 1958, Lorna Margaret, da of Maj-Gen John Simson Stuart Martin, CSI, of Husabost, by Dunvegan, Isle of Skye, and has issue two sons and three das.

DAUGHTERS LIVING OF LIFE BARON

Hon (Sonja) Lois, *b* 19-: *m* 1959, John Godfrey, and has issue two das.
Hon Valentine Harriet Isabella Dione *b* 1930: *m* 1955, Mark Arnold-Forster, DSO, DSC, who *d* 1981, of 115 Blenheim Cres, W11, and has issue three sons and two das.

WIDOW LIVING OF LIFE BARON

NAOMI MARGARET (*Baroness Mitchison*), CBE (Carradale House, Carradale, Campbeltown, Argyll), da of late John Scott Haldane, CH, FRS: Naomi Mitchison, authoress; CBE (Civil) 1985: *m* 1916, Baron Mitchison, CBE, QC (Life Peerage) who *d* 1970, when the title became ext.
Mrs Alec L. M. Molesworth,

MOLESWORTH, VISCOUNT (Molesworth) (Viscount I 1716)

VINCIT AMOR PATRIÆ

The love of my country prevails

RICHARD GOSSET MOLESWORTH, 11th Viscount; *b* 31 Oct 1907; *s* 1961; *ed* Lancing; Middle East 1941-44 with RAF; Freeman of City of London 1978: *m* 1958, Anne Florence (WOMERSLEY), who *d* 1983, da of John Mark Freeman Cohen, of St James's Court, SW1, and has issue.

Arms – Gules, an escutcheon vair, within an orle of eight cross-crosslets or. **Crest** – A dexter arm embowed in armour proper, holding a cross crosslet or. **Supporters** – *Dexter*, a pegasus argent, wings elevated or; *sinister*, a pegasus, wings elevated gules, semée of cross crosslets or.
Residence – Garden Flat, 2 Bishopswood Road, Highgate, N6.

SONS LIVING

Hon ROBERT BYSSE KELHAM, *b* 4 June 1959; *ed* Cheltenham, and Sussex Univ (BA).
Hon William John Charles, *b* 1960; *ed* Cheltenham, and Trin Coll, Camb (MA); LTCL.

COLLATERAL BRANCHES LIVING

Branch from 8th Viscount

Issue of late Hon Arthur Ernest Parnell Molesworth, 3rd son of 8th Viscount, *b* 1870, *d* 1951: *m* 1910, Nellie Maud, JP, who *d* 1956, da of George W. Banks, formerly of Wellington, New Zealand, and widow of Dr George Watson, of S America:—
Frank Ernest Bysse, *b* 1911: *m* 1st, 1934 (*m diss* 1940), Phyllis Margaret Patrick, da of late George Wells; 2ndly, 1943 (*m diss* 1957), Joan, JP, da of A. G. Lethbridge, of Thames Valley and Taranaki, NZ; 3rdly, 1961, Nellie Verdun, da of late Edward Hughes, of Hikurangi, NZ; 4th, 1982, Bernice Sheila Polden Bell, 7th da of George Augustus Hawkes, of NZ, and has issue living, (by 3rd *m*) Helen Deirdre Velvet, *b* 1962. *Address* – 30 Chorley Ave, Massey, Auckland 8, NZ. —— Betty Eleanor Gosset (Los Barrios, Cadiz Province, Andalucia, Spain), *b* 1913: *m* 1948, Frank Geoffrey Harald Allen, late Wing-Cdr RAFVR, who *d* 1985.

Branch from brother of 7th Viscount

Grandson of late Lionel Charles Molesworth, 3rd but only surv son of late Maj Richard Molesworth, eldest son of late Capt Hon Anthony Oliver Molesworth, RA, 3rd brother of 7th Viscount:—
Issue of late Col Roger Bevil Molesworth, RA (ret), *b* 1901, *d* 1974: *m* 1929, Iris, who *d* 1977, da of late Lt-Col Roger Lloyd Kennion, CIE, of Durford Wood, Petersfield:—
Allen Henry Neville (31 Norland Sq, W11 4PU), *b* 1931: *m* 1970, Gail Cheng Kwai, LRAM, ARCM, LGSM, da of L. C. Chan, of 10 Holland Rise, Singapore 10.

Granddaughter of late Col William Molesworth, CIE, CBE, MB, eldest son of late Lt-Col Anthony Oliver Molesworth (infra):—
Issue of late Lieut-Col William Earle Molesworth, MC, *b* 1894, *d* 1955: *m* 1918, Dorothy Loftus, who *d* 1985, da of late Col St George Loftus Steele, CB, of Cheltenham:—
Pamela, *b* 1919: *m* 1950, Robert Anthony Langham, and has issue living, Peter Anthony (Silverdale, Woodmead Rd, Lyme Regis, Dorset), *b* 1953: *m* 1983, Cynthia Maynard, and has issue living, Catherine *b* 1984, — Susan Marie, *b* 1951: *m* 1982, Raymond Purdy, of 100 Upper North St, Brighton, Sussex, and has issue living, Daniel *b* 1982, Lara *b* 1985. *Residence* – 19 Alexandra Road, Reading, Berks.

Grandsons living of late Hugh Wilson Molesworth, CBE (infra)—
Issue of late Hugh Mervyn Molesworth, *b* 1907, *d* 1980: *m* 1st, 1934 (*m diss* 1936), Mary Langhorne, yr da of Harry Langhorne Johnson, CBE, of Hurst Copthorne; 2ndly, 1939, Enid Mary, who *d* 1969, da of late John Utrick Roger Grave, AMICE, of Manchester:—
(By 2nd *m*) Roger (Little Jordans, Colgate, Sussex), *b* 1945; *ed* Marlborough: *m* 1974, Pauline Fay, da of Philip Hunt, of Wood Green, N22. —— Donald (Balmoral, Benenden, Kent), *b* 1948; *ed* Embley Park: *m* 1982, Charlotte Rosalie Penelope, da of J. W. K. Cox, of Green Lane Farm, Challock, Kent.
Issue of late Lt-Col Denys Hope Molesworth, MC, RA, *b* 1910, *d* 1989: *m* 1945, Dorothy May, who *d* 1984, yr da of late William C. Johnston, of Calcutta, India:—
Gillian Tessa, *b* 1946: *m* 1972, Juan Planells, of Ibiza, and has issue living, Nicolas Juan, *b* 1973, — Emma Maria, *b* 1976, — Sara Luisa, *b* 1980. —— Jennifer Margaret, *b* 1948: *m* 1984, Farad Azima, of 9 Madingley Rd, Cambridge, and has issue living, Cyrus Alexander, *b* 1985, — Artemis Natasha, *b* 1986.

Grandchildren of late Lieut-Col Anthony Oliver Molesworth, 4th son of late Capt Hon Anthony Oliver Molesworth, RA (ante):—
Issue of late Hugh Wilson Molesworth, CBE, *b* 1870, *d* 1959: *m* 1903, Dora Hanbury, who *d* 1972, only da of late Maj Sir (Robert) Hanbury Brown, KCMG, of Newlands, Crawley Down, Sussex:—
Eileen Rose, *b* 1904: *m* 1931, Lt-Col Basil Woods Ballard, CIE, MBE, Indian Army (Political Ser), and has issue living, Timothy John (Harpsden Grange, Harpsden Way, Henley, Oxon), *b* 1932; *ed* Marlborough, and Sydney Sussex Coll, Camb (MA); FICE: *m* 1964, Helen Mary Christopherson, and has issue living, Patrick Robert *b* 1975, Bridget Anne *b* 1970, Jennifer Clare *b* 1971, — William Richard (Olivers Cottage, Capel St Mary, Suffolk), *b* 1933: *ed* Marlborough, and Coll of Aeronautics, Cranfield (MSc); CEng, MIMechE: *m* 1967, Marianne Jean Elspeth, da of late Lt-Col Hugh Arbuthnott (*see* V Arbuthnott colls), and has issue living, Hugh William *b* 1968, Andrew James *b* 1976. *Residence* – Shepherds Oak, Crawley Down, Sussex.
Issue of late Col Francis Crofton Molesworth, late RE, *b* 1880, *d* 1955: *m* 1913, Eileen, who *d* 1951, da of late Lieut-Col Richard Denny (Denny, Bt, colls):—
Richard Denny (25 Naunton Way, Cheltenham, Glos) *b* 1919; *m* 1972, Eva Emily Elizabeth Bowler. —— Stephen Lindsay, *b* 1925; 1939-45 War (wounded, despatches); is an ARIBA: *m* 1959, Eve Lovie, and has issue living, Ivan Alexander, *b* 1964, — Anna Cordelia, *b* 1960, — Polly, *b* 1967. —— Beatrix, *b* 1917. *Address* – Chapel Garth, Galphay, Ripon, Yorks.

Grandchildren of late Maj Ernest Kerr Molesworth, 3rd son of late Lt-Col Anthony Oliver Molesworth (ante):—
Issue of late Brownlow David Molesworth, OBE, MRCS, LRCP, *b* 1913, *d* 1986: *m* 1939, Rosemary Katharine, who *d* 1989, da of Lt-Col A. W. Moore, RAMC:—
Patrick David, *b* 1946: *m* 1974, Sheila Doreen Cooling, and has issue living, Peter Patrick, *b* 1983, — Ian David, *b* 1985. —— Anthony Simon, *b* 1955. —— Jenifer Rosemary, *b* 1940: *m* 1960, Peter David Rohde, FRCPsych, FRCP Ed, of 84 Burbage Rd, SE24, and has issue living, Simon Peter, *b* 1962: *m* 1988, Juliette Ann Louise Hinchliff, and has issue living, Florence Rebecca *b* 1992, — Katherine Leslie, *b* 1963: *m* 1991, Paul Simon Bogan, and has issue living, Raphael David *b* 1993. —— Sheila, *b* 1942: *m* 1967, (Charles) Jeremy Harvey, MA, of Obridge House, Obridge Rd, Taunton, Som TA2 7QA, and has issue living, Benjamin David, *b* 1972, — Rachel Claire, *b* 1969, — Joanna Elizabeth, *b* 1970.

Granddaughter of late Rev Anthony Oliver Molesworth, 5th son of Lt-Col Anthony Oliver Molesworth (ante):—
Issue of late Group Capt Anthony Oliver Molesworth, RAF, *b* 1908, *k* on active ser 1944: *m* 1933, Noëlle (B5, Queen Alexandra's Court, Wimbledon, SW19), da of late John Richard Holmes, formerly Pres of District Court, Cyprus:—
Dawn Noëlle, *b* 1934: *m* 1955, Simon Jerrard Findlay Muirhead, of 61, Merton Hall Rd, Wimbledon, SW19, and has issue living, Anthony Oliver Molesworth (3777 Caribeth Drive, Encino, CA 91436, USA), *b* 1957; *ed* Edinburgh Univ (MA): *m* 1985, Cora Ann, only child of Martin D. Seiler, of Studio City, California, USA, and has issue living, Molly Laura *b* 1991, — Lauriston Philip (409 Nowland Av, Sydney, NSW 2641, Australia), *b* 1959; *ed* Newcastle Univ (BSc): *m* 1984, Katherine Barbara, da of late John Rutty, of Kuantan, Malaya, and has issue living, Dauntie Claire *b* 1989, — Imogen Jane, *b* 1963; *ed* Edinburgh Univ (MA, MSc).

Branch from 4th son of 1st Viscount

Granddaughter of late James Murray Molesworth, 3rd son of late Rev William Nassau Molesworth, LLD, eldest son of late Rev John Edward Nassau Molesworth, DD, el son of late John Molesworth, elder son of late Major Hon Edward Molesworth, 4th son of 1st Viscount:—
Issue of late Robert Murray Nassau Molesworth, *b* 1895, *d* 1976: *m* 1st, 1916 (*m diss* 1925), Lucie Amy Gertrude, who *d* 1971, da of late Edward Lawrence, of Clifton, Bristol; 2ndly, 1926, Nora Madelene, da of William John Connell, of Sparkhill, Birmingham; 3rdly, 1955, Clare, widow of T. W. Price:—
(By 2nd *m*) Emily Patricia, *b* 1927: *m* 19—, — Reid, of 100 Park Av North, NW10.

Grandchildren of late William Nassau Molesworth, 5th son of late Rev William Nassau Molesworth, LLD (ante):—
Issue of late Major William Nassau Molesworth, MC, Manchester Regt, *b* 1888, *d* 1959: *m* 1917, Hester Winifred, who *d* 1966, da of late Alfred Watkin, of Danebank, Lymm:—
Rev Canon Anthony Edward Nassau (3 Barrow Hill, Stourton Caundle, Sturminster Newton, Dorset DT10 2LD), *b* 1923; *ed* Haileybury, and Pembroke Coll, Camb (MA) and at Coll of Resurrection, Mirfield; Canon of Pro-Cathedral of St Michael, Eshowe, Zululand 1963-68, and of Dioc of Swaziland 1968-71 (Canon Emeritus of Swaziland); Commissary to Bishop of Swaziland 1973, Rector of Charlton Musgrove with Stoke Trister and Cucklington since 1984: *m* 1969, Susan, SRN, yr da of Prof H. R. B. Fenn, of Weald, Sevenoaks, Kent, and has issue living, Hugh William Nassau, *b* 1972, — Anna Margaret, *b* 1970. —— Gwendolen Clara Nassau (*Lady Lloyd*), *b* 1919; 1939-45 War in WAAF: *m* 1947, Sir (John) Peter (Daniel) Lloyd, and has issue living, David William Molesworth, *b* 1950: *m* 1977, Deborah Armstrong, who *d* 1994, and has issue living, Carson James *b* 1978, Zoë *b* 1980, — John Peter Anthony, *b* 1956: — Judith Mary, *b* 1947: *m* 1st, 1968 (*m diss* 1975), Robert Anthony Hyndes; 2ndly, 1977 (*m diss* 1984), John Paul Kent, and has issue living (by 1st *m*), Anthony Peter *b* 1968, — Angela Hester Olwen, *b* 1940: *m* 1st, 1971, John Gipps Knox-Knight, who *d* 1979; 2ndly, 1983, David Robert Langley, and has issue living (by 1st *m*), Lucy Charlotte *b* 1974, Emily Sarah *b* 1976 (by 2nd *m*), Jessica Penelope *b* 1984, — Penelope, *b* 1953: *m* 1976, Adam Thomson, and has issue living, Edward William *b* 1986, Hugh Lloyd *b* 1988, Alice Clara Margaret *b* 1992, — Sarah Jane, *b* 1955: *m* 1978 (*m diss* 1981), Robert Sheehy and has issue living, Nicholas *b* 1979. *Residence* – 90 Carrington St, Macedon, Victoria 3440, Australia.

Grandson of late Frederick Nassau Molesworth, 2nd son of John Molesworth (*b* 1818), 2nd son of Rev John Edward Nassau Molesworth, DD (ante):—
Issue of late Major John Davenport Newall Molesworth, MC, Roy Corps of Signals (TA), *b* 1884, *d* 1952: *m* 1st, 1909 (*m diss* 1927), Mary (who *d* 1970), da of A. Blake Norman, of Oakham, Rutland; 2ndly, *ca* 1932, Frances Blake, who *d* 1964, of Balcombe, Sussex:—
(By 1st *m*) John Henry Nassau, DSO, DFC, AFC (Beehive Cottage, Eltisley, St Neots, Cambs PE19 4TH), *b* 1913; *ed* Oakham Sch, SE Agric Coll, and London Univ; commnd W/Cdr RAF 1945, 1939-45 War (wounded, despatches, DFC, AFC, DSO); DSO 1945: *m* 1946, Pamela Joan, da of late Frederick William Guildford, of Ramsgate, Kent, and has issue living, Peter John Norman (20 Elgin Park, Bristol BS6 6RX), *b* 1956; *ed* Oakham Sch, and Newcastle Univ (BSc); late Capt Green Howards; Capt Yorks Vol: *m* 1990, Julie A., da of Vince Wicks, of Cairns, Australia, and has issue living, John Henry *b* 1994, Frances Jane *b* 1992.

Grandchildren of late John Molesworth (*b* 1858), 3rd son of late John Molesworth (*b* 1818), 2nd son of late Rev John Edward Nassau Molesworth, DD (ante):—
Issue of late John Molesworth, *b* 1894, *d* 1971; *m* 1927, Dorothy Josephine Mudge (205 Foley St, Junction, Texas, USA):—
John Mudge (PO Box 104, Junction, Texas 76849, USA), *b* 1928: *m* 1951, Joanne Hill, of New York, USA, and has issue living, John, *b* 1952, — Lynn Hill, *b* 1955, — Cynthia, *b* 1953. —— Fred (Route 3, Box 437B, Amarillo, Texas, USA), *b* 1931: *m* 1962, Ann Spoon, of Memphis, Texas, and has issue living, Fred Vance, *b* 1963. —— Dorothy Patricia, *b* 1929: *m* 1949, William Eugene Craft, of Drawer M, Clarendon, Texas, USA, and has issue living, William Patrick, *b* 1952, — John Robert, *b*

1962, — Catherine, b 1950: m 1974, John Throckmorton Keene, of 222, Halcyon, San Antonio, Texas, 78209, USA, and has issue living, Kathleen b 1977, — Christine, b 1957.

Grandchildren of late Reginald Balfour Molesworth, el son of late Cdr George Mill Frederick Molesworth, 4th son of late Rev John Edward Nassau Molesworth, DD (ante):—
Issue of late Rev Gilbert Edmund Nassau Molesworth, b 1895, d 1976: m 1923, Florence Edith Mary (Berrimans, Northam, Bideford, N Devon), da of late Rev Thomas Fisher Maddrell, V of Gulval, Penzance:—
Michael Nassau, b 1924; ed King Edward VI Sch, Birmingham, and Sidney Sussex Coll, Camb (MA); late Sub-Lt RNVR; 1939-45 War: m 1951, Heather, who d 1965, da of late Adm Sir Henry Daniel Pridham-Wippell, KCB, CVO, and has issue living, William Martin Nassau, b 1957, — Peter Timothy Nassau, b 1959, — Susan Claire, b 1961. —— John Edmund Nassau, b 1926; ed King's Sch, Bruton, Sidney Sussex, Coll, Camb, at London Univ, at Middle East Centre of Arab Studies, and at St Luke's Coll, Exeter; Fl-Lt RAF (ret): m 1952, Pamela Anne, da of Harold Richard Summers MacMullen, and has issue living, David Reginald Nassau b 1953; ed Arborfield Coll, Reading, — Carol Anne, b 1956, — Elizabeth Stephanie, b 1958: m 1983, Martin C. Rees, — Hilary, b 1964. —— Richard Mark Nassau (9 Webb Farm Rd, Monroe, NY, USA 10950), b 1930; ed King Edward VI Sch, Birmingham, and Birmingham Univ (BSc): m 1958, Margaret Elizabeth, da of George Thomas Alexander Hastings, MD, and has issue living, Philip Nassau, b 1960, — Richard Nassau, b 1962, — John Nassau, b 1963, — William Nassau, b 1971, — Jennifer Ann, b 1959, — Elizabeth Mary, b 1975. —— Elizabeth Raphael, b 1934: m 19-, Duncan Urquhart, of Grays Hills, Fairlie, NZ, and has issue living, Mark Alexander, b 1967, — Roger David, b 1970, — Lorna Mary, b 1966, — Joanna, b 1968.

Grandchildren of late Rev Rennell Francis Wynn Molesworth, 5th son of late Rev John Edward Nassau Molesworth, DD (ante):—
Issue of late Rev John Hilton Molesworth, b 1856, d 1921: m 1908, Everilda Hamer, who d 1928, el da of late Rev Canon James Hamer Rawdon (Hon Canon of Manchester), of The Hermitage, Stockton-on-Forest, York:—
Rachel Frances Hilton, b 1912: m 1936, Commodore Neil Alexander Mackinnon, RAN, who d 19—, and has issue living, Peter William Alexander (The Old Fox, Lewknor, Oxon), b 1938, — John Hugh Molesworth (19 The Croft, Richmond, Victoria 3121, Australia), b 1941; BA Oxon, — Fiona Margaret, b 1946: m 1970, Ian Horsley, of Gundillawah, Adelong, NSW 2729, Australia. Residence – The Old Fox, Lewknor, Oxon. —— Cecilia Margaret (Lady Mogg), b 1914: m 1939, Gen Sir (Herbert) John Mogg, GCB, CBE, DSO, DL, and has issue living, John Nigel Ballard (Brightwell Park, Brightwell Baldwin, Oxon), b 1940; MA Cantab; Brig late RGJ: m 1967, Tessa Elizabeth, da of late F. D. Wright, of Brightwell Park, Brightwell Baldwin, Oxon, and has issue living, John Peter Francis b 1969; BA, Richard Julian Charles b 1971; BSc, — Patrick Henry Molesworth, b 1942, — Rev Timothy David RAWDON-MOGG (St Andrew's Vicarage, Shrivenham, nr Swindon, Wilts), b 1945; ed St John's Coll, Durham (BA): m 1981, Rachel Mary, da of late Ven D. I. T. Eastman, of 43 Clay Lane, Beaminster, Dorset, and has issue living, Christopher James David b 1984, John Charles Timothy (twin) b 1984, Alice Mary b 1982. Residence – Church Close, Watlington, Oxon OX9 5QR.

Grandsons of late Rev Ernest Hilton Molesworth, 3rd son of Rev Rennell Francis Wynn Molesworth (ante):—
Issue of late Eric Mackinnon Molesworth, MB, ChB, b 1890, d 1963: m 1916, Ethel A., who d 1984, da of late Issac Clark Griffith:—
Selwyn Hilton, MRCS, LRCP (Trevelen, Cots Hill, Stratton, Bude, Cornwall), b 1917; ed Epsom Coll, and Manchester Univ; MRCS, LRCP; Lt RA: m 1949, Margaret Seymour, BA, da of late Percy Arthur Smith, of Dormar, Westridge, Bridlington, E Yorks, and has had issue, †Christopher Roger, b 1951; ed Lancaster Royal Gram Sch, and Nottingham Univ: m 1976, Annette Caroline (2 Colley close, Winchester, Hants), only da of G. C. Holliday, of 206 Rutland Rd, W Bridgeford, Nottingham, and d as the result of a train accident 1988, leaving issue, Steven Richard b 1981, Caroline Patricia b 1980, — William Hugh, b 1952; ed Lancaster R Gram Sch, St Peter's Coll, Oxford, and The Open Univ (BA Hons): m 1977, Angela Jane Walker, only da of Mrs Doreen Smith, of 35 Kennington Rd, Kennington, Oxford, and has issue living, Thomas Edward Alexander b 1978, Benjamin James b 1985, Emma Catherine Seymour b 1981, — Arthur David, b 1956; ed Shebbear Coll, Bristol Univ, and London Univ (MSc). —— Robert Mackinnon (RD4 Whangarei, NZ), b 1923; ed Oundle and Magdalene Coll, Camb (MA); Lt RNVR and an ARIBA: m 1st, 1947 (m diss 1967), Ursula, only da of late Alwin Julius Jaeger, of Thalwil-Zürich, Switzerland; 2ndly, 1967, Mary Craig, el da of late Vice-Adm Sir Maxwell Richmond, KBE, CB, DSO, and has issue living, (by 1st m) Stephen James, b 1961, — (by 2nd m) Peter Maxwell, b 1974, — Elizabeth Anna, b 1968, — Catherine Julia, b 1969. —— David William (37 Lacy Drive, Wimborne Minster, Dorset BH21 1DG), b 1930; ed King's Sch, Canterbury; Sqdn-Ldr RAF: m 1955, Doreen Joyce, da of George Hunter, of Dunelm, Yarborough Cres, Lincoln, and has issue living, Caroline Shona (8 rue des Tieulieres, Montpeyroux 34150, France), b 1956; ed St Helen's Sch, Abingdon, and Univ Coll Hosp (SRN): m 1979, David R. B. Martin, and has issue living, Daniel Russell b 1982, Anna Catherine b 1986, — Melanie Susan (27 Antrobus Rd, Chiswick, W4), b 1958; ed St Helen's Sch, Abingdon: m 1987, Martin Gerald Wesley Dennis, eldest son of J. G. W. Dennis, of Malaga, Spain, and has issue living, George Wesley b 1988, Ralph Wesley b 1992, — Diana Louise (Rua do Regadio 384, Matosinhos 4450, Portugal), b 1964; ed Pipers Sch, High Wycombe, and St Mary's Hosp (RGN, RSCN): m 1989, Roy M. Kirby, eldest son of T. M. Kirby, of Wimborne, Dorset, and has issue living, Jack William Michael b 1992.

Grandson of late Eric Mackinnon Molesworth (ante):—
Issue of late Lieut (E) Richard Charles Victor Molesworth, RN, b 1919, d on active ser: m 1940, Doreen Mary (who m 2ndly, 1967, Bruce Page, of 422 Macquarie St, S Hobart, Tasmania), only da of Joseph Greenwood:—
Eric Richard (422 Macquarie St, S Hobart, Tasmania), b 1942; ed Christ's Hospital, and Southampton Univ; Master Mariner.

Grandchildren of late Rev Rennell Francis Wynn Molesworth (ante):—
Issue of late Theodore Henderson Molesworth, FRCS, b 1872, d 1955: m 1906, Ethel Alexandra, who d 1955, da of late Edward Upton, of The Haven, St Margaret's Bay, near Dover:—
Peter Rennell Henderson (61 Sinah Lane, Hayling Island, Hants), MRCS, LRCP, b 1923; MRCS England and LRCP London 1946: m 1953, Rosemary Ann, da of Cdr R. A. Gould, OBE, RN, of Hayling Island, and has issue living, Simon Peter Henderson (19 The Avenue, Hambrook, Chichester, W Sussex PO18 8TZ) b 1954: m 1975, Joan Lesley Anderson, and has issue living, Alexis Ralph Henderson b 1975, Jason Oliver Henderson b 1978, — David Rennell Henderson, b 1955; ed Dauntsey's Sch: m 1984, Debra C. Dixon, — Nigel Piers Henderson, b 1960; MB BS; ed All Hallows, Lyme Regis. —— Margaret Ethel (1 Vicarage Lane, St Margaret-at-Cliffe, nr Dover, Kent), b 1910. —— Joan Frances, b 1918: m 1944, Lancelot Mitchell Shutte, of 1 Sea View Cottages, St Margarets-at-Cliffe, Dover, and has issue living, Susan Frances, b 1952: m 1st, 1972, Peter Derek Lapage, BSA Police; 2ndly, 1986, J. J. Van Der Walt, of PO Box 248, Gweru, Zimbabwe, and has had issue (by 1st m) Sally Frances b 1975, (by 2nd m) Andrew Mitchell b 1990, d 1991, — Mary Jane, b 1959: m 1980, Selwyn Ronald Danielson, of 18 Bredell St, Edenglen Ext 40, Edenvale 1610, Transvaal, S Africa, and has issue living, Kyle Bruce b 1982, Megan Nicole b 1986.
Issue of late Walter Henderson Molesworth, b 1873, d 1952: m 1910, Theodosia Maud, who d 1920, da of John Chapman, formerly of Ramsdale, Hants:—
Ernest Walter (Little Orchard, Hinton St George, Somerset; RAC, Royal Overseas and Golfers', Clubs), b 1911; ed Dover Coll, and London Univ; 1939-45 War (prisoner of Japanese): m 1947, Irene, da of Rev S. F. Whitehead, of Aston Somerville, Glos. —— Richard Nassau, b 1913. —— Kathleen Janet, b 1915. —— Margery Evelyn, b 1918: m 1st, 1946, Anthony Orde; 2ndly, 1974, Maj Phineas Arthur Jackson, FCIS, FCII, of 70 Creighton Av, N10 1NT.

Granddaughter of late Major Edward Nassau Molesworth, son of late Major Edward Molesworth, eldest son of late Robert Molesworth, 2nd son of late Major Hon Edward Molesworth (ante):—
Issue of late William John Molesworth, *b* 1856, *d* 1937: *m* 1892, Anne Brunette, who *d* 1948, da of late Robert Boyd, MD, of 1 Bolton Row, Mayfair, W:—
Mary Nassau, *b* 1897: *m* 1924, Maj Alfred Charles Stuart Smith, RA (ret), who *d* 1973, and has issue living, Anthony Molesworth Stuart (Whitsend Cottage, Tebay Lane, Ulverston, Cumbria LA12 7SG), *b* 1928: *m* 1952, Dorothy Bennett, and has issue living, Christopher John Stuart *b* 1953, Peter Martin Stuart, *b* 1954, Gillian Eleanor Mary Stuart *b* 1958, — Bridget Mary Stuart, *b* 1927: *m* 1952, Rev Maurice Arthur Reily Collins, of Old Wheatsheaf, Privett, nr Alton, Hants GU34 3NX and has issue living, Jonathan Stuart Reily *b* 1955: *m* 1st, 1985 (*m diss* 1991), Mary Randall; 2ndly, 1991, Christine Barber (and has issue living (by 2nd *m*), Erin Elizabeth Stuart *b* 1993), Edward Charles Reily *b* 1957. *Residence* – Meadow House, West Meon, Hants.

Branch from el son of 7th son of 1st Viscount

Grandchildren of late Arthur Nepean Molesworth (*b* 1856), el son of Arthur Molesworth (*b* 1821), el son of Arthur Nepean Molesworth (*b* 1799), son of Maj Arthur Molesworth, el son of Hon Bysse Molesworth, 7th son of 1st Viscount:—
Issue of late Arthur William Bysse Nepean Molesworth, *b* 1902, *d* 1958: *m* 1922, Ruth Patricia, who *d* 1970, da of late Thomas Gracey, of Moy, co Armagh:—
Guilford Nepean, *b* 1923. *Residence* – 64 Hill Pole, Clawton, Queensland 4019, Australia. —— John Robert, *b* 1930: *m* 1954, Mary, da of Alexander Rodgers, of Montreal, and has issue living, Deborah, *b* 1957, — Kathryn, *b* 1962, — Sandra, *b* 1964. *Residence* – 527 Crumlinside Rd, London, Ontario, Canada. —— Kathleen Violet, *b* 1927. —— Ann, *b* 1928: *m* 1961, Dr Herman Gelber, Scarborough Centenary Hosp, Scarborough, Ont, and has issue living, Sean Roderick (589 Jamaica Court, London, Ontario N6K 1N2, Canada), *b* 1968.

Grandchildren of late Balfour Nepean Molesworth, 2nd son of late Thomas Nepean Molesworth, 2nd son of Arthur Nepean Molesworth (*b* 1799) (ante):—
Issue of late Herbert Nepean Molesworth, *b* 1888, *d* 1978: *m* 1912, Marjorie Kittredge who *d* 1976, da of late W. M. Thompson, of Penetanguishene, Ont, Canada:—
William Herbert (1850, des Chenaux St, Trois-Rivières, Québec, Canada), *b* 1915: *m* 1938, Joan Anne da of late Charles Percival Rudman, of Grand-Mere, Québec, and has issue living, Michael Herbert (101-6th St, Grand-Mere, Québec), *b* 1944: *m* 1982, Sylvie Desbiens, and has issue living, David Alexander Hamilton *b* 1986, Allison Louise *b* 1983, — Patricia Anne, *b* 1942: *m* 1st, 1964 (*m diss* 1978), Clifford Hastings Laurence; 2ndly, 1978, Stephen Alexander Osterman, BSc, DipEd, of 12 Terrasse St, Maurice, Cap-de-la-Madeleine, Québec, and has issue living (by 1st *m*), William Hastings *b* 1966; BA, LLB, Kelly Anne *b* 1965; BCOM, (by 2nd *m*), Michael Alexander *b* 1979, Steven Bradley *b* 1980, Jennifer Joan *b* 1982. —— Robert Nepean (11285 Greenhill Dr, RR2 Ladysmith, BC V0R 2E0, Canada), *b* 1923: *m* 1943, Cecily Elizabeth, da of late Lt-Cdr Cecil Alexander Wade, RN (ret), of Edgeley, Whitchurch, Shropshire, and has issue living, Robert Alexander (4227 Morgan Cres, Prince George, BC, Canada, V2N 3B2), *b* 1946: *m* 1973, Rosalind Anne Stacey, and has issue living, Ryan Jason *b* 1977, Brent Russell *b* 1979, — Gregory Daniel (RR8, Site 13, Comp 5, Prince George, BC, Canada V2N 4M6), *b* 1951: *m* 1st, 1975, Claire Marie Deschambeault; 2ndly, 1985, Terri Kazemir, and has issue living, Danielle Elizabeth *b* 1988, — Susan Elizabeth (721-19th St, Pacific Grove, Calif, USA), *b* 1944: *m* 1st, 1965 (*m diss* 19-) Robert J. Black; 2ndly, 19- (*m diss* 1973), Troy Lee Roper II; 3rdly, 1983, Fraser Thomas Sibbald, of 721-19th St, Pacific Grove 93950, Calif, USA, and has issue living (by 2nd *m*) Troy Lee *b* 1971. —— Marjorie Julia Kittredge, *b* 1919: *m* 1948, John MacLeod Ellis, of Ross Ferry Rd, Boulardarie Bras d'Or, Cape Breton, Nova Scotia, Canada, and has issue living, Marnie MacLeod, *b* 1951: *m* 1987, Peter Douglas Adair Crosby, MD, of 23 Addison Place, Dartmouth, NS, Canada B2U 1G9, and has issue living, Alexander Douglas Judson *b* 1992, William Russel Arthur *b* 1993.

Grandsons of late William Ponsonby Molesworth, yst son of late Thomas Nepean Molesworth (ante):—
Issue of late George Nepean Molesworth, *b* 1885, *d* 1958: *m* 1916, Helen Nelles, who *d* 1954, da of late Sydney Bellingham Sykes, of Toronto:—
John Sydney (74 Second St, Oakville, Ontario L6J 3T3, Canada), *b* 1919: *m* 1946, Barbara Caroline, da of Dr Carswell Marshall, of Leeds, W Yorks, and has issue living, William Marshall, *b* 1949: *m* 1992, Susan Irene Newell, of Whitby, Ontario, — Hugh Carswell, *b* 1952: *m* 1975, Rosemary Druscilla, da of A. Ulch, of Simcoe, Ontario, — James Colin, *b* 1959, — Helen Mary, *b* 1954: *m* 1985, David Weiser, of Houston. Texas, USA. —— David Hugh George (156 Collier St, Toronto, Ontario, Canada), *b* 1927: *m* 1952, Ann DeVeber (4 Sydenham St, Guelph, Ontario, Canada), da of late Major Alfred Clarence Larter, of Toronto, Canada, and has issue living, Ian DeVeber (4 Sydenham St, Guelph, Ontario, Canada), *b* 1956, — Tony Nelles (49 Lawler Av, Toronto, Ontario, Canada), *b* 1958; legally assumed the forename of Tony in lieu of Anthony.

Grandson of late Bevil Hugh Molesworth el son of late Rev Hugh Thomas Molesworth (infra):—
Issue of late Hugh Bevil Alec Molesworth, *b* 1925, *d* 1960: *m* 1959, Patricia (who *m* 2ndly, 1963, Dr Ian Martin, of 40 Carlyle Rd, E Linfield, NSW, 2070), da of late Clive Quinton, of Wahroonga, Sydney, NSW:—
Hugh Bevil Clive, *b* (*posthumous*) 1960: *m* 1989, Karen Roberta, da of Irwin David Staller, of Stockton, California, and has issue living, Maude Clara Felice, *b* 1994. *Residence* – 176 Parnassus Avenue, San Francisco, California 94117, USA.

Grandson of late Rev Thomas Molesworth, son of late Thomas William Ponsonby Molesworth, son of Maj Arthur Molesworth (ante):—
Issue of late Rev Hugh Thomas Molesworth, *b* 1860, *d* 1930: *m* 1889, Alice Marian, who *d* 1939, da of Edward Deshon, CMG, sometime Auditor-Gen of Queensland:—
Guilford Bysse, *b* 1907: *m* 1931, Catherine Maud, da of late Edward Charles Woodward, of Coorparoo, Queensland, and has issue living, William Guilford Hugh (39 Newman Av, Camp Hill, Brisbane, Qld), *b* 1943: *m* 1968, Helen, da of John Edward McCaskie, of Coorparoo, Brisbane, Queensland, and has issue living, Mark William *b* 1975, Peter John *b* 1979. *Residence* – 27 Marriott St, Coorparoo, Brisbane, Queensland.

Branch from 2nd son of 7th son of 1st Viscount

Grandchildren of late Maj-Gen Hickman Thomas Molesworth, el son of Maj-Gen Arthur Molesworth, el son of Capt Robert Molesworth, 2nd son of Hon Bysse Molesworth (ante):—
Issue of late Lieut-Col Hickman Crawford Molesworth, *b* 1858, *d* 1939: *m* 1st, 1883, Margaret Amelia, who *d* 1915, da of late John Hopper, and widow of Surg-Maj M'Lean; 2ndly, 1920, Charlotte Anne, who *d* 1977, da of Alfred Thomas:—
(By 1st *m*) Ivy Frederica (240-857 Rupert Terr, Victoria, BC, Canada V8V 3E5), *b* 1891: *m* 1922, Donald Henry Alexander, who *d* 1976, and has issue living, Douglas Gundry (4453 Torquay Drive, Victoria, BC, Canada V8N 3L3): *m* 1954, Margaret Lindsay Wilson, and has issue living Brian Douglas Alexander *b* 1955: *m* 1978, Carol Martin (and has issue living, Lyndsay Kathleen *b* 1984), Carel Margaret *b* 1957: *m* 1984, James Keith Collins, Janice Eileen *b* 1962, Heather Louise *b* 1965, — Ralph Molesworth (141 Hampton Road, Victoria, BC, Canada), *b* 1929: *m* 1951, Shirley Margaret Boulton, and has issue living, Ross Wayne *b* 1954: *m* 1976, Merry Louise McKinnon, Glen Darryl *b* 1955: *m* 1st, 19—, Cindy Barry; 2ndly, 1989, Barbara Anne Whiteley (and has issue living (by 1st *m*), Shaun Michael *b* 1980), Dean Murray *b* 1970, Laraine Merrill *b*

1960: *m* 1989, Grant Richard McTaggart, of Melbourne, Australia, Julie Marlaine *b* 1965: *m* 1989, David Frederick McCormick.
  Issue of late Lt-Col Robert Everard Molesworth, *b* 1861, *d* 1941: *m* 1st, 1889, Catherine Isabella, who *d* 1904, da of J. Allen; 2ndly 1908, Gladys Eleanor, who *d* 1976, da of late Louis Otto Law:—
(By 2nd *m*) Robert Louis, *b* 1910; formerly Lt Indian Army. —— Marianne Sheila Lindsay, *b* 1914: *m* 1935, Thomas Bogue Alder, of 43 Cadogan Pl, SW1X 9RU, and has issue living, Lucinda Ann, *b* 1936, —— Hermione Sarah, *b* 1941.

  Granddaughter of late Rev Thomas Charles Underwood Molesworth, 5th son of Maj-Gen Hickman Thomas Molesworth (ante):—
    Issue of late Lt-Col Richard Cecil Molesworth, *b* 1898, *d* 1974: *m* 1933, Susan (912, 1 Grosvenor St, London, Ontario, Canada), da of Harry Bazeley, of Bideford, N Devon:—
Gillian Ann, *b* 1935: *m* 1959, Dr John Dupré, of 72 Sherwood Av, London, Ont, Canada, and has issue living, Matthew, *b* 1961, —— Luke, *b* 1972, —— Louisa, *b* 1962.

  Grandsons of late Col Richard Piggot Molesworth, CMG, 6th son of Maj-Gen Hickman Thomas Molesworth (ante):—
    Issue of late Maj Ralph Gerard Lindsay Molesworth, *b* 1910, *d* 1960: *m* 1st, 1933, Eleanor, el da of R. G. Rooke; 2ndly, 1948, Valerie St Claire (10 Richmond Hill, Clifton, Bristol 8), da of Charles Francis Earle:—
(By 1st *m*) Christopher Ralph, *b* 1934. *Address* - Batam Base, McDermott Sea Pte Ltd, Maxwell Rd, PO Box 3034, Singapore. —— Anthony John Lindsay, MBE; *b* 1936; Col, MBE (Mil) 1972. —— (By 2nd *m*) Richard Charles Lindsay, *b* 1950; *ed* Belmont Abbey, and Univ Coll, Wales; LLB (Lond). *Residences* - 1 Town Mills, Church St, Dawlish, Devon; 8 Gloucester Rd, Teignmouth, Devon.

  Granddaughter of late Maj-Gen Hickman Thomas Molesworth (ante):—
    Issue of late Col Herbert Ellicombe Molesworth, CMG, DSO, *b* 1872, *d* 1941: *m* 1914, Eileen Mary, who *d* 1969, da of Col Henry Waugh Renny-Tailyour, of Borrowfield, co Forfar (V Powerscourt):—
Phyllis Eileen, *b* 1914: *m* 1956, Cyril Pickard, of 57 West End, Redruth, Cornwall. —— Betty Lindsay, *b* 1919: *m* 1946, Frederick A. Craswell, of Rising Sun, Boutport St, Barnstaple, Devon, and has issue living, Lindsay, *b* 1951.
    Issue of late Brigadier Alec Lindsay Mortimer Molesworth, CIE, *b* 1881, *d* 1939: *m* 1st, 1915, Esther Alice, who *d* 1935, da of late W. H. Taylor, of Buenos Aires; 2ndly, 1936, Hilda, da of Alfred Henry Miles, OBE, of Wellington, New Zealand:—
(By 1st *m*) Lindsay Diana, *b* 1916: *m* 1940, Com Reginald Nevill Da Costa Porter, MBE, RN, and has issue living, Jeremy Nevill, *b* 1948, —— Valerie Lindsay, *b* 1942. *Residence* - Old Pound Cottage, Chertsey Rd, Chobham, Surrey.

  Grandchildren of Hickman Molesworth (*b* 1842), el son of Sir Robert Molesworth, son of Hickman Blayney Molesworth, 2nd son of Capt Robert Molesworth (ante):—
    Issue of late Surg-Lt Hickman Walter Lancelot Molesworth, FRCS, *b* 1892, *d* 1969: *m* 1923, Caryl Margaret (Bagi-Dua, Rue des Frieteaux, St Martins, Guernsey), da of Stanley Hoare, of 17 Cornwall Terr, Regent's Park, NW:—
Robert Stanley Hickman (23 Pavenham Rd, Carlton, Beds), *b* 1934; solicitor 1963: *m* 1965, Ann, da of A. Metcalfe-Gibson, of Greensidehead, Ravenstonedale, Westmorland, and has issue living, William Metcalfe, *b* 1968, —— Philip Hoare, *b* 1970, —— Catherine Jessie, *b* 1966. —— Richard Baxter (Highland, Framfield, Uckfield, E Sussex), *b* 1939: *m* 1966, Ann Kathleen Duncan, da of late F. N. H. Pexton, and has issue living, Edward James Hickman, *b* 1967, —— Rachel Jane, *b* 1970, —— Victoria Bridget, *b* 1975. —— Bridget Margaret, *b* 1931: *m* 1954, John Omerod Heyworth, of Pucklechurch, Rockshaw Rd, Merstham, Surrey, and has issue living, James Hickman Frederick, *b* 1958, —— Peter Lawrence Ormerod, *b* 1963, —— Caroline Margaret, *b* 1956: *m* 1981, Richard Neil Burnard, son of late Victor Burnard, of Coombe, Kingston upon Thames, Surrey, and has issue living, Olivia Rose Victoria *b* 1988.

  Grandchildren of late Robert Arthur Molesworth, 2nd son of Sir Robert Molesworth (ante):—
    Issue of late John Matheson Molesworth, *b* 1878, *d* 1942: *m* 1906, Elizabeth Flora Frances Hill who *d* 1952, da of late Edwin M. James, MRCSE:—
Richard William Edwin, *b* 1908: *m* 1937, Dirleen Muriel, da of Leslie Sprague, of Charlemont, Geelong, Australia, and has issue living, Michael John Leslie (2 Trinian St, Prahran, Victoria, Australia), BSc, MSc, *b* 1941: *m* 1st, 1967 (*m diss* 1984), Caroline Carse Hay (BA); 2ndly, 19—, Annette Rilton, and has issue living (by 1st *m*), Tamsin Louise *b* 1972, Amanda Frances *b* 1976, Charlotte Marie Louise *b* 1981 (by 2nd *m*) Christopher James Michael *b* 1981, Timothy Mark Richard *b* 1985, Louise Annette Marie *b* 1988, —— Simon Richard (9 Loller St, Brighton, Victoria, Australia), BA, LLB, *b* 1954: Barrister-at-law: *m* 1983, Rosalind Marie Cochrane (BSc), and has issue living, Lachlan James Simon *b* 1984, Anika Genevieve Fleur *b* 1989, —— Corinne Dirleen, BA, *b* 1949: *m* 1981, David Ross Fraser (BA), and has issue living, Hamish Ross Molesworth *b* 1985, Edwina Ross Molesworth *b* 1983. *Residence* - Cowl Cowl, 19 Linacre Road, Hampton, Victoria, Australia. —— John Robert Nassau, DFC, (Ballark, Morrisons, Elaine Victoria, Australia), *b* 1910; S/Ldr RAAF, and a Councillor, Coleraineshire, Victoria; 1939-45 War (DFC): *m* 1940, Sheila Morrell, da of Charles Armytage, of The Wilderness, Coleraine, Victoria, and has issue living, Robert John Armytage (Lindavale, Morrisons, Elaine, Vic 3334, Australia), *b* 1941: *m* 1967, Amanda Grage, and has issue living, Charles John Matheson *b* 1968, Edward Paul *b* 1971, Peter Robert *b* 1976, Katrina Mary *b* 1974, —— John Denis Peter (Ballark, Morrisons, Elaine, Vic 3334, Australia), *b* 1944: *m* 1970, Georgina Mary Pierrepoint, and has issue living, James Robert Beiri *b* 1975, Emma Pamela Pierrepoint *b* 1972, —— Morrell Frances Armytage, *b* 1945: *m* 1967, Michael Guy Earle (*see* Earle, Bt, colls), —— Jackalyn Armytage, *b* 1949: *m* 1974, Barry Lazarus, of 21 Dwyer St, Sunshine Beach, Qld 4567, Australia, and has issue living, James Albert *b* 1982, Georgina Armytage *b* 1979. —— Edwin Noel Waulter (Mittagong, 31 Governor's Drive, Mount Macedon, Vic 3441, Australia), *b* 1916; is a Councillor, and former Pres, Ballanshire, Victoria: *m* 1940, Alison Mary, da of late W. A. Dalrymple, of Glenluce, Gisborne, Victoria, and has issue living, William Anthony Hill, *b* 1941; BAgSc: *m* 1973, Merran Sutherland, and has issue living, Stephen Alexander *b* 1975, Amy Merran Hill *b* 1979, —— Richard Matheson, *b* 1948; BAgSc: *m* 1977, Janet Elaine McIntyre, and has issue living, Louise Elizabeth *b* 1980, Katherine Wendy *b* 1982. —— Mary Margaret Hill (Burlendi, Coleraine, Victoria, Australia) *b* 1922: *m* 1943, Richard Sladen Hope, who *d* 1981, and has issue living, Christopher Sladen (71 Canterbury Rd, Middle Park, Vic, Australia), *b* 1947; MIE, Polar Medal: *m* 1982, Wendy (TPCT, Dip Ed), da of Patrick Jones, of Victoria, and has issue living, Richard Francis Sladen *b* 1984, David William *b* 1986, —— Roland Molesworth, *b* 1949, —— Linden Kenney (Wolta Wolta, Bungower Rd, Moorooduc, Vic), *b* 1954; MB, BS: *m* 1977, Priscilla Jane (BA, LLB), da of Ross Boaden, MSc, of Mount Eliza, Victoria, and has issue living, Edward Charles Kenney *b* 1984, Emily Jane Kenney *b* 1981.

  Grandchildren of late John Matheson Molesworth (ante):—
    Issue of late John Bysse Molesworth, *b* 1912, *d* 1977: *m* 1941, Jessie Martha, da of W. Thomas, of Charters Towers, Queensland:—
David John (25 Meigs Cres, Stuart Park 5790, NT, Australia), *b* 1942: *m* 1965 (*m diss* 1976), Diana Lynette, da of T. E. Mann, of S Caulfield, Victoria, and has issue living, Nicolas Andrew, *b* 1973. —— Judith Hill, *b* 1946; BA: *m* 1st, 1969 (*m diss* 1981), Roger John Young, BEng; 2ndly, 1981, Peter Fleming Terracall, and has issue living (by 1st *m*), Tristan Samuel, *b* 1972, —— Imogen Matilda, *b* 1974, —— (by 2nd *m*) Mikaila Hill, *b* 1981.

PREDECESSORS – **(1)** ROBERT Molesworth, PC, successively MP for Swords, St Michael, Bodmin, and E Retford, Ambassador to Copenhagen, and Commr of Trade Plantations; *cr Baron Philipstown*, of Swords, and *Viscount Molesworth* (peerage of Ireland) 1716; *d* 1925; *s* by his el son **(2)** JOHN, 2nd Viscount; was successively Ambassador to Tuscany,

Sardinia, Florence, Venice, and Turin; *d* 1726; *s* by his brother (3) RICHARD, PC, 3rd Viscount; an eminent soldier, attained the rank of Field-Marshal; sat as MP for Swords 1714; was ADC to Duke of Marlborough (whose life he saved) at Ramillies, Lieut-Gen of the Ordnance 1739, and Com in Ch of the Forces in Ireland 1751; *d* 1758; *s* by his son (4) RICHARD NASSAU, 4th Viscount; *d* unmarried 1793, when the honours reverted to his cousin (5) ROBERT 5th Viscount, el son of Hon William, MP, 3rd son of 1st Viscount; *d* 1813; *s* by his son (6) WILLIAM JOHN, 6th Viscount; a Maj-Gen in the Army; *d* 1815; *s* by his cousin (7) RICHARD PIGOTT, 7th Viscount, el son of Richard, 3rd son of Hon William, MP (ante); *d* unmarried 1875; *s* by his nephew (8) *Rev* SAMUEL (son of Capt John, RN, 3rd son of Richard (ante), by Louisa, da of late Rev Dr Tomkyns), 8th Viscount, *b* 1829; R of St Petrock Minor: *m* 1st, 1862, Georgina Charlotte Cecil, who *d* 1879, da of George Bagot Gosset, formerly of 4th Dragoon Guards; 2ndly, 1883, Agnes, who *d* 1905, da of late Dugald Dove, of Nutshill, Renfrewshire, *d* 1906; *s* by his son (9) GEORGE BAGOT, 9th Viscount; *b* 1867: *m* 1894, Nina Alida, who *d* 1958, da of late Col H. D. Faulkner, 42nd Madras Inf; *d* 1947; *s* by his brother (10) CHARLES RICHARD, 10th Viscount; *b* 1869: *m* 1906, Elizabeth Gladys who *d* 1974, da of late Edward Martin Langworthy; *d* 1961; *s* by his son (11) RICHARD GOSSET, 11th Viscount and present peer; also Baron Philipstown.

MOLLOY, BARON (Molloy) (Life Baron 1981)

WILLIAM JOHN MOLLOY, son of William John Molloy; *b* 26 Oct 1918; *ed* St Thomas, Swansea, and Swansea Coll, Univ of Wales (Hon Fellow); FRGS; Member Transport and General Worker's Union 1936-46; Civil Service Union 1946-52 (Ed Civil Service Review 1949-53); Chm Staff-Side Foreign Office Whitley Council, Germany/Austria Sections, 1950-53; Leader Fulham Borough Council 1959-62 (Member since 1954); formerly Vice-Chm Parl Labour Party Gp for Common Market and European Affairs; Parl Adviser London Trades Council Transport Cttee 1968-70; PPS to Min of Posts and Telecommunication 1969-70; Pres Disabled Drivers Assocn from 1969; Sponsored MP Confederation Health Service Employees 1972; Member European Parl and Council of Europe, WEU 1976-79; Chm Parl Lab Party Social Services Gp 1974; Political Adviser to The Arab League 1981-84, Member Saudi Arabia, Kuwait, Abu Dhabi, Bahrein, Iraq and Dubai Parliamentary Groups; Chm British Tunisian Soc, and Met Area Royal British Legion 1985-93; Nat Vice Pres Royal British Legion since 1994; Hon Life Pres London Univ Soc, Hon Associate British Vetinary Assocn since 1988; served RE 1939-46; MP (*Lab*) Ealing North 1964-79; *cr Baron Molloy*, of Ealing, in Greater London (Life Baron) 1981: *m* 1st, 1946, Eva Lewis, who *d* 1980; 2ndly, 1981 (*m diss* 1987), Doris Paines, and has issue by 1st

m.

Arms – Vert on a rounded mount or an oak tree proper leaved and fructed also or and in base two barrulets wavy argent all within a bordure ermine. **Crest** – Upon rocks thereon oyster shells proper a representation of the Mumbles Lighthouse at Swansea diffusing light from its lantern all proper. **Supporters** – *Dexter*, on a grassy mount proper a dragon passant its tail looped gules tongue and claws or; *sinister*, on a like mount a swan wings displayed inverted and addorsed all proper. **Motto** – Justice and Compassion.
Address – House of Lords, SW1.

DAUGHTER LIVING (By 1st marriage)

Hon Marion Ann, *b* 1947: *m* 1974 (*m diss* 1987), Laurence George Motl, and has issue living, Julia Marion, *b* 1976, — Ann Lillian, *b* 1979. *Residence* – 6225 Idylwood Lane, Edina, Minnesota 55436, USA.

MONCK, VISCOUNT (Monck) Sits as BARON (UK 1866) (Viscount I 1801)

CHARLES STANLEY MONCK, 7th Viscount; *b* 2 April 1953; *s* 1982; *ed* Eton; does not use the title.

Arms – Gules, a chevron between three lions, heads erased argent. **Crest** – A dragon passant wings elevated sable. **Supporters** – *Dexter*, a dragon; *sinister*, a lion; both argent, and holding in the fore paw a branch of laurel resting on the shoulder fructed proper.
Residence – 43 Newbury St, Whitchurch, Hants.

BROTHERS LIVING

Hon GEORGE STANLEY (Yew Tree House, Lea, Malmeslbury, Wilts SN16 9PA), *b* 12 April 1957: *m* 1986, Camilla E.V., 2nd da of late John Naylor, of The Mill House, Bramley, Hants, and has had issue, Henry, *b* and *d* 1991.
Hon James Stanley, *b* 1961.

AUNT LIVING (*Raised to the rank of Viscount's daughter* 1928)

Hon Mary Patricia, *b* 1911: *m* 1935, Brigadier (Charles) Hilary Vaughan Pritchard, DSO, JP, DL (ret), who *d* 1976, having assumed by deed poll 1956 the surname of Vaughan in lieu of his patronymic; late Roy Welch Fus and Parachute Regt, and has issue living, Susan Katharine Vaughan (Shuckburgh House, Naseby, Northampton), *b* 1936: *m* 1957, David Spencer Muirhead, who *d* 1977, — Molly Cecilia Vaughan, *b* 1941: *m* 1962, His Honour Judge Ian Hewitt Davies, TD, c/o Croydon Combined Court Centre, Croydon, Surrey, — Patricia Nesta Vaughan (twin), *b* 1941: *m* 1984, George Engel, who *d* 1987, only son of Max Engel, — Jane Arabella Vaughan, *b* 1945: *m* 1970, David Patrick M. Allen, of Sutton, Dublin. *Residence* – The Old Rectory, Pen Selwood, Wincanton, Somerset.

Boldly, faithfully, successfully

PORTITER FIDELITER FELICITER

WIDOW LIVING OF SIXTH VISCOUNT

BRENDA MILDREDA, da of late George William Adkins, of Bower's Close, Harpenden, Herts: *m* 1st, 1951, as his 2nd wife, the 6th Viscount, OBE, who *d* 1982; 2ndly, 1985, as his 2nd wife, Brig Gerald (Ged) Michael Palmer, MC, of Pilgrims Farm, Overton, Hants.

PREDECESSORS – **(1)** CHARLES STANLEY Monck; *cr Baron Monck*, of Ballytrammon (peerage of Ireland) 1797, and *Viscount Monck* (peerage of Ireland) 1801; *d* 1802; *s* by his el son **(2)** HENRY STANLEY, 2nd Viscount; *cr Earl of Rathdowne* (peerage of Ireland) 1822; *d* 1848, when the earldom expired and the barony and viscountcy devolved upon his brother **(3)** CHARLES JOSEPH KELLY, 3rd Viscount; *b* 1791: *m* 1817, Bridget, da of late John Willington, Esq, of Killoskehane, co Tipperary; *d* 1849; *s* by his son **(4)** CHARLES STANLEY, GCMG, PC, 4th Viscount, *b* 1819; MP for Portsmouth 1852-7; was a Lord of the Treasury 1855-8, Gov-Gen of Canada 1861-7, and of Dominion of Canada 1867-8, Ch Commr in Ireland 1869-81, and Lord-Lieut of co Dublin 1874-92; *cr Baron Monck* (peerage of United Kingdom) 1866: *m* 1844, his cousin, Lady Elizabeth Louise Mary Monck, who *d* 1892, da of 1st Earl of Rathdowne (*ext*); *d* 1894; *s* by his son **(5)** HENRY POWER CHARLES STANLEY, 5th Viscount; *b* 1849; Vice-Lieut co Wicklow (High Sheriff 1887): *m* 1874, Lady Edith Caroline Sophia Scott, who *d* 1929, da of 3rd Earl of Clonmell; *d* 1927; *s* by his grandson **(6)** HENRY WYNDHAM STANLEY, OBE, JP, DL (son of late Capt Hon Charles Henry Stanley Monck, who was *ka* 1914, el son of 5th Viscount), 6th Viscount, *b* 1905; Vice-Chm Nat Asso of Boys' Clubs 1938-78: *m* 1st, 1937 (*m diss* 1951), Eva Maria, Baroness Vreto, 2nd da of Professor Zaunmuller-Freudenthaler, of Vienna; 2ndly, 1951, Brenda Mildreda (who *m* 2ndly, 1985, as his 2nd wife, Brig Gerald (Ged) Michael Palmer, MC, who *d* 1991), only da of late George William Adkins, of Bower's Close, Harpenden, Herts; *d* 1982; *s* by his el son **(7)** CHARLES STANLEY, 7th Viscount and present peer; also Baron Monck.

MONCKTON OF BRENCHLEY, VISCOUNT (Monckton) (Viscount UK 1957)

To spread fame by deeds

FAMAM·EXTENDERE·FACTIS

GILBERT WALTER RIVERSDALE MONCKTON, CB, OBE, MC, 2nd Viscount; *b* 3 Nov 1915; *s* 1965; *ed* Harrow, and Trin Coll, Camb (MA); FSA; Maj-Gen (ret), late 12th R Lancers, formerly 5th R Inniskilling Dragoon Gds; Col 9th/12th R Lancers 1967-73; Hon Col Kent and Sharpshooters Yeo 1974-79; Dep-Chm Gulf Guarantee Bank; Comdg RAC, 3rd Div 1958-63, Dep Dir of Personnel Admin 1962, Dir of Public Relations, War Office 1960-65, and Ch of Staff, HQ, BAOR 1965-67; Pres Kent Assocn of Boys' Clubs 1965-78, and Inst of Heraldic and Genealogical Studies since 1965, of Kent Archaeological Assocn and of Medway Productivity Assocn 1968-74; County Vice-Chm of Scout Assocn (Kent) 1968-74; a DL of Kent; Pres of British Assocn Order of Malta 1974-83; Pres of Anglo-Belgian Union 1973-83; 1939-45 War (MC); Korea 1951-52; a Liveryman of Broderers' Co (Master 1978-79); Baliff Grand Cross of Obedience Sovereign Mil Order of Malta, and KStJ (Chm of Council or Order of St John for Kent 1969-75); Grand Officer of the Order of Leopold II; Cdr of Order of the Crown of Belgium; Bailiff Grand Cross of Justice Constantinian Order of St George; OBE (Mil) 1956, CB (Mil) 1966: *m* 1950, Marianna Laetitia, Dame of Honour and Devotion Sov Mil Order of Malta; Pres St John's Ambulance for Kent 1973-80, Member of SSAFA Central Council since 1968; High Sheriff of Kent (1981); OStJ, da of Cdr Robert Tatton Bower, RN (By Strickland), and has issue.

Arms – Quarterly; 1st and 4th, sable, on a chevron between three martlets or, as many mullets of the field, *Monckton*; 2nd and 3rd, or a chevron gules a chief vair (*St Quintin*). **Crest** – On a wreath sable and or a martlet or. **Supporters** – On either side a horse argent crined and unguled or gorged with a chain gold pendant therefrom an escutcheon sable charged with a rose also argent barbed and seeded proper.
Residence – Runhams Farm, Runham Lane, Harrietsham, Maidstone, Kent, ME17 1NJ. *Clubs* – Brooks's, Cavalry, MCC, Casino Maltese (Valetta).

SONS LIVING

Hon CHRISTOPHER WALTER *b* 14 Feb 1952; *ed* Harrow, Churchill Coll, Camb (MA) and Univ Coll, Cardiff; a DL of Greater London since 1988; OStJ (1973), Kt of Honour and Devotion Sov Mil Order of Malta; a Liveryman of Broderers' Co, leaderwriter Yorkshire Post Newspapers, Ltd, Leeds 1975-77; press officer Conservative Central Office 1977-78; Editor, *The Universe* 1979-81; Sec Economic Accounting Study Group, centre for Policy Studies 1980; Man Ed *The Sunday Telegraph Magazine* 1981-82; Member PM's policy unit 1983-86; Assist Ed *Today* 1986-87, Consulting Ed *Evening Standard* 1987-92; Dir Christopher Monckton Ltd since 1987, Dir Beechwood Clothing Co since 1993; Freeman of City of London: *m* 1990, Juliet Mary Anne, yst da of Jorgen Malherbe Jensen, of Doughty St, WC1. *Residence* – Finnart Lodge, Bridge of Gaur, Rannoch, Perthshire PH17 2QF. *Clubs* – Beefsteak, Brooks's, Pratt's.
Hon Timothy David Robert, *b* 1955; *ed* Harrow, and RAC, Cirencester; Kt of Honour and Devotion, Sov Mil Order of Malta: *m* 1984, Jennifer J., 2nd da of Brendan Carmody, of 72 Ashbourne Rd, W5, and formerly of Sydney Australia, and has issue living, Dominic Walter, *b* 1985, — James Timothy, *b* 1988, — William Henry, *b* 1992. *Residence* – 15 Lombard St, Balgowlah, Sydney 2093, Australia.
Hon Jonathan Riversdale St Quintin (twin), *b* 1955; *ed* Worth; Monk of the Order of St Benedict, Worth Abbey 1975-89: *m* 1992, Carina Therese, da of Brian Beeson, OBE. *Residence* – 90 Innes Gdns, Putney Heath, SW15 3AD.
Hon Anthony Leopold Colyer, *b* 1960; *ed* Harrow, and Magdalene Coll, Camb (MA), comm'd 9th/12th R Lancers 1982, Capt 1984 (ret 1987); 1st Sec Foreign and Commonwealth Office since 1993: *m* 1985, Philippa Susan, yr da of late Gervase Christopher Brinsmade Wingfield (*see* V Powerscourt, colls), and has issue living, Edward Gervase Colyer, *b* 1988, — Camilla Mary, *b* 1989. *Clubs* – MCC and Cavalry and Guards.

DAUGHTER LIVING

Hon Rosamond Mary, *b* 1953; Man Dir Tiffany, London; Freeman of Goldsmith's Co: *m* 1991, as his 2nd wife, Hon Dominic Ralph Campden Lawson, son of Baron Lawson of Blaby, PC (Life Baron), and has issue (*see* B Lawson of Blaby).

SISTER LIVING

Hon Valerie Hamilton (*Senator Hon Lady Goulding*), *b* 1918; Hon LLD, National Univ of Ireland 1968; late Subaltern WRAC (Reserve); Senator of Republic of Ireland; Chm and Man Dir Central Remedial Clinic, Dublin since 1951; Founder Member, Nat Rehabilitation Bd (1955), and Union of Voluntary Organisations for the Handicapped; a Gov St Patrick's Hosp; Member, Management Cttee Mater Hosp, Southern Movement for Peace, etc; Dame of Honour and Devotion, Sov Mil Order of Malta: *m* 1939, Wing Com Sir William Basil Goulding, 3rd Bt, who *d* 1982. *Residence* – Dargle Cottage, Enniskerry, co Wicklow.

PREDECESSOR – (1) *Rt Hon Sir* WALTER TURNER Monckton, GCVO, KCMG, MC, PC, QC, son of Frank William Monckton, of Ightham Warren, Kent; *b* 1891; Attorney-Gen to Duchy Cornwall 1932-47 and 1948-51, Dir-Gen of Min of Information, and an Additional Dep Under-Sec of State for Foreign Affairs 1940, Head of Information Sers Cairo 1941-42, Solicitor Gen 1945, Min of Labour and Nat Ser 1951-55, Min of Defence 1955-56, and Paymaster-Gen 1956-57; MP for Bristol West (*C*) 1951-57; *cr* Viscount Monckton of Brenchley, of Brenchley, co Kent (peerage of UK) 1947: *m* 1914 (*m diss* 1947), Mary Adelaide Somes, who *d* 1964, da of Sir Thomas Colyer Colyer-Ferguson, 3rd Bt; 2ndly, 1947, Bridget Helen, Lady Ruthven of Freeland (in her own right), who *d* 1982, and formerly wife of 11th Earl of Carlisle; *d* 1965; *s* by his only son (2) GILBERT WALTER RIVERSDALE, CB, OBE, MC, 2nd Viscount and present peer.

MONCREIFF, BARON (Moncreiff) (Baron UK 1873, Bt S 1626 and UK 1871)

On hope

HARRY ROBERT WELLWOOD MONCREIFF 5th Baron and 15th Baronet of Moncreiff, and 5th of Tullibole; *b* 4 Feb 1915; *s* 1942: *ed* Fettes Coll; Hon Lt-Col (retired) RASC Burma 1939-45 (despatches): *m* 1952, Enid Marion Watson, who *d* 1985, only da of Major Henry Watson Locke, of Belmont, Dollar, and has issue.

Arms – Quarterly: 1st and 4th argent, a lion rampant gules, armed and langued azure, a chief ermine; 2nd and 3rd argent, an oak tree issuing out of a well in base proper, **Crest** – A demi-lion rampant, as in the arms. **Supporters** – Two men armed cap-a-pie, holdng in the exterior and a spear resting on the shoulder all proper, the breastplate charged with a crescent gules.
Seat – Tullibole Castle, Kinross-shire.

SON LIVING

Hon RHODERICK HARRY WELLWOOD, *b* 22 March 1954: *m* 1982, Alison Elizabeth Anne, only da of late James Duncan Alastair Ross, of West Mayfield, Dollar, Clackmannanshire, and has issue living, Harry James Wellwood, *b* 12 Aug 1986, — James Gavin Francis, *b* 1988.

BROTHER LIVING

Hon Robert Frederick Arthur (26 Croft St, Galashiels, Selkirk), *b* 1924: *m* 1951, Aileen Margaret Marr, da of Robert Marr Meldrum, LDS PhD, and has issue living, Richard Gerard Arthur, *b* 1964, — Gillian Nicola Ann, *b* 1954: *m* 1981, Norman Alexander Stewart, and has issue living, Rory Alexander *b* 1989, Rebecca Jane *b* 1986.

SISTERS LIVING

Hon Lilian Vida Lechmere, *b* 1912: *m* 1942, David Robert Young, and has issue living, Robert Arthur Moncreiff, *b* 1944, — Caroline Vida Rosemary, *b* 1951. *Residence* – Tanworth, Fossoway, Kinross-shire.
Hon Nicola Gladys, *b* 1917: *m* 1st, 1940, Capt Frederick W. Gifford, RA, who was *ka* 1943; 2ndly, 1946, Charles John Derek Renny, who *d* 1970, late Lt RNVR, and has issue living, (by 1st *m*) James Alexander Moncreiff (Fernlee, Banff), *b* 1942: *m* 1967, Patricia Dalton, and has issue living, Robert James Moncreiff *b* 1974, Lucinda Felicity Moncreiff *b* 1971, Samantha Louise Moncreiff *b* 1985, — (by 2nd *m*) Nicholas Charles Moncreiff (USA), *b* 1954: *m* 1982, Carol M., da of Neal R. Ashman, of Home House, St Martin's Guernsey, and has issue living, Alicia Nicola Rose *b* 1985, Emily Ellen Miranda *b* 1987, Abigail Eloise Mateldy *b* 1988, Felicity Alice Prudence *b* 1990, — Susan Miranda Fitzherbert, *b* 1950: *m* 1972, Anthony John O'Donnell, MB, BS, of Le Vieux Rouvet, St Saviours, Guernsey, and has issue living, Nicholas John Renny *b* 1975, Alexa Caroline *b* 1973, Abigail Kate *b* 1978, — Prudence Jane Fitzherbert, *b* 1952: *m* 1977, Paul Lynch, of 8 Kinnaird Av, Chiswick, W4, and has issue living, James Patrick Moncreiff *b* 1980, Harry John Renny *b* 1983. *Residence* – Greenways, Montville Rd, St Peter Port, Guernsey.
Hon Pamela Anne, *b* 1927; MB, ChB Edinburgh 1949: *m* 1st, 1951 (*m diss* 1973), Edward James White; 2ndly, 1979, Ernest Frederic Epps, who *d* 1987, of 13 Barntongate Av, Edinburgh 4, and has issue living (by 1st *m*) Nicholas Alan, *b* 1953, — Douglas Andrew, *b* 1959, — Vivienne Lucy, *b* 1957.

WIDOW LIVING OF SON OF FOURTH BARON

Catriona Sheila, da of James MacDonald, of Devonshaw House, Dollar: *m* 1955, Hon Donald Graham Fitz-Herbert Moncreiff, who *d* 1993, and has issue (see colls, infra). *Residence* – Barrisdale, Comrie, Perthshire.

COLLATERAL BRANCHES LIVING

Issue of late Hon Donald Graham Fitz-Herbert Moncreiff, 2nd son of 4th Baron, *b* 1919, *d* 1993: *m* 1955, Catriona Sheila (ante), da of James MacDonald, of Devonshaw House, Dollar:—
Ranald Patrick MacDonald, *b* 1965. —— Barbara Jane, *b* 1957. —— Frances Catriona FitzHerbert, *b* 1959. —— Theresa Madeline Fitz-Herbert, *b* 1961: *m* 1987, James Stephen Hanna, and has issue living, a da, *b* 1988.

Granddaughter of late Hon James William Moncreiff, 3rd son of 1st Baron:—
Issue of late Edwin Robert Moncreiff, *b* 1877, *d* 1962: *m* 1904, Mary, who *d* 1953, da of late Matthew Montgomerie Bell, WS, of Edinburgh:—
Mary Eileen, *b* 1909: *m* 1st, 1929, Maj John Roy Oakley, Roy Scouts who was *ka* in Palestine 1939; 2ndly, 1939, Capt Charles Philip McLaughlan, architect, and has issue living, (by 2nd *m*) Ian Wellwood, *b* 1940; Maj Scots Guards, — Ann Wellwood, *b* 1944: *m* 1965, David Godfrey-Faussett and has issue living, Katherine Sarah *b* 1971.

Grandchildren of late James Hamilton Moncreiff, yr son of late Hon Francis Jeffrey Moncreiff (infra):—
Issue of late Frederick Henry Wellwood Moncreiff, *b* 1909, *d* 1990: *m* 1939, Gwendolen Alma (Box 98, Haenertsburg, Transvaal, S Africa), da of Patrick Gifford:—
Andrew Malcolm (Greenhills, Fernden Lane, Haslemere, Surrey), *b* 1944; *ed* Pembroke Coll, Camb (MA): *m* 1971, Jennifer Margaret, da of John Chapman, of Johannesburg, and has issue living, Michael Patrick, *b* 1974, — Robert James, *b* 1977. —— Patricia Jane (4 Blandford House, Fentiman Rd, SW8 1LB), *b* 1941.

PREDECESSORS – (1) JOHN Moncreiff, MP, *cr* a *Baronet* 1626 (of Moncreiff) with remainder to his heirs male whatsoever; *d* 1650; *s* by his el son (2) JOHN, 2nd Bt, who in 1663 sold the Moncreiff estates to his cousin Thomas Moncreiff, who in 1685 was *cr* a *Baronet*; *d* 1675; *s* by his brother (3) DAVID, 3rd Bt; *s* by his brother (4) JAMES, 4th Bt, at whose decease the direct line of the 1st Bt expired and the baronetcy reverted to the son of Hugh Moncreiff, yst brother of the 1st Bt. (5) JOHN, 5th Bt; was an eminent Physician; *d* 1710; *s* by his son (6) HUGH, 6th Bt; *d* 1744; *s* by his kinsman, a descendant of Archibald Moncreiff, uncle of 1st Bt (7) *Rev* WILLIAM, 7th Bt; *d* 1767; *s* by his son (8) *Rev* HENRY, DD; was an eminent Divine of the Church of Scotland; assumed the additional surname of Wellwood; *d* 1827; *s* by his son (9) JAMES WELLWOOD, 9th Bt; *b* 1776; was a Lord of Session and Justiciary of Scotland 1829-51: *m* 1808, Ann, who *d* 1843, da of Capt George Robertson, RN; *d* 1851; *s* by his son (10) HENRY WELLWOOD, DD, 10th Bt, was an eminent Divine of the Free Church of Scotland; *dsp* 1883; *s* by his brother (11) JAMES, PC, LLD, 11th Bt, who had previously been *cr* a *Baronet* (of Tulliebole) 1871, and *Baron Moncreiff*, of Tulliebole, co Kinross (peerage of United Kingdom) 1873; *b* 1811; MP for Leith Dist (*L*) 1851-9, for Edinburgh 1859-68, and for Glasgow and Aberdeen Univs 1868-9; was Dean of Faculty of Advocates for Scotland 1858-69, Solicitor-Gen for Scotland 1850-51, Lord Advocate 1851, 1852-8, 1859-66, and Lord Justice-Clerk 1869-88: *m*

1834, Isabella, who *d* 1881, da of Robert Bell, Sheriff of Berwick and Haddington; *d* 1895; *s* by his el son (**12**) HENRY JAMES, 2nd Baron; *b* 1840; Sheriff of Renfrew and Bute 1881-8, and a Judge of Court of Session, Scotland (with title of *Lord Wellwood*) 1888-1905: *m* 1st, 1866, Susan Wilhelmine, who *d* 1869, 3rd da of Sir William H. Dick-Cunyngham, 8th Bt; 2ndly, 1873, Millicent Julia, who *d* 1881, da of late Col Fryer, of Moulton Paddocks, Newmarket; *d* 1909; *s* by his brother (**13**) *Rev* ROBERT CHICHESTER, 3rd Baron; *b* 1843, V of Tanworth 1885-1913: *m* 1871, Florence Kate, who *d* 1926, da of late Lieut-Col Richard Henry FitzHerbert: *d* 1913; *s* by his son (**14**) JAMES ARTHUR FITZHERBERT, 4th Baron ; *b* 1872: *m* 1906, Lucy Vida, who *d* 1973, da of David Lechmere Anderson, LRCP, of Doncaster; *d* 1942; *s* by his el son (**15**) HARRY ROBERT WELLWOOD, 5th Baron and present peer.

MONK BRETTON, BARON (Dodson) (Baron UK 1884)

Successful by favour of Providence

JOHN CHARLES DODSON, 3rd Baron; *b* 17 July 1924; *s* 1933; *ed* Westminster, and New Coll, Oxford: *m* 1958, Zoë Diana, da of Ian Douglas Murray Scott, and has issue.

Arms – Argent, on a fesse raguly plain cotised between six fleurs-de-lis all gules, a sword fesseways point to the dexter proper, pommel and hilt or. **Crest** – Two lion's jambs erased and in saltire gules, entwined by a serpent, head to the dexter proper. **Supporters** – On either side a female figure proper, vested argent, mantle azure, each resting the exterior hand of an antique shield also azure, adorned gold, that on the *dexter* charged with a balance suspended, and that on the *sinister*, with a staff erect entwined by a serpent all or. *Residence* – Shelley's Folly, Cooksbridge, nr Lewes. *Club* – Farmers'.

SONS LIVING

Hon CHRISTOPHER MARK, *b* 2 Aug 1958; *ed* Eton, and Univ of S California (MBA): *m* 1988, Karen L., only da of B. J. McKelvain, of Fairfield, Conn, USA, and has issue living, Ben, *b* 1989—James, *b* 1994, — Emma, *b* 1990.
Hon Henry, *b* 1960; *ed* Eton; BSc (1983) Council for Nat Academic Awards; ARICS 1986.

SISTER LIVING

Hon Priscilla (Balcombe Place, Balcombe, Haywards Heath, W Sussex), *b* 1914: *m* 1935, Maj Claude Thorburn Knight, late Coldm Gds, who *d* 1993, and has issue living, (Christopher) William (82 Lansdowne Rd, W11), *b* 1943: *m* 1969, Jonkvroue Sylvia Caroline, da of Jonkheer Emile van Lennep, of 444 Ruychrocklaan, The Hague, and has issue living, Christopher Thorburn *b* 1973, Alexa Isobel *b* 1971, Louisa Jane *b* 1977, — Caroline Jane, *b* 1935: *m* 1956, Maj Jerome Otway Fane De Salis, Welsh Gds, who *d* 1989, of Bourne House, East Woodhay, Newbury, Berks, and has issue living, Nicholas Charles *b* 1957: *m* 1988, Felicity Anne, da of David Stewart, FRCOG, of Axmouth, Devon, formerly of Harare, Zimbabwe (and has issue living, Alexandra Claire *b* 1991), Rodolph William *b* 1970, Henrietta Jane *b* 1960: *m* 1982, Nigel Ronald Graham (*see* Graham, Bt, *cr* 1662), — Patricia Susan (*Lady Daunt*), *b* 1938: *m* 1962, Sir Timothy Lewis Achilles Daunt, KCMG, and has issue living, Achilles James *b* 1963: *m* 1994, Katherine, da of late Rev Alan Steward, Eleanor *b* 1965: *m* 1990, Dr Marco Puccioni, only son of Dr Marco Puccioni, of Florence, Italy (and has issue living, Emma *b* 1991, Olivia *b* 1993), Alice Louise *b* 1969, — Sarah Georgiana Ann, *b* 1945: *m* 1970, Rear Adm Timothy Michael Bevan, CB, and has issue living, Thomas Loraine *b* 1973, Michael David *b* 1975, Richard John *b* 1977.

PREDECESSORS – (**1**) *Rt Hon* JOHN GEORGE Dodson, CB, only son of late Rt Hon Sir John Dodson LLD, MP for Rye 1819-23; *b* 1825; Dep Speaker and Chm of Committees of House of Commons 1865-72, Financial Sec to Treasury 1873-4, Pres of Lord Govt Board 1880-82, 1874-80, *cr Baron Monk Bretton*, of Conyboro and Hurstpierpoint, co Sussex (peerage of United Kingdom) 1884, Florence, da of W. J. Campion. of Danny, Sussex; *d* 1897; *s* by his son (**2**) JOHN WILLIAM, CB, 2nd Baron; *b* 1869; a JP and DL for E Sussex; Private Sec to Sec of State for Colonies 1900-1903; Chm of London County Council 1929-30: *m* 1911, Ruth, who *d* 1967, da of late Hon Charles Brand; *d* 1933; *s* by his son (**3**) JOHN CHARLES, 3rd Baron and present peer.

MONKSWELL, BARON (Collier) (Baron UK 1885)

PERSEVERE

GERARD COLLIER, 5th Baron; *b* 28 Jan 1947; *s* 1984; *ed* George Heriot's Sch, Edinburgh: *m* 1974, Ann Valeria, da of James Collins, of Liverpool, and has issue.

Arms – Argent, on a chevron azure, between in chief two demi-unicorns courant and in base an elephant's head erased gules, three oak branches slipped, leaved and fructed or. **Crest** – A demiman affrontee proper, holding in the dexter hand an oak branch slipped and leaved proper, fructed or, and resting the sinister hand on an escutcheon azure, charged with two keys saltirewise or. **Supporters** – Two Druids vested argent, wreathed about the temples with laurel leaves vert, each resting the exterior hand on an escutcheon azure, charged with a balance suspended or.
Residence – 513 Barlow Moor Rd, Chorlton cum Hardy, Manchester M21 8AQ.

SONS LIVING

Hon JAMES ADRIAN, *b* 29 March 1977.
Hon Robert William Gerard, *b* 1979.

DAUGHTER LIVING

Hon Laura Jennifer, *b* 1975.

BROTHER LIVING

Neil Adrian José, *b* 1948; *ed* George Heriot's Sch, E Anglia Univ (BSc), and Leicester Univ (Cert Ed): *m* 1st, 1975 (*m diss* 1985), Frances Myra Chapman; 2ndly, 1987, Judith Bosca Brandes, da of late Rico G. Bosca. *Residence* – 1335 Peralta Av, Berkeley, Calif 94702, USA.

HALF-BROTHER LIVING (*son of disclaimed 4th Baron by 3rd wife*)

Benjamino, *b* 1958: *m* 1984, Clare Maria Murphy, and has issue living, Daniel James William Paulo, *b* 1987. *Residence* – Harford House Cottage, Chew Magnor, Avon.

HALF-SISTER LIVING (*daughter of disclaimed 4th Baron by 3rd wife*)

Tiaré Penelope Katherine, *b* 1952. *Residence* – The Clatterway, Bonsall, nr Matlock, Derbys.

UNCLE LIVING (*brother of disclaimed 4th Baron*)

Perceval Gerard, *b* 1915: *m* 1st, 1940 (*m diss* 1947), Lorraine Walker; 2ndly, 1949, Sheila, who *d* 1975, elder da of late Capt Stuart Mackintosh Macpherson, OBE, RAMC, and formerly wife of S/Ldr Robert Francis Doe, DSO and bar, RAF; 3rdly, 1977, Brenda Mary, da of Nathaniel Victor Fortescue, and formerly wife of Geoffrey Dacre Carpenter, and has issue living (by 1st *m*), Anthony Gerard (W/5 Water Rat, T/O Entrepotdok 55, 1018 AD, Amsterdam, Holland), *b* 1942; *ed* Leicester Univ, — (by 2nd *m*), Gavin (113 Mesa Vista 3, Santa Fe, New Mexico 87501, USA), *b* 1951, — Tessa Jill, *b* 1950. *Residence* – Lymington, Hants.

AUNT LIVING (*sister of disclaimed 4th Baron*)

Anna Evangeline, *b* 1918: *m* 1940, Elvin Thorgerson, of 19 Earl St, Cambridge, and has issue living, Storm Elvin, *b* 1944.

DAUGHTER LIVING OF THIRD BARON

Hon Lorna Evelyn (La Chaumière, Camp Lane, W Runton, Cromer, Norfolk NR27 9NE), *b* 1915.

WIDOW LIVING OF FOURTH BARON (*who disclaimed the peerage for life 1964*)

NORA SELBY (*Mrs William A. L. Collier*): *m* 1951, as his 3rd wife, the 4th Baron, who disclaimed his peerage for life 1964, and who *d* 1984. *Residence* – 6 Corona Rd, Cambridge.

MOTHER LIVING

Helen, da of James Dunbar, of Edinburgh (infra): *m* 1st, 1945 (*m diss* 1950), as his 2nd wife, William Adrian Larry Collier, MB, BCh, later 4th Baron Monkswell (until he disclaimed his peerage for life 1964), and who *d* 1984; 2ndly, 1954, Edward Edmund Kemp. *Residence* – 31 Orchard Rd South, Edinburgh EH4 3JA.

COLLATERAL BRANCHES LIVING

Grandchildren of late Hon Gerard Collier, 2nd son of 2nd Baron:—
Issue of late John Bernard Collier, *b* 1920, *d* 1993: *m* 1947, Elsie (12 Argyle Crescent, Portobello, Edinburgh), da of James Dunbar, of Edinburgh (ante):—
Anna Lee (3/7 Magdalene Drive, Edinburgh), *b* 1948: *m* 19— (*m diss* 19—), Michael Gates, and has issue living, Catherine, *b* 1973. —— Sarah, *b* 1950: *m* 1987, John Bett, of East Lodge, Balbirnie, Markinch, Fife, and has issue living, Leo Mark Sean Collier, *b* 1988. —— The late John Bernard Collier also had issue (by Barbara Oriel Markham), Piers Markham COLLIER (11 Northbank Walk, Didsbury, Manchester), *b* 1947: *m* 1973 (*m diss* 1993), Susan Margaret Robinson, and has issue living, Matthew John Samuel, *b* 1978, — Esme Lorraine, *b* 1976.

Grandson of late Hon John Collier, OBE, 2nd son of 1st Baron:—
Issue of late Sir Laurence Collier, KCMG, *b* 1890, *d* 1976: *m* 1917, Eleanor Emma Antoinette, who *d* 1975, only da of late William Luther Watson, S Lancs Regt:—
William Oswald, *b* 1919; *ed* Bradfield Coll, and Balliol Coll, Oxford; FSA; FRHistS: *m* 1st, 1947 (*m diss* 1957), Hon Muriel Joan Lowry Lamb, da of 1st Baron Rochester; 2ndly, 1958, Ina Mary Grace, da of C. Crowne, of Littlehampton, Sussex, and has issue living (by 1st *m*), Sylvia Antoinette, *b* 1952: *m* 1985, Stephen Kenneth Godfrey, — (by 2nd *m*), Jonathan Charles

Laurence, *b* 1959, — Lucy Eleanor Mary, *b* 1961: *m* 1988, David William Hewitt, — Stella Catherine Juliet, *b* 1965. *Residence* – 34 Berwyn Rd, Richmond, Surrey. *Club* – Athenaeum.

PREDECESSORS – **(1)** *Rt Hon Sir* ROBERT PORRETT Collier: was Solicitor-Gen 1863-6, and Attorney-Gen 1868-71; MP for Plymouth (*L*) 1852-71, and a Judge of Judicial Committee of Privy Council; 1871-86; *cr Baron Monkswell*, of Monkswell, co Devon (peerage of United Kingdom), 1885; *b* 1817: *m* 1844, Isabella, who *d* 1886, el da of William Rose Rose, of Wolston Heath, Coventry; *d* 27 Oct 1886; *s* by his el son **(2)** ROBERT, 2nd Baron; *b* 1845; a Lord-in-Waiting to Queen Victoria 1892-5, and Under-Sec of State for War 1895: *m* 1873, Mary Josephine, who *d* 1930, da of late Joseph Alfred Hardcastle, MP: *d* 1909; *s* by his el son **(3)** ROBERT ALFRED HARDCASTLE, 3rd Baron, *b* 1875; 2nd Sec Foreign office 1905-10: *m* 1908, Ursula Mary, who *d* 1915, da of Col Hugh Gurney Barclay, MVO, of Colney Hall, Norwich (B Magheramorne); 2ndly, 1925, Katherine Edith, who *d* 1985, da of William Shaw Harriss Gastrell, of Rockbeare Grange, nr Exeter; *d* 1964; *s* by his nephew **(4)** WILLIAM ADRIAN LARRY, MB, BCh, DPH (son of late Hon Gerard Collier, 2nd son of 2nd Baron), 4th Baron, until he disclaimed his peerage 7 April 1964, *b* 1913; adopted additional christian name of Larry 1932; Member of Halstead UDC 1954-67, and Co Councillor Essex 1958-61; Gen Practitioner, District MO Falmouth, Jamaica; 1939-45 War with RAMC in M-W Europe and Middle East: *m* 1st, 1939 (*m diss* 1945), Erika, da of Dr Edward Kellner, of Vienna; 2ndly, 1945 (*m diss* 1950), Helen, da of James Dunbar, of Edinburgh; 3rdly, 1951, Nora Selby; *d* 1984; *s* by his eldest son **(5)** GERARD, 5th Baron and present peer.

MONSELL, VISCOUNTCY (Eyres Monsell) (Extinct 1993)

SISTER LIVING OF SECOND VISCOUNT

Hon Joan Elizabeth, *b* 1912: *m* 1st, 1939 (*m diss* 1947), William John Rayner CBE; 2ndly, 1968, Patrick Michael Leigh Fermor, DSO, OBE, writer. *Residence* – Kardamyli, Messenia, Greece.

WIDOW LIVING OF FIRST VISCOUNT

ESSEX LEILA HILARY (*Viscountess Monsell*), da of late Lt-Col Hon (Edward) Gerald Fleming French, DSO (*see* E Ypres, colls), and formerly wife of Vyvyan Drury: *m* 1950, as his 2nd wife the 1st Viscount, who *d* 1969.

MONSLOW, BARONY OF (Monslow) (Extinct 1966)

DAUGHTER LIVING OF LIFE BARON (*By 1st marriage*)

Hon Rosemary, *b* 1921: *m* 1948, William Harold Sparks, who *d* 1985, of 41 Trinity St, Rhostyllen, Wrexham, Clwyd.

WIDOW LIVING OF LIFE BARON

JEAN BAIRD (*Baroness Monslow*) (4 Kirklea Circus, Glasgow), da of Rev Angus Macdonald: *m* 1960, as his 2nd wife, Baron Monslow (Life Baron), who *d* 1966.

MONSON, BARON (Monson) (Baron GB 1728, Bt E 1611)
(Name and Title pronounced "Munson")

Ready for my country

JOHN MONSON, 11th Baron, and 15th Baronet; *b* 3 May 1932; *s* 1958; *ed* Eton, and Trin Coll, Camb (BA 1954): *m* 1955, Emma, da of late Anthony Devas, ARA, and has issue.

Arms – Or, two chevronels gules. **Crest** – A lion rampant proper, supporting a column or. **Supporters** – *Dexter*, a lion or; *Sinister*, a griffin wings elevated argent, beaked and membered azure; each gorged with a plain collar azure, charged with three crescents or, and having a line reflexed over the back blue.
Residence – The Manor House, South Carlton, Lincoln.

SONS LIVING

Hon NICHOLAS JOHN, *b* 19 Oct 1955; *ed* Eton: *m* 1981, Hilary, only da of Kenneth Martin, of PO Box 42, Ukunda, Mombasa, Kenya, and has issue living, Alexander John Runan, *b* 1984, — Isabella, *b* 1986. *Residence* – 24 Fentiman Rd, SW8 1LS.
Hon Andrew Anthony John, *b* 1959: *m* 1993, Emily C., yr da of Richard Clement Wheeler-Bennett, of The Mill House, Calstone Wellington, nr Calne, Wilts.
Hon Stephen Alexander John, *b* 1961.

BROTHERS LIVING

Hon Jeremy David Alfonso John, *b* 1934; *ed* Eton, and RMA; Maj Gren Gds (ret 1967); CC Berks 1981-93; High Sheriff of Berks 1994-95: *m* 1958, Patricia Mary, yr da of late Maj George Barker, MFH, of Stanlake Park, Twyford, Berks, and has issue living, John Guy Elmhirst, *b* 1962, — Antonia Debonnaire, *b* 1959. *Residence* – Keepers Cottage, Scarletts Wood, Hare Hatch, nr Reading, Berks RG10 97L.
Hon Anthony John, *b* 1944.

SISTER LIVING

Hon Sandra Debonnaire, *b* 1937: *m* 1958 (*m diss* 1971), Maj (William) Garry Patterson, Life Guards, and has issue living, James William John, *b* 1970, — Debonnaire Jane, *b* 1959: *m* 1984, Count Leopold von Bismarck, yst son of late Prince Otto von Bismarck, of Friedrichsruh, W Germany, and has issue living, Nikolai Leopold Archibald *b* 1986, Tassilo Valentine Christian *b* 1989, Caspar Maximilian Otto *b* 1991, — Juliet Mary, *b* 1963, — Annabel Kate (*Baroness Rayleigh*), *b* 1965: *m* 1991, 6th Baron Rayleigh, of Terling Place, Chelmsford, Essex, and has issue (*see* Rayleigh, B). *Residence* – 23 Lamont Rd, SW10 0HR.

WIDOW LIVING OF TENTH BARON

BETTIE NORTHRUP, da of late Lieut-Col E. Alexander Powell, of Riverain, Falls Village, Connecticut, USA; *m* 1st, 1931, the 10th Baron, who *d* 1958; 2ndly, 1962, Capt James Arnold Phillips, who *d* 1983. *Residence* – La Corderie, Rue St Pierre, St Peter in the Wood, Guernsey, CI.

COLLATERAL BRANCHES LIVING

Granddaughter of late Rev Hon Evelyn John Monson, 6th son of 6th Baron:—
Issue of late Capt Charles Evelyn John Monson, *b* 1878, *d* 1953: *m* 1924, Mabel Gertrude (Orotara, 123 Yarborough Road, Lincoln), da of Edwin Benjamin Pritchard, of Lincoln:—
Rachel Anne, *b* 1926.

Grandchildren of late Alfred John Monson, 3rd son of Rev Thomas John Monson (infra):—
Issue of late Philip Evelyn John Monson, DD, PhD, *b* 1887, *d* 1964: *m* 1st, 1920, Doris Murray, who *d* 1942; 2ndly, 1956, Catherine A.—:—
(By 1st marriage) Philip John, *b* 1928. —— Margaret Enid, *b* 1922.

Grandson of late Rev Thomas John Monson, son of Rev Hon Thomas Monson, 5th son of 2nd Baron:—
Issue of late Henry John Monson, *b* 1862, *d* 1930: *m* 1901, Theodosia Anne Emily, who *d* 1951, da of Rev George Howard-Wright, R of Offord D'Arcy, Hunts (B Denman):—
Thomas Debonnaire John (c/o Lawn Hospital, Union Rd, Lincoln), *b* 1905; *ed* Haileybury: *m* 1934 (*m diss* 1956), Anna Phillipe Bois Clements.

Descendants of late Hon Lewis Monson (2nd son of 1st Baron) who was *cr Baron Sondes* 1760 (*see* Sondes).

PREDECESSORS – (1) *Sir* THOMAS Monson, MP for co Lincoln 1597-8, for Castle Rising 1604-11, and for Cricklade 1614; Master of Armoury and Master of Armoury and Master Falconer to James 1; *cr Baronet* 1611; *d* 1641; *s* by his son (2) *Sir* JOHN, KB, 2nd Bt; MP for Lincoln City 1660 and 1664-78; *d* 1683; *s* by his grandson (3) *Sir* Henry, 3rd Bt; MP for Lincoln City 1679-80; *dsp* 1718; *s* by his brother (4) *Sir* WILLIAM, PC, 4th Bt; *d* 1727; *s* by his nephew (5) *Sir* JOHN, 5th Bt; MP for Lincoln City 1722-8; *cr Baron Monson*, of Burton, co Lincoln (peerage of Great Britain); was Capt of Band of Gentlemen Pensioners 1733, and First Commr of Trade and Plantations 1737; *d* 1748; *s* by his son (7) JOHN, 3rd Baron; *d* 1806; *s* by his son (8) JOHN GEORGE, 4th Baron; *b* 1785, *d* 1809; *s* by his son (9) FREDERICK JOHN, 5th Baron; *dsp* 1841; *s* by his cousin (10) WILLIAM JOHN, 6th Baron; *b* 1796: *m* 1828, Eliza, who *d* 1863, da of late Edmund Larken, of Bedford Square; London; *d* 1862; *s* by his son (11) WILLIAM JOHN, PC, 7th Baron; *b* 1829; MP for Reigate (*L*) 1858-62, Treasurer of HM Queen Victoria's Household 1874, Capt, of HM's Yeomen of the Guard 1880-85 and 1886, Master of the Horse 1892-4, and Militia ADC to HM 1886-96; *cr Viscount Oxenbridge*, of Burton, co Lincoln (peerage of Great Britain) 1886: *m* 1869, Hon Maria Adelaide, who *d* 1897, sister of 1st Earl de Montalt, and widow of 2nd Earl of Yarborough; *d* 1898, when the Viscountcy became ext, and he was *s* in the Barony by his brother (12) DEBONNAIRE JOHN, 8th Baron, *b* 1839; Sergeant-at-Arms to HM Queen Victoria's Household, and Equerry, Comptroller, and Treasurer to HRH the Duke of Saxe-Coburg and Gotha (Duke of Edinburgh); *m* 1861, Augusta Louisa Caroline, who *d* 1936, da of late Lieut-Col Hon Augustus Ellis; *d* 1900; *s* by his son (13) AUGUSTUS DEBONNAIRE JOHN, 9th Baron, *b* 1868: *m* 1903, Romaine Madeleine, who *d* 1943, da of late Gen Roy Stone, of Mendham, New Jersey, USA, and widow of Lawrence Turnure, of New York, *d* 1940; *s* by his son (14) JOHN ROSEBERY, 10th Baron; *b* 1907: Bar Inner Temple 1931, Bettie Northrup (who *m* 2ndly, 1962, Capt James Arnold Phillips, who *d* 1983), da of Lieut-Col E. Alexander Powell, of Journey's End, Chevy Chase, Maryland, USA; *d* 1958: *s* by his el son (15) JOHN, 11th Baron and present peer.

MONTAGU OF BEAULIEU, BARON (Douglas-Scott-Montagu) (Baron UK 1885)
(Title pronounced "Montagu of Bewly")

Let us be judged by our actions

EDWARD JOHN BARRINGTON DOUGLAS-SCOTT-MONTAGU, 3rd Baron; *b* 20 Oct 1926; *s* 1929; *ed* Ridley Coll, St Catharine's, Ontario, Eton, and New Coll, Oxford; Lt Gren Gds 1945-48; Founder Montagu Motor Museum at Beaulieu 1952; Chm Nat Motor Museum Trust since 1972, and Historic Buildings and Monuments Commn 1984-92; Pres Museums Assocn 1982-84; Development Commr 1980-84; Founder Pres Historic Houses Assocn 1973-78, and Pres Union of European Historic Houses 1978-81; Pres Southern Tourist Bd, Assocn Brit Transport and Engr Museums and English Vineyards Assocn; Chancellor Wine Guild of UK; Hon Fellow Museums Assocn; FRSA; Commodore Beaulieu River Sailing Club, Nelson Boat Owners' Club, and Vice Commodore House of Lords Yacht Club; Commodore Royal Southampton Club 1983-86; Vice-Pres Inst of Motor Industry, Pres Historic Commercial Vehicle Soc, Disabled Drivers' Motor Club, and Fedn of British Historic Vehicle Clubs; Founder and publisher of *The Veteran and Vintage* Magazine 1956-79, and author of books on Motoring History, and Historic Houses: *m* 1st 1959 (*m diss* 1974), (Elizabeth) Belinda, only da of late Capt Hon John de Bathe Crossley (*see* B Somerleyton, colls); 2ndly, 1974, Fiona Margaret, da of Richard Herbert, and has issue by 1st and 2nd *m.*

Arms – Quarterly of four: 1st and 4th grand quarter, 1st and 4th argent, three lozenges conjoined in fesse gules, within a bordure sable, *Montagu;* 2nd and 3rd or, an eagle displayed vert, beaked and membered gules, *Monthermer;* 2nd grand quarter argent on a bend azure, an estoile or, between two crescents also or, *Scott;* 3rd grand quarterly, 1st and 4th argent, a human heart gules imperially crowned or, on a chief azure three mullets of the field, *Douglas;* 2nd and 3rd azure, a bend between six crosses crosslet fitchée, the whole within a bordure or, charged with a double tressure flory counterflory, *Mar.* **Crests** – 1st, a griffin's head, couped at the neck or, winged and beaked sable; 2nd, a stag trippant proper; 3rd, a human heart gules, imperially crowned or, between two wings of the second. **Supporters** – Two griffins or, winged and beaked sable, each charged on the shoulder with a cap of maintenance azure.
Seat – Palace House, Beaulieu, Hants SO42 7ZN. **Town Residence** – Flat 11, Wyndham House, 24 Bryanston Sq, W1H 7FJ.

SONS LIVING *(By 1st marriage)*

Hon RALPH, *b* 13 March 1961.

(By 2nd marriage)

Hon Jonathan Deane, *b* 1975.

DAUGHTER LIVING *(By 1st marriage)*

Hon Mary Rachel, *b* 1964.

SISTERS LIVING

Hon Anne Rachel Pearl (*Hon Lady Chichester*), *b* 1921: *m* 1st, 1946, Maj Howel Joseph Moore-Gwyn, Welsh Guards, who *d* 1947; 2ndly, 1950, Sir (Edward) John Chichester, 11th Bt, and has issue living, (by 1st *m*) David John Howel (7 Phillimore Terr, Allen St, W8), *b* 1947: *m* 1974, Alison Frances, yr da of Clifford G. White, and has issue living, Henry John Howel *b* 1975, George Augustus Joseph *b* 1987, Alice Beatrice Rachel *b* 1978, — (by 2nd *m*) (*see* Chichester, Bt). *Residence* – Battramsley Lodge, Lymington, Hants SO41 8PT.
Hon Caroline Cecily, *b* 1925: *m* 1950 (*m diss* 1987) (George) Grainger Weston, and has issue living, Galvin, *b* 1951, — Gregg, *b* 1956, — Graham, *b* 1964, — Sarah, *b* 1953. *Residence* – Santa Clara Ranch, Box 31, Marion, Texas 78124, USA.
Hon Mary Clare *b* 1928: *m* 1st, 1953 (*m diss* 1968), David Bethune, Viscount Garnock (later 15th Earl of Lindsay), who *d* 1989; 2ndly, 1979, Timothy Charles Austin Horn, of Chapel House, Builth Wells, Powys, and has issue (by 1st *m*) (*see* E Lindsay).

HALF-SISTER LIVING.

Hon Elizabeth Susan, *b* 1909: *m* 1962, Col Arthur Noel Claude Varley, CBE, who *d* 1985. *Residence* – By the Mill, Beaulieu, Hants.

WIDOW LIVING OF SECOND BARON

(ALICE) PEARL (*Hon Mrs Edward Pleydell-Bouverie*), da of late Maj Barrington Crake, Rifle Bde: *m* 1st, 1920, as his 2nd wife, the 2nd Baron, who *d* 1929; 2ndly, 1936, Capt Hon Edward Pleydell-Bouverie, MVO, RN, who *d* 1951 (*see* E Radnor). *Residence* – The Lodge, Beaulieu, Brockenhurst, Hants SO42 7YB.

PREDECESSORS – **(1)** HENRY JOHN Douglas-Scott-Montagu, 2nd son of 5th Duke of Buccleuch; *b* 1832; MP for Selkirkshire (*C*) 1861-8, and for S Hampshire 1868-84; sometime Official Verderer of the New Forest; *cr Baron of Beaulieu* (peerage of United Kingdom) 1885: *m* 1865, Hon Cecily Susan Stuart-Wortley, who *d* 1915, sister of 1st Earl of Wharncliffe; *d* 1905; *s* by his el son **(2)** JOHN WALTER EDWARD, KCIE, CSI, 2nd Baron; *b* 1866; Founder *The Car Illustrated* and Editor, and other publications; a Member of Road Board; acted as a Member of War Aircraft Committee March to April 1916, and was Adviser on Mechanical Transport Ser to Govt of India during European War (Hon Brig-Gen); a Member of Mechanical Warfare Board; MP for Hants, New Forest Div (*C*)1892-1905; CSI 1916, KCIE 1919: *m* 1st, 1889, Lady Cecil Victoria Constance, who *d* 1919, el da of 9th Marquess of Lothian; 2ndly, 1920, Alice Pearl (who *m* 2ndly, 1936, Capt Hon Edward

Pleydell-Bouverie, MVO, RN, who *d* 1951), da of late Major Barrington Crake, Rifle Bde; *d* 1929; *s* by his son **(3)** EDWARD JOHN BARRINGTON, 3rd Baron and present peer.

Monteagle, Baron, title of Marquess of Sligo on Roll of HL.

MONTEAGLE OF BRANDON, BARON (Spring Rice) (Baron UK 1839)

Faith does not fear

GERALD SPRING RICE, 6th Baron; *b* 5 July 1926; *s* 1946; *ed* Harrow; Capt (retired) Irish Gds; One of HM's Body Guard of Hon Corps of Gentlemen-at-Arms since 1978; Member London Stock Exchange 1958-76, and of Lloyds since 1978: *m* 1949, Anne, da of late Col Guy James Brownlow, DSO, DL, Rifle Brig, of Ballywhite, Portaferry, co Down, and has issue.

Arms – Quarterly; 1st and 4th, quarterly, 1st and 4th, quarterly 1st and 4th, per pale indented argent and gules, 2nd and 3rd, azure, a lion rampant or; 2nd, or, on a chevron sable, between three mascles, as many mullets argent,; 3rd, paly of six argent and azure, a bend sable. **Crest** – A leopard's head affrontée, ducally crowned or. **Supporters** – Not on record.
Residence – 242A Fulham Rd, SW10. *Clubs* – Cavalry and Guards', Pratt's, Kildare Street and University.

SON LIVING

Hon CHARLES JAMES, *b* 24 Feb 1953: *m* 1987, Mary Teresa Glover, and has issue living, Helena Mairi, *b* 1987, — Charlotte Etain, *b* 1988, — Agnes Imogen, *b* 1991. *Residence* – 26 Malvern Rd, E8 3LP.

DAUGHTERS LIVING

Hon Elinor, *b* 1950: *m* 1974, Myles Clare Elliott, of 41 Ravenscourt Road, W6, and has issue living, Thomas Emerson, *b* 1977, — Nina Anne, *b* 1980, — Emma Clare, *b* 1983.
Hon Angela (twin) *b* 1950; resumed her maiden name 1982: *m* 1st, 1973 (*m diss* 1982), Christopher Richard Seton Sheppard; 2ndly, 1991, Peter Alan Kirby Ottewill of 24 Marney Rd, SW11 5EP, son of Maj W. K. Ottewill, of Rafford, Moray, and has issue living (by 1st *m*), Catherine Christy Seton, *b* 1976.
Hon Fiona, *b* 1957: *m* 1982, Andrew Louis Garber, of 88 Drakefield Rd, SW17, yst son of S. Garber, of St John's Wood, NW8, and has issue living, Rose Anne, *b* 1985, — Eliza Kate, *b* 1987, — Alice Finola, *b* 1991.

BROTHER LIVING

Hon Michael, *b* 1935; *ed* Harrow; late Lieut Irish Gds: *m* 1959, Fiona, yr da of late James Edward Kenneth Sprot, of Natal, and has issue living, Jonathan, *b* 1964, — Kerry (da), *b* 1962. *Residence* – Fosseway House, Nettleton Shrub, Chippenham, Wilts SN14 7NL. *Clubs* – Boodle's, Pratt's, Royal and Ancient Golf, Royal Ashdown Forest Golf and Swinley Forest Golf.

SISTER LIVING

Hon Joan, *b* 1928: *m* 1953, Michael Shears Payne, MC (Harvey, Bt (*cr* 1868) ext), of Scotlands Farm, Cockpole Green, nr Wargrave, Berks, and has issue living, Ashley Desmond, *b* 1956, — Karina, *b* 1954.

PREDECESSORS – **(1)** *Rt Hon* THOMAS Spring Rice; *b* 1790; MP for Limerick 1820-32, Cambridge 1832-9, Under-Sec for Home Depart 1827, Sec of Treasury 1830-4, Sec of State for War and Colonies 1834, Chancellor of the Exchequer 1835-9, and Comptroller Gen of the Exchequer 1835-65; *cr Baron Monteagle of Brandon* co Kerry (peerage of United Kingdom) 1839; *d* 1866; *s* by his grandson **(2)** THOMAS (el son of late Hon Stephen Edmond Spring Rice, el son of 1st Baron, by Ellen Mary, da of late Serjeant William Frere), 2nd Baron; *b* 1849: *m* 1875, Elizabeth, who *d* 1908, da of late Most Rev Rt Hon Samuel Butcher, DD, 90th Lord Bishop of Meath; *d* 1926; *s* by his son **(3)** THOMAS AUBREY, CMG, MVO, 3rd Baron, *b* 1886; in Diplo, Ser; *d* 1934; *s* by his uncle **(4)** FRANCIS (younger son of late Hon Stephen Edmund Spring Rice (*ante*)); *b* 1852; Cdr (ret) RN: *m* 1st, 1882, Elizabeth Ann, who *d* 1922, da of Sir Peter Fitzgerald, 1st Bt (19th Knight of Kerry); 2ndly, 1935, Julia Emma Isabella, who *d* 1936, da of Sir Peter George FitzGerald, 1st Bt (*ante*), and widow of Stephen Edward Spring Rice, CB; *d* 1937; *s* by his son **(5)** CHARLES, 5th Baron, *b* 1887: *m* 1925, Emilie de Kosenko (who *m* 2ndly, 1954, Col Courtenay Fergus Ochoncar Grey Forbes, late Coldstream Guards (*see* L Forbes, colls)), and *d* 1981), da of Mrs Edward Brooks, of New York, USA; *d* 1946; *s* by his son **(6)** GERALD, 6th Baron and present peer.

Montgomerie, Lord; son of Earl of Eglinton and Winton.

Montgomery, Earl of, see Earl of Pembroke and Montgomery.

MONTGOMERY OF ALAMEIN, VISCOUNT (Montgomery) (Viscount UK 1946)

DAVID BERNARD MONTGOMERY, CBE, 2nd Viscount; *b* 18 Aug 1928; *s* 1976; *ed* Winchester, and Trin Coll, Camb; late Lt RTR; a Councillor R Borough of Kensington and Chelsea 1974-78; Chm of Economic Affairs Cttee, Canning House 1973-75; a Dir, Yardley Internat Ltd 1963-74; Man Dir Terimar Services Ltd since 1974; Chm Baring Puma Fund since 1991; Editorial Adviser Vision Interamericana 1974-94; Dir Korn/Ferry Internat 1977-93, Northern Engr Industries 1981-87; Chm Antofagasta (Chili) & Bolivia Rlwy Co 1980-82, and Hispanic & Luso Brasilian Council 1978-80 (Pres 1987-94); Chm, Brasilian Chamber of Commerce in GB 1980-82, Pres Anglo-Argentine Soc 1977-87, Redgrave Theatre Trust 1978-89, Restaurateurs Assocn of GB 1982-90; Pres Centre for Internat Briefing (Farnham Castle) since 1985; CBE (Civil) 1975; Gran Oficial, Orden Bernardo O'Higgins (Chile) 1989; Gran Oficial, Orden Libertador San Martin (Argentina) 1992; Grande Oficial, Orden Nacional Cruzeiro do Sul (Brazil) 1993; Encomienda, Orden de Isabel la Catolica (Spain) 1993; Commander's Cross, Order of Merit (Germany) 1993: *m* 1st, 1953 (*m diss* 1967), Mary Raymond, yr da of late Sir Charles Connell; 2ndly, 1970, Tessa, da of late Lt-Gen Sir Frederick Arthur Montague Browning, GCVO, KBE, CB, DSO (by his late wife, Dame Daphne du Maurier, DBE), and formerly wife of late Maj Peter P. J. de Zulueta, Welsh Gds, and has issue by 1st *m*.

𝕬rms – Azure, two lions passant guardant between three fleurs-de-lys, two in chief and one in base, and two trefoils in fesse all or. 𝕮rest – Issuant from a crescent argent an arm embowed in armour, the hand grasping a broken tilting spear in bend sinister, the head pendent proper. 𝕾upporters – *Dexter*, a Knight in chain armour and surcoat resting his exterior hand on his sword; *sinister*, a soldier in battle dress all propr.
Residence – 54 Cadogan Square, SW1 0JW. *Clubs* – Canning, Garrick, Royal Fowey Yacht.

SON LIVING *(By 1st marriage)*

Hon HENRY DAVID (Bridge House, Combe, nr Presteigne, Powys) *b* 2 April 1954: *m* 1980, Caroline J., da of late Richard Odey, of Hotham Hall, York, and has issue living, Alexa Maud, *b* 1984, — Flora Veronica, *b* 1988, — Phoebe Matilda, *b* 1990.

DAUGHTER LIVING *(By 1st marriage)*

Hon Arabella Clare, *b* 1956: *m* 1982, Jeremy Hugh Stuart-Smith, of Pie Corner, Bedmond, Herts, and has had issue (*see* E Verulam, colls).

PREDECESSOR – (1) *Field Marshal Sir* BERNARD LAW Montgomery, KG, GCB, DSO, son of late Rt Rev Henry Hutchinson Montgomery, KCMG, DD, Preb of St Paul's and Prelate of Order of St Michael and St George, of New Park, Morville, co Donegal; *b* 1887; GOC-in-C 8th Army 1942-43, GOC Allied Army in UK 1944, and 21st Army Group 1944-45; C-in-C BAOR 1945-46; CIGS 1946-48; Chm of W Europe C-in-C Cttee 1948-51; Dep Supreme Cdr, Allied Powers in Europe 1951-58; *cr Viscount Montgomery of Alamein*, of Hindhead, co Surrey (peerage of UK) 1946: *m* 1927, Elizabeth, who *d* 1937, da of late Robert Thompson Hobart, ICS, and widow of Capt Oswald Armitage Carver; *d* 1976; *s* by his only son (2) DAVID BERNARD, CBE, 2nd Viscount, and present peer.

MONTROSE, DUKE OF (Graham) (Duke S 1707, Bt S 1625)

Forget not

JAMES GRAHAM, 8th Duke, and 12th Baronet; *b* 6 April 1935; *s* 1992; *ed* Loretto; Hereditary Sheriff of co Dunbarton; Member Queen's Body Guard for Scotland (Royal Company of Archers) since 1965, Brig since 1976; Member Council Scottish Nat Farmers' Union 1981-86 and 1987-90; OStJ 1978: *m* 1970, Catherine Elizabeth MacDonnell, yst da of late Capt Norman Andrew Thompson Young, Queen's Own Cameron Highlanders of Canada, of Ottawa, and has issue.

Arms – Quarterly: 1st and 4th or, on a chief sable three escallops of the field, *Graham*; 2nd and 3rd argent, three roses gules, barbed and seeded proper, *Montrose*. **Crest** – An Eagle, wings hovering or, preying on a stork on its back proper. **Supporters** – Two storks argent, beaked and membered gules.
Seat – Auchmar, Drymen, Glasgow G63 0AG. *Clubs* – Royal Scottish Pipers' Soc, and Royal Highland Agricultural.

SONS LIVING

JAMES ALEXANDER NORMAN (*Marquess of Graham*), *b* 16 Aug 1973; *ed* Eton, and Edinburgh Univ. *Lord* Ronald John Christopher, *b* 1975; *ed* Eton.

DAUGHTER LIVING

Lady Hermione Elizabeth, *b* 1971; *ed* —Coll, Oxford.

HALF-BROTHERS LIVING

Lord Donald Alasdair, *b* 1956; *ed* St Andrew's Coll, Grahamstown, St Andrews Univ (BSc), and INSEAD (MBA): *m* 1981, his 2nd cousin, Bride Donalda Elspeth, yst da of Maj Allan John Cameron, of Allangrange, Ross and Cromarty (*see* D Montrose, 1976 Edn), and has had issue, Alasdair John Cameron, *b* 1986, *d* 1988, — Caitriana Mary Alice, *b* 1984, — Violet Elizabeth Helen, *b* 1992, — Jennie Alexandra Cameron, *b* 1993. *Residence* – Nether Tillyrie, Milnathort, Kinross-shire KY13 7RW.
Lord Calum Ian, *b* 1958; *ed* St Andrew's Coll, Grahamstown, Cape Town Univ (BSc), and INSEAD (MBA): *m* 1991, Catherine Beatrice, yst da of John Peter Fraser-Mackenzie (*see* Scott, Bt, *cr* 1913). *Address* – Montrose Estate, Drymen, Glasgow G63 0BQ.

SISTER LIVING

Lady Fiona Mary, *b* 1932: *m* 1966, Peter Alexander O'Brien Hannon, 2nd son of late Ven Archdeacon Gordon Hannon, of Ardreigh House, Cultra, co Down, and has issue living, Catherine Mary, *b* 1968: *m* 1991, Mark Tremayne Boobbyer (*see* B Rennell), — Veronica Maeve, *b* 1971: *m* 1992, Jasper E. Bark, son of Roy Bark, of Station Rd, Dalton-in-Furness, Cumbria. *Residence* – The Fort House, Dundooan, Coleraine, co Derry BT52 2PX.

HALF-SISTERS LIVING

Lady Cairistiona Anne (Kirstie), *b* 1955; *ed* Ruskin Sch of Fine Art: *m* 1982, Philip Patrick Saggers, son of Gordon F. Saggers, of PO Box 43, Lockhart 2656, NSW, Australia, and has issue living, Susanna Mary, *b* 1984, — Marina Lilias, *b* 1986, — Georgina Frances, *b* 1989. *Residence* – 42 Cook St, Randwick, NSW 2031, Australia.
Lady Lilias Catriona Maighearad, *b* 1960; *ed* St Andrews Univ (BSc): *m* 1990, Jonathan Dillon Bell, and has issue (*see* Borthwick, Bt, colls). *Address* – c/o Ngaiana, Masterton, New Zealand.

AUNTS LIVING (*daughters of 6th Duke*)

Lady Mary Helen Alma, *b* 1909: *m* 1st, 1931, Maj John Perceval Townshend Boscawen, MBE, Gren Gds, who *d* 1972 (*see* V Falmouth, colls); 2ndly, 1975, Brig Leslie Colville Dunn, TD, DL, who *d* 1990. *Residence* – 8 Wheatfield Rd, Ayr.
Lady Jean Sybil Violet, *b* 1920; DL Ayr and Arran Dist: *m* 1947 (*m diss* 1957), Col John Patrick Ilbert Fforde, CBE, and *d* 1993, and has issue living, Charles John Graham, *b* 1948. *Residence* – Strabane, Brodick, Isle of Arran.

WIDOW LIVING OF SEVENTH DUKE

SUSAN MARY JOCELYN (*Dowager Duchess of Montrose*), da of late Dr John Mervyn Semple, of Gilgil, Kenya, and widow of Michael Raleigh Gibbs, of Nakuru, Kenya: *m* 1952, as his 2nd wife, the 7th Duke, who *d* 1992. *Residence* – Nether Tillyrie, Milnathort, Kinross-shire KY13 7RW.

COLLATERAL BRANCHES LIVING

Issue of late Brig Lord (Douglas) Malise Graham, 2nd son of 5th Duke, *b* 1883, *d* 1974: *m* 1919, Hon Rachael Mary Holland, who *d* 1977, da of 2nd Viscount Knutsford:—
Ivar Malise (The Glen, Coombe Kea, Truro, Cornwall), *b* 1920; *ed* Eton, and Trin Coll, Camb (MA); Archives Dip (London): *m* 1958 (*m diss* 1973), Isabel Mary, da of late C. B. Ewart, of Limpsfield Surrey, and formerly wife of A. W. Carpenter, and has issue living, Alastair David, *b* 1959, — Lucy Helen, *b* 1963. —— Euan Douglas, CB, *b* 1924; *ed* Eton, and Ch Ch, Oxford (MA); CB 1985: *m* 1st, 1954 (*m diss* 1970), Pauline Laetitia, da of late Hon David Francis Tennant (*see* B Glenconner, colls), and formerly wife of Capt Julian Lane Fox-Pitt-Rivers (*see* By Forster, 1980 Edn); 2ndly, 1972, Caroline Esther, da of Sheriff Kenneth W. B. Middleton of Cobblers Cottage, Ledwell, Oxon, and has issue living (by 1st *m*), Andrew Douglas (adopted son), *b* 1964, — (by 2nd *m*), Sarah Caroline, *b* 1973, — Alexandra Katherine, *b* 1976.

Issue of late Lord Alastair Mungo Graham, Capt RN, yst son of 5th Duke, *b* 1886, *d* 1976: *m* 1st 1916, Lady Meriel Olivia Bathurst, who *d* 1936, da of 7th Earl Bathurst; 2ndly, 1944, Sheelagh Violet Edgeworth, who *d* 1985, da of late Essex Edgeworth Reade (B Templemore colls):—
(By 1st *m*) Ian James (Chantry Farm, Campsey Ash, Suffolk), *b* 1923; *ed* Winchester, and Trin Coll, Dublin (BA): Dir, Maya Corpus Program, Peabody Museum, Harvard Univ, Camb, Mass, USA. —— Robin Angus, *b* 1926. —— Lilias Violet, *b* 1917.

—— Margaret Christina, *b* 1919: *m* 1960, Thomas Colin Ernest Campbell-Preston, MC, TD, of 1 Bishop's Way, Stradbroke, Suffolk IP21 5JR, and has an adopted son, Patrick, *b* 1964; *ed* Eton, and Trin Coll, Camb.

PREDECESSORS – (1) PATRICK Graham, on of the Lords of the Regency during the minority of James II, was *cr Lord Graham* (peerage of Scotland) 1445; *d* about 1465; *s* by his son (2) WILLIAM, 2nd Lord; *d* 1472; *s* by his son (3) WILLIAM, 3rd Lord; fought with gallantry at the battle of Sauchyburn 1488; *cr Earl of Montrose* 1505; fell at Flodden 1513; *s* by his son (4) WILLIAM, 2nd Earl; *d* 1571; *s* by his grandson (5) JOHN, 3rd Earl; was Chancellor of Scotland 1599-1604, and Viceroy of Scotland 1604-8; *d* 1608, having *m* 1563, Hon Jean Drummond, and had three sons of whom the 2nd, William, was *cr* a *Baronet* 1625, of Braco while to the Earldom *s* the el son (6) JOHN, 4th Earl; was Pres of the Council in Scotland 1626; *s* by his son (7) JAMES, 5th Earl; having served with the Covenanters 1638-40, espoused the royal cause, and was in 1644 *cr Marquess of Montrose* (peerage of Scotland), and appointed Capt-Gen and Com-in-Ch of all the forces to be raised in Scotland for the King's service; having gained a number of brilliant victories over the Parliamentarians, he was surprised and totally defeated at Philiphaugh 13 Sept 1645; he then left Scotland, and after the execution of the King joined Charles II at the Hague, from whence in 1650 he returned, and having raised a small force was defeatd at Strachan 17 April 1650, and being afterwards taken prisoner was on 20 May following sentenced by the Scottish Parliament to be hanged, &c, which sentence was carried out on the following day and his quartered remains after being exposed were interred beneath the gallows, from whence however they were removed at the Restoration and buried in state in the aisle of the Cathedral Church of St Giles, 14 May 1661; *s* by his son (8) JAMES, PC, 2nd Marquess, who was immediately after the return of Charles II, restored to his honours and estates; appointed an Extraordinary Lord of Session 1668; *s* by his son (9) JAMES 3rd Marquess; was Pres of the Guards and Pres of the Council; *d* 1684; *s* by his son (10) JAMES, KG, PC, 4th Marquess; Lord Pres of the Council in Scotland 1706, a Representative Peer 1707-27, Keeper of the Privy Seal 1709-13, Principal Sec of State to George I, and Keeper of the Great Seal of Scotland 1716-33; resigned the patent Marquess of Montrose, and has a new Charter granted 1706 with various limitations, *cr Lord Aberuthven, Mugdock and Fintrie, Viscount Dundaff, Earl of Kincardine, Marquess of Graham and Buchanan* and *Duke of Montrose* (Peerage of Scotland) 1707; *d* 1742; *s* by his son (11) WILLIAM, 2nd Duke, who had in 1731 *s* his brother David who had in 1722 been *cr Baron Graham* and *Earl Graham* (peerage of Great Britain), with remainder to his brothers; *d* 1790; *s* by his son (12) JAMES, KG, KT, PC, 3rd Duke; was successively MP for Richmond and Great Bedwin, a Lord of the Treasury, Paymaster of the Forces, Master of the Horse, Lord Justice Gen of Scotland, Lord-Lieut of cos Stirling and Dunbarton, Pres of Board of Trade, and Joint Postmaster Gen; *d* 1836; *s* by his son (13) JAMES, KT, 4th Duke; *b* 1799; sat as MP for Cambridge 1826-30, Lord Steward of the Household 1852, Chancellor of the Duchy of Lancaster 1858-9, and Postmaster-Gen 1866: *m* 1836, Hon Caroline Agnes Beresford, who *d* 1894 (having *m* 2ndly, 1876, William Stuart Stirling-Crawford, who *d* 1883; 3rdly, 1888, Marcus Henry Milner), da of 2nd Baron Decies; *d* 1874; *s* by his son (14) DOUGLAS BERESFORD MALISE RONALD, KT, 5th Duke; *b* 1852; Hon Brig-Gen and Lord-Lieut of co Stirling; Lord Clerk Register of Scotland 1890-1925, and Chancellor of the Order of the Thistle 1917-25; High Commr for Gen Assembly of Church of Scotland 1916: *m* 1876 *Dame* Violet Hermione, GBE, LLD, who *d* 1940, da of Sir Frederick Ulrick Graham, 3rd Bt, of Netherby, Cumbria; *d* 1925; *s* by his el son (15) JAMES, KT, CB, CVO, VD, LLD, 6th Duke; *b* 1878; S Africa 1901, attached to Naval Brig, European War 1914-19 with Auxiliary Naval Patrol; Lord-Lieut of co Bute 1920-53; sometime Assist Private Sec (unpaid) to Chancellor of the Exchequer (Rt Hon J. Austen Chamberlain, MP); Lord High Commr to Gen Assembly of Church of Scotland 1942 and 1943: *m* 1906, Lady Mary Louise Douglas-Hamilton, OBE, who *d* 1957, da of 12th Duke of Hamilton; *d* 1954; *s* by his el son (16) JAMES ANGUS, 7th Duke, *b* 1907; Min of Agric, Lands and Natural Resources, S Rhodesia 1962-65, of Agric, Rhodesia 1964-65, and External Affairs and Defence, Rhodesia 1966-68; Lt-Cmdr RNVR 1939-45 War: *m* 1st, 1930 (*m diss* 1950), Isobel Veronica, who *d* 1990, da of late Lt-Col Thomas Byrne Sellar, CMG, DSO; 2ndly, 1952, Susan Mary Jocelyn, da of late Dr John Mervyn Semple, of Gilgil, Kenya, and widow of Michael Raleigh Gibbs; *d* 1992; *s* by his eldest son (17) JAMES 8th Duke and present peer; also Marquess of Montrose, Marquess of Graham and Buchanan, Earl of Montrose, Earl of Kincardine, Earl of Graham, Viscount Dundaff, Lord Graham, and Lord Aberuthven, Mugdock and Fintrie.

Moore, Viscount; son of Earl of Drogheda.

MOORE OF LOWER MARSH, BARON (Moore) (Life Baron 1992)

JOHN EDWARD MICHAEL MOORE, PC, son of Edward Moore, of Brighton; *b* 26 Nov 1937; *ed* Licensed Victuallers' Sch, Slough, and LSE (BSc); late Royal Sussex Regt, Korea 1955-57; Member London Borough Council of Merton 1971-74, Vice-Chm Conservative Party 1975-79, Parly Under Sec for Energy 1979-83, Min of State, Economic Sec at the Treasury June-Oct 1983, Financial Sec 1983-86, Sec of State for Transport 1986-87, Health and Social Services, Social Security, 1988-89; Member of Lloyd's since 1978, Chm Dean Witter Internat Ltd 1975-79 (Dir 1968-79), Energy Saving Trust since 1992, Credit Suisse Asset Management Ltd since 1992, and Monitor Europe since 1992; Dir Swiss American Corporation since 1992, Monitor Inc since 1992; G. Tech since 1992, and Blue Circle Industries since 1993; Member Court of Governors, LSE since 1977 Member Advisory Boards of Sir Alexander Gibb & Ptnrs, and Marvin & Palmer Assocs Inc, Council Member Inst of Dirs; MP Croydon Central (*C*) Feb 1974-92; *cr* PC 1986, and *Baron Moore of Lower Marsh*, of Lower Marsh in the London Borough of Lambeth (Life Baron) 1992: *m* 1962, Sheila Sarah, da of Richard Tillotson, of Illinois, USA, and has issue.

Arms – Azure, a dolphin naiant argent between three bunches of grapes stalked and leaved gold. **Crest** – A griffin statant erect azure billety or and bezanty, beak, forelegs and wings also or, holding in the dexter foreclaw a double-warded key wards upward gold. **Supporters** – On either side a griffin statant erect azure, that to the dexter bezanty, that to the sinister billety or, the beak, forelegs and wings of each also or, the compartment comprising two grassy mounts with marshland between them all proper.

Address – c/o House of Lords, SW1.

SONS LIVING

Hon Martin, *b* 1970.
Hon Richard, *b* 1972.

DAUGHTER LIVING

Hon Stephanie Jane, *b* 1968: *m* 1994, David Mortimer Man, son of William Mortimer Man (*see* Earldom of Jowitt).

MOORE OF WOLVERCOTE, BARON (Moore) (Life Baron 1986)

PHILIP BRIAN CECIL MOORE, GCB, GCVO, CMG, QSO, PC; *b* 6 April 1921, son of late Cecil Moore, ICS; *ed* Cheltenham Coll, and Brasenose Coll, Oxford; Prin Private Sec to First Lord of the Admiralty 1957-58, British Dep High Commr, Singapore 1961-65, Dir of Public Relations, Min of Defence, 1965-66, Assist Private Sec to HM 1966-72, Dep Private Sec 1972-77, Private Sec and Keeper of the Queen's Archives 1977-86; Permanent Lord in Waiting and Extra Equerry to HM The Queen; Chm Trustees King George VI and Queen Elizabeth Foundation of St Catharine's since 1986; 1939-45 War as Fl-Lieut Bomber Comd RAF; *cr* CMG 1966, CB (Civil) 1973, KCB 1976, KCB 1980, GCVO 1983, GCB 1985, and *Baron Moore of Wolvercote*, of Wolvercote, City of Oxford (Life Baron) 1986: *m* 1945, Joan Ursula, da of Capt M. E. Greenop, DCLI, and has issue.

Arms – Gules on a fess between two lions passant guardant or three moorcocks sable crested gules. **Crest** – A moorcock proper gorged with a crown or holding in its dexter claw a quill pen proper. **Supporters** – *Dexter*, a wolf proper crowned or gorged with a collar argent fimbriated or thereon roses gules barbed and seeded proper and cross crosslets sable; *sinister*, a stag proper attired and unguled or crowned also or gorged with a collar argent fimbriated or thereon cross crosslets sable and roses gules barbed and seeded proper therefrom a chain reflexed behind the back ending in a ring gold, the compartment comprising a grassy mount growing therefrom on each side between a thistle and a shamrock both proper a rose gules stalk and leaves vert barbed and seeded to the front thereof on the dexter side a rugby football and similarly on the sinister side a cricket ball proper. **Motto** – Moribus Et Consilio.
Residence – Hampton Court Palace, E Molesey, Surrey. *Clubs* – Athenaeum and MCC.

DAUGHTERS LIVING

Hon Sally Jane, *b* 1949: *m* 1980 (*m diss* 1984), Richard Gerald Grindon Leachman, and has issue living, Lucinda, *b* 1980.
Residence – 20 Marlborough Buildings, Bath, Avon.
Hon Jill Georgina, *b* 1951: *m* 1971 (*m diss* 1990), Peter Gabriel, and has issue living, Anna Marie, *b* 1974, — Melanie, *b* 1976.

MORAN, BARON (Wilson) (Baron UK 1943)

(RICHARD) JOHN McMORAN WILSON, KCMG, 2nd Baron; *b* 22 Sept 1924; *s* 1977; *ed* Eton, and King's Coll, Camb; Sub-Lt RNVR in 1939-45 War; 3rd Sec, British Embassy, Ankara 1948-50, Tel Aviv 1950-53, 2nd Sec, Rio de Janeiro 1953-56, 1st Sec FO 1956-59, Washington 1959-61, FO 1961-65, Counsellor British Embassy, S Africa 1965-68, and Head of W Africa Deptm FCO 1968-73; Ambassador to Chad 1970-73, Hungary 1973-76, and Portugal 1976-81; UK High Commr to Canada 1981-84; Chm Wildlife and Countryside Link, Regional Fisheries Advisory Cttee, Welsh Region, NRA, and Welsh Salmon and Trout Anglers' Association; Pres Radnorshire Wildlife Trust; Vice-Chm Atlantic Salmon Trust; author of *A Life of Sir Henry Campbell-Bannerman* 1973, and *Fairfax* 1985; KCMG 1981: *m* 1949, Shirley Rowntree, da of George James Harris, MC, of Bossall Hall, York, and has issue.
Address – c/o House of Lords, SW1.

SONS LIVING

Hon JAMES McMORAN (65 Upland Rd, Brookline, Mass 02146, USA), *b* 6 Aug 1952; *ed* Eton, and Trin Coll, Camb: *m* 1980, *Hon* (Mary) Jane Hepburne-Scott, yst da of 10th Lord Polwarth and has issue living, David Andrew McMoran, *b* 6 Nov 1990, — Alistair Thomas Hay, *b* 1993.
Hon William Edward Alexander, *b* 1956; *ed* Eton, and Inns of Court Sch of Law; barrister: *m* 1989, Juliette E. C., da of Maj Mungo Walker, of Empshott, Hants (*see* Walker, Bt, *cr* 1868, colls).

DAUGHTER LIVING

Hon Juliet, *b* 1950; *ed* St Mary's Sch, Calne, and Newnham Coll, Camb: *m* 1972, Hon Jeffrey Richard de Corban Evans, of 5 Campden House Court, 42 Gloucester Walk, W8, and has issue (*see* B Mountevans).

BROTHER LIVING

Hon Geoffrey Hazlitt, CVO, *b* 1929; *ed* Eton, and King's Coll, Camb (BA); FCA; late Roy Horse Guards; Chm of Southern Electric plc, Dep Chm of Johnson Matthey plc, Dir Blue Circle Industries and Drayton English and International Trust, Chm of Delta plc 1982-94, formerly Pres British Electrotechnical and Allied Manufacturers Association, Dep Pres Engineering Employers Federation, Chm 100 Group of Finance Directors and Chm of W Midlands and Wales Region of Nat Westminster Bank; CVO 1989: *m* 1955 (Barbara) Jane, only da of late W. E. H. Hebblethwaite, of Itchen Stoke, Alresford, Hants, and has issue living, Nicholas Charles Hazlitt, *b* 1957, — Hugo William Hazlitt, *b* 1963, — and two adopted das, Laura Jane, *b* 1966, — Jessica Harriet, *b* 1967: *m* 1992, Simon C. Newson, yr son of J. A. Newson, of Bury, W Sussex. *Address* – c/o Southern Electric plc, Littlewick Green, Maidenhead, Berks SL6 3QB.

PREDECESSOR – **(1)** CHARLES McMORAN Wilson, MC, MD, FRCP, son of John Forsythe Wilson, MD; *b* 1882; Pres Royal Coll of Physicians, London 1941-50; Consulting Physician to St Mary's Hosp; *cr* Knt 1938, and *Baron Moran*, of Manton, co Wilts (peerage of UK) 1943: *m* 1919, Dorothy, MBE, who *d* 1983, da of Samuel Felix Dufton, DSc; *d* 1977; *s* by his el son **(2)** (RICHARD) JOHN McMORAN, 2nd Baron and present peer.

MORAY, EARL OF (Stuart) (Earl S 1562)
(Title pronounced "Murry")

Salvation through Christ the Redeemer

DOUGLAS JOHN MORAY STUART, 20th Earl; *b* 13 Feb 1928; *s* 1974; *ed* Hilton Coll Natal and Trin Coll, Camb (BA); a JP of Perthshire (1968): *m* 1964, Lady Malvina Dorothea Murray, el da of 7th Earl Mansfield and Mansfield, and has issue.

Arms – Quarterly: 1st and 4th the royal arms of Scotland (a lion rampant within a double tressure flory counterflory gules) surrounded with a bordure componée argent and azure, *Moray*; 2nd or, a fesse checky azure and argent, *Stewart of Doune*; 3rd or, three cushions within a double tressure flory counterflory gules, *Randolph, Earl of Moray*. **Crest** – A pelican in her piety, proper. **Supporters** – Two grey-hounds argent, collared gules.
Residences – Doune Park, Doune, Perthshire; Darnaway Castle, Forres, Morayshire. *Club* – New (Edinburgh).

SON LIVING

JOHN DOUGLAS (*Lord Doune*), *b* 29 Aug 1966.

DAUGHTER LIVING

Lady Louisa Helena, *b* 1968.

BROTHERS LIVING

Hon Charles Rodney Stanford (6 Lynch Rd, Farnham, Surrey; Relugas Mill, Dunphail, Moray), *b* 1933; *ed* Stowe, and McGill Univ, Montreal (B Com 1958); late 2nd Lt The Queen's Bays: *m* 1st, 1961 (*m diss* 1986), Sasha A., el da of Lt-Col R. G. Lewis of The Old Rectory, Upper Swell, Stow on the Wold; 2ndly, 1986, Frauke, only da of Hans Stender, of Marne, Schleswig-Holstein, and has issue living (by 1st *m*), James Benjamin, *b* 1962, — Justin Nicholas Moray, *b* 1964, — Duncan Douglas, *b* 1967.
Hon James Wallace Wilson (twin), *b* 1933; *ed* Stowe, and McGill Univ, Montreal (BA 1958), late 2nd Lieut 13/18th Hussars: *m* 1958, Jane-Scott, only da of Group Capt Henry Gordon Richards, OBE, of Louisville, Kentucky, USA, and has issue living, Elizabeth May, *b* 1967; *ed* Westminster, and Yale Univ. *Residences* – Dunphail, Moray; 67 Cloncurry St, SW6. *Clubs* – Atlantic Cavalry (Montreal), Highland (Inverness).

DAUGHTERS LIVING OF EIGHTEENTH EARL

Lady Mary Anne, *b* 1926: *m* 1st, 1945 (*m diss* 1960), Leonard Byng, ARBS, who *d* 1974; 2ndly, 1961, Col John Bovill Denham, OBE, late Scots Gds, who *d* 1990, only son of late Sir Edward Brandis Denham, GCMG, KBE, and has issue living, (by 1st *m*) Rupert Wingfield, *b* 1946; *ed* Harrow, and New Coll, Oxford: *m* 1987, Mrs Francesca Stewart-Liberty, — Francis John Stuart (Jordan Manor, Widecombe-in-the-Moor, Newton Abbot, Devon TQ13 7PN), *b* 1956; *ed* Eton: *m* 1986, Caroline Margaret, only da of late G. E. Stevenson, of Lymington, Hants, and has issue living, Toby James Findhorn *b* 1986, Maximillian Rupert Stuart *b* 1989 — Charlotte Victoria, *b* 1947: *m* 1991, Julian L. C. de Wette; — Elizabeth, *b* 1949: *m* 1st, 1970, George Sulimirski, yst son of late Prof Tadeusz Sulimirski, of 26 Bishops Mansions, Bishops Park Rd, SW6; 2ndly, 1983, Comte Hervé le Bault de la Morinière, of Knoyle Place, East Knoyle, Salisbury, Wilts SP3 6AF, son of Comte Jean le Bault de la Morinière, and has issue living (by 2nd *m*), Louis Jean Victor *b* 1987, John Hervé *b* 1990, Camilla *b* 1985, — Lucy Anne, *b* 1954: *m* 1st, 1975 (*m diss* 1984), Isidore Brandel; 2ndly, 1990, Francis Robin Christopher Stickney, of Culditch House, Gittisham, Honiton, Devon EX14 0AE, only son of Richard Currier Stickney, and has issue living (by 1st *m*), Lara Rebecca *b* 1977, — (by 2nd *m*), Charles Edward, *b* 1966; *ed* Harrow, and Univ of Kent at Canterbury, — Harriet, *b* 1963. *Residence* – Crabbs Cottage, Gittisham, Honiton, Devon EX14 0AE.
Lady Sarah Gray (*Lady Sarah Stuart*), *b* 1928: *m* 1947 (*m diss* 1977), 4th Baron Hillingdon, who *d* 1978. *Residence* – 62 Pembridge Villas, W11 3ET.
Lady Arabella (*Lady Arabella Stuart*), *b* 1934; resumed the surname of Stuart 1983: *m* 1956 (*m diss* 1981), (Charles) Mark Edward Boxer, cartoonist and publisher, who *d* 1988, and has issue living, Charles Stephen, *b* 1961: *m* 1984, Katie, da of Peter Forshall, — Henrietta Sophia, *b* 1958. *Residence* – 44 Elm Park Rd, SW3 6AX.

WIDOW LIVING OF EIGHTEENTH EARL

BARBARA (*Dowager Countess of Moray*), da of John Archibald Murray, of New York: *m* 1924, the 18th Earl, who *d* 1943. *Residence* – 174 Ebury Street, SW1.

COLLATERAL BRANCHES LIVING

Issue of late Hon James Gray Stuart, CH, MVO, MC, PC (3rd son of 17th Earl) who was *cr Viscount Stuart of Findhorn* 1959 (see that title).

Grandchildren of late Charles Stuart, elder son of late John Alexander Stuart, of Carnock, great-great-grandson of late Archibald Stuart, 3rd son of 4th Earl:—
Issue of late Edgar Francis Stuart, *b* 1864, *d* 1940: *m* 1885, Margaret Jones, who *d* 1935:—
Herbert (Prestwick, Manchester), *b* 1893. —— Francis Gerald, *b* 1896. —— Alan Bruce, *b* 1897. —— Three das.

Granddaughter of late Richard Edgar Stuart, 6th son of late Charles Stuart (ante):—
Issue of late Charles William Stuart, *b* 1895, *d* 1921: *m* 1920, Bessie Lee, da of Walter W. Cook, of Milford, Utah, USA:—
Maxine Charles, *b* (*posthumous*) 1922: *m* 1944, Charles Maxwell Letz, and has issue living, Vicki Diane, *b* 1947.

Grandson of late James Stuart, 4th son of Charles Stuart (ante):—
Issue of late Charles Edward Stuart, *b* 1902, *d* 1982: *m* 1931, Blanche Wilma Bouvette, who *d* 1965:—
James Henry (RR3, Hewlett Rd, Kelowna, BC, Canada V1Y 7R2), *b* 1934: *m* 1955, Anna Frances Ebl, and has issue living, Charles Allan, *b* 1964, — Heather Marie, *b* 1961, — Sheila Christine, *b* 1962: *m* 1983, John Stephen Beliveau.

PREDECESSORS – **(1)** JAMES Stuart, natural son of James V by Margaret, da of 5th Lord Erskine (*de jure* 17th Earl of Mar), *cr Earl of Moray*, and *Lord Abernethy and Strathearn* (peerage of Scotland) 1562; was Regent of Scotland when Queen Mary surrendered her crown to her infant son James VI: *m* 1562, Lady Agnes Keith (who *d* 1588 having *m* 2ndly 1572, Colin Campbell, Lord Lorne, afterwards 6th Earl of Argyll), da of 3rd Earl of Marischal; was murdered by one of his foes, Hamilton of Bothwellhaugh 1570; *s* by his da **(2)** ELIZABETH *Countess of Moray*, who, in 1580, Sir James Stuart, who, in 1590 *s* his father as 2nd *Lord Doune* (see * infra); Sir James on his marriage assumed the earldom, and was known as the "Bonny Earl of Moray"; he was murdered in 1592 by the followers of the 6th Earl (afterwards 1st Marquess) of Huntly; the Countess *d* 1591; *s* by their son **(3)** JAMES, 3rd Earl: *m* 1607, Lady Anne Gordon, da of the instigator of his father's murder, he having previously, through the King's mediation, become reconciled to the Marquess of Huntly, obtained in 1611 from James VI a new investiture of the whole earldom of Moray to himself and his heirs male, and failing which to his brother Sir Francis and the heirs male of his body; *d* 1638; *s* by his son **(4)** JAMES, 4th Earl, who *s* as 3rd *Lord St Colme* 1642/3 (see † infra),: *m* 1627, Lady Margaret Home, who *d* 1683, da of 1st Earl of Home, *d* 1653; *s* by his son **(5)** ALEXANDER, KT, 5th Earl, *b* 1634; was Justice Gen 1675, Lord of the Treasury 1678, Sec of State and an Extraor Lord of Session 1680, and Commr to the Parliament of Scotland 1686: *m* 1658, Emilia, who *d* 1683, da of William Balfour, of Pitcullo; *d* 1700; *s* by his son **(6)** CHARLES, KT, 6th Earl, *b circa* 1660; *cr a Baronet* (Scotland) 1681: *m* 16—, Lady Anne Campbell, who *d* 1734, da of 9th Earl of Argyll, and widow of 4th Earl of Lauderdale; *dsp* 1735, when the baronetcy became ext; *s* by his brother **(7)** FRANCIS, 7th Earl, *b* 1673: *m* 1st, 1698, Elizabeth, da of Sir John Murray of Drumcairn; 2ndly, 1700, Hon Jean Elphinstone, who *d* 1739, da of 4th Lord Balmerinoch; *d* 1739; *s* by his son **(8)** JAMES, KT, 8th Earl, *b* 1708: *m* 1st, 1734, Grace, who *d* 1738, da of George Lockhart of Carnwath, and widow of 3rd Earl of Aboyne; 2ndly, 1740, Lady Margaret Wemyss, who *d* 1779, da of 4th Earl of Wemyss; *d* 1767; *s* by his son **(9)** FRANCIS, 9th Earl, *b* 1737; a Representative Peer 1784-96: *cr Baron Stuart of Castle Stuart* (peerage of Great Britain) 1796: *m* 1763, Hon Jane, who *d* 1786, el da of John, 12th Lord Gray; *d* 1810; *s* by his son **(10)** FRANCIS, KT, 10th Earl, *b* 1771; was Lord Lieut of Elgin: *m* 1st, 1795, Lucy, who *d* 1798, da of Gen John Scott, of Balcomie, co Fife; 2ndly, 1801, Margaret Jane, da of Sir Philip Ainslie, Knt, of Pilton, co Edinburgh; *d* 1848; *s* by his el son **(11)** FRANCIS, 11th Earl: *d* unmarried 1859; *s* by his brother **(12)** JOHN, 12th Earl; a Capt in the Army; *d* unmarried 1867; *s* by his half-brother **(13)** ARCHIBALD GEORGE, 13th Earl; a Lt-Col in the Army; *d* 1872; *s* by his brother **(14)** GEORGE PHILIP, 14th Earl, *b* 1816; *s* to the *Lordship of Gray* (*cr* 1444-5) under special remainder 1878; *d* 1895, when the Lordship of Gray (see that title) was adjudged by the Committee for Privileges of the House of Lords to Eveleen, who *d* 1918, wife of late James Maclaren Smith (who received Roy Licence 1897, to assume for himself and wife the additional surname and arms of Gray), and da of late Lady Jane Pounden, da of Francis, 10th Earl of Moray (ante), and the peerages of 1561, 1581, 1611, and 1796, devolved on his cousin **(15)** EDMUND ARCHIBALD, 15th Earl; *b* 1840; assumed in 1878 the additional surname and arms of Gray, on succeeding to the estates of Margaret, Lady Gray, which he discontinued on his succession to the Earldom: *m* 1877, Anna Mary, who *d* 1915, da of late Rev George J. Collinson, of Clapham; *d* 1901; *s* by his brother **(16)** FRANCIS JAMES, 16th Earl, *b* 1842; assumed in 1895, the additional surname and arms of Gray, which he discontinued in succeeding to the Earldom: *m* 1879, Gertrude Floyer, who *d* 1928, da of late Rev Francis Smith; *d* 1909; *s* by his brother **(17)** MORTON GARY, 17th Earl; assumed the additional surname and arms of Gray on succeeding to the Gray and Kinfauns estates 1901 (relinquished on succession to the title): *m* 1890, Edith Douglas, who *d* 1945, da of Rear-Adm George Palmer; *d* 1930; *s* by his son **(18)** FRANCIS DOUGLAS, MC, 18th Earl; *b* 1892; Lord-Lieut of Morayshire 1935-43; European War 1914-18 as Capt Scottish Horse and RFC (wounded MC): *m* 1924, Barbara da of J. Archibald Murray, of New York; *d* 1943; *s* by his brother **(19)** (ARCHIBALD) JOHN MORTON, 19th Earl: *m* 1922, Mabel Helen Maud, who *d* 1968, da of Ben Wilson, of Battlefields, Zimbabwe; *d* 1974; *s* by his el son **(20)** DOUGLAS JOHN MORAY, 20th Earl and present peer; also Lord Abernethy and Strathearn, Lord Doune, Lord St Colme, and Baron Stuart of Castle Stuart.

Sir JAMES Stuart, of Doune, co Perth was *cr Lord Doune* (peerage of Scotland) 1581, with remainder to his heirs male whatsoever (a charter in confirmation 1588 gave a novodamus of the same with remainder to his heirs male whatsoever bearing the name and arms of Stuart); Extraor Lord of Session, Scotland 1584-6: *m* 1564, Lady Margaret Campbell, who *d* 1592, da of 4th Earl of Argyll; *d* 1590; *s* by his son **(2)** JAMES, 2nd Lord, but styled by courtesy Earl of Moray in right of his wife (see ante).

†HENRY Stuart, yr son of 1st Lord Doune (ante) was *cr Lord St Colme* (peerage of Scotland) 1611 with remainder to his heirs male and assigns whatsoever: *m* 1603, Lady Jean Stuart, (who *d* 1623, having *m* 2ndly, 16—, Nichol Bellenden), da of co-heir of 5th Earl of Atholl; *d* 1612; *s* by his son **(2)** JAMES, *b* 16—; Col in Swedish Ser; *d* 1642/3; *s* by his kinsman **(3)** JAMES, 4th Earl of Moray (see ante).

Moreton, Lord; son of Earl of Ducie.

MORLEY, EARL OF (Parker) (Earl UK 1815)

JOHN ST AUBYN PARKER, 6th Earl; *b* 29 May 1923; *ed* Eton; *s* 1962; Lt-Col (ret) R Fus; NW Europe 1944-45, and Palestine 1945-46, with KRRC, transferred R Fus 1947, Korea 1952-53, Middle East 1953-55, and 56; Comdg 1st Bn R Fus 1965-67; a JP for Plymouth, and a DL for Devon; Vice Lord Lieut of Devon 1978-82, since when Lord Lieut; Pres of Plymouth Incorporated Chamber of Trade and Commerce, since 1970, of West Country Tourist Board 1971-89, and Fedn of Chamber of Commerce and Traders Assocns, Cornwall 1972-79, Chm of Farm Industries Ltd, Truro 1970-85, a Member of Devon and Cornwall Cttee of National Trust 1969-84; Member of Governing Body of Plymouth Polytechnic 1975-82 (Chm 1977-82); Chm Plymouth Sound Ltd since 1974; a Gov of Seale-Hayne Agric Coll 1973-93: *m* 1955, Johanna Katherine, da of Sir John Molesworth-St Aubyn, 14th Bt, and has issue.

Arms – Sable, a buck's head cabossed, between two flaunches, argent. **Crest** – A cubit arm couped below the elbow, the sleeve azure, cuffed and slashed argent, the hand grasping a stag's attire gules. **Supporters** – *Dexter*, a stag argent, collared or, pendant from the collar a shield vert, charged with a horse's head, couped argent, bridled or, *sinister*, a greyhound sable, collared or, pendent from the collar a shield gules, charged with a ducal coronet or.
Seat – Saltram, Plympton, Devon. *Residence* – Pound House, Yelverton, S Devon.

Reward is sure to the faithful

FIDELI CERTA MERCES

SON LIVING

MARK LIONEL (*Viscount Boringdon*), *b* 22 Aug 1956; *ed* Eton; Lt R Green Jackets: *m* 1983, Carolyn Jill, da of Donald McVicar of Meols, Wirral, Cheshire, and has issue:—

DAUGHTERS LIVING—*Hon* Alexandra, *b* 1985, — *Hon* Olivia, 1987, — *Hon* Helena Georgia, *b* 1991.

DAUGHTER LIVING

Lady Venetia Katherine, *b* 1960.

BROTHERS LIVING (*Raised to the rank of an Earl's sons* 1963)

Hon Robin Michael (Saltram, Plympton, Devon), *b* 1925; *ed* Eton; Brig KRRC and RGJ (ret); Palestine 1946-48 (despatches) comdg 2nd Bn RGJ 1967-69.
Hon Nigel Geoffrey, *b* 1931; *ed* Eton, and Trin Coll, Camb; late Grenadier Guards; with Shell Petroleum Co, Ltd 1955-91: *m* 1965, Georgina Jane, el da of Sir Thomas Gordon Devitt, 2nd Bt (*cr* 1916), and has issue living, Edward Geoffrey, *b* 1967; *ed* Eton, and Brasenose Coll, Oxford: *m* 1992, Alice Victoria, da of Thomas Elliott, of Ivy House, Slawston, Leics, — Theresa Hilaria, *b* 1966; *ed* Homerton Coll, Camb: *m* 1994, Simon Maurice William Latham, eldest son of Robert Sidney Latham, of The Old Granary, Reigate, Surrey. *Residence* – Combe Lane Farm, Wormley, Godalming, Surrey.

PREDECESSORS – **(1)** JOHN Parker, MP for Devonshire 1762-84; *cr Baron Boringdon*, of Boringdon, co Devon (peerage of Great Britain) 1784; *d* 1788; *s* by his son **(2)** JOHN, 2nd Baron; *cr Viscount Boringdon* and *Earl of Morley* (Peerage of United Kingdom) 1815; *d* 1840; *s* by his son **(3)** EDMUND, 2nd Earl; *b* 1810: *m* 1842, Harriet Sophia, who *d* 1897, da of Montagu Edmund Parker, of Whiteway, Devon, and widow of William Coryton, of Pentillie Castle, Cornwall; *d* 1864; *s* by his son **(4)** ALBERT EDMUND, PC, 3rd Earl; *b* 1843; as Lord-in-Waiting to HM Queen Victoria 1868-74, Under-Sec for War 1880-85, First Commr of Works 1886, and Chm of Committees and Dep Speaker of House of Lords 1889-1905; *m* 1876, Margaret, who *d* 1908, da of late Robert S. Holford (Lindsay, Bt) of Westonbirt, Gloucestershire; *d* 1905; *s* by his son **(5)** EDMUND ROBERT, 4th Earl; *b* 1877; sometime Capt TF; *d* 1951; *s* by his brother **(6)** MONTAGU BROWNLOW, 5th Earl; *b* 1878; Capt Grenadier Guards; *d* 1962; *s* by his nephew **(7)** JOHN ST AUBYN (el son of late Hon John Holford Parker, by his wife, Hon Marjory Katherine Elizabeth Alexandra St Aubyn, who *d* 1987, da of 2nd Baron St Levan, yst son of 3rd Earl), 6th Earl and present peer; also Viscount and Baron Boringdon.

Mornington, Earl of; grandson of Duke of Wellington.

Morpeth, Viscount; son of Earl of Carlisle.

MORRIS, BARON (Morris) (Baron UK 1918)

MICHAEL DAVID MORRIS, 3rd Baron; *b* 9 Dec 1937; *s* 1975; *ed* Downside: *m* 1st, 1959 (*m diss* 1962), Denise Eleanor, only da of Morley Richards; 2ndly, 1962 (*m diss* 1969), Jennifer, only da of Sq-Ldr Tristram Gilbert; 3rdly, 1980, Juliet Susan, da of Anthony Buckingham, and has issue by 2nd and 3rd *m*.

Arms – Barry wavy of eight argent and azure, two codfish naiant proper, on a chief of the second, a two-masted schooner in full sail, also proper. **Crest** – A caribou's head couped at the neck proper, charged on the neck with a trefoil or. **Supporters** – On either side a caribou charged on the shoulder with a trefoil or.

SONS LIVING (By 3rd marriage)

Hon THOMAS ANTHONY SALMON, *b* 2 July 1982.
Hon James, *b* 1983.

DAUGHTERS LIVING (By 2nd marriage)

Ann Maria (adopted da), *b* 1962.
Hon Michaela Mary, *b* 1965.

(By 3rd marriage)

Always faithful

Hon Lucy Juliet, *b* 1981.

BROTHER LIVING

Hon (Edward) Patrick (twin) (Dormer Cottage, Petham, Canterbury, Kent), *b* 1937; *ed* Downside: *m* 1963, Mary Beryl, el da of Lt-Col D. H. G. Thrush, of Freshwinds, S Canterbury Rd, Canterbury, Kent, and has issue living, Edward Patrick, *b* 1965, — Elizabeth Mary, *b* 1968.

SISTERS LIVING

Hon Aislinn Mary Katharine, *b* 1934; JP: *m* 1954, Capt Angus Jeremy Christopher Hildyard, DL, RA (ret), and has issue living, Nicholas Alexander Cyril (The Elms, Roos, Kingston upon Hull, E Yorks), *b* 1954; *ed* Westminster: *m* 1981, Philippa Clare, only da of Lt-Col Anthony Gillett, TD, DL, of Northfield House, Swanland, E Yorks, and has issue living, Christopher Charles D'Arcy *b* 1984, William George Alexander *b* 1987, — Charlotte (*Lady Tyrwhitt*), *b* 1958: *m* 1984, as his 2nd wife, Sir Reginald Thomas Newman Tyrwhitt, 3rd Bt, and has issue. *Residence* – Goxhill Hall, Barrow upon Humber, S Humberside. *Hon* Clodagh Mary, *b* 1936: *m* 1964, Lt-Col Thomas Hugh Francis Farrell, TD, DL, of 22 Wood Lane, Beverley, North Humberside, and has issue living, James Thomas Hugh, *b* 1966, — Sophia Mary, *b* 1965.

PREDECESSORS – (1) *Rt Hon Sir* EDWARD PATRICK Morris, KCMG, son of Edward Morris, of St John's Newfoundland; *b* 1858; Solicitor, Newfoundland 1884; Bar Newfoundland 1885, and a QC 1896; sat for St John's in Newfoundland Parliament 1885-1919; was a Member of Whiteway Cabinet 1889-97, Acting Attorney-Gen 1890-95, Attorney-Gen and Min of Justice of Newfoundland 1902-07, Prime Min of Newfoundland 1909-18, and a Member of British War Cabinet Feb 1916 to Jan 1918; a Member of Imperial Defence Cttee 1909-18; *cr Baron Morris*, of St John's in the Dominion of Newfoundland, and of City of Waterford (peerage of United Kingdom) 1918: *m* 1901, Isabel Langrishe, who *d* 1934, da of late Rev William Legallais; *d* 1935; *s* by his son (2) MICHAEL WILLIAM, 2nd Baron; *b* 1903; Bar Inner Temple 1925 (disbarred at own request); Solicitor 1931: *m* 1st, 1933 (*m diss* 1946), Jean Beatrice, who *d* 1989, el da of Lt-Col David Edward Maitland-Makgill-Crichton (E Lauderdale, colls); 2ndly, 1960, Mary, who *d* 1991, da of late Rev Alexander Reginald Langhorne, and formerly wife of Anthony Robert Agate, MRCS, LRCP; *d* 1975; *s* by his el son (3) MICHAEL DAVID, 3rd Baron and present peer.

MORRIS OF CASTLE MORRIS, BARON (Morris) (Life Baron 1990)

BRIAN ROBERT MORRIS, son of late Capt William Robert Morris, RN, of Cardiff; *b* 4 Dec 1930; *ed* Cardiff High Sch, and Worcester Coll, Oxford (MA, DPhil); Fellow Shakespeare Inst, Birmingham Univ 1956-58; Lecturer Reading Univ 1960-65, Sr Lecturer York Univ 1967-71, Prof of English Lit Sheffield Univ (also Dep Dean and Public Orator) 1971-80, Principal St David's Univ Coll, Lampeter 1980-91; Chm Museums and Galleries Commn 1985-90 (Member since 1975), Vice-Pres Council for Nat Parks since 1985, Museums Assocn since 1985, Welsh Advisory Cttee, British Council since 1983, and Anthony Panizzi Foundation since 1987; Member of Council, Poetry Soc since 1980, Member Nat Library of Wales 1981-91, and British Library Board 1980-91; Trustee Nat Portrait Gallery since 1977, and Nat Heritage Memorial Fund 1980-91; Gen Ed New Mermaid Dramatists since 1964, and New Arden Shakespeare 1974-82; author and poet; served 1st Batn Welch Regt 1949-51, and 4th Batn Welch Regt (TA) 1951-56; *cr Baron Morris of Castle Morris*, of St Dogmaels, co Dyfed (Life Baron) 1990: *m* 1955, Sandra Mary, da of late Percival Samuel James, and has issue.
Residence – The Old Hall, Foolow, Eyam, Derbys S30 1QR.

SON LIVING

Hon Christopher Justin Robert, *b* 1959.

DAUGHTER LIVING

Hon Lindsay Alison Mary, *b* 1957: *m* 19—,—Boxall.

MORRIS OF GRASMERE, BARONY OF (Morris) (Extinct 1990)

SON LIVING OF LIFE BARON

Hon (Charles) Christopher (Ladywood, White Moss, Ambleside, Cumbria LA22 9SF), *b* 1929: *m* 1951, Cynthia Prudence, da of late Sir (Alfred) Alan Lethbridge Parsons, KCIE, and has issue.

DAUGHTER LIVING OF LIFE BARON

Hon Heather Mary, *b* 1925: *m* 1st, 1946 (*m diss* 1972), Tom Berry Caldwell; 2ndly, 1972, Alfred G. Davey, of Coach House, Kirk Hammerton, York, and has issue (by 1st *m*).

MORRIS OF KENWOOD, BARON (Morris) (Baron UK 1950)

PHILIP GEOFFREY MORRIS, 2nd Baron; *b* 18 June 1928; *s* 1954; *ed* Loughborough Coll; late Flying Officer RAF; a JP for Inner London: *m* 1958, Hon Ruth Joan Gertrude Rahle Janner (a Member Gen Advisory Council IBA since 1987), da of late Baron Janner (Life Baron), and has issue.
Residence – Lawn Cottage, Orchard Rise, Kingston upon Thames, Surrey KT2 7EY.

SON LIVING

Hon JONATHAN DAVID, *b* 5 Aug 1968.

DAUGHTERS LIVING

Hon Diane Susan, *b* 1960, *ed* St Paul's Sch and Central Sch of Speech and Drama (Dip Stage Management): *m* 1981, Cary Haskell Zitcer of 2 Sidmouth Rd, NW2 5JX, and has issue living, Natasha Esther, *b* 1986, — Emily Margaret, *b* 1988.
Hon Caroline Harriet, *b* 1961.
Hon Linda Jane, *b* 1965: *m* 1991, Paul M. Gelernter, of 26A Leighton Gdns, NW10 3PT, son of David Gelernter, and of Mrs Jeanne Canning.

SISTER LIVING

Hon Hilary Zara, *b* 1932: *m* 1964, Ronald Graham Lewis, of Zaraz, Littlewick Green, Maidenhead, Berks.

PREDECESSOR – **(1)** HARRY Morris, son of late Jacob Morris; *b* 1893; was MP for Sheffield Central 1945-50 and for Sheffield Neepsend Feb-March 1950; *cr Baron Morris of Kenwood*, of Kenwood, City of Sheffield (peerage of United Kingdom) 1950: *m* 1924, Florence, who *d* 1982, da of Henry Isaacs, of Leeds; *d* 1954; *s* by his only son **(2)** PHILIP GEOFFREY, 2nd Baron and present peer.

MORRISON, BARON (Morrison) (Baron UK 1945)

DENNIS GLOSSOP MORRISON, 2nd Baron; *b* 21 June 1914; *s* 1953; *ed* Tottenham Co Sch: *m* 1st, 1940 (*m diss* 1958), Florence Alice Helena, da of late August Hennes, of Tottenham, N15; 2ndly, 1959 (*m diss* 1975), Joan Eleanor, da of late William R. Meech, of Acton, W3.
Residence – 7 Ullswater Av, Felixstowe, Suffolk.

PREDECESSOR – **(1)** *Rt Hon* ROBERT CRAIGMYLE Morrison, son of late James Morrison; *b* 1881; was a Town Councillor for Wood Green 1914-19, a co Councillor for Middlesex 1919-24, an Alderman of Tottenham 1935-53, a Member of Metropolitan Water Board 1938-47, Chm of Waste Food Board, Min of Supply 1940-49, a Lord-in-Waiting to HM 1947-8, and Parliamentary Sec to Min of Works 1948-51; sat as MP for N Div of Tottenham (*Lab*) 1922-31 and 1935-45; *cr Baron Morrison*, of Tottenham, co Middlesex (peerage of United Kingdom) 1945: *m* 1910, Grace, who *d* 1983, da of late Thomas Glossop; *d* 1953; *s* by his son **(2)** DENNIS GLOSSOP, 2nd Baron and present peer.

MORRISON OF LAMBETH, BARONY OF (Morrison) (Extinct 1965)

DAUGHTER LIVING OF LIFE BARON (*By 1st marriage*)

Hon Mary Joyce, *b* 1921: *m* 1st, 1941 (*m diss* 1948), Horace Williams (afterwards Hon Horace Williams), son of Baron Williams of Barnburgh (Life Baron); 2ndly, 1948, George Norman Mandelson, who *d* 1988. *Residence* – 12 Bigwood Road, NW11.

WIDOW LIVING OF LIFE BARON

EDITH (*Baroness Morrison of Lambeth*) (Hurstead House, Rochdale, Lancs), da of late John Meadowcroft, of Rochdale: *m* 1955, as his 2nd wife, Baron Morrison of Lambeth (Life Baron), who *d* 1965.

MORTON, EARL OF (Douglas) (Earl S 1458)

Held fast

JOHN CHARLES SHOLTO DOUGLAS, 21st Earl; *b* 19 March 1927; *s* 1976; Property Consultant, Ptnr Dalmahoy Farms, Chm Edinburgh Polo Club; Lord Lieut of W Lothian: *m* 1949, Mary Sheila, da of late Rev Canon John Stanley Gibbs, MC, of Didmarton House, Badminton, Glos, and has issue.

Arms – Quarterly: 1st and 4th argent, a man's heart gules, ensigned with an imperial crown or, on a chief azure, three mullets of the field, *Douglas*; 2nd and 3rd argent, three piles issuing from the chief gules, and in chief two mullets of the field, *Douglas of Lochleven*. Crest – A wild boar proper sticking in the cleft of an oak tree, fructed vert, with a lock holding the clefts of the tree together azure. Supporters – Two savages, wreathed round the temples and waist, and holding in the exterior hand a club reversed, all proper.
Residence – Dalmahoy, Kirknewton, Midlothian.

SONS LIVING

JOHN STEWART SHOLTO (*Lord Aberdour*- pronounced Aberdare) (Haggs Farm, Kirknewton, Midlothian), *b* 17 Jan 1952; Ptnr Dalmahoy Farms: *m* 1985, Amanda Kirsten, yr da of David John Macfarlane Mitchell, of Castle St, Kirkcudbright, and has issue:—

> SON LIVING— *Hon* John David Sholto (*Master of Aberdour*), *b* 28 May 1986.
> DAUGHTERS LIVING—*Hon* Katherine Florence, *b* 1989, — *Hon* Jennifer Mary, *b* 1991.

Hon (Charles) James Sholto, *b* 1954; Ptnr Dalmahoy Farms: *m* 1981, Anne, da of late William Gordon Morgan, of Neapuke, Waikato, NZ, and has issue living, James William Sholto, *b* 1984, — Rebecca Katherine, *b* 1982, — Jillian Rosamond Florence, *b* 1986.

DAUGHTER LIVING

Lady Mary Pamela, *b* 1950: *m* 1973, Richard Callander, of Saughland House, Pathhead, Midlothian, 2nd son of late Maj John David Callander, of Prestonhall, Midlothian, and has issue living, James Edward, *b* 1979, — Sarah Mary, *b* 1977, — Emma Louise, *b* 1981.

HALF-SISTER LIVING

Helen Alice (*Baroness de Mauley*) (Langford, Little Faringdon, Lechlade, Glos), *b* 1921: *m* 1st, 1947, Lt-Col Brian Leslie Abdy Collins, OBE, MC, RE, who *d* 1952; 2ndly, 1954, 6th Baron de Mauley, and has issue living, (by 1st *m*) Thomas Abdy (Willow Cottage, Jumps Rd, Churt, Surrey), *b* 1948: *m* 1982, Anna Mary, el da of Col Ian. R. Critchley, OBE, of Greenden, Farnell, by Breckin, and has issue living, Alice Susanna Abdy *b* 1983, Eleanor Katherine Abdy *b* 1986, Phoebe Helen Abdy *b* 1988, — (Brian) James Douglas (Church Farm, Little Faringdon, Lechlade, Glos), *b* 1952: *m* 1st, 1976 (*m diss* 1988), Philippa Martha Gausel, da of Sir Rowland John Rathbone Whitehead, 5th Bt; 2ndly, 1989, Emma Charlotte, da of late Sir Neill Cooper-Key (*see* V Rothermere), and has issue living (by 1st *m*), Henry James Abdy *b* 1980, Rosie Alice Lousie *b* 1978 (by 2nd *m*), Elspeth Peggy *b* 1990, Cicely Violet *b* 1992, Christabel Lily *b* 1993.

COLLATERAL BRANCHES LIVING

Grandchildren of late Hon (Archibald) Roderick Sholto Douglas (*infra*):—
Issue of late Roderick Walter Sholto Douglas, *b* 1908, *d* 1990: *m* 1st, 1935 (*m diss* 1949), Elizabeth Margaret, who *d* 1977, el da of late Stephen Clement Paston Cooper (*see* Cooper, Bt, colls, cr 1821); 2ndly, 1950, Margaret (Buckstone, Banket, Zimbabwe), da of late J. M. Tennent, of Troon, Ayrshire:—
(By 1st *m*) Alastair Sholto, *b* 1949: *m* 1974, Diane Adams, and has issue living, Michael Bruce Sholto, *b* 1979, — Chantal Bernardene, *b* 1974, — Fay Robyn, *b* 1977. —— Anna Winona, *b* 1936: *m* 1965, Thomas Charles Bushby, of 53A Bannister Rd, Braeside, Harare, Zimbabwe, and has issue living, Lucinda Irene, *b* 1966. —— Juliet Elizabeth, *b* 1941: *m* 1975, Graham Peters, of 40 Parel Vallei Rd, Somerset West, S Africa. —— (By 2nd *m*) Bruce Sholto, *b* 1951.
Issue of late Brig Patrick Sholto Douglas, MC, *b* 1912, *d* 1977: *m* 1st, 1940 (*m diss* 1959), Maude Carol Hermione, da of George Orr, of Kilduff House, Drem, E Lothian; 2ndly, 1963, Alexa Granger (Tanyard Cottage, Fernhurst, Surrey), da of late Adm John Ewan Cameron, CB, MVO, and widow of George Howard Usher Crookshank:—
(By 1st *m*) Katharine Diana (2 Russell Place, Edinburgh), *b* 1942; *m* 1969, Peter Robin Campbell Hendriks, and has issue living, Timothy Ivan Mark, *b* 1970, — Alice Sophie, *b* 1973.

Issue of late Hon (Archibald) Roderick Sholto Douglas, 3rd son of 19th Earl, *b* 1883, *d* 1971: *m* 1907, Winona Constance De Maraisville, who *d* 1951, da of Col Walter Ancell Peake, DSO, of Burrough-on-the-Hill, Leics:—
Peter Frederic Sholto, DSO (Giwonde, Private Bag 7540, Mvurwi, Zimbabwe; New Club, Harare), *b* 1916; *ed* Uppingham; late Maj Argyll and Sutherland Highlanders; 1939-45 War (despatches, DSO 1941; King Haakon VII of Norway's Freedom Cross; American Cert of Merit); Meritorious Service Medal, Rhodesia 1976: *m* 1942, Ursula, da of late Henry Somers Rivers, of Sawbridgeworth, Herts, and has issue living, Roderick Gavin Sholto (40 Maidenhead Lane, Borrowdale, Harare, Zimbabwe), *b* 1944; *ed* Univ Coll of Rhodesia and Nyasaland, and Univ Coll, Lond (School of Library, Archive & Information Studies); BA, Dip Lib (Lond), ALA; Chief Archivist, Nat Archives of Zimbabwe, — Sara, *b* 1947: *m* 1974, Peter David Newbery, of 7 Runnymede Walk, Northwood, Harare, Zimbabwe, and has issue living, Nicholas David *b* 1982, Eloise *b* 1978. —— Rosemary (27 Sefton St, SW15), *b* 1915: *m* 1943, Capt Winfred Marlet Curtis, RM, who *d* 1960, and has issue living, Winona Penelope, *b* 1951: *m* 1973, Richard Granville Peddar, of 12 Lower Richmond Rd, SW15, and has issue living, Adam Winfred Richard *b* 1985, Alexander David Roderick *b* 1987, Theresa Adelina Alice *b* 1980.

Issue of Hon William Sholto Douglas, 4th son of 19th Earl, *b* 1886, *d* 1932: *m* 1914, Hon Ethel Georgiana Frances Somerset, who *d* 1981, da of 3rd Baron Raglan:—

Ian Fitzroy Sholto, *b* 1916: *m* 1st, 1946, Heather Joan, JP, who *d* 1985, da of late Lt-Col Alexander John Hew Maclean of Ardgour (*see* B Inverclyde, 1968 Edn); 2ndly, 1988, Hester Kathleen Lyndon, da of late Maurice Richard Lyndon White, and widow of David McCall-McCowan, of Moniaive, Dumfriesshire, and has issue living (by 1st *m*), William Hew Sholto (21 Moor Rd, Balfron, Stirlingshire), *b* 1947; late Maj 1st Bn Argyll and Sutherland Highlanders: *m* 1986, Frances Mary, da of Brig Robert William Riddle, of Old Harestanes, Blyth Bridge, Peeblesshire, and has issue living, Peter Sholto *b* 1987, Charles Robert Douglas *b* 1989, Andrew William *b* 1993, Kerry Anne Heather *b* 1991, — Peter James (Allandale, High St, New Galloway, by Castle Douglas, Kirkcudbrightshire), *b* 1952, — Elizabeth Heather Winifred, *b* 1948, *m* 1st, 1971 (*m diss* 1983), Edward Inman; 2ndly, 1985, Paul William Alexander Brown, of Five Steps, 14 Froghall Lane, Walkern, Stevenage, Herts ST2 7PH, and has issue living (by 1st *m*), James Michael *b* 1974, Heather Louise *b* 1977, — Jane Charlotte Georgiana, *b* 1950. *Residence* – Balmaclellan House, by Castle Douglas, Kirkcudbrightshire; Puffins (Edinburgh) Club. —— Ronald George Sholto, *b* 1926: *m* 1st, 1952 (*m diss* 1957), Margaret Jean Gai Eliott-Drake, only da of Ivor Herbert McClure, of Sutton, Province of Quebec, Canada; 2ndly, 1960 (*m diss* 1977), Valerie, yr da of William Quarterman, of 104, Cliff Rock Rd, Rubery, Birmingham; 3rdly, 1983, Heather Grey, da of James Philip Law, of Point Chevalier, NZ, and has issue living, (by 1st *m*) Roderick Olaf William Sholto (St Catherine's Lodge, Grange Rd, Edinburgh EH9 1UQ), *b* 1953, — Malcolm David Sholto (25 Culver Rd, Newbury, Berks), *b* 1955: *m* 1979, Barbara Elizabeth, da of Charles Hughes, of Newbury, Berks, and has issue living, James Robert Sholto *b* 1982, Michael Charles Sholto *b* 1984, — Fiona Anne Georgiana, *b* 1956; BSc: *m* 1981, Dr Robert Anderson Somerville, of 16 Grange Rd, Edinburgh EH9 1UJ, son of Charles Somerville, of Edinburgh, and has issue living, Ian Douglas *b* 1986, Anne Margaret *b* 1985, Catherine Mary *b* 1988, — (by 2nd *m*), Shona Fay, *b* 1962; BA: *m* 1983, Dr Roderick McDiarmid Johnstone, of 66 The Lanes, Over, Cambs CB4 5NQ, only son of Dr Robert Douglas Johnstone, of Pitlochry, Perthshire, and has issue living, Peter William Douglas *b* 1993, — Mr Ronald George Sholto Douglas has further issue, Alastair James Sholto Nason, *b* 1968. *Residence* – Dalmahoy, Oneriri Rd, Kaiwaka, N Island, New Zealand. —— Jean Georgiana Ethel, OBE, *b* 1922; OBE (Civil) 1991: *m* 1949, Maj Peter Edward Findlay Heneage, son of late Lt-Col Sir Arthur Pelham Heneage, DSO, and has issue living, Thomas Peter William, *b* 1950: *m* 1980 (*m diss* 1990), Shaunagh Anne Henrietta, el da of George Silver Oliver Annesley Colthurst, of Pitchford Hall, Shrewsbury (*see*Colthurst, Bt), and has issue living, Henry Robert *b* 1983, Elizabeth Anne Sophia *b* 1981, — Charles Arthur (Bailey Hill House, Birdbrook, Essex), *b* 1952: *m* 1978, Sarah Elizabeth, yst da of Col Arthur Harold Newmarch Reade, Queen's Own Hus, of The Post House, Ipsden, Wallingford, Oxon, and has issue living, Frederick Rory Winwood *b* 1990, Sophia Georgiana *b* 1980, Alice Rose *b* 1983, — Robert John (Newport House, North Carlton, Lincoln), *b* 1956: *m* 1984, Maryann Louise, only da of J. N. Milne, of Preston Priory, Ledbury, and has issue living, William *b* 1986, Georgiana *b* 1988, — Katherine Julia, *b* 1960: *m* 1991, Malcolm J. P. Moir, of 31 Poplar Grove, W6 7RF, elder son of Nigel Moir, of Town Farm, Bacton, Suffolk, and has issue living, Jemima Mary *b* 1994. *Residence* – North Carlton Old Hall, Lincoln.

Issue of late Lt Hon Ronald John Sholto Douglas, OBE, RNVR, 5th son of 19th Earl, *b* 1890, *d* 1922: *m* 1920, Alexandra Albertha Jean, who *d* 1974, da of late Adm Sir Frederick Tower Hamilton, GCVO, KCB, (L Belhaven, colls):—

Victoria Maria (Mendham Lodge, Harleston, Norfolk), *b* 1921: *m* 1956, as his 2nd wife, Lt-Col Gillachrist Campbell, RA, who *d* 1975 (V Hawarden, colls), and has issue living, Maria, *b* 1956, — Sophia Frances (Chestnut Cottage, St Margarets, Harleston, Norfolk), *b* 1958, — Catherine, *b* 1959: *m* 1986, Michel Jean Jérôme Corby-Tuech, of 74 rue de Seine, 77250 Veneux les Sablons, France, and has issue living, Jacques Max Gillachrist *b* 1988, Poppy Colette *b* 1987.

Grandchildren of late Capt George Sholto Douglas, only son of Adm Hon George Henry Douglas, 2nd son of 17th Earl:—

Issue of late Brig Archibald Sholto George Douglas, CBE, *b* 1896, *d* 1981: *m* 1928, (Violet) Patricia, who *d* 1989, 4th da of late Maj Arthur Pearson Davison, TD, of 18 Alexander Sq, SW3:—

Colin Sholto Archibald (18 Upshire Gdns, The Warren, Bracknell, Berks RG12 3YZ), *b* 1932; *ed* Eton: *m* 1st, 1958 (*m diss* 1971), Jean, who *d* 1978, da of late Brig George Streynsham Rawstorne, CBE, MC; 2ndly, 1972 (*m diss* 1982), Sally Anne, only da of David Charles Humphrey Townsend, of Grindon, co Durham, and has four children (by 1st *m*), Malcolm Sholto Colin, *b* 1966, — Laura Jean, *b* 1968, — (by 2nd *m*) Archie Sholto James, *b* 1972, — Euan Sholto David, *b* 1975. —— James Sholto Arthur (Good Mondays Farm, Dauntsey, Chippenham, Wilts), *b* 1935; *ed* Eton: Capt 15th/19th Hussars: *m* 1st, 1966 (*m diss* 1979), Tedda Ann, da of Albert Charles Webber, of Litton Cheney, Dorchester, Dorset; 2ndly, 1979, Elizabeth Ann, da of late Maj Montague Howard Crocker, of Minety House, Malmesbury, Wilts, and has four children (by 1st *m*), Justin Sholto James, *b* 1972, — Harry Sholto Gavin, *b* 1974, — Camilla Patricia Ann *b* 1971, — (by 2nd *m*) Toby Sholto Arthur, *b* 1982. —— Gavin Sholto George (Heiton Mill, nr Kelso, Roxburghshire), *b* 1945; *ed* Gordonstoun: *m* 1982, Amanda Jane, elder da of late Christopher Evelyn Twiston Davies, of Drax House, Tilshead, nr Salisbury, and of Mrs Simon Gilbey, of Mains of Solszarie, Bridge of Cally, Perthshire (*see* Gilbey, Bt, colls), and has issue living, Alice Violet, *b* 1983, — Charlotte Rose, *b* 1985. —— Joanna Patricia Margaret, *b* 1948: *m* 1972, Roger D. Day, of Newcotts Farm, N Newton, Bridgwater, Som, and has issue living, Gregory Laramy, *b* 1972, — Lorna Elizabeth, *b* 1974.

Issue of late Capt David Sholto William Douglas, *b* 1899, *d* 1980: *m* 1940, Elizabeth Sarah Ione (Lynwick House, Rudgwick, W Sussex), only da of late Maj George Edward Capel Cure, of Blake Hall, Ongar, Essex:—

Sheena Elizabeth, *b* 1948: *m* 1973, Richard James Wright, of Lynwick House, Rudgwick, W Sussex, only son of George William James Hamilton Wright, of Bessingby Hall, Bridlington, N Yorks, and has issue living, Charles Anthony, *b* 1979. —— The late Capt D. S. W. Douglas also had a da, Ione Lavinia Margaret, *b* 1946: *m* 1983 (*m diss* 1994), Richard Zatloukal, of 3 Burbury Court, 56 Redcliffe Sq, SW10.

Issue of late Lieut-Col John Sholto Henry Douglas, OBE, *b* 1903, *d* 1960: *m* 1955, Celia (Fir Tree Cottage, Broadmeadows, Yarrowford, Selkirk), only da of late Maj J. H. McInnes Skinner, of East Carleton Manor, Norfolk, and widow of Roderick Christopher Musgrave:—

Robin Sholto John (18 Shandon St, Edinburgh EH11 1QH), *b* 1956: *m* 1983, Ann Elisabeth Forssell, and has issue living, James Sholto Edward, *b* 1989, — Anna Louisa Victoria, *b* 1991. —— John Sholto James (59 Grandison Rd, SW11), *b* 1959.

Grandchildren of late Right Rev Hon Arthur Gascoigne Douglas, DD, DCL, Bishop of Aberdeen and Orkney, 5th son of 17th Earl:—

Issue of late Sholto James Douglas, *b* 1866, *d* 1950: *m* 1909, Grace Elizabeth, who *d* 1968, da of Sir James Henry Gibson-Craig, 3rd Bt (Gibson-Craig-Carmichael, Bt):—

Rev Canon Archibald Sholto, TD, *b* 1914; *ed* Selwyn Coll, Camb (MA); formerly V of Siddington, Hon Canon of Chester Cathedral (1978); 3rd class Chap to Forces, Cheshire Regt (TA); formerly Major King's Own Scottish Borderers (TA); appointed Chap to High Sheriff of Cheshire 1960. *Residence* – Monks Heath Hall Farm, Chelford Rd, Nether Alderley, Macclesfield, Cheshire SK10 4SY. —— Hugh Alastair, *b* 1915; formerly Conservator of Forests, Ghana: *m* 1953, Angela Elizabeth, *b* 1956; PhD: *m* 1984, Jeremy Byron Searle, — Coleena Jane, *b* 1958: *m* 1978, Nicholas Hutson Reid. *Residence* – Broadlands House, Brockenhurst, Hants.

Issue of late Rev Canon Archibald William Douglas, *b* 1870, *d* 1955: *m* 1902, Ursula Helen, who *d* 1962, 2nd da of late Capt Robert Watts Davies, RN, of Bloxham, Oxon:—

Joanna Katharine, *b* 1912: *m* 1931, James Utten Todd, who *d* 1981, and *d* 1984, leaving issue, James Donald Utten, *b* 1939: *m* 1962, Susan Mary Briscoe, and has issue living, Robert Alastair Utten *b* 1966, Kate Elizabeth Utten *b* 1971, — William Utten (17 Talbot Rd, Twickenham Green, Middx), *b* 1947: *m* 1976, Frances Margaret Warren, and has issue living, Dylan Utten *b* 1977, — Helen Patrica Utten, *b* 1941: *m* 1962, David Brian Wentworth (RD2, Danville, Penn, USA), and has issue living, Shaun David *b* 1963, James Douglas *b* 1968, Richard Benning *b* 1974, Jennifer Louise *b* 1965.

Descendants of Hon Edward Gordon Douglas-Pennant (brother of 17th Earl), who was *cr Baron Penrhyn* 1866 (see that title).

PREDECESSORS – (1) JAMES Douglas, 4th Feudal Lord of Dalkeith: *m* 1459, Joanna, 3rd da of King James I of Scotland; *cr Earl of Morton* (peerage of Scotland) 1458 *d* 1493; *s* by his son (2) JOHN, 2nd Earl, *b* 1466: *m* 14—, Janet, da of Patrick Crichton, of Cranstoun Riddell; *d* 1513, *s* by his son (3) JAMES, 3rd Earl; not having male issue made an entail of his estate and honours upon James Douglas, husband of his 3rd da Elizabeth: *m* 1507, Katherine Stewart, natural da of King James IV of Scotland; *d* 1548, *s* by his son-in-law (4) JAMES (ante), 4th Earl, *b* 1516; not having male issue he entailed the earldom upon his nephew Archibald Douglas, 8th Earl of Angus, and his heirs male, failing which to William Douglas, of Lochleven; was twice Chancellor and sometime High Adm and also Regent of Scotland: *m* 1543, Elizabeth, da of 3rd Earl (ante); tried for being accessory to the murder of Lord Darnley, and, being found guilty, was publicly executed at the Market Cross, Edinburgh, 2 June 1581, by "The Maiden", a machine he had himself introduced into Scotland; after his execution and forfeiture the Crown conferred the Earldom of Morton upon JOHN, Lord Maxwell, son of Beatrix, 2nd da of 3rd Earl (ante), by her marriage with Robert, Lord Maxwell; the grant of this honour was, however, revoked by the Act of Indemnity in 1585 to the heir of entail, and in recompense he was *cr* Earl of Nithsdale, while the Earldom of Morton passed to his nephew (5) ARCHIBALD Douglas, 5th Earl of (ante) (also 8th Earl of Angus), *b* 1555: *m* 1st, 1573, Mary, who *d* 1575, da of John, Earl of Mar; 2ndly 1575 (*m diss*), Margaret, da of 4th Earl of Rothes; 3rdly, 1587, Jean, da of 8th Lord Glamis *d* 1588; *s* by his kinsman (6) Sir WILLIAM, 6th Earl (a descendant of Sir Harry Douglas of Lugton and Lochleven, 4th son of Sir John Douglas of Dalkeith), *b* 1539-40: *m* 1554, Agnes, da of 4th Earl of Rothes; *d* 1606; *s* by his grandson (7) *Rt Hon* Sir WILLIAM, KG (son of Robert Douglas yr of Lochleven, el son of 6th Earl), 7th Earl, *b* 1582; was Gentleman of the Bedchamber to James VI and Charles I, High Treasurer for Scotland 1630-35, Capt of the Yeomen of the Guard, and 1641 High Chancellor; sold Dalkeith and other estates, and received in return the Islands of Orkney and Zetland, with their whole jurisdiction and royalties redeemable on payment by the Crown of £30,000; in 1638 Aberdour was erected into a burgh of Barony, and his title was altered to *Earl of Morton* and *Lord Aberdour*: *m* 1604, Lady Ann Keith, da of 5th Earl Marischal, *d* 1648; *s* by his son (8) ROBERT, 8th Earl: *m* 16—, Anne, who *d* 1654, da of Sir Edward Villiers of Brokesby; *d* 1649; *s* by his son (9) WILLIAM, 9th Earl; procured a new grant of the Islands of Orkney and Zetland, but the original being contested those islands were annexed to the Crown by Act of Parliament 1669: *m* 1662, Lady Grizel Middleton, who *d* 1666, da of 1st Earl of Middleton; *d* 1681; *s* by his uncle, (10) Sir JAMES, 10th Earl: *m* 16—, Ann, who *d* 1700, da and co heir of Sir James Hay, 1st Bt of Smithfield, *d* 1686: *s* by his son, (11) JAMES, 11th Earl; a strenuous supporter of the Union; *d* unmarried 1715; *s* by his brother, (12) ROBERT, 12th Earl; *d* unmarried 1730; *s* by his brother, (13) GEORGE, 13th Earl, *b* 1662; MP for Orkney and Sutherlandshire 1722-30, Vice-Adm of Scotland 1733-38: *m* 1st, 16—, a da of Alexander Muirhead of Linhouse, co Edinburgh; 2ndly, 17—, Frances, da of William Adderley, of Halstow, Kent; *d* 1738; *s* by his son, (14) JAMES, KT, 14th Earl, *b* 1702, was a Lord of the Bedchamber 1739, a Representative Peer 1739-68; Grand Master Mason of Scotland 1739-40; Lord Clerk Register of Scotland 1761-68; Pres Royal Society 1764-68; arranged finance for Capt James Cooke's 1st voyage of discovery; in 1742 the Earldom of Orkney and Lordship of Zetland were by Act of Parliament disannexed from the Crown, and vested irredeemably in him, a right which he sold to Sir Laurence Dundas, 1st Baron Dundas (M Zetland): *m* 1st, before 1731, Agatha, who *d* 1748, da of James Halyburton of Pitcur; 2ndly, 1755, Bridget, who *d* 1805, da of Sir John Heathcote, 2nd Bt, of Normanton; *d* 1768; *s* by his son (15) SHOLTO CHARLES, 15th Earl; *b* 1732; a Lord of Police: *m* 1758, Katherine, who *d* 1823, da of Hon John Hamilton, 2nd son of 6th Earl of Haddington; *d* 1774; *s* by his son, (16) GEORGE, KT, 16th Earl, *b* 1761; a Representative Peer 1784-91, Chamberlain of the Queen's Household, and Lord-Lieut of co Fife; *cr Baron Douglas of Lochleven* (peerage of Great Britain) 1791: *m* 1814, Susan Elizabeth, da of Sir Francis Buller-Yarde-Buller, 2nd Bt; *dsp* 1827, when the Barony of Douglas became ext and the Scottish peerages devolved upon his cousin, (17) GEORGE SHOLTO, 17th Earl (son of Hon John Douglas, 2nd son of 14th Earl); *b* 1789; was a Representative Peer: *m* 1817, Frances Theodora, who *d* 1879, da of Rt Hon Sir George Henry Rose, GCH; *d* 1858; *s* by his son, (18) SHOLTO JOHN, 18th Earl; *b* 1818, was a Representative Peer: *m* 1st, 1844, Helen, who *d* 1850, da of James Watson of Saughton, Midlothian, 2ndly, 1853, Lady Alice Anne Caroline Lambton, who *d* 1907, da of 1st Earl of Durham; *d* Dec 1884; *s* by his son (19) SHOLTO GEORGE WATSON, 19th Earl, *b* 1844; a Representative Peer for Scotland: *m* 1877, Hon Helen Geraldine Maria Ponsonby, who *d* 1949, da of 2nd Baron de Mauley; *d* 1935; *s* by his grandson (20) SHOLTO CHARLES JOHN HAY (son of Sholto Charles Watson, Lord Aberdour), 20th Earl; *b* 1907; *d* 1976; *s* by his cousin (son of Hon Charles William Sholto Douglas, 2nd son of 19th Earl, *b* 1881, *d* 1960: *m* 1st, 1920, Alice Agnes, who *d* 1924, only da of Lt-Col William Augustus Lane Fox-Pitt, of Presaddfed, Anglesey; 2ndly, 1926, Florence, who *d* 1985, elder da of Maj Henry Thomas Timson, of Stydd House, Lyndhurst) (21) JOHN CHARLES SHOLTO, 21st Earl and present peer; also Lord Aberdour.

MORTON OF HENRYTON, BARONY OF (Morton) (Extinct 1973)

DAUGHTER LIVING OF LIFE BARON

Hon Anne Margaret, *b* 1926, called to the Bar (Lincolns Inn 1979); former Cllr Kensington and Chelsea Borough Cncl 1960-62; Chm Consumer Protection Advy Cttee since 1973; Chm Inner London Juvenile Courts 1970-87 (appointed to panel 1961); Co-Founder and Sec of London Adventure Playground Assn 1962-69; *m* 1947, Peter Andrew Hopwood Viney, DFC (B Southborough), and has issue living, Nicholas Morton, *b* 1948: *m* 1981, Jane Fiona Maud, yr da of Benjamin Bernard Woulfe Goodden, and formerly wife of Graham Holt, — Alison Margaret, *b* 1951: *m* 1970, Christopher Patrick Maguire, — Elizabeth Frances, *b* 1956.

MORTON OF SHUNA, BARON (Morton) (Life Baron 1985)

HUGH DRENNAN BAIRD MORTON, QC, *b* 10 April 1930, son of late Rev Thomas Ralph Morton, DD, by his wife, Janet Maclay MacGregor, da of Hugh Baird, of Glasgow; *ed* Glasgow Acad, and Glasgow Univ (BL); admitted Faculty of Advocates 1965; *cr Baron Morton of Shuna*, of Stockbridge in the District of the City of Edinburgh (Life Baron), 1985; *m* 1956, Muriel, da of Charles Miller, of Edinburgh, and has issue.
Residence – 25 Royal Circus, Edinburgh EH3 6TL.

SONS LIVING

Hon Alistair Charles Ralph, *b* 1958; *ed* R High Sch, Edinburgh, and Glasgow Univ (MA): *m* 1983, Jacqueline Anne, da of William Brown, of Edinburgh.
Hon Kenneth John, *b* 1960; *ed* Broughton High Sch, Edinburgh, and Edinburgh Univ: *m* 1984, Isobel Ann, da of John McLean Cowan, of Greenock.
Hon Douglas William, *b* 1963; *ed* Broughton High Sch, Edinburgh.

MOSTYN, BARON (Lloyd Mostyn) (Baron UK 1831, Bt GB 1778)

My help is from the Lord

ROGER EDWARD LLOYD LLOYD MOSTYN, MC, 5th Baron, and 6th Baronet; *b* 17 April 1920; *s* 1965; *ed* Eton, Capt 9th Queen's R Lancers; 1939-45 War in Middle East (wounded, despatches, MC): *m* 1st, 1943 (*m diss* 1957), Yvonne Margaret, da of A. Stuart Johnson, of Henshall Hall, Congleton, Cheshire; 2ndly, 1957, Sheila Edmondson (SHAW), OBE, DL, da of Maj Reginald Fairweather, of Stockwell Manor, Silverton, Devon, and has issue by 1st *m*.

Arms – Quarterly: 1st and 4th, per bend sinister ermine and ermines, a lion rampant or, *Mostyn*; 2nd and 3rd gules, a Saracen's head affrontée, erased at the neck proper, wreathed about the temples argent and sable, *Lloyd.* **Crests** – 1st, on a mount vert, a lion rampant or; 2nd, a Saracen's head, as in the arms; 3rd a stag trippant proper, attired or, charged on the shoulder with an escutcheon of the second, thereon a chevron of the first, between three men's heads in profile, couped at the neck, also proper. **Supporters** – *Dexter*, a stag proper, attired or, charged on the shoulder with an escutcheon gules, thereon a chevron argent, between three men's heads couped in profile proper; *sinister*, a lion or, charged on the shoulder with an escutcheon argent thereon a cross engrailed and fleurettée sable, between four Cornish choughs proper.
Seat – Mostyn Hall, Mostyn, Flintshire. *Club* – Royal Automobile.

SON LIVING *(By 1st marriage)*

Hon LLEWELLYN ROGER LLOYD (9 Anderson St, SW3), *b* 26 Sept 1948; *ed* Eton; late Capt Army Legal Sers; Bar Middle Temple 1973; in chambers Gray's Inn: *m* 1974, Denise Suzanne, da of Roger Duvanel, and has issue living, Gregory Philip Roger, *b* 31 Dec 1984, — Alexandra Stefanie, *b* 1975.

DAUGHTER LIVING *(By 1st marriage)*

Hon Virginia Yvonne Lloyd, *b* 1946: *m* 1st, 1973, John Robert Hodgkinson; 2ndly, 1983, James R. K. Price, and has issue living (by 1st *m*), Dominic, *b* 1974, — Thomas, *b* 1976.

SISTER LIVING

Hon Elizabeth Mary Gwenllian Lloyd, *b* 1929: *m* 1st, 1950 (*m diss* Jan 1957), David Nicholas Goldsmith Duckham; 2ndly (May) 1957, John Henry Russell, and has issue living (by 1st *m*), Kiloran Mary, *b* 1953. *Address* – Kings of Kinloch, Meigle, Perthshire PH12 8QX.

COLLATERAL BRANCHES LIVING   *(Male line in special remainder to Baronetcy)*

Grandchildren of late Edward Hugh Lloyd Mostyn, el son of late Rev Canon Hon Hugh Wynne Lloyd Mostyn, 5th son of 2nd Baron:—
Issue of late Hugh Wynne Lloyd Mostyn, *b* 1903, *d* 1975: *m* 1933, Eileen Grace, who *d* 1985, da of Arthur Walsh Titherley, DSc PhD, FRIC, of Itchen Abbas Manor, Winchester:—
Roger Hugh Lloyd (42 Lichfield Lane, Mansfield, Notts), *b* 1941; *ed* Lancing; MB, BS London; MRCS England, FRCP London: *m* 1967, Mary Frances, da of Capt Edward Fothergill Elderton, AFRaeS, ACGI, of Ryde, and has issue living, Christopher Edward, *b* 1968, — James William, *b* 1970, — David Thomas, *b* 1981. —— Rosemary Eleanor Lloyd, *b* 1933: *m* 1974, Rev J. D. Thorp, of Lot 264 Johnston St, Mt Helena 6555, W Aust and has issue living, Simon Robin Hugh, *b* 1975. —— Jean Grant Lloyd, *b* 1935: *m* 1956, John Harold Matthews, Film and TV Dir and Producer, of 792 Victoria Rd, Ryde, Sydney, NSW 2112, Australia, and has issue living, Nicholas Stuart, *b* 1958: *m* 1980, Debra Young, and has issue living, Michael Lloyd *b* 1984, Daniel James *b* 1989, — Sarah Jo, *b* 1964: *m* 1988, Dennis Brian Heape.

Grandchildren of late Lt-Col James Pryce Lloyd Mostyn (infra):—
Issue of late Maj Edwyn Inigo Lloyd Mostyn, MC, Scots Gds, *b* 1921, *d* 1978: *m* 1st, 1942 (*m diss* 1964), Avice Louise Trevor, da of Cdr Sir Hugh Trevor Dawson, 2nd Bt, CBE, RN (ret); 2ndly, 1964, Mrs Janet Hope Rutherford, da of late Eric Cecil Barnes, CMG, of Polmear, Frogham, nr Fordingbridge; 3rdly, 1975, Angela, widow of Ralph Leyland:—
(By 1st *m*) James Michael Lloyd, *b* 1952: *m* 1974, Susan Hough, and has issue living, Neil James Lloyd, *b* 1982, — Sarah Louise Lloyd, *b* 1977, — Joanna Mary Lloyd, *b* 1979. —— Caroline Anne Lloyd, *b* 1954: *m* 1979, John J. Baggerman, son of K. J. Baggerman, of Twyford, Hants. —— Louise Avice Lloyd, *b* 1956. —— Annabel Alix Lloyd, *b* 1957.

Grandson of late Rev Canon Hon Hugh Wynne Lloyd-Mostyn (ante):—
Issue of late Lt-Col James Pryce Lloyd Mostyn, *b* 1879, *d* 1968: *m* 1915, Alix Doreen, who *d* 1956, da of late Maj-Gen Inigo Richmund Jones, CVO, CB:—
David Henry Lloyd, *b* 1923, 1939-45 War as Rifleman Rifle Bde, and with Queen's R Regt (invalided): *m* 1956, Betty, da of late James Francis O'Connor, of Applecross, W Aust. *Residence* – 41 Marion Way, Gooseberry Hill, W Australia 6076.

Not in remainder to Barony.
Grandson of late George Llewellyn Lloyd, 2nd son of late William Lloyd (*b* 1824), yr son of Edward Bell Lloyd, el son of Bell Lloyd, next brother of 2nd Bt and 1st Baron:—
Issue of late Llewellyn Bateson Lloyd, *b* 1887, *d* 1952: *m* 1910, Mabel Ellen, who *d* 1961, da of William French:—
†George Llewellyn, *b* 1911: *m* 1948, Marianne, da of Pierre Marcelli, and *d* 1978. *Residence* – Canaja 20, Campile, France.

Grandchildren of late Alfred Norman Mostyn Lloyd (infra):—
Issue of late Cmdr Norman Mostyn Lloyd, RD, RNR, *b* 1911, *d* 1986: *m* 1941, Ethel Kathleen, who *d* 1986, da of late Edward Crouch:—
Edward Mostyn (15 Sussex St, SW1V 4RR), *b* 1943. —— Margaret Gwynedd, *b* 1944: *m* 1966, Douglas Havers, of Svanen, Soren Larson & Sonners, Nykobing Mors, Denmark.

Grandson of late Ven William Henry Cynric Lloyd, yr son of late Bell Lloyd (ante):—
Issue of late Alfred Norman Mostyn Lloyd, *b* 1868, *d* 1941: *m* 1st, 1895, Harriet, who *d* 1904, da of late Canon Crompton, of Breightmet, Pinetown Estate, Natal; 2ndly, 1910, Alice Rivière, who *d* 1944, da of Henry Ainsworth Condron:—
(By 2nd *m*) Alfred Anson, *b* 1914; Doc Econ (Hon Cas); *ed* Michaelhouse: *m* 1941, Elaine, da of late Horace Burdon, and has issue living, Patricia Burdon, *b* 1943, — Barbara Ann, *b* 1948: *m* 1971, Robert John Kendall Slater, of 24 Burleigh Cres,

Durban North 4051, S Africa, and has issue living, Kendall Lloyd *b* 1972, Stuart James *b* 1974. *Residence* – 12 Humber Cresc, Durban North 4051, S Africa.

Granddaughter of late Charles Banastre Lloyd, son of Maj-Gen Benastre Pryce Lloyd, son of Llewelyn Lloyd, yst brother of 2nd Bt and 1st Baron:—
Issue of late Llewelyn Lloyd, *b* 1883, *d* 1960: *m* 1920, Jessie Elizabeth, da of James Thomas Forrester:—
Daphne Ellen Kate, *b* 1921: *m* 19— (*m diss* 1949), — Read, of Johannesburg, and has issue living, Arland Everard, *b* 1944, — Susan, *b* 1946.

PREDECESSORS – (1) EDWARD Lloyd, Secretary of War, *d* 1795, having in 1778 been *cr* a *Baronet*, with remainder to his nephew (2) Sir EDWARD PRYCE Lloyd, 2nd Bt; MP for Flint Borough 1806-07 and 1812-32; *b* 1768; *cr Baron Mostyn*, of Mostyn, co Flint (peerage of United Kingdom) 1831; *d* 1854; *s* by his son (3) EDWARD, 2nd Baron; sat as MP for Flintshire (LC) 1831-37, 1841-42, and 1847-54, and Lichfield 1846-47; was Lord-Lieut of Merionethshire; assumed in 1831 by Roy licence the additional surname of Mostyn; *d* 1884; *s* by his grandson (4) LLEWELYN NEVILLE VAUGHAN (son of late Hon Thomas Edward Mostyn Lloyd-Mostyn, 3rd Baron); *b* 1856; High Sheriff of Flint 1928, and Vice-Adm of N Wales and Carmarthen 1898-1929; bore Royal Standard of the Principality of Wales at Coronation of King George V 1911: *m* 1879, Lady Mary Florence Edith Clements, OBE, who *d* 1933, sister of 4th Earl of Leitrim; *d* 1929; *s* by his son (5) EDWARD LLEWELYN ROGER, 4th Baron *b* 1885; High Sheriff of Flintshire 1928: *m* 1918, Constance Mary, who *d* 1976, only child of late W. H. Reynolds, of Flintshire 1928: *m* 1918, Constance Mary, who *d* 1976, only child of late W. H. Reynolds, of Aldeburgh, *d* 1965; *s* by his el son (6) ROGER EDWARD LLOYD, MC, 5th Baron and present peer.

MOTTISTONE, BARON (Seely) (Baron UK 1933)

I hope in God

DAVID PETER SEELY, 4th Baron, CBE, *b* 16 Dec 1920; *s* 1966; Capt RN (ret); FIERE; FIPM; Hon D Litt; DL of Isle of Wight 1981-1985, since when Lord Lieut, Gov Isle of Wight since 1992; served World War II 1939-40; Special Assist to Ch of Allied Staff, Malta, 1956-58, in Command HMS *Cossack*, Far E Fleet 1958-59; Capt 1960, Dep of Dir of Signals, Admiralty 1961-63, in Command of HMS *Ajax* and 24th Escort Sqdn Far E Fleet (despatches) 1964-65, and Naval Adviser to UK High Comnr in Canada 1965-66; Dir of Distributive Industry Training Board 1969-75; Dir Cake and Biscuit Alliance 1975-82; Chm Bureau of Applied Sciences 1987-91, and Dir Associated Information Services 1987-90: *m* 1944, Anthea Christine, da of Victor McMullan, and has issue.

Arms – Azure, three ears of wheat banded or between two martlets in pale, and as many wreaths of roses in fesse argent. **Crest** – In front of three ears of wheat banded or, the trunk of a tree fesswise eradicated and sprouting to the dexter proper. **Supporters** – On either side a seahorse (hippocampus) azure, gorged with a mural crown and charged on the shoulder with a maple leaf or.
Residence – The Old Parsonage, Mottistone, Isle of Wight. *Clubs* – Royal Yacht Squadron, Royal Cruising, Island Sailing, Royal Commonwealth Society (Fellow), Royal Naval Sailing Association.

SONS LIVING

Hon PETER JOHN PHILIP, *b* 29 Oct 1949: *m* 1972 (*m diss* 1975), Joyce, da of Mrs Ellen Cairns, of St Ninians, Stirling; 2ndly, 1982, Linda, da of W.A. Swain, of Judds House, Bulphan Fen, Upminster, Essex, and has issue living (by 1st *m*), Christopher David Peter, *b* 1 Oct 1974, — (by 2nd *m*), Richard William Anthony, *b* 1988, — Penelope Jane, *b* 1984, — Jennifer Elizabeth, *b* 1986, — Caroline Mary, *b* 1990. *Residence* – Alendale, Uckfield Lane, Hever, Kent TN8 7LJ.
Hon Patrick Michael, *b* 1960; *ed* Harrow, and Trin Coll, Camb: *m* 1984, Susannah Shelley, da of Cdr J. C. Q. Johnson, of Brook, IoW, and has issue living, Thomas Charles Rupert, *b* 1989, — Clementine Mary, *b* 1991. *Residence* – The Old Rectory, Brook, Isle of Wight PO30 4EU.

DAUGHTERS LIVING

Hon Diana Mary, *b* 1954: *m* 1977, Edward Anthony Spours Nicholson, and has issue living, Alexander James Edward, *b* 1988, — Zoë Mary Louisa, *b* 1990. *Residence* – Staple Ash House, Froxfield Green, Petersfield, Hants GU32 1DH.
Hon Victoria Anne, *b* 1957: *m* 1984, Christopher Russell, son of late John Russell, and has issue living, John Hugh *b* 1987, — Emily, *b* 1985, — Kate, *b* 1989, — Alice, *b* 1991. *Residence* – Ningwood Manor, Ningwood, Isle of Wight.

HALF-SISTERS LIVING

Hon Kathleen Mary, *b* 1907: *m* 1946, (Clement) Maxwell Winton Haydon, who *d ca* 1981. *Residence* – Paddock Hill, Lymington, Hants.
Hon Louisa Mary Sylvia, *b* 1913: *m* 1941, Prof Charles Montague Fletcher, CBE, MD, FRCP, FFCM, of 24 West Sq, SE11 4SN, and Coastguard Cottages, Newtown, IoW, only son of late Sir Walter Morley Fletcher, KBE, CB, MD, ScD, FRS, and has issue living, Mark Walter (30 Musgrave Cres, SW6), *b* 1942: *m* 1st, 1968, Amelia Henrietta Rose, yr da of Richard Tyler, of Meesden Hall, Buntingford, Herts; 2ndly, 1988, Mrs Lindy Jones, da of Brig Michael Harbottle, OBE, of Chipping Norton, Oxon, — Susanna Mary (*Lady Lyell*), *b* 1945: *m* 1967, Sir Nicholas Walter Lyell, QC, MP, Attorney Gen since 1992, of Hill Farm, Markyate, Herts, son of Sir Maurice Legat Lyell, — Caroline Anne, *b* 1949: *m* 1974, Christopher Simon Courtenay Stephenson Clarke, QC, of 42 The Chase, SW4 0NH, son of Rev John Stephenson Clarke.

PREDECESSORS – (1) *Rt Hon* JOHN EDWARD BERNARD Seely, CB, CMG, DSO, TD, 4th son of Sir Charles Seely, 1st Bt; *b* 1868; Lord Lt for Hants, Lt-Col and Hon Col 72nd Hampshires Anti-Aircraft Bde RA (TA), and 7th Hussars (Canadian Mil), Maj-Gen in the Army; S Africa 1900-1901, with 4th Bn Imperial Yeo (DSO), 1914-18 War; Under-Sec of State for the Colonies 1908-11, Under-Sec of State for War 1911-12, Sec of State for War and Pres of Army Council 1912-14, Warfare Member of

Munitions Council 1918, Parliamentary Under-Sec to Min of Munitions, and Dep Min of Munitions 1918, and Under-Sec of State for Air 1919; MP for I of W (C) 1900-1906, for Liverpool, Abercromby Div 1906-10, for Ilkeston Div of Derbyshire 1910-22, for I of W (L) 1923-24; *cr Baron Mottistone*, of Mottistone, co Southampton (Peerage of UK) 1933: *m* 1st, 1895, Emily Florence, who *d* 1913, da of Hon Sir Henry George Louis Crichton (E Erne); 2ndly, 1917, Hon Evelyn Izme, JP, who *d* 1976, da of 1st Viscount Elibank, and widow of Capt George Crosfield Norris Nicholson, RFC (*see* Nicholson, Bt, *cr* 1912) *d* 1947, *s* by his el surviving son **(2)** (HENRY) JOHN ALEXANDER, OBE, FRIBA, 2nd Baron, *b* 1899; Surveyor of Fabric, St Paul's Cathedral Architect to St George's Chapel, Windsor; Capt 72nd Hampshire Anti-Aircraft Bde (RA) (TA) 1914-18 War in Italy, 1939-45 War as Fl Lt Aux AF; *d* 1963; *s* by his brother **(3)** (ARTHUR) PATRICK WILLIAM, TD, 3rd Baron, *b* 1905; Lt-Col Anti-Aircraft Regt RA (TA): *m* 1939 (*m diss* 1949), Wilhelmina Josephine Philippa, da of Jonkheer Frans I Van Haeften (Brocklehurst, Bt); *d* 1966; *s* by his half-brother **(4)** DAVID PETER, 4th Baron and present peer.

MOUNTBATTEN OF BURMA, COUNTESS (Knatchbull) (Earl UK 1947)

PATRICIA EDWINA VICTORIA KNATCHBULL, (*Countess Mountbatten of Burma*), CBE, *b* 14 Feb 1924; *s* 1979; Col-in-Ch of Princess Patricia's Canadian LI; CD; DStJ; JP Kent 1971, DL 1973, Vice Lord Lieut 1984; Patron Legion of Frontiersmen of the Commonwealth since 1983; Vice-Pres BRCS; 1939-45 War in WRNS in UK and S-E Asia; CBE (Civil) 1991: *m* 26 Oct 1946, 7th Baron Brabourne, CBE, and has had issue.

Arms – Quarterly: 1st and 4th, azure, a lion rampant double queued barry of ten, argent and gules, armed and langued of the last, crowned or, within a bordure company of the 2nd and 3rd; 2nd and 3rd, argent, two pallets sable charged on the honour point with an escutcheon of the arms of late Princess Alice (namely, the Royal Arms differenced with a label of three points argent, on the centre point charged with a rose gules barbed vert, and each of the other points with an ermine spot sable). **Crests** – 1st, out of a coronet or, two horns barry of ten, argent and gules, issuing from each three linden leaves vert, and from the outer side of each horn four branches barwise, having three like leaves pendant therefrom of the last, *Hesse*; 2nd, out of a coronet or, a plume of four ostrich feathers alternately argent and sable, *Battenberg*. **Supporters** – On either side a lion double queued and crowned all or.
Residences – Newhouse, Mersham, Ashford, Kent TN25 6NQ; 39 Montpelier Walk, SW7 1JH.

SONS LIVING AND DECEASED

NORTON LOUIS PHILIP (*Lord Romsey*) (Broadlands, Romsey, Hants SO51 9ZD), *b* 8 Oct 1947; *ed* Gordonstoun, and Kent Univ; High Steward of Romsey since 1980: *m* 20 Oct 1979, Penelope Meredith, only da of Reginald Eastwood, of Palma de Mallorca, Spain, and has issue:—
   SON LIVING— Hon Nicholas Louis Charles Norton, *b* 15 May 1981.
   DAUGHTERS LIVING AND DECEASED—*Hon* Alexandra Victoria Edwina Diana, *b* 5 Dec 1982, — *Hon* Leonora Louise Marie Elizabeth, *b* 25 June 1986, *d* 22 Oct 1991.
Hon Michael John Ulick KNATCHBULL (9 Queen's Elm Sq, SW3 6ED; Plumpton Farmhouse, Hinkhill, Ashford, Kent TN25 5NT) *b* 24 May 1950; *ed* Benenden, Gordonstoun, and Reading Univ: *m* 1 June 1985, Melissa Clare, only da of Judge Sir John Owen, of Bickerstaff House, Shipston-on-Stour, Warwickshire, and has issue living, Kelly Louise Doreen, *b* 30 March 1988.
Hon Philip Wyndham Ashley KNATCHBULL (41 Montpelier Walk, SW7 1JH) *b* 2 Dec 1961; *ed* Gordonstoun, Kent Univ, and London Internat Film Sch: *m* 16 March 1991, Mrs Atalanta Vereker, da of late John Cowan, and formerly wife of Hugo Dominic Charles Medlicott Vereker (*see* V Gort, colls), and has issue living, Daisy Isadora, *b* 5 Oct 1992.
Hon Nicholas Timothy Charles KNATCHBULL, *b* 18 Nov 1964; *k* with his grandfather, Earl Mountbatten of Burma, and grandmother, Doreen, Lady Brabourne, 1979.
Hon Timothy Nicholas Sean KNATCHBULL, *b* (twin) 18 Nov 1964; *ed* Benenden, Gordonstoun; Atlantic Coll, and Christ's Coll, Camb.

DAUGHTERS LIVING

Lady Joanna Edwina Doreen, *b* 5 March 1955; *ed* Benenden, Atlantic Coll, Kent Univ, and Columbia Univ, USA: *m* 3 Nov 1984, Baron Hubert Henry Francois du Breuil, 2nd son of Baron Bertrand Pernot du Breuil, of 52 Avenue d'Iena, 75116 Paris, and has issue living, Eleuthera Roselyne Patricia, *b* 13 May 1986.
Lady Amanda Patricia Victoria, *b* 26 June 1957; *ed* Benenden, Gordonstoun, Kent Univ, Peking Univ, and Goldsmiths Coll: *m* 31 Oct 1987, Charles V. Ellingworth, of 3 Stowe Rd, W12 2PT, eldest son of William Ellingworth, of Laughton, Leics, and has issue living, Luke John William, *b* 27 Jan 1991, — Joseph Louis Vincent, *b* 2 Dec 1992.

SISTER LIVING

Lady Pamela Carmen Louise, *b* 1929; Lady-in-Waiting to HM The Queen on her tour to Australia and New Zealand 1953-54: *m* 1960, David Nightingale Hicks, and has issue living, Ashley Louis David, *b* 1963: *m* 1990, Allegra Marina, elder da of Dottor Carlo Tondato, of Turin, and has issue living, Angelica Margherita Edwina *b* 1992, — Edwina Victoria Louise, *b* 1961: *m* 1984, Jeremy A. R. Brudenell, of 22 Fulham Park Gdns, SW6 4JX, 2nd son of (John) Michael Brudenell, FRCS, FRCOG, of Hever, Kent, and has issue living, Maddison May *b* 1994, — India Amanda Caroline, *b* 1967. *Residences* – Albany, Piccadilly, W1; The Grove, Brightwell Baldwin, Oxon.

PREDECESSOR – **(1)** *Adm of the Fleet* LOUIS FRANCIS ALBERT VICTOR NICHOLAS Mountbatten, KG, GCB, OM, GCSI, GCIE, GCVO, DSO, PC, FRS (discontinued by R Warrant 1917 the style of HSH and Prince and the appellation of Battenberg, and became known as Lord Louis Mountbatten in lieu of HSH Prince Louis Francis of Battenberg), 2nd son of 1st Marquess of Milford Haven (*see* ROYAL FAMILY), *b* 25 June 1900; Adm of the Fleet 1956, Hon Lt-Gen in the Army and Air Marshal RAF, Col Life Guards, and Col Comdt RM 1965-79; Ch of Combined Operations and a Member of Ch of Staff's Cttee 1942-43; Supreme Allied Cdr SE Asia 1943-47; Viceroy of India March - Aug 1947; Gov-Gen of India 1947-48, Flag Officer Comdg First Cruiser Sqdn 1948-50, Fourth Sea Lord 1950-52, C-in-C Med 1952-54, and C-in-C Allied Forces, Med 1953-54, First Sea Lord 1955-59, Ch of Defence Staff and Chm of Chs of Staff Cttee 1959-65; Gov, Capt, and Steward of Isle of Wight 1965-79, and Lord Lieut 1974-79; *cr Viscount Mountbatten of Burma*, of Romsey, co Southampton (peerage of UK), with remainder to heirs male of his body, and in default of such issue to his el da, Patricia Edwina Victoria, and the heirs male of her body; and in default of such issue to every other da successively in order of seniority of age and priority of birth, and to the heirs male of their bodies 1946, and *Baron Romsey*, of Romsey, co Southampton, and *Earl Mountbatten of Burma* (peerage of UK), with similar special remainders to the above mentioned 1947: *m* 1922, Hon Dame Edwina Cynthia Annette Ashley, CI GBE, DCVO, LLD, who *d* 1960, el da of 1st Baron Mount Temple (ext); assassinated 1979; *s* by his el da **(2)** PATRICIA EDWINA VICTORIA, present peeress; also Viscountess Mountbatten of Burma, and Baroness Romsey.

Mount Charles, Earl of; son of Marquess Conyngham.

MOUNT EDGCUMBE, EARL OF (Edgcumbe) (Earl GB 1789)

AU PLAISIR — FORT — DE DIEU

At the disposal of God

ROBERT CHARLES EDGCUMBE, 8th Earl; *b* 1 June 1939; *s* 1982; formerly farm manager for Lands and Survey, NZ: *m* 1960 (*m diss* 1988), Joan Ivy, da of Ernest Wall, of 3 RD Otorohanga, NZ, and has issue.

Arms – Gules, on a bend ermines, cottised or, three boars' heads argent. **Crest** – A boar statant argent, gorged with a wreath of oak vert, fructed or. **Supporters** – Two greyhounds argent, guttee de poix, and gorged with a collar, dovetailed gules.
Seat – Mount Edgcumbe, Plymouth. *Residence* – Empacombe House, Cremyll, Mount Edgcumbe, Cornwall PL10 1HZ.

DAUGHTERS LIVING

Lady (Valerie) Denise, *b* 1960.
Lady Megan Frances (14 Grey St, Kawerau, Bay of Plenty, NZ), *b* 1962; Horticulturalist.
Lady Tracy Anne, *b* 1966: *m* 1988, Colin Rush, of Opotiki, Bay of Plenty, NZ, and has issue living, Shaun, *b* 1987, — Jamie Lee (da), *b* 1989.
Lady Vanessa Erina Michelle (2 Anderton Quay Cottages, Millbrook, Torpoint, Cornwall PL10 1DU), *b* 1969; has issue living (by Ralph Winsor), Tobias Richard, *b* 1989, — Coral Erina, *b* 1991.
Lady Alison Nicole, *b* 1971.

HALF-BROTHERS LIVING

PIERS VALLETORT, *b* 23 Oct 1946: *m* 1971 (*m diss* 19—), Hilda Warn, and has issue living, Prudence, *b* 1972, — Angela, *b* 1975. *Residence* – 23 Chambord Place, Nelson, New Zealand.
Christopher George Mortimer, *b* 1950: *m* 1985 (*m diss* 1991), Marian Frances, da of Murray Stevenson, and has issue living, Douglas George Valletort, *b* 1985, — Emma Louise (adopted stepda), *b* 1983.

AUNT LIVING (Sister of 7th Earl)

Erina Shelley, *b* 1898: *m* 1930, John Richard Sutton, MICE, of 16 Awatea Rd, Parnell, Auckland, NZ, and has issue living, Gillian Mary Edgcumbe, *b* 1941.

DAUGHTER LIVING OF SIXTH EARL

Lady Hilaria Agnes, *b* 1908: *m* 1933, Lt-Col Denis Lucius Alban Gibbs, DSO, Queen's R Regt, who *d* 1984, and has had issue, Jillianne Bridget, *b* 1935: *m* 1st, 1959 (*m diss* 1973), Maj Martin John Minter-Kemp, RWF (ret); 2ndly, 1974, Anthony Alan Russell Cobbold, of The Vineyard, Weston under Redcastle, Shrewsbury, and *d* 1994, leaving issue (by 1st *m*), Robin John Edgcumbe *b* 1963, Emma Hilaria *b* 1960, Penelope Claire (twin) *b* 1963, — Margaret Hilaria (2516 Top Hill Rd, Louisville, Kentucky 40206, USA), *b* 1937: *m* 1961 (*m diss* 1989), Rev Mark Lyon Thornewill, RN (ret), and has issue living, John-Mark Judah *b* 1961: *m* 1985, Araby Jane Wedekind (and has issue living, Benjamin Aaron *b* 1985, Alice Hilaria *b* 1988), Luke Thomas *b* (twin) 1961, Christopher Shane Kenelm *b* 1968, Jeremy Lyon *b* 1970, Joanna Lilian *b* 1965, — Rosamund Lucia, *b* 1941: *m* 1963, Rear Adm Robert Nathaniel Woodard, RN, of Drift Farm, Constantine, Falmouth, Cornwall TR11 5JN, and has issue living, Rupert Piers Nathaniel *b* 1964, Jolyon Robert Alban *b* 1969, Melissa Lucia Rosamund *b* 1967, — Penelope Mary, *b* 1949: *m* 1st, 1970, Douglas Arthur Dale; 2ndly, 1985, Timothy Roger Douglas-Riley, of 67 Hartismere Rd, SW6 7UE, and has issue living, Henrietta Lucia *b* 1987, Venetia Louise *b* 1988. *Residence* – Aldenham, Deer Park Lane, Tavistock, Devon.

MOTHER LIVING

Meta, da of late Charles Robert Lhoyer, of Nancy, France: *m* 1st, 1935 (*m diss* 1943), George Aubrey Valletort Edgcumbe, brother of 7th Earl, who *d* 1977; 2ndly, 1967, Arthur Edward Blucher, who *d* 1988. *Residence* – Summit Drive, Torbay, Auckland, NZ.

STEPMOTHER LIVING

Una Pamela, da of late Edward Lewis George, of Perth, W Australia: *m* 1st, 1944, as his 2nd wife, George Aubrey Valletort Edgcumbe, brother of 7th Earl, who *d* 1977; 2ndly, 1989, Kenneth Baron. *Residence* – 77 Arapiki Rd, Stoke, Nelson, NZ.

COLLATERAL BRANCHES LIVING

Grandchildren of late Richard Gerald Valletort Edgcumbe, 3rd son of late Edward Mortimer Edgcumbe (infra):—

Issue of late Edward Mortimer Edgcumbe, *b* 1904, *d* 1983: *m* 1941, Mary MacArthur (27 Tuhaere St, Orakei, Auckland, New Zealand), da of John Stone:—
Richard John, *b* 1946. —— Margaret Ann, *b* 1942: *m* 1981, William Kendrick Smithyman, of 66 Alton Ave, Northcote, Auckland, NZ.

Granddaughter of late Edward Mortimer Edgcumbe, yr son of late Hon George Edgcumbe, yst son of 2nd Earl:—
Issue of late Ernest Athole Edgcumbe, *b* 1870, *d* 1937: *m* 1896, Louisa Charlotte, who *d* 1949, da of William Martin, of Auckland, New Zealand:—
Jessie Hilaria, *b* 1911: *m* 1934, Leslie Reeves, who *d* 1986, of Unit 2, 102 Sandwich Rd, Hamilton, NZ and has issue living, Gaynor Hilaria Ann, *b* 1936: *m* 1957, Arthur Herbert Lidington, of 20 Chelsea Place, Hamilton, NZ, and has issue living, Brett Arthur *b* 1961: *m* 1987, Sonia Jane Haines (and has issue living, Reid Arthur *b* 1992), Janine Lesley *b* 1959: *m* 1979, Graeme William Pickering (and has issue living, Samuel Thomas *b* 1987, Hannah Louise *b* 1991).

PREDECESSORS – (1) Rt Hon RICHARD Edgcumbe, PC, many years MP for Cornwall, St Germans, and Plympton, was successively a Lord of the Treasury, Joint Vice-Treasurer, Receiver-Gen, Treasurer of War, Paymaster-Gen, for Ireland, Chancellor of the Duchy of Lancaster, and Lord-Lieut of Cornwall &c; *cr Baron Edgcumbe*, of Mount Edgcumbe, co Devon (peerage of Great Britain) 1742; *d* 1758; *s* by his el son (2) RICHARD, PC, 2nd Baron; MP for Plympton 1747-54, and for Penryn 1754-8; was Lord-Lieut of Cornwall, and successively a Lord Commr of the Admiralty, and Comptroller of the Household, &c; *d* unmarried 1766; *s* by his brother (3) GEORGE, 3rd Baron; and Adm of the Blue; MP for Plympton 1754-61, and Lord-Lieut of Cornwall; *cr Viscount Mount Edgcumbe and Valletort* (peerage of Great Britain) 1781, and *Earl of Mount Edgcumbe* (peerage of Great Britain) 1789; *d* 1795; *s* by his son (4) RICHARD, 2nd Earl; was Lord-Lieut of Cornwall; *d* 1839; *s* by his son (5) ERNEST AUGUSTUS, 3rd Earl; *b* 1797: *m* 1831, Caroline Augusta, da of Rear-Adm Charles Feilding; *d* 1861; *s* by his son (6) WILLIAM HENRY, GCVO, PC, 4th Earl; sat as MP for Plymouth (C) 1859-61; was Lord-Lieut of Cornwall 1877-1917, Lord Chamberlain of HM Queen Victoria's Household 1879-80, Lord High Steward of HM Queen Victoria's Household June 1885 to Jan 1886, and July 1886 to Aug 1892, and ADC to HM Queen Victoria 1887-97; a Member of Council to HRH the Prince of Wales 1901-17, and Keeper of the Seal of the Duchy of Cornwall 1907-17: *m* 1858, Lady Katherine Elizabeth Hamilton, who *d* 1874, da of 1st Duke of Abercorn, KG; 2ndly, 1906, his cousin, Caroline Cecilia, who *d* 1909, da of late Hon George Edgcumbe, and widow of 3rd Earl of Ravensworth; *d* 1917; *s* by his only son, (7) PIERS ALEXANDER HAMILTON, 5th Earl; *b* 1865; Dep Warden of the Stanneries 1913-44: *m* 1911, Lady Edith Villiers, who *d* 1935, da of 5th Earl of Clarendon; *d* 1944; *s* by his kinsman (8) KENELM WILLIAM EDWARD, TD (only son of Richard John Frederick Edgcumbe, MVO, el son of Hon George Edgcumbe, yst son of 2nd Earl), 6th Earl, *b* 1873: *m* 1906, Lilian Agnes, who *d* 1964, da of Col Arthur Chandos Arkwright, of Hatfield Place, Witham, Essex; *d* 1965; *s* by his kinsman (9) EDWARD PIERS (el son of Edward Mortimer Edgcumbe, 2nd son of Hon George Edgcumbe, yst son of 2nd Earl), 7th Earl; *b* 1903: *m* 1944, Victoria Effie, who *d* 1979, yr da of Robert Campbell, of N Ireland and NZ; *d* 1982; *s* by his nephew (10) ROBERT CHARLES (el son of George Aubrey Valletort Edgcumbe, brother of 7th Earl), 8th Earl and present peer; also Viscount Mount Edgcumbe and Valletort, and Baron Edgcumbe.

MOUNTEVANS, BARON (Evans) (Baron UK 1945)

Liberty

(EDWARD PATRICK) BROKE ANDVORD EVANS, 3rd Baron; *b* 1 Feb 1943; *s* 1974; *ed* Rugby, and Trin Coll, Oxford: *m* 1974, Johanna Keyzer, of The Hague.

Arms – Argent two bars wavy azure between three boar's heads sable. **Crest** – Between two cross crosslets fichee sable a demi lion erased reguardant or holding between the paws a boar's head erased also sable. **Supporters** – On either side a king penguin proper.
Address – c/o House of Lords, SW1.

BROTHER LIVING

Hon JEFFREY RICHARD DE CORBAN (5 Campden House Court, 42 Gloucester Walk, W8 4HU), *b* 13 May 1948; *ed* Nautical Coll, Pangbourne, and Pembroke Coll, Camb: *m* 1972, Hon Juliet Wilson, da of the 2nd Baron Moran, and has issue living, Alexander Edward Andvord, *b* 1975, — Julian James Rowntree, *b* 1977.

SISTER LIVING

Hon Lucinda Mary Deirdre EVANS, *b* 1951 (has retained her maiden name); journalist: *m* 1980, John E. Hooper.

UNCLE LIVING (*son of 1st Baron*)

Hon Edward Broke, VRD, *b* 1924; *ed* Wellington Coll; Cdr (E) RNR (ret): *m* 1947, Elaine Elizabeth, da of Capt (S) W. W. Cove, RN, and has issue living, Julian Phillip Broke, *b* 1956, — William Garth, *b* 1959, — Rosemary, *b* 1948. *Residence* – 15 York Mansions, Prince of Wales Drive, SW11.

WIDOW LIVING OF SECOND BARON

DEIRDRE GRACE (*Deirdre, Baroness Mountevans*), da of John O'Connell, of Buxton House, Buxton Hill, Co Cork: *m* 1940, the 2nd Baron, who *d* 1974. *Residence* – 2 Durward House, Kensington Court, W8.

PREDECESSORS – (1) *Adm Sir* EDWARD RATCLIFFE GARTH RUSSELL Evans, KCB, DSC, 2nd son of late Frank Evans, Bar-at-law, of 5 New Square, Lincoln's Inn, WC; *b* 1881; served as Second Officer of relief ship *Morning* during National Antarctic Expedition 1902-4, and made two voyages to Polar regions to relief of *Discovery*; was Second in Command of British Antarctic Expedition 1910, succeeding Capt Scott in command 1912-13; European War 1914-19 with Dover Patrol in command of *Broke* and as Senior Officer, Ostend; Rear-Adm Comdg Roy Australian Navy 1929-31, Com-in-Ch, Africa Station 1933-5, and at The Nore 1935-9; Rector of Aberdeen Univ 1936-42; Regional Commr for London Defence Area 1939-45; *cr Baron Mountevans*, of Chelsea, co London (peerage of United Kingdom) 1945: *m* 1st, 1904, Hilda Beatrice who *d* 1913, da of late Thomas Gregory Russell, Bar-at-law, of Christchurch, New Zealand; 2ndly, 1916, Elsa, who *d* 1963, da of late Richard Andvord, of Oslo, Norway; *d* 1957; *s* by his el son (2) RICHARD ANDVORD, 2nd Baron; *b* 1918; Chm of Norwegian Export

Centre and Anglo-Swedish Parl Group; late Lt RNVR: *m* 1940, Deirdre Grace, da of John O'Connell, of Buxton House, Buxton Hill, Co Cork; *d* 1974; *s* by his el son (3) (EDWARD PATRICK) BROKE ANDVORD, 3rd Baron and present peer.

Mountgarret, Baron, title of Viscount Mountgarret on Roll of HL.

MOUNTGARRET, VISCOUNT (Butler) Sits as BARON (Baron UK 1911) (Viscount I 1550)

I am exalted by depression

RICHARD HENRY PIERS BUTLER, 17th Viscount; *b* 8 Nov 1936; *s* 1966; *hp* to Earldoms of Ormonde and Ossory (*see* M Ormonde); *ed* Eton and RMA, late Capt Irish Guards: *m* 1st, 1960 (*m diss* 1969), Gillian Margaret, only da of Cyril Francis Stuart Buckley, of 41 St Leonard's Ter, SW3; 2ndly, 1970, Jennifer Susan Melville, da of Capt D. M. Wills, of Barley Wood, Wrington, Som, and formerly wife of D. W. Fattorini, of Sawley Hall, Ripon; 3rdly, 1983, Mrs Angela Ruth Waddington, eldest da of Maj Thomas Porter, of Church Fenton, Tadcaster, and has issue by 1st *m*.

Arms – Quarterly, 1st and 4th, perfesse sable and azure, a quadrangular castle with four towers between three martlets all argent, *Rawson*; 2nd and 3rd, or, a chief indented azure, a crescent for difference, *Butler*. **Crests** – 1st, An eagle's head per fesse sable and azure, goutté d'or holding in the beak two annulets interlaced paleways or, *Rawson*. 2nd, out of a ducal coronet or, a plume of five ostrich feathers argent, therefrom a falcon rising of the last, *Butler*. **Supporters** – *Dexter*, a falcon wings inverted argent, armed, membered, and belled or; *sinister*, a male griffin argent, armed, collared , and chained or.
Residence – Stainley House, S Stainley, Harrogate. *Clubs* – White's, Pratt's.

SONS LIVING (By 1st marriage)

Hon PIERS JAMES RICHARD, *b* 15 April 1961.
Hon Edmund Henry Richard, *b* 1962: *m* 1988, Adelle I., only da of M. Lloyd, of New York, USA.

DAUGHTER LIVING (By 1st marriage)

Hon Henrietta Elizabeth Alexandra, *b* 1964: *m* 1991, Robert Cluer, only son of Henry Cluer, of S Africa.

SISTER LIVING

Hon Sarah Elizabeth Ann *b* 1932: *m* 1955 (*m diss* 1976), Geoffrey Kenneth Raynar, and has issue living, Rupert James Geoffrey, *b* 1957, — James Augustine, *b* 1962. *Residence* – 52 St Anne's Drive, Headingley, Leeds.

MOTHER LIVING

(Eglantine Marie) Elizabeth (The Dolphins, Sandwich, Kent), da of late William Lorenzo Christie, of Jervaulx Abbey, Middleham, Yorks: *m* 1931 (*m diss* 1941), the 16th Viscount, who *d* 1966; 2ndly, 1956, Rear Adm Patrick Vivian McLaughlin, CB, DSO, who *d* 1969.

PREDECESSORS – (1) *Hon* RICHARD Butler, 2nd son of 8th Earl of Ormonde; Kt 1547, *cr Viscount Mountgarret* (peerage of Ireland) 1550*: *m* 1st, Eleanor, da of Theobald Butler, of Neigham, co Kilkenny; 2ndly, Catherine, da of Peter Barnewall, of Stackall, co Meath; 3rdly, 1541, Anne, da of 4th Lord Killeen; *d* 1571, *s* by his son (by 1st *m*) (2) EDMUND, 2nd Viscount; sat in Parliament 1585 and was Deputy and Sheriff of co Kilkenny 1576: *m* his 1st cousin, Grizel Fitzpatrick, da of Barnaby, 1st Lord of Upper Ossory; *d* 1602; *s* by his son (3) RICHARD, 3rd Viscount; sat as MP in several Parliaments; was appointed Gen of the Irish Forces 1642, and, having been outlawed, was in 1652, after his death, excepted from pardon; *m* 1st, Margaret, da of Hugh O'Neill, Earl of Tyrone; 2ndly, Thomasine Elizabeth, who *d* 1625, da of Sir William Andrews, of Newport Pagnell, Bucks; 3rdly, Margaret, who *d* 1655, da of Richard Branthwaite, and widow of Sir Thomas Spencer, Bt; *s* by his son (by 1st *m*) (4) EDMUND, 4th Viscount, who in 1660 received a pardon for all treasons, rebellions, etc, from Charles II, and was restored to his estates, &c 1661: *m* 1st, Lady Dorothy Touchet, who *d* 1635, 2nd da of 2nd Earl of Castlehaven; 2ndly, 1635, Anne, da of Sir Thomas Tresham, and widow of William Thatcher; 3rdly, 1637, Elizabeth, da of Sir George Simeon, and widow of William Conyers; *d* 1679; *s* by his son (by 1st *m*) (5) RICHARD, 5th Viscount; Capt Jacobite Army at Siege of Londonderry 4 June 1689: *m* 1st, 1661, Emilia, who *d* 1682, da of William Blundell, of Crosby, Lancs; 2ndly, his 3rd cousin, Margaret, da of Richard Shee, and widow of Gilbert Butler; *d* 1706; *s* by his son (by 1st *m*) (6) EDMUND, 6th Viscount; Lt-Col of Horse in the Irish Army of James II, led the forlorn hope against the City of Londonderry, 1689, and, being taken prisoner, was afterwards outlawed and his estates forfeited; in 1721 claimed his seat in Parliament and took the oath of fidelity; in 1715 the outlawry was reversed: *m* 1st, Mary Buchanan; 2ndly, 1715, Elizabeth, da of John Bryan, and widow of Oliver Grace; *d* 1735; *s* by his el son (7) RICHARD, 7th Viscount: *m* 1711, Catherine, who *d* 1739, da of John O'Neill, of Shanes Castle, co Antrim; *dsp* 1736 *s* by his brother (8) JAMES, 8th Viscount; served in Austrian Army in Campaign on the Rhine 1735: *m* 1736, Margaret, who *d* 1764, 2nd da of 11th Lord Trimlestown; *dsp* 1743; *s* by his brother (9) EDMUND, 9th Viscount: *m* Anne, who *d* 1773, da of Toby Purcell, of Ballymartin, co Kilkenny; *d* 1750; *s* by his son (10) EDMUND, 10th Viscount; *b* 1771; *d* 1779; *m* 1744, Charlotte, who *d* 1778, 2nd da of Sir Simon Bradstreet, 1st Bt; *s* by his son (11) EDMUND, 11th Viscount; MP co Kilkenny 1776-79: *m* 1768, Lady Henrietta Butler, who *d* 1785, 2nd da of 1st Earl of Carrick; *d* 1793; *s* by his son (12) EDMUND, 12th Viscount; *b* 1771; *cr Earl of Kilkenny* (peerage of Ireland) 1793: *m* Mildred, who *d* 1830, *Residence* – eldest da of Most Rev Robert Fowler, Archbishop of Dublin; *d* 1846, when the earldom expired, and the minor honours devolved upon his nephew (13) HENRY EDMUND, 13th Viscount, son of Hon Henry, 3rd son of 11th Viscount, by Anne, da of John Harrison, Esq, of Newton House, co York; *b* 1816; *m* 1843, Frances Penelope, who *d* 1886, only child of Thomas Rawson, of Nidd Hall, Knaresboro'; *d* 1900; *s* by his son (14) HENRY EDMUND, 14th Viscount; *b* 1844; assumed by R Licence 1891 the surname of Rawson-Butler, and the additional arms of Rawson, but in 1902 by R Licence resumed the surname of Butler only; DL and JP W Riding of Yorks, High Sheriff 1895, DL co Kilkenny and for City of York; Lieut 1st LG; *cr Baron Mountgarret*, of Nidd, W Riding of York (peerage of UK) 1911: *m* 1st, 1868, Mary Eleanor, who *d* 1900, da of late St John Chiverton Charlton, of Apley Castle, Shropshire; 2ndly, 1902, Robina Marion, who *d* 1944, el da of Col Edward Hanning Hanning-Lee, JP (formerly Comdg 2nd Life Guards), of The Old Manor House, Bighton, Alresford, Hants; *d* 1912; *s* by his son (**15**) EDMUND SOMERSET, 15th Viscount, *b* 1875: *m* 1897, Cecily, who *d* 1961, (having *m* 2ndly, 1919, as his 2nd wife, Lieut-Col Charles Hoare, DSO, who assumed by R Licence 1927 the surname of Grey in lieu of his patronymic), da of late Arthur Grey; *d* 1918; *s* by his half-brother (**16**) PIERS HENRY AUGUSTINE, 16th Viscount; *b* 1903: *m* 1st, 1931 (*m diss* 1941), Eglantine Marie Elizabeth, da of William Lorenzo Christie, of Jervaulx Abbey, Yorks; 2ndly, 1941, (Elsie) Margarita, who *d* 1968, da of Sir John Nicholson Barran, 2nd Bt; *d* 1966; *s* by his only son (**17**) RICHARD HENRY PIERS, 17th Viscount and present peer; also Baron Mountgarret.

*The 1st Viscount is also said to have been *cr Baron of Kells*, but there is no mention of this title in the grant.

MOUNTMORRES, VISCOUNTCY OF (de Montmorency) (Extinct 1951)

DAUGHTER LIVING OF SEVENTH VISCOUNT

Hon Carolie Madge Warrand, *b* 1920; *ed* Chelsea Coll of Physical Education and W London Sch of Physiotherapy (MCSP); Physiotherapist, Superintendent of Poole Gen Hospital 1965-81; 1939-45 War in WAAF: *m* 1947, Douglas Morris, and has had issue, Andrew John, *b* 1957; 3rd Engr Officer RFA; *ka* S Atlantic Campaign 1982, — Diana Pauline, *b* 1954. *Residence* – Danebury Hill, 15 Greenwood Ave, Lilliput, Poole, Dorset.

Mount Stuart, Lord; son of Marquess of Bute.

MOWBRAY, SEGRAVE and STOURTON, BARON (Stourton) (Baron E 1283; *Baron E 1295; Baron E 1448)
(Title pronounced "Mo-bray, Seagrave and Sturton")

I will be loyal during my life

Badge of the Barons Stourton

CHARLES EDWARD STOURTON,* CBE, 26th Baron Mowbray, 27th Baron Segrave, and 23rd Baron Stourton; *b* 11 March 1923; *s* 1965; *ed* Ampleforth Coll, and Ch Ch, Oxford; Opposition Whip, House of Lords 1967-70 and 1974-78, Deputy Chief Whip 1978-79; a Lord-in-Waiting to HM 1970-74, and 1979-80; Knt of Sovereign Mil Order of Malta; CBE (Civil) 1982; 1939-45 War in NW Europe as Lt Grenadier Gds (wounded); Member Nidderdale RDC 1954-58, and Securicor 1961-64; Dir Securicor (Scotland) Ltd 1964-70; Chancellor Primrose League 1974-83; a Trustee College of Arms since 1975; Dir ERIC (Jersey) Ltd, ERIC (Ghana) Ltd, GDC (Ghana) Ltd, ERIC (Suisse) SA, ERIC (Canada) Inc; Kt of Sacred and Mil Constantinian Order of St George: *m* 1952, Hon Jane Faith de Yarburgh Bateson, only da of 5th Baron Deramore, and has issue.

Arms – Quarterly of six; 1st sable, a bend or between six fountains, *Stourton*; 2nd gules, on a bend between six crosses crosslet argent, an escutcheon or, charged with a demi-lion rampant, pierced through the mouth by an arrow, within a double tressure flory counterflory of the first, *Howard*; 3rd gules, a lion rampant argent, *Mowbray*; 4th sable, a lion rampant argent, ducally crowned or, *Segrave*; 5th gules, three lions passant guardant or, a label of three points argent, *Plantagenet*; 6th gules, a lion, rampant, within a bordure engrailed or, *Talbot*. **Crest** – A demi Monk proper, habited in russet, his girdle or and wielding in his dexter hand a scourge also or, thereon five knotted lashes. **Supporters** – *Dexter*, a lion rampant argent, ducally crowned or; *sinister*, a sea-dog sable, scaled and finned or. **Badges** – A drag or sledge.
Residences – 23 Warwick Sq, SW1; Marcus, by Forfar, Angus. *Clubs* – Pratt's, Turf, White's, Beefsteak.

SONS LIVING

Hon EDWARD WILLIAM STEPHEN (The Stables, Allerton Park, nr Knaresborough, N Yorks), *b* 17 April 1953; *ed* Ampleforth: *m* 1980, Penelope (Nell) Lucy, el da of Dr Peter Brunet, of Paines Hill House, Steeple Aston, Oxon, and has issue living, James Charles Peter, *b* 12 Dec 1991, — (Sarah) Louise, *b* 1982, — Isabel Laura, *b* 1983, — Camilla Charlotte, *b* 1987, — Francesca Jane, *b* 1988.
Hon James Alastair (21 Moreton Place, SW1V 2NL), *b* 1956; *ed* Ampleforth, and Magdalene Coll, Camb (MA); with Sotheby's since 1979; Proprietor, The Stourton Press; Kt of Honour and Devotion Sovereign Mil Order of Malta: *m* 1993, Hon Sophia Ulla Stonor, yst da of 7th Baron Camoys.

SISTER LIVING (*In remainder to the Baronies of Mowbray, Segrave and Stourton*)

Hon Patricia Winifred Mary, *b* 1924; sometime in Foreign Office: *m* 1948, Frederick Petre Crowder, QC, MP (*see* B Petre, colls, 1980 Edn), and has issue living, Richard John (Candie House, Candie St, St Peter Port, Guernsey, CI), *b* 1950; *ed* Eton: *m* 1st, 1973 (*m diss* 19—), Belinda Jane, el da of Capt Matthew Page-Wood (*see* Page-Wood, Bt); 2ndly, 1984, Lucy E., eldest da of Michael Charlesworth, — John George (163 Wakehurst Rd, SW11), *b* 1954; *ed* Eton: *m* 1984, Carolyn, only da of Donald Griffiths, of Elie, Fife, and has issue living, Charles Petre Gordon *b* 1990, Anna Jane *b* 1992.

AUNT LIVING (*Daughter of 24th Baron*)

Hon Charlotte Mary (2 Arthington Av, Harrogate), *b* 1904.

WIDOW LIVING OF SON OF TWENTIETH BARON STOURTON

BEATRICE CICELY (*Hon Mrs Edward P. J. Corbally Stourton*) (Arlonstown Cottage, Dunsany, Navan, co Meath), da of late H. E. Page, of Wragby, Lincs, and Titchwell, Norfolk: *m* 1934, Hon Edward Plantagenet Joseph CORBALLY STOURTON, who *d* 1966, having assumed in 1927, the additional name of Corbally, and has issue (see colls, infra).

COLLATERAL BRANCHES LIVING (*All of whom are in remainder to Baronies of Mowbray, Segrave and Stourton*)

> Issue of late Maj Hon John Joseph Stourton, TD, yr son of 21st Baron Stourton, *b* 1899, *d* 1992: *m* 1st, 1923 (*m diss* 1933), Kathleen Alice, who *d* 1986, da of late Robert Louis George Gunther, of 8 Prince's Gdns, SW, and Park Wood, Englefield Green, Surrey; 2ndly, 1934 (*m diss* 1947), Gladys Leila, who *d* 1953, da of Col Sir William James Waldron, of Ascot Cottage, Winkfield, Berks, and 77 Cromwell Rd, SW7:—
> (By 1st *m*) Michael Godwin Plantagenet, *b* 1926; *ed* Eton; Maj Grenadier Guards (ret); FRICS, QUALAS; ADC to Comdt RMA Sandhurst 1951-52, Adj 1st Bn Grenadier Guards 1953-55, and Staff Capt HQ London Dist 1955-57; Land Agent to HRH the late Duke of Gloucester, Barnwell Manor Estate 1966-71; partner Curtis & Henson 1966-68, since when Savills: *m* 1955, Lady Joanna Lambart, da of FM 10th Earl of Cavan, KP, GCB, GCMG, GCVO, GBE, and has issue living, Thomas Michael John, *b* 1965, — Henry Matthew, *b* 1971, — Julia, *b* 1958: *m* 1987, Simon Anthony Carne Rasch, son of Maj Sir Richard Guy Carne Rasch, 3rd Bt, — Clare Elizabeth, *b* 1962: *m* 1993, Charles Francis Houghton Beckford, HM Foreign Office, 2nd son of Maj Adrian Beckford, of Hook Norton, Oxon. *Residence* – The Old Rectory, Gt Rollright, Oxon. —— John Ralph, *b* 1930; *ed* Eton, and Magdalene Coll, Camb (MA); late Lieut Grenadier Guards; JP co Fermanagh 1977; Dir Liebig's Extract of Meat Co Ltd 1957-68, Brooke Bond Liebig Ltd 1968-74, Interocean Shipping Agency 1974-92: *m* 1st, 1958 (*m diss* 1965), Virginia, twin da of late Basil Colin Shrubra Hordern, of The Old Rectory, Fernhurst, Sussex; 2ndly, 1967, Caroline Honor, yr da of Col J. C. O'Dwyer, of Magheracross, Ballinamallard, co Fermanagh, and has issue living (by 1st *m*), Lucilla Mary, *b* 1959: *m* 1989, John Michael Joseph Royden, elder son of Sir Christopher John Royden, 5th Bt, — (by 2nd *m*) Georgina Caroline, *b* 1969, — Jemima Nicola, *b* 1971: *m* 1992, Marcelo Novoa. *Residence* – The Malthouse Granary, Poulton, Cirencester, Glos GL7 5HN. —— Mary (*Countess of Gainsborough*), *b* 1925: *m* 1947, 5th Earl of Gainsborough. *Residence* – Horn House, Exton, Leics LE15 7QU. —— Monica Kathleen, *b* 1928: *m* 1955, Henry Louis Carron Greig, CVO, CBE, DL, Gentleman Usher to HM, son of late Group Capt Sir Louis Greig, KBE, CVO, and has issue living, Louis Stourton, *b* 1956; *ed* Eton, and St Edmund Hall, Oxford; a Page of Honour to HM 1970-73, — Jonathan, *b* 1958; *ed* Eton, and Downing Coll, Camb, — George Carron, *b* 1960; *ed* Eton, and St Peter's Coll, Oxford, — Laura Monica, *b* (twin) 1960; Lady-in-Waiting to HRH The Princess of Wales since 1989: *m* 1984, James Leopold Somerset Lonsdale (*see* B Raglan, colls, 1990 Edn), and has had issue, Thomas Louis James *b* 1991 *d* 1992, Leonora Diana Fiona *b* 1986, Rosanna Monica *b* 1988. *Residence* – Brook House, Fleet, Hants.

> Issue of late Hon Edward Plantagenet Joseph CORBALLY STOURTON, DSO, 4th son of 20th Baron Stourton, *b* 1880, *d* 1966, having assumed in 1927 the additional name of Corbally: *m* 1934, Beatrice Cicely (ante), da of H. E. Page:—
> Nigel Edward, *b* 1937; late Capt Grenadier Guards: *m* 1960 (*m diss* 1975), Frances Deirdre Morton, da of Patrick Lancaster, of Wapsbourne Manor, Sheffield Park, Sussex, and has issue living, Edward Richard, *b* 1961, — Nicholas Simon, *b* 1963, — Patrick Henry, *b* 1965. *Residence* – 41 St Mary Abbots Court, Warwick Gdns, W14 8RB. —— Vanessa Mary, *b* 1935.

> Granddaughter of late Auberon Joseph Stourton, el son of late Hon Albert Joseph Stourton (infra):—
> Issue of late Eudo Philip Joseph Stourton, *b* 1900, *d* 1975: *m* 1927, Cicely Frances, who *d* 1982, da of late Henry Hyman Haldin, KC, of 17 Montagu Sq, W1 (Leon, Bt):—
> Veronica Philippa, *b* 1929: *m* 1954, Philip Biden Derwent Ashbrooke, who *d* 1993, of La Grande Maison, St John, Jersey, CI, and has issue living, Auberon Francis Biden, *b* 1956; *ed* Ampleforth, and St John's Coll, Camb; Maj King's Royal Hussars, — Sophia Mary Veronica (*Viscountess Stormont*), *b* 1959: *m* 1985, Alexander David Mungo, Viscount Stormont, elder son of 8th Earl of Mansfield and Mansfield.

> Grandchildren of late Capt Herbert Marmaduke Joseph Stourton, OBE, 2nd son of late Hon Albert Joseph Stourton, 6th son of 19th Baron Stourton:—
> Issue of late Sir Ivo Herbert Evelyn Joseph Stourton, CMG, OBE, KPM, *b* 1901, *d* 1985: *m* 1st, 1926, Lilian Margaret, who *d* as a result of enemy action 1942, da of George Dickson; 2ndly, 1945, Virginia (The Old Bakery, Kimpton, Andover, Hants) (who *m* 2ndly, 1986, W. Hilary Young, CMG), da of late Sir Horace James Seymour, GCMG, CVO (*see* M Hertford, colls):—
> (By 1st *m*) Nigel John Ivo, OBE (Arbour Hill, Patrick Brompton, Bedale, N Yorks DL8 1JX), *b* 1929; OBE (Civil) 1981, Knt of Sovereign Mil Order of Malta: *m* 1956, Rosemary Jennifer Rushworth, da of Hon Mr Justice (Sir Myles John) Abbott, Ch Justice of Bermuda, and has issue living, Edward John Ivo (73 Hendham Rd, SW17 7DH), *b* 1957; Knt Sovereign Mil Order of Malta: *m* 1980, Margaret, eldest da of Sir James Napier Finnie McEwen, 2nd Bt, and has issue living, Ivo James Benedict *b* 1982, Thomas Edward Alexander *b* 1987, Eleanor Mary Elizabeth *b* 1984, — Julian Nicolas (26 Lower Addison Gdns, W14 8BG), *b* 1959: *m* 1992, Margaret A., da of late A. J. Barsham, of Broadwater, Weybridge, Surrey, — Christopher Nigel Paul (37 Patience Rd, SW11), *b* 1965: *m* 1992, Melissa, yr da of Hon Sir Richard Storey, 2nd Bt, — Lavinia Margaret Grace, *b* 1962: *m* 1986, Frank D. Nicholson, and has issue (see Lawson-Tancred, Bt). — Simon Nicholas (Wynter House, Dyrham, Chippenham, Wilts), *b* 1932: *m* 1975, Pamela, da of Charles James Baker, of Letcombe Manor, Wantage, Berks, and widow of Alexander J. Scratchley, MC. —— Felicity Magdalen (40 East Witton, Leyburn, N Yorks), *b* 1927. —— (By 2nd *m*) (Barbara) Jane, *b* 1947: *m* 1974, Maj (Archibald) Graham Buchanan-Dunlop, of Broughton Place, Broughton, Biggar, Lanarks, and has issue living, (Archibald) Roderick, *b* 1979, — David Erskine, *b* 1981.
> Issue of late Magdalen Mary Charlotte Stourton, *b* 1899, *d* 1981: *m* 1st, 1925 (*m diss* 1936), Archibald Ashworth Baillie Hay, DSO, MC, who *d* 1965; 2ndly, 1936 (*m diss* USA 1943), Robert Ducas, who *d* 1978; 3rdly, 1947 (*m diss* 1956), William Brian Buchel:—
> (By 2nd *m*) Robert Ivo DUCAS (Flat 10, 24 Lowndes St, SW1 9JE), *b* 1937: *m* 1963, Patricia, who *d* 19—, yr da of P. Provatoroff, of Crippenden Manor, Cowden, Kent, and has issue living, Annoushka, *b* 1966: *m* 1990, John A. C. Ayton, eldest son of Antony Ayton, of Jordans End, Jordans, Bucks, and has issue living, Marina Isobel Provatoroff *b* 1993. —— Magdalen June Ruth (Flat 5, 46 Oakley St, SW3 5HA), *b* 1938: *m* 1959, Hon James Donald Diarmid Ogilvy, and has issue (*see* E Airlie).
> Issue of late Barbara Bertha Mary Stourton, *b* 1900, *d* 1980: *m* 1st, 1924 (*m diss* 1929), Capt Eric Charlton Tunnicliffe, R Welch Fus, who *d* 1937; 2ndly, 1929, Capt Frank Ashton Bellville, who *d* 1937; 3rdly, 1946, Capt Steuart Harrison-Wallace, DSO, RN, who *d* 1963:—
> (By 1st *m*) †Nigel Arthur TUNNICLIFFE, late Gren Gds, *b* 1928: *m* 1957 (*m diss* 1980), Diana Edith, da of late Cdr Peter Du Cane, OBE, RN (*see* Pole, Bt, *cr* 1628, 1985 Edn), and formerly wife of Hon Jeremy John Cubitt (*see* B Ashcombe, colls), and *d* 1982, leaving issue, Brigid Serena, *b* 1963: *m* 1990, Richard L. Pavry, of 19 Dalby Rd, Wandsworth, SW18 1AW. —— Elizabeth Anne, *b* 1926: *m* 1947, William Alexander Mackenzie, of Wakelyns Farm, Fressingfield, Eye, Suffolk, and has issue living, Michael Alexander Edward (Chapel House, Kettlebridge, Cupar, Fife), *b* 1949; *ed* Stanbridge Earls Sch, — Margaret Anne, *b* 1955: *m* 1975, George Champion Streatfeild, of Denmark House, Longtown, Hereford. —— (By 2nd *m*)

Patricia Barbara, *b* 1931: *m* 1965, Alfred Charles Gladitz, of Sadlers House, Hardington Mandeville, Yeovil, Som, and has issue living, Rupert Ivo Charles, *b* 1969; *ed* Ampleforth, and Gonville & Caius Coll, Camb (BA).
    Issue of late Gytha Mary Stourton, *b* 1904, *d* 1992: *m* 1934, Frederick Ramon de Bertodano, 8th Marqués del Moral (Spain), who *d* 1955:—
Alfonso Michael George DE BERTODANO STOURTON (Ferraz 73, Madrid 28008), *b* 1937: *m* 1968, Carolina Garcia de la Riva, da of Abel Garcia, of Murcia, Spain, and has issue living, Miguel Ramon Marcos, *b* 1969, — Ignacio José Roberto, *b* 1970, — Gonzalo Alberto, *b* 1974, — Jaime Felipe, *b* 1982, — Carolina Isabel, *b* 1978. —— Helen Gytha Mary, *b* 1935: *m* 1957, Jean le Goaëc, of Mas de la Condamine, 83570 Cotignac, France, and has issue living, Yann Charles Ramon, *b* 1959, — Michel Patrick Roland, *b* 1962, — Annik Marie Nicole, *b* 1958: *m* 1982, Bruno Gaschet, of 38 bis rue Pascal, 75013 Paris, and has issue living, Guillaume *b* 1986, Astrid *b* 1984, — Katarina Nancy Gytha *b* 1960: *m* 1981, Dr Mark de Caestecker, of 5 Ravenoak Rd, Cheadle Hume, Cheshire, and has issue living, Sebastian *b* 1986, Christian *b* 1990, Cassandra *b* 1983, — Sophie Marie-Helena, *b* 1971, — Isabelle Marie-Anne, *b* 1974.
    Issue of late Mary Jeanne Stourton, *b* 1913, *d* 1987: *m* 1938, 6th Baron Camoys, who *d* 1976:—
See that title.

    Granddaughter of late Hon Albert Joseph Stourton, 6th son of 19th Baron Stourton:—
    Issue of late Bertha Mary Philippa Stourton, *b* 1872, *d* 1958: *m* 1894, Major Frederick Bartholomew Stapleton-Bretherton, who *d* 1938 (B Petre):—
Mary Henrietta STAPLETON-BRETHERTON (18 Stroud Close, Wimborne Minster, Dorset), *b* 1906; resumed maiden name by deed poll 1960: *m* 1940 (*m diss* 1953), Col John Pell Archer-Shee, MC, late 10th Hussars, son of late Lt-Col Sir Martin Archer-Shee, CMG, DSO, and has issue living, Mary Pauline Daphne Therese (44 Cornwall Gdns, SW7), *b* 1941.

BRANCHES FROM YOUNGER SONS OF 17TH BARON STOURTON

    Descendants of late Hon Edward Marmaduke Joseph VAVASOUR (3rd son of 17th Baron Stourton); assumed the surname of Vavasour by sign-manual 1826 in lieu of his patronymic, and was *cr* a *Baronet* 1828:—
See Vavasour, Bt.

    Granddaughter of late Charles Joseph LANGDALE, 3rd son of late Hon Charles Joseph LANGDALE, MP (4th son of 17th Baron Stourton), who assumed the surname of Langdale in lieu of his patronymic 1814:—
    Issue of late Lt-Col Philip Joseph Langdale, OBE, *b* 1863, *d* 1950: *m* 1895, Gertrude, who *d* 1939, da of late Adm Samuel Hoskins Derriman, CB, of Uplands, Sussex, and of 52 Queen's Gate, SW:—
Joyce Elizabeth Mary (*Countess Fitzwilliam*), *b* 1898: *m* 1st, 1922 (*m diss* 1955), 2nd Viscount Fitz Alan of Derwent, who *d* 1962; 2ndly, 1956, 10th Earl Fitzwilliam, who *d* 1979. *Residence* – Milton Park, Peterborough, Cambs.

    Grandsons of late Lt-Col Philip Joseph Langdale (ante):—
    Issue of late Alathea Pauline Mary Alys Langdale, *b* 1902, *d* 1979: *m* 1923 (*m diss* 1936), 2nd Baron Manton, who *d* 1968:—
See that title.
    Issue of late Ursula Dorothy Mary Langdale, *b* 1903, *d* 1969: *m* 1931, Lt-Col Norman Birch, who *d* 1960:—
Michael Edward Stafford BIRCH, *b* 1933. *Residence* – Walkington Park, Beverley, E Yorks. —— Timothy Malcolm Stafford BIRCH, *b* 1937. *Residence* – 1 Little Weighton Rd, Walkington, Beverley, E Yorks.

    Grandchildren of late Dorothy Mary Paula Walpole (*m* 1st, 1919, Maj Austin Edward Scott Murray, MC; 2ndly, 1945, Col Colin Kayser Davy, MC), elder da of late Pauline Mary Langdale (Mrs Horace Walpole) (infra):—
    Issue of late Anne Mary Scott Murray, *b* 1920, *d* 1991: *m* 1944, Maj Rupert Leonard Eversley Milburn, who *d* 1974:—
See Milburn, Bt.

    Granddaughter of late Pauline Mary Langdale (*m* 1887, Col Horace Walpole, KRRC), yr da of late Charles Joseph Langdale (ante):—
    Issue of late Maude Mary Winifred Walpole, *b* 1897, *d* 1968: *m* 1st, 1921, Cyril James Wenceslas Torr, HM Foreign Ser, who *d* 1940; 2ndly, 1946, Vicomte Theophile de Lantsheere, CVO, who *d* 1958:—
(By 1st *m*) Jean Rosita Mary (*Lady Nevile*), MBE, *b* 1923; served 1939-45 War with VAD; MBE (Civil) 1984: *m* 1944, Capt Sir Henry Nicholas Nevile, KCVO, Lord Lieut Lincs since 1975, of Aubourn Hall, Lincoln, and has issue living, Christopher James (Manor Farm, Aubourn, Lincoln; 55 Endell St, WC2H 9AJ), *b* 1954: *m* 1981, Sarah Caroline, yr da of Sir Peter William Youens, KCMG, CMG, OBE, and has issue living, Charles Cato *b* 1990, Zita Stephanie *b* 1984, Nyasa Jane *b* 1986, — Hugh Simon (50 Lonsdale Rd, W11 2DE), *b* 1960: *m* 1989, Joanna Mary, elder da of Timothy Seymour Bathurst (*see* E Bathurst, colls), — Sarah Rosita Mary, *b* 1945: *m* 1968, Roger Hudson, of 38 Kensington Place, W8, and has issue living, Toby *b* 1970, George *b* 1972, — Elizabeth Jane Mary (*Lady Arnold*), *b* 1947: *m* 1st, 1970, Robin Irwin Smithers, who *d* 1979; 2ndly, 1984 (*m diss* 1993), Sir Thomas Richard Arnold, MP, and has issue living (by 1st *m*), Christian Alexander Langley *b* 1971, Lucian James Angelo *b* 1974, (by 2nd *m*) Emily Minna Mary *b* 1986, — Jill Gabriel Anne Mary, *b* 1950: *m* 1982, David Hughes, of 5 Dunsany Rd, W14 0JP, and has issue living, Anthony James Alleyne *b* 1983, Ralph Nicholas Alleyne *b* 1985.

    Grandchildren of late Alfonso Otho GANDOLFI-HORNYOLD, 2nd Duke Gandolfi, elder son of late Thomas Charles Gandolfi Hornyold, 1st Duke Gandolfi, eldest son of late John Vincent Hornyold (formerly Gandolfi), by his wife Charlotte Mary, 2nd da (by 1st *m*) of late Hon Charles Joseph Langdale, MP (ante):—
    Issue of late Maria Teresa Gandolfi-Hornyold, *b* 1910, *d* 1988: *m* 1932, Luigi Acchiappati, who *d* 1972:—
Gianantonio ACCHIAPPATI (33 rue George Sand, 75016 Paris), *b* 1933: *m* 1966, Pierrille, da of Count Alfred de Bertier de Sauvigny, and has issue living, Ugo, *b* 1968, — Gaïa Francesca, *b* 1971. —— Pierluigi (15 via Zenale, 20121 Milan, Italy), *b* 1934: *m* 1968, Chiara, da of Giorgio Bicchi. —— †Elena, *b* 1936: *m* 1964, Francis Buck (18 rue Pierre Brasseur, Luxembourg), and *d* 1977, having had issue, Laurent, *b* 1965; *d* 1976, — Nicolas, *b* 1968, — Frédérique, *b* 1973. —— Nicoletta (33 via Dei Serragli, Florence, Italy), *b* 1937.

    Grandsons of late Thomas Charles GANDOLFI-HORNYOLD, 1st Duke Gandolfi (ante):—
    Issue of late Ralph Vincent GANDOLFI-HORNYOLD, 3rd Duke Gandolfi, *b* 1881, *d* 1938: *m* 1927, Beatrix Purdey (who *d* 1992, having *m* 2ndly, 1940, Lt-Col (Cuthbert) Euan Charles Rabagliati, MC, DFC, late King's Own Yorkshire LI, who *d* 1978, of Villa Valentine, Domaine de la Roseraie, Mougins, France AM), da of Frederick Scott Oliver, of Edgerston, nr Jedburgh, Roxburghshire:—
Antony Frederick Gandolfi HORNYOLD (*Duke Gandolfi*) (Blackmore House, Hanley Swan, Worcester WR8 0ES. *Club* – Brooks's), *b* 1931; *s* his father as 4th Duke Gandolfi (*cr* 1899), and as 17th Marquis (*cr* 1529 and 1899) 1938; *ed* Ampleforth, and Trin Coll, Camb; late 2nd Lieut KOSB; a Knight of Sovereign Mil Order of Malta: *m* 1993, Caroline Mary Katherine, MVO, da of late Maj Patrick Dudley Crichton-Stuart (*see* M Bute, colls). —— Simon Ralph (271 Sandycombe Rd, Kew, Richmond, Surrey), *b* 1933; *ed* Ampleforth; late 2nd Lieut 16th/5th Lancers: *m* 1965, Catherine, da of John Charles Roberts, and has issue living, Anthony Vincent, *b* 1964.

Grandchildren of late Henry HORNYOLD-STRICKLAND, FSA (assumed by Royal Licence 1932 for himself and his issue the addl surname and arms of Strickland: *m* 1920, Hon Mary Constance Elisabeth Christina, CBE, eldest da of 1st Baron Strickland), only son of late Alfred Joseph Hornyold (infra):—
Issue of late Lt-Cdr Thomas Henry HORNYOLD-STRICKLAND, DSC, RN, *b* 1921, *d* 1983; *s* his grandfather (1st Baron Strickland) as 7th Count della Catena (*cr* 1745 by Grand Master (Pinto) of Malta); assumed by Royal Licence 1938 the arms of Matthews quarterly with his own: *m* 1951, Angela Mary, OBE, DL Cumbria (Sizergh Castle, Kendal, Cumbria LA8 8AE), eldest da of late Francis Henry Arnold Engleheart, of The Priory, Stoke-by-Nayland, Suffolk:—
Henry Charles HORNYOLD-STRICKLAND, *b* 1951; *ed* Ampleforth, Exeter Coll, Oxford (BA), and INSEAD Fontainebleau (MBA); 8th Count della Catena; Knight of Honour and Devotion Sovereign Mil Order of Malta: *m* 1979, Claudine Thérèse, da of Clovis Poumirau, of Hossegor, France, and has issue living, Hugo, *b* 1979, — Thomas, *b* 1985. *Residences* – Sizergh Castle, Kendal, Cumbria; 56 Ladbroke Rd, W11 3NW. —— Robert Francis (74 Honeywell Rd, SW11), *b* 1954; *ed* Ampleforth; Knight of Honour and Devotion Sovereign Mil Order of Malta: *m* 1983, Teresa Mary, da of Richard Fawcett, and has issue living, Francis Richard, *b* 1986, — Rollo Michael, *b* 1988, — Zoë Clementine, *b* 1991. —— John Jarrard, *b* 1956; *ed* Ampleforth; Knight of Honour and Devotion Sovereign Mil Order of Malta. —— Edward Thomas, *b* 1960; *ed* Ampleforth. —— Clare Edeline, *b* 1953: *m* 1981, Anthony Prince, of 26 Abingdon Court, Abingdon Villas, W8 6BT. —— Alice Mary, *b* 1959: *m* 1988, Charles Loftie, of Bowerbank, Pooley Bridge, Cumbria, and has issue living, William Thomas Crozier, *b* 1991, — Eleanor Sophie, *b* 1992.
Issue of late Edeline Winifred Hornyold-Strickland, *b* 1922, *d* 1981: *m* 1943, Norman Coppock, who *d* 1982:—
Michael Thomas COPPOCK, *b* 1949; *ed* More House Sch: *m* 1975, Susan Ann, da of John B. Davies, of 41 Mill Lane, Southport, Lancs, and has issue living, David Michael, *b* 1978, — Andrew Joseph, *b* 1983, — Sarah Louise, *b* 1976. *Residence* – 13 Saunders St, Southport, Lancs PR9 0HP.

Granddaughter of late Alfred Joseph HORNYOLD, 3rd son of late John Vincent HORNYOLD (ante):—
Issue of late Dorothy Hornyold, *b* 1892, *d* 1918: *m* 1917, Hon Charles Hugh Clifford (later 11th Baron Clifford of Chudleigh), who *d* 1962:—
See that title.

Grandchildren of late Maj Washington Charles Thomas HIBBERT, elder son of late Mrs Hubert Aloysius Tichborne Hibbert (infra):—
Issue of late Maj Hugh Washington HIBBERT, The Queen's Bays, *b* 1911, *d* 1985: *m* 1st, 1938 (*m diss* 1949), Lady Patricia Margery Kathleen Mackay, who *d* 1973, elder da of 2nd Earl of Inchcape; 2ndly, 1952, Angela Mary, formerly wife of Richard Miles Backhouse (*see* Backhouse, Bt), previously widow of Capt Count Richard Dudley Melchior Gurowski, Scots Gds, and eldest da of late Peter Haig Thomas (*see* E Normanton, 1971 Edn):—
(By 1st *m*) Michael Washington HIBBERT (Westbourne, Alloway, by Ayr), *b* 1946; *ed* Ampleforth: *m* 1972, Gisela, da of Paul Thomsen, of Odense, Denmark, and has issue living, Peter Michael Washington, *b* 1974, — Jasper Erik Washington, *b* 1978. —— †Bridget Anne, *b* 1939: *m* 1966, Edward Alan Mervyn Molyneux Herbert, and *d* 1976, leaving issue (*see* E Carnarvon, colls). —— Elizabeth Caroline (Manor House, Broughton Gifford, Melksham, Wilts), *b* 1943: *m* 1965, Capt Jeremy Michael Porter, RN, who *d* 1985, and has issue (*see* V Charlemont, colls).
Issue of late Violet Margaret Hibbert, *b* 1907, *d* 1986: *m* 1936, Lt-Cdr Llewellyn Somerset Edward Llewellyn, RN (ret), who *d* 1940:—
Virginia Mary LLEWELLYN, *b* 1937. *Residence* – 77 Cadogan Gdns, SW3.

Grandson of late Mrs Francis FFRENCH DAVIS (infra):—
Issue of late Capt Francis Holdsworth FFRENCH DAVIS, *b* 1907, *ka* 1944: *m* 1940, Ingrid Margaret Mary (who *m* 2ndly, 1948, as his 2nd wife, Maj Edmond Myles Pery-Knox-Gore (*see* E Limerick, colls), who *d* 1966), da of late Maj Henry MacDermot, KC, of 19 Fitzwilliam Sq, Dublin:—
Francis Conor FFRENCH DAVIS (Knockharley, Brownstown, Navan, co Meath), *b* 1941: *m* 1962, Prudence Mary Fiona, da of John Evelyn Smith Wright, of Javea, Alicante, Spain, and has issue living, Francis Dermot, *b* 1964, — Dominic John, *b* 1965, — Stephen Luke, *b* 1967, — Michael James, *b* 1969, — Nicola Marguerite, *b* 1977, — Sarah Jane Victoria, *b* 1985.

Grandchildren of late Mary Hornyold (Mrs Hubert Aloysius Tichborne Hibbert), eldest da of late John Vincent Hornyold (ante):—
Issue of late Marguerite Mary Julia Hibbert, *b* 1872, *d* 1964: *m* 1899, Capt Francis ffrench Davis:—
Peter Charles FFRENCH DAVIS (Flat 34, 77 Hallam St, W1N 5LR), *b* 1912; *ed* Ampleforth, and Trin Coll, Camb (BA); late Member London Stock Exchange; served 1939-45 War as Capt Welsh Gds. —— Marguerite Elizabeth Josephine (The Visitation Convent, Waldron, Essex), *b* 1913; a Visitation Nun, as Sister Jane Frances: *m* 1944, Frederick Michael Selmes Jackson, who *d* 1968.
Issue of late Angela Mary Hibbert, *b* 1877, *d* 1972: *m* 1st, 1905, as his 2nd wife, Brig-Gen Paul Aloysius Kenna, VC, DSO, who was *ka* 1915; 2ndly, 1919, Col Allen Victor Johnson, DSO, who *d* 1939 (*see* Johnson, Bt, *cr* 1818, colls, 1939 Edn):—
(By 1st *m*) Kathleen, *b* 1906: *m* 1936, Lt-Cdr Lionel Rupert Knyvet Tyrwhitt, DSO, DSC, RN, who was *ka* 1942, brother of Vera Ruby, Baroness Berners. *Residence* – 23 Fitzmaurice Place, Bradford-on-Avon, Wilts BA15 1EL. —— Celia Mary Ethel, *b* 1909. *Residence* – 23 Fitzmaurice Place, Bradford-on-Avon, Wilts BA15 1EL.

Granddaughter of late Arthur Joseph LANGDALE, 6th son of late Hon Charles LANGDALE, MP (ante):—
Issue of late Gertrude Pietrina Josephine Mary Stourton, *b* 1882, *d* 1915: *m* 1907, Adm James Ughtred Farie, CMG, who *d* 1957:—
Margaret Jean Mary FARIE, *b* 1912; a Benedictine Nun, as Dame Jean Farie, of Stanbrook Abbey, Worcs.

Grandchildren of late Henry Joseph STOURTON, son of late Hon Philip Henry Joseph STOURTON, 6th son of 17th Baron Stourton:—
Issue of late Violet Mary Annette, OBE, *b* 1873, *d* 1961: *m* 1893, Francis Joseph Siltzer, who *d* 1924:—
Derek Henry SILTZER, *b* 1897; *ed* Oratory Sch: *m* 1938, Merlyn Seaforth, da of William Densham, of Melbourne, Australia, and widow of Keith Poulton. *Residence* – 8B Longwood, Darling Point, Sydney, NSW, Australia.

Granddaughter of late Amy Mary Josephine Stourton (Mrs Frederic Dundas Harford), yr da of late Henry Joseph Stourton (ante):—
Issue of late Joan Mary Harford, *b* 1897, *d* 1983: *m* 1920, Lt-Col Sir Alexander Bannerman, 11th Bt, who *d* 1934:—
See that title.

PREDECESSORS – (1) *Sir* JOHN Stourton, Knt, was Sheriff of Wilts 1434, and of co Gloucester 1438, and Treasurer of the Household 1445; served in the Wars of France and Normandy; *cr* Baron Stourton, of Stourton, co Wilts (peerage of England) 1448; *d* 1462; *s* by his son (2) WILLIAM, 2nd Baron; *d* 1478-9; *s* by his el son (3) JOHN, 3rd Baron; *s* by his son (4) FRANCIS, 4th Baron; *d* (young) 1486-7; *s* by his uncle (5) WILLIAM, 5th Baron; *dsp* 1522; *s* by his brother (6) EDWARD, 6th Baron; appointed by Act of Parliament a Justice of the Peace for assessing and collecting £163,000 by a poll-tax; *d* 1535; *s* by his son (7) WILLIAM, 7th Baron; *d* 1548; *s* by his son (8) CHARLES, 8th Baron, was executed 16 March 1557, at Salisbury, in a halter of silk, for murdering two men named Hartgill; *s* by his el son (9) JOHN, 9th Baron; restored in blood by Act of Parliament 1575, and inherited the barony; was one of the peers on the trial of Queen Mary of Scotland; *s* by his brother (10) EDWARD,

10th Baron; *d* 1632; *s* by his son **(11)** WILLIAM, 11th Baron; *s* by his grandson **(12)** WILLIAM, 12th Baron; *s* by his el son **(13)** EDWARD, 13th Baron *dsp* 1720; *s* by his brother **(14)** THOMAS, 14th Baron; *dsp* 1743; *s* by his nephew **(15)** CHARLES, 15th Baron, son of Charles, 3rd son of 12th Baron; *d* 1753-4; *s* by his brother **(16)** WILLIAM, 16th Baron; *m* 1749, Winifred, el da and in her issue co-heir of Philip Howard, cf Buckenham, Norfolk, and in her issue co-heiress of her uncles, the 8th and 9th Duke of Norfolk, to the Baronies of Mowbray and of Segrave (see * infra) and of Howard, Greystock, Ferrers of Wemme, Furnival, Strange of Blackmere, Giffard of Brimmesfield, and Braose of Gower, &c; *d* 1781; *s* by his son **(17)** CHARLES PHILIP, 17th Baron; *d* 1816; *s* by his son **(18)** WILLIAM JOSEPH, 18th Baron; *d* 1846; *s* by his son **(19)** CHARLES, 19th Baron; *b* 1802: *m* 1825, Hon Mary Lucy, da of 6th Baron Clifford; *d* 1872; *s* by his el surviving son **(20)** ALFRED JOSEPH, 20th Baron, in whose favour the abeyances of the Baronies of *Mowbray* and *Segrave* (see ‡ infra) were terminated.

‡**(1)** ROGER de Mowbray was summoned to the Parliament of England as *Baron Mowbray* 1283; having previously been summonded by Simon de Montfort, when in rebellion *temp* Henry III, such summons was declared void by Act of Parliament; *d* 1298; *s* by his son **(2)** JOHN, 2nd Baron; summoned to Parliament in two reigns: *m* Alice, da and co-heir of William, Baron de Braose; was executed at York 1322 for his connection with the rising of the Northern Earls against the Despencers; his estates were forfeited, but an attainder did not follow; *s* by his son **(3)** JOHN, 3rd Baron; served in the wars of Scotland and France, and was summoned to Parliament *temp* Edward III; *d* 1361; *s* by his son **(4)** JOHN, 4th Baron; summoned to Parliament *temp* Edward III: *m* Elizabeth, da and heir of John, 3rd Baron Segrave (see † infra), by which marriage the Segrave estates and the dignity of Lord Segrave were vested in him; slain near Constantinople 1368; *s* by his el son **(5)** JOHN, 5th Baron; *cr Earl of Nottingham* (peerage of England) 1337; *d* unmarried 1382, when the earldom expired; *s* by his half brother **(6)** THOMAS, KG, 6th Baron; summoned as *Earl of Nottingham* (peerage of England) 1383-86; and *cr* Earl Marshal 1386, and *Duke of Norfolk* (peerage of England) 1397: *m* 1st, Elizabeth, da of heir of John, Lord Strange of Blackmere; and 2ndly, Elizabeth, da and co-heir of Richard FitzAlan, Earl of Arundel and Surrey; by the latter he left two sons Thomas and John, and two das Margaret, wife of Sir Robert Howard, and Isabel, wife of James, 6th Lord Berkeley; *d* 1399; *s* by his el son **(7)** THOMAS, 2nd Earl, and Dukedom of Norfolk being erroneously withheld from him, joined the rebellion of the nobles against Henry IV, 1405, and being arrested, was beheaded at York without trial; *dsp*; *s* by his brother **(8)** JOHN, 3rd Duke; in 1425 declared by Parliament to to be entitled to the dukedom; *s* by his son **(9)** JOHN, 4th Duke, obtained a confirmation of the dukedom; went as Ambassador to negotiate peace between England and France: *m* Eleanor, da of William, Baron Bourchier; *s* by his son **(10)** JOHN, 5th Duke; *cr Earl of Warren and Surrey* (peerage of England); *d* 1475, when the Dukedom of Norfolk, and Earldoms of Nottingham, Warren, and Surrey expired, while the Baronies of Mowbray and Segrave devolved upon his da **(11)** ANNE, who in infancy was affianced to Richard, Duke of York, 2nd son of Edward IV; he was murdered with his brother in the Tower 1483, and the Duchess *dsp*, when the baronies became abeyant between the sons of Sir Robert Howard and Lord Berkeley (*see* 6th Baron Mowbray), and remained so until the abeyance was terminated in favour of **(12-22)** JOHN Howard, *cr Baron Howard* (peerage of England) 1470, and *Duke of Norfolk* (peerage of England) 1483, with which peerages the Baronies of Mowbray and Segrave were merged until 1777, when they again became abeyant, and remained so until 1877, when the abeyances were terminated in favour of **(23)** ALFRED JOSEPH Stourton (ante), as senior co-heir of Margaret, wife of Sir Robert Howard (*see* 6th Baron Mowbray); *b* 1829: *m* 1865, Mary Margaret, who *d* 1925, da of late Matthew Corbally, MP; *d* 1893; *s* by his el son **(24)** CHARLES BOTOLPH JOSEPH, 24th Baron Mowbray, 25th Baron Segrave, and 21st Baron Stourton; *b* 1867; claimed as Lord Mowbray to be placed Premier Baron of England, and unsuccessfully claimed ancient Earldom of Norfolk (1312) 1906: *m* 1893, Mary, who *d* 1961, only child of late Thomas Angus Constable, of Manor House, Otley, *d* 1936; *s* by his el son **(25)** WILLIAM MARMADUKE, MC, 25th Baron Mowbray, 26th Baron Segrave, 22nd Baron Stourton, *b* 1895; Capt Grenadier Guards: *m* 1921, Sheila, who *d* 1975, da of late Hon Edward Walford Karslake Gully, CB (V Selby, colls); *d* 1965; *s* by his only son **(26)** CHARLES EDWARD, 26th Baron Mowbray, 27th Baron Segrave, 23rd Baron Stourton and present peer.

† **(1)** NICHOLAS de Segrave, one of the most active leaders of the Baron *temp* Henry III, was summoned to Parliament of England in the King's name as *Baron Segrave* 1295; *d* 1295; *s* by his son **(2)** JOHN, 2nd Baron; summoned to Parliament 1296-1325; was Constable of the English Army in Scotland; taken prisoner at the battle of Bannockburn, and imprisoned by the Scots for a year; *d* 1325; *s* by his grandson **(3)** JOHN, 3rd Baron: *m* Margaret, sole heiress of Thomas de Brotherton, Earl of Norfolk, 5th son of Edward I; *d* 1353; *s* by his da **(4)** ELIZABETH, wife of John, 4th Baron Mowbray (see * ante).

*The question of whether the barony of Segrave was created in 1283 or 1295 is discussed in the preface to *The Complete Peerage*, Vol I.

MOYLE, BARONY OF (Moyle) (Extinct 1974)

SON LIVING OF LIFE BARON (*By 1st m*)

Rt Hon Roland Dunstan (19 Montpelier Row, Blackheath, SE3 0RL), *b* 1928; PC 1978: *m* 1956, Sheleagh Patricia, da of Bernard Hogan.

MOYNE, BARON (Guinness) (Baron UK 1932)

Judge not

JONATHAN BRYAN GUINNESS, 3rd Baron; *b* 16 March 1930; *s* 1992; *ed* Eton (King's Scholar), and Trin Coll, Oxford (MA); Dir Arthur Guinness, Son & Co 1961-88, and Leopold Joseph & Sons 1963-91; Chm Monday Club 1970-72: *m* 1st, 1951 (*m diss* 1963), Ingrid Olivia Georgia, da of late Maj Guy Richard Charles Wyndham, MC (*see* B Egremont, colls); 2ndly, 1964, Suzanne, da of Harold William Denis Lisney, of Cadaqués, Gerona, Spain, and formerly wife of Timothy Phillips, and has issue by 1st and 2nd *m*.

Arms – Per saltire gules and azure, a lion rampant or; on a chief ermine two ducal coronets each enfiling as many arrows in saltire of the third. **Crest** – A boar passant quarterly or and gules charged with a mullet counterchanged. **Supporters** – On either side a Cingalese macaque sejant proper.
Residences – Bosalverne, Greenbank, Alverton, Penzance, Cornwall.
Club – Beefsteak.

SONS LIVING *(By 1st marriage)*

Hon JASPER JONATHAN RICHARD, *b* 9 March 1954; *ed* Eton: *m* 1985, Camilla Alexandra, da of Robie David Corbett Uniacke, and has issue living, Amber, *b* 1989, — Claudia, *b* 1992. *Residence* – Arniano, Murlo, Siena, Italy.
Hon Valentine Guy Bryan, *b* 1959; *ed* Eton, and Ch Ch, Oxford: *m* 1986, Lucinda Jane, only da of Cdr Miles James Rivett-Carnac, RN (*see* Rivett-Carnac, Bt), and has issue living, Tara Victoria, *b* 1991. *Residence* – 87 Hereford Rd, W2 5BB.

(by 2nd marriage)

Hon Sebastian Walter Denis, *b* 1964; *ed* Eton: *m* 1987 (*m diss* 1991), Silvie Dominique, da of Eric A. Fleury, of 7 Chemin de Verdiers, Geneva, Switzerland. *Residence* –

DAUGHTERS LIVING *(By 1st marriage)*

Hon Catherine Ingrid, *b* 1952; resumed her maiden name 1988: *m* 1st, 1983 (*m diss* 1988), James Donald, Lord Neidpath, son of 12th Earl of Wemyss; 2ndly, 1990, Robert Fleetwood Hesketh (*see* E Scarbrough). *Residence* – Meols Hall, Southport, Lancs.

(by 2nd marriage)

Hon Daphne Suzannah Diana Joan, *b* 1967: *m* 1987, Spyros Niarchos, 2nd son of Stavros Niarchos, of Villa Marguns, St Moritz, Switzerland, and has issue living, Nicolas Stavros, *b* 1989, — Alexis Spyros, *b* 1991. *Address* – 41 Park St, W1.

THE THIRD BARON HAS FURTHER ISSUE *(by Susan Mary, da of Ronald Taylor, of Oldham, Lancs)*

Thomas Julian William Jon TAYLOR, *b* 1986. —— Diana Gloria Isolde Rose Dimilo TAYLOR, *b* 1981. —— Aster Sophia Mary TAYLOR, *b* 1984.

BROTHER LIVING

Hon Desmond Walter, *b* 1931; *ed* Gordonstoun, and Ch Ch, Oxford (MA); Hon LLD Trin Coll, Dublin; Pres Irish Georgian Soc 1958-91; author: *m* 1st, 1954 (*m diss* 1981), HSH Princess Marie-Gabrielle (Mariga) Sophie Joti Elizabeth Albertine Almeria, who *d* 1989, eldest da of HSH Prince Albrecht Eberhard Karl Gero-Maria von Urach, Count of Württemberg; 2ndly, 1985, Penelope, da of Graham Cuthbertson, and has issue living (by 1st *m*), Patrick Desmond Karl Alexander, *b* 1956; *ed* Winchester, and Trin Coll, Dublin (MA), — Marina, *b* 1957; *ed* Cranborne Chase. *Residence* – Leixlip Castle, co Kildare.

HALF-BROTHERS LIVING

Hon Finn Benjamin, *b* 1945; *ed* Winchester, Ch Ch, Oxford (MA), and Inst of Animal Genetics, Edinburgh Univ (PhD); Biologist: *m* 1989, Mary Wilson, formerly wife of James Patrick Donleavy, author, and da of late Benjamin Wilson Price, of Baltimore, Maryland, USA. *Residence* – Chute Forest House, Chute, Andover, Hants SP11 9DS.
Hon Kieran Arthur, *b* 1949; *ed* Winchester, and Ch Ch, Oxford (MA); Botanist: *m* 1983, Mrs Vivienne Halban, da of André-Jacques van Amerongen, DFC, MB, BCh, MRCOG, FRCOG, of Grafton House, Blisworth, Northants, and has issue living, Malachy, *b* 1986, — Lorcan, *b* 1989, — Kate, *b* 1985. *Residence* – Knockmaroon House, Castleknock, co Dublin.
Hon Erskine Stuart Richard, *b* 1953; *ed* Winchester, and Edinburgh Univ; Wilts CC 1979-81, MFH Tedworth 1981-84, Farmer, Trustee Guinness Trust Housing Assocn 1979-89: *m* 1984, Louise Mary Elizabeth, only da of late Patrick Dillon-Malone, and has issue living, Hector, *b* 1986, — Arthur, *b* 1991, — Matthew Richard, *b* 1992, — Molly, *b* 1985. *Residence* – Fosbury Manor, Marlborough, Wilts.

HALF-SISTERS LIVING

Hon Rosaleen Elisabeth, *b* 1937; *ed* St Anne's Coll, Oxford (MA): *m* 1965, Sudhir Mulji, and has issue living, Sachin Sudhir, *b* 1967, — Kabir Jayantilal Bryan, *b* 1970, — Sangita Rosaleen, *b* 1966, — Gopali Sharda Elisabeth, *b* 1975. *Residence* – 150 Malcha Marg, New Delhi 110021, India.
Hon Fiona Evelyn, *b* 1940; *ed* Cranborne Chase, and McGill Univ, Canada; Zoologist. *Residence* – Isle of Rhum, Inner Hebrides.
Hon Thomasin Margaret, *b* 1947; *ed* Cranborne Chase, and Farnham Coll of Art; Potter and Painter; has issue living, Luke GUINNESS, *b* 1980. *Residence* – Biddesden House, Andover, Hants.
Hon Catriona Rose, *b* 1950; *ed* Cranborne Chase, Winchester Co High Sch, and LMH Oxford (MA); Botanist and Farm Manager. *Residence* – Biddesden Farm, Andover, Hants.

Hon Mirabel Jane, *b* 1956; *ed* Cranborne Chase, and E Anglia Univ (BA); MFH Tedworth 1986-93; author of *Biddesden Cookery* 1987: *m* 1984, Patrick Ian (Tom) Helme, son of A. R. Helme, of Butcher's Barn, Danehill, Sussex, and has issue living, Toby Anthony Bryan, *b* 1992, — Alice Mirabel, *b* 1987, — Tyga Elisabeth, *b* 1990, — Lily, *b* 1994. *Residence* – Mount Orleans, Collingbourne Ducis, Marlborough, Wilts.

UNCLE LIVING (*son of 1st Baron*)

Hon Murtogh David, *b* 1913: *m* 1949, Nancy Vivien Laura, who *d* 1975, only da of late Cyril Edward Tarbolton, of Hampstead, NW. *Residence* – 117 E 80th St, New York, NY 10021, USA.

AUNT LIVING (*daughter of 1st Baron*)

Hon Grania Maeve Rosaura (*Dowager Marchioness of Normanby*), *b* 1920; Hon LLD Dublin, JP N Yorks 1971-83, Pro Chancellor Dublin Univ since 1985; formerly Section Officer WAAF: *m* 1951, 4th Marquess of Normanby, KG, CBE, who *d* 1994. *Residences* – Lythe Hall, Whitby, N Yorks; Argyll House, 211 King's Rd, SW3.

WIDOW LIVING OF SON OF SECOND BARON

Felicity, only da of Sir Andrew Hunter Carnwath, KCVO, of 37 Riverview Gdns, SW13: *m* 1962, Hon Diarmid Edward Guinness, who *d* 1977, and has issue (see colls, infra). *Residence* – 2 Keats Grove, NW3.

MOTHER LIVING

Hon Diana Freeman-Mitford (*Hon Lady Mosley*), 3rd da of 2nd Baron Redesdale: *m* 1st, 1929 (*m diss* 1934), Hon Bryan Walter Guinness (later 2nd Baron Moyne), who *d* 1992; 2ndly, 1936, Sir Oswald Ernald Mosley, 6th Bt, who *d* 1980. *Residence* – Temple de la Gloire, 91400 Orsay, France.

WIDOW LIVING OF SECOND BARON

ELISABETH (*Dowager Baroness Moyne*), 3rd da of late Capt Thomas Arthur Nelson, of Achnacloich, Connel, Argyll: *m* 1936, as his 2nd wife, the 2nd Baron, who *d* 1992. *Residences* – Biddesden House, Andover, Hants; Knockmaroon House, Castleknock, co Dublin.

COLLATERAL BRANCH LIVING

Issue of late Hon Diarmid Edward Guinness, 3rd son of 2nd Baron, *b* 1938, *d* 1977: *m* 1962, Felicity (ante), only da of Sir Andrew Hunter Carnwath, KCVO, of 37 Riverview Gdns, SW13:—
Ewan Diarmid, *b* 1965; *ed* Eton. ——— Camilla, *b* 1963. ——— Lorna, *b* 1967; *ed* Edinburgh Univ. ——— Harriet, *b* 1970.

PREDECESSORS – **(1)** *Rt Hon* WALTER EDWARD GUINNESS, DSO, TD, 3rd son of 1st Earl of Iveagh; *b* 1880; Lt-Col Suffolk Yeomanry; S Africa 1900-1901 (despatches), 1914-18 War (DSO and Bar); was a County Councillor for London 1907-10, MP for Bury St Edmunds 1907-31, Under-Sec of State for War 1922-23, Financial Sec to Treasury 1923-24 and 1924-25, Min of Agriculture and Fisheries 1925-29 Joint Parliamentary Sec to Min of Agriculture and Fisheries 1940-41, Sec of State for the Colonies and Leader of the House of Lords 1941-42, Dep Min of State in Middle East 1942-44, and Min Resident for United Kingdom in Middle East Jan to Nov 1944; *cr Baron Moyne* of Bury St Edmunds, co Suffolk (peerage of United Kingdom) 1932: *m* 1903, Lady Evelyn Hilda Stuart Erskine, who *d* 1939, da of 14th Earl of Buchan; *d* (assassinated in Cairo) 1944; *s* by his son **(2)** BRYAN WALTER, 2nd Baron; *b* 1905; Bar Inner Temple 1930; formerly Major Royal Sussex Regt; Poet and Novelist, Hon Fellow Trin Coll, Dublin, Member of Irish Academy of Letters, Gov Nat Gallery of Ireland, FRSL: *m* 1st, 1929 (*m diss* 1934), Hon Diana Freeman-Mitford, 3rd da of 2nd Baron Redesdale; 2ndly, 1936, Elisabeth, 3rd da of late Capt Thomas Arthur Nelson, of Achnacloich, Connel, Argyll; *d* 1992; *s* by his eldest son **(3)** JONATHAN BRYAN, 3rd Baron and present peer.

MOYNIHAN, BARONY OF (Moynihan) (Baron UK 1929, Bt 1922) (Dormant 1991)

ANTONY PATRICK ANDREW CAIRNES BERKELEY MOYNIHAN, 3rd Baron, and 3rd Baronet, *d* 1991, and at the time of going to press the succession to the title has not been proved.

DAUGHTERS LIVING OF THIRD BARON (*By 2nd marriage*)

Hon Miranda Dorne Ierne, *b* 1959: *m* 1977 (*m diss* 1985), Horace Harry O'Garrow Omowale X, and has issue living, Saskia Beulegh Ierne *b* 1979.

(*By 3rd marriage*)

Hon Antonita Maria Carmen Fernandez, *b* 1969.
Hon Aurora Luzon Maria Dolores, *b* 1971.
Hon Kathleen Maynila Helen Imogen Juliet, *b* 1974.

HALF-BROTHER LIVING OF THIRD BARON

Hon Colin Berkeley, MP, *b* 13 Sept 1955; *ed* Monmouth Sch, and Univ Coll, Oxford (Pres Oxford Univ Soc 1976); Political Assist to Foreign Sec since 1982; World Gold Medallist for Lightweight Rowing 1978 (Silver 1981), and Olympic Silver Medallist 1980; Freeman City of London 1978, Liveryman Haberdashers' Co 1981; an Under-Sec of State, Dept of Environment (Min of Sport) since 1987; MP for Lewisham East (C) since 1983: *m* 1992, Gaynor-Louise, only da of Paul G. Metcalf, of Healing, S Humberside, and has issue living, Nicholas Ewan Berkeley, *b* 31 March 1994. *Residence* – Flat 42 Buckingham Court, Buckingham Gate, SW1. *Clubs* – Brooks's Royal Commonwealth Soc.

SISTERS LIVING OF THIRD BARON

Hon Imogen Anne Ierne, *b* 1932: *m* 1st 1953 (*m diss* 1965), Michael Edward Peter Williams; 2ndly 1965, Charles Ivan Vance, and has issue living (by 2nd *m*), Jacqueline Belinda Ierne *b* 1963.

Hon Juliet Jane Margaretta, *b* 1934: *m* 1st, 1958, Thomas Edwin Bidwell Abraham, who *d* 1976; 2ndly, 1978, Harry Hougham Sparks, and has issue living (by 1st *m*), James Bidwell, *b* 1959, — John Richard, *b* 1960.

HALF-SISTER LIVING OF THIRD BARON

Hon Melanie June, *b* 1957: *m* 1983, Peter-John Stuart Corbett, of Cedar Cottage, Ludlow Green, Ruscombe, Stroud, Glos GL6 6DH, and has issue living, Edward John Patrick, *b* 1990, — Poppy Ann, *b* 1986, — Daisy Angelica Jak, *b* 1988.

WIDOW LIVING OF SECOND BARON

JUNE ELIZABETH, da of Arthur Stanley Hopkins: *m* 1st, 1952, as his 2nd wife, the 2nd Baron, who *d* 1965; 2ndly, 1967, Neville Barton Hayman, of Burstowe, Shirley Av, Cheam, Surrey.

WIDOW LIVING OF THIRD BARON

JINNA (*Baroness Moynihan*), da of —Sabiaga, of —: *m* 1990, as his 5th wife, the 3rd Baron, who *d* 1991. *Residence* – —.

PREDECESSORS – (1) *Sir* BERKELEY GEORGE ANDREW Moynihan, KCMG, CB, son of late Capt Andrew Moynihan, VC, 8th King's Regt; *b* 1865; and eminent Surg; Pres of Roy Coll of Surgs of England 1926-32; *cr* a *Baronet* 1922, and *Baron Moynihan*, of Leeds, co York (peerage of United Kingdom) 1929: *m* 1895, Isabella Wellesley, who *d* 1936, da of Thomas Richard Jessop, FRCS, JP; *d* 1936; *s* by his son (2) PATRICK BERKELEY, OBE, TD, 2nd Baron, *b* 1906; Chm Exec Cttee, Liberal Party 1947-50, and Chm of N-W Metropolitan Regional Hosp Board 1960-65: *m* 1st, 1931 (*m diss* 1952), Ierne Helen, who *d* 1991, el da of late Cairnes Derrick Carrington Candy; 2ndly, 1952, June Elizabeth (who *m* 2ndly, 1967, Neville Barton Hayman), yr da of Arthur Stanley Hopkins, *d* 1965; *s* by his el son (3) ANTONY PATRICK ANDREW CAIRNES BERKELEY, 3rd Baron, *b* 1936; Lieut Coldstream Gds: *m* 1st, 1955 (*m diss* 1958), Ann, da of Reuben Stanley Herbert, of Greenfield Cottage, Therfield, Royston; 2ndly, 1958 (*m diss* 1967), Shirin Roshan Berry, da of late Ahmed Quereshi; 3rdly, 1968 (*m diss* 1979), Luthgarda Maria Beltran Dela Rosa, da of Alfonzo Fernandez, of 160 P. Gomez, Caloocan City, Philippines; 4thly, 1981 (*m diss* 1990), Editha Eduarda, da of late Maj-Gen Eduardo Ruben, of Bulacan, Philippines; 5thly, 1990, Jinna Sabiaga; *d* 1991, when the title became dormant.

MOYOLA, BARON (Chichester-Clark) (Life Baron 1971)

JAMES DAWSON CHICHESTER-CLARK, PC, son of late Capt James Jackson Lenox-Conyngham Chichester-Clark, DSO, RN (M Donegall, colls); *b* 12 Feb 1923; *ed* Eton; Maj (ret) Irish Gds; 1939-45 War (wounded); a DL of co Derry; a Member of House of Commons of N Ireland 1960-73, Ch Whip 1963-66, Leader 1966-67, Min of Agric 1967-69 and Prime Min 1969-71; *cr* PC 1967, and *Baron Moyola*, of Castledawson, co Londonderry (Life Baron) 1971: *m* 1959, Moyra Maud, da of Brig Arthur de Burgh Morris, CBE, DSO, and widow of Capt T. G. Haughton, and has issue.

Arms – Quarterly, 1st gules three swords erect in pale proper, hilts and pommels or, a canton argent, charged with a trefoil vert, *Clark*; 2ndly, chequy or and gules, a chief vair, *Chichester*; 3rd azure fretty argent *Etchingham*; 4th, azure on a bend or three daws gules, *Dawson*. **Crest** – Out of a mural crown a arm embowed in armour, the hand holding a dagger, all proper, charged with a trefoil vert. **Supporters** – On either side, a heron's wing addorsed and gorged with a baron's coronet proper.
Residence – Moyola Park, Castledawson, co Derry.

DAUGHTERS LIVING

Hon Fiona, *b* 1960: *m* 1994, William Rodney David Fisher, son of Leonard Fisher, of Lurgan, co Armagh.
Hon Tara Olivia, *b* 1962: *m* 1984, Edward Thomas Whitley, son of John Whitley, of Hamsey Lodge, Lewes, Sussex.

MULLEY, BARON (Mulley) (Life Baron 1984)

FREDERICK WILLIAM MULLEY, PC, el son of late William Mulley, of Leamington Spa; *b* 3 July 1918; *ed* Bath Place Church of England Sch, Warwick Sch, and Ch Ch Oxford; served in 1939-45 War (prisoner in Germany 1940-45); Fell of St Catharine's Coll, Cambridge 1948-50; Barrister-at-law, Inner Temple 1954; MP for Park Div of Sheffield 1950-83; PPS to Min of Works 1951; Dep Defence Sec and Min for the Army 1964-65; Min of Aviation 1965-67; Jt Min of State, Foreign and Commonwealth Office 1967-69; Min for Disarmament 1967-69; Min of Transport 1969-70; Min for Transport, Dep of the Environment 1974-75; Sec of State for Education and Science 1975-76; Sec of State for Defence 1976-79; Pres Assembly of Western European Union 1980-83; a Vice-Pres Peace Through NATO since 1985; Mem Nat Executive Cttee, Labour Party 1957-58, 1960-80, Chm Labour Party 1974-75; Dep Chm Sheffield Development Corpn since 1988; *cr* PC 1964, and *Baron Mulley*, of Manor Park, City of Sheffield (Life Baron) 1984: *m* 1948, Joan Doreen, da of Alexander Morris Phillips, of London, and has issue.
Address – c/o House of Lords, Westminster, SW1.

DAUGHTERS LIVING

Hon Deirdre, *b* 1951.
Hon Corinne MULLEY, *b* 1953: *m* 1983, Nicholas Stevens, of Stafford.

MUNSTER, EARL OF (FitzClarence) (Earl UK 1831)

Neither rashly nor fearfully

ANTHONY CHARLES FITZ-CLARENCE, 7th Earl; *b* 21 March 1926; *s* 1983; *ed* St Edward's Sch, Oxford; served RN 1942-47; graphic designer 1950-79; stained glass conservator for Burrell Museum 1979-83, conservator with Chapel Studio 1983-89; MSIA 1960-69, FRSA 1987: *m* 1st, 1949 (*m diss* 1966), Louise Marguerite Diane, da of Louis Delvigne, of Liège, Belgium; 2ndly, 1966 (*m diss* 1979), Mrs Pamela Margaret Hyde, da of Arthur Spooner; 3rdly, 1979, Dorothy Alexa, MusB (Edin), LRAM, da of late Lt-Col Edward Boyd Maxwell, OBE, MC, and has issue by 1st and 2nd *m*.

𝔄rms – The Arms of King William IV (without the escutcheon of the arch-treasurer of the HR empire, and without the crown of Hanover), three debruised by a baton sinister azure, charged with three anchors or. 𝔆rest – On a chapeau, gules, turned up ermine, a lion statant guardant crowned with a ducal coronet or, and gorged with a collar azure, charged with three anchors or. 𝔖upporters – *Dexter*, a lion guardant, ducally crowned or; *sinister*, a horse argent; each gorged with a collar azure, charged with three anchors or.
Residence – Mulberry Cottage, Park Farm, Haxted Rd, Lingfield, Surrey RH7 6DE.

DAUGHTERS LIVING *(By 1st marriage)*

Lady Tara Francesca, *b* 1952: *m* 1979, Ross Jean Heffler, and has issue living, Leo Edward Michael, *b* 1985, — Alexandra Louise, *b* 1982. *Residence* – 146 Ramsden Rd, SW12.
Lady Finola Dominique, *b* 1953: *m* 1981, Jonathan Terence Poynton, yr son of D. R. Poynton, of Woodford, Cheshire, and has issue living, Oliver Maximillian Christo, *b* 1984, — Chloë Nona, *b* 1982. *Residence* – 153 Wellfield Rd, SW16.

(By 2nd marriage)

Lady Georgina, *b* 1966.

WIDOW LIVING OF SIXTH EARL

VIVIAN (*Vivian, Countess of Munster*), da of late Benjamin Schofield, JP, of Greenroyde, Rochdale, Lancs, and stepda of late Judge A. J. Chotzner, MP: *m* 1939, as his 2nd wife, the 6th Earl, who *d* 1983. *Residence* – 1 Arundel Court, Jubilee Place, Chelsea Green, SW3.

COLLATERAL BRANCH LIVING

Granddaughter of late Capt Hon George FitzClarence, 3rd son of 1st Earl:—
Issue of late Lionel Ashley Arthur FitzClarence, *b* 1870, *d* 1936: *m* 1913, Theodora Frances Maclean, who *d* 1948, da of late Evan A. Jack, of 1 The Grove, Boltons, S Kensington, SW:—
Mary Theodora Annette, *b* 1914: *m* 1948, Adam Gluszkiewicz, and has issue living, Anna Judita, *b* 1949. *Residence* – 14 Ellesmere Orchard, Westbourne, nr Emsworth, Hants.

PREDECESSORS – (1) GEORGE FitzClarence, FRS, el natural son of King William IV, by the great comic actress Dorothy Bland, known as Mrs Jordan; *b* 1794: Maj-Gen in the Army, Lieut of the Tower, and Gov of Windsor Castle: *cr Baron Tewkesbury, Viscount FitzClarence* and *Earl of Munster* (peerage of United Kingdom) 1831, with remainder to his brothers, Frederick, Adolphus and Augustus primogeniturely: *m* 1819, Mary Wyndham, who *d* 1842, natural da of George, 3rd Earl of Egremont; *d* 1842; *s* by his son (2) WILLIAM GEORGE, 2nd Earl, *b* 1824; Capt late 1st Life Guards: *m* 1855, Wilhelmina, who *d* 1906, da of late Hon John Kennedy-Erskine; *d* 1901; *s* by his el son (3) GEOFFREY GEORGE GORDON, DSO, 3rd Earl, *b* 1859; Major Lothian Regt; Afghan War 1879-80, S Africa 1881, S Africa 1889-1902 (DSO); *d* 1902; *s* by his brother (4) AUBREY, 4th Earl, *b* 1862; a Gentleman Usher to Queen Victoria and to King Edward VII 1885-1902; *d* 1928; *s* by his nephew (5) GEOFFREY WILLIAM RICHARD HUGH, KBE, PC, (son of late Maj Hon Harold Edward FitzClarence, MC, 7th son of 2nd Earl) 5th Earl *b* 1906; Lord-in-Waiting to HM 1932-38, Paymaster-Gen 1938-39, Under-Sec of State for War 1939, Purl Under-Sec, of State for India and Burma 1943-44, Under-Sec of State for Home Affairs 1944-45, Parl Under-Sec of State for Colonies 1951-54, Min without Portfolio 1954-57, and Lord Lieut of Surrey 1957-73: *m* 1928, Hilary, who *d* 1979, only child of late Edward Kenneth Wilson, of Cannizaro, Wimbledon; *d* 1975; *s* by his kinsman (6) EDWARD CHARLES (son of late Brig-Gen Charles FitzClarence, VC, IG, el son of late Capt Hon George FitzClarence, 3rd son of 1st Earl), 6th Earl, *b* 1899; Capt IG, served 1939-45 War: *m* 1st, 1925 (*m diss* 1930), Monica Sheila Harrington, who *d* 1958, da of Sir Henry Mulleneux Grayson, 1st Bt, KBE; 2ndly, 1939, Mrs Vivian Schofield, da of late Benjamin Schofield, JP, of Greenroyde, Rochdale, Lancs; *d* 1983; *s* by his only son (7) ANTHONY CHARLES, 7th Earl and present peer; also Viscount FitzClarence, and Baron Tewkesbury.

MURRAY OF EPPING FOREST, BARON (Murray) (Life Baron 1985)

LIONEL (LEN) MURRAY, OBE, PC, *b* 2 Aug 1922; *ed* Wellington (Salop) Gram Sch, Univ of London, and New Coll, Oxford (Hon Fellow 1975); Hon DSc Aston 1977, and Salford 1978, Hon LLD St Andrews 1979, and Leeds 1985; Head of Economic Dept TUC 1954-69, Assist-Gen TUC 1969-73, and Gen-Sec 1973-84; OBE (Civil) 1966, PC 1976, and *Baron Murray of Epping Forest*, of Telford, co Shropshire (Life Baron) 1985; *m* 1945, Heather Woolf, and has issue.
Residence – 29 The Crescent, Laughton, Essex.

SONS LIVING

Hon Stephen William, *b* 1959.
Hon David Paul, *b* 1960: *m* 1984, Moira Denise, da of Fl/Lt Patrick Joseph Roche, of Stillorgan, Dublin, and has issue living,
Joseph, *b* 1987, — Elizabeth, *b* 1985. *Address* – PO Box E33, Queen Victoria Terr, Canberra, ACT 2600, Australia.

DAUGHTERS LIVING

Hon Nicola Ruth, *b* 1954.
Hon Sarah Isobel, *b* 1959: *m* 1983, Ian Cook, of 88 Beamish Close, Northweald, Epping, Essex, and has issue living, Georgia,
b 1987, — Jodie, *b* 1990.

MURRAY OF GRAVESEND, BARONY OF (Murray) (Extinct 1980)

SON LIVING OF LIFE BARON

Hon Timothy John, *b* 1966.

DAUGHTER LIVING OF LIFE BARON

Hon Catherine Anne, *b* 1964.

WIDOW LIVING OF LIFE BARON

MARGARET ANNE (*Baroness Murray of Gravesend*) (13 Parrock Rd, Gravesend, Kent), da of Frederick Charles Wakeford: *m*
1960, Baron Murray of Gravesend (Life Baron), who *d* 1980.

MURTON OF LINDISFARNE, BARON (Murton) (Life Baron 1979)

HENRY OSCAR MURTON, OBE, TD, PC, only son of late Henry Edgar
Crossley Murton, of Hexham, Northumberland; *b* 8 May 1914; *ed*
Uppingham Sch; Lt-Col (ret) R Northumberland Fus (TA); Staff Capt
149 Inf Bde (TA) 1937-39, Army Staff Coll Course 1938-39, tsc,
1939-45 War; GSO 1, HQ Salisbury Plain Dist 1942-44; GSO1 SD1,
War Office 1944-46; a JP for Poole, Dorset; Man Dir Henry A.
Murton Ltd, Departmental Stores, Newcastle-upon-Tyne and Sunder-
land 1949-57; MP for Poole (*C*) 1964-79; Sec Conservative Parly
Cttee for Housing, Local Govt and Land 1964-67, Vice-Chm 1967-70;
Chm Conservative Parly Cttee for Public Building and Works 1970;
PPS to Min of Local Govt and Development 1970-71; an Assist Govt
Whip 1971-72; a Lord Commnr HM Treasury 1972-73; Second Dep
Chm of Ways and Means, House of Commons 1973-74, First Dep
Chm 1974, and Dep Speaker and Chm 1976-79; a Dep Chm Cttees,
House of Lords, 1981, and a Dep Speaker, House of Lords, 1983;
Member Joint Select Cttee of Lords and Commons on Private Bill
Procedure 1987-88, Freeman, City of London; Freeman, Wax
Chandlers Co; a Past Master Clockmakers' Co; Chancellor of
Primrose League 1983-88; *cr* OBE (Mil) 1946, TD 1947 (clasp 1951), PC 1976, and *Baron Murton of
Lindisfarne*, of Hexham, co Northumberland (Life Baron) 1979: *m* 1st, 1939, Constance Frances, who *d*
1977, el da of late Fergus O'Loughlin Connell, of Low Fell, co Durham; 2ndly, 1979, Pauline Teresa, yst da
of late Thomas Keenan, of Johannesburg, and has had issue by 1st *m*.

Arms – Argent a lion tricorporate sable on a chief sable three crosses of St Cuthbert argent. **Crest** – In front of a blackcock
drumming proper, three crosses of St Cuthbert argent. **Supporters** – *Dexter*, A lion guardant sable langued and armed gules
gorged with a circlet of St Cuthbert crosses linked argent pendent therefrom an escallop or. *Sinister*, A like lion similarly
gorged pendent therefrom a portcullis gold the compartment comprising a grassy mount proper surrounded by water barry
wavy azure and argent.
Residence – 49 Carlisle Mansions, Carlisle Place, SW1P 1HY.

SON LIVING *(By 1st marriage)*

Hon (Henry) Peter John Connell, *b* 1941: *m* 1962 (*m diss* 1972), Louisa, da of late Maj Percy Montagu Nevile, late The
Green Howards, of Skelbrooke Park, Yorks.

DAUGHTER DECEASED *(By 1st marriage)*

Hon Melanie Frances Isobel Connell, *b* 1946: *m* 1971, Ian Lee Vickery, of Amersham, Bucks, and *d* 1986, leaving issue.

MUSKERRY, BARON (Deane) (Baron I 1781, Bt I 1710)

ROBERT FITZMAURICE DEANE, 9th Baron, and 14th Baronet; *b* 26 March 1948; *s* 1988; *ed* Sandford Park Sch, Dublin, and Trin Coll, Dublin (BA, BAI); Man Dir Stride Mane Ltd, Dir Bridco Ltd, NBUSA Ltd: *m* 1975, Rita Brink, of Pietermaritzburg, S Africa, and has issue.

Arms – Argent, two bars gules. **Crest** – Out of a ducal coronet or, a demi sea-otter proper. **Supporters** – Two angels habited azure, holding in their exterior hands medallions proper.
Seat – Springfield House, Drumcollogher, co Limerick. *Residence* – 74 Bank Terr, Manor Gdns, 4001 Durban, S Africa.

SON LIVING

Hon JONATHAN FITZMAURICE, *b* 7 June 1986.

DAUGHTERS LIVING

Hon Nicola, *b* 1976.
Hon Catherine, *b* 1978.

SISTER LIVING

Nothing is difficult to the strong and faithful

Hon Betty Charlotte, *b* 1951; (BA): *m* 1974, Jonathan Dugdale Sykes, of The Kennels, Springfield, Drumcollogher, co Limerick, and has issue living, Daniel Jonathan, *b* 1980, — Karen Betty, *b* 1985.

WIDOW LIVING OF SON OF SEVENTH BARON

Dorothy, da of late Charles George Cook, of Liverpool: *m* 1st, 1936, Hon Matthew Fitzmaurice Tilson Deane, who *d* 1956; 2ndly, 1968, James Edward Anderton.

WIDOW LIVING OF SEVENTH BARON

MURIEL DOREEN SELLARS (*Muriel, Baroness Muskerry*) (44 Woodlands Rd, Liverpool 17; Cowdray, and Irish Clubs), da of late Arthur Gibson Simpson, of Carlisle: *m* 1964, and his 2nd wife, the 7th Baron, who *d* 1966.

COLLATERAL BRANCH LIVING

Issue of late Hon Hamilton Robert Tilson Grogan Fitzmaurice DEANE- MORGAN el son of 4th Baron, *b* 1873, *d* 1907: *m* 1904, Eva, who *d* 1958 (having *m* 2ndly, 1911, Godfrey William Edward Massy), el da of William Bolton, of The Island, co Wexford:—
Eileen (*posthumous*), *b* 1907.

PREDECESSORS – **(1)** *Sir* MATTHEW Deane, Knt; *cr* a *Baronet* 1710; *d* 1710; *s* by his son **(2)** *Sir* ROBERT, 2nd Bt; *d* 1714; *s* by his son **(3)** *Sir* MATTHEW, 3rd Bt; MP for co Cork; *d* 1747; *s* by his el son **(4)** *Sir* MATTHEW, 4th Bt; MP for Cork City; *s* by his son **(5)** *Sir* ROBERT, PC, 5th Bt; MP for Tallagh; *d* 1770; *s* by his son **(6)** *Sir* ROBERT TILSON, 6th Bt; MP for co Cork; *cr Baron Muskerry* peerage of Ireland; 1781; *d* 1818; *s* by his el son **(7)** JOHN THOMAS FITZMAURICE, CB, 2nd Baron; *dsp* 1824; *s* by his brother **(8)** MATTHEW FITZMAURICE, 3rd Baron; *d* 1868; *s* by his grandson **(9)** HAMILTON MATTHEW TILSON FITZMAURICE, 4th Baron (son of Hon Robert Tilson Fitzmaurice Deane), 2nd son of TILSON FITZMAURICE, 4th Baron (son of Hon Robert Tilson Fitzmaurice, 2nd son of 3rd Baron, by Elizabeth Geraldine, who *d* 19—, da and co-heir of Hamilton Knox Grogan-Morgan, MP, of Johnstown Castle, co Wexford), *b* 1954; a Representative Peer for Ireland: *m* 1st, 1872, Flora Georgina, who *d* 1902, da of late Hon Chichester Thomas Foster-Skeffington; 2ndly, 1905, Lydia, who *d* 1915, only da of J. L. Booth; 3rdly, 1916, Adeline, who *d* 1950, da of late P. Ryan, of The Turrets, Charleville, Ireland; *d* 1929; *s* by his son **(10)** ROBERT MATTHEW FITZMAURICE, 5th Baron; *b* 1874: *m* 1906, Charlotte, who *d* 1960, da of John William Henry Irvine, of Mervyn, Rosslare, co Wexford; *d* 1952; *s* by his brother, **(11)** MATTHEW CHICHESTER CECIL FITZMAURICE, 6th Baron; *b* 1875: *m* 1915, Helen Henrietta Blennerhassett, who *d* 1952, da of late Brig-Surg Lieut-Col Rodolph Harman, Army Med Ser; *d* 1954; *s* by his kinsman, **(12)** MATTHEW FITZMAURICE TILSON (son of late Hon Matthew James Hastings Fitzmaurice Deane, 3rd son of 3rd Baron), 7th Baron; *b* 1874: *m* 1st, 1897, Mabel Kathleen Vivienne, who *d* 1954, da of late Charles Henry Robinson, MD, FRCSI; 2ndly, 1964, Muriel Doreen Sellars, da of late Arthur Gibson Simpson, of Carlisle; *d* 1966; *s* by his yst son **(13)** HASTINGS FITZMAURICE TILSON, 8th Baron; MB, BCh, BAO, DMR (Lond), Consultant Radiologist: *m* 1944, Betty Fairbridge, who *d* (20 Aug) 1988, eldest da of George Wilfred Reckless Palmer, of Glenstone, Grahamstown, S Africa; *d* (14 Oct) 1988; *s* by his only son **(14)** ROBERT FITZMAURICE, 9th Baron and present peer.

MUSTILL, BARON (Mustill) (Life Baron 1992)

MICHAEL JOHN MUSTILL, son of Clement William Mustill, of Sandholme Cottage, Pateley Bridge, Yorks; *b* 10 May 1931; *ed* Oundle, and St John's Coll, Camb; Bar Gray's Inn 1955, QC 1968, Recorder 1972-78, Judge of High Court of Justice (Queen's Bench Div) 1978-92, since when a Lord of Appeal in Ordinary; Chm Civil Service Appeal Tribunal 1971-78; Ktd 1978; *cr Baron Mustill*, of Pateley Bridge, co N Yorks (Life Baron) 1992: *m* 1st, 1960 (*m diss* 1983), Beryl Reid, da of John Alban Davies, of Chandlers Ford, Hants; 2ndly, 1991, Caroline, da of —, and formerly wife/widow of —Phillips, and has issue.
Residence – 8 Prior Bolton St, N1.

Naas, Lord; son of Earl of Mayo.

NAIRNE, LADY (Bigham) (Lordship S 1681)

KATHERINE EVELYN CONSTANCE BIGHAM (Lady Nairne, in her own right) (*Dowager Viscountess Mersey*), *b* 22 June 1912; *s* 1944: *m* 1933, 3rd Viscount Mersey, who *d* 1979, and has issue.

Arms – Quarterly, 1st grand quarter, parted per pale sable and argent, on a chaplet four quatrefoils counterchanged, *Nairne*; 2nd grand quarter, counterquartered, 1st and 4th or, on a fesse gules between three crosses pattee of the second in chief, and a mullet azure in base, three bezants, *Mercer*; 2nd and 3rd argent, a chevron sable between three boars' heads erased gules, *Elphinstone*; 3rd grand quarter, counterquartered, 1st and 4th paly of six, or and sable, 2nd or, a fesse chequy azure and argent, 3rd azure, three mullets argent, with a double tressure flowered and counterflowered of fleur-de-lis or, *Atholl*; 4th grand quarter argent, three martlets sable on a comble azure a cross or, a frane quartier (the mark of distinction of a Military Count of the French Empire) of the 3rd, charged with a sword palewise of the field, hilted and pommelled of the fourth, *Flahault*. **Supporters** – *Dexter*, a pegasus ermine, bridled crined winged and unguled or, charged on the shoulder with a fleur-de-lis azure; *sinister*, a ratch hound proper.
Residence – Bignor Park, Pulborough, Sussex.

SONS LIVING

RICHARD MAURICE CLIVE, *4th Viscount Mersey* (see that title.)
Hon David Edward Hugh (24 Argyll Rd, W8), *b* 1938; *ed* Eton; late Cornet Roy Horse Guards: *m* (Jan) 1965, Anthea Rosemary, el da of Capt Leopold Richard Richard Seymour (*see* M Hertford, colls), and has issue living, Charles Richard Petty, *b* 1967, — Patrick David Hugh, *b* 1969, — James Edward Conway, *b* 1973, — Lucinda Emma, *b* (Nov) 1965.
Hon Andrew Charles, *b* 1941; *ed* Eton, and Worcester Coll, Oxford; late 2nd Lt Irish Gds, assist master Aysgarth Sch, N Yorks, since 1968.

SISTER LIVING

Lady Elizabeth Mary FITZMAURICE, *b* 1927: *m* 1950, Maj Charles William Lambton, Coldm Gds (ret) (*see* E Durham, colls).
Residence – The Old Rectory, Calstone, Calne, Wilts.

COLLATERAL BRANCHES LIVING

Descendants of late Major Lord Charles George Francis MERCER-NAIRNE, MVO, 2nd son of 9th Lord, and 5th Marquess of Lansdowne, *b* 1874, *ka* 1914: *m* 1909, Lady Violet Mary Elliot-Murray-Kynynmound (who *d* 1965, having *m* 2ndly, 1916, Col Hon John Jacob Astor (*see* V Astor)), da of 4th Earl of Minto (*see* M Lansdowne).

Descendants of late Lady Emily Louisa Anne (only da of Emily, Lady Nairne, by the 4th Marquess of Lansdowne), *b* 1855, *d* 1939: *m* 1886, Col Hon Everard Charles Digby, Grenadier Guards, who *d* 1915 (*see* V Hood, colls).

PREDECESSORS – (1) *Sir* ROBERT Nairne, Knt, a Scottish advocate and a zealous partisan of the house of Stuart; was imprisoned in the Tower of London 1651-61; appointed a Lord of Session 1661, and a Lord of Justiciary 1671; *cr Lord Nairne* (peerage of Scotland) 1681, with remainder to the husband of his da Margaret and the heirs of their bodies; *d* 1683; *s* by his son-in-law (ante) (2) *Lord* WILLIAM Murray, 2nd Lord, 4th son of 1st Marquess of Atholl; refused to take the oaths of allegiance or his seat in Parliament until after the Revolution; took part in the rebellion of 1715, was taken prisoner at Preston, and after being confined in the Tower was in 1716 attainted of high-treason and sentenced to be executed, which sentence was however respited; *d* 1725; *s* by his son (3) JOHN, who had previously been attainted for his connection with the rising of 1715; by Act of Parliament 1738, he was enabled to inherit property and to carry on law-suits; engaged in the insurrection of 1745, and was again attainted, having previously been *cr* by the Pretender Viscount Stanley and Earl of Nairne; *d* 1770; *s* by his son (4) JOHN, 4th Lord, a Lieut-Col in the Army; *d* 1782; *s* by his son (5) WILLIAM MURRAY, 5th Lord, who was restored to the family honours by Act of Parliament 1824; *d* 1830; *s* by his son (6) WILLIAM, 6th Lord; *d* unmarried 1837; *s* by his kinswoman (7) MARGARET, who had in 1823 *s* her father in the Barony of Keith (peerage of Ireland, *cr* 1803); *b* 1788: *m* 1817, Auguste Charles Joseph, Comte de Flahault-de-la-Billarderie; *d* 1867, when the Barony of Keith expired, and the Lordship of Nairne devolved upon her el da (8) EMILY JANE, *b* 1819; established her claim to the title 1874: *m* 1843, Henry, 4th Marquess of Lansdowne, who *d* 1866; she *d* 1895; *s* by her el son (9-11) HENRY CHARLES KEITH, 5th Marquess of Lansdowne, the Lordship being merged in the Marquessate until 1945, when, on the death of the 7th Marquess, it devolved upon his sister (12) KATHERINE EVELYN CONSTANCE, present peeress.

NAPIER and ETTRICK, LORD (Napier) (Lord S 1627, Baron UK 1872, Bt S 1666)

FRANCIS NIGEL NAPIER, KCVO, 14th Lord Napier, 5th Baron Ettrick, and 11th Baronet of Thirlestane; Chief of the name of Napier; *b* 5 Dec 1930; *s* 1954; *ed* Eton, and RMA Sandhurst; Hon DLitt Napier Univ 1993. Maj Scots Gds (Reserve), a DL for Ettrick and Lauderdale; a Member of Queen's Body Guard for Scotland (Royal Company of Archers) since 1953; a Freeman of City of London, and Liveryman of Grocers' Co; Pres of London (Prince of Wales') Dist of St John Ambulance Bde 1975-83; served in Malaya 1950-51 (invalided); Adjt 1st Bn Scots Gds 1955-57, Equerry to HRH Prince Henry, Duke of Gloucester 1958-60; Dep Ceremonial and Protocol Sec, Commonwealth Relations Office 1962-66; Conservative Whip, House of Lords 1970-71; on behalf of HM The Queen handed over the Instruments of Independence to Tuvalu (Ellice Islands) 1978; Private Sec, Comptroller and Equerry to HRH The Princess Margaret, Countess of Snowdon since 1973; MVO (4th Class) 1980; CVO 1985; CStJ 1988; KStJ 1991; KCVO 1992: *m* 1958, Delia Mary, yr da of Archibald D. B. Pearson, and has issue.

Arms – Quarterly: 1st and 4th argent, a saltire engrailed cantoned of four roses gules, barbed vert, *Napier*, 2nd and 3rd or, on a bend azure, a mullet pierced between two crescents of the field, within a double tressure flory-counterflory of the second, *Scott of Thirlestane*; below the shield on a compartment, the top of an embattled tower argent, masoned sable, issuant therefrom six lances disposed saltirewise proper, three and three, with pennons azure, *Scott*. **Crest** – A dexter arm erect couped below the elbow proper, grasping a crescent argent, *Napier*. **Supporters** – *Dexter*, an eagle, wings expanded proper; *sinister*, a chevalier in coat of mail and steel cap, all proper, holding in the exterior hand a lance with a pennon azure.
Residences – Forest Lodge, The Great Park, Windsor, Berks; Thirlestane, Ettrick, Selkirkshire: Nottingham Cottage, Kensington Palace, W8. *Clubs* – White's, Pratt's, Royal Caledonian Hunt.

SONS LIVING

Hon FRANCIS DAVID CHARLES (*Master of Napier*), *b* 3 Nov 1962; *ed* Stanbridge Earls; Lloyds: *m* 1993, Zara Jane, only da of Hugh Dermot McCalmont. *Residence* – 23 Poyntz Rd, SW11 5BH. *Club* – Turf.
Hon Nicholas Alexander John, *b* 1971; *ed* Milton Abbey.

DAUGHTERS LIVING

Hon Louisa Mary Constance, *b* 1961: *m* 1987, Alexander Morrison, Maj Scots Gds (Res), elder son of Peter Morrison, and has issue living, Oliver Charles Francis, *b* 1989, — Hugo Peter Alexander, *b* 1992. *Residence* – Yew Tree Cottage, Kingston Lisle, Wantage, Oxon OX12 9QL.
Hon Georgina Helena Katherine, *b* 1969.

BROTHERS LIVING

Hon (Charles) Malcolm (Bardmony House, Alyth, Perthshire; 1 Newton Spicer Drive, Highlands, Harare, Zimbabwe; Cavalry, Turf, Pratt's, Civil Service (Capt Town) Clubs), *b* 1933; *ed* Canford; late Lt 1st R Dragoons, and late Lt Lothians and Border Yeo (TA); served Middle East 1952-53; a Member of Queen's Body Guard for Scotland (Royal Company of Archers); a Dir of Cos, and a Founder Member of Council of Anglo Rhodesian Soc: *m* 1969, Lady Mariota Cecilia Murray, yr da of 7th Earl of Mansfield and Mansfield, and has issue living, Eloise Dorothea, *b* 1970, — Maryel Cecilia, *b* 1973, — Cecilia Frances Stephanie, *b* 1976.
Hon (Hugh) Lenox (The Grange, Balbeggie, by Perth), *b* 1943, *ed* privately.

WIDOW LIVING OF SON OF TWELFTH LORD

Helen Catherine (Kippilaw, St Boswells, Roxburghshire), yr da of late J. M. Sanderson, of Linthill, Melrose: *m* 1967, as his 2nd wife, Cdr Hon Neville Archibald John Watson Ettrick Napier, RN, who *d* 1970.

WIDOW LIVING OF SON OF THIRTEENTH LORD

Juliet Elizabeth Hargreaves (Underhill, Treyford, Midhurst, Sussex), only da of Sir Alexander Charles Durie, CBE: *m* 1968, Hon (John) Greville Napier, who *d* 1988, and has issue (infra).

COLLATERAL BRANCHES LIVING

Issue of late Hon (John) Greville Napier, 3rd son of 13th Lord, *b* 1939, *d* 1988: *m* 1968, Juliet Elizabeth Hargreaves (ante), only da of Sir Alexander Charles Durie, CBE, of The Garden House, Windlesham, Surrey:—
Lucilla Fleur Scott, *b* 1969: *m* 1994, Richard Anthony Agace Ferard (*see* B Biddulph, colls). —— Araminta Elizabeth Muir, *b* 1972.

Issue of late Maj Hon Alastair John George Malcolm Napier, TD, yst son of 12th Lord, *b* 1909, *d* 1984: *m* 1933, Geraldine, who *d* 1983, da of late James Dunlop, of The Bield, Ayr:—
Diana Elizabeth, SRN, *b* 1939: *m* 1967, Maj Robin Edward Doveton Harris, MBE, MC, late 14th/20th King's Hus, of Eden Croft, Wetheral, Carlisle, Cumbria, and has issue living, Gerald Neville Napier, *b* 1975, — Serita Catherine, *b* 1968, — Meralynn Elizabeth, *b* 1970, — Chania Rozanthe, *b* 1973.

Branch from 3rd son of 11th Lord

Grandson of late Com Hon Archibald Lenox Colquhoun William John George Napier, RN, 3rd son of 11th Lord:—

Issue of late William Puleston Scott Napier, *b* 1925, *d* 1986: *m* 1949, Rosemary Heather (Los Arcos, Almeria, Spain), da of late Capt R. H. A. McLaren, of Uphall, Ashill, Norfolk:—
Lenox Scott, *b* 1953; *ed* Rugby: *m*, and has issue living, one son.

Branch from yr sons of 10th Lord

Grandchildren of late Hon Mark Francis Napier, 4th son of 10th Lord:—
Issue of late Major Claude Inverness Napier, *b* 1880, *d* 1946: *m* 1917, Lillian, who *d* 1972, el da of Lt-Com Alfred Francey, RN:—
Mark Francis (Northfield House, Northfield, Somerton, Som, TA11 6SL), *b* 1925: *m* 1951, Mary Frances, da of late Prof A. W. Ling, MSc, and has issue living, Charles Algernon (3 Manor Close, Kingsdon, Somerton, Som), *b* 1953: *m* 1977, Heather, el da of Dennis Harding, and has issue living, Sebastian Charles Bruce *b* 1979, Sophie Ann Frances *b* 1982, — Robert Bruce (37 King Ina Rd, Somerton, Som), *b* 1959: *m* 1980, Susan Ellen, yst da of Ceril Parsley, and has issue living, Matthew Victor Mark *b* 1988, Gemma Marie *b* 1984, — Claudia Frances, *b* 1962. —— Margaret Emily, *b* 1919: *m* 1945, Peter Hincks, of The Hatch, Upton, Langport, Som. —— Eleanor Rosemary Jean, *b* 1921: *m* 1942, Capt Frank Wilson.

Grandson of late Philip Henry Napier, yst son of late Hon Mark Francis Napier (ante):—
Issue of late Nigel Claud Oliver Napier, *b* 1913, *d* 1994: *m* 1st, 1945, Lucy Margaret, who *d* 1980, da of late Capt Arthur Walter Brown, MBE, JP; 2ndly, 1983, Hazel Therese (Thirlstane House, Broughton, Peeblesshire), eldest da of late Joseph Dolan:—
(By 1st *m*) Alastair Denis, *b* 1946; *ed* Stowe.

Branch from 2nd son of 9th Lord

Grandchildren of late Maj Francis Horatio Napier, OBE, LLD, FRCS, el son of late Hon William Napier, 2nd son of 9th Lord:—
Issue of late Maj Archibald John Robert Napier, *b* 1894, *d* 1967: *m* 1926, Lilian Gray Delphin, who *d* 1979, da of Christopher Delphin Petersen, of Oslo:—
William Francis Andrew (22 Rushton Terrace, Armadale, Perth, W Australia 6112), *b* 1927: *m* 1954, Rosemary, da of late Charles William Jacobs, BEM, and has issue living, Stephen Charles Edward, *b* 1955, — Anne-Marie, *b* 1956. —— Robert Anthony Peter (162 Boldmere Rd, Sutton Coldfield, W Midlands), *b* 1940: *m* 1983, Mrs Teresa Dent. —— Charlotte Esmé Mary-Rose, *b* 1930: *m* 1956, Richard Harry Rose, of 7 Church Lane, E Huntspill, Highbridge, Somerset, and has issue living, Nicholas Henry Napier (13 Boulevard Victor, 75015 Paris), *b* 1957: *m* 1989, Laure Anne, da of late Alain Legréau, of Draguignan, France, and has issue living, Dominic Henry *b* 1991, Pierre Anthony *b* 1992, — Alistair Donald *b* 1964, — Yvonne Charlotte, *b* 1958: *m* 1988, Hugh Alexander Norman, of 15 Hay St, Marshfield, Wilts, and has issue living, Alexander Henry *b* 1988, Thomas Martin *b* 1990, — Mary Eleanor, *b* 1961.
Issue of late Cdr Laurence Egerton Scott Napier, DSO, RN, *b* 1896; *d* 1969: *m* 1st, 1921 (*m diss* 19—), Nora Creina, da of Owen Christian, of Port Elizabeth, S Africa; 2ndly, 1930 (*m diss* 19—), Florence Sylvia Jack, who *m* 2ndly, 19—, — Tizzard, of Cape Town:—
(By 2nd *m*) Patricia, *b* 1931: *m* 1952, Robert Louis Moseley, of 1 De Klerks Drive, De Klerkshof, Edenvale, Transvaal.

Granddaughter of late Maj-Gen William John Napier, CB, CMG, 3rd son of late Hon William Napier (ante):—
Issue of late Brig Arthur Francis Scott Napier, *b* 1890, *d* 1971: *m* 1915, Phyllis Grace, who *d* 1978, da of late Edward Fleming:—
Margaret Esmé Scott (Runnymede, 69 Newland, Sherborne, Dorset), *b* 1920: *m* 1st, 1942 (*m diss* 1946), Capt Ephraim Stewart Cook Spence, A & SH; 2ndly, 1946, her cousin, Maj Alexander Napier, Indian Army (ret), who *d* 1954 (infra); 3rdly, 1957, John Whittingdale, FRCS, who *d* 1974, and has issue living (by 2nd *m*) (infra), — (by 3rd *m*) John Flasby Lawrance, OBE, MP, *b* 1959; *ed* Winchester, and Univ Coll, Lond (BSc Econ); Political Sec to Prime Minister 1988-90; MP S Colchester and Maldon (*C*) since 1992; OBE (Civil) 1990: *m* 1990, Ancilla Campbell Murfitt, and has issue living, Henry John Flasby *b* 1993.

Grandsons of late Archibald Scott Napier, yst son of late Hon William Napier (ante):—
Issue of late Maj-Gen Charles Scott Napier, CB, CBE, *b* 1899; *d* 1946: *m* 1927, Ada Kathleen, who *d* 1979, da of V. N. Douétil:—
Rev Michael Scott, *b* 1929; *ed* Wellington Coll, and at Trin Hall, Camb (MA 1955); is in Holy Orders of Church of Rome. *Address* – The Oratory, SW7.
Issue of late Major Alexander Napier, Indian Army, *b* 1904, *d* 1954: *m* 1946, his cousin, Margaret Esmé Scott (Spence) (who *m* 3rdly, 1957, John Whittingdale, who *d* 1974), da of late Brig Arthur Francis Scott Napier (ante):—
Charles Scott, *b* 1947; *ed* Wellington Coll, and Exeter Univ (BA).

Branch from 2nd son of 8th Lord

Granddaughters of late Francis Napier-Clavering, 2nd son of late Rev John Warren Napier-Clavering, 3rd son of Maj Hon Charles Napier, 2nd son of 8th Lord:—
Issue of late Maj-Gen Noel Warren Napier-Clavering, CB, CBE, DSO, *b* 1888, *d* 1964: *m* 1921, Margaret, who *d* 1983, da of T. W. Vigers, of Montville, St Peter Port, Guernsey:—
Diana Margaret (Dressors, Eversley, Hants), *b* 1926: *m* 1950, John Evelyn Gray Todd, Lt RN, who *d* 1978, and has issue living, Michael John Clavering, *b* 1951: *m* 1983, Eileen Margaret Nemoy, of LA, California, and has issue living, Jenna Lauren *b* 1984, — David Matthew, *b* 1953, — Philip Napier, *b* 1956, — Brian William, *b* 1958.
Issue of late Maj Francis Donald Napier-Clavering, MC, *b* 1892, *d* 1969: *m* 1920, Dorothy Avison, who *d* 1979, da of V. A. Holroyd, of Leamington:—
Jean Margaret Avison, *b* 1922; a JP for Leics, DL 1984: *m* 1943, Capt James Gordon Hartridge, RA, of The White House, Groby, Leics, and has issue living, David John, *b* 1944; *ed* Oundle: *m* 1968, Deborah Jane Robson, of Groby, Leics, and has issue living, Andrew Charles Napier *b* 1974, Anthea Frances *b* 1969, Jessica Mary *b* 1972, — Susan Margaret Anne (The Dower House, Shenley Church End, Bucks), *b* 1950; MCSP: *m* 1980, David Peter Hadfield, MICE, of Johannesburg, and has issue living, Christopher John *b* 1984, Alastair David *b* 1987. —— Anne Katherine, *b* 1924: *m* 1948, Eric G. Wood-Hill, of 7 The Garden, N Woodchester, Glos GL5 5PU, and has issue living, Geoffrey Napier (New House Farm, Dorsington, Stratford upon Avon, Warwicks), *b* 1951; MBA, BSc: *m* 1980, Jennifer Margaret Hilton, and has issue living, Joanna Claire *b* 1981, Eve Katherine *b* 1984, — Heather Anne, *b* 1953: *m* 1st, 1978 (*m diss* 1983), Robert David William Reddall, of Barnes, SW13; 2ndly, 1987, Michael Harley, and has issue living (by 2nd *m*), Timothy James Alexander *b* 1987, Victoria Louise *b* 1989. —— Francis Alison Eve (Church Corner House, Michelmersh, Romsey, Hants), *b* 1929: *m* 1951 (*m diss* 1988), Maj Richard Mansel Colvile, RGJ (ret), and has issue living, Julia Francis, *b* 1955: *m* 1977, Nicholas Stephen Gallop, MSc, and has issue living, Katherine Anna *b* 1981, Georgina Claire *b* 1983, — Philippa Katherine, *b* 1957: *m* 1982, George Edward Sampson, of The Cottage, Hall Lane, Taddington, Derbyshire, son of late D. N. Sampson, of Sandiway, Grindleford, Derbyshire, and has issue living, Elizabeth Jill *b* 1986, Claire Joanna *b* 1988, Caroline Louisa *b* 1990, — Joanna Caroline, *b* 1959; BSc: *m* 1980,

Michael Christopher Watkiss, of Row Farm, Keysoe, Bedfordshire, and has issue living, Benjamin Michael *b* 1984, Alistair James *b* 1987, Edward George *b* 1990, Robert David *b* 1993, — Fiona Patricia, *b* 1966.

Grandchildren of late Capt Arthur Lenox NAPIER, OBE, 4th son of late Rev John Warren Napier-Clavering (ante):—

Issue of late Brig John Lenox Clavering Napier, CBE, *b* 1898, *d* 1966: *m* 1925, Grace Edythe Muriel (Puddicombe House, Drewsteignton, Exeter), da of late Col Charles Augustus Young, CB, CMG (V Guillamore, colls):—

Rev Charles John Lenox (The Rectory, Drewsteignton, Exeter, Devon), *b* 1929; *ed* Radley, and at Univ Coll, Oxford (MA): *m* 1964, Jane Noel, da of Rev Gerard Noel Davidson, and has issue living, William John Noel, *b* 1965: *m* 1990, Lynne Margaret, yr da of Geoffrey Wright, of Radnor Cliff, Folkestone, Kent, — Henry Lenox Charles, *b* 1967, — Anna Clare, *b* 1970. —— Gerald William Alistair (Dunterton Glebe House, Milton Abbot, Tavistock, Devon) *b* 1932; *ed* Radley, and Gonville and Caius Coll, Camb (MA); Col late RE (ret): *m* 1962, Marjorie Currie, da of Robert Torrance, and has issue living, Alexander John Robert (38 Hargwyne St, SW9 9RG), *b* 1963: *m* 1988, Nicola, da of late John Sykes, of Penrose Cottage, Stansted, Essex, and has issue living, Jack Alexander Luke *b* 1992, — Mark, *b* 1964, — George, *b* 1967. —— Jean Elizabeth Alison (46 Causewayend, Coupar Angus, Blairgowrie PH13 9DX), *b* 1931: *ed* Roedean; MCSP: *m* 1970 (*m diss* 1988), John Alexander Seivwright.

Granddaughters of late Claude Gerald Napier-Clavering, 6th son of late Rev John Warren Napier-Clavering (ante):—

Issue of late Mark NAPIER, *b* 1898, *d* 1983; discontinued by deed poll 1924 the use of the surname of Clavering: *m* 1st, 1921 (*m diss* 1945), Elizabeth, who *d* 1974, da of late Sir (Samuel) Squire Sprigge, MD, FRCS, FRCP; 2ndly, 1946, Frances Alice (14 William Morgan Dr, Toronto, Ontario, Canada M4H 1E8), da of Dr Henry Allen Turner, of Millbrook, Ontario:—

(By 1st *m*) Julyan (a da), *b* 1922: *m* 1946, Cawthra Falconbridge Mulock, of Falconfield, RR2, Newmarket, Ontario, Canada, and has issue living, Richard Cawthra, *b* 1948; *ed* New Sch, Kings Langley, — Julian Napier, *b* 1950; *ed* Michael Hall, Forest Row: *m* 1993, Andrea Risk, — Mark Ettrick, *b* 1951; *ed* Michael Hall, Forest Row: *m* 1982, Miranda Ramsay, and has issue living, Jonathan *b* 1990, Geoffrey *b* 1992, — Nigel Falcon, *b* 1955; *ed* Sussex Univ (BA). —— Ruth (The Old School House, Fawley, Wantage, Oxon), *b* 1923: *m* 1944, Capt Timothy Algernon Lumley-Smith, 17th/21st Lancers, who *d* 1979, son of Maj Sir Thomas Gabriel Lumley Lumley-Smith, DSO, and has issue living, Elizabeth, *b* 1947, — Sarah, *b* 1949, — Jane, *b* 1951.

Issue of late Alan NAPIER, *b* 1903, *d* 1988, film actor; discontinued the use of the christian name William and the surname of Clavering on being naturalised an American citizen 1952: *m* 1st, 1930 (*m diss* 1944), Nancy Bevill, who *d* 1970, da of Frank Pethybridge; 2ndly, 1944, Aileen Dickens Bourchier, who *d* 1961, da of late Ernest Bourchier Hawksley:—

(By 1st *m*) Jennifer Mary, *b* 1931: *m* 1950, Robert E. Nichols, of Calif, USA, and has issue living, David, *b* 1954, — Christie Catherine, *b* 1952. *Residence* – Millington Green, E Haddam, Conn 06423, USA.

Granddaughter of late Col Edward Napier, 4th son of Maj Hon Charles Napier (ante):—

Issue of late Major Egbert Napier, *b* 1867, *ka* 1916: *m* 1901, Evangeline, who *d* 1936, da of J. G. Dreyer, of Copenhagen, Denmark, and Valschrivierdrift, Orange River Colony:—

Evangeline Mary, *b* 1904: *m* 1925, Percy Henry Vincent Fosbery, and has issue living, Napier, *b* 1926, — Anthony Vincent (T. H. Ranch (Est 1879), Chilcotin Valley, BC, Canada), *b* 1929.

Grandson of late Adm William Rawdon Napier, CB, CMG, DSO, 2nd son of late Com Lenox Napier, RN (infra):—

Issue of late Lieut-Com Mark Napier, RN, *b* 1911, *d* 1962: *m* 1945, Hon Jean Astley (12 Grassmere Close, Felpham, Bognor Regis, W Sussex PO22 7NU), da of 21st Baron Hastings:—

Brian Mark Lenox (119 Kingsmead Av, Worcester Park, Surrey KT4 8UT), *b* 1946: *m* 1970, Melinda, el da of James Prideaux, of 110 East End Rd, Finchley, and has issue living, Mark Anthony Rawdon, *b* 1975, — Jemima Sarah Lenox, *b* 1972.

Granddaughters of late Com Lenox Napier, RN, 6th son of late Maj Hon Charles Napier (ante):—

Issue of late Patrick Ronald Napier, *b* 1879, *d* 1911: *m* 1903, Kathleen Hilda Mary, who *d* 1948, 2nd da of late James O'Reilly Nugent (Nugent, Bt, *cr* 1795, colls):—

Patricia Marion Barbara, *b* 1904; a nun. *Residence* – La Rameé, 5902, Jauchelette, Belgium.

PREDECESSORS – (1) *Rt Hon Sir* ARCHIBALD Napier, PC, son of John Napier, one of the most eminent Philosophers of his age, and inventor of logarithms, of Merchistoun, Midlothian; *b* 1575; Gentleman of the Bedchamber to James VI of Scotland; accompanied the King to England and was one of the Bearers of the Canopy in State Procession of 1603; appointed Treasurer Depute of Scotland for life, and a Lord of Session 1623; Lord Justice-Clerk and Master of Cermonies 1623-4, and an Extraor Lord of Session 1626; *cr* a *Baronet* 1627, and *Lord Napier*, of Merchistoun (peerage of Scotland) 1627: *m* 1619, Lady Margaret Graham, who *d* (circa) 1628, da of 4th Earl of Montrose, and sister of the celebrated 1st Marquess; *d* 1645; *s* by his son (2) ARCHIBALD, 2nd Lord; a zealous Loyalist; distinguished himself in the royal cause during the Civil Wars, and was particularly excluded from Cromwell's Act of Grace and Pardon 1654: *m* 1641, Lady Elizabeth Erskine, who *d* 1683, da of 8th Earl of Mar; *d* 1660; *s* by his son (3) ARCHIBALD, 3rd Lord; Chief of the name of Napier; obtained an extension of the patent with limitation to his heirs female and their heirs male and female, and failing which to his sisters without division and their heirs whatsoever, the female heir being compelled to take the name and arms of Napier; *d* 1683, when the Baronetcy became dormant (see Napier, Bt, *cr* 1627); *s* by his nephew (4) *Sir* THOMAS Nicolson (son of Jean, el da of 2nd Lord by Sir Thomas Nicolson, 3rd Bt, of Carnock), 4th Lord, *b* 1669; *d* unmarried 1686; *s* by his aunt (5) MARGARET Brisbane, Baroness Napier, 2nd da of 2nd Lord: *m* 1676, John Brisbane, who *d* 1684, Sec to Admiralty; *d* 1706; *s* by her grandson (6) FRANCIS (son of Elizabeth (Mistress of Napier), by her marriage with Sir William Scott, 2nd Bt, of Thirlestane, *cr* 1666), 6th Lord, *b* 1705; assumed the name of Napier, and *s* to his father's *Baronetcy of Nova Scotia* 1725; was Lord of Police 1761: *m* 1st, 1729, Lady Henrietta Hope, who *d* 1745, da of 1st Earl of Hopetoun; 2ndly, 1750, Henrietta Maria, who *d* 1795, da of Capt George Johnston; *d* 1773; *s* by his son (7) WILLIAM, 7th Lord, *b* 1730; a Lieut-Col in the Army, and DAG Forces in Scotland: *m* 1754, Hon Mary Anne, who *d* 1774, da of 8th Lord Cathcart; *d* 1775; *s* by his son (8) FRANCIS, DCL, 8th Lord, *b* 1758; was Lord-Lieut and Sheriff Principal of co Selkirk; a Representative Peer 1796, 1802, and 1807; Grand Master Mason of Scotland; 1st Lord High Commr to Gen Assembly of Church of Scotland 1802-16: *m* 1784, Maria Margaret, who *d* 1821, el da of John Clavering, KCB; *d* 1823; *s* by his son (9) WILLIAM JOHN, 9th Lord; *b* 1786; Capt RN; served at Battle of Trafalgar; Representative Peer 1824-32, Ambassador to China 1833, and Lord of Bedchamber to King William IV 1830-33: *m* 1816, Elizabeth, who *d* 1883, da of Hon James Cochrane Johnstone (E Dundonald); *d* 1834; *s* by his son (10) FRANCIS, PC, KT, LLD, 10th Lord, *b* 1819; Envoy Extraor and Min Plen to USA 1857-9 and to The Hague 1859-61, Ambassador to Russia 1861-4 and to Prussia 1864-6, Gov of Madras 1866-72, and Acting Viceroy of India 1872; *cr Baron Ettrick*, of Ettrick, co Selkirk (peerage of United Kingdom) 1872: *m* 1845, Anne Jane Charlotte, CI, da of late Robert Manners, Lockwood, of Dun-y-Greig, Glamorgan; *d* 1898; *s* by his el son (11) WILLIAM JOHN GEORGE, 11th Lord *b* 1846; Sec to Legation at Stockholm 1887-8 and Tokio 1888-91: *m* 1st, 1876, Harriet Blake Armstrong, who *d* 1897, da of late Edward Lumb, of Wallington Lodge, Surrey; 2ndly, 1898, Grace, who *d* 1928, da of late James Cleland Burns; *d* 1913; *s* by his el son (12) FRANCIS EDWARD BASIL, 12th Lord, *b* 1876; *m* 1899, Hon Clarice Jessie Evelyn Hamilton, who *d* 1951, da of 9th Lord Belhaven and Stenton; *d* 1941; *s* by his el son (13) WILLIAM FRANCIS CYRIL JAMES HAMILTON, TD, 13th Lord, *b* 1900; Lieut-Col King's Own Scottish Borderers; 1939-45 Comdg 6th Batn of his Regt; an AAG War Office 1943-44; a Co Councillor for Selkirkshire 1946-48; a Member of Roy Co of Archers (Queen's Body Guard for Scotland): *m* 1928, (Violet) Muir, who *d* 1992, el da of Sir Percy Wilson Newson, 1st Bt, and last; *d* 1954; *s* by his el son **(14)** FRANCIS NIGEL, 14th Lord and present peer; also Baron Ettrick.

The Napiers of Merchistoun are co-heirs general of the Celtic Earls of Lennox. Elizabeth, wife of John Napier of Merchistoun, was grand-da of Margaret (wife of Robert Menteith of Rusky), da of Duncan, 8th Earl of Lennox (executed 1425).

NAPIER OF MAGDALA, BARON (Napier) (Baron UK 1868)
(Title pronounced "Napier of Magdahla")

Break thou the chains

ROBERT ALAN NAPIER, 6th Baron; *b* 6 Sept 1940; *s* 1987; *ed* Winchester, and St John's Coll, Camb (MA): *m* 1964, Frances Clare, eldest da of late Alan Frank Skinner, OBE, of Monks Close, Woolpit, Suffolk, and has issue.

Arms – Gules, on a saltire between two mural crowns in pale, and as many lions passant in fesse or, a rose of the field. **Crest** – Upon a mount vert, a lion passant or, gorged with a collar gules, therefrom a chain reflexed over the back and broken, gold, supporting with the sinister forepaw a flagstaff in bend sinister proper, flowing therefrom a banner argent, charged with a cross couped gules. **Supporters** – *Dexter*, a soldier of the corps of Royal Engineers holding in the exterior hand a musket all proper; *sinister*, a Sikh Sirdar habited and holding in the exterior hand a matchlock all proper.
Residence – The Coach House, Kingsbury St, Marlborough, Wilts SN8 1HU.

SON LIVING

Hon JAMES ROBERT, *b* 29 Jan 1966; *ed* Winchester, and Edinburgh Univ: *m* 1992, Jacqueline, eldest da, A. Stephen, of Inverkeithing, Fife.

DAUGHTER LIVING

Hon Frances Catherine, *b* 1964: *m* 1992, Simon Andrew Cholerton, of 5 Prince St, N Parramatta, NSW 2151, Australia, and has issue living, Nicholas Geoffrey, *b* 1991, — Frances Barbara Clare, *b* 1990.

BROTHERS LIVING

Hon Andrew Perceval, *b* 1947; *ed* Winchester, and Imperial Coll, Lond. *Residence* – 3 Water St, Stamford, Lincs PE9 2NJ.
Hon Michael Elibank, *b* 1953, *ed* Trinity Coll, Glenalmond, St John's Coll, Camb (MA), and Newcastle Univ (PhD). *Residence* – 3 Elswick Dr, Beeston, Nottingham NG9 1NQ.

SISTERS LIVING

Hon Jane Elizabeth, *b* 1942: *m* 1964, Christopher Thomas Butler-Cole, of The Old Manse, Carlops, Penicuik, Midlothian EH26 9NH, and has issue living, Thomas Falcon, *b* 1967, — Emma, *b* 1966: *m* 1988, Philip Stephen Aiken, of 447 Gilmerton Rd, Edinburgh EH17 7JJ, and has issue living, Amanda Joy *b* 1990, Melanie Louise *b* 1992.
Hon Ruth Kathleen (twin), *b* 1947: *m* 1972, John Arthur Self, PhD, of 20 Moorside Rd, Brookhouse, Lancaster LA2 9PJ, and has issue living, Martin David, *b* 1974, — Pamela Clare, *b* 1976.

AUNT LIVING (*Daughter of 4th Baron*)

Hon Ermine Maude, *b* 1907. *Residence* – Boldre House, 35 Manor Rd, Salisbury SP1 1JS.

WIDOW LIVING OF FIFTH BARON

ELIZABETH MARIAN (*Dowager Baroness Napier of Magdala*), yst da of late Edmund Henderson Hunt, FRCS, of Cheniston, Farnham, Surrey; *m* 1939, Brig the 5th Baron, OBE, who *d* 1987. *Residence* – 51 Moorside Rd, Brookhouse, Lancaster LA2 9PJ.

COLLATERAL BRANCHES LIVING

Granddaughters of late Lt-Col Hon Henry Dundas Napier, CMG, 5th son of 1st Baron:—
Issue of late Col Arthur Henry Gurney Napier, OBE, RE, *b* 1900, *d* 1978: *m* 1937, Rosemary Evelyn, who *d* 1993, 2nd da of Charles George Lumley Cator (Blois, Bt):—
Mary-Rose, *b* 1938. —— Angela Marina, *b* 1940: *m* 1979, James Denis Merrik Naper, of Newtown House, Loughcrew, Old-castle, co Meath, eldest son of late Capt Nigel William Ivo Naper, MC (*see* V Valentia, colls, 1973-74 Edn), and has issue living, Merrik Henry Nigel, *b* 1980, — Alexander Denis James, *b* 1981, — Isabel Carola Rosemary, *b* 1983. —— Belinda Jane, *b* 1946: *m* 1968, Michael Alan Fishwick Leather, of Heath Farm House, Heath Lane, Childer Thornton, Wirral, Ches, and has issue living, James Napier Fishwick, *b* 1971, — Giles Napier Fishwick, *b* 1973.

Grandson of late Lt-Col Hon Charles Frederick Hamilton Napier, 7th son of 1st Baron:—
Issue of late Charles Campbell Napier, *b* 1903, *d* 1989: *m* 1931, Violet Mushla Burnie, who *d* 1992:—
Peter Charles Cornelis, *b* 1936: *m* 1962, Violet Walker, da of Charles Kimball-Fitts, of Lincoln, Mass, USA, and has issue living, Arianne Campbell, *b* 1962, — Tanya Kimball, *b* 1968.

Issue of late Hon Sir Albert Edward Alexander Napier, KCB, KCVO, QC, yst son of 1st Baron; *b* 1881, *d* 1973: *m* 1917, Gladys, who *d* 1978, da of late F. M. Sir George Stuart White, VC, GCB, OM, GCSI, GCMG, GCIE, GCVO:—
Patricia Mary Stuart, *b* 1918: *m* 1948, Philip E. R. English, of 14 Milborne Grove, SW10, and has issue living, Georgina Frances, *b* 1958, — Philippa Katharine, *b* 1962.

PREDECESSORS – (1) *Sir* ROBERT CORNELIS Napier, GCB, GCSI, son of Major Charles Frederick Napier, RA, *b* 1810; a distinguished Field-Marshal in British Army, who commanded Abyssinian Expedition 1868, and captured the fortress of Magdāla; Com-in-Ch of Indian Forces 1870-76, and Gov of Gibraltar 1876-82; *cr Baron Napier of Magdāla*, in Abyssinia, and of Caryngton, co Chester (peerage of United Kingdom), 1868: *m* 1st, 1840, Anne Sarah, who *d* 1849, da of George Pearse, DL; 2ndly, 1861, Mary Cecilia, CI, who *d* 1930, da of Maj-Gen Edward William Smyth Scott, RA; *d* 1890; *s* by his el son (2) ROBERT WILLIAM, 2nd Baron, *b* 1845; ADC to Com-in-Ch in India 1870-76, and to Gov of Gibraltar 1876-81, and Assist Mil Sec 1881-82: *m* 1885, Hon Eva Maria Louisa, who *d* 1930, da of 4th Baron Macdonald, and widow of Capt Algernon Langham, Grenadier Guards; *d* 1921; *s* by his brother (3) JAMES PEARSE, 3rd Baron, *b* 1849; Col (ret); Afghanistan 1878-9 (medal): *m* 1876, Mabel Ellen, who *d* 1907, da of late Lieut-Col Windsor Parker, of Clopton Hall, Rattlesden; *d* 1935; *s* by his half-brother (4) EDWARD HERBERT SCOTT, 4th Baron, *b* 1861; formerly Lieut 1st Vol Batn Princess Charlotte of Wales's (Berkshire Regt); in Indian State Railways 1884-1909: *m* 1900, Florence Martha, who *d* 1946, da of late Gen John Maxwell Perceval, CB, of Dillon House, Downpatrick, co Down; *d* 1948; *s* by his son (5) (ROBERT) JOHN, OBE, 5th Baron, *b* 1904, Brig late RE, MICE, served Waziristan 1936-37 (despatches), European War 1939-45 in Sicily and Italy (despatches): *m* 1939, Elizabeth Marian, yst da of late Edmund Henderson Hunt, FRCS, of Cheniston, Farnham, Surrey; *d* 1987; *s* by his eldest son (6) ROBERT ALAN, 6th Baron and present peer.

NATHAN, BARON (Nathan) (Baron UK 1940)

Labour ennobleth

ROGER CAROL MICHAEL NATHAN, 2nd Baron; *b* 5 Dec 1922; *s* 1963; *ed* Stowe, and at New Coll, Oxford (MA), Hon LLD Sussex, FSA, FRSA, FRGS; Solicitor 1950; retired as Senior Partner Herbert Oppenheimer Nathan & Vandyk 1986; Hon Life Associate Member Bar Assocn of City of New York; Chm House of Lords Select Cttee on Murder and Life Imprisonment 1988-89; Pres Jewish Welfare Board 1967-71, Hon Pres Central British Fund for Jewish Relief and Rehabilitation (Chm 1970-77); Chm RSA 1975-77 (Vice-Pres since 1977); Vice-Chm Cancer Research Campaign since 1987 (Chm Exec Cttee 1970-75, Treasurer 1979-87); Member Royal Commission on Environmental Pollution 1979-89 and 1989-92, and House of Lords Select Cttee on European Communities 1983-88; Chm Environment Sub-Cttee 1983-87 and 1989-92; Pres UK Environmental Law Assocn 1987-92, Nat Soc for Clean Air 1987-89, and Vice-Pres since 1992, and Soc of Sussex Downsmen 1987-92; Chm Animal Procedures Cttee 1990-93; Chm Sussex Downs Conservation Board since 1992; Member House of Lords Select Cttee on Science and Technology since 1994; Master Gardeners' Co 1963; 1939-45 War, as Capt 17th/21st Lancers (twice wounded, despatches): *m* 1950, Philippa Gertrude, da of late Maj J. B. Solomon, MC, of Sutton, Sussex, and has issue.

Arms – Or, a fesse cottised sable over all a sword erect gules, on a canton of the second a roll of parchment proper. **Crest** – A kiln enflamed proper. **Supporters** – *Dexter*, a lion; *sinister*, a hind argent; each charged on the shoulder with a grenade sable fired proper.
Residences – Collyers Farm, Lickfold, Petworth, Sussex. *Clubs* – Athenæum, Cavalry and Guards.

SON LIVING

Hon RUPERT HARRY BERNARD, *b* 26 May 1957; *ed* Charterhouse, and Durham Univ (BA): *m* 1987, Ann, da of A. S. Hewitt, of Aldingbourne, Chichester, Sussex.

DAUGHTERS LIVING

Hon Jennifer Ruth, *b* 1952.
Hon Nicola Janet Eleanor, *b* 1954.

SISTER LIVING

Hon Joyce Constance Ina (*Hon Lady Waley-Cohen*), *b* 1920; *ed* St Felix Sch, and at Girton Coll, Camb (MA); a JP for Somerset 1959-87 and formerly of Mddx 1949-59; Member of Board of Govs, Westminster Hosp Group 1952-68, Chm of Westminster Children's Hosp 1952-68, and Chm of Gordon Hosp 1961-68; Chm of Governing Bodies of Girls Schs Assocn 1974-79 (Member since 1963), Member of Indep Schs Information Ser Council and Management Cttee 1972-86, Chm Indep Schs Joint Council 1977-80 and Pres of Indep Schs Info Ser 1981-86; Gov of Taunton Sch 1978-90, Wellington Coll 1979-90 and St Felix Sch, Camb 1945-83 (Chm 1970-83): *m* 1943, Sir Bernard Nathaniel Waley-Cohen, 1st Bt, who *d* 1991. *Residence* – Honeymead, Simonsbath, Minehead, Som TA24 7JX.

PREDECESSOR – (1) HARRY LOUIS Nathan, TD, PC, son of late Michael Henry Nathan, JP; *b* 1889; Under-Sec of State for War and Vice-Pres of Army Council 1945-46, and Min of Civil Aviation 1946-48; MP for NE Div of Bethnal Green (*L*) 1929-35, and for Central Div of Wandsworth 1937-40; 1914-18 War as Maj and Temporary Lt-Col London Regt (severely wounded); *cr Baron Nathan*, of Churt, co Surrey (peerage of UK) 1940, and a PC 1946: *m* 1919, Eleanor Joan Clara, JP, MA, Chm London CC 1948, who *d* 1972, da of late Carl Stettauer: *d* 1963; *s* by his only son (2) ROGER CAROL MICHAEL, 2nd Baron, and present peer.

Neidpath, Lord, son of Earl of Wemyss and March.

NELSON, EARL (Nelson) (Earl UK 1805)

·Palmam ⁜ qui · meruit ferat·

Let him wear the palm who has deserved it

PETER JOHN HORATIO NELSON, 9th Earl, *b* 9 Oct 1941; *s* 1981; Pres R Naval Commando Assocn, and Nelson Soc; Vice Pres Jubilee Sailing Trust; Dir British Navy Pusser's Rum, Chm Retainacar Ltd; Patron Internat Fingerprint Soc, and Clapton Assocn Football Club; Member Cttee of Friends of Nat Maritime Museum: *m* 1st, 1969, Maureen Diana, da of Edward Patrick Quinn, of Kilkenny; 2ndly, 1992, Tracy, da of— Cowie, of—, and has issue by 1st *m*.

Arms – Or, a cross patonce sable surmounted by a bend gules, thereon another bend engrailed of the field, charged with three handgrenades of the second, fired proper; a chief of augmentation wavy argent, thereon waves the sea, from which issuant in the centre a palm tree, between a disabled ship on the dexter and a battery in ruins on the sinister, all proper. **Crests** – 1st, over a naval crown or, the chelenk or diamond plume of triumph, presented to the 1st Lord Nelson, by the Grand Signor, Sultan Selim III; 2nd, the stern of the San Joseph, Spanish man-of-war, floating in waves of the sea proper. **Supporters** – *Dexter*, a sailor habited and armed with a cutlass, with a pair of pistols in his belt proper, his right hand supporting a pike also proper, thereon hoisted a commodore's flag gules, and his left holding a palm branch; *sinister*, a lion reguardant in his mouth two broken staffs, and flowing from the one the Spanish, and from the other the French ensigns, and in the dexter forepaw a palm branch all proper. *Address* – c/o House of Lords, SW1. *Club* – St James's.

SON LIVING (By 1st marriage)

SIMON JOHN HORATIO (*Viscount Merton*), *b* 21 Sept 1971.

DAUGHTER LIVING (By 1st marriage)

Lady Deborah Jane Mary, *b* 1974.

BROTHER LIVING

Francis Edward Horatio, *b* 1947: *m* 1973, —, and has issue living, William, *b* 1975, — Emma, *b* 1974. Resides in New Zealand.

SISTER LIVING

Jane Priscilla, *b* 1944: *m* 1968, Roy Hannant, of 9 Joubert Rd, Green Point, Cape Town, and has issue living, David John Charles, *b* 1972, — Richard Roy, *b* 1974, — Sally Kathleen (twin), *b* 1974.

DAUGHTER LIVING OF EIGHTH EARL

Lady Sarah Josephine Mary, *b* 1947: *m* 1978, Dr John Clive Roberts, MB, BS, FFARCS, of Oak End, Lower Amersham Road, Gerrard's Cross, Bucks.

MOTHER LIVING

Kathleen Mary (306 Chartleigh House, Beach Rd, Sea Point, Cape Town 8001, S Africa), da of William Burr, of Torquay: *m* 1941, Capt Hon John Marie Joseph Horatio Nelson, who *d* 1970.

WIDOW LIVING OF EIGHTH EARL

MARY WINIFRED (*Mary, Countess Nelson*) (9 Pwlldu Lane, Bishopston, Swansea), da of W. Bevan, of Swansea: *m* 1945, the 8th Earl, who *d* 1981.

COLLATERAL BRANCHES LIVING *(The heirs male are in remainder to Earldom)*

Issue of late Lt-Col Hon Charles Sebastian Joseph Horatio Nelson, 3rd son of 5th Earl, *b* 1896, *d* 1964: *m* 1916, Kathleen Cook, who *d* 1980:—
Mary Teresa Muriel, *b* 1917; 1939-45 War with S African Air Force: *m* 1946, Cornelius Johannes Erasmus, and has issue living, Anthony Charles, *b* 1953, — Martina Kathleen, *b* 1947.

Grandchildren of late Rear-Adm Hon Maurice Horatio Nelson, 3rd son of 2nd Earl:—
Issue of late Charles Burrard Nelson *b* 1868, *d* 1931: *m* 1904, Geraldine, who *d* 1969, da of the Rev Ernest Henry Glencross, V of Morval, Cornwall:—
John Charles Horatio, *b* 1905; Com (ret) RN: *m* 1934, Alice Helen, da of late Col Robert Maximilian Rainey-Robinson, CB, CMG, and has issue living, Antony Burrard Horatio, *b* 1935: *m* 1960 (*m diss* 1989), Judith Constance, da of late Brig Thomas Farquharson Ker Howard, DSO, of Goldenhayes, Woodlands, Southampton, and has issue living, Thomas Antony Horatio *b* 1963, Edward Maximilian *b* 1971, Teresa Helen *b* 1962, Rebecca Anne *b* 1975, — Joanna Elizabeth, *b* 1940: *m* 1962, Henry Bruce Milne, of Dowerfield, Long Bredy, Dorchester, and has issue living, Robert Henry *b* 1968, Emma Alice *b* 1970, Sarah Elizabeth *b* 1973, Kate Mary *b* 1978. *Residence* – Pear Trees, Nomansland, Salisbury. —— Emily Geraldine Morval, *b* 1906: *m* 1st, 1928 (*m diss* 1945). Jocelyn Panizzi Preston, who *d* 1970, son of late Sir Frederick George Panizzi Preston, KBE; 2ndly, 1946, Cdr Rowland Kirby, OBE, RNR, who *d* 1971, and has issue living (by 1st *m*) Simon Douglas Nelson (Badsell Park Farm, Matfield, Tonbridge, Kent), *b* 1933: *m* 1962, Celia Mary, da of late Francis Bodenham Thornely, and has issue living, Rupert Robin Nelson, *b* 1963, Adam Bodenham Nelson *b* 1966, John Simon Nelson *b* 1975, Charles Frederick Nelson (twin) *b* 1975, Emma Frances Morval *b* 1965, — (by 2nd *m*) Ben Martin, *b* 1948: *m* 1970, Katharine Alice Mary, da of Alan A. C. Jackson, and has issue living, Henry Rowland *b* 1974, Robin Gerald *b* 1978, Samantha Jane Alice *b* 1972. *Residence* – Bishops Quay, St Martin, Helston, Cornwall, TR12 6DF.

Grandchildren of late Capt George Henry Eyre EYRE-MATCHAM, eldest son of William Eyre Eyre-Matcham, grandson of Catherine Matcham, sister of 1st Baron:—

Issue of late Constance Valentine, *b* 1897, *d* 1984: *m* 1923, Cdr Edmund Valentine Jeffreys, RN:—
George William Eyre JEFFREYS (Newhouse, Redlynch, Salisbury, Wilts), *b* 1931; *ed* Radley: *m* 1960, June, da of Alexander Bennett, of Godshill Wood, Hants, and has issue living, Sarah Kezia Eyre, *b* 1963, — Elizabeth Jemima Eyre, *b* 1964, — Rachel Jane Eyre, *b* 1968. —— Catharine Elizabeth Eyre, *b* 1933: *m* 1953, Anthony William Lane, who *d* 1992, of Over Silton Manor, Over Silton, nr Thirsk, N Yorks, and has issue living, Harriet Elizabeth, *b* 1954: *m* 1974, David Geoffrey Crusher, of Northallerton, N Yorks, — Caroline Mary, *b* 1956 *m* 1986, Gordon Smith, of Leighton Buzzard, Beds, and has issue living, Daniel Harry *b* 1989, Sarah Valentine *b* 1987, — Georgina Margaret, *b* 1959: *m* 1981, William David Owen Bowe, of Northallerton, N Yorks, and has issue living, William David *b* 1983, Matthew George *b* 1990, Emily Jane *b* 1985, Jessica Elizabeth *b* 1987, — Victoria Anne Michell, *b* 1962, — Florence Sophia, *b* 1967.

PREDECESSORS – **(1)** *Sir* HORATIO NELSON, KB, 5th son of late Rev Edmund Nelson, R of Hillborough and of Burnham Thorpe, Norfolk, *b* 1758; one of the most eminent Naval Commanders of any age, having gained the celebrated victory of the Nile on 1 Aug, 1798, was in Nov of the same year *cr Baron Nelson*, of the Nile, and of Burnham Thorpe, co Norfolk (peerage of GB), and in 1799 was *cr Duke of Bronté*, in the kingdom of Sicily, which title he was afterwards permitted to use by royal sanction; on 2 April, 1802, he completely defeated the Danish fleet off Copenhagen, and on May 22 following was *cr Viscount Nelson of the Nile* and *of Burnham Thorpe*, co Norfolk (peerage of UK), and on 18 Aug of the same year was *cr Baron Nelson of the Nile* and *of Hillborough*, co Norfolk, with remainder to his father and the heirs male of his body, and failing them to the heirs male of the body severally and successively of his sisters Mrs Susannah Bolton and Mrs Catherine Matcham; on 21 Oct, 1805, having gained the ever memorable victory of Trafalgar he was mortally wounded, his remains being honoured with a public funeral in St Paul's Cathedral on 9 Jan 1806: *m* 1787, Frances Herbert, da of William Woodward, Sen Judge of Nevis, WI, and widow of Josiah Nisbet, MD; the barony of 1798 and the viscountcy became extinct, and the barony of 1801 and the Dukedom of Bronté devolved upon his brother **(2)** WILLIAM, DD, 2nd Baron; *cr Viscount Merton of Trafalgar* and *of Merton*, co Surrey, and *Earl Nelson*, of Trafalgar and of Merton, co Surrey (peerage of UK) 1805, with a similar remainder to that of the Barony (*cr* 1801); *d* 1835; *s* by his nephew **(3)** THOMAS Bolton, 2nd Earl, el son of Susannah Bolton (ante), who in accordance with the Act of Settlement 46 Geo III, cap 3, assumed the surname of Nelson; *b* 1786: *m* 1821, Frances Elizabeth, da and heir of John Maurice Eyre, of Landford and Brickworth, co Wilts; *d* 1835, when the Duchy of Bronté reverted to Charlotte Mary, only da of the 1st Earl, and wife of Samuel, 2nd Baron Bridport, and the Earldom devolved upon his son **(4)** HORATIO, 3rd Earl, *b* 1823; *m* 1845, Lady Mary Jane Diana Agar, who *d* 1904, da of 2nd Earl of Normanton; *d* 1913; *s* by his el son **(5)** THOMAS HORATIO, 4th Earl; *b* 1857, *d* 1947; *s* by his brother **(6)** EDWARD AGAR HORATIO, 5th Earl; *b* 1860: *m* 1889, Geraldine, who *d* 1936, da of late Henry H. Cave, of Horton Crescent, Rugby; *d* 1951; *s* by his son **(7)** ALBERT FRANCIS JOSEPH HORATIO, 6th Earl; *b* 1890; a lecturer in Astronomy and Anthropology; 1914-19 War with Aust Imperial Force, 1939-44 War as Major: *m* 1st, 1924 (*m diss* 1925), Amelia, who *d* 1937, widow of John C. Scott; 2ndly, 1927 (in Scotland) and 1942 (in England) Marguerite Helen, who *d* 1969, da of Capt J. M. O'Sullivan, of Tipperary; *d* 1957; *s* by his brother **(8)** HENRY EDWARD JOSEPH HORATIO, 7th Earl; *b* 1894; *d* 1972; *s* by his brother **(9)** GEORGE JOSEPH HORATIO, 8th Earl; *b* 1905: *m* 1945, Mary Winifred, da of W. Bevan, of Swansea; *d* 1981; *s* by his nephew **(10)** PETER JOHN HORATIO (son of late Capt Hon John Marie Joseph Horatio Nelson, yst son of 5th Earl), 9th Earl and present peer; also Viscount Merton of Trafalgar, and Baron Nelson of the Nile and of Hillborough.

NELSON OF STAFFORD, BARON (Nelson) (Baron UK 1960, Bt UK 1955)

WHO LEADS SERVES

HENRY GEORGE NELSON, 2nd Baron and 2nd Baronet; *b* 2 Jan 1917; *s* 1962; *ed* Oundle, and at King's Coll, Camb (MA); FEng, FICE, Hon FIMechE, Hon FIEE (Pres 1971), FRAeS; Hon DSc Aston, Keele and Cranfield; Hon LLD Strathclyde; Fellow of Imperial Coll of Science & Tech; Man Dir D. Napier & Son 1942-49, Dir Gen Elec Co, plc 1968-87 (Chm 1968-83) (Dep Man Dir English Elec Co, Ltd 1949-56, Man Dir 1956-62, and Chm and Ch Exec 1962-68, since when Chm), Joint Dep Chm of British Aircraft Corpn 1960-77; Dir of Nat Bank of Australasia, Ltd (London Board of Advice) 1950-81; Chm R Worcester Gp 1978-83, a Dir of Bank of England 1961-87, INCO Ltd (Canada) 1966-88, and Enserch Corpn, USA 1984-89; a Member of Gov Advisory Council on Scientific Policy 1955-58, of Advisory Council on Middle East Trade 1958-63 (Industrial Leader and Vice-Chm 1959-63), of Advisory Council of Technology 1964-70, of Engineering Advisory Council 1958-61, and of Exec Cttee of British Nat Cttee World Energy Conference 1957-87 (Chm 1971-74); Chm Defence Industries Council 1971-77; Pres of Sino-British Trade Council 1973-83; a Trustee of Civic Trust 1962-72; Pres of Electrical Research Assocn 1963-64, of Orgalime (Organisme de Liaison des Industries Métallique Européennes) 1966-70, of British Electrical & Allied Manufacturers Assocn 1966-67, of Locomotive & Allied Manufacturers Assocn 1964-66, and of British Electric Power Convention 1967, and of Soc of British Aircraft Constructors Ltd 1961-62; Vice-Pres of Engineering Employers' Fedn 1963-82; 1st Chancellor of Univ of Aston, Birmingham 1966-79, and a Gov of Commonwealth Inst 1972-74; Member House of Lords Select Cttee on Science and Technology 1984-90; Lord High Steward of Stafford 1966-71; Hon Member of City & Guilds of London Inst; a Liveryman of Goldsmiths Co (a Member of Court since 1974, Prime Warden 1983-84), and Coachmakers and Coach Harness Makers' Co (Assist to Court 1959-62); Benjamin Franklin Medal, Roy Soc of Arts: *m* 1940, Pamela Roy, yr da of late Ernest Roy Bird, MP, of New House Farm, Robertsbridge, Sussex, and has issue.

Arms – Argent, a cross flory sable, a chief gules thereon between a Stafford knot and a rose of the first, barbed and seeded proper, a pale also of the first, charged with a sword erect of the third. **Crest** – An arm embowed resting on the elbow in armour proper, the gauntlet grasping a cross flory fitchée sable between two roses gules, barbed and seeded also proper. **Supporters** – *Dexter*, a lion guardant or charged on the shoulder with a thunderbolt azure; *Sinister*, a grey horse proper gorged with a coronet composed of four fleur-de-lys with chains affixed thereto and reflexed over the back also or, and charged on the shoulder with a Stafford knot gold.
Residences – 244 Cranmer Court, Whiteheads Grove, SW3 3HD; Wincote Farm, Eccleshall, Staffs. *Club* – Carlton.

SONS LIVING

Hon HENRY ROY GEORGE (Eastlands, Tibthorpe, nr Driffield, E Yorks YO25 9LD), *b* 26 Oct 1943; *ed* Ampleforth, and Kings Coll, Camb (MA); CEng, FIMechE, MIEE; Dir TIB plc: *m* 1968, Dorothy, da of Leslie Caley, of Tibthorpe Manor, Driffield, E Yorks, and has issue living, Alistair William Henry, *b* 1973, — Sarah Jane, *b* 1981.
Hon James Jonathan (82 Tachbrook St, SW1V 2NB), *b* 1947; *ed* Ampleforth, and McGill Univ, Canada; Dir Foreign & Colonial Management Ltd since 1974, Man Dir Foreign & Colonial Ventures Ltd since 1985: *m* 1977, Lucy Mary, el da of Roger Gopsill Brown, of Chestnut House, Albrighton, Salop and has issue living, Camilla Amy, *b* 1982, — Lara Kitty, *b* 1986, — Eloise Violet, *b* 1988.

DAUGHTERS LIVING

Hon Caroline Jane, *b* 1942: *m* 1964, Michael John Henry Ford, of Lower Moorhayne Farm, Yarcombe, nr Honiton, Devon EX14 9BE, and has issue living, James Mortimer Henry, *b* 1965, — Andrew Michael Felix, *b* 1967, — Annabel Emma Jane, *b* 1972.
Hon Sally Louise, *b* 1955: *m* 1975, Peter Robert Jolliffe Tritton, of Wease Cottage, Wassel Green, nr Buntingford, Herts, and has issue living, Jonathan James Hedley, *b* 1981, — Emma, *b* 1986.

SISTER LIVING

Hon Margaret Joan, *b* 1915; is a JP Supplementary List Warwickshire: *m* 1941, Edward Michael Price, who *d* 1992, and has issue living, Elizabeth Joan, *b* 1943, — Susan Jane, *b* 1944, — Anne Waldegrave, *b* 1947. *Residence* – Frankton Manor, Frankton, nr Rugby, Warwickshire CV23 9PJ.

PREDECESSOR – **(1)** *Sir* GEORGE (HORATIO) Nelson, son of late George Nelson, of 66 Muswell Hill Rd, N; *b* 1887; Chm of The English Electric Co Ltd, and other Cos; *cr* a Bt 1955, and *Baron Nelson of Stafford*, of Hilcote Hall, co Stafford (peerage of United Kingdom) 1960: *m* 1913, Florence Mabel, who *d* 1962, only da of late Henry Howe, JP, of Leics; *d* 1962; *s* by his only son **(2)** HENRY GEORGE, 2nd Baron and present peer.

NETHERTHORPE, BARON (Turner) (Baron UK 1959)

JAMES FREDERICK TURNER, 3rd Baron; *b* 7 Jan 1964; *s* 1982; *ed* Harrow; Dir UBS London: *m* 1989, (Elizabeth) Curran, da of Edward William Fahan, of Redding, Conn, USA, and has issue.

Arms – Argent on a Cross gules between four garbs vert five millrinds erect or a chief of stone masonry proper. **Crest** – A lion passant guardant gules gorged with a collar sable charged with bezants, supporting with the dexter paw a cornucopia inverted or the fruit proper. **Supporters** – *Dexter*, a bull; *sinister*, a ram, both argent horned and unguled or and gorged with a collar sable charged with bezants.
Residence – Boothby Hall, Boothby Pagnell, Grantham, Lincs NG33 4DQ.

Work itself is pleasing

SON LIVING

Hon ANDREW JAMES EDWARD, *b* 24 March 1993.

BROTHER LIVING

Hon Patrick Andrew, *b* 1971.

SISTERS LIVING

Hon Anna Elizabeth, *b* 1961: *m* 1986, Simon M. Edwards, elder son of late Roland Edwards.
Hon Kate Belinda, *b* 1967: *m* 1993, Rupert J. Ivey, 3rd son of John Ivey, of 1 Bemish Rd, SW15.

UNCLES LIVING (*sons of 1st Baron*)

Hon Edward Neil (The Limes, S Anston, Sheffield), *b* 1941; *ed* Rugby, at Roy Agricultural Coll, Cirencester, and London Univ; FRICS; QALAS; Dip FBA; FBIM; Chm of Edward Turner Cos, and Lazard Smaller Equities Investment Trust; a Member of Yorks and Humberside Regional Economic Planning Council 1975-79; Member S Yorks Residuary Body 1985-89; a Member of Co of Cutlers in Hallamshire; Memb of Council of the BIM 1976-81, 1982-88; Gen Commissioner of Tax since 1973; High Sheriff of S Yorks 1983: *m* 1963, Gillian Mary, el da of late C. J. King, and has issue living, Charles James, *b* 1966: *m* 1992, Sarah Eastwood, — Sara Jane, *b* 1971.
Hon (Philip Noel) Nigel (Parsonage House, Helions Bumpstead, Suffolk), *b* 1949; *ed* Rugby, and Worcester Coll, Oxford; Vice-Pres of The Northern Trust Co 1970-82; Man Dir Barclays Merchant Bank 1983-85, since when Man Dir Lazard Bros & Co Ltd: *m* 1st, 1973, Anne Rachel, da of R. Brown, of Somerton, Oxon; 2ndly, 1988, Mrs Jennifer (Annie) Goodwin, yst da of Capt David Armstrong, of Hepple, Morpeth, Northumberland, and has issue living (by 1st *m*), Lucy Victoria, *b* 1977, — Catherine Louise, *b* 1979, — Georgina Anne, *b* 1983.

WIDOW LIVING OF FIRST BARON

MARGARET LUCY (*Margaret, Baroness Netherthorpe*) (The Garden House, Hadley Hurst, Hadley Common, Barnet, Herts EN5 5QG), da of James Arthur Mattock, of Woodlands, Norfolk Rd, Sheffield: *m* 1935, the 1st Baron, who *d* 1980.

WIDOW LIVING OF SECOND BARON

BELINDA (*Belinda, Baroness Netherthorpe*) (Boothby Hall, Boothby Pagnell, Grantham, Lincs NG33 4DQ), only da of late Frederick Hedley Nicholson, of Boothby Pagnell, Lincs: *m* 1960, the 2nd Baron, who *d* 1982.

PREDECESSORS – (1) JAMES Turner, son of late Albert Edward Mann Turner, of Anston, Yorks; *b* 1908; Pres of NFU 1945-60, R Assocn of British Dairy Farmers and of R Agric Soc; *cr* Knt 1949, and *Baron Netherthorpe*, of Anston, W Riding of Yorkshire (peerage of the UK) 1959: *m* 1935, Margaret Lucy, da of James Arthur Mattock; *d* 1980; *s* by his el son **(2)** JAMES ANDREW, 2nd Baron; *b* 1936; Dep Chm and Ch Exec of Dalgety Ltd, a Dir of Lazard Bros & Co Ltd and of Babcock Internat Ltd: *m* 1960, Belinda, da of Frederick Hedley, of Boothby Pagnell, Lincs; *d* in a motor accident 1982; *s* by his el son **(3)** JAMES FREDERICK, 3rd Baron and present peer.

NEWALL, BARON (Newall) (Baron UK 1946)

Pleasing to God

DEO JUVANTE

FRANCIS STORER EATON NEWALL, 2nd Baron; *b* 23 June 1930; *s* 1963; *ed* Eton, and RMA; Capt (ret) 11th Hussars; Adjt Roy Gloucestershire Hussars 1956-58; a DL of Greater London since 1988; Co Chm and Dir; Chm British Greyhound Racing Board since 1985; Conservative Whip, House of Lords 1976-79; Member Council of Europe and W European Union; Merchant Taylors' Co: *m* 1956, Pamela Elizabeth, el da of Edward Hugh Lee Rowcliffe, TD (*see* Farrington, Bt), and has issue.

Arms – Per pale azure and gules two lions passant guardant in pale or on a chief ermine a rose of the second barbed and seeded between a lotus flower and a sprig of New Zealand fern all proper. **Crest** – Issuant from an astral crown or an eagle wings elevated sable breathing flames proper. **Supporters** – On either side a pegasus gorged with an astral crown or.
Residences – Wotton Underwood, Aylesbury, Bucks; 18 Lennox Gardens, SW1. *Clubs* – Cavalry and Guards'.

SONS LIVING

Hon RICHARD HUGH EATON (11 Burleigh Place, Cambalt Rd, SW15) *b* 19 Feb 1961.
Hon David William Norton, *b* 1963; *ed* Eton, and RMA Sandhurst.

DAUGHTER LIVING

Hon Miranda Jane, *b* 1959: *m* 1986, Timothy Guy Lawson, son of Derek C. Lawson, of Bradford Abbas, Dorset, and has issue living, George Thomas Guy, *b* 1987, — Sam Frederick Guy, *b* 1989, — Eliza Daisy, *b* 1991. *Residence* – Long Acre, Honeycombe Leaze, Fairford, Glos.

SISTERS LIVING AND DECEASED

Hon Georgiana, *b* 1926; *d* as the result of a road accident 1985.
Hon Diana Olive (Tower House, Reybridge, Chippenham, Wilts), *b* 1927: *m* 1956 (*m diss* 1967), John Leonard Joly, and has issue living, Harriet Diana, *b* 1960.

PREDECESSOR – (1) *Marshal of the RAF Sir* CYRIL LOUIS NORTON Newall, GCB, OM, GCMG, CBE, AM, son of late Lt-Col William Potter Newall, Indian Army; *b* 1886; entered Roy Warwickshire Regt 1905, transferred to Indian Army 1909, to RFC 1914 and to RAF 1919; Dir of Operations and Intelligence, Air Min and Dep Ch of Air Staff 1926-31, Comdg Wessex Area, Air Defence 1931, and AOC Middle East 1931-35, Ch of Air Staff 1937-40, and Gov-Gen of New Zealand 1941-46; *cr* 1946, *Baron Newall*, of Clifton-upon-Dunsmoor, Co Warwick (peerage of UK) 1946: *m* 1st, 1922, Mary Dulcie Weddell, who *d* 1924; 2ndly, 1925, Olive Tennyson Foster, who *d* 1988, only da of Horace Tennyson Foster, and Mrs Francis Storer Eaton, of Boston, USA; *d* 1963; *s* by his only son **(2)** FRANCIS STORER EATON, 2nd Baron, and present peer.

NEWBOROUGH, BARON (Wynn) (Baron I 1776, Bt GB 1742)

Gentle in manner, vigorous in action

ROBERT CHARLES MICHAEL VAUGHAN WYNN, DSC, 7th Baron, and 9th Baronet; *b* 24 April 1917; *s* 1965; *ed* Oundle; High Sheriff Merioneth 1963, late 2nd Lt 9th Lancers SR, 5th Inniskilling Dragoon Gds, and Lt 16/5th Lancers 1935-39, invalided 1940, took part in Dunkirk evacuation as civilian, commn'd RNVR in command of MTB 74, St Nazaire (wounded, despatches, DSC, prisoner in Colditz, escaped): *m* 1st, 1945 (*m diss* 1971), Rosamund Lavington, da of late Maj Robert Barbour of Bolesworth Castle, Tattenhall, Chester, 2ndly, 1971, Jennifer Caroline Acland, yst da of late Capt Cecil C. A. Allen, RN, and has issue by 1st *m*.

❦rms – Sable, three fleurs-de-lis-argent. ❧rest – A dexter cubit arm erect, holding in the hand a fleur-de-lis or. ❨upporters – Two lions gules, the *dexter* gorged with a plain collar charged with three fleurs-de-lis or, the *sinister* gorged with a plain collar argent charged with three crosses patée gules.
Residences – Rhug, Corwen, Clwyd, N Wales LL21 0EH. *Clubs* – Naval and Military, Bembridge Sailing.

SON LIVING *(By 1st marriage)*

Hon ROBERT VAUGHAN (Peplow Hall, Peplow, Market Drayton, Shrops), *b* 11 Aug 1949; *ed* Milton Abbey: *m* 1st, 1981, Mrs Sheila Christine Wilson, da of William A. Massey, of Corsley, Wilts; 2ndly, 1988, Mrs Susan E. Hall, da of late Andrew Lloyd, of Malta, and has issue living (by 1st *m*), Lucinda Rosamond, *b* 1982.

DAUGHTERS LIVING *(By 1st marriage)*

Hon (Anne) Patricia Rosamund, *b* 1947: *m* 1970, Anthony George Budgen, of Boreatton House, Baschurch, Shrewsbury, Salop, SY4 2EP, and has issue living, Mark George, *b* 1972, — Nadine Patricia Mary, *b* 1975.
Hon Diana Heather Marion, *b* 1951: *m* 1979, Capt Ralph Peter Kinloch Carmichael, R Scots Dragoon Gds (ret), of The Old Rectory, Woolstaston, Church Stretton, Shropshire, and has issue living, William Ralph, *b* 1983, — Sophie Emma, *b* 1980.

BROTHER LIVING

Hon Charles Henry Romer, *b* 1923; Lt-Com RN (ret): *m* 1947, Hon Angela Hermione Ida Willoughby, da of late 11th Baron Middleton, and has issue living, Antony Charles Vaughan, *b* 1949; *ed* Eton, and Balliol Coll, Oxford: *m* 1973 (*m diss* 1986), Jane Slane Sloan, el da of Rev William Thompson, of Oxnam Manse, Jedburgh, Roxburghshire, — Andrew Guy, LVO (22 The High St, Eton, Windsor, Berks SL4 6AX) *b* 1950: *ed* Eton, Gonville and Caius Coll, Camb; Cdr RN (ret); Equerry to HRH The Duke of Edinburgh 1982-84; LVO 1984: *m* 1st, 1978 (*m diss* 1986), Susanjane, el da of Selwyn Willis Fraser-Smith, CBE, MC; 2ndly, 1988, Shelagh Jean Macsorley, yr da of Prof I.K.M. Smith, of Welwyn Garden City, Herts, and has issue living (by 1st *m*), Alexander Charles Guy *b* 1980. *Residence* – Bunkersland, Withleigh, Tiverton, Devon EX16 8JN.

DAUGHTER LIVING OF FIFTH BARON *(By 2nd m)*

Hon Juno Odette Denisa Palma (changed to Blanche-Neige Juno Palma Odette Denisa), *b* 1940: *m* 1963, Philip Wolfe-Parry, LDS, RCS, of 5 Braemar Ave, Wimbledon Park, SW19, and has issue living, Edward Thomas Wilton, *b* 1972.

WIDOW LIVING OF UNCLE OF SEVENTH BARON

Eleanor Mary Tydfil, yst da of late Arthur Edmund Smith-Thomas: *m* 1943, Hon Rowland Tempest Beresford Wynn, CBE, who *d* 1977.

COLLATERAL BRANCH LIVING

Issue of late Hon Arthur Romer Wynn, brother of 6th Baron, *b* 1885, *d* 1964: *m* 1915, Gladys Catherine, who *d* 1988, da of late Richard Hanbury Joseph Gurney (Buxton, Bt):—
John Christopher Watkin (The School House, Chapel Rd, Roughton, Norwich NR11 8AF), *b* 1917: *m* 1946, Cynthia Maureen, da of late William Dodwell, and has issue living, Nicholas Romer, *b* 1952: *m* 1980, Julie-Ann, elder da of David Turrell, of Pietermartizburg, S Africa, — Gareth Rowland, *b* 1958: *m* 1982, Karen, only da of Kenneth Lake, of Lilongwe, Malawi, — Ann Richenda Dodwell, *b* 1947: *m* 1973 (*m diss* 1983), Thomas William Everett. —— Rosemary Vera Georgina WYNN, *b* 1919; has resumed surname of Wynn: *m* 1st, 1941 (*m diss* 1966), John Richard Boydell; 2ndly, 1966 (*m diss* 1969), John Leicester Goldsmith.

Grandchildren of late Hon Arthur Romer Wynn (ante):—
Issue of late Dennis Gurney Wynn, *b* 1922; *d* 1983: *m* 1950, Joan Edith (The Mount, Ketton, Stamford, Lincs PE9 3TE), da of Alfred Pearman Bentley, of St Mary's Hall, Kings Lynn, Norfolk:—
Simon Charles (80 Chevening Rd, Queen's Park, NW6 6EA), *b* 1952: *ed* R Sch of Mines, Imp Coll: *m* 1984, Alison Rona, only da of Frank Cropper, of Moolham Mill, Ilminster, Som, and has issue living, Victoria Rona, *b* 1987, — Fiona Emily, *b* 1991. —— Mark Gurney, *b* 1957. —— Sarah Frances, *b* 1954. —— Rebecca Helen, *b* 1966.

PREDECESSORS – (1) THOMAS Wynn, Equerry to George II, Clerk to Board of Green Cloth, and MP for Carnarvon 1713-47; *cr* a *Baronet* 1742; *s* by his son (2) Sir JOHN, 2nd Bt, MP for co Carnarvon 1754-61; *s* by his son (3) Sir THOMAS, 3rd Bt; MP for co Carnarvon 1761-74, Lord-Lieut of Carnarvonshire, and Col of Carnarvon Militia; *cr Baron Newborough* (peerage of Ireland) 1776: *m* 2ndly, Maria Stella Patronilla Chiappini; *d* 1807; *s* by his el son (4) THOMAS JOHN, 2nd Baron; MP for Carnarvonshire 1826-31; *d* unmarried 1832; *s* by his brother (5) SPENCER BULKELEY, 3rd Baron, *b* 1803; High Sheriff of Anglesey 1847: *m* 1834, Frances Maria, who *d* 1857, el da of late Rev Walter de Winton, of Hay Castle, Brecon; *d* 1888; *s* by his grandson (6) WILLIAM CHARLES (son of late Hon Thomas John Wynn), 4th Baron; *b* 1873; Lieut Welsh Guards: *m* 1900, Grace Bruce, who *d* 1939, da of late Col Henry Montgomerie Carr; *d* as a result of illness contracted on active ser 1916; *s* by his brother (7) THOMAS JOHN, 5th Baron; *b* 1878; formerly Lieut RNR: *m* 1st, 1907 (*m diss* 1938), Vera Evelyn Mary, who *d* 1940, da of late Capt Philip Montagu, 12th Lancers, of Down Hall, Dorset, and widow of Henry L. Winch; 2ndly, 1939 (*m diss* 1947), Denisa Josephine, who *d* 1987, da of late Lazar Braun, of Subotica, Yugoslavia; 3rdly, 1947, Katherine Rudkin, who *d* 1979, da of Henry Stephen Murray, of Victoria, Australia; *d* 1957; *s* by his cousin (8) ROBERT VAUGHAN, OBE (son of late Hon Charles Henry Wynn, 3rd son of 3rd Baron), 6th Baron, *b* 1877; S Africa 1899-1902 (despatches twice); 1914-18 War with 9th Lancers (despatches four times, Brevet Lt-Col): *m* 1913, Ruby Irene, who *d* 1960, da of late Edmund Wigley Severne; *d* 1965; *s* by his son **(9)** ROBERT CHARLES MICHAEL VAUGHAN, DSC, 7th Baron and present peer.

NEWBURGH, EARL OF (Rospigliosi) (Earl S 1660)
(Title pronounced "Newbrough")

FILIPPO GIAMBATTISTA CAMILLO FRANCESCO ALDO MARIA ROSPIGLIOSI, 12th Earl; *b* 4 July 1942; *s* 1986; 11th Prince Rospigliosi (Holy Roman Empire), 14th Prince of Castiglione, 11th Duke of Zagarolo, Marquis of Giuliana, Count of Chiusa, Baron of La Miraglia and Valcorrente, Lord of Aidone, Burgio, Contessa and Trappeto, and conscribed Roman Noble, Patrician of Venice, Genoa, Pistoia, Ferrara and Ravenna: *m* 1972, Baronessa Donna Luisa, da of Count Annibale Caccia Dominoni, and has issue.

Arms – Not yet matriculated in line of the present Earl.
Residence – Piazza St Ambrogio 16, 20123, Milan, Italy.

DAUGHTER LIVING

Princess BENEDETTA FRANCESCA MARIA (*Mistress of Newburgh*), *b* 4 June 1974.

BROTHER LIVING

Prince Francesco Guido Carlo Antonio Maria, *b* 1947: *m* 1974, Clothilde, da of Henri Rival de Rouville, and has issue living, *Prince* Alessandro Giulio Enrico Francesco, *b* 1978. *Residence* – Viale Elvezia 24, Milan 20154, Italy.

MOTHER LIVING

Donna Giulia (*Giulia, Princess Rospigliosi*), da of Don Guido Carlo dei Duchi Visconti di Modrone, Count of Lonate Pozzolo: *m* 1940, the 11th Earl of Newburgh, Prince Rospigliosi, who *d* 1986. *Residence* – Via Corridoni 3, 20122 Milan, Italy.

COLLATERAL BRANCHES LIVING

Issue of late Princess Elena Rospigliosi (Duchessa Antonio Lante della Rovere), sister of 11th Earl, *b* 1904, *d* 1974: *m* 1926, Duke Antonio Lante Montefeltro della Rovere, who *d* 1954:—
Don Pietro (*Duke Lante della Rovere*) (Fundo Millaray, Casella 176, Rengo, Chile), *b* 1928; a Roman Noble, and Noble of Foligno: *m* 1st, 1953, Marianne La Fourcalde Ithuralde, who *d* 19—; 2ndly, 1989, his cousin, Donna Livia, 6th da of late Don Filippo, Prince Lancellotti, of Rome, and has issue living (by 1st *m*), *Don* Marcantonio Maria Francesco, *b* 1957, — *Donna* Angela Maria, *b* 1956, — *Donna* Patrizia, *b* 1959, — *Donna* Livia Francesca, *b* 1963. —— †*Don* Ludovico, *b* 1931: *m* 1958, Lya Medez Marquez (Calle Los Cortijos, Edificio Country Suites, Urbanization Campoalegro, Caracas, Venezuela), and *d* 1986, leaving issue, *Don* Federico Maria, *b* 1959, — *Donna* Alessandra, *b* 1963, — *Donna* Elena, *b* 1965. —— *Don* Francesco (Via L. Bodio No 10, Rome), *b* 1933: *m* 1957, Carla dei Marchesi Spinola di Pasturana, and has issue living, *Don* Antonio *b* 1962, — *Donna* Silvia, *b* 1965. —— *Don* Alessandro (Via L. Bodio No 10, Rome), *b* 1936: *m* 1964, Marina Punturieri, and has had issue, *Donna* Francesco, *b* 1966: *m* 19—, and *Donna* Lucrezia, *b* 19—. —— *Don* Federico (Calle Rengo 550, Los Angeles, Chile), *b* 1938: *m* 1965, Marcella Sandrez, and has issue living, *Don* Francesco René Maria Baltazar, *b* 1966, — *Don* Pietro Alessandro Maria Gaspar, *b* 1971. —— *Donna* Anna Vittoria (Carmelo delle Tre Madonne, Rome, Italy), *b* 1927; a Carmelite Nun (Sister Maria Carmela del Bambin Gesu). —— *Donna* Angela (Via Bitossi No 34, Rome), *b* 1930: *m* 1950, Massimo Igliori, engineer, who *d* 19—, and has issue living, Ulisse Maria, *b* 1961, — Alessandro, *b* 1963, — Paola, *b* 1952, — Benedetta, *b* 1954, — Maria Gaia, *b* 1959.

Issue of late Prince Francesco Luigi Giuseppe Rospigliosi, uncle of 11th Earl, *b* 1880; *d* 1943: *m* 1914, Laura Macdonald Stallo, who *d* 1972:—
Princess Francesca ROSPIGLIOSI (4000 Cathedral Av NW, Apt 12B, Washington DC 20016, USA), *b* 1921; has resumed her maiden name: *m* 1949, Alexander Clausen Schmidt, who *d* 1972, and has issue living, William Francis (4000 Cathedral Av NW, Apt 518, Washington DC 20016, USA), *b* 1950, — Camillo Alexander (5311 Augusta St, Bethesda, Maryland 20852, USA), *b* 1953, — Laura Maria, *b* 1952: *m* 1988, Joseph Pizzarello, of 8507 Fountain Valley Drive, Gaithersburg, Maryland 20879, USA.

Grandchildren of late Prince Ludovico Guardino Carlo Francesco Rospigliosi, uncle of 11th Earl:—
Issue of late Prince Guglielmo Camillo Carlo Rospigliosi, *b* 1908, *d* 1990: *m* 1933 (*m diss* 1958), Hon Helen Lyon-Dalberg-Acton, da of 2nd Baron Acton:—
Prince Ludovico Giulio Francesco Maria (42 Viale Morin, Forte dei Marmi, Lucca, Italy), *b* 1934; Knt of Honour and Devotion Sovereign Mil Order of Malta, Knt of Justice of Constantinian Order of St George, and Officer of Order of Ad Merito Melitensi: *m* 1960, Giovanna Sallier de la Tour, da of 8th Marquis of Cordon, and has issue living, *Prince* Camillo Carlo Felice Francesco Maria, *b* 1969, — *Princess* Maria Lucrezia Elena Carolina Margherita Vittoria, *b* 1966, — *Princess* Olimpia Francesca Maria, *b* 1975. —— *Prince* Guardino Riccardo Carlo Francesco (119 Whitchurch Rd, Tavistock, Devon), *b* 1938; Knt of Justice of Constantinian Order of St George: *m* 1st, 1961 (*m diss* 1975), Veronica, da of Lt-Col Wilfred York Price, OBE, MC, of Devauden, Chepstow; 2ndly, 1976, Mrs Patricia Harvey, da of Robert Campbell, of Langley, Bucks, and has issue living (by 1st *m*), *Prince* Pericles Stephen Guardino Francesco Maria, *b* 1961: *m* 1987, Pauline Cheriou Lyzette, da of Lloyd Power, and has issue living, *Prince* Caspian Guglielmo Francesco Maria *b* 1988, — *Prince* Saladin Gabriel Charles Francesco Maria, *b* 1964, — *Prince* Joseph Darius Francesco Maria, *b* 1970, — (by 2nd *m*) *Princess* Elissa Alicia Elena Francesca Maria, *b* 1977, — *Princess* Ezinna Margherita Barbara Francesca Maria, *b* 1979. —— *Princess* Giovanna Maria Carolina Annuziata (47 Josephine Av, SW2 2JL), *b* 1935: *m* 1961 (*m diss* 1989), Giles Frere Wordsworth, who *d* 1992, and has issue living, Andrew Guardino Theodore, *b* 1962, — Catherine Columbine Maria Annuziata, *b* 1964, — Anne Lucy Susannah, *b* 1966.

Issue of late Princess Ottavia Rospigliosi, aunt of 11th Earl, *b* 1878, *d* 1968: *m* 1898, Roberto Vimercati Sanseverino, Count of Castel Palazzo, who *d* 1945:—
Count Lionello, *b* 1911: *m* 1936, Oretta dei Conti Ceriana Mayneri, and has issue living, *Count* Ludovico, *b* 1940: *m* 1964, Donna Agnese Tosti dei Duchi di Valminuta, and has issue living, *Count* Ottaviano *b* 1966, *Count* Girolamo *b* 19—, *Countess* Roberta, *b* 1942. —— *Countess* Francesca, *b* 1917: *m* 1939, Enrico Budini Gattai, and has issue living, Antonello, *b* 1940, — Leopoldo, *b* 1942, — Roberto, *b* 1946, — Federico, *b* 1948, — Francesco, *b* 1949, — Ferdinando, *b* 1951, — Ruggero, *b* 1955,

— Rodolfo, *b* 1957, — Giulia, *b* 1938, — Maria Vittoria, *b* 1944, — Nicoletta, *b* 1953, — Cristina, *b* 1957. —— *Countess* Laura, *b* 1923: *m* 1945, Livio Calenda dei Baroni di Tavani, Sqdn-Ldr Italian Air Force, and has issue living, Landolfo, *b* 1946, — Michelangelo, *b* 1953, — Maria Nuvola, *b* 1947, — Maria Gloria, *b* 1951, — Maria Luce (twin), *b* 1951, — Benedetta, *b* 1955, — Candida, *b* 1962.

Grandchildren of late Princess (Maria) Maddalena Clementina Rospigliosi (Countess Ardicino della Porta) (*infra*):—
Issue of late Count Giovanni Ubaldo della Porta, *b* 1914, *d* 1967: *m* 19—, Emma Brugliese (Frontone, nr Pesaro, Italy):—
Count Ferdinando, *b* 1951. —— *Count* Carlo, *b* 1956. —— *Countess* Giuliana, *b* 1947.

Issue of late Princess (Maria) Maddalena Clementina Rospigliosi, aunt of 11th Earl, *b* 1889, *d* 1966: *m* 1909, Ardicino della Porta, Count of Carpine, Biscina and Frontone:—
Count Carlo (Le Carpini, Montone, Perugia, Italy), *b* 1920: *m* 1949, Laura Pignatti Morano, Countess of Custoza, and has issue living, *Count* Giammaria, *b* 1950, — *Count* Roberto, *b* 1955, — *Count* Giulio, *b* 1956, — *Countess* Anna Barbara, *b* 1952, — *Countess* Maria-Camilla, *b* 1962, — *Countess* Maria-Veronica, *b* 1964. —— *Count* Enzo Maria *b* 1922. —— *Countess* Laura, *b* 1911: *m* 1951, Lorenzo Scotti Douglas, Count of Vigoleno, who *d* 1965. —— *Countess* Lucia, *b* 1912: *m* 1938, Professor Gaetano Gentile, and has issue living, Giovanni, *b* 1939: *m* 1964, Giovanna Ferragamo, — Fortunato, *b* 1945, — Maddelena, *b* 1940: *m* 1966, Giuseppe Passetti, — Ludovica, *b* 1943. —— *Countess* Maria, *b* 1917: *m* 1940, Count Josef Forni, and has issue living, *Count* Carlo Francesco Giuseppe Gaetano Ardicino Salvatore, *b* 1941, — *Count* Giulio Maria Giuseppe Pietro Canisio Gaetano Anastasio, *b* 1946, — *Countess* Anna Maria Maddalena d'Pazzi Giulia Francesca de'Paolo Giuseppina Antonia Gaetana, *b* 1942, — *Countess* Teodolinda Maria Assunta Laura Antonia Giuseppina Giocchina, *b* 1943, — *Countess* Maria Cristina Beatrice Paola Giuseppina Antonia Gaetana, *b* 1944, — *Countess* Elena Maria Teresa, *b* 1949.

Grandchildren of late Lady Nicoletta Maria Nazarena Gioacchina Margherita Giustiniani-Bandini, 4th da of 8th Earl, *b* 1863, *d* 1938: *m* 1881, Mario, Duke Grazioli, who *d* 1936:—
Issue of late Pio, Duke Grazioli, *b* 1886, *d* 1954: *m* 1st, 1908, Donna Rufina Lancellotti, who *d* 1942, da of Don Filippo Massimo, 1st Prince Lancellotti; 2ndly, 1948, Cleo Conversi, of Casal de Pazzi, Rome:—
(By 1st *m*) *Don* Caterina, *b* 1913: *m* 1940, Count Gabriele Emo Capodilista Maldura, who *d* 1983, and has issue living, *Count* Giorgio (45 Brunswick Gdns, W8; 32 Via In Piscinula, 00186 Rome), *b* 1941: *m* 1976, Christiane Hoberg, and has issue living, *Count* Alvise Luca *b* 1981, *Count* Pietro Antonio *b* 1990, *Countess* Rufina *b* 1978, *Countess* Beatrix *b* 1984, — *Count* Giovanni (48 Cheyne Walk, SW3), *b* 1944: *m* 1st, 1981 (*m diss* 1988), Lady Arabella Avice Diana Sackville, only da of 10th Earl De La Warr; 2ndly, 1989, Madeleine Maria, yst da of C. J. de Jong, of Glassenbury Park, Kent, and has issue living (by 2nd *m*), *Count* Gabriele Filippo *b* 1990, *Countess* Olimpia *b* 1992. *Residence* – Palazzo Grazioli, 102 Via del Plebiscito, 00186 Rome, Italy. —— (By 2nd *m*) *Don* Riccardo, *b* 1943; Baron of Castelporziano, Nobile di San Marino, and Duke of Magliano: *m* 1st, 19—, Clara Randaccio; 2ndly, 19—, Donna Patrizia Musso di Peralta, and has issue living (by 2nd *m*), *Donna* Giorgiana Pia Olimpia, *b* 1986. *Residence* – Ansedonia V Ginepro 10, Orbetello Scalo, Grosseto, Tuscany, Italy.

Grandchildren of late Pio, Duke Grazioli (*ante*):—
Issue of late Don Massimiliano Grazioli, *b* 1911, kidnapped (presumed *d*) 1977: *m* 1942, Isabella Perrone, who *d* 1988:—
Don Giulio (*Duke Grazioli*), *b* 1943. *Residence* – Palazzo Grazioli, 102 Via del Plebiscito, 00186 Rome, Italy.
Issue of late Donna Anna Grazioli, *b* 1916, *d* 1987: *m* 1942, Don Francesco, Marquis of Caravita, Prince of Sirignano:—
Don Giuseppe, *b* 1944. —— *Don* Alvaro Pietro, *b* 1945. —— *Donna* Nila, *b* 1951: *m* 1975, Ricardo Pintado Rivero, and has issue living, Ricardo Pintado Caravita di Sirignano, *b* 1975, — Tazio Pintado Caravita di Sirignano, *b* 1978, — Diego Pintado Caravita di Sirignano, *b* 1983. *Residences* – Palazzo Grazioli, 102 Via del Plebiscito, 00186 Rome, Italy; Villa Castello, Capri, Naples, Italy; Paseo de la Reforma 1670, 11000 Mexico DF.

Issue of Lady (Maria) Isabella Giovanna Teresa Gioacchina Giustiniani-Bandini, 6th da of 8th Earl, *b* 1867, *d* 1963: *m* 1898, the 1st Baron Howard of Penrith, who *d* 1939 (see that title).

Descendants of the late Lady Elisabetta Bandini (*m* 1841, Marchese Agostino Trionfi), 2nd da of Maria Cecilia, Countess of Newburgh (*see* 1969 and earlier edns).

Descendants of late Lady Cristina Bandini (*m* 1845, Count Marcello Marcelli Fiori), 3rd da of Maria Cecilia, Countess of Newburgh (*see* 1969 and earlier edns).

Descendants of late Lady Maria Bandini (*m* 1849, Federico Pucci Boncambi, Count Palatine, Noble of Perugia), yst da of Maria Cecilia, Countess of Newburgh (*see* 1969 and earlier edns).

PREDECESSORS – (1) Sir JAMES Levingston, a zealous royalist; was *cr Viscount Newburgh* (peerage of Scotland) 1647, and *Lord Levingston*, of Flacraig, *Viscount Kynnaird* and *Earl of Newburgh* (peerage of Scotland) 1660, with remainder to his heirs whatsoever; *d* 1670; *s* by his son (2) CHARLES, 2nd Earl; *d* 1694, when the viscountcy of 1647 expired, and the peerages of 1660 devolved upon his da (3) CHARLOTTE MARIA, who *m* 1st, Thomas, el son of 2nd Baron Clifford, and 2ndly, 1724, Hon Charles Radcliffe, brother of the beheaded 3rd Earl of Derwentwater, who in 1731, on the death of his nephew, assumed the title of 5th Earl of Derwentwater. (Charles Radcliffe was attainted 1716 and imprisoned in Newgate, whence he escaped, but being engaged in the rising of 1745 was taken prisoner and summarily executed on his former attainder): the Countess *d* 1755; *s* by her son (by her 2nd *m*) (4) JAMES BARTHOLOMEW, 4th Earl; unsuccessfully claimed the Derwentwater estates; *d* 1786; *s* by his son (5) ANTHONY JAMES, 5th Earl; in 1788, by Act of Parliament, the Derwentwater estates were charged with £2,500 a year to the Earl and the heirs male of his body; *dsp* 1814; *s* by his kinsman (6) VINCENT, 6th Earl, and 6th *Prince Giustiniani* (*cr* 1644) of the Papal States, son of Cecilia Mahony, only child of Anne Clifford, da of Charlotte Maria, Countess of Newburgh (by her 1st *m*); by Benedict, 5th Prince Giustiniani; he did not take proceedings to establish his claim to the earldom; *d* 1826; *s* by his only da (7) MARIA CECILIA AGATHA ANNA JOSEPHA LAURENTIA DONATA MELCHIORA BALTHASSARA GASPARA, Princess Giustiniani, who *s* her grandfather as Duchess of Mondragone; naturalized by Act of Parliament 1857, and her claims to peerages were allowed 1848: *m* 1815, Charles Bandini, 4th Marquis of Lanciano and Rustano (*cr* 1753) in the Papal States; *d* 1877; *s* by her son (8) SIGISMUND NICHOLAS VENANTIUS GAETANO FRANCIS, 8th Earl, *b* 1818; *cr Prince Giustiniani-Bandini* by Pope Pius IX (with the precedence held by his ancestors the Princes Giustiniani) 1863; *s* as *Duke of Mondragone* (Kingdom of Naples) 1878; assumed in 1850 the additional surname of Giustiniani, as adopted heir to his uncle, James, Cardinal Giustiniani, Bishop of Albano; naturalized by Act of Parliament 1857 (20th and 21st Vic chap 7): *m* 1848, Maria Sophia Angelica, who *d* 1898, da of the Cavaliere Giuseppe Maria Massani; *d* 1908; *s* by his only child (10) MARIA SOFIA GIUSEPPINA, Countess of Newburgh, *b* 1889; Pres Ladies of Charity: *m* 1922, Count Manfredi Gravina di Ramacca, High Commr Danzig, ADC to HM the King of Italy, who *d* 1932; *d* 1977; *s* by her kinsman (11) GIULIO CESARE TADDEO COSIMO, Prince Rospigliosi (son of late Prince Giambattista Pio Sigismondo Francesco Rospigliosi, son of Lady Elena Maria Concetta Isabella Gioacchina Giuseppa Giustiniani-Bandini (*Princess Camillo Rospigliosi*), 3rd da of 18th Earl), 11th Earl of Newburgh, *b* 1907: *m* 1940, Donna Giulia, da of Don Guido Carlo dei Duchi

Visconti di Modrone, Count of Lonate Pozzolo; *d* 1986; *s* by his elder son **(12)** FILIPPO GIAMBATTISTA CAMILLO FRANCESCO ALDO MARIA, Prince Rospigliosi, 12th Earl of Newburgh and present peer; also Viscount Kynnaird and Lord Levingston.

NEWCASTLE, DUKEDOM OF (Pelham-Clinton) (Extinct 1988)

DAUGHTERS LIVING OF NINTH DUKE (*by his 2nd wife, Lady Diana Montagu-Stuart-Wortley-Mackenzie, da of 3rd Earl of Wharncliffe*)

Lady Patricia PELHAM-CLINTON-HOPE, *b* 1949; film actress; resumed maiden name 1974, and again 1983: *m* 1st, 1971 (*m diss* 1974), Alan Pariser; 2ndly, 1981 (*m diss* 1983), Nick Mancuso, actor, of Toronto; has issue living, Dorian Henry Navarr PELHAM-CLINTON-KOLE, *b* 1990. *Residence* – 6901 Washington Rd, W Palm Beach, Florida 33450, USA.
Lady Kathleen Marie Gabrielle PELHAM-CLINTON-HOPE, *b* 1951; has resumed her maiden name: *m* 1st, 1970 (*m diss* 19—), Edward Vernon Reynolds; 2ndly, 19— (*m diss* 19—), a Thai gentleman. *Residence* – The Cottage, Ballinakil, Kilfinny, nr Croom, Limerick.

COLLATERAL BRANCHES LIVING

Granddaughter of late Henry William Pelham-Clinton, 2nd son of late Lord Charles Pelham-Clinton, 2nd son of 4th Duke:—
Issue of late Henry Charles Frederick Pelham-Clinton, *b* 1892, *d* 1968: *m* 1920, Dorothy Charlotte Middleton, who *d* 1969, da of late Capt J. Carlon, Royal Canadian Regt:—
Ethne Mary, *b* 1923: *m* 1951, Jasper Picton Hubbard, and has issue (*see* B Addington, colls). *Residence* – Hammonds, Lewes Heath, Horsmonden, Tonbridge, Kent TN12 8EE.

Granddaughters of late Lord Charles Pelham-Clinton (ante):—
Issue of late Hubert Edward Pelham-Clinton, *b* 1862, *d* 1913: *m* 1st, 1893, Louisa Brooks, who *d* 1911, da of late E. Macaulay Arnaud, of Bath, and widow of Henry Fitzwilliam Browne; 2ndly, 1911, Helen, who *d* 1963, da of James William Halcrow, of Burton-on-Trent:—
(By 2nd wife) Marjorie, *b* 1910: *m* 1940, Edward Date Long, who *d* 1982, and has issue living, Richard Pelham (58 Northcroft Lane, Newbury, Berks RG13 1BN), *b* 1941; *ed* Harrow, Queen's Coll, Camb (MA), and Stanford Univ, Calif (MBA): *m* 1973 (*m diss* 1985), Roslyn Vera, only da of late Capt Gordon Britton, RN, and has issue living, Camilla Elizabeth *b* 1978, Zoë Rebecca *b* 1980, — Alison Jean, *b* 1945: *m* 1969, Gerry Rowe, of 1887 Stonepath Crescent, Mississauga, Ont LAX 1Y1, Canada, and has issue living, Jonathan Oliver *b* 1974, Deborah Elizabeth *b* 1971. —— Georgiana Elizabeth May, *b* 1913; legally adopted 1916 by her aunt, Elizabeth, who *d* 1946, widow of Charles Stapleton Pelham-Clinton: *m* 1951, John Stuart Bordewich, MVO, who *d* 1986, and has issue living, John Peter Pelham, *b* 1955. *Residence* – Highgrove House, 32 Winchester Rd, Worthing, Sussex.

Descendants of Sir Henry Clinton, half-brother of Sir Edward Clinton (great great grandfather of Henry, 2nd Duke of Newcastle, who *s* 1768 by special remainder):—
See E Lincoln, colls.

Newport, Viscount; son of Earl of Bradford.

Newry and Morne, Viscount, see Earl of Kilmorey.

NEWTON, BARON (Legh) (Baron UK 1892)
(Name pronounced "Lee")

On God is my reliance

RICHARD THOMAS LEGH, 5th Baron; *b* 11 Jan 1950; *s* 1992; *ed* Eton, and Ch Ch, Oxford; Solicitor: *m* 1978, Rosemary Whitfoot, yr da of Herbert Whitfoot Clarke, of Eastbourne, Sussex, and has issue.

Arms – Gules, a cross engrailed argent, in the chief point, on an inescutcheon sable, semée of estoiles, an arm in armour embowed of the second, the hand proper holding a pennon silver, all within a bordure wavy or. **Crest** – Issuant out of a ducal coronet or, a ram's head argent, armed or, in the mouth a laurel slip vert; the whole debruised by a pallet wavy azure. **Supporters** – Two mastiffs proper, collared sable.
Residence – Laughton Park Farm, Laughton, Lewes, E Sussex BN8 6BU.

SON LIVING

Hon PIERS RICHARD, *b* 25 Oct 1979.

DAUGHTER LIVING

Hon Alessandra Mary, *b* 1978.

BROTHER LIVING

Hon David Piers Carlis, *b* 1951; *ed* Eton, and RAC Cirencester; FRICS: *m* 1974, Jane Mary, da of John Roy Wynter Bee, of West End, Surrey, and has issue living, Hugo Peter David, *b* 1979, — Thomas John Rowland, *b* 1984, — Charlotte Mary, *b* 1976, — Katherine Anna, *b* 1991. *Residence* – Cubley Lodge, Ashbourne, Derbys DE6 2FB.

WIDOW LIVING OF FOURTH BARON

PRISCILLA, da of late Capt John Egerton-Warburton (*see* Grey-Egerton, Bt, colls), and widow of Maj (William Matthew) Viscount Wolmer, el son of 3rd Earl of Selborne: *m* 1st, 1948, Maj the 4th Baron, who *d* 1992; 2ndly, 1994, as his 2nd wife, Frederick Charles Horace Fryer (*see* E Peel, colls, 1985 Edn). *Residence* – Vernon Hill House, Bishop's Waltham, Hants.

COLLATERAL BRANCHES LIVING

Issue of late Maj Hon Sir Francis Michael Legh, KCVO, yst son of 3rd Baron, *b* 1919, *b* 1984; *m* 1948, Ruadh Daphne, who *d* 1973, da of late Alan Holmes-Watson:—
Nicholas Charles, *b* 1951; *ed* Eton: *m* 1980, Annabel G., da of Peter Hawkings, of Greywell, Hants, and has issue living, Lucy Henrietta, *b* 1982, — Alice Sophia, *b* 1985. *Residence* – Orchard House, Littlestone-on-Sea, New Romney, Kent. ——— Laura Helen (*Hon Mrs Simon Weinstock*) *b* 1954: *m* 1979, Hon Simon Andrew Weinstock, son of Baron Weinstock (Life Baron), and has issue living, Pamela Helen, *b* 1982, — Celia Rose, *b* 1985, — Laetitia Anne Daphne, *b* 1990.

Issue of late Lieut-Col Hon Sir Piers Walter Legh, GCVO, KCB, CMG, CIE, OBE, yr son of 2nd Baron, *b* 1890, *d* 1955: *m* 1920, Sarah Polk, who *d* 1955, da of late Judge James C. Bradford, of Nashville, Tennessee, USA, and widow of Capt Hon Alfred Thomas Shaughnessy (*see* B Shaughnessy):—
Diana Evelyn, *b* 1924; High Sheriff Cornwall 1988-89: *m* 1st, 1945 (*m diss* 1948), 4th Earl of Kimberley; 2ndly, 1951, Lt-Col Norman Robert Colville, MC, FSA, who *d* 1974, and has issue living (by 2nd *m*), James Charles David, *b* 1952; *ed* Eton; a Page of Honour to HM 1966-68: *m* 1983, Fiona, da of John Gaylor, of Bromley, Kent, and has issue living, Robert John James *b* 1984, Sarah Elizabeth Rose *b* 1986, Lucy Isabelle Amy *b* 1988. *Residences* – Penheale Barton, Launceston, Cornwall; 11 Kensington Sq, W8.

PREDECESSORS – (1) WILLIAM JOHN Legh, son of late William Legh; *b* 1828; MP for S Lancashire (*C*) 1859-65 and for Cheshire 1868-85; *cr Baron Newton*, of Newton-in-Makerfield, co Lancaster (peerage of United Kingdom) 1892: *m* 1856, Emily Jane, who *d* 1901, da of late Ven Charles Nourse Wodehouse, Archdeacon of Norwich; *d* 1898; *s* by his el son (2) THOMAS WODEHOUSE, PC, 2nd Baron; *b* 1857; Paymaster-Gen 1915-16, and Assist Under-Sec of State for Foreign Affairs 1916; sat as MP for Lancashire SW, Newton Div (*C*) 1886-1898: *m* 1880, Evelyn, who *d* 1932, da of late William Henry Bromley-Davenport, MP, of Capesthorne, Cheshire; *d* 1942; *s* by his son (3) RICHARD WILLIAM DAVENPORT, TD, 3rd Baron; *b* 1888; Capt Yeo; Hon Attaché at Vienna and Constantinople 1912-14; Hon Col 7th Batn Cheshire Regt (TA) 1939-50: *m* 1914, Hon Helen Winifred Meysey-Thompson, who *d* 1958, da of 1st Baron Knaresborough; *d* 1960; *s* by his el son (4) PETER RICHARD, 4th Baron; *b* 1915; Maj Grenadier Guards; a Lord Commr of the Treasury 1955-57, Vice-Chamberlain HM Household 1957-59, Treasurer 1959-60, Capt Yeomen of the Guard, and Assist Ch Whip House of Lords 1960-62; Joint Parl Sec Min of Health 1962-64, Min of State for Education and Science April to October 1964; MP Petersfield Div of Hants (*C*) 1951-60: *m* 1948, Priscilla (who *m* 2ndly, 1994, as his 2nd wife, Frederick Charles Horace Fryer (*see* E Peel, colls, 1985 Edn)), da of late Capt John Egerton-Warburton (*see* Grey-Egerton, Bt, colls), and widow of Maj (William Matthew) Viscount Wolmer, el son of 3rd Earl of Selborne; *d* 1992; *s* by his elder son (5) RICHARD THOMAS, 5th Baron and present peer.

NICKSON, BARON (Nickson) (Life Baron 1994)

DAVID WIGLEY NICKSON, KBE, son of late Geoffrey Wigley Nickson; *b* 27 Nov 1929; *ed* Eton, and RMA Sandhurst; DL Stirling and Falkirk 1982; FRSE; Brig Queen's Body Guard for Scotland (Royal Company of Archers); Chancellor Glasgow Caledonian Univ since 1993; Hon DUniv Stirling, Napier, and Paisley; Coldstream Guards 1949-54; Dir William Collins plc 1959-76 (Vice-Chm and Group Man Dir 1976-83); Dir Radio Clyde Ltd 1981-85, and Scottish & Newcastle plc since 1981 (Dep-Chm 1982, Chm 1983-89); Chm Clydesdale Bank plc since 1991 (Dir since 1981, Dep-Chm 1990-91); Dep-Chm General Accident plc since 1993 (Dir since 1981); Dir Edinburgh Investment Trust plc 1981-94, Hambros plc, and National Australia Bank since 1991; Pres CBI 1986-88 (Chm for Scotland 1979-81); Chm Countryside Commn for Scotland 1983-85, Member National Economic Devpt Council 1985-88, Sr Salaries Review Body since 1989, Scottish Devpt Agency 1989-91, and Scottish Enterprise 1990-93; Chm Atlantic Salmon Trust since 1988; CBE 1981, KBE 1987; *cr Baron Nickson*, of Renagour, in the District of Stirling (Life Baron) 1994: *m* 1952, (Helen) Louise, da of late Lt-Col Louis William La Trobe Cockcraft, DSO, MVO, and has issue.
Residence – Renagour House, Aberfoyle, Stirling FK8 3TF. *Clubs* – Boodle's, MCC.

DAUGHTERS LIVING

Hon Felicity, *b* 1955: *m* 1980, James Lewis, and has issue living, Emily, *b* 1984, — Sophie, *b* 1986, — Harriet, *b* 1989.
Hon Lucy, *b* 1959: *m* 1984, Melfort Campbell, and has issue living, Iona, *b* 1987, — Araminta, *b* 1988, — Alice, *b* 1990.
Hon Rosemary, *b* 1963: *m* 1st, 1986 (*m diss* 1992), — Petronanos; 2ndly, 1992, Maj Alastair Campbell, and has issue living (by 1st *m*), Andrew, *b* 1988.

NICOL, BARONESS (Nicol) (Life Baroness 1982)

OLIVE MARY WENDY NICOL, da of late James Rowe-Hunter (*d* 1962), by his wife Harriet Hannah (*d* 1932); *b* 21 March 1923; *ed* Cahir Sch, Ireland; Civil Service 1943-48; Trustee United Charities 1967-86; JP (1972)

Cambridge; Member Cambridge City Council 1972-82; Supplementary Benefits Tribunal 1976-78; Careers Service Consultative Panel 1978-81; *cr Baroness Nicol*, of Newnham, co Cambs (Life Baroness) 1982: *m* 1947, Alexander Douglas Ian Nicol, CBE, son of late Alexander Nicol and has issue.
Residence – 39 Grantchester Rd, Newnham, Cambridge CB3 9ED.

SONS LIVING

Hon Adrian Timothy, *b* 4 March 1949: *m* 1st, 1973 (*m diss* 1984), Valerie Joan, da of Alan Gilbert, of Mobberley, Cheshire; 2ndly, 1991, Christine Susan, da of Herbert John Barnes, of Paignton, Devon, and has issue living (by 1st wife), one son and one da, — (by 2nd wife), Thomas Alexander, *b* 1988, — James Edward Jack, *b* 1991.
Hon Colin Douglas, *b* 1950: *m* 1992, June, da of Donald Alexander Smith, of Hull.

DAUGHTER LIVING

Hon Jane Lesley, *b* 1954: *m* 1984, Edward John, only son of J. E. John, of Margam, Port Talbot, W Glam.

NOEL-BAKER, BARONY OF (Noel-Baker) (Extinct 1982)

SON LIVING OF LIFE BARON

Hon Francis Edward (Prokopion, Euboea, Greece *Clubs* – Travellers', Special Forces and Athens) *b* 1920; *ed* Westminster and King's Coll, Camb (Exhibitioner); MP for Brentford and Chiswick (*Lab*) 1945-50, and for Swindon 1955-68; Chm UN Parly Cttee 1966-69 and Parly Lab Party Overseas Devpt Cttee 1964-68; Chm of British Greek Parly Group 1958-69 and of North Euboean Enterprises Ltd from 1963; Hon Pres of Union of Forest Owners of Greece 1968; Dir of Fini Fisheries of Cyprus 1976; Gov of Campion Sch Athens 1974-78; Memb Ecology Party 1978 and Soil Assoc 1979; Pres European Council for Villages and Small Towns (ECOVAST): *m* 1957, Barbara Christina, yr da of late Joseph Sonander, of Swenden, and has issue.

NOEL-BUXTON, BARON (Noel-Buxton) (Baron UK 1930)

MARTIN CONNAL NOEL-BUXTON, 3rd Baron; *b* 8 Dec 1940; *s* 1980; *ed* Bryanston, and at Balliol Coll, Oxford; resumed by deed poll 1964, the surname of NOEL-BUXTON; Solicitor 1966: *m* 1st, 1964 (*m diss* 1968), Miranda Mary, who *d* 1979, el da of Maj Hugo Atherton Chisenhale-Marsh, of Gaynes Park, Epping, Essex; 2ndly, 1972 (*m diss* 1982), Sarah Margaret Surridge, only da of Neil Charles Wolseley Barrett, of Twickenham Rd, Teddington; 3rdly, 1986, Mrs Abigail Marie Granger, da of Eric Philip Richard Clent, and has issue living by 2nd and 3rd *m*.

Arms – Argent, a lion rampant tail elevated and turned over the head sable, between two mullets of the second. **Crest** – A buck's head couped gules, attired or, gorged with a collar of the last, therefrom pendent an escutcheon argent, charged with an African's head sable.
Residence – Little London, Hingham, Norfolk.

SON LIVING *(By 2nd marriage)*

Hon CHARLES CONNAL, *b* 17 April 1975.

DAUGHTERS LIVING *(By 2nd marriage)*

Hon Lucy Margaret, *b* 1977.

(By 3rd marriage)

Hon Antonia Helen, *b* 1989.

BROTHER LIVING

Hon Simon Campden (Abbotsmead, 55 East St, Coggeshall, Essex), *b* 1943; *ed* Bryanston, and Balliol Coll, Oxford: *m* 1981, Alison D., da of S. J. Liddle, of Exmouth, Devon, and has issue living, Christopher John Noel, *b* 1988, — Katherine Helen, *b* 1983.

HALF-BROTHER LIVING

Hon Richard Christopher (29 St Ann's Villas, W11), *b* 1950; *ed* Bryanston: *m* 1988, Annabel, da of Peter Hawker (*see* B Ravensdale, colls), and has issue living, Cecilia, *b* 1990, — a da, *b* 1993.

HALF-SISTER LIVING

Hon Clare Elizabeth Anne, *b* 1954: *m* 1977, Owen Hampden Inskip, only son of His Honour late Judge (John Hampden) Inskip (*see* B Maclay, 1973-74 Edn), and has issue living, Victoria Anne, *b* 1983.

UNCLE LIVING (son of 1st Baron)

Hon Michael Barnett Noel NOEL-BUXTON, *b* 1920; *ed* Harrow, and at Balliol Coll, Oxford; European War 1940-45 with RA; was in Colonial Ser Gold Coast (now Ghana) 1947-59. *Residence* – Stretchney, Diptford, Totnes, S Devon, TQ9 7NN. *Club* – Flyfishers'.

AUNTS LIVING (daughters of 1st Baron)

Hon Jane Elizabeth Noel, *b* 1925; relinquished surname of Noel by Public Declaration, 1957. *Residence* – 27 Redington Rd, Hampstead, NW3.

Hon Sarah Edith Noel NOEL-BUXTON, *b* 1928: *m* 1955, John Goldsborough Hogg, and has issue living, Sarah Jane, *b* 1956: *m* 1981, David Henry Houldsworth (*see* E Morton, colls, 1963 Edn), — Joanna Wynfreda, *b* 1960. *Residence* – Old Broad Oak, Brenchley, Kent.

PREDECESSORS – (1) NOEL EDWARD Noel-Buxton, PC, 2nd son of Sir Thomas Fowell Buxton, 3rd Bt, GCMG, by his wife, Lady Victoria Noel, da of 1st Earl of Gainsborough; *b* 1869; Min of Agriculture and Fisheries Jan to No 1924, and June 1929 to June 1930; sat as MP for Whitby Div of N Riding of Yorkshire (*L*) 1905-6, and for Norfolk, N Div 1910-18, and (*Lab*) 1922-30; assumed by deed poll (enrolled at College of Arms) 1930 the additional surname of Noel before that of Buxton; *cr Baron Noel-Buxton*, of Aylsham, Norfolk (peerage of United Kingdom) 1930: *m* 1914, Lucy Edith, who *d* 1960, da of late Major Henry Pelham Burn; *d* 1948; *s* by his son (2) RUFUS ALEXANDER Buxton, 2nd Baron, *b* 1917; Research Assist, Agricultural Economics Inst, Oxford 1940-43, Lecturer to HM Forces 1942-45, Producer N American Ser, BBC 1946-48, with *Farmers' Weekly* 1950-52: *m* 1st, 1939 (*m diss* 1947), Helen Nancy, who *d* 1949, yr da of late Col Kenneth Hugh Munro Connal, CB, OBE, TD, DL, of Monktonhead, Monkton, Ayrshire; 2ndly, 1948, Margaret Elizabeth, who *d* 1978, el da of Stephanus Abraham Cloete, of Pretoria, S Africa; *d* 1980; *s* by his el son (3) MARTIN CONNAL, 3rd Baron and present peer.

NOLAN, BARON (Nolan) (Life Baron 1994)

MICHAEL PATRICK NOLAN, PC, yr son of James Thomas Nolan, of London; *b* 10 Sept 1928; *ed* Ampleforth, and Wadham Coll, Oxford; RA 1947-49, TA 1949-55; Bar Middle Temple 1953 (Bencher 1975), QC 1968, Member Bar Council 1973-74, and Member Senate of Inns of Court and Bar 1974-81 (Treasurer 1977-79), Bar NI 1974, QC (NI) 1974, Recorder of Crown Court 1975-82, Judge of High Court of Justice (Queen's Bench Div) 1982-91 (Presiding Judge Western Circuit 1985-88), Lord Justice of Appeal 1991-93, since when a Lord of Appeal in Ordinary; *cr* Knt 1982, PC 1991, and *Baron Nolan*, of Brasted, co Kent (Life Baron) 1994: *m* 1953, Margaret, yr da of late Alfred Noyes, CBE, the poet, essayist and critic, and has issue.
Residence – Tanners, Brasted, Westerham, Kent TN16 1NH.

SON LIVING

Hon Michael Alfred Anthony, *b* 1955; *ed* Ampleforth, St Benet's Hall, Oxford (MA), and City Univ (Dip Law); Bar Middle Temple 1981: *m* 1984, Adeline Mei Choo, da of Henry S. H. Oh, of Singapore, and has issue living, Hugh, *b* 1986, — Felix, *b* 1992, — Sophia, *b* 1989. *Residence* – 1 Broomhouse Rd, SW6 3QU.

DAUGHTERS LIVING

Hon Patricia Margaret, *b* 1954: *m* 1979, Col Richard John Morris, and has issue living, Henry John Richard, *b* 1982, — Benjamin Michael Joseph, *b* 1985, — Alice Rose, *b* 1988.

Hon Sheila Mary, *b* 1957: *m* 1981, Charles William Edward Hume, and has issue living, Thomas Charles, *b* 1982, — Joshua Michael, *b* 1986, — Samuel Donald, *b* (twin) 1986, — Lucy Margaret, *b* 1984.

Hon Anne Teresa, *b* 1959.

Hon Clare Elizabeth, *b* 1965.

NORBURY, EARL OF (Graham-Toler) (Earl I 1827)

Faithful to my king and country

NOEL TERENCE GRAHAM-TOLER, 6th Earl; *b* 1 Jan 1939; *s* 1955: *m* 1965, (Rosamund Margaret) Anne, da of late Francis Mathew, and has issue.

Arms – Quarterly: 1st and 4th argent, a cross fleury gules charged with a plain cross couped of the field between four leaves vert, a crescent for difference, *Toler*; 2nd and 3rd argent, a trefoil slipped vert, on a chief sable three escallops or, *Graham*. **Crest** – On a ducal coronet a fleur-de-lis or. **Supporters** – *Dexter*, a horse or, bridled gules; *sinister*, a fawn proper.
Address – Whitefriars Ltd, Coni, Gilbert Sankey, 10 Throckmorton Av, Throckmorton St, EC2N 2DH. *Club* – RAC.

SON LIVING

RICHARD JAMES (*Viscount Glandine*), *b* 5 March 1967.

DAUGHTER LIVING

Lady Patricia Margaret, *b* 1970.

PREDECESSORS – (1) JOHN Toler, KC, 3rd son of late Daniel Toler, of Beechwood, co Tipperary; *b* 1745; Solicitor-Gen for Ireland 1789-98, Attorney-Gen 1798-99, and Ch Justice of Common Pleas 1800-27; MP for Tralee 1776-83, for Philipstown 1783-90, and for Newborough 1790-99; *cr Baron Norbury*, of Ballycrenode, co Tipperary (peerage of Ireland) 1800, and *Viscount Glandine* and *Earl of Norbury*, of Glandine, Kings Co (peerage of Ireland) 1827, with special remainder to his 2nd son, Hector John: *m* 1778, Grace, who *d* 1822 (having been *cr Baroness Norwood*, of Knockalton, co Tipperary (peerage of Ireland) 1797), da of late Hector Graham; *d* 1831; *s* by his son **(2)** HECTOR JOHN, 2nd Earl, *b* 1781, assumed, by Roy licence 1825, the additional surname and arms of Graham; *s* his el brother in his mother's Barony of Norwood and his father's Barony of Norbury 1832: *m* 1808, Elizabeth, who *d* 1859, only child of late William Brabazon; was murdered 1839; *s* by his son **(3)** HECTOR JOHN, 3rd Earl; *b* 1810: *m* 1848, Lady Steuart Lindsay, who *d* 1904, sister of 7th Earl of Lindsay; *d* 1873; *s* by his son **(4)** WILLIAM BRABAZON LINDSAY, 4th Earl; *b* 1862: *m* 1908, Lucy Henrietta Katharine, who *d* 1966, da of late Rev Hon William Charles Ellis (B Howard de Walden); *d* 1943; *s* by his kinsman **(5)** RONALD IAN MONTAGU (son of late Lt-Col James Otway Graham-Toler, son of late Hon Otway Fortescue Graham-Toler, 2nd son of 2nd Earl), 5th Earl; *b* 1893; formerly Capt Roy Inniskilling Fusiliers: *m* 1st, 1919 (*m diss* 1933), Simonne Evangeline Julie Caroline, da of Hans Apeness, of 22 Rue de Thermes, Calais; 2ndly, 1933, Margaret, who *d* 1984, da of John Kevan Greenhalgh, of Hoylake, Cheshire; *d* 1955; *s* by his son **(6)** NOEL TERENCE, 6th Earl and present peer; also Viscount Glandine, Baron Norbury, and Baron Norwood.

NORFOLK, DUKE OF (Fitzalan Howard) (Duke E 1483)

Virtue alone is unconquerable

MILES FRANCIS STAPLETON FITZALAN HOWARD, KG, GCVO, CB, CBE, MC, 17th Duke, and Premier Duke and Earl of England; *b* 21 July 1915; *s* as 12th Baron Beaumont 1971, 4th Baron Howard of Glossop 1972, and 17th Duke of Norfolk, Earl Marshal and Hereditary Marshal of England 1975 (when he assumed the additional forename of Stapleton by deed poll); *ed* Ampleforth, and Ch Ch Oxford (MA); Maj-Gen (ret) late Gren Gds; a DL for W Sussex; Knt of Sovereign Order of Malta; Head of British Mil Mission to Russian Forces in Germany 1957-59, Comdg 70th Bde, King's African Rifles 1961-63, and GOC 1st Div 1963-65, Dir of Management and Support Intelligence, Min of Defence 1965-66, and Dir of Ser Intelligence, Min of Defence 1966-67; a Dir of Robert Fleming & Co, Ltd since 1969; Chm Arundel Castle Trustees Ltd; Pres The Building Societies Assocn 1982-86; Hon Student Ch Ch, Oxford, 1983; Hon Master of Bench Inner Temple since 1984; Hon Joint Treas (with the Duchess of Norfolk) Help the Aged since 1987; 1939-45 War in France, N Africa, Sicily, Italy, and NW Europe (despatches, MC); CBE (Mil) 1960, CB (Mil) 1966, KG 1983, GCVO 1986: *m* 1949, Anne Mary Teresa, CBE, da of late Wing-Cdr Gerald Joseph Constable-Maxwell, MC, DFC, AFC (*see* L Herries of Terregles, colls), and has issue.

Arms – Quarterly: 1st gules, a bend between six cross-crosslets fitchée argent; on the bend an escutcheon or, charged with a demi-lion rampant, pierced through the mouth by an arrow, within a double tressure flory counterflory of the first, *Howard*; 2nd gules, three lions passant guardant in pale or, in chief a label of three points argent, *Thomas of Brotherton*; 3rd checky or and azure, *Warren*; 4th gules, a lion rampant or, *Fitzalan*; behind the shield two gold batons in saltire, enamelled at the ends sable (as *Earl Marshal*). **Crest** – 1st, issuant from a ducal coronet or, a pair of wings gules each charged with a bend between six cross-crosslets fitchée argent; 2nd, on a chapeau gules, turned up ermine, a lion statant guardant with tail extended or, ducally gorged argent, *Thomas of Brotherton*: 3rd, on a mount vert a horse passant argent, holding in the mouth a slip of oak fructed proper. **Supporters** – *Dexter*, a lion argent; *sinister*, a horse argent, holding in his mouth a slip of oak vert, fructed proper.
Seat – Arundel Castle, Sussex BN18 9AB. *Residences* – Carlton Towers, Goole, Yorks DN14 9LZ; Bacres, Hambleden, Henley-on-Thames, Oxon. *Club* – Pratt's.

SONS LIVING

EDWARD WILLIAM (*Earl of Arundel and Surrey*), *b* 2 Dec 1956; *ed* Ampleforth, and Lincoln Coll, Oxford (MA): *m* 1987, Georgina Susan, yr da of John Temple Gore (*see* E Eglinton, 1990 Edn), and has issue:—

SONS LIVING—Henry Miles (*Lord Maltravers*), *b* 3 Dec 1987, — *Hon* Thomas Jack, *b* 1992.
DAUGHTERS LIVING—*Lady* Rachel Rose, *b* 1989, — *Lady* Isabel Serena, *b* 1994.

Seat – Arundel Castle, Sussex BN18 9AB.
Lord Gerald Bernard, *b* 1962; *ed* Ampleforth: *m* 1990, Emma Georgina Egerton, da of late Dr Desmond James Cecil Roberts, of Woodhill, Mayfield, Sussex, and has issue living, Arthur, *b* 1991, — Florence, *b* 1993. *Seat* – Carlton Towers, Goole, Yorks DN14 9LZ.

DAUGHTERS LIVING

Lady Tessa Mary Isabel, *b* 1950: *m* 1971, Roderick Francis Arthur Balfour, and has issue (*see* E Balfour, colls). *Residence* – Burpham Lodge, Burpham, Arundel, Sussex.
Lady Carina Mary Gabriel, *b* 1952: *m* 1983, Sir David Paradine Frost, OBE, author and broadcaster, son of late Rev W. J. Paradine Frost, of Tenterden, Kent, and has issue living, Miles Paradine, *b* 1984, — Wilfred, *b* 1985, — George Paradine, *b* 1987.
Lady Marcia Mary Josephine, *b* 1953, actress (as Marsha Fitzalan): *m* 1977, Patrick Geoffrey Ryecart, actor, yr son of Rev John Reginald Ryecart, of Dovercourt, Essex, and has issue living, Frederick William Hamlet, *b* 1987, — Mariella Celia, *b* 1982, — Jemima Carrie, *b* 1984. *Residence* – Hatchmans House, Hambleden, Henley-on-Thames, Oxon RG9 6SX.

BROTHERS LIVING (*Raised to the rank of a Duke's sons,* 1975)

Lord Michael, GCVO, CB, CBE, MC, *b* 1916; *ed* Ampleforth, and Trin Coll, Camb (MA); Maj-Gen late Scots Gds, and Knight of Sovereign Order of Malta; DL Wilts 1974-93; Ch of Staff London Dist 1958-61, Comdg 4th Guards Bde Group 1961-64, Cdr Allied Command, Europe Mobile Forces (Land Component) 1964-66, Ch of Staff, S Command 1967-68, and GOC London Dist and Maj-Gen Comdg the Household Div 1968-71, Marshal of Diplo Corps 1971-81; Hon Col Camb Univ OTC 1968-71; Col Queen's Lancs Regt 1970-78, Col Life Guards and Gold Stick to HM since 1979; Chm Council of TA & VR Assocs 1973-81, Pres 1981-84, Patron 1984-93; Hon Recorder British Commonwealth Ex-Service League since 1992; Chm Dow Valley Petroleum-UK since 1980; 1939-45 in N-W Europe (despatches, MC), Palestine 1945-46, Malaya 1948-49; MBE (Mil) 1949, MVO (4th class) 1952, CBE (Mil) 1962, CB (Mil) 1968, KCVO 1971, GCVO 1980; Freedom City of London 1985: *m* 1st, 1946, Jean Marion, who *d* 1947, da of Sir Hew Clifford Hamilton-Dalrymple, 9th Bt; 2ndly, 1950, Jane Margaret, da of late Capt W. P. Meade Newman, and has issue living, (by 1st *m*) Jean Mary, *b* 1947; Extra Lady in Waiting to HRH The Princess of Wales 1986-91, since when Lady in Waiting: *m* 1976, Max Eben Lecky Pike, of 12 Alexandra Av, SW11, and has issue living, Molly Ann *b* 1979, Amy Mary *b* 1981, — (by 2nd *m*) Thomas Michael, *b* 1952; *ed* Ampleforth, and Oxford Univ (MA); Lt-Col Scots Gds: *m* 1977 (*m diss* 1992), Penelope Jan, da of Capt David Christopher Richard Walters, RN, and has issue living, Edward Michael *b* 1979, Flora Eleanor Meg *b* 1982, — Richard Andrew *b* 1953; *ed* Ampleforth: *m* 1990, Josephine Nina, da of Peter Johnsen, and has issue living, Lydia Nina *b* 1991, Artemis Cecilia Maria *b* 1993, — Henry Julian Nicholas (103 Abingdon Rd, W8 6QU), *b* 1954; *ed* Ampleforth: *m* 1987, Claire Louise, elder da of Georg Wilhelm von Mallinckrodt (*see* Darell, Bt), and has issue living, George Henry *b* 1991, Marina Katherine *b* 1994, — Alexander Rupert, *b* 1964: *m* 1992, Hon Joanna Elizabeth Venables-Vernon, yr da of 10th Baron Vernon, — Isabel Margaret, *b* 1951: *m* 1975, Peter Christopher Bickmore, of The Old Rectory, Cuxham, Watlington, Oxon (*see* E Perth, colls, 1985 Edn), and has issue living, Andrew Ralph *b* 1979, Rupert Nicholas *b* 1985, Fiona Clare *b* 1981. *Residence* – Fovant House, Fovant, Salisbury, Wilts. *Clubs* – Pratt's, Buck's.

Lord Martin, *b* 1922; *ed* Ampleforth, and Trin Coll, Camb; late Capt Gren Gds; JP N Yorks 1966, and DL 1982; High Sheriff 1979-80; 1939-45 War (wounded), Palestine 1945-46: *m* 1948, Bridget Anne, da of late Lt-Col Arnold Ramsay Keppel (*see* E Albemarle, colls), and has issue living, Philip Arnold Bernard Richard, *b* 1963, — Clare Launa, *b* 1949: *m* 1970, Simon Richard Browne Wood, of Brockfield Farmhouse, York YO3 9XJ, son of Lt-Col B. W. Wood, KOYLI, and has issue living, Charles Browne Martin *b* 1973; *ed* Eton, Alethea Launa Rose *b* 1975, Miranda Bridget Sarah *b* 1978, — Sarah Anne, *b* 1951: *m* 1985, Francis Jacques Roos, of 11 Ennismore Gdns, SW7, only son of Jean Jacques Roos, and has issue living, Theodore Martin *b* 1985, Maximilian Augustus *b* 1985, — Amanda Josephine Margaret, *b* 1953: *m* 1985, Robert C. Pascall, 2nd son of Clive Pascall, of 17 Priory Av, W4, and has issue living, Laurence Blaise Philip *b* 1989, Joshua Ralph Joseph *b* 1992, — Rose Bridget, *b* 1957: *m* 1979, Nicholas ffolliott Woodhead, of The Cottage, Holtby, York, eldest son of Col Michael ffolliott Woodhead, OBE, and has issue living, Christopher Archie ffolliott *b* 1985, Frederick Michael Martin *b* 1986, Hubert Nicholas Philip *b* 1989. *Residence* – Brockfield Hall, York YO3 9XJ.

Lord Mark, OBE, *b* 1934; *ed* Ampleforth; late Coldstream Gds; Chm Assocn of Investment Trust Cos 1981-83; Dir Robert Fleming Holdings Ltd; Treas Scout Assocn since 1986; OBE (1994): *m* 1961, Jacynth Rosemary, da of Sir Martin Alexander Lindsay of Dowhill, 1st Bt, CBE, DSO, and has issue living, Amelia, *b* 1963, — Eliza, *b* 1964: *m* 1987, Timothy Francis Bell, of 26 Melrose Gdns, W6 7RW, yr son of John Bell, and has issue living, Tamara Alexandra *b* 1992. *Residence* – 13 Campden Hill Sq, W8 7LB.

SISTERS LIVING (*Raised to the rank of a Duke's daughters,* 1975)

Lady Mariegold Magdalene, *b* 1919: *m* 1957, Gerald James Auldjo Jamieson, who *d* 1992, son of late Sir Archibald Auldjo Jamieson, KBE, MC, and has issue living, Simon David Auldjo, *b* 1959, — James Gerard, *b* 1963. *Residences* – 32 Cheyne Court, Flood St, SW3; Yarrow House, Elmham, Norfolk.

Lady Miriam, *b* 1924: *m* 1952, Lt-Cdr Theodore Bernard Peregrine Hubbard, RN, and has issue (*see* E Lindsey, colls). *Residence* – Thurston Croft, Thurston, Bury St Edmunds, Suffolk.

Lady Miranda Mary, *b* 1927: *m* 1947, Hon Christopher Anthony Robert Emmet, JP, of Seabeach House, Halnaker, W Sussex, el son of Baroness Emmet of Amberley (Life Baroness), and has issue (*see* By of Emmet).

Lady Mirabel Magdalene, *b* 1931: *m* 1952, Bernard Kelly, el son of late Sir David Victor Kelly, GCMG, MC, and has issue living, Dominic Noël Miles Charles David (Romden Cottage, Smarden, Kent), *b* 1953: *m* 1981, Miranda, da of Lance Macklin, of Alicante, Spain, and has issue living, Sabine Mirabel Jemima Noel *b* 1983, Alice *b* 1985, Celina *b* 1987, — Anthony Noël Francis (Studio 1, 3 Brackenbury Rd, W6 0BE), *b* 1955, — Crispin Bernard Noël (1 Ranelagh Av, SW6), *b* 1956: *m* 1982, Frances, yr da of Sir Charles William Richards Pickthorn, 2nd Bt, and has had issue, Alexander *b* 1985, Christian *b* and *d* 1987, Jessica *b* 1988, — David Mark Noël, *b* 1959: *m* 1992, Alexandra Mary Romana, 3rd da of Joseph Czernin (*see* B Howard de Walden), and has issue living, Natasha Mary Gabriella *b* 1994, — Benedict Bernard Noël d'Arenberg (25 Lavender Gdns, W11 1DH), *b* 1960: *m* 1988, Elizabeth A., yr da of Alexander Eaglestone, of Oxford, and has issue living, Thomas Alexander Noël *b* 1990, Humphrey Martin Noël *b* 1992, — Sebastian Charles Noël, *b* 1972, — Justin Ghislain Octavius Noël, *b* 1974, — Anne-Louise Marie-Noële Miranda Josephine, *b* 1962: *m* 1987, Charles Richard Francis Arkwright, of 52 Bovingdon Rd, SW6, elder son of late Col Peter Arkwright, OBE, of Willersey House, nr Broadway, Worcs, and has issue living, Arabella *b* 1988, Rebecca *b* 1990. *Residences* – 28 Carlyle Sq, SW3 6HA; Romden, Smarden, Kent.

DAUGHTERS LIVING OF SIXTEENTH DUKE

Lady Anne Elizabeth (*Lady Herries of Terregles*), *b* 1938 (see that title).

Lady Mary Katharine, CVO, *b* 1940; *hp* to Lordship of Herries of Terregles; Lady-in-Waiting to HRH Princess Alexandra, Hon Lady Ogilvy, since 1964; CVO 1982: *m* 1986, Gp Capt Anthony Mumford. *Residences* – North Stoke Cottage, N Stoke, Arundel, W Sussex BN18 9LS; Lantonside, Glencaple, Dumfries.

Lady Sarah Margaret, *b* 1941; DL W Sussex 1993: *m* 1988, as his 2nd wife, Nigel Hugh Clutton, yr son of late Robin John Clutton, of Woodcote, Rotherfield, Sussex. *Residence* – The Dover House, Poling, Arundel, W Sussex.

Lady Teresa Jane (*Countess of Ancram*), *b* 1945: *m* 1975, Michael Andrew Foster Jude, Earl of Ancram, MP, elder son of 12th Marquess of Lothian.

DAUGHTERS LIVING OF FIFTEENTH DUKE

Lady Katherine Mary, *b* 1912; has Order of Mercy: *m* 1940, Lieut-Col Joseph Anthony Moore Phillips, DSO, MBE, DL, late King's Dragoon Guards, who *d* 1990, and has had issue, Anthony Bernard Moore, *b* 1953; lost at sea during Whitbread Yacht Race 1989. *Residence* – Lund House, Lund, Driffield, Yorks.

Lady Winefride Alice, *b* 1914: *m* 1943, Lt-Col John Edward Broke Freeman, late Oxfordshire and Buckinghamshire LI, who *d* 1986, son of late Sir Philip Horace Freeman, KCVO, KBE, and has issue living, Charles Philip Broke (Buxhall Vale, Stowmarket, Suffolk), *b* 1947: *m* 1982, Hilary Jane, yr da of Henry Val Faker, of Brentwood, Essex, and has had issue, Thomas *b* 1988, Isabella *b* 1983, Julia *b* 1986 (dec), Cordelia Mary Antonia *b* 1989, and an adopted son, Barnabas *b* 1980, — Mary Gwendoline, *b* 1945: *m* 1967, Martin Richard de Laszlo, of 57 Coniger Rd, SW6, and has issue living, Rupert *b* 1968, Oliver *b* 1971, Lydia *b* 1980, — Virginia Phyllis Theresa, *b* 1949: *m* 1978, Ian Ramsay Hope Henderson, of 20 Westbourne Park Rd, W2, and has issue (*see* B Faringdon, colls). *Residence* – St Catherine's Cottage, Aldingbourne, W Sussex.

WIDOW LIVING OF SIXTEENTH DUKE

LAVINIA MARY, LG, CBE (*Lavinia, Duchess of Norfolk*) (Arundel Park, Sussex), da of 3rd Baron Belper; bore the Queen's Canopy at Coronation of King George VI; Lord Lieut of W Sussex 1975-89; CBE (Civil) 1971, LG 1990: *m* 1937, the 16th Duke, who *d* 1975.

COLLATERAL BRANCHES LIVING

Descendants of late Rt Hon Lord Edmund Bernard Fitzalan-Howard, KG, GCVO, DSO (3rd son of 14th Duke), who was *cr Viscount Fitz Alan of Derwent* 1921:—
See V Fitz Alan of Derwent (ext).

Granddaughter of 2nd Baron Howard of Glossop, 2nd son of Rt Hon Lord Edward George Fitzalan-Howard (who was *cr Baron Howard of Glossop* 1869), 2nd son of 13th Duke:—
Issue of late Hon Philip Granville James Fitzalan Howard, Lt WG, *b* 1895, *d* of wounds received in action 1918: *m* 1916, Gladys Cecily Clara (who *d* 1966, having *m* 2ndly, 1920 (*m diss* 1931), Capt Henry James Fosbery Mills, formerly KRRCR, son of Sir James Mills, KCMG; 3rdly, 1931, Maj P. G. Riviere), da of late Lieut-Col Charles Edward Norton, CMG:—
Philippa Gwendolen Mary (*posthumous*), *b* 1918: *m* 1940, Major Edward Guy Tyler, MC, Irish Guards, and has issue living Peter Edward, *b* 1944; *ed* Ampleforth, — Virginia Anne, *b* 1941: *m* 1965, Carlos de Mejia, of 26 Mallord St, SW1, and has issue living, Carlos-Felipe *b* 1967, Mariana Luisa *b* 1971, Elena Isabel *b* 1975. *Residence* – Hedsor Farm House, Wooburn Green, Bucks.

Grandchildren of late Sir (Edward) Stafford Howard, KCB, 2nd son of late Henry Howard, MP, only son of late Lord Henry Thomas Howard-Molyneux-Howard, MP, brother of 12th Duke:—
Issue of late Maj Sir Algar Henry Stafford Howard, KCB, KCVO, MC, TD, *b* 1880, *d* 1970: *m* 1921, Hon Violet Ethel Meysey-Thompson, who *d* 1960, da of 1st and last Baron Knaresborough, and widow of Capt Alexander Moore Vandeleur:—
Anne Violet, *b* 1923: *m* 1952, John Cahill, of Doneen, Castleisland, co Kerry, and has issue living, John Anthony, *b* 1956, — Colin Algar, *b* 1958, — Peter Francis, *b* 1960, — Elizabeth Mary, *b* 1953, — Alice, *b* 1962, — Angela Violet, *b* 1964, — Rosemary, *b* 1967. —— Elizabeth Helen, *b* 1924: *m* 1958, Harold William Norman Suckling, and has issue living, Penelope Anne, *b* 1959. *Residence* – Camrose, Stockton, Beccles, Suffolk.
Issue of late Capt Stafford Vaughan Stepney Howard, Coldstream Gds (Res), *b* 1915, *d* 1991: *m* 1st, 1936 (*m diss* 1940), Ursula Priscilla Marie Gabrielle, yr da of Lt-Col Sir James Nockells Horlick, 4th Bt, OBE, MC; 2ndly, 1940, (Mary) Gracia (Algar's Garth, Greystoke, Penrith, Cumbria CA11 0TG), da of late George Wilder Neville, of Portsmouth, Virginia, USA:—
(By 1st *m*) Nicholas Stafford (Johnby Hall, Penrith, Cumbria), *b* 1937; *ed* Eton, Magdalen Coll, Oxford, and Churchill Coll, Camb: *m* 1966, Phyllis Bethan, da of late Lewis Duckett, of Essex House, Dursley, Glos, and has issue living, Henry James Stafford, *b* 1972, — Cecilia Charlotte, *b* 1968. —— (By 2nd *m*) (Murray Bernard) Neville Cyprian, OBE (Greystoke Castle, Penrith, Cumbria CA11 0TG), *b* 1942; *ed* Eton, and RMA Sandhurst; Lt-Col Coldstream Gds; OBE (Mil) 1985: *m* 1969, Lavinia Zara, da of late Lt-Col Philip Lewis (*see* E Dartmouth, colls), and has issue living, Alexander Philip Wilder, *b* 1971, — Catherine Anne Cardwell, *b* 1972. —— Amanda Arianwen, *b* 1941: *m* 1967, Michael Noel Francis Cottrell, of Laurenden Forstal, Challock Lees, Canterbury, son of late Sir Edward Baglietto Cottrell, CBE, and has issue living, Edward Stafford Cyprian, *b* 1969; *ed* RMA Sandhurst, — Philip Howard Edward, *b* 1971, — Camilla Mary Josephine, *b* 1973, — Charlotte Lucinda Gracia, *b* 1981. —— Arianwen Catherine Cardwell, *b* (twin) 1942: *m* 1968, Christopher Neville Neve, and has issue living, Thomas Wilder Neville, *b* 1971, — Eleanor Marged Deborah, *b* 1972.

Grandchildren of late Robert Mowbray Howard, 3rd son of late Henry Howard, MP (ante):—
Issue of late Major Henry Ralph Mowbray HOWARD-SNEYD, OBE, *b* 1883, *d* 1950, having assumed by R licence 1950 the additional surname and arms of Sneyd: *m* 1st, 1911 (*m diss* 1931), Helen Millicent (who *d* 1967), da of late William Dodge James CVO (Forbes, Bt, *cr* 1823); 2ndly, 1931, Janet Emma Jameson (HIBBERT), only da of late John Duthie, of Cults House, Aberdeenshire:—
(By 2nd *m*) Thomas Henry Gavin HOWARD-SNEYD (35 Fursecroft, George St, W1; Brooks's Club), *b* 1940: *m* 1963, Serena Patience, yr da of Thomas Lumley, of Ashcombe House, Lewes, and has issue living, Henry Lyulph, *b* 1965, — Justin Andrew *b* 1966, — Antonia Caroline, *b* 1969. —— (By 1st *m*) Diana Katherine *b* 1913: *m* 1938, Richard Marcus Beresford, who *d* 1968, and has issue living, Christopher Charles Howard (Dryden House, Burton's Way, Chalfont St Giles, Bucks HP8 4BW), *b* 1946: *m* 1973, Philippa Susan Yates, and has issue living, Nicholas Charles Marcus *b* 1979, Antonia Charlotte *b* 1975, Fiona Caroline *b* 1977, — Patricia Mary, *b* 1941: *m* 1st, 1964, (*m diss* 1977), Christopher Arthur Rollo Wells; 2ndly, 1978, Cyril Godfrey Lea, of 59 Ember Lane, Esher, Surrey, KT10 8EF, and has issue living (by 1st *m*), Gavin Marcus *b* 1965, Amanda Clare *b* 1967, — Katherine Anne, *b* 1943: *m* 1st, 1965 (*m diss* 1969), Robert Noel Hutchings; 2ndly, 1969, Jeffrey Osman Streäter, of 16 Upstall St, Camberwell, SE5 9JE, and has issue living (by 2nd *m*), Olivia Katherine Nermin *b* 1974. *Residence* – Walnut House, Benefield Rd, Oundle, Peterborough PE8 4EU. —— Pamela Evelyn, *b* 1914: *m* 1939, Ian Reginald Gilfrid Karslake, who *d* 1982, and has issue living, David Ian Howard (6 rue Victor Chevreuil, 75012 Paris), *b* 1944; *ed* Shrewsbury, and Trin Coll, Camb: *m* 1988, Claire Marie, da of Antoine Bonhomme, and has issue living, Charlotte Cordelia Geraldine Leïla *b* 1989, Emma Caroline Adeliza Howard *b* 1994, — Sarah Vivien, *b* 1941; *ed* St Anne's Coll, Oxford: *m* 1976, Peter Fraser Matthews, of The Old Vicarage, Richmond Rd, Lansdown, Bath, and has had issue, Rupert Charles Oliver *b* 1980, *d* 1982, Guy William Rupert *b* 1983, Alexandra Howard *b* 1978, — Elizabeth Ann, *b* 1948: *m* 1993, Jeremy John Hosking, of Frogs Hill Farm, Newenden, Kent, and has issue living, Thomas Frederick Karslake *b* 1992. *Residence* – Oakfield Cottage, Guildford Rd, Cranleigh, Surrey. —— Audrey Elizabeth, *b* 1916: *m* 1940, Ronald John Henry Kaulback, and has issue living, Peter John (108 Byron Av, Ottawa K1Y 3J2, Ont, Canada), *b* 1948: *m* 1973, Elizabeth Jane, da of Maj Douglas Peter Scopes, of Rectory Cottage, Barnwell, Peterborough PE8 5PG, and has issue living, Simon Peter Howard *b* 1980, Marcus Ronald Oliver *b* 1983, Caroline Victoria Margaret *b* 1978, — Bryan Henry (twin), *b* 1948, — Sonia Elizabeth, *b* 1941: *m* 1967, Robin Erskine Waddell, of 453 Earlham Rd, Norwich, — Susan Georgina, *b* 1942: *m* 1969, Mark Edward Hatt-Cook, RD, ADC, Col RMR, of Mascalls, Broad Chalke, Salisbury, Wilts SP5 5HP, and has issue living, Catherine Emma Kaulback *b* 1974, Georgina Alice Kaulback *b* 1977. *Residence* – Ardnagashel House, Bantry, co Cork. —— Joan Margery, *b* 1921: *m* 1945, Hubert Murray Sturges, and has issue living, William Henry (Tythe Farm, Hinton Charterhouse, Bath), *b* 1949: *m* 1973, Virginia Mary, da of Cdr R. FitzGerald, DSC, RN (ret), of Petworth, Sussex, and has issue living, Tom Woody *b* 1979, Robin Millie *b* 1977, — Rosemary Jane, *b* 1946: *m* 1st, 1971 (*m diss* 1975), Alastair William MacDonald; 2ndly, 1977 (*m diss* 1988), Simon John Harley Quantock Shuldham; 3rdly, 1993, Timothy Joseph Minett, of 10 Redwing Rd, Milborne Port, nr Sherborne, Dorset DT9 5DB, and has issue living (by 2nd *m*), Lucinda Clare *b* 1979, Catherine Emma *b* 1981. *Residence* – Springmount, Berwick St John, Shaftesbury, Dorset SP7 0HQ.

Grandsons of late Henry Howard, MP (ante):—
Issue of late Rt Hon Sir Esme William Howard, GCB, GCMG, CVO, who was *cr Baron Howard of Penrith* 1930 (see that title).

Descendants of late Rt Hon Charles Howard (son of late Sir William Howard, son of late Sir Philip Howard, el son of late Lord William Howard, 2nd son of 4th Duke), who was *cr Earl of Carlisle* 1661 (see that title).

Descendants of late Col Sir Francis Howard, 2nd son of late Lord William Howard (ante):—

Grandchildren of late George Howard, son of late Sir Henry Howard, GCMG, KCB, son of late Sir Henry Francis Howard, GCB, son of Henry Howard, 4th in descent from Col Sir Francis Howard (ante):—
Issue of late Capt Henry Howard, Quarter-Master Corps, US Army, *b* 1907, *d* 1955; *m* 1st, 1928 (*m diss* 1930), Vara, da of William Doherty; 2ndly, 1941, Natalie Bayard (Lukeman Lane, Stockbridge, Mass 01262, USA) (who *m* 2ndly, 1956, Kenneth Douglas Robertson, who *d* 1982), da of late Rev Grenville Merrill, of Merillton, Newport, Rhode Island, USA:—
(By 2nd *m*) George, *b* 1944: *m* 1977, Ilse Bay Tarafa, of Hamburg, Germany. *Residence* – 240 North County Rd, Palm Beach, Florida 33480, USA. —— Natalie Bayard, *b* 1942: *m* 1967, Peter Alan Gordon, of Montreal, Canada, and has issue living, Jonathan Kingman, *b* 1970. *Residence* – 49 East 86 St, New York, NY 10028, USA. —— Mary Mowbray, *b* 1948: *m* 1978, Robert Charczuk, of New York, and Russia, and has issue living, William George Howard, *b* 1984. *Residence* – 160 West 16 St, New York, NY 10011, USA.

Grandchildren of late Sir Henry Howard, GCMG, KCB, son of Sir Henry Francis Howard, GCB (ante):—
Issue of late Com Henry Mowbray Howard, OBE, *b* 1873, *d* 1953: *m* 1917, Norah Florence Annie, who *d* 1974, da of Maj John Dunlop Watson:—
Henry Edmund, DSC, RN (The Studio, Roberts Close, Wickham, Hants PO17 5HH), *b* 1923; is Capt (ret); 1939-45 War (DSC): *m* 1945, Sheila, yr da of Colin McNab Brown, of Paisley, and has issue living, Henry Colin Francis, MBE, *b* 1947: *m* 1975, Katharine, da of Kenneth Charles Harold Rowe, MBE, JP, and has issue living, Thomas William *b* 1977, Charles Philip *b* 1979, Jane *b* 1982, — Catherine Jane *b* 1950: *m* 1973, Edward Bruce Williams, of North Corner, Ashford Hill, Berks, and has issue living, Alasdair Edward Bruce *b* 1975, Peter Henry Bruce *b* 1978, Simon Bruce *b* 1982. — Joan Cecilia (4 Lansdowne House, Lansdowne Rd, W11), *b* 1917: *m* 1942, Capt Brent Elworthy Hutton-Williams, MBE, who *d* 1989, and has issue living, Christopher Brent (53 Chatsworth Av, Wimbledon, SW20), *b* 1948: *m* 1974, Caroline Oppenheimer, and has issue living, Beatrice Rose *b* 1980, — Charlotte Fiona Janet *b* 1944: *m* 1st, 1969 (*m diss* 1975), David Fennell; 2ndly, 1975 (*m diss* 19—), Michael Harrison; 3rdly, 1990, John Mather, of 74 Oakley St, SW3, and has issue living (by 1st *m*), Benedict Nicholas *b* 1971 (by 2nd *m*), Toby Lawrence Brent *b* 1978.

(In remainder to Barony of Beaumont only)

Issue of late Hon Ivy Mary Stapleton, yr da of 10th Baron Beaumont, *b* (*posthumous*) 1895; *d* 1967: *m* 1929, Richard Gerald Micklethwait, who *d* 1976, of Ardsley, Barnsley, Yorks:—
Richard Miles MICKLETHWAIT (Preston Hall, Uppingham), *b* 1934; *ed* Ampleforth, and Ch Ch, Oxford; late Capt Grenadier Guards: *m* 1961, Jane Evelyn, da of late William Melville Codrington, CMG, MC (*see* Codrington, Bt (*cr* 1721), colls), and has issue living, Richard John, *b* 1962: *m* 1992, Mrs Fevronia C. Barnard, only da of Michael Read, of Château Rouvres sur Aube, France, — William James, *b* 1964. — Imogen Mary, *b* 1931: *m* 1961, Maj John Lachlan Macdonald of Tote, of Tote House, Isle of Skye, and 50 Chelsea Park Gdns, SW3, and has issue living, Charles Lachlan, *b* 1964: *m* 1994, Juliet E., da of John Drysdale, of Brill House, Brill, Bucks, — Andrew Kenneth, *b* 1965, — Lisabel Mary, *b* 1969.

Grandchildren of late John Stapleton, brother of 8th Baron Beaumont:—
Issue of late Bryan Stapleton, *b* 1871, *d* 1941: *m* 1st, 1912, Geraldine Emma, who *d* 1916, da of late Col John Henry Crowdy, RE; 2ndly, 1918, Ruth Jane, who *d* 1954, da of late Richard James Friel, of Waterford:—
(By 2nd *m*) Thomas, *b* 1920; *ed* Univ Coll, Oxford (BM and BCh, MA, DM); FRCP London; late Capt RAMC. *Residence* – The Foundry Cottage, Lane End, High Wycombe, Bucks. —— (By 1st *m*) Anne Dunscomb, *b* 1914: *m* 1940, David Edwyn Clark, who *d* 1987, and has issue living, Anthony Miles Stapleton (2988 Fleet St, Coquitlam, BC, Canada, V3C 3R8), *b* 1941; PhD Newfoundland: *m* 1970, Ruth Christine, da of Rev Frederick Guy Harrison, of Appleton Roebuck, Yorks, and has issue living, David Crispin Stapleton *b* 1973 (has issue living (by Jennifer Lee, da of Lloyd King, of 1324 Hornby St, Coquitlam, BC, Canada), Aidan Natis Miles KING *b* 1993), Natasha Alexandra *b* 1971: *m* 1993, Scott Charpentier, — Bryan Stapleton (412 Muritai Rd, Eastbourne, Wellington, NZ), *b* 1944: *m* 1971, Nicolien, da of Leslie Lulofs, of 14 Beaumont Rd, Oaklands, Johannesburg, and has issue living, Graham Leslie *b* 1975, Bronwyn *b* 1972, — Geraldine Anne (Apt 1013, 155 Balliol St, Toronto, Ont, Canada, M45 IC4), *b* 1947. *Residence* – 4/378 Muritai Rd, Eastbourne, Wellington, NZ.
Issue of late Louis Henry Stapleton, *b* 1874, *d* 1949: *m* 1908, Annetta Lima Smith, who *d* 1956, da of late A. Perossi:—
Diana Enid Violet Dorothea, *b* 1911: *m* 1939, Dr Allan William Vaughan Eley, late Major RAMC, who *d* 1965, and has had issue, Ian Miles Stanley Vaughan, *b* 1944; *ed* Oratory Sch, Woodcote; *d* 1983, — Nigel Louis Allan, *b* 1949; *ed* Oratory Sch, Woodcote, — Bridget Diana Lilian Annetta, *b* 1940: *m* 1965, Derek Frank Gardner, and *d* 1966. *Residence* – The Cottage, Sonning Common, Oxon.

Granddaughters of late Bryan John Stapleton, half-brother of 8th Baron Beaumont:—
Issue of late Cdr Gregory Stapleton, RN, *b* 1864, *d* 1938: *m* 1904, Marie Marcella, who *d* 1947, el da of Anthony MacDermott, RM, JP:—
Elizabeth Charlotte Josephine, *b* 1907: *m* 1st, 1941, as his 2nd wife, Maj Francis John Angus Skeet, late R Dublin Fus, who *d* 1943; 2ndly, 1945, Maj Casimir Paul Francis Rowland William Blennerhassett (*see* Blennerhassett, Bt, colls), who *d* 1993. *Residence* – 10 Cavendish Court, 38 St George's Rd, Paston Place, Kempstown, Brighton, Sussex BN3 1FU.
Issue of late Christopher Robert Stapleton, PhD, *b* 1870, *d* 1929: *m* 1908, Alice Cicely, who *d* 1950, da of J. J. Sepple:—
Gwendoline Filumena (515 Helen Rd, Mineola, Long Island, New York USA), *b* 1910: *m* 1942, Edward Joseph Battell, who *d* 1964. —— Alice Veronica Enid, *b* 1912: *m* 1930, John Tyler Walls, and has issue living, John Tyler, *b* 1931, — Christopher Stapleton, *b* 1933, — Julian Davis, *b* 1934, — Alice Enid Stapleton, *b* 1941, — Naomi Anne, *b* 1947, — Collette Aurora, *b* 1948.

Grandchildren of late Cdr Gregory Stapleton, RN (ante):—
Issue of late Maj Gregory Joseph Kenneth Stapleton, IA, *b* 1908; *d* 1982: *m* 1945, Margarita (Langton Herring, Weymouth, Dorset), only da of Henry Fitzroy Chamberlayne, of Stonythorpe, Warwick:—
Miles Gregory Rowland (Manor Farm, Pengover, Liskeard, Cornwall), *b* 1948; *ed* Beaumont; formerly Capt Laker Airways; Capt Cyprus Airways: *m* 1973, Delia Felicity Mary, da of Maj Benjamin Harold Dunkey, of 190 Cooden Drive, Bexhill-on-Sea, and has issue living, Zoe Yvonne, *b* 1975, — Margarita Louisa, *b* 1979, — Sarah Jane, *b* 1988.
Issue of late Joseph Mark Hugh Stapleton, *b* 1909; *d* 1967: *m* 1948, Elizabeth (28 Cavendish Rd, Woking, Surrey), da of Sidney M. Vanheems, of Ealing (Papal Chamberlain to Pope Pius XII):—
Elizabeth Mary, *b* 1949: *m* 1973, Michel Paul René Meuret, of 35 Impasse Marcel Aymé, 39000 Lons-le-Saunier, France, and has issue living, Nicolas Mark, *b* 1976, — Caroline Anne, *b* 1982, — Anne-Lise Antoinette, *b* 1985. —— Anne Mary, *b* 1951: *m* 1983, Hendrich Lattul, c/o The British Council, Jakarta, Indonesia, and has issue living, Virginia Helen, *b* 1985. —— Monica Mary, *b* 1953: *m* 1980, Thierry René Wertheimer, of 7 rue du May, 60129 Glaignes, Orrouy, France, and has issue living, Christian Simon, *b* 1982, — Francis Mark, *b* 1985, — Mark Alastair, *b* 1988, — Claire Monica, *b* 1987.
Issue of late Marie Josephine Stapleton, *b* 1905, *d* 1983: *m* 1928, Joseph Gregory Littledale:—
Gregory Bruno LITTLEDALE, *b* 1932; *ed* Beaumont Coll, Old Windsor; late Royal Fus; Fellow Swimming Teachers' Assocn; Member British Computer Soc: *m* 1st, 1957 (*m diss* 1966), Patricia Jane, da of Leonard Howard, of Dover, Kent; 2ndly, 1969, Naomi Abigail, da of G. F. A. Martin, and has issue living (by 2nd *m*), Mark Gregory, *b* 1976, — Joanna Kerra, *b* 1973, — Tamsyn Greer *b* 1983. *Residence* – 56 Dowell Close, Taunton, Som.

Issue of late Antonia Marianne Angela Winefrede Stapleton, *b* 1911, *d* 1969: *m* 1939, Guy George Morris Pritchett, solicitor, of 7 Flower Walk, Guildford (who *m* 2ndly, 1972, Katherine Mary Elfrida, da of Capt John Alick Woodhouse, CBE, RN):—

Malcolm Morris PRITCHETT (19 Hare Hill Close, Pyrford, Woking, Surrey), *b* 1941; *ed* Beaumont and Imperial Coll, London; Consulting Eng; CEng, FIMM: *m* 1963, Lamorna Jill, da of David Bayly Pike, OBE, of Hailsham, Sussex, and has issue living, Clare Marion, *b* 1965: *m* 1987, Charles Croft, of Brighton, — Karen Fiona, *b* 1967, — Sally Antonia, *b* 1970. —— Roger Morris (Canopus, 7 Bramerton Lodge, East Hill Lane, Bramerton, Norfolk NR14 7EQ), *b* 1943; *ed* Beaumont Coll; Solicitor: *m* 1st, 1969 (*m diss* 1990), Vivien, da of Francis Brothers, of Guildford; 2ndly, 1990, Magdelene Joanne Esvyra Sylvyra Margrette, da of late S/Ldr Elbert Bendt Dall, and has issue living (by 1st *m*), Rupert Francis Morris, *b* 1974; *ed* Eton, — Emma Caroline *b* 1977. —— Helen Monica, *b* 1945: *m* 1966, Ian Strickland, FRICS, of 2 Kings Rd, Walton-on-Thames, Surrey, and has issue living, Alexander Peter, *b* 1967, — Matthew Douglas, *b* 1968, — Luke Gregory, *b* 1979, — Natasha Jane, *b* 1970. —— Antonia Mary, *b* 1947: *m* 1971, Philip Roger Wellesley-Davies, of Manor Cottage, Whitchurch-on-Thames, Oxon RG8 7ET, and has issue living, William George, *b* 1971, — Edward James, *b* 1978, — Henry Charles, *b* 1980, — Antonia Louise, *b* 1975.

Issue of late Anne Penrodas Mary Helen Stapleton, *b* 1914, *d* 1986: *m* 1946, Xavier Philip Mary Spruyt de Bay, who *d* 1983:—

Philip Michael SPRUYT DE BAY, *b* 1950: *m* 1st, 1979 (*m diss* 1988), Lucy Therese Frances, yst da of Air Commodore Noel Holroyd Fresson, DFC, RAF, of Sydenham House, Lewdown, Devon; 2ndly, 1993, Elizabeth Jane Stephenson, da of Lt-Col Anthony Loftus St George Stephenson Clarke, of the Manor House, Seend, Wilts. *Residence* – 29 Westover Rd, SW18. —— Helen Mary, *b* 1947: *m* 1971, Jeremy Charles Stewart Fulford Smithies, MBA, CEng, MIMechE, MRAeS, of 20 Boulevard des Pyrénées, 64000 Pau, France, and has issue living, Roland Jeremy Xavier Spruyt de Bay, *b* 1973, — Frances Mary Barbara, *b* 1976.

PREDECESSORS – **(1)** Sir JOHN Howard, KG, an eminent Yorkist, distinguished himself in the French Wars of Henry VI, and in 1468 was appointed Treasurer of the King's Household; summoned to Parliament of England as *Baron Howard* 1470-83, and 1483 was *cr Earl Marshal of England*, and *Duke of Norfolk* (peerage of England), his son and heir being at the same time *cr Earl of Surrey* (peerage of England); as Earl Marshal he was authorized to bear either in the king's presence or absence a golden staff tipped at each end with black, the upper part thereof to be adorned with the royal arms, and the lower with those of his own family, and to support the dignity a grant was made of £20 a year for ever; was subsequently constituted High Steward of England, and Lord Adm of England, Ireland, and Aquitaine for life; killed at Bosworth Field 1485, and was attainted the same year; *s* by his son **(2)** THOMAS, KG, 2nd Duke; having been taken prisoner at Bosworth his Earldom was attainted and he suffered imprisonment three years in the Tower; was restored 1489; appointed Lord Treasurer 1501, and in 1513 commanded the English Army at Flodden Field, when the Scots were routed and James IV slain; *cr Earl Marshal* of England (for life) 1510, and *Duke of Norfolk* (peerage of England) 1514; *d* 1524; *s* by his son **(3)** THOMAS, KG, 3rd Duke; *cr Earl of Surrey* by patent (peerage of England) 1514; was High Admiral 1513, Lord Dep of Ireland 1520, Treasurer of England 1522, Earl Marshal by patent 1533; attainted 1547, imprisoned in the Tower seven years, and restored 1553; *d* 1554; *s* by his grandson **(4)** THOMAS, KG, 4th Duke (son of Henry, KG, Earl of Surrey, a distinguished statesman, soldier, and poet, who was accused of treason and executed during his father's lifetime 1547); restored in blood 1554: being found guilty of high treason for communicating with Mary, Queen of Scots, he was beheaded 1572, when all his honours were forfeited; *s* by his son **(5)** PHILIP, who in right of his mother (Mary, da and heir of Henry Fitzalan, Earl of Arundel) as owner of Arundel Castle became (according to the admission of Parliament 1433) 13th *Earl of Arundel* (a feudal honourpeerage of England), and *Baron Maltravers* (peerage of England) 1330 (see † infra); restored in blood 1581; attainted of high treason 1589 and *d* a prisoner in the Tower 1595; *s* by his son **(6)** THOMAS, 14th Earl, who during the reign of Elizabeth only bore the courtesy title of Lord Maltravers; restored by Act of Parliament 1604 to all the honours and precedence of his father; in 1627 the titles of *Baron FitzAlan, Baron Clun,* and *Baron Oswaldestre* (peerage of England), were annexed by Act of Parliament to the Earldom of Arundel, which peerages were entailed to descend to the heirs male of his body, with remainder to his heirs male, failing which to his heirs general; constituted Earl Marshal 1621, and *cr Earl of Norfolk* 1644; *m* 1606, Alethea, da of 7th Earl of Shrewsbury, becoming in her own right *Baroness Furnivall, Strange of Blackmere and Talbot*; *d* 1646; *s* by his son **(7)** HENRY FREDERICK, 15th Earl of Arundel, who had in 1640 been summoned to Parliament of England as Baron Mowbray; *d* 1652; *s* by his el son **(8)** THOMAS, 16th Earl of Arundel; restored by Act of Parliament 1660 to Dukedom of Norfolk, with precedence of 1st Duke, and in 1661 obtained an Act confirming the same, with remainder to the male issue of his grandfather, and to other collateral branches; *d* unmarried 1677; *s* by his brother **(9)** HENRY, 6th Duke, who in 1669 had been created *Baron Howard*, of Castle Rising, and in 1672 *Earl of Norwich* (peerage of England), with remainder to various collateral branches, and hereditary *Earl Marshal* of England; was Lord-Lieut of cos Berks and Surrey; *d* 1684; *s* by his son **(10)** HENRY, KG, 7th Duke; Constable and Gov of Windsor Castle; *dsp* 1701; *s* by his nephew **(11)** THOMAS, 8th Duke; *dsp* 1732; *s* by his brother **(12)** EDWARD, 9th Duke; *dsp* 1777, when the Earldom of Norwich and Barony of Howard of Castle Rising expired, the Baronies of Mowbray and Segrave (*see* B Mowbray), and the Baronies of Howard, Braose of Gower, Greystock, Ferrers of Wemme, Talbot, Strange of Blackmere, Furnivall, and Giffard of Brimmesfield fell into abeyance, and the dukedom devolved upon his kinsman **(13)** CHARLES, 10th Duke, grandson of Charles, 4th son of 15th Earl of Arundel; *d* 1786; *s* by his son **(14)** CHARLES, PC, 11th Duke; *d* 1815; *s* by his cousin **(15)** BERNARD EDWARD, 12th Duke, great grandson of Charles Bernard, 8th son of 15th Earl of Arundel; by Act of Parliament 1824 the office of Earl Marshal and Hereditary Marshal of England were empowered to be executed by Roman Catholics; *d* 1842; *s* by his son **(16)** HENRY CHARLES, KG, 13th Duke; Master of the Horse 1846-52; *d* 1856; *s* by his son **(17)** HENRY GRANVILLE, 14th Duke; *b* 1815; MP for Limerick 1851-2; assumed by R licence 1842 the additional surname of FitzAlan: *m* 1839, Augusta Mary Minna Catherine, who *d* 1886, da of 1st Baron Lyons; *d* 1860; *s* by his son **(18)** HENRY, KG, PC, GCVO, 15th Duke, *b* 1847; was Postmaster-Gen Aug 1895 to March 1900, and Lord-Lieut of Sussex 1905-17; received Roy Victorian Chain 1911: *m* 1st, 1877, Lady Flora Paulyna Hetty Barbara Abney-Hastings, who *d* 1887, da of late Countess of Loudoun, and of the 1st Baron Donington; 2ndly, 1904, Hon Gwendolen Mary Constable-Maxwell (*Lady Herries of Terregles* in her own right), who *d* 1945, el da of 11th Lord Herries of Terregles; *d* 1917; *s* by his only surviving son (by 2nd *m*) **(19)** BERNARD MARMADUKE KG, GCVO, GBE, TD, PC, 16th Duke; *b* 1908; Joint Parl Sec Min of Agric 1941-45; KG 1937, received R Victorian Chain 1953: *m* 1937, Hon Lavinia Mary Strutt, LG, CBE, da of 3rd Baron Belper; *d* 1975; *s* by his kinsman **(20)** MILES FRANCIS, KG, GCVO, CB, CBE, MC, 17th Duke and present peer; also Earl of Arundel (see † infra), Earl of Surrey, Earl of Norfolk, Baron Maltravers, Baron FitzAlan, Baron Clun, Baron Oswaldestre (Oswestry), Baron Beaumont (see * infra), and Baron Howard of Glossop (†† infra).

†According to the claim of John FitzAlan in 1433, which was upheld by the Crown, the Earldom of Arundel was held by tenure of Arundel Castle, Sussex. William de Albini, of Buckenham, Norfolk, acquired Arundel in 1138 on his marriage to Queen Adeliza of Louvain, widow of Henry I, and was recognized from 1139 variously as Earl of Sussex, Chichester, or (more usually) Arundel **(1)** RICHARD FitzAlan, Lord of Clun and Oswestry, Salop (8th Earl, according to Admission of 1433), grandson of John Fitzalan by Isabel, da of William de Albini, 5th Earl of Arundel and sister and co-heir of Hugh, 6th Earl of Arundel; was summoned to Parliament 1292 as *Earl of Arundel*; served at Carlaverock 1300: *m* before 1285, Alasia di Saluzzo, da of Thomas, Marquis of Saluzzo; *d* 1302; *s* by his son **(2)** EDMUND, 2nd (or 9th) Earl, *b* 1285: *m* 1305, Alice, da of William de Warenne, and sister and heir of John Earl of Surrey; executed and attainted 1326, when the Castle and Honour of Arundel was granted to Edmund, Earl of Kent, son of Edward I, but in 1331, his son **(3)** RICHARD, 3rd Earl, was restored in blood; assumed the Earldom of Surrey 1361 *m* 1st, 1321 (annulled 1344) Isabel, da of Sir Hugh le Despencer; 2ndly, 1345, Lady Eleanor, da of Henry, Earl of Lancaster, and widow of John de Beaumont; *d* 1376; *s* by **(4)** RICHARD, KG, 4th Earl, *b* 1346: *m* 1359, Elizabeth de Bohun, da of William, Earl of Northampton; 2ndly, 1390, Philippa Mortimer, da of Edmund, Earl of March and widow of John Hastings; attainted and executed 1397 when Arundel was granted to John Holand, Duke of Exeter, but in 1400, his son **(5)** THOMAS, KG, 5th Earl, *b* 1381, was restored to the Earldoms of Arundel and Surrey: *m* 1405, Beatrice, da of John I, King of Portugal; *d* 1415, when representation of the Warennes Earls of Surrey

passed to his sister and co-heir, of whom the descendants of the eldest, Elizabeth, Duchess of Norfolk, opposed the claim of the heir male to the Earldom of Arundel; however in 1415 (6) JOHN, *de jure* 6th Earl and Lord Maltravers (§ infra) (grandson of John, 1st Lord Arundel, brother of 4th Earl) *s* to the Castle and Honour of Arundel and said to have been summoned to Parliament as *Earl of Arundel* 1416 but not afterwards: *m* before 1407, Eleanor, da of Sir John Berkeley of Beverstone, Glos; *d* 1421; *s* by his son (7) JOHN, KG, 7th Earl; *b* 1408; Capt of Rouen 1432; his petition to be considered as Earl of Arundel by tenure of Arundel was allowed 1433; *cr* Duke of Touraine (France) 1434; *m* 1st, Constance Cornwall, da of John Lord Fanhope; 2ndly, before 1429, Maud, da of Robert Lovell and widow of Sir Richard Stafford; *d* from wounds at Beauvais 1435; *s* by his son (8) HUMPHREY, 8th Earl; *b* 1429, *d* 1438; *s* by his uncle (9) WILLIAM, KG, 9th Earl, *b* 1417; Warden of Cinque Ports and Constable of Dover Castle: *m* 1438, Joan, da of Richard Nevill, Earl of Salisbury and sister of the Kingmaker; *d* 1487, *s* by his son (10) THOMAS, KG, KB, 10th Earl, *b* 1450; *m* 1464, Margaret Woodville, da of Richard, 1st Earl Rivers; *d* 1524; *s* by his son (11) WILLIAM, KG, KB, 11th Earl, *b c* 1476; *m* 1st, Elizabeth Willoughby, da of Lord Willoughby de Broke: 2ndly, 1511, Anne Percy, da of 4th Earl of Northumberland; *d* 1534; *s* by his son (12) HENRY, KG, PC, 12th Earl, *b* 1512; distinguished at taking of Boulogne; Lord Chamberlain 1546-50, High Constable at Coronations of Edward VI and Mary I: *m* 1st, Catherine Grey, who *d* 1532, da of 2nd Marquess of Dorset; 2ndly, 1545, Mary, da of Sir John Arundell of Lanherne, and widow of Robert Radclyffe, Earl of Sussex; *d* 1580; *s* by his grandson (13) PHILIP Howard, 13th Earl (ante).

§(1) JOHN Maltravers, *b* about 1290; taken prisoner at Bannockburn 1314; Steward of Household to Edward III 1328; summoned to Parliament 1330, by which he is held to be 1st Lord Maltravers; Keeper of Channel Islands 1348: *m* 1st, Milicent, da of Maurice Lord Berkeley; 2ndly, Agnes, da of William de Bereford of Burton, Leics, and widow of (i) Sir John d'Argentine and (ii) Sir John de Nerford; *d* 1364, when the Barony is held to have fallen into abeyance between the two das of his son John who *d* 1349; on the death sp of the elder about 1397, the surviving (2) ELEANOR *s*: *m* 1st, John, son of Richard FitzAlan, 3rd Earl of Arundel; 2ndly, 1384, Reynold, 2nd Baron Cobham of Sterborough; *d* 1405; *s* by their son (3) JOHN, 3rd Baron *b* 1364; not summoned to Parliament: *m* Elizabeth, da of Edward, Baron Le Despencer; *d* 1390; *s* by his son (4) JOHN Lord Arundel and Maltravers, who *s* as 6th Earl of Arundel (ante).

*(1) HENRY de Beaumont, yr son of Louis de Brienne and grandson of John de Brienne, King of Jerusalem, came to England *temp* Edward I and having secured the favour of that monarch obtained high employment from the crown, was rewarded with large territorial grants and made King of the Isle of Man for life; on Mar 4, 1309 he was sworn of the Privy Council and summoned to Parliament as a *Baron of England*: he *m* Alice, da and heiress of Alexander Comyn, Earl of Buchan, in whose right he became Constable of Scotland and was summoned to Parliament (in right of his wife) 1334; *s* by his son (2) JOHN, 2nd Baron; summoned to Parliament as a Baron 25 Feb 1342; *d* 1342, *s* by his son (3) HENRY, 3rd Baron; *d* 1368; *s* by his son (4) JOHN, KG, 4th Baron; summoned to Parliament 1383-93; *d* 1396; *s* by his son (5) HENRY, 5th Baron; *d* 1413; *s* by his son (6) JOHN, KG, 6th Baron; *cr* Viscount Beaumont 1440, being the first person honoured with the title of Viscount in England; was Lord High Chamberlain of England; *s* by his son (7) WILLIAM, 2nd Viscount; *d* 1507, when the Viscountcy expired and the Barony became abeyant between the descendants of his sister Joane and so continued until 1840, when the abeyance was terminated in favour of (8) MILES THOMAS Stapleton, of Carlton, co York, 8th Baron; *b* 1805: *m* 1844, Isabella Anne, who *d* 1916, da of 3rd Baron Kilmaine; *d* 16 Aug 1854; *s* by his son (9) HENRY, 9th Baron, *b* 1848; present at battle of Ulundi 1879: *m* 1888, Violet, OBE, who *d* 1949, only da of Frederick Wootton Isaacson, MP, of 18 Upper Grosvenor Street, W; *d* 1892; *s* by his brother (10) MILES, 10th Baron, *b* 1850; Lieut-Col Comdg 20th Hussars: *m* 1893, Ethel Mary, who *d* 1937, da of Sir Charles Henry Tempest, 1st Bt (*ext*), of Heaton, Lancashire; *d* 1895, when the title remained in abeyance between his two das until 1896, when it was determined in favour of the el da (11) MONA JOSEPHINE TEMPEST, OBE, *b* 1894: *m* 1914, 3rd Baron Howard of Glossop (†† infra), who *d* 1972; *d* 1971; *s* by her el son (12) MILES FRANCIS, KG, GCVO, CB, CBE, MC, 12th Baron, and present peer (also 17th Duke of Norfolk).

††(1) *Lord* EDWARD GEORGE Fitzalan-Howard, PC, 2nd son of 13th Duke of Norfolk; *b* 1818; Vice Chamberlain of HM Household 1846-52, and Dep Earl Marshal 1861-3; MP for Horsham (L) 1848-52, and Arundel 1852-68; *cr* Baron Howard of Glossop (peerage of UK) 1869: *m* 1st, 1851, Augusta, who *d* 1862, only da and heiress of Hon George Henry Talbot (E Shrewsbury); 2ndly, 1863, Winifred Mary, who *d* 1909, da of Ambrose de Lisle, of Garendon Park, Leics; *d* 1883: *s* by his son (2) FRANCIS EDWARD, 2nd Baron, *b* 1859: *m* 1st, 1883, Clara Louisa, who *d* 1887, da of late John Greenwood, MP, of Swarcliffe Hall, Ripley, Yorks; 2ndly, 1891, Hyacinthe, who *d* 1930, da of late William Scott-Kerr, of Chatto and Sunlaws, Roxburghshire; *d* 1924; *s* by his son (3) BERNARD EDWARD, MBE, 3rd Baron, *b* 1885: *m* 1914, Mona Josephine Tempest, *Baroness Beaumont* in her own right, who *d* 1971 (ante); *d* 1972; *s* by his el son (4) MILES FRANCIS, KG, GCVO, CB, CBE, MC, 4th Baron and present peer (also 17th Duke of Norfolk).

NORMAN, BARONY OF (Norman) (Extinct 1950)

WIDOW LIVING OF FIRST BARON

PRISCILLA CECILIA MARIA (WORSTHORNE) (*Baroness Norman*), CBE, da of late Maj Robert Reyntiens, Belgian Artillery (*see* E Lindsey and Abingdon, colls); is a JP: *m* 1933, the 1st Baron, who *d* 1950, when the title became ext; CBE (Civil) 1963. *Residence* – Aubrey Lodge, Aubrey Rd, W8.

NORMANBY, MARQUESS OF (Phipps) (Marquess UK 1838)

Rest in virtue

CONSTANTINE EDMUND WALTER PHIPPS, 5th Marquess; *b* 24 Feb 1954; *s* 1994; *ed* Eton, and Worcester Coll, Oxford; Co Dir and Author: *m* 1990, Mrs Nicola St Aubyn, yr da of Milton Shulman, and formerly wife of Edward St Aubyn (*see* B St Levan, colls), and has issue.

Arms – Quarterly: 1st and 4th sable, a trefoil slipped within an orle of eight mullets argent *Phipps*; 2nd, paly of six argent and azure, a bend gules, *Annesley*; 3rd, the arms of King James II within a border compony ermine and azure (granted to Lady Catherine Darnley). **Crest** – A bear's paw erased and armed gules, holding a trefoil as in the arms. **Supporters** – *Dexter*, an unicorn ermine, armed, unguled, crined, and tufted or, and gorged with a chaplet of roses; *Sinister*, a goat ermine, armed and unguled azure, gorged at the dexter. **Seat** – Mulgrave Castle, Whitby, N Yorkshire YO21 3RJ.

DAUGHTER LIVING

Lady Sibylla Victoria Evelyn, *b* 1992.

BROTHER LIVING

Lord JUSTIN CHARLES, *b* 1 March 1958: *m* 1985, Rachel, da of Charles Stainsby, of The Manse, Chadlington, Oxon, and has issue living, William David, *b* 5 Feb 1990, — Elsie Clare, *b* 1986, — Anna Matilda, *b* 1988, — Katherine Maria, *b* 1991. *Residence* – Cowbridges, Dean, Oxon OX7 3LB.

SISTERS LIVING

Lady Lepel Sophia, *b* 1952: *m* 1975, Richard Kornicki, and has issue living, Edmund Barnaby, *b* 1976, — Dunstan Benedick, *b* 1977, — Aniela, *b* 1979. *Residence* – 12 Amhurst Av, W13 8NQ.
Lady Evelyn Rose, *b* 1955: *m* 1986, James Ernest Buchan, yst son of Hon William de l'Aigle Buchan, and has issue (*see* B Tweedsmuir). *Residence* – 37 Gloucester Crescent, NW1 7DL.
Lady Peronel Katharine, *b* 1959: *m* 1990, Kleber Cruz Jaramillo, son of Jose Domingo Cruz Sarango, of Cruzpamba, Ecuador, and has issue living, Lucas Oswald, *b* 1994. *Residence* – Claymoor Farm, Kettleness, Whitby, N Yorks 2RY.
Lady Henrietta Laura, *b* 1962: *m* 1982, Adam Charles Sedgwick, who *d* 1985, eldest son of late John Humphrey Gerrie Sedgwick, of 49 Novello St, SW6.
Lady Anne Elizabeth Grania, *b* 1965.

WIDOW LIVING OF FOURTH MARQUESS

Hon GRANIA MAEVE ROSAURA GUINNESS (*Dowager Marchioness of Normanby*), da of 1st Baron Moyne: *m* 1951, the 4th Marquess, KG, CBE, who *d* 1994. *Residence* – Lythe Hall, Whitby, N Yorkshire. *Town Residence* – Argyll House, 211 King's Rd, SW3 5EH.

COLLATERAL BRANCHES LIVING

Grandchildren of late Lord Henry George Russell Phipps, 3rd son of 2nd Marquess:—
Issue of late Vivian Louis Augustus Phipps, *b* 1884, *d* 1971: *m* 1921, Marie Elaine, who *d* 1974, da of G. E. Elliott, of the Logan, Qld:—
Vivian Henry Blakeney (52 Beltana Cres, Buddina, Qld 4575, Australia), *b* 1923: *m* 1944, Elizabeth Catherine, da of Hurbert Franklin Blundell, and has issue living, Douglas Vivian (19 Burnett St, Mooloolaba, Qld 4557), *b* 1945: *m* 1st, 1968 (*m diss* 19—), Rosemary Florence McGill; 2ndly, 1980, Robyn Raynor Fraser, and has issue living (by 1st *m*), Justine Danielle *b* 1969, — Paul Russell (17 Tallawa Place, Wurtulla, Qld 4575), *b* 1953: *m* 1977, Robyn Faith Binns, and has issue living, Russell Adam *b* 1980, Lauren Elizabeth *b* 1982, — Catherine Margaret, *b* 1948: *m* 1st, 1969 (*m diss* 1973), — —; 2ndly, 1977, Rolf Christian Schnase, of Kapilano Cres, Mountain Creek, Mooloolaba, Qld 4557, and has issue living (by 1st *m*), Darren DUPREE *b* 1971, (by 2nd *m*) Kelly Anne *b* 1978. —— Maurine Elaine, *b* 1921: *m* 1943, James Fitz-Gibbon Hunter, who *d* 1988, of 43 Lutzow St, Wellers Hill, Qld 4121, and has issue living, Kenneth James, *b* 1955: *m* 1985, Sally-Anne Jefferies, and has issue living, James Richard *b* 1989, Gabrielle Jane *b* 1987, — Ross Vivian, *b* 1961, — Helen Maurine, *b* 1945: *m* 1966, Anthony Beresford Lewis, BEc, ACA, AASA, of 24 Glen St, Hawthorn, Victoria 3122, Australia, and has issue living, Nicholas Anthony Hunter *b* 1971; BCom, Georgia Helen *b* 1969: *m* 1994, Christopher Charles Hoelter, — Barbara Elaine, *b* 1948: *m* 1st, 1969 (*m diss* 1981), Richard Wilfred Armstrong, BEcon; 2ndly, 1981, Antonio Ammendola, — Julie Margaret, *b* 1952: *m* 1977, Roger Murray Harcourt, of 95 Lutzow St, Wellers Hill, Queensland 4121, and has issue living, Andrew Behan *b* 1979, David James *b* 1982, Anthony Roger *b* 1984, Michael Douglas *b* 1986. —— Daphne Margaret, *b* 1929: *m* 1948, Barry E. Valttila, of 3 Michele Place, Turramurra, NSW 2074, and has issue living, Christopher Tony (Box 119 PO, Palm Beach, Queensland 4221), *b* 1953: *m* 1977, Mirja Karina Heimonen, of Helsinki, Finland, and has issue living, Eric Antti *b* 1983, Esa Christian *b* 1978, Elina Carita *b* 1985, Emmanita Aleksandra *b* 1987, — Jan Linda, *b* 1955, — Gaye Helen, *b* 1964.

Grandchildren of late Vivian Louis Augustus Phipps (ante):—
Issue of late Harvey Owen Phipps, *b* 1925, *d* 1982: *m* 1947, Eda Margaret (9 Seaview Terr, Moffatt Beach, Caloundra, Queensland 4551), da of Donald McNab:—
David Owen (4 Ferrar St, Mt Lawley, Perth, W Australia 6050), *b* 1948: *m* 1970, Palma Mary Mammino, and has issue living, Anthony Owen, *b* 1970, — Paul Ryman, *b* 1972. —— John Russell (13 Seaview Terr, Moffat Beach, Caloundra, Qld 4551), *b* 1949: *m* 1972, Elizabeth Gayle Strickland, and has issue living, Elaine Ann, *b* 1973, — Melissa Jane, *b* 1974, — Andra Susan, *b* 1979. —— Wendy Jane, *b* 1950: *m* 1st, 1969 (*m diss* 1981), Michael George Luland; 2ndly, 1981, Roderick Miles Nash, of 6 Greber Rd, Beerwah, Qld 4519, and has issue living (by 1st *m*), Shane Conrad, *b* 1971, — Christopher Michael, *b* 1973, — Katherine Flavelle, *b* 1974, — (by 2nd *m*) Daniel Owen Miles, *b* 1985, — Emma Jane, *b* 1983. —— Susan Margaret, *b* 1955: *m* 1980, John Francis Miguel, of 38 Peachester Rd, Beerwah, Qld 4519, and has issue living, Benjamin John, *b* 1981, — Anna Jane, *b* 1983.

(In remainder to the Earldom of Mulgrave only)

Grandson of late Charles Stewart Phipps (infra):—
Issue of late Charles Francis Douglas Phipps, *b* 1905, *d* 1984: *m* 1935, Kathleen Louise Conlan, who *d* 1982:—
John Douglas Stewart, *b* 1936: *m* 1963, Colleen May, who *d* 1989, da of late James Sinclair Moore, of Cloverdale, BC, and has issue living, Karleen Louise, *b* 1964, — Kimberley Ann, *b* 1966, — Kelly Patricia, *b* 1968: *m* 1989, Craig Douglas Ervin, son of Douglas Allan Ervin, of New Westminster, BC. *Residence* – 1109 London St, New Westminster, BC, Canada V3M 3B9.

Grandchildren of late Maj Charles Edmund Phipps, son of late Col Hon Sir Charles Beaumont Phipps, KCB, 2nd son of 1st Earl of Mulgrave:—
Issue of late Charles Stewart Phipps, *b* 1871, *ka* 1917: *m* 1902, Edith Annie Webber, who *d* 1946, da of late Capt Francis Douglas:—
Emma Doreen Stewart, *b* 1914: *m* 1st, 1936 (*m diss* 1961), Alvah Robert Hager, who *d* 1988; 2ndly, 1964, Ian Hugh Doughty McDiarmid, of 3770 East Blvd, Vancouver, BC, Canada, and has issue living, (by 1st *m*) Robert Stewart (2706 West 50th Av, Vancouver, BC, Canada V6P 1B7), *b* 1937: *m* 1961, Judith Frances, da of Alvin R. Brown, of Vancouver, BC, and has issue living, Leslie Frances *b* 1965, Shelley Bronwyn *b* 1967, — Rosemary Douglas, *b* 1941: *m* 1966, Roger Phillip Thomas, of 212-41st St, Manhattan Beach, Cal 90266, USA, and has issue living, Lisa Michelle *b* 1967, Victoria Mary *b* 1970.
Issue of late Albert Edmund Phipps, *b* 1873, *d* 1945: *m* 1899, Sydney Florence, who *d* 1951, da of Washington Boultbee, of Ancaster, Ontario:—
Stewart Beaumont, *b* 1900: *m* 1st, 1921, Frances Peacey Brown-Constable, who *d* 1951; 2ndly, 1952, Edith Patricia Allison, da of late Dr Allison Smith, and has issue living, (by 1st *m*) Barbara Phyllis, *b* 1923: *m* 1946, Thomas H. Gordon, — Diana Averill, *b* 1937: *m* 1958, Willem Otto Jan Groeneveld Meijer, — (by 2nd *m*) Geoffrey Allison, *b* 1953: *m* 1973, Leslie Elizabeth, da of Douglas D. Clarke, of Vic, BC. —— Norman Ernest, QC, *b* 1907: *m* 1944, Dorothy, da of late Albert Edward Kendal-Quarry, and has issue living, David, *b* 1945, — Penelope, *b* 1948: *m* 1972, Barry E. Tobias. —— Phyllis

Lepel, *b* 1902: *m* 1925, David Eric Cumberland, who *d* 1964, and has issue living, David Keith, *b* 1930: *m* 19—, Mary Fenn. —— Ruth Audrey, *b* 1910.

    Issue of late Augustus Henry Constantine Phipps, *b* 1882, *d* 1946: *m* 1909, Agnes Fraser who *d* 1971, da of late Murdoch Maclachlan, of Kilmun, Scotland:—

Charles Norman (405 Russell Hill Rd, Toronto, Ontario M4V 2V3, Canada), *b* 1912: *m* 1940, Margaret Patricia, da of George F. Saunders, of W Vancouver, British Columbia. —— Harriet Patricia, *b* 1914: *m* 1942, William Henry Brown, who *d* 1971, and has issue living, John Arthur, *b* 1943, — Margaret Evelyn, *b* 1945: *m* 1965, Michael Barclay John Shannon, and has issue living, Michael William *b* 1965. *Residence* – 2250 Bowker Av, Victoria, BC, Canada.

    Grandchildren of late Rt Hon Sir Eric Clare Edmund Phipps, GCB, GCMG, GCVO (infra):—

    Issue of late Lt-Col Mervyn Constantine Sanford Phipps, *b* 1912, *d* 1983: *m* 1941, Joyce Kathleen (1 Stalbridge Rd, Stourton Caundle, Sturminster Newton, Dorset), da of John Patrick Goode, of Foxhall, Letterkenny, co Donegal:—

Magdalene Frances, *b* 1942: *m* 1970, Fergus Rogers, of 12 Holly Mount, Hampstead, NW3. —— Caroline Mary, *b* 1943: *m* 1965, José Vives i López, of Sant Pere 15, 4°, Caldetes, Barcelona, Spain, and has issue living, Alexandre Constantine, *b* 1968, — Catalina Rosa, *b* 1965, — Lucieta, *b* 1967, — Marina, *b* 1974. —— Elizabeth Helen (74b Queenstown Rd, SW11), *b* 1945. —— Dorothy Charlotte (1 Stalbridge Rd, Stourton Caundle, Sturminster Newton, Dorset), *b* 1950: *m* 1979 (*m diss* 1982), Jay Patrick O'Boyle, of 11533 19th Av NE, Seattle, Washington 98124, USA, and has issue living, Marlon Orion Sandford, *b* 1982. —— Mary Ann, *b* 1953: *m* 1973, Nicholas Fforde, of 104 Stonefall Av, Starbeck, Harrogate, N Yorks HG2 7NT, and has issue living, Timothy Constantine, *b* 1977, — Emily Frances, *b* 1973, — Sophie Veronica, *b* 1974, — Sarah Maria, *b* 1980.

    Issue of late Lieut Alan Phipps, RN, *b* 1915, *ka* in Leros 1943: *m* 1940, Hon Veronica Nell Fraser (*Hon Lady Maclean of Dunconnel*) (who *m* 2ndly, 1946, Sir Fitzroy Hew Maclean of Dunconnel, 1st Bt, KT, CBE, *cr* 1957), da of 15th Lord Lovat:—

Jeremy Julian Joseph, *b* 1942; Brig The Queen's Own Hussars: *m* 1974, Susan, da of Lt-Cdr Wilfrid Crawford, RN, of Huntington, Haddington, E Lothian, and has issue living, Jake Shimi Alan, *b* 1975, — Jemma Louise Rose, *b* 1977. —— Susan Rose, *b* 1941: *m* 1st, 1959 (*m diss* 1968), Richard St Clair de la Mare (grandson of late Walter de la Mare, OM, CH); 2ndly, 1968 (*m diss* 1986), Derek Marlowe; 3rdly, 1986, as his 2nd wife, Nicolas Vincent Somerset Paravicini, of Glyn Celyn House, Brecon, Powys, and has issue living (by 1st *m*), Caspar James, *b* 1962, — Adam John, *b* 1964, — Laura Frances Albinia, *b* 1960: *m* 1992, Henry Alexander Boothby (*see* Boothby, Bt, colls), — Selina-Rose, *b* 1963: *m* 1991, Andrew John Harley, of 290 Portobello Rd, W10, — (by 2nd *m*) Benjamin, *b* 1969.

    Grandchildren of late Sir Constantine Edmund Henry Phipps, KCMG, CB, son of late Hon Edmund Phipps, 3rd son of 1st Earl of Mulgrave:—

    Issue of late Rt Hon Sir Eric Clare Edmund Phipps, GCB, GCMG, GCVO, *b* 1875, *d* 1945: *m* 1st, 1907, Yvonne, who *d* 1909, da of late Comte de Louvencourt, of 94 Rue de Courcelles, Paris; 2ndly, 1911, Frances Georgina, who *d* 1988, da of late Herbert Ward:—

(By 2nd *m*) John-Francis (43 Leckford Rd, Oxford), *b* 1933: *m* 1st, 1956 (*m diss* 1972), Charm Alys, yr da of Eric Quick; 2ndly, 1975, Rosemary Carol Anne Tecla (*née* Shirtcliffe), and has issue living (by 1st *m*), Jonathan Eric, *b* 1957, — Anna-Rose, *b* 1959, — Isabel Emma, *b* 1961, — (by 2nd *m*), William Donald *b* 1978, — Sophie Sarita Mary, *b* 1976. —— William Anthony Dominic (31 Chepstow Villas, W11), *b* 1936; late Able Seaman, RCN: *m* 1960, Henrietta Frances, da of late Henry Taylor Lamb, MC, RA (*see* E Longford), and has issue living, Frederick Fabian Aeneas, *b* 1961, — Samuel Cornelius Dominic, *b* 1964: *m* 1990, Clunie Fiona Mary, yst da of Gen Sir (James) Michael Gow, GCB (*see* Scott, Bt, *cr* 1907, colls), and has issue living, Stella Phoebe Scarlett *b* 1991, — Lucian Percy Denis, *b* 1966, — Theresa Pansy Frances, *b* 1963. —— Mary, *b* 1923: *m* 1949, Bonar Sykes, son of late Maj-Gen Rt Hon Sir Frederick Hugh Sykes, GCSI, GCIE, GBE, KCB, CMG, and has issue living, Hugh Bonar, *b* 1950: *m* 1983, Marie-Odile Daulton, — David Eric, *b* 1953, — James Richard, *b* 1956, — Alan Geoffrey, *b* 1960: *m* 1984, Kate Judith Hughes. *Residence* – Conock Manor, nr Devizes, Wilts. —— Margaret Ann, *b* 1925: *m* 1949, George Anthony Cary, who *d* 1953; 2ndly, 1956, Donald Struan Robertson, Emeritus Professor of Greek, Camb Univ, who *d* 1961, and has had issue (by 1st *m*) Christopher Alexander George, *b* 1950: *ed* Westminster, and Trin Coll, Camb: *m* 1973, Joanna Buczkowska, and *d* 1983, leaving issue, Catherine Alexandra Joanna *b* 1979. *Residence* – 2 Richmond Rd, Cambridge CB4 3PU.

PREDECESSORS – (1) CONSTANTINE Phipps; *cr* Baron Mulgrave, of New Ross, co Wexford (peerage of Ireland) 1767; *d* 1775; *s* by his el son (2) CONSTANTINE JOHN, PC, 2nd Baron; Capt RN; went a voyage with a view to discover a NE passage; sat as MP for Newark; was Joint Paymaster of the Forces, and Lord of Trade Commn for Indian Affairs; *cr* Baron Mulgrave, of Mulgrave, co York (peerage of Great Britain) 1790; *d* without male issue 1792, when the English barony became extinct, and the Irish peerage devolved upon his brother (3) HENRY, GCB, 3rd Baron; was a Gen in the Army, Col 31st Foot, and Lord-Lieut of E Riding of York, Chancellor of Duchy of Lancaster, Sec of State for Foreign Affairs, and First Lord of the Admiralty; *cr* Baron Mulgrave, of Mulgrave, co York (peerage of Great Britain) 1794, and Viscount Normanby and Earl of Mulgrave (peerage of United Kingdom) 1812; *d* 1831; *s* by his son (4) CONSTANTINE HENRY, KG, GCB, 2nd Earl; *b* 1797; a distinguished statesman and diplomatist; was Gov-Gen of Jamaica 1832-4, Lord Privy Seal 1834, Lord-Lieut of Ireland 1835-9, Sec of State for the Colonies 1839, and for the Home Depart 1839-41, and Ambassador to France 1846-52, and to Court of Tuscany 1854-8; *cr* Marquess of Normanby (peerage of United Kingdom) 1838: *m* 1818, Hon Maria Liddell, da of 1st Baron Ravensworth; *d* 1863; *s* by his son (5) GEORGE AUGUSTUS CONSTANTINE, PC, GCB, GCMG, 2nd Marquess, *b* 1819; sat as MP for Scarborough (*L*) 1847-51, and 1852-8; was successively Gov of Nova Scotia, Queensland, New Zealand, and Victoria: *m* 1844, Laura, who *d* 1885, da of late Capt Robert Russell, RN; *d* 1890; *s* by his el son (6) Rev CONSTANTINE CHARLES HENRY, 3rd Marquess; *b* 1846; V of St Mark's, Worsley, 1872-90, and Canon of St George's Chapel, Windsor 1891-1907: *m* 1903, Gertrude Stansfield, OBE, who *d* 1948, yr da and co-heiress of late Johnston J. Foster, of Moor Park, Ludlow; *d* 1932; *s* by his son (7) OSWALD CONSTANTINE JOHN, KG, CBE, 4th Marquess, *b* 1912; Lieut 5th Bn Green Howards, 1939-45 War in France (wounded, prisoner, MBE); PPS to Sec of State for Dominion Affairs 1944-45 and to Lord Pres of the Council 1945, a Lord in Waiting to HM King George VI 1945; Chm King's Coll Hospital 1948-78 (Fellow), Lord Lieut and Custos Rotulorum N Riding of Yorks 1965-74 and N Yorks 1974-87, Pres TA&VR Assocn N England 1971-74 and N Yorks and Humberside 1980-83, Hon Col Cmdt Green Howards 1970-82, High Steward York Minster 1980-88: *m* 1951, Hon Grania Maeve Rosaura Guinness, da of 1st Baron Moyne; *d* 1994; *s* by his elder son (8) CONSTANTINE EDMUND WALTER, 5th Marquess and present peer; also Earl of Mulgrave, Viscount Normanby, and Baron Mulgrave.

The Annesley and Darnley quarterings came to this family by the marriage of William Phipps to Lady Catherine Annesley, da and heir of 3rd Earl of Anglesey, by his wife, Lady Catherine Darnley (Duchess of Buckingham), natural da of James II by Catherine Sedley, Countess of Dorchester. William and Lady Catherine Phipps were the parents of 1st Baron Mulgrave.

NORMAND, BARONY OF (Normand) (Extinct 1962)

DAUGHTER LIVING OF LIFE BARON (*By 1st marriage*)

Hon Patricia Drake, *b* 1917: *m* 1948, Douglas William Gourlay, who *d* 1988, and has issue. *Residence* – Goldielea, Dalbeattie Rd, Dumfries.

WIDOW LIVING OF SON OF LIFE BARON

Elizabeth Ann (15 Ravelston Heights, Edinburgh), da of late James Cumming, of Deneholm, Biggar, Lanarkshire: *m* 1945, Hon William Normand, who *d* 1967, and has issue.

NORMANTON, EARL OF (Agar) Sits as BARON SOMERTON (UK 1873) (Earl I 1806)

The beaten path is the safe path

SHAUN JAMES CHRISTIAN WELBORE ELLIS AGAR, 6th Earl of Normanton, and 9th Baron Mendip; *b* 21 Aug 1945; *s* 1967; *ed* Eton, Capt Blues and Royals; patron of three livings: *m* 1970, Victoria Susan, only da of John H. C. Beard, of Turmer House, Somerley, Ringwood, Hants, and has issue.

Arms – Azure, a lion rampant or. **Crest** – A demi-lion rampant or. **Supporters** – Two lions, the *dexter* per bend, and the *sinister* per bend sinister, or and azure, both plain collared and chained gules, each charged on the shoulder with a crescent.
Seat – Somerley, Ringwood, Hampshire BH24 3PL. *Residence* – Flat 6, 28 Hans Place, SW1. *Clubs* – White's, Royal Yacht Squadron.

SON LIVING

JAMES SHAUN CHRISTIAN WELBORE ELLIS (*Viscount Somerton*), *b* 7 Sept 1982.

DAUGHTERS LIVING

Lady Portia Caroline, *b* 1976.
Lady Marisa Charlotte, *b* 1979.

BROTHER LIVING

Hon Mark Sidney Andrew (Inholmes, Woodlands St Mary, Newbury, Berks), *b* 1948; *ed* Gordonstoun; Lt Blues & Royals: *m* 1st, 1973 (*m diss* 1979), Rosemary, da of Maj Philip Marnham; 2ndly, 1985, Arabella Clare, da of late John Gilbert Gilbey (*see* Barwick, Bt, ext, 1985 Edn), and formerly wife of Thomas Charles Blackwell, and has issue living (by 2nd *m*), Max John Andrew *b* 1986, — Charles Christopher Edward, *b* 1989.

PREDECESSORS – (1) CHARLES Agar, DD, 3rd son of Henry Agar, MP, and yr brother of James, 1st Viscount Clifden, was successively Dean of Kilmore, Bishop of Cloyne, Archbishop of Cashel, and Archbishop of Dublin and Primate of Ireland; *cr* *Baron Somerton* (peerage of Ireland) 1795, *Viscount Somerton* 1800, and *Earl of Normanton* (peerage of Ireland) 1806; *d* 1809; *s* by his son (2) WELBORE ELLIS, 2nd Earl; *b* 1778: *m* 1816, Diana, da of 11th Earl of Pembroke; *d* 1868; *s* by his son (3) JAMES CHARLES HERBERT WELBORE ELLIS, 3rd Earl, *b* 1818, MP for Wilton 1841-52: *m* 1856, Hon Caroline Susan Augusta, who *d* 1915, da of 6th Viscount Barrington; *d* 1896; *s* by his el surviving son (4) SIDNEY JAMES, 4th Earl; *b* 1865: *m* 1894, Lady Amy Frederica Alice Byng, who *d* 1961, da of 4th Earl of Stafford; *d* 1933; *s* by his only son (5) EDWARD JOHN SIDNEY CHRISTIAN WELBORE ELLIS, 5th Earl; *b* 1910: *m* 1st, 1937 (*m diss* 1943), Hon Barbara Mary, only da of late Sir Frederick Frankland, 10th Bt, and of Baroness Zouche, and formerly wife of Brig Otho Leslie Prior-Palmer; 2ndly, 1944, Lady Fiona, who *d* 1985, da of 4th Marquess Camden, and formerly wife of Maj Sir (John) Gerard Henry Fleetwood Fuller, 2nd Bt; *d* 1967; *s* by his son (6) SHAUN JAMES CHRISTIAN WELBORE ELLIS, 6th Earl and present peer; also Viscount and Baron Somerton, and Baron Mendip (see * infra).
*(1) Rt *Hon* WELBORE Ellis, FRS, MP, only surv son of Most Rev Welbore Ellis, Bishop of Meath, was Sec at War 1762-65, Treas of the Navy 1777-82, and Sec of State for America and the Colonies 1782; *cr* 1794, *Baron Mendip*, of Mendip, Somerset (peerage of Great Britain) with remainder to the three el sons of his sister Anne by her husband, Henry Agar, of Gowran: *m* 1st, 1747, Elizabeth, who *d* 1761, da and heir of Hon Sir William Stanhope, KB; 2ndly, 1765, Anne, who *d* 1803, sister and heir of the Rt Hon Hans Stanley; *d* 1802; *s* by his gt-nephew (2) HENRY WELBORE Agar-Ellis, 2nd Viscount Clifden, whose father, James Agar, MP, son of Anne (ante) was Postmaster Gen of Ireland, and was *cr Baron Clifden*, of Gowran, co Kilkenny (peerage of Ireland) 1776, and *Viscount Clifden*, of Gowran (peerage of Ireland) 1781; *b* 1761; MP for co Kilkenny 1783-89; assumed the surname of Ellis by Roy licence 1804: *m* 1792, Lady Caroline Spencer, who *d* 1813, da of 4th Duke of Marlborough; his only son, George James Welbore Agar-Ellis, FRS, MP, was *cr Baron Dover* (peerage of UK) 1831: *m* 1822, Lady Georgiana Howard, who *d* 1860, da of 6th Earl of Carlisle; predeceased him in 1833; *d* 1836; *s* by his grandson (3) HENRY, 3rd Viscount, *b* 1825, who had *s* his father in 1833 as 2nd Baron Dover; Gentleman of the Privy Chamber to the Prince Consort: *m* 1861, Eliza Horatia Frederica, VA (Lady of the Bedchamber to Queen Victoria), who *d* 1896, da of Frederick Charles William Seymour; *d* 1866; *s* by his only son (4) HENRY GEORGE, 4th Viscount; *b* 1863; *d* unm 1895; *s* by his uncle (5) LEOPOLD GEORGE FREDERICK, 5th Viscount, *b* 1829; MP for Kilkenny (*L*) 1857-74: *m* 1864, Hon Harriet Stonor, who *d* 1914, da of 3rd Baron Camoys; *d* 1899, when the Barony of Dover became ext, and the other honours passed to his kinsman (6) THOMAS CHARLES Agar-Robartes, 2nd Baron Robartes (son and heir of Thomas James Agar-Robartes, who was *cr* *Baron Robartes*, of Lanhydrock and Truro, Cornwall 1869, son of Hon Charles Bagenal-Agar (who *m* 1804, Anna Maria Hunt, heiress of Lanhydrock, great-niece of Henry Robartes, 3rd Earl of Radnor, Viscount Bodmin, and Baron Robartes of Truro, all of which titles became ext 1757) yst son of 1st Viscount Clifden), 6th Viscount, *b* 1844; Lord-Lieut of Cambs 1906-15, and MP for Cornwall, E (*L*) 1880-82: *m* 1878, Mary, who *d* 1921, da of late Francis Henry Dickinson, of Kingweston, Som; *d* 1930; *s* by his 2nd son (7) FRANCIS GERALD, KCVO, 7th Viscount, *b* 1883; Counsellor of Embassy, Madrid 1926-27, a Member of Council, Duchy of Cornwall 1939-52, and a Lord-in-Waiting to HM 1940-45; *d* 1966; *s* by his brother (8) ARTHUR VICTOR, MC, 8th Viscount, *b* 1887; Lt Gren Gds; acting Maj Gds Machine Gun Regt in 1914-18 War: *m* 1st, 1920 (*m diss* 1945), Patience Mary, who *d* 1956, da of Arthur Francis Basset (Salusbury-Trelawny, Bt); 2ndly, 1948, Margaret, da of Ray Carter of St Louis, USA, formerly wife of John Harvey Thursky, and widow of John Eaton Monins; *d* 1974, when the Viscountcy and Barony of Clifden, and the Barony of Robartes became ext, and the Barony of Mendip devolved upon (9) SHAUN JAMES CHRISTIAN WELBORE ELLIS Agar, 6th Earl of Normanton (ante).

Norreys of Rycote, Lord, son of Earl of Lindsey and Abingdon.

NORRIE, BARON (Norrie) (Baron UK 1957)

God provides for us

GEORGE WILLOUGHBY MOKE NORRIE, 2nd Baron; *b* 27 April 1936; *s* 1977; *ed* Eton, and RMA; commissioned 11th Hussars, 1956; ADC to C-in-C Middle East Command 1961-62; GSO 3 (Int) 4th Guards' Bde 1967-69; Acting Maj Roy Hussars 1969-70; Dir, Fairfield Nurseries (Hermitage), Ltd, Dir Internat Garden Centre (UK) 1984-86, Dir Hilliers (Fairfield) Ltd 1989, Pres British Trust for Conservation Volunteers since 1987, Dir Conservation Practice Ltd 1988-92, House of Lords European Communities sub Cttee F (Environment) 1988, Vice Pres Council for National Parks since 1990, Vice Pres Tree Council since 1990; Pres R British Legion, Newbury Branch: *m* 1964, Celia Marguerite; JP (Berks); da of Maj John Pelham Mann, MC (*see* Mann, Bt, colls), and has issue.

Arms – Quarterly: 1st and 4th, ermine on a pale gules three helmets argent *Norrie*; 2nd and 3rd, or on a chevron azure between two poplar trees eradicated in chief proper and a mullet of six points in base of the second a key the ward downwards of the first *Moke*. **Crests** – An elephant's head erased sable tusked argent supporting with the trunk a garb or; 2nd, a stag's head couped holding in the mouth a branch of poplar proper between the attires a key as in the arms pendent from a chain or. **Supporters** – On either side a dark bay racehorse supporting between the forelegs a frond of New Zealand fern proper.

Residence – East Gate House, Craven Hill, Hamstead Marshall, Newbury, Berks RG15 0JD. *Clubs* – Cavalry and Guards, MCC, White's.

SON LIVING

Hon MARK WILLOUGHBY JOHN, *b* 31 March 1972.

DAUGHTERS LIVING

Hon Clare Marguerite, *b* 1966.
Hon Julia Jocelyn, *b* 1968.

HALF-BROTHER LIVING

Hon Guy Bainbridge (Old Church Farm, Broughton, nr Stockbridge, Hants SO20 8AA; Cavalry & Guards', City of London and White's Clubs), *b* 1940; *ed* Eton; Lt-Col (ret) R Hussars; GSO 1 (DS) Staff Coll, Camberley 1977-8; Member HM Body Guard of Hon Corps of Gentlemen at Arms 1990; Dir Wellington Members Agency Ltd since 1991: *m* 1968, Sarah Georgina, da of Maj George Rudolph Hanbury Fielding, DSO (*see* E Denbigh, colls), and has issue living, Andrew Guy, *b* 1970, — James Adam George, *b* 1973.

SISTER LIVING

Hon Rosemary (*Viscountess Daventry*), *b* 1926: *m* 1959, 3rd Viscount Daventry, and has issue. *Residence* – Temple House, Arbury, Nuneaton, Warwickshire CV10 7PT.

HALF-SISTERS LIVING

Hon Sarah Merryweather, *b* 1943; CGSM: *m* 1974, Charles Lyon Stephenson, TD, of The Cottage, Great Longstone, Bakewell, Derbys (*see* Stephenson, Bt, colls).
Hon Annabel Mary Adelaide (19 Lillyville Rd, SW6 5DP), *b* 1945: *m* 1988, Ian Ronald Malcolm, elder son of late Colin Ronald Malcolm, of Newent, Glos.

WIDOW LIVING OF FIRST BARON

PATRICIA MERRYWEATHER (*Patricia, Baroness Norrie*) (The Old Vicarage, Leckhampstead, Newbury, Berks), da of late Emerson Bainbridge, MP, of Auchnashellach, Ross-shire; DStJ: *m* 1938, as his 2nd wife, the 1st Baron, who *d* 1977.

PREDECESSOR – (1) *Sir* (CHARLES) WILLOUGHBY (MOKE) Norrie, GCMG, GCVO, CB, DSO, MC, son of Maj George Edward Moke Norrie, Duke of Wellington's Regt; *b* 1893; Lt Gen late 11th Hussars and 10th R Hussars, and Hon Col 10th Inf Bn (The Adelaide Rifles); Comd 1st Armoured Div 1940, and 30 Corps 1941-42; Gov of S Aust 1944-52, and Gov Gen of NZ 1952-57; Chancellor of Order of St Michael and St George 1960-68; *cr Baron Norrie*, of Wellington, NZ, and Upton, co Gloucester (peerage of UK) 1957: *m* 1st, 1921, Jocelyn Helen, who *d* 1938, da of late Richard Gosling (Dyer, Bt); 2ndly, 1938, Patricia Merryweather (DStJ), da of late Emerson Bainbridge, MP; *d* 1977; *s* by his el son (2) GEORGE WILLOUGHBY MOKE, 2nd Baron and present peer.

North Lord, son of Earl of Guilford.

NORTH, BARONY OF (North) (Baron E 1554) (Abeyant 1942)

JOHN DUDLEY NORTH, 13th Baron; Lieut RN; *ka* 1941, when the Barony fell into abeyance (see infra).

SISTERS LIVING OF THIRTEENTH BARON (*Co-heiresses to the Barony; raised to the rank of a Baron's daughters* 1947)

Hon DOROTHY ANNE, *b* 4 May 1915: *m* 1st, 1937 (*m diss* 1950), William Robert Alexander Clive Graham, Lieut Sherwood Foresters; 2ndly, 1950, Major John Edward Richard Bowlby, 1st Royal Dragoons (*see* V Valentia, 1985 Edn), and has issue living, (by 1st *m*) Penelope Virginia, *b* 1940, — (by 2nd *m*) Gina Anne, *b* 1954: *m* 1982, Dominic Poole, yr son of Richard Poole, of Ringwood, Hants, and has issue living, Alana *b* 1985, Auriel Martha *b* 1987. *Residence* – 51 Shawfield St, SW3.
Hon SUSAN SILENCE, *b* 19 Jan 1920; assumed by deed poll 1943 the additional surname of Beauchamp: *m* 1944, Frederick Guy Beauchamp, MD, MRCS, who *d* 1981, and has issue living, Susan Donne, *b* 1944: *m* 1965 (*m diss* 1969), Hon Nicholas Charles Cavendish (later 6th Baron Chesham), and has issue living, James North Cavendish *b* 1972, — Sally North, *b* 1945: *m* 1st, 1966 (*m diss* 1967), Michael Robert Parkin; 2ndly, 1973, Bryn Haworth, — Elizabeth Silence, *b* 1950: *m* 1976, Jean-Pierre Guillemet, and has issue living, Lucie Susan Germaine *b* 1977, Alice Elizabeth Felicie *b* 1980.

WIDOW LIVING OF THIRTEENTH BARON

MARGARET, da of R. W. H. Glennie, of Cape Province, S Africa: *m* 1st, 1940, the 13th Baron, who was *ka* 1941; 2ndly, 1943, Lieut Weldon Bernard James, US Marine Corps. Resides in USA.

COLLATERAL BRANCHES LIVING

Grandchildren of late Hon Roger Archibald Percy North, 2nd son of 11th Baron, *b* 1863, *d* 1907: *m* 1896, Robina Ramsay Walker, who *d* 1937, da of late Edwin Barton, of Wallerawang, NSW:—
Issue of late Lt-Col Roger Edward Francis Guilford North, *b* 1897, *d* 1980: *m* 1st, 1927 (*m diss* 1937), Audrey Edith Durani, who *d* 1957, da of late Mr Justice (Alfred Edward) Martineau; 2ndly, 1939, Isabel Floyd-Jones Carpender Burn, who *d* 1983, da of late Noel Lisperard Carpender, of Long Island, USA:—
(By 1st *m*) Roger Robin NORTH (Vine Cottage, Roseacre Gdns, Chilworth, Guildford, Surrey), *b* 1929; *ed* King's Sch, Canterbury; late Lt RASC and King's African Rifles: *m* 1961, Gillian Mary, yr da of late Lt-Col William Augustus Putnam. — Desmond Peter (twin) (The Orchard, Hale St, East Peckham, Tonbridge, Kent), *b* 1929; *ed* King's Sch, Canterbury; late Lt RASC; with Colonial Admin Ser, N Nigeria 1951-55: *m* 1960, Amanda Mary, yr da of Philip Henry Bevington Legge, and has issue living, Rupert Caspar Guilford, *b* 1964; *ed* Cokethorpe: *m* 1988, Sara Catherine Lucy, da of Peter W. Jackson, of Forest Row, Sussex, and has issue living, Caspar John Guilford *b* 1991, — Jason Edward Guilford, *b* 1967; *ed* Sherborne, — Emma Sophie, *b* 1962. — Neil Dermot (17 Clanricarde Gdns, W2), *b* 1932; *ed* King's Sch, Canterbury. — (By 2nd *m*) Edward John (Mossberga Rockneby, Sweden), *b* 1940; *ed* Fettes Coll: *m* 1967, Margreth Ekstrom, of Spanga, Sweden, and has issue living, Tom Nicholas, *b* 1971, — Peter James, *b* 1974.
Issue of late Cdr William Frederic George North, RN, *b* 1898; *d* 1977: *m* 1st, 1924 (*m diss* 1949), Hon Dorothy Hennessy, who *d* 1961, da of 1st Baron Windlesham; 2ndly, 1949, Joan Mabel (Luzborough House, Romsey, Hants), da of late Henry Reginald Fussell, of Southey Hall, Gt Bookham, Surrey, and widow of Wing Cdr Richard Griffith Shaw, of Littlecot, Bartley, Hants:—
(By 1st *m*) Moylena Robin (Sister Frances, Inst of BVM, 47 Fitzjohn's Av, NW3), *b* 1925. — Diana Bridget, *b* 1928: *m* 1st, 1954 (*m diss* 1958), Lt-Col Michael Edward Ovens, MC; 2ndly, 1958 (*m diss* 19—), Afzal Qureshi. — (By 2nd *m*) William Simon Giles (Mossland, Shawford, Winchester), *b* 1950; *ed* Radley: *m* 1980, Angela Joan, da of late John Edward Heslop, of Downs Farm, nr Penarth, S Glamorgan, and has issue living, William James Penarth *b* 1985, — Emma Harriet, *b* 1983. — Jeremy Frederic George (Eldon House, Eldon Lane, Braishfield, Romsey, Hants), *b* 1952; *ed* Radley: *m* 1985, Helen Suzanna Margaret, da of Sidney James Best, of 3 Norman Rd, St Cross, Winchester, and has issue living, Joseph Frederic Jeremy, *b* 1986.

Grandchildren of late Hon Mina Susan Georgina North, eldest da of 11th Baron:—
Issue of late Dudley Francis North FitzGerald, *b* 1891, *d* 1960: *m* 1921, Hermine, who *d* 1955, da of late George Kiely, of Toronto:—
Michael Francis FITZGERALD, *b* 1921; *ed* Dartmouth Coll; Lt-Cdr RN; 1939-45 War: *m* 1943, Anne Lise, da of late Einar Winther, of Copenhagen, and has issue living, Robin Michael (33 Haverfield Gdns, Kew, Richmond, Surrey), *b* 1944; *ed* Downside: *m* 1969, Allessandra Lyn, da of Cecil Davis, of Richmond, Surrey, and has issue living, James Dudley *b* 1972, Sarah Emily *b* 1974, — Christopher Francis (21 Palace Gdns Terr, W8), *b* 1945; *ed* Downside, and Lincoln Coll, Oxford (MA): *m* 1st, 1968 (*m diss* 1984), Jennifer Georgina, da of George Willis, of Sherborne, Dorset; 2ndly, 1986, Jill, da of late Dr Douglas Freshwater, of Upton-upon-Severn, Worcs, and has issue living, (by 1st *m*), Matthew Francis *b* 1973, Francesca Marie *b* 1975, Julia Louise *b* 1978, — Mary Anne Lise (104 Merton Hall Rd, SW19), *b* 1961; *ed* Yeovil Coll, and Surrey Univ (BSc), — Emma Theresa *b* 1967; *ed* Yeovil Coll, and Balliol Coll, Oxford (MA, DPhil): *m* 1990, David Martin Wheeler, of Pinfold House, Frog Lane, Holt, Clwyd LL13 9HJ. *Residence* – 36 Lower Market St, Hove, E Sussex BN3 1AT. — †Gerald Dudley *b* 1922; *ed* Dartmouth Coll; 1939-45 War in RN and as Pilot RAF: *m* 1956, Doreen, who *d* 1969, da of late Alexander Spence Muter, of Middlesborough, and *d* 1987, leaving issue, Susan Hermine (42 Weston Cres, Mount Pleasant, Stockton, Cleveland), *b* 1957.
Issue of late Col John Sidney North FitzGerald, CVO, MBE, MC, *b* 1893, *d* 1976: *m* 1933 (*m diss* 1948), Joyce Mary, da of late Dr Edward William Hedley, MBE, and widow of Thomas Cecil Barber (*see* Barber, Bt, colls):—
Georgiana Mary, *b* 1935: *m* 1956, John Kenneth Humphrey Pettit, JP, of Stepstones, Scotlands Close, Haslemere, Surrey, and has issue living, Timothy John (Woodend, Bramley, nr Guildford, Surrey), *b* 1959: *m* 1987, Susan Julia, da of John Butterfield, and has issue living, Olivia Georgiana Butterfield *b* 1990, Annabel Kathleen *b* 1992, — Richard Kenneth, *b* 1963: *m* 1992, Dyane Lesley, da of Victor Martin Chapman, and has issue living, Isabella Hetty Mary *b* 1993, — Nicola Susan Mary, *b* 1957.

Granddaughter (by 1st *m*) of late Capt Thomas Yates Benyon (infra):—
Issue of late John Wicht Yates Benyon, *b* 1921, *d* 1983: *m* 1966, Joan (9 Avenue Alexandra, Fresnaye, Cape Town, S Africa), da of W. E. Robertson, of Little Brak, S Africa:—
Kendal Joanna YATES BENYON, *b* 1968.

Grandchildren of late Hon Christina Philippa Agnes North, OBE, yst da of 11th Baron, *b* 1869, *d* 1950, having *m* 1st, 1890, Capt Thomas Yates Benyon, formerly 4th Hus, who *d* 1893; 2ndly, 1903, Col Alexander Heirom Ogilvy Spence, CIE, CBE, formerly IA, who *d* 1936:—
Issue of late Capt Thomas Yates Benyon, *b* (*posthumous*) 1893, *d* 1958: *m* 1st, 1918 (*m diss* 1928), Louise, who *d* 1970 da of J. J. Wicht, of Cape Town; 2ndly, 1934, Joan Ida Bishop, da of John Bayley Walters:—
(By 2nd *m*) Thomas Yates BENYON(The Old Rectory, Adstock, Winslow, Bucks, MK18 2HY; Pratt's Club), *b* 1942; *ed* Wellington Sch, and RMA; late Lt Scots Gds; Chm Milton Keynes Health Authority; MP for Abingdon (*C*) 1979-83: *m* 1968, Olivia Jane, yr da of Humphrey Scott-Plummer, of Mainhouse, Kelso, and has issue living, Thomas Yates, *b* 1975, — Oliver William Yates, *b* 1980, — Clare Julia Yates, *b* 1969, — Camilla Lucinda Joan Yates, *b* 1972. — Sarah Joan Yates (1 Gladstone Terr, Ripon, N Yorks HG4 1PR), *b* 1936: *m* 1st, 1956 (*m diss* 1967), Roy Ramsey; 2ndly, 1967 (*m diss* 1985), Andrew Harrison, and has issue living, (by 1st *m*) David Andrew, *b* 1960, — Deborah Jacqueline, *b* 1958, — (by 2nd *m*) Rachel Sarah, *b* 1970. — Belinda Jane Yates, *b* 1939: *m* 1966, John Douglas Lennie, Rosemount, 3 Newbattle Terr, Edinburgh EH10 4RU, and has issue living, Joanna Yates, *b* 1966, — Rosalind Benson, *b* 1969: *m* 1992, Kenneth James Wilson.
Issue of late Christa Marie Margaret Ogilvy Spence, *b* 1907, *d* 1982: *m* 1928, Col Noel Stanley Alington, MC, late IA, and Foreign and Political Dept, India:—
James Giles Roger ALINGTON (46 Atholl Rd, Camps Bay, Cape Province, S Africa), *b* 1929: *m* 1960, Jean Vosloo, da of Thomas Bell, of Harare, Zimbabwe, and has issue living, Julian Giles, *b* 1963.

Grandchildren of late Frederick Keppel North, son of Charles North, el son of late Frederick North, grandson of Fountain North, grandson of Hon Roger North, yst son of 4th Baron:—
    Issue of late Roger North, *b* 1901, *d* 1985: *m* 1934, Pamela Susan (Stable Cottage, Rougham, King's Lynn, Norfolk),
da of late Rev Henry William Leycester O'Rorke, of The Manor House, N Litchfield, Hants:—
Thomas Frederick NORTH (Rougham Hall, King's Lynn, Norfolk), *b* 1942; *ed* Eton, and Trin Coll, Camb; barrister-at-law Inner
Temple 1966: *m* 1974, Sally Catherine, da of late Lt-Col G. M. Strover, of Leigh Delamere House, Leigh Delamere,
Chippenham, Wilts, and has had issue, Charles, *b* 1976; *d* 1993, — Alec Roger, *b* 1979, — Amy, *b* 1977, — Sophie, *b* 1983.
—— Valerie Susan, *b* 1937: *m* 1967, John Ralph Sidney Guinness, of 9 Hereford Sq, SW7, and has issue, Rupert Edward
Roger, *b* 1971, — Peter John Charles, *b* 1974; *d* 1978, — Lucy Arabella, *b* 1970. —— Christine, *b* 1938: *m* 1963, Alan
Blakemore, of Hatchford Park Nurseries, Cobham, Surrey, and has issue living, Emily Jasmine Alice, *b* 1964, — Flora
Marianne Sophie, *b* 1966, — Lily Isabella Katherine Bonnie, *b* 1968, — Jessica Mary Cassandra, *b* 1972. —— Grace
Elizabeth, *b* 1946; BA, MB, BChir: *m* 1975, Alan Barlow, of Janet Cottages, Rougham, Norfolk, and has issue living, Edward
Francis, *b* 1978, — Katherine Clare, *b* 1980.
    Issue of late Charles Percy Frederick North, *b* 1906, *d* 1971: *m* 1937, Judith, who *d* 1991, da of Harry Leon Hamlin,
of Stoneyhill Farm, Amagansett, Long Island, USA:—
Mary Grace (30 Sutton Place, New York City, USA), *b* 1939: *m* 1969, William Ellsworth Clow, who *d* 1970; has issue living,
Miranda Judith, *b* 1980. —— Melissa Judith, *b* 1944: *m* 1976, Michael Nicholas Edmund Chassay, RIBA, of 17 Powis Terr,
W11, and has issue living, Clancy Charles Arcade, *b* 1980, — Dixie Cleopatra, *b* 1976.

Granddaughter of late Charles North (ante):—
    Issue of late Marjoribanks Keppel North, *b* 1865, *d* 1949: *m* 1905, Edith Beatrice, JP, who *d* 1973, only da of Sir
George John Armytage, 6th Bt:—
Arabella, *b* 1909; 1939-45 War as Ch Com ATS: *m* 1950, Louis Euan Babington Morgan, who *d* 1978. *Residence* – Grosvenor
Park, Brookfield Rd, Bexhill-on-Sea, E Sussex TN40 1NY.

Granddaughter of late Marjoribanks Keppel North (ante):—
    Issue of late George Montagu North, *b* 1906, *d* 1953: *m* 1940, June Margaret (who *m* 2ndly, 1956, Robert Burton
Kenward, of Stocks House and Perryfield, Udimore, Sussex), da of late Francis Edward Harrison, OBE, of York:—
Lavinia Keppel, *b* 1940: *m* 1970, Peter Jocelyn Jeffries, of Brownings House, Ide Hill, Sevenoaks, Kent TN14 6JT, and has
issue living, Charles Jocelyn, *b* 1973, — Alexandra Keppel, *b* 1971.

PREDECESSORS – **(1-9)** GEORGE AUGUSTUS NORTH, 9th *Baron North*, of Kirtling, co Camb (by writ of summons 1554) and
3rd Earl of Guilford (*see* E Guilford), *b* 1757; *d* 1802, when the Earldom of Guilford devolved upon his brother, and the
Barony of North became abeyant, and remained so until 1841, when it was terminated in favour of his 2nd da **(10)** SUSAN; *b*
1797: *m* 1835, Col John Sidney Doyle, MP (who in 1838 assumed the surname of North); *d* 1884; *s* by her son **(11)** WILLIAM
HENRY JOHN, 11th Baron, *b* 1836; Bailiff Grand Cross of Sovereign Order of Malta, Pres of that Sovereign Order in Great
Britain, and Hon Pres of Committee of Privileges of Maltese Nobility; *m* 1858, Frederica, who *d* 1915, da of Com R. Howe
Cockerell, RN; *d* 1932; *s* by his son **(12)** WILLIAM FREDERICK JOHN, 12th Baron, *b* 1860: *m* 1885, Arabella Valerie Keppel, who
d 1965, da of late Charles North (E Guilford, colls); *d* 1938; *s* by his grandson **(13)** JOHN DUDLEY (son of late Hon Dudley
William John North, MC, only son of 12th Baron), 13th Baron, *b* 1917; Lt RN: *m* 1940, Margaret (who *m* 2ndly, 1943, Lieut
Weldon Bernard James, US Marine Corps), da of R. W. H. Glennie, of Cape Province, S Africa; *ka* 1941 in HMS *Neptune*,
when the Barony again fell into abeyance.

NORTHAMPTON, MARQUESS OF (Compton) (Marquess UK 1812)
(Name pronounced "Cumpton")

SPENCER DOUGLAS DAVID COMPTON, 7th Marquess; *b* 2 April 1946; *s* 1978; *ed* Eton; patron of nine livings; a DL of Northants: *m* 1st, 1967 (*m diss* 1973), Henriette Luisa Maria Bentinck, only da of late Baron Bentinck, Netherlands Ambassador to France; 2ndly, 1974 (*m diss* 1977), Annette Marie, da of Charles Anthony Russell Smallwood; 3rdly, 1977 (*m diss* 1983), Rosemary Ashley Morritt, only da of P. G. M. Hancock, of Truro, and formerly wife of Hon Lionel John Charles Seymour Dawson-Damer (*see* E Portarlington); 4thly, 1985 (*m diss* 1988), Ellen (Fritzi), only da of late Hermann Erhardt, of Munich, and formerly wife of Hon Michael Orlando Weetman Pearson (*see* V Cowdray); 5thly, 1990, Mrs Pamela Martina Raphaela Kyprios, and has issue by 1st, 3rd and 4th *m*.

Arms – Sable, a lion passant guardant or, between three esquires' helmets argent. **Crest** – On a mount a beacon fired proper, behind it a ribbon inscribed with the words, *Nisi Dominus*. **Supporters** – *Dexter*, a dragon ermine, ducally gorged and chained or; *sinister*, an unicorn argent, horned, maned, hoofed, and tufted sable.
Seats – Castle Ashby, Northampton; Compton Wynyates, Tysoe, Warwick.

SON LIVING *(By 1st marriage)*

DANIEL BINGHAM (*Earl Compton*), *b* 16 Jan 1973.

DAUGHTERS LIVING *(By 1st marriage)*

Lady Lara Katrina, *b* 1968.

(By 3rd marriage)

Lady Emily Rose, *b* 1980.

(By 4th marriage)

Lady Louisa Cecilia, *b* 1985.

BROTHER LIVING

Lord William James Bingham, *b* 1947; *ed* Bryanston: *m* 1973, Marlene, da of late Francis Hosie, and has issue living, James William, *b* 1974, — Clare Victoria Frances, *b* 1980. *Residence* – 50 Bedford Gardens, W8.

SISTERS LIVING

Lady Judith (59 Buckingham Gate, SW1E 6AJ) *b* 1943; *ed* Royal Coll of Music, and London Univ: *m* 1970, Sir Adrian Christopher Swire, and has issue living, Merlin Bingham, *b* 1973, — Samuel Compton, *b* 1980, — Martha Virginia, *b* 1972.
Lady Elizabeth, *b* 1944; DL Ross and Cromarty, Skye and Lochalsh 1990: *m* 1968, Ian Hamish Leslie Melville, and has issue (*see* E Leven and Melville, colls), of Lochluichart, by Garve, Ross-shire IV23 2PZ.

MOTHER LIVING

Virginia Lucie, yst da of late David Rimington Heaton, DSO, of Brookfield, Crownhill, S Devon: *m* 1st, 1942 (*m diss* 1958), as his 2nd wife, the 6th Marquess of Northampton, DSO, who *d* 1978; 2ndly, 1958, as his 3rd wife, Capt Thomas Andrew Hussey, CBE, RN, who *d* 1980. *Residence* – 40 Burghley House, Somerset Rd, London SW19.

COLLATERAL BRANCHES LIVING

Grandchildren of late Lord Alwyne Frederick Compton, DSO, 3rd son of 4th Marquess:—
Issue of late Capt Edward Robert Francis Compton, 2nd Dragoons (R Scots Greys) *b* 1891, *d* 1977: *m* 1st, 1918, Sylvia, who *d* 1950, da of late Lt-Col Alexander Haldane Farquharson (Ross, Bt, *cr* 1672, colls); 2ndly, 1952, Mary Elizabeth, who *d* 1957, da of Sydney Dawson, of Cambridge, and formerly wife of Allen Wilson; 3rdly, 1958, Sallie Whitney, who *d* 1979, da of Dr Leonard Sanford, of New York, and widow of 2nd Baron Sysonby:—
(By 1st *m*) Alwyne Arthur Compton FARQUHARSON OF INVERCAULD, MC (Invercauld, Braemar, Aberdeenshire), *b* 1919; *ed* Eton; Capt R Scots Greys; 1939-45 War (wounded, MC); officially recognised in the surname of Farquharson of Invercauld, and as Chief of Clan Farquharson by warrant of Lord Lyon 1949, and uses his former surname as a third christian name: *m* 1st, 1949, Frances Strickland Lovell (GORDON), who *d* 1991, da of late Robert Pollard Oldham, of Seattle, Washington, USA, and widow of Capt Hon James Henry Bertie Rodney, MC (*see* B Rodney); 2ndly, 1993, Patricia Gabriella Estelle, da of Henry Simms Norman Simms-Adams, of Brancaster Hall, Norfolk, and widow of Nicholas John Dennys Parry de Winton. —— Robert Edward John COMPTON (Newby Hall, Ripon, Yorks), *b* 1922; *ed* Eton; late Maj Coldstream Guards; High Sheriff of N Yorks 1978, and a DL of N Yorks: *m* 1951, Ursula Jane (AITKEN), da of late Maj Robert Orlando Kenyon-Slaney (*see* B Kenyon, colls), and has issue living, James Alwyne (43A Upcerne Rd, SW10; Coombe Cottage, Hanging Langford, Salisbury, Wilts SP3 4NW), *b* 1953: *m* 1st, 1980 (*m diss* 1986), Rebecca, only da of Sir Alan Lewis Wigan, 8th Bt, and formerly wife of John Dominic Spearman (*see* Spearman, Bt, colls); 2ndly, 1989, Lady Tania Frances Meade, yr da of 7th Earl of Clanwilliam, and has issue living (by 1st *m*) Philip *b* 1980, Clephane *b* 1983, Lara Ellen *b* 1985, (by 2nd *m*) Sophie *b* 1993, — Richard Clephane (50 Southerton Rd, W6; The Manor House, Marton-le-Moor, Ripon, N Yorks HG4 5AT), *b* 1957: *m* 1982, Lucinda Jane Astell, yr da of Gerald Arthur Hohler (*see* Stucley, Bt), and has issue living, Orlando Edward de Grey *b* 1986, Ludovic

Hugh *b* 1989, Theodosia Alexandra *b* 1992. —— Mary (twin), *b* 1919: *m* 1st, 1939 (*m diss* 1947), Bernard Henry Richard van Cutsem, who *d* 1975; 2ndly, 1947, Maj William Dalton Henderson, of Ballygown, Ulva Ferry, Mull, and *d* 1989, leaving issue (by 1st *m*), Hugh Bernard Edward (Anmer Hall, King's Lynn, Norfolk PE31 6RW), *b* 1941; *ed* Ampleforth: *m* 1971, Jonkyrouwe Emilie, da of Jonkheer Pieter Quarles van Ufford, of De Dumdoorn, Aerdenhout, Holland, and has issue living, Edward Bernard Charles *b* 1973, Hugh Ralph *b* 1974, Nicholas Peter Geoffrey *b* 1977, William Henry *b* 1979, — Geoffrey Neil (The Old Rectory, Old Somerby, nr Grantham, Lincs; 9A Elm Park Rd, SW3), *b* 1944; *ed* Ampleforth: *m* 1969, Sally, only da of Alastair McCorquodale, of Stoke Rochford, Grantham, Lincs, and has issue living, Sophie *b* 1975, Zara *b* 1978, — (by 2nd *m*), Alexander William, *b* 1948: *m* 1982, Penelope Coates, and has issue living, Edward Alwyne *b* 1985, — Mary Clare, *b* 1951: *m* 1978, Jonathan Martin, of Bentley House, Bentley, Ipswich, Suffolk, and has issue living, Laura *b* 1981, Sophie *b* 1984.

　　　　Issue of late Lt-Cdr Clare George VYNER, RN, *b* 1894, *d* 1989; assumed by Royal Licence the surname of Vyner in lieu of his patronymic, and the arms of Vyner quarterly, 1912: *m* 1923, Lady Doris Hilda Gordon-Lennox, who *d* 1980, da of 8th Duke of Richmond:—

Henry VYNER, *b* 1932: *m* 1st, 1958, Margaret, da of late Capt Ralph Heathcote, DSO, RN, of Gressingham, Lancs, and formerly wife of Hon Hugo John Laurence Phillips (*see* B Milford); 2ndly, 1982, (Charlotte) Claire (Pemberton), da of late Capt Frederick Harold Deming Courtney, and has issue living (by 1st *m*), Harriet de Grey, *b* 1959, — Violet Elizabeth, *b* 1962. *Residence* – Keanchulish, Ullapool, Ross-shire.

PREDECESSORS – (1) *Sir* HENRY Compton, Knt, was summoned to Parliament as *Baron Compton*, of Compton, co Warwick (peerage of England) 1566; in 1587 was at the trial of the Queen of Scots, and was one of the principal commanders of the forces that besieged the Earl of Essex; *d* 1589; *s* by his son (2) WILLIAM, KG, 2nd Baron; Lord Pres of the Marches and dominion of Wales, and Lord-Lieut of Warwickshire; *cr Earl of Northampton* (peerage of England) 1618; *d* 1630; *b* by his son (3) SPENCER, KB, 2nd Earl; was Master of the Robes to Charles, Prince of Wales, and a zealous partisan of James I; *k* at battle of Hopton Heath 1642; *s* by his son (4) JAMES, 3rd Earl; an earnest Royalist; sat as MP for Warwickshire 1640-2; was Lord-Lieut of co Warwick, Constable of the Tower of London and Recorder of Coventry, Tamworth, and Northampton; commanded the Cavalry at first battle of Newbury 1643, and raised the siege of Banbury 1644, etc; *d* 1681; *s* by his son (5) GEORGE, PC, 4th Earl; Constable of the Tower of London, and Lord-Lieut of Warwickshire; bore the King's sceptre and cross at Coronation of William and Mary; *d* 1727; *s* by his el son (6) JAMES, 5th Earl; MP for co Warwick 1710-11, when he was summoned to House of peers in his father's barony of Compton: *m* Elizabeth, in her own right Baroness Ferrers of Chartley, sister and heir of Robert Shirley, Viscount Tamworth; *d* without male issue 1754, when the Barony of Compton devolved upon his da Charlotte (wife of 1st Marquess of Townshend, who also in 1770 inherited from her mother the Baronies of Ferrers of Chartley, Bourchier, Lovaine, and Basset of Drayton), and the Earldom devolved upon his brother (7) GEORGE, 6th Earl; was a Lord of the Treasury 1742; sat as MP for Tamworth 1726-7, and for Northampton 1727-54; *dsp* 1758; *s* by his nephew (8) CHARLES, 7th Earl, son of Hon Charles, MP, 3rd son of 4th Earl; *dsp* 1763; *s* by his brother (9) SPENCER, 8th Earl; sat as MP for Northampton 1761-3; was Lord-Lieut of Northamptonshire, Recorder of Northampton, and a Groom of the Bedchamber; *d* 1796; *s* by his son (10) CHARLES, 9th Earl, *cr Baron Wilmington*, of Wilmington, co Sussex, *Earl Compton*, and *Marquess of Northampton* (peerage of United Kingdom) 1812; *d* 1828; *s* by his son (11) SPENCER JOSHUA ALWYNE, 2nd Marquess; *b* 1790; was Pres of Royal Soc: *m* 1815, Margaret, da of Maj-Gen Douglas Maclean Clephane; *d* 1851; *s* by his son (12) CHARLES, 3rd Marquess; assumed in 1831 by Roy licence the additional and principal surname of Douglas; *dsp* 1877; *s* by his brother (13) WILLIAM, KG, 4th Marquess, *b* 1818; Adm in the Navy; assumed 1851 the additional surname of Maclean, and in 1878 that of Douglas: *m* 1844, Eliza, who *d* 1877, da of late Adm Hon Sir George Elliot, KCB; *d* 1897; *s* by his el surviving son (14) WILLIAM GEORGE SPENCER SCOTT, KG, *b* 1851; Private Sec to Lord-Lieut of Ireland 1880-82 and Lord-Lieut of Warwickshire 1912-13; Special Envoy to Foreign Courts to announce Accession of King George V; MP for Warwickshire, S-W, or Stratford-on-Avon, Div 1885-6, and for Yorkshire, W Riding, S Part, Barnsley Div (*L*) March 1889 to Sept 1897: *m* 1884, Hon Mary Florence Baring, who *d* 1902, da of 2nd Baron Ashburton; *d* 1913; *s* by hs el son (15) WILLIAM BINGHAM, 6th Marquess, DSO, *b* 1885, Maj R Horse Guards; Lt Col Comdg Warwickshire Yeo; a Com of Order of Leopold II of Belgium; CStJ; European war 1914-18 (wounded, DSO 1919): *m* 1st, 1921 (*m diss* 1942), Lady Emma Marjory Thynne, OBE, who *d* 1980, da of 5th Marquess of Bath; 2ndly, 1942 (*m diss* 1958), Virginia Lucie, da of late David Rimington Heaton, DSO, of Brookfield, Crownhill, S Devon; 3rdly, 1958, Elspeth Grace, who *d* 1976, el da of late William Ingham Whitaker, DL (V Melville); *d* 1978; *s* by his el son (16) SPENCER DOUGLAS DAVID, 7th Marquess and present peer; also Earl of Northampton, Earl Compton, and Baron Wilmington.

NORTHBOURNE, BARON (James) (Baron UK 1884, Bt GB 1791)

J'AYME·A·JAMAIS

I love for ever

CHRISTOPHER GEORGE WALTER JAMES, 5th Baron, and 6th Baronet; *b* 18 Feb 1926; *s* 1982; *ed* Eton, and Magdalen Coll, Oxford (MA), FRICS; patron of two livings: *m* 1959, Marie Sygne, el da of Henri Charles Walter Claudel, of Chatou-sur-Seine, and has issue.

Arms – Gules, a dolphin embowed or. **Crest** – An ostrich argent, beaked and legged or. **Supporters** – Two eagles argent, collared gules; each having pendant from the collar a shield charged with the arms. *Seat* – Coldharbour, Northbourne, Deal, Kent. *Residence* – 11 Eaton Place, SW1. *Clubs* – Brook's, Royal Yacht Sqdn.

SONS LIVING

Hon CHARLES WALTER HENRI, *b* 14 June 1960, *ed* Eton, and Magdalen Coll, Oxford: *m* 1987, Catherine Lucy, only da of W. Ralph Burrows, of Prescot, Lancs, and has issue living, Henry Christopher William, *b* 3 Dec 1988, — Anastasia Aliki, *b* 1992. *Residence* – Northbourne Court, Northbourne, Kent.
Hon Anthony Christopher Walter Paul, *b* 1963, *ed* Eton, and Magdalen Coll, Oxford. *Residence* – Evistones, Otterburn, Northumberland.
Hon Sebastian Richard Edward Cuthbert, *b* 1966, *ed* Eton, Magdalen Coll, Oxford, and INSEAD Fontainebleau.

DAUGHTER LIVING

Hon Ophelia Mary Katherine Christine Aliki, *b* 1969; *ed* St Mary's Ascot, King's Sch Canterbury, and Exeter Univ.

SISTERS LIVING

Hon Gwenllian Ellen, *b* 1929: *m* 1st, 1952 (*m* annulled 1960), Michael Hugh Rose (infra); 2ndly, 1960, Thomas Jeffrey Hemsley, of 10 Denewood Rd, Highgate, N6, and has issue living, (by 2nd *m*) William Thomas James, *b* 1962, — Matthew Walter David, *b* 1963, — Michael Richard, *b* 1965.
Hon Elizabeth Sarah, *b* 1933: *m* 1960, Michael Edward Willis-Fleming, and has issue living, John Michael, *b* 1961, — Penelope Katherine, *b* 1965: *m* 1990, Jaume Simon Gispert, of c/o Llado 11-19, Esc Derecha 3° 2A, Badalona, Barcelona, Spain, son of Luis Simon Gispert, of Barcelona. *Residence* – Updown Farm, Betteshanger, Deal, Kent.
Hon Susan Jane, *b* 1936: *m* 1961, Michael Hugh Rose (ante), of Le Sirondole, Panzano-in-Chianti (Florence), Italy, son of late Rt Rev Alfred Carey Wollaston Rose, formerly Bishop of Dover, and has issue living, Michael Justin, *b* 1966, — Nell Susanna, *b* 1961, — Emma Katherine, *b* 1963, — Sophy Elizabeth, *b* 1969.
Hon Katherine Viola, *b* 1940: *m* 1963, John Wharton Hersey, and has issue living, Robert Alexander, *b* 1964, — John Paul, *b* 1966, — Daniel Anthony James, *b* 1971. *Residence* – Thorneyburn Old Rectory, Tarset, Northumberland.

WIDOW LIVING OF SON OF SECOND BARON

Lady Serena Mary Barbara Lumley, da of 10th Earl of Scarbrough: *m* 1923, as his 2nd wife, Hon Robert James, who *d* 1960, and has issue living (see colls, infra). *Residence* – St Nicholas, Richmond, Yorkshire.

COLLATERAL BRANCHES LIVING

Grandchildren of late Lt-Col Hon Cuthbert James, CBE, MP (infra):—
Issue of late Thomas James, *b* 1906, *d* 1976: *m* 1st, 1932 (*m* diss 1940), Lady Germaine Elizabeth Olive Eliot, who *d* 1991, da of 8th Earl of St Germans; 2ndly, 1940 (*m* diss 1953), Julia Mary, who *d* 1974, da of late Charles Solomon, of 36 Queen's Grove, St John's Wood, NW; 3rdly, 1953, Rosemary Heartsease Beare, who *d* 1979, da of late Maj George Frederick Crisp Molineux-Montgomerie (*see* D Beaufort, colls, 1976 Edn), and widow of Capt Reginald Dilworth Howard, RN:—
(By 2nd *m*) Antony Nigel (18 Toorang Av, N Balwyn, Victoria 3104, Australia), *b* 1944: *m* 1973, Therese Macormack, of Melbourne, Aust, and has issue living, Alexander Robert, *b* 1974, — Charles Henry Thomas, *b* 1976, — Francesca Danielle, *b* 1980. —— Georgina Mary, *b* 1948: *m* 1972, Christopher Watts, of 45 Woodley Lane, Cuppernham, Romsey, Hants, SO5 8JR, and has issue living, Ian Charles, *b* 1973, — Mark Andrew, *b* 1976.

Issue of late Lt-Col Hon Cuthbert James, CBE, MP, 2nd son of 2nd Baron, *b* 1872, *d* 1930: *m* 1905, Florence Marion, who *d* 1933, da of late Hussey Packe (E Kimberley):—
Joan Rosamund, *b* 1917: *m* 1949, Maj Launcelot James Francis Brydon, and has issue living, Robert Alexander (49 Melody Rd, SW18 2QW), *b* 1954; *ed* Stowe: *m* 1983 (*m* diss 1987), Francesca Camilla Roberta Ierne, da of Henry John William Phillips, of 46 Hornton St, W8 (*see* B Hothfield, 1985 Edn), and has issue living, Lara Daisy Edina Charlotte *b* 1984, — Nadia Mary BRYDON, *b* 1952: *m* 19— (*m* diss 19—), Sol Alan Saad. *Residence* – The Village House, Brasted, Kent.

Granddaughter of late Hon Robert James (infra):—
Issue of late Arthur Walter James, *b* 1904, *d* 1981: *m* 1st, 1929 (*m* diss 1932), Zita Mary, da of Nico Jungman; 2ndly, 1932, Mary, yr da of late Albany Hawke Charlesworth, and formerly wife of late Lionel Cyril Gibbs:—
(By 2nd *m*) Lucinda Evelyn, *b* 1933: *m* 1st, 1953 (*m* diss 1967), Andrew Duff Tennant (*see* B Glenconner, colls); 2ndly, 1967, Rupert Oliver Steel, of Winterbourne Holt, Newbury, Berks, and has issue living (by 1st *m*) (*see* B Glenconner, colls), — (by 2nd *m*) James Oliver, *b* 1971, — Emily Jane, *b* 1970.

Issue of late Hon Robert James, 3rd son of 2nd Baron, *b* 1873, *d* 1960: *m* 1st, 1900, Lady Evelyn Kathleen Wellesley, who *d* 1922, da of 4th Duke of Wellington; 2ndly, 1923, Lady Serena Mary Barbara Lumley (ante), da of 10th Earl of Scarbrough:—
(By 2nd *m*) Ursula Mary-Rose (*Baroness Westbury*), *b* 1924: *m* 1947, 5th Baron Westbury. *Residence* – Barton Cottage, Malton, Yorks. —— Serena Fay, *b* 1929: *m* 1955 (*m* diss 1963), Colin Griffith Campion, and has issue living, Marcus Robert Guy, *b* 1961, — Georgina Serena, *b* 1955, — Christina Fay, *b* 1957, — Meriona Patricia, *b* 1959. *Residence* – St Nicholas Garden Cottage, Richmond, Yorks.

Issue of late Hon Wilfrid James, 4th son of 2nd Baron, *b* 1874, *d* 1908: *m* 1900, Margaret Anne, who *d* 1957, da of John Stogdon:—

Henry Norman, *b* 1903: *m* 1st, 1933 (*m diss* 1946), Constance Margaret, only da of Capt J. D. Macdonald, of Bucklebury Place, Woolhampton, Berks; 2ndly, 1946, Kathleen Mary, who *d* 1959, da of late Charles William Hewtson; 3rdly, 1967, Marjorie, da of late Charles William Hewtson, and has issue living, (by 2nd *m*) John Henry (Woodlands Farm, Adisham, nr Canterbury, Kent), *b* 1947; *ed* King's Sch, Canterbury: *m* 1970, Karen Lesley, da of Fl Lt Leslie A. Montgomery, MBE, of Ickwell Green, Biggleswade, Beds, and has issue living, Nicholas John *b* 1976, Lisa Maria *b* 1973, — Margaret Anne, *b* 1950: *m* 19—, — Speer, of 3416 Blue Hill, Gallup, New Mexico 87301, USA. *Residence* – Woodlands, Adisham, nr Canterbury, Kent.

PREDECESSORS – **(1)** Sir WALTER JAMES Head, 2nd son of Sir Thomas Head (Knt), of Langley Hall, Berks; was sometime Warden of the Mint; assumed in 1778 by Act of Parliament the surname of James only, and in 1791 was *cr* a *Baronet*; *d* 1829; *s* by his grandson **(2)** Sir WALTER CHARLES, 2nd Baronet (son of late John James, Minister Plenipotentiary to the Netherlands); *b* 1816; MP for Hull (C) 1837-47; *cr Baron Northbourne*, co Kent (peerage of United Kingdom) 1884: *m* 1841, Sarah Caroline, who *d* 1890, da of Cuthbert Ellison, of Hebburn Hall, Durham; *d* 1893; *s* by his son **(3)** WALTER HENRY, 2nd Baron; *b* 1846; MP for Gateshead (L) 1874-93: *m* 1868, Edith Emmeline Mary, who *d* 1929, da of late John Newton Lane, of King's Bromley Manor, Lichfield; *d* 1923; *s* by his son **(4)** WALTER JOHN, 3rd Baron, *b* 1869: *m* 1894, Laura Gwenllian, who *d* 1952 (having *m* 2ndly, 1935, William Curtis Green, RA), da of late Adm Sir Ernest Rice, KCB, of Sibertswold Place, Kent; *d* 1932; *s* by his son **(5)** WALTER ERNEST CHRISTOPHER, 4th Baron, *b* 1896: *m* 1925, Katherine Louise, JP, who *d* 1980, da of George A. Nickerson, of Boston, Mass, USA; *d* 1982; *s* by his son **(6)** CHRISTOPHER GEORGE WALTER, 5th Baron and present peer.

NORTHBROOK, BARON (Baring) (Baron 1866, Bt GB 1793)

By uprightness and labour

FRANCIS THOMAS BARING, 6th Baron and 8th Baronet; *b* 21 Feb 1954; *s* 1990; *ed* Winchester, and Bristol Univ: *m* 1987, Amelia Sharon Elizabeth, elder da of Dr Reginald David Taylor, of Hursley, Winchester, and has issue.

𝕬rms – 1st and 4th, azure, a fesse or, in chief a bear's head proper, muzzled and ringed of the second differenced by a portcullis azure. *Baring*; 2nd and 3rd, gules, a cross patée fitchée or between three fish hauriant argent within an orle of eight cross-crosslets of the second, *Herring*. 𝕮rest – A mullet erminois, two of the points resting on the pinions of a pair of wings conjoined and elevated argent. 𝕾upporters – On either side a bear proper, muzzled and charged on the shoulder with a portcullis or. *Address* – c/o House of Lords, SW1.

DAUGHTERS LIVING

Hon Arabella Constance Elizabeth, *b* 1989.
Hon Venetia Harriet Anne, *b* 1991.

SISTERS LIVING

Hon Laura Anne, *b* 1952: *m* 1982, Ewen Cameron Stewart Macpherson, eldest son of late Brig George Philip Stewart Macpherson, OBE, TD, of The Old Rectory, Aston Sandford, Bucks, and has issue living, James Francis Stewart, *b* 1983, — George Malcolm Stewart, *b* 1985. *Residence* – The Old Rectory, Aston Sandford, nr Aylesbury, Bucks.
Hon Alexandra Grace, *b* 1957: *m* 1981, (Philip) Strone (Stewart) Macpherson, yr son of late Brig George Philip Stewart Macpherson, OBE, TD (ante), and has issue living, Philip Strone Alexander Stewart, *b* 1985, — Temora Anne, *b* 1988, — Clementina Grace, *b* 1989. *Residence* – Armsworth Park House, Old Alresford, Hants SO24 9RH.
Hon Catherine Margaret, *b* 1965: *m* 1992, (Edward) Sherard (Bourchier) Wrey, yr son of Sir (Castel Richard) Bourchier Wrey, 14th Bt. *Residence* – Pink Cottage, Tawstock, Barnstaple, Devon.

AUNT LIVING (*daughter of 5th Baron*)

Hon Anne (Westwood, W Meon, Petersfield, Hants), *b* 1917.

WIDOW LIVING OF FIFTH BARON

ROWENA MARGARET (*Rowena, Baroness Northbrook*), da of late Brig-Gen Sir William Henry Manning, GCMG, KBE, CB: *m* 1951, the 5th Baron, who *d* 1990.

COLLATERAL BRANCHES LIVING (*In remainder to Baronetcy only*)

Grandchildren of late Godfrey Nigel Everard Baring, 4th and yst son of late Thomas Charles Baring, MP, elder son of Rt Rev Charles Baring, DD, Bishop of Durham, 4th and yst son of 2nd baronet:—

Issue of late Desmond Charles Nigel Baring, *b* 1914, *d* 1991: *m* 1938, Mary Eileen, JP (Ardington House, Wantage, Oxon), da of Benjamin Walter Warner:—

PETER (Dower Cottage, Ardington, Wantage, Oxon), *b* 12 Sept 1939; *ed* Eton: *m* 1973, Rose, da of George Nigel Adams, of Fernham Manor, Faringdon, Oxon, and has issue living, Samuel Nigel, *b* 1987, — Mark George, *b* 1990. —— Nigel (The Lodge, Ardington, Wantage, Oxon), *b* 1940; *ed* Eton: *m* 1968, Jane Finola, elder da of Francis Byrne, of 76 Rivermead Court, Hurlingham, SW6, and has issue living, Lorne Benjamin Nigel, *b* 1970; *ed* Eton, and RMA Sandhurst, — Edward Francis Desmond, *b* 1972, — Lucinda Anne, *b* 1980. —— (Margaret) Anne, *b* 1944: *m* 1976, Hugh Barkly Gonnerman Dalgety, of Millards Hill House, Trudoxhill, Frome, Som, and has issue living, Richard Hugh, *b* 1977, — Thomas Arthur, *b* 1984, — Katherine Anne, *b* 1979.

Granddaughter of late Right Rev Charles Baring, DD (ante):—

Issue (by 2nd *m*) of late Rev Francis Henry Baring, *b* 1848, *d* 1914: *m* 1st, 1881, Margaret Ann Borthwick, who *d*

1882, widow of William Elmslie, FRCS, and da of late Rev William Wallace Duncan, of Peebles; 2ndly, 1886, Amy, who *d* 1935, da of late Rev John Alexander Stamper, of Monaline House, Newtownmountkennedy, co Wicklow:— Amy Rose, *b* 1894: *m* 1947, Edwin Daniel Doncaster, who *d* 1950.

Descendants of late Rt Hon Alexander Baring, DCL (2nd son of Sir Francis Baring, 1st Bt), who was *cr Baron Ashburton* 1835:—
See that title.

Descendants of late Lieut-Gen Charles Baring, eldest son of late Henry Bingham Baring, MP, eldest son of late Henry Baring (*d* 1848), 3rd son of Sir Francis Baring, 1st Bt:—
See Baring, Bt.

Descendants of late Edward Charles Baring, 5th son of late Henry Baring (*d* 1848) (ante), who was *cr Baron Revelstoke* 1885:—
See that title.

Granddaughter of late Thomas Baring (infra):—
Issue of late Richard Baring, *b* 1902, *d* 1940: *m* (1 Jan) 1922, Violetta Archer, who *d* 1931; 2ndly, 1932, Margaret, who *d* 1974, da of Henry Thomas Sutton, of Zanesville, Ohio, USA:—
(By 1st *m*) Cecilia Maureen Anne (105 Canfield Gdns, NW6 3DY), *b* (Oct) 1922.

Grandsons of late Thomas Baring, 8th son of Henry Baring (*d* 1848) (ante):—
Issue of late Edward Thomas Baring, *b* 1903, *d* 1980: *m* 1st, 1926 (*m diss* 1949), Virginia, da of John Barry Ryan, of New York; 2ndly, 1950, Pauline Alison, da of late Frank Fawcett Copland, of Sydney, and formerly wife of Timothy Walter Boden:—
(By 1st *m*) Thomas Michael, TD (Westhay House, Axminster, Devon EX13 5XH), *b* 1927; Lt-Col Derbyshire Yeo; Comdg Leics and Derbys Yeo: *m* 1st, 1953 (*m diss* 1965), Hon Sarah Katherine Elinor Norton, da of 6th Baron Grantley, and formerly wife of 3rd Viscount Astor, 2ndly, 1966, Gillian Ann Rosemary, da of Arthur Rupert Woolley, DSO, OBE, of Tisbury, Wilts, and formerly wife of John Graham, and has an adopted son (from 1st *m*), Edward Richard Philip, *b* 1962, — and issue living (by 2nd *m*), Constance Nina, *b* 1970. —— (Edward) Patrick (Old Rectory, Pimperne, Dorset), *b* 1932: *m* 1960, Antonia Miriam, da of late Anthony Wentworth Guinness, of Stoke House, Stoke Albany, Market Harborough, Leics, and has issue living, Anthony Shawn, *b* 1961: *m* 1991, Kirsty A., yst da of Sidney Edmond Jocelyn Ackland (the actor Joss Ackland), — Jonathan Patrick Fortune, *b* 1965, — Sonya Hermione, *b* 1963, — Lucita Catherine Marianne, *b* 1968. —— Christopher John (311 Commonwealth Av, Boston, Mass 02115, USA), *b* 1939: *m* 1971, Katherine Gayle, da of Lee Warren Jones, of Dayton, Ohio, USA.

Descendants of late Rt Hon Sir Evelyn Baring, GCB, OM, GCMG, KCSI, CIE, 9th son of late Henry Baring (*d* 1848) (ante), who was *cr Earl of Cromer* 1901:—
See that title.

Grandsons of late Maj Francis Charles Baring, elder son of late William Henry Baring, only son of late William Baring, MP, 4th and yst son of late Sir Francis Baring, 1st Bt:—
Issue of late Major Thomas Esmé Baring, OBE, *b* 1882, *d* 1957: *m* 1913, Deirdré Mary Hughes, who *d* 1973, da of Hughes Martin, JP, formerly of Tullaghreine, Carrigtwohill, co Cork:—
Maurice Bingham, TD, *b* 1916; *ed* Eton, and at Magdalene Coll, Camb (BA 1939, MA 1949); is Capt Rifle Bde (TA): *m* 1941, Loveday Anne Monica, da of late Capt John Tillie Coryton (V St Vincent, colls), and has issue living, Lynda Anne (16 Cambridge St, SW1), *b* 1944: *m* 1967, Clive Edward Theo Corke, and has issue living, Philip Clive *b* 1979, Shauna Bingham *b* 1972, Anthea Lynda *b* 1973, — Shirley Bingham, *b* 1948. *Residence* – Culmer House, Wormley, nr Godalming, Surrey. —— Hugo Charles, MBE, MC, *b* 1919; *ed* Eton, and at Magdalene Coll, Camb; formerly Maj Rifle Bde; 1939-45 War in Middle East and Italy (despatches, MC, MBE); MBE (Mil) 1945: *m* 1946, Elisabeth Price, who *d* 1977, only da of late Maj John Price Wylie, DSO, Sherwood Foresters, and has issue living, Anthony Hugo (7, 574 New South Head Rd, Point Piper, NSW 2027, Australia), *b* 1947; *ed* Eton: *m* 1976, Anne Crerar, da of late S. G. MacGillivray, of Australia, and has issue living, Nicholas Anthony *b* 1979, Jessica Emily *b* 1977, Eloise Annabelle *b* 1982, — Michael William, *b* 1950; *ed* Eton: *m* 1974, Fayne Smith, and has issue living, Christopher William *b* 1977, Tanya Elizabeth. *Residence* – Koromiko Station, Gladstone, nr Masterton, Wairarapa, NZ.
Issue of late Arthur Francis Charles Baring, *b* 1887, *d* 1964: *m* 1906, Margaret McIntyre, who *d* 1966, da of late George Moore, of Adelaide, S Australia:—
†Ian Douglas, *b* 1915: *m* 1937, Doris Mary Emily Luckhurst, who *d* 1984, and was *k* in a motor accident 1969, leaving issue, Douglas Sydney (10 Bennett Av, Heathmont, Victoria 3135, Australia), *b* 1938: *m* 1960, Jean Melville Leslie, and has issue living, David Ian Alan *b* 1963: *m* 1987, Lisa Joanne Chapman (and has issue living, Trent Andrew Jesse *b* 1990, Joshua David *b* 1992), Jeanette Anne *b* 1965: *m* 1987, Keven Anthony Beekman (and has issue living, Ashley Stewart *b* 1991, Laura Rhiannon *b* (twin) 1991). —— Evelyn Charles, *b* 1924: *m* 1951, Joan Margot Winter, and has issue living, Peter Charles, *b* 1952: *m* 19—, Marie Bernadette Maloney, and has issue living, Eliot FitzRoy *b* 1985, Alexander St John *b* 1989, — Graham John (107 Argyle St, St Kilda, Victoria 3182, Australia), *b* 1954: *m* 1992, Ingrid Frances Draeger, and has issue living, Isabella Tess *b* 1993, — Rodney Alan *b* 1958: has issue living (by Fredariki Josephine Alsop), Oscar Alan *b* 1989. —— Jean Margaret, *b* 1922: *m* 1944, Arthur Gilmour Lees, of 5/4 Broad St, Labrador, Queensland 4215, Australia, and has issue living, Suzanne Leonie Margaret (23 Scala St, London W1), *b* 1949: has issue living, Alexander Lees FAWDREY *b* 1989, Sophie Serena Lees FAWDREY *b* 1992, — Judith Anne, *b* 1951: *m* 1991, Adnan Rashed, of 4/72 Burfitt St, Leichhardt, NSW 2040, Australia.
Issue of late Major Dudley William Baring, Hampshire Regt, and RASC, *b* 1892, *d* 1952: *m* 1919, Cecilia Mary, who *d* 1971, da of late Col Michael Rowan Gray Buchanan, OBE, of Ettrickdale, Isle of Bute (M Bute, colls):—
Francis William, VRD and bar, *b* 1920; *ed* Bradfield Coll; Cdr RNR; 1939-45 War: *m* 1967, Elsie Violet, RD, only da of late William Charles Redding. *Residence* – 71 Clarence Gate Gdns, NW1 6QR.

Granddaughter of late Major Dudley William Baring (ante):—
Issue of late Lieut-Com Michael John Baring, RN, *b* 1921, *d* 1955: *m* 1946, Pamela Anne (The Yews, Swarraton, Alresford, Hants) (who *m* 2ndly, 1959, Capt John Ridgeway Berridge Longden, RN (ret)), da of late Col Frederick Adolphus Fleming Barnardo, CIE, CBE, ESc, MD, MRCP, FRCS:—
†Jeremy Michael Stuart, *b* 1948; *ed* Wellington Coll; *dunm* 1982. —— Angela Jane, *b* 1946: *m* 1969 (*m diss* 1991), William George Stirling Home Drummond Moray (*see* D Buccleuch, colls).

PREDECESSORS – (1) FRANCIS Baring, MP for Grampound 1784-90, for Calen 1796-1802, and for Chipping Wycombe 1802-6; was an eminent London merchant, and a Director of the HEIC 1779-92, and Chairman thereof 1792-3; *cr a Baronet* 1793: *m* 1767, Harriet, da and co-heiress of William Herring, of Croydon, cousin and co-heiress of Thomas Herring, Archbishop of Canterbury; *d* 1810; *s* by his son (2) Sir THOMAS, 2nd Bt; sat as MP for Chipping Wycombe 1806-31; *d* 1848; *s* by his son (3) Sir FRANCIS THORNHILL, 3rd Bt; *b* 1796; sat as MP for Portsmouth 1826-65; was Chancellor of the Exchequer 1839-41, and First Lord of the Admiralty 1849-52; *cr Baron Northbrook*, of Stratton, co Hants (peerage of United Kingdom) 1866: *m* 1st, 1825, Jane, who *d* 1838, da of Hon Sir George Grey, 1st Bt; 2ndly, 1841, Lady Arabella Howard, who *d* 1884, da of 1st Earl of Effingham; *d* 1866; *s* by his son (4) Rt Hon THOMAS GEORGE, GCSI, DCL, LLD; *b* 1826; *cr Viscount Baring* and *Earl of Northbrook* (peerage of United Kingdom) 1876; a Lord of the Admiralty 1857-58, Under-Sec for War 1861, for India

1861-64, and for Home Depart 1864-66, Sec to Admiralty 1866, Under-Sec for War 1868-72, Gov-Gen of India 1872-6, and First Lord of the Admiralty 1880-85; Lord-Lieut of Hampshire; MP for Penryn and Falmouth (*L*) 1857-66; *m* 1848, Elizabeth Harriet, who *d* 1867, da of late Henry Charles Stuart, of Crichel House Dorset; *d* 1904; *s* by his son **(5)** FRANCIS GEORGE, 2nd Earl, *b* 1850; MP for Winchester (*L*) 1880-85, and for N, or Biggleswade, Div of Bedfordshire (LU) 1873-92; High Steward of Winchester and Freeman of that City: *m* 1st, 1894, Ada Ethel Sophie, who *d* 1894, da of Col C. Davidson, CB; 2ndly, 1899, Florence Anita Eyre, CBE, who *d* 1946, da of late Eyre Coote, of West Park, Hants, and widow of Sir Robert John Abercromby, 7th Bt; *d* 1929, when the Earldom and Viscountcy became ext, and the Barony of Northbrook devolved upon his cousin **(6)** FRANCIS ARTHUR (son of late Hon Francis Henry Baring, 3rd son of 1st Baron), 4th Baron; *b* 1882: *m* 1st, 1914, Evelyn Gladys Isabelle, who *d* 1919, da of late John George Charles, of 39 St George's Road, SW1 (*see* M Sligo, 1919 Edn); 2ndly, 1941, Constance Maud, who *d* 1976, da of late Frank Griffin, of Kew Gardens, Surrey; *d* 1947; *s* by his son **(7)** FRANCIS JOHN, 5th Baron, *b* 1915: *m* 1951, Rowena Margaret, da of late Brig-Gen Sir William Henry Manning, GCMG, KBE, CB; *d* 1990; *s* by his only son **(8)** FRANCIS THOMAS, 6th Baron and present peer.

NORTHCHURCH, BARONY OF (Davidson) (Extinct 1985)

SONS AND DAUGHTERS OF LIFE BARONESS

See V Davidson.

NORTHESK, EARL OF (Carnegie) (Earl S 1647)
(Name pronounced "Carneggie")

DAVID JOHN MACRAE CARNEGIE, 14th Earl; *b* 3 Nov 1954; *s* 1994; *ed* Eton: *m* 1979, Jacqueline May, elder (adopted) da of David Lorne Dundas Reid, of Quinta das Murtas, Rua Eduardo van Zeller, Sintra 2710, Portugal (*see* Reid, Bt, colls), and has issue.

Spot without stain

Arms – Quarterly; 1st and 4th, or, an eagle displayed azure, armed, beaked and membered sable and (*as an Honourable Augmentation*) charged on the breast with a naval crown of the field; 2nd and 3rd, argent, a pale gules (*Earldom of Northesk*). **Crests** – 1st, the stem of a battleship of the line with three lanthorns all proper, inflamed gules; 2nd, issuant from a naval crown or a demi-leopard proper holding a rose argent, barbed and seeded vert. **Supporters** – two leopards reguardant proper gorged of three (visible) roses argent, barbed and seeded vert, and each leopard sustaining a banner of Saint George. **Mottoes** – (over the first crest) "Trafalgar"; (over the second crest) "Britannia Victrix"; (below the compartment) "Tache Sans Tache".
Residence – The Firs, Nyewood, nr Petersfield, Hants GU31 5JA.

SON LIVING

ALEXANDER ROBERT MACRAE (*Lord Rosehill*), *b* 16 Nov 1980.

DAUGHTERS LIVING

Lady Sarah Louise Mary, *b* 1982.
Lady Fiona Jean Elizabeth, *b* 1987.
Lady Sophie Margaret Jean *b* 1990.

SISTERS LIVING

Lady Karen Jean, *b* 1951: *m* 1977, Hon Patrick Vavasseur Fisher, Highwayman's Vineyard, Heath Barn Farm, Risby, Bury St Edmunds, Suffolk, and has issue (*see* B Fisher, *cr* 1909).
Lady Mary Barbara, *b* 1953: *m* 1977, William Patrick Stirling Damerell, of Hatchery House, Barrow, Bury St Edmunds, Suffolk, and has issue living, Charles, *b* 1980, — Thomas *b* 1982, — Robert, *b* 1985.

AUNT LIVING (*Daughter of 12th Earl*)

Lady Susan Jean, *b* 1930: *m* 1955, David Blackall Connell, MD, BS, of Lower Wreyland, Lustleigh, Newton Abbot, Devon TQ13 9TS, and has issue living, Timothy Robert, *b* 1956: *m* 1983 (*m diss* 19—), Susanne HAMMER-JENSEN, da of Fru Birthe Jensen, of Hadsund, Denmark, and has issue living, Simon *b* 1984, Emilie *b* 1987, — Alistair Douglas, *b* 1960, — Caroline Lisa, *b* 1958: *m* 1980, David John Wilson, of Duchy Home Farm, Broadfield Farm, Tetbury, Glos, eldest son of Rev John Wilson, of Netherton, Peterborough, and has issue living, Seth Thomas David *b* 1982, Luke Alexander *b* 1984, Joshua Peter Arthur *b* 1987, Benjamin Montague *b* 1990.

WIDOW LIVING OF THIRTEENTH EARL

BROWNIE ELIZABETH (*Dowager Countess of Northesk*), da of Scott Grimason, and widow of Carl L. Heimann: *m* 1989, as his 2nd wife, the 13th Earl, who *d* 1994. *Residence* – Springwaters, Ballamodha, Isle of Man.

COLLATERAL BRANCHES LIVING

Granddaughters of late Isabella Eliza Butter CARNEGY OF LOUR, da of late Patrick Carnegy, CIE, son of late Maj-Gen Alexander Carnegy, CB, 2nd son of late Patrick Carnegy of Lour (*b* 1757), great-grandson of Hon Patrick Carnegie of Lour, 3rd son of 2nd Earl:—

Issue of late Lt-Col Ughtred Elliott Carnegy CARNEGY OF LOUR, DSO, MC, *b* 1886, *d* 1973: *m* 1919, Violet, MBE, who *d* 1965, da of late Henry William Henderson, of West Woodhay House, Newbury, Berks:—
Elizabeth Patricia CARNEGY OF LOUR (*Baroness Carnegy of Lour*), *b* 1925; *cr* Baroness Carnegy of Lour 1982 (see that title). —— Christian Margaret (*Lady Smith*), *b* 1927: *m* 1952, Sir John Lindsay Eric Smith, CH, CBE, FRIBA, of Shottesbrooke Park, White Waltham, Berks, and has had issue, Adam Carnegy Eric, *b* 1953: *m* 1983, Katherine, da of Herbert McDuffee, of Shingle Springs, California, USA, — Bartholomew Evan Eric, *b* 1955: *m* 1987, Catherine Nicola Blanche, da of Gavin Rowan Hamilton, of Stenton, E Lothian (*see* Blakiston, Bt, colls), and has issue living, Matthew John Patrick *b* 1988, Emily (Millie) Blanche Christian *b* 1989, — Emma Victoria Eric, *b* 1956; *ed* St Anne's Coll, Oxford; *d* 1983, — Serena Mary (*Hon Mrs Nicholas Soames*), *b* 1959; *ed* St Anne's Coll, Oxford: *m* 1993, as his 2nd wife, Hon (Arthur) Nicholas Winston Soames, eldest son of Baron Soames (Life Baron), — Clare Elizabeth Dido, *b* 1962; *ed* St Anne's Coll, Oxford.

Grandchildren of Col Charles Gilbert Carnegy, MVO, el son of late Maj-Gen Alexander Carnegy, CB (ante):—
Issue of late Rev Canon Patrick Charles Alexander Carnegy, *b* 1893, *d* 1969: *m* 1928, Joyce Eleanor, da of late W. Percy Townsley, of Roundhay, Leeds:—
Patrick Charles (5 The Causeway, Elsworth, Cambridge), *b* 1940; *ed* Rugby and Trin Hall, Camb (MA). —— Colin David (The Parsonage, Stapleford, Salisbury, Wilts), *b* 1942; *ed* Rugby, and Jesus Coll, Oxford (MA): *m* 1973, Rosemary Frances Deschamps, da of Saunders Edward Chamier, of Wadhurst, Sussex, and has issue living, Charles Alexander, *b* 1975, — Edward William, *b* 1977, — Francis Henry, *b* 1981, — Henrietta Claire, *b* 1983. —— Daphne Joyce (4 Ingram Rd, N2), *b* 1947; *ed* Nottingham Univ (BA).

Granddaughter of late Rev Preb Frederick William Carnegy, 3rd son of late Gen Alexander Carnegy, CB (ante):—
Issue of late Hector David Carnegy, LRAM, *b* 1913, *d* 1982: *m* 1942, Pamela Alice Burnell (9 Browning Av, Bournemouth, Dorset BH5 1NR), da of Henry Stafford Burnell Tubbs, of Winteradeen, Browning Av, Boscombe, Dorset:—
Alison Sandra Christabel, *b* 1944. *Residence* – 9 Browning Av, Bournemouth, Dorset BH5 1NR.

Grandson of late James Souter Carnegy (infra):—
Issue of late Colin Charles Macpherson Carnegy, *b* 1885, *d* 1931: *m* 1922, Mary Teresa, da of Michael Diaz Infante, of Léon, Mexico:—
Charles William, *b* 1923. *Residence* – Guadalajara, Mexico.

Grandchildren of late Charles Carnegy, yst son of Patrick Carnegy of Lour (*b* 1757) (ante):—
Issue of late James Souter Carnegy, *b* 1847, *d* 1915: *m* 1877, Jean Joyce, who *d* 1923, da of late Hon Charles Macpherson, of New Brunswick:—
James William Macpherson, *b* 1893. —— Marguerite Sophia Macpherson: *m* 1910, James Henry Nelson, who *d* 19—. *Residence* – Guadalajara, Mexico.
Issue of late Robert Bower Carnegy, *b* 1849, *d* 1936: *m* 1896, Fanny Jane, who *d* 1949, da of T. A. H. Dodd, formerly of Newcastle-upon-Tyne:—
Francis Anthony Roberts, *b* 1900; *m* 1925, Valentine, who *d* 1969, da of Theodore Taupmann, and has had issue living, †Derek Francis, *b* 1928; Lt-Cdr RN (ret): *m* 1961, Judith, who *d* 1991, only da of late David C. Herbert, and *d* 1993, leaving issue, Miles Bower *b* 1962, Angus (3 Hockley Cottages, Cheriton, Hants) *b* 1964; MB BS: *m* 1992, Mary-Ann Benson, da of Ronald Benson Malam, — Julian Roy (66 Cromford Way, New Malden, Surrey), *b* 1931: *m* 1957, Vivien, da of late Stewart Kay-Menzies, and has issue living, Christopher Roy *b* 1961, Diana Elizabeth *b* 1959: *m* 1983, David John Burchell, of 21 End Gdns, Hotspur Park, New Malden, Surrey. *Residence* – Greathed Manor, Lingfield, Surrey.

PREDECESSORS – (1) Sir JOHN Carnegie, Knt, Sheriff of Forfarshire, was *cr* Lord Lour 1639, and Earl of Ethie 1647, which titles after the Restoration he exchanged for those of *Lord Rosehill and Inglismaldie*, of Rosehill, and Earl of Northesk (peerage of Scotland), with precedence in 1639 and 1647 respectively, and with remainder to heirs male and of entail in his estate; *d* 1667; *s* by his son (2) DAVID, 2nd Earl; *d* 1677; *s* by his son (3) DAVID, 3rd Earl; *d* 1688; *s* by his son (4) DAVID, PC, 4th Earl; a Representative Peer, Lord of Police, and Sheriff of co Forfar; *d* 1729; *s* by his el son (5) DAVID, 5th Earl; *d* unmarried 1741; *s* by his brother (6) GEORGE, 6th Earl; an Adm of the White; *d* 1792; *s* by his son (7) WILLIAM, GCB, 7th Earl; a distinguished Adm, who was 3rd in command at the memorable battle of Trafalgar; *d* 1831; *s* by his son (8) WILLIAM HOPETOUN, 8th Earl; *b* 1794; *m* 1843, Georgina Maria, da of late Adm Hon Sir George Elliot, KCB (E Minto); *d* 1878; *s* by his son (9) GEORGE JOHN, 9th Earl, *b* 1843; a Representative Peer for Scotland: *m* 1865, Elizabeth, who *d* 1933, da of late Adm Sir George Elliot, KCB; *d* 1891; *s* by his el son (10) DAVID JOHN, 10th Earl, *b* 1865; a Representative Peer for Scotland: *m* 1894, Elizabeth Boyle, who *d* 1950, da of late Maj-Gen George Skene Hallowes: *d* 1921; *s* by his son (11) DAVID LUDOVIC GEORGE HOPETOUN, 11th Earl, *b* 1901; a Representative Peer for Scotland 1959-63: *m* 1st, 1923 (*m diss* 1928), Jessica, da of late F. A. Brown, of USA; 2ndly, 1929, Elizabeth, who *d* 1991, da of late Anthony A. Vlasto, formerly of Binfield Park, Bracknell, Berks, *d* 1963; *s* by his kinsman (12) JOHN DOUGLAS (son of late Lt-Col Hon Douglas George Carnegie, 2nd son of 9th Earl), 12th Earl; *b* 1895; 1914-18 War as Maj RFA (despatches): *m* 1920, Dorothy Mary, who *d* 1967, da of Col Sir William Robet Campion, KCMG, DSO (B Byron); *d* 1975; *s* by his yr son (13) ROBERT ANDREW, 13th Earl, *b* 1926; Cattle Breeder, Council Member British Charolais Cattle Soc, Author of *Dairy of an Island Glen*: *m* 1st, 1949, Jean Margaret, who *d* 1989, yr da of Capt John Duncan George MacRae (*see* M Bristol, 1985 Edn); 2ndly, 1989, Mrs Brownie Elizabeth Heimann, da of Scott Grimason, and widow of Carl L. Heimann; *d* 1994; *s* by his only surv son (14) DAVID JOHN MACRAE, 14th Earl and present peer.

NORTHFIELD, BARON (Chapman) (Life Baron 1975)

(WILLIAM) DONALD CHAPMAN, son of William Henry Chapman; *b* 25 Nov 1923; *ed* Barnsley Gram Sch, and Emmanuel Coll, Camb (MA); Snr Scholar of Emmanuel Coll Research into Agric and Econs, Camb 1943-46; Camb City Councillor 1945-47; Gen Sec Fabian Soc 1948-53; G Gibbon Fellow, Nuffield Coll, Oxford 1971-73; Visiting Fellow Centre for Contemporary European Studies, Univ of Sussex since 1973; Chm of HM Development Commnrs 1973-79, and of Telford New Town Development Corpn 1975-87; MP for Northfield Div of Birmingham (*Lab*) 1951-70; *cr Baron Northfield*, of Telford in co Shropshire (Life Baron) 1975.

Northington, Baron; title of Baron Henley on Roll of HL.

Northland, Viscount; son of Earl of Ranfurly

NORTHUMBERLAND, DUKE OF (Percy) (Duke GB 1766, Bt E 1660)

HENRY ALAN WALTER RICHARD PERCY, 11th Duke, and 14th Baronet; *b* 1 July 1953; *s* 1988; *ed* Eton, and Ch Ch Oxford.

Arms – Quarterly: 1st and 4th grand quarters, 1st and 4th counterquartered 1st and 4th or, a lion rampant azure; 2nd and 3rd gules, three lucies hauriant argent, *Lucy;* 2nd and 3rd azure, five fusils conjoined in fesse or, *Percy;* 2nd and 3rd grand quarters quarterly 1st and 4th or, three bars wavy gules, *Drummond;* 2nd and 3rd or, a lion's head erased within a double treasure flory counterflory gules, *Drummond, coat of augmentation.* **Crest** – On a chapeau gules, turned up ermine a lion statant, the tail extended, azure. **Supporters** – *Dexter,* a lion rampant azure; *sinister,* a lion rampant guardant or, ducally crowned of the last, gorged with a collar compony argent and azure.
Seats – Alnwick Castle, Northumberland NE66 1NG; Syon House, Brentford, Middx TW8 8JF. *Club* – Queen's.

Hope in God

BROTHERS LIVING

Lord RALPH GEORGE ALGERNON, *b* 16 Nov 1956; *ed* Eton, and Ch Ch, Oxford; land agent: *m* 1979, (Isobel) Jane M., da of John Walter Maxwell Miller Richard, of Edinburgh, and has issue living, George Dominic, *b* 4 May 1984, — Max Ralph, *b* 1990, — Catherine Sarah, *b* 1982, — Melissa Jane, *b* 1987. *Residence* – Chatton Park, Chatton, nr Alnwick, Northumberland NE66 5RA.
Lord James William Eustace, *b* 1965; *ed* Eton, and Bristol Univ.

SISTERS LIVING

Lady Caroline Mary, *b* 1947: *m* 1974, Count Pierre de Cabarrús, and has issue living, Chiara Therèse Cecilia, *b* 1974, — Diana Marie, *b* 1977. *Residences* – Syon House, Brentford, Middx TW8 8JF; Finca del Alamo, Nijar, Almeria, Spain.
Lady Victoria Lucy Diana, *b* 1949: *m* 1975, (John) Aidan Cuthbert (*see* Milnes Coates, Bt), and has issue living, David Hugh, *b* 1987, — Alice Rose, *b* 1978, — Lucy Caroline, *b* 1982, — Mary Belinda, *b* 1984. *Residence* – Abbeylands, Alnwick, Northumberland NE66 2JY.
Lady Julia Helen, *b* 1950: *m* 1983, Nicholas Robert Craig Harvey (*see* B Somers, colls, 1985 Edn), and has issue living, Christopher Hugh, *b* 1988, — Georgina Elizabeth, *b* 1986, — Laura Mary, *b* 1992. *Residence* – 7 Sibella Rd, SW4 6JA.

AUNT LIVING (*daughter of 8th Duke*)

Lady Elizabeth Ivy, OBE (*Dowager Duchess of Hamilton and Brandon*), *b* 1916; was a Train Bearer to The Queen at Coronation of King George VI; Chm of Lamp of Lothian Collegiate Trust since 1967, Board of Govs, Yehudi Menuhin Sch 1969-89, and Exec Cttee of Friends of St Mary's; DL E Lothian 1984-89; OBE (Civil) 1988: *m* 1937, 14th Duke of Hamilton and Brandon, who *d* 1973. *Residence* – North Port, Lennoxlove, Haddington, E Lothian.

WIDOWS LIVING OF SONS OF EIGHTH DUKE

Hon Clayre Campbell, 2nd da of 4th Baron Stratheden and Campbell, CBE, and formerly wife of Hon Nicholas Ridley, MP (later Baron Ridley of Liddesdale, PC) (*see* V Ridley): *m* 1979, as his 2nd wife, Lord Richard Charles Percy, who *d* 1989. *Residence* – 212 Lambeth Rd, SE1 7JY.
Mary Elizabeth, da of Ralph Lea: *m* 1955, Lord Geoffrey William Percy, who *d* 1984, and has issue (see colls infra). *Residence* – Barton House, Monkleigh, Bideford, N Devon EX39 5JX.

WIDOW LIVING OF TENTH DUKE

Lady Elizabeth Diana Montagu Douglas Scott (*Duchess of Northumberland*), da of 8th Duke of Buccleuch: *m* 1946, the 10th Duke, KG, GCVO, TD, PC, FRS, who *d* 1988. *Residences* – Friar's Well, Alnwick, Northumberland NE66 2LJ; Clive Lodge, Albury, Surrey GU5 9AB.

COLLATERAL BRANCHES LIVING

Issue of late Lord Richard Charles Percy, 3rd son of 8th Duke, *b* 1921, *d* 1989: *m* 1st, 1966, Sarah Jane Elizabeth, who *d* 1978, da of Petre Norton, of The Manor House, Whalton, Northumberland; 2ndly, 1979, Hon Clayre Campbell (*ante*), formerly wife of Hon Nicholas Ridley, MP (later Baron Ridley of Liddesdale, PC) (*see* V Ridley), and 2nd da of 4th Baron Stratheden and Campbell, CBE:—
(By 1st *m*) Algernon Alan, *b* 1969. —— Josceline Richard, *b* 1971.

Issue of late Lord Geoffrey William Percy, 4th and yst son of 8th Duke, *b* 1925, *d* 1984: *m* 1955, Mary Elizabeth (*ante*), da of Ralph Lea:—
Diana Ruth, *b* 1956.

Grandchildren of late Col Lord William Richard Percy, CBE, DSO (infra):—
    Issue of late Henry Edward Percy, *b* 1925, *d* 1985: *m* 1952, Eileen Ruth Morley (Ballygate House, Beccles, Suffolk NR34 9ND), da of late Lt-Col Wilmot-Smyth Caulfeild, MC (*see* V Charlemont, colls):—
George Robert, *b* 1953. —— James Edward Caulfeild, *b* 1958: *m* 1986 (*m diss* 1989), Gay P. Lovell-Badge, da of Mrs John Cator, and stepda of John Cator, of Woodbastwick, Norfolk; 2ndly, 1993, Hon Zara Jane Digby, only da of 12th Baron Digby. —— Lavinia Mary, *b* 1955. —— Susan Clare, *b* 1961: *m* 1990, George M. Woodruff, 2nd son of late James Woodruff, DFC, of Belcombe Court, Bradford-on-Avon, Wilts.

Issue of late Col Lord William Richard Percy, CBE, DSO, 5th son of 7th Duke, *b* 1882, *d* 1963: *m* 1922, Mary, who *d* 1984, da of late Capt George Sitwell Campbell Swinton:—
Gerald (The Granary, Nunnery Place, Thetford, Norfolk IP24 2PZ), *b* 1928: *m* 1st, 1954 (*m diss* 1975), Jennifer, da of John Brougham Home-Rigg, of Eastern Transvaal; 2ndly, 1983, Victoria, da of Dr Roger Henderson, MD, FRCP, and has issue living (by 1st *m*), Richard John (2 Cottesmore Gdns, W8 5PR), *b* 1957: *m* 1987, Deborah Patricia, yr da of Guy Norman, of Brockham, Surrey, and has issue living, Natasha Elizabeth *b* 1988, Sabrina Catherine *b* 1990, — Andrew Alan (2 Cottesmore Gdns, W8 5PR), *b* 1963: *m* 1988, LaNora Lynn, yr da of J. R. Scott, of Scottsdale, Arizona, USA, and has issue living, Ayden Jay *b* 1992, Callum Zane *b* 1994, — Katherine Susan (2 Cottesmore Gdns, W8 5PR), *b* 1955: *m* 1982 (*m diss* 1986), John Bentley, — Diana Mary (2 Cottesmore Gdns, W8 5PR), *b* 1965.

Issue of late Rt Hon Lord Eustace Sutherland Campbell Percy (7th son of 7th Duke), who was *cr Baron Percy of Newcastle* 1952 (see that title, ext 1958).

Grandchildren of late Algernon Hugh Heber-Percy, elder son of late Algernon Heber-Percy (*b* 1845), eldest son of late Algernon Charles Heber-Percy, son of late Rev Hon Hugh Heber-Percy, Bishop of Carlisle, 3rd son of 1st Earl of Beverley, 2nd son of 1st Duke:—
Issue of late Brigadier Algernon George William HEBER-PERCY, DSO, *b* 1904, *d* 1961: *m* 1939 (*m diss* 1950), Daphne Wilma Kenyon, da of late Eustace Bowles (*see* E Macclesfield, colls):—
Algernon Eustace Hugh (Hodnet Hall, Hodnet, Market Drayton, Shropshire TF9 3NN), *b* 1944; *ed* Harrow; late Lt, Grenadier Guards; DL Shropshire 1986, High Sheriff 1987: *m* 1966, Hon Margaret Jane Lever, yst da of 3rd Viscount Leverhulme, KG, and has issue living, Algernon Thomas Lever *b* 1984, — Emily Jane, *b* 1969, — Lucy Ann, *b* 1972, — Sophie Daphne, *b* 1980. —— Zara Mary, *b* 1940: *m* 1st, 1961 (*m diss* 1980), Gavin Nicholas Tait; 2ndly, 1980, Humphrey Swire, and has issue living (by 1st *m*) Lucinda Clare, *b* 1962: *m* 1983 (*m diss* 1994), James Henderson, son of Lt-Col James B. Henderson, and has issue living, Eliza Jennifer Jane *b* 1992, — Arabella Kate Louise, *b* 1965. —— Jane Maude, *b* 1942: *m* 1965, Maj Harold Antony McArthur Pyman, Life Gds, of Windwhistle, Sampford Arundel, Som, son of late Gen Sir Harold English Pyman, GBE, KCB, DSO, and has issue living, Richard Anthony, *b* 1968, — Victoria Clare, *b* 1966.
Issue of late Lt-Col Cyril Hugh Reginald HEBER-PERCY, DSO, MC, *b* 1905, *d* 1989: *m* 1st, 1933 (*m diss* 1944), Anne, yst da of late Charles Tuller Garland, of Moreton Morrell, Warwicks; 2ndly, 1944 (*m diss* 1959), Diana, only da of late Raymond Augustus Edward Radclyffe, of Lew, Oxon; 3rdly, 1959, Pamela (Woodlands Cottage, Ibstone, Bucks), elder da of Kinmont Willie Armstrong-Lushington-Tulloch, of Shanbolard, Moyard, co Galway, widow of Capt Thomas Ansell Fairhurst, The Life Guards, and formerly wife of Maj (George) Derek Cooper, MC, late The Life Guards:—
(By 1st *m*) Alan Cyril (Eyford Knoll, Upper Slaughter, Glos), *b* 1935; *ed* Eton: *m* 1st, 1962, Susan Mary, only da of late Michael Charles St John Hornby (*see* E Dudley, colls, 1985 Edn), and formerly wife of John George Vanderbilt Henry, Marquess of Blandford (later 11th Duke of Marlborough); 2ndly, 1980, Mrs Charlotte Gwynne, 2nd da of late Lt Cdr Sir Cyril Hugh Kleinwort, RNVR (*see* Kleinwort, Bt, colls), and has issue living (by 1st *m*), Larissa Anne, *b* 1968. —— William David, MBE (Lower Cwmgwannon, Clyro, Hay-on-Wye, Hereford), *b* 1939; *ed* Eton; late Assist Adviser, Aden; MBE (Civil) 1966: *m* 1969, Christine, da of Terence Horatio Gates, and has issue living, Peter Hugh, *b* 1971, — Robin Virginia, *b* 1969. —— (By 2nd *m*) Cyril Raymond (Folly Farmhouse, Farmington, Glos), *b* 1945; *ed* Eton: *m* 1st, 1971, Mrs Heather Joan Miller; 2ndly, 1988, Mrs Ann Elizabeth Francis, da of late John Douglas Rowley, of Bristol, Avon, and has issue living (by 1st *m*), Tamara Joan, *b* 1972, — Zara Ana, *b* 1976.
Issue of late Robert Vernon HEBER-PERCY, *b* 1911, *d* 1987: *m* 1st, 1942 (*m diss* 1947), Ann Jennifer Evelyn Elizabeth, only child of Sir Geoffrey Storrs Fry, 1st Bt, KCB, CVO; 2ndly, 1985, Lady Dorothy Lygon, yst da of 7th Earl Beauchamp, KG:—
(By 1st *m*) Victoria Gala, *b* 1943: *m* 1960, Peter Zinovieff, and has issue living, Leo, *b* 1963: *m* 1988, Annabelle Charlotte, only da of Hon Simon Dawson Eccles (*see* V Eccles), and has issue living, Kyril *b* 1991, Aloysha *b* 1988, — Kolinka, *b* 1966, — Sofka, *b* 1961; has issue living (by Vassilis Papadimitriou), Anna Alexandra *b* 1992. *Residences* – 50 Stevenage Rd, SW6; Faringdon House, Faringdon, Berks.

Grandchildren of late Josceline Reginald HEBER-PERCY (infra):—
Issue of late Cdr David Josceline Algernon HEBER-PERCY, DSC, RN, *b* 1909, *d* 1971: *m* 1942, Olivia Mary (Twysden Cottage, Kilndown, Cranbrook, Kent), yr da of late R. W. O'Brien, of Drogheda:—
Michael David (Beechenwood Farm, Hillside, Odiham, Hants), *b* 1943; AADip Hons; ARIBA: *m* 1965, Sarah, yr da of late Alastair Gilmour, and has issue living, Colin Michael (4 Hauteville Court Gdns, Stamford Brook, W6), *b* 1968, — Paul David (Cottage Farm, Old Milverton, Leamington Spa, Warwicks), *b* 1970. —— Carol Margaret Katherine, *b* 1947: *m* 1st, 1970 (*m diss* 1974), Robert Ward Woolner; 2ndly, 1974, Richard Edward Warcup Ashby, Dip Arch RIBA, of Empshott Lodge, Liss, Hants, and has issue living (by 2nd *m*), Sam David Frederick, *b* 1981, — Daisy Katharine, *b* 1974, — Poppy Elizabeth Patricia, *b* 1976, — Holly Patricia, *b* 1979. —— Angela Mary, *b* 1949: *m* 1970, Henry Robert Boileau Fawcett, of Delmonden Manor, Hawkhurst, Kent, and has issue living, Joseph Dylan, *b* 1983, — Emily, *b* 1972, — Kate, *b* 1975.

Granddaughter of late Algernon HEBER-PERCY (*b* 1845) (ante):—
Issue of late Josceline Reginald HEBER-PERCY, *b* 1880, *d* 1964: *m* 1904, Katharine Lousia Victoria, who *d* 1964, da of late Lord Algernon Malcolm Arthur Percy:—
Dorothy Elizabeth (*Elizabeth, Lady Walker-Okeover*) *b* 1913: *m* 1938, Col Sir Ian Peter Andrew Munro Walker-Okeover, 3rd Bt, DSO, TD, JP, who *d* 1982.

Grandsons of late Alan William HEBER-PERCY (infra):—
Issue of late Capt Hugh Alan HEBER-PERCY, OBE, *b* 1897, *d* 1976: *m* 1926, Monica Violet, who *d* 1977, da of late Edmond Waterton Coningsby Erskine (E Mar and Kellie, colls), and widow of Lt-Col G. D. Maynard:—
Robin Erskine (Box 1232, Somerset West, CP 7130, S Africa), *b* 1927; *ed* Hilton Coll, Natal; 1945 War with S African Engineer Corps: *m* 1953, Ann, da of John Gaw. —— Philip Reginald (14 Edgecliffe Park, Bartle Rd, Gillitts, Natal 3610), *b* 1929; *ed* Hilton Coll, Natal; Chartered Accountant: *m* 1952, Cherie, da of Johannes van Wyk, and has issue living, Robyn, *b* 1954: *m* 1976, Anthony David Burgess, of 28 Carnoustie Rd, Muswell Hill, Pietermaritzburg, son of Roy Burgess, and has issue living, Trevor *b* 1983, Bruce *b* 1985, — Julia, *b* 1956: *m* 1993, Andries Burger Laubscher, of 15 Gavin Av, Pine Park 2194, son of Nicholaas Laubscher, — and two adopted das, Renée, *b* 1959: *m* 1981, Dr Andrew Scogings, of 507 Roper St, Baileys Muckleneuk, Pretoria 0181, son of Prof David Scogings, — Kim, *b* 1961: *m* 1985, Peter Adie, of Wedgewood, PO Box 676, Howick 3290, son of Martin Adie. —— John Kellie (34 Kingswood Dr, Chirnside Park, Victoria 3116, Australia), *b* 1935; *ed* Hilton Coll, Natal: *m* 1961, Rosalind Marion, da of late W. H. Gathercole, and has issue living, Gillian Dorothy, *b* 1965: *m* 1987, Michael Alan Heber-Percy (who assumed the surname of Heber-Percy in lieu of his patronymic DIXON), — Helen Marjorie, *b* 1968.

Grandsons of late Algernon Charles Heber-Percy (ante):—
Issue of late Alan William HEBER-PERCY, *b* 1865, *d* 1946: *m* 1st, 1893, Hon Susan Alice Portman, who *d* 1933, da of 2nd Viscount Portman; 2ndly, 1936, Mabel, who *d* 1953, da of late Sir William Darracott, and widow of E. Herbert Hinds:—
(By 1st *m*) Bryan, *b* 1903; formerly Capt RA: *m* 1936, Etelka, da of Istvan Kuiti, of Hungary. —— Peter, OBE, *b* 1908; *ed* Wellington Coll; is Lt Col 55th Anti-Aircraft Regt RA (TA); 1939-45 War in Middle East and Italy (OBE); OBE, (Mil) 1945: *m* 1st, 1930 (*m diss* 1947), (Josephine) Sylvia, who *d* 1990, el da of late Brig-Gen Cyril Randall Crofton, CBE, of Trobridge,

Crediton; 2ndly, 1947, Elsa Maria, da of late Giamcomo Nission, of Pisa, Italy, and has issue living, (by 1st *m*) (Sylvia) Venetia, *b* 1932: *m* 1953, David Gerald Stern, of Bednall Hill, Bednall, Staffs, son of late Lt-Col Sir Albert Gerald Stern, KBE, CMG (Orr-Lewis, Bt), and has had issue, Mark David Robin *b* 1955 *d* 1981, Sylvia Louise *b* 1957, — (Susan) Deirdre, *b* 1938: *m* 1958, Anthony Benedict Xavier Fenwick (*see* B Lilford, colls), — (by 2nd *m*) Sandra Caroline, *b* 19—. *Residence* – Il Gualdo, Punta Ala, Grossetto, Italy.

Grandchildren of late Alan William HEBER-PERCY (ante):—
Issue of late Group Capt John HEBER-PERCY, RAF (ret), *b* 1910, *d* 1975: *m* 1st, 1940 (*m diss* 1949), Eve Robertson; 2ndly, 1950, Marie Elsie Teixeira de Mattos, who *d* 19—:—
(By 1st *m*) *Rev* Christopher John (19 Bellfield Av, Holderness Rd, Kingston-upon-Hull HU8 9DS); *b* 1941; ordained priest 1969: *m* 1964, Lyndis Elizabeth, yst da of Rt Rev John Henry Lawrence Phillips, Lord Bishop of Portsmouth, and has issue living, William John, *b* 1965, — Thomas Henry, *b* 1967, — Anna, *b* 1970. —— Susan Elizabeth, *b* 1943: *m* 1965, Karl John Sabbagh, of 76 Sheen Park, Richmond, Surrey TW9 1UP, and has issue living, Jonathan Christopher, *b* 1978, — Isabella Mary, *b* 1972, — Susanna Jane *b* 1975. —— Josceline Mary, *b* 1946: *m* 1969, Richard Newell, FRCS, of 11 Windsor Terrace, Penarth, S Glamorgan CF64 1AA, and has issue living, Adam Richard Eric, *b* 1971, — Benjamin Rhodri, *b* 1972, — Victoria Claire, *b* 1975, — Charlotte Jessica Eve, *b* 1981.

Granddaughter of late Rev Henry Percy, son of late Rt Rev Hon Hugh Percy, Bishop of Carlisle (ante):—
Issue of late Alfred Percy, *b* 1850, *d* 1907: *m* 1st, 1878, Ada Elizabeth, who *d* 1898, da of late Rev Daniel Packard; 2ndly, 1899, Mary Holmesdale Hyland (who *d* 1962, having *m* 2ndly, 19—, John Kennedy):—
(By 2nd *m*) Mary (19 Cross Rd, Myrtle Bank, S Aust 5064), *b* 1903: *m* 1930, Hugh Bernard Doherty, who *d* 1974, and has issue living, Michael Dominic (104 Beasley St, Torrens, ACT 2607), *b* 1936: *m* 1960, Patricia Mary Hassett, and has issue living, Anthony Michael *b* 1961: *m* 1981, Narelle Christine Sproule (and has issue living, Stephen Anthony *b* 1992), Matthew Michael *b* 1967: *m* 1991, Belinda Maria Hill, Therese Marie *b* 1964: *m* 1st, 1985 (*m diss* 1992), Neil Morgan; 2ndly, 1993, Scott Alan-Boyd McCrohon (and has issue living (by 1st *m*), Nicholas James *b* 1985, Alicia Marie *b* 1988), Noeline Elizabeth *b* 1965: *m* 1983, Colin Andrew Jacob (and has issue living, David Keith *b* 1983, Michael Patrick *b* 1985, Philip John *b* 1991, Naomi Margaret *b* 1988, Rebecca Mary *b* 1993), Louise Gerardine *b* 1968: *m* 1993, Peter Wilhelm Merkel, Catherine Majella *b* 1971, — Brian Hugh (34 Lutana Crescent, Mitchell Park, S Australia 5043), *b* 1938: *m* 1961, Margaret Anne Curran, and has issue living, Andrew Bernard *b* 1962: *m* 1992, Lynn Paul Kemmett (and has issue living, Elizabeth Michele *b* 1994), Michael James *b* 1965: *m* 1991, Moira Teresa Richardson (and has had issue, Mary Teresa *b* and *d* 1993), Joseph Brian *b* 1968, Paul Vincent *b* 1973, Christopher Philip *b* 1975, Catherine Mary *b* 1969: *m* 1990, Robert Leslie Maher (and has issue living, Patrick Leslie *b* 1991, Carmel Margaret *b* 1993), — Maire Rosaleen, *b* 1931: *m* 1957, John William Sunners, of 6 Travers St, Sturt, S Australia 5047, and has issue living, John Bernard *b* 1958: *m* 1980, Helen Maree O'Neill (and has issue living, Damien John *b* 1981, Kylie Maree *b* 1980), Timothy Peter *b* 1959: *m* 1993, Kylie Loudon, David Peter *b* 1961: *m* 1983, Helen Maree Cassidy (and has issue living, Meghann Emily *b* 1988, Nadine Alexandra *b* 1991), Paul Gerard *b* 1963: *m* 1988, Gail Barbara Darling (and has issue living, Maxwell John *b* 1994, Samantha Cara *b* 1989, Kristy Lea *b* 1990, Nicole Mary *b* 1992), Kevin Patrick *b* 1964: *m* 1986, Sherree Michele Coleman (and has issue living, Benjamin William *b* 1989, Abby Louise *b* 1989), Anne Therese *b* 1962 (has issue living, Jessica Rose *b* 1985), Carmel Elizabeth *b* 1962: *m* 1985, Peter David Button (and has issue living, Stephanie Brianna *b* 1991), Claire Louise *b* 1966: *m* 1991, Malcolm McGlashan, Maureen Patricia *b* 1973, — Denise Margaret, *b* 1932: *m* 1956, Leon Thomas Grealy, of 1 Bessie St, Dover Gdns, S Australia 5048, and has issue living, Stephen Matthew *b* 1958: *m* 1979, Heather Joy Rana (and has issue living, Patrick Matthew *b* 1985, Peter John *b* 1987, Christine Anne *b* 1982), Bernadette Anne *b* 1957, Leonie Therese *b* 1962: *m* 1988, Martin Denis Welsh, — Noeline Carmel, *b* 1934: *m* 1957, James Carr, of 3 Short St, Glen Waverley, Victoria 3150, and has had issue, Michael Joseph *b* 1957: *m* 1981, Jennifer Iris Robson (and has issue living, Reuben James *b* 19—, Jemima Rose *b* 1982, Hayley Grace *b* 1983), Damian Peter *b* 1962 (has issue living, by Robyn Patricia Armitage, Ella Rose *b* 1992), Bernard James *b* 1965, Christopher Patrick *b* 1970, Debra Mary *b* 1959: *m* 1993, Ian Anthony Neil, Gerardine Frances *b* 1960: *m* 1990, Geoffrey John Hanson (and has issue living, Merrily Esther *b* 1991, Ginger Bridie *b* (twin) 1991), Paula Maree *b* 1963: *m* 1988, Daniel John Wain (and has issue living, Patrick James *b* 1993, Lewis Peter *b* (twin) 1993), Marita Louise, *b* 1967: *m* 1988 (*m diss* 1993), Robert La Greca, Natalie Ann *b* 1968, Melissa Jane *b* and *d* 1973, — Frances Josephine, *b* 1944: *m* 1st, 1968, Leon Joseph Pasquarelli, who *d* 1979; 2ndly, 1991, John Arthur Dickins, of 6 Pinkwood Drive, Bellevue Park, Southport, Qld 4215, and has issue living (by 1st *m*), Sergio *b* 1975, Maria *b* 1969, Sophia *b* 1971.

Grandchildren of late Josceline Hugh Percy, son of late Rev Henry Percy (ante):—
Issue of late Josceline Richard Percy, *b* 1894, *d* 1971: *m* 1929, Mary, who *d* 1964, da of Harold Nicholson, of Oak House, Farnworth, Bolton:—
Hugh Edward, *b* 1938; *ed* Gonville and Caius Coll, Camb (BA), and Manchester Coll of Commerce; Associate of Library Assocn: *m* 1969, Barbara, only da of —Mulholland, of Lancaster. *Residence* – —. —— Eleanor Mary, *b* 1940: *m* 1962, James Rolf Adams, of 1170 Keeler Av, Berkeley, Cal, USA, and has issue living, Katherine Charlotte, *b* 1963, — Ruth Susannah, *b* 1965.

PREDECESSORS – (1) ALGERNON Seymour, 7th Duke of Somerset (see † infra), was *cr Baron Warkworth*, of Warkworth Castle, co Northumberland and *Earl of Northumberland* (peerage of Great Britain) 1749, with remainder to Sir Hugh Smithson, 4th Bt (see * infra), who in 1740 *m* Lady Elizabeth, the Duke's only surviving child; *d* 1750; *s* by his son-in-law (2) *Sir* Hugh Smithson, KG, 2nd Earl; assumed by Act of Parliament 1750 the surname of Percy, in lieu of his patronymic; *cr Earl Percy* and *Duke of Northumberland* (peerage of Great Britain) 1766, and *Lord Lovaine, Baron of Alnwick* (peerage of Great Britain) 1784, with remainder to his 2nd son Algernon; *d* 1786; *s* by his el son (3) HUGH, KG, 2nd Duke; *d* 1817; *s* by his el son (4) HUGH, KG, 3rd Duke; was Viceroy of Ireland, Lord-Lieut and Vice Adm of Northumberland, and Chancellor of Univ of Cambridge, etc; *dsp* 1847; *s* by his brother (5) ALGERNON, KG, PC, 4th Duke; a distinguished Adm; *cr Baron Prudhoe*, of Prudhoe Castle, co Northumberland (peerage of United Kingdom) 1816; was First Lord of the Admiralty 1852; *d* 1865, when the Barony of Prudhoe became extinct, the Barony of Percy devolved upon the 7th Duke of Atholl, and the Baronetcy, the Earldom of Percy, and Dukedom reverted to his kinsman (6) GEORGE, PC, 5th Duke, el son of Algernon, 2nd Baron Lovaine (ante) who had in 1790 been *cr Earl of Beverley* (peerage of Great Britain); *b* 1778; sat as MP for Beeralston 1808-30; was a Lord of the Treasury 1804-6, and Capt of Yeomen of the Guard 1842-6: *m* 1801, Louisa Harcourt, da of Hon James Archibald Stuart-Wortley (E Wharncliffe); *d* 1867; *s* by his son (7) ALGERNON GEORGE, KG, PC, 6th Duke, *b* 1810; was a Lord of the Admiralty 1858, Vice-Pres of Board of Trade 1859, and Lord-Privy Seal 1878-80; MP for Beeralston (C) 1831-2 and for N Northumberland 1852-65; Lord-Lieut of Northumberland, and of co and city of Newcastle-on-Tyne: *m* 1845, Louisa, who *d* 1890, da of late Henry Drummond, of Albury Park, Surrey; *d* 1899; *s* by his el son (8) HENRY GEORGE (who in 1887 had in his father's lifetime been called to the House of Lords in the Barony of Lovaine), 7th Duke, *b* 1846: *m* 1868, Lady Edith Campbell, who *d* 1913, da of 8th Duke of Argyll, KG, KT; *d* 1918; *s* by his el surviving son (9) ALAN IAN, KG, CBE, MVO, 8th Duke, *b* 1880; Pres of Roy Institution; Lord-Lieut of Northumberland 1918-30: *m* 1911, Lady Helen Magdalen Gordon-Lennox, GCVO, CBE, JP, who *d* 1965, da of 7th Duke of Richmond; *d* 1930; *s* by his el son (10) HENRY GEORGE ALAN, 9th Duke, *b* 1912; Lieut Grenadier Guards; *ka* 1940; *s* by his brother (11) HUGH ALGERNON, 10th Duke, KG, GCVO, TD, PC, FRS, *b* 1914, a Lord-in-Waiting to HM May to June 1940, Lord Steward of HM Household 1973-88, Pres N Area Royal British Legion 1957-84, Hon Treas Royal Nat Life-Boat Inst, Co Councillor Northumberland 1944-55, Alderman 1955-57, Member Hill Farming Advisry Cttee for England and Wales 1946-60, and of other Nat Forestry and Agric Cttees, Pres Court of Durham Univ 1956-63, Master of Percy Fox Hounds 1950-88 Chancellor Univ of Newcastle upon Tyne 1964-88; 1939-45 War as Capt RA, Capt Northumberland Hus (TARO) 1949-64, Hon Col 7th Bn RNF 1948-70, Dep Hon Col Northumbrian Vols TAVR 1971-75, Hon Col 6th (V) Bn RRF 1975-88, Pres TAVR Assocn for N England 1968-71: *m* 1946, Lady Elizabeth Diana Montagu Douglas Scott, da of 8th Duke of Buccleuch; *d* 1988; *s* by his eldest son (12) HENRY ALAN WALTER RICHARD,

11th Duke and present peer; also Earl of Northumberland, Earl Percy, Earl of Beverley, Baron Percy, Baron Warkworth, and Lord Lovaine, Baron of Alnwick.

†(1) ALGERNON Seymour, Earl of Hertford (afterwards 7th Duke of Somerset); summoned to Parliament 1722 by writ on death of his mother, Lady Elizabeth Percy, da and heir of 11th Earl of Northumberland in the erroneous belief that he had inherited the Barony of Percy (cr 1299), which was attainted in 1406, and by sitting in 1723 a barony of writ was thereby created, and he became *Baron Percy* (cr 1723); s by his da (2-5) *Lady* ELIZABETH, who m the 1st Duke of Northumberland (ante), the Barony being merged in the Dukedom until the death of 4th Duke in 1865, when it devolved upon his grand-nephew (6-10) JOHN JAMES HUGH HENRY Stewart-Murray, 7th Duke of Atholl (grandson of Lady Emily Frances Percy, sister of 5th Duke of Northumberland who m the 1st Baron Glenlyon); d 1917, when the Barony became merged in the Dukedom of Atholl until the death of the 9th Duke 1957, when it passed to (11) the 10th Duke of Northumberland (ante).

*(1) HUGH Smithson, a zealous royalist, cr *Baronet* 1660; d 1670; s by his son (2) *Sir* JEROME, 2nd Bt; d 1684; s by his son (3) *Sir* HUGH, 3rd Bt; conformed to doctrines of the Church of England; he having been born a Roman Catholic; d 1729; s by his son (4) HUGH, 4th Bt, who was *cr Duke of Northumberland* (ante).

NORTON, BARON (Adderley) (Baron UK 1878)

Addere legi justitiam decus

It is an honour to add justice to law

JAMES NIGEL ARDEN ADDERLEY, 8th Baron; b 2 June 1947; s 1993; ed Downside: m 1971, Jacqueline Julie, el da of Guy W. Willett, of Sundial House, 24a High St, Alderney, CI, and has issue.

Arms – Argent, on a bend azure, three mascles of the field. **Crest** – On a chapeau azure, turned up ermine, a stork argent. **Supporters** – On either side a stork argent, gorged with a chain or, pendent therefrom an escutcheon azure, charged with a mascle also argent. *Residence* – 1 Picaterre, Alderney, CI.

SON LIVING

Hon EDWARD JAMES ARDEN, b 19 Oct 1982.

DAUGHTER LIVING

Hon Olivia Fleur Elizabeth, b 1979.

BROTHER LIVING

Hon Nigel John, b 1950; ed Downside, and RMA Sandhurst; Maj Life Guards: m 1991, Teresa M. A., da of Maj John Mills, of Vyse House, Winkfield, Berks, and has issue living, Fleur Charlotte Alice, b 1992.

AUNTS LIVING (daughters of 6th Baron)

Hon Rosemary Etheldreda, b 1913: m 1949, Rev John Paul Drake, and has issue living, Simon Francis, b 1956: m 1981, Vanessa, da of Robert Sewell, of Oaklands, Brundall, Norwich, — Catherine Elisabeth, b 1950: m 1974, John William Grace. *Residence* – 3 The Cloisters, Welwyn Garden City, Herts AL8 6DU.

Hon Elisabeth Joan, b 1919: m 1943, Professor (Alexander) Colin Patton Campbell, MB, ChB, MSc, FRCP (Edin), FRCPath, and has had issue, Andrew Colin, b 1943; MA, BM, BCh, D Phil, MRCPath; d 1990, — Richard Hubert Alexander (18 Hillington Rd, Sale, Cheshire), b 1946; MB, ChB, FRCP (Edin), FRCP (Lond): m 1976, Candace, da of Clifford W. Richardson, of Stratford St Andrew, Suffolk, — Rosamund Elizabeth, b 1950; MA Oxon. *Residence* – The Priory House, Ascott-under-Wychwood, Oxon.

Hon Mary, b 1922; European War 1939-45 as 3rd Officer WRNS: m 1950, Hugh Montgomery Campbell, who d 1980, son of late Rt Rev and Rt Hon Bishop Henry Colville Montgomery Campbell, KCVO, MC, PC, DD, formerly Lord Bishop of London, and has issue living, Philip Henry, b 1951; PhD, MSc: m 1980, Judith Margaret, who d 1992, da of Joseph William Yelton, of 7 Park Lane, Earls Colne, Colchester, — Elisabeth Mary, b 1954; — Veronica, b 1958: m 1987, Jeffrey Mark Berman, eldest son of Dolph L. Berman, of Cincinnati, Ohio, USA. *Residence* – 16 Ashworth Rd, W9.

WIDOW LIVING OF SEVENTH BARON

BETTY MARGARET (*Dowager Baroness Norton*), only da of late James McKee Hannah, of Domaine de Fontvieille, Aix-en-Provence, France: m 1946, Major the 7th Baron, OBE, who d 1993. *Residence* – Fillongley Hall, Coventry.

COLLATERAL BRANCH LIVING

Issue of late Group Capt Hon Michael Charles Adderley, OBE, AFC, yr son of 6th Baron, b 1917, d 1992: m 1953, Margrethe Anne, MRCVS, who d 1986, only da of Karl Gerhardt Ornbo:—

Charles Henry, b 1954: m 1982, Jane E—, da of S—Atherton, of Ilkley, W Yorks. —— Anthony John, b 1955. —— David Michael, b 1962. —— Jane Margrethe, b 1957: m 1982, Kenneth Blackburn, of Glen Haven, Long Moss Lane, Whitestake, Preston, Lancs PR4 4XN, and has issue living, Emma Margrethe, b 1986, — Sara Elisabeth, b (twin) 1986.

PREDECESSORS – (1) *Rt Hon Sir* CHARLES BOWYER Adderley, KCMG, el son of late Charles Clement Adderley, of Hams Hall, Warwickshire, and Norton, co Stafford; b 1814; Pres of Board of Health, and Vice-Pres of Committee of Privy Council for Education 1858-9, Under-Sec of State for Colonies 1866-8, and Pres of Board of Trade 1874-8; MP for N Staffordshire (C) 1841-78; cr *Baron Norton*, of Norton-on-the-Moors, co Stafford (peerage of United Kingdom) 1878: m 1842, Hon Julia Anne Eliza, who d 1887, da of 1st Baron Leigh; d 1905; s by his son (2) CHARLES LEIGH, 2nd Baron; b 1846: m 1870, Caroline, who d 1922, da of Sir Alexander Dixie, 10th Bt; d 1925; s by his el son (3) RALPH BOWYER, 3rd Baron, b 1872: m 1899, Mary Louisa, who d 1939, da of Robert Watson, formerly of Ballydarton, co Carlow, and widow of Inglis Brady; d 1933; s by his brother (4) RONALD WOLSTAN FLEETWOOD, 4th Baron, b 1885: m 1931, Hylda, who d 1950, da of late Robert William Tovey, of Cheltenham, and widow of Hilary George Dunbar, of Glasgow; d 1944; s by his uncle (5) HENRY ARDEN (2nd son of 1st Baron), 5th Baron; b 1854: m 1881, Grace, who d 1944, da of late William Bruce Stopford-Sackville, of Drayton House, Thrapston; d 1945; s by his only son (6) HUBERT BOWYER ARDEN, 6th Baron; b 1886; a Lay Guardian of the Sanctuary of Our Lady of Walsingham, Norfolk: m 1912, Elizabeth, who d 1952, da of late William John Birkbeck, of Stratton Strawless Hall,

Norfolk; *d* 1961; *s* by his el son **(7)** JOHN ARDEN, OBE, 7th Baron; *b* 1915; 1939-45 War in N Africa, Sicily and Italy as Major RE (despatches); Assist Master Oundle Sch; a Lay Guardian of the Sanctuary of Our Lady of Walsingham: *m* 1946, Betty Margaret, only da of late James McKee Hannah, of Domaine de Fontvieille, Aix-en-Provence, France; *d* 1993; *s* by his elder son **(8)** JAMES NIGEL ARDEN, 8th Baron and present peer.

NORWICH, VISCOUNT (Cooper) (Viscount UK 1952)

JOHN JULIUS COOPER, CVO, 2nd Viscount; *b* 15 Sept 1929; *s* 1954; *ed* Eton, and at New Coll, Oxford (BA honours 1952); late RN; writer and broadcaster; HM Foreign Ser 1952-64; Third Sec, British Embassy, Belgrade 1956-57, and Second Sec, British Embassy, Beirut 1957-60; CVO 1993: *m* 1st, 1952 (*m diss* 1985), Anne Frances May, el da of late Hon Sir Bede Edmund Hugh Clifford, GCMG, CB, MVO (*see* B Clifford of Chudleigh, colls); 2ndly, 1989, Hon Mrs Mary Philipps, twin da of 1st Baron Sherfield, GCB, GCMG, and has issue by 1st *m*.

Arms – Or three lions rampant gules on a chief azure a portcullis chained between two fleur-de-lys of the first. **Crest** – On the battlements of a tower argent a bull passant sable armed and unguled or. **Supporters** – On either side a unicorn argent gorged with a collar with chain reflexed over the back or pendent from the collar of the dexter a portcullis chained and from that of the sinister a fleur-de-lys both gold. *Residence* – 24 Blomfield Road, W9 1AD. *Clubs* – Beefsteak, Garrick.

SON LIVING (By 1st marriage)

I hate and I love

Hon JASON CHARLES DUFF BEDE, *b* 27 Oct 1959. *Residence* – 14 Alexander St, W2 5NT.

DAUGHTER LIVING (By 1st marriage)

Hon Alice Clare Antonia Opportune (Artemis) COOPER, *b* 1953; writer; prefers to be known as Cooper: *m* 1986, Antony James Beevor, son of late John Grosvenor Beevor, OBE, of 161 Fulham Rd, SW3, and has issue living, Adam John Cosmo, *b* 1993, — Nella, *b* 1990. *Residence* – 54 St Maur Rd, SW6.

PREDECESSOR – **(1)** *Rt Hon Sir* ALFRED DUFF COOPER, GCMG, DSO, PC, son of late Sir Alfred Cooper, FRCS (D Fife); *b* 1890; appointed Private Sec to Parliamentary Under-Sec of State for Foreign Affairs, 1922; was Financial Sec, War Office 1928-29, and again (in National Govt) 1931-33, Financial Sec to Treasury 1934-35, Sec of State for War 1935-37, First Lord of the Admiralty 1937-38, Min of Information 1940-41, Chancellor of Duchy of Lancaster 1941-43, British Envoy to French National Committee in N Africa 1943-44, and Ambassador Extraor and Plen to France 1944-47; European War 1914-19 as Lieut Grenadier Guards (despatches, DSO); sat as MP for Oldham (*C*) 1924-29, and for St George's Div of Westminster 1931-45; *cr Viscount Norwich*, of Aldwick, co Sussex (peerage of United Kingdom) 1952: *m* 1919, Lady Diana Olivia Winifred Maud Manners, who *d* 1986, da of 8th Duke of Rutland; *d* 1954; *s* by his only son **(2)** JOHN JULIUS, 2nd Viscount and present peer.

Nottingham, Earl of, see Earl of Winchilsea and Nottingham.

NUGENT, BARONY OF (Nugent) (Extinct 1973)

WIDOW LIVING OF FIRST BARON

ROSALIE (*Baroness Nugent*) (40 Bramerton St, SW3), da of late Brig-Gen Hon Charles Strathavon Heathcote-Drummond-Willoughby, CB, CMG (*see* Bs Willoughby de Eresby, colls): *m* 1935, the 1st Baron, who *d* 1973, when the title became ext.

Nugent Baron (Austria), see Earl of Westmeath colls.

NUNBURNHOLME, BARON (Wilson) (Baron UK 1906)

For laws and kings

BEN CHARLES WILSON, 4th Baron; *b* 16 July 1928; *s* 1974; *ed* Eton; Maj (ret) R Horse Gds: *m* 1958 (*m diss* 19—), Ines Dolores Jeanne, da of HE Gerard Walravens, of Brussels (sometime Belgian Ambassador to Turkey), and has issue.

𝕬rms – Or, an ancient ship sable, on a chief azure three ducal coronets of the first. Crest – Between two ducal coronets or a demi-wolf sable, holding between the paws a like coronet. Supporters – On either side a Benedictine nun, holding in the anterior hand a rosary, all proper.
Residence – Shillinglee Park, Chiddingfold, Sussex.

DAUGHTERS LIVING

Hon Lorraine Mary Charmaine Nicole, *b* 1959.
Hon Tatiana, *b* 1960: *m* 1988, Nigel L. Dent, of Lake Cottage, Shillinglee Park, Chiddingfold, Sussex, 2nd son of Robin Dent, of Olivers, Painswick, Glos, and has issue living, Frederick, *b* 1989, — Harry Barnaby Nigel, *b* 1991.
Hon Ysabelle, *b* 1963.
Hon Ines Monica (twin), *b* 1963: *m* 1988, Anthony Richard Leslie Garton, yst son of late Anthony Charles Garton, and has issue living, Tristan John Leslie, *b* 1990.

BROTHER LIVING

Hon CHARLES THOMAS (Banco Fonseca y Burnay, Portimao, Portugal; *Club* – White's), *b* 27 May 1935; *ed* Eton and Landgrove Sch; was a Page of Honour to HM King George VI 1950-52; Member of Stock Exchange 1956-66: *m* 1969 (*m diss* 19—), Linda Kay, da of Cyril James Stephens, of Woodlands, Challock Lees, Kent, and has issue living, Stephen Charles, *b* 1973, — Nathalia Ellen, *b* 1971.

HALF-BROTHER LIVING

Hon (David) Mark, *b* 1954; *ed* Eton: *m* 1983, Amanda C, da of Roger Hayward, of Gardiners Hall, Stoke Ash, nr Eye, Suffolk.

SISTER LIVING

Hon Charmaine Elizabeth Violet Cecilia, *b* 1930: *m* 1957, William Rippon Bissill, who *d* 1983, and has had issue, John James Rippon, *b* 1957, *d* 1980, — William Henry, *b* 1960, — Kathleen Mary Florence, *b* 1966: *m* 1991, Mark Adair Hodson (*see* Hodson, Bt). *Residence* – Cranmer House, Aslockton, Notts.

WIDOW LIVING OF THIRD BARON

ALEX, only da of Capt Douglas Hockly, of 10 Eastgate, Tenterden, Kent: *m* 1st, 1953, as his 2nd wife, the 3rd Baron, who *d* 1974; 2ndly, 1975, Harry O. J. C. Jonas.

COLLATERAL BRANCH LIVING

Issue of late Col Hon Guy Greville Wilson, CMG, DSO, TD, 2nd son of 1st Baron, *b* 1877, *d* 1943: *m* 1st, 1904, Lady Isabel Innes-Ker, who *d* 1905, da of 7th Duke of Roxburghe; 2ndly, 1911, Avery, who *d* 1982, da of late Geoffrey Fowell Buxton, CB (*see* Buxton, Bt, colls):—
(By 2nd *m*) Jeremy Charles, DFC, *b* 1923; F/Lt RAF (ret): *m* 1944, June Patricia, da of late Thomas Townsend Bucknill, and has issue living, Peter Richard (The Red House, Hougham, Grantham, Lincs NG32 2JD), *b* 1945, — Thomas Charles (The Old Rectory, Upper Clatford, Andover, Hants SP11 7QP), *b* 1946. *Residence* – Fulmer Cottage, Fulmer, Bucks. —— Malise Joy, *b* 1913; JP: *m* 1942, Lieut-Col Archibald William Antony Smith, DSO, Coldm Gds, who *d* 1989, and has issue living, Antony Luke (28 Beveridge St, Barrow-on-Soar, Loughborough, Leics LE12 8PL), *b* 1943; Maj TAVR: *m* 1985, Penny, da of late Maj David R. W. R. Watts-Russell, of Biggin Hall, Benefield, Northants, — Rupert Malise (273 Trinity Rd, Wandsworth, SW18 3SH), *b* 1944; Coldm Gds (ret): *m* 1978, Angela, yr da of late Dr R. M. Castillo, and has issue living, Rowena Jane *b* 1978, Jessica Malise *b* 1980. *Residence* – Snipe Hall, Wymondham, Melton Mowbray, Leics. —— Alison Ann, *b* 1914: *m* 1938, Brig John Edmund Swetenham, DSO, 5th Dragoon Guards and R Scots Greys, who *d* 1982, and has issue living, (John) Foster (Pound Farmhouse, Rayne, Braintree, Essex), *b* 1939; Capt R Scots Greys (ret): *m* 1964, Marion, yr da of late G. A. Parker, of Bayways, Great Bookham, Surrey, and has issue living, Jeremy Edmund *b* 1967; Maj The Royal Scots Dragoon Gds: *m* 1993, Sandrine, da of Dr Jean-Pierre Martin, of Montgeron, France, Charlotte *b* 1966: *m* 1992, Richard Hamilton Fleetwood Fuller, only son of late Edward Hamilton Fleetwood Fuller, of Weybridge, Surrey. *Residence* – Oak House, Marton, Sinnington, York.

PREDECESSORS – (1) CHARLES HENRY Wilson, son of late Thomas Wilson (*b* 1792), of Cottingham and Hull, Yorkshire, by Susannah West (*b* 1796), da of the Hull Seamen's Orphan Asylum; MP for Kingston-upon-Hull (*L*) 1874-85, and for W Div of Kingston-upon-Hull 1885-1905; *cr Baron Nunburnholme*, of the City of Kingston-upon-Hull (peerage of United Kingdom) 1906: *m* 1871, Florence Jane Helen, OBE, who *d* 1932, da of late Col William Henry Charles Wellesley, formerly 7th Fusiliers; *d* 1907; *s* by his el son (2) CHARLES HENRY WELLESLEY, CB, DSO, 2nd Baron; *b* 1875; S African War 1899-1902, European War 1914-19, Sheriff of Hull 1899-1901, and Lord-Lieut of E Riding of Yorkshire 1908-24; MP for Hull, W Div (*L*) Jan 1906 to Oct 1907: *m* 1901, Lady Marjorie Cecilia, who *d* 1968, da of 1st Marquess of Lincolnshire; *d* 1924; *s* by his el son (3) CHARLES JOHN, 3rd Baron; *b* 1904: *m* 1st, 1927 (*m diss* 1947) Lady Mary Beatrice Thynne, who *d* 1974, da of 5th Marquess of Bath; 2ndly, 1953, Alex (who *m* 2ndly 1975, H. O. J. C. Jonas), only da of Capt Douglas Hockly, of 10 Eastgate, Tenterden, Kent; *d* 1974; *s* by his el son (4) BEN CHARLES, 4th Baron and present peer.

OAKSEY, BARON TREVETHIN AND (Lawrence) (Baron UK 1921 and 1947)

JOHN GEOFFREY TRISTRAM LAWRENCE (*Baron Oaksey*), OBE, 4th Baron Trevethin and 2nd Baron Oaksey; *b* 21 March 1929; *s* 1971; *ed* Eton, New Coll, Oxford, and Yale Univ; late P/O RAFVR and Lt 9th Lancers; OBE 1985: *m* 1st, 1959 (*m diss* 1987), Victoria Mary, el da of Maj John Dennistoun, MBE, of Antwick, Stud House, Letcombe Regis, Berks; 2ndly, 1988, Mrs Rachel Crocker, and has issue by 1st *m*.

Arms – Per chevron argent and gules, two crosses raguly in chief of the last, and a lamb in base holding with the dexter foreleg a banner and staff, all of the first, the banner charged with a cross couped azure. **Crest** – A dragon's head erased sable between two bugle horns counter-embowed or. **Supporters** – *Dexter*, a Guernsey bull; *sinister*, a hart both proper. **Residence** – Hill Farm, Oaksey, Malmesbury, Wilts SN16 9HS. **Club** – Brooks's.

SON LIVING (By 1st marriage)

Hon PATRICK JOHN TRISTRAM, *b* 29 June 1960: *m* 1987, Lucinda H., eldest da of Demetri Marchessini, of Wilton Cres, SW1, and of Mrs Nicholas Peto, of Dean Manor, Charlbury, Oxon, and has issue living, Oliver John Tristram, *b* 17 May 1990, — Calypso Helen, *b* 1987. *Residence* – 21 Dewhurst Rd, W14.

DAUGHTER LIVING (By 1st marriage)

Hon Sara Victoria, *b* 1961: *m* 1987, Mark FitzHerbert Bradstock, eldest son of David FitzHerbert Bradstock, MC, of Clanville Lodge, Andover, Hants. *Residence* – Mabberleys, E Garston, nr Newbury, Berks.

SISTERS LIVING

Hon (Mary) Elizabeth (*Hon Lady Adams*), *b* 1922: *m* 1954, Sir Philip George Doyne Adams, KCMG, HM Foreign Ser (ret), and has issue living, Geoffrey Doyne, *b* 1957: *m* 1985, Anne Louise, yr da of John Jennings, of St Brelade, Jersey, CI, — Justin Alexander, *b* 1961, — Lucy Victoria, *b* 1955, — Harriet Mary, *b* 1959. *Residences* – 54 Sussex Sq, W2; The Malt House, Ditchley, Enstone, Oxon.
Hon (Enid) Rosamond (*Hon Lady Dundas*), *b* 1924: *m* 1950, Group Capt Sir Hugh Spencer Lisle Dundas, CBE, DSO, DFC, RAF (ret) of The Schoolroom, Dockenfield, Farnham, Surrey, and 55 Iverna Court, W8, and has issue (*see* M Zetland, colls).
Hon (Anne) Jennifer, *b* 1926: *m* 1951, Lieut-Col Frederick John Burnaby-Atkins, The Black Watch, and has issue living, John Charles Graham *b* 1961: *m* 1993, Emma Elisabeth, da of James Smith, of Forfar, Angus, — Charlotte Elisabeth Cecily, *b* 1952: *m* 1980, J. Patrick S. Crawford, son of Sir (Robert) Stewart Crawford, GCMG, CVO, of 19 Adam Court, Bell St, Henley-on-Thames, Oxon, and has issue living, Mark Andrew Frederick *b* 1990, Anna Mary Alice *b* 1982, Jessie Susan Charlotte *b* 1985, Harriet Rosamond *b* 1988, — Catherine Rose, *b* 1954, — Rosamond Louise, *b* 1957: *m* 1981, Marc L. J-M. Weemaels, of Brussels, and has issue living, Anthony *b* 1983, John *b* 1985, David *b* 1989. *Residence* – 3 The Street, Oaksey, Malmesbury, Wilts.

COLLATERAL BRANCH LIVING

Issue of late *Hon* Alfred Clive Lawrence, CBE, el son of 1st Baron Trevethin, *b* 1876, *d* 1926: *m* 1924, Mildred Margaret, who *d* 1964, having *m* 2ndly, 1929, 1st Viscount Hailsham, who *d* 1950, da of late Rev Edward Parker Dew, of Breamore, Hants:—
Domini Margaret, *b* 1925: *m* 1979, Arnold Frank Morgan. *Residence* – Teddards, Filching, Polegate, E Sussex BN26 5QA.

PREDECESSORS – (1) *Rt Hon* ALFRED TRISTRAM Lawrence, PC, son of David Lawrence, surg of Pontypool, Monmouthshire, *b* 1843; a Judge of High Court of Justice (King's Beach Div) 1904-21, and Lord Ch Justice of England 1921-2; *cr Baron Trevethin*, of Blaengawney, co Monmouth (peerage of United Kingdom) 1921: *m* 1875, Jessie Elizabeth, who *d* 1931, da of George Lawrence, JP, *d* 1936; *s* by his second son (2) CHARLES TREVOR, 2nd Baron *b* 1879; Lt-Col late RHA and RFA; *d* 1959; *s* by his brother (3) *Rt Hon Sir* GEOFFREY, 3rd Baron, DSO, TD, *b* 1880; Judge of High Court of Jutice (King's Bench Div) 1932-44, Lord Justice of Appeal 1944-47, and Lord of Appeal in Ordinary 1947-57; *cr Baron Oaksey*, of Oaksey, co Wilts (Peerage of UK) 1947: *m* 1921, Marjorie, who *d* 1984, OBE, TD, da of late Cdr Charles Napier Robinson, RN; *d* 1971; *s* by his son (4) JOHN GEOFFREY TRISTRAM, 4th Baron Trevethin, 2nd Baron Oaksey and present peer.

OAKSHOTT, BARONY OF (Oakshott) (Extinct 1975)

SONS LIVING OF LIFE BARON

Hon Sir ANTHONY HENDRIE OAKSHOTT, 2nd Bt, who *s* to baronetcy (*cr* 1959) 1975 (*see* Oakshott, Bt).
Hon Michael Arthur John Oakshott (*see* Oakshott, Bt).

O'BRIEN OF LOTHBURY, BARON (O'Brien) (Life Baron 1973)

LESLIE KENNETH O'BRIEN, GBE, PC, son of late Charles John Grimes O'Brien; *b* 8 Feb 1908; *ed* Wandsworth Sch; Hon DSc City Univ, Hon LLD Univ of Wales; FRCM; entered Bank of England 1927; Ch Cashier 1955-62, Exec Dir 1962-64, Dep Gov 1964-66, and Gov 1963-73; a Liveryman of Mercers' Co, Hon Liveryman of Leathersellers' Co, and a Freeman of City of Lond; *cr* GBE (Civil) 1967, PC, 1970, and *Baron O'Brien of Lothbury*, of City of London (Life Baron) 1973; Cavaliere di Gran Croce al Merito della Republica Italiana 1975, Grand Officer Ordre de la Couronne (Belgium) 1976: *m* 1st, 1932, Isabelle Gertrude, who *d* 1987, da of Francis John Pickett, MBE; 2ndly, 1989, Mrs Marjorie Violet Taylor, da of Albert Cecil Ball, and has issue by 1st *m*.

Arms – Gules bezanty, three lions passant gardant in pale, each per pale or and argent. Crest – In front of two keys in saltire azure, a needle point downwards proper threaded gules. Supporters – On either side a lion gardant per fess or and argent, in the mouth a key or, standing upon a heap of coins or and argent.

Address – 3 Peter Av, Oxted, Surrey RH8 9LG. *Clubs* – Boodle's, Grillions, All England Lawn Tennis.

SON LIVING *(By 1st marriage)*

Hon Michael John (The Lodge, Thursley, nr Godalming, Surrey GU8 6QF) *b* 1933: *m* 1964, Marion Sarah, da of late Walter Graham Blackie, and has issue, — James Leslie Graham, *b* 1967, — Charles John, *b* 1972, — Sarah Christina, *b* 1969.

O'CATHAIN, BARONESS (Bishop) (Life Baroness 1991)

DETTA O'CATHAIN, OBE, da of late Caoimhghin O'Cathain, of Dublin; *b* 3 Feb 1938; *ed* Laurel Hill, Limerick, and Univ Coll, Dublin (BA); formerly Group Economist with Tarmac plc, and Man Dir Milk Marketing Board; Dir Midland Bank plc since 1984, Tesco plc since 1985, and Sears plc 1987; Man Dir The Barbican Centre since 1990; Council Member Industrial Soc since 1987; OBE (Civil) 1983; *cr Baroness O'Cathain*, of The Barbican in the City of London (Life Baroness) 1991: *m* 1968, William Ernest John Bishop.

Residences – Eglantine, Tower House Gdns, Arundel, W Sussex; 121 Shakespeare Tower, Barbican, EC2Y 8DR.

Offaly, Earl of, grandson of Duke of Leinster.

Ogilvy Lord, son of Earl of Airlie.

DEBRETT'S ILLUSTRATED PEERAGE

OGMORE, BARON (Rees-Williams) (Baron UK 1950)

Faithful unto Death

GWILYM REES REES-WILLIAMS, 2nd Baron; *b* 5 May 1931; *s* 1976; *ed* Mill Hill Sch: *m* 1967, Gillian Mavis, da of Maurice Keith Slack, of Hindley, Lancs, and has issue.

Arms – Azure two bars wavy argent on a chief arched of the second between as many hurts, each charged with a quatrefoil or a hurt thereon a sun in splendour of the third. **Crest** – A tiger's head couped proper charged on the neck with three chevronels couped gules. **Supporters** – *Dexter*, a tiger proper charged on the shoulder with three chevronels couped gules; *sinister*, a horse argent.
Residence – 4 Foster Rd, Chiswick, W4 4NY.

DAUGHTERS LIVING

Hon Christine Ann, *b* 1968.
Hon Jennet Elizabeth, *b* 1970.

BROTHER LIVING

Hon MORGAN (50 Novello St, SW6 4JB), *b* 19 Dec 1937; *ed* Mill Hill Sch; Lt R Regt of Wales (TA): *m* 1st, 1964 (*m diss* 1970), Patricia, only da of C. Paris Jones, of Constantine Bay, Padstow; 2ndly, 1972 (*m diss* 1976), Roberta, da of late Capt Alec Stratford Cunningham-Reid, DFC; 3rdly, 1990, Beata, da of Zdislaw Solski, and has issue living (by 3rd *m*), Tudor David, *b* 11 Dec 1991, — Dylan, *b* 1994.

SISTER LIVING

Hon (Joan) Elizabeth HARRIS, *b* 1936; *ed* Croham Hurst Sch, and Mont Olivet, Lausanne; resumed surname of Harris by deed poll 1986: *m* 1st, 1957 (*m diss* 1969), Richard St John Harris, actor; 2ndly, 1971 (*m diss* 1975), Rex Carey Harrison (later Sir Rex Harrison), who *d* 1990, actor; 3rdly, 1981 (*m diss* 1985), Peter Michael Aitken (*see* B Beaverbrook, colls), and has issue living (by 1st *m*), Damian David, *b* 1958: *m* 1981, Annabel Joan, only da of late Robert Noel Brand Brooks (*see* B Crawshaw, colls), and has issue living, Ella *b* 1989, — Jared Francis, *b* 1961: *m* 1961, Jacqueline, yst da of Ralph I. Goldenberg, of Chicago, Illinois, USA, — Jamie St John, *b* 1963. *Residence* – 7 Grove Court, Drayton Gdns, SW10.

WIDOW LIVING OF FIRST BARON

ALICE ALEXANDRA CONSTANCE, (*Constance, Baroness Ogmore*); is a JP for Croydon; da of late Alderman Walter Robert Wills, Lord Mayor of Cardiff 1945-46: *m* 1930, the 1st Baron, who *d* 1976.

PREDECESSOR – (1) *Rt Hon* DAVID REES Rees-Williams, TD, son of late William Rees Williams, FRCVS, of Garth Celyn, Bridgend, Glam; *b* 1903; Parl Under-Sec of State of Colonies 1947-50, and for Commonwealth Relations 1950-51; Min of Civil Aviation June-Oct 1951; MP for S Div of Croydon (*Lab*) 1945-50; carried the coronet at Investiture of HRH The Prince of Wales 1969, *cr Baron Ogmore*, of Bridgend, co Glam (peerage of UK) 1950: *m* 1930, Alice Alexandra Constance, JP, da of late Alderman Walter Robert Wills (Lord Mayor of Cardiff 1945-46); *d* 1976; *s* by his el son (2) GWILYM REES, 2nd Baron, and present peer.

O'HAGAN, BARON (Strachey) (Baron UK 1870)

Buas no bar
Victory or death

Tenez le vraye
Keep the truth

Mihi res non me rebus

CHARLES TOWNELEY STRACHEY, MEP, 4th Baron; *b* 6 Sep 1945; *s* 1961; a Page of Honour to HM 1959-62; *ed* Eton, and New Coll, Oxford (MA); a Member of European Parl since 1973; Independent Member European Parliament 1973-75, Jnr Opposition Whip 1977-79, MEP (*C*) Devon since 1979: *m* 1st, 1967 (*m diss* 1984), HSH Princess Tamara, el da of HSH Prince Michael Imeretinsky, of La Colla, Route de Castellar, Menton, France, and formerly wife of Lt-Cmdr Thomas Mervyn Smith-Dorrien-Smith, of Tresco Abbey, Isles of Scilly; 2ndly, 1985, Mrs Mary Claire Parsons, only da of Rev Leslie Roose-Francis, of Trencoth, Blisland, Bodmin, Cornwall, and has issue by 1st and 2nd *m*.

Arms – Quarterly: 1st and 4th ermine, a bend and on a chief azure a fleur de lis or, *O'Hagan*; 2nd and 3rd argent, a fesse and in chief three mullets sable, *Towneley*. **Crests** – 1st, upon a fasces fessewise proper, a cubit arm vested gules, cuffed ermine, the hand holding a dagger erect, both also proper, *O'Hagan*; 2nd, upon a perch or, a hawk close proper, beaked and belled gold; round the perch a ribbon gules, *Towneley*. **Supporters** – On either side a lion or, collared gemel sable, pendant therefrom an escutcheon argent, charged with a dexter hand couped gules.
Seat – Rashleigh Barton, Wembworthy, Chumleigh, N. Devon.
Residence – 12 Lyndhurst Rd, Exeter, Devon.

DAUGHTERS LIVING (*By 1st marriage*)

Hon Nino Natalia O'Hagan, *b* 1968; *ed* North Foreland Lodge, and Queen's Coll, Oxford.

(by 2nd marriage)

Hon Antonia Philippa Mary, *b* 1986.

BROTHER LIVING (*Raised to the rank of Baron's son* 1963)

Hon RICHARD TOWNELEY, *b* 29 Dec 1950; *ed* Eton, and Bath Acad of Art, Corsham: *m* 1983, Sally Anne, yr da of Frederick Cecil Cross, of Upcompton, Compton Bishop, Somerset.

SISTERS LIVING (*Raised to the rank of a Baron's daughters* 1963)

Hon Frances Towneley, *b* 1948: *m* 1967, Hon Hugh Marcus Thornley Gibson, of The Fold, Parwich, Ashbourne, Derbys (*see* B Gibson).
Hon Jane Towneley STRACHEY, *b* 1953; has reverted to her maiden name: *m* 1972 (*m diss* 1977), William Stone. *Residence* – 24 Kylestrome House, Cundy St, SW1.

AUNT LIVING (*Daughter of 3rd Baron*)

Hon Helen Frances Alice, *b* 1912; late VAD: *m* 1940, Capt Ian Desmond Curry, RA, who *d* 1969, having assumed by deed poll 1942 the surname of Curry-Towneley-O'Hagan, and has issue living, Padraic Desmond (52 Mount Park Rd, W5), *b* 1946: *m* 1971, Judith Patricia, only da of Hon Robin Sandbach Borwick (*see* B Borwick), and has issue living, Fiann James *b* 1974, Dickon Padraic *b* 1977. *Residence* – 24 Burgh St, Islington, N1.

MOTHER LIVING

Lady Mary Sophia Palmer, da of 3rd Earl of Selborne; Lady-in-Waiting to HM when HRH Princess Elizabeth 1944-7, and Extra Lady-in-Waiting 1947-9: *m* 1st, 1944, Hon (Thomas) Anthony Edward Towneley Strachey, who *d* 1955 (having assumed by deed poll 1938, the additional Christian name of Towneley, and his mother's maiden name of Strachey in lieu of his patronymic), only son of 3rd Baron; 2ndly, 1981, as his 2nd wife, (Francis) St John Gore, CBE (*see* Gore, Bt, colls). *Residence* – Grove Farm, Stoke-by-Nayland, Colchester, Essex CO6 4SL.

PREDECESSORS – (1) *Rt Hon Sir* THOMAS O'Hagan, KP, only son of late Edward O'Hagan; *b* 1812; was Solicitor-Gen for Ireland 1860-1, Attorney-Gen 1861-5, a Justice of the Common Pleas in Ireland 1865-8, and Lord Chancellor of Ireland 1868-74 and 1880-1; sat as MP for Tralee (*L*) 1863-5; *cr Baron O'Hagan*, of Tullaghogue, co Tyrone (peerage of United Kingdom) 1870: *m* 1st, 1836, Mary, who *d* 1868, da of Charles Hamilton Teeling, of Belfast; 2ndly, 1871, Alice Mary, who *d* 1921, da and co-heiress of Col Charles Towneley, of Towneley, Lancashire; *d* 1885; *s* by his son (2) THOMAS TOWNELEY, 2nd Baron, *b* 1878; Lieut Grenadier Guards; *d* (in S Africa) 1900: *s* by his brother (3) MAURICE HERBERT TOWNELEY, 3rd Baron; *b* 1882; Hon Major RHA (TA) and Hon Col 4th (Cadet) Batn Essex Regt and 6th Batn Essex Regt (TA), Assist Private Sec (unpaid) to First Lord of Admiralty 1906-7, a Lord-in-Waiting to King Edward VII 1907-10, and Dep Speaker and Dep Chm House of Lords 1950-61; assumed by Roy licence 1909, the additional surname and arms of Towneley: *m* 1st, 1911, Hon Frances Constance Maddalena Strachey, who *d* 1931, only da of 1st Baron Strachie; 2ndly, 1937, Evelyn Violet, who *d* 1965, da of Harry Thornton Ross, and widow of Lt-Col Henry Osbert Samuel Cadogan, R Welch Fusiliers; *d* 1961; *s* by his grandson (4) CHARLES TOWNELEY Strachey (son of late Hon (Thomas) Anthony Edward Towneley Strachey, who assumed by deed poll 1938, the additional Christian name of Towneley, and his mother's maiden name of Strachey in lieu of his patronymic), 4th Baron and present peer.

OLIVER OF AYLMERTON, BARON (Oliver) (Life Baron 1986)

PETER RAYMOND OLIVER, PC, son of late David Thomas Oliver, Fellow of Trin Hall, Camb, by his wife Alice Maud, da of George Kirby; *b* 7 March 1921; *ed* The Leys, and Trin Hall, Camb (Hon Fellow 1980); served in WWII 1941-45, 12th Bn RTR (despatches); Bar Lincoln's Inn 1948, Bencher 1973, QC 1965, Judge of High Court (Chancery Div) 1974-80, a Lord Justice of Appeal 1980-86, a Lord of Appeal in Ordinary 1986-92; Member of Restrictive Practices Court 1976-80; Chm Review Body on Chancery Div of High Court 1979-81; *cr* Kt 1974, PC 1980, and *Baron Oliver of Aylmerton*, of Aylmerton, co Norfolk (Life Baron) 1986: *m* 1st, 1945, Mary Chichester, who *d* 1985, da of late Sir Eric Keightley Rideal, MBE, FRS; 2ndly, 1987, Wendy Anne, widow of late Ivon Lloyd Lewis Jones, and had issue by 1st *m*.

Arms – Per chevron gules and vert in chief two crosses moline or and in base a chaplet of olive also or a bordure ermine. **Crest** – Within a crown pallisado or a grassy mount thereon a representation of the tower of the church of St. John the Baptist at Aylmerton proper issuing therefrom a cubit arm proper holding a crescent ermine. **Supporters** – *Dexter*, a lion purpure the dexter paw in a mail gauntlet argent; *sinister*, an American bald-headed eagle holding in the dexter claw a quill pen all proper. **Motto** – Trwy weithred y dysgir.
Residence – The Canadas, Sandy Lane, Aylmerton, nr Cromer, Norfolk NR27 9ND.

SON LIVING *(By 1st marriage)*

Hon David Keightley Rideal, *b* 1949; *ed* Westminster, and Trin Hall, Camb: *m* 1st, 1972 (*m diss* 1987), Maria Luisa, da of Juan Mirasierras, of Avenida Reina Vittoria, Madrid; 2ndly, 1988, Judith Britannia Caroline, da of David Henry John Griffiths Powell, and has issue living (by 1st *m*), Daniel, *b* 1974, — Thomas, *b* 1976, — (by 2nd *m*) Rhodri, *b* 1990, — Alexander, *b* 1993. *Address* – 13 Old Square, Lincoln's Inn, WC2A 3UA.

DAUGHTER LIVING *(By 1st marriage)*

Hon Sarah Chichester OLIVER, *b* 1951; has resumed her maiden name: *m* 1974 (*m diss* 1983), James Robert Goldsack, and has issue living, Katie Louise, *b* 1980, — Rebecca, *b* 1983.

OLIVIER, BARONY OF (Olivier) (Extinct 1989)

SONS LIVING OF LIFE BARON *(by 1st marriage)*

Hon (Simon) Tarquin, *b* 1936; *ed* Eton, late Coldstream Guards: *m* 1st, 1965 (*m diss* 1975), Riddelle, yr da of Patrick Boyce Riddell Gibson; 2ndly, 1989, (Sahnebat) Zelfa Draz, of Istanbul, and has issue living (by 1st *m*), Tristan, *b* 1966, — Isis, *b* 1967: *m* 1989, Paul D. Fairclough, — Clavelle Athene P., *b* 1972, — (by 2nd *m*) a da, *b* 1989.

(by 3rd marriage)

Hon Richard, *b* 1961; *ed* UCLA; film and theatre dir: *m* 1987, Shelley Marie Dupuis (*née* Herrich), of Canada, and has issue living, Troilus (Troy), *b* 1988, — (Natalie) Alessandra, *b* 1990.

DAUGHTERS LIVING OF LIFE BARON *(by 3rd marriage)*

Hon Tamsin, *b* 1963.
Hon Julianne, Rose H— K— (Julie Kate), *b* 1966.

WIDOW LIVING OF LIFE BARON

JOAN, CBE (*Baroness Olivier*) (the actress Joan Plowright), da of William Ernest Plowright, and formerly wife of Roger Gage: *m* 1961, as his 3rd wife, Baron Olivier, OM (Life Baron), who *d* 1989. *Address* – c/o LOP Ltd, 33-34 Chancery Lane, WC2A 1EN.

O'NEILL, BARON (O'Neill) (Baron UK 1868)

Honours follow us without seeking

The Red Hand of Ireland

RAYMOND ARTHUR CLANABOY O'NEILL, TD, 4th Baron; *b* 1 Sept 1933; *s* 1944; *ed* Eton and R Agric Coll, Cirencester; Maj N Irish Horse (AVR IIA); Lt-Col (RARO), formerly Hon Col D (N Irish Horse) Sqdn RY; a DL for co Antrim; HM Lieut for co Antrim since 1994: *m* 1963, Georgina Mary, da of Lord George Francis John Montagu Douglas Scott (*see* D Buccleuch), and has issue.

Arms – Quarterly: 1st and 4th per fesse wavy, the chief argent, and the base representing waves of the sea, in chief a dexter hand couped at the wrist gules, in base a salmon naiant proper, *O'Neill*; 2nd and 3rd checky, or and gules, a chief vair, *Chichester*. **Crests** – 1st, an arm embowed in armour, the hand grasping a sword, all proper; 2nd, a stork rising, with a snake in its beak, all proper. **Supporters** – On either side a lion gules, gorged with an antique crown argent, pendant therefrom an escutcheon; the *dexter* charged with the arms of O'Neill, and the *sinister* with those of Chichester.
Seat – Shane's Castle, Antrim BT41 4NE. *Club* – Turf.

SONS LIVING

Hon SHANE SEBASTIAN CLANABOY, *b* 25 July 1965.
Hon Tyrone Alexander, *b* 1966.
Hon Rory St John, *b* 1968.

SISTER LIVING

Hon Fionn Frances Bride (182 Ebury St, SW1W 8UP), *b* 1936; *ed* Heathfield, and St Anne's Coll, Oxford: *m* 1961 (*m diss* 1975), John Albert Leigh Morgan, CMG (later Sir John Morgan, KCMG), HM Amb to Mexico (ret 1989), and has issue living, John Edward Rustand, *b* 1964, — Mary Ann Frances, *b* 1962: *m* 1989, Charles Anthony Warneford Gibson, only son of Group Capt Phillip G. Gibson, of Manor Farm House, Sawtry, Cambs, and has issue living, Alexander Shane Warneford *b* 1991, — Frederick John Philip *b* 1993, — Catherine Martha Annabel, *b* 1966.

WIDOW LIVING OF BROTHER OF THIRD BARON

Katharine Jean (*Baroness O'Neill of the Maine*), da of late William Ingham Whitaker, DL, of Pylewell Park, Lymington, Hants: *m* 1944, Baron O'Neill of the Maine, PC (Life Baron), who *d* 1990, and has issue (see colls infra). *Residence* – Lisle Court, Lymington, Hants.

COLLATERAL BRANCHES LIVING

Issue of late Rt Hon Terence Marne O'Neill (*Baron O'Neill of the Maine*), brother of 3rd Baron, *b* 1914, *d* 1990; raised to the rank of a Baron's son 1930, and *cr* Baron O'Neill of the Maine (Life Baron) 1970: *m* 1944, Katharine Jean (ante), da of late William Ingham Whitaker, DL, of Pylewell Park, Lymington, Hants (*see* V Melville, 1970 Edn):—
Hon Patrick Arthur Ingham (48 Forbes St, Newtown, NSW 2042, Australia), *b* 1945; *ed* Eton; Lieut QRI Hussars; Reporter ABC TV, Producer Channel 10 Current Affairs, Councillor Nat Trust of Australia NSW 1986-87: *m* 1st, 1975 (*m diss* 1984), Anne, da of Douglas Lillecrapp, of Adelaide, S Australia; 2ndly, 1984, Stella Mary, da of late Sir Alexander Russell Downer, KBE, of Williamstown, S Australia, and has issue living (by 1st *m*), Sophie Katherine, *b* 1976, — Elizabeth Mary, *b* 1981.
—— *Hon* Penelope Anne, *b* 1947: *m* 1st, 1970 (*m diss* 1982), Christopher William Kerr Devas (*see* M Lothian, colls); 2ndly, 1984, Lt-Cdr William Victor Crutchley, RN (ret), son of Adm Sir Victor Crutchley, VC, KCB, DSC (*see* Parker, Bt, *cr* 1844, 1948 Edn), and has issue living (by 1st *m*), William Thomas, *b* 1975, — (by 2nd *m*) Arthur Percy, *b* 1987, — Daisy Alice, *b* 1986. *Residence* – Mappercombe Manor, Powerstock, Bridport, Dorset.

Issue of late Rt Hon (Robert William) Hugh O'Neill (*Baron Rathcavan*), yst son of 2nd Baron, *b* 1883, *d* 1982; *cr* a Baronet 1929, and Baron Rathcavan 1953:—
See that title.

PREDECESSORS – (1) *Rev* WILLIAM Chichester, el son of Rev Edward Chichester, a descendant of John Chichester, yr brother of 2nd Earl of Donegall (*see* M Donegall, colls) in 1855 succeeded to the estates of his cousin Earl O'Neill (extinct), and in that year assumed by Roy licence the surname of O'Neill; *b* 1813; *cr* Baron O'Neill, of Shanes Castle, co Antrim (peerage of United Kingdom) 1868: *m* 1st, 1839, Henrietta, who *d* 1857, da of late Hon Robert Torrens, a Judge of the Common Pleas in Ireland; 2ndly, 1858; Elizabeth Grace, who *d* 1905, da of the Ven John Torrens, DD, Archdeacon of Dublin; *d* 1883; *s* by his son (2) EDWARD, 2nd Baron, *b* 1839; MP for co Antrim (C) 1863-80: *m* 1873, Lady Louisa Katherine Emma Cochrane, who *d* 1942, da of 11th Earl of Dundonald; *d* 1928; *s* by his grandson (3) SHANE EDWARD ROBERT (el son of late Capt Hon Arthur Edward Bruce O'Neill, MP, Household Cav, *ka* 1914, el son of 2nd Baron), 3rd Baron; *b* 1907; Lieut-Col N Irish Horse: *m* 1932, Anne Geraldine Mary (who *m* 2ndly, 1945 (*m diss* 1952), 2nd Viscount Rothermere; 3rdly, 1952, Ian Lancaster Fleming, who *d* 1964 (Rose Bt, *cr* 1874, colls), and *d* 1981), da of Hon Guy Lawrence Charteris (E Wemyss); *ka* in Italy 1944; *s* by his son (4)RAYMOND ARTHUR CLANABOY, 4th Baron and present peer.

O'NEILL OF THE MAINE, BARONY OF (O'Neill) (Extinct 1990)

SON, DAUGHTER AND WIDOW OF LIFE BARON (*see* B O'Neill)

ONSLOW, EARL OF (Onslow) (Earl UK 1801, Bt E 1674 (with precedency of 1660))

MICHAEL WILLIAM COPLESTONE DILLON ONSLOW, 7th Earl, and 11th Baronet (of 2nd creation); *b* 28 Feb 1938; *s* 1971; *ed* Eton, and Sorbonne; Insurance Broker: *m* 1964, Robin Lindsay, only da of Maj Robert Lee Bullard III, of Atlanta, Georgia, USA, and of Lady Aberconway, and has issue.

Arms – Argent, a fesse gules, between six Cornish choughs proper. **Crest** – An eagle sable, preying on a partridge or. **Supporters** – Two falcons close proper, belled or.
Residence – Temple Court, Clandon Park, Guildford. *Club* – Beefsteak.

SON LIVING

RUPERT CHARLES WILLIAM BULLARD (*Viscount Cranley*), *b* 16 June 1967.

DAUGHTERS LIVING

Lady Arabella Ann Teresa, *b* 1970.
Lady Charlotte Emma Dorothy, *b* 1977.

SISTER LIVING

Quick without impetuosity

Lady Teresa Lorraine, *b* 1940: *m* 1961, Auberon Alexander Waugh, the writer (*see* E Carnarvon, colls, 1973-74 Edn), and has issue living, Alexander Evelyn Michael (2 Souldern Rd, W14 0JE), *b* 1963: *m* 1990, Elizabeth Beatrice, da of Alexander Surtees Chancellor (*see* Paget, Bt, *cr* 1886), and has issue living, Mary Eulalia *b* 1993, — Nathaniel Thomas Biafra, *b* 1968, — (Margaret) Sophia Laura, *b* 1962: *m* 1986, Julian Watson, of 27 Chesterton Rd, W10, only son of Vice Adm Sir Philip Alexander Watson, KBE, LVO, of The Hermitage, Bodicote, Banbury, Oxon, and has issue living, Constance Mary Alabama *b* 1990, Beatrice Teresa Arizona *b* 1992, — Daisy Louisa Dominica, *b* 1967. *Residence* – Combe Florey House, Taunton, Somerset.

WIDOW LIVING OF SIXTH EARL

NINA, MBE (*Jo, Countess of Onslow*) (Sturdee's, Freeland, Oxford), yr da of Thomas Sturdee; MBE (Civil) 1953: *m* 1962, as his 2nd wife, the 6th Earl, who *d* 1971.

COLLATERAL BRANCHES LIVING

Branch from 2nd son of 2nd Earl

Grandchildren of late Arthur Edward Onslow, 4th son of late Lt-Col Arthur Edward Mainwaring-Ellerker-Onslow, 3rd son of late Col Hon Thomas Cranley Onslow, MP, 2nd son of 2nd Earl:—
Issue of late Vivian Isidore Onslow, *b* 1888, *d* 1979: *m* 1st, 1912, Lily, who *d* 1918, elder da of Charles Edward Henson, of Hope House, The Vineyard, Richmond, Surrey; 2ndly, 1919, Annie Dorothea Rose, who *d* 1972, elder da of Frank Charles Davis, of Evercreech, nr Bath:—
(By 2nd *m*) Arthur Charles Vivian (21 Sir John Moore Av, Hythe, Kent CT21 5DE), *b* 1920: *m* 1951, Patricia Taylor, and has had issue, †Robert Charles Vivian, *b* 1952; *d* 1990, — Anthony Ernest Edward, *b* 1955, — David Peter, *b* 1959, — Anne Rose, *b* 1957. —— Denzil Isidore Charles (5 Christopher Way, Shepton Mallet, Som), *b* 1924: *m* 1945, Iris Frances Warren, who *d* 1992, and has issue living, John M. (Little Silvers, Upton Noble, nr Frome, Som), *b* 1948: *m* 1972, Susan Jane Mary Nicholls, and has issue living, Stuart John *b* 1977, — Dennis Raymond (5 Christopher Way, Shepton Mallet, Som), *b* 1949, — Andrew Martin (33 Wyville Rd, Frome, Som), *b* 1954: *m* 1981 (*m diss* 1988), Wendy Jacqueline Baker, and has issue living, Martin Andrew *b* 1983, Matthew John *b* 1984, — Brian S. (34 Blenheim Rd, Street, Som), *b* 1957: *m* 1978, Susan Jane Parsons, and has issue living, Neil Ian *b* 1984, Michelle Claire *b* 1981, — Daphne Carol, *b* 1945: *m* 1st, 19—, — Howell; 2ndly, 1991, Derek Robert Jack, of Knowberry, Whitstone Rd, Shepton Mallet, Som, and has issue living (by 1st *m*), Wayne Lee *b* 1967, Darren Shaun *b* 1970. — Sheila Rose, *b* 1946: *m* 1970, Raymond William Withers, of Home, Weymouth Rd, Evercreech, Som and has issue living, Paul Neil *b* 1970, Mark Andrew *b* 1973, Tony Clive *b* 1980, — Pamela Susan (1 Bolters Lane, Downside, Shepton Mallet, Som), *b* 1952: *m* 1969 (*m diss* 19—), Peter John Gregory, and has issue living, Dean Marcus *b* 1972, Mandy Lea *b* 1969, Tina Clare Angelina *b* 1970, — Christine Ann, *b* 1953: *m* 1975, Glenn Robert Davies, of 34 Wickham Lane, Shepton Mallet, Som, and has issue living, Alan Robert *b* 1975, Gary Martin *b* 1977, — Linda Dawn (16 Westover, Nunney, Frome, Som), *b* (twin) 1954: *m* 1973 (*m diss* 1984), Laurence Vernon Whittaker, and has issue living, Steven Raymond *b* 1974, Timothy Laurence *b* 1977, — Sandra Jane, *b* 1959: *m* 1977, Philip Roy Farmer, of 14 Douglas Drive, Shepton Mallet, Som, and has issue living, Trevor Philip *b* 1979, Jennifer Ann *b* 1980, — Wendy Janice, *b* 1961: *m* 1987, Alan William Coubrough, of 3 Naisholt Rd, Shepton Mallet, Som, and has issue living, Craig William *b* 1990. —— Constance Vivien, *b* 1934: *m* 1st, 1960, Stanley W. Crabb: 2ndly, 19—, — — Tombs.

Branch from 2nd son of 1st Earl

Granddaughter of late Frederick Horace Onslow, son of late Capt Arthur Onslow, son of 2nd son of 1st Earl:—
Issue of late Arthur Onslow, *b* 1871, *d* 1937: *m* 1893, Emily, who *d* 1952, da of W. A. Howe, and has issue living:—
Valentine Charlotte, *b* 1900. *Residence* – Addison House, Niagara-on-the-Lake, Ontario, Canada.

(Male line in remainder to the Barony and Baronetcy)

Branch from 1st son of 1st son of 2nd son of brother of 1st Baron

Grandchildren of late William Cleveland Onslow, son of late Major Pitcairn Onslow, el son of Rev George Walton Onslow, el son of George Onslow, MP (*b* 1721), el son of late Lt-Gen Richard Onslow, nephew of 1st Baron Onslow, and uncle of 1st Earl:—
Issue of late Guy Cleveland Onslow, *b* 1884, *d* 1952: *m* 1916, Angela Mary, who *d* 1974, da of Robert Pearce, of Ripley Court, Surrey:—

Guildford Arthur Richard, *b* 1921: *ed* Camb Univ (BA 19—): *m* 1945, Ilse, only da of Julius Sahm. *Residence* – 7 New Rd, Croxley Green, Rickmansworth, Herts. —— Rose Saltern, *b* 1918. *Residence* – 9 Rose Lane, Ripley, Woking, Surrey.

Branch from 2nd son of 1st son of 2nd son of brother of 1st Baron

Grandchildren of late Maj-Gen James William MACARTHUR-ONSLOW, VD (infra):—
Issue of late James Arthur MACARTHUR-ONSLOW, *b* 1898, *d* 1959: *m* 1925, Constance Faith, who *d* 1962, da of George Herbert of Sydney:—
James William Macleay (9 Pullenvale Rd, Kenmore, Brisbane, Queensland, Aust), *b* 1932; *ed* Knox Gram Sch, Wahroonga, NSW: *m* 1964, Margaret Alice, da of Colin Basil Peter Bell, of Kenmore, Brisbane, Qld, and has issue living, James Stuart Macleay, *b* 1966, — Julienne Elizabeth, *b* 1969. —— Susan Helen, *b* 1935: *m* 1962, Brig Ian Henry Hayman (ret), Austn Staff Corps, of 57 Epping Rd, Double Bay, NSW 2028, Australia, and has issue living, Rosemary Susan, *b* 1963, — Charlotte Elizabeth, *b* 1966. —— Sandra Ruth (9A Cambridge Rd, Artarmon, NSW, Aust), *b* 1936.

Grandsons of late Arthur John MACARTHUR-ONSLOW (ante):—
Issue of late Lt-Col Richard Walton MACARTHUR-ONSLOW, Australian Light Horse, *b* 1904, *d* 1981: *m* 1920, Lois Ruth, who *d* 1976, da of H. B. Greene, of Barncleuth Sq, Sydney, NSW:—
Richard Bowring (Cannanbri, Walcha 2354, NSW), *b* 1934: *m* 1960, Christina Helen Huntly Gordon, da of Ronald Arthur McWilliam, of Vaucluse, Sydney, NSW, and has issue living, Richard Matthew, *b* 1962, — Rohan James, *b* 1964, — Lachlan Robert Hugh, *b* 1972. —— John Walton, *b* 1943. —— William Robert (140 Stock Rd, Gunnedah, NSW), *b* 1945: *m* 1977, Sarah, da of L. B. Bettington, of Fernside, Rylstone, NSW, and has issue living, Felicity Georgina, *b* 1979, — Jane Belinda, *b* 1982.

Grandchildren of late Capt Arthur Alexander Walton Onslow, RN, el son of Arthur Pooley Onslow, el son of Rev Arthur Onslow, 2nd son of George Onslow, MP (ante):—
Issue of late Maj-Gen James William MACARTHUR-ONSLOW, VD, *b* 1867, *d* 1946: *m* 1897, Enid Emma, who *d* 1952, da of Arthur H. Macarthur, of NS Wales:—
Elizabeth Enid, *b* 1903: *m* 1935, Fredrik Ludwig Rothe. *Residence* – 15 Wyuna Rd, Point Piper, Sydney, NSW.
Issue of late Arthur John MACARTHUR-ONSLOW, *b* 1873, *d* 1954, having assumed the additional surname of Macarthur: *m* 1902, Christian Leslie, who *d* 1949, da of late R. Bell, of Golf Hill, Victoria, Australia:—
Rosalind Sibella, *b* 1917: *m* 1944, John Carter, who *d* 1987, and has issue living, Charles John (Kikiamah, Young, NSW), *b* 1950: *m* 1974, Jane Evelyn, da of Dr Ian Barrie, of Kempsey, and has issue living, Charles Ian Onslow *b* 1977, Edward Jack Onslow *b* 1978, Thomas James Onslow *b* 1983, Phoebe Elizabeth Onslow *b* 1981, — Prudence Mary Leslie, *b* 1945: *m* 1970, Hugh Geoffrey O'Neil, of Yamminga, Forbes, NSW, and has issue living, Sophie Christobel Robina *b* 1973, Alice Rosanna *b* 1977. *Residence* – Kikiamah, Young, NSW.
Issue of late Brig-Gen George Macleay MACARTHUR-ONSLOW, CMG, DSO, VD, *b* 1875, *d* 1931: *m* 1907, Violet Marguerite, who *d* 1981, da of late W. F. Gordon, of Manar, near Braidwood, NS Wales:—
Faith MacLeay (Cranmer Cottage, Dorchester-on-Thames, Wallingford, Oxon OX10 7HP), *b* 1910: *m* 1941, Ivan Lloyd Phillips, CBE, DPhil (Oxon), Malayan Civil Ser, who *d* 1984, and has issue living, Hugh Gerard Lloyd (25A Lorne Av, Killara, NSW 2071, Aust), *b* 1946: *m* 1972, Rosalind, da of H. B. Mackenzie-Wood, of Sunninghill, Mt Ousley, NSW, and has issue living, Hugh Edward Paul *b* 1976, Julian Thomas *b* 1979, Clare Elizabeth *b* 1974.

Grandchildren of late Francis Arthur MACARTHUR-ONSLOW, 5th son of Capt Arthur Alexander Walton Onslow, RN (ante):—
Issue of late Maj-Gen Sir Denzil MACARTHUR-ONSLOW, CBE, DSO, ED, *b* 1904, *d* 1984: *m* 1st, 1927 (*m diss* 1950), Elinor Margaret, who *d* 1979, da of late Gordon Caldwell, formerly of 4 Albert Hall Mansions, SW7; 2ndly, 1950, Dorothy Wolseley, AO, MB, BS (Mount Gilead, Campbelltown, NSW, Australia), only child of late W. D. Scott, of Bellevue Hill, NSW:—
(By 1st *m*) (Denzil) Ion (2A Holt St, Double Bay, NSW, Australia), *b* 1928; Lt (ret) R NSW Lancers: *m* 1957, Jenifer Marie, da of late James Crooks, CVO, FRCS, of 46 Harley St, W1, and has issue living, Rupert Gordon *b* 1962, — Sophie Rose, *b* (Nov) 1957: *m* 1st, 1987, Julian Henry Nettlefold, yr son of Edward Michael Nettlefold, of Abbey House, Milton Lilbourne, Pewsey, Wilts; 2ndly, 1993, Peter D. Stork, elder son of Kenneth Stork, of Mayfield, E Sussex, and has issue living (by 1st *m*), Harry Michael Frederick *b* 1989, (by 2nd *m*) James Kenneth Macarthur *b* 1993, — Verena Marie, *b* 1960. —— Neil Gordon, ED (27 Kemmis St, Randwick 2031, NSW, Australia), *b* 1930; Lt-Col comdg 1/15 Armd Regt R NSW Lancers: *m* 1964, Regina de Tessier, da of late Reginald de Tessier Prevost, of Bellevue Hill, NSW, and has issue living, Duncan Reginald, *b* 1966, — Airlie, *b* 1969. —— Euan (East Tinwald, Lochmaben, Dumfriesshire), *b* 1934. —— Diana Florence, *b* 1931: *m* 1952 (*m diss* 1968), Geoffrey Brian Kewley, and has issue living, Robin Geoffrey, *b* 1953, — Martin William, *b* 1959. —— (By 2nd *m*) Lee, *b* 1952; Capt Sydney Univ Regt, Reserve of Officers. —— Katrina (*Lady Hobhouse*), *b* 1953: *m* 1993, Sir Charles John Spinney Hobhouse, 7th Bt, of The Manor, Monkton Farleigh, Bradford-on-Avon, Wilts.
Issue of late Lt-Col Edward Macarthur-Onslow, DSO, ED, Australian Imperial Forces, *b* 1909, *d* 1980: *m* 1932, Winifred Hall, who *d* 1987, da of late William Hall Owen, of Wollongong, NSW:—
Annette Rosemary, *b* 1933. —— Pamela Jane, *b* 1936: *m* 1st, 1958 (*m diss* 1968), Paterson James Saunders; 2ndly, 1971, Arthur Leslie Harrison, of S Shields, co Durham, now of Box 200 PO, Camden, NSW 2570, and has issue living (by 1st *m*), Kirkland Robert Macarthur, *b* 1961, — Christopher Philip, *b* 1962. —— Phoebe (Macquarie Grove, PO Box 2, Camden, NSW 2570), *b* 1939: *m* 1963 (*m diss* 1981), Hugh Geddes Atkinson, and has issue living, Jason Hugh, *b* 1959, — Rachel Ann, *b* 1963.

Grandchildren of late Arthur Loftus Onslow, el son of late Douglas Arthur Onslow, CE (infra):—
Issue of late Douglas Arthur George Onslow, *b* 1901, *d* 1966: *m* 1925, Margaret Forbes Kilgour, who *d* 1985, da of Maj John Merrick Rayner, AMIME, of Maji Chemka, Thomson's Falls, Kenya:—
Richard Douglas Loftus (8 Bridgewater Park, Marais St, PO Box 230, Somerset West 7130, S Africa), *b* 1928; *ed* Michaelhouse, Balgowan, S Africa, and Natal Univ; Kenya 1952-53 with KAR: *m* 1st, 1966 (*m diss* 1968), Mrs Elizabeth Frances Bateman, da of J. Gordon Elsworthy; 2ndly, 1968, Countess Ethel Elisabeth Olga Maria von Rietberg, da of HSH Prince Ferdinand Andreas Joseph Maria of Leichtenstein (Brunner, Bt, colls), and has an adopted da (with 2nd wife), Merith Margaret Andrea, *b* 1972. —— Patricia Margaret Daisy, *b* 1941: *m* 1st, 1960 (*m diss* 1972), Christopher David Kennedy; 2ndly, 1972, Edmond Francis Dorset Fellowes (*see* Twysden, Bt, ext, 1985 Edn), of Seend Green House, Devizes, Wilts, and has issue living (by 1st *m*), Mark Edward Lucian, *b* 1966. —— Prudence Katherine Barbara, *b* 1946: *m* 1970, Lt-Col Robin Timothy Keigwin, Irish Gds, of 36 Cargate Av, Aldershot, Hants GU11 3EW, and has issue living, Richard Skarratt, *b* 1973, — Michael Douglas, *b* 1975.

Grandchildren of late Douglas Arthur George Onslow (ante):—
Issue of late Desmond Merrick Onslow, *b* 1929; *d* 1983: *m* 1954, Syvlia Patricia Melody Wiggins, of PO Box 45, Fourways 2055, S Africa:—
Roger, *b* 1965. —— Debra Susan, *b* 1955: *m* 1977, David Alan Brokenshire, and has issue living, Rhett David, *b* 1982. —— Vanessa Mary, *b* 1960.

Grandsons of late Douglas Arthur Onslow, CE, el son of late Lt-Col William Campbell Onslow, 2nd son of Rev Arthur Onslow (ante):—

Issue of late Francis Robert Douglas Onslow, *b* 1878, *d* 1938: *m* 1925, Mabel, who *d* 1974, da of William Strachan, of Edinburgh:—
Sir Cranley Gordon Douglas, KCMG, MP, *b* 1926; *ed* Harrow, and Oriel Coll, Oxford (MA); late Lt 7th Queen's Own Hussars; a Co Councillor for Kent 1961-64; served in HM Foreign Ser 1951-60, Min of State at Foreign Office 1982-83; MP for Woking Div of Surrey (C) since 1964; *cr* KCMG 1992: *m* 1955, Lady June Ann Hay, da of 14th Earl of Kinnoull, and has issue living, Richard Alan Douglas, *b* 1956; *ed* Harrow, and Oriel Coll, Oxford (MA): *m* 1985, Phyllida K., da of Michael Moore, of Folly Farm, Lindsey, Suffolk, and has issue living, Thomas Cranley Douglas *b* 1992, Isabella *b* 1990, — Sandra (Sue) Dorothy, *b* 1958; *ed* LSE (BSc): *m* 1982, J. Bartlett K. Smith, of Dayton, Ohio, USA, and has issue living, Jonathan Christopher *b* 1990, Claerwen Helen *b* 1988, — Caroline Diana, *b* 1959; *ed* Manchester Univ (BA): *m* 1987, Joseph V. Martino, yr son of late J. Martino, of New York, USA, — Katharine (Kash) Denise, *b* 1961: *m* 1987, Nigel P. Steer, son of Robert Steer, of Liphook, Hants. *Residence* – Highbuilding, Fernhurst, Sussex. —— Ian Denzil, *b* 1929; *ed* Harrow, and Grenoble Univ, France: *m* 1954, Marjorie, da of Albert Domville, of Stockton Heath, and has issue living, Christopher Denzil, *b* 1956; *ed* Harrow: *m* 1st, 1984 (*m diss* 1990), Veronica Jane, yst da of Capt John Stanley Mitcalfe, OBE, VRD, RNR (ret); 2ndly, 1993, Paula Louise Howell, only da of late John Jenkins, MICE, of Inkberrow, Worcs, and has issue living (by 2nd wife), Edward John Denzil *b* 1991, — Mark Loftus Domville, *b* 1958; *ed* Pangbourne: *m* 1983, Judith Heather, da of Peter Smith, of E Grinstead, Sussex, — Michael Piers David, *b* 1963; *ed* Harrow, and Stirling Univ; Capt The Royal Scots (The Royal Regt): *m* 1993, Lesley Alison, eldest da of late Kenneth Jolly, of Gt Baddow, Essex, — Robert Douglas, *b* 1965; *ed* Kings Sch, Bruton, — Victoria Penelope Diana *b* (twin) 1965: *m* 1993, Jolyon Robert Lydall Savill, who *d* (March) 1993, only son of John L. L. Savill. *Residence* – 3 Jubilee Cottages, 43 Middle Rd, Lymington, Hants SO41 9HE.

Granddaughters of late Maj Arthur Hughes-Onslow, el son of late Henry John Hughes-Onslow, 5th son of late Rev Arthur Onslow (ante):—
Issue of late Cdr Sir Geoffrey Henry Hughes-Onslow, KBE, DSC, RN, *b* 1893, *d* 1971: *m* 1918, Hon Eileen Mabel Lowther Crofton, who *d* 1972, da of 4th Baron Crofton:—
Auriole Kathleen, *b* 1919: *m* 1945, Rev Simon Charles David Fergusson, who *d* 1982 (*see* Fergusson, Bt). —— Judith Eileen, *b* 1923: *m* 1945, Lt John Thornton Lorimer, DSO, RNVR, of Kirkangus, Barr, Ayrshire, and has issue living, Patrick James, *b* 1946: *m* 1976, Julia Caroline, da of Alexander Patrick Pringle, DFC, of Gemilston, Kirkmichael, Ayrshire, and has issue living, James Seth Patrick *b* 1979, William Reuben John *b* 1980, Cressida Flora Kate *b* 1984, — Bridget Katharine Eileen (22 Birkbeck Rd, W3), *b* 1948. —— Mary, *b* 1929: *m* 1952, Lt Cdr George Stewart Wright, VRD, RNR, of Wainsford House, Everton, Lymington, Hants, and has issue living, Nicholas Peter, *b* 1960, — Christopher George, *b* 1964.

Grandchildren of late Capt Oliver Hughes-Onslow (infra):—
Issue of late Andrew George Hughes-Onslow, *b* 1920; *d* 1979: *m* 1944, Betty (who *m* 2ndly, 1994, as his 2nd wife, David George Crichton, LVO (*see* E Erne, colls), of 29B Thorney Crescent, Morgans Walk, SW11 3TT), da of late Col Maurice George Lee, MC, RFC, of Christchurch, NZ:—
James Andrew (42 Knatchbull Rd, SE5 9QY; *Club* – Boodle's), *b* 1945; *ed* Eton; journalist: *m* 1982, Christina L., da of Peter Hay, of Melbourne, Australia, and has issue living, Andrew Peter, *b* 1985, — Flora Alice, *b* 1988, — Marina, *b* 1990, — Harriet, *b* 1993. —— Elizabeth Mary, *b* 1949: *m* 1978, John Randolph Hustler, of Ripsley House, Liphook, Hants GU30 7JH, son of late William Mostyn Collingwood Hustler, of 31 Melton Court, SW7, and has issue living, Charles James, *b* 1982, — Frederick Randolph, *b* 1986, — Willa Victoria, *b* 1983. —— Sarah Jane, *b* 1954: *m* 1975, Michael Williams, of Werrington Park, Launceston, Cornwall PL15 8TR, and has issue living, Thomas Edward, *b* 1976, — George Michael, *b* 1979, — Camilla Ruth, *b* 1984.

Grandchildren of late Maj Denzil Hughes-Onslow, 2nd son of Henry John Hughes-Onslow (ante):—
Issue of late Capt Oliver Hughes-Onslow, *b* 1893, *d* 1972: *m* 1916, Helen Ruth, who *d* 1980, da of late Rev George Dods, BD, Min of Barr, Ayrshire:—
Timothy Neil (32 Godfrey St, SW3; White's, Beefsteak, and Brooks's Clubs), *b* 1924; *ed* Eton; Capt (ret), Rifle Bde; 1939-45 War: *m* 1950, Susan, da of Sir William Francis Stratford Dugdale, 1st Bt (*cr* 1936), and has issue living, Archibald Edward Neil (82 Mercers Rd, N19 4PR), *b* 1954; *ed* Eton, BNC Oxford, and Oxford Polytechnic; townplanner; has issue living (by Mary Ryan, solicitor), Daniel *b* 1987, Max *b* 1989, Euan Williams *b* 1991, — Richard Luke (42 Agate Rd, W6 0AH; *Club* – White's), *b* 1958; *ed* Eton: *m* 1988, Christine S., da of Charles Doughty, of Mill House, Denham Bridge, Buckland Monachorum, Devon, and has issue living, Iona Margaret *b* 1992, — Henrietta, *b* 1951: *m* 1980, David W. A. Cole, of 17 Heslop Rd, SW12, son of Sir David Cole, KCMG, MC, and has issue living, Timothy David *b* 1985, Lucy *b* 1983. —— Fergus Erskine (Lower Norsebury, Stoke Charity, Winchester, Hants SO21 3PR; *Clubs* – Boodle's, Pratt's, City of London), *b* 1929; *ed* Eton; Capt (ret) Rifle Bde; a Member of Queen's Body Guard for Scotland (R Company of Archers): *m* 1955, Rose Ariel, da of late Anthony Ewart Ledger Hill, OBE, DL, of Twyford Lodge, Twyford, Hants, and has issue living, Anthony Charles, *b* 1957; Gen Man Broadlands Estate since 19—: *m* 1991, Laura A., da of L. W. Newton, and of Mrs M. A. J. Clark, of W2, and has issue living, Harry Arthur *b* 1992, — Olivia, *b* 1960: *m* 1985, Michael J. W. Winterton, of 55 Tantallon Rd, SW12, son of Cdr David Winterton, RN, of Vale House, Halstock, Yeovil, Som, and has issue living, Xan John *b* 1993, Hermione Rose *b* 1987, Lucy *b* 1989, — Belinda Marion, *b* 1962. —— Virginia Ruth Primrose (Apt 14, Aynhoe Park, Banbury, Oxon OX17 3BQ), *b* 1917: *m* 1st, 1942 (*m diss* 1953), Maj Robert Boothby How, Black Watch, who *d* 1990; 2ndly, 1969, Maurice Oliver Pease, who *d* 1976, and has issue living (by 1st *m*), Denzil Robert Onslow (23 Ladbroke Sq, W11 3NB; White's Club), *b* 1947; *ed* Eton, and Trin Coll, Camb: *m* 1st, 1968 (*m diss* 1985), Sarah Elizabeth, only da of John Ernest Harley Collins, MBE, DSC (*see* B Bicester, 1980 Edn); 2ndly, 1989, Hon Catharine Gina Amita (VEY), da of late Baron Glenkinglas (Life Baron), and has issue living (by 1st *m*), Nicola Jane Audrey *b* 1970, Antonia Clare *b* 1975, Francesca Ruth *b* 1978, Georgina Louise *b* 1981, — Primrose Jean Onslow (47 Queensdale Rd, W11), *b* 1947: *m* 1969 (*m diss* 1993), Andrew Hugh John Muir, and has issue (*see* Muir, Bt), — (Carolyn) Jane Onslow How (9 Wiseton Rd, Wandsworth Common, SW18), *b* 1950; actress; has resumed her maiden name: *m* 1977 (*m diss* 1992), Mark Burns, and has issue living, Jack Louis *b* 1981.

Issue of late Lt-Com Reginald Hughes-Onslow, RN (ret), *b* 1895, *d* 1947: *m* 1934 (*m diss* 1946), Daphne Helen Anne, who *d* 1992, da of late Col Robert Hanbury Brudenell Bruce, DSO (*see* M Ailesbury, colls, 1990 Edn):—
Denzil Jamie (The Old Bake House, Culworth, nr Banbury, Oxon), *b* 1939; *ed* Ampleforth; late 2nd Lt R Armoured Corps: *m* 1973, Chloé Elizabeth, da of Mme Vve de Vic, of St Cloud, Paris, and has issue living, Sophie Anne Rose, *b* 1974.

Branch from 2nd son of 2nd son of brother of 1st Baron

Descendants of late Adm Sir Richard Onslow, GCB, who was *cr* a Bt 1797, 2nd son of late Lt-Gen Richard Onslow (infra):—
See Onslow, Bt.

Branch from 1st son of 3rd son of 2nd son of brother of 1st Baron

Grandchildren of late Maj George Arthur Onslow, 5th and yst son of Capt Andrew George Onslow, of Oxenhall, Newent, eldest son of Richard Foley Onslow, of Stardens, Glos, eldest son of Ven Richard Francis Onslow, Archdeacon of Worcester, eldest son of Very Rev Arthur Onslow, Dean of Worcester, 3rd son of Lt-Gen Richard Onslow, nephew of 1st Baron and uncle of 1st Earl:—
Issue of late Adm Sir Richard George Onslow, KCB, DSO, *b* 1904, *d* 1975: *m* 1932, Kathleen Meriel (Little Ryton House, Ryton, Shrewsbury, Shropshire SY5 7LW), el da of Edmund Taylor, of Longnor Bank House, Shrewsbury:—

Richard Edmund (Preston Bagot House, Preston Bagot, Henley-in-Arden, Warwicks B95 5DR), *b* 1933; Cdr RN: *m* 1961, Mary-Jean, el da of Brig Kenneth James Garner-Smith, OBE, of Aird House, by Inverness, and has issue living, Richard James, *b* 1962; *ed* Eton; Capt Blues & Royals: *m* 1992, Lucinda Caroline, da of Patrick Alexander Campbell Fraser, of Borthwickshiels, Hawick, Roxburghshire, — Robert Denzil, *b* 1965; *ed* Eton, and Magdalen Coll, Oxford; bar-at-law. —— Denzil John (The Bank House, Richards Castle, Salop), *b* 1939: *m* 1967, Susan, da of late B. Leach, and has issue living, Andrew John, *b* 1968, — James Denzil, *b* 1970, — Tamsin Sarah, *b* 1976.

Issue of late Maj John Onslow, Duke of Cornwall's LI, *b* 1906, *d* 1985: *m* 1956, Susan (Oaklea, Vicarage Hill, Loxwood, W Sussex), da of late Roland Percival Neville Towle:—
Andrew George (Rylstone, Grove Park, SE5 8LT), *b* 1957: *m* 1991, (Elizabeth) Jane, yr da of Lt-Col James Barratt Owen, of Beechwood, Bengate, Appleby-in-Westmorland, and formerly wife of — Evans, and has issue living, Harry James Rufus, *b* 1992, — Frederica Jane, *b* 1993. —— Simon John (65 St Margarets Rd, Twickenham, TW1 2LL) *b* 1960, *m* 1993, Clare, da of Norman Lonsdale, of Bridlemere Court, Newmarket, Suffolk. —— Jane Elizabeth, *b* 1958; *d* 1975. —— Sarah Margaret, *b* 1962: *m* 1990, Simon F. Harrison, of Ironstone Cottage, Lower St, Fittleworth, W Sussex, son of R. F. Harrison, of Pulborough, W Sussex, and has issue living, Emily Jane Elizabeth, *b* 1992. —— Rachel Evelyn Mary, *b* 1967.

Issue of late Maj Charles Edward Onslow, MC, *b* 1912, *d* 1969: *m* 1955, Margaret Mary Lee (c/o Mrs P. B. Allen, PO Box 41190, Nairobi, Kenya), da of Rev William Marsh Lee Evans, R of Saxby, Brigg, Lincs:—
John Edward, *b* 1956: *m* 1986, Dora Helen, da of late Christopher Wyborn Armstrong, OBE, of Kwetu Farm, Gilgil, Kenya, and has issue living, Jasper Denzil, *b* 1994. *Address* – Peponi House School, PO Box 23203, Nairobi, Kenya.

Granddaughters of late Capt Andrew George Onslow (ante):—
Issue of late Major George Arthur Onslow, *b* 1876, *d* 1956: *m* 1st, 1902, Charlotte Riou, who *d* 1932, yst da of late Rev Riou George Benson; 2ndly, 1933, Maud Elliot, who *d* 1986, yr da of late George Steele Travers Harris:—
(By 1st *m*) Mary (Hope Cottage, Hayton, Carlisle, CA4 9HT), *b* 1903: *m* 1930, Very Rev William Cyril Mayne, Dean of Carlisle, who *d* 1962. —— Kathleen Theodosia, *b* 1914: *m* 1945, Edward Godfrey Purvis Sherwood, of Applegarth, Hayton, Carlisle, CA4 9HT, and has issue living, Edward Patrick Charles (PO Box 262, Zomba, Malawi), *b* 1946: *m* 1975, Margaret Anne, da of late John Van Vechten Veeder, and has issue living, Edward Godfrey DeWitt *b* 1978, Peter David Onslow *b* 1980, Claire Margaret Letham *b* 1987, — Andrew Godfrey Purvis (2 Pelham Terr, Lewes, E Sussex BN7 1TY), *b* 1950: *m* 1974, Mary Helen, da of Hon Francis Michael Hepburne-Scott (*see* L Polwarth), and has issue living, Gideon *b* 1976, Samuel *b* 1979, Phoebe *b* 1983, — Thomas James Mulso (26 Highclere Rd, New Malden, Surrey KT3 3HJ), *b* 1951: *m* 1980, Barbara, da of Kenneth Walter Emberson, of 2 Newlands Park, Copthorne, Crawley, W Sussex, and has had issue, David Mathew *b* and *d* 1986, Nathan John *b* 1988, Joanna Ruth *b* 1984, — Charlotte Claire, *b* 1947. —— Denzil Octavia (St Andrew's House, 2 Tavistock Rd, W11 1BA), *b* 1919.

Grandchildren of late Augustus Paul Lumsden Onslow, 4th son of Rev Arthur Andrew Onslow, 2nd son of Ven Richard Francis Onslow (ante):—
Issue of late Augustus Charles Albert Foley Onslow, *b* 1888, *d* 1965: *m* 1914, Winifred May, who *d* 1971, da of late W. R. Williams, of Thornton Heath, Surrey:—
Winston Hillier Gopal (108 Culvert Rd, SW11), *b* 1915: *m* 1939, Kathleen Edis, who *d* 1975, and has issue living, Veronica Vivien, *b* 1943: *m* 1969, Alan Roy Wood, Surveyor, of 23 Langdale Rd, Hove, E Sussex, and has an adopted da, Lucille Ann, *b* 1973. —— †Lewis Lumsden William, *b* 1924; Journalist; *d* 1991. —— Patricia Doreen (1 Airey Houses, Scocles Rd, Minster, Isle of Sheppey, Kent), *b* 1927: *m* 1956, Ronald George Coombs, who *d* 1990, and has issue living, Anne Patricia, *b* 1957: *m* 1985, Stephen David Smart, of 32 Minster Rd, Halfway, Sheerness, Kent, and has issue living, Sam Kenneth *b* 1988, Ben *b* 1990.
Issue of late Frederick Hewitt Lumsden Onslow, *b* 1897, *d* 1969: *m* 1939, Olive Eveline (Newgarth Nursing Home, Tower Hill Rd, Dorking, Surrey), da of Ernest Spicer:—
Frederick Winston Lumsden, *b* 1940: *m* 1964, Elizabeth Maude, da of Frank Berenger Benger, and has issue living, Robert Frederick, *b* 1970, — Gillian Elizabeth, *b* 1966, — Vivien Gail, *b* 1967. *Residence* – Red Chimneys, Chalk Lane, E Horsley, Leatherhead, Surrey.

Branch from 3rd son of 3rd son of 2nd son of brother of 1st Baron

Grandchildren of late Henry Phipps Onslow (infra):—
Issue of late Thomas Phipps Onslow, *b* 1907, *d* 1990: *m* 1945, Mrs Pauline Calvert, who *d* 1970, da of Kenneth L. Shoobridge, of Coniston, Glenora, Tasmania:—
William Phipps (Bridge House, Ouse, Tasmania), *b* 1947: *m* 1974, Victoria, da of Paul L. Abbott, of Woodstock, Calder, Tasmania, and has issue living, Fiona Louise, *b* 1975, — Lucie Jane, *b* 1976, — Annabel Rose, *b* 1979. —— Jane Elizabeth, *b* 1945: *m* 1969, Christopher Goodwin Morley, of Bacchus Creek, RMB 303 Kojonup, W Australia 6395, and has issue living, Hamish Charles Thomas, *b* 1977, — Emma Patricia, *b* 1970, — Georgina Joan, *b* 1972.

Granddaughter of late Rev Phipps Onslow, son of late Phipps Vansittart Onslow, yst son of Very Rev Arthur Onslow, DD (ante):—
Issue of late Henry Phipps Onslow, *b* 1869, *d* 1945: *m* 1898, Maisie, who *d* 1959, da of Hon T. Playford, of Drysdale, Norton's Summit, S Australia:—
Margaret Louise, *b* 1921: *m* 1946, Charles Edward Rollins, who *d* 1990, and has issue living, Phillip Charles, *b* 1947: *m* 1970, Suzanne Mary Martin, of Montrose, Tasmania, and has issue living, Richard *b* 1973, Elizabeth *b* 1976, — Susan Louise, *b* 1951. *Residence* – 37 Pioneer Av, Church Hill, New Norfolk, Tasmania.

PREDECESSORS – (1) Sir THOMAS Foote, Knt, Lord Mayor of London 1649; was *cr* a *Baronet* 1660; *d* 1687; his son-in-law (2) ARTHUR Onslow (husband of his da Mary), successively MP for Bramber, Sussex, Surrey, and Guildford; was *cr* a *Baronet* 1674 (with precedency of 1660); *d* 1688; *s* by his son (3) Sir RICHARD, PC, 2nd Bt; was successively MP for Guildford, Surrey, and St Mawes; was a Lord of the Admiralty, Speaker of House of Commons, High Steward of Guildford, Gov of the Levant Co, a Lord of the Treasury, Chancellor and Under-Treasurer of the Exchequer, and a Teller of the Exchequer for life; *cr Baron Onslow*, of Onslow, co Salop, and of Clandon, co Surrey (peerage of Great Britain) 1716, with remaining to his uncle, Denzil Onslow, and aftrwards to the heirs male of his father; *d* 1717; *s* by his son (4) THOMAS, 2nd Baron; *d* 1740; *s* by his son (5) RICHARD, 3rd Baron; *dsp* Oct 1776; *s* by his heir male of his grandfather (6) GEORGE, PC (son of Arthur Onslow, PC, MP, who was Speaker of the House of Commons 1727-61), 4th Baron who in May of the same year had been *cr Baron Cranley*, of Imber Court (peerage of Great Britain); was successively MP for Rye and Surrey Out-Ranger of Windsor Forest, a Lord of the Treasury, Lord-Lieut of Surrey, Treasurer of the Household and a Lord of the Bedchamber; *cr Viscount Cranley* and *Earl of Onslow* (peerage of United Kingdom) 1801; *d* 1814; *s* by his son (7) THOMAS, 2nd Earl; sat as MP for Guildford 1784-1807; *d* 1827; *s* by his son (8) ARTHUR GEORGE, 3rd Earl; *d* 1870, without surviving male issue; *s* by his grandnephew (9) WILLIAM HILLIER, GMCG, PC, (son of George Augustus Cranley (son of Hon Thomas Cranley, 2nd son of 2nd Earl, by Mary Harriet Ann, da of Lieut-Gen William F. B. Loftus)), 4th Earl; *b* 1853; a Lord-in-Waiting to Queen Victoria 1880 and 1886-7, Under-Sec of State for Colonies Feb 1887 to Feb 1888, Parliamentary Sec to Board of Trade Feb to Nov 1888, Gov and Com-in-Chief of New Zealand 1888-92, Under-Sec of State for India July 1895 to Nov 1900, Under-Sec of State for the Colonies 1900-1903, Pres of Board of Agriculture 1903-5, and Dep Speaker and Chm of Committees of House of Lords 1905-11: *m* 1875, Hon Florence Coulstoun, who *d* 1934, da of 3rd Baron Gardner; *d* 1911; *s* by his el son (10) RICHARD WILLIAM ALAN, 5th Earl; *b* 1876; High Steward of Guildford; entered Diplo Ser 1901; was Assist Private Sec of State for Foreign Affairs 1909-11 and Private Sec to Permanent Under-Sec of State for Foreign Affairs (Rt Hon

Nov 1900, Under-Sec of State for the Colonies 1900-1903, Pres of Board of Agriculture 1903-5, and Dep Speaker and Chm of Committees of House of Lords 1905-11: *m* 1875, Hon Florence Coulstoun, who *d* 1934, da of 3rd Baron Gardner; *d* 1911; *s* by his el son **(10)** RICHARD WILLIAM ALAN, 5th Earl; *b* 1876; High Steward of Guildford; entered Diplo Ser 1901; was Assist Private Sec of State for Foreign Affairs 1909-11 and Private Sec to Permanent Under-Sec of State for Foreign Affairs (Rt Hon Sir Arthur Nicolson, Bt, GCB) 1911-13; European War 1915-19 (OBE, Legion of Honour); appointed a Lord-in-Waiting to HM 1919, Civil Lord of the Admiralty 1920, Parliamentary Sec to Min of Agriculture 1921, to Min of Health 1921 and 1923, and to Board of Education 1923 (resigned Jan 1924), Under-Sec of State for War 1924, and Paymaster-Gen 1928 (resigned 1929); Chm of Committees and Dep Speaker in House of Lords 1931-44; became Hon Col 30th (Surrey) Anti-Aircraft Btn, RE (TA) 1927: *m* 1906, Hon Violet Marcia Catherine Bampfylde, CBE, ARRC, who *d* 1954, da of 3rd Baron Poltimore; *d* 1945; *s* by his son **(11)** WILLIAM ARTHUR BAMPFYLDE, KBE, MC, TD, 6th Earl, *b* 1913; Col late RAC, High Steward of Guildford 1947-71, Capt of the Yeoman of the Guard 1951-60: *m* 1st, 1936 (*m diss* 1962), Hon Pamela Louisa Eleanor Dillon, who *d* 1992, only da of 19th Viscount Dillon; 2ndly, 1962, Nina, MBE, da of Thomas Sturdee; *d* 1971; *s* by his son **(12)** MICHAEL WILLIAM COPLESTONE DILLON, 7th Earl and present peer; also Viscount and Baron Cranley, and Baron Onslow.

OPPENHEIM-BARNES, BARONESS (Oppenheim-Barnes) (Life Baroness 1989)

SALLY OPPENHEIM-BARNES, PC, da of late Mark Viner, of Sheffield; *b* 26 July 1930; *ed* Sheffield High Sch, and Lowther Coll, N Wales; former Social Worker with ILEA; Vice-Chm Conservative Parl Prices and Consumer Protection Cttee 1971-73, and Chm 1973-74; Chm Nat Consumer Council 1987-89; Chm Nat Waterways Trust 1988-89; Front Bench Opposition Spokesman on Prices and Consumer Protection 1974-79; Member Shadow Cabinet 1975-79, Min of State for Consumer Affairs, Dept of Trade, 1979-82; Member House of Commons Cttee for Privileges 1986-89, Non-Exec Dir Main Board of Boots Co plc 1982-93, Non-Exec Dir Fleming High Income Investment Trust plc since 1989, Non-Exec Dir HFC Bank plc since 1989, and Nat Vice-Pres Townswomen's Guild 1989-90; former Pres Glos Dist of British Red Cross; MP Gloucester (*C*) 1970-87; *cr* PC 1979, and *Baroness Oppenheim-Barnes*, of Gloucester, co Glos (Life Baroness) 1989: *m* 1st, 1949, Henry Myer Oppenheim, who *d* 1980; 2ndly, 1984, John Barnes, and has issue by 1st *m*.
Residence – Quietways, The Highlands, Painswick, Glos.

SON LIVING (By 1st marriage)

Hon Phillip Anthony Charles Lawrence, MP, *b* 1956; *ed* Harrow, and Oriel Coll, Oxford (MA); MP Amber Valley (*C*) since 1983. *Address* – c/o House of Commons, SW1.

DAUGHTERS LIVING (By 1st marriage)

Hon Carolyn, *b* 1951; *ed* Benenden, and London Univ (BA): *m* 1973, Martin Robert Selman, and has issue living, David Benjamin, *b* 1978, — Victoria Esther Jeanette, *b* 1977, — Henrietta Amy Charlotte, *b* 1982.
Hon Rosanne, *b* 1954: *m* 1st, 1984 (*m diss* 1988), David B. Williams; 2ndly, 1993, Stephen James Mattick, and has issue living (by 2nd *m*), Olivia Daisy Amelia, *b* 1993. *Residence* – Pettett's Barn, Hinxton, Cambs CB10 1RF.

ORAM, BARON (Oram) (Life Baron 1975)

ALBERT EDWARD ORAM, son of late Henry Oram; *b* 13 Aug 1913; *ed* Brighton Gram Sch, and London Univ (BA Hons); Research Officer Co-operative Party 1946-55; MP for East Ham South (*Lab* and *Co-op*) 1955-75; Co-ordinator of Development Programmes Internat Co-operative Alliance 1973-74; Development Administrator Intermediate Tech Development Group 1974-76; a Lord in Waiting to HM 1976-78; *cr Baron Oram*, of Brighton in co of E Sussex (Life Baron) 1975: *m* 1956, Frances Joan, da of Arthur Charles Barber, of Lewes, Sussex, and has issue.
Residence – 19 Ridgeside Av, Patcham, Brighton, BN1 8WD.

SONS LIVING

Hon Mark, *b* 1967.
Hon Robin, *b* 1968.

ORANMORE AND BROWNE, BARON. Sits as BARON MEREWORTH (UK 1926) (Browne) (Baron I 1836)

Boldly and faithfully

DOMINICK GEOFFREY EDWARD BROWNE, 4th Baron; *b* 21 Oct 1901; *s* 1927; *ed* Eton, and Ch Ch, Oxford: *m* 1st, 1925 (*m diss* 1936), Mildred Helen, who *d* 1980, dau of late Hon Thomas Henry Frederick Egerton (*see* D Sutherland, colls); 2ndly, 1936 (*m diss* 1950), Oonagh, da of late Hon Arthur Ernest Guinness (*see* E Iveagh colls), and formerly wife of Hon Philip Leyland Kindersley; 3rdly, 1951, Constance Vera (film actress, Sally Gray), da of late Charles Edward Stevens, and has issue by 1st and 2nd *m*.

Arms – Argent, an eagle displayed with two heads sable, langued gules. **Crest** – A gryphon's head erased argent. **Supporters** – *Dexter*, a knight in ancient armour belted azure, garnished or, holding in his right hand a battle-axe chained proper, charged on the blade with a cross pattee or, on his left an ancient pointed shield gules, charged with two lioncels or, supported by a band from the right shoulder gules, studded and garnished or; *sinister*, a knight, also in chain armour, with a circuit of blue silk, belted gules, leaning his left hand on an ancient two-handed sword, thereon a shield argent, charged with an eagle displayed with two heads sable, langued gules. **Motto** – "Fortiter et fideliter."
Residence – 52 Eaton Place, SW1.

SONS LIVING *(By 1st marriage)*

Hon DOMINICK GEOFFREY THOMAS, *b* 1 July 1929: *m* 1957 (*m diss* 1974), Sara Margaret, da of late Dr Herbert Wright, of 59 Merrion Sq, Dublin.
Hon Martin Michael Dominick, *b* 1931; *ed* Eton: *m* 1958, Alison Margaret, only da of late John Bradford, and has issue living, Shaun Dominick, *b* 1964: *m* 1990, Elizabeth Jane, yr da of Rev Rex Bird, of The Rectory, Monks Eleigh, Suffolk, and has issue living, Ophelia Alexandra *b* 1994, — Cara Margaret, *b* 1961: *m* 1988 (*m diss* 1992), Philip William Howard (*see* Howard-Lawson, Bt).

(By 2nd marriage)

Hon Garech Domnagh, *b* 1939; *ed* Le Rosey: *m* 1981, Princess Harshad Purna Devi (JADEJA) of Morvi, da of late HH Sri Mahendra Maharaja of Morvi, of The New Palace, Morvi, India. *Residences* – 13 rue de la Douzaine, Fort George, St Peter Port, Guernsey, CI; Luggala, Roundwood, co Wicklow.

DAUGHTER LIVING *(By 1st marriage)*

Hon Judith, *b* 1934: *m* 1958 (Ralph) Michael Haslam, and has issue living, Christopher William Dominick, *b* 1960, — David Oliver Myles, *b* 1962, — Carina Judith, *b* 1965. *Residence* – The Orangery, Felix Hall, Kelvedon, Essex CO5 9DG.

WIDOW LIVING OF SON OF FOURTH BARON

Noreen Anne, da of Seán MacSherry, of co Down: *m* 1963, Hon Tara Browne, who was *k* in a motor accident 1966, and has issue living (see colls infra).

COLLATERAL BRANCH LIVING

Issue of late Hon Tara Browne, yst son of 4th Baron, *b* 1945, *k* in a motor accident 1966: *m* 1963, Noreen Anne (ante), da of Seán MacSherry of co Down:—
Dorian Clifford, *b* 1963. —— Julian Dominick, *b* 1965.

PREDECESSORS – (1) DOMINICK Browne, PC, MP for and Lord-Lieut of Co Mayo, was *cr Baron Oranmore and Browne* (peerage of Ireland) 1836; *b* 1787: *m* 1811, Catherine Anne, el da and co-heir of Henry Monck; *d* 1860; *s* by his son (2) GEOFFREY DOMINICK AUGUSTUS FREDERICK, 2nd Baron, *b* 1819; was Representative Peer for Ireland; assumed *vitâ patris* the additional surname of Guthrie on his marriage: *m* 1859, Christina, who *d* 1887, only child and heiress of late Alexander Guthrie, of The Mount, Ayrshire; *d* 1900; *s* by his only son (3) GEOFFREY HENRY BROWNE, KP, PC, 3rd Baron; *b* 1861; a Representative Peer for Ireland, and a Senator for S Ireland; *cr Baron Mereworth*, of Mereworth Castle, Kent (peerage of United Kingdom) 1926: *m* 1901, Lady Olwen Verena Ponsonby, who *d* 1927, da of 8th Earl of Bessborough, KP; *d* 1927; *s* by his son (4) DOMINICK GEOFFREY EDWARD BROWNE, 4th Baron and present peer; also Baron Mereworth.

Orford, Earldom of, see Baron Walpole.

Oriel, Baron, title of Viscount Massereene and Ferrard on Roll of HL.

ORKNEY, EARL OF (Fitz-Maurice) (Earl S 1696)

CECIL O'BRYEN FITZ-MAURICE, 8th Earl; *b* 3 July 1919; *s* 1951 (succession approved by Lyon Court 1955); late Driver RASC; European War 1939-45, Korea 1950-51: *m* 1953, Rose Katherine Durk, da of late J. W. D. Silley, of Brixham, S Devon.

Arms – Quarterly, grand-quartered; 1st and 4th grand-quarters; argent, on a saltire gules a lymphad sails furled or, a chief ermine *Fitz-Maurice*; 2nd grand-quarter, counter-quartered; 1st and 4th, gules, three cinquefoils ermine *Hamilton*; 2nd, argent, a lymphad sails furled sable *Arran*; 3rd argent, a heart gules imperially crowned or, on a chief azure three mullets of the first *Douglas*; over all at the fess point an escallop or for difference *Lord George Hamilton, 1st Earl of Orkney*; 3rd grand-quarter, counter-quartered; 1st and 4th, gules three lions passant guardant per pale or and argent *O'Bryen*; 2nd, argent, three piles meeting in the point issuing from the chief gules; 3rd a pheon azure. **Crests** – 1st, a Sagittarius passant proper; 2nd, an ancient boat or, flagged azure, and issuant therefrom an oak-tree fructed and penetrated by frame-saw proper, the frame or. **Supporters** – *Dexter*, an antelope azure, armed and ducally gorged with chain reflexed across the back or; *sinister*, a stag proper attired and ducally gorged with chain reflexed across the back or, each charged upon the shoulder with a cinquefoil ermine.

Residence – Summerlands, Princes Rd, Ferndown, Dorset.

COLLATERAL BRANCHES LIVING

Grandchildren of late Isabella Annie Fitz-Maurice (*m* 1882, Sir Frederick Robert St John, KCMG), 2nd da of late Capt Hon James Terence Fitz-Maurice, 5th son of 5th Earl:—
(See V Bolingbroke, colls, of whom Dr OLIVER PETER ST JOHN is *hp* to the Earldom of Orkney.)

Grandchildren of late Dorothy Emily Olga St John (*m* 1906, Sir Henry Crofton Lowther, GCVO, KCMG), 2nd da of late Isabella Annie, Lady St John (ante):—
Issue of late Oliver Peter Lowther, *b* 1910, *d* 1990: *m* 1937, Jean (9 Church Close, Bourton, Salisbury SP8 6DU), da of Clarence John Inder, of NZ:—
James Brabazon LOWTHER (Ramridge Dene, Ramridge Park, Weyhill, Andover, Hants SP11 0QP), *b* 1939; *ed* Harrow.

Issue of late Esmée Katalin Lowther, *b* 1913, *d* 1992: *m* 1936, Cmdr John Harry Roughton, RN, who *d* 1970:—
Jeremy John Lowther ROUGHTON *b* 1944. —— Priscilla Dorothy, *b* 1937: *m* 1969, John Paul, of 37 Church Close, Royden, Diss, Norfolk. —— Jacqueline Esmée, *b* 1951: *m* 1973, Gonzalo Amador Salazar, of 14 Kingfisher Drive, Ham, Richmond-on-Thames, Surrey, and has issue living, Rodrigo James, *b* 1977, — Marcel Oliver, *b* 1981, — Andrea Sofia, *b* 1974, — Olympia Gabriella, *b* 1976.

Granddaughter of late Cecil Henry Fitz-Maurice, son of Lt-Col William Edward Fitz-Maurice (son of John, Viscount Kirkwall, el son of Mary, in her own right Countess of Orkney), brother of 5th Earl:—
Issue of late Cecil Edward Arthur Fitz-Maurice, *b* 1871, *d* 1964: *m* 1900, Maude Elizabeth Mary, who *d* 1970, da of late T. G. Waller:—
Mildred Lillian (45 Painters Field, St Cross, Winchester), *b* 1902: *m* 1938, Capt John Major Leslie Bostock, 11th Lancers, who *d* 1959, and has issue living, Christopher John (12 Granton Rd, Edinburgh, EH5 3QH), *b* 1942, *m* 1963, Yvonne Kendrick, and has issue living, Jason Guy *b* 1969, Joanna Clare *b* 1963, Camilla Jane *b* 1967, — Josephine Mary, *b* 1939: *m* 1964, Geoffrey Stonehouse of 7 Parkside Close, E Horsley, Surrey, and has issue living, Nicholas John *b* 1965, Rachel Ann *b* 1967, Stephanie Jane *b* 1969, Sarah *b* 1972.

PREDECESSORS – (1) *Lord* GEORGE Hamilton, KT, PC, 5th son of Lord William Douglas (*cr* Duke of Hamilton for life), by Anne, Duchess of Hamilton, was *cr* Lord Dechmont, Viscount Kirkwall, and *Earl of Orkney* (peerage of Scotland) 1696, with remainder to the heirs whatsoever of his body; was a Field-Marshal in the Army Gov of Edinburgh Castle, Lord-Lieut of Lanarkshire, a Lord of the Bedchamber, Gov of Virginia, and a Representative Peer; *d* 1737; *s* by his da (2) ANNE, wife of William, 4th Earl of Inchiquin; *d* 1756; *s* by her da (3) MARY, 2nd Countess, wife of Murrough, 1st Marquess of Thomond; *d* 1790; *s* by her da (4) MARY, 3rd Countess, wife of Hon Thomas Fitzmaurice, 2nd son of John, Earl of Shelburne, and brother of 1st Marquess of Lansdowne; *d* 1831; *s* by her grandson (5) THOMAS JOHN HAMILTON, 5th Earl; *b* 1803; a Representative Peer: *m* 1826, Hon Charlotte Isabella, who *d* 1883, da of 3rd Baron Boston; *d* 1877; *s* by his son (6) GEORGE WILLIAM HAMILTON, KCMG, 6th Earl, *b* 1827; a Representative Peer: *m* 1872, Amelia, widow of the Baron de Samuel, a peer of Portugal; *d* 1889; *s* by his nephew (7) EDMOND WALTER (son of late Hon Henry Warrender Fitzmaurice, 2nd son of 5th Earl), 7th Earl, *b* 1867; Lieut-Col 3rd Batn Oxfordshire LI: *m* 1829, Constance Macdonald, who *d* 1946, da of late David Gilchrist; *d* 1951; *s* by his kinsman (8) CECIL O'BRYEN (yr son of late Douglas Frederick Harold Fitz-Maurice, son of late Major Douglas Commerell Menzies Fitz-Maurice, el son of late Com Hon Frederick O'Bryen Fitz-Maurice, RN, 3rd son of 5th Earl), 8th Earl and present peer, also Viscount Kirkwall, and Lord Dechmont.

ORMATHWAITE, BARONY OF (Walsh) (Extinct 1984)

SISTERS LIVING OF SIXTH BARON

Hon Jane Emily Mary, *b* 1910; a Lady-in-Waiting to HRH Princess Alice Duchess of Gloucester 1969-75.
Hon Anne Elizabeth, *b* 1911: *m* 1948, as his 2nd wife, Peter Edward Bromley-Martin, who *d* 1968 (Rouse-Boughton, Bt, colls). *Residence* – The Pheasantry, Builth Wells, Powys, LD2 3NP.

COLLATERAL BRANCH LIVING

Issue of late Hon Nigel Christoper Walsh, 6th son of 2nd Baron, *b* 1867, *d* 1931: *m* 1904, Pauline, who *d* 1956, yst da of late Henry Francis Makins, of 180 Queen's Gate, SW:—
Emily Barbara, *b* 1905: *m* 1st, 1940, Peter Clifford Campbell-Martin, MC, RAF Vol Reserve, who was *ka* 1941; 2ndly, 1947, Robert Lewis Paton, of Dreghorn, Tripp Hill, Fittleworth, W Sussex RH20 1ER (son of late Benjamin Lewis Paton, OBE, MD, of Rugeley, Staffs, by his wife, Janet Cowan, grandda of Robert Andrew Macfie, of Dreghorn Castle, Midlothian), and

has issue living (by 2nd *m*), Hermione Ruth, *b* 1948, — Diana Elizabeth, *b* 1950: *m* 1975, Robert Michael Oliver Batty, of 127 Headlands, Kettering, Northants, and has issue living, Michael Robert *b* 1981, Georgina *b* 1976, Marion Elizabeth *b* 1979. —— Geraldine Lettice (9 Abbotsbury House, W14), *b* 1909.

Ormonde, Baron, title of Marquess of Ormonde on Roll of HL.

ORMONDE, MARQUESS OF (Butler) (Marquess I 1825)

As I find.

Butler for ever

JAMES HUBERT THEOBALD CHARLES BUTLER, MBE, 7th Marquess, *b* 19 April 1899; *s* 1971; *ed* Haileybury, and RMC; late Lt KRRC; 1914-18 War (wounded); 31st Hereditary Chief Butler of Ireland; MBE (Mil) 1921: *m* 1st, 1935, Nan, who *d* 1973, da of Garth Gilpin, of USA; 2ndly, 1976, Elizabeth, who *d* 1980, da of Charles B. Rarden, of USA, and has issue by 1st *m*.

Arms – Quarterly: 1st or, chief indented azure *Walter*; 2nd gules, three covered cups or, *Butler*; 3rd argent, a lion rampant gules, on a chief of the second a swan close argent, between two annulets or, *Carrick*; 4th ermine, a saltire gules. **Crest** – Out of a ducal coronet or, a plume of ostrich feathers, issuant therefrom a falcon rising, all argent. **Supporters** – *Dexter*, a falcon argent, legged and beaked or; *sinister*, a male griffin argent, beaked, rayed, collared, and chained or. **Residence** – 6101 S County Line, Burr Ridge, Ill 60521, USA. **Club** – Naval and Military.

DAUGHTERS LIVING (By 1st marriage)

Lady Constance Ann, *b* 1940: *m* 1965, Henry Lea Soukup, of 618 North Washington, Hinsdale, Illinois, USA, and has issue living, Andrew Butler, *b* 1969, — Meghan Ormonde, *b* 1971.
Lady Violet Cynthia Lilah, *b* 1946: *m* 1971, Donald Leroy Robb (2734 North Racine St, Chicago, Illinois 60614, USA).

DAUGHTER LIVING OF SIXTH MARQUESS

Lady Martha, *b* 1926: *m* 1950, Sir Ashley Charles Gibbs Ponsonby, 2nd Bt, MC, late Coldm Gds, of Woodleys, Woodstock, Oxon OX20 1HJ.

COLLATERAL BRANCH LIVING

(In remainder to the Earldoms of Ormonde and Ossory only)

Descendants of the late Hon Richard Butler (yr son of 8th Earl), who was *cr Viscount Mountgarret* 1550, of whom the 17th Viscount is *hp* to Earldoms of Ormonde and Ossory (*see* V Mountgarret).

PREDECESSORS – **(1)** THEOBALD FitzWalter, who accompanied Henry II into Ireland, was *cr Chief Butler of Ireland* 1177; *d* about 1206; *s* by his son **(2)** THEOBALD, 2nd Butler, who in 1221 assumed the surname of Le Botiler or Butler; *d* 1230; *s* by his son **(3)** THEOBALD, 3rd Butler; *d* 1248; *s* by his son **(4)** THEOBALD, 4th Butler; sat as a Baron in the Parliament of Ireland; granted the Prisage of Wines; *d* 1285; *s* by his el son **(5)** THEOBALD, 5th Butler; sat in Parliament of Ireland as a Baron; *s* by his brother **(6)** *Sir* EDMOND, Knt, 6th Butler; was Lord Dep of Ireland 1312, and Ch Gov of Ireland with. title of Lord Justice 1314: received the feodum of Karrik, Macgriffyn, and Roscrea 1315, and sometimes styled Earl of Karryk (Carrick); *d* 1321; *s* by his son **(7)** JAMES, *cr Earl of Ormonde* (peerage of Ireland) 1328; had a renewed grant of the Prisage of Wines, and grant of the Regalities, etc, of co Tipperary, with the rights of a Palatine in that co for life; *d* 1337; *s* by his son **(8)** JAMES, 2nd Earl; was Lord Justice of Ireland; *d* 1382; *s* by his son **(9)** JAMES, 3rd Earl; erected the Castle of Gowran, and was usually known as Earl of Gowran, and afterwards purchased the Castle of Kilkenny; was Lord Justice of Ireland; *d* 1405; *s* by his son **(10)** JAMES, 4th Earl; prevailed upon Henry V to create a King of Arms in Ireland, by the title of Ireland King of Arms (altered by Edward VI to Ulster King of Arms) and he gave lands for ever to the College of Arms, London; was Lord Dep of Ireland 1405, and Lord-Lieut of Ireland 1420, 1425, and 1442; *d* 1452; *s* by his son **(11)** JAMES, KG, 5th Earl, who had in 1449 been *cr Earl of Wiltshire* (peerage of England); was Lord Dep of Ireland 1451; constituted Lord High Treasurer of England 1459; fell into the hands of the Yorkists at Towton, and was beheaded at Newcastle 1461, when both Earldoms were forfeited; *s* by his son **(12)** JOHN, who having been at Towton was attainted; he was afterwards restored in blood, and became 6th Earl of Ormonde; was ambassador to the principal courts of Europe: *d* unmarried 1478; *s* by his brother **(13)** THOMAS, PC, who having been attainted was restored by Act of Parliament became 7th Earl; *d* 1515; *s* by his kinsman **(14)** PIERCE, great-grandson of the 3rd Earl; he assumed the Earldom, but was compelled to relinquish it to Sir Thomas Boleyn (father of Queen Anne, Consort of Henry VIII), who in 1525, was *cr* Viscount Rochford, and in 1529 Earl of Wiltshire, in peerage of England, and in 1527 Earl of Ormonde, in peerage of Ireland; as a recompense for this abandonment he was in 1527 *cr Earl of Ossory* (peerage of Ireland), and in 1538, a year before the death of Thomas Boleyn, *Earl of Ormonde* (ante) without surviving male issue, he was restored to the original Earldom, and became 8th Earl of Ormonde; *d* 1539; *s* by his son **(15)** JAMES, 9th Earl, who in 1536 has been *cr Viscount Thurles*, in 1541 was confirmed by Act of Parliament in Earldom of Ormonde; *d* 1546; *s* by his son **(16)** THOMAS, KG, 10th Earl; was Lord High Treasurer of Ireland; *d* without surviving male issue; *s* by his kinsman **(17)** WALTER, 11th Earl, son of John, 3rd son of 9th Earl; *d* 1632; *s* by his grandson **(18)** JAMES, KG, PC, 12th Earl; was six times Lord-Lieut of Ireland; *cr Marquess of Ormonde* (peerage of Ireland), 1642, *Baron Butler*, of Llanthony, and *Earl of Brecknock* (peerage of England) 1660, *Duke of Ormonde* (peerage of Ireland) 1661, and *Duke of Ormonde* (peerage of England) 1682: *m* Elizabeth Preston in her own right *Lady Dingwall*: *d* 1688; *s* by his grandson **(19)** JAMES, KG, 2nd Duke, who in 1680 had *s* his father as *Baron Butler*, of Moore Park (peerage of England, *cr* 1666), and in 1684 his grandmother as *Lord Dingwall* (peerage of Scotland, *cr* 1609); was Lord High Constable of England at Coronation of William and Mary, Capt Gen and Com in Ch of the Land Forces, Warden of the Cinque Ports, and Constable of Dover Castle; in 1715 was attainted of high treason, all his English honours were forfeited, and an Act was passed to annul the regalities and liberties of the co Palatine of Tipperary; *d* in exile 1745; *s* by his brother (20) CHARLES, who in 1683 had been *cr Baron Butler*, of Werston (peerage of England), and in 1693 *Baron Cloughgrenan, Viscount Tullogh*, and *Earl of Arran* (peerage of Ireland); this nobleman assumed the style of 14th Earl of Ormonde, and did not assume the Irish Dukedom or Marquessate, which had been confirmed upon his father, although the proceedings of the English legislature did not affect the Irish dignities; *d* 1758, when his own honours and the Marquessate and Dukedom of Ormonde became extinct, the Lordship of Dingwall and the Barony of Butler, of Moore Park, reverted to the heir gen (*see* Bs Lucas of Crudwell and Dingwall), and the Earldoms of Ormonde and Ossory and the Viscountcy of Thurles became vested in his kinsman (21) JOHN, great-grandson of Richard, yr brother of the 12th Earl; he did not however assume the titles; *d* 1766; *s* by his cousin (22) WALTER, who did not assume the titles; *d* 1783; *s* by his son (23) JOHN, 17th Earl of Ormonde by decision of House of Lords 1791; *d* 1795; *s* by his el son (24) WALTER, KP, 18th Earl; *cr Baron Butler*, of Llanthony, Mon (peerage of UK) 1801, and *Marquess of Ormonde* (peerage of Ireland) 1816; disposed of the grant of the Prisage of Wines (*see* Theobald, 4th Butler) to the crown for £216,000; *d* 1820, when the Marquessate of Ormonde and the Barony of Butler, of Llanthony, became extinct, and the other honours reverted to his brother (25) JAMES, KP, 19th Earl; *cr Baron Ormonde*, of Llanthony, co Monmouth (peerage of United Kingdom) 1821, and *Marquess of Ormonde* (peerage of Ireland) 1825; was Lord-Lieut of co Kilkenny; *d* 1838; *s* by his son (26) JOHN, KP, 2nd Marquess, *b* 1808: *m* 1843, Frances Jane, da of Gen Hon Sir Edward Paget, GCB (M Anglesey), *d* 1854; *s* by is son (27) JAMES EDWARD WILLIAM THEOBALD, PC, KP, 3rd Marquess, *b* 1844; Commodore Roy Yacht Squadron: *m* 1876, Lady Elizabeth Harriett Grosvenor, who *d* 1928, da of 1st Duke of Westminster; *d* 1919; *s* by his brother (28) JAMES ARTHUR WELLINGTON FOLEY, 4th Marquess; *b* 1849: *m* 1887, Ellen, who *d* 1951, da of late Gen Anson Stager, USA; *d* 1943; *s* by his son (29) JAMES GEORGE ANSON, 5th Marquess, *b* 1890; Major late Life Guards: *m* 1915, Hon Sybil Inna Mildred Fellowes, who *d* 1948, da of 2nd Baron de Ramsey; *d* 1949; *s* by his brother (30) (JAMES) ARTHUR NORMAN, CVO, MC, 6th Marquess *b* 1893: *m* 1924, Jessie Carlos, who *d* 1969, da of late Charles Carlos Clarke; *d* 1971; *s* by his cousin (31) JAMES HUBERT THEOBALD CHARLES, MBE, 7th Marquess and present peer; also Earl of Ormonde, Earl of Ossory, Viscount Thurles, and Baron Ormonde.

ORR-EWING, BARON (Orr-Ewing) (Life Baron 1971 Bt UK 1963)

(CHARLES) IAN ORR-EWING, OBE; Life Baron, and 1st Baronet, son of late Archibald Ian Orr-Ewing (*see* Orr Ewing, Bt, colls, *cr* 1886); *b* 10 Feb 1912; *ed* Harrow, and Trin Coll, Oxford (MA); late Wing-Cdr RAFVR; CEng; PPS to Min of Labour 1952-55, Parl Under-Sec Air Min 1957-59, Parl and Financial Sec to Admiralty 1959, and Civil Lord of Admiralty 1959-63; Joint Vice-Chm of 1922 Cttee 1966-70; Chm Metrication Board 1972-77; 1939-45 War in N Africa, Italy and NW Europe (despatches, OBE); MP (C) for Hendon (North) 1950-70, and *Baron Orr-Ewing*, of Little Berkhamsted, co Hertford (Life Baron) 1971: *m* 1939, Joan Helen Veronica, only da of late Gordon McMinnies, of Talbot Hotel, Stow-on-the-Wold, Glos, and has issue.

Arms – Argent, on a chevron ensigned with a banner between in chief two mullets and in base of representation of the path of two electrons rotating round a nucleus gules a pair of wings conjoined in lure between two lymphads sails furled penons and flags flying or. **Crest** – A demi-lion rampant gules holding in the dexter paw a mullet azure and resting the sinister paw on a portcullis chained or.
Address – c/o House of Lords, SW1A 0PW.

SONS LIVING *(In remainder to Baronetcy only)*

Hon (ALISTAIR) SIMON (29 St James's Gdns, W11), *b* 10 June 1940; *ed* Harrow, Grenoble Univ, and Trin Coll, Oxford, FRICS; *ha* to Baronetcy: *m* 1968, Victoria, da of late Keith Cameron, of Fifield House, Milton-Under-Wychwood, Oxon, and has issue living, Archie Cameron, *b* 1969, — Georgina Victoria, *b* 1971, — Cordelia Victoria, *b* 1974.
Hon (Ian) Colin (The Old Bakehouse, Shalbourne, Hungerford, Berks SN8 3QD), *b* 1942; *ed* Harrow, and Trin Coll, Oxford: *m* 1st, 1973 (*m diss* 1980), Deirdre, el da of Lance Japhet, of Sandhurst, Johannesburg; 2ndly, 1986, Fleur P. M., yr da of late Dr Gavin Knight, of Blackwood, Gwent, and has issue living (by 1st *m*), Francis Ian Lance, *b* 1975, — Bridget Joanna, *b* 1977, — (by 2nd *m*) Cordelia, *b* 1988, — Daisy Caroline, *b* 1990.
Hon Malcolm Archie (The Priory, Syresham, nr Brackley, Northants), *b* 1946; *ed* Harrow, and Munich: *m* 1973, Clare Mary, da of Brig George Robert Flood, MC, of Cheverell Mill, Little Cheverell, Devizes, Wilts, and has issue living, a son, *b* 1990, — Harriet Kate, *b* 1975, — Charlotte Rose, *b* 1978.
Hon Robert James (70 Warwick Gdns, W14), *b* 1953; *ed* Harrow; Bar Inner Temple 1976: *m* 1982, Susannah, da of Mark Bodley Scott, of Uppfield, Sonning-on-Thames, Berks, and has issue living, William Robert, *b* 1985, — Jack Alexander Bodley, *b* 1987, — Alice, *b* 1989.

Orrery, Earl of see Earl of Cork and Orrery.

Ossulston, Lord, son of Earl of Tankerville.

OWEN, BARON (Owen) (Life Baron 1992)

DAVID ANTHONY LLEWELLYN OWEN, CH, PC, son of Dr John William Morris Owen; *b* 2 July 1938; *ed* Bradfield, Sidney Sussex Coll, Camb (Hon Fell 1977), and St Thomas's Hosp (BA, MB BChir, MA);

Neurological and Psychiatric Registrar 1964-66, and Research Fell Med Unit 1966-68, St Thomas's Hosp; PPS to MOD (Admin) 1967, Parly Under Sec of State for Defence for RN 1968-70, Parly Under Sec of State Dept of Health and Social Security 1974, Min of State Dept of Health and Social Security 1974-76, and FCO 1976-77, Sec of State for Foreign and Commonwealth Affairs 1977-79; Founder Memb SDP 1981, Chm SDP Parly Cttee 1981-82, Dep Leader SDP Oct 1982-83, SDP Leader following resignation of Rt Hon Roy Jenkins after election June 1983-87, resigned over merger with Liberal Party 1987, re-elected SDP Leader 1988; Head of European Community's Peace Effort in Yugoslavia since Aug 1992; Gov Charing Cross Hosp 1966-68, Patron Disablement Income Group since 1968, Chm Humanitas and Medecines Sans Frontieres UK; MP Plymouth Sutton (*Lab*) 1966-74, and Plymouth Devonport (*Lab* 1974-81, *SDP* 1981-92); *cr* PC 1976, CH 1994, and *Baron Owen*, of the City of Plymouth (Life Baron) 1992: *m* 1968, Deborah, da of late Kyrill Schabert, of Long Island, NY, and has issue.
Residences – 78 Narrow St, Limehouse, E14 8BP; The Old Rectory, Buttermere, nr Marlborough, Wilts.

SONS LIVING

Tristan Llewellyn (does not use courtesy title), *b* 1970.
Gareth Schabert (does not use courtesy title), *b* 1972.

DAUGHTER LIVING

Lucy Mary (does not use courtesy title), *b* 1979.

OXFORD AND ASQUITH, EARL OF (Asquith) (Earl UK 1925)

JULIAN EDWARD GEORGE ASQUITH, KCMG, 2nd Earl; *b* 22 April 1916; *s* 1928; *ed* Ampleforth, and Balliol Coll, Oxford (Scholar, MA); formerly Lt RE; appointed Assist Dist Commr Palestine 1942, Dep Ch Sec, Tripolitania 1949, Adviser to Prime Min of Libya 1951, Administrative Sec, Zanzibar 1955, and Administrator, St Lucia 1958; Gov and Com-in-Ch of Seychelles 1962-67, and Commr for British Indian Ocean Territory 1965-67; Constitutional Commr Cayman Islands 1971, and Turks and Caicos Islands 1973-74; CMG 1961, KCMG 1964: *m* 1947, Anne Mary Celestine, da of late Sir (Charles) Michael Palairet, KCMG, and has issue.

Arms – Sable, on a fesse between three cross-crosslets argent a portcullis of the field. **Crest** – Issuant out of clouds proper, a mascle gules. **Supporters** – On either side a lion purpure, charged on the shoulder with an open book argent, edged or.
Residence – The Manor House, Mells, Frome.

SONS LIVING

RAYMOND BENEDICT BARTHOLOMEW MICHAEL (*Viscount Asquith*), OBE, *b* 24 Aug 1952; *ed* Ampleforth, and Balliol Coll, Oxford; 1st Sec British Embassy, Moscow 1983-85, Counsellor, British Embassy, Kiev since 1992; OBE (Civil) 1992: *m* 1978, Clare, el da of late Francis Anthony Baring Pollen (*see* Pollen, Bt, colls), and has issue:—
SON LIVING — *Hon* Mark Julian, *b* 13 May 1979.
DAUGHTERS LIVING — *Hon* Magdalen Katharine, *b* 1981, — *Hon* Frances Sophia, *b* 1984, — *Hon* Celia Rose, *b* 1989, — *Hon* Isabel Anne, *b* 1991.
Hon Dominic Anthony Gerard, *b* 1957: *m* 1988, Louise E., only da of John E. Cotton, of Wollaton, Nottingham, and has issue living, Gabriela Elizabeth Louise, *b* 1989.

DAUGHTERS LIVING

Lady (Mary) Annunziata (75 Ladbroke Grove, W11), *b* 1948.
Lady Katharine Rose Celestine (36 Aldridge Road Villas, W11), *b* 1949: *m* 1st, 1970 (*m diss* 1976), Adam Nicholas Ridley (later Sir Adam Ridley) (*see* V Ridley, colls); 2ndly, 1985, (John) Nathaniel Micklem Page, 2nd son of Sir (Arthur) John Page, MP.
Lady Clare Perpetua Frances, *b* 1955.

SISTERS LIVING (*Raised to the rank of an Earl's daughter* 1928).

Lady Helen Frances, OBE (Tynts Hill, Mells, Frome, Som), *b* 1908; BA Somerville Coll, Oxford, 1930; OBE (Civil) 1965.
Lady Perdita Rose Mary (*Perdita, Baroness Hylton*), *b* 1910: *m* 1931, 4th Baron Hylton, who *d* 1967. *Residence* – Church House, Chester Blade, Shepton Mallet, Som BA4 4QX.

COLLATERAL BRANCHES LIVING

Issue of late Hon Herbert Asquith, 2nd son of 1st Earl, *b* 1881, *d* 1947: *m* 1910, Lady Cynthia Charteris, who *d* 1960, da of 11th Earl of Wemyss and March:—
Michael Henry (149 Rusthall Av, W4 1BL), *b* 1914; *ed* Winchester, and Balliol Coll, Oxford (MA); served with Friends Ambulance Unit 1940-5: *m* 1st, 1938 (*m diss* 1952), Diana Eveline Montagu, da of late Lieut-Col Perceval Lawrence Montagu Battye, MC, of 21A Prince Edward Mansions, W1; 2ndly, 1953, Helga Birgitta Ebba Elisabeth, only da of late Dr Walther Sigmund Casimir Ritter, of Carlsbad, and has had issue, (by 1st *m*) Stephen Andrew Romily Michael (Hinchwick Manor, Stow-on-the-Wold), *b* 1944; *ed* Nautical Coll, Pangbourne: *m* 1st, 1963 (*m diss* 1975), Nicola, da of late Lt-Cdr Sir Peter Markham Scott, CBE, DSC; 2ndly, 19—, Clare Frances, eldest da of late Lt-Col John Richard Guy Stanton, MBE, DL, of Snelston Hall, Ashbourne, Derbys (*see* B Castlemaine, 1960 Edn), and formerly wife of Henry Denis Ernest Boyt, and has

issue living (by 1st *m*), Daniel *b* 1964, Emily Rachel *b* 1965: *m* 1988, Mark Charles Francis Derrington Bailey, of 61 Gloucester St, SW1 (*see* St Clair-Ford, Bt, colls, 1985 Edn), Lucy Kate *b* 1967 (by 2nd *m*), Thomas Ivo *b* 1980, Portia *b* 1978, — Peter Edward, *b* 1947, — Annabel Laura Marguerite, *b* 1939; *ed* Somerville Coll, Oxford (BA 1960): *m* 1961, Jasper R. Ungoed-Thomas, of 13 Westbourne Park Rd, W2 5PX, son of late Hon Mr Justice (Sir Lynn) Ungoed-Thomas, and *d* 1971, leaving issue, David Stephen Jerome *b* 1962, Michael Fergus Jonathan *b* 1965, Harry Owen Nathaniel *b* 1969.

Grandchildren of late Hon Herbert Asquith (ante):—
Issue of late Simon Anthony Roland Asquith, *b* 1919, *d* 1973: *m* 1942, Vivien Lawrence (44 Gilpin Av, East Sheen SW14 8QY), da of late Maj Sir Lawrence Evelyn Jones, 5th Bt, MC, TD (*cr* 1831):—
Conrad Robin, *b* 1945; *ed* Westminster, and Ch Ch Oxford: *m* 1977, Patricia, da of L. E. Sproston, of Stoke-on-Trent, and has issue living, Daisy, *b* 1976, — Lily, *b* 1978. *Residence* – 69c Nightingale Lane, Clapham, SW12. —— Ivon Shaun (21 Minster Rd, Oxford OX4 1LY), *b* 1946; *ed* Westminster, and Ch Ch, Oxford: *m* 1982 (*m diss* 1985), Pauline R., da of Lt-Cdr Paul Murray-Jones, RN (ret), and formerly wife of Hon (Maurice) Sebastian Balliol Brett (*see* V Esher), and has issue living, Thomas, *b* 1982, — and further issue (by Katherine Tanya Jury), William, *b* 1985, — Rosamund Eloise, *b* 1991. —— Rosalind Lucy *b* 1948; has issue (by John Fordham), Frederick Simon Asquith FORDHAM, *b* 1985, — Leo Robin Asquith FORDHAM, *b* 1989. *Residence* – 88 Petherton Rd, Highbury, N5 2RG.

Issue of late Brig-Gen Hon Arthur Melland Asquith, DSO, 3rd son of 1st Earl, *b* 1883, *d* 1939: *m* 1918, Hon Betty Constance, who *d* 1962, da of 3rd Baron Manners:—
April Mary (*Hon Mrs W. Keith Rous*) (prefers to be known by her former style), *b* 1919: *m* 1943, as his 2nd wife, 5th Earl of Stradbroke, who *d* 1983, having survived his brother, the 4th Earl, by four days. —— Jean Constance, *b* 1920: *m* 1945, Lawrence Leif Toynbee (*see* E Carlisle, colls, 1956 Edn), and has issue living, Rosalind Catherine, *b* 1946: *m* 1972, Joe Pennybacker, of Ganthorpe Hall, Terrington, York, and has issue living, Thomas Rupert Blaise *b* 1983, Kitty Shushanik *b* 1983, — Celia Jane, *b* 1948: *m* 1966, Jeremy George Marshall Caulton, of 19 Berriman Rd, N7, and has issue living, Elisabeth Amy *b* 1967, — Clare Anne, *b* 1949: *m* 1980, Andrew David Huxley, of 48 Gillespie Rd, N5, and has issue living, Coral Susan Toynbee *b* 1984, — Rachel Mary Agnes, *b* 1950: *m* 1976, Richard Alexander Fletcher, of Low Pasture House, Nunnington, York YO6 5XQ, and has issue living, Humphrey Alexander *b* 1981, Eleanor Constance *b* 1978, Alice Catherine *b* 1983, — Sarah Alice, *b* 1953: *m* 1990, Dr Robert Towler, of 6 Evelyn Mansions, Carlisle Place, SW1, son of — Towler, of King's Lynn, Norfolk, and has issue living, Frederick James Edward *b* 1991, Madeline *b* 1993, — Frances Veronica, *b* 1958: *m* 1987, John Samuel Wilson, of 87 Lambert Rd, SW2. *Residence* – Chapel Cottage, Ganthorpe, Terrington, York. —— Susan Penelope, *b* 1922: *m* 1946, (Evelyn) Basil Boothby, CMG, who *d* 1990 (*see* Boothby, Bt, colls). *Residence* – 23 Holland Park Avenue, W11. —— Christine, *b* 1926: *m* 1952, John Hatch Clark, and has issue living, John Jasper, *b* 1958, — Lucy Caroline, *b* 1953: *m* 1980, William Francis Sebastian Rickett, son of Sir Denis Hubert Fletcher Rickett, KCMG, CB, of 9 The Close, Salisbury, Wilts, and has issue living, Oliver Patrick Oscar *b* 1983, Rosanna Madeleine *b* 1986, — Emma Victoria, *b* 1955. *Residence* – Old Laundry Cottage, Clovelly, N Devon.

Grandchildren of late Rt Hon Sir Cyril Asquith, 4th son of 1st Earl, who was *cr Baron Asquith of Bishopstone* (Life Baron) 1951 (see that title):—
Issue of late Hon Paul Asquith, *b* 1927, *d* 1984: *m* 1st, 1953 (*m diss* 1963), Helena Mary, da of Hon Geoffrey John Orlando Bridgeman, MC (*see* V Bridgeman); 2ndly 1963, Caroline Anne (41 Quarrendon St, SW6), yr da of Sir John Gawen Carew Pole, 12th Bt (*cr* 1628), DSO, TD:—
(By 1st *m*) Jonathan Paul (8 Colinette Rd, SW15 6QQ), *b* 1956: *m* 1984, Sarah Ann, yst da of Peter Noel Negretti (*see* B Eden of Winton), and has issue living, (Paul) William, *b* 1988, — Harriet Mary Rose, *b* 1991. —— (Mary) Clare, *b* 1954: *m* 1986, Rory Patrick Macnamara, of 8 Castello Av, SW15 6EA, elder son of Carroll Macnamara, of Invercharron House, Ross-shire, and has issue living, (Charles) Frederick *b* 1988, — Katharine Rose, *b* 1990, — Flora Mary, *b* 1993. —— (By 2nd *m*) Rupert, *b* 1965. —— Emily Anne, *b* 1964.

PREDECESSORS – (1) *Rt Hon Sir* HERBERT HENRY Asquith, KG, son of late Joseph Dixon Asquith, of Croft House, Morley, Yorkshire, *b* 1852; a KC, High Steward of Oxford, and an Elder Brother of the Trinity House; MP for Fifeshire, E Div (*L*) 1886 to Nov 1918, and for Paisley Feb 1920 to Oct 1924; Sec of State for Home Depart Aug 1892 to June 1895, Chancellor of the Exchequer Dec 1905 to April 1908, Prime Min and First Lord of the Treasury April 1908 to Dec 1916 (also Sec of State for War and Pres of Army Council March to Aug 1914, and Chm of Cabinet War Committee Nov 1915 to Dec 1916), and Leader of Liberal Party 1908-26; *cr Earl of Oxford and Asquith* (peerage of United Kingdom) and *Viscount Asquith*, of Morley, W Riding, co York, Feb 1925: *m* 1st, 1877, Helen Kelsall, who *d* 1891, el da of late Dr Frederick Melland, of Rusholme, Manchester; 2ndly, 1894, Emma Alice Margaret (Margot), who *d* 1945, da of Sir Charles Tennant, 1st Bt; *d* 1928; *s* by his grandson (2) JULIAN, only son of late Raymond Asquith (el son of 1st Earl), who was *ka* in the battle of the Somme 1916, 2nd Earl and present peer; also Viscount Asquith.

OXFUIRD, VISCOUNT OF (Makgill) (Viscount S 1651, Bt NS 1627)
(Title pronounced "Oxfurd" and Name pronounced "McGill")

GEORGE HUBBARD MAKGILL, 13th Viscount and 13th Baronet; *b* 7 Jan 1934; *s* 1986; *ed* St Peter's Sch, Cambridge, NZ, and Wanganui Collegiate Sch; commd RAF GD Branch 1955-58: *m* 1st, 1967 (*m diss* 1977), Alison Campbell, elder da of late Neils Max Jensen, of Randers, Denmark; 2ndly, 1980, Valerie Cunitia Mary, only da of Maj Charles Anthony Steward, of The Platt, Crondall, Farnham, Surrey, and has issue by 1st and 2nd *m*.

Arms – Gules, three martlets argent. **Crest** – a phoenix in flames proper. **Supporters** – *Dexter*, a horse at liberty argent, gorged with a Viscount's coronet, and thereto affixed a chain, maned and hooved or; *sinister*, a bull sable, horned, unguled, collared and chained or.
Address – c/o House of Lords, SW1.

SONS LIVING (By 1st marriage)

Hon IAN ARTHUR ALEXANDER (*Master of Oxfuird*), *b* 14 Oct 1969.
Hon Robert Edward George, *b* 1969 (twin).
Hon Hamish Max Alistair, *b* 1972.

(*by 2nd marriage*)

Hon Edward Anthony Donald, *b* 1983.

SISTER LIVING

Barbara Frances Katherine, *b* 1939. *Residence* – 34 Karaka St, Takapuna, Auckland, NZ.

DAUGHTER LIVING OF TWELFTH VISCOUNT (*By 1st marriage*)

Hon Diana Mary Robina, CVO (Clouds Lodge, E Knoyle, Salisbury, Wilts, and 15 Iverna Court, W8), *b* 1930; FCO 1961-90; Protocol Consultant since 1990; Hon Steward of Westminster Abbey since 1978; Member International Cttee Operation Raleigh; Vice-Chm Women of the Year Luncheon, Action on Addiction; Consultant to Princess Helena College; Freedom of the City of London 1989; Jubilee Medal 1977, MVO 1971, LVO 1983, CVO 1990; Order of Al Kawkab (5th class) (1966), Knight of Order of White Rose of Finland (1969), Order of the Stor (1971), Order of the Sacred Treasure (5th class) (1971), Order of Independence of United Arab Emirates (1989).

WIDOW LIVING OF TWELFTH VISCOUNT

MAUREEN (*Maureen, Viscountess of Oxfuird*), yst da of late Lt-Col Arthur Tilson Shaen Magan, CMG, of co Meath, and formerly wife of Col John Herbert Gillington, OBE, MC: *m* 1955, as his 2nd wife, the 12th Viscount, who *d* 1986. *Residence* – 2 Hillside, Heath Rd, Newmarket, Suffolk CB8 8AY.

COLLATERAL BRANCHES LIVING

Grandchildren of late Capt John Edward Makgill (infra):—
Issue of late Rodney Devereux Makgill, *b* 1901, *d* 1955: *m* 1923, Laura (14 Marei Road, Ellerslie, Auckland, New Zealand), da of late Richard Reynolds, of Cambridge, Auckland, New Zealand:—
Richard John (Matahi Rd, Manawahe, RD, Matata, NZ), *b* 1926: *m* 19—, Marjorie Ann Jamieson, and has issue living, Stuart Rodney, *b* 1956, — Roy Malcolm, *b* 1961, — Janet, *b* 1952, — Yvonne, *b* 1954. —— Patricia Ruth, *b* 1923: *m* 1946, Alfred Bridger, who *d* 1987, of 44 Kiwi Rd, Devonport, Auckland, NZ, and has issue living, Peter James, *b* 1949, — Patricia Ellen, *b* 1947: *m* 1967, Bruce Wallace Nicklin, and has issue living, David John *b* 1969, Jeffrey Bruce *b* 1971, Tracey Rochelle *b* 1973, — Susan, *b* 1957: *m* 1978, Grant Brendan Nauman, and has issue living, Megan Louise *b* 1981, Laura Marie *b* 1982, Raelene Anna *b* 1984, Nicola Lee *b* 1986. —— Muriel Ann, *b* 1927: *m* 1955, Thomas William Tyrwhitt-Drake, and has issue living, Richard William, *b* 1957, — Hugh Charles, *b* 1959, — Penelope Elizabeth, *b* 1964. —— Nancy Margaret (28 Beaumaris Way, Takanani, New Zealand), *b* 1929: *m* 1954, Edward Smith, and has issue living, Nigel, *b* 1957: *m* 1984, Stephanie Littlejohn, — Deborah Ann, *b* 1954: *m* 1986, Fred Hickling, and has issue living, Amy *b* 1988, — Sandra, *b* (twin) 1957: *m* 1981, Glen Pryor, and has issue living, Luke *b* 1986, Kate *b* 1988. —— Elizabeth, *b* 1933: *m* 1968, Capt Thomas Chisholm.
Issue of late Robert John Makgill, *b* 1910, *d* 1983: *m* 1940, Marjorie Wardell-Johnson, who *d* 1981:—
John Wardell (2 Belloc St, Cambridge, NZ), *b* 1944: *m* 1971, Valerie Joan Turner, and has issue living, Braedon, *b* 1973, — Amanda, *b* 1977. —— Hugh Haldane (83 Ngarua Rd, Waitoa, NZ), *b* 1948: *m* 1970, Pamela Ann Jones, and has issue living, Lisa, *b* 1972, — Claudia, *b* 1974, — Joanna, *b* 1977. —— Simon Redding (Lamb St, RD3 Cambridge, NZ), *b* 1949: *m* 1970, Jane Gifford, and has issue living, Matthew Simon, *b* 1977, — Louise Clare, *b* 1973, — Miriam Jane, *b* 1975, — Emily Ann, *b* 1980. —— Robert Cloan (Hemans St, Cambridge, NZ), *b* 1950: *m* 1970, Josephine Mary Uden, and has issue living, Robert, *b* 1971, — Dylan, *b* 1975.

Issue of late Capt John Edward Makgill, 3rd son of 10th baronet, *b* 1874, *d* 1938: *m* 1897, Muriel Ravenscroft, who *d* 1946, da of late Hon Henry de Bohun Devereux (V Hereford, colls):—
Geoffrey Haldane, *b* 1915: *m* 1945, Elizabeth McNiven, of Auckland, New Zealand, and has issue living, Penelope Ann, *b* 1947: *m* 1973, John Bryce Scott, of Puketawa, Roberts Rd, RD2, Cambridge, NZ, and has issue living, William Ruediger Makgill *b* 1975, Geoffrey Robert *b* 1977. *Residence* – 30 Kensington Place, Fairfield, Hamilton, NZ. —— Miriam Isabella, *b* 1903: *m* 1955: *m* 1988, Gael Frances McKitterick, and has issue living, Ben William *b* 1989, Jonathan Guy *b* 1992, — Hensleigh Cathew Marryat Norris, who *d* 1980. *Residence* – c/o Trevellyn Home, Victoria St, Hamilton, NZ. —— Muriel Barbara, *b* 1907. *Residence* – c/o Caswell House, Selwyn Village, Pt Chevalier, Auckland, NZ. —— Margaret Philippa (1/3 Matai Rd, Green Lane, Auckland 5, NZ), *b* 1919: *m* 1946 (*m diss* 1968), Alexander Hamilton Brown.

Issue of late David Makgill, 4th son of 10th baronet, *b* 1880, *d* 1934: *m* 1909, Margaret Elizabeth, who *d* 1948, da of late Ven Archdeacon Palmer:—
John Palmer (40 King St, Waiuku, NZ), *b* 1910: *m* 1938, Lucie Warner, and has issue living, Alan Richard John, *b* 1941: *m* 1985, Heather Dawn, yr da of Norman Douglas, and has issue living, Iona Amie *b* 1987, — Jennifer Ann, *b* 1939, Bruce Hinton, of Te Toro, Waiuku, New Zealand, and has issue living, Stuart Bruce *b* 1963, Wendy Lucille *b* 1960, Barbara Anne *b* 1961. —— David Comins (Highfields, RD3, Waiuku, NZ), *b* 1918: *m* 1949, Ena Thompson, da of Col Keyworth, of Much Wenlock, Salop, and has issue living, Fiona Margaret, *b* 1951: *m* 1979, Donald John Macdonald, of B Westhead Rd, RD3, Waiuku, and has issue living, Scott Donald *b* 1983, Jenny Marie *b* 1981. —— Stephen Stewart (492 Coldstream Drive, Berwyn, Pa 19312, USA), *b* 1929: *m* 1955, Joan Woods, and has issue living, Stephen Stewart (4452 Odessa Dr, Plano, Texas, USA), *b* 1958: *m* 1986, Diane Corcoran, — Kathleen Palmer, *b* 1956: *m* 1981, Gregory Sisk, of 354 Williams St, Marlboro, Mass, USA, — Heather Woods, *b* 1961: *m* 1989, William Lyon, of 12 Arrowhead Rd, Convent Station, NJ, USA, — Allison Ashwell, *b* 1963. —— Margaret May, *b* 1912: *m* 1933, Geoffrey Hall Dadley, and has issue living, David Francis, *b* 1934: *m* 1954 (*m diss* 1969), Joan Muriel Proctor, and has issue living, John David *b* 1954: *m* 1975, Sharon Joy Ludwig (and has issue living, Steven Ronald David *b* 1979, Keri Anne *b* 1978, Jolene Marie *b* 1978), Geoffrey Harold *b* 1956: *m* 1981, Marie Joan Shergold (and has issue living, Adrian Brent *b* 1983), Raewyn Anne *b* 1958: *m* 1982, Lance Noel Worthington (and has issue living, Amber Chanelle *b* 1984), Barbara Joan *b* 1959: *m* 1978, John Kleber Brooks (and has issue living, Chantal Summer *b* 1982), Lorraine Sandra *b* 1961, — Peter Geoffrey, *b* 1936: *m* 1964, Germaine Wormald, and has issue living, Sandra *b* 1965, Helen Deborah *b* 1967, — Marian Rose, *b* 1940: *m* 1962, Keith John Wormald, and has issue living, Geoffrey John *b* 1964, Kirsten Anne *b* 1965, — Robin Margaret, *b* 1943: *m* 1972, Peter Clarke, and has issue living, Michael Anthony *b* 1973, Stephen Matthew *b* 1974, — Rosemary Gwendolyn, *b* 1944, — Katherine Ruth, *b* 1949: *m* 1973, Ian Thornton, and has issue living, Matthew Antony *b* 1983. —— Alice Mary, *b* 1913: *m* 1939, Col Guy Priestley Sanders, DSO, RNZ Engineers (ret), of Meldon, Castor Bay Rd, Auckland, NZ, and has issue living, Guy Makgill, *b* 1940: *m* 1972, Jennifer Chave, and has issue living, Timothy Guy *b* 1982, Stephanie Claire *b* 1977, Katherine Alice *b* 1979, — David William Priestley, *b* 1955: *m* 1988, Gael Frances McKitterick, and has issue living, Ben William *b* 1989, Jonathan Guy *b* 1992, — Philippa Anne, *b* 1944: *m* 1966 (*m diss* 1979), Thomas James Finlayson, and has issue living, Nicholas James *b* 1968, Tobias David *b* 1977, — Penelope Margaret, *b* 1950: *m* 1975, Grant Lyndon Christianson, and has issue living, David Grant *b* 1979, Michael Scott *b* 1981. —— Rose Ashwell, *b* 1916: *m* 1944, Ansel Brooks Smith, Jr, of 3029 Mary Av SE, Grand Rapids, Mich, USA, and has issue living, Haldane Brooks (17639 Walnut Trail, Chagrin Falls, Ohio, USA), *b* 1947, — Byron Whitaker (24 Forest Green Dr, Springfield, Ill, USA), *b* 1950: *m* 1st, 1972 (*m diss* 1978), Leona La Claire; 2ndly, 1981, Mary Kimbo, and has issue living (by 1st *m*), Byron Whitaker *b* 1973, Colin Makgill *b* 1976, — Christopher Carlton (405 Queen St, Woodwind Townhouses, Mauldin, SC, USA), *b* 19—: *m* 1979, Leslie Gaye Booth.

Grandchildren of late Arthur Makgill (infra):—
Issue of late Mungo Ian Makgill, *b* 1911, *d* 1986: *m* 1935, Eugenia Louise (31a View Rd, Waiuku, NZ), da of Samuel Massey, of Belfast:—
Ian James (49 Penny Av, Mt Roskill, NZ), *b* 1946: *m* 1975, Marie Louise Howley, of Auckland, and has issue living, Angela Louise, *b* 1979. — Philippa Suzanne, *b* 1982, — Jennifer Marie, *b* 1986. — Margaret May, *b* 1935. — Elizabeth Marion, *b* 1938. —— Roberta Louise, *b* 1942: *m* 1961, James Samuel Brambley, of 16 Hogan St, Pukekohe, NZ, and has issue living, Douglas James, *b* 1965: *m* 1986, Fiona Thelma McNally, and has issue living, Samuel James *b* 1988, Eli Sean *b* 1992, Renee Vivienne *b* 1989, — Marie-Anne, *b* 1962: *m* 1990 (*m diss* 1993), Michael Walker, — Louise Anne, *b* 1963: *m* 1987, Wayne Robert Callander, and has issue living, Amy Louise *b* 1993, — Vanessa Jane, *b* 1972. —— Colleen Barbara, *b* 1944: *m* 1965, Herbert James Lovell, of 88 Ranfurly Rd, Alfriston, Manurewa, NZ, and has issue living, Scott James, *b* 1966: *m* 1989, Monique Adriana van Meygaarden, and has issue living, Brent William *b* 1991, Shaun Adrian *b* 1994, — Anna Elizabeth, *b* 1968: *m* 1988, Michael John Cutts, — Kirstene Margaret, *b* 1972.

Issue of late Arthur Makgill, 5th son of 10th baronet; *b* 1882; *d* 1954: *m* 1911, Mabel Sophia Elizabeth, who *d* 1932, da of William Marsh:—
Douglas Malcolm, *b* 1922: *m* 1945, Myra Louisa, da of Osborne John Morton Pine, of Sandringham, NZ, and has issue living, Ray Malcolm, *b* 1945: *m* 1969 (*m diss* 1985), Linda Anne Elliment, and has issue living, Daniel Ray *b* 1970, Jamie Douglas *b* 1972, Donna Marie *b* 1974, — Joy Louisa, *b* 1953: *m* 1st, 1973 (*m diss* 1979), Karl Verdun Morris; 2ndly, 1981, Jeffrey John Wills, and has issue living (by 2nd *m*), Kyle Phillip *b* 1985, Ann Marie Frances *b* 1982, Nicola Susan *b* (twin) 1985, — Lynette Jane, *b* 1955: *m* 1979, Peter Leslie Guinibert, of Titirangi, NZ, and has issue living, Matthew John *b* 1985, David James *b* 1987. —— Deborah Elizabeth Mary, *b* 1914: *m* 1939, Capt John Lawrence Clarkson, of 110 Bruce McLaren Rd, Henderson, Auckland, NZ, and has issue living, David John, *b* 1940: *m* 1st, 1965 (*m diss* 19—), Helen Gable, of Toowoomba, Qld; 2ndly, 19—, Catherine de Boer, and has issue living (by 1st *m*), Sean *b* 1969, Fiona *b* 1968 (by 2nd *m*), Euan *b* 1979, — Peter, *b* 1945: *m* 1968, Patricia Goffin, of Howick, Auckland, and has issue living, Stephen *b* 1973, Wayne *b* 1980, Michelle *b* 1971, — Alan Richard, *b* 1946: *m* 1970, Susanne Price, of Otahuhu, Auckland, and has issue living, Jonathan *b* 1977, Melissa *b* 1978, — Christine, *b* 1947: *m* 1971, John Fryer, of Paraparauma, Wellington, and has issue living, Nicholas *b* 1976, Kirsten *b* 1974.

PREDECESSORS – (1) Sir JAMES Makgill of Cranston Riddell, Midlothian, 2nd son of David Makgill of Cranston Riddell; *s* by his el brother David 1619; *cr a Baronet* (Nova Scotia) 1627 with remainder to heirs male whatsoever; Lord of Session 1629; MP for co Edinburgh 1630; *cr Viscount of Oxfuird* and *Lord Makgill of Cousland* (peerage of Scotland) 1651, with remainder to his heirs male of tailzie and provision whomsoever; member of Cttee of Estates 1651; Lord of Session 1661: *m* 1st, 1621, Katherine, el da of John Cockburn of Ormiston; 2ndly, 1646, Christian, who *d* 1664, da of Sir William Livingston of Kilsyth; *d* 1663; *s* by his 6th but 1st surv son (2) ROBERT, 2nd Viscount, *b* 1651; Capt of Militia Troop of Horse, Midlothian 1682: *m* 1st, 1666, Henrietta Livingston, who *d* 1683, da of 2nd Earl of Linlithgow; 2ndly, 1684, Lady Jean Ramsay, who *d* 1696, da of 2nd Earl of Dalhousie, and widow of 11th Lord Ross of Halkhead; *d* 1705, when his Peerages and Baronetcy became dormant; *s* (according to the decision of the Cttee of Privileges of House of Lords 1977) by his kinsman (3) DAVID Makgill of Rankeilour, Fife, *de jure* 3rd Viscount and 3rd Baronet (despite Christian, da of 2nd Viscount having been served heir of tailzie and provision, when in 1706 she wrongly assumed the title of Viscountess Oxfuird and *d* 1707 having married Hon William Maitland, 6th son of the 3rd Earl of Lauderdale, her son and heir Robert Maitland Makgill, voted as Viscount Oxfuird at the election on Representative Peers 1733), only child of Sir James of Rankeilour (*d* 1661), grandson of Sir James of Rankeilour, Clerk Register Lord of Session, Lord Provost of Edinburgh, and an Ambassador to Queen Elizabeth I (*d* 1579), great-uncle of 1st Viscount and 1st Bt: *m* 1693, Janet, da and heir of John Craig of Ramornie, Advocate; *d* 1717; *s* by his el son (4) JAMES, *de jure* 4th Viscount and 4th Bt; *b* 16—: *m* 1720, Jean, da of Sir Robert Anstruther of Balkaskie; *d* 1747; *s* by his kinsman (5) JOHN, *de jure* 5th Viscount and 5th Bt, son of Arthur of Kemback (*d* 1725), son of the Rev John of Kemback (*d* 1673), 3rd son of James, of Rankeilour, Fifeshire (*d* 1661) (ante); *b* 1676: *m* 1706, Agnes, da of John Lindsay of Wormeston, Crail; *d* 1762; *s* by his el son (6) ARTHUR, *de jure* 6th Viscount and 6th Bt; *b* 1709; Capt Comdt Scottish Regt in Dutch Ser; matric arms as heir male of Rankeilour 1771; *d* unm 1733; *s* by his brother (7) GEORGE, *de jure* 7th Viscount and 7th Bt; *b* 1723; joined army of Prince Charles Edward Stuart; pardoned and served as Capt 12th Foot: *m* Agnes, who *d* 1799, da of Major Mungo Law, of Pittilock, Falkland; *d* 1797; *s* by his only son (8) JOHN, *de jure* 8th Viscount and 8th Bt; *b* 1790: *m* 1811, Eliza, who *d* 1860, el da of William Dalgleish of Scotscraig, Fifeshire; *d* 1817; *s* by his son (9) GEORGE, *de jure* 9th Viscount and 9th Bt; *b* 1812: *m* 1833, Harriet, who *d* 1890, da of Amos Strettell, of Binderton House, Sussex; *d* 1878; *s* by her el son (10) JOHN, *de jure* 10th Viscount and 10th Bt; *b* 1836; established his right to the Baronetcy 1906: *m* 1866, Margaret Isabella, who *d* 1920, da of Robert Haldane, of Cloanden, Perthshire; *d* 1906, *s* by his el son (11) GEORGE, *de jure* 11th Viscount and 11th Bt; *b* 1868: *m* 1891, Frances Elizabeth, who *d* 1947, da of Alexander Innes Grant, of Merchiston, Otago, NZ; *d* 1926; *s* by his el son (12) JOHN DONALD ALEXANDER ARTHUR, 12th Viscount, *b* 1899; claim to Viscountcy admitted by Cttee for Privileges of House of Lords, and a writ issued summoning him to Parliament in the Upper House 1977; Hon Maj Coldm Gds: *m* 1st, 1927 (*m diss* 1943), Esther Lilian, da of Sir Robert Bromley, 6th Bt; 2ndly, 1955, Maureen, yst da of Lt-Col Arthur Tilson Shaen Magan, CMG, of co Meath, and formerly wife of Col John Herbert Gillington, OBE, MC; *d* 1986; *s* by his nephew (12) GEORGE HUBBARD (only son of late Sqdn Ldr Richard James Robert Haldane Makgill, RNZAF Air, who was *k* in a flying accident 1948), 13th Viscount and present peer; also Lord Makgill of Cousland.

Oxmantown, Lord, son of Earl of Rosse.

Paget de Beaudesert, Lord; Grandson of Marquess of Anglesey

PAGET OF NORTHAMPTON, BARONY OF (Paget) (Extinct 1990)

WIDOW LIVING OF LIFE BARON

SYBIL HELEN (*Baroness Paget of Northampton*), da of late Sills Clifford Gibbons, widow of Sir John Bridger Shiffner, 6th Bt, and formerly wife of Sir Victor Basil John Seely, 4th Bt: *m* 1931, Baron Paget of Northampton, QC (Life Baron), who *d* 1990. *Residences* – Lubenham Lodge, Market Harborough, Leics; 9 Grosvenor Cottages, SW1.

Pakenham, Baron; title of Earl of Longford, on Roll of HL.

PALMER, BARON (Palmer) (Baron UK 1933, Bt UK 1916)

ADRIAN BAILIE NOTTAGE PALMER, 4th Baron and 4th Baronet; *b* 8 Oct 1951; *s* 1990; *ed* Eton, and Edinburgh Univ; Member Exec Council of Historic Houses Assocn since 1981, Scottish Rep to European Landowning Organisation 1986-92, and Member of Council of Scottish Landowners' Fedn 1986-92; Vice-Chm Historic Houses Assoc for Scotland; Member Queen's Body Guard for Scotland (Royal Company of Archers): *m* 1977, Cornelia Dorothy Katharine, da of Rohan Wadham, DFC, of Dog Kennel, Exning, Newmarket, Suffolk, and has issue.

Arms – Per saltire azure and gules two palmers' staves in saltire between four escallops or. **Crest** – Upon a mount vert in front of a palm tree proper three escallops fesseways or. **Supporters** – On either side a palmer, supporting with the exterior hand a palmer's staff proper.
Seat – Manderston, Duns, Berwickshire.

SONS LIVING

Hon HUGO BAILIE ROHAN, *b* 5 Dec 1980.
Hon George Gordon Nottage, *b* 1985.

DAUGHTER LIVING

Hon Edwina Laura Marguerite, *b* 1982.

BROTHER LIVING (*Raised to the rank of a Baron's son* 1991)

Hon Mark Hugh Gordon, *b* 1954; *ed* Eton: *m* 1982, Irene, da of Guillermo Aranda, of Los Angeles, Calif, USA, and has issue living, Henry Gordon William, *b* 1987, — Olivia Lorna Aranda, *b* 1990. *Residence* – 68 Endlesham Rd, SW12.

DAUGHTERS LIVING AND DECEASED OF THIRD BARON

Hon Amanda Victoria, *b* 1949; *d* 1954.
Hon Carol Lylie (*Lady Wodehouse*), *b* 1951: *m* 1973, John Armine, Lord Wodehouse, son of 4th Earl of Kimberley, and has issue (*see* E Kimberley). *Residence* – Glendalough, Innings Rd, Little Frieth, Henley-on-Thames, Oxon RG9 6NU.
Hon Vanessa Marguerite, *b* 1954: *m* 1977, Robert William St John, son of Lt-Col Charles A. R. L. St John, of Glebe Manor, Pook Lane, Havant, Hants, and has issue living, Edward Robert Cecil, *b* 1982, — Camilla Victoria Celia, *b* 1980, — Laura Zoë Lylie, *b* 1985, — Melissa Lucy Amanda, *b* 1986. *Residence* – 20 Sudbroke Rd, SW12 8TG

AUNT LIVING (*daughter of 2nd Baron*)

Hon Marjorie Elizabeth, *b* 1910: *m* 1945, Frederick Richard Brown, CBE, late Capt RASC, who *d* 1991, and has issue living, Christopher Frederick (42 Strawberry Vale, Strawberry Hill, Twickenham, Middx TW1 4SE), *b* 1946; *ed* Wellington Coll: *m* 1972, Suzanne Ryder, — Ian Cecil Roger (RR2 Raveena, Gibraltar, Ont, Canada N0H 2EO), *b* 1948; *ed* Marlborough, and Fitzwilliam Coll, Camb: *m* 1st, 1981, Grace Rasmussen; 2ndly, 19—, Anne Gowan, — Richard Philip (East Grafton Farm House, East Grafton, Marlborough, Wilts SN8 3DF), *b* 1952; *ed* Marlborough: *m* 1982, Alexandra Margaret Aldcroft, — Jennifer Elizabeth, *b* 1953: *m* 1975, Brian Shephard. *Residence* – 13 Islescourt, Ramsbury, nr Marlborough, Wilts SN8 2QW.

MOTHER LIVING

Lorna Eveline Hope (*Hon Lady Palmer*), DL Berks 1989, da of late Maj Charles William Hugh Bailie, of Manderston, Berwickshire (*see* Miller, Bt, ext, 1942 Edn): *m* 1950, Col Hon Sir Gordon William Nottage Palmer, KCVO, OBE, TD, yr son of 2nd Baron, who *d* 1989. *Residences* – Harris House, Mortimer, Berks; Edrom Newton, Duns, Berwickshire.

WIDOW LIVING OF THIRD BARON

VICTORIA ELLEN (*Victoria, Baroness Palmer*), only da of late Capt Joseph Arthur Ronald Weston-Stevens, of Woolley Cottage, The Thicket, Maidenhead: *m* 1941, the 3rd Baron, OBE, who *d* 1990. *Residence* – Farley Hill House, Farley Hill, Reading RG7 1UP.

COLLATERAL BRANCH LIVING

Issue of late Hon Arnold Nottage Palmer, FRCM, yr son of 1st Baron, *b* 1886, *d* 1973: *m* 1911, Marjorie, who *d* 1966, da of late Alexander Freeland, of Lingfield, Surrey:—
Susan Helen (Fir Tree Farm, Hampstead Norris, Berks), *b* 1912. —— Felicity Amy (Coombe Farm, Frilsham, Hermitage, Newbury, Berks), *b* 1913. —— Nancy Gillian, *b* 1918: *m* 1943, David Charles Bethune Pilkington, OBE, of Appledown, Frilsham, Hermitage (*see* Bethune Bt, 1985 Edn), and has issue living, Julian Alexander Bethune, *b* 1946: *m* 1974, Susan Anne West, and has issue living, Oliver *b* 1975, Louise *b* 1978, Felicity *b* (twin) 1978, — Susan Elizabeth, *b* 1948: *m* 1st, 1969 (*m diss* 1981), John Dallas Scott; 2ndly, 1984, T. Johnson, of Hobart, Tasmania, and has issue living (by 1st *m*), Mungo *b* 1974, Mercedes *b* 1971.

PREDECESSORS – (1) SAMUEL ERNEST Palmer, el son of late Samuel Palmer, of Northcourt, Hampstead, NW; *b* 1858; was a Director of Huntley & Palmers, Ltd, biscuit manufacturers, of Reading, and founder of Roy Coll of Music Patrons' Fund, the Berkshire Scholarship, and Ernest Palmer Fund for Opera Study, also two Scholarships at Guildhall; *cr* a *Baronet* 1916, and *Baron Palmer* of Reading, co Berks (peerage of United Kingdom) 1933: *m* 1881, Amy Christiana, who *d* 1947, only da of late Alderman George Swan Nottage, Lord Mayor of London; *d* 1948; *s* by his son (2) (ERNEST) CECIL NOTTAGE, 2nd Baron; *b* 1882; Dep Chm of Huntley & Palmers Ltd, biscuit manufacturers of Reading: *m* 1909, Marguerite, who *d* 1959, da of late William McKinley Osborne, of USA; *d* 1950; *s* by his son (3) RAYMOND CECIL, 3rd Baron, *b* 1916; Chm Huntley and Palmers Ltd, biscuit manufacturers, of Reading, 1969-80: *m* 1941, Victoria Ellen, only da of late Capt Joseph Arthur Ronald Weston-Stevens, of Woolley Cottage, The Thicket, Maidenhead; *d* 1990; *s* by his nephew (4) ADRIAN BAILIE NOTTAGE (son of late Col Hon Sir Gordon William Nottage Palmer, KCVO, OBE, TD, yr son of 2nd Baron), 4th Baron and present peer.

PALUMBO, BARON (Palumbo) (Life Baron 1991)

PETER GARTH PALUMBO, son of late Rudolph Palumbo; *b* 20 July 1935; *ed* Eton, and Worcester Coll, Oxford (MA); Hon FRIBA; Gov LSE since 1976, Chancellor Portsmouth Univ since 1992; Chm Arts Council of GB 1989-94, Tate Gallery Foundation 1986-87, and Painshill Park Trust Appeal since 1986; Trustee Tate Gallery 1978-85, and Whitechapel Art Gallery Foundation 1981-87; Trustee and Hon Treas Writers' and Scholars' Educational Trust since 1984; National Order of the Southern Cross of Brazil; *cr Baron Palumbo*, of Walbrook, City of London (Life Baron) 1991: *m* 1st, 1959, Denia, who *d* 1986, da of late Maj Lionel Wigram; 2ndly, 1986, Hayat, elder da of late Kamel Morowa, and has issue by 1st and 2nd *m*.

Arms – Vert, a pale or, over all an escarbuncle counterchanged. **Crest** – The top of a dovecot or, perched on its conical roof vert a dove wings elevated and addorsed gold. **Supporters** – *Dexter*, an alsation dog; *sinister*, a fox proper, each resting the exterior foreleg on a rectangular plinth gold, the compartment comprising a circle of paving stones proper.
Residence – Bagnor Manor, Bagnor, Newbury, Berks RG16 8AG. *Clubs* – White's, Turf, Athenaeum, Pratt's

SONS LIVING *(By 1st marriage)*

Hon James Rudolph, *b* 1963.

(by 2nd marriage)

Hon Philip Rudolph, *b* 1992.

DAUGHTERS LIVING *(By 1st marriage)*

Hon Annabella Jane, *b* 1961: *m* 1991, Hugh H. C. Adams, yr son of Geoffrey Adams, of Chilton Foliot, Wilts.
Hon Laura Elizabeth, *b* 1967; *ed* London Univ.

(by 2nd marriage)

Hon Petra Louise, *b* 1989.
Hon Lana Rose, *b* 1991.

PANNELL, BARONY OF (Pannell) (Extinct 1980)

DAUGHTER LIVING OF LIFE BARON

Hon Hilary, *b* 1940.

PARGITER, BARONY OF (Pargiter) (Extinct 1982)

SONS LIVING OF LIFE BARON

Hon Donald (41 Douglas Rd, Maidstone), *b* 1921: *m* 1947.
Hon Russell Ashby (42 Grays Rd, Ferntree, Tasmania 7054), *b* 1924; MB, BS London; a Fellow of Roy Australian and NZ Coll of Psychiatrists; DPM England; FRC Psych; Consultant Psychiatrist, R Hobart Hosp: *m* 1954, Elizabeth Edwina, da of John George Jamieson Coghill.

DAUGHTER LIVING OF LIFE BARON

Hon Isobel, *b* 1931; Pharmaceutical Chemist: *m* 1964, Ernest Cooper-Heyman, who *d* 1982. *Residence* – The Folly, 81 Woodlands Lane, Chichester, W Sussex PO19 3PF.

PARK OF MONMOUTH, BARONESS (Park) (Life Baroness 1990)

DAPHNE MARGARET SYBIL DÉSIRÉE PARK, CMG, OBE, da of late John Alexander Park; *b* 1 Sept 1921; *ed* Rosa Bassett Sch, Somerville Coll, Oxford (MA), and Newnham Coll, Camb; Cdr Women's Transport Ser FANY in NW Europe and N Africa 1943-48; FO 1948, 2nd Sec Moscow 1954, 1st Sec Leopoldville 1959, Lusaka 1964, Consul-Gen Hanoi 1969-70, Chargé d'Affaires Ulan Bator 1972, FCO 1973-79; Principal Somerville Coll, Oxford 1980-89; Member of Board of Sheffield Devpt Corpn 1989-92, Dir Devpt Trust Zoological Soc of London 1989-90; a Gov of BBC 1982-87; Member British Library Board 1981-86, Chm Legal Aid Advisory Cttee to Lord Chancellor 1986-92; pro Vice-Chancellor Oxford Univ, and Chm Royal Commn on Historical Monuments of England 1989-94; Gov Ditchley Foundation since 1989, Trustee Jardine Educational Foundation since 1990; Hon LLD Bristol 1988, Mount Holyoke Coll 1992; Fell of Chatham House, FRSA, OBE (Civil) 1960, CMG 1971, and *Baroness Park of Monmouth*, of Broadway, co Hereford and Worcester (Life Baroness) 1990.
Address – c/o House of Lords, SW1. *Clubs* – Naval and Military, Royal Commonwealth Society, Oxford and Cambridge, Special Forces.

PARKINSON, BARON (Parkinson) (Life Baron 1992)

CECIL EDWARD PARKINSON, PC, son of Sidney Parkinson, of Carnforth, Lancs; *b* 1 Sept 1931; *ed* Royal Lancaster Gram Sch, and Emmanuel Coll, Camb; CA 1960; Chm Hemel Hempstead Conservative Assocn 1966-69, Herts 100 Club 1968-69, Sec Conservative Parly Finance Cttee 1971-72, PPS to Michael Heseltine as Min for Aerospace and Shipping Dept of Trade and Industry 1972-74, Assist Govt Whip 1974, Min of State Dept of Trade 1979-81, Chm Conservative Party and Paymaster Gen 1981-83, Chancellor Duchy of Lancaster 1982-83, Sec of State Trade and Industry June-Oct 1983 (resigned), Sec of State for Energy 1987-89, for Transport 1989-90; MP (C) Enfield W Nov 1970-74, Herts S 1974-83, and Hertsmere 1983-92; *cr* PC 1981, and *Baron Parkinson*, of Carnforth, co Lancs (Life Baron) 1992: *m* 1957, Ann Mary, da of F. A. Jarvis, of Harpenden, Herts, and has issue.

𝕬rms – Quarterly gules and azure, a fret throughout argent, on a chief per pale azure and gules a hart's head caboshed between two lion's heads guardant or, langued argent, all within a bordure ermine. 𝕮rest – A crown palisado, therein a grassy mount and thereon a crane statant proper holding in its beak a rose gules barbed and seeded, slipped and leaved proper. 𝕾upporters – *Dexter*, a crane statant reguardant proper; *sinister*, a hart rampant reguardant also proper, attired or, the compartment comprising a grassy mount proper with on each side and growing therefrom three roses gules barbed and seeded, slipped and leaved all proper.
Clubs - Hawks, Pratt's, Beefsteak, Garrick.

DAUGHTERS LIVING

Hon Mary, *b* 1959.
Hon Emma, *b* 1961: *m* 1991, John Owrid.
Hon Joanna, *b* 1963: *m* 1988, Mark Bamber.

PARMOOR, BARON (Cripps) (Baron UK 1914)

Do not trust in appearances

(FREDERICK ALFRED) MILO CRIPPS, 4th Baron; *b* 18 June 1929; *s* (Oct) 1977; *ed* Ampleforth, and Corpus Christi Coll, Oxford.

Arms – Chequy ermines and argent, on a chevron vert five horseshoes or. **Crest** – An ostrich's head couped argent, gorged with a coronet of fleurs-de-lis, and holding in the beak a horseshoe or. **Supporters** – On either side a seahorse proper, supporting a pennon ermines charged with a swan rousant argent, beaked and legged gules, ducally gorged and lined or.

Residence – Dairy, Sutton Veny, Warminster, Wilts BA12 7A.

COLLATERAL BRANCHES LIVING

Issue of late Major Hon Leonard Harrison Cripps, CBE, 3rd son of 1st Baron, *b* 1887, *d* 1959: *m* 1913, Miriam Barbara, who *d* 1960, da of late Rt Hon Sir Matthew Ingle Joyce:—

(MATTHEW) ANTHONY LEONARD, CBE, DSO, TD, QC, *b* 30 Dec 1913; *ed* Eton and Ch Ch, Oxford (MA); Bar Middle Temple 1938, Inner Temple 1961, QC 1958, Bencher 1965 and Treasurer 1983; Recorder of Nottingham 1961-71; Recorder of Crown Court 1972-87; a Member of Senate of four Inns of Court 1967-71 and 1982-83; Chm of Disciplinary Cttee, of Milk Marketing Board since 1956, and of Home Sec's Advisory Cttee on Ser Candidates 1966-94 (Dep Chm 1965); a Member of Bar Council 1967-69, and 1970-74, and of Min of Agric's Cttees of Inquiry into Foot and Mouth Disease 1968-69, and into Export of Live Animals for Slaughter 1973, Chm Reigate Cons Assocn 1961-64, of Research Cttee, Soc of Cons Lawyers 1963-67 and of Cons Party Research Cttee of Inquiry into Discrimination against Women in Law and Admin 1968-69; a Member of Exec Cttee of Nat Union of Cons Assocns 1964-72, Judge of Canterbury Court of Arches 1969-79; Commr for Local Govt Election Petitions 1978-94; Dep Senior Judge of British Sovereign Bases Area, Cyprus, 1978-94; Chm of RSPCA Legal Advisory Cttee 1977-94; Chm of National Panel of Approved Coal Merchants Scheme 1972-94, author of *The Agricultural Holdings Act, 1948*, and Editor of *Cripps on Compulsory Acquisition of Land*; *Powers, Procedure and Compensation*; 1939-45 War in Norway, North Africa (DSO), and Italy; DSO 1943, CBE (Civil) 1971; Hon Maj R Leics Regt: *m* 1941, (Dorothea) Margaret, who *d* 1992, da of late G. Johnson-Scott, of Hill House, Ashby-de-la-Zouch, and has issue living, Michael Leonard Seddon (Bessemers, Moor Wood, Lane End, High Wycombe, Bucks HP4 3HZ), *b* 1942; *ed* Eton; Bar Middle Temple 1965, Lincoln's Inn 1969, and Inner Temple 1975: *m* 1971, Anne, da of Maj Millward-Shennan, of Moorside, Caldy-in-Wirral, and has issue living, Henry William Anthony *b* 1976, Stephanie Margaret Julia *b* 1974, — Jeremy George Anthony (347 Circular St, Tiffin, Ohio 44883, USA), *b* 1943; *ed* Eton, Case Western Reserve Univ, Cleveland, Ohio (MA), and Union Institute, Cincinnati, Ohio (PhD); FCA; Certified Public Accountant, Ohio, USA; Prof of Accountancy Heidelberg Coll, Tiffin, Ohio: *m* 1972, Mary Elizabeth, only da of Walter Howe, of Golf Manor, Cincinnati, Ohio, USA, and has issue living, Scott Anthony Charles *b* 1978, Clark Robert Leonard *b* 1980, Lynne Margaret *b* 1983, — Richard James Nigel (46 Lilyville Rd, SW6 5DW), *b* 1956; *ed* Eton, and St Catharine's Coll, Camb (MA); Solicitor: *m* 1987, Margaret Jude, 3rd da of late Sam S. Mullin, of Osterville, Mass, and has issue living, Leonard Samuel Anthony *b* 1989, John Richard Charles *b* 1991, Frederick Alfred Michael *b* 1992. *Residence* – Woodhurst, McCrae's Walk, Wargrave, Berks RG10 8LN. *Club* – Brooks's. — Charles Thomas Joyce, *b* 1916; *ed* Eton, and Ch Ch, Oxford; formerly Capt Roy Tank Regt; is a Member of London Stock Exchange: *m* 1941, Noreen, da of late Dr Hugh Pierce, of 24 Upper Duke St, Liverpool, and has issue living, Charles Hugh (136 Sherborne Court, 180 Cromwell Rd, SW5 0SU), *b* 1946; *ed* Eton, — Paul Alfred (7 Pont St, SW1X 9EJ), *b* 1950; *ed* Eton, Sorbonne, and LSE. *Residence* – 41 Somerset Rd, Wimbledon, SW19.

Grandchildren of late Rt Hon Sir (Richard) Stafford Cripps, CH, QC, FRS (infra):—
Issue of late Sir John Stafford Cripps, CBE, *b* 1912, *d* 1993: *m* 1st, 1936 (*m diss* 1971), Ursula, da of late Arthur Cedric Davy, of Whirlow Court, Sheffield; 2ndly, 1971, Ann Elizabeth (*Lady Cripps*) (Fox House, Filkins, Lechlade, Glos), da of Edwin G. K. Farwell, of Swanage, Dorset:—
(By 1st *m*) †David Stafford, *b* 1940; *ed* Bryanston, and Reading Univ: *m* 1968 (*m diss* 1981), Bridget Ayerst, and *d* 1990, leaving issue, Jennifer Bridget, *b* 1969, — Nicola Ann, *b* 1971, — Angela Claire, *b* 1973. — Timothy Francis (10 High St, Harston, Cambridge), *b* 1943; *ed* Eton, and Trinity Coll, Camb *m* 1969, —. — Christopher John (Pear Tree Cottage, Viney Hill, Lydney, Glos), *b* 1947; *ed* Bryanston, King's Coll, Camb, and Architectural Assocn; PhD Liverpool 1981: *m* 1976, Alyson, only da of Cyril Laverick, of 17 Bluebell Grove, Stockton-on-Tees, and has issue living, Joe John Allan, *b* 1978, — Rosie Helen Zoë, *b* 1985. — Richard Andrew (3 Moat Cottages, Filkins, Lechlade, Glos), *b* 1953; *ed* Bryanston, and South-ampton Univ. — Judith Ursula (10 Brookside, Headington, Oxford), *b* 1938; *ed* Somerville Coll, Oxford: *m* 1964, Sarjit Heyer, who *d* 1974, and has issue living, Jasdev Philip, *b* 1968, — Daleep Andrew, *b* 1971, — Amrik Frances, *b* 1967. — Rachel Theresa, *b* 1945; *ed* Sussex Univ: *m* 1969, (James Oriel) Bernard Rosedale, MB BS, of Thornsend, Kingsbury Hill, Marlborough, Wilts, and has issue living, Nicholas Oriel Rupert, *b* 1972, — Lawrence Andrew, *b* 1974, — Benjamin James, *b* 1976, — Katherine Jane, *b* 1978.

Issue of late Rt Hon Sir (Richard) Stafford Cripps, CH, QC, FRS, *b* 1889, *d* 1952, yst son of 1st Baron: *m* 1911, *Dame* Isobel, GBE, who *d* 1979, da of late Com Harold William Swithinbank, DL, of Denham Court, Denham, Bucks:—
Anne Theresa (*Lady Ricketts*), CBE, *b* 1919; CBE (Civil) 1983; Chm Nat Assocn of Citizens Advice Bureaux 1979-84: *m* 1945, Capt Sir Robert Cornwallis Gerald St Leger Ricketts, 7th Bt, late Devonshire Regt. *Residence* – Forwood House, Minchinhampton, Glos. — Enid Margaret (PO Box 829, Kumasi, Ashanti, Ghana), *b* 1921: *m* 1953, Joseph E. Appiah, and has issue living, (Kwame) Anthony Akroma-ampim Kusi (Harvard Univ, Boston, Mass, USA), *b* 1954; *ed* Bryanston, and Clare Coll, Camb; Prof at Harvard Univ, Dept of African American Studies, — Isobel Takyiwah, *b* 1955; *ed* Badminton Sch, and Sussex Univ: *m* 1980, Klaus Endresen, of Statsrad Ihlens Vei 2, 2010 Strømmen, nr Oslo, Norway, and has issue living, Kristian Gyamfi *b* 1981, Anthony Finn *b* 1984, Per Kojo *b* 1987, — Amy Adwoa, *b* 1959; *ed* St Louis Secondary Sch, Kumasi, Roedean, Sussex Univ, and Leeds Univ: *m* 1982, Olawale Edun (4b Hawksworth Rd, Ikoyi, Lagos, Nigeria), and has issue living, Babatunde Adetomiwa Stafford *b* 1984, Adedeji Olamide *b* 1986, Adedamola Oluwatobi *b* 1989, — Theresa Jane (Abena), *b* 1962; *ed* Sidcot Sch, and St Godric's Coll.

PREDECESSORS – (1) *Rt Hon Sir* CHARLES ALFRED Cripps, KCVO, KC, son of late Henry William Cripps, QC, of Beech-wood, Marlow; *b* 1852; appointed Attorney-Gen to successive Princes of Wales 1895, 1901, and 1910 (also a Member of Council), Chancellor and Vicar-Gen to Diocese of York 1900, Chm of Canterbury House of Laymen and a Member of its Committee 1910, a Member of Judicial Committee of Privy Council 1914, British Representative on Council of League of Nations Jan 1924, and Ch British Representative to League of Nations Assembly Sept 1924; was Vicar-Gen of Province of Canterbury 1902-24, First Chm of House of Laity in National Church Assembly 1920-24, Lord Pres of the Council Jan to Nov 1924, and June 1929 to Aug 1931, and Leader of Labour Party in House of Lords Oct 1928 to Aug 1931; sat as MP for Mid, or Stroud, Div of Gloucestershire (C) 1895-1900, for Stretford Div of Lancashire (S-E) 1901-6, and for Bucks, S or Wycombe Div Jan 1910 to Jan 1914; cr Baron Parmoor, of Frieth, co Bucks (peerage of United Kingdom) 1914: m 1st, 1881, Theresa, who d 1893, sixth da of Richard Potter, of Rusland Hall, Lancashire; 2ndly, 1919, Marian Emily, who d 1952, da of late Rt Hon John E. Ellis, of Wrea Head, Scalby, Yorkshire; d 1941; s by his son (2) ALFRED HENRY SEDDON, 2nd Baron; b 1882; Bar Middle Temple 1907; Bursar, Queen's Coll Oxford 1928-45 (Fellow 1929); d (Mar) 1977; s by his brother (3), FREDERICK HEY-WORTH, DSO, TD; b 1885; author of Life's a Gamble, 1958; Lt-Col R Bucks Hussars Yeo, 1914-18 War in Dardanelles, Palestine and France (wounded, DSO and Bar Belgian Croix de Guerre); 1939-45 War as temp Lt-Cdr RNVR: m 1927 (m diss 1951), Violet Mary Geraldine, who d 1983, da of Sir William Nelson, 1st Bt, and formerly wife of (1) George Richard Francis Rowley, and (2) the 2nd Duke of Westminster; d (Oct) 1977; s by his son (4) (FREDERICK ALFRED) MILO, 4th Baron and present peer.

PARRY, BARON (Parry) (Life Baron 1975)

GORDON SAMUEL DAVID PARRY, son of late Rev Thomas Lewis Parry; b 30 Nov 1925; ed Trin Coll, Carmarthen, and Liverpool Univ; House Master Co Secondary Sch, Haverfordwest 1952-62, Inst of Educn, Liverpool Univ 1962-63, House Master Haverford West 1963-67, and Warden of Pembrokeshire Teachers' Centre 1967-1976; Chm Wales Tourist Board 1978 (ret); Member British Tourist Authority 1978-84; Pres: Wales Spastics Soc, Pembrokeshire Spastics Soc, and Pembrokeshire Multiple Sclerosis Soc, former Member of Council of Open Univ (and Chm Educn Cttee); Vice-Pres Mentally Handicapped Soc for Wales, Pres British Inst of Cleaning Science, Pres British Cleaning Council; Pres Milford Docks Co, Pres Tidy Britain Group, Chm Clean World International; Fellow Tourism Soc, FRSA, Fellow Hotel and Catering and Institutional Management Assocn, Hon Fellow James Cook Univ, Australia, Hon Fell Institute of Wastes Management, Hon Fell Trinity Coll, Carmarthen, Hon Fell Univ of Glamorgan, Hon Dr of Education, Swansea Institute of Higher Education; DL Dyfed 1993; cr Baron Parry, of Neyland in co Dyfed (Life Baron) 1975: m 1948, Glenys Catherine, da of Jack Leslie Incledon, and has issue.
Residence – Willowmead, 52 Port Lion, Llangwm, Haverfordwest, Dyfed SA62 4JT.

DAUGHTER LIVING

Hon Catherine Anne, b 1955.

PEARCE, BARONY OF (Pearce) (Extinct 1990)

WIDOWS LIVING OF SONS OF LIFE BARON

(Jennifer) Christine, da of late Rev J. W. G. Westwood, of Eynsham, Oxfordshire: m 1987, as his 2nd wife, Hon (Richard) Bruce (Holroyd) Pearce, QC, who d 1987, and has issue living, Edward William, b 1981, — Erica Harriet, b 1982. Residence – Sweethawes, Kings Sutton, nr Banbury, Oxfordshire.
Julia, yr da of C. D. Hill, of Tyrrellswood, Leatherhead, Surrey: m 1st, 1969, Hon James Edward Holroyd Pearce, QC, who d 1985; 2ndly, 1987, Ian Strickland Ball, and has issue living (by 1st m), Edward b 19—, — Robert, b 19—, — Ianthe, b 19—, — Barbara, b 19—. Residence – Turf Lodge, Sheep Plain, Crowborough, Sussex TN6 3ST.

PEARSON, BARONY OF (Pearson) (Extinct 1980)

SON LIVING OF LIFE BARON

Hon Graham Thomas (Pinette, Whangarei Heads Rd, RD 4, Whangarei, New Zealand), b 1935: m 1963, Diana, da of Vice-Adm Sir Maxwell Richmond, KBE, CB, DSO, of Whangarei Heads, New Zealand, and has issue.

DAUGHTER LIVING OF LIFE BARON

Hon Lois Jean, b 1938: m 1961, Rt Rev Canon Robin Jonathan Norman Smith, of Hertford House, Abbey Mill Lane, St Albans, Herts AL3 4HE, and has issue.

PEARSON OF RANNOCH, BARON (Pearson) (Life Baron 1990)

MALCOLM EVERARD MACLAREN PEARSON, son of late Col John MacLaren Pearson; b 20 July 1942; ed Eton; Founded Pearson Webb Springbett (PWS) Group of Reinsurance Brokers 1964, Chm PWS Holdings plc since 1988; Dir Highland Venison Ltd 1984-89; Chm Rannoch Protection Group since 1979; Founded Rannoch Trust 1984; Member Council for National Academic Awards since 1983 (Hon Treas since 1986); cr Baron Pearson of Rannoch, of Bridge of Gaur, in the District of Perth and Kinross (Life Baron) 1990: m 1st, 1965 (m diss 1970), Francesca Frua, da of Giuseppe Frua de Angeli; 2ndly, 1977, Hon (Francesca) Mary Charteris, only da of Baron Charteris of Amisfield, GCB, GCVO, QSO, OBE, PC (Life Baron), and has issue by 1st and 2nd m.
Residence – Rannock Barracks, Rannoch Station, Perthshire PH17 2QE. Club – White's.

DAUGHTERS LIVING *(By 1st marriage)*

Hon Silvia Maria Francesca, *b* 1966.

(by 2nd marriage)

Hon Marina MacLaren, *b* 1980.
Hon Zara Alexandra Mary, *b* 1984.

PEART, BARONY (Peart) (Extinct 1988)

SON LIVING OF LIFE BARON

Hon Emerson Frederick, *b* 1948: *m* .

WIDOW LIVING OF LIFE BARON

SARAH ELIZABETH *(Baroness Peart)*, da of Thomas Lewis, of Aberystwyth: *m* 1945, Baron Peart (Life Baron), PC, who *d* 1988.

DAUGHTER LIVING *(By 1st marriage)*

Hon Silvia Maria Francesca, *b* 1966.

PEDDIE, BARONY OF (Peddie) (Extinct 1978)

SON LIVING OF LIFE BARON

Hon Ian James Crofton (36 Chiswick Staithe, Hartington Rd, W4 3TP), *b* 1945; *ed* Gordonstoun, and Univ Coll, London (LLB); Bar Inner Temple 1971: *m* 1976, Susan Renee, el da of Edmund John Brampton Howes, of 13 Wheelers Av, Penn, Bucks, and has issue living, Kate Chloe, *b* 1982.

DAUGHTER LIVING OF LIFE BARON

Hon Hilary Aileen (31 Nonsuch Court Av, Ewell, Surrey), *b* 1938: *m* 1959 (*m diss* 19—), Christopher Geoffrey Rudd, and has issue living, Simon Nicholas, *b* 1959, — Susanne Philippa, *b* 1960.

PEEL, EARL (Peel) (Earl UK 1929, Bt GB 1800)

WILLIAM JAMES ROBERT PEEL, 3rd Earl and 8th Baronet; *b* 3 Oct 1947; *s* 1969; *ed* Ampleforth, Tours Univ, France, and Roy Agric Coll, Cirencester; Vice-Chm Game Conservancy Trust since 1990; a Member of the Council of the Prince of Wales, Duchy of Cornwall, since 1993: *m* 1st, 1973, Veronica Naomi Livingston, da of Maj John Alastair Livingston Timpson, MC, Scots Gds (*see* Houstoun-Boswall, Bt); 2ndly, 1989, Hon Mrs Charlotte Clementine Hambro, yr da of late Baron Soames, GCMG, GCVO, CH, CBE, PC (Life Baron), and has issue by 1st and 2nd *m*.

Arms – Argent, three sheaves of as many arrows proper two and one, banded gules, on a chief azure a bee volant or. Crest – A demi-lion rampant argent, gorged with a collar azure charged with three bezants and holding between the paws a shuttle or. Supporters – Dexter, a lion reguardant argent, gorged with a chain or, pendant therefrom an escutcheon azure, thereon a representation of the Speaker's mace erect of the second; sinister, a griffin reguardant or, gorged with a gold chain, pendant therefrom an escutcheon azure, charged with a representation of the Speaker's mace of the first.

Residence – Gunnerside Lodge, Richmond, N Yorks. *Club* – Turf.

SON LIVING *(By 1st marriage)*

ASHTON ROBERT GERARD *(Viscount Clanfield)*, *b* 16 Sept 1976.

DAUGHTERS LIVING *(By 1st marriage)*

Lady Iona Joy Julia, *b* 1978.

(by 2nd marriage)

Lady Antonia Mary Catherine, *b* 1991.

BROTHER LIVING

Hon Robert Michael Arthur, *b* 1950; *ed* Eton, and Hertford Coll, Oxford: *m* 1973, Fiona Natalie, da of Charles Davidson, of Dunhampstead House, Droitwich, Worcs, and has issue living, Kathryn Beatrice, *b* 1978, — Hermione Juliet, *b* 1979, — Eleanor Lindsay, *b* 1981. *Residence* – Berryhill Farm, Coedkernew, Newport, Gwent.

COLLATERAL BRANCHES LIVING *(In remainder to Viscountcy and Baronetcy only)*

Issue of late Major Hon (Arthur) George Villiers Peel, 2nd son of 1st Viscount, *b* 1868, *d* 1956: *m* 1906, Lady Agnes Lygon, who *d* 1960, da of 6th Earl Beauchamp:—
George Frederick, *b* 1921; *ed* Harrow, and at New Coll, Oxford; Personal Assist to Custodian at Pusey Memorial Library, Oxford 1950-52, Assist Custodian thereof 1952-4, and Assist, Faculty of Theology Library, Oxford Univ 1953-4; a Hospital Librarian, Order of St John since 1955, an Asst Archivist USPG 1967-69, since when an Asst Librarian Education Depart, Reading Univ 1969-79; a Life Gov of Corpn of Sons of the Clergy; 1939-45 War with R Berks Regt (invalided); subsequently with Air Min (Flying Training Command): *m* 1960, Elizabeth Mary, only da of late J. V. Coker, of Ruscombe, Berks. *Residence* – 12 Meadow Close, Goring-on-Thames, nr Reading RG8 0AP. *Clubs* – Brooks's, Royal Over-Seas League. —— Juliet Agnes, *b* 1919: *m* 1942, Maj George Thorne, MC, ERD, DL, late Grenadier Guards (B Penrhyn), of 24 Swallowfield Park, Reading, and has issue living, Robert George (Ovington House, Ovington, Alresford, Hants), *b* 1943; *ed* Eton, and RAC, Cirencester; with Barclays Bank: *m* 1990, Sarah Veronica Bond, *née* Priestley, — Ian David Peel (Beauchamp Barn, Kneesall, Newark, Notts NG22 0AS), *b* 1944; *ed* Eton, RMA, and Trin Coll, Oxford; late Capt Grenadier Guards; High Sheriff Notts 1986: *m* 1992, Paula Nkechi Emwezoh, and has issue living, Davina Nkechi Rozelle *b* 1992, — Viola Georgina Juliet, *b* 1948: *m* 1976, Nicholas Guy Halsey, TD, of The Golden Parsonage, Gt Gaddesden, Hemel Hempstead, Herts, and has issue *(see* Halsey, Bt).

Grandchildren of late Rev Hon Maurice Berkeley Peel, MC, 4th son of 1st Viscount:—
Issue of late Major David Arthur Peel, MC, Irish Guards, *b* 1910, *ka* 1944: *m* 1936, Hon Sara Carola Vanneck (Huntingfield Hall, Halesworth, Suffolk, 1P19 0QA), da of 5th Baron Huntingfield:—
Jonathan Sidney, CBE, MC (Barton Hall, Barton Turf, Norwich, NR12 8AU), *b* 1937; *ed* Norwich Sch, Eton, and St Johns Coll, Camb (MA); Capt Rifle Bde (ret); a Page of Honour to HM 1951-53; a Dir Norwich Union Insurance Gp; Chm Pleasureworld plc; Malaya 1957 (MC); Congo 1960-61; JP, DL, CC and Vice Lord-Lieut Norfolk 1980; High Sheriff (1984); Chm National Trust Properties Cttee since 1990, Dep Chm National Trust since 1992, Chm Broads Authority since 1985, Chm County Council Planning and Transport Cttee 1989-93, Chm National Trust E Anglia Region 1981-90, Vice-Pres Norfolk Naturalists Trust, Chm Norwich Sch, and How Hill Trust for Environmental Education; CBE 1994: *m* 1965, Jean Fulton, da of Air Ch Marshal Sir Denis Hensley Fulton Barnett, GCB, CBE, DFC, and has issue living, Robert Denis, *b* 1976, — Ruth Miranda, *b* 1966, — Emily Sara, *b* 1967: *m* 19—, Mario de Pina Antunes, and has issue living, Anibal-Jorge *b* 1991, — Anne Louise, *b* 1970, — Delia Mary, *b* 1974. —— Charles David, *b* 1940; *ed* Eton, and at Norwich Sch; ARIBA: *m* 1973, Catherine Anne, da of Duncan Mackintosh, CBE, of Woodfolds, Oaksey, Wilts, and has issue living, Thomas David *b* 1975, — Elisabeth Alison *b* 1977. —— Julia Victoria Mary, *b* 1939: *m* 1970, Nicholas Longe (High Sheriff of Suffolk 1984-85), of Hasketon Manor, Woodbridge, Suffolk, son of late Lt-Col R. B. Longe, of Hasketon, Lodge, Woodbridge, Suffolk, and has issue living, William Martin Peel, *b* 1972, — David John Hastings, *b* 1975.

(In remainder to Baronetcy only)

Grandchildren of late Lawrence Moore Peel, 3rd son of Capt Robert Moore Peel, el son of late Rt Hon William Yates Peel, MP, 2nd son of 1st baronet:—
Issue of late Lionel Victor Moore Peel, *b* 1901, *d* 1937: *m* 1924, Muriel Mildred (9295 McNaught Rd, Chilliwack, BC, Canada), da of M. A. Murphy, of Chilliwack, BC:—
Robert John (50769 Yale Rd East, RR1, Rosedale, BC, Canada), *b* 1927: *m* 1949, Mona Jean, yst da of A. A. E. Batchelor, and has issue living, Robert Lionel, *b* 1952: *m* 1972, Sheila, 6th da of Austin Byrnes, of Chilliwack, BC, — Rodney Robin, *b* 1955, — Darcy Edward, *b* 1965, — Susan Holly, *b* 1958. —— Lionel Brian, *b* 1931: *m* 1952, Beverly Ann, only da of Harvey G. Cook, of Cultus Lake, BC, Canada, and has issue living, Brian Gregory, *b* 1954: *m* 1973, Sylvia, da of Clarence Hala, of Chilliwack, BC, and has issue living, James Nathan *b* 1974, Jason Randall *b* 1976, — and two adopted das, Kathryn Patricia, *b* 1964, — Kimberley Ann, *b* 1965. —— Iris Patricia, *b* 1929: *m* 1952, Lorne Albert Gehman, and has issue living, Blair Lee, *b* 1957, — Lane Peel, *b* 1958, — Dane Robert, *b* 1959, — Christie Robin, *b* 1962, — Regen Corey Gehman, *b* 1965, — Shannon Dee, *b* 1954.

Grandchildren (by 2nd *m*) of late William Charles Peel (infra):—
Issue of late Frederick William Peel, *b* 1900, *d* 1978; admitted to British nationality 1936; assumed the forename of William in lieu of his second christian name of de Layney: *m* 1924, Martha Grace, da of William Young, of Memphis, Tennessee:—
Frederick William (PO Box 292, Paris, Tennessee, USA), *b* 1925; Lt-Col USAF (ret): *m* 1st, 1945, Clareleen Popham, of Carothersville, USA; 2ndly, 1954, Clare Elizabeth, da of F. B. Hooever, of Enid, Oklahoma, and has issue living (by 1st *m*), Frederick William, *b* 1947, — Martha Frances, *b* 1949, — (by 2nd *m*) John Hoover, *b* 1962: *m* 1985, Karen Denise, da of W. Sanders, of Paris, Tennessee, — Traci de Layney, *b* 1955. —— Robert de Layney (3908 Leon Drive, Plano, Texas 75074, USA), *b* 1939; Lt-Col USAF (ret); Capt Southwest Airlines: *m* 1976, Christine Ann, da of Walter Trimailo, and has issue living, Delaney Anne, *b* 1978, — Kathryn Eve, *b* 1985.

Granddaughters of late Frederick William Peel (*b* 1900) (ante):—
Issue of late Robert Dudley Peel, Major USAF, *b* 1937, *d* 1982: *m* 1963, Mary Elizabeth (2933 Caballero Drive, Jacksonville, Florida 32217, USA), da of Lawrence J. McDonald:—
Elizabeth Anne, *b* 1964: *m* 1987, Jeffrey Alan Styerwalt, and has issue living, Sean William, *b* 1990, — Brian Robert, *b* 1992. —— Mary Martha, *b* 1966: *m* 1991, Christian Simon Bahn. —— Katherine Louise, *b* 1970.

Grandchildren of late Rev Frederick Peel, 3rd son of late Rt Hon William Yates Peel, MP (ante):—
Issue of late William Charles Peel, *b* 1863, *d* 1930: *m* 1st, 1889, Marion Georgiana Frances, who *d* 1897, da of Libert Chandler, of USA; 2ndly, 1900, Leonie Rose, da of Constant Hallu, of Nampeel, France:—
(By 2nd *m*) †Charles William, *b* 1904: *m* 1929, Catherine Veronica, da of S. A. Puskac, of Hamilton, Ohio, USA, and *dsp* 1980. —— †Jack John, *b* 1908; *d* 1917. —— †Evelyn Ker Semer, *b* 1909; assumed the names of Lincoln Henry Tracy in lieu of his christian names: *m* (March) 1946, Hazel Pearl Gener, and *d* 1993, leaving issue, Kevin John (66 Chislehurst Rd, Lesmurdie, W Australia 6076), *b* (Dec) 1946: *m* 1967, Cheryl Anne, da of Albert George Lawrence, of 2 Nereus Place, Madora Bay, W Australia, and has issue living, Gary John *b* 1970, Christopher James *b* 1973. —— †Laurence Donald Tracy, *b* 1917: *m* 1950, Corinne Beatrix Crutchley, and *d* 1983, leaving issue, Suzanne Caroline, *b* 1951: *m* 1970, Paul Raymond Martin, of Oxfootstone House, Low Common, S Lopham, Norfolk IP22 2JS, and has issue living, Philip Andrew *b* 1977, Joanna Corinne Judith *b* 1984. —— Estelle Frances (Cedarwood, Lows Lane, Palgrave, Diss, Norfolk IP22 1AE), *b* 1901: *m* 1st, 19—, T. S. Patterson; 2ndly, 19—, Christopher Lewis, who *d* 1942. —— Dorothy Léonie, *b* 1911: *m* 1938, Donnington Dade, who *d* 1976. —— Xzavia Séréna, *b* 1915: *m* , — , and *dsp* 1989.

Grandchildren of late Capt Francis Peel, 4th son of late Rt Hon William Yates Peel, MP (ante):—

Issue of late Col Robert Francis Peel, CMG, *b* 1874, *d* 1924: *m* 1903, Alice Maude, who *d* 1957, da of Sir Thomas Meyrick, 1st Bt, KCB:—

Chiverton Robert, *b* 1908; *ed* Harrow, and Trin Coll, Camb; Major (ret) Coldstream Guards; European War 1939-41 in France: *m* 1959, Bridget Honoria, who *d* 1994, da of late Edward Hornby Beckwith (*see* Chichester, Bt, 1966 Edn). *Residence* – The Hill, Weare Gifford, near Bideford, N Devon. ——— Hermione Mary, *b* 1912: *m* 1939, Lt Robert Ormsby Oliver, RNVR, who *d* 1973, and has had issue, Lyon Robert, *b* 1949; *ed* Bromsgrove, and Cheltenham Art Coll; artist and designer, — Anne Falkener, *b* 1942; *dum* 1968. *Residence* – Ditton Farm, St Owen's Cross, Hereford.

Grandson of late Col Frederick Peel, 2nd son of late Lt-Col Edmund Yates Peel, 2nd son of Lt-Gen the Rt Hon Jonathan Peel, MP, 5th son of 1st baronet:—

Issue of late Archibald Peel, *b* 1878, *d* 1932: *m* 1908, Mary, da of late Henry Whiteley, of Wakefield, Yorkshire, and adopted da of Reuben Thomas Saunders, formerly of Raskelf, 215 Capstone Road, Bournemouth:—

Maurice (31 Seves St, Altona, Melbourne, Australia), *b* 1910: *m* (March) 1935, Louisa Myrtle, da of late John Newby Carter, and has issue living, Maurice Newby, *b* (Dec) 1935, — Alfred George, *b* 1940, — Stanley Charles, *b* 1946, — Cyril Ronald, *b* 1952, — Violet Ethel, *b* 1937: *m* 1959, Kevin George Anderson, of 59 Bladin St, Laverton, Melbourne, Australia, and has issue living, Kevin John *b* 1960, Brett Lewin *b* 1961, Steven Maurice *b* 1963, Vanessa Lee *b* 1968, — Lorraine Ruth, *b* 1945.

Grandchildren of late Alfred Michael John Russell Peel, 4th son of late Archibald Peel (*b* 1828), 3rd son of late Rt Rev Jonathan Peel, MP (ante):—

Issue of late Archibald John Russell Peel, *b* 1907, *d* 1978: *m* 1946, Patricia Virtue, who *d* 1980, only da of Col Baldwin Millard, of 61 Fitzjohn's Av, NW3:—

Jeremy Robert (Willow Cottages, La Pouquelaye, St Helier, Jersey, CI), *b* 1946: *m* 1st, 1970 (*m diss* 1974), Shirley Ann Brett; 2ndly, 1984, Angela Betty, only da of Edward David Neal, of Red Roofs, St Peter, Jersey, and has issue living (by 1st *m*), Mark Jeremy Russell, *b* 1971. ——— Michael John Russell, *b* 1952. ——— Caroline Georgiana, *b* 1948: *m* 1970, Paul Fisher Bancroft, of Caroline House, South Rd, Oundle, Peterborough, and has issue living, Adam Fisher, *b* 1973, — Oliver Robert, *b* 1976, — Jonathan Guy, *b* 1979, — Imogen Georgiana Patricia, *b* 1984. ——— Elizabeth Francesca (42 Morella Grove, Bridgewater, S Australia 5155), *b* 1950: *m* 1972, Andrew Swart.

Grandsons of late Lt-Col Charles Algernon Peel, only son of late Horace Peel, 3rd son of late Sir Charles Lennox Peel, GCB, eldest son of late Laurence Peel, 6th son of 1st baronet:—

Issue of late Jeremy Charles Peel, *b* 1934, *d* 1988: *m* 1960 (*m diss* 1971), Sheila Mary Rose, da of Capt Charles Elphinstone Fordyce (*see* B Windlesham, 1990 Edn):—

Robert Frederick Charles (6 Terrick Cottages, Terrick, Aylesbury, Bucks), *b* 1962: *m* 1991, Elizabeth Mary, yr da of Geoffrey Green, of Ayr, Ontario, Canada. ——— James Arthur Lennox (The Garden Flat, 120 St John's Hill, SW10), *b* 1964: *m* 1987, Belinda Margaret Emma, yr da of Nicholas Smith, of Charney Bassett, Oxon.

PREDECESSORS – (1) *Rt Hon* ARTHUR WELLESLEY Peel, 5th son of late Rt Hon Sir Robert Peel, 2nd Bt, of Drayton Manor, Staffordshire; *b* 1829; Parliamentary Sec to Poor Law Board 1868-71, and to Board of Trade 1871-3, Patronage Sec to Treasury 1873-4, Under-Sec for Home Depart April to Dec 1880, and Speaker (four times elected to House of Commons Feb 1884 to April 1895); MP for Warwick (*L*) 1865-85, and for Warwick and Leamington 1886-95; *cr Viscount Peel*, of Sandy, co Bedford (peerage of United Kingdom) 1895: *m* 1962, Adelaide, who *d* 1890, da of William Stratford Dugdale, of Merevale, Warwickshire; *d* 1912; *s* by his el son (2) *Rt Hon* WILLIAM ROBERT WELLESLEY, GCSI, GBE, 2nd Viscount; *b* 1867; MP for Manchester (S Div) 1900-1906, and for Taunton 1906-12; appointed Joint Parliamentary Sec (unpaid), National Ser Depart 1917, Under-Sec of State for War 1919, and Chancellor of Duchy of Lancaster 1921 (also Min of Transport (unpaid) 1921); was Sec of State for India 1922-4, and again 1928-9, and Lord Privy Seal Sept to Nov 1931; *cr Viscount Clanfield*, of Clanfield, co Southampton, and *Earl Peel* (peerage of United Kingdom) 1929: *m* 1899, Hon Eleanor (Ella) Williamson, who *d* 1949, da of 1st Baron Ashton (ext); *d* 1937; *s* by his son (3) ARTHUR WILLIAM ASHTON, 2nd Earl *b* 1901; Lord Lt of Lancs 1948-50: *m* 1946, Kathleen, who *d* 1972, da of Michael McGrath of Ballycullane, co Cork; *d* 1969; *s* by his son (4) WILLIAM JAMES ROBERT, 3rd Earl and present peer; also Viscount Peel, and Viscount Clanfield.

*(1) ROBERT Peel, 3rd son of late Robert Peel, of Peele Fold, Lancashire; *b* 1750; was an eminent Cotton Spinner, MP for Tamworth 1790-1818, and contributed £10,000 towards promoting the war with France; *cr* a *Baronet* 1800: *m* 1st, 1783, Ellen, da of William Yates, of Spring Side, near Bury; 2ndly, 1805, Susanna, who *d* 1824, da of late Francis Clerke; *d* 1830; *s* by his el son (2) *Rt Hon* ROBERT, 2nd Bt; *b* 1788; sometime MP for Oxford Univ, and subsequently for Tamworth (*C*); appointed Under-Sec of State for the Colonies 1810, Ch Sec for Ireland 1812, and Sec of State for Home Depart 1828; was First Lord of the Treasury and Prime Minister 1834-5 and 1841-6: *m* 1820, Julia, who *d* 1859, yst da of Gen Sir John Floyd, 1st Bt; *d* 1850; *s* by his el son (3) *Rt Hon Sir* ROBERT, GCB, 3rd Bt; *b* 1822; sat as MP for Tamworth (LC) 1850-80, for Huntingdon (*C*) 1884-5, and for Blackburn 1885-6; was a Lord of the Admiralty 1852-7, and Ch Sec for Ireland 1861-5: *m* 1856, Lady Emily Hay, who *d* 1924, da of 8th Marquess of Tweeddale; *d* 1895; *s* by his only son (4) ROBERT, 4th Bt; *b* 1867: *m* 1897, Mercedes, da of Baron de Graffenried, formerly of Thun, Switzerland; *d* 1925; *s* by his only son (5) ROBERT, 5th Bt; *b* 1898: *m* 1920, Beatrice Gladys, the distinguished comedienne, who *d* 1989, aged 94, da of late John Lillie; *d* 1934; *s* by his only son (6) ROBERT, 6th Bt; *b* 1920; Ordinary Seaman RN; *ka* 1942; *s* by his kinsman (7) ARTHUR WILLIAM ASHTON (ante).

PEMBROKE and MONTGOMERY, EARL OF (Herbert) (Earl E 1551 and 1605)

One I will serve

HENRY GEORGE CHARLES ALEXANDER HERBERT, 17th Earl; *b* 19 May 1939; *s* 1969; *ed* Eton, and Oxford Univ; late RHG; Hereditary Visitor of Jesus Coll, Oxford: *m* 1st, 1966 (*m diss* 1981), Claire Rose, da of Douglas Gurney Pelly (*see* Pelly Bt, colls); 2ndly, 1988, Miranda Juliet, da of Cmdr John Somerville Kendal Oram, of Bulbridge House, Wilton, Salisbury, Wilts (*see* E Cairns, 1985 Edn), and has issue by 1st and 2nd *m*.

Arms – Per pale azure and gules, three lions rampant argent. **Crest** – A wyvern wings elevated vert, holding in the mouth a sinister hand couped at the wrist gules. **Supporters** – *Dexter*, a panther guardant argent, incensed, spotted or, vert, sable azure, and gules, alternately, ducally collared azure; *sinister*, a lion argent, ducally collared or. **Seat** – Wilton House, Salisbury.

SON LIVING *(By 1st marriage)*

WILLIAM ALEXANDER SIDNEY (*Lord Herbert*), *b* 18 May 1978.

DAUGHTER LIVING *(By 1st marriage)*

Lady Sophia Elizabeth, *b* 1966.
Lady Emma Louise, *b* 1969.
Lady Flora Katinka, *b* 1970.

(by 2nd marriage)

Lady Jemima Juliet, *b* 1989.
Lady Alice Mary, *b* 1991.

SISTER LIVING

Lady Diana Mary, *b* 1937.

UNCLE LIVING *(Son of 15th Earl)*

Hon David Alexander Reginald, *b* 1908; *ed* Eton; 1939-45 War as Lt RNVR. *Address* – Box 2024, Tangier (Socco), Morocco.

WIDOW LIVING OF SIXTEENTH EARL

Lady MARY DOROTHEA HOPE, CVO (*Mary, Countess of Pembroke and Montgomery*) (The Old Rectory, Wilton, Salisbury) Hon 1st Officer WRNS; a Lady-in-Waiting to HRH the Duchess of Kent 1934-49 and an Extra Lady-in-Waiting 1949-68; CVO 1947; da of 1st Marquess of Linlithgow: *m* 1936, the 16th Earl, who *d* 1969.

COLLATERAL BRANCHES LIVING

Descendants of late Henry Herbert (el son of late Maj-Gen Hon William Herbert, 5th son of 8th Earl), who was *cr Earl of Carnarvon* 1793 (see that title).

PREDECESSORS – (1) *Sir* WILLIAM Herbert, KG, KB, was Ch Gentleman of the Privy Chamber, Master of the Horse 1549, twice Gov of the Forces sent into Picardy, twice Gov of Calais, and Capt Gen of the Army beyond the Seas, etc; *cr Baron Herbert*, of Cardiff, and *Earl of Pembroke* (peerage of England) 1551; *d* 1570; *s* by his el son (2) HENRY, KG, 2nd Earl; *d* 1601; *s* by his son (3) WILLIAM, KG, 3rd Earl; was Lord Chamberlain of the Household; *d* 1630; *s* by his brother (4) PHILIP, KG, 4th Earl, who in 1605 had been *cr Baron Herbert*, of Shurland, Isle of Sheppey, co Kent, and *Earl of Montgomery* (peerage of England); was Lord Chamberlain to the Household, and Chancellor of Oxford Univ; *d* 1655; *s* by his son (5) PHILIP, 5th Earl; *d* 1669; *s* by his el son (6) WILLIAM, 6th Earl; *d* unmarried 1674; *s* by his half-brother (7) PHILIP, 7th Earl; *d* without male issue 1683; *s* by his brother (8) THOMAS, KG, PC, 8th Earl; was Ambassador to States Gen 1689, Lord Privy Seal 1700, seven times one of the Lord Justices, Lord High Adm of England 1702 and 1708-9, and Lord Pres of the Council 1702; at the Coronation of George I carried the sword styled "Curtana"; *d* 1733; *s* by his son (9) HENRY, 9th Earl; a Lieut-Gen in the Army; *d* 1750; *s* by his son (10) HENRY, 10th Earl; was a Lieut-Gen in the Army, and Col 1st Dragoons; *d* 1794; *s* by his son (11) GEORGE AUGUSTUS, KG, 11th Earl; *d* 1827; *s* by his son (12) ROBERT HENRY, 12th Earl; *d* 1862; *s* by his nephew (13) GEORGE ROBERT CHARLES, 13th Earl of Pembroke, and 10th Earl of Montgomery, who had already in 1861 *s* as 2nd Baron Herbert of Lea (son of Hon Sidney Herbert, 2nd son of 11th Earl, an eminent statesman, who *m* 1846, Elizabeth, da of Lieut-Gen Charles Ashe A'Court; and *d* Aug 1861, having in Jan of that year been *cr Baron Herbert of Lea* (peerage of United Kingdom)), *b* 1850: *m* 1874, Lady Gertrude Frances Talbot, who *d* 1906, da of 18th Earl of Shrewsbury; *d* 1895; *s* by his brother (14) SIDNEY, GCVO, PC, 14th Earl; *b* 1853; a Lord of Treasury 1885-6 and July 1886 to Aug 1892, and Lord Steward of the Household to Queen Victoria July 1895 to Jan 1901, and to King Edward VII 1901-5; MP for Wilton (C) 1877-85, and for Croydon 1886-95: *m* 1877, Lady Beatrix Louisa Lambton, who *d* 1944, da of 2nd Earl of Durham; *d* 1913; *s* by his el son (15) REGINALD, MVO, 15th Earl; *b* 1880; Lieut-Col Roy Horse Guards; Mayor of Wilton 1932-34, 1942-45, and 1954-55: *m* 1904, Lady Beatrice Eleanor, CBE, who *d* 1973, da of late Lord Alexander Victor Paget (M Anglesey); *d* 1960; *s* by his el son (16) SIDNEY CHARLES, CVO, 16th Earl; *b* 1906; Equerry to HRH The Duke of Kent 1935-42; Private Sec and Comptroller to HRH the Duchess of Kent 1942-48; Lord Lieut of Wilts 1954-69: *m* 1936, Lady Mary Dorothea Hope, CVO, da of 1st Marquess of Linlithgow; *d* 1969; *s* by his son (17) HENRY GEORGE CHARLES ALEXANDER, 17th Earl and present peer; also Baron Herbert of Cardiff, Baron Herbert of Shurland, and Baron Herbert of Lea.

PENDER, BARON (Denison-Pender) (Baron UK 1937)

JOHN WILLOUGHBY DENISON-PENDER, 3rd Baron; *b* 6 May 1933; *s* 1965; *ed* Eton; late Capt City of London Yeo (TA); late Lt 10th Hussars; Vice-Pres Royal Sch for the Deaf since 1992: *m* 1962, Julia, da of Richard Nevill Cannon, OBE, of Coombe Place, Lewes, and has issue.

Arms – Quarterly: 1st and 4th gules, on a bend nebuly argent two lions' heads erased of the first, *Pender*; 2nd and 3rd per bend sable and argent two bendlets between a unicorn's head erased in chief and three cross-crosslets in base all counterchanged, *Denison*; **Crests** – 1st, a demi-lion or resting the sinister paw upon a terrestrial globe, and grasping in the dexter paw a seax proper, pomel and hilt gold, *Pender*; 2nd, in front of a sun rising in splendour a dexter arm in bend proper, vested gules gutte-d'eau, cuff erminois, the fore-finger pointing to an estoile or *Denison*. **Supporters** – On either side a figure of Hermes standing on a cable-grapnel, the dexter holding in the exterior hand a Caduceus and the sinister a flash of lightning all proper.
Residence – North Court, Tilmanstone, Kent CT14 0JP. *Clubs* – White's, Pratt's.

I persevere

SON LIVING

Hon HENRY JOHN RICHARD, *b* 19 March 1968.

DAUGHTERS LIVING

Hon Emma Charlotte, *b* 1964: *m* 1992, Matthew Christopher Anthony Brett (*see* V Esher).
Hon Mary Anne Louise, *b* 1965.

BROTHER LIVING

Hon Robin Charles (Jessups, Mark Beech, Edenbridge, Kent; White's Club), *b* 1935; *ed* Eton; late Lt 11th Hussars; High Sheriff Kent 1993; a Member of Stock Exchange: *m* 1966, Clare Nell, da of Lt-Col James Currie Thomson, MBE, TD, JP, DL, of Stable Court, Walkern, Stevenage (*see* Borthwick, Bt, colls), and has issue living, Jocelyn Andrew, *b* 1967, — Peter Robin, *b* 1972, — Sacha Louise, *b* 1969: *m* 1993, Jonathan David Forbes (*see* Ropner, Bt, *cr* 1952).

SISTER LIVING

Hon Ann Camilla (*Hon Lady Dent*), *b* 1931: *m* 1952, Sir Robin John Dent, KCVO, of 44 Smith St, SW3, and has issue living, Annabel Jane, *b* 1954: *m* 1981, James John Meade, of Pitt Vale Farm House, Pitt, Winchester, Hants SO22 5QW, son of J. A. Meade, of 6 Fulham Park House, Chesilton Rd, SW6 5AA, and has issue living, Thomas Edward *b* 1988, Katherine Anne *b* 1984, Susanna Clare *b* 1986, — Jennifer Ann, *b* 1957: *m* 1982, Andrew Everard Martin Smith, elder son of Julian Ronald Martin Smith, of Ringstead Bury, Hunstanton, Norfolk, and has issue living, David Julian *b* 1984, Henrietta Camilla *b* 1986, Rosanna Marcia *b* (twin) 1986.

COLLATERAL BRANCH LIVING

Issue of late Maj Hon Richard Ernest Denison-Pender, TD, yr son of 1st Baron, *b* 1914, *d* 1984: *m* 1939, Louise, who *d* 1973, only da of late Henry Gilbey Riviere:—
James Henry (Denton Foot, Brampton, Cumbria), *b* 1942: *m* 1st, 1971, Gillian, yst da of late John C. Barnett, of Threepwood Hall, Haydon Bridge, Northumberland; 2ndly, 1994, Caroline Anne, da of Maj Timothy Stuart Lewis (*see* V Daventry), and formerly wife of Sir (Frederick Douglas) David Thomson, 3rd Bt, and has issue living (by 1st *m*), Jamie Alexander, *b* 1973, — Nicholas John, *b* 1974. —— Michael Richard (86 Ravenscourt Rd, W6; Middle West Cottage, Sandwich Bay, Kent), *b* (twin) 1942: *m* 1972, Nadine, yr da of late Henri Villiger, of Aigle, Switzerland, and has issue living, Dominic Michael, *b* 1975. —— Linda Louise, *b* 1948: *m* 1973, John Edward Bayman, of Middle Cottage, Sandwich Bay, Kent, and has issue living, Alexander Christian Gray, *b* 1976, — Caroline Louise, *b* 1975.

PREDECESSORS – (1) JOHN CUTHBERT DENISON Denison-Pender, el son of late Sir John Denison-Pender, GBE, KCMG; *b* 1882; sometime Capt in the Army; a County Councillor for London 1910-19; European War 1914-18 in France and Belgium; MP for E, of Newmarket Div, of Cambridgeshire (C) 1913-18, and for Balham and Tooting Div of Wandsworth 1918-22; *cr* *Baron Pender*, of Porthcurnow, co Cornwall (peerage of United Kingdom) 1937: *m* 1906, Irene, who *d* 1943, da of late Sir Ernest de la Rue, KCVO, of 26 Belgrave Square, SW; *d* 1949; *s* by his son (2) JOHN JOCELYN, CBE, 2nd Baron, *b* 1907: *m* 1930, Camilla Lethbridge, who *d* 1988, da of late Willoughby Arthur Pemberton (Lethbridge, Bt, colls); *d* 1965; *s* by his el son (3) JOHN WILLOUGHBY, 3rd Baron and present peer.

PENNEY, BARONY OF (Penney) (Extinct 1991)

SONS LIVING OF LIFE BARON (by 1st marriage)

Hon Martin Charles (16 Gainsborough Court, College Rd, Dulwich, SE21 7LT), *b* 1938; *ed* Cranleigh, and Gonville and Caius Coll, Camb (MA): *m* 1961, Margaret Heather, da of Sqdn-Ldr H. Almond, DSO, DFC, of Basingstoke, and has issue living, Claire Virginia, *b* 1962, — Kathryn Jane, *b* 1964: *m* 1989, Christopher J. Coleman, only son of John Colman, of Monte Carlo, Monaco, and has issue living, Hugo John *b* 1994, Rosanna Eleanor *b* 1991.
Hon Christopher Charles (The Coach House, Langton Way, Blackheath SE3 7TJ), *b* 1941; *ed* Cranleigh, Gonville and Caius Coll, Camb (MA), and Guy's Hosp, FRCP, FRCR: *m* 1968, Margaret, da of Henry Bell Fairley, of Stockport, and has issue living, Richard William, *b* 1970.

WIDOW LIVING OF LIFE BARON

ELEANOR JOAN (*Baroness Penney*), da of George Quennell, of Brentwood, Essex: *m* 1945, as his 2nd wife, Baron Penney, OM, KBE, FRS (Life Baron), who *d* 1991. *Residence* – Orchard House, E Hendred, Wantage, Oxon OX12 8TJ.

PENNOCK, BARONY OF (Pennock) (Extinct 1993)

SON LIVING OF LIFE BARON

Hon David Roderick Michael, *b* 1944; *ed* Rugby, and Merton Coll, Oxford: *m* 1969, Jane Pinhard, and has issue, three sons and one da. *Residence* – Iridge Place, Hurst Green, Sussex TN19 7PN.

DAUGHTERS LIVING OF LIFE BARON

Hon Susan Lorna, *b* 1948: *m* 1970, David Frederick McLaren Selby, of Goodchild's Hill, Stratfield Saye, Reading, Berks, and has issue, two sons and one da.
Hon Claire Elizabeth, *b* 1958: *m* 1985, Peter Vivian Walford, son of Edward Walford, of 108 High St, Norton, Cleveland.

WIDOW LIVING OF LIFE BARON

LORNA (*Baroness Pennock*), da of Percival Pearse, of Morpeth: *m* 1944, Baron Pennock (Life Baron), who *d* 1993. *Residence* – 10 First St, SW3.

PENRHYN, BARON (Douglas-Pennant) (Baron UK 1866)
(Title pronounced "Penrin")

With an even mind

MALCOLM FRANK DOUGLAS-PENNANT, DSO, MBE, 6th Baron; *b* 11 July 1908; *s* 1967; *ed* Eton; Col (ret) late KRRC; 1939-45 in N Africa and N-W Europe; MBE (Mil) 1943, DSO 1945: *m* 1954, Elisabeth Rosemary, da of late Brig Sir Percy Robert Laurie, KCVO, CBE, DSO, and has issue.

Arms – Quarterly: 1st and 4th per bend sinister ermine and ermines, a lion rampant or, *Pennant*; 2nd and 3rd grand quarters quarterly, 1st and 4th argent, a man's heart gules, ensigned with an Imperial crown proper, on a chief azure, three mullets of the field; 2nd and 3rd argent, three piles gules, on the two outer ones a mullet of the field, *Douglas*. **Crests** – 1st, Out of a ducal coronet an antelope's head argent, maned and tufted or, charged on the neck with a cross crosslet sable, for distinction; 2nd a sanglier, statant, between two clefts of an oak tree, with a chain and lock holding them together all proper, and above it the motto *"Lock sicker,"*—(Be secure). **Supporters** – On either side an antelope proper, collared and chain reflexed over the back or, and pendant from the collar of the dexter supporter an escutcheon gules, charged with the bust of a man's head affrontée proper.
Residence – Littleton Manor, Littleton, Winchester SO22 6QU. *Clubs* – Naval and Military; Fly Fishers.

DAUGHTERS LIVING

Hon Gillian Francis, *b* 1955.
Hon Rosemary (*Hon Lady Troubridge*), *b* 1957: *m* 1984, Sir Thomas Richard Troubridge, 7th Bt.

BROTHER LIVING

Hon NIGEL (Brook House, Glemsford, Sudbury, Suffolk), *b* 22 Dec 1909; *ed* Eton, and Clare Coll, Camb (BA 1931); formerly Maj RM: *m* 1st, 1935, Margaret Dorothy, who *d* 1938, da of T. G. Kirkham, of Westholm, Jordanhill, Glasgow; 2ndly, 1940, Eleanor Stewart, who *d* 1987, da of late Very Rev H. N. Craig, Dean of Kildare, and has issue living, (by 1st *m*) Simon (Mulberry House, Old Church Rd, Colwall, Worcs WR13 6HB), *b* 1938; *ed* Eton, and Clare Coll, Camb (BA): *m* 1963, Josephine Maxwell, yr da of late Robert Upcott, and has issue living, Edward Sholto *b* 1966, Hugo Charles *b* 1969, Sophie Margaret *b* 1964: *m* 1989, Michael Robert Trotter, yst son of John Trotter, of London (and has issue living, Hugo William *b* 1991, Archie Milo *b* 1994), Harriet Josephine *b* 1972, — (by 2nd *m*) Philip Morton (Tisbury House, Tisbury, Salisbury), *b* 1947; *ed* Eton: *m* 1975, Sarah Frances Jane, yr da of Maj-Gen Ronald Edward Coaker, CB, CBE, MC, of Seaton Old Rectory, Uppingham, Rutland, and has had issue, Johnny Morton Ronald *b* 1987, Anna Susan *b* 1979; *d* 1993, Camilla Faith *b* 1981, — Brigid Elizabeth, *b* 1943: *m* 1972, Richard H. Peat, of Hockwold Hall, Thetford, Norfolk, and has issue living, Harry Mark Richard *b* 1974, Laura Katharine Alice *b* 1976.

HALF-SISTER LIVING (*Daughter of 5th Baron by 1st marriage*)

Hon Eileen Maud, *b* 1901. *Residence* – Henford House, Warminster, Wilts.

SISTER LIVING

Hon Susan Victoria, *b* 1918. *Residence* – Adam's Cottage, Horningsham, Warminster, Wilts BA12 7LG.

COLLATERAL BRANCHES LIVING

Grandchildren of late Claud Douglas-Pennant (*infra*):—
Issue of late Henry Douglas-Pennant, *b* 1925, *d* 1986: *m* 1957, Pamela (who *m* 2ndly, 1988, Very Rev Patrick Reynold Mitchell, Dean of Windsor, of The Deanery, Windsor Castle, Berks), da of late Alfred Gaspard Le Marchant (*see* Le Marchant, Bt, colls):—
Rupert Henry, *b* 1963. —— †Andrew Claud, *b* 1967; *d* 1993. —— †Edward Alfred, *b* 1967 (twin); *d* 1989. —— Venetia, *b* 1960: *m* 1988, (Charles) Liell Philip Francklin, elder son of Cmdr (Mavourn Baldwin) Philip Francklin, DSO, of Gonalston Hall, Notts, and has issue living, Flora, *b* 1990, — Katharine Josephine, *b* 1992. *Residence* – 62 Brodrick Rd, SW17 7DY.

Granddaughter of late Lieut-Col Hon Archibald Charles Henry Douglas-Pennant, 2nd son of 1st Baron:—
Issue of late Claud Douglas-Pennant, *b* 1867, *d* 1955: *m* 1922, Christian Eleanor Margaret, who *d* 1968, da of Sir Harry (William Henry Neville) Goschen, 1st Bt, KBE:—
Margaret, *b* 1923: *m* 1956, Patrick John Lloyd, of Valaford, W Anstey, S Molton, Devon EX36 3PW, and has issue living, John Philip, *b* 1960, — Phyllida Christian, *b* 1957.

Grandchildren of late Archibald Douglas-Pennant, 5th and yst son of late Lt-Col Hon Archibald Charles Henry Douglas-Pennant (ante):—
Issue of late Ian Douglas-Pennant, *b* 1906, *d* 1941: *m* 1931, Mary, who *d* 1980, da of late Maj John Williams, of Scorrier House, Scorrier, Cornwall:—
Daphne Mary DOUGLAS-PENNANT, *b* 1932; has resumed her maide name: *m* 1st, 1953 (*m diss* 1964), Capt Maurice Douglas Evans, RM (ret); 2ndly, 1965 (*m diss* 1992), Francis Seymour Hurndall-Waldron, and has issue living (by 1st *m*), Jeremy Douglas, *b* 1958, — Claire Douglas, *b* 1954, — Rosemary Douglas, *b* 1956. *Residence* – White Lodge, Kilmington, Warminster, Wilts BA12 6RG.
Issue of late Rodney Archibald Douglas-Pennant, *b* 1913, *d* 1993: *m* 1st, 1945, Mrs Rosemary June Delap, who *d* 1946, da of late John Wilfred Munroe, and formerly wife of Capt William Frederick Delap, of Ol Kalou, Kenya; 2ndly, 1947, Agnes Nydia (Nancye), who *d* 1984, only child of late Arthur Robertson Brailey, FRCS; 3rdly, 1985, Mrs Olivia Joan Herbert (Little White House, Church Lane, Longworth, Oxon OX13 5DX), yst da of late Alexander Henry Melvill Wedderburn, CBE (*see* Wedderburn, Bt, colls), and formerly wife of Richard Weston Herbert:—
(By 2nd *m*) Hugh Archibald, *b* 1951; *ed* Eton: *m* 1st, 1976 (*m diss* 1982), Henrietta, da of Col Olivier Berger, of Warwick Sq, SW1; 2ndly, 1983, Sarah Rosamund, yst da of late Lt-Col Jocelyn Eustace Gurney, DSO, MC, of Tacolneston Hall, Norwich, and has issue living (by 1st *m*), Oliver Andrew, *b* 1979, — Lucy Annabel, *b* 1979, — (by 2nd *m*) Ian Christopher, *b* 1986, — David Arthur, *b* 1989. *Residence* – Churchgate House, Stansfield, Sudbury, Suffolk CO10 8LT. —— Anthea Rose, *b* 1948: *m* 1983, Andrew Lachlan Sutherland, and has issue living, Diana Elizabeth, *b* 1983, — Sarah Felicity, *b* 1985. *Residence* – Hillingdon, RMB 8230, Hamilton, Victoria 3300, Australia.

PREDECESSORS – **(1)** *Hon* EDWARD GORDON Douglas-Pennant, brother of 17th Earl of Morton; *b* 1800; assumed in 1841 by Roy licence the additional surname of Pennant; sat as MP for Carnarvonshire (*C*) 1841-66; was Lord-Lieut of co Carnarvon; *cr Baron Penrhyn*, of Llandegai, co Carnarvon (peerage of United Kingdom) 1866: *m* 1st, 1833, Juliana Isabella Mary, who *d* 1842, el da and co-heiress of George Hay Dawkins Pennant, of Penrhyn Castle; 2ndly, 1846, Lady Maria Louisa FitzRoy, who *d* 1912, 2nd da of 5th Duke of Grafton; *d* 1886; *s* by his son **(2)** GEORGE SHOLTO GORDON, 2nd Baron; *b* 1836; MP for Carnarvonshire (*C*) 1866-8 and 1874-80: *m* 1st, 1860, Pamela Blanche Rushout, who *d* 1869, da of Sir Charles Rushout Rushout, 2nd Bt; 2ndly, 1875, Gertrude Jessy, who *d* 1940, da of late Rev Henry Glynne; *d* 1907; *s* by his el son **(3)** EDWARD SHOLTO, 3rd Baron; *b* 1864; MP for Northamptonshire, S Div (*C*) 1895-1900: *m* 1887, Hon Blanche Georgiana FitzRoy, who *d* 1944, da of 3rd Baron Southampton; *d* 1927; *s* by his son **(4)** HUGH NAPIER, 4th Baron; *b* 1894; Hon Col 6th Batn Roy Welch Fusiliers; Lord-Lieut of Caernarvonshire 1933-41: *m* 1922 (*m diss* 1941), Hon Sybil Mary Hardinge, who *d* 1985, da of 3rd Viscount Hardinge; *d* 1949; *s* by his kinsman **(5)** FRANK (el son of late Lieut-Col Hon Archibald Charles Henry Douglas-Pennant, 2nd son of 1st Baron), 5th Baron; *b* 1865; Lt-Col KRRC: *m* 1st, 1892 (*m diss* 1903), Maud Eleanora, who *d* 1936, da of late Col John Hardy, 9th Lancers; 2ndly, 1905, Alice Nellie, who *d* 1965, da of Sir William Charles Cooper, 3rd Bt, *d* 1967; *s* by hs son **(6)** MALCOLM FRANK, DSO, MBE, 6th Baron and present peer.

PENTLAND, BARONY OF (Sinclair) (Extinct 1984)

See Sinclair, Bt, *cr* 1704.

Perceval, Viscount; son of Earl of Egmont.

PERCY OF NEWCASTLE, BARONY OF (Percy) (Extinct 1958)

DAUGHTERS LIVING OF FIRST BARON

Hon Mary Edith, *b* 1919; *ed* Bristol Univ. *Residence* – Glebe Orchard, Etchingham, Sussex.
Hon Dorothy Anne, *b* 1926; *ed* Durham Univ (MB and BS 1949): *m* 1957, Major Thomas Robert Hales Eustace, Roy Irish Fusiliers, and has issue living, James Maurice Percy, *b* 1960: *m* 1986, Gay Rosemary, da of late Alan Oughton, of The Vale, Findon, Sussex, and has issue living, Henry Alan *b* 1988, David James *b* 1991, — Alicia Mary, *b* 1958, — Katharine (Katrina) Anne, *b* 1965: *m* 1988, Andrew J. McGladdery, only son of Dr John Arthur McGladdery, of 28 Beresford Gdns, Hadleigh, Essex, and has issue living, Charles Eustace *b* 1992. *Residence* – Glebe House, Boughton Aluph, Ashford, Kent.

PERRY OF SOUTHWARK, BARONESS (Perry) (Life Baroness 1991)

PAULINE PERRY, da of late John George Embleton Welch, of Sunderland; *b* 15 Oct 1931; *ed* Girls' High Sch, Wolverhampton, and Girton Coll, Camb (MA); Secondary Sch Teacher, UK, USA and Canada 1953-56 and 1959-61; Lecturer in Philosophy Manitoba Univ 1956-59, and Mass Univ 1961-62, Lecturer in Educn Exeter Univ (part-time) 1963-66, Oxford Univ 1966-70, Access Course Tutor 1966-70; HMI 1970-74, Staff Inspector 1975-81, HM Chief Inspector of Schs 1981-86; Vice-Chancellor South Bank Univ (formerly Polytechnic) 1987-93; Freelance Journalist and Broadcaster; Pres Lucy Cavendish Coll, Camb since 1994, Governing Body of Inst of Development Studies since 1987, British Council's Cttee on Internat Co-operation in Higher Educn since 1987, Economic and Social Research Council 1988-91, Member of Prime Minister's Advisory Panel on the Citizens Charter since 1993; Chm DTI Export Group for the Education and Training Sector 1993; Member of the Nat Advisory Council for Education and Training Targets since 1993, and Board of Governors of the South Bank Centre since 1992; Council Member Foundation for Educn Business Partnerships 1990-91; Rector's Warden Southwark Cathedral since 1990; Freeman of the City of London 1992, Liveryman of the Worshipful Co of Bakers 1992; Companion of the Institute of Management 1993; Hon FCP 1987, Hon FRSA 1988, Hon Fellow Sunderland Polytechnic 1990, Hon LLD Bath 1991; Hon D Litt Sussex 1992; Hon LLD Aberdeen 1994; author; *cr Baroness Perry of Southwark*, of Charlbury, co Oxfordshire (Life Baroness) 1991: *m* 1952, George Walter Perry, and has issue.

𝕬rms – Sable, in dexter chief a sun in splendour issuant and in base a pear slipped and leaved gold (PERRY), on an inescutcheon of pretence argent, a cross of lozenges, in the first quarter a crescent enclosing a quaver and in the fourth quarter a cinquefoil gules (WELCH). 𝕾upporters – *Dexter*, a marmalade tom cat proper; *sinister*, upon a pile of three books, the spines visible bound gules, the pages edged gold, a Persian cat sable, the nose, breast and feet argent, each supporting between the forepaws a quill argent penned or.
Address – House of Lords, London SW1A 0PW.

SONS LIVING

Hon Christopher George, *b* 1953; *ed* Abingdon: *m* 1987, Elizabeth Mary Edwardes, and has issue living, one da.
Hon Timothy John Welch, *b* 1962; *ed* Beckett's Sch, Chesham, Bucks: *m* 1984, Jeannie Ross McKenzie.
Hon Simon Jeremy Welch, *b* 1966; *ed* Sevenoaks.

DAUGHTER LIVING

Hon Hilary Anne Welch, *b* 1955: *m* 1st, 1975 (*m diss* 1990), John Hayward; 2ndly, 1990, Thomas Charles Winstone, and has issue (by 1st *m*), one da, — (by 2nd *m*) two das.

PERRY OF WALTON, BARON (Perry) (Life Baron 1978)

WALTER LAING MACDONALD PERRY, OBE, FRSE, FRS, son of Fletcher S. Perry; *b* 16 June 1921; *ed* Ayr Acad, Dundee High Sch, and St Andrew's Univ (MB ChB, MD, DSc); FRCP (Edin); Dir Dept of Biological Standards, Nat Inst for Medical Research, 1952-58, Prof of Pharmacology, Edinburgh Univ 1958-68 (Vice-Principal 1967-68), Vice-Chancellor The Open Univ 1969-81; Exec Chm Living Tapes Ltd; Consultant United Nations Univ; *cr* OBE (Civil) 1957, Ktn 1974, and *Baron Perry of Walton*, of Walton, co Bucks (Life Baron) 1978: *m* 1st, 1946 (*m diss* 1971), Anne Elizabeth Grant; 2ndly, 1971, Catherine Hilda, da of Ambrose Crawley, and has issue by 1st and 2nd *m*.
Residence – 2 Cramond Rd South, Edinburgh EH4 6AD. *Club* – Savage.

SONS LIVING (By 1st marriage)

Hon Michael John (9 Queens Av, Perth), *b* 1948: *m* 1970, Kathleen Anne Sutherland Elliott, and has issue living, Lindsay, *b* 19—, — Hannah, *b* 19—.
Hon Alan Malcolm (43 Meadway, NW11 7AX) *b* 1950: *m* 1976, Naomi Melanie, da of Dr Abraham Freedman, MD, FRCP, of 21B Chesterford Gdns, NW3, and has issue, three sons.
Hon Niall Fletcher (53 Putnoe Lane, Bedford), *b* 1953: *m* 1978, Sandra Buchanan, and has issue living, two das.

(By 2nd marriage)

Hon Robin Charles Macdonald, *b* 1973.
Hon Colin Stuart Macdonald, *b* 1979.

DAUGHTER LIVING (By 2nd marriage)

Hon Jennifer Joan, *b* 1981.

PERTH, EARL OF (Drummond) (Earl S 1605, Viscount S 1686)

Honour crowns virtue

VI RTUTEM·CORONAT·HONOS

GANG WARILY

JOHN DAVID DRUMMOND, PC, 17th Earl of Perth and 11th (13th but for the attainder) Viscount Strathallan; *b* 13 May 1907; *s* 1951; *ed* Downside, and Camb Univ; Hon LLD St Andrews 1986 (Member of Court 1967-86), Hon FRIBA 1978, Hon FRIAS 1988; a Representative Peer for Scotland 1952-63, Hereditary Thane of Lennox and Hereditary Steward of Menteith and Strathearn; Lt Intelligence Corps; seconded to War Cabinet Officers 1942-43, and to Min of Production 1944-45; Min of State for Colonial Affairs 1957-62; First Crown Estate Commr 1962-77; Chm of the Reviewing Cttee on the Export of Works of Art 1972-76; Trustee of Nat Library of Scotland; PC 1957: *m* 1934, Nancy Seymour, da of Reginald Fincke, of New York City, USA, and has issue.

Arms – Or, three bars wavy gules. **Crest** – A falcon rising proper. **Supporters** – Two wild men wreathed about the temples and loins with oak, and each holding a club resting on his exterior shoulder, proper. *Residences* – 14 Hyde Park Gardens Mews, W2; Stobhall, by Perth. *Clubs* – White's, Puffin's.

SONS LIVING

JOHN ERIC (*Viscount Strathallan*) (46 Tite St, SW3 4JA; *Club* – Boodle's), *b* 7 July 1935; *ed* Downside, Trin Coll, Camb (BA), and Harvard Univ, USA (MBA): *m* 1st, 1963 (*m diss* 1972), Margaret Ann, da of late Robin Gordon; 2ndly, 1988, Mrs Marion V. G. Elliot, and has issue living by 1st *m* :—

    SONS LIVING (*by 1st marriage*)— Hon James David, *b* 24 Oct 1965, — Hon Robert Eric, *b* 1967.

Hon James Reginald (Churchill House, Dinder, nr Wells, Somerset BA5 3RW), *b* 1938; *ed* Downside, and Trin Coll, Camb: *m* 1st, 1961 (*m diss* 1985), Marybelle, da of late Capt Charles Gordon; 2ndly, 1988, Ferelith Alison, da of Mark Palmer (*see* Palmer, Bt, *cr* 1886, colls), and formerly wife of Ashley Gordon Down.

SISTERS LIVING

Lady Angela Alice Maryel, *b* 1912: *m* 1st, 1937 (*m diss* 1959), Count Alessandro Augusto Giovanni Giacinto Barnaba Manassei di Collestatte, who *d* 1962 (Lyle, Bt); 2ndly, 1960, Viggo de Wichfeld (*see* B Massy, colls, 1945 Edn), and has issue living, (by 1st *m*) John Paul James Alessandro Camillo, *b* 1937: *m* 1965 (*m diss* 1975), Hon Susan Barbara, da of the 7th Viscount Sidmouth, and has issue living, Hugo Alexander *b* 1969, Marina Catherine *b* 1967, — Michael David (14 Queen Anne's Grove, W4) *b* 1947: *m* 1978, Vanessa Bettine, who *d* 1985, only da of late Cdr William Gordon Jack, RN (*see* B Tollemache, colls), and has issue living, Nicholas Jason *b* 1980, Polly Teresa *b* 1978, Clare Alexandra *b* 1981, Miranda Frances Vanessa *b* 1985, — Alessandra Mary, *b* 1939: *m* 1959, Francesco Montesi Righetti. *Residences* – Marciana, Marina-Elba, Italy; 41 Lennox Gdns, SW1.
Lady Gillian Mary, *b* 1920: *m* 1946, John Murray Anderson, MC, and bar, who *d* 1991, late Capt Seaforth Highlanders, and has issue living, James Ian (Roro Lodge, Glenlyon, Aberfeldy, Perthshire PH15 2PW), *b* 1952; Member of Queen's Body Guard for Scotland (Royal Company of Archers): *m* 1st, 1981 (*m diss* 1985), Victoria Anne, twin da of late Henry Robert Hildyard, of South Hartfield House, Coleman's Hatch, Sussex (*see* B Kindersley, 1980 Edn); 2ndly, 1988, Hon Emily Mary Astor, da of 3rd Viscount Astor, and formerly wife of Alan Gregory, and has issue living (by 1st *m*), Alice Mona *b* 1983 (by 2nd *m*), Thomas Alexander *b* 1990, Rory John *b* 1991, Liza Kate *b* 1993, Isobel Nancy *b* (twin) 1993, — Sarah Mary, *b* 1947, — Elisabeth Jane, *b* 1949, — Camilla Gillian, *b* 1957: *m* 1st, 1979 (*m diss* 1992), Matthew Aidan Craig Balfour, 2nd son of John Valentine Balfour, of Walnut Tree Farm, Birling (*see* B Plunket, 1968 Edn); 2ndly, 1993, Mark Ronald Shearring, 3rd son of Ronald George Shearring, and has issue living (by 1st *m*), Alexander John *b* 1986, Emily Kate Mary *b* 1984. *Residence* – Wilderwick House, E Grinstead, W Sussex RH19 3NS.

COLLATERAL BRANCHES LIVING

    Issue of late Col Hon Sir Maurice Charles Andrew Drummond, KBE, CMG, DSO, Black Watch, 3rd son of 10th Viscount Strathallan, *b* 1877; *d* 1957: *m* 1904, Ida Mary, who *d* 1966, da of late George James Drummond (see colls, infra):—
Maurice James David, *b* 1907; *ed* Eton; Bar Lincoln's Inn 1952: Hon Lieut-Col (ret) Seaforth Highlanders, and a Member of Queen's Body Guards for Scotland (Royal Company of Archers).

    Issue of late Vice-Adm Hon Edmund Rupert Drummond, CB, CVO, 4th son of 10th Viscount Strathallan, *b* 1884, *d* 1965: *m* 1910, Lady Evelyn Frances Butler, who *d* 1978, da of 4th Marquess of Ormonde:—
Jean Constance (Oxford Beaumont, Boars Hill, Oxford OX1 5DE), *b* 1914; formerly Senior Cdr ATS: *m* 1947, Walter George Finney, TD, late Lt-Col RA (TA), who *d* 1973, and has issue living, Sarah Anne, *b* 1948: *m* 1971, Giles Philip Curtis, and has issue (*see* Curtis, Bt, colls), — Rachel Mary, *b* 1950: *m* 1976, Capt John Jeremy Windham, IG, and has issue (*see* Bowyer-Smyth, Bt, colls), — Elizabeth Jean, *b* 1952: *m* 1979, Andrew William Kennedy Merriam (*see* M Ailsa, 1985 Edn), and has issue living, Alexander George Laurence *b* 1984, Henrietta Jean *b* 1982.

    Granddaughter of late Maj-Gen Lawrence George Drummond, CB, CBE, MVO (infra):—
    Issue of late Lindsay Drummond, *b* 1891, *d* 1951: *m* 1924, Susan Cynthia Frances, who *d* 1981, da of late Alick William Cradock-Hartopp (*see* Cradock-Hartopp, Bt):—
Olivia Joan, *b* 1929: *m* 1957, Maj James Stuart Perry, Special Air Service Regt, and has issue living, Marcus Lindsay, *b* 1957, — Oliver James, *b* 1958. *Residence* – The Mill House, Winchelsea, E Sussex.

    Grandson of late Adm Hon Sir James Robert Drummond, GCB, 2nd son of 6th Viscount Strathallan:—
    Issue of late Maj-Gen Laurence George Drummond, CB, CBE, MVO, *b* 1861; *d* 1946: *m* 1886, Katherine Mary, who *d* 1947, da of late Hugh Lindsay Antrobus (Antrobus, Bt, colls):—
James Arthur Laurence (Rectory House, Ogbourne St George, Wilts), *b* 1905; is Com RN (ret); sometime temporary Flying Officer RAF: *m* 1936, Patricia, who *d* 1990, da of Col Sir Edward Scott Worthington, KCVO, CB, CMG, CIE.

Grandchildren of late Edgar Atheling Drummond, 2nd son of late Andrew Robert Drummond, grandson of Hon Robert Drummond, 3rd son of 4th Viscount Strathallan:—
Issue of late Major Cyril Augustus Drummond, *b* 1873; *d* 1945: *m* 1st, 1897, Edith Belle, who *d* 1917, da of L. I. Wilkins; 2ndly, 1930, Mildred Joan (HARRINGTON) (who *d* 1977, having *m* 3rdly, 1948, Air Commodore John Charles Quinnell, CB, DFC, who *d* 1983), da of late Horace Humphrys:—
(By 2nd *m*) Maldwin Andrew Cyril, OBE, *b* 1932; *ed* Eton; JP 1963 and DL 1976 Hants, and High Sheriff 1980; OBE (Civil) 1990: *m* 1st, 1955 (*m diss* 1977), Susan Dorothy Maria Gabrielle, da of Sir Kenelm Henry Ernest Cayley, 10th Bt; 2ndly, 1978, Gillian Vera, yr da of Charles Gavin Clark (*see* Royden, Bt), and formerly wife of Alexander Graham Athol Turner Laing, and has issue living (by 1st *m*), Frederica Elizabeth, *b* 1957: *m* 1984, Maj Miles Templer, 17th/21st Lancers, son of late Field Marshal Sir Gerald Walter Robert Templer, KG, GCB, GCMG, KBE, DSO, and has issue living, Gerald *b* 1986, (Robert) Benjamin *b* 1987, — Annabella Virginia, *b* 1959: *m* 1980 (*m diss* 1988), Capt Christopher E. Robinson, 17th/21st Lancers, elder son of Edward Robinson, of Summerhill, Withypool, Som, and has issue living, Edward *b* 1982, Jeremy *b* 1984, — (by 2nd *m*), Aldred Robert Alexander, *b* 1978. *Residences* – Cadland, Fawley, Southampton; and Wester Kames Castle, Port Bannatyne, Isle of Bute. *Clubs* – White's, Royal Yacht Squadron. —— Robert Edgar Atheling, *b* 1933; *ed* Eton: *m* 1958 (*m diss* 1967), Mrs Phyllis Field Samper, who *d* 1985, da of Marshall Field, of New York City, USA, and has issue living, Maldwin Marshall, *b* 1959, — Fiona Mary, *b* 1960: *m* 1980, Albemarle John Cator (*see* Cayley, Bt, 1960 Edn), and has issue living, John *b* 1983, Robert *b* 1985, — Bettina, *b* 1963. *Residence* – Stanswood Mews, Fawley, Southampton. —— Annabella Frances Serena, *b* 1938: *m* 1st, 1957 (*m diss* 1961), David Arthur Talbot Rice (*see* B Dynevor, colls); 2ndly, 1961 (*m diss* 1972), Gerardo Hochschild; 3rdly, 1973, John Philip Pochna, of Caherass, Croom, co Limerick, and has issue living (by 2nd *m*) Maurice Leo Robert, *b* 1962, — Fabrizio Gerald Arturo, *b* 1963, — Agustin Emil, *b* 1965.

Grandchildren of late Capt Eric Roderick Brook Drummond, 4th son of late Capt Cecil George Assheton Drummond, 5th and yst son of late Andrew Robert Drummond (ante):—
Issue of late Geoffrey Brook Drummond, *b* 1905, *d* 1976: *m* 1939, Mary Barbara (1 Granville Crescent, Leicester), da of late James Arthur Unitt, MRCS, LRCP, of Quorn, Leics:—
Frederick Brook (Enderby Hall, Enderby, Leics) *b* 1946: *m* 1st, 1974 (*m diss* 1979), Gillian Victoria, da of Donald Leslie Bridges; 2ndly, 1980, Mrs Evelyn Clare Ann Jackson, da of late James Allan, and has issue living (by 1st *m*), Roland Brook, *b* 1975, — (by 2nd *m*) Leigh James Brook, *b* 1981, — Kimberley Brook, *b* 1985. —— Cherry Barbara, *b* 1940: *m* 1959, Derek Cyril Gibbs, of 147 Leicester Rd, Glen Parva, Leicester, and has issue living, Nicholas Cary, *b* 1960, — Alistair Corin, *b* 1972, — Scarlett Kathryn, *b* 1961.

Grandson of late Robert Drummond, eldest son of late Charles Drummond (*b* 1790), eldest son of late Charles Drummond (*b* 1759), yr son of Hon Robert Drummond (ante):—
Issue of late Charles Drummond, *b* 1855, *d* 1932: *m* 1892, Lady Caroline Elizabeth Boyle, who *d* 1958, el da of late Col Gerald Edmund Boyle (E Cork and Orrery):—
Angus Julian, *b* 1910; European War 1939-45 as Lieut (S) RNVR: *m* 1961, Hon Theodosia Beatrix Catherine Mary Meade, who *d* 1990, da of late Richard Charles, Lord Gillford (*see* E Clanwilliam). *Residence* – 62 Ashley Gdns, SW1. *Club* – Travellers'.

Grandchildren of late Gerald Morton Drummond, son of late Rev Morton Drummond, 5th son of late Charles Drummond (*b* 1790) (ante):—
Issue of late Group-Capt Edward Morton Drummond, RAF, *b* 1898, *d* 1993: *m* 1922, Edith Daphne Eunice, who *d* 1989, da of late Wilfred Doneraile Stanhope Taylor (*see* M. Headfort, colls, 1990 Edn):—
David James Morton (Blacklands, Meshaw, S Molton, Devon), *b* 1925; European War 1943-45 as Lieut Black Watch: *m* 1st, 1949 (*m diss* 19—), Cecily Winifred Jillian, only da of Cmdr Alan Douglas Bruford, VRD, RN (ret), of Hailsham, Sussex; 2ndly, 19—, Diana Mary, only da of late Frederick Turner, of Barnstaple, Devon, and has issue living (by 2nd *m*), †James Edward Morton, *b* 1966; *d* 1992, — Lilias, *b* 1962, — Amanda, *b* 1963. —— Charmian Eunice, *b* 1923; 1939-45 War in WAAF: *m* 1951, George Geoffrey Gundry-White, of 49 Tooting Bec Gdns, SW16 1RF, and has had issue, Timothy, *b* 1955, — Patrick, *b* 1957, — Alexander, *b* (twin) 1957; *k* 1989, — Jasper, *b* 1959, — Henry Simon, *b* 1960, — Katherine Jane Louise, *b* 1952, — Madeleine Anne, *b* 1954, — Laura, *b* (twin) 1955. —— Jean, *b* 1927: *m* 1948, Gerald Charles Grenfell Robins, of Wawcott House, Kintbury, Newbury, and has issue living, Charles David Anthony, *b* 1953; *ed* Cookham House, Newbury, — Angela Daphne, *b* 1955, — Marion Gertrude, *b* 1960.

Grandson of late Capt Eric Arthur Drummond, RN (infra):—
Issue of late Ronald Nigel Drummond, *b* 1925, *d* 1978: *m* 1st, 1948 (*m diss* 19—), Josephine Marie, da of Jules Pourbaise, Comte de Bey; 2ndly, 1960, Dinah (41 Glanymor, Aberavon, Dyfed), da of Ralph Adams:—
(By 1st *m*) Iain Stewart, *b* 1950.

Grandchildren of late Lt-Col Arthur Berkeley Drummond, el son of late Rev Arthur Hislop Drummond (infra):—
Issue of late Capt Eric Arthur Drummond, RN, *b* 1900, *d* 1970: *m* 1st, 1924 (*m diss* 1938), Molly Beryl, da of Hugh William Croft, of Ledbury, Herefordshire; 2ndly, 1938 (*m diss* 1947), Elnah Raymond Russell, da of H. R. Wilding, of London; 3rdly, 1954, Mrs Barbara Clarke, who *d* 1972, el da of late Wilfred Barnard Faraday, Recorder of Barnstaple and Bideford:—
(By 1st *m*) John Berwick Lindsay (Stonecroft, Halmonds Frome, Bishops Frome, Worcester WR6 5AX), *b* 1927: *m* 1953, Daphne Mary, el da of Rev Edward Percy Woollcombe, OBE, late R of Sutton, Surrey, and has issue living, Richard John, *b* 1963, — Penelope Anne, *b* 1954, — Sarah Jane, *b* 1958, — Catriona Caroline, *b* 1961. —— Charles Iain (Lochranza, Monument Lane, Chalfont St Peter, Bucks), *b* 1932; *ed* St Edmund Hall, Oxford (BA): *m* 1962, Christine Mary, only da of Eric Stevenson Browne, of Greenleas Rd, Wallasey, Ches, and has issue living, Clare Elizabeth, *b* 1967. —— (By 2nd *m*) Fiona Elnah Russell, *b* 1940: *m* 1st, 1963 (*m diss* 1967), Julian Patrick Selby Ormond; 2ndly, 1967, Robert Adrian Cowell, and has issue living, (by 2nd *m*) John Maximilian Arthur, *b* 1972, — Sophia Russell Lilian, *b* 1969. —— Deirdre Georgina, *b* 1944: *m* 1969, Nigel Builder.

Grandchildren of late Rev Arthur Hislop Drummond, 2nd son of late Rev Arthur Drummond, 4th son of late Charles Drummond (*b* 1759) (ante):—
Issue of late Malcolm Cyril Drummond, *b* 1880; *d* 1945: *m* 1st, 1906, Zina Lilias, who *d* 1931, da of George Macartney Ogilvie, formerly ICS; 2ndly, 1934, Margaret Triquet, who *d* 1988, da of late Rev Arthur Browning, of Pangbourne Rectory, Berks:—
(By 1st *m*) (Arthur Malcolm) James (Wychwood, Logie Coldstone, Aboyne, Aberdeenshire AB34 5NN) *b* 1911; late Capt R Berks Regt: *m* 1st, 1938 (*m diss* 1945), Moyra Blanche, who *d* 1982, da of late Frederick Barnard Elliot, CBE (B Emly); 2ndly, 1954, Patricia, da of late Guy Cave, and has issue living (by 1st *m*), Hamish Guy (PO Box 310, Grand Cayman, BWI), *b* 1939: *m* 1964, Valerie Louise, da of late Tyril McLaughlin, of Cayman Islands, BWI, and has issue living, Andrew Simon Hamish *b* 1970, Katherine Nicola *b* 1966, and two adopted das, Deborah Ann Eileen *b* 1961, Charmaine Alexandra *b* 1963, — (by 2nd *m*), David James, *b* 1960; RAF: *m* 1984, Beverly, da of John Steward, of Camb, and has issue living, Matthew Thomas *b* 1993, Rebecca Gemma *b* 1984, Emily Lisa *b* 1986, Francesca Claire *b* 1989, — Nicola Gesina, *b* 1956, — Alexina Mary, *b* 1957: *m* 1977, Arthur John Menzies, of Coirmoir, Torphins Aberdeenshire, and has issue.

Grandchildren of late George James Drummond, son of George Drummond, el son of George Harley Drumond, el son of George Drummond (b 1758), grandson of Andrew Drummond, next brother of 4th Viscount Strathhallan:—
Issue of late George Henry Drummond, b 1883, d 1963: m 1st, 1917, Helena Kathleen, who d 1933, da of T. Grattan Holt; 2ndly, 1940, Honora Myrtle Gladys (Grand Island Hotel, Ramsay, IoM), da of late Lt-Col Duncan Wilfrid Lambart Spiller, DSO:—
(By 2nd m) George Albert Harley DE VERE DRUMMOND (The Barn, 6 Bannatyne Gdns, Bannatyne, Christchurch, Barbados, W Indies), b 1943: m 1st, 1971 (m diss 1974), Rachel, da of Michael Manley; 2ndly, 1982, Debra Jane, only da of R. B. Hankins, of Hertford, and has issue living (by 1st m), George Manley de Vere b 1971 — (by 2nd m), Sarah Georgina Joy de Vere, b 1982, — Jade Alexandra de Vere, b 1984. —— Annabella Elizabeth, b 1941. —— Omega Margaret (63 Bagley Wood Rd, Kennington, Oxford OX1 5LY), b 1944: m 1961, Robert A. Y. Pouget, and has issue living, Antoine Xavier, b 1962, — Robert Harley, b 1965, — Alexandre, b 1967, — William Francis, b 1975. —— Isobel Camilla (Millie) (Cortijo San Clemente, 18400 Orgiva (Granada), Spain), b 1946.
Issue of late David Robert Drummond, Lt Scots Guards, b 1884, ka 1914: m 1907, Hilda Margaret (who d 1972, having m 2ndly, 1936, Maj John Elgee Gunning, JP, who d 1950), da of late Alfred Hellver Harris, of Donnington, Chichester:—
Joan Cécile, b 1909: m 1st, 1933 (m diss 1939), Maurice James Newcomb; 2ndly, 1942 (m diss 1949), Maj Charles St John Colthurst, RA, who d 1985; 3rdly, 1950 (m diss 1970), Arthur Raywid; 4thly, 1971, Alan James Fuller Eberle, MBE, BM, BCh, who d 1988, of Penton House, Crediton, Devon, and has issue living, (by 1st m) Nicholas James (27 Bishops Court Drive, Bishops Court, Cape 7700, S Africa), b 1935: m 1966, Lorna Faith Maree, and has issue living, Graeme James b 1970, Angela Jean b 1973, — (by 2nd m) Joanna, b 1948: m 1975, Martin Butler, of 43/299 Burns Rd, Lane Cove, NSW 2066, Australia. —— Violet Hilda, b 1911: m 1st, 1933 (m diss 1945), John Peter Pardoe; 2ndly, 1948, Anthony Swetenham, and has issue living, (by 1st m) Julian Hugh (Brinkley House, Newmarket, Suffolk), b 1935; ed Eton: m 1960, Camilla Guendolen, da of Arthur Gruffydd Tudor-Evans, of The Grange, N Rode, Cheshire, and has issue living, Simon David b 1962, Joanna Clare b 1963, Fiona Mary b 1965: m 1994, Nigel M. Powell, yr son of Stephen Powell, of Whaton, Nottingham. Residence – 24 Norfolk Rd, St John's Wood, NW8.
Issue of late Capt Alexander Victor Drummond, b 1888; d 1937: m 1914, Ellen Pauline Matthew (the actress, Pauline Chase), who d 1962, da of Ellis Bliss, of Washington, USA:—
Jane, b 1925: m 1946 (m diss 1968), Irving Howbert, late Lt US Naval Reserve, and has issue living, William Irving, b 1948; ed Emmanuel Coll, Camb, — Anne Noel, b 1950, — Janet Scott, b 1953. Resides in France.

Grandchildren of late Capt Alexander Victor Drummond (ante):—
Issue of late (Alexander) Peter Drummond, b 1927, d 1987: m 1954, Anne Audrey Ruth, da of Frank Seamer, of Leigh, Kent:—
Harrie Malcolm, b 1962. —— Alexandra Elspeth, b 1957. —— (Marina) Jane, b 1959.

Grandchildren of late Capt Algernon Heneage Drummond, only son of Rev Heneage Drummond, Rector of Leckhamstead, yst son of John Drummond (b 1766), yr brother of George Drummond (b 1758) (ante):—
Issue of late Algernon Cecil Heneage Drummond, b 1880, d 1975: m 1917, Janetta, who d 1958, da of late Col John Ormsby Vandeleur, CB (D St Albans, colls):—
Spencer Heneage, DSC (Keeper's Cottage, Petersfield, Hants), b 1922; Capt RN; 1939-45 War (DSC); MPhil: m 1949, Patricia Pauline, da of late Lt-Col Michael Keane, OBE, RAMC, and has issue living, Crispin Heneage (11 Clifton Rd, Winchester, Hants), b 1955: m 1981, Marta A. Tuey, of Boston, Mass, USA, and has issue living, Lewis Spencer Heneage b 1987, Kate Elinor b 1984, Juliet Vandeleur b 1988, — Hereward John Heneage (3 Sleepers Hill Gdns, Winchester, Hants), b 1959: m 1987, Felicia J. B., elder da of George Anthony Shepherd, CMG, of Meonstoke, Hants, and has issue living, Thomas Anthony Heneage b 1988, Frederick Algernon Heneage b 1991, Isabella Mary Heneage b 1989, Lucinda Jane Heneage b 1993, — Deirdre Mary, b 1953: m 1977, Peregrine Tatton Eyre Massey, of Prospect Place, Bilsington, Ashford, Kent, and has issue (see B Massey, colls) — Ianthe Mary, b 1960, — Helena Mhairi, b 1963: m 1990, Andrew P. Johnstone, only son of Rev B. Johnstone, of Clunes, NSW, Australia, and has issue living, William Drummond b 1993. —— John Vandeleur Heneage (9 Upper Wheelan St, Newlands, Cape 7700, S Africa), b 1924; Pilot, E and S African Harbour Sers (ret): m 1951, Annette, da of Dr Alan William Stuart Sichel, MD, LLD, DO, DOMS (Pres BMA 1951-52), of Cape Town, and has issue living, Anthony Christopher Heneage (6 York Rd, Claremont, Cape), b 1954: m 1990, Fiona, da of John Nugent, of Linthorpe, Cleveland, and has issue living, Charlotte b 1992, — Richard Stuart Heneage, b 1962, — Hugo Alistair Heneage (6 Grove Rd, Mowbray, Cape), b 1965: m 1990, Karen, da of Leslie Joubert, of Mowbray, Cape, — Amanda Elizabeth, b 1956. —— Margaret Frederica, b 1926: m 1949, John Ironside Money, of Tanglewood, 72 Skinburness Rd, Silloth, Carlisle, Cumbria CA5 4QF, and has issue living, Paul, b 1950, — Brian, b 1953, — Colin, b 1956, — Olivia Margaret, b 1959.
Issue of late Lieut-Com Geoffrey Heneage Drummond, VC, RNVR, b 1886, d on active ser 1941: m 1918, Maude Aylmer Tindal, who d 1967, da of late Lt-Col Bernard Tindal Bosanquet, of Claysmore, Enfield:—
Geoffrey Mortimer Heneage, RN, b 1920; ed Eton; Lieut-Com; European War 1939-45: m 1956, Sarah Madeline, da of Richard Walter Spencer, of Warsash, Southampton, and has issue living, John Richard Geoffrey, b 1957; ed Eton, and Christ's Coll, Camb (MA); is Cmdr RN, — Charles Mortimer Geoffrey, b 1958, ed Pangbourne, — Caroline Jane, b 1963; ed St Swithuns, and Seale Hayne Agric Coll (BSc). Residence – Faringdon, Hill Head, Hants. Club – Royal Naval. —— Aylmer Merelina, b 1919; is a State Registered Nurse. Residence – 4 Minto St, Newington, Edinburgh EH9 1RG. —— Iris Mary Elizabeth, b 1926; 1939-45 War in WRNS: m 1947, Lt-Cdr John Munro Crosland Fenton, DSC, RN, of Bar Ewing, Balmaclellan, by Castle Douglas, Kirkcudbright, and has issue living, Jeremy John Crosland (2 Royal Crescent, Edinburgh EH3 6PZ), b 1949; ed Glenalmond, and Magdalene Coll, Camb (MA), — James Heneage Crosland (Balfour Cottage, Abernyte, by Inchture, Perthshire PH14 9ST), b 1952; ed Glenalmond, Durham Univ (BSc), and London Univ (PhD); Member British Antarctic Survey 1973-78: m 1986, Susan Claire, da of H. J. Wrenn, of Harmby, Yorkshire, and has issue living, Mairi Alice b 1989, — Geoffrey Eric Crosland (Grove Cottage, Blackford, nr Wedmore, Som BS28 4NG), b 1954; ed Glenalmond, and St John's Coll, Oxford (BA, MSc): m 1980, Elizabeth Tyrie, yst da of Prof J. K. T. L. Nash, of Shandon, Jordans, Bucks, and has issue living, Rosemary Tyrie b 1985, Isabel Shield b 1988, Lucy Crosland b 1991.
Issue of late Maurice John Heneage Drummond, b 1894, d 1975: m 1922, Celia, who d 1964, da of late Rev John Vaughan, Canon of Winchester:—
Rev Christopher John Vaughan (The Rectory, Gt Linford, Milton Keynes, Bucks, MK14 5BD), b 1926; ed Winchester, Magdalen Coll, Oxford (MA) and Ridley Hall, Camb; 1939-45 War in R Signals: m 1960, Gwyneth May, da of George Timmis, of Hanchurch, Staffs, and has issue living, Peter John Vaughan, b 1963, — Gillian Clare b 1961. —— Rev Josceline Maurice Vaughan (3 Fryth Mead, St Albans, Herts), b 1929; ed London Univ (Dip Th BD) and Wycliffe Hall, Oxford; late Lt RN: m 1st 1962, Christine Mary, who d 1987, da of Alfred George Read, of 187 Lower Dale Rd, Derby; 2ndly, 1988, Susan Helena, widow of Rev Canon Andrew Michael Bowman, and da of William Bolitho Rowe, of St Just in Penrith, Cornwall, and has issue living (by 1st m), Andrew Paul Graham, b 1970, — Lydia Rosalind, b 1964: m 1989, Stephen Keith Pierce, of Hastings, Sussex. —— Rosalind Margaret Vaughan, b 1924; MA, PhD; Assoc Prof of English, City Univ, New York: m 1st, 1947 (m diss 1955), Mark Arthur Monson Roberts, MA; 2ndly, 1965, Spencer Depas, of 227 Cumberland St, Brooklyn, New York, NY 11205, USA, and has issue living (by 1st m), Julian Francis; ed Winchester, and Caius Coll, Camb (MA), — (by 2nd m), Sophie Margaret, b 1967.

PREDECESSORS – (1) Hon JAMES Drummond, 2nd son of 2nd Lord Drummond († infra); was cr Lord Maderty (peerage of Scotland) 1609; d 1632; s by his son (2) JOHN, 2nd Lord; joined Montrose after the battle of Kilsyth and was imprisoned; s by his son (3) DAVID, 3rd Lord; resigned his honours 1664, and obtained a new grant with remainder to his heirs male, and failing whom to his nominee and his heirs; d 1684; s by his brother (4) WILLIAM, 4th Lord; held a high command in the army raised in 1648 to rescue Charles I; was taken prisoner at battle of Worcester, but effecting his escape went to Russia, in which country he attained the rank of Lieut-Gen; after the Restoration became Maj-Gen of the Forces in Scotland, Gen of the Ordnance, and a Lord of the Treasury; *cr Lord Drummond of Cromlix*, and *Viscount Strathallan* (peerage of Scotland) 1686, with remainder to the heirs male of his body, which failing, to heirs male whatsoever; *d* 1688; *s* by his son **(5)** WILLIAM, 2nd Viscount; *d* 1702; *s* by his son **(6)** WILLIAM, 3rd Viscount; *dsp* 1711; *s* by his cousin **(7)** WILLIAM, 4th Viscount, son of Hon Sir James, 2nd son of 1st Lord Maderty; having espoused the cause of the Chevalier in 1745, he was slain at Culloden 1746, and the names of himself and eldest son were included in the bill of attainder of that year; *s* by his son **(8)** JAMES, 5th Viscount, who was not attainted until after he had *s* to title; *d* 1766; *s* by his el son **(9)** JAMES; *d* 1775; *s* by his brother **(10)** ANDREW JOHN, a Gen in the Army; petitioned unsuccessfully in 1787 for a restoration of the honours; *d* unmarried 1817; *s* in representation of his family by his cousin **(11)** JAMES ANDREW JOHN LAURENCE CHARLES, 2nd son of Hon William, 2nd son of 4th Viscount; sat as MP for Perthshire 1812-24; was restored to his ancestral honours by Act of Parliament 1824, and was afterwards a Representative Peer; *d* 1851; *s* by his son **(12)** WILLIAM HENRY, 7th Viscount; *b* 1810; was a Representative Peer and a Lord-in-Waiting to HM Queen Victoria: *m* 1833, Christina Maria Hersey, who *d* 1867, da of Robert Baird, of Newbyth; *d* 23 Jan 1886; *s* by his son **(13)** JAMES DAVID, 8th Viscount, *b* 1839; a retired Lieut-Col and a Representative Peer for Scotland: *m* 1st, 1868, Ellen, who *d* 1873, da of late Cudbert B. Thornhill, CIE; 2ndly, 1875, Margaret, who *d* 1920, da of late W. Smythe, of Methven Castle, Perthshire; *d* 1893; *s* by his el son **(14)** WILLIAM HUNTLY, 9th Viscount; *b* 1871; *s* as 15th Earl of Perth 1902 (see infra): *m* 1911, Anna, who *d* 1967, da of Jakob Strauss, of Prague, Czechoslovakia; *d* 1937; *s* by his half-brother **(15)** *Rt Hon* (JAMES) ERIC, GCMG, CB, 16th Earl, and 10th Viscount Strathallan; *b* 1876; a PC (*cr*1933); was Private Sec to Under-Sec for Foreign Affairs 1906-12, and to Prime Min 1912-15, and to Sec of State for Foreign Affairs 1915-19; first Sec-Gen of League of Nations 1919-33; Ambassador Extraor and Plen to Rome 1933-39; sometime Dep Leader of Liberal Party in House of Lords: *m* 1904, Hon Angela Mary Constable-Maxwell, who *d* 1965; yst da of 11th Lord Herries of Terregles; *d* 1951; *s* by his son **(16)** JOHN DAVID, 17th Earl, 11th Viscount Strathallan, and present peer; also Lord Drummond, Lord Maderty, and Lord Drummond of Cromlix.

*****(1)** *Hon* JOHN Drummond, KT, 2nd son of 3rd Earl of Perth, having held several high offices of State, was in 1684 *cr Lord Drummond of Gilstoun*, and *Viscount Melfort* (peerage of Scotland) 1685, and *Lord Drummond of Riccarton, Castlemaine and Gilstoun, Viscount Forth* and *Earl of Melfort* (peerage of Scotland) 1686, with remainder to the heirs male of his body by his second wife, and failing which to the heirs male of his body by his first wife, which Earldom he resigned into the King's hands 1688, when it is said the lands and honours were created into a new Earldom in favour of his wife for life with remainder to John, Viscount Forth, Lord of the Regality of Forth, and the heirs male of his body, whom failing to the heirs female of his body, whom failing to his heirs whatsoever; on the revolution he joined James II in France, and was by him in 1692 *cr Marquess of Forth* and *Duke of Melfort*; and in 1701, Louis XIV accepted the Earl as Duke of Melfort, in the peerage of France; title attainted by Act of Parliament 1695, which attainder, however, did not affect the issue of his first *m*; *d* 1714; *s* by his el son, by 2nd wife **(2)** JOHN, 2nd Earl and Duke of Melfort; *d* 1754; *s* by his son **(3)** JAMES, 3rd Earl and Duke; *d* 1766; *s* by his el son **(4)** JAMES LEWIS, 4th Earl and Duke, who became, on the death of the 12th Earl of Perth (*cr* 1605), heir male to that peerage; *dsp* 1800; *s* by his brother **(5)** CHARLES EDWARD, 5th Earl and Duke of Melfort, and 13th Earl of Perth; a Roman Catholic Prelate; *d* 1840; *s* by his nephew **(6)** GEORGE, 6th Earl and Duke, and 14th Earl of Perth, who, in 1853, was restored in blood by Act of Parliament to the dignities of Earl of Perth (*cr* 1605), Viscount Forth, Lord Drummond, and Lord Drummond of Riccartoun, Castlemains and Gilstoun, he having in 1841 established his right to the French honours; *d* 1902, when the Earldom of Melfort became dormant, and the Lordship of Drummond (*cr* 1487) devolved upon his kinsman **(7)** WILLIAM HUNTLY, 9th Viscount Strathallan (ante), also 15th Earl of Perth (*cr* 1605) (see † infra).

†(1) *Sir* JOHN Drummond of Cargill and Stobhall, PC, Ambassador to England 1483, was in 1487 *cr Lord Drummond* (peerage of Scotland); defeated the Earl of Lennox at Tillymoss 1489; and suppressed the rebellion; was Constable of Stirling Castle and Justiciary of Scotland, *d* 1519; *s* by his great-grandson **(2)** DAVID, 2nd Lord; joined the Association on behalf of Queen Mary at Hamilton 1568; *s* by his son **(3)** PATRICK, 3rd Lord; embraced the reformed religion; *s* by his el son **(4)** JAMES, 4th Baron; was a distinguished courtier *temp* James VI; *cr Earl of Perth* (peerage of Scotland) 1605, it is said with remainder to his heirs male whatsoever, but the patent is not in existence; *s* by his brother **(5)** JOHN, 2nd Earl, as it is said, "heire of tailzie"; joined the Association on behalf of Charles I 1641; *s* by his son **(6)** JAMES, 3rd Earl; joined Montrose 1645, and was taken prisoner at Philiphaugh; *d* 1675; *s* by his son **(7)** JAMES, KT, 4th Earl; was Chancellor of Scotland; said to have had a regrant of his honours after resignation; *cr Earl of Perth, Lord Drummond, Baron Stobhall and Montifex* 1686; in 1693 James II, after his deposition, *cr* him Marquess of Drummond and Duke of Perth (titles acknowledged and confirmed in 1701 by Louis XIV of France), and conferred upon him numerous high offices; *d* 1716; *s* by his son **(8)** JAMES, who was styled "2nd Duke of Perth," and who, having been attainted in 1715, could not succeed to the Earldom of Perth; *s* by his el son **(9)** JAMES, "3rd Duke"; wounded at Culloden; attainted 1746; *s* by his brother **(10)** JOHN, "4th Duke;" attainted 1746; *dsp* 1747; *s* by his uncle **(11)** JOHN, "5th Duke", *d* 1757; *s* by his brother **(12)** EDWARD, "6th Duke"; *dsp* 1760; *s* by his second cousin **(13)** JAMES Lundin, grandson of John, 2nd son of 3rd Earl (see * ante), who assumed the name of Drummond, and also the style of Earl of Perth; *s* by his son **(14)** JAMES, who assumed the Earldom; *cr Lord Perth, Baron Drummond of Stobhall* (peerage of Great Britain) 1797; *d* 1800, when the Lordship of Perth, Baron Drummond of Stobhall became extinct, and the next heir male to the earldom was **(15)** JAMES LEWIS, 4th Duke of Melfort (see * ante); *d* 1800; *s* by his brother **(16)** CHARLES EDWARD, 5th Duke of Melfort; *d* 1840; *s* by his nephew **(17)** GEORGE, 6th Duke of Melfort; in 1841, established his right to the Dukedoms of Melfort and Perth, and to be Comte de Lussan and Baron de Valrose, etc, in France; obtained a reversal of all attainders by Act of Parliament 1853: *m* 1st, 1831, the Baroness Albertine von Rotberg Rheinweiler, who *d* 1842, and widow of Gen Comte Rapp; 2ndly, 1847, Susan Harriet, who *d* 1886, da of Thomas Henry Bermingham Daly Sewell, of Athenry, and widow of Col Burrowes, of Dangan Castle, Meath: *d* 1902, when the French Dukedom became ext; and the Earldom of Melfort, the Viscountcy of Forth, and the Lordship of Drummond of Riccartoun, Castlemaine and Gilstoun became extinct or dormant, while the Lordship of Drummond and the Earldom of Perth passed to his kinsman **(18)** WILLIAM HUNTLY, 9th Viscount Strathallan (ante).

Pestell, see Baron Wells-Pestell.

PESTON, BARON (Peston) (Life Baron 1987)

MAURICE HARRY PESTON, son of Abraham Peston; *b* 19 March 1931; *ed* Bellevue, Bradford, Hackney Downs, London, London Sch of Economics, and Princeton Univ, USA (BSc Econ); Prof of Economics, Queen Mary Coll, London Univ 1965-88, since when Emeritus Prof (Fellow 1992); *cr Baron Peston*, of Mile End, Greater London (Life Baron) 1987: *m* 1958, Helen, da of Joseph Conroy, and has issue.
Address – Queen Mary Coll, London Univ, E1.

SONS LIVING

Hon Robert James Kenneth, *b* 1960.
Hon Edmund Charles Richard, *b* 1964.

DAUGHTER LIVING

Hon Juliet Clare Elaine, *b* 1961.

Petersham, Viscount; son of Earl of Harrington.

PETRE, BARON (Petre) (Baron E 1603)
(Name pronounced "Peter")

SANS DIEU RIEN

Nothing without God

JOHN PATRICK LIONEL PETRE, 18th Baron; *b* 4 Aug 1942; *s* 1989; *ed* Eton, and Trin Coll, Oxford; DL Essex 1991; Officer Brother of the Order of St John of Jerusalem; patron of three livings (but being a Roman Catholic cannot present): *m* 1965, Marcia Gwendolyn, only da of Alfred Plumpton, and has issue.

𝔄rms – Gules, a bend or between two escallops argent. Crest – Two lions' heads erased and addorsed; the dexter or, collared azure; the sinister azure, collared or. Supporters – Two lions reguardant; the *dexter* or, collared azure; the *sinister* azure, collared or.
Seats – Ingatestone Hall, Essex; Writtle Park, Essex.

SONS LIVING

Hon DOMINIC WILLIAM, *b* 9 Aug 1966; *ed* Worth Abbey, and Exeter Univ.
Hon Mark Julian, *b* 1969; *ed* Worth Abbey, and Merton Coll, Oxford.

DAUGHTER LIVING

Hon Clare Helen, *b* 1973; *ed* New Hall, and Royal Holloway Coll, Univ of London.

AUNT LIVING (*daughter of 16th Baron*)

Hon Elisabeth Mary Lionel Margaret, *b* (*posthumous*) 1915: *m* 1935, Robert Peter Healing, who *d* 1991, and has had issue, Michael Lionel Kingsbury, *b* 1936; *ed* Eton; Maj Gren Gds: *m* 1966, Amanda Mary, da of Frank R. Rabone, of Gatcombe Park, Minchinhampton, Glos, and *d* 1970, — Julian Robert Peter (31 Alderney St, SW1; La Maison du Phare, Contis, France; *Clubs* – City of London, White's), *b* 1939: *m* 1970, Sabine Marie Louise Françoise, da of Christian de Sorbier de Pougnadoresse, of Magescq, France, — Susan Elisabeth, *b* 1945: *m* 1966, Edward Reymond Carbutt, of Mount Hall, Gt Horkesley, Colchester, and has issue (*see* de Montmorency, Bt, colls), — Carolyn Margaret (twin), *b* 1945: *m* 1972, Christopher Sands Clayton, son of Archibald Sands Clayton (*see* By of Goddard). *Residence* – The Priory, Kemerton, Glos.

WIDOW LIVING OF SEVENTEENTH BARON

MARGUERITE EILEEN (*Dowager Baroness Petre*), da of late Ion Wentworth Hamilton: *m* 1941, Capt the 17th Baron, who *d* 1989. *Residence* – 32 The Downs, Rosemary Lane, Gt Dunmow, Essex.

COLLATERAL BRANCHES LIVING

Grandchildren of late Francis William Petre, son of late *Hon* Henry William Petre, 2nd son of 14th Baron:—
Issue of late Bernard Francis Petre, *b* 1884, *d* 1942: *m* 1922, Constance, who *d* 1975, yst da of late Capt F. J. Easther, RN, of Dunedin, New Zealand:—
Francis John (18 Ketton Place, St Albans, Christchurch 5, NZ), *b* 1923; Italy 1943-5 with New Zealand Forces: *m* 1947, Patricia Josephine, who *d* 1990, da of Walter Corcoran, of Dunedin, New Zealand, and has issue living, John Bernard (540 Tay St, Invercargill, NZ), *b* 1949: *m* 1972, Kathleen Cullen, and has issue living, Brendan John *b* 1973, Damian Roy *b* 1977, Matthew Patrick *b* 1982, Rebecca Maree *b* 1980, — David Christopher (144 Albert St, Palmerston North, NZ), *b* 1954: *m* 1978, Meryl Kemp, and has issue living, Denis Christopher *b* 1985, Michael Francis *b* 1987, Amy Elizabeth *b* 1981, Josephine Mary *b* 1982, — Gerard Michael (307 Lyttelton St, Spreydon, Christchurch, NZ), *b* 1959, — Frances Mary, *b* 1948: *m* 1974, Michael Pucilowski, of 10 Briar Place, Christchurch, NZ, and has issue living, Anna Gabrielle *b* 1976, Jane Frances *b* 1978, — Philippa Josephine, *b* 1951: *m* 1983, James Frederick Goater, of Nagoya, Japan, and has issue living, Oliver James *b* 1984, Georgina Naomi *b* (twin) 1984. —— Robert Cargill (16 Milburn St, Corstorphine, Dunedin, New Zealand), *b* 1925: *m* 1954, Emily Waiwaha Kohere, and has issue living, Robert Bernard, *b* 1961, — Christopher Andrew, *b* 1962, — Mary Ellen, *b* 1955: *m* 1977, Neville James Forrest, and has issue living, James Andrew *b* 1980, Garth Alan *b* 1982, — Raewyn Kura, *b* 1957: *m* 1979, Martin Allen Hay, and has issue living, Larry Dwain *b* 1981, Kura Anne *b* 1984, — Jennifer Anne, *b* 1965. —— William Bernard (23A Coughtrey St, Dunedin, NZ), *b* 1927: *m* 1974, Margaret Doreen. —— Constance Elizabeth Mary, *b* 1931: *m* 1955, Lambertus Jacobus Gerardus Snellaert, of 4 Bentley Av, Glenfield, Auckland 10, NZ, and has issue living, Peter William, *b* 1957, — Michael John, *b* 1961: *m* 1982, Bernadette Cleary, and has issue living, Sarah Louise *b* 1989, Claire Michelle *b* 1991, — Philip Bernard, *b* 1965, — Jacqueline Mary, *b* 1956: *m* 1978, Daniel Tangata, and has issue living,

Nicholas Tobias *b* 1981, Benjamin Daniel *b* 1991, Helen Frances *b* 1983, Anna Elizabeth *b* 1990, — Catherine Elizabeth, *b* 1959.

Issue of late Joseph Austin Petre, *b* 1893, *d* 1972: *m* 1st, 1921, Eleanor Irene, who *d* 1935, da of late H. H. Norton, of Auckland, NZ; 2ndly, 1940, Leonora Agnes, who *d* 1941, da of late Robert M. Sunley, of Christchurch, NZ:—
(By 2nd *m*) Anthony John (3 Paulus Terr, Cashmere, Christchurch, NZ), *b* 1941: *m* 1967, Barbara Ann, da of late Charles Armstrong, of Geraldine, NZ, and has issue living, Robert Joseph, *b* 1973, — Ruth Leonora, *b* 1968, — Adrienne Joanne, *b* 1970.

Grandchildren of late Sebastian Henry Petre, 4th son of late Hon Henry William Petre (ante):—
Issue of late William Petre, *b* 1888, *d* 1955: *m* 1925, Marjorie Gwladys, who *d* 1982, da of Archibald Dacres Bruce (Smythe, Bt):—
Ann Mary HALES (8 Priory Rd, Cambs), *b* 1926: *m* 1955, John Edward Turner Hales-Tooke, who *d* 1992, and has issue living, Jonathan Petre Turner Paul, *b* 1957: *m* 1994, Breda Flaherty, — Hugh Benedict Milton, *b* 1959, — Giles Anthony Raphael, *b* 1964. —— Mary Elise, *b* 1929: *m* 1951, Leonard Pardoe, and has issue living, Sebastian William Joseph, *b* 1956: *m* 1980, Amanda Walley, and has issue living, Charles Edward Adam *b* 1990, Harry *b* 1993, — Matthew James Wentworth, *b* 1960; Bar Inner Temple 1992, — Louise Mary Anne, *b* 1952; has issue living, Claudia Louise Isobel Chapman *b* 1993. *Residence* – 7 Hereford Sq, SW7.
Issue of late Capt Bernard Francis Petre, *b* 1891, *d* 1977: *m* 1926, Mary Lucy (Ferwood Lea, Oakley, Fife), da of late Archibald Dominic Smith-Sligo, of Inzievar, Oakley, Fife:—
Michael Henry Charles (c/o Royal Over-Seas League, Park Place, SW1), *b* 1930: *m* 1959 (*m diss* 1980), Christian Margaret Lilias, da of John Franc McIntyre (*see* E Perth, colls, 1985 Edn), and has issue living, Benedict Francis Joseph, *b* 1967, — Gavin Ruaraidh Joseph, *b* 1969, — Tanya Mairi, *b* 1961: *m* 1981, Nicholas Lunn, — Helena Mary Alathea, *b* 1964, — Kathryne Maria, *b* 1965, — Elspeth Moira, *b* 1972.

Grandson of late Hon Henry William Petre (ante):—
Issue of late Robert George Petre, *b* 1861, *d* 1922: *m* 1891, Elizabeth Grace, who *d* 1937, da of late Robert Ferguson, of Southbridge, Canterbury:—
Francis William (28 Hautana Sq, Lower Hutt, NZ), *b* 1902: *m* 1st, 1932 (*m diss* 1944), Gertrude Fey, da of Philip Lowry Wright, of Bicton, Napier, NZ; 2ndly, 1947, Athalie Millicent, da of Albert Henry Eaton, of Raumati South, NZ, and has issue living (by 1st *m*), John Lowry (Pariawa, Piopio, NZ), *b* 1934: *m* 1962, Susan Helen, da of Edwin Thomas Durrant, of Auckland, NZ, and has issue living, Michael *b* 1964, Daniel *b* 1966, Sally *b* 1963, — (by 2nd *m*) Robert Bruce, *b* 1952, — Ann Mary Elizabeth, *b* 1948: *m* 1972, Robert Joseph Stella of Lower Hutt, NZ, and has issue living, Daniel John *b* 1976, Nicholas James *b* 1979, Lucy Jane *b* 1982, — Eleanor Jane, *b* 1954: *m* 1976, John Kane, of Wellington, NZ, and has issue living, Alexander John Petre *b* 1985, Eleanor Mary Petre *b* 1989.

Granddaughter of late Capt Hon Frederick Charles Edmund Petre, 3rd son of 11th Baron:—
Issue of late Reginald William Petre, *b* 1851, *d* 19—: *m* 1889, Caroline, da of J. Alexander Preston, of Baltimore, USA:—
Constance Achsah Ridgeley, *b* 1897: *m* 1921, William Carrington Stettinius, and has issue living.

Grandson of late Francis Loraine Petre, OBE, only son of late Hon Edmund George Petre, 5th son of 11th Baron:—
Issue of late Maj-Gen Roderic Loraine Petre, CB, DSO, MC, late Dorset Regt, *b* 1887, *d* 1971: *m* 1922, Katharine Sophia, who *d* 1973, da of Herbert W. Bryans, of The Priory, Bradford-on-Avon, Wilts:—
His Honour Judge Francis Herbert Loraine (The Ferriers, Bures, Suffolk CO8 5DL), *b* 1927; *ed* Downside, and Clare Coll, Camb (BA); Bar Lincoln's Inn 1952; Dep Chm E Suffolk Quarter Sessions 1970; a Circuit Judge since 1972; Regular Judge, Central Criminal Court 1982-93; Chm Police Complaints Authority 1989-92: *m* 1958, Mary Jane, da of late Everard C. X. White, and has issue living, Jonathan Charles Loraine (29 Algarve Rd, SW8), *b* 1959: *m* 1987, Emma Victoria, twin da of Neil Hobson, of London, and has issue living, Robert Francis *b* 1989, Eleanor Mary Rosamond *b* 1993, — William Francis, *b* 1963, — Hugh Robert Edward, *b* 1970, — Harriet Mary, *b* 1961: *m* 1987, Mark William Hinton, of 58 Nasmyth St, W6, elder son of Dr Michael Hinton, of W Burton, Sussex.

Grandchildren of late Sir George Glynn Petre, KCMG, CB, 2nd son of late Henry William Petre, son of 2nd son of 9th Baron:—
Issue of late Alfred William Ralph Petre, *b* 1866, *d* 1959: *m* 1892, Gertrude Briggs, who *d* 1938:—
Charles, *b* 1895. —— Alfred Ralph, *b* 1896.
Issue of late Capt Charles Bernard Petre, formerly King's Roy Rifle Corps, *b* 1870, *d* 1949: *m* (Feb) 1903, Muriel Rosalind, who *d* 1961, da of late W. D. Anderson:—
Robert Charles, *b* 1912; *ed* Harrow, and RMC; Maj Scots Guards; 1939-45 War in Norway and Italy: *m* 1st, 1934, Mary Delphine, el da of late Maj Claude Chichester, of Tunworth Down, Basingstoke; 2ndly, 1975, Sonia Greenish, da of Capt Redfern, and has issue living (by 1st *m*), Charles Henry (Tunworth Down House, Basingstoke, Hants; White's Club), *b* 1936: *m* 1963, Melanie Beatrix, da of Henry Peregrine Hoare (*see* E Cadogan), and has had issue, †(Robert) Henry *b* 1968; *ed* Eton; *d* 1992, Fenella Delphine *b* 1967, — Robert Bernard (54 Westcroft Sq, W6; Boodles's Club), *b* 1938: *m* 1970, Caroline, da of Lt-Col Peter Jackson, of Wappenham, Towcester, and has issue living, Edward Robert *b* 1976, Georgina Sarah *b* 1974, — Claudia Mary Delphine, *b* 1943: *m* 1971, Ambrose Patrick Eustace Scott-Moncrieff, and has issue living, Chlöe *b* 1976. *Residences* – 13 Stafford Terr, W8; Little Bignor Farm, Kirdford, Billinghurst, W Sussex. *Club* – White's. —— Christine Marjorie, *b* 1910: *m* 1st, 1931 (*m diss* 1943), Jerrard Ross Williamson; 2ndly, 1943, Carson Alan Edward Kossatz, and has had issue (by 1st *m*), Charles Antony (Whitehouse Farm, Crowfield, Ipswich, Suffolk), *b* 1933; Lt-Cdr RNR: *m* 1967, Philippa Marie-Theresa, da of late Lt-Col M. R. Braithwaite, and has issue living, Robert Jerrard *b* 1969, Lucy Charlotte *b* 1968, — Timothy Jerrard, *b* 1936; *ed* Marlborough: *m* 1970, Christina, da of Sir Robert Mark, QPM, and *d* 1977, leaving issue, Marcus *b* 1974, Rachell *b* 1971, — Theresa June, *b* 1935: *m* 1961, John Chester, of Clairwood Cottage, London Rd, Camberley, Surrey, and has issue living, Anthony James *b* 1965, — (by 2nd *m*) Robin Martin, *b* 1949: of St George's Coll, Weybridge; *d* 1977. *Residence* – The Coachman's Cottage, Odiham, Hants.
Issue of late Rear-Adm Walter Reginald Glynn Petre, DSO, *b* 1873, *d* 1942: *m* (Jan) 1906, Agnes Marie, who *d* 1963, yst da of Capt Eugene Cadic, of Rennes, France:—
Walter George Glynn (La Mouette, Sark, Channel Isles), *b* (Oct) 1906; *ed* Oratory Sch; Sqdn-Ldr RAF: *m* 1939, Myra Millicent, who *d* 19—, only da of late Arthur Willows, of Rushton Manor, near Kettering, and has issue living, Michael Bernard (Four Winds, Cookham Dene, Berks), *b* 1946: *m* 1978, Pauline Carole McCormack, da of late Lionel Alfred Weston, and has issue living, Nicholas *b* 1980, Simon Robert Glynn *b* 1983, — Geraldine Marie, *b* 1944: *m* 1st, 1967, David Robin Petre-Mears; 2ndly, 1992, Michael Guest, of Baytree Cottage, Sark, Channel Isles, and has issue living (by 1st *m*), Edward Petre *b* 1968, Justin *b* 1972, — Anne Rosalie, *b* 1949. —— †Henry Edward, *b* 1907; *ed* Oratory Sch: is Lt-Cdr RNR: *m* 1939, Rosemary Sonia (10 Camden Rd, Eastbourne, E Sussex), da of late Benjamin Gottschalk of 26 Ulster Place, NW1, and *d* 1994, leaving issue, Cecilia Marie, *b* 1940: *m* 1964, Douglas Milton Wiggins, MBE, of Sydenham House, Adderbury, Oxon, and has issue living, Nicholas James Petre *b* 1974, Emma Jane *b* 1966: *m* 1988, David Hamish Easdale, son of Hamish Easdale, of Polkerris, Camp Rd, Gerrards Cross, Bucks, Katherine Blanche *b* 1968, Henrietta Clare *b* 1969, — Teresa Jane Glynn, *b* 1944: *m* 1976, George Andrew Hutchinson, of 3 Westdean Cottages, Westdean, Seaford, Sussex, and has issue living, Rupert Charles Petre *b* 1981, Amanda Jane Petre *b* 1979, — Sonia Rosemary, *b* 1946: *m* 1966, Dr Robert Hancock, of 8 Daisy Lane, Hurlingham, SW6, and has issue living, Benjamin Charles Petre *b* 1971, Toby Charles Petre *b* 1974, Bertie

Petre Oliver *b* 1979, Scarlett *b* 1981. —— Mary Katherine Gabrielle, *b* 1909. —— Marie Madeleine Ethel, *b* 1913: *m* 1944, Maj-Gen Desmond Alexander Bruce Clarke, CB, CBE, late RA, who *d* 1986, of Elm Cottage, Caldbeck, Cumbria, and has issue living, Desmond Walter Robert (Old Dairy Cottage, Winchester Hants), *b* 1945; Capt RA: *m* 1970, Fiona, da of John Harrison, of The Barn Cottage, Wilmington, Sussex, and has issue living, Duncan Robert Petre *b* 1971, Sebastian Alexander *b* 1982, Philippa Kate *b* 1975, — Dominic Michael Bernard (15 Norfolk Mansions, Prince of Wales Drive, SW11), *b* 1949, — Damian Anthony John (4 School Terrace, Reading, Berks), *b* 1958: *m* 1986, Imogen, da of Rev David Cooke, of The Rectory, Stone, Bucks, and has issue living, Edward *b* 1986, Henry *b* 1988, George *b* 1989, — Antoinette Marie Edwina, *b* 1947: *m* 1978, David Ward, of The Green, Caldbeck, Cumbria, and has issue living, Andrew *b* 1981, Robin *b* 1982, Rachel *b* 1979, — Amicie Mary Bernadette, *b* 1950, *m* 1972, David Heath Thompson, of Northfields, Sudbury, Suffolk, and has issue living, Joseph Andrew *b* 1975, Toby *b* 1977, Benedict *b* 1985, Jessica *b* 1983. —— Monica, *b* 1919. *Residence* – Kenmare, Southbourne, Hants.

    Grandson of late Rear-Adm Walter Reginald Glynn Petre, DSO (ante):—
    Issue of late Major Gerard Malcolm Mary Laurence Petre, Essex Regt, *b* 1916; *ka* in France 1944: *m* 1941, Pamela Marian (who *m* 2ndly, 1946, Major Desmond John H. Bannister, MC, Devonshire Regt), da of Capt G. B. Pratt, RA (ret):—
Andrew Charles Malcolm Glynn, *b* 1944; *ed* Downside.

    Grandsons of late Lt-Col Oswald Henry Philip TURVILLE-PETRE, el son of Edward Henry Petre, 3rd son of Henry William Petre (ante) *b* 1862, *d* 1941 (having assumed for himself and issue by Roy licence 1907, the additional surname and arms of Turville):—
    Issue of late Prof Edward Oswald Gabriel TURVILLE-PETRE, *b* 1908, *d* 1978: *m* 1943, Joan Elizabeth (18 Hungate St, Aylsham, Norfolk), da of Sam Blomfield, of Colchester:—
Thorlac Francis Samuel (c/o Dept of English, Nottingham University, Nottingham), *b* 1944; *ed* Magdalen Coll Sch, Oxford, and Jesus Coll, Oxford (MA, BLitt): *m* 1967, Ingrid Elisabeth, da of Rudolf Zimmerlund, of Stockholm, and has issue living, Francis Gustaf, *b* 1971, — Crispin Gabriel, *b* 1974. —— Merlin Oswald, *b* 1946: *m* 1973, Christine Margaret, da of Ivor Lee-Smith, of Newbury, Berks, and has issue living, Daisy Kate, *b* 1975, — Martha Amanda, *b* 1978. —— †Brendan Arthur Auberon, *b* 1948; *d* 1981.

    Granddaughter of late Edward Henry Petre, 3rd son of late Henry William Petre (ante):—
    Issue of late Lieut-Col Oswald Henry Philip TURVILLE-PETRE, *b* 1862, *d* 1941 (having assumed for himself and issue by Roy licence 1907, the additional surname and arms of Turville): *m* 1899, Margaret, who *d* 1954, da of late Laurence Trent Cave, of Ditcham Park, Petersfield, and 13 Lowndes Square, SW:—
Mary Alethea Elizabeth Evelyn, *b* 1904: *m* 1940, Major David Turville-Constable-Maxwell, TD, Anti-Aircraft Regt, RA, who *d* 1985 (*see* L Herries, colls). *Residence* – Penthouse, Bosworth Hall, Husbands Bosworth, Lutterworth, Leics.

    Grandchildren of late Maj Myles Seymour Edward Petre, Duke of Cornwall's LI (infra):—
    Issue of late Martin Anthony Chaworth Petre, *b* 1940, *d* 1991: *m* 1968, Selina Frances Gladstone (c/o Cross House, Henstridge, Templecombe, Som), da of Brig Philip William Gladstone Pope, DSO, MC, of Cross House, Henstridge, Som:—
Edward Myles Chaworth, *b* 1971. —— Henrietta Claire Gladstone, *b* 1969. —— Isabel Mary Hartshorne, *b* 1973.

    Grandson of Bertram Edward Petre, yr son of Edward Henry Petre (ante):—
    Issue of late Major Myles Seymour Edward Petre, Duke of Cornwall's LI, *b* 1913, *ka* 1942: *m* 1938, Audrey Catherine, who *d* 1982, da of Col John Nevile Chaworth-Musters, DSO, OBE, TD, of Annesley Park, Nottingham:—
Robin David Oswald (Flaxbourne, Blenheim, NZ), *b* 1942; *ed* Ampleforth, and RMAS; Maj (ret) 17th/21st Lancers: *m* 1968, Cecily Constance, el da of late Simon Scrope, of Flaxbourne House, Gt Ouseburn, Yorks, and has issue living, Diana Audrey Constance, *b* 1969, — Nicola Mary Catherine, *b* 1971.

    Grandchildren of late Louis William Henry Petre, son of Philip William Petre, yr son of late Hon George William Petre, 2nd son of 9th Baron:—
    Issue of late Edward Philip William Petre, *b* 1869, *d* 1923: *m* 1890, Zoila Rosa del Carmen Larenas, who *d* 1953:—
Luis Enrique, *b* 1898; is a Bank Director: *m* 19—, Else Newman Etienne, and has issue living, Agnes Petre Newman, *b* 1924: *m* 1945 (*m diss* 1952), Fernando Zilleruedo Vargas, Lieut Chilean Air Force, and has issue living, Fernando *b* 1951, Marie-Agnes *b* 1946, Marie-Luz *b* 1948. —— Anna Lucie, *b* 1894: *m* 1923, Col Aquiles Vergara Vicuña, Bolivian Army. *Residence* –

PREDECESSORS – (1) *Sir* JOHN Petre, Knt, only son of Sir William Petre, a Sec of State to Henry VIII and Edward VI; MP for Essex 1584-87; *cr Baron Petre*, of Writtle, co Essex (peerage of England) 1603; *d* 1613; *s* by his son (2) WILLIAM, 2nd Baron; MP for Essex 1597-1601; *d* 1637; *s* by his son (3) ROBERT, 3rd Baron; *d* 1638; *s* by his el son (4) WILLIAM, 4th Baron; *d* a prisoner in the Tower 1683; *s* by his brother (5) JOHN, 5th Baron; *d* unmarried; *s* by his brother (6) THOMAS, 6th Baron; Lord-Lt of Essex; *d* 1707; *s* by his son (7) ROBERT, 7th Baron; *d* 1713, *s* by his son (8) ROBERT JAMES, 8th Baron; *d* 1742; *s* by his son (9) ROBERT EDWARD, 9th Baron: *m* Anne Howard, niece of Edward, 9th Duke of Norfolk, and who became at his death a co-heir to the Baronies of Howard, Furnivall, Strange of Blackmere, Talbot, Braose of Gower, Dacre of Gillesland, Greystock, Ferrers of Wemme, Gifford of Brimsfield and Verdon; *d* 1801; *s* by his son (10) ROBERT EDWARD, 10th Baron; *d* 1809; *s* by his son (11) WILLIAM HENRY FRANCIS, 11th Baron; *d* 1850; *s* by his el son (12) WILLIAM BERNARD, 12th Baron; *b* 1817; *m* 1843, Mary Teresa, el da of Hon Charles Thomas Clifford; *d* 4 July 1884; *s* by his el son (13) *Right Rev* WILLIAM JOSEPH, 13th Baron, *b* 1847; Domestic Prelate at the Court of the Vatican; *d* 1893; *s* by his brother (14) BERNARD HENRY PHILIP, 14th Baron, *b* 1858: *m* 1899, (Etheldreda Mary) Audrey, who *d* 1959, da of Rev William Robinson Clark, MA, DD, LLD, DCL, FRS (Canada), formerly V of Taunton, Preb of Wells, and Professor of Philosophy in Trin Coll, Toronto; *d* 1908; *s* by his brother (15) PHILIP BENEDICT JOSEPH, 15th Baron; *b* 1864: *m* 1888, Julia Mary, who *d* 1931, el da of late George Cavendish Taylor, of 42 Elvaston Place, SW; *d* 1908; *s* by his son (16) LIONEL GEORGE CARROLL, 16th Baron; *b* 1890; Capt Coldstream Guards: *m* 1913, Catherine Margaret (who *m* 2ndly, 1921, Col Sir Frederic Carne Rasch, 2nd Bt, CVO, DSO (*d* 1963), and *d* 1983), da of Hon John Boscawen; *d* of wounds received in action 1915; *s* by his only son (17) JOSEPH WILLIAM LIONEL, 17th Baron; *b* 1914; Capt Essex Regt: *m* 1941, Marguerite Eileen, da of Ion Wentworth Hamilton; *d* 1989; *s* by his only son (18) JOHN PATRICK LIONEL, 18th Baron and present peer.

PEYTON OF YEOVIL, BARON (Peyton) (Life Baron 1983)

JOHN WYNNE WILLIAM PEYTON, PC, son of late Ivor Eliot Peyton, by his wife Dorothy Helen; *b* 13 Feb 1919; *ed* Eton and Trin Coll, Oxford; served in 1939-45 War with 15/19 Hussars (PoW 1940-45); Barrister-at-law, Inner Temple 1945; MP for Yeovil Divn of Somerset 1951-83; Min of Transport 1970; Min for Transport Industries DoE 1970-74; Chm Texas Instruments Ltd 1974-90; *cr* PC 1970, and *Baron Peyton of Yeovil,* of Yeovil, co Somerset (Life Baron) 1983: *m* 1st, 1947 (*m diss* 1966), Diana, da of late Douglas Clinch, of Durban; 2ndly, 1966, Mary Constance, da of late Col Hon (Everard) Humphrey Wyndham, MC (*see* Egremont, B), and previously wife of Ralph Hamilton Cobbold, and has issue living, by 1st *m.*

Arms – Sable a cross engrailed in the first quarter a mullet Or. **Crest** – A griffin sejant or. **Supporters** – *Dexter,* on a mount vert with four oak sprigs growing therefrom fructed or a bull rampant reguardant in trian aspect sable armed membered the tail tuft and muzzle or unguled gules holding in the mouth an oak sprig fructed or and a shamrock slipped vert; *sinister,* on a mount vert growing therefrom four shamrocks slipped proper a griffin segreant reguardant or grasping in the beak a shamrock slipped proper and an oak sprig fructed gold.

·PATIOR·POTIOR·

Residences – The Old Malt House, Hinton St George, Somerset TA17 8SE; 6 Temple West Mews, West Square, SE11 4TJ.

SON LIVING *(By 1st marriage)*

Hon Thomas Richard Douglas, *b* 1950; *ed* Eton: *m* 1981, Vivien, da of Dr Jack Birks, CBE, and has issue living, Joseph Anthony Charles, *b* 1986.

DAUGHTER LIVING *(By 1st marriage)*

Hon Sarah Grenville, *b* 1948: *m* 1971, Dugald Graham-Campbell, and has issue. *Residence* – Gifford House, Fonthill Gifford, Salisbury, Wilts SP3 6PX.

PHILLIMORE, BARON (Phillimore) (Baron UK 1918, Bt UK 1881)

Pray for a brave soul

FRANCIS STEPHEN PHILLIMORE, 5th Baron and 5th Baronet; *b* 25 Nov 1944; *s* 1994; *ed* Eton, and Trin Coll, Camb: *m* 1971, Nathalie, da of late Michael Anthony Pequin, of Paris, and has issue.

Arms – Sable, three bars indented erminois, in chief an anchor between two cinquefoils or. **Crest** – In front of a tower argent, thereon a falcon volant proper holding in the beak a lure gold, three cinquefoils fessewise or. **Supporters** – On either side an owl proper, each charged with an anchor or.
Residence – Coppid Hall, Binfield Heath, nr Henley-on-Thames, Oxon.

SONS LIVING

Hon TRISTAN ANTHONY STEPHEN, *b* 18 Aug 1977. —— *Hon* Julian Michel Claud, *b* 1981.

DAUGHTER LIVING

Hon Arabella Maroussia Eleanor, *b* 1975.

SISTER LIVING

Hon (Marion) Miranda, *b* 1946: *m* 1973 (*m diss* 1985), Thomas Walter Montagu Douglas Scott, and has issue (*see* D Buccleuch, colls). *Residence* – 65 Cloncurry St, Bishop's Park, SW6 6DT.

AUNT LIVING *(Daughter of 2nd Baron)*

Hon Phœbe Margaret Dorothy (*Hon Lady Rose*), *b* 1912: *m* 1937, Sir Charles Henry Rose, 3rd Bt (*cr* 1909), who *d* 1966. *Residence* – Hardwick Hall, Whitchurch, Oxon.

SISTER LIVING OF THIRD BARON *(raised to the rank of a Baron's daughter 1949)*

Hon Frances Phoebe, *b* 1938: *m* 1st, 1961 (*m diss* 1978), Colin John Francis Lindsay-MacDougall of Lunga (*see* E Crawford, colls); 2ndly, 1980, Joseph Peter Gibson, son of Charles Gibson, of Kelty Hill, Kelty, Fife, and has issue (by 1st *m*) (*see* E Crawford, colls). *Residence* – Quinta das Madres, Ulgueira, Colras, 2710 Sintra, Portugal.

WIDOWS LIVING OF SONS OF SECOND BARON

Anne Julia, da of late Maj-Gen Sir Cecil Edward Pereira, KCB, CMG: *m* 1934, Capt Hon Anthony Francis Phillimore, who was *ka* 1940, and has issue (ante). *Residence* – Coppid Hall, Henley-on-Thames, Oxon.
Sheila Bruce, da of John Farquhar MacLeod, JP, MB, ChB, of Peterculter, Aberdeenshire: *m* 1944, Col Hon Robert George Hugh Phillimore, OBE, who *d* 1984, and has issue (see colls infra). *Residence* – Brook Cottage, Mill Road, Shiplake, Oxon.

Margaret, da of late Gibson Lamb Caldwell, of Kenwood Place, Wheeling, W Virginia, USA: *m* 1946, Hon Miles Godfrey Walter Phillimore, who *d* 1972, and has issue (see colls infra). *Residence –*

WIDOW LIVING OF THIRD BARON

MARIA (*Maria, Baroness Phillimore*), da of Ilya Slonim, by his wife Tatiana Litvinov: *m* 1983, as his 2nd wife, the 3rd Baron, who *d* 1990. *Residence –* Crumplehorn Barn, Corks Farm, Dunsden Green, nr Reading, Berks.

WIDOW LIVING OF FOURTH BARON

ANNE ELIZABETH (*Dowager Baroness Phillimore*), da of late Maj Arthur Algernon Dorrien-Smith, DSO, of Tresco Abbey, Isles of Scilly: *m* 1944, the 4th Baron, who *d* 1994. *Residences –* 39 Ashley Gdns, SW1; Rymans, Apuldram, Chichester, W Sussex.

COLLATERAL BRANCHES LIVING

Issue of late Col Hon Robert George Hugh Phillimore, OBE, 3rd son of 2nd Baron, *b* 1913, *d* 1984: *m* 1944, Sheila Bruce (ante), da of John Farquhar MacLeod, JP, MB, BCh, of Peterculter, Aberdeenshire:—
Annabel Margaret, *b* 1947: *m* 1978, Hugo Massey Gamble, of The Mill House, Rotherfield Greys, Henley-on-Thames, and has issue living, James Hugo Phillimore, *b* 1979, — Lucinda Diana MacLeod, *b* 1981, — Rosemary Leigh Phillimore, *b* 1984. —— Lindsay Mary MacLeod (Ellanore House, Ellanore Lane, West Wittering, Sussex PO26 8AN), *b* 1951: *m* 1977, Charles F. Dewhurst, son of late Col F. W. Dewhurst, of Pound Cottage, Buckland Monachorum, Yelverton, S Devon, and has issue living, Robert Edward Charles, *b* 1984, — Anna Elizabeth MacLeod, *b* 1987. —— (Sheila) Leigh, *b* 1952: *m* 1978, Matthew W. J. Thorne, of The Mount, Bannerdown Rd, Batheaston, Bath BA1 8EG, son of Robin Thorne, CMG, OBE, of The Old Vicarage, Old Heathfield, Sussex, and has issue living, Robin Lindsey Phillimore, *b* 1983, — Andrew Robert Wadman, *b* 1986, — Edward, *b* 1989, — Aelene Elizabeth, *b* 1981, — Marini Annabel, *b* 1992. —— Elizabeth Anne Haig, *b* 1955: *m* 1978, Timothy H. S. Brutton, of Greenmoor Hill Farm, Woodcote, Reading, Berks RG8 0RT, son of Rev R. S. Brutton, of 7 North St, Langton Matravers, Dorset, and has issue living, Emma Penelope Phayre, *b* 1981, — Victoria Anne Haig, *b* 1983, — Clare Elizabeth Macleod, *b* 1986.

Issue of late Hon Miles Godfrey Walter Phillimore, 4th and yst son of 2nd Baron, *b* 1915, *d* 1972: *m* 1946, Margaret (ante), da of late Gibson Lamb Caldwell, of Kenwood Place, Wheeling, W Virginia:—
Dorothy Eleanor Barbara, *b* 1940: *m* 1st, 1973, Robert William Drumm; 2ndly, 1982, Wayne Amos Rayfield.

PREDECESSORS – (1) *Rt Hon Sir* ROBERT JOSEPH Phillimore, DCL; 1810; *cr a Baronet* 1881; MP for Tavistock (LC) 1855-7, and Judge of the High Court of Admiralty 1867-83, and of Court of Arches 1867-75: *m* 1844, Charlotte Anne, who *d* 1892, da of late John Denison, MP, of Ossington, Newark, and sister of 1st Viscount Ossington; *d* 1885; *s* by his el son (2) *Rt Hon* WALTER GEORGE FRANK, GBE, DCL, LLD, 2nd Bt; *b* 1845; was a Judge of the High Court of Justice 1897-1913, and a Lord Justice of Appeal 1913-16; Pres English Church Union 1919-20; Chm of Naval Prize Tribunal 1918-28; *cr Baron Phillimore*, of Shiplake, Oxfordshire (peerage of United Kingdom)1918: *m* 1870, Agnes, who *d* 1929, el da of late Charles Manners Lushington, MP for Canterbury (E Iddesleigh); *d* 1929; *s* by his son (3) GODFREY WALTER, MC, 2nd Baron; *b* 1879; Capt late Highland LI; European War 1914-16 (MC): *m* 1st, 1905, Dorothy Barbara, who *d* 1915, el da of Lieut-Col Arthur Balfour Haig, CVO, CMG; 2ndly, 1923, Marion (BRYCE), who *d* 1950, da of late Maj-Gen Cecil Robert St John Ives; *d* 1947; *s* by his grandson (4) ROBERT GODFREY son of late Capt Hon Anthony Francis Phillimore (*ka* 1940) (el son of 2nd Baron), 3rd Baron, *b* 1939; late Lieut 9th/12th Royal Lancers: *m* 1st, 1974 (*m diss* 1982), Amanda, da of Carlo Hugo Gonzales-Castillo, by his wife Aida Aramburu; 2ndly, 1983, Maria, da of Ilya Slonim, by his wife Tatiana Litvinov; *d* 1990; *s* by his uncle (5) CLAUD STEPHEN (2nd son of 2nd Baron), 4th Baron, *b* 1911: *m* 1944, Anne Elizabeth, da of Maj Arthur Algernon Dorrien Smith, DSO, of Tresco Abbey, Isle of Scilly; *d* 1994; *s* by his son (6) FRANCIS STEPHEN, 5th Baron and present peer.

PHILLIPS, BARONY OF (Phillips) (Extinct 1992)

SON LIVING OF LIFE BARONESS

Hon Morgan David, *b* 1939; *ed* St Paul's Sch, and at Downing Coll, Camb (BA); PGCE, Univ of London.

DAUGHTER LIVING OF LIFE BARONESS

Hon Gwyneth Patricia, MP (113 Cromwell Tower, EC2), *b* 1930; *ed* Fulham Co Secondary Sch, and Convent of Nôtre Dame, Battersea; MP for Exeter (*Lab*) 1966-70, for Crewe since 1974, and for Crewe and Nantwich since 1983: Parl Sec to Board of Trade 1967-70; a Dir of Film Production Assocn of Gt Britain: *m* 1954 (*m diss* 1975), John Elliott Orr Dunwoody, MB, BS, and has issue.

PIERCY, BARON (Piercy) (Baron UK 1945)

JAMES WILLIAM PIERCY, 3rd Baron; *b* 19 Jan 1946; *s* 1981; *ed* Shrewsbury, and Edinburgh Univ (BSc); AMIEE, FCCA.

Arms – Per fesse indented gules and argent in chief three pierced mullets of the last and in base a lion rampant guardant sable. **Crest** – Issuant from a bezant in front of two spears in saltire points upwards proper a demi lion guardant sable charged on the shoulder with a pierced mullet argent. **Supporters** – Not recorded at time of going to press.
Residence – 13 Arnold Mansions, Queen's Club Gdns, W14 9RD.

BROTHER LIVING

Hon MARK EDWARD PELHAM, *b* 30 June 1953; *ed* Shrewsbury, and New Coll, Oxford; Barrister-at-law (Lincoln's Inn): *m* 1979, Vivien Angela, da of His Honour Judge Evelyn Faithfull Monier-Williams, and has issue living, William Nicholas Pelham, *b* 11 March 1989, — Katherine Henrietta, *b* 1982, — Olivia Charlotte, *b* 1984, — Harriet Lavinia, *b* 1987. *Residence* – 39 Carson Rd, W Dulwich, SE21 8HT.

SISTERS LIVING

Hon Charlotte Mary, *b* 1947; *ed* Badminton Sch, Arts degree at Univ of Florence: *m* 1st, 1966 (*m diss* 1985), Paolo Emilio Taddei; 2ndly, 1985, as his 2nd wife, (William Guy) David Ropner (*see* Ropner, Bt, *cr* 1904, colls), and has issue living (by 1st *m*), Guido, *b* 1970, — Caroline Rachel, *b* 1967, — (by 2nd *m*) (*see* Ropner, Bt, *cr* 1904, colls).
Hon Lavinia Caroline, *b* (twin) 1947: *ed* Badminton Sch, and St Hugh's Coll, Oxford (MA): *m* 1971, Nicholas John Elliot Sealy, FCA, of Timber Hill, Chobham, Surrey (*see* E Chichester, colls), and has issue living, Edward John Pelham, *b* 1975, — Lucinda Clare, *b* 1977.
Hon Henrietta Jane, *b* 1951; *ed* Badminton Sch, and St Andrew's Univ (MA): *m* 1985, Tullio Luigi Guiseppe Tomba, of via Corona 40, Campoformido (UD), Italy, and has issue living, Tommaso Piercy, *b* 1987, — Francesco Piercy, *b* 1989.

AUNTS LIVING (*Daughters of 1st Baron*)

Hon Penelope Katherine, CBE (Charlton Cottage, Tarrant Rushton, Blandford Forum, Dorset DT11 8SD), *b* 1916; *ed* St Paul's, and Somerville Coll, Oxford; CBE (Civil) 1968.
Hon Joanna Elizabeth (Gable Cottage, 55 Witney St, Burford, Oxon OX18 4RZ), *b* 1923; *ed* St Paul's, and Somerville Coll, Oxford: *m* 1968, James Francis Turner.
Hon Priscilla Jane, *b* 1926; *ed* Downe House, and at London Sch of Economics: *m* 1950 (*m diss* 1972), Rev Thomas Fish Taylor, and has issue living, Francis Nicholas, *b* 1954, — Ann Clemency, *b* 1952, — Helen Mary, *b* 1957, — Bridget Jane, *b* 1961. *Residence* – 14 Union St, Wells, Somerset BA5 2PU.

WIDOW LIVING OF FIRST BARON

VERONICA (*Veronica, Baroness Piercy*) (Fair View House, Marton, Sinnington, York Y06 6RD), da of late John Hordley Warham: *m* 1964, as his 2nd wife, the 1st Baron, who *d* 1966.

PREDECESSORS – (1) WILLIAM Piercy, CBE, son of late (Augustus) Edward Piercy; *b* 1886; Economist and Financier; Chm of Industrial & Commercial Finance Corporation Ltd 1945-64, a Dir of Bank of England 1946-56, and Chm Wellcome Trust 1960-65; *cr Baron Piercy*, of Burford, co Oxford (peerage of UK) 1945: *m* 1st, 1915, Mary Louisa, OBE, who *d* 1953, da of late Hon Thomas Henry William Pelham, CB (E Chichester, colls); 2ndly, 1964, Veronica, da of John Hordley Warham; *d* 1966; *s* by his son (2) NICHOLAS PELHAM, 2nd Baron, *b* 1918: *m* 1944, Oonagh Lavinia, JP, who *d* 1990, da of late Maj Edward John Lake Baylay, DSO; *d* 1981; *s* by his el son (3) JAMES WILLIAM, 3rd Baron and present peer.

PIKE, BARONESS (Pike) (Life Baroness 1974)

IRENE MERVYN PARNICOTT PIKE, DBE, da of Ivan Samuel Pike, of Okehampton, Devon; *b* 16 Sept 1918; *ed* Hunmanby Hall, E Yorks; and Reading Univ (BA); 1939-45 War with WAAF: MP for Melton Div of Leics (*C*) 1956-74; Assist Postmaster-Gen 1959-63, and Joint Parl Under-Sec of State, Home Office 1963-64; Chm WRVS 1974-81; a co Councillor W Riding of Yorks 1955-57; a Dir of Watts, Blake and Bearne since 1964; Chm Broadcasting Complaints Commn 1981-85; *cr Baroness Pike*, of Melton, co Leicestershire (Life Baroness) 1974, and DBE (1981).

Arms – Or on a cross gules a churchwarden's staff headed of a mitre or on a chief sable a castleford fine stoneware teapot proper. **Supporters** – On either side a fox, that on the dexter gorged with a wreath of ivy, and that on the sinister with a wreath of rosemary proper, and each resting the interior hind foot on a portcullis or, the compartment comprising a grassy mount proper.
Residence – Hownam, Kelso, Roxburgh.

PILKINGTON, BARONY OF (Pilkington) (Extinct 1983)

SON LIVING OF LIFE BARON (By 1st marriage)

Rev Hon John Rowan, *b* 1932; *ed* Rugby, and Magdalene Coll, Camb (MA); V of St Mark's, Darlington, since 1989: *m* 1964, Celia Collison, and has issue.

DAUGHTER LIVING OF LIFE BARON (By 1st marriage)

Hon Jennifer Margaret, *b* 1933: *m* 1958, Dennis Jones, of Swallow Cottage, Burbage, Leics and has issue.

WIDOW LIVING OF LIFE BARON

Mavis Joy Doreen (*Baroness Pilkington*), da of Gilbert Caffrey, of Woodleigh, Lostock Park, Bolton, and formerly wife of Dr John Hesketh Wilding: *m* 1961, as his 2nd wife, Baron Pilkington (Life Baron), who *d* 1983. *Residence* – Windle Hall, St Helens, Merseyside.

PITT OF HAMPSTEAD, BARON (Pitt) (Life Baron 1975)

David Thomas Pitt, MB, ChB, son of Cyril S. L. Pitt, of St David's, Grenada, W1; *b* 3 Oct 1913; *ed* St David's RC Sch, Grenada, Grenada Boys' Secondary Sch, and Edinburgh Univ (MB, ChB), First Jr Pres Student Rep Council Edinburgh Univ 1936-37; DCH London; JP of Great London; Dist Med Officer, St Vincent, W1 1938-39, House Phys San Fernando Hosp, Trinidad 1939-41, Gen Practitioner San Fernando 1941-47, and London since 1947; Dep Mayor San Fernando 1946-47; Pres W Indian Nat Party (Trinidad) 1943-47; a Member of London Co Council 1961-65, and of GLC 1964-77 (Dep Chm 1969-70, Chm 1974-75); a Member of Nat Cttee for Commonwealth Immigrants 1965-67, and Chm of Campaign Against Racial Discrimination 1965; a Dep Chm of Community Relations Commn 1968-77; *cr Baron Pitt of Hampstead*, of Hampstead, Greater London, and Grenada (Life Baron) 1975: *m* 1943, Dorothy Elaine, da of Aubrey Alleyne, and has issue.
Clubs – Royal Commonwealth Society (W Indian), MCC.

SON LIVING

Hon Bruce Michael David, *b* 19—

DAUGHTERS LIVING

Hon Phyllis Leonora, *b* 19—
Hon Amanda, *b* 19—

PLANT, BARONY OF (Plant) (Extinct 1986)

SONS LIVING OF LIFE BARON

Hon John Sydney Sampson (6 Swallow Croft, Leek, Staffs), *b* 1931: *m* 1953, Mary, da of John Clayton, and has issue.
Hon Christopher Victor Howe (Flat 4, 178 Dyke Rd, Brighton, E Sussex), *b* 1945: *m* 1966, Marian, da of John Parkes, and has issue.

DAUTHTER LIVING OF LIFE BARON

Hon Jennifer Edna Jane, *b* 1939: *m* 1973, Raymond John Brian Pilbeam, and has issue living, Nicholas Colin Emmerton, *b* 1962, — Sarah Jane Emmerton, *b* 1964. *Residence* –

PLANT OF HIGHFIELD, BARON (Plant) (Life Baron 1992)

Raymond Plant, son of late Stanley Plant; *b* 19 March 1945; *ed* Havelock Sch, Grimsby, King's Coll, London (BA), and Hull Univ (PhD); Sr Lecturer in Philosophy Manchester Univ 1967-69, Prof of Politics Southampton Univ since 1979; Master of St Catherine's Coll, Oxford since 1994; Stevenson Lecturer Glasgow Univ 1981, Agnes Cumming Lecturer Univ Coll, Dublin 1988, Stanton Lecturer Camb Univ 1989-90 and 1990-91, Sarum Lecturer Oxford Univ 1991, Ferguson Lecturer Univ of Manchester 1994; Hon D Litt Guildhall Univ, Hon D Litt Hull Univ; Chm Labour Party Commn on Electoral Systems since 1991; author and contributor to *New Statesman and Society*, *The Independent*, *The Times*, etc; *cr Baron Plant of Highfield*, of Weelsby, co Humberside (Life Baron) 1992: *m* 1967, Katherine Sylvia, da of late Jack Dixon, and has issue.
Residence – 6 Woodview Close, Bassett, Southampton S02 8P2.

SONS LIVING

Hon Nicholas, *b* 1969.
Hon Matthew, *b* 1971.
Hon Richard, *b* 1976.

PLATT, BARONY OF (Platt) (Extinct 1978)

SON LIVING OF LIFE BARON

Hon Sir PETER PLATT, 2nd Bt, who *s* to Baronetcy (*cr* 1959), 1978 (*see* Platt, Bt).

DAUGHTERS LIVING OF LIFE BARON

(see Platt, Bt)

WIDOW LIVING OF LIFE BARON

(*see* Platt, Bt)

PLATT OF WRITTLE, BARONESS (Platt) (Life Baroness 1981)

BERYL CATHERINE PLATT, CBE, da of Ernest Myatt; *b* 18 April 1923; *ed* Westcliffe High Sch for Girls, and Girton Coll, Camb, MA and Hon Fellow; Hon DSc City Univ, Salford, Cranfield Inst and Nottingham Trent, Hon D Univ Open Univ, Middlesex Univ and Essex Univ, Hon DEng Bradford, Hon D Tech Brunel and Loughborough, Hon LLD Cantab, Hon FIMechE, FRAeS, Eur Ing, Hon Fellow Wales Poly, Ealing Coll of Higher Educn, UMIST, Manchester Poly, FRSA, FITD, Hon FCP, FEng, FRAeS, Hon Fell Women's Engineering Soc; elected Chelmsford RDC 1959-74; elected Essex CC 1965 (Alderman 1969-74); Vice-Chm Educn Cttee 1969-71, Chm 1971-80; Chm Further Educn Sub-Cttee 1969-71; Vice-Chm County Council, and Chm Co-Ordinating & Finance Cttee 1980-83; Member of Court, Essex Univ and Brunel Univ 1985-92; Member of Court, Cranfield Univ; Member City and Guilds of London Inst Council 1974 and Camb Univ Appointment Bd 1975-79; Chm Equal Opportunities Commn 1983-88, Pres Inst of Training and Development 1985-87, Chm Women's Working Group of Industry Matters 1986-90, Member Careers Research and Advisory Centre 1983-93, and Engrg Council 1981-90; Chancellor of Middlesex Univ since 1994; President of Pipeline Industries Guild; Liveryman of Worshipful Co of Engineers, Freeman of the City of London; Dir British Gas since 1988; a DL of Essex since 1983; CBE 1978; *cr Baroness Platt of Writtle*, of Writtle, co Essex (Life Baroness) 1981: *m* 1949, Stewart Sydney Platt, and has issue.

Arms – Vert, four seaxes in cross their blades outwards proper hilts quillons and pommels or and as may aerofoils in saltire argent all between four plates. **Supporters** – *Dexter*, Perched upon the stock of an anchor a kingfisher, wings elevated and addorsed proper. *Sinister*, A lion, the wings also elevated and addorsed, supporting a patriarchal cross gules the compartment comprising a grassy mount springing therefrom founts of water proper. **Motto** – Love God and everyone.
Address – The House of Lords, SW1.

SON LIVING

Hon Roland Francis (Headley House, 40 Headley Chase, Brentwood, Essex CM14 5BN), *b* 1951; FCA: *m* 1982, Louise M., yr da of Lionel Jackson, of 56 Chelmsford Rd, Shenfield, Essex, and has issue, one son and two das.

DAUGHTER LIVING

Hon Victoria Catherine, *b* 1953; MA, FCA, ATII: *m* 1984, Rhodri Davies, son of His Honour Judge John Davies, QC, and has issue, three das.

PLOWDEN, BARON (Plowden) (Life Baron 1959)

EDWIN NOEL PLOWDEN, GBE, KCB, Roger H. Plowden, of Strachur Park, Argyll; *b* 6 Jan 1907; *ed* Switzerland, and Pembroke Coll, Camb (Hon Fellow); Hon DSc Pennsylvania State Univ, and Aston Univ, Hon D Litt Loughborough Univ, Visiting Fellow of Nuffield Coll, Oxford 1956-64; in Min of Economic Warfare 1939-40, in Min of Aircraft Production 1940-46 (Ch Executive and a Member of Aircraft Supply Council 1945-46); in Treasury as Ch Planning Officer and Ch of Economic Planning Board 1947-53, Vice-Chm Temporary Council Cttee of NATO 1951-52, Adviser on Atomic Energy Organisation 1953-54, and Chm UK Atomic Energy Authority 1954-59, of Cttee on Control of Public Expenditure 1959-61, of Cttee of Enquiry into Organisation of Representational Sers Overseas 1963-64, of Cttee of Enquiry into future of UK Aircraft Industry 1964-65, of Standing Advisory Cttee on Pay of Higher Civil Ser 1968-70, of Cttee of Enquiry into Structure of Electricity Supply Industry 1974-75, and of Cttee of Enquiry into CBI's aims and organisation 1974-75, Pres of Tube Investments, Ltd since 1976 (Chm 1963-76), of Equity Capital for Industry Ltd 1976-83 and of Police Complaints Board 1976-81, Dep Chm Cttee of Inquiry on the Police 1977-79, Independent Chm Police Negotiating Board 1979-82, and Chm Top Salaries Review Body 1981-89 (Member 1977-81) and Pres of London Graduate Sch of Business Studies since 1976 (Chm of Governing Body 1964-76); Dir C. Tennant, Sons & Co Ltd 1938-49, Commercial Union Assurance Co Ltd 1946-78, and Nat West Bank Ltd 1960-77; Member Ford European Advisory Council 1976-83, Internat Advisory Board SE Bank NA 1982-87, Chm CBI Cos Cttee 1976-80, Vice-Chm CBI Presidents Cttee 1977-80; *cr* KBE (Civil) 1946, KCB (Civil) 1951, GBE (Civil) 1987, and *Baron Plowden*, of Plowden, co Salop (Life Baron) 1959: *m* 1933, Dame Bridget Horatia, DBE, JP, da of late Adm Sir Herbert William Richmond, KCB (Bell, Bt, *cr* 1885), and has issue.

𝕬rms – Azure a fesse dancettee, the upper points terminating in fleurs-de-lys or. 𝕮rest – A buck passant sable, attired or.
Residences – Martels Manor, Dunmow, Essex; 11 Abingdon Gdns, Abingdon Villas, W8 6BY. *Club* – Brooks's.

SONS LIVING

Hon William Julius Lowthian (49 Stockwell Park Rd, SW9), *b* 1935; *ed* Eton, King's Coll, Camb, and California Univ: *m* 1960, Veronica Mary, only da of Lieut-Col Derek Ernest Frederick Orby Gascoigne (*see* B O'Neill, 1990 Edn), and has issue living, Benedict Edmund, *b* 1963, — Luke Piers, *b* 1967, — Frances Helen, *b* 1965, — Eleanor Mary, *b* 1969.
Hon Francis John (44 Hasker St, SW3), *b* 1945; *ed* Eton, and Trin Coll, Camb: *m* 1984, Mrs Geraldine Miles, elder da of late Gerald Wickman, of Orton Longueville, Peterborough.

DAUGHTERS LIVING

Hon Anna Bridget (46 Brixton Water Lane, SW2), *b* 1938; *ed* Newhall, Chelmsford, and at Institute of Archæology, London Univ.
Hon Penelope Christina (43 Lansdowne Gdns, SW8), *b* 1941; *ed* St Mary's Convent, Ascot, and New Hall, Camb: *m* 1st, 1965 (*m diss* 1975), Christopher Roper (*see* E Lovelace, colls, 1985 Edn); 2ndly, 1981, Rees T. Martin, and has issue living (by 2nd *m*), Henry, *b* 1984.

PLUMB, BARON (Plumb) (Life Baron 1987)

(CHARLES) HENRY PLUMB, son of Charles Plumb, of Ansley Warwicks, by his wife Louise, da of Henry Fisher, of Over Whitacre, Warwicks; *b* 27 March 1925; *ed* King Edward VI Sch, Nuneaton; Hon DSc Cranfield (1983); DL Warwick 1977; FRSA 1970, FRAgS 1974; Member of Council NFU since 1959, Vice Pres 1964-65, Dep Pres 1966-69, Pres 1970-79; Chm British Agricultural Council 1975-79; Member Duke of Northumberland's Cttee of Enquiry on Foot and Mouth Disease 1967-68; Dep Pres Royal Agricultural Soc of England, etc; Pres Nat Fedn of Young Farmers' Clubs 1976-86; MEP (*C*) The Cotswolds 1979-86, Chm Agricultural Cttee 1979-82, Leader European Democratic Group 1982-87, since when Pres European Parl; *cr* Kt 1973, and *Baron Plumb*, of Coleshill, co Warwicks (Life Baron) 1987: *m* 1947, Marjorie Dorothy, da of Thomas Victor Dunn, of Bentley, Warwicks, and has issue.
Residence – The Dairy Farm, Maxstoke, Coleshill, Warwicks B46 2QJ.

SON LIVING

Hon John Henry, *b* 1951; *ed* Solihull Sch, Wye Coll and London Univ (BSc 1973): *m* 1975, Beatrix, da of David Somoza, of Buenos Aires, Argentina, and has issue living, David Henry, *b* 1979, — Alison Ruth, *b* 1976, — Liliane, *b* 1983. *Residence* – Southfields, Coleshill, Warwicks B46 3EJ.

DAUGHTERS LIVING

Hon Elizabeth Marjorie, *b* 1948: *m* 1971 (*m diss* 19—), Robin Arbuthnot: 2ndly, 1982, Maj Anthony Holman, and has issue living (by 2nd *m*), Thomas Henry, *b* 1984, — Charles Anthony, *b* 1986. *Residence* – 9 Wilderness Mount, Seal Hollow Rd, Sevenoaks, Kent.

Hon Christine Mary, *b* 1950: *m* 1973, Benjamin John Mayo, FEng, and has issue living, Katharine Elizabeth, *b* 1977, — Sarah Louise, *b* 1979, — Stephanie Caroline, *b* 1983. *Residence* – The Garth, Kirkby Lane, Great Broughton, N Yorks.

PLUMER, VISCOUNTCY OF (Plumer) (Extinct 1944)

DAUGHTERS LIVING OF SECOND VISCOUNT

Hon (Anne) Cynthia Veronica Tempest, *b* 1921: *m* 1952, John Frederick Martyn Leapman, and has issue living, Joanna Mary Martyn, *b* 1953: *m* 1978, Colin Denis Keogh, of The Manor Farm, North Oakley, nr Basingstoke, Hants RG26 5TT, only son of J. D. Keogh, of 87 St Andrew's Rd, Hurlingham, Johannesburg, and has issue, Thomas Henri John *b* 1983, William Edward Colin *b* 1987, Katharine Emma *b* 1984, Georgina Ann *b* 1990, — Emma Hilda Martyn, *b* 1956: *m* 1982, Nicholas Richard Hunter Jones, of 69 Calbourne Rd, SW12, yst son of Col H. E. Hunter Jones, of Church Farm, Langham, Essex, and has issue living, Samuel *b* 1984, Timothy *b* 1987, Theodore *b* 1991, — Sarah Anne Martyn, *b* 1961: *m* 1987, Frederick Ellyer Cohen, only son of late Sebag Cohen, of Loge de Tisserand, Trinity, Jersey, CI, and has issue living, Harry *b* 1990, Charles *b* 1992, Emily *b* 1988. *Residence* – Highcliff, St John, Jersey.
Hon Rosemary Diana Lavinia, *b* 1929: *m* 1949, Frederick Henry Lowry-Corry (see E Belmore, colls). *Residence* – Edwardstone Hall, Boxford, Suffolk.

PLUMMER OF ST MARYLEBONE, BARON (Plummer) (Life Baron 1981)

(ARTHUR) DESMOND (HERNE) PLUMMER, TD, son of late Arthur Herne Plummer; *b* 25 May 1914; *ed* Hurstpierpoint Coll, and Coll of Estate Management; JP co London, DL Greater London; Member of St Marylebone Borough Council 1952-65 (Mayor 1958-59), LCC for St Marylebone 1960-65, ILEA 1964-76, GLC for Cities of London and Westminster 1964-73 and for St Marylebone 1973-76; Opposition Leader 1966-67 and 1973-74; Leader GLC 1967-73; Member of Court, Lond Univ, 1967-77; Member of Lloyd's; Chm Horserace Betting Levy Board 1974-82, Epsom and Walton Downs Training Grounds Man Board 1974-82 and National Stud 1975-82; Pres London Anglers' Assocn since 1976, Thames Angling Preservation Soc since 1970, and Metropolitan Assocn of Building Societies 1983-89; KStJ 1986 FAI; FRICS; FRSA; served 1939-46 with RE, Lt-Col (Temp); *cr* Knt 1971, and *Baron Plummer of St Marylebone*, in the City of Westminster (Life Baron) 1981: *m* 1941, Ella Margaret, da of Albert Holloway, and has issue.

𝔄rms – Barry wavy argent and azure on a chief vert three stirrups argent. 𝔠rest – On the battlements of a tower proper two surveyor's ranging rods in saltire compony argent and gules enfiling a stirrup argent. 𝔖upporters – Two herons proper standing on a grassy mount and extending the inner leg above a portcullis chained gold and set amid madonna lilies growing from each mount proper. 𝔐otto – Erectus non elatus
Residence – 4 The Lane, St John's Wood, NW8 0PN *Clubs* – Carlton, RAC and MCC.

DAUGHTER LIVING

Hon Sally Jane PLUMMER, *b* 19—; has retained her maiden name: *m* 1991, Richard F. Lowe, son of late W. Lowe, of Danehill, W Sussex

PLUNKET, BARON (Plunket) (Baron UK 1827)

ROBIN RATHMORE PLUNKET, 8th Baron, *b* 3 Dec 1925; *s* 1975; *ed* Eton; late Capt Rifle Bde: *m* 1951, Jennifer Bailey, da of Bailey Southwell, of Crocodile Leap Farm, Olivenhoutpoort, S Africa.

Arms – Sable, a bend between in sinister chief a tower and in dexter base a portcullis, all or. **Crest** – A horse passant argent, charged on the side, with a portcullis sable. **Supporters** – *Dexter*, an antelope or; *sinister*, a horse argent; each gorged with a collar, and pendent therefrom by a chain a portcullis sable.
Residences – Rathmore, Chimanimani, Zimbabwe; 39 Lansdowne Gdns, SW8.

– FESTINA·LENTE –

Quick, without impetuosity

BROTHER LIVING

Hon SHAUN ALBERT FREDERICK SHERIDAN (11 Ennismore Gdns, SW7. *Club* – White's), *b* 5 April 1931; *ed* Eton and L'Institut de Touraine; formerly Lt Irish Gds, and Dist Comdt, Kenya Police (Reserve); a Fellow of Institute of Directors: *m* 1st, 1961 (*m diss* 1979), Judith Ann, el da of late Gerard Patrick Power of Lapworth, Warwickshire; 2ndly, 1980, Elisabeth, who *d* 1986, da of late Helge Drangel, of Stockholm, and formerly wife of late Thomas de Sancha; 3rdly, 1989, Andrea Barbara, da of late Andre Milos, of Budapest, and formerly wife of Sheldon Reynolds, and has issue living (by 1st *m*), Tyrone Shaun Terence, *b* 1966; a Page of Honour to HM The Queen (ret 1979), — Loelia Dorothée Alexandra, *b* 1963.

WIDOW LIVING OF SON OF FIFTH BARON

Pamela Mary (16 Town Hill, W Malling, Kent ME19 6QN), da of late James Watherston, of Christchurch, NZ: *m* 1962, Hon (Denis) Kiwa Plunket, who *d* 1970.

COLLATERAL BRANCHES LIVING

Issue of late Flight-Lieut, Hon Brinsley Sheridan Bushe Plunket, RAF Vol Reserve, 2nd son of 5th Baron, *b* 1903, *d* on active ser 1941: *m* 1927 (*m diss* 1940), Aileen Sibell Mary PLUNKET (she *m* 2ndly, 1956, Valerian Stux-Rybar), da of late Hon Arthur Ernest Guinness (*see* E Iveagh, colls):—
Doon Aileen (*Countess Granville*), 1931: *m* 1958, 5th Earl Granville. *Residence* – Callernish, N Uist, Western Isles.

Grandchildren of late David Pierce Conyngham Plunket (infra):—
Issue of late Simon Patrick Conyngham Plunket, Lt 12th Lancers, *b* 1932, *d* 1968: *m* 1955, Susan Diana (who *m* 2ndly, 1972, Martin John Faber Morrison; and 3rdly, 1979, Maj Richard Harden, of Hunters Hill Farm, Nether Silton, nr Thirsk, N Yorks), da of late Robert Vivian Fairney, of Hartley End House, Hartley Wintney, Hants:—
Piers Robert Conyngham, *b* 1959: *m* 1989, Cordelia M., da of Colin Hart, of Charlbury, Oxon, and of Hon Mrs Patrick Penny (*see* V Marchwood), and has issue living, Simon Tuam Conyngham, *b* 1991, — Oliver David Conyngham, *b* 1994. —— Sara Doon, *b* 1957: *m* 1979, Luca Matteo Cumani, son of Sergio Cumani, of Milan, and has issue living, Matthew Sergio Simon, *b* 1981, — Francesca Deepsea, *b* 1983. *Residence* – Bedford House, Bury Rd, Newmarket, Suffolk.

Grandsons of late Most Rev Hon Benjamin John Plunket, DD, Bishop of Meath 1919-25, 2nd son of 4th Baron:—
Issue of late David Pierce Conyngham Plunket, *b* 1908, *d* 1956: *m* 1930, Sybil Marjorie, who *d* 1982, yr da of late Alfred German Archer, of Seaford, Sussex:—
David Archer Lee (Flat 2, 57 Sinclair Rd, W14 0NR; Cavalry Club), *b* 1936; *ed* St Columba's Coll, Dublin: *m* 1964, Philippa Susan, yr da of late Capt Brian St George Daly, Lancashire Fus, of Templeogue House, co Dublin, and has issue living, Emma Elizabeth Lee, *b* 1966, — Arabella Susan, *b* 1969.
Issue of late Benjamin William Alan Plunket, MVO, *b* 1912, *d* 1981: *m* 1943, Pamela, who *d* 1990, da of Charles Whatley, of Burderop, Swindon:—
Charles Patrick Benjamin, *b* 1947; *ed* Harrow: *m* 1990, Fiona, yr da of Gerald James, of Aston Rowant, Oxfordshire, and has issue living, Emily Lee, *b* 1991, — Olivia Kate, *b* 1993. *Residence* – Belle Isle, Lisbellaw, co Fermanagh.

Granddaughter of late Hon Charles Bushe Plunket, 2nd son of 3rd Baron:—
Issue of late David Darley Donnybrook Plunket, *b* 1869, *d* 1956: *m* 1900, Helen Rosanna, who *d* 1951, da of late Thomas Greene, of 49 St Stephen's Green, Dublin:—
Rosamond Sylvia, *b* 1908: *m* 1939, Air Commodore Henry Sam Francis Temple Jerrard, CBE, RAF, who *d* 1961, and has issue living, David Grattan (Hillside, Newcourt Av, Bray, co Wicklow), *b* 1944: *m* 1969, Noreen, da of Alphonsus Reginald Timothy Nolan, of Alvenor, Meath Rd, Bray, co Wicklow, — Helen Frances, *b* 1941: *m* 1962, John Patrick Roe. *Residence* – Hillside, Newcourt Av, Bray, co Wicklow.

Grandchildren of late Hon Arthur Cecil Crampton Plunket, 4th son of 3rd Baron:—
Issue of late Henry Coote Lifford Plunket, *b* 1875, *d* 1955: *m* 1912, Emily Evelyn Marjorie, who *d* 1968, da of late Severne Rowlands, of Ipswich, Queensland:—
Arthur Robert Lifford, *b* 1914: *m* 1938, Elies, da of Hugo Krieger, of Prague. *Residence* – 130 Sevenoaks Rd, Borkwood Park, Orpington, Kent.
Issue of late Archibald John Lifford Plunket, *b* 1877, *d* 1940: *m* 1909, Mary Calvert, who *d* 1937, da of late Henry Frederick Swan, CB, of Prudhoe Hall, Northumberland:—
Norah Mary Lifford, *b* 1912: *m* 1939, Hugh Honner Sancroft Baker, late Capt RE, of 198 Middle Drive, Darras Hall, Ponteland, Newcastle-upon-Tyne, and has issue living, Terence Sancroft, *b* 1941: *m* 1980, Anne Dorothy Hicklin, and has issue living, Nicholas Sancroft *b* 1981, Daniel Sancroft *b* 1983.

PREDECESSORS – (1) WILLIAM CONYNGHAM Plunket, MP for Charlemont in Irish Parliament 1798-1800, and for Dublin Univ 1812-27, Ch Justice of the Common Pleas in Ireland 1827-30, and Lord Chancellor of Ireland 1830-34 and 1835-41; *cr Baron Plunket*, of Newtown, co Cork (peerage of United Kingdom) 1827; *d* 1854; *s* by his el son (2) THOMAS SPAN, DD, 2nd Baron; was Lord Bishop of Tuam, Killala and Achonry 1839-66; *s* by his brother (3) JOHN, QC, 3rd Baron; *b* 1793: *m* 1824,

Charlotte, who *d* 1886, da of Rt Hon Charles Kendal Bushe, Lord Ch Justice of Ireland; *d* 1871; *s* by his son **(4)** *Most Rev* WILLIAM CONYNGHAM, DD, 4th Baron, *b* 1828; Bishop of Meath 1876-84 and Archbishop of Dublin 1884-97: *m* 1863, Anne Lee, who *d* 1889, da of Sir Benjamin Lee Guinness, 1st Bt, and sister of 1st Barons Ardilaun and Iveagh; *d* 1897; *s* by his el son **(5)** WILLIAM LEE, GCMG, KCVO, KBE, 5th Baron, *b* 1864; Gov of New Zealand 1904-10; Bore Standard of the Dominion of New Zealand at Coronation of King George V 1911: *m* 1894, Lady Victoria Alexandrina Hamilton-Temple-Blackwood, who *d* 1968, da of 1st Marquess of Dufferin and Ava; *d* 1920, *s* by his el son **(6)** TERENCE CONYNGHAM, 6th Baron; *b* 1899; Lt Rifle Brig (Reserve); European War 1918: *m* 1922, Dorothé Mabel, who *d* 1938, da of late Joseph Lewis, and widow of Capt Jack Barnato, RAF; *d* 1938: *s* by his el son **(7)** PATRICK TERENCE WILLIAM SPAN, KCVO; 7th Baron; *b* 1923; Lt-Col Irish Gds; Equerry to King George VI 1948-52 and to Queen Elizabeth II 1952-75; Dep Master of the Household 1954-75; *d* 1975; *s* by his brother ROBIN RATHMORE, 8th Baron and present peer.

PLURENDEN, BARONY OF (Sternberg) (Extinct 1978)

DAUGHTERS LIVING OF LIFE BARON

Hon Rosanne Monica Michelle STERNBERG, *b* 1960; has retained her maiden name: *m* 19—, Robert William Kenneth Harris, elder son of K. A. Harris, of Lanwardleigh, Devon, and has issue living, Jessica Rosanne, *b* 1990.
Hon Francesca Nicola, *b* 1962: *m* 1989, Douglas G. Allen, eldest son of B. G. Allen, of Scott City, Kansas, USA.

WIDOW LIVING OF LIFE BARON

DOROTHEE MONICA (*Baroness Plurenden*) (Lidostrasse 63, 6314 Unterägeri, Switzerland), da of Maj Robert Bateman Prust, OBE, of Vancouver, BC, Canada: *m* 1951, Baron Plurenden (Life Baron), who *d* 1978.

PLYMOUTH, EARL OF (Windsor-Clive) (Baron E 1529, Earl UK 1905)

I trust in God

OTHER ROBERT IVOR WINDSOR-CLIVE, 3rd Earl; *b* 9 Oct 1923; *s* 1943; *ed* Eton, and Trin Coll, Camb; late Capt Coldstream Guards; is a KStJ, a DL Shropshire, and an FRSA: *m* 1950, Caroline Helen, only da of Edward Rice, of Dane Court, Eastry, Kent, and has issue.

Arms – Quarterly: 1st and 4th argent, on a fesse sable, three mullets or, *Clive*; 2nd and 3rd gules, a saltire argent, between twelve cross crosslets or, *Windsor*. **Crest** – 1st, a griffin statant argent, gorged with a ducal crown gules; 2nd, a stag's head at gaze, couped at the neck argent, attired or. **Supporters** – On either side an unicorn argent, horned, maned, and hoofed or.
Residences – The Stables, Oakly Park, Ludlow, Shropshire; 48 Burton Court, SW3.

SONS LIVING

IVOR EDWARD OTHER (*Viscount Windsor*) (Oakly Park, Ludlow, Shropshire; 6 Oakley St, SW3), *b* 19 Nov 1951; *ed* Harrow: *m* 1979, Caroline Anne, da of Frederick Nettlefold (*see* Scarsdale, V), and has issue:—
　　　　SONS LIVING — *Hon* ROBERT OTHER IVOR, *b* 25 March 1981, — *Hon* Frederick John Richard, *b* 1983.
　　　　DAUGHTER LIVING — *Hon* India Harriet, *b* 1988.
Hon Simon Percy, *b* 1956; *ed* Harrow.
Hon David Justin (29 Cheyne Court, Flood St, SW3), *b* 1960: *ed* Harrow, and RAC Cirencester; Commodity Broker: *m* 1986, Camilla Jane, eldest da of John Squire, of Marbella, Spain, and of Mrs John Ticehurst, of 43 Smith Terr, SW3, and has issue living, Alexander, *b* 1993.

DAUGHTER LIVING

Lady Emma WINDSOR CLIVE, *b* 1954; has resumed her maiden name: *m* 1975 (*m diss* 1992), Robert Arthur Smith-Dorrien-Smith, and has issue living, Adam Robert, *b* 1978, — Michael Horace, *b* 1987, — Frances Marcella, *b* 1980. *Residence* – The Granary, Yeabridge, S Petherton, Som TA13 5LW.

BROTHER LIVING

Hon Richard Archer Alan, *b* 1928; *ed* Eton, and Trin Coll, Camb; late Lieut RA; Chm of Bayfine Ltd 1973-85: *m* 1st, 1955 (*m diss* 1968), Joanna Mary, el da of Edward Corbet Woodall, OBE (Crawley-Boevey, Bt colls); 2ndly, 1968, Hon (Mary) Alice Chancellor, da of 4th Baron Hylton, and has issue living (by 1st *m*), Stephen Miles, *b* 1956; *ed* Eton, — Cathryn Harriet, *b* 1958: *m* 1983, Thomas P. Macfarlane, son of late Craig Macfarlane, and has issue living, Cosmo *b* 1987, Ivo *b* 1988, Rose *b* 1990, — (by 2nd *m*) Nell, *b* 1974. *Residence* – Combe, Nettlecombe, Taunton, Somerset.

SISTERS LIVING

Lady Clarissa, *b* 1931: *m* 1953, Major Keith Maclean Forbes Egleston, late Rifle Bde, of 7 Ernest Gdns, W4, and has issue living, Hugo Vivyan, *b* 1955; *ed* Eton, — Sarah Caroline, *b* 1956, — Harriet Gilian, *b* 1962: *m* 1988, Simon Richard Alsop, only son of B. G. P. Alsop, of Ashtead, Surrey.
Lady Rosula Caroline, *b* 1935; OStJ: *m* 1962, Maj Sir Alan Glyn, ERD, of 17 Cadogan Place, SW1X 9SA, late Royal House Guards, MP for Clapham Division of Wandsworth 1959-64 and for Berkshire Division of Windsor and Windsor and Maidenhead 1970-92, son of late John Paul Glyn, RHG, and has issue living, Mary Caroline, *b* 1963: *m* 1993, Capt Adrian John Weale, son of Dr K. E. Weale, of Elmwood Rd, Chiswick, W4 and has issue living, Robert Kenneth *b* 1994, — Anne Serena, *b* 1964.

COLLATERAL BRANCHES LIVING (*In remainder to Barony of Windsor only*)

Issue of late Lady Gillian Mary Windsor-Clive, da of 2nd Earl, *b* 1922, *d* 1961: *m* 1st, 1941 (*m diss* 1947), Wilfred Wooller, Lieut RA; 2ndly, 1947, Lieut Albertus Jacobus de Haan, DFC (Netherlands), Croix de Guerre (Belgium), R Netherlands Navy, who *d* 1991:—
(By 2nd *m*) Julian Jan Ivor (Southfield House, Forthampton, Glos GL19 4RA), *b* 1948; *ed* Gresham's Sch, Holt; CA: *m* 1972, Juliet Clare, da of late Maj Henry Benjamin van der Gucht, MC, and has issue living, Luke Archer, *b* 1973; *ed* Eton, Cheltenham, and Reading Univ, — Tom Julian, *b* 1976; *ed* Cheltenham, — Sophia Gillian, *b* 1979; *ed* Malvern Girls' Sch. —— Archer Anthony (Cookeridge Farm, Bromfield, Ludlow, Shropshire), *b* 1950; *ed* Gresham's Sch, Holt: *m* 1st, 1975 (*m diss* 1987), Amanda Ball; 2ndly, 1987, Vivien Whittall, and has issue living (by 1st *m*), Toby Archer, *b* 1976, — Laura Mary Emma, *b* 1979, — (by 2nd *m*) Frances Catherine, *b* 1988, — Hannah Gillian, *b* (twin) 1988. —— Andrew David (Thameside Cottage, Longworth, Oxon), *b* 1954; *ed* Northease Manor, Lewes: *m* 1981, Emma Katherine, yst da of Cdr Christopher William Stuart Dreyer, DSO, DSC. —— Valentine Nicholas, *b* 1956; *ed* Stanbridge Earls Sch.

Issue of late Lady Phyllis Windsor-Clive, only da of 1st Earl, *b* 1886, *d* 1971; *m* 1924, Maj Hugh Gordon Benton, 2nd Lancers (Indian Cav), who *d* 1931:—
(Caroline Rose) Melissa BENTON, *b* 1928.

Grandsons of late Lt-Col Hon George Herbert Windsor Windsor-Clive, son of late Harriet, Baroness Windsor:—
Issue of late Lt-Col George Windsor-Clive, CMG, *b* 1878, *d* 1968: *m* 1912, Sidney Guendolen, who *d* 1935, da of Charles Carmichael Lacaita, of Selham, Sussex (Doyle, Bt):—
Robert Charles (The Pleck, Ashford Carbonel, Ludlow, Shropshire SY8 4DB), *b* 1919; *ed* Eton, and RMC; Brig (ret) late Coldm Gds; 1939-45 War (wounded despatches): *m* 1949, Olive Mary, yr da of Lt-Col Francis Longueville, DSO, MC, and has issue living, George Francis (Balak Farm, Marridge Hill, Ramsbury, Wilts), *b* 1954; *ed* Eton, and RAC Cirencester; late Lt Coldm Gds, Maj (TA) Royal Yeo; Man Dir Christopher Stephenson Int Ltd: *m* 1988, Anna Georgina, da of Antony Leaf, of Cleeve House, Ampney St Peter, Cirencester, Glos, and has issue living, Thomas Robert *b* 1992, John Antony *b* 1993, — Annabel Mary, *b* 1951: *m* 1979, Mark Savage, of Castlett Farm Cottage, Guiting Power, Cheltenham, Glos, son of G. A. R. Savage, of 179 Gloucester St, Cirencester, and has issue living, Gabriel Frances *b* 1984, Victoria Mary *b* 1987. —— Francis Archer (Toneys, Bromsberrow, nr Ledbury, Herefordshire), *b* 1922; *ed* Eton; late Capt Coldm Gds; 1939-45 War (wounded, despatches): *m* 1945, Anne Gertrude, el da of late Lt-Col Francis Longueville, DSO, MC, and has issue living, Edward Archer (54 Oxberry Av, SW6), *b* 1946; *ed* Ampleforth, and RMA Sandhurst; Maj late Coldm Gds: *m* 1982, Grania M. S., da of M. E. F. S. FitzGerald, of Hill Place, Haywards Heath, Sussex, and has issue living, Robert *b* 1985, Sophie Anne *b* 1983, — Robert Ivor (Cefn Ceist, Michaelchurch, Escley, Herefordshire), *b* 1950; *ed* Ampleforth, and RAC Cirencester: *m* 1980 (*m diss* 1990), Aricelli Romero, and has issue living, Francisco Alexis *b* 1982, Ana Willow *b* 1984, — Other John, *b* 1958; *ed* Ampleforth, and RMA Sandhurst; Maj Coldm Gds, — William Henry (Bury Court, Redmarley, Glos), *b* 1960; *ed* Belmont Abbey, and RAC Cirencester: *m* 1989, Jane, da of J. R. Lawther, of Little Arley, Birtsmorton, nr Malvern, Worcs, and has issue living, Harriet Ann *b* 1990, Phoebe Jane *b* 1993, — Frances Anne, *b* 1948; BEd (Cantab): *m* 1972, Maj Andrew Stow, RE, of Perrins Court, Bromsberrow, nr Ledbury, Herefordshire, and has issue living, Catherine Mary *b* 1974, Isobel Anne *b* 1976, Elizabeth Rose (twin) *b* 1976. —— Everard Ivor (The Leys, Stoke Bliss, Tenbury Wells, Worcs), *b* 1925; *ed* Eton; late Col Coldm Gds; 1939-45 War.

PREDECESSORS – (1) Sir ANDREWS Windsor, KB, distinguished himself in the French wars of Henry VIII, and was made a Knight Banneret at the battle of the Spurs 1513; summoned to Parliament of England as *Baron Windsor*, of Stanwell, co Bucks 1529; *d* 1543; *s* by his son (2) WILLIAM, KB, 2nd Baron; *d* 1558; *s* by his son (3) EDWARD, 3rd Baron; distinguished himself at St Quentin, and in 1566 entertained Queen Elizabeth at his seat at Bradenham; *d* 1574; *s* by his el son (4) FREDERICK, 4th Baron; *d* unmarried 1585; *s* by his brother (5) HENRY, 5th Baron; *d* 1605: *s* by his son (6) THOMAS, KB, 6th Baron; was a Rear-Adml; *dsp* 1642; *s* by his nephew (7) THOMAS Windsor-Hickman, PC, 7th Baron, son of Hon Elizabeth Windsor by her marriage with Dixie Hickman, of Kew; assumed the additional surname of Windsor; commanded a Regt of Horse at Naseby 1646; was Lord-Lieut of Worcestershire, and Gov of Jamaica 1661-2; *cr Earl of Plymouth* (peerage of England) 1682; *d* 1687; *s* by his grandson (8) OTHER, 2nd Earl; *d* 1727; *s* by his son (9) OTHER, 3rd Earl; *d* 1732; *s* by his son (10) OTHER LEWIS, 4th Earl; was Custos Rotulorum of cos Flint, Glamorgan, and Cheshire; *d* 1777; *s* by his son (11) OTHER HICKMAN, 5th Earl; *d* 1799; *s* by his son (12) OTHER ARCHER, 6th Earl; *dsp* 1833, when the Barony of Windsor became abeyant between his sisters Maria, wife of 2nd Marquess of Downshire, and Harriet, wife of Hon Robert Henry Clive (E Powis), and the earldom reverted to his uncle (13) ANDREWS, 7th Earl; *d* unmarried 1837; *s* by his brother (14) HENRY, 8th Earl; *dsp* 1843, when the earldom became extinct. In 1855 the abeyance of the Barony of Windsor was terminated in favour of (15) HARRIET Clive (ante); *b* 1797; assumed in 1855 by Roy licence the additional surname of Windsor: *m* 1819, Hon Robert Henry Clive, MP, 2nd son of 1st Earl of Powis; *d* 1869; *s* by her grandson (16) ROBERT GEORGE Windsor-Clive, GBE, CB, PC, 1st Earl, only son of Hon Robert, MP, by Lady Mary Selina Louisa Bridgeman, da of 2nd Earl of Bradford; *b* 1857; Lord-Lieut of Glamorganshire 1890-1923; Paymaster-Gen 1891-2, and 1st Commr of Works 1902-5; *cr Viscount Windsor*, of St Fagans, co Glamorgan, and *Earl of Plymouth*, in co Devon (peerage of United Kingdom) 1905: *m* 1883, Alberta Victoria Sarah Caroline, who *d* 1944, da of late Rt Hon Sir Augustus Berkeley Paget, PC, GCB; *d* 1923; *s* by his son (17) IVOR MILES, PC, 2nd Earl; *b* 1889; was Parliamentary Private Sec (unpaid) to Sec of State for Home Depart (Rt Hon W. C. Bridgeman, MP), 1922, and Under-Sec of State for Dominion Affairs Jan to June 1929; became Parliamentary Sec to Min of Transport (in National Govt) Nov 1931, and Parliamentary Under-Sec, Colonial Office Sept 1932; Parliamentary Under-Sec, Foreign Office July 1936; Hon Freeman of Cardiff 1936; elected Pro-Chancellor of Univ of Wales 1941; bore Standard of Wales at Coronation of King George VI; sat as MP for Shropshire, Ludlow Div (C) Jan 1922 to Mar 1923: *m* 1921, Lady Irene Corona Charteris, who *d* 1989, da of 7th Earl of Wemyss; *d* 1943; *s* by his son (18) OTHER ROBERT IVOR, 3rd Earl and present peer; also Baron Windsor, and Viscount Windsor.

Pollington, Viscount; son of Earl of Mexborough.

POLTIMORE, BARON (Bampfylde) (Baron UK 1831, Bt E 1641)

MARK COPLESTONE BAMPFYLDE, 7th Baron, and 12th Baronet; *b* 8 June 1957; *s* 1978; *ed* Radley: *m* 1982, Sally Anne, da of Dr Norman Miles, of The Old House, Caythorpe, Lincs, and has issue.

Arms – Or, on a bend gules, three mullets argent. **Crest** – A lion's head erased sable ducally crowned or. **Supporters** – Two lions reguardant, sable, ducally crowned gules, gorged with a collar gemelle or, and pendant therefrom an escutcheon of the arms of Bampfylde.
Residence – Ridgemoor Farmhouse, West St, Burghclere, Newbury, Berks RG15 9LD.

To rejoice in the Lord

SONS LIVING

Hon HENRY ANTHONY WARWICK, *b* 3 June 1985.
Hon Oliver Hugh Coplestone, *b* 1987.

DAUGHTER LIVING

Hon Lara Fioan Brita, *b* 1990.

SISTER LIVING

Christine Margaret Hermione, *b* 1948: *m* 1st, 1970 (*m diss* 1977), Peter William Denby Roberts (*see* Roberts, Bt, colls, cr 1909); 2ndly, 1977, Patrick Joseph Scott Plummer, of Mainhouse, Kelso, Roxburghshire (*see* B Kinross).

UNCLE LIVING (*son of 6th Baron*)

Hon David Cecil Warwick (Coombe Lea, Malmesbury, Wilts), *b* 1924; *ed* Eton; late Capt KRRC, 1939-45 War (wounded): *m* 1950, Jean Margaret, da of late Lt-Col Patrick Kinloch Campbell, and has issue living, Michael Hugh Warwick (Tower Farm Cottage, Towerhead Rd, Banwell, Avon BS24 6PQ), *b* 1951; *ed* Milton Abbey; late Capt Queen's Own Hus: *m* 1981, Sarah Fenella, da of Cdr Michael Edward St Quintin Wall, RN, of Ivy House, Lambourn, Berks RG16 7PB (*see* B de Mauley, colls), and has issue living, Edward David Warwick *b* 1986, Laura Margaret *b* 1989, — Richard Ian David (31 Fernhurst Rd, SW6 7JN), *b* 1953; *ed* Milton Abbey; late Capt 15th/19th R Hus: *m* 1st, 1980 (*m diss* 1989), Sara, da of late Maj Kenneth Spicer Few, of Cambridge; 2ndly, 1990, Charlotte Mary, yr da of late Lt-Col John Monsell Christian, MC, and formerly wife of John Angus Harcourt Gold (*see* By Trent), and has issue living (by 2nd *m*) Camilla *b* 1994, — John Spencer Warwick (56 Ames St, Paekakariki, Wellington, NZ), *b* 1960; *ed* Radley, and Bristol Univ; MBA Cranfield: *m* 1990, Mrs Nicola Duffain, yr da of Sir Charles Henry McLeod, 3rd Bt.

DAUGHTER LIVING OF FOURTH BARON (*By 1st marriage*)

Hon Sheila Margaret Warwick (*Hon Lady Stucley*) (Hartland Abbey, N Devon), *b* 1912; Patron of two livings: *m* 1932, Maj Sir Dennis Frederic Bankes Stucley, 5th Bt, R Devon Yeo and Gren Gds, who *d* 1983, and has issue (*see* Stucley, Bt).

MOTHER LIVING

Brita Yvonne (Stable Cottage, Donnington Grove, Newbury, Berks), only da of late Baron (Rudolph) Cederström (*see* B De Ramsey, 1972-73 Edn): *m* 1st, 1947, Capt Hon Anthony Gerard Hugh Bampfylde, who *d* 1969; 2ndly 1975, Guy Elmes, and has issue by 1st *m*.

COLLATERAL BRANCHES LIVING

Granddaughter of late Hon Charles Warwick Bampfylde (infra):—
Issue of late Richard Warwick Bampfylde, *b* 1903, *d* 1942: *m* 1932, Ethe (who *m* 2ndly, 19—, Joseph Sweeney), da of late Mauris Edwards:—
Sonya, *b* 1937: *m* 1959, Ronald Patrick Trevor Lyttle. *Residence* – 1070A Avenue Rd, Toronto 12, Ontario, Canada.

Issue of late Hon Charles Warwick Bampfylde, 2nd son of 2nd Baron, *b* 1867, *d* 1931: *m* 1891, Edith Anne, who *d* 1959, da of Edward Browne:—
Barbara Warwick, *b* 1898: *m* 1921, George Phillips-Smith, and has issue living, Nigel Derek, *b* 1922, — Phillippa, *b* 1924, — June Denzilla Haidee, *b* 1927: *m* 1953, David Thomas. *Residence* – Bridge House, 3 Broad Oak Rd, Weston-super-Mare.

Issue of late Hon Francis Warwick Bampfylde, 3rd son of 2nd Baron, *b* 1885, *d* 1940: *m* 1911, Margaret Harriet, who *d* 1968, da of late Robert Martin, of Belfast:—
Caroline Warwick, *b* 1920: *m* 1st, 1942 (*m diss* 1951), Wing-Cdr Dean Lenthal Swift, Roy Australian Air Force; 2ndly, 1951 (*m diss* 1984), Edward Foster James, CMG, OBE, HM Foreign Ser, and has issue living, (by 2nd *m*) David Peter (18 Girdlers Rd, W14), *b* 1954, — Susan Alexandra Caroline JAMES, *b* 1952; HM Foreign Ser; has resumed her maiden name: *m* 1979 (*m diss* 1984), Timothy Ison, — Penelope Sarah (twin), *b* 1954: *m* 1981, Christopher Wyndham Hume Stewart-Moore (*see* Llewellyn, Bt, cr 1922). *Residence* – Springfield House, W Clandon, Surrey.

PREDECESSORS – (1) JOHN Bampfylde; MP for Penryn 1640; *cr a* Baronet 1641; *s* by his son (2) *Sir* COPLESTONE, 2nd Bt; *d* 1691; *s* by his grandson (3) *Sir* COPLESTONE WARWICK, 3rd Bt; MP for Exeter and Devon; *d* 1727; *s* by his son (4) *Sir* RICHARD WARWICK, 4th Bt; MP for Devon; *d* 1776; *s* by his son (5) *Sir* CHARLES WARWICK, DCL, 5th Bt; MP for Exeter; was assassinated 1823; *s* by his son (6) *Sir* GEORGE, 6th Bt; *b* 1786; was Vice-Lieut of Devon, and a Lord-in-Waiting to Queen Victoria; *cr Baron Poltimore* of Poltimore, co Devon (peerage of United Kingdom) 1831: *m* 2ndly, 1836, Caroline, da of Gen Frederick William Buller; *d* 1858; *s* by his son (7) AUGUSTUS FREDERICK GEORGE WARWICK, PC, 2nd Baron; *b* 1837; Treasurer of Queen Victoria's Household 1872-4: *m* 1858, Florence Sara Wilhelmine, who *d* 1909, da of late Richard Brinsley Sheridan, of Frampton Court, Dorset; *d* 1908; *s* by his son (8) COPLESTONE RICHARD GEORGE WARWICK, 3rd Baron; *b* 1859: *m* 1881, Hon Margaret Harriet Beaumont, who *d* 1931, da of 1st Baron Allendale; *d* 1918; *s* by his son (9) GEORGE WENTWORTH WARWICK, 4th Baron, *b* 1882: *m* 1st, 1910, Cynthia Rachel, who *d* 1961, da of late Hon Gerald William Lascelles (E Harewood, colls); 2ndly, 1962, Barbara Pitcairn (WALKER), who *d* 1969, da of Peter Nicol, of Kirkintilloch; *s* by his brother (10) ARTHUR BLACKETT WARWICK, 5th Baron, *b* 1883: *m* 1st, 1916, Catharine Frances Graham, who *d* 1938, da of late Gen Hon Sir David Macdowell Fraser, GCB (L Saltoun, colls); 2ndly, 1939 (*m diss* 1948), Mrs Mabel Violet Blanche Meyrick, da of late Col Arthur Hill Sandys Montgomerie, of Grey Abbey, co Down; *d* 1967, *s* by his brother (11) HUGH DE BURGH WARWICK, 6th Baron; *b* 1888: *m* 1918, Margaret Mary, who *d* 1981, da of 4th Marquis de la Pasture (*cr* France 1768); *d* 1978, *s* by his grandson **(12)** MARK COPLESTONE (son of late Capt Hon Anthony Gerard Hugh Bampfylde, el son of 6th Baron), 7th Baron and present peer.

POLWARTH, LORD (Hepburne-Scott (Lord S 1690)
(Name pronounced "Hebburn-Scott")

The moon will replenish her horns

FIDES·PROBATA·CORONAT

Approved faith crowns

HENRY ALEXANDER HEPBURNE-SCOTT, TD, 10th Lord; *b* 17 Nov 1916; *s* 1944; *ed* Eton, and King's Coll, Camb (MA); Hon LLD, St Andrews, Aberdeen, Hon DLitt, Heriot Watt; D Univ Stirling; FRSE; FRSA, Hon FRIAS; a Representative Peer for Scotland 1945-63; a Member of Queen's Body Guard for Scotland (Royal Company of Archers), Vice-Lord Lt Borders Region (Roxburgh, Ettrick and Lauderdale); a partner in the firm of Chiene & Tait, chartered accountants 1950-68; Chm Scottish Council (Development & Industry) 1956-66 (Pres 1966-72), and General Accident Insurance Gp 1968-72; Min of State Scottish Office 1972-74; Chancellor Aberdeen Univ 1966-86; a Dir of Bank of Scotland 1950-71 and 1974-87 (Gov 1968-72) of ICI Ltd 1969-72 and 1974-81; a Dir of Canadian Pacific Ltd 1975-86, Sun Life Assurance Co of Canada 1975-84, Halliburton Co 1974-87, The Weir Group Ltd, and Commonwealth Development Finance Co Ltd; Member Franco-British Council, Chm Scottish Forestry Trust since 1987, Member House of Lords Select Cttee on Overseas Trade 1984-85; 1939-45 War as Capt Lothians and Border Horse: *m* 1st, 1943 (*m diss* 1969), Caroline Margaret, who *d* 1982, da of late Capt Robert Athole Hay (*see* Hay, Bt, colls, *cr* 1635, 1980 Edn); 2ndly, 1969, Jean, da of Adm Sir Angus Edward Malise Bontine Cunninghame Graham of Gartmore and of Ardoch, KBE, CB, and formerly wife of Charles Eliot Jauncey, QC (later Lord Jauncey of Tullichettle, Life Baron), and has issue by 1st *m*.

Arms – Quarterly, 1st and 4th grand quarters quartered; 1st, vert, a lion rampant argent *Hume*; 2nd, argent, three papingoes vert *Pepdie*; 3rd, gules; three piles engrailed argent *Polwarth*; 4th, argent, a cross engrailed azure *St Clair of Herdmanston*, over all on an escutcheon azure, an orange with the stalk erect, slipped proper, and over it an Imperial Crown; 2nd grand quarter or, two mullets and a crescent in base azure *Scott of Harden*; 3rd grand quarter quartered; 1st and 4th gules, on a chevron argent a rose between two lioncels combatant of the first *Hepburne of Humbie*; 2nd and 3rd argent, three dock leaves vert *Foulis* **Crest** – 1st, a lady richly attired holding in her dexter hand the sun and in her sinister a half-moon all proper *Scott of Harden*; 2nd issuing out of a man's heart, or, an arm from the elbow proper, brandishing a scimitar of steel, with cross and pommel of gold, *Polwarth*; 3rd an oak tree proper, and a horse passant argent, saddled and bridled gules *Hepburne of Humbie* **Supporters** – *Dexter*, a lion rampant reguardant argent, lanuged gules; *sinister*, a mermaid — holding in her sinister hand and resting on her shoulder a mirror all proper.
Residence – Easter Harden, Hawick, Roxburghshire TD9 7LP. *Clubs* – Brooks's, Pratt's, New (Edinburgh).

SON LIVING *(By 1st marriage)*

Hon ANDREW WALTER (*Master of Polwarth*) (72 Cloncurry St, SW6), *b* 30 Nov 1947; *ed* Eton and Trin Hall, Camb: *m* 1971, Isabel Anna, da of Maj John Freville Henry Surtees, OBE, MC, of Down House, Wylye, Wilts, and has issue living, William Henry, *b* 1973, — Robert Mungo, *b* 1974, — Georgina Mary, *b* 1979, — Caroline Rose, *b* 1983.

DAUGHTERS LIVING *(By 1st marriage)*

Hon Sarah Margaret, *b* 1944: *m* 1977, John Alexander Hamish Macnab of Barravorich, of 16 Cupar Rd, SW11, and has issue living, Lucy Margaret, *b* 1978, — Clare Sarah, *b* 1980.
Hon Diana Mary, *b* 1946: *m* 1977, Richard James Bradshaw, of 397 Wellesley St East, Toronto, Ontario, Canada M4X 1H5, and has issue living, James Edward Merton, *b* 1983, — Jenny Alexandra, *b* 1979.
Hon Mary Jane, *b* 1955: *m* 1980, Hon James McMoran Wilson, of 65 Upland Rd, Brookline, Mass 02146, USA, el son of 2nd Baron Moran, KCMG, and has issue (*see* B Moran).

BROTHER LIVING *(Raised to the rank of a Baron's son 1945)*

Hon Francis Michael, MC, *b* 1920; *ed* Eton, and King's Coll, Camb; a FRICS; sometime Maj Lothians and Border Horse, 1939-45 War; a Consultant Smiths Gore, Chartered Surveyors; 1939-45 War (MC): *m* 1946, Marjorie Hamilton, da of Horatio John Ross (Lighton, Bt), and has issue living, James Patrick (Larkhill, Lauder, Berwickshire), *b* 1947; *ed* Eton; late Capt The Black Watch: *m* 1972, Christian Diana, da of Maj John Freville Henry Surtees, OBE, MC, of Down House, Wylye, Wilts, and has issue living, Walter Robert *b* 1974, George James *b* 1983, Emily May *b* 1977, — Michael Francis (Wester Newhouse, Lilliesleaf, Melrose, Roxburghshire), *b* 1959: *m* 1984, Viola Susan, da of Christopher Heywood, of 3 The Drive, SW20, and has issue living, Francis Hedley *b* 1987, Malcolm Ross *b* 1988, — Mary Helen, *b* 1949: *m* 1974, Andrew Godfrey Purvis Sherwood (*see* E Onslow, colls) *Residence* – Newhouse, Lilliesleaf, Melrose, Roxburghshire.

COLLATERAL BRANCHES LIVING

Issue of late Hon Patrick John Hepburne-Scott, yst son of 9th Lord, *b* 1899; *d* 1982: *m* 1st, 1925, Cona, who *d* 1961, da of late Cyril Fielding Smith, of Dublin; 2ndly, 1963, Margaret Mary, who *d* 1982, da of late Arthur George Riddell, of Harrow, Middx:—

(By 1st *m*), Patricia Mary, *b* 1926: *m* 1966, Peter Rudolph Ramm. —— Ann Harriet, *b* 1929: *m* 1963, Colin Andrew Baxter, of Red Tiles, West Linton, Peeblesshire, and has issue living, Patrick Ian (Girwoodend Farm, Auchengray, Lanarkshire), *b* 1968.

Grandsons of late Hon Henry Robert Hepburne-Scott, 2nd son of 7th Lord:—

Issue of late James Cospatrick Hepburne-Scott, *b* 1882, *d* 1942: *m* 1907, Lady Isobel Alice Adelaide Kerr, who *d* 1975, da of 9th Marquess of Lothian:—

Michael Henry (13 Hamlet Court, W6), *b* 1909; Maj late 16th/5th Lancers; late Dep Assist Dir of Army Legal Sers, War Office: *m* 1st, 1931 (*m diss* 1949), Frances Elizabeth, who *d* 1984, da of late Rev George Victor Collier, of Sotwell, Wallingford, Berks; 2ndly, 1949, Mrs Rohilla Ada May Pelz, da of Albert Smith, and has had issue (by 1st *m*), David Michael Cospatrick, *b* 1935; *ed* Eton and King's Coll, Camb (MA); Assist Master, Westminster Sch; *d* 1992, —— Walter Francis (Pantiles, Beeches Rd, Farnham Common, Bucks SL2 3PS), *b* 1944; *ed* Eton; MB BS, MRCGP, LLB: *m* 1st, 1968 (*m diss* 1977), Fiona Mary, da of Frey Richard Ellis, MD, of 27 Links Rd, Epsom, Surrey, 2ndly, 1983, Teresa Gail, da of Frederick John Major, and has issue living (by 1st *m*), Henry Walter *b* 1970, George Walter *b* 1971, Edward Walter *b* 1974, — (by 2nd *m*), Angela Susan, *b* 1949: *m* 1973, Othmar Schimek, of Imberg Stiege 4, Salzburg, Austria 5020, and has issue living, Othmar *b* 1974, Isabelle Alice *b* 1983. —— Walter Schomberg, *b* 1910; is an ARIBA, and Capt late RE: *m* 1945, Deborah, who *d* 1993, only child of late Tudor Ralph Castle, Lt Queen's Roy Regt (D Norfolk, colls), and has issue living, James Ralph Schomberg, *b* 1947; *ed* Nautical Coll, Pangbourne, — Lyulph Mark Esme, *b* 1949: *m* 1980, Jane Anne, elder da of Peter Telford, of 11 Grange Close, Southam, Leamington Spa, Warwicks. *Residence* – Northfield, Prestonpans, E Lothian.

PREDECESSORS – (1) *Rt Hon Sir* PATRICK Hume, PC, and Extraor Lord of Session 1693 Lord High Chancellor of Scotland 1696, and First Lord of the Treasury and of the Admiralty etc, was *cr Lord Polwarth*, of Polwarth, co Berwick (peerage of Scotland) 1690, and *Earl of Marchmont, Viscount Blasonberry, and Lord Polwarth*, of Polwarth, Redbraes and Greenlaw peerage of Scotland) 1697: *d* 1724; *s* by his son (2) ALEXANDER, KT, PC, 2nd Earl; was a Senator of the College of Justice, and Ambassador to Denmark and Prussia; *d* 1740; *s* by his son (3) HUGH, 3rd Earl; was First Lord of Police in Scotland; *d* 1793, when the earldom, viscountcy and lordship of 1697 became extinct, and the lordship of 1690 became vested in the grandda of the 3rd Earl of Marchmont (4) ANNE, *de jure* Lady Polwarth (da of Sir John Paterson), 3rd Bt, who *m* Anne, el da of the 3rd Earl of Marchmont; she *d* 1822, before any decision regarding her claim to the Lordship had been reached; her aunt (5) DIANA (yst da of 3rd Earl of Marchmont), became *de jure* Lady Polwarth: *m* 1754, Walter Scott, MP, of Harden, co Roxburgh, Chieftain of the Scotts of Sinton, *d* 1827; her only son and heir (6) HUGH Scott, was MP for Berwick 1780-4; assumed the additional surname of Hepburne; in 1835 he claimed and was allowed the peerage becoming 6th Lord; *d* 1841; *s* by his son (7) HENRY FRANCIS, 7th Lord; was a Representative Peer, Lord-Lieut of Selkirkshire, and a Lord-in-Waiting to Queen Victoria; *d* 1867; *s* by his son (8) WALTER HUGH, 8th Lord, *b* 1838; Capt Roy Co of Archers (King's Body Guard for Scotland); Lord-Lieut of co Selkirk 1878-1919: *m* 1st, 1863, Lady Mary Hamilton-Gordon, who *d* 1914, da of 5th Earl of Aberdeen; 2ndly, 1915, Katherine Grisell, who *d* 1938, da of late Rev Hon John Baillie; *d* 1920; *s* by his el son (9) WALTER GEORGE, 9th Lord; *b* 1864: *m* 1888, Edith Frances, who *d* 1930, da of Sir Thomas Fowell Buxton, 3rd Bt; *d* 1944; *s* by his grandson (10) HENRY ALEXANDER (son of late Capt Hon Walter Thomas Hepburne-Scott), 10th Lord and present peer.

PONSONBY OF SHULBREDE, BARON (Ponsonby) (Baron UK 1930)

For the king, the law, and the people

FREDERICK MATTHEW THOMAS PONSONBY, 4th Baron; *b* 27 Oct 1958; *s* 1990; *ed* Holland Park Sch, Univ Coll, Cardiff, and Imperial Coll, London; a Cllr London Borough of Wandsworth since 1990.

Arms – Gules, a chevron between three combs argent. **Crest** – Out of a ducal coronet azure three arrows, points downwards, one in pale and two in saltire, entwined at the intersection by a snake proper.

SISTERS LIVING AND DECEASED

Hon Julia Mary, *b* 1960.
Hon Charlotte, *b* 1961; *d* 1979.
Hon Rachel Elizabeth Emma, *b* 1964.

AUNTS LIVING (*daughters of 2nd Baron*)

Hon Laura Mary, *b* 1935. *Residence* – 17 South End, Kensington Sq, W8.
Hon Rose Magdalen, *b* 1940: *m* 1966, Brian David Owen-Smith, MB, FRCP, DPhys Med, of 48 Westgate, Chichester, Sussex PO19 3EU, and has issue living, Timothy Clive Owen, *b* 1968, — Emma Elizabeth Jane, *b* 1971.
Hon Catherine Virgina, *b* 1944: *m* 1972, Ian Macdonald Affleck Russell, of Shulbrede Priory, Lynchmere, Haslemere, Surrey, and has issue living, Harriet Mary, *b* 1977, — Joanna Elizabeth, *b* 1979.

MOTHER LIVING

Ursula Mary, yr da of Cdr Thomas Stanley Lane Fox-Pitt, OBE, RN (ret) (*see* Lowther, Bt, *cr* 1824, 1964 Edn): *m* 1st, 1956 (*m diss* 1973), Hon Thomas Arthur Ponsonby (later 3rd Baron Ponsonby of Shulbrede), who *d* 1990; 2ndly, 1974, as his 2nd wife, John Ingham Brooke (*see* Hewett, Bt).

WIDOW LIVING OF THIRD BARON

MAUREEN ESTELLE (*Baroness Ponsonby of Shulbrede*), da of Alfred William Windsor, and formerly wife of Dr Paul Campbell-Tiech: *m* 1973, as his 2nd wife, the 3rd Baron, who *d* 1990.

PREDECESSORS – (1) ARTHUR AUGUSTUS WILLIAM HARRY Ponsonby, son of late Gen the Rt Hon Sir Henry Frederick Ponsonby, GCB, PC (E Bessborough, colls); *b* 1871; in Diplo Ser 1894-1903, Private Sec to Prime Min (Rt Hon Sir Henry Campbell-Bannerman GCB, MP) 1905-08, Under-Sec of State for Foreign Affirs Jan to Nov 1924, and leader of the Opposition in House of Lords Sept 1931 to Sept 1935; appointed Under-Sec of State for Dominion Affairs June 1929, Parliamentary Sec to Min of Transport Nov 1929, and Chancellor of Duchy of Lancaster March 1931 (resigned Aug 1931); sat as MP for Stirling Dist (*L*) May 1908 to Nov 1918, and for Sheffield, Brightside Div (*Lab*) Nov 1922 to Jan 1930; *cr* Baron Ponsonby of *Shulbrede*, of Shulbrede, Sussex (peerage of United Kingdom) 1930: *m* 1898, Dorothea, who *d* 1963, da of late Sir Charles Hubert Hastings Parry, 1st Bt (ext); *d* 1946; *s* by his only son (**2**) MATTHEW HENRY HUBERT, 2nd Baron; *b* 1904: *m* 1929, Hon Elizabeth Mary Bigham, who *d* 1985, da of 2nd Viscount Mersey; *d* 1976; *s* by his only surviving son (**3**) THOMAS ARTHUR, 3rd Baron, *b* 1930; a Councillor Royal Borough of Kensington 1956-65, an Alderman Royal Borough of Kensington and Chelsea 1964-74, an Alderman GLC 1970-77 (Chm of Council 1976-77), Opposition Chief Whip, House of Lords, 1982-90, a Gov of LSE 1970-90: *m* 1st, 1956 (*m diss* 1973), Ursula Mary, yr da of Cdr Thomas Stanley Lane Fox-Pitt, OBE, RN (*see* Lowther, Bt, *cr* 1824, 1964 Edn); 2ndly, 1973, Maureen Estelle, da of Alfred William Windsor, and formerly wife of Dr Paul Campbell-Teich; *d* 1990; *s* by his only son (**4**) FREDERICK MATTHEW THOMAS, 4th Baron and present peer.

Ponsonby of Sysonby, Baron; title of Earl of Bessborough on Roll of HL.

POOLE, BARON (Poole) (Baron UK 1958)

DAVID CHARLES POOLE, 2nd Baron; *b* 6 Jan 1945; *s* 1993; *ed* Gordonstoun, Ch Ch Oxford, and INSEAD Fontainebleau; Member Stock Exchange: *m* 1st, 1967 (*m diss* 19—), Fiona, da of John Donald, of 69 Rivermead Court, SW6; 2ndly, 1975, Philippa, da of late Mark Reeve, of Lower Brook House, King's Somborne, Hants, and has issue by 1st *m*.

Arms – Per saltire or, and barry undy argent and azure, in chief and in base a portcullis chained also azure. **Crest** – A lion's gamb erased or, enfiled by a crown composed of four trident heads set upon a rim azure. **Supporters** – On either side a crane proper about the neck a purse azure garnished gold.
Residence – 7 Farmer St, W8; *Clubs* – Buck's, Royal Yacht Squadron, Groucho's.

SON LIVING (By 1st marriage)

Hon OLIVER JOHN, *b* 30 May 1972; *ed* Eton, and St Anne's Coll, Oxford.

DAUGHTERS LIVING OF FIRST BARON (by 1st marriage)

Hon Caroline (*Hon Lady Lucas-Tooth*), *b* 1934: *m* 1955, Sir Hugh John Lucas-Tooth, 2nd Bt. *Residences* – 41 Lancaster Rd, W14 1QJ; Parsonage Farm, E Hagbourne, Didcot, Oxon.
Hon Alison Victoria, *b* 1936: *m* 1961, Dr Fitz Zankel, and has issue living, Michael Rudolph, *b* 1962, — Thomas Joseph, *b* 1964, — Olivia, *b* 1977. *Residence* – Staudgasse 75, Vienna.
Hon Sheila Marian, *b* 1940: *m* 1st, 1966 (*m diss* 19—), Anthony William Paul (Cob) Stenham; 2ndly, 1980, George Ian Kenneth Ireland. *Residence* – 74 Clancarty Rd, SW6.

WIDOW LIVING OF FIRST BARON

BARBARA ANN (*Dowager Baroness Poole*), only da of E. A. Taylor, of Kinsbourne Green, Harpenden, Herts: *m* 1966, as his 3rd wife, the 1st Baron, CBE, TD, PC, who *d* 1993. *Residence* – 24 Campden Hill Gate, Duchess of Bedford Walk, W8 7QH.

PREDECESSOR – (**1**) *Rt Hon* OLIVER BRIAN SANDERSON Poole, CBE, TD, son of late Donald Louis Poole, of Lloyd's; *b* 1911; an Underwriting Member of Lloyd's, Chm Lazard Bros & Co, Dir S. Pearson & Sons, etc; Joint Hon Treas Conservative Party 1952-55, Chm 1955-57, Dep Chm 1957-59, Joint Chm May-Oct 1963, and Vice-Chm 1963-64; commn'd Life Guards 1932, Warwickshire Yeo 1933-45, Lt-Col (Hon Col) TA, served 1939-45 War (despatches thrice, American Legion of Merit, etc); MP Oswestry Div of Shropshire (*C*) July 1945-Feb 1950; MBE (Mil) and OBE (Mil) 1943, CBE (Mil) 1945, *cr* Baron Poole, of Aldgate, City of London (peerage of United Kingdom) 1958, and PC 1963: *m* 1st, 1933 (*m diss* 1951), Betty Margaret, who *d* 1988, yr da of late Capt Dugald Stewart Gilkison, Cameronians (Scottish Rifles) (*see* B Vernon, colls, 1969 Edn); 2ndly, 1952 (*m diss* 1965), Mrs Daphne Wilma Kenyon Heber-Percy, da of late Eustace Bowles (*see* E Macclesfield, colls); 3rdly, 1966, Barbara Ann, only da of E. A. Taylor, of Kinsbourne Green, Harpenden, Herts; *d* 1993; *s* by his only son (**2**) DAVID CHARLES, 2nd Baron and present peer.

POPPLEWELL, BARONY OF (Popplewell) (Extinct 1977)

SON LIVING OF LIFE BARON

(*Hon*) John Arnold, *b* 1928: *m* 1951.

WIDOW LIVING OF LIFE BARON

LAVINIA (*Baroness Popplewell*), OBE, da of Samuel Rainbow, of Sherburn-in-Elmet: *m* 1922, Baron Popplewell (Life Baron), who *d* 1977.

Porchester, Lord; son of Earl of Carnarvon.

PORRITT, BARONY OF (Porritt) (Extinct 1994)

For widow, sons and daughter of Life Baron, *see* Porritt, Bt.

PORTAL OF HUNGERFORD, VISCOUNTCY OF (Portal) (Extinct 1990)

WIDOW LIVING OF FIRST VISCOUNT

JOAN MARGARET (*Viscountess Portal of Hungerford*) (West Ashling House, nr Chichester), da of Sir Charles Glynne Earle Welby, CB, 5th Bt: *m* 1919, the 1st Viscount, who *d* 1971, when the Viscountcy became ext.

PORTARLINGTON, EARL OF (Dawson-Damer) (Earl I 1785)

Virtue is the way of life

GEORGE LIONEL YUILL SEYMOUR DAWSON-DAMER, 7th Earl; *b* 10 Aug 1938; *s* 1959; *ed* Eton; a patron of two livings; a Page of Honour to HM 1953-55; a Dir G. S. Yuill & Co Pty Ltd, of Sydney, Austn Stock Breeders Co Ltd, Brisbane, and other Cos: *m* 1961, Davina, el da of late Sir Edward Henry Windley, KCMG, KCVO (V Brookeborough, colls), and has issue.

Arms – Azure, a chevron ermine, between three arrows points downwards, or, barbed and flighted proper; on a chief argent three martlets sable, and on a canton gules a mullet or. **Crest** – A cat's head erased at the neck, and affrontée, or a tabby colour, holding in the mouth a rat sable. **Supporters** – Two heraldic tigers proper.
Residence – 19 Coolong Rd, Vaucluse, NSW, 2030.

SONS LIVING

CHARLES GEORGE YUILL SEYMOUR (*Viscount Carlow*), *b* 6 Oct 1965; Page of Honour to HM the Queen 1979-81; *ed* Eton. *Address* – c/o John Swire & Sons (HK) Ltd, GPO Box 1, Hong Kong.
Hon Edward Lionel Seymour, MVO, *b* 1967; Capt; Equerry to HM Queen Elizabeth the Queen Mother 1992-94; MVO 1994.
Hon Henry Lionel Seymour, *b* 1971.

DAUGHTER LIVING

Lady Marina Davina, *b* 1969. *Residence* – 76 Burton Court, Franklins Row, SW3.

BROTHER LIVING

Hon Lionel John Charles Seymour (1 Rose Bay Av, Bellevue Hill, NSW 2023), *b* 1940; *ed* Eton: *m* 1st, 1965 (*m diss* 1975), Rosemary Ashley Morrett, da of P. G. M. Hancock, of Trenowth, Grampound Rd, Truro; 2ndly, 1982, Ashley, da of W/Cdr W. Mann, of W Australia.

PREDECESSORS – (1) WILLIAM HENRY Dawson, MP for Portarlington and for Queen's Co; *cr Baron Dawson*, of Dawsons' Court, Queen's co (peerage of Ireland) 1770, and *Viscount Carlow* (peerage of Ireland) 1776; *d* 1779; *s* by his son (2) JOHN, 2nd Viscount; *cr Earl of Portarlington* (peerage of Ireland) 1785; sat as MP for Portarlington; *d* 1798; *s* by his son (3) JOHN, 2nd Earl; was Col 23rd Dragoons; present at numerous battles in the Peninsula, and Waterloo; in 1808 *s* to the estates of George Damer, 2nd and last Earl of Dorchester; *d* unmarried 1845; *s* by his nephew (4) HENRY JOHN REUBEN, KP, 3rd Earl, son of Capt Hon Henry Dawson (who assumed by sign manual the additional surname of Damer), by Eliza, da of Capt Edmund Joshua Moriarty, RN, and grandda of 1st Earl of Carhampton, *b* 1822; was a Representative Peer: *m* 1847, Lady Alexandrina Octavia Maria Vane, who *d* 1874, da of 3rd Marquess of Londonderry: *d* 1889; *s* by his cousin (5) LIONEL SEYMOUR WILLIAM (son of late Col Rt Hon George Lionel Dawson-Damer, 3rd son of 1st Earl), 4th Earl, *b* 1832; MP for Portarlington (C) 1857-65: *m* 1855, Hon Harriet Lydia Montagu, da of 6th Baron Rokeby (*ext*); *d* 1892; *s* by his el son (6) GEORGE LIONEL HENRY SEYMOUR, 5th Earl; *b* 1858: *m* 1881, Emma Andalusia Frere, who *d* 1929, da of late Lord Nigel Kennedy; *d* 1900; *s* by his son (6) LIONEL ARTHUR HENRY SEYMOUR, 6th Earl; *b* 1883; formerly Lt Irish Gds: *m* 1907, Winnafreda, only child of late George Skelton Yuill, of, 37 Chesham Place, SW; *d* 1959; *s* by his grandson (7) GEORGE LIONEL YUILL SEYMOUR (el son of late Air Commodore George Lionel Seymour, Viscount Carlow, only son of 6th Earl), 7th Earl and present peer; also Viscount Carlow, and Baron Dawson.

PORTER OF LUDDENHAM, BARON (Porter) (Life Baron 1990)

GEORGE PORTER, OM, FRS, son of late John Smith Porter; *b* 6 Dec 1920; *ed* Thorne Gram Sch, Leeds Univ (BSc), and Emmanuel Coll, Camb (MA, PhD, ScD); RNVR Radar Officer 1941-45; Demonstrator in Physical Chemistry, Camb Univ, 1949-52, Assist Dir of Research in Physical Chemistry, Camb Univ, and Fellow Emmanuel Coll 1952-54; Assist Dir British Rayon Research Assocn 1954-55; Prof of Physical Chemistry, Firth Prof and Head of Dept of Chemistry, Sheffield Univ, 1955-66; Dir The Royal Institution

1966-86, Pres The Royal Society 1985-90; Research Prof Imperial Coll since 1987; Chm Centre for Molecular Sciences since 1990, and Chancellor Leicester Univ since 1986; Hon Doctorates Oxford (DSc), Cambridge (LLD) and 30 other Univs in UK and abroad; Nobel Prize (joint) for Chemistry 1967, Faraday Medal (Royal Soc of Chemistry) 1981, Davy Medal 1971, Rumford Medal 1978 and Copley Medal 1990 (Royal Society); author and contributor to learned journals; *cr* Knt 1972, OM 1989, and *Baron Porter of Luddenham*, of Luddenham, co Kent (Life Baron) 1990: *m* 1949, Stella Jean, da of late Col George Arthur Brooke, of Leeds, Maidstone, Kent, and has issue.
Residences – The Old Rectory, Luddenham, Faversham, Kent ME13 0TE; 53 Prince's Gdns, Exhibition Rd, SW7. *Club* – Athenaeum.

SONS LIVING

Hon John Brooke, *b* 1952; *ed* Oundle, Emmanuel Coll, Camb (BChir 1977, MB 1978), and Univ Coll Hosp, London; MRCP (UK) 1980, MRCPath 1988: *m* 1989, Suzanne Margaret, da of late David William Church, of Beaconsfield, Bucks, and has issue living, William John, *b* 1991. *Residence* – 18 St Paul's Place, Islington, N1 2QF.
Hon Andrew Christopher George, *b* 1955; *ed* Oundle, Westminster, Bristol Univ and Linacre Coll, Oxford (PhD). *Residence* – 24 Stanley Rd, Oxford OX4 1QZ.

PORTLAND, EARL OF (Bentinck) (Earl GB 1689)

HENRY NOEL BENTINCK, 11th Earl; *b* 2 Oct 1919; *s* 1990; *ed* Harrow; a Mediatised Count of the Holy Roman Empire; formerly Lieut Coldstream Guards; 1939-45 War (twice wounded): *m* 1st, 1940, Pauline, who *d* 1967, da of late Frederick William Mellowes, of Penn House, Reynolds Close, Hampstead, NW; 2ndly, 1974, Jenifer, only da of late Reginald Hopkins, of 91 Kingsley Way, N2, and has issue by 1st *m*.

Arms – Azure, a cross-moline argent. **Crest** – Two arms counter-embowed, vested gules, on the hand gloves, or, each holding an ostrich feather argent. **Supporters** – Two lions double queued, the *dexter* or; the *sinister* sable.

SON LIVING (By 1st marriage)

TIMOTHY CHARLES ROBERT NOEL (*Viscount Woodstock*) (3 Stock Orchard Crescent, Islington, N7 9SL), *b* 1 June 1953; *ed* Harrow, and E Anglia Univ (BA); a Mediatised Count of the Holy Roman Empire; actor: *m* 1979, Judith Ann, da of John Robert Emerson, of 70 Queen St, Cheadle, Staffs, and has issue:—

SONS LIVING- *Hon* William Jack Henry, *b* 19 May 1984, — *Hon* Jasper James Mellowes, *b* 1988.

DAUGHTERS LIVING (By 1st marriage)

Lady Sorrel Deirdre BENTINCK, *b* 1942; resumed her maiden name 1990: *m* 1972 (*m diss* 1988), Sir John Philip Lister Lister-Kaye, 8th Bt, and has issue. *Residence* – 18 Rankeillor St, Edinburgh EH8 9SL.
Lady Anna Cecilia BENTINCK, *b* 1947; has resumed her maiden name: *m* 1st, 1965 (*m diss* 1974), Jasper Hamilton Holmes; 2ndly, 1975 (*m diss* 1977), Nicholas George Spafford Vester; has issue living (by Arnold George Francis Cragg, son of Rt Rev Kenneth Cragg, of Ascott-under-Wychwood, Oxon), Gulliver Jack Bentinck CRAGG, *b* 1978. — George Finn Gareth Bentinck CRAGG, *b* 1980, — Charlotte-Sophie Camden Bentinck CRAGG, *b* 1988. *Residence* – 64 Croftdown Rd, NW5 1EN.

SISTER LIVING

Countess Brydgytte Blanche (Rykstraatweg, 242 Haren, Groningen, Holland), *b* 1916: *m* 1937, Jonkheer Adriaan Hendrik Sibble Van der Wyck, who *d* 1973, Capt Royal Netherlands Horse Artillery (Res), and Attorney to the Queen of the Netherlands, and has issue living, *Jonkheer* Evert Rein Robert Henry, *b* 1945, — *Jonkheer* Douglas Roderick Arthur Duncan, *b* 1955, — Caroline Norah Frédérique Adrienne, *b* 1938: *m* 1961, K. J. A. Baron Collot d'Escury, Estate Agent of Crown Property, Zeeland, and has issue living, Guyon Adolf André *b* 1962, Robert Willem Frederick *b* 1970, Juliette Brydgytte Blanche *b* 1963, Marina Caroline Norah *b* 1965, — Brydgytte Agnes Dawn (Boerenstreek 1, Gaast, Friesland, Holland), *b* 1940: *m* 1968 (*m diss* 1990), Paul Heinz Maria Dirk Vermeer, and has issue living, Robert Paul Adriaan Henry Simon *b* 1968, Fiona Victoria Regina Brydgytte *b* 1970, Nadia Norah Noel *b* 1971, — Reina Jeanne Woltera, *b* 1942; a nurse: *m* 1973, H. W. van Harrenveld, Judge of the Courts of Justice at Zutphen, of De Buitenhof, Brummen, Geldersland, and has issue living, Hugo Johannes Hendrik *b* 1974, Diederik Godard Adriaan Roelant *b* 1980, Wendela Blanche Catherine *b* 1977.

DAUGHTER LIVING OF NINTH DUKE OF PORTLAND (*by 1st marriage*)

Lady Mary Jane, *b* 1929: *m* 1st, 1963 (*m diss* 1978), Alexander Constantine Georgiades, of Pilton, Oundle, Northants; 2ndly, 1978, Prof Stephen Richards Graubard, and has issue living (by 1st *m*), William James, *b* 1967, — David Constantine, *b* 1969. *Residence* – 8 Maple Av, Cambridge, Mass 02139, USA.

DAUGHTER LIVING OF SEVENTH DUKE OF PORTLAND

Lady Alexandra Margaret Anne CAVENDISH-BENTINCK, *b* 1916; CStJ. *Seats* – Welbeck Abbey, Worksop, Notts; Welbeck Woodhouse, Worksop, Notts; Langwell, Berriedale, Caithness; Bothal Castle, Northumberland.

WIDOW LIVING OF EIGHTH DUKE OF PORTLAND

GWYNETH ETHEL (*Gwyneth, Duchess of Portland*), MBE, da of late John Wesley Edward, of Chettlewood Estate, and Montpellier, Jamaica, BWI, and widow of Col David Alexander John Bowie, MC, RA: *m* 1950, as his 2nd wife, the 8th Duke, KBE, CMG, MC, who *d* 1980. *Address* – Muthaiga, PO Box 47311, Nairobi, Kenya.

WIDOW LIVING OF NINTH DUKE OF PORTLAND

KATHLEEN ELSIE (*Duchess of Portland*), da of Arthur Barry, of Montreal, and formerly wife of Arthur Richie Tillotson: *m* 1948, as his 2nd wife, the 9th Duke, CMG, who *d* 1990. *Residence* – 21 Carlyle Sq, SW3.

COLLATERAL BRANCHES LIVING

Granddaughters of late William Charles Philip Otto Aldenburgh-Bentinck, 6th Count Bentinck (great great grandson of Hon William Bentinck, yr son of 1st Earl), Count of the Holy Roman Empire, who received 1886 a Royal Licence to bear in England the title of Count of the Holy Roman Empire, with permission for all other descendants, both male and female, of his father to bear the title of Count or Countess before their christian names:—

Issue of late William Frederick Charles Henry Aldenburg-Bentinck, 7th Count Bentinck; *b* 1880, *d* 1959: *m* 1923, Adrienne (LABOUCHERE), da of late Philip Ernst Vegelin van Claerbergen, of The Hague:—

Countess Sophie Mechtild Marie, *b* 1924: *m* 1950, Count Enrico Gaetani dell'Aquila d'Aragona, and has issue living, *Donna* Benedetta Rita Maria, *b* 1953, — *Donna* Jacobella Immacolata Scolastica, *b* 1956, — *Donna* Giovannella Maria, *b* 1961. *Residence* – 43 Pizzofalcone, Naples, Italy. —— *Countess* Isabelle Adrienne, *b* 1925: *m* 1951, Count Aurel Ladislaus Franz Heinrich Ernst zu Ortenburg, and has issue living, *Count* Franz Wilhelm Friedrich Ladislaus, *b* 1953, — *Count* Philipp Wilhelm, *b* 1955, — *Countess* Nadine Marie Elisabeth Johanna, *b* 1957: *m* 1981, Count Albrecht von Brandenstein-Zeppelin. *Residences* – 8601 Schloss Birkenfeld, Germany; Kasteel Middachten, De Steeg, Holland.

Granddaughter of late Count Godard John George Charles Aldenburg-Bentinck, yst son of Lt-Gen Charles Anthony Ferdinand Aldenburg Bentinck, 4th Count Bentinck:—

Godard Adrian Henry Jules (9th Count Bentinck, and Baron Aldenburg), *b* 1887, *d* 1968: *m* 1st, 1921, Jacoba, who *d* 1949, da of late Jacobus Johannes van den Heuvel; 2ndly, 1961, Alida (22 Saxen Weimarlaan, Amsterdam, Holland), da of late Frits Vlieger:—

(By 1st *m*) *Countess* Louise Andrienne Jacoba, *b* 1923: *m* 1954, George Léon Alex de Brauwere dit de Steelant, who *d* 1992, and has issue living, Alain George Francois (25 Kazernestraat, The Hague), *b* 1961; attorney (Bar of Supreme Court of Netherlands): *m* 1994, Gemma Anna Maria Wilhelmina Bakx, — Jemima Sophie Adrienne, *b* 1958: architect: *m* 1980, Ir G. R. Scherpbier, of Delft. *Residence* – Zuylestein, Leersum, Utrecht, Holland.

PREDECESSORS – **(1)** HANS WILLIAM Bentinck, KG, PC (whose el brother Eusebius Borchard was Baron Bentinck of Diepenheim and Schoonheten in the Netherlands), having first served William, Prince of Orange, as a Page of Honour, eventually became his confidential adviser, and after that Prince's accession to the British throne, was appointed Groom of the Stole and First Gentleman of the Bedchamber; commanded a Dutch Regt of Horse Guards, and as a Lieut-Gen took a distinguished part at the battle of the Boyne 1690; *cr Baron Cirencester, Viscount Woodstock*, and *Earl of Portland* (peerage of Great Britain) 1689; *d* 1709; *s* by his son **(2)** HENRY, 2nd Earl; was Gov and Capt Gen of Jamaica, and sometime MP for Southampton; *cr Marquess of Titchfield* and *Duke of Portland* (peerage of Great Britain) 1716: *m* 1704, Elizabeth da of the 2nd Earl of Gainsborough (*cr* 1682); *d* 1726; *s* by his son **(3)** WILLIAM HENRY, 2nd Duke; *d* 1762; *s* by his son **(4)** WILLIAM HENRY CAVENDISH, KG, 3rd Duke; was MP for Weobley 1761-2, Viceroy of Ireland 1782, First Lord of the Treasury 1783 and 1807, Sec of State for Home Depart 1794, Pres of the Council 1801, Chancellor of Oxford Univ, High Steward of Bristol, and Lord Lieut of Notts; assumed the additional surname of Cavendish by Roy licence 1801; *d* 1809; *s* by his son **(5)** WILLIAM HENRY, PC, DCL, FRS, 4th Duke; was Lord-Lieut of Middlesex; assumed by Roy licence in 1795 the additional surname of Scott; *d* 1854; *s* by his son **(6)** WILLIAM JOHN Cavendish-Bentinck-Scott, 5th Duke, *b* 1800; sat as MP for Lynn 1824-6; *d* 1879; *s* by his kinsman **(7)** WILLIAM JOHN ARTHUR CHARLES JAMES, KG, GCVO, TD, PC (el son of late Lieut-Gen Arthur Cavendish-Bentinck, 2nd son of Lord William Charles Augustus Cavendish-Bentinck, 3rd son of 3rd Duke), 6th Duke; *b* 1857; Hon Col 4th and 7th Batns Sherwood Foresters; sometime Lord-Lieut of Notts; Master of the Horse 1886-92 and 1895-1905, and Chancellor of Order of the Garter 1937-43; received Roy Victorian Chain 1953; *m* 1889, *Dame* Winifred, DBE, who *d* 1954, only da of late Thomas Yorke Dallas-Yorke, of Walmsgate, Louth; *d* 1943; *s* by his el son **(8)** WILLIAM ARTHUR HENRY, KG, 7th Duke; *b* 1893; Junior Lord of the Treasury 1927-29, and 1932; MP for Newark Div of Notts (U) 1922-43; Chancellor of Nottingham Univ 1927-29; Lt-Col Cmdg Notts Yeo (Sherwood Rangers) 1933-36; Lord Lieut of Notts 1939-62: *m* 1915, Hon Ivy Gordon-Lennox, DBE (Maid of Honour to Queen Alexandra 1912-15), who *d* 1982, da of Lord Algernon Charles Gordon-Lennox (D Richmond); *d* 1977; *s* by his kinsman **(9)** FERDINAND WILLIAM, KBE, CMG, MCel son of (William George) Frederick Cavendish-Bentinck, grandson of Maj-Gen Lord Frederick Cavendish-Bentinck, CB, MP (4th son of 3rd Duke), 8th Duke, *b* 1888; Private Sec to Gov of Uganda 1925-27; Member for Agric and Natural Resources in Kenya; Speaker of Kenya Legislative Council: *m* 1st, 1912 (*m diss* 1950), Wentworth Frances, who *d* 1964, da of late William James Hope-Johnston (E Annandale and Hartfell, colls); 2ndly, 1950, Gwyneth Ethel, MBE, da of late John Wesley Edward, of Chettlewood Estate, and Montpellier, Jamaica, BWI and widow of Col David Alexander John Bowie, MC, RA; *d* 1980; *s* by his brother **(10)** VICTOR FREDERICK WILLIAM, CMG, 9th Duke, *b* 1897; Chm Joint Intelligence Sub Cttee on Chs of Staff 1939-45, Foreign Office Advisor to Dir of Plans 1942-45, and Ambassador to Poland 1945-47: *m* 1st, 1924 (*m diss* 1948), Clothilde Bruce, who *d* 1984, da of late James Bruce Quigley, of Dallas, Texas; 2ndly, 1948, Kathleen Elsie, da of Arthur Barry, of Montreal, and formerly wife of Arthur Richie Tillotson; *d* 1990, when the Dukedom became extinct and the Earldom passed to his kinsman **(11)** HENRY NOEL, 11th Earl and present peer; also Viscount Woodstock and Baron Cirencester.

◆ The 1st Earl of Portland had issue a 2nd son, Hon William Bentinck, who was *cr* a Count of the Holy Roman Empire by Charles VI of Austria 1732, for himself and his descendants. In 1845 by decree of the German Diet, the Counts Bentinck obtained recognition of their right to the dignities and privileges of the Mediatised Houses (Reichsunmittelbar) of Germany with the style of *Erlaucht*. His great great grandson, Lt-Col Count Henry Charles Adolphus Frederick William Aldenburg-Bentinck, 5th Count Bentinck, resigned his rights as head of the family 1874 to his yr brother, William Charles Philip Otho Aldenburg-Bentinck. The 5th Count *d* 1903, leaving issue, Count Robert Charles Bentinck, *b* 1875: *m* 1915, Lady Norah Ida Emily Noel, who *d* 1939, da of 3rd Earl of Gainsborough, and *d* 1932, leaving issue an only son, *Count* Henry Noel Bentinck, who *s* 1990 his kinsman as 11th Earl of Portland (ante).

PORTMAN, VISCOUNT (Portman) (Viscount UK 1873)

EDWARD HENRY BERKELEY PORTMAN, 9th Viscount; *b* 22 April 1934; *s* 1967; *ed* Canford, and Roy Agric Coll, Cirencester: *m* 1st, 1956 (*m diss* 1966), Rosemary Joy, el da of Charles Farris, of Coombe Bissett, Wilts; 2ndly, 1966, Penelope Anne Hassard, yr da of Trevor Allin, of N Moreton, Berks, and has had issue by 1st and 2nd marriages.

Arms – Quarterly: 1st and 4th or, a fleur-de-lis azure, *Portman*; 2nd and 3rd gules, a chevron ermine, between ten crosses patée argent, six in chief and four in base, *Berkeley.* **Crests** – 1st, a talbot sejeant or; 2nd, a unicorn passant gules, armed and crined or. **Supporters** – *Dexter*, a savage, wreathed about the head and waist with ivy, in his dexter hand a club resting on the shoulder, proper; *sinister*, a talbot or.
Residence – Clock Mill, Clifford, Hereford HR3 5HB. *Clubs* – White's, British Racing Drivers.

SONS LIVING AND DECEASED (*By 1st marriage*)

Hon CHRISTOPHER EDWARD BERKELEY, *b* 30 July 1958: *m* 1st, 1983, Caroline, da of Terence Ivan Steenson, of Caversham, Berks; 2ndly, 1987, Patricia Martins, elder da of Bernardino Pim, of Rio de Janeiro, Brazil, and has issue living (by 1st *m*), Luke Oliver Berkeley, *b* 31 Aug 1984, — (by 2nd *m*) Matthew Bernardo Berkeley, *b* 1990.

(*By 2nd marriage*)

Hon Alexander Michael Berkeley, *b* 1967: *m* 1992, Emma Esma, da of Christopher Morgan, of Ste Saturnin-les-Apt, Vaucluse, France.
Hon Justin Trevor Berkeley, *b* 1969.
Hon Piers Richard Berkeley, *b* 1971.
Hon Matthew Gerald Berkeley, *b* 1973; *d* as the result of a motorcycle accident 1990.

DAUGHTER LIVING (*By 1st marriage*)

Hon Claire Elizabeth, *b* 1959: *m* 1983, (Anthony) Henry Robinson (*see* B Heytesbury, 1990 Edn), and has issue living, Anthony, *b* 1984, — James, *b* 1985, — Patrick, *b* 1987.

HALF-SISTER LIVING

Suna (Synöve Isobel) PORTMAN (Portman Lodge, Durweston, Blandford, Dorset DT11 0QA), *b* 1939; has reverted to her maiden name: *m* 1st, 1968 (*m diss* 1970), Martin George Anthony Wilkinson; 2ndly, 1970 (*m diss* 1981), Simon Thomas Paul Boyle, and has issue living (by 1st *m*), Heron Berkeley, *b* 1968, — (by 2nd *m*) Kestrel Berkeley, *b* 1970, — Storm Simon, *b* 1979.

DAUGHTERS LIVING OF FIFTH VISCOUNT

Hon Sheila Constance (*Viscountess Knutsford*), *b* 1927: *m* 1951, 6th Viscount Knutsford. *Residence* – Broadclyst House, Exeter.
Hon Rosemary, *b* 1931: *m* 1951, Derrick Allix Pease (*see* Pease, Bt, cr 1920). *Residence* – 2 Britten St, SW3; Upper Woodcott, Whitchurch, Hants.

WIDOW LIVING OF EIGHTH VISCOUNT

NANCY MAUREEN (*Nancy, Viscountess Portman*), (Sutton Waldron House, Blandford, Dorset), da of Capt Percy Herbert Franklin, RN (ret): *m* 1946, as his 2nd wife, the 8th Viscount, who *d* 1967.

COLLATERAL BRANCHES LIVING

Grandson of late Berkeley Portman, el son of late Hon Maurice Berkeley Portman (infra):—
　　Issue of late Com Maurice Percy Berkeley Portman, RN, *b* 1884, *d* 1928: *m* 1918, Joan Wycliffe, who *d* 1971, da of late Maj-Gen Charles William Thompson, CB, DSO:—
Berkeley Charles Berkeley, *b* 1919; *ed* Wellington Coll; late Lt RN: *m* 1944, Sheila Margaret Penelope, da of late Capt F. D. Mowat, RN, and has issue living, Rodney John Berkeley (3 Harley Gdns, SW10) *b* 1947; *ed* Wellington Coll, and Trin Coll, Camb: *m* 1976 (*m diss* 1992), Angela, only da of Maj John Cartwright Pringle, MC, of Pyt House, Tisbury, Wilts, and has issue living, Guy Seymour Berkeley *b* 1977; *ed* Stowe, John Berkeley *b* 1982, Olivia Joan *b* 1979. — Celia Rose Berkeley, *b* 1946: *m* 1972, Anthony William Charlton Edwards, of Salterton House, nr Salisbury, Wilts, and has issue living, Berkeley Humfrey Charlton *b* 1978, Marcella Louise Charlton *b* 1973, Imogen Patricia Charlton *b* 1975, Hermione Celia Charlton *b* 1982, — Lucy Joan Berkeley, *b* 1953: *m* 1983, Ian Parsons, of Newmains, Stenton, Dunbar, E Lothian EH42 1TQ, eldest son of Edward Victor Parsons, of Harlow, Essex, and has issue living, Hugh Stanley *b* 1988, Jessie Catherine *b* 1986, Elspeth Caroline *b* 1990, — Edwina Penelope Berkeley, *b* 1956: *m* 1986, Timothy J. Hicks, yst son of William Hicks, of Church Farm, Leckhampton, Glos, and has issue living, James *b* 1988, Frederick *b* 1991, Camilla *b* 1986, Chloë *b* 1989, — Rachel Mary Berkeley, *b* 1961. *Residence* – Danley Hill, Lynchmere, nr Haslemere, Surrey. *Clubs* – Army and Navy, Royal and Ancient.

Grandchildren of late Com Maurice William Portman, 2nd son of late Hon Maurice Berkeley Portman (infra):—
　　Issue of late Brigadier Guy Maurice Berkeley Portman, CB, TD, *b* 1890, *d* 1961; *m* 1922, Miriam Katharine, who *d* 1975, da of George William Taylor (*see* E Wilton, 1953 Edn):—
Anthony Seymour Berkeley, *b* 1928; *ed* Eton; late Lieut Dorset Regt; High Sheriff Hants 1992: *m* 1961, Penelope Helen Kathleen, da of Derrick Warner Candy, of Kingston Warren, Wantage, Oxon, and has issue living, Michael Henry Berkeley, *b* 1962: *m* 1992, Alison G. S., only da of R. A. Bench, of Minchinhampton, Glos, — Jonathan Guy Berkeley, *b* 1965. *Residence* – Rushmore Farm, Upton, Andover, Hants. *Club* – Boodle's. —— Lusia Edwina, *b* 1931: *m* 1952, Christopher David Howard, who *d* 1991, of Ryton Corner, Ryton, Shrewsbury, and has issue living, Davinia Elizabeth, *b* 1953: *m* 1981, James William Vernon, elder son of Sir Nigel John Douglas Vernon, 4th Bt and has issue (*see* Vernon, Bt), — Belinda Jane, *b* 1956: *m* 1981, Timothy Michael Evans, elder son of Geoffrey Evans, of Stanyeld, Church Stretton, Shropshire, and has issue living, Alice Valerie Katherine *b* 1983, Camilla Rose Lusia *b* 1986, Florence Diana Elizabeth *b* 1991.

Granddaughter of late Hon Maurice Berkeley Portman, 3rd son of 1st Viscount:—
Issue of late Cecil Berkeley Portman, *b* 1869, *d* 1915: *m* 1902, Florence Wyndham, who *d* 1967, da of late Maj Lachlan Forbes:—

Marigold Florence Lavinia, *b* 1903: *m* 1929, Raymond Patterson, who *d* 1984, and has issue living, Alan Noel (c/o 2685 Queenswood Drive, Victoria, BC, Canada), *b* 1936: *m* 1965 (*m diss* 1975), Mary Elizabeth Ann, da of Jeffrey Boys, of Vancouver, and has issue living, Jeremy Patrick *b* 1967, Samantha Jeanne *b* 1969, Jennifer Anne *b* 1970, — Robert George (745 Greenlea Drive, Victoria, BC), *b* 1944: *m* 1974, Susan Veronica Mary, da of Henry Martyn, of Falmouth, Cornwall, and has issue living, Mark Richard Murray *b* 1978, Claire Elizabeth Olive *b* 1980, — Janet Murray, *b* 1930: *m* 1949, David Blanchet, who *d* 1981, of 1230 Gladwin Drive, North Vancouver, British Columbia, and has issue living, Julia Claire Janet *b* 1949. *Address* – 2685 Queenswood Drive, Victoria, British Columbia.

Grandson of late Montagu Berkeley Portman, yst son of late Hon Maurice Berkeley Portman (ante):—
Issue of late Lieut-Col Gerald Berkeley Portman, RA, *b* 1903, *d* 1954: *m* 1st, 1928 (*m diss* 1945), Joan, da of late Col G. Turner; 2ndly, 1945 (*m diss* 1950), Cicely Falkener, da of Godfrey Oliver, of Port Hill, Northam, Devon; 3rdly 1950, Mai Elisabeth, who *d* 1979, da of Samuel Wohlin, of Lidingo, Brevik, Sweden:—

(By 2nd *m*) Michael Berkeley (Port Hill, Northam, Devon; *Clubs* – Cavalry and Guards', MCC), *b* 1947; *ed* Wellington Coll, and RMA; Lt-Col Light Dragoons: *m* 1979, Penelope Jane, elder da of Brig Harry Wilkinson Bishop, FRCVS, of Holm Wykeham, W Malvern, Worcs, and has issue living, Edward Berkeley, *b* 1983, — Lucy Serena, *b* 1985.

PREDECESSORS – (1) EDWARD BERKELEY Portman, son of Edward Berkeley Portman, of Bryanston; *b* 1799; sat as MP for Dorsetshire (*L*) 1823-32, and for Marylebone 1833; was *cr Baron Portman*, of Orchard Portman, co Somerset, 1837, and *Viscount Portman* (peerage of United Kingdom) 1873: *m* 1827, Lady Emma Lascelles, who *d* 1865, da of 2nd Earl of Harewood; *d* 1888; *s* by his el son (2) WILLIAM HENRY BERKELEY, GCVO, 2nd Viscount, *b* 1829; MP for Shaftesbury 1852-7, and Dorsetshire (*L*) 1857-85: *m* 1st, 1855, Hon Mary Selina Charlotte Wentworth-Fitzwilliam, who *d* 1899, da of late Viscount Milton, son of 5th Earl Fitzwilliam; 2ndly, 1908, Frances Maxwell, who *d* 1939, da of late Boyd Alexander Cuninghame, RN, of Craigends, co Renfrew, and widow of Andrew James J. Livingstone Learmonth; *d* 1919; *s* by his el son (3) HENRY BERKELEY, 3rd Viscount, *b* 1860: *m* 1901, Emma Andalusia Frere, who *d* 1929, da of late Lord Nigel Kennedy, and widow of the 4th Earl of Portarlington; *d* 1923; *s* by his brother (4) CLAUD BERKELEY, 4th Viscount, *b* 1864: *m* 1st, 1888 (*m diss* 1897), Mary Ada, who *d* 1900, da of late Major Francis Hastings Toone Gordon Cumming (Gordon Cumming, Bt, colls); 2ndly, 1898, Harriette Mary, who *d* 1939, da of late William Stevenson; *d* 1929; *s* by his son (5) EDWARD CLAUD BERKELEY, 5th Viscount, *b* 1898; Capt Life Guards: *m* 1926, Hon Sybil Mary Douglas-Pennant, who *d* 1975, da of 3rd Baron Penrhyn; *d* 1942; *s* by his uncle (6) SEYMOUR BERKELEY (5th son of 2nd Viscount), 6th Viscount; *b* 1868; *d* 1946; *s* by his brother (7) GERALD BERKELEY, 7th Viscount, *b* 1875: *m* 1902, Dorothy Marie Isolde, who *d* 1964, da of Sir Robert Sheffield, 5th Bt: *d* 1948: *s* by his el son (8) GERALD WILLIAM BERKELEY, 8th Viscount, *b* 1903: *m* 1st, 1926 (*m diss* 1946), Marjorie Josephine Wernham Bentley, who *d* 1981, da of George Bentley Gerrard, of Montreal; 2ndly, 1946, Nancy Maureen, da of Capt Percy Herbert Franklin, RN (ret); *d* 1967; *s* by hs nephew (9) EDWARD HENRY BERKELEY (el son of late Hon Michael Berkeley Portman, yr son of 7th Viscount), 9th Viscount and present peer; also Baron Portman.

PORTSMOUTH, EARL OF (Wallop) (Earl GB 1743)

QUENTIN GERARD CAREW WALLOP, 10th Earl; *b* 25 July 1954; *s* (Oct) 1984; *ed* Eton, and Millfield; Hereditary Bailiff of Burley, New Forest; Pres Basingstoke Conservative Assocn since 1992; Dir Grainger Trust plc: *m* 1st, 1981 (*m diss* 1985), Candia Frances Juliet, writer, da of late Colin Edgar McWilliam, of Edinburgh; 2ndly, 1990, Annabel, eldest da of Dr Ian Fergusson, of Tudor Place, Richmond Green, Surrey, and has issue by 1st and 2nd *m*.

Arms – Argent, a bend wavy sable. **Crest** – A mermaid holding in the dexter hand a mirror, in the other a comb, all proper. **Supporters** – Two chamois or wild goats sable. (These arms were resumed (and Royal Licence applied for in 1993) by the 5th Earl, together with the family surname of Wallop).
Seat – Farleigh House, Farleigh Wallop, Basingstoke, Hants RG25 2HT.
Clubs – Buck's, International Assocn of Cape Horners, and Royal Yacht Sqdn.

In following the truth

SON LIVING (By 1st marriage)

OLIVER HENRY RUFUS (*Viscount Lymington*), *b* 22 Dec 1981.

DAUGHTERS LIVING (By 1st marriage)

Lady Clementine Violet Rohais, *b* 1983.

(by 2nd marriage)

Lady Rose Hermione Annabel, *b* 1990.

SISTERS LIVING

Hon Lucinda Ruth, *b* 1956: *m* 1984, as his 2nd wife, Patrick Anthony Ewen Bellville, only surv son of late Anthony Seymour Bellville, of The White House, Bembridge, Isle of Wight, and has issue living, Blaise Anthony Valentine, *b* 1985, — Oscar Rupert Kintzing, *b* 1986, — Archie Seymour, *b* 1988. *Residence* – Manor Farm House, Cliddesden, Basingstoke, Hants.
Hon Emma Geraldine Anne, *b* 1958: *m* 1981, Gerald Thomas Cordingley, son of late Thomas Cordingley, and has issue living, Katie Madelaine, *b* 1983, — Venetia Ruth, *b* 1985, — Jennifer Rose, *b* 1991. *Residence* – Cheesecombe Farm, Hawkley, nr Liss, Hants.

HALF-UNCLE LIVING (son of 9th Earl by 2nd marriage)

Hon Nicholas Valoynes Bermingham (15 Tregunter Rd, SW10), *b* 1946; *ed* Stowe: *m* 1969, Lavinia, only da of David Karmel, CBE, QC, of 108 Eaton Place, SW1, and has issue living, Henry Robert Newton, *b* 1974, — Victoria Urania Sophia, *b* 1972.

AUNT LIVING (Daughter of 9th Earl by 1st marriage)

Lady (Anne) Camilla Eveline, *b* 1925: *m* 1944, Lord Rupert Charles Montacute Nevill, Life Guards, who *d* 1982, and has had issue (*see* M Abergavenny). *Residences* – Old House Farm, Glynde, Lewes, Sussex; 35 Upper Addison Gdns, W14.

HALF-AUNT LIVING (Daughter of 9th Earl by 2nd marriage)

Lady Jane Alianora Borlase, *b* 1939. *Residence* – 1 Broadmere, Farleigh Wallop, Basingstoke, Hants.

WIDOW LIVING OF SON OF NINTH EARL

Julia (*Viscountess Lymington*), only da of late W. Graeme Ogden, DSC, of The Old Manor, Rudge, Frome, Somerset, and formerly wife of Peter Robin Kirwan-Taylor: *m* 1974, as his 3rd wife, Oliver Kintzing, Viscount Lymington, elder son of 9th Earl, who *dvp* (June) 1984. *Residence* – 5 Venner House, 47 Bourne St, SW1W 8UR.

COLLATERAL BRANCHES LIVING

Issue of late Hon Oliver Malcolm Wallop, yr son of 8th Earl, *b* 1905, *d* 1980: *m* 1st, 1929, Jean, who *d* 1943, da of Edward Small Moore, of New York; 2ndly, 1944 (*m diss* 1954), Mrs Alberta Jannopolis Hines; 3rdly, 1954, Carolyn, who *d* 1973, da of Harvey Parker Towle, MD, and formerly wife of Henry Sturgis Russell:—
(By 1st *m*) Edward John (68 Hanna Creek Rd, Big Horn, Wyoming 82833, USA), *b* 1930: *m* 1st, 1952 (*m diss* 1959), Carrol Robertson; 2ndly, 1962, Victoria Neison, only da of H. Lyman Stebbins, of New York; 3rdly, 1986, Tessa Janet, only da of late Douglas Neale Dalton, of Bridgnorth, Shropshire, and has issue living (by 1st *m*), John Michael, *b* 1955, — (by 2nd *m*), Andrew Gerard, *b* 1965, — Sam Huntington, *b* 1972, — Harriet Walker, *b* 1968 (adopted da), — Alexandra Marcina, *b* 1969. —— Malcolm, *b* 1933: *m* 1st, 1955 (*m diss* 1966), Josephine Vail Stebbins; 2ndly, 1967, Judith Warren, formerly wife of —Goodwin, and has issue living (by 1st *m*), Malcolm Moncreiffe (Henry), *b* 1957, — (Oliver) Mathew, *b* 1960, — Paul Stebbins, — Amy Vail, *b* 1962. —— Jean Margaret (*Countess of Carnarvon*), *b* 1934: *m* 1956, 7th Earl of Carnarvon, KCVO, KBE. —— Carolyn Walker, *b* 1939: *m* 1963, Irving Newman Alderson, of Bones Brothers Ranch, Birney, Montana, USA, and has issue living, Natalie Moore, *b* 1963, — Jean, *b* 1965, — Mary Roberts, *b* 1968.

Grandchildren of late Maj Barton Newton Wallop William-Powlett, late Royal Fusiliers (City of London Regt), only son of late Maj William Barton Powlett Wallop William-Powlett, son of Rev Hon Barton Wallop, brother of 2nd Earl:—
Issue of late Capt Newton James Wallop William-Powlett, DSC, RN, *b* 1896, *d* 1963: *m* 1929, Barbara Patience (*Lady William-Powlett*), who *m* 2ndly, 1966, Vice Adm Sir Peveril Barton Reibey Wallop William-Powlett, KCB, KCMG, CBE, DSO (infra), da of Sir Bernard Eyre Greenwell, 2nd Bt, MBE:—
Oliver Newton Wallop, *b* 1933; *ed* Eton; Lieut RNR; JP, DL and High Sheriff Devon 1989. *Residence* – Cadhay, Ottery St Mary, Devon EX11 1QT. —— Ann Patience Wallop, *b* 1930: *m* 1953, Maj Thomas Noel Thistlethwayte, late 60th Rifles, of Summerhayes, Throwleigh, Okehampton, Devon EX20 2HX, and has issue living, Rupert Thomas Newton (3 Court Lane Gdns, SE21 7DZ), *b* 1955: *m* 1982, Elisabeth Anne, only da of Francis Cator (*see* Storey, Bt), and has issue living, Emma *b* 1983, Katharine *b* 1985, — Jane Camilla, *b* 1957: *m* 1991, Timothy L. S. Dodd, of 56 Chancellor's Rd, W6 9RS, only son of Lewis Dodd, of Newport, Dyfed, and has issue living, Peter Alexander *b* 1992. —— Sara Elisabeth Wallop (*Hon Mrs David Bruce*), *b* 1936: *m* 1960, Hon Edward David Bruce, of Blairhill, Rumbling Bridge, Kinross, and has issue (*see* E Elgin).
Issue of late Vice Adm Sir Peveril Barton Reibey Wallop William-Powlett, KCB, KCMG, CBE, DSO, *b* 1898, *d* 1985: *m* 1st, 1923, Helen Constance, who *d* 1965, da of late J. Forbes Crombie, of Aberdeen; 2ndly, 1966, Barbara Patience (Cadhay, Ottery St Mary, Devon), widow of his elder brother, Capt Newton James Wallop William-Powlett, DSC, RN (ante):—
(By 1st *m*) Olivia Pansy Wallop, *b* 1925: *m* 1950, Lt-Col John Clairmont Wood, of Coombe Down, Beaminster, Dorset, and has issue living, Giles Powlett Clairmont, *b* 1954: *m* 1988, Frances Mary Catherine Stewart, and has issue living, Robert *b* 1991, Rollo *b* 1992, — Charlotte Knollys Olivia, *b* 1953: *m* 1977, Philip Gilbert Herbert Bradley, and has issue living, William *b* 1980, Piers *b* 1982, Timothy *b* 1985, — Louisa Ella Delamotte, *b* 1959: *m* 1987, Richard Charles Hawker, who *d* 1992, and has issue living, John Henry Gore *b* 1988, Constance Rose Knollys *b* 1990. —— Helen Vernon Wallop, *b* 1927: *m* 1951, Lt Cdr Henry Victor Bruce, RN, of Barley Down House, Ovington, Alresford, Hants, and Sallachy, Lairg, Sutherland, and has issue (*see* E Elgin, colls). —— Judith Jean Wallop (*Lady Colman*), *b* 1936: *m* 1955, Sir Michael Jeremiah Colman, 3rd Bt, of Malshanger, Basingstoke, Hants, and has issue.
Issue of late Maj Peter de Barton Vernon Wallop William-Powlett, MC, *b* 1903, *d* 1988: *m* 1935, Hon Katherine Elizabeth Keyes (22 St Leonard's Terr, SW3), da of 1st Baron Keyes:—
Barton Roger Wallop (Piercewebbs, Clavering, Saffron Walden, Essex), *b* 1938: *m* 1962, Judith, elder da of Colin Silk, of 13 Highdown Rd, Lewes, and has issue living, Patrick Henry Wallop, *b* 1964, — Thomas Wallop, *b* 1968, — Katherine Wallop, *b* 1965: *m* 1990, Dr D. Joshua Danziger, of 31 Goodge St, W1, son of Dr Arnold M. Danziger, of Wilmslow, Cheshire. —— Mary Wallop, *b* 1936: *m* 1957, Jonathan Janson, Lieut RNVR, of Howgate Farm, Bembridge, I of W PO35 5QN, and has issue living, Nicola Claire Wallop, *b* 1959: *m* 1985, Richard Henry Alexander Southby, of The Red House, Overbury, Tewkesbury, Glos GL20 7PB, and has issue (*see* Southby, Bt), — Lucinda Katrina, *b* 1961: *m* 1991, Andrew Peter Watt, of 33 Chaldon Rd, SW6 7NH, 2nd son of Cdr Alexander Strachan Watt, of Ditcheatt, Somerset, and has issue living, Georgiana Louisa Janson *b* 1993, — Sara Arabella, *b* 1965.

PREDECESSORS – (1) JOHN Wallop, MP for Hants 1714-20; was a Lord of the Treasury 1747, Lord-Lieut of Hants, Lord Warden and Keeper of the New Forest, Vice-Adm of Hants, and Vice-Adm and Gov of the Isle of Wight; *cr Baron Wallop*, of Farley Wallop, co Southampton, and *Viscount Lymington* (peerage of Great Britain) 1720, and *Earl of Portsmouth* (peerage of Great Britain) 1743; *d* 1762; *s* by his grandson (2) JOHN, 2nd Earl; *d* 1797; *s* by his el son (3) JOHN CHARLES, 3rd Earl; *dsp*, 1853; *s* by his brother (4) NEWTON, 4th Earl; *b* 1772; assumed by Roy licence in 1794 for himself and issue the surname and arms of Fellowes only: *m* 2ndly, 1820, Lady Catherine, da of 1st Earl Fortescue; *d* 1854; *s* by his son (5) ISAAC NEWTON, 5th Earl, *b* 1825; resumed (but without Roy licence) the family surname and arms of Wallop: *m* 1855, Lady Eveline Alicia Juliana Herbert, who *d* 1906, el da of the Earl of Carnarvon; *d* 1891; *s* by his el son (6) NEWTON, 6th Earl, *b* 1856, MP for Barnstaple. (*L*) 1880-85, and for Devon, N, or S Molton Div 1885-91: *m* 1885; Beatrice Mary, who *d* 1935, only child of late Edward Pease, of Summer House, Bewdley, and Greencroft West, Darlington; *d* 1917; *s* by his brother (7) JOHN FELLOWES, 7th Earl, *b* 1850; *d* 1925; *s* by his brother (8) OLIVER HENRY, 8th Earl; *b* 1861: *m* 1897, Marguerite, who *d* 1938, da of late S. J. Walker, of Frankfort, Kentucky, and Chicago, Illinois, USA; *d* 1943; *s* by his son (9) GERARD VERNON, 9th Earl; *b* 1898; 1914-18 War as Lieut 2nd Life Gds and Guards Machine Gun Regt; MP for Basingstoke Div of Hants (*C*) May 1929-Feb 1934; Chm Country Landowners' Assocn 1947-49; Vice-Pres European Electors' Union, Kenya 1952, Pres 1953; Chm Forestry Advisory Cttee, Kenya 1954-61; Vice-Chm E Africa Natural Resources Cttee 1964-84: *m* 1st, 1920 (*m diss* 1936), Mary Lawrence, who *d* 1964, da of Waldron Kintzing Post, of Bayport, LI, USA; 2ndly, 1936, Bridget Cory (OStJ), who *d* 1979, only da of late Capt Patrick Bermingham Crohan, RN, of Owlpen Old Manor, Uley, Glos; *d* (Oct) 1984; *s* by his grandson **(10)** QUENTIN GERARD CAREW (only son of Oliver Kintzing, Viscount Lymington, *b* 1923: *m* 1st, 1952 (*m diss* 1954), Maureen, only da of Lt-Col Kenneth Bridges Stanley, of 58 Kingston House, Princes Gate, SW7; 2ndly, 1954 (*m diss* 1974), Ruth Violet, who *d* 1978, yr da of Brig-Gen Gerald Carew Sladen, CB, CMG, DSO, MC (*see* Ewing, Bt, colls, 1964 Edn); 3rdly, 1974, Julia, only da of W. Graeme Ogden, DSC, of The Old Manor, Rudge, Frome, Somerset, and formerly wife of Peter Robin Kirwan-Taylor; *dvp* (June) 1984), 10th Earl and present peer; also Viscount Lymington, and Baron Wallop.

POULETT, EARLDOM OF (Poulett) (Extinct 1973) (Barony of Poulett of Hinton St George, E 1627, Extinct or Dormant 1973)

WIDOW LIVING OF EIGHTH EARL

MARGARET CHRISTINE (*Countess Poulett*), (Le Cercle, Rue du Croquet, St Aubin, Jersey), da of Wilfred John Peter Ball, of Reading: *m* 1968, as his 3rd wife, the 8th Earl, who *d* 1973, when the Earldom became extinct and the Barony became extinct or dormant.

Powell, see Baron Baden-Powell.

Powerscourt, Baron; title of Viscount Powerscourt on Roll of HL.

POWERSCOURT, VISCOUNT (Wingfield) Sits as BARON POWERSCOURT (UK 1885) (Viscount I 1743)
(Name pronounced "Poërscourt")

Fidelity is of God

MERVYN NIALL WINGFIELD, 10th Viscount; *b* 3 Sept 1935; *s* 1973; *ed* Stowe; late Lt Irish Gds: *m* 1st, 1962, (*m diss* 1974), Wendy Ann Pauline, elder da of Ralph C. G. Slazenger; 2ndly, 1979, Pauline, da of W. P. Van, of San Francisco, USA, and has issue by 1st *m*.

Arms – Argent, on a bend gules, three pairs of wings conjoined in lure of the field. **Crest** – A demi-eagle wings displayed argent, gazing on the sun proper. **Supporters** – Two pegasi argent, maned, hoofed, and wings addorsed or.

SON LIVING (By 1st marriage)

Hon (MERVYN) ANTHONY, *b* 21 Aug 1963.

DAUGHTER LIVING (By 1st marriage)

Hon Julia Margaret, *b* 1965.

BROTHER LIVING

Hon Guy Claude Patrick (PO Box 186, Applegate, Calif 95703-0186, USA), *b* 1940; *ed* Millfield.

SISTER LIVING

Hon Grania Sybil Enid (*Hon Lady Langrishe*), *b* 1934: *m* 1955, Sir Hercules Ralph Hume Langrishe, 7th Bt, of Ringlestown House, Kilmessan, co Meath.

COLLATERAL BRANCHES LIVING

Issue of late Maj-Gen Hon Maurice Anthony Wingfield, CMG, CVO, DSO, yst son of 7th Viscount, *b* 1883, *d* 1956: *m* 1906, Sybil Frances, who *d* 1967, only da of F. D. Leyland, formerly of The Vyne, Basingstoke:—
Anthony Desmond Rex, DSO, MC, *b* 1908; *ed* Eton, and RMC; Brigadier (ret) late 10th Hussars; sometime Com, 22nd Armoured Bde; Assist Racing and Stud Manager to HM 1957-63, and Stud manager 1963; 1939-45 War in Middle East and N-W Europe (wounded MC, DSO, Order of Leopold of Belgium, Belgian Croix de Guerre); DSO 1943: *m* 1935, Juliet Constance, who *d* 1980, da of late William Burroughs Stanley, DL, of Coolamber Manor, Westmeath, and Lillybrook, Budleigh Salterton, and has issue living, Deidre Jocelyn, *b* 1936: *m* 1969, Basil Tiernay Pegg (The White House, Chaddleworth, Berks), and has issue living, Jonathan Mark *b* 1973, Camilla Louise *b* 1971. *Residence* – Brownstown Park, Navan, co Meath. —— Jocelyn Sybil Julia, *b* 1913: *m* 1st, 1940, Lt-Col Clifford Willoughby (Peter) Hordern, who *d* 1966; 2ndly, 1970, Ralph Hamilton Cobbold, who *d* 1987, of Broom House, Sudbourne, Woodbridge, Suffolk, and 8 Pont St, SW1, and has had issue (by 1st *m*), Peter Anthony, *b* 1941; *d* 1953, as the result of an accident at cricket.

Grandchildren of late Richard William Wingfield (infra):—

Issue of late Richard Mervyn Wingfield, MC, b 1894, d 1951: m 1918, Lynette Agnes, da of late Major Sydney Cowper, CMG, JP, of Wynberg, Cape Provine, S Africa:—
Elizabeth Sonia, b 1925: m 1st, 1944 (m diss 1945), Basil Wilson, Lt, S African Air Force, 2ndly, 194—, Fl Lt M. J. Dunne, and has issue living, (by 1st m) Sandra Lynn Wingfield, b 1945, — (by 2nd m) Richard Matthew Wingfield, b 1948, — Lesley Clare Wingfield, b 1952, — Robin Elizabeth Wingfield, b 1954.
Issue of late Noel Sparks Wingfield, b 1907, d (Feb) 1992: m 1933, Mary Joan, who d (Sept) 1992, da of R. H. Wood:—
Patrick Noel (Belvedere North, PO Goromonzi, Zimbabwe), b 1934: m 1st, 1960 (m diss 1971), Jean, da of David Morris Williams, of Blantyre, Nyasaland; 2ndly, 1973, Margaret, da of J. H. McKenzie Finch, of Canterbury, Kent, and has had issue, (by 1st m) Richard David Noel, b 1966, — Sandra Joan, b 1963, d 1976, — (by 2nd m) Jeremy James, b 1974, — Clare Muriel, b 1975. —— Jenepher Cynthia (44 Cambridge Rd, Avondale, Harare, Zimbabwe), b 1937: m 1961, Guy Colin Hensman, who d 1993, and has issue living, David Guy, b 1965, — Bridget Ann, b 1963.

Granddaughter of late Richard Robert Wingfield, el son of late Rev Hon Edward Wingfield, 3rd son of 4th Viscount:—
Issue of late Richard William Wingfield, b 1849, d 1918: m 1889, Jessie Emily (who d 1936, having m 2ndly, 1920, Thomas Edward Broster, who d 1941), da of Benjamin Mitchell Kennedy:—
Clare Mary Sophia (64 Jabulani, Sutton Lane, Warner Beach, Amanzimoti, S Africa), b 1904: m 1926, Sydney William Hall Kennard, who d 1970, and has issue living, David George (Private Bag 1325, Grahamstown 6140, S Africa), b 1929; ed Hilton Coll, Natal: m 1956, Isabelle, da of late Maurice Henry de Vere Pennefather, of Fort Victoria, Zimbabwe, and has issue living, Roland Derek b 1958, Nigel Hugh b 1961, Kate Ellen b 1971, — Desmond Richard (2 Wharncliffe Gdns, Beacon Bay, S Africa), b 1935; ed Hilton Coll, Natal: m 1956, Cynthia Norma, da of late Dr William Beck, of Potchefstroom, and has issue living, Mark William b 1959, Grant Richard b 1961, Brett Wingfield b 1964, Leigh Mary b 1957.

Grandchildren of late Capt Anthony Edward Foulis Wingfield, elder son of Sir Anthony Henry Wingfield, elder son of George John Wingfield, 2nd son of Rev Hon Edward Wingfield (ante):—
Issue of late Gervase Christopher Brinsmade Wingfield, b 1931, d 1964: m 1958, Mary Margaret (Hackney Lodge, Melton, Woodbridge, Suffolk) (who m 2ndly, 1973, Dennis Henry Bagshaw Neal), da of Dennis McGuinn, of Haverford, Penn, USA:—
Andrew Nicholas Brinsmade, ED, b 1959; ed Worth, and Bristol Univ; Maj Royal Hong Kong Regt (The Volunteers), and The Royal Yeo; Solicitor: m 1989, Caroline Jane Victoria, yst da of John Francis Felix Porter, of The Old Bakery, Martock, Som, and has issue living, Edward Nicholas Anthony, b 1991, — Henry John Gervase, b 1994. Club - Cavalry and Guards'. —— Nicola Caroline McGuinn, b 1961: m 1986, Mark Godfrey Jerram, of Van Cottage, Compton Chamberlayne, Salisbury, Wilts SP3 5DB, only son of Maj Geoffrey Forster Jenner Jerram, of Lower Wraxall Farmhouse, nr Dorchester, Dorset, by his wife, Anne (née Brigg) (see Prince-Smith, Bt, 1970 Edn), and has issue living, Alexander Geoffrey Wingfield, b 1989, — Dominic Alistair, b 1990. —— Philippa Susan (Hon Mrs Anthony Monckton), b 1962: m 1985, Capt Hon Anthony Leopold Colyer Monckton, yst son of 2nd Viscount Monckton of Brenchley, and has issue.

Grandchildren of late Edward Rhys Wingfield, el son of late Capt Edward Ffolliott Wingfield (infra):—
Issue of late Lieut-Col Mervyn Edward George Rhys Wingfield, Gloucestershire Regt, b 1872, d 1952: m 1919, Florence Marguerite Erle, who d 1990, da of late Col Richard Erle Benson, E Yorkshire Regt:—
Charles Talbot Rhys, b 1924; ed Eton, and Ch Ch, Oxford; late Lieut Coldstream Guards; a DL of Glos and High Sheriff 1962; France 1944 (wounded): m 1954, Hon Cynthia Merial Hill, da of 6th Baron Sandys, and has issue living, Richard Mervyn Rhys, b 1967, — Venetia Blanche, b 1956: m 1978, Richard Crosbie Dawson (see Sutton Bt, colls, 1985 Edn), and has issue living, Anthony Charles b 1983, George Robert b 1985, Charlotte Rose b 1990, — Olivia Patricia, b 1958, — Diana Mary, b 1961: m 1986, Robert Anthony Copley, and has issue (see Cs Loudoun, colls). Residence - Barrington Park, Burford, Oxon. Club - Guards'. —— David de Cardonnel Ffolliott Rhys, b 1933; ed Bradfield Coll: m 1982, Mrs Mary Ann E. L. Harrison. —— Jonathan Fitzuryan Rhys (Edifico Mediterraneo, Fuengirola, Malaga, Spain), b 1935; ed Eton: m 1970, Judith, da of Albert George James Gibbons, of Mount Pleasant, Stocklane, Langford, Bristol, and widow of Hon Philip John Inman (see B Inman), and has issue living, Annabel Lucy, b 1973, — Felicity Jane, b 1975. —— Mary Florence Eleanor, b 1920: m 1945, Sqdn-Ldr Neville Thomas Cole, RAF, and has issue living, Michael Duncan Mervyn, b 1946, — Edward Charles Ffolliott George, b 1954, — Rachel Elizabeth Rosemary, b 1948. Residence - Windrush Lodge, Nazeing, Essex. —— Elizabeth Marguerite, b 1926.

Grandsons of late Maj William Jocelyn Rhys Wingfield, 2nd son of late Edward Rhys Wingfield (ante):—
Issue of late Maj William Thomas Rhys Wingfield, TD, Northamptonshire Yeo b 1907, d 1976: m 1936, Patricia (Angel House, Elton, Peterborough, Cambs), only child of late Maj-Gen Sir (William) James (Norman) Cooke-Collis, KBE, CB, CMG, DSO:—
Jocelyn James (18 Chiddingstone St, SW6 3TG), b 1937; ed Eton; Maj (ret) LI; Divisional Dir Overseas (Latin America, Middle East, Pacific), Save the Children Fund: m 1968, Sara Elizabeth, only da of Sir (Edward John) Patrick (Boschetti) ffolkes, 6th Bt, and has issue living, Serena Geraldine Rhys, b 1969, — Camilla Patricia Rhys, b 1971. —— Robert Talbot Rhys (The Spring House, Grimston, nr Melton, Leics LE14 3BZ), b 1940; ed Stowe and Trin Coll, Dublin (PhD); with British Geological Survey: m 1969, Anne Mary, da of Lt-Col T. W. Hamilton, of Nunholm House, Dumfries, and has issue living, James Hamilton Rhys, b 1971, — Charles Timothy Rhys, b 1974. —— George Anthony Rhys (Hearne House, North Wootton, Shepton Mallet, Som), b 1942; ed Eton and Trin Coll, Dublin; with IBM: m 1968, Gloria, da of Bernard Bolingbroke-Kent, of Cerne Easter, Westerham, Kent, and has issue living, Rupert Bolingbroke Rhys, b 1972; ed Eton, — Michael Somerset Rhys, b 1975; ed Blundell's.

Granddaughter of late Edward Rhys Wingfield (ante):—
Issue of late Sir Charles John Fitzroy Rhys Wingfield, KCMG, b 1877, d 1960: m 1905, Lucy Evelyn, who d 1977, da of late Sir Edmund Douglas Veitch Fane, KCMG, of Boyton Manor, Wilts:—
Diana Evelyn, b 1907: m 1935, Baron Alessandro Corsi di Turri, who d 1987, and has issue living, Baron Raimondo (Via Rovani 6, 20052 Monza, Italy), b 1937; Kt of Honour and Devotion Sov Mil Order of Malta, Kt of Justice Sacred Mil Constantinian Order of St George: m 1964, Donna Maria Francesca di Lorenzo, and has issue living, Carlo Alessadro b 1965, Diana Lucrezia b 1970, — Antonio Giuliano (Via Massimi 27, 00136 Rome, Italy), b 1941: m 1st, 1967 (m diss 1978), Maria Grazia Barbiani; 2ndly, 1979, Giovanna Attanasio, and has issue living (by 1st m), Flavio Alessandro b 1968, (by 2nd m) Benedetta Lucy, b 1983. Residence - 1 Via Masaccio, 00196 Rome, Italy.

Grandchildren of late Capt Cecil John Talbot Rhys Wingfield, 5th and yst son of late Edward Rhys Wingfield (ante):—
Issue of late Maj Edward William Rhys Wingfield, KRRC, b 1905, d 1984: m 1935, Lady Norah Beryl Cayzer Jellicoe (Salterbridge, Cappoquin, co Waterford), da of 1st Earl Jellicoe:—
Philip John (Salterbridge, Cappoquin, co Waterford), b 1938; ed Eton: m 1971, Susan Johanna, da of late Maj-Gen Ronald Edward Coaker, CB, CBE, MC, of Seaton Old Rectory, Uppingham, and has issue living, Edward Mervyn, b 1973, — Venetia Sophie, b 1975, — Sarah Jane, b 1978. —— Jacqueline, b 1936: m 1967, Brig Anthony Chester Vivian, CBE, ADC, Col RWF, of 22 Henning St, Battersea, SW11 3DR. —— Elizabeth Jane, b 1941.

Granddaughters of late Major Charles George Lewis Wingfield, 2nd son of late Capt Edward Ffolliott Wingfield, 3rd son of late Rev Hon Edward Wingfield (ante):—
Issue of late Charles Trevor Wingfield, b 1889, d 1924: m 1914, Liliane Laure Agnes, who d 1979, only child of late Vladimir Czerny, of Petrograd, Russia:—
Tatiana Elianore Lucile Beatrice b 1916: m 1947, Brig Alan Godfrey Drake-Brockman, OBE, who d 1976, and has issue living, Trevor Vivian, b 1950. —— Yvonne Angéle Primrose Czerny (61 Prevost Martin, Geneva, Switzerland), b 1917.

Grandchildren of late Lt-Col Rev William Edward Wingfield, DSO (infra):—
Issue of late John Anthony David Wingfield, b 1905, d 1983: m 1934, Eileen Earle, who d 1982, da of late Hugh Melville, of Durban, S Africa:—
Anthony Richard Melville, b 1941; ed St Andrews, Grahamstown. —— John Mervyn (4 Lewis Cres, Gt Abingdon, Cambs CB16 AG), b 1944; ed St Andrews, Grahamstown, Rand Univ (BSc), and Trin Coll, Camb (BA): m 1970, Diana Kay, da of F. C. Harris, of Newlands, Cape Town, and has issue living, Richard John, b 1972, — David Mervyn, b 1975, — Christopher Robert, b 1978. —— Robert Edward Melville (9918-227th Place SW, Edmonds, Washington 98020, USA), b 1950; ed St Andrews, Grahamstown, and Rand Univ (BSc); Civil Engr: m 1979, Carol, da of P. Jansen, of Seattle, USA, and has issue living, Jeremy, b 1981, — Joanna Ruth, b 1980. —— Elizabeth Melville, b 1936; BSc (Hons) Rand Univ, MSc London: m 1963, Hugh Vincent Williams, MSc, of 04 Glen St, Kenmare, Krugersdorp, Transvaal, and has issue living, Katharine Elizabeth, b 1965, — Julia Margaret Frances, b 1969, — Susan Eileen Isabella, b 1970.

Grandson of late Capt Richard Thomas Wingfield, el son of late Rev Hon William Wingfield, 4th son of 4th Viscount:—
Issue of late Lieut-Col Rev William Edward Wingfield, DSO, b 1867, d 1927: m 1896, Elizabeth Mary, who d 1939, a da of late George Frederic Trench (B Ashtown, colls):—
Mervyn Robert George, DSO, DSC, b 1911; Capt RN (ret); an ADC to HM 1962-67; formerly Naval Attaché, British Embassy, Athens, and Dir of Underwater Weapons at Admiralty; 1939-45 War (DSO, DSC and Bar, despatches); DSO 1942: m 1936, Sheila Mary, da of late Maj J. H. P. Leschallas, formerly of Lynchmere House, Lynchmere, Sussex, and has issue living, Richard Mervyn (Chiltern House, Hardwick Rd, Whitchurch, Pangbourne, Berks, RG8 7HW), b 1942; ed Wellington, Pembroke Coll, Camb (MA) and Southampton Univ (MSc); CEng; MICE: m 1969, Diana, da of P. M. Longhurst, of Lodsworth, Sussex, and has issue living James Richard b 1973, Caroline Sarah b 1976, — William Peter (47 Combemartin Rd, SW18), b 1948; ed Wellington Coll, and Sussex Univ (BA): m 1975, Patricia Jane, da of G. A. Slatter, of Hastings, Sussex, — Cicely (2 Spencer Rd, S Croydon), b 1940: m 1964, David Barry Knowles, Lt-Cdr RN, who d 1967, and has issue living, Alastair David b (Nov) 1964, Melanie Kathleen b 1966. Residence – Fair Winds, Highfield Cres, Hindhead, Surrey.

Granddaughter of late Brig-Gen Cecil Vernon Wingfield-Stratford, CB, CMG, 3rd son of late John Wingfield-Stratford, only son of Hon John Wingfield Stratford, 2nd son of 3rd Viscount:—
Issue of late Esmé Cecil Wingfield-Stratford, DSc, b 1882, d 1971: m 1915, Barbara Elizabeth, who d 1976, da of late Lt-Col Francis Henry Lancelot Errington (B Congleton):—
Roshnara Barbara WINGFIELD-STRATFORD-JOHNSTONE, b 1916; assumed by deed poll 1970, for herself and her issue by 2nd m the surnames of Wingfield-Stratford-Johnstone: m 1st, 1941 (m diss 1949), Maj Richard John Wrottesley, MC (later 5th Baron Wrottesley); 2ndly, 1950, Lt-Col Norman David Melville Johnstone, MBE, Gren Gds, of Park House, Gaddesby, Leics, and has issue living, (by 1st m) (see B Wrottesley), — (by 2nd m) Esmé Edward Melville (Chateau de Sours, 33750 St Quentin de Baron, France), b 1950: m 1972, Sara, da of Maj Richard Francis Birch Reynardson, and has issue living, Rupert Leo Esmé b 1975, Dickon b 1978, Harry Crocker b 1983, — Victoria Rose Charlotte, b 1954: m 1982, William John Corby, only son of R. A. Corby, of Kilbracken, Hudnall Common, Berkhamsted, Herts, and has issue living, Roshnara b 1983, Diana b 1986, Christina b 1988.

Grandchildren of late Francis Mervyn Wingfield-Stratford, 7th and yst son of late John Wingfield-Stratford, only son of late Hon John Wingfield Stratford, 2nd son of 3rd Viscount (ante):—
Issue of late Mervyn Verner Wingfield-Stratford, b 1907; d 1982: m 1935, Anne Helen, da of late Douglas Charles Stewart-Sandeman, of Martins Heron, Bracknell, Berks:—
(Mervyn) Peter Douglas (28 Lansdowne Rd, Holland Park, W11), b 1936; LIM Citizen and Goldsmith of London: m 1969, Jane, da of late Dr Edward Worsley Burstal, of Lutterworth, and has issue living, James Richard Mervyn, b 1973, — Annabel Jane, b 1971. —— Georgina Isabel, b 1939: m 1962, John L. M. Modley, Lt RE, and has issue living, Drummond, b 1963, — Alexander, b 1968.

PREDECESSORS – (1) RICHARD Wingfield, MP for Boyle; cr Baron Wingfield, of Wingfield, co Wexford, and Viscount Powerscourt (peerage of Ireland) 1743; d 1751; s by his el son **(2)** EDWARD, 2nd Viscount; MP for Stockbridge 1756-61; d unmarried; s by his brother **(3)** RICHARD, 3rd Viscount; d 1788; s by his son **(4)** RICHARD, 4th Viscount; d 1809; s by his son **(5)** RICHARD, 5th Viscount; d 1823; s by his son **(6)** RICHARD, 6th Viscount, b 1815; many years MP for Bath: m 1836, Lady Elizabeth Frances Charlotte Jocelyn, who d 1884, da of 3rd Earl of Roden; d 1844; s by his son **(7)** MERVYN, KP, PC, 7th Viscount; was a Representative Peer; cr Baron Powerscourt, of Powerscourt, co Wicklow (peerage of United Kingdom) 1885: m 1864, Lady Julia Coke, who d 1931, el da of 2nd Earl of Leicester; d 1904; s by his son **(8)** MERVYN RICHARD, KP, MVO, 8th Viscount, b 1880; was Comptroller of the Household to Lord-Lieut of Ireland 1906-7; appointed Lieut of co Wicklow 1901; elected a Member of Senate of S Ireland 1921: m 1903, Sybil, who d 1946, da of late Walter Pleydell-Bouverie; d 1947; s by his son **(9)** MERVYN PATRICK, 9th Viscount, b 1905: m 1932, Sheila Claude, writer, who d 1992, da of late Lt-Col Claude Beddington, of 33 Grosvenor St, W1; d 1973; s by his el son **(10)** MERVYN NIALL, 10th Viscount and present peer; also Baron Wingfield, and Baron Powerscourt.

POWIS, EARL OF (Herbert) (Earl UK 1804)
(Title pronounced "Po-is")

JOHN GEORGE HERBERT, 8th Earl; *b* 19 May 1952; *s* 1993; *ed* Wellington Coll, and McMaster Univ, Ontario, Canada (MA, PhD); formerly Lecturer McMaster Univ, and Assist Prof of English Literature Redeemer Coll, Ontario 1990-92; patron of twelve livings: *m* 1977, Marijke Sophia, eldest da of Maarten N. Guther, of Ancaster, Ontario, Canada, and has issue.

Arms – Per pale azure and gules, three lions rampant argent. **Crest** – A wyvern wings elevated addorsed vert, gorged with a ducal coronet or, holding in the mouth a sinister hand couped at the wrist gules. **Supporters** – *Dexter*, an elephant argent; *sinister*, a griffin, wings elevated, argent, ducally gorged gules, and charged with five mullets in saltire sable.
Seat – Powis Castle, Welshpool, Powys. *Residence* – Walcot, Chirbury, Montgomery, Powys.

Ung je serviray
One will I serve

SON LIVING

JONATHAN NICHOLAS WILLIAM (*Viscount Clive*), *b* 5 Dec 1979.

DAUGHTERS LIVING

Lady Stephanie Moira Christina, *b* 1982.
Lady Samantha Julie Esther, *b* 1988.

BROTHERS LIVING

Hon Michael Clive, *b* 1954, *ed* Wellington Coll, Christ's Coll, Camb, and London Business Sch: *m* 1978, Susan Mary, da of late Guy Baker, of Welshpool, Powys, and has issue living, Thomas Guy Clive, *b* 1981, — Mark Philip Clive, *b* 1983, — Joanna Frances Clare, *b* 1987. *Residence* – Wicken Hall, Wicken, Ely, Cambs CB7 5XT.
Hon Peter James, *b* 1955; *ed* Wellington Coll; MSI: *m* 1978, Terri, yr da of Sean McBride, of Callan, co Kilkenny, and has issue living, Oliver George Laurie, *b* 1983, — Sophie Louise Mary, *b* 1980, — Lucy Alison Julia, *b* 1988. *Residence* – 9 Turnberry Court, Iona Way, Haywards Heath, W Sussex R16 3TD.
Hon Edward David, *b* 1958; *ed* Bryanston, Lancaster Univ (BSc), and Spurgeon's Coll (BA); ACMA: *m* 1985, Diana Christine, eldest da of Cedric Shore, and has issue living, David Andrew, *b* 1988, — Joy Sarah, *b* 1986.

ADOPTIVE SISTERS

Lorraine Elizabeth, *b* 1961: *m* 1981, Roger Samuel Jones, and has issue living, Martin William, *b* 1986, — Caroline Lorraine, *b* 1989. *Residence* – Three Brooks, Harthall, Tenbury Wells, Worcs.
Nicola Wendy, *b* 1962: *m* 1985, Robert Thomas Buxton, and has issue living, Kim Sally, *b* 1991. *Residence* – Bridge House, Chirbury, Montgomery, Powys.

UNCLES LIVING (*brothers of 7th Earl*) (*Raised to the rank of an Earl's sons,* 1991)

Hon David Mark, *b* 1927; *ed* Rugby, and Trin Coll, Camb (MA); formerly Assist Master at Christ's Hospital; Publisher and Writer: *m* 1955, Monica Brenda, only da of Laurence Edmund Swann, of The Cottage, Bilting Lane, Ashford, Kent, and has an adopted son and da, Charles Clive, *b* 1959; *ed* Bryanston, and William Ellis Sch, — Emma Katherine Elaine, *b* 1961: *m* 1985, Simon Smyth Hore, son of Julian Smyth Hore, of Grenfell, Australia. *Residence* – 46 Northchurch Rd, N1 4EJ. *Club* – Garrick.
Hon Andrew Clive, *b* 1933; *ed* Repton; late Capt Royal Norfolk Regt; Film Dir, Editor and Producer: *m* 1st, 1963 (*m diss* 1971), Carol Mae, yr da of late John Charlton; 2ndly, 1983, Edith Ann, yr da of late Alexander Dominguez, of Glendale, Calif, USA, and has had issue (by 1st *m*), Nicholas Mark, *b* 1963, — †Hugo Clive, *b* 1965; *d* 1985, — (by 2nd *m*), Timothy James, *b* 1987, — Amanda Colleen, *b* 1983.

AUNT LIVING (*sister of 7th Earl*) (*Raised to the rank of an Earl's daughter,* 1991)

Lady Elizabeth Barbarina, *b* 1928: *m* 1948, Maj Hubert Robert Holden, MC, late Royal Norfolk Regt, who *d* 1987, and has issue living, Robert David (34 Nevern Place, SW5; Sibdon Castle, Craven Arms, Shropshire), *b* 1956: *ed* Eton: *m* 1988, Susan Emily Frances, only da of Sir Joshua Francis Rowley, 7th Bt (*cr* 1786), — Caroline Elizabeth (Holmleigh Cottage, Chirbury, Powys), *b* 1950: *m* 1971 (*m diss* 1981), Richard Matthew Pieckielon-Slowik, and has issue living, Daniel George Robert *b* 1973, Amy Elizabeth *b* 1976, — Sarah Barbarina, *b* 1953: *m* 1974, Alan Hodgson, of 8 Ashburnham Grove, Bradford 9, W Yorks, and has issue living, Matthew William *b* 1976, Thomas Edward *b* 1983, Emily Barbarina *b* 1979, — Jane Amanda, *b* 1954: *m* 1978, Robert Glyn Jones, of Garthmyl House, Garthmyl, nr Beriew, Powys, son of Robert Jones, of Johannesburg, S Africa, and has issue living, William Edward Robert *b* 1981, Samuel Bruno *b* 1982, Flora Nancy Sarah *b* 1990. *Residence* – Meadows End Cottage, Long Meadow End, Craven Arms, Shropshire SY7 8ED.

DAUGHTER LIVING OF FOURTH EARL

Lady Hermione Gwladys, *b* 1900: *m* 1924, Conte Roberto Lucchesi Palli, 11th Duca della Grazia, and 13th Principe di Campofranco, Bailiff Grand Cross of the Sovereign Mil Order of Malta, Knight of San Gennaro and the Ordine Constantiniano, who *d* 1979, and has issue living, *Donna* Violet Maria Carolina Sidonie (Avenue Chailly 84c, Lausanne, Switzerland), *b* 1930. *Residence* – Hotel Beaurivage, 1006 Lausanne, Switzerland.

WIDOW LIVING OF SON OF FOURTH EARL

VIDA, only da of late Capt James Harold Cuthbert, DSO, Scots Guards; is an OStJ; appointed a Lady-in-Waiting to HRH the Duchess of Gloucester 1944: *m* 1st, 1934, Squadron-Leader Viscount Clive, RAF (17th Baron Darcy de Knayth) who was *ka* 1943, only surviving son of 4th Earl, 2ndly, 1945, Brig Derek Schuldham Schreiber, MVO, who *d* 1972 (B Faringdon), and has issue, (by 1st *m*) (*see* Bs Darcy de Knayth). *Residences* – 59 Cadogan Place, SW1; Fir Hill, Droxford, Hants.

WIDOW LIVING OF SEVENTH EARL

Hon KATHARINE ODEYNE DE GREY (*Dowager Countess of Powis*), da of 8th Baron Walsingham: *m* 1949, the 7th Earl of Powis, who *d* 1993. *Residence* – Marrington Hall, Chirbury, Montgomery, Powys.

COLLATERAL BRANCHES LIVING

Issue of late Squadron-Leader Mervyn Horatio Herbert, RAF (*Viscount Clive*) (only surviving son of 4th Earl), who *s* his mother as 17th *Baron Darcy de Knayth* 1929 (see that title).

Descendants of late Hon Robert Henry Clive (2nd son of 1st Earl) who *m* 1819 Harriet, *Baroness Windsor* in her own right (*see* E Plymouth).

PREDECESSORS – (1) ROBERT Clive (el son of Richard Clive of Styche, Salop), having served three years in the Civil Service of the HEIC, he entered that Co's Military Ser and subsequently became one of its most distinguished Generals, and to him England owed, to a very substantial extent, the establishment of her dominion in India. He avenged the outrage of the "Black Hole of Calcutta" by completely routing, in the Grove of Plassey, the forces of the Surajah Dowlah amounting to 70,000, and by dethroning the Surajah, events which gave rapid ascendency to the British power. When Gov of Calcutta he defeated the Dutch by sea and land and obtained from them a beneficial treaty for the E India Co. He was subsequently Pres of Bengal, and sat as MP for Shrewsbury 1760-74; *cr Baron Clive*, of Plassey, co Clare (peerage of Ireland) 1762; KB 1764; *d* 1774; *s* by his son (2) EDWARD, 2nd Baron; was Lord-Lieut of cos Salop and Montgomery; *cr Baron Clive*, of Walcot, co Salop (peerage of Great Britain) 1794, and *Baron Powis*, of Powis Castle, co Montgomery, *Baron Herbert of Chirbury*, co Salop, and *Viscount Clive* and *Earl of Powis* (peerage of United Kingdom) 1804: *m* 1784, Henrietta Antonia, who *d* 1830, da of Herbert Arthur Herbert, Earl of Powis (and sister and heiress of George Edward Henry Arthur, the last Earl of Powis of the family of Herbert); *d* 1839; *s* by his son (3) EDWARD, KG, 2nd Earl; *b* 1785; assumed the surname and arms of Herbert by Roy licence 1807; was Lord-Lieut of co Montgomery: *m* 1818, Lady Lucy Graham, da of 3rd Duke of Montrose; *d* 1848; *s* by his son (4) EDWARD JAMES, 3rd Earl; *b* 1818; MP for N Shropshire (*C*) 1843-8; Lord-Lieut of Montgomeryshire; *d* 1891; *s* by his nephew (5) GEORGE CHARLES (son of late Lt-Gen the Rt Hon Sir Percy Egerton Herbert, KCB, MP, 2nd son of 2nd Earl), 4th Earl; *b* 1862; Hon Col 4th Batn, S Wales Borderers, a GCStJ; sometime Prior for Wales, Order of St John; was Lord-Lieut for Salop 1896-1951: *m* 1890, Hon Violet Ida Eveline Lane-Fox (*Baroness Darcy de Knayth* in her own right), who *d* 1929, da and co-heiress of 12th Baron Conyers; *d* 1952; *s* by his kinsman (6) EDWARD ROBERT HENRY, CBE, TD (son of late Col Edward William Herbert, CB, son of late Hon Robert Charles Herbert, 4th son of 2nd Earl), 5th Earl; *b* 1889: *m* 1932, Ella Mary, who *d* 1987, da of late Col William Hans Rathborne, formerly wife of Col Frank Alan George Macartney, OBE, MC, DL, IA, and previously widow of Capt Peter Douglas Colin Eliot, IA; *d* 1974; *s* by his brother (7) CHRISTIAN VICTOR CHARLES, 6th Earl; *b* 1904; Maj RAOC, Bar Inner Temple 1932, Private Sec to Gov and C-in-C British Honduras 1947-55, and to Gov of British Guiana 1955-64, author of a monograph on The Dog in Sherlock Holmes; *dunm* 1988; *s* by his kinsman (8) GEORGE WILLIAM (son of late Rt Rev Percy Mark Herbert, KCVO, DD, son of late Maj-Gen Hon William Henry Herbert, 5th son of 2nd Earl), 7th Earl; *b* 1925; FRICS, Fellow Land Agents' Soc: *m* 1949, Hon Katharine Odeyne de Grey, da of 8th Baron Walsingham; *d* 1993; *s* by his eldest son (9) JOHN GEORGE, 8th Earl and present peer; also Viscount Clive, Baron Herbert of Chirbury, Baron Powis, and Baron Clive.

PRENTICE, BARON (Prentice) (Life Baron 1992)

REGINALD ERNEST PRENTICE, PC, son of Ernest George Prentice, of Thornton Heath, Surrey; *b* 16 July 1923; *ed* Whitgift Sch, and LSE (BSc); RA 1942-46, served Italy and Austria 1944-46; JP Croydon 1961; Min of State Dept of Educn and Science 1964-66, Min of Public Building and Works 1966-67, Min of Overseas Devpt 1967-69, Alderman GLC 1970-71, Opposition Spokesman on Employment 1972-74, Sec of State for Educn and Science 1974-75, Min for Overseas Dept 1975-76, Min for Social Security 1979-81; Member Exec Cttee Nat Union of Conservative Assocs 1988-90, Pres Assocn of Business Execs since 1983; Co Dir and Consultant on Public Affairs; MP East Ham North (*Lab*) 1957-74, Newham North East (*Lab*) 1974-77, Newham North East (*C*) 1977-79, and Daventry (*C*) 1979-87; *cr* PC 1966, Knt 1987, and *Baron Prentice*, of Daventry, co Northants (Life Baron) 1992: *m* 1948, (Vera May) Joan, da of Mrs Rosa Godwin, of Hatfield Heath, Herts, and has issue.
Residence – Wansdyke, Church Lane, Mildenhall, Marlborough, Wilts SN8 2LU.

DAUGHTER LIVING

Hon Christine Ann, *b* 1951.

PRIOR, BARON (Prior) (Life Baron 1987)

JAMES MICHAEL LEATHES PRIOR, PC, son of late Charles Bolingbroke Leathes Prior, of Norwich; *b* 11 Oct 1927; *ed* Charterhouse, and Pembroke Coll, Camb; Parl Private Sec to Pres of Board of Trade 1963, to Min of Power 1963-64, to Rt Hon Edward Heath (as Leader of Opposition) 1965-70; Min of Agriculture, Fisheries and Food 1970-72, Lord Pres of Council and Leader of House of Commons 1972-74, Opposition front bench spokesman on Employment 1974-79, Sec of State for Employment 1979-81, for Northern Ireland 1981-84; a Dep Chm Conservative Party 1972-74 (Vice-Chm 1965); Dir United Biscuits (Holdings) 1984, Barclays Bank 1984-89, Barclays International 1984-89, J. Sainsbury 1984-92, Chm The General Electric Co plc since 1984; Chm Allders plc, East Anglian Radio plc, and Royal Veterinary Coll; Member Tenneco European Advisory Council and American International Group Advisory Council; commn'd Royal Norfolk Regt 1946, served in India and Germany; farmer; MP Lowestoft (Suffolk) (*C*) 1959-83, and Waveney 1983-87; *cr* PC 1970, and *Baron Prior*, of Brampton, Suffolk (Life Baron) 1987: *m* 1954, Jane Primrose Gifford, 2nd da of late Air Vice-Marshal Oswyn George William Gifford Lywood, CB, CBE, and has issue.
Address – House of Lords, SW1A 0PW.

SONS LIVING

Hon David Gifford Leathes, *b* 1954: *m* 1987, Caroline, da of Peter Holmes, of The Old Rectory, Shotesham, Norwich, and has issue living, Nicholas James Peter, *b* 1988, — Helena Caitlin Elizabeth, *b* (twin) 1988. *Residence* – Swanington Manor, Norwich, Norfolk NR9 5NR.
Hon Simon Gilman Leathes, *b* 1956 *m* 1985, Vivien Ann, da of Peter George Keely, of The Cottage, Ringsfield Rd, Beccles, Suffolk, and has issue living, Alice Rebecca, *b* 1986. *Residence* – Church Farm, Shadingfield, Beccles, Suffolk NR34 8DF.
Hon Jeremy James Leathes, *b* 1962: *m* 1988, Camilla Sarah, elder da of Julian Riou Benson, of The Old Rectory, Abbots Ann, Andover, Hants, and has issue living, Oliver James Leathes, *b* 1991, — Edward Thomas Leathes, *b* 1993. *Residence* – The Moat House, Old Hall, Brampton, Beccles, Suffolk NR34 8EE.

DAUGHTER LIVING

Hon Sarah-Jane Leathes, *b* 1959: *m* 1982, David Alexander Roper, and has issue living, Lucy Victoria, *b* 1987, — Alexandra Florence, *b* (twin) 1987, — Rosanna Jane, *b* 1989. *Residence* – Widbrook House, Sutton Rd, Cookham, Berks SL6 9RD.

PRITCHARD, BARON (Pritchard) (Life Baron 1975)

DEREK WILBRAHAM PRITCHARD, son of Frank Wheelton Pritchard, of Didsbury, Lancs; *b* 8 June 1910; *ed* Clifton Coll; 1939-45 War; Col RA in Far East, and Dir of Radar Procurement Combined Chs of Staff, Washington; Chm of BNEC 1966-68 (Chm 1965-66), of Allied Breweries Ltd 1968-70, of Carreras Ltd, 1970-72 and of Rothmans Internat 1972-75: Pres of Inst of Dirs 1968-74; Chm of Dorchester Hotel 1976-80 and a Dir of Midland Bank Samuel Montagu & Co Ltd, Philips Electronic & Associated Industries Ltd since 1978; Chm Tiedemann-Goodnow Internat Investment Co since 1984, and Thoroughbred Holdings Internat Ltd since 1984, and other cos; Pres, Abbeyfield Soc for Aged, Northants Red Cross Soc and British Export Houses Assocn etc; Gov Clifton Coll since 1969; Vice-Pres of Wine and Spirit Assocn of Gt Britain (Pres 1962-64) and Inst of Export, of Northants Youth Club Assocn since 1965 and of East of England Agric Soc since 1974: former DL of Northants, former Chm Pytchley Hunt; *cr* Knt 1968, and *Baron Pritchard*, of West Haddon, Northants (Life Baron) 1975: *m* 1941, Denise Arfor, da of Frank Huntbach, and has issue.

Arms – Argent five roses in chevron gules barbed and seeded proper. **Crest** – A talbot rampant sable in the mouth a rose gules, barbed, seeded, slipped and leaved proper. **Supporters** – On either side a talbot reguardant sable, in the mouth a rose gules barbed, seeded, slipped and leaved proper.
Residence – West Haddon Hall, West Haddon, Northampton, NN6 7AU.

DAUGHTERS LIVING

Hon Rosemary Gail, *b* 1946: *m* 1st, 1967 (*m diss* 1971), Ernest Raymond Anthony Travis; 2ndly, 1980 (*m diss* 1984), Ian Barby; 3rdly, 1985, Michael Withers, of PO Box N7776, Nassau, Bahamas, and has issue (by 2nd and 3rd *m*).
Hon Diana Gillian Amanda (The Gate House, Stoneleigh Abbey, Kenilworth, Warwicks CV8 2LF), *b* 1948: *m* 1st, 1969 (*m diss* 1977), David Huntington Williams; 2ndly, 1984 (*m diss* 1993), Harry Johnson, only son of Henry Edward Johnson, of Offchurch Bury, Warwicks, and has issue by both marriages.

PRYS-DAVIES, BARON (Prys-Davies) (Life Baron 1982)

GWILYM PRYS PRYS-DAVIES, son of William Davies, by his wife Mary Matilda; *b* 8 Dec 1923; assumed by Deed Poll 1982 the surname of Prys-Davies in lieu of his patronymic; *ed* Towyn Sch, and Univ Coll of Wales, Aberystwyth; served in RN 1942-46; Faculty of Law, Univ Coll of Wales, Aberystwyth 1946-52; admitted Solicitor 1956; Partner, Morgan Bruce & Nicholas, Solicitors, Cardiff, Pontypridd and Porth since 1957; Special Adviser to Sec of State for Wales 1974-78; Chm Welsh Hosps Bd 1968-74; Member Welsh Council 1967-69; Member Economic and Social Cttee, EEC 1978-82; OStJ; *cr Baron Prys-Davies*, of Llanegryn, co Gwynedd (Life Baron) 1982: *m* 1951, Llinos, da of Abram Richard Evans, and has issue, three das.
Residence – Lluest, 78 Church Road, Tonteg, Pontypridd, Mid Glamorgan.

DAUGHTERS LIVING

Hon Catrin Prys, *b* 1957: *m* 1980, Andrew Peter Waugh, and has issue living, Matthew Prys, *b* 1989, — Owen Prys, *b* 1992.
Hon Ann Prys, *b* 1959.
Hon Elin Prys, *b* 1963.

PYM, BARON (Pym) (Life Baron 1987)

FRANCIS LESLIE PYM, MC, PC, only son of late Leslie Ruthven Pym, MP, of Penpergwm Lodge, Abergavenny, Mon, and Hazells Hall, Sandy, Beds; *b* 13 Feb 1922; *ed* Eton, and Magdalene Coll, Camb; a DL for Cambs since 1973; Hon Fell Magdalene Coll, Camb 1979; served World War II 1941-45 as Capt 9th Queen's Royal Lancers (despatches, MC 1945); Memb Herefords CC 1958-62, MP for Cambs (*C*) 1961-83, and for Cambs South East 1983-87; Parl Sec to Treasury and Govt Chief Whip 1970-73, Sec of State Northern Ireland 1973-74, Opposition Spokesman: Agriculture 1974-76, House of Commons Affairs and Devolution 1976-78, Foreign and Commonwealth Affairs 1978-79; Sec of State for Defence 1979-81; Chancellor of Duchy of Lancaster, Paymaster Gen and Leader of House of Commons 1981, Lord Pres of the Council and Leader of House of Commons 1981-82, Foreign Sec 1982-83, Pres Atlantic Treaty Assocn 1985-88; Chm English-Speaking Union 1987-92; *cr* PC 1970, and *Baron Pym*, of Sandy, co Beds (Life Baron) 1987: *m* 1949, Valerie Fortune, elder da of Francis John Heaton Daglish, and has issue.

Arms – Quarterly, 1st and 4th sable on a fesse engrailed between three owls or a trefoil slipped vert between two cross crosslets of the first all within a bordure of the second (*Pym*); 2nd vert on a cross engrailed ermine a lion rampant reguardant sable in the dexter canton a mullet or (*Kingsley*); 3rd sable three salmon haurient per pale argent and or (*Orde*). **Crest** – Upon a mount vert a hind's head erased or gorged with a collar nebuly azure and holding in the mouth a trefoil slipped vert. **Supporters** – *Dexter*, rampant upon a sandy mount with tussocks of grass proper a warhorse in trian aspect sable mane tail and hooves or on its head a chanfron and on the neck a crinet both argent gorged with a double chain pendent therefrom a portcullis gold; *sinister*, rampant upon a like mount a bull in trian aspect sable armed and unguled or also gorged with a double chain and pendent therefrom a portcullis gold. **Motto** – Ubi Seritur Ibi Floreat.
Residence – Everton Park, Sandy, Beds SG19 2DE. *Clubs* – Cavalry and Guards', Buck's.

SONS LIVING

Hon (Francis) Jonathan, *b* 1952; *ed* Eton, and Magdalene Coll, Camb; Partner, Travers Smith Braithwaite, Solicitors since 1984: *m* 1981, Laura Elizabeth Camille, yr da of Robin Alfred Wellesley, and has issue living, (Francis) Matthew, *b* 1984, — Oliver Quintin, *b* 1988, — Katharine Camille, *b* 1985. *Residence* – 53 Ridgway Place, SW19 4SP. *Clubs* – Garrick, City of London, Roehampton.
Hon Andrew Leslie, *b* 1954; *ed* Eton, and RAC Cirencester: *m* 1976, Ruth Alison, da of Benjamin Peter Skelton, and has issue living, Benjamin Ruthven, *b* 1979, — Jessica Mary, *b* 1982. *Residence* – The Elms, Everton, Sandy, Beds SG19 2JV.

DAUGHTERS LIVING

Hon Charlotte Hazell, *b* 1950: *m* 1984, Ian Nye Lightbody, and has issue living, Thomas Hugh, *b* 1986, — Helena Rosamund, *b* 1988.
Hon Sarah Lucy, *b* 1958: *m* 1985, Peter Walton, and has issue living, James Peter, *b* 1986, — Victoria Lucy, *b* 1988. *Residence* – Thockrington, Colwell, Hexham, Northumberland NE48 4DH.

QUEENBOROUGH BARONY OF (Paget) (Extinct 1949)

DAUGHTER LIVING OF FIRST BARON (*By 2nd marriage*)

Hon Cicili Carol, *b* 1928: *m* 1949, Capt Robert Victor John Evans, and has had issue, John Almeric, *b* 1950: *m* 1980, Patricia L., da of R. W. Westall, of Birchfield Farm, Sundridge, Kent, and has issue living, William *b* 1983, James *b* 1986, — Michael Hugh, *b* 1956: *m* 1989, Penelope M., da of David Rosling, of Hammerwood, Sussex, — Camilla Carol, *b* 1952; *d* 1963, — Patricia Antoinetta, *b* 1959. *Residence* – Gainsford House, Cowden, Kent.

Queensberry, Duke of; title borne by Duke of Buccleuch.

QUEENSBERRY, MARQUESS OF (Douglas) (Marquess S 1682, Bt S 1668)

DAVID HARRINGTON ANGUS DOUGLAS, 12th Marquess, and 11th Baronet; *b* 19 Dec 1929; *s* 1954; *ed* Eton; late 2nd Lieut Roy Horse Guards; Prof of Ceramics, Roy Coll of Art since 1959; Sr Fell Royal Coll of Art 1990: *m* 1st, 1956 (*m diss* 1969), Ann, da of Maurice Sinnett Jones, and formerly wife of George Arthur Radford; 2ndly, 1969 (*m diss* 1986), Alexandra Mary Clare Wyndham, da of Guy Wyndham Sich, and has issue by 1st and 2nd wives.

𝔄rms – Quarterly: 1st and 4th argent, a King's heart crowned gules, on a chief azure, three stars of The first, *Douglas*; 2nd and 3rd azure, a bend between six cross crosslets fitchée or, *Mar*: the whole within a bordure or, charged with the double tressure flory-counter gules. ℭrest – A heart gules, crowned and winged. 𝔖upporters – Two flying horses argent winged or.
Residence – 24 Brook Mews North, W2 3BW.

SONS LIVING (*By 2nd wife*)

SHOLTO FRANCIS GUY (*Viscount Drumlanrig*), *b* 1 June 1967.
Lord Milo Luke Dickon, *b* 1978.

DAUGHTERS LIVING (*By 1st wife*)

Lady Emma Cathleen, *b* 1956.
Lady Alice, *b* 1965.

(*By 2nd wife*)

Lady Kate Cordelia Sasha, *b* 1969.

HALF-BROTHER LIVING

Lord Gawain Archibald Francis (2 Archery Sq, Walmer, Deal), *b* 1948; *ed* Downside, and Royal Acad of Music; LRAM: *m* 1971, Nicolette, yr da of Col Frank Alfred Eustace, OBE, RM, of Hong Kong, and has issue living, Jamie Sholto, *b* 1975, — Dalziel Frances, *b* 1971, — Elizabeth Meriel, *b* 1974, — Natasha Rose, *b* 1976, — Margarita Consuela, *b* 1978, — Mary Anne, *b* 1981.

SISTER LIVING

Lady Jane Katherine, *b* 1926: *m* 1949 (*m diss* 1985), David Arthur Cory-Wright (*see* Cory-Wright, Bt). *Residence* – 11 Stowe Rd, W12 8BQ.

COLLATERAL BRANCHES LIVING

Issue of late Lord Cecil Charles Douglas, 2nd son of 10th Marquess, *b* 1898, *d* 26 Feb 1981: *m* 1927, Ruby, who *d* 9 May 1981, formerly wife of — St Bede Kirkley, 2nd da of George de Vere Fenn:—
Susan Jean, *b* 1939: *m* 1965, Baron (Joachim) Botho Carl Waldemar Georg Hasso von Bose, Kt of Justice, Johanniterorden (Bailiwick of Brandenburg). *Residence* – Apt 1203, 1166 Bay St, Toronto, Ont M5S 2X8, Canada. *Club* – White's.

Grandchildren of late Lord Sholto George Douglas, 4th son of 9th Marquess:—
Issue of late Sholto Augustus Douglas, *b* 1900 (became a French citizen 1938), *d* 1950: *m* 1925, Isabelle, who *d* 1993, da of late François Raymon:—
Douglas Bruce Georges, *b* 1926. —— Robert, *b* 1933: *m* 1963, Nicole Bourgeois, and has issue living, Marie Christine, *b* 1965. —— Noel (son), *b* 1939. —— Elisabeth Georgette, *b* 1927: *m* 1952, Jean Masoin, artist, and has issue living, Sybil Elisabeth, *b* 1953: *m* 1985, Daniel Rohemer, and has issue living, Alexandre *b* 1988, Aurelia *b* 1986. —— Sybil, *b* 1931: *m* 1966, Nigel Paul Mitchell-Carruthers, of 308, Route de Grasse, Vence, 06 France, and has issue living, Bruce Nigel Lawrence, *b* 1968, — Cecilia Elisabeth, *b* 1973. —— Marquerite Jeannette, *b* 1941: *m* 1st, 1969 (*m diss* 1973), Jean Demol; 2ndly, 1974, Count Xavier de Chagny, and has issue living (by 1st *m*), Ysabelle, *b* 1965, — (by 2nd *m*), Godefroy, *b* 1975. —— Marie-Jeanne, *b* 1944: *m* 1st, 1970, Horace Warren Hastings-Hodgkins, who *d* 1972; 2ndly, 1978, Wesley Alan Christie, of 44 Howard Rd, Wokingham, Berks RG11 2BX, and has issue living (by 1st husband), Warren Sholto Olivier, *b* 1966; MA Cantab: *m* 1992, Pamela, da of Kuldip Khosla, — Julian Percy Herbert, *b* 1967, — Alistair John Hughes, *b* 1970, — (by 2nd husband), Michael Ian Jerôme, *b* 1974, — Jasmine Elisabeth Céline, *b* 1976.

Grandson of late Arthur Henry Johnstone-Douglas, son of Robert Johnstone-Douglas, son of Henry Alexander Douglas, brother of 6th and 7th Marquesses:—
Issue of late Robert Sholto Johnstone-Douglas, *b* 1871, *d* 1958: *m* 1913, Bettina, who *d* 1961, da of late Harman Grisewood:—
Robert Arthur, *b* 1914. —— Elizabeth Gwendolen Teresa, *b* 1916: *m* 1st, 1954, as his 2nd wife, 6th Earl of Craven, who *d* 1965; 2ndly, 1966, Kenneth Harmood Banner, of Peelings Manor, Pevensey, Sussex.

Grandson of late Right Rev Henry Alexander Douglas, Bishop of Bombay, son of late Henry Alexander Douglas (ante):—
Issue of late Archibald Charles Douglas, *b* 1861, *d* 1939: *m* 1896, Betty, who *d* 1960, da of Andrew S McClelland, CA:—
Archibald Andrew Henry (4 The Mews, Amesbury Abbey, Amesbury, Wilts SP4 7EX), *b* 1902; *ed* Clifton, and Glasgow Univ (BSc): *m* 1935 (*m diss* 1980), Marjorie Gordon, who *d* 1992, el da of late Dr Grey Brown, and has issue living, Archibald Sholto Gordon (10 Coleford Rd, Wandsworth, SW18) *b* 1937: *m* 1984, Mrs Victoria Ann Adam, only da of late James Bonnyman, of Sarasota, Florida, — Ian Andrew McClelland (6 Ansley Rd, Houghton, Cambs PE17 2DQ), *b* 1939; W/Cmdr RAF: *m* 1967, Jennifer Merrett, of Plymouth, and has issue living, Andrew James Sholto *b* 1973, Kirsten Lucy *b* 1969, — Katherine Veronica, *b* 1943: *m* 1963, Richard Ninian Barwick Clegg, QC, of The Old Rectory, Brereton, via Sandbach, Ches, only son of late Sir Cuthbert Barwick Clegg, TD, and has issue living, Aidan Charles Barwick *b* 1966, Sebastian James Barwick *b* 1969, Flavia Mary Rosabel *b* 1968, — Ursula Rosemary, *b* (twin) 1943: *m* 1968, William Harvey Righter, of 10 Quick St, N1, Reader in English and Comparative Lit, Warwick Univ.

Grandchildren of late (Hon) John Douglas, CMG (infra):—
Issue of late (Hon) Edward Archibald Douglas, b 1877, d 1947: m 1907, Annette Eileen, who d 1966, 2nd da of Hon
Mr Justice Virgil Power (a Puisne Judge of Supreme Court, Queensland), of Rockhampton, Queensland:—
Sir Edward Sholto, b 1909; ed St Ignatius Coll, Sydney; 1939-45 War as Major Austn Imperial Force; Kt 1977: m 1939, Mary
Constance, da of late C. M. Curr, of Buckie, NS Wales. Residence – 81 Markwell Street, Hamilton, Brisbane, Queensland.
—— Gavin James, b 1926; ed Downlands Coll, Toowoomba, and Queensland Univ (MB and BS 1948); FRACS 1955; m 1951,
Clare, da of J. H. McHugh of Townsville Queensland, and has issue living, Edward John, b 1952, — Andrew Benedict, b
1957, — Gavin Gerard, b 1958, — Christopher James, b 1962, — Margot Anne, b 1953, — Helen Penny, b 1955, — Annette
Josepa, b 1960, — Mary Patrice, b 1964. Residence – 107 Stanley St, North Ward, Townsville, Queensland. —— Andrew
Brice, b 1931; ed Downlands Coll, Toowoomba: m 1957, Lorraine, da of R. J. Lawson, of Brisbane, and has issue living, Rev
Sholto Francis, b 1958; ed Downlands Coll, Toowoomba, Queensland Univ (BA 1980), Monash Univ (Dip Ed 1987), and
Melbourne Univ (B Theol 1988); ordained priest 1988, — David James, b 1960; ed Downlands Coll, Toowoomba, and
Queensland Univ (B Comm 1983), ASA 1989: m 1991, Karen, da of B. H. Emerson, of Dover, UK, and has issue living,
Alexandra Helena b 1993, — Maxwell Richard, b 1966; ed St Joseph's Coll, Brisbane, and Queensland Univ (BSc 1986), —
Andrew Brice Christopher, b 1968; ed St Joseph's Coll, Brisbane, and Queensland Univ (BA 1988); LLB 1991. Residence – 17
Sutherland Av, Ascot, Brisbane, Queensland 4007.
Issue of late Henry Alexander Cecil Douglas, b 1879, d 1952: m 1st, 1910, Flora Isabel, who d 1910, da of Charles
Hugh Macdonald, formerly of Kilcoy, Queensland; 2ndly, 1914, Catherine Cecilia, who d 1977, da of late T. C.
Beirne, MLC, of Queensland:—
(By 2nd m) Alexander Michael (17 Palm Av, Ascot, Brisbane, Queensland), b 1926; ed Downlands Coll, Queensland: m 1954,
Morna Therese, da of Michael Patrick O'Rourke of Brisbane, Queensland, and has issue living, Henry Alexander Michael, b
1955; ed St Joseph's Coll, Brisbane, and Queensland Univ (MB BS) 1978: m 1984, Frances Michelle, da of Eric Donnelly, of
Brisbane, and has issue living, Eric Michael b 1987, Joseph Henry b 1988, Alexandra Kate b 1991, — Richard John, b 1957;
ed St Joseph's Coll, Brisbane, and Queensland Univ (BCom, LLB), Bar Q'land 1980: m 1981, Rosemary Nerida, da of R.
Wylie, of Brisbane, — Alexander Rodney, b 1958; ed St Joseph's Coll, Brisbane, and Queensland Univ (MB BS) 1981: m
1983, Susan Kim, da of C. Primmer, of Rockhampton, Queensland, — Andrew Beirne, b 1960; ed St Joseph's Coll, Brisbane,
and Queensland Univ (BCom) 1982, — James Patrick, b 1965; ed St Joseph's Coll, Brisbane. —— Sybil Catherine b 1918: m
1943, Alan B. Bryan, FCA, Lt Cdr R Aust Navy (ret), and has issue living, Alan Douglas, b 1944; MB BS, FRACP: m 1972,
Margaret Suzanne van Rompaey, and has issue living, Thomas Charles b 1975, Sophie Elizabeth b 1973, Olivia Catherine b
1977, Chloe Margaret b 1979, — Henry Beirne, b 1947; MB BS: m 1982, Patricia Mary Johnson, and has issue living, Henry
William b 1986, Michael Charles b 1987, Brigid Catherine Cecilia b 1984, — Edward Alan, b 1954; BComm: m 1st, 1982 (m
diss 1990), Heather Joy Killen; 2ndly, 1990, Felicity York Sharples, and has issue living (by 2nd m), Isobel Rose b 1992, —
Neil Beirne, b 1959; BBus: m 1983, Lisa Marie Walsh, and has issue living, Edward George Peter b 1986, George Bernard
Joseph b 1990, Lucy Cecilia b 1985, Harriet Catherine b (twin) 1986, Annie Beatrice b 1992, Charlotte Mary b (twin) 1992, —
Mary Christine, b 1949: m 1973, David Walter Drake, BComm, FCA, and has issue living, Alexander Bryan b 1974, Nicholas
Thomas b 1977, Douglas Romeo b 1983, Elizabeth Sybil b 1980. Residence – 14 Inverness St, Ascot, Brisbane, Queensland
4007.
Issue of late Hugh Maxwell Douglas Lieut Australian Forces, b 1881, d of wounds received in action 1918: m 1904,
Hannah Elizabeth, 2nd da of E. L. Thornton, formerly of Warwick, Queensland:—
Henry Alexander (37 Ormond St, Ascot, Brisbane, Queensland), b 1908: m 1938, Ethel Audrey, da of late Dr A. E. Malaher,
and has issue living, Henry John, b 1942: m 1966, Susan da of E. Clark, of Balgowlah Heights, Sydney, and has issue living,
Geoffrey Peter b 1970, Ian Andrew b 1971, Elizabeth Jane b 1967: m 1989, Conrad Cholakos, Kathryn Ann b 1973, —
Kathrine, b 1938: m 1961 (m diss 1982), John Francis Douglas, and has issue living, Andrew b 1963, Grahame b 1965, James
b 1968. —— Edward Octavius, b 1913. Residence – 91 Uplancaster Rd, Ascot, Brisbane, Qld.

Grandchildren of late (Hon) John Douglas, CMG, 7th son of Henry Alexander Douglas (brother of 6th and
7th Marquesses), 3rd son of Sir William Douglas, 4th Bt:—
Issue of late (Hon) Robert Johnstone Douglas, b 1883, d 1972; Puisne Judge of Supreme Court of Qld: m 1912,
Alice Mary (18 Lawson St, Hermit Park, Townsville 4812, Qld), da of late Andrew Ball, of Townsville, Qld:—
Robert Andrew, AM (18 Lawson St, Hermit Park, Townsville, Qld), b 1915; ed St Joseph's Coll, Nudgee, and Melbourne Univ
(MB, BS); FRACP 1967; FRCP Lond 1979; formerly Maj Australian Army Med Corps Middle East, New Guinea, and Tarakan
1940-45; AM (1984): m 1949, Barbara, da of late Rev John Shaw, of Adelaide, S Australia, and widow of Harry Buzolich, of
Melbourne, and has issue living, Robert John (13 Drewett St, Surrey Hills, Melbourne, Vic 3127), b 1950; ed James Cook
Univ (BA), and Melbourne Univ (MBA): m 1983, Lynne, da of late Capt James Erskine Muirhead of Melbourne, and has
issue living, James Robert b 1986, Sarah Jane b 1984, — Sholto James Shaw, b 1962, — Catriona b 1952: m 1983, Geoffrey
Charles Beames, MB BS, FRANZCP, and has issue living, Alexander Thomas b 1986, Michael Robert Charles b 1988,
Catherine Alice b 1990, — Barbara Selina, b 1953: m 1974, Philip William Hale, and has issue living, Nathan Alexander b
1974, Emily Angela b 1975, — Sarah, b 1955. —— Beatrice Rose Mary, b 1919: m 1947, Cornelius James Howard, who d
1980, of 984 Burke Rd, Deepdene, Melbourne, Aust, and has issue living, Catherine Mary, b 1952: m 1977, Peter Capell
Dobson, MB, BS, MRCOG, FRCS Ed, FRACOG, and has issue living, Michael Howard b 1980, Elizabeth Mary b 1978, Sarah
Catherine b 1982, Alice Jane b 1985, — Elizabeth Anne, b 1953: m 1978, Christopher John Dawson, of 33 Dorking Rd, Box
Hill, Victoria, Australia, and has issue living, Emma Catherine b 1984, Juliet Beatrice b 1986, Maria Irene b 1988, Tess
Elizabeth b 1992.

Grandchildren of late (Hon) Robert Johnstone Douglas (ante):—
Issue of late (Hon) James Archibald Douglas, b 1917; Puisne Judge of Supreme Court of Queensland, Maj AIF; d
1984: m 1943, Marjorie Mary (Greyleaves, Morgan St, Ascot, Brisbane, Queensland), da of late James Campbell
Ramsay, of Ballarat:—
Robert Ramsay, RFD (18 Towers Street, Ascot, Brisbane, Qld), b 1944; ed Villanova Coll, Coorparoo, and Qld Univ (LLB);
Bar Qld 1968; QC 1982; W Comm'r RAAF Res; Judge Advocate, Aust Defence Forces; Knight of Honour and Devotion
Sovereign Mil Order of Malta: m 1970, Jennifer Farmar, da of Frank Wilmot Horton, of Blenheim, NZ, and has issue living,
Robert Horton, b 1970, — William John Archibald, b 1975, — Charlotte Mary, b 1972. —— Francis Maxwell (4 Wiston
Gardens, Double Bay, Sydney, NSW), b 1946; ed Villanova Coll, Coorparoo, Qld Univ (BA, LLB), and Camb Univ (LLB); Bar
Qld 1969, Bar NSW 1975, QC 1988: m 1972, Sigrun Baldvinsdottir, da of Baldvin Einarsson, of Rekjavik, Iceland, and has
issue living, James Baldvin b 1974, — Helga Sigrun, b 1979, — Sara Kristin b 1989. —— James Sholto (9 Lucinda Street,
Taringa, Brisbane, Qld), b 1950; ed Villanova Coll, Coorparoo, Qld Univ (BA, LLB), and Camb Univ (LLB); Bar Qld 1973,
QC 1980: m 1980, Margaret Anne, da of Francis Xavier Kennedy, of Brisbane, and has issue living, Francis Sholto, b 1983,
— Hannah Mary, b 1986. —— Catherine Alice Mary (9 Glostermin, Whyenbah St, Hamilton, Qld), b 1948; BA, LTCL,
ASDA: m 1974 (m diss 1977), Roger John Stredwick; 2ndly, 1981, William Charles Edward McCourt, of Brisbane.

Grandson of late Walter Douglas-Irvine, 3rd son of late Lord William Robert Keith Douglas, MP (infra):—
Issue of late Rev Henry Archibald Douglas (who reverted to that surname only 1919), b 1883, d 1962: m 1913,
Beatrice Alice, who d 1976, da of Thomas William Gratrix, of Liverpool:—
Walter Francis Edward (32 St Leonard's St, Stamford, Lincs), b 1917; ed Exeter Coll, Oxford (BA 1938, MA 1950): m 1944,
Eugenie Nellie, who d 1988, yst da of Gustave Chaudoir, of Highgate, N, and has issue living, Francis Gustave (12 Wood-
lands, Kerry Pike, co Cork), b 1946; ed New Univ of Ulster (BSc 1971, MA 1976), and Univ of Hull (PhD 1993): m 1976,
Hilary Agnes, only child of G. A. Deane, of Armoy, co Antrim, and has issue living, Niall Edward b 1978, Aoife Lucy b 1983,
— Mark Gavin (94 Paston Lane, Peterborough), b 1958: m 1981, Sally Knew, — Ruth Mary, b 1947; ed St Martin's Coll of
Art (Dip AD 1969), and Goldsmiths' Coll (PGCE 1988, MA 1992): m 1971, William Francis Wright of 10A Tower Av,

Chelmsford, Essex, and has issue living, Henry Joseph *b* 1967, Francis Reuben *b* 1973, Barnabas Mark *b* 1981, Rebecca Elizabeth *b* 1976, — Josephine Eugenie, *b* 1950: *m* 1st, 1973 (*m diss* 1981), Alan Michael Locker; 2ndly, 1984, Peter John Jarmakowiecz (uses surname of Jakins), and has had issue, (by 1st *m*), Benjamin Harvey *b* 1974, Joseph Charles *b* 1978, Samuel William *b* and *d* 1980, — Rachel Margaret, *b* 1954: *m* 1974, Richard David Palmer, and has issue living, George Richard *b* 1982, Thomas Jonathan *b* 1983, John Henry *b* 1987.

Grandchildren of late Charles Irvine Douglas, 4th son of late Lord William Robert Keith Douglas, MP (who was raised to the rank of a Marquess's yr son 1837), 4th son of Sir William Douglas, 4th Bt, and brother of 6th and 7th Marquesses:—

Issue of late Robert Keith Douglas, *b* 1874, *d* 1917: *m* 1902, Louisa Mary (who *m* 2ndly, 1924, Major Hugh Fraser, late Rifle Brig), yst da of late Rev Horace Charles Ripley, sometime V of Minster-Lovell, Witney, Oxon:—

Archibald William (Le Chalet Du Moine, St John, Jersey JE3 4FP), *b* 1907; *ed* Malvern, and Brasenose Coll Oxford (MA); late Maj Int Corps; 1939-45 War: *m* 1934, Barbara Middlemost, who *d* 1970, yr da of late Herbert Pratt Bairstow, and has issue living, Janet Valerie, *b* 1937: *m* 1959, His Honour Judge (John Percival) Harris, DSC, of Tudor Court, Fairmile Park Rd, Cobham, Surrey, and has issue living, Steven Oliver *b* 1965; *ed* Wellington Coll, and Bristol Univ (BSc): *m* 1993, Diana Elizabeth Jonas, Juliet Caroline, *b* 1961: *m* 19—, Alistair Charles Timms, of Heath End, Bowlhead Green, Godalming, Surrey GU6 6NW (and has issue living, Charles Benjamin Alistair *b* 1991, Amelia Charlotte *b* 1993), Charlotte Beatrice, *b* 1963: *m* 19—, Nicholas Michael Frederick Fuller, of 12 Ruvigny Gdns, SW15 1JR, — Alison Rosemary, *b* 1939: *m* 1967, Brian Woodcock, of La Cohue, Hérupe, St John, Jersey, and has issue living, James William *b* 1970; *ed* Uppingham, and Buckingham Univ (BA), Sara Jane *b* 1969

Issue of late John Campbell Douglas, *b* 1876, *d* 1960: *m* 1910, Violet Douglas, who *d* 1972, da of late C. J. Daniell, of Cuyim, Punta del Este, Uruguay:—

(Charles) Sholto, *b* 1915; European War 1939-45 as Major King's Own Scottish Borders: *m* 1941, Christian Frances, who *d* 1990, da of late Maj-Gen Francis James Marshall, CB, CMG, DSO, and has issue living, Helen Frances *b* 1942: *m* 1971, Clive Eden Walker (37 Hans Schoeman St, Malanshof, Randburg 2194, S Africa), and has issue living, Alice Megan *b* 1973, Mary Louise *b* 1976, — Katharine Ann, *b* 1943: *m* 1st, 1969 (*m diss* 1983), Timothy MacDermot-Roe; 2ndly, 1984, Robert Athelston Price, of Urlar Farm, Aberfeldy, Perthshire, and has issue living (by 1st *m*), Charles Alexander *b* 1974, Katherine Emma *b* 1972, (by 2nd *m*) Robert John Crossley *b* 1984, Sarah Margaret *b* 1986, — Margaret Jean, *b* 1945: *m* 1976, David Eric Short, of PO Box 880, Harrismith 9880, S Africa, and has issue living, Alan Douglas *b* 1977, Brian Eric *b* 1979. *Residence* – Old School House, Little Ballinluig, Grandtully, Perthshire. ——Violet Katherine, *b* 1910: *m* 1st, 1935, John Griffith O'Donoghue, who *d* 1976; 2ndly, 1982, Brig F. W. Sandars, DSO, of La Guarida, Jesús Pobre, Gata de Gorgos, Alicante, Spain, and has issue living (by 1st *m*), Susan *b* 1936: *m* 1956, A. L. K. Liddle, and has issue living, Nicholas John Kestell *b* 1958, Alan Digby Simon *b* 1959, Juliet Susan *b* 1965, — Margaret Ann (Peggy), *b* 1938: *m* 1960, Christopher James Waller, Queen's Roy Irish Hussars, and has issue living, Sarah Louise *b* 1961, Celia Katherine *b* 1963. *Residence* – Drumcowie, Malin, co Donegal. ——Margaret Elizabeth, *b* 1918: *m* 1945, John Craigmyle Cooper, and has issue living, Ian Alexander Douglas, *b* 1947. — Peter Craigmyle *b* 1952, — Margaret Jane, *b* 1948. *Residence* – Cherryhill Farm, RR1, Freelton, Ontario, Canada.

Granddaughter of late Sir John Douglas KCMG, 7th son of late Gen Sir James Dawes Douglas, son of Maj James Sholto Douglas, grandson of Sir John Douglas, 3rd Bt:—

Issue of late Francis William Douglas; *b* 1874, *d* 1953; *m* 1908, Violet Eleanor Jane, who *d* 1956, da of late John More O'Ferrall:—

Helen Sholto, *b* 1910: *m* 1st, 1932, Edward William Eric Mann, who was *ka* 1943; 2ndly, 1950, Wilfred Harry Levita, of 6 Hans Crescent, SW1.

PREDECESSORS – (1) Sir WILLIAM Douglas, 9th Feudal Baron of Drumlanrig; entertained James VI at his mansion; *cr Lord Douglas of Hawick and Tibbers*, and *Viscount Drumlanrig* (peerage of Scotland) 1628, and *Earl of Queensberry* (peerage of Scotland) 1633, with remainder to his heirs male bearing the surname and arms of Douglas; *d* 1640; *s* by his son (2) JAMES, 2nd Earl; a zealous Royalist; *d* 1671; *s* by his son (3) WILLIAM, PC, 3rd Earl; Justice-Gen of Scotland 1680-2, Extraordinary Lord of Session 1681, and High Treasurer of Scotland and Constable and Gov of Edinburgh Castle 1682; *cr Lord Douglas of Kinmont, Middlebie and Dornoch, Viscount Nith, Torthorwald and Ross, Earl of Drumlanrig and Sanquhar*, and *Marquess of Queensberry* (peerage of Scotland) 1682, with remainder to his heirs male whatsoever, and *Marquess of Dumfriesshire*, and *Duke of Queensberry* (peerage of Scotland) 1683, with remainder to heirs male; *d* 1695: *s* by his el son (4) JAMES, KG, 2nd Duke; Lord High Treasurer of Scotland, Sec of State and Lord High Commr, and First Commr on the part of Scotland to discuss the measure of the Union; in 1806 surrendered the Marquessate of Dumfriesshire and the Dukedom of Queensberry, and in the same year received a new grant of those honours extending the remainder to the heirs of entail descended from William, 1st Earl of Queensberry; *cr Baron Ripon, Marquess of Beverley* and *Duke of Dover* (peerage of Great Britain) 1708 with special remainder to his 2nd son Charles and yr sons in tail male; *d* 1711; *s* (according to decision of House of Lords 1812) by his el surviving son in the Marquessate and Earldom of Queensberry, the Viscountcy of Drumlanrig, and the Lordship of Douglas of Hawick and Tibbers, these not being mentioned in the resignation and regrant of 1706, were not affected by it and descended according to the original limitation, and in the Dukedom and other titles (by his nomination) by his second surviving son, Charles (infra) (5) JAMES, 3rd Marquess; an idiot, probably from birth, who never used the titles; *d* 1715; *s* by his brother (6) CHARLES, 3rd Duke, who had in 1706 been *cr Viscount Tibbers* and *Earl of Solway* (peerage of Scotland), with remainder to the heirs of his father not in succession to the Dukedom of Queensberry; *d* without surviving issue 1778, when the English honours expired and the Scottish peerage devolved upon (7) WILLIAM, KT (only son of William, 2nd Earl of March, el son of William, 1st Earl of March, 2nd son of 1st Duke, who had been *cr Earl of March, Viscount Peebles, and Lord Douglas of Neidpath, Lyne and Munard* (peerage of Scotland) 1697, with remainder to heirs male of body, failing which to heirs to entail of the Lordships and lands of Neidpath), 4th Duke, who in 1731 had *s* his father as 3rd Earl of March (ante), and in 1748 his mother as 4th *Earl of Ruglen* (peerage of Scotland, *cr* 1665); *cr Baron Douglas of Amesbury* (peerage of Great Britain) 1768; *d* 1810, when the Barony of Douglas of Amesbury and the Earldom of Ruglen became ext, and the Earldom of March and inferior dignities (*cr* 1697) passed to the 8th Earl of Wemyss (grandson of Lady Anne Douglas, daughter of 1st Duke of Queensberry and sister of 1st Earl of March, on whom the lordships and lands of Neidpath were entailed), the Dukedom of Queensberry, Marquessate of Dumfriesshire, Earldom of Drumlanrig and Sanquhar, Viscountcy of Nith, Torthorwald, and Ross, and Lordship of Douglas of Kinmont, Middlebie and Dornoch reverted to the 3rd Duke of Buccleuch (grandson of Lady Jane Douglas, el da of 2nd Duke of Queensberry), and the Marquessate and Earldom of Queensberry, Viscountcy of Drumlanrig, and Lordship of Douglas of Hawick and Tibbers devolved upon his kinsman and heir male (8) Sir CHARLES Douglas, 5th Bt of Kelhead (4th in descent from Sir James Douglas of Kelhead, who was created a baronet of Nova Scotia 1668 with remainder to heirs of his body, el surviving son of Col Sir William Douglas of Kelhead, 2nd son of 1st Earl of Queensberry), who became the 6th Marquess of Queensberry; *cr Baron Solway*, of Kinmount, co Dumfries (peerage of United Kingdom) 1833; *dsp* 1837, when the Barony of Solway became ext, and he was *s* in the Scottish honours by his brother (9) JOHN, 7th Marquess; *d* 1856; *s* by his son (10) ARCHIBALD WILLIAM, PC, 8th Marquess; *b* 1818: *m* 1840, Caroline Margaret, who *d* 1904, da of Gen Sir William Robert Clayton, 5th Bt; was MP for Dumfriesshire (LC) 1847-56, and Comptroller of the Household 1853-6; *d* 1858; *s* by his son (11) JOHN SHOLTO, 9th Marquess, *b* 1844: *m* 1st, 1866 (*m diss* 1887) Sibyl, who *d* 1935, da of late Alfred Montgomery; 2ndly, 1893 (*m diss* 1894), Ethel, da of Edward Charles Weeden, of Eastbourne; *d* 1900; *s* by his el surviving son (12) PERCY SHOLTO, 10th Marquess, *b* 1868: *m* 1st, 1893, Anna Maria, who *d* 1917, da of late Rev Thomas Walters, V of Boyton, Cornwall; 2ndly, 1918, Mary Louise, who *d* 1956, da of late Richard Bickel, of Cardiff, and widow of Ernest Morgan; *d* 1920; *s* by his el son (13) FRANCIS ARCHIBALD KELHEAD, 11th Marquess, *b* 1896; Capt Black Watch (Roy Highlanders); European War 1914-19 (twice wounded); sometime a representative Peer for Scotland: *m* 1st, 1917 (*m diss* 1925), Irene Clarice, da of H. W. Richards, of Regent's Park, NW;

2ndly, 1926 (*m diss* 1946), Kathleen Sabine, who *d* 1959, da of late Harrington Mann; 3rdly, 1947, Muriel Beatrice Margaret (CHUNN), who *d* 1992, da of late Arthur John Rowe Thornett; *d* 1954; *s* by his el son (14) DAVID HARRINGTON ANGUS, 12th Marquess and present peer; also Earl of Queensberry, Viscount Drumlanrig, and Lord Douglas of Hawick and Tibbers.

QUIBELL, BARONY OF (Quibell) (Extinct 1962)

DAUGHTER LIVING OF FIRST BARON (*By 1st marriage*)

Hon Edith Ellen, *b* 1904: is Pres of Roy So for Prevention of Cruelty to Animals, Scunthorpe, a Dir of Quibell & Hardy Ltd, builders and contractors, and a JP for Parts of Lindsey, Lincolnshire; was Mayoress of Scunthorpe 1953-4: *m* 1954, Eric Bennard Cuthbert, who assumed by deed poll 1962 the surname of Bennard in lieu of his patronymic. *Residence –*

QUINTON, BARON (Quinton) (Life Baron 1982)

ANTHONY MEREDITH QUINTON, FBA, son of late Surgeon Capt Richard Frith Quinton, RN (*d* 1935), by his wife, late Gwenllyan Letitia (*d* 1978); *b* 25 March 1925; *ed* Stowe, and Ch Ch Oxford (BA 1948); served 1939-45 War with RAF; Fell of All Souls Coll Oxford 1949-55; Fell of New Coll Oxford 1955-78; Pres of Trin Coll Oxford 1978-87; Member Arts Council of Great Britain 1979-82; FBA 1977; *cr Baron Quinton*, of Holywell, City of Oxford and co Oxfordshire (Life Baron) 1982; *m* 1952, Marcelle, da of late Maurice Wegier, of New York, and has issue.

Arms – Argent a tilting spear in bend sable grip butt and coronal or between two bends also sable and in chief three roses Gules barbed and seeded proper and in base as many martlets also gules. **Crest** – A quintain proper **Supporters** – *Dexter*, a fox rampant proper; *sinister*, a griffin segreant per fess azure and or both gorged with a coronet flory gold.
Residence – The Mill House, Turville, Henley-on-Thames, Oxon RG9 6QL. *Club* – Garrick.

SON LIVING

Hon Edward Frith, *b* 1957; *ed* Winchester, and Imp Coll, London: *m* 1987, Sarah Eve, da of A. W. Travis, of Western Samoa. *Residence* – Byfield House, Byfield, nr Daventry, Northants.

DAUGHTER LIVING

Hon Joanna, *b* 1955, *m* 1st 1974 (*m diss* 1981), Francis Joseph Fitzherbert-Brockholes (*see* B De Freyne, 1971 Edn); 2ndly, 1981, Jonathan Nelson, of New York, NY, USA.

RADNOR, EARL OF (Pleydell-Bouverie) (Earl GB 1765, Bt GB 1714)

(Name pronounced "Pleddel-Booverie")

My country is dear; liberty is dearer

JACOB PLEYDELL-BOUVERIE, 8th Earl, and 11th Baronet; *b* 10 Nov 1927; *s* 1968; *ed* Harrow, and Trin Coll, Camb; patron of two livings: *m* 1st, 1953 (*m diss* 1962), Anne Garden Farquharson, da of Donald Farquharson Seth-Smith, MC; 2ndly, 1963 (*m diss* 1985), Margaret, da of late Robin Fleming, of Catter House, Drymen; 3rdly, 1986, Mrs A. C. Pettit, previously wife of late Anthony Pettit, and has issue by 1st and 2nd *m*.

Arms – Quarterly: 1st and 4th, per fesse or and argent, an eagle displayed, with two heads sable, on the breast an escutcheon gules, charged with a bend vair, *Bouverie* 2nd and 3rd, argent a bend gules, guttée d'eau between two ravens sable, a chief checky, or and sable, *Pleydell*. **Crest** – A demi-eagle with two heads displayed sable, ducally gorged or, and charged on the breast with a cross crosslet argent. **Supporters** – Two eagles reguardant, wings elevated sable, ducally gorged or, each charged on the breast with a cross crosslet argent.
Residence – Longford Castle, Salisbury, Wilts SP5 4EF.

SONS LIVING (*By 1st marriage*)

WILLIAM (*Viscount Folkestone*), *b* 5 Jan 1955; *ed* Harrow, and RAC Cirencester.

Hon Peter John, *b* 1958; *ed* Harrow, and Trin Coll, Camb: *m* 1986, Hon Jane Victoria Gilmour, only da of Baron Gilmour of Craigmillar, PC (Life Baron), and has issue living, Timothy, *b* 1987, — Jamie, *b* 1989, — Lara Caroline, *b* 1993, — Clare Anne, *b* (twin) 1993. *Residences* – Newcourt Farmhouse, Downton, Wilts; 38 Queensdale Rd, W11 4SA. *Club* – Pratt's.

DAUGHTERS LIVING *(By 2nd marriage)*

Lady Lucy, *b* 1964.
Lady Martha, *b* (twin) 1964.
Lady Belinda, *b* 1966.
Lady Frances, *b* 1973.

BROTHER LIVING

Hon Reuben (Bleak House, Slindon, W Sussex BN18 0RP), *b* 1930; *ed* Harrow: late 2nd Lt Roy Scots Greys: *m* 1956, Bridget Jane, el da of late John Fowell Buxton (*see* Buxton, Bt, colls), and has issue living, Edward (29 Malcolm St., Fremantle, Western Australia), *b* 1957: *m* 1984, Nichola, da of Dr John Wood, of Blackheath, SE3, and has issue living, Nathan John *b* 1987, Joshua Edward *b* 1989, Monica Alice *b* 1990, Jessica Anne *b* 1994, — Jasper John (29 Clapham Common Southside, SW4), *b* 1964: *m* 1991, Katherine Jane, only da of Richard Christopher Wordsworth Pelly (*see* Pelly, Bt, colls), — Rosalind Mary, *b* 1960: *m* 1988, Dr Jonathan Hugh Higham, of 30 Princes St, Dunstable, Beds, eldest son of J.A.E. Higham, of New York, and Chichester, Sussex.

HALF-BROTHER LIVING

Hon Richard Oakley (Lawrence End, Peters Green, Luton, Beds), *b* 1947; *ed* Harrow, and RAC Cirencester; DL Herts 1992: *m* 1978, Victoria M., yr da of late Frank Waldron, of Pond House, Kidmore End, nr Reading, and has issue living, David Oakley, *b* 1979, — Bartholomew Richard, *b* 1981, — Harriot Isobel, *b* 1984.

SISTERS LIVING

Lady Jane, *b* 1923: *m* 1945, Richard Anthony Bethell, of Manor Farm House, Long Riston, Hull (Cotterell, Bt), and has issue living, Hugh Adrian (Rise Park, Hull) *b* 1952; *ed* Eton, and Exeter Univ: *m* 1983, Sarah Elizabeth, eldest da of Maj Thomas Edward St Aubyn, CVO, of Dairy House Farm, Ashford Hill, Newbury, Berks (*see* B St Levan, colls), and has issue living, Oliver Anthony *b* 1985, Edward *b* 1987, Nicholas *b* 1990, — William Anthony (Arnold Manor, Long Riston, nr Hull), *b* 1957: *m* 1983, Elizabeth Anne, yr da of Lt-Col Charles Samuel Madden, of co Dublin, and has issue living, Christopher Frederick *b* 1988, Harriet Primrose *b* 1986, — Camilla, *b* 1946: *m* 1966, Peter Charles Freeman Gregory-Hood (*see* V Hood, colls), — Sarah, *b* 1948: *m* 1966, David Ratcliffe Brotherton, of Whitwell-on-the-Hill, York.
Lady Phœbe (Water's Edge, 1 New Bridge Rd, Salisbury, Wilts), *b* 1932: *m* 1955 (*m diss* 1963), Hubert Beaumont Phipps, and has issue living, Hubert Grace, *b* 1958, — Melissa Adeane, *b* 1955.
Lady Harriot, *b* 1935: *m* 1965, Mark Iain Tennant, of 30 Abbey Gdns, NW8 9AT, and Balfluig Castle, by Alford, Aberdeenshire (*see* B Glenconner, colls).

AUNTS LIVING *(Daughters of 6th Earl)*

Lady Margaret, *b* 1903: *m* 1923, Lt-Col Gerald Barry, MC, who *d* 1977 (*see* Barry, Bt, colls).
Lady Helen, OBE, *b* 1908; OBE (Civil) 1946, DL Berks: *m* 1931, Major Hon David John Smith, CBE, who *d* 1976 (*see* V Hambleden). *Residence* – King's Copse House, Bucklebury, Berks.

WIDOW LIVING OF SON OF SIXTH EARL

(Alice) Pearl, da of late Major Barrington Crake, Rifle Brig, and widow of 2nd Baron Montagu of Beaulieu: *m* 1936, Capt Hon Edward Pleydell-Bouverie, MVO, RN, who *d* 1951, and has issue living (*see* colls, infra). *Residence* – The Lodge, Beaulieu, Brockenhurst, Hants SO42 7YB.

WIDOW LIVING OF SON OF SIXTH EARL

Audrey (Bodenham House, Salisbury, Wilts), da of late Capt Archibald Glen Kidston, JP, of Tyrcelyn, Builth Wells, Radnorshire, and Gwenyfed, Three Cocks, Breconshire, and formerly wife of Anthony Seymour Bellville: *m* 1947, as his 2nd wife, Maj Hon Peter Pleydell-Bouverie, KRRC, who *d* 1981, and has issue living (*see* colls infra.)

WIDOW LIVING OF SEVENTH EARL

Anne Isobel Graham, OBE, DL Wilts 1987 (*Dowager Countess of Radnor*) (Avonturn, Alderbury, Salisbury), da of Lt-Col Richard Oakley, DSO, and widow of Richard Thomas Reynolds Sowerby: *m* 1943, as his 2nd wife, the 7th Earl, who *d* 1968.

COLLATERAL BRANCHES LIVING

Issue of late Capt Hon Edward Pleydell-Bouverie, MVO, RN, 2nd son of 6th Earl, *b* 1899, *d* 1951: *m* 1936, (Alice) Pearl (ante), da of late Major Barrington Crake, Rifle Brig, and widow of 2nd Baron Montagu of Beaulieu:—
Robin (20 Manson Mews, SW7 5AF; Curles Close, Bucklers Hard, Hants SO42 7XA), *b* 1937: *m* 1st, 1960 (*m diss* 1975), Anne-Louise, da of Bruce Durham; 2ndly, 1978, Felicity Ruth, yr da of David Towers Downer, DFC, of Holland Park, W11, and has issue living (by 2nd *m*), Nicholas Edward, *b* 1983, — Camilla, *b* 1981.

Issue of late Hon Bartholomew Pleydell-Bouverie, 3rd son of 6th Earl, *b* 1902, *d* 1965: *m* 1st, 1927, Lady Doreen Clare Hely-Hutchinson, who *d* 1942, da of 6th Earl of Donoughmore; 2ndly, 1949, Mrs Katharine Bradley Martin, who *d* 1977, da of late Robert E. Tod, of New York:—
(By 1st *m*) Simon (The Castle House, Deddington, Oxon), *b* 1928; *ed* Harrow: late 2nd Lt Life Guards: *m* 1961, Vivien Eleanor, only da of Sir Richard Michael Keane, 6th Bt, and has issue living, David Archie, *b* 1964, — Grania Clare, *b* 1962: *m* 1991, Niels David Scott, son of Wolf Scott, of Geneva, Switzerland, and of Fredensborg, Denmark, and has issue living, Finn *b* 1992, — Juliet Rose, *b* 1968, — Alice Susan, *b* 1970. —— Penelope Jane, *b* 1932: *m* 1955, Michael Francis Meredith-Hardy, of Radwell Mill, Baldock, Herts SG7 5ET, and has issue living, Richard, *b* 1957; *ed* Eton, and Birmingham Poly: *m* 1987, Nicola Louise, eldest da of Hugh Morgan Lindsay Smith, of Bank Farm, Brandon Creek, Downham Market, Norfolk, and has issue living, Hugo *b* 1994, Alexandra *b* 1990, Isobel *b* 1992, — Luke, *b* 1959: *m* 1987, Clare M, yst da of late William T. Minogue, of Kew, Melbourne, Australia, and has issue living, William Michael, *b* 1992, Katherine Jane *b* 1988, Georgina Ann *b* 1990, — John Octavian, *b* 1962, — Paul Bartholomew, *b* 1966.

Issue of late Maj Hon Peter Pleydell-Bouverie, KRRC, yst son of 6th Earl, *b* 1909, *d* 1981: *m* 1st, 1938 (*m diss* 1946), Audrey Evelyn, who *d* 1968, da of late William Dodge James, CVO, JP, DL, of West Dean Park,

Sussex (Forbes, Bt), formerly wife of Marshall Field, of Chicago, USA, and previously widow of Capt Muir Dudley Coats, MC; 2ndly, 1947, Audrey (Bodenham House, Salisbury, Wilts), da of late Capt Archibald Glen Kidston, JP, of Tyrcelyn, Builth Wells, Radnorshire, and Gwenyfed, Three Cocks, Breconshire, and formerly wife of late Anthony Seymour Bellville:—
(By 2nd *m*) James, *b* 1950; *ed* Harrow.

Granddaughter of late Col Hon Stuart Pleydell-Bouverie, DSO, OBE, TD (infra):—
Issue of late Christopher Pleydell-Bouverie, *b* 1901, *d* 1949: *m* 1930 (*m diss* 1939), Kathleen Adele, who *d* 1981, da of late William Henry Carpenter Gelshenen, of New York, and 7 Cadogan Gardens, SW:—
Anne Patricia, *b* 1933: *m* 1953, Peter James Grant, Lieut Queen's Own Cameron Highlanders (TA Reserve), and has issue living, Charles Ludovic, *b* 1956; *ed* Eton, — Laura Marguerite, *b* 1959. *Residence* – Standon House, Standon, Herts.

Issue of late Col Hon Stuart Pleydell-Bouverie, DSO, OBE, TD, 2nd son of 5th Earl, *b* 1877, *d* 1947: *m* 1900, Edith Dorothy, who *d* 1949, da of late Albert Vickers, of 14 Cadogan Square, SW:—
David, *b* 1911; *ed* Charterhouse: *m* 1946 (*m diss* 1952), Mrs Alice Astor Harding, who *d* 1956, da of late Col John Jacob Astor, and formerly wife of (1) Prince Serge Obolensky (2) Raimund von Hofmannsthal, and (3) Philip John Ryves Harding. *Residence* – The Valley of the Moon, Glen Ellen, California, USA.

Issue of late Hon Kenelm Pleydell-Bouverie, 6th son of 4th Earl, *b* 1852, *d* 1921: *m* 1905, Evelyn Bertie Charlotte, who *d* 1936, da of late David Maitland Makgill-Crichton (E Lauderdale, colls):—
Bertrand Eric (Middle Leaze, Coleshill, Swindon, Wilts), *b* 1914; *ed* Trin Coll, Camb (BA 1939); 1939-45 War (despatches): *m* 1950, Pamela, adopted da of late Lt-Col Roderick William Macdonald, CIE, DSO, and has issue living, Rupert William (Waverley House, Monkwood, Alresford, Hants SO24 0HB), *b* (Dec) 1950; *ed* Harrow; FCA: *m* 1978, Evelyn Marie, da of Capt John A. Conlon, of Manor Croft, W Ayton, Yorks, and has issue living, Matthew Alexander *b* 1979, Edward Richard *b* 1984, — Nigel Justin (Middle Leaze, Coleshill, Highworth, Wilts), *b* 1955; *ed* Harrow, Univ of BC, Canada and Cardiff Univ, — Prunella Sarah, *b* 1952: *m* 1976, Thomas Paul Miller, of 44 Bloomfield Terrace, SW1, and Lyemarsh Farmhouse, Mere, Wilts, and has issue living, Thomas Bertrand *b* 1984, Jessica Frances *b* (twin) 1984.

Granddaughter of late Walter Pleydell-Bouverie, only son of late Rt Hon Edward Pleydell-Bouverie, 2nd son of 3rd Earl:—
Issue of late Major Humphrey Pleydell-Bouverie, MBE, *b* 1883, *d* 1958: *m* 1922, Margaret Elfrida, who *d* 1976, da of R. H. Holden, formerly of Talton House, Stratford-on-Avon:—
Ann, *b* 1923: *m* 1st, 1943 (*m diss* 1953), Lieut-Col Eric Charles Twelves-Wilson, VC, late E Surrey Regt, Colonial Administration, Tanganyika; 2ndly, John Kennett Walker, who *d* 1954, and has issue living, (by 1st *m*) Michael Charles Bouverie, *b* 1947, — Anthony, *b* 1949, — (by 2nd *m*) Diana, *b* 1954. *Residence* – Chorley, Lancashire.

Grandchildren of late Wilfred Pleydell-Bouverie, 2nd son of late Adm Frederick William Pleydell-Bouverie, el son of late Rev Hon Frederick Pleydell-Bouverie, 4th son of 2nd Earl:—
Issue of late Hugh Wyndham Pleydell-Bouverie, *b* 1900, *d* 1979: *m* 1926, Viola Elizabeth, da of Walter Holloway Usher:—
Robin Wyndham (Longford (Private Bag), Harding, Natal), *b* 1935: *m* 1960, Jean Elizabeth Vermaak, and has issue living, Kim Wyndham, *b* 1965, — Penelope Ann, *b* 1961, — Carolyn, *b* 1963, — Lynn Michelle, *b* 1968. —— Peter Hugh, *b* 1943. —— Joy, *b* 1927: *m* 1950, Neville Ramsay Barrett, of 15 Pepworth, Rd, Scottsville, Pietermaritzburg 3201, S Africa, and has issue living, Roger Hugh (8 Dan Pienaar Rd, Port Shepstone 4240, S Africa), *b* 1950: *m* 1974, Sally Taylor, and has issue living, Mark Hugh *b* 1975, Leigh *b* 1977, — Maureen, *b* 1953: *m* 1978, Neil Maxwell (c/o PO Box 1, Winterton 3340, S Africa), and has issue living, Greg *b* 1985, Kirsty *b* 1983, — Judy, *b* 1959: *m* 1981, Wadham Hewstone Hull, of 39 Fir Tree Av, Cleland, Pietermaritzburg 3201, S Africa, and has issue living, Lindsay *b* 1984, Tarryn *b* 1986. —— Monica Viola, *b* 1937: *m* 1960, Norman Alexander John Herring, of Chertsey, Cedarville, Natal 4720, S Africa, and has issue living, Kerry, *b* 1961: *m* 1986, Gavan Gray, of 17 Cowan Rd, Hilton, Natal 3245, S Africa, and has issue living, Darren Alexander *b* 1993, Hayley *b* 1991, — Deborah, *b* 1963: *m* 1984, Graeme Holloway, of 61 Dennis Rd, Hayfields, Pietermaritzburg, Natal 3201, S Africa, and has issue living, Christy *b* 1988, Tatum *b* 1991.

Grandchildren of late Seymour Pleydell-Bouverie, 2nd son of Philip Pleydell-Bouverie, son of Hon Philip Pleydell-Bouverie, MP, 5th son of 2nd Earl:—
Issue of late Lieut-Com Philip Hales Pleydell-Bouverie, RNVR, *b* 1900, *d* 1951: *m* 1st, 1923 (*m diss* 1927), Alice Margaret, da of William Alfred Ingram, of 5 Highbury Grove, N5; 2ndly, 1927, Beth Olivia, who *d* 1948, adopted da of late Brig-Gen Ronald Maclachlan, Rifle Brig, and formerly wife of John Fitzhardinge Berkeley Gage (*see* V Gage, colls); 3rdly, 1945, Kathleen, who *d* 1982, da of J. T. Fell, of Bristol:—
(By 1st *m*) Patricia, *b* 1924: *m* 1949, John Marshall, Solicitor, and has issue living, Roland, *b* 1950; *ed* Bloxham Sch, — Richard James, *b* 1954; *ed* Radley; has issue living, Angus *b* 1982, Hamish *b* 1984, — Sheila Ann, *b* 1953. *Residence* – Hill House, Andover Road, Newbury. —— (By 2nd *m*) Lois, *b* 1928: *m* 1950, Gunther Wolff, and has issue living, Adrian, *b* 1957: *m* 1982, Mary Anne Schuetter, and has issue living, Adam David *b* 1986, Kirsten Marie *b* 1988. *Residence* – RR3 Huron Line Rd, Windsor, Ontario, Canada N9A 6Z6. —— Xenia, *b* 1929: *m* 1964, Alec Ronald Ayliffe, of RD3 Drury, NZ, and has issue living, Gillian Xenia, *b* 1966.

PREDECESSORS – (1) WILLIAM Des Bouveries, an eminent Turkey merchant; *cr a Baronet*, 1714; *d* 1717; *s* by his el son (2) *Sir* EDWARD, 2nd Bt; *d* 1736; *s* by his brother (3) *Sir* JACOB, 3rd Bt; was MP for and Recorder of New Sarum; *cr Lord Longford*, Baron of Longford, and *Viscount Folkestone* (peerage of Great Britain) 1747; *d* 1761; *s* by his son (4) WILLIAM, 2nd Viscount; *cr Baron Pleydell-Bouverie*, of Coleshill, co Berks, and *Earl of Radnor* (peerage of Great Britain) 1765, with remainder to the earldom in default of male issue to the male descendants of his father; *d* 1776; *s* by his son (5) JACOB, 2nd Earl; *d* 1828; *s* by his son (6) WILLIAM, 3rd Earl; *b* 1779; sat as MP for Salisbury 1802-28: *m* 2ndly, Anne Judith, da of Sir Henry Paulet St John Mildmay, 3rd Bt; *d* 1869; *s* by his son (7) JACOB, 4th Earl, *b* 1815; was Lord-Lieut of Wilts: *m* 1840, Lady Mary Augusta Frederica Grimston, who *d* 1879, da of 1st Earl of Verulam; *d* 1889; *s* by his son (8) WILLIAM, 5th Earl, *b* 1841; was Treasurer of the Household 1885-6 and 1886; sat as MP for Wiltshire S (C) 1874-85, and for Enfield Div of Middlesex 1885-9: *m* 1866, Helen Matilda, who *d* 1929, da of late Rev Henry Chaplin, of Blankney, Lincoln; *d* 1900; *s* by his el son (9) JACOB, CIE, CBE, 6th Earl, *b* 1868; MP for Wilts S, or Wilton, Div (C) 1892-1900, and Lord-Lieut for Wilts 1925-30: *m* 1891, Julian Eleanor Adelaide, who *d* 1946, da of late Charles Balfour, of Newton Don; *d* 1930; *s* by his son (10) WILLIAM , KG, KCVO, 7th Earl, *b* 1895; Keeper of Privy Seal to Prince of Wales 1933; Lord Warden of the Stannaries 1933-65; Chm of Rothamsted Experimental Station 1938-64, and Forestry Commn 1952-63; Official Verderer of New Forest 1964-66: *m* 1st, 1922 (*m diss* 1942), Helena Olivia (*d* 1985) (who *m* 2ndly, 1943, Brig Montacute William Worrell Selby-Lowndes, DSO, who *d* 1972), da of late Charles Robert Whorwood Adeane, CB (B Leconfield, colls); 2ndly, 1943, Anne Isobel Graham, OBE, da of Lt-Col Richard Oakley, DSO, and widow of Richard Thomas Reynolds Sowerby; *d* 1968; *s* by his son (11) JACOB, 8th Earl and present peer; also Viscount Folkestone, Baron Longford (peerage of GB), and Baron Pleydell-Bouverie.

RADSTOCK, BARONY OF (Waldegrave) (Extinct 1953)

GRANDDAUGHTERS LIVING OF FIFTH BARON

Issue of late Com Hon John Montagu Granville Waldegrave, DSC, RN, only son of 5th Baron, *b* 1905, *k* on active ser 1944: *m* 1940, Lady Hersey Margaret Boyle (who *d* 1993, having *m* 2ndly, 1947, John Goring (see Goring, Bt, colls), who *d* 1990), da of 8th Earl of Glasgow:—
Horatia Marion, *b* 1941: *m* 1970, Oliver John Diggle, of Waterfall House, Swanton Morley, Dereham, Norfolk NR20 4QD, and has issue living, John Wyndham Hugh, *b* 1974, — Rowena Mary, *b* 1972, — Emma Georgiana, *b* 1977.　— Griselda Hyacinthe, *b* 1943: *m* 1967, Charles D. S. Drace-Francis, CMG (c/o FCO (Lisbon), King Charles St, SW1), and has issue living, James, *b* 1969, — Alexander John, *b* 1971, — Teresa, *b* 1979.

RAGLAN, BARON (Somerset) (Baron UK 1852)

FITZROY JOHN SOMERSET, 5th Baron; *b* 8 Nov 1927; *s* 1964; *ed* Westminster, and Magdalen Coll, Oxford; Capt Welsh Guards (Reserve of Officers); JP, and a DL for Mon; Chm of Cwmbran New Town Development Corpn; a Crown Estate Commr since 1970: *m* 1973 (*m diss* 19—), Alice, yr da of Peter Baily, of Great Whittington, Northumberland.

𝕬rms – Quarterly: 1st and 4th azure, three fleurs-de-lis or, *France*; 2nd and 3rd gules, three lions passant guardant in pale or, *England*; the whole within a bordure company argent and azure. 𝕮rest – A portcullis or, nailed azure, with chains pendant therefrom gold. 𝕾upporters – *Dexter*, a panther argent, spotted of various colours, fire issuant from the mouth and ears proper, gorged with a plain collar and chained or; *sinister*, a wyvern, wings endorsed, vert, holding in the mouth a sinister hand, couped at the wrist, gules.
Seat – Cefntilla Court, Usk, Gwent.

MUTARE · VEL · TIMERE · SPERNO

I scorn to change or fear

BROTHER LIVING

Hon GEOFFREY, *b* 29 Aug 1932; *ed* Westminster, and Roy Agricultural Coll; is Lt Grenadier Guards (Reserve); a co Councillor of Berks 1966-75, District Councillor of Newbury 1978-83, and co-Councillor of Oxon 1988-93: *m* 1956, Caroline Rachel, da of Col Edward Roderick Hill, DSO, JP (E St Aldwyn, colls), and has issue living, Arthur Geoffrey, *b* 27 April 1960, — Belinda Caroline, *b* 1958: *m* 1989, Nicholas Grant Boyd, eldest son of Cmdr Christopher Dennis Boyd, DSC, RN, of London, — Lucy Ann, *b* 1963. *Residence* – Manor Farm, Stanford-in-the-Vale, Faringdon, Oxon.

SISTER LIVING

Hon Cecily, *b* 1938: *m* 1961, Jonkheer Jan T. P. Steengracht van Moyland, Capt late Irish Guards, and has issue living, Jonkheer Henry Jan Berrington, *b* 1963, — Jonkvrowe Suzanna Cecily, *b* 1968.

COLLATERAL BRANCHES LIVING

Issue of late Brig Hon Nigel FitzRoy Somerset, CBE, DSO, MC, 3rd and yst son of 3rd Baron, *b* 1893, *d* 1990: *m* 1922, Phyllis Marion Offley, who *d* 1979, da of late Dr Henry Offley Irwin, of Boulder, W Australia:—
David Henry FitzRoy (White Wickets, Boars Head, Crowborough, Sussex TN6 5HE), *b* 1930; *ed* Wellington Coll, and Peterhouse, Camb (BA 1952, MA 1956); Chief Cashier of Bank of England 1980-88, since when Fellow of Peterhouse: *m* 1955, Ruth Ivy, da of Wilfred Robert Wildbur, of Kings Lynn, Norfolk, and has issue living, Henry Robert FitzRoy (53 Winsham Grove, SW11 6NB), *b* 1961; *ed* Wellington Coll, and Trin Hall, Camb (BA 1983, MA 1988): *m* 1992, Jane Laird, da of Dr Peter Gordon, of Currie, Edinburgh, and has issue living, Alice Caroline Laird *b* 1993, — Louise Charlotte, *b* 1956; *ed* Girton Coll, Camb (BA 1978, MA 1982): *m* 1981, John Roberts Beach, of Coppice Cottage, Ashton-under-Hill, Worcs, son of Gen Sir Hugh Beach, GBE, KCB, MC, and has issue living, Charles Thomas FitzRoy *b* 1993, Georgiana Emily Estelle *b* 1989.　— Susan Mary, *b* 1923: *m* 1953 (*m diss* 1977), Patrick William Mackenzie Dean, and has issue living, James FitzRoy, *b* 1954: *m* 1987, Charlotte Janet Rose Unwin, and has issue living, — Julia Mary Mackenzie, *b* 1956: *m* 1986, Alexander Archibald Scott, and has issue living, — Veronica Jane Somerset, *b* 1958: *m* 1984, Peter Francis Howard Stephens and has issue living, — Rosemary Elizabeth, *b* 1964.

PREDECESSORS – (1) *Field-Marshal Lord* FITZROY JAMES HENRY Somerset, GCB, son of 5th Duke of Beaufort; *b* 1788; distinguished himself in the Peninsula, and lost an arm at Waterloo; was many years Mil Sec to Duke of Wellington, and Master-Gen of the Ordnance 1854; commanded the English troops in the Crimea 1854-5, and gained the victories of the Alma, Inkerman, and Balaclava; *cr Baron Raglan*, of Raglan, co Monmouth (peerage of United Kingdom) 1852: *m* 1814, Lady Emily Harriet, da of 3rd Earl of Mornington; *d* 28 June 1855, whilst commanding the troops before Sebastopol; *s* by his son (2) RICHARD HENRY FITZROY, 2nd Baron, *b* 1817: *m* 1st, 1856, Lady Georgiana Lygon, who *d* 1865, da of 4th Earl Beauchamp; 2ndly, 1871, Mary Blanche, who *d* 1916, da of Sir Walter Rockliff Farquhar, 3rd Bt; *d* 3 May 1884; *s* by his son (3) GEORGE FITZROY HENRY, GBE, CB, 3rd Baron, *b* 1857; Under-Sec of State for War Nov 1900 to Aug 1902, and Lieut-Gov of the Isle of Man 1902-19: *m* 1883, Lady Ethel Jemima Ponsonby, who *d* 1940, da of 7th Earl of Bessborough; *d* 1921; *s* by his el son (4) FITZROY RICHARD, 4th Baron, *b* 1885; Maj Grenadier Guards; Lt-Col and Brevet Col Monmouthshire Militia 1930-35, Lord-Lieut of Monmouthshire 1942-64, and Pres, National Museum of Wales 1957-62: *m* 1923, Hon Julia Hamilton, who *d* 1971, da of 11th Lord Belhaven and Stenton; *d* 1964; *s* by his 2nd son (5) FITZROY JOHN, 5th Baron, and present peer.

Ramsay, Lord; son of Earl of Dalhousie.

RAMSEY OF CANTERBURY, BARONY OF (Ramsey) (Extinct 1988)

WIDOW LIVING OF LIFE BARON

JOAN ALICE CHETWODE (*Baroness Ramsey of Canterbury*), da of late Lt-Col Francis Alexander Chetwode Hamilton, MC, The Cameronians (Scottish Rifles): *m* 1942, Baron Ramsey of Canterbury, PC, DD, who *d* 1988.
Residence – St John's Home, St Mary's Rd, Oxford OX4 1QE.

Ranfurly, Baron; title borne by Earl of Ranfurly on Roll of HL.

RANFURLY, EARL OF (Knox) Sits as BARON RANFURLY (UK 1826) (Earl I 1831)

I move and prosper

GERALD FRANCOYS NEEDHAM KNOX, 7th Earl; *b* 4 Jan 1929; *s* 1988; *ed* Wellington Coll; Lt Cdr RN (ret); Stockbroker, Sr Ptnr Brewin Dolphin & Co 1982: *m* 1955, Rosemary, only da of late Air Vice-Marshal Felton Vesey Holt, CMG, DSO, and has issue.

Arms – Gules, a falcon volant or, within an orle, wavy on the outer, and engrailed on the inner edge, argent. Crest – A falcon close, standing on a perch proper. Supporters – Two falcons, wings inverted proper, beaked, membered, belled, ducally collared and lined, or.
Residence – Maltings Chase, Nayland, Colchester, Essex.

SONS LIVING

EDWARD JOHN (*Viscount Northland*), *b* 21 May 1957; *ed* Leys Sch, and Loughborough Univ (BA): *m* 1st, 1980 (*m diss* 1984), Rachel Sarah, da of Frank Hilton Lee; 2ndly, 1994, Johanna Humphrey, da of late Sqdn Ldr Harry Richard Walton. *Residence* – 62 Crooms Hill, SE10.
Hon Rupert Stephen, *b* 1963; *ed* Ipswich Sch.

DAUGHTERS LIVING

Lady Elizabeth Marianne, *b* 1959: *m* 1986, Simon Empson, and has issue living, Lucy, *b* 1987, — Victoria, *b* 1989, — Alice, *b* 1993.
Lady Frances Christina, *b* 1961: *m* 1981, Henry Gordon-Jones, and has issue living, Alexandra, *b* 1983, — Susannah, *b* 1985, — Louise, *b* 1988.

BROTHER LIVING

Rev Thomas Anthony, *b* 1931; *ed* Wellington Coll, and St Chad's Coll, Durham (BA): *m* 1959, Susan Phoebe, da of late Arthur Pollard Matthews, of Mount Creek Manor, Chattanooga, Tennessee, USA, and has issue living, James Michael (Focus Windsurfing, Magharees, Castlegregory, co Kerry, Republic of Ireland), *b* 1962, — David Andrew (125 Oswald Rd, Manchester), *b* 1965, — Anne Margaret, *b* 1960: *m* 1991, Herbert Musisi, of 87 Dorset Rd, E7. *Residence* – The Rectory, 41 Leighton Rd, Toddington, Beds.

DAUGHTER LIVING OF SIXTH EARL

Lady Caroline, *b* 1948: *m* 1975, John Edward Simmonds, and has issue living, Lucy, *b* 1976, — Zara, *b* 1980, — Rose, *b* 1987.

WIDOW LIVING OF SIXTH EARL

HERMIONE (*Hermione, Countess of Ranfurly*, OBE, CStJ), eldest da of Griffith Robert Poyntz Llewellyn, of Baglan Hall, Abergavenny: *m* 1939, the 6th Earl, KCMG, who *d* 1988. *Residence* – Great Pednor, Chesham, Bucks.

COLLATERAL BRANCHES LIVING

Grandchildren of late Octavius Newry Knox, 3rd son of Hon John Henry Knox, MP, 3rd son of 1st Earl:—
Issue of late Leonard Needham Knox, *b* 1879, *d* 1956: *m* 1924, Berthe Hélène, who *d* 1982, da of late Henri Joseph Brel:—
Sir John Leonard (*Hon Mr Justice Knox*), *b* 1925; *ed* Radley, Worcester Coll, Oxford (BA 1951, MA 1958), and Paris Univ: Bar Lincoln's Inn 1953; Bencher 1977; Attorney-Gen to Duchy of Lancaster 1984-85, Judge of High Court of Justice (Chancery Div) since 1985, Dep Chm Parl Boundary Commn for England since 1987, Judge of Employment Appeal Tribunal since 1989; late Lieut RA; Knt 1985: *m* 1st, 1953, Anne Jacqueline, who *d* 1991, da of Herbert Mackintosh, of Frensham, Surrey; 2ndly, 1993, Benedicta Eugenie, da of late Léon Jean Goossens, CBE, FRCM, and widow of Robin Philip Cooksey, and has issue living (by 1st *m*), Thomas Francis Needham, *b* 1964, — Diana Jane, *b* 1957: *m* 1981, John Martyn Gurney Barclay, of 18 King Edward Rd, Jordanhill, Glasgow G13 1QW, yst son of Oliver Rainsford Barclay, of 8a Southland Rd, Leicester, and has issue living, Robert James *b* 1986, David Timothy *b* 1988, Frances Elizabeth *b* 1991, — Catherine Mary, *b* 1959: *m* 1983, David Alan Robinson, of 11 Parkway Gdns, Chandlers Ford, Hants, and has issue living, Edward John *b* 1989, Thomas George *b* 1991, Alistair David *b* 1993, — Margaret Lucy, *b* 1960: *m* 1986, Philip Stack Hanson Budden, of 45 Ethelbert Av, Swaythling, Southampton, and has issue living, Peter James *b* 1993, Lucy Anne *b* 1992. *Address* – c/o Royal Courts of Justice, Strand, WC2A 2LL. —— Lucy Mary, *b* 1927: *m* 1960, Peter James Denholm, and has issue living, William Leonard, *b* 1962, — John Peter, *b* 1964, — Eva Mary, *b* 1969. *Residence* – Lot 5, Phillips Rd, Byford, W Aust 6201.

(In remainder to Viscountcy of Northland)

Granddaughter of late Vesey Edmond Knox, el son of Rev Francis Edmond Knox, 2nd son of Hon Vesey Knox, 3rd son of 1st Viscount Northland:—
Issue of late Charles Thomas Gisborne Knox, *b* 1868, *d* 1957: *m* 1893, Ethel Flora, who *d* 1935, da of Surg-Gen Archibald Henry Fraser:—
Ethel Eileen, *b* 1894: *m* 1941, Benjamin Joseph Redding.

Grandchildren of late Rev Charles Beresford Beresford-Knox, son of late Rev James Spencer Knox, son of late Rt Rev Hon William Knox, DD, Bishop of Derry, 4th son of 1st Viscount Northland:—
Issue of late Rev Charles Edward Leslie Beresford Knox, *b* 1864, *d* 1956: *m* 1903, Ethel Margaret, who *d* 1952, da of late Rev Francis John Dickson, of Ribchester, Lancashire:—
Charles Francis BERESFORD-KNOX (5 Dukes Meadow, Stapleford, Cambridge CB2 5BH), *b* 1917; *ed* Tonbridge and Keble Coll, Oxford (BA 1939, MA 1985); late Capt RA: *m* 1941, Margaret Eugenie Morgan, and has issue living, Richard Charles (8 Finches Close, Stapleford, Camb CB2 5BL), *b* 1944: *m* 1967, Doris Frey, and has issue living, Christopher David *b* 1982, Nicholas James *b* 1984, — John Edward BERESFORD-KNOX (14 Park Rd, Limpsfield, Oxted, Surrey RH8 OAW), *b* 1949: *ed* Keble Coll, Oxford (BA 1971), and Nottingham Univ (MA 1973): *m* 1979, Jacqueline Rosalind Wildash, and has issue living, Anna Louise *b* 1983, Lucy Elizabeth *b* 1985. —— Margaret Leslie BERESFORD-KNOX (2 Quarry Close, Hansford Sq, Bath, BA2 5LP), *b* 1904. —— Christina Kathleen Mary BERESFORD-KNOX (Chestnut Lodge, 43 Glenwood Rd, West Moore, Wimborne, Dorset BH22 0BN), *b* 1910.

Grandson of late Rev Thomas Knox, son of late Ven Hon Charles Knox, 6th son of 1st Viscount Northland:—
Issue of late Com Vesey Knox, RN, *b* 1847, *d* 18-: *m* 1885, Helen, da of late Benjamin William Leigh, of Manchester and Valparaiso:—
Albert Vesey Bent, *b* 1887. *Residence* –

PREDECESSORS – (1) THOMAS KNOX, MP for Dungannon; *cr Baron Welles*, of Dungannon, co Tyrone (peerage of Ireland) 1781, and *Viscount Northland* (peerage of Ireland) 1791; *d* 1818: *s* by his son (2) THOMAS, 2nd Viscount; *cr Baron Ranfurly* (peerage of United Kingdom) 1826, and *Earl of Ranfurly* (peerage of Ireland) 1831; *d* 1840; *s* by his son (3) THOMAS, 2nd Earl; *d* 1858; *s* by his son (4) THOMAS, 3rd Earl; *b* 1816; *m* 1848, Harriet, who *d* 1891, da of James Rimington, Esq, of Broomhead Hall, co York; *d* 1858; *s* by his el son (5) THOMAS GRANVILLE HENRY STUART, 4th Earl; *b* 1875; *s* by his brother (6) UCHTER JOHN MARK, GCMG, PC, 5th Earl, *b* 1856; a Lord-in-Waiting to Queen Victoria 1895-7, and Gov of New Zealand 1897-1904: *m* 1880, Hon Constance Caulfeild, who *d* 1932, da of 7th Viscount Charlemont; *d* 1933; *s* by his grandson (7) THOMAS DANIEL, KCMG (son of late Capt Thomas Uchter Caulfeild, Viscount Northland, only son of 5th Earl), 6th Earl, *b* 1913; ADC to Gov and Com-in-Ch of Commonwealth of Australia 1936-38, Gov and Com-in-Chief of the Bahamas 1953-56; co-founder, with wife, of the Ranfurly Library Service: *m* 1939, Hermione, OBE, da of Griffith Robert Poyntz Llewellyn, of Abergavenny; *d* 1988; *s* by his kinsman (8) GERALD FRANCOYS NEEDHAM (son of late Capt John Needham Knox, RN (by his wife Monica, only da of late Maj-Gen Sir Gerald Kitson, KCVO, CB, CMG), elder son of late Edward Knox, OBE, grandson of late Hon John Knox, MP, 3rd son of 1st Earl), 7th Earl and present peer; also Viscount Northland, Baron Welles, and Baron Ranfurly.

RANK, BARONY OF (Rank) (Extinct 1972)

DAUGHTERS LIVING OF FIRST BARON

Hon Ursula Helen, *b* 1919: *m* 1952, Lance Robert Newton, who *d* 1969, and has issue living, Joseph Robert (Hall Farm Stonesby, Melton Mowbray, Leics), *b* 1956: *m* 1978, Emma Finola, da of late Maj Richard Shelley, CVO, and has issue living, Chloe *b* 1984, Willa *b* 1990. — Carol, *b* 1953: *m* 1985, Stephen Andrew Taylor, of The Cottage, Burrough on the Hill, nr Melton Mowbray, Leics, elder son of late E. Taylor, and has issue living, James William Arthur *b* 1990, Sarah Amanda *b* 1988, — Nicola Jane, *b* 1960: *m* 1982, Paul Robert Carey Morrison, of Burnhouse Stud, Gainford, Darlington, co Durham, and has issue living, Lucy Elizabeth *b* 1985, Georgina Alice *b* 1989. *Residence* – Church Farm, Saltby, Melton Mowbray, Leics.
Hon Shelagh Mary, *b* 1923: *m* 1st, 1945 (*m diss* 1955), Fred M. Packard, late Lieut Signal Corps US Army; 2ndly, 1957, Major Rosslyn Fairfax Huxley Cowen, MBE, and has issue living, (by 1st *m*) Frederick Arthur Rank, *b* 1949, — Susan Mary, *b* 1947, — (by 2nd *m*) Andrew Edward (Manor Farm, E Wretham, Thetford, Norfolk), *b* 1958: *m* 1985, Nicola, yr da of D. Baker, of Park Lane, Reigate, and has issue living, Fergus *b* 1988, Lucy *b* 1986, — Stuart Huxley, *b* 1960. *Residence* – Shawdon, Glanton, Northumberland.

RANKEILLOUR, BARON (Hope) (Baron UK 1932)

But hope is unbroken

PETER ST THOMAS MORE HENRY HOPE, 4th Baron; *b* 29 May 1935; *s* 1967; *ed* Ampleforth.

Arms – Azure, on a chevron or between three bezants, a bay leaf slipped vert, a bordure ermine. **Crest** – A broken globe surmounted of a rainbow proper. *Residence* – Achaderry House, Roy Bridge, West Inverness-shire.

SISTER LIVING

Hon Anne Mary, *b* 1936: *m* 1958, John Stephen Dobson, JP, and has issue living, Dominic Stephen Christopher Charles, *b* 1959, — Philippa Mary, *b* 1961, — Catherine Teresa, *b* 1962: *m* 1988, Hamish Lindsay McNair, only son of Archibald Alister Jourdan (Archie) McNair, of Hurlingham Court, SW6, and of Istan, Malaga, Spain, and has issue living, Mungo Alexander *b* 1992. *Residence* – Papplewick Lodge, Nottinghamshire.

DAUGHTERS LIVING OF SECOND BARON

Hon Bridget (25 Kings Court North, Kings Rd, SW3 5EQ), *b* 1920: *m* 1942, Lt-Col George Henry Hugh Coles, Prince of Wales Own Regt of Yorks, who *d* 1992, and has issue living, Caroline Mary, *b* 1942: *m* 1965, Lt-Col Rodney Gilbert Stapleton Cotton, RA, and has issue living, Nicholas Henry Stapleton *b* 1968; Capt The Queen's Royal Lancers, Martha Louise *b* 1966, — Elisabeth Helena Anne *b* 1944: *m* 1967, Maj Hugh Rollo Gillespie, Queens R Irish Hussars, of The Old Rectory, Kirby Wiske, Thirsk, Yorks, and has issue living, Simon Rollo *b* 1970, James Hugh *b* 1973, Alice Catherine Mary *b* 1976, — Mary-Jane, *b* 1948: *m* 1987, Timothy C. Gibson, son of Henry L. Gibson, of the Old Vicarage, Little Missenden, Bucks, and has issue living, Benjamin Henry *b* 1987, Kate Louise *b* 1989.
Hon Jean Margaret (*Hon Lady Wilson*), *b* 1923: *m* 1st, 1942 (*m diss* 1955), Capt Anthony Paul; 2ndly, 1958, Lt-Gen Sir Alexander James Wilson, KBE, MC, of 151 Rivermead Court, Ranelagh Gdns, SW6 3SF (*see* Starkey, Bt, 1985 Edn), and has had issue (by 1st *m*) (Anthony) Hugh (23 Ludlow, Birch Hill, Bracknell, Berks RG12 7BZ), *b* 1951: *m* 1973, Jacqueline Anne, da of Richard Francis Winstone, and has issue living, Nicholas Anthony *b* 1975, Richard James *b* 1980, — Sarah Margaret, *b* 1943: *m* 1st, 1965 (*m diss* 1980), Nigel John Kington Blair-Oliphant; 2ndly, 1981, Peter Tait, son of Lt-Col W. E. Tait, of Bromsgrove, Worcs, and has issue living (by 1st *m*), Richard Mark *b* 1967, David Iain *b* 1969, — Susan Carolina *b* 1949, *d* 1986, — (by 2nd *m*) William Robert Bevil (6 Roundmead Av, Loughton, Essex), *b* 1959: *m* 1994, Lisa, only da of Colin Roby, of Cleveleys, Lancs, — Rupert James, *b* 1961.
Hon Barbara Mary, *b* 1930: *m* 1954, William Edward Peter Louis Drummond-Murray of Mastrick, Slains Pursuivant of Arms (E Perth, colls), and has issue living, Andrew Philip, *b* 1958: *m* 1981, Susan Fiona Dorinthea, da of Prof Donald Michie, DPhil (*see* B Aberconway), and has issue living, John Douglas *b* 1986, Jessica Katharine *b* 1983, Laura Catriona *b* 1988, — James, *b* 1959: *m* 1989, Namkhang, da of Mak Tonwong, of Thailand, — Robert, *b* 1965, — Walter David, *b* 1973, — Isabel Mary, *b* 1966. *Residence* – 67 Dublin St, Edinburgh EH3 6NS.

WIDOW LIVING OF THIRD BARON

MARY SIBYL (*Baroness Rankeillour*), da of late Lt-Col Wilfred Ricardo, DSO, of Hook Hall, Surrey: *m* 1933, the 3rd Baron, who *d* 1967. *Residence* – Papplewick Lodge, Papplewick, Notts.

COLLATERAL BRANCH LIVING

Issue of late Hon Richard Frederick Hope, OBE, yst son of 1st Baron, *b* 1901, *d* 1964: *m* 1938, Helen Sybil Mary, who *d* 1971, da of late Alfred Charlemagne Lambart (E Cavan, colls):—
MICHAEL RICHARD, *b* 21 Oct 1940; *ed* Downside: *m* 1964, Elizabeth Rosemary, el da of Col Francis H. Fuller, of Wakelins, Genesis Green, Wickhambrook, Newmarket, Suffolk, and has issue living, James Francis, *b* 1968, — Henrietta Mary, *b* 1965, — Louisa Mary, *b* 1966. —— Simon James (103 Frescade Cres, Basingstoke, Hants), *b* 1941; *ed* Downside. —— Margaret Mary, *b* 1945: *m* 1966, Neil Arnold Slater, of Marshborough House, Woodnesborough, Sandwich, Kent, and has issue living, Richard Benjamin Arnold, *b* 1968, — Katherine Helen, *b* 1970.

PREDECESSORS – (1) *Rt Hon* JAMES FITZALAN Hope, son of late James Robert Hope-Scott QC (*see* M Linlithgow, colls); *b* 1870; was Parliamentary Private Sec (unpaid) to successive Postmaster-Gens (Duke of Norfolk and Marquess of Londonderry) 1896-1901, to Pres of Board of Trade (Rt Hon G. W. Balfour, MP) 1901, and to Colonial Sec (Rt Hon A Lyttelton, MP) 1904-5, Treasurer of HM's Household 1915-16, a Junior Lord of the Treasury 1916-18, Financial Sec to Min of Munitions 1919-21, and Chm of Committees and Dep Speaker in House of Commons 1921-4 and 1924-9; sat as MP for Sheffield, Brightside Div (C) 1900-1906, and for Sheffield, Central Div 1908-29; *cr Baron Rankeillour*, of Buxted, co Sussex (peerage of UK) 1932: *m* 1st, 1892, Mabel Helen, OBE, who *d* 1938, da of Francis Riddell, of Cheeseburn Grange, Northumberland; 2ndly, 1941, Lady Beatrice Minnie Ponsonby Moore, who *d* 1966, da of 9th Earl of Drogheda, and widow of Capt Struan Robertson Kerr-Clark, Seaforth Highlanders; *d* 1949; *s* by his son (2) ARTHUR OSWALD JAMES, GCIE, MC, 2nd Baron; *b* 1897; was Parliamentary Private Sec (unpaid) to Min of Mines 1924-9, a Junior Lord of the Treasury 1935-7, Treasurer of HM's Household 1937-9, Gov of Madras 1940-46, and MP for Warwickshire, Nuneaton Div (C) 1924-29, and for Birmingham, Aston Div 1931-9; European War 1914-18 as Capt Coldstream Guards (MC): *m* 1919, Grizel, who *d* 1975, da of Brig-Gen Sir Robert Gordon Gilmour, 1st Bt, CB, CVO, DSO; *d* 1958; *s* by his brother (3) HENRY JOHN, 3rd Baron; *b* 1899; Lt-Col Scots Guards: *m* 1933, Mary Sibyl, da of late Lt-Col Wilfred Ricardo, DSO, of Hook Hall, Surrey; *d* 1967; *s* by his only son (4) PETER ST THOMAS MORE HENRY, 4th Baron and present peer.

RATHCAVAN, BARON (O'Neill) (Baron UK 1953, Bt UK 1929)

PHELIM ROBERT HUGH O'NEILL, PC (NI), 2nd Baron and 2nd Baronet; *b* 2 Nov 1909; *s* 1982; *ed* Eton; late Maj RA; MP (UU) for N Antrim (UK Parl) 1952-59, and in Parl of NI 1959-73 (U and later Alliance) (Parl suspended March 1972); Min of Educn 1969 and Agric 1969-71; PC (NI) 1969: *m* 1st, 1934 (*m diss* 1944), Clare Désirée, who *d* 1956, da of Detmar Blow (*see* B Tollemache, colls); 2ndly, 1953, Bridget Doreen, formerly wife of Thomas Richard Edwards-Moss (*see* Edwards-Moss, Bt), and da of late Maj Hon Richard Coke (*see* E Leicester, colls), and has issue by 1st and 2nd *m*.

Arms – Quarterly: 1st and 4th per fesse wavy, the chief argent, and the base representing waves of the sea, in chief a dexter hand couped at the wrist gules, in base a salmon naiant proper. *O'Neill*; 2nd and 3rd checky, or and gules, a chief vair, *Chichester*; a mullet for difference. **Crest** – 1st, an arm embowed in armour, the hand grasping a sword, all proper; 2nd a stork rising, with a snake in its beak, all proper. **Mottoes** – Invitum sequitur honos (Honours follow us without seeking), and Lamh dearg Eirin (*The Red hand of Ireland*). **Supporters** – On either side a heron proper standing on a billet fessewise wavy argent charged with a bar wavy azure.
Residence – Killala Lodge, Killala, co Mayo.

SON LIVING (By 1st marriage)

Hon HUGH DETMAR TORRENS, *b* 14 June 1939; *ed* Eton; Capt IG: *m* 1983, Mrs Sylvie Marie-Therese Chittenden, da of late Georges Wichard, of Provence, France, and has issue living, François Hugh Nial, *b* 26 June 1984. *Residences* – 14 Thurloe Place, SW7 2RZ, and Cleggan Lodge, Ballymena, co Antrim BT43 7JW. *Clubs* – Beefsteak, Garrick.

DAUGHTERS LIVING (By 1st marriage)

Hon Mary-Rose, *b* 1935: *m* 1960, David Stewart Wellesley Blacker (E Peel), and has issue living, Barnaby Stewart Hugh, *b* 1961: *m* 1988, Colleen M., eldest da of Alexander McConnell, of Palmerston North, NZ, and has issue living, Julia Adelaide *b* 1989, — William O'Neill, *b* 1962, — Rohan David Peel, *b* 1966.

(By 2nd marriage)

Hon Rosetta Anne, *b* 1954: *m* 1977, Maj John Michael Anthony Paxman, Coldstream Gds, and has issue living, Truscote Phelim, *b* 1985, — Musidora Anne, *b* 1980, — Zena Binny Lavinia, *b* 1982. *Residence* – Ballylina House, Borissokane, co Tipperary.
Hon Moira Louisa, *b* 1961.
Hon Grania Elizabeth, *b* 1963.

WIDOWS LIVING OF SONS OF FIRST BARON

Anne-Marie (*Hon Lady O'Neill*), da of late Bertil Ljungström, of Stockholm, and formerly wife of M. Lindberg: *m* 1961, as his 3rd wife, Hon Sir Con Douglas Walter O'Neill, GCMG, who *d* 1988. *Residence* – 45 Godfrey St, SW3.
Virginia Lois, da of late John Douglas Legge, MC (*see* E Dartmouth, colls): *m* 1966, Hon Nial Arthur Ramleh O'Neill, who *d* 1980. *Residence* – Crowfield House, Crowfield, Ipswich, Suffolk IP6 9TP.

COLLATERAL BRANCH LIVING

Issue of late Hon Sir Con Douglas Walter O'Neill, GCMG, 2nd son of 1st Baron, *b* 1912, *d* 1988: *m* 1st, 1940 (*m diss* 1954), Rosemary Margaret, only da of late Harold Pritchard, FRCP; 2ndly, 1954, Baroness Carola Hertha Adolfine Emma Harriet Luise (Mady), who *d* 1960, eldest da of late Baron Max von Holzing-Berstett, and widow of Baron Wilhelm Pleikart Marschall von Bieberstein; 3rdly, 1961, Mrs Anne-Marie Lindberg (ante), da of late Bertil Ljungstöm, of Stockholm, and formerly wife of M. Lindberg:—
(By 1st *m*) Rowan Peter Hugh (Jerome House, Front St, Churchill, Bristol), *b* 1944; *ed* Eton, and Worcester Coll, Oxford (BA 1966); Capt The Parachute Regt, commn'd 1967: *m* 1990, Mrs Elizabeth A. Wilson, da of late Edgar Goad, of Oxshott, Surrey. —— Onora Sylvia O'NEILL (11a Stonefield St, N1 0HW), *b* 1941; has resumed her maiden name: *m* 1963 (*m diss* 1976), Edward Nell, of Brooklyn, NY, USA, and has issue living, Adam, *b* 1967, — Jacob, *b* 1969.

PREDECESSORS – (1) *Rt Hon* (ROBERT WILLIAM) HUGH O'Neill, PC, 3rd son of 2nd Baron O'Neill; *b* 1883; Bar Inner Temple 1909; Maj Roy Irish Rifles; HM's Lieut for co Antrim 1948-59; European War 1915-17 in Roy Irish Rifles, and on Staff, Palestine 1918, as Dep Judge Advocate-Gen; Chm of Conservative Private Members 1922 Cttee in House of Commons 1935-39, and Under-Sec of State for India and Burma 1939-40; Pro Chancellor Queen's Univ, Belfast 1922; unsuccessfully contested Stockport (*C*) Jan 1906; sat as MP for Antrim County, Mid Antrim Div (*U*) Feb 1915-Oct 1922, for Antrim County Nov 1922-Feb 1950, and for N Div of Antrim Feb 1950-Oct 1952; sat for Antrim County (Parliament of N Ireland) May 1921-April 1929 (was first Speaker of that Parliament June 1921-May 1929); *cr* PC (Ireland) 1921, (N Ireland) 1922, and (GB) 1937, a *Baronet* 1929, and *Baron Rathcavan*, of The Braid, co Antrim (peerage of UK) 1953: *m* 1909, Sylvia, who *d* 1972, da of Walter A Sandeman, of Morden House, Royston; *d* 1982; *s* by his el surv son (2) PHELIM ROBERT HUGH, 2nd Baron and present peer.

RATHCREEDAN, BARON (Norton) (Baron UK 1916)

You may break but shall not bend me

CHRISTOPHER JOHN NORTON, 3rd Baron; *b* 3 June 1949; *s* 1990; *ed* Wellington Coll, and RAC Cirencester: *m* 1978, Lavinia Anne Ross, da of Alan George Ross Ormiston, of Coln Orchard, Arlington, Bibury, Glos (*see* E Harewood, colls), and has issue.

Arms – Per fesse or and azure, in chief a lion passant sable and in base a maunch ermine. **Crest** – A tiger's head couped at the neck, holding in the mouth a broken spear in bend proper. **Supporters** – On either side a tiger reguardant proper, collared and chained argent, the collar of that on the dexter side charged with three roses gules, and that on the sinister side with three trefoils vert.
Residence – Waterton Farm House, Ampney Crucis, Cirencester, Glos. *Club* – Turf.

DAUGHTERS LIVING

Hon Jessica Charlotte, *b* 1983.
Hon Serena Clare, *b* 1987.

BROTHER LIVING

Hon ADAM GREGORY, *b* 2 April 1952: *m* 1980, Hilary Shelton, only da of Edmon Ryan, of Anchorage, Kentucky, USA, and has issue living, Emily Beatrice, *b* 1984, — Georgina Christine Ryan, *b* 1988. *Residence* – 60 Marmora Rd, E Dulwich, SE22. *Club* – Savile.

SISTER LIVING

Hon Elizabeth Ann, *b* 1954: *m* 1988, Alistair Scott, elder son of Prof James S. Scott, of Byards Lodge, Knaresborough, N Yorks.

WIDOW LIVING OF SECOND BARON

ANN PAULINE (*Dowager Baroness Rathcreedan*), JP, da of late Surg-Capt William Bastian, RN: *m* 1946, Maj the 2nd Baron Rathcreedan, TD, who *d* 1990. *Residence* – Church Field, Fawley, Henley-on-Thames, Oxon RG9 6HZ.

PREDECESSORS – (1) CECIL WILLIAM Norton, son of late William Norton, R of Baltinglass, Ireland; *b* 1850; a Junior Lord of the Treasury 1905-10, Assist Postmaster-Gen 1910-16, and Assist Parliamentary Sec (unpaid), Min of Munitions and Supply in the House of Lords 1919-21; MP for W Div of Newington July 1892 to Jan 1916; *cr Baron Rathcreedan*, of Bellehatch Park, Oxon (peerage of United Kingdom) 1916: *m* 1st, 1880, Cecilia Lafayette, who *d* 1948, da of James Kennedy, of The Limes, co Down, and widow of William Thomas Cavendish, of Thornton Hall, Bucks, and Crakemarsh Hall, Stafford; 2ndly, 1903, Margurete Cecil, who *d* 1955, da of Sir Charles Philip Huntington, 1st Bt; *d* 1930; *s* by his son (2) CHARLES PATRICK, TD, 2nd Baron, *b* 1905, Bar Inner Temple 1931, Solicitor 1936, Maj 4th Batn Oxford and Bucks LI (TA), European War 1939-45 (prisoner): *m* 1946, Ann Pauline, da of late Surg-Capt William Bastian, RN; *d* 1990; *s* by his elder son (3) CHRISTOPHER JOHN, 3rd Baron and present peer.

RATHDONNELL, BARON (McClintock-Bunbury) (Baron I 1868)

Power is stronger by unity

THOMAS BENJAMIN MCCLINTOCK-BUNBURY, 5th Baron; *b* 17 Sept 1938; *s* 1959; *ed* Charterhouse, and RNC Dartmouth: *m* 1965, Jessica Harriet, da of George Gilbert Butler (*see* B Dunboyne, colls) and has issue.

Arms – Quarterly: 1st and 4th argent, on a bend sable, three chess-rooks of the field; 2nd and 3rd per pale gules and azure, a chevron ermine, between three escallops argent. **Crest** – 1st, two swords in saltire argent, hilted or, pierced through a leopard's face of the last; 2nd, a lion passant proper. **Supporters** – *Dexter*, a lion; *sinister*, a leopard; both proper, each gorged with a collar ermine, and charged on the shoulder with an escallop argent.
Seat – Lisnavagh, Rathvilly, co Carlow.

SONS LIVING

Hon WILLIAM LEOPOLD, *b* 6 July 1966.

Hon George Andrew Kane, *b* 1968.
Hon James Alexander Hugh, *b* 1972.

DAUGHTER LIVING

Hon Sasha Anne, *b* 1976.

SISTERS LIVING

Hon Katharine Alexandra (Coole Stables, Rathvilly, co Carlow), *b* 1940: *m* 1960, James Joseph Doyle, who *d* 1993.
Hon Hermione Jane, *b* 1943: *m* 1988, Callum Macleod, of 34 Newell St, Pt Chevalier, Auckland, NZ.
Hon Pamela Rosemary (The Middle Lodge, Kilruddery, Bray, co Wicklow), *b* 1948.

PREDECESSORS – (1) JOHN M'CLINTOCK, MP for co Louth 1857-9; *b* 1798; was Lord-Lieut of co Louth and Col Louth Militia; *cr Baron Rathdonnell*, of Rathdonnell, co Donegal (peerage of Ireland) 1868, with remainder to the issue male of his deceased brother, Capt William Bunbury McClintock-Bunbury, RN, MP; *d* 1879; *s* by his nephew (2) THOMAS KANE (son of late Capt M'Clintock-Bunbury, RN, MP) (ante), by Pauline Caroline Diana Mary, da of Sir James Stronge, 2nd Bt, 2nd Baron, *b* 1848; was HM's Lieut for co Carlow 1890-1929 (High Sheriff 1876), and a Representative Peer: *m* 1874, Katherine Anne, who *d* 1925, da of Right Hon Henry Bruen, PC, of Oak Park, co Carlow; *d* 1929; *s* by his son (3) THOMAS LEOPOLD, MBE, 3rd Baron, *b* 1881; High Sheriff of Carlow 1908-9; *m* 1912, Ethel Synge, who *d* 1922, da of late Robert Wilson Ievers, CMG; *d* 1937; *s* by his son (4) WILLIAM ROBERT, MC, 4th Baron; *b* 1914; Major 15th/19th Hussars: *m* 1937, Pamela (who *d* 1989, having *m* 2ndly, 1961, Major Hugh Caruthers Massy, who *d* 1987), el da of late John Malcolm Drew, of Eversley, near Milnthorpe, Westmorland; *d* 1959; *s* by his son (5) THOMAS BENJAMIN, 5th Baron and present peer.

RAVENSDALE, BARON (Mosley) (Baron UK 1911, Bt GB 1781)

Custom rules the law

NICHOLAS MOSLEY, MC, 3rd Baron, and 7th Baronet; *b* 25 June 1923; *s* 1966; *ed* Eton, and Balliol Coll, Oxford; 1939-45 War in Italy (MC) as Capt, Rifle Bde; writer, author of *Accident, Hopeful Monsters* (Whitbread Book of the Year Award 1991), etc: *m* 1st, 1947 (*m diss* 1974), Rosemary Laura, who *d* 1991, da of late Marshal of the RAF Sir John Maitland Salmond, GCB, CMG, CVO, DSO (*see* B Lucas of Crudwell); 2ndly, 1974, Verity Elizabeth, 2nd da of late N. J. B. (Jack) Raymond, of Winslade Down, Basingstoke, Hants, and formerly wife of (John) Adrian Bailey, and has issue by 1st and 2nd *m*.

Arms – Quarterly, 1st and 4th, sable, a chevron between three pickaxes argent, *Mosley*; 2nd and 3rd argent, on a bend sable, three popinjays or, collared gules, *Curzon.* **Crest** – An eagle displayed ermine. **Supporters** – *Dexter*, a raven proper; *sinister*, a popinjay proper collared gules.
Residence – 2 Gloucester Crescent, NW1 7DS.

SONS LIVING *(By 1st marriage)*

Hon SHAUN NICHOLAS, *b* 5 Aug 1949; *ed* Bryanston, and Hertford Coll, Oxford: *m* 1978, Theresa Clifford, and has issue living, Daniel Nicholas, *b* 10 Oct 1982, — Matthew, *b* 1985, — Francis, *b* 1988, — Aidan, *b* 19—.
Hon Ivo Adam Rex, *b* 1951; *ed* Bryanston, and New Coll, Oxford: *m* 1977, Xanthe Jennifer Grenville, yst da of Sir Michael Bernard Grenville Oppenheimer, 3rd Bt, and has issue living, Nathaniel Inigo, *b* 1982, — Felix Harry, *b* 1985, — Scipio Louis, *b* 1988, — Noah Billy, *b* 1990. *Residence* – Courtyard, Neopardy, Crediton, Devon.
Hon Robert, *b* 1955; *ed* Bedales: *m* 1980, Victoria McBain, and has issue living, Gregory, *b* 1981, — Vija, *b* 1985.

(By 2nd marriage)

Hon Marius, *b* 1976.

DAUGHTER LIVING *(By 1st marriage)*

Hon Clare Imogen, *b* 1959.

BROTHER LIVING *(Raised to the rank of a son of a Baroness 1967)*

Hon Michael (Durham Cottage, Christchurch St, SW3), *b* 1932; *ed* Eton, and London Sch of Economics.

HALF-BROTHERS LIVING

(Oswald) Alexander (31 rue de l'Université, Paris 75007, France), *b* 1938; *ed* St Martin de France, Pontoise, and Ohio State Univ: *m* 1975, Charlotte Diana, da of George Gosselin Marten, MVO, DSC (*see* By Alington), and has issue living, Louis, *b* 1983.
Max Rufus, *b* 1940; *ed* Stein an der Traun, Germany, and Ch Ch, Oxford; Barrister-at-law, Gray's Inn 1964; Pres Internat Motor Sports Fedn since 1991; Pres Federation Internationale de l'Automobile 1993: *m* 1960, Jean Marjorie, da of James Taylor, and has issue living, Alexander James, *b* 1970, — Patrick Max, *b* 1972.

SISTER LIVING *(Raised to the rank of a daughter of a Baroness 1967)*

Hon Vivien Elisabeth (11 Mulberry Walk, SW3); *b* 1921: *m* 1949, Desmond Francis Forbes Adam, who *d* 1958 (*see* Adam, Bt, colls, *cr* 1917).

AUNT LIVING *(Daughter of 1st Baron Ravensdale and 1st Marquess Curzon of Kedleston) (In special remainder to the Barony only)*

Lady Alexandra Naldera, CBE (65 Eaton Place, SW1), *b* 1904; a CStJ; Order of Merit (4th Class) of Italy, Order of Merit of Merit of Italian Republic (4th Class), and Cross of Merit (1st Class) of Sovereign Mil Order of Malta; CBE (Civil) 1975: *m* 1925 (*m diss* 1955), Maj Edward Dudley Metcalfe, MVO, MC, Indian Army (ret), who *d* 1957, and has issue living, David Patrick (15 Wilton St, SW1. *Clubs* – White's, Buck's), *b* 1927; *ed* Eton; late Lt Irish Guards; Member of Lloyd's: *m* 1st, 1957 (*m diss* 1964), Alexandra Irene, who *d* 1966, da of Michael Boycun, of Fort William, Ontario, and widow of Sir Alexander Korda; 2ndly, 1968 (*m diss* 1973), Anne, Countess Chauvigny de Blot; 3rdly, 1979, Mrs Sally Howe, da of Edward E. Cullen, of Philadelphia, USA, and has issue living, (by 1st *m*) Julian Edward *b* 1959, Charles Michael *b* 1962, Zara Naldera *b* 1957: *m* 1989, as his 2nd wife, Jonathan Halsey Luke Colchester, of New Place, Ickham, Kent, son of Rev Halsey Sparrowe Colchester, CMG, OBE, of Oxford, (by 2nd *m*) Edward George Anthony *b* 1961. — Davina Naldera, *b* 1930: *m* 1966, as his 2nd wife, (John) Hugo Eastwood, of The Pheasantry, Bramshill Park, Bramshill, Hants, and of 4 Lydon Rd, Clapham Old Town, SW4, son of late John F. Eastwood, OBE, KC, and has issue living, Philip Hugo *b* 1966, Emma Alexandra *b* 1969, —

Linda Mary (14 Elvaston Place, SW7 5QF; 239 Tangier Av, Palm Beach, Florida 33480, USA), *b* (twin) 1930: *m* 1965, Henry Tilford Mortimer, who *d* 1993, son of Stanley Grafton Mortimer, of Tuxedo Park, New York, USA, and has issue living, John Metcalfe *b* 1966, Alexander Dudley *b* 1969.

WIDOW LIVING OF SIXTH BARONET

Hon DIANA (*Hon Lady Mosley*) (1 rue des Lacs, 91400 Orsay, France), da of 2nd Baron Redesdale, and formerly wife of Hon Bryan Walter Guinness (afterwards 2nd Baron Moyne): *m* 1936, as his 2nd wife, Sir Oswald Ernald Mosley, 6th Bt, who *d* 1980.

COLLATERAL BRANCHES LIVING   (*In remainder to the Baronetcy only*)

Issue of late Edward Heathcote Mosley, 2nd son of 5th baronet, *b* 1899, *d* 1980: *m* 1st, 1923 (*m diss* 1932), Sylvia, who *d* 1977, da of late Lt-Col Herbert Alfred Johnson, of Allestree Hall, Derby; 2ndly, 1943, Edith Victoria, who *d* 1990, da of late Thomas Leach, of Malvern.
(By 1st *m*) John Ronald (Flat 31, Chestnut House, East St, Blandford Forum, Dorset, DT11 7DU), *b* 1926; *ed* Stowe: *m* 1st, 1956 (*m diss* 1970), Primrose Antoinette, 2nd da of late F. G. Hadwen; 2ndly, 1972, Caroline Rosalind, da of late H. H. S. Hillier, and has issue living (by 1st *m*), Clare, *b* 1958: *m* 1985, Mark Bicknell, of 56 Camberwell Grove, SE5, son of F. A. Bicknell, of Putney, and has issue living, Augustus Ivo Guy *b* 1990, Cecilia *b* 1994, — Charlotte Louise, *b* 1960.
—— Veronica, *b* 1924: *m* 1954, Peter Hawker, of Coln House, Coln Rogers, Cheltenham, Glos, and has issue living, Annabel (*Hon Mrs Richard Buxton*), *b* 1957: *m* 1988, Hon Richard Christopher Buxton, son of 2nd Baron Noel-Buxton.

Issue of late John Arthur Noel Mosley, yst son of 5th baronet, *b* 1901, *d* 1973: *m* 1st, 1925 (*m diss* 1936), Caroline Edith Sutton, who *d* 1986, da of late Lt-Col George D. Timmis of Matson House, Glos; 2ndly, 1936, Anne Marie Vaudescal-Vartejanu (92 Rue Raynonard, Paris XVI):—
(By 1st *m*) †Timothy John Oswald, *b* 1926; *ed* Eton; late Lt Coldm Gds: *m* 1st, 1955, Pamela, da of R. Kirk Askew, of New York; 2ndly, 1958, Hon Brighid Sarah, who *d* 1985, da of late Lt-Col Hon Michael Thomas Henderson (*see* B Faringdon, 1985 Edn), and *d* 1993. —— Simon James (Flat 4, 59 Onslow Gdns, SW7), *b* 1927; *ed* Eton and Ch Ch, Oxford (MA); Solicitor 1957, ret 1993; late Lt Coldm Gds: *m* 1957, Maria, da of Iraklis Zeri, of Athens, and has issue living, George Christopher (23 The Little Boltons, SW10 9SU), *b* 1959; *ed* Eton: *m* 1992, Ana-Maria, da of Miguel Rincon, of Jerez, Spain, and of Mrs V. Anderson, of London, and has issue living, Oliver Simon *b* 1994, — Claire Amalia, *b* 1964.

Granddaughter of late Capt John William Paget Mosley, only son of late Lt-Col John Edward Paget Mosley, 2nd son of Capt William Bayley Mosley, 3rd son of Rev John Peploe Mosley, 2nd son of 1st baronet:—
Issue of late John Herbert Mosley, *b* 1912, *d* 1986: *m* 1st, 1935 (*m diss* 1947), Ethel Marcia Hancock; 2ndly, 1949 (*m diss* 1950), Mrs Elaine Verna Savory; 3rdly, 1951 (*m diss* 1955), Elizabeth Anna Maria Stefak; 4thly, 1962 (*m diss* 1973), Lyla Fay Hemus, of Auckland, NZ:—
(By 1st *m*) Christine Ann, *b* 1941: *m* 1964, Clive Dearden, of 76 Hillsway, Littleover, Derby, and has issue living, Rosemary Ann, *b* 1969, — Heather Jane, *b* 1971.

Grandsons of late Rev Oswald Henry Mosley, 4th son of Capt William Bayley Mosley (ante):—
Issue of late Oswald Feilden Mosley, *b* 1880, *d* 1946: *m* 1912, Ida, da of late William Palmer, of St Mary Church, Torquay:—
Oswald Henry Feilden, *b* 1913; late Capt Roy Armoured Corps: *m* 1st, 1941, Mary Angela, da of late Louis de Las Cassas (Heathcoat-Amory, Bt); 2ndly, 1952, Olga Marie Noelie, da of George Ackroyd, and has issue living, (by 1st *m*) Sheila Dorothy, *b* 1942: *m* 1970, Paul Brissault Minet, of Old Knowle, Frant, Kent TN3 9EJ, and has issue living, Isobel Louise *b* 1971, Anthea *b* 1973. —— Robert Anthony (Immeuble Victoria, 13 Blvd Princess Charlotte, Monte Carlo, Monaco. *Club* – RAF), *b* 1920; formerly Sqdn Ldr RAF; is a Dir of Vieux Temps of Monte Carlo: *m* 1944 (*m diss* 1954), Renee Carmen Cecily Assouad, and has had issue, Anthony Noel, *b* 1949, — Bertha Mary Isobel, *b* 1945: *m* 1968, Alistair Maciver, and *d* 1988, leaving issue, Neil Anthony *b* 1970, Katherine Anne May *b* 1968.

PREDECESSORS – **(1)** GEORGE NATHANIEL Curzon, KG, GCSI, GCIE, PC, FRS, el son of 4th Baron Scarsdale; *b* 1859; Under-Sec of State for India 1891-92, Under-Sec of State for Foreign Affairs 1895-8, Viceroy and Gov-Gen of India 1898-1904 and again 1904-5, Lord Privy Seal 1915-16, Lord Pres of the Council and Leader of the House of Lords, and Sec of State for Foreign Affairs 1919-24 (also Leader of House of Lords), and again Lord Pres of the Council and Leader of the House of Lords 1924-52; *cr Baron Curzon of Kedleston*, co Derby (peerage of Ireland) 1898, and *Baron Ravensdale*, of Ravensdale, co Derby, with special remainder, in default of issue male, to his el da and the heirs male of her body, failing which to his other das in like manner in order of primogeniture, *Viscount Scarsdale*, of Scarsdale, co Derby, with special remainder in default of issue male, to his father (the 4th Baron Scarsdale, whom he succeeded in the Barony) and the heirs male of his body, *Earl Curzon of Kedleston*, co Derby (all in peerage of UK) 1911, and *Earl of Kedleston*, co Derby, and *Marquess Curzon of Kedleston* (peerage of UK) 1921; *s* as 5th Baron Scarsdale and 9th Baronet (both of Scotland and England) 1916: *m* 1st, 1895, Mary Victoria, CI, who *d* 1906, el da of late Levi Zeigler Leiter, of Washington, USA; 2ndly, 1917, *Dame* Grace Elvina Trilla, GBE, who *d* 1958, da of late J. Monroe Hinds, of Alabama, USA, and widow of Alfred Duggan, of Buenos Aires; *d* 1925, when the Irish Barony of 1898, the Earldom of 1911, and the Marquessate of 1921, became ext, while the Barony (*cr* 1761) and the Viscountcy of Scarsdale, together with the two Baronetcies, devolved upon his nephew, Richard Nathaniel Curzon (see that title), and the Barony of Ravensdale devolved by special remainder upon his el da **(2)** MARY IRENE; *b* 1896; Treasurer of Musicians' Benevolent Fund; *cr Baroness Ravensdale of Kedleston*, of Kedleston, co Derby (Life Baroness) 1958; *d* 1966, when the Barony of Ravensdale (*cr* 1911) devolved on her nephew **(3)** NICHOLAS Mosley, MC (el son of Lady Cynthia Blanche Mosley (2nd da of 1st Marquess Curzon of Kedleston and 1st Baron Ravensdale), who *d* 1933, having *m* 1920, as his 1st wife, Sir Oswald Ernald Mosley, 6th Bt), 3rd Baron, and present peer.
*(1) JOHN PARKER MOSLEY, son of Nicholas Mosley; *cr* a *Baronet* 1781; *s* by his grandson **(2)** *Sir* OSWALD, 2nd Bt; MP for N Div of Staffs; *d* 1871; *s* by his son **(3)** *Sir* TONMAN, 3rd Bt; *d* 1890; *s* by his son **(4)** *Sir* OSWALD, 4th Bt; High Sheriff of Staffs; *d* 1915; *s* by his son **(5)** *Sir* OSWALD, 5th Bt; *d* 1928; *s* by his son **(6)** *Sir* OSWALD, 6th Bt; leader of *New Party* Feb 1931; *d* 1980; *s* by his son **(7)** *Sir* NICHOLAS, 7th Bt, who succeeded as 3rd Baron Ravensdale (see ante).

RAVENSWORTH, BARON (Liddell) (Baron UK 1821, Bt E 1642)

One and the same

ARTHUR WALLER LIDDELL, 8th Baron, and 13th Baronet; *b* 25 July 1924; *s* 1950; *ed* Harrow; formerly Radio Engineer, British Broadcasting Corporation: *m* 1950, Wendy, adopted da of J. Stuart Bell, of Studio House, Cookham, Berks, and has issue.

Arms – Argent, fretty gules, on a chief of the second three leopards' faces or. **Crest** – A lion rampant sable, semée of billets or, and crowned with an Eastern coronet gold. **Supporters** – On either side a leopard or, semée of golps, gorged with a mural crown purpose.
Seat – Eslington Park, Whittingham, Alnwick, Northumberland.

SON LIVING

Hon THOMAS ARTHUR HAMISH, *b* 27 Oct 1954; *ed* Gordonstoun, and RAC Cirencester: *m* 1983, Linda, da of late Henry Thompson, of Hawthorn Farm, Brunton Lane, Gosforth, Newcastle-upon-Tyne, and has issue living, Henry Arthur Thomas, *b* 27 Nov 1987, — Alice Lorina, *b* 1986. *Residence* – Mountain, Whittingham, Northumberland.

DAUGHTER LIVING

Hon Jane Alice, *b* 1952: *m* 1984, Michael James Crowhurst Rubie, only son of late Henry Edward Rubie, of Rustington, W Sussex, and has issue living, Sophia Amy Elizabeth, *b* 1986, — Isabel Emma Mary, *b* 1988, — Francesca Louise, *b* 1991. *Residence* – Red Briars, 35 Drax Av, SW20 0EQ.

SISTER LIVING (Raised to the rank of a Baron's daughter 1951)

Hon Sophie Harriet, *b* 1927: *ed* Central High Sch, Newcastle-on-Tyne, and King's Coll, Durham Univ; ordained Deaconess 1980, Deacon 1987: *m* 1981, Leslie Charles William Woodhams, of 31 Hanover Close, Shaftgate Av, Shepton Mallet, Som BA4 5YQ.

SISTER LIVING OF SEVENTH BARON

Hon Beatrice Sophie, *b* 1906: *m* 1931, Edward Richard Speyer, and has issue living, Jocelyne Isolda, *b* 1933: *m* 1958, Alan Richard Tait, and has issue living, Matthew Edward *b* 1960, — Valentine Antonia, *b* 1938: *m* 1974, Nicholas John Windsor Gaffney, of Flat 1, 13 South Hill Park Gdns, Hampstead, NW3. *Residence* –

COLLATERAL BRANCHES LIVING

Grandchildren of late Capt Augustus Frederick Liddell, CVO, son of late Col Hon George Augustus Liddell, 6th son of 1st Baron:—
Issue of late Guy Maynard Liddell, CB, CBE, MC, *b* 1892, *d* 1958: *m* 1926 (*m diss* 1943), Hon Calypso Baring, who *d* 1974, da of 3rd Baron Revelstoke:—
Peter Lorillard (Nym House, Oakdale Rd, Tunbridge Wells, Kent), *b* 1927, *ed* Oxford Univ (MA 1954): *m* 1st, 1951 (*m diss* 1966), Anne Jamieson, da of Capt F. M. Cannon, US Naval Res Med Corps, of San Rafael, California, USA; 2ndly, 1970, Joan Frances Hopkinson, and has issue living, (by 1st *m*) Peter Guy, *b* 1952; *ed* Sevenoaks: *m* 1st, 1977 (*m diss* 1989), Elaine Patricia, eldest da of Harold Mountford Wenzel, of 41 Sedley Rise, Loughton, Essex; 2ndly, 1993, Hilary Lazenby, and has issue living, (by 1st wife) Thomas Edward *b* 1984, (by 2nd wife) Rose Alice *b* 1992, — John David, *b* 1954; *ed* Sevenoaks: *m* 1994, Jana Berg, — Thomas Andrew, *b* 1960, — Alice, *b* 1958: *m* 1987, Paul Richard Wells, son of Fl Cmdr Oliver Wells, of Ickwell, Beds, and has issue living, Harry Augustus *b* 1992, Georgina Charlotte *b* 1988. —— Elizabeth Gay, *b* 1928: *m* 1st, 1946 (*m diss* 1970), Carl Paulson; 2ndly, 1973, Alexander van de Pol, of 615 Palos Verdes Drive West, Palos Verdes Estates, CA 90274, USA, and has issue living (by 1st *m*), Jay, *b* 1950: *m* 1982, Diane Plummer, and has issue living, Kyle *b* 1983, Scott *b* 1985, Derek *b* 1987, — Mark, *b* 1957, — Sandra, *b* 1947: *m* 1977, Harry Reese. —— Anne Jennifer, *b* 1931: *m* 1951 (*m diss* 19—), Joseph Enzensperger, and has issue living, Joseph, *b* 1952, — Janet, *b* 1957, — Ann, *b* 1959.

(The male line is in remainder to Baronetcy)

Grandchildren of late Edward Henry Liddell, son of late Very Rev Henry George Liddell, DD, son of late Rev Henry George Liddell, 2nd son of 5th Bt:—
Issue of late Lieut-Col Geoffrey William Liddell, DSO, *b* 1884, *d* 1955: *m* 1915, his 2nd cousin, Mary Sophia who *d* 1987, da of late Charles Lyon Liddell (infra):—
Charles Henry, MC (Fullerton Grange, Andover, Hants SP11 7LA), *b* 1917; *ed* Eton, and RMC Sandhurst; Maj (ret) The Rifle Bde, and a JP for Hants (High Sheriff 1975); 1939-45 War (wounded, MC): *m* 1944, Pamela Mary, da of late Maj Antony Hubert Gibbs, JP, of Pytte, Clyst St George, Devon, and has issue living, James Edward Cory (Cottonworth House, Fullerton, Andover, Hants), *b* 1947; *ed* Eton, and RAC Cirencester: *m* 1970, Rachel Anne, yr da of Maj George De Pree, late 60th Rifles, KRRC, of Little Knelle Farm, Beckley, Rye, Sussex (see E Galloway, colls), and has issue living, Tom Edward Charles *b* 1977; *ed* Milton Abbey, Hugh Geoffrey *b* 1980; *ed* Milton Abbey, Georgie Sophia *b* 1975, — (Mary) Susan, *b* 1944: *m* 1964, Rev Antony Michael Ansell, of 10 Durand Gdns, SW9 0PP (Fuller, Bt), son of late Col Sir Michael Picton Ansell, CBE, DSO, and has issue living, Michael James Kirkpatrick *b* 1970; *ed* Harrow, Harriet Mary *b* 1966, Alexandra Jane *b* 1968: *m* 1991, Andrew Dunnett, son of Rev Robert Dunnett, — Alice Margaret, *b* 1950: *m* 1973, Christopher Nicholas Allen, of Newman Street Farm, Doulting, Shepton Mallet, Somerset, son of Douglas Allen, and has issue living, Luke Llewellyn Liddell *b* 1985, Jack Basil Charles Liddell *b* 1987, Gus Douglas Oliver Liddell *b* 1989. —— Thomas Lyon, *b* 1920; *ed* Radley, and Worcester Coll, Oxford; 1939-45 War as Capt Rifle Bde: *m* 1951, Susan Mary, da of late C. R. V. Coutts, of the Court Lodge, Chelsfield, Kent, and has issue living, Edward Henry (97 Narbonne Av, SW4), *b* 1953; *ed* Eton, and Magdalen Coll, Camb: *m* 1988, Hon Anna Kinnaird, 2nd da of 13th Lord Kinnaird, and has issue living, Patrick Edward Charles *b* 1991, — Roderick William (29 rue de la Gare, Marienthal Haguenaux, 67500 France), *b* 1955; *ed* Eton, and Worcester Coll, Oxford: *m* 19—, Marie Françoise, yst da of Cmdt Michel Dujol, of Calaman, Cahors, France, and has issue living, Loïc *b* 1979, Theo Antonin Thomas *b* 1981, — David Lyon (17 Klea Av, SW4), *b* 1959; *ed* Eton, and Trin Coll, Camb: *m* 1990, Chloë Camilla Margot, yst da of Dennis Percy Bertlin, of Castlefield, Bletchingley, Surrey, and has issue living, Freya Margot *b* 1994, — Emma Mary, *b* (twin) 1955; *ed* Wycombe Abbey, and St Hilda's Coll, Oxford: *m* 1981, Charles William Taaffe Munro Mackenzie, of 4 Vicarage Rd, SW14, 2nd son of John Hugh Munro Mackenzie of Mornish, and has issue living, Charles Alexander Munro *b* 1983, Kenneth Thomas Munro *b* 1986, Charlotte Annabella Jemima *b* 1990. *Residence* – Dorman's Corner, Lingfield, Surrey. —— William Adrian (Westover, Goodworth Clatford, Andover, Hants), *b* 1924; *ed* Radley, and Magdalen Coll, Camb (BA 19-, MA 19-); late Lt RNVR; 1939-45 War (despatches): *m* 1956, Anne Primrose, da of late Group Capt R. W. G. Lywood, of

Bay Cottage, Scilly, Kinsale, co Cork, and has issue living, William George, *b* 1958; *ed* Eton, — Mary Clare, *b* 1960: *m* 1992, Ralph Wynne Griffith, — Caroline Sophia, *b* 1962: *m* 1988, Dominick Percival Ian Reyntiens (*see* Bruce, Bt, *cr* 1628, colls). —— Geoffrey Andrew (12 Frewin Rd, Wandsworth Common, SW18), *b* 1926; *ed* Radley; late RN; 1939-45 War: *m* 1958, Jillian Mary (CLIFTON-BROWNE), da of David Walkinshaw, of The Lodge, Highfield, Haslemere, Surrey, and has issue living, Charles David Andrew (2 Louisville Rd, SW17 8RW), *b* 1960; *ed* Marlborough: *m* 1986, Victoria Elizabeth, da of Geoffrey Herbert Jolly, of The Old Vicarage, New Chapel Lane, Horwich, Bolton, Lancs, and has issue living, Marcus Andrew *b* 1988, Caitlin Alice *b* 1991.

Granddaughter of late Very Rev Henry George Liddell, DD (ante):—
Issue of late Sir Frederick Francis Liddell, KCB, KC, *b* 1865, *d* 1950: *m* 1901, Mabel Alice, who *d* 1959, da of late Arthur Magniac:—
Bridget Elvira (The Old Cottage, Bulls Head Green, Ewhurst, Surrey), *b* 1908: *m* 1st, 1931 (*m diss* 1937), Peter Lockwood Smith-Dorrien, who was *k* in the bomb explosion at the King David Hotel, Jerusalem, 1946; 2ndly, 1939, Lewis Civval, who *d* 1973; 3rdly, 1979, John Reeder Blandy, OBE, of Old Cottage, Ewhurst, Surrey, and has issue living, (by 2nd *m*) Martha Bridget Liddell, *b* 1941: *m* 1st, 1966, George Patrick Francis Ennor; 2ndly, 1988, E. J. Ivory, of Lyfield House, Ewhurst, Cranleigh, Surrey, and has issue living (by 1st *m*), Julian George *b* 1970, Daniel Lewis *b* 1974, Charlotte Annabella *b* 1968, — Julia Jane (35 Fabian Rd, SW6), *b* 1942: *m* 1974 (*m diss* 1988), Oliver James Malim Case, — Camilla Frances, *b* 1946: *m* 1974, Philip Lee Malim Case, of Halls Farm, Silchester, Berks, and has had issue, Benjamin James Civval *b* 1978, Thomas Henry Civval *b* 1980, Alice Philippa Liddell *b* 1975, *d* 1983.

Grandchildren of late Sir Frederick Francis Liddell, KCB, KC (ante):—
Issue of late Henry George Magniac Liddell, *b* 1902, *d* 1985: *m* 1932, Amelia Lydia, who *d* 1981, da of William Albert Walker, of Gadzema, Rhodesia:—
Eric Henry George, *b* 1935: *m* 1958, Jane-Anne, da of late Walter John Hoskins, RA, of Elston, Shrewton, Wilts, and has issue living, Karen Anne, *b* 1961, — Jacqueline Toni, *b* 1962: *m* 1987, Rodney Alan Penaluna, — Bridget Alice, *b* 1964. *Address* – 6 Stirling Rd, PO Box 67555, Bryanston 2021, Transvaal, S Africa.
Issue of late Maurice Arthur Liddell, OBE, *b* 1905, *d* 1976: *m* 1937, Alix, OBE, who *d* 1981, da of late Adm Mark Edward Frederick Kerr, CB, MVO (*see* M Lothian, colls):—
Virginia Sarah Alix, *b* 1941: *m* 1962, Simon Claude Ashton, CBE, FCA, who *d* 1986, of 27 Newton Rd, W2, and has issue living, Guy Julian Claude, *b* 1964: *m* 1991, Claire Chapman, — Melanie Isabel, *b* 1967: *m* 1994, Hugh Giles Keyworth Broughton, — Jessica Alix, *b* 1970. —— Judith Rose, *b* 1944: *m* 1968, David Mark Jackson, BM, BCh, FFARCS, of The Old Vicarage, Church Walk, Ashton Keynes, Wilts, and has issue living, Luke Hadley, *b* 1970, — Felix Mark, *b* 1973.

Granddaughter of late Lionel Charles Liddell, MVO, yst son of late Very Rev Henry George Liddell, DD (ante):—
Issue of late Philip Liddell, *b* 1904, *d* 1976: *m* 1944, Elizabeth Jane Boret (The Cottage, 26 Lisburn Rd, Newmarket, Suffolk), da of late Colledge Leader, of Newmarket:—
Susan Jane, *b* 1946: *m* 1970, Anthony Gatehouse Hide, of Machell Place, Newmarket, Suffolk, and has issue living, Philip Edward, *b* 1973, — Timothy David, *b* 1982, — Lucinda Jane, *b* 1971.

PREDECESSORS – (1) THOMAS Liddell, a zealous supporter of Charles I; *cr Baronet* 1642; *d* 1650; *s* by his son (2) *Sir* THOMAS, 2nd Bt; *d* 1697; *s* by his son (3) *Sir* HENRY, 3rd Bt; *d* 1723; *s* by his grandson (4) *Sir* HENRY, 4th Bt; MP; *cr Baron Ravensworth*, of Ravensworth Castle (peerage of Great Britain) 1747; *d* 1784, when the barony became extinct, and the baronetcy devolved upon his nephew (5) *Sir* HENRY GEORGE, 5th Bt; *d* 1791; *s* by his son (6) *Sir* THOMAS HENRY, 6th Bt; *cr Baron Ravensworth* (peerage of United Kingdom) 1821; *d* 1855; *s* by his son (7) HENRY THOMAS, 2nd Baron; *b* 1797; MP for Northumberland (*C*) 1826-39, for N Durham 1837-47, and for Liverpool 1853-5; *cr Baron Eslington*, of Eslington Park, co Northumberland, and *Earl of Ravensworth* (peerage of United Kingdom) 1874: *m* 1820, Isabella Horatia, da of late Lord George Seymour (M Hertford); *d* 1878; *s* by his son (8) HENRY GEORGE, 2nd Earl, *b* 1821; MP for Northumberland S (*C*) 1852-78: *m* 1st, 1852, Diana, who *d* 1890, da of late Orlando Gunning-Sutton, RN; 2ndly, 1892, Emma Sophie Georgiana, who *d* 1939 (having *m* 3rdly, 1904, James William Wadsworth), da of late Hon Richard Denman, and widow of Capt Oswin Cumming Baker Cresswell; *d* 1903; *s* by his brother (9) ATHOLE CHARLES, 3rd Earl, *b* 1833: *m* 1866, Caroline Cecilia (who *d* 1909, having *m* 2ndly, 1906, as his 2nd wife, her cousin, 4th Earl of Mount Edgcumbe), da of late Hon George Edgcumbe; *d* 1904, when the Earldom became ext, but the Barony of Ravensworth passed to his cousin (10) ARTHUR THOMAS (son of late Rev Hon Robert Liddell, 5th son of 1st Baron), 5th Baron, *b* 1837: *m* 1866, Sophia Harriett, who *d* 1918, da of Sir Thomas Walker, 2nd Bt; *d* 1919; *s* by his el son (11) GERALD WELLESLEY, 6th Baron, *b* 1869: *m* 1899, Isolda Blanche, who *d* 1938, da of Charles Glyn Prideaux Brune, of Prideaux Place, Cornwall; *d* 1932; *s* by his son (12) ROBERT ARTHUR, ED, 7th Baron, *b* 1902; Major RA (TA); *d* 1950; *s* by his cousin (13) ARTHUR WALLER (son of late Hon Cyril Arthur Liddell, 2nd son of 5th Baron), 8th Baron and present peer.

RAWLINSON OF EWELL, BARON (Rawlinson) (Life Baron 1978)

PETER ANTHONY GRAYSON RAWLINSON, PC, QC, son of late Lt Col Arthur Richard Rawlinson, OBE, of Ferring, Sussex (*see* Grayson, Bt, 1990 Edn), who *d* 1984; *b* 26 June 1919; *ed* Downside and Christ's Coll, Camb (Exhibitioner, Hon Fellow); Bar Inner Temple 1946, QC 1959; Recorder of Salisbury 1961-62, Solicitor-Gen 1962-64, and Attorney Gen 1970-74; Chm of Senate of Four Inns and Bar 1975-76, Pres 1986, Recorder of Kingston upon Thames since 1975; Chm of the Bar 1975-76; Leader of Western Circuit 1975-82; Treas Inner Temple 1984; Hon Fellow Coll of America's Trial Lawyers, and Hon Member America's Bar Assocn; MP for Epsom (*C*) 1955-74, and Epsom and Ewell 1974-78; 1939-45 War as Maj Irish Gds in N Africa (despatches); *cr Knt* 1962, PC 1964, and *Baron Rawlinson of Ewell*, of Ewell, co Surrey (Life Baron) 1978: *m* 1st, 1940 (*m diss* 1954) (*m* annulled by Sacred Rota, Rome), Haidee da of late Gerald Kavanagh; 2ndly, 1954, Elaine Angela, da of late Vincent Luis Dominguez, of Rhode Island, USA (*see* Grayson, Bt, 1980 Edn), and has issue by 1st and 2nd *m*.

Arms – Or between three towers sable each charged with a sword point upwards argent a pall reversed sable thereon in chief a lymphad argent and in chevron a lion head erased or between two roses argent barbed and seeded proper. **Crest** – On a mount vert within a circlet of acorns and harps or a duck proper holding in the beak an escallop argent. **Supporters** – *Dexter*, a pegasus sable, maned, hooved and crowned gold; *sinister*, a llama or gorged with a ribbon blue celeste and argent the ends flottant upwards.
Residence – 9 Priory Walk, SW10 9SP. *Clubs* – Whites, Pratts, MCC.

SONS LIVING *(By 2nd marriage)*

Hon Michael Vincent, *b* 1957: *m* 1982, Maria Alexandra Hilda Madeline de Lourdes, only da of late Anthony Charles Garton.
Hon Anthony Richard, *b* 1963.

DAUGHTERS LIVING *(By 1st marriage)*

Hon Mikaela, *b* 1941: *m* 1964, Jonathan Irwin, of Sandymount House, Digby Bridge, Sallins, co Kildare, and has issue living, Charles, *b* 1965, — Luke, *b* 1967, — Jago, *b* 1972, — Samson, *b* 1982.
Hon Dariel, *b* 1943: *m* 1965, Harry John Gerard Garnett, of 32 Northumberland Pl, W2, and has issue living, Sophia, *b* 1968: *m* 1994, Tim Beddow, son of late C. M. Beddow, — Natasha, *b* 1970.
Hon Haidée, *b* 1948: *m* 1st, 1968, Richard Annesley; 2ndly, 1985, Maj Ralph Cowdy, and has issue living (by 1st *m*), Peter, *b* 1970, — Arabella, *b* 1972.

(By 2nd marriage)

Hon Angela Lorraine, *b* 1962: *m* 1991, Mathew Steinmann.

RAYLEIGH, BARON (Strutt) (Baron UK 1821)

Tenax propositi
Tenacious of purpose

JOHN GERALD STRUTT, 6th Baron; *b* 4 June 1960; *s* 1988; *ed* Eton, RMA Sandhurst, and RAC Cirencester; late Lieut Welsh Gds: *m* 1991, Annabel Kate, yst da of Maj (William) Garry Patterson, Life Guards (*see* B Monson), and has issue.

Arms – Azure, on a chevron argent, between three cross-crosslets fitchée or, as many leopards' faces proper. **Crest** – A demi-lion azure, gorged with a mural crown, holding in the dexter paw a cross-crosslet fitchée or, and resting the sinister on a shield sable, charged with a chevron argent, between three cross-crosslets fitchée also or. **Supporters** – *Dexter*, a reindeer or, collared and attired sable; *sinister*, a monkey proper, banded round the loins and chained, chain reflexed over the back or.
Seat – Terling Place, Chelmsford, Essex.

SON LIVING

Hon JOHN FREDERICK, *b* 29 March 1993.

SISTERS LIVING

Anne Caroline (*Hon Mrs Bernard Jenkin*), *b* 1955: *m* 1988, Hon Bernard Christison Jenkin, yr son of Baron Jenkin of Roding, PC (Life Baron).
Mary Jean, *b* 1957: *m* 1981, Roderick Joseph Fraser, and has issue (*see* L Lovat, colls). *Residence* – Berwicks Farm House, Hatfield Peverel, Chelmsford, Essex.

UNCLE LIVING *(son of 4th Baron by 1st marriage)*

Hon Hedley Vicars, *b* 1915; *ed* Eton, and Trin Coll, Camb; Capt (ret) Scots Guards. *Residence* – Mulroy, Carrigart, Letterkenny, co Donegal. *Club* – Brooks's.

HALF-UNCLE LIVING *(son of 4th Baron by 2nd marriage)*

Hon Guy Robert, *b* 1921; *ed* Eton, and Trin Coll, Camb (BA 1943). *Residence* – The Old Rectory, Terling, Chelmsford, Essex CM3 2QE.

AUNT LIVING *(daughter of 4th Baron by 1st marriage)*

Hon Daphne (*Dowager Baroness Acton*), *b* 1911: *m* 1931, 3rd Baron Acton, who *d* 1989. *Residence* – 46 Clarence Rd, Moseley, Birmingham B13 9UH.

MOTHER LIVING

Hon Jean Elizabeth Davidson, da of 1st Viscount Davidson: *m* 1952, Hon Charles Richard Strutt, 2nd son of 4th Baron, who *d* 1981. *Residence* – Berwick Place, Hatfield Peverel, Chelmsford, Essex.

COLLATERAL BRANCHES LIVING

Grandson of late Hon Richard Strutt, 3rd son of 2nd Baron:—
Issue of late Capt Geoffrey St John Strutt, CBE, *b* 1888, *d* 1971: *m* 1912, Sybil Eyre, who *d* 1975, da of Sir Walpole Lloyd Greenwell, 1st Bt:—
Antony Geoffrey, OBE, *b* 1913; *ed* Winchester; Wing Cdr RAF; OBE (Mil) 1952: *m* 1st, 1939 (*m diss* 1951), Ebba, da of Lief Lunderbye, of Oslo; 2ndly, 1951, Millicent (Molly) Edith, da of Aubrey Stephen Waters, of London, and has issue living (by

1st wife), Vivienne Ebba, *b* 1940: *m* 1968, Richard Maitland Sands, of Hill Farm House, Thorpe Morieux, Bury St Edmunds, Suffolk, and has issue living, Richard Jonathan Neville *b* 1974, — (by 2nd wife) Peter Antony (37 Bearwood Rd, Wokingham, Berks RG11 4TB), *b* 1949, — Stephen Nigel (Caixa Postal 5155, Campinas, Brazil), *b* 1952, — Michael Geoffrey, *b* 1958: *m* 1992, Barbara —, — Ian David, *b* 1965, — Denise Olivia (14 East St, Ashburton, Devon), *b* 1955: *m* 1975 (*m diss* 1990), Richard Lyndale, — Pamela Jane, *b* 1957: *m* 1980 (*m diss* 1994), Ian Fielding. *Residence* – Flat 1, Park House, Ridgeway Rd, Torquay, S Devon TQ1 2ES.

Grandsons of late Capt Geoffrey St John Strutt, CBE (ante):—
Issue of late Lt Stephen Alistair Strutt, RNVR, *b* 1918, *d* 1949: *m* 1941, Felicity Anne (who *m* 2ndly, 1959, Brig David Campbell Mullen, CBE, who *d* 1968), da of Mervyn Sorley MacDonnell:—
Paul Alistair, *b* 1944; *ed* Ampleforth; Maj: *m* 1977, Charlotte Yvonne, da of Brig Mortimer Cecil Lanyon, MBE, MC (*see* B Amherst of Hackney, colls), and has issue living, Richard Alistair Robert, *b* 1986, — Louisa Anne, *b* 1982. *Residence* – Flaxmans, W Tytherley, nr Salisbury, Hants SP5 1NR. —— Stephen Mark Alistair, *b* 1948; *ed* Ampleforth, and RAC Cirencester; late Maj Gren Gds: *m* 1980, Christina Mary Amoroso, da of Dr Eric Amoroso Centeno, and has issue living, Edward Alistair James, *b* 1985, — Catherine Mary Felicity Erica, *b* 1983. *Residence* – St Catherine's, Bath, Som BA1 8HA. —— Lucinda Alistaire, *b* 1942: *m* 1976, Lt-Col Angus Iain Ramsay, and *dsp* 1986.

Grandchildren of late Hon Edward Gerald Strutt, CH, 5th son of 2nd Baron:—
Issue of late Gerald Murray Strutt, *b* 1880, *d* 1955: *m* 1910, Rhoda, OBE, who *d* 1968, 2nd da of late Collingwood Hope, CBE, KC, formerly Recorder of Bolton, of Crix, Hatfield Peverel, Essex:—
Pamela, *b* 1911: *m* 1935, Richard Gatty, JP, who *d* 1975, yr son of late Sir Stephen Herbert Gatty, KC, and has had issue, Jonathan *b* 1937: *m* 1st, 1962 (*m diss* 1984), Valerie Cynthia, da of Alfred H Adcock; 2ndly, 1984, Cheryll, (Pepper Arden, Northallerton, N Yorks), da of George Mansfield, of Risca, Gwent, and *d* 1991, leaving issue (by 1st *m*), Fiona Katherine Adelaide *b* 1963: *m* 1992, Maj Torquil MacLeod, The Black Watch (RHR) (and has issue living, Alexander Jonathan Hardine *b* 1994, Sophie *b* 19—), Philippa Margaret *b* 1965: *m* 1988, John Lanteri-Laura, (by 2nd *m*) Richard George *b* 1984, — Jessica Margaret, *b* 1938, — Rhoda Pamela, *b* 1943: *m* 1964, John David Bucknill, of The Grange, Grateley, Andover, Hants SP11 8JR and has issue living, Stephen *b* 1965: *m* 1993, Amanda Jane Cotton, Gemma Martha *b* 1967: *m* 1990, Michael Anthony Hughes, Charlotte *b* 1969. *Residence* – Pepper Arden, Northallerton, N Yorks. —— Ursula Joyce, *b* 1917; 1939-45 War in WRNS: *m* 1948, Maj James Richard Edwards Harden, OBE, DSO, MC, DL, and has issue living, David James (Nanhoron, Pwllheli, Gwynedd), *b* 1954: *m* 1983, Bettina Clare Lascelles, only da of Col Brian C. L. Tayleur, OBE, of Nairobi, Kenya, and has issue living, Edward Richard *b* 1986, Matilda Claire *b* 1984, — Thérèse Annabella, *b* 1949: *m* 1st, 1972 (*m diss* 1979), Charles Herbert Pelham (*see* E Chichester, colls); 2ndly, 1980, Lt-Cdr Nigel John Pearson, RN, and has issue living (by 2nd *m*), James Nicholas *b* 1985, Lucinda Christine *b* 1987, — Carolyn Emily, *b* 1952: *m* 1986, Colin Ransford Galloway, and has issue living, Miles Malcolm Ransford *b* 1989, Tanya *b* 199-, Zoë *b* 1992. *Residence* – Hendy, Nanhoron, Pwllheli, Gwynedd.
Issue of late John James Strutt, *b* 1881, *d* 1968: *m* 1914, Hon Agnes Roger Dewar, who *d* 1919, da of 1st Baron Forteviot:—
Joan Eleanor (173 Cranmer Court, SW3), *b* 1916.
Issue of late Capt Edward Jolliffe Strutt, *b* 1884, *d* 1964: *m* 1912, Amélie, who *d* 1954, da of late Frederic Devas:—
Sir Nigel Edward, TD (Sparrows, Terling, Chelmsford, Essex; Brooks's and Farmers' Clubs), *b* 1916; *ed* Winchester, and Wye Coll (Fellow 1970); Maj Essex Yeo (ret); a DL for Essex; High Sheriff 1966; Hon Fellow of Roy Agric Soc of England 1971 (Pres 1982-83); Hon DSc Cranfield 1979, Hon DUniv Essex 1981, Hon D Ph Anglia Poly Univ 1993, Johann Heinrich von Thünen Gold Medal, Kiel Univ, 1974; Massey Ferguson Award for sers to Agriculture 1976; 1939-45 War as Capt 104th (Essex) Yeo RHA (TA); Middle East 1939-45 (wounded, prisoner); Knt 1972. —— Gillian Leonora, *b* 1918: *m* 1st, 1941 (*m diss* 1959), Rt Hon Harold Anthony Nutting (later 3rd Bt); 2ndly, 1961, Brig Oliver George Brooke, CBE, DSO, of The Manor House, Gt Cheverell, Devizes (*see* V Brookeborough, colls, 1985 Edn), who *d* 1987.

Granddaughter of late Capt Edward Jolliffe Strutt (ante):—
Issue of late Lt-Col Mark Frederic Strutt, MC, TD, *b* 1913, *d* 1982: *m* 1946, Estelle Elaine, da of Capt Sir Thomas Reedham Berney, 10th Bt, MC, and widow of Maj Kenneth William Bols, IA (Strickland-Constable, Bt, colls):—
Charlotte Olivia, *b* 1947: *m* 1969, Bruce Dudley Ryder, of Crix, Hatfield Peverel, Essex, and has issue living (*see* E Harrowby, colls).

PREDECESSORS – (1) *Lady* CHARLOTTE MARY GERTRUDE FITZGERALD, da of James, 1st Duke of Leinster, and wife of Col Joseph Holden Strutt, MP for Maldon 1790-1827, was *cr Baroness Rayleigh*, of Terling Place, co Essex (peerage of United Kingdom) 1821; *s* by her son (2) JOHN JAMES, 2nd Baron; *b* 1796: *m* 1842, Clara Elizabeth Latouche, who *d* 1900, da of late Capt Richard Vicars, RE; *d* 1873; *s* by his son (3) JOHN WILLIAM, OM, PC, DCL, LLD, DSc, FRS, 3rd Baron, *b* 1842; sometime Lord-Lieut of Essex; the eminent scientist; Nobel Prizeman, Chancellor of Camb Univ, Hon Professor of Natural Philosophy at Roy Institution, and Scientific Adviser to the Trinity House; four years Professor of Experimental Physics in Camb Univ: *m* 1871, Evelyn Georgiana Mary, who *d* 1934, da of late James Maitland Balfour, of Whittingehame, Prestonkirk; *d* 1919; *s* by his son (4) ROBERT JOHN, 4th Baron; *b* 1875; a FRS; Pres of British Asso 1938, and of Roy Institution 1945: *m* 1st, 1905, Lady Mary Hilda Clements, who *d* 1919, da of 4th Earl of Leitrim; 2ndly, 1920, Kathleen Alice, OBE, who *d* 1980, da of late John Coppin-Straker, of Stagshaw House, Northumberland, and widow of Capt James Harold Cuthbert, DSO, Scots Guards; *d* 1947; *s* by his son (5) JOHN ARTHUR, 5th Baron, *b* 1908: *m* 1934, Ursula Mary, who *d* 1982, da of late Lt-Col Richard Hugh Royds Brocklebank, DSO, of 18 Hyde Park Sq, W; *d* 1988; *s* by his nephew (6) JOHN GERALD (only son of late Hon Charles Richard Strutt, 2nd son of 4th Baron), 6th Baron and present peer.

RAYNE, BARON (Rayne) (Life Baron 1976)

MAX RAYNE, el son of Phillip Rayne; *b* 8 Feb 1918; *ed* Central Foundation Sch, and Univ Coll, London (Hon LLD; Hon Fellow 1966); served with RAF 1940-45; Chm First Leisure Corporation plc since 1992; Dir Housing Corporation (1974) Ltd 1974-78, and Dir of other companies; Gov of St Thomas's Hosp 1962-74, Special Trustee of St Thomas's Hosp 1974-92; Gov of Royal Ballet Sch 1966-79; Gov of Centre for Environmental Studies 1967-73; Member of Gen Council of King Edward VII's Hospital Fund for London since 1966; Trustee of Henry Moore Foundation since 1988; Hon Vice-Pres of Jewish Care since 1966; Vice-Pres of Yehudi Menuhin Sch since 1987 (Gov 1966-87); Chm Royal Nat Theatre 1971-88; Founder Patron of The Rayne Foundation since 1962; Hon Fell of Darwin Coll, Camb 1966, Univ Coll London 1966, LSE 1974, Royal Coll of Psychiatrists 1977, King's Coll Hosp Med Sch 1980, Univ Coll, Oxford 1982, King's Coll, London 1983, Westminster Sch 1989, Royal Coll of Physicians 1992, UMDS, Guy's and St Thomas's 1992; Officier, Légion d'Honneur 1987 (Chevalier 1973); *cr* Knt 1969, and *Baron Rayne*, of Prince's Meadow in Greater London (Life Baron) 1976: *m* 1st, 1941 (*m diss* 1960), Margaret, da of Louis Marco, of London; 2ndly, 1965, Lady Jane Antonia Frances Vane-Tempest-Stewart, el da of 8th Marquess of Londonderry, and has issue by 1st and 2nd *m*.

Arms – Per fess dancetty azure and gules a caduceus between in chief two roses or. **Crest** – Upon a wreath or and azure issuant from a circlet or a mount vert thereon a lion passant gold murally crowned azure holding in the dexter forepaw a key erect wards outwards or. **Supporters** – *Dexter*, a lion or crowned and gorged with a chain pendant therefrom two triangles interlaced azure; *sinister*, a lion azure crowned and gorged with a like chain pendant therefrom a fleur-de-lys gold. *Residence* – 33 Robert Adam St, W1M 5AH.

SONS LIVING *(By 1st marriage)*

Hon Robert Anthony, *b* 1949: *m* 1973, Jane, da of late Robert Blackburn, and has issue.

(By 2nd marriage)

Hon Nicholas Alexander, *b* 1969.
Hon Alexander Philip, *b* 1973.

DAUGHTERS LIVING *(By 1st marriage)*

Hon Madeleine Barbara, *b* 1943: *m* 1964, Alan Rayner.
Hon Susan Ann, *b* 1945: *m* 1965 (*m diss* 1974), John Rubin.

(By 2nd marriage)

Hon Natasha Deborah, *b* 1966: *m* 1992, Nicholas J. Capstick-Dale, son of J. R. Capstick-Dale.
Hon Tamara Annabel, *b* 1970.

RAYNER, BARON (Rayner) (Life Baron 1983)

DEREK GEORGE RAYNER, only son of George William Rayner; *b* 30 March 1926; *ed* City Coll, Norwich, and Selwyn Coll, Camb (Hon Fellow 1983); joined Marks and Spencer 1953, Dir 1967, Jt Man Dir 1973, and Jt Vice-Chm 1982, Chief Exec since 1983; Chm 1984-91; Chief Exec (Procurement Exec) MOD 1971-72; Member of Design Council 1973-75, and of UK Permanent Security Commn 1977-80; Dep-Chm Civil Service Pay Board 1978-80; Adviser to PM on improving efficiency and eliminating waste in Gvt 1979-83; *cr Baron Rayner*, of Crowborough, co E Sussex (Life Baron) 1983.
Address – Michael House, Baker St, W1.

Raynham, Viscount; son of Marquess Townshend.

REA, BARON (Rea) (Baron UK 1937, Bt UK 1935)
(Name pronounced "Ree")

Ready for everything

(JOHN) NICOLAS REA, 3rd Baron and 3rd Baronet, *b* 6 June 1928; *s* 1981; *ed* Dartington Hall, Dauntsey's Sch, and Christ's Coll, Camb (MA, MD); DPH, DCH, DObst, FRCGP: *m* 1st, 1951 (*m diss* 1991), Elizabeth Anne, da of late William Hensman Robinson, of Woking; 2ndly, 1991, Judith Mary, da of late Norman Powell, of Lytham St Anne's, Lancs, and has issue by 1st *m*.

Arms – Or, on a fesse wavy azure between three stags courant gules, a lymphad sails furled of the field. **Crest** – A stag at gaze gules, resting the dexter foreleg on an anchor or. **Supporters** – On either side a stag gules, charged on the shoulder with a bezant, thereon an anchor azure.
Residence – 11 Anson Rd, N7 0RB.

SONS LIVING

Hon MATTHEW JAMES, *b* 28 March 1956; *ed* William Ellis Sch, and Sheffield Univ; has issue living, Ivan REA *b* 1992, Ellis Kelsey Haslam REA (a da), *b* 1989.
Hon Daniel William, *b* 1958; *ed* William Ellis Sch, and Bristol Univ, and UCH Medical Sch: *m* 1983, Hon Rebecca Llewelyn Davies, yst da of late Baron Llewelyn-Davies (Life Baron), and has issue living, William Alexander, *b* 8 Oct 1991, — Edward Inigo *b* 1994. *Residence* – 4 Queensgate Villas, Victoria Park Rd, E9.
Hon Quentin Thomas, *b* 1961; *ed* William Ellis Sch, and Manchester Univ.
Hon John Silas Nathaniel, *b* 1965; *ed* William Ellis Sch.

BROTHER LIVING (*Raised to the rank of a Baron's son,* 1989)

Hon Charles Julian (62 Dukes Av, N10), *b* 1931: *m* 1st, 1951 (*m diss* 1964), Bridget, da of late Montagu Slater; 2ndly, 1964, Anne, da of William Robson, and has issue living (by 1st *m*), Steven, *b* 1956, — Julia, *b* 1952, — (by 2nd *m*), William, *b* 1965, — James, *b* 1968, — Lucy, *b* 1966, — Kate, *b* 1972.

AUNT LIVING (*Daughter of 1st Baron*)

Hon Elisabeth Russell (*Hon Lady Clapham*), *b* 1911; *ed* Newnham Coll, Camb (MA); a JP of London: *m* 1935, Sir Michael John Sinclair Clapham, KBE, son of late Sir John Harold Clapham, CBE, and has had issue, Adam John (254 Alexandra Park Rd, N22), *b* 1940; *ed* Bryanston, and Grenoble Univ, — Charles Marcus (27 Jeffreys St, NW1), *b* 1942; *ed* Marlborough, and King's Coll, Camb (MA); FRMetS: *m* 1971 (*m diss* 1980), Margaret Golledge, and has issue living, Nicolas *b* 1972, — Giles Sinclair, *b* 1946; *d* 1990, — Antonia, *b* 1938; *ed* Cranborne Chase, and Newnham Coll, Camb: *m* 1966, Barry Till, MA, of 44 Canonbury Sq, N1, and has issue living, Lucy Rose Victoria *b* 1969, Emily Caroline Rose 1971. *Residence* – 26 Hill St, W1X 7FU.

WIDOW LIVING OF SON OF FIRST BARON

Helen Margaret, da of late Bernhard Hermann Richardson, of Edinburgh, and formerly wife of Donald Crawford Reid: *m* 1959, as his 3rd wife, Hon Findlay Russell Rea, who *d* 1984. *Residence* – Weald Cottage, Weald, Sevenoaks, Kent TN14 6PY.

COLLATERAL BRANCH LIVING

Issue of late Hon Findlay Russell Rea, 3rd son of 1st Baron, *b* 1907, *d* 1984: *m* 1st, 1932 (*m diss* 1946), (Margaret) Hermione, eldest da of late Col Kenneth Hope Bruce, DSO; 2ndly, 1947 (*m diss* 1959), Eileen, da of late Lt-Col Isaac Wardle, IA, and formerly wife of John Lionel Clemence; 3rdly, 1959, Helen Margaret (ante), da of late Bernhard Hermann Richardson, of Edinburgh, and formerly wife Donald Crawford Reid:—
(By 1st *m*) Benjamin Russell (Trevereux House, Limpsfield Chart, Oxted, Surrey), *b* 1936: *ed* Bryanston, and Trin Coll, Oxford: *m* 1st, 1964 (*m diss* 1972), Angela, only da of Arthur Jackson Bradley; 2ndly, 1973, Dorinda Anne, da of Stanley Cutting, of Bath, Avon, and has issue living (by 1st *m*), Susannah, *b* 1968, — (by 2nd *m*) James Russell, *b* 1973, — Thomas Russell, *b* 1975. —— Joanna (Foxgloves, Wood Lane, Parbold, Wigan, Lancs WN8 7TH), *b* 1934; JP Ormskirk: *m* 1st, 1957 (*m diss* 1982), Robert Cecil Seeckts, yr son of late George Seeckts; 2ndly, 1984, Peter John Bartram, el son of late George Hylton Bartram, of Sunderland, and has issue living (by 1st *m*), Richard Philip, *b* 1966, — Rosemary Anne, *b* 1958, — Sarah Elizabeth, *b* 1960, — Katherine Mary, *b* 1963.

PREDECESSORS – (1) WALTER RUSSELL REA, son of late Rt Hon Russell Rea, MP of Tanhurst, Dorking, Surrey, and Dean Stanley Street, SW1; *b* 1873; a Merchant Banker, and Pres of Free Trade Union; was Comptroller of HM's Household 1931-2; sat as MP for Scarborough (*L*) 1906-18, for N Div of Bradford 1923-4, and for Dewsbury 1931-5; *cr* a *Baronet* 1935, and *Baron Rea*, of Eskdale, co Cumberland (peerage of United Kingdom) 1937: *m* 1st, 1896, Evelyn, who *d* 1930, da of J. J. Muirhead, JP, of Edinburgh; 2ndly, 1931, Jemima, who *d* 1964, da of Rev Alexander Ewing; *d* 1948; *s* by his el son (2) PHILIP RUSSELL, OBE, PC, 2nd Baron, *b* 1900; Foreign Office 1945-50; Liberal Leader in House of Lords 1955-67; Pres of Liberal Party 1955; a Dep Speaker House of Lords 1950-78; 1939-45 War as Lt-Col KRRC attached Special Forces (despatches): *m* 1922, Lorna, who *d* 1978, da of late Lewis O. Smith, of Glasgow; *d* 1981; *s* by his nephew, (JOHN) NICOLAS (son of late Hon James Russell Rea, 2nd son of 1st Baron), 3rd Baron and present peer.

READING, MARQUESS OF (Rufus Isaacs) (Marquess UK 1926)

Either do not attempt or complete

SIMON CHARLES HENRY RUFUS ISAACS, 4th Marquess; *b* 18 May 1942; *s* 1980; *ed* Eton, and Tours Univ France; Lt 1st The Queen's Dragoon Gds 1961-64; Member of London Stock Exchange 1970-74; Management Consultant: *m* 1979, Melinda Victoria, yr da of Richard J. G. Dewar, of Shoelands House, Seale, Surrey, and has issue.

Arms – Sable, a bend between two leopards' faces or, on a chief argent a fasces fessewise proper. **Crest** – In front of a leopard's head couped sable, a faces as in the arms. **Supporters** – On either side a leopard proper, round the neck a collar or, pendent therefrom an escutcheon argent charged with a human head affrontée proper, erased at the neck, ducally crowned or.
Residence – Jaynes Court, Bisley, Glos GL6 7BE. *Clubs* - Cavalry and Guards'; MCC; All England Lawn Tennis.

SON LIVING

JULIAN MICHAEL (*Viscount Erleigh*), *b* 26 May 1986.

DAUGHTERS LIVING

Lady Sybilla Alice, *b* 1980.
Lady Natasha Rose Eleanor, *b* 1983.

BROTHERS LIVING

Lord Antony Ian Michael (9723 Oak Pass Rd, Beverly Hills, CA 90210, USA), *b* 1943; *ed* Gordonstoun: *m* 1st, 1972 (*m diss* 1976), Ann Pugsley; 2ndly, 1983, Heide Lund, of Vancouver, BC, and has issue living (by 2nd *m*), Tallulah Elke Margot, *b* 1987, — Ruby Jacqueline Kirsten, *b* 1989.
Lord Alexander Gerald (2132 Century Park Lane, Apt 109, LA, CA 90067, USA), *b* 1957; *ed* St Paul's Sch, and Oriel Coll, Oxford (MA); Bar (Middle Temple) 1982; California Bar 1988: *m* 1993, Marjorie Frances BACH, da of Howard Goldbach, of LA, USA.

SISTER LIVING

Lady Jacqueline Rosemary Margot, *b* 1946: *m* 1976, Mark Wilfrid Home Thomson, of 42 Glebe Place, SW3, only son of Sir Ivo Wilfrid Home Thomson, 2nd Bt (*cr* 1925).

AUNTS LIVING (*Daughters living of 2nd Marquess*)

Lady Joan Alice Violet (*Baroness Zuckerman*), *b* 1918; formerly a JP for Birmingham and Hunstanton: *m* 1939, Prof Baron Zuckerman, OM, KCB, FRS (Life Baron), who *d* 1993. *Residence* - The Shooting Box, Burnham Thorpe, King's Lynn, Norfolk.
Lady Elizabeth Anne Mary, *b* 1921: formerly Junior Com ATS: *m* 1945, Maj Derek Francis Hornsby, KRRC, who *d* 1971 (B Belper), and has issue living, Richard Gerald (8 Bovingdon Rd, SW6 2AP), *b* 1948: *m* 1980, Maria Lara, of San Francisco, California, and has issue living, Simon Daniel *b* 1983, Rachael Sarah *b* 1982, Annabel *b* 1991, — David Julian (7395 Sir Francis Drake Blvd, Lagunitas, California 94938, USA), *b* 1953: *m* 1975, Julie Ann Witford, and has issue living, Alexander Keith *b* 1977, Samuel Florian *b* 1985, Michael David *b* 1987. *Residence* - 29 Warwick Sq, SW1V 24B.

WIDOW LIVING OF THIRD MARQUESS

MARGOT IRENE (*Dowager Marchioness of Reading*) (Glebe Farm House, Cornwell, nr Chipping Norton, Oxon OX7 67X), yr da of late Percival Augustus Duke, OBE: *m* 1941, the 3rd Marquess, MBE, MC, who *d* 1980.

PREDECESSORS – (1) *Sir* RUFUS DANIEL ISAACS (later Rufus Isaacs), GCB, GCSI, GCIE, GCVO, PC, son of late Joseph Michael Isaacs, merchant and shipbroker, of London; *b* 1860; sat as MP for Reading (*L*) 1904-13; appointed Solicitor-Gen March 1910, Attorney-Gen Oct 1910 (with a seat in the Cabinet from June 1912), and Lord Chief Justice of England 1913-21; Pres Anglo-French Mission to USA 1915, Special British Representative to USA 1917, High Commr in USA, and Ambassador Extraor and Plen on Special Mission 1918-19, Viceroy of India 1921-6, and Sec of State for Foreign Affairs (in National Government) Aug to Nov 1931, became Capt of Deal Castle 1926, and Lord Warden of the Cinque Ports 1934; *cr Baron Reading*, of Erleigh, Berks (peerage of United Kingdom) 1914, *Viscount Reading*, of Erleigh, Berks (peerage of United Kingdom) 1916, *Viscount Erleigh*, of Erleigh, Berks, and *Earl of Reading* (peerage of United Kingdom) Nov 1917, and *Marquess of Reading* (peerage of United Kingdom) 1926: *m* 1st, 1887, *Dame* Alice Edith, GBE, CI, who *d* 1930, da of Albert Cohen, merchant, of London; 2ndly, 1931, *Dame* Stella, GBE (*Baroness Swanborough*), who *d* 1971, da of the late Charles Charnaud; *d* 1935; *s* by his son (2) GERALD, GCMG, CBE, MC, TD, PC, QC, 2nd Marquess; *b* 1889; a Bencher and Treasurer of Middle Temple; was Joint Parliamentary Under-Sec of State for Foreign Affairs 1951-53, and Joint Min of State for Foreign Affairs 1953-7: Hon Col Inns of Court Regt (TA) 1947-59: *m* 1914, Hon Eva Violet Mond, CBE, JP, who *d* 1973, da of 1st Baron Melchett; *d* 1960; *s* by his son (3) MICHAEL ALFRED, MBE, MC, 3rd Marquess *b* 1916; Major Queen's Bays and on Staff; served in World War II *m* 1941, Margot Irene, yr da of late Percival Augustus Duke, OBE, of Watts Close, Tadworth, Surrey; *d* 1980; *s* by his son (4) SIMON CHARLES HENRY, 4th Marquess and present peer, also Earl of Reading, Viscount Erleigh, and Baron Reading.

REAY, LORD (Mackay) (Lord S 1628, Bt NS 1627)
(Name pronounced "Ray")

HUGH WILLIAM MACKAY, 14th Lord and 14th Baronet; *b* 19 July 1937; *s* 1963; *ed* Eton, and Ch Ch, Oxford; is Chief of the Clan Mackay, and Baron Mackay van Ophemert in the Netherlands; Member of European Parl, Strasbourg, since 1973; a Lord in Waiting since 1989, Under-Sec Dept of Trade and Industry 1989-92: *m* 1st, 1964 (*m diss* 1978), Hon Annabel Térèse Fraser, da of 15th (*de facto*) Lord Lovat; 2ndly, 1980, Hon Victoria Isabella Warrender, only da of 1st Baron Bruntisfield, and has issue by 1st and 2nd *m*.

Arms – Azure, on a chevron argent, between three bears' heads couped argent, muzzled gules, a roebuck's head erased, between two hands grasping daggers, the points turned towards the buck's head, all proper. **Crest** – A dexter arm erect couped at the elbow, the hand grasping a dagger also erect proper. **Supporters** – *Dexter*, a pikeman armed at all points; *sinister*, a musketeer, both proper.
Residences – Ophemert in Gelderland, Netherlands; 98 Oakley St, SW3. *Clubs* – Turf, Beefsteak, Puffin's, Pratt's.

SONS LIVING *(By 1st marriage)*

Hon ÆNEAS SIMON (*Master of Reay*), *b* 20 March 1965; *ed* Westminster, and Brown Univ, USA.
Hon Edward Andrew, *b* 1974.

DAUGHTERS LIVING *(By 1st marriage)*

Hon Laura Elizabeth, *b* 1966.

(by *2nd marriage*)

Hon Antonia Alexandra, *b* 1981.
Hon Isabel Violet Grace, *b* 1985.

SISTERS LIVING

Hon Elizabeth Mary, *b* 1938: *m* 1962 (*m diss* 1979), Nicholas Hardwick Fairbairn, QC, MP (later Sir Nicholas Fairbairn), and has issue living, Charlotte Elizabeth, *b* 1963, — Anna-Karina, *b* 1966, — Francesca Katharine Nichola, *b* 1969. *Residence* – 38 Moray Pl, Edinburgh.
Hon Margaret Anne (Upper Huntlywood, Earlston, Berwickshire), *b* 1941: *m* 1976, Allen Leslie Christian, of Upper Huntlywood, Earlston, Berwicks, and Buttonwood Bay AA8, Key Largo, Florida, USA.

UNCLE LIVING *(Son of 12th Lord)*

Baron (and *Hon*) Alexander Willem Rynhard (De Lindenlaan, 76 Schapendrift, Blaricum, Netherlands), *b* 1907.

WIDOW LIVING OF THIRTEENTH LORD

CHARLOTTE MARY (*Charlotte, Lady Reay*) (Southbank, Melrose, Roxburghshire, Bowden, TD6 OST), da of late William Younger, of Ravenswood, Melrose: *m* 1936, the 13th Lord, who *d* 1963.

COLLATERAL BRANCHES LIVING

Granddaughter of late Baron Theodoor Philip Mackay, 2nd son of Johan François Hendrik Jacob Ernestus Mackay, brother of 10th Lord:—
Issue of late Baron Constantyn Willem Ferdinand Mackay, *b* 1870, *d* 1955: *m* 1st, 1898, Jonkvrouw Petronella Adamina Hoeufft, who *d* 1933; 2ndly, 1937, Dr C. Frida Katz, who *d* 1963:—
Baroness Margaretha Clara Françoise, *b* 1909: *m* 1937, Rev Henri Jean Louis André Couvée, who *d* 1969, and has issue living, Jean Pierre Henri, *b* 1939, — Petronella Adamina, *b* 1941, — Agnès Madeleine Adélaide, *b* 1943. *Residence* – 61 Joh, Bildersstraat, The Hague.

Grandchildren of late Baron Æneas Mackay (infra):—
Issue of late Lt-Col Baron Daniel Mackay, *b* 1900, *d* 1969: *m* 1927, Henriette Constance Adèle, who *d* 1986, da of Dr Alfred Joan Labouchere, of Zeist, Netherlands:—
Baron Donald (279 Irislaan, 2343 CM Oegstgeest, Netherlands), *b* 1928; Lt-Col RNAF (ret): *m* 1968 (*m diss* 1987), Danielle Christine da of Dr Hendrik Gerrit Beins. —— Baron Alfred Alexander (248 Parkweg, Voorburg, Netherlands), *b* 1930: *m* 1965, Diana Margaret, da of Sydney Jesty Elwin, of Strathfield, NSW, and has issue living, Baron Andrew Robert, *b* 1967, — Baroness Caroline Jane, *b* 1969. —— Baron Hugo Carel Æneas (175 Burg. Fabiuspark, Bilthoven, Netherlands), *b* 1936: *m* 1st, 1967, Gwendoleen, who *d* 1973, da of Elbert Waller; 2ndly, 1989, Hanna, da of late Isaac Samuel Brouwer. —— Baron Eric Joan Maurits (Van Calcarlaan 21, Wassenaar, Netherlands), *b* 1938: *m* 1963, Susan Jane, da of Francis McNeill, and has issue living, Baron Patrick Joan, *b* 1967, — Baroness Alexandra, *b* 1966, — Baroness Helen Danielle, *b* 1969, — Baroness Madeline, *b* 1971.
Issue of late Baron Reinhold Alexander Mackay, *b* 1903, *d* 1990: *m* 1930, Greta Ernestina (Flat 15, 81 Schouwweg, Wassenaar, Netherlands), da of Jan Adrian Smits, of The Hague:—
Baroness Sonja Gratia, *b* 1931: *m* 1953, Hendrick Willem Balthasar Croiset van Uchelen, and has issue living, Eric Alexander, *b* 1958, — Helen Astrid, *b* 1955.

Grandchildren of late Baron Theodoor Philip Mackay (ante):—
Issue of late Baron Æneas Mackay, *b* 1872, *d* 1932; Jonkvrouwe Hermina Clasina, who *d* 1945, da of Lieut-Gen Jonkheer J. C. C. den Beer Poortugael, Min of War, and Privy Councillor:—
Baron Theodoor Philip (Provinciënlaan 3-53, Heemstede, Netherlands), *b* 1911: former Burgomaster: *m* 1941, Zsófia Friderika Emma, da of late Dr Andor Henrik Ráthonyi Reusz, of Budapest, Hungary, and has issue living, Baron Æneas (Anton

Mauvelaan 8, 1401 CK Bussum, Netherlands), *b* 1942; is a Dir: *m* 1975, Yvonne Marie-Blanche, da of Frans Wyers, and has issue living, *Baron* Randolph Philip *b* 1977, *Baron* Patrick James *b* 1979, — *Baroness* Marguerite Louise, *b* 1943: *m* 1964, Dr Bernhard Rudolf Grüninger, of La Chaux de Fonds, Rue de la Prairie 76, Switzerland, and has issue living, Daniel Robert *b* 1966, Marie-Anne *b* 1968, — *Baroness* Lilian Mary, *b* 1945: *m* 1970, Jan Willem Stuart, of Heemstede, and has issue living, Wendelien *b* 1972, Marguérite *b* 1974, — *Baroness* Zsófia Alexandra, *b* 1951: *m* 1979, Dr Frederik Christiaan Musch, Secretary of Bank of International Settlements, Basle, Switzerland, and has issue living, Willem Heiko *b* 1980, Onno Frederick Roger *b* 1984, Clare Alexandra *b* 1982. —— *Baroness* Louisa Wilhelmina Elizabeth Amarantha, *b* 1906. —— *Baroness* Erica, *b* 1916: *m* 1974, Jonkheer Gerard Beelaerts van Blokland former Netherlands Ambassador to Russia, of Jan Muschlaan 203, The Hague.

Issue of late Baron Edward Mackay, *b* 1873, *d* 1950: *m* 1902, Ina Petronella Lyckholt, wie Nyeholt, who *d* 1903:—
Baroness Catherine Margaretha Elisabeth, *b* 1903: *m* 1923, Ernest Johannes Désandré, who *d* 1988, of 444 Saratoga Av, Apt 24-H, Santa Clara, Cal 95050, USA, and has issue living, Edward Ernest, *b* 1929, — Ina Catherina Elisabeth, *b* 1932.

Issue of late Baron Dirk Rijnhard Johan Mackay, *b* 1876, *d* 1960: *m* 1st, 1906, Johanna Elisabeth Blaauw, who *d* 1920; 2ndly, 1927 (*m diss* 1937), Violet, da of Edward Egerts; 3rdly, 1939, Helena Esme Egerts, who *d* 1990, sister of his 2nd wife:—
(By 1st *m*) *Baron* Johan Jacob (Casilla 116, Talca, Chile), *b* 1909: *m* 1936, Elisabeth E., da of William Clarence Holman, and has issue living, *Baron* Derrik Philip (Casilla 116, Talca, Chile), *b* 1937: *m* 1964, Juanita Carmiña Hederra Sepulveda, da of Agusto Hederra Silva, and has issue living, *Baron* Cristian Andrès *b* 1965: *m* 1993, Maria Consuelo Diaz, da of Patricio Diaz Carrasco (and has issue living, *Baroness* Maria Consuelo Magdalena *b* 1994), *Baron* Alexandro Andrès *b* 1967, *Baron* Matias Andrès *b* 1972, — *Baron* John Hugo (Casilla 116, Talca, Chile), *b* 1941: *m* 1971, Sylvia Bravo Perucca, da of Ladislao Bravo, and has issue living, *Baron* John Donald, *b* 1973, *Baroness* Sylvia Francisca *b* 1972, — *Baroness* Johanna Elizabeth, *b* 1939: *m* 1970, German del Rio, and has issue living, German Andrès *b* 1971, Juan Ignacio *b* 1972, — *Baroness* Marie Louise, *b* 1952. —— *Baron* Johan Hugo (29 Ary Schefferstr, 2597 VN, The Hague, Holland), *b* 1914, Commodore, RNN (ret): *m* 1945, Margaret, da of Pearse John Herbert, and has issue living, *Baron* Alexander Rijnhard *b* 1950: *m* 1972 (*m diss* 1987), Maria Paula Hermanna, da of Bernardus Petrus Maria Marquering, and has issue living, *Baron* Robert Bernard *b* 1975, *Baron* Michiel Christiaan *b* 1978, — *Baron* Donald Johan, *b* 1964, — *Baroness* Carol Huguette, *b* 1954: *m* 1991, Dr Eric Paul Jozef Myjer, and has issue living, Florian Hugo Bob *b* 1992, Sandrijn Margaret Maria *b* 1988. —— *Baron* Eric Rijnhard Alexander, *b* 1917: *m* 1943, Gertrud, da of Paul Moritz Robert Ernst Brückmann, and has issue living, *Baron* Æneas, *b* 1944: *m* 1971, Joke, da of Eduard Strelitski, and has issue living, *Baron* Alexander *b* 1975, *Baroness* Fleur *b* 1977, — *Baron* Paul, *b* 1946: *m* 1st, 1971 (*m diss* 1974), Cornelie Elisabeth, da of Dr Jan Cornelis Steye Marie Nijenbandring de Boer; 2ndly, 1982, Ulrike Borgwardt, and has issue living, (by 2nd *m*) *Baron* Laurens Johannes *b* 1985, *Baron* Ernst Julian *b* 1987, *Baron* Rembert Helins *b* 1990, — *Baron* Eric, *b* 1953: *m* 1982, Geertje, da of Dr Boschma, and has issue living, *Baron* Barthold *b* 1987, *Baron* Christiaan *b* 1991, *Baroness* Charlotte *b* 1985. —— *Baroness* Helene Gérardine, *b* 1907: *m* 1926, Rodney Frederick Jarrett Sterwin, who *d* 1981, and has issue living, Peter Philip, *b* 1930, — Angela Helen, *b* 1929. —— *Baroness* Anna Maria, *b* 1913: *m* 1st, 1933 (*m diss* 1948), George Eschauzier, of The Hague, Holland; 2ndly, 1949, Herman B. Baruch, former American Ambassador to The Netherlands, who *d* 1953; 3rdly, 1958, Rolf Robert, of 120 Harbor View Lane, Largo, Florida, USA, and has issue living, (by 1st *m*) Pierre George, *b* 1940, — Hilda Susan, *b* 1934, — Johanna Elisabeth, *b* 1936. —— (By 2nd *m*) *Baroness* Patricia, *b* 1928: *m* 1951 (*m diss* 1959), Leonard Johannes Mens, and has issue living, Edward Maarten, *b* 1955.

Grandchildren of late Baron Daniel Mackay (*b* 1878) (infra):—
Issue of late Baron Donald Theodoor Mackay, *b* 1910, *d* 1992: *m* 1st, 1939 (*m diss* 1945), Jonkvrouwe Alexandra Frederica, da of Jonkheer Bonifacius Christiaan de Savornin Lohman; 2ndly 1945, Kathleen, da of Percy Shaw Pearce:—
(By 2nd *m*) *Baron* Niall (Hadhams, Hogs Lane, Chrishall, Herts SG8 8RN), *b* 1956: *m* 1985, Jennifer Mary, da of Hugh Butcher, and has issue living, *Baron* Calum Hugh, *b* 1989, — *Baroness* Georgia Kathleen, *b* 1992. —— *Baroness* Moira, *b* 1952.

Grandchildren of late Baron Theodoor Philip Mackay (ante):—
Issue of late Baron Daniel Mackay, *b* 1878, *d* 1962: *m* 1st, 1906 (*m diss* 1921), Helene Hommel; 2ndly, 1921, Marie Françoise, who *d* 1959, da of Hugo François Lamaison; 3rdly, 1960, Anna Minke, da of Johannes Weyer:—
(By 1st *m*) *Baroness* Maria Christine Jeanette, *b* 1907. —— (By 2nd *m*) *Baroness* Maria Constantia (Voorsterweg 153, Tonden, 6975 AD Tonden, Gelderland, Holland), *b* 1922: *m* 1947, (*m diss* 1961) Johan Barthold Frans Bosch Ridder van Rosenthal, and has issue living, Lodewijk Hendrik Nicolaas, *b* 1948: *m* 1972, Erica van Hoorn, and has issue living, Eelco *b* 1976, Saskia *b* 1974, — Roelina Gijsbertha Gerardina, *b* 1951: *m* 1978, Christiaan van Haersma Buma, and has issue living, Michiel *b* 1981, Robert *b* 1983, — Nicolette, *b* 1953: *m* 1975, Pieter Roodenburgh, and has issue living, Frederiek *b* 1980, Roelien Anne *b* 1978. —— *Baroness* Juliana Anna (Houtlaan 50, Leiden, Holland) *b* 1925: *m* 1950 (*m diss* 1960), Count Rutger Jan Moritz Albert Schimmelpenninck, and has issue living, *Count* Gerrit Marius, *b* 1951, — *Countess* Marie Danielle, *b* 1952.

Granddaughter of late Baron Willem Karel Mackay, yst son of late Johan François Hendrik Jacob Ernestus Mackay (ante):—
Issue of late Baron Barthold Mackay, *b* 1871, *d* 1945: *m* 1898, Jonkvrouwe Alpheda Louise, who *d* 1935, da of Jonkheer Cornelis Charles van der Wyck:—
Baroness Johanna Elisabeth, *b* 1907: *m* 1st, 1936, Capt Patrick Alexander Agnew, Seaforth Highlanders (TA) (*ka* 1943) (*see* Agnew, Bt *cr* 1629, colls); 2ndly, 1944 (*m diss* 1965), Lt-Col William Stanley Baird. *Residence* - Laan van Rijnwijk/Flat 35c, Zeist, Holland.

PREDECESSORS - (1) Sir DONALD Mackay, Knt, el son of Huistean Du of Farr, and Strathnaver; *b* 1590; a distinguished royalist soldier, was *cr* a *Baronet* 1627, and *Lord Reay* peerage of Scotland, 1628, with remainder to his heirs male for ever bearing the name and arms of Mackay: *m* 1st, 1610, Barbara Mackenzie, sister of 1st Earl of Seaforth; 2ndly, before 1631, (marriage annulled) Rachel Winterfield or Harrison; 3rdly, Elizabeth, da of Robert Thomson, of Greenwich; 4thly, Marjorie, da of Francis Sinclair of Stirkoke; *d* 1649; *s* by his son (2) JOHN, 2nd Lord, who espoused the royal cause: *m* 1st, 1636, Isabel Sinclair; 2ndly, Barbara, da of Col Hugh Mackay of Scourie; *d* about 1681; *s* by his grandson (3) GEORGE, FRS (son of late Donald Mackay, Master of Reay), 3rd Lord: *m* 1st, 1702, Margaret, da of Lt-Gen Hugh Mackay of Scourie; 2ndly, Janet, da of John Sinclair of Ulbster and widow of Benjamin Dunbar, yr, of Hempriggs; 3rdly, 1713, Mary, da of John Doull of Thuster, WS; *d* 1748; *s* by his son (4) DONALD, 4th Lord: *m* 1st, 1732, Marion, who *d* 1740, da of Sir Robert Dalrymple; 2ndly, 1741, Christian, who *d* 1763, da of James Sutherland, of Pronsie; *d* 1761; *s* by his el son (5) GEORGE, 5th Lord: *m* 1st, 1758, his cousin, Marion, who *d* 1759, da of late Col Hon Hugh Mackay; 2ndly, 1760, Elizabeth, who *d* 1780, da of late John Fairlie, Collector of Customs at Ayr; *d* 1768; *s* by his half-brother (6) HUGH, *d* unmarried 1797; *s* by his cousin (7) ERIC (son of late Hon George Mackay, 3rd son of 3rd Lord); 7th Lord; *b* 1773; *d* 1847; *s* by his brother (8) ALEXANDER, 8th Lord; *b* 1775: *m* 1809, Marion, who *d* 1865, da of Col Gall, and widow of David Ross; *d* 1863; *s* by his son (9) ERIC, 9th Lord; *d* unmarried 1875; *s* by his kinsman (10) ÆNEAS (son of Barthold John Christiaan Mackay (who was *cr* Baron Mackay van Ophemert, of the Netherlands), great-grandson of the Hon Æneas Mackay, Brig-Gen in Dutch Ser, 2nd son of 2nd Lord), 10th Lord; *b* 1806; was Min of State, and Vice-Pres of Privy Council of the Netherlands: *m* 1837, Mary Catherine Anne Jacoba, who *d* 1886, da of Baron Fagel, Privy Councillor of the Netherlands; *d* 1876; *s* by his son (11) DONALD JAMES, KT, GCSI, GCIE, PC, 11th Lord; *b* 1839; naturalized by Act of Parliament 1877, and *cr* Baron Reay, of Durness (peerage of United Kingdom) 1881; Lord-Lieut of co Roxburgh 1892, Gov of Bombay 1885-90, Under-Sec of State for India 1894-5, and first Pres of British Acad 1902-7: *m* 1877, Fanny Georgiana Jane, CI, who *d* 1917, da of late Richard Hasler, of Aldingbourne,

Sussex, and widow of Capt Alexander Mitchell, MP, of Stow; *d* (Aug) 1921, when the United Kingdom Barony (*cr* 1881) became ext, and he was *s* in the Scottish titles by his cousin **(12)** *Baron* ERIC (only son of late Baron Æneas Mackay, son of Johan François Hendrik Jacob Ernestus Mackay, brother of 10th Lord), 12th Lord, *b* 1870: *m* 1901, Baroness Maria Johanna Bertha Christina Van Dedem, who *d* 1932; *d* (Nov) 1921; *s* by his el son **(13)** ÆNEAS ALEXANDER, 13th Lord; *b* 1905; naturalized a British subject 1938; in Foreign Office 1939-47; a Representative Peer 1955-9: *m* 1936, Charlotte Mary, da of late William Younger, of Ravenswood, Melrose; *d* 1963; *s* by his only son **(14)** HUGH WILLIAM, 14th Lord and present peer.

REDCLIFFE-MAUD, BARONY OF (Redcliffe-Maud) (Extinct 1982)

SON LIVING OF LIFE BARON

Hon Sir Humphrey John Hamilton MAUD, KCMG (31 Queen Anne's Grove, W4), *b* 1934; *ed* Eton, and King's Coll, Camb; Instructor in Classics, Minnesota Univ 1958-59; entered Foreign Service 1959, Madrid 1961-63, Havana 1963-65; FO 1966-67; Cabinet Office 1968-69; Paris 1970-74; Nuffield Coll, Oxford (Econs) 1974-75; Head of Financial Relations Dept, FCO 1975-79; Minister, Madrid 1979-82, HM Ambassador to Luxembourg 1982-85, Assist Under-Sec of State (Econ & Commercial Affairs) 1985-88, High Commr to Cyprus 1988-90, HM Ambassador to Argentina 1990-93, Commonwealth Sec-Gen (Econ & Social Affairs) since 1993; CMG 1982, KCMG 1993: *m* 1963, Maria Eugenia Gazitua, and has issue living, three sons. *Residence* – 31 Queen Anne's Grove, Bedford Park, Chiswick W4 1HW. *Clubs* – United Oxford and Cambridge Univ.

DAUGHTERS LIVING OF LIFE BARON

Hon Caroline Mary Stewart, *b* 1939: *m* 1967, Very Rev Dean Joel Wilson Pugh, of The Deans House, 320 W 18th St, Little Rock, Arkansas 72206, USA.

REDESDALE, BARON (Mitford) (Baron UK 1902)

God careth for us

RUPERT BERTRAM MITFORD, 6th Baron; *b* 18 July 1967; *s* 1991; *ed* Milton Abbey, Highgate, and Newcastle Univ (BA).

Arms – Quarterly; 1st and 4th argent, a fesse between three moles sable, *Mitford*; 2nd and 3rd azure, three lozenges conjoined in fesse or, a canton ermine, *Freeman*. **Crest** – 1st, two hands couped at the wrist proper, grasping a sword erect piercing a boar's head erased sable, *Mitford*; 2nd, a demi-wolf argent, charged on the shoulder with a fesse dancettée gules, and holding between the paws a lozenge or, *Freeman*. **Supporters** – On either side an eagle wings expanded sable, beaked and membered or, charged on the breast with a lozenge also or, and gorged with a wreath of shamrock vert.
Residences – 2 St Mark's Sq, NW1 7TP; The School House, Rochester, Newcastle upon Tyne NE19 1RH; The School House, Exbury, nr Southampton, Hants SO4 1AE.

SISTERS LIVING AND DECEASED

Hon Emma, *b* 1959: *m* 1985, George Frederick Wady, of Green Batt House, The Pinfold, Alnwick, Northumberland, yr son of George Wady, of Frinton-on-Sea, Essex, and has issue living, Alexander Bertram, *b* 1989, — Philippa Bryony, *b* 1992.
Hon Tessa, *b* 1960: *m* 1990, Paul Dominic Priestman, of 19 Pembridge Mews, W11 3EQ, yr son of Martin Priestman, of Great Gransden, Cambs.
Hon Georgina Kathryn Mercia (Kate), *b* 1961; *d* 1985.
Hon Victoria-Louise, *b* 1962: *m* 1988, Patrick James Padgett, of 2 St Mark's Sq, NW1 7TP, yr son of James Padgett, of Asheville, N Carolina, USA.
Hon Henrietta Jane, *b* 1965.
Hon Georgina Clementine, *b* 1968.

GREAT AUNT LIVING (*Daughter of 1st Baron*)

Hon Daphne (*Dowager Baroness Denham*), *b* (twin) 1895: *m* 1919, 1st Baron Denham, who *d* 1948. *Residence* – Dunsland House, Shrublands Rd, Berkhamsted, Herts.

DAUGHTERS LIVING OF SECOND BARON

Hon Diana (*Hon Lady Mosley*), *b* 1910: *m* 1st, 1929 (*m diss* 1934), Hon Bryan Walter Guinness (afterwards 2nd Baron Moyne), who *d* 1992; 2ndly, 1936, as his 2nd wife, Sir Oswald Ernald Mosley, 6th Bt, who *d* 1980. *Residence* – Temple De La Gloire, 91400 Orsay, France.
Hon Jessica Lucy, *b* 1917: *m* 1st, 1937, Esmond Marcus David Romilly, Pilot Officer Roy Canadian Air Force, who was *ka* 1941; 2ndly, 1943, Robert Edward Treuhaft, of New York, USA, and has issue living (by 2nd *m*) Benjamin (Piano Shop, 2005 Stuart St, Berkeley, Calif 94703, USA), *b* 1947, — (by 1st *m*) Anne Constancia, *b* 1941: *m* 1st, 1964 (*m diss* 1975), James Rufus Forman; 2ndly, 1980, Edwin Terrance Weber, of 979 Eden Avenue SE, Atlanta, Georgia 30316, USA, and has issue living (by 1st *m*), James Robert Lumumba *b* 1967, Chaka Esmond Fanon *b* 1970. *Residence* – 6411 Regent St, Oakland, California 94618, USA.
Hon Deborah Vivien (*Duchess of Devonshire*), *b* 1920: *m* 1941, 11th Duke of Devonshire. *Residences* – Chatsworth, Bakewell, Derbyshire; 4 Chesterfield Street, W1 7HG.

WIDOW LIVING OF FIFTH BARON

SARAH GEORGINA CRANSTOUN (*Baroness Redesdale*), yr da of Brig Alston Cranstoun Todd, OBE, of Bramblehurst, Limes Lane, Buxted, Sussex: *m* 1958, the 5th Baron, who *d* 1991. *Residences* – 2 St Mark's Sq, NW1 7TP; The School House, Rochester, Newcastle-upon-Tyne NE19 1RH; The School House, Exbury, nr Southampton, Hants SO4 1AE.

COLLATERAL BRANCH LIVING

Issue of late Major Hon Clement Bertram Ogilvy Freeman-Mitford, DSO, el son of 1st Baron, *b* 1876, *ka* 1915: *m* 1909, Lady Helen Alice Willington Ogilvy, (who *d* 1973, having *m* 2ndly, 1918 (*m diss* 1931), Capt Henry Courtney Brocklehurst, who was *ka* 1942 (Brocklehurst, Bt), and 3rdly, 1933, Lt-Col Harold Bligh Nutting), da of 11th Earl of Airlie:—

Rosemary Ann, *b* 1911: *m* 1932, Cdr Richard James Bailey, OBE, RN, who *d* 1969, and has issue living, Richard Lee Clement (49 Lawrence Gdns, Mill Hill, NW7), *b* 1933; *ed* Charterhouse: *m* 1959, Barbara Joyce, el da of S. G. Ede, of Fowey, Cornwall, and has issue living, Samantha Kate *b* 1967, — Michael Lee George (48 Kingshill Park, Dursley, Glos) *b* 1934; *ed* Charterhouse: *m* 1st, 1964 (*m diss* 1976), Diana Jane, da of late Maj Laurence Deacon; 2ndly, 1979, Diana Maria Teresa, who *d* 1986, da of Bruno Cainero, of Udine, Italy, and has issue living (by 1st *m*), Anthony Michael George *b* 1966, Clementine Jane *b* 1969 (by 2nd *m*) Francesca Diana *b* 1980, — Ann Clementine, *b* 1936: *m* 1964, Peter Calver, of Whitcliffe Grange Farm, Ripon, N Yorks, only son of late Sir Robert Henry Sherwood Calver, QC, — Diana Penelope (6 South St, Osney, Oxford), *b* 1940: *m* 1960 (*m diss* 1979), William Henry Gordon Leaf, and has issue living, James-William Richard Tyrrell *b* 1963, Jessica Frances Rosemary *b* 1961, — Lavinia Jessica Iris, *b* 1944: *m* 1st, 1965 (*m diss* 1974), Antony Carlson; 2ndly, 1975, Hugh Brewis Bailey, MRCS, LRCP, of Hillcrest, 214 Newmarket Rd, Norwich, NR4 7LA, and has issue living (by 1st *m*), Sarah Rosemary Iris *b* 1967: *m* 1992, Spiros Mouzakitis, of Avliotes, Corfu, Greece, Lucy *b* 1969, (by 2nd *m*), David Andrew Robert *b* 1977, — Annabel Lee Christine, *b* 1945: *m* 1974, Malcolm Valentine (23 Aspen Way, Cringleford, Norwich, Norfolk NR4 6UA) and has issue living, Richard William *b* 1976, Clare Rosemary *b* 1978. *Residence* – Mitford Cottage, Westwell, Burford, Oxon OX8 4JU. —— Clementine Mabell Kitty (*Lady Beit*), *b* (*posthumous*) 1915: *m* 1939, Sir Alfred Lane Beit, 2nd Bt, who *d* 1994. *Residences* – Russborough, Blessington, co Wicklow; 137 Beach Rd, Gordon's Bay, Cape Province, S Africa; 2 Little Boltons, SW10.

PREDECESSORS – (1) This family descends from John Mitford of London, merchant (*d* 1720), 3rd son of Robert Mitford of Mitford Castle, Northumberland. John Mitford, Speaker of House of Commons and Lord Chancellor of Ireland; was *cr* Baron Redesdale 1802. His son was *cr* Earl of Redesdale 1877, both titles becoming ext 1886. The latter devised his estates to his cousin Algernon Bertram Mitford. (1) *Sir* Algernon Bertram Freeman-Mitford, GCVO, KCB, son of Henry Reveley Mitford, of Exbury House, Hants; *b* 1837; Sec to HM's Commrs of Public Works and Buildings 1874-6; MP for Stratford-on-Avon (*C*) 1892-5; assumed by Roy licence 1886 the additional surname and arms of Freeman; *cr Baron Redesdale*, of Redesdale, co Northumberland (peerage of UK) 1902: *m* 1874, Lady Clementine Gertrude Helen Ogilvy, who *d* 1932, da of 7th Earl of Airlie; *d* 1916; *s* by his el surviving son (2) David Bertram Ogilvy, 2nd Baron; *b* 1878; Capt late Northumberland Fusiliers; a Member of Select Committee of Peerages in Abeyance 1925: *m* 1904, Sydney, who *d* 1963, da of late Thomas Gibson Bowles (sometime MP for King's Lynn), of 25 Lowndes Sq, SW; *d* 1958; *s* by his brother (3) Bertram Thomas Carlyle Ogilvy, DSO, 3rd Baron; *b* 1880; Capt RN; High Sheriff of Oxon 1935: *m* 1925, Mary Margaret, who *d* 1967, da of late Thomas Cordes, JP, DL; *d* 1962; *s* by his brother (4) John Power Bertram Ogilvy, 4th Baron, *b* 1885: *m* 1914 (marriage annulled in Germany on her petition 1914), Marie Anne, da of Friedrich Viktor von Friedlander-Fuld, of Berlin; *d* 1963; *s* by his nephew (5) Clement Napier Bertram (son of Hon (Ernest) Rupert Bertram Ogilvy Freeman-Mitford, 5th son of 1st Baron), 5th Baron, *b* 1932; commn'd The Black Watch 1951, served 4th Bn King's African Rifles in Kenya and Uganda, and 3rd Bn in Malaya; Pres Guild of Cleaners and Launderers 1968-70; Chm Mitford's Advertising 1970-77, Vice-Pres Corporate Communications Europe, Africa and Middle East, Chase Manhattan Bank: *m* 1958, Sarah Georgina Cranstoun, yr da of Brig Alston Cranstoun Todd, OBE, of Bramblehurst, Limes Lane, Buxted, Sussex; *d* 1991; *s* by his only son (6) Rupert Bertram, 6th Baron and present peer.

REDMAYNE, BARON (Redmayne) (Extinct 1983)

Hon Sir Nicholas John Redmayne, 2nd Bt, who *s* to baronetcy (*cr* 1964), 1983 (*see* Redmayne, Bt).

REES, BARON (Rees) (Life Baron 1987)

Peter Wynford Innes Rees, PC, son of late Maj-Gen Thomas Wynford Rees, CB, CIE, DSO, MC, Indian Army, of Goytre Hall, Abergavenny; *b* 9 Dec 1926; *ed* Stowe, and Ch Ch, Oxford; Scots Guards 1945-48; Bar 1953, QC 1969, Oxford Circuit; PPS to Solicitor-Gen 1972; Min of State, HM Treasury 1979-81, Min for Trade 1981-83, Chief Sec to Treasury and Member of Cabinet 1983-85; Member of Court and Council of Museum of Wales; Chm and Dir of Companies, Dep Chm Leopold Joseph plc; MP Dover (*C*) 1970-74, Dover and Deal 1974-83, and Dover 1983-87; *cr* PC 1983, and *Baron Rees*, of Goytre, co Gwent (Life Baron) 1987: *m* 1969, Mrs Anthea Peronelle Wendell, da of late Maj Hugh John Maxwell Hyslop, Argyll and Sutherland Highrs, and formerly wife of Maj Jac Wendell, Gren Guards.

Arms – Argent two chevrons ermines between three ravens proper. **Crest** – Upon a chapeau turned up ermines a peacock holding in its beak an oak sprig proper. **Supporters** – Two Bengal tigers rampant, the *Dexter* on a grassy mount growing therefrom two tea-plant flowers, and the *Sinister* on a like mount growing therefrom as many lotus flowers all proper.
Residences – Goytre Hall, Abergavenny, Gwent; 39 Headfort Place, SW1X 7DE.
Clubs – Boodle's, Beefsteak, White's.

REES-MOGG, BARON (Rees-Mogg) (Life Baron 1988)

WILLIAM REES-MOGG, son of late Edmund Fletcher Rees-Mogg, JP, of Cholwell House, Som; *b* 14 July 1928: *ed* Charterhouse, and Balliol Coll, Oxford (MA, Pres Oxford Union 1951); Visiting Fell Nuffield Coll, Oxford, 1968-72, Hon LLD Bath 1977; High Sheriff Somerset 1978; with Financial Times 1952-60, Chief Leader Writer 1955-60, Assist Ed 1957-60, joined Sunday Times 1960, City Ed 1960-61, Political and Economic Ed 1961-63, Dep Ed 1964-67, Ed the Times 1967-81; Treas Inst of Journalists 1960-63, 1966-68 (Pres 1963-64), Vice-Chm Conservative Party's Nat Advisory Cttee on Political Educn 1961-63, Pres English Assocn 1983-84, Dir The Times Ltd 1968-81, Times Newspapers Ltd 1978-81, Vice-Chm Board of Govs BBC 1981-86; Chm Pickering & Catto (Publishers) since 1983, and Sidgwick & Jackson 1985-88; Chm Arts Council 1982-89; Chm Broadcasting Standards Council 1988-93; author of *His Majesty Preserved* (1954), *Sir Anthony Eden* (1956), *How to Buy Rare Books* (1985), etc; *cr* Kt 1981, and *Baron Rees-Mogg*, of Hinton Blewitt, co Avon (Life Baron) 1988: *m* 1962, Gillian Shakespeare, yr da of Thomas Richard Morris, JP, Mayor of St Pancras 1962, of 53 Queen Alexandra Mansions, WC1, and has issue.

Arms – Quarterly: 1st and 4th, on a fesse pean between six ermine spots, the two exterior in chief and the centre spot in base, surmounted by a crescent gules, a cock or, *Mogg*; 2nd and 3rd, gules, a chevron engrailed erminois between three swans argent, wings elevated or.*Rees.* **Crests** – *Mogg*, between two spearheads erect sable a cock proper; *Rees*, a swan argent, wings elevated or, holding in the beak a water-lily slipped proper. **Motto** – Cura pii Diis sunt.
Residences – The Old Rectory, Hinton Blewitt, nr Bristol, Avon; 17 Pall Mall, SW1. *Club* – Garrick.

SONS LIVING

Hon Thomas Fletcher, *b* 1966; *ed* Downside.
Hon Jacob William, *b* 1969; *ed* Eton, and Trinity Coll, Oxford.

DAUGHTERS LIVING

Hon Emma Beatrice, *b* 1962; *ed* St Hugh's Coll, Oxford: *m* 1990, David William Hilton Craigie (who assumed the surname of Craigie in lieu of his patronymic 1990), son of late Maj Robin Brooks, and of Mrs Brian Ford, of London, and has issue living, Maud, *b* 1991.
Hon Charlotte Louise, *b* 1964; *ed* Heythrop Coll, London Univ.
Hon Annunziata Mary, *b* 1979.

Reidhaven, Viscount; son of Earl of Seafield.

REIGATE, BARON (Vaughan-Morgan) (Life Baron 1970, Bt UK 1960)

JOHN KENYON VAUGHAN-MORGAN, PC; *Life Baron* and 1st *Baronet*, son of late Sir Kenyon Pascoe Vaughan-Morgan, OBE, MP; *b* 2 Feb 1905; *ed* Eton, and Ch Ch, Oxford, (MA); Chm of Board of Govs of Westminster Hosp 1963-74; a Member of Court of Assistants of Merchant Taylors' Co (Master 1970); a Dir of Morgan Crucible Co Ltd; Hon Freeman of Reigate; Parl Sec, Min of Health Jan to Sept 1957, and Min of State Board of Trade 1957-59; MP for Reigate (*C*) 1950-70; Dep Chm S Westminster Magistrates Bench 1966-74; 1939-45 War as Lt-Col Welsh Gds, and GSOI, HQ, 21st Army Group (despatches); *cr* PC 1961, a *Baronet* 1960, and *Baron Reigate*, of Outwood, co Surrey (Life Baron) 1970: *m* 1940, Emily Redmond, da of late William Redmond Cross, of New York City, USA, and has issue.

Arms – Quarterly; 1st and 4th, or, five lozenges conjoined in fesse gules between three lymphads, sails furled sable colours flying of the second, *Morgan*; 2nd and 3rd, sable on a chevron or, between three boys' heads couped at the shoulders proper crined or enwrapped about the neck with a snake as many spear heads embrued proper. *Vaughan.* **Crest** – 1st, argent and sable a cock gules resting the dexter claw on a bundle of twigs banded proper; 2nd, in front of a boy's head, as in the Arms, two spears saltirewise proper. **Supporters** – *Dexter*, a dragon gules; *sinister*, a camel or, with one hump.
Residence – 36 Eaton Sq, SW1. *Clubs* – Brooks's, Beefsteak, Hurlingham.

DAUGHTERS LIVING

Hon Julia Redmond, *b* 1943; *ed* Courtauld Inst of Art, London Univ (BA), and Oxford Poly (Dip Publ); author of *The Flowering of Art Nouveau Graphics*, 1990: *m* 1st, 1962 (*m diss* 1978), Henry Walter Wiggin; 2ndly, 1986, Dr Joseph Austin King, son of late William Thayer King, of Kingsport, Tennessee, USA, and has issue (by 1st *m*) (*see* Wiggin, Bt colls).
Hon Deborah Mary, *b* 1944: *m* 1966, Michael Whitfeld, of Querns, Goring Heath, Reading, RG8 7RH (E Howe, colls), and has issue living, Nicholas John, *b* 1968, — Mark David, *b* 1971, — Melanie Katherine, *b* 1976.

REILLY, BARONY OF (Reilly) (Extinct 1990)

DAUGHTER LIVING OF LIFE BARON (*By 1st marriage*)

Hon Victoria Wentworth, *b* 1941: *m* 1973, Daniel Špička, of U Mrázovky 7, Prague 5, The Czech Republic, and has issue living, Katherine Wentworth, *b* 1974, — Lucie Wentworth, *b* 1977.

WIDOW LIVING OF LIFE BARON

ANNETTE ROSE (*Baroness Reilly*), da of late Brig-Gen Clifton Inglis Stockwell, CB, CMG, DSO: *m* 1952, as his 2nd wife, Baron Reilly (Life Baron), who *d* 1990. *Residence* – 3 Alexander Place, SW7 2SG.

REITH, BARONY OF (Reith) (Baron UK 1940, disclaimed 1972)

Whatsoever

CHRISTOPHER JOHN REITH, *b* 27 May 1928; *s* as 2nd Baron 16 June 1971, disclaimed his peerage for life 21 April 1972; *ed* Eton, and Worcester Coll, Oxford (MA); late RN: *m* 1969, (Penelope Margaret) Ann, el da of late Henry Rowland Morris, of Beeston, Notts, and has issue.

Arms – Or, a cross engrailed sable between four mullets gules, on a chief of the last a lion passant of the field. **Crest** – An eagle rising reguardant proper. **Supporters** – (borne by Barons Reith) Two eagles, wings addorsed proper.
Residence – Whitebank Farm, Methven, Perthshire.

SON LIVING

Hon JAMES HARRY JOHN, *b* 2 June 1971.

DAUGHTER LIVING

Hon Julie Katharine, *b* 1972.

SISTER LIVING

Hon Marista Muriel, *b* 1932; *ed* St George's, Ascot, and St Andrews Univ (MA); Ist Dir Insite Trust for Consultancy and Training in Heritage Interpretation: *m* 1960, Rev Robert Murray Leishman, MA, Chap Roy Edinburgh (Psychiatric) Hosp; Lecturer New Coll, Edinburgh; and has issue living, Mark Murray, *b* 1962, — Iona Marista, *b* 1963, — Martha Katharine, *b* 1965, — Kirsty Jane, *b* 1969. *Residence* – 9/1 St Leonards Crag, Edinburgh EH8 9SP.

PREDECESSOR – (1) *Rt Hon Sir* JOHN CHARLES WALSHAM REITH, KT, GCVO, GBE, CB, TD, DCL, LLD, 5th son of late Very Rev George Reith, DD, of Aberdeen, and Glasgow; *b* 1889, first Gen Man and Man Dir of British Broadcasting Co Ltd 1922-26, Dir Gen of BBC 1926-38; Min of Information, Jan to May 1940; Min of Transport, May to Oct 1940; Min of Works and Bidgs, and 1st Commr of Works 1940-42; *cr Baron Reith*, of Stonehaven, co Kincardine (peerage of UK) 1940: *m* 1921, Muriel Katharine, who *d* 1977, yr da of late John Lynch Odhams, of Southwick, Sussex; *d* 1971; *s* by his only son (2) CHRISTOPHER JOHN, 2nd Baron, until he disclaimed his peerage 1972.

REMNANT, BARON (Remnant) (Baron UK 1928, Bt UK 1917)

Let him who has deserved the palm bear it

JAMES WOGAN REMNANT, CVO, 3rd Baron, and 3rd Baronet; *b* 23 Oct 1930; *s* 1967; *ed* Eton; National Service Lt Coldstream Guards; FCA; Partner, Touche Ross & Co 1958-70; Chm of Institutional Investors Cttee 1977-78; a Church Commnr for England 1976-84; Chm of Assocn of Investment Trust Cos 1977-79; Pres Nat Council of YMCAs; Past Pres London Central YMCA, Trustee Royal Jubilee Trusts (previously Hon Treas and Chm); Chm Nat Provident Inst, Dir Bank of Scotland (and London Bd), TR Technology plc, London Merchant Securities plc, previously Chm Touche, Remnant & Co, TR City of London Trust plc, TR Energy plc, TR Pacific Investment Trust plc, Dep Chm Ultramar plc, Dir Union Discount Co of London plc, Australian Mercantile Land and Finance Co Ltd, Australia and New Zealand Banking Group and other cos; Pres Nat Florence Nightingale Foundation; Chm Learning Through Landscapes Trust; Bailiff of Egle of Order of St John; CVO 1979, GCStJ 1993: *m* 1953, Serena Jane, only da of Cdr Sir Clive Loehnis, KCMG, RN (ret) (*see* E Harrowby, colls), and has issue.

Arms – Sable, a bend vair between two sheldrakes proper all within two flaunches argent and charged with a cinquefoil gules. **Crest** – Between rushes a sheldrake proper, holding in the beak a rose gules, barbed, seeded, leaved and slipped proper. **Supporters** – On either side a dolphin proper charged with a cinquefoil gules.
Residence – Bear Ash, Hare Hatch, Reading, Berks RG10 9XR. *Club* – White's.

SONS LIVING

Hon PHILIP JOHN (36 Stevenage Rd, SW6 6ET), *b* 20 Dec 1954; *ed* Eton and New Coll, Oxford: *m* 1977, Caroline Elizabeth Clare, da of late Capt Godfrey Herbert Richard Cavendish (*see* D Devonshire, colls), and has issue living, Edward James, *b* 2 July 1981, — Eleanor Clare, *b* 1983, — Sophie Caroline, *b* 1986.
Hon Robert James (Jardine Pacific Vietnam Ltd, 16 Han Thuyen St, Hai Ba Trung Dis, Hanoi, Socialist Republic of Vietnam) *b* 1956; *ed* Eton: *m* 1981 (*m diss* 1991), Sherrie, el da of Frederick Cronn, and has issue living, Christopher Michael, *b* 1982, — Jack Preston, *b* 1989. Mr Remnant has adopted (1987) his step-son, Shannon Lynn, *b* 1973.
Hon Hugo Charles (55 Northbrook St, Newbury, Berks), *b* 1959; *ed* Eton, and Newcastle Univ (BSc): *m* 1993, Annabelle Rachel, only da of T. R. Reynolds, of Tollard. Royal, Dorset.

DAUGHTER LIVING

Hon Melissa Clare, *b* 1963; *ed* Wycombe Abbey, and Exeter Univ: *m* 1990, David Wilson Bradley, of 1 Thessaly Lodge, Gloucester Rd, Stratton, Cirencester, Glos GL7 2LJ, yr son of J. W. A. Bradley, of Halls Court, Chesterton, Cambs.

SISTER LIVING

Hon Susan Frances, *b* 1938: *m* 1967, Alan Tyser, of West Hanney House, Wantage, Oxon OX12 0LN, and has issue living, Harry, *b* 1968.

COLLATERAL BRANCH LIVING

Issue of late Hon Peter Farquharson Remnant, yr son of 1st Baron, *b* 1897, *d* 1968: *m* 1923, Betty, who *d* 1965, da of late William George Tanner, of Frenchay, Glos:—
Dawn, *b* 1927: *m* 1951, Anthony Stewart Hooper, and has issue living, Susan Jane, *b* 1952, — Mary Sandra, *b* 1953, — Carol Ann, *b* 1956. —— Merrial, *b* 1934: *m* 1st, 1954 (*m diss* 1960), Arthur James Wesley-Smith; 2ndly, 1962, Henry James Stockley, who *d* 1967: 3rdly, 1968, Ivor John Crosthwaite, DSO, and has issue living, (by 1st *m*) Shane, *b* 1955, — Linda, *b* 1957, — (by 2nd *m*) Marian Julia, *b* 1963.

PREDECESSORS – **(1)** JAMES FARQUHARSON Remnant, CBE, son of late Frederick William Remnant, of Southwold, Suffolk; *b* 1863; a Member of Select Committee on Taxation of Land Values (Scotland) 1904, of Roy Commn on Canals and Inland Navigation 1906-10, of Select Committee on Police Day of Rest 1908-9, of Home Office Committee on Conditions and Pay of Police 1919, and of Rating Machinery Committee 1924; MP for Holborn Div of Finsbury (*C*) March 1900 to Nov 1918, and for Holborn (*U*) Dec 1918 to June 1928; *cr* a *Baronet* 1917, and *Baron Remnant*, of Wenhaston, co Suffolk (peerage of United Kingdom) 1928: *m* 1892, Frances Emily, who *d* 1944, da of late Robert Gosling, of Hassobury, Essex; *d* 1933; *s* by his el son **(2)** ROBERT JOHN FARQUHARSON, MBE, 2nd Baron, *b* 1895: *m* 1924, Norah Susan, who *d* 1990, da of late Lt-Col Alexander John Wogan-Browne; *d* 1967; *s* by his only son **(3)** JAMES WOGAN, 3rd Baron and present peer.

RENDLESHAM, BARON (Thellusson) (Baron I 1806)
(Name pronounced "Tellusson")

By labour and honesty

CHARLES ANTHONY HUGH THELLUSSON, 8th Baron; *b* 15 March 1915; *s* 1943; *ed* Eton; late Capt R Signals: *m* 1st, 1940 (*m diss* 1947), Margaret Elizabeth, da of Lt Col Robin Rome; 2ndly, 1947, Clare, who *d* 1987, da of late Lt-Col D. H. G. McCririck, and has issue by 1st and 2nd *m*.

Arms – Quarterly, wavy or and argent: in the 1st and 4th quarters, two wings barwise in pale and expanded towards the dexter sable, each charged with a trefoil slipped in fesse, the point towards the sinister or; in the 2nd and 3rd quarters, an oak tree eradicated vert, thereon an escutcheon placed bendwise gules, an charged with three guttés argent. **Crest** – A demi-greyhound salient argent, collared sable, between two wings elevated and expanded sable, each charged with a trefoil slipped or. **Supporters** – Two greyhounds reguardant argent, plain collared sable.
Residence – Glebe Pl, SW3.

SON LIVING (By 2nd marriage)

Hon CHARLES WILLIAM BROOKE, *b* 10 Jan 1954; *ed* Eton: *m* 1983, Susan, yst da of E. R. Fielding, of Monte Carlo, Monaco.

DAUGHTERS LIVING (By 1st marriage)

Hon Caroline, *b* 1941: *m* 1960 (*m diss* 19—), Sir William Burton Nigel Goring, 13th Bt. *Residence* – 25 Queen's Gate Terrace, SW7.

(By 2nd marriage)

Hon Sarah Ann, *b* 1949: *m* 1989, Keir H. Helberg, of Washington, DC, USA.
Hon Antonia, *b* 1956: *m* 1981, Hugo Giles Stephen Astley Kirby, eldest son of Giles Kirby, of The Manor House, S Harting, Petersfield, Hants, and has issue living, Nicholas Charles Astley, *b* 1983, — Natasha Alexandra, *b* 1985. *Residence* – 17 Wetherby Gdns, SW5.
Hon Jaqumine, *b* 1960: *m* 1987, Charles Nigel Bromage (*see* Cayzer, Bt, colls, 1990 Edn), and has issue living, Maximilian Charles *b* 1993.

BROTHER LIVING (Raised to the rank of a Baron's son 1945)

Hon Peter Robert, *b* 1920; *ed* Eton; is Capt KRRC: *m* 1st, 1947 (*m diss* 1950), Pamela, who *d* 1968, da of late Oliver Ivan Parker (E Macclesfield, colls), and formerly wife of Maj Timothy Tufnell, MC; 2ndly, 1952, Celia, da of James Walsh, and has issue living, (by 2nd *m*) James Hugh, *b* 1961, — Peter Richard, *b* 1962.

PREDECESSORS – (1) PETER ISSAC THELLUSSON, son of Peter Thellusson, MP for Malmesbury 1796-7, a wealthy London merchant, and the descendant of a French Protestant nobleman; *cr* Baron Rendlesham (peerage of Ireland) 1806; *d* 1808; *s* by his el son (2) JOHN, 2nd Baron; *d* 1832; *s* by his brother (3) WILLIAM, 3rd Baron; was in Holy Orders; *d* 1839; *s* by his brother (4) FREDERICK, 4th Baron; *b* 1798: *m* 1838, Eliza Charlotte, da of Sir George Beeston Prescott, 2nd Bt, and widow of James Duff, *d* 1852; *s* by his son (5) FREDERICK WILLIAM BROOK, 5th Baron *b* 1840; MP for Suffolk E (C) 1874-85: *m* 1861, Lady Egidia Montgomerie, who *d* 1880, da of 18th Earl of Eglinton, KT; *d* 1911; *s* by his el son (6) FREDERICK ARCHIBALD CHARLES, *b* 1868: *m* 1st, 18—, Lillian, who *d* 1931, da of late J. Manly, JP, of Kingston, Jamaica; 2ndly, 1931, Dolores Olga, who *d* 1959, da of Sir William Lewis Salusbury-Trelawny, 10th Bt, and widow of Henry Harcourt Williams; *d* 1938; *s* by his brother (7) PERCY EDWARD, 7th Baron; *b* 1874; *m* 1922, Gladys Dunlop, OBE, who *d* 1933, da of Andrew Vans Dunlop Best; *d* 1943; *s* by his nephew (8) CHARLES ANTHONY HUGH (son of late Lieut-Col Hon Hugh Edmund Thellusson, DSO, 3rd son of 5th Baron), 8th Baron and present peer.

Renfrew, Baron of; title borne by Prince of Wales.

RENFREW OF KAIMSTHORN, BARON (Renfrew) (Life Baron 1991)

(ANDREW) COLIN RENFREW, son of late Archibald Renfrew, of Giffnock, Glasgow; *b* 25 July 1937; *ed* St Alban's Sch, and St John's Coll, Camb (BA, PhD, ScD); Hon D Litt Sheffield Univ 1987, D (honoris causa) Athens Univ 1991, FSA 1968, FSAScot 1970, FBA 1980; RAF 1956-58; Reader in Prehistory & Archaeology Sheffield Univ 1965-72, Research Fellow St John's Coll, Camb 1965-68, Bulgarian Govt Scholarship 1966, Visiting Lect California Univ at Los Angeles 1967, Prof of Archaeology and Head of Dept Southampton Univ 1972-81, since when Disney Prof of Archaeology and Head of Dept Camb Univ; Fellow St John's Coll, Camb 1981-86, since when Master Jesus Coll, Camb; Member Royal Commn for Historic Monuments of England 1977-87, Historic Buildings and Monuments Commn Advisory Board since 1983, Historic Buildings and Monuments Commn Science Panel 1983-89; Chm Nat Curriculum Art Working Group 1990-91; Freeman City of London; author; *cr* Baron Renfrew of Kaimsthorn, of Hurlet, District of Renfrew (Life Baron) 1991: *m* 1965, Jane Margaret, da of Ven Walter Frederick Ewbank, of Penrith, Cumbria, and has issue.

Residence – The Master's Lodge, Jesus College, Cambridge CB5 8BL. *Clubs* – Athenaeum, United Oxford and Cambridge.

SONS LIVING

Hon Alban, *b* 1970.
Hon Magnus, *b* 1975.

DAUGHTER LIVING

Hon Helena, *b* 1968.

RENNELL, BARON (Rodd) (Baron UK 1933)

(JOHN ADRIAN) TREMAYNE RODD, 3rd Baron, *b* 28 June 1935, *s* 1978; *ed* Downside, and RNC Dartmouth; Lieut RN, former Scottish Rugby International, Dir Tremayne Ltd: *m* 1977, Phyllis Caroline, da of Thomas David Neill, of Portadown co Armagh, and has issue.

Arms – Argent, two trefoils slipped sable on a chief of the second, three crescents of the first. **Crest** – A representation of the Colossus of Rhodes, over the shoulder a bow, in the dexter hand an arrow and in the sinister a cup, all proper. **Supporters** – On the either side a Cornish chough, wings elevated and addorsed proper, charged on the breast with a trefoil slipped argent.
Address – c/o White's Club, 37 St James's St, SW1.

SON LIVING

Hon JAMES RODERICK DAVID TREMAYNE, *b* 9 March 1978.

DAUGHTERS LIVING

Recte omnia duce Deo
With God for guide, all is right

Hon Sophie Mary Jane *b* 1981.
Hon Rachel, *b* 1987.
Hon Lilias, *b* 1989.

DAUGHTERS LIVING OF SECOND BARON

Hon Joanna Phoebe, *b* 1929: *m* 1966, Comte Gérard de Renusson d'Hauteville, yr son Marquis d'Hauteville. *Residences* – 9 rue Puget, 06100 Nice, France; 10 rue François Mouthon, 75015 Paris. *Hon* Juliet Honor, *b* 1930: *m* 1957, Brian Boobbyer, and has issue living, Philip Christopher, *b* 1963, — Mark Tremayne, *b* 1967: *m* 1991, Catherine Mary, elder da of Peter Alexander O'Brien Hannon (*see* D Montrose). *Residence* – Little Rodd, Presteigne, Powys.
Hon Mary Elizabeth Jill, *b* 1932: *m* 1st, 1954, Michael William Langan Dunne; 2ndly, 1985, Christopher Bridges Daniell, and has issue living (by 1st *m*), John Francis Jeremy, *b* 1957, — Stephen Michael Damian, *b* 1961, — Mary Jemima, *b* 1955, — Teresa Mary Claire, *b* 1962: *m* 1993, Thomas A. Calvert, yr son of David J. Calvert, of Wetmore, Shropshire, — Miranda Mary *b* 1966. *Residence* – Ashley Farm, Stansbatch, Pembridge, Herefordshire.
Hon Rachel Georgiana, *b* 1935: *m* 1964, Richard Douglas Blythe, of 14 Lawson Way, Darlington, Perth, W Aust, and has issue living, Joseph Matthew Gerard, *b* 1968, — Matthew Francis, *b* 1970.

PREDECESSORS – **(1)** Rt Hon Sir (JAMES) RENNELL RODD, GCB, GCMG, GCVO, son of late Major James Rennell Rodd; *b* 1858; was Envoy Extraor and Min Plen to Stockholm 1904-8, and Ambassador Extraor and Min Plen to Italy 1908-19; sat as MP for St Marylebone 1928-32 (*C*); *cr Baron Rennell*, of Rodd, co Hereford (peerage of United Kingdom) 1933: *m* 1894, Lilias Georgina, who *d* 1951, da of late James Alexander Guthrie, of Craigie, Forfar; *d* 1941; *s* by his el son **(2)** FRANCIS JAMES RENNELL, 2nd Baron, KBE, CB, 2nd Baron; *b* 1895, Pres R Geographical Soc 1945-48, Visiting Fellow of Nuffield Coll, Oxford: *m* 1928, Hon Mary Constance Vivian Smith, who *d* 1981, da of 1st Baron Bicester; *d* 1978; *s* by his nephew **(3)** (JOHN ADRIAN) TREMAYNE, 3rd Baron and present peer (only surv son of late Cdr Hon Gustaf Guthrie Rennell Rodd, OBE, RN, yst son of 1st Baron).

RENTON, BARON (Renton) (Life Baron 1979)

Virtue is in action

DAVID LOCKHART-MURE RENTON, KBE, TD, PC, QC, son of late Maurice Waugh Renton, MD CM, DPH; *b* 12 Aug 1908; *ed* Oundle, and Univ Coll Oxford (BCL, MA); Bar Lincoln's Inn 1933, Member of Bar Council 1939, QC 1954, a Bencher 1962, and Treasurer 1979; a Member of Senate of Inns of Court 1967-71 and 1975-79; a DL of Cambs; Parl Sec Min of Fuel and Power 1955-57, and of Min of Power 1957-58, Joint Parl Under-Sec of State, Home Office 1958-61, Min of State, Home Office 1961-62; Recorder of Rochester 1963-68, and of Guildford 1968-71; Pres Conservation Soc 1970-71; Pres Statute Law Soc since 1980; Pres National Council for Civil Protection 1980-91; Joint-Pres Parl Arts and Heritage Council since 1992; a Member Commn on the Constitution 1971-73; Chm of Cttee on the Preparation of Legislation 1973-75; Chm Nat Soc for Mentally Handicapped Children 1977-82, Pres 1982-88; 1939-45 War as Maj RA; MP for Hunts (*C*) 1945-79; Patron National Law Library; Patron Hunts Div Conservative Assocn; Patron DEMAND (Design & Manufacture for Disability), Royal British Legion (Hunts), and Ravenswood Foundation; *cr* PC 1962, KBE (Civil) 1964, and *Baron Renton*, of Huntingdon in co Cambs (Life Baron) 1979: *m* 1947, Claire Cicely, who *d* 1986, yst da of late Walter Atholl Duncan, and has issue.

Arms – Azure a horse forcene on a chief or a sword point to the dexter gules between a portcullis chained and hunting horn stringed azure. **Crest** – In front of a horse's head erased or a hunting horn stringed azure. **Supporters** – *Dexter*, a lion guardant purpure gorged with a fine chain pendant therefrom a millrind gold. *Sinister*, a stag guardant proper gorged with a like chain pendant therefrom a fetterlock enclosing a heart gold.
Residences – Moat House, Abbots Ripton, Huntingdon; 16 Old Buildings, Lincoln's Inn, WC2. **Clubs** – Carlton; Pratt's.

DAUGHTERS LIVING

Hon Caroline Mary, *b* 1948: *m* 1st, 1970 (*m diss* 1974), Peter Dodds Parker; 2ndly, 1977, Robin Warwick Antony Parr, of Port Mary House, Dundrennan, Kirkcudbright, and has issue living by both *m*.
Hon Clare Olivia (11 Flodden Rd, SE5), *b* 1950; Barrister-at-law: *m* 1982, Timothy John Whittaker Scott, and has issue.
Hon Davina Kathleen, *b* 1954.

RENWICK, BARON (Renwick) (Baron UK 1964, Bt UK 1927)

To work is to pray

HARRY ANDREW RENWICK, 2nd Baron and 3rd Baronet; *b* 10 Oct 1935; *s* 1973; *ed* Eton: *m* 1st, 1965 (*m diss* 1989), Susan Jane, da of late Capt Kenneth Stephen B. Lucking, Cheshire Regt; 2ndly, 1989, Mrs Homayoun Mazandi, da of late Maj Mahmoud Yazdanparst Pakzad, and formerly wife of Joe Mazandi, of LA, Calif, USA, and has issue by 1st *m*.

Arms – Argent, a husbandman in the act of sowing-proper, on a chief azure a thunderbolt between two bulls, heads caboshed or. **Crest** – a thunderbolt or. **Supporters** – *Dexter*, a black poodle proper; *sinister*, a tabby cat proper.
Residence – 47 Cheyne Walk, SW3.

SONS LIVING (By 1st marriage)

Hon ROBERT JAMES, *b* 19 Aug 1966.
Hon Michael David, *b* 1968.

SISTERS LIVING AND DECEASED

Hon Susan Mary, *b* 1930; a JP for Hants: *m* 1955 (*m diss* 1984), Hon Sir John Francis Harcourt Baring (later 7th Baron Ashburton). *Residence* – 13 Alexander St, W2.
Hon Jennifer, *b* 1932: *m* 1st, 1954 (*m diss* 1967), Antony Duncan Rowe; 2ndly, 1973 (*m diss* 1978), Roy Philip Arthur, who *d* 1994; 3rdly, 1978 (*m diss* 1989), Robert Ian MacDonald, and *d* 1989, leaving issue (by 1st *m*), Giles Timothy Robert (Flat 4, 38 Redcliffe Gdns, SW10), *b* 1956: *m* 1986 (*m diss* 1991), Karma Nabulsi, — Antonia Tanya, *b* 1959: *m* 1983, Henry James Stone, of Fairviews, Honeysuckle Close, S Pool, Kingsbridge, S Devon, and has issue living, Benjamin James *b* 1986, Liam Henry *b* 1988, Jacob Antony *b* 1991, Harry Edward *b* 1993, Gemma Elizabeth *b* 1984.
Hon Belinda Anne, *b* 1934: *m* 1959, as his 2nd wife, John Horatio Gordon Shephard, formerly Capt Gren Gds, who *d* 1993, of The Barn, Elcot, Newbury, Berks, and has issue living, William, *b* 1962, — Sarah, *b* 1959: *m* 1st, 1988 (*m diss* 1993), Stephen P.M. Clarke; 2ndly, 1993, Alexander J. H. Scrimgeour, of 103 Strathville Rd, SW18.

MOTHER LIVING

Dorothy Mary (Miserden House, Stroud, Glos), da of late Maj Harold Parkes, of the Dial House, Alveston, Stratford-on-Avon: *m* 1st, 1929 (*m diss* 1953), Sir Robert Burnham Renwick, KBE, 2nd Bt (later 1st Baron Renwick), who *d* 1973; 2ndly, 1953, John FitzAdam Ormiston, who *d* 1994.

WIDOW LIVING OF FIRST BARON

(Edith) Joan (*Joan, Baroness Renwick*) (Herne's Cottage, Windsor Forest, Berks), only da of late Sir Reginald Clarke, CIE, and widow of Maj John Ogilvy Spencer, WG: *m* 1953, as his 2nd wife, the 1st Baron, who *d* 1973.

PREDECESSORS – (1) HARRY BENEDETTO Renwick, KBE, son of Andrew Renwick, of Windsor, *b* 1861; *cr* a Baronet 1927: *m* 1897, Frederica Louisa, da of Robert Laing, of Stirling; *d* 1932; *s* by his only son (2) Sir ROBERT BURNHAM, KBE, 2nd Bt *b* 1904; Industrialist; Chm of Airbourne Forces, 1943-45; Controller of Communications Air Min and Communications Equipment, Min of Aircraft Production 1942-45; Chm Asso TV 1961; *cr Baron Renwick*, of Coombe, co Surrey (peerage of UK) 1964: *m* 1st, 1929 (*m diss* 1953), Dorothy Mary, da of late Maj Harold Parkes, of the Dial House, Alveston, Stratford-on-Avon; 2ndly, 1953, Edith Joan, only da of late Sir Reginald Clarke, CIE; and widow of Maj John Ogilvie Spencer, WG; *d* 1973; *s* by his only son (3) HARRY ANDREW, 2nd Baron and present peer.

REVELSTOKE, BARON (Baring) (Baron UK 1885)

By uprightness and labour

RUPERT BARING, 4th Baron; *b* 8 Feb 1911; *s* 1934; *ed* Eton; formerly 2nd Lt Roy Armoured Corps (TA): *m* 1934 (*m diss* 1944), Hon Florence (Flora) Fermor-Hesketh, who *d* 1971, da of 1st Baron Hesketh, and has issue. The 4th Baron *d* 18 July 1994.

Arms – Azure, a fesse or, in chief a bear's head proper, ringed or, differenced by a hurt, thereon a mullet erminois. **Crest** – A mullet erminois, between two wings argent. **Supporters** – *Dexter*, a bull argent; *sinister*, a bear proper, muzzled or, each charged on the shoulder with a mullet erminois. *Residence* – Lambay Island, Rush, co Dublin.

SONS LIVING

Hon JOHN, *b* 2 Dec 1934; *ed* Eton.
Hon James Cecil, *b* 1938; *ed* Eton: *m* 1st, 1968, Aneta, yr da of late Erskine A. H. Fisher, 2ndly, 1983, Sarah, da of William Edward Stubbs, MBE, and has issue living (by 1st *m*), Alexander Rupert, *b* 1970, — Thomas James, *b* 1971, — (by 2nd *m*) Flora Aksinia, *b* 1983. *Residence* –

COLLATERAL BRANCHES LIVING

Issue of late Brig-Gen Hon Everard Baring, CVO, CBE, 4th son of 1st Baron, *b* 1865, *d* 1932: *m* 1904, Lady Ulrica Duncombe, who *d* 1935, da of 1st Earl of Feversham:—
Helen, *b* 1906: *m* 1939, as his 2nd wife, Maj Gordon Bentley Foster, who *d* 1963, and has issue living, Rosanna (*Hon Mrs Oliver James*), *b* 19—: *m* 1965, Hon Oliver Francis Wintour James, and has issue (*see* B James of Rusholme), — Mary Helen, *b* 1942: *m* 1981, John Duncan, of The Old Vicarage, Salton, York. *Residence* – Sleightholmedale, Kirkbymoorside, York. —— Audrey, *b* 1909: *m* 1st, 1933 (*m diss* 1948), Lt-Col Sir Charles Frederick Richmond Brown, 4th Bt; 2ndly, 1947, Lt-Col Campbell K. Finlay, of West Ardhu, Dervaig, Isle of Mull.

Grandchildren of late Hon Hugo Baring, OBE, yst son of 1st Baron:—
Issue of late Francis Anthony Baring, *b* 1909, *ka* 1940: *m* 1933, Lady Rose Gwendolen Louisa McDonnell, DCVO, who *d* 1993, da of 7th Earl of Antrim:—
Nicholas Hugo (43 Sutherland Place, W2 5BY; The Old Rectory, Ham, Marlborough, Wilts SN8 3QR) *b* 1934; *ed* Eton, and Magdalene Coll, Camb; late Lieut Coldstream Gds; Trustee Nat Gallery since 1989 (Chm since 1991): *m* 1972, Diana, da of late Lt-Col Charles Crawfurd, and has issue living, Francis Charles, *b* 1973, — Tobias Keith Alexander, *b* 1976, — Edward Randal, *b* 1979. —— Peter (29 Ladbroke Sq, W11), *b* 1935; *ed* Eton, and Magdalene Coll, Camb: *m* 1960, Teresa Anne, da of late Hon Sir Maurice Richard Bridgeman, KBE (*see* V Bridgeman), and has issue living, Guy Francis, *b* 1965, — Max Maurice, *b* 1967, — Hugo John, *b* 1970. —— Susan Violet, *b* 1938: *m* 1962, Henry Joseph Rogaly, of 56 Croftdown Rd, NW5, and has issue living, Benjamin Nelson, *b* 1963, — Sarah Rose, *b* 1965, — Rachel Frances, *b* 1968, — Jessica Hilary, *b* 1971.

PREDECESSORS – (1) EDWARD CHARLES Baring, son of late Henry Baring, MP (*see* B Northbrook, colls); *b* 1828; was head of mercantile firm of Baring Brothers and Co Bishopsgate Street, EC; *cr Baron Revelstoke*, of Membland, co Devon (peerage of United Kingdom) 1885: *m* 1861, Louisa Emily Charlotte, who *d* 1892, da of John Crocker Bulteel, of Flete, Devon; *d* 1897; *s* by his son (2) JOHN, 2nd Baron, GCVO, *b* 1863; a partner in the firm of Baring Bros and Co (Limited), and a Director of Bank of England; a Member of Council of HRH the Prince of Wales 1907-29, Receiver-Gen of Duchy of Cornwall 1908-29, and Lord-Lieut for Middlesex 1926-9; *d* 1929; *s* by his brother (3) CECIL, 3rd Baron; *b* 1864: *m* 1902, Maude, who *d* 1922, da of late Pierre Lorillard, *d* 1934; *s* by his son (4) RUPERT, 4th Baron and present peer.

RHODES, BARONY OF (Rhodes) (Extinct 1987)

DAUGHTERS LIVING OF LIFE BARON

Hon Pamela JUDSON-RHODES (18 Aiken Ave, Princeton, NJ 08540, USA), *b* 1927: *m* 1st, 1953 (*m diss* 1969), Walter L. Hemphill; 2ndly, 1990, S. Sheldon Judson, and has issue (by 1st *m*).
Hon Helen, *b* 1929: *m* 1954, John Sutcliffe, JP, DL, of Lower Carr, Diggle, Dobcross, nr Oldham, Lancs, and has issue.

RICHARD, BARON (Richard) (Life Baron 1990)

IVOR SEWARD RICHARD, QC, son of Seward Thomas Richard, of 30 Heol Nant Castan, Rhiwbina, Cardiff; b 30 May 1932; ed Cheltenham, and Pembroke Coll, Oxford (BA 1953, MA 1970, Hon Fellow 1981); Bar Inner Temple 1955, QC 1971, Bencher 1985; Delegate at Assembly for Council of Europe 1965-68, and Western European Union 1965-68; PPS to Sec of State for Defence 1966-69, Parly Under-Sec of State for Defence (Army) 1969-70, Opposition Spokesman Broadcasting, Posts and Telecommunications 1970-71, Dep Opposition Spokesman Foreign Affairs 1971-74, UK Permanent Rep to UN 1974-79, Chm Rhodesia Conference, Geneva, 1976, UK Commr to Commn of European Communities 1981-85; Opposition Leader of House of Lords since 1992; Member Fabian Soc and Lab Lawyers; MP Barons Court (*Lab*) 1964-74; *cr Baron Richard*, of Ammanford, co Dyfed (Life Baron) 1990: *m* 1st, 1956 (*m diss* 1962), Geraldine Maude, da of Alfred Moore, of Hartlepool, co Durham; 2ndly, 1962 (*m diss* 1985), Alison Mary, da of Joseph Imrie, of Alverstoke, Hants; 3rdly, 1989, Janet, da of John Jones, of Oxford, and has issue by 1st, 2nd and 3rd *m*. *Address* – 2 Paper Buildings, Temple, EC4.

SONS LIVING *(By 1st marriage)*

Hon David Seward, *b* 1959.

(by 2nd marriage)

Hon Alun Seward, *b* 1963.

(by 3rd marriage)

Hon William John, *b* 1990.

DAUGHTER LIVING *(By 2nd marriage)*

Hon Isobel Margaret Katherine, *b* 1966.

RICHARDSON, BARON (Richardson) (Life Baron 1978, Bt UK 1963)

JOHN SAMUEL RICHARDSON, LVO, *Life Baron* and 1st *Baronet*, son of late Maj John Watson Richardson, of Sheffield (Roberts, Bt) (*cr* 1919); *b* 16 June 1910; *ed* Charterhouse, and Trin Coll, Camb (MA BChir, MD, Hon Fellow 1979) Hon DSc, NUI Hull, Hon DCL Newcastle, Hon LLD Nottingham, Liverpool; FRCP London; Hon FRCP Ed; Hon FRCP Glasgow; Hon FRCPsych; Hon FRCS; Hon FRCGP; Hon FFCM; a Consulting Physician St Thomas's Hosp since 1947, to Metropolitan Police 1957-80, to Army 1964-75, and to London Transport 1964-80; Chm Council for Postgraduate Med Educ in England and Wales 1972-80; Hon Master of The Bench of Gray's Inn 1974; Pres of Gen Med Council 1973-80, Chm of Joint Consultants Cttee 1967-72; Pres of R Soc of Medicine 1969-71, and British Med Assocn 1970-71; Master of Soc of Apothecaries of London 1971-72; Pres of International Soc of Internal Med 1966-70; 1939-45 War, as Lt-Col RAMC; LVO 1943; Knt 1960; *cr* a *Baronet* (UK, of Ecclesall, West Riding, co York) 1963, and *Baron Richardson*, of Lee, co Devon (Life Baron) 1978: *m* 1933, Sybil Angela Stephanie, who *d* 1991, da of A. Ronald Trist, of Stanmore, Middx, and has issue.

Arms – Sable on a fess engrailed or between in chief an open book proper bound gules edged gold between two mullets and in base a swan argent, a lion passant guardant also gules. **Crest** – The head of a rhinoceros erased sable behind the horn a scroll inscribed with words "Till time ceases" (in letters gules). **Supporters** – Two horses reguardant the dexter a Grey, with Saddlecloth of the Metropolitan Police Force, the sinister also a Grey, with Saddlecloth of the Royal Army Medical Corps, both saddled, bridled, with headstall, horse-hair plume and breast girth all with silver buckles and bosses proper.
Residence – Windcutter, Lee, nr Ilfracombe, N Devon.

DAUGHTERS LIVING

Hon Elizabeth-Ann, *b* 1937: *m* 1st, 1960 (*m diss* 1970), Angus Gavin Lockhead Jack (*see* Inglefield-Watson, Bt, colls); 2ndly, 1971, Gregory Edmund Stafford, LLB, of 49 Deodar Rd, SW15, and has issue living (by 1st *m*—*see* Inglefield-Watson, Bt, colls), — (by 2nd *m*), Samuel, *b* 1975.
Hon Susan Clare, *b* 1940: *m* 1970, Robert Wales, of 2 Thorne St, SW13, and has issue living, Duncan John Richardson, *b* 1970.

RICHARDSON OF DUNTISBOURNE, BARON (Richardson) (Life Baron 1983)

GORDON WILLIAM HUMPHREYS RICHARDSON, KG, MBE, PC, el son of late John Robert Richardson; *b* 25 Nov 1915; *ed* Nottingham High Sch, and Gonville and Caius Coll, Camb (BA, LLB); 1939-45 War as Maj S Notts Hus Yeo, RHA; Bar Gray's Inn 1946; Hon Bencher 1973; Chm Pilgrim Trust 1984-89; a Member of Bar Council 1951-55; Chm J. Henry Schroder Wagg & Co Ltd 1962-72, and Schroders Ltd 1966-73; Chm of Industrial Development Advisory Board 1972-73; a Dir of Bank of England 1967-75; Gov of Bank of England 1973-83; Chm R Inst of Internat Affairs 1984-87; one of HM Lieuts City of London since 1974, and a DL of Glos; *cr* MBE (Mil) 1944, PC (1976), KG (1983), and *Baron Richardson of Duntisbourne*, of Duntisbourne, co Glos (Life Peer) 1983; *m* 1941, Margaret Alison, el da of late Very Rev Hugh Richard Lawrie Sheppard, Canon and Precentor of St Paul's Cathedral, and has issue.

Arms – Argent a fess wavy bleu celeste between in chief three swords in pale points upwards fesswise gules and in base a pair of scales sable on a bordure also gules eight bezants. **Crest** – A seated female figure representing the Bank of England proper habited argent crined and murally crowned or resting the sinister hand on an oval cartouche carved or the field argent thereon a cross gules and holding in the palm of the extended dexter hand a terrestrial globe also proper. **Supporters** – On either side a griffin segreant gules the wings elevated and bezantly gorged with coronet of sword hilts gold.
Address – c/o Morgan Stanley International, Kingsley House, 1A Wimpole St, W1M 7AA. *Clubs* – Athenaeum, Brooks's.

SON LIVING

Hon Simon Bruce Sheppard, *b* 1944: *m* 1979, Miriam Ann, da of George Harrison Gibson. *Residence* – River House, Bromham Park, Bromham, Beds MK43 8HH.

DAUGHTER LIVING

Hon Sarah (*Hon Lady Riddell*), LVO, *b* 1942; LVO 1993: *m* 1969, Sir John Charles Buchanan Riddell, 13th Bt, CVO, DL, and has issue. *Residences* – Hepple, Morpeth, Northumberland; 49 Campden Hill Sq, W8 7JR.

RICHMOND and GORDON, DUKE OF (Gordon Lennox) (Duke (Richmond) E 1675, Duke (Lennox) S 1675, Duke (Gordon) UK 1876)

CHARLES HENRY GORDON LENNOX, 10th Duke of Richmond and Lennox, and 5th Duke of Gordon; also Duke of Aubigny in France; *b* 19 Sept 1929; *s* 1989; *ed* Eton, and William Temple Coll, Rugby; Hereditary Constable of Inverness Castle; Lord Lieut W Sussex 1989-94; late 2nd Lt KRRC; Chancellor Sussex Univ since 1985; a Chartered Accountant; formerly Member of House of Laity of General Synod for Diocese of Chichester, and of Central and Exec Cttee of World Council of Churches, and Chm of Board for Mission and Unity of General Synod; a Church Commr: *m* 1951, Susan Monica, da of Col Cecil Everard Montague Grenville-Grey, CBE (*see* Morrison-Bell, Bt (*cr* 1905), colls), and has issue.

Arms – Quarterly: 1st and 4th grand quarters, the Royal arms of Charles II (viz quarterly; 1st and 4th, France and England quarterly; 2nd, Scotland; 3rd Ireland), the whole within a bordure compony argent and gules charged with eight roses of the second, barbed and seeded proper, *Lennox*; over all an escutcheon gules, three buckles or, *Aubigny*; 2nd and 3rd grand quarters quarterly, 1st azure, three boars' heads couped or, *Gordon*; 2nd or, three lions, heads erased gules, *Badenoch*; 3rd or, three crescents within a double tressure counterflory gules, *Seton*; 4th azure, three cinquefoils argent, *Fraser*. **Crests** – 1st, a bull's head erased sable horned or, *Lennox*; 2nd, on a chapeau gules, turned up ermine, a lion statant guardant or, ducally crowned gules, and gorged with a collar compony of four pieces, argent and gules charged with eight roses of the last, *Richmond*; 3rd, out of a ducal coronet, a Stag's head affrontée proper, attired with ten tynes or. **Supporters** – *Dexter*, a unicorn argent, armed, crined and unguled, or; *sinister*, an antelope argent, also crined, and unguled, or, each supporter gorged with a collar compony as the crest.
Seat – Goodwood, Chichester, West Sussex PO18 OPX.

SON LIVING

CHARLES HENRY (*Earl of March and Kinrara*), *b* 8 Jan 1955; *ed* Eton: *m* 1st, 1976 (*m diss* 1989), Sally, da of late Maurice Clayton; 2ndly, 1991, Hon Janet Elizabeth Astor, da of 3rd Viscount Astor, and has issue:—

DAUGHTER LIVING (by 1st *m*)—*Lady* Alexandra, *b* 1985.

DAUGHTERS LIVING

Lady Ellinor Caroline, *b* 1952.
Lady Louisa Elizabeth, *b* 1967.

ADOPTED DAUGHTERS LIVING

Maria, *b* 1959. —— Naomi, *b* 1962.

BROTHER LIVING

Lord Nicholas, KCMG, KCVO, *b* 1931; *ed* Eton and Worcester Coll, Oxford; HM Diplomatic Ser (Paris) 1975-79; HM Amb to Spain 1984-89; a Gov of BBC since 1990; late 2nd Lt KRRC; MVO (4th class) 1957, CMG (Civil) 1978, KCMG 1986, KCVO 1988: *m* 1958, Mary, only da of late Brig Hudleston Noel Hedworth Williamson, DSO, MC (*see* Williamson, Bt, colls), and has issue living, Anthony Charles, *b* 1969, — Sarah Caroline, *b* 1960: *m* 1988, Dominic Caldecott, yst son of Andrew Caldecott, of Ramsbury, Wilts, and has issue living, Frederick Arthur Nicholas *b* 1989, Thomas Andrew *b* (twin) 1989, Rufus George *b* 1993, — Henrietta Mary, *b* 1962: *m* 1992, Michael J. Lindsell, son of W. M. Lindsell, of Lymington, Hants, and has issue living, Albert *b* 1993, — Lucy Elizabeth, *b* 1965. *Residence* – South Nore, W Wittering, Chichester, Sussex PO20 8AT.

COLLATERAL BRANCHES LIVING

Grandchildren of late Brig-Gen Lord Esmé Charles Gordon Lennox, KCVO, CMG, DSO (infra):—
Issue of late Capt Reginald Arthur Charles Gordon Lennox, OBE, *b* 1910, *d* 1965: *m* 1942, Pamela Cicely (1103 Balnagask, Banket St, Johannesburg, S Africa), da of Capt Christopher Digby Leyland, Life Gds (Cotterell, Bt):—
James David Charles *b* 1944: *m* 1973 (*m diss* 1979), Sally Cooper, da of John Roger Cooper Brain, and has issue living, Henry, *b* 1976. —— Clare Evelyn, *b* 1946: *m* 1967, Edmund Clive Lardner-Burke.

Issue of late Brig-Gen Lord Esmé Charles Gordon Lennox, KCVO, CMG, DSO, 2nd son of 7th Duke, *b* 1875, *d* 1949: *m* 1st, 1909 (*m diss* 1923), Hon Hermione Frances Caroline Fellowes, who *d* 1971, da of 2nd Baron De Ramsey; 2ndly, 1923, Rosamond Lorys, who *d* 1961, da of late Vice-Adm Norman Craig Palmer, CVO:—
(By 2nd *m*) Sara Carolyn (*Lady Fergusson*), *b* 1933: *m* 1st, 1956, Sir William Andrew Malcolm Martin Oliphant Montgomery Cuninghame, 11th Bt, who *d* 1959; 2ndly, 1959, Sir Ewen Alastair John Fergusson, GCMG, GCVO, son of late Sir Ewen Macgregor Field Fergusson, and has issue living, (by 2nd *m*) Ewen Alexander Nicholas, *b* 1965, — Anna Rosamund Harriot, *b* 1961, — Iona Frances, *b* 1967. *Address* – c/o Coutts & Co, 440 Strand, WC2R 0QS.

Grandsons of late Maj Lord Bernard Charles Gordon Lennox, 3rd son of 7th Duke:—
Issue of late Lt-Gen Sir George Charles Gordon Lennox, KBE, CB, CVO, DSO, *b* 1908, *d* 1988: *m* 1931, Nancy Brenda, who *d* 1993, da of Maj Sir Lionel Edward Hamilton Marmaduke Darell, 6th Bt, DSO:—
Bernard Charles, CB, MBE (Hill House, Eversley, Hants), *b* 1932; *ed* Eton, a Page of Honour to HM 1946-49; Maj-Gen late Gren Gds; Senior Army Member Royal Coll of Defence Studies 1986-88, Lieut-Col Gren Gds 1989; Chm Guards' Polo Club since 1992; MBE (Mil) 1968, CB (Mil) 1986: *m* 1958, Sally-Rose, only da of late John Weston Warner, of The Old Rectory, Stanton, nr Broadway, Worcs, and has issue living, Edward Charles, *b* 1961; a Page of Honour to HM 1974-77; Capt Gren Gds: *m* 1989, Katharine Elizabeth, eldest da of (Robert) Martin Mays-Smith, of Chaddleworth House, Chaddleworth, Newbury, Berks, and has issue living, Alexander Charles *b* 1990, Rosie Jennifer *b* 1992, — Angus Charles, *b* 1964: *m* 1990, Camilla Douglas, elder da of Ian Alan Douglas Pilkington (*see* B Faringdon, colls), and has issue living, Iona Alice *b* 1993, — Charles Bernard, *b* 1970. —— David Henry Charles (Saxham Hall, Bury St Edmunds, Suffolk IP29 5JW), *b* 1935; *ed* Eton; Col Gren Gds: *m* 1982, Elizabeth C., da of late Gen Sir William Gurdon Stirling, GCB, CBE, DSO, and has issue living, Flora, *b* 1983.

Issue of late Rear Adm Sir Alexander Henry Charles Gordon Lennox, KCVO, CB, DSO, *b* 1911, *d* 1987: *m* 1936, Barbara, who *d* 1987, da of late Maj-Gen Julian Steele:—
Michael Charles, *b* 1938; *ed* Eton, and RNC Dartmouth; Capt RN: *m* 1974, Jennifer Susan, da of late Capt Hon Vicary Paul Gibbs (*see* B Aldenham, colls), and has issue living, Hamish Charles, *b* 1980, — Lucinda Jean, *b* 1975, — Charlotte Louise, *b* 1978. *Residence* – Fishers Hill, Iping, Midhurst, W Sussex. —— Andrew Charles, *b* 1948; *ed* Nautical Coll, Pangbourne, and RNC Dartmouth; Cdr RN: *m* 1973, Julia Jane Neill, da of late Dr J. Neill Morrison, and has issue living, Simon Charles, *b* 1978, — Hugo Charles, *b* 1980. *Residence* – Bridge House, Westbourne, Emsworth, Hants.

Grandson of late Rt Hon Lord Walter Charles Gordon Lennox, 4th son of 6th Duke:—
Issue of late Capt Victor Charles Hugh Gordon Lennox, *b* 1897, *d* 1968: *m* 1st, 1923 (*m diss* 1928), Mrs Anne Dorothy Bridge, who *d* 1963, da of late Edward Cazalet Browne; 2ndly, 1932 (*m diss* 1940), Diana Elizabeth Constance, who *d* 1982, da of late Adm Sir Charles Edmund Kingsmill, of Ballybeg, Ottawa; 3rdly, 1958, Norah Julia Wensley, who *d* 19—, da of Edward Guy Schofield, of Leeds:—
(By 2nd *m*) (Henry) George Charles, *b* 1934: *m* 1958, Odile Steinmann, of Grenoble, France, and has issue living, Ian Charles (5 Ave du Bijou, 01210 Ferney-Voltaire, France), *b* 1958: *m* 1989, Jeltje, elder da of Owen Aukema, of Holland, Michigan, USA, — Philip George Hugh (Yoyogi Terrace Apt 216, 1-32-27 Shibuya-Ku, Tokyo 151, Japan), *b* 1962: *m* 1987, Junko, da of late Prof Tomio Higuchi, and has issue living, Thomas Charles *b* 1991, Alec George *b* 1993, — Geneviève Ann (Stutzstrasse 11, 8353 Elgg, Switzerland), *b* 1961: *m* 1993, Rainer Frick, son of Wilhelm Frick, of Basel, Switzerland.

PREDECESSORS – (1) CHARLES Lennox, KG, illegitimate son of King Charles II, by Louise Renée de Penancoet de Kerouaille (who was *cr* by HM *Baroness Petersfield, Countess of Fareham*, and *Duchess of Portsmouth* for life, and by Louis XIV of France Duchess d'Aubigny); *b* 1672; *cr Baron of Settrington*, of Settrington, co York, *Earl of March, Duke of Richmond* (peerage of England) 1675, and *Lord of Torboulton*, of Torbolton, *Earl of Darnley and Duke of Lennox* (peerage of Scotland) 1675; *d* 1723; *s* by his son (2) CHARLES, KG, KB, PC, 2nd Duke, *b* 1701; was High Constable of England at coronation of George II, Master of the Horse and on four occasions a Lord Justice to administer the government during the absence of the king; in 1734, on the death of his grandmother, he became *Duke d'Aubigny* (cr 1684) in France; *d* 1750; *s* by his son (3) CHARLES, KG, 3rd Duke, *b* 1735; carried the sceptre at the Coronation of George III; was Ambassador to France 1765, Principal Sec of State 1766, and Master-Gen of the Ordnance 1782; *dsp* 1806; *s* by his nephew (4) CHARLES, KG, 4th Duke, *b* 1764; a Gen in the Army; MP for Sussex 1790-1806; was Lord-Lieut of Ireland 1807-13, and Gov-Gen of Canada 1818-19: *m* Charlotte, da of Alexander, 4th Duke of Gordon; *d* 1819; *s* by his son (5) CHARLES, KG, PC, 5th Duke; *b* 1791; was Lord-Lieut of Sussex; assumed in 1836 by patent the additional surname of Gordon; the title of Duke D'Aubigny was confirmed to him and registered by Parliament of France 1777, and re-confirmed 1816 by Louis XVIII; *m* 1817, Lady Caroline Paget, da of

1st Marquess of Anglesey; *d* 1860; *s* by his son **(6)** CHARLES HENRY, KG, PC, DCL, LLD, 6th Duke of Richmond and Lennox; *b* 1818; Lord-Lieut of co Banff, and an Elder Brother of Trinity House; MP for W Sussex (*C*) 1841-60; ADC to Com-in-Ch (Duke of Wellington and Viscount Hardinge) 184-54, Pres of Poor Law Board 1859, and of Board of Trade 1867-8 and 1885, Lord Pres of Council 1874-80, *ex officio* Keeper of the Great Seal of Scotland, Sec for Scotland and Vice-Pres of Committee of Council on Education in Scotland 1885-6; *cr Earl of Kinrara*, and *Duke of Gordon* (peerage of United Kingdom) 1876: *m* 1843, Frances Harriet, who *d* 1887, el da of late Algernon Frederic Greville; *d* 1903; *s* by his son **(7)** CHARLES HENRY, KG, GCVO, CB, 7th Duke; *b* 1845; sat as MP for W Sussex (*C*) 1869-85, and for SW, or Chichester, Div of Sussex 1885-8; Hereditary Constable of Inverness Castle, an ADC to Queen Victoria, King Edward VII, and King George V 1896-1920, Lord-Lieut and Custos Rotulorum of cos Elgin and Banff 1903-28, and Chancellor of Aberdeen Univ 1917-28; bore Sceptre with Dove at Coronation of King George V 1911: *m* 1st, 1868, Amy Mary, who *d* 1879, el da of late Percy Ricardo, of Bramley Park, Guildford; 2ndly, 1882, Isabel Sophie, who *d* 1887, da of William George Craven; *d* 1928; *s* by his son **(8)** CHARLES HENRY, DSO, MVO, 8th Duke, *b* 1870; Lieut-Col Reserve of Officers; S Africa 1900 (despatches, DSO); accompanied Special Mission to Foreign Courts to announce Accession of King George V 1910; appointed Lord Lt of co Elgin 1928: *m* 1893, Hilda Madaleine, DBE, who *d* 1971, el da of Henry A. Brassey, of Preston Hall, Aylesford; *d* 1935; *s* by his son **(9)** FREDERICK CHARLES, 9th Duke, *b* 1904; 1939-45 War as Fl Lt RAF; bore Sceptre with the Dove at Coronations of King George VI and Queen Elizabeth II; *m* 1927, Elizabeth Grace, who *d* 1992, da of late Rev Thomas William Hudson, formerly V of Wendover, Bucks; *d* 1989; *s* by his elder son **(10)** CHARLES HENRY, 10th Duke and present peer; also Earl of March, Earl of Darnley, Earl of Kinrara, Baron of Settrington, and Lord of Torboulton.

RIDLEY, VISCOUNT (Ridley) (Viscount UK 1900, Bt GB 1756)

Constant in loyalty

MATTHEW WHITE RIDLEY, KG, GCVO, TD, 4th Viscount, and 8th Baronet; *b* 29 July 1925; *s* 1964; *ed* Eton, and Balliol Coll, Oxford; ARICS; Hon Col Queen's Own Yeomanry (TA); HM's Lord Lieut and Custos Rotulorum of Northumberland since 1984, a DL, JP, and Alderman for Northumberland; Lord Steward of HM Household since 1989; Chm of Northumberland Co Council 1967-79; Chancellor of Univ of Newcastle-upon-Tyne since 1989; Chm of Internat Dendrology Soc 1988-93; Pres ACC 1979-84; Member of Council of TAVRAS 1984-93; ADC to Gov of Kenya 1952-53; *cr* KG 1992, GCVO 1994, KStJ: *m* 1953, Lady Anne Katherine Lumley, da of 11th Earl of Scarbrough, and has issue.

Arms – Gules, on a chevron argent between three falcons proper, as many pellets. **Crest** – A bull passant the tail turned over the back gules. **Supporters** – Two bulls gules, each gorged with a collar gemelle or and charged on the shoulder with three mullets, pierced argent.
Seat – Blagdon, Seaton Burn, Newcastle-upon-Tyne.

SON LIVING

Hon MATTHEW WHITE, *b* 7 Feb 1958: *m* 1989, Anya Christine, da of Dr Robert Hurlbert, of Houston, Texas, and has issue living, Matthew White, *b* 27 Sept 1993.

DAUGHTERS LIVING

Hon Cecilia Anne, *b* 1953: *m* 1978, Berkeley Arthur Cole (*see* E Enniskillen).
Hon Rose Emily, *b* 1956: *m* 1980, Owen William Paterson, yr son of A. D. Paterson, of Oaklands, Tarporley, Cheshire, and has issue living, Felix Charles, *b* 1986, — Edward Owen, *b* 1988, — a da, *b* 1992.
Hon Mary Victoria, *b* 1962: *m* 1991, John James, son of P. L. James, of Meesden Hall, Herts.

BROTHER DECEASED

†*Rt Hon* Nicholas, *b* 1929; *cr Baron Ridley of Liddesdale* (Life Baron) 1992 (see that title); *d* 1993.

COLLATERAL BRANCHES LIVING

Grandson of late Major Hon Sir Jasper Nicholas Ridley, KCVO, OBE, 2nd son of 1st Viscount:—
  Issue of late Jasper Alexander Maurice Ridley, Lieut King's Roy Rifle Corps, *b* 1913, *d* on active ser in Italy 1943: *m* 1939, (Helen Laura) Cressida Bonham Carter (Keeper's Cottage, Gt Bottom, Stockton, Warminster, Wilts), da of Baroness Asquith of Yarnbury (Life Baroness):—
Sir Adam Nicholas, *b* 1942, *ed* Eton, and Balliol Coll, Oxford; Kt 1985; *m* 1st, 1970 (*m diss* 1976), Lady Katherine Rose Celestine Asquith, da of 2nd Earl of Oxford and Asquith; 2ndly, 1981, Margaret Anne (Biddy), yst da of Frederic L. Passmore, of Cobbetts, Virginia Water, Surrey, and has issue living (by 2nd *m*), Jasper, *b* 1987, — Luke, *b* (twin) 1987, — Jo (a son), *b* 1988.

(In remainder to the Baronetcy only)

Grandson of late Henry Colborne Maunoir Ridley, only son of late Rev William Henry Ridley, el son of late Rev Henry Colborne Ridley, 3rd son of 2nd baronet:—
  Issue of late Capt William Henry Wake Ridley, OBE, RN, *b* 1887, *d* 1955: *m* 1913, Vera, who *d* 1965, da of Charles Walker, formerly of Launceston, Tasmania, and widow of Gerald Stuart Eardley-Wilmot (Eardley- Wilmot, Bt, colls):—
William Terence Colborne, CB, OBE, *b* 1915; Rear-Adm; Port Adm HM Naval Base, Rosyth, 1971-72; 1939-45 War in SW Pacific (despatches twice); OBE (Mil) 1954, CB (Mil) 1968: *m* 1st, 1938, Barbara, who *d* 1989, da of R. L. Allen, of Hartford, Cheshire; 2ndly, 1993, Joan Elaine, née Dowding, widow of Rev John William Leneve Norman, and has issue living (by 1st *m*), Peter William Wake (24 Entry Hill Park, Bath, Avon BA2 5ND), *b* 1939; Capt RN: *m* 1965, Jenifer, da of Capt W. J. M. Teale, RN, and has issue living, Timothy Jaspar William *b* 1967, Nicolas Henry Sumner *b* 1971. *Residence* – 4 Hill View Rd, Bath, Avon BA1 6NX.

Granddaughter of late Arthur William Ridley, 3rd son of Rev Nicholas James Ridley, 2nd son of Rev Henry Colborne Ridley (ante):—

Issue of late Mervyn Adrian Toucher Ridley, b 1886, d 1951: m 1920, Sybil Henrietta, who d 1966, da of late Capt Charles Robert Kennet Fergusson, late Cameron Highlanders (Fergusson, Bt, colls), and widow of Capt Malcolm Cosmo Bonsor (Bonsor, Bt):—

Susan Frances, b 1921: m 1949, Major Richard Mark Chaplin, Coldstream Guards, and has issue living, David Frank, b 1951, — Mervyn Henry, b 1958, — Serena Jane, b 1954. Residence – Littlefield Farm, East Carlton, Market Harborough.

Grandson of late Rev Oliver Matthew Ridley, 3rd son of late Rev Henry Colborne Ridley (ante):—

Issue of late Major Edward Keane Ridley, b 1861, d 1947: m 1903, Ethel Janet, who d 1962, da of late Alexander Forbes Tweedie:—

Edward Alexander Keane, CB (c/o Coutts & Co, 440 Strand, WC2), b 1904; ed Wellington, and Keble Coll, Oxford (BA 1925, MA 1955); Solicitor 1928; Principal Assist Treasury Solicitor 1956-69; CB (Civil) 1963.

Grandchildren of late Frank Colborne Ridley, 5th son of late Rev Oliver Matthew Ridley (ante):—

Issue of late Keith Vivian Colborne Ridley, b 1904, d 1977: m 1933, Joan Madeline Marling (8 Mill Place, Lisvane, Cardiff CF4 5TF), da of late Rev Ernest Marling Roberts:—

Richard Nicholas (53 Pelham St, SW7 2NJ), b 1939: m 1st, 1963 (m diss 1973), Susan Gwynne, da of R. E. Haddingham; 2ndly, 1974 (m diss 1982), Penelope Anne, da of Roger Melville Brewer; 3rdly, 1984, Wendy Ann, da of Denis Hand-Bowman, of Pippins, Old Lane, Crowborough, E Sussex, and has issue living (by 1st m), Caroline Lois, b 1964, — Jacqueline Claire, b 1966, — (by 2nd m) Michael James, b 1976, — Nicholas Mark, b 1980, — (by 3rd m) Serena Eloise, b 1988. —— Henry Colborne (835, W Wolfram, Chicago, Ill, 60657, USA), b 1944: m 1969, Mary Randall, da of Alfred Acierto, of Chicago, and has issue living, Emily Marling, b 1971, — Elisa Acierto, b 1975. —— Gillian Elizabeth, b 1937: m 1st, 1960 (m diss 1980), John Hunt; 2ndly, 1983, Peter Dignus Garside, of 30 Cyncoed Rd, Cardiff, and has issue living (by 1st m), Graham (46 Northumberland Court, 2 Duke St, Banbury, Oxon OX16 8NJ), b 1961: m 1986 (m diss 1993), Cheryl Haidon, da of Gordon Taylor, of Stratford-upon-Avon, — Adam Christopher Jonathan, b 1974, — Robin Nicholas Andrew, b 1976, — Natalie Victoria, b 1962: m 1988, Simon Halling.

Granddaughter of late Rev Oliver Matthew Ridley (ante):—

Issue of late Clarence Oliver Ridley, OBE, b 1869, d 1951: m 1st, 1896, Anne Arabella, who d 1898, da of Gregory William Eccles, formerly of 6 Melrose Road, Southfields, SW; 2ndly, 1900, Gertrude Henrietta, who d 1951, second da of Henry Houseman (ante):—

(By 2nd m) Barbara Frances, b 1907: m 1937, Thomas C. S. Bullick, who d 1976, and has issue living, Timothy John, b 1938: m 1965, Tessa Mary Garstang, and has issue living, David Christopher b 1973, Claire Elizabeth b 1966, Judith Catherine b 1969, — Caroline Bridget, b 1941: m 1965, Anthony Townsend Parker, of 9 Holton Rd, Buckingham, and has issue living, Rachel b 1966, Alison b 1968, Jessica b 1971, — Sheila Mary, b 1945: m 1969, Geoffrey Scott Clark, RN, of 1 Mount Way, Princes Risborough, Bucks HP17 9BQ, and has issue living, Jeremy Scott b 1971, Jonathan Thomas b 1974. Residence – The Leys, Tarrant Keynston, Blandford, Dorset DT11 9JE.

PREDECESSORS – (1) MATTHEW WHITE, only surviving son of Matthew White, Sheriff of Northumberland 1756; cr a Baronet 1756, with remainder to the heirs-male of his sister, Elizabeth, wife of Matthew Ridley, of Heaton; d 1763; s by his nephew (2) Sir MATTHEW WHITE RIDLEY, 2nd Bt; b 1745: MP, for Newcastle-upon-Tyne: m 1777, Sarah, da of Benjamin Colborne, of Bath; d 1813; s by his el son (3) Sir MATTHEW WHITE, 3rd Bt; b 1778; MP for Newcastle-upon-Tyne: m 1803, Laura, da of George Hawkins; d 1836; s by his el son (4) Sir MATTHEW WHITE, 4th Bt; b 1807; MP for Northumberland N (C) 1859-60: m 1841, Cecilia Anne, da of Sir James Parke (who became subsequently Lord Wensleydale); d 1877; s by his el son (5) Sir MATTHEW WHITE, 5th Bt; b 1842; cr Viscount Ridley and Baron Wensleydale, of Blagdon and Blyth, co Northumberland (peerage of United Kingdom) 1900; MP for Northumberland N (C) 1868-85, and for Blackpool Div of Lancashire N Aug 1886 to Dec 1900; Under Sec of State for Home Depart 1878-80, Financial Sec to Treasury 1885-6, and Sec of State for Home Depart 1895-1900: m 1873, Hon Mary Georgina Marjoriebanks, who d 1899, da of 1st Baron Tweedmouth; d 1904; s by his son (6) MATTHEW WHITE, 2nd Viscount; b 1874; MP for Stalybridge (C) 1900-1904: m 1899, Hon Rosamond Cornelia Gladys Guest, who d 1947, da of of 1st Baron Wimborne; d 1916; s by his el son (7) MATTHEW WHITE, CBE, 3rd Viscount, b 1902; Chm of Northumberland Co Council 1940-46 and 1949-52, and Regional Controller, N Region, Min of Production 1942-49; Hon Col Northumberland Hussars (TA) 1962-64: m 1924, Ursula, OBE, who d 1967, da of Sir Edwin Landseer Lutyens, OB, KCIE, PRA, LLB (E Lytton); d 1964; s by his el son (8) MATTHEW WHITE, 4th Viscount and present peer; also Baron Wensleydale.

RIDLEY OF LIDDESDALE, BARONY OF (Ridley) (Life Baron 1992 Extinct 1993)

NICHOLAS RIDLEY, PC, yr son of 3rd Viscount Ridley; b 17 Feb 1929; ed Eton, and Balliol Coll, Oxford; late Capt Northumberland Hussars (TA); Joint Parl Sec Min of Technology June-Oct 1970, Parl Under-Sec of State Dept of Trade and Industry 1970-72, Min of State FCO 1979-81, Financial Sec to Treasury 1981-83, Sec of State for Transport 1983-86, for the Environment 1986-89, and for Trade and Industry 1989-90; MICE; MP for Cirencester and Tewkesbury (C) 1959-92; cr PC 1982, and Baron Ridley of Liddesdale, of Willimontswick, co Northumberland (Life Baron) 1992: m 1st, 1950 (m diss 1974), Hon Clayre Campbell, da of 4th Baron Stratheden and Campbell; 2ndly, 1979, Judith Mary, da of Dr Ernest John Coponet Kendall, of Epsom, Surrey, and d 4 March 1993, leaving issue by 1st m.

DAUGHTERS LIVING (By 1st marriage)

Hon Jane, b 1953: m 1986, Stephen Francis Thomas, yr son of Capt Sir William James Cooper Thomas, 2nd Bt (cr 1919), and has issue, two sons. Residence – 4 Scraesburgh Cottages, Jedburgh, Roxburghshire.

Hon Susanna, b 1955: m 1987, Charles Christopher Hugh Rickett, son of Christopher Owen Rickett, of Little Benhams, Rusper, Sussex, and has issue living, Benjamin Christopher, b 1988, — Matthew Charles, b 1991, — William Oliver Nicholas, b (twin) 1991.

Hon Jessica Clayre, b 1957: m 1991, David M. G. Fletcher, son of Col Derek Fletcher, and has issue living, Daisy Columba, b 1992. Residence – 46 Bolingbroke Rd, W14.

RIPPON OF HEXHAM, BARON (Rippon) (Life Baron 1987)

FRANGAS·NON·FLECTES·

(AUBREY) GEOFFREY FREDERICK RIPPON, PC, QC, son of late Arthur Ernest Sydney Rippon, of Surbiton, Surrey; b 28 May 1924; ed King's Coll, Taunton, and Brasenose Coll, Oxford (Hon Fellow); Bar Middle Temple 1948, QC 1964; Councillor of Surbiton 1945-54 (Mayor 1951-52), a Memb London Co Council 1952-61, Leader Conservative Party Group 1957-59, PPS to Min of Housing and Local Govt 1956-57, and to Min of Defence 1957-59, Parliamentary Sec to Min of Aviation 1959-61, Joint Parliamentary Min of Housing and Local Govt 1961-62, Min of Public Buildings and Works 1962-64 (Cabinet 1963-64), Min of Tech June to July 1970, Chancellor of Duchy of Lancaster 1970-72, Sec of State for the Environment 1972-74, Chm Conservative Foreign Affairs Cttee 1974-75; Chm Uni Chem plc, Dun & Bradstreet (UK) Ltd, and other Cos; Chm Court of London Univ since 1991; Grand Cross Order of Merit (Liechtenstein) 1967, Knight Grand Cross Order of North Star (Sweden) 1982; MP for Norwich South (C) 1955-64, and for Hexham 1966-87; cr PC 1962, and Baron Rippon of Hexham, of Hesleyside, co Northumberland (Life Baron) 1987: m 1946, Ann Leyland, da of Donald Yorke, MC, of Prenton, Cheshire, and has issue.

Arms – Barry wavy of fourteen argent and azure a cross patonce between in dexter chief and sinister base a hunting horn stringed sable. Crest – A stag's head erased and per fess wavy gules and argent in the argent two bars wavy azure attired gules each attire charged with two bars gold. Supporters – Dexter, on a mount of rocky moorland proper a bull gardant gules unguled or gorged with an ancient crown also or the horns gules each charged with two bars gold; sinister, on a like mount proper a stag gardant gules unguled or gorged with an ancient crown also or attired gules each attire charged with two bars gold. Motto – Frangas Non Flectes.
Residence – The Old Vicarage, Broomfield, nr Bridgwater, Somerset. Clubs – White's, Pratt's, MCC.

SON LIVING

Hon Anthony Simon Yorke, b 1959.

DAUGHTERS LIVING

Hon Fiona Carolyn, b 1947.
Hon Sarah Lovell, b 1950; ed Sherborne Girls' Sch, St Paul's Girls' Sch, and St Anne's Coll, Oxford (MA); Solicitor 1978, Bar New York 1980: m 1978 (m diss 1988), Michael Taylor, and has issue living, James Geoffrey Bethune, b 1979, — Alexander Edward Yorke, b 1982.
Hon Penelope Anne, b 1953: m 1984, Simon Rae, and has issue living, Albertine Helen Yorke, b 1985.

RITCHIE-CALDER, BARONY OF (Calder) (Extinct 1982).

SONS LIVING OF LIFE BARON

Hon Nigel David Ritchie (26 Boundary Rd, Northgate, Crawley, Sussex RH10 2BJ), b 1931; ed Merchant Taylors' Sch, and at Sidney Sussex Coll, Camb (MA); author and television script writer; Editor of New Scientist 1962-66: m 1954, Elisabeth, da of Alfred James Palmer and has issue.
Hon Angus Lindsay Ritchie, b 1942; ed Wallington Co Sch, King's Coll, Camb (MA), and Univ of Sussex (D Phil): an author, Reader in Literature and staff tutor in arts, Open Univ in Scotland 1979-93: m 1st, 1963 (m diss 1983), Jennifer, da of Prof David Daiches; 2ndly, 1986, Catherine Kyle, and has issue.
Hon Allan Graham Ritchie, b 1944; ed New Sherwood Sch, Ewell Tech Coll, and London Univ (BSc, PhD); Balloon Pilot and Mathematician: m 1st, 1967, Anne Margaret, da of Robert A. Wood; 2ndly, 1983, Lilian Lydia, da of Edward Godfrey, and has issue.

DAUGHTERS LIVING OF LIFE BARON

Hon Fiona Catherine Ritchie, b 1929; ed Rosebery Co Sch, Epsom, London Sch of Economics (BSc Econ); writer: m 1949, Ernest Rudd, DSc (Econ), PhD, of 19 South Parade, York YO2 2BA, and has issue.
Hon Isla Elizabeth Ritchie CALDER (38 Well Court, Edinburgh EH4 3BE) b 1947; ed Nonsuch Co Sch, Cheam, St George's, Edinburgh, Froebel Inst of Education, Roehampton, and Open Univ (BA); business consultant; resumed surname of Calder by deed poll: m 1971 (m diss 1983), Alan Evans.

WIDOW LIVING OF LIFE BARON

MABEL JANE FORBES (Baroness Ritchie-Calder) (4/57 Gillsland Rd, Edinburgh EH10 5BW), da of Dr David McKail, of Glasgow: m 1927, Baron Ritchie-Calder, CBE, (Life Baron), who d 1982.

RITCHIE OF DUNDEE, BARON (Ritchie) (Baron UK 1905)

Honour is acquired by virtue

(HAROLD) MALCOLM RITCHIE, 5th Baron; *b* 29 Aug 1919; *s* 1978; *ed* Stowe and Trin Coll, Oxford (MA); 1939-45 War as Capt KRRC: *m* 1948, Anne, da of late Col C. G. Johnstone, MC, of Durban, S Africa, and has issue.

Arms – Argent, an anchor sable, on a chief of the last three lions' heads erased of the first of the first. **Crest** – Out of an Eastern crown or a unicorn's head argent, armed of the first and charged on the neck with an anchor sable. **Supporters** – On either side a unicorn gules, gorged with an Eastern Crown or, the *dexter* charged on the shoulder with a purse or, the *sinister* with a balance, also or.
Residence – The Roundel, Springsteps, Winchelsea, Sussex.

SON LIVING

Hon CHARLES RUPERT RENDALL, *b* 15 March 1958: *m* 1984, Tara, da of Howard J. Koch, jr, of USA.

DAUGHTER LIVING

Hon Philippa Jane, *b* 1954.

SISTER LIVING

Hon Margaret Ruth, *b* 1913: *m* 1943, Major (William Arthur) Martin Chippindale, Worcestershire Regt (ret) (B Sandys), and has issue living, Philip John, *b* 1949: *m* 1978, Sally, da of Maurice J. Ashworth, of Fairlight, Sussex, — Jean Margaret, *b* 1945. *Residence* – 5 Fair Meadow, Playden, Rye, Sussex TN31 7NL.

COLLATERAL BRANCH LIVING

Grandchildren of late Lt-Col Hon Harold Ritchie, DSO (*infra*):—
Issue of late Maj Ian Charles Ritchie, RA, *b* 1908, *d* 1983: *m* 1st, 1931 (*m diss* 1946), Ann Dundas, da of late Gen Sir Robert Dundas Whigham, GCB, KCMG, DSO; 2ndly, 1946, Mrs Pamela Eveleen Elizabeth White (Highway House, Hog's Back, Seale, Farnham, Surrey), only da of Reginald Vickers, of Broomwood, Kettlewell Hill, Woking:—
(By 1st *m*) Harold Bruce (PO Box 431, Eltham, Victoria 3095, Australia), *b* 1933; *ed* Repton: *m* 1st, 1967 (*m diss* 1975), Shirley Anne, da of Gordon Steele, of Bury St Edmunds; 2ndly, 1977, Nancy Leith, da of Frank Richard Andrewartha, of Maryborough, Victoria, Australia, and has issue living, (by 1st *m*) Ian Angus Dundas, *b* 1972, — (by 2nd *m*) Fionnah Alice Ellen, *b* 1979. —— Fiona, *b* 1934: *m* 1967 (*m diss* 1975), Kenneth Stewart Donaldson, and *d* 1992.

Issue of late Lieut-Col Hon Harold Ritchie, DSO (with Bar), The Cameronians (Scottish Rifles), yr son of 1st Baron, *b* 1876, *ka* 1918: *m* 1907, Ella, who *d* 1956 (she *m* 2ndly, 1922, Surg-Lieut-Col Evelyn John Hansler Luxmoore, MC, Life Guards, who *d* 1955), da of late Robert Chambers Priestley, of Terriers House, High Wycombe, Bucks:—
William Nigel, *b* 1914; is a Flt-Lt RAF Vol Res: *m* 1939, Baroness Sibylla, da of late Baron von Hirschberg of Murnau, Bavaria, and has issue living, James Antony Gregor (108A Dartmouth Rd, NW2), *b* 1945; *ed* Harrow, and Ch Ch Oxford, — Andrew William (53 Egerton Gdns, SW3), *b* 1947; *ed* Harrow, and Trin Coll, Camb, — Caroline Elisabeth (*Hon Mrs Hugh Gathorne-Hardy*) *b* 1943: *m* 1971, Hon Hugh Gathorne- Hardy (*see* E Cranbrook). *Residence* – Mariners, Bradfield, Berks.

PREDECESSORS – (1) *Rt Hon* CHARLES THOMSON Ritchie, PC (whose el brother was *cr* a *Baronet* 1903), son of late William Ritchie, of Rockhill, Broughty Ferry, *b* 1838; MP for Tower Hamlets (C) Feb 1874 to Nov 1885, for Tower Hamlets, St George Div·1885 to 1892, and for Croydon May 1895 to Dec 1905; Sec to the Admiralty June 1885 to Jan 1886, Pres of Local Govt Board Aug 1886-1892 (with a seat in the Cabinet from April 1887), Pres of Board of Trade (with seat in the Cabinet) June 1895 to Oct 1900, Sec of State for Home Depart Oct 1900 to Aug 1902, and Chancellor of the Exchequer Aug 1902 to Sept 1903; *cr Baron Ritchie of Dundee*, of Welders, Chalfont St Giles, co Buckingham (peerage of United Kingdom) Dec 1905: *m* 1858, Margaret, who *d* 1906, da of late Thomas Ower, of Perth; *d* Jan 1906; *s* by his el surviving son (2) CHARLES, 2nd Baron; *b* 1866; was Chm of Port of London Authority 1925-41, and Pres of Dock and Harbour Authorities Asso 1938-41: *m* 1898, Sarah Ruth, who *d* 1950, da of late Louis Jennings MP: *d* 1948; *s* by his el surviving son (3) JOHN KENNETH, PC, 3rd Baron; *b* 1902; Chm of London Stock Exchange 1959-65: *m* 1945, Joan Beatrice, who *d* 1963, da of late Rev Henry Charles Lenox Tindall, of Peasmarsh, Sussex; *d* 1975; *s* by his brother (4) COLIN NEVILLE OWER, 4th Baron; *b* 1908; Headmaster of Brickwall Sch, E Sussex: *m* 1943, Anne Petronill, who *d* 1989, da of Henry Curteis Burra, of Rye, and formerly wife of John Francis Burra Huntley; *d* 1978; *s* by his brother (5) HAROLD MALCOLM, 5th Baron, and present peer.

RIVERDALE, BARON (Balfour) (Baron UK 1935, Bt UK 1929)

Faithful in difficulties

ROBERT ARTHUR BALFOUR, 2nd Baron, and 2nd Baronet; *b* 1 Sept 1901; *s* 1957; *ed* Aysgarth, and at Oundle; late Lt Cdr RNVR; Pres of Balfour & Darwins, Ltd, and a Dir of subsidiary Cos of the Group, Patron of Sheffield Savings Bank (Gov 1948-58), Town Trustee of Sheffield Town Trust, a DL of S Yorks county; elected Master of Cutlers' Co of Sheffield 1946; appointed Consul for Belgium for Sheffield area 1945; Pres of Milling Cutter and Reamer Trade Assocn 1936-54 (Vice-Pres 1954-57, Hon Vice-Pres 1958), of Twist Drill Traders' Assocn 1946-55, and of Nat Federation of Engineers' Tool Manufacturers 1951-57 (Hon Vice-Pres since 1957), and Chm of British Council of Australian Assocn of British Manufacturers 1954-57; Pres of Sheffield Chamber of Commerce 1950 (Joint Hon Sec since 1957), and Member of British National Cttee, International Chamber of Commerce, of National Production Advisory Cttee, and of W Hemisphere Exports Council (formerly Dollar Exports Council) 1957-61; a Member of Management Cttee of High Speed Steel Assocn 1947-65, of Executive Council of Assocn of British Chambers of Commerce since 1950 (Vice-Pres 1952-54, Chm of Overseas Cttee 1953-57, Dep Pres 1954-57, Pres 1957-58), of Crucible and High Speed Steel Conference, Standing Cttee since 1951, and Guardian of Standard of Wrought Plate within City of Sheffield since 1948; Commodore of Roy Cruising Club 1961-66; 1939-45 War as Lt-Cdr RNVR; a Chevalier of Order of the Crown of Belgium, Officer of Order of Leopold II of Belgium, and Medaille Civique de Première Classe of Belgium: *m* 1st 1926, Nancy Marguerite, who *d* 1928, da of late Engineer Rear-Adm Mark Rundle, DSO; 2ndly 1933, Christian Mary, who *d* 1991, da of late Maj Arthur Rowland Hill (*see* V Hill, colls), and has issue by 1st and 2nd *m*.

Arms – Per chevron argent and sable, in chief two crosses pattée of the second and in base a sun in splendour per pale or and of the first. **Crest** – In front of a dragon's head sable a sun as in the arms. **Supporters** – On either side a dragon sable, each charged on the wing, the dexter with a garb, and the sinister with a cross pattée or.
Residence – Ropes, Grindleford, near Sheffield. *Clubs* – Bath, Royal Cruising, Sheffield.

SONS LIVING *(By 1st marriage)*

Hon MARK ROBIN, *b* 16 July 1927; *ed* Aysgarth Sch, Yorks, and Trin Coll Sch, Port Hope, Canada; Chm of Ashdell Sch Trust Ltd, Fingland Services Ltd, and Yorkshire Cancer Research Campaign; Pres of Nat Federn of Engineer's Tool Manufacturers 1974-76; Chm of Sheffield Rolling Mills Ltd 1969-75, and Balfour Darwins Ltd 1971-75; A Member of Exec Cttee of BISPA 1967-75; Pres Nat Fedn of Engineers Tool Manufacturers 1974; Dir of Overseas Operations, Edgar Allen Balfour Ltd, Chm of Eagle & Globe Steel Ltd, Aust, Eagle & Globe Products Pty Ltd Aust, Eagle & Globe (Hong Kong) Ltd, Hong Kong, Arthur Balfour Ltd Canada until 1979; Chm Export Year Cttee for S Yorks; Pres of Sheffield Chamber of Commerce 1978; a Member of Aust British Trade Assocn Council, and Aust and NZ Trade Advisory Cttee until 1986; a Consul for Finland; a Member of Blacksmiths' Co, Master of Cutler's Co 1969-70 and Freeman of City of London; Order of Lion of Finland 1975, Silver Jubilee Medal 1977: *m* 1959, Susan Ann, el da of R. P. Phillips, of The Mews, 48 Ivy Park Rd, Sheffield, and has issue living, Anthony Robert, *b* 1960, — Nancy Ann, *b* 1963, — Kate Frances, *b* 1967. *Residence* – Fairways, Saltergate Lane, Bamford, nr Sheffield, Derbys S30 2BE. *Club* – Sheffield.

(By 2nd marriage)

Hon David Rowland, *b* 1938; *ed* Harrow, and Queens' Coll, Camb.

DAUGHTER LIVING *(By 2nd marriage)*

Hon Frances Christian, *b* 1946; *ed* Wycombe Abbey, and New Hall, Camb.

BROTHER LIVING

Hon Francis Henry, TD, *b* 1905; *ed* Oundle; late Maj RA (TA); Knt of Order of Dannebrog of Denmark; Vice-Consul for Denmark 1947-60: *m* 1st, 1932, Muriel Anne, who *d* 1970, da of late Eng Rear-Adm Ralph Berry; 2ndly, 1971, Daphne Cecelia, da of A. C. Moss, of Rochfort, Bathampton, Bath, and has issue living, (by 1st *m*) Arthur Michael (Wynthrop, Chorleywood Rd, Rickmansworth, Herts), *b* 1938; *ed* Oundle, and Bristol Univ (BSc 1960); a GIMechE: *m* 1962, Rita Ann, el da of L. C. Fance, of 21 Ashley Close, Charlton Kings, Cheltenham, and has issue living, Edward Francis *b* 1965, James Henry *b* 1966, Anna Louise *b* 1971, — Jeremy Ralph (151 Knowle Lane, Brentry, Bristol), *b* 1948; *ed* Oundle, and Plymouth Polytechnic (BSc): *m* 1974, Wendy May, da of W. H. Seal, of 153 Southdown Rd, Bath, and has issue living, Robert Henry *b* 1980, Rebecca Anne *b* 1983, — Bridget Anne, *b* 1933: *m* 1957, Ewan Peter Graham, of 8 Shrimpton Close, Knotty Green, Beaconsfield, Bucks, and has issue living, Philip James *b* 1959, Stephen Paul *b* 1960, Adam Timothy *b* 1964, — Frances Elizabeth, *b* 1934: *m* 1958, Charles David Plows, MB, and has issue living, Ian Julian *b* 1960, Christopher Mark *b* 1962. *Residence* – Holcombe Cottage, Holcombe Lane, Bathampton, Bath BA2 6UN.

SISTER LIVING

Hon Primrose Keighley, *b* 1913: *m* 1st, 1933, Oliver Grahame Hall, who *d* 1974, having assumed by deed poll 1945 the christian name of Claude in lieu of Oliver, and the surname of Muncaster in lieu of his patronymic; 2ndly, 1975, Robert John Minnitt, CMG, and has issue living, (by 1st *m*), Martin Grahame Muncaster (Clouds Hill, Lynchmere, Haslemere), *b* 1934: *m* 1959, Iona Gilbert, and has issue living, Timothy Grahame MacGeoch *b* 1960, Oliver Martin Keighley *b* 1964, Miranda Jane *b*

1962, — Clive Muncaster (c/o Whitelocks, Sutton, Pulborough, Sussex), *b* 1936: *m* 1959, Ursula Mary, el da of late Capt Edward Brotherton-Ratcliffe, and has issue living, Maximilian Nicholas Clive *b* 1960, Peregrine Luke (96 West Hill, Hitchin, Herts SG5 2HX) *b* 1962: *m* 1986, Catherine Margaret, da of Michael Andrew Holford, of Icknield House, Westmill Lane, Ickleford, Hitchin, Herts (and has issue living, Dominic Peregrine *b* 1992, Harriet Mary *b* 1988, Georgina Margaret *b* 1990), Crispin Claude *b* 1965, Caspar Amadeus *b* 1967, Quentin Augustine *b* 1971. *Residence* – Whitelocks, Sutton, Pulborough, Sussex. *Club* – Lansdowne.

PREDECESSOR – (1) ARTHUR Balfour, GBE, son of late Herbert Balfour; *b* 1873; a Steel Manufacturer, Chm of Arthur Balfour & Co, Ltd, and of C Meadows & Co, Ltd, of Sheffield, Chm of Advisory Council for Scientific and Industrial Research 1937-57, Vice-Consul for Denmark 1899-1947, Master Cutler of Sheffield 1911-12, Pres of Asso of British Chambers of Commerce 1923-4, and of British Council 1947-50; *cr* KBE (Civil) 1923, a *Baronet* 1929, *Baron Riverdale*, of Sheffield, co York (peerage of United Kingdom) 1935, and GBE (Civil) 1942: *m* 1899, Frances Josephine Keighley (a CStJ), who *d* 1960, da of late Charles Henry Bingham; *d* 1957: *s* by his el son (2) ROBERT ARTHUR, 2nd Baron and present peer.

RIX, BARON (Rix) (Life Baron 1992)

BRIAN NORMAN ROGER RIX, CBE, son of late Herbert Dobson Rix, of E Yorks; *b* 27 Jan 1924; *ed* Bootham Sch, York; Hon MA Hull 1981, Open Univ 1983, Hon DUniv Essex 1984, Hon LLD Manchester 1986, Hon DSc Nottingham 1987, Hon LLD Dundee 1994; served 1939-45 War in RAF also a Bevin Boy; actor-manager 1948-77 (particularly noted for a series of successful farces at the Whitehall Theatre), actor in films and on television, BBC TV and Radio presenter; Dir and Theatre Controller Cooney-Marsh Group 1977-80; Sec-Gen Royal Soc for Mentally Handicapped Children and Adults (MENCAP) 1980-87, Chm since 1988; Chm Independent Development Council for People with Mental Handicap 1981-88; Member Arts Council 1986-93 (Chm Drama Panel until 1993), Member Barbican Centre Cttee since 1993, Chm Friends of Normansfield since 1976, Chm Libertas since 1987; Hon Vice-Pres Radio Soc of GB; DL Greater London 1987, Vice Lord Lieut since 1988; author; *cr* CBE (Civil) 1977, Knt 1986, and *Baron Rix*, of Whitehall, in the City of Westminster, and of Hornsea in Yorkshire (Life Baron) 1992: *m* 1949, Elspet Jeans (actress as Elspet Gray), da of late James MacGregor-Gray, of Surrey, and has issue.

Arms – Per chevron double arched points upwards gules and or, in chief a rose argent between two suns in splendour also or and in base chevronwise a Greek mask of comedy vert and a like mask of tragedy sable. **Crest** – The upper part of a ship's wheel or, standing thereon an avocet wings elevated proper, gorged with a cronal studded gold, pendant therefrom a cross crosslet fitchy sable. **Supporters** – On either side a labrador dog or, the compartment comprising a grassy mount proper, growing therefrom roses argent barbed and seeded proper, slipped and leaved vert.
Residence – 8 Ellerton Rd, Wimbledon Common, SW20 0EP. *Clubs* – Garrick, Lord's Taverners (Pres 1970), MCC.

SONS LIVING

Hon James MacGregor, *b* 1958; *ed* St Paul's Sch, and Univ of Kent at Canterbury (BA): *m* 1980, Helen Middleton Murry, and has issue living, Benjamin, *b* 1982, — Jack, *b* 1984. *Residence* – 47 Ritherdon Rd, SW17 8QE.
(*Hon*) Jonathan Robert MacGregor, *b* 1960; does not use courtesy title; *ed* St Paul's Sch, and Warwick Univ (BEd): *m* 1991, Caroline Cook.

DAUGHTERS LIVING

Hon Elspet Shelley, *b* 1951. *Residence* – 8/10 Woodham Crescent, Whitton, Middx.
Hon Louisa MacGregor, *b* 1955; *ed* Queen's Gate Sch, and LAMDA; actress: *m* 1981 (*m diss* 1992), Jonathan Coy, actor, and has issue living, Jolyon, *b* 1985, — Charlotte Elizabeth, *b* 1983. *Residence* – 13 Combemartin Rd, Southfields, SW18 5PP.

ROBBINS, BARONY OF (Robbins) (Extinct 1984)

SON LIVING OF LIFE BARON

Hon Richard, *b* 1927; *ed* Dauntsey's Sch, and New Coll, Oxford: *m* 1st, 1952 (*m diss* 1961); 2ndly, 1961, Mrs Brenda Dorothy Rooker Roberts, da of late Douglas Edward Clark, and has issue by 1st *m*. *Residence* – 50 Highbury Hill, N5 1HP.

DAUGHTER LIVING OF LIFE BARON

Hon Anne *b* 1925; *ed* N London Collegiate Sch, and Univ Coll, London: *m* 1958, Christopher Johnson, of 39 Wood Lane, N6, and has issue.

WIDOW LIVING OF LIFE BARON

IRIS ELIZABETH (*Baroness Robbins*) (Southwood Hall, N6), da of A. G. Gardiner, of The Spinney, Whiteleaf, Bucks: *m* 1924, Baron Robbins, CH, CB (Life Baron), who *d* 1984.

ROBENS OF WOLDINGHAM, BARON (Robens) (Life Baron 1961)

ALFRED ROBENS, PC, son of late George Robens, of Manchester; *b* 18 Dec 1910; Hon DCL Newcastle; Hon LLD Leicester and Manchester; Hon MIMinE; a Fellow of Manchester Coll of Science and Tech; a Member of Manchester City Council 1942-45, PPS to Min of Transport 1945-47, Parl Sec to Min of Fuel and Power 1947-51, Min of Labour and National Ser April to Oct 1951, and Dep Chm of National Coal Board Oct 1960 to Feb 1961, and Chm 1961-71; a Member of Roy Commn on Trade Unions and Employers' Assocns 1965-68, a Gov of Queen Elizabeth Training Coll for Disabled since 1951, and of London Sch of Economics since 1965, Chm of Board of Govs, Guy's Hosp since 1965, a Dir of Bank of England, and of Times Newspapers since 1966; Pres of Advertising Assocn 1963-67; Chm of Joint Steering Cttee for Malta 1967; Chancellor of Univ of Surrey 1966-77. Chm of Council of Manchester Business Sch since 1964, a Member of NEDC 1962-72, Dep Chm of Foundation on Automation and Human Development since 1962, Chm of Special Cttee of Enquiry into Health and Safety of Persons in Employment, of Vickers Ltd, and of Johnson Matthey Ltd; R Soc of Arts, Albert Medal 1977; MP for Wansbeck Div of Northumberland (*Lab*) 1945-50, and for Blyth 1950-60; *cr* PC 1951, and *Baron Robens of Woldingham*, of Woldingham, co Surrey (Life Baron) 1961: *m* 1936, Eva, da of Frederick Powell, of Manchester.
Residence – Salcombe Court, Cliff Rd, Salcombe, Devon TQ8 8JQ.

ROBERTHALL, BARONY (Hall) (Extinct 1988)

DAUGHTERS LIVING OF LIFE BARON (*By 1st marriage*)

Hon Felicity Margaret, *b* 1936; *ed* Oxford High School for Girls, and Lady Margaret Hall, Oxford; Dir Urban Inst Press, Washington DC: *m* 1957, Thomas Skidmore, of 44 Halsey St, Providence, Rhode Island 02706, USA, and has issue.
Hon Anthea Mary, *b* 1939; *ed* Oxford High Sch for Girls, and Lady Margaret Hall, Oxford; Journalist: *m* 1966, (David) Max Wilkinson, 112 Hemingford Rd, N1 1DE, and has issue.

WIDOW LIVING OF LIFE BARON

PERILLA THYME (*Baroness Roberthall*), da of late Sir Richard Vynne Southwell, and formerly wife of Patrick Horace Nowell-Smith: *m* 1968, as his 2nd wife, Baron Roberthall, KCMG, CB (Life Baron), who *d* 1988. *Residence* – Quarry, Trenance, Newquay, Cornwall.

Roberts, see Baron Goronwy-Roberts.

ROBERTSON OF OAKRIDGE, BARON (Robertson) (Baron UK 1961 Bt UK 1919)

WILLIAM RONALD ROBERTSON, 2nd Baron, and 3rd Baronet; *b* 8 Dec 1930; *s* 1974; *ed* Charterhouse; Maj (ret) R Scots Greys: *m* 1972, Celia Jane, yr da of William Elworthy, of the Manor House, Winterborne Monkton, Dorchester, Dorset, and has issue.

Arms – Gules, two swords in saltire argent, hilted and pommelled gold, the points downwards, between in chief a sun in splendour, in base a fleur-de-lis or, and in fesse two wolves' heads erased of the second. **Crest** – Issuant from a coronet of fleur-de-lis or, a demi-wolf argent, gorged with an Eastern crown gold supporting with the dexter paw a lance proper thereon a pennon per fesse gules and argent. **Supporters** – *Dexter*, a grey charger in review order; *sinister*, a springbok proper.

SON LIVING

Hon WILLIAM BRIAN ELWORTHY, *b* 15 Nov 1975.

SISTERS LIVING

Hon Christine Veronica Helen, *b* 1927: *m* 1949, Col Robert Hugh Cuming, MBE, JP, DL, R Scots Greys (ret) and has issue living, Brian Hugh Douglas, *b* 1950; Lt-Cdr RN: *m* 1977, M. Jane, da of Capt R. N. Heard, RN, and has issue living, Alexander Hugh Robert *b* 1983, Hamish Arthur Brian *b* 1984, Victoria Helen *b* 1980, — Alastair Nicholas, *b* 1958; Capt R Scots Dragoon Gds (ret), — Frances Mary Christine, *b* 1952: *m* 1981, Cdr Francis John Cadman Bradshaw, LVO, RN (*see* B Cadman).
Hon (Catherine) Fiona, *b* 1939: *m* 1965, Allan Claude Chapman, DL, and has issue living, Caroline Fiona, *b* 1968, — Katharine Jean, *b* (twin) 1968: *m* 1993, David J. Cook.

AUNT LIVING

Helen Millicent (*Helen, Lady Vincent*), *b* 1905: *m* 1938, Sir Lacey Eric Vincent, 2nd Bt (*cr* 1936), who *d* 1963.

PREDECESSOR – **(1)** *Field-Marshal Sir* WILLIAM ROBERT Robertson, GCB, GCMG, GCVO, DSO, son of late Thomas Charles Robertson; *b* 1860; enlisted in 16th Lancers 1877; commissioned as 2nd Lieut 3rd Dragoon Guards 1888; Chitral Relief Force 1895 (severely wounded DSO), S Africa 1900 as DAAG, Army Head Quarters, European War 1914-19, becoming Ch of Imperial Gen Staff (Legion of Honour, KCB, Lieut-Gen, Croix de Guerre, Orders of Crown of Italy, of White Eagle of Serbia with Swords, of Chia Ho of China, of St Alexander Nevsky of Russia and of Rising Sun of Japan, GCMG, thanked by Parliament, granted £10,000); *cr* a *Baronet* 1919: *m* 1894, Mildred Adelaide, who *d* 1942, da of late Lieut-Gen T. C. Palin, Indian Army, *d* 1933; *s* by his son **(2)** BRIAN HUBERT, GCB, GBE, KCMG, KCVO, DSO, MC, 2nd Bt, *b* 1896; mil Gov of British Zone, Germany 1947-49, UK High Commr for Germany 1949-50, C-in-C, MELF 1950-53, Chm of British Transport Commn 1953-61; Col Comdr RE 1950-60, and REME 1951-61; *cr Baron Robertson of Oakridge*, of Oakridge, Glos (peerage of UK) 1961: *m* 1926, Edith Christina, OStJ, who *d* 1982, da of James Black Macindoe, of Glasgow; *d* 1974; *s* by his son **(3)** WILLIAM RONALD, 2nd Baron and present peer.

ROBINS, BARONY OF (Robins) (Extinct 1962)

DAUGHTERS LIVING OF FIRST BARON

Hon Diana Mary Wroughton, *b* 1920: *m* 1940, Col John Offley Crewe-Read, OBE, of Croft House, Aston Tirrold, nr Didcot, Oxon, and has issue living, David Offley (Werg's Farm, Old Burghclere, Hants), *b* 1944: *m* 1966, Lisa, elder da of H. J. Dyer, of Odiham, and has issue living, Caspian Dante David Offley *b* 1967, Daniel Osiris John *b* 1972, Gabriella Diana *b* 1974, — Christopher Thomas Malcolm, *b* 1951: *m* 1980 (*m diss* 1989), Belinda, yst da of Sir Reginald Bennett, VRD, of 30 Strand-on-the-Green, W4, and has issue living, Chloe Evelyn *b* 1985, Madeleine Brittain *b* 1988, — Joanna Christina (17 The Little Boltons, SW10 9LJ), *b* 1941: *m* 1st 1962 (*m diss* 1969), Capt John Anthony Frank Morton, late RHA; 2ndly, 1974, Alasdair James Hew Saunders (*see* Culme-Seymour Bt, colls), and has issue living (by 1st *m*), Dominic Jonathan Ellis *b* 1964, Serena Mary Louise *b* 1966, (by 2nd *m*) Thomas Alasdair *b* 1978, Alice Elizabeth *b* 1975.
Hon Philippa Mary Ellis, *b* 1923: *m* 1946, Col Patrick James Danvers McCraith, MC, TD, DL, and has issue living, Michael Ellis, *b* 1949: *m* 1981, Sarah Anne, el da of William Bromley, of Apperley, Gerrards Cross, Bucks, and has issue living, Flora Kate Mary *b* 1982, Alice Clementine *b* 1985, — Sally Victoria, *b* 1947: *m* 1971, Patrick George Francis Lort-Phillips, Capt 9th/12th Lancers (V Cobham, colls, 1972-73 Edn), and has issue living, Harry Patrick Francis *b* 1975, Charles Arthur Ellis *b* 1980, Alexandra Mary *b* 1972. *Residence* – Cranfield House, Southwell, Notts.

ROBINSON, BARONY OF (Lister Robinson) (Extinct 1952)

DAUGHTER LIVING OF FIRST BARON

Hon Mary Teresa, *b* 1914; *m* 1st, 1939 (*m diss* 1951), Wing Cdr Paul Henry Mills Richey, DFC, who *d* 1989; 2ndly, 1979, Peter Leighton Ryde, of 4 Phene St, SW3, and has issue living (by 1st *m*), Peter Michael (The White House, Lee, nr Ilfracombe, N Devon), *b* 1945, — Simon Anthony (145 Brecknock Rd, N19), *b* 1947: *m* 1976, Christine Anne Fox, and has issue living, Anna Colette *b* 1979, — Ann Mary Teresa, *b* 1941: *m* 1st, 1960, (*m diss* 1969), Alistair Norris Cowin; 2ndly, 1975, Peter Mavrogordato, of School Cottage, Hardmead, Bucks, and has issue living, (by 1st *m*), Amanda Mary Theresa *b* 1961, Emma Mary Teresa *b* 1963, — Pauline Mary (9 Alacross Rd, W5), *b* 1943: *m* 1967 (*m diss* 1983), Antony Michael Lawson-Smith, and has issue living, Dominic Antony *b* 1968, Michael Charles *b* 1971. *Residence* – 4 Phene St, SW3.

ROBOROUGH, BARON (Lopes) (Baron UK 1938, Bt UK 1805)

Do to another as you would be done by

HENRY MASSEY LOPES, 3rd Baron, and 6th Baronet; *b* 2 Feb 1940; *s* 1992; *ed* Eton; late Lieut Coldstream Guards: *m* 1st, 1968 (*m diss* 1986), Robyn Zenda Carol, eldest da of John Bromwich, of Stamford Hill, Bacchus Marsh, Victoria, Australia; 2ndly, 1986, Sarah Anne Pipon, 2nd da of Colin Baker, of The Glebe House, Peter Tavy, Tavistock, Devon, and has issue by 1st and 2nd *m*.

Arms – Quarterly: 1st and 4th, azure, a chevron or charged with three bars gemells; gules between three eagles rising of the second on a chief of the second five lozenges of the first; 2nd and 3rd, in a landscape field a fountain proper, thereout issuing a palm-tree also proper. **Crests** – 1st, a lion sejant erminois gorged with a collar gemelle gules, the dexter forepaw resting on a lozenge azure; 2nd, a dexter arm couped and embowed, habited purpure, purtled and diapered or, cuffed argent, holding in the hand proper a palm-branch vert. **Supporters** – *Dexter*, a lion proper gorged with a collar gemel and charged on the shoulder with a lozenge azure; *sinister*, a bull also proper, charged on the shoulder with a like lozenge.
Seat – Maristow, Roborough, S Devon. *Residence* – Bickham House, Roborough, S Devon.

SONS LIVING (By 1st marriage)

Hon MASSEY JOHN HENRY, *b* 22 Dec 1969; *ed* Eton, and — Coll, Durham.
Hon Andrew James, *b* 1971; *ed* Plymouth Coll: *m* 1993, Kristina Marie Overbeck.

DAUGHTERS LIVING *(By 1st marriage)*

Hon Katie Victoria, *b* 1976.
Hon Melinda Claire, *b* 1978.

(by 2nd marriage)

Hon Emily Jane, *b* 1987.
Hon Louisa Constance, *b* 1989.

BROTHER LIVING

Hon George Edward, *b* 1945; *ed* Eton, and RAC Cirencester: *m* 1975, Hon Sarah Violet Astor, da of 2nd Baron Astor of Hever, and has issue living, Harry Marcus George, *b* 1977; *ed* Eton, — Lorna Violet, *b* 1979, — Sabrina Helen, *b* 1983. *Residence* – Gnaton Hall, Yealmpton, Plymouth, Devon PL8 2HU.

WIDOW LIVING OF SECOND BARON

HELEN (*Helen, Baroness Roborough*), only da of late Lt-Col Edward Alfred Finch Dawson, Rifle Bde, of Launde Abbey, Leics: *m* 1936, Maj the 2nd Baron, who *d* 1992. *Residence* – Bickham Barton, Roborough, S Devon.

PREDECESSORS – (1) MANASSEH MASSEY Lopes, son of late Mordecai- Rodrigues Lopes, of Clapham, SW; *b* 1755; was successively MP for Evesham, South Devon, Barnstaple, and Westbury; *cr* a *Baronet* 1805 with special remainder to his nephew, Ralph Franco, son of his yr sister, Esther, wife of Abraham Franco, of London: *m* 1795, Charlotte, who *d* 1833, da of late John Yeates, of Monmouthshire; *d* 1831; *s* by his nephew (2) RALPH (ante), 2nd Bt; *b* 1788; assumed by Roy licence 1831 the surname of Lopes in lieu of his patronymic and the arms of Lopes quarterly with those of Franco; sat as MP for Westbury (*C*) 1832-7 and 1841-7, and for South Devonshire (*C*)1849-54: *m* 1817, Susan Gibbs, who *d* 1870, el da of late A. Ludlow, of Heywood House, Wilts; *d* 1854; *s* by his el son (3) (LOPES) MASSEY, PC, 3rd Bt; *b* 1818; sat as MP for Westbury (*C*) 1857-68, and Devonshire, S Div 1868-85, and was a Civil Lord of the Admiralty 1874-80: *m* 1st, 1854, Hon Bertha Yarde-Buller, who *d* 1872, da of 1st Baron Churston: 2ndly, 1874, Louisa, who *d* April 1908, da of Sir Robert William Newman, 1st Bt (*cr* 1836); *d* Jan 1908; *s* by his only son (4) HENRY YARDE BULLER, 4th Bt; *b* 1859; sat as MP for Grantham (*C*) 1892-1900; *cr Baron Roborough*, of Maristow, co Devon (peerage of United Kingdom) Jan 1938: *m* 1891, Lady Albertha Louisa Florence Edgcumbe, who *d* 1941, da of 4th Earl of Mount Edgcumbe; *d* April 1938; *s* by his only son (5) MASSEY HENRY EDGCUMBE, 2nd Baron; *b* 1903, Major Royal Scots Greys, Hon Col Devon Army Cadet Force, 1939-45 War with RAC (wounded twice), ADC to Gov-Gen of S Africa 1936, DL Exeter 1946, Vice-Lieut 1951-58, Lord Lieut and Custos Rotulorum 1958-78, High Steward Barnstaple, 1st Pres Devon Historical Buildings Trust 1965-78, and Memb of Duchy of Cornwall Council 1958-68: *m* 1936, Helen, only da of late Lt-Col Edward Alfred Finch Dawson, Rifle Bde, of Launde Abbey, Leics; *d* 1992; *s* by his elder son (6) HENRY MASSEY 3rd Baron and present peer.

ROBSON OF KIDDINGTON, BARONESS (Robson) (Life Baroness 1974)

INGA-STINA ROBSON, da of Erik R. Arvidsson, of Stockholm; *b* 20 Aug 1919; Pres Women's Liberal Fedn 1968-69 and 1969-70; Pres Liberal Party Organisation 1970-71; former Chm of Liberal Party Environment Panel; former Chm Queen Charlotte's and Chelsea Hosps Special Trustees, and former Chm of S-W Thames Regional Health Authority; Chm Anglo-Swedish Soc 1982-92; *cr Baroness Robson of Kiddington*, of Kiddington in Oxfordshire (Life Baroness) 1974: *m* 1940, Sir Lawrence William Robson, FCA, FCMA, JDipMA, who *d* 1982, and has issue.

Arms – Or, a Viking ship, oars in action sable, between two fleurs-de-lys azure. **Supporters** – *Dexter*, a sea stag argent attired and finned or. *Sinister*, a sea horse also argent, crined and finned or, the tails proper and each gorged with a Baron's coronet also proper.
Residences – The Dower House, Kiddington, Woodstock, Oxon OX20 1BU; 1 Whitehall Place, SW1.

SON LIVING

Hon (Erik) Maurice William (Kiddington Hall, Woodstock, Oxon; Erchless Castle, Struy, by Beauly, Inverness), *b* 1943; *ed* Eton, and Ch Ch, Oxford (MA); FCA: *m* 1985, Chloe Annabel, elder da of Richard Arthur Edwards, of Ipswich, Suffolk (*see* B Hylton, colls), and has issue living, James Patrick, *b* 1990, — Natasha Lilly, *b* 1993.

DAUGHTERS LIVING

Hon Kristina Elizabeth, *b* 1946: *m* 1967, Iain McLaren Mason, of 17 Crick Rd, Oxford.
Hon Vanessa Jane, *b* 1949: *m* 1973, Jonathan Martin Potter, of Tyler Hall, Tyler Hill, Canterbury, Kent.

ROCHDALE, VISCOUNT (Kemp) (Baron UK 1913, Viscount UK 1960)

I hope for light

ST JOHN DURIVAL KEMP, 2nd Viscount; *b* 15 Jan 1938; *s* 1993; *ed* Eton: *m* 1st, 1960 (*m diss* 1974), Serena Jane, da of late (James Edward) Michael Clark-Hall, of Wissenden, Bethersden, Kent; 2ndly, 1976, Elizabeth, da of Robert Norman Rossiter Boldon, and formerly wife of James Michael Anderton, and has issue by 1st *m*.

Arms – Argent, a chevron engrailed gules between two estoiles in chief azure, and a rose of the second in base barbed and seeded proper. **Crest** – A cubit arm erect, vested argent, cuffed azure, the hand proper grasping a chaplet vert encircling a rose as in the arms. **Supporters** – On either side a ram or, charged on the shoulder with a rose gules, slipped and leaved proper.
Address – c/o House of Lords, SW1A 0PW.

SONS LIVING (By 1st marriage)

Hon JONATHAN HUGO DURIVAL, *b* 10 June 1961; *ed* Stowe: *m* 1994, Ming Xian, only da of Mr and Mrs Zhu, of Shanghai.
Hon Christopher George, *b* 1969.

DAUGHTERS LIVING (By 1st marriage)

Hon Joanna Victoria, *b* 1964.
Hon Susanna Jane, *b* 1965.

SISTER DECEASED

Hon Bryony Joy, *b* 1947; *d* as the result of a riding accident 1963.

WIDOW LIVING OF FIRST VISCOUNT

ELINOR DOROTHEA, CBE, JP (*Elinor, Viscountess Rochdale*), da of late Ernest Hubert Pease, of Mowden, Darlington: *m* 1931, Col the 1st Viscount, OBE, TD, who *d* 1993. *Residence* – Lingholm, Keswick, Cumbria CA12 5UA.

PREDECESSORS – (1) GEORGE Kemp, CB, son of late George Tawke Kemp, of Beechwood, Rochdale; *b* 1866; Chm of Kelsall & Kemp, Ltd, woollen manufacturers, and Lord-Lieut of Middx; S Africa 1900-1902 with Imperial Yeo (despatches), 1914-19 War in Gallipoli and Egypt as Brig-Gen; MP for Heywood Div of Lancs (L) 1895-1906, and for N-W Div of Manchester 1910-12; *cr Baron Rochdale*, of Rochdale, co Palatine of Lancaster (peerage of United Kingdom) 1913: *m* 1896, Lady Beatrice Mary Egerton, MBE, who *d* 1966, da of 3rd Earl of Ellesmere; *d* 1945; *s* by his son (2) JOHN DURIVAL, OBE, TD, 1st Viscount; *b* 1906; 1939-45 War in Europe, Pacific (US Forces) and India (despatches), Col late RA (TA), Hon Brig; DL Cumbria 1948-83; Chm Kelsall & Kemp, Rochdale, 1950-71, Dep-Chm W Riding Worsted & Woollen Co Ltd, 1969-72, Williams & Glyn's Bank Ltd, 1973-77, and other Cos; *cr Viscount Rochdale*, of Rochdale, co Palatine of Lancaster (peerage of UK) 1960: *m* 1931, Elinor Dorothea, CBE, da of late Ernest Hubert Pease, of Mowden, Darlington; *d* 1993; *s* by his only son (3) ST JOHN DURIVAL, 2nd Viscount and present peer; also Baron Rochdale.

ROCHE, BARONY OF (Roche) (Extinct 1956)

SON LIVING OF LIFE BARON

Hon Thomas Gabriel, QC, *b* 1909; *ed* Rugby, and Wadham Coll, Oxford; Bar Inner Temple 1932, and a QC 1955; appointed Recorder of Worcester 1959, and a Church Commr for England 1961; 1939-45 War as Lt-Col RA (despatches). *Residence* – Ashcroft House, Chadlington, Oxford. *Club* – United University.

ROCHESTER, BARON (Lamb) (Baron UK 1931)

FOSTER CHARLES LOWRY LAMB, 2nd Baron; *b* 7 June 1916; *s* 1955; *ed* Mill Hill, and Jesus Coll, Camb (MA); formerly Capt 23rd Hussars; joined ICI Ltd 1946, Labour Manager, Alkali Div 1955-63, Mond Div 1964-72; Personnel Manager, Mond Div, ICI; Pro-Chancellor of Univ of Keele 1976-86; DL Cheshire 1979; DUniv Keele 1986: *m* 1942, Mary Carlisle, BA, da of Thomas Benjamin Wheeler, CBE, and has issue.
Residence – The Hollies, Hartford, Ches.

SONS LIVING

Hon DAVID CHARLES, *b* 8 Sept 1944; *ed* Shrewsbury and Sussex Univ: *m* 1969, Jacqueline, da of John Alfred Stamp, of Torquay, and has issue living, Daniel, *b* 1971, — Joe, *b* 1972. *Residence* – The Anchorage, 1 Beresford Av, Twickenham, Middx TW1 2PY.
Hon Timothy Michael, *b* 1953; *ed* Shrewsbury, and The Queen's Coll, Oxford; formerly a professional cricketer, Cricket Sec, Test and County Cricket Board, since 1988: *m* 1978, Denise Ann, da of John Buckley, of Frinton-on-Sea, Essex, has issue living, Nicholas, *b* 1985, — Sophie, *b* 1983. *Residence* – 12 Park Av, St Albans, Herts AL1 4PB.

DAUGHTER LIVING

Hon Elizabeth Mary, *b* 1951: *m* 1974, Thomas Meredith McIlroy, and has issue living, Samuel, *b* 1975, — Duncan, *b* 1977, — John Benjamin, *b* 1979, — Catherine, *b* 1989.

BROTHERS LIVING

Rev Hon Roland Hurst Lowry, *b* 1917; *ed* Mill Hill, and Jesus Coll, Camb, (BA 1938, MA 1942); sometime Chap RAF; Gen Sec of British Evangelical Council 1967-82: *m* 1943, Vera Alicia, da of late A. H. Morse, and has issue living, Andrew Michael (5 Flint Lane, South Darley, Matlock, Derbys), *b* 1951: *m* 1974, Helen, da of late Eric Mitchell, of 30 Fisher Av, Rugby, and has issue living, Benjamin James *b* 1980, Rebecca Mary Alicia *b* 1982, — Rosemary Elizabeth, *b* 1947: *m* 1969, David Pike, of 3 Laburnum Rd, Weston-super-Mare, and has issue living, Martin John *b* 1973, Sarah Louise *b* 1971, — Hilary Jennifer, *b* 1949: *m* 1972, Dr Howard Jackson, of 11 Fox Hill, Selly Oak, Birmingham, and has issue living, Nathan Dieter *b* 1976, Kirsten Renate *b* 1978, Lydia Ruth *b* 1985, — Valerie Judith, *b* 1955: *m* 1978, Joseph George Unsworth, of 73 Elwyn Drive, Halewood Village, Liverpool, and has issue living, Joseph Jonathan *b* 1993, Jodi Ann *b* 1980, Amy Ruth *b* 1983, Mia Dawn *b* 1986. *Residence* – 13 Eversleigh Rise, Darley Bridge, Matlock, Derbys DE4 2JW.
Hon Kenneth Henry Lowry, CBE, *b* 1923; *ed* Harrow, and Trin Coll, Oxford (BA 1944, MA, 1949); Sec to Church Commrs 1980-85; formerly Instructor-Lt RN; Head of Religious Broadcasting, BBC 1963-66; Sec of BBC 1967-68; Dir Public Affairs BBC 1969-77, Special Adviser Broadcasting Research 1977-80; Commonwealth Fund Fellow, Harvard Univ, USA, 1953-55: *m* 1952, Elizabeth Anne, da of late D. A. Saul, and has issue living, Stephen Ernest Henry, *b* 1957: *m* 1993, Sue M., elder da of W. J. Turner, of Clevedon, Avon, — Sarah Elizabeth Hurst, *b* 1955, — Caroline Mary Anne, *b* 1966: *m* 1992, Lieut Paul J. O. Knight, RN, son of Dr Peter Knight, of Austin, Texas. *Residence* – 25 South Terr, SW7 2TB.

SISTER LIVING

Hon Muriel Joan Lowry, *b* 1921; *ed* Oxford Univ (BA 1943, MA 1957); Senior Lecturer in Education, Loughborough Coll of Education; PT tutor counsellor, Open Univ, 1977-84; formerly 3rd Sec, British Embassy, Oslo: *m* 1947 (*m diss* 1957), William Oswald Collier (*see* B Monkswell, colls). *Residence* – 26 George St, Cambridge.

PREDECESSORS – (1) Ernest Henry Lamb, CMG, el son of late Benjamin Lamb, of Thorndown, Windlesham, Surrey, and Shorne, Rochester, Kent, *b* 1876; a retired Transport Contractor; was Paymaster-Gen (in National Govt) 1931-35; represented Min of Labour in House of Lords 1931-5; Vice-Pres of Methodist Church 1941-2, and of British Council of Churches 1942-4; sat as MP for Rochester (L) 1906-10, and 1910-18; *cr Baron Rochester*, of Rochester, co Kent (peerage of United Kingdom) 1931: *m* 1913, Rosa Dorothea, who *d* 1979, yr da of late William John Hurst, JP, of Drumaness, Ballynahinch, co Down; *d* 1955; *s* by his el son (2) Foster Charles Lowry, 2nd Baron and present peer.

ROCKLEY, BARON (Cecil) (Baron UK 1934)

Late, but in earnest

James Hugh Cecil, 3rd Baron; *b* 5 April 1934; *s* 1976; *ed* Eton, and New Coll, Oxford: *m* 1958, Lady Sarah Primrose Beatrix Cadogan, el da of 7th Earl Cadogan, and has issue.

Arms – Barry of ten argent and azure, over all six escutcheons, three, two, and one, sable, each charged with a lion rampant of the first, and for difference a crescent gules charged with another crescent or, a crescent gules for difference. **Crest** – Six arrows in saltire or, barbed and flighted argent, girt together with a belt gules, buckled and garnished gold, over the arrows a morion cap proper. **Supporters** – On either side a lion ermine, gorged with a collar or pendent therefrom an escutcheon, the dexter sable a lion argent, and the sinister gules, three tilting spears erect or, headed argent.
Residence – Lytchett Heath, Poole, Dorset BH16 6AE.

SON LIVING

Hon Anthony Robert, *b* 29 July 1961; *ed* Eton, and Camb Univ: *m* 1988, Katherine Jane, da of G. A. Whalley, of Chipperfield, Herts, and has issue living, Emily Sarah, *b* 1991, — Lydia Elizabeth, *b* 1994.

DAUGHTERS LIVING

Hon Caroline Anne, *b* 1960: *m* 1985, Mark G. Preston, yr son of Simon Preston, of Lowfield Farm, Tetbury, Glos, and has issue living, Hugh Simon, *b* 1987, — Edward James, *b* 1989, — Lucy Camilla, *b* 1991.
Hon Camilla Sarah, *b* 1965.

BROTHER LIVING

Hon Charles Evelyn (Wilcote House, Charlbury, Oxon), *b* 1936; *ed* Eton: *m* 1965, Jennifer Anne, da of Duncan Mackinnon, of Swinbrook House, Burford, Oxon, and has issue living, David *b* 1971, — Arabella Elizabeth, *b* 1967, — Lucinda, *b* 1970.

SISTER LIVING

Hon Elizabeth Anne, *b* 1939: *m* 1961, Capt Andrew Lyon Wills, late Life Guards (*see* Wills, Bt (*cr* 1904), colls). *Residence* – Middleton House, Longparish, Andover, Hants.

PREDECESSORS – (1) *Rt Hon Sir* Evelyn Cecil, GBE, el son of late Lieut-Col Lord Eustace Brownlow Henry Gascoyne Cecil (M Salisbury, colls); *b* 1865; MP for Herts E, or Hertford Div (C) 1898-1900, for Aston Manor 1900-1918, and for Aston Div of Birmingham 1918-29; *cr Baron Rockley*, of Lytchett Heath, co Dorset (peerage of United Kingdom) 1934: *m* 1898, Hon Alicia Margaret Amherst, CBE, who *d* 1941, da of 1st Baron Amherst of Hackney; *d* 1941; *s* by his son (2) Robert William Evelyn, 2nd Baron; *b* 1901: *m* 1933, Anne Margaret, who *d* 1980, da of late Adm Hon Sir Herbert Meade-Featherstonhaugh, GCVO, CB, DSO (E Clanwilliam, colls); *d* 1976; *s* by his el son (3) James Hugh, 3rd Baron and present peer.

RODEN, EARL OF (Jocelyn) (Earl I 1771, Bt E 1665)

FÁIRE MON DEVOIR

To do my duty

ROBERT JOHN JOCELYN, 10th Earl, and 14th Baronet; *b* 25 Aug 1938; *s* 1993: *m* 1st, 1970 (*m diss* 1982), Sara Cecilia, da of late Brig Andrew Dunlop, of Que Que, Zimbabwe; 2ndly, 1989, Ann Margareta Maria, da of late Dr Gunnar Albert Philip Henning, of Göteborg, Sweden, and has issue by 1st and 2nd *m*.

Arms – Azure, a circular wreath or torse argent and sable, with four hawks' bells conjoined thereto in quadrangle or. Crest – A falcon's leg erased at the thigh proper, belled or. Supporters – Two falcons proper, wings inverted belled or.
Seat – Bryansford, co Down. *Residence* – 4 The Boltons, SW10 9TB.

SON LIVING *(By 2nd marriage)*

SHANE ROBERT HENNING (*Viscount Jocelyn*), *b* 9 Dec 1989.

DAUGHTER LIVING *(By 1st marriage)*

Lady Cecilia Rose, *b* 1976.

BROTHER LIVING

Hon James Michael, *b* 1943; *ed* Stowe, and Trin Coll, Dublin. *Residence* – Glynsk, Cashel, Connemara, co Galway.

COLLATERAL BRANCH LIVING

Issue of Lt-Cdr Hon Thomas Alan Jocelyn, RN, 2nd son of 9th Earl, *b* 1941, missing, feared lost at sea, 1991: *m* 1966 (*m diss* 1982), Fiona Alice, da of Capt Rudland Dallas Cairns, DSC, RN (*see* Simpson, Bt, ext):—
Charles Patrick, *b* 1978. —— Moira Anne, *b* 1969. —— Caragh Clodagh, *b* 1975.

PREDECESSORS – (1) ROBERT Jocelyn, successively Solicitor-Gen, Attorney-Gen, and Lord High Chancellor of Ireland, and twelve times a Lord Justice in the absence of the Viceroy, was *cr Baron Newport*, of Newport (peerage of Ireland) 1743, and *Viscount Jocelyn* (peerage of Ireland) 1755; *d* 1756; *s* by his son (2) ROBERT, 2nd Viscount; was MP for Old Leighlin 1743, and Auditor-Gen of Ireland 1750; *s* by his kinsman as 5th Bt 1770 (see * infra); *cr Earl of Roden*, of High Roding, co Tipperary (peerage of Ireland) 1771; *d* 1797; *s* by his son (3) ROBERT, KP, 2nd Earl; was MP for Dundalk, and joint Auditor-Gen for Ireland; *d* 1820; *s* by his son (4) ROBERT, KP, PC, 3rd Earl, *b* 1788; was MP for Dundalk, Auditor-Gen of the Exchequer in Ireland, and Custos Rotulorum of co Louth; *cr Baron Clanbrassil*, of Hyde Hall, co Herts (peerage of United Kingdom) 1821; *s* by his grandson (5) ROBERT, 4th Earl; was a Lord-in-Waiting to HM 1874-80; *d* unmarried 1880; *s* by his uncle (6) JOHN STRANGE, 5th Earl (2nd son of 3rd Earl), *b* 1823: *m* 1851, Hon Sophia Hobhouse, who *d* 1916, 2nd da of 1st Baron Broughton; *d* 1897, when the Barony of Clanbrassil became ext and the Barony of Newport passed to his kinsman (7) WILLIAM HENRY (son of late Hon John Jocelyn, 4th son of 2nd Earl), 6th Earl, *b* 1842; *d* 1910; *s* by his brother (8) ROBERT JULIAN, 7th Earl, *b* 1845; Lieut-Col in the Army: *m* 1882, Ada Maria, who *d* 1931, da of late Col Soame Gambier Jenyns, CB; *d* 1915; *s* by his son (9) ROBERT SOAME, 8th Earl; *b* 1883; Capt (ret) N Irish Horse, and a Representative Peer: *m* 1905, Elinor Jessie, who *d* 1962, da of late Joseph Charlton Parr; *d* 1956; *s* by his son (10) ROBERT WILLIAM, 9th Earl; *b* 1909; Capt RN, served European War 1939-45 (despatches thrice): *m* 1937, Clodagh Rose, who *d* 1989, da of late Edward Robert Kennedy (*see* Kennedy, Bt, colls, 1990 Edn); *d* 1993; *s* by his eldest son (11) ROBERT JOHN, 10th Earl and present peer; also Viscount Jocelyn and Baron Newport.
*(1) ROBERT Jocelyn, of Hyde Hall; *cr a Baronet* 1665; *d* 1712; *s* by his son (2) Sir STRANGE 2nd Bt; *d* 1734; *s* by his el son (3) Sir JOHN, 3rd Bt; *d* unmarried 1741; *s* by his brother (4) Sir CONVERS, MD, 4th Bt; Sheriff of Hertford 1745; *d* unmarried 1770; *s* by his kinsman (5) ROBERT, 2nd Viscount Jocelyn (see ante) grandson of Thomas, 3rd son of 1st Bt.

RODGER OF EARLSFERRY, BARON (Rodger) (Life Baron 1992)

ALAN FERGUSON RODGER, son of late Prof Thomas Ferguson Rodger, CBE, of Glasgow; *b* 18 Sept 1944; *ed* Kelvinside Academy, Glasgow, Glasgow Univ (MA, LLB), and New Coll, Oxford (DCL, MA, DPhil); Hon Bencher Lincoln's Inn 1992; Research Fellow Balliol Coll, Oxford 1969-70, Fellow and Tutor in Law New Coll, Oxford 1970-72, Member Faculty of Advocates 1974, Clerk of Faculty 1976-79, Standing Jr Counsel (Scotland) to Dept of Trade 1979, QC 1985, Advocate Depute 1985-88, Home Advocate Depute 1986-88, Solicitor Gen for Scotland 1989-92, since when Lord Advocate of Scotland; Member Mental Welfare Commn for Scotland 1982-85, Maccabaean Lect British Academy 1991; FBA 1991, FRSE 1992; *cr Baron Rodger of Earlsferry*, of Earlsferry in the District of NE Fife (Life Baron) 1992.
Address – Lord Advocate's Chambers, Regent Rd, Edinburgh EH7 5BL. *Club* – Athenaeum.

RODGERS OF QUARRY BANK, BARON (Rodgers) (Life Baron 1992)

WILLIAM THOMAS RODGERS, PC, son of William Arthur Rodgers, of Liverpool; *b* 28 Oct 1928; *ed* Quarry Bank High Sch, Liverpool, and Magdalen Coll, Oxford; Parl Under Sec Dept of Economic Affairs 1964-67, Foreign Office (Leader of UK Delegation to Council of Europe & Assembly of Western European Union) 1967-68, Min of State Board of Trade 1968-69, Treasury 1969-70, Min of Defence 1974-76, Sec of State for Transport 1976-79; Gen-Sec Fabian Soc 1953-60 (member until 1981); Chm Expenditure Cttee Trade &

Industry 1971-74; Dir-Gen RIBA 1987-94; MP for Stockton-on-Tees (*Lab* 1962-81, *SDP* 1981-83) 1962-74, and Teesside, Stockton 1974-83; author of *Hugh Gaitskell* (1963), *The People into Parliament* (1966), *The Politics of Change* (1982), *Government and Industry* (1986), etc; *cr* PC 1975, and *Baron Rodgers of Quarry Bank*, of Kentish Town in the London Borough of Camden (Life Baron) 1992: *m* 1955, Silvia, da of Hirsch Szulman, of London, and has issue, three das.
Residence – 43 North Hill, N6 4BE. *Club* – Garrick.

RODNEY, BARON (Rodney) (Baron GB 1782, Bt GB 1764)

NON·GENERANT·AQUIL·ÆCOLUMBAS

Eagles do not bring forth doves

GEORGE BRYDGES RODNEY, 10th Baron, and 10th Baronet; *b* 3 Jan 1953; *s* 1992; *ed* Eton.

Arms – Or: three eagles displayed with wings inverted purpure. **Crest** – On a ducal coronet or, an eagle, wings displayed and inverted purpure. **Supporters** – Two eagles, wings inverted purpure, beaked and membered or, each sustaining with the interior claw a banner of St George, the staves proper, each enfiled with a naval coronet gold.
Residence – 38 Pembroke Rd, W8 6NU.

SISTER LIVING

Hon Anne, *b* 1955; resumed her maiden name 1982: *m* 1st, 1982 (*m diss* 19—), Hugh Lusted, PhD, of San Francisco, Calif, USA; 2ndly, 1991, Alexander Constantine Basil D'Janoeff, son of late Constantine V. D'Janoeff, of Windsor, Berks. *Residence* – 3 Avenue Court, Draycott Av, SW3.

AUNT LIVING (*daughter of 8th Baron*)

Hon Diana Rosemary (5222 Sark Rd, Victoria, BC, Canada V8Y 2M3), *b* 1924; *ed* Havergal Coll, and McGill Univ, Canada (BA 1949); served World War II with WRCNS 1943-45.

WIDOW LIVING OF SON OF EIGHTH BARON

Penelope Jane, da of late Capt Eric S. Garner, of Easton, Northants: *m* 1974, as his 2nd wife, Hon Michael Christopher Rodney, who *d* 1993. *Address* – PO Box 11, Pender Is, BC, Canada V0N 2M0.

WIDOW LIVING OF NINTH BARON

REGINE ELISABETH LUCIENNE THERESE MARIE GHISLAINE (*Baroness Rodney*), yr da of late Chevalier Robert Egide Marie Ghislain Pangaert d'Opdorp, of Château Rullingen, Looz, Belgium: *m* 1951, the 9th Baron, who *d* 1992. *Residence* – 38 Pembroke Rd, W8 6NU.

COLLATERAL BRANCHES LIVING

Issue of late Hon Michael Christopher Rodney, yst son of 8th Baron, *b* 1926, *d* 1993: *m* 1st, 1953 (*m diss* 1973), Anne, da of David Yuile, of Montreal, Canada; 2ndly, 1974, Penelope Jane (ante), da of late Capt Eric S. Garner, of Easton, Northants:—
(By 1st *m*) Patricia Anne, *b* 1955. —— Jocelyn Marjorie, *b* 1959. —— Jennifer Susan, *b* 1964.

Grandchildren of late Lt-Cdr Mervyn Harley Rodney, eldest surv son of late Hon Robert William Henry Rodney (infra):—
Issue of late Cdr Nigel Robert Harley Rodney, RN, *b* 1917, *d* 1992: *m* 1946, Patricia Ann Merlyn (Ashen House, Northleigh, Colyton, Devon), da of late Lt-Col Harley Wentworth Ashburner, DSO:—
NICHOLAS SIMON HARLEY (17 rue da Labruyere, 78000 Versailles, France), *b* 20 Dec 1947: *m* 1973, Maité Bernadette Edith, da of Henri Pinet des Ecots, of Château de Curty, Imphy, 58 Nièvre, France. —— Christopher Lossie Charles, *b* 1957. —— Julia Diana, *b* 1951. —— Emma Gabrielle, *b* 1952: *m* 1975, Charles Ainslie Guest, of Glebe House, Southleigh, Colyton, Devon, son of Dennis William Guest, of 20A Watchwell St, Rye, Sussex, and has issue living, Henry Harley, *b* 1983, —— Charles Humphrey, *b* 1985, —— Oliver Hugh, *b* 1987.
Issue of late Maj John Armand Rodney, MC, *b* 1921, *d* 1992: *m* 1951, Gertrude Evelyn (147 Gloucester Rd, SW7 4TH), yr da of late Capt Simon John James:—
Peter Miles, *b* 1953; *ed* Radley: *m* 1980, Marianne Hilary, da of George Robert Downes, and has issue living, Lydia Jane Louise, *b* 1983, —— Katharine Amelia Laura, *b* 1985. —— David James (74 Cicada Rd, SW18 3QN), *b* 1965; *ed* Haileybury, and RMA Sandhurst; commn'd Coldm Gds 1985: *m* 1989, Sally L— M—, elder da of Dr David Norman Howell Owen, of Bryn-y-Mor, Fishguard, Pembrokeshire, and has issue living, Harry John Melville, *b* 1992.

Granddaughters of late Hon Robert William Henry Rodney, 2nd son of 6th Baron:—
Issue of late Group Capt Ivor Morgan Rodney, OBE, RAF (ret), *b* 1896, *d* 1954: *m* 1931, Althea Caroline Winifred, who *d* 1978, el da of late Sir Gerald Woods Wollaston, KCB, KCVO, FSA, late Garter Principal King of Arms:—
Sarah Patience, *b* 1933: *m* 1959, Brian Woodard, of 69 Bernham Rd, Hellesdon, Norwich, and has issue living, Anthony John, *b* 1960, —— Paris Morgan, *b* 1962, —— Craig Charles, *b* 1963: *m* 1987, Linda Christine Heasman, and has issue living, Ritchie Craig *b* 1990, Kimberley Linda *b* 1988, —— Helen Mary, *b* 1961: *m* 1st, 1979 (*m diss* 1985), Lloyd Haydn Anthony Evans; 2ndly, 1994, Gerard Martin Kavanagh, of Toronto, Canada, and has issue living (by 1st *m*), Stephanie Sarah *b* 1980. —— Prudence Jane, *b* 1936: *m* 1960, Keith Hyde Wollaston, TD, of 105 Valiant House, Vicarage Crescent, SW11 3LX and 1 Beach Court, The Beach, Walmer, Deal, Kent, and has issue living, Andrew James Rodney, *b* 1961: *m* 1991, Alison Wishart, —— Rachel Althea Rodney, *b* 1963, —— Frances Jane Rodney, *b* 1964: *m* 1993, Said El Moumni, —— Catherine Mary Rodney, *b* (twin) 1964: *m* 1991, Robert Dickson, and has issue living, Wendy Elizabeth *b* 1992. —— Alicia Henrietta Althea, *b* 1937: *m* 1960, David John Pentin, of 16 St Dunstan's Terrace, Canterbury, Kent, and has issue living, John Mark, *b* 1964, —— Richard

Harley, *b* 1969, — Caroline Louise, *b* 1962: *m* 1987, Mark Kendall Blamey, and has issue living, Jacob John *b* 1992, — Edward Michael, *b* 1971.

Grandson of late Frederick James Rodney, son of late Hon Mortimer Rodney, 7th son of 2nd Baron:—
Issue of late Reginald George Rodney, *b* 1873, *d* 1933: *m* 1916, Patricia Lissette du Châstel, who *d* 1964, da of late William James MacGrath, of co Tipperary:—
Philip Harley Brydges (61 Knighton Rd, Wembury, Plymouth), *b* 1917: *m* 1951, Janet Barker, and has issue living, Julie Rose Patricia, *b* 1954: *m* 1976, Andrew George Lewis Leftley, and has issue living, Ian Andrew Philip *b* 1985, Nicola Caroline *b* 1979, — Faye Jessica Frances Corisande, *b* 1958: *m* 1991, Graham George Tongue.

PREDECESSORS – (1) *Adm Sir* GEORGE BRYDGES Rodney, (son of Henry Rodney, greatgrandson of Sir John Rodney, by Jane (cousin german to Edward VI), da of Sir Henry Seymour, brother of 1st Duke of Somerset and Queen Jane Seymour), an eminent Naval Commander, who, having gained numerous victories, eventually in 1782 defeated the French fleet under the Comte de Grasse, whom he took prisoner, the result of this success was the peace of Versailles 20 Jan 1783; *cr Baronet* 1764, and *Baron Rodney*, of Rodney Stoke, co Somerset (peerage of Great Britain) 1782; granted by Parliament a pension of £2,000 a-year to himself and his successors (commuted 1924); successively MP for Saltash, Okehampton, Penrhyn, and Northampton; *d* 1792; *s* by his son (2) GEORGE, 2nd Baron; sat as MP for Northampton; *d* 1802; *s* by his el son (3) GEORGE, 3rd Baron; was Lord-Lieut of Radnor; *d* 1842; *s* by his brother (4) THOMAS JAMES, 4th Baron; assumed the additional surname and arms of Harley by Roy licence 1805; *d* unmarried 1843; *s* by his brother (5) SPENCER, 5th Baron; was Rector of Elmley, Kent; *d* unmarried 1846; *s* by his nephew (6) ROBERT DENNETT, 6th Baron, son of Capt Hon Robert, RN, 4th son of 2nd Baron; *b* 1820: *m* 1850, Sarah, who *d* 1882, da of late John Singleton; *d* 1864; *s* by his son (7) GEORGE BRIDGES HARLEY DENNETT, 7th Baron; *b* 1857: *m* 1st, 1891 (*m diss* 1902), Hon Corisande Evelyn Vere Guest, who *d* 1943, da of 1st Baron Wimborne; 2ndly, 1903, Charlotte Eugenia, who *d* 1939, da of late Edmund Probyn, of Longhope and Huntley, Gloucestershire; *d* 1909; *s* by his el son (8) GEORGE BRIDGES HARLEY GUEST, 8th Baron; *b* 1891: *m* 1917, Lady Marjorie Lowther, who *d* 1968, da of 6th Earl of Lonsdale; *d* 1973; *s* by his 2nd son (9) JOHN FRANCIS, 9th Baron; *b* 1920; 1939-45 War as Lieut Commandos (despatches); Delegate to Council of Europe and Western European Union: *m* 1951, Régine Elisabeth Lucienne Thérèse Marie Ghislaine, yr da of late Chevalier Robert Egide Marie Ghislain Pangaert d'Opdorp, of Château Rullingen, Looz, Belgium; *d* 1992; *s* by his only son (10) GEORGE BRYDGES, 10th Baron and present peer.

ROLL OF IPSDEN, BARON (Roll) (Life Baron 1977)

ERIC ROLL, KCMG, CB, son of Mathias Roll; *b* 1 Dec 1907; *ed* Birmingham Univ (BCom, PhD), Hon DSc, Hull, Hon DSoc Sci Birmingham, Hon LID Southampton; Prof of Economics and Commerce, Univ Coll of Hull (1935-46); Special Rockefeller Foundation Fellow, USA 1939-41; Member, later Dep Head Brit Food Mission to N America, and UK Dep Member and UK Exec Officer, Combined Food Board, Washington 1941-46; Assist Sec, Min of Food, 1946-47; Under-Sec HM Treasury 1948, Min UK Delegation to OEEC, 1949, Dep Head, UK Delegation to NATO, Paris 1952-53, Under Sec Min of Agric, 1953-57, Exec Dir Internat Sugar Council 1957-59; Chm UN Sugar Conference 1958; Dep Sec Min of Agric 1959-61; Dep Leader, UK Delegation for negotiations with the EEC, 1961-63; Econ Min and Head of UK Treasury Delegation, Washington, Exec Dir for the UK Internat Monetary Fund and Internat Bank for Reconstruction and Development 1963-64 and Permanent Under-Sec of State, Dept of Economic Affairs, 1964-66; Dir of Bank of England 1968-77, Chm and later Hon Chm Book Development Council since 1967; Dir Times Newspapers Ltd 1967-83, and Indep Member NEDC 1971-80; Chancellor, Southampton Univ 1974-84; Chm S. G. Warburg & Co Ltd and Mercury Securities Ltd 1974-84, and a Dir of other Cos; Pres S. G. Warburg Group plc; *cr* CMG 1949, CB (Civil) 1956, KCMG 1962, *Baron Roll of Ipsden*, of Ipsden, co Oxford (Life Baron) 1977: *m* 1934, Winifred, only da of Elliott Taylor, and has issue.
Club – Brooks's.

DAUGHTERS LIVING

Hon Joanna, *b* 1944.
Hon Elizabeth, *b* 1946: *m* 1st, 1970 (*m diss* 1975), Hon Robin James Greenhill, who *d* 1986, yr son of Baron Greenhill of Harrow, GCMG, OBE; 2ndly, 19—, Peter Foldes, and has issue.

ROLLO, LORD (Rollo) (Lord S 1651, and Baron UK 1869)

Fortune makes way through everything

ERIC JOHN STAPYLTON ROLLO, 13th Lord; *b* 3 Dec 1915; *s* 1947; *ed* Eton; Capt late Grenadier Guards; a JP of Perthshire; 1939-45 War: *m* 1938, Suzanne, da of W. H. B. Hatton, of Broome House, Clent, Worcs, and has issue.

Arms – Or, a chevron between three boars heads erased azure, armed proper langued gules. **Crest** – A stag's head couped at the neck proper. **Supporters** – Two stags proper.
Residence – Pitcairns, Dunning, Perthshire. *Club* – Guards'.

SONS LIVING

Hon DAVID ERIC HOWARD (*Master of Rollo*) (20 Draycott Av, SW3), *b* 31 March 1943; *ed* Eton; Capt Gren Gds: *m* 1971, Felicity Anne Christian, only da of Lt-Cdr John Bruce Lamb, DSC, RN, of Burrow House, Tywardreath, Cornwall, and has issue living, James David, William, *b* 1972, — Thomas Stapylton, *b* 1975, — William Eric John, *b* 1978.
Hon James Malcolm, *b* 1946; *ed* Eton, and Ch Ch, Oxford (BA): *m* 1968, Henrietta Elizabeth Flora, da of Maj Alasdair David Forbes Boyle (*see* E Glasgow, colls), and has issue living, Malcolm Howard, *b* 1981, — Helen Beatrice, *b* 1985.

DAUGHTER LIVING

Hon (Erica) Helen Susan, *b* 1939: *m* 1970, Valentine Edward Dillon, of 45 Sandford Rd, Dublin.

HALF-BROTHERS LIVING (*Son of 12th Lord by 2nd marriage*)

Hon John Dunning, *b* 1931.

(*Son of 12th Lord by 3rd marriage*)

Hon Simon David Paul (Hollyburn, Bankfoot, Perth PH1 4AB; 60 Green Leas, Sunbury on Thames, Middx TW17 7PG), *b* 1939; *ed* Eton: *m* 1964, Valerie, yr da of R. W. G. Willis, of Newton Green, Sudbury, Suffolk, and has issue living, Michelle Leila, *b* 1971, — Dominique Ruth, *b* 1977.

SISTER LIVING

Hon Jean Helen, *b* 1926: *m* 1952, Lt-Col Robert Henry Heywood-Lonsdale, MBE, MC, DL, Grenadier Gds, of Mount Farm, Churchill, Oxon (V Valentia), and has issue living, Thomas Norman, *b* 1953; *ed* Eton: *m* 1987, Sara Lonsdale, da of Strachan Bongard, of Toronto, and has issue living, James Alexander *b* 1989, Oliver Robert *b* (twin) 1989, Edward David *b* 1990, — Helen Jane, *b* 1957, — Clare Jean, *b* 1961: *m* 1987, James Hugh Leslie Melville, only son of Maj Hon George David Leslie Melville (*see* E Leven and Melville), — Emma Lucinda, *b* 1962: *m* 1989, Matthew Donald Knight, eldest son of Nicholas P. Knight, of Eltham, SE9 and has issue living, Laura Emma *b* 1991, Sophie Lucinda *b* 1993.

WIDOW LIVING OF BROTHER OF TWELFTH LORD

Diana Joan (Barley Thorpe, Oakham, Rutland), da of late Edward Castell Wrey (*see* Wrey Bt): *m* 1st 1932 (*m diss* 1946), Jocelyn Abel Smith, who *d* 1966; 2ndly, 1946, as his 2nd wife, Hon William Hereward Charles Rollo, MC (who was raised to the rank of a Baron's son 1946), who *d* 1962.

WIDOW LIVING OF SON OF TWELFTH LORD

Bridget Mary (30 King St, Nairn), da of Brig James Erskine Stirling, DSO (*see* D Devonshire colls, 1980 Edn): *m* 1948, Capt Hon David Ian Rollo, MBE, MC, who *d* 1981, and has issue living (*see* colls infra).

COLLATERAL BRANCHES LIVING

Issue of late Capt Hon David Ian Rollo, MBE, MC, yst son of 12th Lord, *b* 1921; *d* 1981: *m* 1948, Bridget Mary (ante), da of late Brig James Erskine Stirling, DSO (*see* D Devonshire, colls, 1980 Edn):—
(Norman) Hamish (Burnbrae, Burghclere, Newbury, Berks), *b* 1955: *m* 1979, Nicole, yst da of Vincent J. Sullivan, of Larchdale, Ashford, Kent, and has issue living, Andrew David, *b* 1981, — Euan Christopher, *b* 1983. —— Joanna Mary (3 Jenner Rd, N16), *b* 1949. —— Carolyn Louise, *b* 1952: *m* 1st, 1973, Gordon Wilson; 2ndly, 1981, Ronald Mitchell, of Kinsteary Cottage, Auldearn, Nairn, and has issue living, (by 1st *m*) Kirsty Jane MITCHELL, *b* 1974, — (by 2nd *m*), Jake David, *b* 1984, — Abigail Betty, *b* 1982. —— Harriet Clarissa Jane, *b* 1960: *m* 1983, Julian P. Spencer, of 12 Streathbourne Rd, SW17 8QX, elder son of late Michael Spencer, and has issue living, George Hector, *b* 1990, — Alexander James, *b* 1993.

Issue of late Hon William Hereward Charles Rollo, MC (who was raised to the rank of a Baron's son 1946), yr brother of 12th Lord, *b* 1890, *d* 1962: *m* 1st, 1917 (*m diss* 1946), Lady Kathleen Nina Hill, who *d* 1960, da of 6th Marquess of Downshire; 2ndly, 1946, Mrs Diana Joan Abel Smith (ante), da of late Edward Castell Wrey (*see* Wrey Bt):—
(By 1st *m*) (Peter) Andrew, MBE (Cold Blow, Oare, Marlborough, Wilts), *b* 1919, Lieut RN (ret); Far East 1945; MBE (Mil) 1946 *m* 1953, Patricia Mary, who *d* 1985, da of late Capt Charles Cairn Best, and has issue living, William Raoul, *b* 1955; *ed* Eton; Maj the Blues and Royals: *m* 1987, Annabel Evadne, only da of Lt-Cdr Sir Howard Christian Sheldon Guinness, VRD, RNR, of The Manor House, Glanvilles Wootton, Sherborne, Dorset (*see* Smith-Marriott, Bt, colls, 1973-74 Edn), and has issue living, a da *b* 1989, a da *b* 1991, — Susan Rose, *b* 1957.

Grandchildren of late Hon Gilbert de Ste Croix Rollo, yst son of 10th Lord:—
Issue of late Alexander David Rollo, *b* 1909, *d* 1974: *m* 1st, 1934 (*m diss* 19—), Maud Mary Venn; 2ndly, 1952, Margaret Valmai, who *d* 1961, only da of William Slaney Wilmot:—
(By 2nd *m*) Calum John Slaney *b* 1953: *m* 1980, Lindsay Froggatt.
Issue of late Maj Robert Duncan Rollo, *b* 1911, *d* 1986: *m* 1936, Violet Augustine (The Close, Boscombe Village, Salisbury, Wilts), da of late Russell Charles Stanhope (*see* E Harrington, colls):—

Gilbert Mark (Monadhliath House, Aviemore, Inverness-shire PH22 1QT), *b* 1937: *m* 1968, his first cousin once removed, Paulette Beatrice, da of Lt-Col Aubrey Charles Stanhope, USAF (*see* E Harrington, colls), and has issue living, Duncan Andrew, *b* 1971, — Catherine Ann, *b* 1969, — Clare Elizabeth, *b* 1976, — Caroline Jane, *b* 1979. —— Charles (21 Countess Rd, Amesbury, Wilts), *b* 1950. —— Mary Rose, *b* 1938: *m* 1st, 1960, Noel Keaveney, of Cork; 2ndly, 1988, John Curry, of 2 Rosery Court, Dinton, Wilts, and has issue living (by 1st *m*), Catherine Ruth, *b* 1961, — Deborah Maeve, *b* 1963.

PREDECESSORS – **(1)** Sir Andrew Rollo; *cr* Lord Rollo, of Duncrub (peerage of Scotland) 1651, with remainder to his heirs male whatsoever; *s* by his son **(2)** James, 2nd Lord; *d* 1669; *s* by his son **(3)** Andrew, 3rd Lord; *d* 1700; *s* by his son **(4)** Robert, 4th Lord; was implicated in the rising of 1715, but having surrendered he obtained the benefit of the Act of Grace 1716; *d* 1758; *s* by his el son **(5)** Andrew, 5th Lord; served as Brig-Gen in the first American War; *d* without surviving issue 1765; *s* by his brother **(6)** John, 6th Lord; *d* 1783; *s* by his son **(7)** James, 7th Lord; *d* 1784; *s* by his son **(8)** John, 8th Lord; served with the Guards in Flanders 1793-5; *d* 1846; *s* by his son **(9)** William 9th Lord; *b* 1809: *m* 1834, Elizabeth, da of John Rogerson; *d* 1852; *s* by his son **(10)** John Rogerson, 10th Lord; *b* 1835; was a Representative Peer for Scotland 1860-68; *cr Baron Dunning* (peerage of UK) 1869: *m* 1857, Agnes Bruce, who *d* 1906, el da of Lt-Col Trotter, of Ballindean House, co Perth; *d* 1916; *s* by his el son **(11)** William Charles Wordsworth, CB, 11th Lord; *b* 1860; formerly Lt-Col and Hon Col 3rd Batn Black Watch (Roy Highlanders): *m* 1882, Mary Eleanor, who *d* 1929, da of late Beaumont Williams Hotham; *d* 1946; *s* by his nephew **(12)** John Eric Henry (son of late Hon Eric Norman Rollo, 2nd son of 10th Lord), 12th Lord; *b* 1889: *m* 1st, 1915, Helen Maud, who *d* 1928, da of late Frederick Chetwynd-Stapylton; 2ndly, 1930 (*m diss* 1936), Phyllis Carina, only da of late Bernard Sanderson; 3rdly, 1937, Mrs Lily Marie Cockshut (who *d* 1989, having *m* 3rdly, 1949, Richard Andrew Perceval Leach, who *d* 1981), da of Max Seiflow, of Hatch End, Middlesex; *d* 1947; *s* by his el son **(13)** Eric John Stapylton, 13th Lord and present peer; also Baron Dunning.

ROMILLY, BARONY OF (Romilly) (Extinct 1983)

WIDOW LIVING OF FOURTH BARON

Marion Elizabeth Jessie, da of late Charles M. Clover, of Pilgrim's Way, Blewbury, Berks, formerly wife of Geoffrey Adams, and widow of Capt Lionel Cecil (M Salisbury): *m* 1966, as his 3rd wife, Maj 4th Baron Romilly, Coldstream Gds, who *d* 1983, when the title became ext; 4thly, 1986, as his 2nd wife, Col Edward John Sutton Ward, LVO, MC (*see* E Dudley, colls), who *d* 1990. *Residence* – Chilton, Hungerford, Berks.

ROMNEY, EARL OF (Marsham) (Earl UK 1801, Bt E 1663)

Michael Henry Marsham, 7th Earl, and 13th Baronet; *b* 22 Nov 1910; *s* 1975; *ed* Sherborne; formerly Maj RA; 1939-45 War: *m* 1939, Frances Aileen, da of late Maj James Russell Landale, Indian Army.

Arms – Argent, a lion passant in bend gules, between two bendlets azure. **Crest** – A lion's head erased gules. **Supporters** – Two lions azure, semée of cross crosslets and each gorged with a naval coronet or.
Residence – Wensum Farm, West Rudham, King's Lynn, Norfolk PE31 8SZ.

SISTER LIVING (*Raised to the rank of an Earl's daughter* 1976)

Lady Anne Rhoda (c/o The Earl of Romney, Wensum Farm, West Rudham, King's Lynn, Norfolk PE31 8SZ), *b* 1909; 1939-45 War as Section Officer, WAAF; Kenya Police Reserve 1952-60.

COLLATERAL BRANCHES LIVING

Not for himself, but for his country

Grandchildren of late Hon Sydney Edward Marsham, yst son of 4th Earl:—
Issue of late Col Peter William Marsham, MBE, *b* 1913, *d* 1970: *m* 1946, Hersey (Waterloo Cottage, Gayton, King's Lynn, Norfolk), da of late Maj Hon Richard Coke (*see* E Leicester, colls):—
Julian Charles (Gayton Hall, King's Lynn, Norfolk), *b* 28 March 1948; *ed* Eton: *m* 1975, Catriona Ann, da of Robert Christie Stewart, of Arndean, Dollar, Perthshire (*see* B Cochrane of Cults, colls), and has issue living, David Charles, *b* 1977, — Michael Julian, *b* 1979, — Laura Jane, *b* 1984. —— Lavinia, *b* 1950: *m* 1973, Simon James Macdonald Lockhart of The Lee, of Crosshill House, Auchterarder, Perthshire, and has issue (*see* E Ducie, colls). —— Sarah, *b* 1954: *m* 1982, Maxwell Colin Bernard Ward, of Stobshiel House, Humbie, East Lothian, and has issue (*see* E Bangor, colls).

Grandchildren of late Walter John Marsham, 2nd son of late Rev Hon John Marsham (infra):—
Issue of late John Edward Marsham, *b* 1910, *d* 1990: *m* 1st, 1937 (*m diss* 1970), Jean Frances, da of late Reginald Cambden Clare Hayward; 2ndly, 1970, Mrs Evelyn Moore (16 Barchester Rd, Langley, Bucks), da of Lesley George Rush:—
(By 1st *m*) Richard John, *b* 1946: *m* 1964, Janet Anne Wilson, and has issue living, Gary Frederick, *b* 1964: *m* 1988, his cousin, Celaine Margaret, da of late Donald James Griffin (infra), and has issue living, Cassandra Dawn *b* 1989, — Stephen John, *b* 1967. —— Gillian Dawn (1 Belmont Vale, Maidenhead, Berks), *b* 1938: *m* 1st, 1956, Donald James Griffin, who *d* 1959; 2ndly, 1961 (*m diss* 1964), Alan Henry Craig; 3rdly, 1968, Abdul Hanif Rashid, who *d* 1971; 4thly, 19— (*m diss* 1979), Thomas William McConnell; 5thly 1980 (*m diss* 1985, re-*m* 1990), David Alfred Forisky, and has issue living (by 1st *m*), Pauline Elizabeth, *b* 1956; has issue living, Darrell Colin Griffin *b* 1981, John Bushnell *b* 1986, Gillian Dawn Griffin *b* 1976, — Celaine Margaret, *b* 1959: *m* 1988, her cousin, Gary Frederick Marsham, and has issue (ante), — (by 3rd *m*) Kris Hanif, *b* 1970; assumed forename of Kris by deed poll 19— in lieu of Aftab.

Grandchildren of late Rev Hon John Marsham, 2nd son of 3rd Earl:—
Issue of late Capt Cyril Montagu Charles Marsham, DCM, *b* 1871; *d* 1943: *m* 1911, Gladys Helen, who *d* 1965, da of late Douglas Kingsford, Bar-at-law:—

Peter (Kings Acre, Coddington, Ledbury, Herefordshire), *b* 1912: *m* 1938, Margaret, da of Benjamin Harral, of Cawthorne, Barnsley, Yorkshire, and has issue living, John Kingsford, OBE, *b* 1942; Lt-Col 3rd LI; OBE (Mil) 1993: *m* 1978, Olwen, da of late Joshua Adamson, of Brisbane, Australia, and has issue living, Robert Edward Harral *b* 1981, Anne Kingsford *b* 1979, — Robert Harral, *b* 1946, — Marion Caroline, (2 Marshall Place, Oakley Green, Windsor, Berks), *b* 1939: *m* 1st, 1961 (*m diss* 1978), Richard Naylor; 2ndly, 1981 (*m diss* 1989), Dr George Richard Castellain Walton, and has issue living (by 1st *m*), Charles Gray Marsham *b* 1962, Michael Harry Richard *b* 1970, Margaret Kingsford *b* 1964. —— Richard Douglas Hollinshead (Llwynglas, Penrhiwllan, Llandyssul, Dyfed), *b* 1913; Maj (ret) Worcester Regt: *m* 1947 (*m diss* 1981), Shirley, da of late John Hannah, of The Mill House, Mathon, Malvern, Worcestershire, and has issue living, Richard Charles Hannay, *b* 1948, — David John Hollinshead, *b* 1954, — Catherine Elizabeth, *b* 1952.

 Granddaughters of late Hugh Sydney Marsham-Townshend, el son of late Hon Robert Marsham-Townshend, 2nd son of 2nd Earl:—
Issue of late Capt Thomas Marsham-Townshend, Scots Guards, *b* 1915, *ka* 1944: *m* 1940, Averil Innes (who *d* 1993, having *m* 2ndly, 1945, Col John Robert Stephenson Clarke, OBE, MC, Scots Guards, who *d* 1993), da of late Major Lewis Frederic Innes Loyd:—
June (*Lady Rankin*), *b* 1942: *m* 1st, 1962, Bryan Montagu Norman; 2ndly, 1980, Sir Ian Niall Rankin, 4th Bt, of 63 Marlborough Pl, NW8, and has issue (by 2nd *m*) (*see* Rankin, Bt, colls), and an adopted da (from 1st *m*), Emily Kate, *b* 1975. —— Susan (*posthumous*), *b* 1944: *m* 1972, Dr Piero Studiati Berni, of Molina di Quosa, Pisa, Italy, and has issue living, Cesare Studiati, *b* 1972, — Viola, *b* 1975.

(In remainder to Barony of Romney and Baronetcy)

 Grandson of late Robert Henry Bullock-Marsham, 2nd son of late Robert Bullock-Marsham, el son of late Rev John Jacob Marsham, DD, 3rd son of 2nd Baron:—
Issue of late Major Charles George FIELD-MARSHAM, *b* 1872, *d* 1956; assumed by deed poll 1920 the surnames of Field-Marsham in lieu of his patronymic: *m* 1904, Mary Dorothea, who *d* 1970, only child of Edward Knight, of Keswick Old Hall, Norfolk:—
Robert Edward, *b* 1905; *ed* Eton; Major The Bays: *m* 1st, 1936 (*m diss* 1950), Geraldine Hamilton; 2ndly, 1950, Joan Helen, who *d* 1988, da of late Percy Llewellyn Nevill (*see* M Abergavenny, colls), and widow of Charles Austen Field-Marsham (infra). *Residence* – Tophill Farm, Langton Green, Kent.

 Grandson of late Major Charles George FIELD-MARSHAM (ante):—
Issue of late Charles Austen FIELD-MARSHAM, Lieut Life Guards, *b* 1910, *ka* 1941: *m* 1935, Joan Helen (who *m* 2ndly, 1950, as his 2nd wife, Major Robert Edward Field-Marsham), The Bays (ante), and *d* 1988, da of late Percy Llewellyn Nevill (*see* Abergavenny, colls):—
Rupert Charles Edward (29 Roxborough St West, Toronto, Canada), *b* 1938; *ed* Eton, and McGill Univ; 2nd Lt R Armoured Corps: *m* 1st, 1963 (*m diss* 1973), Marilyn, da of Dr G. B. Maugham, of Westmount, Montreal; 2ndly, 1973, Lindsay Ruth, da of late Robert Dale-Harris (by his wife, Leslie, da of late Leslie Howard, the actor), and has issue living (by 1st *m*), Robert Scott, *b* 1964, — Rupert Charles, *b* 1968, — (by 2nd *m*), George Edward, *b* 1975, — Mark Austen, *b* 1977, — Jacob Edward, *b* 1979.

 Grandsons of late Robert Anstruther MORRIS-MARSHAM, yr son of Robert Henry Bullock-Marsham (ante):—
Issue of late Richard Henry Anstruther Morris-Marsham, *b* 1905, *d* 1975: *m* 1st, 1929 (*m diss* 1951), Iris Rose Sophia, da of Capt Dennis Larking, CMG, RN; 2ndly, 1951, Eileen Reba (Jacaranda, 4 Chiltley Lane, Liphook, Hants), only da of late Victor di Halfalla Nahum, of Italy, and formerly wife of Neville Blond, CMG, OBE:—
(By 1st *m*) David Charles Robert (32 Alderbrook Rd, Clapham, SW12 8AE), *b* 1930; *ed* Eton and Merton Coll, Oxford: *m* 1976, Margaret Lindelia, da of late Robert Crawford, and has issue living, Victoria Harriet, *b* 1978, — Charlotte Rose, *b* 1979. —— Jack Richard (Brookside, Ewen, Cirencester, Glos GL7 6BU), *b* 1936; *ed* Eton: *m* 1st, 1963 (*m diss* 1978), Agnes Margaret (Molly), da of late Maj-Gen Walter Rutherfoord Goodman, CB, DSO, MC; 2ndly, 1978, Ann Christine Humphreys, who *d* 1980, da of Howard Sargent Backhouse; 3rdly, 1983, Serena Sybil Newmark, da of Gp Capt Geoffrey Kinglake Fairtlough, and has issue living (by 1st *m*), James Jonathan (6 Dairy Farm, Gosditch, Ashton Keynes, Wilts SN6 6NZ), *b* 1964: *m* 1991, Susan Marie, elder da of Henry Menzel, of Falmouth, Cornwall, and has issue living, Jessica Rose *b* 1993, — Dominic Rutherfoord, *b* 1967, — Tiffany Jane, *b* 1969.

 Grandchildren of late Rev Cloudesley Dewar Bullock-Marsham, 3rd son of Robert Bullock-Marsham (ante):—
Issue of late Cloudesley Henry Bullock-Marsham, *b* 1879, *d* 1928: *m* 1911, Algitha, who *d* 1972, da of late Rev Hon Algernon Robert Parker (E Macclesfield, colls):—
Cloudesley George (Horton Cottage, Rolvenden Layne, Cranbrook, Kent TN17 4WP), *b* 1917; *ed* Eton; Maj 297th (Kent Yeo) Field Regt RA (TA); 1939-45 War (prisoner): *m* 1941, Suzanne, da of Dudley Holloway. —— Algernon James (Langton House, 42 The Street, Appledore, Ashford, Kent TN26 2BX), 1919; *ed* Eton, and Ch Ch, Oxford; Capt KRRC; 1939-45 War (prisoner): *m* 1948, Elizabeth, da of Air Vice-Marshal Malcolm Henderson, CB, CIE, DSO, and has issue living, Charles James Lessels, *b* 1950; *ed* Eton. —— Vere Frances, *b* 1913: *m* 1932, (George) Ronald Pigé Leschallas, who *d* 1991, and has issue living, Anthony George, *b* 1933: *m* 1954, Marie-Louise Yvonne Renner, and has issue living, Anthony Simon *b* 1955: *m* 1987, Amanda Nanci, da of Maj James Le Coq, of Seething, Norfolk (and has issue living, Marie-Clair *b* 1988), William Henry *b* 1963: *m* 1992, Emma C., elder da of David Huxtable, of Bosham, W Sussex, Marie-Louise Sophie *b* 1957, Joanna Clare *b* 1960: *m* 1989, Edward Anthony Morys Berry (*see* V Kemsley, colls), — James Ronald Percy, *b* 1943: *m* 1967, Rosemary Elizabeth, only da of late Rev Hon Andrew Charles Victor Elphinstone, and has issue (*see* L Elphinstone), — Lavinia Frances, *b* 1934: *m* 1965, Christopher William Trelawny Hare, and has issue living, Henry William Trelawny *b* 1966, Jonathan Christopher Trelawny *b* 1968, James Frederick Trelawny *b* 1971, — Suzanne Vere (*Lady Jones*), *b* 1939: *m* 1965, Gen Sir (Charles) Edward Webb Jones, KCB, CBE, late Royal Green Jackets, and has issue living, Hume Richard Webb *b* 1967; Capt The Royal Green Jackets, Benjamin Edward Webb *b* 1978, Jemma Suzanne *b* 1971.

PREDECESSORS – (1) Sir JOHN Marsham, MP, one of the six Clerks of the Court of Chancery 1638-44 and 1660-80; *cr* a *Baronet* 1663; *s* by his son (2) Sir JOHN, 2nd Bt; *d* 1692; *s* by his son (3) Sir JOHN, 3rd Bt; *d* unmarried 1696; *s* by his uncle (4) Sir ROBERT, Knt, 4th Bt; was one of the six clerks in Chancery 1680-95; sat as MP for Maidstone 1698-1703; *d* 1703; *s* by his son (5) Sir ROBERT, 5th Bt; was Gov of Dover Castle; sat as MP for Maidstone 1708-16; *cr Baron of Romney*, of Romney, co Kent (peerage of Great Britain) 1716; *d* 1724; *s* by his son (6) ROBERT, DCL, FRS, 2nd Baron; *d* 1793; *s* by his son (7) CHARLES, 3rd Baron, successively MP for Maidstone and Kent; in 1799 entertained George III at the Mote, when HM reviewed about 6,000 of the Kentish Volunteers; was Lord-Lieut of Kent; *cr* Viscount Marsham and *Earl of Romney* (peerage of UK) 1801; *d* 1811; *s* by his son (8) CHARLES, 2nd Earl; was successively MP for Hythe and Downton; *d* 1845; *s* by his son (9) CHARLES, 3rd Earl; *b* 1808; sat as MP for W Kent (*C*) 1841-5: *m* 1832, Lady Margaret Harriet Montagu-Douglas-Scott, who *d* 1846, da of 4th Duke of Buccleuch; *d* 1874; *s* by his son (10) CHARLES, 4th Earl; *b* 1841; was a Lord-in-Waiting to HM Queen Victoria 1889-92: *m* 1863, Lady Frances Augusta Constance Muir-Campbell-Rawdon-Hastings, who *d* 1910, da of 2nd Marquess of Hastings; *d* 1905; *s* by his el son (11) CHARLES, 5th Earl; *b* 1864; Hon Lieut-Col (ret) 4th Batn Bedfordshire Regt, and Pres of Marine So: *m* 1890, Anne Louisa, who *d* 1936, da of Sir Edward Henry Scott, 5th Bt (*cr* 1821); *d* 1933; *s* by his son (12) CHARLES, 6th Earl; *b* 1892: *m* 1918, Marie Henrietta, who *d* 1976, da of Sir Colin Richard Keppel, GCVO,

KCIE, CB, DSO (E Albemarle, colls); *d* 1975; *s* by his cousin (**13**) MICHAEL HENRY (son of Lt-Col Hon Reginald Hastings Marsham, OBE, 2nd son of 4th Earl), 7th Earl and present peer; also Viscount Marsham, and Baron Romney.

Romsey, Lord; son of Countess Mountbatten of Burma.

Ronaldshay, Earl of; son of Marquess of Zetland.

ROOTES, BARON (Rootes) (Baron UK 1959)

Forwards into the Future

NICHOLAS GEOFFREY ROOTES, 3rd Baron; *b* 12 July 1951; *s* 1992; *ed* Harrow; Journalist, Author and Copywriter: *m* 1976, Dorothy Anne, formerly wife of Jonathan Burn-Forti, of Barnes, SW, and da of Cyril Wood, of Swansea.

Arms – Ermine within an orle azure a bugle horn sable garnished or stringed gules. **Crest** – On a wreath argent and vert a cubit arm bendwise in armour or the hand proper grasping a spear in bend also proper flying therefrom a forked pennon barry argent and azure semée of plates and bezants. **Supporters** – On either side a horse argent gorged with a chain pendent therefrom a wheel or. *Residence* – 2 Cedars Rd, Barnes, SW13 0HP.

SISTER LIVING

Hon Sally Hayter, *b* 1947: *m* 1968, Andrew Beauchamp St John, of Cul-na-Cloich, Glenalmond, Perthshire (*see* B St John of Bletso, colls).

WIDOW LIVING OF SON OF FIRST BARON

Elizabeth Margaret (The Old Farmhouse, Ramsbury, Wilts), da of late Rev Humphrey Gordon Barclay, CVO, MC, and widow of Lt Norman Lewis Philips (E Ducie, colls): *m* 1944, Hon Brian Gordon Rootes, who *d* 1971, and has issue (*see* colls infra).

WIDOW LIVING OF SECOND BARON

MARIAN (*Marian, Baroness Rootes*), da of late Lt-Col Herbert Roche Hayter, DSO, and widow of Wing-Cdr James Hogarth Slater, AFC, RAF: *m* 1946, the 2nd Baron, who *d* 1992. *Residence* – North Standen House, Hungerford, Berks RG17 0QZ.

COLLATERAL BRANCH LIVING

Issue of late Hon Brian Gordon Rootes, yr son of 1st Baron, *b* 1919, *d* 1971: *m* 1944, Elizabeth Margaret (ante), da of late Rev Humphrey Gordon Barclay, CVO, MC, and widow of Lt Norman Lewis Philips (E Ducie, colls):—

WILLIAM BRIAN (Belhie House, Aberuthven, Auchterarder, Perthshire, PH3 1EH), *b* 8 Nov 1944: *m* 1969, Alicia Graham, yst da of late Frederick Graham Roberts, OBE, of East Farm House, Piddlehinton, Dorset, and has issue living, Talitha Alice Louise, *b* 1973, — Annabel Catherine Natasha, *b* 1976.

PREDECESSORS – (**1**) *Sir* William Edward Rootes, GBE, son of late William Rootes, of Hawkhurst, Kent; *b* 1894; Chm of Rootes, Ltd; Chm of Dollar Exports Council 1951-60, and of successor body, W Hemisphere Exports Council 1961-64: *m* 1st, 1916 (*m diss* 1951) Nora, who *d* 1964, da of Horace Press; 2ndly, 1951, Ruby Joy (Ann), who *d* 1968, da of Capt Gordon Duff, widow of Sir Charles Thomas Hewitt Mappin, 4th Bt, and formerly wife of Sir Francis Henry Grenville Peek, 4th Bt; *d* 1964; *s* by his el son (**2**) (WILLIAM) GEOFFREY, 2nd Baron, *b* 1917; Chm Chrysler UK Ltd (formerly Rootes Motors Ltd) 1967-73, Pres Inst of Motor Industry 1973-75, etc; Member Council of Warwick Univ 1956-74, Vice-Pres Game Conservancy 1975-79: *m* 1946, Marian, da of late Lt-Col Herbert Roche Hayter, DSO, and widow of Wing-Cdr James Hogarth Slater, AFC, RAF; *d* 1992; *s* by his only son (**3**) NICHOLAS GEOFFREY, 3rd Baron and present peer.

ROSEBERY, EARL OF (Primrose) (Earl S 1703 Bt S 1651)

By faith and trust

NEIL ARCHIBALD PRIMROSE, 7th Earl, and 9th Baronet; *b* 11 Feb 1929; *s* 1974; *ed* Stowe, and New Coll, Oxford; patron of three livings; a DL for Midlothian: *m* 1955, (Alison Mary) Deirdre, da of late Ronald William Reid, MS, FRCS (*see* Chaytor, Bt, colls, 1980 Edn), and has issue.

𝕬rms – Quarterly: 1st and 4th vert three primroses within a double tressure flory counterflory or *Primrose*; 2nd and 3rd argent, a lion rampant, double queued sable *Cressy*. 𝕮rest – A demilion gules holding in the dexter paw a primrose or. 𝕾upporters – Two lions or.
Seat – Dalmeny House, South Queensferry, W Lothian.

SON LIVING

HARRY RONALD NEIL (*Lord Dalmeny*), *b* 20 Nov 1967: *m* 1994, Caroline J., eldest da of Ronald Daglish and of Mrs William Wyatt-Lowe, of Hemel Hempstead.

DAUGHTERS LIVING

Lady Lucy Catherine Mary, *b* 1955: *m* 1976, (Anthony Gavin) Charles Luis Garton, 2nd son of late Anthony Charles Garton, of West Hyde House, W Hyde, Herts, and has issue living, James Anthony Leo, *b* 1986, — Camilla Mary Eva, *b* 1982.
Lady Jane Margaret Helen, *b* 1960: *m* 1989, Michael S. E. Kaplan, son of R. Kaplan, of Cambridge, Mass, USA, and has issue living, Felix Balthazar Inigo, *b* 1991.
Lady Emma Elizabeth Anne, *b* 1962: *m* 1984, William G. Lamarque, yr son of late W. G. Lamarque, and has issue living, Victor George, *b* 1986, — Francesca, *b* 1988.
Lady Caroline Sara Frances, *b* 1964.

HALF-SISTER LIVING

Lady Helen Dorothy, *b* 1913: *m* 1933, Hon Hugh Adeane Vivian Smith, who *d* 1978 (*see* B Bicester). *Residence* – The Old Rectory, Souldern, Bicester, Oxon.

COLLATERAL BRANCHES LIVING

(Not in remainder to United Kingdom Earldom)

Grandchildren of late Ralph Gore Primrose, son of late Edward Montagu Primrose, son of late Hon Francis Ward Primrose, MP, 2nd son of 3rd Earl:—
　Issue of late Gerald Edward David Primrose, *b* 1914, *d* 1988: *m* 1950, Anne Loletta (350 La Prenda, Millbrae, Calif 94030, USA), da of late James Ranney Broughton, of Atwood, Ontario, Canada:—
James Ralph, *b* 1952: *m* 1983, Jane Porter, da of Lewis Weyburn Saxby, Jr, of Toledo, Ohio, and has issue living, Andrew Gerald, *b* 1988, — Nicholas James, *b* 1991. *Residence* – 242 Sydney Dr, Walnut Creek, Calif 94595, USA.
　Issue of late Neil Primrose, *b* 1918, *d* 1979: *m* 1944, Margaret Verna (14560 Sunset Drive, White Rock, BC, Canada V4B 2V9), da of late Henry James Francis, of Portsmouth:—
David Neil (2278 Midas St, Abbotsford, BC, Canada V2S 4R2), *b* 1945; CGA: *m* 1966, Anna Joyce, da of late F. C. Walters, of White Rock, BC, and has issue living, David Francis Neil, *b* 1966: *m* 1989, Cynthia Lee, da of Dennis C Rumpel, of Abbotsford, BC, — Douglas James Baird, *b* 1974, — Amy Irene, *b* 1979, — Tanya Margaret, *b* 1983. —— Margaret Jane Elizabeth, *b* 1948: *m* 1971, Robert Noboru Maikawa, of 5382 Frances St, Burnaby, BC, Canada V5B 1T5, and has issue living, Paul Robert, *b* 1974, — Steven Anthony, *b* 1976, — Andrea Margaret, *b* 1979. —— Deirdre Katherine, *b* 1951: *m* 1971, Thomas Kevin Ruffen, of 812 East 51st Av, Vancouver, BC, Canada V5X 1E5, and has issue living, Jessica Kirsten, *b* 1973. —— Ann Jennifer, *b* 1954: *m* 1973, Christopher John Barber, of Box 34 Morello Rd, RR1, Nanoose Bay, BC, Canada V0R 2R0, and has issue living, Matthew John, *b* 1975, — Daniel Morgan, *b* 1977, — Jennifer Erin, *b* 1978.

PREDECESSORS – (1) ARCHIBALD Primrose, Clerk of the Privy Council, *cr* a *Baronet* (NS) by Charles II, 1651, and after the Restoration (1661) was appointed a Lord of Session and Lord Clerk Register with the title of Lord Carrington; *d* 1679; *s* by his son (2) *Sir* WILLIAM, 2nd Bt; was Clerk of the Notaries; *d* 1687; *s* by his son (3) *Sir* JAMES, 3rd Bt; MP for Edinburghshire 1702-3; *cr Lord Primrose and Castlefield*, and *Viscount Primrose* (peerage of Scotland) 1703, with remainder to the heirs male of his father; *d* 1706; *s* by his el son (4) ARCHIBALD, 2nd Viscount; *d* unmarried 1716; *s* by his brother (5) HUGH, 3rd Viscount; a Lieut-Col in the Army; *dsp* 1741, when the peerages expired, and the baronetcy devolved upon his kinsman (6) JAMES, 6th Bt, who had in 1723 *s* his father as *2nd Earl of Rosebery* (see*infra); *d* 1755; *s* by his son (7) NEIL, KT, 3rd Earl; a Representative Peer 1768-84; *d* 1814; *s* by his son (8) ARCHIBALD JOHN, KT, PC, 4th Earl, *b* 1783; was unsuccessively MP for Helston and Cashel, and Lord-Lieut of Linlithgowshire; *cr Baron Rosebery*, of Rosebery, co Edinburgh (peerage of United Kingdom) 1828: *m* 1st, 1808, Harriet, da of Hon Bartholomew Bouverie (E Radnor); *d* 1868; *s* by his grandson (9) ARCHIBALD PHILIP, KG, KT, PC (el son of Archibald, Lord Dalmeny, MP, by Lady Catherine Lucy Wilhelmine Stanhope, da of 4th Earl Stanhope), 5th Earl; *b* 1847; Lord-Lieut of cos Linlithgow 1873-1929, and Edinburgh 1884-1929, an Elder Brother of Trinity House, Lord Rector of Aberdeen Univ 1878-81, Under-Sec of State for Home Depart 1881-3, Lord Rector of Edinburgh 1882-5, Lord Privy Seal and First Commr of Works and Public Buildings Feb to June 1885, temporary Keeper of the Great Seal of Scotland 1885, Sec of State for Foreign Affairs 1886 and Aug 1892 to March 1894, and Premier, First Lord of the Treasury, and Lord Pres of the Council March 1894 to June 1895, and Lord Rector of Glasgow 1899-1902; Special Envoy to Court of Vienna to announce Accession of King George V 1910; held Conspic at Coronations of Kings Edward VII and George V: *cr* KG 1892, KT 1895, *Baron Epsom*, of Epsom, co Surrey, and *Viscount Mentmore*, of Mentmore, and *Earl of Midlothian* (peerage of United Kingdom) 1911; received Victorian Chain 1917: *m* 1878, Hannah, who *d* 1890, da and heiress of the late Baron Meyer de Rothschild; *d* 1929; *s* by his son (10) ALBERT EDWARD HARRY MAYER ARCHIBALD, KT, DSO, MC, PC, 6th Earl; *b* 1882; doyen of British Turf as racehorse owner, and breeder, Steward of Jockey Club 1929-32, and 1945-48; MP for Midlothian (*L*) 1906-10; Regional Commr for Scotland 1941-45; Sec of State for Scotland 1945; Chm of Nat Liberal Party 1945-47: *m* 1st, 1909 (*m diss* 1919), Lady Dorothy Alice Margaret Augusta Grosvenor, who *d* 1966, sister of 3rd Duke of Westminster; 2ndly, 1924, Hon Dame Eva Isabel Marian Strutt, DBE, JP, LLD, who *d* 1987, da of 2nd Baron Aberdare, and formerly wife of 3rd Baron Belper; *d* 1974, *s* by his yr son (11) NEIL ARCHIBALD, 7th Earl and present peer; also Earl of Midlothian, Viscount Rosebery, Viscount Inverkeithing, Viscount Mentmore, Lord Primrose and Dalmeny, Lord Dalmeny and Primrose, Baron Rosebery, and Baron Epsom.

*(1) ARCHIBALD Primrose, 4th son of Sir Archibald Primrose, 1st Bt (ante), MP for Edinburgh 1695, Gentleman of the Bedchamber to Prince George of Denmark, and a Commr for the Treaty of the Union, was *cr Lord Primrose and Dalmeny* and *Viscount of Rosebery* (peerage of Scotland) 1700, with remainder to his issue male and female successively, and in default thereof to the heirs of entail in the lands of Rosebery; and *Lord Dalmeny and Primrose, Viscount Inverkeithing*, and *Earl of*

Rosebery (peerage of Scotland) 1703, with remainder to his issue male and female successively; was a Representative Peer 1708- 14; *d* 1723; *s* by his son (2) JAMES, 2nd Earl, *b* 1741; *s* as 6th Bt (see ante).

Rosehill, Lord; son of Earl of Northesk.

ROSKILL, BARON (Roskill) (Life Baron 1980)

EUSTACE WENTWORTH ROSKILL, PC, yst son of late John Roskill, KC (Dilke, Bt); *b* 6 Feb 1911; *ed* Winchester (Fell 1981-86), and Exeter Coll, Oxford (MA, Hon Fellow 1963); Bar Middle Temple 1933, QC 1953, and Bencher 1961; Dep Chm of Hants Quarter Sessions 1951-60, and Chm 1960-71; Vice-Chm Parole Board 1967-69; Chm 3rd London Airport Commn 1968-70; Pres Senate of Four Inns of Court 1972-74; Treas Middle Temple, Hon Bencher Inner Temple 1980; Chm Lond Internat Arbitration Trust 1981-88, Fraud Trials Cttee 1983-85, and Take Over Panel Appeal Cttee 1987-93; DL for Hants; a Judge of High Court of Justice (Queen's Bench Div) 1962-71, *cr* Knt 1962, PC 1971; a Lord Justice of Appeal 1971-80, a Lord of Appeal in Ordinary 1980-86 with title of *Baron Roskill*, of Newtown, co Hants (Life Baron) 1980: *m* 1947, Elisabeth Wallace, 3rd da of late Thomas Frame Jackson, and has issue.

Arms – Gules a lion rampant quarterly argent and or in chief two green woodpeckers respectant proper. **Crest** – A sword erect proper pommel and hilt or enfiled through a hank of cotton proper.
Residence – Heatherfield, Newtown, Newbury, Berks.

SON LIVING

Hon Julian Wentworth (8 Leigh Rd, N5), *b* 1950; *ed* Winchester; Solicitor 1974: *m* 1975, Catherine Elizabeth, 2nd da of Maj William Francis Garnett, of Quernmore Park, Lancaster, and has issue, Matthew Wentworth, *b* 1979, — Oliver Wentworth, *b* 1981.

DAUGHTERS LIVING

Hon Jane Elisabeth Sybil, *b* 1948: *m* 1973, David Christopher Roberts, of 133 Albert Street, NW1.
Hon Katharine Lucy, *b* 1953: *m* 1977, Nicholas Richard Melville Williams, of 37 Perrymead St, SW6, and has issue, George Nicholas Melville, *b* 1981, — Olivia Katharine Elisabeth, *b* 1978.

ROSS OF MARNOCK, BARONY OF (Ross) (Extinct 1988)

WIDOW LIVING OF LIFE BARON

ELIZABETH JANE ELMA (*Baroness Ross of Marnock*), BEM, da of J. Aitkenhead, of Ayr: *m* 1948, Baron Ross of Marnock, MBE, PC, who *d* 1988, and has issue two das. *Residence* – 10 Chapelpark Rd, Ayr.

ROSS OF NEWPORT, BARONY OF (Ross) (Extinct 1993)

SONS LIVING OF LIFE BARON

Hon James Gibb, *b* 1956. *Residence* – 65 Brocklehurst St, SE19.
Hon Huw Weston, *b* 1960. *Residence* – 61B Pyle St, Newport, IoW.

DAUGHTERS LIVING OF LIFE BARON

Hon Lesley Priscilla, *b* 1950: *m* 19—, Finian O'Sullivan, of 44 Station Rd, Netley, Southampton, Hants.
Hon Judith Caroline, *b* 1952: *m* 1983, Theodore Kiendl, of 65 Tyrwhitt Rd, Brockley, SE14.

WIDOW LIVING OF LIFE BARON

BRENDA MARIE (*Baroness Ross of Newport*), da of Arthur Ivor Hughes, of Stanmore, Middx: *m* 1949, Baron Ross of Newport (Life Baron), who *d* 1993. *Residence* – Herb Cottage, Skyborry Green, Knighton, Powys LD7 1TW.

ROSSE, EARL OF (Parsons) (Earl I 1806, Bt I 1677)

For God and the king

WILLIAM BRENDAN PARSONS, 7th Earl and 10th Baronet; *b* 21 Oct 1936; *s* 1979; *ed* Grenoble Univ, and Ch Ch, Oxford (MA); late 2nd Lt Irish Guards; Admin Officer UN Ghana, 1963-65; Assist Resident Representative, UN Development Programme, Dahomey 1965-68, Area Officer for Mid-West Africa 1968-70, Assist Resident Representative, Iran 1970-75, Dep Resident Representative, Bangladesh 1975-78, and of Algeria 1978-80; Dir Historic Irish Houses and Gardens Assoc 1980-91, Agency for Personal Services Overseas 1981-89, Birr Scientific and Heritage Foundation since 1985, and Lorne House Trust since 1993; Memb of Irish Govt's Advisory Council on Development Co-operation 1983-88; Fell of Institution of Engineers of Ireland 1994: *m* 1966, Alison Margaret, el da of late Maj John Davey Cooke-Hurle, of Startforth Hall, Barnard Castle, co Durham, and has issue.

Arms – Gules, three leopards' faces argent. **Crest** – A cubit arm proper, grasping a poleaxe gules. **Supporters** – Two ounces argent, spotted sable, and gorged with a plain collar gules, charged with four bezants. *Seat* – Birr Castle, Birr, co Offaly.

SONS LIVING

(LAURENCE) PATRICK (*Lord Oxmantown*), *b* 31 March 1969; *ed* Aiglon Coll, Switzerland.
Hon Michael John Finn, *b* 1981.

DAUGHTER LIVING

Lady Alicia Siobhan Margaret Nasreen, *b* 1971; *ed* Kingston Univ (B Eng 1993).

BROTHER LIVING

Hon Desmond Oliver Martin (Womersley Park, Doncaster), *b* 1938; *ed* Eton: *m* 1965, Aline Edwina, da of George Alexander Macdonald, MB, of Gable End, Priors Marston, Rugby, and has issue living, Rupert Alexander Michael, *b* 1966, — Desmond Edward Richard, *b* 1968.

COLLATERAL BRANCHES LIVING

Grandchildren of late Hon Richard Clere Parsons, 5th son of 3rd Earl:—
Issue of late Lieut-Col William Frederic Parsons, DSO, *b* 1879, *d* 1956: *m* 1915, Clara Helena who *d* 1972, da of late Hon Edward Gerald Strutt (B Rayleigh, colls):—
(Desmond) Richard (Flat 5, 113 Ifield Rd, SW10 9AS), *b* 1916; *ed* Lancing, and Trin Coll, Camb (BA 1938); late 2nd Lieut Essex Regt. —— Nancy Olivia, *b* 1919.
Issue of late Arthur David Clere Parsons, *b* 1881, *d* 1955: *m* 1914, Doris, who *d* 1970, da of late Norman Charles Cookson, of Oakwood, Wylam, Northumberland:—
(Arthur) Christopher (Hatchwood House, Odiham, Hants; Army and Navy, and City of London Clubs), *b* 1919; 1939-45 War as Maj RA: *m* 1945, Veronica Rosetta de Courcy, el da of Maj-Gen Sir Guy de Courcy Glover, KBE, CB, DSO, MC (B Kingsale, colls), and has issue living, John Christopher, LVO (19 Melrose Gdns, W6 7RN; Brooks's Club), *b* 1946; Dep Treas to HM since 1987; LVO 1992: *m* 1982, Hon Anne Constance Manningham-Buller, yst da of 1st Viscount Dilhorne, and has issue living, Michael Reginald *b* 1983, David Guy *b* 1985, Lilah Veronica *b* 1988, — Rosemary Anne, *b* 1948: *m* 1975, John Bernard Burke, of Western House, Lowick, Berwick-upon-Tweed, Northumberland TD15 2UD, — Daphne Phoebe, *b* 1951: *m* 1971, Hugh Richard Oliver-Bellasis, of Wootton House, Wootton St Lawrence, Basingstoke, Hants RG23 8PE, and has issue living (*see* Bates, Bt, *cr* 1880, colls). —— Norman Charles (Pigdon House, nr Morpeth, Northumberland, NE61 3SE), *b* 1925: *m* 1953, Katharine Alison, who *d* 1992, 2nd da of Col H. H. Gardiner, MC, late RA, and has had issue, Giles Randal, *b* 1957: *d* 1983, — Deborah Anne, *b* 1954: *m* 1988, Timothy Harvey Noel Martin, of 154 Loughborough Rd, Nottingham NG2 7JE, and has issue living, Toby Charles *b* 1991, — Clare Elizabeth, *b* 1959: *m* 1991, Emanuele Trullo, of 107 Marchmont Rd, Edinburgh EH9 1HA, — Katharine Mary, *b* 1963: *m* 1987, Alexander Bruce Gentles, of Montgomery House, Stukeley Park, Great Stukeley, Huntingdon, Cambs PE17 5AQ. —— Theodora Phoebe, MBE, *b* 1915; MBE (Civil) 1989: *m* 1939, Lt-Cdr James Bertram Everard Wainwright, DSO, OBE, RN, who *d* on active serv 1943, and has had issue, Andrew Christopher James, *b* 1943, — Susan Rosalind, *b* 1941, *d* 1989: *m* 1967, Richard Edward Dawson. *Residence* – Sycamore, Lord's Hill Common, Shamley Green, Guildford, Surrey GU5 0UZ. —— Phyllis Rosemary, *b* 1918: *m* 1st, 1945, as his 2nd wife, Capt Ian Stanley Akers-Douglas, Berks Yeo, who *d* 1952 (*see* V Chilston, colls); 2ndly, 1965, John Anthony Cobham Shaw, of Heath Green Farmhouse, Hattingley, Alton, Hants (*see* By Cobham).
Issue of late Rev Canon Richard Edward Parsons, *b* 1888, *d* 1971: *m* 1917, Hester Katherine, who *d* 1954, da of late Maj John William Ainslie Drummond (E Perth, colls):—
Rev Desmond John (The Vicarage, Limpsfield, Surrey), *b* 1925; *ed* Eton; Late Lt Irish Gds; Organising Sec and Dep Warden, Moor Park Coll for Adult Education 1950-61, and a Gov 1961: *m* 1968, Althea Hermione, da of Charles Anthony Stanley Prowse (*see* Millais, Bt), and has issue living, Benedict Desmond Drummond, *b* 1969, — Francesca Catherine, *b* 1972. —— Agnes Mary, *b* 1918: *m* 1941, Maj Cosmo Rex Ivor Russell (*see* B Ampthill, colls). —— Hester Clere, *b* 1920: *m* 1940, David Hastings Gerald Russell, late Lt RNVR (*see* B Ampthill, colls). —— Elizabeth Frances, *b* 1923. —— Rachel Anne (38 Ridgeway Rd, Farnham, Surrey), *b* 1927.

Grandchildren of late Rev Randolph Cecil Parsons (infra):—
Issue of late John Cecil Lawrence Parsons, *b* 1905, *d* 1978: *m* 1940 (*m diss* 1958), Mary Lovell:—
Michael Charles (12 Addicott Rd, Weston-super-Mare), *b* 1950. —— Cynthia, *b* 1948: *m* 1967, John Ryman, and has issue living, Julie Angela, *b* 1968.

Granddaughter of late Hon Lawrence Parsons, son of 2nd Earl:—
Issue of late Rev Randolph Cecil Parsons, *b* 1852, *d* 1941: *m* 1901, Florence Emily, who *d* 1946, da of William Ashton:—
Joan Mary (12 Addicott Rd, Weston-super-Mare), *b* 1906; LRAM.

PREDECESSORS – (1) LAWRENCE Parsons; *cr* a *Baronet* 1677; was attainted by King James's Parliament 1689, and sentenced to death; *d* 1698; *s* by his son (2) Sir WILLIAM, 2nd Bt; *d* 1740; *s* by his grandson (3) Sir LAWRENCE, 3rd Bt; was MP for King's Co 1741; *d* 1749; *s* by his son (4) Sir WILLIAM, 4th Bt; was MP for King's Co; *d* 1791; *s* by his son (5) Sir LAWRENCE, 5th Bt; successively MP for Dublin University and King's Co; in 1807 *s* his father's half-brother as 2nd *Earl of Rosse* (see *infra); was a Representative Peer, and last Joint Postmaster-Gen for Ireland; *d* 1841; *s* by his son (6) WILLIAM, KP, 3rd Earl; *b* 1800; sat as MP for King's Co (L) 1821-34; was a Representative Peer, Pres of Royal Soc, Chancellor of Dublin Univ; erected upon his estate at Parsonstown between the years 1828 and 1845 an enormous telescope at the cost of more than £20,000: *m* 1836, Mary, who *d* 1885, da and el co-heir of John Wilmer Field, of Heaton Hall, co York; *d* 1867; *s* by his son (7) LAWRENCE, KP, DCL, FRS, 4th Earl; *b* 1840; a Representative Peer and Chancellor of Dublin Univ; Lieut and Custos Rotulorum of King's Co (High Sheriff 1867): *m* 1870, (Frances) Cassandra, who *d* 1921, da of 4th Baron Hawke; *d* 1908: *s* by his son (8) WILLIAM EDWARD, 5th Earl, *b* 1873; a Representative Peer, and Lieut and Custos Rotulorum of King's co; Major Irish Guards: *m* 1905, Frances Lois, who *d* 1984, having *m* 2ndly, 1920, 5th Viscount de Vesci (*d* 1958), da of Sir Cecil Edmund Lister-Kaye, 4th Bt; *d* of wounds received in action 1918; *s* by his son (9) LAURENCE MICHAEL HARVEY, KBE, 6th Earl; *b* 1906; FSA, FRSA, FRAS, Hon FRIBA, MRIA, VMH, Vice-Chancellor Dublin Univ 1949-64, Chm Georgian Group 1947-68, and Standing Commn on Museums and Galleries; Dep Chm National Trust: *m* 1935, Anne, who *d* 1992, only da of late Lt-Col Leonard Charles Rudolph Messel, OBE, TD (and granddaughter of Linley Sambourne, in whose house at 18 Stafford Terr, W8, she assembled the Victorian Soc 1957), and formerly wife of late Ronald Owen Lloyd Armstrong-Jones, MBE, QC (*see* E Snowdon); *d* 1979; *s* by his son (10) WILLIAM BRENDAN, 7th Earl and present peer; also Baron Oxmantown.

*(1) LAWRENCE Parsons, 2nd son of Sir Lawrence, 3rd Bt (ante), was *cr* Baron Oxmantown (peerage of Ireland) 1792, with remainder to his nephew Sir Lawrence Parsons, 5th Bt (ante), *Viscount Oxmantown* (peerage of Ireland) 1795, without the special remainder, and *Earl of Rosse* (peerage of Ireland) 1806, with remainder to his nephew aforesaid; *d* 1807, when the Viscountcy became ext, and he was *s* in the other honours by his nephew (2) Sir LAWRENCE, 2nd Earl and 5th Bt (ante).

ROSSLYN, EARL OF (St Clair-Erskine) (Earl UK 1801, Bt S 1666)

PETER ST CLAIR-ERSKINE, 7th Earl, and 10th Baronet; *b* 31 March 1958; *s* 1977; *ed* Eton, and Bristol Univ (BA); Metropolitan Police 1980-94, Thames Valley Police since 1994: *m* 1982, Helen M., eldest da of C. R. Watters, of Christ's Hospital, Sussex, and has issue.

Arms – Quarterly: 1st, argent, a cross engrailed sable, *St Clair*, 2nd, argent, a pale sable, *Erskine*; 3rd azure, a bend between six cross crosslets fitchée or, *Mar*, 4th argent, on a chevron between three roses gules, a fleur-de-lis of the field, *Wedderburn*. **Crest** – A demi-phoenix in flames, wings expanded and elevated proper. **Supporters** – Dexter, an eagle, wings inverted proper, gorged with a plain collar argent, thereon a rose gules; *sinister*, a griffin, wings elevated proper, beaked and membered or.
Address – c/o House of Lords, SW1A 0PW.

SON LIVING

JAMIE WILLIAM (*Lord Loughborough*), *b* 28 May 1986.

DAUGHTERS LIVING

Lady Alice, *b* 1988.
Lady Lucia, *b* 1993.

SISTER LIVING

Lady Caroline, *b* 1956: *m* 1991, Michael Francis Marten, son of Lt-Col Francis William Marten, CMG, MC (*see* B Vernon, 1964 Edn).

MOTHER LIVING

Athenaïs, da of late Louis Victor de Mortemart, Duc de Vivonne: *m* 1955 (*m diss* 1962), 6th Earl of Rosslyn, who *d* 1977.

COLLATERAL BRANCH LIVING

Issue of late Maj Hon David Simon St Clair Erskine, Royal Scots, 3rd and yst son of 5th Earl, *b* 1917, *d* 1985: *m* 1948 (*m diss* 1959), Antonia Mary, who *d* 1965, da of late Adm of the Fleet Sir John Donald Kelly, GCB, GCVO:—
Jonathan Harry, *b* 1949: *m* 1980, Mrs Christine Moore, da of Frederick Inch, of Huntingdon.

PREDECESSORS – (1) *Rt Hon* ALEXANDER Wedderburn, PC, MP for the Ayr Burghs 1761-8, for Castle Rising 1774, for Okehampton 1774-8, and for Bishops Castle 1778-80, having been Solicitor-Gen, and Attorney-Gen was in 1780 *cr Baron Loughborough*, of Loughborough, co Leicester (peerage of Great Britain); was Lord High Chancellor of Great Britain 1793-1801; *cr Baron Loughborough*, of Loughborough, co Surrey (peerage of Great Britain) 1795, with remainder to his nephew Sir James Erskine, 6th Bt (see *infra) and *Earl of Rosslyn* (peerage of United Kingdom) 1801, with similar remainders; *dsp* 1805; *s* by his nephew (2) JAMES, GCB, PC, 2nd Earl; assumed the additional surname of St Clair by Roy licence 1805; sat as MP for Castle Rising 1782-84, for Morpeth 1784-90 and for Kirkcaldy 1796-1805; was Director-Gen of Chancery in Scotland 1785-1837, a Lieut-Gen in the Army, Lord-Lieut of Fifeshire, and Lord Pres of the Council 1834-5; *d* 1837; *s* by his son (3) JAMES ALEXANDER, PC, 3rd Earl; *b* 1802; was a Gen in the Army, Col 7th Hussars, Master of the Buckhounds 1841-6, and Under-Sec of State for War 1859: *m* 1826, Frances, da of Lieut-Gen William Wemyss; *d* 1866; *s* by his son (4) FRANCIS ROBERT, PC, 4th Earl; *b* 1833; High Commr to Gen Assembly of Church of Scotland 1874, 1878, 1879, and 1880, and Capt of Corps of Gentlemen-at-Arms 1886-90; *d* 1890: *m* 1866, Blanche Adeliza, who *d* 1933, da of Henry FitzRoy, and widow of Col Hon Charles Henry Maynard; *s* by his el son (5) JAMES FRANCIS HARRY, 5th Earl, *b* 1869: *m* 1st, 1890 (*m diss* in Scotland 1902), Violet Aline, who *d* 1945, da of late Robert Charles de Grey Vyner (B Lucas, colls); 2ndly, 1905 (*m diss* 1907), Georgeiana, then a member of the dramatic profession, who *d* 1917, yr da of George Robinson, of Minneapolis, USA; 3rdly 1908, Vera Mary, who *d* 1975, da of late Eric Edward Bayley, formerly Lt 17th Lancers; *d* 1939; *s* by his grandson (6) ANTHONY HUGH FRANCIS HARRY (son of late Francis Edward Scudamore, Lord Loughborough, el son of 5th Earl), 6th Earl, *b* 1917: *m* 1955 (*m diss* 1962), Athenaïs de Mortemart, only da of late Louis Victor, Duc de Vivonne, and *d* 1977; *s* by his only son (7) PETER, 7th Earl and present peer; also Baron Loughborough.

*(1) CHARLES Erskine, successively MP for cos Clackmannan and Stirling; *cr* a *Baronet* 1666: *s* by his el son (2) *Sir* JAMES, 2nd Bt; *k* at battle of Landen 1693, unmarried; *s* by his brother (3) *Sir* JOHN, 3rd Bt; MP for Clackmannan; *d* 1739; *s* by his el son (4) *Sir* CHARLES, 4th Bt; *k* at battle of Laffeldt 1747, unmarried; *s* by his brother (5) *Sir* HENRY, 5th Bt; a Lieut-Gen in the Army; sat as MP for Ayr and for Anstruther: *m* Janet, da of Peter Wedderburn (Lord Chesterhall), a Lord of Session; *s* by his son (6) *Sir* JAMES, 6th Bt, who *s* his uncle as 2nd Earl of Rosslyn (ante).

ROSSMORE, BARON (Westenra) (Baron I 1796 and UK 1838)

After battles, rewards

WILLIAM WARNER WESTENRA, 7th Baron; *b* 14 Feb 1931; *s* 1958; *ed* Eton, and Trin Coll, Camb (BA 1957); is 2nd Lieut Somerset LI: *m* 1982, Valerie Marion, da of Brian Tobin, of Ballough, Riverstown, Birr, co Offaly, and has issue.

𝕬rms – Quarterly: 1st and 4th per bend or and argent, in chief a tree eradicated vert, and in base waves of the sea, therein a sea-horse naiant, reguardant, all proper, *Westenra*; 2nd and 3rd quarterly, 1st and 4th azure, three mullets argent, *Murray*; 2nd and 3rd gules, three martlets within a bordure or, *Cairnes*. 𝕮rest – A lion rampant proper. 𝕾upporters – *Dexter*, a trooper of the 5th Dragoons in uniform, and holding in his right hand a sword, point downwards; *sinister*, a black charger of the same regiment, caparisoned proper.
Address – c/o Lloyds Bank plc, 6 Pall Mall, SW1.

SON LIVING

Hon BENEDICT WILLIAM, *b* 6 March 1983.

SISTER LIVING

Hon Brigid Mary WESTENRA , *b* 1928; has resumed her maiden name: *m* 1956 (*m diss* 1969), Hon Jonathan Alan Howard (*see* B Strathcona and Mount Royal).

COLLATERAL BRANCH LIVING

Issue of late Hon Richard Westenra, 2nd son of 5th Baron, *b* 1893, *d* 1944: *m* 1st, 1919 (*m diss* 1936), Alice Florence, who *d* 1975, da of Maxwell Vandeleur Blacker-Douglas, of Seafield, Millbrook, Jersey, Channel Islands; 2ndly, 1936, Mrs Margaret Cecilia Sullivan Hope, who *d* 1979, da of Rev George Sullivan Edgcombe:—
(By 1st *m*) Cynthia Zia Hester, *b* 1920: *m* 1947 (*m diss* 1957), Eric Miles, son of Alfred Shakespear Miles, of Buenos Aires, Argentina, and has issue living, Richard Christopher (37 St Peter's Sq, W6 9NW), *b* 1955: *m* 1982, Sarah Dawson, and has issue living, Robert Henry Shakespear *b* 1988, Henry Blacker Shakespear *b* 1990, Katharine Westenra *b* 1985, — Caroline Rose, *b* 1948: *m* 1970, James Peter Stansfeld-Huelin, of La Vallonerie, La Blinerie, St Clements, Jersey, CI, and has issue living, Alicia Antoinette *b* 1975, Rosanna Arlette *b* 1978, — Sylvia Claire, *b* 1950: *m* 1979, Guy Robert William Woods, of Homestead, Rue De La Fontaine, St Lawrence, Jersey, CI (*see* Pelly, Bt, 1990 Edn), and has issue living, Serena Sylvia *b* 1982.

PREDECESSORS – (1) ROBERT Cuninghame, son of late Col David Cuningham; *b* 17-; a Gen in the Army, and Col 5th Dragoons; MP for Tulske 1751-60, for Armagh 1761-8, for Monaghan 1769-96, and for E Grinstead 1788-9; *cr Baron Rossmore*, of Monaghan, co Monaghan (peerage of Ireland) 1796, with remainder to his wife's nephews, Henry Alexander Jones (who *dsp*) and Warner William and Henry Westenra: *m* 1754, Elizabeth, who *d* 1824, 2nd da and co-heiress of the late Col John Murray; *d* 1801; *s* by his nephew (2) WARNER WILLIAM Westenra, 2nd Baron; *b* 1765; MP for co Monaghan 1800-1801; *cr Baron Rossmore*, of co Monaghan (peerage of United Kingdom) 1838: *m* 1st, 1791, Marianne, who *d* 1807, da of late Charles Walsh, of Walsh Park, co Tipperary; 2ndly, 1819, Lady Augusta Charteris, who *d* 1840, da of Francis, Lord Elcho; *d* 1842; *s* by his el son (3) HENRY ROBERT, 3rd Baron; *b* 1792; was MP for co Monaghan 1818-32 and 1834-42, and afterwards Lord-Lieut thereof: *m* 1st, 1844; 2ndly, 1846, his cousin, Julia Ellen Josephine, who *d* 1912, da of Henry Lloyd, of Farinrory, co Tipperary; *d* 1860; *s* by his el son (4) HENRY CAIRNES, 4th Baron; Cornet 1st Life Guards; *d* 1874; *s* by his brother (5) DERRICK WARNER WILLIAM, 5th Baron; Lieut of co Monaghan: *m* 1882, Mittie, OBE, who *d* 1953, da of Richard Christopher Naylor, of Hooton Hall, Cheshire; *d* 1921; *s* by his el son (6) WILLIAM, 6th Baron; *b* 1892; European War 1914-18, European War 1939-45 as Lieut RNVR: *m* 1927, Dolores Cecil, who *d* 1981, formerly wife of late Col Maurice George Lee, and da of late Lieut-Col James Alban Wilson, DSO, Indian Army, of West Barton, Yorkshire; *d* 1958; *s* by his only son (7) WILLIAM WARNER, 7th Baron, and present peer.

ROTHERMERE, VISCOUNT (Harmsworth) (Viscount UK 1919, Bt UK 1910)

He who acts diligently acts well

VERE HAROLD ESMOND HARMSWORTH, 3rd Viscount, and 3rd Baronet; *b* 27 Aug 1925; *s* 1978; *ed* Eton, and Kent Sch, Conn, USA; FBIA; FRSA; Trustee of Reuters since 1970, and Chm of Asso Newspapers Ltd since 1970; launched new *Daily Mail* 3 May 1971, and *Mail on Sunday* 1982; Chm of Newsvendors' Benevolent Inst Festival Appeal 1963, Pres of Nat Advertising Benevolent Soc 1964-65, of Cttee of Advertising Assoc 1965, Festival Pres Newspaper Press Fund 1966, Pres Newspaper Press Fund 1967; Pres Printers' Charitable Corp 1975-76; Pres Commonwealth Press Union 1983-89; patron of three livings; Cdr of Order Merit of Republic of Italy 1977; Cdr Order of Lion of Finland 1978; Cdr Order of the Southern Cross of Republic of Brazil 1993: *m* 1st, 1957, Patricia Evelyn Beverley, who *d* 1992, da of John William Matthews, FIAS, and formerly wife of Capt Christopher John Brooks (*see* B Crawshaw); 2ndly, 1993, Maiko Joeong-shun Lee, of Kyoto, Japan, and has issue by 1st *m*.

Arms – Azure, two scrolls of paper in saltire or, banded in the centre gules, between four bees volant of the second. **Crest** – Between two ostrich feathers or a cubit arm erect proper, the hand grasping a roll of paper or. **Supporters** – On either side a gladiator fully habited and accoutred, the dexter holding in the exterior hand a sword, and the sinister holding on the exterior arm a shield all proper, each charged on the breast with a fountain.

Residence – 36 Rue du Sentier, Paris 75002. *Clubs* – Boodle's, Roy Yacht Sqdn, Beefsteak, The Brook (New York), Travellers' (Paris).

SON LIVING (By 1st marriage)

Hon (HAROLD) JONATHAN ESMOND VERE, *b* 3 Dec 1967: *m* 1993, Claudia C., da of T. J. Clemence, of Wilton Crescent, SW1.

DAUGHTERS LIVING (By 1st marriage)

Hon Geraldine Theodora Mary Gabriel, *b* 1957: *m* 1981 (*m diss* 1990), David John, Lord Ogilvy, el son of 13th Earl of Airlie.
Hon Camilla Patricia Caroline, *b* 1964: *m* 1989, Andrew R. Yeates, and has issue living, Sebastian Andrew Alexander Vere, *b* 1990, — Alexander Samuel Jonathan Vere, *b* 1993.

HALF BROTHER LIVING

Hon Esmond Vyvyan, *b* (June) 1967.

SISTERS LIVING

Hon Lorna Peggy Vyvyan (*Hon Lady Cooper-Key*), *b* (Oct) 1920: *m* 1941, Sir (Edmund Mc) Neill Cooper-Key, who *d* 1981 (*see* Wigram, Bt, colls, 1973-74 Edn), and has had issue, Adrian Astley Vere, *b* 1942; *ed* Eton; *d* as the result of a motor accident in Spain 1963, — (Kevin) Esmond Peter, *b* 1943; *ed* Le Rosey, Millfield, and Carleton Univ, Canada: *m* 1st, 1971 (*m diss* 1976), Lady Mary Gaye Georgiana Lorna Curzon, da of 6th Earl Howe; 2ndly, 1980, Anna (who *m* 2ndly, 1987, Thomas C. U. M. Lundstrom, of Hurdcott House, Hurdcott, Winterbourne Earls, Salisbury, Wilts), da of Count Wilhelm Wachtmeister, Swedish Ambassador to USA, and *d* 1985, leaving issue (by 1st *m*), Pandora Lorna Mary *b* 1973, (by 2nd *m*) Cosmo *b* 1980, Cara *b* 1981, — Emma Charlotte, *b* 1958: resumed her maiden name until re-marriage: *m* 1st, 1985 (*m diss* 19—), Hilary Ord Chittenden, son of late N. G. Chittenden; 2ndly, 1989, (Brian) James Douglas Collins, and has issue (by 2nd *m*) (*see* E Morton). *Residence* – Floralies, Ave de Grande Bretagne, Monte Carlo, Monaco.
Hon Esme Mary Gabriel, CVO, *b* 1922; a Lady of the Bedchamber to HM 1967-71, and an Extra Lady of the Bedchamber to HM, 1974-93, since when an Extra Woman of the Bedchamber to HM; CVO 1980: *m* 1st, 1942, 3rd Earl of Cromer, KG, GCMG, MBE, PC, who *d* 1991; 2ndly, 1993, as his 2nd wife, (Reinier) Gerrit Anton van der Woude, late Capt Gren Guards.

PREDECESSORS – (1) *Rt Hon* HAROLD SIDNEY Harmsworth, 2nd son of late Alfred Harmsworth, Bar-at-Law; *b* 1868; sometime Ch Proprietor of the *Daily Mail, Evening News*, etc, Chm of Associated Newspapers, Ltd, and a Director of the Amalgamated Press, Ltd; was Director-Gen of Roy Army Clothing Depart 1916, and Pres of Air Council 1917-18; *cr* a *Baronet*, 1910, *Baron Rothermere*, of Hemstead, co Kent (peerage of UK) 1914, and *Viscount Rothermere*, of Hemsted, co Kent (peerage of UK) 1919: *m* 1893, Mary Lilian, who *d* 1937, da of George Wade Share, of Forest Hill, SE; *d* 1940; *s* by his 3rd but only surviving son (2) ESMOND CECIL, 2nd Viscount; *b* 1898, was MP Isle of Thanet Div, Kent 1919-29; Chm of Assoc Newspapers, and *Daily Mail* and General Trust, Pres Newspaper Press Fund 1935-37, Chm Newspaper Proprietors' Assoc 1934-61, Chm Newsprint Supply Co 1940-59, Trustee Reuters New Agency: *m* 1st, 1920 (*m diss* 1938), Margaret Hunam, who *d* 1991 (having *m* 2ndly, 1938 (*m diss* 1946), as his 2nd wife, Capt Thomas Andrew Hussey, CBE, RN, who *d* 1980, and 3rdly, 1947, as his 2nd wife, Sir John Lionel Reginald Blunt, 10th Bt, who *d* 1969), da of late William Lancelot Redhead, of Carville Hall, Brentford; 2nd, 1945 (*m diss* 1952), Ann Geraldine Mary, who *d* 1981, el da of Hon Guy Lawrence Charteris (*see* E Wemyss), and widow of 3rd Baron O'Neill; 3rdly 1966, Mary, who *d* 1993, el da of Kenneth Murchison, of Dallas, Texas, and formerly wife of Richard Ohrstrom, of The Plains, Virginia; *d* 1978; *s* by his el son (3) VERE HAROLD ESMOND, 3rd Viscount and present peer; also Baron Rothermere.

ROTHERWICK, BARON (Cayzer) (Baron UK 1939, Bt UK 1924)

(HERBERT) ROBIN CAYZER, 2nd Baron, and 2nd Baronet; *b* 5 Dec 1912; *s* 1958; *ed* Eton, and Ch Ch Oxford (BA 1935); formerly Major The Greys (Supplementary Reserve); Dep Chm Caledonia Investments plc; Middle East 1939-45: *m* 1952, Sarah Jane, who *d* 1978, only da of Sir Michael Nial Slade, 6th Bt, and has issue.

ᴀrms – Per chevron azure and argent, two estoiles or and an ancient ship with three masts, sails furled sable, pinions flying gules; a chief invected of the third charged with a rose gules barbed and seeded proper between two fleurs-de-lis of the first. Ϲrest – A sea-lion erect proper, gorged with a naval crown and holding in his dexter paw an estoile gold. ᴤupporters – *Dexter*, a lion; and *sinister*, a Bengal tiger proper; each gorged with a naval crown or, and grasping a flagpole also proper, flying therefrom a banner gules, thereon a lozenge argent charged with a lion rampant, also gules.
Residence – Rangers Lodge, Charlbury, Oxon OX7 3HL. *Club* – White's.

SONS LIVING

Hon (HERBERT) ROBIN, *b* 12 March 1954: *m* 1982, Sara Jane, only da of Robert James McAlpine, of Tilstone Lodge, Tarporley, Cheshire (*see* McAlpine, Bt, colls), and has issue living, Herbert Robin, *b* 10 July 1989, — Henry Alexander, *b* 1991, — Harriette Jane, *b* 1986. *Residence* – Cornbury Park, Charlbury, Oxford OX7 3EH.
Hon Charles William, *b* 1957: *m* 1985, Amanda C.S., 2nd da of John Squire, of Marbella, Spain, and has issue living, (Charles) William, *b* 1991, — Victoria Amanda, *b* 1989. *Residence* – Finstock Manor, Finstock, Oxon OX7 3DG.
Hon Avon Arthur, *b* 1968.

DAUGHTER LIVING

Hon Robina Jane, *b* 1953: *m* 1981, Olivier Debarge, of 3 Redesdale St, SW3, and has issue living, Alexandra Jane *b* 1982, — Iona Amelia, *b* 1986.

SISTER LIVING

Hon Molly Angela (*Hon Lady Wyldbore-Smith*), *b* 1917: *m* 1944, Maj-Gen Sir Francis Brian Wyldbore Wyldbore-Smith, CB, DSO, OBE (*see* Smith-Marriott, Bt, colls). *Residence* – Grantham House, Grantham, Lincs, NG31 6SS.

WIDOW LIVING OF SON OF FIRST BARON

Baroness Sybille de Selys Longchamps: *m* 1982, as his 2nd wife, Hon (Michael) Anthony (Rathbone) Cayzer, who *d* 1990.

COLLATERAL BRANCH LIVING

Issue of late Hon (Michael) Anthony (Rathbone) Cayzer, yr son of 1st Baron, *b* 1920, *d* 1990: *m* 1st, 1952, Hon Patricia Helen Browne, who *d* 1981, da of 4th Baron Oranmore and Browne; 2ndly, 1982, Baroness Sybille de Selys Longchamps (ante):—
(By 1st *m*) (Linda) Kinvara, *b* 1953: *m* 1st, 1979 (*m diss* 1989), Timothy James Douro Hoare, eldest son of Michael Douro Hoare, of Downland Court, Ditchling, Sussex; 2ndly, 1994, Alan Holder, and has issue living (by 1st *m*), Sam Patrick Douro, *b* 1981. *Residence* – Model Farm, Kings Langley, Herts. —— Rosanne (*Hon Mrs Hugh Tollemache*), *b* 1956: *m* 1986, Hon Hugh John Hamilton Tollemache, yst son of 6th Baron Tollemache, and has issue. *Residence* – Sandbourne House, Earl's Croome, Worcs WR8 9GD. —— Verena Brigid, *b* 1961: *m* 1985, R. Ian Molson, 3rd son of William M. Molson, of Montreal, Canada, and has issue living, Edward Charles, *b* 1987, — Camilla Rose, *b* 1989.

PREDECESSOR – (1) HERBERT ROBIN Cayzer, 5th son of Sir Charles (William) Cayzer, 1st Bt (*cr* 1904), of Gartmore, Perthshire; *b* 1881; Chm British & Commonwealth Steamship Co Ltd, Clan Line Steamers Ltd, Union Castle Mail Steamship Co Ltd, and other Cos; MP for S Div of Portsmouth (*C*) 1918-22, and 1923-39; *cr* a *Baronet* 1924, and *Baron Rotherwick*, of Tylney, co Southampton (peerage of United Kingdom) 1939: *m* 1911, Freda Penelope, who *d* 1961, da of late Col William Hans Rathbone, formerly of Scripplestown and of Kilcogy, co Cavan; *d* 1958; *s* by his el son (2) (HERBERT) ROBIN, 2nd Baron and present peer.

ROTHES, EARL OF (Leslie) (Earl S before 1457)
(Title pronounced "Roth-ez")

IAN LIONEL MALCOLM LESLIE, 21st Earl; *b* 10 May 1932, *s* 1975; *ed* Eton; late Sub-Lieut RNVR: *m* 1955, Marigold, only da of late Sir David Martyn Evans Bevan, 1st Bt, and has issue.

Arms – Quarterly: 1st and 4th, Argent on a bend azure three buckles or, *Leslie*; 2nd and 3rd or, a lion rampant, gules, debruised by a ribbon sable, *Abernethy*. **Crest** – A demi-griffin proper. **Supporters** – Two griffins proper.
Residence – Tanglewood, W Tytherley, Salisbury, Wilts.

SONS LIVING

JAMES MALCOLM DAVID (*Lord Leslie*), *b* 4 June 1958.
Hon Alexander John, *b* 1962; *ed* Eton: *m* 1990, Tina L., da of Dr T. E. Gordon, of Westmoreland Drive, Orlando, Florida, USA. *Residence* – Berryside, by Leven, Fife KY8 5PH.

SISTERS LIVING

Lady Jean, *b* 1927: *m* 1949, Roderick Robin Mackenzie (Troubridge, Bt). *Residence* – Kingfisher House, Ampfield, Hants.
Lady Evelyn, *b* 1929: *m* 1949, Gerard William Mackworth Mackworth-Young (*see* Young, Bt *cr* 1813, colls), who *d* 1984. *Residence* – Fisherton Mill, Fisherton de la Mere, Warminster, Wilts BA12 OPZ.

WIDOW LIVING OF SON OF NINETEENTH EARL

Coral Angela, da of late George Henry Pinckard, JP, of Combe Court, Chiddingfold, Surrey, and 9 Chesterfield St, W1: *m* 1932, Hon John Wayland Leslie, late Flight-Lieut RAF Vol Reserve, who *d* 1991. *Residence* – Guildford House, Castle Hill, Farnham, Surrey GU9 7JG.

COLLATERAL BRANCHES LIVING

Issue of late Hon John Wayland Leslie, late Flight-Lieut RAF Vol Reserve, yr son of 19th Earl, *b* 1909, *d* 1991: *m* 1932, Coral Angela (ante), da of late George Henry Pinckard, JP, of Combe Court, Chiddingfold, Surrey, and 9 Chesterfield St, W1:—
Alastair Pinckard, TD, *b* 1934; *ed* Eton; formerly Capt RSF (TA); Member Queen's Body Guard for Scotland (Royal Company of Archers): *m* 1963, Rosemary, da of late Cdr Hubert Wyndham Barry, RN, of Hill House, Broughton, Hants (*see* Barry, Bt, colls), and has had issue, †David John, *b* 1967, *d* 1989, — Fiona Jane, *b* 1965: *m* 1990, Richard Alan Patrick de Klee, yst son of Col Murray de Klee, OBE, of Auchnacraig, Isle of Mull, and has issue living, Frederick Leslie Blair *b* 1993, — Ann Mary, *b* 1973. *Residence* – Seasyde House, by Errol, Perthshire PH2 7TA. —— Amber Elizabeth, *b* 1939: *m* 1964, Beresford Robert Winder White, and has issue living, Rupert Beresford, *b* 1966, — Alexander Richard Beresford, *b* 1968. *Residence* – Dumpford Manor House, Trotton, nr Rogate, Petersfield, Hants.

Issue of late Hon Edward Courtenay Haworth-Leslie, 2nd son of Mary Elizabeth, Countess of Rothes, *b* 1840, *d* 1911: *m* 1890, Caroline Edith, who *d* 1948, da of Thomas Tregenna Biddulph, of The Earee, Shoalhaven, NS Wales:—
Edward Biddulph, *b* 1895; 1914-18 War as Cpl AIF in France. —— Martin Tregenna, *b* 1896; Lt Australian Reserve of Officers; 1914-18 War in Egypt, Gallipoli, and France (wounded): *m* 1st, 1928, Nettie Margaret, who *d* 1943, da of William Harper, of Napier, NZ; 2ndly, 1945, Joyce Enid, da of Rev Alfred James Gardner, of Chatswood, NSW, and widow of Rev L. M. Dunstan, and has issue living, (by 1st *m*), Mary Haworth, *b* 1936. —— Norman Evelyn, *b* 1898: *m* 1944, Helen Thomson, da of James Thomson Robertson.

PREDECESSORS – (1) GEORGE Leslie, *cr* Lord Leslie (peerage of Scotland 1445), and *Earl of Rothes* (peerage of Scotland) before 1457; *d* 1488; *s* by his grandson (2) GEORGE, 2nd Earl; *d* 1513; *s* by his brother (3) WILLIAM, 3rd Earl; killed at Flodden 1513; *s* by his son (4) GEORGE, 4th Earl, Extraordinary Lord of Session; *d* 1558; *s* by his son (5) ANDREW, 5th Earl; *d* 1611; *s* by his grandson (6) JOHN, 6th Earl, one of the first signatories of National Covenant 1638; *d* 1641; *s* by his son (7) JOHN, 7th Earl; carried the Sword of State at the Coronation of Charles II at Scone 1651; was taken a prisoner at battle of Worcester, his estates were forfeited, and he was kept in confinement 1651-8; on the Restoration he was constituted Pres of the Council, and an Extraordinary Lord of Session, was High Commr to the Parliament at Edinburgh 1663, and Keeper of the Privy Seal 1664, Gen of the Forces in Scotland 1666, and Lord High Chancellor for life 1667; obtained in 1663 a charter conferring the *Earldom of Rothes*, and the Lordship of Leslie, regranted as *Leslie and Ballenbreich* in default of male issue upon his el da and her descendants male and female, with the stipulation that the Earldoms of Rothes and Haddington should not be united, and in 1680 was *cr Lord Auchmuty and Caskieberry, Viscount Lugtown, Earl of Leslie, Marquess of Ballenbreich*, and *Duke of Rothes* (peerage of Scotland); *d* without male issue 1681, when the peerages of 1680 expired, and the Earldom of Rothes and inferior honours devolved upon his el da (8) MARGARET, wife of Charles, 5th Earl of Haddington; *d* 1700; *s* by her el son (9) JOHN Hamilton, 9th Earl; assumed the surname of Leslie; appointed a Scottish Representative Peer 1708; *d* 1722; *s* by his son (10) JOHN, KT, 10th Earl; a Lieut-Gen in the Army, and Com-in-Ch of the Forces in Ireland and a Representative Peer; *d* 1767; *s* by his son (11) JOHN, 11th Earl; *dsp* 1773; *s* by his el sister (12) JANE ELIZABETH, wife of George Raymond Evelyn; *d* 1810; *s* by her son (13) GEORGE WILLIAM, 13th Earl; *d* 1817; *s* by his da (14) HENRIETTA ANNE, wife of George Gwyther; assumed the name of Leslie; *d* 1819; *s* by her son (15) GEORGE WILLIAM EVELYN, 15th Earl; *b* 1809: *m* 1831, Louisa, who *d* 1886, da of Col Anderson Morshead, RE; *d* 1841; *s* by his son (16) GEORGE WILLIAM EVELYN, 16th Earl; *d* unmarried 1859; *s* by his sister (17) HENRIETTA ANDERSON MORSHEAD: *m* 1861, Hon George Waldegrave, who assumed the additional surname of Leslie, yst son of 8th Earl Waldegrave; *dsp* 10 Feb 1886; *s* by her aunt (18) MARY ELIZABETH (2nd da of Henrietta Anne (ante No 14)), *b* 1811: *m* 1835, Martin E. Haworth, who *d* Nov 1886, having in March of that year assumed the additional surname of Leslie; *d* 1893; *s* by her grandson (19) NORMAN EVELYN (son of late Martin Leslie Haworth, who *d* before his mother *s* to the Earldom), 19th Earl, *b* 1877; a Representative Peer for Scotland: *m* 1900, Lucy Noël Martha (who *d* 1956, having *m* 2ndly, 1927, Col Claud Macfie, DSO, who *d* 1963), only child of late Thomas Dyer-Edwardes, of Prinknash Park, Gloucester, and Charmandean, Broadwater, Sussex; *d* 1927; *s* by his son (20) MALCOLM GEORGE DYER EDWARDES, 20th Earl *b* 1902; Representative Peer for Scotland 1931-59; Member Queen's Body Guard for Scotland (Royal Company of Archers), Maj Gen List 1940; Dir of Tyres 1941-45, Chm Trinidad Petroleum Co Ltd, Butterworth & Co (Publishers) Ltd, Nat Mutual Life Assurance Soc, Dep Chm British Electric Traction Ltd, Dir Inst of Opthalmology,

Rothes Chair in Public Health Opthalmology established at London Univ 1977: *m* 1926, Beryl Violet, who *d* 1994, only da of James Lionel Dugdale, of Crathorne Hall, Yorks; *d* 1975; *s* by his son **(21)** IAN LIONEL MALCOLM, 21st Earl and present peer; also Lord Leslie and Ballenbreich.

Rothesay, Duke of; title borne by Prince of Wales.

ROTHSCHILD, BARON (Rothschild) (Baron UK 1885, Bt UK 1847)

Concord, integrity, industry

(NATHANIEL CHARLES) JACOB ROTHSCHILD, 4th Baron, and 5th Baronet; *b* 29 April 1936; *s* 1990; *ed* Eton, and Ch Ch, Oxford; Chm J. Rothschild Holdings plc since 1971, Chm Board of Trustees National Gallery since 1985, Member of Council RCA since 1986, Chm Nat Heritage Memorial Fund since 1991; Cdr of Order of Henry the Navigator (Portugal) 1985: *m* 1961, Serena Mary, da of Sir Philip Gordon Dunn, 2nd Bt (ext), and has issue.

Arms – Quarterly: 1st or, an eagle displayed sable langued gules; 2nd and 3rd azure, issuing from the dexter and sinister sides of the shield, an arm embowed proper, grasping five arrows points to the base argent; 4th or, a lion rampant proper, langued gules, over all an escutcheon gules, thereon a target, the point to the dexter proper. **Crest** – 1st (*centre*), issuant from a ducal coronet or, an eagle displayed sable; 2nd (*dexter*), out of a ducal coronet or, between open buffalo horns per fesse or and sable, a mullet of six points or; 3rd (*sinister*), out of a ducal coronet or, three ostrich feathers, the centre one argent, the exterior ones azure. **Supporters** – (of the Austrian Barony), — *Dexter*, a lion rampant or; *sinister*, an unicorn argent.
Residences – 28 Warwick Av, W9; Stowell Park, Marlborough, Wilts; *Club* – White's.

SON LIVING

Hon NATHANIEL PHILIP VICTOR JAMES, *b* 1971; *ed* Wadham Coll, Oxford.

DAUGHTERS LIVING

Hon Hannah Mary, *b* 1962.
Hon Beth Matilda, *b* 1964: *m* 1991, Antonio Tomassini, son of Georgio Tomassini, and has issue living, a son, *b* 1992.
Hon Emily Magda, *b* 1967.

HALF-BROTHER LIVING

Hon Amschel Mayor James, *b* 1955; *ed* Leys Sch, and City Univ, London: *m* 1981, Anita Patience, 3rd da of James Edward Alexander Rundel Guinness, of 36 Phillimore Gdns, W8, and has issue living, James Amschel Victor, *b* 1985, — Kate Emma, *b* 1982, — Alice Miranda, *b* 1983. *Residence* – 11 Herschel Rd, Cambridge CB3 9AG.

SISTERS LIVING

Hon Sarah, *b* 1934; *ed* St Hilda's Coll, Oxford: *m* 1st, 19— (*m diss* 19—), James Douglas-Henry, of London; 2ndly, 19—,— Daniel, and has issue living (by 1st *m*), Thomas James DANIEL, *b* 19—; has assumed surname of Daniel in lieu of his patronymic: *m* 1993, Emma Louise Gilmour, yr da of John Robert Purvis, CBE, of Gilmerton, St Andrews, Fife, — Sharon, *b* 19—: *m* 19—, Da'ad de Gunzbourg, and has issue living, Patrice *b* 19—. *Residence* – 72 Victoria Park, Cambridge.
Hon Miranda, *b* 1940.

HALF-SISTERS LIVING

Hon Emma Georgina, *b* 1948; *ed* Somerville Coll, Oxford.
Hon Victoria Katherine, *b* 1953; *ed* Bedford Coll, London.

AUNT LIVING (*sister of 3rd Baron*) (*Raised to the rank of a Baron's daughter* 1938)

Hon Miriam Louisa, CBE, FRS (1985), *b* 1908; DScP (Oxon); Hon DSc Leicester, Hull, Goteborg, North Western Univ, Open Univ; Prof Roy Free Hosp, and a Trustee of British Museum; CBE (Civil) 1982: *m* 1943 (*m diss* 1957), George Lane, MC, and has issue living, Charles Daniel, *b* 1948, — Mary Rozsika, *b* 1945, — Charlotte Theresa, *b* 1951, — Johanna Miriam, *b* 1951. *Residence* – Ashton Wold, Peterborough PE8 5LZ.

WIDOW LIVING OF THIRD BARON

TERESA GEORGINA, MBE (*Teresa, Baroness Rothschild*), da of late Robert John Grote Mayor, CB, of 26 Addison Av, W11: *m* 1946, as his 2nd wife, the 3rd Baron, GBE, GM, FRS, who *d* 1990. *Residence* –

COLLATERAL BRANCHES LIVING

(In remainder to Baronetcy only)

Grandchildren of late Leopold DE ROTHSCHILD, CVO, son of late Baron Lionel Nathan Rothschild, el brother of 1st baronet:—
Issue of late Major Lionel Nathan DE ROTHSCHILD, OBE, *b* 1882, *d* 1942: *m* 1912, Marie-Louise Eugenie, who *d* 1975, da of late Edmond Beer, of Paris:—

Edmund Leopold, TD, *b* 1916; *ed* Harrow, and Trin Coll, Camb (MA); Hon LLD Memorial Univ of Newfoundland 1961, Hon DSc Salford Univ; Order (1st Class) of the Sacred Treasure of Japan; Major RA (TA); Dir of N. M. Rothschild & Sons Ltd; 1939-45 War (wounded): *m* 1st, 1948, Elizabeth Edith, who *d* 1980, da of late Marcell Lentner, of Vienna, Austria; 2ndly, 1982, Anne Evelyn, JP, widow of Lt-Col J. Malcolm Harrison, OBE, TD, and has issue living (by 1st *m*), Nicholas David, *b* 1951: *m* 1985, Caroline J. L., da of late Lawrence Darvall, of Reading, Berks, and has an adopted da, Chloe Alix Irina *b* 1990, — (David) Lionel, *b* 1955: *m* 1991, Louise de C., yst da of late Dr P. M. de C. Williams, of Boar's Hill, Oxford, and has issue living, Leopold James *b* 1994, Elizabeth Naomi *b* 1992, — Katherine Juliette, *b* 1949: *m* 1971, Marcus Ambrose Paul Agius, of 7 South Terr, SW7 2TB, and has issue living, Marie-Louise Eleanor *b* 1977, Lara Sophie Elizabeth *b* 1980, — Charlotte Henrietta, *b* (twin) 1955: *m* 1990, Nigel S. Brown, yr son of late Michael G. H. Brown. *Residence* – Exbury House, Exbury, Southampton. —— Leopold David, CBE, *b* 1927; *cr* CBE (Civil) 1985; Member of Council of Winston Churchill Memorial Trust since 1990. —— Rosemary Leonora, *b* 1913: *m* 1st, 1934 (*m diss* 1942), Maj Hon Denis Gomer Berry, TD, Gren Gds, who *d* 1983, (*see* V Kemsley); 2ndly, 1942, John Antony Seys, who *d* 1989, of Yew Tree Cottage, Blackheath, Guildford, Surrey GU4 8QU, and has issue living (by 1st *m*) (*see* V Kemsley), — (by 2nd *m*) David Godfrey Antony (Aston House, Blackheath, Guildford, Surrey, GU4 8RD), *b* 1947: *m* 1978, Nicola Barrington Baird, and has issue living, Philip Christopher Hugh *b* 1984. —— Naomi Louisa Nina, *b* 1920: *m* 1st, 1941, Jean Pierre Reinach, who was *ka* 1942; 2ndly, 1947, Bertrand Goldschmidt, and has issue living, (by 1st *m*) Jocelyne Marguerite Marie Louise, *b* 1942: *m* 1965, Claude Brice, of Paris, — (by 2nd *m*) Paul Lionel, *b* 1952: *m* 1982, Cynthia Hampton, — Emma Louise, *b* 1955: *m* 1987, David Machover. *Residence* – 11 Boulevard Flandrin, Paris, XVI.

Issue of late Anthony Gustav DE ROTHSCHILD, *b* 1887, *d* 1961: *m* 1926, Yvonne (Ascott Cottage, Wing, Leighton Buzzard, Bedfordshire), da of late Robert Cahen d'Anvers, of Paris:—
Sir Evelyn Robert Adrian (Ascott, Wing, Leighton Buzzard, Beds), *b* 1931; *ed* Harrow and Trin Coll, Camb; Kt 1989: *m* 1st, 1966 (*m diss* 1971), Jeanette, who *d* 1981, da of late Ernest Bishop; 2ndly 1973, Victoria, da of Lewis Schott, and has issue living (by 2nd *m*), Anthony James, *b* 1977, — David Mayer, *b* 1978, — Jessica, *b* 1974. —— Renée Louis Marie, *b* 1927: *m* 1955, Peter David Robeson. *Residence* – Fences Farm, Tyringham, Newport Pagnell, Bucks.

PREDECESSORS – **(1)** ANTHONY de Rothschild, second son of Nathan Mayer Rothschild, of Frankfort-on-Main, who was *cr* a Baron of the Austrian Empire 1822; *b* 1810; a merchant and banker in London; *cr* a *Baronet* 1847 with remainder to the issue of the sons of his elder brother Lionel: *m* 1840, Louise, who *d* 1910, da of late Abraham Montefiore, of Stamford Hill, Middlesex; *d* 1876; *s* by his nephew **(2)** NATHANIEL MAYER, GCVO, PC (el son of late Baron Lionel Nathan de Rothschild, MP, the first Member of the Jewish persuasion to enter Parliament), 2nd baronet; *s* by special remainder, his uncle, Sir ANTHONY, as 2nd Baronet 1876, and *cr Baron Rothschild*, of Tring, co Hertford (peerage of United Kingdom) 1885; Lord-Lieut of Bucks 1887-1915; MP for Aylesbury (*L*) 1865-85: *m* 1867, Emma Louisa, who *d* 1935, da of Baron Carl de Rothschild, of Frankfort-on-Main; *d* 1915; *s* by his el son **(3)** LIONEL WALTER, 2nd Baron, *b* 1868; a Trustee of British Museum, Lieut for City of London; FRS; MP for Bucks, Mid, or Aylesbury Div (LU) 1899-1910; *dunm* 1937; *s* by his nephew **(4)** NATHANIEL MAYER VICTOR, GBE, GM, FRS (only son of Hon (Nathaniel) Charles Rothschild, 2nd son of 1st Baron), 3rd Baron, *b* 1910, Col Intelligence Corps 1939-45 War, Assist Dir of Research, Zoology Dept, Camb Univ 1950-70, Chm Agricultural Research Council 1948-58, Chm N. M. Rothschild and Sons 1975-76, and Rothschild Continuation Ltd 1976-88, Chm Shell Research Ltd 1963-70, etc, Dir Gen Central Policy Review Staff, Cabinet Office, 1971-74, author: *m* 1st, 1933 (*m diss* 1945), Barbara, who *d* 1989 (having *m* 2ndly, 1949 (*m diss* 19—), Rex Warner, who *d* 1986, and 3rdly, 1961, Nico Hadjikyriakou-Ghika), da of late St John Hutchinson, KC, Bar-at-law, Recorder of Hastings; 2ndly, 1946, Teresa Georgina, MBE, da of late Robert John Grote Mayor, CB, of 26 Addison Av, W11; *d* 1990; *s* by his elder son **(5)** (NATHANIEL CHARLES) JACOB, 4th Baron and present peer.

ROWALLAN, BARON (Corbett) (Baron UK 1911)

God feeds the ravens

JOHN POLSON CAMERON CORBETT, 4th Baron; *b* 8 March 1947; *s* 1993; *ed* Eton, and RAC Cirencester; ARICS: *m* 1st, 1971 (*m diss* 1983), Susan Jane Dianne, da of James A. Green, of New Farm House, South Linden, Longhorsley, Northumberland; 2ndly, 1984 (*m diss* 1994), Sandrew Filomena, da of William Bryson, of Holland Green, Kilmaurs, Ayrshire, and has issue by 1st and 2nd *m*.

Arms – Quarterly, 1st and 4th argent, a key fesse-wise, wards downwards between two ravens sable, *Corbett*; 2nd and 3rd, azure, a chevron or between two bears' heads couped argent muzzled gules in chief, and in base a cross moline of the third, *Polson*. Crest - A branch of an oak proper, thereon a raven sable. Supporters – *Dexter*, a salmon proper, holding in its mouth a jewelled ring or; *sinister*, a seal also proper.
Residence – Meiklemosside, Fenwick. Ayrshire KA3 6AY.

SONS LIVING *(By 1st marriage)*

Hon JASON WILLIAM POLSON CAMERON, *b* 21 April 1972; *ed* Glenalmond, and RAC Cirencester.

(By 2nd marriage)

Hon (Jonathan Arthur) Cameron, *b* 1985.

DAUGHTERS LIVING *(By 1st marriage)*

Hon Joanna Gwyn Alice Cameron, *b* 1974.

(By 2nd marriage)

Hon Soay Mairi Cameron, *b* 1988.

SISTERS LIVING

Hon Sarah Elizabeth Cameron, *b* 1949: *m* 1968, (Lachlan) Roderick Maclean, and has issue living, Iona Charlotte, *b* 1969, — Sophy Emma, *b* 1972. *Residence* – 8 Elthiron Rd, SW6.
Hon Anne Mary Cameron, *b* 1953: *m* 1972, Rodney John Turner, and has issue living, James Anthony, *b* 1975; *ed* Milton Abbey, — Charles Rory, *b* 1981, — Nicola Anne Maria, *b* 1974, — Arabella Mary Claire, *b* 1984. *Residence* – Littlebrook House, Exbridge, nr Dulverton.

Hon Rosalind Eleanor Cameron, *b* 1958: *m* 1977, Jeremy Michael Sacher, and has issue living, Harry, *b* 1987, — Chloe Emma, *b* 1979, — Charlotte Daisy, *b* 1982. *Residence* – 11 Lansdowne Crescent, W11 2NJ.

UNCLES LIVING *(Sons of 2nd Baron)*

Hon Joseph Mervyn, *b* 1929; *ed* Eton, and Corpus Christie Coll, Camb (BA 1953); late 2nd Lieut Royal Scots Fusiliers: *m* 1960, Hon Catherine Lyon-Dalberg-Acton, da of 3rd Baron Acton, CMG, MBE, TD, and has issue living, Sebastian Antony (Chittlegrove, Rendcomb, nr Cirencester, Glos GL7 7DG), *b* 1963; *ed* Eton, and RAC Cirencester: *m* 1991, Mrs Doran Elizabeth Ann McPherson, only da of late Alan Leary, and has issue living, George Alan Cameron *b* 1993, — Victoria, *b* 1961: *m* 1988, Hugh Merrill, MVO, of 21 Bristol Gdns, W9 2JQ, son of Eric Merrill, of Monkseaton, Tyne & Wear, and has issue living, James Joseph *b* 1989, Guy Charles *b* 1992. *Residence* – The Old Rectory, Coates, nr Cirencester, Glos.
Hon Robert Cameron, *b* 1940; *ed* Eton, and Ch Ch, Oxford. *Residence* – Cankerton, Stewarton, Ayrshire. *Clubs* – White's, Beefsteak, Turf, Pratt's, Puffin's (Edinburgh).

AUNT LIVING *(Daughter of 2nd Baron)*

Hon Fiona Elizabeth Cameron, *b* 1942: *m* 1st, 1966 (*m diss* 1972), David Richard Amherst Cecil (*see* B Amherst of Hackney, colls); 2ndly, 1974, William Garry Patterson, late Maj Life Guards, and has issue living (by 1st *m*) (*see* B Amherst of Hackney, colls), — (by 2nd *m*), Joseph Robert William, *b* 1981. *Residence* – Kisby's Farm, Ecchingswell, Newbury, Berks RG15 8TS; 43 Holland Villas Rd, W14.

MOTHER LIVING

Eleanor Mary, da of late George Frederic Boyle (*see* E Glasgow, colls): *m* 1st, 1945 (*m diss* 1962), Capt Hon Arthur Cameron Corbett, late 3rd Baron Rowallan), who *d* 1993; 2ndly, 1963, Col (Richard) Derek Cardiff, late Scots Guards. *Residence* – Flat 1, 13 Embankment Gdns, SW3 4LW.

PREDECESSORS – **(1)** ARCHIBALD CAMERON Corbett, son of late Thomas Corbett, JP, of South Park, Cove, Dunbartonshire; *b* 1856; sat as MP for Tradeston Div of Glasgow (*L*) 1885-1911; *cr Baron Rowallan*, of Rowallan, co Ayr (peerage of United Kingdom) 1911: *m* 1887, Alice Mary, who *d* 1902, only da of John Polson, of Castle Levan, by Gourock; *d* 1933; *s* by his son **(2)** THOMAS GODFREY POLSON, KT, KBE, MC, TD, 2nd Baron, *b* 1895; Lt-Col RSF; Ch Scout of British Commonwealth and Empire 1945-59, Gov of Tasmania 1959-63; Hon Freeman of Edinburgh 1957: *m* 1918, Gwyn Mervyn (CStJ), who *d* 1971, da of Joseph B. Grimond, of St Andrews, Fife, *d* 1977; *s* by his son **(3)** ARTHUR CAMERON, 3rd Baron, *b* 1919; Capt Ayrshire Yeo; 1939-45 War (despatches, Croix de Guerre): *m* 1st, 1945 (*m diss* 1962), Eleanor Mary, da of late George Frederic Boyle (*see* E Glasgow, colls); 2ndly, 1963 (*m* annulled 1970), April Ashley; *d* 1993; *s* by his eldest son **(4)** JOHN POLSON CAMERON, 4th Baron and present peer.

ROWLEY, BARONY OF (Henderson) (Extinct 1968)

WIDOW LIVING OF LIFE BARON

MARY ELIZABETH (*Baroness Rowley*), (POB 5, Miami Shores, Florida 33153, USA), da of Ernest Verrall Barnes, of Finchley, N, and widow of Harold Gliksten, of London: *m* 1958, Baron Rowley (Life Baron), who *d* 1968.

ROXBURGHE, DUKE OF (InnesKer) (Duke S 1707, Bt S 1625)
(Title pronounced "Roxborough", Name pronounced "InnezCarr" Seat pronounced "Fleurs")

For Christ and country danger is sweet

GUY DAVID INNES-KER, 10th Duke, 11th Baronet, and Premier Baronet of Scotland or Nova Scotia; *b* 18 Nov 1954; *s* 1974; *ed* Eton, Magdalene Coll, Camb, and RMA; Lt Blues and Royals (RHG and 1st Dragoons): *m* 1st, 1977 (*m diss* 1990), Lady Jane Meriel Grosvenor, da of 5th Duke of Westminster; 2ndly, 1992, Virginia Mary, elder da of David Wynn-Williams, and of Mrs Christopher Edwards, and has issue by 1st *m*.

Arms – Quarterly: 1st and 4th grand quarters counter quartered, 1st and 4th, vert on a chevron between three unicorn's heads erased argent, as many mullets sable; 2nd and 3rd, gules, three mascles or, 2nd and 3rd grand quarters, argent three stars of five points azure. **Crests** – 1st, a unicorn's head erased argent, armed and maned or: 2nd, a boar's head erased proper, langued gules. **Supporters** – Two savages wreathed about the head and middle with laurel, and holding in their exterior hands a club resting on the shoulder all proper.
Seat – Floors Castle, Kelso, Roxburghshire.

SONS LIVING *(By 1st marriage)*

CHARLES ROBERT GEORGE (*Marquess of Bowmont and Cessford*), *b* 18 Feb 1981.
Lord Edward Arthur Gerald, *b* 1984.

DAUGHTER LIVING *(By 1st marriage)*

Lady Rosanagh Viola Alexandra, *b* 1979.

BROTHER LIVING

Lord Robert Anthony, *b* 1959; *ed* Gordonstoun; Lieut Blues and Royals; served in S Atlantic Campaign (despatches), 1982. *Residence* – 6 Fawcett St, SW10.

COLLATERAL BRANCHES LIVING

Issue of late Lieut-Col Lord Alastair Robert Innes-Ker, CVO, DSO, 2nd son of 7th Duke, *b* 1880, *d* 1936: *m* 1907, Anne, who *d* 1959, da of late William Lawrence Breese, of New York:—
(Eloise) Jean Horatia, *b* 1915: *m* 1940, Reginald Baron Black, late Sqdn-Ldr RAFVR, and has issue living, Nicola Jean-Anne, *b* 1943: *m* 1972, Archibald Donald Orr Ewing, of 13 Warriston Crescent, Edinburgh, and has issue (*see* Orr Ewing, Bt). *Residence* – Brook House, Fovant, Salisbury, Wilts.

Descendants of Thomas Ker, of Ferniehirst, brother of Walter Ker, great-great-grandfather of 1st Earl of Roxburghe:—
See M Lothian.

(In remainder to Baronetcy only)

Descendants of Alexander Innes, yr brother of James Innes, of Cromey, great-grandfather of 1st baronet:—

Grandchildren of late Arthur Charles Innes-Cross (who assumed the additional surname of Cross by Roy Licence 1888), son of Arthur Innes, of Dromantine, co Down, 8th in descent from Alexander Innes:—
Issue of late Arthur Charles Wolseley Innes, MC, Irish Guards, who relinquished the additional surname of Cross 19—; *b* 1888, *d* 1940: *m* 1915, Etta Maud, who *d* 1971, da of William Bradshaw, of Ordley Hill:—
William Anthony Wolseley, *b* 1935; *ed* Eton. *Residence* – 35 Whittingstall Rd, SW6. ——— Anne, *b* 1929: *m* 1959, Roger I. C. Ryland, and has issue living, Charles John, *b* 1962: *m* 1990, Jane M., elder da of Prof Charles Fowler Cullis, of Cuckfield, Sussex, and has issue living, Anna Elizabeth *b* 1991, Arabella Kate *b* 1994, — Anna, *b* 1960. *Residence* – 32a Pembroke Sq, W8.

PREDECESSORS – **(1)** Sir ROBERT Ker, Knt; *cr Lord Roxburghe* peerage of Scotland, before 31 March 1600, *Lord Ker of Cessford and Cavertoun*, and *Earl of Roxburghe* (peerage of Scotland) 1616, which honours in 1648 were by charter confirmed in remainder to his grandson Hon William Drummond, who was 4th son of his da Jean by her marriage with the 2nd Earl of Perth, and after him upon the three sons successively of his grand-da Jean, by her marriage with the 3rd Earl of Wigton, with the express stipulation that whoever should succeed should marry Jean, the da of his deceased son Harry, and failing her the next eldest da Anne, and failing her the next da Margaret, and a final remainder to heirs male whatsoever; was Keeper of the Privy Seal 1637; *d* 1650; *s* by his grandson (ante) **(2)** WILLIAM Drummond, 2nd Earl; assumed the surname of Ker, and *m* his cousin Jean, according to the stipulation of the remainder; *d* 1675; *s* by his son **(3)** *Rt Hon* ROBERT, 3rd Earl; *d* 1682; *s* by his el son **(4)** ROBERT, 4th Earl; *d* unmarried 1693; *s* by his brother **(5)** JOHN, KG; was Sec of State 1704; *cr Viscount Broxmouth, Earl of Kelso, Marquess of Bowmont and Cessford*, and *Duke of Roxburghe* (peerage of Scotland) 1707, with remainder to the heirs who should inherit the Earldom of Roxburghe; *d* 1741; *s* by his son **(6)** ROBERT, 2nd Duke, who in 1722 had been *cr Baron Ker*, of Wakefield, co York, and *Earl Ker* (peerage of Great Britain); *d* 1755; *s* by his son **(7)** JOHN, KG, KT, 3rd Duke; *d* unmarried 1804 when the peerages of Great Britain (*cr* 1722) expired, and the Scottish honours devolved upon his kinsman **(8)** WILLIAM, 4th Duke, who in 1797 had *s* as 7th *Lord Bellenden of Broughton*, peerage of Scotland, *cr* 1661; *dsp* 1805, when the Lordship of Bellenden of Broughton became extinct and the Scottish peerages remained dormant until 1812, when they were successfully claimed by **(9)** JAMES Innes, great-grandson of Lady Margaret (ante), 3rd grand-da of the 1st Earl, by her marriage with Sir James Innes, 3rd Bt (see†infra), assumed in 1767 by Roy licence the additional surname of Norcliffe, and relinquished it in 1807 on the death of his first wife; *d* 1823; *s* by his only son by his 2nd *m* **(10)** JAMES HENRY ROBERT, KT, 6th Duke; *b* 1816; *cr Earl Innes* (peerage of United Kingdom) 1837; was Lord-Lieut of Berwickshire, and a Lieut-Gen of Royal Co of Archers: *m* 1836, Susanna Stephania, da of Lieut-Gen Sir James Charles Dalbiac, KCH, *d* 1879; *s* by his son **(11)** JAMES HENRY ROBERT, 7th Duke, *b* 1839; MP for Roxburghshire (*L*) 1870-74; Lord-Lieut of co Roxburgh, and one of HM Queen Victoria's Body Guard of Scotland: *m* 1874, Lady Emily Anne Spencer-Churchill, OBE, VA, who *d* 1923, da of 6th Duke of Marlborough; *d* 1892; *s* by his el son **(12)** HENRY JOHN, KT, MVO, 8th Duke, *b* 1876; bore Queen Consort's Crown at Coronation of King Edward VII 1902, and St Edward's Staff at Coronation of King George V 1911; was Chancellor of the Order of the Thistle: *m* 1903, Mary, who *d* 1937, da of late Ogden Goelet, of Newport, USA; *d* 1932; *s* by his only son **(13)** GEORGE VICTOR ROBERT JOHN, 9th Duke, *b* 1913: *m* 1st, 1935 (*m diss* 1953), Lady Mary Evelyn Hungerford Crewe-Milnes, da of 1st Marquess of Crewe (ext); 2ndly, 1954, (Margaret) Elisabeth (who *m* 3rdly, 1976, as his 2nd wife, Jocelyn Olaf Hambro, MC, and *d* 1983), da of late Capt Frederick Bradshaw McConnel, Gordon Highlanders, of Knockdalian, Colmonell, Ayrshire, and formerly wife of Lt-Col James Cunningham Church, MC; *d* 1974; *s* by his el son **(14)** GUY DAVID, 10th Duke, and present peer; also Marquess of Bowmont and Cessford, Earl of Roxburghe, Earl of Kelso, Earl Innes, Viscount Broxmouth, Lord Roxburghe, and Lord Ker of Cessford and Cavertoun.
†**(1)** *Rt Hon Sir* ROBERT Innes (19th Baron of Innes, co Moray, from 1160); MP for Elgin and Forres-shire 1639-41; *cr a Baronet* with remainder to heirs male whatsoever 1625; *d* 1658; *s* by his son **(2)** Sir ROBERT, 2nd Bt; MP for Moray 1661-78; *s* by his son **(3)** Sir JAMES, 3rd Bt: *m* Lady Margaret Ker (ante), da of Harry, son of 1st Earl of Roxburghe; *s* by his son **(4)** Sir HARRY, 4th Bt; MP for Moray in Union Parliament 1707; *d* 1721; *s* by his son **(5)** Sir HARRY, 5th Bt; *d* 1762; *s* by his son **(6)** Sir JAMES, 6th Bt, who *s* as 5th Duke of Roxburghe (ante).

ROYLE, BARONY OF (Royle) (Extinct 1975)

DAUGHTER LIVING OF LIFE BARON

Hon Joan Mary (Abbotswell, Frogham, Fordingbridge, Hants), *b* 1920: *m* 1st, 1942 (*m diss* 1963), Gordon Dixon; 2ndly, 1975, Albert Ralph Roberts, who *d* 1980; 3rdly, 1987, Rev John Atcherley Davies, of the Vicarage, Hyde, Fordingbridge, Hants SP6 2QJ, and has issue (by 1st *m*), one son.

RUFFSIDE, VISCOUNTCY OF (Brown) (Extinct 1958)

DAUGHTER LIVING OF FIRST VISCOUNT

Hon Audrey Pellew, *b* 1908; *cr Baroness Hylton-Foster* (Life Baroness) 1965 (see that title).

RUGBY, BARON (Maffey) (Baron UK 1947)

ROBERT CHARLES MAFFEY, 3rd Baron; *b* 4 May 1951; *s* 1990; *ed* —; a Farmer: *m* 1974, Anne Penelope, yr da of David Hale, of Somerden, Chiddingstone, Kent, and has issue.

Arms – Ermine, a fort with two towers proper, issuant from the base a pile reversed sable, a chief dancette or, surmounted by a pile azure, charged with an increscent argent. **Crest** – A gauntlet fessewise grasping a lantern proper. **Supporters** – On either side an Afghan hound proper gorged with a collar with chain reflexed over the back or.
Residence – Grove Farm Cottage, Frankton, Rugby.

SONS LIVING

Hon TIMOTHY JAMES HOWARD, *b* 23 July 1975; *ed*
Hon Philip Edward, *b* 1976; *ed*

BROTHERS LIVING

Hon Christopher Alan, *b* 1955; *ed* Malvern: *m* 1st, 1977 (*m diss* 1981), Barbara Anne, yr da of Guthrie Stewart, of Auckland, NZ; 2ndly, 1982, Katherine, elder da of Viv Rutherfurd, of Waiuku, Auckland, NZ, and has issue living (by 2nd *m*), Aaron John, *b* 1983, — Leigh Alan, *b* 1984. *Residence* – Hamiltons Rd, RD4, Waiuku, NZ.
Hon Mark Andrew, *b* 1956; *ed* Harrow, and Ecole de Commerce, Neuchâtel, Switzerland: *m* 1983, Angela Mary, da of Derek J. Polton, of The Pennies, Draycote, Rugby, and has issue living, Thomas Henry, *b* 1988, — Georgina Louise, *b* 1986. *Residence* – The Flat, Grove Farm, Frankton, Rugby.

SISTERS LIVING

Hon Selina Penelope, *b* 1952; has issue living, Tamas Henry, *b* 1990, — Angelica Helena, *b* 1986. *Residence* – McDougal Rd, Julatten, Queensland 4880, Australia.
Hon Alicia Dorothy, *b* 1960: *m* 1981 Richard M. Morton, 2nd son of John Morton, of Draycote, Rugby, and has issue living, Samuel Richard, *b* 1986, — John Alan Kynaston, *b* 1990, — Eleanor Margaret, *b* 1984. *Residence* – Manor Farm, Draycote, Rugby.

UNCLE LIVING (*son of 1st Baron*)

Hon Simon Chelmsford Loader (Charterhouse, EC1), *b* 1919; *ed* Rugby; formerly Lt Coldstream Guards; 1939-45 War in France (wounded): *m* 1949 (*m diss* 1962), Andrée Norma, da of George Middleton, of London, and has issue living, Penelope Anne, *b* 1950: *m* 1973, Richard Patrick James Lacy, of 16 Huron Rd, SW17, and has issue living (*see* Tyrwhitt, Bt).

AUNT LIVING (*daughter of 1st Baron*)

Hon Penelope Loader (*Hon Lady Aitken*), MBE (2 North Court, Great Peter St, SW1), *b* 1910; MBE (Civil) 1955; JP: *m* 1938, Sir William Traven Aitken, KBE, MP, who *d* 1964, and has issue living, Jonathan William Patrick, MP, *b* 1942; *ed* Eton, and Ch Ch, Oxford (MA); Dir TV-am 1981-88; Min of State for Defence since 1992; MP for Thanet South (*C*) since 1974: *m* 1979, Lolicia Olivera, da of O. A. Azucki, of Zürich, Switzerland, and has issue living, William *b* 1982, Victoria *b* 1980, Alexandra *b* (twin) 1980, — Maria Penelope Katharine, *b* 1945; actress: *m* 1st, 1968, Mark Richard Durden-Smith; 2ndly, 1972 (*m diss* 1980), Nigel Davenport; 3rdly, 1991, Patrick J. McGrath, and has issue living (by 2nd *m*), Jack *b* 1973.

WIDOW LIVING OF SECOND BARON

MARGARET (*Margaret, Baroness Rugby*), da of Harold Bindley, of Burton-on-Trent: *m* 1947, the 2nd Baron, who *d* 1990. *Residence* – Grove Farm, Frankton, Rugby.

PREDECESSORS – (1) *Sir* JOHN LOADER Maffey, GCMG, KCB, KCVO, CSI, CIE, son of late Thomas Maffey, of Rugby; *b* 1877; entered ICS 1899, Priv Sec to HE The Viceroy 1916-20, Ch Cmmr NWFP India 1921-24, Gov-Gen of the Sudan 1926-33; Permanent Under-Sec of State for Colonies 1933-37; UK Rep res in Eire 1939-49; *cr Baron Rugby*, of Rugby, co Warwick (peerage of UK) 1947: *m* 1907, Dorothy Gladys, OBE, who *d* 1973, da of late Charles Lang Huggins, JP, of Hadlow Grange, Buxted; *d* 1969; *s* by his el son (2) ALAN LOADER, 2nd Baron, 1939-45 War as Fl Lt RAF, Farmer: *m* 1947, Margaret, da of Harold Bindley, of Burton-on-Trent; *d* 1990; *s* by his 2nd son (his eldest son, Hon John Richard, *b* 1949, *dvp* in Egypt 1981), ROBERT CHARLES, 3rd Baron and present peer.

RUNCIE, BARON (Runcie) (Life Baron 1991)

Rt Rev and *Rt Hon* ROBERT ALEXANDER KENNEDY RUNCIE, MC, PC, son of late Robert Dalziel Runcie, of Crosby, Merseyside; *b* 2 Oct 1921; *ed* Merchant Taylors', Crosby, Brasenose Coll, Oxford (MA), and Westcott House, Camb (Dip Theol); served European War 1939-45 Scots Guards (MC 1945); Hon Bencher Gray's Inn 1981; Hon DD Oxford 1980, Camb 1981, St Andrews 1989, Yale 1989, London 1990, and other Univs, Hon DLitt Keele 1981, Hon DCL Kent 1982, and Hon LittD Liverpool 1983; ordained priest 1949, Curate All Saints Gosforth 1950-52, Chaplain and Vice-Pres Westcott House, Camb, 1953-56, Dean Trin Coll, Camb, 1956-60, Principal Cuddesdon Theol Coll 1960-70, Bishop St Albans 1970-80, Archbishop of Canterbury 1980-91, since when High Steward Camb Univ; Anglican Chm Anglican-Orthodox Joint Doctrinal Commn 1973-80; Teape Lecturer Delhi Univ 1962, and Nobell Lecturer Harvard Univ 1987; Freeman Cities of London, Canterbury and St Albans; Freeman Merchant Taylors' Co, Grocers' Co and Butchers' Co; author; PC 1980, Royal Victorian Chain 1991; *cr Baron Runcie*, of Cuddesdon, co Oxfordshire (Life Baron) 1991: *m* 1957, (Angela) Rosalind, da of late J. W. Cecil Turner, MC, of Cambridge, and has issue.

Arms – Argent, on a fess sable between three roses gules barbed and seeded proper as many crosses patonce also argent. **Crest** – A horse statant argent, crined, maned, unguled and the tail sable, gorged with a chaplet of roses gules barbed and seeded proper, resting the dexter foreleg upon a millrind gold. *Residence* – 26a Jennings Rd, St Albans, Herts AL1 4PD. *Clubs* – Athenaeum, Cavalry and Guards', and MCC.

SON LIVING

Hon James (36 Liverpool Rd, St Albans, Herts AL1 3UJ), *b* 1959; *ed* Marlborough, and Trin Hall, Camb (MA): *m* 1985, Mrs Marilyn Elsie Kellagher, da of late John Campbell Imrie, of Redroofs, Markinch, Fife, and has issue living, Charlotte Susan Elizabeth, *b* 1989.

DAUGHTER LIVING

Hon Rebecca (86B Broxash Road, SW11 6AB), *b* 1962; *ed* St Albans High Sch for Girls, Haileybury, and St Mary's Coll, Durham: *m* 1994, T. M. Christopher Tabor, only son of G. M. Tabor, of South Cerney, Glos.

RUNCIMAN OF DOXFORD, VISCOUNT (Runciman) (Viscount UK 1937 Bt UK 1906)

WALTER GARRISON RUNCIMAN, CBE, 3rd Viscount; *b* 10 Nov 1934; *s* 1989; *ed* Eton, and Trin Coll, Camb (Fellow 1959-63, and since 1971); Hon DSc (Soc Sci) Edinburgh, Hon D. Univ York; Chm Andrew Weir & Co Ltd and Runciman Investments Ltd; Jt Dep Chm Securities & Investments Board; Pres of Gen Council of British Shipping 1986-87; CBE 1987, FBA: *m* 1963, Ruth, OBE, da of Joseph Hellman, of Johannesburg, and has issue.

Arms – Per fesse or and azure a lymphad oars in action, the sail charged with a thistle leaved and slipped proper, flags flying to the dexter gules. **Crest** – A seahorse erect gules, holding in the fore fins a thistle as in the arms. **Supporters** – On either side a seahorse or gorged with a chain pendent therefrom a grappling iron azure. *Seat* – Doxford, Chathill, Northumberland. *Residence* – 44 Clifton Hill, NW8 0QE. *Club* – Brooks's.

SON LIVING

Hon DAVID WALTER, *b* 1 March 1967; *ed* Eton, and Trin Coll, Camb.

DAUGHTERS LIVING

Hon Lisa, *b* 1965.
Hon Catherine, *b* 1969.

UNCLE LIVING (*son of 1st Viscount*)

Hon Sir James Cochran Stevenson (*Hon Sir Steven Runciman*), CH, *b* 1903; *ed* Eton, and Trin Coll, Camb (MA, Fellow); Hon LittD, Oxford, and Camb, Hon LLD Glasgow; Hon DLitt Durham, London, St Andrews, and Birmingham; Hon DPh Salonika 1951; Hon DD, Wabash, Indiana, and Ball State, Indiana, Hon DHL Chicago and New York, and Author, a FBA, and a Knight Cdr of Order of Phoenix of Greece; Prof of Byzantine Art and History at Istanbul Univ 1942-45; Representative of British Council in Greece 1945-47; Knt 1958, CH 1983. *Residence* – Elshieshields, Lockerbie, Dumfriesshire.

AUNT LIVING (*daughter of 1st Viscount*)

Hon Katharine (*Hon Lady Lyell*), *b* 1909: *m* 1st, 1931, 4th Baron Farrer, who *d* 1954; 2ndly, 1955, Sir Maurice Legat Lyell, who *d* 1975. *Residence* – Puddephats Farm, Markyate, Herts.

PREDECESSORS – **(1)** WALTER Runciman, son of late Walter Runciman, of Dunbar; *b* 1847; head of firm of Walter Runciman & Co, Ltd, shipowners of Newcastle, London, etc, Chm of Anchor Line, Ltd, Glasgow, and a Member and Chm of various other shipping organisations; MP for Hartlepool (*L*) 1914-18; *cr* a *Baronet* 1906, and *Baron Runciman*, of Shoreston, co Northumberland (peerage of United Kingdom) 1933: *m* 1868, Ann Margaret, who *d* 1933, el da of late John Lawson, of Blakemoor Northumberland; *d* Aug 1937; *s* by his only son **(2)** WALTER, 2nd Baron; *b* 1870; Chm of United Kingdom Provident Institution 1920-31; Pres of Chamber of Shipping of United Kingdom 1926; was Parliamentary Sec to Local Govt Board 1905-07, Financial Sec to the Treasury 1907-08, Pres of Board of Education 1908-11, Pres of Board of Agriculture and Fisheries, and Commr of HM Woods, Forests, and Land Revenues 1911-14, Pres of Board of Trade 1914-16, again Pres of Board of Trade (in National Govt) 1931-7, and Lord Pres of the Council 1938-9; Head of Mission to Czechoslovakia 1938; sat as MP (*L*) for Oldham 1899-1900, for Dewsbury 1902-18, for Swansea, W Div 1924-9, and for St Ives Div of Cornwall 1929-37; *cr Viscount Runciman of Doxford*, of Doxford, co Northumberland (peerage of United Kingdom) June 1937: *m* 1898, Hilda (MP for Cornwall, St Ives Div (*L*) 1928-9), who *d* 1956, da of late James Cochran Stevenson (sometime MP for South Shields), of Westoe, South Shields: *d* 1949; *s* by his el son **(3)** WALTER LESLIE, OBE, AFC, AE, 2nd Viscount; *b* 1900, Elder Brother of Trinity House, Hon Air Commodore, Chm of Council of Armstrong Coll, Durham 1935-37, Dir-Gen British Overseas Airways Corporation 1940-43, Air Attaché British Embassy, Teheran 1943-46, Pres Royal Inst of Naval Architects 1951-61, Pres Chamber of Shipping of UK 1952, Chm of Trustees Nat Maritime Museum 1961-72, Chm British Hall-Marking Council 1974-83, and Pres Marine Soc 1974-89: *m* 1st, 1923 (*m diss* 1928), Rosamond Nina, who *d* 1990, da of late Rudolph Chambers Lehmann, of Fieldhead, Bourne End, Bucks; 2ndly, 1932, Katharine Schuyler, who *d* 1993, aged 90, yst da of late William R. Garrison, of New York; *d* 1989; *s* by his only son **(4)** WALTER GARRISON, 3rd Viscount and present peer; also Baron Runciman.

RUNCORN, BARONY OF (Vosper) (Extinct 1968)

WIDOW LIVING OF LIFE BARON

HELEN NORAH, da of late Sir (Joseph) Crosland Graham, of Clwyd Hall, Ruthin, Denbighshire; a JP for SW London, a Member of Merton Sutton and Wandsworth Area Health Authority (Teaching), and of Westminster Hosp (Special Trustee 1974-88; a Gov of Westminster Hosp Teaching Group 1972-74; Member of R Dental Hosp Sch Council 1978-82), and Roehampton Trustee 1976-1989; Chm Richmond, Twickenham and Roehampton Health Authority, and Member Charing Cross and Westminster Medical Sch Council 1982-88; Member Hammersmith and Queen Charlotte's Special Health Authority 1988-94; Member Council for Action since 1988; Member of Industrial Tribunal, London South since 1989: *m* 1st, 1966, as his 2nd wife, Baron Runcorn (Life Baron), who *d* 1968; 2ndly, 1976, Dr James Earle, FRC Path, MD, of 18 Hillside, Wimbledon SW19.

RUSHCLIFFE, BARONY OF (Betterton) (Extinct 1949)

DAUGHTERS LIVING OF FIRST BARON

Hon Averil Diana, *b* 1914: *m* 1st, 1939, Major Richard Wyndham-Quin Going, KOSB, who was *ka* in Normandy 1944; 2ndly, 1946, Col Charles Walter Philipps Richardson, DSO, KOSB (Foley-Philipps, Bt), who *d* 1993, and has issue living, (by 1st *m*) Christopher Wyndham (15 Wycombe Place, SW18), *b* 1944, Capt 9th/12th Royal Lancers (POW's): *m* 1975 (*m diss* 1989) Elisabeth Susan, da of James Christie Brownlow, of Ballydugan House, Downpatrick, co Down, and has issue living, Richard Wyndham *b* 1980, Emily Sarah *b* 1978, — Penelope Clare, *b* 1942: *m* 1965, Col Arthur David Bentley Brooks, The Queen's R Irish Hussars, of Higher Barns, Malpas, Cheshire, and has issue living, Jonathan Wyndham *b* 1970, Emma Frances *b* 1968, — (by 2nd *m*) Mark Rushcliffe (Priors Court, W Hanney, Wantage, Oxon), *b* 1947: *m* 1973, Cherry Victoria, yst da of Sidney Smart, of Oak Ash, Chaddleworth, Newbury, and has issue living, Hugo Charles Rushcliffe *b* 1981, Melanie Clare *b* 1974, Davina Kate *b* 1976. *Residence* – Quintans, Steventon, Hants.

Hon Claudia Violet, *b* 1917: *m* 1937, Maj Derek Swithin Allhusen, CVO, 9th Lancers, and has issue living, Timothy Frederick (Capstitch House, Compton Abbas, Shaftesbury, Dorset), *b* 1942: *m* 1965, Annabel Victoria, only da of late John Creighton Morris, and has issue living, Nicolas Christian *b* 1970, Alexia Suzanne *b* 1966, Lara Victoria *b* 1968, — Rosemary Claudia, *b* 1944: *m* 1973, Maj Jeremy Grimble Groves, 17th/21st Lancers, of Cole Henley Manor, Whitchurch, Hants RG28 7QD and has issue living, Anthony Grimble, *b* 1975, Clare Nicola Claudia *b* 1977. *Residence* – The Manor House, Claxton, Norwich.

RUSSELL, EARL (Russell) (Earl UK 1861)

What will be, will be

CONRAD SEBASTIAN ROBERT RUSSELL, 5th Earl; *b* 15 April 1937; *s* 1987; *ed* Eton, and Merton Coll, Oxford; Reader in History, Bedford Coll, London Univ until 1979; Prof of History, Yale Univ 1979-84, Astor Prof of British History, Univ Coll, London 1984-90, since when Prof of British History, King's Coll, London; Sir Henry Savile Visiting Prof, Merton Coll Oxford 1994-95; Ford's Lecturer Oxford Univ 1987-88: *m* 1962, Elizabeth, da of Horace Sanders, of 43 Stockwood Rd, Chippenham, Wilts, and has issue.

Arms – Argent, a lion rampant gules, on a chief sable, three escallops of the field, over the centre escallop a mullet. **Crest** – A goat stantant argent, armed and unguled or. **Supporters** – *Dexter*, a lion gules; *siniser*, an heraldic antelope gules, armed, unguled, tufted, ducally gorged and chained, the chain reflexed over the back or; each supporter charged on the shoulder with a mullet argent.
Address – c/o House of Lords, SW1A 0PW.

SONS LIVING

NICHOLAS LYULPH (*Viscount Amberley*), *b* 12 Sept 1968; *ed* William Ellis Sch, Camden.
Hon John Francis, *b* 1971; *ed* William Ellis Sch, Camden.

DAUGHTER LIVING OF FOURTH EARL

Lady Sarah Elizabeth, *b* 1946.

HALF-SISTER LIVING

Lady Katharine Jane, *b* 1923: *m* 1948, Rev Charles William Stuart Tait, and has issue living, David Alexander, *b* 1951, — Jonathan Francis, *b* 1955, — Andrew Michael Philip, *b* 1961, — Benjamin Peter, *b* 1965, — Anne Elizabeth, *b* 1953.

MOTHER LIVING

Patricia Helen, da of Harry Evelyn Spence: *m* 1936 (*m diss* 1952), as his 3rd wife, the 3rd Earl, who *d* 1970.

PREDECESSORS – (1) *Lord* JOHN Russell, KG, 3rd son of 6th Duke of Bedford; *b* 1792; sat as MP for Tavistock (*L*) 1813-17, 1818-19, and 1830-2, for Huntingdonshire 1820-6, for Bandon 1826-30, for S. Devonshire 1832-5, for Stroud 1835-41, and for London 1841-61; was Sec for Home Depart 1835-9, for the Colonies 1839-41 and 1855, Sec for Foreign Affairs 1852-3 and 1859-65, Premier and First Lord of the Treasury 1846-52 and 1865-6, and Lord Pres of the Council 1854-5; *cr Viscount Amberley* and *Earl Russell* (peerage of United Kingdom) 1861: *m* 1st, 1835, Adelaide, who *d* 1838, da of Thomas Lister, of Armitage Park, and widow of 2nd Baron Ribblesdale; 2ndly, 1841, Lady Frances Anna Maria Elliot, da of 2nd Earl of Minto, GCB; *d* 1878; *s* by his grandson (2) JOHN FRANCIS STANLEY (son of John, Viscount Amberley, MP, by Hon Katherine Louisa, da of 2nd Baron Stanley of Aderley), 2nd Earl, *b* 1865; tried by his Peers at Westminster 1901 (free pardon granted by His Majesty and recorded in proceedings of House of Lords July 1911): Parliamentary Sec to Min of Transport June 1929, and Under Sec of State for India Dec 1929-31: *m* 1st 1890 (*m diss* 1901), Mabel Edith, who *d* 1908, da of Sir Claude Edward Scott, 4th Bt (*cr* 1821); 2ndly, 1901 (*m diss* 1915), Mollie, da of George Cooke; 3rdly, 1916, Mary Annette (an authoress), who *d* 1941, da of H. Herron Beauchamp, and widow of Count (Henning August) Von Arnim; *d* 1931; *s* by his brother (3) BERTRAND ARTHUR WILLIAM OM, 3rd Earl, *b* 1872; Philosopher and Mathematician: *m* 1st, 1894 (*m diss* 1935), Alys Whitall who *d* 1951, da of late Robert Pearsall Smith; 2ndly, 1921 (*m diss* 1935), Dora Winifred, MBE, who *d* 1986, da of late Sir Frederick William Black, KCB; 3rdly, 1936 (*m diss* 1952), Patricia Helen, da of Henry Evelyn Spence; 4thly, 1952, Edith, who *d* 1978, da of late Edward Bronson Finch, of New York; *d* 1970; *s* by his son (4) JOHN CONRAD, 4th Earl, *b* 1921; served RNVR, Admin Assist HM Treasury: *m* 1946 (*m diss* 1955), Susan Doniphan, da of late Nicholas Vachel Lindsay, American poet; *d* 1987; *s* by his half-bro (5) CONRAD SEBASTIAN ROBERT, 5th Earl and present peer; also Viscount Amberley.

RUSSELL OF KILLOWEN, BARONY OF (Russell) (Extinct 1986)

SONS LIVING OF LIFE BARON (*By 1st marriage*)

See Russell, Bt (*cr* 1916), colls.

DAUGHTER LIVING OF LIFE BARON (*By 1st marriage*)

See Russell, Bt (*cr* 1916), colls.

WIDOW LIVING OF LIFE BARON

See Russell, Bt (*cr* 1916), colls.

RUSSELL OF LIVERPOOL, BARON (Russell) (Baron UK 1919)

SIMON GORDON JARED RUSSELL, 3rd Baron; *b* 30 Aug 1952; *s* 1981; *ed* Charterhouse, Trin Coll, Camb, and INSEAD, France: *m* 1984, Gilda F., yst da of F. Albano, of Salerno, Italy, and has issue.

Arms – Per saltire sable and or, in chief an estoile argent, two roses in fesse gules, barbed and seeded proper, and in base a thistle leaved and slipped of the second. **Crest** – An owl wings expanded argent, beaked and legged or, resting the dexter claw on an estoile azure. **Supporters** – On either side an owl argent beaked and legged or, gorged with a chaplet of roses gules, leaved vert.
Address – c/o House of Lords, SW1A 0PW.

SONS LIVING

Hon EDWARD CHARLES STANLEY, *b* 2 Sept 1985.
Hon William Francis Langley, *b* 1988.

DAUGHTER LIVING

Hon Leonora Maria Kiloran, *b* 1987.

BROTHERS LIVING (*Raised to the rank of a Baron's sons, 1983*)

Hon Adam Mark Haslingden, *b* 1957.
Hon Daniel Charles Edward, *b* 1962.

SISTERS LIVING (*Raised to the rank of a Baron's daughters, 1983*)

Hon Emma Kiloran, *b* 1955.
Hon Annabel Tacy, *b* 1959: *m* 1987, Lt-Col Mark Ralph Michael Eliot, 1st Queen's Dragoon Gds, son of Maj Morrell Geffery Eliot, MBE, and has issue living, Caspar Laurence Robin, *b* 1989, — Ralph Morrell Arthur, *b* 1992.
Hon Lucy Leonora Catherine, *b* 1968.

AUNT LIVING (*Daughter of 2nd Baron by 1st marriage*)

Hon Anne Philippa *b* 1924: *m* 1947, Gershom Radcliffe Layton Warren, late Maj Canadian Army, who *d* 1991, of 15 Williams St, Taupo, NZ.

HALF-AUNT LIVING (*Daughter of 2nd Baron by 2nd marriage*)

Hon Crystal (Ann Boleyn's Cottage, Grandmother's Rock Lane, Beach, Bittern, nr Bristol, Avon), *b* 1936: *m* 1955 (*m diss* 1969), John Mark Essington-Boulton, and has issue living, James Clive, *b* 1958, — Nicolette, *b* 1956.

MOTHER LIVING

Kiloran Margaret (*Hon Mrs Langley G. H. Russell*) (Ash Farm, Stourpaine, Blandford, Dorset), da of late Hon Sir Arthur Jared Palmer Howard, KBE, CVO (*see* B Strathcona and Mount Royal, colls): *m* 1951, Capt Hon Langley Gordon Haslingden Russell, MC, who *d* 1975.

PREDECESSORS – (1) *Sir* EDWARD RICHARD Russell, son of late Edward Haslingden Russell, of London; *b* 1834; editor of *Liverpool Daily Post and Mercury*, MP for Glasgow, Bridgeton Div (*L*) 1885-7; *cr Baron Russell of Liverpool*, of Liverpool, co Palatine of Lancaster (peerage of United Kingdom) 1919: *m* 1st, 1858, Eliza Sophia, who *d* 1901, da of Stephen Bradley, of Bridge, Canterbury; 2ndly, 1902, Jean Stewart, who *d* 1927, da of late Alexander Macdonald, of Campbeltown, Argyllshire, and Joseph, and widow of Joseph McFarlane; *d* 1920; *s* by his grandson (2) EDWARD FREDERICK LANGLEY, CBE, MC (son of late Richard Henry Langley Russell, 2nd son of 1st Baron), 2nd Baron, *b* 1895; Bar Gray's Inn 1931; Brig The King's Regt (Liverpool) and 20th Lancers (IA); Assist Judge Advocate Gen British Expeditionary Force 1930-40, Dep Judge Advocate Gen at 1st Army Headquarters 1942-43, and Allied Force Headquarters 1943-45, to Middle East Forces 1945-46, and to British Army of the Rhine 1946-51, and Assist Judge Advocate Gen 1951-54; an author: *m* 1st, 1920 (*m diss* 1933), Constance Claudine, who *d* 1974, yr da of late Col Philip Cecil Harcourt Gordon, CMG, RAMC; 2ndly, 1933 (*m diss* 1946), (Joan) Betty, da of late David Ewart, OBE, MD, FRCS, of Chichester; 3rdly, 1946, Alix, who *d* 1971, only da of late Marquis de Bréviaire d'Alaincourt, and widow of Comte de Richard d'Ivry; 4thly, 1972, Selma, who *d* 1977, da of —, and widow of A. W. Brayley; *d* 1981; *s* by his grandson (3) SIMON GORDON JARED (son of late Capt Hon Langley Gordon Haslingden Russell, MC, only son of 2nd Baron), 3rd Baron and present peer.

Ruthven of Canberra, Viscount; son of Earl of Gowrie.

Ruthven of Freeland, Lord (Ruthven) (Lordship S 1651); see Carlisle, Earl of.

(Name pronounced "Rivven")

RUTLAND, DUKE OF (Manners) (Duke E 1703)

In order to accomplish

CHARLES JOHN ROBERT MANNERS, CBE, 10th Duke; *b* 28 May 1919; *s* 1940; *ed* Eton, and Trin Coll, Camb (BA); Capt Gren Gds, and patron of eleven livings; Chm of E Midlands Economic Planning Council since 1971; CBE (Civil) 1962: *m* 1st, 1946 (*m diss* 1956), Anne Bairstow da of late Major William Cumming Bell, of Binham House, Edgerton, Huddersfield; 2ndly, 1958, Frances Helen, da of late Charles Sweeny, of 70 South Audley St, W1, and has issue by 1st and 2nd *m*.

Arms – Or, two bars azure, a chief quarterly, azure and gules; in 1st and 4th quarters two fleurs-de-lis, and in the 2nd and 3rd a lion passant guardant, all or. **Crest** – On a chapeau gules, turned up ermine, a peacock in pride proper. **Supporters** – Two unicorns, armed, ungules, maned and tufted, or. *Seats* – Haddon Hall, Bakewell, Derby; Belvoir Castle, Grantham.

SONS LIVING *(By 2nd marriage)*

DAVID CHARLES ROBERT (*Marquess of Granby*), *b* 8 May 1959: *m* 1992, Emma L., da of John Watkins, of Heartsease, Knighton, Powys, and has issue:—
    DAUGHTER LIVING— *Lady* Violet Diana Louise, *b* 1993.
Lord Edward John Francis, *b* 1965.

DAUGHTERS LIVING *(By 1st marriage)*

Lady Charlotte Louisa, *b* 1947.

(By 2nd marriage)

Lady (Helen) Teresa Margaret (17 Belgrave Pl, SW1), *b* 1962.

BROTHERS LIVING

Lord John, *b* 1922; *ed* Eton, and New Coll, Oxford; formerly Capt Life Guards, and 2nd Special Air Ser Regt: *m* 1957, Mary Diana, yst da of late Lieut-Col Lancelot Geoffrey Moore, DSO, and has issue living, Richard John Peveril, *b* 1963, — Elizabeth (Libby) Diana, *b* 1959: *m* 1986, Alexander Charles Thomas Wriothesley Russell, and has issue living (*see* D Bedford, colls), — Lucy Rachel, *b* 1961; appointed an Extra Lady in Waiting to HRH The Duchess of York 1989. *Residences* – Reservoir Cottage, Knipton, Grantham, Lincolnshire; Haddon Hall, Bakewell, Derbyshire.
Lord Roger David (Belcombe Court, Bradford-on-Avon), *b* 1925; *ed* Eton; formerly 2nd Lt Grenadier Guards: *m* 1965, Finola St Lawrence, only da of Thomas Edward Daubeney, and has issue living, Moira Violet Joanna, *b* 1966, — Phœbe Constance Adeliza, *b* 1968.

SISTERS LIVING

Lady Ursula Isabel, *b* 1916; was a Train Bearer to the Queen at Coronation of King George VI: *m* 1st, 1943 (*m diss* 1948), Anthony Freire Marreco, late Lieut RNVR; 2ndly, 1951, Robert Erland Nicolai d'Abo, who *d* 1970, and has issue living, (by 2nd *m*) John Henry Erland, *b* 1953; *ed* Eton, — Richard Winston Mark, *b* 1956; *ed* Eton, — Louisa Jane (*Hon Mrs John P. Ramsay*), *b* 1955: *m* 1981, Hon John Patrick Ramsay, yst son of 16th Earl of Dalhousie. *Residences* – West Wratting Park, Cambs; 29 Kensington Sq, W8.
Lady Isabel Violet Kathleen, *b* 1917: *m* 1st, 1936 (*m diss* 1951), as his 2nd wife, Group Capt (Thomas) Loel Evelyn Bulkeley Guinness, OBE, Auxiliary Air Force (Reserve), who *d* 1988; 2ndly, 1953, Sir Robert George Maxwell Throckmorton, 11th Bt, who *d* 1989, and has issue living, (by 1st *m*) William Loel Seymour, *b* 1939: *m* 1971, Agnes Elizabeth Lynn, only da of Ian T. M. Day, and has issue living, Sheridan William *b* 1972, Thomas Seymour *b* 1973, — Serena Belinda Rosemary (*Marchioness of Dufferin and Ava*), *b* 1941: *m* 1964, 5th Marquess of Dufferin and Ava, who *d* 1988. *Residences* – Coughton Court, Alcester, Warwickshire; Molland, South Molton, N Devon.

COLLATERAL BRANCHES LIVING

Grandchildren of late Rev William Manners-Sutton, 2nd son of late Frederick Manners-Sutton, 3rd son of late Capt John Manners-Sutton, MP, 2nd son of late Lord George Manners-Sutton, 3rd son of 3rd Duke:—
    Issue of late Frederick William Manners-Sutton, *b* 1865, *d* 1946: *m* 1902, Winifred Grace Richardson, who *d* 1970:—
John Lumley, *b* 1914: *m* 1949, Elizabeth Mary Gylda Eliot, da of A. N. G. Irving, of Lesmurdie, W Aust, and has issue living, John Frederick, *b* 1955, — Elizabeth Marjorie Inez (61 Riley Rd, Dalkeith, Western Australia 6009, Australia), *b* 1950: *m* 1987, Barry Spencer Clements, MB ChB, MRCP, only son of Sydney Ernest Clements, of Johannesburg, and has issue living, Christopher James *b* 1989, Michael Alexander *b* 1992, — Melanie Grace, *b* 1952: *m* 1978, Robert James Champion de Crespigny, of 1 Edwin Terr, Gilberton 5081, Adelaide, S Australia and has issue living, Stuart James *b* 1980, Angus Robert *b* 1982, Lachlan Thomas *b* 1984, James John *b* 1987, Georgina Melanie *b* 1993. *Residence* – 3 Buckingham St, Gilberton 5081, Adelaide, S Australia. —— Freda Grace, *b* 1905: *m* 1925, Keith Lee Roberts, who *d* 1949, and has issue living, Christopher Manners (184 Sladen St, Cranbourne, Victoria, Australia), *b* 1932: *m* 1964, Beverley Anne Jensen, and has issue living, Andrew Lee Christian *b* 1971, Adam Keith Llewellyn *b* 1972, — Antony John (Maranup, Roberts Rd, Leongatha, S Gipsland, Victoria, Australia), *b* 1938: *m* 1960, Margaret Mary Carra, and has issue living, Timothy Keith *b* 1961, Jonathan Antony *b* 1963, Caroline Margaret *b* 1966, — Joanna Margaret, *b* 1935: *m* 1962, Keith Clive Andrews, of Treweeks Rd, Blampied, Victoria, Australia, and has issue living, Michael Keith *b* 1963, Christopher Bernard *b* 1968, Jane Elizabeth *b* 1964, Kerrie Anne *b* 1966. *Residence* – Bendon, 19 Fernhurst Grove, Kew, Melbourne, Australia. —— Evelyn Mabel (Tarcoola, Shepparton, Victoria, Australia), *b* 1909: *m* 1928, John Kenneth Finlay, MBE, who *d* 1970, and has issue living, Chester Manners, *b* 1932, — Warwick Henry (Campbells Bend, Murchison, Victoria, Australia), *b* 1934: *m* 1973, Anne Elizabeth Jones, and has issue living, Gareth John *b* 1974, Jocelyn Edwina *b* 1976, — John Lexton (Thalia, RMB 4067, Violet Town, Victoria 3669, Australia), *b* 1936: *m* 1961, Sandra Marion, elder da of Donald Hugh Bayne, of Barambah, Nagambie, Victoria, Australia, and has issue living, Mark John *b* 1966, Sarah Elizabeth *b* 1961, Catherine Deborah *b* 1963.

Descendants of late Rt Hon Thomas Manners-Sutton, 5th son of late Lord George Manners-Sutton (*ante*), who was *cr Baron Manners* 1807 (see that title).

PREDECESSORS – **(1)** *Sir* THOMAS Manners, KG, 13th Baron de Ros (*see* B de Ros), was *cr Earl of Rutland* (peerage of England) 1525; *d* 1543; *s* by his son **(2)** HENRY, KG, 2nd Earl; was Constable of Nottingham Castle, and Pres of the North; he completed the re-building of Belvoir Castle; *d* 1563; *s* by his son **(3)** EDWARD, KG, 3rd Earl; *d* 1587 without male issue, when the Barony of de Ros reverted to his da Elizabeth, wife of Lord Burleigh (*see* M Exeter), and the earldom devolved upon his brother **(4)** JOHN, 4th Earl; *d* 1588; *s* by his el son **(5)** ROGER, 5th Earl; *dsp* 1612; *s* by his brother **(6)** FRANCIS, KG, 6th Earl; who in 1616 had been *cr Baron Roos*, of Hamlake (peerage of England); in 1618 *s* his cousin, son of Elizabeth, Baroness de Ros (ante), as 17th Baron de Ros; *d* 1632, when the Barony of Roos of Hamlake expired, and the other honours devolved upon his brother **(7)** GEORGE, 7th Earl; *dsp* 1641, when the Barony of de Ros reverted to Katherine, wife of George Villiers, 1st Duke of Buckingham (*cr* 1623), and the earldom devolved upon his cousin **(8)** JOHN, 8th Earl; *d* Sept, 1679; *s* by his son **(9)** JOHN, 9th Earl, who in April, 1679, had been summoned to Parliament as *Baron Manners of Haddon*, co Derby (peerage of England); was Lord-Lieut of Leicestershire; *cr Marquess of Granby* and *Duke of Rutland* (peerage of England) 1703; *d* 1711; *s* by his son **(10)** JOHN, KG, 2nd Duke; *b* 1676; successively MP for Derbyshire, Leicestershire, and Grantham, and Lord-Lieut of Leicestershire: *m* 1st, 1693, Catharine Russell, who *d* 1711, da of William, Lord Russell, 2nd son of 1st Duke of Bedford; 2ndly, 1713, Hon Lucy Sherard, who *d* 1751, da of 2nd Baron Sherard; *d* 1721; *s* by his son **(11)** JOHN, KG, PC, 3rd Duke; *b* 1696; was Lord-Lieut of co Leicester 1721-79, Chancellor of Duchy of Lancaster, Lord Steward of the Household 1755-61, and Master of the Horse 1761-66: *m* 1717, Hon Bridget Sutton, who *d* 1734, da of 2nd Baron Lexinton; *d* 1779; *s* by his grandson **(12)** CHARLES, KG, PC (son of late John, Marquess of Granby, el son of 3rd Duke), 4th Duke; was MP for Camb Univ 1774-9, and Viceroy of Ireland 1784-7: *m* 1775, Lady Mary Isabella Somerset, who *d* 1831, da of 4th Duke of Beaufort; *d* 1787; *s* by his son **(13)** JOHN HENRY, KG, 5th Duke; *b* 1778; was Lord-Lieut of co Leicester, Recorder of Grantham, Cambridge, and Scarborough, and Col Leicestershire Militia: *m* 1799, Lady Elizabeth Howard, who *d* 1825, da of 5th Earl of Carlisle, KG; *d* 1857; *s* by his son **(14)** CHARLES JOHN CECIL, KG, 6th Duke; *b* 1815; sat as MP for Stamford (*C*) 1837-52, and for N Leicestershire 1852-7; *d* 1888; *s* by his brother **(15)** JOHN JAMES ROBERT, KG, GCB, PC, DCL, LLD, 7th Duke, First Commr of Works (with a seat in the Cabinet) 1852, 1858-9 and 1866-7, Postmaster-Gen 1874-80 and 1885-6, and Chancellor of Duchy of Lancaster July 1886 to Aug 1892; sat as MP for Newark (*C*) 1841-7, for Colchester 1850-57, for Leicestershire N 1857-85, and for E, or Melton, Div of Leicestershire 1885-8; *cr Baron Roos of Belvoir*, co Leicester (peerage of United Kingdom) 1896: *m* 1st, 1851, Catherine Louisa, who *d* 1854, da of late Col George Marlay, CB; 2ndly, 1862, Janetta, who *d* 1899, da of Thomas Hughan, of Airds; *d* 1906; *s* by his son **(16)** HENRY JOHN BRINSLEY, KG (who had been called to the House of Lords in his father's Barony of Manners of Haddon 1896, and *s* as 8th Duke of Rutland and 2nd Baron Roos of Belvoir 1906), 8th Duke; *b* 1852; Principal Private Sec to Marquess of Salisbury June 1885 to Jan 1886, and Aug 1886 to March 1888; Lord-Lieut of Leicestershire 1900-25; MP for E, or Melton, Div of Leicestershire (*C*) 1888-95: *m* 1882, Marion Margaret Violet, who *d* 1937, da of late Col Hon Charles Hugh Lindsay, CB; *d* 1925; *s* by his yr son, **(17)** JOHN HENRY MONTAGU, 9th Duke; *b* 1886: *m* 1916, Kathleen, who *d* 1989, da of Francis John Tennant (B Glenconner, colls); *d* 1940; *s* by his el son **(18)** CHARLES JOHN ROBERT, 10th Duke and present peer; also Marquess of Granby, Earl of Rutland, Baron Manners of Haddon, and Baron Roos of Belvoir.

RYDER OF EATON HASTINGS, BARON (Ryder) (Life Baron 1975)

SYDNEY THOMAS (DON) RYDER, son of John Ryder; *b* 16 Sept 1916; *ed* Ealing County Gram Sch; Editor of *Stock Exchange Gazette* 1950-60; Joint Man Dir Kelly Iliffe Holdings, and Associated Iliffe Press Ltd 1961-63, Man Dir 1961-63, Dir IPC 1963-70, Man Dir Reed Paper Gp 1963-68 and Chm and Ch Exec Reed Internat, Ltd (formerly Reed Gp, Ltd) 1968-75; Pres of Nat Materials Handling Centre 1970-75; Vice-Pres of Roy Soc of Prevention of Accidents 1973-88, Dir of Metropolitan Estate and Property Corpn, Ltd 1972-75, Member of Council BIM 1970-75, of British Gas Board 1972-78, and Reserve Pension Board 1973-75, of UK S Africa Trade Assocn 1974-75, and Govt Ch Industrial Adviser 1975-77; *cr* Knt 1972, and *Baron Ryder of Eaton Hastings*, of Eaton Hastings, Oxon (Life Baron) 1975: *m* 1950, Eileen, da of William Dodds, and has issue.

𝔄rms – Not exemplified at time of going to press.

SON LIVING

Hon Michael John, *b* 1953.

DAUGHTER LIVING

Hon Jill Patricia, *b* 1950.

RYDER OF WARSAW, BARONESS (Cheshire) (Life Baroness 1978)

(MARGARET) SUSAN CHESHIRE, CMG, OBE, da of late Charles Ryder; *b* 3 July 1923; *ed* Benenden; Hon LLD Liverpool 1973, Exeter 1980, London 1981, Hon DLitt Reading 1982, Hon LLD Leeds 1984, Hon DCL Kent 1986, Hon LLD Cambridge 1989, DUniv Essex 1993: Founder and Social Worker, Sue Ryder Foundation for the Sick and Disabled of all age groups; co-Founder of The Ryder-Cheshire Foundation, and Trustee of The Leonard Cheshire Foundation; 1939-45 War with FANY and Special Operations Executive: Polonia Restituta (1965), Golden Order of Merit of Poland (1976); Medal of Yugoslav Flag with Gold Wreath and Diploma (1971), Polish Order of Smile (1981), Cdr's Cross of the Order of Polonia Restituta 1992, and Author of *And The Morrow is Theirs*, 1975; *cr* OBE (Civil) 1957, CMG 1976, and *Baroness Ryder of Warsaw*, of Warsaw in Poland and of Cavendish, co Suffolk (Life Baroness) 1978: *m* 1959, Group Capt (Geoffrey) Leonard Cheshire (*Baron Cheshire*) (Life Baron), VC, OM, DSO, DFC, who *d* 1992, and has issue (*see* B Cheshire).
Address – Sue Ryder Home, Cavendish, Sudbury, Suffolk CO10 8AY.

SACKVILLE, BARON (Sackville-West) (Baron UK 1876)

LIONEL BERTRAND SACKVILLE-WEST, 6th Baron; *b* 30 May 1913; *s* 1965; *ed* Winchester, and Magdalen Coll, Oxford (BA); late Capt Coldm Guards, and a Member of Lloyd's; patron of eleven livings; 1939-45 War (prisoner): *m* 1st, 1953, Jacobine Napier, who *d* 1971, da of J. R. Menzies-Wilson, of Fotheringhay Lodge, Nassington, Peterborough, and widow of Capt John Hichens, RA; 2ndly, 1974 (*m diss* 1983), Arlie Roebuck, who *d* 1991, da of Charles Woodhead, of Romany Rye, Brisbane, Aust, widow of Maj Hugh Dalzell Stewart, W Yorks Regt, and formerly wife of Maj-Gen Sir Francis Wilfred de Guingand, KBE, CB, DSO; 3rdly, 1983, Jean, da of late Arthur Stanley Garton, of Danesfield, Marlow, Bucks, and widow of Maj Sir Edward Henry Bouhier Imbert-Terry, 3rd Bt, and has issue by 1st *m*.

Arms – Quarterly: 1st and 4th argent, a fesse dancette sable, *West*; 2nd and 3rd or and gules, a bend vair, *Sackville*. Crests – 1st, out of a ducal coronet or, a griffin's head azure, beaked and eared gold; 2nd out of a coronet composed of a fleur-de-lis or, an estoile argent. Supporters – On either side a griffin azure, beaked and eared or, ducally gorged gold, therefrom pendent an escutcheon, that on the dexter charged with the arms of West, and that on the sinister with the arms of Sackville.
Seat – Knole, Sevenoaks, Kent.

The day of my life

DAUGHTERS LIVING *(By 1st marriage)*

Hon Teresa, *b* 1954: *m* 1979 (Alastair) Rupert Marlow, of 11 Gladstone St, SE1, son of Capt C. N. Marlow, RN, of Greenhill House, Upper Westwood, Wilts, and has issue living, Sebastian Edward, *b* 1985, — Julia Catherine, *b* 1982, — Rebecca Clare, *b* 1983.
Hon Catherine Jacobine SACKVILLE-WEST (36 Iffley Rd, W6), *b* 1956; resumed her maiden name 1984: *m* 1980 (*m diss* 1983), Stuart Cooper Bennett, elder son of H. M. Bennett, of Pasadena, Calif, USA.
Hon Sophia Anne, *b* 1957: *m* 1988, Guy R. Elliott, of 11 Sinclair Gdns, W14, only son of Robert Elliott, of Little Ashley Farm, Bradford-on-Avon, Wilts.
Hon Victoria Mary, *b* 1959: *m* 1989, Jonathan G. F. Lang, of 61 Richbourne Terr, SW8, yr son of John Lang, of Nairobi, Kenya, and has issue living, Leo John Bertrand, *b* 1993, — Clementine Jacobine Eva, *b* 1991.
Hon Sarah Elizabeth, *b* 1960: *m* 1992, (Edward) Simon Rendall, yr son of Peter Godfrey Rendall, of Burford, Oxon.

BROTHER LIVING

HUGH ROSSLYN INIGO, MC (Knole, Sevenoaks, Kent; Brooks's Club), *b* 1 Feb 1919; *ed* Winchester, and Magdalen Coll, Oxford (MA); late Capt R Tank Regt; ARICS; Admin Officer, N Nigeria 1946-59; 1939-45 War (wounded, MC, French Croix de Guerre): *m* 1957, Bridget Eleanor da of Capt Robert Lionel Brooke Cunliffe, CBE, RN (*see* Cunliffe, Bt, colls), and has issue living, Robert Bertrand (Gardener's Cottage, Knole, Sevenoaks, Kent TN15 0RP), *b* 1958: *m* 1st, 1985 (*m diss* 1992), Catherine Dorothea, elder da of Geoffrey Bennett, of Smelthouses, N Yorks; 2ndly, 19—, (Margot) Jane, da of Mark MacAndrew, of Holmwood House, Holmwood, Dorking, Surrey, — William Lionel Cunliffe (Flat 9, Cleveland Court, 90 Cleveland St, W1P 5DR), *b* 1967: *m* 1993, Annika, da of Kurt Lennartsson, of Västeras, Sweden, and of Birgitta Dellastrand, of Köping, Sweden, — Mary Cecilie, *b* 1960, — Elizabeth Anne, *b* 1962, — Jane Eleanor, *b* 1964.

PREDECESSORS – (1) *Hon* MORTIMER Sackville-West (4th son of 5th Earl De La Warr); *b* 1820; held several high appointments in Royal Household, and was *cr Baron Sackville*, of Knole, co Kent (peerage of United Kingdom), 1876, with special remainder, failing heirs male of his body, to his brothers Lionel and William Edward respectively in like manner (*see* E De La Warr, colls): *m* 1st, 1847, Fanny Charlotte, da of late Maj-Gen William Dickson, CB; 2ndly, 1873, Elizabeth, da of late Charles William Faber, Esq, of Northaw House, Barnet; *d* 1888; *s* by his brother (2) LIONEL SACKVILLE, GCMG, 2nd Baron; *b* 1827; was Min to Argentine Republic 1872-8, to Madrid 1878-81, and to Washington 1881-8; *dspl* 1908, when a suit was brought by Henri Ernest Jean Baptist Sackville-West under the Declaration of Legitimacy Act, claiming to be el legitimate son of the 2nd Baron by Josephine Duran de Ortega (Pepita), but in 1910 the petition was dismissed, and then *s* to the Barony under the special remainder the 2nd Baron's nephew (3) LIONEL EDWARD (el son of late Lieut-Col Hon William Edward Sackville-West), 3rd Baron, *b* 1867; a Director of Bank of Liverpool and Martins: *m* 1890, his cousin, Victoria Sackville-West, who *d* 1936, natural da of 2nd Baron Sackville; *d* 1928; *s* by his brother (4) CHARLES JOHN, KBE, CB, CMG, 4th Baron, *b* 1870; Maj-Gen, late King's Roy Rifle Corps; British Representative at Supreme War Council, Versailles 1918 and 1919, Mil Attaché at Paris 1920-4, and Lieut-Gov of Guernsey 1925-9: *m* 1st, 1897, Maud Cecilia, who *d* 1920, da of late Matthew John Bell, of Bourne Park, Kent (B St Leonards); 2ndly, 1924, Anne (BIGELOW), who *d* 1961, da of late William Meredith, of New York; *d* 1962; *s* by his son (5) EDWARD CHARLES, 5th Baron, *b* 1901, *d* 1965; *s* by his cousin (6) LIONEL BERTRAND (el son of Hon Bertrand George Sackville-West, yst brother of 4th Baron), 6th Baron and present peer.

SAINSBURY, BARON (Sainsbury) (Life Baron 1962)

ALAN JOHN SAINSBURY, el son of late John Benjamin Sainsbury; *b* 13 Aug 1902; *ed* Haileybury; Hon Fellow of Inst of Food Science and Techn; Joint Pres of J. Sainsbury plc, Grocery and Provision Merchants; Vice-Pres of Roy Soc for Encouragement of Arts, Manufactures and Commerce 1962-66, and Pres of Multiple Shops Federation 1963-65, of Grocers' Inst 1963-66, and of Internat Assocn of Chain Stores 1965-68, and Chm of Min of Health Cttee of Inquiry into relationship of Pharmaceutical Industry with Nat Health Ser 1965-67, a Member of NEDC for Distributive Trades 1964-68, Pres of Roy Inst of Public Health and Hygiene 1965-70, and a Gov of City Literary Inst 1967-69; Chm of Trustees, Uganda Asian Relief Trust 1972-74; Pres of Pestalozzi Children's Village Trust since 1963, Member of Food Research Advisory Cttee 1960-70 (Chm 1965-70), Vice-Pres of Assocn of Agric 1965-73, a Member of Court of Univ of Essex 1966-76, and Chm of Trustees Overseas Students Advisory Bureau since 1969; Pres Distributive Trades Education and Training Council 1975-83; Vice-Pres International Voluntary Ser 1977-81: a Member of Exec Cttee of PEP 1970-76; *cr Baron Sainsbury*, of Drury Lane, Borough of Holborn (peerage of UK) 1962: *m* 1st, 1925 (*m diss* 1939), Doreen Davan, who *d* 1985, da of Leonard Adams; 2ndly, 1944, Anne Elizabeth (Babette), who *d* 1988, da of Paul Lewy, and has issue by 1st and 2nd *m*.

Arms – Azure, on a fess dancetty between three cornucopiae bendwise or, as many lyres gules. Crest – A mural crown azure, thereon a leopard sejant proper supporting a corinthian column gold.
Address – Stamford House, Stamford St, SE1 9LL.

SONS LIVING *(By 1st marriage)*

Hon Sir John Davan, *b* 1927; *cr Baron Sainsbury of Preston Candover* (Life Baron) 1989 (see that title).
Hon Simon David Davan, *b* 1930; *ed* Eton, and Trin Coll, Camb; formerly Vice-Chm and a Director of J. Sainsbury Ltd; a Trustee Nat Gallery since 1991.
Rt Hon Timothy Alan Davan, MP (c/o House of Commons, SW1A 0AA; Boodle's Club), *b* 1932; *ed* Eton, and Worcester Coll, Oxford; MP for Hove (*C*) since 1973; Govt Whip 1983-87, Parl Under-Sec Min of Defence 1987-89, Parl Under-Sec of State Foreign & Commonwealth Office 1989-90, since when a Min of State, Dept of Trade & Industry; PC 1992: *m* 1961, Susan Mary, da of Brig James Alastair Harry Mitchell, CBE, DSO, and has issue living, (Timothy) James, *b* (Feb) 1962, — Alexander, *b* 1968, — Camilla Davan, *b* (Dec) 1962: *m* 1987, Shaun Anthony Woodward, yst son of Dennis Woodward, and has issue living, one son and two das, — Jessica Mary, *b* 1970.

DAUGHTER LIVING *(By 2nd marriage)*

Hon Paulette Ann, *b* 1946: *m* 1970, James Anderson, and has issue.

SAINSBURY OF PRESTON CANDOVER, BARON (Sainsbury) (Life Baron 1989)

JOHN DAVAN SAINSBURY, KG, eldest son of Baron Sainsbury (Life Baron); *b* 2 Nov 1927; *ed* Stowe, and Worcester Coll, Oxford (Hon Fell 1982); Hon Bencher Inner Temple 1985, Hon FIGD 1973, Hon DSC Econ London 1985, Hon DLitt South Bank Univ 1992, Hon LLD Bristol 1993, Hon FRIBA 1993, Albert Medal RSA 1989; Dir J Sainsbury plc 1958-92, Vice-Chm 1967-69, Chm 1969-92, since when Pres; Dir The Royal Opera House, Covent Garden, 1969-85, Chm 1987-91, Chm Friends of Covent Garden 1969-81, Dir The Royal Opera House Trust 1974-84, and since 1987; Chm Benesh Inst of Choreology 1986-87, and Dulwich Picture Gallery since 1994; Gov Royal Ballet Sch 1965-76, and 1987-91, Gov Royal Ballet since 1987; Dir The Economist 1972-80; Joint Hon Treas European Movement 1972-75, Memb Council Retail Consortium 1975-79, Nat Cttee for Electoral Reform 1976-85, and President's Cttee CBI 1982-84; Vice-Pres Contemporary Arts Soc since 1984 (Hon Sec 1965-71, Vice-Chm 1971-74), Trustee National Gallery 1976-83, Westminster Abbey Trust 1977-83, Tate Gallery 1982-83, Rhodes Trust since 1984, Prince of Wales Inst of Architecture since 1992 etc; *cr Kt* 1980, *Baron Sainsbury of Preston Candover*, of Preston Candover, co Hants (Life Baron) 1989, and KG 1992: *m* 1963, Anya (Anya Linden, Royal Ballet ballerina), formerly wife of Igor Tamarin, and da of George Charles Eltenton, and has issue.

Arms – Azure, on a fess dancetty between three cornucopiae bendwise or, as many lyres gules. Crest – A mural crown azure, thereon a leopard sejant proper supporting a corinthian column gold. Supporters – On either side rampant upon a cornucopia or a leopard proper, the compartment comprising a grassy mount all proper.
Address – Stamford House, Stamford St, SE1. *Club* – Garrick.

SONS LIVING

Hon John Julian, *b* 1966.
Hon Mark Leonard, *b* 1969.

DAUGHTER LIVING

Hon Sarah Jane, *b* 1964: *m* 1990, Robert Joseph Neville Galmoye Butler-Sloss, elder son of Hon Mr Justice (Joseph William Alexander) Butler-Sloss.

ST ALBANS, DUKE OF (Beauclerk) (Duke E 1684)
(Name pronounced "Bo-clare")

AUSPICIUM MELIORIS ÆVI

A pledge of better times

MURRAY DE VERE BEAUCLERK, 14th Duke; *b* 19 Jan 1939; *s* 1988; *ed* Tonbridge; a Chartered Accountant, a Liveryman of Drapers' Co; patron of two livings, Hereditary Grand Falconer, and Hereditary Registrar of Court of Chancery; Gov-Gen Royal Stuart Soc: *m* 1st, 1963 (*m diss* 1974), Rosemary Frances, only da of Dr Francis Harold Scoones, JP, MRCS, LRCP, of 83 Abbotsbury Rd, W14; 2ndly, 1974, Cynthia Theresa Mary, da of late Lt-Col William James Holdsworth Howard, DSO, and formerly wife of Sir Anthony Robin Maurice Hooper, 2nd Bt, and has issue by 1st *m*.

Arms – Quarterly: 1st and 4th grand quarters the royal arms of King Charles II, 1st and 4th France and England, quarterly; 2nd Scotland; 3rd Ireland; the whole debruised by a baton sinister gules, charged with three roses argent, *Beauclerk*; 2nd and 3rd grand quarters quarterly gules and or, in the 1st quarter a mullet argent *de Vere*. Crest – On a chapeau gules, turned up ermine, a lion statant guardant or, ducally crowned per pale argent and gules, and gorged with a plain collar gules, charged with three roses argent. Supporters – *Dexter*, an antelope argent, armed and unguled or; *sinister*, a greyhound argent, each collared as the crest.
Residence – 3 St George's Court, Gloucester Rd, SW7. *Club* – Hurlingham.

SON LIVING *(By 1st marriage)*

CHARLES FRANCIS TOPHAM DE VERE (*Earl of Burford*), *b* 22 Feb 1965; *ed* Sherborne, Hertford Coll, Oxford (MA), and Edinburgh Univ; founder De Vere Soc; Vice-Pres Royal Stuart Soc since 1989; Liveryman Drapers' Co 1990. *Residence* – Canonteign, Exeter, Devon EX6 7RH. *Club* – Brooks's.

DAUGHTER LIVING *(By 1st marriage)*

Lady Emma Caroline de Vere, *b* 1963; *ed* Roedean, St John's Coll, Camb (BA), and Univ of E Anglia: *m* 1991, David Craig Shaw Smellie, son of late Prof (Robert) Martin Stuart Smellie, of Hyndland, Glasgow. *Residence* – 2 Kingsgate, Red Lion Sq, WC1R 4RB.

HALF-BROTHERS LIVING

Lord Peter Charles de Vere, *b* 1948; *ed* Eton: *m* 1972 (*m diss* 19—), Beverley June, da of late Alva Edwin Bailey, of Cal, USA, and has had issue, Robin, *b* 1971; *d* 1973, — Angela Grace de Vere, *b* 1974. *Residence* – 2726 Shelter Island Drive 332, San Diego, California 92106, USA.
Lord James Charles Fesq de Vere (Barn House, Midgham, Reading, Berks RG7 5UG), *b* 1949; *ed* Eton.
Lord John William Aubrey de Vere, *b* 1950; *ed* Eton: *m* 1986, Carolyn Ann Heath, da of Mrs B. Wilkinson, of Isle of Wight, and has issue living, Kiatsi Sofia, *b* 1984. *Address* – c/o Save The Children Fund (Mongolia), 17 Grove Lane, SE5 8SP.

HALF-SISTER LIVING

Lady Caroline Anne de Vere, *b* 1951; *ed* Fritham House, and Queen's Gate Sch: *m* 1970 (*m diss* 1986), Neil St John ffrench Blake, and has issue living, Clare Eleanor de Vere, *b* 1972, — Kate Juliana de Vere, *b* 1977. *Residence* – Barn House, Midgham, Reading, Berks RG7 5UG.

WIDOW LIVING OF THIRTEENTH DUKE

SUZANNE MARIE ADELE (*Dowager Duchess of St Albans*), da of late Emile William Fesq, of Mas Mistral, Vence, France AM: *m* 1947, as his 2nd wife, Col the 13th Duke, OBE, who *d* 1988. *Residence* – 64 West St, Newbury, Berks RG13 1BD.

COLLATERAL BRANCHES LIVING

Granddaughter of late William Nelthorpe Beauclerk, JP, DL, LLD, el son of Capt Lord Frederick Charles Peter Beauclerk, JP, RN, 2nd surv son of 8th Duke:—
Issue of late Major Aubrey Nelthorpe Beauclerk, *b* 1879, *d* 1916: *m* 1911, Vera Eileen May, who *d* 1975, having *m* 2ndly, 1919, Capt Gerald Andrew Greig, late R Scots Fusiliers, who *d* 1950, da of late Capt W. H. Francis, formerly 28th Regt:—
Daphne Diana de Vere, *b* 1911: *m* 1933, Count Claude Antoine Chauvin de Précourt, who *d* 1971, and has issue living, François Charles Christian (36 rue de la Résistance, 78150 Le Chesnay, France), *b* 1936: *m* 1962, Sabine, da of the late Comte de Vautibault, of Laval, Mayenne, France and has issue living, Claude Henri Aubrey *b* 1963, Rémy François Xavier *b* 1972, Ghislaine *b* 1967: *m* 1991, Jean du Puytison, of Versailles (and has issue), — Philippe Etienne (27 Rue Borgnis-Desbordes, Versailles, 78000, France), *b* 1938: *m* 1st, 1961, Marie-Noelle, who *d* 1989, da of René Gasquet, of Neuilly-sur-Seine, France; 2ndly, 1992, Catherine, da of Robert Treppier, of Paris, and has issue living (by 1st *m*), Aude Emilie *b* 1962:

m 1989, Geoffrey de Monteynard, son of Comte Jean de Monteynard, of Versailles (and has issue), Laure Sabine Pierrette *b* 1963, Clarisse Agnes *b* 1966: *m* 1991, Nicolas Demont, of Versailles (and has issue), Marguerite *b* 1972, — Jean Yves (Le Bouscatel, Bouchet de la Lauze, Ponteils par Génolac, 30, France), *b* 1943: *m* 1970, Nathalie, da of Dr Dubel, of France, and has issue living, Jeremy Adrian *b* 1978, Penelope *b* 1971, — Anne Victoria (18 Bina Gdns, SW5), *b* 1944. *Residence* – Kennards, Amberley, Sussex.

Grandchildren of late Maj Aubrey Nelthorpe Beauclerk (ante):—
Issue of late Hermione de Vere Beauclerk, *b* 1915, *d* 1969: *m* 1939, James Dewar, MBE, GM, AE, FCA, who *d* 1983:—
Peter de Vere BEAUCLERK-DEWAR, RD and bar (45 Airedale Av, Chiswick, W4 2NW, and Holm of Huip, by Stronsay, Orkney; New (Edinburgh), and Puffins Clubs), *b* 1943; recognised in the surname and arms of Beauclerk-Dewar by Lyon Court 1965; *ed* Ampleforth; Lt-Cdr RNR; RD 1980 and bar 1990; Member Queen's Body Guard for Scotland (Royal Co of Archers); Falkland Pursuivant Extraor 1975, 1982, 1984, 1986, 1987, 1991 and 1994; Silver Stick Usher at HM Silver Jubilee Thanksgiving Ser 1977; Usher at HM Queen Elizabeth the Queen Mother's 80th Birthday Thanksgiving Ser 1980; JP (Inner London), FSA Scot, FIMgt, FFA, FHG (Hon); co-author of *The House of Nell Gwyn* 1974, and author *The House of Dewar* 1991; a Liveryman of Haberdashers' Co; OStJ, Kt of Sovereign Mil Order of Malta, Kt of Sacred Mil Order of Constantine St George, Cdr of Merit with Swords 'Pro Merito Melitensi' 1989: *m* 1967, Sarah Ann Sweet Verge, el da of Maj Lionel John Verge Rudder, late DCLI, of the Old Dairy Barn, Bibury, Glos, and has issue living, James William Aubrey de Vere (1 Sterndale Rd, W14 0HT), *b* 1970; *ed* Ampleforth, — Alexandra Hermione Sarah, *b* 1972, — Emma Diana Peta, *b* 1973, — Philippa Caroline Frances, *b* 1982. —— Gillian de Vere BEAUCLERK (Lamberts, Stourton Caundle, Dorset DT10 2JJ), *b* 1944; assumed surname of Beauclerk by deed poll 1990: *m* 1st, 1964 (*m diss* 1978), Peter John Lawrence Silley, of Park House, Eynsford, Kent; 2ndly, 1978 (*m diss* 1990), Robert Erskine Beveridge, and has had issue (by 1st *m*), Natasha Margaret, *b* 1965, — Tanya Anne, *b* 1967; *d* 1984.

Grandchildren of late Charles Robert Beauclerk, son of late Charles George Beauclerk, grandson of late Lord Sydney Beauclerk, 5th son of 1st Duke:—
Issue of late William Topham Sidney Beauclerk, *b* 1864, *d* 1950: *m* 1910, Lola de Penalver, who *d* 1972, da of Enrique, Conde de Penalver y Marqués de Arcos in Spain:—
Rafael Charles, MBE (31 Marryat Rd, Wimbledon Common, SW19 5BE), *b* 1917; *ed* Downside; 1939-45 War as Capt Intelligence Corps (MBE (Mil) 1945, French Croix de Guerre); Marques Valero de Urria in Spain; MBE (Mil) 1945: *m* 1957, Noirine Mary, el da of J. Bowen, of Bowen's Cross, co Cork, and has issue living, William Rafael (6 Queen Anne Gdns, Leatherhead, Surrey KT22 7JE; 15 rue de Breteuil, 78670 Medan, France), *b* 1961; *ed* Worth; Lieut RN (ret) served in HMY *Britannia*; ARICS: *m* 1986, Margaret Eleanor, da of Lesley James Mountjoy, of Totteridge, London, and has issue living, Alexander Charles *b* 1990, Cameron *b* 1993, Charlotte *b* 1987, — Dolores Mary, *b* 1958; SRN: *m* 1981, Dr Richard M. Makower, son of C.S. Makower, MC, of 37 Piercing Hill, Theydon Bois, Essex, and has issue living, Timothy *b* 1984, Oliver William *b* 1992, Emily Elizabeth *b* 1987. —— Diana Mary, *b* 1924. *Residences* – Villa Etchè Biskiak, Av des Chênes, Biarritz, France; 31 Marryat Rd, Wimbledon, SW19.

PREDECESSORS – (1) *Sir* CHARLES Beauclerk, KG, FRS, natural son of Charles II, by Eleanor Gwyn; *b* 1670; *cr Baron Heddington*, co Oxford, and *Earl of Burford* (peerage of England) 1676, and *Duke of St Albans* (peerage of England) 1684; Hereditary Registrar of the Court of Chancery 1698; Hereditary Master Falconer of England 1685; Capt of Band of Gentlemen Pensioners; a Lord of the Bedchamber, Lord Lieut of Berks, High Steward of Windsor and of Wokingham and Col of Princess Anne of Denmark's Regt of Horse: *m* 1694, Lady Diana de Vere (1st Lady of the Bedchamber and Lady of the Stole to Caroline, Princess of Wales, later Queen Caroline), who *d* 1742, el da and heir of 20th and last Earl of Oxford, KG; *d* 1726; *s* by his son (2) CHARLES, KG, KB, 2nd Duke; *b* 1696; successively MP for Bodmin and Windsor, Constable and Gov of Windsor Castle and Lord Warden of the Forests; a Lord of the Bedchamber; Lord Lieut of Berks and High Steward of Windsor and of Wokingham: *m* 1722, Lucy, who *d* 1752, da of Sir John Werden, 2nd Bt; *d* 1751; *s* by his son (3) GEORGE, 3rd Duke; *b* 1730; a Lord of the Bedchamber, Lord Lieut of Berks and High Steward of Windsor: *m* 1752, Jane who *d* 1778, da and heir of Sir Walter Roberts, 6th Bt; *dsp* 1786; *s* by his 1st cousin once removed (4) GEORGE (grandson of Lord William, 2nd son of 1st Duke), 4th Duke; *b* 1758; Lt-Col 3rd Foot Gds; *d unm* 1787; *s* by his 1st cousin once removed (5) AUBREY, (son of Adm Lord Vere of Hanworth, 3rd son of 1st Duke, who *d* 1781, having in 1750 been *cr Baron Vere of Hanworth* (peerage of GB)), 5th Duke; *b* 1740; successively MP for Thetford and Aldborough: *m* 1763, Lady Catherine Ponsonby, who *d* 1789, da of 2nd Earl of Bessborough; *d* 1802, *s* by his son (6) AUBREY, 6th Duke; *b* 1765; Lt-Col 34th Foot: *m* 1st, 1788, Jane, who *d* 1800, da of John Moses, of Hull; 2ndly, 1802, Louisa Grace, who *d* 1816, da of John Manners, MP, of Grantham Grange, Lincs, by Lady Louisa Manners (later Tollemache), Countess of Dysart; *d* 1815; *s* by his son (7) AUBREY, 7th Duke; *b* 1815; *d* 1816; *s* by his uncle (8) WILLIAM, 8th Duke; *b* 1766; Cdr RN; High Sheriff of Denbigh and Lincs: *m* 1st, 1791, Charlotte, who *d* 1797, da of Rev Robert Carter Thelwall, of Redbourne Hall, Lincs; 2ndly, 1799, Maria Janetta, who *d* 1822, da of John Nelthorpe, of Little Grimsby Hall, Lincs; *d* 1825; *s* by his son (9) WILLIAM AUBREY DE VERE, 9th Duke; *b* 1801; LLD Cantab: *m* 1st, 1827, Harriet (actress), da of Matthew Mellon, and widow of Thomas Coutts, banker of London; 2ndly, 1839, Elizabeth Catherine, who *d* 1893, da of Gen Joseph Gubbins, of Kilfrush, co Limerick; *d* 1849; *s* by his son (10) WILLIAM AMELIUS AUBREY DE VERE, PC, 10th Duke; *b* 1840; Lord Lieut Notts; Capt of HM's Yeomen of the Guard 1873-74 Col 1st Notts (Robin Hood) Rifle Vols; offered but declined KG 1875: *m* 1st, 1867, Sybil Mary, who *d* 1871, da of Gen Hon Charles Grey; 2nd, 1874, Grace, who *d* 1926, da of Ralph Bernal Osborne, MP, of Newtown Anner, co Tipperary; *d* 1898; *s* by his el son (11) CHARLES VICTOR ALBERT AUBREY DE VERE, 11th Duke; *b* 1870; Capt S Notts Yeo, formerly Lieut R Scots; *dunm* 1934; *s* by his half-brother (12) OSBORNE DE VERE, TD, 12th Duke, *b* 1874; Capt 17th Lancers and Maj S Notts Hussars; High Sheriff and DL co Waterford: *m* 1918, Lady Beatrix Frances, GBE, who *d* 1953, da of the 5th Marquess of Lansdowne, KG, and widow of 6th Marquess of Waterford, KP; *dsp* 1964; *s* by his 2nd cousin (13) CHARLES FREDERIC AUBREY DE VERE, OBE (only son of Aubrey Topham Beauclerk, 3rd son of late Charles Beauclerk, 5th surv son of 8th Duke), 13th Duke, *b* 1915; Col Intelligence Corps, 1939-45 War in Mediterranean, Dir Films Div, Central Office of Information, Gov-Gen Royal Stuart Soc: *m* 1st, 1938 (*m diss* 1947), Nathalie Chatham, who *d* 1985, da of late Percival Field Walker, of Rythe Court, Thames Ditton, Surrey; 2ndly, 1947, Suzanne Marie Adèle, da of Emile William Fesq, of Mas Mistral, Vence, France AM; *d* 1988; *s* by his eldest son (14) MURRAY DE VERE, 14th Duke and present peer; also Earl of Burford, Baron Hedington, and Baron Vere of Hanworth.

ST ALDWYN, EARL (Hicks Beach) (Earl UK 1915, and Bt E 1619)

All in good time

MICHAEL HENRY HICKS BEACH, 3rd Earl, and 11th Baronet; *b* 7 Feb 1950; *s* 1992; *ed* Eton, and Ch Ch Oxford (MA): *m* 1982, Gilda Maria, only da of late Barão Saavedra, of Rua Paula Freitas 104, Copacabana, Rio de Janeiro, and has issue.

Arms – Quarterly: 1st and 4th, vaire, argent and gules, a canton azure charged with a pile or, *Beach*; 2nd and 3rd, gules, a fesse wavy between three fleurs-de-lis or, a crescent for difference, *Hicks*. **Crest** – A demi-lion rampant argent, ducally gorged or, and holding in the paws an escutcheon azure, charged with a pile or. **Supporters** – *Dexter*, a knight armed cap-à-pie in the middle of the fourteenth century, his jupon charged with the arms of *Beach*, namely, vaire argent and gules, on a canton azure a pile or; *sinister*, a knight similarly vested, his jupon charged with the arms of *Hicks*, namely, gules a fesse wavy between three fleur-de-lis, or, a crescent argent for difference.
Residences – Williamstrip Park, Cirencester, Gloucestershire GL7 5AT; 17 Hale House, 34 De Vere Gdns, W8 5AQ. **Clubs** – Leander, White's, Pratt's.

DAUGHTERS LIVING

Lady Atalanta Maria, *b* 1983.
Lady Aurora Ursula, *b* 1988.

BROTHERS LIVING AND DECEASED

Hon Peter Hugh, *b* 1952; *ed* Eton; painter; *dunm* 1990.
Hon DAVID SEYMOUR, *b* 25 May 1955; *ed* Eton; a Page of Honour to HM 1969-71: *m* 1993, Katrina (Kate) Louise Susannah, da of Michael Henriques, of Winson Manor, Cirencester, Glos. *Residence* – The Upper Mill, Coln St Aldwyns, Glos GL7 5AJ. *Club* – Pratt's.

AUNT LIVING (*sister of 2nd Earl*) (*raised to the rank of an Earl's daughter* 1920)

Lady Delia Mary, *b* 1910: *m* 1934, Brigadier Sir Charles Michael Dillwyn-Venables-Llewellyn, 3rd Bt, MVO, who *d* 1976. *Residence* – Llysdinam, Newbridge-on-Wye, Powys.

COLLATERAL BRANCHES LIVING (*In remainder to the Baronetcy only*)

Grandson of late William Frederick Hicks Beach, 2nd son of 8th Bt:—
Issue of late Michael Hicks Beach, *b* 1872, *d* 1953: *m* 1907, Helène, who *d* 1941, da of Arthur Des Fosses, formerly of Montreal:—
Michael, *b* 1909: *m* 1st, 1932, Dorothy, da of late Robert Stratton, formerly of Nottingham; 2ndly, 1944, Eunice, who *d* 1973, da of late Rudolph J. Thanisch, of Boston, Mass, USA; 3rdly, 1974, Grace Vera, da of late Henry Moos, Sr, of Union City, NJ, USA, and widow of Charles Arthur Rankin, and has issue living (by 1st *m*), Heather Diane HICKS BEACH (417 Hampton Court, Falls Church, Va 22046, USA), *b* 1935; has reverted to maiden name: *m* 1957 (*m diss* 1970), Edward Lionel Peck, and has issue living, Brian Michael *b* 1960, Heather Anne *b* 1959: *m* 1989, Michael Lindner (and has issue living, Noah William *b* 1994). *Residence* – 9538 Ash St, Apt 111, Overland Park, Kansas 66207, USA.

Grandchildren of late Michael Hicks Beach (*ante*):—
Issue of late Frederick Edward Hicks Beach, *b* 1911, *d* 1972: *m* 1st, 1933 (*m diss* 1947), Harriet Green (who *m* 2ndly, 1947, Oren Clark Burt); 2ndly, 1947, Lois (5230 101st St, Jacksonville, Florida, 32210, USA), da of John W. Lainhart, of Washington, DC, USA:—
(By 1st *m*) Frances Helene BURT (934 East 40th St, Brooklyn, NY 11210), *b* 1942; has issue living, Liam Christopher, *b* 1981.
Issue of late John Hugh Hicks Beach, *b* 1915, *d* 1982: *m* 1945, Jeanne Potter (55 Clinton Rd, Bedford Hills, New York, USA), da of Herbert McGuhy, of Bedford Hills:—
John Hugh, *b* 1960. —— Lucinda, *b* 1948: *m* 1971, Timothy F. Quinn, of Jonathan Way, Brewster, NY 10509, USA, and has issue living, Tressan Lucinda, *b* 1977. —— Holly Bebhinn, *b* 1979. —— Priscilla, *b* 1950: *m* 1982, Ferdinand Travis Hopkins IV, of 416 Benedict Av, Tarrytown, NY 10591, USA.

Grandchildren of late Ellis Hicks Beach (*infra*):—
Issue of late Maj William Whitehead Hicks Beach, TD, *b* 1907, *d* 1975: *m* 1939, Diana (Witcombe Park, Gloucester), da of Christopher Gurney Hoare:—
Mark William (Witcombe Farm, Great Witcombe, nr Glos), *b* 1943: *m* 1966, Cecilia Ruth, el da of Douglas Allan Wright, of Gannymede, Ashford, Kent, and has issue living, Andrew William, *b* 1970, —— Frederick David, *b* 1980, —— Lucinda Jane, *b* 1975. —— Elizabeth Anne, *b* 1940: *m* 1962, Simon Erne St Houlston Clarke, and has issue living, Martin, *b* 1963, —— Timothy, *b* 1965. —— Rosemary Gillian, *b* 1944: *m* 1965, Maj Gen David Murray Naylor, CB, late Scots Gds (see Holt, Bt, *cr* 1935, 1985 Edn), and has issue living, Nicholas John, *b* 1967, —— Duncan Hugh, *b* 1968, —— Christopher William, *b* 1972. *Residence* – South Warnborough Manor, nr Basingstoke, Hants RE25 1RR.

Grandchildren of late William Frederick Hicks Beach (*ante*):—
Issue of late Ellis Hicks Beach, *b* 1874, *d* 1943: *m* 1903, Nancy, who *d* 1942, da of Spencer Whitehead, sometime a Master of Supreme Court:—
Letitia, *b* 1909: *m* 1st, 1931 (*m diss* 1939), Horace Alfred Townsend; 2ndly, 1947 (*m diss* 1960), George Miles; 3rdly, 1960, John Messent Grover, solicitor, of 57 Lyndhurst Grove, SE15, and has issue living, (by 1st *m*) John (23 Aldersmead Rd, Beckenham, Kent), *b* 1934: *m* 1957, Andrina Hume, — Tomazin, *b* 1933: *m* 1953, Stanley John Geller, of 120 Harwich Rd, Mistley, Manningtree, Essex CO11 2DG, — (by 2nd *m*) George Rufus, *b* 1948, — Richard Josef, *b* 1951.
Issue of late Edward Howe Hicks Beach, *b* 1875, *d* 1967: *m* 1903, Alberta Louise, who *d* 1946, da of William Penn Jaynes, of Vancouver:—
Edward Adryan, *b* 1915: *m* 1st, 1936 (*m diss* 1940), Evelyn, da of Clarence Dale, of Los Angeles, Cal, USA; 2ndly, 1940, Linnea Maria, da of late Andrew Holst, of Los Angeles, Cal, USA, and has issue living, (by 1st *m*) Edward Erick, *b* 1941, — Frederick Howe, *b* 1944. —— Clara Violet Louise, *b* 1905: *m* 1954, Ralph Elmer Wilson, of 4181 Lincoln Av, Culver City, Cal 90230, USA. —— Doris Margaret, *b* 1910: *m* 1934, Harry Roderic Theodore Marble, and has issue living, Harry Arthur, *b* 1936: *m* 1966, Marilyn Francis, da of Francis A. Schneider, of Oxford, Iowa, USA, and has issue living, Daniel Edward *b* 1966, Timothy John *b* 1968, Joseph Harry *b* 1975, Karen Margaret *b* 1971, — William Edward *b* 1947, — Michael Stephen (twin), *b* 1947, — Linnea Louise, *b* 1940: *m* 1st, 1959 (*m diss* 19—), Charles Bartl Adams; 2ndly, 1977, Garrith Dale Perrine, and has issue living, (by 1st *m*) Gregory Walter *b* 1962, Brian Roderic *b* 1965, Steven Edward *b* 1968.

Grandson (by 1st *m*) of late William Guy Hicks Beach (infra):—
Issue of late Michael William Bramston Hicks Beach, DSC, RNVR, *b* 1919, *d* 1985: *m* 1940, Kathleen Edyth Doreen
Augusta, who *d* 1985, da of Sir Brodrick Cecil Denham Arkwight Hartwell, 4th Bt:—
Michael Brodrick, *b* 1942: *m* 1st, 1970 (*m diss* 19—), Carolyn Anne, only da of Sir Richard Ashton Beaumont, KCMG, OBE;
2ndly, 1979, Mrs Eugenia Anne Garton.

Grandsons of late Maj Archibald William Hicks Beach, son of late Rt Hon William Wither Bramston
Beach, MP, son of late William Beach, MP, son of 2nd son of 6th Bt:—
Issue of late William Guy Hicks Beach, *b* 1891, *d* 1953: *m* 1st, 1914 (*m diss* 1932), Fanny Muriel, da of Ninian B.
Stewart, of Dunloe, Wemyss Bay, and 14 Park Circus, Glasgow; 2ndly, 1932, Mrs Beatrice Mary Uniacke, who *d*
1975, da of Arthur Johnstone, formerly Indian Police:—
(By 1st *m*) Peter Stewart, OBE (Boscobel, Hammer Lane, Grayshott, Hindhead, Surrey), *b* 1924; Capt RN; 1939-45 War
(despatches); OBE (Mil) 1968: *m* 1950, Victoria Margaret, who *d* 1986, da of Ralph Victor Nelson, and has had issue,
Richard Stewart Nelson, *b* 1951; *d* 1966, — Sally Elizabeth, *b* 1953: *m* 1980, Anthony Michael Farnfield, and has issue living,
Johanna *b* 1983. ——— Geoffrey Robert Wither (Cucumber Hall, Fressingfield, Suffolk), *b* 1925: *m* 1952, Rosemary Wendy
Wolseley-Charles, and has issue living, Nicholas Charles, *b* 1960, — Fiona Susan, *b* 1955: *m* 1981, Anthony Arthur Edwards,
of 107 Mycenae Rd, SE3, son of A. A. Edwards, of Swansea, and has issue living, Benjamin Nicholas Owen *b* 1984, Samuel
Dafydd William *b* 1989, Rosamund Margretta Victoria *b* 1986.

PREDECESSORS – **(1)** WILLIAM Hicks of Beverston Castle, co Gloucester, only son of Sir Michael Hicks, descended from
Robert Hicks of Bristol, a merchant in London, and father of the famous Sir Baptist Hicks, created (1628) Viscount
Campden, from whom spring the Noels, Earls of Gainsborough; *b* 1596; *cr* a *Baronet* 1619; *d* 1680; *s* by his son **(2)** WILLIAM,
2nd Bt; *d* 1703; *s* by his son **(3)** HENRY, 3rd Bt; twice *m*; *d* 1755; *s* by his only son **(4)** ROBERT, 4th Bt; *d* 1768; *s* by his
cousin **(5)** JOHN BAPTIST (son of Charles Hicks), 5th Bt; *d* 1792: *s* by his cousin **(6)** HOWE (son of Howe Hicks, of Witcombe,
Gloucestershire), 6th Bt; *b* 1722: *m* 1739; *d* 1801; *s* by his son **(7)** WILLIAM, 7th Bt; *b* 1754: *m* 1st, 1785, Judith, who *d* 1787,
da of Edward Witcombe; 2ndly, 1793, Anne Rachael, da of T. L. Chute, who *d* 1839; *d* 1834; *s* by his great nephew **(8)**
MICHAEL (son of Michael Hicks-Beach, of Netheravon, Wilts, whose father assumed the additional surname of Beach), 8th
Bt; MP for E Gloucestershire 1854: *m* 1832, Harriet Victoria, who *d* 1900, da of John Stratton, of Farthinghoe Lodge; *d* 1854;
s by his son **(9)** MICHAEL EDWARD, PC, DCL, *b* 1837; MP for E Gloucestershire (*C*) 1864-85, and for W Div of Bristol 1885-
1906; Parl Sec to Poor Law Board March to Aug 1868, Under-Sec for Home Office Aug to Dec 1868, Ch Sec for Ireland
1874-8, Sec of State for the Colonies 1878-80, a Member of Committee of Council on Education in Scotland and Chancellor
of the Exchequer 1885-6, again Ch Sec for Ireland July 1886 to March 1887, Pres of Board of Trade Feb 1888 to Aug 1892,
a Church Estates Commr 1892-5, and again Chancellor of the Exchequer 1895-1902; *s* to the Baronetcy 1854, and was *cr*
Viscount St Aldwyn, of Coln St Aldwyn, co Gloucester (peerage of the United Kingdom) 1906, and *Viscount Quenington*, of
Quenington, co Gloucester, and *Earl of St Aldwyn*, of Coln St Aldwyn, co Gloucester (peerage of United Kingdom) 1915: *m*
1st, 1864, Caroline Susan, who *d* 1865, da of late John Henry Elwes, of Colesborne Park, Cheltenham (Bromley-Wilson, Bt);
2ndly, 1874, Lady Lucy Catherine Fortescue, who *d* 1940, da of 3rd Earl Fortescue; *d* 1916; *s* by his grandson **(10)** MICHAEL
JOHN, GBE, TD, PC (son of late Capt Michael Hugh, Viscount Quenington, MP, Gloucestershire Hussars Yeo, son of 1st
Earl, *ka* 1916, by his wife, Marjorie, who *d* 1916, da of late John Henry Dent Brocklehurst, of Sudeley Castle, Winchcombe), 2nd
Earl, *b* 1912; Major 1st Royal Gloucestershire Hussars; JP and DL Glos, and Vice-Lieut 1981-87; Min of Agriculture, Fisheries
and Food 1955-58, Chief Whip House of Lords, and Capt Hon Corps of Gentlemen-at-Arms 1958-64 and 1970-74: *m* 1948,
Diana Mary Christian (SMYLY), who *d* (10 July) 1992, da of late Henry Christian George Mills (*see* B Hillingdon, colls, 1990
Edn); *d* (29 Jan) 1992; *s* by his eldest son **(11)** MICHAEL HENRY, 3rd Earl and present peer; also Viscount St Aldwyn, and
Viscount Quenington.

St Andrews, Earl of; son of Duke of Kent.

ST AUDRIES, BARONY OF (Fuller-Acland-Hood) (Extinct 1971)

(See also Fuller-Acland-Hood, Bt, ext)

WIDOW LIVING OF SON OF FIRST BARON

Phyllis Lily Frances (Wootton House, nr Glastonbury, Somerset), da of late Dr Denys B. I. Hallett, of 2 Old Palace Terr, The
Green, Richmond, Surrey: *m* 1939, Hon (Arthur) John Palmer Fuller-Acland-Hood, who *d* 1964, and has issue living (see
colls, infra).

COLLATERAL BRANCH LIVING

Issue of late Hon (Arthur) John Palmer Fuller-Acland-Hood, yr son of 1st Baron, *b* 1906, *d* 1964: *m* 1939,
Phyllis Lily Frances (ante), da of late Dr Denys Bouhier Imbert Hallett, of 2 Old Palace Terr, The Green,
Richmond, Surrey:—
Elizabeth Periam (*Lady Gass*) (Fairfield, Stogursey, Bridgwater, Som) *b* 1940; High Sheriff Som 1994: *m* 1975, Sir Michael
David Irving Gass, KCMG, who *d* 1983. ——— Mary Mildred ACLAND-HOOD (9 Fentiman Rd, SW8), *b* 1941; has resumed the
surname of Acland-Hood: *m* 1st, 1961, Timothy Stephen (Toby) Hodder-Williams, who *d* 1969; 2ndly, 1975, Frank Thomas
Blackaby, and has issue living (by 2nd *m*), John Christopher ACLAND-HOOD, *b* 1979, — Susan Elizabeth ACLAND-HOOD, *b*
1977. ——— Sylvia (The Rectory, Exford, Minehead, Som), *b* 1944: *m* 1991, Rev Robin J. Ray.

SAINT BRIDES, BARONY OF (James) (Extinct 1989)

SON LIVING OF LIFE BARON (*By 1st marriage*)

Hon Roderick Morrice, *b* 1956; *ed* Emmanuel Coll, Camb: *m* 1981, Harriet Sophie, yst da of Cdr John Benians, RN, of Waterfield, Headley, Hants, and has issue living, Caspian, *b* 1985, — Pasco, *b* 1987. *Residence* – Hopkiln Cottage, Gracious St,
Selborne, Hants.

DAUGHTERS LIVING OF LIFE BARON (By 1st marriage)

Hon Laura Catherine, *b* 1948; *ed* Sussex Univ (BA): *m* 1981, Robert Lacy Tatton Sykes, elder son of Geoffrey Sykes, of Kirribilli, NSW, Australia. *Residence* – 6 Hans Crescent, SW1X 0LJ.
Hon Clare Veronica JAMES, *b* 1950; *ed* London Univ (BSc); has resumed her maiden name: *m* 1970 (*m diss* 1978), Dr Patrick Duncan, son of late Patrick Baker Duncan, and has issue living, Patrick, *b* 1973. *Residence* – Köpenhamnsgatan 24, S-164 42 Kista, Sweden.

WIDOW LIVING OF LIFE BARON

GENEVIEVE CHRISTIANE (*Baroness Saint Brides*), da of late Robert Henri Houdin, and widow of Prof Reymond Sarasin: *m* 1968, as his 2nd wife, Baron Saint Brides, GCMG, CVO, MBE, PC (Life Baron), who *d* 1989. *Residence* – Cap Saint-Pierre, 83990 Saint-Tropez, France.

St Cyres, Viscount; son of Earl of Iddesleigh.

ST DAVIDS, VISCOUNT (Philipps) (Viscount UK 1918, Bt E 1621)

Patriotism my motive

COLWYN JESTYN JOHN PHILIPPS, 3rd Viscount, and 15th Baronet; *b* 30 Jan 1939; *s* 1991; *ed* Sevenoaks Sch, and King's Coll, London (Cert Advanced Mus Studies 1989); late 2nd Lieut Welsh Guards; a Lord in Waiting to HM since 1992: *m* 1965, Augusta Victoria Correa Larrain, da of late Don Estantislao Correa Ugarte, of Santiago, Chile, and has issue.

Arms – Argent, a lion rampant sable, ducally gorged and chained or, langued and taloned gules. **Crest** – A lion as in the arms. **Supporters** – *Dexter*, a knight vested in chain armour, the jupon charged with the arms of *Philipps* and resting his exterior hand upon the hilt of his sword; *sinister*, a knight vested in plate armour, his jupon charged with arms of *Wogan* (or, on a chief sable, three martlets of the field) and resting the exterior hand upon the hilt of the sword; both standing upon a battlemented wall, all proper.
Address – c/o House of Lords, SW1.

SONS LIVING

Hon RHODRI COLWYN, *b* 16 Sept 1966; *ed* Worth.
Hon Roland Augusto Jestyn Estantislao, *b* 1970; *ed* Downside.

SISTERS LIVING

Hon Rowena Frances (418 Wellington St, Clifton Hill, Vic 3068, Australia), *b* 1940: *m* 1959 (*m diss* 1977), David Elford, and has had issue, Richard, *b* 1962; *d* 1990. — Wendy, *b* 1960, — Suzanne, *b* 1964, — Leone, *b* 1965.
Hon Myfanwy Ann (23 Pyrland Rd, Islington, N5), *b* 1944: *m* 1968, Anthony John Frederick Smith, and has issue living, Tobias Peter John, *b* 1971, — Benjamin Cosby, *b* 1973.
Hon Rhiannon Elizabeth (106 Prince of Wales Rd, NW5 3NE), *b* 1946: *m* 1974 (*m. diss* 1991), Donald Hudson Chapman.
Hon Eiddwen Sara, *b* 1948: *m* 1986, Clive Geoffrey Owen, of 4 Quarry Rd, Kenilworth, Warwicks CV8 1AE, and has issue living, David James, *b* 1987, — Philip Michael, *b* 1990.

WIDOW LIVING OF SECOND VISCOUNT

EVELYN MARJORIE (*Marjorie, Viscountess St Davids*), only da of late Dr John Edmund Guy Harris, of The Heritage, Bray-on-Thames, Berks: *m* 1959, as his 3rd wife, the 2nd Viscount, who *d* 1991. *Residence* – 15 St Mark's Crescent, Regent's Park, NW1 7TS.

COLLATERAL BRANCHES LIVING

(Male line in remainder to Baronetcy only)

Issue of late Owen Cosby Philipps (*cr Baron Kylsant* 1923), 3rd son of 12th Baronet, *b* 1863, *d* 1937, when the Barony became extinct (see that title).
Issue of late Laurence Richard Philipps (*cr Baron Milford* 1939), 6th son of 12th Baronet, *b* 1874, *d* 1962 (see that title)

(In remainder to Baronies of Strange of Knokin, Hungerford and de Moleyns)

Issue of late Hon Lelgarde de Clare Elizabeth Rawdon Hastings, only da of 1st Viscount St Davids, by his 2nd wife, Elizabeth Frances, Baroness Strange of Knokin, Hungerford and de Moleyns (in her own right), *b* 1918, *d* 1984: *m* 1950 (*m diss* 1967), Colin Charles Evans:—
Roland Anthony Christopher EVANS (78 Dundela Park, Sandycove, co Dublin), *b* 1951; *ed* Portora Royal Sch: *m* 1978, Annette Matilda, da of Alfred Hunter, of Carrick Henry, co Sligo, and has issue living, Rebecca Lara, *b* 1982. ▬ William Harold Sandford EVANS (Aglish, The Curragh, Castlebar, co Mayo), *b* 1953; *ed* St George's Sch, Nenagh: *m* 1979, Elizabeth Ann, da of Sean James Smith, of Castlebar, co Mayo, and has issue living, Billy Sean, *b* 1980, — Kayleigh Elizabeth, *b* 1988, — Bronwyn Mary, *b* 1990. ▬▬ (Lorna) Susan (11 Fairoak Chase, Brockla, Whitchurch, Bridgend, Glamorgan), *b* (twin) 1953.

PREDECESSORS – This family is of great antiquity in South Wales. Among its ancestors was Sir Aaron ap Rhys, who attended Richard I into the Holy Land 1190, where he behaved so gallantly against the Saracens, that he is said to have received from Richard the Knighthood of the Sepulchre of Our Saviour, his arms of a lion rampant sable, and the addition of a "Crown and Chain". Sir Thomas Philipps, Knt, of Picton Castle, accompanied Henry VIII twice to France. His descendant **(1)** *Sir* JOHN Philipps, Knt, of Picton, co Pembroke; MP for Pembroke 1597-98 and Oct-Dec 1601; *cr* a *Baronet* 1621: *m* Anne, da of Sir John Perrott, of Haroldston; *d* 1629; *s* by his el son **(2)** RICHARD, 2nd Bt: *m* Elizabeth, da of Sir Erasmus Dryden, Bt; *d* 16—; *s* by his son **(3)** ERASMUS Philipps, 3rd Bt; MP for Pembroke 1654-55 and Jan-April, 1659: *m* 1st, Cicely, da of Thomas, Earl of Winchilsea; 2ndly, Katharine, el da and co-heir of Edward D'Arcy, of Newhall, co Derby; *d* 1697; *s* by his 2nd son **(4)** JOHN, 4th Bt; MP for Pembroke 1695-1702, and for Haverfordwest 1718-1722: *m* 1697, Mary, da of Anthony Smith; *d* 1736; *s* by his el son **(5)** ERASMUS, 5th Bt; MP for Haverfordwest 1726-43; *d* 1743; *s* by his brother **(6)** JOHN, 6th Bt; MP for Carmarthen 1741-47, for Petersfield 1754-61, and for co Pembroke 1761-64: *m* Elizabeth, da of Henry Shepperd; *d* 1764; *s* by his only son **(7)** RICHARD, 7th Bt; MP for co Pembroke 1765-70 and 1786-1812, Lord-Lieut of co Pembroke 1786; *cr Baron Milford* 1776: *m* 1764, Mary, da of James Philipps, of Penty Park; *d* 1823, when the Barony of Milford became ext and the Baronetcy passed to his kinsman **(8)** ROWLAND HENRY Philipps-Laugharne-Philipps (descendant of Hugh Philipps, 3rd son of 1st Bt), 8th Bt: *m* 1812, Elizabeth, who *d* 1834, da of James Frampton; *d* 1823; *s* by his brother **(9)** WILLIAM, 9th Bt; *b* 1794: *m* 1829, Elizabeth, who *d* 1865, da of George White; *d* 1850; *s* by his only son **(10)** GODWYN, 10th Bt; *b* 1840; *d* 1857; *s* by his kinsman **(11)** *Rev Sir* JAMES EVANS Philipps, 11th Bt; *b* 1793: *m* 1822, Mary Anne, who *d* 1833, da of Benjamin Bickley; *d* 1873; *s* by his son **(12)** *Rev Sir* JAMES ERASMUS, 12th Bt; *b* 1824; V of Warminster 1859-1897, and Canon of Salisbury: *m* 1859, Hon Mary Margaret, who *d* 1913, da of late Rev Hon Samuel Best; *d* 1912; *s* by his el son **(13)** JOHN WYNFORD, 13th Bt; *b* 1860; *cr Baron St Davids*, of Roch Castle, co Pembroke (peerage of UK) 1908, and *Viscount St Davids*, of Lydstep Haven, co Pembroke (peerage of UK) 1918: *m* 1st, 1888, Nora, who *d* 1915, da of late I. Gestenberg, of Stockleigh House, Regent's Park, NW; 2ndly, 1916, Lady Elizabeth Frances (*Baroness Strange of Knokin, Hungerford, and de Moleyns* in her own right), who *d* 1974 (see † infra), da of late Maj Hon Paulyn Francis Cuthbert Rawdon-Hastings; *d* 1938; *s* by his 3rd but only surviving son **(14)** JESTYN REGINALD AUSTEN PLANTAGENET, 2nd Viscount; *b* 1917; Lieut RNVR; founder Regent's Boat Club 1966, co-founder Inland Waterways Assocn, Cttee Memb House of Lords Yacht Club, and founder and patron Pirate Club; Queen Elizabeth II's Silver Jubilee Medal: *m* 1st, 1938 (*m diss* 1954), Doreen Guinness, who *d* 1956, only da of Capt Arthur Craven Jowett, of Coverdale, Toorak, Melbourne, Australia; 2ndly, 1954 (*m diss* 1959), Elisabeth Joyce, elder da of Dr E. Alec Woolf, of Hove, Sussex; 3rdly, 1959, (Evelyn) Marjorie, only da of Dr John Edmund Guy Harris, of The Heritage, Bray-on-Thames, Berks; *d* 1991; *s* by his only son **(15)** COLWYN JESTYN JOHN, 3rd Viscount and present peer; also Baron Strange of Knokin, Hungerford and de Moleyns, and Baron St Davids.

†**(1)** *Sir* WALTER Hungerford, KG; served with distinction in France; was Steward of the Household to Henry VI; summoned to Parliament of England as *Baron Hungerford* 1426-49; *d* 1449; *s* by his son **(2)** ROBERT, 2nd Baron; summoned to Parliament 1450-5: *m* Margaret, only da of William, *Baron Botreaux* (peerage of England, *cr* 1368); *d* 1458; *s* by his son **(3)** ROBERT, 3rd Baron, who had previously 1445-52 been summoned to Parliament of England as *Baron de Moleyns* (or *Molines*); was never summoned as Baron Hungerford; joined the Lancastrian interests, and being made prisoner at the battle of Hexham his honours and estates were attainted, and he was beheaded at Newcastle 1463; *s* by his son **(4)** THOMAS, who espoused the cause of Edward IV, but subsequently exerted his influence for the restoration of Henry VI, he was seized and beheaded as a traitor 1479: he left issue by his first *m* **(5)** MARY, who obtained the reversal of her father's and grandfather's attainders, and was styled Baroness Hungerford, Botreaux, and Molines (or de Moleyns); she *m* Edward Hastings, son and heir of William, 1st *Baron Hastings* (peerage of England, *cr* 1461); *s* by her son **(6-15)** GEORGE, 6th Baron; *cr Earl of Huntingdon* 1529; in which peerage these Baronies of Hungerford, Botreaux, de Moleyns (or Molines) and Hastings were merged until 1789, when the 10th Earl *dsp*, and was *s* by his sister **(16)** ELIZABETH, wife of John Rawdon, 1st *Earl of Moira* (peerage of Ireland, *cr* 1762); *d* 1808; *s* by her son **(17)** FRANCIS, KG, GCB, who in 1793 had *s* his father as 2nd Earl of Moira; a Gen in the Army, Lord-Lieut of the Tower Hamlets, Constable of the Tower of London, and successively Gov-Gen of India and Gov and Com-in-Ch of Malta; assumed the name of Hastings in addition to that of Rawdon; *cr Baron Rawdon*, of Rawdon, co York (peerage of Great Britain) 1783, and *Viscount Loudoun, Earl of Rawdon*, and *Marquess of Hastings* (peerage of United Kingdom) 1816: *m* Flora Mure-Campbell, *Countess of Loudoun*, in her own right; *d* 1826; *s* by his son **(18)** GEORGE AUGUSTUS FRANCIS, 2nd Marquess, who in 1840 *s* his mother as 7th Earl of Loudoun: *m* 1831, Barbara, *Baroness Grey de Ruthyn* (peerage of England, *cr* 1324); he *d* 1844; *s* by his el son **(19)** PAULYN REGINALD SERLO, 3rd Marquess; *d unm* 1851; *s* by his brother **(20)** HENRY WEYSFORD CHARLES PLANTAGENET, 4th Marquess, who in 1858 *s* to his mother's Barony of Grey de Ruthyn; *d* 1868, when the Barony of Rawdon, the Viscountcy of Loudoun, the Earldoms of Moira and Rawdon, and the Marquessate of Hastings became extinct and the Baronies of Grey de Ruthyn, Hastings, Hungerford, Botreaux, and de Moleyns (or Molines) became abeyant between his sisters, and the Earldom of Loudoun and minor Scottish honours devolved upon his el sister **(21)** EDITH MAUD Abney-Hastings, in whose favour in 1871, the abeyance of the Baronies of Hastings, Hungerford, Botreaux and de Moleyns (or Molines) was terminated; *b* 1833: *m* Charles Frederick Clifton, who in 1859 assumed the names of Abney-Hastings, and in 1880 was *cr Baron Donington*, of Donington Park, co Leicester (peerage of United Kingdom); she *d* 1874; *s* by his son **(22)** CHARLES EDWARD HASTINGS, 11th Earl of Loudoun, *b* 1855; an Hereditary Bearer of one of the Golden Spurs: *m* 1880, Hon Alice Mary Elizabeth Fitzalan-Howard, who *d* 1915, da of 1st Baron Howard of Glossop; *d* 1920, when the Barony of Donington devolved upon his brother Gilbert Theophilus Clifton Clifton-Hastings-Campbell, and the Earldom of Loudoun upon his niece, Edith Maud, el da of late Major Hon Paulyn Francis Cuthbert Rawdon-Hastings, while the Baronies of Botreaux, de Moleyns (or Molines), Hungerford, and Hastings fell into abeyance between the das of late Major Hon Paulyn Francis Cuthbert Rawdon-Hastings, brother of 11th Earl of Loudoun, the abeyance in the Baronies of Hungerford and de Moleyns, as well as in the Barony of Strange of Knokin (*cr* by writ 1299) (see * infra) being shortly afterwards in Feb 1921 terminated in favour of the el **(23)** ELIZABETH FRANCES, Viscountess St Davids (ante).

*(1)** JOHN le Strange, son of John le Strange, of Knokin, co Salop, was summoned by writ to Parliament 1299 and 1308-9 as *Lord Strange de Knokin*; *d* 1309; *s* by his son **(2)** JOHN; summoned to Parliament 1311; *d* 1311; *s* by his son **(3)** JOHN; summoned to Parliament 1312-13; *d* 1323; *s* by his brother **(4)** ROGER; summoned to Parliament 1341-47; *d* 1349; *s* by his son **(5)** ROGER; summoned to Parliament 1355-82; *d* 1382; *s* by his son **(6)** JOHN; summoned to Parliament 1383-97: *m* Maud, da and co-heir of John, Lord Mohun de Dunster (*cr* 1299); *d* 1387; *s* by his son **(7)** RICHARD, *b* 1381; in 1431 became (through his mother) *Lord Mohun de Dunster*, *d* 1449; *s* by his son **(8)** JOHN; summoned to Parliament 1446-72; *d* 1477; *s* by his only da **(9)** JOAN: *m* 1482, George, Lord Stanley, KG, son of the 1st Earl of Derby, who in right of his wife was summoned to Parliament as Lord Strange de Knokin 1482-96; *d* 1513; *s* by her el son **(10)** THOMAS, *b* 1485, who in 1504 had *s* as 2nd Earl of Derby, as well as to the Barony of Stanley (*cr* 1456); *d* 1521; *s* by his son **(11)** EDWARD, 3rd Earl, *b* 1509; *d* 1572; *s* by his son **(12)** HENRY, 4th Earl, *b* 1521; summoned to Parliament in his father's Barony of Strange of Knokin 1558-75; *d* 1593; *s* by his son **(13)** FERDINANDO, 5th Earl, *b* 1559; summoned to Parliament in his father's Barony of Strange de Knokin 1588-92; *d* 1594; when the Earldom of Derby devolved upon his brother, and the Baronies of Strange de Knokin, Mohun de Dunster, and Stanley fell into abeyance between his daughters and co-heirs, until in 1921 the abeyance in the Barony of Strange de Knokin was determined in favour of **(14)** ELIZABETH FRANCES, Viscountess St Davids (ante).

ST GERMANS, EARL OF (Eliot) (Earl UK 1815)

PEREGRINE NICHOLAS ELIOT, 10th Earl; *b* 2 Jan 1941; *s* 1988; *ed* Eton; patron of three livings: *m* 1st, 1964 (*m diss* 1990), Hon Jacquetta Jean Frederica Lampson, da of 1st Baron Killearn; 2ndly, 1991, Elizabeth Mary Williams, and has issue by 1st *m*.

Arms – Argent, a fesse gules, between double cottises wavy azure. **Crest** – An elephant's head argent, plain collared gules. **Supporters** – Two eagles reguardant, wings displayed and inverted proper, each charged on the breast with an ermine spot sable.
Seat – Port Eliot, St Germans, Cornwall.

SONS LIVING *(By 1st marriage)*

JAGO NICHOLAS ALDO (*Lord Eliot*), *b* 24 March 1966; *ed* Millfield.
Hon Louis Robert, *b* 1968; *ed* Eton.
Hon Francis Michael, *b* 1971; *ed* Eton.

SISTER LIVING

Lady Frances Helen Mary, *b* 1943: *m* 1965 (*m diss* 1987), Charles Maurice, Earl of Shelburne, el son of 8th Marquess of Lansdowne.

Press close upon those who take the lead

DAUGHTER LIVING OF SIXTH EARL

Lady Cathleen Blanche Lily, *b* 1921; a co-heir to Baronies of Botetourt and Herbert (*see* Botetourt and Herbert, B*y*): *m* 1st, 1946 (*m diss* 1956), Capt John Seyfried, Roy Horse Guards; 2ndly, 1957, Sir Havelock Henry Trevor Hudson, and has issue living (by 1st *m*), David John (39 Chiddingstone St, SW6 3TQ), *b* 1952; *ed* Harrow: *m* 1975, Jane Angela Bishop, and has issue living, Oliver Richard *b* 1976; *ed* Harrow, Charlotte Sophia Caroline *b* 1977, — Sarah Diana, *b* 1949: *m* 1975, Peter Michael Smith, — (by 2nd *m*) Michael Guy Havelock, *b* 1962, — Louise Deborah, *b* 1958. *Residence* – The Old Rectory, Stanford Dingley, Berks.

WIDOW LIVING OF SON OF EIGHTH EARL

Marie Frances Richmond, da of late Geoffrey Mervyn Cooper, of Preston Candover, Hants (*see* Cooper, Bt, *cr* 1863, colls), and widow of A. R. Lusk, of Comrie, Perthshire: *m* 2ndly, 1983, Capt Hon (Montagu) Robert (Vere) Eliot, Gren Gds (ret), who *d* 1994. *Residence* – Lux Cross House, Liskeard, Cornwall PL14 3EL.

WIDOW LIVING OF NINTH EARL

MARY BRIDGET (*Bridget, Countess of St Germans*), only child of late Sir Thomas Shenton Whitelegge Thomas, GCMG, OBE, and formerly wife of Lt-Col Jack Leslie Larry Lotinga: *m* 1965, as his 3rd wife, the 9th Earl, who *d* 1988. *Residence* – Penmadown, St Clement, Truro, Cornwall TR1 1SZ.

COLLATERAL BRANCHES LIVING

Issue of late Lieut-Col Hon Christian Edward Cornwallis Eliot, OBE, brother of 7th and 8th Earls, *b* 1872, *d* 1940: *m* 1st, 1897, Laura Grey, who *d* 1938, da of Lieut-Col Sir George Chetwode, 6th Bt; 2ndly, 1938, Daisy Blossom Roberts, who *d* 1965, da of late Alexander Elkan:—
(Frederica) Betty Cornwallis (*Betty, Lady Markham*) (PO Box 583, Mbabane, Swaziland), *b* 1900: *m* 1923 (*m diss* 1929), Capt Robert Wigram Crawford, formerly King's R Rifle Corps; 2ndly, 1942, as his 3rd wife, Sir Charles Markham, 2nd Bt, who *d* 1952.

Issue of late Hon Edward Granville Eliot, brother of 7th and 8th Earls, *b* 1878, *d* 1950: *m* 1907, Clare Louisa, who *d* 1927, da of late William Robert Phelips (E Bessborough, colls):—
Ven Canon Peter Charles, MBE, TD, *b* 1910; *ed* Wellington Coll, and at Magdalene Coll, Camb, (MA); admitted a Solicitor 1934; late Lt-Col 297th (Kent Yeo) Light Anti-Aircraft Regt, RA (TA); Assist Curate of St Martin-in-the-Fields, WC2, 1954-57, and V of Cockermouth 1957-61, Rural Dean of Cockermouth and Workington 1960-61, and V of Cropthorne with Charlton 1961-65, Archdeacon of Worcester 1965-75 and Residentiary Canon of Worcester 1965-75; MBE (Mil) 1945: *m* 1934, Lady Alethea Constance Dorothy Sydney, da of 1st Earl Buxton (ext). *Residence* – The Old House, Kingsland, Leominster, Herefordshire HR6 9QS. —— Margaret Augusta, *b* 1914: *m* 1943, Richard Alan John Asher, MD, FRCP, who *d* 1969, and has issue living, Peter, *b* 1944; *ed* Westminster; record producer: *m* 1st, 19— (*m diss* 19—) Betsy Doster; 2ndly, 1983, Wendy Worth, and has issue living (by 2nd *m*), Victoria Jane *b* 1984, — Jane, *b* 1946; actress and author: *m* 19—, Gerald Scarfe, artist, and has issue living, Alexander David *b* 1981, Rory Christopher *b* 1983, Katie Geraldine *b* 1974, — Clare, *b* 1948: *m* 1975, John Gillies, of 6 Hillbury Rd, SW17 8JT, and has issue living, Sarah *b* 1978, Helen *b* 1980. *Residence* – 6A Hillbury Rd, SW17.

PREDECESSORS

– (1) EDWARD Eliot, MP for Cornwall, and Receiver Gen of Duchy of Cornwall; *cr Baron Eliot*, of St Germans, Cornwall (peerage of Great Britain) 1784; assumed the additional surname of Craggs by Roy licence 1789; *d* 1804; *s* by his son (2) JOHN, 2nd Baron; *cr Earl of St Germans* (peerage of United Kingdom) 1815, with remainder to his brother; *dsp* 1823; *s* by his brother (3) WILLIAM, 2nd Earl; was successively Ambassador to the States Gen and to Munich, MP for Liskeard, and a Lord of the Treasury; *d* 1845; *s* by his son (4) EDWARD GRANVILLE, GCB, PC, 3rd Earl; *b* 1798; sat as MP for Liskeard 1824-32, and for Cornwall, E (C) 1837-45; was a Lord of the Treasury 1827-32, Envoy to Spain 1835, Ch Sec for Ireland 1841-5, Postmaster-Gen 1845, Lord-Lieut of Ireland 1852-5, Lord Steward of the Household 1857-8 and 1859-66, and Special Dep Warden of Stannaries 1852-77: *m* 1824, Lady Jemima Cornwallis, da and co-heiress of 2nd and last Marquess Cornwallis; *d* 1877; *s* by his son (5) WILLIAM GORDON CORNWALLIS, 4th Earl; sat as MP for Devonport (L) 1866-8; called to the Upper House in his father's Barony of Eliot 1870; *d unm* 1881; *s* by his brother (6) HENRY CORNWALLIS, 5th Earl, *b* 1835; in RN 1848-53 and Foreign Office 1855-81: *m* 1881, Hon Emily Harriet Labouchere, who *d* 1933, da of 1st Baron Taunton (ext); *d* 1911; *s* by his yr son (7) JOHN GRANVILLE CORNWALLIS, 6th Earl; *b* 1890; Capt R Scots Greys: *m* 1918, Lady Blanche Linnie Somerset, who *d* 1968, da of 9th Duke of Beaufort, *d* 1922; *s* by his cousin (8) GRANVILLE JOHN (el son of Col Hon Charles George Cornwallis Eliot, CVO, 6th son of 3rd Earl), 7th Earl; *b* 1867; *d* 1942; *s* by his brother (9) MONTAGUE CHARLES, KCVO, OBE, 8th Earl; *b* 1870; a Gentleman Usher to King Edward VII 1901-8, and a Groom in Waiting 1908-10, a Gentleman Usher to King George V 1911-36, Groom of the Robes 1920-36, and an Extra Groom in Waiting 1924-36, and 1937-60; European War 1914-19 as Lieut-Com RNVR: *m* 1910, Helen Agnes, who *d* 1962, da of late Arthur Post, of New York; *d* 1960; *s* by his el son (10) NICHOLAS RICHARD MICHAEL, 9th Earl *b* 1914; Capt Duke of Cornwall's LI, served European War 1939-45:

m 1st, 1939 (*m diss* 1947), Helen Mary, who *d* 1951, yr da of late Lt-Col Charles Walter Villiers, CBE, DSO (E Clarendon, colls); 2ndly, 1948 (*m diss* 1959), Margaret Eleanor, who *d* 1967, only da of late Lt-Col William Francis George Wyndham, MVO, of Heathfield Lodge, Midhurst, Sussex, and formerly wife of (i) Hugh Wharton Earle, and (ii) Basil Francis Eyston; 3rdly, 1965, (Mary) Bridget, da of late Sir Thomas Shenton Whitelegge Thomas, GCMG, OBE, and formerly wife of Lt-Col Jack Leslie Larry Lotinga; *d* 1988; *s* by his only son (**11**) PEREGRINE NICHOLAS, 10th Earl and present peer; also Baron Eliot.

ST HELENS, BARON (Hughes-Young) (Baron UK 1964)

RICHARD (RORY) FRANCIS HUGHES-YOUNG, 2nd Baron; *b* 4 Nov 1945; *s* 1980; *ed* Nautical Coll, Pangbourne: *m* 1983, Mrs Emma R. Talbot-Smith, and has issue.

Arms – Or three piles sable each charged with a fountain. **Crest** – A dexter cubit arm proper charged with a fountain a hand grasping an arrow fesswise proper. **Supporters** – *Dexter*, a wolf gules; *sinister*, a griffin sable; each charged on the shoulder with a portcullis or.
Residence – Marchfield, Binfield, Berks.

SON LIVING

Hon HENRY THOMAS, *b* 7 March 1986.

DAUGHTER LIVING

Hon Lara Elizabeth, *b* 1987.

SISTERS LIVING

Hon Henrietta Maria, *b* 1940: *m* 1970, Brian Turnbull Julius Stevens, of Sutton Warbington, Long Sutton, Hants, and has issue living, (Flora) Matilda Julius, *b* 1973, — Harriet Maria Julius, *b* 1975, — Louisa Elizabeth Julius, *b* 1976.
Hon Selina Lilian, *b* 1944: *m* 1969, Jonathan Basil Morton Peto (*see* Peto, Bt, colls, *cr* 1927), of Bealings House, Woodbridge, Suffolk.
Hon Louisa Nina, *b* 1949: *m* 1974, Maj James Francis Arbuthnott, Black Watch (*see* V Arbuthnott, colls), of Stone House Cottage, Stone, Kidderminster, Worcs.

PREDECESSOR – (**1**) MICHAEL HENRY COLIN Hughes-Young, MC, son of Brig-Gen Henry George Young, CIE, DSO, of Skeffington Lodge, Antrim; *b* 1912; Lt-Col The Black Watch; a Lord Commnr of Treasury 1958-62, Dep Govt Ch Whip 1959-64, Treasurer to HM Household 1962-64; MP for Central Div of Wandsworth (*C*) 1955-64; *cr Baron St Helens*, of St Helens co Palatine of Lancaster (Peerage of UK) 1964: *m* 1939, Elizabeth Agnes, who *d* 1956, yst da of Capt Richard Blakiston-Houston (Blakiston, Bt); *d* 1980; *s* by his only son (**2**) RICHARD FRANCIS, 2nd Baron and present peer.

St John, Viscount; title borne by Viscount Bolingbroke.

ST JOHN OF BLETSO, BARON (St John) (Baron E 1559, Bt E 1660)
(Title pronounced "Sinjun of Bletso")

Following his allotted fate

ANTHONY TUDOR ST JOHN, 21st Baron, and 18th Baronet; *b* 16 May 1957; *s* 1978; *ed* Diocesan Coll, Cape Town, Cape Town Univ (BA, BSc, and London Univ (LLM)); Solicitor; Consultant to Smith New Court plc, and Chm Eurotrust Internat; Cross Bencher, House of Lords.

𝕬rms – Argent, on chief gules, two mullet, or. 𝕮rest – On a mount vert, a falcon rising or, belled of the last, ducally gorged gules. 𝕾upporters – Two monkeys proper.
Residences – 10 Pencombe Mews, Denbigh Rd, W11 2SJ; Woodlands, Llanishen, nr Chepstow, Gwent NP6. *Club* – Hurlingham.

AUNT LIVING (*Sister of 20th Baron*)

(*Raised to the rank of a Baron's daughter, 1977*)

Hon Elaine Julia Barbara, *b* 1921: *m* 1939, Lt-Col John Francis Whidborne (ret), RA, and has had issue, Stephen Barham, *b* 1940; *ed* Blundell's; *dunm* 1965, — Richard St John, MBE (14 Berrylands, Liss Forest, Liss, Hants GU33 7DB), *b* 1942; *ed* Blundell's; Maj (ret) AAC; Air Accidents Investigation Branch, Dept of Transport; MBE (Mil) 1973, FRAeS 1993: *m* 1st, 1965, Linda Beverley, who *d* 1975, da of Cyril Trevor Sherwood, of Child Okeford, Dorset; 2ndly, 1978, Jennifer, da of F. E. Gould, of Sempringham House, Sleaford, Lincs, and has issue living (by 1st *m*), Nicholas St John *b* 1969, James Oliver St John *b* 1973, — Julia Lauretta, *b* 1943. *Residence* – Holly Mount, Pethybridge, Lustleigh, Devon TQ13 9TG.

DAUGHTERS LIVING OF EIGHTEENTH BARON

Hon Helen Evelyn (c/o Balfour & Manson, Solicitors, 58 Frederick St, Edinburgh, EH2 1LS), *b* 1906.
Hon Katherine Barbara, *b* 1907: *m* 1945, George William Uttley, MA, BSc, late Fl-Lt RAF, and has issue living, Alathea St John, *b* 1947.

WIDOW LIVING OF TWENTIETH BARON

KATHERINE (*Baroness St John of Bletso*) (By The Sea, Kalk Bay, Cape, S Africa), yst da of late Alfred von Berg, of Gonville House, Manor Fields, SW15: *m* 1955, the 20th Baron, who *d* 1978.

COLLATERAL BRANCHES LIVING

Granddaughters of late Lt-Col Hon Rowland Tudor St John, Durham LI, 3rd son of 16th Baron:—
Issue of late Rev Oliver John Frank Lockwood St John, DSC, *b* 1914, *d* 1972: *m* 1938, Elva Rosemary (29 Bay Rd, Alverstoke, Hants), da of Alfred John Skinn, MB, ChB, of Hong Kong:—
Vyvian Elaine, *b* 1940: *m* 1972, Patrick Nelson Maudsley, of 18 Tudor Way, Wellingborough, Northants, and has issue living, Ruth Claire, *b* 1973. — Juliet Rosemary, *b* 1943; SRN: *m* 1967, Brian William Ellis Johnson, ARIBA, of 131 Grosvenor Av, N5, and has issue living, George St John, *b* 1969, — Hugh William Nicholas, *b* 1979, — Katherine Alice (twin), *b* 1969. —— Diana Hazel Susan, *b* 1946; BA: *m* 1970, Ewart John Holmes, ARIBA, MRTPI, of Harpers Cottage, Main St, Avebury, Marlborough, Wilts SN8 1RF, and has issue living, Rowland St John, *b* 1973, — Oliver John, *b* 1975, — Genevieve Anne, *b* 1979. —— Margaret Vanessa Lucy, *b* 1948: *m* 1969, George Marlay Spencer, BA (c/o Royal Bank of Scotland, Whitehall, SW1), and has issue living, Rachel Marlay, *b* 1972, — Abigail, *b* 1974.

Grandchildren of late Rev Hon Edmund Tudor St John, 3rd son of 14th Baron:—
Issue of late Col Edmund Farquhar St John, CMG, DSO, *b* 1879, *d* 1945: *m* 1921, Henrietta Frances (7 Inverleith Terrace, Edinburgh), da of late Col James Alexander Dalmahoy, MVO, WS:—
(EDMUND) OLIVER, WS, *b* 13 Oct 1927; *ed* Trin Coll, Glenalmond; WS 1953: *m* 1959, Elizabeth Frances, only da of Lieut-Col H. R. Nicholl, of High Lipwood, Haydon Bridge, Northumberland, and has issue living, Charles Henry Oliver, *b* 1963: *m* 1991, Emma Catherine Sewell, elder da of Henry Moore, of Shucknall Court, Hereford, — Nicola Rosemary, *b* 1960, — Emma Harriet, *b* 1968. *Residence* – Spittal, Biggar, Lanarkshire. —— Frances Dalmahoy, *b* 1931. *Residence* – Bletsoe, 26 St Andrew's St, Brechin, Angus.
Issue of late Maj Beauchamp Tudor St John, *b* 1880, *d* 1965: *m* 1910, Madeleine Ethel, who *d* 1982, da of late J. Ellis Goodbody, of Thornville, Limerick:—
Roger Ellis Tudor, CB, MC (Harelaw, Virginia Water, Surrey), *b* 1911; *ed* Wellington Coll; Maj-Gen (ret); Dep Col (Northumberland) R Regt of Fusiliers 1968-69; Comd, British Army Staff and Mil Attaché Washington 1963-65, and Pres of Regular Commns Board 1965-67; 1939-45 War (despatches, MC), Kenya 1955 (despatches); CB (Mil) 1965: *m* 1943, Rosemary Jean Douglas, da of late Ronald Vickers, and has issue living, Henry Edward Tudor (68 Lonsdale Rd, Oxford), *b* 1949; *ed* Eton, and Coll of Estate Management (BSc, FRICS), Partner Cluttons, Chartered Surveyors: *m* 1983, Kerra, eldest da of John Lockhart, of Calgary, Alberta, Canada, and has issue living, Oliver Tudor Lockhart *b* 1984, Atlanta Victoria *b* 1987, — Angela Lucy, *b* 1944: *m* 1970, Maj Christopher Rohan Delacombe, late R Scots, only son of late Maj-Gen Sir Rohan Delacombe, KCMG, KCVO, KBE, CB, DSO, and has issue living, Caroline May *b* 1971, Sophie Clare *b* 1973, Katharine Joyce *b* 1975, — Jane Margaret, *b* 1946, — Alice Rosemary, *b* 1950: *m* 1974, Hugh Martyn Williams, of Lower Willsworthy, Peter Tavy, Tavistock, Devon PL19 9NB, and has issue living, Patrick *b* 1986, Emily *b* 1979, Florence *b* 1980, Martha *b* 1985, Veronica *b* 1991. —— Michael Beauchamp, DSC (The Old Thatch, Leggs Lane, Heyshott, nr Midhurst, Sussex), *b* 1915; Cdr (ret) RN; 1939-45 War with Submarines (DSC): *m* 1944, Pamela Patience, da of late Sir Arthur Rundell Guinness, KCMG, and has issue living, Andrew Beauchamp (Cul-na-Cloich, Glenalmond, Perthshire), *b* 1945: *m* 1968, Hon Sally Hayter Rootes, da of 2nd Baron Rootes, — Clare Pamela, *b* 1947: *m* 1968, David Waldorf Astor, of Bruern Grange, Milton-under-Wychwood, Oxon (*see* V Astor), — Hermione Patience, *b* 1951: *m* 1973, William Stanhope Owen, of Merriscourt Farm House, Churchill, Oxon OX76 6QX, and has issue living, Sam Arthur Stanhope *b* 1975, Georgina Hermione *b* 1974.

Grandchildren of late Cdr Richard St John, RN, 4th and yst son of late Rev Hon Edmund Tudor St John (ante):—

Issue of late Capt John Richard St John, *b* 1917, *d* 1988: *m* 1st, 1943 (*m diss* 1951), Helen Mary, da of late H. O. Coleman; 2ndly, 1952, Diana Elwell (40 Arkwright Rd, NW3 6BH), yst da of late Col Edward Stockley Sinnott, CMG, TD:—
(By 1st *m*) Tudor Richard, *b* 1946: *m* 1977, Marlyn, only da of G. Foster. —— Lucinda Jill, *b* 1944; ARCM: *m* 1968, Andrew Jon Cameron-Beaumont, FRICS, and has issue living, Richard Peregrine, *b* 1973, — Charlotte Lucinda, *b* 1971; BSc. *Residence* – Tideford Farmhouse, Tideford, Cornwall. —— (By 2nd *m*) Clare Sylvia, *b* 1955. —— Katharine Elinor Margaret, *b* 1957: *m* 1st, 1976 (*m diss* 1986), Erik Austin Flakoll; 2ndly, 1993, Albert Sidney Griffin, of Kentucky, USA.

Grandchildren of Richard Fleming St Andrew St John, son of Henry St Andrew St John, son of Rev John Francis Seymour St John, 2nd son of the Very Rev Hon St Andrew St John, DD, 2nd son of 10th Baron:—
Issue of late Winstan St Andrew St John, MRCS, LRCP, *b* 1872, *d* 1962: *m* 1909, Violet Julia Louisa, da of late Henderson James Twigg, of Petane Grange, Petane, Hawks Bay, New Zealand:—
Orford Henderson St Andrew, *b* 1910; *ed* Wellington Coll, and at Hertford Coll, Oxford (BA 1932); 1939-45 War as Capt Gen List (Movement Control, attached Intelligence). Resides in Spain.
Issue of late Major Edward Churchill St John, *b* 1878, *d* 1956: *m* 1906, Irene, who *d* 1956, da of Col Charles Edward Shepherd, formerly Indian Army:—
Catherine Margaret, *b* 1907.
Issue of late Lieut-Com Arthur Beauchamp St John, RN (ret), *b* 1884, *d* 1948: *m* 1914, Lucinda Mary Stanley, da of late Hon John French, of Miramar, Queenstown, co Cork, and Rotra House, Frenchpark, co Roscommon:—
Œnône Mary, *b* 1917: *m* 1st, 1943, John Francis Elton Watkins; 2ndly, 1953, Leslie James Ashton, of 1 Victoria Flats, Livingstone Av, Gwelo, Zimbabwe, and has issue living (by 1st *m*), Mary Veronica, *b* 1946: *m* 1969, Donald Hodder (c/o Standard Bank, Cecil Sq, Harare, Zimbabwe). —— Deirdre Mary, *b* 1919: *m* 1944, Harold Drummond-Hay Oxenham Leach, of PO Box 1409, Port Shepstone 4240, Natal, S Africa, and has issue living, Susan Mary, *b* 1945: *m* 1965, Christopher Forbes Johnson (PO Box 125, Fort Victoria, Zimbabwe), and has issue living, Russell Forbes *b* 1968, Catherine Amber *b* 1966, — Peta Mary, *b* 1947: *m* 1967, Clive Charles Lilford, and has issue living, Grant Charles *b* 1968, Karen *b* 1970, — Lucinda Margaret, *b* 1950, — Mary Louisa, *b* 1951.

Granddaughters of late Maj Edward Churchill St John (ante):—
Issue of late Lt-Col Edward Richard Gordon St John, RA, *b* 1911, *d* 1986: *m* 1943, Mary Aderyn, who *d* 1993, da of Rev H. Jones-Davies:—
Catherine Aderyn, *b* 1944: *m* 1968, Friedrich Kuebart, of 463 Bochum, Plasshofstr 21, W Germany. —— Margaret Joan, *b* 1949. *Residence* – 19 Selwyn Rd, Birmingham 16.

Granddaughters of late George Beauchamp Fleming St John, son of Rev George St John, son of Rev John Francis Seymour St John (ante):—
Issue of late Harry Beauchamp St John, *b* 1886, *d* 1957: *m* 1919, Mary Katherine, who *d* 1947, da of late Moreton Hyde Fitzhardinge, of Sydney, NSW:—
Barbara Margaret (Unit 20, Chatswood Garden Village, 5 Hart St, Lane Cove 2066, NSW, Australia), *b* 1920. —— Gladys, *b* 1922; 1939-45 War in AWAS: *m* 1945, Norman Wycliffe Fairfax, who *d* 1986, and has issue living, John Beauchamp, *b* 1949, — Helen Margaret, *b* 1947. *Residence* – 133 Woodburn St, Evans Head, NSW 2473, Australia.

Grandchildren of late Rev Harris Fleming St John, son of late Fleming St John, son of late Rev John Francis Seymour St John (ante):—
Issue of late Oliver Stukeley Fleming St John, *b* 1881, *d* 1955: *m* 1st, 1913, Agnes Jane, who *d* 1916, da of Arthur Jenkins, of Pencombe, Herefordshire; 2ndly, 1924, Elizabeth Sarah Ross, who *d* 1933:—
(By 2nd *m*) Paul Fleming, *b* 1928: *m* 1953, Lesley Patricia, yst da of Albert Edwin Marsh, of Perth, W Australia, and has issue living, Brian Fleming, *b* 1954, — Peter Michael, *b* 1957: *m* 1981, Loretta Anne-Marie, elder da of John Toniolo, of Perth, W Australia, — Nola Margaret, *b* 1955: *m* 1980, Stewart Parkinson, yr son of John Parkinson, of Perth, and has issue living, Hannah Jane *b* 1983, — Pauline Maree Teresa, *b* 1960: *m* 1979, Graham Leslie Waddell, of Perth, — Julie Frances, *b* 1964. *Residence* – 6 Kinsella St, Joondanna, Perth, W Australia 6060. —— Rev Oliver Peter Fleming (St Joseph's Presbytery, PO Box 45, Kulin, W Australia 6535), *b* 1929. —— Michael Fleming, *b* 1932: *m* 1958, Teresa Josephine, da of Thomas W. Murphy, of Finchley, N3, and has issue living, Nicholas Fleming, *b* 1961: *m* 1989, Catherine Clare, da of James Smith, of Winton House, Westcliff-on-Sea, Essex, — Andrew Thomas *b* 1963, — Philip Ambrose, *b* 1965: *m* 1986, Catherine Anne, da of Stanley John Simpson, of Perth, W Australia, — Robert Oliver, *b* 1968. *Residence* – 9 Victoria Av, Finchley, N3. —— Joan Fleming, *b* 1925: *m* 1947, Stanley John Simpson, of 13 Byron St, Leederville, Perth, W Australia 6007 and has issue living, Christopher John, *b* 1950, — Peter James, *b* 1952, — John Andrew, *b* 1957, — Richard Stephen Francis, *b* 1960, — Pauline Mary, *b* 1948: *m* 1968, Kenneth Gerald Glasgow (c/o BP Australia, Port-Hedland, W Aust), — Catherine Anne, *b* 1966. —— (By 1st *m*) Evelyn Mary Fleming (31 Mayfield Rd, Crouch End, N8), *b* 1915: *m* 1943, Daniel Reidy, who *d* 1969, and has issue living, Richard Daniel Kenneth, *b* 1944.

Grandchildren of late Lt-Col Sir Henry Beauchamp St John, KCIE, CBE, Indian Army, only son of late Col Sir Oliver Beauchamp Coventry St John, KCSI, el son of Oliver St John, 2nd son of late Thomas St John (*b* 1765), 3rd son of Very Rev Hon St Andrew St John, DD (ante):—
Issue of late Lt-Col Oliver Charles Beauchamp St John, CMG, *b* 1907; *d* 1976: *m* 1st, 1935, Elizabeth Mary, who *d* 1957, da of Philip Lambton; 2ndly, 1966, Mary (Masseys, East Boldre, Brockenhurst, Hants, SO42 DWE), da of John Greenway, and widow of John Gillum Maxwell-Gumbleton:—
(By 1st *m*) Simon Lambton Beauchamp (65 Linda Lane, Bethel, Connecticut 06801, USA), *b* 1940: *m* 1971, Margaret Lee, step-da of Perry Leslie Owen, of Tampa, Florida, USA, and has issue living, Ryan Christopher Beauchamp, *b* 1972, — Erin Elizabeth, *b* 1975. —— Sarah Mary (23 Fir Tree Close, Aldrington Rd, SW16 1TF), *b* 1937: *m* 1957 (*m diss* 1980), Michael Geoffrey Morvaren Mayhew, and has issue living, Nicholas Morvaren, *b* 1959; Lt Cmdr RN: *m* 1987, Katherine Cherry, — Charles Geoffrey, *b* 1966: *m* 1989, Michele Crosby, and has issue living, Joshua Charles *b* 1991, Emily Victoria *b* 1992, — Hamish St John, *b* 1968: *m* 1993, Julia A. Jarvis, — Amanda Elizabeth, *b* 1962. —— Victoria Anne, *b* 1942: *m* 1983, Brian Richard Easton, of 17 Abbots Way, Beckenham, Kent. —— Vanessa Margaret, *b* 1944: *m* 1964, Nicholas John Connolly, of Monks Gate Cottage, Monks Gate, Horsham, and has issue living, Rupert St John, *b* 1965; *ed* — Coll, Oxford (MA), and Warwick Univ (MSc), — Philippa Joan, *b* 1964; *ed* Leeds Univ, and Penn State Univ, USA; MEng, CEng MICE, MIStructE, — Victoria Maria, *b* 1967; MA (Oxon).

Grandchildren of late Philip George St John, 5th and yst son of late Lt-Col Oliver Henry Beauchamp St John, el son of Lt-Gen Robert St John, 3rd son of Thomas St John (*b* 1765), 3rd son of Very Rev Hon St Andrew St John, DD (ante):—
Issue of late Capt Anthony Philip St John, RA, *b* 1925, *d* 1990: *m* 1st, 1947 (*m diss* 1951), Joyce Elizabeth, who *d* 1988, da of late George Edward Alleyne Dawes; 2ndly, 1959, Shelagh Marie James (Christophers, Budleigh Salterton, Devon):—
(By 1st *m*) David Warren (4 Nottingham Rd, Somercotes, Derbys DE55 4JJ), *b* 1950: *m* 1977, Dawn Yvonne, da of John Barry Price, of Bareen, Hilcote Lane, Derbys. —— (By 2nd *m*) Oliver Philip, *b* 1959. —— Trudie Sophia, *b* 1961. —— Katherine Emma, *b* 1963.

Grandchildren of late Com Thomas Charles St Andrew St John, 3rd son of late Lt-Gen Robert St John (ante):—
Issue of late Robert Henry Beauchamp St John, b 1878, d 1956: m 1st, 1901, Agnes Mary Sybil, who d 1915, da of late Capt Frederick Shelton, Argyll and Sutherland Highlanders; 2ndly, 1916, Edith Mary, da of late Capt Cape Hutton, of Ives, Bucks:—
(By 1st m) Dorothy Mary Beaufort, b 1902: m 1962, Magnus Karl Olof Friman, of 24 Sheepfold Lane, Amersham, Bucks.
Issue of late St John St Andrew Newell St John, b 1884, d 1962: m 1910, Mary Audrey, who d 1957, da of C. E. Hicks, of North Battlefold, Saskatchewan, Canada:—
Andrew Charles, b 1927: m 1952, Cecile Marie, da of W. J. Calnan, of Vancouver, British Columbia and has issue living, Marie Patricia, b 19—, — Janet Mary, b 1956, — Jillian Eleanor, b 1966. —— Mary Cecilia, b 1912: m 1932, Walter Davidson. —— Ella Monica, b 1917: m 1942, W. H. Davis, Pilot Officer Roy Canadian Air Force, and has issue living, Ralph Austin, b 1947, — Marion Elizabeth, b 1950, — Anne Roberta, b 1954. —— Hilda Margaret, b 1925: m 1949, Victor Leon Charbonneau, and has issue living, Kenneth Lawrence, b 1960, — Susan Hilda, b 1952, — Catherine Ann, b 1962.

Grandchildren of late Rev Canon Frederick de Porte St John (infra):—
Issue of late Roland Tyrwhitt St John, MBE, b 1914, d 1992: m 1st, 1949, Margaret, who d 1972, da of late Ven Archdeacon Reginald Beatty Massey; 2ndly, 1976, Marjorie Jean (6 Campbell St, Toowoomba, Queensland 4350, Australia), widow of Rev D J. T. Richardson:—
(By 1st m) David Henry (7 Raine Terr, Winthrop, W Australia 6150), b 1951; ed Qld Univ (BSc, PhD); Research Manager in Materials Science at CRA Advances Tech Devpt, Perth: m 1976, Helen Jennifer, da of Donald McLeod, of Brisbane, and has issue living, Andrew Timothy, b 1980, — Robin Thomas, b 1983. —— Paul Michael (2/170 Dornoch Terr, Highgate Hill, Queensland 4101), b 1953; ed Qld Univ (BSc): m 1987, Frances Julia, da of John Thompson McDonald, of Toowoomba. —— Nigel Alexander, b 1958; ed Qld Inst of Technology (BAppSc). —— Julian Andrew, b 1963. —— Philippa Robin, b 1955; ed Qld Univ (BA): m 1988, Kim Graham Grady, of 15 Delville Av, Moorooka, Queensland 4015, and has issue living, Alicia St John, b 1988.

Grandchildren of late Henry St John (b 1852), yst son of late Frederick St John, 5th and yst son of Very Rev Hon St Andrew St John, DD (ante):—
Issue of late Rev Canon Frederick de Porte St John, b 1879, d 1963: m 1908, Hannah Phœbe Mabel, who d 1950, da of late Samuel Lucas Charles Pyrke, JP, of Tamworth, NS Wales:—
Edward Henry, QC (40 Alexandra Cres, Bayview, NSW, Australia 2104; Mt Elliot, Holgate, NSW), b 1916; ed Sydney Univ (BA, LLB); Bar-at-law 1940, and a QC 1956; sometime Capt AIF; Austn Parl as Member for Warringah 1966-69; Pres, International Commn of Jurists, Austn Section 1961-73; a Member of Intern Commn of Jurists, Geneva 1966; author of *A Time to Speak* (1969), and numerous articles in learned and literary journals; Austn delegate to Commonwealth and Empire Law Conference, London, 1955, and to Congresses of Intern Commn of Jurists, New Delhi 1959, Rio de Janeiro 1962, and Bangkok 1965; official observer at S African Treason Trials on behalf of British Section of Intern Commn of Jurists 1959, and Member of Malta Constitutional Commn 1960; 1939-45 War in Middle East, and New Guinea; Visiting Fell, Univ of NSW 1984: m 1st, 1940, Sylvette, who d 1954, da of Jean Meer Cargher, of Alsace; 2ndly, 1955, Valerie Erskine, da of Henry John Winslow, late of London, and has issue living, (by 1st m) Madeleine ST JOHN (53E Colville Gdns, W11 2BA), b 1941; ed Univ of Sydney (BA); resumed her maiden name 1972: m 1965 (m diss 1972), Christopher Roger Tillam, BA, — Colette, b 1944: m 1980, Stephen Louis Lippincott, and has issue living, Aaron b 1985, — (by 2nd m) Oliver Winslow, b 1956, — Edward Erskine, b 1960: m 1988, Susan Elizabeth, da of Sydney Young, of Albury, and has issue living, Henry William b 1993, — Patrick Graeme, b 1963; ed NSW Univ (BComm, LLB): m 1992, Karen Leanne, da of late Peter John Reginald O'Loughlin, of Sydney. —— Florence Anne, b 1924; ed Sydney Univ: m 1955, Frank Heller, BSc, PhD, of 84 Wood Vale, N10, and has issue living, Michael Guy St John, b 1957, — Juliet Margarethe, b 1961, — Clare Andrea, b 1964. —— Pamela Mary ST JOHN (River Glen, 1/590 Riversdale Rd, Camberwell, Vic 3124, Aust), b 1925; BA (Melb), BEd (Melb); Dip Adv Studies in Ed; Cert KTC (Adelaide); resumed the surname of St John 1972; Lecturer at Inst of Early Childhood Development, Melbourne, 1967-84: m 1st, 1946 (m diss 1959), Ronald Fry, late RN, who d 1971; 2ndly, 1976 (m diss 1977), Edward John Minchin, solicitor, and has issue living (by 1st m), Jeremy William ST JOHN (205 William St, Melbourne, Vic, Australia), b 1952; ed Melbourne Univ (LLB); Bar and Solicitor 1975; Bar-at-law 1983: m 1st, 1978 (m diss 1985), Christine Fay Barrow; 2ndly, 1990, Jillian Margaret Rivers, and has issue living (by 1st m), Emily Catherine b 1980, Polly Louise b 1982, (by 2nd m) Thomas Rivers b 1994, Rhoebe Rivers b 1991, — Jennifer Jane, b 1949; BEd (Special Educn) Melbourne, TITC (Melbourne), TTCTD (Melbourne): m 1977, Jonathan Hugh Beverley Crosskill, and has issue living, Nicholas William b 1980, Richard Campbell b 1982, Edward Daniel b (twin) 1982, — Catherine Mary, b 1957; BEd, Melbourne: m 1st, 1978 (m diss 1981), David Kenneth Hitchcock; 2ndly, 1981 (m diss 1992), Kim Leigh Mark Savery, and has issue living (by 2nd m), Elliot Henry b 1986, Amelia Kate b 1983.
Issue of late Ambrose St John, b 1896, d 1968: m 1925, Mary Kathleen (34 Kemp St, Port Macquarie, NSW 2444), da of Peter Gaffney, of Sydney, NSW:—
Kevin Joseph (34 Kemp St, Port Macquarie, NSW 2444), b 1926. —— Desmond Henry, b 1932: m 19—, Mavis Duncan, of Rockhampton, Qld, and has issue living, Lorelle b 19—, — Deborah, b 19—, — Sandra, b 1963. —— Marlene Illina, b 1936: m 1962, David Steuart, of 6/25 Banksia Rd, Caringbah, NSW 2229, and has issue living, Jason, b 1967, — Nicole, b 1963.

Granddaughters of late Oliver St John (infra):—
Issue of late Oliver Beauchamp St John, b 1895, d 1970: m 1st, 1921 (m diss 19—) Winifred Lyndall Fox, of Hastings, Sussex; 2ndly, 1944, Josephine Lorna, who d 1969, da of W. Kurtze, of Saskatoon, Canada:—
(By 1st m) Patricia Jocelyn (3171 Henderson Rd, Victoria, BC, Canada V8P 5A3), b 1922: m 1941, Prof John Alexander McCarter, PhD, FRSC, and has issue living, David Graham (511 Hibiscus Av, London, Ont, Canada), b 1946: m 1968, Janice Evelyn, da of R. E. Yates, of Walkerton, Ont, Canada, and has issue living, Robert Alexander b 1974, — Robert Malcolm, b 1948: m 1971, Bonnie Gail, da of Lorne E. Davis, of London, Ont, — William Alexander, b 1955, — Patricia Lyndall, b 1953. —— Josephine Lyndall (11713 Brookmere Court, Maple Ridge, BC, Canada V2X 9G3), b 1925: m 1947 (m diss 1974), Walter H. Cudmore, and has issue living, Rodney William, b 1949: m 19—, Leonora Marie Dixon, — Donald MacKenzie, b 1953, — Richard Michael, b 1957, — Diane Louise, b 1962.

Granddaughters of late Frederick St John (ante):—
Issue of late Oliver St John, b 1857, d 19—: m 1891, Alice, da of late Samuel Richardson, of Ingatestone, Essex:—
Olive Alice, b 1892: m 1913, Gordon Thomson, and has issue living, Jack, b 1916: m and has issue, — David, b 1920: m and has issue, — Margaret, b 1915: m 1934, A. Ambridge, of Ottawa, Ont, and has issue, — Ruth, b 1918: m and has issue, — Beth, b 1922: m and has issue. —— Constance Muriel, b 1893: m 1914, Bernard Freeman, and has issue living, John Lynn (3316 Ivanhoe Rd, Pittsburgh, Penn, USA), and has issue living, Jack b 1952, Richard b 1955, — Bernard Keith, (Santa Barbara, Cal USA): m 1st, 1939, (m diss 1971), Florence Pozzi; 2ndly, 1971, Mildred Stockton, and has issue living (by 1st m) Ronald Keith b 1942: m and has issue, — Oliver Franklin (437 Princeton Av, Ventura, Cal, USA), b 1922: m 1946, Marjorie Smith, and has issue living, Kim Donna, b 1954, Cindy b 1955, — Constance Mary, b 1924: m 1948, John A. Pusateri, and has issue living, John Freeman b 1952, Keith David, b 1957, Marilyn b 1949: m and has issue, Kathleen Alice b 1950: m, Jill Anne b 1964, Lisa Mary b 1966.

Descendants, if any, of Capt Hon Henry St John, RN (b 17—), and Rev Hon Ambrose St John (b 1743), 3rd and 4th sons of 10th Baron.

PREDECESSORS – **(1)** OLIVER St John (descended from John St John, el son of Sir Oliver St John of Bletso, who *m* Margaret, great-granddaughter of Roger de Beauchamp, who was summoned to Parliament of England as *Baron Beauchamp of Bletshoe* 1363-79, since when that title has not been assumed), *cr Baron St John of Bletso*, co Beds (peerage of England) 1559; *d* 1592; *s* by his el son **(2)** JOHN, 2nd Baron; was one of the peers who sat on the trial of Mary, Queen of Scots; *d* without male issue 1596, when the Barony of Beauchamp devolved upon his da Anne, wife of William, Lord Howard, el son of the 1st Earl of Nottingham, and the Barony of St John devolved upon his brother **(3)** OLIVER, 3rd Baron; *d* 1618; *s* by his el son **(4)** OLIVER, 4th Baron; *cr Earl of Bolingbroke* (peerage of England) 1624; *d* 1646; *s* by his grandson **(5)** OLIVER, 2nd Earl; *d* 1688; *s* by his brother **(6)** PAULET, 3rd Earl; *d* unm 1711, when the earldom became extinct and the barony devolved upon his kinsman **(7)** PAULET ST ANDREW, 7th Baron, who had previously *s* his father as 4th Bt (see * infra); *d* 1714; *s* by his uncle **(8)** WILLIAM, 8th Baron; *d* unm 1720; *s* by his brother **(9)** ROWLAND, 9th Baron; *d* unm 1722; *s* by his brother **(10)** JOHN, 10th Baron; *d* 1757; *s* by his son **(11)** JOHN, 11th Baron; *d* 1767; *s* by his el son **(12)** HENRY BEAUCHAMP, 12th Baron; *d* 1805; *s* by his brother **(13)** ST ANDREW, 13th Baron; *d* 1817; *s* by his son **(14)** ST ANDREW BEAUCHAMP, 14th Baron; *b* 1811: *m* 1838, Eleanor, who *d* 1899, da of late Vice-Adm Sir Richard Hussey-Hussey, GCMG, KCB; *d* 1874; *s* by his son **(15)** ST ANDREW, 15th Baron, *b* 1840: *m* 1868, Ellen Georgiana, who *d* 1890, da of late Edward Senior, Poor Law Commr, Ireland; *d* 1887; *s* by his brother **(16)** BEAUCHAMP MOUBRAY, 16th Baron; *b* 1844; Lord-Lieut of Bedfordshire: *m* 1st, 1869, Helen Charlotte, who *d* 1909, 2nd da of late Harry Thornton, of Kempston Grange, Beds; 2ndly, 1911, Ethel Susan, who *d* 1945, da of late John Habington Barneby Lutley, of Brockhampton, Herefordshire; *d* 1912; *s* by his son **(17)** HENRY BEAUCHAMP OLIVER, 17th Baron; *b* 1876; *d* 1920; *s* by his son **(18)** MOUBRAY ST ANDREW THORNTON, 18th Baron; *b* 1877: *m* 1st, 1905, Evelyn Geraldine, who *d* 1918, yst da of late Capt Andrew Hamilton Russell (formerly 58th Regt), of The Heath House, Petersfield, Hants; 2ndly, 1923, Elizabeth May, who *d* 1978, da of Lloyd Griffith, of Hurst Court, Ore, Hastings, and widow of Col Edward Charles Ayshford Sanford, CMG, of Nynehead Court, Som; *d* 1934; *s* by his only son **(19)** JOHN MOUBRAY RUSSELL, 19th Baron; *b* 1917; *d* 1976; *s* by his cousin **(20)** ANDREW BEAUCHAMP, TD (3rd son of Lt-Col Hon Rowland Tudor St John, DLI, 3rd son of 16th Baron), 20th Baron; *b* 1918: *m* 1955, Katharine, yst da of late Alfred von Berg, of 5 Gonville House, Manor Fields, SW15; *d* 1978; *s* by his only son **(21)** ANTHONY TUDOR, 21st Baron and present peer.

*The Hon Sir Rowland St John, 4th son of the 3rd Baron St John of Bletso (see ante), had, with other issue **(1)** OLIVER, *cr* a *Baronet* 1660; *d* 1661; *s* by his son **(2)** *Sir* ANDREW, 2nd Bt; *d* 1708; *s* by his son **(3)** *Sir* ST ANDREW, 3rd Bt; *s* by his son **(4)** *Sir* PAULET ST ANDREW, 4th Bt, who succeeded as 7th Baron St John of Bletso (see ante).

ST JOHN OF FAWSLEY, BARON (St John-Stevas) (Life Baron 1987)

NORMAN ANTONY FRANCIS ST JOHN-STEVAS, PC, son of late Stephen S. Stevas, by his wife, late Kitty St John O'Connor; *b* 18 May 1929; *ed* Ratcliffe, Fitzwilliam Coll, Camb (BA 1950, MA 1954), Ch Ch, Oxford (BCL 1954), and Yale Univ; Bar Middle Temple 1952; jurisprudence tutor Ch Ch 1953-55, and Merton Coll 1955-57; legal, ecclesiastical and political correspondent on *The Economist* 1959-64; Min of State for Educn and Science with special responsibility for the Arts 1973-74, Opposition Spokesman for the Arts 1974, Member Shadow Cabinet, Min for the Arts 1979-81, Leader of House of Commons and Chancellor of Duchy of Lancaster 1979-81, Member Parly Select Cttee on Foreign Affairs since 1983; Chm Booker McConnell Prize 1985, Vice-Pres Theatres Advisory Council since 1983, Member of Council of RADA since 1983, Nat Soc for Dance since 1983, Nat Youth Theatre since 1983, RCA since 1985, etc; Trustee: Royal Soc of Painters in Watercolours since 1984, Decorative Arts Soc since 1984, and Royal Philharmonic Orchestra since 1985, Chm Royal Fine Art Commn since 1985; Master Emmanuel Coll, Camb since 1991; author and editor, *Walter Bagehot* (1959), and subsequently edited his literary, historical and political works; MP Chelmsford (*C*) 1964-87; OStJ 1980, Order of Merit (Italy) 1965, FRSL 1966; *cr* PC 1979, and *Baron St John of Fawsley*, of Preston Capes, co Northants (Life Baron) 1987.

Arms – Tierced in fesse azure, gules and azure per pale counterchanged, in the azure an open crown or, in the gules a lion passant guardant gold, armed and langued azure. **Crest** – A fallow deer's head erased proper, in the mouth a chaplet of laurel vert, the attires per fesse, the dexter azure and gules, the sinister gules and azure. **Supporters** – *Dexter*, a monkey proper; *sinister*, a lion argent winged or, both crowned with a crown rayonny also or and each rampant on a grassy mount, the dexter having a primrose growing therefrom, the sinister a lily all proper.
Residences – 27 Charles St, W1; The Old Rectory, Preston Capes, Daventry, Northants. *Clubs* – White's, Garrick, Pratt's.

ST JUST, BARONY OF (Grenfell) (Extinct 1984)

DAUGHTERS LIVING OF SECOND BARON (By 1st marriage)

Hon Laura Clare, *b* 1950: *m* 1980, Hayden Phillips, CB, Permanent Sec, Dept of Nat Heritage, and has issue living, Thomas Peter, *b* 1987, — Florence Leslie, *b* 1981, — Louisa Henrietta, *b* 1984.

(By 2nd marriage)

Hon Kathrine (Katya), *b* 1957; resumed her maiden name 1985: *m* 1st, 1981 (*m diss* 1985), Oliver John Gilmour (later Hon Oliver John Gilmour); 2ndly, 1990, Roger N. Middleton, and has issue (by 1st *m*) (*see* B Gilmour of Craigmillar).
Hon Natasha Jeannine Mary, *b* 1959.

ST LEONARDS, BARONY OF (Sugden) (Extinct 1985)

NATURAL BROTHERS LIVING OF FOURTH AND LAST BARON

Arthur Herbert (1 Abbey Park, Killester, Dublin 5), *b* 1942: *m* 1967, Phyllis, da of late Patrick Muldoon, of Whitehall, and has issue living, Arthur John, *b* 1968.
Philip Hugh (17 Craigford Drive, Artane, Dublin 5), *b* 1944: *m* 1965, Roseanna Mary da of Michael Hill, of Clonshaugh, and has issue living, Philip Hugh, *b* 1966, — Mark Anthony, *b* 1974, — Edward Charles, *b* 1977, — Derek Peter, *b* 1978, — Rebecca Julie, *b* 1969.
Hugh David (1 Merchants Rd, East Wall, Dublin 3), *b* 1947: *m* 1983, Caroline, da of Denis Galavan, of Artane, Dublin.

MOTHER LIVING OF FOURTH AND LAST BARON

Julia Sheila (17 Craigford Drive, Artane, Dublin 5), da of late Philip Wyatt, of Curragh, co Kildare: *m* 1949, Arthur Herbert Sugden, who *d* 1958.

ST LEVAN, BARON (St Aubyn) (Baron UK 1887, Bt UK 1866)

IN · SE · TERES ·

Exact in himself

JOHN FRANCIS ARTHUR ST AUBYN, DSC, 4th Baron, and 5th Baronet; *b* 23 Feb 1919; *s* 1978; *ed* Eton, and Trin Coll, Camb (BA); Fellow of Roy Soc for Encouragement of Art, FRSA 1974; admitted a solicitor 1948; sometime Lt RNVR; High Sheriff of Cornwall 1974, DL 1977, Vice Lord Lieut since 1992; Pres Cornwall Branch, Council for Protection of Rural England since 1975, Friends of Plymouth City Museums and Art Gallery since 1985, London Cornish Assocn since 1987, Penzance YMCA, Royal Bath and SW Cos Soc (Vice Pres 1989), Truro Branch Royal Naval Assocn; Vice Pres Royal Cornwall Agric Assocn (formerly Pres); CStJ; author *Illustrated History of St Michael's Mount*: *m* 1970, Susan, yr da of late Maj-Gen Sir John Noble Kennedy, GCMG, KCVO, KBE, CB, MC.

Arms – Ermine, on a cross gules, five bezants, all within a bordure wavy of the second. **Crest** – A rock proper, therefrom a Cornish chough rising sable, the whole debruised with a bendlet sinister wavy ermine. **Supporters** – Two lions or, each gorged with a chain proper and pendant therefrom an escutcheon, that of the dexter, per fesse azure and argent, in chief a naval crown between two laurel branches saltirewise or, in base the frame of a vessel proper; that of the sinister, sable, charged with five bezants.
Residence – St Michael's Mount, Marazion, Cornwall, TR17 0HT. *Clubs* – Brooks's, Royal Yacht Squadron.

BROTHERS LIVING

Hon (OLIVER) PIERS, MC, *b* 12 July 1920; *ed* Wellington Coll, and St James's Sch, Maryland, USA; High Sheriff of E Sussex 1982-83; 1939-45 War as Capt 60th Rifles and Parachute Regt (despatches, MC): *m* 1948, Mary Bailey, who *d* 1987, da of Bailey Southwell, of Crocodile Leap Farm, Olievenhoutpoort, S Africa, and has issue living, James Piers Southwell (The Manor House, Ringmore, Kingsbridge, Devon TQ7 4HJ), *b* 1950; *ed* Eton, and Magdalen Coll, Oxford: *m* 1981, Mary Caroline, yst da of Peter Ward Bennett, OBE, of Dene House, Glynde, Sussex, and has issue living, Hugh James *b* 14 June 1983, Felix John *b* 1992, Clemency Lara *b* 1985, Louisa Mary *b* 1987, — Nicholas Francis (Golden Manor, Grampound, Truro, Cornwall TR2 4DF), *b* 1955; *ed* Eton: *m* 1980, Jane Mary, only da of William F. Brooks, of Bishopswood House, Bishopswood, Herefordshire, and has issue living, Henry Francis *b* 1981, Katharine Mary *b* 1983, Alice Jane *b* 1986, Camilla Bailey *b* 1990, — Fiona Mary, *b* 1952: *m* 1987, Robert William Boyle, of 30 Durand Gdns, SW9 0PP, and has issue (*see* E Cork).
Residence – Hogus House, Ludgvan, Penzance, Cornwall TR20 8EZ. *Clubs* – Brooks's, House of Lords Yacht.
Hon Giles Rowan, LVO, *b* 1925; *ed* Wellington Coll, at Glasgow Univ, and at Trin Coll, Oxford; FRSL; 1939-45 War as Ordinary Seaman RN (invalided); LVO 1977. *Residences* – Cornwall Lodge, Cambridge Park, St Peter Port, Guernsey, CI. *Clubs* – Beefsteak, House of Lords Yacht.

SISTERS LIVING

Hon Jessica Gwendolen, *b* 1918: *m* 1939, John Patrick Koppel, late Maj Welsh Gds, and has issue living, Patrick Anthony (1727 Valley Vista, Houston, Texas, USA), *b* 1944: *m* 1st, 1967 (*m diss* 1971), Jacqueline Ann, da of J. N. Fairrie; 2ndly, 1974, Jerry, da of Cecil White, — Lamorna Jessica, *b* 1940: *m* 1st, 1964 (*m diss* 1974), Ian Clinton Elliot; 2ndly, 1974, Alastair Michael Hyde Villiers (*see* D Roxburghe, 1968 Edn), of 17 Lansdowne Crescent, W11, and has issue living (by 1st *m*), Patrick Ian *b* 1965, Shane Robert *b* 1970, (by 2nd *m*) Katherine Alexandra Hyde *b* 1979, — Susan Katherine Dorothy, *b* 1942: *m* 1963, Richard Noël Dobbs, of 19 Haygarth Place, Wimbledon Village, SW19 5BX, and has issue living, Richard Francis Conway *b* 1966, Alexander Noel *b* 1967, Jessica Katherine Ann *b* 1971. *Residence* – Goodworth House, Goodworth Clatford, Andover, Hants.
Hon Philippa Catherine, *b* 1922: *m* 1948, Evelyn Charles Lacy Hulbert-Powell, late Lieut Queen's Roy Regt, who *d* 1985, and has issue living, Charles George Lacy (Old Place Farm, Mayfield, E Sussex): *b* 1952: *m* 1978, Sara Mary Philomena, el da of Michael Walter Bonn, of Oaklands, St Peter, Jersey (*see* Buxton, Bt), and has issue living, John Charles Lacy *b* 1984, Catherine Mary Lacy *b* 1980, Emma Sara Lacy *b* 1982, Victoria Elizabeth Lacy *b* 1987, — Francis Peter Lacy, *b* 1961, — Elizabeth Catherine Lacy, *b* 1950: *m* 1976, Lt-Cdr Richard Charles Harden, RN, and has issue (*see* Ingram, Bt), — Veronica Mary Lacy, *b* 1954: *m* 1979, John Robert Maclean, DL, of Westfield House, Spynie, Elgin, Morayshire, and has issue living, Hugh Charles *b* 1984, Charlotte Louise *b* 1982, Anastasia Mary *b* 1986, — Teresa Philippa Lacy, *b* 1956: *m* 1993, Paul H. C. T. Isolani-Smyth, only son of C. T. Isolani, CBE, LVO, of Pont St, SW1. *Residence* – Old Place Farm Bungalow, Mayfield, Sussex TN20 6PN.

WIDOW LIVING OF THIRD BARON

Hon CLEMENTINA GWENDOLEN CATHARINE (*Dowager Baroness St Levan*) (Avallon, Green Lane, Marazion, Cornwall), da of 1st Baron Carnock; a JP: *m* 1916, 3rd Baron St Levan, who *d* 1978.

COLLATERAL BRANCHES LIVING

Grandchildren of Hon Lionel Michael St Aubyn, MVO (infra):—
Issue of late Lt-Cdr Geoffrey Piers St Aubyn *b* 1922, *d* 1964: *m* 1958, Valerie Elizabeth, who *d* 1964, only da of late Wing-Cdr B. W. T. Hare, of Curtisknowle, Totnes:—
Michael Piers, *b* 1959: *m* 1987, Astrid E., da of Richard Edward Walter Lumley, of Roundwood, Windlesham, Surrey, and has issue living, Thomas Piers, *b* 1991, — Matilda Elizabeth, *b* 1994. *Residence* – Lower Part Farm, Water Eaton, Cricklade, Wilts. —— Rupert Trelawny, *b* 1963. —— Camilla Elizabeth, *b* 1961: *m* 1988, Jonathan Chiam Elichaoff, elder son of Michael Elichaoff, of Finchley, N3.

Issue of late Capt Hon Lionel Michael St Aubyn, MVO, yst son of 1st Baron, *b* 1878, *d* 1965: *m* 1915, Lady Mary Theresa Parker, who *d* 1932, da of 3rd Earl of Morley:—
Thomas Edward, CVO (Dairy House Farm, Ashford Hill, Newbury, Berks), *b* 1923; late Maj 60th Rifles; Lieut HM Body Guard of Hon Corps of Gentlemen at Arms 1990-93; High Sheriff Hants 1979, DL 1984; CVO 1993: *m* 1953, Henrietta Mary, only da of Sir Henry Grey Studholme, 1st Bt, CVO, MP, and has issue living, Sarah Elizabeth, *b* 1955: *m* 1983, Hugh Adrian Bethell (*see* E Radnor), — Caroline Mary, *b* 1957: *m* 1980, Andrew H. Llewellyn, of Church Acre, Rhode Lane, Uplyme, Lyme Regis, Dorset, — Judith Clare, *b* 1962.

(In remainder to the Baronetcy only)

Granddaughter of late Col Edward St Aubyn (infra):—
Issue of late Lieut-Col Guy Stewart St Aubyn, OBE, *b* 1870, *d* 1924: *m* 1899, Florita, who *d* 1925, da of late Pascoe du Pre Grenfell, of Wilton Park, Bucks:—
Violet Susan May, *b* 1929, Raymond Lort-Phillips, Capt Scots Guards, who *d* 1980, and has had issue, Guy Stewart (Camellia Cottage, Gorey Hill, Jersey, Channel Isles), *b* 1930; *ed* Eton; late Capt Welsh Guards: *m* 1956, Norah Eugenie, who *d* 1986, da of late Hans Rodolphe de Jenner, of Schloss Landshütte, nr Berne, Switzerland, and formerly wife of Patrick O'Leary, and has issue living, Piers Wickham *b* 1957: *m* 1986, Virginia, da of late Ronald Hodgson, of Vaucluse, Sydney, Australia (and has issue living, Harry Burgess *b* 1991), Giles Raymond *b* 1958: *m* 1985, Kathleen, da of Sydney Miles, of Randfontein, S Africa (and has issue living, Guy Dylan *b* 1986, Ben Raymond *b* 1988), Edward St Aubyn *b* 1966, — †Peregrine Edward Grenfell, *b* 1937; *ed* Charterhouse, and at Trin Coll, Camb (BA Hons); Solicitor 1962: *m* 1st, 1963 (*m diss* 1981), Carolyn Diana Brougham, only da of late George A. B. Docker, of 13 Prospect Place, Watlington, Oxon; 2ndly, 1984, Lamorna (who *m* 3rdly, 1990, Michael F. Good), da of Roger St Aubyn (infra), and formerly wife of Capt David Julian Cotton, and *d* 1988, leaving issue (by 1st *m*), Penelope Samantha *b* 1964, Venetia Nike *b* 1968, — Anthony Frederick Fitzroy (70 Roseville St, St Helier, Jersey, CI), *b* 1944; *ed* Eton, and RMA Sandhurst; late Capt Gren Gds: *m* 1971, Saranne Frances, who *d* 1984, da of James Harold Alexander, of co Dublin, and formerly wife of 10th Baron Calthorpe. *Residence* – Camellia Cottage, Gorey, Jersey.

Grandchildren of late Col Edward Geoffrey St Aubyn, DSO, 2nd son (by 2nd *m*) of Col Edward St Aubyn (infra):—
Issue of late Roger St Aubyn, *b* 1906, *d* 1985: *m* 1st, 1939 (*m diss* 1957), Baroness Sophie Helene, da of Baron Heinrich von Puthon; 2ndly, 1957 (*m diss* 1968), Lorna, elder da of Capt Alastair Mackintosh:—
(By 1st *m*) Lamorna, *b* 1944: *m* 1st, 1965 (*m diss* 1983), David Julian Cotton, Capt RGJ, TAVR; 2ndly, 1984, Peregrine Edward Grenfell Lort-Phillips, who *d* 1988 (ante); 3rdly, 1990, Michael Frankland Good, of Brick Kiln Cottage, Outwick, Breamore, nr Fordingbridge, Hants SP6 2BT, and has issue living (by 1st *m*), Caroline Mary Sophie, *b* 1966: *m* 1990, Julian Chamberlen, eldest son of Nicholas Chamberlen, of Ryders Wells House, Ringmer, E Sussex. —— Diana, *b* 1945: *m* 1970, Daniel Romer-Lee, of 35 Napier Av, SW6 3PS, and has issue living, Christopher Daniel, *b* 1972, — Serena Isabel Hilaria, *b* 1974. —— (By 2nd *m*) Edward (Le Petit Canadeau, Le Plan du Castellet, Var 83330, France), *b* 1960: *m* 1987 (*m diss* 1990), Nicola, yr da of Milton Shulman, writer. —— Alexandra, *b* 1958.

Issue of late Col Edward St Aubyn, 4th son of 1st baronet, *b* 1837, *d* 1914, *m* 1st, 1866, Edith, who *d* 1875, da of late Adm Hon Keith Stewart, CB, son of 8th Earl of Galloway; 2ndly, 1879, Eugenia Susannah, who *d* 1886, da of David Barclay Chapman, of Downshire House, Roehampton, and widow of George Henry FitzRoy; 3rdly, 1891, Ada Mary, who *d* 1948, da of late Col Sir Robert Thomas White-Thomson, KCB (Ferguson-Davie, Bt):—
(By 3rd *m*) Hildegarde Ada, *b* 1894.

PREDECESSORS – **(1)** EDWARD ST AUBYN, *b* 1799 (son of Sir John St Aubyn, FRS, FSA, FLS, 5th and last Bt (*cr* 1671), by Miss Juliana Vinicombe, whom he *m* 1822); *cr* a *Baronet* 1866: *m* 1828, Emma, who *d* 1887, da of Gen Knollys; *d* 1872; *s* by his son **(2)** JOHN 2nd Bt; *b* 1829; MP for Cornwall W (*L*) 1858-85, and for W, or St Ives, Div of Cornwall (LU) 1885-7; Mayor of Devonport 1890 and 1891; *cr* Baron St Levan, of St Michael's Mount, Cornwall (peerage of United Kingdom) 1887: *m* 1856, Lady Elizabeth Clementina Townshend, who *d* 1910, da of 4th Marquess Townshend: *d* 1908; *s* by his son **(3)** JOHN TOWNSHEND, CB, CVO, 2nd Baron, *b* 1857; Col and Hon Brig-Gen late Grenadier Guards, and Dep Warden of the Stannaries of Cornwall and Devon: *m* 1st, 1892, Lady Edith Hilaria Edgcumbe, who *d* 1931, da of 4th Earl of Mount Edgcumbe; 2ndly, 1933, Julia Georgiana Sarah, who *d* 1938, da of Sir George Orby Wombwell, 4th Bt, and widow of 2nd Earl of Dartrey; *d* 1940; *s* by his nephew **(4)** FRANCIS CECIL (son of late Hon Arthur James Dudley Stuart St Aubyn, 4th son of 1st Baron), 3rd Baron, *b* 1895: *m* 1916, Hon Clementina Gwendolen Catharine Nicolson, JP, da of 1st Baron Carnock; *d* 1978; *s* by his el son JOHN FRANCIS ARTHUR, 4th Baron, and present peer.

ST OSWALD, BARON (Winn) (Baron UK 1885)

All for God and my country

DEREK EDWARD ANTHONY WINN, 5th Baron; *b* 9 July 1919; *s* 1984; *ed* Stowe; a DL W Yorks 1987; formerly Lieut KRRC (Supplementary Res); Capt Parachute Regt (Regular Army Res); European War 1939-45 in Middle East and N Africa (wounded); ADC to Gov-Gen of NZ 1943-45, Malayan Police Service 1948-51: *m* 1954, Charlotte Denise Eileen, only da of late Wilfrid Haig Loyd (*see* Oakeley, Bt, 1985 Edn), and has issue.

Arms – Ermine, on a fesse vert, three eagles displayed or. **Crest** – A demi-eagle or, collared ermine. **Supporters** – Two dragons reguardant vert, each gorged with a cord or, and pendant therefrom an escutcheon gules, each charged with a rose argent.
Seat – Nostell Priory, Wakefield, W Yorks. *Residence* – The Old Rectory, Bainton, Driffield, E Yorks YO25 9NG. *Clubs* – Lansdowne, Special Forces.

SON LIVING

Hon CHARLES ROWLAND ANDREW, *b* 22 July 1959; *ed* New School, King's Langley: *m* 1985, Louise Alexandra, da of Stewart MacKenzie Scott, and has issue living, Rowland Charles Sebastian Henry, *b* 15 April 1986, — Henrietta Sophia Alexandra, *b* 1993.

DAUGHTER LIVING

Hon Geva Charlotte Caroline, *b* 1955: *m* 1987, (John) Simon Blackett, and has issue (*see* Blackett, Bt, colls). *Residence* – Clunie Cottage, Braemar, Aberdeenshire AB35 5XQ.

WIDOW LIVING OF SON OF SECOND BARON

Alice, da of late Moncure Perkins, of Virginia, USA: *m* 1924, Maj Hon Reginald Henry Winn, Gren Gds, who *d* 1985, and has issue (see colls infra). *Residence* – 59 Whitelands House, Cheltenham Terr, SW3.

COLLATERAL BRANCHES LIVING

Issue of late Hon Charles John Frederic Winn, 2nd son of 2nd Baron, *b* 1896, *d* 1968: *m* 1st, 1919 (*m diss* 1925), Hon Olive Cecilia Paget, who *d* 1974, da of 1st Baron Queenborough; 2ndly, 1929 (*m diss* 1938), Katherine, da of Henry Van Hevkelom; 3rdly, 1938, Mrs Theodora Thorpe Dixon, who *d* 1978:—
(By 1st *m*) Susan Mary Sheila, *b* 1923: *m* 1st, 1946 (*m diss* 1971), Capt Hon Geoffrey Denis Erskine Russell, late Irish Guards, now 4th Baron Ampthill; 2ndly, 1972, Col Edward Remington-Hobbs, DSO, OBE, of 3 Lyall Mews, SW1, and has issue (by 1st *m*) (*see* B Ampthill). —— (By 2nd *m*) Michael Peter Anthony (301 East 69th St, New York, 10021, NY, USA), *b* 1933: *m* 1963, Caroline Knowlton Lipscomb, of New York, and Southport, Conn, USA, and has issue living, Charles Michael Anthony, *b* 1967.

Issue of late Maj Hon Reginald Henry Winn, Gren Gds, 3rd son of 2nd Baron, *b* 1899, *d* 1985: *m* 1924, Alice (ante), da of late Moncure Perkins, of Virginia, USA:—
Elizabeth Susan (Neville House, 15 Onslow Gdns, SW7), *b* 1925. —— Anne, *b* 1926: *m* 1947 (*m diss* 19—), Hon Mark Hugh Wyndham, MC, 12th R Lancers, and has issue (*see* B Egremont). *Residence* – Thatched Cottage, Chilson, Charlbury, Oxon.

Grandchildren of late Hon Cecil Henry Winn (infra): —
Issue of late Maj Henry John Winn, DSO, MC, *b* 1914, *d* 1991: *m* 1960, Pamela Sylva (Exelby House, Exelby, Bedale, N Yorks), only da of late Ernest Charles de Rougemont, CBE:—
Martin John (93 Palace Rd, SW2), *b* 1961: *m* 1986, Caroline Anne, da of Douglas da Costa, of 6 Clifton Gdns, W9, and has issue living, Hugo John, *b* 1991, — Hannah Louise, *b* 1993. —— Fiona Jane, *b* 1962: *m* 1988, Bruce J. Moriarty, of 7 Habgood St, E Fremantle, W Australia 6158, son of Donald Moriarty, of Halifax, Nova Scotia, Canada.

Issue of late Hon Cecil Henry Winn, 5th son of 1st Baron, *b* 1866, *d* 1934: *m* 1913, Alice Marjorie Iris, who *d* 1964, da of late Henry Darley, of Aldby Park, York:—
(Geoffrey) Mark Victor, *b* 1918; late Capt RE; 1940-45 War in NW Europe and SE Asia: *m* 1958, Alice Alexandra, who *d* 1991, da of late Peter Haig-Thomas (*see* E Normanton, 1971 Edn), and has issue living, Geoffrey George WINN-DARLEY, *b* 1966, assumed the additional surname and arms of Darley by Royal licence 1985, — Alice Rosemary *b* 1960: *m* 1993, Christopher Milan Nenadich, of The Mole Hole, Ocle Pychard, Hereford, and has issue living, Megan Rose *b* 1993, — Iris Alexandra, *b* 1964. *Residence* – Aldby Park, Buttercrambe, York.

PREDECESSORS – (1) ROWLAND Winn (el son of late Charles Winn, of Nostell Priory, Yorkshire, and Appleby Hall, Lincolnshire); *b* 1820; MP for N Lincolnshire (C) 1868-85; a Lord of the Treasury 1874-85; was *cr Baron St Oswald*, of Nostell, co York (peerage of United Kingdom) 1885; *m* 1854, Harriet Maria Amelia, who *d* 1926, da of late Col Henry Dumaresq; *d* 1893; *s* by his el son (2) ROWLAND, 2nd Baron; *b* 1857; sat as MP for Pontefract (C) 1885-93: *m* 1892, Mabel Susan, who *d* 1919, da of Sir Charles Forbes, 4th Bt, of Newe, Aberdeenshire; *d* 1919; *s* by his son (3) ROWLAND GEORGE, 3rd Baron; *b* 1893; Capt Coldm Gds: *m* 1915, Eve Carew, who *d* 1976, da of Charles Greene; *d* 1957; *s* by his el son (4) ROWLAND DENYS GUY, 4th Baron, *b* 1916; Maj King's R Irish Hus, DL of W Riding of Yorks and of York; a Lord in Waiting 1959-62; Joint Parliamentary Sec, Min of Agric, Fisheries and Food 1962-64; Member European Parliament, Strasbourg 1973-84; served Middle East 1940-44, SE Asia 1945 (wounded, despatches), Korea 1950-52 (MC): *m* 1st, 1952 (*m diss* 1955), Laurian, da of Sir (George) Roderick Jones, KBE; 2ndly, 1955, Marie Wanda, who *d* 1981, yr da of late Sigismund Jaxa-Chamiec, of Filtrowa, Warsaw, Poland; *d* 1984; *s* by his brother (5) DEREK EDWARD ANTHONY, 5th Baron and present peer.

ST VINCENT, VISCOUNT (Jervis) (Viscount UK 1801)

RONALD GEORGE JAMES JERVIS, 7th Viscount; *b* 3 May 1905; *s* 1940; *ed* Sherborne; 1939-45 War as acting Lt-Cdr RNVR; JP Som 1950-55: *m* 1945, Constance Phillida Anne, only da of late Lieut-Col Robert Hector Logan, OBE, late Loyal Regt, and has issue.

Arms – Sable, a chevron ermine, between three martlets argent. **Crest** – Out of a naval coronet or, encircled round the rim by a wreath of laurel vert, a demi-pegasus argent, wings elevated azure, thereon a fleur-de-lis gold. **Supporters** – *Dexter*, an eagle, wings elevated, grasping in the left claw a thunderbolt, all proper; *sinister*, a pegasus argent, wings elevated azure, thereon a fleur-de-lis or. *Residence* – Les Charrières, St Ouen, Jersey.

SONS LIVING

Hon EDWARD ROBERT JAMES, *b* 12 May 1951; *ed* Radley: *m* 1977, Victoria Margaret, only da of late Wilton J. Oldham, of Jersey, and has issue living, James Richard Anthony, *b* 1982, — Emma Margaret Anne, *b* 1980. *Residence* – Colinas Verdes 26, Bensafrim, Lagos 8600, Algarve, Portugal.
Hon Ronald Nigel John, *b* 1954; *ed* Eton, and Durham Univ: *m* 1983, Gillian Lois, da of Geoffrey Sharp, and has issue living, David Stephen, *b* 1988, — Sarah Frances, *b* 1986, — Ruth Margaret, *b* 1991. *Residence* – The Brooms, Congleton, Cheshire.

DAUGHTER LIVING

Hon Cassandra Phillida Anne RINGSELL, *b* 1949: reverted to her former married surname by deed poll 1980: *m* 1st, 1970 (*m diss* 1976), Martyn Leslie Ringsell; 2ndly, 1979 (*m diss* 1981), James E. M. Colbeck-Welch, and has issue living (by 1st *m*), Brett George Jervis, *b* 1972, — Christopher Charles Robert, *b* 1974. *Residence* – O'Quintal, 8500 Mexhiloera Grande, Portimao, Algarve, Portugal.

COLLATERAL BRANCHES LIVING

Issue of late Col Hon St Leger Henry Jervis, DSO, 5th son of 3rd Viscount, *b* 1863, *d* 1952: *m* 1905, Hilda Maud, who *d* 1942, only da of late Thomas Collier:—
Hilda Violet Ursula, *b* 1909: *m* 1934 (*m diss* 1949), Lieut-Col John Alexander Goschen, OBE, Gren Gds (afterwards 3rd Viscount Goschen), who *d* 1977. *Residence* – Pitminster Lodge, Taunton, Som.

Grandsons of Edward St Vincent Parker-Jervis, son of late Edward John Parker-Jervis, el son of late Hon Edward Swynfen Parker-Jervis, yst son of 2nd Viscount:—
Issue of late Lieut St Vincent John Parker-Jervis, RNVR, *b* 1891, *d* 1931: *m* 1917, Marianita (who *m* 2ndly, 19—, John Frederick Harker), yr da of late C. T. Roller, of Burnham, Bucks:—
Antony St Vincent, *b* 1919; *ed* Ampleforth Coll; Capt Roy Canadian Horse Artillery; head of Mathematics Dept, St George's Sch, BC, since 1961: *m* 1942, Doris Beauchamp, da of late George Beauchamp Taverner, of Winryl, East Close, Middleton-on-Sea, Sussex, and Midhurst, Longwood Drive, Roehampton, SW, and has issue living, Nicholas St Vincent (6474 109th St, Delta, BC, Canada V4E IH3), *b* 1943; *ed* Univ of BC (BA) and Oxford Univ (Dip Ed): *m* 1st, 1967 (*m diss* 1976), Patsy K., da of Masao Hayashi, of Steveston, BC; 2ndly, 1976, Hazel Anne, da of Edward Lester Pierrot, and widow of Robert Frank Wright, and has issue living (by 2nd *m*), John St Vincent *b* 1980, Laura Anne *b* 1978, — Antony Leigh (3337 William St, Vancouver, BC, Canada V5K 224), *b* 1947: *m* 1981, Lisa Robbyn Marie, da of George Edmond Joseph Ayotte, and has issue living, Sarah Marie Grace *b* 1983, — Hilary Anne, *b* 1950. —— Noel John, *b* 1920: *ed* Ampleforth, and Univ of British Columbia (BA); formerly Prof of English, Univ of Alberta; late Lance-Bombardier, Roy Canadian Artillery: *m* 1st, 1950 (*m diss* 1954), Jean Mary Columbus; 2ndly, 1956, Betty, 3rd da of late Jasper Rutherford, and has issue living, (by 2nd *m*) Jonathan Rutherford, *b* 1962. *Residence* – 3549 Cardiff Place, Victoria, BC, Canada.

Granddaughters of late Maj Edward Mainwaring Parker-Jervis, MC (infra):—
Issue of late Robert St Vincent Parker-Jervis, *b* 1908, *d* 1973: *m* 1st, 1936 (*m diss* 1946), Lucy, who *d* 1966, only da of Maj William Edward Burrill, of the Green, Masham, Ripon; 2ndly, 1946, Pamela Violet, who *d* 1981, da of late Capt Alexander Moore Vandeleur, Life Gds (By Knaresborough), and formerly wife of Lt-Col Lennox John Livingstone-Learmonth, DSO, MC:—
(By 1st *m*) Diana Elizabeth, *b* 1937: *m* 1958, Roger Parker-Jervis (infra). —— (By 2nd *m*) Linda, *b* 1946: *m* 1970, Brig Michael Lord, of Orchard Farm, Tutts Clump, nr Reading, Berks, and has issue living, Simon James Austin, *b* 1972, — Guy Robert Thomas, *b* 1974, — Patrick Michael Jervis, *b* 1977. —— Sally Anne *b* 1947: *m* 1981, John William Parsons, CBE, of Townsend House, Corfe Castle, Dorset, son of late Frederick John Parsons, of Wareham, Dorset, and has issue living, Timothy John Jervis, *b* 1987. —— Angela, *b* 1949: *m* 1984, (Peter) Jeremy Woodland Payne, of 50 Narbonne Av, SW4 9JT, son of Dr R. F. Payne, of Huxtable Farm, Devon, and has issue living, Christopher William, *b* 1992, — Emily Louise, *b* 1989.

Granddaughter of late William Robert Parker Jervis, 3rd son of late Hon Edward Swynfen Parker-Jervis, yst son of 2nd Viscount:—
Issue of late Major Edward Mainwaring Parker-Jervis, MC, *b* 1880, *d* 1935: *m* 1906, Eleanor Dora, who *d* 1955, da of Alfred Charles Lyon, formerly of Albrighton Hall, Albrighton, Salop:—
Rosemary Eleanor, *b* 1914: *m* 1940, Brig Francis Peter Barclay, DSO, MC, late Royal Norfolk Regt, who *d* 1992, and has had issue, Robin Peter, *b* 1943; *ed* Harrow, and RMA Sandhurst, 2nd Lieut 1st East Anglian Regt; *d* 1964 as a result of a mountain accident while serving in Aden, — Christopher Thomas, *b* 1946; *ed* Harrow. *Residence* – Little Dunham Lodge, King's Lynn, Norfolk.

Grandchildren of late Humphrey Parker-Jervis (infra):—
Issue of late Capt John Humphrey Parker-Jervis, RE, *b* 1923, *d* 1989: *m* 1956, Elizabeth Margaret (Martens Hall Farm, Longworth, Abingdon, Oxon), da of Richard Durrant Trotter, of Brin House, Flichity, Inverness:—
Simon Humphrey, *b* 1961. —— Fiona Mary, *b* 1965. —— Mary Clare, *b* 1966: *m* 1993, Andrew Hank Shaw, son of Stephen Shaw, of Crockham Hill, Kent.

Grandsons of late Thomas Swynfen Parker-Jervis, 8th son of late Hon Edward Swynfen Parker-Jervis (ante):—
Issue of late Humphrey Parker-Jervis, *b* 1889, *d* 1948: *m* 1922, Helen Frances (Brook Cottage, Uley, Dursley, Gloucestershire), da of Sir John Ralph Starkey, 1st Bt:—

Christopher Thomas (Lane Cottage, Watledge, Nailsworth, Glos), *b* 1929; *ed* Radley; Lt-Cdr RN (ret): *m* 1959, Gillian Bowden, and has issue living, Edward Christopher, *b* 1960; *ed* Abingdon, and St Catherine's Coll, Oxford: *m* 1990, Sarah Jane, only da of Rev John Musgrave Shorrock, of Bredgar Vicarage, Sittingbourne, Kent, — William Thomas, *b* 1965; *ed* Abingdon, — Sarah Belinda, *b* 1967.
    Issue of late George Parker-Jervis, *b* 1895, *d* 1973: *m* 1924, Ruth Alice, who *d* 1990, da of late Charles Edward Farmer:—
James (Templewood, Brechin, Angus DD9 7PT), *b* 1926; *ed* Eton; Lt-Cdr RN (ret): *m* 1956, Sybil Anne, da of late Thomas Prain Douglas Murray, MBE, TD, of Templewood, Brechin, Angus, and widow of Hon John Michael Inigo Cross (*see* V Cross), and has issue living, Andrew Swynfen (Studland House, Causeway End, Felsted, Dunmow, Essex CM6 3LS), *b* 1959; *ed* Eton, and Edinburgh Univ: *m* 1990, Victoria L., yst da of late Rowan B. Hutchison, and of Mrs D. Allen, of Rendham Court, Saxmundham, Suffolk, and has issue living, Holly Audrey *b* 1993, — Harriet Anne, *b* 1957: *m* 1985, Frederick Gibson, son of late F. W. Gibson, and has issue living, James Frederick *b* 1989, Rosie Alice *b* 1993. —— Nicholas (The Manor House, South Littleton, Evesham, Worcs), *b* 1927; *ed* Eton, and at Magdalene Coll, Camb: *m* 1960, Elisabeth Henley, da of J. T. Morgan, of Llaneinydd, St Nicholas, Glam, and has issue living, George Rhidian, *b* 1961, — Thomas Fabyan, *b* 1974, — Catherine Elisabeth, *b* 1964. —— Roger, *b* 1931; *ed* Eton, and Magdalene Coll, Camb: *m* 1958, Diana Elizabeth, da of late Robert St Vincent Parker-Jervis (ante), and has issue living, Edward Swynfen, *b* 1959, — Guy, *b* 1960: *m* 1985, Linda Johnston, — Lucy Alice, *b* 1966: *m* 1989, Julian Guy Rutherford, yr son of Ian Rutherford, of Childwickbury, Herts, and has issue living, Laura Diana *b* 1992. *Residence* – The Old Schoolhouse, Brill, Bucks.

PREDECESSORS – (1) *Adm Rt Hon Sir* John Jervis, GCB, 2nd son of late Swynfen Jervis, of Meaford, Staffordshire; *b* 1734; a celebrated Naval Commander, who in 1797 obtained a splendid victory over the Spanish Fleet at Cape St Vincent; First Lord of the Admiralty 1801-4; MP for Launceston 1783-4, for Great Yarmouth 1784-90, and for Chipping Wycombe 1790-94: *m* 1783, his cousin, Martha, who *d* 1816, da of late Rt Hon Sir Thomas Parker, Lord Ch Baron of the Exchequer; *cr Baron Jervis*, of Meaford, co Stafford, and *Earl of St Vincent* (peerage of Great Britain) 1797, and *Viscount St Vincent*, of Meaford, co Stafford (peerage of United Kingdom) 1801, with remainder to his nephews, William Henry Ricketts and Edward Jervis Ricketts successively, and after them to his niece Mary, wife of 7th Earl of Northesk, and her heirs male; *d* 1823, when the barony and earldom became extinct and the viscountcy devolved upon his surviving nephew (2) Edward Jervis Ricketts, 2nd Viscount; *b* 1767; assumed by Roy licence 1823 the surname of Jervis only; *d* 1859; *s* by his grandson (3) Carnegie Robert John, 3rd Viscount; *b* 1825: *m* 1848, Lucy Charlotte, who *d* 1900, da of John Baskervyle Glegg, of Withington Hall, Cheshire; *d* 1879; *s* by his son (4) John Edward Leveson, 4th Viscount; *b* 1850; *d* of wounds received at battle of Abu Klea Jan 1885; *s* by his brother (5) Carnegie Parker, 5th Viscount; *b* 1855: *m* 1885 (*m diss* 1896), Rebecca May, da of late James Baston, of Barrow-in-Furness; *d* 1908; *s* by his brother (6) Ronald Clarges, 6th Viscount; *b* 1859: *m* 1894, Marion Annie, who *d* 1911, da of late James Brown, of Orchard, Carluke, and Petit Menage, Jersey; *d* 1940; *s* by his son (7) Ronald George James, 7th Viscount and present peer.

SALISBURY, MARQUESS OF (Gascoyne-Cecil) (Marquess GB 1789)

Late, but seriously

Robert Edward Peter Gascoyne-Cecil, 6th Marquess; *b* 24 Oct 1916; *s* 1972; *ed* Eton; DL Dorset 1974; patron of seven livings, Capt Gren Gds; MP for W Bournemouth (*C*) 1950-54: *m* 1945, Marjorie Olein, da of late Capt Hon Valentine Maurice Wyndham-Quin, RN (*see* E Dunraven), and has had issue.

Arms – Quarterly: 1st and 4th barry of ten argent and azure, over all six escutcheons, three, two, and one, sable, each charged with a lion rampant of the first, a crescent gules for difference, *Cecil*; 2nd and 3rd argent, on a pale sable, a conger's head erased and erect or, charged with an ermine spot, *Gascoyne*. **Crests** – 1st, six arrows in saltire or, barbed and feathered argent, banded gules, buckled and garnished gold, surmounted by a morion or steel cap proper; 2nd, a conger's head erased and erect or, charged with an ermine spot. **Supporters** – On either side a lion ermine.
Seat – Hatfield House, Hatfield.

SONS LIVING AND DECEASED

Robert Michael James (*Viscount Cranborne*) (The Manor House, Cranborne, Wimborne, Dorset), *b* 30 Sept 1946; *ed* Eton, and Ch Ch Oxford; MP for Dorset South (*C*) 1979-87; DL Dorset 1988; called to House of Lords in his father's Barony of Cecil 1992: *m* 1970, Hannah Ann, da of Lt-Col William Joseph Stirling of Keir (*see* Stirling-Maxwell, Bt, dormant), and has issue:—
    Sons Living— *Hon* Robert Edward William, *b* 18 Dec 1970; a Page of Honour to HM 1983-86, — *Hon* James Richard, *b* 1973.
    Daughters Living— *Hon* Elizabeth Ann, *b* 1972, — *Hon* Georgiana, *b* 1977, — *Hon* Katherine, *b* 1977 (twin).

Lord Richard Valentine, *b* 1948; *ed* Eton; Capt Gren Gds (despatches 1973); *d* 1978.
Lord Charles Edward Vere (21 Hollywood Rd, SW10), *b* 1949; *ed* Eton, and Ch Ch Oxford: *m* 1993, Virginia Edith, yr da of late Paul Zervudachi, of Morges, Switzerland, and Levanto, Italy.
Lord Valentine William (11 Shalcomb St, SW10), *b* 1952; *ed* Eton; a Page of Honour to HM Queen Elizabeth The Queen Mother 1966-67; Maj Gren Gds.
Lord Michael Hugh (PO Box 49428, Nairobi, Kenya), *b* 1960; *ed* Eton; Gren Gds: *m* 1986, Camilla Julia, yr da of late Maj Richard Jervoise Scott, TD (*see* Scott, Bt, *cr* 1962, colls), and has issue living, Hubert George, *b* 1992, — Daisy Alice Julia, *b* 1989.

DAUGHTER LIVING

Lady Rose Alice Elizabeth Cecil, *b* 1956; has retained her maiden name: *m* 1985, Mark Flawn Thomas, yst son of Peter Flawn Thomas, of Shortbridge Mill, Piltdown, Sussex.

COLLATERAL BRANCHES LIVING

    Issue of late Lord (Edward Christian) David Cecil, CH, CLit, author, yr son of 4th Marquess, *b* 1902, *d* 1986: *m* 1932, Rachel, who *d* 1982, da of late Sir Desmond McCarthy:—

Jonathan Hugh, *b* 1939; *ed* Eton, and New Coll, Oxford; actor: *m* 1st, 1963 (*m diss* 19—), Vivien Sarah Frances, el da of late David Granville Heilbron, of 2 Clevedon Dr, Glasgow, W2; 2ndly, 1976, Anna Sharkey. —— Hugh Peniston (The University, Leeds, Yorks), *b* 1941; *ed* Eton, and New Coll Oxford (BA): *m* 1972, Mirabel, da of Richard Walker, OBE, of The Close, Withington, Glos, and has issue living, Conrad Richard James, *b* 1973, — David Edward Hugh, *b* 1978, — Clementine Rachel Amelia, *b* 1975, — Stella, *b* 1984. —— Alice Laura, *b* 1947: *m* 1975, Angelo Hornak, and has issue living, Leo David, *b* 1979, — Francesca Rachel, *b* 1982.

Grandchildren of late Rt Rev Lord William Rupert Ernest Gascoyne-Cecil, DD, Bishop of Exeter (infra):—
Issue of late Randle William Gascoyne-Cecil, *b* 1889, *ka* 1917: *m* 1st, 1914 (*m diss* 1916), Dorothy Janaway, who *d* 19—; 2ndly, 1916, Elizabeth Claire, who *d* 1972, da of George Turner:—
(By 2nd *m*) Anne Mary (*posthumous*), *b* 1918; 1939-45 War as 2nd Officer WRNS: *m* 1945, David Bryce Wilson, Lt-Cdr RCNVR, and Canadian Foreign Ser (ret), and has issue living, Andrew David Randle (Canadian Foreign Ser, 13 Lynhaven Crescent, Nepean, Ontario K2E 5K3), *b* 1956: *m* 1988, Susan Blyth-Schofield, — Elizabeth Anne, *b* 1946: *m* 1982, Bruno Fascinato, of 52 Manitoba St, Guelph, Ontario, Canada N1E 3B9, and has issue living, Francesco Bruno Bruce *b* 1989, David Tullio Charles *b* 1986, — Carolyn Susan Mary, *b* 1948: *m* 1972, Simon Roger Williams (c/o Canadian High Commn, Canberra, Australia), — Jennifer Laura Eve *b* 1951: *m* 1982 (*m diss* 1994), Nyle Belkov, — Deborah Rosalind Louise (702 Parkdale Av, Ottawa, Ontario K1Y 1J4), *b* 1952. *Residence* – 371 Daly Av, Ottawa, Ontario, Canada K1N 6G8.
Issue of late Maj Victor Alexander Gascoyne-Cecil, *b* 1891, *d* 1977: *m* 1915, Fairlie Estelle Caroline, who *d* 1980, da of late Lt-Col Arthur Watson, of Dublin:—
Rupert Arthur Victor CECIL, DFC, *b* 1917; MA Oxon; DPh; Wing-Cdr (ret) RAFVR; relinquished by deed poll 1955, the surname of Gascoyne; Vice-Prin of Linacre Coll, Oxford; 1939-45 War (DFC and Bar): *m* 1st, 1940 (*m diss* 1974), Helen Moira Rosemary Phillips, only child of late Col Roland Luker, CMG, MC; 2ndly, 19—, Anna Teresa, da of Donald Hodson, of 10 Wood Lane, Highgate, N6 (*see* V Arbuthnott, 1970 Edn), and has issue living (by 1st wife), Desmond Hugh (c/o Nat Westminster Bank, E Molesey and Hampton Court Branch, 13 Bridge Rd, E Molesey, Surrey KT8 9EZ), *b* 1941; *ed* Magdalen Coll Sch, Queen's Coll, Oxford (MA), and Berne Univ; Counsellor, HM Dip Serv (British Embassy, Vienna): *m* 1964, Ruth Elizabeth, da of Dr Werner Sachs, of 19 Tideswell Rd, SW15, and has issue living, Thomas Desmond *b* 1966, Nicholas David *b* 1968, Andrew Peter *b* 1971, Sarah Ruth *b* 1972, — Timothy Rupert (27 Kay's Rd, Flitwick, Bedford), *b* 1944; *ed* Magdalen Coll Sch, Exeter Coll, Oxford (MA), and Munich Univ: *m* 1977, Ursula Margaret, da of John Christopher Rotton, of Compton, Sussex, and has issue living, Robert *b* 1977, Thomas *b* 1979, — June Elizabeth (4 Pleasant Place, Bathford, Bath BA1 7TL), *b* 1946: *m* 1968 (*m diss* 1994), Michael Durnford Robb, and has issue living, Geoffrey Edward *b* 1972, Joanna Frances *b* 1970, — (by 2nd wife) Flora, *b* 1971, — Maud, *b* 1972. —— Anthony Robert (Woodlands, Butts Green, Sandon, Chelmsford, Essex), *b* 1921: *m* 1st, 1944 (*m diss* 1951), Mary Hood, only da of late Rev Ernest James Simpson, of Great Burstead Vicarage, Billericay, Essex; 2ndly, 1952, Alison Julia, only da of late H. C. Foster, of Little Baddow, Essex, and has issue living (by 1st *m*), Michael Anthony (12 School Rd, Downham, Essex), *b* 1946: *m* 1969 (*m diss* 1990), Carol Ann, only da of Samuel Oxford, and has issue living, Jonathan Michael *b* 1971, Christopher Anthony *b* 1973, Victoria Ruth *b* 1976, Elizabeth Carol *b* 1980, — Jennifer Jean Mary, *b* 1947: *m* 1981, John Warwick Mills, of Thorington Hall, Wherstead, Ipswich, Suffolk, and has issue living, George Frederick Cecil *b* 1986, Eleanor Mary Cecil *b* 1984, — (by 2nd *m*) Richard David (Chestnut Cottage, Butts Green, Sandon, Chelmsford, Essex), *b* 1953: *m* 1978, Judith Westhorp, only da of Geoffrey Roberts, OBE, of 5 Arley Close, Chester, and has issue living, James Anthony *b* 1981, Andrew Peter *b* 1985, Helen Elizabeth *b* 1982, — Caroline Alison, *b* 1955, — Rosalind Julia, *b* 1962: *m* 1993, David Platt, of 2 Ilgars Cottage, Mosses Lane, S Woodham Ferrers, Chelmsford, Essex, son of Malcolm Platt, of The Wirral, Merseyside.

Issue of late Rt Rev Lord William Rupert Ernest Gascoyne-Cecil, DD, Bishop of Exeter, 2nd son of 3rd Marquess, *b* 1863, *d* 1936: *m* 1887, Lady Florence Mary Bootle-Wilbraham, who *d* 1944, da of 1st Earl of Lathom:—
Eve Alice, *b* 1900: *m* 1929, Vice-Adm Richard Benyon, CB, CBE, who *d* 1968 (*see* Shelley, Bt, *cr* 1611, colls). *Residence* – The Brew House, Englefield, Reading.

Grandchildren of late Lieut-Col Lord Eustace Brownlow Henry Gascoyne-Cecil, 3rd son of 2nd Marquess:—
Issue of late Rt Hon Evelyn Cecil, GBE, who was *cr Baron Rockley* 1934:—
(See that title)

Grandson of late Lord Arthur Cecil, 6th son of 2nd Marquess:—
Issue of late Capt Arthur William James Cecil, *b* 1875, *d* 1936: *m* 1906, Hon Beatrice Susan Theodosia Stuart Wortley, who *d* 1973, da of 1st Baron Stuart of Wortley (ext):—
Robert Arthur, *b* 1921; *ed* Winchester; formerly Capt King's Royal Rifle Corps. *Residence* – 11 Duke St, W1.

PREDECESSORS – **(1)** *Rt Hon Sir* ROBERT Cecil, KG, PC, yr son of William Cecil, 1st Baron Burghley (*see* M Exeter); was Sec of State 1596-1612, Chancellor of Duchy of Lancaster 1597-9, Lord Privy Seal 1597-1612, and Lord High Treasurer 1608-12; *cr Baron Cecil*, of Essendon, co Rutland (peerage of England) 1603, *Viscount Cranborne* (peerage of England) 1604, and *Earl of Salisbury* (peerage of England) 1605; *d* 1612; *s* by his son **(2)** WILLIAM, KG, 2nd Earl; *d* 1668; *s* by his grandson **(3)** JAMES, KG, 3rd Earl; *d* 1683; *s* by his son **(4)** JAMES, 4th Earl; having become a convert to the Roman Catholic faith the House of Commons in 1689 resolved that he be impeached for high treason, but the prosecution was not proceeded with; *d* 1694; *s* by his son **(5)** JAMES, 5th Earl; carried King Edward's staff at the coronation of George I; *d* 1728; *s* by his son **(6)** JAMES, 6th Earl; *d* 1780; *s* by his son **(7)** JAMES, KG, 7th Earl; *cr Marquess of Salisbury* (peerage of Great Britain) 1789; sat as MP for Bedwin; was Lord Chamberlain of the Household 1783-1804, and Lord-Lieut of Herts; *d* 1823; *s* by his son **(8)** JAMES BROWNLOW, KG, PC, DCL, 2nd Marquess; *b* 1791; was Lord Pres of the Council 1858-9, and Lord-Lieut of Middlesex; in 1821 assumed by Roy licence the additional surname of Gascoyne: *m* 1821, Frances Mary, da and heir of late Bamber Gascoyne; 2ndly, 1847, Lady Mary Catherine Sackville-West, da of 5th Earl De la Warr; *d* 1868; *s* by his 2nd son **(9)** ROBERT ARTHUR TALBOT, KG, GCVO, PC, 3rd Marquess; *b* 1830; MP for Stamford (*C*) 1853-68; Sec of State for India 1866-7 and 1874-8, and for Foreign Affairs 1878-80, Special Ambassador at Conference on Eastern Affairs held at Constantinople 1876-7, 2nd Plen for Great Britain at Congress of Berlin 1878, Prime Minister and Sec of State for Foreign Affairs June 1885 to Feb 1886, Prime Minister and First Lord of the Treasury June 1886 to Jan 1887, Prime Minister and Sec of State for Foreign Affairs Jan 1887 to Aug 1892, and again Prime Minister and Sec of State for Foreign Affairs June 1895 to Nov 1900, and Prime Minister and Lord Privy Seal 1900-1902: *m* 1857, Georgina, CI, VA, who *d* 1899, da of late Hon Sir Edward Hall Alderson, a Baron of the Court of Exchequer; *d* 1903; *s* by his son **(10)** JAMES EDWARD HUBERT, KG, GCVO, CB, PC, 4th Marquess; *b* 1861; sometime High Steward of Westminster and Hertford; served in Herts Yeo, Bedfordshire Regt (TA), and RA (TA), becoming Maj-Gen; S Africa 1900 (despatches, CB); was Under-Sec of State for Foreign Affairs 1900-1903, Lord Privy Seal 1903-5, Lord Privy Seal and Pres of Board of Trade 1905, and Lord Pres of the Council and Dep Leader of the House of Lords (also temporary Chancellor of the Duchy of Lancaster) 1922-4, and again Lord Privy Seal 1924-9 (also Leader of the House of Lords 1925-9, and of Opposition 1929-31); appointed Lord High Steward 1937; bore St Edward's Crown at Coronation of King George VI; sat as MP for Darwen Div of N-E Lancashire (*C*) 1885-92 and for Rochester 1893-1903: *m* 1887, Lady Cicely Alice Gore, who *d* 1955, second da of 5th Earl of Arran; *d* 1947; *s* by his son **(11)** ROBERT ARTHUR JAMES, KG, PC, 5th Marquess *b* 1893; MP for S Dorset (*C*) 1929-41; called to House of Lords in his father's Barony of Cecil 1941; Sec of State for Dominions Affairs 1940-42 and 1943-45, for Colonies 1942 and for Commonwealth Relations 1952, Lord Privy Seal 1942-43 and 1951-52, and Lord Pres of the Council 1952-57; Leader of House of Lords 1942-43 and 1951-57; Chancellor Liverpool Univ 1951-71; Chancellor of Order of the Garter 1960-72: *m* 1915, Elizabeth Vere, who *d* 1982, da of late Col Rt Hon Lord Richard

Frederick Cavendish, CB, CMG (D Devonshire); *d* 1972; *s* by his son **(12)** ROBERT EDWARD PETER, 6th Marquess and present peer; also Earl of Salisbury, Viscount Cranborne, and Baron Cecil.

SALMON, BARONY OF (Salmon) (Extinct 1991)

SON LIVING OF LIFE BARON

Hon David Neville Cyril (Holne Cott, Holne, nr Ashburton, Devon), *b* 1935: *m* 1st, 1958 (*m diss* 1972), Heather Turner-Laing; 2ndly, 1973, Mrs Sarah Harrison, da of Herman L. Eberts, of Montreal, Canada, and formerly wife of Noel Harrison, and has issue living, Alexander, *b* 19—, — Marc, *b* 19—.

DAUGHTER LIVING OF LIFE BARON

Hon Gai Rencie, *b* 1933: *m* 1st 1955, Martin Treves, who *d* 1970; 2ndly, 1973, Geoffrey Robinson, CBE, of Salts End, Ash, nr Canterbury, Kent, and has issue (by 1st *m*), William Martin, *b* 1960, — George Thomas, *b* 1963, — Toby Charles, *b* 1966, — Emma Elizabeth Rencie, *b* 1959.

Saltersford, Baron; title of Earl of Courtown on Roll of HL.

SALTOUN, LADY (Fraser) (Lordship S 1445)
(Title pronounced "Salton")

FLORA MARJORY FRASER, *Lady Saltoun*; *b* 18 Oct 1930; *s* 1979; Chief of the name of Fraser: *m* 6 Oct 1956, Capt Alexander Arthur Alphonso David Maule Ramsay of Mar, Grenadier Guards (ret) (*see* E Dalhousie, colls), and has issue.

Arms – Azure, three fraises argent. **Crests** – *Dexter*, on a mount a flourish of strawberries leaved and fructed proper. *Sinister*, an ostrich holding in its beak a horseshoe proper. **Supporters** – Two angels proper with wings expanded and vested in long garments or.
Residence – Cairnbulg Castle, Fraserburgh, Aberdeenshire AB43 5TN.

DAUGHTERS LIVING

Hon KATHARINE INGRID MARY ISABEL FRASER, *b* 11 Oct 1957; assumed the surname and arms of Fraser by Warrant of Lord Lyon King of Arms 1973: *m* 3 May 1980, Capt Mark Malise Nicolson, Irish Guards, only son of Malise Allen Nicolson, MC, of Frog Hall, Tilston. Malpas, Cheshire, and has issue living, Alexander William Malise FRASER *b* 5 July 1990, — Louise Alexandra Patricia, *b* 1984, — Juliet Victoria Katharine, *b* 1988. *Residence* – 41 Napier Av, SW6 3PS.
Hon Alice Elizabeth Margaret, *b* 8 July 1961: *m* 1990, David Ramsey, yr son of Ronald Ramsey, of St James, Barbados, and has issue living, Alexander David, *b* 1991, — Victoria Alice, *b* 1994.
Hon Elizabeth Alexandra Mary RAMSAY OF MAR, *b* 15 April 1963.

WIDOW LIVING OF SON OF EIGHTEENTH LORD

Margaret Elizabeth (Luxilyan, 15 Louw Av, Somerset West, Cape Province, S Africa), da of Reginald Barnes, of St Ermin's, Westminster: *m* 1934, as his 2nd wife, Rear Adm Hon George Fraser, DSO, RN, who *d* 1970, and has issue living (see colls infra).

COLLATERAL BRANCHES LIVING

Issue of late Rear Adm Hon George Fraser, DSO, RN, 2nd son of 18th Lord, *b* 1887, *d* 1970: *m* 1st, 1920, Elizabeth FRASER SPENCER STANHOPE, who *d* 1964, having assumed by Roy licence 1945, the additional surnames of Spencer Stanhope, da of late John Montague Spencer-Stanhope (Milborne-Swinnerton-Pilkington, Bt, colls); 2ndly, 1934, Margaret Elizabeth (ante). da of Reginald Barnes, of St Ermin's, Westminster:—
(By 1st *m*) Simon Walter (Tom-a-Ghiuthais, Appin, Argyllshire; New Club), *b* 1924; *ed* Eton: *m* 1st, 1950 (*m diss* 1962), Jean Madeline Frances, da of late Prof John Masson Gulland, FRS, of 8 Great Stuart St, Edinburgh; 2ndly, 1962 (*m diss* 1971), Yvonne, da of Edwin Valère Newby; 3rdly, 1971 (*m diss* 1976), Cheryl Mary Eleanor, da of David McNeil Williams of Summerfield House, Cheshire, and formerly wife of Richard Charles Sheffield (*see* Sheffield, Bt, colls); 4thly, 1976 (*m diss* 1983), Meryl, da of John Ingham, of Halifax, W Yorks; 5thly, 1987, Marjorie, widow of late Neil W. Cameron, MD, ChB, and da of late Sydney Donaldson, and has issue living (by 1st *m*) Isabel Madeline, *b* 1951, — Elspeth Caroline, *b* 1954, — (by 2nd *m*) Alistair John, *b* 1963: *m* 1989, Marie-Catherine Elizabeth, da of James Sigston, of Prenton, Wirral, — Deborah Gail, *b* 1965, — (by 3rd *m*) James David, *b* 1971, — William Alexander, *b* 1972. ——— (By 2nd *m*) Robert Andrew Gerard (Suikerbos, Gordons Bay, Cape Province), *b* 1935: *m* 1964, Sarah Elizabeth, da of Brig Gerald Edward Peck, CBE, DSO, and has issue living, David Alexander George, *b* 1966, — Fiona Elizabeth, *b* 1965. ——— Patrick George (Silverhill, Kenilworth, Cape Province, S Africa), *b* 1938: *m* 1975, Patricia Aletta, da of late Dr Peter John Frost, and has issue living, Alexandra Nelle, *b* 1979, — Sophie Elizabeth, *b* 1981, — Camilla Mary, *b* 1981.

Issue of late Brig Hon William Fraser, DSO, MC, yst son of 18th Lord, *b* 1890, *d* 1964: *m* 1919, Pamela Cynthia who *d* 1975, da of late Cyril Francis Maude (V Hawarden, colls), and widow of Maj William La Touche Congreve, VC, DSO, MC:—

Sir David William, GCB, OBE (Vallenders, Isington, Alton, Hants; Turf and Pratt's Clubs), *b* 1920; Gen late Gren Gds; *ed* Eton, and Ch Ch, Oxford; Hon DLitt Reading 1992; 1939-45 War; Malaya 1948: Cyprus 1958, Cameroun 1961, and Borneo 1964; GOC 4th Div 1969-71, Asst Ch of Defence Staff 1971-73, and Vice-Ch of Gen Staff 1973-75, UK Mil Rep to NATO 1975-77, Comdt R Coll of Defence Studies 1977-80; ADC (Gen) 1977; Col Royal Hampshire Regt 1981-87; Chm of Treloar Tst and Gov body of Treloar Coll 1982-93; OBE (Mil) 1952, KCB (Mil) 1973, GCB (Mil) 1980; a DL of Hants since 1982: *m* 1st, 1947 (*m diss* 1952), Anne, da of late Brig Edward William Sturgis Balfour, CVO, DSO, OBE, MC (E Balfour); 2ndly, 1957, Julia Frances Oldridge, da of late Maj C. James Oldridge de la Hey, and has issue living, (by 1st *m*) Antonia Isabella, *b* 1949: *m* 1st, 1972 (*m diss* 1975), Thomas Harney; 2ndly 1975 (*m diss* 1979), Thomas Bantock; 3rdly, 1981, Timothy Hanbury, and has issue living (by 2nd *m*), Amaryllis Eva *b* 1975, (by 3rd *m*) Edan William Samson *b* 1985, — (by 2nd *m*) Alexander James, *b* 1960, — Simon William David, *b* 1963: *m* 1991, Lucinda Anne, elder da of Thomas Edward Sydney Egerton, of Chaddleworth, Newbury, Berks, and has issue living, a son *b* 1994, — Arabella Katharine, *b* 1958: *m* 1984, Lt-Col Gordon Thomas Riddell Birdwood, Blues and Royals, son of Lt-Col Richard Birdwood, MC, DL, of Horwood House, Horwood, Bideford, Devon, — Lucy Caroline (*Hon Mrs Alexander Baring*), *b* 1965: *m* 1992, Hon Alexander Nicholas John Baring, yr son of 7th Baron Ashburton, KCVO.

Issue of late Hon Mary Alexandra Fraser, da of 18th Lord, *b* 1892, *d* 1969: *m* 1st, 1918, Lt-Cdr John Robert Auber Codrington, RN, who *d* 1918 (V Hambleden); 2ndly, 1928, Maj Arthur Balcarres Wardlaw Ramsay, DL, JP (B Magheramorne, colls), who *d* 1956:—

(By 2nd *m*) Euphan Mary, *b* 1931: *m* 1955, Richard Hanbury-Tenison, JP, Lord Lieut of Gwent, of Clytha Park, Gwent, and has issue living, John Wardlaw, *b* 1957: *m* 1993, Laura Katharine, only da of Sir Robert Lucian Wade-Gery, KCMG, KCVO, of 7 Rothwell St, NW1, — William Ayscough, *b* 1962, — Capel Thomas, *b* 1965: *m* 1992, Beatrice Hannah, eldest da of Alan Hutchison, of Wern-y-Cwm, Abergavenny, and has issue living, William Augustus *b* 1992, — Sarah, *b* 1956: *m* 1984, Dr Martin S. Tolley, yr son of Canon George Tolley, of Dore, Sheffield, and has issue living, Thomas *b* 1986, Sophie Margaret *b* 1989, Felicity Ruth *b* 1993, — Laura Mary, *b* 1966: *m* 1991, A. John Femi-Ola. —— Elizabeth Mary, *b* 1934: *m* 1955, Simon Anthony Helyar Walker-Heneage, of The Old Rectory, Wanstrow, Shepton Mallet, Somerset BA4 4TQ, and has issue living, James Arthur, *b* 1957: *m* 1987, Charlotte Elizabeth, da of late Roland Shott, of North Farm House, Ashmore, Wilts, and has issue living, Eliza Mary *b* 1993, — Celia Mary, *b* 1956: *m* 1990, Paul Maxwell Gurowich, of 6 Loder Rd, Brighton, son of Peter Gurowich, of 10 Godwin Close, Winchester, and has issue living, Timothy Peter *b* 1991, — Arabella Jane, *b* 1959: *m* 1985, Nicholas David Douro Hoare, of 66 Winchedon Rd, SW6, son of Michael Douro Hoare, of Downsland Court, Ditchling, Hassocks, Sussex, and has issue living, Thomas *b* 1988, — Sophie Dionysia, *b* 1962: *m* 1988, Nicholas John Gibson Wright, son of David John Vernon Wright, of 11 Davenant Rd, Oxford, and has issue living, Flora Clemence Elizabeth *b* 1990, Lily Dionysia *b* 1992, — Sarah Phoebe, *b* 1974.

PREDECESSORS – (1-6) *Sir* LAURENCE Abernethy; *cr Lord Saltoun*, of Abernethy (peerage of Scotland) 1445, and the title passed in regular succession for five generations; in 1587 the 6th Lord was *s* by his son (7) GEORGE, 7th Lord; *s* by his son (8) JOHN, 8th Lord; *s* by his son (9) ALEXANDER, 9th Lord; *dsp* 1668; *s* by his cousin (10) ALEXANDER, 10th Lord, son of Margaret, da of 7th Lord, by her *m* with Alexander Fraser, of Philorth; title confirmed by patent 1670 and ratified by Parliament; wounded at battle of Worcester; *d* 1693; *s* by his grandson (11) WILLIAM, 11th Lord; *d* 1716; *s* by his son (12) ALEXANDER, 12th Lord; *d* 1748; *s* by his el son (13) ALEXANDER, 13th Lord; *d* unm 1751; *s* by his brother (14) GEORGE, 14th Lord; *d* 1782; *s* by his son (15) ALEXANDER, 15th Lord; *d* 1793; *s* by his son (16) ALEXANDER GEORGE, 16th Lord; a Lieut-Gen in the Army, and Representative Peer; *dsp* 1853; *s* by his nephew (17) ALEXANDER, 17th Lord, son of Hon William, 3rd son of 15th Lord; was a Representative Peer: *m* 1849, Charlotte, 2nd da of Thomas Browne Evans, Esq, of Dean House, Oxfordshire; *d* 31 Jan 1886; *s* by his son (18) ALEXANDER WILLIAM FREDERICK, CMG, 18th Lord; *b* 1851; a Representative Peer for Scotland, and Capt King's Body Guard for Scotland (Roy Co of Archers): *m* 1885, Mary Helena, who *d* 1940, sister of Sir Henry Christopher Grattan-Bellew, 3rd Bt; *d* 1933; *s* by his el son (19) ALEXANDER ARTHUR, MC, 19th Lord; *b* 1886; a Representative Peer for Scotland 1935-63; Capt Gordon Highlanders; a Member of Roy Co of Archers (Queen's Body Guard for Scotland); 1914-18 War (prisoner, MC): *m* 1920, Dorothy Geraldine, who *d* 1985, da of Sir Charles Glynne Earle Welby, 5th Bt, CB; *d* 1979; *s* by his only da (20) FLORA MARJORY, present peeress.

SAMUEL, VISCOUNT (Samuel) (Viscount UK 1937)

TURN NOT ASIDE

DAVID HERBERT SAMUEL, 3rd Viscount; *b* 8 July 1922; *s* 1978; *ed* Balliol Coll, Oxford (MA); PhD Hebrew Univ, Jerusalem 1953; Sherman Prof Emeritus of Physical Chemistry Weizmann Inst of Science, Rehovot, Israel, and Pres Shenkar Coll of Textile Technology and Fashion, Ramat Gan, Israel; Research Fellow, Chemistry Dept, Harvard Univ, Camb, Mass, USA 1957-58; Research Fell, Chemical Biodynamics Lab (LRL), Univ of California, Berkeley 1965-66; Visiting Royal Soc Prof, Zoology Dept (MRC Neuroimmunology Unit), Univ Coll, London 1974-75; Visiting Prof, Pharmacology Dept, Yale Univ Sch of Medicine 1983-84; McLaughlin Prof, Medical Sch McMaster Univ, Hamilton, Ont 1984; Dep Chm of Scientific Council Weizmann Inst 1963-65; Dean, Faculty of Chemistry, Weizmann Inst 1971-73, Dir Centre for Neurosciences and Behavioural Research, Weizmann Inst, 1977-87; Member US-Israel Educational (Fulbright) Foundation Bd 1969-74 (Chm 1974-75); Member Advisory Bd, Bat-Sheva de Rothschild Foundation for the Advancement of Science in Israel 1970-83; Academic Advisory Cttee, Everyman's (Open) Univ 1976-83; Bd of Governors, Bezallel Acad of Arts and Design since 1976; Council, Israel Chemical Soc 1977-83; Member Israel Exec Cttee, America-Israel Cultural Foundation 1978-88 (Chm 1985-88); a Gov Tel-Aviv Museum since 1980; Member Council Anglo-Israel Assoc, London since 1982; titular Member Cttee for Chemical Education of Internat Union of Pure and Applied Chemistry 1982-91; Member Advisory Cttee and Bd of Trustees, Israel Centre for Psychobiology since 1973, and Bd of Trustees, Menninger Foundation, Topeka, KS, USA; co-editor of *Aging of the Brain* (1983), Member Editorial Bd of *Journal of Labelled Compounds and Radiopharmaceuticals*; *Brain Behaviour and Immunity; Alzheimer Disease and Related Disorders*, and author or co-author of over 300 scientific publications; 1939-45 War as Capt RA in India, Burma and Sumatra (despatches): *m* 1st, 1950 (*m diss* 1957), Esther, da of late J. Berelowitz, of Cape Town, S Africa; 2ndly, 1960 (*m diss* 1979), Mrs Rinna Dafni, da of late Meir Grossman, of Herzliyah, Israel; 3rdly, 1980 (*m diss* 1993), Mrs Veronika Engelhardt Grimm, da of late Ernest Engelhardt, of Toronto, Canada, and has issue by 1st and 2nd *m*.

Arms – Or, a bend between two caps of liberty gules, on a chief sable a balance of the first. **Crest** – In front of a sun rising or a dove wings elevated and addorsed, holding in the beak an olive branch proper. **Supporters** – On either side a lion or, the *dexter* gorged with a collar gules and resting the interior hind leg on a stump of oak eradicated and sprouting proper; the *sinister* gorged with an Eastern Crown also gules and resting the interior hind leg on a stump of olive eradicated and sprouting also proper.
Address – 54 Rehov Hanasi, Harishon, Rehovot, Israel.

DAUGHTERS LIVING (By 1st marriage)

Hon Judith (prefers to be known as *Hon Mrs Samuel-Daliot*), *b* 1951; *ed* Technion-Israel Inst of Technology, and Architectural Assocn London (BArch 1972): *m* 1987, Dr Daniel Daliot, MD, and has issue living, Jonathan, *b* 1988, — Talya, *b* 1990. *Residence* – 5 Lipsky St, Tel Aviv, Israel.

(By 2nd marriage)

Hon Naomi Rachel (prefers to be known as *Hon Mrs Samuel-Wilf*), *b* 1962; *ed* Hebrew Univ, Jerusalem Law Sch (LLB 1987); with Legal Dept, Israel Police Force since 1990: *m* 1992, Nir Wilf, and has issue living, Ittamar, *b* 1994. *Residence* – 43 Hatishbi St, Haifa, Israel.

BROTHER LIVING

Hon DAN JUDAH (154 Hillspoint Rd, Westport, CT 06880, USA; The Barns, Old Mill Farm, Mill Hamlet, Sidlesham, Sussex.), *b* 25 March 1925; *ed* Rugby, and at Balliol Coll, Oxford (MA); formerly Maj Yorkshire Hussars; with Sch of Advanced Intern Studies, Wash 1950-51; Gen Manager of Shell Co of Thailand 1962-66, with Shell Oil Co, New York 1966-67, Pres of Belgian Shell Co 1967-70, Gen Man, Regional Marketing, Shell Internat Chemical Co, London 1971-72, Marketing Co-ordinator (Oil) 1973-75, Group Personnel Co-ordinator 1976-77, Regional Co-ordinator W Hemisphere 1977-81, and a Dir of Shell Internat Petroleum Co, London 1973-81; Pres and Chief Exec Offr Scallop Corpn, New York 1981-86; Business Consultant, Member Bd of Directors Witco Corpn, New York, and of Canadian Overseas Packaging Industries; Chm Board of Management SEATO Graduates Sch of Eng, Bangkok 1963-66, and UK Trustee of Asian Inst of Technology 1966-68, and 1973-91; Member Bd of Directors Council of the Americas, New York 1981-86, British-American Educational Foundation, New York, and Foundation for Management Educn, London 1975-77; Cdr of Order of Roy Crown of Thailand; Officer Order of Crown of Belgium: *m* 1st, 1957 (*m diss* 1977), Nonni (Esther), da of late Max Gordon, of Johannesburg, S Africa; 2ndly, 1981 (*m diss* 1992), Heather, da of late Angus Cumming, of Haywards Heath, and has issue living (by 1st *m*), Jonathan Herbert, *b* 1965, — Lia Miriam, *b* 1961: *m* 1987, Glenn H. Album, — Maia Tessa, *b* 1963, — (by 2nd *m*), Benjamin Angus, *b* 1983, — Sasha Tamar, *b* 1982.

UNCLE LIVING

Hon Philip Ellis Herbert, *b* 1900; *ed* Westminster, and at Trin Coll, Camb; 1939-45 War with Hong Kong Vol Defence Corps (prisoner). *Address* – c/o Royal Institution, 21 Albemarle St, W1X 4BS. *Clubs* – Royal Overseas League, Victory Services, Devonshire (Eastbourne).

AUNT LIVING

Hon Nancy Adelaide, *b* 1906; *ed* Oxford Univ (BA 1928, MA 1955): *m* 1935, Arthur Gabriel Salaman, MB, BCh, MRCS, LRCP, and has issue living, John Redcliffe (25 Heol Don, Whitchurch, Cardiff), *b* 1937; *ed* Bedales, and at Clare Coll, Camb (MA) MB, MChir, FRCS: *m* 1961, Patricia Faith, da of Edward G. Burkett, and has issue living, Robert Arthur *b* 1965, Janet Susan *b* 1967, Mary Elizabeth *b* 1967, — William Herbert, *b* 1940; *ed* Bedales, and at Clare Coll, Camb (BA): *m* 1963, Alison Spears, da of Dr Philippe Sidney de Quetteville Cabot, and has issue living, Clare Rachel *b* 1966, Rachel Isabel *b* 1968, — Susan Caroline (23a High St, Littleport, Ely, Cambs CB6 1HE), *b* 1936: *m* 1960, Reginald Valentine Clery, — Juliet Miriam, *b* 1942: *m* 1961, Reuben Selek, and has issue living, Gull *b* 1963, Oren *b* 1965, Netta *b* 1971, Tal *b* 1979. *Residence* – 45 Havenfield, Cambridge.

PREDECESSORS – (1) *Sir* HERBERT LOUIS SAMUEL, GCB, OM, GBE, PC, son of late Edwin Louis Samuel, of Claremont, Prince's Park, Liverpool, and 9 Kensington Gore, SW, banker; *b* 1870; Under-Sec of State of Home Dept 1905-9, Chancellor of Duchy of Lancaster, 1909-10, Postmaster Gen 1910-14, Pres of Local Govt Board 1914-16, again Postmaster Gen 1915, again Chancellor of Duchy of Lancaster 1915-16, Sec of State for Home Dept 1916, British Special Commr to Belgium 1919, High Commr for Palestine 1920-25, again Sec of State for Home Dept 1931-2; MP for Cleveland Div, N Riding of Yorks (*L*) 1902-18, and for Darwen Div of Lancs 1929-35; Chm Liberal Party Organization 1917-29, Leader of Liberal Parliamentary Party 1931-35, and Dep Leader of Liberal Party in the House of Lords 1941-4, and Leader 1944-55; *cr Viscount Samuel*, of Mount Carmel and of Toxteth, City of Liverpool (peerage of UK) 1937: *m* 1897, Beatrice, who *d* 1959, yst da of late Ellis Abraham Franklin; *d* 1963; *s* by his el son (2) EDWIN HERBERT, CMG, 2nd Viscount; *b* 1898; Palestine Civil Ser 1920-48; Dir of Broadcasting, Palestine 1945-48, Prin of Inst of Public Admin in Israel 1945-78; Senior Lecturer in British Instns, Hebrew Univ, Jerusalem 1954-69; author of *A Lifetime in Jerusalem, A Cottage in Galilee*, and other short stories: *m* 1920, Hadassah, who *d* 1986, da of Judah Goor, of Tel Aviv; *d* 1978; *s* by his el son (3) DAVID HERBERT, 3rd Viscount and present peer.

SAMUEL OF WYCH CROSS, BARONY (Samuel) (Extinct 1987)

DAUGHTER LIVING OF LIFE BARON

Hon Carole, *b* 1942: *m* 1963, Geoffrey Clive Henry Lawson, and has issue.
Hon Marion, *b* 1944: *m* 1964, Guy Antony Naggar.

WIDOW LIVING OF LIFE BARON

EDNA (*Baroness Samuel of Wych Cross*), da of Harry Nedas, of London: *m* 1936, Baron Samuel of Wych Cross (Life Baron), who *d* 1987.

SANDERSON OF AYOT, BARONY OF (Sanderson) (Baron UK 1960, disclaimed 1971)

ALAN LINDSAY SANDERSON, *b* 12 Jan 1931; *s* as 2nd Baron 15 Aug 1971, disclaimed his peerage for life 28 Sept 1971; *ed* Uppingham; MB, BS London; MRCP London; MRC Psych: *m* 1959, Gertrud, da of Herman Bocshsler, and has issue.

Arms – Paly of six argent and azure on a bend sable a mullet of the first between two annulets or. **Crest** – A talbot passant argent pied and eared sable resting the dexter forepaw on an annulet or. **Supporters** – (borne by Barons Sanderson of Ayot). On either side a talbot sejant erect argent pied and eared sable.
Residence – 2 Caroline Close, W2.

SON LIVING

Hon MICHAEL, *b* 6 Dec 1959; *ed* St Paul's Sch, York Univ (BA), and The Wharton Sch, Pennsylvania (MBA).

DAUGHTERS LIVING

Hon Evelyn, *b* 1961.
Hon Frances, *b* 1963.
Hon Andrea, *b* 1964.
Hon Stephanie, *b* 1970.

BROTHER LIVING

Hon Murray Lee (twin) (PO Box 20516, Kitwe, Zambia), *b* 1931; *ed* Rugby, at Trin Coll, Oxford, and at King's Coll, Camb; a Co Dir; Admin Officer, Kenya, 1956-63: *m* 1st, 1966 (*m diss* 1972), Muriel, da of late George Williams; 2ndly, 1973, Eva, da of Rev David Simfukwe, and has issue living, (by 2nd *m*) Basil, *b* 1974, — Constance, *b* 1976.

SISTER LIVING

Hon Pauline Maud, *b* 1929; MA Oxford; Dr de l'Université de Paris: *m* 1952, Robert Henry Matarasso, who *d* 1982, and has issue living, Pascale, *b* 1955, — Antoine, *b* 1957, — François, *b* 1958, — Veronique, *b* 1964.

PREDECESSORS – **(1)** BASIL Sanderson, MC, son of Harold Arthur Sanderson, of Jenkyn Place, Bentley, Hants; *b* 1894; Dir of Shipping in Port, Min of Shipping 1939-41, Head of Port Transit Control, Min of War Transport 1941-45, and Man Dir of Shaw Sevill & Albion Co, Ltd 1945-59, and Chm 1947-63; *cr Baron Sanderson of Ayot*, of Welwyn, co Hertford (peerage of UK) 1960: *m* 1927, Evelyn Constance, who *d* 1940, da of Joseph Bruce Ismay, of Costelloe, co Galway, and London; *d* 1971; *s* by his el son **(2)** ALAN LINDSAY, 2nd Baron, until he disclaimed his peerage, 1971.

SANDERSON OF BOWDEN, BARON (Sanderson) (Life Baron 1985)

(CHARLES) RUSSELL SANDERSON, son of Charles Plummer Sanderson, by his wife, Martha Evelyn, da of Joseph Gardiner, of Glasgow; *b* 30 April 1933; *ed* Trin Coll, Glenalmond, Scottish Coll of Textiles, Galashiels, and Bradford Coll; commn'd R Signals 1952, served 51 (Highland) Inf Div Signal Regt (TA) 1953-56, KOSB (TA) 1956-58; DL Ettrick and Lauderdale 1989; Chm Central & Southern Area, Scottish Conservative Unionist Assocn, 1974-75, Vice-Pres 1975-77, Pres 1977-79; Vice-Chm Nat Union of Conservative Assocns 1979-81 (Member Exec Cttee since 1977), Chm Exec Cttee 1981-86; Gov St Mary's Sch, Melrose, 1977-87, and Scottish Coll of Textiles 1980-87, Member of Council Trin Coll, Glenalmond, since 1982; Ptnr Chas P. Sanderson, Wool and Yarn Merchants, Melrose, 1978-87; Chm Edinburgh Financial Trust (Yorkshire and Lancashire Trust, renamed 1984) 1983-87, Chm Shires Investment Trust 1984-87, Member Scottish Council Independent Schools 1984-87, Member Cttee Gvng Bodies Assocn 1984-87, Dir Clydesdale Bank 1985-87; Commr Gen Assembly Church of Scotland 1972; a Min of State, Scottish Office, 1987-90; Chm Scottish Conservative Party 1990-93; Chm Scottish Mortgage Trust since 1993; Dir United Auctions Ltd, Watson & Philip plc, Edinburgh Woollen Mills Ltd since 1993, and Woolcombers Ltd since 1991; *cr* Kt 1981, and *Baron Sanderson of Bowden*, of Melrose in the District of Ettrick and Lauderdale (Life Baron) 1985: *m* 1958, Frances Elizabeth, da of Donald Alfred Ramsden Macaulay, of Rylstone, Skipton, Yorks, and has had issue.

Arms – Per pale, dexter bendy sable and or, sinister azure, a chevron per pale azure and or, in dexter chief a ram's head affrontee argent horned gules, in sinister chief a fleur de lys issuant from a crescent argent. **Crest** – a cock or armed, crested and wattled sable supporting in the dexter claw a buckle of the first. **Supporters** – *Dexter* a Connemara pony proper; *Sinister* – a Cashmere goat proper. **Motto** – Persevere.
Residence – Becketts Field, Bowden, Melrose, Roxburgh TD6 OST

SONS LIVING AND DECEASED

Hon (Charles) David Russell, *b* 1960; *ed* Glenalmond, and Leeds Univ (BA): *m* 1990, Laura, yr da of H. G. Purdie, of Coatbridge, Lanarks. *Residence* – Deansyde, Denholm Hawick, Roxburghshire.
Hon Andrew Bruce Plummer, *b* 1968; *ed* Glenalmond; *d* 1991.

DAUGHTERS LIVING

Hon (Evelyn) Claire, *b* 1961; *ed* St Leonard's Sch, Newnham Coll, Camb (BA), and Edinburgh Univ; MRChB: *m* 1986, Thomas M. Walker, only son of K. P. Walker, of Glenairlie, Kilmalcolm.
Hon (Frances) Georgina, *b* 1963; *ed* St Leonard's Sch, and Queen Margaret's Coll, Edinburgh: *m* 1990, Peter James Holland Riley, son of Maj J. C. Riley, of Chislehurst, Kent.

SANDFORD, BARON (Edmondson) (Baron UK 1945)

Rev JOHN CYRIL EDMONDSON, DSC, 2nd Baron; *b* 22 Dec 1920; *s* 1959; *ed* Eton; Cdr RN (ret); 1939-45 War with Eastern Med Fleet, Allied Landings in N Africa, Sicily and Normandy (DSC); on Staff of C-in-C Far East 1951-53, and Cdr Home Fleet Flagship 1955-56; Curate of St Nicholas, Harpenden, 1958-63; Exec Chap to Bishop of St Albans 1965-68; Conservative Whip, House of Lords 1966-70; a Parl Sec, Min of Housing and Local Govt June to Oct 1970, and a Parl Under-Sec of State Dept of Environment 1970-73, and of Dept of Education and Science 1973-74, Chm of Herts Council of Social Ser 1966-69, and Chm of Church Army Board 1969-70; Pres of Council for Environmental Education 1975-84; Chm of Community Task Force 1977-82; Pres Assoc of District Councils 1980-86, since when a Vice-Pres; Church Commissioner 1981-88; Dir Ecclesiastical Insurance Office 1978-89; Chm Redundant Churches 1982-89; Founder Sandford Award for Heritage Educn, and Heritage Educn Trust; Chm Conference on SE Regional Planning 1981-88; Pres Anglo-Swiss Soc 1976-83; Vice-Pres of Youth Hostels Assocn 1977-89: *m* 1947, Catharine Mary, da of Rev Oswald Andrew Hunt, and has issue.

Arms – Azure, a cross couped and pointed between, in chief two lions combatant, and in base as many swans, wings elevated and addorsed respectant, all or. **Crest** – In front of a portcullis or a dexter arm embowed in armour fessewise, the hand clenched proper. **Supporters** – On either side a pikeman of Honourable Artillery Company armed and accoutred supporting with the exterior hand a pike erect proper, the dexter charged with a portcullis chained or, and the sinister with an oak tree eradicated and fructed also proper, the trunk pierced by three arrows or flighted azure (the badge of the Edmondson family).
Residence – 27 Ashley Gdns, Ambroseden Av, SW1P 1QD.

SONS LIVING

Hon JAMES JOHN MOWBRAY (1023 East 21st St, Vancouver, BC V5V IS6, Canada), *b* 1 July 1949; *ed* Eton, and York Univ; school counsellor: *m* 1st, 1973 (*m diss* 1986), Ellen Sarah, da of Jack Shapiro, of Toronto; 2ndly, 1986, Linda, da of Michael Wheeler, of Nova Scotia, and has issue living (by 1st *m*), Sarah Juliette, *b* 1977, — (by 2nd *m*) Devon John, *b* 1986.
Hon Nicholas Mark (237 Abbotsfield Rd, Pitsmoor, Sheffield), *b* 1956; *ed* Eton: *m* 1983, Joanna, da of Gordon Snee, of Willingham, Lincs, and has issue living, Rachel Alice, *b* 1986, — Amber May, *b* 1989.

DAUGHTERS LIVING

Hon Margaret Catharine, *b* 1947; *ed* Downe House Sch, Trin Coll, Dublin, and Bristol Univ; social worker: *m* 1977, (Charles Alan) Simon Holland, of Barncroft, Brightwell-cum-Sotwell, Wallingford, Oxon, and has issue living, Hereward Julian, *b* 1984, — Hannah Catharine, *b* 1979, — Venetia Frances, *b* 1981.
Hon Frances Mary, *b* 1953; *ed* Downe House Sch, and Bristol Univ; research scientist: *m* 1979, Geoffrey Wharton, of Vorgebirgstrasse 5, 50677 Köln, Germany, elder son of Robert Wharton, of Grand Forks, N Dakota, USA, and has issue living, Lionel Thomas, *b* 1982, — John Lorenz, *b* 1984.

BROTHER LIVING

Hon Anthony James Kinghorn (Stable Cottage, Barkers Hill, Semley, Shaftesbury, Dorset SP7 9BJ), *b* 1924; *ed* Eton, and Harvard Univ; Capt (ret) Gren Gds: *m* 1st, 1947 (*m diss* 1969), Olivia Charlotte, yst da of late Rev Oswald Andrew Hunt; 2ndly, 1969, Hilary Pauline, da of late Lt-Col Edward Shirley Trusler, OBE, and has had issue (by 1st *m*), Charles Anthony (Burhill, Buckland, nr Broadway, Worcs WR12 7LY), *b* 1949; *ed* Shrewsbury: *m* 1978 (*m diss* 1989), Isabella, da of Thomas Wright, of Glasgow, and has issue living, Andrew James *b* 1982, Sarah Isabella *b* 1979, Gemma Lavinia *b* 1981, and (by Rhian Cowles), Toby Benjamin *b* 1994, — Simon Andrew (Conde de Aranda, No 3 4th Floor, 28001 Madrid, Spain), *b* 1955; MA; MFA: *m* 1981 (*m diss* 1988), Louise Caroline Marion, da of Donald Alistair Blair, of 9 Roedean Terrace, Brighton; 2ndly, 1992, Maria Martin Hernandez-Cañizares, da of Cristobal Martin Garcia, of Madrid, — Anthony James (Somerford Lakes Reserve, Somerford Keynes, Cirencester, Glos), *b* 1957: *m* 1987 (*m diss* 19—), Olivia, 5th da of Dr Charles Dansie, of Welwyn, Herts, — Elizabeth Anne (14 Davies Drive, Bishops Cannings, Devizes, Wilts SN10 2RL), *b* 1951: *m* 1979 (*m diss* 19—), Nigel A. Urquhart, el son of Sir Andrew Urquhart, KCMG, MBE, — (by 2nd *m*) Rupert James Kinghorn, *b* 1972, *d* 1979.

PREDECESSOR – (1) *Sir* ALBERT JAMES Edmondson, son of late James Edmondson, of Weston, Herts; *b* 1886; Major Hon Artillery Co; Parliamentary Private Sec to Min of Pensions 1924-29 and 1931-34, an Assist Govt Whip 1937, a Junior Lord of the Treasury 1939, Vice-Chamberlain of HM's Household 1939, Treasurer of HM's Household 1942-5, Dep Ch Whip 1942-5, and High Steward of Banbury 1947; sat as MP for Banbury Div of Oxfordshire (*C*) 1922-45; *cr Baron Sandford*, of Banbury, co Oxford (peerage of United Kingdom) 1945: *m* 1911, Edith Elizabeth, who *d* 1946, da of George James Freeman; *d* 1959; *s* by his el son (2) *Rev* JOHN CYRIL, 2nd Baron and present peer.

SANDHURST, BARON (Mansfield) (Baron UK 1871)

(JOHN EDWARD) TERENCE MANSFIELD, DFC, 5th Baron; *b* 4 Sept 1920; *s* 1964; *ed* Harrow; 1939-45 War as Flight-Lt, RAFVR Bomber Command (DFC): *m* 1st, 1942 (*m diss* 1946), Priscilla Ann, who *d* 1970, da of late J. Fielder Johnson; 2ndly, 1947, Janet Mary, el da of late John Edward Lloyd, of Long Island, New York, USA, and has issue by 2nd *m*.

Arms – Argent, on a chevron embattled azure, between three maunches sable an Eastern crown or; on a chief enrailed of the third a lion of the fourth combatant with a tiger cowed proper. **Crest** – Out of an Eastern crown argent, a griffin's head sable beaked or, between two branches of laurel proper. **Supporters** – *Dexter*, A horse argent mane and tail sable, charged on the shoulder with a rose gules barbed and seeded proper, holding in the mouth a branch of laurel vert; *sinister*, a tiger cowed proper, gorged with a collar therefrom a chain reflexed over the back sable.
Residence – La Volière, Les Ruisseaux, St Brelade, Jersey, CI. *Clubs* – RAF, United (Jersey), MCC.

SON LIVING *(By 2nd marriage)*

Hon GUY RHYS JOHN (1 Crown Office Row, Temple, EC4Y 7HH; Leander Club, MCC; United (Jersey)), *b* 3 March 1949; *ed* Harrow, and Oriel Coll, Oxford (MA); Bar Middle Temple 1972, QC 1994, Recorder of the Crown Court since 1993: *m* 1976, Philippa St Clair, el da of late Digby Everard Verdon-Roe, of 5 Hameau de Bosquet, 41 Avenue Victoria, 06110 Le Cannet, France, and has issue living, Edward James, *b* 12 April 1982, — Alice Georgina, *b* 1980.

DAUGHTER LIVING *(By 2nd marriage)*

Hon Victoria Elizabeth, *b* 1957; *ed* Benenden, and Univ of Bordeaux: *m* 1978, (Charles) James Sharp Bentley, and has issue living, James William Nicholas, *b* 1982, — Sophie Katharine, *b* 1985. *Residence* – South Fen House, Fen End, Kenilworth, Warwicks CV8 1NQ.

SISTER LIVING

Hon Valerie (*Dowager Countess of Macclesfield*), *b* 1918: *m* 1938, 8th Earl of Macclesfield, who *d* 1992. *Residence* – Shirburn Castle, Watlington, Oxfordshire OX9 5DL.

WIDOW LIVING OF SON OF FOURTH BARON

Evelyn Cecil, yr da of late Sir Ronald Barry Keefe: *m* 1961, as his 2nd wife, Hon Ralph Geoffrey Knyvet Mansfield, 2nd son of 4th Baron, who *d* 1983, and has issue (see colls infra). *Residence* – 12 Grove Walk, Norwich NR1 2QF.

COLLATERAL BRANCH LIVING

Issue of late Hon Ralph Geoffrey Knyvet Mansfield, 2nd son of 4th Baron, *b* 1926, *d* 1983: *m* 1st, 1952 (*m diss* 1960), Hélène Gertrude, who *d* 1975, only da of late James Montague Coutts Duffus of Dalclaverhouse, of The Mansion House, Claverhouse, by Dundee; 2ndly, 1961, Evelyn Cecil (ante), yr da of late Sir Ronald Barry Keefe:—
(By 1st *m*) (Penelope) Sara Hélène, *b* 1953: *m* 1983, Dr C. Neale Muir, of Sheldon Park, Forrestdale, W Australia 6112. —— Trudé Charlotte Victoria, *b* 1955; MPS: *m* 1983, M. Timothy Borrett, of Beckwith Farm, Great Holland, Essex, and has issue living, Alexandra Victoria, *b* 1984, — Katherine Frances, *b* 1986. —— Tessa Emily Henrietta, *b* 1959: *m* 1981, Steven Williams, of Middleton Cheney, Banbury, Oxon. —— (By 2nd *m*) Morley Rafael Kate, *b* 1965: *m* 1988, Bernard Reignier, ingénieur, of Château Malard, Bordeaux, France, and has issue living, Sheldon, *b* 1992.

PREDECESSORS – (1) *Gen Rt Hon Sir* WILLIAM ROSE Mansfield, GCB, GCSI, PC, DCL, *b* 1819; Col 38th Foot; served in Sutlej Campaign 1845-6, commanded 53rd Regt in the Punjab 1848-9; employed in Peshawar operations 1851-2; appointed responsible military adviser to ambassador at Constantinople 1855, and accompanied Lord Stratford de Redcliffe to the Crimea; was Ch of Staff during Indian Mutiny Campaign 1857-9, Com-in-Ch in India 1865-70, and Com of Forces in Ireland 1870-5; *cr Baron Sandhurst*, of Sandhurst, co Berks (peerage of United Kingdom) 1871: *m* 1854, Margaret, da of Robert Fellowes, of Shotesham Park, Norfolk; *d* 1876; *s* by his son (2) WILLIAM, GCSI, GCIE, GCVO, PC, 2nd Baron, *b* 1855; a Lord-in-Waiting to HM Queen Victoria 1880-85, Under-Sec of State for War 1886 and 1892-5, and Gov of Bombay 1895-1900; appointed Lord Chamberlain of the Household 1912, a Member of Govt Committee for Employment of Disabled Soldiers and Sailors 1915, and again Lord Chamberlain of the Household 1916 and Jan 1919; Treasurer of St Bartholomew's Hospital 1908-21; *cr Viscount Sandhurst*, of Sandhurst, Berks (peerage of United Kingdom) 1917: *m* 1st, 1881, Lady Victoria Alexandrina Spencer, CI, who *d* 1906, da of 4th Earl Spencer; 2ndly, 1909, Eleanor Mary Caroline, OBE, who *d* 1934, da of late Matthew Arnold, and widow of Hon Armine Wodehouse, CB, MP; *d* 1921, when the Viscountcy became ext, and he was *s* in the Barony by his brother (3) JOHN WILLIAM, 3rd Baron, *b* 1857: *m* 1888, Edith Mary, who *d* 1939, da of late John Higson, JP, of Oakmere Hall, Hartford, Cheshire; *d* 1933; *s* by his son (4) RALPH SHELDON, OBE, 4th Baron, *b* 1892: *m* 1917, Victoria Morley, who *d* 1961, da of Edward Berners Upcher, formerly of Kirby Cane, Sheringham; *d* 1964; *s* by his el son (5) JOHN EDWARD TERENCE, 5th Baron and present peer.

Sandon, Viscount; son of Earl of Harrowby.

SANDWICH, EARLDOM OF (Montagu) (Earl E 1660, disclaimed 1964)

(ALEXANDER) VICTOR EDWARD PAULET MONTAGU, *b* 22 May 1906; *s* as 10th Earl 15 June 1962, disclaimed his peerages for life, 24 July 1964; *ed* Eton, and at Trin Coll, Camb (BA 1928, MA 1941); 1939-45 War with 5th (Hunts) Bn Northamptonshire Regt in France, and as Maj, Gen Staff, Home Forces; Private Sec to Rt Hon Stanley Baldwin, MP, 1932-34, Treasurer, Junior Imperial League 1934-35, Chm of Tory Reform Cttee, House of Commons 1943, MP for S Div of Dorset (*C*) 1941-62; Pres Anti-Common Market League 1962-84; Chm Conservative Trident Gp 1973: *m* 1st, 1934 (*m diss* 1958), (Maud) Rosemary, da of late Maj Ralph Harding Peto (*see* Peto, Bt, *cr* 1855, colls); 2ndly, 1962 (*m* annulled 1965), Lady Anne, MBE, who *d* 1981, yst da of 9th Duke of Devonshire, formerly wife of late Lt-Col Henry Philip Hunloke, and widow of Christopher John Holland-Martin, MP, and has issue by 1st *m*.

Arms – Quarterly: 1st and 4th argent three fusils, conjoined in fesse gules within a bordure sable, *Montagu*; 2nd and 3rd or, an eagle displayed vert, beaked and membered gules, *Monthermer*. **Crest** – A griffin's head couped at the neck or, wings elevated sable. **Supporters** – (borne by Earls of Sandwich)—*Dexter*, a triton proper, crowned with an Eastern crown or, and holding in his right hand a trident sable; *sinister*, an eagle with wings expanded vert, beaked and membered gules.
Residence – Mapperton, Beaminster, Dorset.

SONS LIVING (By 1st marriage)

JOHN EDWARD HOLLISTER (has not used courtesy title of Viscount Hinchingbrooke since 1970), *b* 11 April 1943; *ed* Eton, and at Trin Coll, Camb (MA): *m* 1968, (Susan) Caroline, da of Rev Canon Perceval Ecroyd Cobham Hayman, of 3 East St, Beaminster, Dorset, and has issue living, Luke Timothy Charles, *b* 1969, — Orlando William, *b* 1971, — Jemima Mary, *b* 1973.
Hon (George Charles) Robert (The Old Manor, Evershot, Dorset DT2 0JR), *b* 1949; *ed* Eton: *m* 1970, Donna Marzia, da of Conte Brigante Colonna, and has issue living, Oliver Drogo, *b* 1974, — Cosimo Ralph, *b* 1988, — Fiamma Fleur, *b* 1971, — Bona Frances, *b* 1972.

DAUGHTERS LIVING (By 1st marriage)

Sarah Jane Helen (does not use courtesy title) (Podere dell'Uccello, Via Montetermine 2, Polveretto, 50020 San Pancrazio, FI Italy), *b* 1935: *m* 1959 (*m diss* 1971), Alessandro Ballarin, and has issue living Caterina Teresa, *b* 1960, — Antonia Barbara, *b* 1964.
Elizabeth Anne (does not use courtesy title), *b* 1937: *m* 1961, Torquil Patrick Alexander Norman (*see* Norman, Bt, *cr* 1915).
Lady Katharine Victoria, *b* 1945: *m* 1965, Nicholas Victor Hunloke (*see* D Devonshire, 1980 Edn), of The Old Rectory, Poulshot, Devizes, Wilts and has issue living, Edward Perceval, *b* 1969, — Henrietta Yvery, *b* 1968, — Matilda Anne, *b* 1972.
Lady Julia Frances, *b* 1947: *m* 1st, 1972 (*m diss* 1976), Martin Lee Oakley; 2ndly, 1976, Peter Gerald Edward Body, of 31 Ouseley Rd, Wraysbury, Berks TW19 5JB, and has issue living (by 2nd *m*), Timothy, *b* 1982.

SISTER LIVING

Lady Elizabeth, *b* 1917. *Residence* – 11 York Mansions, Prince of Wales Drive, SW11.

COLLATERAL BRANCH LIVING

Issue of late Hon (William) Drogo Sturges Montagu, Flying Officer Auxiliary Air Force, 2nd son of 9th Earl, *b* 1908, *k* in an aeroplane accident on active ser 1940: *m* 1st, 1931 (*m diss* 1935), Tanis Eva Bulkeley, who *d* 1993, da of late Benjamin Seymour Guinness; 2ndly, 1935, Hon Janet Gladys (CAMPBELL) (who *d* 1988, having *m* 3rdly, 1942, Major Thomas Edward Dealtry Kidd, MBE, Roy Canadian Artillery), da of 1st Baron Beaverbrook:—
(By 1st *m*) John Dru (1 Netherton Grove, SW10), *b* 1932; is Lt RNR: *m* 1st, 1958, Sarah Maria (Sari), da of Manolo de Palacio, of Serrano 39, Madrid; 2ndly, 1977, Maria Elena (Minna), eldest da of late Richard Guy Buckmaster, and has issue living (by 1st *m*), Sophie, *b* 1959, — Bridget Doon, *b* 1961, — Claire Mary, *b* 1962, — Sarah Tanis, *b* 1965, — (by 2nd *m*), Paul Patrick Drogo, *b* 1979, — Kyra, *b* 1978. ——— (By 2nd *m*) William Drogo (Garland Cottage, Beard's Yard, Langport, Som), *b* 1936: *m* 1969, Edna Maud Ahlers, and has issue living, Nicola Lilian, *b* 1971, — Monette Edna, *b* 1973.

PREDECESSORS – (1) *Rt Hon Sir* EDWARD Montagu, KG, PC, son of late Sir Sidney Montagu, yst brother of 1st Earl of Manchester; *b* 1625; a distinguished Parliamentary Gen, and afterwards Lord High Adm of England, in which capacity he induced the whole fleet to support the Restoration of 1660; MP for Huntingdonshire 1644-7; *cr Baron Montagu*, of St Neots, Hunts, *Viscount Hinchingbrooke* and *Earl of Sandwich* (peerage of England) 1660: *m* 1642, Hon Jemima Crewe, who *d* 1674, da of 1st Baron Crewe; *ka* 1672 in the great sea-fight with the Dutch off Sole Bay; *s* by his son (2) EDWARD, 2nd Earl; *b* 1648; was Ambassador at Lisbon 1678: *m* 1668, Hon Mary Boyle, who *d* 1671, da of 2nd Earl of Cork; *d* 1689; *s* by his son (3) EDWARD, 3rd Earl; *b* 1670; was Lord-Lieut of co Huntingdon: *m* 1689, Hon Elizabeth Wilmot, who *d* 1757, da of 2nd Earl of Rochester; *d* 1729; *s* by his grandson (4) JOHN, 4th Earl; *b* 1718; was successively a Sec of State and First Lord of the Admiralty; sponsored the voyages of discovery made by Capt James Cooke, who named the Sandwich Islands in his honour; *d* 1792; *s* by his son (5) JOHN, 5th Earl; *b* 1744; *d* 1814; *s* by his son (6) GEORGE JOHN, 6th Earl; *b* 1773; *d* 1818; *s* by his son (7) JOHN WILLIAM, PC, 7th Earl; *b* 1811; was Master of the Buckhounds, 1858-9, and Lord-Lieut of Huntingdonshire: *m* 1st, 1838, Lady Mary Paget, who *d* 1859, da of 1st Marquess of Anglesey, KG; 2ndly, 1865, Lady Blanche Egerton, da of 1st Earl of Ellesmere; *d* 1884; *s* by his son (8) EDWARD GEORGE HENRY, KCVO, 8th Earl, *b* 1839; Lord-Lieut of Hunts 1891-1916; MP for Huntingdon (*C*) 1876-84; *d* 1916; *s* by his nephew (9) GEORGE CHARLES (son of late Rear-Adm Hon Victor Alexander Montagu, CB, 2nd son of 7th Earl), 9th Earl; *b* 1874; Assist Private Sec to Board of Agriculture 1898-1900; MP for S Div of

Hunts (C) 1900-6: *m* 1st, 1905, Alberta, who *d* 1951, da of late William Sturges, of New York; 2ndly, 1952, Ella Lillian (Amiya), who *d* 1986, da of late George Sully, of N Petherton, Somerset; *d* 1962; *s* by his elder son (**10**) ALEXANDER VICTOR EDWARD PAULET, 10th Earl, also Viscount Hinchingbrooke, and Baron Montagu, until he disclaimed his peerage 1964.

SANDYS, BARON (Hill) (Baron UK 1802)
(Title pronounced "Sands")

RICHARD MICHAEL OLIVER HILL, 7th Baron; *b* 21 July, 1931; *s* 1961; late Lieut R Scots Greys; a DL of Worcs; FRGS; patron of one living; a Lord-in-Waiting to HM Jan to March, 1974; Opposition Whip, House of Lords 1974-79; Dep Ch Whip and Capt Yeomen of the Guard 1979-83: *m* 1961, Patricia Simpson, da of late Capt Lionel Hall, MC, of Parkgate, Lower Beeding, Sussex.

Probum non pænitet

The honest man has not to repent

Arms – Quarterly: 1st and 4th or, a fesse dancettée, between three cross crosslets fitchée gules, *Sandys*; 2nd and 3rd sable, on a fesse argent, between three leopards passant guardant or, spotted of the field, as many escallops gules, *Hill*. **Crests** – 1st, a griffin segreant per fesse or and gules, *Sandys*; 2nd, a reindeer's head couped at the neck gules, attired and plain collared or, *Hill*. **Supporters** – Two griffins, with wings elevated per fesse, or and gules, each gorged with a collar dancettée, of the last.
Seat – Ombersley Court, Droitwich, Worcestershire. *Club* – Cavalry and Guards'.

SISTER LIVING

Hon Cynthia Meriel, *b* 1929: *m* 1954, Charles Talbot Rhys Wingfield (*see* V Powerscourt, colls). *Residence* – Barrington Park, Burford, Oxon.

PREDECESSORS – (**1**) MARY, wife of 2nd Marquess of Downshire, inherited the estates of her uncle, Edwin, 2nd and last Baron Sandys, *cr* 1743, and was *cr Baroness Sandys*, of Ombersley, co Worcester (peerage of United Kingdom) 1802, with remainder to her sons Arthur Moyses William, Arthur Marcus Cecil, Arthur Augustus Edwin, and George Augustus successively, and failing them to her el son Arthur Blundell; *d* 1836; *s* by her 2nd son (**2**) ARTHUR MOYSES WILLIAM, 2nd Baron; a Lieut-Gen in the Army; *d* unm 1860; *s* by his brother (**3**) ARTHUR MARCUS CECIL, PC, 3rd Baron; assumed in 1861 by Roy licence the surname of Sandys, in lieu of Hill: *m* 1837, Louisa, who *d* 1886, da of Joseph Blake; *d* 1863; *s* by his son (**4**) AUGUSTUS FREDERICK ARTHUR, 4th Baron, *b* 1840: *m* 1872, Augusta, who *d* 1903, da of Sir Charles Des Vœux, 2nd Bt; *d* 1904; *s* by his brother (**5**) MICHAEL EDWIN MARCUS, 5th Baron, *b* 1855: *m* 1886, Marjorie Clara Pentreath, who *d* 1929, da of late John Morgan, of Brighton; *d* 1948; *s* by his kinsman (**6**) ARTHUR FITZGERALD SANDYS HILL (son of late Arthur Blundell George Sandys Hill, el son of late Lord George Augustus Hill, MP, 5th son of Mary, Baroness Sandys), 6th Baron; *b* 1876; Lieut-Col RE: *m* 1924, Cynthia Mary, who *d* 1990, da of late Col Frederic Richard Thomas Trench-Gascoigne, DSO; *d* 1961; *s* by his son (**7**) RICHARD MICHAEL OLIVER, 7th Baron and present peer.

Savernake, Viscount; grandson of Marquess of Ailesbury.

SAVILE, BARON (Lumley-Savile) (Baron UK 1888)

GEORGE HALIFAX LUMLEY-SAVILE, 3rd Baron; *b* 24 Jan 1919; *s* 1931; *ed* Eton; a DL for W Yorks, a JP for Dewsbury and patron of two livings; CStJ; formerly Capt Duke of Wellington's Regt; Burma 1943-44 attached Lincolnshire Regt.

Arms – Argent, on a bend sable, three owls affrontée of the first, within a bordure wavy of the second. **Crest** – An owl affrontée argent, debruised by a bendlet sinister wavy sable. **Supporters** – Two talbots ermine, each gorged with a collar wavy sable, pendent therefrom an escutcheon or charged with a popinjay vert, collared gules.
Seat – Walshaw, Hebden Bridge, W Yorks. *Residence* – Gryce Hall, Shelley, via Huddersfield, W Yorks. *Club* – Brooks's.

BROTHER LIVING

Hon HENRY LEOLINE THORNHILL (*Clubs* - White's, Buck's, Guards'); *b* 2 Oct 1923; *ed* Eton; late Lieut Grenadier Guards; European War 1939-45 (wounded); *m* 1st, 1946 (*m diss* 1951), Presiley June, only da of Maj G. H. E. Inchbald, of 28/2 Porchester Gdns, W2; 2ndly, 1961. Caroline Jeffie, who *d* 1970, da of Peter Julian Clive, of Biarritz, France (*see* By Muir-Mackenzie, 1970 Edn); 3rdly, 1972, Margaret Ann, ARCM, da of Edward Matthew Phillips, of Vancouver, BC, and widow of Peter Alexander Bruce (*see* E Elgin, colls, 1970 Edn), and has issue living, (by 1st *m*) John Anthony Thornhill, *b* 1947, — (by 3rd *m*), James George Augustus, *b* 1975, — Peter Edward Henry (triplet), *b* 1975, — Robin William Matthew (triplet), *b* 1975.

SISTER LIVING

Hon Deirdre Barbara Elland, *b* 1928: *m* 1948, Col Kent Kane Parrot, US Air Force (ret), and has issue living, Jonathan Kent (483 Peregrine Drive, Indialantic, Florida 32903, USA), *b* 1950: *m* 1976, Theresa Marie Mell, — Richard Halifax (1210 West 27th St, No 8, Los Angeles, Calif 90007, USA), *b* 1952, — Barbara Elland, *b* 1959: *m* 1982, Howard R. Katz, of 5507 Grove St, Chevy Chase, Maryland 20815, USA. *Residence* – 5506 Grove St, Chevy Chase, Maryland 20815, USA.

PREDECESSORS – (1) JOHN Savile, GCB, PC, natural son of 8th Earl of Scarbrough, *b* 1818; Envoy Extraor and Min Plen to Saxony 1866-67, to Swiss Confederation 1867-68, and to Brussels 1868-83, and Ambassador Extraor and Min Plen to Italy 1883-88; assumed by Roy licence 1887 the surname of Savile in lieu of Lumley; *cr Baron Savile*, of Rufford, Notts (peerage of United Kingdom) 1888, with remainder, in default of male issue, to his nephew, John Savile Lumley, only son of late Rev Frederick Savile-Lumley; *d* 1896; *s* under the special remainder by his nephew (2) JOHN, KCVO, 2nd Baron, *b* 1853; served in Foreign Office and Diplo Ser; assumed by Roy licence 1898 the surname of Savile after that of Lumley, and the arms of Savile only: *m* 1st, 1894, Gertrude Violet, who *d* 1912, da of late Charles Francis Webster-Wedderburn, and widow of Horace Augustus Helyar, of Coker Court, Somersetshire; 2ndly, 1916, Esmé Grace Virginia, who *d* 1958, only da of late John Hyem Wolton, and formerly wife of Capt Claude Levita; *d* 1931; *s* by his el son (3) GEORGE HALIFAX, 3rd Baron and present peer.

SAYE and SELE, BARON (Fiennes) (Baron E 1447 and 1603)
(Name pronounced "Fines")

Ask for a brave spirit

NATHANIEL THOMAS ALLEN FIENNES, 21st Baron; *b* 22 Sept 1920; *s* 1968; *ed* Eton, and New Coll, Oxford; relinquished by deed poll 1965 the additional surnames of Twisleton and Wykeham; 1939-45 War in Rifle Bde (despatches twice); a DL Oxon 1979: *m* 1958, Mariette Helena, only da of late Maj-Gen Sir (Arthur) Guy Salisbury-Jones, GCVO, CMG, CBE, MC (*see* de Bunsen, Bt, ext), and has issue.

Arms – Quarterly: 1st and 4th azure, three lions rampant or, *Fiennes*; 2nd and 3rd argent, a chevron between three moles sable, *Twisleton*. **Crests** – 1st, a wolf sejant proper, gorged with a spiked collar, the line therefrom reflexed over the back or, *Fiennes*; 2nd, an arm embowed, vested sable, cuffed argent, holding in the hand proper a mole spade or, headed and armed of the second, *Twisleton*. **Supporters** – Two wolves argent, gorged and lined as the crest.
Seat – Broughton Castle, Banbury, Oxon.

SONS LIVING

Hon RICHARD INGEL, *b* 19 Aug 1959.
Hon Martin Guy, *b* 1961.
Hon William John, *b* 1970.

DAUGHTER LIVING

Hon Susannah Hersey (twin), *b* 1961.

BROTHER LIVING

Very Rev Hon Oliver William TWISLETON-WYKEHAM-FIENNES (Home Farm House, Colsterworth, Lincs), *b* 1926; *ed* Eton, and New Coll, Oxford (MA); late Lt Rifle Bde; Chap St J; Dean of Lincoln 1968-89, Dean Emeritus 1989: *m* 1956, Juliet, yr da of late Dr Trevor Heaton, of 3 St Martins Sq, Chichester, and has issue living, Adam Hugh, *b* 1961, — James William, *b* 1964, — Celia Ruth, *b* 1957: *m* 1979, James Long-Howell, only son of Lt-Col J. D. Howell, of Maenillar, Pembrey, Dyffd, and has issue living, George David Henry *b* 1992, Emily Myfanwy *b* 1987, Charlotte *b* 1990, — Laura Charlotte, *b* 1959: *m* 1988, Roger Hughes, yr son of late Gordon Hughes, of Chapeltown, Lancs, and has had issue, Charles Oliver *b* 1989, Robert Roger *b* and *d* 1992.

COLLATERAL BRANCHES LIVING

Grandchildren of late Hon Eustace Edward Twisleton-Wykeham-Fiennes (2nd son of 17th Baron), who was *cr* a *Baronet* 1916:—
See Twisleton-Wykeham-Fiennes, Bt.

Grandchildren of late Gerard Yorke Twisleton-Wykeham-Fiennes (infra):—
Issue of late Gerard Francis Gisborne Twisleton-Wykeham-Fiennes, OBE, *b* 1906, *d* 1985: *m* 1st, 1934, Norah, who *d* 1960, el da of Thomas Davies, of Llangollen; 2ndly, 1962, Jean (29 Wentworth Rd, Aldeburgh, Suffolk), formerly wife of — Kerridge, and da of late James Valentine, of Dovercourt:—
(By 1st *m*) Jeremy (36 Montpelier Grove NW5 2XE), *b* 1937; *ed* Winchester, and Clare Coll, Camb: *m* 1st, 1962 (*m diss* 19??), Else Brekke, da of Niels Larsen, of Knuthenborg Park, Bandholm, Denmark; 2ndly, 19??, —, and has issue living (by 1st *m*), Sine, *b* 1962, — Nicole Juana, *b* 1968. —— Michael Wynn (Burcott Manor, nr Wells, Som), *b* 1941; *ed* Winchester, New Coll, Oxford, and Harvard: *m* 1966, Rosalie Ruth, da of Stanley Sheppard, of Street, Som, and has issue living, Rupert Yorke, *b* 1969, — Hugo Barnabas, *b* 1971, — Joshua Gisborne, *b* 1974, — Ivo Martindale, *b* 1978. —— Gerard Ivor, *b* 1946; *ed* Winchester and Hertford Coll, Oxford: *m* 1973, Jane, da of Neil Digney, of Wimbledon, and has issue living, David Gerard *b* 1982, Clare Elizabeth *b* 1976. —— Joslin Mary, *b* 1939; *ed* Newnham Coll, Camb: *m* 1963, Pierre Michael Landell-Mills, of 2954 Macomb St, NW Washington, DC 20008, USA, and has issue living, Julius Paul, *b* 1965, — Nicholas Vladimir, *b* 1967, — Natalia Norah, *b* 1972. —— Bronwen Margaret, *b* 1944: *m* 1967, Oliver Addis, of 389 Bobbin Head Rd, N Turramurra, NSW 2074, Australia, and has issue living, Thomas Oliver, *b* 1970, — Helen Mary, *b* 1968, — Harriet Jane, *b* 1972, — Sarah *b* 1974.
Issue of late Richard Nathaniel Twisleton-Wykeham-Fiennes, MRCVS, *b* 1909, *d* 1988: *m* 1st, 1941 (*m diss* 1948), Mary Morwenna Daphne, da of late Rev James Rashleigh Hale, sometime V of Yalding, Maidstone; 2ndly, 1948, Alice Isobel, who *d* 1986, da of late William Cowie, of Singapore, and formerly wife of Robert Tremlett, of Mbale, Uganda:—
(By 2nd *m*) (Richard) George, *b* 1950; *ed* Winchester, and Coll of Estate Mgmnt (BSc), ARICS: *m* 1974, Julia Florence, da of Raymond Humphrey, of Winchester, and has issue living, Felix George, *b* 1978, — Eleanor Florence, *b* 1983, — Isobel Joanna, *b* 1986, — Arabella Julia, *b* 1988. —— Frances Elizabeth, *b* 1947; *ed* St Paul's Girls' Sch, and York Univ (BA); JP: *m* 1969, Col Michael Philip Kenneth Beatty, CBE, TD, DL (Staffs 1980), High Sheriff 1994-95, late Royal Mercian and Lancastrian Yeo, of Tixall Farmhouse, Tixall, Stafford ST18 0XT, and has issue living, Geraldine Alice Martindale, *b* 1971, — Rosanna Mary Gisborne, *b* 1973, — Katherine Margaret Barrett, *b* 1980, — Caroline Diana Charlotte, *b* 1986.

Grandchildren of late Rev Hon Wingfield Stratford Twisleton-Wykeham-Fiennes, 4th son of 16th Baron:—
Issue of late Gerard Yorke Twisleton-Wykeham-Fiennes, CBE, *b* 1864, *d* 1926: *m* 1905, Gwendolen, who *d* 1968, da of late Francis Gisborne of Holme Hall, Bakewell:—
Sir John Saye Wingfield, KCB, QC, *b* 1911; *ed* Winchester, and Balliol Coll, Oxford (BA); Bar Middle Temple 1936; Bencher 1969; QC 1972; First Parl Counsel 1968-72; CB (Civil) 1953; KCB (Civil) 1970: *m* 1937, Sylvia Beatrice, who *d* 1979, da of late Rev Charles Robert Loraine McDowall (Burdett, Bt, *cr* 1665), and has issue living, Nicholas John (21 Chalfont Rd, Oxford OX2 6TL), *b* 1940; *ed* Winchester, and Merton Coll, Oxford: *m* 1st, 1969 (*m diss* 1990), Vicki Karen, da of W. Alan Thomas, of Stourbridge, Worcs; 2ndly, 1993, Angela Helen, only da of late Rev Geoffrey Walker Ellison, of Withington, Glos, and has issue living (by 1st *m*), Alexander William *b* 1971, John Edward *b* 1973, Katherine Margaret *b* 1974, — William Gerard (April Cottage, Main Street, Clanfield, Oxon OX18 2QH), *b* 1946; *ed* Winchester, New Coll, Oxford, and Imperial Coll, London: *m* 1976, Rosalind Dalzel, da of William Dalzel Pritchard, of Alderton, Glos, and has issue living, Timothy Gerard *b* 1985, Lucy Anne *b* 1981, — Judith Mary (5 Parliament Court, Parliament Hill, NW3 2TS), *b* 1938. *Residence* – Mill House, Preston, Sudbury, Suffolk CO10 9ND. —— †Michael Yorke, *b* 1912; *ed* Winchester, and New Coll, Oxford; 1939-45 War as Capt RA: *m* 1940, Jacqueline (Woodcote, Oaks Rd, Tenterden, Kent), da of Rev Edward Montmorency Guilford, and *d* 1989, leaving issue, Toby Jonathan (20 Kitsbury Rd, Berkhamstead, Herts HP4 3EG), *b* 1961: *m* 1989, Hilary Linda, elder da of D. T. McGladdery, of Newton Abbot, Devon, — Peter Guilford, *b* 1963: *m* 1993, Anna, only da of Martin Graham, of Highgate, N6.
Issue of late Alberic Arthur Twisleton-Wykeham-Fiennes, *b* 1865, *d* 1919: *m* 1895, Gertrude Theodosia, who *d* 1934, da of late Henry Fitz-George Colley (V Harberton, colls):—
Sir Maurice Alberic, *b* 1907; *ed* Repton; CEng, MIMechE; Knt 1965: *m* 1st, 1932 (*m diss* 1964), Sylvia, da of Maj David Finlay, late 7th Dragoon Gds; 2ndly, 1967, Erika Hueller, da of Dr Herbert Hueller von Huellenried, of Vienna, and has issue living, (by 1st *m*) Mark (29 Therapia Rd, SE22 0SF), *b* 1933; *ed* Eton: *m* 1962, Jennifer Anne Mary Alleyne, who *d* 1993, da of late Brig Henry Alleyne Lash, Indian Army, of Bridge End, Churt, Surrey, and has issue living, Ralph Nathaniel *b* 1962; actor (as Ralph Fiennes): *m* 1993, Alexandra Elizabeth, da of Anthony Charles Edward Kingston, of Betchworth, Surrey, Magnus Hubert *b* 1965, Jacob Mark *b* 1970, Joseph Alberic (twin) *b* 1970, Martha Maria *b* 1964, Sophia Victoria *b* 1967, — Alberic George (5 Narborough St, SW6), *b* 1947; *ed* Lyceum Alpinum, Zuoz; MS, FRCS: *m* 1985, Louise Emily Jane, eldest da of Gordon Bidlake, of Dorking, Surrey, and has issue living, Emily Elizabeth *b* 1989, Alice Henrietta *b* 1991, — Elizabeth (c/o National Westminster Bank, 27 Horseferry Rd, SW1P 2AZ) *b* 1935: *m* 1965, Lt-Col Richard James Heslop Randall, MA (Oxon), who *d* 1984, and has issue living, William Basil *b* 1966, Michael Matthew Shaun *b* 1968, Roland Patrick James *b* 1970, — Antonia Susan Maria (c/o Barclay's Bank, 1 Pall Mall East, SW1), *b* 1939: *m* 1970 (*m diss* 1989), John Houlton Ewing Mocatta, and has issue living, Antonia Irena Maria *b* 1971, Marie-Gabrielle *b* 1974, — Henrietta Celia, *b* 1943: *m* 1987, Stephen René Molivadas, DFC, of 4701 Willard Av, Suite 703, Chevy Chase, Maryland 20815, USA, son of late Constantine Molivadas, of Corfu, Greece. *Residence* – 11 Heath Rise, Kersfield Rd, SW15 3HF. —— Audrey Gertrude, *b* 1899. —— Celia Mary, *b* 1902: *m* 1932, Noel Rooke, who *d* 1953. *Residence* – The Green, Culworth, Banbury, Oxon.

Grandsons (by 2nd *m*) of late Maj Cecil Wingfield Twisleton-Wykeham-Fiennes (infra):—
Issue of late Anthony Patrick Twisleton-Wykeham-Fiennes, *b* 1927, *d* 1989: *m* 1966, Prudence Jane (Manor Farm, Duddington, Stamford, Lincs), da of late George Woodward Pearce:—
Nicholas Mark, *b* 1969. —— Nathaniel Woodward, *b* 1973.

Grandchildren of late Caryl Wentworth Twisleton-Wykeham-Fiennes, 3rd son of Rev Hon Wingfield Stratford Twisleton-Wykeham-Fiennes (ante):-
Issue of late Maj Cecil Wingfield Twisleton-Wykeham-Fiennes, RMLI, *b* 1897, *d* 1972: *m* 1st, 1920, Margaret Annie, who *d* 1921, da of Philip Robinson, of Egginton, Derby; 2ndly, 1923 (*m diss* 1936), Jessie Mary Goddard, who *d* 1993, da of Nicholas Goddard Jackson, of Duddington, Northants; 3rdly, 1940, Elizabeth Stockton, who *d* 1961, da of George Perry Fiske, of New York:—
(By 2nd *m*) (Kathleen) Patricia, *b* 1925: *m* 1958, Richard Graham Shedden, MC, of Bowers Barn, Blandford Forum, Dorset, and has issue living, Simon Rory Lindesay, *b* 1963, — Emma Lavinia, *b* 1959.

Granddaughter of late Rev Hon Wingfield Stratford Twisleton-Wykeham-Fiennes (ante):—
Issue of late Lt-Col John Temple Twisleton-Wykeham-Fiennes, *b* 1877; *d* 1970: *m* 1929, Constance Astbury; who *d* 1939, da of late David Ross, of Holywood, co Down:—

Bridget Susan Winifred, *b* 1935: *m* 1956, Melvin Marriott, and has issue living, Crispin John Fiennes, *b* 1966, — Josephine Susan, *b* 1957, — Esmeralda Jane, *b* 1959, — Prudence Ann, *b* 1964, — Samantha Sara, *b* 1968.

PREDECESSORS – (1) *Sir* JAMES Fiennes, Constable of Dover, Warden of the Cinque Ports and Lord Treasurer of England; summoned to Parliament 1446-7-9, and said to have been *cr Lord Saye and Sele* by patent 1447; was imprisoned in the Tower as a partisan of the Duke of Suffolk, and in 1450 was beheaded by Jack Cade's mob at the Standard in Cheapside; *s* by his son (2) WILLIAM, 2nd Lord; was Constable of Porchester and Pevensey Castles, and Vice-Adm of England; summoned to Parliament 1451-69; killed at the Battle of Barnet 1471; *s* by his son (3) HENRY, 3rd Lord; bore the title of Lord Saye but was not summoned to Parliament; *d* 1476; *s* by his son (4) RICHARD, *de jure* 4th Lord; was not summoned to Parliament; *s* by his son (5) EDWARD, *de jure* 5th Lord; did not assume the title; *s* by his son (6) RICHARD, *de jure* 6th Lord, who did not assume the title; *d* 1573; *s* by his son (7) RICHARD, KB; obtained confirmatory recognition of his claim to the Barony, and in 1603 was *cr* by letters patent *Baron Saye and Sele* (peerage of England), with remainder to his heirs-gen with precedence of that date; *d* 1613; *s* by his son (8) WILLIAM, 8th Baron; was a Commr of the Public Safety, and a distinguished leader in the contest between the Parliament and Charles I, and at his residence at Broughton the secret discussions of resistance to the Court took place; *cr Viscount Saye and Sele* (peerage of England) 1624; *d* 1662; *s* by his el son (9) JAMES, 2nd Viscount; *d* 1674 without surviving male issue, when the barony became abeyant between his das, Elizabeth, wife of John Twisleton, and Frances, wife of Andrew Ellis, and the viscountcy devolved upon his nephew (10) WILLIAM, 3rd Viscount, son of Col Hon Nathaniel Fiennes, Speaker of Cromwell's Upper House, who was 2nd son of the 8th Baron; *d* 1696; *s* by his son (11) NATHANIEL, 4th Viscount; *d* unm 1710; *s* by his cousin (12) LAWRENCE, 5th Viscount (son of Col Hon John, one of Cromwell's Lords, who was 3rd son of 8th Baron); *dsp* 1742; *s* by his cousin (13) RICHARD, 6th Viscount (son of Rev Richard Fiennes); *d* 1781, when the viscountcy expired, and the abeyance of the barony of Saye and Sele, which owing to the death of one of the two co-heirs had belonged de jure since 1715 to (14) CECIL, *de jure* Baroness Saye and Sele (da of John Twisleton, of Barley Hall, ante), then to her son (15) FIENNES, *de jure* 11th Baron Saye and Sele, and subsequently to his son (16) JOHN, *de jure* 12th Baron Saye and Sele was terminated in favour of the latter's son (17) THOMAS Twisleton, 13th Baron, great-great-grandson of Elizabeth, da of 2nd Viscount (ante); Gen in the Army and Col 9th Foot; *d* 1788; *s* by his son (18) GREGORY WILLIAM, 14th Baron; assumed in 1825 the additional surnames of Fiennes and Eardley; *d* 1844; *s* by his son (19) WILLIAM THOMAS, 15th Baron; *d* unm 1847; *s* by his cousin (20) FREDERICK, DCL, 16th Baron, 3rd son of the Ven Hon Thomas James Twisleton, DD, by Anne, da and co-heir of Benjamin Ashe; *b* 1799; assumed by Roy licence 1849 the additional surnames of Wykeham-Fiennes: *m* 1st, 1827, Hon Emily Wingfield, who *d* 1837, da of the 4th Viscount Power-scourt; 2ndly, 1857, Hon Caroline Leigh, da of the 1st Baron Leigh; *d* 1887; *s* by his el son (21) JOHN FIENNES, 17th Baron, *b* 1830: *m* 1856, Lady Augusta Sophia Hay, who *d* 1915, da of 10th Earl of Kinnoull; *d* 1907; *s* by his el son (22) GEOFFREY CECIL, 18th Baron; *b* 1858; was Comptroller of HM's Household 1912-15: *m* 1884, Marion Ruperta Murray, who *d* 1946, da of late Major Robert Bartholomew Lawes, of Old Park, Dover; *d* 1937; *s* by his el son (23) GEOFFREY RUPERT CECIL, 19th Baron; *b* 1884; Bar Inner Temple 1911; *d* 1949; *s* by his brother (24) IVO MURRAY, OBE, MC, 20th Baron; *b* 1885; Lt-Col RA; High Steward of Banbury 1959-68: *m* 1919, Hersey Cecilia Hester, who *d* 1968, da of late Capt Sir Thomas Dacres Butler, KCVO (E Minto, colls); *d* 1968; *s* by his el son (25) NATHANIEL THOMAS ALLEN, 21st Baron and present peer.

SCANLON, BARON (Scanlon) (Life Baron 1978)

HUGH PARR SCANLON, son of Hugh Scanlon; *b* 26 Oct 1913; *ed* Stretford Elem Sch and Nat Council of Labour Colls; Hon DCL Univ of Kent at Canterbury 1988; Pres Amalgamated Engineering Union 1967-78; Chm Engineering Industry Training Board since 1975; Member British Gas Corpn since 1977; *cr Baron Scalon*, of Davyhulme, co Greater Manchester (Life Baron) 1978: *m* 1943, Nora, da of James Markey, and has issue living, two das.
Residence – 23 Seven Stones Dr, Broadstairs, Kent.

SCARBROUGH, EARL OF (Lumley) (Earl E 1690)

RICHARD ALDRED LUMLEY, 12th Earl; *b* 5 Dec 1932; *s* 1969; *ed* Eton, and Magdalen Coll, Oxford; late Lt Queen's Own Yorks Dragoons, and 2nd Lt 11th Hussars; Hon Col 1st Bn Yorkshire Vols since 1975; Pres Northern Area, R British Legion since 1984; DL S Yorks 1974: *m* 1970, Lady Elizabeth Ramsay, da of 16th Earl of Dalhousie, and has issue.

Arms – Argent, a fesse gules, between three popinjays vert, collared of the second. **Crest** – A pelican in her piety, proper. **Supporters** – Two parrots, wings expanded, vert beaked and membered gules.
Residence – Sandbeck Park, Maltby, Rotherham, S Yorks. *Clubs* – White's, Pratt's, Jockey.

A sound conscience is a wall of brass

SONS LIVING

RICHARD OSBERT (*Viscount Lumley*), *b* 18 May 1973.
Hon Thomas Henry, *b* 1980.

DAUGHTER LIVING

Lady Rose Frederica Lily, *b* 1981.

SISTERS LIVING

Lady Mary Constance, OBE, *b* 1923; a DStJ; OBE (Civil) 1974: *m* 1952, Col Roger Fleetwood Hesketh, OBE, TD, DL, who *d* 1987, and has had issue, Robert Fleetwood, *b* 1956; *ed* Eton: *m* 1990, Hon Catherine Ingrid Guinness, eldest da of 3rd Baron Moyne, and formerly wife of James Donald, Lord Neidpath, and has issue living, a son *b* 1992, Anna *b* 1991, Violet *b* (twin) 1991, — Laura, *b* 1953: *m* 1981, Anthony Blond, publisher, of 42 New Concordia Wharf, Mill St, SE1, and has an adopted son, Ajith Charminda, *b* 1981, — Sarah Frances, *b* 1954: *m* 1980, Patrick Anthony Ewen Bellville, and *d* 1984. *Residence* – Meols Hall, Southport, Lancs.

Lady Elizabeth (*Baroness Grimthorpe*), CVO, *b* 1925; appointed a Lady of the Bedchamber of HM Queen Elizabeth, The Queen Mother 1973; CVO 1983: *m* 1954, 4th Baron Grimthorpe. *Residence* – Westow Hall, York.

Lady Anne Katharine (*Viscountess Ridley*), *b* 1928: *m* 1953, 4th Viscount Ridley, KG. *Residence* – Blagdon, Seaton Burn, Northumberland.

Lady (Jane Lily) Serena, *b* 1935: *m* 1963, Hugh Wiley of Oak Hill, Palmyra, Virginia, USA, and has issue living, Justin Hugh, *b* 1964, — Marcus Thomas, *b* 1966, — Peter Alexander, *b* 1971.

DAUGHTER LIVING OF TENTH EARL

Lady Serena Mary Barbara, *b* 1901; is a DStJ, and a JP for Richmond: *m* 1923, Hon Robert James, who *d* 1960 (*see* B Northbourne, colls). *Residence* – St Nicholas, Richmond, Yorkshire.

PREDECESSORS – **(1)** *Sir* RICHARD Lumley, Knt, garrisoned Lumley Castle on behalf of the Royal cause, and was a principal commander under Prince Rupert; *cr Viscount Lumley* (peerage of Ireland) 1628; *s* by his grandson **(2)** RICHARD, PC, 2nd Viscount; commanded a regt of Horse at Battle of Sedgemoor 1685; was a Gentleman of the Bedchamber to Prince of Orange, Lieut-Gen of Forces in Flanders, Lord-Lieut of Durham and Northumberland, and Chancellor of the Duchy of Lancaster, etc; *cr Baron Lumley*, of Lumley Castle, co Durham (peerage of England) 1681, and *Viscount Lumley* and *Earl of Scarbrough* (peerage of England) 1690; *d* 1721; *s* by his son **(3)** RICHARD, KG, 2nd Earl; *d* unm 1740; *s* by his brother **(4)** THOMAS, KB, 3rd Earl; assumed the surname of Saunderson by Roy licence 1723; *d* 1752; *s* by his son **(5)** RICHARD, PC, 4th Earl; was Cofferer of the Household, Dep Earl Marshal of England, and Joint Vice-Treasurer of Ireland; *d* 1782; *s* by his el son **(6)** GEORGE AUGUSTUS, 5th Earl; *d* unm 1807; *s* by his brother **(7)** RICHARD, 6th Earl; sat as MP for Lincoln city; *d* 1832; *s* by his brother **(8)** JOHN, 7th Earl; assumed the surname of Savile by Act of Parliament; was Preb of York and Rector of Winteringham; *d* 1835; *s* by his son **(9)** JOHN, 8th Earl; assumed by Roy licence 1836 the additional and principal surname of Savile; was Lord-Lieut of Nottinghamshire; *d* unm 1856; *s* by his cousin **(10)** RICHARD Lumley, 9th Earl, son of Frederick Lumley-Savile (5th son of 4th Earl); *b* 1813: *m* 1846, Frederica Mary Adeliza, who *d* 1907, da of late Andrew Robert Drummond; *d* 1884; *s* by his son **(11)** ALDRED FREDERICK GEORGE BERESFORD, KG, GBE, KCB, TD, 10th Earl, *b* 1857; late Hon Col (sometime Comdg) Yorkshire Dragoons (Yeo), and Bailiff Grand Cross of Order of St John of Jerusalem (Sub-Prior thereof 1923-43); Lord-Lieut of W Riding of Yorkshire 1892-1904; S Africa 1900 with Imperial Yeo; Director-Gen of Territorial and Vol Forces 1917-21 with rank of Maj-Gen: *m* 1899, Lucy Cecilia, who *d* 1931, el da of Cecil Dunn Gardner, and widow of Robert Ashton; *d* 1945; *s* by his nephew **(11)** (LAWRENCE) ROGER, KG, GCSI, GCIE, GCVO, Royal Victorian Chain, TD, PC (son of late Brig-Gen Hon Osbert Victor George Atheling Lumley, CMG, 3rd son of 9th Earl), 11th Earl, *b* 1896; World War I 1915-18 with 11th Hus; MP for E Hull 1922-29 and for York 1931-37; Gov of Bombay 1937-43; Lord Lieut W Riding 1948-69; Lord Chamberlain 1952-63; Grand Master of United Grand Lodge of English Freemasons 1951-67, and Pro Grand Master 1967-69; a Permanent Lord-in-Waiting to HM 1963-69; Chancellor of Durham Univ; High Steward of York Minster: *m* 1922, Katharine Isabel, DCVO, who *d* 1979, da of late Robert Finnie McEwen, of Bardrochat, Ayrshire, and Marchmont, Berwickshire (B Napier of Magdala); *d* 1969; *s* by his only son **(12)** RICHARD ALDRED, 12th Earl and present peer; also Viscount and Baron Lumley.

SCARMAN, BARON (Scarman) (Life Baron 1977)

LESLIE GEORGE SCARMAN, OBE, PC, son of late George Charles Scarman; *b* 29 July, 1911; *ed* Radley, and Brasenose Coll, Oxford (MA, Hon Fellow 1966); Hon LLD Exeter, Glasgow, London, Keele, Freiburg, Warwick and Bristol; Bar Middle Temple 1936; QC 1957; Bencher 1961; a Judge of High Court of Justice (Probate, Divorce and Admiralty Div, now Family Div) 1961-72; Chm Law Commn 1965-72; Lord Justice of Appeal 1972-77, since when a Lord of Appeal in Ordinary; Chancellor, Warwick Univ since 1978; author of *Pattern of Law Reform*, 1967, and *English Law — The New Dimension*, 1975; 1939-45 War as Wing Cdr RAFVR (OBE); *cr* OBE (Mil) 1945, Knt 1961, PC 1972, and *Baron Scarman*, of Quatt, co Salop (Life Baron) 1977: *m* 1947, Ruth Clement, da of late Clement Wright, ICS.

Address – c/o House of Lords, SW1.

ADOPTED SON LIVING

John Clement, *b* 1946.

SCARSDALE, VISCOUNT (Curzon) (Baron GB 1761. Viscount UK 1911, Bt (S) 1636 and (E) 1641)

Justly and mildly

FRANCIS JOHN NATHANIEL CURZON, 3rd Viscount, 7th Baron, and 11th Baronet; *b* 28 July 1924; *s* 1977; *ed* Eton; late Capt Scots Gds; 30th Lord of Kedleston, and patron of three livings (but being a Roman Catholic cannot present): *m* 1st, 1948 (*m diss* 1967), Solange Yvonne Palmyre Ghislaine, who *d* 1974, da of late Oscar Hanse, of Mont-sur-Marchienne, Belgium; 2ndly, 1968, Mrs Helene Gladys Frances Lubbock, only da of late Maj William Ferguson Thomson, of Kinellar, Aberdeenshire, and has issue by 1st and 2nd *m*.

𝖆rms – Argent, on a bend sable, three popinjays or, collared gules. 𝕮rest – A popinjay rising, wings displayed and inverted or, collared gules. 𝕾upporters – Two female figures, the *dexter*, representing Prudence, habited argent, mantled azure, holding in her sinister hand a javelin, entwined by a remora proper; the *sinister* representing Liberality, habited argent mantled purpure, and holding in both hands a cornucopia proper. 𝕸ottoes – Let Curzon holde what Curzon helde; Recte et suaviter.
Seat – Kedleston, Derby. *Residence* – 53 Rutland Gate, SW7. *Club* – County (Derby).

SONS LIVING (*By 1st marriage*)

Hon PETER GHISLAIN NATHANIEL (Battle Barn Farm, Sedlescombe, Sussex), *b* 6 March 1949; *ed* Ampleforth: *m* 1983, Mrs Karen Osborne, and has issue living, Danielle Solange, *b* 1983.
Hon David James Nathaniel (33 Lingfield Rd, SW19), *b* 1958; *ed* Stowe: *m* 1981, Ruth, da of late John Ernest Linton, of Wavertree, Liverpool, and has issue living, Andrew Linton Nathaniel, *b* 1986, — Emma Rachel, *b* 1983.

(*By 2nd marriage*)

Hon Richard Francis Nathaniel, *b* 1969; *ed* Shiplake, and RAC Cirencester.
Hon James Fergus Nathaniel, *b* 1970; *ed* Eton, and Edinburgh Univ (MA).

DAUGHTER LIVING (*By 1st marriage*)

Hon Annette Yvonne, *b* 1953: *m* 1979, Capt Hani Talaat Latief, of 7 Dr Ismaeel Ghanem St, Nozha Geddida, Heliopolis, Cairo, and has issue living, Sagi, *b* 1982.

SISTER LIVING (*Raised to the rank of a Viscount's daughter*, 1980)

Hon Christian Avril (The House of the Pines, Virginia Ave, Virginia Water, Surrey), *b* 1923.

DAUGHTERS LIVING OF SECOND VISCOUNT

Hon Anne Mildred (Hill Farm, Garsdale, Sedbergh, Cumbria), *b* 1923; 1942-44 War in ATS: *m* 1942 (*m diss* 1960), Maj Walter James Latimer Willson, DSO, Gren Gds, who *d* 1994, son of Sir Walter Stuart James Willson, and has issue living, Simon James Curzon (104 Kensington Church St, W8), *b* 1942: *m* 1st, 1968, Sarah, el da of Douglas Ferris Hewat Jaboor, MB, of La Maison De la Fontaine, Mont Perrine, St Lawrence, Jersey (*see* Aykroyd, Bt, *cr* 1920, 1985 Edn); 2ndly, 1979, Sandra, da of Harold Singer, of Tillsonburg, Canada, and has issue living, (by 1st *m*), Alexander James Alfred Curzon *b* 1969, Benjamin William Curzon *b* 1971, — Jacqueline Anne Curzon, *b* 1945: *m* 1967, Anthony Julian Bavin.
Hon Juliana Eveline (Castledown, Portroe, Nenagh, co Tipperary), *b* 1928: *m* 1st, 1948 (*m diss* 1952), George Derek Stanley Smith, who *d* 1963; 2ndly, 1953 (*m diss* 1956), Frederick Nettlefold; 3rdly, 1956 (*m diss* 1962), as his 2nd wife, Sir Dudley Herbert Cunliffe-Owen, 2nd Bt; 4thly, 1962 (*m diss* 1972), as his 2nd wife, John Roberts (*see* Roberts, Bt, colls, *cr* 1909), and has issue living, (by 1st *m*) Charles Peregrine, *b* 1952; *ed* Eton, — Venetia Mary, *b* 1950, — (by 2nd *m*) Caroline Anne (*Viscountess Windsor*), *b* 1954: *m* 1979, Ivor Edward Other, Viscount Windsor, el son of 3rd Earl of Plymouth, — (by 3rd *m*) (*see* Cunliffe-Owen, Bt), — (by 4th *m*) (*see* Roberts, Bt, colls, *cr* 1909).
Hon Diana Geraldine, *b* 1934.

DAUGHTER LIVING OF FIRST VISCOUNT SCARSDALE AND FIRST MARQUESS CURZON OF KEDLESTON

See B Ravensdale.

WIDOW LIVING OF SECOND VISCOUNT

OTTILIE MARGARETE JULIE (*Ottilie, Viscountess Scarsdale*) (The Dower House, Rowler Manor, Croughton, Brackley, Northants), da of late Charles Pretzlik, of Lowfield Park, Crawley, Sussex, and formerly wife of James Harris; formerly Ensign FANY: *m* 1946, as his 2nd wife, the 2nd Viscount, who *d* 1977.

COLLATERAL BRANCH LIVING

(*In remainder to Baronetcies only*)

Descendants of Assheton Curzon (2nd son of 4th baronet), who was *cr Viscount Curzon* 1802 (*see* E Howe).

PREDECESSORS – From the muniments at Kedleston this family can trace descent from Robert de Courson, Seigneur of Courson, nr Lisieux, Normandy, who was granted Fishead, Oxon, W Lockinge, Berks, etc by William I. His grandson, Richard de Courson, was granted Knights' fees of Croxall, Kedleston, Edinghall and Twyford, cos Derby and Stafford. Richard's 2nd son Stephen (who *m* Elfrica, da of Olav King of Man) held Fauld, Staffs. The senior line terminated in Mary, da and heir of Sir George Curzon of Croxall, who *m* c 1612, Edward Sackville, 4th Earl of Dorset, KC, the second line being Curzon of Kedleston, and the third, Curzon of Waterperry (Bts ext 1750); **(1)** JOHN Curzon (*cr* a *Baronet* of Scotland 1636 and of England 1641), el son of John Curzon of Kedleston, MP for Derbys; *d* 1686; *s* by his son **(2)** *Sir* NATHANIEL, 2nd Bt;

d 1718; *s* by his el son **(3)** *Sir* JOHN, 3rd Bt; sat as MP for Derbyshire 1702-27; *d* unmarried 1727; *s* by his brother **(4)** *Sir* NATHANIEL, 4th Bt; sat as MP for Derbyshire 1727-58; his 2nd son was *cr* Viscount Curzon (*see* E Howe); *d* 1758; *s* by his el son **(5)** *Sir* NATHANIEL, 5th Bt; *cr Baron Scarsdale*, of Scarsdale, co Derby (peerage of Great Britain) 1761; was Chm of Cttees in House of Lords 1775-90; *d* 1804; *s* by his son **(6)** NATHANIEL, 2nd Baron; *d* 1837; *s* by his el son **(7)** NATHANIEL, 3rd Baron; *d* unmarried 1856; *s* by his nephew **(8)** *Rev* ALFRED NATHANIEL HOLDEN, 4th Baron (2nd son of the Rev Hon Alfred Curzon, 2nd son of 2nd Baron), *b* 1831; R of Kedleston: *m* 1856, Blanche, who *d* 1875, da of Joseph Pocklington Senhouse, of Netherhall, Cumberland; *d* 1916; *s* by his el son **(9)** GEORGE NATHANIEL, KG, GCSI, GCIE, PC, FRS, 5th Baron, 1st Earl and 1st Marquess Curzon of Kedleston; *b* 1859; Under-Sec of State for India Nov 1891 to Aug 1892, Under-Sec of State for Foreign Affairs 1895-98, Viceroy and Gov-Gen of India 1898-1904, and again 1904-5, Lord Warden of the Cinque Ports and Constable of Dover Castle 1904-5, Lord Privy Seal 1915-16, Pres of first Air Board May to Dec 1916 (also became a Member of Cabinet War Council July 1916), Lord Pres of the Council and Leader of the House of Lords (with a seat in the War Cabinet) Dec 1916 to Nov 1919, and Sec of State for Foreign Affairs Nov 1919 to Jan 1924 (also Leader of the House of Lords), and again Lord Pres of the Council and Leader of the House of Lords Nov 1924 to March 1925; sat as MP for SW Lancashire, Southport Div (*C*) 1886-98; bore Standard of Empire of India at Coronation of King George V 1911; *cr Baron Curzon of Kedleston*, co Derby (peerage of Ireland) 1898, *Baron Ravensdale*, of Ravensdale, co Derby, with special remainder in default of issue male to his el da and the heirs of her body, failing whom to his other das in like manner in order of primogeniture, *Viscount Scarsdale*, of Scarsdale, co Derby, with special remainder in default of issue male, to his father (the 4th Baron Scarsdale, whom he succeeded in the Barony) and the heirs male of his body, and *Earl Curzon of Kedleston*, co Derby (all in peerage of UK) 1911; KG 1916; *cr Earl of Kedleston*, co Derby and *Marquess Curzon of Kedleston* (peerage of UK) 1921; *s* as 5th Baron Scarsdale and as 9th Baronet (both of Scotland and England) 1916; received Roy Victorian Chain 1903: *m* 1st, 1895, Mary Victoria, CI, who *d* 1906 (had Kaisar-i-Hind gold medal), el da of Levi Zeigler Leiter, of Dupont Circle, Washington, USA; 2ndly, 1917, *Dame* Grace Elvina Trilla, GBE, who *d* 1958, da of J. Monroe Hinds, of Alabama, USA, widow of Alfred Duggan, (M Curzon of Kedleston (ext)); *d* 1925, when the Irish Barony of 1898, the Earldom of 1911, and the Marquessate and Earldom of 1921 became ext, and the Barony of Ravensdale devolved by special remainder upon his el da Mary Irene, and the Barony (*cr* 1761) and Viscountcy of Scarsdale, together with the two Baronetcies, passed to his nephew **(10)** RICHARD NATHANIEL (son of late Col Hon Alfred Nathaniel Curzon, 2nd son of 4th Baron Scarsdale and in special remainder to the Viscountcy), 2nd Viscount; *b* 1898, 1914-18 War with R Scots Greys; 1939-45 War as Maj RA in Middle East; sometime Hon Attaché Diplo Ser, and Vice-Pres British Boxing Board of Control: *m* 1st, 1923 (*m diss* 1946), Mildred Carson, who *d* 1969, da of William Roland Dunbar, of Huyton, Lancs; 2ndly, 1946, Ottilie Margarete Julie, da of late Charles Pretzlik, of 155 Sloane St, SW1, and formerly wife of James Harris; *d* 1977; *s* by his first cousin **(11)** FRANCIS JOHN NATHANIEL (son of late Hon Francis Nathaniel Curzon, 3rd son of 4th Baron), 3rd Viscount and present peer; also Baron Scarsdale.

SCHON, BARON (Schon) (Life Baron 1976)

FRANK SCHON, son of late Dr Frederick Schon, of Vienna; *b* 18 May 1912; *ed* Rainer Gymnasium, Vienna, and Vienna and Prague Univs; Hon DCL Durham; Co-founder Marchon Products Ltd 1939; Solway Chemicals 1943 (Chm and Man Dir of both Cos until 1967); Dir Albright & Wilson Ltd 1956-67; a Member of Council, King's Coll, Durham Univ 1959-63, and Newcastle upon Tyne Univ 1963-66; a Member of Court, Newcastle upon Tyne Univ 1963-78; Chm Cumberland Development Council 1964-68, a Member of Northern Economic Planning Council 1965-68, and of Industrial Reorganisation Corpn 1966-71; a Dir of Blue Circle Industries plc 1967-82; a Member of Board of Nat Research Development Corpn 1967-79 (Chm 1969-79); Hon Freeman of Whitehaven; *cr* Knt 1966, and *Baron Schon*, of Whitehaven, co Cumbria (Life Baron) 1976: *m* 1936, Gertrude, who *d* 1993, da of late Abraham Secher, and has issue.

Arms – Per chevron chequly vert and or and lozengy of the same overall a comet in bend argent, on a bordure also or six annulets sable. **Crest** – In front of two factory chimneys smoking proper on three mounts conjoined proper a griffin segrant argent. **Supporters** – *Dexter*, a Plant Chemist wearing a white coat and protective eye shield and gloves, holding in dexter hand, a beaker and in sinister a flask; *Sinister*, a Process Worker habited in overalls and wearing a protective helmet and holding a sinister hand a work sheet all proper.
Residence – Flat 82, Prince Albert Court, 33 Prince Albert Rd, NW8 7LU.

DAUGHTERS LIVING

Hon Susan Henriette, *b* 1941: *m* 1964, Richard Henry Keller, of Hillmorton, Wills Grove, Mill Hill Village, NW7.
Hon Yvonne Catherine, *b* 1944: *m* 1979, Norman Saville, of 21 Hillview Rd, Mill Hill Village, NW7.

Scrymgeour, Lord; son of Earl of Dundee.

SEAFIELD, EARL OF (Ogilvie-Grant) (Earl S 1701)

IAN DEREK FRANCIS OGILVIE-GRANT, 13th Earl; *b* 20 Mar 1939; *s* 1969; *ed* Eton; recognised in the surname of Ogilvie-Grant by warrant of Lord Lyon 1971: *m* 1st, 1960 (*m diss* 1971), Mary Dawn Mackenzie, el da of Henry Illingworth, of 35 Gloucester Sq, W2; 2ndly, 1971, Leila, da of Mahmoud Refaat, of Cairo, and has issue by 1st *m*.

Arms – Quarterly; 1st and 4th grand quarters, quarterly, 1st and 4th, argent, a lion passant guardant gules, crowned with an imperial crown or, and 2nd and 3rd, argent, a cross engrailed sable, *Ogilvie*; 2nd and 3rd grand quarters, gules, three antique crowns or, *Grant*. **Crests** – *Dexter*, a lady richly attired from the waist upwards proper wearing a pointed fifteenth century head-dress argent, *Ogilvie*; *sinister*, a burning hill between two Scots Pine saplings proper, *Grant*. **Supporters** – *Dexter*, a lion rampant guardant or, armed gules: *sinister*, a savage or naked man bearing upon his shoulder a club proper and wreathed about the head and middle with a laurel vert.
Seat – Old Cullen, Cullen, Banffshire.

SONS LIVING (By 1st marriage)

Hon JAMES ANDREW (*Viscount Reidhaven and Master of Seafield*), *b* 30 Nov 1963; *ed* Harrow.
Hon Alexander Derek Henry, *b* 1966; *ed* Eton.

SISTER LIVING

Lady Pauline Anne, *b* 1944: *m* 1st, 1964 (*m diss* 1970), James Henry Harcourt Illingworth; 2ndly, 1972 (*m diss* 1976), Sir William Gordon Gordon-Cumming, 6th Bt; 3rdly, 1976, Hugh Richard Sykes; 4thly, 1989, David John Nicholson, of Revack Lodge, Grantown-on-Spey, Morayshire, and has issue living (by 3rd *m*), Harry Peter Derek, *b* 1977.

COLLATERAL BRANCHES LIVING *In remainder to the Earldom, the Barony of Strathspey, and the Baronetcy (cr 1625)*

Descendants of late Trevor Ogilvie Grant (2nd son of 10th Earl), who *s* as 4th Baron Strathspey 1915 (see that title).

Grandchildren of late William Robert Ogilvie-Grant, son of late Capt Hon George Henry Essex Ogilvie-Grant, 6th son of 6th Earl:—
　　Issue of late Eleanora Ogilvie-Grant, *b* 1892, *d* 1956: *m* 1st, 1913 (*m diss* 1926), Lt-Com Reginald William Blake, RN (ret), who *d* 1927; 2ndly, 1926, Lt-Com Sir Roger Thomas Twysden, 10th Bt, who *d* 1934:—
(By 1st *m*) Pamela Rosemary, *b* 1916: *m* 1937, Col Leslie Brindley Bream Beuttler, OBE, Duke of Wellington's Regt, who *d* 1978, and has had issue, †Michael Simon Brindley Bream, *b* 1940; *d* 1988, — Nicholas Randolph Kerr (Château de la Môle, La Môle 83129, France), *b* 1943: *m* 1979, Martine Andriveau, — Caroline Jane (*Hon Mrs Alan Clark*), *b* 1942: *m* 1958, Rt Hon Alan Kenneth McKenzie Clark, of Saltwood Castle, Hythe, Kent (see B Clark, ext), and has issue living, James Alasdair Kenneth *b* 1960: *m* 1st, 1985 (*m diss* 1988), Sarah Marian, yst da of A. Dawes, of Wexham Place, Fulmer, Bucks; 2ndly, 1988, Sally Ruth, da of late Peter Smith, of Codsall, Staffs, Andrew McKenzie *b* 1962: *m* 1993, Sarah G., da of Nigel Harris, of Muscat, Sultanate of Oman. *Residence* – Finca Villordo, Benalmádena-Pueblo, Malaga, Spain. ——— Lavinia Elizabeth, *b* 1921: *m* 1954, Lt-Col Charles Edward Morton, TD, City of London Yeo (TA) (Durrant, Bt), who *d* 1988, of Printstile, Bidborough, Tunbridge Wells, and has issue living, Roger Thomas, *b* 1957, — Louise Jean, *b* 1955.
　　Issue of late Marjorie Elspeth Ogilvie-Grant, *b* 1894, *d* 1967: *m* 1921, Capt Ronald Fitzhardinge Speir, formerly RE (B Gifford):—
(John Hugh) Anthony SPEIR (PO Box 1, Paardekraal 1752, S Africa), *b* 1925: Capt S African Inf Corps: *m* 1st 1946 (*m diss* 1952), Isobel, da of James Snart, of Leicester; 2ndly, 1974, Joan Margaret, da of A. Valentine, of Krugersdorp, S Africa, and has issue living (by 1st *m*), Helen Joanna, *b* 1948: *m* 1969, David George Thomson, of 35 Edgewood Rd, Chatham, NJ 07928, USA, and has issue living, Iain James Speir *b* 1973, Caroline Louise Speir *b* 1976, — Fiona Margaret, *b* 1951: *m* 1973, Michael John Haughey, of 11 Blenheim Rd, Bedford Park, W4 1VB, and has issue living, Barnaby Michael Fitzhardinge Speir *b* 1975, Tobias John Thomas Speir *b* 1983, Michael Gabriel Bartholomew Speir *b* 1986, Rachel Mary Speir *b* 1974, Bethany Joy Speir *b* 1978, Tamara Jane Speir *b* 1979. ——— Elizabeth Jean (Flat 5, 13 Upper Phillimore Gdns, W8 7HF), *b* 1922. ——— Diana Marigold (1 North St, St Andrews, Fife), *b* 1932.
　　Issue of late Alison Jean Ogilvie-Grant, *b* 1896, *d* 1970: *m* 1923, Capt Reginald Cornwallis Hargreaves, MVO, MC, formerly Rifle Bde, who *d* 1974:—
Basil John Alexander HARGREAVES (c/o National Westminster Bank, 19 High St, Heathfield, E Sussex), *b* 1925: *m* 1st, 1960 (*m diss* 1972), Anne Mary Beatrice Stacey; 2ndly, 1980, Mrs Barbara Ann Baker (*née* Court), and has issue living (by 1st *m*), Charles John Cornwallis, *b* 1966. ——— Alison June (Swallowfield, Enton Green, Godalming, Surrey), *b* 1928: *m* 1978, Ronald Burns.

PREDECESSORS – (1) *Sir* WALTER Ogilvie, Knt, was *cr* Lord Ogilvie of Deskford (peerage of Scotland) 1616; *s* by his son (2) JAMES, 2nd Lord; *cr* Earl of Findlater (peerage of Scotland) 1638, and obtained in 1641 a new patent with remainder to his daughter Elizabeth and her husband Sir Patrick Ogilvy, who at his death became (3) PATRICK and ELIZABETH, Earl and Countess of Findlater; *s* by his son (4) JAMES, 3rd Earl, *d* 1711; *s* by his son (5) JAMES, 4th Earl, who had in 1698 been *cr* Lord Ogilvy of Cullen and Viscount Seafield (peerage of Scotland), with remainder, failing heirs male of the body, to heirs of entail, and in 1701 Lord Ogilvy of Deskford, and Cullen, Viscount Reidhaven, and Earl of Seafield (peerage of Scotland), with the same special remainder; was an eminent lawyer, and held successively the offices of Solicitor Gen and Sec of State for Scotland, Lord Chief Baron of the Exchequer, High Commr to the Gen Assembly of the Church, Keeper of the Great Seal in Scotland, and Pres of the Court of Session; *d* 1730; *s* by his son (6) JAMES, 5th Earl of Findlater and 2nd Earl of Seafield; *d* 1764; *s* by his son (7) JAMES, 6th Earl of Findlater and 3rd Earl of Seafield; *d* 1770; *s* by his son (8) JAMES, 7th Earl of Findlater and 4th Earl of Seafield; *d* 1811, when the Earldom of Findlater expired, and the peerages of 1698 and 1701 reverted to his heir-general (9) *Sir* LEWIS ALEXANDER Grant of Grant, 9th Bt, who became 5th Earl of Seafield; assumed 1811 the additional surname of Ogilvie; MP for Elginshire 1790-96; *d* unmarried 1840; *s* by his brother (10) FRANCIS WILLIAM, 6th Earl of Seafield; MP for various Scottish constituencies 1802-40; was Lord-Lt of co Inverness, and a Representative Peer; *d* 1853; *s* by his son (11) JOHN CHARLES, KT, 7th Earl, *b* 1815; having been a Representative Peer, was *cr* Baron Strathspey, of Strathspey, cos Inverness and Moray (peerage of UK) 1858: *m* 1850, Hon Caroline Henrietta Stuart, who *d* 1911 (having succeeded in 1884 to the Grant and Seafield estates, and having devised them in trust for the 11th Earl and his successors in the title), da of 11th Lord Blantyre; *d* 1881; *s* by his son (12) IAN CHARLES, 8th Earl, *b* 1851; *dsp* 1884, when the Barony of Strathspey became ext *s* in Scottish peerages of 1698 and 1701 by his kinsman (13) JAMES, 9th Earl, 4th son of 6th Earl, by Mary Anne, da of John Charles Dunn, of St Helena and Higham House; *b* 1817; sat as MP for Elgin and Nairnshire (C) 1868-74; *cr* Baron Strathspey (peerage of UK) 1884: *m* 1st, 1841, Caroline Louisa, who *d* 1850, da of late Eyre

Evans, of Ash Hill Towers, Limerick; 2ndly, 1853, Constance Helena, who *d* 1872, da of Sir Robert Abercromby, 5th Bt; 3rdly, 1875, Georgiana Adelaide, da of late Gen Frederick Nathaniel Walker, KCH, of Manor House, Bushey, and widow of William Stuart, of Aldenham Abbey, Herts; *d* 1888; *s* by his el son **(14)** FRANCIS WILLIAM, 10th Earl, *b* 1847: *m* 1874, Ann (Nina) Trevor Corry, who *d* 1935, da of late Maj George Thomas Evans, of Ash Hill Towers, co Limerick, and Clooneavin, Otago, NZ; *d* 1888; *s* by his el son **(15)** JAMES, 11th Earl, *b* 1876; 30th Chief of the Clan Grant; Capt Queen's Own Cameron Highlanders: *m* 1898, Mary Elizabeth Nina, who *d* 1962, da of late Joseph Henry Townend, MD, JP, of Christchurch, NZ; *ka* 1915, when the Barony of Strathspey and the Baronetcy devolved upon his brother, but in the Scottish Peerages he was *s* by his only child **(16)** NINA CAROLINE, Countess of Seafield, *b* 1906: *m* 1930 (*m diss* 1957), Derek Studley-Herbert (who *d* 1960, having assumed by deed poll 1939, the additional surnames of Ogilvie-Grant), F/O RAFVR, and late Gren Gds; *d* 1969; *s* by her only son **(17)** IAN DEREK FRANCIS, 13th Earl, and present peer; also Viscount Seafield, Viscount Reidhaven, Lord Ogilvie of Cullen, and Lord Ogilvie of Deskford and Cullen.

Seaford, Baron; see Baron Howard de Walden and Seaford.

SECCOMBE, BARONESS (Seccombe) (Life Baroness 1991)

JOAN ANNA DALZIEL SECCOMBE, DBE, da of late Robert John Owen, of Solihull, W Midlands; *b* 3 May 1930; *ed* St Martin's Sch, Solihull; JP Solihull 1968, Chm of Bench 1981-84, Chm Lord Chancellor's Advisory Cttee Solihull 1978-93, CC W Midlands 1977-81; Chm Trading Standards Cttee 1979-81, Midlands Electrical Consultative Council 1981-90, Conservative Women's Nat Cttee 1981-84, and Nat Union of Conservative and Unionists Assocn 1987-88 (Vice-Chm 1984-87), Vice-Chm Conservative Party since 1987; Member W Midlands Police Cttee 1977-81, and 1985-91; Gov Nuffield Hosps since 1988, Chm of Trustees Nuffield Hosps Pension Fund; *cr* DBE 1984, and *Baroness Seccombe*, of Kineton, co Warwicks (Life Baroness) 1991: *m* 1950, Henry Lawrence Seccombe, and has issue.

Arms – Per pale gules and vert, a chevron ermine between three bugle horns argent, stringed or, on a chief per pale vert and gules three roses argent barbed or, on each another rose gules barbed and seeded proper.
Residence – Trethias, Norton Grange, Little Kineton, Warwicks CV35 0DP.

SONS LIVING

Hon Philip Stanley, *b* 1951; *ed* Rugby, and RAC Cirencester: *m* 1977, Isabel Elizabeth Urquhart, and has issue living, Charles Stanley, *b* 1981, — Olivia Elizabeth, *b* 1984.
Hon Robert Murray, *b* 1954; *ed* Stowe, and Brasenose Coll, Oxford.

SEEAR, BARONESS (Seear) (Life Baroness 1971)

BEATRICE NANCY SEEAR, PC, da of late Herbert Charles Seear, of Croydon; *b* 7 Aug 1913; *ed* Croydon High Sch, Newnham Coll, Camb, and LSE; Pres of Liberal Party Organisation 1965-66; Reader in Personnel Management, LSE 1946-78; Leader of the Liberal Party, House of Lords 1984-88, since when Dep Leader Social Liberal Democrats, House of Lords; *cr Baroness Seear*, of Paddington, City of Westminster (Life Baroness) 1971.
Residence – 189B Kennington Rd, SE11 6ST. *Club* – Royal Commonwealth Society.

SEEBOHM, BARONY OF (Seebohm) (Extinct 1990)

SONS LIVING OF LIFE BARON

Hon Richard Hugh, *b* 1933; *ed* Winchester, Magdalene Coll, Camb (MA 1964), and Magdalen Coll, Oxford (DPhil 1964); late 2nd Lieut RA; Tube Investments Ltd 1960, HM Treasury 1968, Department of Trade and Industry 1982; a Reference Sec Monopolies and Mergers Commn 1990-93: *m* 1966, Margaret Evelyne, da of late Cdr Edward Rolf Frederick Hok, OBE, RN, of Long Crendon, Aylesbury, Bucks, and has issue living, Henrietta Lucy, *b* 1967, — Sophia Kate, *b* 1968, — Charlotte Emily, *b* 1970, — Laura Frances Harriet, *b* 1973. *Residence* – Stable Cottage, Flatford Lane, E. Bergholt, Colchester, Essex C07 6UN.

DAUGHTERS LIVING OF LIFE BARON

Hon Victoria, *b* 1937; author and journalist (as Victoria Glendinning): *m* 1st, 1958 (*m diss* 1981), Prof Oliver Nigel Valentine Glendinning; 2ndly, 1982, Terence de Vere White, who *d* 1994, and has issue living (by 1st *m*), Paul Alexander, *b* 1959, — Hugo Frederic, *b* 1961, — Matthew Nigel, *b* 1962, — Simon Benjamin, *b* 1964. *Address* – c/o David Higham Assocs, 5-8 Lower John St, W1R 4HA.
Hon Caroline, *b* 1940; writer: *m* 1st, 1962 (*m diss* 1967), Roger John Smith; 2ndly, 1974 (*m diss* 1993), Walter H. Lippincott, and has issue living (by 2nd *m*), Hugh, *b* 1983, — Sophie, *b* 1979. *Residence* – 19 River Drive, Titusville, NJ 08560, USA.

SEFTON OF GARSTON, BARON (Sefton) (Life Baron 1978)

WILLIAM HENRY SEFTON, son of George Sefton; *b* 5 Aug 1915; *ed* Duncombe Rd Sch, Liverpool; Liverpool Co Council 1953 (Leader 1964-78); Chm and Leader, Merseyside Co Council 1974-77, since when a Member, Dep Chm Runcorn Development Corpn 1967-74, since when Chm; a Member of NW Economic Planning Corpn since 1975; *cr Baron Sefton of Garston*, of Garston, co Merseyside (Life Baron) 1978: *m* 1940, Phyllis, da of — Kerr.
Residence – 88 Tramway Rd, Liverpool L17 7AZ.

SEGAL, BARONY OF (Segal) (Extinct 1985)

DAUGHTERS LIVING OF LIFE BARON

Hon Maureen, *b* 1935: *m* 1956, Jeremy Hadfield, who *d* 1988, of 19 Christchurch Hill, NW3, and has issue.
Hon Valery, *b* 1943: *m* 1967, Paul Nicholas David Pelham, of Manor Farm House, Manningford Bohun, nr Pewsey, Wilts, and has issue.

SELBORNE, EARL OF (Palmer) (Earl UK 1882)

JOHN ROUNDELL PALMER, KBE, 4th Earl; *b* 24 March 1940; *s* 1971; *ed* Eton, and Ch Ch, Oxford (MA); DL Hants 1982; FIBiol, FRAgS, Hon LLD Bristol 1989; FRS; Vice Chm of The Apple and Pear Development Council 1971-73; Treas of Bridewell Royal Hosp (King Edward's Sch, Witley) 1972-83, and Chm Hops Marketing Board 1978-82; Chm Agricultural and Food Research Council 1983-89; Pres South of England Agric Soc 1984, and Royal Agric Soc of England 1988; Chm Joint Nature Conservation Cttee since 1991; Memb Royal Commn on Environmental Pollution since 1993; Chm House of Lords Select Cttee on Science and Technology since 1993; *cr* KBE (Civil) 1987: *m* 1969, Joanna Van Antwerp, yr da of Evan James, of Upwood Park, Abingdon, Oxon, and has issue.

The palm is for virtue

Arms – Argent, two bars sable, charged with three trefoils slipped of the field; in chief a greyhound courant of the second, collared or. **Crest** – A mount vert, thereon a greyhound sejant sable, collared or, charged on the shoulder with a trefoil slipped argent. **Supporters** – On either side a greyhound sable, collared or, and charged on the shoulder with a trefoil slipped argent.
Residence – Temple Manor, Selborne, Alton, Hants. *Clubs* – Brooks's, Farmers'.

SONS LIVING

WILLIAM LEWIS (*Viscount Wolmer*), *b* 1 Sept 1971; *ed* Eton, and Ch Ch Oxford.
Hon George Horsley, *b* 1974; *ed* Eton.
Hon Luke James (twin), *b* 1974; *ed* Eton.

DAUGHTER LIVING

Lady Emily Sophia, *b* 1978.

BROTHER LIVING

Hon Henry William (Burhunt Farm, Selborne, Alton, Hants), *b* 1941; *ed* Eton, and Ch Ch, Oxford (MA); Dir The Centre for Interfirm Comparison since 1985; FBIM: *m* 1968, Minette, el da of late Sir Patrick William Donner, of Hurstbourne Park, Whitchurch, Hants, and has issue living, Benjamin Matthew, *b* 1970, — Robert Henry, *b* 1972, — Charles William, *b* 1978, — Laura Cecilia, *b* 1976.

SISTER LIVING (*raised to the rank of an Earl's daughter* 1985)

Lady Katherine Elizabeth, *b* 1938: *m* 1958, Hon David Laurence Robert Nall-Cain, of Ballacleator, St Judes, Isle of Man (*see* B Brocket).

AUNTS LIVING (*Daughters of 3rd Earl*)

Lady Anne Beatrice Mary, *b* 1911; *ed* Somerville Coll, Oxford (BA 1934): *m* 1935, Rev John Salusbury Brewis, who *d* 1972 (Duckworth-King, Bt, colls), and has issue living, Thomas William (West Garth, Bailes Lane, Normandy, Guildford, Surrey GU3 2AX) *b* 1937; *ed* Eton: *m* 1983, Susan Alison Virginia, da of late Lt-Col J. A. Mackay, — Robert Salusbury (Benham's Farm, Benham's Lane, Blackmoor, Liss, Hants), *b* 1939; *ed* Eton: *m* 1965, Irena, el da of late Wiktor Grubert, and has issue living, Paul William Salusbury *b* 1966, Edward George *b* 1969, Eleanor Anne *b* 1975, — Mary Elizabeth Maud, *b* 1947: *m* 1970, David Allison Osborne Tweedie, Solicitor (1 Bedford Row, WC1), of 23 Kilmaine Rd, SW6, eldest son of late Dr Reid Tweedie, of Sungei Siput, Perak, Malaysia, and has issue living, Jeannie Anne Cecilia *b* 1973; *ed* Exeter Univ, Katherine Grace *b* 1975; *ed* St Andrews Univ, — Susan Amy, *b* 1949; *ed* King's Coll, London: *m* 1975, Edward Crispin Akers Martineau, of Moorland, Box End Rd, Bromham, Bedford. *Residence* – Benham's House, Benham's Lane, Blackmoor, Liss, Hants.
Lady Laura Mary, *b* 1915; Lambeth Diploma in Theology 1944; was Chaplain's Assist to ATS 1944-6; Sec to Women's Land Army (Hampshire) 1940-42: *m* 1948, Rt Rev Cyril Eastaugh, MC, 34th Bishop of Peterborough 1961-72, who *d* 1988, and has issue living, Andrew Nathaniel (South Cove House, Wrentham, nr Beccles, Suffolk NR34 7JD), *b* 1954; MB BS, MRCS Eng,

LRCP Lond 1978, MRCP (UK), MRCGP: *m* 19—, Alice M., yr da of Cyril Hopkins, of Glutières, Switzerland, and has issue living, Rose Frances *b* 1983, Charlotte Laura *b* 1985, Sophia Mary *b* 1988, — Laura Jane Catherine, *b* 1949: *m* 1st, 1972, William McDonell Eddis; 2ndly, 1981, Giichi Inoue, of Apt 111, 4-3-16 Nakarokugo, Ota-Ku, Tokyo 144, Japan, and has issue living (by 1st *m*), Nathalie *b* 1973, (by 2nd *m*) Marina *b* 1984, — Elisabeth Mary, *b* 1951: *m* 1976, Rev Canon Mark Bryant, of 35 Wood Lane, Shilton, Coventry CV7 9LA, and has issue living, Simon Mark *b* 1978, Christopher Nathaniel *b* 1984, Helen Elisabeth *b* 1981. *Residence* – 9 Blackmoor House, Blackmoor, Liss, Hants 9U33 6DA.

Lady Mary Sophia, *b* 1920: Lady-in-Waiting to HRH Princess Elizabeth 1944-7, and Extra Lady-in-Waiting 1947-9: *m* 1st, 1944, Maj Hon (Thomas) Anthony Edward Towneley Strachey, who *d* 1955, only son of 3rd Baron O'Hagan; 2ndly, 1981, as his 2nd wife, (Francis) St John Gore, CBE (*see* Gore, Bt, colls), and has issue (by 1st *m*) (*see* B O'Hagan). *Residence* – Grove Farm, Stoke-by-Nayland, Colchester, Essex C06 4SL.

MOTHER LIVING

Priscilla, da of late John Egerton-Warburton (*see* Grey-Egerton, Bt, colls): *m* 1st, 1936, William Matthew, Maj Viscount Wolmer, who *d* on active ser 1942; 2ndly, 1948, 4th Baron Newton, who *d* 1992; 3rdly, 1994, as his 2nd wife, Frederick Charles Horace Fryer (*see* E Peel, colls, 1985 Edn). *Residence* – Vernon Hill House, Bishop's Waltham, Hants.

COLLATERAL BRANCHES LIVING

Issue of late Maj Hon Robert Jocelyn Palmer, MC, late Coldstream Guards, 3rd son of 3rd Earl, *b* 1919, *d* (30 Nov) 1991: *m* 1950, Anne Rosemary, Baroness Lucas of Crudwell, and Lady Dingwall (in her own right), who *d* (31 Dec) 1991:—

Ralph Matthew, *b* 1951, who *s* his mother as *Baron Lucas of Crudwell and Lord Dingwall* 1991 (see those titles). —— *Hon* Timothy John (West Woodyates Manor, Salisbury, Wilts), *b* 1953; *ed* Eton, and Balliol Coll, Oxford: *m* 1984, Adèle Cristina Sophia, 4th da of late Lt-Col Hon Henry Anthony Camillo Howard (*see* B Howard of Penrith, colls), and has issue living, Henry Jocelyn, *b* 1987, — Robert Dominic, *b* 1993, — Nan Cristina, *b* 1985, — Isabella Spring, *b* 1989. —— *Hon* Anthea Amabel, *b* 1956; assumed by deed poll 1963 the additional christian name of Amabel.

Issue of late Hon Edward Roundell Palmer, yst son of 3rd Earl, *b* 1926, *d* 1974: *m* 1957, Joanna Constance (who *d* 1994, having *m* 2ndly, 1982, John Bernard Bruce), el da of Sir Edmund Castell Bacon, 14th Bt, KG, KBE, TD:—

Francis Mark Bacon, *b* 1958. —— Matthew Roundell, *b* 1965. —— Henrietta Cecilia, *b* 1960. —— Lucinda Beatrice, *b* 1962.

Grandsons of late Hon (William Jocelyn) Lewis Palmer (infra):—
Issue of Rev Stephen Roundell Palmer, *b* 1923, *d* 1990: *m* 1952, Joyce (21 Windy Ridge, Beaminster, Dorset DT8 3SP), da of Rev Walter Darling Topping:—
William Jocelyn, *b* 1953. —— Andrew Nicholas, *b* 1955.

Issue of late Hon (William Jocelyn) Lewis Palmer, yst son of 2nd Earl, *b* 1894, *d* 1971: *m* 1922, Hon Dorothy Cecily Sybil Loder, who *d* 1986, da of 1st Baron Wakehurst:—
Penelope Jane, *b* 1925: *m* 1965, David George Jamison, BM, of Les Fontenelles, Forest, Guernsey, CI.

PREDECESSORS – **(1)** Rt Hon Sir ROUNDELL Palmer, PC, *b* 1812; MP for Plymouth (*L*) 1847-52 and 1853-7, and for Richmond 1861-72; was Solicitor-Gen 1861-3, Attorney-Gen 1863-6, and Lord High Chancellor 1872-4, and 1880-85; *cr Baron Selborne*, of Selborne, co Southampton (peerage of United Kingdom) 1872, and *Viscount Wolmer* and *Earl of Selborne* (peerage of United Kingdom) 1882: *m* 1848, Lady Laura Waldegrave, who *d* 1885, 3rd da of 8th Earl Waldegrave; *d* 1895; *s* by his ony son **(2)** WILLIAM WALDEGRAVE, KG, PC, GCMG, 2nd Earl, *b* 1859; was Under-Sec of State for Colonies 1895-1900, First Lord of the Admiralty 1900-05, High Commr for S Africa and Gov of Transvaal 1905-10, and Pres of Board of Agriculture and Fisheries 1915-16; sat as MP for E or Petersfield Div of Hampshire (LU) 1885-92, and for W Div of Edinburgh 1892-5: *m* 1883, Lady Beatrix Maud Cecil, who *d* 1950, da of 3rd Marquess of Salisbury; *d* 1942; *s* by his son **(3)** ROUNDELL CECIL, CH, PC, 3rd Earl, *b* 1887; Asst Postmaster-Gen 1924-29; Min of Economic Warfare 1942-45; MP for Newton Div, SW Lancs (LU) 1910-18, and Aldershot (*C*) 1918-40; called to House of Lords in his father's Barony of Selborne 1941: *m* 1st, 1910, Hon Grace Ridley, who *d* 1959, da of 1st Viscount Ridley; 2ndly, 1966, Mrs Valerie Irene Josephine Margaret de Thomka Bevan, who *d* 1968, da of late J. A. N. de Thomka de Thomkahaza, Sec of State for Hungary; *d* 1971; *s* by his grandson **(4)** JOHN ROUNDELL (el son of late William Matthew, Maj Viscount Wolmer, el son of 3rd Earl), 4th Earl and present peer, also Viscount Wolmer, and Baron Selborne.

SELBY VISCOUNT (Gully) (Viscount UK 1905)

MICHAEL GUY JOHN GULLY, 4th Viscount; *b* 15 Aug 1942; *s* 1959; *ed* Harrow; FCA: *m* 1965, Mary Theresa, da of late Capt Thomas F. Powell, of 10 Pelham Cres, SW7, and has issue.

Arms – Argent, a lion rampant sable between four escallops gules, on a chief of the last as many escallops or. **Crest** – Between two wings erect or, an arm vested sable, cuffed argent, the hand grasping a sword erect proper. **Supporters** – *Dexter*, an owl sable, charged with a balance or; *sinister*, an eagle sable, charged with a portcullis or.
Seat – Shuna Castle, Island of Shuna, Argyll. *Residence* – Ardfern House, by Lochgilphead, Argyll.

Nec temere nec tarde

Neither rashly nor slowly

SON LIVING

Hon EDWARD THOMAS WILLIAM, *b* 21 Sept 1967; *ed* Harrow: *m* 1992, Charlotte Catherine, yr da of Rolph Brege, of Lomma, Sweden, and has issue living, Christopher Rolf Thomas, *b* 18 Oct 1993.

DAUGHTER LIVING

Hon Catherine Mary Albinia, *b* 1971.

BROTHER LIVING

Hon James Edward Hugh Grey (Island of Shuna, Arduaine, by Oban, Argyll; Dunmor, Easdale, Isle of Seil, by Oban, Argyll), *b* 1945; *ed* King's Sch, Canterbury: *m* 1971, Fiona Margaret, only da of late Ian Strathaird Mackenzie, of Iona, and has issue living, James Ian Mackenzie, *b* 1975, — Andrew Donald Mackenzie, *b* 1977.

SISTER LIVING

Hon (Helen) Alexandra Briscoe (*Hon Lady Roche*), *b* 1934: *m* 1st, 1952 (*m diss* 1965), Roger Moreton Frewen, who *d* 1972; 2ndly, 1971, Sir David O'Grady Roche, 5th Bt, and has had issue (by 1st *m*), Jonathan Briscoe Moreton, *b* 1953: *m* 1979, Anita Louise, yr da of late Nils J. L. Grebstad, of Sykkylven 6230, Norway 66, and has issue living, Antonia *b* 1987, — Robert Edward Jerome (Park Hall, Healaugh, Richmond, N Yorks), *b* 1957: *m* 1989, Rolline Charlotte, yr da of late Alexander Fergus Forbes Williamson (*see* B Forres, colls), and has issue living, Jennie Selina McMorrough *b* 1992, — Charles Grey Justin, *b* 1959, — Selina Veronica Clara, *b* 1955; *k* in a motor accident 1972, — (by John Foster) Emma Catherine GULLY, *b* 1964: *m* 1985, Jonathan Colin Fraser Bower, only son of Colin Bower, of 6 Hestercombe Av, SW6, — (by 2nd *m*) (*see* Roche, Bt). *Residences* – Bridge House, Starbottom, Skipton, N Yorks BD23 5HY; 36 Coniger Rd, SW6 3TA.

AUNT LIVING (*Daughter of 2nd Viscount*)

Hon Signe Evelyn, *b* 1909: *m* 1938, Max Brandenstein, who assumed the name of Mark Leslie Brandon, and has issue living, Lionel Roderick Evelyn, *b* 1939, — Vanessa Maxine, *b* 1947: *m* 1976, Gilbert Thompson-Royds (*see* Thompson, Bt, *cr* 1890). *Residence* – Seymour House, Market St, Charlbury, Oxon.

WIDOW LIVING OF THIRD VISCOUNT

VERONICA CATHERINE BRISCOE (*Dowager Viscountess Selby*), da of late J. George: *m* 1933, the 3rd Viscount, who *d* 1959. *Residence* – The Dower House, Island of Shuna, Argyll.

PREDECESSORS – **(1)** *Rt Hon* WILLIAM COURT Gully, son of late James Manby Gully, MD of The Priory, Great Malvern, *b* 1835; Recorder of Wigan 1886-95, and Speaker of the House of Commons 1895-1905; MP for Carlisle (*L*) 1886-1905; *cr* Viscount Selby, of the City of Carlisle (peerage of United Kingdom) 1905: *m* 1865, Elizabeth Anne Walford, who *d* 1906, el da of late Thomas Selby, of Whitley and Wimbish, Essex; *d* 1909; *s* by his el son **(2)** JAMES WILLIAM HERSCHELL, 2nd Viscount; *b* 1867: *m* 1st, 1893 (*m diss* 1909), Ada Isabel, who *d* 1931, da of late Alexander George Pirie, of Stoneywood House, Aberdeen; 2ndly, 1909, Dorothy Evelyn, who *d* 1951, da of late Sir William Grey, KCSI; *d* 1923; *s* by his son **(3)** THOMAS SUTTON EVELYN, 3rd Viscount; *b* 1911; Paymaster Lieut-Com RNR (ret): *m* 1933, Veronica Catherine Briscoe-George, da of late J. George; *d* 1959; *s* by his son **(4)** MICHAEL GUY JOHN, 4th Viscount and present peer.

SELKIRK, EARL OF (Douglas-Hamilton) (Earl S 1646)

GEORGE NIGEL DOUGLAS-HAMILTON, KT, GCMG, GBE, AFC, PC, AE, QC, 10th Earl; *b* 4 Jan 1906; *s* 1940; *ed* Eton, at Balliol Coll, Oxford (BA and MA 1933), and Paris, Bonn, Vienna, and Edinbugh (LLB 1933) Univs; a Scottish Representative Peer 1945-63; Advocate, Scotland 1934, and a QC 1959; Group-Capt Auxiliary Air Force, Commanded 603 City of Edinburgh Sqdn of AAF 1934-38, a Member of Queen's Body Guard for Scotland (Roy Co of Archers), Dep Keeper of the Palace of Holyrood House 1937-72, and a Freeman of Hamilton; was a Member of Edinburgh Town Council 1935-40, a Commr (unpaid) of Gen Board of Control for Scotland 1936-39, Commr for Special Areas in Scotland 1937-39, a Lord-in-Waiting to HM Nov 1951 to Nov 1953, and Paymaster-Gen 1953 to Dec 1955, Chancellor of Duchy of Lancaster Dec 1955 to Jan 1957, First Lord of the Admiralty Jan 1957 to Oct 1959, and UK Commr for Singapore and Commr-Gen S-E Asia 1959-63; Chm of Conservative Commonwealth Council 1965-72; Pres of Building Socs Assocn since 1965-82, of Roy Central Asian Soc 1966-76, and of Nat Ski Fedn of Great Britain 1965-68; Chm of Victoria League 1971-77; Hon Chief, Salteaux Indians 1967; Hon Citizen of Winnipeg (Manitoba) 1982; 1939-45 War (despatches, OBE), OBE (Mil) 1941, PC 1955, GCMG 1960, GBE 1963, KT 1976; *m* 1949, Audrey Durell, da of late Maurice Drummond-Sale-Barker.

Arms – Quarterly: 1st and 4th grand quarters, argent, a heart gules imperially crowned proper, on a chief azure three mullets argent, *Douglas*; 2nd grand quarter, counter-quartered, 1st azure a lion rampant argent, crowned or, *Galloway*; 2nd or a lion rampant gules, surmounted of a ribband sable, *Abernethy*; 3rd argent three piles gules, *Jedforest*; 4th or, a fess chequy azure and argent surmounted of a bend gules charged with three buckles or, *Stewart*; 3rd grand quarter, counter-quartered, 1st and 4th gules, three cinquefoils ermine, *Hamilton*; 2nd and 3rd argent, a lymphad, sails furled, sable flagged gules, *Arran*; over the grand quarters at the fesspoint a crescent sable. **Crest** – On a chapeau gules furred ermine a salamander in flames, proper. **Supporters** – *Dexter*, a savage wreathed about the head and middle with laurel, holding in his exterior hand a club, resting in a brandished posture on his shoulder, all proper; *sinister*, an antelope argent, armed and unguled or, gorged with an earl's coronet proper and having a chain reflexed over the back, also or.
Residences – Rose Lawn Coppice, Wimborne, Dorset; 60 Eaton Place, SW1X 8AT.

COLLATERAL BRANCH LIVING

Issue of late Lord Malcolm Avondale Douglas-Hamilton, OBE, DFC, next brother of 10th Earl, and 3rd son of 13th Duke of Hamilton, *b* 1909, *d* 1964: *m* 1st, 1931 (*m diss* 1952), (Clodagh) Pamela, only child of late Lt-Col Hon Malcolm Bowes-Lyon, CBE (*see* E Strathmore, colls); 2ndly, 1953, Natalie, CBE, da of Maj Nathaniel Brackett Wales, of New York, and Boston, USA, and widow of Edward Bragg Paine, of New York:—
(By 1st *m*) (*see* D Hamilton, colls) of whom ALASDAIR MALCOLM, *b* 10 Sept 1939, is *hp* to the Earldom.

PREDECESSORS – (1) *Lord* WILLIAM Douglas, KG, PC, 4th son of 1st Marquess of Douglas; *b* 1634; a Commr of Treasury 1686-89 and an Extraor Lord of Session 1686-89 and 1689-94; *cr Lord Daer and Shortcleuch* and *Earl of Selkirk* (peerage of Scotland) 1646, and *Duke of Hamilton; Marquess of Clydesdale, Earl of Arran, Lanark and Selkirk, Lord Aven, Machansire, Polmont and Daer* (peerage of Scotland) 1660 for life only; having resigned his Lordships and Earldom into the King's hands, who in 1688 re-conferred them, with the precedence of 1646, upon his 3rd son, Charles, and his yr sons primogeniturely (provided that, if the said son Charles, or any of his brothers or the heirs male of their bodies succeeded to the Dukedom of Hamilton, *cr* 1643, the Earldom should pass to the then Duke's next brother), and with further remainder to his Grace's other heirs male; in conformity with the new patent the 3rd son (2) CHARLES, PC, *b* 1662, became 2nd Earl; was Lord Clerk Register 1696 and 1733, a Lord of the Bedchamber and a Representative Peer; *d* 1739; *s* by his brother (3) JOHN, 3rd Earl, *b* 1664, who in 1697 had been *cr Lord Hilhouse, Viscount Riccartoun*, and *Earl of Ruglen* (peerage of Scotland) with remainder to heirs of his body whatsoever; *d* 1744; *s* in Earldom of Ruglen, and in peerages of 1697 by his da Anne, while the honours of 1646 reverted to his grand-nephew (4) DUNBAR Hamilton (grandson of Lord Basil, 6th son of 1st Earl), 4th Earl, *b* 1722; resumed the paternal surname of Douglas, was a Representative Peer: *m* 1758, Helen, who *d* 1802, da of late Hon John Hamilton; *d* 1799; *s* by his 7th son (5) THOMAS, 5th Earl, *b* 1771; a Representative Peer; founder of Red River Settlement in Manitoba: *m* 1807, Isabella, who *d* 1871, da of Andrew Blackburn; *d* 1820; *s* by his son (6-9) DUNBAR JAMES, 6th Earl; *d* 1886; *s* by his kinsman the 12th Duke of Hamilton, the Earldom being held in fiduciary fee until 1940, when it devolved under the terms of special destination upon (10) (GEORGE) NIGEL (2nd son of 13th Duke of Hamilton) 10th Earl and present peer; also Lord Daer and Shortcleuch.

SELSDON, BARON (Mitchell-Thomson) (Baron UK 1932, Bt UK 1900)

God will provide

MALCOLM MCEACHARN MITCHELL-THOMSON, 3rd Baron, and 4th Baronet; *b* 27 Oct 1937; *s* 1963; *ed* Winchester: *m* 1965, Patricia Anne, da of Donald Smith, and has issue.

𝔸rms – Per pale argent and gules between three mascles a stag's head cabossed all counter-changed. ℭrest – A dexter hand couped at the wrist proper grasping a cross-crosslet fitchée in bend sinister gules. 𝔖upporters – Two sea-horses proper, crined sable, finned or.
Address – c/o House of Lords, SW1.

SON LIVING

Hon CALLUM MALCOLM MCEACHARN, 7 Nov 1969.

SISTER LIVING

Hon Mary Gail, *b* 1939: *m* 1963, Patrick John O'Kelly, MB, BCh, and has issue living, Sebastian Patrick Sean, *b* 1964, — Shane, *b* 1968, — Niall, *b* 1970.

HALF-SISTER LIVING

Hon Petrina Frances Anne, *b* 1945: *m* 1967, James Geoffrey Lennox Pugh, late Gren Gds, of Whitelands, Rudford, Glos, and has issue living, Henry William Geoffrey, *b* 1974, — Emma Louise, *b* 1969.

PREDECESSORS – (1) *Sir* MITCHELL Thomson, 4th son of late Andrew Thomson, of Seafield, Alloa, by Janet, da of William Mitchell, *b* 1846; was Lord Provost of Edinburgh 1897-1900; assumed by Roy licence 1900 the additional surname of Mitchell; *cr* a *Baronet* 1900: *m* 1st, 1876, Eliza Flowerdew, who *d* 1877, da of late William Lowson, of Balthaycock, Perthshire; 2ndly, 1880, Eliza Lamb, who *d* 1926, da of late Robert Cook, shipowner, of Leith; *d* 1918; *s* by his son (2) *Rt Hon Sir* WILLIAM LOWSON, KBE, 2nd Bt, *b* 1877; was Parliamentary Sec to Min of Food 1920-21, and to Board of Trade 1921-2, and Postmaster-Gen 1924-9; MP for N-W Div of Lanarkshire (*U*) 1906-10, for N Down Div of co Down 1910-18, for Mary-hill Div of Glasgow 1918-22, and for S Div of Croydon 1923-32; *cr Baron Selsdon*, of Croydon, co Surrey (peerage of United Kingdom) 1932: *m* 1st, 1909 (*m diss* 1932), Anne Madeleine, who *d* 1946, da of late Sir Malcolm Donald McEacharn, of Galloway House, Garlieston, and Goathland, Melbourne; 2ndly, 1933, Effie Lilian Loder, who *d* 1956, da of late Lieut-Col Charles Brennan, of Mullingar; *d* 1938; *s* by his son (3) PATRICK, 2nd Baron *b* 1913: *m* 1st, 1936 (*m diss* 1944), Phoebette, who *d* 1991, da of Crossley Swithinbank, of Donnington Grove, Newbury; 2ndly, 1944, Dorothy (who *m* 2ndly, 1972, Charles Larking, and *d* 1988), da of late Frederick John Greenish, of Honnington Hall, Lincoln; *d* 1963; *s* by his only son (4) MALCOLM MCEACHARN, 3rd Baron and present peer.

SELWYN-LLOYD, BARONY OF (Lloyd) (Extinct 1978)

DAUGHTER LIVING OF LIFE BARON

Hon Joanna Elizabeth, *b* 1952.

SEMPILL, LADY (Sempill) (Lordship S 1489)

ANN MOIRA SEMPILL, *b* 19 March 1920; *s* 1965; late Petty Officer WRNS: *m* 1st, 1941 (*m diss* 1945), Capt Eric Holt, Manchester Regt; 2ndly, 1948, Lt-Col Stuart Whitemore Chant-Sempill, OBE, MC, late Gordon Highlanders (who *d* 1991, having assumed by decree of Lyon Court 1966 the additional name of Sempill) and has issue by 1st and 2nd marriages.

𝔸rms – Argent, a chevron checky gules and of the field, between three hunting horns sable, garnished and stringed of the second. ℭrest – A stag's head argent, attired with ten tines azure, collared with a Prince's crown or. 𝔖upporters – Two greyhounds argent collared gules.
Residences – East Lodge, Druminnor, Rhynie, Aberdeenshire; 15 Onslow Court, Drayton Gdns, SW10.

SONS LIVING *(By 2nd marriage)*

Hon JAMES WILLIAM STUART WHITEMORE SEMPILL (*Master of Sempill*), *b* 25 Feb 1949; *ed* Oratory Sch, St Clare's Hall, Oxford (BA), and Hertford Coll, Oxford: *m* 1977, Josphine Ann Edith, da of Joseph Norman Rees, of Kelso, and has issue living, Francis, *b* 1979, — Cosima, *b* 1983. *Residence* – 18 Brandon Terrace, Edinburgh EH3 5DZ.
Hon Ian David Whitemore CHANT-SEMPILL, *b* 1951; *ed* Oratory Sch; Lt-Col Gordon Highlanders: *m* 1980, Amanda, yr da of Anthony Dallas, of Blackmoor, Burghfield, Berks, and has issue living, Hamish, *b* 1987, — Clementine Ann Constance, *b* 1985.

DAUGHTER LIVING *(By 1st marriage)*

Hon Frances Marion CHANT-SEMPILL, *b* 1942: *m* 1976, David Ian Russell (*see* Russell, Bt, *cr* 1916). *Residence* – 25 Eddiscombe Rd, SW10.

HALF SISTERS LIVING

Hon Janet Cecilia FORBES-SEMPILL, *b* 1942. *Residence* – Keil Cottage, Muir of Fowlis, nr Alford, Aberdeenshire.
Hon Kirstine Elizabeth DARANYI-FORBES-SEMPILL, *b* 1944: *m* 1st, 1968 (*m diss* 1989), John Michael Forbes-Cable (who assumed by deed poll 1968 the additional surname of Forbes); 2ndly, 1990, Béla Peter de Daranyi, and has issue living (by 1st *m*), William Richard Craigievar, *b* 1970, — Malcolm Dunbar Craigievar, *b* 1972. *Residence* – Flat 8, 17-20 Embankment Gdns, SW3.
Hon Brigid Gabriel, *b* 1945: *m* 1983 (*m diss* 19—), Hon Jeremy Menuhin (Life Baron), OM, KBE, and has issue living, Petroc Forbes, *b* 1988, — Nadja Cecilia *b* 1985.

COLLATERAL BRANCHES LIVING

Issue of late Rear Adm Hon Arthur Lionel Ochoncar Forbes-Sempill, yst son of 17th Lord:—
See Forbes, Bt (*cr* 1630), of Craigievar, Aberdeenshire.

Grandchildren of late Alexander William Pirie, 2nd son of late Hon Evelyn Courtenay Forbes-Sempill (Hon Mrs Pirie) (infra):—
Issue of late Ridley Gordon Pirie, *b* 1936, *d* 1984: *m* 1962, Eva Maria Lenel (28 Hubert Rd, Winchester, Hants):—
Edward Duncan PIRIE, *b* 1968. —— Fernanda, *b* 1964.

Issue of late Hon Evelyn Courtenay Forbes-Sempill, da of 17th Lord, *b* 1868, *d* 1934: *m* 1894, Lieut-Col Duncan Vernon Pirie, OBE, JP, DL, a Member of King's Body Guard for Scotland (Royal Company of Archers), who *d* 1931:—
Douglas Gordon PIRIE, *b* 1910; *ed* Winchester, and Edinburgh Univ; is a Member of Queen's Body Guard for Scotland (Royal Company of Archers); 2nd Lieut Coldm Gds (SR) 1935, Private Sec and ADC to Gov of Mauritius 1937-40, Private Sec to Gov of Kenya 1946-47, in Colonial Office 1947-50, and in HM Foreign Ser 1950-53; 1939-45 War as Lt-Col Coldm Gds (despatches, Legion of Honour): *m* 1954, Jean Frances Caroline Alicia Dorothea Grant, yst da of late Evelyn George Massey Carmichael of Carmichael, OBE, JP, FSA (Colquhoun, Bt), and has had issue, †Douglas Alastair Carmichael *b* 1957; *d* 1989. *Residences* – The Old House, Milland, Liphook, Hants; 70 Pelham Court, Fulham Rd, SW3. *Club* – Boodle's. —— Valérie Marguerite (Old Rectory House, Coombe Bissett, Salisbury, Wilts), *b* 1906: *m* 1962, Henry Ernest Spry, CBE, who *d* 1967.

Grandchildren living of late Hon Evelyn Courtenay Forbes-Sempill (ante):—
Issue of late Evelyn Jean-Gordon Pirie, *b* 1895, *d* 1981: *m* 1926, Col Owen Evelyn Wynne, OBE, RE, who *d* 1974, son of Gen Sir Arthur Singleton Wynne, GCB:—
Robert Owen WYNNE (18 Britten St, SW3), *b* 1930; *ed* Wellington, and RMA Sandhurst; late Lieut KOYLI, served in Malaya 1950-51. —— Evelyn Valerie, *b* 1928; *ed* St Andrews Univ (MA 1950): *m* 1957, Thomas Syme Drew, of Fossens House, Methill Rd, Alyth, Perthshire, son of late Maj-Gen Sir James Syme Drew, KBE, CB, DSO, MC, and has issue living, Rachel Jean, *b* 1961: *m* 1986, John David Barstow, of Thorpe Hall, Ampleforth, N Yorks, and has issue living, Marcus Thomas James *b* 1990, Julia Victoria *b* 1992.

Grandchildren of late Lt-Col James Ochoncar Forbes (infra):—
Issue of late Lt-Col Patrick Walter Forbes, OBE, *b* 1914, *d* 1979: *m* 1939, Margaret Hawthorne (Gardeners Cottage, Breda, Alford AB3 8NN, Aberdeenshire), da of C. H. Lydall, of Brightling, Sussex:—
Andrew Iain Ochoncar, *b* 1945; MA (Oxon); Maj (ret) Gordon Highlanders; *hp* to baronetcy of Forbes of Craigievar (*cr* 1630). —— Mhairi Margaret, *b* 1942. —— Shelagh Anne, *b* 1948.

Grandson of late Hon James Ochoncar Forbes, brother of 17th Lord:—
Issue of late Lieut-Col James Ochoncar Forbes, *b* 1867, *d* 1945: *m* 1912, Nora Maude, who *d* 1958, da of late Douglas Charles Abercromby (Abercromby, Bt, colls):—
David Ochoncar, *b* 1917. *Residence* – Park Neuk, Corse, Lumphanan, Aberdeenshire.

Granddaughter of late Charlotte Elizabeth Henrietta Grant of Druminnor (who *m* 1886, Philip Alexander Holland, both of whom and their issue assumed in 1896 the surname of Grant), only surviving da and heir of Hon Elizabeth Forbes, el sister of 17th Lord, who *m* 1864, Robert Grant of Druminnor:—
Issue of late Alexander Philip Foulerton Grant of Druminnor, MBE, *b* 1887, *d* 1961: *m* 1916, Maud Annie, who *d* 1963, da of late John Dyer, of Cheltenham:—
Rachel Ann, *b* 1922: *m* 1941, Maurice Richard Pope, and has issue living, Richard John, *b* 1953, — Diana Mary Ann, *b* 1955: *m* 1978, Laramy Walter Badcock Day, of Tuckerton Farm, N Newton, Bridgwater, Som.

Grandchildren of late Alexander Mansfield Forbes, son of Hon Sarah Forbes 2nd sister of 17th Lord, who *m* 1852, Duncan Forbes (*see* Forbes, Bt (*cr* 1630), of Craigievar, colls):—
Issue of late Duncan Alexander Forbes, *b* 1888, *d* 1964: *m* 1918, Sybil Dorothy, who *d* 1948, da of late John Mitchell, of Ceylon:—
Duncan, MC (18 Thornton Close, Girton, Cambridge), *b* 1922; Emeritus Reader in History of Modern Political Thought, Camb Univ, and a Fellow of Clare Coll, Camb: *m* 1947, Sheila, da of Rev Clement John Morton, and has issue living, Duncan Alastair (80 Southfield Rd, Oxford), *b* 1949; Fellow and Bursar, Mansfield Coll, Oxford: *m* 1971, Angela, da of Francis Ralph Sargent, and has issue living, Joy Mary *b* 1972, Katherine Dorothy *b* 1976, — Ian (twin) (Peat Hill, Westgate, Bishop Auckland, co Durham), *b* 1949: *m* 1973, Pamela, da of Dr Douglas Bailey, and has issue living, Nicholas Iain *b* 1973, Helen Catherine *b* 1977, Susan Claire *b* 1980, — Helen Morag, *b* 1954: *m* 1986, Mark Fitton, and has issue living, Jessica Elisabeth *b* 1990, Ruth *b* 1992. —— Katharine Ann (Inveroy, Roy Bridge, Inverness-shire), *b* 1926: *m* 1947, Albert Cook, (*m diss* 1956), and has issue living, Rosemary Ann, *b* 1948: *m* 1979, Timothy Cresswell Skipper, of Gyfeile, Maesymeillion, Llandysul, Dyfed, and has issue living, Andrew James *b* 1979, Peter Timothy *b* 1983, — Valerie, *b* 1952: *m* 1986, Timothy Dix, of 2 Drimsdale, S Uist, Western Isles, and has issue living, Alasdair John *b* 1987, Iain Timothy *b* 1989.
Issue of late Mhari Margaret Forbes, *b* 1891, *d* 1975: *m* 1st, 1918 (*m diss* 1935), Arthur Haydn Parry, who *d* 1944; 2ndly, 1935, Maj Stuart Frederick Maxwell Ferguson, MC, RA, who *d* 1975:—
(By 1st *m*) Mhari Elisabeth Forbes (Broadmead Copse, Wanborough, Guildford, Surrey), *b* 1921.

Grandchildren of late Most Rev Walter John Forbes Robberds, DD, son of Rev Frederick Walter Robberds and Hon Caroline Anne Forbes, yst sister of 17th Lord:—
Issue of late Ethel Margaret Robberds, *b* 1901, *d* 1984: *m* 1938, John Whitehead, who *d* 1985:—
Janet Margaret, *b* 1939; *ed* St Andrews Univ (MA): *m* 1968, Peter John Low, of 21 Corbar Rd, Buxton, Derbys, and has issue living, Caroline Margaret, *b* 1969, — Elizabeth Hilary, *b* 1971, — Polly Alexandra, *b* 1973.

Issue of late Katharine Frances Robberds, *b* 1904, *d* 1980: *m* 1924, Francis David Jefferson Buist, who *d* 1980:— Mary (Beech Cottage, 1 Glen Court, Dunblane, Perthshire FK15 0DY), *b* 1926: *m* 1st, 1945 (*m diss* 1966), Roland Sydney Hill, who *d* 1972; 2ndly, 1967, William James Drysdale, who *d* 1979, and has issue living (by 1st *m*), Andrew Forbes (Leask Cottage, Collieston, Aberdeenshire), *b* 1955; MA (Hons) Edinburgh; FSA Scot: *m* 1983, Linda Joan Knox, — David Jefferson, *b* 1957, — Susan Frances, *b* 1946: *m* 1969, Donald Drysdale, CA, of Ardlochan, 49 Roselea Drive, Milngavie, Glasgow, and has issue living, Michael Christopher *b* 1972, Alastair Nicholas *b* 1974, Lisa Jane *b* 1977, — Alison Margaret, *b* 1949; MA Edinburgh: *m* 1st, 1971, Iain Taylor Carruthers, who *d* 1986; 2ndly, 1988, Eugene Charles Henry O'Neale, of 23 Warriston Cres, Edinburgh EH3 5LB, and has issue living (by 1st *m*), Angus St John Hornsby *b* 1983, Catherine Lucy Forbes *b* 1974, Jessica Rose *b* 1977. —— Margaret Brora, *b* 1930: *m* 1954, Charles Richard Butterworth, of Maus House, Hilton, Dornoch, Sutherland IV25 3PW, and has issue living, Emma Mary, *b* 1955: *m* 1980, Francis Anderson Murray, of 21 Victoria Av, Surbiton, Surrey KT6 5DL, and has issue living, Angus Francis Hugh *b* 1984, Frederick Richard Finnbarr *b* 1986, Lucy Anne *b* 1983, — Charlotte Clunes, *b* 1958: *m* 1981, Gordon Bruce Dickie, of Poundland, Moniaive, Dumfriesshire, and has issue living, Alice Katharine Brora *b* 1983, Arabella Rose *b* 1984, Flora Sophia Elizabeth *b* 1988.

PREDECESSORS – (1) *Sir* JOHN Sempill, Knt, *cr* Lord Sempill (peerage of Scotland) about 1489; *k* at Flodden 1513; *s* by his son (2) WILLIAM, 2nd Lord; *d* about 1550; *s* by his son (3) ROBERT, 3rd Lord, known as "The Great Lord Sempill"; *s* by his grandson (4) ROBERT, 4th Lord; was Ambassador from James VI to Spain 1596; *s* by his son (5) HUGH, 5th Lord; *d* 1639; *s* by his el son (6) FRANCIS, 6th Lord; *dsp* 1644; *s* by his brother (7) ROBERT, 7th Lord; *d* 1675; *s* by his son (8) FRANCIS, 8th Lord; *dsp* 1684; *s* by his sister (9) ANNE, wife of Robert Abercromby, who in 1685 was *cr* Lord Glassford for life; obtained in 1688 a new charter settling the Lordship of Sempill, in default of male issue, upon her daughters without division by her then or any future husband; *d* 1695: *s* by her el son (10) FRANCIS, 10th Lord; *d* unmarried; *s* by his brother (11) JOHN, 11th Lord; *d* unmarried 1716; *s* by his brother (12) HUGH, 12th Lord; commanded left wing of Govt Army at Culloden 1746; *d* 1746; *s* by his son (13) JOHN, 13th Lord; *d* 1782; *s* by his son (14) HUGH, 14th Lord; *b* 1758: *m* 1787, Maria, da of Charles Mellish, of Ragnal, Notts: *d* 1830; *s* by his son (15) SELKIRK, 15th Lord; *d* unmarried 1835; *s* by his sister (16) MARIA JANET: *m* 1836, Edward Candler, who were both allowed by Roy Licence 1853 to assume the name and arms Sempill only; *dsp* 1884; *s* by her kinsman (17) *Sir* WILLIAM Forbes, 8th Bt of Craigievar, grandson of Hon Sarah, el da of 13th Lord, *b* 1836; assumed in 1885, the additional and principal surname of Sempill: *m* 1st, 1858 (*m diss* 1861), Caroline Louisa, who *d* 1872, da of Sir Charles Forbes, 3rd Bt, of Newe; 2ndly, 1862, Frances Emily, who *d* 1887, da of Sir Robert Abercromby, 5th Bt; 3rdly, 1890, Mary Beresford, who *d* 1930, da of late Henry Sherbrooke, of Oxton, Notts; *d* 1905; *s* by his son (18) JOHN, 18th Lord, *b* 1863; Hon Col 5th Bn Gordon Highlanders (TA), a Representative Peer for Scotland: *m* 1892, Gwendolen, who *d* 1944, da of late Herbert Prodgers, of Hington St Michael, Chippenham, Wilts; *d* 1934; *s* by his son (19) WILLIAM FRANCIS, AFC, 19th Lord, *b* 1893; a Representative Peer for Scotland, Wing-Cdr RNAS and Col RAF, a pioneer in aviation: *m* 1st, 1919, Eileen Marion, who *d* 1935, da of Sir John Lavery, RA; 2ndly, 1941, Cecilia Alice, who *d* 1984, da of B. E. Dunbar-Kilburn, of Ledwell, Sandford St Martin, Oxon; *d* 1965; *s* in the baronetcy of Forbes of Craigievar by his brother Sir Ewan Forbes of Brux, 11th Bt (*see* Forbes, Bt), and in the Lordship by his el da (20) ANN MOIRA, Lady Sempill and present peeress.

SEROTA, BARONESS (Serota) (Life Baroness 1967)

BEATRICE SEROTA, DBE, da of Alexander Katz; *b* 15 Oct 1919; *ed* London Sch of Economics (BSc Econ); a JP of Inner London; a Member of LCC 1954-65 (Chm of Children's Cttee 1958-65) and of GLC (Lambeth) 1964-67; a Member of Advisory Council in Child Care and Central Training Council in Child Care 1958-68, of Advisory Council on Penal System 1966-68; Chm of Health Education Council 1967-69, a Baroness in Waiting to HM 1968-69, and Min of State, Dept of Health and Social Security 1969-70; Pres of National Council for Unmarried Mother and Her Child since 1971; a Member of Community Relations Comm 1971; *cr* Baroness Serota, of Hampstead in Greater London (Life Baroness) 1967, and DBE 1992: *m* 1942, Stanley Serota, FICE, and has issue.
Residence – The Coach House, 15 Lyndhurst Terr, NW3.

SON LIVING

Nicholas Andrew (does not use courtesy title), *b* 1946; *ed* Haberdashers' Askes Sch, Christ's Coll, Camb (BA), and Courtauld Inst of Art (MA); Dir Whitechapel Art Gallery 1976-88, Trustee Public Art Development Trust 1983-88, Dir Tate Gallery since 1988: *m* 1973, Angela Mary Beveridge, and has issue, two das.

DAUGHTER LIVING

Hon Judith Alexandra Anne, *b* 1948; *ed* Royal Manchester Coll of Music: *m* 1973, Francis John Pugh, and has issue living, Rebecca Sarah, *b* 1975, — Ellen Martha, *b* 1978.

Seymour, Lord; son of Duke of Somerset.

SHACKLETON, BARON (Shackleton) (Life Baron 1958)

By endurance we conquer

EDWARD ARTHUR ALEXANDER SHACKLETON, KG, OBE, PC, son of late Sir Ernest Henry Shackleton, CVO, OBE, Antarctic explorer; *b* 15 July 1911; *ed* Radley, and Magdalen Coll, Oxford (MA, Hon Fellow 1986); FRS; Hon LLD Newfoundland; Hon DSc Warwick and Southampton; an Author, Lecturer and Broadcaster; accompanied Expeditions to Borneo and Sarawak, 1932, and to Ellesmere Land 1934-35, a Dir of John Lewis Partnership 1955-64, Pres Arctic Club 1960, and Pres of R Geographical Soc 1971-74 (Vice-Pres 1962-67, and 1969-71); Chm of RTZ Development Enterprises Ltd 1973-83, and Dir of Corpn of RTZ 1973-82, Dep Chm 1975-82; Min of Defence for RAF 1964-67, Min without Portfolio, and Dep Leader House of Lords, 1967-68, Lord Privy Seal Jan to April 1968, Paymaster-Gen April to Nov 1968, and again Lord Privy Seal 1968-70; Leader of House of Lords 1968-70, and Leader of the Opposition, House of Lords 1970-74; Min in Charge of Civil Ser Dept 1968-70; Cuthbert Peek Award (RGS) 1933; Ludwig Medallist (Munich Geog Soc) 1938; Freedom of Stanley, Falkland Is, 1988; Hon AC 1990; Royal Scottish Geographical Soc Medal 1990; Special Gold Medal, RGS, 1990; 1939-45 War as Wing-Cdr RAFVR in Intelligence Branch (despatches twice, OBE); MP for Preston (*Lab*) 1946-50, and for Preston S Div 1950-55; *cr* OBE (Mil) 1945, *Baron Shackleton*, of Burley, co Southampton (Life Baron) 1958, PC 1966, and KG 1974: *m* 1938, Betty Muriel Marguerite, da of late Capt Charles E. Homan, Elder Brother of Trinity House, and has had issue.

Arms – Or, on a fesse fules, three lozengy buckles tongues palewise gold, on a canton of the second a cross humettée of the third. **Crest** – A poplar tree proper, charged with a buckle as in the arms.
Address – House of Lords, SW1A 0PW. *Club* – Brooks's.

DAUGHTER LIVING

Hon Alexandra Mary Swinford, *b* 1940; *ed* Trin Coll, Dublin: *m* 1969, Richard Charles Bergel, MB, BS, of Dolphin House, Beaver Lane, Yateley, Hants, and has issue.

WIDOW LIVING OF SON OF LIFE BARON

Lady Caroline Harriet Hastings, da of 15th Earl of Huntingdon: *m* 1970, Hon Charles Edward Ernest Shackleton, who *d* 1979. *Address* – c/o Coutts & Co, 16 Cavendish Sq, W1.

SHAFTESBURY, EARL OF (Ashley-Cooper) (Earl E 1672, Bt E 1622)

ANTHONY ASHLEY-COOPER, 10th Earl, and 11th Baronet; *b* 22 May 1938; *s* 1961; *ed* Eton, and Ch Ch, Oxford; late Lt 10th Hussars; Hon Citizen S Carolina, USA; Chm London Philharmonic Orchestra Council 1966-80; patron of five livings: *m* 1st, 1966 (*m diss* 1976), Mrs Bianca Maria Le Vien, da of late Gino de Paolis; 2ndly, 1976, Mrs Christina Eva Casella, da of Nils Montan, and has issue by 2nd *m*.

Arms – Quarterly: 1st and 4th argent, three bulls passant sable, armed and unguled or. *Ashley;* 2nd and 3rd gules, a bend engrailed between six lions rampant or, *Cooper.* **Crest** – On a chapeau gules, turned up ermine, a bull statant sable, armed, unguled and ducally gorged or. **Supporters** – *Dexter*, a bull sable, armed, unguled, ducally gorged and chain reflexed over the back or; sinister, a talbot azure, ducally gorged or.
Residence – St Giles's House, Wimborne, Dorset, BH21 5NH. *Clubs* – Turf, Pratt's.

SONS LIVING *(By 2nd marriage)*

ANTHONY NILS CHRISTIAN (*Lord Ashley*), *b* 24 June 1977.
Hon Nicholas Edmund Anthony, *b* 1979.

SISTER LIVING *(Raised to the rank of an Earl's daughter 1962)*

Lady Frances Mary Elizabeth (La Combe, 30126 Tavel, Gard, France), *b* 1940.

WIDOW LIVING OF SON OF NINTH EARL

Julian, da of late Capt George Gerald Petherick (*see* E Radnor, 1976 Edn): *m* 1946, Maj Hon (Anthony) John Percy Hugh Michael Ashley Cooper, yr son of 9th Earl, who *d* 1986, and has issue (see colls infra). *Residence* – Nine Yews House, Wimborne, Cranborne, Dorset BH21 5PW.

MOTHER LIVING

Françoise, da of George Souilier: *m* 1st, 1937, as his 2nd wife, Lord Ashley, who *d* 1947, el son of 9th Earl; 2ndly, 1947, Col François Goussault, French Air Force, who *d* 1984. *Residence* – 6 Square d'Astorg, Residence St Honoré, 78150 Le Chesnay, France.

COLLATERAL BRANCH LIVING

Issue of late Maj Hon (Anthony) John Percy Hugh Michael Ashley Cooper, yr son of 9th Earl, *b* 1915, *d* 1986: *m* 1946, Julian (Nine Yews House, Wimborne, Cranborne, Dorset BH21 5PW), da of late Capt George Gerald Petherick (*see* E Radnor, 1976 Edn):—
Susan Mary Jeane, *b* 1946. —— Caroline Sibell, *b* 1948. —— Elizabeth Julian, *b* 1950. —— Mary Patricia, *b* 1953: *m* 1984, Robert John Elkington, son of J. D. R. Elkington, of Haworth House, Kintbury, Berks, and has issue living, Edwina Amy Charlotte, *b* 1989.

PREDECESSORS – (1) *Sir* JOHN Cooper, sometime MP for Poole; *cr Baronet* 1622, *d* 1631; *s* by his son (2) *Sir* ANTHONY ASHLEY, PC, an able and prominent statesman, who having originally espoused the royal cause, afterwards joined the Parliamentarians, and eventually assisted to restore the monarchy; *cr Baron Ashley*, of Wimborne St Giles, co Dorset (peerage of England) 1661, and *Baron Cooper*, of Paulett, co Somerset, and *Earl of Shaftesbury* (peerage of England) 1672; was Lord-Lieut of Dorset, Chancellor of the Exchequer 1667-72, Lord High Chancellor of England 1672-3, and Lord Pres of the Council 1679; *d* 1683; *s* by his son (3) ANTHONY ASHLEY, 2nd Earl; *d* 1699; *s* by his son (4) ANTHONY, 3rd Earl; designated by Voltaire as the boldest English philosopher; *d* 1713; *s* by his son (5) ANTHONY, 4th Earl; *d* 1771; *s* by his el son (6) ANTHONY ASHLEY, 5th Earl; *d* 1811; *s* by his brother (7) CROPLEY ASHLEY, 6th Earl; *b* 1768; was Chm of Committees in House of Lords; *d* 1851; *s* by his son (8) ANTHONY Ashley-Cooper, KG, PC, 7th Earl; was Lord-Lieut of Dorsetshire; sat as MP for Woodstock (C) 1826-30, for Dorchester 1830, for Dorsetshire 1831-46 and for Bath 1847-51; *d* 1 Oct 1885; *s* by his son (9) ANTHONY, 8th Earl; *b* 1831; sat as MP for Hull (LC) 1857-9, and for Cricklade 1859-65: *m* 1857, Lady Harriet Augusta Anne Seymourina Chichester, who *d* 1898, only da of 3rd Marquess of Donegall; *d* 1886; *s* by his son (10) ANTHONY, KP, GCVO, CBE, PC, 9th Earl; *b* 1869; Capt 10th Hussars; Lieut-Col and Hon Col Comdg N Irish Horse 1902-12, and HM's Lieut for co Antrim 1911-16; Hon Brig-Gen Hon Col Special Cav, and RGA; was Mil Sec to Gov of Victoria (Baron Brassey) 1896-8, Lord Mayor of Belfast 1907-8, HM's Lieut 1903-11, Commr of Congested Dists Board for Ireland 1902-14, Chamberlain to Queen Mary (when Princess of Wales) 1901-10, Lord Chamberlain to Queen Mary 1910-22, Chm of National Advisory Council for Juvenile Employment (England and Wales) 1928-31, and Lord Steward of HM's Household 1922-36; Chancellor of Belfast Univ 1910-23; Lord-Lieut for Dorset 1916-52; European War 1914-18; Chm of Dorset Co Council 1924-46: *m* 1899, Lady Constance Sibell Grosvenor (a DJStJ), who *d* 1957, da of late Earl Grosvenor; *d* 1961; *s* by his grandson (11) ANTHONY (son of late Anthony, Lord Ashley, el son of 9th Earl), 10th Earl and present peer; also Baron Ashley, and Baron Cooper.

SHANNON, EARL OF (Boyle) Sits as BARON CARLETON (GB 1786) (Earl I 1756)

Virtue outlives the grave

POST FUNERA VIVIT VIRTUS

SPECTEMUR • AGENDO

Let us be judged by our actions

RICHARD BENTINCK BOYLE, 9th Earl; *b* 23 Oct 1924; *s* 1963; late Capt Irish Guards: *m* 1st, 1947 (*m diss* 1955), Donna Catherine Irene Helen (Katie Boyle, the broadcaster), da of the Marchese Demetrio Imperiali di Francavilla; 2ndly, 1957 (*m diss* 1979), Susan Margaret, da of late John Russell Hogg (M Lothian); 3rdly, 1994, Almine, da of late Rocco Catorsia de Villiers, of Cape Town, S Africa, and has issue by 2nd *m*.

Arms – Per bend embattled argent and gules, a crescent for difference. **Crest** – Out of a ducal coronet or a lion's head per pale embattled argent and gules, and charged with a crescent for difference. **Supporters** – Two lions, the *dexter* per pale embattled gules and argent, the *sinister* per pale embattled argent and gules, each charged with a crescent for difference.
Residence – Pimm's Cottage, Man's Hill, Burghfield Common, Berks RG7 3BD. *Club* – White's.

SON LIVING (By 2nd marriage)

RICHARD HENRY JOHN (*Viscount Boyle*), *b* 19 Jan 1960.

DAUGHTERS LIVING (By 2nd marriage)

Lady Georgina Susan, *b* 1961.
Lady Caroline Mary Victoria, *b* 1965: *m* 1990, Mark Nowell Waters, only son of P.N. Waters, of Guildford, Surrey, and has issue living, Oliver Robert Nowell, *b* 1991, — Max Alexander, *b* 1993. *Residence* – White Wey Cottage, Unstead Wood, Peasmarsh, Guildford, Surrey GU3 1NG.

COLLATERAL BRANCHES LIVING

Grandchildren of late Vice-Adm Hon Robert Francis Boyle, MVO, 3rd son of 5th Earl:—
Issue of late Cdr Vivian Francis Boyle, RN, *b* 1902, *d* 1962: *m* 1929, Margaret Ruth Howard, da of Charles Howard Tripp, of Timaru, New Zealand:—
Robert Francis (McDowell St, Rotorua, NZ), *b* 1930; logging consultant: *m* 1956, Janet Eleanor Ashley, da of Selwyn Ashley Cooper, of Rotorua, NZ, and has issue living, David de Crespigny, *b* 1959, — Robert Andrew, *b* 1961, — Judith Eleanor, *b* 1957: *m* 1987 (*m diss* 1992), Abid Ilahi. —— Moyra Anne, *b* 1936: *m* 1960, William Francis Leonard, of 4 Gifford St, St Heliers, Auckland, NZ, and has issue living, Mark Francis, *b* 1961, — Philippa Jane, *b* 1962: *m* 1988, Alastair Salmond, of Wellington, NZ, — Virginia Anne, *b* 1965.

Grandsons of Capt Hon Edward Spencer Harry Boyle, RN, 5th son of 5th Earl:—
Issue of late Lt-Cdr Patrick Spencer Boyle, RNVR, *b* 1905, *d* 1978: *m* 1st, 1932, Vera Maude Radcliffe Agnew, who *d*

(Feb) 1940, da of Daniel Radcliffe, JP, LLD, of Pen-y-Lan, Cardiff; 2ndly, (Aug) 1940, Rita (13 Springfield, E Oakley, Basingstoke, Hants), da of late Cecil Behrens, JP:—
(By 1st *m*) Michael Patrick Radcliffe (Forest Lodge, Ashe Park, Basingstoke, Hants), *b* 1934; *ed* Eton; Capt (ret) IG; CC Hants 1970, and DL 1982: *m* 1962, Lady Nell Carleton Harris, da of 6th Earl of Malmesbury, and has issue living, Robert Algernon Radcliffe (Boodle's Club), *b* 1963; *ed* King's Sch, Bruton; Capt Irish Gds: *m* 1987, Fiona Elisabeth Maule, yst da of Col George Patrick Maule Ramsay (*see* E Dalhousie, colls), — Rupert, *b* 1968, — Maria, *b* 1964. —— (By 2nd *m*) David Spencer (2 St John's Gdns, W11 2NO), *b* 1942; *ed* Winchester, and Trin Coll, Camb: *m* 1980, Melanie Georgiana, only da of late William Robert Brudenell Foster (*see* M Ailesbury, colls, 1976 Edn), and has issue living, James Patrick W., *b* 1983, — Fennella, *b* 1982.

PREDECESSORS – (1) HENRY BOYLE, PC, MP for co Cork 1715-56, Speaker of the Irish House of Commons, fifteen times Lord Justice of Ireland, and Chancellor of the Exchequer and Commr of the Treasury; *cr Baron Castle Martyr, Viscount Boyle,* and *Earl of Shannon* (peerage of Ireland) 1756; *d* 1764; *s* by his son (2) RICHARD, KP, PC, 2nd Earl; was successively MP for Dungarvan and for co Cork, Master-Gen of the Ordnance 1766-70, and Vice-Treasurer of Ireland 1781, etc; *cr Baron Carleton,* of Carleton, co York (peerage of Great Britain) 1786; *d* 1807; *s* by his son (3) HENRY, KP, 3rd Earl; was Custos Rotulorum of co Cork, and Clerk of the Pells in Ireland; *d* 1842; *s* by his son (4) RICHARD, 4th Earl; *b* 1809: *m* 1832, Emily Henrietta, da of Lord George Seymour (M Hertford); *d* 1868; *s* by his son (5) HENRY BENTINCK, 5th Earl. *b* 1833: *m* 1st, 1859, Lady Blanche Emma Lascelles, who *d* 1863, da of 3rd Earl of Harewood; 2ndly, 1868, Julia Charlotte, who *d* 1921, da of Sir William Edmund Cradock-Hartopp, 3rd Bt; *d* 1890; *s* by his el son (6) RICHARD HENRY, 6th Earl, *b* 1860: *m* 1895, Nellie, who *d* 1910, da of late Charles Thompson, of 14 Park Sq, NW; *d* 1906; *s* by his el son (7) RICHARD BERNARD, 7th Earl, *b* 1897; Lt Roy Fusiliers; (*ka* 1917); *s* by his brother (8) ROBERT HENRY, 8th Earl; *b* 1900; Capt Indian Army; ADC to Gov of Madras 1923: *m* 1923, Marjorie, who *d* 1981, da of S. A. Walker, of Ootacamund, India; *d* 1963; *s* by his only son (9) RICHARD BENTINCK, 9th Earl and present peer; also Viscount Boyle, Baron Castle Martyr, and Baron Carleton. (*Note,* this title derived from Shannon Park, co Cork and *not* the River Shannon.)

SHARP OF GRIMSDYKE, BARONY OF (Sharp) (Life Baron 1989, Extinct 1994)

ERIC SHARP, CBE, son of Isaac Sharp; *b* 17 Aug 1916; *ed* LSE (BSc Econ, Hon Fellow 1986); Chm Cable & Wireless since 1980 (Chief Exec since 1981), Monsanto Ltd since 1975 (Dep-Chm 1973-74), and Polyamide Intermediates since 1975; Member Economic Devpt Cttee Chemical Industry since 1980, and Central Electricity Generating Board since 1980; Freeman City of London 1982; *cr* CBE 1980, Knt 1984, and *Baron Sharp of Grimsdyke,* of Stanmore, in the London Borough of Harrow (Life Baron) 1989: *m* 1950, Marion, da of — Freeman, of —, and *d* 1994, having had issue.

Arms – Azure, in pale a pallet fracted at fess point double endorsed argent between two arrows points upwards gold. **Crest** – A beaver sejant guardant or supporting a sphere per pale azure and paly argent and azure, overall a barrulet cotised argent.

SON LIVING

Hon Richard Simon, *b* 1956.

DAUGHTERS LIVING AND DECEASED

Nicola Rosemary, *b* 1954; *d* 19—.
Hon Victoria Madeleine, *b* 1956 (twin): *m* 19—, — Chappatte.

SHARPLES, BARONESS (Swan) (Life Baroness 1973)

PAMELA SWAN, da of Keith William Newall; *b* 11 Feb 1923; *ed* Southover Manor, Lewes; 1939-45 War as LACW with WRAF; *cr Baroness Sharples,* of Chawton, in Hampshire (Life Baroness) 1973: *m* 1st, 1946, Sir Richard Christopher Sharples, KCMG, OBE, MC, Gov of Bermuda, who *d* (assassinated in Bermuda) 1973; 2ndly, 1977, Patrick David de Laszlo, who *d* 1980; 3rdly, 1983, Robert Douglas Swan, and has issue by 1st *m*.

Arms – Argent, a chevron vert between in chief two copper beech trees eradicated, and in base a white tailed tropicbird (Phaethon Lepturus), a volant proper, for *Sharples,* on an escutcheon of pretence the Arms of *Newall,* Per saltire argent and gules, a crozier in fesse or between three bustards, wings elevated and addorsed, counterchanged. **Supporters** – On either side a Great Dane dog, resting the interior hind foot proper on a portcullis or.
Residence – Nunswell, Higher Coombe, Shaftesbury, Dorset.

SONS LIVING *(By 1st marriage)*

Hon Christopher John SHARPLES (72 Elm Park Rd, SW3), *b* 1947: *m* 1975, Sharon, el da of late Robert Sweeny, of Montague Sq, W1; and has issue.
Hon David Richard SHARPLES, *b* 1955: *m* 1981 (*m diss* 1988), Annabel (Anna), 2nd da of Col Thomas Armitage Hall, OBE, of Chiselhampton House, Oxford.

DAUGHTERS LIVING *(By 1st marriage)*

Hon Fiona, *b* 1949: *m* 1981 (*m diss* 1982), Alexander Paterson; has issue living, Natalie Louise SHARPLES, *b* 1975.
Hon Miranda, *b* 1951: *m* 1981, Nicholas Larkins, elder son of Dr N. Larkins, of Sydney, Australia, and has issue living, Harry Claud, *b* 1985, — Amelia Kate (Kitty), *b* 1989. *Residence* – The Old Rectory, Stoke Wake, Blandford, Dorset.

SHAUGHNESSY, BARON (Shaughnessy) (Baron UK 1916)

With a strong hand

WILLIAM GRAHAM SHAUGHNESSY, CD, 3rd Baron; *b* 28 Mar 1922; *s* 1938; *ed* Bishop's Coll Sch, Bishop's Univ, Lennoxville, Canada, and Columbia Univ, New York; Major (ret) Canadian Gren Gds; Dir Arbor Memorial Services Inc, Toronto, since 1972, Memb Joint Select Cttee on Statutory Instruments since 1985, and Delegated Powers Scrutiny Cttee (Hoel) since 1993; Executive Assist to Canadian Min of Finance 1949-51; Pres of Royal Commonwealth Soc, Montreal, Canada 1959-61; Trustee, The Last Post Fund; 1939-45 War in NW Europe (despatches); CD 1955: *m* 1944, Mary, only da of late John Whitley, of Letchworth, and has had issue.

Arms – Per fesse gules and azure, in chief two mill-rinds, and in base an ancient harp or, within a bordure engrailed ermine. **Crest** – Issuing from an antique crown or, a dexter cubit arm in armour and gauntleted, grasping a two-headed battle-axe, all proper. **Supporters** – *Dexter*, an Irish wolfhound proper, gorged with a collar argent charged with three trefoils vert; *sinister*, a beaver proper, gorged with a collar argent, charged with three maple leaves gules.
Address – c/o House of Lords, SW1A 0PW.

SONS LIVING AND DECEASED

†*Hon* Patrick John, *b* 1944; *d* 1982.
Hon MICHAEL JAMES, *b* 12 Nov 1946.

DAUGHTERS LIVING

Hon Brigid Mary, *b* 1948.
Hon Marion Kathleen, *b* 1951.

COLLATERAL BRANCH LIVING

Granddaughters of late Capt Hon Alfred Thomas Shaughnessy (infra):—
Issue of late Capt Thomas Bradford Shaughnessy, *b* 1915, *d* 1994: *m* 1949, Margot, who *d* 1991, da of late William D. Chambers, of Montreal:—
Amanda Marguerite Polk, *b* 1951. —— Roxane Elizabeth, *b* 1952: *m* 1984, Thomas Herbert McGreevy, son of John McGreevy, of Quebec City, Canada, and has issue living, Julian Thomas Gray, *b* 1989, — Sarah Paige, *b* 1986, — Madeleine Claire Elizabeth, *b* 1989. —— Tara Evelyn, *b* 1954: *m* 1983, Alain Du Bois, of 50 Tunstall Av, Senneville, Quebec H9X 1T2, Canada, son of Leopold Du Bois, of Magog, Quebec, Canada, and has issue living, Louis Shaughnessy, *b* 1985, — Chella Evelyn, *b* 1988.

Issue of late Capt Hon Alfred Thomas Shaughnessy, Canadian Expeditionary Force, yr son of 1st Baron, *b* 1887, *ka* 1916: *m* 1912, Sarah Polk, who *d* 1955 (having *m* 2ndly, 1920, Lieut-Col Hon Sir Piers Walter Legh, GCVO, CMG, CIE, OBE, who *d* 1955 (*see* B Newton, colls)), da of late Judge James C. Bradford, formerly of Nashville, Tennessee, USA:—
Alfred James (*posthumous*), *b* 1916; is Capt, Gren Gds (Reserve): *m* 1948, Jean Margaret, da of late George Lodge, of Kirkella, Yorks and has issue living, Charles George Patrick, *b* 1955: *m* 1983, Susan, da of Sydney Fallender, of Los Angeles, Cal, USA, and has issue living, Jenny Johanna *b* 1990, — David James Bradford, *b* 1957: *m* 1985, Anne-Marie, da of Thomas Schoettle, of Indianapolis, USA, and has issue living, Amy Jean *b* 1990, Kathryn Anne *b* 1992. —— Elizabeth Sarah Polk (Flat 1, Durham House, Durham Place, SW3 4ET), *b* 1913: resumed the surname of Stafford 1976 until re-marriage: *m* 1st, 1932 (*m diss* 1946), 2nd Baron Grenfell, who *d* 1976; 2ndly, 1946, Maj Berkeley Buckingham Howard Stafford, KRRC, who *d* 1966; 3rdly, 1969 (*m diss* 1975), Trevor Walton King; 4thly, 1983, Cdr (Arnold) Derek Arthur Lawson, RN, who *d* 1984, and has issue living (by 1st *m*) (*see* B Grenfell).

PREDECESSORS – (1) THOMAS GEORGE Shaughnessy, KCVO, son of Thomas Shaughnessy, of Limerick; *b* 1853 (Milwaukee, USA); was Pres Canadian Pacific Railway 1899-1918 (Chm of Board of Directors); also a Director of all this Co's allied lines; *cr Baron Shaughnessy*, of City of Montreal, Dominion of Canada, and of Ashford, co Limerick (peerage of United Kingdom) 1916: *m* 1880, Elizabeth Bridget, who *d* 1937, da of N. Nagle, of Milwaukee, USA; *d* 1923; *s* by his son (2) WILLIAM JAMES, KC, 2nd Baron; *b* 1883; KC Canada; a Director of Canadian Pacific Railway Co, of Canadian Bank of Commerce, and other Cos: *m* 1911, Marion Laura, who *d* 1936, da of late Robert Kilgour Graham, of Montreal, Canada; *d* 1938; *s* by his only son (3) WILLIAM GRAHAM, 3rd Baron and present peer.

SHAWCROSS, BARON (Shawcross) (Life Baron 1959)

HARTLEY WILLIAM SHAWCROSS, GBE, PC, QC, son of late John Shawcross, MA; *b* 4 Feb 1902; *ed* Dulwich Coll and Geneva; Hon LLM Liverpool; Hon LLD Columbia (USA), Bristol, Michigan, Lehigh (USA), Sussex, London and Liverpool; Hon DCL New Brunswick, and Hull; Hon Member Royal Coll of Surgeons, and Royal Coll of Obstetricians & Gynaecologists; Bar Gray's Inn 1925, Bencher 1939, KC 1939, and Treasurer 1955; a Member of Bar Council (Chm 1952-57), Hon Fellow of American Bar Foundation, and Hon Member of American and New York Bars; Recorder of Salford 1941-45, and Kingston upon Thames 1946-61; Attorney-Gen 1945-51 and Pres of Board of Trade April to Oct 1951; a Prin Delegate for UK to Assemblies of UN 1945-49, Ch Prosecutor for UK before Internat Mil Tribunal Nuremberg 1945-46, and UK Member of Permanent Court of Arbitration, The Hague 1950-67, Chm Royal Commn on the Press 1961-62, Med Research Council 1961-65, Sussex Discharged Prisoners' Aid Soc 1962-66, and City Panel on Take-Overs and Mergers 1968-80; a JP for Sussex; Dir: Caffyns Ltd (Dep Chm); sometime Dir Observer Newspapers Ltd, Shell Transport & Trading Co Ltd, Morgan et Cie SA, Hawker Siddeley Group Ltd, Times Newspapers Ltd, Thames Television Ltd (Chm 1969-74), Upjohn (UK) Ltd (Chm), Rank Hovis Macdougall Ltd; sometime Consultant to Hawker Siddeley, Rank Hovis, and J.P. Morgan; Chm Morgan Guaranty Trust Co's Internat Advisory Council 1967-74; Past Pres of Rainer Foundation (formerly London Police Court Mission), and of British Hotels and Restaurants Assocn; a sometime Member of Exec of Internat Commn of Jurists, and of Council of Internat Chamber of Commerce; Chm of Friends of Atlantic Union, Internat Law Section, British Inst of Internat & Comparative Law, and Justice (British Branch Internat Commn of Jurists); Member of Court, London Univ; Chancellor of Sussex Univ 1965-85; Indep Chm of Press Council 1974-78; MP for St Helens (*L*) 1945-58; *cr* Knt 1945, PC 1946, *Baron Shawcross*, of Friston, co Sussex (Life Baron) 1959, and GBE (Civil) 1974: *m* 1st, 1924, Rosita Alberta, who *d* 1943, da of William Shyvers, of Upminster Lodge, Essex; 2ndly, 1944, Joan Winifred, who *d* 1974, da of Hume Mather, of Carlton Lodge, Tunbridge Wells, and has issue by 2nd *m*.

ᴀrms – Per pale azure and gules on a saltire between four annulets argent an ermine spot sable. ᴄrest – Upon the battlements of a tower proper a martlet gules holding in the beak a cross paty fitchy or. Supporters – *Dexter*, a lion argent gorged with a chain sable pendant therefrom an escutcheon also sable charged with a balance or; *sinister*, a griffin sable armed and langued azure gorged with a chain, pendent therefrom a portcullis or.
Residences – Friston Place, Sussex; Anchorage, St Mawes, Cornwall; I-One Albany, Piccadilly, W1V 9RP. *Address* – 60 Victoria Embankment, EC4Y 0JP. *Clubs* – Buck's, White's, Garrick, Pratt's, Royal Automobile, Royal Cornwall Yacht, Royal Yacht Squadron, New York Yacht, and Travellers' (Paris).

SONS LIVING *(By 2nd marriage)*

Hon William Hartley Hume (46 Blomfield Rd, W9), *b* 1946; *ed* Eton, and Univ Coll, Oxford: *m* 1st, 1972 (*m diss* 1980), Marina Sarah, da of late Col Esmond Pelham Warner, TD, of Cambridge; 2ndly, 1981 (*m diss* 19—), Michal E., da of A. J. Levin, of London; 3rdly, 1993, Hon Mrs Olga Polizzi, eldest da of Baron Forte (Life Baron), and has issue living (by 1st *m*), Conrad Hartley Pelham, *b* 1977, — (by 2nd *m*) Eleanor Joan Georgina, *b* 1983.
Hon Hume, *b* 1953; *ed* Eton.

DAUGHTER LIVING *(By 2nd marriage)*

Hon Joanna, *b* 1948; *ed* Benenden, and St Bartholomew's Hosp Med Sch: *m* 1986, Charles Russell Peck, eldest son of Russell Peck, of Cambridge, Mass, USA, and has issue living, Henry Russell Hartley, *b* 1988, — Alice Joan, *b* 1989. *Residence* – Flint Cottage, Friston Place, nr Eastbourne, Sussex BN20 0AN.

Sheffield and Stanley of Alderley, Baron (see Stanley of Alderley).

Shelburne, Earl of; son of Marquess of Lansdowne.

SHEPHERD, BARON (Shepherd) (Baron UK 1946)

MALCOLM NEWTON SHEPHERD, PC, 2nd Baron; *b* 27 Sept 1918; *s* 1954: Capt of HM Body Guard of Hon Corps of Gentlemen-at-Arms 1964-67; Dir Mitchell Cotts & Co (FE) Ltd 1946-50, Chm and Man Dir Fielding, Brown and Finch (FE) Ltd 1950-64; Dep Speaker and Ch Whip, House of Lords 1964-67; a Min of State Commonwealth Office 1967-70, and Dep Leader House of Lords 1968-70; Lord Privy Seal and

Leader of the House of Lords 1974-76; Dep Chm of Sterling Group of Cos since 1976; Chm of Practice and Procedure Select Cttee House of Lords 1976-78, of Medical Research Council 1973-79, of Civil Ser Pay Research Unit Board since 1978, of Packaging Council since 1978, Chm National Bus Co 1978; Pres Centre Européen de L'Enterprise Publique 1984-85, and Inst of Road Transport Engrs since 1987; Chm House of Lords Cttee European Community Affairs, Telecom.-Transport-Energy, 1987-89; Internat Consultant, Sun Hung Kai Securities, Sun Hung Kai Bank, Hong Kong; 1939-45 War as Lt RASC in N Africa, Sicily, and Italy; PC 1965: *m* 1941, Allison, da of Patrick Redmond, of 56 Carrick Knowe, Parkway, Edinburgh, and has issue.
Residence – 29 Kennington Palace Court, Sancroft St, SE11.

SONS LIVING

Hon GRAEME GEORGE, *b* 6 Jan 1949: *m* 1971, Eleanor, da of —, and has issue living, Patrick Malcolm, *b* 19—.
Hon Douglas Newton, *b* 1952.

SISTER LIVING

Hon Margaret Eleanor, *b* 1922: *m* 1949, Theodore Leonard Bates, and has issue living, Andrew Michael, *b* 1952, — Suzanne Katherine Michele, *b* 1960. *Residence* – Justacott, 3 Victoria Cottages, Lydiate Lane, Lynton, N Devon.

PREDECESSOR – **(1)** *Rt Hon* GEORGE ROBERT Shepherd, PC, son of late George Robert Shepherd of Spalding, Lincolnshire, *b* 1881; Ch Opposition Whip, and a Dep-Speaker, House of Lords and a Member of Parliamentary Committee of Labour Party; National Agent of Labour Party 1928-46; was a Lord-in-Waiting to HM Oct 1948 to July 1949; Capt of Yeomen of the Guard July to Oct 1949, and Capt of Gentlemen-at-Arms and Ch Govt Whip in House of Lords Oct 1949 to Oct 1951; *cr* PC 1951, *Baron Shepherd*, of Spalding, co Lincoln (peerage of UK) 1946: *m* 1915, Ada, who *d* 1975, da of late Alfred Newton, of Halstead, Essex; *d* 1954; *s* by his son **(2)** MALCOLM NEWTON, 2nd Baron and present peer.

SHERBORNE, BARONY OF (Dutton) (Extinct 1985)

WIDOW LIVING OF SON OF SIXTH BARON

Pauline Stewart (*Hon Mrs George E. Dutton*) (Kings Thorn, Hereford), yr da of late Maj Stewart Robinson, of Lyonshall, Hereford, and formerly wife of Michael Shephard, MC and bar: *m* 1959, as his 2nd wife, Hon George Edward Dutton, yr son of 6th Baron, who *d* 1981.

COLLATERAL BRANCH LIVING

Issue of late Vice-Adm Hon Arthur Brandreth Scott Dutton, CB, CMG (raised to rank of a Baron's son 1920), brother of 6th Baron, *b* 1876, *d* 1932: *m* 1914, Doriel, who *d* 1941, da of Sir John Adam Hay, 9th Bt (*cr* 1635):—

Julia Meliora, *b* 1914: *m* 1939, Bertram Salisbury Butler, formerly Sqdn-Ldr RAFVR, of Burton Manor, Pulborough, Sussex, and has issue living, Doriel Julia Primrose, *b* 1941: *m* 1964, Gavin Fleming Crawford, of 7 Woodsford Sq, Addison Rd, W14, and has issue living, Charles William Norrie *b* 1970, Caroline Doriel *b* 1966, Sarah Elizabeth *b* 1968. —— (Doriel) Rowena, *b* 1916: *m* 1940, Ian Norman Bayles, DFC, Wing-Cdr RAFVR, of Chatsworth Park, Tabilk, Vic, Aust, and has issue living, Alastair Ian (Chatsworth Park, Tabilk, Victoria 3607, Aust) *b* 1941: *m* 1967, Judith Alison, el da of Geoffrey Ryan, of Willowmavin, Vic, Aust, and has issue living, Emma Rowena *b* 1970, Fiona Alison *b* 1973, — Archibald James Norman (Pevensey Station, Hay, NSW, Australia), *b* 1948: *m* 1975, Sally Ishbel, el da of Sir Alec (Alexander Reid) Creswick, of Allanvale, Avenel, Vic, Aust, and has issue living, Timothy James Creswick *b* 1981, Edward Ian Alexander *b* 1984, — Aprilla Rowena, *b* 1946: *m* 1st, 1968 (*m diss* 1979), John Beaufort Somerset; 2ndly, 1979, Anthony George Hodgson, of S Yarra, Melbourne, Aust, and has issue living (by 1st *m*), Sarah Penelope *b* 1970, Catherine Rowena *b* 1971, — Amanda Mary, *b* 1951: *m* 1st, 1976 (*m diss* 1987), Capt David Maurice Stirling Home Drummond Moray, Scots Gds (ret) (*see* D Buccleuch, colls); 2ndly, 1987, John Dorman Elliott, of Toorak, Melbourne, Aust, and has issue living (by 1st *m*) (*see* D Buccleuch, colls) (by 2nd *m*) Alexandra Louisa Amanda *b* 1989, — Ayliffe Julia (twin), *b* 1951: *m* 1977, John Wallis Caldwell, of Milong, Yourg, NSW, and has issue living, William John Bayles *b* 1982, Hugh Ian Wallis *b* 1984, Camilla Ayliffe *b* 1980. *Residence* – Chatsworth Park, Tabilk, Vic, Aust.

SHERFIELD, BARON (Makins) (Baron UK 1964)

ROGER MELLOR MAKINS, GCB, GCMG, FRS, 1st Baron, son of late Brig-Gen Sir Ernest Makins, KBE, CB, DSO; *b* 3 Feb 1904; *ed* Winchester, and Ch Ch, Oxford; a DL of Hants; Hon DCL Oxford, Hon LLD Sheffield and London, DIC, Hon FICE, Fellow of All Souls' Coll, Oxford; Fellow of Winchester Coll 1963-79, Warden 1974-79; Hon Student Ch Ch Oxford, and Hon DLitt Reading; Bar Inner Temple 1927; Min at Washington 1945-47, Assist Under-Sec of State, Foreign Office 1947-48, Dep Under-Sec of State 1948-52, Ambassador to USA 1952-56, Joint Permanent Sec to The Treasury 1956-60, and Chm of UK Atomic Energy Authority 1960-64; Chm Board of Govs, Imperial Coll of Science and Technology 1962-74, Industrial and Commercial Finance Corporation 1964-74, Hill Samuel & Co, Ltd, 1966-70, A. C. Cossor 1968-82, Raytheon Europe International Co 1970-82, Wells-Fargo Ltd 1972-84, Ditchley Foundation 1962-65, Marshall Aid Commemoration Commn 1965-73, and House of Lords Select Cttee on Science and Technology 1984-87, and other cos; Pres Parliamentary and Scientific Cttee 1969-72, British Standards Instn 1970-72, and The Centre for Internat Briefing 1972-85; Chancellor of Reading Univ 1970-92, since when Chancellor Emeritus; FRS 1986; *cr* CMG 1944, KCMG 1949, KCB (Civil) 1953, GCMG 1955, GCB (Civil) 1960 and *Baron Sherfield*, of Sherfield-on-Loddon, co Southampton (Peerage of UK) 1964: *m* 1934, Alice Brooks, who *d* 1985, el da of late Hon Dwight F. Davis, and has issue.

𝕬rms – Argent or a fesse embattled counter embattled gules between in chief two falcons proper belled or, and in base a lion's face of the second, an annulet or between two besants. 𝕮rest – A dexter arm embowed in armour proper encircled by an annulet or and holding a flagstaff, therefrom flowing a banner argent charged with a lion's face gules. 𝕾upporters – *Dexter*, a lion sable pendent from a chain about the neck or a bezant charged with a model representing an atom of lithium 6 sable, *Sinister*, a bald headed eagle rising proper adorned likewise about the neck the bezant charged with a lawn tennis racquet erect gules.
Residences – Ham Farm House, Ramsdell, nr Basingstoke, Hants; 81 Onslow Sq, SW7.
Clubs – Boodle's, Pratt's, MCC.

SONS LIVING

Hon CHRISTOPHER JAMES (3034 P St NW, Washington, DC, USA), *b* 23 July 1942; *ed* Winchester and New Coll, Oxford; Fellow of All Souls Coll, Oxford; HM Foreign Ser 1964-74: *m* 1975, Wendy Cortesi, and has issue.
Hon Dwight William, *b* 1951; *ed* Winchester, and Ch Ch, Oxford: *m* 1983, Penelope Jane, da of D. R. L. Massy Collier.

DAUGHTERS LIVING

Hon Mary (*Viscountess Norwich*), *b* 1935: *m* 1st 1959 (*m diss* 1984), as his 2nd wife, Hon Hugo John Laurence Philipps (later 3rd Baron Milford); 2ndly, 1989, as his 2nd wife, 2nd Viscount Norwich, CVO, and has issue (by 1st *m*) (*see* B Milford).
Residence – 24 Blomfield Rd, W9.
Hon Cynthia (twin), *b* 1935: *m* 1967, Oliver James Colman, of 7 Tor Gdns, W8, and has issue (*see* Colman, Bt, *cr* 1907).
Hon Virginia, *b* 1939; *ed* Lady Margaret Hall, Oxford: *m* 1972, David Michael Shapiro, of 14 Woodstock Rd, W4, and has issue, three sons.
Hon Patricia, *b* 1946: *m* 1st, 1966, Michael Ordway Miller, of Muir Beach, Cal, USA; 2ndly, 1980, Loring Sagan, of 488 Old County Rd, Tahoe City, Cal, USA, and has issue.

SHINWELL, BARONY OF (Shinwell) (Extinct 1986)

SON LIVING OF LIFE BARON

Hon Samuel, *b* 19—.

DAUGHTER LIVING OF LIFE BARON

Hon Mrs P. Sellers.

SHREWSBURY AND WATERFORD, EARL OF (Chetwynd-Talbot) (Earl E 1442, I 1446, and GB 1784)

Ready to accomplish

CHARLES HENRY JOHN BENEDICT CROFTON CHETWYND CHETWYND-TALBOT, 22nd Earl, and Premier Earl (on the Roll) in peerages both of England and Ireland; *b* 18 Dec 1952; *s* 1980; *ed* Harrow; is Hereditary Lord High Steward of Ireland, and patron of eleven livings: *m* 1974, Deborah Jane, only da of Noel Staughton Hutchinson, of Ellerton House, Sambrook, Shropshire, and has issue.

Arms – Quarterly, 1st and 4th, gules, a lion rampant, within a bordure engrailed or, *Talbot*; 2nd and 3rd azure, a chevron between three mullets or, *Chetwynd*. **Crest** – 1st, on a chapeau gules, turned up ermine, a lion statant, with the tail extended or, *Talbot*; 2nd, a goat's head erased argent, attired or, *Chetwynd*. **Supporters** – Two talbots argent. **Badge** – A talbot passant argent.
Seat – Wanfield Hall, Kingstone, Uttoxeter, Staffs.

SONS LIVING

JAMES RICHARD CHARLES JOHN (*Viscount Ingestre*), *b* 11 Jan 1978.
Hon Edward William Henry Alexander, *b* 1981.

DAUGHTER LIVING

Lady Victoria Jane, *b* 1975.

BROTHER LIVING

Hon Paul Alexander Anthony Bueno, *b* 1957; *ed* Eton, and Ch Ch, Oxford (BA): *m* 1982, Sarah Elizabeth, da of Simon Hildebrand Melville Bradley, of Thundridge, Ware, Herts (*see* V Hampden), and has issue living, Harry, *b* 1985, — Jack, *b* 1987. *Residence* – Gunville House, Grateley, nr Andover, Hants SP11 8JQ.

SISTERS LIVING

Lady Charlotte Sarah Alexandra, *b* 1938: *m* 1965, Camillo Cavazza dei Conti Cavazza, of S Felice del Benaco, Brescia, Italy, who *d* 1981, and has issue living, Sigmar, *b* 1966, — Eric, *b* 1969, — Christian, *b* 1979, — Lars-Patrick, *b* (twin) 1979, — Livia, *b* 1967, — Ilona, *b* 1972, — Alberta, *b* 1977.
Lady (Josephine) Sylvia-Rose, *b* 1940: *m* 1965, Stafford Antony Saint, and has issue living, Stafford Alexander Antony Talbot, *b* 1970, — Helen Elizabeth Charlotte, *b* 1966, — Victoria Nadine Mary, *b* 1968. *Residence* – Ledburn Farm, Ledburn, Leighton Buzzard, Beds.
Lady Catharine Laura, *b* 1945; LRAM: *m* 1966, Richard Sebastian Endicott Chamberlain, and has issue living, Thomas Endicott, *b* 1973; *ed* Radley, — Sophie Anne Zacyntha *b* 1968, — Caroline Amy, *b* 1971. *Residence* – Stocks Farm, Burley St, nr Ringwood, Hants.
Lady Marguerite Mary, *b* 1950: *m* 1st, 1970 (*m diss* 1984), Guy William Brisbane; 2ndly, 1984, Andrew Wynne, and has issue living (by 1st *m*), Duncan Guy Talbot, *b* 1975; *ed* Berkhamsted. *Residence* – 18 Campbell Drive, Beaconsfield, Bucks HP9 1TF.

AUNT LIVING (*Granddaughter of* 20th *Earl*) (*Raised to the rank of an Earl's daughter* 1921)

Lady Victoria Audrey Beatrice, *b* 1910: *m* 1st, 1932 (*m diss* 1936), 6th Baron Sheffield; 2ndly, 1945, His Honour Judge (Gwyn Rhyse Francis) Morris, QC, who *d* 1982.

MOTHER LIVING

Nadine Muriel, yr da of late Brig-Gen Cyril Randell Crofton, CB, of Trobridge, Crediton, Devon: *m* 1936 (*m diss* 1963), as his 1st wife, the 21st Earl, who *d* 1980. *Residence* – The House, Lower Ascott, Leighton Buzzard, Beds.

COLLATERAL BRANCHES LIVING

Grandson of late Brig-Gen Arthur Hervey Talbot, son of late Charles Arthur Talbot, elder son (by 1st *m*) of late Rev Hon Arthur Chetwynd-Talbot, 3rd son of 2nd Earl Talbot:—
Issue of late Lieut-Col Douglas Hervey Talbot, DSO, MC, *b* 1882, *d* 1927: *m* 1914, Dorothy Helen Roylance, who *d* 1978, da of late William Roylance Court, JP (Walker, Bt, *cr* 1886):—
Bryan Hervey (Aston Lodge, Aston, Runcorn, Cheshire), *b* 1916; *ed* Marlborough Coll; 1940-46 War as Fl Lt RAFVR: *m* 1940, Katherine, who *d* 1977, da of R. J. Hughes, of Llandudno, and has issue living, Andrew Hervey (White Cottage, Aston Heath, Runcorn, Chesh), *b* 1946: *m* 1st, 1972 (*m diss* 1976), Hilda Margaret Priscilla Williams, SRN; 2ndly, 1979, Danielle Claude, yst da of Roger Basil Boulay, of La Promenade, Aubige-Racan 72420, France, and has issue living, Jessie Sarah *b* 1983, — Howard Douglas (Burnt Thatch, Aston, Runcorn, Chesh), *b* 1948: *m* 1972, Christine Anne, da of W. A. A. Dutton, of Hoole Bank, Chester, and has issue living, Charles Aston Hervey *b* 1981, Bridget Louisa *b* 1975, Sophie Katharine *b* 1977, — Marie Luize, *b* 1942: *m* 1966, John Bernard Haycraft, of The Pipings, Pebworth, Warwicks, and has issue living, Alexander Richard *b* 1969, Oliver Talbot *b* 1972, Simon Hervey *b* 1973, — Wendy Robina Roylance, *b* 1949: *m* 1973, Rodger Price, of Hilltop, Sutton Weaver, Runcorn, Cheshire, and has issue living, Hannah Roylance *b* 1975, Madeleine Kate *b* 1977.

Grandson of late Col Hervey Talbot, yr son (by 1st *m*) of late Rev Hon Arthur Chetwynd-Talbot (ante):—
Issue of late Arthur Aston Talbot, *b* 1881, *d* 1918: *m* 1912, Mary Winifred, who *d* 1964, da of late A. Battiscombe, of Hinton Court, Hereford:—
Patrick Edward Aston (1941 Arrowhead Drive, St Petersburg, Florida 33703, USA), *b* 1913; RAF 1934-38, RAE 1939-46: *m* 1936, Gwyneth, yr da of late Lt-Col Herbert Gaussen Sargeaunt, RA, and has issue living, David Nugent Aston (Ontario, Canada), *b* 1939: *m* 1st, 1962 (*m diss* 1971), Carole, da of Oakley Pawson, of Ontario; 2ndly, 1979, Rachel, who *d* 1988, yr da of Dr Frank Edmund Hampton, of Grimsby, Lincs, and has issue living (by 1st *m*), John Oakley Aston *b* 1964, Jeanne Davida *b* 1962, Rachel Millicent *b* 1966, (by 2nd *m*) Georgina Amy *b* 1980, — Maryan Gwyneth, *b* 1938; BA Hons (1959): *m* 1974, John Roberts, of Douro Terrace, St Helier, Jersey, CI.

Grandchildren of late Rev Arthur Henry Chetwynd-Talbot, yst son (only son by 2nd *m*) of late Rev Hon Arthur Chetwynd-Talbot (ante):—

Issue of late Sqdn-Ldr John Arthur Chetwynd-Talbot, AFC, *b* 1905, *d* 1993: *m* 1st, 1929 (*m diss* 1963), Helen Mary, who *d* 1969, eldest da of late Adm Cyril Samuel Townsend, CB; 2ndly, 1963, Betty Verral (Stoke End Cottage, Stoke Green, Stoke Poges, Bucks), yr da of late Rev Augustus George Allton:—

(By 1st *m*) John Edward (46 Swan St, Kingsclere, Newbury, Berks), *b* 1934; *ed* Harrow; Sub-Lieut (A) RNVR 1955-57: *m* 1st, 1959 (*m diss* 1964), Sonja Ann, da of late Roger Walker, of South Corner, Duncton, Sussex; 2ndly, 1967, Belinda Bess, yr da of Maj Euan James Leslie Warren Gilchrist, MC, DFC, RA, of Monk Sherborne House, Monk Sherborne, Hants, and has issue living (by 1st *m*), Jane Sonja, *b* 1960: *m* 1984, Simon Barkes, of Fawler End, Kingston Lisle, Wantage, Oxon, son of B. R. Barkes, of Wimbledon, and has issue living, Benjamin *b* 1989, Harriet Maria Eleanora *b* 1987, Serena Jane *b* 1991, — Sarah Ann, *b* 1962: *m* 1983, Michael W. Morris, son of M. E. Morris, of Myrtle Cottage, Llandogo, Gwent, and has issue living, Rebecca Sarah *b* 1984, Chloe *b* 1985, — (by 2nd *m*) Edward John, *b* 1969, — Mary Rowena, *b* 1968, — Prudence Ankaret, *b* (twin) 1969. —— Susan Mary, *b* 1930: *m* 1954, William Byars Thomson, of Holt Valley Farm, Clayton, Hassocks, Sussex, and has issue living, Geoffrey Charles Byars, *b* 1958, — *Rev* Richard William Byars, *b* 1960, — Mary Rose Byars, *b* 1962; MB BS: *m* 1987, Peter George Shears, of 109 Bonchurch Rd, Brighton. —— Ankaret Helen, *b* 1932: *m* 1955, John Orcheston Dean, of 1054 Burnhamthorpe Rd, RR1, Oakville, Ontario, Canada, and has issue living, John Anthony, *b* 1962, — Joanna Elizabeth, *b* 1956: *m* 1979, David Knight Wilson, of 60 Evelyn Av, Ottawa, Ontario, Canada, and has issue living, Lucas Knight *b* 1983, Amanda Helen *b* 1981, — Philippa Ankaret, *b* 1958: *m* 1979, Russel Ray Pedley, of RR1, S Slocan, BC, Canada, and has issue living, Sidney Matthew *b* 1982, Jasmine Ankaret *b* 1981, — Louise Helen, *b* 1960: *m* 1979, Douglas William Moody, of 354 Queen St, Midland, Ontario, Canada, and has issue living, Jonathan William *b* 1979, Adam Douglas *b* 1982, Simon Jeffrey *b* 1984.

Issue of late Rev Arthur Charles Ashton Chetwynd-Talbot, *b* 1907, *d* 1987: *m* 1945, Pamela Mountjoy (Flat 2, Park Lodge, 2 Blackwater Rd, Eastbourne BN21 4JE), da of late Hugh John Say, of Dartford, Kent:—

Clare Eveline (29 Holloway, Bath, Avon), *b* 1946: *m* 1968 (*m diss* 1976), Malcolm Garfield Green, and has issue living, Timothy Ashton Garfield, *b* 1969, — Caroline Anne, *b* 1971.

Grandchildren of late Rt Hon Sir George John Talbot, eldest son of late Rt Hon John Gilbert Talbot, elder son of late Hon John Chetwynd-Talbot, QC, 4th son of 2nd Earl Talbot:—

Issue of late Capt Thomas George Talbot, CB, QC, *b* 1904, *d* 1992: *m* 1933, Hon Cynthia Edith Guest (The Small House, Falconhurst, Markbeech, Edenbridge, Kent), yr da of 1st Viscount Wimbourne:—

Charles John, *b* 1947: *m* 1st, 1978 (*m diss* 1992), Phyllida R., eldest da of late Rev Michael McCormick; 2ndly, 1993, Nicola Mary, da of late George Boulton, of Upland, Hillydeal Rd, Otford, Sevenoaks, Kent, and has issue living (by 1st *m*), Richard Charles, *b* 1980, — Francis Michael, *b* 1982, — Hugo Peter, *b* 1983, — (by 2nd *m*) George Thomas, *b* 1992. *Residence* – Falconhurst, Markbeech, Edenbridge, Kent TN8 5NR. —— Meriel Cornelia, *b* 1935: *m* 1966, Prof Robert David Hugh Boyd, MB, FRCP, of The Stone House, Skellorn Green, Adlington, Macclesfield, Cheshire, and has issue living, Thomas Dixon, *b* 1957, — Diana Charlotte, *b* 1969, — Lucy Madeleine, *b* 1974. —— Joanna, *b* 1938: *m* 1964, Alan Malcolm Smith, of Edells, Markbeech, Edenbridge, Kent, and has issue living, Bertram Thomas, *b* 1967, — Emily Mary, *b* 1965, — Flora, *b* 1971. —— Mary Gertrude (13 Ufton Grove, N1), *b* 1942.

Grandchildren of late John Edward Talbot, 3rd son of late Rt Hon John Gilbert Talbot (ante):—

Issue of late Lt-Col Evan Arthur Christopher Talbot, MBE, Gren Gds, *b* 1903, *d* 1975: *m* 1926, Felicite Annette Cynthia, who *d* 1985, da of Lt-Col William Edward Long:—

Christopher Michael Edward, *b* 1928; late Lt RN: *m* 1962, Suzanne Barbara, el da of late Arthur Dulley, and has issue living, Sarah Josephine, *b* 1964: *m* 1990, Hugh S. Muirhead, son of Richard Muirhead, of Greenfields, Plumpton, Sussex, — Miranda Meriel, *b* 1966, — Alice Elizabeth, *b* 1969. —— Catherine (11 rue Maitre Cornille, 13990 Fontvieille, France), *b* 1930: *m* 1958 (*m diss* 1978), Clement Francis Kelly, and has issue living, Anthea Jane, *b* 1959: *m* 1981 (*m diss* 1991), C. Coulson, — Felicity Ankaret, *b* 1962: *m* 1992, Gordon Jones.

Granddaughter of late Rt Rev Edward Stuart Talbot, DD, Lord Bishop of Winchester, son of late Hon John Chetwynd-Talbot, QC (ante):—

Issue of late Rt Rev Neville Stuart Talbot, MC, DD, Bishop of Pretoria 1920-32, *b* 1879, *d* 1943: *m* 1918, Cecil Mary, who *d* 1921, da of William Seymour Eastwood, of West Stoke House, Chichester:—

Elizabeth, *b* 1919; late Flight Officer WAAF; is a JP: *m* 1946, Fl Lt Ronald Arthur Chalk, who *d* 1993, and has issue living, Gilbert John, *b* 1947: *m* 1975, Gillian Frances Audrey, only da of Sir Gervase Ralph Edmund Blois, 10th Bt, MC, and formerly wife of Hugh Christopher Riddle, and has issue living (*see* Blois, Bt), — Sarah Elizabeth, *b* 1950: *m* 1982, Nicholas John Squire, and has issue living, Guy Charles *b* 1985, Hugo Edward John *b* 1987, Amanda Elizabeth *b* 1984, Octavia Clare *b* 1991. *Residence* – 12 Loudwater House, Rickmansworth, Herts.

Granddaughter of late George Canning Talbot, son of late Rev Hon George Gustavus Chetwynd-Talbot (infra):—

Issue of late Major John Arthur William Talbot, *b* 1876, *d* 1918: *m* 1906, Barbara Grace, who *d* 1938, el da of late Rowland Ticehurst, of Crickley, St Witcombe, Gloucestershire:—

Lettice Mary, *b* (Dec) 1907: *m* 1934, George Butt Miller, who *d* 1958, and has issue living, Thomas Butt (La Planque, Torteval, Guernsey), *b* 1935; *ed* Eton, and New Coll, Oxford (MA); Solicitor 1966: *m* 1965, Jane Mary, only da of late C. C. Roberts, of Bepton Old Rectory, Midhurst, — Robert Cottrell Butt (80 Alderney St, SW1), *b* 1947; *ed* Worksop Coll, Trin Coll, Dublin (BA), and Edinburgh Univ (M Litt): *m* 1971, Patricia Georgina, da of Dr G. McBrien, of Bath, and has issue living, George Talbot *b* 1974; *ed* Sherborne, and Reading Univ, Caroline Mary *b* 1978, — John Richard Butt (The Glebe House, Kilninor, Gorey, co Wexford), *b* 1950; *ed* Stanbridge Sch, and Duke Univ, N Carolina, — Barbara Blanche, *b* 1938, — Mary Ruth (Calebrook House, Charlton Musgraove, Wincanton, Som), *b* 1939: *m* 1989, George Blaug. *Residence* – Berrywood House, Donhead, Shaftesbury, Dorset.

Granddaughters of late Lieut-Col Gerald Francis Chetwynd-Talbot, 3rd son of late Rev Hon William Whitworth Chetwynd-Talbot, 6th son of 2nd Earl Talbot:—

Issue of late Stafford Cecil Chetwynd-Talbot, *b* 1880, *d* 1950: *m* 1905, Ethel Lilian Caroline Leslie, who *d* 1963, da of late Robert Leslie Gault, of Montreal:—

Charlotte Henrietta Dorwin, *b* 1908: *m* 1935, Richard Charles Powys-Smith, late Lieut-Cdr RNR, and has issue living, Richard Talbot, *b* 1941: *m* 1970, Lavinia Susan Sanderson, and has issue living, James Robert Talbot *b* 1972, Mark William Talbot *b* 1975. *Residence* – Church Place, E Hendred, Wantage, Oxon.

Issue of late Sir Gerald Francis Chetwynd-Talbot, KCVO, CMG, OBE, *b* 1881, *d* 1945: *m* 1920, Hélène, who *d* 1975, da of S. Jarislowsky, of Paris, and widow of Capt Charles Labouchere, French Army:—

Isobel Helen Henrietta, *b* 1923: *m* 1942, Antony Mackenzie Smith, OBE, MC, and has issue living, Peter (British Council, London) *b* 1946: *m* 1973, Sandra Gay-French, and has issue living, Helen Sarah *b* 1974, Alexandra Anne *b* 1976, Harriet Isobel *b* 1981, — Duncan John Gerald (10c Windsor Rd, W5), *b* 1951, — Jane Elizabeth, *b* 1947: *m* 1972, Robin Martin, and has issue living, James Benedict *b* 1973, Edward Barnaby *b* 1975, Peter Nicholas *b* 1983, — Catherine Isobel, *b* 1957; MD Sydney 1982: *m* 1979, Dr Simon Hawke, of Corner House, High St, Islip, Oxon OX5 2RX, and has issue living, Henrietta *b* 1984, Charlotte *b* 1986. *Residence* – Backfields End, Winchelsea, Sussex.

Grandchildren living of late Gilbert Edward Chetwynd-Talbot (infra):—

Issue of late Maj Patrick Gilbert Murray Chetwynd-Talbot, *b* 1905, *d* 1979: *m* 1928, Audrey (The Dower House, Headbourne Worthy, Winchester), yst da of late Julius Ernst Guthe, JP, of Kepwick Hall, Northallerton, Yorks:—

Humphrey John Patrick (The Three Horseshoes, 31 Staploe, St Neots, Cambs PE19 4JA), *b* 1930; *ed* Winchester, and Univ Coll, Oxford (MA): *m* 1953, Anne, twin da of late Capt Edward Glyn de Styrap Jukes-Hughes, CBE, RN, of Stourbridge House, Milton-on-Stour, Gillingham, Dorset, and has issue living, Kathryn Helen Anne, *b* 1957: *m* 1979, Sidney Anthony George Abrahams, and has issue living, Thomas Anthony Talbot *b* 1985, Annika Kathryn Anne *b* 1983, Harriett Laila *b* 1988, — Jennifer Mary, *b* 1958; *ed* St Hugh's Coll, Oxford (MA); MBA: *m* 1983, Martin Paul Rigby, late Capt RGJ, son of John Rigby, of Camberley, Surrey, and has issue living, Dominic John Vaughan *b* 1992, Eloise Jennifer *b* 1989, Alice Helen Elizabeth *b* 1992, — Annabel Jean, *b* 1961; *ed* Exeter Univ (B Ed Hons). ——Michael Gilbert (Langford Court Farm Cottage, Bath Rd, Upper Langford, Avon BS18 7DG), *b* 1931; *ed* Eton, and RMA Sandhurst; late Capt RA: *m* 1956 (*m diss* 19—), Bridget Adele, yr da of late Sidney Terence Evelyn Pook Ennion, of Colbourne, IoW, and has issue living, Rupert Edward Terence Gilbert, *b* 1962, — Tobias John Michael, *b* 1963, — Juliet Emma Serena, *b* 1958. ——Janet Ivory Audrey, *b* 1932: *m* 1954, Donald Craufurd Robertson, of 45 Park Rd, Chiswick, W4, and has issue living, James Craufurd, *b* 1958, — William Alexander, *b* 1959, — David Kenneth Craufurd, *b* 1964.

Grandson of late Col Hon Sir Wellington Patrick Manvers Chetwynd-Talbot, KCB, 8th son of 2nd Earl Talbot:—
Issue of late Gilbert Edward Chetwynd-Talbot, *b* 1876, *d* 1950: *m* 1905, Geraldine Mary, who *d* 1953, da of late Rev Frederick William Murray, R of Stone and Canon of Rochester (D Atholl, colls):—
Edward Hugh Frederick, MBE (Mead Acre, Milton Lilbourne, Pewsey, Wilts), *b* 1909; *ed* Haileybury; is Capt late RA; 1939-45 War (MBE), MBE (Mil) 1945: *m* 1935, Cynthia Phœbe Duncan, da of late Noel McGrigor Phillips, of Stoke d'Abernon Manor, Cobham, and has issue living, Mark Patrick (Scencliffe Grange, Coxwold, York 1) *b* 1941; Maj late Coldm Gds: *m* 1970, Elizabeth Ann, da of Sacheverel O. F. Bateman, of Mortham Tower, Barnard Castle, co Durham, and has issue living, Nicholas John *b* 1971, Lara Katherine *b* 1973, — Anthea, *b* 1939: *m* 1963, Philip Simon Antill, of Scofton Farm House, Worksop, Notts, and has issue living, Vanessa Cicely *b* 1964: *m* 1989, Andrew Robinson (and has issue living, Thomas *b* 1992, Abigail *b* 1994), Juliet Willa *b* 1966, Helen Meriel *b* 1969, Jemima Louise *b* 1971, — Meriel *b* 1944: *m* 1964, Mark Alexander Wyndham Baker, of The Old School, Fyfield, Abingdon, Oxon, and has issue (*see* Macnaghten, Bt, colls).

Grandchildren of late Charles Fleming Chetwynd Chetwynd-Talbot (infra):—
Issue of late Charles John Huyshe Chetwynd Chetwynd-Talbot, *b* 1910, *d* 1991: *m* 1936, Jane (VAUGHAN), who *d* 1989, eldest da of late David Wheldon Jones, of Blaenyddol, Ffestiniog, N Wales:—
John Vaughan Chetwynd (8 Kinecroft, Wallingford, Oxon), *b* 1941; *ed* Eton; Page to Earl of Shrewsbury at Coronation of HM Queen Elizabeth II. ——Frances Elizabeth, *b* 1947: *m* 1974, Peter Henry Mayes, of Blakenhall Lodge, The Green, Barton-under-Needwood, Staffs, and has issue living, Tomasine Lucy, *b* 1977, — Rebecca Jane, *b* 1979.

Grandchildren of late Charles Alexander Price Chetwynd-Talbot, son of Hon Gerald Chetwynd-Talbot, 9th son of 2nd Earl Talbot:—
Issue of late Charles Fleming Chetwynd Chetwynd-Talbot, *b* 1879, *d* 1933: *m* 1906, Margaret Dorothy, who *d* 1969, da of Lt-Col Dunbar Fraser Huyshe, formerly RHA:—
Gilbert Alexander Lucius Chetwynd, *b* 1918; *ed* Eton: Lt-Col (ret) late Comdg 14th/20th King's Hussars; formerly Assist Mil Sec to C-in-C, Middle East; Sec, Albany, Piccadilly, 1967-83; 1939-45 War in Iraq, Syria, Persia (despatches), and Italy. *Residences* – Mansion Basement, Albany, Piccadilly, W1; Pleasant Cottage, Brightwell-cum-Sotwell, Wallingford, Oxon. *Club* – Cavalry. ——Geraldine Cecil Barbara, *b* 1907; formerly Subaltern First Aid Nursing Yeo. *Residences* – Mansion Basement, Albany, Piccadilly, W1; Pleasant Cottage, Brightwell-cum-Sotwell, Wallingford, Oxon.
Issue of late Gilbert Patrick Chetwynd-Talbot, *b* 1887, *d* 1958: *m* 1921 (*m diss* 1929), Alice Alethea, da of C. H. Christopher Moller, of Lindsey House, Cheyne Walk, Chelsea, SW:—
Christopher Patrick Chetwynd, RD (The Old Farm House, Godshillwood, Fordingbridge, Hants SP6 2LP), *b* 1922; *ed* Harrow, and Corpus Christi Coll, Camb; 1939-45 War as Lieut RNVR; Lt-Cdr RNR (ret) 1957-81: *m* 1955, Rosalind Mary, da of Air Vice-Marshal Christopher Neil Hope Bilney, CB, CBE, and has two adopted children, Patrick Nicholas Chetwynd, *b* 1958, — Harriet Susan, *b* 1959. ——Barbara Maud Mary, *b* 1924: *m* 1949, Douglas Scott. *Residence* – Nigg Mains, Nigg, Ross-shire.

Grandchildren of late Maj Henry Charles Talbot, son of Rev Henry George Talbot, el son of Very Rev Charles Talbot, son of 3rd son of 1st Baron:—
Issue of late Capt Henry Fitzroy George Talbot, DSO, RN, *b* 1874, *d* 1920: *m* 1904, Susan Blair Athol, who *d* 1951, only da of late William Allison:—
Sir (Arthur Allison) FitzRoy, KBE, CB, DSO, *b* 1909; Vice-Adm (ret); formerly Naval Attaché, Moscow; Commodore RN Barracks, Portsmouth 1957-59; Flag Officer, Arabian Seas and Persian Gulf 1960-62, C-in-C, Atlantic, and S American Station 1962-65, and of Plymouth Command 1965-67; 1939-45 War, operations off Norway and Dieppe (wounded); DSO 1940 (Bar 1944), CB (Mil) 1961, KBE (Mil) 1964: *m* 1st, 1940, Joyce Gertrude, who *d* 1981, el da of late Frank Edward Linley, of 28 Lower Sloane St, SW1, and Fowey, Cornwall; 2ndly, 1983, Elizabeth Mary, widow of Sir Esmond Otho Durlacher, formerly wife of Capt Richard Steel, RN, and da of Rupert Handley Ensor, and has issue living (by 1st *m*), Anthea Jane, *b* 1944: *m* 1969, James A. H. Charrington, of Cherry Orchard, Shaftesbury, Dorset, and has issue living, Melissa Clare *b* 1970, Lucinda Rose *b* 1973, — Elizabeth, *b* 1945: *m* 1969, Michael Shuttleworth, of Hathersage, Derbys, and has issue living, Ashton FitzRoy *b* 1972, Henry Ashton *b* 1974. *Residence* – Wooton FitzPaine Manor, Bridport, Dorset DT6 6NF. *Club* – United Service. ——Nesta Cecil, *b* 1905: *m* 1929, Capt John Hext Lewes, OBE, KStJ, RN (ret), Lord Lieut of Cardiganshire 1956-74, Lieut of Dyfed 1974-77, who *d* 1992, of Llanllyr, nr Lampeter, Cardiganshire, and has issue living, John William Talbot, RN (Y Fron, Maesycrugiau, Pencader, Carmarthenshire). *Club* – United Service), *b* 1931; is Lt-Cdr; Korea 1950-51; *m* 1st, 1954 (*m diss* 1963), Mary Georgiana, who *d* 1992, da of late Pascoe Anthony George Glyn (*see* B Wolverton, colls, 1990 Edn); 2ndly, 1967, Margaret Jane, da of Owen Fenner Clayton, of Sydney, NSW, Australia and has issue living, (by 1st *m*) John Pascoe *b* 1955, James Glyn *b* 1959: *m* 1984, Helen Lohmann, of Reading, Penn, USA (and has issue living, Maxwell John Pascoe *b* 1985), Alice Mary Rhiannon *b* 1957, (by 2nd *m*) Owain Vaughan *b* 1967, Angharad Hope *b* 1972, — Loveday Elisabeth Talbot, *b* 1932: *m* 1956, Robert George Gee, of Llanllyr, Talsarn, Lampeter, Dyfed, and has issue living, Matthew George Cooper *b* 1960, Patrick Robert Cooper *b* 1963: *m* 1991, Miranda Whitelaw Dunn (and has issue living, William Benedict Robert Cooper *b* 1992), Emma Louise Moya *b* 1962: *m* 1990, Nicholas Eric Hugh Barran (and has issue: *see* Barran, Bt, colls), — Gwenllian Anne Talbot, *b* 1934: *m* 1955, Capt John Franklin Kidd, RN, of Llanfair, Llandyssul, Dyfed, and has issue living, John Christopher William *b* 1957, Elisabeth Ceridwen *b* 1958.

Grandsons of late Maj Edward Frederick Talbot-Ponsonby, 3rd but eldest surv son of late Charles William Talbot-Ponsonby (infra):—
Issue of late Lt-Col John Arthur Talbot-Ponsonby, *b* 1907, *d* 1969: *m* 1st, 1931 (*m diss* 1956), Frances Elizabeth, who *d* 1980, only da of late Douglas H. Fraser; 2ndly, 1957, Daphne TALBOT-PONSONBY (who *d* 1976, having *m* 2ndly, 1972, Capt Thomas Hanbury), el da of late Percival Augustus Duke, OBE, and formerly wife of Capt Jack Brittain-Jones, CBE:—
(By 1st *m*) Michael Clement (10 Westmoreland Pl, SW1; Hinton Manor, Hinton Parva, nr Swindon, Wilts), *b* 1932: *m* 1956, Judith Katharine Gibson, who *d* 1985, and has issue living, Caroline Frances, *b* 1958: *m* 1990, Patrick E. F. Pilkington, eldest son of late Maj Nigel Pilkington, of Purley, Surrey, and has issue living, Hubert Edward *b* 1991, John Nigel *b* 1993, Patrick Cecil *b* 1994, — Charlotte Jane, *b* 1963: *m* 1992, William M. E. O'Leary, eldest son of David O'Leary, — Lucy Elizabeth, *b* 1965, — Katherine Louisa, *b* 1967. ——Peter William (Tocknells House, Painswick, Glos GL6 6TR), *b* 1938: *m* 1st, 1962 (*m diss* 1988), Sarah Vansittart, da of late Sir Eric Vansittart Bowater; 2ndly, 1988, Jane Faye, da of Jean Lancelot d'Espeissis, of

Perth, W Australia, and has issue living (by 1st *m*), Nina, *b* 1964, — Jessica, *b* 1965: *m* 1987, Andrew J. Saunders, of 19 Ensor Mews, SW7, — Eila, *b* 1972, — (by 2nd *m*) Frederick James, *b* 1990.

Grandchildren of late Charles William TALBOT-PONSONBY (who assumed by Roy Licence 1866, the additional surname of Ponsonby), el son of late Adm Sir Charles Talbot, KCB, 2nd son of late Very Rev Charles Talbot (ante):—
Issue of late Charles George Talbot-Ponsonby, *b* 1874, *d* 1937: *m* 1914, Violet Mary, who *d* 1945, da of Capt Raymond Parr (B Dunsany):—
Edward FitzRoy, *b* 1916; *ed* Harrow: *m* 1st, 1938 (*m diss* 1960), Bertha Marie Louise Muriel, da of H. C. Barber, of Trinity Hill, Jersey; 2ndly, 1960 (*m diss* 1967), Shirley Rhona Mearns; 3rdly, 1967, Anja Edith Boudewijn, of Cowes, and has issue living, (by 1st *m*), Nigel Edward Charles (Langrish Lodge, Langrish, Petersfield, Hants), *b* 1946: *m* 1977, Robina Helen, el da of Lt-Cdr Henry Victor Bruce, RN (ret) (*see* E Elgin, colls), and has issue living, Charles Henry FitzRoy *b* 1981, James Nigel Edward *b* 1986, Alexander John Bruce *b* 1987, — Suzanne Molly, *b* 1959: *m* 1957 (*m diss* 1973), Lt James Granville Lucas, RN (*see* Lucas, Bt, colls). *Residence* – East Lodge, Rogate, Petersfield, Hants.
Issue of late Com Frederick William Talbot-Ponsonby, RN, *b* 1879, *d* 1930: *m* 1913, Hannah, who *d* 1952, da of late John Ritchie Findlay, of Aberlour, Banffshire:—
Evelyn John, *b* 1915; *ed* Harrow, and Trin Coll, Camb (MA); formerly Lieut RNVR: *m* 1943, Hilary, da of T. Kingsley Curtis, of 82 Highgate West Hill, N6, and has issue living, *Rev Preb* Andrew (Leintwardine Rectory, nr Craven Arms, Shropshire), *b* 1944; *ed* Harrow: *m* 1st, 1968, Alice Margaret, who *d* 1989, da of Raymond Whittier Baldwin, of Alderley Edge, Ches (*see* Barlow, Bt, *cr* 1902, colls); 2ndly, 1991, Rev Jill, da of Cecil Frank Robert Sims, of Shirley, Southampton, and has issue living (by 1st *m*), Daniel Frederick *b* 1971; *ed* Shrewsbury, and Oriel Coll, Oxford (BA), Thomas Martin *b* 1973; *ed* Shrewsbury, William Peter *b* 1975; *ed* Shrewsbury, Henry James *b* 1981, — Christopher, *b* 1950, — Simon (West Barns, Home Farm, Abbots Leigh, Bristol), *b* 1952; *ed* Harrow, and Nottingham Univ (BSc); CEng: *m* 1976 (*m diss* 1990), Hilary, da of Eric Cropper, — Elizabeth Hannah, *b* 1945: *m* 1969, Dr John Michael Beck, of 4 St Mary's Av, Harrogate, and has issue living, Mark Thomas Coulton *b* 1972, George Samuel Curtis *b* 1975, Charles Edward Frank *b* 1979, Tess Adwoa Margaret Nora *b* 1970, Ruth Mary Ann *b* 1977, — Celia, *b* 1947: *m* 1971, David McTeer, G/Capt RAF, and has issue living, Stuart Paul *b* 1973, Ian James *b* 1975, Philip John *b* 1977. *Residence* – 38 Kitsbury Rd, Berkhamsted, Herts HP4 3EA. —— Felicity Philippa (*Lady Scott*), *b* 1918: *m* 1951, Lt-Cdr Sir Peter Markham Scott, CH, CBE, DSC, FRS, late RNVR, who *d* 1989 (Bruce, Bt, *cr* 1804, colls), and has issue living, Richard Falcon (The Depot, Weeton Lane, Dunkeswick, Harewood, Leeds LS17 9LP), *b* 1954: *m* 1981 (*m diss* 1992), Jillian Elizabeth Gomersall, and has issue living, Lucy Jane Elizabeth *b* 1983, — Dafila Kathleen, *b* 1952: *m* 1980, Dr Timothy Clutton-Brock, of White Roses, Reach, Cambs, and has issue living, Peter *b* 1983, Amber *b* 1981. *Residence* – The New Grounds, Slimbridge, Gloucestershire GL2 7BS.

Grandchildren of late Maj Francis Arthur Bouverie Talbot, 2nd son of late Adm Sir Charles Talbot, KCB (ante):—
Issue of late Vice-Adm Sir Cecil Ponsonby Talbot, KCB, KBE, DSO, *b* 1884, *d* 1970: *m* 1912, Bridget, who *d* 1960, da of late R. B. D. Bradshaw, of Fairfield, Barrow-in-Furness:—
John (Lodge House, Smeeth, Ashford, Kent TN25 6QZ), *b* 1925; *ed* Radley; Lt-Col RA (ret), formerly Defence Attaché Sofia, then Vienna: *m* 1954, Janet Wyndham, da of late Lt-Gen Sir William Wyndham Green, KBE, CB, DSO, MC, and has issue living, David John (Schlehenring 115, D85551 Kirchheim bei München, Germany), *b* 1960: *m* 1983, Margret Manson, da of Douglas Gordon McKenzie Cameron, of Dunfermline, Fife, and has issue living, Charles Edward Cameron *b* 1987, James Alexander St John *b* 1989, Sholto Richard John *b* 1993, — Anthony Francis Wyndham (124 East 65th St, New York, NY 10021, USA), *b* 1961: *m* 1989, Melody Jane, da of Peter Sidney Hallett, of 6 Loxton Place, Forestville 2087, NSW, Australia, and has issue living, Imogen Primrose Claire *b* 1993, — Peter Charles (178 Underwood St, Paddington, Sydney, Australia), *b* 1964: *m* 1990, Jacqueline Margaret, da of David Parkes, of The Old Rectory, Wrington, Bristol. —— Barbara Bridget, *b* 1919: *m* 1940, Cdr Richard Molyneux Favell, DSC, JP, DL, RN, of Shell Cottage, Penberth, St Buryan, Cornwall (High Sheriff Cornwall 1963), and has issue living, Frances Barbara Molyneux (*Lady Banham*), *b* 1943: *m* 1965, Sir John Michael Middlecott Banham, of Penberth, St Buryan, N Penzance, and has issue living, Mark Richard Middlecott *b* 1968, Serena Frances Tamsin *b* 1970, Morwenna Bridget Favell *b* 1972, — Bridget Alathea, *b* 1946: *m* 1970, David Llewelyn Hugh-Jones, of The Thatched Cottage, Penberth, St Buryan, N Penzance, and has issue living, Tristan Llewelyn *b* 1973, Rupert Favell *b* 1977, Demelza Alice *b* 1971, Carenza Bridie *b* 1978, — Julia Alice, *b* 1949: *m* 1976, Derek Robin Bryant, of Chynance, St Buryan, N Penzance, and has issue living, Frank Ingram *b* 1981, Rebecca Sophie *b* 1978, Rachel Jessica *b* 1980.

Granddaughter of late George Ponsonby Talbot, son of Adm Sir Charles Talbot, KCB (ante):—
Issue of late Vice-Adm Arthur George Talbot, CB, DSO, *b* 1892, *d* 1960: *m* 1923, Doris, who *d* 1972, da of late Charles Fremantle Branson:—
Diana Maud Ponsonby, *b* 1921: *m* 1942, Major Leslie Alban Harris, OBE, DSC, RM (Fleet Air Arm) (ret), and has issue living, Nicholas Graham Talbot (The Granary, Milborne Port, Sherborne, Dorset), *b* 1947; *ed* Sherborne; Lt-Cdr RN: *m* 1971, Jennifer Jane Stuart, da of Capt Justin Mallinson, of Bredy, Burton Bradstock, Dorset, and has issue living, Charles Justin Talbot *b* 1983, Antonia Diana Stuart *b* 1975, Francesca Louise Talbot *b* 1979. *Residence* – 39 South St, W1.

Grandson of late Col George Reginald Fitzroy Talbot (infra):—
Issue of late Col Granville FitzRoy Talbot, *b* 1908, *d* 1978: *m* 1938, Kathleen Betty (Lapworth Cottage, Elstead, Surrey), only da of Gerald Townend, of Woking:—
John FitzRoy (Daggers House, Hope, Derbyshire), *b* 1945; *ed* Uppingham, and St Thomas's Hosp, London; MB, BS, FRCS, FRC Ophth, LRCP; Consultant Ophthalmic Surg and Hon Lecturer, Sheffield Med Sch: *m* 1972, Esmé, yst da of late Dr Robert de Brath Ashworth, of Holdfast Hall, Warfield, Berks (*see* B Ravensdale, colls, 1990 Edn), and has issue living, Fleur Katharine FitzRoy, *b* 1978, — Emily Sarah FitzRoy, *b* 1980, — Ann Adele FitzRoy, *b* 1987.

Granddaughter of late Maj-Gen FitzRoy Somerset Talbot, son of late Col George Talbot, yst son of late Very Rev Charles Talbot (ante):—
Issue of late Col George Reginald Fitzroy Talbot, *b* 1870, *d* 1931: *m* 1902, Eleanor Morwenna, who *d* 1949, only da of late Rev Roger Granville, MA, Sub-dean of Exeter, of Pilton House, Pinhoe, near Exeter:—
Gwendoline Betty Alice, *b* 1905.

PREDECESSORS – **(1)** *Sir* GILBERT Talbot, Lord Chamberlain to Edward III, was summoned to Parliament of England 1331; *d* 1346; *s* by his son **(2)** RICHARD, 2nd Baron, and a Knight Banneret; was summoned to Parliament 1331-55; *d* 1356, possessed of immense estates; *s* by his son **(3)** GILBERT, 3rd Baron; summoned to Parliament 1362-86; *d* 1387; *s* by his son **(4)** RICHARD, 4th Baron; summoned to Parliament as Ricardo *Talbot de Blackmere* in his father's lifetime 1387: *m* Ankaret, da and heiress of John, 5th Baron *Strange of Blackmere*; *d* 1396; *s* by his son **(5)** GILBERT, 5th Baron; *d* 1419; *s* by his da **(6)** ANKARET; *d* unmarried 1431; *s* by her uncle **(7)** JOHN, KG, 7th Baron, who having *m* 1408, Maud (*suo jure* Baroness Furnivall), da of Thomas (Nevill) Lord Furnivall, in 1409 had been summoned to Parliament as *Johann Talbot de Furnyvall*; became Lord Justice of Ireland 1412, and was Lord-Lieut thereof 1414-21; was a celebrated warrior and gloriously sustained the cause of Henry VI throughout his French realm; his successes were, however, in 1429, checked by the Maid of Orleans at Patay, when his army was routed and himself taken prisoner; he was soon exchanged and again pursued a career of victory; *cr* Earl of Shrewsbury (peerage of England) 1442, and *Earl of Waterford* (peerage of Ireland) 1446; was Ambassador to France 1443: appointed Lieut of the Duchy of Aquitaine 1453, and on 20 July of that year was killed at the battle of Castillon; *s* by his son **(8)** JOHN, KG, KB, 2nd Earl; was Lord Chancellor of Ireland 1446, and Lord High Treasurer of

England 1457; *k* at the battle of Northampton 1460, while fighting for the Red Rose; *s* by his son **(9)** JOHN, 3rd Earl; *d* 1473; *s* by his son **(10)** GEORGE, KG, 4th Earl; served with distinction at the battle of Stoke; *d* 1528; *s* by his son **(11)** FRANCIS, KG, PC, 5th Earl; summoned to Parliament in lifetime of his father; was one of the few public men who, having served Queen Mary, was admitted to the Privy Council of Elizabeth; *d* 1560; *s* by his son **(12)** GEORGE, KG, 6th Earl; had the charge of Mary, Queen of Scots, for many years, and assisted at her execution; appointed Lord High Steward of England at the arraignment of the Duke of Norfolk, and Earl Marshal after the Duke's execution; *d* 1590; *s* by his son **(13)** GILBERT, KG, 7th Earl; *d* without male issue, when the Baronies of Talbot, Furnivall, and Strange of Blackmere became abeyant between his three daughters, eventually devolving upon the last surviving Alathea, wife of Thomas, 14th Earl of Arundel; *s* in the earldom by his brother **(14)** EDWARD, 8th Earl; *d* 1617; *s* by his kinsman **(15)** GEORGE, 9th Earl, descendant in the 4th generation of Sir Gilbert, 3rd son of 2nd Earl; *d* 1630; *s* by his nephew **(16)** JOHN, 10th Earl; *d* 1653; *s* by his son **(17)** FRANCIS, 11th Earl; killed in a duel with George Villiers, 2nd Duke of Buckingham, 1667; *s* by his son **(18)** CHARLES, KG, 12th Earl; held some of the most important offices in the state, and was a prominent statesman *temp* William and Mary, Anne, and George I; conformed to the Protestant cause 1679; *cr Marquess of Alton* and *Duke of Shrewsbury* 1694; *dsp* 1717, when the marquessate and dukedom expired and the earldom reverted to his cousin **(19)** GILBERT, 13th Earl, son of Hon Gilbert, 2nd son of 10th Earl; was in Holy Orders of Church of Rome; *d* 1743; *s* by his nephew **(20)** GEORGE, 14th Earl; *dsp* 1787; *s* by his nephew **(21)** CHARLES, 15th Earl; *dsp* 1827; *s* by his nephew **(22)** JOHN, 16th Earl; *d* 1852; *s* by his cousin **(23)** BERTRAM ARTHUR, 17th Earl; *d* 1856; *s* by his kinsman **(24)** HENRY JOHN Chetwynd-Talbot (*infra*), CB, PC, 18th Earl; who, in 1849, had *s* as 3rd *Earl Talbot* and 5th *Baron Talbot* (see * infra); was an Adm and Capt of Corps of Gentlemen-at-Arms, etc; *d* 1868; *s* by his son **(25)** CHARLES JOHN, 19th Earl; *b* 1830; sat as MP for N Staffordshire 1859-65, and for Stamford 1868; was Capt of Hon Corps of Gentlemen-at-Arms 1874-7: *m* 1855, Anne Theresa, who *d* 1912, da of Com Richard Howe Cockerell, RN; *d* 1877; *s* by his son **(26)** CHARLES HENRY JOHN, KCVO, 20th Earl; *b* 1860; was Lord High Steward of Ireland: *m* 18 June 1882, Ellen Mary, who *d* 1940, da of late Charles Rowland Palmer-Morewood (B Byron), and former wife of Alfred Edward Miller Mundy, of Shipley Hall, Derby; *d* 1921; *s* by his grandson **(27)** JOHN GEORGE CHARLES HENRY ALTON ALEXANDER CHETWYND (son of late Charles John Alton Chetwynd, Viscount Ingestre, MVO, who *d* 1915), 21st Earl, *b* 1914; Staff-Lieut to HRH The Duke of Gloucester 1940-42; served in World War II as Capt RA in Middle East and Italy 1942-44; Pres Staffordshire Agric Soc, and Assoc of Agric: *m* 1st, 1936 (*m diss* 1963), Nadine Muriel, yr da of late Brig-Gen Cyril Randell Crofton, CB; 2ndly, 1963, Doris Aileen Mortlock, who *d* 1993; *d* 1980; *s* by his el son **(28)** CHARLES HENRY JOHN BENEDICT CROFTON CHETWYND, 22nd Earl and present peer; also Earl of Waterford, Earl Talbot, Viscount Ingestre, and Baron Talbot.

***(1)** CHARLES Talbot, PC, eighth in descent from Hon Sir Gilbert Talbot, 3rd son of 2nd Earl of Shrewsbury; sat successively as MP for Tregony and Durham; was an eminent lawyer, and in 1723 attained the summit of his profession on being constituted Lord High Chancellor of England; *cr Baron Talbot*, of Hensol, co Glamorgan (peerage of Great Britain) 1723; *d* 1737; *s* by his son **(2)** WILLIAM, PC, 2nd Baron; was Lord Steward of the Household; *cr Earl Talbot* (peerage of Great Britain), 1761, and *Baron Dinevor*, of Dynevor, co Carmarthen (peerage of Great Britain), 1780, with remainder to his da Cecil, wife of George Rice, MP, and her issue male; *d* 1782, when the earldom expired, the barony of Dinevor passed to his da (ante), and the Barony of Talbot reverted to his nephew **(3)** JOHN CHETWYND, 3rd Baron; sat as MP for Castle Rising; *cr Viscount Ingestre* and *Earl Talbot* (peerage of Great Britain) 1784, and assumed by Roy licence the additional surname and arms of Chetwynd; *d* 1793; *s* by his son **(4)** CHARLES, KG, 2nd Earl; was Viceroy of Ireland, and Lord-Lieut of Staffordshire; *d* 1849; *s* by his son **(5)** HENRY JOHN (ante) 3rd Earl, who in 1856 *s* as 18th Earl of Shrewsbury.

Shute, Baron; title borne by Viscount Barrington on Roll of HL.

SHUTTLEWORTH, BARON (Kay-Shuttleworth) (Baron UK 1902, Bt UK 1850)

Kind kin when known keep

CHARLES GEOFFREY NICHOLAS KAY-SHUTTLEWORTH, 5th Baron, and 6th Baronet; *b* 2 Aug 1948; *s* 1975; *ed* Eton; DL Lancs 1986; Chm Rural Development Commn since 1990, Chm National & Provincial Building Soc since 1994; FRICS: *m* 1975, Ann Mary, da of James Whatman, of Northcote Hill, Shamley Green, Surrey, and formerly wife of late Daniel Henry Barclay, and has issue.

Arms – Quarterly; 1st and 4th, argent, three shuttles sable, tipped and threaded or; 2nd and 3rd, argent, two bendlets sable between as many crescents azure, between the bendlets three ermine spots. **Crests** – 1st, a cubit arm in armour proper, grasping in the gauntlet a shuttle as in the arms, *Shuttleworth*; 2nd, on a crescent azure a goldfinch proper, *Kay*. **Supporters** – *Dexter*, a weaver habited in cap and apron proper, holding in the exterior hand a shuttle as in the arms; *sinister*, a seaman holding in his exterior hand a ship's lamp, all proper. **Residences** – Leck Hall, Carnforth, Lancs; 14 Sloane Av, SW3 3JE.

SONS LIVING

Hon THOMAS EDWARD, *b* 29 Sept 1976.
Hon David Charles, *b* 1978.
Hon William James, *b* 1979.

BROTHERS LIVING

Hon Robert James, *b* 1954; *ed* Eton; late Lieut Coldsteam Guards Res.
Hon Edward Roger Noël, *b* 1962; *ed* Eton.

SISTER LIVING

Hon Sarah Rachel Jane, *b* 1950: *m* 1st, 1970 (*m diss* 1984), Richard Francis Foster (*see* M Ailesbury, colls, 1976 Edn), 2ndly, 1988, Peter Figgins, and has issue living (by 1st *m*), Edward William Thomas *b* 1978, — Henrietta Victoria, *b* 1973, — Georgiana Pamela, *b* 1975, — (by 2nd *m*) Tom, *b* 1990. *Residence* – Flat 15, 16 Pembridge Sq, W2 4EH.

COLLATERAL BRANCH LIVING

Issue of late Robert Kay-Shuttleworth, 2nd son of 1st Baronet, *b* 1847, *d* 1934: *m* 1896, Ethel Clementina, who *d* 1962, da of late Alfred J. Freeman, MD, of Villa delle Palme, San Remo, Italy:—
Helen Victoria (Whitefolds, 28 Dorset Rd South, Bexhill-on-Sea), *b* 1905: *m* 1936, Major Wynyard Montagu Hall, late W Yorkshire Regt, who *d* 1949.

PREDECESSORS – (1) *Sir* JAMES PHILLIPS Kay-Shuttleworth, el son of late Robert Kay, of Brookshaw, Bury, Lancashire; *b* 1804; was Sec to the Committee of the Privy Council on Education 1839-49; *cr* a Baronet 1850: *m* 1842, Janet, who *d* 1872, only child and heiress of Robert Shuttleworth, of Gawthorpe Hall, whose surname he assumed by Roy licence in addition to his patronymic; *d* 1877: *s* by his el son (2) *Sir* UGHTRED JAMES, PC, 2nd Bt, *b* 1844; Under-Sec of State for India Feb to April 1886, Chancellor of Duchy of Lancaster April to Aug 1886, Parliamentary Sec to Admiralty 1892-5, and Lord-Lieut and Custos Rotulorum of Lancashire 1908-28; MP for Hastings (L) 1869-80, and for Clitheroe Div of N-E Lancashire 1885-1902; *cr Baron Shuttleworth*, of Gawthorpe, co Palatine of Lancaster (peerage of United Kingdom) 1902: *m* 1871, Blanche Marion, who *d* 1924, da of late Sir Woodbine Parish, KCH; *d* 1939; *s* by his grandson (3) RICHARD UGHTRED PAUL (son of late Capt Hon Lawrence Ughtred Kay-Shuttleworth), RFA (el son of 1st Baron), who was *ka* 1917, 2nd Baron, *b* 1913; Flying Officer RAF Vol Reserve, and a JP and Co Councillor for Lancashire; *ka* during Battle of Britain 1940; *s* by his brother (4) RONALD ORLANDO LAWRENCE, 3rd Baron, *b* (*posthumous*), 1917; Capt RA (TA); *ka* in N Africa 1942; *s* by his cousin (5) CHARLES UGHTRED JOHN, MC (son of late Capt Hon Edward James Kay-Shuttleworth) (2nd son of 1st Baron), who *d* (accidentally *k* during 1914-18 War) 1917, 4th Baron; *b* 1917: *m* 1947, Anne Elizabeth, who *d* 1991, da of late Col Geoffrey Francis Phillips, CBE, DSO (*see* V Ridley, colls, 1971 Edn); *d* 1975; *s* by his el son (6) CHARLES GEOFFREY NICHOLAS, 5th Baron and present peer.

SIDMOUTH, VISCOUNT (Addington) (Viscount UK 1805)

Liberty under a pious king

JOHN TONGE ANTHONY PELLEW ADDINGTON, 7th Viscount; *b* 3 Oct 1914; *s* 1976; *ed* Downside, and Brasenose Coll, Oxford; Colonial Ser E Africa 1938-54; Cttee Chm and Council Member, Nat Farmers Union 1962-69; Member Agric Research Council 1964-74; Member Central Council for Agric Co-operation 1970-73; Kt of Malta: *m* 1st, 1940, Barbara Mary Angela, who *d* 1989, el da of Bernard Rochford, OBE, of 7 Prince's Gate, SW7; 2ndly, 1993, Marie Thérèse, da of His Honour late Sir Joseph (Alfred) Sheridan, and widow of Francis Anthony Baring Pollen (*see* Pollen, Bt, colls), and has had issue.

Arms – Per pale ermine and ermines, a chevron charged with five lozenges counter-changed, between three fleurs-de-lis or. **Crest** – A cat-a-mountain sejant guardant proper, bezantée, the dexter forepaw resting on an escutcheon azure, charged with a mace erect, surmounted with a regal crown or, within a bordure engrailed argent. **Supporters** – Two stags, the *dexter* ermines, the *sinister* ermine, both attired and gorged with a chain, pendent therefrom a key, all or. *Residence* – 12 Brock St, Bath, Avon BA1 2LW.

SONS LIVING AND DECEASED (By 1st marriage)

Hon Christopher John, *b* 1941; *ed* Downside, and Brasenose Coll, Oxford: *m* 1963, Clio Mona, who *d* (8 April) 1986, only da of John Peristiany, of 15 Karneadou St, Athens, and *d* (2 June) 1986.
Hon JEREMY FRANCIS, *b* 29 July 1947; *ed* Ampleforth: *m* 1st, 1970, Grete, da of — Henningsen, of Randers, Denmark; 2ndly, 1986, Una, eldest da of James Coogan, of 54 Compton Bassett, Calne, Wilts, and of Mrs Susana Newman, and has issue living (by 1st wife), Steffan, *b* 1966, — Laura Grete, *b* 1975, — (by 2nd wife) John, *b* 29 Nov 1990, — Anna Frances, *b* 1988. *Residence* – Highway Manor, nr Calne, Wilts SN11 8SR.

DAUGHTERS LIVING (By 1st marriage)

Hon Veronica Mary, *b* 1944: *m* 1st, 1982 (*m* annulled 1987), Allan Gilfillan (Sam) Mainds, eldest son of late George Mainds; 2ndly, 1989, Michael Jeremy Hodges, only son of late Capt Michael Hodges, RN; has issue living, Philippa Clare, *b* 1969. *Residences* – 54a Cornwall Gdns, SW7 4BG; 1 The Cottage, Berwick St James, Salisbury, Wilts SP3 4TN.
Hon Susan Barbara (27 Ellerby St, SW6), *b* 1945: *m* 1st, 1965 (*m diss* 1975), Count John Paul James Alessandro Camillo Manassei di Collestatte (*see* E Perth); 2ndly, 1990, as his 2nd wife, Anthony Andrew Ward Kimpton (*see* B Hazlerigg, 1990 Edn), and has issue (by 1st *m*) (*see* E Perth).
Hon Janet Teresa, *b* 1949: *m* 1972, Anthony Goodman, of 30 Benmore Rd, Morningside, Sandton 2057, S Africa, and has issue living, Joanna Louise, *b* 1973, — Frances Julia, *b* 1975, — Isabel Alice *b* 1979.
Hon Pauline Rosemary, *b* 1951: *m* 1973, Paul Cristopher Clare, of Glenarth, Aberarth, Aberaeron, Dyfed, and has issue living, Tomas Aeron, *b* 1980, — John Joseph, *b* 1988, — Jennifer Rose, *b* 1982.
Hon Mary Margaret (Kidge), *b* 1956: *m* 1978, James Alexander Burns, and has issue living, Julia Isabel, *b* (Feb) 1985, — Miriam Janet, *b* (Dec) 1985. *Residence* – 51 Brynmaer Rd, SW11.

BROTHERS LIVING

Hon Hiley William Dever, *b* 1917; Lt-Cdr RN (ret); 1939-45 War: *m* 1st, 1942, Brenda Swanney, who *d* 1990, da of late Robert Charles Wallace, CMG, PhD, DSc, Principal of Queen's Univ, Kingston, Canada; 2ndly, 1993, Rita, widow of Alec T. Cousins, and has issue living (by 1st *m*), Robert Hiley, *b* 1944, — Charles Haviland, *b* 1949, — Frances Clare, *b* 1947. *Residence* – 1420 Sylvan Court, Sarnia, Ontario, Canada N7S 4A3.
Hon Raymond Thomas Casamajor, MC, *b* 1919; *ed* Downside; Major (ret) RHA, 1939-45 War in Commandos (MC): *m* 1947, Veronique, who *d* 1970, da of Emile Wirtz, of Antwerp, Belgium, and has issue living, Peter John Gerald (Highway Farm, Calne, Wilts SN11 8SR), *b* 1948: *m* 1977, Rosemary Anita, da of Richard Anthony Lamb, of Knighton Manor, Broadchalke, Wilts, and has issue living, Paul Anthony *b* 1979, Michael Peter *b* 1980, Edmund John *b* 1983, Raleigh Thomas *b* 1987, — Donald Emile (216 Varsity Estates Link, Calgary, Alberta, Canada T3B 4C9), *b* 1949: *m* 1973, Jean Margaret, da of David Alexander Baikie, and has issue living, Jack Alexander *b* 1974, Leo Nicholas *b* 1976, Oliver Thomas *b* 1979, Zoe Veronica *b* 1977, — Francis Henry, *b* 1955, — Lucy Anne *b* 1952, — Carol Jacqueline, *b* 1953, — Tonia Veronica, *b* 1956, — Edwina Gillian, *b* 1959: *m* 1983, Yokinobu Mori, of Tokyo, Japan, and Riyadh, Saudi Arabia, and has issue living, Henry Addington *b* 1984, George Addington *b* 1987. *Residence* – Strattons, Highway, nr Calne, Wilts SN11 8SR.

Hon Gurth Louis Francis, *b* 1920; *ed* Downside, and Brasenose Coll, Oxford (MA); 1939-45 War with RAF (Air Crew): *m* 1950, Patience Gillian, da of late Col L. E. Travers, RE, and has issue living, Martin Gerald Francis (6 Palm Av, Palmerston North, NZ), *b* 1952: *m* 1978, Lynne Elizabeth Mautner, and has issue living, Benjamin Richard Francis *b* 1980, Lauren Elizabeth *b* 1982, — David Anthony Brian (32 Aitken Av, Queenscliff, Sydney, NSW 2096, Australia), *b* 1955: *m* 1979, Mary-Anne Delmont, and has issue living, Daniel Anthony Travers *b* 1985, Emma Teresa *b* 1982, — Mark Nicholas Guy, *b* 1957, — Mary Clare, *b* 1951: *m* 1975, Trevor Roberts, of 2 Millbank, Ecton Brook, Northants NN3 5HJ, and has issue living, Dafydd Wynn *b* 1982, Owen Wynn *b* 1986, Gareth Wynn *b* 1988, Halina Clare *b* 1980, — Catherine Dorothy, *b* 1953: *m* 1975, Richard James Lumley, of 3 Edwards Bay Rd, Mosman, Sydney, NSW 2088, Australia, and has issue living, Roger Gurth *b* 1988, Justine Molly *b* 1982, Rebecca Patience *b* 1984, Philippa Catherine *b* 1986, — Deirdre Anne (twin), *b* 1955: *m* 1981, Derek Trow, of 370 Lords Place, Orange, NSW 2800, Australia, and has issue living, Gareth Michael Addington *b* 1986, Miriam Johanna Addington *b* 1987, — Monica Jane (twin), *b* 1957: *m* 1983, Glenn Richard Batchelor, of 33 Piedmont St, Box Hill South, Melbourne, Vic 3128, Australia, and has issue living, Richard Mark *b* 1989, Kate Betty *b* 1986, Jessica Patience *b* 1988, — Barbara Mary, *b* 1961: *m* 1987, John William Waugh, of 7 Wisdom Place, Hughes, ACT 2605, Australia, and has issue living, Henry William Addington *b* 1990, Olivia Charlotte *b* 1988, Cecilia Jane *b* 1992, — Jane Margaret, *b* 1964: *m* 1984, Stephen Hall, of 199 Onewa Rd, Birkenhead, Auckland, NZ, and has issue living, Edward James *b* 1989. *Residence* – 11 Edwin St, Fairlight, NSW 2094, Australia.

Hon Leslie Richard Bagnall, DFC; *b* 1923; *ed* Downside; Lt-Col (ret) late RA; Comdg Essex Yeo 1965-66; Malaya 1948, Korea 1951-52 (DFC): *m* 1955, Anne, el da of Capt Trevor Hume (Lacy, Bt), and has issue living, William Leslie Hume, *b* 1956: *m* 1981, Sally Jane, da of Brig D. G. Russell, of Fletching, Sussex, and has issue living, Alexander William Russell *b* 1987, Jason Robin Mark *b* 1989, — Richard Charles Raymond, *b* 1958: *m* 1989, Deryn Victoria, da of Col R. H. Johnson, of San Antonio, Texas, USA, and of Mrs Joan Pepita Nell Brown, of Bourton on the Hill, Glos, and has issue living, Constance Victoria Nell *b* 1993, — Sarah Anne Clare, *b* 1961, — Alice Mary Cynthia, *b* 1964: *m* 1992, Julian Guy Rogers-Coltman, elder son of Lt-Cdr Wyndham Julian Rogers-Coltman, RN, of Berryburn, Ancroft, Northumberland. *Residence* – Polebridge, Sutton Veny, Warminster, Wilts. *Club* – Army and Navy.

SISTERS LIVING

Hon Prudence Mary, *b* 1916: *m* 1939, Lieut-Com Hugo Edward Forbes Tweedie, DSC, RN, who *d* 1986, son of late Adm Sir Hugh Justin Tweedie, KCB, and has issue living, Alexander Hugh Carmichael (5 St Mary's Rd, Wimbledon, SW19), *b* 1942; *ed* Downside, Christ's Coll Camb (BA Agric), and Stanford Univ (MA Agric Econs): *m* 1966, Wendy, da of Basil Henry Francis Templer, and has issue living, Michael Hugh Quarter *b* 1970, Richard *b* 1976, Lisa Ann *b* 1967, Jessica Margret *b* 1968, — Dominic James Drumelzier, *b* 1945; *ed* Downside: *m* 1st, 1972, Maia Knoetzer; 2ndly, Dr Judith Atkinson, and has issue living (by 2nd *m*), James *b* 1975, Hugh *b* 1976, — Julian Michael Forbes (Mombiti, Manston Rd, Rixon, Sturminster Newton, Dorset DT10 1BQ), *b* 1947; *ed* Downside: *m* 1970, Shirley, da of late Leslie Mousley, of Machakos, Kenya, and has issue living, Nicola *b* 1976, — Rev Stephen John Oliver, *b* 1952; *ed* Downside, and Leeds Univ (BA); monk of Downside Abbey; ordained priest by HH Pope John Paul II at Manchester 31 May 1982, — Teresa Frances, *b* 1940: *m* 1964, Nicolas Alexander Victor Garratt Carp (Selwood Lodge, Frome, Somerset BA11 2JX), and has issue living, Sarah Frances *b* 1965, Juliet Anne *b* 1967, Victoria Teresa *b* 1970, Lucy Beatrice *b* 1973, — Monica Mary, *b* 1954; *ed* St Mary's Convent, Shaftesbury, and Hull Univ (BA): *m* 1978, Ian Richard Newbery, of 17 Braidley Rd, Bournemouth, Dorset BH2 6JX, and has issue living, Guy Francis *b* 1983, John Forbes *b* 1985, — Prudence Margaret, *b* 1956; SRN. *Residence* – 14 Fernbank, St Stephen's Rd, Bournemouth, Hants BH2 6JP.

Hon Mary Octavia, *b* 1927: *m* 1st, 1953, David Christopher Leeming; 2ndly, 1959, David Tilling Wroth, who *d* 1986; 3rdly, 1989, Maj R. William Ingall, DSO, and has issue living, (by 1st *m*) Toby, *b* 1955. *Residence* – Santiani, Moscari, Mallorca, Spain.

Hon Elizabeth Clare, *b* 1928. *Residence* – Coachmans Cottage, Pewsey, Wilts.

PREDECESSORS – (1) *Rt Hon* HENRY Addington; MP for Devizes 1784-1805, Speaker of the House of Commons 1789-1801, First Lord of the Treasury (Prime Minister) and Chancellor of the Exchequer 1801-4, Pres of the Council 1805-6, Lord Privy Seal 1806, Home Sec 1812-22, High Steward of Westminster and Reading, Gov of the Charterhouse, and Dep Ranger of Richmond Park, etc; *cr Viscount Sidmouth* (peerage of United Kingdom) 1805; *d* 1844; *s* by his son (2) WILLIAM LEONARD, 2nd Viscount; *b* 1794; was in Holy Orders: *m* 1820, Mary, who *d* 1894, el da of Rev John Young, Rector of Thorpe Malsor, co Northampton; *d* 1864; *s* by his son (3) WILLIAM WELLS, 3rd Viscount; *b* 1824; MP for Devizes 1863-4: *m* 1848, Georgiana Susan, who *d* 1896, da of late Very Rev Hon George Pellew, DD; *d* 1913; *s* by his el son (4) GERALD ANTHONY PELLEW BAGNALL, 4th Viscount, *b* 1854: *m* 1881, Ethel Mary, who *d* 1954, only da of late Capt Louis Charles Henry Tonge, RN; *d* 1915; *s* by his el son (5) GERALD WILLIAM, 5th Viscount, *b* 1882; Capt Devonshire Regt and Chm of Honiton Rural Dist Council; European War 1914-18 in India, Mesopotamia, Aden and Salonika: *m* 1915, Mary Murdoch, who *d* 1983, da of late Sir Donald Campbell Johnstone, formerly Ch Judge of Ch Court, Punjab; *d* 1953; *s* by his brother, (6) RAYMOND ANTHONY, 6th Viscount; *b* 1887: *m* 1913, Gladys Mary Dever, who *d* 1983, da of late Thomas Francis Hughes, Commr of Imperial Chinese Customs; *d* 1976; *s* by his el son (7) JOHN TONGE ANTHONY PELLEW, 7th Viscount and present peer.

SIEFF, BARONY OF (Sieff) (Extinct 1972)

SON LIVING OF LIFE BARON

Hon Sir Marcus Joseph, OBE, *b* 1913: *cr Baron Sieff of Brimpton*, 1979 (see that title).

WIDOW LIVING OF SON OF LIFE BARON

Elizabeth, da of late William Norman Pitt, of Hampton, Middx: *m* 1975, as his 2nd wife, Hon Michael David Sieff, CBE, who *d* 1987.

GRANDCHILDREN OF LIFE BARON

Issue of late Hon Michael David Sieff, CBE, el son of late Baron Sieff, *b* 1911, *d* 1987: *m* 1st, 1932 (*m diss* 1975), Daphne Madge Kerin, who *d* 1988 (having *m* 2ndly, 1976, Sir Michael Hadow, KCMG, who *d* 1993), da of Cyril Aaron Michael, of London; 2ndly, 1975, Elizabeth (ante), da of late William Norman Pitt, of Hampton, Middx:—

(By 1st *m*) Jonathan, *b* 1933; *ed* Marlborough: *m* 1st, 1959 (*m diss* 1966), Nicole, only da of Francis Moschietto, of 8 Avenue St Michael, Monte Carlo; 2ndly, 1966 (*m diss* 19—), Angela, da of Brig Douglas Pringle, of 14c The Precincts, Canterbury; 3rdly, 1986, Candy Seymour-Smith, and has issue living (by 1st *m*), Mark, *b* 1959, — Patrick, *b* 1963, — (by 2nd *m*) Rebecca, *b* 1967. —— (By 2nd *m*) Daniel Marcus, *b* 1977. —— Elizabeth Anne, *b* 1980.

SIEFF OF BRIMPTON, BARON (Sieff) (Life Baron 1980)

MARCUS JOSEPH SIEFF, OBE, yr son of late ISRAEL MOSES, Baron Sieff (Life Baron *cr* 1966), *b* 2 July 1913; *ed* Manchester Gram Sch, St Paul's, and Corpus Christi Coll, Camb (BA); Hon LLD St Andrews 1983, Hon Dr Babson Coll, Mass, 1984, Hon DLitt Reading 1986, D Univ Stirling 1986, Hon Dr of Laws Leicester 1988; Marks and Spencer Ltd, Vice-Chm and Assist Managing Dir 1965-67, Vice-Chm 1965, Joint Managing Dir 1967-83, Dep Chm 1971, Chm 1972-84, Pres 1984-85, since when Hon Pres; Chm First Internat Bank of Israel Trust Ltd since 1983, Non-Exec Chm *The Independent* since 1986, Non-Exec Dir Wicks plc, and Sock Shop Internat plc; a Member of BNEC 1965-71; Chm of Export Cttee for Israel 1965-68; Hon Pres of Joint Israel Appeal since 1984, Vice Pres Policy Studies Inst (formerly PEP) since 1975, Pres Anglo-Israel Chamber of Commerce 1975; a Trustee Nat Portrait Gallery 1986-92; Hon Master of the Bench Inner Temple 1987, Hon FRCS 1984; Col RA, 1939-45 War in Middle East and Italy (despatches); OBE (Mil) 1944; *cr* Knt 1971, and *Baron Sieff of Brimpton*, of Brimpton, co Berks (Life Baron) 1980: *m* 1st, 1937 (*m diss* 1947), Rosalie Fromson; 2ndly, 1951 (*m diss* 1953), Elsie Florence Gosen; 3rdly, 1956 (*m diss* 1962), Brenda Mary Beith; 4thly, 1963, Mrs Pauline Lily Moretzki, da of Friedrich Spatz, and has issue by 1st, 3rd and 4th *m*.

Arms – Sable a lion rampant argent crowned with an Eastern Crown and holding between forepaws 2 triangles interlaced and eradiated or, on a chief argent a lyre azure between 2 pairs paintbrushes in a saltire proper. **Supporters** – *Dexter*, a lion holding aloft two interlaced triangles or, depressing a cornucopia replenished proprer and gorged with a plain collar sable tied about with a fishing line knotted in front and pendent there from a "Grey Wulf" trout fly proper. *Sinister*, an Owl proper gorged with a like collar tied about with a fishing line knotted in front and pendent there from a "Red Wulf" trout fly proper. **Crest** – A demi-lion as in the arm supporting a caduceus or. **Motto** – "Without knowledge there is no understanding". *Address* – Michael House, Baker St, W1A 1DN.

SON LIVING *(By 1st marriage)*

Hon David Daniel, *b* 1939; *ed* Repton: *m* 1962, Jennifer, da of H. Walton, of Salford Priors, Worcs, and has issue living, Simon Marcus, *b* 1965, — Jonathan David, *b* 1966.

DAUGHTERS LIVING *(By 3rd marriage)*

Hon Amanda Jane, *b* 1958.

(By 4th marriage)

Hon Daniela Frederica, *b* 1965.

Silchester, Baron; title of Earl of Longford on Roll of HL.

SILKIN, BARONY OF (Silkin) (Baron UK 1950, disclaimed 1972)

ARTHUR SILKIN, *b* 20 Oct 1916; *s* as 2nd Baron 11 May 1972, disclaimed his peerage for life 18 May 1972; *ed* Dulwich Coll, and Peterhouse, Camb (BA honours); formerly with Civil Ser Coll (ret 1976); 1939-45 War as F/O RAF: *m* 1969, Audrey, da of late Thomas Bennett. *Residence* – 33 Woodnook Rd, SW16 6TZ.

WIDOWS LIVING OF SONS OF FIRST BARON

Sheila Marian (*Baroness Silkin of Dulwich*) (see that title).
Rosamund John, actress, da of Frederick Jones, and formerly wife of Lt-Cdr Russell Lloyd, RNVR: *m* 1950, Rt Hon John Ernest Silkin, MP, yst son of 1st Baron, who *d* 1987. *Residence* – Vine House, Staplehurst, Kent.

COLLATERAL BRANCHES LIVING

Issue of late Rt Hon Samuel Charles (*Baron Silkin of Dulwich*), QC, PC, 2nd son of 1st Baron, *b* 1918; *cr* Baron Silkin of Dulwich (Life Baron) 1985; *d* 1988: *m* 1st, 1941, Elaine Violet, who *d* 1984, da of late Arthur Stamp, of London; 2ndly, 1985, Sheila Marian (ante), da of A. E. Jeal, and widow of Walter Swanston:—
(By 1st *m*) (*see* By Silkin of Dulwich).

Issue of late Rt Hon John Ernest Silkin, MP, yst son of 1st Baron, *b* 1923, *d* 1987: *m* 1950, Rosamund John (ante), formerly wife of Lt-Cdr Russell Lloyd, RNVR, and da of Frederick Jones:—
Rory Lewis, *b* 1954.

PREDECESSOR – (1) *Rt Hon* LEWIS Silkin, CH; *b* 1889: Min of Town and Country Planning 1945-50, Dep Leader of Labour Party, House of Lords 1955, and MP for Peckham Div of Camberwell (*Lab*) 1946-50; *cr Baron Silkin*, of Dulwich, co London (peerage of UK) 1950: *m* 1st, 1915, Rosa Neft, who *d* 1947; 2ndly, 1948, Frieda M., who *d* 1963, da of late Rev Canon Pilling, of Norwich, and widow of J. F. F. Johnson; 3rdly, 1964, Marguerite Schlageter, who *d* 1975; *d* 1972; *s* by his el son (2) ARTHUR, 2nd Baron, until he disclaimed his peerage 1972.

SILKIN OF DULWICH, BARONY OF (Silkin) (Extinct 1988)

SONS LIVING OF LIFE BARON

Hon CHRISTOPHER LEWIS, *b* 12 Sept 1947; *hp* to his uncle Baron Silkin (disclaimed 1972); *ed* Dulwich, and Middlesex Tech Coll (LLB); admitted a solicitor 1977.
Hon Peter David Arthur, *b* 1952; *ed* Dulwich, and Sussex Univ (MA); Member of Inst of Public Finance and Accountancy 1985: *m* 1974 (div 1982), Frances, da of Dr Patrick Kemp, of Woking. *Residence* – 28 Phoebeth Rd, SE4 1JP.

DAUGHTERS LIVING OF LIFE BARON

Hon Charlotte Ann, *b* 1944; *ed* James Allen's Girls Sch, and Lady Spencer Churchill Coll, Oxford (BEd): *m* 1965, Francis Josephs, MA, and has issue living, Thomas Daniel, *b* 1972, — Anna Frances, *b* 1975.
Hon Patricia Jane SILKIN, *b* (twin) 1947; *ed* James Allen's Girls Sch, and Sussex Univ (BA); has reverted to her maiden name: *m* 1970, Michael Johnson, BA, PhD.

WIDOW LIVING OF LIFE BARON

SHEILA MARIAN (*Baroness Silkin of Dulwich*), da of A. E. Jeal, and widow of Walter Swanston: *m* 1985, as his 2nd wife, Baron Silkin of Dulwich, QC, PC, who *d* 1988. *Residence* – The Croft, The Green, East End, North Leigh, Oxon.

SILSOE, BARON (Eve) (Baron UK 1963, Bt UK 1943)

DAVID MALCOLM TRUSTRAM EVE, QC, 2nd Baron, and 2nd Baronet, *b* 2 May 1930; *s* 1976; *ed* Winchester, Ch Ch, Oxford (MA), and Columbia Univ, New York; Bar Inner Temple 1955; Bar Auditor Inner Temple 1965-70; Bencher 1970; QC 1972; late 2nd Lt RWF, and Lt, Queen Victoria's Rifles (TA): *m* 1963, Bridget Min, da of Sir Rupert Charles Hart-Davis, of The Old Rectory, Marske-in-Swaledale, Richmond, N Yorks, and has issue.

Arms – Sable, two swords, points upwards, in saltire argent pommels and hilts or, on a chief of the second a closed book gules, garnished of the third, between two torteaux. **Crest** – Issuant from a mural crown or, an apple tree fructed, the trunk entwined by a serpent proper. **Supporters** – On either side a Kashmir goat argent, horned winged and gorged with a mural crown or.
Residence – Neals Farm, Wyfold, Reading, Berks, RG4 9JB.

SON LIVING

Hon SIMON RUPERT TRUSTRAM, *b* 17 April 1966.

DAUGHTER LIVING

Hon Amy Comfort Trustram, *b* 1964.

BROTHER LIVING

Hon Peter Nanton Trustram, OBE, (twin) (Barton End Court, nr Nailsworth, Glos GL6 0QQ; Flat D, 163 Pavilion Rd, SW1; Ski Club of Great Britain and Anglo-Belgian), *b* 1930; *ed* Winchester, and Ch Ch, Oxford (MA); Col R Green Jackets (ret); late 2nd Lt RWF, and Lt Queen Victoria's Rifles (TA); US Armed Forces Staff Coll 1972, British Army Staff, Washington 1972-73, Cmdg Officer Oxford Univ Officers Training Corps 1973-75; Defence and Mil Attaché, Brussels 1980-83; Gen Man Churchill Hosp 1985-88; OBE (Mil) 1978: *m* 1961, Petronilla Letiere Sheldon, da of late Jannion Steele Elliott, of Dowles Manor, Bewdley, Worcs, and has issue living, Richard Malcolm Jannion Trustram, *b* 1963: *m* 1988, Albinia Julia, elder da of late Maj Christopher Wyndham Diggle (*see* Thompson, Bt, colls, *cr* 1890), and has issue living, Alexander Christopher Peter Trustram *b* 1993, — Nicholas Dominic Peter Trustram, *b* 1965.

PREDECESSOR – (1) *Sir* (ARTHUR) MALCOLM TRUSTRAM Eve, GBE, MC, TD, QC, son of late Sir Herbert Trustram Eve, KBE; *b* 1894; Chm of War Damage Commn 1941-49, of War Works Commn 1945-49, and of Burnham Cttees on Teachers' Salaries 1950-53; First Crown Estate Commr 1954-62, and First Church Estates Commr 1954-69; *cr a Baronet* 1943, and *Baron Silsoe*, of Silsoe, co Bedford (peerage of UK) 1963: *m* 1st, 1927, Marguerite, who *d* 1945, da of late Sir Augustus Meredith Nanton; 2ndly, 1946, Margaret Elizabeth, who *d* 1993, da of late Henry Wallace Robertson, of Ayton, Berwicks; *d* 1976; *s* by his el son (2) DAVID MALCOLM TRUSTRAM, 2nd Baron, and present peer.

SIMEY, BARONY OF (Simey) (Extinct 1969)

SON LIVING OF LIFE BARON

Hon Thomas Iliff (Coed Nant Gain, Cilcain Rd, Pontnewydd, Mold, Clwyd CH7 5NJ), *b* 1938; *ed* St Christopher's Sch, Letchworth; Chartered Architect 1965; Consultant in Community Building Initiatives, Lesotho, 1977-86: *m* 1963, Fiona, da of A. G. Porteous, of Menstrie, Clackmannanshire, and has issue.

WIDOW LIVING OF LIFE BARON

MARGARET BAYNE (*Baroness Simey*), (3 Blackburne Terr, Blackburne Pl, Liverpool L8 7PJ), da of John Aiton Todd: *m* 1935, Baron Simey (Life Baron), who *d* 1969.

SIMON, VISCOUNT (Simon) (Viscount UK 1940)

JAN DAVID SIMON, 3rd Viscount, *b* 20 July 1940; *s* 1993; *ed* Westminster, Dept of Navigation, Southampton Univ, and Sydney Technical Coll: *m* 1969, Mary Elizabeth, da of John Joseph Burns, of Sydney, NSW, Australia, and has issue.

Arms – Gules three lotus flowers in pale proper between two flaunches or each charged with a lion rampant of the field. **Crest** – Upon a well proper an eagle rising or. **Supporters** – *Dexter*, a guillemot; *sinister*, a monal proper.
Residence – Rose Cottage, Parsonage Lane, Barnston, Gt Dunmow, Essex CM6 3PA.

Such is my name

DAUGHTER LIVING

Hon Fiona Elizabeth Christie, *b* 1971.

SISTER LIVING

Hon Gemma Louise, *b* 1934: *m* 1956, Brian Hunter, and has issue living, Ian *b* 1957, — Alan, *b* 1958.

WIDOW LIVING OF SECOND VISCOUNT

(JAMES) CHRISTIE (*Dowager Viscountess Simon*), da of William Stanley Hunt: *m* 1930, 2nd Viscount, CMG, who *d* 1993. *Residence* – 2 Church Cottages, Abbotskerwell, Newton Abbot, Devon TQ12 5NY.

PREDECESSORS – (1) *Rt Hon Sir* JOHN ALLSEBROOK SIMON, GCSI, GCVO, OBE, PC, QC, only son of late Rev Edwin Simon, a Congregational Min; *b* 1873; was Solicitor-Gen 1910-13, Attorney-Gen (with a seat in the Cabinet) 1913-15, Sec of State for Home Depart 1915-16, Sessional Chm and Dep Leader of Ind Liberal Party in House of Commons 1922-4, and Chm of Indian Statutory Commn 1927-30, R101 Airship Inquiry 1930, and Roy Commn on Population 1943-6; appointed Sec of State for Foreign Affairs (in National Govt) 1931, Sec of State for Home Affairs and Dep Leader of House of Commons 1935, and Chancellor of the Exchequer 1937 (also Member of War Cabinet 1939); Lord High Chancellor 1940-45; sometime Leader of Liberal National Party; High Steward of Oxford Univ; European War 1917-18 as Maj RAF (despatches); sat as MP for SW or Walthamstow, Div of Essex (*L*) 1906-18; and for Yorkshire W Riding, Spen Valley Div 1922-40; *cr Viscount Simon*, of Stackpole Elidor, co Pembroke (peerage of United Kingdom) 1940: *m* 1st, 1899, Ethel Mary, who *d* 1902, da of Gilbert Venables; 2ndly, 1917, Kathleen, DBE, who *d* 1955, da of Francis Eugene Harvey, of Wexford, and widow of T. Manning, MD; *d* 1954; *s* by his only son (2) JOHN GILBERT, CMG, 2nd Viscount, *b* 1902; Manager P & O London 1936-40, with Min of War Transport 1940-46, Man Dir (later Joint Dep Chm) P & O 1947-58, Chm Port of London Authority 1958-71, sometime Pres Chamber of Shipping, Royal Inst of Naval Architects, Inst of Naval Engrs, Internat Assocn of Ports and Harbours, and Royal National Inst for the Deaf, etc; Memb N Atlantic Assembly, Dep Speaker House of Lords: *m* 1930, (James) Christie, da of William Stanley Hunt; *d* 1993; *s* by his only son (3) JAN DAVID, 3rd Viscount and present peer.

SIMON OF GLAISDALE, BARON (Simon) (Life Baron 1971)

JOCELYN EDWARD SALIS SIMON, PC, son of late Frank Cecil Simon, of 51 Belsize Park, NW3; *b* 15 Jan 1911; *ed* Gresham's Sch, Holt, and Trin Hall, Camb; Bar Middle Temple 1934, KC 1951, and Bencher 1958; Joint Parl Under-Sec of State, Home Office 1957-58, Financial Sec to the Treasury 1958-59, Solicitor-Gen 1959-62, Pres of Probate, Divorce and Admiralty Div of High Court 1962-71, and a Lord of Appeal in Ordinary 1971-77; 1939-45 War as Maj RTR, and Lt-Col Staff; MP for W Middlesbrough (*C*) 1951-62; *cr* Knt 1959, PC 1961, and *Baron Simon of Glaisdale*, of Glaisdale, in N Riding, co York (Life Baron) 1971: *m* 1st, 1934, Gwendolen Helen, who *d* 1937, da of E. J. Evans; 2ndly, 1948, Fay Elizabeth Leicester, JP, da of Brig H. Guy A. Pearson, of Jersey, and has issue by 2nd *m*.

Arms – Per saltire sable and ermine, a pair of scales or between in fess two roses argent barbed and seeded proper, and in pale two crescents ermine. **Crest** – A cock's head erased azure combed and wattled gules between two palm branches vert, holding in the beak two roses argent clipped leaved barbed and seeded proper. **Supporters** – *Dexter*, a man habited in the robes of a Doctor of Civil Law in the University of Cambridge proper, and holding in his dexter hand a book or; *sinister*, a man habited in the robes of the President of the Probate Divorce and Admiralty Division of the High Court proper.
Address – c/o House of Lords, SW1.

SONS LIVING (By 2nd marriage)

Hon Peregrine Charles Hugo, *b* 1950; *ed* Westminster, and Trin Hall, Camb (MA); Bar Middle Temple 1973, QC 1991: *m* 1980, Francesca, da of Maj T. W. E. Fortescue Hitchins, of Border Lodge, Brewham, Som, and has issue, Alexander Edward Orlando, *b* 1986, — Ferdinand William Hugo, *b* 1989, — Polly Harriet Artemis, *b* 1982, — Lucy Persephone Frances, *b* 1984. *Residence* – Midge Hall, Glaisdale, Whitby, N Yorks.
Hon (Benedict) Mark Leicester, *b* 1953; *ed* Marlborough, Trin Hall, Camb (MA), and Wolfson Coll, Oxford (BLitt): *m* 1980, Patricia, da of Ricardo Hernandez Amozurrutia, of Mexico City, and has issue, Isaak David, *b* 1989, — Jael Daniela, *b* 1984. *Residence* – 33 South Parade, Oxford.
Hon (Dominic) Crispin Adam, *b* 1958; *ed* Westminster, and Lincoln Coll, Oxford (MA): *m* 1983, Georgina Frances, da of R. G. Brown, of Chestnut House, Albrighton, Shropshire, and has issue, Freddie, *b* 1991, — Clementine, *b* 1993. *Residence* – Cotte Farm, Combe Hay, Bath, Avon.

SIMON OF WYTHENSHAWE, BARON (Simon) (Baron UK 1947)

ROGER SIMON, 2nd Baron, *b* 16 Oct 1913; *s* 1960 (but does not use the title); *ed* Gresham's Sch, Holt, and at Gonville and Caius Coll, Camb; European War 1940-45: *m* 1951 (Anthea) Daphne, da of Sidney George William May, and has issue.
Residence – Oakhill, Chester Avenue, Richmond, Surrey.

SON LIVING

MATTHEW (does not use courtesy title), *b* 10 April 1955; *ed* St Paul's Sch, and Balliol Coll, Oxford (BA, PhD); Lecturer; CEng, MIMechE.

DAUGHTER LIVING

Hon Margaret, *b* 1953.

BROTHER LIVING

Hon Brian, *b* 1915; *ed* Gresham's Sch, Holt, and Trin Coll, Camb; European War 1940-45: *m* 1941, Joan Home, da of late Capt Home Peel, DSO, MC (By Emmott), and has had issue, †Alan, *b* 1943; *d* 1991, — Martin, *b* 1944. *Residence* – 11 Pendene Rd, Leicester.

PREDECESSOR – (1) ERNEST DARWIN Simon, son of late Henry Simon, of Lawnhurst, Didsbury; *b* 1879; an Engineer and Contractor, and Pres of Simon Carves Ltd, and of Henry Simon Ltd; Lord Mayor of Manchester 1921-2; Parliamentary Sec to Min of Health (in National Govt) Sept to Oct 1931; was Chm of British Broadcasting Corporation 1947-52; sat as MP for Withington Div of Manchester (*L*) 1923-4 and 1929-31; *cr Baron Simon of Wythenshawe*, of Didsbury, City of Manchester (peerage of United Kingdom) 1947: *m* 1912, Shena Dorothy, who *d* 1972, da of John Wilson Potter, of Westminster, SW1; *d* 1960; *s* by his el son (2) ROGER, 2nd Baron and present peer.

SINCLAIR, LORD (St Clair) (Lord S about 1449, confirmed 1488-9)
(Title pronounced "Sinclair" and name pronounced "St Clair")

CHARLES MURRAY KENNEDY ST CLAIR, CVO, 17th Lord; *b* 21 June 1914; *s* 1957; *ed* Eton, and Magdalene Coll, Camb; a Representative Peer for Scotland 1959-63; Major late Coldstream Guards; is a Member of Queen's Body Guard for Scotland (Roy Co of Archers); HM's Lord Lieut for Dumfries and Galloway (District of Stewartry) 1982-89; Portcullis Pursuivant of Arms 1949-57, and York Herald 1957-68; Hon Genealogist to Roy Victorian Order 1960-68; an Extra Equerry to HM Queen Elizabeth the Queen Mother since 1953; Palestine 1939 (despatches), 1939-45 War (wounded); LVO 1953, CVO 1990: *m* 1968, Anne Lettice, yr da of Sir Richard Charles Geers Cotterell 5th Bt, CBE, TD, and has issue.

Arms – Argent, a cross engrailed azure. **Crest** – A swan, wings expanded and elevated proper gorged with a ducal coronet and chained or. **Supporters** – Two gryphons sable, armed and beaked and winged or, beaked and membered or.
Residence – Knocknalling, St John's Town of Dalry, Castle Douglas DG7 3ST.

SON LIVING

Hon MATTHEW MURRAY KENNEDY (*Master of Sinclair*), *b* 9 Dec 1968.

DAUGHTERS LIVING

Hon Laura Anne, *b* 1972.
Hon Annabel Lettice, *b* 1973.

SISTER LIVING

Hon Patricia Mary (Three Ways, Yelverton Rd, Norwich) *b* 1912: *m* 1940, Lt-Col Charles Archibald Richard Coghill, OBE, Scots Gds (ret), who *d* 1975, and has issue living, Hugh Murray Charles (Lodge Farm, Castle Acre, King's Lynn, Norfolk) *b* 1950: *m* 1973, (Elisabeth Ann) Edwina, yr da of Rev Mark Wynn-Eyton Wells, and has issue living, Charles Edward Mark *b* 1976, Harry Robert Murray *b* 1978, Benjamin Michael Richard *b* 1981, — Sarah, *b* 1948: *m* 1972, Peter Grosvenor Hopkins, and has issue living, James Richard Grosvenor *b* 1972, Laura Sarah *b* 1975, Catherine Jane *b* 1978, — Patricia Jane *b* 1949: *m* 1970, Graham Merrison, of Ivy Cottage, Iden Green, Benenden, Kent, and has issue living, Rupert Alexander James *b* 1973, Alexander Toby Charles *b* 1974, Edward Nicholas Harry *b* 1976, Annabel Sophie Louise *b* 1978.

COLLATERAL BRANCHES LIVING

Grandchildren of late Hon Lockhart Matthew St Clair, CIE, CBE, 4th son of 14th Lord:—
Issue of late Maj-Gen George James Paul St Clair, CB, CBE, DSO, *b* 1885, *d* 1955: *m* 1911, Charlotte Theresa Orme, who *d* 1961, da of late Major Archibald Cosmo Little (E Shrewsbury):—
Malcolm Archibald James, TD, *b* 1927; *ed* Eton; is a Farmer; MP for S-E Div of Bristol (C) 1961-63; Lt-Col Comdg R Glos Hussars (TA) 1967-69: *m* 1955, Mary-Jean, only da of Wing-Cdr Caryl Liddell Hargreaves, of Broadwood House, Sunningdale, Berks (B Ravensworth, colls), and has issue living, Hugh Alan Charles (The Priory, Long Newnton, Tetbury, Glos), *b* 1957; *ed* Eton, and USA; writer: *m* 1988, Raffaella F., elder da of late George Barker, of Bintry House, Itteringham, Norfolk, and has issue living, Roman George *b* 1988, Lorne Patrick *b* 1991, — Andrew David Paul, *b* 1960; *ed* Eton, — Vanessa Alice Rosabelle, *b* 1971; *ed* St Mary's Calne, and Manchester Univ (BA). *Residence* – The Priory, Long Newnton, Tetbury, Glos. *Club* – White's. —— Rosabelle Evelyn Teresa, *b* 1919. —— Guendolen Helen Charlotte (Berkley House, The Chipping, Tetbury, Glos), *b* 1920: *m* 1966, Maurice Owen Griffith Cleaver, who *d* 1975.

Grandchildren of late Adm William Home Chisholme St Clair, el son of late Com Hon Charles St Clair (infra):—
Issue of late Capt Frederic Cathcart Guy St Clair, RN, *b* 1878, *d* 1931: *m* 1913, Maude Sophie Childers, who *d* 1962, yr da of Capt S. H. Childers Thompson, RN (ret), formerly of Taplow, Bucks:—
Derek Charles ST CLAIR-STANNARD, MBE, *b* 1919; formerly in HM Foreign Ser; Public Relations Officer to Roy Agricultural Soc of England 1960-70; 1939-45 War as Lt RNVR (MBE); assumed by deed poll 1939, the additional surname of Stannard; MBE (Mil) 1945: *m* 1953, Elizabeth Ann, da of Douglas Charles Baskett, and has issue living, Matthew Peter, *b* 1954: *m* 1981, Sally Elizabeth, eldest da of Capt R. Heptinstall, RN, and has issue living, Guy Roger *b* 1982, Oliver Simon Charles *b* 1984, Chloe Elizabeth *b* 1989, — Lucie, *b* 1955: *m* 1981, Richard John Shelbourne, yr son of G. R. Shelbourne, of Langore, Cornwall, and has issue living Frederick John Philip *b* 1988, India Lucie *b* 1982, Arabella Frances *b* 1984, Tatiana Francesca Sophia *b* 1993, — Sophie Alexandra, *b* 1958: *m* 1985, Richard Sean de Courcy O'Grady, eldest son of late Patrick de Courcy O'Grady, and has issue living, Ludovic Patrick *b* 1989, Harriet Rose *b* 1987, — Josephine Camilla, *b* 1965. *Residence* – The Priory, 33 Church St, Godalming, Surrey GU7 1EL.

Grandchildren of late Percival James St Clair, el son of James Andrew St Clair (infra):—
Issue of late Rodney Samuel St Clair, *b* 1919, *d* 1964: *m* 1942, Beatrice Wyatt Walker (Trefusis, Boomi, NS Wales):—
Malcolm Clive, *b* 1943: *m* 1971, Julie Murphy, and has issue living, Rodney James, *b* 1973, — Timothy, *b* 1975. —— Rosslyn Violet, *b* 1947: *m* 1971, Iain Couper, and has issue living, Samuel Boyd *b* 1971, Rachel Kate *b* 1974. —— Linda Helen, *b* 1953: *m* 1974, Ronald Coulton, and has issue living, Christopher Ronald, *b* 1980, — Sarah Jane, *b* 1977.

Granddaughters of late James Andrew St Clair, 5th son of Hon Charles St Clair, 3rd son of 13th Lord:—
Issue of late Charles Archibald St Clair, *b* 1878, *d* 1917: *m* 1913, Madeline Smith:—
Joan Madeline, *b* 1914.
Issue of late Christopher Fenwick St Clair, *b* 1882, *ka* 1918: *m* 1914, Ethel Maud Cheesbrough:—
Erica Webster, *b* 1916: *m* 1940, Duncan Cannon McConnel, and has issue living, Christopher David, *b* 1951: *m* 1984, Susan Jane Underdown, and has issue living, Caitlin Jane St Clair *b* 1990, — Rosemary Robina St Clair, *b* 1941: *m* 1987, Graham Kensley Neumann, — Diana Rose, *b* 1946: *m* 1968, Arthur Edmund de Norbury Rogers, and has issue living, Andrew de Norbury *b* 1970, Scott McConnel *b* 1972, James McConnel *b* 1974. *Residence* – Cressbrook, Toogoolawah, Queensland.

PREDECESSORS – **(1)** WILLIAM Sinclair, 3rd Earl of Orkney (*cr* 1379); a Lord of Parliament as *Lord Sinclair* about 1449; *cr Earl of Caithness* 1455; resigned the Earldom of Orkney to the Crown 1470 and the Earldom of Caithness later; *s* by his son **(2)** WILLIAM; *s* by his son **(3)** HENRY, who in 1488 was confirmed as a Peer of Parliament as *Lord Sinclair* (peerage of Scotland); *k* at Flodden Field 1513; *s* by his son **(4)** WILLIAM, 4th Lord; *d* 1570; *s* by his son **(5)** HENRY, 5th Lord; *d* 1601; *s* by his grandson **(6)** HENRY, 6th Lord; *d* 1602; *s* by his brother **(7)** JAMES, 7th Lord; *d* 1607; *s* by his brother **(8)** PATRICK, 8th Lord; *d* 1617; *s* by his son **(9)** JOHN, 9th Lord; *d* 1676; *s* by his grandson **(10)** HENRY (son of John St Clair by Catherine, Mistress of Sinclair, da of 9th Lord Sinclair), 10th Lord; obtained a charter under the Great Seal 1677 confirming all the honours, precedence, and dignities, etc, enjoyed by his predecessors, with remainders respectively to his brother Henry and his father's brothers Robert, George, and Matthew, and failing them to his own heirs male whatsoever; *d* 1723, his el son **(11)** JOHN, having been engaged in the Rebellion of 1715 was attainted, and never assumed the title; *dsp* 1750; his brother **(12)** JAMES also did not assume the title; a Gen in the Army and a distinguished diplomatist; *d* 1762, when the Lordship became dormant and remained so until 1782, when through **(13)** CHARLES (son of Matthew (ante)), *de jure* 11th Lord; *s* by his son **(14)** ANDREW, *de jure* 12th Lord, the House of Lords confirmed the claim of his son **(15)** CHARLES, who thus became 13th Lord, and the first of his line who held the title without descent from the original Lords; was a Representative Peer, *d* 1863; *s* by his son **(16)** JAMES, 14th Lord; *b* 1803; a Representative Peer: *m* 1830, Jane, da of Archibald Little, Esq, of Shabden Park, Surrey, *d* 1880; *s* by his son **(17)** CHARLES WILLIAM, 15th Lord, *b* 1831; a Representative Peer; Col in Army; Crimean Campaign 1854-55: *m* 1870, Margaret Jane, who *d* 1935, da of James Murray, of 16 Bryanston Square, W; *d* 1922; *s* by his son **(18)** ARCHIBALD JAMES MURRAY, MVO, 16th Lord; *b* 1875; Extra Equerry to HRH Prince Arthur of Connaught 1914-38; a Representative Peer for Scotland: *m* 1906, Violet Frances, who *d* 1953, da of late Col John Murray Kennedy, MVO, of Knocknalling, Dalry, Galloway; *d* 1957; *s* by his only son **(19)** CHARLES MURRAY KENNEDY, 17th Lord and present peer.

SINCLAIR OF CLEEVE, BARON (Sinclair) (Baron UK 1957)

JOHN LAWRENCE ROBERT SINCLAIR, 3rd Baron; *b* 6 Jan 1953; *s* 1985; *ed* Winchester, Bath Univ and Manchester Univ; teacher.

Arms – Or a cross engrailed sable in the first quarter a sword erect proper on a chief also sable three martlets gold. **Crest** – In front of a saltire argent a dove proper beaked and legged gules in the beak an olive branch also proper. **Supporters** – *Dexter*, a griffin sable; *sinister*, a unicorn argent. Each gorged with a chaplet or white may leaved and flowered proper.

SISTERS LIVING

Hon Juliet, *b* 1951: *m* 1983, A. Philip Wallis, only son of A. P. Wallis, of Beaumont, Essex.
Hon Jane, *b* 1955: *m* 1982, Robert Anthony John Holliday, son of R. F. Holliday, of Ashwellthorpe, Norfolk, and has issue living, James Robert Sinclair, *b* 1984, — Fiona Jane, *b* 1987. *Residence* – Larkfield, Hawstead, Bury St Edmunds, Suffolk.

WIDOW LIVING OF SECOND BARON

PATRICIA (*Baroness Sinclair of Cleeve*), da of Lawrence Hellyer, of The Hawke, Lockerbie, Dumfriesshire: *m* 1950, Lt-Col, the 2nd Baron, OBE, who *d* 1985.

PREDECESSORS – **(1)** ROBERT JOHN SINCLAIR, KCB, KBE, son of Robert Henry Sinclair, *b* 1893, Pres of Imperial Tobacco Co Ltd; Chm Finance Corp for Industry and of Bristol Waterworks Co; Dir-Gen of Army Requirements, War Office 1939-42; Ch Executive, Min of Production 1943-45; Pres of Fedn of British Industries 1949-51; a Member of Security Commn 1966-77; Pro-Chancellor of Bristol Univ 1946-70, and High Sheriff Som; *cr Baron Sinclair of Cleeve*, of Cleeve, co Somerset (peerage of UK) 1957: *m* 1917, Mary Shearer, who *d* 1984, da of late Robert Shearer Barclay; *d* 1979; *s* by his son **(2)** JOHN ROBERT KILGOUR, OBE, 2nd Baron, *b* 1919; Lt-Col Queen's Own Highlanders, Mil Attaché, Leopoldville 1960-63, with SHAPE 1964-66, and Min of Defence 1967-69; served 1939-45 War (despatches): *m* 1950, Patricia, da of Lawrence Hellyer, of The Hawke, Lockerbie, Dumfriesshire; *d* 1985; *s* by his only son **(3)** JOHN LAWRENCE ROBERT, 3rd Baron and present peer.

SINHA, BARON (Sinha) (Baron UK 1919)

Susanta Prasanna Sinha, 4th Baron; *b* 1953; *s* 1989; tea broker: *m* 1972, Patricia Orchard, and has had issue.

Arms – Argent, on a chevron ermine between in chief two lotus flowers and in base an Adjutant bird, three fountains all proper. **Crest** – A demi-tiger supporting a fasces erect proper. **Supporters** – On either side an Adjutant bird proper, collared or.
Residence – 7 Lord Sinha Road, Calcutta, India.

SON DECEASED

Shane Patrick, *b* 1974; *d* 1978.

DAUGHTERS LIVING AND DECEASED

Hon Caroline, *b* 1973.
Sharon Patricia, *b* 1975; *d* 1978.

SISTERS LIVING

Hon Manjula, *b* 1947; *m* 19— (*m diss* 19—), Tobgye Dorji, son of late Jigme Dorji, Prime Minister of Bhutan, and has issue living, Jigme Tobgye, *b* 19—.
Hon Anjana, *b* 1950.

UNCLE DECEASED (*son of 2nd Baron*) (*by 2nd m*)

Hon Anindo Kumar, *b* 18 May 1930; *ed* Charterhouse; *d* before 1993, in India.

HALF AUNTS LIVING (*daughters of 2nd Baron by 1st m*)

Hon Bina, *b* 1917.
Hon Gita, *b* 1918.

AUNT LIVING (*daughter of 2nd Baron by 2nd m*)

Hon Sheila, *b* 1923.

GREAT UNCLE LIVING (*son of 1st Baron*)

Hon Tarun, *b* 1899; *ed* Hertford Coll, Oxford (BA).

GREAT AUNT LIVING (*daughter of 1st Baron*)

Hon Kamala, *b* 1892; *m* 1st, 1910 (*m diss* 1943), Ashoke Chandra Gupta, OBE, Accountant-Gen (ret), Central Revenue, India; 2ndly, 1943, J. Burnier, and has issue living, (by 1st *m*) Anil Kumar, *b* 1918. *Address* – Paris.

WIDOW LIVING OF THIRD BARON

Madhabi (*Dowager Baroness Sinha*), da of late Monoranjan Chatterjee, of Calcutta, India: *m* 1945, the 3rd Baron, who *d* 1989.
Residence – 7 Lord Sinha Rd, Calcutta, India.

COLLATERAL BRANCHES LIVING

Issue of late Hon Sisir Sinha, 2nd son of 1st Baron, *b* 1890, *d* 1950: *m* 1917 — (Lord Sinha Rd, Calcutta, India) da of —:—
Indrajit (7/1, Lord Sinha Rd, Calcutta, India), *b* 18 Aug 1918; presumed heir: *m* 1951, Sunanda, da of late S. Seu, of Calcutta, and has issue living, Premola, *b* 1954. —— Anita, *b* 1921.

Issue of late Hon Sushil Kumar Sinha, 3rd son of 1st Baron, *b* 1895, *d* 1968: *m* 1st, (Oct) 1919, a da (who *d* Dec 1919), of late Sir Atul Chandra Chatterjee, GCIE, KCSI, ICS; 2ndly, 1921, Romola (Alipore, Calcutta, India), da of D. S. K. Mullick:—
(By 2nd *m*) Arun, *b* 1939. —— Leila, *b* 1937.

PREDECESSORS – (1) *Rt Hon Sir* Satvendra Prasanna Sinha, KCSI, PC, KC (the first Indian to be created a peer), son of Siti Kanatha Sinha, of Raipur, Birbhum, Bengal, *b* 1864; was a Member of Viceroy's Council 1909-10, Advocate-Gen and a MLC, Bengal 1916-19; Under-Sec of State for India Jan 1919 to Nov 1920, and Gov of Bihar and Orissa Nov 1920 to Nov 1921; represented India at Special War Conference 1917 and 1918; appointed a Member of Judicial Committee of Privy Council 1926; *cr Baron Sinha*, of Raipur, Presidency of Bengal (peerage of United Kingdom) 1919: *m* 1880, Gobindo Mohini, who *d* 1938, da of Krislo Chunder Mitter, Zemindar of Maheta, District Burdwan, India; *d* 1928; *s* by his son (2) Aroon Kumar, 2nd Baron; *b* 1887; writ of summons to House of Lords granted 1939: *m* 1st, 1916, Pryatama (Rani), who *d* 1919, el da of Rai Bahadur Lalit Mohan Chatterjee; 2ndly, 1919, Nirpuama, yr da of Rai Bahadur Lalit Mohan Chatterjee (ante); *d* 1967; *s* by his son (3) Sudhindro Prosanno, 3rd Baron; *b* 1920: *m* 1945, Madhabi, da of late Monoranjan Chatterjee, of Calcutta; *d* 1989; *s* by his son (4) Susanta Prasanna, 4th Baron and present peer.

SKELMERSDALE, BARON (Bootle-Wilbraham) (Baron UK 1828)

In the haven there is rest

ROGER BOOTLE-WILBRAHAM, 7th Baron; *b* 2 April 1945; *s* 1973; *ed* Eton, Lord Wandsworth Coll, Basingstoke; Proprietor of Broadleigh Gdns 1972, Man Dir Broadleigh Nurseries, Ltd 1973; a Lord in Waiting to HM 1980-86, Parliamentary Under-Sec Dept of Environment 1986-87, Dept of Health and Social Security 1987-88, Dept of Social Security 1988-89, N Ireland Office 1989-90, since when Consultant in Parl Affairs; Dir Broadleigh Nurseries Ltd: *m* 1972, Christine Joan, only da of Phillip Roy Morgan, of Evercreech, Somerset, and has issue.

Arms – Quarterly: 1st and 4th argent, three bendlets wavy azure, *Wilbraham*; 2nd and 3rd gules, on a chevron engrailed, between three combs argent, as many crosses partée fitchée, of the field. *Bootle*. **Crest** – 1st, a wolf's head erased argent; 2nd, a demi-lion reguardant proper, holding in the paws an escutcheon gules, charged with a cross flory argent. **Supporters** – *Dexter*, a wolf argent; gorged with a plain collar azure, and pendent thereform an escutcheon charged with the ancient arms of Wilbraham, viz azure, two bars argent, and a canton sable, thereon a wolf's head erased argent; *sinister*, a wolf proper, collared or, and from the collar pendent an escutcheon as the dexter. *Address* – c/o House of Lords, SW1A 0PW.

SON LIVING

Hon ANDREW, *b* 9 Aug 1977.

DAUGHTER LIVING

Hon Carolyn Ann, *b* 1974.

SISTERS LIVING

Hon Lavinia, *b* 1937: *m* 1969, Robert Brian Noel Massey, of Waterstone House, Itchenor, nr Chichester, Sussex, and has issue living, Harry, *b* 1975, — Archibald Edmonds, *b* 1977.
Hon Olivia, *b* 1938: *m* 1961 (*m diss* 1975), Anthony John Hoole Lowsley-Williams (*see* Makins, Bt, 1967 Edn), and has issue living, Richard Edward, *b* 1962, — (Hugh) Sebastian, *b* 1964, — Benjamin Christopher, *b* 1968.
Hon Daphne, *b* 1946: *m* 1980 (*m diss* 1992), Jocelyn Peter Gore Graham, son of Brig Peter Alastair John Gore Graham, of Chalkpit Cottage, Blewbury, Oxon, and has issue living, Tamsin Christobel, *b* 1985. *Residence* – 11 Rosenau Rd, SW11.

PREDECESSORS – (1) EDWARD Bootle-Wilbraham; *b* 1771; MP for Westbury 1795-6, for Newcastle-under-Lyme 1796-1812, and for Dover 1818-28; *cr Baron Skelmersdale* (peerage of United Kingdom) 1828; *d* 1853; *s* by his grandson (2) EDWARD, GCB, PC (son of Hon Richard Bootle-Wilbraham, MP), 2nd Baron; *b* 1837; Lord-in-Waiting to HM Queen Victoria 1866-8, Capt of Yeomen of the Guard 1874-80, and Lord Chamberlain of HM's Household 1885-6, 1886-92, and 1895-8; *cr Earl of Lathom* (peerage of United Kingdom) 1880: *m* 1860, Lady Alice Villiers, who *d* 1897, 2nd da of 4th Earl of Clarendon; *d* 1898; *s* by his el son (3) EDWARD GEORGE, 2nd Earl, *b* 1864: *m* 1889, Lady Wilma Pleydell-Bouverie, who *d* 1931, only surviving da of 5th Earl of Radnor; *d* 1910; *s* by his only son (4) EDWARD WILLIAM, 3rd Earl; *b* 1895: *m* 1927, Marie Xenia, who *d* 1974, da of E. W. de Tunzelman, of Singapore, and formerly wife of Ronald William Morrison; *d* 1930, when the Earldom of Lathom became ext, and the Barony of Skelmersdale devolved upon his kinsman (5) ARTHUR GEORGE, MC (el son of late Col Arthur Bootle-Wilbraham, a grandson of 1st Baron), 5th Baron; *b* 1876; *d* 1969; *s* by his cousin (6) LIONEL, DSO, MC (only son of Lionel Bootle-Wilbraham, grandson of 1st Baron), 6th Baron, *b* 1896; Lt-Col Coldm Gds: *m* 1936, Ann, who *d* 1974, da of late Percy Cuthbert Quilter (Quilter, Bt, colls); *d* 1973; *s* by his son (7) ROGER, 7th Baron and present peer.

SKIDELSKY, BARON (Skidelsky) (Life Baron 1991)

ROBERT JACOB ALEXANDER SKIDELSKY, son of late Boris Jacob Skidelsky, of Vladivostock, Russia; *b* 25 April 1939; *ed* Brighton Coll, and Jesus Coll, Oxford (MA, DPhil); Research Fellow Nuffield Coll, Oxford 1965-68, British Acad 1968-70, Assoc Prof of History John Hopkins Univ, USA 1970-76, Head of Dept of History, Philosophy and European Studies N London Poly 1976-78, Prof of Internat Studies Warwick Univ 1978-90, since when Prof of Pol Ec Warwick Univ; Chm Charleston Trust 1987-92; Member Policy Cttee SDP 1988-90, and Lord Chancellor's Advisory Council on Public Records 1988-93; Chm Social Market Foundation since 1989; Pres Hands Off Reading Campaign since 1994; FRHistS 1973, FRSL 1978; author; *cr Baron Skidelsky*, of Tilton, co E Sussex (Life Baron) 1991: *m* 1970, Augusta Mary Clarissa, da of late John Humphrey Hope, of E Harptree, Som, and has issue.
Residence – Tilton House, Firle, E Sussex. *Club* – United Oxford and Cambridge.

SONS LIVING

Hon Edward, *b* 1973; *ed* Eton.
Hon William, *b* 1976; *ed* Eton.

DAUGHTER LIVING

Hon Juliet, *b* 1981.

Slane, Viscount; grandson of Marquess Conyngham.

SLATER, BARONY OF (Slater) (Extinct 1977)

SON LIVING OF LIFE BARON

Hon Brian, *b* 1948. *Residence* – 30 Corscombe Close, Rudds Hill, Ferryhill, co Durham.

DAUGHTER LIVING OF LIFE BARON

Hon Elizabeth, *b* 1934: *m* 1955, Frank Davison, of 1 Seymour Grove, Eaglescliffe, Cleveland.

WIDOW LIVING OF LIFE BARON

HILDA (*Baroness Slater*) (32 The Garth, Church Lane, Ferryhill, co Durham), da of Gilbert James Clement: *m* 1928, Baron Slater (Life Baron), who *d* 1977.

SLIGO, MARQUESS OF (Browne) (Marquess I 1800) Sits as BARON MONTEAGLE (UK 1806)

Follow the right

JEREMY ULICK BROWNE, 11th Marquess; *b* 4 June 1939; *s* 1991; *ed* St Columba's Coll, and RAC Cirencester: *m* 1961, Jennifer June Lushington, only da of Maj (George) Derek Cooper, MC, late The Life Guards, of Dunlewey, Gweedore, co Donegal, and of Mrs Cyril Heber-Percy, and has issue.

Arms – Sable, three lions passant in bend between four bendlets argent. **Crest** – An eagle displayed vert. **Supporters** – *Dexter*, a talbot proper, gorged with a baron's coronet; *sinister*, a horse argent.
Seat – Westport House, Westport, co Mayo.

DAUGHTERS LIVING

Lady Sheelyn Felicity, *b* 1963.
Lady Karen Lavinia, *b* 1964.
Lady Lucinda Jane, *b* 1969.
Lady Clare Romane, *b* 1974.
Lady Alannah Grace, *b* 1980.

AUNTS LIVING (sisters of 10th Marquess) (raised to the rank of a Marquess's daughters 1953)

Lady Sheelah Annette, *b* 1908: *m* 1930, John Dalrymple Winn Treherne, who *d* 1972, and has had issue, Roland Dalrymple, *b* 1935; *ed* Eton; *d* 1992, — Oona Cicely (Long Meadow, Hasketon, Woodbridge, Suffolk), *b* 1930: *m* 1950 (*m diss* 1973), Christopher Paul Mansel Campbell Methuen-Campbell, and has issue (*see* B Methuen, colls). *Residence* – Long Meadow, Hasketon, Woodbridge, Suffolk.
Lady Noreen, *b* 1910: *m* 1931, Clive Ali Chimmo Branson, who was *ka* in Far East 1944, and has issue living, Rosa (46 Southwood Av, Highgate, N6), *b* 1933: *m* 1st, 1954 (*m diss* 1966), Alan Hopkins; 2ndly, 1971, Henry Joseph Hooper, who *d* 1990, and has issue living (by 1st *m*), Michael Stephen *b* 1958: *m* 1986, Eileen Jane Eccles, Peggy Anne *b* 1955: *m* 1st, 1975 (*m diss* 1983), Thomas Aquineas Prendeville; 2ndly, 1987, Anthony George Francis Godfrey, of 10 Colmans Court, 46 Morris Rd, E14 (and has issue living (by 2nd *m*) Isolde Iona Hephzibah *b* 1989). *Residence* – 46 Southwood Av, Highgate, N6.

WIDOW LIVING OF BROTHER OF TENTH MARQUESS

Fiona, da of late John Glenn, of E Grinstead, Sussex: *m* 1962, as his 2nd wife, Capt Lord Ulick Browne, RA (who was raised to the rank of a Marquess's son 1953), who *d* 1979, and has issue (see colls infra). *Residence* – 32 The Little Boltons, SW10.

WIDOW LIVING OF TENTH MARQUESS

JOSÉ (*Dowager Marchioness of Sligo*), da of late William Gauche, of —: *m* 1930, the 10th Marquess, who *d* 1991. *Residence* –

COLLATERAL BRANCHES LIVING

Issue of late Capt Lord Ulick Browne, RA (raised to the rank of Marquess's son 1953), brother of 10th Marquess, *b* 1915, *d* 1979: *m* 1st, 1942, Mrs Elma Valerie Warren, who *d* 1959, da of Capt Andrew Burmanoff, Russian Hussars; 2ndly, 1962, Fiona (ante), da of late John Glenn, of E Grinstead, Sussex:—
(By 2nd *m*) SEBASTIAN ULICK, *b* 27 May 1964; *ed* Rugby: *m* 1984 (*m diss* 1992), Christina Maria, yst da of late Luis Suaznabar, of Bolivia, and has issue living, Christopher Ulick, *b* 14 Nov 1988, — Camilla, *b* 1986. —— Ulicia Catherine, *b* 1962: *m* 1993, Giles P. T. Edwards, only son of Peter Guy Edwards, of Low Walworth Hall, Darlington, co Durham.

Grandsons of late Major Percy Howe Browne, 2nd son of Lord Richard Howe Browne (infra):—
Issue of late Lieut-Com Anthony Howe Browne, RN, *b* 1905, *ka* 1940: *m* 1931, Joyce Mary Le Roy (who *d* 1981, having *m* 2ndly, 1946, Squadron Leader Graham Doody, ACA, who *d* 1981), da of John Collin, of Trumpington, Cambridge:—
Patrick Ulick Anthony Howe (27 Lanhill Rd, W9; Brook Farm, Fowlmere, nr Royston, Herts), *b* 1935; *ed* Eton; and Magdalene Coll, Camb: *m* 1962, Gerd, da of Anders Hamer, of Norway, and has issue living, Patrick Alexander Howe, *b* 1965, — Anthony Howe, *b* 1967, — Cecilie Howe, *b* 1963. —— Michael John Le Roy (27 Lanhill Rd, W9), *b* 1936: *m* 1959 (*m diss* 1969), Sarah Ruth, da of James Edward Kenneth Sprot, of Natal, and has issue living, Richard Howe, *b* 1962, — Jeremy Ulick, *b* 1963.

Granddaughters of late Lord Richard Howe Browne, 6th son of 2nd Marquess:—
Issue of late Cyril Edward Browne, OBE, *b* 1873, *d* 1960: *m* 1902, Alice Christina, who *d* 1962, da of Frederick Thomas Lewin, DL, of Castlegrove, near Tuam, co Galway, and Cloghans, co Mayo:—
Phyllis Marion Alice, *b* 1913; *ed* Trin Coll, Dublin (Mod BA): *m* 1st, 1941, Harold Hugh Brodie Ind, who *d* 1977; 2ndly, 1982, Kingsmill Pennefather, of Elsinore, Delgany, co Wicklow, and has issue living (by 1st *m*), Peter Lewin Brodie (18 Oak Apple Close, Cowfold, W Sussex), *b* 1944; *ed* Eton, and Trin Coll, Dublin (BA): *m* 1982, Peta Mary Wildbore (*née* Butler), and has issue living, Lisa Peta Alice *b* 1983, — Christina Isabel Mary, *b* 1942; *ed* Trin Coll, Dublin (BA): *m* 1970, W/Cdr Robin Worthington Scott, of Throstlenest, Summer Bridge, Harrogate, York, and has issue living, Gervase Roderick John *b* 1971; *ed* Repton, and Edinburgh Univ, Nicholas Hugo Howe *b* 1972; *ed* Repton, and Edinburgh Univ, — Miranda Eleanor Phyllis (Ashleagh, Knockroe, Greystones, co Wicklow), *b* 1946: *m* 1971, John Morris O'Connor, Assist Prof of Philosophy, Case Western Reserve Univ, Cleveland, and has issue living, Amanda Evelyn Alice *b* 1974. —— Marjory Maud, *b* 1916: *m* 1954, Charles Hastings Doyne, and has issue living, Charles Philip (Greenside House, Hampsthwaite, Harrogate, N Yorks HG3 2EU), *b* 1955; *ed* Sherborne, and Aston Univ (BSc): *m* 1987, Sarah Mary, da of Michael S. Benson, of High Pines, Dane Hill, Sussex, and has issue living, Samuel Charles Michael *b* 1992, Alice Mary Sarah *b* 1990. *Residence* – Cotes des Vallees, Castel, Guernsey, CI.

(In remainder to Earldom of Altamont, Viscountcy of Westport, and Barony of Mount Eagle only)

Grandchildren of late Capt Perceval Altamont Browne, only surv son of John Denis Browne, 4th son of Rt Hon Denis Browne, MP, 2nd son of 2nd Earl of Altamont:—
Issue of late Percy Frederick Browne, *b* 1872, *d* 1959: *m* 1904, Ruth Reynolds, who *d* 1957, da of John Reynolds Warren, of Berea, Durban, S Africa:—
Nancye Maud (The Cottage, 12 Mayfair Av, Newlands, Cape Town 7700, S Africa), *b* 1905: *m* 1945, Maj Aubrey James Rous, and has issue living, Patrick James (106, 1124 North Kings Rd, Los Angeles, Calif 90069, USA), *b* 1947. —— Moya Lennox (1005-2012 Fullerton Av, N Vancouver, BC, Canada V7P 3P3), *b* 1917: *m* 1944, Richard Read Birtwistle, who *d* 1983, and has issue living. Susan Lennox, *b* 1947: *m* 1972, Capt Dan Collinson Koch, of 1945 Russel Way, W Vancouver, BC V7V 3B3, Canada, and has issue living, Michael Richard Collinson *b* 1975, Christopher John Collinson *b* 1978, James Daniel Collinson *b* 1990.

Grandchildren of late Percy Frederick Browne (ante):—
Issue of late Patrick Warren Browne, *b* 1908, *d* 1944: *m* 1936, Ada Elizabeth Minnie Barnes, who *m* 2ndly, 1946 (*m diss* 1954), Charles Edward Hatton Duprez, and has resumed the surname of Browne:—
Michael Lewis, *b* 1940. —— (Phillip) Anthony (1537 30th St NW, Washington DC 20007, USA), *b* 1941. —— Patricia Ruth, *b* 1937: *m* 19—, David Heather, and has issue living, Lucy, *b* 19—.

Grandchildren of late George Robert Browne, eldest son of Rev George Browne, 5th son of late Rt Hon Denis Browne, MP (ante):—
Issue of late George Denis Gun Browne, *b* 1874, *d* 1946: *m* 1901, Gertrude Bessie, who *d* 1953, yst da of John Robert Sutton Hudson:—
Denis George Robert Anthony Gun, *b* 1907: *m* 1960, Violet Ailsa, da of Charles Henry Stewart-Hess, of Wallasey, Cheshire. —— Gertrude Frances Hester, *b* 1905: *m* 1st, 1931, George Ryder Runton, who *d* 1935; 2ndly, 1945, Roger Sydney McCulloch (PO Box 200, Selukwe, Zimbabwe), and has issue living, (by 1st *m*) Aileen Frances (Paarl, Cape Prov, S Africa), *b* 1932: *m* 1950, John Geoffrey Harrison, who *d* 1975, and has issue living, Michael John *b* 1952, Rosemary Ann *b* 1954, — (by 2nd *m*) Jane Ann Louise, *b* 1946: *m* 1968, Marie Denise Guiot-Pascau, of Natal, and has issue living, Daniel François *b* 1973, Grant Ivan *b* 1975, Heal Gregory *b* 1977.

Grandchildren of late Robert Denis Browne, eldest son of late Rev Robert Browne, 2nd son of late Rev George Browne (ante):—
Issue of late Robert John Denis Browne, FRCGP, *b* 1907, *d* 1985: *m* 1949, Norah Mary (1536 Pershore Rd, Stirchley, Birmingham, W Midlands), da of David Haywood, of Burton-on-Trent:—
Stephen Denis, *b* 1950; MRCGP: *m* 1978, Patricia Marian, da of William George Delahaye, of Birmingham, and has issue living, Elizabeth Anne, *b* 1979, — Sarah Jayne, *b* 1981. —— Anthony David, *b* 1958; MSc: *m* 1983, Susan Elizabeth, da of John Frederick Hole, of Stourbridge, and has issue living, David Alexander, *b* 1989, Daniel Benjamin *b* 1991. —— Margaret, *b* 1952: *m* 1973, John Charles Williams, and has issue living, Rachel, *b* 1977, — Ruth Emma, *b* 1979.
Issue of late Terence Francis Denis Browne, *b* 1910, *d* 1987: *m* 1947, Avril Honor, who *d* 1973, da of William T. Thompson, of Rustington, Sussex:—
Peter Malyon Denis, *b* 1953. —— Ian Anthony Denis (20 Woodfield Lane, Ashtead, Surrey KT21 2BE), *b* 1956.

Grandson of late Rev Robert Browne (ante):—
Issue of late Rev Cyril George Denis Browne, *b* 1873, *d* 1952: *m* 1906, Sarah H. J., who *d* 1952, da of Charles Crooks Higby:—
Rev Cyril Theodore Martin *b* 1912; sometime R of Tilston and Shocklach. *Residence* – 14 St Philip's Court, Sandhurst Rd, Tunbridge Wells, Kent TN2 3SW.
Issue of late Ambrose George Denis Browne, *b* 1875, *d* 1954: *m* 1st, 1915, Alice Winifred who *d* 1938, da of late Sir William Henry White, KCB, 2ndly, 1941, Gertrude Mariana, who *d* 1973, yr da of late Rev John Kipling Quarterman, MA, of Blackheath, SE3:—
(By 1st *m*) William Robert Anthony Denis (1334 St Patrick St, Oak Bay, Vic, Vancouver, BC, Canada), *b* 1924; FRICS, RI (BC); European War with RM: *m* 1st, 1949 (*m diss* 1967), Eileen Beatrice Louise, da of Horace Hugh Perceval Hunt, of High Ham, Somerset; 2ndly, 1967, Hildegard, da of Johann Cremer, of Dorsetn, W Germany, and has issue living (by 1st *m*), James Anthony Ulick Denis, *b* 1956, — Caroline Elizabeth Anne Denis, *b* 1952, — (by 2nd *m*) Andrew Christopher Denis *b* 1972. —— Winifred Anne Denis, *b* 1921: *m* 1950, John Henry Bateman, MA, of The Orchard, 18A Chapel Lane, Wilmslow, Ches.

Grandchildren of late Henry Browne, 2nd son of late George Browne, 3rd son of late Maj John Browne, el son of Col Rt Hon Arthur Browne, MP, 2nd son of 1st Earl of Altamont:—
Issue of late Ernest Henry Browne, *b* 1863, *d* 1928: *m* 19—, Beatrice Brownrigg, who *d* 1964:—
Ernest Henry (126 Ohiro Bay Parade, Wellington, S2, NZ), *b* 1913. —— Beatrice Mary (92 Cabra Park, Phibsborough, Dublin), *b* 1911.

Granddaughter of late Rev John Denis Browne, son of late George Townshend Browne, son of late Col Rt
Hon Arthur Browne, MP (ante):—
Issue of late Rev Valentine John Augustus (altered by deed poll 1897 to Valentine Denis) Browne, b 1843, d 1933:
m 1884, Frances Elizabeth, da of late William Rose, Bar-at-law:—
Rosalind Frances, b 1885.

PREDECESSORS – (1) JOHN Browne, son of Peter Browne of Westport, grandson of Sir John Browne, 1st Bt (cr 1636) (see
B Kilmaine), was MP for Castlebar 1749-60; cr Baron Mount Eagle, co Mayo (peerage of Ireland) 1760, Viscount
Westport (peerage of Ireland) 1768, and Earl of Altamont (peerage of Ireland) 1771; d 1776; s by his son **(2)** PETER, 2nd Earl,
sat as MP for co Mayo; d 1780, s by his son **(3)** JOHN DENIS, KP, PC, 3rd Earl; sat as MP for co Mayo; cr Marquess of Sligo
(peerage of Ireland) 1800, and Baron Monteagle, of Westport, co Mayo (peerage of United Kingdom) 1806; d 1809; s by his
son **(4)** HOWE PETER, KP, PC, 2nd Marquess, b 1788: m 1816, Hester Catherine, el da of 13th Earl of Clanricarde; d 1845; s
by his son **(5)** GEORGE JOHN, 3rd Marquess, b 1820: m 1st, 1847, Louisa Ellen Frances Augusta Smythe, who d 1852, da of
6th Viscount Strangford; 2ndly, 1858, Julia Catherine Anne Nugent, who d 1859, el da of 9th Earl of Westmeath; 3rdly, 1878,
Isabelle, who d 1927, da of late Vicomte de Peyronnet; d 1896; s by his brother **(6)** JOHN THOMAS, 4th Marquess; b 1824; sat
as MP for co Mayo 1857-68; d 1903; s by his brother **(7)** HENRY ULICK, 5th Marquess; b 1831: m 1855, Catharine Henrietta,
who d 1914, da of late William Stephens Dicken, Dep Inspector-Gen Indian Med Ser; d 1913; s by his el son **(8)** GEORGE
ULICK, 6th Marquess; b 1856; in 1916 s to Earldom of Clanricarde (cr 1800) (see * infra); appointed Lieut and Custos
Rotulorum for co Mayo 1914: m 1887, Agatha Stewart, who d 1965, da of late J. Stewart Hodgson, of Haslemere; d 1935; s by
his only son **(9)** ULICK DE BURGH, MC, 7th Marquess; b 1898; Capt (ret) The Greys; European War 1914-19 (MC); d 1941; s
by his uncle **(8)** ARTHUR HOWE, KBE, CB (3rd son of 5th Marquess), 8th Marquess; b 1867; Col late S Staffordshire Regt
and Roy Munster Fusiliers; on Gen Staff, Special Intelligence Directorate, War Office 1914-19 (KBE); Principal Assist Sec,
Imperial War Graves Commn 1919-30: m 1919, Lilian Whiteside, who d 1953, da of Charles Chapman, and widow of Major A.
F. Mann; d 1951; s by his brother **(9)** TERENCE MORRIS, 9th Marquess; b 1873; was Sup Bengal Police 1894-1907, d 1952; s by
his nephew **(10)** DENIS EDWARD (el son of late Lieut-Col Lord Alfred Eden Browne, DSO, 5th son of 5th Marquess), 10th
Marquess; b 1908: m 1930, José, da of William Gauche; d 1991; s by his only son **(11)** ULICK, 11th Marquess, and
present peer; also Earl of Altamont, Earl of Clanricarde, Viscount Westport, Baron Mount Eagle, and Baron Monteagle.

***(1)** ULICK BURKE or de Burgh, great grandson of Ulick de Bourke, MacWilliam Eighter, feudal Lord of Clanricarde,
collateral heir male of Earls of Ulster; Gov of Connaught; cr Baron of Dunkellin, and Earl of Clanricarde (peerage of Ireland)
1543; d 1544; s by his son **(2)** RICHARD, 2nd Earl; was Lord-Lieut of Ireland; d 1582; s by his son **(3)** ULICK, 3rd Earl; his 4th
son, John, was cr Viscount Burke, of Clanmories, co Mayo (peerage of Ireland) 1629, with remainder to the issue male of his
father, which title, on the death of the 2nd Viscount, merged into the Earldom; d 1601; s by his son **(4)** RICHARD, 4th Earl;
cr Baron Somerhill and Viscount Tunbridge (peerage of England) 1624, and Earl of St Albans (peerage of England) 1628; d
1635; s by his son **(5)** ULICK, 5th Earl; cr Marquess of Clanricarde (peerage of Ireland) 1646; d without male issue 1658,
when the English peerages and the Marquessate became extinct, and the Irish Earldom devolved upon his cousin **(6)**
RICHARD, 6th Earl, el son of Sir William Burke, 3rd son of 3rd Earl; d 1666; s by his brother **(7)** William, 7th Earl; d 1687; s
by his son **(8)** RICHARD, 8th Earl; s by his brother **(9)** JOHN, 9th Earl, Col of a regiment of foot in the army of James II;
being taken prisoner at the battle of Aghrim 1691, was outlawed and attainted, and his estates were forfeited; his children
however claimed their several remainders prior to the sale of the forfeitures and recovered the same; in 1701 the Earl was,
by Act of Parliament, acquitted of his treasons and attainder; and restored to his estates; d 1722; s by his son **(10)** MICHAEL,
10th Earl; d 1726; s by his son **(11)** JOHN SMITH, 11th Earl; resumed by sign manual the ancient surname of De Burgh, d
1782; s by his son **(12)** HENRY, KP, PC, 12th Earl; Gov of co Galway; cr Marquess of Clanricarde (peerage of Ireland) 1789;
dsp 1795, when the Marquessate became extinct; s in Earldom by his brother **(13)** JOHN THOMAS, 13th Earl; a Gen in the
Army and Gov of co Galway; cr Earl of Clanricarde (peerage of Ireland) 1800, with remainder to his two daughters and their
issue male according to priority of birth; d 1808; s by his son **(14)** ULICK JOHN, KP, PC, 14th Earl; b 1802; was Under-Sec for
Foreign Affairs 1826-7, Ambassador at St Petersburg 1838-40, Postmaster-Gen 1846-52, Lord Privy Seal 1858, and Lord-Lieut
of co Galway, etc; cr Marquess of Clanricarde (peerage of Ireland) 1825, and Baron Somerhill, of Somerhill, co Kent (peerage
of United Kingdom) 1826: m 1825, Hon Harriet, who d 1876, da of Rt Hon George Canning and of his wife Viscountess
Canning in her own right; d 1874; s by his son **(15)** HUBERT, 2nd Marquess; b 1832; assumed in 1862 the additional
surname of Canning, by Roy licence, as heir of his maternal uncle, the 1st Earl Canning; MP for co Galway (L) 1867-71; d
1916, when the Marquessate of Clanricarde and the Barony of Somerhill became ext, and the Barony of Dunkellin, and Earldom of Clanricarde (cr 1543), and the Viscountcy of Bourke became ext, while the Earldom of Clanricarde (cr 1800)
devolved under special remainder upon his cousin **(16)** GEORGE ULICK, 6th Marquess of Sligo (ante).

SLIM, VISCOUNT (Slim) (Viscount UK 1960)

JOHN DOUGLAS SLIM, OBE, 2nd Viscount; b 20 July 1927; s 1970; Lt-
Col (ret) A&SH and Special Air Ser Regt; DL Greater London 1988;
FRGS 1983; cr OBE (Mil) 1973: m 1958, Elisabeth, da of Arthur
Rawdon Spinney, CBE, and has issue.

Arms – Gules semée of swords erect argent a lion rampant or, on a canton
quarterly azure and also argent a mullet of seven points gold. **Crest** - Out of a
Crown Vallary or a peacock in its pride proper gorged with a collar and with
line reflexed over the back gold. **Supporters** – Dexter, a British soldier in jungle-
green battle dress with web equipment the exterior hand supporting a rifle with
bayonet affixed; Sinister, a Gurkha rifleman in North-West Frontier dress with
web equipment the exterior hand supporting a rifle all proper.
Address – c/o Lloyds Bank, 6 Pall Mall, SW1. **Clubs** – White's, Special Forces.

A recompense is fairer from a depth

Bristol.

SONS LIVING

Hon MARK WILLIAM RAWDON, b 13 Feb 1960: m 1992, Harriet Laura, yr da of
Jonathan Harrison, of Beds.
Hon Hugo John Robertson, b 1961; ed Eton, and St John's Coll, Oxford (MA);
Senior Research Officer, Save The Children Fund, London; FRGS: m 1991, M.
B. Rebecca, da of late Prof Philip Abrams, and of Mrs Derek Greenwood, of

DAUGHTER LIVING

Hon Mary Ann, b 1964; BA.

SISTER LIVING

Hon Una Mary, *b* 1930: *m* 1st, 1953 (*m diss* 1979), Maj Peter Nigel Stewart Frazer, Grenadier Guards; 2ndly, 1980, Ronald Rowcliffe, of Bamson, Puddington, Tiverton, Devon, and has issue living (by 1st *m*), Sarah Juliet, *b* 1953: *m* 1978, Robert M. Whyte, — (Jennifer) Jane, *b* 1956: *m* 1989, Colin P. G. Farrant, son of Michael Farrant, of Crawley, Hants, and has issue living, Luke *b* 1991, Annabel Mary *b* 1993, — Emma Mary, *b* 1965.

PREDECESSORS – **(1)** *Sir* WILLIAM JOSEPH SLIM, KG, GCB, GCMG, GCVO, GBE, DSO, MC, son of late John Slim of Bristol; *b* 1891; Field Marshal; GOC-in-C 14th Army 1943-45, Allied Land Forces, SE Asia 1945-46, Dep Chm Rly Exec 1948, CIGS 1948-53, Gov-Gen of Aust 1953-60, and Gov and Constable Windsor Castle 1964-70; *cr Viscount Slim*, of Yarralumla, ACT, and of Bishopston, City and Co of Bristol (peerage of UK) 1960: *m* 1926, Aileen, who *d* 1994, da of Rev J. A. Robertson, of Edinburgh; *d* 1970; *s* by his son **(2)**JOHN DOUGLAS, 2nd Viscount and present peer.

SLYNN OF HADLEY, BARON (Slynn) (Life Baron 1992)

GORDON SLYNN, son of late John Slynn; *b* 17 Feb 1930; *ed* Sandbach Sch, Goldsmiths' Coll, and Trin Coll, Camb; Hon Fellow Buckingham 1982, St Andrew's Coll Sydney Univ 1991, Liverpool Poly 1992, and Goldsmiths' Coll 1993, Hon LLD Birmingham 1983, Buckingham 1983, Exeter 1985, Univ of Technology Sydney 1991, Bristol Poly 1992, Sussex 1992, and Stetson, USA 1993, Hon DCL Durham 1989, Hon Decanus Legis Mercer Univ USA 1986, Hon Fellow American Coll of Trial Lawyers 1992, Memb American Law Inst 1993; Bar Gray's Inn 1956 (Treasurer 1988), Recorder 1971, Hon Recorder Hereford 1972-76, Junior Counsel to Treasury 1968-74, QC 1974, Leading Counsel to Treasury 1974-76, a Judge of the High Court of Justice (Queen's Bench Div) 1976-81, Pres Employment Appeal Tribunal 1978-81, Advocate-Gen Court of Justice European Communities 1981-88, Judge 1988-92, since when a Lord of Appeal in Ordinary; Visiting Prof of Law Durham Univ 1981-88, Univ of Technology Sydney since 1990, and National Univ of India since 19—; Chief Steward Hereford since 1978; Gov Internat Students' Trust 1979-85, and since 1992, Chm Exec Council Internat Law Assocn since 1988; Member Court of Broderers' Co; Commandeur d'honneur de Bontemps de Medoc et des Graves, Commandeur Confrerie de St Cumbert, Chevalier de Tastevin; contributor to learned journals, and author of *Introducing a European Legal Order*, *cr* Knt 1976, and *Baron Slynn of Hadley*, of Eggington, co Beds (Life Baron) 1992: *m* 1962, Odile Marie Henriette, da of late Pierre Boutin.

Arms – Argent, on a chevron gules between three leopards' heads proper as many garbs or, on a chief azure three saltires couped argent. **Crest** – Within a crest coronet or a tawny owl holding in the dexter claw a quill erect proper, the leg ringed or.
Address – Royal Courts of Justice, Strand, WC2. *Clubs* – Athenaeum, Beefsteak, Garrick.

SMITH, BARON (Smith) (Life Baron 1978)

(EDWIN) RODNEY SMITH, KBE, MS, FRCS, only son of Dr Edwin Smith; *b* 1914; *ed* Westminster and London Univ; MB, BS London 1937; MRCS, LRCP 1937; FRCS England 1939; MS London 1941; Pres, Roy Coll of Surgs 1973-77; Chm Conference of Roy Colls (UK) 1976-78; Pres, Roy Soc of Medicine 1978-80; 1939-45 War as Lt-Col RAMC in Egypt, N Africa and Italy; *cr* KBE (Civil) 1975, and *Baron Smith*, of Marlow, co Buckinghamshire (Life Baron) 1978: *m* 1st, 1938 (*m diss* 1971) Mary Rodwell; 2ndly, 1971, Susan, da of Dr Rowdon Marrian Fry, and has issue by 1st *m*.

Arms – Gules in chief two fleams the blades outwards, and in base a lyre or, a border ermine. **Crest** – An eagle close regardant sable, beaked and legged or, holding in the dexter claw a bugle horn or, by its strings sable. **Supporters** – *Dexter*, a Burmese cat; *sinister*, a greyhound sable, both collared or, each collar charged with a thistle proper.
Residence – Dower Cottage, Marlow Common, Bucks. *Club* – MCC.

SONS LIVING *(By 1st marriage)*

Hon Martin Rodney, *b* 1942.
Hon Andrew Edward Rodney, *b* 1948.
Hon Robert Aidan Rodney, *b* 1956.

DAUGHTER LIVING *(By 1st marriage)*

Hon Elinor, *b* 1950.

SNOW, BARONY OF (Snow) (Extinct 1980)

SON LIVING OF LIFE BARON

Hon Philip Charles Hansford, *b* 1952; *ed* Eton, and Balliol Coll, Oxford; writer; Member Royal Inst of Internat Affairs, and Council Member China Soc: *m* 1987, Amanda C., elder da of Sir Clive Anthony Whitmore, of E Sussex, and has issue living, Renata Maria Hansford, *b* 1992. *Residence* – 39 Alderney St, SW1V 4HH.

SNOWDON, EARL OF (Armstrong-Jones) (Earl UK 1961)

What God wills will be

ANTONY CHARLES ROBERT ARMSTRONG-JONES, GCVO, 1st Earl, son of late Ronald Owen Lloyd Armstrong-Jones, MBE, QC, of Plas Dinas, Caernarvonshire; *b* 7 Mar 1930; *ed* Eton, and Jesus Coll, Camb; Hon DLitt Portsmouth 1993; Constable of Caernarvon Castle since 1963; *cr Viscount Linley*, of Nymans, co Sussex, and *Earl of Snowdon* (peerage of UK) 1961; GCVO 1969: *m* 1st, 6 May 1960 (*m diss* 1978), HRH The Princess Margaret Rose, yr da of HM late King George VI; 2ndly, 1978, Lucy Mary, only da of Donald Brook Davies, of Enniskerry, co Wicklow, and formerly wife of Michael Lindsay-Hogg (*see* Lindsay-Hogg, Bt), and has issue by 1st and 2nd *m*.

Arms – Sable on a chevron argent, between in chief two fleurs-de-lis, and in base an eagle displayed or, four pallets gules. **Crest** – A stag statant gules attired collared and unguled or between two arms embowed in armour the hands proper each grasping a fleur-de-lis gold. **Supporters** – *Dexter*, a griffin, and *sinister*, an eagle, each with wings elevated and addorsed or.
Residence – 22 Launceston Place, W8 5RL. *Clubs* – Buck's, Leander, Hawkes, Oxford and Cambridge.

SON LIVING (By 1st marriage)

DAVID ALBERT CHARLES (*Viscount Linley*), *b* 3 Nov 1961; *ed* Bedales: *m* 8 Oct 1993, Hon Serena Alleyne Stanhope, only da of Charles Henry Leicester, Viscount Petersham (*see* E Harrington).

DAUGHTERS LIVING (By 1st marriage)

Lady Sarah Frances Elizabeth, *b* 1964; *ed* Bedales, and Royal Academy Sch: *m* 1994, Daniel Chatto, yr son of late Thomas Chatto.

(By 2nd marriage)

Lady Frances, *b* 1979.

SOAMES, BARONY OF (Soames) (Extinct 1987)

SONS LIVING OF LIFE BARON

Hon (Arthur) Nicholas Winston, *b* 1948; *ed* Eton; 2nd Lieut 11th Hussars (PAO) 1967-70; Extra Equerry to HRH the Prince of Wales 1970-72; Memb Select Cttee on European Legislation 1983-84; MP for Crawley (*C*) since 1983; Parl Private Sec to Min of State for Employment and Chm Conservative Party (Mr John Gummer) 1984-92, since when Parly Sec, Dept of Agriculture, Fisheries and Food: *m* 1st, 1981 (*m diss* 1988), Catherine N., eldest da of Capt Anthony E. Weatherall, of Cowhill Tower, Dumfries; 2ndly, 1993, Serena Mary, da of Sir John Lindsay Eric Smith, CH, CBE (*see* E Northesk, colls), and has issue living (by 1st *m*), Arthur Harry David, *b* 1985.
Hon Jeremy Bernard, *b* 1952; *ed* Eton: *m* 1978, Susanna, elder da of (James) David (Agar) Keith, of W Barsham Hall, Fakenham, Norfolk, and has issue living, Archie Christopher Winston, *b* 1988, — Gemma Mary, *b* 1979, — Flora Caroline, *b* 1982.
Hon Rupert Christopher, *b* 1959; *ed* Eton: *m* 1988, Camilla Rose, eldest da of Thomas Raymond Dunne, of Gatley Park, Leominster, Herefords, and has issue living, Arthur Christopher, *b* 1990, — Daisy, *b* 1992.

DAUGHTERS LIVING OF LIFE BARON

Hon Emma Mary SOAMES, *b* 1949; has resumed her maiden name; journalist; editor of *Tatler* 1988-90, and *ES* Magazine since 1992: *m* 1981 (*m diss* 1989), James N. M. MacManus, eldest son of Dr Niall MacManus, of 8 Warwick Sq, SW1, and has issue living, Emily Fiona, *b* 1983. *Residence* – 26 Eland Rd, SW11.
Hon Charlotte Clementine (*Countess Peel*), *b* 1954: *m* 1st, 1973 (*m diss* 1982), (Alexander) Richard Hambro, 2nd son of Jocelyn Olaf Hambro, MC; 2ndly, 1989, as his 2nd wife, 3rd Earl Peel, and has issue (by 1st *m*), Clementine Silvia, *b* 1976, — (by 2nd *m*) (*see* E Peel). *Residence* – Gunnerside Lodge, Richmond, N Yorks.

WIDOW LIVING OF LIFE BARON

Hon MARY SPENCER-CHURCHILL, DBE (*Baroness Soames*), yst da of late Rt Hon Sir Winston Leonard Spencer-Churchill, KG, OM, CH, TD, FRS (*see* D Marlborough, colls), and of late Baroness Spencer-Churchill, GBE: *m* 1947, Baron Soames, GCMG, GCVO, CH, CBE, PC (Life Baron), who *d* 1987.

SOMERLEYTON, BARON (Crossley) (Baron UK 1916, Bt UK 1863)

All good is from above

SAVILE WILLIAM FRANCIS CROSSLEY, KCVO, 3rd Baron and 4th Baronet; *b* 17 Sept 1928; *s* 1959; *ed* Eton; Capt (ret) Coldstream Guards; co Councillor E Suffolk 1967-73; DL Suffolk 1964; JP Lowestoft 1969; a Lord in Waiting to HM The Queen 1978-92, and Master of the Horse to HM since 1991; a Dir of E Anglian Water Co; Chm E Anglia Regional Branch, Historic Houses Assocn, and of Assocn of Masters of Harriers and Beagles, Pres of E Region, YMCA, and Gov Lowestoft Coll of Further Education; patron of one living; KCVO 1994: *m* 1963, Belinda Maris, only da of late Capt Vivian Loyd, RFA, of Kingsmoor, Ascot, and has issue.

Arms – Gules, a chevron indented ermine between two cross-crosslets in chief, and a saltire coupled in base or. **Crest** – A demi-hind erased proper, charged with two bars holding between the feet a cross-crosslet or. **Supporters** – On either side a hind proper, semée of cross-crosslets or.
Seat – Somerleyton Hall, Lowestoft, Suffolk. *Clubs* – White's, Pratt's.

SON LIVING

Hon HUGH FRANCIS SAVILE, *b* 27 Sept 1971; a Page of Honour to HM The Queen 1983-84.

DAUGHTERS LIVING

Hon Isabel Alicia Claire, *b* 1964: *m* 1991, Mark Cator (*see* Storey, Bt).
Hon Camilla Mary Lara, *b* 1967: *m* 1993, William Aldwin (Sandy) Soames, eldest son of Robert Harold Soames, of Toppesfield, Essex.

Hon Alicia Phyllis Belinda, *b* 1969.
Hon Louisa Bridget Vivien, *b* 1974.

BROTHER LIVING

Hon (Richard) Nicholas, TD (Westfield Farm, Settrington, Malton, York. *Clubs* – Cavalry and Guards', Pratt's); *b* 1932; *ed* Eton and RMA; DL N Yorks 1988, High Sheriff 1989; Capt 9th Queen's R Lancers (ret); Maj Queens Own Yeo (TA); Comdg Officer Queens Own Yeomanry (TA) 1973-76, Col Gen Staff (TA) 1978; appointed Aide-de-Camp TAVR to HM The Queen 1980; a Member of Hon Corps of Gentlemen-at-Arms: *m* 1958, Alexandra Anne Maitland, who *d* 1990, only da of W/Cdr Charles Donald Graham Welch, RAF of Perrot Farm, Graffham, Sussex, and has issue living, John Dickon Francis, *b* 1966; *ed* Eton, and RMA Sandhurst; Capt 9/12th Royal Lancers, — Amanda Carolyn, *b* 1960: *m* 1st, 1984, Patrick James Auchinleck Darling, only son of Gerald Ralph Auchinleck Darling, RD, QC, of Crevenagh, Omagh, co Tyrone; 2ndly, 1992, Edward P. U. Mead, son of Humphrey Mead, of Normandy, and of Mrs Peter Cadbury, of Alresford, Hants, and has issue living (by 1st *m*), Shaunagh Edwina Auchinleck *b* 1986, (by 2nd *m*) Arthur Silas *b* 1993, Leila Alexandria *b* (twin) 1993, — Lucinda Mary, *b* 1962: *m* 1980, Masood Oloumi, of Yazdi, and has issue living, Lilly *b* 1985, Rose *b* 1989.

SISTER LIVING

Hon Mary, *b* 1926; JP Huntingdon and Peterborough 1966: *m* 1950, Maj William Birkbeck, DL, Coldm Gds (ret), of Bainton House, Stamford, Lincs, and has issue living, Anthony William Savile, *b* 1956; *ed* Eton: *m* 1991, Hon Davina Mary Bewicke-Copley, yr da of 6th Baron Cromwell, and has issue living, Elizabeth (Beth) *b* 1993, — Victoria Mary, *b* 1951: *m* 1981, Adauto Santos, of Rio de Janeiro, *b* 1952: *m* 1987, Diana Kenneth Scott Moncrieff, elder son of David Charles Scott Moncrieff, CVO, TD, WS, of 23 Cluny Drive, Edinburgh, and has issue living, Robert David *b* 1991, Iona Mary *b* 1988, Isabel Ann *b* 1989, — Rosetta Sybil, *b* 1958: *m* 1987, Iain James Russell, only son of James Russell, of Croyard House, Beauly, Inverness-shire, and of Seafield, co Waterford, and has issue living, Oliver George Seckham *b* 1988, Alastair William James *b* 1991, Patrick Alexander Bazaine *b* 1993.

COLLATERAL BRANCH LIVING

Issue of late Capt Hon John de Bathe Crossley, 2nd son of 1st Baron, *b* 1893, *d* 1935: *m* 1st, 1918 (*m diss* 1930), Dorothy Frances who *d* 1955, da da of Capt Sir George Everard Cayley, 9th Bt; 2ndly, 1930, Sybelle Winifred, who *d* 1963, da of Cyril Augustus Drummond (E Perth, colls):—
(By 1st *m*) Anthony Everard Savile (Milima, MSF 115 Gympie, Qld 4570, Aust), *b* 1920: *m* 1956, Jean Margaret Gillian, el da of D. O. Russell, of Kipkarren River, Kenya and has issue living, John de Bathe, *b* 1958: *m* 1982, Yvonne van Tongeren, — Timothy Elgon Savile, *b* 1963. — Marguerite, *b* 1957: *m* 1982, William Anthony Peat Darbyshire, — Julia, *b* 1960. —— Charles John (Linda Cruises, Cosgrove Lock, Milton Keynes, Bucks, MK19 7JR), *b* 1921: *m* 1957, Catherine Adelaide Anne da of late Gabriel Noel Dyer (*see* Legard, Bt, colls, 1971 Edn), and formerly wife of Capt John Henry Mark Fane, MBE (*see* B Clinton). —— (By 2nd *m*) (Elizabeth) Belinda (Kings Rew, Blackfield, Southampton), *b* 1932: *m* 1959 (*m diss* 1974), 3rd Baron Montagu of Beaulieu.

PREDECESSORS – (1) FRANCIS Crossley, son of John Crossley, of Halifax, *b* 1817; MP for Halifax (*L*) 1852-9, and for the North-West Riding of Yorkshire 1859-72; *cr* a *Baronet* 1863: *m* 1845, Martha Eliza, who *d* 1891, da of Henry Brinton; *d* 1872; *s* by his only son (2) *Sir* SAVILE BRINTON, GCVO, PC, 2nd Bt; *b* 1857; MP for N, or Lowestoft, Div of Suffolk (LU) 1885-92, and for Halifax 1900-1906; Paymaster-Gen 1902-5, and a Lord-in-Waiting to HM 1918-24; *cr* Baron Somerleyton, of Somerleyton, co Suffolk (peerage of United Kingdom) 1916: *m* 1887, Phyllis, CBE, yst da of Gen Sir Henry Percival de Bathe, KCB, 4th Bt; *d* 1935; *s* by his son (3) FRANCIS SAVILE, MC, 2nd Baron; *b* 1889; Major late 9th Lancers and a Director of John Crossley & Sons Ltd, of Halifax: *m* 1924, Bridget, MBE, who *d* 1983, da of William Douro Hoare, CBE, of Guessons, Welwyn, Herts; *d* 1959; *s* by his el son (4) SAVILE WILLIAM FRANCIS, 3rd Baron, and present peer.

SOMERS, BARON (Cocks) (Baron GB 1784, Bt GB 1772)

(Title pronounced "Summers")

JOHN PATRICK SOMERS COCKS, 8th Baron, and 8th Baronet; *b* 30 April 1907; *s* 1953; BMus; ARCM; Prof Roy Coll of Music; Dir of Music, Epsom Coll, 1949-53: *m* 1st, 1935, Barbara Marianne, who *d* 1959, da of Charles Henry Southall, of Norwich; 2ndly, 1961, Dora Helen, who *d* 1993, da of late John Mountfort.

Arms – Quarterly; 1st and 4th sable, a chevron between three stags' attires argent, *Cocks*; 2nd and 3rd vert, a fesse dancettée ermine, *Somers*. **Crest** – On a mount vert, a stag lodged and reguardant argent, attired and hoofed sable. **Supporters** – Two lions, each gorged with a collar dancettée vert.
Address – c/o Musicians Benevolent Fund, Dulas Court, Herefordshire.

To be useful, rather than conspicuous

COLLATERAL BRANCHES LIVING

Grandchildren of late Philip Alphonso Somers Cocks, CMG, son of late Hon John James Thomas Somers Cocks, brother of 5th Baron:—
Issue of late John Sebastian Somers Cocks, CVO, CBE, *b* 1907, *d* 1964: *m* 1946, Marjorie Olive (19 Kempson Rd, SW6), da of late Arthur Julius Weller:—
PHILIP SEBASTIAN SOMERS (19 Kempson Rd, SW6), *b* 4 Jan 1948. —— Anne (Anna) Gwenllian Somers, *b* 1950; *ed* St Anne's Coll, Oxford (MA), and Courtauld Inst, London Univ (MA); writer: *m* 1st, 1971 (*m diss* 1978), John Julian Savile Lee Hardy; 3rdly, 1991, Umberto Allemandi, c/o Reform Club, 104 Pall Mall, SW1, and has issue living (by 2nd *m*), Maximilian John Lee, *b* 1980, — Katherine Isabella Eugenia, *b* 1982. —— Frances Mary Somers, *b* 1953.

Grandchildren of late Rev Canon Philip John Cocks, 3rd son of late Rev Henry Bromley Cocks (infra):—
Issue of late Henry Bromley Cocks, *b* 1896, *d* 1967: *m* 1922, Edith Hazel, who *d* 1976, da of late F. H. Melville Walker, of Christchurch, NZ:—
Alan Bromley (55 La Trobe St, Pakuranga, Auckland, NZ), *b* 1930: *m* 1955, Pamela Fay, da of A. H. Gourlay, of Christchurch, NZ, and has issue living, Martin Bromley (10 Clipper Place, Cockle Bay, Auckland, NZ), *b* 1957: *m* 1982, Janice Anne, da of A. L. White, of Auckland, NZ, and has issue living, Jonathan Bromley *b* 1985, Stephen Michael *b* 1987, — Lynette Marguerite, *b* 1960: *m* 1981, Kevin Mark Steadman, of 13 Darcy Place, Royal Heights, Auckland, and has issue living, Ryan David *b* 1990, Rachel Marguerite *b* 1993, — Gillian Fay, *b* 1962: *m* 1989, Christian Leonard Mitchell, of 8434 Greenstone Drive, Dallas, Texas 75243, USA, — Judith Grace Somers *b* 1973. —— Pamela Somers, *b* 1927; *ed* Canterbury Coll, NZ (MA): *m* 1968, Allan John Hall, LLB, of 6 Ann St, Gisborne, NZ, and has issue living, Veronica Ann, *b* 1970; LLB, — Rosemary Megan, *b* 1972.
Issue of late John Reginald Cocks, *b* 1898, *d* 1973: *m* 1920, Mary Dillworth, who *d* 1973, da of late Charles Dilworth Fox, of Christchurch, NZ:—
John Alexander (RD, Turua, NZ), *b* 1921. —— Timothy Charles (2 Beach Rd, Manly, Whangaparaoa, NZ), *b* 1923: *m* 1949, June Alice, da of J. C. Fantham, and has issue living, Ross Basil (RD1, Bruntwood, Cambridge, NZ), *b* 1951: *m* 1972, Janice Evelyn, yst da of late Pat Russell, of Silverdale, and has issue living, Wayne Gregory *b* 1976, Michael Bryce *b* 1977, Joananna Karen *b* 1982, — Barry John, (58 Citrus Av, Wahi Beach, Auckland, NZ), *b* 1954: *m* 1980, Raewyn Louisa, da of R. P. Gavin, of Tuakau, and has issue living, Philip Gavin *b* 1984, Ryan John *b* 1987, — Helen Julie, *b* 1958: *m* 1984, William Roy McCready, of Yarborough Station, RD1, Kohu Kohu, NZ, and has issue living, Richard James *b* 1987, Daniel Thomas *b* 1992, Carol Anne *b* 1985. —— Kathleen Mary, *b* 1922: *m* 1946, Archibald Stewart Gray, of 22 Hillcrest St, Tirau, Waikato, NZ, and has issue living, Peter Stewart (Parapara Rd, Tirau, Waikato, NZ), *b* 1946: *m* 1984, Mary Elizabeth, da of Robert Hyndman, of Hamilton, NZ, and has issue living, Simon Peter *b* 1988, — Sidney Charles (Long Gully, Takitimu, RD1, Te Anau, South Island, NZ), *b* 1948: *m* 1976, Susan Mary, 2nd da of Robin Sim, of Queenstown, NZ, and has issue living, Rebekah Susan *b* 1978, Catherine Amy *b* 1980, — Mary Kathleen, *b* 1949: *m* 1971, John Edward Bray, of PO Ahaura, West Coast, South Island, NZ, and has issue living, Rachael Janine *b* 1975, Helen Mary *b* 1977, Carissa Anne *b* 1979, — Barbara Elizabeth, *b* 1951: *m* 1974, Ian Goodall, of 48 Orakei Rd, Remuera, Auckland 5, NZ, and has issue living, Elizabeth Anne *b* 1976, Hilary Jean *b* 1978. —— Phoebe Somers, *b* 1925: *m* 1949, Roland Hunter, of 7B Waerenga Rd, Otaki, NZ, and has issue living, James Reginald (11 Matthew Rd, Wainuiomata, NZ), *b* 1953: *m* 1975, Anna Margaret, only da of Michael Malanchak, of Lower Hutt and has had issue, James Michael Roland *b* and *d* 1977, David James Robert *b* 1979, Brian Benjamin *b* 1980, Roseanna Marie *b* 1985, — Roger Paul (RD Turua, NZ), *b* 1956: *m* 1984, Stephanie Gaye, yst da of Colin William Wallace, — Ann Helen, *b* 1950: *m* 1st, 1970 (*m diss* 1987), Brian Edward Turner; 2ndly, 1987, Peter Terrance Spicer, of 208 Chapel St, Masterton, NZ, and has issue living (by 1st *m*), Pamela Ann *b* 1972, Melanie Rose *b* 1973, — Janet Clair, *b* 1951: *m* 1971, Randall John Papworth, of 115 Te Pene Av, Titahi Bay, NZ, and has issue living, Michael Randall *b* 1974, Susanne Mary *b* 1971, Elizabeth Carol *b* 1972, — Peggy Jane, *b* 1958: *m* 1977, Steven Daryl Mathie, of 2 Bermer Rd, Belmont, Lower Hutt, and has issue living, Bruce Thomas *b* 1981, Jennifer Louise *b* 1983.
Issue of late Ven Hubert Maurice Cocks, BD, *b* 1901: *m* 1928, Mary (13 Jackson's Rd, Christchurch, NZ), da of C. D. Matson of Fendalton, Christchurch, NZ:—
Rev Michael Dearden Somers *b* 1930; *ed* Canterbury Coll, NZ and Oxford (MA); V of Hororata, Canterbury, NZ: *m* 1958, Barbara Phyllis, el da of Hector Frank Allan, of Nelson, NZ, and has issue living, Richard Martin, *b* 1966, — Charlotte Elizabeth, *b* 1959, — Andrea Jane, *b* 1961, — Stephanie Anne, *b* 1963. —— Jonathan Somers (113 Worcestor St, Ashhurst, Manawatu, NZ), *b* 1933: *m* 1st, 1962, Audrey Geraldine, who *d* 1987, da of Aubrey William Scott, of Burnham, NZ; 2ndly, 1991, Jennifer Marianne, da of William Rudd Pratt, of Apiti, NZ, and has issue living (by 1st *m*), Jeremy Andrew Somers, *b* 1964, — Jennifer Mary, *b* 1963.

Grandchildren of late Frederic Armine Cocks (infra):—
Issue of late Douglas Edgar West Cocks, *b* 1901, *d* 1981: *m* 19—, Olive May, da of late Joseph Messines:—
Peter Douglas, *b* 1937: *m* 19—, Joan, da of John Brentnall Lees, of Christchurch, NZ, and has issue living, Paul Brentnall, *b* 1964, — Sheryll Anne, *b* 1962. *Residence* – Adams Rd, RD6, W Melton, Christchurch, NZ. —— Patricia Somers, *b* 1928: *m* 1953, Walter Percival Ussher, and has issue living, Simon Walter, *b* 1956, — Julie Helen, *b* 1960: *m* 1983, Paul Raymond Quinn, of Boxhill North, Melbourne 3129, Australia, and has issue living, Jarrod Jeffrey *b* 1984, Alistair Paul *b* 1986, Bradley David *b* 1988. *Residence* – 6 Burrows Av, Karori, Wellington, NZ. —— Helen Marion (4 Roberta Drive, Spreydon, Christchurch 2, NY), *b* 1930: *m* 1952 (*m diss* 1976), Kenneth William Barr, and has issue living, Deborah Jane, *b* 1956: *m* 19—, Stuart Stephenson, and has issue living, Dominic Robert *b* 1988, Simon Salvatore *b* 1990, Tobias Douglas Stuart *b* 1993, — Janine Patricia, *b* 1959: *m* 1988, Alistair James, — Elizabeth Kaye, *b* 1962: *m* 1989, Beat Gasser.

Grandchildren of late Rev Henry Bromley Cocks, son of Rev Henry Somers Cocks, only child of Hon Reginald Cocks, 4th son of 1st Baron:—
Issue of late Frederic Armine Cocks, *b* 1871, *d* 1966: *m* 1900, Mary Louisa, who *d* 1951, da of late Capt. —— Parsons, of Rangiora, NZ:—

Armine Christopher Somers (113 Cranford St, Christchurch 1, NZ), *b* 1903: *m* 1936, Ella, da of J. Buzan, and has issue living, Robin Fraser (17 Ashbrook Lane, Lower Cashmere, Christchurch 2, NZ), *b* 1944: *m* 1969, Anita Josephine, da of K. A. J. Smith, of Christchurch, NZ, and has issue living, Rodney Somers *b* 1969, Calvin James *b* 1972, Penelope Jane *b* 1974, — Denis Somers (97 Mount Pleasant Rd, Mount Pleasant, Christchurch 8, NZ), *b* 1947; BA: *m* 1971, Allison Elspeth, da of late D. W. Cook, of Dacre, Southland, NZ, and has issue living, Bede Somers *b* 1979, Gretchen Emma *b* 1976, — Diane Beverley, *b* 1939: *m* 1962, Douglas Bernard Charles Williams, of 85 Breezes Rd, Christchurch 7, NZ, and has issue living, Shane Douglas *b* 1962, Brent Charles *b* 1965, — Juliet Elizabeth, *b* 1940; NZRN: *m* 1964, Donald Martin Stirton, of 7 Searells Rd, Christchurch 5, NZ, and has issue living, Rachel *b* 1972, Sally Somers NZ 1976. ——— †Charles John Somers, *b* 1904: *m* 1932, Hazel, da of William Steel, of Christchurch, NZ, and *d* 1975, leaving issue, Geoffrey Somers (9 Rossall St, Christchurch, NZ), *b* 1934: *m* 1st, 1959, Madeline Mary, who *d* 1980, da of R. J. Coulter, of Ashburton, NZ; 2ndly, 1985, Sharon May Fountain, and has issue living (by 1st *m*), Richard Somers *b* 1962, Mark Somers *b* 1967, Elizabeth Mary *b* 1968, Charlotte Ann *b* 1972, — Ian Somers (45 Fendalton Rd, Christchurch, NZ), *b* 1940; APANZ: *m* 1961, Beverley Claire, da of G. W. Kearney, of Christchurch, NZ, and has issue living, Tracey Jane *b* 1962, Sarah Hilary *b* 1964, — Sandra Christine, *b* 1944; *ed* Canterbury Univ, NZ (BA): *m* 1970, Thomas Desmond Keenan, MD, ChB, of 7 St Andrews Sq, Christchurch, NZ, and has issue living, Timothy James *b* 1969. ——— Patrick Somers (20B Glenharrow Av, Avonhead, Christchurch 4, NZ), *b* 1905: *m* 1943, Evelyn May, da of Lealand Bertram Iles, and has issue living, Barbara Mary, *b* 1944: *m* 1975, Graeme Clifford Wynn, of 3550 W 19th Av, Vancouver, BC, Canada, and has issue living, Jonathan Blakeley Somers *b* 1984, Louise Jane *b* 1978, — Yvonne Dawn (21050 Sitting Bull, Apple Valley, Cal 92307, USA), *b* 1946: *m* 1967 (*m diss* 1983), — Newton, and has issue living, John Patrick *b* 1975, Roxanne Leah *b* 1972, — Cynthia Joan, *b* 1950, — Marion Elizabeth, *b* 1952: *m* 1st, 1970 (*m diss* 1978), Kenneth Michael Tate; 2ndly, 1979, Dennis Erwyn Young, of 23 Meadowville Av, Spreydon, Christchurch, NZ, and has issue living, (by 1st *m*) Rachael Marion, *b* 1971, (by 2nd *m*) Heather Jane, *b* 1980.

    Issue of late Charles Richard Cocks, *b* 1877, *d* 1944: *m* 1926, Fanny (71 Garden Road, Fendalton, Christchurch, New Zealand), da of S. E. Hubbard, of Dunedin, New Zealand:—

Charles Bromley, *b* 1928; *ed* Canterbury Coll, New Zealand (LLB 1956).

PREDECESSORS – (1) CHARLES Cocks, MP for Reigate; *cr* a *Baronet* 1772, and *Baron Somers*, of Evesham, co Worcester (peerage of Great Britain) 1784; *d* 1806; *s* by his son (2) JOHN SOMERS, 2nd Baron; MP for Grampound, Lord-Lieut of Herefordshire, and Recorder of Gloucester; *cr Viscount Eastnor* and *Earl Somers* (peerage of United Kingdom) 1821; *d* 1841; *s* by his son (3) JOHN SOMERS, 2nd Earl; *b* 1788; was Lord-Lieut of Herefordshire, and Col Hereford Militia: assumed the additional surname of Somers by Roy licence 1841; *d* 1852; *s* by his son (4) CHARLES SOMERS, 3rd Earl; *b* 1819; sat as MP for Reigate (C) 1852-7: *m* 1850, Virginia, who *d* 1910, da of late James Pattle, BCS; *d* 1883, when the viscountcy and earldom became extinct and the barony devolved upon his kinsman (5) PHILIP REGINALD Cocks, 5th Baron (son of late Lieut-Col Hon Philip James Cocks, MP, 3rd son of 1st Baron), *b* 1815: *m* 1859, Camilla, who *d* 1904, da of late Rev William Newton, V of Old Cleeve, Somerset; *d* 1899; *s* by his grand-nephew (6) ARTHUR HERBERT TENNYSON, KCMG, DSO, MC (son of late Herbert Haldane Somers Cocks, a descendant of 3rd son of 1st Baron), 6th Baron; *b* 1887; Lieut-Col late 1st Life Guards; was a Lord-in-Waiting to HM King George V 1924-6, and Gov of Victoria, Australia 1926-31; Ch Scout of United Kingdom and the British Commonwealth 1941-4; European War 1914-19 (MC, DSO): *m* 1921, (Daisy) Finola, CBE, who *d* 1981, da of late Capt Bertram Meeking; *d* 1944; *s* by his uncle (7) ARTHUR PERCY SOMERS (4th son of late Arthur Herbert Cocks, CB, brother of 5th Baron), 7th Baron; *b* 1864; European War 1915-17 with Canadian Forces: *m* 1896, Benita, who *d* 1950, da of late Major Luther Sabin, of USA; *d* 1953; *s* by his son (8) JOHN PATRICK SOMERS, 8th Baron and present peer.
*John Somers, Lord Chancellor 1697-1700, *cr Baron Somers*, of Evesham 1697, and *d* 1716 when his title became ext. His sister and co-heir, Mary, *m* Charles Cocks, of Worcester, by whom she was mother of John Cocks, father of 1st Baron, of second creation (ante).

SOMERSET, DUKE OF (Seymour) (Duke E 1547, Bt E 1611)

JOHN MICHAEL EDWARD SEYMOUR, 19th Duke and 17th Baronet; *b* 30 Dec 1952; *s* 1984; *ed* Eton; DL Wilts 1993 FRICS; patron of two livings: *m* 1978, Judith-Rose, elder da of John Hull, of 33 Edwardes Sq, W8, and has issue.

Arms – Quarterly: 1st and 4th or, on a pile gules, between six fleurs-de-lis azure, three lions of England; 2nd and 3rd gules, two wings conjoined in lure or, *Seymour*. **Crest** – Out of a ducal coronet or, a demi-phoenix in flames proper. **Supporters** – *Dexter* a unicorn argent, armed, unguled, and crined, or, gorged with a ducal coronet, per pale azure and gold, and chained of the last; *sinister*, a bull azure, armed, unguled, ducally gorged and chained, or. **Seats** – Maiden Bradley, Warminster, Wilts; Berry Pomeroy, Totnes, S Devon.

FOY · POVR · DEVOIR

Faith for duty

SONS LIVING

SEBASTIAN EDWARD (*Lord Seymour*), *b* 3 Feb 1982.
Lord Charles Thomas George, *b* 1992.

DAUGHTERS LIVING

Lady Sophia Rose, *b* 1987.
Lady Henrietta Charlotte, *b* 1989.

BROTHER LIVING

Lord Francis Charles Edward (27 Palliser Rd, W14), *b* 1956; *ed* Eton; solicitor: *m* 1982, Paddy, da of Col Anthony John Irvine Poynder, MC, RE, of Gassons, Slindon, Sussex, and has issue living, Webb (a son), *b* 1990, — Poppy Hermione Alexandra, *b* 1988.

SISTER LIVING

Lady Anne Frances Mary, *b* 1954.

AUNT LIVING (*Daughter of 17th Duke*)

Lady Susan Mary, *b* 1913; late Divisional Pres British Red Cross So, Warminster. *Residence* – Sunnyside, Maiden Bradley, Wilts.

GWENDOLINE COLLETTE (JANE) (*Jane, Duchess of Somerset*), da of late Maj John Cyril Collette Thomas, N Staffordshire Regt, of Burn Cottage, Bude, Cornwall: *m* 1951, Maj the 18th Duke, who *d* 1984. *Residence* – Maiden Bradley, Warminster, Wilts.

COLLATERAL BRANCHES LIVING

Descendants of late Rt Hon Francis Seymour-Conway (4th son of Hon Sir Edward Seymour, 4th Bt, grandfather of 8th Duke), who was *cr* Baron Conway of Ragley 1703 (*see* M Hertford).

PREDECESSORS – **(1)** Sir EDWARD Seymour, KG, KB, PC, el surv son of Sir John Seymour of Wolf Hall, Wilts (by Marjorie, da of Sir Henry Wentworth, KB, of Nettlestead, Suffolk, a descendant of Edward III) and brother of Queen Jane Seymour; *b* c 1500: *m* 1st, c 1527, Katherine (whom he repudiated and who probably *d* before 1535), da and co-heir of Sir William Fillol, of Woodlands, Dorset; 2ndly, c 1535, Anne (who *d* 1582, having *m* 2ndly, Francis Newdegate), da of Sir Edward Stanhope, of Rampton Notts; *cr Viscount Beauchamp* (peerage of England), with remainder to heirs male of his body *hereafter* to be begotten, 1536, and *Earl of Hertford* (peerage of England) with remainder to his issue male by his present or any future wife 1537, *Baron Seymour* and *Duke of Somerset* (peerage of England) with a special remainder to his issue male by his 2nd wife, failing which to his male descendants by his 1st and any other wife 1547; Protector of the Realm to his nephew Edward VI 1547-1549; found guilty of felony 1 Dec 1551, and executed on Tower Hill, 22 Jan 1552; attainted 12 April 1552, by Act of Parliament, and all his honours forfeited. His el surv son by his 2nd wife **(2)** Sir EDWARD, KB; *b* 1539; *cr Baron Beauchamp* and *Earl of Hertford* (peerage of England) 1559; Ambassador to Brussels 1605: *m* 1st (secretly) 1560, Lady Katherine (sister of Lady Jane Grey), da of Henry Grey, Duke of Suffolk; on discovery of this marriage he was fined £15,000 (later remitted to £3,000) "for seducing a virgin of the blood royal" and he and his wife imprisoned in the Tower; the *m* was pronounced invalid 1561, but validity was established in 1606; she *d* 1568 in captivity at Cockfield Hall, Suffolk; he *m* 2ndly c 1595, Frances Howard, who *d* 1598, da of 1st Lord Howard of Effingham; 3rdly, 1601, Frances Howard (who *d* 1639, having *m* 3rdly Ludovic Stuart, 1st Duke of Richmond), da of 1st Viscount Howard of Bindon, and widow of Henry Pranell; *d* 1621; *s* by his grandson **(3)** WILLIAM, KG, KB, PC (2nd but eventually el son and heir of Edward Lord Beauchamp, who *d* 1612, el son of 1st Earl by 1st wife) 2nd Earl; *b* 1587; bore King Edward's staff at Coronation of Charles I 1626; Gov of Prince of Wales (Charles II) 1641-43; Royalist Lt-Gen of South-West and S Wales 1642-43; restored to Barony of Seymour and Dukedom of Somerset 1660: *m* 1st (secretly) 1610, Lady Arabella Stuart, da and heir of 5th Earl of Lennox and 1st cousin of James I, for which they were both imprisoned in the Tower, where she *dsp* 1615; 2ndly, 1617, Lady Frances Devereux, who *d* 1674, sister and co-heir of 3rd Earl of Essex: *d* 1660; *s* by his grandson **(4)** WILLIAM, 3rd Duke (son and heir of Henry, Lord Beauchamp); *b* 1652; *d* unm 1671; *s* by his uncle **(5)** JOHN, 4th Duke, *b* 1629; *m* 1661, Sarah (who *d* 1692, having *m* 3rdly, 1682, 2nd Baron Coleraine) da and co-heir of Sir Edward Alston, MD, and widow of George Grimston; *d* 1675, when the Marquessate of Hertford became ext and his estates passed to his niece Elizabeth (sister of 3rd Duke) who *m* 1676 the 2nd Earl of Ailesbury; *s* by his kinsman **(6)** FRANCIS (3rd Baron Seymour of Trowbridge) 5th Duke (son of Charles 2nd Baron, son of Francis 1st Baron (*cr* 1641), yr brother of 2nd Duke) *b* 1658; *d* 1678, having been shot at the door of his inn at Lerice, Italy, by Horatio Botti, a Genoese nobleman, who alleged his wife had been insulted by the Duke's companions; *s* by his brother **(7)** CHARLES, KG, 6th Duke ("The Proud Duke") *b* 1662; Master of the Horse 1702-12 and 1714-15: *m* 1st, 1682, Lady Elizabeth Percy (Mistress of the Robes to Queen Anne), who *d* 1722, da and heir of 11th Earl of Northumberland and widow of Henry Cavendish, Earl of Ogle, and Thomas Thynne of Longleat; 2ndly, 1726, Lady Charlotte Finch, who *d* 1773, da of 7th Earl of Winchilsea and 2nd Earl of Nottingham; *d* 1748; *s* by his son **(8)** ALGERNON, 7th Duke; *b* 1684; summoned to Parliament as *Lord Percy* 1722 under the erroneous belief that this Barony had been vested in his mother, and took his seat, by which the Barony of Percy was *cr* by writ; *cr Baron Warkworth*, of Warkworth Castle, co Northumberland, and *Earl of Northumberland* (peerage of Great Britain) 1749, with remainder to his son-in-law, Sir Hugh Smithson, and *Baron Cockermouth*, of Cockermouth Castle, and *Earl of Egremont*, with remainder to his nephews, Sir Charles Wyndham, Bt, and Percy O'Brien (who was afterwards *cr* Earl of Thomond): *m* 1715, Frances, who *d* 1754, da of Hon Henry Thynne, son of 1st Viscount Weymouth; *d* 1750, when the Earldom of Hertford, and the Baronies of Beauchamp and Seymour of Trowbridge expired, the Barony of Warkworth and Earldom of Northumberland devolved upon his son-in-law Sir Hugh Smithson, the Barony of Cockermouth and Earldom of Egremont reverted to his nephew Sir Charles Wyndham, the Barony of Percy (*cr* 1722), passed to his da Lady Elizabeth, wife of Sir Hugh Smithson (ante), and the Barony of Seymour and Dukedom of Somerset descended to the heir male of the 1st Duke by his 1st *m* **(9)** EDWARD, 8th Duke, who had previously *s* as 6th Bt (see * infra); *b* 1695; MP for Salisbury 1741: *m* 1717, Mary, who *d* 1768, da and heir of Daniel Webb of Malksham, Wilts; *d* 1757; *s* by his el son **(10)** EDWARD, 9th Duke; *b* 1718, *d* unm 1792; *s* by his brother **(11)** WEBB, 10th Duke; *b* 1718: *m* 1769, Anna Marie, who *d* 1802, da and heir of John Bonnell; *d* 1793; *s* by his son **(12)** EDWARD ADOLPHUS, 11th Duke; *b* 1775: *m* 1800, Lady Charlotte Douglas-Hamilton, da of 9th Duke of Hamilton and Brandon; *d* 1855; *s* by his son **(13)** EDWARD ADOLPHUS, KG, 12th Duke, *b* 1804; MP for Totnes (*L*) 1834-55; First Lord of the Admiralty 1859-66; *cr Earl of St Maur* (peerge of UK) 1863; *d* 1885, when the Earldom of St Maur became extinct, and the Dukedom of Somerset and Barony of Seymour passed to his brother **(14)** ARCHIBALD HENRY ALGERNON, 13th Duke, *b* 1810; *d* 1891; *s* by his brother **(15)** ALGERNON PERCY BANKS, 14th Duke, *b* 1813: *m* 1845, Horatia Isabella Harriet, who *d* 1915, da of John Philip Morier, HM Min at Dresden; *d* 1894; *s* by his el son **(16)** ALGERNON, 15th Duke *b* 1846; bore the Orb at Coronations of King Edward VII and King George V: *m* 1877, Susan Margaret, who *d* 1936, yr da of Charles Mackinnon; *d* 1923; *s* by his cousin **(17)** EDWARD HAMILTON, KBE, CB, CMG (son of late Rev Francis Payne Seymour), 16th Duke, *b* 1860; Brig-Gen; in March 1925 he established before the Cttee for Privileges of the House of Lords his right to the Dukedom as grandson of Capt Francis Edward Seymour, RN, el son of Col Francis Compton Seymour (grandson of 8th Duke), who *m* 1787, Leonora, widow of John Hudson (who *d* 1786 in Calcutta): *m* 1881, Rowena, who *d* 1950, da of George Wall, of Colombo; *d* 1931; *s* by his son **(18)** EVELYN FRANCIS EDWARD, DSO, OBE, 17th Duke, *b* 1882; Lt-Col (ret) R Dublin Fusiliers and Devonshire Regt, Col Gen Staff, and Lord-Lieut for Wilts; S Africa 1901-02 (Queen's medal with five clasps), 1914-18 War (despatches, DSO, OBE); bore the Sceptre at Coronation of King George VI: *m* 1906, Edith Mary, who *d* 1962, only child of W. Parker, JP, of Whittington Hall, Derbyshire; *d* 1954; *s* by his only son **(19)** PERCY HAMILTON, 18th Duke, *b* 1910; Maj Wilts Regt, DL and Pres British Legion for Wilts: *m* 1951, Gwendoline Collette (Jane), da of late Maj John Cyril Collette Thomas, N Staffordshire Regt, of Burn Cottage, Bude, Cornwall; *d* 1984; *s* by his elder son **(20)** JOHN MICHAEL EDWARD, 19th Duke and present peer; also Baron Seymour.

***(1)** EDWARD Seymour, MP for Devon (el son of Sir Edward Seymour, who was el son of 1st Duke of Somerset by his 1st *m*); *cr* a *Baronet* 1611; *d* 1613; *s* by his son **(2)** *Sir* EDWARD, KB, 2nd Bt; was MP for Devon; *d* 1659; *s* by his son **(3)** EDWARD 3rd Bt; sat as MP for Devon; *d* 1688; *s* by his son **(4)** *Sir* EDWARD, PC; promoted the impeachment of Lord Clarendon, and was Speaker of the Long Parliament, *d* 1708; *s* by his son **(5)** *Sir* EDWARD, 5th Bt; *d* 1741; *s* by his son **(6)** *Sir* EDWARD, 6th Bt, who *s* as 8th Duke of Somerset (ante).

Somerton, Viscount; son of Earl of Normanton.

Somerton, Baron; title of Earl of Normanton on Roll HL.

SONDES, EARL (Milles-Lade) (Earl UK 1880)

Be what you seem to be

HENRY GEORGE HERBERT MILLES-LADE, 5th Earl; *b* 1st May 1940; *s* 1970; *ed* Eton, and La Rosey: *m* 1st, 1968 (*m diss* 1969), Primrose Anne, da of late Lawrence Stopford Llewellyn Cotter (*see* Cotter, Bt, colls), and formerly wife of Richard Hugh Nicholas Creswell; 2ndly, 1976 (*m diss* 1982), Silvia-Gabrielle (Sissy), da of Hans Otto Scheid, and widow of Hugo 6th Prince and Altgraf zu Salm-Reifferscheidt-Raitz; 3rdly, 1981 (*m diss* 1984), Sharon McCluskey; 4thly, 1986, Phyllis Kane Schmertz.

Arms – Ermine, a fer de moulin between two martlet in pale sable; on a chief engrailed azure, two marlion's wings conjoined or. Crest – A lion rampant erminois, holding between the paws a fer de moulin, as in the arms. Supporters – Dexter, a griffin wings elevated argent, gorged with a marquess' coronet or; sinister, a bear proper, gorged with a belt argent, rimmed, buckled and charged with two crescents, or.
Residences – Stringman's Farm, Badlesmere, Faversham, Kent; 38 Chester Sq, SW1.

PREDECESSORS – (1) *Hon* LEWIS Monson, 2nd son of 1st Baron Monson, assumed the surname of Watson on succeeding to the estates of his cousin Thomas, 3rd and last Earl of Rockingham; *cr Baron Sondes*, of Lees Court, co Kent (peerage of Great Britain), 1760; *d* 1795; *s* by his son (2) LEWIS THOMAS Watson, 2nd Baron; *d* 1806; *s* by his son (3) LEWIS RICHARD, 3rd Baron; *d* unmarried 1836; *s* by his brother (4) GEORGE JOHN, 4th Baron; *b* 1794; in 1820 assumed by Roy licence the surname of Milles only: *m* 1823, Eleanor, who *d* 1883, da of Sir Edward Knatchbull, 8th Bt; *d* 1874; *s* by his son (5) GEORGE WATSON Milles, 5th Baron, *b* 1824; MP for E Kent (*C*) 1866-74; *cr Viscount Throwley*, of co Kent, and *Earl Sondes*, of Lees Court, co Kent (peerage of United Kingdom) 1880: *m* 1859, Charlotte, who *d* 1927, da of Sir Henry Stracey, 5th Bt; *d* 1894, *s* by his el son (6) GEORGE EDWARD, 2nd Earl, *b* 1861; *d* 1907; *s* by his brother (7) LEWIS ARTHUR, 3rd Earl, *b* 1866: *m* 1913, Emma Beatrice, who *d* 1935, da of late Percy Hale-Wallace, and widow of James Meakin, of Westwood Manor, Staffordshire; *d* 1941; *s* by his nephew (8) GEORGE HENRY (only son of late Hon Henry Augustus Milles-Lade, 4th son of 1st Earl), 4th Earl; *b* 1914: *m* 1939, Pamela, who *d* 1967, da of Lt-Col Herbert McDougall, of Cawston Manor, Norfolk, and 23 Wilton Cres, Belgrave Sq, SW1; *d* 1970; *s* by his son (9) HENRY GEORGE HERBERT, 5th Earl and present peer; also Viscount Throwley, and Baron Sondes.

SOPER, BARON (Soper) (Life Baron 1965)

Rev DONALD OLIVER SOPER, son of Ernest Frankham Soper, of Wandsworth, SW; *b* 31 Jan 1903; *ed* Aske's Sch, Hatcham, at St Catharine's Coll, Camb (MA), Wesley House, Camb, and London Sch of Economics (PhD), DD (Camb); Min of South London Mission 1926-29 and of Central London Mission 1929-36; Supt Min of W London Mission 1936-78: Chm of Shelter 1974-78; *cr Baron Soper*, of Kingsway, London Borough of Camden (Life Peerage) 1965: *m* 1929, Marie Gertrude, who *d* 1994, da of Arthur Dean, of Norbury, and has issue.
Address – 19 Thayer St, W1M 5LJ.

DAUGHTERS LIVING

Hon Ann Loveday Dean, *b* 1931; BSc: *m* 1952 (*m diss* 1979), Prof Gabriel Horn, MD. *Residence* – 54 St Barnabas Rd, Cambridge.
Hon Bridget Mary Dean, *b* 1933: *m* 1956, Owen H. Kemmis, MA (*dec*). *Residence* – Garden Flat, 30 Parliament Hill, NW3 2TN.
Hon Judith Catharine Dean, *b* 1942; BSc: *m* 1970, Alan Jenkins, BEd. *Residence* – 12 Brookland Hill, NW11.
Hon Caroline Susan Dean, *b* 1946; BA: *m* 1975, Terence Blacker, MA, el son of Gen Sir Cecil Hugh Blacker, KCB, OBE, MC (*see* Buxton, Bt, colls). *Residence* – 91 Wendell Rd, W12.

SORENSEN, BARONY OF (Sorensen) (Extinct 1971)

DAUGHTER LIVING OF LIFE BARON

Hon Moira Muriel, *b* 1917: *m* 1951, Derek Gerald Clark, JP, of 15 Crossing Rd, Epping, Essex, CM16 7BQ, and has issue.

WIDOW LIVING OF SON OF LIFE BARON

Jennifer (37 Nassington Rd, NW3), da of Alan Adams, of Stocksfield, Newcastle-upon-Tyne: *m* 1960, Hon Michael Malcolm Reginald Sorensen, who *d* 1978.

SOULBURY, VISCOUNT (Ramsbotham) (Viscount UK 1954)

Not by force but by virtue

JAMES HERWALD RAMSBOTHAM, 2nd Viscount; 21 March 1915; *s* 1971; *ed* Eton, and Magdalen Coll, Oxford: *m* 1949, Anthea Margaret, who *d* 1950, da of late David Wilton.

Arms – Sable on a chevron or between three plates each charged with a cross pattée gules a ram's head erased of the field. **Crest** – A plate charged with a ram's head erased per pale gules and sable. **Supporters** – On either side a raven proper charged with a plate thereon a cross pattée gules. *Address* – c/o House of Lords, SW1.

BROTHER LIVING

Hon Sir PETER EDWARD, GCMG, GCVO, *b* 8 Oct 1919; *ed* Eton, and Magdalen Coll, Oxford; NW Europe 1944-45 as Lt-Col Intelligence Corps (despatches, Croix de Guerre with palm); a Member of HM Diplo Ser; British High Commr in Cyprus 1969-71, Ambassador to Iran 1971-73, and Ambassador to USA 1974-77; Gov and C-in-C Bermuda 1977-80; CMG 1964, KCMG 1972, GCVO 1976, GCMG 1977: *m* 1st, 1941, Frances Marie, who *d* 1982, da of Hugh Massie Blomfield; 2ndly 1985, Dr Zaida Mary Hall, previously wife of late Ruthven Hall, and has issue living (by 1st *m*), Oliver Peter (11 Silverless St, Marlborough), *b* 1943: *m* 1965, Meredith Anne, only da of Brian Jones, of The White House, Easton Royal, Pewsey, Wilts, and has issue living, Edward Herwald *b* 1966, Benedict *b* 1967, Alexander *b* 1969, — Simon Edward (36 Bensham Lane, Croydon), *b* 1949: *m* 1976, Sandra Cayley, and has issue living, David Peter *b* 1981, Elizabeth Sarah *b* 1978, Allison Frances *b* 1983, — Mary Frances, *b* 1945: *m* 1st, 1981, Charles Gray, who *d* 1982; 2ndly, 1993, Christopher Coulston, of 1 The Fairway, Rowner, Gosport, Hants. *Residence* – East Lane, Ovington, Alresford, Hants SO24 0RA.

SISTER LIVING

Hon Joan Eleanor, *b* 1917: *m* 1950, Major Robert Hardress Standish O'Grady, MC, Irish Guards, and has issue living, Jeremy Robert (32 Addison Av, W11 4QR), *b* 1953, — Jane Elizabeth (The Cottage, 141 St Mark's Rd, W10), *b* 1952, — Selina Joan (29 Linden Gdns, W2), *b* 1956. *Residences* – 32 Addison Av, Holland Park, W11; Midford Place, Midford, Bath, Avon.

PREDECESSORS – **(1)** *Rt Hon Sir* HERWALD Ramsbotham, GCMG, GCVO, OBE, MC, son of Herwald Ramsbotham, JP, of London; *b* 1887; Min of Pensions 1936-39, 1st Commr of Works 1939-40, Pres of Board of Education 1940-41, Chm of Assistance Board 1941-48, and Gov-Gen of Ceylon 1949-54; MP for Lancaster (*C*) 1929-41; *cr Baron Soulbury*, of Soulbury, co Buckingham (peerage of UK) 1941, and *Viscount Soulbury*, of Soulbury, co Buckingham (peerage of UK) 1954; *m* 1st, 1911, Doris Violet, CStJ, who *d* 1954, da of Sinauer de Stein; 2ndly, 1962, Ursula, who *d* 1964, da of late Amand Jerome, and widow of Frederick Wakeham; *d* 1971; *s* by his el son **(2)** JAMES HERWALD, 2nd Viscount and present peer; also Baron Soulbury.

SOULSBY OF SWAFFHAM PRIOR, BARON (Soulsby) (Life Baron 1990)

ERNEST JACKSON LAWSON SOULSBY, son of William George Lawson Soulsby; *b* 23 June 1926; *ed* Queen Elizabeth Gram Sch, Penrith, and Edinburgh Univ; MRCVS, DVSM, PhD, MA (Cantab), Fellow Wolfson Coll, Camb; Veterinary Officer City of Edinburgh 1949-52, Lecturer in Clinical Parasitology Bristol Univ 1952-54, and Animal Pathology Camb Univ 1954-63, Prof of Parasitology Pennsylvania Univ 1964-78, since when Prof of Animal Pathology Camb Univ; Pres Royal Coll of Veterinary Surgeons 1984, Sr Vice-Pres 1985; Ford Foundn Visiting Prof at Ibadan Univ 1964, Richard Merton Guest Prof at Justus Liebig Univ 1974-75; Expert Advisor and Consultant for many Scientific Groups and Organisations; lecturer and contributor to learned journals; Hon AM 1972, Hon DSc (Pennsylvania Univ 1984), Hon DVSM (Edinburgh 1991); R. N. Chaudhury Gold Medal, Calcutta Sch of Tropical Medicine, 1976, Behring-Bilharz Prize, Cairo 1977, Ludwig-Schunk Prize, Justus Liebig Univ 1979, etc; *cr Baron Soulsby of Swaffham Prior*, of Swaffham Prior, co Cambs (Life Baron) 1990: *m* 1962, Georgina Elizabeth Annette, da of John Whitmore Williams, of Cambridge, and has issue.

Residence – Old Barn House, Swaffham Prior, Cambs CB5 0LD. *Clubs* – Farmers', and United Oxford & Cambridge University.

SON LIVING

Hon John Angus Lawson, *b* 1954.

DAUGHTER LIVING

Hon Katrina Yvonne, *b* 1950: *m* 19—, — Bulloch.

SOUTHAMPTON, BARON (FitzRoy) (Baron GB 1780)

The ornament and recompense of virtue

CHARLES JAMES FITZROY, 6th Baron; *b* 12 Aug 1928; *s* 1989; *ed* Stowe; Master of Easton Harriers 1968-69 and 1970-71, and of Blankney Foxhounds 1971-72: *m* 1951, Pamela Anne, da of late Edward Percy Henniker, of Clematis, Yelverton, S Devon, and has had issue.

Arms – Quarterly: 1st and 4th, France and England quarterly; 2nd, Scotland; 3rd, Ireland; the whole debruised by a baton sinister compony argent and azure, and with a crescent for difference. **Crest** – On a chapeau gules, turned up ermine, a lion statant guardant or, ducally crowned azure, and gorged with a collar counter compony argent and azure. **Supporters** – (borne by Barons Southampton) *Dexter*, a lion guardant or, ducally crowned azure, gorged with a collar compony argent and blue; *sinister*, a greyhound argent gorged as the dexter. *Residence* – Stone Cross, Chagford, Newton Abbot, Devon.

SONS LIVING AND DECEASED

Charles, *b* 1954; *ed* Gresham's Sch, Holt: *m* 1975, Joanna Dana (who *m* 2ndly, 1977, Paul Farrant), da of late Chandos Robert Henry Brudenell-Bruce (*see* M Ailesbury, colls), and was *k* in a motor accident (Oct) 1975, *sp*.

Hon EDWARD CHARLES, *b* 8 July 1955; *ed* Gresham's Sch, Holt, and RAC Cirencester: *m* 1978, Rachel Caroline Vincent, 2nd da of Peter John Curnow Millett, of West Underdown, Drewsteignton, Devon, and has issue living, Charles Edward Millett, *b* 18 Jan 1983, — Fiona Joan Margaret, *b* 1979, — Sarah Barbara Sibell, *b* 1981, — Julia Rachel Caroline, *b* 1984. *Residence* – Venn Farm, Morchard Bishop, Crediton, Devon EX17 6SQ.

DAUGHTER LIVING

Hon Geraldine Anne, *b* 1951: *m* 1st, 1969 (*m* diss 19—), Gavin Prescott; 2ndly, 1977, Richard G. Fuller, and has issue living (by 2nd *m*), Joshua FitzRoy, *b* 1978, — Oliver, *b* 1981, — Victoria, *b* 1983. *Residence* – Strete House, Strete, Whimple, nr Exeter, Devon.

AUNT LIVING (*daughter of 4th Baron*)

Hon Ismay Hilda Margaret, *b* 1908: *m* 1928, Brig Walter Morley Sale, CVO, OBE, late R Horse Gds, who *d* 1976, and has issue living, Charles Richard Walter (Garey Manor, Lezayre, Ramsey, IoM), *b* (Nov) 1928; late Capt R Horse Gds: *m* 1958, Marian Eleanor, da of Maj John Darling Young, of Thornton Hall, Bletchley, Bucks, and has issue living, Nigel Richard *b* 1962, Lucinda Marian *b* 1965, — Caroline Ismay Maud, *b* 1934. *Residence* – 15 St Paul's Mews, Ramsey, IoM.

COLLATERAL BRANCHES LIVING

Descendants of late Capt Rt Hon Edward Algernon FitzRoy, MP (Speaker of House of Commons 1928-43), 2nd son of 3rd Baron, *d* 1943: *m* 1891, Muriel, CBE, da of late Lieut-Col Hon Archibald Charles Henry Douglas-Pennant (*see* B Penrhyn, colls), who was *cr Viscountess Daventry* 1943 (see that title).

Grandson of late Maj-Gen William FitzRoy, el son of late William Simon Haughton FitzRoy, el son of late Lieut-Gen Hon William FitzRoy, 7th son of 1st Baron:—
Issue of late Capt Frederick Henry FitzRoy, RD, RNR, *b* 1872, *d* 1937: *m* 1904, Eleanor, who *d* 1969, da of late William Allan, of Avondale, Gosforth:—
William Wentworth STEWART-FITZROY (1137 Westmoreland Rd, Alexandria, Virginia 22308, USA), *b* 1907; Capt RN (ret); late Commodore Supt, HM Dockyard, Singapore, and HM's Naval Attaché at Belgrade; appointed Naval ADC to HM 1961; Admiralty Regional Officer, Scotland, 1962-72; Hon Sheriff for Sutherland 1974; he and his issue assumed by deed poll 1958 the additional surname of Stewart before their patronymic: *m* 1st, 1934, Margaret Patricia, who *d* 1984, da of late Douglas Stewart Grant, of New York, USA; 2ndly, 1988, Evelyn, widow of Col John Fogg Twombly III, US Army, and da of late James Wallace Nichol, of Washington, DC, and has issue living (by 1st *m*), Allan Wentworth (12 St Georges Av, Warblington, Havant, Hants), *b* 1935; Cdr RN: *m* 1960, Susan Elizabeth, da of Capt Horace Gerald Southwood, CBE, DSC, RN, and has issue living, Louise *b* 1962: *m* 1988, Maj Michael John Stone, Duke of Wellington's Regt (and has issue living, Arthur Maxallan John *b* 1994, Alexandra Susan Joy *b* 1990), Jane *b* 1964: *m* 1987, Rupert John Eastell (and has issue living, Tom Jonathan *b* 1992, Georgina Jane *b* 1994), Helen *b* 1967, — Douglas James Fitzflaad (51 Brondesbury Villas, Kilburn, NW6 6AJ), *b* 1943, — Roderick Charles FITZROY, *b* 1947; relinquished surname of Stewart by deed poll 1976: *m* 1972, Susan Mary, da of H. C. Ruse, of Arbroath, and has issue living, James *b* 1973, Amanda Jane *b* 1976, — Anne Patricia (135 E 50th St, NY 10022, USA), *b* 1936; MBA, CPA.

Grandson of late Capt George Dartmouth FitzRoy, 2nd son of late William Simon Haughton FitzRoy (ante):—
Issue of late Gordon Duncan Seymour FitzRoy, *b* 1868, *d* 1936: *m* 1st, 1891, Marie E., who *d* 1894, widow of Howell Turner, MD, of Norwich; 2ndly, 189—, N. Adalia Leasure, of Arkansas City, Kansas, USA:—
(By 2nd *m*) Francis George, *b* 1903.

Grandchildren of late Lt-Col Ferdinand FitzRoy, RA, 3rd son of late William Simon Haughton FitzRoy (ante):—
Issue of late Ferdinand Trevor FitzRoy, of Ard-Falen, Alexandria, Victoria, Australia, *b* 1857, *d* 1928: *m* ca 1904, Maud Harvey Hamilton:—
Eric Hamilton, *b* ca 1906. —— Herbert Cromwell, *b* ca 1907. —— Kathleen Mary, *b* ca 1904. —— Elizabeth Lorraine, *b* ca 1912.

PREDECESSORS – (1) Lieut-Gen CHARLES FitzRoy, 2nd son of Lord Augustus FitzRoy (D Grafton); *cr Baron Southampton*, of Southampton, co Hants (peerage of Great Britain) 1780; *d* 1797; *s* by his son (2) GOERGE FERDINAND, 2nd Baron, was a Lieut-Gen in the Army and Col 34th Regt; *d* 1810; *s* by his son (3) CHARLES, 3rd Baron; *b* 1804; was Lord-Lieut of Northampton: *m* 1st, 1826, Harriet, who *d* 1860, da of late Henry FitzRoy Stanhope; 2ndly, 1862, Ismania Catherine, VA, who *d* 1918, da of late Walter Nugent, a Baron of the Austrian Empire; *d* 1872: *s* by his son (4) CHARLES HENRY, OBE, 4th Baron, *b* 1867; Capt 10th Hussars, and Lieut-Col Yorkshire Regt: *m* 1892, Lady Hilda Mary Dundas, who *d* 1957, da of 1st Marquess of Zetland; *d* 1958; *s* by his son (5) CHARLES, 5th Baron, *b* 1904; late Royal Horse Guards, and Pioneer Corps; Jt Master Grove Foxhounds 1930-32; disclaimed his peerage for life 1964: *m* 1st, 1927, Margaret, who *d* 1931, da of Rev Preb Herbert

Mackworth Drake, V of Berry Pomeroy, Devon; 2ndly, 1940 (*m diss* 1944), Mrs Phyllis Joan Leslie, da of Francis Archibald Lloyd; 3rdly, 1951, Rachel Christine, who *d* 1985, da of Charles Zaman, of Lille, France; *d* 1989; *s* by his only son **(6)** CHARLES JAMES, 6th Baron and present peer.

SOUTHBOROUGH, BARONY OF (Hopwood) (Extinct 1992)

ADOPTED DAUGHTER LIVING OF FOURTH BARON

Anne Mary, *b* 1960: *m* 1992, John Charles Cunningham-Jardine, of Fourmerkland, Lockerbie, Dumfriesshire (*see* Nairn, Bt, 1985 Edn), and has issue living, Serena Moyna, *b* 1993. *Residence* – Tinwald House, Tinwald, Dumfriesshire DG1 3PW.

SISTER LIVING OF FOURTH BARON

Hon Moira, *b* 1919: *m* 1st, 1940, Peter Anthony Stanley Woodwark, Fl/Lieut RAF Vol Res, who was *ka* 1943, son of late Col Sir (Arthur) Stanley Woodwark, CMG, CBE, MD, FRCP; 2ndly, 1946, Joseph McArthur Rank, Hon FRCP, and has issue living (by 1st *m*), Caroline Nicola, *b* 1943: *m* 1966, Richard Hugh Payne, of West End, Shipton Moyne, Tetbury, Glos, and has issue living, Alexander Richard *b* 1971, Hugo Frederick *b* 1981, Samantha *b* 1969, Selina Francesca *b* 1978, — (by 2nd *m*) Colin Rowland Hopwood (The Old Forge, Kemble, Glos), *b* 1948: *m* 1972, Lavinia Ruth Phillips, and has issue living, James Benjamin *b* 1974, Nicola Emily 1976, Rachel Margaret *b* 1978, — Camilla Moira, *b* 1953: *m* 1971, Jeremy Allan Jennings, of 21 Bramerton St, SW3, and has issue living, Joseph Piers *b* 1975, Timothy David *b* 1977, Katharine Moira *b* 1979, Serena Margaret *b* 1993. *Residence* – 22 Coulson St, SW3.

WIDOW LIVING OF THIRD BARON

AUDREY EVELYN DOROTHY (*Baroness Southborough*), da of late Edgar George Money: *m* 1918, the 3rd Baron, who *d* 1982. *Residence* – Kemblewood House, Church Rd, Kemble, Glos.

Southesk, Earl of; son of Duke of Fife

SOUTHWELL, VISCOUNT (Southwell) (Viscount I 1776, Bt I 1662)
(Title pronounced "Suthell")

Not an unknown knight

PYERS ANTHONY JOSEPH SOUTHWELL, 7th Viscount, and 10th Baronet; *b* 14 Sept 1930; *s* 1960; Capt (ret) 8th Hussars: *m* 1955, Barbara Jacqueline, da of A. Raynes, and has issue.

Arms – Argent, three cinquefoils pierced gules, charged on each leaf with an annulet or the field. **Crest** – A demi-Indian goat argent, armed and eared gules, ducally gorged or, and charged on the body with three annulets in bend also gules. **Supporters** – Two Indian goats argent, ducally collared, chained, and charged on the body with three annulets gules.
Address – c/o House of Lords, SW1.

SONS LIVING

Hon RICHARD ANDREW PYERS, *b* 15 June 1956.
Hon Charles Anthony John *b* 1962.

SISTERS LIVING

Evelyn Mary Elizabeth, *b* 1926: *m* 1952, Harold Hope, and has issue living, Carol, *b* 1953, — Valerie, *b* 1956. *Residence* – 19 Mortlake Street, Islington, Christchurch, New Zealand. —— Barbara Frances Magdalene, *b* 1928: *m* 1949, Peter Fowler, and has issue living, Simon Peter, *b* 1965, — Vivienne Anne, *b* 1951, — Gillian Clare, *b* 1953, — Sarah Elizabeth, *b* 1959. *Residence* – Beech Tree House, Market Drayton, Salop.

DAUGHTER LIVING OF SIXTH VISCOUNT

Hon Susan Mary, *b* 1926: *m* 1951, Keith Francis MacRae, of 27 Dennis Rd, Slacks Creek, via Brisbane, Queensland, and has issue living, John Francis, *b* 1952, — Paul Finlay, *b* 1955.

WIDOW LIVING OF SON OF FIFTH VISCOUNT

Daphne Lewin, da of Sir Geoffrey Lewin Watson, 3rd Bt (*cr* 1918, ext): *m* 1932, Lieut Com Hon John Michael Southwell, RN, who was *ka* 1944. *Residence* – Buckclose, Longparish, Andover, Hants.

COLLATERAL BRANCHES LIVING

Grandchildren of late Walter Stedman Southwell (*infra*):—
Issue of late Capt Bertie Charles Sydney Stedman Southwell, late 59th Bn AIF, *b* 1882, *d* 1984: *m* 1921, Elsie Annie, da of late J. S. Wenden:—

Evelyn John Stedman (2 Terry St, Balwyn, Victoria 3103, Australia), *b* 1923; late 2nd Commando Squad 2/AIF: *m* 1951, Shirley Jean, da of Robert Ingram Kennison, of 94 Prospect Rd, Geelong, and has issue living, Robert John, *b* 1953, — Anne Heather, *b* 1957. —— Alec James, QC (7 Euston St, Malvern, Victoria 3144, Australia), *b* 1926; late RANR; Judge Supreme Court, Victoria: *m* 1957, Margot Rose, da of late Frank Tracy, of Mount Eliza, Victoria, and has issue living, Peter James, *b* 1961, — Kay Tracy, *b* 1962. —— Mary Joy, *b* 1924: *m* 1949, Edward Russell Wilmoth, MC, late Lt-Col AIF, of 16 Haverbrack Av, Malvern, Victoria 3144, Australia, and has issue living, Stephen Guy Russell, *b* 1952, — Peter Charles Russell, *b* 1960, — Wendy Anne, *b* 1950, — Rosemary Susan, *b* 1954, — Jennifer Mary, *b* 1959, — Sarah Jane, *b* 1962.

Granddaughter of late Charles Josiah Southwell, el son of late Josiah Southwell, 2nd son of late Thomas Southwell, son of Hon John Southwell, 4th son of 1st Baron:—
Issue of late Walter Stedman Southwell, *b* 1853, *d* 1939: *m* 1881, Janet, who *d* 1951, da of late William Renton:—
Maida Lyttelton, *b* 1898: *m* 1st, 1932, Baden McIntyre, who *d* 1977; 2ndly, 1984, Arthur Pritchard Townshend Robins, of Melbourne, who *d* 1989, and has issue living (by 1st *m*), John Southwell (1 Keating St, Black Rock, Melbourne, Vic, Aust), *b* 1936: *m* 1st, 1959 (*m diss* 1966), Patricia Agnes, da of Francis Carney; 2ndly, 1967, Margaret Ruth, da of John Moore Wilson, of 76 Hall St, Ormond, Mel, Aust, and has issue living, (by 1st *m*) Colin John Southwell *b* 1960, Lynn Rebecca *b* 1963, (by 2nd *m*) Stephen David *b* 1971, Matthew James *b* 1975, Lachlan Robert *b* 1976, — Mary Ursula, *b* 1933: *m* 1954, Rev William Booth Gill, of 19 Clanbrae Av, Burwood, Victoria 3125, Aust, and has issue living, Andrew William Booth (19 Clanbrae Av, Burwood, Vic) *b* 1986, Lorraine, da of Anthony O'Brien, of Melbourne (and has issue living, William Booth *b* 1985, Julian Andrew *b* 1990, Elizabeth Susan *b* 1984), Shirley Elizabeth *b* 1955, Barbara Marie *b* 1958: *m* 1982, Ross Edwin Mallett, of 14 Jell's Rd, Wheeler's Hill, Vic (and has issue living, Cameron Ross *b* 1985, Stephen Alexander *b* 1987, Cassandra Skye *b* 1992), Teresa Margaret *b* 1960: *m* 1979, Simon William Plant (and has issue living, Justin David William *b* 1980, Christopher James *b* 1982, Matthew Kyle *b* 1990, Melissa Therese *b* 1978, Alana Louise *b* 1986, Courtney Elizabeth *b* 1987), Jennifer Rose *b* 1961, Dulcie Robyn (twin) *b* 1961: *m* 1979, Andrew Williams (and has had issue, Daniel Andrew *b* 1990, Kathryn Dulcie *b* 1980; *d* 1992, Tracey Anne *b* 1982), Christine Anne *b* 1962, Nicole Joy *b* 1966: *m* 1992, Stephen Anthony Liddell, Angelique Faith *b* 1968. *Residence* – 4/210, Warrigal Rd, Burwood, Vic, Aust, 3125.

Granddaughter of late Thomas Martin Southwell, JP, 2nd son of late Josiah Southwell (ante):—
Issue of late Frank Marven Southwell, *b* 1859, *d* 1935: *m* 1887, Florence Isabel, who *d* 1930, da of late Rev Henry James Cotton (V Combermere, colls):—
Gladys Florence, *b* 1888. *Residence* – Alexandra House, Poyner Rd, Ludlow, Shropshire.

PREDECESSORS – (1) Sir THOMAS Southwell, Knt; *cr Baronet* 1662: *s* by his grandson (2) Sir THOMAS, PC, 2nd Bt; sat as MP for co Limerick 1702-17; *cr Baron Southwell*, of Castle Mattress (peerage of Ireland) 1717; *d* 1720; *s* by his son (3) Sir THOMAS, 2nd Baron; *d* 1766; *s* by his son (4) THOMAS GEORGE, 3rd Baron; sat as MP for Enniscorthy; *cr Viscount Southwell* (peerage of Ireland) 1776; *d* 1780; *s* by his son (5) THOMAS ARTHUR, 2nd Viscount; *d* 1796; *s* by his son (6) THOMAS ANTHONY, KP, 3rd Viscount; *d* 1860; *s* by his nephew (7) THOMAS ARTHUR JOSEPH, KP, 4th Viscount; *b* 1836; was Lord-Lieut of co Leitrim: *m* 1871, Charlotte Mary Barbara, da of Sir Pyers Mostyn, 8th Bt; *d* 1878; *s* by his son (8) ARTHUR ROBERT PYERS JOSEPH MARY, 5th Viscount; *b* 1872: *m* 1897, Hon Dorothy Katharine Walrond who *d* 1952, da of 1st Baron Waleran; *d* 1944; *s* by his son (9) ROBERT ARTHUR WILLIAM JOSEPH, 6th Viscount; *b* 1898; Com RN: *m* 1st, 1926 (*m diss* 1931), Violet Mary Weldon, da of Paymaster-Com Francis Weldon Walshe, MVO, OBE, RN (ret); 2ndly, 1943, Josephine, who *d* 1973, da of Denis Joseph de la Mole, and formerly wife of Capt Henry Noel Marryat Hardy, DSO, RN; *d* 1960; *s* by his nephew (10) (PYERS) ANTHONY Joseph (son of Hon Francis Joseph Southwell, 2nd son of 5th Viscount), 7th Viscount and present peer; also Baron Southwell.

SPENCER, EARL (Spencer) (Earl GB 1765, Viscount UK 1905)

God defend the right

CHARLES EDWARD MAURICE SPENCER, 9th Earl; *b* 20 May 1964; *s* 1992; *ed* Eton, and Magdalen Coll, Oxford; Patron of twelve livings; Page of Honour to HM 1977-79: *m* 1989, (Catherine) Victoria, only da of John Lockwood, of Barnes, SW14, and has issue.

Arms – Quarterly argent and gules, in the 2nd and 3rd quarters a fret or, over all on a bend sable three escallops of the first. **Crest** – Out of a ducal coronet or, a griffin's head argent, gorged with a collar gemelle gules, between two wings expanded and elevated, also argent. **Supporters** – *Dexter*, a griffin wings elevated per fesse ermine and erminois; *sinister*, a wyvern wings elevated ermine; each chained and gorged with a collar sable, flory and counterflory, charged with three escallops, argent.
Seat – Althorp, Northampton. *Clubs* – Brooks's, White's.

SON LIVING

LOUIS FREDERICK (*Viscount Althorp* - pronounced Altrup), *b* 14 March 1994.

DAUGHTERS LIVING

Lady Kitty Eleanor, *b* 1990, — *Lady* Eliza Victoria, *b* 1992, — *Lady* Katya Amelia, *b* 1992 (twin).

SISTERS LIVING

Lady (Elizabeth) Sarah Lavinia, *b* 1955: *m* 1980, Neil Edmund McCorquodale, High Sheriff Lincs 1987 (*see* E Westmorland, colls, 1969 Edn), and has issue living, George, *b* 1984, — Emily, *b* 1983, — Celia, *b* 1989. *Residence* – Stoke Rochford, Grantham, Lincs.
Lady (Cynthia) Jane, *b* 1957: *m* 1978, Rt Hon Sir Robert Fellowes, KCB, KCVO (*see* V Hampden, colls), and has issue living, Alexander Robert, *b* 1983, — Laura Jane, *b* 1980, — Eleanor Ruth, *b* 1985. *Residence* – 5a The Old Barracks, Kensington Palace, W8.
Lady Diana Frances (*HRH The Princess of Wales*), *b* 1 July 1961: *m* 29 July 1981, HRH The Prince Charles Philip Arthur George, KG, KT, GCB, PC, Prince of Wales, and has issue (*see* ROYAL FAMILY). *Residence* – Kensington Palace, W8 4PU.

AUNT LIVING (daughter of 7th Earl)

Lady Anne, *b* 1920; sometime 3rd Officer WRNS, served 1939-45 War: *m* 1944, Capt Christopher Baldwin Hughes Wake-Walker, DL, RN, and has issue (*see* Walker, Bt, *cr* 1856, colls). *Residence* – East Bergholt Lodge, Suffolk.

GREAT AUNT LIVING (daughter of 6th Earl)

Lady (Alexandra) Margaret Elizabeth, *b* 1906: *m* 1931 (*m diss* 1947), Hon Henry Montagu Douglas-Home, MBE, who *d* 1980, and has issue (*see* B Home of the Hirsel). *Residence* – The New Cottage, Burnham Market, Norfolk.

MOTHER LIVING

Hon Frances Ruth Burke, yr da of 4th Baron Fermoy: *m* 1st, 1954 (*m diss* 1969), Edward John, Viscount Althorp, LVO (later 8th Earl Spencer), who *d* 1992; 2ndly, 1969 (*m diss* 1990), Peter Shand Kydd. *Residence* – Ardencaple, Isle of Seil, by Oban, Argyll.

WIDOW LIVING OF EIGHTH EARL

RAINE, da of late Alexander George McCorquodale, of The White Lodge, Speen, Berks, and of Dame Barbara Cartland, DBE, of Camfield Place, Hatfield, Herts, and formerly wife of 9th Earl of Dartmouth: *m* 2ndly, 1976, as his 2nd wife, the 8th Earl Spencer, LVO, who *d* 1992; 3rdly, 1993, Count Jean-François de Chambrun. *Residence* – 24 Farm St, W1X 7RE.

COLLATERAL BRANCH LIVING

Issue of late Capt Hon George Charles Spencer, 3rd son of 6th Earl, *b* 1903, *d* 1982: *m* 1st, 1931 (*m diss* 1962), Barbara, who *d* 1978, only da of Benjamin Blumenthal, of Paris; 2ndly, 1966, (Kathleen Elisabeth) Sheila, who *d* 1968, yr da of late J. J. Henderson, and formerly wife of (i) William Geoffrey Lowndes, and (ii) Lt-Col Robert Fitzroy Hamilton Pascoe Stuart-French:—
(By 1st *m*) George Cecil Robert Maurice, *b* 1932; *ed* Eton; late Lieut 11th Hus. *Residence* – 314 Almeria Rd, West Palm Beach, Florida 33405, USA. *Club* – Cavalry and Guards.

PREDECESSORS – Hon John Spencer, MP, 3rd son of 3rd Earl of Sunderland (D Marlborough), had issue **(1)** JOHN, sometime MP for Warwick; *cr* Baron Spencer, of Althorp, co Northampton, and *Viscount Spencer* (peerage of Great Britain) 1761, and *Viscount Althorp* and *Earl Spencer* (peerage of Great Britain) 1765; *d* 1783; *s* by his son **(2)** GEORGE JOHN, KG, 2nd Earl; was First Lord of the Admiralty 1794-1801, and Sec of State for Home Depart 1806-7; *d* 1834; *s* by his el son **(3)** JOHN CHARLES, 3rd Earl; MP for Northamptonshire S, and Chancellor of the Exchequer 1830-4; *d* 1845; *s* by his brother **(4)** FREDERICK, KG, CB, 4th Earl; *b* 1798; Rear-Adm; Lord Chamberlain 1846-8, and Lord Steward of the Household 1854-7: *m* 1st, 1830, Elizabeth Georgina, da of William Stephen Poyntz, MP, of Cowdray, Sussex; 2ndly, 1854, Adelaide Horatia Elizabeth, da of Sir Horace Beauchamp Seymour (M Hertford); *d* 1857; *s* by his son **(5)** JOHN POYNTZ, KG, PC, DCL, LLD, 5th Earl, *b* 1835; Groom of the Stole to the Prince Consort 1859-61, and to King Edward VII when Prince of Wales 1862-6, Lord-Lieut of Ireland 1868-74 and 1882-5, and of Northamptonshire 1872-1908, Lord Pres of Council 1880-83 and 1886, and First Lord of Admiralty 1892-95; MP for S Northamptonshire (L) 1857; Member of Council of Prince of Wales 1898-1910, and Member of Council of Duchy of Cornwall and Keeper of its Privy Seal 1901-7: *m* 1858, Charlotte Frances Frederica, VA, who *d* 1903, 4th da of Frederick Charles William Seymour (M Hertford, colls); *d* 1910; *s* by his half-brother **(6)** CHARLES ROBERT, KG, GCVO, PC, *b* 1857 (who had been *cr* Viscount Althorp, of Great Brington, co Northampton, peerage of United Kingdom 1905), 6th Earl; was Parliamentary Groom-in-Waiting to Queen Victoria Jan to July 1886, Vice-Chamberlain to the Household Aug 1892 to June 1895, Lord Chamberlain of the Household 1905-12, and Lord-Lieut of Northants 1908-22; MP for N Northamptonshire (L) April 1880 to Nov 1885, and for Mid Div of Northamptonshire 1885-95 and Oct 1900 to Dec 1905: *m* 1887, Hon Margaret Baring, who *d* 1906, da of 1st Baron Revelstoke; *d* 1922; *s* by his el son **(7)** ALBERT EDWARD JOHN, TD, DLitt, 7th Earl; *b* 1892; Capt 1st Life Gds; Lord Lieut of Northants 1952-67; Chm Advisory Council, Victoria & Albert Museum 1961-69: *m* 1919, Lady Cynthia Ellinor Beatrix Hamilton, DCVO, OBE (Lady of the Bedchamber to HM Queen Elizabeth the Queen Mother), who *d* 1972, da of 3rd Duke of Abercorn; *d* 1975; *s* by his only surv son **(8)** EDWARD JOHN, LVO, 8th Earl, *b* 1924; temp Equerry to HM King George VI 1950-52, and HM Queen Elizabeth II 1952-54, ADC to Gov of S Aust 1947-50, Dep Hon Col The Royal Anglian Regt (Northants) TAVR, late Capt Royal Scots Greys, served 1939-45 War (despatches), DL, Co Councillor and High Sheriff Northants: *m* 1st, 1954 (*m diss* 1969), Hon Frances Ruth Burke Roche, da of 4th Baron Fermoy; 2ndly, 1976, Raine, da of late Alexander George McCorquodale, of The White Lodge, Speen, Berks, and formerly wife of 9th Earl of Dartmouth; *d* 1992; *s* by his only surv son **(9)** CHARLES EDWARD MAURICE, 9th Earl and present peer; also Viscount Althorp, and Viscount and Baron Spencer.

Spencer-Churchill, Barony of (Ext 1977); see Marlborough, Duke of.

SPENS, BARON (Spens) (Baron UK 1959)

PATRICK MICHAEL REX SPENS, 3rd Baron; *b* 22 July 1942; *s* 1984; *ed* Rugby, and Corpus Christi Coll, Camb (MA, FCA); formerly Man Dir Henry Ansbacher & Co Ltd, a Dir of Morgan Grenfell & Co Ltd: *m* 1966, Barbara Janet Lindsay, da of Rear Adm Ralph Lindsay Fisher, CB, DSO, OBE, DSC, and has issue.

Arms – Quarterly, 1st and 4th, or, a lion rampant gules within a bordure of the last charged with eight roses argent, *Spens of Lathallan*, in the dexter chief point a heart ensigned with an Imperial crown, both proper; 2nd and 3rd, gyronny of eight, or and sable, charged of a quarter in dexter chief per bend argent and azure, *Campbell of Glendouglas*; over all on an inescutcheon or, a lion rampant gules surmounted by a bend sable charged with three mascles argent, which inescutcheon is ensigned with the circlet of a Lord-Baron's coronet, *Spens*. **Crest** – A hart's head erased proper. **Supporters** – *Dexter*, an elephant; *Sinister*, a mallard wings close, both proper.
Residence – Gould, Frittenden, Kent.

SON LIVING

Hon PATRICK NATHANIEL GEORGE, *b* 14 Oct 1968; *ed* Rugby.

DAUGHTER LIVING

Hon Sarah Helen, *b* 1970; *ed* Benenden, and Bristol Univ (MA).

BROTHER LIVING

Hon William David Ralph (Marsh Mills Cottage, Over Stowey, Som), *b* 1943; *ed* Rugby, and Corpus Christi Coll, Camb (MA); Bar Inner Temple 1972: *m* 1967, Gillian Mary, only da of Albert Edwin Jowett, OBE, MD, FRCS, of the Old Rectory, Over Stowey, and has issue living, James Michael William, *b* 1969, — Tamsin Caroline, *b* 1971.

SISTER LIVING

Hon Mallowry Ann (Lambden, Pluckley, Ashford, Kent), *b* 1949.

AUNTS LIVING (*Daughters of 1st Baron*)

Hon Patricia Mary, *b* 1919: *m* 1946, Anthony MacGregor Grier, CMG, who *d* 1989, late Overseas Civil Ser, and has issue living, Anthony Richard MacGregor (79 Somerset Rd, Wimbledon, SW19), *b* 1948: *m* 1976, Sally, el da of K. H. Ong, of Singapore, and has issue living, Alexander Anthony MacGregor *b* 1978, Cristelle Patricia *b* 1983, — Francis John Roy, *b* 1955: *m* 1st, 1976, Shelagh Elizabeth, da of Alec John Frederick Banks; 2ndly, 1990, Anjali, da of Joseph D'Souza, and has issue living (by 2nd *m*), Savitri Patricia *b* 1992, — Lynda Mary, *b* 1947: *m* 1981, John D. Payne, of The Gable House, Abbots Morton, Worcs WR7 4NA, son of late Percy Jennings Payne, and has issue, Robert John *b* 1983, David Roy Christopher *b* 1984. *Residence* – Mulberry House, Abbots Morton, Worcester WR7 4NA.
Hon Emily Susan, MBE, *b* 1924; WRNS 1941-46; Foreign & Commonwealth Office 1956-72; Internat Atomic Energy Agency 1972-82; MBE (Civil) 1970. *Residence* – 47 The Drive, Hove, Sussex BN3 3JE.

WIDOW LIVING OF FIRST BARON

KATHLEEN ANNIE FEDDEN (*Dowager Baroness Spens*), (Gould, Frittenden, Kent), da of late Roger Dodds, of Bath, and Northumberland: *m* 1963, as his 2nd wife, the 1st Baron, who *d* 1973.

WIDOW LIVING OF SECOND BARON

JOAN ELIZABETH (*Joan, Baroness Spens*) (Lambden, Pluckley, Ashford Kent), da of late Reginald Goodall; *m* 1941, the 2nd Baron, who *d* 1984.

COLLATERAL BRANCH LIVING

Issue of late Capt Robert Richard Patrick Spens, MC, Roy Norfolk Yeo, yr son of 1st Baron, *b* 1917, *ka* 1942: *m* 1939, Elisabeth Clare (who *d* 1990, having *m* 2ndly, 1955, Francis David Corbin, TD), da of George Catterall Leach:—
Charmian Helen, *b* 1940: *m* 1960, William Thomas Scott, of Meiklewood, Stirling FK8 3AF, and has issue living, Thomas Robert George, *b* 1973, — Elisabeth Charlotte, *b* 1962, — Alexandra Mary, *b* 1965: *m* 1987, Hugh Colin Graham-Watson, yr son of Charles Fitzjames Graham-Watson, of La Massana, Andorra, and has issue living, Archibald Edward *b* 1990, Amber Isobel *b* 1989.

PREDECESSORS – *Rt Hon Sir* (WILLIAM) PATRICK Spens, KBE, son of late Nathaniel Spens, of 1 St Mary Abbot's Court, Kensington, W; *b* 1885, Bar Inner Temple; Commr of Imperial War Graves Comm 1931-43 and 1949-65; Ch Justice of India 1943-47; Chm of Arbitral Tribunal for India and Pakistan 1947-48; MP for Ashford, Kent (*C*) 1933-43, and S Kensington 1950-59; *cr Baron Spens*, of Blairsanquhar, co Fife (peerage of UK) 1959: *m* 1st, Hilda Mary, who *d* 1962, da of Lt-Col Wentworth, Grenville Bowyer (B Denham, colls); 2ndly, 1963, Kathleen Annie Fedden, da of Roger Dodds, of Bath and Northumberland; *d* 1973; *s* by his el son (2) WILLIAM GEORGE MICHAEL, 2nd Baron *b* 1914; Bar Inner Temple 1945; Maj RA: *m* 1941, Joan Elizabeth, da of late Reginald Goodall, *d* 1984 *s* by his elder son (3) PATRICK MICHAEL REX, 3rd Baron and present peer.

STAFFORD, BARON (Fitzherbert) (Baron E 1640)

One I will serve

FRANCIS MELFORT WILLIAM FITZHERBERT, 15th Baron; *b* 13 March 1954; *s* 1986; *ed* Ampleforth; patron of one living (but being a Roman Catholic cannot present): *m* 1980, Katharine Mary, 3rd da of John Codrington, of Barnes, SW13, and has issue.

Arms – Argent, a chief vairée or and gules, over all a bend sable, *Fitzherbert*. **Crest** – A dexter cubit arm in armour erect, the hand appearing clenched within the gauntlet. **Supporters** – *Dexter*, a lion argent; *sinister* a swan, wings inverted argent, gorged with a ducal coronet per pale gules and sable.
Seat – Swynnerton Park, Stone, Staffordshire.

SONS LIVING

Hon BENJAMIN JOHN BASIL, *b* 8 Nov 1983.
Hon Toby Francis, *b* 1985.

DAUGHTERS LIVING

Hon Teresa Emily, *b* 1987.
Hon Camilla Rose Jane, *b* 1989.

BROTHERS LIVING

Hon Thomas Alastair, *b* 1955; *ed* Ampleforth; late Capt Scots Gds: *m* 1982, Deborah Susan, yr da of late Peter Alan Beak, of Brazil, and has issue living, Rory, *b* 1989, — Tamara Frances, *b* 1986, — Purdita Aileen, *b* 1987.
Hon Philip Basil, *b* 1962; *ed* Ampleforth, and Durham Univ (BA): *m* 1991, Caroline T., yr da of Michael Hadcock, of Bodedern, Isle of Anglesey.

SISTERS LIVING

Hon Aileen Mary, *b* 1953: *m* 1980, Antony Robin Walhouse Littleton, and has issue (*see* B Hatherton). *Residence* – Old Walls, Hannington, Hants.
Hon Caroline Fiona, *b* 1956: *m* 1981, William Kirkland Tellwright, eldest son of late William Tellwright, of Park Springs, Shropshire, and has issue living, Turia Mary, *b* 1984, — Laura Caroline, *b* 1987. *Residence* – The Sydnall Farm, Woodseaves, Market Drayton, Shropshire.
Hon Wendy Helen, *b* 1961: *m* 1983, Jeremy John Maurice Hill, eldest son of late Lt-Col Colin Hill, of Coley Court, E Harptree, Avon, and has issue living, Thomas Colin Evelyn, *b* 1985, — Nicholas Jeremy John, *b* 1987. *Residence* – 66 Scarsdale Villas, W8.

WIDOW LIVING OF FOURTEENTH BARON

MORAG NADA (*Dowager Baroness Stafford*), DStJ, yr da of late Lt-Col Alastair Campbell, of Altries, Milltimber, Aberdeenshire: *m* 1952. the 14th Baron, who *d* 1986. *Residence* – Beech Farm House, Beech, Stoke-on-Trent, Staffs.

COLLATERAL BRANCHES LIVING

Grandchildren of late Hon Mary Beatrice Theresa Fitzherbert, eldest sister of 12th and 13th Barons, *b* 1862, *d* 1949: *m* 1895, as his 2nd wife, Sir Trevor John Chichele Chichele Plowden, KCSI, who *d* 1905:—
Issue of late Hester Mary Beatrice Chichele-Plowden, *b* 1902, *d* 1993: *m* 1922, Cdr Kenneth Gordon Poland, RNVR, who *d* 1970:—
Trevor Peter Gordon (3 Cheyne Gdns, SW3), *b* 1923; Lt-Cdr RN (ret): *m* 1st, 1944, June Mary, who *d* 1969, eldest da of Henry Bowlby, of 100 Elm Park Gdns, SW10 (*see* V Combermere, colls, 1960 Edn); 2ndly, 1969, Lorette Elizabeth Johanna, da of late Dr J. M. Durr, of Cape Town, S Africa, and has issue living (by 1st *m*), Peter Kenneth, *b* 1945, — Jill, *b* 1948, — (by 2nd *m*) Sophie Victoria, *b* 1982. ——— John Michael (Fermain, W Wittering, Chichester, Sussex), *b* 1925; *ed* Downside, and Trin Coll, Camb: *m* 1952 (*m diss* 1983), Diana Mary Angela Forbes, da of late Leo Forbes O'Connor (*see* B Byron, 1985 Edn), and has issue living, Simon John Joseph, *b* 1957, — Jonathan David, *b* 1958, — Matthew John, *b* 1963, — Sara Daphne Mary, *b* 1954, — Lucy Mary, *b* 1959: *m* 1987, (Geoffrey Roger George) Chandos Elletson, yr son of late Daniel Hope Elletson, of Parrox Hall, Leics, and has issue living, Frederick Chandos John *b* 1990. ——— †David Kenneth, *b* 1929; *ed* Downside: *m* 1st, 1958 (*m diss* 1967), Joanna Mary, eldest da of late Capt J. B. Hall, RN; 2ndly, 1967, Isie Suzetli, only da of late Maj Louis Esselen, of S Africa, and *d* 1982, leaving issue (by 1st *m*), Kevin John, *b* 1959, — Jeremy David, *b* 1961, — (by 2nd *m*) Caroline Mary, *b* 1969. ——— Michael Desmond (Lower Preshaw House, Upham, Southampton SO3 1HP), *b* 1937; *ed* Downside; *m* 1st, 1969 (*m diss* 1980), Elizabeth, da of late Philip Asprey, of Perry, Worplesdon, Surrey; 2ndly, 1981, Mrs Carolyn Mary Denison, 2nd da of late W/Cdr William James Maitland Longmore, CBE (*see* B Forres), and has issue living (by 1st *m*), Lara Hester Mary, *b* 1969, — Emma Elizabeth, *b* 1970, — Liza Evelyne Theresa, *b* 1973, — Anna Louise, *b* 1974. ——— Daphne Elizabeth Beatrice, *b* 1933: *m* 1960, Edward Kendall Thorneycroft, MBE, TD, DL, of Tigbourne Farm, Wormley, Surrey, and has issue living, Tom Edward, *b* 1962, — Mary Louise, *b* 1961: *m* 1985, Jeremy Campbell-Lamerton, of The Old Rectory, Rendlesham, Woodbridge, Suffolk, eldest son of Col Michael John Campbell-Lamerton, of Shipston-on-Stour, Warwicks, and has issue living, Harry Alexander *b* 1987, Alice Louisa *b* 1988, Olivia Rose *b* 1990, Poppy Camilla *b* 1993.

Grandchildren of late Hon Alice Mary Wilhelmina Trappes-Lomax, 3rd sister of 12th and 13th Barons: *m* 1894, Maj Richard Trappes-Lomax, JP:—
Issue of late Brig Basil Charles Trappes-Lomax, MC, *b* 1896, *d* 1963: *m* 1929, Diana Mary (131 Southgate St, Bury St Edmunds), da of late Capt A. E. Silvertop, RN:—
†David Edward (Great Hockham Hall, Thetford), *b* 1930; *ed* Downside; Maj Scots Guards: *m* 1980, Gillean Hill, and *dsp* 1993. ——— John Michael (131 Southgate St, Bury St Edmunds, Suffolk), *b* 1947; *ed* Downside, and Gonville and Caius Coll, Camb. ——— Alice Mary, *b* 1938: *m* 1959, John Edward Benedict Wells, of Creaber, Gidleigh, nr Newton Abbot, Devon, and has issue living, Benedict Swithin (c/o BFPO 17), *b* 1960; The King's Royal Hussars: *m* 1989, Vicki Caroline, da of Stanley Alexander Maitland, of Firs Hill, High Rd, Chipstead, Surrey, and has issue living, James Edward Benedict *b* 1994, Sophie Louise Cameron *b* 1990, Georgia Rose *b* 1991, Juliet Katherine *b* 1993, — Thomas Edward (83 Fellows Rd, NW3), *b* 1962: *m* 1990, Katherine J. Rich, — Katherine Mary Horatia, *b* 1959: *m* 1988, John Collingwood Almond, of 1 Elthiron Rd, SW6, and has issue living, Edward *b* 19—, Lucy Horatia *b* 1991.

Issue of late Col Nicholas Hugh Trappes-Lomax, *b* 1911, *d* 1969: *m* 1938, Gertrude Maisie, who *d* 1994, da of late Lt-Col Hugh Charles Stockwell, OBE:—
Hugh Richard Nicholas (28 Blackford Av, Edinburgh EH9 2PH), *b* 1943: *m* 1968, Jocelyn Nchekei, da of Johnson Karandi, of Meru, Kenya, and has issue living, Simon Mwenda, *b* 1968: *m* 1993, Marie-Christine Michaela, da of late Michael Edward Skrutkowski, of Bromma, Sweden, — Robert Kimathi, *b* 1981, — Catherine Nkirote, *b* 1970, — Helen Kagendo, *b* 1977. — Mark Clement, *b* 1946. —— Tessa Margaret, *b* 1941. —— Nicola Frances, *b* 1944: *m* 1964, Anthony Miles Trevor Eastwood, of Foulscales House, Newton-in-Bowland, Clitheroe, Lancs, and has issue living, Anthony Charles, *b* 1965, — Benjamin Miles, *b* 1966, — Carl Hugh, *b* 1968.

Issue of late Maj Stephen Richard Trappes-Lomax, MC, TD, *b* 1913; *d* 1982: *m* 1952, Alison Marjorie Gundrede (The Farm House, Little London, N Walsham, Norfolk), only da of late George Algernon Perkins, of Bure House, Lamas, Norwich:—
Francis George, *b* 1955: *m* 1986, Annette Chalkley, and has issue living, Christopher Michael, *b* 1990, — Catherine Ruth, *b* 1988. *Residence* - Croft Cottage, Cann's Lane, Hethersett, Norwich NR9 3JE. —— Richard Nicholas Henry, *b* 1960. —— Mary Alison Catherine, *b* 1953: *m* 1984, Alexander Cockburn, of Rosedene, Aylsham Rd, Swanton Abbott, Norwich, elder son of Denison Cockburn, of Chipping Campden, Glos, and has issue living, George Stephen Denison, *b* 1986, — Alastair William Richard, *b* 1989. —— Clare Gundrede, *b* 1957: *m* 1983, Brian Ronald Weir Gibson, of Longworth House, Gt Wolford, Shipston-on-Stour, Warwicks, son of late Ronald Gibson, of Lowood, S Queensferry, W Lothian, and has issue living, Emma Clare, *b* 1987.

Descendants, in the female line, of brothers of 8th Baron:—
See 1969 and earlier edns.

PREDECESSORS – (1) Sir WILLIAM Howard, KB (3rd son of Thomas Howard, *cr* Earl of Norfolk 1644); *m* Mary, only sister of Henry, 5th (or but for attainder 14th) Baron de Stafford; in 1640 he and his wife were *cr Baron* and *Baroness Stafford* (peerage of England), with remainder, in default of heirs male of the body, to the heirs of their bodies, and *Viscount Stafford* (peerage of England) with remainder to his issue male; subsequently tried for complicity in Titus Oates plot, attainted 1678 and executed 1680; his wife was *cr Countess of Stafford* 1688 for life; she *d* 1693; *s* by her son (2) HENRY STAFFORD, *de jure* 2nd Baron; *cr Earl of Stafford* (peerage of England) 1688, with remainder to his brothers John and Francis; *dsp* 1719; *s* by his nephew (3) WILLIAM, 2nd Earl, and *de jure* 3rd Baron Stafford, el son of the Hon John (ante); *s* by his son (4) WILLIAM MATTHIAS, 3rd Earl, and *de jure* 4th Baron Stafford; *dsp* 1750; *s* by his uncle (5) JOHN PAUL STAFFORD, 4th Earl, and *de jure* 5th Baron Stafford; *dsp* 1762, when the earldom expired, and the barony vested in (6-7) Mary, wife of Sir George Jerningham, 5th Bt, only child of Mary Plowden, sister of 4th Earl; attainder of the 1st Viscount was reversed 1824, and on 6 July 1825, the House of Lords resolved that (8) Sir GEORGE WILLIAM Jerningham, 7th Bt (*cr* 1621), had made out his claim to be 8th Baron Stafford; unsuccessfully claimed the Barony of Stafford, *cr* 1299; assumed 1826 by Roy licence additional surname and arms of Stafford; *d* 1851; *s* by his son (9) HENRY VALENTINE, 9th Baron; *b* 1802; *d* 30 Nov 1884; *s* by his nephew (10) AUGUSTUS FREDERICK FITZHERBERT, son of Hon Edward (2nd son of 8th Baron), 10th Baron, *b* 1830: *d* 1892; *s* by his brother (11) FITZHERBERT EDWARD, 11th Baron, *b* 1832; *d* 1913; *s* by his nephew (12) FRANCIS EDWARD Fitzherbert-Stafford, DSO (son of late Basil Thomas Fitzherbert, of Swynnerton Park, Stone (who *m* 2ndly, 1887, Emma Eliza, Baroness Stafford, who *d* 1912), by Emily Charlotte, who *d* 1881, sister of 10th and 11th Barons), 12th Baron, *b* 1859: was Lord High Steward of Stafford; assumed by Roy licence 1913 for himself and issue the additional surname of Stafford: *m* 1903, Dorothy Hilda, who *d* 1958, 3rd da of late Albert Octavius Worthington, JP, DL, of Maple Hayes, Lichfield; *d* 1932; *s* by his brother (13) EDWARD STAFFORD JOSEPH Fitzherbert, KCB, 13th Baron; *b* 1864; Adm; Com-in-Chief African Station 1918-20; *d* 1941; *s* by his nephew (14) BASIL FRANCIS NICHOLAS (son of late Capt Hon Thomas Charles Fitzherbert, AM, brother of 13th Baron), 14th Baron, *b* 1926; Lt Scots Gds: *m* 1952, Morag Nada, yr da of late Lt-Col Alastair Campbell, of Altries, Milltimber, Aberdeenshire; *d* 1986; *s* by his elder son (15) FRANCIS MELFORT WILLIAM, 15th Baron and present peer.

STAIR, EARL OF (Dalrymple) (Earl S 1703, Bt S 1664 and 1698)

JOHN AYMER DALRYMPLE, KCVO, MBE, 13th Earl, and 14th Baronet of Stair and 10th of Killock; *b* 9 Oct 1906; *s* 1961; *ed* Eton; is Col late Scots Guards, Capt Gen Queen's Body Guard for Scotland (Royal Company of Archers), Gold Stick for Scotland, and formerly Lord-Lt of Wigtownshire; 1939-45 War in Middle East and Central Mediterranean (despatches, MBE); MBE (Mil) 1941, CVO 1964, KCVO 1977: *m* 1960, Davina Katharine, da of late Hon Sir David Bowes-Lyon, KCVO (*see* E Strathmore, colls), and has issue.

Arms – Quarterly: 1st, or, on a saltire azure nine lozenges of the field, *Dalrymple*; 2nd or, a chevron chequy sable and argent between three water bougets of the second, *Ross*; 3rd grand quarter, quarterly, 1st and 4th counterquartered, 1st and 4th gules, three cinquefoils ermine, 2nd and 3rd, argent, a galley sails furled sable, the whole within a border compony argent and azure, the first charged with hearts gules, and the second with mullets argent, *Hamilton of Bargany*; 2nd and 3rd gules, on a fesse between three crescents or, as many mullets azure, de *Franguetot*; 4th grand quarter, quarterly, 1st and 4th gules, on a chevron between three cinquefoils argent, as many round buckles azure, *Hamilton of Fala*; 2nd and 3rd gules, three martlets argent, *Makgill*. **Crest** – A rock proper. **Supporters** – Two storks holding in their beaks, a fish, all proper.
Seat – Lochinch Castle, Stranraer, Wigtownshire. *Clubs* – Guards', Turf.

SONS LIVING

JOHN DAVID JAMES (*Viscount Dalrymple*), *b* 4 Sept 1961.
Hon David Hew, *b* 1963.
Hon Michael Colin, *b* 1965: *m* 1991, Harriet Lucy, elder da of Lt-Cdr Jocelyn Charles Roden Buxton, VRD, RNVR (*see* Buxton, Bt, colls), and has issue living, William Hew, *b* 1992, — a son, *b* 1993.

BROTHERS LIVING

Hon Hew North, TD, *b* 1910; *ed* Eton; formerly Capt 2nd Batn Black Watch (TA); is a Member of Queen's Body Guard for Scotland (Royal Company of Archers); DL Ayrshire 1955; N Africa and Burma 1943-5 (twice wounded): *m* 1st, 1938, Mildred Helen, who *d* 1980, da of late Hon Thomas Henry Frederick Egerton (D Sutherland, colls); 2ndly, 1983, Helen M. W. Phillips, and has issue living (by 1st *m*), Robert Hew, *b* 1946: *m* 1976, Caroline Anne, da of (Charles) Patrick (Maule) Hunting, CBE, TD, FCA, of The Old House, Birch Grove, Horsted Keynes, Sussex, and has issue living, Hamish Hew *b* 1979, Alastair North *b* 1982. *Residence* – Castlehill, Ballantrae, Ayrshire.

Hon Colin James, *b* 1920: *ed* Eton, and Trin Coll, Camb (BA 1941): Major (ret) Scots Guards, a Member of Queen's Body Guard for Scotland (Royal Company of Archers); DL Midlothian 1961, and JP; Italy 1944-5: *m* 1st, 1945 (*m diss* 1954), Pamela Mary, only da of Major Lamplugh Wickham, CVO; 2ndly, 1956, Fiona Jane, only da of late Adm Sir Ralph Alan Bevan Edwards, KCB, CBE, and has issue living (by 1st *m*), Andrew David, *b* 1959: *m* 1987, Bryony W., da of W. A. Major, of Shilston Barton, Modbury, S Devon, and has issue living, Hew William James *b* 1993, Louisa Alice Clare *b* 1990, — (by 1st *m*) Caroline Mary, *b* 1946: *m* 1973, Michael Scott, ARICS, of Troloss, Elvanfoot, Lanarkshire, son of M. M. Scott, of Cakemuir Castle, Tynehead, Midlothian, and has issue living, Alexander James *b* 1975, Camilla Rose *b* 1978, — (by 2nd *m*) Serena Jane, *b* 1957: *m* 1979, Maj James Peter Greenwell, The Blues and Royals (ret), and has issue (*see* Greenwell, Bt), — Rose Joanna, *b* 1962: *m* 1987, Charles Leighton Dudgeon, of Fala Mains, Blackshiels, Midlothian, son of John Dudgeon, of Humbie, Kirkliston, W Lothian, and has issue living, Edward John *b* 1993, Sara Rose *b* 1991. *Residence* – Oxenfoord Mains, Dalkeith, Midlothian. *Club* – New (Edinburgh).

SISTERS LIVING

Lady Jean Margaret, DCVO, *b* 1905; appointed a Woman of the Bedchamber to HM Queen Elizabeth The Queen Mother 1947; CVO 1957, DCVO 1969: *m* 1931, Lt-Col (Arthur) Niall Talbot Rankin, Scots Guards, who *d* 1965 (*see* Rankin, Bt, colls *cr* 1898). *Residence* – House of Treshnish, Calgary, Isle of Mull.

Lady Marion Violet, *b* 1908; a JP of Pembrokeshire; has Order of Mercy; FRAgS; *m* 1930, Major Hon Richard Hanning Philipps, MBE, Welsh Guards (*see* B Milford). *Residence* – Picton Castle, Haverfordwest, Pembrokeshire.

COLLATERAL BRANCHES LIVING   *(In special remainder to Earldom)*

Grandchildren of late Col Hon North de Coigny DALRYMPLE-HAMILTON, MVO, 2nd son of 10th Earl:—
Issue of late Adm Sir Frederick Hew George Dalrymple-Hamilton of Bargany, KCB; *b* 1890, *d* 1974: *m* 1918, Gwendolen, who *d* 1974, da of Sir Cuthbert Edgar Peek, 2nd Bt:—

North Edward Frederick DALRYMPLE-HAMILTON OF BARGANY, CVO, MBE, DSC (Lovestone House, Bargany, Girvan, Ayrshire, KA26 9RF. *Clubs* – Pratt's, MCC, New (Edinburgh)), *b* 1922; *ed* Eton; Capt RN (ret) and Lieut Queen's Body Guard for Scotland (Royal Company of Archers); DL Ayrshire 1973, JP 1980; 1940-45 War (DSC), Korea 1952-53 (MBE); MBE (Mil) 1953, MVO (4th class) 1954, CVO 1961: *m* 1st, 1949, Hon Mary Helen Colville, who *d* 1981, el da of 1st Baron Clydesmuir; 2ndly, 1983, Geraldine Inez Antoinette, widow of Maj Rowland Beech, MC, of Park Leaze, Ewen, Cirencester, and da of late Maj Frank Harding, and has issue living (by 1st *m*), North John Frederick, OBE, TD (Houdston, Girvan, Ayrshire KA26 9PH), *b* 1950; *ed* Eton, and Aberdeen Univ (MA Hons); a Page of Honour to HM Queen Elizabeth The Queen Mother 1964-66; Member Queen's Body Guard for Scotland (Royal Company of Archers), Col late Queen's Own Yeo (TA); TD 1986, OBE (Mil) 1992: *m* 1980, Sally-Anne, da of Robert Boothby How, of Ladies Lake, St Andrews, Fife, and has issue living, Hew North Robert *b* 1981, Edward *b* 1986, Catherine Mary Anne *b* 1982, — James Hew Ronald, *b* 1955: ARICS: *m* 1986, Pippa M. D., only da of Maj David Metcalfe, of Minchinhampton, Glos, and has issue living, Frederick David George *b* 1990, Jack Louis Robert *b* 1994, Clementine Mary *b* 1989. —— Christian Margaret, MBE, *b* 1919; a DL of Wigtown; MBE 1989. *Residence* – Cladyhouse, Cairnryan, Stranraer, Wigtown. —— Graeme Elizabeth, *b* 1926: *m* 1948, Alexander Grant Laing, MC, who *d* 1988, of Relugas, Forres, Moray IV36 0QL (Grant, Bt, *cr* 1924), and has issue living, Alasdair North Grant (Logie House, Forres, Moray IV36 0QN), *b* 1949; *ed* Eton; Lt Scots Guards: *m* 1979, Hon Lucy Ann Anthea Low, yr da of 1st Baron Aldington, and has issue living, Alexander William Grant *b* 1982, Frederick Charles Grant *b* 1985, Emma Mary Grant *b* 1980, — Fergus Hew Grant (Craggan, Grantown on Spey, Morayshire), *b* 1951; *ed* Gordonstoun: *m* 1979, Priscilla Mary, yr da of late Michael Telfair Keith, TD, of Hoe Hall, Dereham, Norfolk (*see* Mann, Bt), and has issue living, Michael Hew Grant *b* 1984, Iona Rose Grant *b* 1982, Henrietta Mary Grant *b* 1986, Elizabeth Ruby Grant *b* 1988, — Carolyn Margaret Grant, *b* 1952: *m* 1981, Capt James Melville John Balfour, RGJ (*see* E Harewood, colls, 1972-73 Edn), and has issue living, Edward James Melville *b* 1982, Laura Elizabeth *b* 1984, Margaret Carolyn *b* 1985, — Fiona Mary Grant (*Hon Mrs Jonathan Warrender*), *b* 1954: *m* 1979, Hon Jonathan James Warrender, of Minuntion, Pinmore, Girvan, Ayrshire KA26 0TE, yr son of 2nd Baron Bruntisfield, and has issue.

Granddaughter of late George North Dalrymple, el son of Hon George Grey Dalrymple, 2nd son of 9th Earl:—
Issue of late Maj Walter Grey North Hamilton Dalrymple, *b* 1896, *d* 1969: *m* 1929 (*m diss* 1946), Melisande Germaine Violet Craigie, who *d* 1969, da of Robert G. Hunter, of London:—
Dawn Mary Kathleen, *b* 1930: *m* 1956, Peter Humphrey Methuen, of Elliston, St Boswells, Roxburghshire, and has issue living, Piers Harry North Dalrymple, *b* 1966.

Granddaughter of late Walter Francis Dalrymple, yr son of Hon George Grey Dalrymple (ante):—
Issue of late Basil Walter Dalrymple, *b* 1891, *d* 1977: *m* 1st, 1920, (*m diss* 1925), Aileen Eugenie, only da of late Maj Charles May Hayes-Newington, late King's and Cheshire Regts; 2ndly, 1930, Erica Isolde, who *d* 1977, da of late Lt-Col P. N. G. Reade, RA:—
(By 1st *m*) Elizabeth Mary Wetherell (11 Rylstone Rd, Eastbourne, Sussex), *b* 1920; late Com ATS: *m* 1945 (*m diss* 1954), Anthony Edward Home Phillips, Sub-Lt RNVR, only son of late Sir Herbert Phillips, KCMG, OBE, and has issue living, Anthony Jeremy Herbert Home, *b* 1947.

Descendants of late Hon Sir Hew Dalrymple, MP (3rd son of 1st Viscount Stair), who was *cr* a *Baronet* 1698:—
See Hamilton-Dalrymple, Bt.

Descendants of late Robert Dalrymple-Horn-Elphinstone (2nd son of late Robert Dalrymple-Horn-Elphinstone, el son of late Hew Dalrymple, 2nd son of late Hon Sir Hew Dalrymple (ante)), who was *cr* a *Baronet* 1828:—
See Elphinstone-Dalrymple, Bt.

PREDECESSORS – (**1**) JAMES Dalrymple, a Lord of Session as Lord Stair, was *cr* a *Baronet* (of Stair) 1664; appointed Pres of Court of Session 1671; removed from that office 1681, and reappointed in 1688, after the revolution; *cr Lord Glenluce and Stranraer* and *Viscount Stair* (peerage of Scotland) 1690; *d* 1695; *s* by his son (**2**) JOHN, PC, 2nd Viscount; was Lord Justice Clerk, Lord Advocate for Scotland, and a Principal Sec of State, which latter office he resigned in consequence of the part he took in the massacre of Glencoe; *cr Lord Newliston, Glenluce* and *Stranraer, Viscount Dalrymple* and *Earl of Stair* (peerage of Scotland) 1703, with remainder to the heirs male of his father; *d* 1707; *s* by his son (**3**) JOHN, KT, 2nd Earl; an eminent military commander; attained the rank of Field Marshal, and was sometime ambassador to France; his brother Hon

William (heir presumptive), having *m* the Countess of Dumfries, a peeress in her own right, he in 1707 surrendered all his honours to the Crown, and obtained a new charter empowering him to name as his successor any male descendant of the 1st Viscount, and in virtue of this authority he in 1747, shortly before his death, nominated by deed his nephew John, 2nd son of his 2nd brother George; this nomination was contested, and the House of Lords decided in favour of the 2nd son of Hon William and the Countess of Dumfries (ante) viz **(4)** JAMES, 3rd Earl: *dsp* 1760: *s* by his el brother **(5)** WILLIAM, 4th Earl, who had previously *s* as 4th *Earl of Dumfries; dsp* 1768, when the Earldom of Dumfries devolved upon his nephew Patrick Macdowal, Esq, and the Earldom of Stair passed to his cousin **(6)** JOHN, 5th Earl, who had been nominated for the title by the 2nd Earl; *d* 1789; *s* by his son **(7)** JOHN, 6th Earl; a Representative Peer, and sometime Ambassador to Prussia, *dsp* 1821; *s* by his cousin **(8)** JOHN WILLIAM HENRY, 7th Earl, son of Gen William Dalrymple, Lieut-Gov of Chelsea Hospital; *dsp* 1840; *s* by his kinsman **(9)** JOHN HAMILTON, KT, 8th Earl, who had previously *s* as 5th Bt (see * infra); was a Gen in the Army; *cr Baron Oxenfoord*, of Cousland, co Edinburgh (peerage of United Kingdom) 1841, with remainder to his brother; *d* 1853; *s* by his brother **(10)** NORTH HAMILTON, 9th Earl; *b* 1776: *m* 1st, 1817, Margaret, da of J. Penny, of Arrad; *d* 1864; *s* by his son **(11)** JOHN HAMILTON, KT, 10th Earl, *b* 1819; sat as MP for Wigtownshire 1841-56; was Lord High Commr to Gen Assembly of Church of Scotland 1869-71; many years Lord-Lieut of Ayrshire and Lord-Lieut of co Wigtown: *m* 1846, Louisa Jane Henrietta Emily, who *d* 1896, da of the Duc de Coigny; *d* 1903; *s* by his son **(12)** JOHN HEW NORTH GUSTAVE HENRY, 11th Earl, *b* 1848; Provost of Stranraer 1900-1909, and Lord High Commr to Gen Assembly of Church of Scotland 1910: *m* 1878 (*m diss* 1905), Susan Harriet, who *d* 1946, da of Sir James Grant-Suttie, 6th Bt; *d* 1914; *s* by his son **(13)** JOHN JAMES, KT, DSO, 12th Earl; *b* 1879; formerly Lieut-Col Scots Guards; MP for Wigtownshire (C) 1906-14; Lord High Commr to Church of Scotland 1927 and 1928, and Lord-Lieut of Wigtownshire 1935-61; European War 1914-19 (DSO): *m* 1904, Violet Evelyn, JP, who *d* 1968, da of Col Frederick Henry Harford; *d* 1961; *s* by his son **(14)** JOHN AYMER, 13th Earl and present peer; also Viscount Stair, Viscount Dalrymple, Lord Glenluce and Stranraer, Lord Newliston, and Baron Oxenfoord.

*****(1)** *Hon* JAMES Dalrymple, 2nd son of 1st Viscount: *cr* a *Baronet* (of Killock) 1698; *s* by his son **(2)** *Sir* JOHN, 2nd Bt; *d* 1740; *s* by his son **(3)** *Sir* WILLIAM, 3rd Bt; *d* 1771; *s* by his son **(4)** *Sir* JOHN, 4th Bt; was a Baron of the Court of Exchequer in Scotland: *m* his cousin Elizabeth Macgill, the heir and representative of the Viscount Oxenfoord, and assumed the surnames of Hamilton and Macgill; *d* 1810; *s* by his son **(5)** *Sir* JOHN HAMILTON Dalrymple, 5th Bt, who *s* as 8th Earl of Stair (ante).

STALLARD, BARON (Stallard) (Life Baron 1983)

ALBERT WILLIAM STALLARD, son of Frederick Stallard, of Tottenham; *b* 5 Nov 1921; *ed* Low Waters Public Sch, and Hamilton Academy, Scotland; engineer 1937-65; Technical Training Officer 1965-70; mem St Pancras Borough Council 1953-59; Alderman 1962-65; mem Camden Borough Council 1965-70; Alderman since 1971; MP for St Pancras North 1970-74 and for Camden Divn of St Pancras North 1974-83; PPS Min of Agric 1973-74; PPS Min of Housing and Construction 1974-76; Assistant Govt Whip 1976-78; a Lord Commr of HM Treasury 1978-79; *cr Baron Stallard* of St Pancras, London Borough of Camden (Life Baron) 1983: *m* 1944, Julie, da of William Cornelius Murphy, of co Kerry, and has issue.
Residence – 2 Belmont Street, Chalk Farm, NW1.

SON LIVING

Hon Richard, *b* 1945; *ed* Richard Acland Sch, London; *m* 1969, Carol, da of William Packman, of Swanley, Kent, and has issue.

DAUGHTER LIVING

Hon Brenda, *b* 1949, *m* 1971 (*m diss* 1987), Colin Hills, and has issue.

STAMP, BARON (Stamp) (Baron UK 1938)

TREVOR CHARLES BOSWORTH STAMP, 4th Baron; *b* 18 Sept 1935; *s* 1987; *ed* Leys Sch, Gonville and Caius Coll, Camb (BA 1956), and Yale Univ, USA (MSc 1957); St Mary's Hosp Med Sch, London; MB BChir 1961, MD 1972, FRCP 1978 (Lond): *m* 1st, 1963 (*m diss* 1971), Anne Carolynn, da of John Kenneth Churchill, of Tunbridge Wells, Kent; 2ndly, 1975, Carol Anne, da of Robert Keith Russell, of Farnham, Surrey, and has issue by 1st and 2nd *m*.

Arms – Gules between two garbs or three bezants in bend each charged with a horse passant sable. Crest – Issuant from a mount vert bezantee a demi-horse argent. Supporters – On either side a horse argent resting the interior hind leg on a bezant.
Residence – Pennyroyal, Hedgerley, Bucks SL2 3UY.

FIDEI · COMMISSA · TENEO

I hold in trust that which is trusted to me

SON LIVING *(By 2nd marriage)*

Hon NICHOLAS CHARLES TREVOR, *b* 1978.

DAUGHTERS LIVING *(By 1st marriage)*

Hon Catherine Anne Louise, *b* 1963.
Hon Emma Caroline, *b* 1968.

(by 2nd marriage)

Hon Lucinda Jane, *b* 1976.

BROTHER LIVING

Hon Josiah Richard, *b* 1943; *ed* Winchester, and Queens' Coll, Camb (BA). *Residence* – Flat B, 11 Lymington Rd, NW6 1HX.

UNCLE LIVING *(son of 1st Baron)*

Hon (Jos) Colin, *b* 1917; *ed* Leys Sch, and Queens' Coll, Camb (MA); late Lt RNVR: late Dir of Marketing Sers for Europe of American Express Internat: *m* 1st, 1940 (*m diss* 1956), Althea, da of late Mrs William Dawes, of Evanston, Illinois, USA; 2ndly, 1958, Gillian Penelope, da of late Guy St J. Tatham, of Johannesburg, SA, and has issue living, (by 1st *m*) Olive Judith *b* 1941; *ed* Wellesley Coll, Mass, USA (BA): *m* 1963 (*m diss* 1975), Eugene Humphrey, and has issue living, Eugene Jos *b* 1971, Alison Dudley *b* 1968, — Althea Patricia Dawes, *b* 1943; *ed* Wellesley Coll, Mass, USA (BA), and York Univ, Toronto (PhD 1981): *m* 1981, Stephen Katz, of Toronto, — Ann Jocelyn, *b* 1945, — Rowena Jane, *b* 1953: *m* 1977, Patrick Olwell, of Nellysford, Va, and has issue living, Matthew *b* 1978, Aaron *b* 1981, — (by 2nd *m*) Robert Colin, *b* 1960; *ed* St Paul's, and Corpus Christi Coll, Camb (BA): *m* 1988, Susan Caroline, da of late John F. Lester, and has issue living, Samuel Robert Josiah *b* 1990, Olivia Joscelyne Isabel *b* 1993, — Jonathan Guy, *b* 1963; *ed* St Paul's, and Balliol Coll, Oxford (BA). *Residence* – 12 Ullswater Rd, SW13 9PJ. *Club* – Naval.

DAUGHTERS LIVING OF SECOND BARON

Hon Nancy Elizabeth (11 Harpes Rd, Summertown, Oxford), *b* 1931; *ed* St Andrews Univ (MA 1953).
Hon Veronica, *b* 1934; MRCS, and LRCP 1960: *m* 1961, Richard Alfred Hugh McWatters, of The Grove, Dundry, Bristol, son of late Sir Arthur Cecil McWatters, CIE, and has issue living, Rupert Charles, *b* 1967, — Philippa Mary, *b* 1964, — Bridget Penelope, *b* 1965.
Hon Jessica Catherine, *b* 1936; *ed* London Univ (BA 1958): *m* 1961, John Edward Chalmers Dow, and has issue living, Charlotte Mary, *b* 1963: *m* 1990, Kevin John Davis, eldest son of F. J. Davis, of Worcester Park, Surrey, and has issue living, Emily Jessica Lycett *b* 1992, — Juliette Elizabeth Chalmers, *b* 1966. *Residence* – 30 Norfolk Farm Rd, Pyrford, Woking, Surrey GU22 8LH.

WIDOW LIVING OF SON OF FIRST BARON

(Alice) Mary (1 Holly Oaks, Wormingford, Colchester, Essex), elder da of late Walter Richards, and formerly wife of John Hagon: *m* 1944, as his 2nd wife, Lt-Col Hon (Arthur) Maxwell Stamp, who *d* 1984.

WIDOW LIVING OF THIRD BARON

FRANCES DAWES (*Frances, Baroness Stamp*), da of late Charles Henry Bosworth, of Evanston, Illinois, USA: *m* 1932, the 3rd Baron, who *d* 1987. *Address* – c/o The Lord Stamp, The Flat, Pennyroyal, Village Lane, Hedgerley, Bucks SL2 3YU.

COLLATERAL BRANCH LIVING

Issue of late Lt-Col Hon (Arthur) Maxwell Stamp, 3rd son of 1st Baron, *b* 1915, *d* 1984: *m* 1st, 1938 (*m diss* 1943), Janet Tyler, da of B. Tyler Bryan, of Beaumont, Texas, USA; 2ndly, 1944, (Alice) Mary (ante), elder da of late Walter Richards, and formerly wife of John Hagon:—
(By 2nd *m*) Anthony Philip Josiah (Bonds Cottage, Wormingford, Colchester, Essex), *b* 1947; *ed* Winchester, and Jesus Coll, Camb (BA): *m* 1970, Rosemary Ann, only da of Hume Boggis-Rolfe, CB, CBE, of 22 Victoria Sq, SW1, and has three adopted children, Joseph Anthony, *b* 1975, — Marianna Rose, *b* 1977, — Laura Dorothea, *b* 1982. —— Marian Ellina, *b* 1945; *ed* Somerville Coll, Oxford (MA, DPhil): *m* 1967 (*m diss* 1984), Clinton Richard Dawkins, only son of Clinton John Dawkins, of Over Norton Park, Chipping Norton, Oxon. —— Alison Mary, *b* 1950; *ed* Somerville Coll, Oxford (BA): *m* 1980, Richard Cooke, of Sudbury House, Wrotham, Kent, elder son of late Canon Alfred Gordon Cooke, of The Rectory, St Columb Major, Cornwall, and has issue living, Maxwell Richard Gordon *b* 1985, Florence Mary *b* 1982, Hannah Marian *b* 1984.

PREDECESSORS – (1) *Sir* JOSIAH CHARLES Stamp, GCB, GBE, DSc, son of late Charles Stamp, of Yomah, Bexley; *b* 1880; was Assist Sec to Board of Inland Revenue 1916-19, Sec and Director Nobel Industries, Ltd 1919-26, and a Director of Imperial Chemical Industries, Ltd 1927-8; appointed a Member of Roy Commn on Income Tax 1919, British Member of Reparations Expert ("Dawes") Committee 1924, a Member of Coal Mins Enquiry Court 1925, a Reparation Expert for Great Britain 1929, and Chm Canadian Grain Futures Enquiry 1931; Chm and Pres of Executive of London, Midland and Scottish Railway, a Director of Bank of England, Adviser of Economic Co-ordination, Past Pres Roy Statistical So, and Pres National Institute of Economic Research and of So of Genealogists, Col Comdg Engineer and Railway Staff Corps (TA) and Hon Col Transportation, RE (Supplementary Reserve); Charter Mayor of Beckenham 1935, and Pres British Asso for Advancement of Science 1936: *m* 1903, Olive Jessie, who *d* as a result of enemy action during World War II, 16 April 1941, da of Alfred Marsh; *cr Baron Stamp*, of Shortlands, co Kent (peerage of United Kingdom) 1938; *d* as a result of enemy action during World War II, 16 April 1941; *s* by his el son (by decision of House of Lords 10 Sept 1941, and approved by HM King George VI, the decision being analogous to the Law of Property Act 1925, which provides that where two persons have died in circumstances rendering it uncertain which of them survived the other, such deaths should be presumed to have occurred in order of seniority) (2) WILFRID CARLYLE, 2nd Baron, *b* 1904: *m* 1929, Katharine Mary, who *d* 1985, da of Tom Wickett, of Redruth; *d* as a result of enemy action during World War II, 16 April 1941; *s* by his brother (3) TREVOR CHARLES, 3rd Baron, *b* 1907, MD, MRCS England and LRCP London, FRCPath, Prof Emeritus of Bacteriology, Lond Univ: *m* 1932, Frances Dawes, da late Charles Henry Bosworth, of Evanston Illinois, USA; *d* 1987; *s* by his elder son (4) TREVOR CHARLES BOSWORTH, 4th Baron and present peer.

Stanhope, Earldom of; see Chesterfield and Stanhope.

Stanley, Barony of (cr 1456); see Loudoun, Countess of.

STANLEY OF ALDERLEY, BARON SHEFFIELD AND (Stanley) (Baron I 1783, UK 1839 and 1848 and Bt E 1660)

Without changing

THOMAS HENRY OLIVER STANLEY (*Baron Stanley of Alderley*), 8th Baron Sheffield, 8th Baron Stanley of Alderley, and 14th Baronet; *b* 28 Sept 1927; *s* 1971; *ed* Wellington Coll; Capt (ret), Coldm Gds; DL Gwynedd 1985; Member Cttee of Management RNLI since 1981, Chm Fund Raising since 1985; Gov St Edward's Sch, Oxford: *m* 1955, Jane Barrett, da of late Ernest George Hartley, of Lower Farm, Milton-under-Wychwood, Oxon, and has issue.

Arms – Argent, on a bend azure, three bucks' heads cabossed or: a crescent for difference. **Crest** – On a chapeau gules, turned up ermine, an eagle with wings expanded or preying upon an infant proper, swaddled gules, handed argent. **Supporters** – (appertaining to the Barony of Stanley of Alderley) — *Dexter*, a stag or, gorged with a ducal crown, line reflexed over the back, and charged on the shoulder with a mullet azure; *sinister*, a lion reguardant proper, gorged with a plain collar argent charged with three escallops gules.
Residence – Trysglwyn Fawr, Rhos y Bol, Amlwch, Anglesey.

SONS LIVING

Hon RICHARD OLIVER, *b* 24 April 1956; *ed* St Edward's Sch, Oxford, and Univ Coll, London (BSc): *m* 1983, Carla Mary Angela, el da of Dr Kenneth Thomas Clyde McKenzie, of 14 The Crescent, Solihull, and has had issue, Oliver Richard Hugh, *b* 1986, *d* 1989, — Maria Elizabeth Jane, *b* 1988, — Imogen Alexandra Ruth, *b* 1990, — Hermione Helena Rose, *b* 1992.
Hon Charles Ernest, *b* 1960; *ed* St Edward's Sch, Oxford, and Nottingham Univ (BA): *m* 1989, Beverley Ann, elder da of Michael Emmitt, of Swineshead, Lincs, and has issue living, Venetia Jane, *b* 1992. *Residence* – 34 Rosaline Rd, SW6 7QT.
Hon Harry John, *b* 1963; *ed* St Edward's Sch, Oxford, Univ Coll, London (LLB), and Camb Univ (LLM).

DAUGHTER LIVING

Hon Lucinda Maria, *b* 1958: *m* 1983, Peter Brazel, son of late Benedict Brazel, of Lyndhurst, S Australia, and has issue living, Thomas Owen, *b* 1984, — Harry Jack, *b* 1987, — Jack Alexander, *b* 1988. *Residence* – 1 Clarence St, Shepparton, Victoria 3630, Australia.

BROTHER LIVING (*Raised to the rank of a Baron's son* 1973)

Hon Richard Morgan Oliver, *b* 1931; *ed* Winchester and New Coll, Oxford: *m* 1956, Phyllida Mary Katharine, da of Lt-Col Clive Grantham Austin, RHA, JP, DL (E Scarbrough), and has issue living, Martin Thomas Oliver (Raegetenstrasse 18, CH-6318 Walchwil, Switzerland), *b* 1957; *ed* Harrow; 17th/21st Lancers (ret): *m* 1982, Georgina Mary Victoria, only da of George Grimm, of 10 Radnor Walk, SW3 and has issue living, Oliver George *b* 1984, Hugh Richard Timothy *b* 1992, Clementine Masha *b* 1986, Isabella Kate *b* 1988, — Oliver Hugh (42 Franconia Rd, SW4), *b* 1959; *ed* Harrow; Coldstream Gds (ret): *m* 1985, Sophie Elizabeth, da of Nicholas Holmes, of Hook Norton Manor, Banbury, Oxon, and has issue living, Arabella Anne *b* 1989, Sabrina Laura *b* 1992, Susannah Rose *b* 1994, — Serena Emma Rose (PO Box 305, Madang, Papua New Guinea), *b*

1961: *m* 1987, Matthew Hilary Jebb (*see* Pollen, Bt, colls), and has issue living, Edwin Francis *b* 1988, a son *b* 1990, Theodore Philip *b* 1992, — Laura Sylvia Kathleen, *b* 1968. *Residence* – Wood End House, Ridgeway Lane, Lymington, Hants S041 8AA.

DAUGHTER LIVING OF SIXTH BARON

Hon Edwina Maureen, *b* 1933: *m* 1st, 1953 (*m diss* 1966), John Dawnay Innes, who *d* 1966 (V Downe, colls); 2ndly, 1968, J Philip Epstein, and has issue living, (by 1st *m*), Thomas John Stanley (64 Monnow St, Monmouth), *b* 1954; *ed* Eton: *m* 1989, Irma Fingal-Rock, and has issue living, Oliver Edward Zachariah FINGAL-ROCK INNES *b* 1984, Aphrodite Irma Emilie Clementine FINGAL-ROCK INNES *b* 1987, — Richard James (57 Walham Grove, SW6), *b* 1955: *m* 1987, Auriol I., yr da of R. H. F. Stanton, of Bungay, Suffolk, and has issue living, Archibald John Stanton *b* 1992, Dominic Robert *b* 1994, — Mary Clementine Adelaide, *b* 1960: *m* 1986, Alexander Nikolaevich Drewchin, of Box 920, RD1 Honesdale, Pennsylvania 18431, USA. *Residence* – 146 Benhill Rd, SE5 7LZ.

DAUGHTER LIVING OF FIFTH BARON

Hon Victoria Venetia, *b* 1917: *m* 1942, Lt-Cdr James Douglas Woods, Roy Canadian Naval VR, and has issue living, Virginia Louise, *b* 1943, — Teresa Clare, *b* 1946. *Residence* – 31 Boswell Av, Toronto 180, Ont, Canada.

WIDOW LIVING OF SIXTH BARON

KATHLEEN MARGARET (*Kathleen, Baroness Stanley of Alderley*) (1 Links Court, Grouville, Jersey), da of late Cecil Murray Wright, of Malden, Surrey, and widow of Sir Edmund Frank Crane: *m* 1961, as his 4th wife, the 6th Baron, who *d* 1971.

PREDECESSORS – (1) Rt Hon JOHN Holroyd, MP for Coventry: *cr Baron Sheffield*, of Dunnamore, co Meath (peerage of Ireland) 1781, *Baron Sheffield*, of Roscommon (peerage of Ireland) 1783 with remainder to the das of his 1st *m* and their heirs male, *Baron Sheffield*, of Sheffield, co York (peerage of United Kingdom) 1802, and *Viscount Pevensey* and *Earl of Sheffield* (peerage of Ireland) 1816; Pres of Board of Agriculture 1803, and Lord of Board of Trade, etc; *d* 1821; *s* by his son (2) GEORGE AUGUSTUS FREDERICK CHARLES, 2nd Earl; *b* 1802; a Lord-in-Waiting to HM Queen Victoria 1858-9: *m* 1825, Harriet, da of 2nd Earl of Harewood; *d* 1870; *s* by his son (3) HENRY NORTH, 3rd Earl; *b* 1832; MP for Sussex E (C) 1857-65; *d* 1909, when the Irish Barony (*cr* 1781), the United Kingdom Barony (*cr* 1802), and the Earldom (*cr* 1816) became *ext*; *s* in the Irish Barony (*cr* 1783) under the special remainder by his kinsman (4) EDWARD LYULPH, PC, 4th Baron Stanley of Alderley (grandson of Lady Maria Josepha Holroyd, da of 1st Earl of Sheffield) (see * infra); *b* 1839; in 1909 *s* to *Barony of Sheffield* (*cr* 1783): MP for Oldham (*L*) 1880-85: *m* 1873, Mary Katharine, CBE, who *d* 1929, da of late Sir (Isaac) Lowthian Bell, 1st Bt; *d* 1925; *s* by his son (5) ARTHUR LYULPH, KCMG, 5th Baron; *b* 1875; was Director of National Bank of Australasia and of Australian Mercantile, Land, and Finance Co (Limited); formerly a Member of Woods and Forests Committee; sometime Parliamentary Private Sec (unpaid) to Postmaster-Gen (Rt Hon S. C. Buxton, MP), Private Sec (unpaid) Office of Woods and Forests, and a Member of Select Committee on Peerages in abeyance: Gov of Victoria 1914-20: MP for Cheshire, Eddisbury Div (*L*) Jan 1906 to Jan 1910; *m* 1905, Margaret Evelyn, who *d* 1964, da of Henry Evans Gordon, of 59 Cadogan Gdns, SW; *d* 1931; *s* by his son (6) EDWARD JOHN, 6th Baron; *b* 1907: *m* 1st, 1932 (*m diss* 1936), Lady Victoria Audrey Beatrice Chetwynd-Talbot, da of late Charles John Alton Chetwynd, Viscount Ingestre, MVO (E Shrewsbury); 2ndly, 1944 (*m diss* 1948), Louise Sylvia, who *d* 1977, da of Arthur Hawkes, and widow of Douglas Fairbanks, Sr; 3rdly, 1951 (*m diss* 1957), Thérèse, da of Gen Husson, of Toulon, France; 4thly, 1961, Kathleen Margaret, da of late Cecil Murray Wright, and widow of Sir Edmund Frank Crane; *d* 3 March 1971, *s* by his brother (7) LYULPH HENRY VICTOR OWEN, 7th Baron *b* 1915, *d* 23 June 1971; *s* by his cousin (8) THOMAS HENRY (3rd son of Lt-Col Hon Oliver Hugh Stanley, DSO, yst son of 4th Baron), 8th Baron and present peer; also Baron Stanley of Alderley, and Baron Eddisbury.

*(1) THOMAS Stanley, Bar-at-law, descended from Hon Sir John Stanley, 3rd son of 1st Baron Stanley (*see* E Derby); *cr* a *Baronet* 1660; *s* by his son (2) Sir PETER, 2nd Bt; was High Sheriff of Cheshire 1678; *d* 1701; *s* by his son (3) Sir THOMAS, 3rd Bt; *d* 1721; *s* by his el son (4) Sir JAMES, 4th Bt; *d* 1746; *s* by his brother (5) Sir EDWARD, 5th Bt; *d* 1755; *s* by his son (6) Sir JOHN THOMAS, 6th Bt; was a Gentleman of the Privy Chamber and Clerk of the Cheque of the Yeomen of the Guard; *d* 1807; *s* by his son (7) Sir JOHN THOMAS, 7th Bt; *cr Baron Stanley of Alderley* (peerage of United Kingdom) 1839: *m* Lady Maria Josepha Holroyd, da of 1st Earl of Sheffield; *d* 1850; *s* by his son (8) EDWARD JOHN, PC, 2nd Baron, who in 1848 had been *cr Baron Eddisbury*, of Winnington (peerage of United Kingdom); *b* 1802; sat as MP for Hendon 1831, and for N Cheshire 1832-41, and 1847-8; was Under-Sec of Home Dept 1834, Sec to Treasury 1835-41, Under-Sec for Foreign Affairs 1846-52, Vice-Pres of Board of Trade 1852, Pres of Board of Trade 1855-8, and Postmaster-Gen 1859-66: *m* 1826, Hon Henrietta Maria, who *d* 1895, da of 13th Viscount Dillon; *d* 1869; *s* by his son (9) HENRY EDWARD JOHN, 3rd Baron; *b* 1827; Sec of Legation at Athens 1854-9; *dsp*; *s* by his brother (10) EDWARD LYULPH, PC, 4th Baron, who *s* as 4th Baron Sheffield 1909 (ante).

STANSGATE, VISCOUNTCY OF (Benn) (Viscount UK 1942, disclaimed 1963)

Rt Hon ANTHONY (NEIL) WEDGWOOD BENN, MP, *b* 3 April 1925; *s* as 2nd Viscount 17 Nov 1960, but made it known that he did not wish to claim the Viscountcy; disclaimed his peerage for life 31 July 1963, having unsuccessfully attempted to renounce his right of succession 1955 and 1960; *ed* Westminster, and New Coll, Oxford (MA); CIEE; FRSA; Hon LLD Strathclyde; Hon DTech Bradford; Hon DSc Aston; late PO RAFVR, and Sub-Lt Fleet Air Arm; 1939-45 War; Postmaster-Gen 1964-66, and Min of Tech 1966-70; Chm of Labour Party 1971-2; Sec of State for Industry, and Min of Posts and Telecommunications 1974-75, Sec of State for Energy 1975-79; MP for SE Div of Bristol (*Lab*) 1950-60; re-elected May 1961, but debarred from sitting by judgement of Election Court 1961; MP for SE Div of Bristol 1963-83, and for Chesterfield since 1984; PC 1964: *m* 1949, Caroline Middleton, MA, da of late James Milton De Camp, of Handasyde Court, Cincinnati, USA, and has issue.

Arms – See Benn, Bt (*cr* 1914), not used.
Residence – 12 Holland Park Av, W11.

SONS LIVING

STEPHEN MICHAEL WEDGWOOD, *b* 21 Aug 1951: *m* 1988, Ishika Nita, da of Stuart Ashley Bowes, of Tel Aviv Univ, Ramat Hashaaron, Israel, and has issue living, Daniel, *b* 10 Dec 1991, — Emily, *b* 1989.
Hilary James Wedgwood, *b* 1953: *m* 1st, 1973, Rosalind Retey, who *d* 1979; 2ndly, 1982, Sally Clark, and has issue, three sons and one da.
Joshua William Wedgwood, *b* 1958: *m* 1984, Elizabeth Feeney, and has issue, one son.

DAUGHTER LIVING

Melissa Anne Wedgwood, *b* 1957.

BROTHER LIVING

Hon David Julian Wedgwood, *b* 1928; *ed* Balliol Coll, Oxford (BA honours 1951): *m* 1959, June Mary, MA Oxon, el da of late Ernest Charles Barraclough, and has issue living, Piers Michael Wedgwood, *b* 1962, — Cordelia Frances Margaret Wedgwood, *b* 1964. *Residences* – 4 Liskeard Gdns, Blackheath, SE3; Stansgate Cottage, nr Steeple, Southminster, Essex.

PREDECESSOR – (1) (WILLIAM) WEDGWOOD Benn, DSO, DFC, PC, 2nd son of Sir John William Benn, 1st Bt (*cr* 1914); *b* 1877; Sec of State for India 1929-31, and Sec of State for Air 1945-46; sat as MP for St Geroge's Div of Tower Hamlets (L) 1906-18, for Leith 1918-27, for Aberdeen, N Div (Lab) 1928-31, and Gorton Div of Manchester 1937-41; *cr Viscount Stansgate*, of Stansgate, co Essex (peerage of United Kingdom) 1942: *m* 1920, Margaret Eadie, who *d* 1991, da of late Daniel Turner Holmers, formerly MP for Govan Div of Lanarkshire; *d* 1960; *s* by his 2nd son (2) ANTHONY (NEIL) WEDGWOOD, 2nd Viscount, until he disclaimed his Peerage 1963.

STEDMAN, BARONESS (Stedman) (Life Baroness 1974)

PHYLLIS STEDMAN, OBE, da of Percy Adams; *b* 14 July 1916; *ed* County Gram Sch, Peterborough; a Member of Board of Peterborough Development Corpn 1972-75, and Vice-Chm of Cambs County Council 1973-75: appointed a Baroness-in-Waiting to HM 1975; Govt spokesman in House of Lords on Transport, Environment and Trade: Parl Under Sec at Dept of the Environment 1979-80; Vice-Pres Nat PHAB, Assoc of District Councils, and Assoc of Local Councils; mem Council of Fire Services Nat Benevolent Fund: *cr* OBE (Civil) 1956, and *Baroness* Stedman, of Longthorpe, in City of Peterborough (Life Baroness) 1974: *m* 1941, Henry William Stedman, who *d* 1988.
Residence – 1 Grovelands, Thorpe Rd, Peterborough, Cambs PE3 6AQ.

STERLING OF PLAISTOW, BARON (Sterling) (Life Baron 1991)

JEFFREY MAURICE STERLING, CBE, son of Harry Sterling; *b* 27 Dec 1934; *ed* Reigate Gram Sch, Preston Manor County Sch, and Guildhall Sch of Music; Advisor, Paul Schweder & Co, Stock Exchange, 1955-57, and G. Eberstadt & Co 1957-62, Finance Dir Gen Guarantee Corpn 1962-64, Man Dir Gula Investments Ltd 1964-69, Chm Sterling Guarantee Trust plc 1969-85, when it merged with P&O Steam Navigation Co, Chm P&O Steam Navigation Co since 1983; Member British Airways Bd 1979-82; Special Advisor to Sec of State for Industry 1982-83, since when to Sec of State for Trade & Industry; Chm Organisation Cttee World ORT (Organisation for Rehabilitation by Training) Union 1969-73 (Member Exec since 1966), Chm ORT Technical Services since 1974, Vice-Pres British ORT since 1978; Pres Gen Council of British Shipping 1990-91; Dep-Chm and Hon Treas London Celebrations Cttee, HM's Silver Jubilee, 1975-83; Chm Young Vic Co 1975-83, Chm of Govs Royal Ballet Sch since 1983, Gov Royal Ballet since 1986; Vice-Chm and Chm of Exec Motability since 1977; Hon Fell Inst of Marine Engrs 1991; CBE 1977, Knt 1985, and *Baron Sterling of Plaistow*, of Pall Mall, City of Westminster (Life Baron) 1991: *m* 1985, Dorothy Ann, da of — Smith, and has issue, one da.

𝕬rms – Chequy argent and sable, three lyres bendwise in bend gules. 𝕮rest – A salamander statant upon its hind legs sable, enflamed proper, and holding between the forefeet the Hebrew letter chaim argent.
Residence – 17 Brompton Sq, SW3. *Office*- The Peninsular and Oriental Steam Navigation Company, Peninsular House, 79 Pall Mall, SW1Y 5EJ. *Clubs* – Garrick, Carlton, Hurlingham.

STEVENS OF LUDGATE, BARON (Stevens) (Life Baron 1987)

DAVID ROBERT STEVENS, son of (Arthur) Edwin Stevens, CBE, of Esher, Surrey, by his wife Kathleen Alberta, da of Charles James; *b* 26 May 1936; *ed* Stowe, and Sidney Sussex Coll, Camb (MA); Dir Philip Hill Higginson Erlangers 1959-68, Hill Samuel Securities since 1968, Drayton Group 1968-74, Samuel Montagu (Man Dir) 1974-85, Chm City & Foreign since 1976, Drayton Far East since 1976, English & Internat since 1976, Consolidated Venture (formerly Montagu Boston) since 1979, Drayton Consolidated since 1980, Drayton Japan since 1980, Chm EDC for Civil Engrs 1984-86, United Newspapers since 1981 (Dir since 1974), Express Newspapers since 1985, and Chm and Chief Exec MIM Britannia Ltd (formerly Montagu Investment Management Ltd) since 1980; *cr Baron Stevens of Ludgate*, of Ludgate, in the City of London (Life Baron) 1987: *m* 1st, 1961 (*m diss* 1970), Patricia Ann, da of George Warren Rose, of St George's Hill, Weybridge, Surrey; 2ndly, 1977, Mrs Melissa Sadoff, who *d* 1989, da of Milos Milicevic and of Countess Andrassy; 3rdly, 1990, Mrs Meriza Giori, and has issue by 1st *m*.

Arms – Argent a bear rampant proper and a chief embattled azure. **Crest** – A triple mount vert thereon a crest coronet or the lesser finials (two manifest) pearled proper statant within the same a swan wings displayed proper about the neck two ribands nowed and the ends flotant to the rear gules and argent. **Supporters** – *Dexter*, a lion sejant erect and guardant or; *sinister*, a cairn terrier also sejant erect and guardant proper, the compartment comprising a grassy mount also proper. **Motto** – Perseverance.
Address – 11 Devonshire Sq, EC2M 4YR. *Club* – White's.

SON LIVING *(By 1st marriage)*

Hon Andrew David, *b* 1966.

DAUGHTER LIVING *(By 1st marriage)*

Hon Judith Ann, *b* 1964.

STEWARTBY, BARON (Stewart) (Life Baron 1992)

(BERNARD HAROLD) IAN (HALLEY) STEWART, RD, PC, only son of Prof Harold Charles Stewart, CBE (grandson of late Sir Halley Stewart, *see* Stewart, Bt, *cr* 1937); *b* 10 Aug 1935; *ed* Haileybury, and Jesus Coll, Camb (MA, DLitt 1978); RNVR 1954-56, Lieut-Cdr RNR (RD 1972); Dir Brown Shipley & Co (Merchant Bankers) 1971-83, Brown Shipley Holdings 1981-83, and Victory Insurance 1976-83; PPS to Rt Hon Sir Geoffrey Howe (as Chancellor of the Exchequer) 1979-83, Under-Sec MOD (Defence Procurement) Jan-Oct 1983, Economic Sec Treasury 1983-87, Min of State for the Armed Forces 1987-88, and for NI 1988-89; Chm Throgmorton Trust plc since 1990, Member Public Expenditure Cttee 1977-79, Public Accounts Cttee 1991-92, and British Academy Cttee for Sylloge of Coins of British Isles since 1967; Vice-Chm Westminster Cttee for the Protection of Children since 1975, Life Gov Haileybury 1977, Trustee Sir Halley Stewart Trust since 1978, Vice-Pres St John's Ambulance for Herts since 1977, CStJ 1986, KStJ 1992; FBA 1981, FRSE 1986, FSA, FSA(Scot); author; MP Hitchin (C) 1974-83, and N Herts 1983-92; *cr* PC 1989, Kt Bach 1991, and *Baron Stewartby*, of Portmoak, in the District of Perth and Kinross (Life Baron) 1992: *m* 1966, Deborah Charlotte, da of Hon William de l'Aigle Buchan (*see* B Tweedsmuir), and has issue.

Arms – Or, a fess chequy azure and argent between a portcullis with chains in chief, and a lymphad, sails furled, oars in action sable, flagged gules in base all within a bordure azure, a label of three points gules. **Crest** – A lymphad as in the shield between two fleurs-de-lys or. **Supporters** – *Dexter*, a stag proper attired or gorged with a collar engrailed gules; *sinister*, a lion proper gorged with a collar engrailed chequy argent and gules.
Address – c/o House of Lords, SW1A 0PP. *Clubs* – MCC, Hawks, RAC.

SON LIVING

Hon Henry Ernest Alexander Halley, *b* 1972; *ed* Haileybury, and Jesus Coll, Camb; 2nd Lieut Royal Scots.

DAUGHTERS LIVING

Hon Lydia Barbara Rose Anna Phoebe, *b* 1969.
Hon (Dorothy) Louisa Charlotte Amabel, *b* 1970.

STOCKS, BARONY OF (Stocks) (Extinct 1975)

DAUGHTERS LIVING OF LIFE BARONESS

Hon Mary Ann, *b* 1915: *m* 1942, Arthur Patterson, CMG, and has issue.
Hon Helen Jane, JP, *b* 1920. *Residence* – 44 Regent's Park Rd, NW1.

STOCKTON, EARL OF (Macmillan) (Earl UK 1984)

ALEXANDER DANIEL ALAN MACMILLAN, 2nd Earl; *b* 10 Oct 1943; *s* 1986; *ed* Eton, Univ of Paris, and Strathclyde Univ; Chm Macmillan Publishing Ltd since 1980: *m* 1970 (*m diss* 1991), Hélène Birgitte (Bitta), da of late Alan Douglas Christie Hamilton, of Stable Green, Mitford, Northumberland, and has issue.

Arms – Argent a chief or overall between three open books proper edged or and bound azure those in chief inscribed respectively in letters sable $'Miseres' and $'Discere' and that in base also in letters sable inscribed $'Succo' and as many mullets azure a lion rampant sable. **Crests** – Upon a helm with a wreath or azure and sable within sprigs of oak fructed or a dexter cubit arm and a sinister arm embowed both proper the dexter hand gauntletted or and with the other brandishing a two handed sword proper hilt pommel and quillons sable. **Supporters** – *Dexter* a lion rampant gules; *sinister* an American bald headed eagle proper the compartment comprising a crenelated wall proper in the portal thereof an anchor azure and joined on either side by two bars wavy azure to a grassy mount growing from that on the dexter a long branch and from that on the sinister a thistle both proper.
Residence – 35 Cheyne Court, SW3 5TR; *Office* - 4 Little Essex St, WC2R 3LF.

SON LIVING

DANIEL MAURICE ALAN (*Viscount Macmillan of Ovenden*), *b* 9 Oct 1974.

DAUGHTERS LIVING

Lady Rebecca Elizabeth, *b* 1980.
Lady Louisa Alexandra, *b* 1982.

BROTHERS LIVING AND DECEASED

Joshua Edward Andrew, *b* 1945; *ed* Balliol Coll, Oxford; *dunm* 1965.
Hon Adam Julian Robert, *b* 1948; *ed* Eton, and Univ of Strasbourg: *m* 1982, Sarah Anne Mhuire, yr da of late Dr Brian Mac-Greevy, of 85 Onslow Sq, SW7, and has issue living, Frederick Maurice Brian, *b* 1990, — Sophia Elizabeth Katherine, *b* 1985, — Alice Charlotte Rose, *b* 1987. *Residence* – 65 Cambridge St, SW1V 4PS.
Hon David Maurice Benjamin, *b* 1957; *ed* Harrow.

SISTER DECEASED

Hon Rachael Mary Georgina, *b* 1955: *m* 1982 (*m diss* 1986), Leith Corbett, only son of H. M. Corbett, of Sydney, NSW, Australia; *dsp* 1987.

AUNT LIVING (*Daughter of 1st Earl*)

Lady (Ann) Caroline, *b* 1923: *m* 1944, Julian Tufnell Faber (Fisher's Gate, Withyham, Hartfield, E Sussex TN7 4BB; Flat 4, 17-21 Sloane Court West, SW3), son of late Alfred Faber, and has had issue, Michael David Tufnell (2A Lyall Mews, SW1; Bay House, Sandwich, Kent), *b* 1945; *ed* Eton, and Trin Coll, Camb: *m* 1968, Catherine Suzanne, da of Comte Robert de Braine, of Cannes, France, and has issue living, Richard Julian Robert *b* 1974, Elizabeth Anne Catherine *b* 1971, — Mark James Julian, *b* 1950; *ed* Eton, and Balliol Coll, Oxford: *m* 1983, Ann (12 Tite St, SW3), da of Christopher Griffith, of Natal, South Africa, and *d* 1991, leaving issue, Alexander John Julian *b* 1986, Luke Christopher Michael *b* 1990, Thomas Mark Nicholas, *b* (*posthumous*) 1992, — David James Christian, MP (House of Commons, SW1), *b* 1961; *ed* Eton, and Balliol Coll, Oxford; MP Westbury (*C*) since 1992: *m* 1988, Sally Elizabeth, elder da of Mrs Kenneth J. Gilbert, of Yelverton, Devon, and has issue living, Henry Mark Tufnell *b* 1992, — James Edwin Charles (30 Harcourt Terr, SW10), *b* 1964; *ed* Eton, and Edinburgh Univ, — Anne Christine Adriane (27 Tregunter Rd, SW10), *b* 1944; JP Inner London 1994: *m* 1970 (*m diss* 1981), Michael Roger Lewis Cockerell, and has issue living, William Michael Victor Lewis *b* 1973, Sophia Charlotte Evelyn *b* 1970.

MOTHER LIVING

Hon Katharine Margaret Alice Ormsby-Gore (*Viscountess Macmillan of Ovenden*), DBE, 2nd da of 4th Baron Harlech, KG, GCMG, PC: *m* 1942, Maurice Victor, Viscount Macmillan of Ovenden, PC, MP, who *dvp* 1984, only son of 1st Earl. *Residence* – 9 Warwick Square, SW1.

PREDECESSORS – **(1)** Rt Hon (MAURICE) HAROLD Macmillan, OM, PC, FRS, 3rd and yst son of late Maurice Crawford Macmillan, *b* 1894, served 1914-18 War as Capt Gren Gds (thrice wounded), MP for Stockton-on-Tees 1924-29 and 1931-45, and for Bromley 1945-64, Parlimentary Sec Min of Supply 1940-42, Under-Sec of State for the Colonies Feb-Dec 1942, Min Resident in N Africa Dec 1942 — May 1945, Sec of State for Air May-July 1945, Min of Housing and Local Govt 1951-54, of Defence 1954-55, Sec of State for Foreign Affairs April-Dec 1955, Chancellor of the Exchequer 1955-57, Prime Minister and First Lord of the Treasury 1957-63, Chancellor of Oxford Univ 1960-86, Pres Macmillan Ltd 1974-86, Hon Freeman City of London 1961; *cr Viscount Macmillan of Ovenden*, of Chelwood Gate, in the County of E Sussex, and of Stockton-on-Tees, in the County of Cleveland, and *Earl of Stockton* (peerage of United Kingdom) 1984: *m* 1920, Lady Dorothy Evelyn Cavendish, GBE, who *d* 1966, 3rd da of 9th Duke of Devonshire, KG, GCMG, GCVO, PC; *d* 1986; *s* by his grandson **(2)** ALEXANDER DANIEL ALAN (eldest son of Maurice Victor, Viscount Macmillan of Ovenden, only son of 1st Earl), 2nd Earl and present peer; also Viscount Macmillan of Ovenden.

STODART OF LEASTON, BARON (Stodart) (Life Baron 1981)

JAMES ANTHONY STODART, PC, son of late Col Thomas Stodart, CIE, IMS; *b* 6 June 1916; *ed* Wellington; Under-Sec of State for Scotland 1963-64, Parl Sec Min of Agric, Fisheries and Food 1970-72, Min of State Min of Agric, Fisheries and Food 1972-74; MP for Edinburgh West (*C*) 1959-74; Chm Agric Credit Corpn 1975-87; Chm Cttee of Enquiry into Local Govt in Scotland 1980; *cr* PC 1974, and *Baron Stodart of Leaston*, of Humbie, in the District of E Lothian (Life Baron) 1981: *m* 1940, Hazel Jean, da of Lieut Ronald James Usher, DSC, RN (*see* Usher, Bt, colls).
Residence – Lorimers, N Berwick, E Lothian. *Clubs* – New (Edinburgh), Farmers'.

STODDART OF SWINDON, BARON (Stoddart) (Life Baron 1983)

DAVID LEONARD STODDART, son of late Arthur Leonard Stoddart, by his wife Queenie Victoria Price; *b* 4 May 1926; *ed* St Clement Danes and Henley Gram Schs; mem Reading County Borough Council 1954-72; MP for Swindon 1970-83; an Assistant Govt Whip 1975; a Lord Commr for HM Treasury 1976-77; *cr Baron Stoddart of Swindon*, of Reading in the Royal County of Berkshire (Life Baron) 1983: *m* 1st, 1946 (*m diss* 1960), Doreen M. Maynard; 2ndly, 1961, Jennifer, adopted da of late Mrs Lois Percival-Alwyn, of Battle, Sussex, and has issue by 1st and 2nd *m*.
Residence – Sintra, 37A Bath Road, Reading, Berks.

SONS LIVING *(By 2nd marriage)*

Hon Howard David, *b* 1966; *ed* Alfred Sutton Boys' Sch, Reading.
Hon Mathwyn Hugh, *b* 1969; *ed* Alfred Sutton Boys' Sch, Reading.

DAUGHTER LIVING *(By 1st marriage)*

Hon Janet Victoria, *b* 1947, *m* 1967, Jack Pudney, of 3 Delbridge Drive, Kenwick, Western Australia, and has issue.

STOKES, BARON (Stokes) (Life Baron 1969)

DONALD GRESHAM STOKES, TD, son of Harry Potts Stokes, of Rock Towers Hotel, Looe; *b* 22 March 1914; *ed* Blundell's Sch, and Harris Inst of Technology, Preston; F Eng; FIMechE; MSAE; FIMI; FCIT; FIRTE; Hon LLD Lancaster; Hon DTech Loughborough; Hon DSc Southampton, and Salford; late Lt-Col REME; DL for Lancs; Gen Sales Manager Leyland Motors Ltd, 1950, Dir 1954, Chm and Managing Dir Leyland Motor Corpn, 1967, and of British Leyland Motor Corpn Ltd 1968, Ch Exec 1973 (Pres 1977-79); Chm Dutton-Forshaw Motor Group Ltd and Jack Barclay Ltd 1980-90; a Member of NW Economic Planning Council 1965-70; Chm NEDC for Electronics Industry 1966-68; a Dir of National Westminster Bank 1969-81; Chm of British Arabian Advisory Co 1977-85, Vice-Pres of Employers' Eng Fedn, a Member of Council CBI, a Member of Soc of Motor Manufacturers & Traders; Dir KBH Communications Ltd since 1985; Dir Scottish & Universal Investments Ltd 1980-92, and GWR Group since 1990; Chm Two Counties Radio Ltd since 1979; Dir Beherman Auto-Transports NV (Belgium) 1982-89; Fell of Keble Coll, Oxford since 1968; Pres Manchester Univ Inst of Science and Technology 1968-76; Chm The Dovercourt Motor Co Ltd 1982-90; Liveryman of Carmen Co; Officer of Order of Crown of Belgium; Cdr of the Order of Leopold II of Belgium; *cr* Knt 1965, and *Baron Stokes*, of Leyland, co Palatine of Lancaster (Life Baron) 1969: *m* 1939, Laura Elizabeth Courteney, da of Frederick C. Lamb, and has issue.

Arms – Gyronny of eight or and sable, a lion rampant double queued ermine, on a chief or an estoc erect between two speedwell flowers stalked and leaved proper. **Crest** – A demi lion double queued ermine, holding between the paws a piston with connecting rod argent, the crown inflamed proper. **Supporters** – *Dexter*, a lion reguardant double queued ermine; *sinister*, a horse argent, crined and unguled sable.
Residence – Branksome Cliff, Westminster Road, Poole, Dorset, BH13 6JW. *Club* – Royal Motor Yacht.

SON LIVING

Hon Michael Donald Gresham, *b* 1947; *ed* Southampton Univ (BSc): *m* 1st, 1970 (*m diss* 1980), Inger Anita, yr da of Douglas Percy, of Hotspur House, Hythe, Hants; 2ndly, 1986, Theresa, da of late John Edgar Papworth, and has issue. *Residence* – Longfield House, Mill Bank, Fladbury, Worcs WR10 2QA.

STONE, BARONY OF (Stone) (Extinct 1986)

SON LIVING OF LIFE BARON

Hon Richard Malcolm Ellis, (15 Blenheim Rd, NW8 0LU), *b* 1937; MA (Jurisprudence) Oxford; BM BCh, MRCGP: *m* 1970, Ruth Perry, and has isuse living, one son and two das.

DAUGHTER LIVING OF LIFE BARON

Hon Adrianne Barbara Ellis, *b* 1934; LCST: *m* 1957, Clive M. Marks, of 39 Farm Av, NW2.

STONEHAM, BARONY OF (Collins) (Extinct 1971)

SON LIVING OF LIFE BARON

Hon Ian Grenville (Mallards, Mileham, Kings Lynn, Norfolk), *b* 1941; *ed* Queen's Coll Taunton, and Kingston Gram Sch: *m* 1968, Sandra Felicity Bell, and has issue.

Stopford, Viscount; son of Earl of Courtown

STOPFORD OF FALLOWFIELD, BARONY OF (Stopford) (Extinct 1961)

SON LIVING OF LIFE BARON

Hon Thomas, *b* 1921; *ed* Manchester Gram Sch, and at Manchester Univ; European War 1939-45 as Capt RA: *m* 1943, Mary Howard, da of late Alfred James Small, of Manchester, and has issue. *Residence* – 16 Rhos Manor, Colwyn Avenue, Rhos-on-Sea, Clwyd LL28 4NP.

Stormont, Viscount; son of Earl of Mansfield and Mansfield.

Stourton, Baron; see Baron Mowbray, Segrave and Stourton.

STOW HILL, BARONY OF (Soskice) (Extinct 1979)

SONS LIVING OF LIFE BARON

Hon David William, *b* 1941; *ed* Winchester, and Trin Coll, Oxford: *m* 1966, Alison, da of Walter Black, and has issue.
Hon Oliver Cloudesley Hunter, *b* 1947; *ed* Winchester, and Trin Hall, Camb: *m* 1982, Janet L., el da of A. M. Martin, of St Louis, Missouri, USA, and has issue.

WIDOW LIVING OF LIFE BARON

SUSAN ISABELLA CLOUDESLEY (*Baroness Stow Hill*) (Church Row, Hampstead, NW3), da of William Auchterlony Hunter, of Spean Bridge, Inverness-shire: *m* 1940, Baron Stow Hill, PC, QC (Life Baron), who *d* 1979.

STRABOLGI, BARON (Kenworthy) (E 1318)
(Title pronounced "Strabogie")

Without noise

DAVID MONTAGUE DE BURGH KENWORTHY, 11th Baron; *b* 1st Nov 1914; *s* 1953; *ed* Gresham's Sch, Holt, Chelsea Sch of Art, and Paris; a co-heir to the Baronies of Cobham and Burgh; 1939-45 War in France and Middle East as Maj and acting Lt-Col RAOC; Capt of Queen's Bodyguard of Yeomen of the Guard and Dep Chief Whip, House of Lords 1974-79; Parl Priv Sec to Lord Privy Seal 1969-70; Assist Opposition Whip, House of Lords 1970-74, a Dep Speaker and Dep Chm of Cttees, House of Lords since 1986; Member British Section, Franco-British Council 1981; Dep Chm Bolton Building Soc 1983 (Chm 1986-87); Freeman City of London; Officier de la Légion d'Honneur: *m* 1st 1939 (*m diss* 1946), Denise, yr da of Jocelyn William Godefroi, MVO; 2ndly, 1947 (*m diss* 1951), Angela, only child of George Street, of Barton Lawn, nr Elstree, Herts; 3rdly, 1955 (*m diss* 1961), Myra Sheila Litewka; 4thly, 1961, Doreen Margaret, el da of late Alexander Morgan, of Ashton-under-Lyne, Lancs.

Arms – Argent, an eagle displayed gules surmounted by a bend vert, thereon three fleur-de-lis or. **Crest** – An eagle displayed argent, collared gules, holding in either claw a fleur-de-lis gold. *Address* – House of Lords, SW1.

BROTHER LIVING

Hon Basil Frederick da la Pole, TD (Hurlingham, Istanbul and Oxford Carlton Clubs, Anglo-Turkish Society), *b* 1920; *ed* Oundle, and Lincoln Coll, Oxford (MA); FInstPet; MInstT; Capt RA (TA Reserve); 1939-45 War in Norway, Greece, Crete, Middle East, India and Germany (prisoner); a Member of Turco-British Assocn, Oxford Union Soc, British Field Sports Soc and of Lincoln Soc: *m* 1948 (*m diss* 1965), Chloë, da of late Henry Gerard Walter Sandeman (*see* B Newton, 1985 Edn), and has issue living, Forflissa Viola, *b* 1949: *m* 1970, William John Healey, of Preston Lodge, Watermill Lane, Bexhill, Sussex, and has issue living, Patrick Joseph *b* 1975, Charlotte Eleanor *b* 1977, Megan Jane Florence *b* 1981, Rachel Lilian *b* 1983, — Nicolette Elizabeth, *b* 1950: *m* 1972, Prof John Russell Vincent, of 8 Charlotte St South, Bristol 1, and has issue living, Leo Jonathan *b* 1984, — Emma Yseult, *b* 1958: *m* 1988, P. Sebastian Kent, only son of late Maj Leonard Kent, of Amesbury, Wilts, and has issue living, Miranda Jacket *b* 1992.

SISTER LIVING

Hon Ferelith Rosemary Florence (*Hon Lady Hood*), *b* 1918: *m* 1946, Sir Harold Josph Hood, TD, 2nd Bt. *Residence* – 31 Avenue Rd, St John's Wood, NW8 6BS.

WIDOW LIVING OF SON OF TENTH BARON

Victoria HEWITT: *m* 1963, as his 2nd wife, Rev the Hon Jonathan Malcolm Atholl Kenworthy, who *d* 1991, and has issue (see colls infra).

COLLATERAL BRANCHES LIVING

Issue of late Rev the Hon Jonathan Malcolm Atholl Kenworthy, 2nd son of 10th Baron, *b* 1916, *d* 1991: *m* 1st, 1943, Joan Marion, who *d* 1963, da of late Claude Gilbert Gaster, of Tunbridge Wells; 2ndly, 1963, Victoria Hewitt (ante):—
(By 1st *m*) Elizabeth Joan, *b* 1944: *m* 1st, 1964 (*m diss* 1977), Geoffrey Greetham; 2ndly, 1978 (*m diss* 1986), David Woodman, and has issue living (by 1st *m*), Jonathan, *b* 1967, — Matthew, *b* 1968, — Alexander, *b* 1971, — (by 2nd *m*) Edward, *b* 1980, — Kathrine, *b* (twin) 1980. —— Brenda Marion, *b* 1946: *m* 1974, Geoffrey Collins, and has issue living, Ian Gareth, *b* 1981. —— (By 2nd *m*) ANDREW DAVID WHITLEY, *b* 25 Jan 1967. —— †James Atholl, *b* 1971; *d* 1993. —— Penelope Ruth, *b* 1964: *m* 1986, Dr Samuel B. P. Bass, son of late P. A. Bass, and has issue living, Oliver William, *b* 1993, — Laura Charlotte, *b* 1992.

Grandchildren of late Rev Hon Cuthbert Reginald Leatham Kenworthy, 2nd son of 9th Baron:—
Issue of late Maj Cuthbert Reginald D'Isney Kenworthy, Gordon Highlanders, *b* 1914, *d* 1987: *m* 1st, 1941 (*m diss* 1947), Patricia Kathleen, only da of late Brig Sir Francis William Crewe Fetherston-Godley, OBE, of St Lawrence, Jersey, CI; 2ndly, 1947 (*m diss* 1958), Joan Mary, da of Lt-Col R. A. G. Stewart, RM (ret), of Winthorpe House, Newark; 3rdly, 1960, Mrs Peggy Owtram (Rose Cottage, Jubilee Lane, Boundstone, Farnham, Surrey GU10 4TA):—
(By 1st *m*) David Patrick Francis, *b* 1942. —— (By 2nd *m*) Duncan Alexander D'Isney, *b* 1950: *m* 1975, Alwyn Jean Flack, and has issue living, Stewart Alexander D'Isney, *b* 1982, — Kirsten Jane, *b* 1979. *Residence* – 3 Grasslees, Rickleton, Washington, Tyne & Wear NE38 9JA. —— Sheena Mary, *b* 1948: *m* 1969, Allan de Jager, of 8 Allambic St, The Gap, Brisbane, Queensland 4061, Australia.

PREDECESSORS – **(1)** MADACH, 1st Earl of Atholl (*cr* S, *circa* 1122), was nephew of Malcolm III and Duncan I, Kings of Scotland; *s* by his son **(2)** MALCOLM, 2nd Earl; *s* by his son **(3)** HENRY, 3rd Earl; *s* by his da **(4)** ISABELLA, Countess of Atholl: *m* Thomas of Galloway (*jure uxoris* Earl of Atholl); *s* by her son **(5)** PATRICK, 5th Earl; murdered 1242; *s* by his aunt **(6)** FERELITH, Countess of Atholl, yr da of 3rd Earl: *m* David Hastings (*jure uxoris* Earl of Atholl); one of the Guarantors of the Treaty of Peace with Henry III 1244: *s* by her da **(7)** ADA, Countess of Atholl: *m* John of Strabolgi (or Strabogie), son of David of Strabolgi, and grandson of Duncan, Earl of Fife, who granted the lands of Strathbogie to the above-mentioned David; *s* by her son **(8)** DAVID, 8th Earl; joined the 7th Crusade under Louis IX of France; *d* of the plague at Carthage 1270; *s* by his son **(9)** JOHN, 9th Earl; taken prisoner by the English at Battle of Methven 1306, and subsequently executed in London: *m* Margery, da of Donald, Earl of Mar, and sister of Isabel, wife of Robert Bruce, King of Scotland; *s* by his son **(10)** DAVID (de Strabolgi), 10th Earl; summoned to Parliament as Lord Strabolgi 1318; *d* 1326; *s* by his el son **(11)** DAVID, 11th Earl of Atholl, and 2nd Lord Strabolgi; summoned to Parliament as Lord Strabolgi 1329-34; a famous soldier; accompanied his kinsman, Lord Balliol, in invasion of Scotland, when a much larger force of their opponents was defeated at battle of Dupplin Moor (tactics employed became model for English armies, and also affected military procedure on the Continent); *k* at battle of Kilblane 1335; *s* by his only son **(12)** DAVID, 12th Earl of Atholl and 3rd Lord Strabolgi; summoned

to Parliament as Lord Strabolgi 1335-1369; went to the wars in France with the Black Prince in 1355: *m* Catherine, da of 2nd Lord Ferrers of Groby; *dsp* 1369, when the Scottish Earldom of Atholl (*cr circa* 1122) ceased to be borne in England, and the English Barony of Strabolgi fell into abeyance between his das and co-heirs, and so remained until 1496, when it is held to have passed to the sole surviving representative of the co-heirs (13) Sir EDWARD Burgh, *de jure* 4th Baron (son of Thomas Burgh temp 1431-95); MP for co Lincoln: *m* 1477, Anne, da of Sir Thomas Cobham of Sterborough Castle, and widow of 2nd Baron Mountjoy; *d* 1528; *s* by his son (14) THOMAS, *de jure* 5th Baron; summoned to Parliament as Lord Burgh 1529: *m* 1st, 1497, Agnes, da of Sir William Tyrwhitt; 2ndly, 15—, Alice, da of William London, and widow (i) of Sir Thomas Bedingfeld and (ii) of Sir Edmund Rokewood; *d* 1550; *s* by his el surviving son (15) WILLIAM, 2nd Baron Burgh, and *de jure* 6th Baron Strabolgi; summoned to Parliament as Lord Burgh 1551-80: *m* 15—, Catherine, da of Edward, Earl of Lincoln; *d* 1584; *s* by his el surviving son (16) THOMAS, KG, 3rd Baron Burgh, and *de jure* 7th Baron Strabolgi; summoned to Parliament as Lord Burgh 1584-97; Ambassador to Scotland 1593, and Lord Dep of Ireland 1597: *m* 15—, Frances, da of John Vaughan, of Sutton-on-Derwent; *d* 1597; *s* by his el surviving son (17) ROBERT, 4th Baron Burgh, and *de jure* 8th Baron Strabolgi; *dsp* (about) 1600, when the Baronies fell into abeyance between his four sisters, among whose descendants they so remained until the abeyances were determined in 1916, the Barony of Strabolgi being called out of abeyance in favour of (18) CUTHBERT MATTHIAS Kenworthy (only surviving son of late Rev Joseph Kenworthy, R of Acworth, co York, by Harriet Elizabeth, da of Capt William Henry Cockerell Leatham, of Kirkham Abbey, Carleton, Yorkshire, and a co-heiress to the Barony), 9th Baron Strabolgi, *b* 1853; established his claim as a co-heir to the Baronies of Burgh and Cobham 1912; *m* 1884, Elizabeth Florence, who *d* 1951, da of George Buchanan Cooper, of Sacramento, California, USA; *d* 1934; *s* by his el son (19) JOSEPH MONTAGUE, RN, 10th Baron Strabolgi: *b* 1886; Lieut-Com (ret); with Grand Fleet, on Admiralty War Staff, and Assist Chief of Staff, Gibraltar during European War 1914-18; was Ch Opposition Whip in House of Lords 1937-45; sat as MP for Kingston-upon-Hull, Central Div (*L* afterwards *Lab*) 1919-29: *m* 1st, 1913 (*m diss* 1941), Doris Whitley, who *d* 1988, only child of late Sir Frederick Whitley-Thomson, JP, MP; 2ndly, 1941, Mrs Geraldine Mary (HAMILTON), who *d* 1970, da of late Maurice Francis; *d* 1953; *s* by his el son (20) DAVID MONTAGUE DE BURGH, 11th Baron Strabolgi and present peer.
(The title of Strabolgi is derived from the Aberdeenshire district of Strathbogie, being the valley of the river Bogie, which flows into the Deveron; and Strathbogie Castle was the seat of the Earls of Atholl.)

STRADBROKE, EARL OF (Rous) (Earl UK 1821, Bt E 1660)

JE·VIVE·EN·ESPOIR

(ROBERT) KEITH ROUS, 6th Earl and 11th Baronet; *b* 25 March 1937; *s* 1983; *ed* Harrow: *m* 1st, 1960 (*m diss* 1976), Dawn Antoinette, da of Thomas Edward Beverley, of Brisbane; 2ndly, 1977, Roseanna Mary, da of late Francis Reitman, MD (*see* B Lyveden, colls), and has issue living by 1st and 2nd *m*.

Arms – Sable, a fesse dancettée or, between three crescents argent. Crest – A pyramid of bay leaves, in the form of a cone vert. Supporters – *Dexter*, a lion, gorged with a wreath of olive proper; *Sinister*, a seahorse, gorged with a wreath of olive proper, the tail resting on an anchor azure.
Seat – Henham, Wangford, Beccles, Suffolk. *Address* – Mount Fyans, RSD Darlington, Victoria 3271, Australia.

SONS LIVING (*By 1st marriage*)

ROBERT KEITH (*Viscount Dunwich*), *b* 15 Nov 1961.
Hon Wesley Alexander, *b* 1972.

(*By 2nd marriage*)

Hon Hektor Fraser, *b* 1978.
Hon Maximilian Otho, *b* 1981.
Hon Henham Mowbray, *b* 1983.
Hon Winston Walberswick, *b* 1986.
Hon Yoxford Ulysses Uluru, *b* 1989.
Hon Ramsar Fyans, *b* 1992.

DAUGHTERS LIVING (*By 1st marriage*)

Lady Ingrid Arnel, *b* 1963, has issue living, Sam, *b* 1994.
Lady (Sophia) Rayner, *b* 1964; has issue living, Jake, *b* 1993, — Olivia, *b* 1990, — Kaylon, *b* 1991, — Cerana, *b* 1992.
Lady Heidi Simone, *b* 1966: *m* 1991, Timothy Crick, and has issue living, Joshua William, *b* 1992, — Thomas Oscar, *b* 1993.
Lady Pamela Keri, *b* 1968.
Lady Brigitte Aylena, *b* 1970.

(*By 2nd marriage*)

Lady Zea Katherina, *b* 1979.
Lady Minsmere Mathilda, *b* 1988.

BROTHER LIVING

Lt-Gen Hon Sir William Edward, KCB, OBE (RHQ Coldm Gds, Wellington Barracks, SW1), *b* 1939; *ed* Harrow, Angers Univ and RMA Sandhurst; Brig; commn'd Coldm Gds 1959, commanded 2nd Bn Coldm Gds 1979-81, and 1st Inf Bde 1983-84, Dir of Public Relations (Army) 1985-87, GOC 4 Armoured Div 1987-89, Comdt Staff Coll 1990-91, Mil Sec 1991-94, since when QMG; 27th Col Coldm Gds 1994; MBE (Mil) 1974, OBE (Mil) 1980, KCB (Mil) 1992: *m* 1970, Judith Rosemary, da of late Maj Jocelyn Arthur Persse, Rifle Bde, and has issue living, James Anthony Edward, *b* 1972, — Richard William Jocelyn, *b* 1975.

HALF-BROTHER LIVING

Hon John, *b* 1950; *ed* Gordonstoun, and Kent Univ (BA): *m* 1984, Zeenat, da of late Dr K. Hameed, of Lucknow, and has issue living, Maha Magdalene, *b* 1987, — Zoya Constance, *b* 1990. *Residences* – Clovelly Court, Bideford, Devon; 83 Flood St, SW3.

HALF-SISTERS LIVING

Lady (Christine) Caroline Catherine, *b* 1946; *ed* Cranborne Chase, Zambia Univ, and London Univ (BSc, PGCE, Dip Ed): *m* 1978, John Francis Burnett Armstrong, who *d* 1992, and has issue living, Henry Francis Arthur Rous, *b* 1978, — John George William Rous, *b* 1982, — Catherine Julia Cecily, *b* 1986. *Residence* – Dalby, Terrington, N Yorks.
Lady Henrietta Elizabeth, *b* 1947. *Residences* – 6 Cadogan Mansions, Sloane Sq, SW1; Clovelly Court, Bideford, Devon.
Lady Virginia, *b* 1954: *m* 1974, Antony William Hew Gibbs, and has issue (*see* Hamilton Dalrymple, Bt). *Residence* – Home Farm, Barrow Gurney, Bristol.

DAUGHTERS LIVING OF FOURTH EARL

Lady Marye Violet Isolde, *b* 1930. *Residence* – Sacaba Beach, Malaga 29004, Spain.
Lady Penelope Anne, *b* 1932: *m* 1st, 1950 (*m diss* 1960), Com Ian Dudley Stewart Forbes, DSC, RN, who *d* 1992, and has issue (*see* Forbes, Bt, colls, *cr* 1823); 2ndly, 1961 (*m diss* 1969), John Cator (*see* Cayley, Bt, 1960 Edn); 3rdly, 1984, as his 3rd wife, Anthony James Gilbey (*see* M Linlithgow, colls, 1990 Edn). *Residence* – White Lion House, Wangford, Beccles, Suffolk NR34 8RL.

UNCLE LIVING (*son of 3rd Earl*)

Hon Peter James Mowbray (Malvern House, Box 44, Mvurwi, Zimbabwe), *b* 1914; *ed* Harrow, and Melbourne Gram Sch; Maj (ret) 16th/5th Lancers; 1939-45 War (Italy Star): *m* 1942, Elizabeth Alice Mary, who *d* 1968, da of late Maj Hon Alastair Thomas Joseph Fraser, DSO (L Lovat, colls), and has had issue, Michael James Mowbray (57 Parma Crescent, SW11 1LU), *b* 1944; *ed* Elston Hall, and St George's Coll, Salisbury: *m* 1989, Isabelle M. B., eldest da of François Le Chevallier, of Paris 75015, — Peter George Anthony Mowbray, *b* 1948, *d* as the result of an accident 1952, — Simon Roderick (Burston, Dulverton, Somerset), *b* 1950; *ed* St George's Coll, and Trin Coll, Camb (MA): *m* 1978, Carol A., da of Robert Dawson, of Bolton, Lancs, and has issue living, Oliver Mowbray Abdel Rahman *b* 1981, Clare Elizabeth Khalida *b* 1979, Rebecca Mary Alice *b* 1987, Henrietta Florence *b* 1988, — (John) Sebastian (Kamusha, Box 25, Mvurwi, Zimbabwe), *b* 1953: *m* 1980, Valda Louise, da of Alastair Guy Waterhouse, of Middleton Hall, Youlgrave, Derbys, and has issue living, Justin Henry *b* 1980, William James *b* 1984, Julia Louise *b* 1982, — Edmund Felix, *b* 1954: *m* 1982, Jane N., elder da of Derek Willshaw, of Sussex, and has issue living, Sebastian James *b* 1985, Emma Jade *b* 1982, Elizabeth Frances *b* 1988, — Peter Joseph, *b* 1956, — Christopher Hugh (PO Box 432, Upperville, Virginia 22176, USA), *b* 1958: *m* 1987, Elisabeth Christman, only da of Dr Stokes Jerome Smith, of Spartanburg, S Carolina, USA, and has issue living, Simon Joseph *b* 1990, Katherine Elisabeth *b* 1988, — Petronilla, *b* 1943: *m* 1966, (Thomas) Peter John Cockin, of 13 The Ferns, Carlton Rd, Tunbridge Wells TN1 2JT, and has had issue, James Francis John *b* 1968, John Joseph *b* 1970, Charles Hereward John *b* and *d* 1974, Michael Hereward John *b* 1975, Antonia Patricia Mary *b* 1967: *m* 1993, Nicholas Edward Osborne, of 24 Fair Health, 43 Putney Hill, SW15, — Helena Sibyl, *b* 1947: *m* 1977, Michael Clive Rashleigh Beasley, of 83 Beaumont Rd, W4, and has issue living, Thomas *b* 1979, George *b* 1983, Charlotte *b* 1981, — Elizabeth Anne, *b* 1951: *m* 1977, Bruce Lewis Hamilton Powell, of Broadhatch House, Bentley, Alton, Hants, and has issue living, Louis Edmund *b* 1983, Jemima Anne *b* 1978, Camilla (Millicent) Mary Augusta *b* 1979, Harriet Elizabeth Maud *b* 1980, — Philippa Mary Katherine, *b* 1960: *m* 1986, Anthony John Stratford Eyre, of Poppy Cottage, Driffield, Cirencester GL7 5PY, yr son of Raymond John Eyre, of London, and has issue living, Edmund Anthony Bobo *b* 1988, Giles Peter Dusmet *b* 1989, Hew Raymond Bundu *b* 1991, Elena Alice *b* 1993.

WIDOW LIVING OF FIFTH EARL

(APRIL) MARY (*Hon Mrs W. Keith Rous*) (prefers to be known by her former style), da of late Hon Arthur Melland Asquith (*see* E Oxford and Asquith, colls): *m* 1943, as his 2nd wife, the 5th Earl, who *d* 1983 (having survived his elder brother, the 4th Earl, by four days). *Residence* – Clovelly Court, Bideford, N Devon.

COLLATERAL BRANCH LIVING

Issue of late Maj Hon George Nathaniel Rous, 3rd son of 3rd Earl, *b* 1911; *d* 1982: *m* 1949, Joyce, who *d* 1985, yst da of late Maj Charles Harpur, OBE:—
Robert Charles, *b* 1953; *ed* Harrow, and Trin Coll, Camb (MA); Lay Canon of St Edmundsbury Cathedral; ARICS: *m* 1976, Teresa Mary Mercedes, da of David Keith Ford Heathcote, of Badlingham Manor, Chippenham, Cambs (*see* Sykes, Bt, *cr* 1783, 1990 Edn), and has issue living, Peter George *b* 1984, — Laura Frances, *b* 1982. *Residence* – Dennington Hall, Woodbridge, Suffolk. —— Georgina Alice, *b* 1951; *ed* Heathfield: *m* 1975, Charles H. W. Holloway, and has issue living, George Henry Rous, *b* 1983, — Edward Charles, *b* 1986, — Alice Victoria Pendrill, *b* 1980. —— Veronica Rose, *b* 1958; *ed* Heathfield: *m* 1989, James H. A. Maberly, eldest son of late Lt-Col J. E. A. Maberly, and has issue living, Edward George Astley, *b* 1991, — Harry Robert Astley, *b* 1993. —— Frances Diana (*Hon Mrs Charles R. Boscawen*), *b* 1961; *ed* Heathfield: *m* 1985, Hon Charles Richard Boscawen, 3rd son of 9th Viscount Falmouth, and has issue (*see* V Falmouth).

PREDECESSORS – This family descends from Sir Peter Rous, of Dennington, near Stradbroke, Suffolk, *temp* early 14th century. Henham became the principal seat in 1544. (**1**) JOHN ROUS, MP for Dunwich; *cr* a *Baronet* 1660; *s* by his son (**2**) *Sir* JOHN, 2nd Bt; High Sheriff of Suffolk *d* 1730; *s* by his son (**3**) *Sir* JOHN, 3rd Bt; *d* unmarried; *s* by his half-brother (**4**) *Sir* ROBERT, 4th Bt; *s* by *Sir* JOHN, 5th Bt; was MP for Suffolk; *d* 1771; *s* by his son (**6**) *Sir* JOHN, 6th Bt; sat as MP for Suffolk 1780-96; *cr* *Baron Rous*, of Dennington, co Suffolk (peerage of Great Britain) 1796, and *Viscount Dunwich* and *Earl of Stradbroke* (peerage of United Kingdom) 1821: *m* 2ndly, 1792, Charlotte Maria, da of Abraham Whittaker; *d* 1827; *s* by his son (**7**) JOHN EDWARD CORNWALLIS, 2nd Earl; *b* 1794; was Lord-Lieut of Suffolk; served in Coldm Gds in Peninsular War (medal with five clasps) and in Belgian Campaign 1815: *m* 1857, Augusta, da of the Rev Sir Christopher John Musgrave, 9th Bt, and widow of Col Bonham; *d* 27 Jan 1886; *s* by his son (**8**) GEORGE EDWARD JOHN MOWBRAY, KCMG, CB, CVO, CBE, 3rd Earl; *b* 1862; Lord-Lieut and Vice-Adm of Suffolk; Gov of Victoria, Australia 1920-26, and Parliamentary Sec to Min of Agriculture and Fisheries 1928-9; European War 1914-19 (CBE): *m* 1898, *Dame* Helena Violet Alice, DBE, who *d* 1949, da of late Lieut-Gen James Keith Fraser, CMG; *d* 1947; *s* by his son (**9**) JOHN ANTHONY ALEXANDER, 4th Earl, *b* 1903; Lay Canon of St Edmundsbury Cathedral; FRSA; Cdr RN, Hon Col 660th Heavy Anti-Aircraft Regt RA (TA); Lord-Lt of Suffolk 1948-78; Agriculturalist and Forester; Vice-Pres of R British Legion (Pres Eastern Area); Vice-Pres of Assocn of Land Drainage Authorities; a CC for E Suffolk 1931-45, and an Alderman 1953-64: *m* 1929, Barbara, who *d* 1977, yr da of late Lord Arthur High Grosvenor (D Westminster, colls); *d* (14 July) 1983; *s* by his brother (**5**) (WILLIAM) KEITH, 5th Earl, *b* 1907; Lt (E) RN; Lt RNVR; 1939-45 War, commanded HMS *Amethyst*, HMS *Lady Lilian* and HMS *Coltfoot* 1940-43: *m* 1st, 1935 (*m diss* 1941), Pamela Catherine Mabell, who *d* 1972, da of late Capt Hon Edward James Kay-Shuttleworth (B Shuttleworth, colls); 2ndly, 1943, April Mary, da of late Brig-Gen Hon Arthur Melland Asquith, DSO (*see* E Oxford and Asquith, colls); *d* (18 July) 1983; *s* by his el son (**6**) (ROBERT) KEITH, 6th Earl, and present peer; also Viscount Dunwich, and Baron Rous.

STRAFFORD, EARL OF (Byng) (Earl UK 1847)

I will defend

THOMAS EDMUND BYNG, 8th Earl, *b* 26 Sept 1936; *s* 1984; *ed* Eton, and Clare Coll, Camb: *m* 1st, 1963 (*m diss* 1981), Jennifer Mary Denise, elder da of Rt Hon William Morrison May, MP, of Mertoun Hall, Holywood, co Down; 2ndly, 1981, Julia Mary, formerly wife of Derek Nicholas Howard, and yr da of late Sir Dennis Pilcher, CBE, of Brambles, Batts Lane, Mare Hill, Pulborough, W Sussex, and has issue by 1st *m*.

𝔄rms – Quarterly: sable and argent, in the first quarter a lion rampant of the second; over all in bend sinister, a representation of the Regimental Colour of the 31st Regt of Foot. ℭrest – 1st, out of a mural crown or, an arm, embowed gules, curfed azure, grasping the Regimental Colour of the said Regt, and pendent from the wrist by a crimson riband, the gold cross awarded to the 1st Lord Strafford, and on an escroll, the word "Mouguerre", 2nd, an heraldic antelope statant ermine, attired and crined or. 𝔖upporters – *Dexter*, an heraldic antelope ermine, attired and crined or; *sinister*, a lion or.
Residence – Apple Tree Cottage, Easton, Winchester.

SONS LIVING *(By 1st marriage)*

WILLIAM ROBERT *(Viscount Enfield)*, *b* 10 May 1964; *ed* Winchester.
Hon James Edmund, *b* 1969; *ed* Winchester.

DAUGHTERS LIVING *(By 1st marriage)*

Lady Georgia Mary Caroline, *b* 1965: *m* 1990, Daniel S. Chadwick, yr son of Lynn Chadwick, of Lypiatt, Glos.
Lady (Harriet Clare) Tara, *b* 1967: *m* 1994, T. Christopher Wilbur, son of late Richard Wilbur, of Hawaii, and of Mrs Richard Anger, of Calif, USA.

BROTHER LIVING

Hon Julian Francis, *b* 1938; *ed* Eton; Capt Queen's R Rifles (TA): *m* 1st, 1966 (*m diss* 1983), Ingela Brita, da of Axel Berglund, of Stockholm; 2ndly, 1984, Mrs Prudence Mary Kent, da of late Albert Edward Delany, of Queensland, Australia, and has issue living (by 1st *m*), Francis Gustaf, *b* 1968; *ed* Eton, — (George Michael) Alexander, *b* 1973; *ed* Eton.

MOTHER LIVING

Maria Magdalena Elizabeth, da of late Henry Cloete, CMG, of Alphen, S Africa: *m* 1st, 1934 (*m diss* 1947), Robert Cecil Byng (later 7th Earl of Strafford), who *d* 1984; 2ndly, 1954, as his 2nd wife, James Henry Royds (*see* E Perth, 1959 Edn).
Residence – Cedar Falls, Bishop Lydeard, nr Taunton, Som.

COLLATERAL BRANCH LIVING

Issue of late Major Hon Lionel Frances George Byng, 6th son of 2nd Earl, *b* 1858, *d* 1915: *m* 1902, Lady Eleanor Mable Howard, who *d* 1945 (having *m* 2ndly, 1922, Henry Ernest Atkinson, who *d* 1926), da of 18th Earl of Suffolk and Berkshire:—
Eleanor Myrtle Howard, *b* 1908. *Residence* – Cranford, Lyddington, Oakham, Rutland.

PREDECESSORS – (1) *Sir* JOHN BYNG, GCB, GCH, PC (great-grandson of the 1st Viscount Torrington, and of Thomas Wentworth, 1st Earl of Strafford of 2nd creation 1711) was one of the most distinguished military commanders during the Peninsular War; *b* 1772; *cr Baron Strafford* (peerage of United Kingdom) 1835, and *Viscount Enfield* and *Earl of Strafford* (peerage of United Kingdom) 1847: *m* 1st, 1804, Mary Stevens, who *d* 1806, da of Peter Mackenzie, of Grove House, Middlesex; 2ndly, 1808, Marianne, who *d* 1845, da of Sir Walter James James (formerly Head) 1st Bt; *d* 1860; *s* by his son (2) GEORGE STEVENS, PC, FRS, 2nd Earl; *b* 1806; sat as MP for Milborne Port (*L*) 1831, the Poole 1835-7, and for Chatham 1837-52; was a Lord of the Treasury 1834, Comptroller and Treasurer of HM Queen Victoria's Household 1841, and Sec of Board of Control 1846-7: *m* 1st, 1829, Lady Agnes Paget, who *d* 1845, da of 1st Marquess of Anglesey, KG; 2ndly, 1848, Hon Harriet Elizabeth Cavendish, da of 1st Baron Chesham; *d* Oct 1886; *s* by his son (3) GEORGE HENRY CHARLES, 3rd Earl, *b* 1830; called to the House of Lords in his father's Barony of Strafford 1874; Parliamentary Sec to Poor Law Board 1865-6, Under-Sec of State for Foreign Affairs 1870-74, a Lord-in-Waiting to HM Queen Victoria 1880, Under-Sec of State for India 1880-83, and First Civil Ser Commr (unpaid) 1880-88; Lord-Lieut of Middlesex: *m* 1854, Lady Alice Harriet Frederica Egerton, who *d* 1928, da of 1st Earl of Ellesmere, KG; *d* 1898; *s* by his brother (4) HENRY WILLIAM JOHN, KCVO, CB, 4th Earl, *b* 1831; Page of Honour to HM Queen Victoria 1840-47, Groom-in-Waiting 1872-4, and Equerry 1874-99: *m* 1st, 1863, the Countess Henrietta Daneskiold Samsoe, who *d* 1880; 2ndly, 1898, Cora, who *d* 1932, widow of S. Colgate, of USA; *d* 1899; *s* by his brother (5) FRANCIS EDMUND CECIL, 5th Earl, *b* 1835; V of St Peter's, S Kensington 1867-89, and Chap to Speaker of House of Commons 1874-89: *m* 1st, 1859, Florence Louisa, who *d* 1862, da of Sir William Miles, 1st Bt; 2ndly, 1866, Emily Georgina, who *d* 1929, el da of late Adm Lord Frederick Herbert Kerr; *d* 1918; *s* by his son (6) EDMUND HENRY, 6th Earl; *b* 1862; a Co Alderman for Middlesex and Herts: *m* 1894, Mary Elizabeth, who *d* 1951, da of Sir Thomas Edward Colebrooke, 4th Bt; *d* 1951; *s* by his nephew (7) ROBERT CECIL (son of late Hon Ivo Francis Byng, 4th son of 5th Earl), 7th Earl; *b* 1904: *m* 1st, 1934 (*m diss* 1947), Maria Magdalena Elizabeth, da of Henry Cloete, CMG, of Alphen, S Africa; 2ndly, 1948, Clara Evelyn, who *d* 1985, da of Sir Nusserwanjee Nowrosjee Wadia, KBE, CIE; *d* 1984; *s* by his son (8) THOMAS EDMUND, 8th Earl and present peer; also Viscount Enfield, and Baron Strafford.

STRANG, BARON (Strang) (Baron UK 1954)

COLIN STRANG, 2nd Baron: *b* 12 June 1922; *s* 1978; *ed* Merchant Taylors' Sch, and St John's Coll, Oxford (MA, BPhil); *m* 1st, 1948, Patricia Marie, da of Meiert C. Avis, of Johannesburg, S Africa; 2ndly, 1955,

Barbara Mary Hope, who *d* 1982, da of Frederick Albert Carr, of Wimbledon, SW; 3rdly, 1984, Mary Shewell, da of Richard Miles, of Sheffield, and has issue living by 2nd *m*.
Residence – Gorton School House, Bruichladdich, Isle of Islay PA49 7UN.

DAUGHTER LIVING *(By 2nd marriage)*

Hon Caroline Jane, *b* 1957.

PREDECESSORS – **(1)** WILLIAM STRANG, GCB, GCMG, MBE, was British Rep on European Advisory Commn with rank of Ambassador 1943-45, Political Advisor to Com-in-Ch, British Forces in Germany 1945-47, Permanent Under-Sec of State, Foreign Office (German Sect) 1947-49, Permanent Under-Sec of State, Foreign Office 1949-53, Chm of National Parks Commn 1954-66; a Dep Speaker of House of Lords 1962-78; *b* 1893; *cr Baron Strang* of Stonesfield, co Oxford (peerage of UK) 1954: *m* 1920, Elsie Wynne, who *d* 1974, da of late J. E. Jones, of Addiscombe; *d* 1978; *s* by his son **(2)** COLIN, 2nd Baron and present peer.

STRANGE, BARONESS (Drummond of Megginch) (Baron E 1628)

(JEAN) CHERRY DRUMMOND OF MEGGINCH (*Lady Strange*) *b* 17 Dec 1928; *s* (on termination of abeyance) 1986; *ed* St Andrews (MA) and Camb Univs; FSA (Scot); Pres War Widows' Assocn since 1990; senior heir-general of Aubrey de Vere, Master Chamberlain to King Henry I: *m* 1952, Capt Humphrey ap Evans, MC, who assumed the name of Drummond of Megginch by decree of Lord Lyon 1966, son of Maj James John Pugh Evans, MBE, MC, JP, DL, of Lovesgrove, Aberystwyth, Cardiganshire, and has issue.

Arms – Parted per fess waved or and gu. **Crest** – Two arms ppr drawing an arrow to the head of a bow or. **Supporters** – *Dexter*, a naked savage wreathed about the head and middle with oak leaves, holding over his dexter shoulder a club all ppr; *sinister*, a knight armed at all points, the visor of his helmet up, a spear resting on his sinister arm and a shield hanging thereon all ppr. **Motto** – Marte et arte. **Badge** – holly.
Seat – Megginch Castle, Errol, Perthshire. *Town Residence* – 160 Kennington Rd, SE11.

SONS LIVING

Hon ADAM HUMPHREY, *b* 20 April 1953; *ed* Eton, and RMA Sandhurst: *m* 1988, Hon Mary Emma Jeronima Dewar, eldest da of 4th Baron Forteviot, and has issue living, John Adam Humphrey, *b* 3 Nov 1992, — Sophia Frances, *b* 1991.
Dr the Hon Humphrey John Jardine, *b* 1961; *ed* Eton, and Imperial Coll, London (BSc 1981); PhD 1988, DIC, MRSC, CChem, ARCS. *Residence* – 33 Drummond St, S Windsor, NSW 2756, Australia.
Hon John Humphrey Hugo, *b* 1966; *ed* Eton, and St John's Coll, Camb (MA); ACA 1993. *Residence* – 160 Kennington Rd, SE11.

DAUGHTERS LIVING

Hon Charlotte Cherry, *b* 1955; *ed* Heathfield, and Dundee Coll of Commerce. *Residence* – 222, 2500 Q St NW, Washington, DC 20007, USA.
Hon Amélie Margaret Mary, *b* 1963; *ed* Heathfield, Dundee Coll of Commerce, and London Poly: *m* 1990, as his 2nd wife, Philippe, 8th Marquis de MacMahon, 4th Duc de Magenta, and has issue living, Maurice Marie Patrick Bacchus Humphrey (Comte de MacMahon de Magenta), *b* 1992, — Pélagie Jeanne Marie Marguerite Charlotte Natalie, *b* 1990. *Residence* – Château de Sully, 71360 Epinac, Saone-et-Loire, France.
Hon Catherine Star Violetta, *b* 1967; *ed* Heathfield, Dundee Coll of Commerce, and Hertfords Univ.

SISTERS LIVING

Hon Heather Mary, *b* 1931: *m* 1954, Lt-Cdr Andrew Christian Currey, RN, of The Mill House, Santon, Isle of Man, only son of late Rear Adm Harry Philip Currey, CB, OBE, and has issue living, Robert James Drummond (99 Ritherdon Rd, SW17), *b* 1955; *ed* Eton, and at London Polytechnic (BSc): *m* 1983, Diana Jane, da of Kenneth Garrod, of Aldeburgh, Suffolk, and has issue living, Cosmo Charles Drummond *b* 1985, Francesca Rose *b* 1989, — John Andrew Fairbridge, *b* 1959; *ed* Stowe, — Arabella Mary Christian, *b* 1958; *ed* Hampden House: *m* 1987, Reiner Friedhelm Gustav Gerland, son of Karl Heinz Gerland, of Kassel, W Germany, and has issue living, Oskar Gustav Christian *b* 1987.
Hon Margaret April Irene (*Hon Lady Agnew-Somerville*), *b* 1939: *m* 1963, Sir Quentin Charles Somerville Agnew-Somerville, 2nd Bt, of Mount Auldyn, Jurby Rd, Ramsey, Isle of Man, and has issue.

PREDECESSORS – **(1)** JAMES Stanley, later 7th Earl of Derby, was summoned to Parliament by writ 1628 as *Baron Strange*. The Barony followed succession of the Earldom **(2-3)** until the death of 9th Earl of Derby 1702, when it fell into abeyance between his two daughters, Lady Henrietta and Lady Elizabeth Stanley. On the death of Lady Elizabeth in 1714, the barony devolved on her sister **(4)** *Lady* HENRIETTA: *m* 1st, 1706, 4th Earl of Anglesey, who *d* 1710; 2ndly, 1714, 1st Earl of Ashburnham, who *d* 1737, and *d* 1718; *s* by her da (by 2nd *m*) **(5)** *Lady* HENRIETTA BRIDGET Ashburnham, *dunm* 1732; *s* by her great uncle **(6)** JAMES Stanley, 10th Earl of Derby, and 6th Baron Strange, who *dsp* 1736; *s* as Baron Strange and in the sovereignty of the Isle of Man by his kinsman **(7)** JAMES Murray, 2nd Duke of Atholl, KT, and 7th Baron Strange (grandson of Lady Amelia Sophia Stanley, da of 7th Earl of Derby and 1st Baron Strange, who *m* 1659, John Murray, 1st Marquess of Atholl); *d* 1764; *s* in the Barony of Strange and in the sovereignty of the Isle of Man by his da **(8)** *Lady* CHARLOTTE, *b* 1731: *m* 1753, her cousin, John Murray, 3rd Duke of Atholl; *d* 1805; disposed of sovereignty of the Isle of Man to British Govt in 1765 for £70,000; *s* by her eldest son **(9)** JOHN, 4th Duke of Atholl, and 9th Baron Strange, from whom it followed succession of the Dukedom **(10-14)** to JAMES THOMAS, 9th Duke and 14th Baron Strange; *dunm* 1957, when the Barony of Strange fell into abeyance between the representatives of the three daughters of the 4th Duke (i) Lady Charlotte Murray, who *m* 1st, 1797, Sir John Menzies, 4th Bt, who *d* 1800; 2ndly, 1801, Adm Sir Adam Drummond of Megginch, KCH, (ii) Lady Amelia Sophia Murray, who *m* 1809, 6th Viscount Strathallan (E Perth), and (iii), Lady Elizabeth Murray, who *m* 1808, Maj-Gen Sir Evan John Murray MacGregor, 2nd Bt, and so continued until 1964, when the abeyance was terminated (after petition to HM the Queen) in favour of **(15)** JOHN Drummond of Megginch (only son of Capt Malcolm Drummond, JP, DL, 9th of Megginch, and great grandson of Lady Charlotte Drummond), 15th Baron, *b* 1900; author (as John Drummond) of ten books of fact and fiction: *m* 1928, Violet Margaret Florence, who *d* 1975, formerly wife of Capt Edmund Owen Ethelstone Peel, MC, and only da of Sir Robert William Buchanan-Jardine, 2nd Bt; *d* 1982, when the barony again fell into abeyance between his three daughters, and so continued until 1986, when the abeyance was terminated (after petition to HM The Queen) in favour of the eldest da **(16)** (JEAN) CHERRY Drummond of Megginch, Baroness Strange, the present peeress.

Strange of Knokin, Hungerford, and de Moleyns, Baron; see Viscount St Davids.

Strathallan, Viscount; son of Earl of Perth.

STRATHALMOND, BARON (Fraser) (Baron UK 1955)

WILLIAM ROBERTON FRASER, 3rd Baron; *b* 22 July 1947; *s* 1976; *ed* Loretto; CA; Man Dir London Wall Members Agency 1986-91, and Dir London Wall Holdings 1986-91, since when Chm R. W. Sturge Ltd: *m* 1973, Amanda Rose, yr da of Rev Gordon Clifford Taylor, of St Giles-in-the-Fields Rectory, Gower St, WC1, and has issue.

Arms – Tierce in pairle azure gules and sable cinquefoils or. **Crest** – In front of a bezant gutté d'huile a stag's head erased proper. **Supporters** – *Dexter*, a pheasant; *sinister*, a grouse proper. *Residence* – Holt House, Elstead, Godalming, Surrey GU8 6LF

SONS LIVING

Hon WILLIAM GORDON, *b* 24 Sept 1976.
Hon George Edward, *b* 1979.

DAUGHTER LIVING

Hon Virginia Audrey Hart, *b* 1982.

SISTERS LIVING

Hon Cordelia, *b* 1949: *m* 1981 (*m diss* 1986), Ralph Lyman Brown. *Residence* – 75 Carthew Rd, W6 0DU.
Hon Christina, *b* 1954: *m* 1974, Timothy Andrew Lebus, and has issue living, David Oliver, *b* 1983. *Residence* – 70 Ellerby St, SW6 6EZ.

AUNT LIVING (*Daughter of 1st Baron*)

Hon Mary Joan (*Hon Lady Westbrook*), *b* 1922: *m* 1945, Sir Neil Gowanloch Westbrook, and has issue living, Fraser Gownaloch, *b* 1946: *m* 1971 (*m diss* 1993), Jane Bray, — Mary Joan, *b* 1950: *m* 1974, Robert Michael John Keene. *Residence* – White Gables, Prestbury, Ches.

WIDOW LIVING OF SECOND BARON

LETITIA (*Letitia, Baroness Strathalmond*), da of late Walter Martin Krementz, of Morristown, New Jersey, USA: *m* 1945, the 2nd Baron, who *d* 1976. *Residence* – 155 Fawn Lane, Portola Valley, Calif 94025, USA.

PREDECESSORS – **(1)** Sir WILLIAM Fraser, CBE, son of late William Fraser, of Glasgow; *b* 1888; Chm of British Petroleum Co, Ltd, 1941-56; *cr* Knt 1939, and Baron Strathalmond, of Pumpherston, co Middlothian (peerage of UK) 1955: *m* 1913, Mary Roberton, who *d* 1963, da of late Thomson McLintock, of Glasgow; *d* 1970; *s* by his son **(2)** WILLIAM, CMG, OBE, TD, 2nd Baron; *b* 1916; Man Dir of Kuwait Oil Co 1959-62 and Dir of British Petroleum Co Ltd 1962-74: *m* 1945, Letitia, da of late Walter Martin Krementz, of Morristown, New Jersey, USA; *d* 1976; *s* by his only son **(3)** WILLIAM ROBERTON, 3rd Baron and present peer.

STRATHCARRON, BARON (Macpherson) (Baron UK 1936, Bt UK 1933)

DAVID WILLIAM ANTHONY BLYTH MACPHERSON, 2nd Baron, and 2nd Baronet; *b* 23 Jan 1924; *s* 1937; *ed* Eton, and Jesus Coll, Camb; formerly Fl-Lt RAFVR; motoring correspondent of *The Field*; a Partner in the firm of Strathcarron & Co, a Dir of Kirchoffs (London) Ltd, of Seabourne World Express Group plc, and of Kent Internat Airport Ltd; Fellow Inst of Motor Industry, and of Chartered Inst of Transport; Chm All-Party Parl Motorcycle Group; Pres Vehicle Builders & Repairers Assocn, Driving Instructors Assocn, and Nat Breakdown Recovery Club; Pres of Guild of Motoring Writers; Chm The Order of the Road; author of *Motoring for Pleasure*: *m* 1st (Feb) 1947 (*m diss* 1947), Valerie Cole; 2ndly, 1948, Diana Hawtry, who *d* 1973, da of late Cdr R. H. Deane, of Cooden, Sussex, and formerly wife of J. N. O. Curle; 3rdly, 1974, Mary Eve, da of late John Comyn Higgins, CIE, and formerly wife of Hon Anthony Gerald Samuel (*see* V Bearsted), and has issue by 2nd *m*.

Arms – Per fesse or and azure a galley of the first, masts, oars, and tackling proper, flagged gules, in the dexter chief point a hand couped fesseways holding a dagger paleways, and in the sinister a cross-crosslet fitchée of the last; over all a fese chequy of the second and argent. **Crest** – A cat-a-mountain sejant guardant, and having its dexter paw raised proper. **Supporters** – *Dexter*, a private soldier of the Cameron Highlanders in field service dress of the period 1916-18; *sinister*, a Macpherson clansman of the period 1745.

Residences – 22 Rutland Gate, SW7 1BB; Otterwood, Beaulieu, Hants.

SONS LIVING *(By 2nd marriage)*

Hon IAN DAVID PATRICK, *b* 31 March 1949. *Residence* – Flat 1, 26 Old Church St, SW3 5BY.
Hon Andrew Charles James, *b* 1959.

SISTERS LIVING

Hon Fiona (*Hon Lady Runge*), *b* 1917: *m* 1935, Sir Peter Francis Runge, who *d* 1970, and has issue living, Anthony Peter, *b* 1937; *ed* Eton, and Trin Coll, Oxford: *m* 1970, Mrs Susan Grievson, da of Denis Cooil, of Struan, Balla Salla, I of Man, and has issue living, Lucy Victoria *b* 1971, — Charles David, *b* 1944; *ed* Eton, and Ch Ch, Oxford: *m* 1st, 1967 (*m diss* 1980), Harriet, da of John Bradshaw, of Withers, Inkpen, Berks; 2ndly, 1981, Jil, only da of John Liddell, of Greenock, and has issue living (by 1st *m*), Thomas Peter *b* 1971, Louise Dele *b* 1973, (by 2nd *m*) Emma Virginia *b* 1986, — Michael Robert, *b* 1947: *m* 1986, Misae Yeggie, and has issue living, Robert Andrew *b* 1987, — Julia Norah, *b* 1939: *m* 1st, 1958 (*m diss* 1973), Michael D'Arcy Stephens (B McGowan); 2ndly, 1982, James Connell, and has issue living (by 1st *m*), D'Arcy Mark *b* 1965, Katherine Alison *b* 1960. *Residence* – 4 Lammas Way, Lane End, High Wycombe, Bucks, HP14 3EX.
Hon Ann Patricia (*Hon Lady Lowson*) (Oratory Cottage, 33 Ennismore Gdns Mews, SW7 IH2) *b* 1919; is an OStJ: *m* 1936, Sir Denys Colquhoun Flowerdew Lowson, 1st Bt, who *d* 1975.

PREDECESSOR – (1) *Rt Hon* (JAMES) IAN Macpherson, PC, KC, son of James Macpherson, JP, of Inverness; *b* 1880; MP for Ross and Cromarty (*L*) 1911-18, and for Inverness-shire, Ross-shire and Cromarty, Ross and Cromaty Div 1918-35; successively Parliamentary Under-Sec of State for War, Dep Sec of State and Vice-Pres of Army Council, Ch Sec for Ireland, and Min of Pensions; *cr* a *Baronet* 1933, and *Baron Strathcarron*, of Banchor, co Inverness (peerage of United Kingdom) 1936: *m* 1915, Jill, who *d* 1956, da of Sir George Wood Rhodes, JP, 1st Bt; *d* 1937; *s* by his son (2) DAVID WILLIAM ANTHONY BLYTH 2nd Baron and present peer.

STRATHCLYDE, BARON (Galbraith) (Baron UK 1955)

A leader of men

THOMAS GALLOWAY DUNLOP DU ROY DE BLICQUY GALBRAITH, 2nd Baron; *b* 22 Feb 1960; *s* 1985; *ed* Wellington Coll, Univ of E Anglia, and Univ of Aix-en-Provence; a Lord in Waiting 1988-89; Parl Under-Sec of State Dept of Employment, and Min for Tourism 1989-90, Under Sec of State Dept of Environment July-Sept 1990, Under Sec of State Scottish Office, Min of Agric and Fisheries 1990-92, Parl Under Sec of State Dept of Environment 1992-93, Under Sec of State Dept of Trade and Industry 1993-94, since when Min of State, Min for Consumer Affairs and Small Firms: *m* 1992, Jane, elder da of John Skinner, of Chenies, Herts, and has issue.

Arms – Gules, three bears' heads erased argent, muzzled azure, within a bordure indented or charged with three mullets of the third, a crescent of the second for difference. **Crest** – A bear's head erased gules, muzzled argent. **Supporters** – Two bears gules, muzzled argent. *Address* – c/o House of Lords, SW1.

DAUGHTER LIVING

Hon Elizabeth Ida Skinner, *b* 1993.

BROTHER LIVING (*raised to the rank of Baron's son* 1987)

Hon CHARLES WILLIAM DU ROY DE BLICQUY, *b* 20 May 1962; *ed* Wellington Coll, and St Andrews Univ: *m* 1992, Bridget Anne, da of Brian Reeve, of Marford, Clwyd. *Residence* – 59 Cleaver Sq, SE11 4EA.

SISTER LIVING (*raised to the rank of a Baron's daughter* 1987)

Hon (Anne Marie) Ghislaine (du Roy), *b* 1957: *m* 1989, Peter Dilworth Kennerley, TD, of 112 Streathbourne Rd, SW17 8QY, son of John Dilworth Kennerley, of Whitchurch, Canonicorum, Dorset, and has issue living, Samuel John Maximilian, *b* 1992, — Sarah Marie Louise, *b* 1991.

UNCLES LIVING (*sons of 1st Baron*)

Hon James Muir Galloway, CBE, *b* 1920; *ed* RN Coll, Dartmouth, Ch Ch, Oxford (MA) and R Agric Coll, Cirencester; FRICS; late Lt RN; 1939-45 War in destroyers (wounded); Co Councillor Dumfries-shire 1951-52; JP Inverness-shire 1953-54; a Dir of Buccleuch Estates Ltd since 1964; Member Home Grown Timber Advisory Cttee 1978-90; Chm Timber Growers UK 1980-83, and Chm Forestry Industry Cttee of GB 1987-90; Chm Scottish Forestry Trust since 1990; CBE 1984: *m* 1945, Anne, el da of late Maj Kenneth Paget, of Old Rectory House, Itchen Abbas, Hants, and has issue living, Brodie Thomas Paget (13 Trowlock Av, Teddington, Middx), *b* 1948: *ed* Wellington Coll and Besançon Univ; late Capt The Queen's Own Hussars: *m* 1983, Fawziah Mohammad, and has issue living, Alexander *b* 1988, Diana *b* 1984, Selina *b* 1986, — James Muir Paget (7 Saxe-Coburg Place, Edinburgh EH3), *b* 1955; *ed* Eton and RAC, Cirencester; ARICS; Member Queen's Body Guard for Scotland (Royal Company of Archers): *m* 1990, Mrs Antoinette C. Hudson, da of late Brig Peter Robert Ashburner, CBE, MC, of Wamil Hall, Mildenhall, Bury St Edmunds, Suffolk, — John Kenneth Paget (Belses Muir, Ancrum, Roxburghshire), *b* 1956; *ed* Eton: *m* 1983, Dorothy, da of John P. S. Hunter, JP, of Torbeag, Banavie, Inverness-shire, and has issue living, Donald *b* 1983, Jock *b* 1993, Anna *b* 1985, Emily *b* 1987, Flora *b* 1991, — Sara Caroline Paget, *b* 1950: *m* 1977, John Barry Ernest McCorkell, of Clanmurry House, Dromore, co Down, eldest son of Col Michael McCorkell, OBE, of Ballyarnett, Londonderry, and has issue living, Harry *b* 1988, Rosanna *b* 1985. *Residence* – Rawflat, Ancrum, Roxburghshire TD8 6UW. *Clubs* – Naval and Military, Army and Navy, New (Edinburgh).
Hon Norman Dunlop Galloway, *b* 1925; *ed* Wellington Coll; a Dir of Ben Line Steamers Ltd 1968-86; 1939-45 War as Sub-Lieut RNVR: *m* 1950, Susan Patricia, el da of late Com J. H. F. Kent, of La Coupe, St Martin, Jersey, Channel Islands, and has issue living, Norman Thomas Galloway (Hopefield Farm, Tranent, E Lothian EH33 2AL), *b* 1955; *ed* Wellington Coll, and Newcastle Univ; FRICS: *m* 1987, Quona Rose, da of late Maj Cecil Geoffrey Braithwaite, of Lochmalony, Cupar, and has issue living, Jake Geoffrey Kent *b* 1990, James Jan Kent *b* 1991, Ann Rose Braithwaite *b* 1990, — Patricia Jane, *b* 1951: *m* 1981, Christopher J. Rowe, of Withy Shaw House, Goring Heath, nr Reading, Oxon RG8 7RJ, and has issue living, John Edward *b* 1983, Hamish Patrick Rowe *b* 1990, — Diana Susan, *b* 1954: *m* 1976, Andrew Guy Windham, and has issue (*see* Bowyer-Smyth, Bt). *Residence* – Over Newton, Gifford, by Haddington, E Lothian.
Hon David Muir Galloway, *b* 1928; *ed* Wellington Coll, and Roy Agricultural Coll, Cirencester: *m* 1967, Marion Bingham, da of Maj Bruce Bingham Kennedy, TD, of Doonholm, Ayr, and has issue living, William James Kennedy *b* 1970; *ed* Glenalmond, Newcastle Univ (BSc), and RMA Sandhurst; Capt Royal Scots Dragoon Gds, — Fiona Jane Kennedy, *b* 1968: *m* 1991, Andrew P. Robinson, son of R. L. Robinson, of Top Cottage, Thornyflat Farm, Ayr, — Mary Ida Galloway, *b* 1973, — Alice Sylvia Kennedy, *b* 1976. *Residence* – Burnbrae Lodge, Mauchline, Ayrshire.

AUNTS LIVING (*Daughters of 1st Baron*)

Hon Ida Jean Galloway, *b* 1922; 1939-45 War as 3rd Officer WRNS.
Hon Heather Margaret Anne Galloway, *b* 1930.

PREDECESSORS – (1) THOMAS DUNLOP Galbraith, PC, 1st Baron, son of late William Brodie Galbraith, JP, of Overton, Kilmacolm, Renfrewshire; *b* 1891; Hon FRCP Edinburgh 1960, and Hon Fellow, Roy Coll of Physicians and Surgeons, Glasgow 1961; Com RN, a Chartered Accountant, and an Hon Gov of Glasgow Acad; was a Member of Glasgow Corporation 1933-40, and Magistrate 1938-40, Joint Parliamentary Under-Sec of State for Scotland May to Aug 1945, and again Nov 1951 to April 1955, and Min of State, Scottish Office April 1955 to Oct 1958; a Gov of Wellington Coll 1947-61; Chm of North of Scotland Hydro-Electric Board 1959-67; European War 1914-18, in HMS *Audacious* and HMS *Queen Elizabeth* at Gallipoli Landings and surrender of German High Seas Fleet; European War 1939-45 on Staff of Com-in-Ch, Coast of Scotland, and as Dep British Admiralty Supply Representative in USA; MP for Pollock Div of Glasgow (*U*) 1940-55; a Freeman of Dingwall and Aberdeen; *cr* PC 1953 and *Baron Strathclyde*, of Barskimming, co Ayr (peerage of United Kingdom) 1955: *m* 1915, Ida Jean, who *d* 1985, da of late Thomas Galloway, JP, of Auchendrane, Ayrshire; *d* 1985; *s* by his grandson (2) THOMAS GALLOWAY DUNLOP DU ROY DE BLICQUY (son of late Hon Sir Thomas Galloway Dunlop Galbraith, KBE), 2nd Baron and present peer.

STRATHCONA AND MOUNT ROYAL, BARON (Howard) (Baron UK 1900)

DONALD EUAN PALMER HOWARD, 4th Baron; *b* 26 Nov 1923; *s* 1959; *ed* Eton, at Trin Coll, Camb, and McGill Univ., Montreal; late Lt RNVR; a DL for Angus; Vice-Chm Maritime Trust, and Pres of UK Pilots Assocn and Steamboat Assocn of Great Britain; a Lord in Waiting to HM and a Govt Whip 1973-74, and Parl Under-Sec of State for RAF Jan to March 1974; Joint Dep Leader of the Opposition House of Lords since 1976; Min of State, MOD, since 1979: *m* 1st, 1954 (*m diss* 1977), Lady Jane Mary Waldegrave, da of 12th Earl Waldegrave; 2ndly, 1978, Patricia, da of late Harvey Evelyn Thomas, and widow of John Middleton, and has issue by 1st *m*.

Arms – Quarterly, 1st and 4th argent, on a bend indented between four cross-crosslets gules, three maple leaves or; 2nd and 3rd gules, on a fess argent, between a demi-lion rampant or in chief, and a canoe of the last with four men rowing proper, in the stern a flag of the second flowing towards the dexter inscribed flag of the second flowing towards the dexter inscribed with the letters NW sable, in base a hammer surmounted of a nail in saltire of the last. **Crest** – On a mount vert, a beaver eating into a maple tree proper. **Supporters** – *Dexter*, a trooper of the Regiment of Strathcona's Horse peroper; *sinister*, a navvy standing on a railway sleeper, chaired and railed all proper. *Seat* – Isle of Colonsay, Argyll. *Residence* – 16 Henning St, SW11 3DR. *Clubs* – Brooks's, Pratt's, Royal Yacht Squadron.

SONS LIVING *(By 1st marriage)*

Hon (DONALD) ALEXANDER SMITH, *b* 24 June 1961; *ed* Gordonstoun, and London Business Sch (MBA): *m* 1992, Jane Maree, da of R. Shaun Gibb, of Sydney, Australia.
Hon Andrew Barnaby, *b* 1963: *m* 1994, Katharine E., eldest da of C. Oldfield, of Uplyme, Devon.

DAUGHTERS LIVING *(By 1st marriage)*

Hon Jane Elizabeth Stirling, *b* 1955; *ed* Sherborne Sch for Girls, and Somerville Coll, Oxford: *m* 1987, Nigel Morris Jones, only son of M. H. Morris Jones, of Tarvin, Cheshire, and has issue living, Sophia Venetia, *b* 1989, — Lydia Iona, *b* 1991, — Kiloran Imogen, *b* 1993, — Eloïse Georgia, *b* (twin)1993. *Residence* – 143 Portland Rd, W11 4LR.
Hon Katharine Mary, *b* 1956: *m* 1st, 1975, Gavin Michael Jasper Strachan; 2ndly, 1982, William Evelyn Hinton Joll (*see* Agnew, Bt (*cr* 1895), 1985 Edn), and has issue living (by 2nd *m*), Harry Augustus, *b* 1983, — Flora Katharine Kiloran, *b* 1985, — Hannah Olympia, *b* 1988. *Residence* – 17 Durand Gdns, SW9 0PS.
Hon Caroline Anne, *b* 1959.
Hon Emma Laura Louise (twin), *b* 1963.

BROTHERS LIVING

Hon Barnaby John, *b* 1925; *ed* Eton, and Trin Coll, Camb (BA Law 1948, MA 1954); appointed Commr, S Rhodesian Forestry Commn 1957; European War 1943-45 as Sub-Lt RNVR (Air Branch): *m* 1st, 1952 (*m diss* 1967), Elizabeth, da of late Frank M. Mayfield, of St Louis, Missouri, USA; 2ndly, 1970, Mary-Jane Bishop, who *d* 1994, da of late Ambrose Chambers, and has had issue (by 1st *m*) †Alan Stirling, *b* 1956; *d* 1992, — Elizabeth Kiloran, *b* 1957: *m* 1982, Vicomte Philippe de Lapérouse, of 2 White Gate Lane, St Louis, Missouri 63124, USA, eldest son of Count Bertrand de Lapérouse, of Fairhaven, NJ, USA, and has issue living, Patrick Henri Louis Léon Marie *b* 1985, Kiloran Elizabeth Diana Marie *b* 1986, Isabelle Marthe Jeanne Marie *b* 1990, — Sarah Ann Catriona, *b* 1962: *m* 1983, Dr Jeffrey Lee Thomasson, MD, of 7218 Maryland Av, St Louis, MO 63130, USA, and has issue living, Robert Howard *b* 1987, Alan Mayfield *b* 1988, Patricia Delzell *b* 1991. *Address* – 1224 River Rd, Orange Park, Florida 32073, USA; St Ann's Bay, Englishtown, Nova Scotia, Canada, BOC 1HO. *Clubs* – Brooks's, Queen's, Mill Reef (Antigua), Bedford Golf & Tennis.
Hon Jonathan Alan, *b* 1933; *ed* Eton, Trin Coll, Camb, R Inst of Tech, Stockholm, and Stockholm Univ; late 2nd Lt Coldstream Guards, and Argyll & Sutherland Highlanders (TA): *m* 1st, 1956 (*m diss* 1969), Hon Brigid Mary Westenra, da of 6th Baron Rossmore; 2ndly, 1970 (*m diss* 1981), Cecilia Philipson, and has issue living (by 1st *m*), Nicola Charlotte, *b* 1958, — Kiloran Emma, *b* 1959, — (by 2nd *m*) Olof Philipson, *b* 1970. *Address* – PACIM, PO Box 98, Mindelo, Cape Verde Is.

SISTER LIVING

Hon Diana Catriona, *b* 1935: *m* 1956, Michael Leslie Ogilvie Faber, of The Combe, Glynde, Lewes, Sussex BN8 6RP, and has issue living, Rory Valdemar, *b* 1956, — Guy Donald George, *b* 1959, — Laura Diana, *b* 1958: *m* 1993, John R. Percival, son of Michael Percival, of SW1, — Charlotte Victoria (twin), *b* 1958: *m* 1990, John Marais, and has issue living, Edward John *b* 1991, Maria-del-Mar *b* 1989.

COLLATERAL BRANCH LIVING

Issue of late Capt Hon Sir Arthur Jared Palmer Howard, KBE, CVO, yst son of Margaret Charlotte, Baroness Strathcona and Mount Royal, *b* 1896, *d* 1971: *m* 1922, Lady Leonora Stanley Baldwin, who *d* 1989, da of 1st Earl Baldwin of Bewdley:—
Alexander (Poronui Station, RD3 Taupo, NZ), *b* 1930; *ed* Eton, and Trin Coll, Camb (MA); Scots Gds: *m* 1959, Penelope Joanna, da of Gershom Radcliffe Layton Warren, of Saanichton BC, Canada, and has issue living, Shamus Alexander, *b* 1962, — Harry Alexander, *b* 1967, — Rory Jared, *b* 1973. ——— Kiloran Margaret (*Hon Mrs Langley G. H. Russell*), *b* 1926: *m* 1951, Hon Langley Gordon Haslingden Russell, MC, who *d* 1975 (*see* B Russell of Liverpool). ——— Jill, *b* 1934: *m* 1958, Peter James Scott Lumsden, and has issue living, James Herbert, *b* 1962, — Alice Margaret, *b* 1961, — Susanna Helen, *b* 1965.

PREDECESSORS – (1) Sir DONALD ALEXANDER Smith, GCMG, GCVO, DCL, LLD, FRS, son of late Alexander Smith, of Archieston, Scotland, *b* 1820; entered Hudson Bay Co's Ser at an early age, and was last Resident Gov of that Corporation as a governing body; was Special Commr during 1st Riel Rebellion in Red River Settlements 1869-70 (thanked by Gov-Gen in Council); appointed a MEC (first) of NW Territory 1870; represented Winnipeg and St John's in Manitoba Legislature 1871-84; elected MP for Selkirk in Canadian House of Commons 1871, 1872, 1874, and 1878, and for Montreal West 1887 and 1891, which constituency he represented until 1896; sworn PC Canada 1896, and was appointed High Commr in Great Britain for the Dominion 1896; raised a body of mounted troops — Strathcona's Horse — for service in S Africa 1900; *cr* GCMG 1896, GCVO 1908, *Baron Strathcona and Mount Royal*, of Glencoe, co Argyll, and Mount Royal, Quebec, Canada (peerage of United Kingdom) 1897, and *Baron Strathcona and Mount Royal*, of Mount Royal, Quebec, Canada, and Glencoe, co Argyll (peerage of UK) 1900, with special remainder in default of male issue to his only da Margaret Charlotte, and her heirs male: *m* 1853, Isabella Sophia, who *d* 1913, da of late Richard Hardisty, of Canada; *d* 1914, when the Barony (*cr* 1897) became ext, while in that of 1900 he was *s* under the special remainder by his only da (2) MARGARET CHARLOTTE Howard, *b* 1854: *m* 1888, Robert Jared Bliss Howard, OBE, FRCS, who *d* 1921; *d* 1926; *s* by her son (3) DONALD STIRLING PALMER Howard, 3rd Baron; *b* 1891; Major London Scottish (TA); was MP for Cumberland, N Div (*U*) 1922-26, Parliamentary Private Sec (unpaid) for Parliamentary Sec to Min of Labour 1923-4, Parliamentary Private Sec to First Lord of the Admiralty 1925-7, and Under-Sec of State for War and Vice-Pres of Army Council 1934-39; appointed Capt of Yeomen of the Guard 1931; *m* 1922, Hon Diana Evelyn Loder, who *d* 1985, da of 1st Baron Wakehurst; *d* 1959; *s* by his son (4) DONALD EUAN PALMER, 4th Baron and present peer.

STRATHEDEN AND CAMPBELL, BARON (Campbell) (Baron UK 1836)

Boldly and openly

DONALD CAMPBELL, 6th Baron; *b* 4 April 1934; *s* 1987; *ed* Eton: *m* 1957, Hilary Ann Holland, who *d* 1991, da of late Lt-Col William Derington Turner, of Simonstown, S Africa, and has issue.

𝖆rms – Gyronny of eight or and sable, within a bordure engrailed quarterly, or and azure charged with eight buckles counterchanged. 𝕮rest – A boar's head erased, gyronny or eight, or and sable. 𝕾upporters – (*Barony of Stratheden*) On either side a buck argent, attired and hoofed or, that on the dexter gorged with a collar counter-compony gules and of the second, therefrom pendent an escutcheon gyronny of eight or and sable and that on the sinister gorged with a collar or, therefrom pendent an escutcheon gold, charged with three chaplets of laurel two and one proper. ——— (*Barony of Campbell*) On either side a lion guardant gules, that on the *dexter* gorged with a collar or, pendant therefrom an escutcheon azure, charged with a saltire argent, and that on the *sinister* gorged with a wreath of shamrocks proper, therefrom an escutcheon checky or and gules.
Residence – Ridgewood, MS 401, Cooroy, Queensland 4563, Australia.

SON LIVING

Hon DAVID ANTHONY, *b* 13 Feb 1963; *ed* Queensland, Australia: *m* 1993, Jennifer Margarett Owens. *Residence* – 6 Lawnville Rd, Cooroy, Queensland 4563, Australia.

DAUGHTERS LIVING

Hon Tania Ann CAMPBELL, *b* 1960; has resumed her maiden name: *m* 1984, Paul Hamment, of Melbourne. *Residence* – 36 Charles Kurg Drive, Worongary, Queensland 4213, Australia.
Hon Wendy Meriel, *b* 1969.
Hon Joyce Margaret, *b* 1971.

DAUGHTERS LIVING OF FOURTH BARON

Hon Moyra Jean, *b* 1924. *Residence* – Scraesburgh, Jedburgh, Roxburghshire.
Hon Clayre (*Lady Richard Percy*), *b* 1927: *m* 1st, 1950 (*m diss* 1974), Hon Nicholas Ridley, MP (later Baron Ridley of Liddesdale, PC, Life Baron), who *d* 1993; 2ndly, 1979, as his 2nd wife, Lord Richard Charles Percy (*see* D Northumberland), who *d* 1989. *Residence* – 212 Lambeth Rd, SE1 7JY.
Hon Fiona, *b* 1932. *Residence* – 158 Lambeth Rd, SE1 7DF.

WIDOW LIVING OF FOURTH BARON

NOEL CHRISTABEL (*Noël, Baroness Stratheden and Campbell*), da of late Capt Conrad Viner, and formerly wife of George Vincent: *m* 1964, as his 2nd wife, the 4th Baron, CBE, who *d* 1981.

PREDECESSORS – (1) JOHN Campbell, PC; *b* 1779; a distinguished lawyer, judge, and biographical writer; sat successively as MP for Stafford, Dudley, and Edinburgh (*L*), and having held for many years the offices of Solicitor-Gen and Attorney-Gen was in 1841 appointed Lord Chancellor of Ireland, and *cr Baron Campbell*, of St Andrews, co Fife (peerage of United Kingdom); was Chancellor of the Duchy of Lancaster 1846, Lord Ch Justice of England 1850-9, and Lord High Chancellor of Great Britain 1859-61: *m* 1821, Hon Mary Elizabeth Scarlett (da of 1st Baron Abinger), who in 1836, was *cr* in her own right *Baroness Stratheden*, of Cupar, co Fife (peerage of United Kingdom); *d* 1861; *s* by his son (2) WILLIAM FREDERICK, 2nd Baron, who in 1860 had *s* his mother as 2nd Baron Stratheden, *b* 1824; MP for Cambridge (*L*) 1847-52, and for Harwich 1856-60; *d* 1893; *s* by his brother (3) HALLYBURTON GEORGE, 3rd Baron, *b* 1829: *m* 1865, Louisa Mary, who *d* 1923, el da of late Rt Hon Alexander James Beresford-Hope, MP; *d* 1918; *s* by his grandson (4) ALASTAIR, CBE (son of late Capt Hon John Beresford Campbell, DSO, son of 3rd Baron), 4th Baron, Brig Coldstream Gds, Capt Queen's Body Guard for Scotland (Roy Co of Archers); Chm Edinburgh and E Scotland Coll of Agric 1956-70, and Hill Farming Research Organisation 1958-69; Convenor Roxburgh Co Council 1960-68, Pres Assocn of Co Councils in Scotland 1966-68; Chm Historic Buildings Council for Scotland 1969-76: *m* 1st, 1923, Jean Helen St Clair, CBE, who *d* 1956, da of Col William Anstruther-Gray (Anstruther, Bt, colls); 2ndly, 1964, Mrs Noël Christabel Vincent, da of late Capt Conrad Viner; *d* 1981; *s* by his brother (5) GAVIN, 5th Baron, *b* 1901; Maj KRRC and Lieut-Col 19th (Kenya) Battn King's African Rifles: *m* 1933, Evelyn Mary Austen, who *d* 1989, da of late Col Herbert Austen Smith, CIE; *d* 1987; *s* by his only son (6) DONALD, 6th Baron and present peer; also Baron Campbell.

STRATHMORE AND KINGHORNE, EARL OF (Bowes Lyon) (Earl S 1606 and 1677, Earl UK 1937)

In Thee, O Lord, have I put my trust

MICHAEL FERGUS BOWES LYON, 18th Earl; *b* 7 June 1957; *s* 1987; a Page of Honour to HM Queen Elizabeth the Queen Mother 1971-73; a Lord in Waiting 1989-91, and again since 1992, Capt Yeomen of the Guard (Dep Chief Whip) since 1991; DL Angus 1994; Pres The Boys Brigade since 1994: *m* 1984, Isobel Charlotte, yr da of Capt Anthony E. Weatherall, of Cowhill, Dumfries, and has issue.

Arms – Quarterly: 1st and 4th argent, a lion rampant azure, armed and langued gules, within a double tressure flory counterflory of the second, *Lyon*; 2nd and 3rd ermine, three bows, strings palewise proper, *Bowes*. **Royal Augmentation** (granted to the holder of the Earldom only) — An inescutcheon en surtout azure, thereon a rose argent, barbed vert, seeded or, ensigned with an Imperial Crown proper, within a double tressure flory-counterflory of the second, the said inescutcheon ensigned with an Earl's coronet proper. **Crest** – Between two slips of laurel, a lady to the girdle, habited, and holding in her right hand a thistle all proper. **Supporters** – *Dexter*, a unicorn argent, armed, unguled, maned, and tufted or; *sinister*, a lion per fesse or and gules.

Seat – Glamis Castle, Forfar, co Angus. *Clubs* – Turf, Pratt's, Perth, White's.

SONS LIVING

SIMON PATRICK (*Lord Glamis*), *b* 18 June 1986.
Hon John Fergus, *b* 1988.
Hon George Norman, *b* 1991.

SISTERS LIVING

Lady Elizabeth Mary Cecilia, *b* 1959; *ed* St Hilda's Coll, Oxford: *m* 1990, Antony Richard Leeming, eldest son of late Richard Leeming, of Skirsgill Park, Penrith, Cumbria, and has issue living, Richard Fergus, *b* 1992, — Teresa Mary, *b* 1994. *Residence* – Skirsgill Park, Penrith, Cumbria.
Lady Diana Evelyn, *b* 1966.

UNCLE LIVING (*Brother of 17th Earl; raised to the rank of an Earl's son* 1974)

Hon (Michael) Albemarle, *b* 1940; *ed* Eton, and Magdalen Coll, Oxford; Dir Coutts & Co 1969-93; Gov Peabody Trust since 1982, Hon Treasurer Family Service Units since 1976.

AUNTS LIVING (*Sisters of 17th Earl; raised to the rank of an Earl's daughters* 1974)

Lady Mary Cecilia, *b* 1932; an Extra Lady-in-Waiting to HRH Princess Alexandra, Hon Lady Ogilvy, since 1970: *m* 1951, Timothy James Alan Colman, of Bixley Manor, Norwich NR14 8SJ, and has issue living, James Russell, *b* 1962: *m* 1994, Sacha L., da of Robert Cotterell, of Upper Norton, Herefords, and of Mrs Elizabeth Rawlings, of Chaddleworth, Berks, — Matthew Geoffrey, *b* 1966, — Sarah Rose, *b* 1953; Lady-in-Waiting to HRH The Duchess of Kent since 1990: *m* 1977, Peter John Charles Troughton, of The Lynch House, Upper Wanborough, Swindon, Wilts SN4 0BA, eldest son of late Sir Charles Hugh Willis Troughton, CBE, MC, TD, of Little Leckmelm, Ullapool, Ross-shire (*see* Fowler, Bt (ext 1933), 1966 Edn), and has issue living, Michael *b* 1981, Rose *b* 1979, Lucy *b* 1984, — Sabrina Mary, *b* 1955: *m* 1976, Christopher Arthur Penn, yr son of late Lt-Col Sir Eric Charles William MacKenzie Penn, GCVO, OBE, MC, and has issue living, Rory *b* 1980, Louisa *b* 1983, — Emma Elizabeth, *b* 1958: *m* 1986 (*m diss* 1994), Richard Henry Ramsbotham, yst son of Lt-Gen Sir David Ramsbotham, CBE, and has issue living, Sophie *b* 1987.
Lady Patricia Maud (twin) (Abbey Lodge, Wymondham, Norfolk), *b* 1932: *m* 1964 (*m diss* 1970), Oliver Robin Tetley, and has issue living, Alexander, *b* 1965; *ed* Eton, Univ of Wales, and RMA Sandhurst; Capt Scots Guards; Equerry to HRH The Duke of Kent since 1993.

GREAT AUNT LIVING (*Daughter of 14th Earl*)

Lady Elizabeth Angela Marguerite (*HM Queen Elizabeth The Queen Mother*), *b* 4 Aug 1900 (*see* ROYAL FAMILY): *m* 26 April 1923, HM King George VI, who *d* 6 Feb 1952. *Residences* – Clarence House, SW1; Royal Lodge, Windsor Great Park, Berkshire; Castle of Mey, Caithness.

WIDOW LIVING OF SON OF FOURTEENTH EARL

Rachel Pauline (*Hon Lady Bowes Lyon*), da of late Col Rt Hon Herbert Spender Clay, CMG, MC, MP (V Astor): *m* 1929, Hon Sir David Bowes Lyon, KCVO, who *d* 1961, and has issue living (see colls, infra). *Residence* – St Pauls Walden Bury, Hitchin, Herts.

WIDOW LIVING OF SEVENTEENTH EARL

MARY PAMELA (*Mary, Countess of Strathmore and Kinghorne*), DL Angus 1989, yr da of Brig Norman Duncan McCorquodale, MC, of Maxton House, St Boswell's, Roxburghshire: *m* 1956, the 17th Earl, who *d* 1987. *Residence* – Glamis House, Forfar, co Angus.

COLLATERAL BRANCHES LIVING

Issue of late Hon John Herbert Bowes Lyon, 2nd son of 14th Earl, *b* 1886, *d* 1930: *m* 1914, Hon Fenella Hepburn-Stuart-Forbes-Trefusis, who *d* 1966, da of 21st Baron Clinton:—
Katherine, *b* 1926.

Issue of late Hon Sir David Bowes Lyon, KCVO, yst son of 14th Earl, *b* 1902, *d* 1961: *m* 1929, Rachel Pauline (ante), da of late Col Rt Hon Herbert Spender-Clay, CMG, MC, MP (V Astor):—
Simon Alexander (St Pauls Walden Bury, Hitchin, Herts), *b* 1932; *ed* Eton; Lord Lieut of Hertfordshire 1986: *m* 1966, Caroline Mary Victoria, da of late Rt Rev Victor Joseph Pike, CB, CBE, former Bishop Suffragan of Sherborne, and has issue living, Fergus Alexander, *b* 1970, — David Victor, *b* 1973, — Andrew Simon *b* 1979, — Rosemary Pema, *b* 1968.

—— Davina Katharine (*Countess of Stair*), *b* 1930: *m* 1960, 13th Earl of Stair. *Residence* – Lochinch Castle, Stranraer, Wigtownshire.

(Not in remainder to UK Earldom)

Grandchildren of late Capt Geoffrey Francis Bowes-Lyon (infra):—
Issue of late Maj-Gen Sir Francis James Cecil Bowes-Lyon, KCVO, CB, OBE, MC, *b* 1917, *d* 1977: *m* 1941, Mary (Beltingham House, Bardon Mill, Hexham, Northumberland), da of late Sir Humphrey Edmund de Trafford, MC, 4th Bt:—
John Francis, *b* 1942; *ed* Ampleforth. *Residence* – D5 Albany, Piccadilly, W1. *Clubs* – Buck's, Pratt's. —— David James, *b* 1947; *ed* Ampleforth; DL Midlothian 1992: *m* 1976, (Elizabeth) Harriet, da of late Sir John Rupert Colville, CB, CVO (*see* V Colville of Culross, colls), and has issue living, James Francis John, *b* 1979; Page of Honour to HM since 1991, —— Charles David, *b* 1989, — Georgina Alice, *b* 1977, — Alexandra Violet, *b* 1986. *Residence* – Heriot Water, Heriot, Midlothian. *Club* – White's. —— Fiona Ann, *b* 1944: *m* 1966, Joseph Henry Goodhart, of Great Givendale, Pocklington, York, and has issue living, James Henry, *b* 1970, — David Andrew, *b* 1971, — Camilla Bridget, *b* 1968: *m* 1994, (David) Benjamin Ridgwell, yr son of Dr Stanley Ridgwell, of London.

Granddaughters of late Hon Francis Bowes-Lyon, 2nd son of 13th Earl:—
Issue of late Capt Geoffrey Francis Bowes-Lyon, Black Watch (Roy Highlanders), *b* 1886, *d* 1951: *m* 1914, Edith Katharine, who *d* 1971, da of Sir Lewis Amherst Selby-Bigge, 1st Bt, KCB:—
Caroline Anne Lindsay, *b* 1916: *m* 1939, Llewellyn Ross Llewellyn, who *d* 1988, and has issue living, Llewellyn Charles (44 Drayton Gdns, SW10 9SA), *b* 1943: *m* 1966, Kathleen Mary, da of late John Charles Roche, of Nairobi, Kenya, and has issue living, Sophie Anita *b* 1971, Eleanor Loveday Caroline (Daisy) *b* 1976, — Simon Lindsay, *b* 1945: *m* 1970 (*m diss* 1992), Stella Willis, and has issue living, Fergus John *b* 1975, Emma *b* 1977. *Residence* – Casa Al Ghaba, Alfeição, 8100 Loulé, Algarve, Portugal. —— Susannah Sarah, *b* 1920: *m* 1940, Peter Hugh Dudley Ryder, MBE, Hon Lt-Col late R Armoured Corps TA Reserve, who *d* 1993 (*see* E Harrowby, colls). *Residence* – Ardmore, Riverbank Rd, Ramsey, Isle of Man.

Grandchildren of late Hon Ernest Bowes-Lyon, 3rd son of 13th Earl:—
Issue of late Hubert Ernest Bowes-Lyon, *b* 1883, *d* 1959: *m* 1st (Jan) 1905, Mary Agnes, who *d* 1914, da of James Hay Smeaton; 2ndly, 1919, Margaret, who *d* 1966, da of Frank Nuttall, of Belfast, and widow of James Graham:—
(By 1st *m*) Hubert Ernest Malcolm, *b* 1907; Fl-Lieut RAF Reserve: *m* 1943 (*m diss* 1964), Fanny Rose, who *d* 1969, da of late Simon Jacobs, of S Africa, and has issue living, Jennifer Merrill, *b* 1944; *ed* Tel Aviv Univ (BA): *m* 19—, Stephen Byk, and has issue living, a da *b* 1977. —— Douglas Ian Gordon, *b* 1912; Lieut CAC (ret); served World War II: *m* 1942, Charlotte, da of late Norman Herbert Gardner, and has issue living, Douglas Malcolm (1474 Lloyd George, Verdun, Quebec, Canada H4H 2P5), *b* 1946: *m* 1975, Diana Frechette, — David Gordon (780 Edgewood Rd, Pickering, Ontario, Canada L1V 2Z9), *b* 1949; *ed* Concordia Univ (B Comm): *m* 1974, Elizabeth, da of Donald Allan Rodier, and has issue living, Marianne Elizabeth *b* 1978, Andrea Lynn *b* 1980, — Charlotte Mary Diane, *b* 1943: *m* 1965, Jean D. Wagner, of 127 Chartwell Crescent, Beaconsfield, Quebec, Canada H9W 1C2, and has issue living, Richard Steven *b* 1968, Ian Gordon *b* 1982, Andrew James *b* 1983, Heidi *b* 1970, — Deborah Jane (PO Box 1300, St John's, Newfoundland, Canada A1C 8H8), *b* 1958. *Residence* – 1245 Clemenceau Av, Verdun, Quebec, Canada H4H 2P9. —— (By 2nd *m*) Sonia Gabrielle, *b* 1922: *m* 1948, Lt-Col Stephen Otteran Murphy, MBE, of Higher Polgrain, St Wenn, Bodmin.

Issue of late Hon Patrick Bowes-Lyon, 5th son of 13th Earl, *b* 1863, *d* 1946: *m* 1893, Alice Wiltshire, who *d* 1953, ward of late Capt Arthur Lister-Kaye, of Manor House, Stretton-on-Dunsmore:—
Margaret Anne, *b* 1907: *m* 1945, Lieut-Col Francis Arthur D'Abreu, ERD, ChM, FRCS, late RAMC, and has issue living, Anthony Patrick John, *b* 1946; *ed* Stonyhurst, and London Univ (BA 1970): *m* 1967 (*m diss* 1976), Rachel Jane, da of late Maj W. Green, and has issue living, James Simon Francis, *b* 1970, Catherine Jane Ann *b* 1967, — Francesca Ann, *b* 1948: *m* 1970, Kieran Patrick Fogarty, — Anna Teresa, *b* 1950: *m* 1977 (*m diss* 1990), Nicholas Robin Le Fowne Hurt, and has issue living, (Cassandra) Isobel Ann *b* 1980. *Residences* – 36 Cumberland Terr, Regents Park, NW1 4HP; Thatch Cottage, Hambleden, Henley-on-Thames.

Issue of late Lieut-Col Hon Malcolm Bowes-Lyon, CBE, yst son of 13th Earl; *b* 1874, *d* 1957: *m* 1907, Winifred, who *d* 1957, da of Hector John Gurdon-Rebow, JP, formerly of Wyvenhoe Park, Essex:—
Clodagh Pamela (*Pamela, Lady Lever*) (Lessudden, St Boswells, Roxburghshire), *b* 1908: *m* 1st, 1931 (*m diss* 1952), Lord Malcolm Avondale Douglas-Hamilton, OBE, DFC, RAF, who *d* 1964 (*see* D Hamilton and Brandon); 2ndly, 1962, Sir Tresham Joseph Philip Lever, 2nd Bt, who *d* 1975.

PREDECESSORS – (1) PATRICK Lyon, PC, grandson of Sir John Lyon, of Forteviot, and afterwards of Glamis, co Forfar (who *m* Jean, da of King Robert II of Scotland); was one of the hostages to the English 1424-7 for the ransom of King James I; *cr* Lord Glamis 1445, and appointed Master of the Household 1452; *d* 1459; *s* by his son (2) ALEXANDER, 2nd Lord; *dsp* 1485; *s* by his brother (3) JOHN, PC, 3rd Lord; was Justice Gen of Scotland; *d* 1497, *s* by his son (4) JOHN, 4th Lord; *d* 1500; *s* by his el son (5) GEORGE, 5th Lord; *d* 1505; *s* by his brother (6) JOHN, 6th Lord; *d* 1528; his son Lord Glamis, his widow, a kinsman; and an old priest were indicted for designs against the life of James V by poison or witchcraft; Lady Glamis was condemned to the flames and suffered on the Castle Hill at Edinburgh, July 17th, 1537, Lord Glamis was sentenced to be executed and his estates forfeited, but was respited until he attained his majority; the accuser, however, having confessed that the whole story was a fabrication his lordship was released, and in 1543 was restored by Act of Parliament to his honours and estates, and *s* as (7) JOHN, 7th Lord; *d* 1558; *s* by his son (8) JOHN, 8th Lord; was Lord Chancellor of Scotland 1575; *d* 1578; *s* by his son (9) PATRICK, PC, 9th Lord; was Capt of the Guard; *cr* Earl of Kinghorne (peerage of Scotland) 1606; *d* 1615; *s* by his son (10) JOHN, 2nd Earl; *d* 1647; *s* by his son (11) PATRICK, PC, 3rd Earl; was a Lord of the Treasury, an Extraordinary Lord of Session; obtained in 1672 a new charter extending the remainder to his heirs and assigns whatsoever, and in 1677 another charter providing that he and each successive inheritor of the title should be styled *Lord Glamis, Tannadyce, Sidlaw and Strathdichtie, Viscount Lyon*, and *Earl of Strathmore and Kinghorne*; *d* 1695; *s* by his son (12) JOHN, 4th Earl; *d* 1712; *s* by his el son (13) JOHN, 5th Earl, was slain in the rebellion of 1715 at battle of Sheriffmuir; *s* by his brother (14) CHARLES, 6th Earl; *b* 17—: *m* 1725; *d* 1728; *s* by his brother (15) JAMES, 7th Earl; *b* 1702: *m* (May) 1731, Mary, who *d* (Sept) 1731, da of Dr Charles Oliphant; *d* 1735; *s* by his brother (16) THOMAS, 8th Earl; *b* 1704: *m* 1736, Jean, who *d* 1778, da of James Nicholson, of West Rainton, co Durham; *d* 1753: *s* by his son (17) JOHN, 9th Earl; assumed by Act of Parliament 1767 the surname of Bowes: *m* 1767, Mary Eleanor, who *d* 1800, da and heir of George Bowes of Streatlam Castle, co Durham; *d* 1776; *s* by his el son (18) JOHN, 10th Earl; *cr* Baron Bowes, of Streatlam Castle (peerage of United Kingdom) 1815; *d* 1820; *s* by his brother (19) THOMAS, 11th Earl; resumed the surname of Lyon before that of Bowes: *m* 1800, Mary Elizabeth Louisa Rodney, who *d* 1811, da and heir of George Carpenter, of Redbourn, Herts; *d* 1846; *s* by his grandson (20) THOMAS GEORGE, 12th Earl, son of George, Lord Glamis, by Charlotte, da of Joseph Valentine Grimstead; was a Representative Peer; *d* 1865; *s* by his brother (21) CLAUDE, 13th Earl; *b* 1824; Lord-Lieut of co Forfar; a Representative Peer 1870-87; assumed the surname of Bowes Lyon in lieu of Lyon Bowes; *cr* Baron Bowes, of Streatlam Castle (peerage of United Kingdom) 1887: *m* 1852, Frances Dora, who *d* 1922, da of Oswald Smith, of Blendon Hall, Kent; *d* 1904; *s* by his son (22) CLAUDE GEORGE, KG, KT, GCVO, 14th Earl; *b* 1855; 32 years Lord Lieut, of co Angus; *cr* Earl of Strathmore and Kinghorne (peerage of United Kingdom) 1937: *m* 1881, Cecilia Nina, GCVO, who *d* 1938, da of late Rev Charles William Cavendish Bentinck (D Portland, colls); *d* 1944; *s* by his son (23) PATRICK, 15th Earl, *b* 1884: *m* 1908, Lady Dorothy Beatrix Osborne, who *d* 1946, da of 10th Duke of Leeds; *d* 1949; *s* by his son (24) TIMOTHY PATRICK, 16th Earl, *b*

1918: *m* 1958, Mary Bridget, who *d* 1967, da of Peter Brennan, of Clonasee, co Leix; *d* 1972; *s* by his cousin **(25)** FERGUS MICHAEL CLAUDE (el son of Hon Michael Claude Hamilton Bowes Lyon, 5th son of 14th Earl), 17th Earl, *b* 1928; late Capt Scots Gds, and Member of Queen's Body Guard for Scotland (Royal Company of Archers); Vice Lieut co Angus 1979-87; Dir T. Cowie plc, Sunderland, co Durham: *m* 1956, Mary Pamela, yr da of Brig Norman Duncan McCorquodale, MC; *d* 1987; *s* by his only son **(26)** MICHAEL FERGUS, 18th Earl and present peer; also Earl of Strathmore and Kinghorne (*cr* UK 1937), Viscount Lyon, Lord Glamis, Tannadyce, Sidlaw and Strathdichtie, and Baron Bowes.

Strathnaver, Lord; son of Countess of Sutherland.

STRATHSPEY, BARON (Grant of Grant) (Baron UK 1884, Bt NS 1625)
(Title pronounced "Strathspay")

JAMES PATRICK TREVOR GRANT OF GRANT, 6th Baron, and 18th Baronet; *b* 9 Sept 1943; *s* 1992; *ed* abroad; is 33rd Chief of Clan Grant: *m* 1966 (*m diss* 1984), Linda, da of David Piggott, of Forfar; 2ndly, 1985 (*m diss* 1993), Margaret, da of Robert Drummond, of Fife, and has issue by 1st *m*.

Arms – Gules, three antique crowns or. **Crest** – A burning hill proper. **Supporters** – Two savages or naked men wreathed about the head and middle with laurel, each bearing on his exterior shoulder a club, proper.
Address – The School House, Lochbuie, Isle of Mull, Argyllshire.

DAUGHTERS LIVING (By 1st marriage)

Hon Carolyn Anne Maclean, *b* 1967.
Hon Philippa Jane, *b* 1971.
Hon Victoria Louise, *b* 1976.

HALF-BROTHER LIVING

Hon MICHAEL PATRICK FRANCIS, *b* 22 April 1953; *ed* Harrow, and Oriel Coll, Oxford; ARICS. *Residence* – 3 Ifield Rd, SW10 9AZ.

SISTERS LIVING

Hon (Geraldine) Janet GRANT OF GRANT, *b* 1940; resumed surname of Grant of Grant 1972: *m* 1963 (*m diss* 1972), Neil Hamish Cantlie, yr son of late Adm Sir Colin Cantlie, KCB, CB, DSC. *Address* – c/o Royal Bank of Scotland, 14 George St, Edinburgh EH2 2YF.
Hon Jacqueline Patricia, *b* 1942: *m* 1966, Malcolm Usheen Lingen Hutton. *Residence* – Borrowstone House, Kincardine O'Neil, Aberdeenshire AB34 5AP.

HALF-SISTER LIVING

Hon Amanda Caroline, *b* 1955; *ed* St Margaret's Sch, Bushey, and Central Sch of Art and Design, London. *Residence* – 10 Nevern Place, SW5 9PR.

MOTHER LIVING

Alice, only child of late Francis Bowe, of Timaru, NZ: *m* 1st 1938 (*m diss* 1951), as his 1st wife, the 5th Baron, who *d* 1992; 2ndly, 1953, Brig Alasdair Gillean Lorne Maclean of Pennycross, who *d* 1973.

WIDOW LIVING OF FIFTH BARON

OLIVE (*Dowager Baroness Strathspey*), only da of late Wallace Henry Grant, of Norwich: *m* 1951, as his 2nd wife, the 5th Baron, who *d* 1992. *Residence* – Elms Ride, W Wittering, Sussex.

COLLATERAL BRANCHES LIVING (*In remainder to Baronetcy only*) (*See* E Seafield, colls.)

PREDECESSORS – **(1-5)** *Sir* HUMPHREY Colquhoun, 5th Bt, of Luss (*cr* 1625), obtained 1704 a new patent with original precedence giving remainder to his son-in-law, James Grant; *d* 1718; *s* by his son-in-law **(6)** *Sir* JAMES, 6th Bt; *d* 1747; *s* by his son **(7)** *Sir* LUDOVICK, 7th Bt; sat as MP for co Moray 1741-61: *m* 2ndly, Lady Margaret Ogilvie, da of Earl of Findlater; *d* 1773; *s* by his son **(8)** *Sir* JAMES, 8th Bt; sat as MP for Elgin and Forres 1761-8, and was Lord-Lieut of Inverness-shire; *d* Feb 1811; *s* by his son **(9)** *Sir* LEWIS ALEXANDER Grant of Grant, 9th Bt, who in Oct 1811 *s* as 5th Earl of Seafield; assumed in 1811 the additional surname of Ogilvie; MP for Elginshire 1790-96; *d* unmarried 1840; *s* by his brother **(10)** FRANCIS WILLIAM, 6th Earl; MP for various Scottish constituencies 1802-40; Lord-Lieut of co Inverness, and a Representative Peer; *d* 1853; *s* by his son **(11)** JOHN CHARLES, KT, 7th Earl, *b* 1815; a Representative Peer; *cr Baron Strathspey*, of Strathspey, cos Inverness and Moray (peerage of United Kingdom) 1858: *m* 1850, Hon Caroline Henrietta Stuart, who *d* 1911, da of 11th Baron Blantyre; *d* 1881; *s* by his son **(12)** IAN CHARLES, 8th Earl, *b* 1851; *dsp* 1884, when the Barony of Strathspey became ext; *s* in Scotch peerages of 1698 and 1701 by his uncle **(13)** JAMES, 9th Earl (3rd son of 6th Earl, by Mary Anne, da of John Charles Dunn, of St Helena and Higham House), *b* 1817; MP for Elgin and Nairnshire (*C*) 1868-74; *cr Baron Strathspey* (peerage of United Kingdom) 1884: *m* 1st, 1841, Caroline Louisa, who *d* 1850, da of late Eyre Evans, of Ash Hill Towers,

Limerick; 2ndly, 1853, Constance Helena, who *d* 1872, da of Sir Robert Abercromby, 5th Bt; 3rdly, 1875, Georgiana Adelaide, da of late Gen Frederick Nathaniel Walker, KCH, of Manor House, Bushey, and widow of William Stuart, of Aldenham Abbey, Herts; *d* 1888; *s* by his el son (14) FRANCIS WILLIAM, 10th Earl, *b* 1847: *m* 1874, Ann (Nina) Trevor Corry, da of Major George Thomas Evans, of Clooneavin, Otago, New Zealand; *d* 1888; *s* by his el son (15) JAMES, 11th Earl, *b* 1876; Capt Queen's Own Cameron Highlanders: *m* 1898, Mary Elizabeth Nina, da of late Joseph Henry Townend, MD, JP, of Christchurch, New Zealand; *ka* 1915, when the Earldom of Seafield devolved upon his only da, and he was *s* in the Barony of Strathspey and the Baronetcy by his brother (16) TREVOR, 4th Baron, *b* 1879: *m* 1st, 1905, Alice Louisa, who *d* 1945, da of late Thomas Masterman Hardy Johnston, MICE, of London, and subsequently Christchurch, New Zealand; 2ndly, 1947 El-frida Minnie Fass, who *d* 1949, da of late Gordon William Alexander Cloete, JP, of Cape Prov, S Africa, and widow of Lt-Col George Capron, York and Lancaster Regt; *d* 1948; *s* by his son (17) DONALD PATRICK TREVOR, 5th Baron, *b* 1912; Lieut-Col Gen List; recognised in the surname of Grant of Grant by decree of Lord Lyon 1950; Assist Chief Land Agent Defence Lands Sers: *m* 1st, 1938 (*m diss* 1951), Alice, only child of late Francis Bowe, of Timaru, NZ; 2ndly, 1951, Olive, only da of late Wallace Henry Grant, of Norwich; *d* 1992; *s* by his eldest son (18) JAMES PATRICK TREVOR, 6th Baron and present peer.

STRAUSS, BARONY OF (Strauss) (Extinct 1993)

SONS LIVING OF LIFE BARON (By 1st marriage)

Hon Roger Anthony, *b* 1934.
Hon Brian Timothy, *b* 1935.

DAUGHTER LIVING OF LIFE BARON (By 1st marriage)

Hon Hilary Jane, *b* 1937.

WIDOW LIVING OF LIFE BARON

Mrs BENITA ELEONORA ARMSTRONG (*Baroness Strauss*): *m* 1987, as his 2nd wife, Baron Strauss, PC (Life Baron), who *d* 1993. *Residence* – 1 Palace Green, W8.

Stuart, Viscount; son of Earl Castle Stewart.

STUART OF FINDHORN, VISCOUNT (Stuart) (Viscount UK 1959)

DAVID RANDOLPH MORAY STUART, 2nd Viscount; *b* 20 June 1924; *s* 1971; *ed* Eton; late Lt KRRC; Maj 6/7th R Welch Fus (TA); FRICS; Page of Honour to HM 1938-40; DL of Caerns 1963-68: *m* 1st, 1945, Grizel Mary Wilfreda, who *d* 1948, da of late Theodore Fyfe, and widow of Michael Gillilan; 2ndly, 1951 (*m diss* 1979), Marian, da of late Gerald Wilson, of Kint-bury, Berks; 3rdly, 1979, Margaret Anne, yr da of Cdr Peter Du Cane (*see* Pole, Bt, *cr* 1628, 1985 Edn), and has issue by 1st and 2nd *m*.

Arms – Quarterly: 1st, or, a lion rampant within a double tressure flory counterflory gules, all within a bordure compony azure and argent, *Stuart*; 2nd, or, a fess chequy azure and argent, *Stewart of Downe*; 3rd, or, three cushions within a double tressure flory counterflory gules, *Randolph*; 4th gules, a lion rampant within a bordure engrailed argent, *Gray*, all within a bordure or for difference. **Crest** – In a nest vert a pelican feeding her young or, about her neck a collar engrailed gules. **Supporters** – Two capercailzie proper, their wings closed. *Residence* – 38 Findhorn, Findhorn, Moray.

SONS LIVING (By 1st marriage)

Hon (JAMES) DOMINIC, *b* 25 March 1948; *ed* Eton: *m* 1979, Yvonne Lucienne, da of Edgar Després, of Ottawa. *Residence* – 15 Stowe Rd, W12.

(By 2nd marriage)

Hon Andrew Moray, *b* 1957.

DAUGHTERS LIVING (By 2nd marriage)

Hon Chloe Anne-Marie, *b* 1952.
Hon Rosalie Jane, *b* 1954.
Hon Vanessa Mary, *b* 1960.

SISTER LIVING

Hon Jean Davina (Tannachie, Findhorn, Forres, Moray IV36 0JY), *b* 1932: *m* 1st, 1951, John Reedham Erskine Berney, Lt Roy Norfolk Regt, who was *ka* in Korea 1952, son of Major Sir Thomas Reedham Berney, MC, 10th Bt; 2ndly, 1954, Percy William Jesson; 3rdly, 1985, Michael Denison Ritchie, and has issue living, (by 1st *m*) (*see* Berney, Bt), — (by 2nd *m*) Rayner Charles Percy (13 Basing St, W11), *b* 1954: *m* 1987, Gordana, da of Veljko Simakovic, of Sarajevo, Yugoslavia, — James Gray (6 Bishop's Av, E13), *b* 1959, — Arabella Clare Lucy, *b* 1962: *m* 1984, Barry Ball, of 27 Observatory Rd, SW17 7QB.

PREDECESSOR – (1) *Rt Hon* JAMES GRAY Stuart, CH, MVO, MC, 3rd son of 17th Earl of Moray; *b* 1897; Ch Conservative Whip 1941-48, Sec of State for Scotland 1951-57, Chm of Unionist Party in Scotland 1950-62, and MP for Moray and Nairn 1923-59; *cr Viscount Stuart of Findhorn*, of Findhorn, co Moray (peerage of UK) 1959: *m* 1923, Lady Rachel Cavendish, who *d* 1977, da of 9th Duke of Devonshire; *d* 1971; *s* by his el son (2) DAVID RANDOLPH MORAY, 2nd Viscount and present peer.

SUDELEY, BARON (Hanbury-Tracy) (Baron UK 1838)

MERLIN CHARLES SAINTHILL HANBURY-TRACY, 7th Baron; *b* 17 June 1939; *s* 1941; *ed* Eton, and Worcester Coll, Oxford (BA); Lay Patron Prayer Book Soc, Pres Monday Club, and Vice-Chancellor Monarchist League; FSA; co-author of *The Sudeleys, Lords of Toddington* (1987): *m* 1980 (*m diss* 1988), Hon Mrs Elizabeth Mairi Villiers, el da of late Derek William Charles Keppel, Viscount Bury (*see* E Albemarle), and formerly wife of Alastair Michael Hyde Villiers (*see* D Roxburghe, 1968 Edn).

Arms – Quarterly: 1st and 4th or, an escallop in the chief point sable, between two bendlets gules, *Tracy*; 2nd and 3rd or, a bend engrailed vert plain cotised sable, *Hanbury*. **Crest** – 1st, on a chapeau gules, turned up ermine, an escallop sable, between two wings or; 2nd, out of a mural coronet sable, a demi-lion rampant or, holding in the paws a battle-axe sable, helved gold. **Supporters** – On either side a falcon, wings elevated proper, beaked and belled or. **Badge** – A fire beacon, and in front thereof and chained thereto a panther ducally gorged, the tail nowed.
Residence – 25 Melcombe Court, Dorset Square, NW1 6EP.

MEMORIA · PII · ÆTERNA

The pious are held in everlasting remembrance

Badge of the
Barons Sudeley

WIDOW LIVING OF SIXTH BARON

ELIZABETH MARY (*Lady Collins*), da of Rear-Adm Sir Arthur Bromley, KCMG, KCVO, 8th Bt: *m* 1st, 1940, the 6th Baron, who *d* on active service 1941; 2ndly, 1965, Maj Sir Arthur James Robert Collins, KCVO, of 38 Clarence Terr, Regent's Park, NW1 4RD; and Kirkman Bank, Knaresborough, N Yorks.

COLLATERAL BRANCHES LIVING

Granddaughter of late Hon Felix Charles Hubert Hanbury Tracy, 3rd son of 4th Baron:—
Issue of late Ninian John Frederick Hanbury Tracy, *b* 1910, *d* 1971: *m* 1st, 1935 (*m diss* 1954), Hon Blanche Mary Arundell, who *d* 1993, da of 15th Baron Arundell of Wardour; 2ndly, 1954, Daphne Mary Christian, who *d* 1983, da of late Lt-Col Vivian Henry, CB (Milbank, Bt), and widow of Maj Charles Scott:—
(By 1st *m*) Jennifer Avril, *b* 1941: *m* 1964, Martin Robert Morland, CMG, HM Ambassador to Burma 1986-90, of 50A Britannia Rd, SW6, el son of Sir Oscar Charles Morland, GBE, KCMG, and has issue living, William, *b* 1965, — Anthony, *b* 1967, — Catherine Mary, *b* 1966.

Grandchildren of late Maj Eric Thomas Henry Hanbury-Tracy, OBE, only surv son of late Lt-Col Hon Frederick Stephen Archibald Hanbury Tracy, MP, 5th son of 2nd Baron:—
Issue of late Maj Claud Edward Frederick HANBURY-TRACY-DOMVILE, TD, *b* 1904, *d* 1987; assumed by deed poll 1961 the additional surname of Domvile: *m* 1st, 1927 (*m diss* 1948), Veronica May, who *d* 1985, da of late Cyril Grant Cunard (Cunard, Bt, colls); 2ndly, 1954, Marcella Elizabeth, who *d* 1983, da of late Canon John Willis Price, Rector of Croughton, Brackley, Northants:—
(By 1st *m*) (DESMOND) ANDREW JOHN HANBURY-TRACY, *b* 30 Nov 1928; *ed* Sherborne, and RAC Cirencester: *m* 1st, 1957 (*m diss* 1966), Jennifer Lynn, only da of Dr Richard Christie Hodges, of Elizabethan House, Warwick; 2ndly, 1967, Lillian, da of late Nathaniel Laurie; 3rdly, 1988, Mrs Margaret Cecilia White, da of late Alfred Henry Marmaduke Purse, and has issue living (by 1st *m*), Nicholas Edward John, *b* 1959, — (by 2nd *m*), Timothy Christopher Claud, *b* 1968. —— Charles William Justin HANBURY-TRACY (c/o Barclays Bank plc, Whitehall, SW1A 2EA), *b* 1938; *ed* Sherborne: *m* 1969 (*m diss* 1983), Sarah Jane, da of late Lt-Col George Ashley, The Cameronians (Scottish Rifles), of Rosamundford Lodge, Aylesbeare, Devon, and has issue living, Justin, *b* 1970, — Edward Claud, *b* 1976, — Emily, *b* 1971. —— Mary Claudia Elizabeth, *b* 1953, Robert Singlehurst Cross, of West End House, 1 Step Terrace, Winchester SO22 5BW, only son of late Lt-Col Charles Norman Cross, MC and bar, of Park House, Market Drayton, Shropshire, and has issue living, Edward Robert, *b* 1956, — Lucy Cunard, *b* 1954, — Sylvia Mary, *b* 1961, — Anna Elizabeth, *b* 1964.

PREDECESSORS – (1) CHARLES Hanbury, 3rd son of late John Hanbury, of Pontypool Park, Mon (deriving from the same source as the Barons Bateman); *b* 1777; MP for Tewkesbury; Chm of Commn to Judge Designs for new Houses of Parliament 1835; *cr Baron Sudeley* of Toddington, co Gloucester (peerage of UK) 1838: *m* 1798, Hon Henrietta Susanna, who *d* 1839, only child and heir of Henry, 8th and last Viscount Tracy, who in the same year took by sign manual the surname and arms of Tracy in lieu of his patronymic, and assumed the surname of Hanbury-Tracy; *d* 1858; *s* by his son (2) THOMAS CHARLES, 2nd Baron; *b* 1801; assumed by Roy licence the surname of Leigh 1806, which name in 1839 he discontinued by

Roy licence, and again assumed the surname of Hanbury: *m* 1831, Emma Eliza Alicia, who *d* 1888, da of late George Hay Dawkins-Pennant, of Penrhyn Castle, co Caernarvon; *d* 1863; *s* by his el son (3) SUDELEY CHARLES GEORGE, 3rd Baron; *d* 1877; *s* by his brother (4) CHARLES DOUGLAS RICHARD, PC, FRS, 4th Baron; *b* 1840; MP for Montgomery Dist (*L*) 1863-77; a Lord-in-Waiting to Queen Victoria 1880-85, and Capt Hon Corps of Gentlemen-at-Arms 1886: *m* 1868, Ada Maria Katherine, who *d* 1928, da of late Hon Frederick James Tollemache (Cs Dysart); *d* 1922; *s* by his el son (5) WILLIAM CHARLES FREDERICK, 5th Baron, *b* 1870: *m* 1905 (*m diss* 1922), Edith Celandine who *d* 1975, da of late Lieut Lord Francis Horace Pierrepont Cecil, RN (M Exeter); *d* 1932; *s* by his nephew (6) RICHARD ALGERNON FREDERICK (son of late Major Hon Algernon Henry Charles Hanbury-Tracy, CMG, 2nd son of 4th Baron), 6th Baron; *b* 1911; Major Roy Horse Guards: *m* 1940, Elizabeth Mary, da of Rear-Adm Sir Arthur Bromley, KCMG, CVO: *d* on active service 1941; *s* by his kinsman (7) MERLYN CHARLES SAINTHILL (son of late Capt (Michael) David Charles Hanbury Tracy, who *d* on active service 1940, grandson of 4th Baron), 7th Baron and present peer.

Sudley, Baron; title of Earl of Arran on Roll of HL.

Sudley, Viscount; son of Earl of Arran.

SUFFIELD, BARON (Harbord-Hamond) (Baron GB 1786, Bt GB 1745)

Even mindedly

ANTHONY PHILIP HARBORD-HAMOND, MC, 11th Baron, and 12th Baronet; *b* 19 June 1922; *s* 1951; *ed* Eton; Maj Coldm Gds (ret); Member HM Body Guard of Hon Corps of Gentlemen-at-Arms 1973-92; 1942-45 War in N Africa and Italy; Malaya 1948-50 (MC): *m* 1952, Elizabeth Eve, el da of late Judge (Samuel Richard) Edgedale, QC, of Field Lodge, Crowthorne, Berks, and has issue.

Arms – Quarterly: 1st and 4th quarterly, azure and gules, four lions rampant argent, and in the entre an imperial crown or, *Harbord*; 2nd and 3rd argent, a fleur-de-lis gules, *Morden*. **Crest** – On a chapeau gules turned up ermine, a lion couchant argent. **Supporters** – *Dexter*, a lion or, charged on the shoulder with a fleur-de-lis gules, and gorged with a crown flory, chain reflexed over the back, azure; *sinister*, a leopard guardant proper, gorged with a similar coronet and chain or. *Residence* – Park House, Gunton Park, Hanworth, Norfolk NR11 7HL. *Clubs* – Army and Navy, Pratt's.

SONS LIVING

Hon CHARLES ANTHONY ASSHETON, *b* 3 Dec 1953; *ed* Eton; formerly Capt Coldm Gds; temp Equerry to HM 1977: *m* 1983 (*m diss* 19—), Lucy Lennox Scrope, yr da of Com A. S. Hutchinson, of Langford Grange, Lechlade, Glos. *Residence* – 12B Albert Bridge Rd, SW11 4PY. *Clubs* – Pratt's, City of London.
Hon John Edward Richard, *b* 1956: *m* 1983, Katharine Margaret Lucy, only child of Maj George Raymond Seymour, CVO, of The Old Vicarage, Bucklebury, Reading, Berks (*see* M Hertford, colls), and has issue living, Sam Charles Antony, *b* 1989, — George Edward Seymour, *b* 1991, — Alice Mary, *b* 1986. *Residence* – 28 Swanage Rd, SW18 2DY.

Hon Robert Philip Morden, *b* 1964: *m* 1994, Sarah, only da of Derek Stevens. *Residence* – Harbord House, Cromer, Norfolk.

DAUGHTER LIVING

Hon Caroline Mary Elaine, *b* 1960: *m* 1985, Audley William Twiston Davies (*see* Archdale, Bt, colls). *Residences* – 43 Chester Sq, SW1W 9EA; The Mynd, Much Dewchurch, Ross-on-Wye.

SISTER LIVING

Hon Charity Patricia, *b* 1917. *Residence* – Westleigh, Froghall Lane, Hadleigh, Suffolk.

COLLATERAL BRANCHES LIVING

Issue of late Maurice Assheton Harbord, yst brother of 10th Baron, *b* 1874, *d* 1954: *m* 1st, 1905 (*m diss* 1918), Isabel Jessie Lowth, 4th da of Baron Frederick von Wurzburg Schade, and widow of Richard Hedley Robinson, of Kirkby Mallory Hall, Leicestershire; 2ndly, 1929, Ethel Florence, who *d* 1992, da of George William Goldsmith, of Hastings, and widow of Francis Tungwell Cowley:—
(By 2nd *m*) Patrick Rupert Shirley, *b* 1930: *m* 1955, Jean Shirley, da of Reginald George Webb, of Pebsham Farm Cottage, Bexhill-on-Sea, and has issue living, Alan Anthony (Brookwood, 44 Wadhurst Close, St Leonards-on-Sea, E Sussex), *b* 1956: *m* 1977, Nicola, only da of R. Greenhalf, of 75 Mount Rd, Hastings, and has issue living, Matthew Aaron *b* 1984, Stacey Jane *b* 1977, — Shirley Ann, *b* 1958: *m* 1984, Roy Anthony Jennings, of Owls Roost, 9 Aviemore Dr, Oakley, Basingstoke, Hants, only son of Lawrence Hamilton Jennings, of Gt Yarmouth, Norfolk. *Residence* – 16 Clarence Road, Bohemia, St Leonards-on-Sea. —— Ralph Assheton Edward, *b* 1932: *m* 1959, Angela, only da of S. D'Eath, of 5 Conqueror Road, St Leonards, Sussex, and has issue living, Richard, *b* 1964. *Residence* – Scotsford Cottage, 12 New Town, Uckfield, E Sussex.

Grandchildren of late Capt Edward Ralph Harbord, DSO, MC (*infra*):—

Issue of late William Edward Harbord, *b* 1908, *d* 1992: *m* 1st, 1938 (*m diss* 1949), Vivien Sylvia, da of late Lt-Col Foster Newton Thorne, Royal Sussex Regt; 2ndly, 1950 (*m diss* 1959), Christine Winifred, da of late Alan Higham, of Richmond Surrey:—
(By 1st *m*) Charles Francis (Torres du Colegio, Monte Judeu, 8600 Lagos, Portugal), *b* 1943; *ed* Harrow: *m* 1st, 1973, Honor Lois, da of Tom Saul, of Seacroft, Lincs; 2ndly, 1980, Sarah Juliet, da of late Peter Blandy, of Jubilee Place, SW3, and has issue living (by 2nd *m*), Astrid Anne Sylvia, *b* 1981, — Davina Auriol Bridget, *b* 1986. —— †David Ralph Foster, *b* 1947; *ed* Worksop Coll; Capt 15/19th Royal Hussars: *m* 1971, Lauretta Chinty (who *m* 2ndly, 1978, Nicholas Charles Wetherill Ridley), only da of Sir Hervey John William Bruce, 6th Bt (*cr* 1804), and *d* 1974. —— (By 2nd *m*) Christopher Evelyn, *b* 1953; *ed* Albury, NSW. —— Gay Diana, *b* 1951.
Issue of late Ralph Evelyn Harbord, *b* 1915, *d* (9 May) 1993: *m* 1950, Madeleine Betty Kezia, who *d* (23 Oct) 1993, da of late Robert Finlay-Greig:—
Robert Ralph, *b* 1950; *ed* Eton; late Lieut Royal Green Jackets: *m* 1984, Clare Mary Petre, da of late Capt Thomas Hornsby (*see* By Furnivall), and has issue living, Harry Robert Thomas, *b* 1991, — Charles Edward Ralph, *b* 1994. —— Jeremy Julian (*Clubs* - Swinley Forest, St Mortiz Tobagganing), *b* 1953; *ed* Eton; late Capt The Life Guards: *m* 1984, Monique Katherine Marie, elder da of Maj Theobald Henry Robert Fetherstonhaugh, and has issue living, James Henry Sebastian Charles *b* 1988, — Sophie India Charlotte, *b* 1986.

Granddaughters of late Hon Ralph Harbord, 6th son of 3rd Baron:—
Issue of late Capt Edward Ralph Harbord, DSO, MC, *b* 1870, *d* 1950: *m* 1906, Annie Evelyn, who *d* 1980, da of Henry Herbert Riley-Smith, of Toulston, Tadcaster Yorks:—
Bridget, *b* 1907: *m* 1931, Noel Fraser Nickols, who *d* 1966. *Residence* – 2 Beech Court, Harrogate, N Yorks HG2 0EU. —— Elizabeth Mary, *b* 1912; 1939-45 War as Ch Officer WRNS; a CSU: *m* 1946, Capt John Michael Hodges, DSO, RN (ret), who *d* 1987, son of late Adm Sir Michael Henry Hodges, KCB, CMG, MVO, of The White House, Thatcham, Berks, and has issue living, Patrick Michael (Bentworth Place, Bentworth, Alton, Hants GU34 5JP), *b* 1948; *ed* Eton: *m* 1974, Alison Mary, da of Wing-Cdr Roy Dossetter, RAF, of Andover, Hants, and has issue living, Rupert Henry *b* 1982, Catherine Mary *b* 1978, — Judith Evelyn, *b* 1952; *ed* Roedean: *m* 1982, Maj William F. A. Heal, late Royal Anglian Regt, of Burgh Parva Hall, Melton Constable, Norfolk NR24 2PU, son of Lt-Col W. A. Heal, OBE, of Denston, Suffolk, and has issue living, Jeremy William Austin *b* 1984, Olivia Claire Evelyn *b* 1983. *Residence* – 31 Marlborough Court, Pembroke Rd, W8 6DE. —— (Dorothy) Primrose, *b* 1919: *m* 1939, Maj Edward d'Abo, KOYLI (Reserve), and has issue living, Philip Edward (Windwood House, High Drive, Oxshott, Surrey KT22 0NG), *b* 1941; *ed* Harrow: *m* 1972, Fay Mary St Claire, da of late William Barbour, and has issue living, Camilla Sophie Louise *b* 1973, Lucy Dorothy *b* 1977, — Michael David (29 Middle St, Stroud, Glos GL5 1DZ), *b* 1944; *ed* Harrow: *m* 1st, 1966 (*m diss* 1982), Margaret Evelyn, da of George Lyndon, of Chelmsford; 2ndly, 1982 (*m diss* 1993), Karen Sue, da of William Gilbert, of Michigan, USA, and has issue living, (by 1st *m*) Benjamin Byron *b* 1967, Olivia Jane *b* 1969, (by 2nd *m*) Bruno George *b* 1984, — (Andrew Gerard) Noel (187 Amesbury Av, SW2 3BJ), *b* 1948; *ed* Harrow: *m* 1980, Caroline Lydia Susan, yr da of Edward Burnham, of Chelwood Beacon Cottage, Haywards Heath, W Sussex, and has issue living, Polly Primrose *b* 1983, Phoebe Rose *b* 1989, — (Penelope) Carol (twin), *b* 1948: *m* 1970, Nicholas Brian Baker, MP N Dorset, son of late Col Harold Stanley Baker, OBE, and has issue living, Matthew Ronald Nicholas *b* 1976, Annabel Dorothy Primrose *b* 1980. *Residence* – 18 White Rock House, White Rock Rd, Hastings, E Sussex TN4 1LE. —— Molly, *b* 1921: *m* 1st, 1941 (*m diss* 1946), Roy Laird-Macgregor, Lt RA; 2ndly, 1953, John Cecil Atkinson Clark, who *d* 1969 (Meyrick, Bt), and has issue living (by 2nd *m*), George Evelyn (Ewingston, Humbie, E Lothian EH36 5PE), *b* 1960; *ed* Eton; Capt The Queen's Own Yeo (TA); Member Queen's Body Guard for Scotland (Royal Company of Archers): *m* 1986, Hon Sarah Anne Elliott, twin da of Baron Elliott of Morpeth (Life Baron), and has issue living, Edward George *b* 1988, Henry William *b* 1993, Sophie Catherine *b* 1990. *Residence* – 1c Edificio El Chambel, Calle Miguel Caño 15, Marbella 29600, Spain.

PREDECESSORS – (1) *Sir* WILLIAM Morden, KB, was *cr* a Baronet 1745; assumed by Roy licence the surname of Harbord in lieu of his patronymic; *d* 1770; *s* by his son (2) *Sir* HARBORD Harbord, 2nd Bt; was MP for Norwich; *cr Baron Suffield*, co Norfolk (peerage of Great Britain) 1786; *d* 1810; *s* by his el son (3) WILLIAM ASSHETON, 2nd Baron; *d* 1821; *s* by his brother (4) EDWARD, 3rd Baron; *b* 1781: *m* 1st, 1809, Hon Georgiana, da and heiress of George, 2nd Baron Vernon; 2ndly, 1826, Emily Harriet, da of Evelyn Shirley, of Ettington Park, Warwickshire; *d* 1835; *s* by his son (5) EDWARD VERNON, 4th Baron; *dsp* 1853; *s* by his half-brother (6) CHARLES, GCVO, KCB, PC, 5th Baron; *b* 1830; Lord-in-Waiting to Queen Victoria 1868-72, Lord of Bedchamber to Prince of Wales 1872-1901, and Permanent Lord-in-Waiting to King Edward VII 1901-10: *m* 1st, 1854, Cecilia Annetta, who *d* 1911, da of late Henry Baring; 2ndly, 1911, Frances Amelia Jessie, who *d* 1934, only da of late Major Robert Poole Gabbatt, RA, and widow of Col Charles C. Rich, RHA; *d* 1914; *s* by his el son (7) CHARLES, CB, MVO, 6th Baron, *b* 1855; a Groom-in-Waiting to HM Queen Victoria 1895-1901: *m* 1896, Evelyn Louisa, JP, who *d* 1951, da of late Capt Eustace John Wilson-Patten (*see* B Winnarleigh); *d* 1924; *s* by his el son (8) VICTOR ALEXANDER CHARLES, 7th Baron; *b* 1897: *m* 1925 (*m diss* 1937), Hon Olwen Gwynne Philipps, da of 1st Baron Kylsant (ext); *d* 1943; *s* by his brother (9) JOHN, 8th Baron; *b* 1907; *d* 1945; *s* by his kinsman (10) GEOFFREY WALTER (3rd son of late Hon William Harbord, 4th son of 3rd Baron; *b* 1861: *m* 1902, Eliza Jane, who *d* 1933, da of John Mills, and widow of A. R. Beaumont, 16th Lancers; *d* 1946, *s* by his cousin (11) RICHARD MORDEN (son of late Rev Hon John Harbord, 5th son of 3rd Baron), 10th Baron; *b* 1865; Adm; Egyptian War 1882, European War 1914-19; assumed by Roy Licence 1917 the additional surname of Hamond: *m* 1913, Nina Annette Mary Crawfuird, who *d* 1955, el da of John William Hutchison of Laurieston Hall, and Edingham, Kirkcudbright; *d* 1951; *s* by his only son (12) ANTHONY PHILIP, 11th Baron and present peer.

SUFFOLK AND BERKSHIRE, EARL OF (Howard) (Earl Suffolk E 1603 and Berkshire E 1626)

We will maintain

MICHAEL JOHN JAMES GEORGE ROBERT HOWARD, 21st Earl of Suffolk and 14th Earl of Berkshire; *b* 27 March 1935; *s* 1941; *ed* Winchester; Nat Service Lieut RNVR: *m* 1st, 1960 (*m diss* 1967), Mme Simone Paulmier, da of Georges Litman, of Paris; 2ndly, 1973 (*m diss* 1980), Anita Robsahm, yr da of late Robin Robsahm Fuglesang, of Cuckfield, Sussex; 3rdly, 1983, Linda Jacqueline, da of Lt-Col Vincent Rudolph Paravicini, of Nutley Manor, Basingstoke, and formerly wife of 4th Viscount Bridport, and has issue living by 2nd and 3rd *m*.

Arms – Quarterly: 1st gules, a bend between six cross-crosslets fitchée argent, on the bend an escutcheon or, charged with a demi-lion rampant, pierced through the mouth with an arrow, and within a doubletressure flory-counter-flory gules, *Howard*; 2nd gules, three lions passant guardant in pale or, and a label of three points argent, *Thomas of Brotherton*; 3rd, checky or and azure, *Warren*; 4th gules, a lion rampant argent, *Mowbray*; in the centre of the four quarterings a crescent for difference. **Crest** – On a chapeau gules, turned up ermine, a lion statant guardant tail extended or, gorged with a ducal coronet argent, and charged on the body with a crescent for difference. **Supporters** – Two lions argent, each charged on the shoulder with a crescent sable.
Seat – Charlton Park, Malmesbury, Wilts, SN16 9DG.

SON LIVING (By 2nd marriage)

ALEXANDER CHARLES MICHAEL WINSTON ROBSAHM (*Viscount Andover*), *b* 17 Sept 1974.

DAUGHTERS LIVING (By 2nd marriage)

Lady Katharine Emma Frances Anita Robsahm, *b* 1976.

(By 3rd marriage)

Lady Philippa Mimi Jacqueline Henrietta, *b* 1985.
Lady Natasha Rose Catherine Linda, *b* 1987.

BROTHERS LIVING

Hon Maurice David Henry (3 Walpole St, SW3), *b* 1936; *ed* Eton; served with RN (Suez) 1955-57: *m* 1978, C. M. Vicky, el da of G. B. Summers, of Newcastle upon Tyne, and has issue living, Annabel Frances Victoria, *b* 1979.
Hon Patrick Greville (Far Upton Wold, Moreton-in-Marsh, Glos GL56 9TG), *b* 1940; *ed* Eton, Grenoble (France) and Heidelberg Univs, and Peterhouse, Camb (BA); Lt R Wiltshire Yeo: *m* 1966, Mary Elizabeth, da of Dr Clarence Laverne Johnson, of 140 Park Lane, W1 (*see* Royden Bt, 1980 Edn), and has issue living, Jason Patrick, *b* 1968: *m* 1991, Amanda Jane, da of Sir (James) Gerard Waterlow, 4th Bt (*cr* 1930), — Rory Alexander, *b* 1970, — Timothy Charles, *b* 1973, — Charles Edward, *b* 1974.

WIDOW LIVING OF SON OF NINETEENTH EARL

Frances Drake, da of late Edwin Morgan Dean, of Newcastle, Northumberland, and Toronto, Canada: *m* 1939, Hon Cecil John Arthur Howard, who *d* 1985. *Residence* – 1511 Summit Ridge Drive, Beverly Hills, Calif, USA.

COLLATERAL BRANCHES LIVING

Issue of late Lt-Cdr Hon Greville Reginald Howard, yst son of 19th Earl, *b* 1909, *d* 1987: *m* 1945, Mary, who *d* 1994, da of late William Smith Ridehalgh, of Broughton Lodge, Cartmel, N Lancs:—
Caroline Margaret, *b* 1947: *m* 1st, 1965, Nigel William Stacey; 2ndly, 1970, Robert Mark Goodden. *Residence* – Polkanugga Farm, St Martin, Helston, Cornwall.

Issue of late Hon James Knyvett Estcourt Howard, 2nd son of 18th Earl, *b* 1886, *d* 1964: *m* 1925, Nancy Induna Frances Caroline, who *d* 1972, el da of late Edgar Lubbock, LLB (B Avebury, colls):—
Virginia Mary Eloise, *b* 1926: *m* 1948, Capt David John Richard Ker, MC, DL, late Coldm Gds, and has issue living, David Peter James (85 Bourne St, SW1W 8HF; *Clubs* – White's, Turf, Beefsteak, Pratt's, The Brook (NY)); *b* 1951; Founder and Proprietor David Ker Fine Art 1980: *m* 1974, Alexandra Mary, da of Vice-Adm Sir Dymock Watson, KCB, CBE, DL, of Trebinshwyn, Brecon, and has had issue, David Edward Richard *b* 1979; *d* 1980, David Humphry Rivers *b* 1982, Clare Rose *b* 1977, — Caroline Moira, *b* 1949: *m* 1968 (*m diss* 1972), Thomas William Fellowes (*see* V Hampden, colls), — Camilla Rosanna Gian, *b* 1959. —— Priscilla Margaret, *b* 1930: *m* 1954, Jeremy Porter.

Grandchildren of late Brig Sir Charles Alfred Howard, GCVO, DSO, yr son of Hon Greville Theophilus Howard, 2nd son of 17th Earl:—
Issue of late Lt-Col Henry Redvers Greville Howard, KRRC, *b* 1911, *d* 1978: *m* 1st 1940 (*m diss* 1946), Patience, da of Lt-Col Charles Rice Iltyd Nicholl, TD, of 52 Queen's Gate, SW7; 2ndly 1948, Odette (Castle Rising, King's Lynn, Norfolk), da of Henry Clark, of Ventnor, Isle of Wight, and widow of Fl-Lt Gordon Crosby, RAF:—
(By 1st *m*) Greville Patrick Charles (Castle Rising, King's Lynn, Norfolk), *b* 1941: *m* 1st, 1968 (*m diss* 1972), Zoë, yr da of Douglas Walker, of 65 Pont St, SW1, and Paris; 2ndly, 1978, Mary Rose, who *d* 1980, yst da of Sir (Edward) John Chichester, 11th Bt; 3rdly, 1981, Mary Cortland, da of Robert Culverwell, of Bridges Court, Luckington, Wilts, and has issue living (by 3rd *m*), Thomas Henry Greville, *b* 1983, — Charles Edward John, *b* 1986, — Annabel Rosemary Diana, *b* 1984. —— Amanda Susan Diana (Castle Rising, King's Lynn, Norfolk), *b* 1943: *m* 1968, Alexander Simon James Montague Burton, who *d* 1972, and has issue living, Michael Alexander Greville James, *b* 1971, — Sophie Amelia Sarah, *b* 1970. —— (By 2nd *m*) Katherine Venetia, *b* 1948.

PREDECESSORS – **(1)** *Lord* THOMAS Howard, KG, PC, 2nd son of Thomas, 4th Duke of Norfolk, was summoned to Parliament in right of his mother as *Baron Howard de Walden* (peerage of England) 1597, and in 1603 was *cr Earl of Suffolk* (peerage of England); was a Commr for executing the office of Earl Marshal of England, in which capacity he was mainly instrumental in discovering the Gunpowder Plot; elected Chancellor of Cambridge University 1613; was Lord High Treasurer of England 1613-18; *d* 1626; *s* by his son **(2)** THEOPHILUS, KG, PC, 2nd Earl; summoned to Parliament in his father's Barony of Howard de Walden; was Lord Warden of the Cinque Ports, Constable of Dover Castle, and Capt of the Band of Gentlemen Pensioners; *d* 1640; *s* by his el son **(3)** JAMES, KB, 3rd Earl; *d* 1689 without male issue, when the Barony of Howard de Walden went into abeyance between his daughters, and the Earldom devolved upon his brother **(4)** GEORGE, 4th Earl, who *dsp* 1691; *s* by his next brother **(5)** HENRY, 5th Earl; *d* 1709; *s* by his son **(6)** HENRY, 6th Earl, who in 1706 had been *cr Baron Chesterford*, Co Essex and *Earl of Bindon*, Co Dorset (peerage of England); was sometime Dep Earl Marshal, in which capacity in 1707 he held a Court of Chivalry; *d* 1718; *s* by his son **(7)** CHARLES WILLIAM, 7th Earl; *dsp* 1722, when the Barony of Chesterford and the Earldom of Bindon expired, and the Earldom of Suffolk devolved upon his uncle **(8)** EDWARD, 8th Earl; *d* unmarried 1731; *s* by his brother **(9)** CHARLES, 9th Earl; *d* 1733; *s* by his son **(10)** HENRY, 10th Earl; *dsp* 1745; *s* by his kinsman **(11)** HENRY BOWES, PC, 11th Earl, who had previously *s* as 4th *Earl of Berkshire* (see * infra); appointed Dep Earl Marshal of England 1708; *d* 1757; *s* by his grandson **(12)** HENRY, 12th Earl; *d* 1779; *s* by his son **(13)** HENRY, 13th Earl; *d* 1779; *s* by his great-uncle **(14)** THOMAS, 14th Earl, 3rd son of 11th Earl; *dsp* 1783; *s* by his kinsman **(15)** JOHN, 15th Earl, great-grandson of Hon Philip, 7th son of 1st Earl of Berkshire; was a Gen in the Army; *d* 1820; *s* by his son **(16)** THOMAS, 16th Earl; *d* 1851; *s* by his son **(17)** CHARLES JOHN, 17th Earl; *b* 1804; sat as MP for Malmesbury (*L*) 1832-41: *m* 1829, Isabella, who *d* 1891, da of Lord Henry Howard and niece of 12th Duke of Norfolk; *d* 1876; *s* by his son **(18)** HENRY CHARLES, 18th Earl of Suffolk and 11th Earl of Berkshire, *b* 1833; MP for Malmesbury (*L*) 1859-68: *m* 1868, Mary Eleanor Lauderdale, who *d* 1928, da of late Hon Henry Amelius Coventry; *d* 1898; *s* by his el son **(19)** HENRY MOLYNEUX PAGET, 19th Earl of Suffolk and 12th Earl of Berkshire, *b* 1877; Maj RFA: *m* 1904, Marguerite Hyde, who *d* 1968, da of late Levi Zeigler Leiter, of Dupont Circle, Washington, USA: *ka* 1917; *s* by his el son **(20)** CHARLES HENRY GEORGE, GC, 20th Earl of Suffolk, and 13th Earl of Berkshire; *b* 1906: *m* 1934, Mimi, who *d* 1966, da of late Alfred George Forde-Pigott; *d* on active service 1941; *s* by his el son **(21)** MICHAEL JOHN JAMES GEORGE ROBERT, 21st Earl of Suffolk, and 14th Earl of Berkshire and present peer; also Viscount Andover, and Baron Howard of Charlton.

*****(1)** *Hon* THOMAS Howard, KG, 2nd son of the 1st Earl of Suffolk was *cr Baron Howard of Charlton*, co Wilts, and *Viscount Andover* (peerage of England) 1625, and *Earl of Berkshire* (peerage of England) 1626; *d* 1660; *s* by his son **(2)** CHARLES, 2nd Earl; was summoned to Parliament in his father's Barony of Howard; *d* 1679; *s* by his brother **(3)** THOMAS, 3rd Earl; *d* 1706; *s* by his great-nephew **(4)** HENRY BOWES, 4th Earl (grandson of Hon William, 4th son of 1st Earl), who *s* as 11th Earl of Suffolk (ante).

Suirdale, Viscount; son of Earl of Donoughmore.

SUMMERSKILL, BARONY OF (Summerskill) (Extinct 1980)

SON LIVING OF LIFE BARONESS

Hon Michael Brynmôr SUMMERSKILL (4 Millfield Lane, N6), *b* 1927; *ed* St Paul's Sch, and Oxford Univ (BCL MA); Bar Middle Temple 1952: *m* 1st, 1951, Florence Marion Johnston, da of Sydney Robert Elliott, of Glasgow; 2ndly, 1972, Audrey Alexandra Brontë Blemings; 3rdly, 1983, Maryly Blew La Follette, da of Earle Blew, and has issue (by 1st *m*), Ben Jeffrey Peter, *b* 1961, — Anna Felicity, *b* 1959, — Clare Aracea Elliott, *b* 1961.

DAUGHTER LIVING OF LIFE BARONESS

Hon Shirley Catherine Wynne SUMMERSKILL, *b* 1931; *ed* St Paul's Girls' Sch, and Somerville Coll, Oxford (BM, BCh and MA); MP for Halifax (*Lab*) 1964-83; an Under-Sec of State Home Office 1974-79: *m* 1957 (*m diss* 1971), John Ryman, Bar-at-law.

Sunderland, Earl of; grandson of Duke of Marlborough

SUTHERLAND, COUNTESS OF (Sutherland) (Earl S about 1235)

ELIZABETH MILLICENT SUTHERLAND (*Countess of Sutherland*), 24th holder of the peerage, Chief of Clan Sutherland, *b* 30 Mar 1921; *s* 1963; adopted the surname of Sutherland under Scots Law 1963: *m* 1946, Charles Noel Janson, late Welsh Guards, and has issue.

Arms – Gules, three mullets or (as the ancient arms of Sutherland of that Ilk), on a bordure of the second a double tressure flory-counterflory of the first (as an Honourable Augmentation). **Crest** – A Cat-a-mountain sejant rampant proper. **Supporters** – *Dexter*, a savage man wreathed about the head and loins with laurel proper, holding in his exterior hand a club Gules resting upon his shoulder, *sinister*, another like savage sustaining in his sinister hand and against his shoulder, upon a staff ensigned by the coronet of an Earl, a bannerette gules, charged of three mullets or.
Seat – Dunrobin Castle, Golspie, Sutherland. *Residences* – 39 Edwardes Sq, W8; House of Tongue, by Lairg, Sutherland.

SONS LIVING

ALISTAIR CHARLES ST CLAIR SUTHERLAND (*Lord Strathnaver*) (Sutherland Estates Office, Golspie, Sutherland), *b* 7 Jan 1947; *ed* Eton, and Ch Ch, Oxford; Master of Sutherland; Vice Lord Lieut of Sutherland since 1993; Metropolitan Police 1969-74; IBM UK Ltd 1975-78: *m* 1st, 1968 (*m diss* 19—), Eileen Elizabeth, only da of Richard Wheeler Baker, of Princeton, USA; 2ndly, 1980, Gillian Margaret St Clair, el da of late Robert Murray, of 23 Cloch Rd, Gourock, Renfrewshire, and has issue by 1st and 2nd *m*:—

SON LIVING (*By 2nd m*) *Hon* Alexander Charles Robert, *b* 1 Oct 1981.
DAUGHTERS LIVING (*By 1st m*) *Hon* Rachel Elizabeth, *b* 1970, — *Hon* Rosemary Millicent, *b* 1972, — (*by 2nd m*) *Hon* Elizabeth Murray St Clair, *b* 1984.

Hon Martin Dearman SUTHERLAND JANSON (twin), *b* 1947; *ed* Eton: *m* 1974, Hon Mary Ann Balfour, da of 1st Baron Balfour of Inchrye, and has issue living, James Charles Harold, *b* 1975, — Nicholas George, *b* 1977, — Benjamin Edward, *b* 1979, — Alexander Martin, *b* 1981, — Christopher David, *b* 1984. *Residence* – Meadow Cottage, Christmas Common, Watlington, Oxon.

DAUGHTER LIVING

Lady Annabel Elizabeth Hélène SUTHERLAND, *b* 1952: *m* 1982, John Vernon Bainton, of Charleton, Bungunya, N Queensland, Australia, only son of late John Richard Bainton, of Point Piper, Sydney, and has issue, Edward John, *b* 1983, — Nicholas John, *b* 1988, — Alice Elizabeth, *b* 1985. *Residence* – 9 Eaton Sq, SW1.

COLLATERAL BRANCHES LIVING

Descendants of late Lady Rosemary Millicent Sutherland-Leveson-Gower, RRC, yr da of 4th Duke, *b* 1893, *d* 1930: *m* 1919, Viscount Ednam, afterwards 3rd Earl of Dudley, who *d* 1969:—
See E Dudley.
Descendants of late Lord Francis Leveson-Gower, 2nd son of 3rd Duke, who *s* his mother as 2nd Earl of Cromartie:—
See E Cromartie.
Descendants of late Lady Florence Leveson-Gower, elder da of 3rd Duke, *b* 1855, *d* 1881: *m* 1876, Rt Hon Henry Chaplin, afterwards 1st Viscount Chaplin, who *d* 1923:—
See V Chaplin (ext).
Grandchildren of late Hon Edith Helen Chaplin, DBE, elder da of late Lady Florence Chaplin (ante), *b* 1879, *d* 1959: *m* 1899, 7th Marquess of Londonderry, who *d* 1949:—
See M Londonderry.
Grandchildren of late Hon Florence Chaplin (Hon Mrs Hoare) (infra):—
Issue of late Charles Hugh Hoare, *b* 1923, *d* 1981: *m* 1949, Gillian Leith (High Farm, Alexton, Uppingham, Leics), da of Samuel Ernest Chesterman:—
Richard Mark HOARE, *b* 1955: *m* 1986, Alison Wendy Allen (*née* McDonald), and has issue living, Edward Hugh Richard, *b* 1986. *Residence* – Wardley, Stonehouse, Oakham, Leics. —— Stephen Robin HOARE, *b* 1959. —— Caroline (Amanda) HOARE, *b* 1952.

Issue of late Hon Florence Chaplin, yr da of late Lady Florence Chaplin (ante), *b* 1881, *d* 1949: *m* 1920, Charles Richard Hoare, who *d* 1933:—
Helen HOARE, *b* 1921. *Residence* – Wardley House, Wardley, Oakham, Leics.

Descendants of late Lady Elizabeth Georgiana Leveson-Gower, VA, CI, el da of 2nd Duke, *b* 1824, *d* 1878: *m* 1844, 8th Duke of Argyll, who *d* 1900 (*see* that title).
Descendants of the late Lady Evelyn Leveson-Gower, 2nd da of 2nd Duke, *b* 1825, *d* 1869: *m* 1843, 12th Lord Blantyre, who *d* 1900 (*see* Baird, Bt, *cr* 1809, colls).
Descendants of late Lady Caroline Leveson-Gower, 3rd da of 2nd Duke, *b* 1827, *d* 1887: *m* 1847, 4th Duke of Leinster, who *d* 1887 (see that title).
Descendants of late Lady Constance Gertrude Leveson-Gower, yst da of 2nd Duke, *b* 1834, *d* 1880: *m* 1852, 1st Duke of Westminster (see that title).
Descendants of late Lord Francis Leveson-Gower (*cr Earl of Ellesmere*), 3rd son of Elizabeth, Countess of Sutherland and 1st Duke (*see* D Sutherland).
Descendants of late Lady Charlotte Sophia Leveson-Gower, el da of Elizabeth, Countess of Sutherland and 1st Duke, *b* 1788, *d* 1870: *m* 1814, 13th Duke of Norfolk (see that title).
Descendants of late Lady Elizabeth Mary Leveson-Gower, yr da of Elizabeth, Countess of Sutherland and 1st Duke, *b* 1797, *d* 1891: *m* 1819, 2nd Marquess of Westminster, who *d* 1869 (*see* D Westminster).

PREDECESSORS – (1) WILLIAM of Murray (Moray, the vast northern province of which his family were the leading barons at end of 12th century) afterwards called William of Sutherland, el son of Hugh Freskin or de Moray, Lord of Duffus in Moray; *s* his father as Lord Sutherland before 1222; *cr* Earl of Sutherland after 1232; *d* 1248; *s* by his son **(2)** WILLIAM Sutherland, 2nd Earl; defeated Norse invaders of Sutherland 1263; *d* 1306/7; *s* by his el son **(3)** WILLIAM, 3rd Earl, attended Parliament at St Andrews 1308/9 as an adherent of King Robert Bruce; *d* 1330; *s* by his brother **(4)** KENNETH, 4th Earl: *m* (according to Sir Robert Gordon) Mary, da of Donald, Earl of Mar; *k* at Halidon Hill 1333; *s* by his el son **(5)** WILLIAM, 5th Earl; taken prisoner at Nevill's Cross 1346; had a blood feud with the Mackays of Strathnaver that lasted three centuries: *m* 1st, 1342, Margaret, who *d* 1346, da of King Robert I; 2ndly, 1347, Joan, da of Sir John Menteith of Rusky, and widow of Malise, 7th Earl of Strathearn, of John Campbell, Earl of Atholl, and of Maurice Moray, Earl of Strathearn; *d* about 1371; *s* by his el surv son (by 2nd wife) **(6)** ROBERT, 6th Earl, after whom his castle of Dunrobin ("Robert's Castle") was named; mentioned by Froissart as a leader of invasion of England 1388: *m* 1389, Margaret Stewart, nat da of Alexander, Earl of Buchan, "the Wolf of Badenoch", 4th son of King Robert II; *d* about 1427; *s* by his el son **(7)** JOHN, 7th Earl; knighted on battlefield near Liège 1408; resigned Earldom to his son John, Master of Sutherland 1456: *m* Margaret, who *d* 1509/10, da of Sir William Baillie of Lamington; *d* about 1460; his el surv son **(8)** JOHN, 8th Earl; *s* 1456; became an idiot 1494: *m* 1st, (according to Sir Robert Gordon) da of Alexander Macdonald, Lord of the Isles and Earl of Ross; 2ndly, Fingole, said to have been da of William, Thane of Cawdor, and widow of Sir John Munro, 11th of Foulis; 3rdly, Catherine; *d* about 1508; *s* by his son, by his first wife **(9)** JOHN, *de jure* 9th Earl; also became mentally incapable, so was ward of the Crown, his estates being administered by High Treasurer; his service as heir was opposed by his half-brother Alexander (son of 2nd marriage), who in 1509 resigned his claim; *d* 1514; *s* by his sister **(10)** ELIZABETH, Countess of Sutherland: *m* about 1500 Adam Gordon of Aboyne (who *d* 1538), *jure uxoris* 10th Earl of Sutherland, 2nd son of 2nd Earl of Huntly; constantly at war with her half-brother, who seized Dunrobin Castle; she resigned Earldom, with consent of her husband in favour of her son Alexander 1527, who was infeft in reversion; *d* 1535; *s* by their grandson **(11)** JOHN Gordon (el son of Alexander Gordon, Master of Sutherland, who *m* Lady Janet Stewart, da of 2nd Earl of Atholl, and *d* 1529/30) 11th Earl; *b* 1525; accompanied Queen Dowager to France 1550, and *cr* Knt of St Michael there; involved in Earl of Huntly's revolt, and dignities and titles forfeited 1563, when he fled to Flanders; restored by Parliament in 1567; assisted at Queen Mary's marriage to Bothwell: *m* 1st, 1545/46, Lady Elizabeth Campbell, who *dsp* about 1548, da of 3rd Earl of Argyll, and widow of James, Earl of Moray, nat son of James IV; 2ndly, 1548, Lady Helen Stuart, who *d* 1564, da of 12th Earl of Lennox and widow of 6th Earl of Erroll; 3rdly, Marion Seton, who *d* (poisoned) 1567, da of 4th Lord Seton, and widow of 4th Earl of Menteith; *d* (poisoned) at Dunrobin 1567; *s* by his only surviving son **(12)** ALEXANDER, 12th Earl, *b* 1552; Hereditary Sheriff of Inverness; acquired Lordship of Strathnaver from Earl of Huntly in exchange for Aboyne; made peace treaties with his ancestral enemies the Mackay chief and Earl of Caithness: *m* 1st, 1567 (*m diss* 1572) Lady Barbara Sinclair, el da of 4th Earl of Caithness; 2ndly, 1573, Lady Jean Gordon (who *m* 3rdly, 1599 Alexander Ogilvie of Boyne, and *d* 1629), da of 4th Earl of Huntly, and formerly wife of 4th Earl of Bothwell (afterwards husband of Mary, Queen of Scots); *d* 1594; *s* by his el son **(13)** JOHN, 13th Earl, *b* 1576, bore the Sword of State before the King at Rising of Parliament 1597, which he claimed as his hereditary right; encouraged industry in Sutherland, opening coalpits at Brora; obtained 1601 a novodamus of Earldom, which was erected into a Regality, with grant of Hereditary Shrievalty of Sutherland (his territories being specially erected into a sheriffdom), in favour, failing heirs male of his body, of his brothers and their issue male, whom all failing, to Adam Gordon; 3rd son of 1st Marquess of Huntly and his heirs male whatsoever: *m* 1600, the Hon Agnes Elphinstone, who *d* 1617, el da of 4th Lord Elphinstone; *d* 1615; *s* by his 4th but el surv son **(14)** JOHN, 14th Earl, *b* 1609; was the first man to sign the National Covenant 1638; active Covenanter during Civil War (Commr for Sutherland); Col of Horse and Foot, Sutherland; Lord Privy Seal (for Cromwell) 1656-58; bore the Sceptre at opening of 1st Parliament of Charles II 1661; obtained 1662 a novodamus of Earldom in favour of his son George, Lord Strathnaver: *m* 1st, 1632, Lady Jean Drummond, who *d* 1637, da of 1st Earl of Perth; 2ndly, 1659, Hon Anne Fraser, who *dsp* 1658, da of 7th Lord Lovat; *d* 1679; *s* by his el surv son **(15)** GEORGE, 15th Earl, *b* 1633; Commr of Great Seal (for William III) 1689; obtained 1681 a novodamus of Earldom in favour of his el son and their heirs male of the body, whom failing, to Lord Strathnaver's el da and other heirs named: *m* 1659, Lady Jean Wemyss, who *d* 1715; da and heir of line of 2nd Earl of Wemyss, and widow of Archibald, Earl of Angus, son of 1st Marquess of Douglas; *d* 1703; *s* by his son **(16)** JOHN Gordon, (later Sutherland) KT, PC, 16th Earl, *b* 1661; secured Inverness for William III; raised his own Regt of Foot, which he commanded in Flanders campaign 1694; later Lt-Gen; Commr for the Union 1706; was elected one of the first 16 Representative Peers; as Lord-Lt of all the six northern counties, he held them for George I against Jacobite Rising 1715; resumed ancient surname of Sutherland about 1670; obtained 1706 a novodamus of Earldom in favour of his son Lord Strathnaver and himself, and their heirs male of the body, whom failing the heirs female of the body of Lord Strathnaver without division, and their issue male, whom failing the Earl's heirs female: *m* 1st, 1680, Helen Cochrane, who *d* 1690, da of William Lord Cochrane (E Dundonald); 2ndly, Lady Katherine Tollemache, who *d* about 1705, da of Countess of Dysart (Duchess of Lauderdale) and widow of James, Lord Doune (E Moray); 3rdly, 1727, Frances, who *d* 1732, da of Sir James Hodgson of Bramwith Hall, Yorks, and widow of Sir Thomas Travell; *d* 1733; *s* by his grandson **(17)** WILLIAM, 17th Earl (son of William, Lord Strathnaver, by Katherine, da of William Morison of Prestongrange, E Lothian); *b* 1708; a Representative Peer; supported Govt 1745-46, present at Culloden; received £1,000 in compensation for abolition of Hereditary Shrievalty of Sutherland 1747: *m* 1734, Lady Elizabeth Wemyss who *d* 1747, da of 3rd Earl of Wemyss; *d* 1750; *s* by his only son **(18)** WILLIAM, 18th Earl *b* 1735; Lt-Col Comdt of a Bde of Highlanders; a Representative Peer: *m* 1761, Mary, who *d* 1766, da and co-heir of William Maxwell, of Preston, Kirkcudbright; *d* 1766; *s* by his only surv da **(19)** ELIZABETH, Countess of Sutherland, *b* 1765; her right to the Peerage, which was opposed by Sir Robert Gordon, descendant of 2nd son of 12th Earl, as heir male of body of Adam Gordon, Earl of Sutherland, husband of Elizabeth Countess of Sutherland **(20 ante)**, and by George Gordon of Forse, as heir male of 1st Earl, was confirmed by House of Lords 1771; raised Sutherland Fencibles 1779 and 1793: *m* 1785, the 1st Duke of Sutherland; *d* 1839 **(20-23)**; succession followed the Dukedom of Sutherland until the death of 5th Duke 1963; he was *s* in the Earldom by his niece **(24)** ELIZABETH MILLICENT (only da of late Lord Alistair St Clair Sutherland-Leveson-Gower, MC, 2nd son of 4th Duke), Countess of Sutherland and present peeress; also Lady Strathnaver.

SUTHERLAND, DUKE OF (Egerton) (Duke UK 1833, Bt E 1620)

Thus until

JOHN SUTHERLAND EGERTON, 6th Duke; *b* 10 May 1915; *s* as 5th Earl of Ellesmere 1944, and as 6th Duke of Sutherland 1963; *ed* Eton, and Trin Coll, Camb; late Capt Roy Armoured Corps (TA), and a DL for Berwickshire; 1939-45 War (prisoner): *m* 1st, 1939, Lady Diana Evelyn Percy, who *d* 1978, da of 8th Duke of Northumberland; 2ndly, 1979, Evelyn Mary, da of Maj Robert Moubray (*see* Morrison-Bell, Bt, colls).

Arms – Argent, a lion rampant gules between three pheons sable. **Crest** – On a chapeau gules, turned up ermine, a lion rampant of the first, supporting an arrow or, feathered and headed argent. **Supporters** – *Dexter*, a horse argent, ducally gorged or; *sinister*, a griffin or, ducally gorged azure.
Seats – Mertoun, St Boswell's, Roxburghshire; Lingay Cottage, Newmarket, Suffolk. *Clubs* – Jockey, White's, Turf.

SISTERS LIVING

Lady Susan Alice, *b* 1913: *m* 1933 (*m diss* 1966), Maj John Marjoribanks Askew, Gren Gds, and has issue living, Henry John (Ladykirk House, Berwick-upon-Tweed TD15 1SU; 77 Chester Row, SW1W 8JL), *b* 1940; *ed* Eton: *m* 1978, Rosemary Eileen da of Dr (Charles) Edmunds Darby Taylor, of Alnwick House, Little Shelford, Cambridge, and has issue living, Jack *b* 1984, George *b* 1986, William *b* 1992, — Sarah Caroline (*Baroness Faringdon*), *b* 1936: *m* 1959, 3rd Baron Faringdon, of Barnsley Park, Cirencester, and 30 Phillimore Gdns, W8. *Residence* – Stone House, Sprouston, Kelso, Roxburghshire.
Lady Margaret, *b* 1918; sometime Junior Comm ATS; was a Lady-in-Waiting to HRH Princess Elizabeth 1946-49, Extra Lady-in-Waiting to HM Queen Elizabeth the Queen Mother: *m* 1948, Sir John Rupert Colville, CB, CVO, who *d* 1987 (*see* V Colville of Culross, colls). *Residence* – The Close, Broughton, nr Stockbridge, Hants.

WIDOW LIVING OF FIFTH DUKE

CLARE JOSEPHINE (DUNKERLEY) (*Clare, Duchess of Sutherland*), da of late Herbert O'Brien, of Calcutta: *m* 1944, as his 2nd wife, the 5th Duke, who *d* 1963.

COLLATERAL BRANCHES LIVING

Issue of late Capt Lord Alistair St Clair Sutherland-Leveson-Gower, MC, 2nd son of 4th Duke, *b* 1890, *d* 1921: *m* 1918, Elizabeth Helène, who *d* 1931 (having *m* 2ndly, 1931, Col Baron George Osten Driesen), da of Warren Gardener Demarest of New York City:—
Elizabeth Millicent (*Countess of Sutherland*); *s* as Countess of Sutherland 1963 (see that title).

Grandchildren of late Hon Francis William George Egerton, 2nd son of 3rd Earl of Ellesmere:—
Issue of late Cyril Reginald Egerton, *b* 1905, *d* 1992: *m* 1st, 1934, Mary, who *d* 1949, da of Rt Hon Sir Ronald Hugh Campbell, GCMG; 2ndly, 1954, Mary Truda, who *d* 1982, only da of late Sir (Thomas) Sydney Lea, 2nd Bt:—
(By 1st *m*) FRANCIS RONALD, *b* 18 Feb 1940; *ed* Eton, and RAC Cirencester: *m* 1974, Victoria Mary, da of Maj-Gen Edward Alexander Wilmot Williams, CB, CBE, MC, of Herringston, Dorset (*see* B Addington, 1968 Edn), and has issue living, James Granville, *b* 1975, — Henry Alexander, *b* 1977. *Residence* – Ley Farm, Stetchworth, Newmarket, Suffolk CB8 9GX. —— Lucy Helen, *b* 1937: *m* 1958, Michael Alan Pelham, JP, of Old Way House, Beaulieu, Hant SO42 7YL, and has issue living, Charles Peregrine (12A Charleville Mansions, Charleville Rd, W14 9JB), *b* 1959: *m* 1990, Clare Johanna Marina, da of Wallace Earl Britton, of 1842 Calypso Drive, Aptos, CA 95003, USA, and has issue living, Henry Cyril *b* 1992, George Marcus *b* 1994, — Laura Mary (10 Hollywood Court, Hollywood Rd, SW10 9HR), *b* 1962. —— Katharine Mary, *b* 1942: *m* 1979, Franklin Watts, of 42 Chiddingstone St, SW6, and has issue living, Angus William, *b* 1982, — Camilla Mary, *b* 1984. —— Alice Marian, *b* 1946: *m* 1971, Thomas David Fremantle, and has issue (*see* B Cottesloe, colls).

Issue of late Hon Thomas Henry Frederick Egerton, 3rd son of 3rd Earl of Ellesmere, *b* 1876, *d* 1953: *m* 1902, Lady Bertha Anson, who *d* 1959, da of 3rd Earl of Lichfield:—
Pamela Katharine, *b* 1918: *m* 1940, Lieut-Col Ralph Capel Stockley, Roy Northumberland Fusiliers, who was *ka* 1944, and has issue living, Jane Margaret, *b* 1942: *m* 1974, Gerard Balfour Chichester, of Llangoed, Erwood, Builth Wells, Powys, and has issue living, Henry Ralph *b* 1977, Charles Edmond *b* 1978, — Sally Elizabeth, *b* 1944: *m* 1978, Dr Christopher John Tudor Lewis, of Malt Office Farm, Metfield, Harleston, Norfolk, and has issue living. Beatrice Emily Frances *b* 1979, and an adopted son, John Claude *b* 1976 (adopted 1983). *Residence* – Owls, Middle Hill, Englefield Green, Surrey.

Grandsons of late Capt Francis Egerton (infra):—
Issue of late Anthony Francis Egerton, *b* 1921, *d* 1985; late Lieut 60th Rifles and Fl Lieut RAF: *m* 1946, Pauline Clodagh (Old Hoyle, Heyshott, Midhurst, Sussex), da of late Trevor Toulmin Seaton Leadam, of Colebrooke, Watersfield, Sussex:—
Simon Francis Cavendish, *b* 1949; *ed* Milton Abbey: *m* 1990, Juliet Susannah, only da of Robert Assheton Barrett, of Widford, Herts (*see* B Clitheroe, 1972-73 Edn), and has issue living, Isabella Louise Greville *b* 1994. *Residence* – Old Hoyle, Heyshott, Midhurst, Sussex GU29 0DX. —— Fulke Charles Granville, *b* 1952; *ed* Stanbridge Earls. *Address* – c/o Wells Fargo Bank, Sunnyvale, Calif, USA.
Issue of late Michael Godolphin Egerton, *b* 1924, *d* 1979: *m* 1st, 1951, (Pamela) Nicolette, yr da of Giulio Giorgio de Gardiol, of La Fontana, and Luserna San Giovanni, Turin, Italy, and formerly wife of Patrick William Meade-Newman; 2ndly, 1957, Elizabeth Anne Bowring, who *d* 1994, only da of Leslie Bowring Wimble, of Romany Ridge, N Chailey, Lewes, Sussex:—
(By 2nd *m*) Mark William Godolphin (Mijas, Malaga, Spain), *b* 1958: *m* 1st, 1979 (*m diss* 1983), Nicola J. Hawkes; 2ndly, 1991, Mercedes Abadia Gomez, of Fuengirola, Spain, and has issue living (by 1st *m*), Sophia Annabel Godolphin, *b* 1983, — (by 2nd *m*) Sacha Louise, *b* 1993. —— †Robin Michael Bowring, *b* 1962: *m* 1985, Suzanne, da of John Edward Liversidge, of Field Cottage, Westlands, Birdham, nr Chichester, Sussex, and *d* 1988, as the result of a motor accident, leaving issue, Kathryn Rebecca, *b* 1986, — Charlotte Louise, *b* 1987. —— Nicholas, *b* 1967.

Grandson of late William Francis Egerton, son of late Adm Hon Francis Egerton, 2nd son of 1st Earl of Ellesmere:—

Issue of late Capt Francis Egerton, b 1896, d 1935: m 1921, Hon Doris Mary Pottinger Meysey-Thompson (who d 1953, having m 2ndly, 1938, Major John Humphrey Allison Seed, TD, DL, JP, Yorkshire Hussars (Yeo)), da of 1st Baron Knaresborough:—

David William, b 1930; ed Stowe; Capt (ret) 17th/21st Lancers: m 1956, Patricia Mary Treharne, da of late Archibald Allen Treharne Thomas, formerly wife of late William Rippon Bissill, and has issue living, Francis David, b 1959; ed Stowe, RAC Cirencester (ARICS), and Keble Coll, Oxford (BA). Club – Cavalry and Guards'.

Granddaughters of late Claude Francis Arthur Egerton, 3rd son of late Lt-Col Hon Arthur Frederick Egerton, 4th son of 1st Earl of Ellesmere:—

Issue of late Lt-Col Scrope Arthur Francis Sutherland Egerton, b 1902, d 1986: m 1933, Marjorie, who d 1992, da of late Hugh Morrison, MP (see E Granville, 1934 Edn):—

Sarah Jane Mary, b 1934. —— Susan Alexandra, b 1936: m 1957, David John Yorke, of Hall Foot, Clitheroe, Lancs, and has issue (see B Clitheroe). —— Katharine Rose, b 1946: m 1973, Peter John Sanguinetti, of Sand Hall, Wedmore, Som, and has issue living, Edward Francis b 1979, Charlotte Emma Georgiana b 1983.

(In remainder to Marquessate of Stafford)

Descendants of late Rt Hon Lord Granville Leveson-Gower, GCB (yst son of 1st Marquess of Stafford), who was cr Earl Granville 1833 (see that title).

(In remainder to Earldom of Gower)

Grandchildren of late Lt-Col Harold Boscawen Leveson-Gower (infra):—

Issue of late Charles Murrough Leveson-Gower, b 1933, d 1983: m 1960, Rosemary Anne (who m 2ndly, 1987, Ronald Patrick Thorburn, FRICS, of Straloch, by Blairgowrie, Perthshire), da of late Maj Charles John Frederick Platt, 3rd Hussars, of Muirhouselaw, St Boswells, Roxburghshire:—

Mark Broke, b 1961: m 1987, Emma Joy, elder da of Desmond O'Conor Cameron, of Horsegrove House, Rotherfield, Sussex, and has issue living, Hugh Charles, b 1993. —— Henry Boscawen Boddington, b 1962; has assumed his wife's maiden name as an additional forename: m 1992, Paula Ruth, DPhil, yr da of David Boddington, of Poole, Dorset, and has issue living, Reuben Boddington, b 1993. Residence – 8 Holroyd St, Watson, ACT 2602, Australai. —— Alice Victoria, b 1966: m 1993, Mark W. V. Mathewson, yr son of Niel Mathewson, of Cullaloe, Fife.

Granddaughter of late Col Charles Cameron Leveson-Gower, CMG, OBE, el son of late Capt Hugh Broke Boscawen Leveson-Gower, 2nd son of John Leveson-Gower, el son of Gen John Leveson-Gower, el son of Adm Hon John Leveson-Gower, yst son of 1st Earl Gower:—

Issue of late Lt-Col Harold Boscawen Leveson-Gower, b 1905, d 1973: m 1930, Kathleen May, OBE, who d 1984, da of late Sir Murrough John Wilson, KBE (B Inchiquin, colls):—

Anastasia (Anastasia, Lady Studd), b 1931: m 1958, Sir Robert Kynaston Studd, 3rd Bt, who d 1977, and has issue (see Studd, Bt).

Issue of late Brig-Gen Philip Leveson-Gower, CMG, DSO, DL, yr son of Capt Hugh Broke Boscawen Leveson-Gower (ante), b 1871, d 1939: m 1899, Eleanor Marcia, who d 1975, da of Christopher R Nugent, JP, formerly of The Hall, Pinner, Middx:—

Elizabeth Ellen b 1915: m 1945, Mark William Harford, who d 1969, and has issue living, Philip Hugh (Horton Hall Farm, Horton, Chipping Sodbury, Avon BS17 6QN), b 1946: m 1982, Willa, yr da of late William Joseph Franklin, of St Mary's Mead, Witney, Oxon, and has issue living, William Scandrett b 1984, Harriet Kate Isabel b 1987, — Gerald Mark (Trewyn, Abergavenny NP7 7PG), b 1948: m 1985, Camilla Margaret, eldest da of Alistair Allan Horne, of The Old Rectory, Turville, Oxon (see D Buccleuch, 1976 Edn), and has issue living, Auriol Louise b 1987, Elizabeth Mida b 1989. Residence – 8 Court St, Sherston, Malmesbury, Wilts SN16 0LL.

Granddaughter of late Brig-Gen Philip Leveson-Gower, CMG, DSO, DL (ante):—

Issue of late Brig Hugh Nugent Leveson-Gower, b 1900, d 1979: m 1st, 1934 (m diss 1948), Avril Joy, who was k in a motor accident in Mexico 1978, da of late Sir John Ashley Mullens, and formerly wife of Prince George Imeritinsky; 2ndly, 1949, Rachel, who d 1981, yst da of Maj Harold Hunter Grotrian, of North Stainley Hall, Ripon, and formerly wife of Michael Humphrey Wilkins:—

(By 1st m) Lucinda Gaye (Lady Le Marchant), b 1935: m 1955, Sir Spencer Le Marchant (see Le Marchant, Bt), who d 1986. Residences – 29 Rivermill, Grosvenor Rd, SW1; The Saltings, Yarmouth, I o Wight.

Grandson of late Granville William Gresham Leveson-Gower, el son of late William Leveson-Gower (b 1806), el son of William Leveson-Gower (b 1779), 3rd son of Adm Hon John Leveson-Gower (ante):—

Issue of late Rev Frederick Archibald Gresham Leveson-Gower, b 1871, d 1946: m 1st, 1897, Cecil Eyre, who d 1939, da of Sir Walpole Lloyd Greenwell, 1st Bt; 2ndly, 1940, Elizabeth, who d 1964, da of late George Dodds, of Newcastle-on-Tyne:—

(By 1st m) Humphrey Leigh Gresham (4 Merrion Court, 55 Bournemouth Rd, Parkstone, Poole, Dorset), b 1908: m 1st, 1929 (m diss 1941), Tracy, da of late R. Hughes; 2ndly, 1942, Cecily Marion, who d 1980, da of Henry Saxe-Wyndham.

Grandchildren of late Evelyn Marmaduke Gresham Leveson-Gower, 6th son of late Granville William Gresham Leveson-Gower (ante):—

Issue of late Alastair Marmaduke Gresham Leveson-Gower, b 1907, d 1990: m 1st, 1934, Marjorie Blackburn, who d 1936, da of late Herbert Cawtheray; 2ndly, 1939, Barbara (3 Briarwood Rd, St Johns, Woking, Surrey), da of William George Higgins:—

(By 1st m) Anthony Gresham (24A Oak Tree Rd, Whitehill, Bordon, Hants GU35 9DF), b 1934. —— (By 2nd m) Robert Alastair (3 Briarwood Rd, St Johns, Woking, Surrey GU21 1XD), b 1946.

Issue of late Rupert Evelyn Gresham Leveson-Gower, Capt King's Own Royal Regt, b 1911, d 1985: m 1956, May (Manor Farm, Standlake. Witney, Oxon), da of William Humphrey Clinkard, of Great Leys Farm, Garsington, Oxon:—

Charles William Gresham, b 1959. —— Catherine Anne Gresham, b 1957.

PREDECESSORS – (1) Sir THOMAS Gower, Knt; cr a Baronet 1620; s by his son (2) Sir THOMAS, 2nd Bt; a zealous partisan of Charles I; s by his grandson (3) Sir THOMAS, 3rd Bt; a Col of Foot; d unmarried 1689; s by his uncle (4) Sir WILLIAM Leveson-Gower, 4th Bt; sat for many years as MP for Newcastle-under-Lyme; d 1691; s by his son (5) Sir JOHN, 5th Bt; was Chancellor of the Duchy of Lancaster cr Baron Gower, of Sittenham, co York (peerage of Great Britain) 1703; d 1709; s by his son (6) JOHN, PC, 2nd Baron; was Lord Privy Seal, twice one of the Lords Justice during the King's absence, and Custos Rotulorum of Staffordshire; cr Viscount Trentham and Earl Gower (peerage of Great Britain) 1746; d 1754; s by his son (7) GRANVILLE, KG, 2nd Earl; sat successively as MP for Bishop's Castle, Westminster, and Lichfield; was a Lord of the

Admiralty 1749, Lord-Lieut of Staffordshire, Lord Privy Seal 1755-7, Master of the Horse 1757, Keeper of the Great Wardrobe 1760, Lord Chamberlain 1763-5, and Pres of the Council 1768-79 and 1783-94; *cr Marquess of Stafford* (peerage of Great Britain) 1786; *d* 1803; *s* by his son (8) GEORGE GRANVILLE, KG, PC, 2nd Marquess; was summoned to Parliament in his father's Barony of Gower 1799; was Ambassador to Paris 1790-2: *m* 1785, Elizabeth, in her own right *Lady Strathnaver* and *Countess of Sutherland* (peerage of Scotland, see Css Sutherland, ante); *cr Duke of Sutherland* (peerage of United Kingdom) 1833; *d* 1833; *s* by his son (9) GEORGE GRANVILLE, KG, 2nd Duke; summoned to Parliament in his father's Barony of Gower 1826, and in 1839 *s* his mother as Baron Strathnaver and Earl of Sutherland; *b* 1786; sat as MP for St Mawes 1808; was Lord-Lieut of co Sutherland, and Custos Rotulorum of Staffordshire: *m* 1823, Harriet Elizabeth Georgiana, VA, da of 6th Earl of Carlisle; *d* 1861; *s* by his son (10) GEORGE GRANVILLE, KG, 3rd Duke, *b* 1828; MP for Sutherland (*L*) 1852-61; Lord-Lieut of Cromartie and Sutherland; *m* 1st, 1849, Anne, VA (*cr Countess of Cromartie, Viscountess Tarbat of Tarbat, Baroness Castlehaven of Castlehaven and Baroness Macleod of Leod* (peerage of United Kingdom) 1861, with remainder to her second surviving son Francis, and the heirs male of his body, to each other her yr sons in like manner in priority of birth, to said Francis and the heirs of his body, to each other her yr sons in like manner in priority of birth, to her daughter Florence and the heirs of her body, and to each other of her daughters in like manner in priority of birth), who *d* 1888 (when the Earldom of Cromartie devolved, in accordance with the special remainder upon her second surviving son, Francis), only child of John Hay Mackenzie; 2ndly, 1889, Mary Caroline, who *d* 1912, da of Rev Richard Mitchell, DD, and widow of Arthur Kindersley Blair, 71st Highland LI; *d* 1892; *s* by his el son (11) CROMARTIE, KG, 4th Duke; *b* 1851; Mayor of Longton 1895; MP for Sutherland (*L*) 1874-86; KG 1902: *m* 1884, Lady Millicent Fanny St Claire-Erskine, who *d* 1955 (having *m* 2ndly, 1914 (*m diss* 1919), Brig-Gen Percy Desmond Fitzgerald, DSO, 11th Hussars, and 3rdly, 1919, Lieut-Col Geoffrey Ernest Hawes, DSO, MC, Roy Fusiliers (ret), who *d* 1945), da of 4th Earl of Rosslyn; *d* 1913; *s* by his el son (12) GEORGE GRANVILLE SUTHERLAND, KT, PC, 5th Duke, *b* 1888; Lord High Commr to Gen Assembly of Ch of Scotland 1921 and 1922, Under Sec of State for Air 1922-24, Paymaster-Gen 1925-28, Lord Steward of HM Household to King Edward VIII 1936, and High Steward of Kingston upon Thames 1953-63: *m* 1st, 1912, Lady Eileen Gwladys Butler, who *d* 1943, da of 7th Earl of Lanesborough; 2ndly, 1944, Mrs Clare Josephine Dunkerly, da of late Herbert O'Brien, of Calcutta; *d* 1963; *s* in the Earldom of Sutherland and Lordship of Strathnaver by his niece, Elizabeth Millicent, da of late Capt Lord Alistair St Clair Sutherland-Leveson-Gower, MC, 2nd son of 4th Duke, and wife of Charles Noel Janson (*see* Cs Sutherland), and in his other honours by his kinsman (13) JOHN SUTHERLAND Egerton, 5th Earl of Ellesmere (see infra *), 6th Duke, and present peer; also Marquess of Stafford, Earl Gower, Earl of Ellesmere, Viscount Trentham, Viscount Brackley, and Baron Gower.

*(1) *Lord* FRANCIS Leveson-Gower, KG, PC, yr surv son of 1st Duke; MP for Sutherland, 1826-31 and for S Lancashire 1835-36; a Lord of the Treasury 1827, Ch Sec for Ireland 1828, and Lord-Lieut of Lancashire; assumed the name of Egerton by Roy licence on succeeding to the estates of the 3rd and last Duke of Bridgwater; *cr Viscount Brackley* and *Earl of Ellesmere* (peerage of UK) 1846; *d* 1857; *s* by his son (2) GEORGE GRANVILLE FRANCIS, 2nd Earl, *b* 1823: *m* 1846, Lady Mary Louisa Campbell, who *d* 1916, da of 1st Earl Cawdor; *d* 1862; *s* by his son (3) FRANCIS CHARLES GRANVILLE, 3rd Earl, *b* 1847: *m* 1868, Lady Katharine Louisa Phipps, who *d* 1926, da of 2nd Marquess of Normanby; *d* 1914; *s* by his el son (4) JOHN FRANCIS GRANVILLE SCROPE, MVO, 4th Earl, *b* 1872: *m* 1905, Lady Violet Lambton, who *d* 1972, da of 4th Earl of Durham; *d* 1944; *s* by his only son (5) JOHN SUTHERLAND, 5th Earl, and afterwards 6th Duke of Sutherland (ante).

SWANN, BARONY OF (Swann) (Extinct 1990)

SONS LIVING OF LIFE BARON

Hon Richard Meredith (1 Carmel Court, Holland St, W8), *b* 1944, *ed* The Edinburgh Academy, Trin Coll, Camb, and Univ Coll, London; architect: *m* 1969, Julia, da of Ronald Coke-Steel, and has issue, Robert Edward Meredith, *b* 1973.
Dr the Hon (Gavin Michael) Peter (28 Winscombe Cres, W5), *b* 1955; *ed* The Edinburgh Academy, St Andrews Univ, Bristol Univ, and LSE; Associate Prof, London Business Sch: *m* 1989, Jenny R., yr da of Prof Walter Elkan, and has issue living, Caroline Susan Teresa, *b* 1991, — Emma Frances Ruth, *b* 1992.

DAUGHTERS LIVING OF LIFE BARON

Hon Sylvia Jane, *b* 1947: *m* 1970, Christopher William Maxwell Garnett, of Henden Hall, Biddenden, Kent TN27 8BB, and has issue living, Simon Michael John, *b* 1978, — Lucy Teresa Emma, *b* 1973, — Emma Caroline Barbara, *b* 1975.
Hon Catriona Mary Antonia, *b* 1953: *m* 1976, Robert Noble Watson, of Ballingall, nr Leslie, Fife, and has issue, James Richard, *b* 1982, — Teresa Janet, *b* 1978.

WIDOW LIVING OF LIFE BARON

TERESA ANN (*Baroness Swann*), da of late Prof Reginald Morier Yorke Gleadowe, CVO: *m* 1942, Baron Swann, FRS (Life Baron), who *d* 1990. *Residences* – Tallat Steps, Coln-St-Denys, Cheltenham, Glos; 23 Sheffield Terr, W8.

SWANSEA, BARON (Vivian) (Baron UK 1893, Bt UK 1882)

Live by the spirit of God

JOHN HUSSEY HAMILTON VIVIAN, 4th Baron, and 4th Baronet; *b* 1 Jan 1925; *s* 1934; *ed* Eton, and Trin Coll, Camb; a DL for Powys; CStJ: *m* 1st, 1956 (*m diss* 1973), Miriam Antoinette, who *d* 1975, da of A. W. F. Caccia-Birch, MC, of Guernsey Lodge, Marton, New Zealand; 2ndly, 1982, Mrs Lucy Temple-Richards, da of Rt Rev Hugh Rowlands Gough, CMG, OBE, TD, DD of Forge House, Over Wallop, Stockbridge, Hants (*see* B Kinnaird), and has issue by 1st *m*.

ᴀrms – Or, on a chevron azure, between three lions' heads erased proper, as many annulets gold; on a chief embattled gules, a wreath of oak or, between two martlets argent. ᴄrests – 1st, a lion's head erased proper charged with two bezants palewise and gorged with a collar gules, thereon three annulets or, with a chain of the last; 2nd, issuant from a bridge of one arch embattled and having at each end a tower proper, a demi-hussar, in the uniform of the 18th Reg, holding in his right hand a sabre and in his left a red pennon flying to the sinister. ᴥupporters – *Dexter*, a dragon wings elevated gules, gorged with a collar or charged with three torteaux; *sinister*, a horse argent, saddle and bridle proper, trappings gules, gorged with a collar sable charged with three bezants. *Residence* – 16 Cheyne Gdns, SW3 5QT.

SON LIVING *(By 1st marriage)*

Hon RICHARD ANTHONY HUSSEY, *b* 24 Jan 1957; *ed* Eton, and Durham Univ.

DAUGHTERS LIVING *(By 1st marriage)*

Hon Amanda Ursula Georgina, *b* 1958: *m* 1985, Hugh William Lowther, and has issue (*see* Lowther, Bt, colls, *cr* 1824). *Residence* – Nortoft Grange, Guilsborough, Northants NN6 8QB.
Hon Louisa Caroline Sarah, *b* 1963: *m* 1990, Paul David Vincent, only son of Peter Vincent, of 16 Gaddum Rd, Bowdon, Cheshire.

SISTER LIVING

Hon Averil, *b* 1930; a JP for Herts: *m* 1953, Alexander William Houston, and has issue living, Peter Richard Vivian (Faith House, South Stoke Lane, Bath, Avon), *b* 1954: *m* 1979, Susan Caroline, yr da of Maj Robert Evelyn Russell Smallwood (*see* Birkmyre, Bt), — Charles Robson Hamilton, *b* 1959: *m* 1987, Emma Woodbine, yst da of Michael Woodbine Parish, MC (*see* By Trent), and has issue living, Michael Charles Woodbine *b* 1991, Florence Rose Woodbine *b* 1989, Roselle Azalea Woodbine *b* 1992, — Claire Mary, *b* 1956: *m* 1985, Patrick Charles Archibald Mansel Lewis, of Capel Isaf, Manordeilo, Llandeilo, Dyfed, and has issue (*see* E Wharncliffe). *Residence* – The Little House, Datchworth, Knebworth, Herts.

PREDECESSORS – **(1)** HENRY HUSSEY Vivian, el son of John Henry Vivian, MP, brother of 1st Baron Vivian; *b* 1821; MP for Truro (*L*) 1852-7, for Glamorganshire 1857-85, and for Swansea Dist 1885-93; *cr* a *Baronet* 1882,and *Baron Swansea*, of Singleton, co Glamorgan (peerage of United Kingdom) 1893: *m* 1st, 1847, Jessie Dalrymple, who *d* 1848, da of Ambrose Goddard, MP, of The Lawn, Swindon; 2ndly, 1853, Caroline Elizabeth, who *d* 1868, da of Sir Montague John Cholmeley, MP, 2nd Bt; 3rdly, 1870, Averil, who *d* 1934, da of Capt Richard Beaumont, RN; *d* 1894; *s* by his el son **(2)** ERNEST AMBROSE, 2nd Baron; *b* 1848; *d* 1922; *s* by his half-brother **(3)** ODO RICHARD, DSO, MVO, TD, 3rd Baron; *b* 1875; European War 1914-18 as Lieut-Col Cmdg 14th Batn Roy Irish Rifles (DSO); *m* 1906, Hon Winifred Hamilton, who *d* 1944, da of 1st Baron Holm Patrick; *d* 1934; *s* by his only son **(4)** JOHN HUSSEY HAMILTON, 4th Baron and present peer.

SWAYTHLING, BARON (Montagu) (Baron UK 1907, Bt UK 1894)

DAVID CHARLES SAMUEL MONTAGU, 4th Baron and 4th Baronet; *b* 6 Aug 1928; *s* 1990; *ed* Eton, and Trin Coll, Camb (BA); formerly Chm Rothmans International plc; Pres Asso for Jewish Youth: *m* 1951, Christine Françoise (Ninette), da of late Edgar Dreyfus, of 5 rue de Chaillot, Paris, and has had issue.

ᴁrms – Or, on a mount proper, a tent argent between on the dexter a staff proper, flowing therefrom a pennon azure, charged with a lion rampant of the field, and on the sinister a palm tree also proper. ℭrest – A stag statant holding in the mouth a sprig of palm proper, in front of a flagstaff also erect proper, therefrom flowing to the dexter a banner azure, charged with a lion rampant or. ᴥupporters – On either side a figure representing a soldier of ancient Judea. *Residence* – 14 Craven Hill Mews, Devonshire Terr, W2 3DY.

SWIFT · YET · SURE

SON LIVING

Hon CHARLES EDGAR SAMUEL, *b* 20 Feb 1954.

DAUGHTERS LIVING AND DECEASED

Fiona Yvonne, *b* 1952, *d* 1982.
Hon Nicole Mary, *b* 1956: *m* 1987, Nicholas C. W. Campbell, yst son of late Prof Wilson Campbell, of Warkworth, Northumberland. *Residence* – 33 Parkers Rd, Sheffield, Yorks S10 1BN.

BROTHER LIVING

Hon Anthony Trevor Samuel, *b* 1931; *ed* Eton; Chm Abingworth plc, 26 St James's St, SW1: *m* 1962, Deirdre Bridget, yr da of late Brig Ronald Henry Senior, DSO, TD (*see* B Joicey, 1985 Edn), and has issue living, Rupert Anthony Samuel, *b* 1965, — Damian William Samuel, *b* 1970, — Georgina Mary, *b* 1963. *Residence* – 78 Chelsea Park Gds, SW3.

SISTER LIVING

Hon Jean Mary, *b* 1927: *m* 1951, Lintorn Trevor Highett, MC, and has issue living, Paul Lintorn, *b* 1958, — Clare Joanna, *b* 1956: *m* 1977, Nigel Godfrey Powell Day, and has issue living, Peter *b* 1986, Emma Louise *b* 1984, — Stephanie Jane, *b* 1963. *Residence* – 2A Gore St, SW7.

WIDOW LIVING OF SON OF SECOND BARON

Iris Rachel (24 Montrose Court, Exhibition Rd, SW7 2QQ), da of Solomon Joseph Solomon, RA, formerly of Hyde Park Gate, W: *m* 1925, Hon Ewen Edward Samuel Montagu, CBE, QC, who *d* 1985.

MOTHER LIVING

Mary Violet, eldest da of late Maj Walter Henry Levy, DSO (*see* V Bearsted, 1962 Edn): *m* 1st, 1925 (*m diss* 1942), the 3rd Baron, who *d* 1990; 2ndly, 1945, Henry Elliott-Blake, TD, FRCS, who *d* 1983. *Residence* – 17 Cadogan Sq, SW1.

COLLATERAL BRANCHES LIVING

Issue of late Ewen Edward Samuel Montagu, CBE, QC, 2nd son of 2nd Baron, b 1901, d 1985: m 1925, Iris Rachel (ante), da of Solomon Joseph Solomon, RA, formerly of 18 Hyde Park Gate, W:—

Jeremy Peter Samuel (171 Iffley Rd, Oxford OX4 1EL), b 1927; ed Hotchkiss Sch, USA, Gordonstoun, Trin Coll, Camb, and Guildhall Sch of Music; museum curator: m 1955, Gwen Ellen, da of Jack Ingledew, of Westhouses, Derby, and has issue living, Simon Joseph Samuel, b 1959: m 1st, 1983 (m diss 1989), Judith, da of Charles Lowy, of 14 Edgware Court, High St, Edgware; 2ndly, 19—, Hepzibah, da of Mordecai Cohen, of Jerusalem, and has issue living (by 1st m), Avital Rose b 1986, (by 2nd m) Aviad Mordecai b 1992, Ahinoam Rachel b 1993, — Rachel Mary, b 1956; Rabbi: m 1990, Francis Samuel, son of Werner Treuherz, of Rochdale, and has issue living, Eliezer Michael b 1993, — Sarah Ruth, b 1958: m 1980, Mark Roseman, and has issue living, Jacob Edward James b 1981, Abigail Shoshana b 1984, Kate Nechama b 1987. —— Jennifer Iris Rachel b 1931; ed Lady Margaret Hall, Oxford (BA), and London Univ (PhD 1960); art historian.

Issue of late Hon Gerald Samuel Montagu, 3rd son of 1st Baron, b 1880, d 1956: m 1909, Florence, who d 1961, da of Percy M. Castello, formerly of 20 Chalfont Court, Clarence Gate, NW1:—

Bryan de Castro Samuel, b 1916; ed Stowe; European War 1939-45 as Capt RA: m 1950, Elcie, da of late John Weiser, of 5 Rowan Walk, N2, and has a son and a da, Robert de Castro Samuel (6 Groveside, Gt Bookham, Surrey KT23 4LD), b 1956: m 1983, Claire Strettell, and has issue living, James de Castro Samuel b 1990, Charlotte Claire b 1992, — Lydia, b 1959: m 1989, Ian Leonard Coltman, of 44 Normanton Av, Wimbledon Park, SW19 8BB, elder son of William A. Coltman, of Catterick, N Yorks. Residence – 9 Hesper Mews, SW5 0HH.

PREDECESSORS – (1) Montagu Samuel-Montagu, son of late Louis Samuel, watchmaker of Liverpool; b 1832; founder of the banking firm of Samuel Montagu and Co, of Old Broad Street, EC; granted Roy licence 1894 to assume surnames of Samuel-Montagu (surname of Samuel not now used by descendants); MP for Tower Hamlets, Whitechapel Div (L) 1885-1900; cr a Baronet 1894, and Baron Swaythling, of Swaythling, co Southampton (peerage of United Kingdom) 1907: m 1862, Ellen, who d 1919, da of late Louis Cohen, of the Stock Exchange; d 1911; s by his el son (2) Louis Samuel, 2nd Baron, b 1869; head of the banking firm of Samuel Montagu and Co, of Old Broad Street, EC: m 1898, Gladys Helen Rachel, OBE, who d 1965, da of Col Albert Edward Williamson Goldsmid, MVO; d 1927; s by his son (3) Stuart Albert Samuel, OBE, 3rd Baron, b 1898; Dir Samuel Montagu & Co Ltd, Bankers; Pres English Guernsey Cattle Soc 1950-51, and 1971-72, and of Royal Assocn of British Dairy Farmers 1972-73 (Dep Pres 1970-72 and 1973-74): m 1st, 1925 (m diss 1942), Mary Violet, eldest da of late Maj Walter Henry Levy, DSO (see V Bearsted, 1962 Edn); 2ndly, 1945, Jean Marcia, CBE, who d 1993, da of late G. C. Leith Marshall, and formerly wife of late S/Ldr G. R. M. Knox, RAF; d 1990; s by his elder son (4) David Charles Samuel, 4th Baron and present peer.

SWINFEN, BARON (Eady) (Baron UK 1919)

Roger Mynors Swinfen Eady, 3rd Baron; b 14 Dec 1938; s 1977; ed Westminster; late Lt R Scots; ARICS: m 1962, Patricia Anne, only da of late J. D. Blackmore, of Doone, Highfield Park, Dundrum, co Dublin, and has issue.

Through difficulties to the heights

Arms – Per pale argent and vert, on a chevron between three battle-axes, as many ermine spots, all counter-charged. Crest – A demi-lion rampant vert, charged on the body with a battle-axe erect, and holding a like axe in bend argent. Supporters – Dexter, a lion guardant vert charged with a battle-axe argent; sinister, a lion guardant argent charged with a battle-axe vert. Address – c/o House of Lords, SW1.

SON LIVING

Hon Charles Roger Peregrine Swinfen, b 8 March 1971.

DAUGHTERS LIVING

Hon Georgina Mary Rose Swinfen, b 1964: m 1990, Capt Robin Edgar Douglas Liley, 2nd son of Capt Robert Liley, of Deal, Kent, and has issue living, Sophie Anne Clare, b 1994.
Hon Katherine Anne Dorothy Swinfen, b 1966: m 1993, Capt Gareth Huw Davies, RTR, son of Dr Cyril Davies, of Bath.
Hon Arabella Victoria Eleanor Swinfen, b 1969: m 1994, Capt Charles E. A. Mayo, The Light Dragoons, son of Col John Mayo.

BROTHER LIVING

Hon (Hugh) Toby, b 1941; ed Bryanston, and Wadham Coll, Oxford.

MOTHER LIVING

Mary Aline, da of late Col Harold Mynors Farmar, CMG, DSO: author under the name of Mary Wesley: m 1st, 1937 (m diss 1945) the 2nd Baron, who d 1977; 2ndly, 1952, Eric Otto Siepmann, journalist, who d 1970.

WIDOW LIVING OF SECOND BARON

Averil Kathleen Suzanne (Averil, Baroness Swinfen) (Keentlea, Clifden Hill, Corofin, co Clare) da of late Maj William Marshall Hickman Humphreys, of Broomfield House, Midleton, co Cork, and formerly wife of Lt Col Andrew Knowles, TD: m 1950, as his 2nd wife, the 2nd Baron, who d 1977.

PREDECESSORS – (1) Rt Hon Sir Charles Swinfen Eady, son of George John Eady, of Chertsey, b 1851; a Judge of High Court of Justice 1901-13, a Lord Justice of Appeal 1913-18, and Master of the Rolls 1918-19; cr Baron Swinfen, of Chertsey, co Surrey (peerage of United Kingdom), 1 Nov 1919: m 1894, Blanche Maude, who d 1946, da of late S. W. Lee of Dereham, Putney Hill, SW; d 15 Nov 1919; s by his only son (2) Charles Swinfen, 2nd Baron; b 1904; Bar-at-law, Inner Temple: m 1st, 1937 (m diss 1945), Mary Aline, da of Col Harold Mynors Farmar, CMG, DSO; 2ndly, 1950, Averil Kathleen

Suzanne, da of late Maj William Marshall Hickman Humphreys, of Broomfield House, Midleton, co Cork, and formerly wife of Lt-Col Andrew Knowles, TD; *d* 1977; *s* by his el son **(3)** ROGER MYNORS SWINFEN, 3rd Baron and present peer.

SWINTON, EARL OF (Cunliffe-Lister) (Earl UK 1955)

DAVID YARBURGH CUNLIFFE-LISTER, 2nd Earl; *b* 21 March 1937; *s* 1972; *ed* Winchester, and Roy Agric Coll, Cirencester; JP and DL N Yorks; CC N Riding of Yorks 1961-74, and N Yorks 1973-77; Dep Ch Whip 1982-86, and Capt of the Queen's Body Guard of Yeomen of the Guard 1982-86: *m* 1959, Susan Lilian Primrose (*Baroness Masham of Ilton*) (Life Baroness), yr da of late Sir Ronald Norman John Charles Udny Sinclair, 8th Bt (*cr* 1704), and has two adopted children.

Arms – Quarterly; 1st and 4th ermine, on a fesse sable three mullets or and (for distinction) a cross crosslet of the second, *Lister*; 2nd, sable, three conies courant argent, and (for distinction) a cross crosslet of the last, *Cunliffe*; 3rd, or, two chevronels sable, on a chief of the second three escallops of the first, *Greame*. **Crests** – 1st, a stag's head proper, erased or, attired sable, charged on the neck (for distinction) with a cross crosslet sable, *Lister*; 2nd a greyhound sejant argent, collared with a ring attached sable, charged on the shoulder (for distinction) with a cross crosslet sable, *Cunliffe*; 3rd, two wings endorsed semee of escallops sable, *Graeme*. **Supporters** – On either side a stag proper, the dexter gorged with a chain or, suspended from the dexter a rose argent, barbed and seeded proper and from the sinister an escallop also argent.
Residence – Dykes Hill House, Masham, Ripon, Yorks HG4 4NS.

ADOPTED SON LIVING

John Charles Yarburgh, *b* 1967.

ADOPTED DAUGHTER LIVING

Clare Caroline, *b* 1965.

BROTHER LIVING (*Raised to the rank of an Earl's son* 1974)

Hon NICHOLAS JOHN (Glebe House, Masham, Ripon, Yorks), *b* 4 Sept 1939; *ed* Winchester, and Worcester Coll, Oxford; late 2nd Lt WG; Solicitor 1966: *m* 1966, Hon (Elizabeth) Susan Whitelaw, eldest da of 1st Viscount Whitelaw, and has issue living, Mark William Philip, *b* 1970, — Simon Charles, *b* 1977; *s* his kinsman Marcus William Wickham-Boynton in Burton Agnes, E Yorks, 1989, — Lorna Mary, *b* 1968.

COLLATERAL BRANCH LIVING

Issue living of late Hon Philip Ingram Cunliffe-Lister, DFC, DSO, yr son of 1st Earl, *b* 1918, *d* 1956: *m* 1st, 1940 (*m diss* 1947), Rosina Gladys, da of A. G. Emburey, of Cambridge; 2ndly, 1947, Mary Stewart (who *d* 1978, having *m* 3rdly, 1958 (*m diss* 1969), Robert Alexander Pleasant Craigie, and resumed the surname of Cunliffe-Lister by deed poll 1973; *m* 4thly, 1977, Maj Patrick Robert Reid, MBE, MC, who *d* 1990), da of late Robert G. Leggatt, of Hamilton, Lanarks, and formerly wife of Robert Noel Stewart-Humphries:—
(By 2nd *m*) (Julian) Michael (64 Hill Rd, Eastbourne, E Sussex BN20 8SN), *b* 1949; *ed* Uppingham: *m* 1976 (*m diss* 1989), Penelope Susan, only da of Lt-Col David A. Pinner, of White Cottage, Sandhurst Lane, Little Common, Bexhill, E Sussex, and has issue living, Constance Alexandra Elise, *b* 1979. —— (By 1st *m*) Simone Philippa Judith Clare, *b* 1943; resumed her maiden name 1976: *m* 1st, 1965 (*m diss* 1980), Jack Frederick Deakin; 2ndly, 1986, Keith Howell, and has issue living (by 1st *m*), Lorna-Jane CUNLIFFE-LISTER, *b* 1970, — Deborah Simone Jackeline CUNLIFFE-LISTER, *b* 1971. *Residence* – Mole Corner, Summer Gardens, E Molesey, Surrey KT8 9LT. —— (By 2nd *m*) Madeline Frances Anne, *b* 1950. *Residence* – 76 South St, Lewes, E Sussex.

PREDECESSORS – **(1)** *Rt Hon Sir* PHILIP Cunliffe-Lister, GBE, CH, MC, son of late Lt-Col Yarburgh George Lloyd-Greame, of Sewerby House, Bridlington; *b* 1884; assumed by Roy licence 1924 the surname of Cunliffe-Lister; Pres of Board of Trade 1922-24, 1924-29, and 1931; Sec of State for Colonies 1931-35, and for Air 1935-38; Min Resident in W Africa 1942-44; Min of Civil Aviation 1944-45; Chancellor of The Duchy of Lancaster and Min of Materials 1951-52, and Sec of State for Commonwealth Relations 1952-55; MP for Hendon (*C*) 1918-35; *Viscount Swinton*, of Masham, co York (peerage of UK) 1935, and *Baron Masham*, of Ellington, co York and *Earl of Swinton* (peerage of UK) 1955: *m* 1912, Mary Constance, who *d* 1974, da of late Rev Charles Ingram William Boynton (Boynton, Bt colls); *d* 1972; *s* by his grandson **(2)** DAVID YARBURGH (son of late Maj Hon John Yarburgh Cunliffe-Lister, el son of 1st Earl), 2nd Earl, and present peer; also Viscount Swinton and Baron Masham.

SYSONBY, BARON (Ponsonby) (Baron UK 1935)

For the king, the law, and the people

JOHN FREDERICK PONSONBY, 3rd Baron; *b* 5 Aug 1945; *s* 1956.

Arms – Gules, a chevron between three combs argent. **Crest** – Out of a ducal coronet azure three arrows, points downwards, one in pale and two in saltire, entwined at the intersection by a snake proper. **Supporters** – On either side a lion guardant crowned with a Saxon crown or, and charged on the shoulder with a key, wards downwards and inwards azure.
Address – c/o Birch Cullimore, Solicitors, Friars, White Friars, Chester CH1 1XS.

SISTER LIVING

Hon Carolyn Mary, *b* 1938.

PREDECESSORS – (1) *Rt Hon Sir* FREDERICK EDWARD GREY Ponsonby, GCB, GCVO, son of late Gen the Rt Hon Sir Henry Frederick Ponsonby, GCB, GCVO (E Bessborough, colls); *b* 1867; formerly Major and Brevet Lieut-Col Grenadier Guards; was an Equerry-in-Ordinary to Queen Victoria 1894-1901, Assist Keeper of the Privy Purse and Assist Private Sec to Queen Victoria 1897-1901, and Equerry-in-Ordinary, an Assist Keeper of the Privy Purse, and an Assist Private Sec to King Edward VII 1901-10; appointed an Equerry-in-Ordinary to HM King George V 1910, Keeper of HM's Privy Purse and an Extra Equerry 1914, Treasurer to the King and Keeper of the Privy Purse 1920, and Lieut-Gov of Windsor Castle and Constable of the Round Tower 1928; Receiver-Gen of Duchy of Lancaster; S Africa 1901-2, European War 1914; *cr Baron Sysonby*, of Wonersh, co Surrey (peerage of United Kingdom) June 1935: *m* 1889, Victoria Lily Hegan, who *d* 1955, da of late Col Edmund Hegan Kennard of 25 Bruton Street, W; *d* Oct 1935; *s* by his son (2) EDWARD GASPARD, DSO, 2nd Baron, *b* 1903; Lieut-Col 5th Batn Queen's Roy Regt (TA); European War 1939-40 (DSO): *m* 1936, Sallie Whitney, who *d* 1979, having *m* 3rdly, 1958, Maj Edward Robert Francis Compton (M Northampton, colls), da of Dr Leonard Cutler Sanford, of New York, USA, and formerly wife of George Edward Monkland; *d* 1956; *s* by his only son (3) JOHN FREDERICK, 3rd Baron and present peer.

Talbot, Earl of, title borne by Earl of Shrewsbury.

TALBOT OF MALAHIDE, BARON (Arundell) (Baron I 1831)

Strong and faithful

(REGINALD) JOHN RICHARD ARUNDELL, 10th Baron; *b* 9 Jan 1931; *s* 1987; *ed* Stonyhurst; DL Wilts 1983; KStJ; Hereditary Lord Admiral of Malahide and Adjacent Seas: *m* 1st, 1955, Laura Duff, who *d* 1989, da of late Group-Capt John Edward Tennant, DSO, MC (*see* B Glenconner, colls); 2ndly, 1992, Mrs Patricia Mary Blundell-Brown, eldest da of late John Cuthbert Widdrington Riddell, OBE, of Felton Park, and Swinburne Castle, Northumberland, and formerly wife of late Maj Geoffrey Thomas Blundell-Brown, MBE, and has issue by 1st *m*.

Arms – Quarterly: 1st and 4th, sable six martlets three two and one argent, *Arundell*; 2nd and 3rd, gules a lion rampant or within a bordure engrailed erminois, *Talbot*. **Crests** – 1st, a wolf passant argent, *Arundell* 2nd, on a chapeau gules doubled ermine a lion passant erminois, *Talbot* **Supporters** – *Dexter*, a talbot or; *sinister*, a lion gules. **Motto** – Deo data.
Seat – Malahide Castle, co Dublin. *Residence* – Hook Manor, Donhead St Andrew, nr Shaftesbury, Dorset SP7 9EU.

SON LIVING (By 1st marriage)

Hon RICHARD JOHN TENNANT, *b* 28 March 1957; *ed* Stonyhurst, and RAC Cirencester; commn'd Royal Wessex Yeo (TA) 1979: *m* 1984, Jane Catherine, da of Timothy Heathcote Unwin, MFH, and has issue living, Isabel Mary, *b* 1986, — Emily Rose, *b* 1988, — Frances Laura, *b* 1990, — Lucinda Jane, *b* 1991. *Residence* – Park Gate Farm, Donhead, Shaftesbury, Dorset.

DAUGHTERS LIVING (By 1st marriage)

Hon Juliet Anne Tennant, *b* 1959: *m* 1987, Simon James Teakle, son of John Anthony Teakle, MRCVS, of Southover Old House, Lewes, Sussex, and has issue living, Humphrey, *b* 1990, — George, *b* 1991, — Sophie, *b* 1988, — Laura, *b* 1993.
Hon Catherine Mary Tennant, *b* 1960: *m* 1993, Andrew G. Allwood, only son of C. M. Allwood, of Ferndown, Dorset.
Hon Caroline Rose Tennant, *b* 1962.
Hon Lucy Veronica Tennant, *b* 1965: *m* 1991, Christopher S. Daniel, only son of Lt Cdr J. J. S. Daniel, of W Meon, Hants.

BROTHER LIVING (Raised to the rank of a Baron's son 1991)

Hon Edward Renfric, *b* 1933; *ed* Oratory Sch, and RMA Sandhurst; commn'd Duke of Cornwall's LI; Maj: *m* 1961, Margaret Ann Honoria, da of Brig John Francis Macnab, CBE, DSO, and has issue living, Lucinda Margaret Beatrice, *b* 1962: *m* 1987, Dr Steven Roy Nash, MB BS, MRCGP, son of Roy Nash, of Liskeard, Cornwall, and has issue living, Edward Mungo Steven *b* 1990, Emma Margaret Alice *b* 1988, Tertia Mary *b* 1993, — Camilla Edwina Clare, *b* 1965, — Nicola Marina Merry, *b* 1967: *m* 1992, Dominic Peter Craven Chambers, of 1 Dorncliffe Rd, SW6 (*see* L Herries, colls). *Residence* – 82 Edith Grove, SW10 0NH.

DAUGHTER LIVING OF EIGHTH BARON

Hon Ann Cecily Mary, *b* 1931: *m* 1955, Col Edward Reginald Edwards, and has issue living, Edward David, *b* 1956, — John Llewellyn, *b* 1958, — Richard Reginald, *b* 1973. *Residence* – Malahide, Whiteway, Litton Cheney, Dorchester, Dorset DT2 9AG.

SISTER LIVING OF SEVENTH BARON (*Raised to the rank of a Baron's daughter* 1949)

Hon Rose Maud (Malahide, Fingal, Tasmania, Australia 7214), *b* 1915.

COLLATERAL BRANCHES LIVING

Grandson of late Reginald Aloysius Talbot, 3rd son of late John Reginald Francis George Talbot, elder son of Adm Hon Sir John Talbot, GCB, 3rd son of 1st Baroness:—
Issue of late Joseph Hubert Edward Pius Talbot, *b* 1903, *d* 1975: *m* 1943, Mercia Cecelia, da of late Capt H. C. Cowell:—
Clive Richard (41 Headland Av, Seaford, E Sussex), *b* 1943: *m* 1965, Pamela Maureen, da of Basil Coxwell, of Bahia, Brazil, and has issue living, Richard Paul, *b* 1966; *ed* RNC Dartmouth; Lieut RN, — Anthony John, *b* 1967; *ed* Reading Univ (BSc), — Michael Hugh Arnold, *b* 1977, — Stephen Edward, *b* 1981, — Nicola Louise Cecilia, *b* 1970; *ed* Essex Univ (BSc), — Frances Mary, *b* 1984.

Grandchildren of late John Reginald Francis George Talbot (ante):—
Issue of late Reginald Aloysius Talbot, *b* 1870, *d* 1922: *m* 1898, Mabile Mary, who *d* 1942, da of late Hon Robert Arthur Arundell (B Arundell of Wardour, colls):—
Robert Peter Frederick Gerard (602 Hanworth Rd, Hounslow, Middlesex), *b* 1916: *m* 1944 (*m diss* 1983), Blanche Edna, da of late Herbert Albert Caseley, and has issue living, Anthony Robert John (59 Vandyke, Great Hollands, Bracknell, Berks), *b* 1946: *m* 1970, Patricia Ayliffe Doris, da of Arthur Edward Davis, and has issue living, Christopher Anthony Matthew *b* 1979, Claire Elizabeth Patricia *b* 1976, — Catherine Blanche Mary, *b* 1944. —— Lucy Geraldine Mary (Visitation Convent, Bridport, Dorset), *b* 1907. —— (Hilda Mary) Clare (27 Mulberry Gdns, Church St, Fordingbridge, Hants), *b* 1913: *m* 1972, Lt-Col Peter Coventry Grant, RE (ret), who *d* 1973, yr son of late Maj-Gen Sir Philip Gordon Grant, KCB, CMG, RE (E Coventry, colls).

PREDECESSORS – Richard Talbot, of Malahide Castle, heir male of the ancient Lords of Malahide (barons by tenure): *m* **(1)** MARGARET, el da of James O'Reilly, Esq, of Ballinlough, co Westmeath (of the Milesian princely house of Breffney); she was *cr* 1831 *Baroness Talbot of Malahide* and *Lady Malahide of Malahide*, co Dublin (peerage of Ireland), with remainder to her issue male by her late husband Richard Talbot; *d* 1834; *s* by her el son **(2)** RICHARD WOGAN, 2nd Baron; *cr Baron Furnival* (peerage of United Kingdom) 1839; *d* 1849; without surviving male issue, when the Barony of Furnival became extinct, and the Barony of Talbot of Malahide devolved upon his brother **(3)** JAMES, 3rd Baron; *b* 1767; *d* 1850; *s* by his son **(4)** JAMES, LLD, FRS, 4th Baron; *b* 1805; sat as MP for Athlone (*L*) 1832-5; *cr Baron Talbot de Malahide* (peerage of United Kingdom) 1856: *m* 1842, Maria Margaretta, who *d* 1873, da of Patrick Murray, of Simprim, Forfarshire; *d* 1883; *s* by his son **(5)** RICHARD WOGAN, 5th Baron; *b* 1846: *m* 1st, 1873, Emily Harriet, who *d* 1898, da of Sir James Boswell, 2nd Bt (*ext*); 2ndly, 1901, Dame Isabel Charlotte, DBE, who *d* 1932, da of late Robert Blake Humfrey, of Wroxham House, Norwich, and widow of John Gurney, of Sprowston Hall, Norfolk; *d* 1921; *s* by his son **(6)** JAMES BOSWELL, 6th Baron; *b* 1874: *m* 1924, Joyce Gunning, who *d* 1980, da of late Frederick Kerr, formerly of 84 Coleherne Court, SW5 *d* 1948; *s* by his cousin **(7)** MILO JOHN REGINALD, CMG (son of late Col Hon Milo George Talbot, CB, 4th son of 4th Baron), 7th Baron; *b* 1912; Ambassador to Laos 1955-56; *d* 1973, when the UK *Barony of Talbot de Malahide* became ext; *s* in the Irish peerage of *Baron Talbot of Malahide*, by his Kinsman **(8)** REGINALD STANISLAUS VICTOR, MC (2nd son of John Reginald Charles Talbot, grandson of Adm Hon Sir John Talbot, GCB, 3rd son of 1st Baroness), 8th Baron; *b* 1897: *m* 1924, Cecily Elizabeth, who *d* 1976, da of Maj Garstang Hodgson, of Clevedon, Som; *d* 1975; *s* by his brother **(9)** JOSEPH HUBERT GEORGE, 9th Baron; *b* 1899; Lieut Coldm Gds: *m* 1st, 1924, Hélène, who *d* 1961, da of M. Gouley, of Bessancourt, Seine-et-Oise, France; 2ndly, 1962 (*m diss* 1970), Beatrice Bros, of 20 rue Frederic, Passy, Nice; *d* 1987; *s* by his 1st cousin once removed **(10)** REGINALD JOHN RICHARD ARUNDELL (son of late Reginald John Arthur ARUNDELL, who assumed the surname and arms of Arundell in lieu of his patronymic, by Royal Licence 1945, eldest son of late Reginald Aloysius Talbot (grandson of Adm Hon Sir John Talbot, 3rd son of 1st Baroness), by his wife Mabile Mary, da of Hon Robert Arthur Arundell, 4th son of 9th Baron Arundell of Wardour), 10th Baron and present peer.

Tamworth, Viscount; son of Earl Ferrers.

TANGLEY, BARONY OF (Herbert) (Extinct 1973)

SON LIVING OF LIFE BARON

Hon Peter Meldrum, *b* 1936: *m* 1961, Annabel Evelyn, da of Stephen Binnie, and has issue living, Julian Tangley, *b* 1964, — James Meldrum, *b* 1965; Lieut 6th QEO Rifles: *m* 1990, Helen S., only da of Peter Palmer, of White Beeches, Moss Green Lane, Brayton, N Yorks.

DAUGHTERS LIVING OF LIFE BARON

Hon Elizabeth Ann, *b* 1933; *ed* Oxford Univ (MA, BM, BCh): *m* 1960, Hon Michael Cottrell Brain, DM, of 131, Northshore Blvd E, Burlington, Ontario, Canada (*see* B Brain).
Hon Jane Katherine, *b* 1938; GRSM, LRAM: *m* 1964, George Kenneth Beattie, CBE, RD, DL, of Big Oak, Churt, Farnham, Surrey, who *d* 1994, and has issue.
Hon Alison Margaret, *b* 1943; LRAM, ARCM: *m* 1965, John Michael Bradshaw, of Cherrydale, W Clandon, Surrey, and has issue.

TANKERVILLE, EARL OF (Bennet) (Earl GB 1714)

PETER GREY BENNET, 10th Earl; *b* 18 Oct 1956; *s* 1980; *ed* Grace Cathedral Sch (chorister), San Francisco, and Oberlin Conservatory, Ohio (B Mus), MA (Mus) San Francisco State Univ.

Arms – Gules, three demi-lions rampant argent, in the centre point a bezant. **Crest** – 1st, out of a mural coronet or, a lion's head gules, charged on the neck with a bezant; 2nd, a scaling ladder or. **Supporters** – Two lions argent, ducally crowned or, and charged on the shoulder with a torteau.
Seat – Chillingham Castle, Alnwick, Northumberland.
Residence – 139 Olympia Way, San Francisco, Cal 94131, USA.

To serve the king with good will

SISTERS LIVING AND DECEASED

Lady Alexandra Katherine, *b* 1955; *d* 1993.
Lady Anne Thérèse *b* (twin) 1956: *m* 1981, Timothy Michael Poirier.

UNCLE LIVING (son of 8th Earl by 1st m)

Rev Hon GEORGE ARTHUR GREY (112 Norwich Rd, Wymondham, Norfolk NR18 0SZ), *b* 12 March 1925; *ed* Radley, and Corpus Christi Coll, Camb (MA); V in Shaston Team Min 1973-80; Rector of Redenhall, Harleston, Wortwell and Needham 1980-90; author of *Electricity and Modern Physics* (1965), *Progress through Lent* (1993): *m* 1957, Hazel (Jane) G., da of late Ernest W. G. Judson, of Bishopswood, Chard, Somerset, and has issue living, Adrian George, *b* 1958: *m* 1st, 1984 (*m diss* 1991), Lucinda Mary, eldest da of Ashley Bell, of Weetwood Hall, Wooler, Northumberland; 2ndly, 1991, Karel Ingrid Juliet Wensby-Scott, — Neil Robert, *b* 1961, — Helen Jane, *b* 1964.

HALF-UNCLE LIVING (son of 8th Earl by 2nd marriage)

Hon Ian (Estate House, Chillingham, Alnwick, Northumberland), *b* 1935; *ed* Radley, and Corpus Christi Coll, Camb (MA); Lt RNR.

HALF-AUNT LIVING (daughter of 8th Earl by 2nd marriage)

Lady Corisande, *b* 1938: *m* 1963, Lt-Cdr Timothy Bain Smith, RN, of Wickens Manor, Charing, Kent, and has issue living, James, *b* 1964; *ed* Winchester, — Charles, *b* 1966; *ed* Winchester: *m* 1993.

WIDOW LIVING OF EIGHTH EARL

VIOLET (*Dowager Countess of Tankerville*), (Estate House, Chillingham, Alnwick, Northumberland), da of Erik Pallin, of Stockholm; JP of Northumberland; has Order of Vasa of Sweden: *m* 1930, as his 2nd wife, the 8th Earl, who *d* 1971.

WIDOW LIVING OF NINTH EARL

GEORGIANA LILIAN MAUDE (*Countess of Tankerville*) (139 Olympia Way, San Francisco, Cal, USA), da of late Gilbert Wilson, DD, MA, PhD, of Vancouver, BC: *m* 1954, as his 2nd wife, the 9th Earl, who *d* 1980.

PREDECESSORS – (1) *Sir* JOHN Bennet, KB, el son of late Sir John Bennet, of Dawley; *cr Baron Ossulston*, of Ossulston, co Middlesex (peerage of England) 1682; he and the heirs male of his body are in special remainder to the titles of his younger brother Henry, who was *cr Baron Arlington*, of Arlington, co Middlesex, *Viscount Thetford* and *Earl of Arlington* (peerage of England) 1672: *m* 1st, 1661, Lady Elizabeth, who *d* 1672, da of 1st Earl of Middlesex, and widow of 2nd Earl of Mulgrave; 2ndly, 1673, Bridget, who *d* 1703, da of John Grubham Howe, of Langar, Nottingham: *d* 1682; *s* by his son (2) CHARLES, KT, 2nd Baron: *m* 1695, Lady Mary Grey, da and heiress of 1st and last Earl of Tankerville (*cr* 1695), and after the demise of his father-in-law he was *cr Earl of Tankerville* (peerage of Great Britain) 1722; *s* by his son (3) CHARLES, KT, 2nd Earl; filled several high positions about the Court 1728-40: *m* 17-, Camilla, who *d* 1775, da of late Edward Colville, of Whitehouse, Durham; *d* 1753; *s* by his son (4) CHARLES, 3rd Earl; MP for Northumberland 1748-53: *m* 1742, Alicia, who *d* 1775, da of Sir John Astley, 2nd Bt (*cr* 1662, ext); *d* 1767: *s* by his son (5) CHARLES, 4th Earl: *m* 1771, Emma, who *d* 1836, da of Sir James Colebrook, Bt; *d* 1822; *s* by his son (6) CHARLES AUGUSTUS, PC, 5th Earl; *b* 1776; Joint Postmaster-Gen 1782-3 and 1784-6: *m* 1806, Corisande Armandine Sophie Léonice Helene, who *d* 1865, da of Antoine, Duke de Gramont; *d* 1859; *s* by his son (7) CHARLES, 6th Earl; *b* 1810; MP for N Northumberland (C) 1832-59, Capt Hon Corps of Gentlemen-at-Arms 1866-7, and Lord Steward of the Household 1867-8; summoned to House of Lords in his father's Barony of Ossulston 1859: *m* 1850, Lady Olivia Montagu, who *d* 1922, el da of 6th Duke of Manchester; *d* 1899; *s* by his second son (8) GEORGE MONTAGU, 7th Earl, *b* 1852: *m* 1895, Leonora Sophia, who *d* 1949, da of late J. G. van Marter, sometime of New York; *d* 1931; *s* by his el son (9) CHARLES AUGUSTUS KER, 8th Earl, *b* 1897: *m* 1st, 1920 (*m diss* 1930), Roberta, who *d* 1992, da of Julian Nolan, of Chicago, USA, and step-da of Dr Percy Mitchell; 2ndly, 1930, Violet, JP, da of Erik Pallin, of Stockholm; *d* 1971; *s* by his son (10) CHARLES AUGUSTUS GREY, 9th Earl, *b* 1921: *m* 1st, 1943 (*m diss* 1950), Virginia, da of late Louis M. Diether, of Vancouver, and formerly wife of — Morris; 2ndly, 1954, Georgiana Lilian Maude, da of late Gilbert Wilson, DD, MA, PhD, of Vancouver, BC; *d* 1980; *s* by his only son (11) PETER GREY, 10th Earl and present peer; also Baron Ossulston.

TANLAW, BARON (Mackay) (Life Baron 1971)

SIMON BROOKE MACKAY, yst son of 2nd Earl of Inchcape; *b* 30 March 1934; *ed* Eton, and Trin Coll, Camb (MA); Dir of Inchcape & Co, Ltd 1966-92; Chmn and Man Dir of Private Group of Cos since 1973; Hon Treasurer, Scottish Peers Assoc 1979-85; Pres Sarawak Assocn 1972-75; Member Council of Management, Univ of Buckingham since 1973 (Hon Fellow 1981); Member Court of Governors of London Sch of Economics and Political Science since 1980; *cr Baron Tanlaw*, of Tanlawhill, co Dumfries (Life Baron) 1971: *m* 1st, 1959, Joanna Susan, only da of late Maj John Henry Hirsch, of Sungrove Lodge, Newbury; 2ndly, 1976, Rina Siew Yong, yst da of late Tiong Cha Tan, of Kuala Lumpur, Malaysia, and has had issue by 1st and 2nd *m*.

Arms – Parted per chevron azure and argent, in chief two lymphads of the 2nd and in base a tiger's face affrontée proper, on a chief or a cross engrailed per cross indented azure and sable. **Crest** – A falcon proper, hooded gules, issuant out of a five-pointed Eastern crown or. **Supporters** – *Dexter*, a Prejevalski's mare proper; *sinister*, a roe deer also proper.

Residences – Tanlawhill, Eskdalemuir, Dumfries-shire DG13 0PQ; 31 Brompton Sq, SW3 2AE.

SONS LIVING AND DECEASED *(By 1st marriage)*

Hon James Brooke, *b* 1961: *m* 1993, Anne-Marie, yr da of Michael Barrett, of Midsomer Norton, Som.
Joshua Alexander Brooke, *b* 1964; *d* 1967.

(By 2nd marriage)

Hon Brooke Brooke, *b* 1982.

DAUGHTERS LIVING *(By 1st marriage)*

Hon Iona Hélöise MACKAY, *b* 1960; has resumed her maiden name: *m* 1978 (*m diss* 1988), Stephen P. Hudson.
Hon Rebecca Alexandra, *b* 1967.

(By 2nd marriage)

Hon Asia Brooke, *b* 1980.

Tarbat, Viscount; son of Earl of Cromartie.

Tavistock, Marquess of; son of Duke of Bedford.

TAYLOR, BARONY OF (Taylor) (Extinct 1988)

SON LIVING OF LIFE BARON

Hon Jeremy Stephen (12 Wymond St, Putney, SW15 1DY), *b* 1940; *ed* Highgate; a Television Executive: *m* 1964, Christina, yr da of late John Bruce Holmes, of 37 Redington Rd, NW3 (*see* L Forbes, colls, 1968 edn), and has issue.
Hon Charles Richard Herbert (3911 Argyle Terr NW, Washington DC 20011, USA), *b* 1950; *ed* Highgate, King's Coll, Camb, Queen's and St Antony's Colls, Oxon, and Wharton Business Sch, Univ of Pennsylvania; Economist, Group of Thirty: *m* 1977, Mary-Ellen, da of late John Feeney, of 1543 North Hills Av, Willow Gr, Pa 19090, USA, and has issue.

DAUGHTER LIVING OF LIFE BARON

Hon Elizabeth Trilby Charity, *b* 1943; *ed* Univ of Sussex; Librarian, British Technology Group Ltd: *m* 1st, 1971 (*m diss* 1986), Paul Stephen Masterman; 2ndly, 1986, Alan George Woodruff, of 26 Lucastes Lane, Haywards Heath, W Sussex RH16 1LD.

WIDOW LIVING OF LIFE BARON

(MAY DORIS) CHARITY (*Baroness Talyor*), MB, BS, MRCS, LRCP, da of late Wron George Clifford: *m* 1939, Baron Taylor, MRCS, LRCP, MRCP, FRCP, FRCGP, FFOM (Life Baron), who *d* 1988. *Residence* – 10 Clover Court, Church Rd, Haywards Heath, W Sussex RH16 3UF.

TAYLOR OF BLACKBURN, BARON (Taylor) (Life Baron 1978)

THOMAS TAYLOR, CBE, son of James Taylor, *b* 10 June 1929; *ed* Blakey Moor Higher Grade Sch; Member of Blackburn Town Council 1954-76 (Leader 1972-76, and Chm Policy and Resources Cttee 1972-76); a Member of N-W Economic Planning Council, N-W and Area Health Authority; Dept Pro-Chancellor of Lancaster Univ since 1974; (Member of Council and Founder Member); a Member of Council for Education and Technology in UK, of Nat Foundation for Educational Research in England and Wales, and of Schs Council; author of Taylor Report on problems at Lancaster Univ 1973; Chm, Govt Cttee of Enquiry into Management and Govt of Schs, and of Nat Foundation for Visual Aids; JP of Blackburn, Lancs; Past Chm of Juvenile Bench; Sunday Sch Supt 1947-59, and Pres Free Church Council 1962-68; Elder of United Reform Church; Treas, Blackburn Labour Party 1964-76; Member of Norweb Board and consultant, Shorrock Security Systems Ltd, Chm Thames Internat plc and other cos: *cr* OBE (Civil) 1969, CBE (Civil) 1974, and *Baron Taylor of Blackburn*, of Blackburn, co Lancaster (Life Baron) 1978: *m* 1950, Kathleen, da of John Edward Nurton, and has issue.

Arms – Argent a bar wavy cottised wavy sable between three roses gules barbed and seeded proper all within a bordure vert thereon eight bees volant proper. **Crest** – Statant on a grassy mount proper a lion or supporting with the dexter forepaw at its base growing from the front of the mount a rose branch proper reflexed over the lion's back and ending in three roses gules barbed and seeded proper on the mid-most a bee also proper. **Supporters** – *Dexter*, a dragon statant erect gules eyed langued clawed and the barb of its tail or gorged with a bar wavy sable fimbriated argent and in its jaws an olive branch proper; *Sinister*, a bull statant erect in trian aspect gules armed and unguled and the tuft of its tail or also gorged with a bar wavy sable fimbriated argent and also holding in its mouth an olive branch proper.
Residence – 34 Tower Rd, Feniscliffe, Blackburn, Lancs.

SON LIVING

Hon Paul Nurton (1 Risdale Grove, Blackburn), *b* 1953: *m* 1978, Diane Brindle.

TAYLOR OF GOSFORTH, BARON (Taylor) (Life Baron 1992)

PETER MURRAY TAYLOR, PC, son of late Herman Louis Taylor, of Newcastle upon Tyne; *b* 1 May 1930; *ed* Newcastle Royal Gram Sch, and Pembroke Coll, Camb (Hon Fellow 1992); Hon LLD Newcastle Univ 1990; Bar Inner Temple 1954, QC 1967, Recorder of Huddersfield 1969, Teesside 1970-71 and Crown Court 1972-80, Dep Chm Northumberland Quarter Sessions 1970, Bencher 1975, Chm of the Bar 1980, a Judge of the High Court (Queen's Bench Div) 1980-87, Presiding Judge NE Circuit 1984-87, a Lord Justice of Appeal 1987-92, Pres Inns of Court 1991-92, since when Lord Chief Justice; Chm Hillsborough Disaster Inquiry 1989, Controller Royal Opera House Devpt Land Trust since 1990, Chm Trinity Coll of Music 1991-92; *cr* Knt 1980, PC 1988, and *Baron Taylor of Gosforth*, of Embleton, co Northumberland (Life Baron) 1992: *m* 1956, Irene Shirley, da of Lionel Harris, of Newcastle, and has issue.
Address – c/o Royal Courts of Justice, Strand, WC2.

SON LIVING

Hon David Louis, *b* —.

DAUGHTERS LIVING

Hon Ruth Diana, *b* 1958.
Hon Deborah Frances, *b* 1959: *m* 1987, Michael Stevenson, and has issue living, one son.
Hon Judith Claire, *b* 1961: *m* 1986, Paul Bridge, and has issue living, one da.

TAYLOR OF GRYFE, BARON (Taylor) (Life Baron 1968)

THOMAS JOHNSTON TAYLOR, son of John Sharp Taylor, of Glasgow; *b* 27 April 1912; *ed* Ballahouston Acad, Glasgow; Chm of Forestry Commn 1970-76, and of Morgan Grenfell (Scotland), Ltd; Chm of Economic Forestry Group 1976-82; Fellow R Soc of Edinburgh since 1977; DL, LLD (Strathclyde) since 1974; a Member of Exec Cttee, Scottish Council (Development and Industry) since 1964, of British Railways Board, and a Board Member of Scottish Television Ltd 1968-82, and of Friends Provident and Century Group 1972-82; a Dir Whiteways Laidlaw & Co 1971-88, Chm Isaac and Edith Wolfson Trust, Trustee Dulverton Trust, Chm Scottish Peers Assocn, and Scottish Metropolitan Property Co Ltd since 1972; *cr* *Baron Taylor of Gryfe*, of Bridge of Weir, Renfrewshire (Life Baron) 1968: *m* 1943, Isobel, da of Williams Wands, and has issue.
Residence – The Cottage, Auchenames, Kilbarchan, Renfrewshire, PA10 2PM. *Clubs* – Caledonian (London); Royal & Ancient.

DAUGHTERS LIVING

Hon Jill, *b* 1945: *m* 1st, 1969, Dr Thomas Egli; 2ndly, 1976, Hans Wäber.
Hon Joyce (1 Woodland Rise, Muswell Hill, N10 3UP), *b* 1948: *m* 1st, 1969 (*m diss* 1980), Alan Begbie; 2ndly, 1982, John Huw Lloyd Richards, and has issue living (by 1st *m*).

TAYLOR OF HADFIELD (Taylor) (Life Baron 1983)

FRANCIS (FRANK) TAYLOR, son of late Francis Taylor, by his wife Sarah Ann Earnshaw; *b* 7 Jan 1905; Hon DScc Salford 1973; FIOB (Hon Fellow 1979) founded Taylor Woodrow, Building, Civil & Mechanical Engineering Contractors 1921 (Public Company 1935); Man Dir 1935-79, Chm 1937-74, and Pres and Executive Dir 1979-90, since when life Pres; mem Advisory Council to Min of State 1954-55; Chm Export Group for Constructional Industries 1954-55; Pres Provident Inst of Builders' Foremen and Clerks of Works 1950; Dir Freedom Federal Savings and Loan Assoc, Worcester, Mass 1972-82; Dir BOAC 1958-60; Vice-Pres Aims since 1978; Gov Queenswood Sch for Girls 1948-77; Fell Chartered Inst of Building; Knt 1974; *cr Baron Taylor of Hadfield*, of Hadfield, co Derbys (Life Baron) 1983: *m* 1st, 1929 (*m diss* 1956), Evelyn Woodrow; 2ndly, 1956, Christine Enid, da of Charles Hughes, and has issue by 1st and 2nd *m*.

Arms – Argent in front of a representation of Aitoff's Projection of the globe azure the land masses argent a mullet of four points gyronny of eight argent and sable the fesswise points extended on a chief gules four workmen hauling on a rope argent. **Crest** – In front of a representation of Aitoff's Projection of the globe a mullet as in the arms. **Supporters** – *Dexter*, A surveyor supporting by the exterior hand a theodolite. *Sinister*, A carpenter holding in the exterior hand a tenon saw, each wearing a safety helmet all proper. **Motto** – Conjuncti laboramus.
Address – c/o House of Lords, SW1A 0PW.
Clubs – Royal Automobile, Queen's, Hurlingham, All England.

DAUGHTERS LIVING *(By 1st marriage)*

Hon Audrey Evelyn, *b* 1932: *m* 1952, Brian S. L. Trafford, and has had issue, John Tarleton Leigh, *b* 1960; *d* 1985, — David Jeremy Mallory, *b* 1962: *m* 1985, Stephanie Vivien Ffooles, and has issue living, George William Leigh *b* 1991, Henry John Jeremy *b* 1993, — Judy Evelyn (*Lady Scott*), *b* 1952: *m* 1st, 1972, Andrew Lyndon-Skeggs; 2ndly, 1982, Sir James Jervoise Scott, 3rd Bt (*cr* 1962) and has issue living, (by 1st *m*) Vanessa Evelyn *b* 1975, Tessa Angela *b* 1979, (by 2nd *m*) (*see* Scott, Bt, *cr* 1962), — Diana Barbara (*Viscountess Melgund*), *b* 1954: *m* 1983, Gilbert Timothy George Lariston, Viscount Melgund son of 6th Earl of Minto. *Residence* – Tismans, Rudgwick, Sussex.
Hon Gillian Doreen, *b* 1934: *m* 1st, 1955, Simon Edward Anthony Kimmins, VRD, of Geneva; 2ndly, 1980, Robin Marlar, and has issue living (by 1st *m*), Andrew Simon Taylor, *b* 1958, — Martin Charles Anthony, *b* 1965: *m* 19—, Charlotte Louise, eldest da of Raymond Haslam, of Turton, Lancs, and has issue living, Thomas Charles Anthony *b* 1991, — Robyn Elizabeth Frances, *b* 1957, — Joanna Mary Verena, *b* 1960. *Residence* – Brantyngeshay, Sample Oak Lane, Chilworth, Surrey.

(By 2nd marriage)

Hon C. Sarah A., *b* 1961: *m* 1987, David M. Melville, son of Murray Melville, of Lymington, Hants, and has issue living, John Edward Charles, *b* 1992, — Mary Diana Christine, *b* 1993.

TAYLOR OF MANSFIELD, BARONY OF (Taylor) (Extinct 1991)

SON LIVING OF LIFE BARON

Hon Bernard Alfred (3 Sycamore Close, Rainworth, nr Mansfield, Notts NG2 0FX), *b* 1922: *m* 1952, Mary K. Green.

TAYSIDE, BARONY OF (Urquhart) (Extinct 1975)

SONS LIVING OF LIFE BARON

Hon William James Lauchlan (West Kilmany House, Kilmany, Cupar, Fife), *b* 1944; *ed* Fettes Coll, and Glasgow Univ (BSc Hons); CA; Member of Inst of Taxation; *m* 1967, Wendy Helen Cook, and has issue, three das.
Hon Ronald Douglas Lauchlan (Cherrills, Wonersh Park, Guildford, Surrey GU5 0QP; Caledonian Club, London, and Hong Kong Club), *b* 1948; *ed* Fettes Coll, and Edinburgh Univ (LLB); CA: *m* 1975, Dorothy May Jackson.

DAUGHTER LIVING OF LIFE BARON

Hon Hilda Louise Lauchlan, *b* 1950; *ed* St Leonards Sch, St Andrews, and Bedford Coll of Physical Education: *m* 1978, John Alexander Dalgety, of 9 Merlin Park, Dollar, Clackmannanshire.

WIDOW LIVING OF LIFE BARON

HILDA GWENDOLINE, BSc (*Baroness Tayside*) (Kallisté, 30 Turfbeg Place, Forfar, Angus), da of John Thomson Harris, of Dundee: *m* 1939, Baron Tayside (Life Baron), who *d* 1975.

TEBBIT, BARON (Tebbit) (Life Baron 1992)

NORMAN BERESFORD TEBBIT, CH, PC, 2nd son of Leonard Albert Tebbit, of Enfield, Middx; *b* 29 March 1931; *ed* Edmonton Co Gram Sch; RAF 1949-51, RAuxAF 1952-55; Airline Pilot 1953-70; Member Select Cttee Science and Technology, Chm Conservative Aviation Cttee, Vice Chm and Sec Conservative Housing and Construction Cttee, Sec New Town MPs, PPS to Min of State for Employment 1972-73, Parly Under Sec of State for Trade 1979-81, Min of State for Industry 1981, Sec of State for Employment 1981-Oct 1983, Sec of State for Trade and Industry Oct 1983-85, Chancellor of Duchy of Lancaster 1985-87, and Chm of Conservative Party 1985-87; MP Epping (*C*) 1970-74, and Waltham Forest, Chingford 1974-92; author and Co Dir; *cr* PC 1981, CH 1987 and *Baron Tebbit*, of Chingford, in the London Borough of Waltham Forest (Life Baron) 1992: *m* 1956, Margaret Elizabeth, da of Stanley Daines, of Chatteris, Isle of Ely, and has issue.

Address – c/o House of Lords, SW1 0PW.

SONS LIVING

Hon John Beresford, *b* 1958: *m* 1984, Penelope Robinson, and has issue living, one son and two das.
Hon William Mark, *b* 1965: *m* 1992, Vanessa Hurrell.

DAUGHTER LIVING

Hon Alison Mary, *b* 1960: *m* 1981, Raymond Shakespeare Smith, and has issue living, one son and one da.

TEDDER, BARON (Tedder) (Baron UK 1946)

ROBIN JOHN TEDDER, 3rd Baron;; *b* 6 April 1955; *s* 1994; Man Dir Australian Gilt Securities: *m* 1st, 1977, Jennifer Peggy, who *d* 1978, da of John Mangan, of New Zealand; 2ndly, 1980, Rita Aristea, yr da of John Frangidis, of Sydney, NSW, Australia, and has issue by 2nd *m*.

Arms – Sable, a sword enflamed palewise all proper in chief an eagle affronty volant head to sinister or. **Crest** – Issuant from an astral crown or a lion sejant guardant sable, armed and langued or, holding in the sinister fore-paw a sword enflamed as in the Arms. **Supporters** – Two representations of the God Horus all proper.
Residence – 11 Kardinia Rd, Clifton Gds, Sydney, NSW, Australia.

SONS LIVING *(By 2nd marriage)*

Hon Benjamin John, *b* 1985.
Hon Christopher Arthur, *b* 1986.

DAUGHTER LIVING *(By 2nd marriage)*

Hon Jacqueline Christina, *b* 1988.

BROTHER LIVING

Hon Andrew Jonathan (Sydney, NSW, Australia), *b* 1958.

SISTER LIVING

Hon Anne Rosalinde, *b* 1963: *m* 1989, Euan Angus Johnston, son of David Johnston, of Leuchars, Fife, and has issue living, Jade, *b* 1991.

HALF-UNCLE LIVING *(son of 1st Baron by 2nd marriage)*

Hon Richard Seton (W Buckland, Luddesdown, nr Meopham, Kent), *b* 1946: *m* 1st, 1975 (*m diss* 1987), Ann-Marie Adams; 2ndly, 1989, Lesley Anne, yr da of John Coster, of Luddesdown, Kent.

AUNT LIVING *(daughter of 1st Baron by 1st marriage)*

Hon Mina Una Margaret (Openfields, Barnyards, Kilconquhar, Fife), *b* 1920: formerly Assist Librarian, British Embassy, Wash, USA; BBC, TV 1954-7, and Scottish TV Glasgow 1957-65; Dist Commr, Nat Savings, Alnwick, Northumberland.

WIDOW LIVING OF SECOND BARON

PEGGY EILEEN (*Dowager Baroness Tedder*), yr da of Samuel George Growcott, of Birmingham: *m* 1952, 2nd Baron Tedder, who *d* 1994. *Residence* – Little Rathmore, Kennedy Gdns, St Andrews, Fife.

PREDECESSORS – (1) *Marshal of the RAF Sir* ARTHUR WILLIAM Tedder, GCB, yr son of Sir Arthur John Tedder, CB; *b* 1890; 1914-18 War with Dorset Regt, and RFC; ACC Far East, Singapore 1936-38, Dir-Gen of Research and Development, Air Min 1938-40, Dep Air Member for Development and Production 1940, Dep AOC in C Middle East 1940-41, AOC in C Middle East 1941-42, AOC in C Mediterranean 1943, Dep Supreme Cdr SHAEF 1943-45, Ch of Air Staff 1946-49, and Chm of British Joint Sers Mission, Washington USA 1950; Chancellor of Camb Univ 1950-67; *cr Baron Tedder*, of Glenguin, co Stirling (peerage of UK) 1946: *m* 1st, 1915, Rosalinde, who *d* 1943, da of William McIntyre Maclardy, of Sydney, NSW; 2ndly, 1943, Mrs Marie de Seton Black, who *d* 1965, da of Col Sir Bruce Gordon Seton, CB, 9th Bt (*cr* 1663); *d* 1967: *s* by his 2nd son, (2) JOHN MICHAEL, 2nd Baron: *b* 1926; FRSE; FRIC; Purdie Prof of Chemistry, Univ of St Andrews: *m* 1952, Peggy Eileen, yr da of Samuel George Growcott, of Birmingham; *d* 1994: *s* by his elder son, (3)ROBIN JOHN, 3rd Baron and present peer.

TEIGNMOUTH, BARONY OF (Shore) (Extinct 1981)

DAUGHTER LIVING OF SIXTH BARON

Hon Elizabeth Mary, *b* 1916: *m* 1942, Maj Charles John Patrick Barnwell, Somerset LI, and has had issue, Patrick Hugh Lowry (Pounsell House, Huish Episcopi, Langport, Somerset), *b* 1948: *m* 1st, 1975, Julia-Anne, only da of Peter Charnley, of Port Elizabeth, S Africa; 2ndly, 1986, Barbara Claire Patricia, yr da of late Sidney Warneford James Pestell, of Weston-super-Mare, — Robin Charles Lowry, *b* 1953, *d* 1970. *Residence* – Standerwick, Fivehead, Taunton, Somerset.

WIDOW LIVING OF SEVENTH BARON

PAMELA (*Baroness Teignmouth*) (108 Kensington Church St, W8 4BH), da of late Henry Edmonds-Heath, of Hungerford, Berks, and formerly wife of George Anthony Meyer: *m* 1979, as his 2nd wife, the 7th Baron, DSC and Bar, who *d* 1981, when the title became extinct.

TEMPLE OF STOWE, EARL (Temple-Gore-Langton) (Earl UK 1822)

(WALTER) GRENVILLE ALGERNON TEMPLE-GORE-LANGTON, 8th Earl; *b* 2 Oct 1924; *s* 1988; *ed* Nautical Coll, Pangbourne: *m* 1st, 1954, Zillah Ray, who *d* 1966, da of James Boxall, of Tillington, Petworth, Sussex; 2ndly, 1968, (Margaret) Elizabeth Graham, only da of late Col Henry William Scarth of Breckness, of Skaill House, Orkney, and has issue by 1st *m*.

Arms – Quarterly: 1st and 4th grand quarters, quarterly sable and or, a bend argent, *Langton*: 2nd grand quarter, gules, a fesse between three cross-crosslets fitchée or, *Gore*: 3rd grand quarter, quarterly, 1st and 4th or, an eagle displayed sable; 2nd and 3rd argent, two bars sable, each charged with three martlets or, *Temple*. **Crest** – 1st, An eagle or and a wyvern vert, their necks entwined reguardant, *Langton*; 2nd, on a mount vert, an heraldic tiger salient argent, ducally gorged or, *Gore*; 3rd on a ducal coronet or, a martlet gold, *Temple*.
Supporters – *Dexter*, a lion per fesse nebuly or and gules, gorged with a ribbon of the last, pendant therefrom an escutcheon of the arms of *Langton; sinister*, a horse argent, semée of eaglets displayed sable, gorged with a ribbon gules, pendent therefrom an escutcheon of the arms of *Gore*.
Residences – The Cottage, Easton, Winchester, Hants; Garth, Outertown, Stromness, Orkney.

SONS LIVING (By 1st marriage)

JAMES GRENVILLE (*Lord Langton*), *b* 11 Sept 1955; *ed* Winchester.
Hon Robert Chandos, *b* 1957; *ed* Eton; journalist: *m* 1985, Susan Penelope, elder da of David Cavender, of The Manor House, Dowlish Wake, Ilminster, Somerset, and of Mrs Jennifer Neubauer, of Smallcombe House, Bath, and has issue living, Louis Grenville, *b* 1990, — Christopher Chandos, *b* 1993, — Georgia Ray, *b* 1989. *Residence* – 33 Horsford Rd, SW2 5BW.

DAUGHTER LIVING (By 1st marriage)

Lady Anna Clare, *b* 1960.

SISTER LIVING

Elspeth Dorina, *b* 1926: *m* 1950, Thomas Alfred Spry Carlyon, and has issue living, William Thomas Alfred, *b* 1951; *ed* Stowe: *m* 1988, Mrs Alison Jean Humphreys, da of C. H. J. Bellingham, of Cornworthy, Devon, and has issue living, Sam *b* 1991, Thomas *b* (triplet) 1991, Sophie *b* (triplet), 1991, — Nicola Elspeth, *b* 1954. *Residence* – The Glebe, Colan, Newquay, Cornwall TR8 4NB.

SISTER LIVING OF SEVENTH EARL (*Raised to the rank of an Earl's daughter* 1941)

Lady Elizabeth Ann, *b* 1908: *m* 1927, Group-Capt Peter Bathurst, RAF, who *d* 1970 (*see* E Bathurst, colls). *Residence* – 12A Northanger Court, Grove St, Bath, Avon BA2 6PE.

COLLATERAL BRANCHES LIVING

Grandchildren of late Cdr Hubert Edwin Gore Langton, DSO, RN, 3rd son of late Col Hon Henry Powell Gore Langton, brother of 4th Earl:—
Issue of late Lt-Cdr Alaric Hubert St George Gore Langton, RN, *b* 1918, *d* 1987: *m* 1946, Margaret Edwina (Hatch Park, Hatch Beauchamp, Somerset), elder da of Lt-Col Donald McLeod Douglas, MC, of Sanderstead, Surrey:—
Chandos Alaric Graham, *b* 1949; *ed* Taunton Sch, and St Catherine's Coll, Oxford: *m* 1978, S. Fiona, da of Bernard Collins, of Pitsham Place, Midhurst, Sussex, and has issue living, Chandos James Brydges, *b* 1987, — Emma Lucilla Clare, *b* 1983, — Lucy Fiona Alice, *b* 1985. —— Grenville Julian Brydges, *b* 1954; *ed* Millfield. —— Clare Margaret, *b* (twin) 1954: *m* 1984,

Peter E. Jordan, yr son of late Maj H. J. Godfrey Jordan, of Thornhill, Kiltimagh, co Mayo, and has issue living, Henry James Bourke, *b* 1987, — Oliver Charles d'Exeter, *b* (twin) 1987.

Grandchildren of late Robert Lancelot Gore-Langton (infra):—
Issue of late Montagu Grenville Gore-Langton, *b* 1919, *d* 1968: *m* 1944, Wilda Handlen, who *m* 2ndly, 1971, Geoffrey D. Smiley, of 3396, Hilton Rd, Duncan, BC, Canada:—
Robert Edward (650 Grandview, London, Ont, Canada N6K 3G6), *b* 1950; *ed* Victoria Univ, BC (BSc), and Trin Hall, Camb (PhD): *m* 1989, Dr Susan Anne Jennifer Daniel, and has issue living, Jonathan Kent, *b* 1990, — Jena Anne Catherine, *b* 1992. —— Gillian Dixie GORE-LANGTON (588A, 4678 Elk Drive, Victoria, BC V8Z 5MI, Canada), *b* 1945; has resumed her maiden name: *m* 1st, 1963 (*m diss* 1968), George Clifford Madill; 2ndly, 1971 (*m diss* 1978), John Molloy; 3rdly, 1985 (*m diss* 19—), Stanley Moritz, and has issue living, (by 1st *m*) Michael George, *b* 1964, — Lance Maurice, *b* 1967, — Susan Lorraine, *b* 1965, — (by 2nd *m*) Shannon Marie, *b* 1973.

Grandchildren of late Col Hon Henry Powell Gore-Langton (ante):—
Issue of late Robert Lancelot Gore-Langton, *b* 1885, *d* 1948: *m* 1914, Winifreda Lilian Margaret, who *d* 1987, da of late Capt Arthur G. Nixon, Rifle Bde (Prince Consort's Own):—
Margaret Coëline, *b* 1920: *m* 1944, Andrew William Stewart, RCAF, of 2326 Lincoln Rd, Victoria, BC V8R 6A4, Canada, and has issue living, Ronald David, *b* 1961, — Heather Margaret, *b* 1948: *m* 1969 (*m diss* 1988), Peter John Lund, RCMP, of Ottawa, Ont, and has issue living, David Alexander *b* 1974, Wendy Anne *b* 1969, — Victoria Ann, *b* 1953: *m* 1976, Michael Reginald Ziegler, of Victoria, BC, and has issue living, Tristan Brooks *b* 1983. —— Gillian Mary, *b* 1925: *m* 1st, 1950, Hugo Wuerzer, who *d* 1984; 2ndly, 1986, George Arthur Barr, and has issue living (by 1st *m*), Nigel John, *b* 1955; *ed* St Edward's Sch, Oxford, Bath Univ and Birmingham Univ: *m* 1984, Sheila Marion, da of E. F. Thorpe, of Taunton, Som, and has issue living, James Lewis *b* 1985, Laura Jane *b* 1988, — Robert Guy, *b* 1959; *ed* Wellington Sch, Som, — Wendy Margaret, *b* 1951: *m* 1976, Lt-Col David H. Keenan and has issue living, Nicholas Edward *b* 1983, Rosalind Jane *b* (twin) 1983, — Jane Felicity, *b* 1956. *Residences* – 620 Braemar Av, RR2, Sidney, VI V8L 5G5, Canada; 7 Killams Crescent, Taunton, Somerset.
Issue of late Richard Gerald Gore-Langton, *b* 1892, *d* 1978: *m* 1st, 1925 (*m diss* 1936), Laura Edith Pryor, da of late Herbert W. Bevan; 2ndly, 1936, Doreen Audrey (5421 Old West Rd, Victoria, BC, Canada), da of Aubrey H. Davies, MB, MRCS, LRCP:—
(By 1st *m*) Richard Eric Bevan (5465 Alderley Rd, Victoria, BC, Canada), *b* 1933: *m* 1957, Marjorie Joyce, da of late Thomas A. Boag, and has issue living, Richard Thomas, *b* 1959, — Laura Gay, *b* 1961: *m* 1993, Mark Joseph Ahern. —— (By 2nd *m*) Gerald Hugh, *b* 1947. —— Norman Guy, *b* 1950. —— Dorothy Veronica, *b* 1952.

PREDECESSORS – **(1)** RICHARD Temple-Nugent-Grenville, KG, 2nd Marquess of Buckingham (*see* V Cobham); assumed 1799, by Roy licence, the additional surnames of Brydges, Chandos; was *cr Earl Temple of Stowe* (with remainder to his grandda Anna Eliza Mary, afterwards wife of William Henry Powell Gore-Langton, MP), *Marquess of Chandos*, and *Duke of Buckingham and Chandos* (peerage of United Kingdom) 1822, **(2-3)** in which title the Earldom of Temple was merged until the death of the 3rd Duke of Buckingham and Chandos (*ext*) in 1889, when it devolved upon his nephew **(4)** WILLIAM STEPHEN Gore-Langton (son of late William Henry Powell Gore-Langton, MP (ante)), 4th Earl, *b* 1847; MP for Mid Somerset (C) 1878-85; assumed by Roy licence 1892 the additional surname and arms of Temple: *m* 1870, Helen Mabel, who *d* 1919, 2nd da of Sir Graham Graham-Montgomery, 3rd Bt; *d* 1902; *s* by his son **(5)** ALGERNON WILLIAM STEPHEN, 5th Earl; *b* 1871; *m* 1913, Agnes Florence Regina, who *d* 1941, da of Charles K. de Laporte, and widow of Alfred Burrows, of Melbourne; *d* 1940; *s* by his nephew **(6)** CHANDOS GRENVILLE (son of late Capt Hon Chandos Graham Temple-Gore-Langton, 2nd son of 4th Earl); 6th Earl; *b* 1909: *m* 1st, 1934 (*m diss* 1940), Frances Vauriel Fenton, da of Maj Francis Vivian Lister, OBE, of Ashwick Grove, Oakhill, Bath; 2ndly, 1943, Joan Helen, who *d* 1977, da of Charles Abbott, of Penn, Bucks; *d* 1966; *s* by his brother **(7)** RONALD STEPHEN BRYDGES, 7th Earl; *b* 1910; travelling salesman in Australia; did not use the title; *dunm* 1988; *s* by his cousin **(8)** WALTER GRENVILLE ALGERNON (only son of late Cdr Hon Evelyn Arthur Grenville Temple-Gore-Langton, DSO, RN, yst son of 4th Earl) 8th Earl and present peer.

TEMPLEMAN, BARON (Templeman) (Life Baron 1982)

SYDNEY WILLIAM TEMPLEMAN, MBE, PC, son of late Herbert William Templeman; *b* 3 March 1920; *ed* Southall Gram Sch, and St John's Coll, Camb; Bar Middle Temple and Lincoln's Inn 1947, QC 1964, Bencher Middle Temple 1969 (Treas 1987); a Member Bar Council 1961-65 and 1970-72; Attorney Gen Duchy of Lancaster 1970-72, a Judge of High Court of Justice (Chancery Div) 1972-78; a Member Tribunal to inquire into matters relating to Vehicle & Gen Insurance Co 1971-72; a Member R Commn on Legal Services 1976-79; a Lord Justice of Appeal 1978-82, since when a Lord of Appeal in Ordinary; 1939-45 War as Maj 4/1st Gurkha Rifles in India and Burma (despatches); *cr* MBE (Mil) 1946, Knt 1972, PC 1978, and *Baron Templeman*, of White Lackington, co Somerset (Life Baron) 1982: *m* 1946, Margaret Joan, who *d* 1988, da of Morton Rowles, and has issue.

Arms – Per pale azure and gules a fess raguly between a lion passant in chief and in base a fleur-de-lys bourgeonny gold. **Crest** – An eagle or, beaked and legged and wings displayed gules, gorged with a coronet its finials of roses also gules, and supporting by the dexter claw a kukri erect with the point of the blade outwards proper. **Supporters** – Dexter a cock pheasant. Sinister a hen pheasant both guardant and in the beak of each a grain of wheat proper.
Residence – Manor Heath, Knowl Hill, Woking, Surrey.

SONS LIVING

Rev Hon Peter Morton, *b* 1949: *m* 1973, Ann Joyce, da of Peter Williams, and has issue.
Hon Michael Richard, *b* 1951: *m* 1974, Lesley Frances, da of Henry Davis, and has issue.

TEMPLETOWN, VISCOUNTCY OF (Upton) (Extinct 1981)

DAUGHTER LIVING OF FIFTH VISCOUNT

Hon (Alleyne Evelyn) Maureen Louisa, *b* 1921; late ATS: *m* 1st, 1947, Maj John Hackett, late RAOC; 2ndly, 1961 (*m diss* 1983), Michael Starkey, and has issue living (by 1st *m*), Charles John, *b* 1948. *Residence* – 13 Malbrook Rd, SW15 6UH.

TENBY, VISCOUNT (Lloyd George) (Viscount UK 1957)

WILLIAM LLOYD GEORGE, 3rd Viscount; *b* 7 Nov 1927; *s* 1983; *ed* Eastbourne Coll, and St Catharine's Coll, Camb (Exhibitioner, BA Hons); RWF (TA); a JP for Hants: *m* 1955, Ursula, yst da of late Lt-Col Henry Edward Medlicott, DSO, and has issue.

Arms – Azure over water barry wavy in base a bridge of one arch proper, on a chief argent a portcullis sable between two daffodils stalked and leaved also proper. **Crest** – A demi-dragon gules holding between the claws a portcullis sable. **Supporters** – *Dexter*, a dragon gules; *sinister* a lion or each gorged with a collar compony argent and vert; pendent from that of the dexter an escutcheon argent charged with a martlet sable, and from that of the sinister an escutcheon gules charged with a port between two towers also argent.
Residence – Triggs, Crondall, nr Farnham, Surrey.

SON LIVING

Hon TIMOTHY HENRY GWILYM, *b* 19 Oct 1962; *ed* Downside, and Univ Coll of Wales, Aberystwyth.

DAUGHTERS LIVING

Hon Sara Gwenfron, *b* 1957.
Hon Clare Mair, *b* 1961.

PREDECESSORS – (1) GWILYM Lloyd George, TD, PC, 2nd son of 1st Earl Lloyd George of Dwyfor; *b* 1894; MP for Pembrokeshire (*L*) 1922-24 and 1929-50, and N Newcastle-upon-Tyne (*L and C*) 1951-57; Min of Fuel and Power 1942-45, Min of Food 1951-54, and Home Sec and Min for Welsh Affairs 1954-57; *cr Viscount Tenby*, of Bulford, co Pembroke (Peerage of UK) 1957: *m* 1921, Edna Gwenfron, who *d* 1971, da of David Jones, of Gwnfa, Denbigh; *d* 1967; *s* by his el son (2) DAVID, 2nd Viscount, *b* 1922; *d* 1983; *s* by his brother (3) WILLIAM, 3rd Viscount and present peer.

TENNYSON, BARON (Tennyson) (Baron UK 1884)

Look backward and forward

MARK AUBREY TENNYSON, DSC, 5th Baron; *b* 28 March 1920; *s* 1991; *ed* RNC Dartmouth; Cdr RN 1939-45 War (despatches, DSC): *m* 1964, Deline Celeste, da of Arthur Harold Budler, of Cradock, S Africa.

Arms – Gules, a bend nebuly or, thereon a chaplet vert, between three leopards' heads jessant de lys of the second. **Crest** – A dexter arm in armour, the hand in a gauntlet or, grasping a broken tilting spear enfiled with a garland of laurel. **Supporters** – Two leopards rampant guardant gules, semée de lys and ducally crowned or.
Residence – Mellaston, Cumnor Av, Kenilworth, Cape Town 7700, S Africa. *Clubs* – White's Royal Yacht Squadron, RAC.

COLLATERAL BRANCHES LIVING

Grandchildren of late Hon Lionel Tennyson, 2nd son of 1st Baron:—

Issue of late Alfred Browning Stanley Tennyson, *b* 1878, *d* 1952: *m* 1912, Hon Margaret Cicely Drummond, who *d* 1963, da of 10th Viscount Strathallan (E Perth):—

JAMES ALFRED, DSC (222A Karori Rd, Wellington 5, NZ), *b* 26 Nov 1913; Lieut-Cdr RN (ret); formerly in New Zealand Govt Ser; European War 1939 (despatches, DSC): *m* 1954, Beatrice Aventon, eldest da of Alexander Tolhurst Young, of Wellington, NZ, and has issue living, David Harold Alexander, *b* 4 June 1960; *ed* Scot's Coll, and Canterbury Univ, NZ (ME), — Alan James Drummond, *b* 1965; *ed* Scot's Coll, and Otago and Auckland Univs, NZ (MSc): has issue living (by Susanna Ruth Brow), Andrew Barnard TENNYSON, *b* 1992. —— Aubrey Drummond (Urb el Salze No 3, Escas, La Massana, Andorra), *b* 1920; Capt late Essex Regt and Sudan Defence Force; attached Sudan Govt: *m* 1966, Mai Chin Yau, and has issue living, Davina May, *b* 1969; *ed* Edgehill Coll, Devon, and Liverpool Univ (BSc), — Georgina Cicely, *b* 1979; *ed* Culford Sch, Bury St Edmunds. —— Eleanor Rachel (41 Alver Quay, Gosport, Hants PO12 1SR), *b* 1915; an artist and former art teacher at Atherley Sch, Southampton; formerly Prof of Art, Baylor Univ, Waco, Texas, USA: *m* 1st, 1945 (*m diss* 1954), Maj David Rainsford Moore, Essex Regt; 2ndly, 1967 (*m diss* 19——), William Charles Bigg, RAF (ret).

Grandchildren of late Sir Charles Bruce Locker Tennyson, CMG (infra):—

Issue of late Capt Charles Julian Tennyson, *b* 1915, *ka* in Burma 1945: *m* 1937, Yvonne (who *m* 2ndly, 1947, Michael Jeans), da of Col R. B. le Cornu:—

Simon, *b* 1939. —— Penelope (40 Kent Gdns, W14), *b* (twin) 1939.
    Grandson of late Hon Lionel Tennyson (ante):—
    Issue of late Sir Charles Bruce Locker Tennyson, CMG, *b* 1879, *d* 1977: *m* 1909, Ivy Gladys, OBE, who *d* 1958, da
of late Walter J. Pretious:—
Hallam Augustine (1 Berkeley Rd, N8), *b* 1920; *ed* Eton, and Balliol Coll, Oxford; author and broadcaster: *m* 1945 (*m diss*
1971), Margot, da of late Gustav Wallach, and has issue living, Charles Jonathan Penrose, *b* 1955; *ed* Bootham Sch, York;
Lecturer in Physics at London Univ: *m* 1985, Janice Hopson, and has issue living, Alexander Hallam Hopson *b* 1986,
Matthew James *b* 1988, Frederick Penrose *b* 1991, —— (Sita) Rosalind Joanne, *b* 1950; Dir Marylebone Centre Trust 1989-91:
m 1980, Richard Grover.

PREDECESSORS – (1) ALFRED Tennyson, DCL, FRS, son of late Rev George Clayton Tennyson, LLD, R of Somersby, *b*
1809; Poet Laureate 1850-92; *cr Baron Tennyson*, of Aldworth, Sussex, and Freshwater, Isle of Wight (peerage of United
Kingdom) 1884: *m* 1850, Emily, who *d* 1896, da of Henry Sellwood, of Berkshire; *d* 1892; *s* by his el son (2) HALLAM,
GCMG, PC, 2nd Baron, *b* 1852; Gov and Com-in-Ch of S Australia 1899-1902, and Gov-Gen of Commonwealth of Australia
1902-4; appointed Dep Gov and Steward of the Isle of Wight 1913: *m* 1st, 1884, Audrey Georgiana Florence, who *d* 1916, da
of late Charles John Boyle; 2ndly, 1918, Mary Emily, who *d* 1931, da of Charles Robert Prinsep, Advocate-Gen of Calcutta,
and widow of Andrew Hichens; *d* 1928; *s* by his el son (3) LIONEL HALLAM, 3rd Baron, *b* 1889; Major Rifle Brig, and Hon Col
51st (London) Anti-Aircraft Brig RA (TA): *m* 1st, 1918 (*m diss* 1928), Hon Clarissa Madeline Georgiana Felicité, who *d* 1960,
da of 1st Baron Glenconner, and formerly wife of Capt William Adrian Vincent Bethell, 2nd Life Guards; 2ndly, 1934 (*m diss*
1943), Carroll, da of Howard Elting, of Chicago, USA, and widow of Joseph William Donner, of Buffalo, USA; *d* 1951; *s* by
his el son (4) HAROLD CHRISTOPHER, 4th Baron, *b* 1919; Co-Founder with Sir Charles Tennyson of Tennyson Research Centre,
Lincoln; *d* 1991; *s* by his brother (5) MARK AUBREY 5th Baron and present peer.

TENTERDEN, BARONY OF (Abbott) (Extinct 1939)

DAUGHTER LIVING OF FOURTH BARON

Hon Gwen Elfrida Penelope, *b* 1908: *m* 1941, William Fisher, and has issue living, Robert Anthony Abbot, *b* 1942, —— David
James Abbott *b* 1951: *m* 1980, Sarah McAdoo, da of R. Wheatland II, of Boston, Mass, USA.

TERRINGTON, BARON (Woodhouse) (Baron UK 1918)

Labour conquers all things

JAMES ALLEN DAVID WOODHOUSE, 4th Baron; *b* 30 Dec 1915; *s*
1961; *ed* Winchester, and RMC Sandhurst; Major (ret) Roy
Norfolk Regt and Queen's Westminster Rifles (King's Roy
Rifle Corps) TA; formerly a Member of London Stock
Exchange, and a partner in the firm of Sheppards and
Chase, Clements House, Gresham St, EC2; formerly Vice-
Chm of London Group of Oxford Cttee for Famine Relief,
and former Dep Chm of Wider Share Ownership Council
(now Council Member); a Dep Chm of Cttees, House of
Lords 1961-63; Member Ecclesiastical Cttee since 1979; Vice-
Pres Small Farmers' Assocn, formerly Dep-Chm Nat Listen-
ing Library, Talking Books for the Disabled (now Member
of Board); Member Internat Advisory Board of the American
Univ, Washington DC; an ADC to GOC Madras 1940;
1939-45 War in India, N Africa, and Middle East (wounded):
m 1942, Suzanne, da of Col T. S. Irwin, JP, DL, late Roy
Dragoons, of Justicetown, Carlisle, and Mill House, Holton,
Suffolk, and has issue.

Arms – Per fesse or and azure, issuant in chief a hurst of oak trees
proper, in base two bars wavy argent. **Crest** – A demi-woodman proper
issuant out of a wreath of roses argent, barbed and seeded also proper,
supporting in the dexter hand an axe or. **Supporters** – On either side
an Airedale terrier proper, gorged with a ducal coronet or.
Residence – The Mill House, Braemore, Fordingbridge, Hants. *Clubs* –
Boodle's, Pratt's.

DAUGHTERS LIVING

Hon Lavinia Valerie, *b* 1943: *m* 1974, Nicholas George Bolton, of Sevenhampton House, Sevenhampton, Highworth, Wilts,
son of Sir George Lewis French Bolton, KCMG, and has issue living, Carina Suzanne, *b* 1976, —— Sophie Davina, *b* 1979.
Hon Georgina Caroline (Flat 12, 5 Elm Park Gdns, SW10 9QQ), *b* 1946; Interior Designer.
Hon Davina Mary (*Countess Alexander of Tunis*), LVO, *b* 1955; Pres SOS, Member of General Council, Friends of the Elderly
and Gentlefolks' Help; Lady in Waiting to HRH The Princess Margaret, Countess of Snowdon, 1975-79, since when Extra
Lady in Waiting; LVO 1991: *m* 1981, as his 2nd wife, 2nd Earl Alexander of Tunis, and has issue (*see* E Alexander of Tunis).

BROTHER LIVING

Hon (CHRISTOPHER) MONTAGUE, DSO, OBE, *b* 11 May 1917; *ed* Winchester and New Coll, Oxford (MA); FRSL 1951; Fellow
Trin Hall, Camb 1950 and Visiting Fellow of Nuffield Coll, Oxford 1956-64, since when Visiting Prof of Kings Coll, Lond
1978, Special memb of Acad of Athens 1980, Director-Gen of Roy Inst of International Affairs 1955-59 and Dir of Studies
1955-59; Parl Sec to Min of Aviation 1961-62 and Joint Parl Under-Sec of State for Home Dept 1962-64; Dir of Education and
Training CBI 1966-70; 1939-45 War in Middle East as temporary Col Intelligence Corps (despatches twice, DSO, OBE),
organised resistance in occupied Greece; has American Legion of Merit, and Order of Phoenix of Greece with Swords; MP

for Oxford (C) 1959-66, and 1970-74; DSO 1943, OBE (Mil) 1944: *m* 1945, Lady Davidema Katharine Cynthia Mary Millicent Bulwer-Lytton, da of 2nd Earl of Lytton, and widow of the 5th Earl of Erne, and has issue living, Christopher Richard James (14 Crescent Grove, SW4), *b* 1946; *ed* Winchester, and Guy's Hosp Med Sch MB, FRCS, FEBU: *m* 1975, Hon Anna Margaret Philipps, elder da of 3rd Baron Milford, and has issue living, Jack Henry Lehmann *b* 1978, Constance Margaret Davina *b* 1982, — Nicholas Michael John (72 Kingston Rd, Oxford), *b* 1949; *ed* Winchester, and Ch Ch Oxford: *m* 1973, Mary Jane Stormont, da of D. M. Stormont Mowat, of Long Crendon, Bucks, and has issue living, Thomas Duncan *b* 1987, — Emma Davina Mary, *b* 1954: *m* 1981, Christopher Ian Johnson-Gilbert, of 41 Bromfelde Rd, SW4 6PP, son of T. I. Johnson-Gilbert, of 5 Blenheim Rd, NW8, and has issue living, Hugh Christopher Ian *b* 1991, Cordelia Mary *b* 1983, Jemima Catherine *b* 1985, Imogen Alice *b* 1990. *Residence* – Willow Cottage, Latimer, Chesham, Bucks HP5 1TW.

PREDECESSORS – **(1)** JAMES THOMAS Woodhouse, son of James Woodhouse, of Flamborough, ER Yorks; *b* 1852; MP for Huddersfield (*L*) 1895-1906; a Railway and Canal Traffic Commr 1906-21, and Chm Losses under Defence of the Realm Commn 1915-21; *cr* Knt 1895, and *Baron Terrington*, of Huddersfield, co York (peerage of United Kingdom) 1918: *m* 1876, Jessie, who *d* 1942, da of W. J. Reed, formerly of Skidby, Yorkshire; *d* 1921; *s* by his el son **(2)** HAROLD JAMES SELBORNE, OBE, 2nd Baron, *b* 1877: *m* 1st, 1918 (*m diss* 1926), Vera Florence Annie (MP for Bucks, Wycombe Div (*L*) 1923-4), da of H. G. Bousher, and widow of Guy Ivo Sebright, son of Sir Guy Thomas Saunders Sebright, 12th Bt; 2ndly, 1927, Rena de Vere, who *d* 1973, da of late Capt William Molyneux Shapland-Swiny, 42nd Roy Highlanders (The Black Watch), and sometime ADC to HRH the late Duke of Edinburgh, of Ballymurrogh and Cloghamon, co Wexford; *d* 1940; *s* by his brother **(3)** HORACE MARTON, KBE, 3rd Baron, *b* 1887; Bar Inner Temple 1911, Principal Assist Sec, Min of Labour and National Ser 1941-4, Dep Speaker and Dep Chm of Committee, House of Lords 1949: *m* 1st, 1914, Valerie, who *d* 1958, da of late George Allen Phillips of Leyden House, Edenbridge, Kent; 2ndly, 1959, Mrs Phyllis Mary Haggard, who *d* 1971, da of late W. W. Drew, ICS; *d* 1961; *s* by his son **(4)** JAMES ALLEN DAVID, 4th Baron and present peer.

TEVIOT, BARON (Kerr) (Baron UK 1940)

Late, but in earnest

CHARLES JOHN KERR, 2nd Baron; *b* 16 Dec 1934; *s* 1968; *ed* Eton: *m* 1965, Patricia Mary, da of late Alexander Harris, and has issue.

Arms – Quarterly: 1st and 4th gules, on a chevron argent three mullets of the field, *Kerr of Ferniehurst*; 2nd and 3rd per fess gules and vert, on a chevron argent between three mascles in chief or and a unicorn's head in base of the third, horned of the fourth, three mullets of the first, *Kerr of Cessford*; in the centre of the quarters a rose or. **Crest** – A stag's head erased proper. **Supporters** – Two border terriers proper. *Residence* – 12 Grand Av, Hassocks, Sussex.

SON LIVING

Hon CHARLES ROBERT, *b* 19 Sept 1971.

DAUGHTER LIVING

Hon Catherine Harriet, *b* 1976.

PREDECESSOR – **(1)** CHARLES IAIN Kerr, DSO, MC, son of Charles Wyndham Rudolph Kerr (M Lothian, colls); *b* 1874; Lt-Col R Horse Guards; Junior Lord of the Treasury 1937-39, Comptroller of HM's Household 1939-40, Chm of Liberal National Party 1940-56, Ch Whip of Liberal National Party in House of Lords 1945; MP for Montrose (*L*) 1932-40; *cr Baron Teviot*, of Burghclere, co Southampton (peerage of UK) 1940: *m* 1st, 1911 (*m diss* 1930), Muriel Constance, da of late William Gordon-Canning, of Hartpury, Glos; 2ndly, 1930, Florence Angela, who *d* 1979, da of late Lt-Col Charles Walter Villiers, CBE, DSO (E Clarendon, colls); *d* 1968; *s* by his only son **(2)** CHARLES JOHN, 2nd Baron, and present peer.

TEYNHAM, BARON (Roper-Curzon) (Baron E 1616)
(Title pronounced "Tenham")

SPES MEA IN DEO

My hope is in God

JOHN CHRISTOPHER INGHAM ROPER-CURZON, 20th Baron; *b* 25 Dec 1928; *s* 1972; *ed* Eton; late Capt The Buffs (TA), and 2nd Lt Coldm Gds; Land Agent; OStJ; ADC to Gov of Bermuda 1953 and 1955 to Gov of Leeward Is 1955-56 (Private Sec 1956) and to Gov of Jamaica 1962; Palestine 1948; Pres of Inst of Commerce: *m* 1964, Elizabeth, yr da of late Lt-Col Hon David Scrymgeour-Wedderburn, DSO, Scots Gds (*see* E Dundee, colls), and has issue.

Arms – Quarterly: 1st and 4th argent, on a bend sable, three popinjays or, collared gule *Curzon*; 2nd and 3rd per fesse azure and or, a pale counterchanged, and three stags' heads eased of the second, *Roper.* **Crest** – 1st a popinjay rising, wings displayed and inverted or collared gules, *Curzon*; 2nd, a lion rampant sable, supporting on the dexter forepaw a ducal coronet or, *Roper.* **Supporters** – *Dexter*, a buck or; *sinister*, an heraldic tiger regardant argent.
Residences – The Walton Canonry, Cathedral Close, Salisbury, Wilts; Pylewell Park, Lymington, Hants. *Clubs* – Turf, House of Lords Yacht, Puffin's (Edinburgh), Ocean Cruising.

SONS LIVING

Hon DAVID JOHN HENRY INGHAM, *b* 5 Oct 1965: *m* 1985, Lucinda L., eldest da of Maj-Gen Sir Christopher John Airy, KCVO, CBE, and has had issue, Henry Christopher John Ingham (Alexis), *b* 5 Feb 1986, — Jack, *b* and *d* 1990, — (Elizabeth) Poppy, *b* 1989.
Hon Jonathan Christopher James, *b* (twin) 1973.
Hon Peter Michael Alexander, *b* 1977.
Hon William Thomas, *b* 1980.
Hon Benjamin Alexander, *b* 1982.

DAUGHTERS LIVING

Hon Emma Elizabeth, *b* 1966: *m* 19—, Robert A. Murphy, yr son of Christopher Murphy, of 17 Napier Av, SW6, and has issue living, Doone, *b* 1989, — Willow, *b* 1990, — a da, *b* 1992.
Hon Sophie Patricia, *b* 1967.
Hon Lucy Elspeth, *b* 1969: *m* 1991, Benjamin Hugh Fraser (*see* L Lovat, colls).
Hon Hermione Marie Hilda Edith, *b* (twin) 1973.
Hon Alice Penelope Rachael, *b* 1983.

BROTHER LIVING

Hon Michael Henry, *b* 1931; Lt (ret) RN; an OStJ: *m* 1964 (*m diss* 1967), Maria, only da of late Maj R. V. Taylor, 16th/5th Queen's R Lancers. *Residence* – 75 Eccleston Square Mews, SW1.

HALF SISTERS LIVING

Hon Henrietta Margaret Fleur, *b* 1955. *Residence* – 165 Walmer Rd, W11 4EW.
Hon Holly Anne-Marie, *b* 1963. *Residence* – 19 Breer St, SW6 3HE.

WIDOW LIVING OF NINETEENTH BARON

ANNE RITA (Inwood House, Sarisbury Green, Hants), da of late Capt Leicester Charles Assheton St John Curzon-Howe, MVO, RN (*see* E Howe, colls): *m* 1st, 1955, as his 2nd wife, the 19th Baron, who *d* 1972, 2ndly, 1975, Dr Ian Edwards, who *d* 1988.

COLLATERAL BRANCHES LIVING

Grandchildren of late Blayney Tenison Roper (*b* 1853), elder son of Blayney Tenison Roper (*b* 1811), yst son of Very Rev Henry Roper, DD, eldest son of Rev Hon Richard Henry Roper, yst son of 8th Baron:—
Issue of late Lt-Col Richard Blayney Roper, *b* 1897, *d* 1964: *m* 1930, Elmslie, who *d* 1962, da of late William Forbes-Garden:—
Christopher Blayney (40 Northumberland Av, Craighall Park, Johannesburg 2196, S Africa), *b* 1932; late 2nd Lt RE; CEng; an Asso of Camborne Sch of Mines: *m* 1963, Elizabeth Garthorne, 2nd da of late Andrew Ian Dalglish Brown, of Johannesburg, and has issue living, Katherine Elizabeth, *b* 1966; *ed* Univ of Witwatersrand (BSc): *m* 1989, Ian Frederick Burman, of 22D Guildford Rd, Tunbridge Wells, Kent TN1 1LS, — Margaret Jennifer, *b* 1967; *ed* Univ of Witwatersrand (BPrim Ed, BEd), — Philippa Garthorne, *b* 1969. —— Margaret Elizabeth, *b* 1935: *m* 1959, Maj John David Cousins (65 Harvey St, Taupo, NZ), late 10th Princess Mary's Own Gurkha Rifles, and has issue living, Terence David, *b* 1969; MB, ChB, — Elizabeth Mary, *b* 1972.

Grandson of late Capt Charles Cadwaladr Trevor-Roper, el son of late George Edward Trevor-Roper, 3rd son of Charles Blayney Trevor-Roper, el son of Cadwallader Blayney TREVOR-ROPER, 2nd son of Rev Hon Richard Henry Roper, yst son of 8th Baron:—
Issue of late Flight-Lieut Richard Dacre Trevor Roper, DFC, DFM, RAF, *b* 1915, *ka* over Germany 1944: *m* 1942, Patricia Audrey Edwards, who *m* 2ndly, 1949, Frank Marvin, and 3rdly, 1955, John Derick Straight, of 292 Reading Rd, Winnersh, Berks:—
Charles Anthony (Brookdale House, North Huish, nr Totnes, S Devon), *b* 1943; *ed* Wellington, and Reading Univ (BSc, PhD): *m* 1967, Carol Elizabeth, da of Charles James Pape, of 4 Vauxhall Drive, Woodley, Reading, and has issue living, Dacre Gabriel, *b* 1969, — Mathew Blayney *b* 1977.

Granddaughter of late George Edward Trevor-Roper (ante):—

Issue of late Capt Charles Cadwaladr Trevor-Roper, Hampshire Regt, *b* 1884, *d* of wounds received in action 1917: *m* 1913, Gertrude Alice, who *d* 1962 (having *m* 2ndly, 1925, Major Robert Hugh Poyntz, MC, late The King's Shropshire LI, who *d* 1931), da of W. G. Clabby, Indian Police:—
Anne, *b* 1916: *m* 1941, Josiah Maddocks, of 8 Northgate, Goosnargh, Preston, Lancs, and has issue living, Richard James (8 Lindle Close, Hutton, Preston, Lancs), *b* 1943: *m* 1965, Dorothy Suzanne Pallett, and has issue living, John Charles James *b* 1967, Valerie Suzanne *b* 1966, — David Hugh *b* 1950.

Grandchildren of late Arthur Messeena Trevor-Roper (infra):—
Issue of late Richard Teynham Trevor-Roper, *b* 1903, *d* 1968: *m* 1928, Lilian M. Prestwood, who *d* 1978:—
Richard Eric (14 Groby Rd, Glenfield, Leics), *b* 1928: *m* 1st, 1954 (*m diss* 1959), Patricia Anne McClintock; 2ndly, 1964, Marilyn Elizabeth Fox, and has issue living (by 1st *m*), Richard Patrick (64 Hinau St, Wanganui, NZ), *b* 1955: *m* 1977, Michelle Anne Lhonneux, and has issue living, Michael Patrick *b* 1980, Jason Charles *b* 1982, Ryan Paul *b* 1986. —— Kathleen Edith, *b* 1931: *m* 1951, Kenneth Leslie Jones, of 139 Leicester Rd, Thurcaston, Leics, and has issue living, Nigel Kenneth, *b* 1952: *m* 1972, Gillian Ann Hardy, and has issue living, Nicola Marie *b* 1976, Abbie Eileen *b* 1978.

Grandchildren of Richard Henry Trevor-Roper, 4th son of Charles Blayney Trevor-Roper (ante):—
Issue of late Arthur Messeena Trevor-Roper, *b* 1876, *d* 1966: *m* 1902, Mary Wynifred, who *d* 19—, da of James Keel, of Froglands, Cheddar, Somerset:—
Cyril Peter (Pixholme Cottage, Pixham Lane, Dorking, Surrey), *b* 1916: *m* 1940, Lorna Eileen, da of late Harry J. Smith, of Hillside Terr, Dorchester, Dorset, and has issue living, Virginia Yvonne, *b* 1943, — Sandra Victoria, *b* 1946, — Susan Brenda, *b* 1952. —— Kathleen Victoria, *b* 1911: *m* 1940, George Stanley White. —— Margaret Elizabeth, *b* 1923: *m* 1946, Niels Peter Nielsen, of 23 Hampshire Rd, Aylsestone, Leicester, LE2 8HF.
Issue of late Bertie William Edward Trevor-Roper, MB, MRCS, *b* 1885, *d* 1978: *m* 1910, Kathleen Elizabeth, who *d* 1964, da of William Davison:—
Hugh Redwald (*Baron Dacre of Glanton*), *b* 1914; *cr* Baron Dacre of Glanton 1979 (see that title). —— Patrick Dacre, MB, BCh, (3 Park Sq West, NW1. *Clubs* – Athenaeum, Beefsteak), *b* 1916; *ed* Charterhouse, and Clare Coll, Camb (CMB, ChB, MA): FRCS England; Ophthalmic Surg, Westminster and Moorfields Eye Hosps, and late Capt New Zealand Med Corps.

Grandchildren of late Dacre Trevor-Roper, 5th son of Charles Blayney Trevor-Roper (ante):—
Issue of late Lennard Carew Trevor-Roper, *b* 1876, *d* 1948: *m* 1st, 1898, Margaret Helen, who *d* 1901, da of late James Laffan, of Killarney; 2ndly, 1909, Lisbeth Rankin, who *d* 1970 da of Alexander Knight Stein:—
(By 2nd *m*) Lennard Dacre, *b* 1910: *m* 1935, Constance May, da of John H. Barr, of Abergele, Denbighshire. —— Janet Rankin, *b* 1911; formerly 3rd Officer, WRNS: *m* 1942, Major Vivian M. E. Bateson, King's (Liverpool) Regt, who *d* 1959, and has issue living, Simon Vivian Ranulf, *b* 1946, — Julia Janet, *b* 1948: *m* 1965, John Read, and has issue living, Sean *b* 1965, Amber Ruth *b* 1966. *Residence* – 8 South Close, Green Lane, Morden, Surrey.
Issue of late Rev Ranulph Dacre Trevor-Roper, *b* 1893, *d* 1975: *m* 1916, Joan Fraser, who *d* 1976 da of late Robert Fraser Woodcock, MRCS, of Wigan:—
Helen Bennetta, *b* 1919: *m* 1st, 1940, Richard Stoate; 2ndly, 1957, Terence H. Summers, of 15 Pigeon House Lane, Freeland, Oxford. —— Joan Everilda (4 Wetherell Pl, Bristol, B58 1AR), *b* 1923: *m* 1940 (*m diss* 1968), Owen John Howell, ARIBA, and has issue living, Robin John (91 Kingsdown Parade, Bristol 6), *b* 1941: *m* 1963, Pamela Ann, da of Alfred Raymond Reader, of Northampton, and has issue living, Jonathan Raef *b* 1964, Nicholas Dacre *b* 1966, Christopher Noel *b* 1969, Benjamin James *b* 1970, — Jennifer Eve, *b* 1949: *m* 1970, Anthony Stephen Duval, and has issue living, Simon Joseph *b* 1975, Timothy James *b* 1978.

Grandchildren of late Rev Ranulph Dacre Trevor-Roper (ante):—
Issue of late Capt Anthony Dacre Trevor-Roper, MC, *b* 1921, *d* 1986: *m* 1954, Amy Frances (The Flat, Great Oakley Hall, Great Oakley, Corby, Northants), yst da of late Capt John Douglas Collins, of Burton Bradstock, Dorset:—
Julian Dacre, *b* 1956. —— Christopher Charles ffarington, *b* 1964. —— Mary Anne *b* 1954: *m* 1982, Michael John Frederick Charles Buswell, and has issue living, Jonathan Charles, *b* 1982. —— Susan Elizabeth, *b* 1958; *ed* Imperial Coll of Science (BSc), ARCS 1980: *m* 1982, Nicholas Mark Palmer, 2nd son of B. E. Palmer, of Hadley Green, Herts.

Grandson of late William Roper (*b* 1837), son of late Charles Roper, son of William Roper (*b* 1768) (infra):—
Issue of late William Trevor Roper, *b* 1880, *d* 1956: *m* 1st, Elsie Beatrice, who *d* 1934, da of Thomas Holt, of Oxton, Cheshire; 2ndly, 1938, Janet Pegman, of Clontarf, Dublin:—
(By 1st *m*) Dacre Alexander (Kings Shade, 70 The Street, Capel, Dorking, Surrey RH5 5LA), *b* 1921; 1939-45 War as Lt RNVR: *m* 1st, 1945, Sylvia Mary, da of Thomas H. Jameson, of Dublin; 2ndly, 1987, Joan Hodges, of Beare Green, Surrey, and has issue living (by 1st *m*), Lynda Susan, *b* 1948.

Granddaughter of late William Trevor Roper (ante):—
Issue of late Trevor Holt Roper, *b* 1914, *d* 1988: *m* 1938, Hylda Florence (203 Rosses Court, Dun Laoghaire, co Dublin), da of Charles T. Marks:—
Penelope Margaret, *b* 1944: *m* 1968, David Allengame Proger, of Crowe Abbey House, Killincarrig, Delgany, co Wicklow, and has issue living, Lizanne Margaret, *b* 1969, — Philippa Jane, *b* 1972, — Nicola Kate, *b* 1980.

Grandson of late Hon Sir Henry Roper, son of late William Roper (*b* 1768), son of late Rev Hon Richard Henry Roper (ante):—
Issue of late Henry Charles Roper, *b* 1850, *d* 1916: *m* 1912, Hilda Kate Marguerite Collen, who *d* 1966, da of Alfred John Stearn, formerly of Bythe Church, Cambridge:—
Alexander John Henry, TD, *b* 1913; *ed* King's Coll, London (BSc 1934); is Capt RA: *m* 1st, 1947, Marjorie Edith, who *d* 1981, da of Henry Broom Vines, formerly of Lower Field, Bourton, Berks; 2ndly, 1983, Evelyn Joan, da of Herbert Vines, of Petwick Farm, Challow, Berks, and has issue living (by 1st *m*), Richard Henry, *b* 1948, — Margaret Hilda Jane, *b* 1950. *Residence* – 7 Orchard Hill, Faringdon, Oxon SN7 7EH.

PREDECESSORS – (1) Sir JOHN Roper, Knt, was *cr Baron Teynham*, of Teynham, co Kent (peerage of England) 1616; *d* 1618; *s* by his son (2) CHRISTOPHER, 2nd Baron; *d* 1622; *s* by his son (3) JOHN, KB, 3rd Baron; *d* 1627; *s* by his son (4) CHRISTOPHER; 4th Baron; *d* 1673; *s* by his son (5) CHRISTOPHER, 5th Baron; was Lord-Lieut of co Kent; *d* 1692; *s* by his el son (6) JOHN, 6th Baron; *d* unmarried; *s* by his brother (7) CHRISTOPHER, 7th Baron; *d* unmarried; *s* by his brother (8) HENRY, 8th Baron; conformed to the Established Church, and took his seat in the House of Lords 1715; was a Lord of the Bedchamber to George I; *d* 1722; *s* by his el son (9) PHILIP, 9th Baron; *d* unmarried 1727; *s* by his brother (10) HENRY, 10th Baron; *d* 1781; *s* by his son (11) HENRY, 11th Baron; *d* 1786; *s* by his el son (12) HENRY, 12th Baron; *d* unmarried 1806; *s* by his brother (13) JOHN, 13th Baron; *d* unmarried 1824; *s* by his cousin (14) HENRY FRANCIS, 14th Baron, son of Hon Francis Roper, 4th son of 10th Baron; *b* 1768; assumed in 1788 by Roy licence the surname of Curzon in lieu of his patronymic, and in 1813 by Roy licence he assumed the surnames of Roper-Curzon, in lieu of his then name: *m* 1788, Bridget, da and heiress of Thomas Hawkins, of Nash Court; *d* 1842; *s* by his el son (15) HENRY, 15th Baron; *dsp* 1842; *s* by his brother (16) GEORGE HENRY, 16th Baron, *b* 1798: *m* 1st, 1822, Eliza, who *d* 1871, da of William Joynes, of Sevenoaks; 2ndly, 1873, Elizabeth, da of late William Jay, Lieut RA; *d* 1889; *s* by his son (17) HENRY GEORGE, 17th Baron, *b* 1822: *m* 1860, Harriet Anne Lovell, who *d* 1916, da of the Rev Thomas Heathcote; *d* 1892; *s* by his el son (18) HENRY JOHN PHILIP SYDNEY, 18th

Baron, *b* 1867: *m* 1895, Mabel, who *d* 1937, da of late Lt-Col Henry Green Wilkinson, Scots Guards; *d* 1936; *s* by his el son **(19)** CHRISTOPHER JOHN HENRY, DSO, DSC; 19th Baron; *b* 1896; Capt RN; Dep Chm of Cttees, House of Lords 1946-59, and Chancellor of Primrose League 1948: *m* 1st, 1927 (*m diss* 1954), Elspeth Grace, who *d* 1976, el da of William Ingham Whitaker (V Melville); 2ndly, 1955, Anne Rita (who *m* 2ndly, 1975, Dr Ian Edwards), da of Capt Leicester Charles Assheton St John Curzon-Howe, MVO, RN (E Howe); *d* 1972; *s* by his el son **(20)** JOHN CHRISTOPHER INGHAM, 20th Baron and present peer.

THATCHER, BARONESS (Thatcher) (Life Baroness 1992)

MARGARET HILDA THATCHER, OM, PC, yr da of late Alfred Roberts, of Grantham, Lincs; *b* 13 Oct 1925; *ed* Grantham Girls' Sch, and Somerville Coll, Oxford (MA, BSc, Hon Fell 1970); Bar Lincoln's Inn 1954 (Hon Bencher 1975); FRS 1983, Freedom of Borough of Barnet 1980, Hon Freeman Grocers' Co 1980, Freedom Falkland Is 1983, Donovan Award USA 1981, US Medal of Freedom 1991; Chancellor Buckingham Univ since 1992; Joint Parly Sec Min of Pensions and National Insurance 1961-64, Memb Shadow Cabinet 1967-70, Chief Opposition Spokesman on Educn 1969-70, Sec of State Educn and Science (and co-Chm Women's National Commn) 1970-74, Chief Opposition Spokesman on the Environment 1974-75, Leader of the Opposition Feb 1975-79, Prime Min and First Lord of the Treasury (first woman to hold this office) 4 May 1979-28 Nov 1990, Min for the Civil Ser 1981-90; Chancellor, William and Mary Coll, Williamsburg, Virginia, since 1994; MP Finchley (*C*) 1959-74, Barnet, Finchley 1974-83, 1983-87 and 1987-90; *cr* PC 1970, OM 1990 and *Baroness Thatcher*, of Kesteven, co Lincs (Life Baroness) 1992: *m* 1951, Sir Denis Thatcher, 1st Bt, MBE, TD, and has issue.

Arms – Per chevron azure and gules, in chief two lions rampant guardant, the dexter contourny, supporting between them a double-warded key wards upward or and in base a tower also or, its portal sable, therein a portcullis gold. **Supporters** – *Dexter*, on a mount of tussocks of grass proper a male figure representing an Admiral of the Fleet on active service holding in his exterior hand a pair of binoculars all proper; *sinister*, on a grassy mount vert a male figure representing Sir Isaac Newton holding in his exterior hand a pair of scales all proper.
Address – c/o House of Lords, SW1A 0PW.

SON LIVING

Hon Mark, *b* 1953; *ed* Harrow: *m* 1987, Diane, only da of T. C. Burgdorf, of Dallas, Texas, USA, and has issue living, Michael *b* 1988, — a da, *b* 1993.

DAUGHTER LIVING

Hon Carol, *b* (twin) 1953; journalist and broadcaster.

THOMAS, BARONY OF (Thomas) (Extinct 1980)

SON LIVING OF LIFE BARON

Hon (William) Michael Webster *b* 1926: *m* 1952, Ann, da of late Col Philip Kirby-Green, and has issue.

DAUGHTER LIVING OF LIFE BARON

Hon Sheila, *b* 1925: *m* 1948, Julian von Bergen, of Ellicombe, Minehead, Som, and has issue.

THOMAS OF GWYDIR, BARON (Thomas) (Life Baron 1987)

PETER JOHN MITCHELL THOMAS, PC, QC, only son of late David Thomas, solicitor, of Llanrwst, Denbighshire; *b* 31 July 1920; *ed* Epworth Coll, Rhyl, and Jesus Coll, Oxford (MA); served 1939-45 War in RAF, Pilot, Bomber Command (prisoner 1941-45); Bar Middle Temple 1947, QC 1965, Bencher 1971 (Emeritus 1991), Member Wales and Chester Circuit, Dep-Chm Cheshire Quarter Sessions 1966-70, and Denbighshire Quarter Sessions 1968-70, Recorder of Crown Court 1974-88; PPS to Solicitor-Gen 1955-59, Parl Sec Min of Labour 1959-61, Parl Under-Sec of State for Foreign Affairs 1961-63, and Min of State for Foreign Affairs 1963-64, Chm Conservative Party Orgn 1970-72, and Sec of State for Wales 1970-74, Pres of Nat Union of Conservative Assocns 1973-75; a JP of Cheshire and Denbighshire; MP for Conway (*C*) 1951-66, and for Hendon South 1970-87; *cr* PC 1964, and *Baron Thomas of Gwydir*, of Llanrwst, co Gwynedd (Life Baron) 1987: *m* 1947, Frances Elizabeth Tessa, who *d* 1985, only da of late Basil Dean, CBE, theatrical producer (*see* E Warwick, 1968 Edn), and has issue.

Arms – Per pale vert and gules in pale a sword point upwards argent hilt pommel and quillons or between in chief two portcullisses also or all within a bordure engrailed of the last thereon eight pellets. **Crest** – A grassy mount proper statant thereon a stag armed and unguled or resting the dexter foreleg upon a staff raguly also or and between the attires a cross engrailed gold. **Supporters** – *Dexter*, a dragon statant erect tail nowed gules gorged with a crown rayonny gold; *Sinister*, a lamb statant erect or gorged with a crown rayonny gules.
Residences – 37 Chester Way, SE11; Millicent Cottage, Elstead, Surrey. *Club* – Carlton.

SONS LIVING

Hon David Nigel Mitchell, *b* 1950. *Residence* – 72 Jerningham Rd, SE14.
Hon Huw Basil Maynard Mitchell, *b* 1953. *Residence* – 1 Regent St, Oxford.

DAUGHTERS LIVING

Hon Frances Jane Mitchell, *b* 1954: *m* 1982, Jeffrey Alex Clargo, and has issue, two sons and one da. *Residence* – 33 Oxford Rd, Putney, SW15.
Hon Catherine Clare Mitchell, *b* 1958: *m* 19—, —Howe. *Residence* – 39 Culver Rd, St Albans, Herts.

THOMAS OF SWYNNERTON, BARON (Thomas) (Life Baron 1981)

HUGH SWYNNERTON THOMAS, son of Hugh Whitelegge Thomas, CMG (*d* 1960), by his wife Margery Angelo Augusta, da of Frederick R. Swynnerton; *b* 21 Oct 1931; *ed* Sherborne, and Queens' Coll, Camb; Historian; *cr Baron Thomas of Swynnerton*, of Notting Hill in Greater London (Life Baron) 1981: *m* 1962, Hon Vanessa Mary Jebb, el da of 1st Baron Gladwyn, and has issue.

Arms – Quarterly argent and or cross formy flory sable surmounted of a dragon's head erased gules. **Crest** – Upon a helm with chapeau gules turned up ermine, issuant from the top of a representation of the Torre d'Arnolfo on the Palazzo Vicariale at Scarperia in Italy, argent a bull's head sable armed or. **Supporters** – Upon a compartment composed of a grassy mound proper thereon a bar embowed proper or charged with a like barrulet wavy azure, a pair of falcons wings expanded and addorsed argent, beaked, armed and belled or, legged gules, gorged with a torse or and gules and holding in the beak a quill argent penned or.
Residence – 29 Ladbroke Grove, W11. *Clubs* – Garrick, Travellers' (Paris).

SONS LIVING

Hon Charles Inigo Gladwyn, *b* 1962; *ed* Latymer Upper Sch, and Univ of East Anglia.
Hon (Henry) Isambard (Tobias), *b* 1964 *ed* Latymer Upper Sch, London Coll of Printing, and St Martin's Sch of Art.

DAUGHTER LIVING

Hon Isabella Pandora, *b* 1966; *ed* St Paul's Girls' Sch, and Newnham Coll, Camb.

THOMSON OF FLEET, BARON (Thomson) (Baron UK 1964)

KENNETH ROY THOMSON 2nd Baron; *b* 1 Sept 1923; *s* 1976; *ed* Upper Canada Coll, and Camb Univ (MA); Chm Pres and Dir, Thomson Newspapers Ltd, (Owners of 40 daily newspapers in Canada), and Thomson Newspapers (Owners of 82 newspapers in USA); Chm and Dir, Internat Thomson Organisation plc Ltd, of London, Internat Thomson Organisation Ltd, and Thomson British Holdings Ltd; formerly Co-Pres, Times Newspapers Ltd; Pres and Dir of Dominion-Consolidated Holdings Ltd, The Evening Telegram Ltd, Fleet Street Publishers Ltd, Kenthom Holdings Ltd, 96015 Ontario Ltd, 373075 Ontario Ltd, Ontario Newspapers Ltd, The Standard St Lawrence Co Ltd, Thomson Internat Corp Ltd, and other Cos; 1939-45 War with RCAF: *m* 1956, Nora Marilyn, da of Albert Vernard Lavis, of Toronto, and has issue.

Arms – Argent, a stag's head cabossed proper on a chief azure between two mullets a hunting-horn of the first, stringed gules. **Crest** – A beaver sejant erect proper, blowing upon a hunting-horn argent, slung over his dexter shoulder by a ribband of the Dress Tartan proper to Thomson of that Ilk and his dependers. **Supporters** – *Dexter*, a Mississauga Indian, habited in the proper costume of his tribe, holding in his dexter hand a bow all proper; *sinister*, a shepherd, bearing in his sinister hand a shepherd's crook, on his head a bonnet all proper, and wearing a kilt of the usual tartan proper to Thomson of that Ilk and his dependers.

Residences – 8 Kensington Palace Gdns, W8; 8 Castle Frank Rd, Toronto 5, Ont, Canada M4W 2Z4.

SONS LIVING

Hon DAVID KENNETH ROY, *b* 12 June 1957.
Hon Peter John, *b* 1965.

DAUGHTER LIVING

Hon Lesley Lynne, *b* 1959.

SISTER LIVING

Hon Phyllis Audrey (c/o Thomson Organisation Ltd, PO Box 4YG, 4 Stratford Place, W1A 4YG), *b* 1917: *m* 1947, Clarence Elwood Campbell, and has issue living, Linda Christine *b* 1949, — Patricia Gay, *b* 1951, — Susan Elaine, *b* 1954.

PREDECESSORS – (1) *Sir* ROY HERBERT THOMSON, GBE, son of Herbert Thomson; *b* 1894; Joint Chm of Thomson Organisation (and subsidiaries including *The Times* and *The Sunday Times*) and of The Thomson Newspapers Ltd, Toronto, Canada, and founder of The Thomson Foundation; *cr Baron Thomson of Fleet*, of Northbridge, City of Edinburgh (peerage of UK) 1964: *m* 1916, Edna Alice, who *d* 1951, da of late John Irvine, of Drayton, Ont; *d* 1976; *s* by his only son (2) Kenneth Roy, 2nd Baron, and present peer.

THOMSON OF MONIFIETH, BARON (Thomson) (Life Baron 1977)

GEORGE MORGAN THOMSON, KT, PC, son of late James Thomson, of Monifieth, Angus; *b* 16 Jan 1921; *ed* Grove Acad, Dundee; DL Kent 1992; Hon LLD Dundee; Hon DLitt Heriot Watt; Hon DSc Aston, Hon DCL Kent; 1939-45 War with RAF; MP for E Dundee (*Lab*) 1952-72; Min of State FO 1964-66, Chancellor of Duchy of Lancaster 1966-67, and again 1969-70, Sec of State for Commonwealth Affairs 1967-68, and Min without Portfolio 1968-69; a Member of Commn of European Communities, with special responsibility for Regional Policy, and of enlarged EEC (Regional Policy) 1973-77; First Crown Estate Commissioner 1977-80; Chm Independent Broadcasting Authority 1981-88, Chm Leeds Castle Foundation; *cr* PC 1966, and *Baron Thomson of Monifieth*, of Monifieth in the district of the city of Dundee (Life Baron) 1977; KT (1981): *m* 1948, Grace, da of Cunningham Jenkins, of Glasgow, and has issue.
Address – House of Lords, SW1A 0PW. *Club* – Brooks's.

DAUGHTERS LIVING

Hon Caroline Agnes Morgan, *b* 1954: *m* 1st, 1977 (*m diss* 1981), Ian C. Bradley; 2ndly, 1983, Roger Liddle, and has issue living (by 2nd *m*), Andrew *b* 1988.
Hon Ailsa Ballantyne, *b* 1956: *m* 1978, Richard Newby, and has issue living, Mark, *b* 1985, — Roger, *b* 1987.

THORNEYCROFT, BARONY OF (Thorneycroft) (Life Baron 1967; extinct 1994)

(GEORGE EDWARD) PETER THORNEYCROFT, CH, PC, son of late George Edward Mervyn Thorneycroft, DSO, of Dunston Hall, Stafford (Cs Dysart, colls); *b* 26 July 1909; *ed* Eton; Parl Sec to Min of War Transport May to July 1945, Pres of Board of Trade 1951-57, Chancellor of the Exchequer Jan 1957, resigned Jan 1958, Min of Aviation 1960-62, Min of Defence 1962-64; Sec of State for Defence, April to Oct 1964; Chm of Trust Houses Forte 1971-81, Pres since 1981; Chm of Pirelli UK Ltd since 1983; Chm British Reserve

Insurance Co Ltd since 1980; Chm Cinzano (UK) Ltd since 1982; MP for Stafford (*C*) 1938-45, and for Monmouth 1945-66; Chm of Conservative Party 1975-81; 1st Class Order of the Sacred Treasure (Japan) 1983; *cr* PC 1951, CH 1979, and *Baron Thorneycroft*, of Dunston, co Stafford (Life Baron) 1967: *m* 1st, 1938 (*m diss* 1949), Sheila Wells, da of E. W. Page, Tettenhall; 2ndly, 1949, Countess Carla Roberti, da of late Count Malagola Cappi, of Ravenna, Italy, and *d* 4 June 1994, leaving issue by 1st and 2nd *m*.

SON LIVING *(By 1st marriage)*

Hon John Hamo, LVO, *b* 1940; LVO 1992: *m* 1971, Delia, yst da of William Lloyd, of Penallt, Mon, and has issue living, Richard William Henshaw *b* 1977, Eleanor Blanche *b* 1974. *Residence* – 21 St Peters St, Islington, N1 8JD.

DAUGHTER LIVING *(By 2nd marriage)*

Hon Victoria Elizabeth Anne, *b* 1951: *m* 1975, Richard H. Nathanson, and has issue living, Daniel, *b* 1978, — Alexander, *b* 1980, — Susannah, *b* 1985. *Residence* – 35 Enmore Rd, SW15.

THURLOW, BARON (Hovell-Thurlow-Cumming-Bruce) (Baron GB 1792)

We have been — *Faith is the sister of Justice* — *Wherever fate may call*

FRANCIS EDWARD HOVELL-THURLOW-CUMMING-BRUCE, KCMG, 8th Baron; *b* 9 March 1912; *s* 1971; *ed* Shrewsbury Sch and Trin Coll, Camb (MA); Dept of Agric for Scotland 1935-37; Sec to British High Commn in NZ 1939-44, and Canada 1944-45, Private Sec to Sec of State for Commonwealth Relations 1947-49, Counsellor; British High Commn in New Delhi 1949-52; Adviser to Gov of Gold Coast 1955, Dep High Commr in Ghana 1957, and in Canada 1958; High Commr for UK in NZ 1959-63, and in Nigeria 1963-66, Dep Sec in Diplo Ser 1966-68, and Gov of Bahamas 1968-72; KStJ; CMG 1957, KCMG 1961: *m* 1949, Yvonne Diana, who *d* 1990, da of late Aubyn Wilson, of Westerlees, St Andrews, Fife, and has had issue.

Arms – Quarterly: 1st or, a saltire gules, on a chief of the last in the sinister canton a mullet of the first, charged with a crescent of the second, and for distinction a cross crosslet gold, *Bruce*; 2nd azure, three garbs or, and for distinction in the centre chief point a cross crosslet of the last, *Cumming*; 3rd argent, upon a chevron between two chevronels sable, three portcullises, with chains and rings of the field, *Thurlow*; 4th or, a cross sable, *Hovell*. **Crest** – 1st, upon a cap of maintenance proper, a dexter arm in armour from the shoulder, resting on the elbow also proper, the hand holding a sceptre erect or, the arm charged for distinction with a cross crosslet gules; 2nd a lion rampant or, holding in the dexter paw a dagger proper, charged on the shoulder for distinction with a cross crosslet azure; 3rd a raven proper, with a portcullis hung round her neck argent; 4th a greyhound couchant or, collared and line reflexed over the back sable. **Supporters** – Two greyhounds or, collared and lined sable.
Residences – 102 Leith Mansions, Grantully Rd, W9 1LJ; Philham Water, Hartland, Bideford, N Devon EX69 6EZ. *Club* – Travellers'.

SONS LIVING AND DECEASED

Hon ROUALEYN ROBERT, *b* 13 April 1952; *ed* Milton Abbey: *m* 1980, Bridget Anne Julia, only da of (Hugh) Bruce Ismay Cheape, TD, of South Lodge, Isle of Mull, and had issue living, Nicholas Edward, *b* 16 Feb 1986, — George Patrick Ranelagh, *b* 1990, — Tessa Iona, *b* 1987, — Lorna Belinda, *b* 1991. *Residence* – Old Vicarage, Mapledurham, Oxon.
†*Hon* Peter Torquil Francis, *b* 1962, *ed* Shrewsbury; *d* 1985.

DAUGHTERS LIVING

Hon (Diana) Miranda, *b* 1954: *m* 1981, Michael J. Gurney, son of late J. C. Gurney, of 19a Marloes Rd, W8, and has issue living, Mungo *b* 1982, — Rowan (a da), *b* 1984. *Residence* – Broad Lane House, Brancaster, Norfolk.
Hon Aubyn Cecilia, *b* 1958: *m* 1986, Frederick March Phillipps de Lisle, elder son of Gerard March Phillipps de Lisle, of Quenby Hall, Leics, and has issue living, James Gerard, *b* 1987, — Ralph Francis, *b* 1989, — Rosalie, *b* 1991.

BROTHERS LIVING

Hon Sir (James) Roualeyn (*Rt Hon Lord Justice Cumming-Bruce*), *b* (twin) 1912; *ed* Shrewsbury, and Magdalene Coll, Camb; Bar Middle Temple 1937, a Bencher 1959, and Treas 1975; Chancellor of Diocese of Ripon 1954-57, Recorder of Doncaster 1957-59 and of York 1959-61 and Junior Counsel, Treasury (Common Law) 1959-64, a Judge of High Court of Justice (Divorce, Probate and Admiralty Div) 1964-76 and a Lord Justice of Appeal 1977-85; 1939-45 War as Lt-Col RA in Iraq, Syria, Egypt, N Africa, and E Mediterranean; Knt 1964, PC 1977: *m* 1955, Lady (Anne) Sarah Alethea Marjorie Savile, who *d* 1991, da of 6th Earl of Mexborough, and has issue living, Edward Simon (33 Malward Rd, SW12 8EN), *b* 1958: *m* 1984, Antonia Mary, elder da of Christopher Stephen Gaisford-St Lawrence, of Howth Castle, co Dublin (see Mostyn, Bt, colls, 1985 Edn), and has issue living, Michael Alastair *b* 1985, William James Christopher *b* 1987, Isabelle *b* 1990, — Richard Henry, *b* 1963, — Jane Mary, *b* 1956: *m* 1980, Josslyn Henry Robert Gore-Booth, and has issue (see Gore-Booth, Bt). *Residence* – 1 Mulberry Walk, SW3. *Clubs* – Pratt's, United Universities.
Hon Alexander Pascoe, OBE, *b* 1917; *ed* Shrewsbury Sch, and at Trin Coll, Camb (MA); Colonial Admin Ser 1941-60, and Home Civil Ser 1961-78; OBE (Civil) 1960: *m* 1942, Catherine Agnes, da of Rev Hamilton Blackwood, of Scalby, Yorks, and has issue living, Charles Hamilton (Leazes Cottage, Leazes Place, Claypath, co Durham), *b* 1947; *ed* Gordonstoun, and

Exeter Univ (BA Hons): *m* 1982, Dr Vimala Valencia Herman, da of late Nicholas Herman, — Nicholas Christian, *b* 1949, — Catherine Veronica, *b* 1943: *m* 1970, George Nikolaou Yannoulopoulos, and has issue living, Nicholas Alexis *b* 1970.

COLLATERAL BRANCHES LIVING

(Male line was in special remainder to Barony)

Granddaughters of late Lt-Col Hugh Hovell Thurlow, son of late Rev Charles Augustus Thurlow, son of late Rev Edward South Thurlow, son of late John Thurlow, yst brother of 1st Baron:—

Issue of late Brig (Edward) Guy (Lethbridge) Thurlow, CBE, DSO, *b* 1881, *d* 1966: *m* 1912, Margaret Merry, who *d* 1952, da of Lt-Col E. H. Vaughan:—

Nancy Katharine, *b* 1914: *m* 1940, Henry George Willis, of Ellesboro, Brushford, Dulverton, Som, and has issue living, Nicholas Michael Thurlow (via Cantonale 31, CH-6537 Grono, Switzerland), *b* 1942; *ed* Harrow, and London Univ (BA): *m* 1972, Ann Catherine, da of Harvey Roy (Jack) Callaway, of 5 Chestnut Circle, Mount Hope, W Virginia, USA, and has issue living, Caroline Fiona *b* 1973, Rebecca Margaret *b* 1977, — Ian Henry (Chapel Barn, Goodworth Clatford, Andover, Hants SP11 7QY), *b* 1946; *ed* Harrow, RMA Sandhurst, and Ch Ch, Oxford (BA, BPhil); Capt 4/7th Dragoon Guards (ret): *m* 1978, Mary Catherine Ileana Camilla, elder da of Radu Tilea, of 7 Kenil Court, Clinton Lane, Kenilworth, Warwicks (*see* E Carnarvon, colls), and has issue living, Nicholas Henry David *b* 1984, Edward Tilea *b* 1986, Sophie Catherine Glory *b* 1989. — Rosemary Margaret, *b* 1919; formerly Junior Cdr ATS; has Territorial Efficiency Medal: *m* 1st, 1947, Maj Jasper John Ogilvie, MBE, Somerset LI, who *d* 1974; 2ndly, 1976, Lt-Cdr James Henry de Courcy Hughes, RN (ret), of The Old Rectory, Hinton St George, Som, and has issue living (by 1st *m*), Philip John (The Old Rectory, Hinton St George, Som; Paseo del Parque 100, 11310 Sotogrande, Cadiz, Spain), *b* 1948; FCA; *ed* Ampleforth: *m* 1981, Loreto, da of Col Eduardo Vega de Seoane y Barroso, of Madrid, and has issue living, Ian Alexander *b* 1985, William Jasper Charles *b* 1988, James Edward George *b* 1990, — David Jasper, *b* 1952; *ed* Millfield.

PREDECESSORS – (1) Rt Hon EDWARD Thurlow, having been Solicitor-Gen and Attorney-Gen, was in 1778 appointed Lord High Chancellor of England, and *cr Baron Thurlow*, of Ashfield, co Suffolk (peerage of Great Britain); held the Great Seal from June 1778 till April 1783 and from Dec 1783 to 1792, when he was *cr Baron Thurlow*, of Thurlow, co Suffolk (peerage of Great Britain), with remainder to his brothers; *d* unmarried 1806, when the Barony of Thurlow, of Ashfield expired, and the Barony of Thurlow, of Thurlow, devolved upon his nephew (2) EDWARD, 2nd Baron, el son of Rt Rev Thomas Thurlow, Lord Bishop of Durham; assumed in 1814 by Roy licence the additional surname of Hovell; *d* 1829; *s* by his son (3) EDWARD, 3rd Baron; *b* 1814: *m* 1836, Sarah, who *d* 1840, only da of Peter Hodgson; *d* 1857; *s* by his el son (4) EDWARD THOMAS, 4th Baron; *d* 1874; *s* by his brother (5) THOMAS JOHN, PC, 5th Baron; *b* 1838; a Lord-in-Waiting to Queen Victoria 1880-85, High Commr to Gen Assembly of Church of Scotland 1886, and Paymaster-Gen 1886; assumed in 1873 by Roy licence the additional surname of Bruce, and in 1874 the additional surname of Cumming: *m* 1864, Lady Elma Bruce, who *d* 1923, da of 8th Earl of Elgin, KT; *d* 1916; *s* by his son (6) *Rev* CHARLES EDWARD, 6th Baron; *b* 1869; V of St Andrew, and Rural Dean, Bishop Auckland 1913-22, Rural Dean of Liverpool N 1926-30, and R of Sedgefield, co Durham 1930-39: *m* 1909, Grace Catherine, who *d* 1959, da of late Rev Henry Trotter, formerly V of Ch Ch, Barnet; *d* 1952, *s* by his el son (7) HENRY CHARLES, CB, CBE, DSO, 7th Baron, *b* 1910: Maj-Gen late Seaforth Highlanders; GOC Troops, Malta 1962-63, *d* 1971; *s* by his brother (8) FRANCIS EDWARD, 8th Baron and present peer.

THURSO, VISCOUNT (Sinclair) (Viscount UK 1952, Bt GB 1786)

ROBIN MACDONALD SINCLAIR, 2nd Viscount and 5th Baronet; *b* 24 Dec 1922; *s* 1970; *ed* Eton, New Coll, Oxford, and Edinburgh Univ; a JP for Caithness since 1959; CC for Caithness 1949-61 and 1965-73, Town Councillor Thurso 1957-61 and 1965-73, Baillie 1960 and 1969, Dean of Guild 1968, Police Judge 1971; Pres Highland Soc 1980-82, Brigade Pres The Boy's Brigade since 1985; a DL for Caithness 1952-64, Vice-Lt 1964-73, since when Lord Lt; 1939-45 War as Fl-Lt RAF: *m* 1952, Margaret Beaumont, da of late Col Josiah James Robertson, DSO, TD, DL, JP, of Norwood, Wick, Caithness, and widow of Lt Guy Warwick Brokensha, DSC, RN, and has issue.

Arms – Quarterly: 1st, azure, a ship at anchor, her oars erected in saltire, within the royal tressure or; 2nd and 3rd or, a lion rampant gules; 4th azure, a ship under sail or; over all dividing the quarters, a cross engrailed quarterly argent and sable, all within a bordure quartered or and gules, the last charged with three stars of the first. **Crest** – A star of six points waved argent, rising from a cloud proper. **Supporters** – Two red deer proper.
Seat – Dalnawillan, Altnabreac, Caithness. *Residence* – Thurso East Mains, Caithness. *Clubs* – RAF, New (Edinburgh).

SONS LIVING

Hon JOHN ARCHIBALD, yr of Ulbster, *b* 10 Sept 1953; *ed* Eton; Dir Lancaster Hôtel 1981-85, Cliveden House Ltd 1987-93, Savoy Hotel plc since 1993; FHCIMA 1991, Master Innholder 1991: *m* 1976, Marion, da of Louis D. Sage, of Connecticut, USA, and has issue living, James Alexander Robin, *b* 14 Jan 1984, — George Henry MacDonald, *b* 1989, — Louisa Ticknor Beaumont, *b* 1980.
Hon Patrick James, *b* 1954; *ed* Fettes: *m* 1974 (*m diss* 1984), Carol North, and has issue living, Jody Fergus Peter North, *b* 1976, — Luke Robin, *b* 1979. Mr Sinclair also has issue, Celeste Jennifer, *b* 1981. *Residence* – Woodford, Eel Pie Island, Twickenham, Middx.

DAUGHTER LIVING

Hon Camilla Janet, *b* 1957: *m* 1983, Robert Bruce Sanson, of Puketotara Rd, RD3, Whangarei, NZ.

BROTHER LIVING

Hon Angus John, *b* 1925; *ed* Eton, and New Coll, Oxford; formerly Lt Scots Gds; NW Europe 1945; BBC 1950-54, Nigerian Broadcasting Corporation 1954-58, Central Office of Information 1959-85, British Council 1985-90, Man Dir Universal Aunts Ltd since 1991: *m* 1st, 1955 (*m diss* 1967), Pamela Karen, da of Dallas Bower; 2ndly, 1968 (*m diss* 1992), Judith Anne Percy; 3rdly, 1992, Kate, da of late William Fry, and widow of Leonard Hunting, and has issue living, (by 2nd *m*) Isaiah William Columba Stroma, *b* 1971. *Residence* – 19 The Chase, SW4. *Club* – Pratt's.

SISTER LIVING

Hon Catherine, *b* 1919: *m* 1957, Kazimierz Zielenkiewicz, who *d* 1988, and has issue living, Clementina Stewart, *b* 1958: *m* 1st, 1981 (*m diss* 1984), Roberto Lucarini, only son of Alvaro Lucarini, of Prato-in-Toscana, Italy; 2ndly, 1990, Alain Stiegler, son of Mme Colette Stiegler, of Le Grand Pressigny, Touraine, and has issue living (by 2nd *m*), Max Casimir *b* 1990. *Residence* – The Mill House, Isle Brewers, Taunton.

COLLATERAL BRANCHES LIVING   *(In remainder to Baronetcy only)*

Grandchildren of late Ven John Stewart Sinclair, son of Rev William Sinclair, 5th son of 1st baronet (infra):—
    Issue of late Very Rev Ronald Sutherland Brook Sinclair, MC, *b* 1894, *d* 1953: *m* 1924, Patience Penelope, who *d* 1988, da of Herbert Chitty, FSA:—
Christopher Ronald (5 Fentiman Rd, SW8), *b* 1936; *ed* King's Sch, Canterbury, and at Exeter Coll, Oxford; Dir Adcomm Ltd: *m* 1969, Penelope Ann, da of Edwin Alfred Springett, and has issue living, Sophie Letitia, *b* 1971.
    Issue of late Maj-Gen Sir John Alexander Sinclair, KCMG, CB, OBE, *b* 1897, *d* 1977: *m* 1927, Esmé Beatrice, who *d* 1983, da of late Ven Thomas Karl Sopwith, Archdeacon of Canterbury:—
Ian Alexander Charles (The Old Vicarage, Great Totham, nr Maldon, Essex), *b* 1938; *ed* Eton and Worcester Coll, Oxford (BA, PhD): *m* 1969, Elma Elizabeth, da of late Charles Henry Williams, of Braunton, Devon, and has issue living, Andrew George, *b* 1970. — John Charles, *b* 1972, — Elizabeth Beatrice, *b* 1974. —— Roderick John (Downgate Farm, Petersfield, Hants), *b* 1944: *m* 1st, 1970 (*m diss* 1976), Lucinda Mary, da of late Eric Martin Smith, MP; 2ndly, 1977, Sarah Margaret, da of Brig Cyril Edwin Harold Dolphin, CBE, of 78 Heath Rd, Petersfield, Hants and has issue living (by 2nd *m*), James Alexander, *b* 1984, — Natasha Esmé, *b* 1981. —— Jean Esmé, *b* 1929: *m* 1961, Christopher Bruce Seagrim, of Hill Farm, Pulborough, Sussex, and has issue living, John Christopher, *b* 1965, — Victoria Esmé, *b* 1962. —— Iona (*Lady Carnegie*), *b* 1931: *m* 1955, Lt-Gen Sir Robin Macdonald Carnegie, KCB, OBE, DL, yr son of late Sir Francis Carnegie, CBE, and has issue living, Rupert Alexander, *b* 1959, — Catriona Jean, *b* 1957: *m* 1982, Simon J. N. Heale, son of James Heale, and has issue living, James Newton *b* 1985, Charlotte Esmè Serena *b* 1987, Anna Frances *b* 1989, — Rachel Clare *b* 1962: *m* 1989, Mark Goldring, and has issue living, Natasha *b* 1992.

Grandchildren of late Rev William Sinclair, 5th son of 1st baronet:—
    Issue of late Ven John Stewart Sinclair, *b* 1853, *d* 1919: *m* 1893, Clara Sophia, who *d* 1948, da of J. Dearman Birchall, JP, of Bowden Hall, Gloucestershire:—
Diana Clara, *b* 1899: *m* 1923, Thomas Elcho Vardon Ross-Ross, who *d* 1960, and has issue living, John Durnford Sinclair, *b* 1927. *Residence* – 23 Little London, Chichester, Sussex.

PREDECESSORS – **(1)** *Rt Hon* John Sinclair, only son of George Sinclair; *b* 1754; a PC and Founder of the Board of Agriculture; *cr* a *Baronet*, 1786, with remainder, in default of his own male issue, to male issue of his daughters respectively: *m* 1st, 1776, Sarah, who *d* 1785, da of late Alexander Maitland, of Stoke Newington; 2ndly, 1788, Hon Diana Macdonald of Macdonald, who *d* 1845, da of 1st Baron Macdonald; *d* 1835; *s* by his son **(2)** *Sir* George, 2nd Bt; *b* 1790; MP for Caithness-shire (L) 1811-18 and 1831-41: *m* 1816, Lady Catherine Camilla Tollemache, who *d* 1863, sister of 8th Earl of Dysart; *d* 1868; *s* by his only surviving son **(3)** *Sir* John George Tollemache, 3rd Bt; *b* 1824; sometime Page of Honour to Queen Adelaide; MP for Caithness-shire (L) 1869-85: *m* 1853 (*m diss* 1878), Emma Isabella Harriet, who *d* 1889, da of late William Standish Standish, of Duxbury Park, Lancashire; *d* 1912; *s* by his grandson **(4)** Archibald Henry Macdonald, KT, CMG, PC (son of late Clarence Granville Sinclair, el son of 3rd baronet), 4th Bt *b* 1890; Sec of State for Scotland (Nat Govt) 1931-32, Leader of Liberal Party in House of Commons 1935-45, Lord Rector of Glasgow Univ, 1938-45, Sec of State for Air 1940-45, MP for Caithness and Sutherland (L) 1922-45; *cr Viscount Thurso*, of Ulbster, co Caithness (peerage of UK) 1952: *m* 1918, Marigold, who *d* 1975, da of late Lt-Col James Stewart Forbes (Forbes, Bt, colls, *cr* 1823); *d* 1970, *s* by his el son **(5)** Robin Macdonald, 2nd Viscount and present peer.

Tiverton, Viscount; son of Earl of Halsbury.

TODD, BARON (Todd) (Life Baron, 1962)

ALEXANDER (ROBERTUS) TODD, OM, FRS, son of late Alexander Todd, JP, of Glasgow; *b* 2 Oct 1907; *ed* Allan Glen's Sch, Glasgow (DSc), Frankfurt-am-Main (PhD), and Oxford (DPhil) Univs; MA, Camb; Hon LLD Glasgow, Melbourne, Edinburgh, Manchester, and California; Hon DSc Durham, and other Univs; a FRS, and an Hon Fellow of Oriel Coll, Oxford, Darwin Coll, Camb, and Churchill Coll, Camb; Sir Samuel Hall Prof of Chemistry, Manchester Univ 1938-44; Chm of Advisory Council on Scientific Policy 1952-64, and Roy Commn on Med Education 1965-68, Pres of Chemical Soc 1960-62, Pres Soc Chemical Ind 1981-82, and Master of Salters' Co 1961-62; Prof of Organic Chemistry, Camb Univ 1944-71; Managing Trustee of Nuffield Foundation 1951-79 (Chm since 1973); Master of Christ's Coll, Camb 1963-78, First Chancellor of Strathclyde Univ since 1963; Pres of Royal Society 1975-80; Nobel Prize for Chemistry 1957; Chm Croucher Foundation, Hong Kong 1980-88, since when Pres; awarded Soviet Academy's Lomonosov Gold Medal 1979; *cr* Knt 1954, *Baron Todd*, of Trumpington, Cambs (Life Baron) 1962, and OM 1977: *m* 1937, Alison Sarah, who *d* 1987, el da of Sir Henry Hallett Dale, OM, GBE, MD, FRCP, FRS, and has issue.

Arms – Gules a chevron between in chief two foxes' masks, and in base a serpent embowed biting the tail or. **Crest** – In front of an open book proper bound or, a fox passant guardant gules. **Supporters** – *Dexter*, an ounce, and *Sinister*, a fox, each sable bezanty and gorged with a Ducal Coronet, with chain reflexed over the back or, pendant from the coronet by a like chain an escutcheon blue celeste.
Residence – 9 Parker St, Cambridge CB1 1JL. *Club* – Athenaeum.

SON LIVING

Hon Alexander Henry (The Chestnuts, Lower Peover, Knutsford, Cheshire), *b* 1939; *ed* The Leys Sch, Camb, and at Oriel Coll, Oxford (D Phil): *m* 1st, 1967 (*m diss* 19—), Joan Margaret, da of Frederick Wilbur Koester, of Campbell, Cal, USA; 2ndly, 1981, Patricia Mary, da of late Brig A. Harvey Jones, of Somerford Booths, Cheshire.

DAUGHTERS LIVING

Hon Helen Jean, *b* 1941; *ed* Somerville Coll, Oxford: *m* 1963, Philip Edgar Brown, of 124 Edge Hill, Darras Hall, Ponteland, Newcastle-upon-Tyne NE20 9JL, and has issue.
Hon Hilary Alison, *b* 1946.

TOLLEMACHE, BARON (Tollemache) (Baron UK 1876)

(Name and Title pronounced "Tolmash")

I trust and am content

TIMOTHY JOHN EDWARD TOLLEMACHE, 5th Baron, *b* 13 Dec 1939; *s* 1975; *ed* Eton; late Lt Coldstream Gds; DL Suffolk 1984, and Vice Lord Lieut 1994; Chm CLA Suffolk 1990-93, Dir Fortis (UK) Ltd, and other cos; Pres Suffolk Assocn of Local Councils since 1978; Chm Council of St John in Suffolk 1982-89; Pres Friends of Ipswich Museums since 1980; Chm Historic Houses Assoc (E Anglia Region) 1979-83; Chm St Edmundsbury Cathedral Appeal 1986-90; Pres Suffolk Family History Soc since 1988; Vice-Pres Cheshire Red Cross since 1980; Vice-Pres Suffolk Preservation Soc since 1992; Patron Suffolk Accident Rescue Service since 1984; Patron Suffolk Association for the Blind since 1992; Pres Cheshire Cereal Society since 1983, and Suffolk Agricultural Assocn 1988; a patron of four livings: *m* 1970, Alexandra Dorothy Jean, da of late Col Hugo Meynell, MC (*see* E Halifax, colls) and has issue.

Arms – Argent, a fret sable. **Crest** – A horse's head erased argent, between two wings or, pelletty. **Supporters** – On either side a stag guardant proper, gorged with a collar flory counterflory or.
Seat – Helmingham Hall, Stowmarket, Suffolk IP14 6EF. *Clubs* – White's, Pratt's, Special Forces.

SONS LIVING

Hon EDWARD JOHN HUGO, *b* 12 May 1976; a Page of Honour to HM The Queen 1988-90.
Hon James Henry Timothy, *b* 1980.

DAUGHTER LIVING

Hon Selina Karen, *b* 1973.

BROTHERS LIVING

Hon (John) Nicholas Lyonel (1114 San Ysidro Drive, Beverly Hills, Calif 90210, USA), *b* 1941; *ed* Eton and Trin Coll, Camb (MA) and Harvard Univ, USA (MBA): *m* 1st, 1971 (*m diss* 1974), Heide Eva Marie, da of Gunther Wiedeck, of Bonn; 2ndly, 1982, Dietlinde Hannelore, da of Hannelore Riegel, of Munich, W Germany.

Hon Michael David Douglas (Framsden Hall, Stowmarket, Suffolk IP14 6HL; White's Club), *b* 1944; *ed* Eton, and Trin Coll, Camb (MA); Dir Michael Tollemache Ltd since 1967, David Carritt Ltd since 1983, and Artemis Fine Art (UK) Ltd since 1983: *m* 1969, Theresa, da of Peter Bowring, of London, and has issue living, Lyonel John Peter, *b* 1973, — Archibald Robert Bowring (twin), *b* 1973, — Melissa Natasha, *b* 1971.

Hon Hugh John Hamilton (Sandbourne House, Earl's Croome, Worcs WR8 9DG), *b* 1946; *ed* Eton; Man Dir Beshara Press Ltd: *m* 1986, Rosanne, 2nd da of late Hon (Michael) Anthony (Rathborne) Cayzer, of Great Westwood, King's Langley, Herts (*see* B Rotherwick), and has issue living, Thomas Anthony Hamilton, *b* 1987, — David Charles John, *b* 1989, — John Edward Hugh, *b* 1992.

DAUGHTERS LIVING OF THIRD BARON *(by 1st marriage)*

Hon Dorothy Ceciley, *b* 1907: *m* 1942, Air Commodore Reynell Henry Verney, CBE, RAF, who *d* 1974 (B Willoughby de Broke, colls). *Residence* – Stone House, Bishop's Hill, Lighthorne, Warwick.

(by 2nd marriage)

Hon Sybil Diana, *b* 1930: *m* 1966, Harold Diehl.

WIDOW LIVING OF FOURTH BARON

DINAH SUSAN (*Dinah, Baroness Tollemache*) (The Home Farm, Peckforton, Tarporley, Cheshire), da of late Sir Archibald Auldjo Jamieson, KBE, MC: *m* 1939, the 4th Baron, who *d* 1975.

COLLATERAL BRANCHES LIVING *(All of whom are in remainder to the Earldom of Dysart)*

Grandchildren of late Henry Robert Tollemache, yr son of late Hon Hamilton John Tollemache, 4th son of 1st Baron:—
Issue of late Sqdn Ldr Anthony Henry Hamilton Tollemache, GC, RAuxAF, *b* 1913, *d* 1977: *m* 1st, 1947 (*m diss* 1960), Françoise, da of Comte Jean de Hauteclocque, French Ambassador to Canada; 2ndly, 19—, Cecilia Vernon Mary, who *d* 1993, da of late Bryce Cochrane, of McLaren Rd, Edinburgh:—
(By 1st wife) Richard Lionel (41 Lochaline St, W6), *b* 1950: *m* 1978, Caroline, da of Capt Edward Maxwell Cunningham Walker, OBE, RN, and has issue living, Max Philip Anthony, *b* 1987, — Stephanie Elizabeth Louise, *b* 1985. —— Gregory Marmaduke Anthony (6 Elm Walk, Totnes, Devon TQ9 5YQ), *b* 1954: *m* 1976, Karin —, and has issue living, Eugene Anthony, *b* 1976. —— Catherine, *b* 1948: *m* 1970, Malcolm Woolff, of The Old Granary, Malton Rd, Orwell, Herts SG8 5QN, and has issue living, Nicholas Elliot, *b* 1974, — Georgina Juliet, *b* 1975. —— Juliette, *b* 1956: *m* 1979, Jonathan Brian Cottam, of 2 Lindfield Rd, Ealing, W5 1QR, and has issue living, Alexie Juliette Daisie, *b* 1982, — Harriet Rosie Madeleine, *b* 1986. —— (By 2nd wife) Alexander Anthony, *b* 1958; *ed* Stowe, and Exeter Univ: *m* 1987, Nobuko Kida.
Issue of late Karin Irene Elizabeth Tollemache, *b* 1916, *d* 1981: *m* 1945, Cdr William Gordon Jack, RN, who *d* 1992:—
Michael Anthony Gordon JACK, *b* 1946; *ed* Charterhouse, and Lincoln Coll, Oxford: *m* 1980, Anne, da of Hugh Fletcher, of Cape Province, S Africa, and has issue living, Julia, *b* 1981, — Diana, *b* 1984. —— †David Lionel, *b* 1954; *ed* Eton, and Bristol Univ; *d* as the result of an accident in Bermuda 1985. —— †Vanessa Bettine, *b* 1948; *ed* East Haddon Hall, and Univ of E Anglia: *m* 1978, Michael Manassei di Collestatte, and *d* 1985, leaving issue (*see* E Perth).

Grandchildren of late Hon Hamilton James Tollemache (ante):—
Issue of late Marguerite Emily Tollemache, *b* 1880, *d* 1968: *m* 1906, Lt-Col George Cecil Minett Sorel-Cameron, CBE, late Queen's Own Cameron Highlanders, who *d* 1947:—
Robert SOREL-CAMERON, CBE, AFC, *b* 1911; *ed* Wellington Coll, and Edinburgh Univ; Air Commodore (ret) RAF; Air Attache Athens 1960-62, SE Asia 1945-47 (AFC, CBE): *m* 1939, Henrietta Grace, da of late Capt John Radford-Norcop, of The Brand Hall, Market Drayton, Shropshire, and has issue living, Alistair (49 Montgomery Rd, W4 5LZ), *b* 1940: *m* 1981, Ann Kristine, da of Kenneth Cole Harkess, MBE, of 4 Copperfields Close, Kemsing, Kent, and has issue living, George Jack *b* 1988, Henrietta Eve *b* 1986, — James (50 Main St, St Bees, Cumbria), *b* 1948: *m* 1972, Bridget Susan, eldest da of Alan Henry Dring, of Tinkley Lodge, Nympsfield, Stonehouse, Glos, and has issue living, Robert James *b* 1975, Peter Alan *b* 1982, Matthew George *b* 1984, Catriona Jane *b* 1973, Joanna Helen *b* 1979, — Victoria, *b* 1943: *m* 1968, Sayyid Rifaat, of The Old Bakery, Yattendon, Berks, and has issue living, Tariq Sayyid *b* 1971, Rashid Ali *b* 1973, Samir *b* 1975, Sasha Amy *b* 1979. *Residence* – The White House, Whitwell, Norfolk NR10 4RF. —— Hester Marguerite (*Lady Dick-Lauder*), *b* 1920: *m* 1945, Maj Sir George Andrew Dick-Lauder, 12th Bt, who *d* 1981.

Grandchildren of late Marguerite Emily Tollemache (Mrs George C. M. Sorel-Cameron) (ante):—
Issue of late Brig John Sorel-Cameron, CBE, DSO, *b* 1907, *d* 1986: *m* 1937, Catherine Nancy (Sally), who *d* 1984, yr da of late Frank Lee, of Well Head, Halifax:—
Catriona, *b* 1940: *m* 1st, 1963, Allan Carruthers; 2ndly, 1968, Maurice Cleary, and has issue living (by 1st *m*), Rupert Harry Edgell, *b* 1963, — (by 2nd *m*) Angus Peter, *b* 1968. *Residence* – 4 Holbein Mews, SW1.
Issue of late Agnes Sorel-Cameron, *b* 1909, *d* 1986: *m* 1933, Lt-Col Cyril Hugh Kerr-Smiley, TD, who *d* 1980:—
See Smiley, Bt, colls.

Grandchildren of late Winifred Gertrude Tollemache (Mrs Detmar Blow) (infra):—
Issue of late Richard Purcell Blow, *b* 1915, *d* 1963: *m* 1st, 1939 (*m diss* 1956), Diana Hermione, who *d* 1967 (having *m* 2ndly, 1961, Marco Blow), da of late Capt William Adrian Vincent Bethell (*see* B Glenconner, 1960 Edn); 2ndly, 1957, Catherine, who *d* 1992, da of late Donald MacAskill, of 23 Borve, Berneray, Inverness-shire:—
(By 1st *m*) (Richard) David Detmar BLOW (7 Heathview Gdns, SW15), *b* 1942: *m* 1988, Laurence Marie, da of George Lécallier, of 11 rue Parmentier, Neuilly, Paris, and has issue living, John, *b* 1989. —— (Adrian) Simon (35 Great Queen St, WC2), *b* 1943; writer. —— (By 2nd *m*) Catherine Anne, *b* 1960.
Issue of late Jonathan Oliver Tollemache Blow, *b* 1919, *d* 1977: *m* 1962, (Elaine) Helga (The Chalet Hotel, Kandy, Sri Lanka; Hilles Edge, Stroud, Glos GL6 6NW), da of late Edmund Frederick Lorenz de Silva, MBE, of Kandy, Sri Lanka, sometime MP for Kandy, Ceylonese Ambassador to France and Memb of Executive Board of UNESCO:—
Detmar Hamilton Lorenz Arthur BLOW (199 Strand, WC2R 1DR; 67 Elizabeth St, SW1W 9JP; Hilles, Edge, Stroud, Glos GL6 6NW. *Club* – Brooks's), *b* 1963; *ed* Harrow, and LSE (BA); Bar Middle Temple 1989: *m* 1989, Isabella Delves, eldest da of

Sir Evelyn Delves Broughton, 12th Bt. —— Amaury Hugh John Jellings (Edge Farm, Edge, Stroud, Glos), *b* 1965; *ed* Mill-field. —— Selina Jane (67 Elizabeth St, SW1W 9JP; Cherry Hill Cottage, Spoonbed Vale, Edge, Stroud, Glos), *b* 1966; *ed* Hatherop Castle, and Queen's Coll; fashion designer.

      Issue of late Clare Desirée Blow, *b* 1914, *d* 1956: *m* 1st, 1934 (*m diss* 1944), Hon Phelim Robert Hugh O'Neill (later 2nd Baron Rathcavan); 2ndly, 1944, Lt-Col Lewis Stanton Starkey, of Huttons Ambo Hall, York:—
(By 1st *m*) (*See* B Rathcavan). —— (By 2nd *m*) †Kathleen Mary, *b* 1946: *m* 1972, John Fitzgerald Willcox Jenyns, yr son of Roger Soame Jenyns, of Bottisham Hall, Cambridge, and *d* 1994, leaving issue, Clare Eulalia Starkey, *b* 1974. *Residence* – The Grange, Huttons Ambo, York.

           Granddaughter of late Hon Hamilton James Tollemache (ante):—
      Issue of late Winifred Gertrude Tollemache, *b* 1882, *d* 1954: *m* 1910, Detmar Blow, JP, FRIBA, who *d* 1939:—
Lucilla, *b* 1923: *m* 1948, Philip Warre-Cornish, of The Tower, Woolstone, Faringdon, Oxfordshire SN7 7QL, and has issue living, Alexander Philip Hubert Detmar (le Sage ten Broeklaan 81, Eindhoven, The Netherlands), *b* 1949; *ed* Eton: *m* 1983, Penelope Ann, da of Dr Philip Canning Farrant, of 8 High View Rd, Sidcup, Kent, and has issue living, Katherine Mary *b* 1985, Harriet Jane *b* 1988, Anna Belinda *b* 1991, — James Damian, *b* 1952.

      Issue of late Hon Stanhope Alfred Tollemache, 6th son of 1st Baron, *b* 1855, *d* 1934: *m* 1905, Elizabeth, who *d* 1958, da of W Monks:—
Rhona Elizabeth, *b* 1906: *m* 1st, 1935, George Harrison of Johannesburg, who *d* 1935; 2ndly, 1944, Wlodzimierz Jan Zbrowski, late of Warsaw, Poland, who in 1950 assumed the name of John Vladimir Moreton Monks, and who *d* 1981. *Residence* – Bentley Cottage, St Just-in-Roseland, Truro. —— Ina Elaine (Hanby, 94A High Rd West, Felixstowe, Suffolk), *b* 1916.

           Grandchildren of late Maj Hon Douglas Alfred Tollemache (infra):—
      Issue of late Capt Humphrey Douglas Tollemache, RN, *b* 1893, *d* 1970: *m* 1924, Elsie Violet, who *d* 1981, da of late William George Raphael (Goldsmid, Bt):—
Michael Humphrey (Tollemache Hall, Offton, Ipswich, IP8 4RT), *b* 1930; *ed* Eton: *m* 1968, Gay Rosemary D. O'Grady, da of H. E. O'Grady Thompson, of Castle Garde, co Limerick, and has issue living, Rosamond Sybil, *b* 1969: *m* 1993, Ashley P. de Laroque, only son of Charles de Laroque, of Lyndale Cottage, Chalfont St Peter, Bucks, — Juliet Elsie, *b* 1974. —— Jean Margherita (*Baroness Tweedsmuir*) *b* 1927: *m* 1st, 1953, Sir Francis Cullen Grant, 12th Bt, who *d* 1966; 2ndly, 1980, as his 2nd wife, 2nd Baron Tweedsmuir, CBE, CD, of Kingston Bagpuize House, Kingston Bagpuize, Oxon OX13 5AX.

      Issue of late Major Hon Douglas Alfred Tollemache, 8th son of 1st Baron, *b* 1862, *d* 1944: *m* 1887, Alice Mary, who *d* 1959, el da of late John Head:—
Angela Mariota, *b* 1900; appointed Hon Col 307 (N Command) Btn WRAC (TA) 1956: *m* 1st, 1923, as his 2nd wife, 3rd Baron Belper, who *d* 1956; 2ndly, 1958, Norman Tollemache (formerly Wrigley). *Residence* – Bentley House, Ipswich.

      Issue of late Hon Ranulph Carteret Tollemache, 10th son of 1st Baron, *b* 1866, *d* 1960: *m* 1889, Annie Mary, who *d* 1923, da of late William Smith, of Haverstock Hill, NW:—
Devereux John Rex, *b* 1891: *m* 1914, Gladys Victoria, who *d* 1960, da of John Waddington of 19 Brunswick Terr, Hove, Sussex, and Waddington Old Hall, Yorks.

           Grandchildren of late Hon Ranulph Carteret Tollemache, 10th son of 1st Baron:—
      Issue of late Com Lawrence Lionel Tollemache, RN, *b* 1894, *d* 1954: *m* 1926, Violet Mary (who *m* 2ndly, 1956, Laurence Reid), da of John Bayly A'Deane:—
Margaret Ngaire Ngaskyl A'Deane, *b* 1928: *m* 1955, Antony Percy Jackson, of White Pines, Takapau, Hawkes Bay, New Zealand, and has issue living, Peter Lawrence, *b* 1956, — Timothy, *b* 1959, — Ashley, *b* 1961, — Alison, *b* 1958, — Ngaianne, *b* 1962. —— Annette A'Deane, *b* 1950: *m* 1st, 1974 (*m diss* 1981), Andrew Berne Vallance; 2ndly, 1984, Bryan Chesney Philpott, of Ashcott Station, RD Takapau, Hawkes Bay, NZ, and has issue living (by 1st *m*), Natasha A'Deane, *b* 1978, — (by 2nd *m*) Tamarin Mary A'Deane, *b* 1983.
      Issue of late Harold Vincent Tollemache, *b* 1895, *d* 1989: *m* 1937, Marjorie Violet, who *d* 1990, da of late W. H. Lonsdale, of Rangoon:—
Laurence Ranulph (46 Preston Grove, Faversham, Kent), *b* 1938: *m* 1960, Maureen Elizabeth, da of Harold Hex, of Taunton, Som, and has issue living, Paul Laurence, *b* 1965, — Clare Elizabeth, *b* 1968.

           Grandchildren of late Leila Mary Cartwright (infra):—
      Issue of late Sir Charles Mortimer Tollemache Smith-Ryland, KCVO, *b* 1927, *d* 1989: *m* 1952, Hon Jeryl Marcia Sarah (*Hon Lady Smith-Ryland*) (Sherbourne Park, Warwick), da of late Hon Robert Brampton Gurdon (*see* B Cranworth):—
Robin Charles SMITH-RYLAND, *b* 1953: *m* 1st, 1982 (*m diss* 1985), Eliza S., da of late Cdr James George Greville Dugdale, RN; 2ndly, 1985, Baroness Helène von Ludinghausen. —— David James, *b* 1961. —— Sarah Yoskyl, *b* 1955: *m* 1983 (Luke Edward) Timothy Hue Williams, and has issue living, Charles Luke, *b* 1991, — Sophie, *b* 1984, — Laura, *b* 1987. —— Joanna, *b* 1959. —— Petra Louisa, *b* 1970.

           Granddaughter of late Hon Mortimer Granville Tollemache, yst son of 1st Baron:—
      Issue of late Leila Mary Tollemache, *b* 1896, *d* 1971: *m* 1st, 1919, Charles Ivor Phipson Smith-Ryland, Capt Warwickshire Yeo, and Lieut Coldstream Gds Res of Officers, who *d* 1929; 2ndly, 1933, Victor Hamilton Aubrey Cartwright:—
(By 1st *m*) June, *b* 1924: *m* 1946, Robert W. Bensley, of Kahdena Rd, Morristown, NJ, USA, and has issue living, Robert Ward, *b* 1954, — Charles Ivor, *b* 1958, — Leila Hannah, *b* 1947.

PREDECESSORS – (1) JOHN JERVIS Tollemache of Helmingham Hall, Suffolk, son of late Adm John Richard Delap Tollemache (formerly Halliday), maternal grandson of 4th Earl of Dysart, sat as MP for Cheshire S (C) 1841-68, and for Cheshire W 1868-72, and was *cr Baron Tollemache*, of Helmingham, co Suffolk (peerage of United Kingdom) 1876; *b* 1805: *m* 1st, 1825, Georgina Louisa, who *d* 1846, da of Thomas Best; 2ndly, 1850, Eliza-Georgiana, who *d* 1918, da of James Duff; *d* 1890; *s* by his el son (2) WILBRAHAM FREDERICK, 2nd Baron; *b* 1832; MP for Cheshire W (C) 1872-85: *m* 1st, 1858, Lady Emma Georgina Stewart, who *d* 1869, 2nd da of 9th Earl of Galloway; 2ndly, 1878, Mary, who *d* 1939, da of late Rt Hon Lord Claude Hamilton (*see* D Abercorn, colls); *d* 1904; *s* by his grandson (3) BENTLEY LYONEL JOHN (son of late Hon Lyonel Plantagenet Tollemache, el son of 2nd Baron), 3rd Baron; *b* 1883; Capt 3rd Batn Cheshire Regt, Lieut-Com RNVR, and Capt RGA: *m* 1st, 1902, Wynford Rose, who *d* 1926, only da of late Gen Sir Arnold Burrowes Kemball, KCB, KCSI; 2ndly 1928, Lynette, MBE, who *d* 1982, da of Alfred Vincent Pawson, of Nynehead Court, Somerset; *d* 1955; *s* by his kinsman (4) JOHN EDWARD HAMILTON, MC (only son of late Maj-Gen Edward Devereux Hamilton Tollemache, DSO, MC, el son of late Hon Hamilton James Tollemache, 4th son of 1st Baron), 4th Baron; *b* 1910; Maj Coldm Gds: *m* 1939, Dinah Susan, da of late Sir Archibald Auldjo Jamieson, KBE, MC; *d* 1975; *s* by his el son (5) TIMOTHY JOHN EDWARD, 5th Baron and present peer.

TOMBS, BARON (Tombs) (Life Baron 1990)

FRANCIS LEONARD TOMBS, son of Joseph Tombs; *b* 17 May 1924; *ed* Elmore Green Sch, Walsall, Birmingham Coll of Technology, and London Univ (BSc); Hon LLD Strathclyde Univ (Chancellor since 1991), Hon DSc Aston Univ, Lodz Univ (Poland), Cranfield Inst of Technology (Pro-Chancellor and Chm of Council 1985-91), City of London Univ, Bradford Univ, Queen's Univ (Belfast), Surrey Univ and Nottingham Univ, Hon DTech Loughborough Univ of Technology, Hon DEd CNAA, Hon DSc Camb 1989, FEng, Hon FIEE, Hon FIMechE, Hon FICE, Hon FIChemE, Hon FIProdE, Hon Member British Nuclear Energy Soc; Chm Electricity Council for England and Wales 1977-80, Weir Group plc 1981-83, Turner & Newall plc 1982-89, Rolls-Royce plc 1985-92 (Dir since 1982), The Eng Council 1985-88, The Advisory Council on Science and Technology 1987-90, and Molecule Theatre Co 1985-92; Dir N M Rothschild & Sons Ltd since 1981, Turner & Newall Int Ltd 1982-89, Turner & Newall Welfare Trust Ltd 1982-89, and Shell UK Ltd since 1983; Liveryman and Assist Warden Goldsmiths' Co, Freeman City of London; *cr* Knt 1978, and *Baron Tombs*, of Brailes, co Warwicks (Life Baron) 1990: *m* 1949, Marjorie, da of Albert Evans, of Walsall.

Arms – Azure, on a saltire azure fimbriated argent a sun, its four rays in saltire extended and tipped with flame all gold. **Crest** – Out of a crown rayonny or, each straight ray ending in a mullet or, a dexter arm embowed vested azure the hand proper holding two keys in saltire bows upwards gold. **Supporters** – *Dexter*, a unicorn argent, armed, unguled, bearded, maned and tufted or, sejant erect upon a grassy mount proper between two double roses growing therefrom argent on gules and both barbed and seeded, stalked and leaved proper; *sinister*, a bear proper, clawed and muzzled or, sejant erect upon a like mount between two thistles growing therefrom also proper.
Residence – Honington Lodge, Honington, Shipston-upon-Stour, Warwicks CV36 5AA.

DAUGHTERS LIVING

Hon Catherine Barbara, *b* 1950.
Hon Elisabeth Jane, *b* 1952.
Hon Margaret Clare, *b* 1958.

TOMLIN, BARONY OF (Tomlin) (Extinct 1935)

DAUGHTER LIVING OF LIFE BARON

Hon Helen Rosa, *b* 1906: *m* 1932, Prof Frank Goldby, MD, FRCP, of 1 St Mark's Court, Barton Rd, Cambridge.

TONYPANDY, VISCOUNT (Thomas) (Viscount UK 1983)

(THOMAS) GEORGE THOMAS, PC, 1st Viscount, son of late Zachariah Thomas, of Tonypandy (*d* 1932); *b* 29 Jan 1909; *ed* Tonypandy Gram Sch, and Univ Coll, Southampton; MP for Central Cardiff 1945-50 and for Cardiff West 1950-83; Parl Under-Sec of State, Home Office 1964-66; Min of State, Welsh Office 1966-67 and Commonwealth Office 1967-68; Sec of State, Welsh Office 1968-70; Dep Speaker and Chm of Ways and Means 1974-76; Speaker of the House of Commons 1976-83; Vice-Pres Methodist Conference 1959-60; Pres of Coll of Preceptors 1984-88 and British Heart Foundation 1984-90; Chm Nat Children's Home 1983-90, since when Pres; Freeman of Borough of Rhondda 1970, City of Cardiff 1974, City of London 1980, Borough of Port Talbot 1991, and Paphos, Cyprus 1988; *cr* PC 1968, and *Viscount Tonypandy*, of Rhondda, co Mid Glamorgan (Peerage of UK) 1983.

Arms – Or an open book proper bound sable garnished gules, on a chief of the last between two portcullises or a pale per pale argent and or, charged with three chevrons gules. **Crest** – A miner's lamp between two daffodils slipped and leaved proper. **Supporters** – *Dexter*, A coal miner circa 1930 in his working clothes wearing a cloth cap proper and holding in his exterior hand a miner's lamp also proper. *Sinister*, A serjeant at arms habited in court dress as worn on state occasions his cocked hat under his exterior arm the hand thereof gloved and grasping the hilt of his sword proper.
Residence – Tilbury, 173 King George V Drive East, Cardiff.

TORDOFF, BARON (Tordoff) (Life Baron 1981)

GEOFFREY JOHNSON TORDOFF, son of Stanley Acomb Tordoff, of Marple, Cheshire, *b* 11 Oct 1928; *ed* Manchester Gram Sch, and Manchester Univ; Chm Liberal Party 1976-79, Pres 1983-84; *cr Baron Tordoff*, of Knutsford, co Cheshire (Life Baron) 1981: *m* 1953, Mary, da of Thomas Swarbrick, of Leeds, and has issue.

Residence – c/o House of Lords, SW1.

SONS LIVING

Hon Nicholas Gregory, *b* 1958.
Hon Mark Edmund, *b* 1962.

DAUGHTERS LIVING

Hon Mary Catherine, *b* 1954.
Hon Frances Jane, *b* 1956.
Hon Paula Mary, *b* 1960.

TORPHICHEN, LORD (Sandilands) (Lord S 1564)
(Title pronounced "Tor-fikken")

I hope for better things

SPERO · MELIORA

JAMES ANDREW DOUGLAS SANDILANDS, 15th Lord, *b* 27 Aug 1946; *s* 1975: *m* 1976, Margaret Elizabeth, only da of late William A. Beale, of Boston, Mass, USA, and has issue.

Arms – Quarterly: 1st and 4th argent, on a chief an Imperial crown or, in base a thistle vert, flowered gules; 2nd and 3rd grand quarters, 1st and 4th argent, a bend azure, *Sandilands*; 2nd and 3rd argent, a man's heart proper, ensigned by an Imperial crown gules, on a chief azure, three mullets of the field, *Douglas*. **Crest** – An eagle displayed proper. **Supporters** – Two wild men, wreathed about the temples and loins with oak leaves, each holding on the exterior shoulder a club proper.
Seat – Calder House, Mid-Calder, West Lothian EH53 0HN.

DAUGHTERS LIVING

Hon Margaret Elizabeth Grizel, *b* 1979.
Hon Mary Christian Sarah, *b* 1981.

SISTER LIVING

Hon Alison Mary, *b* 1944: *m* 1966, David Maurice Baldwin, and has issue living, Emma Alison, *b* 1968, — Petra Josephine, *b* 1972.
Residence – 30 Rochford Av, Shenfield, Essex.

MOTHER LIVING

Mary Thurstan, only da of Randle Henry Neville Vaudrey, of Edgbaston, Birmingham: *m* 1943 (*m diss* 1952), Hon James Bruce Sandilands, Master of Torphichen (later 14th Lord Torphichen), who *d* 1975.

WIDOW LIVING OF FOURTEENTH LORD

PAMELA MARY (*Pamela, Lady Torphichen*) (16 Moore St, SW3), da of late John Howard Snow, and widow of Thomas Hodson-Pressinger: *m* 1973, as his 3rd wife, the 14th Lord, who *d* 1975.

COLLATERAL BRANCHES LIVING

Issue of late Hon Walter Alexander Sandilands, yst son of 12th Lord, *b* 1888, *d* 1966: *m* 1918 (*m diss* 1930), Nancy Margaret, da of Hubert Powell, of Lewes:—
DOUGLAS ROBERT ALEXANDER (*Master of Torphichen*) (109 Royal George Rd, Burgess Hill, W Sussex); *b* 31 Aug 1926; a Driving Instructor: *m* 1st, 1949, Ethel Louise Burkitt; 2ndly 19—, Suzette Vera (*née* Pernet), and has issue living (by 1st *m*), Robert Powell, *b* 1950: *m* 1974, Cheryl Lin Watson, of Eastbourne, (by 2nd *m*), Bruno Charles, *b* 1977, — Edward Louis, *b* 1979. —— Jean Eleanor, *b* 1920: *m* 1st, 1947 (*m diss* 1950), Edward Cecil Doudney, who *d* 1955; 2ndly, 1955, as his 2nd wife, Col Richard Greville Acton Steel, TD, who *d* 1981, of 11 Eastleach Turville, Cirencester, Glos, and has issue living (by 2nd *m*) James Alexander Drummond, *b* 1958. —— Jonet Christian, *b* 1924: *m* 1st, 1944, Capt John Osborne Wigg, RN; 2ndly, 19—, John Hine (*dec*), of Houston, Texas, and has issue living (by 1st *m*), Anthony John Osborne, *b* 1955, — Coralie Ann Osborne *b* 1945: *m* 1965, Keith Clement, — Nina Jonet Osborne, *b* 1947: *m* 1966 (*m diss* 1983), Roderic Erskine Swift, and has issue living, Damien John Erskine *b* 1968, Julian James Sheridan *b* 1971, Amanda Jane Osborne *b* 1966: *m* 1986, Peter Dyke.

Granddaughters of late Hon John Hope Sandilands (*raised to the rank of a Baron's son* 1870), brother of 12th Lord:—
Issue of late James Bruce Sandilands, *b* 1883, *d* 1951: *m* 1909, Aline, who *d* 1972, da of F. G. Taylor, of Uralla, NSW:—
Helen Lucy, *b* 1909: *m* 1936, Richard Riley Trevitt, of Braeside, Uralla, NSW, and has issue living, Richard John (Sandon, Uralla, NSW), *b* 1938: *m* 1961, Mollie Juanita Blomfield, of Quirindi, NSW, and has issue living, Marcus John *b* 1964, Justin

James *b* 1966, Annette *b* 1963, — Simon Bruce, *b* 1942: *m* 1965, Robyn Anne Brown, of Uralla, NSW, and has issue living, Shaun Richard *b* 1967, Fiona Jane *b* 1969, — Robin Ann Lucy, *b* 1939: *m* 1965, David Edward Moore, of Perth, and has issue living, Richard Edward *b* 1966, Andrew Geoffrey *b* 1968, Amanda Gillian *b* 1969. —— Aline Dorothy, *b* 1920: *m* 1st, 1941, Godfrey Rees-Jones, RAAF, who was *ka* over Germany 1942; 2ndly, 1955, (Arthur) Harold Roberts, and has issue living, (by 2nd *m*) Marc Bruce (Flat 1 Shawfields, 41 Cranley Rd, Guildford, Surrey), *b* 1959: *m* 1991, Deborah Lee Scott, — Ian Geoffrey, *b* 1964, — Julie Aline, *b* 1957: *m* 1979, Glenn Raymond Johns, of 5 Robyn Avenue, French's Forest, Sydney, NSW 2086, and has issue, Lee Michael *b* 1981, Matthew Marc *b* 1982, Adam Glenn *b* 1984. *Residence* – 8 Ocean View Drive, Alstonville, NSW 2477.

Granddaughter of late James Bruce Sandilands (ante):—
Issue of late Geoffrey Bruce Hope Sandilands, Roy Australian Air Force, *b* 1922, *k* on active ser 1944: *m* 1944, Dorothy Mary (who *m* 2ndly, 1952, Henry Myron Carlson, of 3,000 Quadra Street, Victoria, British Colombia), da of George Nelson Joyce, of Victoria, BC:—
Joyce Hope SANDILANDS (4444 Tremblay Drive Victoria, BC, Canada V8N 4W5), *b* (*posthumous*) 1945; has resumed her maiden name: *m* 1964 (*m diss* 1979), D. L. Atchison, CA, and has issue living, James Geoffrey, *b* 1965, — Christine Anne, *b* 1967: *m* 1990, Steven Falconer, of Victoria, BC, Canada, and has issue living, Shayla Christine *b* 1994.

PREDECESSORS – (1) *Sir* JAMES Sandilands, 2nd son of the 6th feudal Baron of Calder, a Knight of Malta and Chief of that Order in Scotland, having resigned the property of the Knights of St John to Queen Mary, was *cr Lord Torphichen* (peerage of Scotland) 1564, with remainder to his heirs and assigns whatsoever; *dsp* 1579; *s* by his great-nephew, the 8th feudal Baron of Calder (2) JAMES, 2nd Lord; *d* 1617; *s* by his el son (3) JAMES, 3rd Lord; *d* unmarried 1622; *s* by his brother (4) JOHN, 4th Lord; *d* 1637; *s* by his el son (5) JOHN, 5th Lord; *d* unmarried 1649; *s* by his brother (6) WALTER, 6th Lord; *d* 1690; *s* by his son (7) JAMES, 7th Lord; a zealous supporter of the Scottish Union; was Commr of Police; *d* 1753; *s* by his son (8) WALTER, 8th Lord; *d* 1765; *s* by his son (9) JAMES, 9th Lord; was a Representative Peer; *dsp* 1815; *s* by his cousin (10) JAMES, 10th Lord; el son of Hon Robert, 8th son of 7th Lord; *d* 1862 *s* by his son (11) ROBERT, 11th Lord; *d* 1869; *s* by his nephew (12) JAMES WALTER, 12th Lord (el son of Rev the Hon John, 2nd son of 10th Lord, by Helen, da of James Hope, Clerk to the Signet), *b* 1846; a Representative Peer: *m* 1881, (*m diss* 1890) Francis Ellen, el da of late Lieut-Gen Charles Parke Gordon CB; *d* 1915; *s* by his second son (13) JOHN GORDON, 13th Lord; *b* 1886: *m* 1st, 1916, Grace Douglass, who *d* 1948, da of Winslow Pierce, of Bayville, Long Island, New York; 2ndly, 1950, Isabel Fernandez, who *d* 1976, da of Richard Bowden Daniel, of Jacksonville, Fla, USA, and widow of Richard Youel Phillips, of Greystones, Nanyuki, Kenya; *d* 1973; *s* by his son (14) JAMES BRUCE, 14th Lord; *b* 1917: *m* 1st, 1943 (*m diss* 1952) Mary Thurstan, only da of Randle Henry Neville Vaudrey, of Edgbaston, Birmingham; 2ndly, 1955 (*m diss* 1967), Margaret Dawson, of New York City, USA; 3rdly, 1973, Pamela Mary, da of late John Howard Snow, and widow of Thomas Hodson-Pressinger; *d* 1975; *s* by his only son (15), JAMES ANDREW DOUGLAS, 15th Lord and present peer.

TORRINGTON, VISCOUNT (Byng) (Viscount GB 1721, Bt GB 1715)

I will defend

TIMOTHY HOWARD ST GEORGE BYNG, 11th Viscount, and 11th Baronet; *b* 13 July 1943; *s* 1961; *ed* Harrow and St Edmund Hall, Oxford: *m* 1973, Susan Honour, da of Michael George Thomas Webster, of Little Manor Farm, Dummer, Hants (M Conyngham), and has issue.

Arms – Quarterly, sable and argent, in the 1st quarter a lion rampant of the second. **Crest** – An heraldic antelope ermine. **Supporters** – *Dexter*, an heraldic antelope ermine, armed, unguled, maned and tufted or, standing on a ship's gun proper; *sinister*, a sea-horse also proper also on a ship's gun.
Residence – Great Hunts Place, Owslebury, Winchester, Hants. *Clubs* – White's, Pratt's, Muthaiga, Kenya.

DAUGHTERS LIVING

Hon Henrietta Rose, *b* 1977.

Hon Georgina Isabel, *b* 1980.
Hon Malaika Anne, *b* 1982.

AUNT LIVING (*Daughter of 10th Viscount*)

Hon Honor (26 Swan Court, SW7), *b* 1912: *m* 1937 (*m diss* 1951), Lisle Marles Humphreys.

HALF AUNT LIVING (*Daughter of 10th Viscount*)

Hon (Rosamond Stella) Frances (2 St Boniface Rd, Ventnor, Isle of Wight), *b* 1937: *m* 1st, 1960 (*m diss* 1985), Antony B. Cobb; 2ndly, 1991, Frank Stephen Cross, and has issue living (by 1st *m*), Dorian Byng, *b* 1965, — Michelle Pandora, *b* 1961.

MOTHER LIVING

Anne Yvonne, da of late Capt R. G. P. Wood, Dragoon Guards, of Durban, Natal: *m* 1st, 1942, Paymaster-Lieut Hon George Byng, RN, who *d* on active service 1944, only son of 10th Viscount; 2ndly, 1951, Howard Henry Masterton Carpenter, who *d* 1976; 3rdly, 1991, Michael Ingram Bostock. *Residence* – 12 Southgate Villas, St James Lane, Winchester, Hants SO23 9SG.

COLLATERAL BRANCHES LIVING

Grandson of late Lt-Col Alfred Molyneux Cranmer-Byng, el son of Capt Henry Byng, RN (infra):—
Issue of late Capt Launcelot Alfred Cranmer Byng, *b* 1872, *d* 1945: *m* 1st, 1894, Harriet, who *d* 1913, da of Issac Hammersley; 2ndly, 1916, Daisy Elaine, who *d* 1981, da of N. B. Beach, of Chelmsford:—
(By 2nd *m*) JOHN LAUNCELOT, MC, *b* 18 March 1919; MA 1944; Prof of History, Toronto Univ; formerly Lecturer in History at Univ of Hong Kong; 1939-45 War as Maj Airborne Forces (MC): *m* 1955, Margaret Ellen, da of R. H. Hardy, of Sevenoaks, Kent, and has issue living, Colin Hugh, *b* 1960, — Alison Caroline, *b* 1956, — Sheila Margaret, *b* 1962. *Residence* – 190 Glengrove Av, Toronto, Canada.

Granddaughters of late John Anstruther Byng (infra):—

Issue of late Arthur Maitland Byng, *b* 1917, *d* 1983: *m* 1965, Joan Stuart Marr (Glenbucket, Box 1146, Rustenburg 0300, Transvaal, S Africa):—

Joanne Rachel, *b* 1969. —— Ann Maitland, *b* 1970.

Granddaughters of late Major Arthur Hervey Byng, son of Capt Henry Byng, RN, eldest son of Vice-Adm Hon Henry Dilkes Byng, 4th son of 5th Viscount:—

Issue of late John Anstruther Byng, *b* 1877, *d* 1960: *m* 1915, Rachel Wyllie, da of William Hampden Brodie, of Glenbucket, Scotland:—

Julienne Wyllie, *b* 1919: *m* 1st, 1941, John Duncan, who *d* 19—; 2ndly, 1965, Courtice Jocelyn Leigh-Hunt, who *d* 1976, of No 6 Golden Pond, off Somerset Place, 3245 Hilton, Natal, and has issue living (by 1st *m*), Annette Jenifer, *b* 1943, — Patricia Jane, *b* 1945. — Julienne Rachel, *b* 1947. —— Norah Cranmer, *b* 1921: *m* 1949, John Winnall Franklin Hampton (decd). —— Mary Maitland, *b* 1923: *m* 1946, Arthur Harold Hampshire Davison, and has issue living, Ian Hampshire *b* 1948, — Neil Torrington, *b* 1953, — Bruce Dale, *b* 1958.

Descendants of late Rt Hon Sir John Byng, GCB, GCH (3rd son of late George Byng, MP, el son of late Hon Robert Byng, 3rd son of 1st Viscount), who was *cr Earl of Strafford* 1847 (see that title).

PREDECESSORS – (1) *Adm Sir* GEORGE Byng, Knt, an eminent naval commander, knighted 1704; *cr a Baronet* 1715, and *Baron Byng*, of Southill, co Bedford, and *Viscount Torrington* (peerage of Great Britain) 1721; sat as MP for Plymouth 1705-21, and was Treasurer of the Navy 1725, and First Lord of the Admiralty 1727; *d* 1733; s by his el son (2) PATTEE PC, 2nd Viscount; sat successively as MP for Plymouth and Bedfordshire; was Treasurer of the Navy 1724-7, and sometime Vice Treasurer and Paymaster-Gen for Ireland, and Capt of the Yeomen of the Guard; *d* 1747; s by his brother (3) GEORGE, 3rd Viscount; a Maj-Gen in the Army; *d* 1750; s by his el son (4) GEORGE, 4th Viscount; *d* 1812; s by his brother (5) JOHN, 5th Viscount; *d* 1813; s by his son (6) GEORGE, 6th Viscount; *b* 1768; was a Vice-Adm; *d* 1831; s by his son (7) GEORGE, DCL, 7th Viscount; *b* 1812; was Gov of Ceylon 1847-50, a Lord-in-Waiting to HRH the Prince Consort 1853-9, and to HM Queen Victoria 1859-84; *d* 26 April 1884; s by his nephew (8) GEORGE STANLEY, 8th Viscount (son of late Major Hon Robert Barlow Palmer Byng, 3rd son of 6th Viscount, and Elizabeth Maria Lowther (who *m* 2ndly, 1861, Rev William Winchester), da of Col Gwatkin) *b* 1841; a Lord-in-Waiting to HM Queen Victoria: *m* 1st, 1882, Alice Arabella, who *d* 1883, da of James Jameson, of Airfield, Dublin; 2ndly, 1885, Emmeline St Maur, who *d* 1912, da of Rev Henry Seymour; *d* 1889; s by his son (9) GEORGE MASTER, 9th Viscount, *b* 1886; was a Page of Honour to Queen Victoria and to King Edward VII 1899-1903; sometime a Railway and Canal Commr: *m* 1st, 1910 (*m diss* 1921), Eleanor, who *d* 1931, el da of late Edwin Souray, of Long Ditton, Surrey; 2ndly, 1923, Norah Elizabeth Ursula (FERENS), who *d* 1968, da of late Capt Robert Wood-Pottle, 5th R Irish Lancers; *d* 1944; s by his cousin (10) ARTHUR STANLEY (son of late Hon Sydney Byng, brother of 8th Viscount), 10th Viscount; *b* 1876; Lt-Col RASC; S Africa 1899-1902 (DCM), 1914-18 War (Officer of Legion of Honour): *m* 1st, 1909 (*m diss* 1936), Louise Annette, da of Joseph Rawlins; 2ndly, 1936 (*m diss* 1952), Rosamund Ella, da of late Vice-Adm Alexander Percy Davidson, DSO; *d* 1961; s by his grandson (11) TIMOTHY HOWARD ST GEORGE (only son of late Paymaster-Lt Hon George Byng, RN, only son of 10th Viscount), 11th Viscount and present peer; also Baron Byng.

TOWNSHEND, MARQUESS (Townshend) (Marquess GB 1787, Bt E 1617)

HÆC·GENERI·INCREMENTA·FIDES

Faith obtained these honours for our race

GEORGE JOHN PATRICK DOMINIC TOWNSHEND, 7th Marquess, and 12th Baronet; *b* 13 May 1916; *s* 1921; *ed* Harrow; is Patron of thirteen livings; DCL, FRSA; Chm of Anglia Television Group plc 1976-86, Anglia Television Ltd 1958-86, Anchor Enterprises Ltd 1967-88, AP Bank Ltd 1975-87, Raynham Farm Co since 1957, Norfolk Agricultural Station 1974-87, and Survival Anglia Ltd 1971-86; Vice Chm Norwich Union Life Insurance Society 1973-86, and Fire Insurance Soc 1975-86; Dir Scottish Union and National Insurance Co 1968-86, Maritime Insurance Co Ltd 1968-86, London Merchant Securities plc since 1964, D E Longe & Co since 1962 (Chm since 1981), Napak Ltd since 1968 (Chm since 1981), E Coast Grain Ltd since 1962 (Chm since 1981), Dir Anglia Radio Ltd until 1986, and Norwich Union Holdings 1981-86; a Gov of Roy Agric Soc of England; 55 (Suffolk and Norfolk Yeo) Anti Tank Regt 1936, ADC to GOC-in-C, E Command 1936-39, Personal Assist to CIGS 1939-40, Scots Gds 1940-45: *m* 1st, 1939 (*m diss* 1960), Elizabeth Pamela Audrey, who *d* 1989, only da of Maj Thomas Luby, late Judicial Commr, ICS; 2ndly, 1960, Ann Frances, who *d* 1988, only da of late Arthur Pellew Darlow, and has issue by 1st and 2nd *m*.

Arms – Azure, a chevron ermine between three escallops argent. **Crest** – A stag statant proper, attired and unguled or. **Supporters** – *Dexter*, a stag sable attired and unguled or: *sinister*, a greyhound argent.

Seat – Raynham Hall, Norfolk. **Clubs** – White's, Norfolk, MCC.

SONS LIVING (By 1st marriage)

CHARLES GEORGE (*Viscount Raynham*) (Pattesley House, Fakenham, Norfolk; 22 Ebury St, SW1), *b* 26 Sept 1945; *ed* Eton: *m* 1st, 1975, Hermione, who *d* 1985 in a motor accident, da of Lt-Cdr Robert Martin Dominic Ponsonby (*see* E Bessborough, colls); 2ndly, 1990, Mrs Alison Marshall, yr da of late Sir Willis Ide Combs, KCVO, CMG, of Wadhurst Park, E Sussex, and has issue:—

SON LIVING (by 1st *m*), — Hon THOMAS CHARLES, *b* 2 Nov 1977.

DAUGHTER LIVING (by 1st *m*), — Hon Louise Elizabeth *b* 1979.

(By 2nd marriage)

Lord John Patrick, *b* 1962; *ed* Eton, and London Univ: *m* 1987 (*m diss* 1991), Rachel Lucy, da of FM Sir John Chapple, GCB, KBE, ADC Gen. *Residence* – 31 Coleherne Rd, SW10 9BS.

DAUGHTERS LIVING *(By 1st marriage)*

Lady Carolyn Elizabeth Ann TOWNSHEND, *b* 1940; has resumed her maiden name: *m* 1st, 1962 (*m diss* 1971), Antonio Capellini; 2ndly, 1973 (*m annulled* 1974), Edgar Miles Bronfman, and has issue living (by 1st *m*), Vincenzo Charles TOWN-SHEND, *b* 1963. *Residence* – 89 Elizabeth St, SW1W 9PG.

Lady Joanna Agnes TOWNSHEND, *b* 1943: *m* 1st, 1962 (*m diss* 1968), Jeremy George Courtenay Bradford; 2ndly, 1978 (*m diss* 1984), James Barry Morrissey; 3rdly, 1991, Christian Marc Boegnor, son of late Etienne Boegnor, and has issue living (by 1st *m*), Francis James Patrick, *b* 1963. *Residence* – 120 East 87th St, New York, NY 10128, USA.

(By 2nd marriage)

Lady Katherine Ann *b* 1963: *m* 1991, Piers W. Dent, yst son of Robin Dent, of Olivers, Painswick, Glos, and has issue living, Lucia, *b* 1992.

COLLATERAL BRANCHES LIVING

Grandsons of late Ferrars Ernest Osborne Townshend, only son of late George Ferrars Townshend (infra):—
Issue of late Henry George Townshend, *b* 1911, *d* 1979; *m* 1943, Elaine Florence, da of T. E. Frith, of Melbourne, Australia:—
Ferrars Edwin, *b* 1944: *m* 1980, Gillian Adams. *Residence* – Pitua Rd, Tauranga, NZ. ⸺ Anthony Stuart, *b* 1956.

Grandchildren of late Rev Lord George Osborne Townshend, yr brother of 4th Marquess:—
Issue of late George Ferrars Townshend, *b* 1854, *d* 1942: *m* 1st, 18—, Elizabeth Brenda Baillie, who *d* 1891; 2ndly, 18—, Clara Jenkins, of Auckland, New Zealand:—
(By 2nd *m*) Rua Hildyard Bute (18 Tautari St, Orakei, Auckland 5), *b* 1902: *m* 1st, 1927 (*m diss* 1934), Vivian Herbert Judd; 2ndly, 1934, Robert Hanna, who *d* 1975, and has issue living (by 1st *m*), Raynham George HANNA, *b* 1928 (assumed step-father's surname by deed poll), ⸺ Ross Townshend HANNA, *b* 1930, ⸺ Mason Townshend HANNA, *b* 1930 (twin). ⸺ Rere, *b* 1904: *m* 1924, Digby Felix McGarry, of 201 Victoria Av, Remuera, Auckland 5, and has issue living, Digby Rochefort Dillon, *b* 1925: *m* 1954, Katherine Mary Palmer. ⸺ Rata Victoria, *b* 1912: *m* 1934, Jack Mason Norling, of 158 Coates Av, Orakei, Auckland 5, and has issue living, Michael Holmden Mason, *b* 1935.

Granddaughter of late George Ferrars Townshend (ante):—
Issue of late George Ferrars Vere Townshend, *b* 1897, *d* 1957: *m* 1921, Fanny Elizabeth, da of James Matthew Brassington, of Staffordshire:—
Diana Vere, *b* 1927: *m* 1949, Noel Trevor Gedye, MI StructE, AMNZIE, and has issue living, Christopher John, *b* 1950: *m* 1973, Ranee Joy Murphy, and has issue living, Sharl Justin *b* 1980, Nichole Jade *b* 1984, ⸺ Stephen Warren, *b* 1953: *m* 1977, Roseann Hare, ⸺ Michael Jonathan, *b* 1957: *m* 1984, Victoria Ruth Ohms. *Residence* – 1/19 Selwyn Av, Mission Bay, Auckland 5, New Zealand.

Grandsons of late Ernest Edwin Townshend, 3rd son of late Rev Lord George Osborne Townshend (ante):—
Issue of late Clifford Edwin Townshend, *b* 1884, *d* 1958: *m* 1915, Rose Evelyn, MBE, da of John Abraham Greensill, of Picton, Marlborough, New Zealand:—
John Edwin (PO Box 736, Napier, NZ), *b* 1918; 1939-45 with RNZAF: *m* 1943, Mary, da of William Joseph Curran Sharp, and has issue living, Keith Edwin (38A Symonds St, Onehunga, Auckland 6, NZ), *b* 1948: *m* 1981, Margaret Johanna, da of Joseph Boldero, of Kawhia, NZ, and has issue living, David John Edwin *b* 1982, James Raynham *b* 1983, ⸺ Margaret Ann TOWNSHEND (1019 Hood St, Hastings, NZ), *b* 1944; has resumed the surname of Townshend: *m* 1st, 1963 (*m diss* 1972), Earl Dudley Gee; 2ndly, 1974 (*m diss* 1982), John Leslie Taylor, and has issue living, (by 1st *m*) Richard John Earl TOWNSHEND *b* 1969; assumed surname of Townshend by deed poll in lieu of his patronymic, Michelle Margaret *b* 1963: *m* 1984, Neville McAlister, of 11A Woodfield Av, Palmerston North, NZ, Lisa Ann *b* 1966. ⸺ George Maling, MBE (2/26 Rothesay Bay Rd, Auckland, NZ), *b* 1921; *ed* Marlborough Coll, NZ; a JP, and a City Councillor of Napier; 1939-45 War with RNZAF: *m* 1st, 1944, Alice Joyce, who *d* 1986, el da of Alfred Wilfred Nye, of Long Bay Rd, Coromandel, NZ; 2ndly, 1987, Heather Joan Pallesen, 3rd da of Douglas Brown, of Hastings, NZ, and has issue living (by 1st *m*), Colin David (7 Edgecumbe St, Hamilton, NZ), *b* 1948: *m* 1969, Jennifer Pearl, da of Ian Alfred Madsen, of Napier, NZ, and has issue living, Glen David *b* 1971, Zane Colin *b* 1972, Tara Jean *b* 1974, ⸺ Yvonne Joy, *b* 1946: *m* 1971, Brett Denize, of 27 Haseler Cres, Howick, Auckland, NZ, and has issue living, Donna Joy *b* 1972, Rowena Helen *b* 1975.

Grandchildren of late Clifford Edwin Townshend (ante):—
Issue of late Charles Roberts Townshend, *b* 1926, *d* 1987: *m* 1952, Dorothy Winifred (11 Whakarire Av, Westshore, Napier, NZ), da of Frederick Leo Luks, of Auckland, NZ:—
Robert Paul, *b* 1965. ⸺ Denise Kaye, *b* 1955: *m* 1980, Stephen Alexander Greer, solicitor, of 10 Matai Place, Tamatea, Napier, NZ, and has issue living, Alexander Townshend, *b* 1982, ⸺ Charles Townshend, *b* 1989, ⸺ Rebecca Ellen, *b* 1984.

PREDECESSORS – **(1)** ROGER Townshend, MP for Norfolk 1627; *cr* a *Baronet* 1617; *d* 1637; *s* by his el son **(2)** *Sir* ROGER; 2nd Bt; *s* by his brother **(3)** *Sir* HORATIO, 3rd Bt a zealous royalist, who rendered valuable assistance in restoring the monarchy; was sometime MP for Norfolk; *cr Baron Townshend*, of Lynn Regis (peerage of England) 1661, and *Viscount Townshend*, of Rainham (peerage of England) 1682; *d* 1687; *s* by his son **(4)** CHARLES, KG, PC, 2nd Viscount; was Lord-Lt of Norfolk, Capt of Yeomen of the Guard 1707-11, Ambassador to the Hague 1709-10, a Lord Justice, Principal Sec of State 1714-16 and 1721-30, and Pres of the Council 1720; *d* 1738; *s* by his son **(5)** CHARLES, 3rd Viscount, who in 1723 had been summoned to Parliament in his father's Barony of Lynn; was Lord of the Bedchamber, Custos Rotulorum of Norfolk, and Master of the Jewels; *d* 1767; *s* by his son **6** GEORGE, PC, 4th Viscount; a Field-Marshal in the Army and a successful military commander, was *cr Marquess Townshend* (Peerage of Great Britain) 1787; sat as MP for Norfolk, Lt-Gen of the Ordnance 1763-67, and Master-Gen 1772-82, Viceroy of Ireland 1767, Gov of Jersey, &c, Lord-Lieut of Norfolk, &c: *m* 1st 1751, Charlotte, who *d* 1770, in her own right (through her mother) Baroness Ferrers of Chartley, and (through her father) Baroness Compton; 2ndly, 1773, Anne, who *d* 1819, da of Sir William Montgomery, 1st Bt; *d* 1807; *s* by his son **(7)** GEORGE, 2nd Marquess, who following the death of his mother 1770, was summoned to Parliament as *Baron Ferrers de Chartley*, and in 1784 had been *cr Earl of Leicester* (peerage of Great Britain); was Postmaster-Gen 1794-8, and Lord Steward of the Household 1799-1802; *d* 1811; *s* by his son **(8)** GEORGE FERRERS, 3rd Marquess; *dsp* 1855, when the Earldom of Leicester became extinct, the Baronies of Ferrers of Chartley, Compton, &c became abeyant, and the Barony, Viscountcy, and Marquessate of Townshend devolved upon his cousin **(9)** JOHN, 4th Marquess; *b* 1798; was a Rear-Adm: *m* 1825, Elizabeth Jane, who *d* 1877, da of Rear-Adm Lord George Stuart, CB (M Bute); *d* 1863; *s* by his son **(10)** JOHN VILLIERS Stuart, 5th Marquess; MP for Tamworth (L) 1856-63: *m* 1865, Lady Anne Elizabeth Clementina Duff, who *d* 1925, da of 5th Earl of Fife; *d* 1899; *s* by his only son **(11)** JOHN JAMES DUDLEY STUART, 6th Marquess; *b* 1866: *m* 1905, Gladys Ethel Gwendolen Eugénie (who *d* 1959, having *m* 2ndly, 1946, Bernard le Strange), eldest da of late Thomas Sutherst, Bar-at-law; *d* 1921; *s* by his son **(12)** GEORGE JOHN PATRICK DOMINIC, 7th Marquess and present peer; also Viscount Townshend, of Rainham, and Baron Townshend, of Lynn Regis.

TRAFFORD, BARONY OF (Trafford) (Extinct 1989)

SON LIVING OF LIFE BARON

Hon Mark Russell, *b* 1966; *ed* Lancing, and Lincoln's Inn.

DAUGHTER LIVING OF LIFE BARON

Hon Tanya Helen, *b* 1968; *ed* Deepdene Sch Sandhurst Military Acad.

WIDOW LIVING OF LIFE BARON

HELEN (*Baroness Trafford*), da of Ralph Chalk, of Cambs; Hon DSc Univ of Sussex 1991; Member of Univ Court 1992; Founder Trafford Centre for Medical Research; Dir South Downs Health NHS Trust, Trustee Nurses Welfare Service, Brighton Health Care Arts Trust, Trafford Renal Research Trust, etc: *m* 1960, Baron Trafford (Life Baron), who *d* 1989. *Residence* – 18 Ponsonby Place, SW1.

TRANMIRE, BARONY OF (Turton) (Extinct 1994)

SONS LIVING AND DECEASED OF LIFE BARON

Hon Michael Andrew, *b* 1929.
†*Hon* Timothy Robert Scott, *b* 1934; *ed* RNC Dartmouth, and Balliol Coll, Oxford; Bar Inner Temple 1956; *d* 1989.
Hon Gerald Christopher (Park House, Upsall, N Yorks), *b* 1937; *ed* Eton, and RAC Cirencester; a farmer: *m* 1967, Alexandra Susan, da of Lt-Col S. Oliver, of 12 Maison Dieu, Richmond, Yorks, and has issue living, Robert Edmund, *b* 1971, — Natalia Maud Elizabeth, *b* 1969, — Alexandra Christian, *b* 1974.

DAUGHTER LIVING OF LIFE BARON

Hon Gillian Hermione Christian, *b* 1930: *m* 1960, David Poulett Wells, BM, BCh, FRCGP, of Hilperton House, Hilperton, Trowbridge, Wilts, and has had issue, Quinton Robert, *b* 1962, — Nicholas Michael, *b* and *d* 1966, — Fiona Mary, *b* 1963, — Olivia Rosalind, *b* 1969.

WIDOW LIVING OF LIFE BARON

RUBY CHRISTIAN (*Baroness Tranmire*), da of late Robert Thomas Scott, of Beechmont, Sevenoaks, Kent: *m* 1928, Baron Tranmire, KBE, MC, PC (Life Baron), who *d* 1994. *Residence* – Upsall Castle, Thirsk, N Yorks YO7 2NU; 15 Greycoat Gdns, SW1.

TREDEGAR, BARONY OF (Morgan) (Extinct 1962)

WIDOW LIVING OF SIXTH BARON

JOANNA, only da of Walter Henry Law-Smith, of Adelaide, S Australia: *m* 1st, 1938 (*m diss* 1954), Cdr A. B. Russell, DSO, RN; 2ndly, 1954, the 6th Baron, who *d* 1962, when the title became ext; 3rdly, 1967, the 9th Baron Wharton, who *d* 1969; 4thly, 1971, Bruce Yorke, of Casa Le Concha, Rocio de Naguëles, Marbella (Malaga), Spain.

TREFGARNE, BARON (Trefgarne) (Baron UK 1947)

DAVID GARRO TREFGARNE, PC, 2nd Baron; *b* 31 March 1941; *s* 1960; *ed* Haileybury, and Princeton Univ, USA; awarded Roy Aero Club Bronze Medal (jointly) for flight UK to Aust and back in light aircraft 1963; Opposition Whip, House of Lords 1977-79; Lord in Waiting to HM 1979-81; Under Sec, Dept of Trade 1981; Under Sec, Foreign & Commonwealth Office 1981-82; Under Sec Dept of Health & Social Security 1982-83; Under Sec for Armed Forces 1983-85, Min of State for Defence (Support) 1985-86, and (Procurement) 1986-89, Min for Trade Dept of Trade & Industry 1989-90; Company Dir and Pres of Metcom; PC 1989: *m* 1968, Hon Rosalie Lane, da of Baron Lane of Horsell (Life Baron), and has issue.

Arms – Or, a dragon rampant gules, over all a bend azure charged with a leek of the first between two thistles stalked and leaved proper. **Crest** – A palm tree, suspended therefrom by a strap proper an escutcheon or, charged with a portcullan chained gules. **Supporters** – On either side is a Herefordshire bull proper, charged on the shoulder with an escutcheon or, thereon a portcullis chained sable.
Address – c/o Barclays Bank, Woking, Surrey GU21 1AE.

SONS LIVING

Hon GEORGE GARRO, *b* 4 Jan 1970.

Hon Justin Peter Garro, *b* 1973.

DAUGHTER LIVING

Hon Rebecca Rosalie, *b* 1976.

BROTHERS LIVING

Hon Trevor Garro, *b* 1944; *ed* Cheltenham; Cranfield Sch of Management 1968-69; Chm, Nesco Investments plc 1979-87; Dir of other cos: *m* 1st, 1967, (*m diss* 1979), Diana Elizabeth, 2nd da of Michael Edward Gibb; 2ndly, 1979, Caroline France, da of Michael Gosschalk, of 12 Boulevard de Suisse, Monte Carlo, and has issue living (by 1st *m*), Rupert Michael Garro, *b* 1972, — Oliver Edward Garro, *b* 1974, — Susannah Julia, *b* 1976, — (by 2nd *m*) Mark Michael Garro, *b* 1982, — Camilla Amélie, *b* 1988.

Hon Gwion George Garro (Cherry Croft, Hewelsfield, Lydney, Glos), *b* 1953; *ed* Milton Abbey, and Merrist Wood & Usk Agric Colls; Tree Surgeon: *m* 1986, Jacqueline Louise, da of Alan Rees, of Woodspring, Brockweir, Chepstow, Gwent, and has issue living, Samuel Ivor Garro, *b* 1987, — Hannah Elizabeth, *b* 1989.

SISTER LIVING

Hon Mary Elizabeth, *b* 1946; Bar (Gray's Inn) 1971.

PREDECESSOR – (1) GEORGE MORGAN Trefgarne, son of late Rev David Garro-Jones of Milford Haven; *b* 1894; assumed by deed poll (enrolled at College of Arms) 1954 the surname of Trefgarne in lieu of his patronymic; was Parliamentary Sec, Min of Production 1942-5, Chm of Television Advisory Committee 1945-9, and Founder Chm of Colonial Development Corporation 1947-50; sat at MP for S Div of Hackney (*L*) 1924-9, and for N Div of Aberdeen (*Lab*) 1935-45; *cr Baron Trefgarne*, of Cleddau, co Pembroke (peerage of UK) 1947: *m* 1940, Elizabeth (who *m* 2ndly, 1962 (*m diss* 1966), Com Anthony Tosswill Courtney, OBE, who *d* 1988, and 3rdly, 1971, Hugh Cecil Howat Ker, and *d* 1987), yst da of late Charles Edward Churchill, of Ashton Keynes, Wilts; *d* 1960; *s* by his el son (2) DAVID GARRO, 2nd Baron and present peer.

TRENCHARD, VISCOUNT (Trenchard) (Viscount UK 1936, Bt UK 1919)

Know thyself

HUGH TRENCHARD, 3rd Viscount and 3nd Baronet; *b* 12 March 1951; *s* 1987: *ed* Eton, and Trin Coll, Camb (BA 1973); Capt 4th Royal Green Jackets, TA (1973-80); Member General Affairs Cttee, Japan Security Dealers Assocn 1987-88, Japan Assocn of Corporate Execs since 1987, and Executive Cttee British Chamber of Commerce in Japan since 1993; Chm Securities Cttee, European Business Community in Japan since 1993; Dir Dover Japan KK 1985-87, and Kleinwort Benson Ltd, since 1986: *m* 1975, Fiona Elizabeth, da of Hon James Ian Morrison (*see* B Margadale), and has issue.

Arms – Per Pale argent and azure, on the first three pallets sable, all within a bordure of the last. **Crest** – A cubit arm erect, vested azure, cuffed argent, holding in the hand a Cinqueda sword, both proper. **Supporters** – On either side an eagle close gules, each charged on the neck, the dexter with a thistle slipped and leaved and the sinister with truncheon erector.
Residence – 7-10 Shirogane 4-chome, Minato-ku, Tokyo 108, Japan.

SONS LIVING

Hon ALEXANDER THOMAS, *b* 26 July 1978; *ed* Eton; a Page of Honour to HM The Queen 1990-93.
Hon William James, *b* 1986.

DAUGHTERS LIVING

Hon Katherine Clare, *b* 1980.

Hon Laura Mary, *b* 1987.

BROTHERS LIVING

Hon John, *b* 1953; *ed* Eton: *m* 1983, Clare, yst da of Edward Chandos de Burgh Marsh, of The Old Rectory, Salcott, Essex, and has issue living, Thomas Edward, *b* 1988, — Emma Clare, *b* 1991.
Hon Thomas Henry, *b* 1966; *ed* Haileybury.

WIDOW LIVING OF SECOND VISCOUNT

PATRICIA SCOTT (*Dowager Viscountess Trenchard*), da of late Adm Sir Sidney Robert Bailey, KBE, CB, DSO: *m* 1948, the 2nd Viscount, MC, who *d* 1987. *Residence* – Abdale House, North Mymms, Hatfield, Herts.

PREDECESSORS – (1) *Marshal of the RAF Sir* HUGH MONTAGUE Trenchard, GCB, OM, GCV0, DSO, son of late Capt Henry Montague Trenchard; *b* 1873; S Africa 1900-02 with Imperial Yeo, Bushman Corps, and Canadian Scouts (dangerously wounded), S Nigeria 1904 in command (despatches), 1904-05 Comdg patrol through Ibibio and Kwa country, 1905-6 in command of Bendo-Onitsha Hinterland Expedition (despatches, DSO), 1914-18 War as Gen Officer Comdg Mil Wing of RFC as Ch of Air Staff (RAF) and as GOC-in-C, Inter-Allied Indep Air Force, thanked by Parliament, *cr* a Baronet, granted £10,000; Ch of Air Staff and Member of Air Council 1918 and 1918-30. Prin Air ADC to HM 1921-25, and Commr of Metropolitan Police 1931-35; bore Third Sword at Coronation of King George VI; *cr* a Baronet 1919, *Baron Trenchard*, of Wolfeton, co Dorset (peerage of UK) 1930, and *Viscount Trenchard*, of Wolfeton, co Dorset (peerage of UK) 1935: *m* 1920, Katherine Isabel Salvin, who *d* 1960, da of late Edward Salvin Bowlby, of Gilston Park, Herts, and Knoydart, Inverness-shire, and widow of Capt Hon James Boyle; *d* 1956; *s* by his yr son (2) THOMAS, MC, 2nd Viscount, *b* 1923; served 1939-45 War as Capt KRRC; Dir T. Wall & Sons Ltd 1953-66, Chm Walls Meat Co Ltd 1960-66, Dir Unilever Ltd, and Unilever NV 1967-77, and other Cos; Pres Royal Inst of Public Health and Hygiene 1970-79; Member Agric Research Council 1970-79; Pres of Grocery Distribution 1974-77; Min of State Dept of Industry 1979-81, for Defence Procurement 1981-83; Chm Schlumberger Measurement & Control (UK) Ltd 1985-87: *m* 1948, Patricia Scott, da of late Adm Sir Sidney Robert Bailey, KBE, CB, DSO; *d* 1987; *s* by his eldest son (3) HUGH, 3rd Viscount and present peer; also Baron Trenchard.

TREND, BARONY OF (Trend) (Extinct 1987)

SONS LIVING OF LIFE BARON

Hon Michael St John, *b* 1952; *ed* Westminster, Oriel Coll, Oxford and in Athens (Greek Govt scholarship); MP (*C*) Windsor and Maidenhead since 1992, Parly Priv Sec Dept of the Environment since 1993: *m* 1987, Jill Elizabeth, elder da of L. A. Kershaw, of Oldham, Lancs, and has issue living, Edward St John, *b* 1990, — Faith Charlotte, *b* 1988, — Mary Cecilia, *b* 1994.
Dr the Hon Patrick St John, *b* 1955: *m* 1989, Susan F., da of late R. W. Saunders, of Meanwood, Leeds, and has issue living, Alexander *b* 1992, — Hector, *b* 1993.

DAUGHTER LIVING OF LIFE BARON

Hon Catharine Julia, *b* 1950: *m* 1966, Colin James Rawlinson.

WIDOW LIVING OF LIFE BARON

PATRICIA CHARLOTTE (*Baroness Trend*), da of late Rev Gilbert Shaw: *m* 1949, Baron Trend, GCB, CVO, PC, who *d* 1987.

TRENT, BARONY OF (Boot) (Extinct 1956)

DAUGHTERS LIVING OF SECOND BARON

Hon Barbara Jacqueline (Wilton Lodge, Lovel Rd, Winkfield, Berks), *b* 1915: *m* 1934 (*m diss* 1973), Maj Willoughby Rollo Norman, and has issue living (*see* Norman, Bt).

Hon Joceleyne Mary, *b* 1917: *m* 1947, Maj Harcourt Michael Scudamore Gold, MC, of Wheathill, Sparsholt, nr Winchester, Hants, who *d* 1982, and has issue living, John Angus Harcourt, *b* 1958: *m* 1982 (*m diss* 19—), Charlotte Mary, yr da of late Lt-Col John Monsell Christian, MC, — Charmian Joy, *b* 1950: *m* 1st, 1969 (*m diss* 1973), Frederick James Meynell (*see* E Halifax, colls); 2ndly, 1974 (*m diss* 19—), James Richard Nicholson (*see* Nicholson Bt, *cr* 1912); 3rdly, 1982, Timothy Gilbert Culcheth Holcroft (*see* Holcroft, Bt, colls).

Hon (Margaret) Anne, *b* 1920: *m* 1st, 1940 (*m diss* 1948), Major John Edward Jocelyn Davie, Derbyshire Yeo; 2ndly, 1949, Air Vice-Marshal Somerled Douglas MacDonald, CB, CBE, DFC, who *d* 1979, and has issue living, (by 1st *m*) Simon John (55 Sutherland St, SW1), *b* 1941, — (Anne) Clare (18 Quarrendon St, SW6), *b* 1943: *m* 1964 (*m diss* 1975), Robin Gerard d'Abo. *Residence* – Thane, Kintbury, Newbury, Berks.

Hon Elizabeth Campbell, *b* 1927: *m* 1947, Major Michael Woodbine Parish, MC, Notts Yeo, and has issue living, Clement Robin Woodbine, *b* 1950, — Suzanne Woodbine, *b* 1948: *m* 1983, S. B. Kumaramangalam, of Dharmapuri, Tamil Nadu, India, and has issue living, Kim *b* 1983, Melissa Zoë *b* 1984, — Caroline Woodbine, *b* 1953: *m* 1979, George Constantine Zegos, of Villa Primrose, Grammou St, Kaki-Vigla, Salamina, Greece, and has issue living, Constantine George *b* 1979, Elizabeth Miriam *b* 1984, Dimitra Winifred *b* 1986, Rose Athina *b* 1988, — Emma Woodbine, *b* 1957: *m* 1987, Charles Robson Hamilton Houston, and has issue living (*see* B Swansea). *Residence* – Walcot Hall, Lydbury North, Shropshire.

TREVELYAN, BARONY OF (Trevelyan) (Extinct 1985)

DAUGHTERS LIVING OF LIFE BARON

Hon Susan Anne, *b* 1941: *m* 1961, Harald Busse (c/o Ministry of Foreign Affairs, Bonn, Germany), and has issue living, Allan George, *b* 1962, — Jan Michael, *b* 1963, — Nicola Andrea, *b* 1967.

Hon Catherine Mary, OBE, *b* 1943; OBE (Civil) 1977: *m* 1990, as his 3rd wife, Robert Kee.

WIDOW LIVING OF LIFE BARON

Violet Margaret (*Baroness Trevelyan*) (24 Duchess of Bedford House, W8 7QN), da of late Gen Sir William Henry Bartholomew, GCB, CMG, DSO: *m* 1937, Baron Trevelyan, KG, GCMG, CIE, OBE (Life Baron), who *d* 1985.

Trevethin and Oaksey, Baron, see Oaksey.

TREVOR, BARON (Hill-Trevor) (Baron UK 1880)

Charles Edwin Hill-Trevor, 4th Baron; *b* 13 Aug 1928; *s* 1950; *ed* Shrewsbury; is patron of two livings, a JP for Denbighshire, Chm Berwyn PS Div; Trustee R Forestry Soc of England, Wales and N Ireland, and an OStJ: *m* 1967, Susan Janet Elizabeth, da of Ronald Ivor Bence, DSC, URD, BM, of 13 Bournbrook Rd, Selly Oak, Birmingham, and has issue.

Arms – Quarterly: 1st and 4th per bend sinister ermine and ermines, a lion rampant or, *Trevor.* 2nd and 3rd sable, on a fesse argent, between three leopards passant guardant or, spotted of the field, as many escallops gules, *Hill.* Crest – 1st, a wyvern, wings addorsed sable, *Trevor;* 2nd, a reindeer's head couped at the neck gules, attired and plain collared or, *Hill.* Supporters – *Dexter,* a lion ermines, gorged with a ducal coronet and chained or, the chain reflexed over the back; pendent from the collar a shield argent, charged with the crest of Trevor; *sinister* a leopard or, spotted sable, gorged with a ducal coronet and chained or, the chain reflexed over the back; pendent from the collar a shield ermines charged with the crest of Hill.
Seats – Brynkinalt, Chirk, Wrexham; Auch, Bridge of Orchy, Argyllshire. *Clubs* – Flyfishers; E India.

SONS LIVING

Hon Marke Charles, *b* 8 Jan 1970.
Hon Iain Robert, *b* 1971.

BROTHER LIVING

Hon Nevill Edward (Plas Lledrod, Llansilin, Clwyd), *b* 1931; *ed* Shrewsbury; Flying Officer RAF (ret); a DL for Clwyd (High Sheriff 1965-66); ADC to Com-in-Ch Fighter Command, 1958-59; ADC to Ch of Air Staff 1960-61: *m* 1963, Deborah, only da of late W. T. B. Jowitt, of Killinghall, Harrogate, and has issue living, Caroline Anne, *b* 1965, — Diana Rosemary, *b* 1967.

PREDECESSORS – (1) *Lord* Arthur Edwin Hill, 3rd son of 3rd Marquess of Downshire, KP; *b* 1819; MP for co Down (*C*) 1845-80; assumed the additional surname of Trevor 1862, on succeeding to the estates of Viscount Dungannon; *cr Baron Trevor,* of Brynkinalt, co Denbigh (peerage of United Kingdom) 1880: *m* 1st, 1848, Mary Emily, who *d* 1855, el da of Sir Richard Sutton, 1st Bt; 2ndly, 1858, Hon Mary Catherine Curzon, who *d* 1911, sister of 4th Baron Scarsdale; *d* 1894; *s* by his el son (2) Arthur William, 2nd Baron, *b* 1852; Lieut-Col 1st Life Guards, and Vice-Lieut for Denbighshire; Comdt Denbighshire Vol Regt 1917-20 (Hon Col): *m* 1st, 1894, Hon Annie Mary Eleanor Fraser, who *d* 1895, da of 17th Baron Saltoun, and formerly wife of 15th Baron Zouche; 2ndly, 1897, Rosamond, MBE, who *d* 1942, da of late Hon Edmund George Petre (*see* B Petre, colls), and widow of 4th Earl of Bantry (*ext*); *d* 1923; *s* by his half-brother **(3)** CHARLES EDWARD, 3rd Baron, *b* 1863: *m* 1927, Phyllis, who *d* 1990, da of J. A. Sims, of Ings House, Kirton-in-Lindsey, Lincolnshire; *d* 1950; *s* by his el son **(4)** CHARLES EDWIN, 4th Baron and present peer.

TRIMLESTOWN, BARON (Barnewall) (Baron I 1461)

I had rather die than be disgraced

ANTHONY EDWARD BARNEWALL, 20th Baron; *b* 2 Feb 1928; *s* 1990; *ed* Ampleforth; late Irish Guards: *m* 1st, 1963 (*m diss* 1973), Lorna Margaret Marion, who *d* 1988, da of late Charles Douglas Ramsay; 2ndly, 1977, Mary Wonderly, elder da of late Judge Thomas F. McAllister, of Grand Rapids, Michigan, USA.

Arms – Ermine, a bordure engrailed gules. **Crest** – A plume of five ostrich feathers or, gules, azure, vert, and argent, and issuant therefrom a demifalcon rising of the last. **Supporters** – *Dexter*, a griffin argent; *sinister*, a lion gules. *Address* – PO Box 215, Ada, Michigan 49301, USA.

BROTHER LIVING

Hon RAYMOND CHARLES (Autumn Cottage, Chiddingfold, Surrey), *b* 29 Dec 1930; *ed* Ampleforth.

SISTER LIVING

Hon Diana, *b* 1929: *m* 1954, Anthony Gerard Astley Birtwistle, and has issue living, Caroline Muriel Mary, *b* 1955: *m* 1982, Stewart Oliver, of Creek Farm, Brancaster, King's Lynn, Norfolk, son of S/Ldr H. W. Oliver, OBE, RAF, of Staithe House, Brancaster Staithe, King's Lynn, Norfolk, and has issue living, Alexander Charles James *b* 1985, George Anthony Andrew *b* 1989, Charlotte Mary Rose *b* 1983, — Emma Frances Mary, *b* 1957: *m* 1982, Oliver John Woodforde Pawle, of 33 Blenkarne Rd, SW11 6HZ, son of late Roger Pawle, OBE, of Parkstone, Dorset, and has issue living, James Roger Woodforde *b* 1985, Lucy Diana Mary *b* 1988, Victoria Louise Maria *b* 1992, — Lucinda Jane Mary, *b* 1960: *m* 1986, P. Malcolm G. Reid, of 30 Melody Rd, SW18 2QF, yst son of Dr Kenneth Reid, of Rest Harrow, Cooden, Sussex, and has issue living, Charles Anthony Gilmore *b* 19—, Emily Louise Mary *b* 1988, — Sophia Louise Mary, *b* 1964.

PREDECESSORS – **(1)** Sir ROBERT Barnewall, was *cr Baron Trimlestown*, of Trimlestown, co Meath (peerage of Ireland) 1461; *s* by his son **(2)** CHRISTOPHER, 2nd Baron; *s* by his el son **(3)** JOHN; appointed Vice-Treasurer of Ireland 1522 High Treasurer 1524, and Lord High Chancellor 1534; *d* 1538; *s* by his son **(4)** PATRICK, 4th Baron; *s* by his el son **(5)** ROBERT, 5th Baron; *dsp* 1573; *s* by his brother **(6)** PETER 6th Baron; *d* 1598; *s* by his son **(7)** ROBERT, 7th Baron; *d* 1639; *s* by his grandson **(8)** MATTHIAS (el son of Hon Christopher Barnewall, el son of 7th Baron), 8th Baron; *d* 1667; *s* by his el son **(9)** ROBERT, 9th Baron; *d* 1687; *s* by his el son **(10)** MATTHIAS, 10th Baron; *dsp* 1692; *s* by his brother **(11)** JOHN, 11th Baron: *m* 1703, Margaret, da and heiress of Sir John Barnewall; *s* by his el son **(12)** ROBERT, 12th Baron; *d* 1779; *s* by his only son **(13)** THOMAS, 13th Baron; a Knight of Malta; *dsp* 1796; *s* by his cousin **(14)** NICHOLAS (son of Hon Richard Barnewall, 3rd son of 11th Baron), 14th Baron; *b* 1726; was twice *m*; *d* 1813; *s* by his only son **(15)** JOHN THOMAS, 15th Baron, *b* 1773: *m* 1793, Maria Theresa, da of R. Kirwan; *d* 1839; *s* by his son **(16)** THOMAS, 16th Baron, *b* 1796; *m* 1836, Margaret Randalina, who *d* 1872, da of Philip Roche; *d* 1879, when the title became dormant until claimed in 1891 by his kinsman **(17)** CHRISTOPHER PATRICK MARY, *de jure*, 17th Baron, son of Charles Barnewall, of Meadstown, co Meath, and great-grandson of Richard Barnewall, of Fyanstown (a descendant of Hon Patrick Barnewall, 2nd son of the 7th Baron), on whom the 14th Baron, failing his own issue male, entailed his estates: he *d* 1891, before he had established his right to vote at the Election of Representative Peers; *s* by his brother **(18)** CHARLES ALOYSIUS, 18th Baron; *b* 1861; adjudged 18th Baron Trimlestown by Committee for Privileges of House of Lords in 1893: *m* 1st, 1889, Margaret Theresa, who *d* 1901, da of Richard John Stephens, of Brisbane; 2ndly, 1907, Mabel Florence, who *d* 1914, da of William Robert Shuff, of Torquay, Devon; 3rdly, 1930, Josephine Francesca, who *d* 1945, da of Rt Hon Sir Christopher John Nixon, PC, MD, 1st Bt; *d* 1937; *s* by his only surviving son **(19)** CHARLES ALOYSIUS, 19th Baron; *b* 1899, Lieut Irish Guards: *m* 1st, 1926, Muriel, who *d* 1937, da of Edward Oskar Schneider, of Mansfield Lodge, Whalley Range, Manchester; 2ndly, 1952, Freda Katheen, who *d* 1987, da of late Alfred Watkins, of Ross-on-Wye; *d* 1990; *s* by his elder son **(20)** ANTHONY EDWARD, 20th Baron and present peer.

TRUMPINGTON, BARONESS (Barker) (Life Baroness 1980)

JEAN ALYS BARKER, PC, da of late Arthur Edward Campbell-Harris; *b* Oct 23 1922; *ed* Privately; Camb City Councillor 1963-73, Cambs Co Councillor 1973-75, Mayor of Camb 1971-72, JP South Westminster 1976-82; Member Airline Users Cttee 1973-80 (Chm 1979-80); UK Representative to UN Status of Women 1979-82; Baroness in Waiting (Govt Whip) 1983-85, and 1991-92; Parl Under Sec of State DHSS 1985-87, Parl Sec Agriculture 1987-92; *cr Baroness Trumpington*, of Sandwich, co Kent (Life Baroness) 1980, and PC 1992: *m* 1954, William Alan Barker, who *d* 1988, and has issue.

Arms – Gyronny of eight ermine and azure, three hedgehogs two and one, gold. **Supporters** – *Dexter*, a boxer bitch; *Sinister*, a bay colt, both proper. *Address* – c/o House of Lords, SW1.

SON LIVING

Hon Adam Campbell, *b* 1955: *m* 1985, Elizabeth M., elder da of Eric Marsden, of Stourpaine Manor, Blandford, Dorset, and has issue living, Virginia Giverny, *b* 1987. *Residence* – Rose Cottage, King St, Sandwich, Kent.

TRYON, BARON (Tryon) (Baron UK 1940)

DO RIGHT AND FEAR NOT

ANTHONY GEORGE MERRIK TRYON, 3rd Baron; *b* 26 May 1940; *s* 1976; *ed* Eton; a Page of Honour to HM 1954-56; Capt R Wilts Yeo; DL Wilts 1993: *m* 1973, Dale Elizabeth, el da of Barry Harper, of Melbourne, Vic, Aust, and has issue.

Arms – Azure a fesse embattled between in chief three estoiles and in base a portcullis chained or. **Crest** – Issuant from a coronet composed of four roses set upon a rim or a bear's head sable charged with seven stars in the form of the constellation ursa major gold. **Supporters** – *Dexter*, an army pensioner in hospital uniform; *sinister*, a postman holding with the exterior hand a letter sack over his shoulder proper.
Residence – The Manor House, Great Durnford, Salisbury.

SONS LIVING

Hon CHARLES GEORGE BARRINGTON, *b* 15 May 1976; a Page of Honour to HM since 1988.
Hon Edward Henry, *b* 1979

DAUGHTERS LIVING

Hon Zoë Elizabeth, *b* 1974.
Hon Victoria Clementine *b* 1979 (twin).

SISTER LIVING

Hon Patricia Joan Kathleen, *b* 1942: *m* 1973, C. Ranald Macdonald, of 103 Caroline St, S Yarra, Vic 3141, Aust, and has issue living, Hamish Aylmer Syme, *b* 1977, — Laura Christina, *b* 1974.

UNCLE LIVING (*son of 1st Baron*)

Hon Aylmer Douglas (Kingfisher Mill, Great Durnford, nr Salisbury; Boodle's Club), *b* 1909; *ed* Eton, and Trin Coll, Camb (BA); formerly Capt Grenadier Guards.

WIDOW LIVING OF SECOND BARON

ETHELREDA JOSEPHINE (*Dreda, Baroness Tryon*) (Church Farm, Great Durnford, Salisbury), da of Sir Merrik Raymond Burrell, 7th Bt, CBE: *m* 1939, the 2nd Baron, who *d* 1976.

PREDECESSORS – **(1)** *Rt Hon* GEORGE CLEMENT Tryon, son of late Vice-Adm Sir George Tryon, KCB, *b* 1871; was Min of Pensions Oct 1922 to Jan 1924, Nov 1924 to June 1929, and Sept 1931 to June 1935, Postmaster-Gen June 1935 to April 1940, Chancellor of Duchy of Lancaster April to May 1940, First Commr of Works May to Oct 1940, and Parliamentary Sec to Min of Pensions Oct to Nov 1940; sat as MP for Brighton (*C*) 1910-40; *cr Baron Tryon*, of Durnford, co Wilts (peerage of UK) 1940: *m* 1905, Hon Averil Vivian, who *d* 1959, da of 1st Baron Swansea; *d* 1940; *s* by his son **(2)** CHARLES GEORGE VIVIAN, GCVO, KCB, DSO, PC, 2nd Baron, *b* 1906; Assist Keeper of HM's Privy Purse 1949-52, Keeper of The Privy Purse and Treas to HM the Queen 1952-71, and a Lord-in-Waiting to HM 1971-76: *m* 1939, Ethelreda Josephine, da of Sir Merrik Raymond Burrell, 7th Bt, CBE; *d* 1976; *s* by his son **(3)** ANTHONY GEORGE MERRIK, 3rd Baron and present peer.

TUGENDHAT, BARON (Tugendhat) (Life Baron 1993)

CHRISTOPHER SAMUEL TUGENDHAT, elder son of late Dr Georg Tugendhat, of London; *b* 23 Feb 1937; *ed* Ampleforth, and Gonville and Caius Coll, Camb; Leader and Feature Writer *Financial Times* 1960-70; Dir Sunningdale Oils 1971-76, Consultant Phillips Petroleum Internat Ltd 1972-76, British EEC Commr 1977-81, and Vice-Pres Commn of European Communities 1981-85; Dep-Chm National Westminster Bank 1990-91 (Dir 1985-91), Chm Abbey National plc since 1991; Non-Exec Dir The BOC Group, Commercial Union Assurance plc 1988-91, LWT (Holdings) plc, Eurotunnel plc, etc; MP Cities of London and Westminster (*C*) 1970-74, and City of London and Westminster South 1974-76; *cr Knt* 1990, and *Baron Tugendhat*, of Widdington, co Essex (Life Baron) 1993: *m* 1967, Julia Lissant, da of Kenneth D. Dobson, of Keston, Kent, and has issue.
Residences – 35 Westbourne Park Rd, W2 5QD. *Club* – Buck's.

SONS LIVING

Hon James Walter, *b* 1971.
Hon Angus George Harry, *b* 1974.

TURNER OF CAMDEN, BARONESS (Turner) (Life Baroness 1985)

MURIEL WINIFRED TURNER, da of Edward Price; *b* 18 Sept 1927; Assist Gen Sec Assocn of Scientific, Technical and Managerial Staffs (ASTMS) 1970-87; Chm Ombudsman Council, Personal Investment Authority since 1994; Member: TUC Gen Council, Equal Opportunities Commn, Occupational Pensions Bd, Central Arbitration Cttee and Brokers' Registration Council; Hon LLD (Leicester Univ) 1992, *cr Baroness*

Turner of Camden, of Camden in Greater London (Life Baroness) 1985: *m* 1955, Reginald Thomas
Frederick Turner, MC, DFC, DFC (USA), late W/Cdr RAF.
Residence – 87 Canfield Gdns, Hampstead, NW6.

TWEEDDALE, MARQUESS OF (Hay) (Marquess S 1694)

EDWARD DOUGLAS JOHN HAY, 13th Marquess; *b* 6 Aug 1947; *s*
1979; presumed heir to Baronetcy of Hay of Smithfield and
Haystoun (*cr* 1635); *ed* Milton Abbey Sch, and Trin Coll,
Oxford (BA Hons); insurance broker; Hereditary
Chamberlain of Dunfermline.

Arms – Quarterly: 1st and 4th, argent, three inescutcheons gules, *Hay*;
2nd, gules, three bars ermine, *Gifford of Yester*; 3rd, azure, three
cinquefoils argent, *Fraser*. **Crest** – A goat's head erased argent, horned
or. **Supporters** – Two bucks proper, attired or, collared azure, the
collars charged with three cinquefoils argent.
Address – c/o House of Lords, SW1.

BROTHERS LIVING

Lord CHARLES DAVID MONTAGU (4D Muirhouse Place East, Edinburgh
EH4 4PW), *b* (twin) 6 Aug 1947; *ed* Milton Abbey Sch, and Trin Coll,
Oxford.
Alistair James Montagu (does not use courtesy title), *b* 1955; *ed* Eton,
and Univ Coll, Oxford (MA, DPhil); Botanist; has taken Australian
citizenship. *Residence* – 32 Copeland St, Alexandria, NSW 2015,
Australia.

HALF-BROTHERS LIVING

Lord Andrew Arthur George, *b* 1959; *ed* Fettes Coll, and RAC
Cirencester: *m* 1986, Rosanna Meryl, 2nd da of John Brabazon Booth,
of Darver Castle, Dundalk, co Louth, and has issue living, Angus, *b*
1991, — Rory, *b* 1993.
Lord Hamish David Montagu (Cadland Court, Ocean Village, South-
ampton), *b* (twin) 1959; *ed* Fettes Coll, Wadham Coll, Oxford (BA), and King's Coll Hosp (MB, BS, DA).

AUNT LIVING (*Sister of 12th Marquess*) (*Raised to the rank of a Marquess's daughter* 1970)

Lady Marioth Christina HAY (Forbes Lodge, Gifford, E Lothian) *b* 1918, resumed by deed poll the surname of Hay 1971: *m*
1st, 1940 (*m diss* 1954), Lt-Col George Richard Trotter, R Scots Greys, who *d* 1970 (E Eglinton); 2ndly, 1954, as his 2nd
wife, Sir Gifford Wheaton Grey Fox, 2nd Bt, who *d* 1959, when the title became extinct; 3rdly, 1963 (*m diss* 1971), Sir John
Hastings James, KCVO, CB, who *d* 1980, and has issue living, (by 1st *m*) Richard Reginald (52 Leander Av, Hillside,
Bulawayo, Zimbabwe), *b* 1941; *ed* Eton: *m* 1974, Marion M., el da of Lt-Col Ralph Maxwell Campbell, of Chasehayes, Stockland, Devon, and has issue living, Georgina Maryoth Maxwell *b* 1978, — Edward George (The Cottage, Bohunt Manor, Liphook, Hants GU30 7DL), *b* 1943: *m* 1973, Jemima Rachel McLay, el da of Niel Mills, of Upton Grey House, Hants (*see* B
Hazlerigg, 1990 Edn), and has issue living, George *b* 1977, Joanna *b* 1975, — Bridget Mary, *b* 1944: *m* 1981, John Ellwood,
of 2 McLaren Rd, Edinburgh EH9 2BH, son of late Capt Victor Ellwood, RFC, of 88 Harley St, W1, and has issue living,
Sophy Catherine *b* 1982.

HALF-AUNT LIVING (*Half-sister of 12th Marquess*) (*Raised to the rank of a Marquess's daughter* 1970)

Lady Caroline Susan Elizabeth, *b* 1930: *m* 1st, 1953 (*m diss* 1970), Richard Noel Marshall Armitage, who *d* 1986, 2ndly, 1970,
Reginald Charles Tyrrell, of Capplegill, Moffat, Dumfries-shire, and has issue living, (by 1st *m*) Charles Edward Marshall, *b*
1954: *m* 1987, Judith A., only da of F. Reed, of Hampton, Middx, — Alexander James (81 Lonsdale Rd, SW13), *b* 1958; *ed*
Eton: *m* 1987, Carolyn Margery, da of Peter Allen, of Portsmouth, and has issue living, Sophie Claire *b* 1987, Daisy Elizabeth
Collette *b* 1990.

DAUGHTERS LIVING OF ELEVENTH MARQUESS

Lady Hélène Candida (*Viscountess Kemsley*) (Field House, Lubenham, Market Harborough, Leics LE16 9TR); a DStJ, *b* 1913:
m 1933, 2nd Viscount Kemsley.
Lady (Marguerite) Georgina Christine, *b* 1916: *m* 1941, Capt Arthur Nicholas Coleridge, late Irish Guards (*see* B Coleridge,
colls), who *d* 1988. *Residence* – 33 Peel Street, W8.
Lady (Christine) Daphne, *b* 1919: *m* 1st, 1939 (*m diss* 1947), Lieut-Col David Morley-Fletcher, TD, Rifle Brig; 2ndly, 1957,
Lieut-Col Francis Robert Cameron Stewart, late Indian Army, el son of late Sir Francis Hugh Stewart, CIE, and has issue
living, (by 1st *m*) Hugo David Montagu (The Old Vicarage, Padbury, Buckingham), *b* 1940; *ed* Stowe, and Trin Coll, Camb
(MA); FSA: *m* 1st, Josceline Mary, yr da of late Rt Hon Lord Justice (Sir Henry Josceline) Phillimore, OBE; 2ndly, 1980,
Belinda Mary, da of William Miles David, of Little Smeaton, Pontefract, Yorks, and has issue living (by 1st *m*), Gifford
Henry Montagu *b* 1969, Hester Mary Victoria *b* 1972, (by 2nd *m*) Isabella Frances *b* 1981, — Victoria Catherine Margaret, *b*
1942. *Residence* – 5 Brewery Court, Haddington, E Lothian.
Lady Frances Elizabeth Ann, *b* 1926: *m* 1956, Nigel Arthur Pearson, who *d* 1975, son of Sir Neville Arthur Pearson, 2nd Bt.
Residence – Coedsaithpren, Nantgaredig, Carmarthen, Dyfed.

MOTHER LIVING

Hon Sonia Mary, da of 1st Viscount Ingleby: *m* 1st, 1946 (*m diss* 1958), 12th Marquess of Tweeddale, GC, who *d* 1979;
2ndly, 1966, Maj Michael William Vernon Hammond-Maude, JP, 5th R Inniskilling Dragoon Guards (ret), of Mitton Cottage,
Arncliffe, Skipton, N Yorks.

WIDOW LIVING OF TWELFTH MARQUESS

NELLA DOREEN (*Marchioness of Tweeddale*) (Isle of Mull), da of M. Dutton: *m* 1959, as his 2nd wife, 12th Marquess, GC, who *d* 1979.

COLLATERAL BRANCHES LIVING

Issue of late Capt Lord Arthur Vincent Hay, 2nd son of 9th Marquess, *b* 1886, *ka* at battle of the Aisne 1914: *m* 1911, Menda, who *d* 1959 (having *m* 2ndly, 1916, Lieut-Col Robert Edward Kennard Leatham, DSO, who *d* 1948), da of late Ambrose Ralli, of 24 Gloucester Square, Hyde Park, W.:—

Jean (*Jean, Lady Makins*), *b* 1912: *m* 1932, Lt-Col Sir William Vivian Makins, 3rd Bt, Welsh Guards, who *d* 1969. *Residence* – Martyrwell, Cheriton, Alresford, Hants.

Grandchildren of late Maj Malcolm Vivian Hay, of Seaton House, Aberdeen (infra):—
Issue of late Maj James Malcolm Hay of Seaton, *b* 1907, *d* 1987: *m* 1941, Mary Eleanora Basset (Edinglassie, Huntly, Aberdeenshire), da of late Charles Ernest Basset Lothian Curzon (*see* E Howe, colls):—

Malcolm Charles HAY OF SEATON (24 Hendrick Av, SW12), *b* 1956; *ed* Ampleforth, and Magdalene Coll, Camb: *m* 1983, Deborah Louise, da of Lt-Cdr Derek Malcolm Rouse, MBE, RN (ret), of The Dell, Bonchurch, IoW, and has issue living, James Malcolm Douglas, *b* 1985, — Oliver Charles Quintin, *b* 1987, — Georgina Eileen, *b* 1990, — Isabella Jane, *b* 1993, — Katharine Louise, *b* (twin) 1993. —— Elizabeth Mary, *b* 1942: *m* 1977, David Buchanan Gillespie, of Snipe Cottage, Kingsley Green, Haslemere, Surrey, and has issue living, Hamish Peregrine Curzon, *b* 1979. —— Joanna Margaret, *b* 1945: *m* 1973, Brig Ewen Duncan Cameron, OBE, The Black Watch (*see* Rugge-Price, Bt) and has issue living, Louisa Mary, *b* 1976, — Clare Elizabeth, *b* 1977. —— Nicola Anne, *b* 1958: *m* 1983, Andrew Lachlan Rattray, yst son of Capt James Silvester Rattray of Rattray (28th Chief), and has issue living, Thomas Alexander, *b* 1987, — Hew Lachlan, *b* 1989, — Flora Mary, *b* 1992.

Grandchildren of late James Gordon Hay, el son of Lt-Gen Lord James Hay, 2nd son of 7th Marquess:—
Issue of Maj Malcolm Vivian Hay, of Seaton House, Aberdeen, *b* 1881, *d* 1962: *m* 1st, 1902, Florence, who *d* 1943, da of George Erlington, of Paris; 2ndly, 1956, Alice Ivy DStJ, who *d* 1974, da of Herbert John Wigmore, of Perth, W Australia, and widow of Walter Moncrieff Paterson, of Tilliefoure, Aberdeenshire:—

(By 1st *m*) Peter Brian (Titford Hold, Awliscombe, Honiton, Devon), *b* 1918; Maj Gordon Highlanders (ret); 1939-45 War (despatches, prisoner): *m* 1946, Marigold Armatrude, da of Col A. G. Eden, of Culver, nr Exeter, and has issue living, Angus Malcolm (Cavalry and Guards), *b* 1947; late Capt Scots Greys, and late Capt Abu Dhabi Defence Force (Arabian Gulf): *m* 1978 (*m diss* 1984), Miranda Mary, da of late Anthony Seymour Bellville, of The White House, Bembridge, I of Wight, — James Andrew, *b* 1949: *m* 1975 (*m diss* 1979), Emma, da of (Rondle) Owen (Charles) Stable, QC, of Buckler's Hall, Much Hadham, Herts, — Charlotte Jerardine, *b* 1959: *m* 1988, John Paul Deacon, of 1 Kildare Terrace, W2, and has issue living, Maximilian James *b* 1989, Georgia Florence *b* 1991, Jessica Charlotte *b* (twin) 1991. —— Elizabeth Charlotte Sarah (*Lady Hodson*) (Middle Farm, Dinder, Wells, Somerset), *b* 1904: *m* 1928, Sir Arnold Wienholt Hodson, KCMG, who *d* 1944, and has issue living, Jean Rosemary, *b* 1930: *m* 1st 1958 (*m diss* 1972), John Wilfrid Gillams, 2ndly, 1977, John Allister Nutt, of Filbert House, E Ilsley, Newbury, Berks, and has issue living (by 1st *m*), Judith Elizabeth *b* 1960; FRCS: *m* 1987, Luc Mella, airline pilot, of 45 Potter St, Melbourne, Derby (and has issue living, Sophie Louise *b* 1988, Stephanie Laurie *b* 1990, Florence Emily *b* 1992), Charlotte Louise *b* 1963; MB: *m* 1993, Owen Francis Boyd, MB, — Elisabeth Anne *b* 1934: *m* 1st, 1963 (*m diss* 1983), Anthony Arthur Verrier; 2ndly, 19—, Francis Floyd, of Middle Farm, Dinder, Wells, Somerset, and has issue living (by 1st *m*), Charles Simpson *b* 1966, Frances Joan *b* 1968. —— Georgiana Catherine, *b* 1910: *m* 1941, George Richard Williams, late RAMC, who *d* 1993, and *d* 1989, having had issue, Malcolm George, *b* 1948, *d* 1956, — Olga Georgiana, *b* 1942; has issue living, Sarah Georgiana *b* 1978, — Maureen Elizabeth, *b* 1943, — Ann Catherine, *b* 1945: *m* 1970, Ronald Thorne, of 708 Gilbert St W, Whitby, Ontario, Canada, and has issue living, Christopher Malcolm *b* 1970, Jaimie Ronald George *b* 1974, Robin Francis *b* 1978. —— Frances Mary *b* 1914: *m* 1941, Arthur Ernest Parker, of 40 Bedford Rd, Hitchin, Herts, and has issue living, John Francis, *b* 1944, — Anthony David, *b* 1947, — Gerald Stephen, *b* 1953, — Robert Charles, *b* 1955, — Sara Laura, *b* 1942: *m* 1964, Nicholas McConochie.

Issue of late Capt Cuthbert Joseph Hay, *b* 1882, *d* 1970: *m* 1908, Letitia Griffith, who *d* 1982, da of Frederick Heylighter Fausset, of Willsborough, co Sligo:—

Ronald Cuthbert, DSO, DSC (South Mill, Amesbury, Wilts) *b* 1916; *ed* Ampleforth; Cdr RN; 1939-45 War, (DSO, DSC and Bar); DSO 1944: *m* 1944, Barbara, da of Lt-Col George Rochfort Grange, of Strathblane, Stirlingshire, and has issue living, Charles Edward Ronald (A10 Habitat, Lot 1106, DD 217 Pak Sha Wan, Sai Kung, N.T., Hong Kong), *b* 1948; *ed* Ampleforth: *m* 1975, Susan Rodica, da of Terence Prendergast, of Steeple Claydon, Bucks, and has issue living, Jeremy Charles *b* 1976, Hannah Rodica Barbara *b* 1980, — James Philip Burness, *b* 1957, — Penelope Rochfort, *b* 1946: *m* 1977, Maj John Julius Rogers, R Hussars (PWO), and has issue living, Katherine Philippa *b* 1978, Vanessa Victoria *b* 1981, Olivia Hilary *b* 1983, — Sara Elizabeth, *b* 1951: *m* 1980, Alastair Macrae, and has issue living, Calum Andrew *b* 1980, Athene Hope *b* 1983. —— John Malcolm (Mirrabooka, 56 Mugga Way, Red Hill, Canberra, ACT), *b* 1918; *ed* Ampleforth; Lt-Cdr RN; 1939-45 War: *m* 1952, Alicia Gertrude Maria, da of Herbert Moore, of Sydney, NSW, and has issue living, Richard Malcolm (Characene Park, RMB 605, Summer Hill Rd, Bungendore 2621, NSW, Australia), *b* 1953: *m* 1972, Maureen Loretta, da of Walter Larkin, of San Francisco, Calif, USA, and has issue living, David Richard Hay *b* 1983, Katie Elizabeth Hay *b* 1985. —— Vivien Mary (Fiveways, Cookham, Berks) *b* 1909: *m* 1st, 1937, M. John Ripley, who *d* 1947; 2ndly, 1960, Samuel K. Jerome, who *d* 1966, and has issue living, (by 1st *m*) Michael, *b* 1939. —— Mary Charlotte, *b* 1915: *m* 1947, Lt-Col Neil Sylvester Smith, RAF Signals, who *d* 1981, and has issue living, Stephen Neil, *b* 1948: *m* 1984, his cousin, Jaqueline Mary, yr da of Sqdn-Ldr W.D.K. Franklin, by his wife Margaret Patricia, 2nd da of late Capt Cuthbert Joseph Hay (ante), and has issue living, Ashley Christopher *b* 1984, Simon Matthew *b* 1987, Sophia Gilliam *b* 1990, — Graham John, *b* 1957, — Diana Mary, *b* 1949: *m* 1st, 1969 (*m diss* 1976), Peter John Thompson; 2ndly, 1978, Brian Barbrec Campbell, of 139 Orange Valley Rd, Lesmurdie 6076, W Australia, and has issue living (by 1st *m*), Bentley Warrick James *b* 1972, Grant Peter *b* 1974, (by 2nd *m*) Reuben Gregory Barbrec *b* 1980, Zoe Louise *b* 1983. *Residence* – 5 Wiese Way, Esperance 6450, W Australia.

Granddaughters of late Capt William Drummond Ogilvy-Hay-Newton, el son of John Stuart Hay-Newton, grandson of Richard Hay Newton, uncle of 7th Marquess:—
Issue of late Lieut-Col Stuart Hay, DSO, *b* 1876, *d* 1960: *m* 1908, Inna Vera Evelyn, who *d* 1971, da of late Hon Louis Guy Scott (E Clonmell, colls):—

(Inna) Veronica Adeline, *b* 1909: *m* 1966, Brig Stanley Oswald Jones, OBE, MC, late RWF, of The Orchard, Stoke Trister, Wincanton, Somerset. —— Vera Jean (Woodhouse Farm, Marsh, Aylesbury, Bucks), *b* 1910. —— Evelyn Sheelagh (twin), *b* 1910.

Grandchildren of late William Hope Hay, el son of Maj-Gen Alexander Charles Hay (infra):—
Issue of late Lt-Col George Harold Hay, DSO, *b* 1893, *d* 1967: *m* 1935, Patricia Mary (106 Polwarth Terrace, Edinburgh), da of Maj Etienne Hugonin, of Edinburgh:—

Alexander Douglas (Duns Castle, Berwickshire, TD11 3NW), *b* 1948: *m* 1973, Aline Mary, da of Robert Macdougall, of Edinburgh, and has issue living, Robert Alexander, *b* 1976, — Caroline Laura, *b* 1978. —— Philip Antony, *b* 1950: *m* 1975, Helena Anne, da of Frank Sim, of Alloa, and has issue living, George Francis, *b* 1979, — Felicity Patricia, *b* 1977. —— Caroline Mary, *b* 1944: *m* 1967, George Michael Mackinnon Thomson, and has issue living, George Jolyon Hay, *b* 1970, — Mary Emma Julia (twin), *b* 1970. —— Barbara Elizabeth, *b* 1947: *m* 1979, Dr Michael John Chevalier Asher.

Granddaughter of late Maj-Gen Alexander Charles Hay, son of late William Hay, son of late Robert Hay (*b* 1731), grandson of late Hon William Hay, 2nd son of 1st Earl:—

Issue of late Edward George Hay, *b* 1879, *d* 1945: *m* 1917, Ascelin Frances Collett, da of late James Collett-Mason, JP, of Ashurst Place, Langton Green, Kent:—

Nora Margaret, *b* 1922: *m* 1942, John Robertson Campbell, and has issue living, David Michael Hay, *b* 1944, — Christopher William John, *b* 1949, — Stuart Calvin, *b* 1953, — Tessa Margaret, *b* 1946, — Lynn Nora Mary, *b* 1952, — Sally Anne Frances, *b* 1956.

Grandchildren of late Robert William Seton Hay (infra):—

Issue of late Robert Dino James Hay, *b* 1901, *d* 1977: *m* 1942, Laura, who *d* 1984, da of Gen N. Fochetti:—

William Robert Alexander, *b* 1947. —— Patricia Caterina Maria *b* 1944. *Residence* – Via di Trasone 5, 00199 Rome, Italy.

Grandson of late Robert James Alexander Hay, son of Robert Hay (*b* 1799), son of Robert Hay (*b* 1731) (ante):—

Issue of late Robert William Seton Hay, *b* 1878, *d* 1965: *m* 19—, Maria, who *d* 1961, da of Antonio Baratti:—

Alexander Giuseppe (4 S Lorenzo di Rabatta, 06070 Perugia, Cenerente, Italy), *b* 1906: *m* 1937, Giovanna Bice, da of Cdr Mario Dasso, and has issue living, Andrew Alexander Mario (6 Favorita Rubbiano, 06070 Perugia Cenerente, Italy), *b* 1941: *m* 1966, Maria Pia Antonietta Mancini, and has issue living, Alexander *b* 1966, Massimo *b* 1971, Maurizio *b* 1973, — Mary Grace Alexandra, *b* 1939, — Roberta Alexandra, *b* 1942, — Jane Alexandra, *b* 1948, — Daniela Alexandra, *b* 1953.

Descendants of late James Hay (4th in descent from Hon John Hay, 2nd son of 3rd Lord Hay of Yester), who was *cr* a *Baronet* 1635:—

See Hay, Bt, *cr* 1635.

PREDECESSORS – (1) JOHN HAY; *cr* Lord Hay of Yester (peerage of Scotland) 1488; *s* by his son (2) JOHN, 2nd Lord; fell at Flodden 1513; *s* by his son (3) JOHN, 3rd Lord; *s* by his son (4) JOHN, 4th Lord; was imprisoned for some years in the Tower of London, having been taken prisoner at the battle of Pinkie 1547; *d* 1557; *s* by his son (5) WILLIAM, 5th Lord; *s* by his el son (6) WILLIAM, 6th Lord; *s* by his brother (7) JAMES, 7th Lord; *s* by his son (8) JOHN, 8th Lord; commanded a Regt in the Royal Army 1639; *cr* Earl of Tweeddale (peerage of Scotland) 1646; *d* 1654; *s* by his (9) JOHN, PC, 2nd Earl; sat as MP for Haddingtonshire in Cromwell's Parliament; assisted at Coronation of Charles II at Scone; having been a Commr of the Treasury and an Extra Lord of Session was in 1692 appointed Lord Chancellor of Scotland; *cr* Viscount Walden, Earl of Gifford, and Marquess of Tweeddale (peerage of Scotland) 1694, with remainder to his heirs male whatsoever; *d* 1697; *s* by his son (10) JOHN, PC, 2nd Marquess; was High Treasurer of Scotland 1695, High Commr to the Scottish Parliament 1704, Lord Chancellor of Scotland 1704-5, and sometime a Representative Peer; *d* 1713; *s* by his son (11) CHARLES, 3rd Marquess; was Pres of Court of Police, Lord-Lieut of Haddingtonshire, and a Representative Peer; *d* 1715; *s* by his son (12) JOHN, PC, 4th Marquess; was a Representative Peer, the last person who held the office of Extraordinary Lord of Session, Sec of State for Scotland 1742-6, Principal Keeper of the Signet, and in 1761 Justice-Gen of Scotland; *d* 1762; *s* by his son (13) GEORGE, 5th Marquess; *d* 1770; *s* by his uncle (14) GEORGE, 6th Marquess; *d* unmarried 1787; *s* by his kinsman (15) GEORGE, 7th Marquess, grandson of Lord William, 3rd son of 2nd Marquess; was Lord-Lieut of Haddington, and a Representative Peer; *d* 1804; *s* by his son (16) GEORGE, KT, GCB, 8th Marquess; *b* 1787: a Field-Marshal; served with distinction in the Peninsular War; a Representative Peer, Gov and Com in Ch at Madras 1842-48, Col 2nd Life Guards, and Lord-Lieut of Haddingtonshire; *m* 1816, Lady Susan Montagu, da of 5th Duke of Manchester; *d* 1876; *s* by his son (17) ARTHUR, 9th Marquess; *b* 1824; Lieut-Col Grenadier Guards: *m* 1st, 1857, Helena Eleanora Charlotte Augusta, who *d* 1871, da of Count Adolf August Friedrich von Kielmansegge; 2ndly, 1873, Julia Charlotte Sophia, who *d* 1937 (having *m* 2ndly, 1887, Rt Hon Sir John Rose, GCMG, PC, 1st Bt, who *d* 1888; 3rdly, 1892, Major Sir William Eden Evans-Gordon, who *d* 1913), da of Keith Stewart Mackenzie; *d* 1878; *s* by his brother (18) WILLIAM MONTAGU, KT, 10th Marquess; *b* 1826: in BCS, 1845-62; MP for Taunton (*L*) 1865-8, and for Haddington Dist 1878; Lord High Commr for the Gen Assembly of Church of Scotland 1889-92, 1896, *cr* Baron Tweeddale, of Yester, co Haddington (peerage of United Kingdom) 1881: *m* 1878, Candida Louise, CBE, who *d* 1925, da of Vincenzo Bartolucci, of Cantiano, Italy; *d* 1911; *s* by his el son (19) WILLIAM GEORGE MONTAGU, 11th Marquess; *b* 1884; Lord-Lt of E Lothian 1944-67: *m* 1st, 1912, Marguerite Christine Ralli, who *d* 1944, step-da of Lewis Einstein; 2ndly, 1945, Marjorie Helen, who *d* 1977, da of late Henry John Wagg, OBE, and formerly wife of Lt-Col Joseph Henry Nettleford; *d* 1967; *s* by his nephew (20) DAVID GEORGE MONTAGU, GC son of Lt-Col Lord Edward Douglas John Hay (3rd son of 10th Marquess), and Violet Florence Catherine Bridget, da of Maj Cameron Barclay (B Decies), 12th Marquess; *b* 1921; AM 1941, Lloyd War Medal for bravery at sea and Royal Life Saving Medals: *m* 1st, 1946 (*m diss* 1958), Hon Sonia Mary Peake, da of 1st Viscount Ingleby; 2ndly, 1959, Nella Doreen, da of M. Dutton; *d* 1979; *s* by his son (21) EDWARD DOUGLAS JOHN, 13th Marquess and present peer; also Earl of Gifford, Earl of Tweeddale, Viscount Walden, Lord Hay of Yester, and Baron Tweeddale.

TWEEDMOUTH, BARONY OF (Majoribanks) (Extinct 1935)

DAUGHTER LIVING OF THIRD BARON

Hon Moyra, *b* 1902: *m* 1st, 1923, Lieut-Col Reginald Francis Heyworth, 1st Roy Dragoons, who was *ka* 1941; 2ndly, 1943, Major Reginald Brodrick Freeman-Thomas, King's Own Yorkshire LI, and has issue living, (by 1st *m*) John (Bradwell Grove, Burford, Oxon), *b* 1925; *ed* Eton; High Sheriff Oxon 1962: *m* 1950, Susan Elizabeth Hamersley, da of Sir John Henry Burder, ED, and has issue living, Reginald *b* 1961, Caroline *b* 1952: *m* 1976, Roger Alexander Eckersley, of Woodside Farm, Bradwell Grove, nr Burford, Oxon OX8 4JL (and has issue living, William Peter *b* 1980, Fergus John *b* 1983, Olivia Mary *b* 1986), Jane (*Countess of Haddington*) *b* 1953: *m* 1984, as his 2nd wife, 13th Earl of Haddington, Joanna *b* 1957, — Anne (*Lady Pease*) *b* 1924: *m* 1st, 1946 (*m diss* 1955), Flight-Lieut David Henry Lewis Wigan, RAFVR; 2ndly, 1956, Sir Richard Thorn Pease, 3rd Bt (*cr* 1920), of Hindley House, Stocksfield, Northumberland, and has issue living (by 1st *m*), Anthony John (Serrada de Janes, Rua 19 Novembre, Malveira de Serra, 2750 Cascais, Portugal) *b* 1947; *ed* Eton: *m* 1st, 1970 (*m diss* 1980), Amanda, elder da of Maj Geoffrey Edward Ford North, MC (*see* B Walsingham); 2ndly, 19—, Patrizia Maria, da of Stefan Ludwig Borbas, of Gottfried Kellerg 2, 1030 Vienna, Austria (and has issue living, Orlando Henry Lewis *b* 1981, James Gino Anthony *b* 1983, Tara Luciana Martha Dinah *b* 1986), Susan Anne, *b* 1949: *m* 1971, Richard Angus Bonsor, and has issue (*see* Bonsor, Bt). *Residence* – Kingswall House, nr Malmesbury, Wilts.

TWEEDSMUIR, BARON (Buchan) (Baron UK 1935)

Not following meaner things

JOHN NORMAN STUART BUCHAN, CBE, CD, 2nd Baron; *b* 25 Nov 1911; *s* 1940; *ed* Eton, and Brasenose Coll, Oxford (MA); Hon LLD Aberdeen 1948, and Queen's, Ontario 1955; is a FRSE, a FRGS, a FRSA, and FZS; was Assist Dist Officer, Uganda 1934-36, and in Hudson's Bay Co's Ser 1937-39; elected Rector of Aberdeen Univ 1948; Pres of Federation of Commonwealth and British Empire Chambers of Commerce 1955-57, and of Inst of Export 1963-67, and a Member of Board BOAC 1955-64; a Gov of Commonwealth Inst 1958-77, Trustee since 1977; Chm Council on Tribunals 1973-80; Hon Col Hastings and Prince Edward Regt (Canadian Mil) 1955-60; 1939-45 War in Sicily, Italy, and NW Europe as Lt-Col Hastings and Prince Edward Regt (Canadian Mil) and on Staff (wounded, despatches twice, OBE); Order of Orange Nassau of the Netherlands with Swords; OBE (Mil) 1945; CBE (Civil) 1964: *m* 1st, 1948, Rt Hon Priscilla Jean Fortescue (*Baroness Tweedsmuir of Belhelvie*, PC), who *d* 1978, da of Brig Alan Fortescue Thomson, DSO, and widow of Maj Sir Arthur Lindsay Grant, 11th Bt (*cr* 1705); 2ndly, 1980, Jean Margherita, da of late Capt Humphrey Douglas Tollemache, RN (*see* B Tollemache, colls), and widow of Capt Sir Francis Cullen Grant, 12th Bt (*see* Grant, Bt, *cr* 1705), and has issue by 1st *m*.

Arms – Azure, a fesse between three lions' heads erased argent. **Crest** – A sunflower proper. **Supporters** – *Dexter*, a stag proper, attired or, collared gules; *sinister*, a falcon proper, jessed, belled, and beaked or, armed and collared gules. *Residence* – Kingston House, Kingston Bagpuize, Oxfordshire OX13 5AX. *Clubs* – Travellers', Carlton, Pratt's, Flyfishers'.

DAUGHTER LIVING (*By 1st marriage*)

Hon Priscilla Susan (*Lady James Douglas-Hamilton*) *b* 1949: *m* 1974, Lord James Alexander Douglas-Hamilton, MP, and has issue (*see* D Hamilton and Brandon).

BROTHER LIVING

Hon WILLIAM DE L'AIGLE, *b* 10 Jan 1916; *ed* Eton, and at New Coll, Oxford; is Sqdn-Ldr RAF Vol Reserve: *m* 1st, 1939 (*m diss* 1946), Nesta, only da of Lt-Col C. D. Crozier; 2ndly, 1946 (*m diss* 1960), Barbara Howard, who *d* 1969, da of E. N. Ensor, of 24 Chivelston Court, Wimbledon Parkside, SW; 3rdly, 1960, Sauré Cynthia Mary, da of late Maj G. E. Tatchell, R Lincs Regt, and has issue living, (by 1st *m*) Perdita Caroline, *b* 1940: *m* 1968 (*m diss* 1977), Edward Connolly, of Concord Academy, Concord, Mass 01742, USA, and has issue living, Cressida *b* 1969, — (by 2nd *m*) John William Howard de l'Aigle (Toby) (c/o Lloyds Bank, Wallingford, Oxon), *b* 25 May 1950: *m* 1977, Amanda Jocelyn, 2nd da of Sir Gawain Westray Bell, KCMG, CBE, of Hidcote Bartrim Manor, Chipping Campden, Glos, and has issue living, John Alasdair Gawain *b* 20 Nov 1986, Christopher Charles Westray *b* 1988, — (Charles Walter) Edward (Ralph) (53 Lillieshall Rd, SW4 0LW), *b* 1951: *m* 1982, Fiona J., yr da of Paul Carlisle, of Penyrwrlodd, Llanigon, Hay-on-Wye, Hereford, and has issue living, William Edward Francis Ewelme *b* 1984, Annabel *b* 1986, Laura *b* 1988, — James Ernest (37 Gloucester Crescent, NW1 7DL), *b* 1954: *m* 1986, Lady Evelyn Rose Phipps, 2nd da of 4th Marquess of Normanby, and has issue living, Nicholas Adam *b* 1992, Elizabeth Blanche *b* 1989, — Deborah Charlotte (*Baroness Stewartby*), *b* 1947; JP: *m* 1966, Baron Stewartby, RD, PC (Life Baron), and has issue (*see* B Stewartby), — Laura Mary Clare, *b* 1953: *m* 1980, Robin Chanter, of Maison Bacchus, Gajan, 37030 St Mamert du Gard, France, and has issue living, Bacchante Pallas-Athene *b* 1981, Artemis Helen Bacchante *b* 1982, Aphrodite Barbara Bacchante *b* 1984, Demeter Violetta Bacchante *b* 1988, — Ursula Margaret Bridget, *b* (twin) 1953: *m* 1979, Charles Thomas Wide, of Church Cottage, Main St, Glapthorn, Northants, yr son of Nicholas Wide, and has issue living, Thomas *b* 1984, Emily *b* 1982, — (by 3rd *m*) Alexander Edward, *b* 1961. *Residence* – West End House, Hornton, Banbury, Oxfordshire. *Club* – Travellers'.

WIDOW LIVING OF SON OF FIRST BARON

Hope (The Old Swan, Brill, Bucks), da of late David Gordon Gilmour, of Ottawa, Canada: *m* 1942, Prof Hon Alastair Francis Buchan, CBE, who *d* 1976, and has issue (see colls infra).

COLLATERAL BRANCH LIVING

Issue of late Prof Hon Alastair Francis Buchan, CBE, yst son of 1st Baron; *b* 1918; *d* 1976: *m* 1942, Hope (ante), da of late David Gordon Gilmour, of Ottawa, Canada:—
David John Brian Washington, OBE (45 Oakley Road, N1) *b* 1947; OBE 1993: *m* 1st, 1974 (*m diss* 1980), Sarah, da of George L. Cawkwell, of 8 Moreton Rd, Oxford; 2ndly, 1981, Eugenie Elisabeth, da of Prof Charles Maechling, Jr, of Washington, DC, USA, and has issue living (by 2nd *m*), Charles, *b* 1986, — Susannah Janet, *b* 1983. —— Benjamin William Alastair (6 Franconia Rd, SW4), *b* 1948: *m* 1974, Elizabeth, da of Maj Peter Oakleigh-Walker, of The Meade, Crondall, Surrey, and has issue living, Adam Peter Alastair, *b* 1980, — Eleanor Rose, *b* 1983. —— (Anna) Virginia Pauline, *b* 1953: *m* 1983, Kenneth David Peake, of 103 The Bowery, New York City, NY 10002, USA, son of Kenneth Peake, of Penyffordd, N Wales.

PREDECESSOR – (1) Rt Hon JOHN BUCHAN, GCMG, GCVO, CH, son of late Rev John Buchan, of Glasgow; *b* 1875; a well-known Author; sat as MP for Edinburgh, St Andrews, Glasgow and Aberdeen Univs (C) 1927-35; was Lord High Commr to Gen Assembly of Church of Scotland 1933 and 1934, and Gov-Gen and Com-in-Ch Dominion of Canada 1935-40; *cr Baron Tweedsmuir*, of Elsfield, co Oxford (peerage of United Kingdom) 1935: *m* 1907, Susan Charlotte, who *d* 1977, da of Capt Hon Norman de l'Aigle Grosvenor (B Ebury); *d* 1940; *s* by his son (2) JOHN NORMAN STUART, 2nd Baron and present peer.

TWEEDSMUIR OF BELHELVIE BARONY OF (Thomson) (Extinct 1978)

DAUGHTERS LIVING OF LIFE BARONESS

(By 1st m) *(see* Grant, Bt, *cr* 1705).
(By 2nd m) *(see* Tweedsmuir, B).

TWINING, BARONY OF (Twining) (Extinct 1967)

SONS LIVING OF LIFE BARON

Hon John Peter (3 The Ridgeway, Guildford), *b* 1929; *ed* Charterhouse, and Brasenose Coll, Oxford; Colonial Ser 1953-63; an Admin Officer, City and Guilds of London Inst; 1963-78; Chm Guildford Educational Services Ltd: *m* 1954, Mary Avice, da of late Brig Joseph Hector Dealy Bennett, CBE, and has issue.
Hon William Lawrence (10 Mill Lane, Iffley, Oxford), *b* 1934; *ed* Charterhouse, Brasenose Coll, Oxford, and Chicago Univ; Prof of Law, Queen's Univ, Belfast 1965-72 Prof of Law Univ of Warwick 1972-82; Quain Prof of Jurisprudence, Univ Coll, London since 1983: *m* 1957, Penelope Elizabeth, da of Richard Wall Morris, of Dublin, and has issue.

Tyrone, Baron, title of Marquess of Waterford on Roll of HL.

Tyrone Earl of; son of Marquess of Waterford.

ULLSWATER, VISCOUNT (Lowther) (Viscount UK 1921)

NICHOLAS JAMES CHRISTOPHER LOWTHER, 2nd Viscount; *b* 9 Jan 1942; *s* 1949; *ed* Eton, and Trin Coll, Camb; Capt Wessex Yeo (ret); Parl Under-Sec Dept of Employment since 1990: *m* 1967, Susan, da of James Howard Weatherby, of Cleeve House, E Knoyle, Salisbury, Wilts *(see* Wake, Bt), and has issue.

Arms – Or, six annulets, three, two, and one, sable, a crescent for difference. **Crest** – A dragon passant argent. **Supporters** – On either side a horse argent, gorged with a wreath of laurel vert and charged on the shoulder with a portcullis chained or.
Residence – The Old Rectory, Docking, King's Lynn, Norfolk PE31 8LJ.

SONS LIVING

Hon BENJAMIN JAMES, *b* 26 Nov 1975.
Hon Edward John, *b* 1981.

DAUGHTERS LIVING

Hon Emma Mary, *b* 1968.
Hon Clare Priscilla, *b* 1970.

The office shows the man

SISTER LIVING *(Raised to the rank of a Viscount's daughter* 1951)

Hon Kirstin Elizabeth, *b* 1939: *m* 1st, 1966, Capt Caledon Alexander, late 7th Queen's Own Hussars; 2ndly, 1976, Antony Edward Ord Welton, and has issue living (by 1st *m*), James Caledon, *b* 1969, — Charlotte Jane, *b* 1968.

HALF-AUNTS LIVING *(Raised to the rank of a Viscount's daughters* 1950)

Hon Rosemary, *b* 1922: *m* 1945, Lt Douglas Cyril Aubrey Goolden, RNVR, and has issue living, Michael Cyril Christopher (Foxes Bank Farm, Wadhurst, E Sussex TN5 6LN), *b* 1947: *m* 1977, Siegrith, yr twin da of late Basil Vickers, of Skelmorlie, Ayrshire, and has issue living, Freya Polly Tamsin *b* 1980, Camilla Sophia Marique *b* 1984, Chloë Florence Basilia *b* 1988, — Alastair Richard Lowther, *b* 1954, — Jill Priscilla, *b* 1949: *m* 1984, Paul Douglas Marshall, son of Frank Marshall, of Hampton. *Residence* – Forge Cottage, Withyham, Sussex.
Hon Jennifer LOWTHER, *b* 1932; resumed her maiden name 1989: *m* 1st, 1954 (*m diss* 1962), as his 2nd wife, 7th Earl of Lonsdale; 2ndly, 1962 (*m diss* 1972), Flt-Lt William Edward Clayfield, DFC, RAF; 3rdly, 1976 (*m diss* 1979), Rev Oswald Dickin Carter, who *d* 1986; 4thly, 1981, James Cornelius Sullivan. *Residence* – 19 Minster Yard, Lincoln LN2 1PY.

PREDECESSOR – (1) *Rt Hon Sir* JAMES WILLIAM Lowther, GCB, son of late Hon William Lowther, brother of 3rd Earl of Lonsdale; *b* 1855; Bar Inner Temple 1879, and a Bencher 1906; was 4th (unpaid) Charity Commr 1887-91, Under-Sec of State for Foreign Affairs 1891-2, Chm of Committee of Ways and Means and Dep Speaker of House of Commons 1895-1905, and Speaker 1905-21; Chm of Political Honours Commn 1923-4; sat as MP for Rutland (C) 1883-5, for Mid, or Penrith, Div of Cumberland 1886-1918, and for Cumberland, Penrith and Cockermouth Div 1918-21; *cr Viscount Ullswater*, of Campsea Ashe, co Suffolk (peerage of UK) 1921: *m* 1886, Mary Frances, who *d* 1944, da of late Right Hon Alexander James Beresford-Hope, MP, of Bedgebury Park, Cranbrook; *d* 1949; *s* by his great-grandson (2) NICHOLAS JAMES CHRISTOPHER (son of late Lt John

Arthur Lowther, MVO, RNVR, son of late Maj Hon Christopher William Lowther, el son of 1st Viscount), 2nd Viscount and present peer.

Ulster, Earl of; son of Duke of Gloucester.

UNDERHILL, BARONY OF (Underhill) (Extinct 1993)

SONS LIVING OF LIFE BARON

Hon Terry Leonard (Fairlight, Mill Cross, Rattery, South Brent, Devon), *b* 1938: *m* 1960, Dorothy, da of late Edwin Askew, and has issue, three sons.
Hon Robert (4 Hall Rd, Wilmslow, Cheshire SK9 5BW), *b* 1948: *m* 1970, Christine Ann, da of Ernest Edward Lawrence Vinsen, of 19 Cherrydown Close, E4, and has issue, one son and one da.

DAUGHTER LIVING OF LIFE BARON

Hon Joan Evelyn (88 Mansfield Rd, Selston, Notts NG9 6AH), *b* 1944; CC Notts, Chm Social Services Cttee, and Chm Social Services Cttee Assocn of CCs: *m* 1st, 1965 (*m diss* 1973), Edwin Fennell; 2ndly, 1973 (*m diss* 1989), Ian Robert Taylor; 3rdly, 1993, John Robert Stocks, and has issue (by 1st *m*), one son, — (by 2nd *m*), two sons.

WIDOW LIVING OF LIFE BARON

FLORA JANET (*Baroness Underhill*), da of Leonard George Philbrick: *m* 1937, Baron Underhill, CBE (Life Baron), who *d* 1993. *Residence* – 94 Loughton Way, Buckhurst Hill, Essex IG9 6AH.

Uxbridge, Earl of; son of Marquess of Anglesey.

VAIZEY, BARONY OF (Vaizey) (Extinct 1984)

SONS LIVING OF LIFE BARON

Hon Thomas Peter John, *b* 1964; *ed* St Paul's, Worcester Coll, Oxford (BA), and City Univ (Dip Law); Bar Inner Temple 1988.
Hon Edward, *b* 1968; *ed* St Paul's (Scholar), and Merton Coll, Oxford.

DAUGHTER LIVING OF LIFE BARON

Hon Polly, *b* 1962; *ed* St Paul's Girls' Sch, and Lady Margaret Hall, Oxford: *m* 1991, Charles Gavin McAndrew, elder son of Nicolas McAndrew, of Blairquhosh House, Blanefield, Stirlingshire.

WIDOW LIVING OF LIFE BARON

MARINA ALANDRA (*Baroness Vaizey*); author, Gov South Bank Board since 1993; Trustee Imperial War Museum since 1991; Ed Publications National Art Collections Fund since 1991; da of Lyman Stansky, of New York, USA: *m* 1961, Baron Vaizey (Life Baron), who *d* 1984. *Residence* – 24 Heathfield Terr, W4 4JE.

VALENTIA, VISCOUNT (Annesley) (Viscount I 1642, with precedence of 1622, Bt I 1620)

By the love of virtue

VIRTUTIS · AMORE

(Name pronounced "Ansley")

RICHARD JOHN DIGHTON ANNESLEY, 15th Viscount and Premier Baronet of Ireland; *b* 15 Aug 1929; *s* 1983; *ed* Marlborough; Capt RA (ret): *m* 1957, Anita Phyllis, only da of William Arthur Joy, of Bristol, and has had issue.

𝔄rms – Paly of six argent and azure, over all a bend gules. ℭrest – A Moor's head in profile couped proper, wreathed about the temples argent and azure. 𝔖upporters – *Dexter*, a Roman soldier in armour or, short sleeves and apron gules, face, arms, and legs bare, the latter sandalled, argent: on his head a helmet gold, on the top three feathers of the second, holding in his exterior hand a shield, thereon a female's head; *sinister*, a Moorish prince proper, in armour or, wreathed round the temples argent and azure, short sleeves and apron gules, boots gold, behind him a sheaf of arrows proper, fastened by a pink ribbon, in his exterior hand a bow proper.
Residence – East Range Farm, Chinhoyi, Zimbabwe.

SONS LIVING AND DECEASED

Hon FRANCIS WILLIAM DIGHTON, *b* 29 Dec 1959; *ed* Falcons, Bulawayo: *m* 1982, Shaneen Hobbs, and has issue living, Kirsten, *b* 1986, — Sarah Ashleigh, *b* 1989.
†*Hon* Richard Dighton, *b* 1962; *ed* Falcons, Bulawayo; *d* 1989.
Hon Peter John, *b* 1967; *ed* Falcons, Bulawayo.

DAUGHTER LIVING

Hon Sarah Joy, *b* 1958: *m* 1980, Mark K. Frewen, of Hillside Farm, N Bergersdorp, NE Cape, S Africa, and has issue living, Matthew, *b* 1991, — Samantha, *b* 1987.

SISTERS LIVING

Hon Elizabeth Mary Jean, *b* 1926: *m* 1948, Maj James Terence Ralph Sylvester Bradley, MA, CEng, MIERE, who *d* 1987, of Knighton Manor, Durweston, Blandford, Dorset, and has issue living, Charles Robin (9 Pembroke Rd, Westbourne, Bournemouth), *b* 1959: *m* 1985, Jennifer Roberts, and has issue living, Jolyon *b* 1986, Christabel Morwenna *b* 1990, — Fiona Elizabeth (195A Quemerford, Calne, Wilts SN11 8JX), *b* 1949, — Heather Mary, *b* 1951: *m* 1978, Michael Dias do Nascimento, BVMS, MRCVS, of Quinta dos Sobreiros, Faxelhas, Apartado 75, 8300 Silves, Algarve, Portugal, and has issue living, Charles James *b* 1979, Edward Michael *b* 1980, Jorge Norman *b* 1988, — Catherine Alison, *b* 1957: *m* 1984, Toby C. Goddard, of Knighton Manor, Durweston, Blandford, Dorset, son of Keith Goddard, FRICS, FSVA, of Lane End, Broad Oak, Sturminster Newton, Dorset, and has issue living, Hamish Toby *b* 1989, Alexandra Catherine *b* 1987.
Hon Susan Margaret, *b* 1931: *m* 1954, Peter Lindsay Milln, and has issue living, Jeremy James, *b* 1956, — Teresa Clare, *b* 1958: *m* 1983, John Joseph Doran, of Mullingar, co Westmeath, and has issue living, Fabian James *b* 1985, Jonathan Lindsay *b* 1988, — Eleanor Eve, *b* 1961: *m* 1987, John Courtnay Channon, eldest son of George H. Channon, of Herons Lake, Polbrook, Bodmin, Cornwall, — Jesica Rose, *b* 1964. *Residence* – Nanterrow, Tregongeeves Lane, Polgooth, St Austell, Cornwall.
Hon Helen Jennifer Frances, *b* 1935: *m* 1957, Simon FitzRoy Casswell, and has issue living, Edward FitzRoy, *b* 1958: *m* 19—, Rosemary Tassel, and has issue living, James FitzRoy *b* 1987, Mark *b* 1989, — Jane Elizabeth, *b* 1962, — Karen Mary, *b* 1969. *Residence* – The Limes Barn Farm, Smarden, nr Ashford, Kent.

WIDOW LIVING OF THIRTEENTH VISCOUNT

GLADYS MAY KATHLEEN (*Gladys, Viscountess Valentia*), da of late Uriah Fowler; *ed* Ridley Hall, Camb: *m* 1938, the 13th Viscount, who *d* 1951. *Residences* – Wassall House, Wincanton, Somerset; Monckton, 34 Uphills, Bruton, Somerset.

COLLATERAL BRANCHES LIVING

Issue of late Philip de Vere Annesley, brother of 13th Viscount, *b* 1879, *d* 1949: *m* 1907, Christabel Charlotte, BEM, who *d* 1955, da of late John Christopher Tomson:—
Anne Christabel de Vere (*Lady Thompson*), *b* 1909; assumed by deed poll 1941 the additional christian name of Anne: *m* 1939, Sir Richard Hilton Marler Thompson, 1st baronet (*cr* 1963), of Rhodes House, Sellindge, Ashford, Kent.

Granddaughter of late Lt-Col Clifford Reginald Templeman Annesley, DSO (infra):—
Issue of late Reginald Clifford Martin Annesley, *b* 1909, *d* 1994: *m* 1940, Ann Isabella, who *d* 1986, el da of John Robert Strachan, of Firthview, Tain, Ross-shire:—
Kathleen Elaine Vere, *b* 1941: *m* 1966, Beverley Aldington Bird, and has issue living, Clive Robert, *b* 1982, — Glynnis Ann, *b* 1970: *m* 1989, Henry Kevin Botes, and has issue living, Dean Stephen *b* 1989, Matthew Ryan *b* 1992, — Jane Claire, *b* 1972. — Sheila Rosalind, *b* 1945: *m* 1964, Michael Stuart Allen, late BSA Police, and has issue living, Stuart David, *b* 1969, — Christopher Michael, *b* 1985, — Deborah Michelle, *b* 1966: *m* 1989, Paul Whitechurch, and has issue living, Gary Paul *b* 1990, Ashleigh Lara *b* 1994, Kirsten Michelle *b* (twin) 1994, — Nicole Paula, *b* 1983.

Grandchildren of late Lt-Col Reginald Carey Annesley, son of George, yst son of late Rev Arthur Annesley, son of late Rev Arthur Henry Annesley, DD, great-grandson of late Hon Francis Annesley, 4th son of 1st Viscount:—
Issue of late Lt-Col Clifford Reginald Templeman Annesley, DSO, *b* 1877, *d* 1971: *m* 1907, Clara Mabel, who *d* 1954, el da of Lt-Col Samuel Martin Gully, Norfolk Regt:—
Vere Bessie Mabel (18 Wykeham Place, Lymington, Hants), *b* 1910.
Issue of late Maj Martin Tyndale Annesley, *b* 1896, *d* 1965: *m* 1935, Marjorie Jex Blake, who *d* 1980, el da of Lt-Col B. E. Winter, of Lowestoft:—
Richard Bruce (Bledlow House, Church End, Bledlow, Aylesbury), *b* 1937: *m* 1972, Elizabeth Mary Emily, da of late Thomas Doyle, of Armanagh, Glenbrook, co Cork, and has issue living, Charlotte Mary, *b* 1973, — Philippa Vere, *b* 1975, — Sophie Elizabeth, *b* 1977.

Descendants of late William Annesley, MP (3rd son of Hon Francis Annesley, 4th son of 1st Viscount), who was *cr Viscount Glerawly* 1766 (*see* E Annesley).

PREDECESSORS – **(1)** *Rt Hon Sir* FRANCIS Annesley, filled during forty years numerous high official positions in Ireland, and sat for sometime as MP for Armagh; *cr* a *Baronet* 1620; in 1621 obtained by patent a reversionary grant to the peerage of *Viscount Valentia* (peerage of Ireland) at the decease of the then viscount; *cr Baron Mountnorris*, of Mountnorris, co Armagh (peerage of Ireland) 1628; in 1635 he publicly offended Lord Strafford, the Lord Deputy of Ireland, and for this offence he was tried, and found guilty, and sentenced to deprivation of military rank and to be shot or beheaded at the pleasure of the General; the capital punishment was not carried out, but he suffered a long imprisonment in Dublin Castle; *d* 1660; *s* by his son **(2)** ARTHUR, 2nd Viscount; was Treasurer of the Navy 1667, and Lord Privy Seal 1673; *cr Baron Annesley*, of Newport Pagnel, co Bucks, and *Earl of Anglesey* (peerage of England) 1661; *d* 1686; *s* by his son **(3)** JAMES, 2nd Earl; *d* 1690; *s* by his el son **(4)** JAMES, 3rd Earl; *d* 1702; *s* by his brother **(5)** JOHN, 4th Earl; *d* 1710; *s* by his brother **(6)** ARTHUR, 5th Earl; *d* 1737; *s* by his kinsman **(7)** RICHARD, 6th Earl, who had previously *s* as 5th *Baron Altham* (peerage of Ireland, *cr* 1680), he being 2nd son of the 3rd Baron Altham, who was 3rd son of the 1st Earl; after the assumption of the earldom by this peer a Mr James Annesley claimed the earldom as son of Arthur, 4th Baron Altham, and alleged that in his infancy he had been kidnapped by his uncle Richard (6th Earl), and in 1743 he commenced a suit of law to recover the property from his uncle and obtained a verdict, though he did not further pursue his claim to the earldom, and his uncle continued to be recognised as earl; *d* 1761; *s* by his son **(8)** ARTHUR, 8th Viscount, whose claims to the Baronies of Mountnorris, Altham, and the Viscountcy of Valentia were twice confirmed by the Irish Parliament, whilst his claim to the Barony of Annesley and Earldom of Anglesey was refused by the English Parliament; *cr Earl of Mountnorris* (peerage of Ireland) 1793; *d* 1816; *s* by his son **(9)** GEORGE, second Earl; *d* 1844 when the Barony of Altham and Earldom of Mountnorris expired; *s* in the Baronetcy, Barony of Mountnorris, and Viscountcy of Valentia by his kinsman **(10)** ARTHUR, 10th Viscount, 5th in descent from Francis, 4th son of 1st Earl; *d* 1863; *s* by his grandson **(11)** ARTHUR, KCVO, CB, 11th Viscount, son of Hon Arthur Annesley (el son of 10th Viscount by Flora Mary, who *d* 1884, da of Lt-Col James Macdonald of Clanranald); Comptroller of the Household to Queen Victoria 1898-1901, and to King Edward VII 1901-05, and a Lord-in-Waiting to King George V 1915-24; *cr Baron Annesley of Bletchington*, co Oxford (peerage of UK) 1917: *m* 1878, Laura Sarah, who *d* 1933, da of Daniel Hale Webb, of Wykeham Park, and widow of Sir Algernon William Payton, 4th Bt; *d* 1927; *s* by his son **(12)** CARYL ARTHUR JAMES, CVO, 12th Viscount; *b* 1883; Maj 1st R Dragoons; High Steward of Banbury 1932-47; Private Sec to HRH Prince Arthur of Connaught 1922-38; *d* unm 1949, when the Barony of Annesley of Bletchington (peerage of UK) became ext; *s* in his other titles by his kinsman **(13)** *Rev* WILLIAM MONCKTON, 13th Viscount (el son of Rev Henry Arthur Annesley, el son of Arthur Annesley, great-grandson of Rev Martin Annesley, DD, grandson of Hon Francis Annesley, 4th son of 1st Viscount); *b* 1875; V of Brewham-cum-Redlynch, Somerset, and Cottonian Family Trustee of British Museum: *m* 1938, Gladys May Kathleen, da of late Uriah Fowler; *d* 1951; *s* by his cousin **(14)** FRANCIS DIGHTON, MC, MRCS, LRCP (son of late George Dighton Annesley, uncle of 13th Viscount); 14th Viscount, *b* 1888; established his succession 1959; MRCS, LRCP 1914; Brig RAMC; Cottonian Family Trustee of British Museum; European War 1914-18 (MC, Belgian Croix de Guerre), Afghanistan 1919, Waziristan 1922-23, European War 1939-45: *m* 1925, Joan Elizabeth, who *d* 1986, da of late John J. Curtis, of Sunnybrook, Sandhurst; *d* 1983; *s* by his only son **(15)** RICHARD JOHN DIGHTON, 15th Viscount and present peer; also Baron Mountnorris.

Vane, Earl, title of Marquess of Londonderry on Roll of HL.

VANSITTART, BARONY OF (Vansittart) (Extinct 1957)

DAUGHTER LIVING OF FIRST BARON (*By 1st m*)

Hon Cynthia, *b* 1922: *m* 1st, 1942 (*m diss* in California, USA 1954), Frederick C. Whitman; 2ndly, 1955, Edward Hart Mackay, and has issue living, (by 1st *m*) Michael Robert Vansittart (2518 Buchanan St, San Francisco, Calif 94115, USA), *b* 1944, — Jonathan Crocker (2199 Jackson St, San Francisco, Calif 94115, USA), *b* 1948, — Kevin Crocker (46 West 69th St, New York, NY 20023, USA), *b* 1950, — Tania Vansittart (2109 Baker St, San Francisco, Calif 94115, USA), *b* 1942, — (by 2nd *m*) Robert Vansittart, *b* 1958, — Donald James Edward, *b* 1961. *Residence* – 2655 Clay St, San Francisco, USA.

VARLEY, BARON (Varley) (Life Baron 1990)

ERIC GRAHAM VARLEY, PC, son of Frank Varley, of Poolsbrook, Derbys; *b* 11 Aug 1932; *ed* Ruskin Coll, Oxford; DL Derbys 1989; Engineer's Turner 1952-55, Mining Industry (Coal) Craftsman 1955-64; Assist Govt Whip 1967-68, PPS to PM (Rt Hon Harold Wilson) 1968-69, Min of State Min of Technology 1969-70, Sec of State for Energy 1974-75, for Industry 1975-79; Chief Opposition Spokesman on Employment 1978-83; Treasurer Lab Party 1981-83; Visiting Fellow Nuffield Coll 1977-81; Chm and Chief Exec Coalite Group since 1984; Steward and Bailiff of the Manor of Northstead since 1984; MP for Chesterfield (*Lab*) 1964-84; *cr* PC 1974, and *Baron Varley*, of Chesterfield, co Derbys (Life Baron) 1990: *m* 1955, Marjorie, da of Alfred Turner, of Duckmanton, Derbys, and has issue.
Residence – 189 Middlecroft Rd, Staveley, Chesterfield, Derbys.

SON LIVING

Hon —, *b* 19—.

Vaughan, Viscount; son of Earl of Lisburne.

VAUX OF HARROWDEN, BARON (Gilbey) (Baron E 1523)
(Title pronounced "Vawks of Harrowden")

Today, not tomorrow

JOHN HUGH PHILIP GILBEY, 10th Baron; *b* 4 Aug 1915; *s* 1977; *ed* Ampleforth Coll, and at Ch Ch Oxford (BA 1937); Maj Duke of Wellington's Regt (ret): *m* 1939, Maureen, da of late Hugh Gilbey, of Shellwood Bend, Leigh, Reigate, Surrey, and has issue.

Arms – Quarterly, 1st and 4th gules, a fesse nebulée or, in chief a horse rampant between two estoiles and the like in base, all of the last, *Gilbey*; 2nd and 3rd: Per bend sinister ermine and erminois a lion rampant or, *Mostyn*. **Crest** – In front of a tower proper issuant from the battlements thereof a dragon's head gules, a fleur-de-lis or, all between two ostrich feathers argent. **Supporters** – *Dexter*, a griffin sable beaked or the forelegs gold; *sinister*, a buck or each gorged with a torse argent and gules pendant therefrom by a ring gold an escutcheon of the Arms of Vaux (checky, or and gules, on a chevron azure, three roses gold).
Residence – Cholmondeley Cottage, 2 Cholmondeley Walk, Richmond, Surrey.

SONS LIVING

Hon ANTHONY WILLIAM (Rusko, Gatehouse of Fleet, Kirkcudbrightshire), *b* 25 May 1940; FCA; *ed* Ampleforth: *m* 1964, Beverley Anne, only da of late Charles Alexander Walton, of Cooden, Sussex, and has issue living, Richard Hubert Gordon, *b* 16 March 1965, — Philip Alexander Charles, *b* 1967, — Victoria Caroline, *b* 1969, — Elizabeth Muriel Emma, *b* 1989.
Hon William John (The Grange, Waltham St Lawrence, Twyford, Berks), *b* 1944, *ed* Ampleforth: *m* 1971, Caroline, da of Alan Ball, of The Old Mill, Ramsbury, Wilts, and has issue living, Thomas Edward, *b* 1972, — James William, *b* 1978, — Charlotte Katharine, *b* 1974.
Hon Michael Christopher (Pheasants Ridge, Hambleden, Henley, Oxon RG9 6SD), *b* 1949, *ed* Ampleforth, and St Andrew's Univ (MA); ARICS: *m* 1971, Linda, yst da of late Arthur Sebastian Gilbey (*see* Gilbey, Bt, colls), and has issue living, Henry John, *b* 1973, — Julian Sebastian, *b* 1975, — William Michael, *b* 1979.

DAUGHTER LIVING

Hon Penelope Margaret, *b* 1942: *m* 1965, John Charles Haynes, of Evelith Mill, Shifnal, Shropshire, and has issue living, Charles Thomas Francis, *b* 1967, — Edward Hugh Gordon, *b* 1976, — Alexandra Louise, *b* 1966: *m* 1991, Christopher John Courage, of Edgcote, Banbury, Oxon (*see* Reynolds, Bt), — Bridget Clare, *b* 1969.

SISTER LIVING

Hon Mary Agnes Margaret, *b* 1928. *Residence* – Dolphins, Gt Harrowden, Wellingborough.

COLLATERAL BRANCHES LIVING

Grandchildren of late Hon Harold Plantagenet Mostyn, yr brother of 7th Baron:—
Issue of late George Anthony Mostyn, *b* 1898, *d* 1972: *m* 1924, Catharine Sibylla, who *d* 1983, da of late Bernard Henry Holland, CB (*see* V Knutsford, colls):—
Richard Anthony Mostyn (3 Flamingo Drive, Greenside, Mutari, Zimbabwe), *b* 1927; *ed* RNC Dartmouth; Lt RN (ret); FIAC (SA); LIMTA (SA): *m* 1961, Mary, da of J. J. Michie, of Marian Hill, Natal, and has issue living, Anthony Damian, *b* 1964; CA (Zim), — Christopher Francis Joseph, *b* 1966, — Nicola Mary, *b* 1961: *m* 1981, Grant Taylor, of Redcliffe, Queensland, Australia, and has issue living, Grant Alexander *b* 1994, Alana Clare *b* 1986, — Clare Sibylla, *b* 1963: *m* 1983, Morgan Hore, of Dagenham, Essex, and has issue living, Mark Patrick *b* 1983, Kevin Anthony *b* 1987. —— Valentine Francis (50 Cranley Mews, SW7), *b* 1925: *m* 1925: *ed* Oxford Sch of Architecture, and Canterbury Sch of Architecture (Dip Arch); ARIBA: *m* 1974, Gay, da of H. Field (PO Box 1167, Malibu, Calif 90265), and has issue living, Amy Clare, *b* 1974, — Sarah Jane, *b* 1977. —— Juliet Veronica, *b* 1925: *m* 1952, Anthony Lightfoot, of Valley Cottage, Brundish, nr Woodbridge, Suffolk, and has issue living, Edward Jude, *b* 1953: *m* 1st, 1977 (*m diss* 1982), Hilary Diane Carver; 2ndly, 1983, Gaynor Alison Clark, and has issue living (by 2nd *m*), Alexander Richard *b* 1985, — Jessica Louise *b* 1954, — Dominic Anthony, *b* 1955, — Paul Jerome, *b* 1956: *m* 1982, Claudia Cecilia, only da of Claude Vaux Miéville (*see* B Hatherton, 1985 Edn), — Mary Victoria, *b* 1959, — Catherine Lucy, *b* 1966: *m* 1992 (*m diss* 1993), James Hartley Berwick, of Bruisyard, Suffolk. —— Joan Elizabeth Verena Mostyn, *b* 1948; *ed* Royal Coll of Art (MA): *m* 1971 (*m diss* 1977), Anthony John Dyson; has issue living (by Douglas Jones, of San Francisco, Calif), Santiago Alexis Kanjuchi Sadiq Mostyn, *b* 1981. *Residence* – No 8 Cockington Rd, Mandara, Harare, Zimbabwe.

Issue of late Hon Gladys Flora Mostyn, 2nd da of 7th Baron, *b* 1889, *d* 1975: *m* 1911, George Victor Bellasis Charlton, who *d* 1943:—
Eleanor Margaret Mary, *b* 1912. —— †Anne Mary Georgina, *b* 1913: *m* 1948, Hugh Dougal Fyfe Baird, who *d* 1979, and *d* 1994, leaving issue, (Rosemary) Gillian (1 Boghead Cottages, Mintlaw, Peterhead, Aberdeen), *b* 1950: *m* 1st, 1974 (*m diss* 1980), Barry Lambert; 2ndly, 1981, Charles Davies King, and has issue living (by 2nd *m*), Patrick Charles *b* 1987. —— Joan Mary Winifrede, *b* 1916: *m* 1st, 1940, Ian Alexander Bruce Johnstone, P/O RAF, who was *ka* 1942; 2ndly, 1945, Harry James Hubert Ripper, F/O RAF, of 18 School Rd, Sible Hedingham, Essex CO9 3NR, and has issue living (by 2nd *m*), Christopher James (24 Gills Hill, Radlett, Herts WD7 8BZ), *b* 1946; *ed* Blackfriars Sch, Laxton, Northants: *m* 1974, Julie Margaret Long, of Sydney, Australia, and has issue living, Georgina Louise *b* 1977, Annabel Merry *b* 1979, Holly Charlton *b* 1981, — Judith Caroline (51 Begbroke Crescent, Begbroke, Oxon OX5 1RW), *b* 1949: *m* 1971 (*m diss* 1993), Philip William Ford, and has issue living, Adam George *b* 1973, Samantha Anne *b* 1973. —— Dorothy Mary Amy, *b* 1919: *m* 1958, Digby Michael Auden, of Dolphin House, Hardingstone, Northampton NN4 6BX, and has had issue, †Julian Michael, *b* 1961; *k* in an accident 1973, — Penelope Clare, *b* 1960: *m* 1986, Paul Radford, of 6 Darwin Close, Porterswood, St Albans, Herts AL3 6LH, and has issue living, Michael Julian Auden *b* 1988, Dominic Peter Auden *b* 1990, Sebastian Thomas Auden *b* 1992, Catriona Helen Margaret Auden *b* 1987. —— Frances Mary Elizabeth, *b* 1924: *m* 1947, Stephen Louis Dudley Ripper, of Orchard House, High St Green, Sible Hedingham, Essex CO9 3LG, and has had issue, Anne Mary Frances, *b* 1948: *m* 1983, Anton Brooke Shellim, of 12 Moreton Av, Harpenden, Herts AL5 2ET, and has issue living, Alexander Brooke *b* 1985, Rebecca Frances *b* 1987, — †Susan Mary Margaret, *b* 1951: *dunm* 1990, — Catherine Mary Alison, *b* 1955: *m* 1st, 1974 (*m diss* 1980), George Hales; 2ndly, 1989, John Alexander Malone, of 8 Greenbank Crescent, Edinburgh EH10 5SG, and has issue living (by 2nd *m*), Martin John *b* 1988, Amy Frances *b* 1984.

Descendants of late Barbara Maria Mostyn, sister of 6th Baron, who *m* 1833, Sir Frederick William Slade, QC, 2nd Bt:—

See Slade, Bt.

PREDECESSORS – **(1)** *Sir* NICHOLAS Vaux, a distinguished soldier and statesman, was summoned to Parliament of England as *Baron Vaux of Harrowden*, 1523; *d* 1523; *s* by his son **(2)** THOMAS, 2nd Baron; *d* 1562; *s* by his son **(3)** WILLIAM, 3rd Baron; was summoned to Parliament 1563-89; *d* 1595; *s* by his grandson **(4)** EDWARD, 4th Baron; summoned to Parliament 1620; *dsp* 1661; *s* by his brother **(5)** HENRY, 5th Baron; *d* unmarried 1662, when the barony became abeyant between his surviving sister Joyce, and the heirs of his sisters Mary (Lady Symeon) and Catherine (Baroness Abergavenny), and remained so until 1838, when the abeyance was terminated in favour of the heir of Mary, the el sister **(6)** GEORGE Mostyn, 6th Baron, son of Mary Lucinda, née Butler, by her *m* to Charles Browne-Mostyn, 2nd son of Sir Edward Mostyn, 5th Bt; *d* 1883; *s* by his grandson **(7)** HUBERT GEORGE CHARLES (el son of late Major Hon George Charles Mostyn), 7th Baron; *b* 1860; appointed Attache in Diplo Ser 1884, became a 3rd Sec 1886, and a 2nd Sec 1891; retired 1899: *m* 1st, 1886, Eleanor Margaret, who *d* 1896, da of Sir Alexander Matheson, MP, 1st Bt; 2ndly, 1902, Margaret Annette Jane Chichele, who *d* 1922, da of late Sir William Chichele Plowden, KCSI (Bass, Bt); 3rdly, 1924, Mary Winefride Teresa (Freyda), who *d* 1944, da of Sir Joseph Edward Radcliffe, 4th Bt, and widow of Capt Thomas Cecil de Trafford, Roy Fusiliers (de Trafford, Bt, colls); *d* 1935, when the Barony again fell into abeyance between his three das, and so remained until July 1938, when it was terminated by Letters Patent in favour of the el **(8)** GRACE MARY ELEANOR Mostyn, *b* 1887: *m* 1911, William Gordon Gilbey who *d* 1965; *d* 1958; *s* by her el son **(9)** *Rev* PETER HUBERT GORDON, 9th Baron, in Holy Orders of Church of Rome, a Monk of Ampleforth Abbey, *d* 1977; *s* by his brother **(10)** JOHN HUGH PHILIP, 10th Baron and present peer.

VENTRY, BARON (Daubeny de Moleyns) (Baron I 1800, Bt I 1797)
(Name pronounced "demmoleens")

To conquer is to live enough

ANDREW WESLEY DAUBENEY DE MOLEYNS, 8th Baron and 8th Baronet; *b* 28 May 1943; *s* 1987; assumed by deed poll 1966 the surname of Daubeny de Moleyns; *ed* Aldenham: *m* 1st, 1963 (*m diss* 1979), Nelly Edouard Renée, da of Abel Chaumillon, of Loma de los Riseos, Villa Angel, Torremolinos, Malaga, Spain; 2ndly, 1983, Jill Rosemary, da of Cecil Walter Oram, and has issue by 1st and 2nd *m*.

Arms – Quarterly, 1st and 4th sable, on a chief ermine three fusils gules; 2nd and 3rd per pale or and sable, two chevronels between three griffins passant counterchanged. **Crests** – 1st, a savage's head couped at the shoulders and affrontée, proper; 2nd, a goat's head erased, per chevron or and sable, attired of the 2nd, in the mouth a branch of laurel proper. **Supporters** – Two lions or, ducally collared and chained azure.
Residence – Hill of Errol House, Errol, Perthshire PH2 7TQ.

SON LIVING (By 1st marriage)

Hon FRANCIS WESLEY, *b* 1 May 1965; *ed* Gordonstoun.

DAUGHTERS LIVING (By 1st marriage)

Hon Elizabeth-Anne Stuart, *b* 1964: *m* 1990, Justin D. Byford, only son of T. J. Tyford, of Belgrade, Yugoslavia, and of Mrs J. D. Campane, of Barnes, SW14. *Residence* – 8 Regina Rd, W Ealing, W13 7PW.
Hon Brigitte Catherine, *b* 1967.

(by 2nd marriage)

Hon Lisa, *b* 1985.

SISTER LIVING

Sally Joan, *b* 1940: *m* 1964, Robin Hart, son of George Hart, of Beaulieu, Mitton Grove, Shrewsbury, and has issue living, Christopher, *b* 1965; *ed* Shrewsbury, — Penelope, *b* 1966, — Caroline, *b* 1968, — Rachel, *b* 1970. *Residence* – Ruan Mill, Ruan Lanihorne, Truro, Cornwall TR2 5NU.

HALF-SISTER LIVING

Valentia, *b* 1928: *m* 1950, Capt Nathaniel Duncan Spry Grant-Dalton, RHA, High Sheriff of Cornwall 1986, and has issue living, Kevin Duncan Spry, *b* 1952; *ed* Radley: *m* 1980, Amanda Charlton, da of F. E. de Smitt, of 45 Drax Av, SW20, and has issue living, Samuel Duncan Spry *b* 1985, Jolyon *b* 1991 Pippa Charlton *b* 1988, — Miranda Jane, *b* 1955: *m* 1983, Simon James Forrester, elder son of Maj-Gen Michael Forrester, CB, CBE, DSO, MC, of West Worldham, Hants, and has issue living, Nicholas Francis *b* 1985, Frederick Richard George *b* 1990, — Nicola Frances, *b* 1957: *m* 1979, Ian Adair Campbell, of 11 Burcote Rd, SW18, 2nd son of Lt-Col Robert Adair Campbell, of Altries, Maryculter, Aberdeenshire, and has issue living, Hamish Adair *b* 1982, Oliver Alistair *b* 1985, Robert Francis *b* 1988. *Residence* – Place house, St Anthony-in-Roseland, Portscatho, Cornwall TR2 5EZ.

MOTHER LIVING

Joan, eldest da of Harold Wesley, of the The Wilderness, E Molesey, Surrey, and widow of Fl-Lieut H. G. Adams, RAF: *m* 1938 (*m diss* 1952), Hon Francis Alexander Innys Eveleigh-Ross-de-Moleyns, who *d* 1964; 3rdly, 1952, Nigel Eric Springett. *Residence* – Fieldfare, Rackenford, nr Tiverton, Devon.

STEP-MOTHER LIVING

Olivia Phœbe (has reverted to her former style of *Lady John Conyngham*), da of Capt Percy Neave Leathers, of Fayre Cottage, Robertsbridge, Sussex, and widow of Lord John Victor Albert Blosse Conyngham, son of 6th Marquess Conyngham: *m* 1963, as his 4th wife, Hon Francis Alexander Innys Eveleigh-Ross-de-Moleyns, who *d* 1964. *Residence* – Windmill Cottage, Yapton Rd, Barnham, Bognor Regis, W Sussex.

COLLATERAL BRANCHES LIVING

Grandchildren of late Hon John Gilbert Eveleigh-de-Moleyns (infra):—
Issue of late John Andrew WAUCHOPE, *b* 1900, *d* 1956, having assumed the surname of Wauchope in lieu of his patronymic 1945: *m* 1923, Rosemary Eve, who *d* 1975, da of late Rear-Adm John Arthur Tuke:—
Andrew Dermod (Lochtower Cottage, Kelso), *b* 1932: *m* 1957, Jennifer Siggers, and has issue living, James Andrew, *b* 1963, — Ian Simon (twin) *b* 1963, — Fiona Jane, *b* 1958, — Nicola Anne, *b* 1959. —— Œnone Eileen Frances, *b* 1931: *m* 1952, Timothy Robert Crum Willis, of Meadowcroft, Station Rd, Great Ayton, Middlesbrough, Cleveland TS9 6HB, and has issue living, Robert Nigel Crum, *b* 1954: *m* 1984, Paula Carol Hamilton, and has issue living, Simon Robert Crum *b* 1987, Deborah Carol Jane *b* 1988, — Andrew James Scott, *b* 1956: *m* 1992, Linda Marinaro, and has issue living, Robin Christopher Scott *b* 1994, — John Douglas Charles, *b* 1960, — Michael Philip Bruce, *b* 1966: *m* 1993, Karen Edwick.

Issue of late Hon John Gilbert Eveleigh-de-Moleyns, brother of 6th Baron *b* 1878, *d* 1928: *m* 1899, Marguerite, who *d* 1982, aged 103, da of George Edward Noon:—
Eileen Mildred Alice, *b* 1912: *m* 1939, Harold Alan Coldham, LLB, and has issue living, Simon Frederick Russell (La Bastia, Propriano, France), *b* 1940; MA, PhD, — Christopher Alan, *b* 1943, — Marie Audrey (twin), *b* 1943.

Granddaughter of late Rev William Bishop de Moleyns, 2nd son of late Major Hon Edward de Moleyns, 5th son of 1st Baron:—
Issue of late Rev Alured Bayfield de Moleyns, *b* 1851, *d* 1925: *m* 1888, Mary Louisa, who *d* 1908, el da of John Lyon (retired Fleet Paymaster, RN):—
Alice Louisa Eveleigh, *b* 1889.

PREDECESSORS – (1) THOMAS Mullins; *cr* a *Baronet* 1797, and *Baron Ventry*, of Ventry, co Kerry (peerage of Ireland) 1800; *d* 1824; *s* by his son (2) WILLIAM TOWNSEND, 2nd Baron; *d* 1827; *s* by his nephew (3) THOMAS TOWNSEND AREMBERG, 3rd Baron; *b* 1786; resumed the ancient family name of De Moleyns by Roy licence 1841: *m* 1821, Eliza Theodora, da of Sir John Blake, 10th Bt; *d* 1868; *s* by his son (4) DAYROLLES BLAKENEY, 4th Baron, *b* 1828; a Representative Peer; assumed 1874 the additional surname and arms of Eveleigh: *m* 1860, Harriet Elizabeth Frances, who *d* 1906, da of Andrew Wauchope, of Niddrie Marischal, Midlothian; *d* 1914; *s* by his el son (5) FREDERICK ROSSMORE WAUCHOPE, DSO, 5th Baron, *b* 1861; *d* 1923; *s* by his brother (6) ARTHUR WILLIAM, 6th Baron, *b* 1864: *m* 1897, Evelyn Muriel Stuart, who *d* 1966, da of Lansdowne Daubeney, of Norton Malreward, Somerset, *d* 1936; *s* by his el son (7) ARTHUR FREDERICK DAUBENEY, 7th Baron, *b* 1898, assumed addl christian name of OLAV, received King Haakon's Freedom Medal, served in World War I in Irish Guards and RAF (Airship Branch), and World War II in Balloon Cmd and Intelligence, late Hon A/Cdre No 902 (Co of London) Balloon Sqdn AAF and Fl Lieut RAFVR; *d* 1987; *s* by his nephew (8) ANDREW WESLEY (son of late Hon Francis Alexander Innys Eveleigh-Ross-de Moleyns, yr son of 6th Baron), 8th Baron and present peer.

This family descends from Col Frederick Mullins of Burnham, Norfolk, who settled in Ireland about 1666, and *m* Jane, da and co-heir of Very Rev John Eveleigh, Dean of Ross. The Mullins family claim descent from the de Moleyns, though the descent remains to be proved. They may have taken their name from Moulins la Marche, Orne, Normandy; *see* The Complete Peerage, Vol IX, p 43, for a note on the origin of this family.

VERNON, BARON (Venables-Vernon) (Baron GB 1762)

or
Ver non semper viret
Vernon always flourishes; or
The spring does not always flourish

JOHN LAWRANCE VENABLES-VERNON, 10th Baron; *b* 1 Feb 1923; *s* 1963; *ed* Eton, and Magdalen Coll, Oxford; Bar Lincoln's Inn 1949; a JP for Derbys; served in Cabinet Office 1953-57, Colonial Office, Kenya 1957-58, and Foreign Office 1958-60; 1939-45 War as Capt Scots Gds: *m* 1st, 1955 (*m diss* 1982), Sheila Jean, yr da of W. Marshall Clark, OBE, of Johannesburg, S Africa; 2ndly, 1982, Sally June, el da of Robin Stratford, QC, and formerly wife of (i) Colin Fyfe-Jamieson and (ii) Sir (John) Jeremy Eustace Tennyson d'Eyncourt, 3rd Bt, and has had issue by 1st *m*.

Arms – Quarterly: 1st and 4th grand quarters quarterly 1st and 4th argent, a fret sable; 2nd and 3rd or, on a fesse azure, three garbs of the field, *Vernon*; 2nd and 3rd azure, two bars argent, *Venables*. **Crests** – 1st, a boar's head erased sable, ducally gorged or, *Vernon*; 2nd, a wyvern, with wings endorsed, standing on a fish weir or trap, devouring a child, and pierced through with an arrow in fesse, all proper, *Venables*. **Supporters** – *Dexter*, a lion gules, collared, and chain reflexed over the back or; *sinister*, a boar sable, ducally gorged, and chain reflexed over the back or.

Seat – Sudbury House, Sudbury, Derby. *Residence* – 10 Ringmer Av, SW6. *Club* – Boodle's.

DAUGHTERS LIVING AND DECEASED (By 1st marriage)

Hon Georgina Frances, *b* 1963; *ed* Cranborne Chase, and — Coll, Camb; author (as Frances Vernon) of *Privileged Children* 1982, *Gentlemen and Players* 1984, *A Desirable Husband* 1987, *The Bohemian Girl* 1988, and *The Marquis of Westmarch* 1989; *d* 1991.
Hon Joanna Elizabeth, *b* 1965: *m* 1992, Alexander Rupert Fitzalan Howard (*see* D Norfolk).

COLLATERAL BRANCHES LIVING

Granddaughter of late Rt Hon Sir William George Granville Venables-Vernon-Harcourt, KC, MP, 2nd son of late Rev William Harcourt, 4th son of the Most Rev Hon Edward Harcourt, Archbishop of York, 3rd son of 1st Baron:—

Issue of late Robert Venables-Vernon-Harcourt, who discontinued the use of the surnames of Venables-Vernon, *b* 1878, *d* 1962: *m* 1911, Margorie Laura, who *d* 1977, da of late William Samuel Cunard (Cunard, Bt, colls):—

Mary Elizabeth, *b* 1922: *m* 1950, Com Ian Rochfort Johnston, RN, of 8 Pembroke Gardens Close, W8, and has issue living, Sarah Elizabeth, *b* 1956: *m* 1979, William James Archer Ziegler (*see* B Brownlow, colls), — Laura Catherine, *b* 1960.

Granddaughter of late Augustus George Vernon-Harcourt, FRS, el son of Adm Frederick Edward Vernon-Harcourt (infra):—

Issue of late Simon Evelyn Vernon-Harcourt, *b* 1882, *d* 1966: *m* 1916, Dorothy Margaret, MBE, who *d* 1987, da of late Sir Robert Hudson, GBE:—

Anne, *b* 1925.

Grandson of late Leveson Francis Vernon-Harcourt, MICE, 2nd son of Adm Frederick Edward Vernon-Harcourt, 5th son of late Most Rev Hon Edward Harcourt (ante):—

Issue of late Leveson William Vernon-Harcourt, *b* 1871, *d* 1909: *m* 1899, Rose Adelaide (who *d* 1959, having *m* 2ndly, 1914, Matthew Liddell, who *d* 1934), da of Frederick Lawrence:—

WILLIAM RONALD DENIS, OBE, *b* (*posthumous*) 4 May 1909; *ed* Eton, and Magdalene Coll, Camb (BA 1930); Col (ret) late S Wales Borderers; Civil Defence Officer, S-E Hants 1958-68; Burma 1941-42 (despatches); OBE (Mil) 1947: *m* 1937, Nancy Everil, only child of late Lt-Col Bertram Henry Leatham, DSO, and has issue living, Anthony William (Monks Farm, Debden Green, Saffron Walden, Essex), *b* 1939: *m* 1966, Cherry Stanhope, da of late Thomas Corbin, of Lime Tree House, Spaldwick, Hunts, and has issue living, Simon Anthony *b* 1969, Edward William *b* 1973, Oliver Thomas *b* 1977, Charlotte Lucy *b* 1968, — Anne Dorothy (The Old School, Clanfield, Hants), *b* 1945: *m* 1st, 1967 (*m diss* 1974), Nicholas Bloxam; 2ndly, 1983, Peter George Cobb, and has issue living (by 1st *m*), Richard William *b* 1971, David Vernon *b* 1974. *Residence –* Quoin Cottage, Southwick Rd, Denmead, Portsmouth, Hants P07 6LA.

Granddaughters of late Edward Evelyn Harcourt-Vernon, eldest son of late Rev Evelyn Hardolph Harcourt-Vernon, 2nd son of late Granville Harcourt-Vernon, 7th son of Most Rev Hon Edward Harcourt (ante):—

Issue of late Capt Egerton Gervase Edward Harcourt-Vernon, MC, Gren Gds, *b* 1899, *d* 1976: *m* 1932, Norma, da of G. W. Hatherly:—

Anne Letitia, *b* 1933. —— Pamela Teresa Marygold, *b* 1938; *ed* Bedgebury Park, Medway Coll of Technology (BSc London), and Newnham Coll, Camb (MA): *m* 1961, Antony Dawson Cox, FRCP, FRCPsych, of Wenlsey Hall, nr Matlock, Derbys DE4 2LL, and has issue living, Simon, *b* 1962: *m* 1989, Antonia, da of E. Feuchtwanger, and has issue living, George Leo Vernon *b* 1994, — Nicholas, *b* 1964, — Hugo Francis *b* 1967. —— Rosalind Elizabeth Ida, *b* 1942: *m* 1966, Christopher Howell, of 36 Guards Club Rd, Maidenhead, and has issue living, Candida Justine, *b* 1969, — Madeleine Theresa, *b* 1977.

Grandchildren of late Herbert Evelyn Harcourt-Vernon, yst son of late Rev Evelyn Hardolph Harcourt-Vernon (ante):—

Issue of late Arthur Arundel Harcourt-Vernon, *b* 1895, *d* 1971: *m* 1925, Alice Margaret, who *d* 1977, da of late Rev Edward Cartwright Cayley (*see* Cayley, Bt, colls):—

Granville Patrick (57 Glengowan Rd, Toronto, Ont, Canada M4N IG3), *b* 1926; BA (Toronto), LLB, QC: *m* 1954, Deborah Perry Smith, and has issue living, Geoffrey William (20 Elmer Av, Toronto, Ont, Canada), *b* 1958; BA (Toronto), BLA (Guelph): *m* 1980 (*m diss* 1994), Cynthia Jane Gunn, and has issue living, Caitlin Elizabeth Gunn *b* 1988, Julia Robin Gunn *b* 1991, — Catherine Harcourt, *b* 1956; BA (Queens), MBA (Western Ont): *m* 1987, Robert Bruce McFarran Martin, of 71 Rosedale Heights Drive, Toronto, Ont, Canada, and has issue living, Richard Harcourt *b* 1988, Stephen Taylor *b* 1990, Scott Edward *b* 1993, — Susan Elizabeth *b* 1961; BSc (Queens), MBA (INSEAD): *m* 1992, Denis Pellerin, of 38 Av Albine, Bat B 78, 600, Maisons-Laffitte, France. —— Hugh, *b* 1930: *m* 1st, 1953, Elizabeth Virginia Richardson; 2ndly, 1978, Mrs Shirley Rose Archer, da of Cecil Ernest Woodford, of Prestatyn, co Clwyd, and has issue living (by 1st *m*), Christopher Hugh, *b* 1956, — Nancy Margaret, *b* 1960, — Tannis Elizabeth, *b* 1964. —— John Anthony, *b* 1938: *m* 1975, Susan Elaine, da of Thomas Tinniswood Vaulkhard, of Victoria, BC, and has issue living, Mark Nicholas, *b* 1984, — Stephen Andrew, *b* 1984, — Marin Georgina, *b* 1982. —— Joy, *b* 1934. —— Rosemary, *b* 1935: *m* 1960, Rev John Francis Moorhead (21 Winslow St, Chatham, New Brunswick, Canada), and has issue living, Margaret Patricia, *b* 1961, — Nancy Catherine, *b* 1967, — Cynthia Mabel, *b* 1970.

PREDECESSORS – (1) GEORGE Vernon, son of Henry Vernon of Sudbury, Derby, and Anne, da and heir of Thomas Pigott by Mary, sister and heir of Sir Peter Venables, Baron of Kinderton, Cheshire; MP for Lichfield; assumed in 1728 by Roy licence the additional surname of Venables and in 1762 was *cr Baron Vernon, Baron of Kinderton,* co Chester (peerage of Great Britain), *d* 1780; *s* by his el son **(2)** GEORGE, 2nd Baron; sat as MP for Glamorganshire 1774; *d* 1818; *s* by his half-brother **(3)** HENRY, 3rd Baron; *d* 1829; *s* by his son **(4)** GEORGE CHARLES, 4th Baron; *d* 1838; *s* by his son **(5)** GEORGE JOHN, 5th Baron; *b* 1803; assumed in 1837 by sign manual the surname of Warren only for himself and subsequent issue; *d* 1866; *s* by his son **(6)** AUGUSTUS HENRY, 6th Baron; *b* 1829: *m* 1851, Lady Harriet Frances Maria Anson, who *d* 1898, da of 1st Earl of Lichfield: *d* 1883; *s* by his son **(7)** GEORGE WILLIAM HENRY, PC, 7th Baron, *b* 1854; Capt Hon Corps of Gentlemen-at-Arms 1892-4: *m* 1885, Frances Margaret, who *d* 1940, da of Francis Lawrance, of New York; *d* 1898; *s* by his el son **(8)** GEORGE FRANCIS AUGUSTUS, 8th Baron, *b* 1888; (*ka* as Capt Derbyshire Yeo 1915); *s* by his brother **(9)** FRANCIS WILLIAM LAWRANCE, 9th Baron; *b* 1889; Lt-Cdr RN: *m* 1915, Violet Miriam Nightingale, who *d* 1978, da of late Lt-Col Charles Herbert Clay; *d* 1963; *s* by his only son **(10)** JOHN LAWRANCE, 10th Baron and present peer.

VERULAM, EARL OF (Grimston) (Earl UK 1815, Bt E 1629)

Moderate things are stable

JOHN DUNCAN GRIMSTON, 7th Earl and 14th Baronet; *b* 21 April 1951; *s* 1973; *ed* Eton, and Ch Ch, Oxford: *m* 1976, Dione Angela, el da of Jeremy Fox Eric Smith, of The Old Rectory, Slaugham, Handcross, W Sussex (*see* Burrell, Bt), and has issue.

Arms – Quarterly: 1st and 4th argent, on a fesse sable, three rowels of six points or pierced gules; in the dexter chief an ermine spot sable, *Grimston*; 2nd sable, a fesse dancettée between two leopards' faces or, *Luckyn*; 3rd argent, three bugle horns sable, stringed gules, *Forrester*. **Crest** – A stag's head erased proper, attired or. **Supporters** – *Dexter*, a stag reguardant proper, attired or; *sinister*, a griffin reguardant or. **Seat** – Gorhambury, St Albans, Herts.

SONS LIVING

JAMES WALTER (*Viscount Grimston*), *b* 6 Jan 1978.
Hon Hugo Guy Sylvester, *b* 1979.
Hon Sam George, *b* 1983.

DAUGHTER LIVING

Lady Flora Hermione, *b* 1981.

SISTERS LIVING

Lady Hermione Frances GRIMSTON (Old Pondyards, Redbourn Rd, St Albans, Herts), *b* 1941; resumed the surname of Grimston: *m* 1st, 1965 (*m diss* 1971), Richard John Perronet Thompson; 2ndly, 1971 (*m diss* 1982), James Darell Dickson Thompson-Schwab.
Lady Romayne Bryony, *b* 1946: *m* 1973, John Roberts Bockstoce, of 1 Hill St, S Dartmouth, Mass 02748, USA, and has issue living, John Grimston, *b* 1976.
Lady Iona Charlotte (*Countess of Mount Charles*), *b* 1953: *m* 1985, as his 2nd wife, Henry Vivian Pierpoint, Earl of Mount Charles, eldest son of 7th Marquess Conyngham. *Residence* – Slane Castle, co Meath.

WIDOW LIVING OF SIXTH EARL

MARJORIE RAY (*Dowager Countess of Verulam*) (Pré Mill House, Redbourn Rd, St Albans, Herts), da of late Walter Atholl Duncan: *m* 1938, the 6th Earl, who *d* 1973.

COLLATERAL BRANCHES LIVING

(In remainder to Lordship of Forrester of Corstorphine only)

Issue of late Lady Elisabeth Hariot Grimston, eldest da of 6th Earl, *b* 1939, *d* 1987: *m* 1958 (*m diss* 1972), John Christopher George, Viscount Pollington (later 8th Earl of Mexborough):—
See E Mexborough.

Issue of late Lady Helen Grimston, eldest da of 3rd Earl, *b* 1879, *d* 1947: *m* 1908, Rt Hon Sir Felix Cassel, 1st Bt, who *d* 1953:—
See Cassel, Bt.

Issue of late Lady Hermione Grimston, 2nd da of 3rd Earl, *b* 1831, *d* 1924: *m* 1904, Cdr Bernard Buxton, DSO, RN, who *d* 1923:—
See Buxton, Bt, colls.

Grandchildren of late Lady Aline Grimston, 3rd da of 3rd Earl:—
Issue of late (Peter) Cedric Barnett, *b* 1910, *d* 1980: *m* 1941, Sylvia Irina, OBE (7 Upper Belgrave St, SW1), da of Lt-Col William David Kenny, OBE, of Dun Laoghaire, co Dublin:—
Ulric David BARNETT, *b* 1942; *ed* Eton, and Magdalen Coll, Oxford: *m* 1969, Marie-Jane, da of Capt de Frégate Jean Levasseur, and has issue living, Rory Nicholas, *b* 1971, — Oliver Louis, *b* 1979, — Natalie Aline, *b* 1974. *Residence* – Towersey Manor, Thame, Oxon OX9 3QR. —— Patricia (26 Stanhope Gdns, SW7), *b* 1945: *m* 1st, 1968 (*m diss* 1975), Oscar Jorge Potier; 2ndly, 1975 (*m diss* 1979), Dennis Nagle; 3rdly, 1979, Samuel Kenneth Henry Goodenough, who *d* 1983, yst son of Sir William Macnamara Goodenough, 1st Bt, and has issue living (by 1st *m*), Rupert Alexander, *b* 1969, — (by 2nd *m*), Patricia, *b* 1975. —— Susan, *b* 1947: *m* 1967, Capt Charles Temple Blackwood, late Gren Gds, of Brickworth Park, White-parish, Salisbury, and has issue living, James Temple, *b* 1969, — Jonathan Charles, *b* 1971.

Grandchildren (by 1st *m*) of late Lady Elizabeth Motion (infra):—
Issue of late Maj Michael Hesketh-Prichard, RA, *b* 1909, *d* 1988: *m* 1938, Venetia Alice, who *d* 1992, da of late Sir Frederick Daniel Green:—
Richard Michael HESKETH-PRICHARD (1703 Calveryman Lane, Katy, Texas 77449, USA), *b* 1939; *ed* Fettes: *m* 1965 (*m diss* 1981), Elizabeth Susan, da of late John Cuthbert Ottaway, MBE, TD, of Beech Bottom, St Albans, and has issue living, James Michael, *b* 1966; *ed* Pembroke Coll, Camb, — Thomas Richard Edward, *b* 1969, — Rebecca Sophie Venetia, *b* 1971; *ed* Exeter Univ. —— Cicely Elizabeth Theodosia (Hill Cottage, Thurloxton, Taunton, Som), *b* 1942: *m* 1966 (*m diss* 19—), Martin Charles Jacoby, FLS, and has issue living, Charles John, *b* 1967, — Katherine Venetia, *b* 1970. —— Venetia, *b* 1948; *ed* Trin Coll, Dublin (BA): *m* 1972, David Richard Lascelles, of 60 Talbot Rd, Highgate, N6, and has issue living, Harry Francis, *b* 1978, — Alice Virginia, *b* 1976.

Issue of late Lady Elizabeth Grimston, 4th da of 3rd Earl, *b* 1885, *d* 1975: *m* 1st, 1908, Maj Hesketh Vernon Hesketh-Prichard, DSO, MC, who *d* 1922; 2ndly, 1927, Maj Thomas Augustus Motion, JP, who *d* 1942:—
(By 2nd *m*) Joan Elizabeth Mary (*Lady Stuart-Smith*), *b* 1929; *ed* St Anne's Coll, Oxford; JP, DL, High Sheriff Herts 1983: *m* 1953, Rt Hon Sir Murray Stuart-Smith, Lord Justice of Appeal, of Serge Hill, Abbots Langley, Herts, and has issue living, Jeremy Hugh (Pie Corner, Abbots Langley, Herts), *b* 1955; *ed* Radley, and Camb Univ (Corpus Scholar): *m* 1982, Hon

Arabella Clare Montgomery, da of 2nd Viscount Montgomery of Alamein, and has had issue, Edward Murray *b* 1988, Sam Nicholas *b* 1990, Luke David *b* 1993, Emma *b* 1984, Laura *b* 1986 *d* 1987, — Mark, *b* 1958; *ed* Radley, and Corpus Christie Coll, Camb, — Thomas Richard Steven Peregrine (The Barn, Serge Hill, Abbots Langley, Herts), *b* 1960; *ed* Radley, and Camb Univ (Corpus Scholar): *m* 1986, Dr Susan Jane Evans, da of late Bryan Evans, of Ardnadam House, Ardnadam, by Dunoon, Strathclyde, and has issue living, Benjamin *b* 1989, Harry Horatio *b* 1992, Rose *b* 1987, — Katherine, *b* 1957: *m* 1992, Dr David Docherty, of 16 Upper Addison Gdns, W14, and has issue living, Flora Olivia Annie *b* 1993, — Jane, *b* 1961: *m* 1992, Hugh Jonathan Earle Raven, of 14 Avondale Park Gdns, W11, — Elizabeth (twin), *b* 1961: *m* 1990, Adam Beck, elder son of Sir Philip Beck.

Issue of late Lady Sibyl Grimston, 5th da of 3rd Earl, *b* 1887, *d* 1968: *m* 1915, Maj Hon Alastair Thomas Joseph Fraser, DSO, who *d* 1949:—
See L Lovat, colls.

Issue of late Lady Vera Grimston, SRN, yst da of 3rd Earl, *b* 1890, *d* 1970: *m* 1922, Maurice Francis Headlam, CB, CMG, who *d* 1956:—
Anthony Francis HEADLAM (c/o Child & Co, 1 Fleet St, EC4), *b* 1923; *ed* Eton (KS), and King's Coll, Camb (Scholar); 1939-45 War with KRRC: *m* 1956 (*m diss* 1977), Jill Caroline, da of late Bruce R. Campbell, of Sydney, Aust, and has issue living, Hugh Francis, *b* 1960; *ed* Eton, — Caroline Ann, *b* 1963. —— †Christopher Grimston, *b* 1925; *ed* Eton (KS), and King's Coll, Camb (Scholar); 1939-45 War with RNVR: *m* 1959, Sarah, da of late Sir John Richard Hobhouse, MC, and *d* 1989, leaving issue, Thomas Walter, *b* 1962, — Catherine Sophia, *b* 1960. —— James Nicholas, *b* 1926; *ed* Eton, and New Coll, Oxford (Scholar): *m* 1966, Elizabeth Jane, da of Sir Peter William Shelley Yorke Scarlett, KCMG, KCVO, and has issue living, Anthony John Nicholas, *b* 1969, — Fenella Jane, *b* 1967, — Mary Amelia, *b* 1973.

(Male line in remainder to all peerages)

Grandchildren of late Rev Canon Hon Robert Grimson, 3rd son of 2nd Earl:—
Issue of late Sir Robert Villiers Grimston, *b* 1897, *d* 1979; *cr* a *Baronet* 1952, and *Baron Grimston of Westbury* 1964:—
See B Grimston of Westbury.

Grandson of late George Sylvester Grimston, son of late Rev Hon Francis Sylvester Grimston, 5th son of 1st Earl:—
Issue of late Francis Sylvester Grimston, CIE, *b* 1876, *d* 1969: *m* 1907, Eleanor Vincent, who *d* 1960, da of late Arthur W. L. Reddie:—
Francis Brian Sylvester (Lyn Cottage, Hound St, Sherborne, Dorset DTG 3AA; Royal Thames & Ocean Racing Clubs), *b* 1908; *ed* Cheltenham; late S/Ldr RAFVR: *m* 1940 (*m diss* 1954), Monica Katherine, who *d* 1978, da of late Col Hon Sir Maurice Charles Andrew Drummond, KBE, CMG, DSO (*see* E Perth, colls, 1980 Edn).

PREDECESSORS – (1) WILLIAM Luckyn (MP for St Albans), great-nephew of Sir Samuel Grimston, 3rd Bt (ext), whose surname he assumed on succeeding to the estates, was *cr Baron Dunboyne* and *Viscount Grimston* (peerage of Ireland) 1719, and in 1736 *s* his brother as 5th Bt (*cr* 1629); *d* 1756; *s* by his son (2) JAMES, 2nd Viscount; *d* 1773; *s* by his son (3) JAMES BUCKNALL, 3rd Viscount; *cr Baron Verulam*, of Gorhambury, co Herts (peerage of Great Britain) 1790; *d* 1809; *s* by his son (4) JAMES WALTER, 4th Viscount, who in 1808 had *s* his maternal cousin Anna Maria as 10th *Lord Forrester of Corstorphine* (see*infra*); *b* 1775; MP for St Albans 1802-8; Lord-Lieut of co Herts; *cr Earl of Verulam* (peerage of United Kingdom) 1815: *m* 1807, Lady Charlotte Jenkinson, da of 1st Earl of Liverpool; *d* 1845; *s* by his son (5) JAMES WALTER, 2nd Earl, *b* 1809; MP for St Albans (C) 1830, for Newport 1831; and for Hertfordshire 1832-45; a Lord-in-Waiting to HM Queen Victoria 1852 and 1858-9, sometime Lord-Lieut of Herts: *m* 1844, Elizabeth Joanna, who *d* 1886, da of Richard Weyland, of Woodeaton, Oxford; *d* 1895; *s* by his el son (6) JAMES WALTER, 3rd Earl, *b* 1852; MP for Mid, or St Albans, Div of Herts (C) 1885-92: *m* 1878, Margaret Frances, who *d* 1927, da of Sir Frederic Ulric Graham, 3rd Bt, of Netherby; *d* 1924; *s* by his son (7) JAMES WALTER, 4th Earl, *b* 1880: *m* 1909, Lady Violet Constance Maitland Brabazon, who *d* 1936, da of 12th Earl of Meath; *d* 1949; *s* by his son (8) JAMES BRABAZON, 5th Earl; *b* 1910; Mayor of St Albans 1956-7; *d* 1960; *s* by his brother (9) JOHN, 6th Earl, *b* 1912; MP for St Albans (C) 1943-45 and 1950-59: *m* 1938, Margaret Ray, da of Walter Duncan; *d* 1973; *s* by his son (10) JOHN DUNCAN, 7th Earl and present peer; also Viscount Grimston, Baron Verulam, Baron Dunboyne, and Lord Forrester of Corstorphine.

*(1)** GEORGE Forrester of Corstorphine, Midlothian, el son of Henry Forrester of Corstorphine; *cr Lord Forrester of Corstorphine* (peerage of Scotland) 1633, with remainder to his heirs male whatsoever; on the death of his only son without issue, he resigned his peerage and obtained a re-grant thereof 1651 with remainder to James Baillie, husband of his fifth da Joanna and their issue in tail male, remainder to William Baillie, husband of Lilias his sixth and yst da and their issue in tail male, remainder to the issue of James and William by their said wives, in tail general, the el da of such issue to be heir of line, with a final remainder to James Baillie and his heirs male or of entail made by him, all parties to bear the name and arms of Forrester jointly with his own: *m* 1606, Christian, da of Sir William Livingston of Kilsyth; *d* 1652; *s* by his son-in-law (2) JAMES Baillie (afterwards Forrester), 2nd Lord; *b* 1629; was fined £2,500 under Cromwell's Act of Grace 1654: *m* 1st, 1649, Joanna, da of 1st Lord Forrester of Corstorphine (ante); 2ndly, 1661, Janet, 3rd da and co-heir of Patrick Ruthven, 1st Earl of Forth and Brentford; *d* 1679; *s* by his brother (3) WILLIAM, *de jure* 3rd Lord; *b* 1632; did not assume the title: *m circa* 1650 Lilias, yst da of 1st Lord Forrester of Corstorphine (ante); *d* 1681; *s* by his son (4) WILLIAM, 4th Lord; *b* 16—: *m circa* 1684, Margaret, da of Sir Andrew Birnie, of Saline, Judge of Court of Session; *d* 1705; *s* by his son (5) GEORGE, 5th Lord; *b* 1688; Lt-Col 26th Foot (Cameronians), and Col 30th Foot, and of Horse Grenadier Guards: *m circa* 1724, Charlotte, who *d* 1743, da of Anthony Rowe; *d* 1727; *s* by his son (6) GEORGE, 6th Lord; *b* 1724; Capt RN; *d unm* 1748; *s* by his cousin (7) WILLIAM (son of Capt Hon John Forrester, RN, yst son of 4th Lord), 7th Lord: *m* 17—, Hannah—, who *d* 1825; *d* 1763; *s* by his cousin (8) CAROLINE, el sister of 6th Lord (who *s* under terms of special remainder); *b* 17—: *m* 17—, Capt George Cockburn of Ormiston, RN, who *d* 1770; *d* 1784; *s* by her da (9) ANNA MARIA: *b* 17—; *d unm* 1808; *s* by her cousin (10) JAMES WALTER Grimston, son of James Bucknall Grimston, 3rd Viscount Grimston, by Harriet, da and heir of Edward Walter, and Hon Harriet Forrester, yst da of 5th Lord, who in 1809 *s* as 4th Viscount Grimston (ante).

VESTEY, BARON (Vestey) (Baron UK 1922, Bt UK 1913)

SAMUEL GEORGE ARMSTRONG VESTEY, 3rd Baron, and 3rd Baronet; *b* 19 March 1941; *s* 1954; *ed* Eton; Lt Scots Gds; patron of one living; DL Glos 1982; GCStJ, Chancellor Order of St John 1988-91, since when Lord Prior: *m* 1st, 1970 (*m diss* 1981), Kathryn Mary, el da of John Eccles, of Moor Park, Herts; 2ndly, 1981, Celia Elizabeth, da of late Maj (Hubert) Guy Broughton Knight, MC, of Lockinge Manor, Wantage, Oxon, and has issue by 1st and 2nd *m*.

Arms – Azure, in base barry wavy of four argent and of the first an iceberg issuant proper, on a chief of the second three eggs also proper. **Crest** – In front of a springbok's head couped at the neck proper three mullets fessewise azure. **Supporters** – *Dexter*, a sheep proper; *sinister*, a bull argent.
Residence – Stowell Park, Northleach, nr Cheltenham, Glos GL54 3LE.

From labour stability

SONS LIVING *(By 2nd marriage)*

Hon WILLIAM GUY, *b* 27 Aug 1983.
Hon Arthur George, *b* 1985.

DAUGHTERS LIVING *(By 1st marriage)*

Hon Saffron Alexandra, *b* 1971.
Hon Flora Grace, *b* 1978.

(By 2nd marriage)

Hon Mary Henrietta, *b* 1992.

BROTHER LIVING

(Raised to the rank of a Baron's son 1955)

Hon Mark William (Foxcote Manor, Andoversford, Glos), *b* 1943; *ed* Eton; 2nd Lt Scots Guards: *m* 1975, Rose Amelia, da of Lt-Col Peter Thomas Clifton, *CVO*, DSO (*see* Bruce, Bt, *cr* 1804), and has issue living, Benjamin John, *b* 1979, — Tamara Pamela, *b* 1976, — Carina Patricia, *b* 1982.

MOTHER LIVING *(Raised to the rank of a Baron's Widow 1955)*

(HELEN) PAMELA FULLERTON (MELBA) (*Pamela, Baroness Vestey*), da of late George Nesbitt Armstrong (*see* Armstrong, Bt, *cr* 1841, colls): *m* 1939, Capt Hon William Howarth Vestey, Scots Guards, who was *ka* in Italy 1944. *Residence* – Coombe Cottage, Coldstream, Vic, Australia.

COLLATERAL BRANCHES LIVING

Issue of late Hon George Ellis Vestey, 2nd son of 1st Baron, *b* 1884, *d* 1968: *m* 1909, Florence May, who *d* 1964, da of Thomas Webster, of Melling, Lancs:—
Florence Mary (Vines Cottage, Kidmore End, Reading, Berks), *b* 1913: *m* 1945, Anthony Hugh Stevens, TD, late Maj RA, who *d* 1979, and has issue living, Hugh Charles (The Hall, Thorpe Arnold, Melton Mowbray, Leics LE14 4RU), *b* 1946; *ed* Winchester, and Univ of Michigan (BA): *m* 1st, 1972 (*m diss* 1993), Nicola Priscilla, da of John Bridgman, of Woodroffes, Marchington Woodlands, Staffs; 2ndly, 1993, Gabriele Maria Irmingard Nuesslein, of Munich, and has issue living (by 2nd wife), Delia Mary Susanne *b* 1991, Sophie Clara Charlotte *b* 1993, — Angela Mary, *b* 1948: *m* 1972, Aubrey John Adams of Vines Farm, Kidmore End, Reading, Berks, and has issue living, Katherine Mary Alicia *b* 1975, Sara Angela Rose *b* 1978, Felicity Nichole Elizabeth *b* 1983. —— Norah (Knockarron, Enniskerry, co Wicklow) *b* 1916: *m* 1944, Maj William Bellingham Denis Dobbs, R Ulster Rifles (ret), who *d* 1982, and has issue living, George Denis Kildare, *b* 1947: *m* 1975, Prunella Osborne, da of Osborne David Philips, of Sheephill, Dunganstown, co Wicklow, and has issue living, Kildare Denis David *b* 1979, Edward George *b* 1982, Emily Norah *b* 1977, — Rosemary Florence, *b* 1944: *m* 1971, David Michael Cochrane Elsworth Steen (*see* Cochrane, Bt), — Susan Norah, *b* 1951: *m* 1978, Nigel Atkinson, of 43 Bramerton St, SW3, and has issue living, Anna Venetia *b* 1980, Camilla Mary *b* 1983. —— Alice (Appleton House, Appleton-le-Street, Malton, N Yorks, YO17 0PG), *b* 1918: *m* 1st, 1939, William Ernest Legard, F/O, RAF, who was *ka* 1940 (*see* Legard, Bt, colls); 2ndly, 1943, Col Basil Perry Beale, OBE, MC, DL, RASC, who *d* 1967, and has issue living, (by 1st *m*) (*see* Legard, Bt, colls), — (by 2nd *m*) Richard Basil William, *b* 1944: *m* 1981, Siao-Li Liao, and has issue living, Jennifer Mary Alice *b* 1982, Alice Elizabeth May *b* 1985, — Stephen Dudley Norman, *b* 1950: *m* 1st, 1972 (*m diss* 1978), Elizabeth Helen, da of Peter Green, of The Rookery, Kirkby Malham, Skipton, Yorks; 2ndly, 1978, Jo-Anna Mary Munt, da of Arthur Harry Cook, of Church Farm, Wavendon, Bucks, and has issue living (by 1st *m*), Zoë Helen *b* 1973, (by 2nd *m*) Rollo Basil Arthur *b* 1982, — Elizabeth Alice, *b* 1947: *m* 1975, Anthony David Stanbury, of Lewcombe Manor, E Chelborough, Dorchester, Dorset, and has issue living, Alexander George Basil *b* 1978, Edward Samuel Joseph *b* 1982, Caroline Alice *b* 1976, Victoria Elizabeth Sophie *b* 1984.

Issue of late Hon Leonard Vestey, 3rd son of 1st Baron, *b* 1888, *d* 1954: *m* 1st, 1919 (*m diss* 1931), Hilda Dorothy, da of Thomas Thompson; 2ndly, 1931, Eleanor Margery (who *d* 1972, having *m* 3rdly, 1955, Dr Richard Taylor, and 4thly, 19—, Frank Fisher), widow of Capt F. W. H. Simpson, RA:—
(By 1st *m*) Joyce (19 Elamang Av, Kirribilli, Sydney, NSW 2061), *b* 1920: *m* 1st, 1949 (*m diss* 1953), Henry Willis Maxwell Telling, who *d* 1993; 2ndly, 1966, Dr Thomas Hugh Strong, who *d* 1988, and has issue living, (by 1st *m*) Michael Henry Maxwell *b* 1950: *m* 1st, 1978 (*m diss* 1981), Alison Ruth Webber; 2ndly, 1981, Monika Elizabeth, who *d* 1983, da of Louis Zumsteg, of Santa Rosa, Calif, USA, and has issue living (by 1st *m*), Matthew James Maxwell *b* 1979. —— Elizabeth Anne (26 Eldon Rd, W8), *b* 1923: *m* 1946 (*m diss* 1962), Lt-Cdr Patrick Brougham, RN, and has issue living, Christopher John (34 Launceston Place, W8), *b* 1947; *ed* Radley, and Worcester Coll, Oxford (BA); Bar Inner Temple 1969, QC 1988: *m* 1974, Mary Olwen, da of Timothy Traherne Corker, of 19 Park Sq East, NW1, and has issue living, William Charles Rupert *b* 1977, Emily Clarissa *b* 1979, Miranda Jane Thérèse *b* 1982, Deborah Anne Rosemary *b* 1988, — Nicholas Dominic Leonard (Ampfield House, Blackheath, Guildford, Surrey GU4 8RD), *b* 1954; *ed* Radley: *m* 1982, Susan, da of Thomas Frederick Vernon Mason, of Carbery Lodge, Farley Green, Albury, Surrey, and has issue living, Thomas Edward Alexander *b* 1988, Caroline Fiona Jane *b* 1984, Claire Emma Louise *b* 1986, — Margaret Elizabeth Jane, *b* 1948: *m* 1st, 1970 (*m diss* 1982), Hugh Robert John Simpson; 2ndly, 1982, John Arthur William Webber, of 8 Elm Rd, Beckenham, Kent, BR3 4JB, and has had issue (by 1st *m*), Antony John *b* 1972 *d* 1986, Tracey Jane *b* 1975.

PREDECESSORS – (1) WILLIAM Vestey, el son of Samuel Vestey, of Liverpool; *b* 1859; was Joint Head of Blue Star Line; *cr* a *Baronet* 1913, and *Baron Vestey*, of Kingswood, co Surrey (peerage of United Kingdom) 1922: *m* 1st, 1882, Sarah, who *d* 1923, da of George Ellis; 2ndly, 1924, Evelyn, who *d* 1941, da of H. Brodstone, of Superior, Nebraska, USA; *d* 1940; *s* by his el son (2) SAMUEL, 2nd Baron; *b* 1882; High Sheriff of Gloucestershire 1953: *m* 1908, Frances Sarah, who *d* 1969, da of John Richard Howarth, of Freshfield, Lancs; *d* 1954; *s* by his grandson (3) SAMUEL GEORGE ARMSTRONG (son of late Capt Hon William Howarth Vestey, only son of 2nd Baron), 3rd Baron and present peer.

Villiers, Viscount; son of Earl of Jersey.

VINSON, BARON (Vinson) (Life Baron 1985)

NIGEL VINSON, LVO, son of late Ronald Vinson, of Nettlestead Place, Wateringbury, Kent, by his 2nd wife, Bettina Myra Olivia, da of Dr Gerald Southwell-Sanders; *b* 27 Jan 1931; *ed* RNC Pangbourne; Lieut Queen's Royal Regt 1949-51; DL Northumberland 1990; foundation donor Martin Mere Wildfowl Trust; founder (Chm 1952-72) Plastic Coatings Ltd; Dir Centre for Policy Studies 1974-80; Hon Dir Queen's Silver Jubilee Appeal 1976-78; Chm Rural Development Commn 1980-90, and Industrial Participation Assocn 1971-79; Dep Chm Electra Investment Trust plc since 1989, Chm of Trustees of the Inst of Economic Affairs since 1989, and Trustee St George's House Windsor Castle since 1989; FRSA; *cr* LVO 1979, and *Baron Vinson*, of Roddam Dene, co Northumberland (Life Baron) 1985: *m* 1972, Yvonne Ann, da of Dr Olaf Collin, of Forest Row, Sussex, and has issue.

Arms – Per pale gules and azure, a cross formy argent, on a chief per pale azure and gules two bull's heads caboshed argent armed or and crowned with a crown rayonny each straight ray ensigned by a mullet gold. Crest – Upon a helm with a wreath argent, azure and gules within a garland of vine leaves or a demi-ounce azure. Supporters – *dexter*— An ounce rampant sable semy of mullets or gorged with a garland of vine leaves gold; *sinister*— A horse rampant argent also gorged with a garland of vine leaves gold, the compartment comprising two grassy hillocks and in the valley between them water barry wavy of six azure and argent.

Residence – Roddam Hall, by Alnwick, Northumberland. *Address* – 34 Kynance Mews, SW7. *Club* – Boodle's.

DAUGHTERS LIVING

Hon Bettina Claire, *b* 1974.
Hon Rowena Ann, *b* 1977.
Hon Antonia Charlotte, *b* 1979.

VIVIAN, BARON (Vivian) (Baron UK 1841, Bt UK 1828)

Live, as one about to live hereafter

NICHOLAS CRESPIGNY LAURENCE VIVIAN, 6th Baron, and 6th Baronet; *b* 11 Dec 1935; *s* 1991; *ed* Eton, and Madrid Univ; commn'd 3rd Carabiniers 1955, Royal Scots Dragoon Gds 1971, Comdg Officer 16/5th The Queen's Royal Lancers 1976-79, Col MOD 1979-84, Dep Cmdr Land Forces Cyprus, and Ch of Staff 1984-87, Cmdr British Communication Zone NW Europe 1987-90, ret 1990 as Brig: *m* 1st, 1960 (*m diss* 1972), Catherine Joyce, yst da of James Kenneth Hope, CBE, DL, of West Park, Lanchester, co Durham; 2ndly, 1972, Carol, elder da of late (Frederick) Alan Martineau, MBE, JP, of Valley End House, Chobham, Surrey, and has issue by 1st and 2nd *m*.

Arms – Or, a chevron azure, between three lions' heads erased proper, as many annulets gold; on a chief embattled gules, a wreath of oak or, between two medals, that on the dexter representing the gold medal and clasp given to the first baron for his services in the actions of Sahagun, Benevente and Orthes; and that on the sinister the silver Waterloo medal. Crest – Issuant from a bridge of one arch embattled, and having at each end a tower, a demi-hussar, in the uniform of the 18th Regt holding in his right hand a sabre, and in his left a pennon flying to the sinister gules, and inscribed with gold letters, "Croix d'Orade". Supporters – *Dexter*, a grey horse caparisoned, thereon mounted a hussar of the 7th Regt of Light Dragoons (Hussars) habited, armed and accoutred, his sword drawn proper; *sinister*, a bay horse guardant, caparisoned, thereon mounted a lancer of the 12th Regt of Lancers, habited, armed and accoutred, supporting his lance, also proper.

Clubs - White's, Cavalry and Guards'.

SONS LIVING *(By 1st marriage)*

Hon CHARLES CRESPIGNY HUSSEY, *b* 20 Dec 1966; *ed* Milton Abbey.

DAUGHTERS LIVING *(By 1st marriage)*

Hon Henrietta Mary, *b* 1963: *m* 1984, Philip John Hoyland, son of Dr Hugh James Hoyland, of Clarelands, Painswick, Glos, and has issue living, Jack Nicholas Hope, *b* 1985, — George Hugh James, *b* 1991, — Francesca Mary Jane, *b* 1986. *Residences* – 14 Starmead Drive, Wokingham, Berks; Box Green, Box, Nailsworth, Glos.

(by 2nd marriage)

Hon Natasha Sarah, *b* 1973.
Hon Camilla Harriet, *b* 1976.

BROTHER LIVING

Hon Victor Anthony Ralph Brabazon, *b* 1940; *ed* Nautical Coll, Pangbourne, and Southampton Univ; late Merchant Navy: *m* 1966, Inger Johanne, yr da of Advokat Per Gulliksen, of Sandfjord, Norway, and has issue living, Thomas Crespigny Brabazon, *b* 1971; *ed* Marlborough, and Grenoble Univ, — Arabella Victoria, *b* 1973. *Residence* – 26 Roehampton Close, Roehampton Lane, SW15 5LU.

SISTER LIVING

Hon Sally Ann Marie Gabrielle, *b* 1930: *m* 1st, 1954 (*m diss* 1962), (William) Robin Charles Edward Cecil Lowe, son of late John Muir Lowe (actor, as John Loder); 2ndly, 1963, Charles William Munro Wilson, son of late Charles Skinner Wilson, and has issue living (by 2nd *m*), Alexander Vivian, *b* 1965; *ed* Shiplake Coll. *Residence* – 150 Cranmer Court, Whiteheads Grove, SW3 3HF.

AUNT LIVING *(daughter of 4th Baron)*

Hon Daphne Winifred Louise, *b* 1904; author and biographer, *Mercury Presides, The Duchess of Jermyn Street: The Life and Times of Rosa Lewis, The Adonis Garden, Emerald and Nancy, The Nearest Way Home, The Rainbow Picnic: A Portrait of Iris Tree, The Face on the Sphinx: A Portrait of Gladys Deacon, Duchess of Marlborough*, etc: *m* 1st, 1926 (*m diss* 1953), 6th Marquess of Bath, who *d* 1992; 2ndly, 1953 (*m diss* 1978), Maj Alexander (Xan) Wallace Fielding, DSO, who *d* 1991. *Residence* – Old Laundry, Badminton, Avon.

WIDOW LIVING OF SON OF FOURTH BARON

Mary Alice (Monastery Garden, Edington, Westbury, Wilts), da of late Francis John Gordon Borthwick, WS (*see* L Borthwick, colls): *m* 1943, Lt-Cdr Hon Douglas David Edward Vivian, DSC, RN, who *d* 1973, and has issue (see colls infra).

COLLATERAL BRANCHES LIVING

    Issue of late Lt-Cdr Hon Douglas David Edward Vivian, DSC, RN, yr son of 4th Baron, *b* 1915, *d* 1973: *m* 1943, Mary Alice (ante), da of late Francis John Gordon Borthwick, WS (*see* L Borthwick, colls):—
Deborah Mary, *b* 1944; JP: *m* 1971, Nicholas John Hinton, CBE, of 22 Westmoreland Place, SW1V 4AE, and has issue living, Josephine Mary Vivian, *b* 1984. —— Rose Emma Margaret, *b* 1945: *m* 1st, 1965 (*m diss* 1973), James Collet Norman; 2ndly, 1973, Benjamin B. W. Goodden, of Ferryside, Riverside, Twickenham, Middx, and has issue living (by 1st *m*), Rupert Montagu, *b* 1966, — Jason Douglas, *b* 1968, — Melissa Rose, *b* 1970, — (by 2nd *m*) Timothy Simon, *b* 1980. —— Eugenie Nancy (Pear Tree Cottage, Bratton, nr Westbury, Wilts), *b* 1947: *m* 1966 (*m diss* 1988), Capt Simon N. J. Burne, 9th/12th R Lancers, and has issue living, Thomas Edward Francis, *b* 1980, — Lucy Caroline, *b* 1970. —— Victoria Alice (twin), *b* 1947: *m* 1972, Nicholas Charlton Dudley Craig, of Piper Close, Corbridge, Northumberland, and has issue living, Richard Nicholas Dudley, *b* 1976, — Edward Douglas Charlton, *b* 1977, — George David Vivian, *b* 1982. —— Charlotte Claire, *b* 1950: *m* 1971, Charles Robert Dimpfl, of 19 Gledhow Gdns, SW5 0AZ, and has issue living, Francesca Mary, *b* 1979, — Daisy Charlotte, *b* 1985, — Nancy Alice Rose, *b* 1990.

    Granddaughter of late Lieut-Col Claud Esmé Vivian, MC (infra):—
    Issue of late Capt Claud Panton Vivian, RHA, *b* 1920, *d* of wounds received in action in Normandy 1944: *m* 1943, Margaret Eleanor (who *m* 2ndly, 1947, Charles Dundas Lawrie, of Plâs Gwyn, Pentraeth, Anglesey), only da of Alec E. Baird, OBE, of Hailes Brae, Colinton, Edinburgh:—
Amanda Mary Panton, *b* 1944.

    Grandchildren of late Hon Claud Hamilton Vivian, 4th son of 2nd Baron:—
    Issue of late Lieut-Col Claud Esmé Vivian, MC, *b* 1882, *d* 1928: *m* 1914, Emily, da of late Col Michael Rowan Gray Buchanan, OBE (M Bute, colls):—
Elizabeth Frederica Amesbury, *b* 1916: *m* 1947, Maj Claude Fanning-Evans, JP, DL, late Durham LI. *Residence* – Plas Cadnant, Menair Bridge, Anglesey. —— Ann (Cae Du, Dwyran, Anglesey), *b* 1923: *m* 1953, Desmond Brennan, MB, who *d* 1970, and has issue living, Vincent Patrick Esme, *b* 1958, — Claire Patricia Ann, *b* 1956, — Hazel Mary, *b* 1961.
    Issue of late Capt Eric Paul Vivian, RN, *b* 1891, *d* 1961: *m* 1922, Evelyn Audrey (Hook Cottage, Hambledon, Hants), el da of Capt Thomas Pryse Arthur Holford, late 10th Hussars, of Duntish Court, Buckland Newton, Dorset:—
†Desmond Walter Paul, *b* 1925; *ed* Harrow; Capt 12th Lancers; served 1939-45 War (despatches twice): *m* 1949, Rose (Langford Gate, Sydling St Nicholas, Dorset), da of Capt Charles Houssemayne du Boulay, RN, of Exton House, Exton, Hants, and *d* 1974, leaving issue, Christopher John Desmond, *b* 1956; *ed* Harrow: *m* 1984, Alice Camilla, yst da of John Brian Hollingsworth, of Cruea, Llanfrothen, Penrhyndeudraeth, Gwynned, and has issue living, Alastair Desmond *b* 1991, — Vanda Rose, *b* 1950, — Clare Veronica, *b* 1952. —— Patrick Cyril, *b* 1929; *ed* Camb Univ (BA 1950, MA 1958, MB and BCh 1953, DRCOG 1958); late Capt RAMC: *m* 1961, Pamela Mary, da of Lieut-Col Richard Rees Davies, JP, DL, of Ceris, Bangor, Caernarvonshire, and has issue living, Simon Paul Richard, *b* 1962: *m* 1988, Rose Rookmin, da of Dr Balideo Bisseru, of Lusaka, Kenya, and of Bromley, Kent, — Susan Caroline, *b* 1964. *Residence* – Pumney, Sutton Courtenay, nr Abingdon, Berks. —— Charles Evelyn, *b* 1937. *Residence* – Hook Cottage, Hambledon, Hants.
    Issue of late Capt Robert Crespigny Gwynedd Vivian, LG, *b* 1898, *d* 1984: *m* 1925, Violet Clinton, who *d* 1993, da of Clinton Holme, of Ruthin, N Wales:—
Robin Audley Clinton (B92 Res Amiral, Marina Baie des Anges, 06270 Villeneuve-Loubet, France), *b* 1936; *ed* Eton: *m* 1961, Alice Penelope, only da of late Lt Caesar Charles Hawkins, DSC, RN (*see* Hawkins, Bt, colls), and has issue living, Rupert James, *b* 1970, — Claire Jennifer, *b* 1971. —— Edith Evelyn CLINTON (Hawthorne Cottage, Pitmore Lane, Sway, Lymington, Hants), *b* 1926: *m* 1954 (*m diss* 1975), Arnold Euston More Bloomer, and has issue living, Anthony Leonard Clinton, *b* 1964: *m* 1993, Harriet Ann, only da of Timothy George Kirkbride (*see* Baker Wilbraham, Bt), — Angela Gwyneth More, *b* 1960: *m* 1988, John Jardine Hearne Slater.

PREDECESSORS – **(1)** *Sir* RICHARD HUSSEY Vivian, GCB, GCMG, GCH, PC, etc; *b* 1775; a Lt-Gen in the Army, and a distinguished soldier, cmdg 7th Lt Dragoons throughout the Peninsula Campaign and the Light Cavalry Bde at Waterloo; was Col 1st R Dragoons, Com of the Forces in Ireland, MP for Windsor, Equerry to George IV, and Master Gen of Ordnance 1835-41; *cr* a *Baronet* 1828, and *Baron Vivian*, of Glynn, and of Truro, co Cornwall (peerage of United Kingdom) 1841: *m* 1st, 1804, Eliza, da of Philip Champion de Crespigny, of Aldborough, Suffolk; *d* 1842; *s* by his son **(2)** CHARLES CRESPIGNY, 2nd Baron; sat as MP for Bodmin (*L*) 1837-42: was Lord-Lieut of Cornwall 1856-77: *m* 1st, 1833, Arabella, who *d* 1837, da of Rev John Middleton Scott, of Ballygannon, co Wicklow; 2ndly, 1841, Mary Elizabeth, who *d* 1907, el da of Jones Panton, of Plasgwyn, Anglesey; *d* 24 April 1886; *s* by his son **(3)** HUSSEY CRESPIGNY, GCMG, CB, PC, 3rd Baron, *b* 1834; Agent and Consul-Gen in Moldavia and Wallachia 1874-6, and in Egypt 1876-9, Min at Berne 1879-81, Envoy Extraor and Min Plen to Swiss Confederation 1881, to Denmark 1881-4, and at Brussels 1884-9, and Ambassador Extraor and Plen to Rome 1891-3: *m* 1876, Louisa Alice, who *d* 1926, da of Robert George Duff, of Wellington Lodge Ryde; *d* 1893: *s* by his only son **(4)** GEORGE CRESPIGNY BRABAZON, DSO, 4th Baron, *b* 1878; Col (ret) TA; sometime Major 17th Lancers; S Africa 1900-01, European War 1914-18 (DSO): *m* 1st, 1903 (*m diss* 1907), Barbara, da of late William Atmar Fanning; 2ndly, 1911, Nancy Lycett, MBE, who *d* 1970, da of Sir Edward Lycett Green, 2nd Bt (*cr* 1886), and widow of Capt Adrian Rose, Roy Horse Guards; *d* 1940; *s* by his son **(5)** ANTHONY CRESPIGNY CLAUD, 5th Baron; *b* 1906; European War 1939-40 in RA, Special Constabulary and War Correspondent; Theatrical Impressario: *m* 1930, Victoria Ruth Mary Rosamond, who *d* 1985, da of Capt Henry Gerard Laurence Oliphant, DSO, MVO, RN; *d* 1991; *s* by his elder son **(6)** NICHOLAS CRESPIGNY LAURENCE, 6th Baron and present peer.

WADDINGTON, BARON (Waddington) (Life Baron 1990)

DAVID CHARLES WADDINGTON, GCVO, PC, QC, son of late Charles Waddington, JP, of The Old Vicarage, Read, Lancs; *b* 2 Aug 1929; *ed* Sedbergh, and Hertford Coll, Oxford; DL Lancs 1991; 2nd Lieut 12th Royal Lancers 1951-53; Bar Gray's Inn 1951, QC 1971, Recorder 1972, Bencher 1985; sometime Dir J. J. Broadley Ltd, J. and J. Roberts Ltd, and Wolstenholme Rink Ltd; MP Nelson and Colne (*C*) 1968-74, Clitheroe 1979-83, Ribble Valley 1983-90; Lord Commr HM Treasury 1979-81, Parly Under Sec Employment 1981-83, Min of State Home Office 1983-87, Govt Chief Whip 1987-89, Home Sec 1989-90, Lord Privy Seal and Leader House of Lords 1990-92, since when Gov of Bermuda; *cr* PC 1987, GCVO 1994, and *Baron Waddington*, of Read, co Lancs (Life Baron) 1990: *m* 1958, Gillian Rosemary, da of Alan Green, CBE, of The Stables, Sabden, Lancs, and has issue.

𝕬rms – Ermine on a cross azure a lions' head gardant or langued gules between four roses gules barbed and seeded proper. 𝕮rest – An arm embowed vested azure issuing from the sleeve of a silk's gown sable the hand proper holding a wreath of four roses gules barbed and seeded proper enfiled by a sword point upwards argent, hilt, pommel and quillons gold. 𝕾upporters – *dexter*— A lion in trian aspect; *sinister*— A griffin, both or, armed and langued gules, gorged with a bar dancetty ermine edged azure, each statant erect amid reeds growing from a grassy mount proper.
Residences – Government House, Bermuda; Whins House, Sabden, nr Blackburn, Lancs; 9 Denny St, SE11. *Club* – Cavalry and Guards'.

SONS LIVING

Hon James Charles, *b* 1960.
Hon Matthew David, *b* 1962.
Hon Alistair Paul, *b* 1965.

DAUGHTERS LIVING

Hon Jennifer Rosemary, *b* 1965.
Hon Victoria Jane, *b* 1971.

WADE, BARONY OF (Wade) (Extinct 1988)

SONS LIVING OF LIFE BARON

Hon Donald William Mercer, *b* 1941, *ed* Silcoates Sch, and at Trin Hall, Camb (MA).
Hon Robert Alexander Mercer (The Old Rectory, Barwick-in-Elmet, Leeds, W Yorks), *b* 1943; *ed* Mill Hill, and Trin Coll, Camb (MA, LLM); Solicitor 1968: *m* 1st 1967, Jennifer Jane, da of Leslie Elliott, of Grantley Grange, High Grantley, Ripon; 2ndly, 1978, Elizabeth, da of James Lobban, of 24 Lintrathen Gdns, Dundee, and has issue living, (by 1st *m*) Michael Richard, *b* 1968, — Juliet Helen, *b* 1970, — (by 2nd *m*) Alistair James Mercer, *b* 1982, — Katherine Elizabeth, *b* 1985.

DAUGHTERS LIVING OF LIFE BARON

Hon Helen Mary, *b* 1933: *m* 1963, Rev Dr Lionel Wickham, of The Vicarage, West Wratting, Cambridge, and has issue living, three sons, and one da, of whom, the 2nd son Henry J., *b* 1966: *m* 1991, Madeleine S., eldest da of David Townley, of Wimbledon.
Hon Rosalind Beatrice, *b* 1937: *m* 1961, Richard David Morrish, solicitor, of 34 St Margaret's Rd, Horsforth, Leeds, and has issue living, Jonathan R., *b* 1964: *m* 1992, Katharine L. Brown, and has issue living, one da, — Thomas Wade, *b* 1966: *m* 1993, Sarah J. Challinor, — a da.

ELLENORA BEATRICE (*Baroness Wade*), da of F. H. Bentham, of Bradford: *m* 1932, Baron Wade (Life Baron), who *d* 1988. *Residence* – Meadowbank, Wath Rd, Pateley Bridge, N Yorks.

WADE OF CHORLTON, BARON (Wade) (Life Baron 1990)

WILLIAM OULTON WADE, son of Samuel Norman Wade, of Chester; *b* 24 Dec 1932; *ed* Birkenhead Sch, and Queen's Univ, Belfast; CC Cheshire 1973-77; Dir Murray Vernon (Holdings) Ltd, John Wilman Ltd, Millers Damsell Ltd, Inward, and Fletchers Stores Ltd, Chm Marlow Wade and Partners Ltd, Consultants, Nimtech Ltd, and P.I. Political Consultants Ltd; Chm English Cheese Export Council 1982-84; Chm Parly Rural Economy Group; JP Cheshire 1967, Freeman City of London 1980, Liveryman Farmers' Co since 1980; Joint Treasurer Conservative Party 1982-90; *cr* Knt 1982, and *Baron Wade of Chorlton*, of Chester, co Cheshire (Life Baron) 1990: *m* 1959, Gillian Margaret, da of Desmond Leete, of Buxton, Derbys, and has issue.
Residence – Chorlton Lodge Farm, Chorlton-by-Backford, Chester CH2 4DB. *Clubs* – Carlton, Farmers', St James's (Manchester), City (Chester).

SON LIVING

Hon Christopher James, *b* 1961.

DAUGHTER LIVING

Hon Alexandra Jane, *b* 1964.

WAKEFIELD OF KENDAL, BARONY OF (Wakefield) (Extinct 1983)

DAUGHTERS LIVING OF FIRST BARON

Hon Joan Rosemary, OBE, *b* 1920; OBE (Civil) 1981: *m* 1944, Capt Antony Edward Montague Raynsford, RN (ret), DL, who *d* 1993, and has issue living, Richard Wakefield, *b* 1945: *m* 1979, Rosemary, da of late Brig Thomas Hayward Evill, CBE, DSO, and has issue living, Thomas Lindsay Wakefield *b* 1980, Clementina Daisy *b* 1982, — Julia Daphne (*Lady Boyd*), *b* 1948: *m* 1977, Sir John Dixon Iklé Boyd, KCMG, and has issue living, Jessica *b* 1978, Alice Clara *b* 1979, Olivia Wakefield *b* 1982. *Residences* – Milton Malsor Manor, Northampton NN7 3AR; The Old House, Kendal, Cumbria.
Hon Mary Sheila, OBE, *b* 1922; OBE 1992: *m* 1945, Brig Richard Frank Bradshaw Hensman, CBE, who *d* 1988, and has issue living, Peter Richard Wavell, *b* 1948: *m* 1973, Claire Theresa, da of Peter Wallace Henderson, MC, BM, BCh, and has issue living, Roger Edward Wavell *b* 1981, Lucinda Carolyn Barrett *b* 1978, Joanna Mary Bradshaw *b* 1980, — Suzannah Mary, *b* 1953: *m* 1977, William Ian Simpson, and has issue living, Thomas James *b* 1981, Victoria Jane *b* 1979. *Residence* – Lindum Holme, Stricklandgate, Kendal, Cumbria LA9 4QG.
Hon Ruth Isabel, *b* 1932: *m* 1st, 1955, Maj Nigel James Clarkson Webb, who *d* 1987; 2ndly, 1992, Paul Anthony Adorian, and has issue living (by 1st *m*), Edward James, *b* 1966, — Georgina Anne, *b* 1957: *m* 1981, Christopher Campbell Townsend, eldest son of Eric L. Townsend, of Sandford Orcas, Sherborne, Dorset, and has issue living, Alexander Peard *b* 1984, Rosanna Campbell *b* 1987, — Carolyn Mary, *b* 1958: *m* 1983, Jeremy Simon Seel, yst son of Kenneth Seel, of Great Rollright Manor, Chipping Norton, Oxon, and has issue living, Annabel Lucy *b* 1987, Natasha Mary *b* 1989. *Residence* – Buckstone House, Carnforth, Lancs.

WAKEHAM, BARON (Wakeham) (Life Baron 1992)

JOHN WAKEHAM, PC, son of late Maj Walter John Wakeham, of Godalming, Surrey; *b* 22 June 1932; *ed* Charterhouse; JP Inner London 1972; CA, Member of Lloyd's, sometime Sec Small Businesses Cttee, Govt Whip 1979, Lord Commr to the Treasury 1981, Under Sec of State for Industry 1981-82, Min of State Treasury 1982-83, Parly Sec to the Treasury and Chief Whip 1983-87, Lord Privy Seal 1987-88, Lord Pres of the Council 1988-89, Leader of the House of Commons 1987-89, Sec of State for Energy July 1989-92, since when Lord Privy Seal, and Leader of the House of Lords; MP Maldon (*C*) 1974-83, and Colchester S and Maldon 1983-92; *cr* PC 1983, and *Baron Wakeham*, of Maldon, co Essex (Life Baron) 1992: *m* 1st, 1965, Anne Roberta, who was *k* in the bomb explosion at the Grand Hotel, Brighton, 1984, da of late Harold Edwin Bailey; 2ndly, 1985, Alison Bridget, MBE, yr da of Ven Edwin James Greenfield Ward, LVO (*see* Buxton, Bt, colls, 1985 Edn), and has issue by 1st and 2nd *m*.

Arms – Per fesse embattled azure and argent, a pale counter-changed, in the azure a lion's head guardant or, langued gules, and in the argent a bugle horn azure, garnished and stringed gold. **Crest** – A greyhound statant or, crowned with a mural crown checky azure and argent and supporting by the dexter fore-leg a cross raguly argent, nailed of three gold. **Supporters** – *Dexter*, a sea-lion azure, mane and head in trian aspect argent, langued gules, crowned with a crown trident gold; *sinister*, a sea-horse azure, head and neck argent and crowned also with a crown trident gold, the compartment comprising three bars wavy azure, argent and azure, in front thereof a grassy mount, growing therefrom three double roses argent upon gules, barbed and seeded, stalked and leaved proper.
Address – c/o House of Lords, SW1. **Clubs** – Buck's, Carlton, Garrick, Royal Yacht Squadron, St Stephen's Constitutional.

SONS LIVING *(By 1st marriage)*

Hon Jonathan Martin, *b* 1972; *ed* Charterhouse.
Hon Benedict Ian, *b* 1975; *ed* Charterhouse.

(by 2nd marriage)

Hon David Robert, *b* 1987.

WAKEHURST, BARON (Loder) (Baron UK 1934)

A sound conscience is a wall of brass

(JOHN) CHRISTOPHER LODER, 3rd Baron; *b* 23 Sept 1925; *s* 1970; *ed* Eton, King's Sch, nr Sydney, NSW, and Trin Coll, Camb (MA, LLB); Bar Inner Temple 1950; Chm Anglo & Overseas Trust plc since 1968, The Overseas Investment Trust plc since 1980, and Morgan Grenfell Equity Income Trust plc since 1991, Dir Morgan Grenfell Latin American Companies Trust plc since 1994, Dep Chm London and Manchester Group plc since 1970; a CStJ; late Sub-Lt RANVR and RNVR; 1939-45 in W Pacific: *m* 1st, 1956, Ingeborg, who *d* 1977, da of Walter Krumbholz; 2ndly, 1983, Brigid, yr da of William Noble, of Cirencester, Glos, and has issue by 1st *m*.

Arms – Quarterly; 1st and 4th grand quarters; Azure, on a fesse between in chief a portcullis chained and in base a martlet or, three stags' heads caboshed proper, *Loder*; 2nd grand quarter, quarterly, the Royal Arms of Charles II, 1st and 4th, France and England quarterly, 2nd, Scotland, 3rd, Ireland, and overall a baton sinister gules charged with three roses argent, barbed and seeded proper, *Beauclerk*; 3rd grand quarter, quarterly gules and or, in the first a mullet argent, *de Vere*. **Crest** – A stag's head caboshed transfixed by an arrow bendwise point downwards all proper, between two escallops or. **Supporters** – *Dexter*, A Russian brown bear proper; *sinister*, a greyhound argent gorged with a collar checky of the last and azure.
Residence – 26 Wakehurst Rd, SW11 6BY.

SON LIVING *(By 1st marriage)*

Hon TIMOTHY WALTER (26 Wakehurst Rd, SW11 6BY), *b* 28 March 1958; *ed* Millfield: *m* 1987, Susan Elaine Hurst.

DAUGHTER LIVING *(By 1st marriage)*

Hon Christina Anne (Wiveton Hall, Wiveton, Holt, Norfolk NR25 7TE), *b* 1959: *m* 1993, Desmond James MacCarthy (*see* Buxton, Bt, colls).

BROTHERS LIVING

Hon (James) David Gerald (Flat C, 45 Chesterton Rd, W10 6ES), *b* 1928; *ed* Geelong Gram Sch, Victoria, and Trin Coll, Camb (BA); Bar Inner Temple 1952; OStJ; late Lt Coldstream Guards.
Hon Robert Beauclerk, CBE (14 Ladbroke Grove, W11 3BQ), *b* 1934; *ed* Eton, and Trin Coll, Camb (BA); Chm Mental

Health Foundation since 1982; CBE (Civil) 1990: *m* 1973, Josette, da of Josef Bromovsky (*see* Dunn, Bt, ext), of Ottmanach, Pisheldorf, Kärnten, Austria, and has issue living, John James (Jan), *b* 1977, — Nicolai, *b* 1986, — Nell Marguerite, *b* 1983.

SISTER LIVING

Hon Henrietta Marguerite Jean, *b* 1922; *ed* Univ of Sydney (Dip Social Studies): *m* 1953, John Wilmot Reader-Harris, who *d* 1975, and has issue living, Michael John (26 Mansefield Av, Cambuslang, Glasgow G72 8NZ), *b* 1957: *m* 1985, Susan Mary, eldest da of Lt-Col J. L. Wilson Smith, OBE, of Cumledge, Duns, Berwickshire, and has issue living, Peter John *b* 1989, Rachel Katharine Hope *b* 1992, — Sarah Margaret, *b* 1959: *m* 1982, Erik Van Hove, and has issue living, Hannah Jean *b* 1987, Rebecca Claire *b* 1989, Laura Iris *b* 1991. *Residence* – 35 The Close, Salisbury, Wilts SP1 2EL.

WIDOW LIVING OF SECOND BARON

Dame MARGARET, DBE (*Margaret, Baroness Wakehurst*) (31 Lennox Gdns, SW1X ODE); Hon LLD Belfast; GCStJ; DBE (Civil) 1965; da of Sir Charles Tennant, 1st Bt (*see* B Glenconner): *m* 1920, the 2nd Baron, who *d* 1970.

PREDECESSORS – (1) GERALD WALTER ERSKINE Loder, 5th son of Sir Robert Loder, 1st Bt; *b* 1861; was an Assist Private Sec to Pres of Local Govt Board 1888-92, and to Sec of State for India 1896-1901; sat as MP for Brighton (C) 1889-1905; *cr* Baron Wakehurst, of Ardingly, co Sussex (peerage of United Kingdom) 1934: *m* 1890, Lady Louise de Vere Beauclerk, who *d* 1958, el da of 10th Duke of St Albans: *d* 1936; *s* by his only son (2) JOHN DE VERE, KG, KCMG, 2nd Baron, *b* 1895; MP for E Leicester (C) 1924-29, and Lewes 1931-36; Gov of NSW 1937-46, and N Ireland 1952-64: *m* 1920, Dame Margaret, DBE, da of Sir Charles Tennant, 1st Bt (B Glenconner); *d* 1970; *s* by his el son (3) (JOHN) CHRISTOPHER, 3rd Baron and present peer.

WALDEGRAVE, EARL (Waldegrave) (Earl GB 1729, Bt E 1643)
(Name and Title pronounced "Wallgrave")

Press forward

GEOFFREY NOEL WALDEGRAVE, KG, GCVO, TD, 12th Earl, and 16th Baronet; *b* 21 Nov 1905; *s* 1936; *ed* Winchester, and Trin Coll, Camb; Hon LLD Bristol; Chm of Agricultural Exec Cttee for Somerset 1948-51, a Co Alderman for Somerset 1949-58, Liaison Officer to Min of Agriculture and Fisheries 1952-57, and Vice-Lt for Somerset 1955-60; Joint Parly Sec to Min of Agriculture, Fisheries and Food 1957-62; Chm of Forestry Commn 1963-65; a Member of Prince's Council, Duchy of Cornwall 1951-58; Lord Warden of the Stanneries 1965-76; 1939-45 War as Maj RA (TA); Officer of the American Legion of Merit; *cr* KG 1971, GCVO 1976: *m* 1930, Mary Hermione, da of late Lt-Col Arthur Morton Grenfell, DSO (V Cobham, colls), and has issue.

Arms – Per pale argent and gules. **Crest** – Out of a ducal coronet or, a plume of five ostrich feathers, the first two argent, the third per pale argent and gules, and the last two gules. **Supporters** – Two talbots sable, ears or, each gorged with a mural coronet argent.
Residence – Chewton House, Chewton Mendip, Bath BA3 4LQ.

SONS LIVING

JAMES SHERBROOKE (*Viscount Chewton*) (West End Farm, Chewton Mendip, Bath BA3 4LQ), *b* 8 Dec 1940; *ed* Eton, and Trin Coll, Camb: *m* 1986, Mary Alison Anthea, da of late Sir Robert Furness, of Little Shelford, Camb, and has issue:—

SONS LIVING—*Hon* Edward Robert, *b* 10 Oct 1986, — *Hon* Robert Arthur Riversdale, *b* 1989.

Rt Hon William Arthur, MP (c/o House of Commons, SW1), *b* 1946; *ed* Eton, Corpus Christi Coll, Oxford, and Harvard Univ; Quondam Fellow of All Souls Coll, Oxford; CPRS 1971-73; Head of Rt Hon Edward Heath's Political Office 1974-75; GEC Ltd 1975-81; Member IBA Advsy Council 1980-81 Under Sec of State DES (for higher education) 1981-83, Under Sec of State, Dept of Environment, 1983-85, Min of State: Dept of Environment, 1985-88, Foreign & Commonwealth Office 1988-90, Dept of Health and Social Security 1990-92, since when Chancellor of the Duchy of Lancaster; JP; MP for Bristol West (C) since 1979; PC 1990: *m* 1977, (Linda Margaret) Caroline, yr da of Maj Richard Burrows, of 2a Royal Chase, Tunbridge Wells, Kent, and has issue living, James Victor, *b* 1984, — Katharine Mary, *b* 1980, — Elizabeth Laura, *b* 1983, — Harriet Horatia, *b* 1988.

DAUGHTERS LIVING

Lady Sarah Caroline, *b* 1931: *m* 1955: Ernest George Wright, GM, CPM, late Sr-Supt Colonial Police Service (Kenya) of Honibere Farmhouse, Burton, Stogursey, Somerset, and has issue living, Thomas Geoffrey, *b* 1956; late RGJ: *m* 1986, Sophia Louise, yst da of late J. F. P. Tate, of The Old Rectory, Boscombe, Salisbury, Wilts, — David James *b* 1957.
Lady Jane Mary HOWARD (17 Durand Gdns, SW9 0PS), *b* 1934: *m* 1st 1954 (*m diss* 1977), 4th Baron Strathcona and Mount Royal; 2ndly 1977 (*m diss* 1979), Duncan McIntosh, OBE, AFC.
Lady Elisabeth Jeronima (*Baroness Forteviot*), *b* 1936: *m* 1963, 4th Baron Forteviot, of Aberdalgie House, by Perth.
Lady Anne Hermione, *b* 1937: *m* 1971, Sir John Dennis (Jack) Boles, MBE (High Sheriff Devon 1993), of Rydon House, Talaton, nr Honiton, Devon EX5 2RP.
Lady Susan Katharine, DCVO, *b* 1939; appointed a Woman of the Bedchamber to HM The Queen 1960; CVO 1971, DCVO 1984: *m* 1959, Marmaduke James Hussey, Chm BBC since 1986, of Flat 15, 47 Courtfield Rd, SW7, and has issue living, James Arthur, *b* 1961; a Page of Honour to HM The Queen 1975-76: *m* 1st, 1988 (*m diss* 1993), Jacqueline, da of Dr (George) Hugh Barrington Baker, of Sutton, Surrey; 2ndly, 1993, Emma, da of John Shelley, of Wimbledon, — Katharine Elizabeth (*Lady Brooke*) *b* 1964: *m* 1989, Sir Francis George Windham Brooke, 4th Bt, and has issue.

SISTER LIVING

Lady (Gabrielle) Sophia Annette, *b* 1908: *m* 1935, John Stephen Schilizzi (*see* Ralli, Bt, 1952 Edn), who *d* 1985, and has issue living, Stephen Noel John, *b* 1937: *m* 1959, Diana, only da of Eustace Allfrey, of Chacombe Priory, near Banbury, Oxon, — Gabrielle Anne Mary, *b* 1936: *m* 1957, Capt Gordon Shafto Hedley, late 17th/21st Lancers of Turweston Glebe, Brackley, Northants, and has issue living, Nicholas Edward John *b* 1962, Caroline Mary *b* 1957: *m* 1984, George Adam Traill, Anne Penelope *b* 1959: *m* 1983, Timothy Christopher Thompson-Royds, and has issue (*see* Thompson, Bt, *cr* 1890, colls), — Helena Margaret, *b* 1939. *Residence* – The Old Vicarage, Chacombe, near Banbury, Oxon.

COLLATERAL BRANCH LIVING

Descendants of Adm Hon Sir William Waldegrave, GCB (2nd son of 3rd Earl), who was *cr Baron Radstock* 1800 (see that title).

PREDECESSORS – (1) *Sir* EDWARD Waldegrave, Knt, sometime MP for Sudbury; when 70 years of age took up arms in the royal cause; *cr* a *Baronet* 1643; afterwards eminently distinguished as a military leader; *s* by his son (2) *Sir* HENRY, 2nd Bt; *d* 1658; *s* by his son (3) *Sir* CHARLES, 3rd Bt; *s* by his son (4) *Sir* HENRY, 4th Bt; *cr Baron Waldegrave*, of Chewton, co Somerset (peerage of England) 1686; was Comptroller of the King's Household; *d* 1689; *s* by his son (5) JAMES, KG, PC, 2nd Baron; conformed to the Church of England and took his seat in the House of Lords 1722; was Ambassador to Emperor of Germany 1727-37: *cr Viscount Chewton and Earl Waldegrave* (peerage of Great Britain) 1729; *d* 1741; *s* by his el son (6) JAMES, KG, PC, 2nd Earl; was successively a Lord of the Bedchamber, Steward of the Duchy of Cornwall, Gov to George Prince of Wales and to Prince Edward, Duke of York, and Teller of the Exchequer, &c; *d* 1763; *s* by his brother (7) JOHN, KG, 3rd Earl; sat as MP for Oxford and Newcastle-under-Lyme; was Master of the Horse, Gov of Plymouth, a Groom of the Bedchamber, and Lord-Lieut of Essex: *d* 1784; *s* by his son (8) GEORGE, 4th Earl; was Col 14th Regt: *m* his cousin, Lady Elizabeth Laura Waldegrave, da of the 2nd Earl; *d* 1789; *s* by his el son (9) GEORGE, 5th Earl; *d* 1794; *s* by his brother (10) JOHN JAMES, 6th Earl; a Lt-Col in the Army *d* 1835; *s* by son (11) GEORGE EDWARD, 7th Earl; *dsp* 1846; *s* by his uncle (12) WILLIAM, CB (4th son of 4th Earl), 8th Earl; was a Vice-Adm; *d* 1859: *s* by his grandson (13) WILLIAM FREDERICK, PC (el son of William Frederick, Viscount Chewton, by Frances, VA, da of late Capt John Bastard, RN), 9th Earl, *b* 1851; a Lord-in-Waiting to Queen Victoria Aug 1886 to Aug 1892 and July 1895 to Aug 1896, Capt of the Yeomen of the Guard 1896-1906, and Ch Conservative Whip in the House of Lords 1896-1911: *m* 1874, Lady Mary Dorothea Palmer, DBE, da of 1st Earl of Selborne; *d* 1930; *s* by his only son (14) WILLIAM EDWARD SEYMOUR, 10th Earl, *b* 1882; *d* 1933; *s* by his uncle (15) *Rev* HENRY NOEL (2nd son of William Frederick, Viscount Chewton), 11th Earl, *b* 1854; Rector of Stoke d'Abernon, Surrey, of Marston Bigot, nr Frome, Somerset, and of Orchardleigh with Lullington: *m* 1892, Anne Katharine, who *d* 1962, da of late Rev William Pollexfen Bastard, of Buckland Court, Ashburton and Kitley, Devon; *d* 1936; *s* by his only son (16) GEOFFREY NOEL, 12th Earl and present peer; also Viscount Chewton, and Baron Waldegrave.

WALERAN, BARONY OF (Walrond) (Extinct 1966)

WIDOW LIVING OF SECOND BARON

VALENTINE (*Baroness Waleran*) (42A Cathcart Rd, SW10), da of late Eric Oswald Anderson, CBE: *m* 1954, as his third wife, the 2nd Baron, who *d* 1966, when the title became ext.

WALES, PRINCE OF, see Royal Family.

Walker, see Baron Gordon-Walker.

WALKER OF WORCESTER, BARON (Walker) (Life Baron 1992)

PETER EDWARD WALKER, MBE, PC, son of Sydney Walker; *b* 25 March 1932; *ed* Latymer Upper Sch; Member Nat Exec of Conservative Party since 1956, PPS to Leader of House of Commons 1963-64, Min of Housing and Local Govt June-Oct 1970, Sec of State for Environment 1970-72, for Trade and Industry 1972-74, Min of Agriculture, Fisheries and Food 1979-83, Sec of State for Energy 1983-87, and for Wales 1987-90; Chm Walker Young & Co Ltd, Lloyd's Brokers, non-exec Dir British Gas plc, Worcester Group plc, Tate & Lyle plc, Smith Court plc, Dalgety plc, Chm The Thornton Group, and Cornhill Insurance Co; author of *The Ascent of Britain* 1977, *Trust the People* 1987, and *Staying Power* 1991; MP Worcester (*C*) 1961-92; *cr* MBE (Civil) 1950, PC 1970, and *Baron Walker of Worcester*, of Abbots Morton, co Hereford and Worcester (Life Baron) 1992: *m* 1969, Tessa, da of Geoffrey Ivan Prout, and has issue.

Arms – Per pale sable and or semy of portcullises and three-turreted towers all counterchanged. **Crest** – Growing from a grassy mound proper, over which curls a footpath, a cedar tree all proper irradiated or. **Supporters** – *Dexter*, a dragon gules; *sinister*, a sea lion proper, the head and mane or, supporting a trident also proper; a compartment per bend dexter a grassy mound, growing therefrom red and yellow cowslips all proper, sinister water barry-wavy azure and argent, over all in bend a footpath proper.
Residence – Abbots Morton Manor, Gooms Hill, Abbots Morton, Worcs WR7 4LT. *Clubs* – Buck's, Pratt's, Carlton.

SONS LIVING

Hon Jonathan Peter, *b* 1970; *ed* St Paul's and Balliol Coll, Oxford.
Hon Timothy Rupert, *b* 1975; *ed* St Paul's.
Hon Robin Caspar, *b* 1978; *ed* St Paul's.

DAUGHTERS LIVING

Hon Shara Jane, *b* 1971; *ed* Francis Holland Sch, and Brasenose Coll, Oxford.
Hon Marianna Clare, *b* 1985; *ed* Francis Holland Sch.

WALL, BARONY OF (Wall) (Extinct 1980)

SONS LIVING OF LIFE BARON

Hon Martin John, *b* 1948: *m* 1976, Margaret, da of L. J. Scott, of Alton, Hants.
Hon Robin John, *b* (twin) 1948: *m* 1977, Catharine Joan, da of H. Sara, of Salisbury.

DAUGHTER LIVING OF LIFE BARON

Hon Yvonne Marie, *b* 1942: *m* 1970, Hugh Walker.

WIDOW LIVING OF LIFE BARON

GLADYS EVELYN (*Baroness Wall*) (Wychwood, Coombe End, Coombe Hill, Kingston upon Thames, Surrey KT2 7DQ), da of William Edward Wright. *m* 1939, Baron Wall, OBE (Life Baron), who *d* 1980.

WALLACE OF CAMPSIE, BARON (Life Baron 1974)

GEORGE WALLACE, son of John Wallace; *b* 13 Feb 1915; *ed* Queen's Park Secondary Sch, and Glasgow Univ; a DL and JP of Co of City of Glasgow; KStJ; Hon Sheriff Substitute of Lanarkshire at Hamilton 1971; established Wallace, Cameron & Co, Ltd 1948 (Chm and Man Dir 1948-77); Pres Wallace Cameron (Holdings) Ltd since 1977; a Dir of Smith & Nephew Asso Cos, Ltd 1973-77; Chm of E Kilbride & Stonehouse Development Corpn 1969-75, and Pres of Glasgow Chamber of Commerce 1974-76; 1939-45 War as F/O RAF; *cr Baron Wallace of Campsie*, of Newlands, co of City of Glasgow (Life Baron) 1974.
Residence – 14 Fernleigh Rd, Glasgow G43 2UE. *Club* – Royal Scottish Automobile.

WALLACE OF COSLANY, BARON (Wallace) (Life Baron 1974)

GEORGE DOUGLAS WALLACE, son of late George Wallace, of Cheltenham; *b* 18 April 1906; *ed* Cheltenham Central Sch; 1939-45 War as Sgt RAF; Govt Whip 1947-50 and Oppn Whip 1979-86; PPS to Lord Pres of Council 1964-66, to Sec of State for Commonwealth Affairs 1966-67, and to Min of State for Housing and Local Govt 1967-68; Speaker's Panel of Chairman 1970-74; a Lord in Waiting to HM 1977-79; Pres Radio Soc of GB 1977, Pres Friends of Queen Mary's Hosp Sidcup; MP for Chislehurst (*Lab*) 1945-50, and for Norwich North 1964-74; *cr Baron Wallace of Coslany*, of Coslany, City of Norwich (Life Baron) 1974: *m* 1932, Vera, da of William Joseph Randall, of Guildford, Surrey, and has issue.

𝕬rms – Or a turkey oak tree eradicated vert in base a portcullis chained orle-wise azure on a chief of the last a representation of Norwich Castle argent masoned proper its portal or closed by a portcullis azure all between in the flanks two roses gules barbed and seeded stalked and leaved proper. 𝕮rest – Statant within a chaplet of turkey oak vert a lion in trian aspect gules head mane and tail tufts or supporting the shaft of a spear gules headed or pendent therefrom on a crossbar by a cord azure and or a gonfalon of the arms. 𝕾upporters – *Dexter*, a horse argent; *sinister*, a lion or head and mane gules, each rampant on a hillock of two grassy mounts the innermost higher than the other both within a circular wall proper masoned or growing from the dexter hillock between two double roses argent upon gules an oak sprig proper fructed or and from the sinister hillock between two like oak sprigs another double rose argent upon gules all three roses barbed seeded stalked and leaved proper. 𝕸otto – Usque ad finem.
Residence – 44 Shuttle Close, Sidcup, Kent, DA15 8EP.

SON LIVING

Hon Michael George (17 Leamington Av, Orpington, Kent), *b* 1944: *m* 1974, Susan, da of Henry William Price, of Orpington, Kent, and has issue.

DAUGHTER LIVING

Hon Elizabeth Anne (44 Shuttle Close, Sidcup, Kent), *b* 1933; Dep Headmistress of St Mary's C of E Sch, Swanley, ret 1993.

WALPOLE, BARON (Walpole) (Baron GB 1723 and 1756)

Let him be true to himself

ROBERT HORATIO WALPOLE, 10th Baron Walpole, and 8th Baron Walpole of Wolterton; *b* 8 Dec 1938; *s* 1989; *ed* Eton, and King's Coll, Camb; JP; patron of six livings: *m* 1st, 1962 (*m diss* 1979), Sybil Judith, who *d* 1993, da of Theodore Thomas Schofield, FDS, MRCS, LRCP, of Harpenden, Herts; 2ndly, 1980, Laurel Celia, only da of S. T. Ball, of Swindon, Wilts, and has issue by 1st and 2nd *m*.

𝕬rms – Or, on a fesse, between two chevrons sable three cross-crosslets of the field. 𝕮rest – A Saracen's head in profile, couped at the shoulders proper, ducally crowned or, and from the coronet flowing a red cap turned down in front, tasselled, and charged with a catherine-wheel gold. 𝕾upporters – *Dexter*, an antelope argent; *sinister*, a stag argent, each gorged with a collar checky or and azure, and therefrom a chain reflexed over the back gold.
Seat – Wolterton Hall, Erpingham, Norwich, NR11 7LY; *Residence* – Mannington Hall, Norwich, Norfolk NR11 7BB.

SONS LIVING *(By 1st marriage)*

Hon JONATHAN ROBERT HUGH, *b* 16 Nov 1967; *ed* Eton, and Manchester Univ.
Hon Benedict Thomas Orford, *b* 1969; *ed* Eton.

(by 2nd marriage)

Hon Roger Horatio Calibut, *b* 1980.
Hon Henry William, *b* 1982.

DAUGHTERS LIVING *(By 1st marriage)*

Hon Alice Louise, *b* 1963, *ed* Norwich High Sch, and New Hall, Camb: *m* 1990, Dr Angel Cesar Carro Castrillo, yr son of Herminio Carro Castrillo, of Geneva.
Hon Emma Judith, *b* 1964; *ed* Norwich High Sch, and Durham Univ.

(by 2nd marriage)

Hon Grace Mary, *b* 1986.

SISTER LIVING

Hon Phillida Ann, *b* 1950: *m* 1st, 1973 (*m diss* 1981), Clive Grainger Morgan-Evans; 2ndly, 1983, Anthony Hurn, of Beck Farm, Calthorpe, Norwich NR11 7NG, and has issue living (by 1st *m*), Edward Grainger, *b* 1973; *ed* Framlingham Coll, — Daniel Rupert, *b* 1977; *ed* Framlingham Coll.

DAUGHTER LIVING OF FIFTH EARL OF ORFORD

Lady Anne Sophia, *b* 1919; VMH 1986, Hon FRHS 1988; Hon Dr Sc Exeter 1990; Chm Internat Dendrology Soc 1982-87, Vice-Pres Internat Dendrology Soc for England since 1988; JP 1964-80: *m* 1st, 1939, Col Joseph Eric Palmer, CBE, TD, DL, who *d* 1980; 2ndly, 1990, Robert James Berry, of Tiniroto, Gisborne, NZ, and has issue living (by 1st *m*), John Robert Walpole (Kirkmichael House, Blairgowrie, Perthshire), *b* 1943: *m* 1st, 1971, Carolyn, da of W. H. Atkinson-Clark, of Ashintully Castle, Kirkmichael, Blairgowrie; 2ndly, 1979, Mrs Alison Ann Allinson, da of Dr Noel Ian Bartholomew, of The Old Vicarage, Norton Bavant, Warminster, Wilts, — Anthony Eric Fletcher, *b* 1945: *m* 1969, Nicola Mary, da of H. Maude, of Gisborne, NZ. *Address* – Hackfalls, PO Box 3, Tiniroto, via Gisborne, NZ.

WIDOW LIVING OF SEVENTH BARON

NANCY LOUISA, OBE (*Nancy, Baroness Walpole*), da of late Frank Harding Jones, of 21 Abingdon Court, W8; OBE (Civil) 1977; JP: *m* 1937, Capt the 7th Baron, TD, who *d* 1989. *Residence* – Nelson House, Aldborough, Norfolk NR11 7AA.

COLLATERAL BRANCH LIVING

Grandchildren of late Sir Horatio George Walpole, KCB, el son of late Rt Hon Spencer Horatio Walpole, QC, 2nd son of late Thomas Walpole (*b* 1755), son of Hon Thomas Walpole, 2nd son of 1st Baron Walpole of Wolterton:—

Issue of late Maj Robert Spencer Hobhouse Walpole, *b* 1881; *d* 1975: *m* 1923, Edith Winifred, who *d* 1978, da of late S. H. Keeling, of Parkfield, Kenilworth:—

Horace Jeremy Spencer (Old Forge, Ashton Keynes, Swindon, Wilts), *b* 1924; Lt-Cdr RN: *m* 1950, Mary Elizabeth Bruce Kidman, and has issue living, Robert Charles Spencer (2 Churnside Cottages, Preston, nr Cirencester, Glos), *b* 1955: *m* 1st, 1975 (*m diss* 1986), Diana Rosemary Bishop; 2ndly, 1987, Judith, da of Carrick McLelland, of Wester Housebyes, Melrose, Roxburghshire, and has issue living, (by 1st *m*) Daniel Nicholas Spencer *b* 1977, Thomas James *b* 1980, Theresa *b* 1975 (by 2nd *m*) Catherine Mary *b* 1992, — Caroline Mary Bruce, *b* 1951 — Elizabeth Jane Bruce, *b* 1953; has issue (by Dr Peter Lawrence), Emma Victoria *b* 1990, Charlotte Alice *b* 1991, — Lucy Margaret Bruce *b* (twin) 1955: *m* 1974, Stephen Ashcroft, of 1 Down Ampney, Glos, and has issue living, Simon James *b* 1975, Christopher Andrew Jeremy *b* 1981, Caroline Jennifer *b* 1978, — Charlotte Victoria Bruce, *b* 1960: *m* 1987, James Ronald Trumper, of The Bothy, The Whiteway, Cirencester, Glos, son of William Trumper, of Bloxham, Oxon, and has issue living, Fiona Jane *b* 1991.

PREDECESSORS – (1) *Sir* ROBERT Walpole, KG, KB, a distinguished statesman; sat as MP for Lyme Regis 1702-42; was successively a Lord of the Treasury, Chancellor of the Exchequer, a Lord Justice, sole Sec of State, and Prime Minister; made a KG 1726, while a Commoner; *cr Baron Walpole*, of Houghton, *Viscount Walpole* and *Earl of Orford* (peerage of Great Britain) 1742; *d* 1745; *s* by his son (2) ROBERT, KB, 2nd Earl, who had in 1723 been *cr Baron Walpole*, of Walpole, co Norfolk (with remainder to his brothers Edward and Horace, and in default thereof to the heirs male of his father, and in default thereof to the heirs male of his grandfather): *m* 1724, Margaret, afterwards in her own right Baroness Clinton; the Earl *d* 1751; *s* by his son (3) GEORGE, 3rd Earl, who in 1781 *s* his mother as 16th *Baron Clinton* (peerage of England, *cr* 1332); was a Lord of the Bedchamber and Ranger of St James's and Hyde Parks; *d* 1791, when the Barony of Clinton reverted to his kinsman, Robert George William Trefusis (see B Clinton), and the Earldom devolved upon his uncle (4) HORACE, 4th Earl; sat successively as MP for Collington, Castle Rising, and King's Lynn, but was more distinguished for literary than political attainments; was Usher of the Receipt of the Exchequer, Comptroller of the Great Roll, and Keeper of the Foreign Receipts, having retired from public life he purchased a villa at Twickenham and transformed it into the celebrated Gothic mansion known as Strawberry Hill, where he printed his own works and many curious pieces; *d* unmarried 1797, when all the honours expired except the Barony of Walpole of Walpole (*cr* 1723), which devolved upon his first cousin (5) HORATIO, 4th Baron, who in 1757 had *s* his father, who was brother of 1st Earl, as 2nd *Baron Walpole of Wolterton* (peerage of Great Britain, *cr* 1756), sat as MP for Lynn Regis 1747-57; *cr Earl of Orford* (peerage of United Kingdom) 1806; *d* 1809; *s* by his son (6) HORATIO, 2nd Earl; MP for Wigan 1780-4, and for King's Lynn 1784-1809; *d* 1822; *s* by his son (7) HORATIO, 3rd Earl; *b* 1783; was High Steward of Lynn, and Col W Norfolk Militia: *m* Mary, da of late William Augustus Fawkener, of Brocton Hall, Salop; *d* 1858; *s* by his son (8) HORATIO WILLIAM, 4th Earl, *b* 1813; MP for Norfolk 1835-7: *m* 1841, Harriet Bettina Frances, who *d* 1886, da of late Hon Sir Fleetwood Broughton Reynolds Pellew; *d* 1894; *s* by his nephew (9) ROBERT HORACE (son of late Hon Frederick Walpole, MP, 3rd son of 3rd Earl), 5th Earl, *b* 1854: *m* 1st, 1888, Louise Melissa, who *d* 1909, da of D. C. Corbin, of New York; 2ndly, 1917, Emily Gladys, who *d* 1988, da of Rev Thomas Henry Royal Oakes, R of Thurgarton, Norwich; *d* 1931, when the Earldom of Orford became ext, and the Baronies of Walpole and Walpole of Wolterton devolved upon his cousin (10) ROBERT HENRY MONTGOMERIE (son of late Horatio Spencer Walpole, descended from late Hon Thomas Walpole, brother of 1st Earl of Orford, *cr* 1806), 9th Baron, *b* 1913, Capt RA, TD: *m* 1937, Nancy Louisa, OBE, da of late Frank Harding Jones, of 21 Abingdon Court, W8; *d* 1989; *s* by his elder (but only surv) son (11) ROBERT HORATIO, 10th Baron, and present peer; also Baron Walpole of Wolterton.

WALSINGHAM, BARON (de Grey) (Baron GB 1780)

To be spirited, not inactive

JOHN DE GREY, MC, 9th Baron; *b* 21 Feb 1925; *s* 1965; *ed* Wellington Coll, Aberdeen Univ, and at Magdalen Coll, Oxford (MA); Lt-Col (ret) RA; patron of three livings; 1939-45 War, Palestine 1947, Korea 1951-52 (MC), Malaya 1954-56, Cyprus and Suez 1956, Aden 1957-58 and 1961-63, Far East (Borneo) 1963-65: *m* 1963, Wendy Elizabeth, elder da of Edward S. Hoare, of Southwick, Sussex, and has issue.

Arms – Barry of six argent and azure, in chief three annulets gules. **Crest** – A wyvern's head, or. **Supporters** – Two wyverns regardant argent, collared azure, chained or, and charged on the breast with three annulets gules. *Residence* – Merton Hall, Thetford, Norfolk 1P25 6QJ. *Clubs* – Army and Navy, Farmers', Norfolk County (Norwich) Special Forces.

SON LIVING

Hon ROBERT, *b* 21 June 1969; *ed* Exeter Univ (BSc 1992).

DAUGHTERS LIVING

Hon Sarah Jane, *b* 1964; *ed* London Univ (BA 1986): *m* 1990, Bryan Muggeridge, yr son of Percy Muggeridge, of Paarl, Cape Province, S Africa.
Hon Elizabeth Anne, *b* 1966; *ed* Durham Univ (BA 1989): *m* 1993, Stefan Jones, only son of Roger Jones, of Yarnton House, Peopleton, Worcs.

SISTERS LIVING

Hon Lavender Hyacinth, *b* 1923; European War 1942-45 with First Aid Nursing Yeo in N Africa, Italy, India and Ceylon: *m* 1946, Col William d'Arcy Garnier, late RA, who *d* 1989, and has issue living, James Hugh, *b* 1948: *m* 1984, Katherine Hale, yr da of late John Hale Puckle, of Foxton House, Foxton, Cambs, and has issue living, Louisa Hale *b* 1986, Sophia Elizabeth *b* 1988, Georgina Sarah *b* 1989, Olivia Caroline *b* 1991, — Richard Charles, *b* 1950: *m* 1986, Melissa (Minnie) Mary, eldest da of Anthony Meyrick Denny, of Rose Cottage, Hattingley, Alton, Hants, and has issue living, William *b* 1989, Robert Anthony *b* 1993, — Edward Henry (1 Brick Court, Temple, EC4), *b* 1952; *ed* Wellington Coll, and Jesus Coll, Oxford (MA); Bar Middle Temple 1976; MP for Harborough (C) since 1992: *m* 1982, Anna Caroline, el da of late Michael James Mellows (*see* Heathcote, Bt, of London), and has issue living, George Edward *b* 1986, James William *b* 1991, Eleanor Katharine Rose *b* 1983, — Katharine Juliet, *b* 1958: *m* 1985, Anthony Richard Ashmore Wolstenholme, elder son of Michael Ashmore Wolstenholme, of Fitzgeorge Av, W14, and has issue living, Florence Maud *b* 1990, Edwina Lavender *b* 1991. *Address* – College Farm, Thompson, Thetford, Norfolk.
Hon Margaret Isolda, *b* 1926; European War 1943-45 in WRNS: *m* 1950, Major Geoffrey Edward Ford North, MC, High Sheriff Devon 1990, and has issue living, David John Ford (8 Egliston Rd, SW15 1AL), *b* 1959: *m* 1986, Sarah Jane, da of Gerald Barrow, of Gustard Wood, Wheathampstead, Herts, and has issue living, George Peter Ford *b* 1988, Rosanna Katharine *b* 1990, Perdita Alexandra *b* 1991, — Amanda (*Lady Weldon*), *b* 1951: *m* 1st, 1970 (*m diss* 1980), Anthony John Wigan (*see* By Tweedmouth); 2ndly, 1980, Sir Anthony William Weldon, 9th Bt, of Easton Manor, Easton Royal, Pewsey, Wilts, — Joanna Katharine (*Hon Mrs Kim Fraser*), *b* 1953: *m* 1975, Hon Kim Maurice Fraser (*see* L Lovat), — Belinda Jane, *b* 1955. *Residence* – Holmingham Hall, Bampton, Tiverton, Devon.
Hon Katharine Odeyne (*Dowager Countess of Powis*), *b* 1928: *m* 1949, 7th Earl of Powis, who *d* 1993. *Residence* – Marrington Hall, Chirbury, Montgomery, Powys.

COLLATERAL BRANCHES LIVING

Grandsons of late Nigel de Grey, CMG, OBE (infra):—
Issue of late John de Grey, *b* 1911, *d* 1973: *m* 1939, Averil Mary (Oliver House, Buckden, Cambs), da of late Herman Walter de Zoete, of Sproughton, Suffolk:—
Michael John (42 Murray Rd, W5 4XS), *b* 1942: *m* 1st, 1966 (*m diss* 1988), Carolyn Althea Jane, da of late John Ernest Haldane Blackie, CB, of The Bell House, Alconbury, Cambs; 2ndly, 19—, Charlotte Ashe, and has issue living, (by 1st *m*) Rachel Emma, *b* 1969, — Helen Sarah, *b* 1970, — (by 2nd *m*) Annabel, *b* 1994. —— Anthony (8 Rosenthorpe Rd, SE15 3EG), *b* 1948: *m* 1975 (*m diss* 1985), Miranda Jane, da of Robert Clive Murdoch, of Westerhill, Linton, Maidstone, Kent, and of Mrs Patrick Meredith-Hardy, and has issue living, Nigel John, *b* 1981, — Alexandra Mary Carena, *b* 1984.

Grandchildren of late Rev Hon Arnald de Grey, 3rd son of 5th Baron:—
Issue of late Nigel de Grey, CMG, OBE, *b* 1886, *d* 1951: *m* 1910, Florence Emily Frances, who *d* 1963, da of late Spencer William Gore (E Arran, colls):—
Sir Roger, KCVO, *b* 1918; *ed* Eton; Hon DLitt Reading 1992; Capt Roy Armoured Corps; NW Europe, 1944-45 (wounded, Bronze Star of USA); ARA 1962; Pres Royal Academy 1984-93: *m* 1942, Flavia Hatt, da of late Lt-Col Clinton Irwin, MC, of Silver Bridge, Chideock, Dorset, and has issue living, Spencer Thomas, *b* 1944: *m* 1977, Hon Amanda Lucy Annan, el da of Baron Annan (Life Peer), and has issue living, Felix Nicholas *b* 1992, Georgia Catherine *b* 1988, — Robert Fulke, *b* 1948: *m* 1974, Muriel Janik, da of Jean-Paul Schoendoerffer, of Paris, and has issue living, Thomas George *b* 1981, Elisa Catherine *b* 1976, Alice Rose *b* 1979, — Emilia Jane Mary, *b* 1952: *m* 1975, Timothy Crawford, son of James Crawford, of Post House, Stroud, Hants, and has issue living, George *b* 1979, Joseph *b* 1988, Harriet *b* 1982. *Residence* – 5-6 Camer St, Meopham, Kent.

PREDECESSORS – (1) Sir WILLIAM de Grey, Knt, having filled the offices of Solicitor-Gen, Attorney-Gen and Ch Justice of the Common Pleas, was *cr Baron Walsingham*, of Walsingham, co Norfolk (peerage of Great Britain) 1780; sat as MP for Newport, Cornwall, 1762-8, and for Cambridge University 1770; *d* 1781; *s* by his son (2) THOMAS, 2nd Baron; was for 20 years Chairman of Committees of House of Lords; *d* 1818; *s* by his el son (3) GEORGE, 3rd Baron; Lieut-Gen Peninsular Campaign; he was burned to death 26 April, 1831, his wife dying the following day; *s* by his brother (4) THOMAS, 4th Baron; was Archdeacon of Surrey, and Prebendary of Winchester, &c; *d* 1839; *s* by his son (5) THOMAS, 5th Baron; *b* 1804: *m* 1st, Augusta Louisa, da of Sir Robert Frankland Russell, 7th Bt; 2ndly, Hon Emily Elizabeth Julia Thellusson, da of 2nd Baron Rendlesham; *d* 1870; *s* by his son (6) THOMAS, 6th Baron, *b* 1843; MP for Norfolk (C) 1865-70, and a Lord-in-Waiting to Queen Victoria 1874-5: *m* 1st, 1877, Augusta Selina Elizabeth (Leila), who *d* 1906, da of late William Locke (*see* Cs Dysart, colls), widow of Ernest, Lord Burghersh (E Westmorland), and formerly wife of Don Luigi Caracciolo, Duke of San Teodoro; 2ndly, 1908, Marion Gwytherne-Williams, of Belvedere, St Lawrence, Isle of Wight, who *d* 1913, da of late Thomas Rhys Withers; 3rdly, 1914, Agnes Baird, who *d* 1926, da of late Frederick Shand Hemming, and widow of Richard Dawson, of Lealands, Hellingly; *d* 1919; *s* by his half-brother (7) JOHN AUGUSTUS, 7th Baron; *b* 1849; a Metropolitan Police Magistrate 1905-19; *m* 1st, 1883, Elizabeth Henrietta, who *d* 1927, da of Patrick Grant, HEICS; 2ndly, 1928, Marguerite, who *d* 1931, da of late Walter Vernon, of Trematon Lodge, Anerley, SE, and widow of Thomas Godley, of Scarborough; *d* 1929; *s* by his son

(8) George, DSO, OBE, 8th Baron, *b* 1884; Lt-Col, R Norfolk Regt 1914-18 War (thrice wounded): *m* 1919, Hyacinth Lambart, who *d* 1968, da of late Lt-Col Lambart Henry Bouwens, RHA; *d* 1965; *s* by his son **(9)** John, MC, 9th Baron and present peer.

WALSTON, BARONY OF (Walston) (Extinct 1991)

SONS LIVING OF LIFE BARON (*By 1st marriage*)

Hon Oliver (Thriplow Farm, Thriplow, Royston, Herts) *b* 1941: *m* 1st, 1966, Leslie, da of Milton A. Gordon, of New York; 2ndly, 1969, Anne Dunbar, of Washington, DC, and has issue.
Hon William (34 Alpha Terrace, Trumpington, Cambridge) *b* 1942: *m* 1st, 1963 (*m diss* 1988), Hilary Blanche, da of William Osselton Galbraith; 2ndly, 1989, Barbara Catherine, da of Michael James Jardine, and has issue by both marriages.
Hon James Patrick Francis (Via del Biscione 78, 00186, Rome, Italy) *b* 1949, *ed* Eton, Ampleforth and Jesus Coll Camb: *m* 1987, Nora Emilia Antonia Maria, da of Vincenzo Galli de'Paratesi.

DAUGHTERS LIVING OF LIFE BARON (*By 1st marriage*)

Hon Anne Sheridan (who has resumed name of Brewin since 1982) (Clare Cottage, Northfield End, Henley-on-Thames, Oxon RG9 2JL), *b* 1937: *m* 1st, 1960 (*m diss* 1972), Charles Edward Brewin; 2ndly, 1978 (*m diss* 1982) Edward McCririe-Hallman, and has issue by 1st *m*.
Hon Susan (RMB31, Marlee, NSW, Australia) *b* (twin) 1942.

WIDOW LIVING OF LIFE BARON

Elizabeth Rosemary (*Baroness Walston*), da of late Robert Bissett-Robinson, and formerly wife of Nicholas Paul Scott, MBE, MP (later Rt Hon Nicholas Scott): *m* 1979, as his 2nd wife, Baron Walston, CVO (Life Baron), who *d* 1991. *Residences* – Selwood Place, Bath, Avon; Marquis, St Lucia, W Indies.

WALTON OF DETCHANT, BARON (Walton) (Life Baron 1989)

John Nicholas Walton, TD, son of Herbert Walton; *b* 16 Sept 1922; *ed* Alderman Wraith Gram Sch, and King's Coll Med Sch, Durham Univ (MD); late Col RAMC, Comdg Offr 1 (N) Gen Hosp (TA) 1963-66, Hon Col 201 (N) Gen Hosp (TAVR) 1968-73; Consultant Neurologist Newcastle Univ Hosps 1958-83, Prof of Neurology Newcastle Univ 1968-83, Chm Muscular Dystrophy Group of GB since 1970, Member Gen Med Council since 1971 (Chm Educn Cttee 1975-82, Pres 1982-89), Pres BMA 1980-82, Assocn for Study of Med Educn 1982-94, and Assocn of British Neurologists 1987-88, first Vice-Pres World Fedn of Neurologists 1981-89, since when Pres, and Pres Royal Soc of Medicine 1984-86; Warden Green Coll, Oxford 1983-89; FRCP, DSc Newcastle; TD 1962; *cr* Knt 1979, and *Baron Walton of Detchant*, of Detchant, co Northumberland (Life Baron) 1989: *m* 1946, Mary Elizabeth, da of Joseph Harrison, of Spennymoor, co Durham, and has issue, one son and two das.

Arms – Paly wavy argent and gules, a castle triple-towered purpure, on a chief of the last three crosses formy quadrate gold. Crest – Issuant from clouds proper a seahorse argent the piscine part proper, crined and finned or, holding between the forelegs a cross formy quadrate fitchy at the foot purpure. Supporters – *Dexter* — A boar gold suspended from the neck by a riband purpure a clarion, pipes downward, gules; *sinister* — A greylag goose proper.
Residence – 13 Norham Gdns, Oxford OX2 6PS. *Clubs* – Athenaeum, United Oxford and Cambridge.

WARD OF WITLEY, VISCOUNTCY OF (Ward) (Extinct 1988)

DAUGHTER LIVING OF FIRST VISCOUNT

See E Dudley, colls.

WARDINGTON, BARON (Pease) (Baron UK 1936)

Peace and hope

CHRISTOPHER HENRY BEAUMONT PEASE, 2nd Baron; *b* 22 Jan 1924; *s* 1950; *ed* Eton; late Capt Scots Guards; a partner in the firm of Hoare, Govett, Ltd 1950-86; an Alderman of City of London 1960-63; Member of Council of the Stock Exchange 1963-81; Member of Corporation of Foreign Bond Holders since 1967, and of Public Works Loan Board 1964-69; Chm Athlone Trust; Chm Friends of the British Library; Trustee of Royal Jubilee Trusts; 1939-45 War (wounded): *m* 1964, Audrey (DUNFEE), da of late John White, and has one adopted son and two adopted das.

Arms – Per fesse azure and gules, a fesse nebuly ermine between two lambs passant in chief argent, and in base upon a mount proper a dove rising argent, holding in the beak a pea stalk, the blossom and pods proper. Crest – Upon the capital of an Ionic column a dove rising, holding in the beak a pea stalk as in the arms. Supporters – On either side a fox or, charged on the shoulder with a bugle horn stringed sable.
Seat – Wardington Manor, Banbury, Oxon OX17 1SW. *Residence* – 29 Moore Street, SW3 2QW.

SON LIVING

Christopher William Beaumont, *b* 1970.

DAUGHTERS LIVING

Lucy Anne, *b* 1966: *m* 1991, John Vallance Petrie, eldest son of Neil Petrie, of Sulphur Wells, NZ, and has issue living, Christopher Beaumont, *b* 1993.
Helen Elizabeth, *b* 1967.

BROTHER LIVING

Hon WILLIAM SIMON, *b* 15 Oct 1925; *ed* Eton, New Coll, Oxford (MA), and St Thomas's Hosp Med Sch; MB and BS London; FRCS England; late Capt Gren Gds; late Consultant ENT Surgeon, Central Middx and Northwick Park Hosps: *m* 1962, Hon Elizabeth Jane Ormsby-Gore, da of 4th Baron Harlech. *Residences* – 29 Upper Addison Gdns, W14; Lepe House, Exbury, Southampton. *Club* – Royal Yacht Squadron.

PREDECESSOR – (1) JOHN WILLIAM BEAUMONT Pease, 1st Baron, son of late John William Pease, DCL, of Pendower, Newcastle-upon-Tyne, and Nether Grange, Alnmouth, Northumberland; *b* 1869; Chm of Lloyds Bank 1922-45, and of Bank of London and S America 1922-47; *cr Baron Wardington* of Alnmouth, co Northumberland (peerage of United Kingdom) 1936: *m* 1923, Hon Dorothy Charlotte, who *d* 1983, da of 1st Baron Forster, and widow of Capt Hon Harold Fox Pitt Lubbock, Grenadier Guards (*see* B Avebury); *d* 1950; *s* by his el son (2) CHRISTOPHER HENRY BEAUMONT, 2nd Baron and present peer.

WARNOCK, Baroness (Warnock) (Life Baroness 1985)

(HELEN) MARY WARNOCK, DBE, da of late Archibald Edward Wilson, of Winchester, by his wife, Ethel Mary, eldest da of Sir Felix Otto Schuster, 1st Bt; *b* 14 April 1924; *ed* St Swithun's, Winchester, and Lady Margaret Hall, Oxford (Hon Fellow 1984); has Hon Degrees from Univs of Essex, Exeter, Melbourne, St Andrews, Manchester, York, etc Fellow and Tutor in Philosophy, St Hugh's Coll, Oxford 1949-66 (Senior Research Fellow 1976-84, Hon Fellow 1985); Headmistress, Oxford High Sch 1966-72; Member, IBA 1973-81, Cttee of Inquiry into Special Educn 1974-78, R Commn on Environmental Pollution 1979-84 (Chm), Advisory Cttee on Animal Experiments (Chm 1979-86), and Cttee of Inquiry into Human Fertilization 1982-84 (Chm); Mistress of Girton Coll, Camb 1985-92; author of philosophical and educational works; *cr* DBE (Civil) 1984, and *Baroness Warnock*, of Weeke, in the City of Winchester (Life Baroness) 1985: *m* 1949, Sir Geoffrey James Warnock, Prin Hertford Coll, Oxford, 1971-88, and Vice-Cllr, Oxford Univ 1981-85, and has issue.
Residence – Brick House, Axford, Wilts.

SONS LIVING

Hon Felix Geoffrey, *b* 1952; *ed* Winchester, and R Coll of Music: *m* 1975, Juliet, da of Arthur Robert Lehwalder, of 5047-18-NE, Seattle, Washington, USA, and has issue living, Daniel Arthur Richard, *b* 1985, — Eleanor Denise, *b* 1982, — Polly Patricia, *b* 1986. *Residence* – 5 Kingsbridge Rd, W10 6PU.
Hon James Marcus Alexander, *b* 1953; *ed* Winchester, and E Anglia Univ: *m* 1986, Fiona Margaret, da of Matthew Stewart Hair, and has issue, one son and one da. *Residence* – 5 Cheltenham Av, Liverpool 17 2AR.

DAUGHTERS LIVING

Hon Kathleen, *b* 1950; *ed* Oxford High Sch, and St Hugh's Coll, Oxford.
Hon Stephana (Fanny), *b* 1956; *ed* Downe House, Oxford High Sch, and Guildhall Sch of Music: *m* 1987, David E. (Bruno) Branson, son of W. E. Branson, of South Hill, Beds, and has issue living, Abigail Brigitte Edith, *b* 1989. *Residence* – 7 St Ruald's Close, Wallingford, Oxon.
Hon (Grizel) Maria, *b* 1961; *ed* Oxford High Sch, and W Surrey Sch of Art and Design: *m* 1994, Paul Jenkins, son of Keith Jenkins, of Kidlington, Oxford. *Residence* – 32 Sidney Rd, Rochester, Kent ME1 3HF.

WARWICK, EARL BROOKE AND OF (Greville) (Earl GB 1746)

I scarcely call these things our own

DAVID ROBIN FRANCIS GUY GREVILLE, 8th Earl, *b* 15 May 1934; *s* 1984; *ed* Eton; Warwickshire Yeo (TA), late 2nd Lieut LG: *m* 1956 (*m diss* 1967), Sarah Anne Chester, da of Alfred Chester Beatty, of Owley, Wittersham, Kent, and has issue.

Arms – Sable, on a cross, engrailed or five pellets, all within a bordure engrailed of the second or. Crests – 1st, out of a ducal coronet gules, a demi-swan, with wings expanded and elevated argent beaked of the first; 2nd, a bear sejant argent, muzzled gules, supporting a ragged staff of the first. Supporters – Two swans, wings inverted, argent legged, beaked, and ducally gorged gules.
Residences – Pelican Point, PO Box 203, Providenciales, Turks and Caicos Islands, West Indies; 43 Rue du Colisée, Paris 75008; 43 Fifth Avenue, New York City, NY 10003, USA. *Clubs* – White's, The Brook (New York City), The Eagle (Gstaad).

SON LIVING

GUY DAVID (*Lord Brooke*) *b* 30 Jan 1957; *ed* Eton: *m* 1981, Susan McKinley, da of George William McKinley Wilson, of Melbourne, Australia, and formerly wife of Nicholas Sydney Cobbold, and has issue:—

　　　SON LIVING— *Hon* Charles Fulke Chester, *b* 27 July 1982.
Residence – 4 Walter St, Claremont 6010, Perth, Australia.

DAUGHTER LIVING

Lady Charlotte Anne, *b* 1958: *m* 1979, Hon Andrew Roy Matthew Fraser, who was *k* in a hunting accident, 1994, and has issue (*see* L Lovat). *Residence* – Calle Betis 63, Seville 41010, Spain.

WIDOW LIVING OF SEVENTH EARL

JANINE (*Countess of Warwick*), da of Georges Detry de Mares: *m* 1963, as his 3rd wife, the 7th Earl, who *d* 1984. *Residence* – 201 Via Appia Antica, Rome, Italy.

COLLATERAL BRANCHES LIVING

Issue of late Hon Maynard Greville, yst son of 5th Earl, *b* 1898, *d* 1960: *m* 1918, Dora, who *d* 1957, da of late Edward Pape, of Moor Hall, Battle, and 26 Portland Place, W.:—
Felice, *b* 1919: *m* 1940, Eric J. Spurrier, who *d* 1984. *Residence* – Perryfields, Easton Lodge, Dunmow, Essex.

(In remainder to Barony of Brooke only)

Grandchildren of late Lt-Col Guy George Frederick Fulke Greville, DSO, HLI (infra):—
Issue of late Capt Guy Eric Fulke Greville, MC, ERD, RTR, *b* 1911, *d* 1986: *m* 1st, 1934 (*m diss* 1968), Mary Henrietta d'Arcy, who *d* 1982, da of Col Sir Harry Waechter, 1st Bt, CMG; 2ndly, 19—, Rosalind Jessie Gwavas (Treetops, Llandividdy Lane, Polperro, nr Looe, Cornwall PL13 2RT), widow of John Mostyn-Walker, and da of late George Larritt Polsue:—
(By 1st wife) Guy Jonathan Fulke, *b* 1940; *ed* privately. —— René Brooke Fulke (Fressingfield Hall, Fressingfield, Suffolk), *b* 1947; *ed* privately: *m* 1976, Marion Pearl Emma, only child of H. E. Ings, of Harrow Weald, Middx, and has issue living, Beaufort Henry d'Arcy, *b* 1977, — Brooke Southwell Guy, *b* 1981. —— Priscilla Mary Caroline, *b* 1935: *m* 1957, Dr Richard Michael Holmes, only son of Prof Eric Gordon Holmes, of Mivanza, Tanganyika, and has issue living, Guy Aladar, *b* 1960, — Michael Aristide, *b* 1966, — Jacquetta Noël Barbara, *b* 1959. —— Charlotte Anne Esther, *b* 1937: *m* 1954, Bernard Morton-Stevens, of 39 Greys Rd, Eastbourne, Sussex, son of Bernard Morton-Stevens, of Highgate, N6, and has issue living, Robert Guy *b* 1956, — Dominic Peter, *b* 1962, — Veronica Mary, *b* 1955, — Lesley Anne, *b* 1959. —— (By 2nd wife) Brooke Peregrine Fulke, *b* 1966. —— Hugh Tristan Maynard, *b* 1968.

Grandson of late Brooke Southwell Greville, el son of Maj Southwell Greville, brother of 1st Baron Greville, 2nd son of late Algernon Greville, great-grandson of Hon Algernon Greville, MP, 2nd son of 5th Baron Brooke:—
Issue of late Lt-Col Guy George Frederick Fulke Greville, DSO, HLI, *b* 1884, *d* 1966: *m* 1911, Esther Hope, who *d* 1968, da of Henry Erskine Girard:—
Hugh Edward Arderne Fulke, *b* 1914.

Granddaughters of late Maj Southwell Greville (ante):—
Issue of late Brooke Southwell Greville, *b* 1855, *d* 1945: *m* 1879, Charlotte Priscilla, who *d* 1933, da of late E. B. Clough, of Pietermaritzburg, Natal:—
Charlotte Caroline Muriel, *b* 1880: *m* 1901, George McKechnie. —— Irene Fanny Gwendoline Gertrude, *b* 1888. —— Cecil Violet Enid, *b* 1896: *m* 1927, Wing-Cdr Edward Irvine Russell, RAF.

Grandson of late Stapleton Fulke Greville, el son of late Rear-Adm Stapleton John Greville, grandson of Lt-Col Henry Francis Greville, yr brother of Capt William Fulke Greville, RN, MP, grandson of Hon Algernon Greville, MP (ante):—
Issue of late John Algernon Fulke Greville, *b* 1896, *d* 1968: *m* 1929, Frances Alice, who *d* 1989, da of Harry Bird Harper:—
John Brooke Fulke (314 Robin Hood Lane, Hall Green, Birmingham, 28), *b* 1930: *m* 1958, Maureen Constance, da of L. A. Parkhouse, and has issue living, Robert John Fulke, *b* 1960.

Granddaughter of late Rear-Adm Stapleton John Greville (ante):—
Issue of late Henry Brooke Macartney Crewe Greville, *b* 1870, *d* 1944: *m* 1906, Cecilia Ada, who *d* 1959, da of Lieut-Col Sir Frederick Thomas Arthur Hervey-Bathurst, 4th Bt:—
Margaret Ishla, *b* 1914. *Residence* – Ridge Hill Cottage, Kingscote, E Grinstead, Sussex.

PREDECESSORS – **(1)** *Rt Hon Sir* FULKE Greville, *de jure* 5th Lord Willoughby de Broke, a favourite courtier of Queen Elizabeth I, was successively keeper of the signet to the Council in the Marches of Wales, Treasurer of the Navy, and Chancellor of the Exchequer; obtained, *temp* James I, a grant of Warwick Castle and its dependencies; *cr Baron Brooke*, of Beauchamp's Court, co Warwick (peerage of England) 1621, with remainder to his cousin, Robert, son of Fulke Greville, of Thorpe Latimer, co Lincoln; *d* (stabbed by a servant) unmarried 1628; *s* by his kinsman **(2)** ROBERT, 2nd Baron, son of Fulke (ante); sat as MP for Warwick; was a distinguished Gen in the Parliamentary Army during the Civil Wars; *k* at the assault of Lichfield 1642; *s* by his el son **(3)** FRANCIS, 3rd Baron; *s* by his brother **(4)** ROBERT, 4th Baron; was one of the Commrs deputed to invite the return of Charles II; *d* 1676; *s* by his brother **(5)** FULKE, 5th Baron; was Recorder of Warwick; *d* 1710; *s* by his grandson **(6)** FULKE, 6th Baron; *d* unmarried; *s* by his brother **(7)** WILLIAM, 7th Baron; was Recorder of Warwick; *d* 1727; *s* by his son **(8)** *Sir* FRANCIS, KT, 8th Baron; was Recorder of Warwick, and Lord-Lieut of Warwickshire; *cr Earl Brooke* (peerage of Great Britain) 1746, and *Earl of Warwick* (peerage of Great Britain) 1759; *d* 1773; *s* by his son **(9)** GEORGE, 2nd Earl; sat as MP for Warwickshire; was a Lord of Trade and Recorder of Warwick; *d* 1816; *s* by his son **(10)** HENRY RICHARD, KT, 3rd Earl; *b* 1779; was Lord-Lieut of Warwickshire: *m* 1816, Sarah, widow of 3rd Baron Monson, and da of 2nd Earl of Mexborough; *d* 1853; *s* by his son **(11)** GEORGE GUY, 4th Earl, *b* 1818; MP for S Warwickshire (C) 1846-53: *m* 1852, Lady Anne Charteris, da of 8th Earl of Wemyss and March; *d* 1893; *s* by his el son **(12)** FRANCIS RICHARD CHARLES GUY, 5th Earl, *b* 1853; MP for Somerset E (C) 1879-85, and for Colchester 1888-92; Lord-Lieut of Essex 1901-19: *m* 1881, Frances Evelyn, who *d* 1938, da of late Col Hon Charles Henry Maynard (V Maynard (*ext*), colls); *d* 1924; *s* by his el son **(13)** LEOPOLD GUY FRANCIS MAYNARD, CMG, MVO, 6th Earl; *b* 1882; Capt 1st Life Guards; Hon Brig-Gen Overseas Mil Forces of Canada, Hon Lieut-Col TF Reserve; S African War 1900, European War 1914-19 as ADC to Com-in-Ch, and Comdg 4th and 12th Canadian Inf Brigs; Reuter's Special Correspondent during Russo-Japanese War 1904-5: *m* 1909, Elfrida Marjorie, who *d* 1943, da of Sir William Eden, 7th Bt; *d* 1928; *s* by his el son **(14)** CHARLES GUY FULKE, 7th Earl, *b* 1911, a Gov Birmingham Univ, Warwicks Kings Sch, R Shakespeare Theatre and Univ Coll Hosp; Mayor of Warwick 1951-52: *m* 1st, 1933 (*m diss* 1938), Rose, who *d* 1972, da of late David Cecil Bingham (*see* E Lucan, colls); 2ndly, 1942 (*m diss* 1949), Mary Kathleen, el da of late Percy Clifford Hopkinson, of Seabarn, Kingston Gorse, Sussex, and formerly wife of Harold Edward Bell; 3rdly, 1963, Mme Janine Detry de Marès; *d* 1984; *s* by his only son **(15)** DAVID ROBIN FRANCIS GUY, 8th Earl and present peer; also Baron Brooke.

Waterford, Earl of; title borne by Earl of Shrewsbury.

WATERFORD, MARQUESS OF (Beresford) Sits as BARON TYRONE (GB 1786) (Marquess I 1789, Bt I 1665)

No dependence but in the Cross

JOHN HUBERT DE LA POER BERESFORD, 8th Marquess, and 12th Baronet; *b* 14 July 1933; *s* 1934; *ed* Eton; Lieut Roy Horse Guards Supplementary Reserve: *m* 1957, Lady Caroline Olein Geraldine Wyndham-Quin, da of 6th Earl of Dunraven and Mount-Earl, and has issue.

Arms – Quarterly: 1st and 4th argent, semée of cross crosslets fitchée and three fleurs-de-lis within a bordure engrailed sable, *Beresford*; 2nd and 3rd argent, a chief indented sable, *De la Poer*. **Crest** – A dragon's head erased azure, the neck pierced with a broken tilting spear, and holding the point broken off in the mouth. **Supporters** – Two angels, habited in white robes reaching to the ankles, hair and wings inverted or, the exterior arm extended and holding a sword erect proper, pommel and hilt gold.
Seats – Curraghmore, Portlaw, co Waterford; Glenbride Lodge, Valleymount, co Wicklow. *Club* – White's.

SONS LIVING

HENRY NICHOLAS DE LA POER (*Earl of Tyrone*), *b* 23 March 1958: *m* 1986, Amanda, da of Norman Thompson, of The Castle, Borris-in-Ossary, co Leix, and has issue:—

> SONS LIVING— Richard John (*Baron Le Poer*), *b* 19 Aug 1987, — *Hon* Marcus Patrick, *b* 1990.

Residence – Little Oak, Hilcot End, Ampney Crucis, Cirencester.
Lord Charles Richard de la Poer (Estancia el Pucara, 6409 Tres Lomas, Prov de Buenos Aries), *b* 1960: *m* 1984, Maria Teresa, da of Sr Gabriel Donoso Phillips, and Sra Maria Isabelle Donosa Rosselot, of Geronimo de Molina 4900, Santiago, Chile, and has issue living, William, *b* 1990, — Carolina, *b* 1989.

Lord James Patrick de la Poer, *b* 1965: *m* 1989, Avril, da of Louis Murphy, of Baylough, Portlaw, co Waterford.

DAUGHTER LIVING

Lady Alice Rose de la Poer, *b* 1970.

BROTHER LIVING

Lord Patrick Tristram de la Poer, *b* 1934; *ed* Eton; Capt (ret) RHG: *m* 1964 (*m diss* 1971), Julia, formerly wife of Capt Darel Saumarez Carey, RHG, and da of late Col Thomas Cromwell Williamson, DSO, and has issue living, Valentine Tristram, *b* 1965: *m* 1993, Evelyne D., 2nd da of John Hoskin, of Harlow, Essex, — Samantha Julia *b* 1969. *Residence* – Fairview Cottage, Wicks Green, Binfield, Bracknell, Berks RG12 5PF.

WIDOW LIVING OF SON OF SIXTH MARQUESS

Rachel (Thatched Cottage, Church Lane, Stradbally, co Waterford), da of George Kennett Page, of Upton Lodge, Bursledon, Hants: *m* 1945, Maj Lord William Mostyn de la Poer Beresford, who *d* 1973, and has issue (see colls infra).

COLLATERAL BRANCHES LIVING

(Branch from 2nd son of 6th Marquess of Waterford)

Issue of late Maj Lord William de la Poer Beresford, 2nd son of 6th Marquess, *b* 1905, *d* 1973: *m* 1945, Rachel (ante), da of George Kennett Page, of Upton Lodge, Bursledon, Hants:—
Meriel, *b* 1948: *m* 1970, Joseph Power, of Old Town House Stud, Shanballymore, co Cork, and has issue living, James Anthony, *b* 1972, — Richard Joseph, *b* 1982, — Rosemarie Ann, *b* 1970, — Jennifer, *b* 1986. ——— Nicola, *b* 1951: *m* 1976 (legally separated 1993), Andreas Minihan, of Englishtown, Stradbally, co Waterford, eldest son of Andrew Minihan, of Kylebeg, New Ross, co Wexford, and has issue living, Andrew Peter Mark de la Poer, *b* 1977, — Ian Michael de la Poer, *b* 1980, — William David de la Poer, *b* 1983, — Anna Rachel, *b* 1984.

(Branch from 2nd son of 1st Earl of Tyrone) (*Male line in remainder to Earldom of Tyrone*)

Grandchildren of late George Stuart de la Poer Beresford, 2nd son of Arthur George de la Poer Beresford, 2nd son of George William de la Poer Beresford, el son of John Beresford (*b* 1796), el son of Rt Rev George de la Poer Beresford, 2nd son of Rt Hon John de la Poer Beresford (*b* 1738), 2nd son of 1st Earl of Tyrone:—
Issue of late Arthur de la Poer Beresford, *b* 1903, *d* 1931: *m* 1926, Helen, who *d* 1973, da of late Thomas Cull, of Perth, W Australia:—
John de la Poer (5A Shark Court, Sorrento 6020, Perth, Western Australia), *b* 1927; Snr Technical Officer, Commonwealth Scientific and Industrial Research Organisation (ret 1986): *m* 1951, Pamela, da of late Glen J. Sloman, of Applecross, W Aust, and has issue living, Marcus de la Poer (Villa 7, 11 Malcolm St, N Beach, W Australia 6020), *b* 1952, — Graham de la Poer (Justin Drive & Porteus St, Sorrento 6020, Western Australia), *b* 1954: *m* 1981, Josephine Vasallo, and has issue living, Lauren Louise *b* 1987, — Simon Stuart de la Poer, *b* 1961, — Shelley Louise, *b* 1957: *m* 1980, Graham Ekert, of 10 Boya Crescent, Boya, W Australia 6056, and has issue living, Cassandra Claire *b* 1985, Melissa Louise *b* 1987. ——— Margaret Pamela de la Poer, *b* 1930: *m* 1953, Lt-Col Eric McPherson McCormick, R Australian Regt (ret), of 12 Hawkesbury Cres, Farrer, ACT 2607, Australia, and has issue living, Gordon Rory (54 Matina St, Narrabundah, ACT 2604, Australia), *b* 1954: *m* 1982, Alice Jeanette Robinson, and has issue living, Fergus George *b* 1984, Harriet Faith *b* 1986, — Peter James (11 McManus Place, Calwell, ACT 2905, Australia), *b* 1956: *m* 1983, Jennifer Louise Spence, and has issue living, Rory Michael *b* 1984, Mitchell James *b* 1986, Georgia Mae *b* 1991, — Angus Roy (231 Namatjira Drive, Fisher, ACT 2611, Australia), *b* 1957: *m* 1985, Dianna Marie McKeough, and has issue living, Thomas John *b* 1990, Ashleigh Louise *b* 1987, — Hamish John, *b* 1961.
Issue of late Major Brian de la Poer Beresford, MC, Australian Forces, *b* 1910, *ka* in New Guinea 1942: *m* (April) 1942, Valmai, only da of Merlyn B. Jones, of Perth, W Australia:—
Brian George de la Poer (*posthumous*) (3 Circe Circle, Dalkeith, W Australia), *b* 1943; Bar-at-law and Solicitor, Australia: *m* 1964, Deborah Frances, only da of Albert Francis Gamble, of Evalley, Koorda, W Australia, and has issue living, Brian James de la Poer, *b* 1967, — Victoria Jane, *b* 1965.

Grandchildren of late Arthur George de la Poer Beresford (ante):—
Issue of late George Stuart de la Poer Beresford (twin), *b* 1877, *d* 1965: *m* 1st, 1900, Margaret, who *d* 1920, da of late Edward Hooper, of Melbourne, Victoria; 2ndly, 1923, Kathleen, who *d* 1950, da of late Thomas Cull, of Perth, W Australia; 3rdly, 1950, Faith, who *d* 1984, da of Rev F. G. O'Halloran, of Perth, W Australia, and widow of Sqdn Ldr Preston Williams, MC:—
(By 1st *m*) Rosemary de la Poer, *b* 1917: *m* (Feb) 1948, Flight Lt Reginald Harold Sutton, DFC, RAAF, of Must St, Portland, Victoria, Australia, and has issue living, David Beresford, *b* 1953: *m* 1980, Catherine Anne Brewster, and has issue living, Hannah Catherine *b* 1986, Brigitte Rose *b* 1989, — Georgia Jane, *b* (Dec) 1948: *m* 1979, Peter Jonathan Schofield, of Cottage Farm, Obi Obi Road, Mapleton, Qld, — Rosemary Ann, *b* 1950: *m* 1974, William Richard Kilpatrick, of Allanvale, Great Western, Victoria, Aust, and has issue living, Jane Regina *b* 1977, Catharine Ann *b* 1979, Annabel Clare *b* 1984.
Issue of late Marcus John de la Poer Beresford, *b* 1882, *d* 1952: *m* 1st, 1910, Alice Janet Schmidt, who *d* 1935, of Victoria, Australia; 2ndly, 1936, Edith, da of late Capt George Wilkins, of Young, NS Wales:—
(By 1st *m*) Marcus de la Poer, *b* 1912: *m* 1936, Marie Helmers, and has issue living, Marcus Edward de la Poer, *b* 1937, — Brian de la Poer, *b* 1942. ——— John de la Poer, *b* 1913; S-W Pacific 1944-45 with Australian Imperial Force: *m* 1936, Helen Wilson, and has issue living, John de la Poer, *b* 1942, — Helende la Poer, *b* 1937, — Barbara de la Poer, *b* 1940. *Residence* – Turramurra, NS Wales.
Issue of late Henry Mayo de la Poer Beresford, *b* 1889, *d* 1948: *m* 1921, Nathalie, who *d* 1963, da of late Robert Muir, of Middle Brighton, Victoria, Australia:—
Joan de la Poer (Corner Cottage, Sandy Lane, Kingswood, Surrey KT20 6LZ), *b* 1922: *m* 1965, Ralph Louis Bewick, MBE, TD, R Fusiliers (TA) (ret), who *d* 1985. ——— Judith de la Poer, *b* 1954 (*m diss* 1983), Lt-Col Robin William Hone, R Australian Regt (ret), who *d* 1992, and has issue living, David Christopher, *b* 1958: *m* 1993, Wendy Jane, da of Barry Moss, — Carolyn Louise, *b* 1963: *m* 1984, Andrew John McLean (1 Mitchell Rd, Mosman 2088, NSW, Australia), and has issue living, Christopher Andrew *b* 1987, Alexandra Louise *b* 1993, Anastasia Leah *b* 1994. *Address* – Unit 1, 16 Alpha St, Kensington Park, S Aust 5068.
Issue of late Capt William Russell de la Poer Beresford, MC, *b* 1893; *d* 1938: *m* 1923, Marie Isobel, who *d* 1914, da of Samuel Cowper Ward of Adelaide, S Australia:—
Diana Mary de la Poer (139 Stanley St, N Adelaide, S Australia), *b* 1924: *m* 1946, Arthur John Watson, AM, who *d* 1991, and has issue living, Christopher John Beresford (69 Highlever Rd, W10), *b* 1948: *m* 1st 1970 (*m diss* 1976), Georgiana Henry; 2ndly, 1977, Lalita Georgiana Williams, da of W. Peter Halliday, MBE, and has issue living (by 1st *m*), Michaela *b* 1970 (by 2nd *m*) Adelaide Elizabeth Beresford *b* 1982, Francesca Mary Beresford *b* 1984, — Johanna Mary Beresford *b* 1950: *m* 1st, 1972 (*m diss* 1979), Rolf Alexander Detmering; 2ndly, 1992, Geoffrey Robert Scott, of 11 Ferdinand St, Hunters Hill, NSW, Australia, and has issue living, (by Ian Darnton Hill) Phoebe Jane Beresford *b* 1981, (by 2nd *m*) Georgia Anne Beresford *b* 1992, — Robina Anne Beresford, *b* 1960: *m* 1986, Richard Goldsmith Daw, of 40 Melville St, Hawthorn, Victoria, Australia. ——— Marie Suzanne de la Poer, *b* 1925: *m* 1st, 1946, Murray Frew Bonnin, solicitor, late Austn Imperial Forces, who *d* 1978; 2ndly, 1979, David Hans Heysen, of Heysen Rd, Hahndorf, S Australia 5245, son of late Sir Hans Heysen, and has issue living (by 1st *m*), John Frew, *b* 1951, — David Frew, *b* 1952: *m* 1st, 1976, Jennifer Crowe; 2ndly, 1989, Angela Jane Dunstan, and has issue living (by 2nd *m*), William Frew *b* 1990, Annabel Beresford *b* 1992.

Grandchildren of late Richard de la Poer Beresford, 3rd son of George William de la Poer Beresford (ante):—
Issue of late Claude Richard de la Poer Beresford, *b* 1888, *d* 1945: *m* 1915, Edith Marion, who *d* 1977, da of Christopher Beaven, of Adelaide, S Aust:—
Ben Richard de la Poer, *b* 1927; late RAN; ASA; Member of Australian Stock Exchange: *m* 1955, Janet Marcia, da of John Essington Grime, of The Pines, Green Point, NSW, and has issue living, William Richard de la Poer (472 Argyle St, Moss Vale, NSW 2577, Australia), *b* 1959; BVSc: *m* 1987, Sally Isobel, da of John Walsh, of Sutton Forest, NSW, and has issue living, Samantha Jane *b* 1988, Georgia Kate *b* 1993, — John Ben de la Poer, *b* 1965, — Charles Patrick de la Poer (3 Charles St, Prospect, S Australia), *b* 1966; LLB: *m* 1992, Sarah Jane, da of Colin Hagger, of North Adelaide, S Australia, — Mary Lynne de la Poer, *b* 1956; B app Sc (Physio): *m* 1977, Stewart Graham Teague, of 354A Kensington Rd, Erindale, S Australia, and has issue living, Nicholas James *b* 1982, Andrew Graham *b* 1984, James Robert *b* 1986, Benjamin Stewart *b* 1988, Sarah

Jane *b* 1980. *Residence* – 36 Brunswick St, North Walkerville, S Aust 5081. —— Donald Charles de la Poer (55/186 Sutherland St, Paddington, NSW 2021, Australia), *b* 1933: *m* 1962 (*m diss* 1979), Ruth Tisdall, and has issue living, Peter Mark de la Poer, *b* 1965, —— Susan Jane de la Poer, *b* 1964. —— Sydney May de la Poer (116 Walkerville Terr, Walkerville, S Australia 5081), *b* 1917: *m* 1937, Leonard Arthur Ranson Evans, who *d* 1989, and has issue living, Michael John de la Poer Beresford (17 William St, Hawthorn, S Australia 5062), *b* 1941: *m* 1971, Rachel Anne Wyndham, and has issue living, (David) Michael Wyndham *b* 1974, (Kathryn) Mary *b* 1973, —— Elizabeth Jane, *b* 1946: *m* 1971 (*m diss* 1993), Whalley de Quetteville Robin, and has issue living, Ben de Quetteville *b* 1975, Anne Sutton *b* 1973, Mary de Quetteville *b* 1978. —— Molly Clodagh de la Poer (50 Second Av, St Peters, S Australia 5069), *b* 1920: *m* 1940, Harold de Vall Amphlett, who *d* 1988, and has issue living, John de Vall, *b* 1949: *m* 1976, Margaret, da of Robert Stokes, SM and has issue living, Scott Francis *b* 1980, Mark John de Vall *b* 1982, Alice Louise *b* 1988, —— Margaret de Vall, *b* 1947: *m* 1968, Daniel Knight, and has issue living, Andrew de Vall *b* 1971, (Rebecca) Anne *b* 1974.

Issue of late Guy Erroll de la Poer Beresford, *b* 1889, *d* 1944: *m* 1921, Dorothy Margaret, who *d* 1956, da of W. T. McCoy, of Adelaide:—

Richard de la Poer (5 George St, Norwood 5067, S Australia), *b* 1922; 1939-45 War in RAAF: *m* 1945, Elizabeth Leitch, and has issue living, Marcus Richard de la Poer (145 Drayton St, Bowden 5007, S Australia), *b* 1950, —— Melaine de la Poer, *b* 1948. —— Margaret de la Poer, *b* 1925; *m* 1947, Jan Edgar Marr, late AIF, and has issue living, Carolyn Ann, *b* 19—, —— Stephanie Jane, *b* 19—, —— Katrina Louise, *b* 19—.

Grandson of late Edward Beresford, yr son of George de la Poer Beresford, el son of Rt Hon and Most Rev Marcus Gervais Beresford, DD, Archbishop of Armagh, 2nd son of Rt Rev George de la Poer Beresford (ante):—

Issue of late George Henry William de la Poer Beresford, *b* 1904, *d* 1961: *m* 1926 (*m diss* 1949), Mary Isobel, who *d* 1989, da of George Richardson, of Molesley:—

John George de la Poer (Aubawn, Lamorna Cove, Penzance, Cornwall TR19 6XW), *b* 1927: *m* 1960, Jeanne Frances, da of William Steward, of London, and has issue living, Stephen de la Poer, *b* 1961: *m* 1991, Aline Rogers, —— Mark de la Poer, *b* 1962: *m* 1989, Sophie Grissa, and has issue living, Justin de la Poer *b* 1989, Eloise *b* 1992, —— Clare Jeanne, *b* 1964.

Grandchildren of late George Henry William de la Poer Beresford (ante):—

Issue of late Timothy Edward de la Poer Beresford, *b* 1931, *d* 1964: *m* 1955, Mary Thom Leburn (Maureen) (who *m* 2ndly 1965, Maj Matthew Alexander Forrester, of Little Etchden, Bethersden, Kent TN26 3DS), only child of late John Waugh, of Edinburgh:—

Michael John de la Poer, *b* 1957. —— Karen Mary de la Poer, *b* 1959: *m* 1984, Gordon James Findlay, elder son of James Findlay, of 13 Courthope House, Hartington Rd, SW8. Resides in Portugal.

Grandson of late Lt-Col Kennedy Beresford, el son of Maj Henry Marcus Beresford, yr son of Rt Hon and Most Rev Marcus Gervais Beresford, Archbishop of Armagh (ante):—

Issue of late Col Gervais de la Poer Beresford, MBE, MC, DSM, *b* 1895, *d* 1979: *m* 1st, 1927, Nada Celina, who *d* 1956, da of Harry L. Wormald, of Bramhall, Cheshire; 2ndly, 1957, Rosemary Helen Arnaud Gange, da of late Lt-Col G. E. Painter, RE, of Epsom, Surrey:—

(By 1st *m*) Michael Marcus Gervais de la Poer (26 Ladbroke Sq, W11), *b* 1928; *ed* Marlborough, and at Birmingham Univ; Lt 8th Hussars (Reserve): *m* 1975, Ann Veronica Nieburg, of S Africa.

Grandson of late Col William Randal Hamilton Beresford-Ash, 3rd son of late John Barré Beresford (infra):—

Issue of late Maj Douglas Beresford-Ash, *b* 1887, *d* 1976: *m* 1930, Lady Betty Helena Joanna Rous, who *d* 1969, da of 3rd Earl of Stradbroke:—

John Randal (Ashbrook, co Londonderry; Carlton Club), *b* 1938; *ed* Eton: *m* 1968, Agnès Marie Colette, da of Count Guy de Lamberterie, of Ensouleiada, Avenue de Benefiat, Cannes, and has issue living, Melanie Anne Helena Charlotte, *b* 1968, —— Louisa-Jane Marie Caroline, *b* 1971, —— Angélique Mary Elisa, *b* 1978.

Granddaughter of late John Barré Beresford, el son of Henry Barré Beresford, yst son of Rt Hon John de la Poer Beresford (*b* 1738) (ante):—

Issue of late Lieut-Col Marcus John Barré de la Poer Beresford, DSO, *b* 1868, *d* as a result of enemy action 1944: *m* 1914, Alma, who *d* 1968, da of David Methven, of Hillside, 31 Elsworthy Rd, Regent's Park, NW3:—

Patricia Douglas Methven, *b* 1924: *m* 1974, Maurice William Alfred Carter, of Worthing, Sussex.

(Branch from 3rd son of 1st Earl of Tyrone)

Descendants of late Most Rev Hon William Beresford, DD (3rd son of 1st Earl of Tyrone), who was *cr Baron Decies* 1812 (see that title).

PREDECESSORS – (1) Sir TRISTRAM Beresford, MP for Londonderry, was *cr* a Baronet 1665; *d* 1673; *s* by his son (2) Sir RANDAL, 2nd Bt; *s* by the son (3) Sir TRISTRAM, 3rd Bt; commanded a Regt of Foot against James II, and was attainted by Parliament; *d* 1701; *s* by his son (4) Sir MARCUS, 4th Bt: *m* 1717, Lady Catharine Poer (*Baroness La Poer* in her own right, *cr* by writ of summons 1375 *et seq*), da and heiress of James, 3rd Earl of Tyrone and Baron La Poer; *cr Baron Beresford*, of Beresford, co Cavan, and *Viscount Tyrone* (peerage of Ireland) 1720, and *Earl of Tyrone* (peerage of Ireland) 1746; *d* 1763; *s* by his son (5) GEORGE DE LA POER, 2nd Earl, who in 1769 *s* by his mother in the Barony of De La Poer; *cr Baron Tyrone*, of Haverfordwest, co Pembroke (peerage of Great Britain) 1786, and *Marquess of Waterford* (peerage of Ireland) 1789; *d* 1800; *s* by his son (6) HENRY DE LA POER, KP, PC, 2nd Marquess was Gov of co Waterford and Col of Waterford Militia; *d* 1826; *s* by his el son (7) HENRY DE LA POER, KP, 3rd Marquess; *d* 1859; *s* by his brother (8) JOHN DE LA POER, 4th Marquess; *b* 1814; was in Holy Orders, a Rural Dean, and incumbent of Mullaghbrack: *m* 1843, Christiana, da of Charles Powell Leslie, MP, of Glaslough, co Monaghan; *d* 1866; *s* by his son (9) HENRY DE LA POER, PC, KP, 5th Marquess, *b* 1844; Lord-Lieut of co Waterford; MP for Waterford Co (C) 1865-6, and Master of the Buckhounds 1885-6: *m* 1st, 1872, Florence Grosvenor, who *d* 1873, da of Major George Rowley, Bombay Army, and divorced wife of Hon John C. W. Vivian; 2ndly, 1874, Lady Blanche Elizabeth Adelaide, da of 8th Duke of Beaufort; *d* 1895; *s* by his only son (10) HENRY DE LA POER, KP, 6th Marquess, *b* 1875: *m* 1897, Lady Beatrix Frances Fitzmaurice, GBE, who *d* 1953 (having *m* 2ndly, 1918, 12th Duke of St Albans), da of 5th Marquess of Lansdowne; *d* 1911; *s* by his el son (11) JOHN CHARLES DE LA POER, 7th Marquess, *b* 1901: *m* 1930, Juliet Mary (who *d* 1987, having *m* 2ndly, 1946, Lieut-Col John Eric Durnford Silcock), da of Major David Balcarres Lindsay; *d* 1934; *s* by his el son (12) JOHN HUBERT DE LA POER, 8th Marquess and present peer; also Earl of Tyrone, Viscount Tyrone, Baron Le Poer, Baron Beresford, and Baron Tyrone.

WATERPARK, BARON (Cavendish) (Baron I 1792, Bt GB 1755)

FREDERICK CARYLL PHILIP CAVENDISH, 7th Baron, and 8th Baronet; *b* 6 Oct 1926; *s* 1948; *ed* Eton; late Lieut Grenadier Gds; Assist Dist Comdt Kenya Police Reserve 1952-54; Dir CSE Aviation 1962, Dep Chm since 1983: *m* 1951, Danièle Alice, da of Roger Guirche, of Paris, and has issue.

Arms – Sable, three stags' heads cabossed argent, attired or, within a bordure of the second. **Crest** – On a ducal coronet or, a serpent nowed fessewise proper. **Supporters** – *Dexter*, a stag, per fesse indented gules and sable, attired and unguled or; *sinister*, a stag proper, attired and unguled or, and gorged with a chaplet of four roses argent and azure, alternatively.
Residence – 74 Elm Park Rd, SW3 6AU; Park House, Bletchington, Oxon. **Club** – Cavalry and Guards.

Secure by caution

SON LIVING

Hon RODERICK (RORY) ALEXANDER, *b* 10 Oct 1959: *m* 1989, Anne, da of Hon Luke Asquith (*see* By Asquith of Bishopstone), and has issue living, Luke Frederick, *b* 17 Sept 1990.

DAUGHTERS LIVING

Hon Caroline Laurence Patricia, *b* 1952: *m* 1979, Richard Michael George Goulding, and has issue living, William Roderick Ossian, *b* 1983, — Laura Yasuko Danielle, *b* 1986.
Hon Juliet Enid Marie Gabrielle, *b* 1953: *m* 19—, Charles Dumaresq Nicholson, yr son of late Arthur Wilfrid Nicholson, of Hartham Park, Corsham, Wilts, and has issue living, Isabel, *b* 1986, — Claire, *b* 1988.

SISTER LIVING

Patricia Enid (Broadlands Stud, Somerset West, CP, S Africa), *b* 1925: *m* 1st, 1950 (*m diss* 1954), Frank Thomas O'Neill; 2ndly, 1958, Count Aymon de Roussy de Sales; 3rdly, 1969, Frank Thomas O'Neill (ante).

DAUGHTERS LIVING OF SIXTH BARON (By 1st marriage)

Hon Cecilia Claribel, *b* 1903: *m* 1933, James Mitchell Anderson, MD, ChB, who *d* 1963, and has issue living, Isabel Juliet Cavendish, *b* 1937: *m* 1957, Clifford Anthony Broom, and has issue living, Nicholas James *b* 1959, Christopher David *b* 1961, — Annabel Fiona Macpherson Cavendish, *b* 1940: *m* 1st, 1962 (*m diss* 1970), Manfred Seifert; 2ndly, 1971, Haven Lemar Dunn, and has issue living (by 1st *m*), Jenny Elisabeth *b* 1965. *Residence* – Courtenay Beach, Kingsway, Hove, Sussex.

(By 2nd marriage)

Hon Margaret, *b* 1907: *m* 1934, Wallace Edward Thomas Leaver, BSc who *d* 1972, and has issue living, Diana Cavendish, *b* 1938: *m* 1961, Charles Peter Parnell Wiggins, of East Cross, Tenterden, Kent, and has issue living, Rupert Alexander Cavendish *b* 1963, Philippa Cavendish *b* 1962, — Elizabeth Cavendish, *b* 1942. *Residence* – St Benets, Beech Hill, Bridge, Canterbury.
Hon Winifred *b* 1909: *m* 1929, Albert Frank Tribe, Trinity House Pilot, who *d* 1962, having assumed by deed poll 1944 the additional surname of Cavendish, and by letters patent, 1944 the Arms of Cavendish quarterly with Tribe, and has issue living, Barrie Cavendish (27 Strickmere, Stratford St Mary, Colchester, Essex), *b* 1930: *m* 1957, Jane McGeorge, only da of late Surg Rear-Adm David Duncan, CB, OBE, and has issue living, Eur Ing Alan Cavendish *b* 1960; BSc Eng, C Eng, MI Mech E, M Weld Inst, Sonia Cavendish *b* 1963; BSc Chem. *Residence* – Saxons Beech Hill, Bridge, nr Canterbury, Kent.

COLLATERAL BRANCH LIVING

Grandsons of late Charles Tyrell Cavendish, second son of late Hon Richard Cavendish, 2nd son of 2nd Baron:—
Issue of late Tyrell William Cavendish, *b* 1875, *d* 1912: *m* 1906, Julia Florence, who *d* 1963, only child of Henry Siegel, of New York:—
Henry Siegel, *b* 1908; *ed* Eton, and Trin Coll Camb; European War 1939-45 as Squadron-Leader Auxiliary Air Force: *m* 1940, Diana Linda, da of Edward Hewish Ryle, and has issue living, William Henry Tyrell, *b* 1940; *ed* Eton. *Residence* – 15 Cadogan Lane, SW1. —— Geoffrey Manners (7 Gema Close, Allestree, Derby, DE22 2UL), *b* 1910; *ed* Stowe; CEng; MIEE; Member of Institution of British Radio Engineers; Diploma of Faraday House Engineering Coll; late Air Min Examiner in Scientific and Electrical Section of Aeronautical Inspection Directorates: *m* 1st, 1937, Caecilia Frances Patricia, who *d* 1968, da of Godfrey Pharazyn, of Waewaepa, Dannevirke, Hawkes Bay, NZ; 2ndly, 1967, Mrs Pamela Newman, and has issue living (by 1st *m*) Caroline Anne, *b* 1938: *m* 1964, Charles Grellan Aliaga-Kelly, BArch, ARIBA, FRTPI, FRIAI, Dublin Planning Officer (ret), of Clare Villa, Coliemore Rd, Dalkey, co Dublin, and has issue living, William John *b* 1967; *ed* Univ Coll, Dublin, — Caecilia Bridget, *b* 1941: *m* 1979, Ralph Rokeby Johnson, of Kelsey Farm, PO Box 2001, Stellenbosch, Cape 7601, S Africa; and Arthingworth, PO Box 1513, Rancho Santa Fé, Calif 92067, USA, and has issue living, Henry Ralph Cavendish *b* 1979.

PREDECESSORS – (1) *Rt Hon* HENRY Cavendish, PC; MP for Lismore, Teller of the Exchequer in Ireland, Collector for Cork, and a Commr for Revenue (Ireland); *cr* a *Baronet* 1755; *d* 1776; *s* by his son (2) *Sir* HENRY, PC, 2nd Bt; sat as MP for Lostwithiel; was Receiver-Gen in Ireland: *m* 1757, Sarah, da and heir of Richard Bradshaw, which lady was in 1792 *cr Baroness Waterpark*, 5th Baron, co Cork (peerage of Ireland), with remainder to her issue male by Sir Henry Cavendish; she *d* 1807; *s* by her son (3) RICHARD, 2nd Baron, who in 1804 had *s* his father as 3rd Bt; *d* 1830; *s* by his son (4) HENRY MANNERS, 3rd Baron; *b* 1793; was Col Derbyshire Militia, and a Lord-in-Waiting: *m* 1837, Hon Eliza Jane, VA, who *d* 1894, da of 1st Viscount Anson; *d* 1863; *s* by his son (5) HENRY ANSON, 4th Baron; *b* 1839: *m* 1873, Emily, who *d* 1925, da of late John Stenning; *d* 1912; *s* by his son (6) HENRY FREDERICK, 5th Baron; *b* 1883; *d* 1932; *s* by his cousin (7) HENRY SHEPPARD HART (el son of late William Thomas Cavendish, grandson of 2nd Baron), 6th Baron; *b* 1876; was a hunter and explorer in Africa, Patagonia, Australia, Solomon Islands, and Canada: *m* 1st, 1902 (*m diss* 1906), Isabel Emilie (an actress), who *d* 1927, da of John Wimburn Jay; 2ndly, 1906 (*m diss* 1913), May, who *d* 1969, da of William Ernest Burbridge, of Bromley, Kent; 3rdly, 1913 (*m diss* 1919), Elise, da of Emmanuel Adolphe Herran, formerly Sec to French Embassy in London: 4thly, 1920 (*m diss* 1929), Georgette, da of Ivan Zlateffmoloff Chandronnier of Bulgaria; 5thly, 1929, Jeanne, who *d* 1968, da of Pierre Lassallette;

d 1948; *s* by his nephew **(8)** FREDERICK CARYLL PHILIP (only son of late Brig-Gen Frederick William Laurence Sheppard Hart Cavendish, brother of 6th Baron), 7th Baron and present peer.

WATKINS, BARONY OF (Watkins) (Extinct 1983)

WIDOW LIVING OF LIFE BARON

BRONWEN RICHARDS (*Baroness Watkins*), da of late Thomas Stather, of Talgarth: *m* 1936, Baron Watkins (Life Baron), who *d* 1983.
Residence – Bronafon Penyfan Rd, Brecon, Powys.

WATKINSON, VISCOUNT (Watkinson) (Viscount UK 1964)

HAROLD ARTHUR WATKINSON, CH, PC, 1st Viscount, son of Arthur G. Watkinson, of Walton-on-Thames; *b* 25 Jan 1910; *ed* Queen's Coll, Taunton, and King's Coll, London; PPS to Min of Transport and Civil Aviation 1951-52; Parl Sec to Min of Labour and National Ser 1952-55, Min of Transport and Civil Aviation 1955-59, and Min of Defence 1959-62, and Chm of Cttee for Exports to USA 1964-67; Managing Dir of Schweppes Group 1963-68, Chm Cadbury Schweppes, Ltd, 1969-74, and of BIM 1968-70; Pres of Inst of Grocery Distribution 1972-73; Pres CBI 1976-77; 1939-45 War as Lt-Cdr RNVR; MP for Woking Div of Surrey (C) 1950-64; *cr* PC 1955, CH 1962, and *Viscount Watkinson*, of Woking, co Surrey (peerage of UK) 1964: *m* 1939, Vera, da of John Langmead, of Northwood, Ford, Sussex, and has issue.

Arms – Vert fretty and three fleeces or. **Crest** – A ram passant proper on an antique cannon sable garnished or. **Supporters** – *Dexter*, a weaver holding in the exterior hand a shuttle; *sinister* a shepherd holding with the exterior hand a crook all proper.
Residence – Tyma House, Bosham, Chichester, Sussex. *Clubs* – RNVR, Royal Southern Yacht Club.

DAUGHTERS LIVING

Hon Sarah Margaret, *b* 1944: *m* 1965, David Bethune Spicer, of Vingers, West Harting, Petersfield, Hants GU31 5NX, and has issue living, Mary Bethune, *b* 1966, — Joanna Margaret, *b* 1968, — Eliza Jane, *b* 1970, — Alice Bethune, *b* 1985.
Hon Rosemary Jane, *b* 1947: *m* 1976, Barrie Robert Musgrave, of Droridge Barn, Dartington, Totnes, Devon TQ9 6JG, and has issue living, Oliver Robert, *b* 1977, — Rowan Gill, *b* 1979.

WAVELL, EARLDOM OF (Wavell) (Extinct 1953)

DAUGHTERS LIVING AND DECEASED OF FIRST EARL

Lady (Eugénie) Pamela, *b* 1918: *m* 1942, Arthur Francis Walter Humphrys, OBE, only son of Lieut-Col Sir Francis Humphrys, GCMG, GCVO, KBE, CIE, and has issue living, Francis Wavell Harold James, *b* 1944, — (Henry) Owen Rookhurst, *b* 1946. — (Eugénie) Cecilia, *b* 1950.
Lady Felicity Ann, *b* 1921: *m* 1947, Major Peter Maitland Longmore, MC, RA (Maitland, Bt colls), who *d* (22 April) 1994, and *d* (19 June) 1994, having had issue, Richard Martin Wavell *b* 1948, *d* 1982, Andrew Nigel Murray, *b* 1953: *m* 1976, Jane, el da of Dr B. G. Morgan, of 29 Gerard Rd, Wallasey Merseyside, and has issue living, Anna *b* 1980, Jessica *b* 1982, — Ann Christina, *b* 1950 *m* 1971 (*m diss* 1985), Angus McDonagh, and has issue living, Amber *b* 1977, and further issue (by John D. Colvin), Rhiannon COLVIN *b* 1989, Kieran COLVIN *b* 1992, — Fiona Elaine, *b* 1963: *m* 19—, (Bengt) Joacim Holgersson.
Lady Joan Patricia Quirk, *b* 1923: *m* 1st, 1943, Capt Hon Simon Nevill Astley, 7th Hussars, who *d* 1946 (*see* B Hastings); 2ndly, 1948, Maj Harry Alastair Gordon, MC, Gordon Highlanders, who *d* 1965; 3rdly, 1973, Maj Donald Struan Robertson, Scots Gds, who *d* 1991, of Winkfield Plain Farm, Winkfield, Windsor, Berks, SL4 4QU, and has issue living (by 1st *m*) (*see* B Hastings), — (by 2nd *m*) Anthea Leila, *b* 1949: *m* 1st, 1970 (*m diss* 1980), Timothy Hanbury; 2ndly, 1982, William D. Dalton, of 155 Chadwick Rd, SE15 4PY, and has issue living (by 1st *m*), Jesse *b* 1974, Griffin *b* 1975, Luella *b* 1977, — Patricia, *b* 1951: *m* 1977 (*m diss* 1990), Sir John Auld Mactaggart, 4th Bt, of 19 Chelsea Sq, SW3, and of Ardmore House, Ardtalla Estate, Islay, Argyll.

WAVERLEY, VISCOUNT (Anderson) (Viscount UK 1952)

JOHN DESMOND FORBES ANDERSON, 3rd Viscount; *b* 31 Oct 1949; *s* 1990; *ed* Malvern: *m* 1994, Her Excellency Dr Ursula Helen Barrow, LLM, PhD, High Commr for Belize, da of Raymond Hugh Barrow, SC, Bar-at-law, of Belize City.

Arms – Argent, a saltire engrailed between a mullet in chief and a lotus flower in base, and in each flank a crescent gules; on a chief sable three martlets of the field. **Crest** – A demi-lion rampant or, armed and langued azure, holding in his dexter forepaw a branch of olive proper. **Supporters** – Two horses argent, crined and unguled or.
Address – c/o House of Lords, SW1A 0PW

SISTERS LIVING AND DECEASED

Hon Ida Christina Romaine, *b* 1952; *k* in a motor accident in Africa 1972.
Hon Patricia Mairead Janet, *b* 1955; resumed her maiden name 1983: *m* 1st, 1979 (*m diss* 1983), Charles R. Roberts; 2ndly, 1989, Leon Clifton, of Colorado, USA, and has issue living (by 2nd *m*), William Scott, *b* 1990, — India Rose Veronica Romaine, *b* 1994. *Residence* – Chanders, Aldworth, Berks RG8 9RU.

AUNT LIVING (*daughter of 1st Viscount*)

Hon Dame Mary Mackenzie, DBE, *b* 1916; Brig WRAC; Dir WRAC; and Hon ADC to HM, 1967-70; MBE (Mil) 1958, DBE (Mil) 1970: *m* 1973, Frithjof Pihl, of Engö, Tjøme, Norway, who *d* 1988. *Residence* – 7 Kiln Gardens, Hartley Wintney, Hants RG27 8RG.

WIDOW LIVING OF SECOND VISCOUNT

LORNA MYRTLE ANN (*Dowager Viscountess Waverley*), da of late Lt-Col Frederick Hill Ledgerwood, late IA: *m* 1948, the 2nd Viscount, who *d* 1990. *Residence* – Chanders, Aldworth, Berks RG8 9RU.

PREDECESSORS – (1) *Rt Hon Sir* JOHN ANDERSON, GCB, OM, GCSI, GCIE, FRS, son of late David A. P. Anderson, of Westland House, Eskbank, Midlothian; *b* 1882; entered Colonial Office 1905, became Principal Clerk National Health Insurance Commn 1912, Sec thereto 1913, Joint Min of Shipping 1917-19, Second Sec Min of Health 1919, Chm and a Commr of Board of Inland Revenue 1919, Joint Under-Sec for Ireland 1920, and Permanent Under-Sec of State for Home Depart 1922; Gov of Bengal 1932-37, Lord Privy Seal 1938-9, Sec of State for Home Depart and Min of Home Security 1939-40, Lord Pres of the Council (Member of War Cabinet) 1940-43, and Chancellor of the Exchequer 1943-45; Chm of Port of London Authority 1946-58; sat as MP for Edinburgh, St Andrews, Glasgow, and Aberdeen Univs (*National*) 1938-50; *cr* Viscount Waverley, of Westdean, co Sussex (peerage of United Kingdom) 1952: *m* 1st, 1907, Christina, who *d* 1920, da of late Andrew Mackenzie, of Edinburgh; 2ndly, 1941, Ava, who *d* 1974, da of late J. E. C. Bodley, and widow of Ralph Wigram, CMG; *d* 1958; *s* by his only son (2) DAVID ALASTAIR PEARSON, 2nd Viscount; *b* 1911, MRCS England and LRCP London 1936, MRCP 1946, FRCP 1957, Consultant Physician, Royal Berkshire Hospital, Reading: *m* 1948, Lorna Myrtle Ann, da of late Lt-Col Frederick Hill Ledgerwood, late IA: *d* 1990; *s* by his only son (3) JOHN DESMOND FORBES, 3rd Viscount and present peer.

WEATHERILL, BARON (Weatherill) (Life Baron 1992)

(BRUCE) BERNARD WEATHERILL, PC, son of late Bernard Weatherill, of Spring Hill, Guildford; *b* 25 Nov 1920; *ed* Malvern; Hon DCL Univ of William and Mary, Williamsburg, Virginia, USA 1988, Hon DCL Univ of Kent at Canterbury 1990, and Hon DL Open Univ 1993; Hon Bencher, Lincoln's Inn 1990; DL Kent 1992; commn'd 4/7th Royal Dragoon Guards 1940, transferred to IA (19th King George V's Own Lancers) and served 1939-45 War in Burma and NW Europe; Bernard Weatherill Ltd, Tailors, of Savile Row 1946-70 (Man Dir 1957-70), Pres since 1992; Lord Commr HM Treasury 1970-71, Vice-Chamberlain Royal Household 1971-72, Comptroller 1972-73, Treasurer and Dep Chief Whip 1973-74, Chm Ways and Means and Dep Speaker 1979-83, Speaker of the House of Commons 1983-92; Chm Commonwealth Speakers and Presiding Officers 1986-88; Chm Guildford Conservative Assocn 1959-63, and Member Nat Union of Conservative Party 1963-64; Chm The Parliamentary Channel 1993; Chm The Industry and Parliament Trust 1994; Alternate Convenor of Cross Bench Peers in House of Lords 1993; High Bailiff Westminster Abbey since 1989; Vice Chancellor Order of St John of Jerusalem since 1992; Freeman City of London; MP Croydon NE (*C*) 1964-92; *cr* PC 1980, and *Baron Weatherill*, of NE Croydon, London Borough of Croydon (Life Baron) 1992: *m* 1949, Lyn, da of late Henry Thomas Eatwell, of Whitehall, Sandwich Bay, Kent, and has issue.

Arms – Azure, a cross floretty or surmounting two lances in saltire proper, flying from each a forked pennon per fess gules and argent. **Crest** – A horse rampant argent supporting a mace erect or. **Supporters** – *Dexter*, a Captain in the 19th King

George V's Own Lancers (Indian Army); *sinister*, a Knight of Justice of the Most Venerable Order of the Hospital of St John of Jerusalem both proper.

SONS LIVING

Hon Bernard Richard, *b* 1951; *ed* Malvern: *m* 1977, Sally Maxwell Fisher, and has issue living, Thomas Bernard, *b* 1984, — Julia Rosemary, *b* 1982.

Hon Henry Bruce, *b* 1953; *ed* Malvern: *m* 1978, Susan Mary Dutton, and has issue living, James Edward Bruce, *b* 1983, — Benjamin Harry Charles, *b* 1986, — Sophie, *b* 1989.

DAUGHTER LIVING

Hon Virginia, *b* 1955: *m* 1982, Alan Charles Lovell, and and has issue living, Emma Charlotte, *b* 1985, — Lucinda Mary, *b* 1986.

WEDDERBURN OF CHARLTON, BARON (Wedderburn) Life Baron (1977)

KENNETH WILLIAM WEDDERBURN, son of Herbert John Wedderburn; *b* 13 April 1927; *ed* Aske's (Hatcham) Gram Sch, Whitgift Sch, and Queen's Coll, Camb (MA, LLB), Hon D Giur, Pavia 1990, Hon D Econ, Siena 1991; Bar Middle Temple 1953, QC 1990; Fellow Clare Coll, Camb 1952-64, Cassel Professor of Commercial Law, London Univ (LSE) 1964-92, since when Emeritus, Professor of Law; Visiting Professor Harvard Law School 1969-70; Gen Editor, *Modern Law Review* 1970-88; Chm TUC Indep Review Cttee since 1976; Pres Inst of Employment Rights since 1989; FBA (1981); Fl Lt RAF 1951; *cr Baron Wedderburn of Charlton*, of Highgate, Greater London (Life Baron) 1977: *m* 1st, 1951 (*m diss* 1962), Nina, da of Dr Myer Salaman; 2ndly, 1962 (*m diss* 1969), Dorothy Enid, da of Frederick C. Barnard, and formerly wife of William A. Cole; 3rdly, 1969, Frances Ann, da of Basil F. Knight, and has issue by 1st and 3rd *m*. *Residence* – 29 Woodside Av, Highgate, N6 4SP.

SONS LIVING *(By 1st marriage)*

Hon David Roland *b* 1956; BSc, ACA.

(By 3rd marriage)

Hon Jonathan Michael, *b* 1972.

DAUGHTERS LIVING *(By 1st marriage)*

Hon Sarah Louise, *b* 1954: *m* 1st, 1975 (*m diss* 1985), Michael Walsh; 2ndly, 1992, Hugh Edmund Brooke Faulkner, of 3 Birley Rd, N20 0HB. *Hon* Lucy Rachel, *b* 1960.

WEDGWOOD, BARON (Wedgwood) (Baron UK 1942)

I split asunder obstacles

3rd Baron, who *d* 1970.

PIERS ANTHONY WEYMOUTH WEDGWOOD, 4th Baron, *b* 20 Sept 1954; *s* 1970; *ed* Marlborough; late Capt Royal Scots: *m* 1985, Mary Regina Margaret Kavanagh, da of late Edward Quinn, of Philadelphia, Pa, USA, and has issue.

Arms – Gules four mullets in cross and a canton argent. **Crest** – On a ducal coronet, a lion passant argent. **Supporters** – On either side a lion rampant queue fourchée argent supporting a staff raguly gules. *Residence* – 152 Ashley Gdns, SW1.

DAUGHTER LIVING

Hon Alexandra Mary Kavanagh, *b* 1987.

SISTERS LIVING

Hon Susan Margaret, *b* 1950: *m* 1994, Hubert Ribeiro de Santana. *Hon* Sarah Jane Edith, *b* 1958: *m* 1982, Paul J. Bitove, of Toronto, Canada, son of James Bitove, of Toronto, Canada, and has issue living, Olivia Charlotte, *b* 1988.

WIDOW LIVING OF THIRD BARON

JANE WEYMOUTH (*Dowager Baroness Wedgwood*), (Harewood Cottage, Chicksgrove, Tisbury, Wilts), da of William James Poulton, of Kenjockety, Molo, Kenya: *m* 1949, as his 2nd wife the

COLLATERAL BRANCH LIVING

Issue of late Hon Josiah Wedgwood, yr son of 1st Baron; *b* 1899; *d* 1968: *m* 1919, Dorothy Mary, OBE, who *d* 1974, da of Percy James Winser, of Knutsford:—
JOHN, CBE (156 Ashley Gdns, Thirleby Rd, SW1P 1HW; Athenaeum Club), *b* 1919; *ed* Abbotsholme and Camb Univ (MA, BCh, MD); FRCP; 1939-45 War, as Surg-Lt RNVR in Europe and Far East; Emeritus Consultant Physician at Middx Hospital (ret 1980) since when, Dir Roy Hospital & Home for Incurables; Hon Sr Lectr Middx Hospital Med Sch 1980-86, and Dir Wedgwood Ltd 1967-87; CBE (Civil) 1987: *m* 1st, 1943 (*m diss* 1971), Margaret, da of Alfred S. Mason of Bury St Edmunds, Suffolk; 2ndly, 1972, Jo Alice Tamlyn, da of late Harold Swann Ripsher, and has issue living (by 1st *m*), Antony John (10 Milner Place, N1; Athenæum Club), *b* 1944; *ed* Marlborough, and Trin Coll, Camb (MA); FCA; partner in KPMG Peat Marwick: *m* 1970, Angela Margaret Mary Page, and has issue living, Thomas *b* 1978, Elizabeth *b* 1975, Caroline *b* 1981, — Simon James Josiah, *b* 1949, — Nicholas Ralph, *b* 1951, — Judith Margaret Susannah, *b* 1946: *m* 1st, 1966 (*m diss* 1986), Christopher Anthony Wingfield Tracy; 2ndly, 1986, (Kevin) Dominic Hall Brennan, and has issue living (by 1st *m*), Emma *b* 1970, Victoria *b* 1974, Charlotte *b* 1976, (by 2nd *m*) Alexander *b* 1987, Roland *b* (twin) 1987, , — Katherine Sarah, *b* 1955: *m* 1988, Ian R. Stanbury, and has issue living, Jack *b* 1988, Matthew *b* 1990. —— Josiah Ralph (3717 41st Av NE, Seattle, Washington 98105-5436, USA), *b* 1924; *ed* Bedales, Putney Sch, Putney, Vermont, Harvard Univ, and Harvard Med Sch (MD); naturalized US citizen 1951; Prof Univ of Washington, Seattle since 1963: *m* 1943, Virginia Lloyd, da of late Edward Eyre Hunt, of Washington, DC, and has had issue, Josiah Francis, *b* 1950: *m* 1982, Ruth Anne, da of Morris Glushien, of Gt Neck, LI, USA, — †James Cecil, *b* 1951; *d* 1973, — Jeffrey Galton, *b* 1953: *m* 1st, 1974 (*m diss* 1984), Cynthia Baird; 2ndly, 1985, Susan S., da of Pierce D. Smith, of Darien, Conn, USA, and has issue living (by 2nd *m*), Josiah Smith *b* 1986, Grace Madeleine *b* 1989, — John Ralph Christopher, *b* 1964: *m* 1987, Kathleen, da of William Turner of Kirkland, WA, USA.

PREDECESSORS – (1) *Col Rt Hon* JOSIAH CLEMENT WEDGWOOD, DSO, 2nd son of late Clement Francis Wedgwood, master potter, of Barlaston, Staffordshire, *b* 1872; S Africa 1899-1902, European War 1914-19 as Col (DSO); Chancellor of Duchy of Lancaster (also Ch Civil Commr) Jan to Nov 1924; sat as MP for Newcastle-under-Lyme (*L, Lab,* and *Ind*) Jan 1906 to Jan 1942; *cr Baron Wedgwood*, of Barlaston, co Stafford (peerage of United Kingdom) 1942: *m* 1st, 1894 (*m diss* 1919), Hon Ethel Kate, who *d* 1952, da of 1st Baron Bowen; 2ndly, 1919, Florence Ethel, who *d* 1969, da of late Edward Guy Willett; *d* 1943; *s* by his son (2) FRANCIS CHARLES BOWEN, 2nd Baron; *b* 1898; an Artist: *m* 1920, Edith May, who *d* 1977, da of William Telfer, of Glasgow; *d* 1959; *s* by his only son (3) HUGH EVERARD, 3rd Baron, *b* 1921: *m* 1st, 1945 (*m diss* 1947), Jeno Annette Heather, only child of Ralph S Leake, of Bournemouth; 2ndly, 1949, Jane Weymouth, da of William James Poulton, of Kenjockety, Molo, Kenya; *d* 1970; *s* by his only son (4) PIERS ANTHONY WEYMOUTH, 4th Baron and present peer.

WEEKS, BARON (Weeks) (Extinct 1960)

DAUGHTERS LIVING OF FIRST BARON

Hon Pamela Rose, *b* (Nov) 1931: *m* 1957, Lieut-Com Henry Walter Plunkett-Ernle-Erle-Drax, RN (ret) (*see* B Dunsany, colls).
Residence – Charborough Park, Wareham, Dorset.
Hon Venetia Daphne (*Venetia, Hon Lady Troubridge*), *b* 1933: *m* 1954, Lt-Cdr Sir Peter Troubridge, RN (ret), 6th baronet, who *d* 1988. *Residence* – The Manor House, Elsted, Sussex.

WEIDENFELD, BARON (Weidenfeld) (Life Baron 1976)

(ARTHUR) GEORGE WEIDENFELD, son of late Max Weidenfeld; *b* 13 Sept 1919; *ed* Piaristen Gymnasium, Vienna, Vienna Univ, and Konsular Akademie (Diplomatic Coll); Chm of Weidenfeld & Nicolson Ltd, since 1948; Gov The South Bank Board Ltd, and Trustee Nat Portrait Gallery since 1988; Member English Nat Opera Board; Vice-Chm Campaign for Oxford; *cr* Knt 1969, and *Baron Weidenfeld*, of Chelsea in Greater London (Life Baron) 1976: *m* 1st, 1952, Jane, da of J. Edward Sieff; 2ndly, 1956 (*m diss* 1961), Mrs Barbara Connolly, da of Maj George Skelton; 3rdly, 1966 (*m diss* 1973), Sandra, da of Charles Shipman Payson; 4thly, 1992, Annabelle, da of late Cdr Nicholas Whitestone, and has issue by 1st *m*.

Arms – Per fess or and vert, a fess embattled argent masoned proper, overall a weeping willow eradicated. **Crest** – a demi-wolf regardant sable holding in its mouth a scroll argent. **Supporters** – *Dexter*, an old man proper bearded argent habited in a gown and cap sable supporting in his exterior hand a tablet proper; *Sinister*, a youth proper habited in a blouse argent and breeches or, boots and peaked cap sable, a rapier the scabbard sable.
Residence – 9 Chelsea Embankment, SW3.

Arms must yield to the gown

CEDANT ARMA TOGAE

DAUGHTER LIVING (By 1st marriage)

Hon Laura Miriam Elizabeth, *b* 1953: *m* 1976, Christopher Andrew Barnett, of Haling House, South Croydon and has issue living, Benjamin, *b* 1979, — Rowan, *b* 1981, — Nathaniel Peter Edward, *b* 1984, — Clara Aurjana, *b* 1986.

WEINSTOCK, BARON (Weinstock) (Life Baron 1980)

ARNOLD WEINSTOCK, son of Simon Weinstock; *b* 29 July 1924; *ed* London Univ (BSc Econ); FSS; Hon FRCR, Hon DSc Salford, Aston, Bath and Reading Univs, Hon LLD Leeds Univ, and Wales Univ; Hon D Tech Loughborough Univ; Hon Fell of Peterhouse, Camb, and LSE; Hon Master of the Bench, Gray's Inn; Man Dir General Electric Co Ltd since 1963, and a Dir Rolls-Royce (1971) Ltd 1971-73; Trustee British Museum since 1985; *cr* Knt 1970 and *Baron Weinstock*, of Bowden, co Wilts (Life Baron) 1980: *m* 1949, Netta, da of late Sir Michael Sobell, and has issue.

Arms – Dancetty argent and gules on each of three piles, two issuant in chief and one in base azure, a sun in splendour its straight rays each tipped with flame gold. **Crest** – Upon a wreath argent, or and azure on a mount vert two musical pipes saltirewise or between two stakes entwined by vines fructed proper and ensigned by a crown rayonny gules. **Supporters** – *Dexter*, a male griffin azure beaked, rayed and gorged with a crown tridenty and forelegs or; *sinister*, a horse or gorged with a wreath of trefoils the stalks entwined vert.

SON LIVING

Hon Simon Andrew, *b* 1952; *ed* Winchester, and Magdalen Coll, Oxford (MA): *m* 1979, Laura Helen, only da of Maj Hon Sir Francis Michael Legh, KCVO, and has issue (*see* B Newton).

DAUGHTER LIVING

Hon Susan Gina, *b* 1955; *ed* Cranbourne Chase, St Hilda's Coll, Oxford, and LSE (PhD): *m* 1980, Laurent Lacroix, and has issue living, Jerome Humphrey Andrew, *b* 1992, — Clare Marguerite Pamela, *b* 1985, — Karis Anne, *b* 1989.

WEIR, VISCOUNT (Weir) (Viscount UK 1938)

WILLIAM KENNETH JAMES WEIR, 3rd Viscount, *b* 9 Nov 1933; *s* 1975; *ed* Eton and Trin Coll, Camb (BA), Hon D Eng Glasgow, Hon F Eng; Chm The Weir Group plc since 1983 (Vice Chm 1981-83; Chm and Chief Exec 1972-81); Vice-Chm St James's Place Capital plc, Chm The Great Northern Investment Trust Ltd 1975-82; a Dir Hambro Life 1984-86; Dep Chm BICC plc, of The British Bank of the Middle East 1977-79, British Steel Corpn 1972-76, Canadian Pacific Ltd since 1989; Member of the London Advisory Cttee of the Hong Kong and Shanghai Banking Corpn 1980-92, of the Engineering Industries Council 1975-81, and a Member of Court, Bank of England 1972-84, a Member of Queen's Body Guard for Scotland (Roy Co of Archers): *m* 1st, 1964 (*m diss* 1974), Diana Lucy, da of late Peter Lewis MacDougall, of Rockcliffe, Ont, Canada; 2ndly, 1976 (*m diss* 19—), Jacqueline Mary, el da of late Baron Louis de Chollet, of Fribourg, Switzerland, and formerly wife of Donald Alexander Cameron Marr; 3rdly, 1989, Marina, da of late Marc Sevastopoulo, of 1150 Fifth Av, New York City, and has issue by 1st and 3rd *m*.

Arms – Azure, a cogwheel or, winged argent, in chief the sun in his splendour of the second. **Crest** – A wing argent, charged with a thistle slipped proper. **Supporters** – Two winged horses argent, armed and crined or. *Residence* – Rodinghead, Mauchline, Ayrshire KA5 5HU. *Club* – White's.

SON LIVING (By 1st marriage)

Hon JAMES WILLIAM HARTLAND, *b* 6 June 1965.

(By 3rd marriage)

Hon Andrew Alexander Marc, *b* 1989.

DAUGHTER LIVING (By 1st marriage)

Hon Lorna Elizabeth, *b* 1967.

BROTHERS LIVING

Hon Douglas Nigel (47 Spey Terrace, Edinburgh), *b* 1935; *ed* Eton and Trin Coll, Camb: *m* 1964, Penelope Anne, da of Group Capt John Whitehead, of Bent Mead, Waltham St Lawrence, Berks, and has issue living, Juliet Anne, *b* 1964, — Lucy, *b* 1966, — Nicola Jean, *b* 1969, — Joanna, *b* 1978.
Hon George Anthony (Kilmany House, Kilmany, Cupar, Fife) *b* 1940; *ed* Winchester, at Trin Coll, Camb (BA), and at Mass Inst of Technology, USA (SM, PhD): *m* 1962 (*m diss* 1992), Hon Jane Caroline Anstruther-Gray, da of late Baron Kilmany

(Life Baron) (*see* Anstruther of that Ilk, Bt, colls), and has issue living, William John, *b* 1971, — Edward Kenneth, *b* 1972, — Belinda Jane, *b* 1974.
Hon James Richard Canning (25 Chester St, SW1), *b* 1949; *ed* Winchester, and Strathclyde Univ (BA): *m* 1977, Haude Chantal Gabrielle, da of Marc Charpentier, of Paris, and has issue living, Victoria Dorothy Sabine, *b* 1978, — Kate, *b* 1980.

SISTER LIVING

Hon Janet Sibella, *b* 1947: *m* 1978, Francis Anthony Brinsley (James) Valentine (*see* E Lanesborough, 1985 Edn), and has issue living, Robert Harris, *b* 1983, — Sibella Margaret, *b* 1981. *Residence* – The Gate House, Astrop, nr Banbury, Oxon.

WIDOW LIVING OF SECOND VISCOUNT

DOROTHY (*Dorothy, Viscountess Weir*), da of late William Yerrington Dear, and widow of Edward F. Hutton: *m* 1973, as his 2nd wife, the 2nd Viscount, who *d* 1975. *Residence* – Little Pennbrook, Lake Rd, Far Hills, NJ, USA 07931.

PREDECESSORS – (1) *Rt Hon Sir* WILLIAM DOUGLAS Weir, GCB, son of late James Weir, of Over Courance, Dumfriesshire; *b* 1877; Hon Pres of G & J Weir Holdings, Ltd, and a Director of International Nickel Co of Canada; was Scottish Director of Munitions 1915-16, Controller of Aeronautical Supplies; and a Member of Air Board 1917-18, Director-Gen of Aircraft Production, Min of Munitions 1918, Sec of State and Pres of Air Council April to Dec 1918, Director-Gen of Explosives and Chemical Supplies, Min of Supply 1939-41, and Chm of Tank Board 1943; *cr Baron Weir*, of Eastwood, co Renfrew (peerage of UK) 1918, and *Viscount Weir*, of Eastwood, co Renfrew (peerage of UK) 1938: *m* 1904, Alice Blanche, who *d* 1959, da of late John MacConnachie of Glasgow; *d* 1959; *s* by his only son (2) (JAMES) KENNETH, 2nd Viscount, *b* 1905; Engineer; (Chm of Weir Group, Ltd of Glasgow), 1955-72: *m* 1st, 1929 (Dorothy Isabel), Lucy, who *d* 1972, only da of James Fuidge Crowdy, MVO, Asst Sec to Gov Gen of Canada; 2ndly, 1973, Dorothy, da of William Yerrington Dear, and widow of Edward F. Hutton; *d* 1975: *s* by his el son (3) WILLIAM KENNETH JAMES, 3rd Viscount and present peer; also Baron Weir.

WELLINGTON, DUKE OF (Wellesley) (Duke UK 1814)

Fortune is the companion of valour

ARTHUR VALERIAN WELLESLEY, KG, LVO, OBE, MC, 8th Duke, Prince of Waterloo in the Netherlands (*cr* 1815), Duque da Vittoria and Marques de Torres Vedras (*cr* 1812) and Conde do Vimeiro (*cr* 1811) in Portugal, and Duque de Ciudad Rodrigo (*cr* 1812), and a Grandee (1st class) in Spain, which he became on the renunciation by his father (published in Official Gazette Madrid, 20 Feb 1968); *b* 2 July 1915; *s* 1972: *ed* Eton, and New Coll, Oxford; patron of four livings; Brig (ret) late RHG; OC RHG 1954-58, Silver Stick-in-Waiting, and Lt-Col Comdg Household Cav 1959-60, and Comdg 22nd Armd Bde 1960-61, CRAC, 1st British Corps 1962-64, and Defence Attaché Madrid 1964-67; Col C-in-C The Duke of Wellington's Regt since 1974; late Hon Col 2nd Br Wessex Regt TAVRA; Co Councillor for Hants 1967-73; DL for Hants (1975); Pres SE Branch of R British Legion, Member of Council, RASE, and Dep Pres 1993, Pres Atlantic Salmon Trust, Trustee Thames Salmon Trust and Lawes Agricultural Trust; a Gov of Wellington Coll since 1965; Pres of Rare Breeds Survival Trust from 1982. HM The Queen's Member of Bd of Trustees of the Armouries since 1983; Member of Advisory Cttee, Centre for Agricultural Strategy at Reading Univ; Chm of the Pitt Club; 1939-45 War in Middle East, Italy, and NW Europe (MC 1941); LVO 1952, OBE (Mil) 1957, KG 1990: *m* 1944, Diana Ruth, only da of late Maj-Gen Douglas Fitzgerald McConnel, of Knockdolian, CB, CBE, DSO, of Ayrshire, and has issue.

Arms – Quarterly: 1st and 4th gules, a cross argent, in each quarter five plates in saltire, *Wellesley*: 2nd and 3rd or, a lion rampant gules, ducally collared gold, *Cowley*. over all, in the centre chief point, an escutcheon of augmentation charged with the Union badge. **Crest** – Out of a ducal coronet or, a demi-lion rampant gules, holding in the paws a forked pennon argent, flowing to the sinister, charged with the cross of St George, the ends gules. **Supporters** – Two lions gules, gorged with Eastern coronets, and chained or.
Seat – Stratfield Saye House, Reading, RG7 2B2. *Town Residence* – Apsley House, Piccadilly, W1V 9FA.

SONS LIVING

ARTHUR CHARLES VALERIAN (*Marquess of Douro*) (Apsley House, 149 Piccadilly, W1V 9FA; The Old Rectory, Stratfield Saye, Reading, RG7 2DA), *b* 19 Aug 1945; *ed* Eton, and Ch Ch, Oxford; Dep-Chm Vendôme Luxury Group plc since 1993, Dir Sun Life Assurance Soc since 1988, Transatlantic Holdings plc since 1983, Chm Dunhill Holdings plc 1990-93, Dir Rothmans International plc 1990-93, Dep Chm Guinness Mahon Holdings plc 1988-91, Dir Continental & Industrial Trust plc 1987-90, Deltec Panamerica SA 1968-89 (late Dep-Chm), Eucalyptus Pulp Mills plc 1979-88, and GB Papers 1981-84; Member of Council Royal Coll of Art since 1992; Basingstoke Borough Councillor 1978-79; MEP (C) 1979-89; *m* 1977, Antonia Brigid Elizabeth Luise, yr da of HRH the late Prince Friedrich Georg Wilhelm Christoph of Prussia (*see* Royal Family), and has issue living:—

    SONS LIVING—Arthur Gerald (*Earl of Mornington*), *b* 31 Jan 1978, — Lord Frederick Charles, *b* 1992.
    DAUGHTERS LIVING—Lady Honor Victoria, *b* 1979, — Lady Mary Luise, *b* 1986, — Lady Charlotte, *b* 1990.

Lord Richard Gerald (Knockdolian, Colmonell, Girvan, Ayrshire), *b* 1949; *ed* Eton and RAC Cirencester: *m* 1973, Joanna, el da of John Sumner, of Marston St Lawrence, Oxon, and has issue living, Natasha Doone, *b* 1975, — Davina Chloe, *b* 1977.
Lord John Henry (15 Ensor Mews, SW7 3BT), *b* 1954; *ed* Eton: *m* 1977, Corinne, da of HE Baron Vaes, KCMG, formerly Belgian Ambassador, and has issue living, Gerald Valerian, *b* 1981, — Alexandrina Sofia, *b* 1983.
Lord (James) Christopher Douglas, *b* 1964: *m* 1994 Laura Elizabeth, only da of T. E. Wedge.

DAUGHTER LIVING

Lady (Caroline) Jane (42 Clarendon Rd, W11), *b* 1951.

SISTER LIVING

Lady Elizabeth (Oliver's Farm, Bramley, Basingstoke, Hants), *b* 1918: *m* 1939 (*m diss* 1960), Capt Thomas Clyde, Royal Horse Guards, and has issue living, Jeremy, *b* 1941: *m* 1970, Vanessa, da of Harold Field, — William Jonathan, *b* 1949.

DAUGHTER LIVING OF FIFTH DUKE

Lady Anne Maud, *b* 1910; *s* her brother (6th Duke of Wellington) as Duquesa de Ciudad Rodrigo and a Grandee (1st class) in Spain (*cr* 1812) 1943, but relinquished this title in favour of her uncle the 7th Duke of Wellington 1949: *m* 1933 (*m diss* 1963), Capt Hon David Reginald Rhys, Welsh Gds, who *d* 1991 (*see* B Dynevor). *Residence* –

COLLATERAL BRANCHES LIVING

Issue of late Capt Lord Richard Wellesley, 2nd son of 4th Duke, *b* 1879, *ka* 1914: *m* 1908, Louise Nesta Pamela, who *d* 1946, having *m* 2ndly (in New York), 1917, his younger brother, Major Lord George Wellesley, MC (ante), da of Sir Maurice FitzGerald (20th *Knight of Kerry*), CVO, 2nd Bt:—
Mary (*posthumous*), *b* 1915. *Residence* – 12 Clarence Terr, NW1 4RD.

Grandchildren (by 1st *m*) of Lt-Col late Lord George Wellesley, MC, 4th son of 4th Duke:—
Issue of late Maj Richard Wellesley, MC, DL, *b* 1920, *d* 1984: *m* 1st, 1948 (*m diss* 1970), Ruth, da of late Peter Haig-Thomas (*see* E Normanton, 1971 Edn); 2ndly, 1970, Jill (Buckland Mead, Buckland, Faringdon, Oxon, SN7 8QR), da of late G/Capt E. Burton, RAF:—
(By 1st *m*) Charles (The Dower House, Buckland, nr Faringdon, Oxon SN7 8QR), *b* 1955: *m* 1981, Louise Charlotte, da of late Cdr Allan Miles Brittain Buxton, and has issue living, Rosanna *b* 1989, — Charlotte, *b* 1992. —— John, *b* 1962. —— Nesta, *b* 1951: *m* 1985, Richard Sidney Hawes, of St Mary's, Latton, Swindon, Wilts SN6 6DS, only son of Sidney Hawes, of Cirencester, Glos, and has issue living, a son, *b* 1992, — a son, *b* (twin) 1992. —— Lucy, *b* 1953.

(*In remainder to Earldom of Mornington Viscounty of Wellesley and Barony of Mornington only*)

Granddaughters of late Lt-Col Frederic Henry Burton Wellesley, yr son of Lt-Col Gerald Valerian Wellesley, 2nd son of Col William Henry Charles Wellesley, 2nd son of Hon Gerald Valerian Wellesley, DD, 4th son of 1st Earl of Mornington:—
Issue of late Maj Frederic Henry Valerian Wellesley, *b* 1908; *d* 1978: *m* 1938, Nancy Evelyn (Church Hill, Crayke, Yorks), yr da of late Percy Saunders:—
Evelyn Angela Juliana, *b* 1938: *m* 1961, John Albert Searle. *Residence* – Southlands, Market Bosworth, Leics CV13 0LS. —— Helen Christabel Kate, *b* 1947: *m* 1975, Daniel Levasseur. *Residence* – Church Hill, Crayke, York. —— Rosalind Jane, *b* 1954: *m* 1978, Alfred Peter Walshaw. *Residence* – The Cottage, 1 High Mickley, Stocksfield, Northumberland.

Granddaughter of late Gerald Valentine Wellesley, elder son of late Edmond Ernest Charles Wellesley, 3rd son of late Col William Henry Charles Wellesley (ante):—
Issue of late Philip Vernon Charles Wellesley, *b* 1921, *d* 1992: *m* 1952, Marguerite Victoria (50A Ellerslie Rd, N Barnstaple, Devon), da of Alfred Cameron Clark, of Barnstaple: —
Barbara Victoria, *b* 1958: *m* 1985, Roger John Sandwell, of 25 Lydhurst Av, Barnstaple, Devon.

Granddaughters of late Col William Henry Charles Wellesley (ante):—
Issue of late Major Cecil George Wellesley, OBE, *b* 1869, *d* 1932: *m* 1906, Winifred Mary (who *d* 1959, having *m* 2ndly, 1933, Lieut-Col Clifford Charles Horace Twiss, DSO, who *d* 1947), da of late Hon Reginald Parker (E Macclesfield, colls):—
Lettice Jane Katherine, *b* 1908: *m* 1930, Peter Jocelyn Lambert, MC, who *d* 1970, and has issue living, (Peter) Miles (Ash Tree Farm, Wissett, Halesworth, Suffolk), *b* 1931; late Maj Gren Gds: *m* 1959, Armorel Madeleine Frances Tress, da of Maj Sir Rupert Rodney Francis Tress Barry, 4th Bt, and has issue living, Peter Tobin *b* 1966, Annabel Madeleine Jane *b* 1960: *m* 1992, Jonathan Reinier Manuel, of 64 Ridgway Place, Wimbledon, SW19 (and has issue living, Olivia Victoria Greta *b* 1993), Miranda Caroline Tress *b* 1962, — April Daphne Claire, *b* 1934: *m* 1954, Michael Gascoigne Falcon, CBE, DL, of Keswick Old Hall, Norwich, and has issue living, Michael *b* 1956: *m* 1983, Katharine Miranda, da of Peter Thomas Thistlethwayte, of East Donyland Hall, Colchester, Essex (*see* V Monck, 1985 Edn) (and has issue living, Emily *b* 1987, Isabella *b* 1989, Amy Lucinda *b* 1993), Andrew *b* 1958: *m* 1991, Victoria, only da of Maj Peter Noel de Bunsen (*see* B Carrington) (and has issue living, Ruby *b* 1993), Claire Isabella *b* 1960: *m* 1990, Simon N. Garrett, of Ffynnon Felen, Cwm Bach, Whitland, Dyfed, son of J. Garrett, and Mrs R. Quint, of Ventura, Calif, USA (and has issue living, George Francis *b* 1993, Isabel *b* 1991). —— Pamela (White Gate, Acrise, nr Folkestone, Kent), *b* 1909: *m* 1938, Maj-Gen Edward Noel Keith Estcourt, DSO, OBE, late RA, who *d* 1982, and has issue living, Edward James (c/o Lloyds Bank, Yorktown Branch, London Rd, Camberley, Surrey), *b* 1939; Lt-Col RA: *m* 1963, Jennifer Clare, da of Lt-Col C. A. McLaren, of High Torr, Cornwood, Ivybridge, S Devon, and has issue living, Edward Rory Charles *b* 1965, Angus James *b* 1968, — Adrian Charles (Sunnycroft, Petworth Rd, Chiddingfold, Surrey), *b* 1942; late Lt Parachute Regt: *m* 1967 (*m diss* 1991), Judith Mary, da of Col G. W. Preston, of Beck Cottage, Menethorpe, Malton, Yorks, and has issue living, Suzannah Jane *b* 1970, Charlotte Pamela *b* 1972, — Hermione Jessica Jane *b* 1947: *m* 1970, Christopher Hugh James Cousins, of White Gate, Acrise, nr Folkestone, Kent, and has issue living, Elizabeth Pamela Juliet *b* 1977, Victoria Edwina Jane *b* 1982.

Descendants of late Hon Sir Henry Wellesley (5th son of 1st Earl of Mornington), who was *cr Baron Cowley* 1828 (see E Cowley).

PREDECESSORS – (1) *Rt Hon Sir* ARTHUR Wellesley, KG, GCB, etc, 3rd son of 1st Earl of Mornington, *b* 1769; entered 73rd Regt 1787; became a Gen 1808, and a Field-Marshal 1815; sat as MP for Trim in the Irish Parliament; *cr Baron Douro*, of Wellesley, co Somerset, and *Viscount Wellington of Talavera and of Wellington*, co Somerset (peerage of United Kingdom) 1809, *Earl of Wellington*, co Somerset (peerage of United Kingdom) 1812, *Marquess of Wellington* (peerage of United Kingdom) 1812, *Marquess Douro* and *Duke of Wellington* (peerage of United Kingdom) 1814, *Count of Vimeiro* in Portugal 1811, *Duke of Ciudad Rodrigo* (and a Grandee of the 1st class) in Spain 1812, *Duke of Vittoria* and *Marques of Torres Vedras* in Portugal 1812, and *Prince of Waterloo*, in the Netherlands 1815; the brilliant services of the "Great Duke" are unrivalled in military history, but they are too varied to be particularized in this volume; in recognition of these services he was awarded the highest honours that could be conferred, besides large pecuniary awards, while the Sovereigns of various European countries conferred upon him their highest titles of nobility; was Premier 1828-30 and 1834-5, Chancellor of University of Oxford, Lord High Constable of England, Lord Warden of the Cinque Ports, Constable of the Tower and of Dover Castle, Lord-Lieut of Hants, Chief Ranger of Hyde, St James's and other Parks, Com in Chief, Col of Grenadier Guards, Col-in-Chief of Rifle Brigade, etc: *m* 1806, Hon Catherine Sarah Dorothea Pakenham, who *d* 1831, 2nd da of 2nd Baron Longford; *d* 14 Sept 1852; *s* by his son (2) ARTHUR RICHARD, 2nd Duke, *b* 1807; sat as MP for Aldborough (*C*) 1829-30 and 1831, and for

Norwich 1837-52; was Master of the Horse 1853-8, a Lieut-Gen in the Army and Lord, Lieut of Middlesex; s in 1863 as 6th Earl of Mornington (see infra *); dsp 13 Aug 1884: s by his nephew (3) HENRY, 3rd Duke, el surviving son of Maj-Gen Lord Charles Wellesley, MP (2nd son of 1st Duke), by Augusta Sophia Anne, only child of the Right Hon Henry Manvers Pierrepont (E Manvers), b 1846, MP for Andover (C) 1874-80: m 1882, Evelyn Katrine Gwenfra, who d 1939, da of late Col Thomas Peers Williams MP, of Temple House, Great Marlow; d 1900; s by his brother (4) ARTHUR CHARLES, KG, GCVO, 4th Duke, b 1849; Col (ret) late Grenadier Guards; bore Union Standard at Coronations of Edward VII 1902, and George V 1911: m 1872, Kathleen Emily Bulkeley Williams, who d 1927, da of late Robert Griffith Williams (Williams-Bulkeley, Bt, colls); d 1934; s by his el son (5) ARTHUR CHARLES, 5th Duke, b 1876: m 1909, Hon Lilian Maud Glen Coats, who d 1946, da of 1st Baron Glentanar; d 1941; s by his only son (6) HENRY VALERIAN GEORGE, 6th Duke, b 1912; Capt Duke of Wellington's Regt and Commando; ka 1943, when he was s in the Dukedom of Ciudad Rodrigo and as a Grandee (1st class) in Spain (cr 1812) by his sister, Lady Anne Maud, wife of Hon David Reginald Rhys, and in the British and Portuguese titles by his uncle (7) GERALD, KG, 3rd son of 4th Duke, 7th Duke, b 1885; Lt-Col Gren Gds; Surveyor of HM's Works of Art 1936-44; Chancellor of Southampton Univ 1951-62; Gov, Capt and Steward of Isle of Wight 1957-65: m 1914, Dorothy, who d 1956, da of late Robert Ashton, of Croughton, Cheshire; d 1972, s by his son (8) ARTHUR VALERIAN, 8th Duke and present peer; also Marquess of Wellington, Marquess Douro, Earl of Mornington (I), Earl of Wellington, Viscount Wellesley (I), Viscount Wellington of Talavera and Wellington, Baron Mornington (I), and Baron Douro; Prince of Waterloo in Netherlands (cr 1815) Duque da Vittoria and Marques de Torres Vedras (cr 1812) and Conde do Vimeiro (cr 1811) in Portugal, and Duque de Ciudad Rodrigo and a Grandee (1st class) in Spain (cr 1812).

*(1) RICHARD, MP, son of Henry Colley, MP, assumed in 1728 by Roy licence the surname of Wesley; sat as MP for Trim 1729-46; cr Baron of Mornington (peerage of Ireland) 1746; d 1758; s by his son (2) GARRET, 2nd Baron; sat as MP for Meath 1757-8; cr Viscount Wesley (changed to Wellesley by his son ca 1798) and Earl of Mornington (peerage of Ireland) 1760; d 1781; s by his son (3) RICHARD, KG, KP, 2nd Earl: sat as MP for Trim, 1780-1, Beeralston 1784-6, Saltash 1786-7, Windsor 1787-96 and Sarum 1796-7; was Gov-Gen of India 1798-1805, Ambassador to Spain 1809, Ch Sec of State for Foreign Affairs 1809-12, Lord-Lieut of Ireland 1821, 1833-4; cr Marquess Wellesley (peerage of Ireland) 1799; dsp 1842, when the Marquessate became extinct; s by his brother (4) WILLIAM, GCH, PC, 3rd Earl; assumed in 1778 the surname of Wellesley-Pole: sat as MP for Trim 1783-90, East Looe 1790-94, and Queen's Co 1801-21; was Postmaster-Gen in 1835; cr Baron Maryborough (peerage of UK) 1821; d 1845; s by his son (5) WILLIAM POLE, 4th Earl; assumed in 1812 the additional surnames of Tylney-Long; d 1857; s by his son (6) WILLIAM ARTHUR, 5th Earl; d unmarried 1863, when the Barony of Maryborough became ext and the honours of the first Earl devolved upon his cousin (7) ARTHUR RICHARD, 6th Earl, who had previously succeeded as 2nd Duke of Wellington (see ante).

WELLS-PESTELL, BARONY OF (Wells-Pestell) (Extinct 1991)

SONS LIVING OF LIFE BARON

Hon Philip (7 Woodberry Av, Winchmore Hill, N21), b 1941: m 1965, Holly, da of Lorne Hopkins, of Conn, USA, and has issue.
Hon Richard (2 Queen's Mansions, Queen's Av, Muswell Hill N10), b 1945: m 1973, (m diss 1977), Claudia Marseille, step-da of Prof John Gerhart, of Berkeley, Calif, USA.

WEMYSS AND MARCH, EARL OF (Charteris) (Earl S 1633 and 1697)

This is our Charter

(FRANCIS) DAVID CHARTERIS, KT, 12th Earl of Wemyss and 8th Earl of March; b 19 Jan 1912; s 1937; ed Eton, and Balliol Coll, Oxford (BA); Hon LLD, St Andrews 1953 and Hon D Univ Edinburgh, 1983; a JP for E Lothian; Lord Lieut 1967-87; Lord High Commr to Gen Assembly of Church of Scotland 1959, 1960 and 1977; Lieut in the Queen's Body Guard for Scotland (R Co of Archers); Lord Clerk Register of Scotland and Keeper of HM Signet for Scotland since 1974; Chm of Roy Commn on Ancient and Historical Monuments of Scotland 1949-84, and of Scottish Cttee of Marie Curie Memorial Foundation; Vice-Chm of Marie Curie Memorial Foundation, Pres of the National Trust for Scotland and Pres Emeritus since 1991, Hon Pres of the Thistle Foundation for Severely Disabled Scottish Ex-Servicemen; Pres of National Bible Soc of Scotland 1960-83; a Consultant of Wemyss and March Estate Management Co Ltd; late Capt Lovat Scouts (TA Reserve); Colonial Admin Ser, Basutoland 1937-44; Middle East 1941-44 with Basuto Troops as Maj: KT 1966: m 1940, Mavis Lynette Gordon, who d 1988, el da of late Edwin E. Murray, of Hermanus, Cape Province, S Africa, and has issue.

Arms – Quarterly: 1st and 4th argent, a fesse azure, within a double tressure flory counterflory gules, Charteris; 2nd and 3rd or, a lion rampant gules, armed and langued azure, Wemyss. Crest – A dexter hand holding up a dagger paleways proper. Supporters – Two swans, wings elevated proper, gorged with earl's coronets about their necks. Residence – Gosford House, Longniddry, East Lothian EH32 0PX. Club – New (Edinburgh).

SON LIVING

JAMES DONALD (*Lord Neidpath*), *b* 22 June 1948; *ed* Eton, Univ Coll, Oxford (BA 1969), St Antony's Coll, Oxford (D Phil 1975), and RAC Cirencester (Diploma 1978); ARICS 1984; Page of Honour to HM Queen Elizabeth the Queen Mother 1962-64; author of *The Singapore Naval Base and the Defence of Britain's Eastern Empire 1919-41*: *m* 1983 (*m diss* 1988), Catherine Ingrid, el da of Hon Jonathan Bryan Guinness (later 3rd Baron Moyne), and has issue:
SON LIVING—*Hon* (Francis) Richard, *b* 15 Sept 1984.
DAUGHTER LIVING— *Hon* Mary Olivia, *b* 1987.
Residence – Stanway, Cheltenham, Glos. *Clubs* – Brooks's, Pratt's, Puffin's (Edinburgh), Ogniesko Polski.

DAUGHTER LIVING

Lady Elizabeth Mary, *b* 1941: *m* 1964, David Holford Benson, of 11 Brunswick Gdns, W8, son of late Lt-Col Sir Reginald (Rex) Lindsay Benson, DSO, MVO, MC, and has issue living, Matthew James, *b* 1966, — Henrietta Katharine, *b* 1969, — Katharine Emma, *b* 1972.

BROTHER LIVING

Rt Hon Sir Martin Charles, GCB, GCVO, OBE, QSO, PC (*Baron Charteris of Amisfield*), *b* 1913: *cr* Baron Charteris of Amisfield 1977 (see that title).

WIDOW LIVING OF SON OF ELEVENTH EARL

Violet (The Old House, Didbrook, Winchcombe, Glos), da of late Alfred Charles Masterton Porter, of Dundee: *m* 1945, as his 2nd wife, Capt Hon Guy Laurence Charteris, who *d* 1967.

COLLATERAL BRANCHES LIVING

Grandchildren of late Capt Hon Guy Laurence Charteris, 2nd son of 11th Earl:—
Issue of late Capt Hugo Francis Guy Charteris, MC, *b* 1922, *d* 1970: *m* 1948, Virginia Mary Forbes (The Elms, Church St, Bubwith, Selby, Yorks), da of late Colin Gurdon Forbes Adam, CSI (*see* Adam, Bt, *cr* 1917):—
James Hugo Desmond, *b* 1958: *m* 1990, Kathryn Helen., only da of G. B. Shaw, of Fourstones, Hexham, Northumberland, and has issue living, Felix Guy, *b* 1992. —— Frances Irene Anne, *b* 1950: *m* 1983, Val Chong, of 705 Driggs Av, Brooklyn, New York, USA, and has issue living, Ayinde (a son), *b* 1981, — Chinue Amelia, *b* 1987. —— Virginia Jane, *b* 1953: *m* 1984, Peter Charles Clark, elder son of F. C. Clark, of Streatham, SW16. —— Perdita Rosemary, *b* 1955: *m* 1978, Jeremy Rupert Beckett, and has had issue (*see* Beckett, Bt).

Grandchildren of late Capt Hon Frederick William Charteris, RN, 5th son of 9th Earl:—
Issue of late Col Nigel Keppel Charteris, CMG, DSO, OBE, *b* 1878, *d* 1967: *m* 1904, Katharine Margaret, who *d* 1961, el da of Sir John Walter Buchanan Riddell, 11th Bt:—
John Douglas (Glen Lorne House, Muirfield Drive, PO Chisipite, Harare City, Zimbabwe), *b* 1914; *ed* Radley; Maj R Scots (ret); Palestine 1936-38; 1939-45 War (despatches): *m* 1st, 1943, Mrs Catherine Pitcairn Colley, who *d* 1957, da of late Capt W. P. Nunneley, Black Watch; 2ndly, 1958 (*m diss* 1971), Jean Haigh, of Umtali, Rhodesia; 3rdly, 1982, Mrs Rosemary Gillian Druscilla Perry (*neé* Edmonds), of Zimbabwe, and has issue living, (by 1st *m*) Sarah Keppel, *b* 1945: *m* 1970, Peter Guthrie Brown, and has issue living, Robert Guthrie *b* 1973, Christopher John *b* (twin) 1973, — (by 2nd *m*) Martin Ian (Wingtip Farm, Marondera, Zimbabwe), *b* 1960: *m* 1989, Dr Helen Heath, and has issue living, Michael Samuel *b* 1991, Andrew Phillip *b* 1992, — Bridget Alison, *b* 1958: *m* 1983, Ian Donovan, of 3 Lightfoot Cottages, Penshurst Rd, Leigh, Kent, and has issue living, Matthew John *b* 1989, Emma Clare *b* 1985. —— David Nigel (Longstones Cottage, South St, Little Avebury, nr Marlborough, Wilts SN8 1QX), *b* 1920; *ed* Lancing; late Lt RNVR: *m* 1st, 1952, Euphemia Mary, who *d* 1969, da of Maj-Gen Sir (John) Drummond Inglis, KBE, CB, MC; 2ndly, 1982, Astrid Henrietta Vivian Alys (*neé* Cooper), widow of Dr A. Henderson-Begg and has issue living (by 1st *m*), Nigel Drummond Keppel (c/o P.O. Box BW358, Borrowdale, Harare, Zimbabwe), *b* 1958: *m* 1988, Philippa Margaret, da of Maj Robert Edward Paton, of Harare, Zimbabwe, and has issue living, James David *b* 1992, Alice Fiona *b* 1990, — Angela Katharine Keppel, *b* 1953: *m* 1980, Nigel A. C. Butler, of Mufaro, 56 Kent Rd, Chisipite, Harare, Zimbabwe, and has issue living, Katharine Emma *b* 1981, Sabrina Charlotte *b* 1983, Belinda *b* 1986, Joanna Mary *b* 1988, — Helen Mary Keppel, *b* 1956: *m* 1984, Richard William Lewis Groves (c/o The Hong Kong & Shanghai Banking Corpn, 1 Queens Rd, Central, Hong Kong), son of Capt P. W. Groves, of Whitchurch, Cardiff, and has issue living, Charlotte Elizabeth *b* 1985, Francesca Katharine *b* 1987, Georgina *b* 1993. —— Margaret Olive (Clare Park, Crondall, Farnham, Surrey), *b* 1905: *m* 1st, 1930, Lt-Cdr Michael Richard Hallam Murray, RN (ret), who *d* 1938; 2ndly, 1954, Maj Eric Cecil Lewis Copner, Devon Regt, who *d* 1968, and has issue living, (by 1st *m*) Christopher Philip Hallam (Manor Farm, Little Barugh, Malton, N Yorks YO17 0UY), *b* 1937: *m* 1967, Judith Mary, da of late Lt-Col I. D. MacInnes, and has issue living, James Michael Hallam *b* 1968, Justin Richard Hallam *b* 1973, Harriet Alexandra Hallam *b* 1970, — Susan Barbara (69 Redcliffe Gdns, SW10), *b* 1930: *m* 1974, Leslie Max Pritchard, who *d* 1990, — Katharine Bridget (19 Gray Close, Henbury, Bristol BS10 7SZ), *b* 1934: *m* 1956, Lt John Charles Brian Taite, RN, who *d* 1975, and has issue living, Roderick Michael James *b* 1966, Clare Bridget *b* 1959, Caroline Rachel *b* 1960. —— Anne Louisa, *b* 1909: *m* 1939, John Arkwright Bonham-Carter, CVO, DSO, OBE, ERD, KStJ, FCIT, MA, Col Engineer & Transport Staff Corps RE (TA) (Alleyne, Bt), of Redbridge House, Crossways, Dorchester, Dorset, and has issue living, Richard Francis (16 South Rd, Hagley, Stourbridge, W Midlands), *b* 1940: *m* 1968, Josephine Ann Gallimore, and has issue living, Nicola Jane *b* 1969, Claire Helen *b* 1972, — Nigel John (Dowlands, Thorndon, Eye, Sussex) *b* 1945.

Grandsons living of late Randolph Gordon Erskine Wemyss, el son of James Hay Erskine Wemyss, MP, el son of Lt-Gen William Wemyss, MP, el son of Hon James Wemyss, MP, 3rd son of 5th Earl:—
Issue of late Capt Michael John Wemyss of that Ilk, *b* 1888; *d* 1982; recognised as Chief of the name of Wemyss by Lord Lyon 1910: *m* 1918, Lady Victoria Alexandrina Violet Cavendish Bentinck, CVO, who *d* 1994, aged 104, da of 6th Duke of Portland:—
David WEMYSS OF THAT ILK, *b* 1920; *ed* Eton, and Magdalene Coll, Camb; formerly Capt Roy Corps of Signals: *m* 1945, Lady Jean Christian Bruce, da of 10th Earl of Elgin and Kincardine, and has issue living, Michael James (Wemyss Castle, Easter Wemyss, Fife), *b* 1947; *ed* Gordonstoun, and RAC Cirencester; DL; FRICS 1985: *m* 1975, Charlotte Mary, da of late Lt-Col Royle Bristowe, of Brookhampton Hall, Ickleton, Cambs, and has issue living, Hermione Mary *b* 1982, Leonora Anne *b* 1986, — Charles John (Tillyochie, House, by Kinross, Kinross-shire), *b* 1952; *ed* Eton: *m* 1978, Fiona Elizabeth, only da of late Lt-Col Sir Eric Charles William Mackenzie Penn, GCVO, OBE, MC, of Sternfield House, Saxmundham, Suffolk, and has issue living, James Michael *b* 1987, Mary Victoria *b* 1981, Elizabeth Katherine *b* 1985. *Residence* – Invermay, Forteviot, Perthshire. —— Andrew Michael (Torrie House, Newmills, Dunfermline, Fife), *b* 1925; *ed* Eton: *m* 1967, Janet Alethea, only da of John Swire Scott, of Eredine Dalmally, Argyll, and has issue living, William John, *b* 1970, — Isabella Alethea, *b* 1968.

PREDECESSORS – (1) *Rt Hon* JOHN Wemyss, was *cr* by Charles I a *Baronet of Nova Scotia* 1625, *Lord Wemyss of Elcho* (peerage of Scotland) 1628, and *Lord Elcho and Methel* and *Earl of Wemyss* (peerage of Scotland) 1633; he eventually espoused the cause of the Covenant; *d* 1649; *s* by his son (2) DAVID, 2nd Earl; constructed at his own cost the harbour of Methil, in 1672 resigned his honours to the crown in return for a new patent with original precedence and extending the limitation to his da; *d* 1679, when the baronetcy expired and the peerages devolved upon his 2nd surv da **(3)** MARGARET; *d* 1705; *s* by her son **(4)** DAVID, PC, 4th Earl; was Lord High Adm of Scotland, a Commr for concluding the Treaty of Union, and a Representative Peer: *d* 1720; *s* by his son **(5)** JAMES, 5th Earl; *d* 1756; *s* by his el son **(6)** DAVID, *de jure* 6th Earl, who having been attainted in 1746 did not succeed to the titles and they remained dormant; *dsp* 1787, when the peerages but for the attainder would have devolved upon his younger brother **(7)** FRANCIS, *de jure* 7th Earl; *b* 1725; assumed the surname of Charteris in lieu of that of Wemyss on being made his heir by his maternal grandfather, Col Francis Charteris, of Amisfield, who *d* 1732; enabled by Act of Parliament in 1771 to retain the surname, arms and estates of Charteris of Amisfield, notwithstanding the devolution upon him of the Earldom of Wemyss, or any other title, which under the will of Col Charteris had been prohibited; assumed the Earldom of Wemyss on the death of his el brother in 1787; *d* 1808; *s* by his grandson **(8)** FRANCIS 8th Earl; *b* 1772; in 1810 on the death of the 4th Duke of Queensberry, who was also 3rd Earl of March he *s* (under special remainder, being the lineal heir male of Lady Anne Douglas, sister of 1st Earl of March) (see *infra), as 4th *Earl of March*, and in 1821 was *cr Baron Wemyss*, of Wemyss, co Fife (peerage of United Kingdom); obtained a reversal of the attainder in 1826; was Lord-Lieut of co Peebles, *d* 1853; *s* by his son **(9)** FRANCIS, 9th Earl; *b* 1796; was Lord-Lieut of Haddingtonshire: *m* 1817, Lady Louisa Bingham, who *d* 1882, da of 2nd Earl of Lucan; *d* 1 Jan 1883; *s* by his son **(10)** FRANCIS, GCVO, LLD, 10th Earl; *b* 1818; was Scotch Lord of the Treasury 1853-5, and an ADC to Queen Victoria 1881-1901, to King Edward VII 1901-10, and to King George V 1910-14; MP for E Gloucestershire (LC) 1841-6, and for Haddingtonshire 1847-83: *m* 1st, 1843, Lady Anne Frederica Anson, who *d* 1896, da of 1st Earl of Lichfield; 2ndly, 1900, Grace, who *d* 1946, da of late Major Blackburn; *d* 1937; *s* by his el surviving son **(11)** HUGO RICHARD, 11th Earl; *b* 1857; MP for Haddingtonshire (C) 1883-5, and for Ipswich 1886-95: *m* 1883, Mary Constance, who *d* 1937, da of late Hon Percy Scawen Wyndham; *d* 1937; *s* by his grandson **(12)** FRANCIS DAVID (son of late Capt Hugo Francis Lord Elcho), who was *ka* 1916, 12th Earl and present peer; also Earl of March, Viscount of Peebles, Lord Elcho and Methel, Lord Douglas of Neidpath, Lyne, and Munard, Lord Wemyss of Elcho, and Lord Wemyss of Wemyss.

*(1) Lord WILLIAM DOUGLAS, 2nd son of 1st Duke of Queensberry, *b* circa 1665; Gov of Edinburgh Castle 1702-4; received from his father on his marriage the lands of Neidpath and others in Peeblesshire; *cr Lord Douglas of Neidpath, Lyne, and Munard, Viscount of Peebles*, and *Earl of March* (peerage of Scotland) 1697, with remainder to heirs male of his body, failing which to his other heirs male and of tailzie; *m* 1693, Lady Jane Hay, who *d* 1729, da of 1st Marquess of Tweeddale; *d* 1705; *s* by his son **(2)** WILLIAM, 2nd Earl; *b* circa 1696; *m* 17-, Lady Anne Hamilton (who *s* her father as Countess of Ruglen 1744 and who *m* 2ndly, 1747, Anthony Sawyer, and *d* 1748), da of 3rd Earl of Selkirk and 1st Earl of Ruglen; *d* 1731; *s* by his son **(3)** WILLIAM, KT, 3rd Earl, *b* 1725, *s* his kinsman as 4th Duke of Queensberry 1778, and his mother as 4th Earl of Ruglen 1748; *cr Baron Douglas of Amesbury*, co Wilts (peerage of Great Britain) 1768; *d* unm 1810, when the Barony of Douglas of Amesbury and the Earldom of Ruglen became ext, the Dukedom of Queensberry reverted to the 3rd Duke of Buccleuch, the Marquessate and Earldom of Queensberry passed to his kinsman Sir Charles Douglas, 5th Bt, of Kelhead, and the Earldom of March devolved on his kinsman **(4)** FRANCIS 4th Earl (great-great-grandson of Lady Anne Douglas, wife of 4th Earl of Wemyss, and sister of 1st Earl of March), who had *s* as 8th Earl of Wemyss 1808, but on account of his predecessor's forfeiture none of the titles was recognised by the Crown until his attainder was reversed in 1826 (ante).

West, see Baron Granville-West.

WESTBURY, BARON (Bethell) (Baron UK 1861)

Ap Ithel (the old Welsh family name)

DAVID ALAN BETHELL, CBE, MC, 5th Baron; *b* 16 July 1922; *s* 1961; *ed* Harrow, and RMC Sandhurst; Capt Scots Guards; a DL (for N Yorks 1973); Equerry to HRH the Duke of Gloucester 1947-49; KStJ 1977, Bailiff of Egle, Order of St John 1988-92, Bailiff Grand Cross 1988; 1939-45 War in N Africa and Italy (thrice wounded, despatches, MC); CBE 1994: *m* 1947, Ursula Mary-Rose, da of late Hon Robert James (*see* B Northbourne, colls), and has issue.

Arms – Argent, on a chevron engrailed azure between three boars' heads couped sable, an estoile or, all within a bordure of the third. **Crest** – Out of a crown vallery or, an eagle's head sable, between two wings azure, charged on the breast with an estoile as in the arms. **Supporters** – On either side an eagle, wings addorsed azure, ducally crowned, collared, and charged on the breast with an estoile or.
Residences – Barton Cottage, Malton, Yorkshire; 8 Ropers Orchard, Danvers St, SW3. *Club* – Jockey.

SONS LIVING

Hon RICHARD NICHOLAS, MBE, *b* 29 May 1950; *ed* Harrow, and RMA Sandhurst; Maj Scots Guards; MBE (Mil) 1979; served in NI and S Atlantic Campaign 1982 (despatches twice, wounded); Officer Brother, Order of St John; *m* 1st, 1975 (*m diss* 1991), Caroline Mary, da of Richard John Palmer, of Queen Anne's Mead, Swallowfield, Berks (*see* V Churchill); 2ndly, 1993, Charlotte Bruce, and has issue living (by 1st *m*), Alexander, *b* 21 Dec 1986, — Alice Mary, *b* 1979, — Rose *b* 1984.
Hon JAMES DAVID WILLIAM, *b* 1952: *m* 1st, 1974, Emma Hermione, yr da of Malise Allen Nicolson, MC, of Frog Hall, Tilston, Malpas, Cheshire; 2ndly, 1987, Mrs Sally Le Gallais, da of John Roberts (*see* Roberts, Bt, *cr* 1909, colls) and has issue living, (by 1st *m*), Clare Angelina Serena, *b* 1977, — Lucinda Emma, *b* 1979, — (by 2nd *m*) Edward David John, *b* 1994, — Jessica Mary, *b* 1988. *Residence* – Clarendon House, Manor House Stables, Middleham, Leyburn, N Yorks DL8 4QL.

DAUGHTER LIVING

Hon (Celia) Mary, *b* 1955: *m* 1980, as his 2nd wife, (Lionel) Brook Holliday, yr son of late Maj Lionel Brook Holliday, OBE, TD, of Copgrove Hall, Yorks, and has issue living, Lucy, *b* 1983, — Serena, *b* 1990. *Residence* – Mount St John, Felixkirk, Thirsk, Yorks.

SISTER LIVING (Raised to the rank of a Baron's daughter 1930)

Hon Veronica Wenefryde Nefertari, *b* 1917: *m* 1941, Lieut-Col James Innes, Coldstream Guards (ret) (E Lonsdale), and has issue living, James Richard (Romanys, Lawbrook Lane, Peaslake, Guildford, Surrey) *b* 1943; Lt-Col Coldm Gds, — Peter David (Boon House, Lauder, Berwicks), *b* 1952; Capt Coldm Gds: *m* 1980, Carolyn Ann Darley, da of Julian Blackwell, of

Osse Field, Appleton, Oxon, and has issue living, James David *b* 1982, Sarah Clementine *b* 1984, Laura Mary *b* 1987, — Elizabeth Mary, *b* 1947: *m* 1st, 1967 (*m diss* 1972), James Keith Alan Rugge-Price (*see* Rugge-Price, Bt); 2ndly, 1973, Edward Rice Nicholl, of Trewhitt Hall, Thropton, Northumberland NE65 7ET, and has issue (by 1st *m*) (*see* Rugge-Price, Bt), (by 2nd *m*), Katherine Sarah *b* 1974, Emily Mary *b* 1977. *Residence* – 25 Beaufort Close, SW15 3TL.

COLLATERAL BRANCHES LIVING

Grandchildren of late Lionel Beresford Bethell, 3rd son of late Hon Slingsby Bethell, CB, 2nd son of 1st Baron:—

Issue of late Maj Vivian Lionel Slingsby Bethell, *b* 1897, *d* 1967: *m* 1928, Joan Ker, da of late John Manwell:—

Richard Ker Slingsby, OBE (Court Farm House, Nunney, Frome, Somerset; *Club* – Army and Navy) *b* 1928; Capt RN, OBE (Mil) 1973; DL Somerset 1991: *m* 1953, Anne, da of H. Frost, and has issue living, Helena Susan Mary, *b* 1955: *m* 1978, Cdr Nicholas J. G. Harland, RN, of Quinces, Piddle Hinton, Dorset, and has issue living, Rupert Slingsby *b* 1981, Francesca *b* 1984, — Theresa Jane, *b* 1956: *m* 1979, Michael J. Stephenson, of Napier Lodge, Napier Av, SW6, and has issue living, Edward *b* 1982, Emily *b* 1984, — Jane Ker, *b* 1959: *m* 1979, David F. Fletcher, of 18 Rusholme Rd, Putney, SW15, and has issue living, Charles *b* 1992, Rosanna *b* 1987. —— Deirdre Ann, *b* 1929: *m* 1st, 1952 (*m diss* 1964), Sir Hugo Giles Edmund Sebright, 14th Bt, who *d* 1985; 2ndly, 1965, Anthony Melbourne-Hart, who *d* 1988.

Grandchildren of late Hon Slingsby Bethell, CB (ante):—

Issue of late Llwelyn Slingsby Bethell, *b* 1889, *d* 1971: *m* 1914, Margery Gladys, who *d* 1985, aged 99, da of late George Stanley Farnell, Prin of Victoria Coll, Jersey:—

Margaret Eve Slingsby, *b* 1915: *m* 1939, Cdr Warwick Bracegirdle, DSC, RAN, and has issue living, Simon Warwick Slingsby, *b* 1941, — Nicholas, *b* 1944, — Phillada Ann, *b* 1946.

Issue of late Lt-Cdr Richard Alfred Slingsby Bethell, RN (ret), *b* 1892, *d* 1975: *m* 1930, Frances Elizabeth (Frome House, Dorchester, Dorset), da of late Lt-Col Charles Maxwell Shurlock Henning, of Frome House, Dorchester, Dorset:—

Maxwell Slingsby (Oakenclough, Higher Sutton, Macclesfield, Ches), *b* 1931; *ed* Wellington Coll, and Camb Univ (MB and BCh, MA, DPM): *m* 1953, Pamela Mary, da of late Hubert Fletcher, and has issue living, Charles Maxwell Slingsby, *b* 1957, — Nicola Slingsby, *b* 1953: *m* 19–, Nicholas Winer, and has issue living, a son *b* 1982, — Juliet Slingsby, *b* 1955, — Zoe Melisende Slingsby, *b* 1958. —— David Slingsby (Frome House, Dorchester), *b* 1934; *ed* Camb Univ (MA): *m* 1964, Sadie Melfort, da of Lt-Col G. M. Baldwin, of Culver House, Payhembury, Devon, and has issue living, Richard Slingsby, *b* 1965, — Christopher Maunsell Slingsby, *b* 1966, — Zillah Slingsby, *b* 1968.

PREDECESSORS – (1) *Rt Hon Sir* RICHARD Bethell, DCL; sat as MP for Aylesbury 1851-9, and for Wolverhampton 1859-61; was Solicitor-Gen 1852-6, Attorney-Gen 1856-8 and 1859-61, and Lord Chancellor of England 1861-5; *cr Baron Westbury*, of Westbury (peerage of United Kingdom) 1861; *d* 1873; *s* by his son (2) RICHARD AUGUSTUS, 2nd Baron; *b* 1830; was a Registrar in Bankruptcy: *m* 1851, Mary Florence, who *d* 1901, da of Rev Alexander Fownes-Luttrell; *d* 1875; *s* by his son (3) RICHARD LUTTRELL PILKINGTON, 3rd Baron; *b* 1852: *m* 1882, Lady Agatha Manners Tollemache, who *d* 1941, sister of 9th Earl of Dysart; *d* 1930; *s* by his grandson (4) RICHARD MORLAND TOLLEMACHE (son of late Capt Hon Richard Bethell, only son of 3rd Baron), 4th Baron; *b* 1914; European War 1939-45 as Major RE; *d* 1961; *s* by his brother (5) DAVID ALAN, 5th Baron and present peer.

WESTER WEMYSS, BARONY OF (Wemyss) (Extinct 1933)

DAUGHTER LIVING OF FIRST BARON

Hon Alice Elizabeth Millicent, *b* 1906: *m* 1953, Major Francis Henry Cunnack, RA (ret), who *d* 1974. *Residence* –

WESTMEATH, EARL OF (Nugent) (Earl I 1621)

I have resolved

WILLIAM ANTHONY NUGENT, 13th Earl; *b* 21 Nov 1928; *s* 1971; *ed* Marlborough and RMA Sandhurst; late Capt RA; sometime Senior Master, St Andrews Sch, Pangbourne (ret 1988): *m* 1963, Susanna Margaret, only da of His Hon Judge (James Charles Beresford Whyte) Leonard, of Cross Trees, Sutton Courtenay, Berks, and has issue.

Arms – Ermine, two bars gules. **Crest** – A cockatrice, wings elevated and displayed, vert. **Supporters** – Two cockatrices, wings elevated, vert. *Residence* – Farthings, Rotten Row Hill, Tutts Clump, Bradfield, Berks.

SONS LIVING

SEAN CHARLES WESTON (does not use courtesy title), *b* 16 Feb 1965; *ed* Ampleforth.

Hon Patrick Mark Leonard, *b* 1966; *ed* Douai.

SISTER LIVING

Lady Pamela Joan, *b* 1921; sometime Section Officer WAAF: *m* 1950, Lieut-Col Peter John Barbary, OBE, GM, TD, DL, FRIBA, who *d* 1969, and has issue living, Michael John Nugent, *b* 1951, — Joanna Clare Nugent, *b* 1955. *Residence* – Briar Rose Cottage, 17 Landeryon Gdns, Penzance, Cornwall.

COLLATERAL BRANCHES LIVING

Granddaughter of late Maj-Gen St George Mervyn Nugent, son of late Christopher Edmund John Nugent, a descendant of late Oliver Nugent, brother of 13th Baron Delvin:—

Issue of late Maj-Gen Sir Oliver Stewart Wood Nugent, KCB, DSO, *b* 1860, *d* 1926: *m* 1899, Catherine Percy, who *d* 1970, da of late Thomas Evans Lees, of Betley Hall, Ches:—

Alison Joan Elliott, *b* 1909: *m* 1947, Harry Gerhard Hirschberg, LLD, of Cullentragh, Mount Nugent, co Cavan.

(In remainder to Barony of Delvin)

Grandchildren of late Brig-Gen Frank Henry Burnell-Nugent, CB, DSO, OBE, yst son of Albert Llewellyn Nugent, 4th son of Walter Nugent (*cr* Baron of Austria 1859, with remainder to issue male and female), 10th in descent from Andrew Nugent of Clonlost, yr son of Andrew Nugent of Donore, brother of 11th Baron Delvin:—

Issue of late Cdr Anthony Frank Burnell-Nugent, DSC, RN (ret), *b* 1906, *d* 1976: *m* 1941, Gian Mary, da of late Rear-Adm Charles Otway Alexander, of Wilford Rise, Woodbridge, Suffolk:—

Charles Anthony (*Baron Nugent*) (10 Radley Lodge, 25 Inner Park Rd, Wimbledon SW19 6DG), *b* 1942; *s* his cousin as 8th Baron Nugent 1988; *ed* Brickwall. —— James Michael, *b* 1949; *ed* Stowe, and Corpus Christi Coll, Camb; Capt RN: *m* 1973, Henrietta Mary, yst da of Rt Rev Robert Wilmer Woods, KCMG, KCVO, Bishop of Worcester, and has issue living, Anthony James, *b* 1980, — Rupert Michael, *b* 1982, — Henrietta Marie, *b* 1978. —— Mary, *b* 1947: *m* 1967, John Richard Conway Lloyd, of Argent Manor, Sutton, Ipswich, and has issue living, John Conway, *b* 1970, — Lucy Ellen, *b* 1972. —— Sheila Jane, *b* 1951: *m* 1980, Marino Gianella, of Florence, Italy, and has issue living, Francesco, *b* 1981.

PREDECESSORS – (1) Richard Nugent, 12th Baron of Delvin, and Lord Dep of Ireland 1528, was summoned to Parliament of Ireland 1486, 1490, and 1493; *d* 1538; *s* by his grandson (2) Richard, 13th Baron; *d* 1559; *s* by his son (3) Christopher, 14th Baron; *d* 1602; *s* by his son (4) Richard, 15th Baron; *cr Earl of Westmeath* (peerage of Ireland) 1621; *d* 1641; *s* by his grandson (5) Richard, 2nd Earl; *d* 1684; *s* by his grandson (6) Richard, 3rd Earl; was a Capuchin Friar; *d* 1714; *s* by his brother (7) Thomas, 4th Earl; having been outlawed for his adhesion to the cause of James II, the outlawry was afterwards reversed and his honours and estates restored; *d* 1752; *s* by his brother (8) John, 5th earl; a Major-Gen in the Army; *d* 1754; *s* by his son (9) Thomas, KP, 6th Earl: conformed to the Established Church; *d* 1792; *s* by his son (10) George Frederick, 7th Earl; *d* 1814; *s* by his son (11) George Thomas John, 8th Earl; was Lord-Lieut of co Westmeath, and a Representative Peer; *cr Marquess of Westmeath* (peerage of Ireland) 1822; *d* 1871, when the marquessate became extinct, and the earldom devolved upon his kinsman (12) Anthony Francis, 9th Earl, descendant of Thomas, 2nd son of 2nd Earl, whose father was called 4th Lord Riverston (a title that had been conferred by James II after his deposition); *b* 1805; established his claim to the Earldom 1871; *d* 1879; *s* by his son (13) William St George, 10th Earl, *b* 1832: *m* 1866, Emily Margaret, who *d* 1906, da of late Andrew William Blake, JP, DL, of Furbough, co Galway; *d* 1883; *s* by his son (14) Anthony Francis, 11th Earl, *b* 1870; a Representative Peer for Ireland; *d* 1933: *s* by his brother (15) Gilbert Charles, 12th Earl, *b* 1880: *m* 1915, Doris, who *d* 1968, da of late Charles Imlach, of Liverpool; *d* 1971; *s* by his son (16) William Anthony, 13th Earl and present peer, also Baron Delvin.

WESTMINSTER, DUKE OF (Grosvenor) (Duke UK 1874, Bt E 1622)

VIRTVS · NON · STEMMA

Virtue, not ancestry

Gerald Cavendish Grosvenor, 6th Duke, and 15th Baronet; *b* 22 Dec 1951; *s* 1979; *ed* Harrow, and Sunningdale Sch; DL Cheshire 1982; Lt-Col and OC Queen's Own Yeo (TAVR) 1992; Dir Grosvenor Estate Holdings, Marcher Sound Ltd, Sutton Ridge Pty Ltd, North West Business Leadership Team, and Business in the Community; Pres Royal Nat Inst for the Blind since 1986, The Spastics Soc, Arthritis Care, Game Conservancy, Abbeyfield Soc, BLESMA, Youth Clubs UK, BASC, and Drug and Alcohol Foundn; Pres of Royal Agric Soc of England; Chancellor Manchester Metropolitan Univ; Trustee TSB, Foundn for England and Wales, and The Civic Trust; Member of Council of National Army Museum; Freeman of City of Chester in 1971 and of London 1981; KStJ 1991: *m* 1978, Natalia Ayesha, yst da of late Lt-Col Harold Pedro Joseph Phillips, FRGS (*see* Wernher, Bt), and has issue.

Arms – Quarterly: 1st and 4th azure, a portcullis with chains pendant or, on a chief of the last, between two united roses of York and Lancaster a pale, charged with the arms of King Edward the Confessor *City of Westminster* (Augmentation); 2nd and 3rd azure, a garb or, *Grosvenor*. **Crest** – A talbot statant or. **Supporters** – Two talbots reguardant or, collared azure.
Seat – Eaton Hall, Eaton, Chester. *Clubs* – Cavalry and Guards'; MCC; Brooks's; Roy Yacht Sqdn.

SON LIVING

Hugh Richard Louis (*Earl Grosvenor*), *b* 29 Jan 1991.

DAUGHTERS LIVING

Lady Tamara Katherine, *b* 1979.
Lady Edwina Louise, *b* 1981.
Lady Viola Georgina, *b* 1992.

SISTERS LIVING

Lady Leonora Mary (*Countess of Lichfield*), *b* 1949: *m* 1975 (*m diss* 1986), 5th Earl of Lichfield. *Residence* – 80 Eaton Sq, SW1.
Lady Jane Meriel (*Lady Jane Grosvenor*), *b* 1953; has reverted to her former style: *m* 1977 (*m diss* 1990), 10th Duke of Roxburghe. *Residence* – Cherrytrees, Keslo, Roxburghshire TD5 8BY.

DAUGHTER LIVING OF SECOND DUKE (*by 1st marriage*)

Lady Mary Constance, *b* 1910. *Residence* – Saighton Lodge, Saighton, Chester.

WIDOW LIVING OF SECOND DUKE

ANNE WINIFRED (*Anne, Duchess of Westminster*), only da of late Brig-Gen Edward Langford Sullivan, CB, CMG, of Glanmire House, co Cork: *m* 1947, as his fourth wife, the 2nd Duke, who *d* 1953. *Residence* – Eaton Lodge, Eccleston, Chester.

COLLATERAL BRANCHES LIVING

Granddaughter of late Lord Arthur Hugh Grosvenor, 9th son of 1st Duke:—
Issue of late Robert Arthur Grosvenor, MC, *b* 1895, *d* 1953: *m* 1925, Doris May, who *d* 1975, da of late Frederick William Wignall (Tate, Bt, colls):—
Robina Jill, *b* 1930: *m* 1st, 1951 (*m diss* 1961), Michael Phillip Forsyth-Forrest; 2ndly, 1961, Ronald Mills of Court Farm, Kenchester, Hereford, and has issue living, (by 1st *m*) Anita, *b* 1952, — Tessa (*Hon Mrs Harry Fane*), *b* 1955: *m* 1984, Hon Harry St Clair Fane, yr son of 15th Earl of Westmorland, — (by 2nd *m*), Robin, *b* 1962, — Serena Laura Rosanna, *b* 1965.

(In remainder to the Marquessate)

Descendants of late Rt Hon Lord Thomas Grosvenor, GCH, DCL (2nd son of 1st Marquess), who *s* his maternal grandfather (under special remainder) as 2nd *Earl of Wilton* 1814 (see that title).

Descendants of late Rt Hon Lord Robert Grosvenor (3rd son of 1st Marquess of Westminster), who was *cr Baron Ebury* 1857 (see that title).

PREDECESSORS – **(1)** *Sir* RICHARD Grosvenor, Knt, of Eaton, Cheshire, MP for Cheshire, was *cr a Baronet* 1622; *d* 1645; *s* by his son **(2)** *Sir* RICHARD, 2nd Bt; *d* 1664; *s* by his grandson **(3)** *Sir* THOMAS, 3rd Bt; sat as MP for Chester; *d* 1700; *s* by his el son **(4)** *Sir* RICHARD, 4th Bt; was Grand Cupbearer at the coronation of George II, *dsp* 1732; *s* by his brother **(5)** *Sir* THOMAS, 5th Bt; was MP for Chester; *d* 1733; *s* by his brother **(6)** *Sir* ROBERT, 6th Bt; sat as MP for Chester; *d* 1755; *s* by his son **(7)** *Sir* RICHARD, 7th Bt; *cr Baron Grosvenor*, of Eaton, co Chester (peerage of Great Britain) 1761, and *Viscount Belgrave* and *Earl Grosvenor* (peerage of Great Britain) 1784: *m* 1776, Henrietta (who *m* 2ndly, 1802, 6th Baron de Hochepied, and *d* 1828), da of Henry Vernon, of Hilton Park, Staffs; *d* 1802; *s* by his son **(8)** ROBERT, 2nd Earl; *cr Marquess of Westminster* (peerage of United Kingdom) 1831; was Lord-Lieut of Flintshire: *m* 1794, Lady Eleanor Egerton, who *d* 1846, da of 1st Earl of Wilton; *d* 1845; *s* by his son **(9)** RICHARD, KG, PC, 2nd Marquess; *b* 1795; was Lord-Lieut of Cheshire: *m* 1819, Elizabeth Mary, who *d* 1891, da of 1st Duke of Sutherland; *d* 1869, *s* by his son **(10)** HUGH LUPUS, 3rd Marquess; *b* 1825; Lord-Lieut of Cheshire, and of co London; Master of the Horse 1880-85; MP for Chester (*L*) 1847-69; *cr Duke of Westminster* (peerage of United Kingdom) 1874: *m* 1st, 1852, Lady Constance Gertrude Leveson-Gower, who *d* 1880, da of 2nd Duke of Sutherland, KG; 2ndly, 1882, Hon Katharine Caroline Cavendish, CBE, who *d* 1941, da of 2nd Baron Chesham; *d* 1899; *s* by his grandson **(11)** HUGH RICHARD ARTHUR, GCVO, DSO (only son of Victor Alexander, Earl Grosvenor), 2nd Duke; *b* 1879; S Africa 1900-02, and 1914-18 War: *m* 1st, 1901 (*m diss* 1919), Constance Edwina, CBE, who *d* 1970, da of late Col William Cornwallis-West (E De La Warr); 2ndly, 1920 (*m diss* 1926), Violet Mary Geraldine, who *d* 1983, da of Sir William Nelson, 1st Bt; 3rdly, 1930 (*m diss* 1947), Hon Lœlia Mary Ponsonby, who *d* 1993, da of 1st Baron Sysonby; 4thly, 1947, Anne Winifred, only da of late Brig-Gen Edward Langford Sullivan, CB, CMG, of Glanmire House, co Cork; *d* 1953; *s* by his cousin **(12)** WILLIAM (son of late Lord Henry George Grosvenor, 3rd son of the 1st Duke), 3rd Duke; *d* 1963; *s* by his cousin **(13)** GERALD HUGH, DSO, PC (el son of late Capt Lord Hugh William Grosvenor, 6th son of 1st Duke) 4th Duke; *b* 1907; Lt-Col 9th Lancers; Col 9th/12th Lancers 1961-67; High Sheriff of Cheshire 1959; Lord Steward of HM Household 1964-67: *m* 1945, Sally PERRY, who *d* 1990, natural twin da of late Roger Ackerley (by Muriel Perry); *d* 1967; *s* by his brother **(14)** ROBERT GEORGE, TD, 5th Duke, *b* 1910; Col N Irish Horse; Lord Lieut co Fermanagh 1977-79, High Sheriff 1952, PPS to Sec of State for Foreign Affairs 1957-59, MP for Fermanagh and S Tyrone (*U*) 1955-64 and Senator, N Ireland 1964-67: *m* 1946, Hon Viola Maud Lyttelton, who was *k* in a motor accident 1987, da of 9th Viscount Cobham; *d* 1979; *s* by his only son **(15)** GERALD CAVENDISH, 6th Duke and present peer; also Marquess of Westminster, Earl Grosvenor, Viscount Belgrave, and Baron Grosvenor.

WESTMORLAND, EARL OF (Fane) (Earl E 1624)

Disgrace not the altar

ANTHONY DAVID FRANCIS HENRY FANE, 16th Earl; *b* 1 Aug 1951; *s* 1993; *ed* Eton; FRGS: *m* 1985, Mrs Caroline Eldred Fairey, da of Keon Hughes, and formerly wife of Charles Fairey, and has issue.

𝕬rms – Azure, three dexter gauntlets back affrontée or. 𝕮rest – Out of a ducal coronet or, bull's head of a brindled colour, armed gold, and charged with a rose gules. 𝕾upporters – *Dexter*, a griffin, per fesse argent and or, collared, and line reflexed over the back sable; *sinister*, a pied or brindled bull, collared and lined or, at the end of the line a ring and three staples of the last.
Residence – 31 Langton St, SW10 0JL. *Club* – Turf.

DAUGHTER LIVING

Lady Daisy Caroline, *b* 1989.

BROTHER LIVING

Hon HARRY ST CLAIR, *b* 19 March 1953; *ed* Harrow; Page of Honour to HM 1966-68: *m* 1984, Tessa, da of Capt Michael Philip Forsyth-Forrest (*see* D Westminster, colls), and has issue living, Sam Michael David, *b* 1989, — Sophie Jane, *b* 1987. *Residences* – 14 Trevor St, SW7; The Barn House, Eastcourt, Malmesbury, Wilts.

SISTER LIVING

Lady Camilla Diana, *b* 1957: *m* 1985, Howard J. Hipwood, and has issue living, Sebastian John, *b* 1988, — Rosanna Charlotte, *b* 1986. *Residence* – New Priory Farm, Kington St Michael, Chippenham, Wilts SN14 6JP.

UNCLE LIVING (*son of 14th Earl*)

Hon Julian Charles, *b* 1927; *ed* Harrow; Author; FRSL 1974: *m* 1976, Gillian, yr da of late John Kidston Swire, DL, of Hubbards Hall, Harlow, Essex. *Residence* – Rotten Row House, Lewes, E Sussex BN7 1TN.

WIDOW LIVING OF FIFTEENTH EARL

BARBARA JANE (*Dowager Countess of Westmorland*), da of Lt-Col Sir Roland Lewis Findlay, 3rd Bt: *m* 1950, the 15th Earl, GCVO, who *d* 1993. *Residences* – The Old Rectory, Badminton, Avon; 26 Laxford House, Cundy St, SW1.

COLLATERAL BRANCHES LIVING

Issue of late Lt-Col Hon Mountjoy John Charles Wedderburn Fane, TD, 2nd son of 13th Earl, *b* 1900, *d* 1963: *m* 1926, Agatha Isabel, who *d* 1993, da of late Lt-Col Arthur Acland-Hood-Reynardson, OBE (*see* Fuller-Acland-Hood, Bt, colls, 1990 Edn):—
Antony Charles Reynardson (Ridgemead House, Shrubbs Hill Lane, Sunningdale, Berks SL5 OLD), *b* 1927; Lt-Cdr RN (ret): *m* 1956, Caroline Mary Rokeby, da of late Hugh D. Holland, of The Crossways, Englefield Green, Surrey, and has issue living, Edward Hugh Reynardson (15 Kyrle Rd, SW11 6BD), *b* 1957: *m* 1982, Suki Serena, only da of Sir David Mitchell, MP, of Berry Horn Cottage, Odiham, Hants, and has issue living, Arthur Charles Reynardson *b* 1992, Elizabeth Helen Clementine *b* 1986, Helena Evelyn Cecily *b* 1988, — Olivia Mary Rokeby, *b* 1960: *m* 1st, 1982 (*m diss* 1992), Adam Nicolson (*see* B Carnock, colls); 2ndly, 1993, (Richard) Mark Pemberton, of 17 Melbourne Place, Cambridge, 2nd son of Christopher Henry Pemberton, of Place Farmhouse, Bardwell, Bury St Edmunds, Suffolk (*see* Riddell, Bt), — Charlotte Evelyn Langham, *b* 1967. —— Daphne Sybil, *b* 1929.

Grandchildren of late Col William (Vere Reeve) KING-FANE, only son of late William Dashwood Fane, 5th son of late Hon Henry Fane, MP, yr son of 8th Earl:—
Issue of late Capt Henry William Newman Fane, OBE, *b* 1897, *d* 1976: *m* 1946, Dorothy Mary, who *d* 1986, only da of late Alexander Findlay, of Llantarnam, Gwent:—
Mary Helen, *b* 1947: *m* 1982, Michael Robin Fry, and has issue living, Marcus Fane, *b* 1985, — Samuel Henry Fane, *b* 1987. *Residence* – Fulbeck Hall, Grantham, Lincs.
Issue of late Lt Francis Christopher Fane, RN, *b* 1900, *d* 1947: *m* 1931, Joyce Patricia (Scots Hill, Fulbeck, Grantham, Lincs) (who *m* 2ndly, 1957, Maj Vincent Tofts, TD, late Indian Army, who *d* 1983), da of late Rev W. Hugh Hancock:—
Julian Francis, *b* 1938; *ed* Marlborough and Emmanuel Coll, Camb (MA), High Sheriff of Lincolnshire 1981: *m* 1965, Mary Julia, da of Michael W. Allday, of The Shrubbery, Hartlebury, Worcs, and has issue living, Andrew Julian, *b* 1967; *ed* Marlborough, — Alexandra Julia, *b* 1969. *Residence* – Fulbeck Manor, Grantham. —— Susan Cicely, *b* 1932: *m* 1953, Lt-Col John Lindley Marmion Dymoke, MBE, DL, late R Anglian Regt, 34th Queen's Champion of England (By Lindley, ext), High Sheriff Lincs 1979, Vice-Lord Lieut 1991, and has issue living, Francis John Fane Marmion (Scrivelsby Grange, Horncastle, Lincs), *b* 1955: *m* 1982, Rosalie Mary, only da of Maj Antony Goldingham, of Marsh Farm, Uley, Glos, and has issue living, Henry Francis Marmion *b* 1984, Thomas Antony Marmion *b* 1989, Emily Rachel Marmion *b* (twin) 1994, — Philip Henry Marmion, *b* 1957; Maj WG: *m* 1982, Arabella, yr da of Sir Ralph Jordan Dodds, 2nd Bt, and has issue living, Edward *b* 1985, William *b* 1988, — Charles Edward Marmion, *b* 1961: *m* 1990, Kathryn Jane, yst da of Rex Topham, of Otford, Kent, and has issue living, Jasper Rex Fane *b* 1993. *Seat* – Scrivelsby Court, Horncastle, Lincs. *Club* – United Service. —— Rosemary Lillias, *b* 1934; BA (Soc Sci 1987) JP: *m* 1954, Derek Cecil Stevenson, MB BS, MRCS, LRCP, FRCS, and has issue living, Christopher Peter, *b* 1956; B Juris, LLB, LLM (Lond): *m* 1985, Evelyn Bowen, MB BS, DObst (RCOG), and has issue living, Richard Vere *b* 1990, Harry Bowen *b* 1994, Georgina Bowen *b* 1988, — Melody Jane, *b* 1958: *m* 1980, Christopher John Chipper, and has issue living, Simon Derek *b* 1984, Jasmin Melody *b* 1982, — Catherine Fane, *b* 1960: *m* 1985, Peter Charles Kiel, MB BS, and has issue living, Michael William *b* 1989, David Peter Fane *b* 1991, Sarah Jane Mary *b* 1987, — Mary-Louise, *b* 1969; BSc: *m* 1993, Russell Paul Hardwick. *Residence* – 7 Muller St, N Beach, W Aust. —— Belinda Joyce (26a Cumberland Way, Bessenden, Western Australia), *b* (twin) 1938; ThA 1976, ThDip 1988: *m* 1971 (*m diss* 1981), Gary Douglas Phillips.
Issue of late Charles William Fane, *b* 1904; *d* 1976: *m* 1st, 1931 (*m diss* 1966), Pauline Margaret, da of Rt Rev Ernest Morell Blackie, Dean of Rochester; 2ndly, 1966, Pamela Mary, who *d* 1987, da of late Capt Robert Millington Synge (*see* Synge, Bt, colls):—

(By 1st wife) Peter William (22 Cheyne Row, SW3; Garrick Club and MCC), *b* 1939; *ed* Eton; High Sheriff of Lincs 1983-84: *m* 1969, Ruth, da of late John Paske Yeomans, and has an adopted son, Maximilian William, *b* 1978. —— Angela Pauline, *b* 1936: *m* 1964, Lt-Cdr Kenneth Patrick Bruce-Gardyne, RN, of The Old Rectory, Meonstoke, Hants, and has issue living, James Patrick, *b* 1965, — Vere Alexander, *b* 1973, — Victoria Sophie, *b* 1969. —— (By 2nd wife) Eleanor Mary, *b* 1965. —— Georgina Rachel, *b* 1966. —— Rose Christabel, *b* 1968.

Granddaughter of late William Dashwood Fane (ante):—
Issue of late Col William (Vere Reeve) KING-FANE, *b* 1868, *d* 1943 (having assumed by Roy licence 1920 the surname of King in addition to and before that of Fane): *m* 1895, Helen Beatrice, who *d* 1962, da of late Thomas Holdsworth Newman (Newman, Bt, *cr* 1836, colls):—
Elizabeth Christine (121 Gloucester Court, Kew Rd, Richmond, Surrey TW9 3DY), *b* 1906: *m* 1931, Col Jeffrey Maurice Lambert, OBE, late RE, who *d* 1967, and has issue living, John Alexander, *b* 1932; *ed* St Lawrence Coll, Ramsgate: *m* 1961, Iris Elaine, only da of late James Balfour Craig, of Belfast, and has issue living, Alastair James *b* 1966, Rachel Elizabeth *b* 1962, — Janetta, *b* 1936.

Grandchildren of late Cecil Francis William Fane, 2nd son of late Robert George Cecil Fane, 7th son of late Hon Henry Fane, MP (ante):—
Issue of late John Lionel Richards Fane, *b* 1884, *d* 1945: *m* 1928 Barbara Kathleen (who *d* 1980, having *m* 3rdly, 1947, Bryan Northam Gibbs, MBE, who *d* 1965, and 4thly, 1969, John Sidney Mason, who *d* 1974), da of late Falconer Lewis Wallace, OBE, of Candacraig, Aberdeenshire (M Anglesey, colls), and formerly wife of late Capt Oliver Henry Douglas Vickers:—
Vere John Alexander (18 Empire House, Thurloe Place, SW7; White's Club), *b* 1935; *ed* Eton, and Trin Coll, Camb; late Lt Coldm Gds: *m* 1964, Tessa Helen Murray, only da of late John Murray Prain, DSO, OBE, DL, of Longrigg, St Andrews, Fife, and has issue living, Rupert John Alexander, *b* 1967, — Miranda Helen, *b* 1968. —— Venetia Sophia Diana (Drumwhill, Mossdale, by Castle Douglas, Kirkcudbrightshire DG7 2NL), *b* 1930.

Grandchildren of late Major John Augustus Fane, el son of late Col John William Fane, MP, son of John Fane, MP (*b* 1775), el son of John Fane, MP, son of Henry Fane, yr brother of 8th Earl:—
Issue of late Francis Luther Fane, *b* 1865, *d* 1954: *m* 1st, 1906, Mary, who *d* 1927, da of late John Henry Horris of Ballarat, Victoria, Australia; 2ndly, 1929, Beatrice Jane, who *d* 1961, el da of late Harry Coppleston, of Lostwithiel, Cornwall:—
(By 2nd *m*) John Coppleston Luther (MCC, Cavalry and Guards' Club), *b* 1933; *ed* Harrow, and Emmanuel Coll, Camb; late Lt Welsh Guards; High Sheriff of Oxfordshire 1977. —— Anne Isabel (Castle Minor, Tintagel, Cornwall), *b* 1931: *m* 1954 (*m diss* 1976), Colin Irvin Richmond-Watson, and has had issue, Harry Fane, *b* 1956, — Angus Colin John, *b* 1958; *d* 1984, — Elizabeth Frances Aves, *b* 1960; has resumed her maiden name: *m* 1978 (*m diss* 1982), Stuart Hogan, and has issue living, Gareth Michael Colin *b* 1978, — Sarah Eleanor, *b* 1962: *m* 1987 (*m diss* 1992), Kerry C. Baxley, of New York.

Grandchildren of late Sydney Algernon Fane, 2nd son of late Maj John Augustus Fane (ante):—
Issue of late Capt Gerard William Reginald Fane, DSC, *b* 1898, *d* 1979: *m* 1st, 1919, Constance Rhoda Elizabeth, who *d* 1969, da of Sir Nicholas Henry Bacon, 13th Bt; 2ndly, 1970, Phyllis Jane (Feering Place, Kelvedon, Colchester), da of late Hugh Jackson, of Chevington:—
(By 1st *m*) Julian Raymond, *b* 1925.
Issue of late Cdr Nigel Loftus Henry Fane, RNR, *b* 1904, *d* 1973: *m* 1st, 1935 (*m diss* 1959), Catharine Henrietta, who *d* 1968, da of Henry P. Hussey, of Bricklehurst Manor, Stonegate, Sussex; 2ndly, 1960 (*m diss* 1971), Dorothy Mai, da of John Farrington, and widow of Borras Noel Hamilton Whiteside (*see* L Belhaven and Stenton, colls, 1980 Edn):—
(By 1st *m*) Patricia Margaret, *b* 1936: *m* 1958, Charles Henry David Denning, of the Old Vicarage, Stonegate, Wadhurst, Sussex, yr son of Lt-Gen Sir Reginald Francis Stewart Denning, KBE, CB, and has issue living, James Henry, *b* 1959, — Guy William, *b* 1962, — Sophia Jane, *b* 1964, — Venetia Mary, *b* 1966.

Grandchildren of late Hubert William Fane (infra):—
Issue of late Maj Robert William Augustus Fane, MBE, *b* 1913, *d* 1989: *m* 1940, Elinor Valerie (Hoo House, Hoo, Woodbridge, Suffolk), da of late Hon William Borthwick (*see* Borthwick, Bt, colls):—
Andrew William Mildmay, *b* 1949; *ed* Radley, and Emmanuel Coll, Camb: *m* 1989, Clare Lucy, MB BS, FRCS, yr da of Francis Marx, of Coventry, Warwicks. —— Peter Robert Spencer, *b* 1956; *ed* Radley. —— Priscilla Margaret, *b* 1943: *m* 1975, Christopher Brewer, of Ballards Cottage, Ballards Lane, Limpsfield, Surrey, and has issue living, Simon Robert, *b* 1976, — Charles Thomas, *b* 1979. —— Lavinia Anne, *b* 1947: *m* 1974, Stephen Wright, PhD, and has issue living, Matthew David Robert, *b* 1975, — Catherine Frances, *b* 1977. —— Angela Elizabeth, *b* 1954.

Grandchildren of late Capt Henry George Fane, 2nd son of Col John William Fane, MP (ante):—
Issue of late Hubert William Fane, *b* 1878, *d* 1911, Tilda, who *d* 1953, da of late A. von Adametz:—
Dorothy Louisa (25 Amesbury Crescent, Hove, E Sussex BN3 5RD), *b* 1917: *m* 1st, 1938, Capt Frederick James Colville, Gordon Highlanders, who was *ka* 1940 (V Colville of Culross, colls); 2ndly 1941 (*m diss* 1962), Lt-Cdr Clifford John Maddocks, RNVR, MIME; 3rdly, 1962 (*m diss* 1974), Lt-Col John Anthony Russell Freeland, late Queen's R Regt, who *d* 1989, and has issue living (by 2nd *m*), Cynthia Diana, *b* 1944: *m* 1967, John Charles Johnson Orchard, of Honington Glebe, Honington, nr Shipston-on-Stour, Warwicks, and has issue living, Alaister Mildmay Heywood *b* 1971, Alexandra Rosemary Fane *b* 1969, — Anne Susan, *b* 1948: *m* 1st, 1968 (*m diss* 1988), Richard Fullerton Evetts; 2ndly, 1989, Christopher Corder Litten, of The Lodge, Bovingdon Green, Bovingdon, Herts HP3 0LD, and has had issue (by 1st *m*), Toby James Fullerton *b* 1970, David Jason Clifford *b* and *d* 1974.
Issue of late Francis John Fane, *b* 1885, *d* 1963: *m* 1915, Violet, who *d* 1970, da of late G. Clifford Bower, of Newquay, Bromley, Kent:—
Peter Francis George (Wildermere, Haughurst Hill, Baughurst, Hants. *Club* – Carlton), *b* 1917; *ed* Marlborough, and Emmanuel Coll, Camb (MA 1939); Capt (ret) RA; 1939-45 War (prisoner): *m* 1939, Diana, only da of late Col George Holden Hodgkinson, and has issue living, Francis Michael George (80 Mathews Green Rd, Wokingham, Berks RG11 1JT), *b* 1941; *ed* Peterhouse, Rhodesia, and Emmanuel Coll, Camb (MA): *m* 1st, 1967 (*m diss* 1989), Anne Bridget, da of late Maj John Alfred Gordon, Gribble; 2ndly, 1989, Irene, da of late Maurice Frederick Osborne Johnston, of 27 Sefton Drive, Maghull, Merseyside, and has issue living (by 1st *m*), Thomas Francis *b* 1968, Suzanne *b* 1972, — Victoria, *b* 1947; BSc 1993: *m* 1966, Martin Richard Cardale, of Castle View Hotel, Chepstow, Gwent, and has issue living, George Martin *b* 1970, Miranda Lucy *b* 1968; *ed* Exeter Univ (BA 1989): *m* 1994, Stuart James Nicholson, of 6 Malcolm Rd, Borrodale, Harare, Zimbabwe, Zara Diana *b* 1980, — Sarah Lucy *b* 1962; *ed* Exeter Univ (BA 1984). —— Elizabeth Daphne (Alderley, Pine Av, Camberley, Surrey) *b* 1916: *m* 1940, Lt-Col John David Logan Dickson, MC, RHA, who *d* 1958, and has issue living, Jeremy David Fane (8 Alan Rd, Wimbledon, SW19), *b* 1941; *ed* Marlborough, and Emmanuel Coll, Camb (MA): *m* 1965, Patricia, da of Laurence Cleveland Martin, MD, FRCP, and has issue living, James David Laurence *b* 1970, Lucy Camilla *b* 1971, — Sally Ann, *b* 1942: *m* 1975, Lt-Col John Alan Cubitt Blakiston, 13th/18th Royal Hus, and has issue (*see* Blakiston, Bt, colls).

Grandsons of late Francis John Fane (ante):—
Issue of late Maj Henry John Fane, MC, RA, *b* 1919, *d* 1993: *m* 1st, 1945 (*m diss* 1970), Agatina, da of Onorevole, Count Severio d'Ayala, of Rome; 2ndly, 1980, Mrs Anne Barclay Fane (Redlands, Duncton, Petworth, Sussex), da of

late Lt-Col Henry Gamble, OBE, of Instow, N Devon, formerly wife of Lt-Cdr Anthony Stuart Melville-Ross, DSC, RN, and widow of his kinsman, Peter Gerald Scrope Fane, RNVR (*see* 1976 Edn):—
(By 1st *m*) Richard John George, *b* 1946; *ed* The Oratory: *m* 1989, Anne L., yst da of Peter Knox, of 27 The Rise, Sevenoaks, Kent. —— Patrick Henry, *b* 1949; *ed* The Oratory: *m* 1976, Stephanie Anne, eldest da of A.R. Matanle, of East Wing, Beedings Castle, Nutbourne, Sussex, and has issue living, Edward Henry, *b* 1978, —— George Arthur, *b* 1981, —— Heloise Anne, *b* 1982.

Granddaughter of late Col John William Fane, MP (ante):—
Issue of late Cecil Fane, *b* 1859, *d* 1948: *m* 1st, 1892, Alice Mary, who *d* 1899, da of Rev Thomas Ward Goddard, formerly V of Nazeing, Essex; 2ndly 1913, Florence Marjorie, who *d* 1967, d of William Ferrand (B Bolton, colls):—
(By 2nd *m*) Winifred Anne, *b* 1917; late Flight Officer WAAF: *m* 1949, Philip William Dacre Stuart, and has issue living, Peter Robin (17 Wellington St, Goderich, Ont, Canada N7A 2W6), *b* 1953: *m* 1979, Susan Blaker Clinkard, and has issue living, Tyler John *b* 1985, Amanda Michelle *b* 1981, —— Penelope Anne, *b* 1951: *m* 1970, Eric Douglas Honsberger, of 90 Quantrell Trail, Scarborough, Ont, Canada M1B 1L8, and has issue living, Philip John Walter *b* 1974, Stuart Douglas *b* 1979, Margaret Anne *b* 1972, Alison Michelle *b* 1976. *Residence* – 35 Front St South, Apt 1806, (Port Credit) Mississauga, Ontario, Canada L5H 2C6.

Grandchildren of late Cecil Fane, 4th and yst son of late Col John William Fane, MP (ante):—
Issue of late Adrian Cecil Fane, *b* 1916, *d* 1987: *m* 1952, Eliabeth Muriel (Carrickmanor Haven, Carrickbrennan Rd, Monkstown, co Dublin), da of Henry Wheeler, of Garbally, Bruff, co Limerick:—
Henry Cecil (Lawrenny Castle Hotel, High Street, Neyland, Pembrokeshire SA73 1SR), *b* 1954; *ed* Kilkenny Coll: *m* 1st, 1979 (*m diss* 1991), Roisin Elizabeth, da of Donald Mooney, of Delgany, co Wicklow; 2ndly, 1991, Mrs Celia Margaret Wreford, da of Brian Councell, of Clevedon, Avon, and formerly wife of Anthony Wreford, and has issue living (by 1st *m*), Edwyn Charles *b* 1979, —— Gareth John, *b* 1981. —— Gwendoline Ann, *b* 1953: *m* 1988, Michael John Harrison, of 36 Pearson St, Narara, NSW 2250, Australia.
Issue of late John William Fane, *b* 1919; *d* 1982: *m* 1st, 1944 (*m diss* 19-), Doreen, da of Albert Lawrence, of Waltham Abbey, Essex; 2ndly, 1964, Gwendoline-Ann, widow of Gerald Francis Kelly (84 Addison Rd, Enfield, Middlesex):—
(By 1st *m*) Anthony John, *b* 1948. —— Sheila Rosamond, *b* 1951: *m* 19—, John Johnson, of 3 Manton Rd, Lincoln LN2 2JL.

Granddaughters of late Col Frederick John Fane, son of late Rev Frederick Adrian Scrope Fane, 2nd son of late John Fane, MP (*b* 1775) (ante):—
Issue of late Frederick Luther Fane, MC, *b* 1875, *d* 1960: *m* 1938, Edna Mary, who *d* 1982, da of late Henry James Meads, of Eastbourne:—
Elizabeth Anne, *b* 1946. —— Rosemary Enid, *b* 1952. *Residence* – Hoo House, Hoo, Woodbridge, Suffolk.

Grandchildren of late Charles Eugene Fane (infra):—
Issue of late Charles Irwin Fane, *b* 1912, *d* 19—: *m* 1942, Gwendoline Jolyn (Safe Box 610, Darwin, Northern Territory, Australia 5970), da of Ernest Stainton, of Broome, WA:—
Michael, *b* 1949. —— Fifi Antoinette, *b* 1943. —— Tania, *b* 1952.

Grandchildren of late Charles Augustus Fane, of Carnarvon, W Australia, elder son of late George Augustus Scrope Fane, 3rd son of late John Fane, MP (ante):—
Issue of late Charles Eugene Fane, *b* 1872, *d* 1955: *m* 1909, Florence Beatrice Yeates:—
Alexander Eugene, *b* 1913: *m* 1942, Nancy Lorna, da of Ray Carron, of Brighton, Vic, and has issue living, Russell (21 Knox Dr, Barwon Heads, Victoria), *b* 1952, —— Sylvia, *b* 1943: *m* 1966, Donald B. Shaw, of 37 Kent St, Gladstone, Qld, —— Gwendoline (13 Haines St, Hawthorn, Victoria), *b* 1948: *m* 1966 (*m diss* 1981), Ray Leggett. *Residence* – 48 Doulberg St, Ocean Grove, Victoria, Australia. —— George Augustus, *b* 1916: *m* 1st, 19— (*m diss* 19—), Eileen Byers: 2ndly, 19—, Lena Campbell, and has issue living (by 1st *m*), Brenda, *b* 19—, — Joy, *b* 19—, — (by 2nd *m*) Peter Eugene (230 Barker Rd, Subiaco, W Australia), *b* 1959; *ed* Univ of Western Australia, and Australia Nat Univ: *m* 1983, Debra Barnes, and has issue living, Kristy Caroline *b* 1983, — Donald Lorne (4 Lazarus St, Geraldton 6530, W Australia), *b* 1960: *m* 1982, Gae Pepperell, — Shirlee Margaret, *b* 1956: *m* 1983, Allan Rose, of 8 Duclas Place, Geraldton 6530, W Australia. *Residence* – 159 George Rd, Geraldton 6530, W Australia. —— Iolanthe Florence, *b* 1918: *m* 1945, Ronald LeGrange Dunlop, and has issue living, Diana Iolanthe, *b* 1946: *m* 1970, John Joseph Pauley, of 10 Rainbow View, Ocean Reef 6027, W Australia, and has issue living David John *b* 1974, Helen Diana *b* 1973, — Margaret Chase, *b* 1950: *m* 1979, John Robin Lanyon, of Yarrabee, One Tree Hill Rd, Ferny Creek, Victoria 3786, Australia, and has issue living, James John *b* 1982, Thomas Charles *b* 1985. *Residence* – 130 Abbett St, Scarborough, W Australia. —— Beatrice Mary, *b* 1922: *m* 1944, Laban Johnson-Head, and has issue living, Stephen Johnson (207 Windward Passage, Slidell, Louisiana 70458, USA), *b* 1945: *m* 1970 (*m diss* 1985), Betsy Holter, and has issue living, Charles Johnson *b* 1974, —— Susan Gail (5134 Timber Trail, Atlanta, Georgia 30342, USA), *b* 1947: *m* 1st, 1976 (*m diss* 1983), Elgin M. Wells, jr; 2ndly, 1988, Brian Wealand Kreider, and has issue living (by 1st *m*), Laurel Brooke *b* 1978, — Julia Kathleen, *b* 1952: *m* 1980, Charles David Adams, Capt USAF, of 2839 Tahoe Drive, Merced, California 95340, USA, and has issue living, Royce Henry *b* 1988. Capt and Mrs Charles D. Evans also have adopted children, Quinton Lee *b* 1984, Royal Dawn *b* 1980, Jennifer Réne *b* 1982 *Residence* – 1046 McConnell Drive, Decatur, Georgia 30033, USA. —— Gloria Sybil, *b* 1924: *m* 1958, Noel Gleed. *Residence* – 12 Grosvenor Rd, Meltham 6053, W Australia. —— Deborah Kathleen *b* 1927: *m* 1951, Murray Henderson, and has issue living, Murray, *b* 1953, — John, *b* 1955, — Fiona, *b* 1957. (Mrs Henderson also has issue, Margaret Enid FANE (15B, 55 Herdsman Parade, Wembley, WA 6014, Australia), *b* 1950; SFO (Third Order of St Francis); legally resumed the surname of Fane 1982: *m* 1973 (*m diss* 1981), Steven James Kirkman, and has issue living, James Murray *b* 1977, Genevieve Margaret *b* 1974, Priscilla Norma (39 Mistral St, Falcon, WA 6210, Australia) *b* 1976, Kathleen Deborah *b* 1979). *Residence* – MS 115, Harchs Rd, Gympe 4570, Queensland, Australia. —— Mary Patricia, *b* 1929: *m* 1955, Donald Whiteford McLaren, who *d* 1976. *Residence* – 104 Nollamara Av, Nollamara, W Australia 6061.

PREDECESSORS – (1) Sir FRANCIS Fane, was *cr Baron Burghersh* and *Earl of Westmorland* (peerage of England) 1624, and in 1626 *s* his mother as *Baron Le Despencer* (see V Falmouth); *d* 1628; *s* by his son (2) MILDMAY, KB, 2nd Earl; *d* 1665; *s* by his el son (3) CHARLES, 3rd Earl; *dsp* 1691; *s* by his half-brother (4) VERE, KB, 4th Earl; *d* 1693; *s* by his el son (5) VERE, 5th Earl; *d* unmarried 1699; *s* by his brother (6) THOMAS, 6th Earl; *dsp* 1736; *s* by his brother (7) JOHN, 7th Earl, a Lieut-Gen in the Army and a distinguished military officer under the Duke of Marlborough; *cr Baron Catherlough* (peerage of Ireland) 1733: *d* 1762 when the Barony of Catherlough became extinct, the Barony of Le Despencer passed to Sir Francis Dashwood, Bt (see V Falmouth) and the Barony of Burghersh and Earldom of Westmorland devolved upon his kinsman (8) THOMAS, MP, the descendant of Sir Francis Fane, 3rd son of 1st Earl; *d* 1771: *s* by his son (9) JOHN, 9th Earl; *d* 1774; *s* by his son (10) JOHN, KG, 10th Earl; *d* 1841; *s* by his son (11) JOHN, GCB, GCH, 11th Earl; *b* 1784; a Gen in the Army and a distinguished military officer, was afterwards Ambassador at Berlin 1841, and at Vienna 1851, and Special Commr at Conference at Vienna 1855: *m* 1811, Lady Priscilla Anne Wellesley, da of 3rd Earl of Mornington; *d* 1859; *s* by his son (12) FRANCIS WILLIAM HENRY, CB, 12th Earl, *b* 1825; Col Coldstream Guards: *m* 1857, Lady Adelaide Ida Curzon, 2nd da of 1st Earl Howe, GCB; *d* 1891; *s* by his only surviving son (13) ANTHONY MILDMAY JULIAN, CBE, 13th Earl, *b* 1859; Col, and an ADC to HM; S Africa 1902: *m* 1st, 1892, Lady Sybil Mary St Clair-Erskine, who *d* 1910, da of 4th Earl of Rosslyn; 2ndly, 1916, Catherine Louise, who *d* 1973, da of late Rev John S. Geale; *d* 1922; *s* by his el son (14) VERE ANTHONY FRANCIS ST CLAIR, 14th Earl, *b* 1893; Lt (ret) RN: *m* 1923, Hon Diana Lister, who *d* 1983, da of 4th Baron Ribblesdale (ext), and widow of (i) Percy Lyulph Wyndham, Lt Coldstream Gds (E Leconfield), and (ii) Capt Arthur Edward Capel, CBE; *d* 1948; *s* by his el son (15) DAVID ANTHONY THOMAS, GCVO, 15th Earl, *b* 1924; Capt Royal Horse Gds, 1939-45 War (wounded); Chm Sothebys 1980-82 (Dir since 1965); Lord in Waiting to HM 1955, Master of the Horse 1978-91; *m* 1950, Barbara Jane, da of Lt-Col Sir Roland Lewis Findlay, 3rd Bt; *d* 1993; *s* by his elder son (16) ANTHONY DAVID FRANCIS HENRY, 16th Earl and present peer; also Baron Burghersh.

WESTWOOD, BARON (Westwood) (Baron UK 1944)

WILLIAM GAVIN WESTWOOD, 3rd Baron; *b* 30 Jan 1944; *s* 1991; *ed* Fettes: *m* 1969, Penelope, FCA, eldest da of Charles Edgar Shafto, VRD, MB, of 67 Jesmond Park West, Newcastle upon Tyne NE7 7BX, and has issue.

Arms – Argent, a lion rampant gules, between three lymphads sable, flags flying to the dexter of the second. **Crest** – A mullet argent, charged with a thistle slipped and leaved proper. **Supporters** – On either side a sea-lion argent, charged on the shoulder with two anchors in saltire sable.
Residence – Ferndale, Clayton Rd, Newcastle upon Tyne NE2 1TL.

SONS LIVING

Hon WILLIAM FERGUS, *b* 24 Nov 1972; *ed* Royal Gram Sch, Newcastle.
Hon Alistair Cameron, *b* 1974; *ed* Royal Gram Sch, Newcastle.

BROTHER LIVING

Hon Nigel Alistair, *b* 1950; *ed* Fettes; FRICS, FRSA; Hon Royal Norwegian Consul: *m* 1977, Joan Elizabeth, yr da of Reginald Ibison, CBE, of Gosforth, Newcastle-upon-Tyne, and has issue living, David Alistair, *b* 1983, — Peter Robert, *b* 1986. *Residence* – 7 Fernville Rd, Gosforth, Newcastle upon Tyne NE3 4HT.

AUNT LIVING (*daughter of 1st Baron*)

Hon Margaret Taylor Young, MBE, *b* 1913; formerly 3rd Officer, WRNS: *m* 1st, 1934, William B. Lynn; 2ndly, 1945 (*m diss* 1974), John Bruce Campbell, formerly Roy Canadian Artillery, and has issue living, (by 2nd *m*), Robert Bruce, *b* 1948, — Helen Jean Laura, *b* 1946. *Residence* – 2 Ethorpe Cresc, Gerrards Cross, Bucks SL9 8PW.

WIDOW LIVING OF SECOND BARON

MARJORIE (*Dowager Baroness Westwood*), only child of Arthur Bonwick, of Heaton, Newcastle upon Tyne: *m* 1937, the 2nd Baron, who *d* 1991. *Residence* – 55 Moor Court, Westfield, Newcastle upon Tyne NE3 4YD.

COLLATERAL BRANCHES LIVING

Adopted da of late Hon Douglas Wilkie Westwood, 2nd son of 1st Baron, *b* 1910, *d* 1968: *m* 1939, Mary Katherine, who *d* 1987, da of John Carter:—
Carol Margaret, *b* 1945: *m* 1st, 1966 (*m diss* 1978), Maj Stephen Ralli, Rifle Bde (ret); 2ndly, 1978, Robert Alexander Karl Constantin, Baron Staël von Holstein, and has issue living (by 1st *m*) Charles Douglas Stephen, *b* 1968; *ed* Sherborne.

Issue of late Hon James Young Shaw Westwood, yst son of 1st Baron, *b* 1915, *d* 1989: *m* 1941 (*m diss* 1969), Joan, only child of Raymond Potts:—
Roger Douglas, *b* 1943; *ed* Westminster, and New Coll, Oxford (MA, Dip Ed); P/O RAFVR. *Residence* – Swallowtail Cottage, Beckley, E Sussex TN31 6TT.

PREDECESSORS – (1) WILLIAM Westwood, OBE, son of late William Westwood, of Dundee; *b* 1880; was National Supervisor of Ship Constructors' and Shipwrights' Asso 1913-29, and Gen Sec thereof 1929-45, Ch Industrial Adviser 1942-45, a Lord-in-Waiting to HM 1945-47, and Chm of Mineral Development Committee under Min of Fuel and Power 1946-49; *cr Baron Westwood*, of Gosforth, co Northumberland (peerage of United Kingdom) 1944: *m* 1st, 1905, Margaret Taylor, who *d* 1916, da of late William Young, of Dundee; 2ndly, 1918, Agnes Helen Flockhart, who *d* 1952 da of late James Downie, of Dundee; *d* 1953; *s* by his el son (2) WILLIAM, 2nd Baron, *b* 1907, FRSA, FCIS, Life Member and Former Pres Football League: *m* 1937, Marjorie, only child of Arthur Bonwick, of Heaton, Newcastle upon Tyne; *d* 1991; *s* by his elder son (3) WILLIAM GAVIN, 3rd Baron and present peer.

Weymouth, Viscount; son of Marquess of Bath.

WHADDON, BARON (Page) (Life Baron 1978)

(JOHN) DEREK PAGE, son of John Page; *b* 14 Aug 1927; *ed* St Bedes Coll, Manchester; BSc (Sociology) London; Dir, Cambridge Chemical Co Ltd since 1962, and Rindalbourne Ltd 1983-90; Chm Daltrade Ltd since 1983, and Skorimpex-Rind Ltd since 1986; MP for Kings Lynn (*Lab*) 1964-70; *cr* Baron Whaddon of Whaddon Co Cambridge (Life Baron) 1978: *m* 1st, 1948, Catherine Audrey, who *d* 1979, da of John William Halls; 2ndly, 1981, Angela Rixson, da of Luigi della Bella, of Treviso, Italy, and has issue by 1st *m*.

Arms – Quarterly vert and or on a fess engrailed ermine between in dexter chief a mullet and in sinister base a harp or and in sinister chief and dexter base a rose gules barbed and seeded proper three garbs gold. **Crest** – Upon a wreath or, vert and gules a crown vallary or issuing therefrom, within a chaplet vert set with roses gules barbed and seeded proper, a triple trefoil slipped vert. **Supporters** – *Dexter*, a lion guardant proper winged or; *sinister*, a mermaid proper crined and with a tail fin or, a round shield with its boss gold on her forearm and holding in the hand proper a sword point upward argent hilt, pommel and quillons gold.
Residence – The Old Vicarage, Whaddon, Royston, Herts. *Club* – Reform.

SON LIVING *(By 1st marriage)*

Hon John Keir *b* 1955: *m* 1976, Gale Masterman.

DAUGHTER LIVING *(By 1st marriage)*

Hon Eve-Ann, *b* 1952: *m* 1972, Patrick Prentice.

WHARNCLIFFE, EARL OF (Montagu Stuart Wortley) (Earl UK 1876)

RICHARD ALAN MONTAGU STUART WORTLEY, 5th Earl; *b* 26 May 1953; *s* 1987; *ed* Wesleyan Univ, Conn; builder: *m* 1979, Mary Elizabeth, da of Rev William Wellington Reed, of Keene, NH, and has issue.

Arms – Quarterly: 1st and 4th argent, on a bend between six martlets gules three bezants, a canton or charged with a fesse checky azure and argent within a double tressure flory counterflory gules, *Wortley*; 2nd or, a fesse checky azure and argent within a double tressure flory counterflory gules, *Stuart*; 3rd argent, three lozenges conjoined in fesse gules within a bordure sable, *Montagu*. **Crests** – 1st, a demi-lion gules, and in an escrol over the motto 'Nobilis Ira', *Stuart*; 2nd, an eagle's leg erased or, issuant therefrom three ostrich feathers proper, charged on the thigh with a fesse checky azure and argent, *Wortley*; 3rd, a griffin's head couped or, wings endorsed and beak sable, *Montagu*. **Supporters** – *Dexter*, a horse argent, bridled and gorged with a collar, flory counterflory gules; *sinister*, a stag proper gorged as the dexter.
Residence – 270 Main St, Cumberland, Maine 04021, USA.

He flourishes with the honour of his ancestors

SONS LIVING

REED (*Viscount Carlton*), *b* 5 Feb 1980.
Hon Christopher James, *b* 1983.

BROTHER LIVING

William Ralph, *b* 1959: *m* 1985, Dorothea Jane, da of Ronald Riley, of Rochester, NH, USA, and has issue living, Brian Alan, *b* 1988, — Dorothea Jayme, *b* 1987.
Residence – 18 Nola Av, Rochester, NH, USA.

SISTER LIVING

Anne Steele, *b* 1955: *m* 1987, Robert Losty, son of Bruce Losty, of Cheshire, Conn, USA, and has issue living, Michelle Anne, *b* 1988. *Residence* – 278 Old Stage Coach Rd, Meriden, Conn, USA.

AUNT LIVING

Joan Isabella, *b* 1928: *m* 1951, Harry Atwater Bishop, Jr, and has issue living, Harry Atwater (III) (15 Burnside St, Lancaster, NH 03584, USA), *b* 1957; *ed* Univ of NH, Plymouth: *m* 1982, Julie Sayre, da of Leonard Mulligan, and has issue living, Alex MacKenzie *b* 1986, Erin Sayre *b* 1984, — Alan Stuart Wortley, *b* 1959; *ed* Syracuse Univ (BA), — Wendy Anne Isabella, *b* 1952; *ed* Univ of NH, Durham (BA): *m* 1975, Dennis Charles Gillespie, and has issue living, Kelly Anne Isabella *b* 1977, Meghan Therese *b* 1980, — Linda Walters, *b* 1953; *ed* Springfield Coll, Mass (BS, MSM): *m* 1981, Nicolo Bimbo, of 76 Center St, Groveland, Mass 10834, USA, and has issue living, Katherine Anne, *b* 1985. *Residence* – 18 Webber Av, Bath, Maine 04530, USA.

DAUGHTERS LIVING AND DECEASED OF FOURTH EARL

Lady Joanna Margaret, *b* 1959; *k* in a motor accident 1981.
Lady Rowena STUART WORTLEY HUNT, *b* 1961: *m* 1986, John Hunt, son of Dr H. G. Hunt, of Greenwich, and has issue living, Somerset Carlton Gerald, *b* 1987. *Residence* – Minety House, Minety, nr Malmesbury, Wilts.

DAUGHTERS LIVING OF THIRD EARL

Lady Ann Lavinia Maud, *b* 1919; 1939-45 War in Mechanised Transport Corps: *m* 1939, as his 2nd wife, Cdr Vivian Russell Salvin Bowlby, RN (ret), who *d* 1972, and has issue living, Michael Robin Salvin, *b* 1947; *ed* Malvern. *Residence* – Sutton Stables, Felixkirk Rd, Sutton-under-Whitestonecliffe, Thirsk, N Yorks YO7 2PU.

Lady (Mary) Diana, *b* 1920; 1939-45 War in Mechanised Transport Corps: *m* 1946 (*m diss* 1959), as his second wife, 9th Duke of Newcastle. *Residence* – Cortington Manor, Warminster, Wilts.

Lady Barbara Maureen, *b* 1921; formerly in Women's Land Army, and Remount Depot, Melton Mowbray: *m* 1943, David Cecil Ricardo, Lieut (ret) 8th King's Roy Irish Hussars, and has issue living, Dorrien Harry Ralph *b* 1952; *ed* Scarborough Coll, — Richard Michael David, *b* 1955; *ed* Ackworth: *m* 1986, (Charlotte) Miranda, da of Michael Evelyn Brown, of East Bergholt, Suffolk, and has issue living, Frederick Michael David *b* 1989, Corisande Barbara Emily *b* 1991. *Residence* – Carlton Lodge, Wortley, Sheffield S30 4DG.

Lady Mary Rosemary Marie-Gabrielle, OBE, *b* 1930; JP 1974; OBE (Civil) 1983: *m* 1953, David Courtenay Mansel Lewis, JP, KStJ, Lord Lieut of Dyfed (*see* Warner, Bt, 1985 Edn), and has issue living, Patrick Charles Archibald Mansel (Capel Isaf, Manordeilo, Llandeilo, Dyfed), *b* 1953; *ed* Eton: *m* 1985, Claire Mary, only da of (Alexander) William Houston, of The Little House, Datchworth, Herts (*see* B Swansea), and has issue living, Edward Vivian *b* 1987, Robert William *b* 1989, John David *b* 1992, — Catherine Maud Leucha, *b* 1955: *m* 1985, Christopher N. Hamilton, of The Old Vicarage, Cwmyoy, Abergavenny, Gwent, son of P. N. Hamilton, of Via dei Bentaccordi 4, Florence, Italy, and has issue living, Archie Balthazar *b* 1985, — Annabel Lilian Elfrida, *b* 1962: *m* 1990, Guy W. C. Herbert, elder son of H. R. Herbert, of Alderbury, Wilts, and has issue living, Ben *b* 1991. *Residence* – Stradey Castle, Llanelli, Dyfed SA15 4PL.

WIDOW LIVING OF SON OF SECOND EARL

Lucy, da of — Perrin: *m* 1st, 1921, Hon Edward Thomas Montagu Stuart Wortley, who *d* 1923; 2ndly, 1925, Frank Leslie Russell. *Residence* –

MOTHER LIVING

Virginia Ann, da of (William) Martin Claybaugh, of Brownsville, Penn, USA: *m* 1952, Alan Ralph Montagu Stuart Wortley, who *d* 1986. *Residence* – 486 Coleman Rd, Cheshire, Conn 06410, USA.

WIDOW LIVING OF FOURTH EARL

ALINE MARGARET (*Aline, Countess of Wharncliffe*), da of late Robert Fernie Dunlop Bruce, of Dyson Holmes House, Wharncliffe Side, nr Sheffield: *m* 1957, the 4th Earl, who *d* 1987. *Residence* – Wharncliffe House, Wortley, Sheffield.

PREDECESSORS – (1) *Rt Hon* JAMES ARCHIBALD Stuart Wortley Mackenzie (grandson of 3rd Earl of Bute, KG), successively MP for Bossiney and Yorkshire, and Lord-Lieut of co York; was *cr Baron Wharncliffe*, of Wortley, co York (peerage of United Kingdom) 1826, was Lord Privy Seal 1834 and Lord Pres of the Council 1841; *d* 1845; *s* by his son (2) JOHN, 2nd Baron; *b* 1801: *m* 1825, Lady Georgiana Elizabeth, da of 1st Earl of Harrowby; *d* 1884, da of 1st Earl of Harrowby; *d* 1855; *s* by his son (3) EDWARD MONTAGU STUART GRANVILLE, 3rd Baron, *b* 1827; *cr Viscount Carlton* and *Earl of Wharncliffe* (peerage of United Kingdom) 1876, with remainder to his brother, Francis Dudley; assumed in 1880 by Roy licence the additional surname of Montagu: *m* 1855, Lady Susan Charlotte Lascelles, who *d* (da of 3rd Earl of Harewood); *d* 1899; *s* by his nephew (4) FRANCIS JOHN (el son of late Hon Francis Dudley Montagu Stuart Wortley), 2nd Earl, *b* 1856: *m* 1886, Ellen, who *d* 1922, da of late Lieut-Gen Sir Thomas Lionel John Gallwey, KCMG; *d* 1926; *s* by his son (5) ARCHIBALD RALPH, 3rd Earl; *b* 1892; sometime Capt Life Guards: *m* 1918, Lady Maud Lilian Elfrida Mary Wentworth-Fitzwilliam, who *d* 1979, da of 7th Earl Fitzwilliam; *d* 1953; *s* by his only son (6) ALAN JAMES, 4th Earl, *b* 1935; Master of Ecclesfield Beagles: *m* 1957, Aline Margaret, da of late Robert Fernie Dunlop Bruce, of Dyson Holmes House, Wharncliffe Side, Sheffield; *d* 1987; *s* by his kinsman (7) RICHARD ALAN MONTAGU (elder son of late Alan Ralph Montagu Stuart Wortley, only son of late Ralph Montagu Stuart Wortley, only son of late Hon Ralph Granville Montagu Stuart Wortley, brother of 2nd Earl), 5th Earl and present peer; also Viscount Carlton, and Baron Wharncliffe.

WHARTON, BARONESS (Robertson) (Baron E 1544-5)

MYRTLE OLIVE FELIX (ZIKI) (*Baroness Wharton*); *b* 20 Feb 1934; *s* (on termination of abeyance) 1990: *m* 1958, Henry MacLeod Robertson, Composer and Film Producer, and has issue.
Residence – 9 Gipsy Lane, SW15.

SONS LIVING

Hon MYLES CHRISTOPHER DAVID, *b* 1 Oct 1964; *ed* King's Coll, Wimbledon.
Hon Christopher James, *b* 1969; *ed* Clayesmore.
Hon Nicholas Charles, *b* (twin) 1969; *ed* Clayesmore.

DAUGHTER LIVING

Hon Patricia Lesley, *b* 1966.

SISTER LIVING

Hon Caroline Elizabeth, *b* 1935: *m* 1970, Capt Jonathan Cecil Appleyard-List, CBE, RN, and has issue living, Zoë, *b* 1973. *Residence* – Birches, Stanford Common, Pirbright, Surrey.

WIDOW LIVING OF NINTH BARON

JOANNA, only da of Walter Henry Law-Smith, of Adelaide, S Australia, widow of 6th Baron Tredegar, and formerly wife of late Cmdr Archibald Boyd Russell, DSO, RN: *m* 3rdly, 1967, the 9th Baron, who *d* 1969; 4thly, 1971, Bruce Yorke. *Residence* – Casa La Concha, Rocio de Naguèles, Marbella (Malaga), Spain.

PREDECESSORS – (1) Sir THOMAS Wharton, *b* 1495; MP for Appleby 1529-36, and Cumberland 1542-4; Warden of West Marches 1537, and Gov of Carlisle Castle 1541, and of Berwick Castle 1557; summoned to Parliament 1544-5 to 1566: *m* 1st, Helen, da of Sir Bryan Stapleton, of Whighill; 2ndly, 1561, Anne, widow of 2nd Baron Braye, and da of 5th Earl of Shrewsbury; *d* 1568; *s* by his son (2) THOMAS, 2nd Baron; MP for Cumberland 1544-5 and 1547-52, for Headon 1554, and for Northumberland 1555-9; summoned to Parliament 1571-2: *m* 1547, Anne, who *d* 1561, da of 1st Earl of Sussex; *d* 1572; *s* by his only son (3) PHILIP, 3rd Baron: summoned to Parliament 1580-1625: *m* 1st, 1577, Frances, who *d* 1592, da of 2nd Earl of Cumberland; 2ndly, 1597, Dorothy, da of Thomas Colley, of Sherfield, and widow of (i) John Tamworth, of Leek, and (ii) *Sir* Francis Willoughby, of Wollaton; *d* 1625; *s* by his grandson (4) PHILIP (son of Sir Thomas Wharton, of Aske), 4th Baron; summoned to Parliament 1639-85; Lord-Lieut. of cos Lancaster, Buckingham, and Westmorland; Speaker of the House of Lords 1642-5: *m* 1st, (about) 1632, Elizabeth, da of Sir Rowland Wandesford, of Pickhill; 2ndly, 1637, Jane, da of Arthur Goodwin; 3rdly, 1661, Anne, da of William Carr, of Ferneyhurst, Roxburghshire, and widow of Col Edward Popham; *d* 1695; *s* by his son (5) THOMAS, 5th Baron; *b* 1648; MP for Wendover 1673-9 and Bucks 1679-96; Comptroller of the Household to William of Orange 1689-1702; one of the Commrs for Union with Scotland; *cr Viscount Winchendon*, of co Bucks, and *Earl of Wharton*, co Westmorland 1706; served as Lord-Lieut of Ireland 1708-10; *cr Baron of Trim*, co Meath, *Earl of Rathfarnham*, co Dublin, and *Marquess of Catherlough* Jan 1714-15, and *Marquess of Wharton*, co Westmorland, and *Marquess of Malmesbury*, co. Wilts, Feb 1714-15: *m* 1st, 1673, Anne, who *d* 1685, da of Sir Henry Lee, 5th Bt, of Ditchley, Oxon; 2ndly, 1692, Lucy, who *d* 1717, da of 1st Viscount Lisburne (*cr* 1685); *d* 1715; *s* by his only son (6) PHILLIP, 6th Baron; *cr Duke of Wharton*, co Westmorland 1718; outlawed for high treason 1728 (but declared void on a writ of error in Court of Queen's Bench 1845, and so declared by the Committee for Privileges 1915): *m* 1st, 1714, Martha, who *d* 1726, da of Maj-Gen Richard Holmes; 2ndly, 1726, Maria Theresa O'Beirne, who *d* 1777, da of Col Henry O'Beirne; *d* 1731, when all dignities became ext, except (according to the decision of the Committee for Privileges) the Barony of Wharton, which they decided fell into abeyance between his two sisters, the elder of whom survived, when the Barony devolved upon her (7) JANE, *de jure* Baroness Wharton: *m* 1st, 1723, John Holt, who *d* 1728; 2ndly, 1733, Robert Coke, of Hillingdon, Middlesex; *dsp* when, according to the decision in 1915, the Barony again fell into abeyance among the representatives of the 4th Baron; from Mary, the second of whom, by her second marriage in 1678 with Sir Charles Kemeys, 3rd Bt., of Cefn Mably, is descended (through her da Jane, who *m* Sir John Tynte, 2nd Bt) (8) CHARLES THEODORE HALSWELL Kemeys-Tynte, 8th Baron, *b* 1876; the abeyance was determined in his favour Feb 1916: *m* 1899, Dorothy, who *d* 1944, da of the late Maj-Gen Sir Arthur Edward Augustus Ellis, GCVO, CSI; *d* 1934; *s* by his son (9) CHARLES JOHN HALSWELL, 9th Baron; *b* 1908: *m* 1967, Joanna (who *m* 4thly, 1971, Bruce Yorke), da of Walter Henry Law-Smith, of Adelaide, S Australia, widow of 6th Baron Tredegar, and formerly wife of late Cmdr Archibald Boyd Russell, DSO, RN; *d* 1969; *s* by his sister (10) ELIZABETH DOROTHY, Baroness Wharton; *b* 1906: *m* 1st, 1933 (*m diss* 1946), David George Arbuthnot, who *d* 1985 (*see* Arbuthnot, Bt, colls); 2ndly, 1946 (*m diss* 1958), St John Vintcent; *d* 1974, when the barony again fell into abeyance between her two das, Hon Myrtle Olive Felix Robertson, and Hon Caroline Elizabeth Appleyard-List, and so continued until 1990, when the abeyance was terminated in favour of the elder da (11) MYRTLE OLIVE FELIX, present peeress.

WHEATLEY, BARONY OF (Wheatley) (Extinct 1988)

SONS LIVING OF LIFE BARON

Hon John Francis (Braefoot Farmhouse, Fossoway, Kinross-shire), *b* 1941; *ed* Mount St Mary's Coll, and Edinburgh Univ (BL); called to Scots Bar 1966; Advocate-Depute 1974-78; Sheriff of Perthshire and Kinross-shire since 1980: *m* 1970, Bronwen Catherine, da of Alastair Fraser of 25 Strachan Cres, Dollar, and has issue living.
Hon Patrick, *b* 1943: *m* 1968, Sheena, da of late Douglas James Lawrie.
Hon Anthony, *b* 1945; *ed* Mount St Mary's Coll, Sheffield, Fordham Univ, New York, and Holy Cross Academy, Edinburgh.
Hon Michael (Millburn, Old Phillipstoun, W Lothian, EH49 7RY; MCC), *b* 1949; *ed* Mount St Mary's Coll: *m* 1971, Anne, da of Thomas Barry.

DAUGHTER LIVING OF LIFE BARON

Hon Kathleen Mary Agnes, *b* 1937; *ed* Convent of the Sacred Heart, Aberdeen, and Edinburgh Univ (MA 1960); Member of Royal Fine Art Commission for Scotland and Ancient Monuments Board: *m* 1963, (Thomas) Tam Dalyell of The Binns, MP, 11th Bt (but does not use the title), of the Binns, Linlithgow.

WIDOW LIVING OF LIFE BARON

AGNES (*Baroness Wheatley*), da of Samuel Nichol, of Tollcross, Glasgow: *m* 1935, Baron Wheatley, PC (Life Baron), who *d* 1988. *Residence* – 91/16 Morningside Rd, Edinburgh EH10 4DB.

WHITE, BARONESS (White) (Life Baroness 1970)

EIRENE LLOYD WHITE, da of late Thomas Jones, CH, LLD, of Brynhir, Aberystwyth; *b* 7 Nov 1909; *ed* St Paul's Girls' Sch, and Somerville Coll, Oxford (Hon Fellow 1966); Min of Labour Officer 1933-37, and 1941-45; Political Correspondent *Manchester Evening News* 1945-49; a Member of Nat Exec Cttee Labour Party 1947-53, and 1958-72 (Chm 1968-69); Parl Sec, Colonial Office 1964-66, Min of State for Foreign Affairs 1966-67, and Min of State, Welsh Office 1967-70; Dep Chm, Metrication Board 1972; a Dep Speaker House of Lords 1979-89; Member of Royal Commission on Environmental Pollution; Pres of Nat Council of Women (Wales); MP for E Flint (*Lab*) 1950-70; *cr Baroness White*, of Rhymney, co Monmouth (Life Baroness) 1970: *m* 1948, John Cameron White, who *d* 1968.
Residences – 64 Vandon Court, Petty France, SW1H 9HF; Treberfydd, Bwlch, Brecon, Powys LD3 7PX.

WHITE OF HULL, BARON (White) (Life Baron 1991)

(VINCENT) GORDON LINDSAY WHITE, KBE, son of late Charles White, of Hull, Yorks; *b* 11 May 1923; *ed* De Aston Sch, Lincs; Hon Fell St Peter's Coll, Oxford 1984, Hon DSc Hull 1988; 1939-45 War as Capt SOE Force; Chm Welbecson Ltd 1947-65, Dep-Chm Hanson Trust 1965-73, Chm Hanson Industries since 1983; Gov BFI 1982-84; Member Bd of British Airways plc since 1989; Member and Chm Internat Cttee USA Congressional Award since 1984, Council Member Police Rehabilitation Appeal 1985, Member Bd of Dirs Shakespeare Theatre, Folger Library, Washington, since 1987, Council Member City Technology Colls Trust Ltd since 1987; Chm Zoological Soc of London Devpt Trust 1988-91; Aims of Industry Free Enterprise Award (with Lord Hanson) 1985, etc; *cr* KBE 1979, and *Baron White of Hull*, of Hull, co Humberside (Life Baron) 1991: *m* 1st, 1958 (*m diss* 1968), Ann Elisabeth, da of Carl Gustav Kalen; 2ndly, 1974 (*m diss* 1979), Virginia Anne, da of Allen Northorp; 3rdly, 1992, Victoria Ann Tucker, and has issue by 1st and 2nd *m*.

Arms – Azure, an equestrian figure in plate armour brandishing a sword in bend sinister, his helm crested by a plume of five ostrich feathers, his horse salient and with trapper and chanfron all argent and within a bordure of the last charged with thirteen mullets azure. **Crest** – Issuing out of a circlet of roses argent, barbed and seeded proper, set upon a rim or, an American eagle's head proper and a lion's head addorsed or. **Supporters** – *Dexter*, a bear proper; *sinister*, a lion or, on the head of each a baron's coronet proper.
Residence – 410 Park Ave, New York, NY 10022, USA. *Clubs* – Special Forces, Brook (NY), Explorers' (NY).

SON LIVING *(By 1st marriage)*

Hon Lucas Charles, *b* 1974.

DAUGHTERS LIVING *(By 1st marriage)*

Hon Carolina, *b* 1959.
Hon Ana Luisa, *b* 1961.

WHITELAW, VISCOUNT (Whitelaw) (Viscount UK 1983)

WILLIAM STEPHEN IAN WHITELAW, KT, CH, MC, PC, 1st Viscount, son of late William Alexander Whitelaw, of Monkland, Nairn (*ka* 1919); *b* 28 June 1918; *ed* Winchester, and Trin Coll Camb (MA); Major (ret) Scots Guards; served in 1939-45 War with Scots Guards Tank Bn in Normandy, Germany and Palestine (despatches); MP for Penrith and the Border 1955-83; Lord Commr of the Treasury 1961-62; Parl Sec to Min of Labour 1962-64; Opposition Chief Whip 1964-70; Lord Pres of the Council and Leader of the House of Commons 1970-72; Sec of State for Northern Ireland 1972-73; Sec of State for Employment 1973-74; Dep Leader of the Opposition 1975-79; Home Sec 1979-83; Lord Pres of the Council and Leader of the House of Lords 1983-88; Chm Govs of St Bees Sch, Cumbria, since 1984, Chm Carlton Club since 1986; Pres GB-USSR Assocn since 1988; DL (1967) Cumbria; MC 1944; *cr* PC 1967, CH 1974, KT 1990, and *Viscount Whitelaw*, of Penrith, co Cumbria (peerage of UK) 1983: *m* 1943, Cecilia Doriel, yr da of late Major Mark Sprot, R Scots Greys, of Riddell, by Melrose, Roxburghshire, by his wife Meliora, da of Sir John Adam Hay, 9th Bt (*cr* 1635), and has issue.

Arms – Sable a chevron engrailed or between three boars' heads couped argent armed and langued or. **Crest** – A bee erect proper. **Supporters** – On either side a Charolais bull in trian aspect proper each with a garland about the shoulder of roses gules barbed and seeded slipped and leaved and thistles stalked and leaved proper and interlaced in front with two pairs of golf clubs fretted saltirewise gold, the compartment comprising three mounts of moorland proper growing from each of those to the fore two roses and as many thistles the roses gules barbed and seeded stalked and leaved proper and the thistles stalked and leaved also proper.
Residence – Ennim, Penrith, Cumbria. *Clubs* – White's, Carlton, County (Carlisle), and Royal and Ancient Golf Club of St Andrews (Captain 1969-70).

DAUGHTERS LIVING

Hon (Elizabeth) Susan, *b* 1944, *m* 1966, Hon Nicholas John Cunliffe-Lister, of Glebe House, Masham, Ripon, Yorks, and has issue (see E Swinton).
Hon Carolyn Meliora, *b* 1946, *m* 1st, 1973 (*m diss* 1979), Robert Donald Macleod Thomas; 2ndly, 1983, Michael Francis Graves-Johnston, of 54 Stockwell Park Road, SW9, and has issue living (by 1st *m*), Miranda Cecilia, *b* 1974, — Rhoda Mary Macleod, *b* 1977, — (by 2nd *m*) Cleopatra Frances, *b* 1985, — Helen Mercedes, *b* 1987.
Hon Mary Cecilia, *b* 1947, *m* 1972, David Alexander Coltman, of Haystoun House, Peebles, yr son of Col Thomas Alexander Hamilton Coltman, OBE, DL, RA (*see* B Hothfield), and has issue living, Susannah Mary Lavinia, *b* 1987.

Hon Pamela Winifred, *b* 1951, *m* 1974, Malise Charles Richard Graham, of The Cottage, Sproxton, Melton Mowbray, Leics, and has issue (*see* Graham, Bt, *cr* 1783).

WICKLOW, EARLDOM OF (Forward-Howard) (Extinct 1978)

WIDOW LIVING OF EIGHTH EARL

Eleanor (*Countess of Wicklow*), architect, mem Irish Senate 1948-52; da of late Prof Rudolph M. Butler, of Dublin: *m* 1959, the 8th Earl, who *d* 1978.

COLLATERAL BRANCH LIVING

Issue of late Hon Hugh Melville Forward-Howard, 3rd son of 6th Earl, *b* 1883; *d* 1919: *m* 1908, Mary
Emily, who *d* 1941, da of Benjamin Aymar Sands, of New York, and Southampton, Long Island, USA:—
Katharine Frances Theodosia (Kiltennel House, Gorey, co Wexford), *b* 1910.

WIDGERY, BARONY OF (Widgery) (Extinct 1981)

ANN (*Baroness Widgery*) (56 Jubilee Place, SW3 3QT), da of late William Edwin Kermode, of Peel, Isle of Man: *m* 1948, Baron Widgery, OBE, TD, PC (Life Baron), who *d* 1981.

WIGG, BARONY OF (Wigg) (Extinct 1983)

DAUGHTERS LIVING OF LIFE BARON

Hon Mary Cecilia, *b* 1930: *m* 1958, Robert Cartlidge, of Abilene, Princes St, Huntly, Aberdeenshire AB5 5HA, and has issue, three das.
Hon Jean Audrey, *b* 1932: *m* 1955, Andrew Huggins, of Ty Eiddew, Garndolbenmaen, Gwynedd, N Wales, and has issue, three das.
Hon Maureen Ann, *b* 1934: *m* 1964, Alfred John Mudge, who *d* 1987, of 940 Melton Drive, Mississauga, Ont, Canada L4Y 1L1.

WIGODER, BARON (Wigoder) (Life Baron 1974)

BASIL THOMAS WIGODER, QC, son of Philip I. Wigoder, LRCPI, LRCSI, of 2 St John St, Deansgate, Manchester 3; *b* 12 Feb 1921; *ed* Manchester Gram Sch, and Oriel Coll, Oxford (MA); Bar Gray's Inn 1946, Bencher 1972 (Master of the Bench 1972), Treasurer 1989; a Member of Gen Council of the Bar 1970-74, a memb Crown Court Rules Cttee 1971-77, and a Recorder of the Crown Court 1972-84; Chm Liberal Party Exec 1963-65, and Liberal Party Organising Cttee 1965-66, Vice-Pres of Liberal Party 1966; Chm of Health Sers Board 1977-80, Chm of BUPA and Dir of BUPA Hospitals 1981-92, since when Vice-Pres BUPA; Ch Liberal Whip in House of Lords 1977-84; Pres of Oxford Union 1946, 1939-45 War, as Lt RA, in Middle East, Italy, and Greece; *cr Baron Wigoder*, of Cheetham, in City of Manchester (Life Baron) 1974: *m* 1948, Yoland, da of Ben Levinson, and has issue.

𝔄rms – Gules a chevron engrailed ermine between three wigs or a chief or. ℭrest – On a wreath or and gules, upon a mount vert a gosling or, supporting by the dexter foot a daffodil proper, mantled gules doubled argent. 𝔖upporters – *Dexter*, a seahorse; *sinister*, a sea-griffin; both or, their piscine parts azure scaled, finned and tailed or, each gorged with a collar sable, pendent therefrom a chain ending in a broken ring sable.
Address – c/o House of Lords, SW1. *Clubs* – National Liberal, MCC.

SONS LIVING

Hon Justin, *b* 1951: *m* 1981, Heather J., da of late J. H. Bugler, and has issue living, Annabel Miriam Jane, *b* 1986, — Charlotte Abigail Lucy, *b* 1991.
Hon Charles Francis, *b* 1960: *m* 1988, Elizabeth Sophia, only da of Elmar Duke-Cohan, of Totteridge, and has issue living, Benjamin Marcus James, *b* 1990, — Natasha Sarah, *b* 1992.
Hon Giles, *b* 1963: *m* 1993, Louisa eldest da of Prof Gerald Westbury.

DAUGHTER LIVING

Hon Carolyn (twin), *b* 1963.

WIGRAM, BARON (Wigram) (Baron UK 1935)

Sweet is the love of one's country

(GEORGE) NEVILLE (CLIVE) WIGRAM, MC, 2nd Baron; *b* 2 Aug 1915; *s* 1960; *ed* Winchester, and Magdalen Coll, Oxford; late Lt-Col Gren Gds; a JP and a DL for Glos; a Page of Honour to HM 1925-32, and Mil Sec and Comptroller to Gov-Gen of NZ 1946-49; a Gov of Westminster Hosp 1967; 1939-45 War: *m* 1941, Margaret Helen, who *d* 1986, da of late Gen Sir Augustus Francis Andrew Nicol Thorne, KCB, CMG, DSO (B Penrhyn), and has issue.

𝕬rms – Argent, on a pale gules three escallops or; over all a chevron engrailed counterchanged, and on the chief waves of the sea, thereon a ship representing an English vessel of war of the 16th century, with four masts, sails furled proper, colours flying gules. 𝕮rest – On a mount vert, a hand in armour in fesse couped at the wrist proper, charged with an escallop holding a fleur-de-lis erect or. 𝕾upporters – On either side a Bengal Lancer holding in the exterior hand a lance proper.
Residence – Poulton Fields, Cirencester, Gloucestershire. *Clubs* – Cavalry and Guards', MCC.

SON LIVING

Hon ANDREW FRANCIS CLIVE, MVO (Poulton Fields Farms, Cirencester, Glos. *Clubs* – Leander and Farmers), *b* 18 March 1949; *ed* Winchester, RMA, and RAC Cirencester; Maj Gren Gds; Extra Equerry to HRH The Duke of Edinburgh 1982-86: *m* 1974, Gabrielle Diana, yst da of late R. D. Moore, of Wellington, NZ, and has issue living, Harry Richard Clive, *b* 20 May 1977, — Robert Christopher Clive, *b* 1980, — William Michael Clive, *b* 1984, — Alice Poppy Louise, *b* 1989.

DAUGHTERS LIVING

Hon Margaret Cherry, *b* 1942: *m* 1972 (*m diss* 1993), Lt-Col Greville John Wyndham Malet, OBE, R Hussars, of The Walled House, Hatherop, Cirencester, Glos, and has issue (*see* Malet, Bt, colls).
Hon Anne Celia, *b* 1945: *m* 1973, Brig Evelyn John Webb-Carter, OBE, late Gren Gds, of Horcott House, Fairford, Glos (V Hood, colls), and has issue living, Alexander Clive, *b* 1975, — Helen Celia, *b* 1978, — Rose Evelyn *b* 1983.

PREDECESSOR – (1) CLIVE WIGRAM, GCB, GCVO, CSI, PC, son of late Herbert Wigram (see Wigram, Bt, colls), *b* 1873; Lieut-Col and Brevet Col (ret) Indian Army; was an Extra Equerry-in-Waiting to Prince of Wales 1906-10, an Equerry-in-Waiting and Assist Private Sec to King George V 1910-31, Private Sec and an Extra Equerry 1931-36 (also Keeper of HM's Privy Purse 1935-36) and Keeper of HM's Archives 1936-45; acted as Assist to Ch of Staff of the Prince of Wales during tour in India 1905-6; S Africa 1900, with Kitchener's Horse; Dep Constable and Lieut-Gov of Windsor Castle 1936-45; Permanent Lord-in-Waiting to HM King George VI 1936-52, and to HM Queen Elizabeth II 1952-60; *cr Baron Wigram*, of Clewer, co Berks (peerage of United Kingdom) 1935: *m* 1912, Nora Mary, who *d* 1956, da of late Col Sir Neville Francis Fitzgerald Chamberlain, KCB, KCVO, *d* 1960; *s* by his son (2) (GEORGE) NEVILLE (CLIVE), 2nd Baron and present peer.

WILBERFORCE, BARON (Wilberforce) (Life Baron 1964)

RICHARD ORME WILBERFORCE, CMG, OBE, PC, son of Samuel Wilberforce, of Lavington House, Petworth, Sussex; *b* 11 March 1907; *ed* Winchester, and New Coll, Oxford; Hon DCL Oxford 1967; Hon LLD London 1972 and Bristol Univ 1983; Bar Middle Temple 1932, and QC 1954; a Judge of High Court of Justice (Chancery Div) 1961-64; a Lord of Appeal in Ordinary 1964-82; High Steward of Oxford Univ 1967-90 and Chllr of Hull Univ 1978-94; appointed Chm of Court of Inquiry into power workers' dispute 1970; Fell of All Souls Coll, Oxford since 1932; Hon Fellow, New Coll, Oxford since 1965; Hon Fellow Wolfson Coll Oxford 1990; 1939-45 War as Brig late RA in Norway and Germany (OBE); *cr* OBE (Mil) 1944, CMG 1956, Knt 1961, PC 1964, and *Baron Wilberforce*, of city and co of Kingston-upon-Hull (Life Baron) 1964: *m* 1947, Yvette Marie, da of Roger Lenoan, of Paris, and has issue.
Residence – 8 Cambridge Place, W8. *Club* – Athenæum.

SON LIVING

Hon Samuel Herbert, *b* 1951; *ed* Eton: *m* 1978, Mrs Sarah L. Scorer, da of late Arthur Allen, of Northampton.

DAUGHTER LIVING

Hon Anne Catherine, *b* 1948: *m* 1975, Lindsay Stuart Burn.

WILLIAMS, BARONY OF (Williams) (Extinct 1966)

DAUGHTER LIVING OF FIRST BARON

Hon Gweneth Mary, *b* 1927: *m* 1st, 1947 (*m diss* 1958), Hugh Sharp Eadie, AMIEE; 2ndly, 1961, Donald Walter Alexander Brown, MB, ChB, and has issue living (by 1st *m*), Graham Edward, *b* 1949, — Dianne Claire, *b* 1951.

WIDOW LIVING OF FIRST BARON

LAVINIA (*Baroness Williams*), da of Charles Northam, of Plumstead, SE18: *m* 1921, the 1st Baron, who *d* 1966, when the title became ext.

WILLIAMS OF BARNBURGH, BARON (Williams) (Extinct 1967)

WIDOW LIVING OF SON OF LIFE BARON

Margaret Dick Chisholm (*Hon Mrs Horace Williams*), da of William Green: *m* 1952, as his 2nd wife, Hon Horace Williams, who *d* 1993. *Residence* – Flat 3, 2 Chichester Terrace, Kemptown, Brighton, Sussex.

DAUGHTER LIVING OF LIFE BARON

Hon Doris (346 Thorne Rd, Doncaster), *b* 1916: *m* 1939, Robert Kesteven Lee, who *d* 1967.

WILLIAMS OF CROSBY, BARONESS (Williams) (Life Baroness 1993)

SHIRLEY VIVIEN TERESA BRITTAIN NEUSTADT, PC, da of late Prof Sir George Edward Gordon Catlin, by his late wife, Vera Brittain; *b* 27 July 1930; *ed* Summit Sch, Minnesota, USA, St Paul's Girls' Sch, Somerville Coll, Oxford (Hon Fellow), and Columbia Univ, New York; PPS to Min of Health 1964-66, Parl Sec Min of Labour 1966-67, Min of State for Educn and Science 1967-69, Min of State Home Office 1969-70, Sec of State for Prices and Consumer Protection 1974-76 (also Paymaster-Gen), Sec of State for Educn and Science 1976-79; Chm Fabian Soc 1980 (Gen Sec 1960-64); Member Lab National Executive Cttee 1970-81; Co-Founder SDP 1981, Pres 1982-88; MP for Hitchin (*Lab*) 1964-74, Hertford and Stevenage (*Lab*) 1974-79, and Crosby (SDP) 1981-83; Fellow Inst of Politics Harvard 1979-80, OECD Examiner since 1979, Prof and Fellow Policy Studies Inst 1979-85, Public Service Prof of Elective Politics, Kennedy Sch of Government, Harvard since 1988, and Member Senior Advisory Cttee Inst of Politics Harvard; FBA; *cr* PC 1974, and *Baroness Williams of Crosby*, of Stevenage, co Herts (Life Baroness) 1993: *m* 1st, 1955 (*m diss* 1974), Prof Bernard Arthur Owen Williams; 2ndly, 1987, Prof Richard E. Neustadt, and has issue by 1st *m*.

𝔄rms – Per chevron azure and or, three lions passant guardant in pale counter-changed, a bordure engrailed ermine.
Residence – The Well House, Causeway, Furneaux Pelham, Buntingford, Herts SG9 0LN.

DAUGHTER LIVING (*By 1st marriage*)

Hon Rebecca Clare, *b* 1961.

WILLIAMS OF ELVEL, BARON (Williams) (Life Baron 1985)

CHARLES CUTHBERT POWELL WILLIAMS, CBE, *b* 9 Feb 1933, son of late Dr Norman Powell Williams, DD, by his wife, Muriel de Lérisson, only surv da of late Arthur Philip Cazenove, of 51 Cadogan Pl, SW1; *ed* Westminster, and Ch Ch, Oxford, and LSE; British Petroleum Co Ltd 1958-64, Bank of London and Montreal 1964-66, Eurofinance SA, Paris 1966-70, Baring Brothers & Co Ltd 1970-77 (Man Dir 1971-77), Chm Price Commn 1977-79, Man Dir Henry Ansbacher & Co Ltd 1980-82, Ch Exec Henry Ansbacher Holdings plc, Chm Henry Ansbacher & Co Ltd 1982-85, Pres Campaign for the Protection of Rural Wales since 1989; *cr* CBE (Civil) 1980, and *Baron Williams of Elvel*, of Llansantffraed in Elvel, co Powys (Life Baron) 1985: *m* 1975, Jane Gillian, da of Lt-Col Gervase Edward Portal, and formerly wife of Gavin Bramhall Bernard Welby.
Residence – 48 Thurloe Sq, SW7 2SX. *Clubs* – Reform, and MCC.

WILLIAMS OF MOSTYN, BARON (Williams) (Life Baron 1992)

GARETH WYN WILLIAMS, son of late Albert Thomas Williams; *b* 5 Feb 1941; *ed* Rhyl Gram Sch, and Queens' Coll, Camb (MA, LLM); Bar Gray's Inn 1965, Recorder Crown Court 1978, QC 1978, Leader Wales and Chester Circuit 1987-90, Bencher Gray's Inn 1991, Member Bar Council since 1986 (Chm since 1992); *cr Baron Williams of Mostyn*, of Great Tew, co Oxon (Life Baron) 1992: *m* 1962, Pauline, da of late Ernest Clarke, and has issue.

Arms – Ermine, on a pile flory at the point sable a lion rampant or, armed and langued gules. **Crest** – A portcullis or in front of an arm embowed vested and the cuff braided sable, frilled at the wrist, the hand proper holding by its blade upwards argent a sword palewise to the front of the portcullis, its hilt, pommel and quillons gold. **Supporters** – *Dexter*, upon a grassy mount, growing therefrom two sweet pea flowers proper, a griffin statant erect gold; *sinister*, upon a like mount a dragon statant erect also gold, both armed and langued gules.
Residence – 36 Great Tew, Oxon OX7 4AL. *Chambers* – Farrar's Building, Temple, EC4Y 7BD.

SON LIVING

Hon Daniel, *b* 1969.

DAUGHTERS LIVING

Hon Martha, *b* 1963.
Hon Emma, *b* 1966.

WILLIAMSON, BARONY OF (Williamson) (Extinct 1983)

DAUGHTER LIVING OF LIFE BARON

Hon Milba Hartley, *b* 1926: *m* 1952, Jack Fleming Eccles, CBE, of Terange, 11 Sutton Rd, Alderley Edge, Cheshire SK9, and has issue.

WILLIS, BARONY OF (Willis) (Extinct 1992)

SON LIVING OF LIFE BARON

(*Hon*) John Edward, *b* 1946; does not use courtesy title; *ed* Eltham Coll, Fitzwilliam Coll, Camb (MA), and Bristol Univ (Postgrad Cert in Radio, Film and TV); writer and director, dir *Johnny Go Home*, etc; Dir of Programmes for Channel Four Television since 1993: *m* 1972, Janet, da of Kenneth Sperrin, and has issue living, Thomas, *b* 1975, — Beth, *b* 1978.

DAUGHTER LIVING OF LIFE BARON

Hon Sally Ann Hale, *b* 1951: *m* 1974, Robin James Murray, and has issue living, James Edward, *b* 1980, — Alice Louise, *b* 1982, — Helen Jane, *b* (twin) 1982.

WIDOW LIVING OF LIFE BARON

AUDREY MARY (*Baroness Willis*), da of Alfred Hale: *m* 1944, Baron Willis (Life Baron), who *d* 1992.

WILLOUGHBY DE BROKE, BARON (Verney) (Baron E 1491)
(Title pronounced "Willoughby de Brook")

Virtue prevails

(LEOPOLD) DAVID VERNEY, 21st Baron; *b* 14 Sept 1938; *s* 1986; *ed* Le Rosey, and New Coll, Oxford; patron of two livings: *m* 1965, Petra Daphne, 2nd da of late Col Sir John Renton Aird, 3rd Bt, MVO, MC, and has issue.

Arms – Quarterly: 1st and 4th, gules, three crosses recercellé or, a chief vair ermine and ermines; 2nd and 3rd, quarterly argent and gules, a bear sejant sable. **Crests** – 1st, a Saracen's head, affrontée, couped at the shoulders proper, ducally crowned or; 2nd, a demi-bear sable, holding in his paws a lozenge, pierced or. **Supporters** – Two antelopes argent, semée of torteaux, armed and unguled or.
Residences – Ditchford Farm, Moreton in Marsh, Glos GL56 9RD. *Club* – White's.

SONS LIVING

Hon RUPERT GREVILLE, *b* 4 March 1966.
Hon John Mark, *b* 1967.
Hon Edmund Peyto, *b* 1973.

SISTER LIVING

Hon Susan Geraldine, *b* 1942: *m* 1st, 1964 (*m diss* 1969), Jeremy James Wagg (*see* Horlick, Bt, 1969 Edn); resumed her maiden name by deed poll 1969; 2ndly, 1972, and his 2nd wife, Capt Robie David Corbett Uniacke; 3rdly, 1990, as his 2nd wife, Rupert John Orlando Lascelles (*see* E Harewood, colls), and has had issue (by 2nd *m*), Caspar John, *b* 1973, — Kate Rachel, *b* 1975; *d* 1979. *Residence* – Tarrant Abbey, Blandford, Dorset DT11 9HU.

COLLATERAL BRANCHES LIVING

Issue of late Hon Blanche Verney, el da of 18th Baron, *b* 1872, *d* 1947: *m* 1898, Capt Michael Granville Lloyd Lloyd-Baker, Gloucestershire Yeo, who was *ka* 1916:—
Audrey Pamela Lloyd, *b* 1908.

Issue of late Hon Patience Verney, 2nd da of 18th Baron, *b* 1873, *d* 1965: *m* 1896, Lt-Col Basil Hanbury, who *d* 1933 (Mackenzie, Bt, *cr* 1702, colls):—
Harold Greville, QC *b* 1898; *ed* Charterhouse, and at Brasenose Coll, Oxford (DCL); Bar Inner Temple 1922; Hon Bencher 1951, and a QC 1960; late Lt Warwickshire Yeo; Vinerian Prof Emeritus of English Law; Fellow of Lincoln Coll, Oxford 1921-49 (Hon Fellow 1949); Fellow of All Souls Coll, Oxford 1949-64; Dean of Faculty of Law, and Visiting Prof, Univ of Ife 1962-63, and Univ of Nigeria 1964-66: *m* 1927, Anna Margaret Geelmuyden, da of late Hannibal Dreyer (Adviser to Post & Telegraph Dept, Thailand), of Copenhagen.

PREDECESSORS – (1) *Sir* ROBERT Willoughby, Knt, who took part in the victory of Bosworth, was summoned to the Parliament of England as *Lord Willoughby de Broke* 1491; was Capt Gen of the Forces sent to aid the Duke of Brittany against the French, *temp* Henry VII and subsequently Marshal of the English Army sent into France: *m circa* 1475, Blanche, da and co-heir of Sir John Champernowne, of Beer Ferrers, Devon; *d* 1502; *s* by his son (2) ROBERT, 2nd Baron; summoned to Parliament 1511: *m* 1st, Elizabeth, who *d* 1503, da and co-heir of 2nd Baron Beauchamp of Powyk; 2ndly, Lady Dorothy Grey (who *m* 2ndly, 15—, William Blount, 4th Baron Mountjoy, and *d* 1553), da of 1st Marquess of Dorset; *d* 1522; when the barony fell into abeyance between the three das of his el son Edward Willoughby, and so remained until 1558, when the sole surviving grand-da (her sisters dying without issue) (3) ELIZABETH, became *de jure* Baroness: *m circa* 1534, as his second wife, Sir Fulke Greville; *d* 1560; *s* by her el son (4) *Sir* Fulke, *de jure* 4th Baron, *b* 1535; MP for Warwick 1586: *m circa* 1553, Lady Anne Nevill, da of 4th Earl of Westmorland; *d* 1606; *s* by his only son (5) *Sir* FULKE, *de jure* 5th Baron; *b circa* 1554; *cr* Baron Brooke, of Beauchamp's Court, co Warwick 1621, with remainder to his cousins Robert and William Greville; *d* 1628, when the Barony of Brooke passed to Robert Greville (see E Warwick) and the right to the Barony of Willoughby de Broke devolved on his sister (6) MARGARET, *de jure* Baroness; *b circa* 1561: *m* before 1584, Sir Richard Verney, of Compton Verney, co Warwick; *d* 1631; *s* by her el son (7) *Sir* GREVILLE, *de jure* 7th Baron; *b circa* 1587: *m* 1618, Catherine, da of Sir Robert Southwell, of Woodrising, Norfolk; *d* 1642; *s* by his el son (8) GREVILLE, *de jure* 8th Baron; *b circa* 1620: *m* 16—, Hon Elizabeth Wenman, who *d* 1649, da of 2nd Viscount Wenman of Tuam; *d* 1648; *s* by his only child (9) *Sir* GREVILLE, KB, *de jure* 9th Baron, *b* (posthumously) 1649: *m* 1667, Lady Diana Russell (who *m* 2ndly, 1675 the 3rd Baron Alington of Killard, and *d* 1701), da of 1st Duke of Bedford; *d* 1668; *s* by his only child (10) WILLIAM, *de jure* 10th Baron, *b* 1668; *d* 1683; *s* by his great-uncle (11) *Sir* RICHARD (3rd son of *de jure* 7th Baron), 11th *de jure* Baron, *b* 1621; established his claim to the Barony before the House of Lords 1696: *m* 1st, before 1658, Elizabeth, da and heir of George Turpin; 2ndly, circa 1677, Frances, da of Thomas Dove; *d* 1711; *s* by his son (12) GEORGE, 12th Baron; *b* 1659; was Dean of Windsor: *m* 1688, Margaret, who *d* 1729, da and heir of Sir John Heath; *d* 1728; *s* by his son (13) RICHARD, 13th Baron; *b* 1693: *m* 1st, 17—, Penelope, who *d* 1718, da of Clifton Packe; 2ndly, before 1735, Elizabeth, who *d* 1767, da of Nathaniel Williams; *dsp* 1752; *s* by his nephew (14) JOHN, 14th Baron, son of Hon John Verney, 3rd son of 12th Baron; *b* 1762; assumed in 1772 the additional surname of Peyto: *m* 1761, Lady Louisa North, who *d* 1798, da of 1st Earl of Guilford; *d* 1816; *s* by his son (15) JOHN, 15th Baron; *b* 1762; *d unm* 1820; *s* by his brother (16) HENRY, 16th Baron; *dsp* 1852; *s* by his nephew (17) ROBERT JOHN, 17th Baron, son of Hon Louisa, da of 14th Baron, by her marriage to the Rev Robert Barnard; *b* 1809; assumed in 1852 the surname of Verney in lieu of his patronymic: *m* 1842, Georgiana Jane, who *d* 1889, da of Maj-Gen Thomas William Taylor, CB, of Ogwell, Devon; *d* 1862; *s* by his son (18) HENRY, 18th Baron; *b* 1844: *m* 1867, Geraldine, who *d* 1894, el da of late James H. Smith-Barry, Esq, of Marbury Hall, Cheshire, and Fota Island, Cork; *d* 1902; *s* by his son (19) RICHARD GREVILLE, 19th Baron, *b* 1869; MP for Warwickshire, SE, or Rugby Div (C) 1895-1900: *m* 1895, Marie Frances Lisette, OBE, who *d* 1941, da of late Charles Addington Hanbury; *d* 1923; *s* by his son (20) JOHN HENRY PEYTO, MC, AFC, AE, 20th Baron, *b* 1896, JP, DL and Lord Lieut Warwicks 1939-67; Member Jockey Club (Steward 1944-47, and 1954-56), and National Hunt Cttee (Steward 1942-44, 1950-53 and 1964-67), Chm Tattersall's Cttee 1948-53, Pres Hunters' Improvement Soc 1957-58, Member Council of Order of St John 1946-67; Capt 17th/21st Lancers, Air Commodore RAuxAF, Cdr 605 (Co Warwick) Sqdn AAF 1936-39 (Air Efficiency Award, AFC), Hon Col Queen's Own Warwicks and Worcs Yeo (TA) 1942-63, served 1914-18 War (wounded MC), and 1939-45 War (despatches); Dep Dir Public Relations Air Min 1941-44 (Dir 1945-46): *m* 1933, Rachel, who *d* 1991, only child of Sir (Robert) Bourchier Sherard Wrey, 11th Bt; *d* 1986; *s* by his only son (21) LEOPOLD DAVID, 21st Baron and present peer.

WILLOUGHBY DE ERESBY, BARONESS (Heathcote-Drummond-Willoughby) (Baron E 1313)

(NANCY) JANE MARIE HEATHCOTE-DRUMMOND-WILLOUGHBY, *Baroness Willoughby de Eresby*; *b* 1 Dec 1934; *s* 1983; Joint Hereditary Lord Great Chamberlain of England; a Train Bearer to HM The Queen at the Coronation 1953; Patron King Edward VI Sch, Spilsby, Lincs, since 1987.

Arms – Quarterly, — 1st and 4th, or fretty azure, *Willoughby*; 2nd, or three bars wavy gules, *Drummond*; 3rd, ermine three pomais each charged with a cross or, *Heathcote*.
Seat – Grimsthorpe Castle, Bourne, Lincs; Drummond Castle, Crieff, Perthshire.

AUNTS LIVING (*Daughters of 2nd Earl of Ancaster*)

(Co-heiresses presumptive)

Lady CATHERINE MARY CLEMENTINA, *b* 25 Sept 1906: *m* 1st, 1935 (*m* diss 1948), John St Maur Ramsden, who *d* 1948, el son of Sir John Frencheville Ramsden, 6th Bt; 2ndly, 1948, Charles Wedderburn Hume, who *d* 1974, and has issue (by 1st *m*) (see Ramsden, Bt, colls). *Residence* – Hunting Ridge Farm, 2670 Ridge Rd, Charlottesville, Virginia 22901, USA.
Lady PRISCILLA, *b* 29 Oct 1909: *m* 1939, Col Sir John Renton Aird, 3rd Bt, MVO, MC, Gren Gds, who *d* 1973, and has issue (see Aird, Bt). *Residence* – Wingrove House, Chipping Campden, Glos.

COLLATERAL BRANCHES LIVING (*All in remainder*)

Granddaughter of late Brig-Gen Hon Charles Strathavon Heathcote-Drummond-Willoughby, CB, CMG (infra):—
Issue of late Charles Peregrine Heathcote-Drummond-Willoughby, *b* 1905, *d* 1965: *m* 1939, Anne Eveline, who *d* 1983, da of late James Fitzsimmons:—
(Anne) Leueen WILLOUGHBY, *b* 1949; continues to be styled by her maiden name: *m* 1985, David Reid Brown, and has issue living, Peregrine WILLOUGHBY-BROWN, *b* 1985, — Breanne WILLOUGHBY-BROWN, *b* 1988. *Residence* – 509 Broadview Av, Toronto, Canada M4K 2N5.

Issue of late Brig-Gen Hon Charles Strathavon Heathcote-Drummond-Willoughby, CB, CMG, son of 1st Earl, *b* 1870, *d* 1949: *m* 1903, Lady Muriel Agnes Stuart Erskine, who *d* 1967, da of 14th Earl of Buchan:—
Rosalie (*Baroness Nugent*) (40 Bramerton St, SW3), *b* 1908: *m* 1935, 1st Baron Nugent, who *d* 1973, when the title became extinct.

Grandchildren of late Lady Margaret Mary Heathcote-Drummond-Willoughby (infra):—
Issue of late Margaret Evelyn Rutherford, *b* 1903, *d* 1984: *m* 1930 (*m* diss 1944), Lt-Cdr Reginald Arthur Forbes, RN (ret), who *d* 1975:—
See Stuart-Forbes, Bt.

Issue of late Lady Margaret Mary Heathcote-Drummond-Willoughby, 2nd da of 1st Earl, *b* 1866, *d* 1956: *m* 1902, Gideon Macpherson Rutherford, Bar-at-law, who *d* 1907:—
Christine Jane, *b* 1906: *m* 1934, Group Capt W. H. Poole, AFC, MM, RAF, who *d* 1971, and has issue living, David Rutherford (Wanebridge House, Malt Hill, Warfield, Bracknell, Berks RG12 6PL), *b* 1939; *ed* Charterhouse; MA: *m* 1962, Julie Anne Hoskins, and has issue living, Jennifer Alice *b* 1968. *Residence* – Ascot, 7 Thamesfield Court, Wargrave Rd, Henley-on-Thames, Oxon RG9 2ND.

Issue of late Lady Mary Adelaide Heathcote-Drummond-Willoughby, yst da of 1st Earl, *b* 1878, *d* 1960: *m* 1903, 14th Earl of Dalhousie, who *d* 1928:—
See E Dalhousie.

PREDECESSORS – (1) ROBERT Willoughby, having been actively engaged in the French and Scottish wars of Edward I, was summoned to Parliament of England as Baron 1313; *s* by his son (2) JOHN, 2nd Baron; was one of the principal commanders at the battle of Crécy; summoned to Parliament 1332-49; *s* by his son (3) JOHN, 3rd Baron; served at Poitiers; *d* 1373; *s* by his son (4) ROBERT, 4th Baron; *d* 1390; *s* by his son (5) WILLIAM, 5th Baron; was a Peer of Parliament when Richard II made a formal resignation in 1399; *s* by his son (6) ROBERT, KG, 6th Baron; an eminent military commander, *temp* Henry VI; *cr Baron Willoughby of Monblay and Beaumesguil and Earl of Vendome and Beaumont*, in France, which titles expired at his death in 1452; *s* in Barony of Willoughby de Eresby by his da (7) JOAN, wife of Sir Richard Welles, Knt, who in right of his wife was summoned to Parliament as 7th Baron Willoughby de Eresby 1455-66; his lordship was only son of Leo, 6th Baron Welles (*cr* 1299), who was killed at the battle of Towton Field 1461, and at his decease his estates and honours were attainted; in 1468 the attainders were reversed and he became 7th Baron Welles; having become through his son involved in the vibrating fortunes of the red and white roses he was treacherously beheaded by the order of King Edward IV 1469; *s* by his son (8) ROBERT, 8th Baron, who having heard of the king's treachery attacked the royal army, but being defeated he was taken prisoner and immediately beheaded; *s* in both baronies by his sister (9) JOANE, wife of Richard Hastings, who was summoned to Parliament as Baron Welles 1482-3; he *d* 1503 when his Barony of Welles became extinct; the Baroness *d* 1506 when the old Barony of Welles became abeyant and still remains so, while the Barony of Willoughby de Eresby passed to (10) WILLIAM Willoughby, 10th Baron, lineal descendant of Sir Thomas Willoughby, 2nd son of 5th Baron; *d* 1525; *s* by his da (11) KATHERINE: *m* 1st, Charles Brandon, KG, 1st Duke of Suffolk, and 2ndly, Richard Bertie; *d* 1580; *s* by her son by her 2nd marriage (12) PEREGRINE Bertie, 12th Baron; summoned to Parliament 1581; *d* 1601; *s* by his son (13) ROBERT, KG, 13th Baron; established (through his mother, sister and heiress of 17th Earl of Oxford) his right to be hereditary Lord Great Chamberlain of England; *cr Earl of Lindsey* (peerage of England) 1626; *s* by his son (14) MONTAGU, KG, 2nd Earl; *d* 1666; *s* by his son (15) ROBERT, 3rd Earl; *d* 1701; *s* by his son (16) ROBERT, 4th Earl; summoned to Parliament as Baron Willoughby de Eresby in his father's lifetime; *cr Marquess of Lindsey* (peerage of Great Britain) 1706, and *Duke of Ancaster and Kesteven* (peerage of Great Britain) 1715; *d* 1723; *s* by his son (17) PEREGRINE, 2nd Duke; *d* 1742; *s* by his son (18) PEREGRINE, 3rd Duke; *d* 1778; *s* by his son (19) ROBERT, 4th Duke; *d* unmarried 1779, when the dukedom and all honours except the Barony of Willoughby de Eresby passed to his uncle Brownlow (see E Lindsey), and the Barony of Willoughby fell into abeyance between his grace's sisters, Priscilla, wife of 1st Baron Gwydyr, and Georgiana, wife of 1st

Marquess of Cholmondeley, each of whom became Joint Hereditary Great Chamberlain; in 1780 the abeyance was terminated in favour of the former **(20)** PRISCILLA BARBARA ELIZABETH: *m* 1779, Sir Peter Burrell, Bt, who in 1796 was *cr* Baron Gwydyr; she *d* 1828; *s* by her son **(21)** PETER ROBERT, 21st Baron, who in 1820 had *s* his father as 2nd Baron Gwydyr; assumed in 1807 by sign manual the additional surname of Drummond: *d* 1865; *s* by his son **(22)** ALBERIC, 22nd Baron; was Joint Hereditary Great Chamberlain of England; *d* unmarried 1870, when the Barony of Gwydyr devolved upon his cousin Peter Robert Burrell, and the Barony of Willoughby de Eresby fell into abeyance between his sisters, Clementina, wife of 1st Baron Aveland, and Charlotte, wife of 2nd Baron Carrington each of whom became entitled to a moiety of the office of Joint Hereditary Great Chamberlain; in 1871 the abeyance was terminated in favour of **(23)** CLEMENTINA ELIZABETH, *b* 1809; assumed in 1870 by Roy licence the additional surname and arms of Drummond, and in 1872, the additional surname of Willoughby: *m* 1827, the 1st Baron Aveland; *d* 1888; *s* by her el son **(24)** GILBERT HENRY, 2nd Baron Aveland (infra), 24th Baron Willoughby de Eresby; *b* 1830; in 1872, assumed by Roy licence the additional surnames of Willoughby and Drummond; MP for Boston (*L*) 1852-56, and for Rutland 1856-67; *cr Earl of Ancaster*, in co Lincoln (peerage of United Kingdom) 1892: *m* 1863, Lady Evelyn Elizabeth Gordon, who *d* 1921, 2nd da of 10th Marquess of Huntly; *d* 1910; *s* by his son **(25)** GILBERT, GCVO, TD, 2nd Earl, *b* 1867; Parliamentary Sec to Min of Agriculture and Fisheries 1921-4 (also Dep Min therefor from Oct 1921), Lord-Lieut of Rutland 1921-51; Joint Hereditary Lord Great Chamberlain (acting for reign of King George VI) 1936-50; sat as MP (*C*) for Lincolnshire, S Lindsey or Horncastle Div 1894-1910: *m* 1905, Eloise, OBE, JP, who *d* 1953, el da of late W. L. Breese, of New York, USA; *d* 1951; *s* by his el son **(26)** (GILBERT) JAMES, KCVO, TD, 3rd Earl, *b* 1907; Maj RA (TA); Joint Hereditary Lord Chamberlain (acting for reign of King George VI); European War 1939-45 (despatches); Lord Lieut of Lincs 1950-75, and an Alderman for Kesteven Co Council 1954-75; bore St Edward's Staff at Coronation of Queen Elizabeth II; MP for Rutland and Stamford Div of Parts of Kesteven and Rutland (*C*) Nov 1933 — Feb 1950; called to House of Lords in his father's Barony of Willoughby de Eresby Jan 1951: *m* 1933, Hon (Nancy) Phyllis Louise Astor, who *d* 1975, da of 2nd Viscount Astor; *d* 1983, when the Earldom of Ancaster and Barony of Aveland became ext, and the baronetcy of Heathcote passed to his kinsman (*see* Heathcote, Bt, of London), and he was *s* in the Barony of Willoughby de Eresby by his only surv child (his only son, Timothy Gilbert, Lord Willoughby de Eresby, *b* 1936, disappeared at sea between Cap Ferrat and Corsica 1963) **(27)** (NANCY) JANE MARIE, Baroness Willoughby de Eresby, present peeress.

WILSON, BARON (Wilson) (Baron UK 1946)

PATRICK MAITLAND WILSON, 2nd Baron; *b* 14 Sept 1915; *s* 1964; *ed* Eton, and King's Coll, Camb; 1939-45 War in Greece and Middle East (despatches), *m* 1945, Storeen Violet, who *d* 1990, da of late Maj James Hamilton Douglas Campbell of Blythswood, OBE (B Clarina, ext).

Arms – Sable, a wolf salient or, on a chief of the last a pale of the first charged with a fleur-de-lys argent between two pellets. **Crest** – A demi wolf or, the sinister paw resting on a pellet charged with a fleur-de-lys gold. **Supporters** – *Dexter*, a rifleman; *sinister*, a bugler, both of the Rifle Brigade, in full dress proper. *Address* –

SISTER LIVING

Hon Maud Maitland, *b* 1917. *Residence* – 8 Cumberland Lodge Mews, Windsor Great Park, Berks.

PREDECESSOR – **(1)** *Sir* HENRY MAITLAND Wilson, GCB, GBE, DSO, son of Arthur Maitland Wilson, OBE, of Stowlangtoft Hall, Suffolk; *b* 1881; Field Marshal late Rifle Bde (OC 1st Bn 1927-30), and Col Comdt 1939-51; GOC-in-C British Troops in Egypt 1939-41, Mil Gov and GOC-in-C Cyrenaica, GOC-in-C British Troops in Greece, GOC, British Troops in Palestine and Transjordan, GOC, Allied Forces in Syria, and GOC 9th Army 1941, GOC-in-C, Persia and Iraq 1942-43, and Middle East 1943-44, Supreme Allied Comd in Mediterranean Theatre 1944-45 and Head of British Joint Staff Mission, Washington 1945-47, Constable of HM Tower of London 1955-60; *cr Baron Wilson*, of Libya and of Stowlangtoft, co Suffolk (Peerage of UK) 1946: *m* 1914, Hester Mary, who *d* 1979, da of Philip James Digby Wykeham, late of Tythrop House, Oxon; *d* 1964; *s* by his only son **(2)** PATRICK MAITLAND, 2nd Baron and present peer.

WILSON OF HIGH WRAY, BARONY OF (Wilson) (Extinct 1980)

WIDOW LIVING OF LIFE BARON

VALERIE FRANCES ELIZABETH (*Baroness Wilson of High Wray*) (Gillinggate House, Kendal, Cumbria LA9 4JB), da of late William Baron Fletcher, of Cape Town: *m* 1935, Baron Wilson of High Wray, OBE, DSC, FSA (Life Baron), who *d* 1980.

WILSON OF LANGSIDE, BARON (Wilson) (Life Baron 1969)

HENRY STEPHEN WILSON, PC, QC, son of late James Wilson of Glasgow, Solicitor; *b* 21 March 1916; *ed* Glasgow High Sch, and Glasgow Univ (MA, LLB); Bar Scotland 1946, QC 1965; Advocate Depute 1948-51, Sheriff Substitute of Greenock 1955-56, and Glasgow 1956-65, Solicitor-Gen for Scotland 1965-67, and Lord Advocate 1967-70; Sheriff of Glasgow 1971-75, and Sheriff Principal of Glasgow and Strathkelvin 1975-77;

Dir Scottish Courts Admin 1971; Joint Chm of "Scotland is British" 1977; 1939-45 War with HLI and RAC (Commnd 1940, demobilized as Capt 1946); *cr* PC 1967, and *Baron Wilson of Langside*, of Broughton, in co Edinburgh (Life Baron) 1969: *m* 1942, Jessie Forrester, da of late William Nisbet Waters, of Paisley. *Residence* – Dunallan, Kippen, Stirlingshire. *Club* – RSAC (Glasgow).

WILSON OF RADCLIFFE, BARONY OF (Wilson) (Exinct 1983)

DAUGHTER LIVING OF LIFE BARON

Hon Moyra Christine, *b* 1943: *m* 1964, Dr Arthur Crowther, who *d* 1979; 2ndly, 1983, Joseph Levey, of 8 Delfur Rd, Bramhall, Cheshire.

WIDOW LIVING OF LIFE BARON

FREDA (*Baroness Wilson of Radcliffe*), da of Jessie Mather, of Bolton: *m* 1976, as his second wife, Baron Wilson of Radcliffe (Life Baron), who *d* 1983. *Residence* – 4 Hey House Mews, off Lumb Carr Rd, Holcombe, nr Bury, Lancs BL8 4NS.

WILSON OF RIEVAULX (Wilson) (Life Baron 1983)

(JAMES) HAROLD WILSON, KG, OBE, PC, FRS, only son of late James Herbert Wilson, of Rievaulx, Biscovey, Par, Cornwall, formerly of Huddersfield and of Manchester (*d* 1971); *b* 11 March 1916; *ed* Milnsbridge Council Sch, and Royds Hall Sch, Huddersfield, Wirral Gram Sch, Bebington, Cheshire, and Jesus Coll Oxford; Lecturer in Economics, New Coll Oxford 1937; Fell of Univ Coll 1938; Praelector in Economics and Domestic Bursar 1945; MP for Ormskirk Divn of Lancs 1945-50 and for Huyton Divn of Lancs 1950-83; Pres Bd of Trade 1947-51; Chm Labour Party Exec Cttee 1961-62; Leader of Labour Party 1963-76; Prime Minister and First Lord of the Treasury 1964-70 and 1974-76; Leader of the Opposition 1963-64 and 1970-74; an Elder Brother of Trinity House 1968; Hon Fell of Jesus and Univ Colls Oxford 1963; Hon Freeman of the City of London 1975; Pres of Royal Shakespeare Theatre Co since 1976; Hon LLD Lancaster, Liverpool, Nottingham and Sussex Univs; Hon DCL Oxford; Hon DTech Bradford; D Univ of Essex and Open Univ; author; FRS 1969; *cr* OBE (Civil) 1945, PC 1947, KG 1976, and *Baron Wilson of Rievaulx*, of Kirklees, co W Yorks (Life Baron) 1983: *m* 1940, (Gladys) Mary, da of late Rev Daniel Baldwin, of The Manse, Duxford, Cambridge, and has issue.

Arms – Argent an ancient ship proper on a chief gules a stag's head caboshed or between two water bougets argent. **Crest** – Upon a rock a lighthouse in front thereof a spade blade downwards and a quill point downwards in saltire all proper. **Supporters** – *Dexter*, A winged lion purpure charged on the wing with three roses argent barbed and seeded proper. *Sinister*, A griffin or charged on the wing with three roses gules barbed and seeded proper
Residence – 5 Ashley Gardens, Ambrosden Avenue, SW1.

SONS LIVING

Hon Robin James, *b* 1943, *ed* Univ Coll Sch, Balliol Coll, Oxford (MA), Univ of Pennsylvania (MA, PhD), and Massachusetts Inst of Technology: *m* 1968, (Margaret Elizabeth) Joy, da of Brian Crispin, of Dawlish, and has issue, Jennifer, *b* 1975, — Catherine, *b* (twin) 1975. *Residence* – 15 Chalfont Road, Oxford.
Hon Giles Daniel John, *b* 1948; *ed* Univ Coll Sch, Brighton Coll of Education, and Open Univ (BA). *Residence* – 5 Ashley Gdns, Ambrosden Avenue, SW1.

WILSON OF TILLYORN, BARON (Wilson) (Life Baron 1992)

DAVID CLIVE WILSON, GCMG, son of late Rev William Skinner Wilson; *b* 14 Feb 1935; *ed* Trin Coll, Glenalmond, Keble Coll, Oxford (MA), Hong Kong Univ, Columbia Univ (visiting scholar), and London Univ (PhD); Hon LLD Aberdeen Univ 1990, Hon DLitt Sydney Univ 1991; HM Diplomatic Ser since 1958, ed The China Quarterly Contemporary Inst SOAS London Univ 1968-74, Cabinet Office 1974-77, Political Adviser to Gov of Hong Kong 1977-81, Head S European Dept FCO 1981-84, Assist Under Sec of State responsible for Asia and the Pacific, FCO 1984-87, Govr and C-in-C Hong Kong 1987-92; Chm Scottish Hydro-Electric plc, Chancellor's Assessor, Univ of Aberdeen, and Chm Scottish Cttee of British Council since 1993; *cr* CMG 1985, KCMG 1987, GCMG 1991, and *Baron Wilson of Tillyorn*, of Finzean, in the District of Kincardine and Deeside and of Fanling in Hong Kong (Life Baron) 1992: *m* 1967, Natasha Helen Mary, da of late Bernard Gustav Alexander, and has issue.

Arms – Sable, on a chevron argent between a dragon passant guardant or in chief, and a demi-wolf argent holding in its forepaws a pearl proper in base, a Celtic cross azure. **Crest** – A talbot's head erased sable langued gules gorged of a collar argent charged with two mullets gules.
Residence – Tillyorn, Finzean, Aberdeenshire AB31 3PN. *Clubs* – Athenaeum, Alpine, New (Edinburgh).

SONS LIVING

Hon Peter Michael Alexander, *b* 1968.
Hon Andrew Marcus William, *b* 1969.

WILTON, EARL OF (Egerton) (Earl UK 1801)

I trust to virtue, not to arms

SEYMOUR WILLIAM ARTHUR JOHN EGERTON, 7th Earl; *b* 29 May 1921; *s* 1927; *ed* Eton: *m* 1962, Diana Elizabeth Lea (NAYLOR-LEYLAND), da of Roy Galway, of St Ronans, Winkfield Row, Ascot, Berks.

Arms – Argent, a lion rampant gules, between three pheons, points downwards sable. **Crest** – Three arrows, points downwards, one in pale and two in saltire or, barbed and fledged sable, band gules, and tasseled or. **Supporters** – *Dexter*, a wyvern, wings inverted or; *sinister*, a lion argent, ducally crowned or.
Address – c/o Messrs Warrens Boyes and Archer, 20 Hartford Rd, Huntingdon, Cambs PE18 6QE. *Club* – White's.

COLLATERAL BRANCH LIVING (*In special remainder*)

Descendants of late Lord Robert Grosvenor (3rd son of 1st Marquess of Westminster), who was *cr Baron Ebury* 1857 (see that title):—

Of whom FRANCIS EGERTON (*Baron Ebury*), *b* 8 Feb 1934; is *hp* to the Earldom.

PREDECESSORS – (1) *Sir* THOMAS Egerton, 7th Bt, of Oulton, was *cr Baron Grey de Wilton*, of Wilton Castle, co Hereford (peerage of Great Britain) 1784, and *Viscount Grey de Wilton* and *Earl of Wilton* (peerage of United Kingdom) 1801, with remainder to the 2nd and all the younger sons successively of his da Eleanor, wife of Lord Belgrave, afterwards 1st Marquess of Westminster; *d* 1814, when the Barony of Grey de Wilton expired, the baronetcy reverted upon the lineal descendant of the 1st Bt (see Grey-Egerton, Bt), and the viscountcy and earldom devolved upon his grandson (2) Rt Hon THOMAS Grosvenor, GCH, DCL, 2nd Earl; *b* 1799; was Lord Steward of the Household; assumed in 1821 by sign manual the surname of Egerton in lieu of Grosvenor: *m* 1st, 1821, Lady Mary Margaret Stanley, da of 12th Earl of Derby; 2ndly, 1863, Isabella, who *d* 1916, da of late Major Elton Smith, of Ilminster: *d* 1882; *s* by his el son (3) ARTHUR EDWARD HOLLAND GREY, 3rd Earl; *b* 1833; sat as MP for Weymouth (C) 1859-65, and for Bath 1873-4: *m* 1858, Lady Elizabeth Charlotte Louisa Craven, who *d* 1919, da of 2nd Earl of Craven; *cr Baron Grey de Radcliffe* (peerage of United Kingdom) 1875; *dsp* 19 Jan 1885, when the Barony of Grey de Radcliffe became extinct, and the peerage of 1801 devolved upon his brother (4) SEYMOUR JOHN GREY, 4th Earl; *b* 1839; *m* 1862, Laura Caroline, who *d* 1916, da of late William Russell; *d* 1898; *s* by his son (5) ARTHUR GEORGE, 5th Earl, *b* 1863: *m* 1895, Hon Mariota Thelluson, who *d* 1924, da of 5th Baron Rendlesham; *d* 1915; *s* by his el son (6) SEYMOUR EDWARD FREDERICK, 6th Earl; *b* 1896: *m* 1917, Brenda, who *d* 1930, da of late Sir William Petersen, KBE, of Eigg, Inverness; *d* 1927; *s* by his son (7) SEYMOUR WILLIAM ARTHUR JOHN, 7th Earl and present peer; also Viscount Grey de Wilton.

Wiltshire, Earl of; son of Marquess of Winchester.

WIMBORNE, VISCOUNT (Guest) (Viscount UK 1918, Baron UK 1880 and 1910, Bt UK 1838)

By iron, not by the sword

IVOR MERVYN VIGORS GUEST, 4th Viscount, and 6th Baronet; *b* 19 Sept 1968; *s* 1993; *ed* Eton.

Arms – Azure, on a chevron or, between three swan's heads erased proper, as many crosses moline sable. **Crest** – A swan's head, erased proper, gorged with a collar or, and charged underneath with a cross moline as in the arms, between two ostrich feathers or. **Supporters** – On either side a figure habited as Vulcan, resting his exterior hand on an anvil and holding in front thereof a sledge hammer, all proper. **Address** – c/o House of Lords, SW1A 0PW.

HALF-SISTER LIVING

Hon Ilona Charlotte, *b* 1985.

UNCLES LIVING (*sons of 2nd Viscount*)

Hon JULIAN JOHN, *b* 12 Oct 1945; *ed* Stowe: *m* 1st, 1970 (*m diss* 1978), Emma Jane Arlette, elder da of Cdr Archibald Gray, DSO, RN, of Tilbridge, Gt Staughton, St Neots, Hunts; 2ndly, 1983, Jillian, da of late Ninian Stuart Gray Bannatine. *Address* – c/o White's Club, St James's, W1.

Hon Charles James, *b* 1950; *ed* Harrow, and RMA Sandhurst; commn'd 9th/12th Royal Lancers (Prince of Wales's) 1973, late Capt Royal Wessex Yeo; Member of Securities Institute, with Neilson Cobbold Ltd: *m* 1976, Simone Katherine, yst da of Patrick Whinney, of Grand Havre, Guernsey, CI, and has issue living, Henry Charles, *b* 1978, — William Patrick, *b* 1981, — Catherine Elizabeth, *b* 1987. *Residence* – Truckwell Manor Farm, Lydeard St Lawrence, Taunton, Som TA4 3PT; *Club* – White's.

AUNT LIVING (*daughter of 2nd Viscount*)

Hon Frances Ann, *b* 1942: *m* 1st, 1971 (*m diss* 1987), Ernest Martin Johnson; 2ndly, 1991, Rao Gaddipati. *Residence* – Apt 6R, 5440 Little Neck Parkway, Little Neck, NY 11362, USA.

GREAT-AUNT LIVING (*Daughter of 1st Viscount*)

Hon Cynthia Edith, *b* 1908: *m* 1933, Capt Thomas George Talbot, CB, QC, who *d* 1992 (*see* E Shrewsbury and Talbot, colls), of The Small House, Falconhurst, Markbeech, Edenbridge, Kent.

MOTHER LIVING

Victoria Ann, only da of late Col Mervyn Doyne Vigors, DSO, MC, 9th Bengal Lancers (Hodson's Horse): *m* 1st, 1966 (*m diss* 1981), the 3rd Viscount Wimborne, who *d* 1993; 2ndly, 1982, Vincent Poklewski-Koziell.

WIDOW LIVING OF SECOND VISCOUNT

Lady MABEL EDITH FOX-STRANGWAYS (*Dowager Viscountess Wimborne*) (Magnolia House, Candie, St Peter Port, Guernsey), da of 6th Earl of Ilchester: *m* 1938, the 2nd Viscount, who *d* 1967.

WIDOW LIVING OF THIRD VISCOUNT

VENETIA MARGARET (*Viscountess Wimborne*), da of Richard Bridges St John Quarry, of Orchard House, Odiham, Hants, and formerly wife of Capt Frederick Grant Barker, late 11th Hus: *m* 1983, as his 2nd wife, the 3rd Viscount, who *d* 1993. *Residence* – Fontaine l'Abbé, 27470 Serquigny, France.

COLLATERAL BRANCHES LIVING (*In remainder to the Barony of Wimborne and the Baronetcy only*)

Issue of late Lieut-Col Hon (Christian) Henry Charles Guest, 2nd son of 1st Baron, *b* 1874, *d* 1957: *m* 1911, Hon Frances Henrietta Lyttelton, who *d* 1918, da of 8th Viscount Cobham:—
John Spencer Churchill, *b* 1913: *m* 1948, Margaret Hetherington, da of late Henry Craft Houck, of Schenectady, New York, USA, and has issue living, Richard Lyttelton (5 James St, Norwalk, Connecticut, USA), *b* 1954: *m* 1983, Cynthia Rogers, da of William Shelton Vaiden, of Los Osos, Cal, USA, and has issue living, Sarah Frances Vaiden *b* 1984, — Cornelia Schermerhorn, *b* 1952: *m* 1986, Robert Allan Mitchell, of 148 June Rd, North Salem, NY, USA, and has issue living, Andrew Moses Leonard *b* 1993, John Henry Guest *b* (triplet) 1993, Aune Elizabeth Houck *b* (triplet) 1993. *Residence* – 839 Weed St, New Canaan, Connecticut 06840-4023, USA.

Grandchildren of late Capt Rt Hon Frederick Edward Guest, CBE, DSO, MP (infra):—
Issue of late Capt Winston Frederick Churchill Guest, US Marines, *b* 1906, *d* 1982: *m* 1st, 1934 (*m diss* 1944), Helena Woolworth, da of Charles Edward Francis McCann, of New York; 2ndly, 1947, Lucy Douglas (651 North Country Rd, Palm Beach, Fla 33480, USA), da of late Alexander Lynde Cochrane, of Boston, Mass:—
(By 1st *m*) Winston (152 Wells Rd, Palm Beach, Fla 33480, USA), *b* 1936: *m* 1967, Helen, da of Joseph V. Shields, of New York, and has issue living, Winston Frederick Churchill, *b* 1968, — Spencer Randolph Harrison, *b* 1984, — Helena Woolworth, *b* 1970. —— Frederick Edward (II) (c/o Bessemer Trust Co, 630 5th Ave, New York City 10111, USA), *b* 1938: *m* 1st, 1963, Stephanie, da of late Walter F. Wanger, by his late wife, Joan Bennett, the film actress; 2ndly, 1988, Carole, da of Frank Baldoff, of Pittsburgh, Penn, and has issue living (by 1st *m*), Frederick Edward (III), *b* 1975, — Andrew Churchill, *b* 1976, — Victoria Woolworth, *b* 1966, — Vanessa Wanger, *b* 1973. —— (By 2nd *m*) Alexander Michael Dudley Churchill (11 Knollwood Drive, Mendham, NJ 07845, USA), *b* 1954: *m* 1986, Elizabeth, da of Cyril Geacintov, and has issue living, Gregory Winston Churchill, *b* 1990.
Issue of late Raymond Richard Guest, sometime Senator of Virginia, and US Amb to Ireland 1965-69, *b* 1907, *d* 1991: *m* 1st, 1935, Elizabeth Sturgis, who *d* 1990, da of Frank Lyon Polk; 2ndly, 1953, Mrs Ellen Tuck Astor, da of Francis Ormond French, and formerly wife of John Jacob Astor; 3rdly, 1960, HH Princess Caroline Cécile

Alexandrine Jeanne (Powhatan Plantation, King George, Virginia, USA), yr da of HH late Prince Alexandre Michel Eugène Joachim Napoléon Murat:—

(By 1st *m*) Raymond Richard (Jr) (Rock Hill Farm, Front Royal, Virginia, USA), *b* 1939: *m* 1st, 1962, Patricia, da of David R. Donovan; 2ndly, 1979, Mary Scott, da of Butler Carbon Derrick, and has issue living (by 1st *m*), Raymond Richard (III), *b* 1965, — Mary Elizabeth, *b* 1964. —— Elizabeth Polk, *b* 1937: *m* 1st, 1958, Edward B. Condon; 2ndly, 1965, George C. Stevens, Jr, of 3050 Avon Lane NW, Washington DC 20007, USA, and has issue living (by 1st *m*), Caroline, *b* 1959, — (by 2nd *m*) Michael Murrow, *b* 1966, — David Averill, *b* 1968. —— Virginia, *b* 1946: *m* 1st, 1975 (*m diss* 1978), William L. Van Alen, Jr, of Newtown Sq, Penn; 2ndly, 1991, E. Massie Valentine, of 102 Tonbridge Rd, Richmond, Virginia 23221, USA. —— (By 3rd *m*) Achille Murat, *b* 1961. —— Laetitia Amelia (68 Blvd de Courcelles, 75017 Paris, France), *b* 1965.

Issue of late Capt Rt Hon Frederick Edward Guest, CBE, DSO, MP, 3rd son of 1st Baron, *b* 1875, *d* 1937: *m* 1905, Amy, who *d* 1959, da of Henry Phipps:—

Diana, *b* 1909; resumed the surname of Guest in lieu of Sevastopoulo by deed poll 1938: *m* 1st, 1934 (*m diss* 1937), Marc Sevastopoulo; 2ndly, 1943, Count Jean de la Valdène; 3rdly, 1970, Allen Manning, and has issue living, (by 1st *m*) Diane Lorraine, *b* 1935: *m* 1st, 1955, Pierre Firmin-Didot; 2ndly, 1967, Arthur Peter Perkins, of Wimborne Farm, Winchester Rd, Pàris, Kentucky 40361, USA, and has issue living (by 1st *m*), Isabelle Marie *b* 1962, Christine Aimée *b* 1963: *m* 1987, Antonio Bulridge, — (by 2nd *m*) Guy Winston (Count de Gaillard de la Valdène) (146 Dunbar Rd, Palm Beach, Florida 33480, USA), *b* 1944: *m* 1965, Thérèse Anderson, and has issue living, Jean Pierre *b* 1967, Valery Elaine *b* 1966, — Lorraine Aimée, *b* 1946: *m* 1978, Christian Odasso, of 201 West Indies Drive, Palm Beach Florida 33480, USA, and has issue living, Fréderick Christian *b* 1978, Diana Melody Christina *b* 1979. *Residence* – Domaine de Saint Georges, 27710 Saint-Georges-Motel, France.

Issue of late Major Hon (Oscar) Montague Guest, yst son of 1st Baron, *b* 1888, *d* 1958: *m* 1924, Kathleen Susan, who *d* 1982, da of late Graham Paterson (E Huntingdon):—

Bertie Warner (Cabalva House, Whitney-on-Wye, Hereford), *b* 1925: *m* 1949, (*m diss* 1970), Margaret Rose, da of Charles Lamond Henderson, QC, and has issue living, Jonathan Bertie, *b* 1952, — Veronica Susan GUEST, *b* 1953; resumed her maiden name 19—: *m* 1978 (*m diss* 1989), J. Crowder, — Harriet Clare, *b* 1955, — Diana Charlotte, *b* 1959: *m* 1988, Charles Hicks. — Patrick Henry, *b* 1927: *m* 1951, Juliet Marian, da of late H. M. James, and has issue living, Peter Hugh, *b* 1952: *m* 1988, Donna Jean, da of late Donald Lee Macfarlane, of Piedmont, Calif, USA, — Matthew James, *b* 1954, — David Christian, *b* 1960: *m* 1986, Henrietta Mary, da of John Giles Selby Coode-Adams, of Feeringbury Manor, Feering, Essex (*see* Buxton, Bt, colls, 1980 Edn), and has issue living, Imogen Victoria *b* 1993. *Residences* – 14 Hobury St, SW10; Lower Bettws Farm, Whitney-on-Wye, Herefords. — Cornelia Rowena, *b* 1928: *m* 1st, 1949 (*m diss* 1955), Hugh Dearman Janson; 2ndly, 1957, Peter Frederick Arthur Denman (see B Denman, colls), and has issue living, (by 1st *m*) Charles James, *b* 1952, — Sarah, *b* 1950, — (by 2nd *m*) (see B Denman, colls). *Residence* – Duke's House, 23 Lawrence St, SW3. —— Revel Sarah, *b* 1931; co-author of *Lady Charlotte; a Biography of the Nineteenth Century* (1989): *m* 1963, Robert Alan Albert, and has issue living, Justin Thomas (Cabalva Farmhouse, Whitney-on-Wye, Hereford), *b* 1965: *m* 1991, Hester Amanda Jessica, eldest da of Michael Selby Gray, of Argyll, — Corisande Charlotte, *b* 1967. *Residence* – Cabalva House, Whitney-on-Wye, Hereford HR3 6EX.

Granddaughters of late Arthur Edward Guest, brother of 1st Baron:—

Issue of late (Arthur) Rhuvon Guest, *b* 1869, *d* 1946: *m* 1901, Hilda Eugenia, who *d* 1959, da of late Adm Hon Keith Stewart, CB (E Galloway, colls):—

Mary Adeline (39 Argyll Rd, W8), *b* 1904: *m* 1929, Capt Henry T. W. Bousfield, late Indian Army, who *d* 1967. —— Pamela Margaret (Windrush Cottage, Inkpen, Berks), *b* 1905.

PREDECESSORS – (1) JOSIAH JOHN Guest, son of late Thomas Guest, of Dowlais, Glamorgan; *b* 1785; MP for Honiton 1825-31, and for Merthyr Tydvil 1832-52; *cr a Baronet* 1838: *m* 1st, 1817, Maria Elizabeth, who *d* 1818, da of William Ranken; 2ndly, 1833, Lady Charlotte Elizabeth Bertie, who *d* 1895 (having *m* 2ndly, 1855, Charles Schreiber, MP, who *d* 1884), da of 9th Earl of Lindsey: *d* 1852; *s* by his son (2) Sir IVOR BERTIE, 2nd Bt, *b* 1835; *cr Baron Wimborne*, of Canford Magna, Dorset (peerage of United Kingdom) 1880: *m* 1868, Lady Cornelia Henrietta Maria Spencer-Churchill, who *d* 1927, el da of 7th Duke of Marlborough; *d* 1914; *s* by his el son (3) IVOR CHURCHILL, PC, 2nd Baron, *b* 1873; MP for Plymouth (*L*) 1900-1906, and for Cardiff 1906-10; Paymaster-Gen 1910-12, a Lord-in-Waiting to HM 1913-15, and Lord-Lieut of Ireland 1915-18; *cr Baron Ashby St Ledgers*, of Ashby St Ledgers, co Northampton (peerage of United Kingdom) 1910, and *Viscount Wimborne*, of Canford Magna, Dorset (peerage of United Kingdom) 1918: *m* 1902, Hon Alice Katherine Sibell Grosvenor, who *d* 1948, da of 2nd Baron Ebury; *d* 1939; *s* by his only son (4) IVOR GROSVENOR, OBE, 2nd Viscount. *b* 1903; PPS to Under-Sec of State for Air 1943-45; MP for Breconshire 1935-39: *m* 1938, Lady Mabel Edith Fox-Strangways, da of 6th Earl of Ilchester; *d* 1967; *s* by his son (5) IVOR FOX-STRANGWAYS, 3rd Viscount, *b* 1939; Chm Harris & Dixon Ltd 1972-76, Chm Harris & Dixon Holdings Ltd 1977-93; Joint Master Pytchley Hounds 1968-76: *m* 1st, 1966 (*m diss* 1981), Victoria, only da of late Col Mervyn Doyne Vigors, DSO, MC, 9th Bengal Lancers (Hodson's Horse); 2ndly, 1983, Mrs Venetia Margaret Barker, da of Richard Bridges St John Quarry, of Gaddeshill House, Everley, Hants, and formerly wife of Capt Frederick Grant Barker, late 11th Hus; *d* 1993; *s* by his only son (6) IVOR MERVYN VIGORS, 4th Viscount and present peer; also Baron Ashby St Ledgers, and Baron Wimborne.

WINCHESTER, MARQUESS OF (Paulet) (Marquess E 1551)

Love loyalty

NIGEL GEORGE PAULET, 18th Marquess, and Premier Marquess of England; *b* 22 Dec 1941; *s* 1968; Dir Rhodesia Mineral Ventures (Pvt) Ltd, Sani-Dan Services (Pvt) Ltd, and Rhodesia Prospectors (1969) (Pvt) Ltd: *m* 1967, Rosemary Anne, da of Maj Aubrey John Hilton, of Harare, Zimbabwe, and has issue.

Arms – Sable, three swords in pile, points downwards, proper, pommels and hilts, or. **Crest** – A falcon, wings displayed or, belled of the same, and ducally collared gules. **Supporters** – Two hinds purpure, semée of estoiles, and ducally gorged or.
Residence – 6A Main Rd, Irene 1675, Transvaal, S Africa.

SONS LIVING

CHRISTOPHER JOHN HILTON (*Earl of Wiltshire*), *b* 30 July 1969.
Lord Richard George, *b* 1971.

DAUGHTER LIVING

Lady Susan, *b* 1976.

BROTHER LIVING *(Raised to the rank of a Marquess's son* 1970)

Lord Timothy Guy, *b* 1944: *m* 1973, Gilian Margaret, da of late Capt Thomas Preacher, 8th Bn DLI, and has issue living, Timothy Guy, *b* 1975, — Michael Raoul, *b* 1976.

SISTER LIVING *(Raised to the rank of a Marquess's daughter* 1970)

Lady Jane Angela, *b* 1939: *m* 1972, Christopher John Fisher.

AUNT LIVING

Violet Susan Mary (Lydford Hall, Lydford-on-Fosse, Somerton, Somerset), *b* 1903.

SISTER LIVING OF SEVENTEENTH MARQUESS *(Raised to the rank of Marquess's daughter* 1970)

Lady Eileen Cecil Theo, *b* 1916: *m* 1st, 1941, Harry Evan Martin, who *d* 1946; 2ndly, 1949, Joseph Fitton, of 470 Sonora Crescent, Campbell River, BC, Canada V9W 6V3, and has had issue (by 1st *m*), Gillian Jane (1193 S Alder St, Campbell River, BC, Canada V9W 1Z8), *b* 1942: *m* 1964, Lipot Gyula Winter, and has issue living, Edward Steven *b* 1966, Robert Ferenc *b* 1974, Peter James *b* 1978, Elizabeth Jane *b* 1964, — Elizabeth Susan, *b* 1945: *m* 19—, — de Assis Correia, of 21 Kenton Gdns, Kenton, Harrow, Middx HA3 8BE, — (by 2nd *m*) Francis Peter (Box 454, Quathiaski Cove, Quadra Is, BC, Canada V0P 1NO), *b* 1949: *m* 1985, Victoria Lynn, da of Donald Ralph Gregory, and has issue living, Kala Louise *b* 1985, Deanna Eileen *b* 1987, — Jonathan Paul (359 Simms Rd, Campbell River, BC, Canada V9W 1P2), *b* 1952: *m* 1991, Lona Dianne, da of Reuben Emil Croissant; has issue living, Jeffrey Duggan *b* 1983, William Elliot *b* 1984, — Theresa Mary, *b* 1951: *m* 1992, Neil Andrew Marson, of 500 Quadra St, Campbell River, BC, Canada V9W 6V1, — Margaret Anne, *b* 1956: *m* 1982, Kenneth Dodd Clippingdale, of Box 203, Heriot Bay, BC, Canada V0P 1H0, and has issue living, Robert Nathan *b* 1974, Andrew Dodd *b* 1983, — Catherine Louise, *b* 1958, — Judith Ellen, *b* 1961; *d* 19—.

WIDOW LIVING OF SIXTEENTH MARQUESS

BAPSY *(Bapsy, Marchioness of Winchester)*, da of late Most Rev Khurshedi Pavry, High Priest of the Parsees in India; MA Columbia Univ, New York 1925; a Member of Council of World Alliance for International Peace through Religion, and Author of "Heroines of Ancient Iran" 1930; instituted Dasturzada Doctor Jal Pavry Memorial Lectureship Endowment at Univ of Bombay and Dasturzada Doctor Jal Pavry Memorial Award Fund at Oxford Univ in area of International Peace and Understanding in perpetuity to commemorate the memory or her late brother 1989; instituted Bapsybanoo Marchioness of Winchester Award Fund at Oxford Univ in area of International Relations in perpetuity 1991; has Order of Merit of Iran: *m* 1952, as his 3rd wife, the 16th Marquess, who *d* 1962. *Address* – P.O. Box 122, Bombay 400 038, India.

COLLATERAL BRANCH LIVING

Issue of late John Valentine Paulet, uncle of 18th Marquess, *b* 1909, *d* 1970: *m* 1945, Mira Elizabeth, da of Edmund Francis Smith, of Mossel Bay, Cape Province:—
Pamela Elizabeth, *b* 1947.

PREDECESSORS – **(1)** *Sir* WILLIAM Paulet, KG, and *cr Baron St John of Basing* (peerage of England) 1539, *Earl of Wiltshire* (peerage of England) 1550, and *Marquess of Winchester* (peerage of England) 1551, and *Marquess of Winchester* (peerage of England) 1551; was an executor to the will of Henry VIII, and Lord Treasurer of England *temp* Edward VI and Queens Mary I and Elizabeth I; *d* 1572; *s* by his son **(2)** JOHN, 2nd Marquess; summoned to Parliament in his father's barony of St John; *d* 1576; *s* by his son **(3)** WILLIAM 3rd Marquess; summoned to Parliament in his father's barony of St John; *d* 1598; *s* by his son **(4)** WILLIAM, 4th Marquess; entertained Queen Elizabeth with magnificence at his seat at Basing, by which and other expenses he became involved in pecuniary difficulties; *d* 1628; *s* by his son **(5)** JOHN, 5th Marquess, a zealous partisan of Charles I; his seat at Basing was after a protracted siege by the Parliamentarians burned to the ground, when property of the value of £200,000 was destroyed; *d* 1675; *s* by his son **(6)** CHARLES, 6th Marquess; *cr Duke of Bolton* (peerage of England) 1689; *d* 1699; *s* by his son **(7)** CHARLES, 2nd Duke; was Lord-Lieut of Ireland 1717; *d* 1722; *s* by his el son **(8)** CHARLES, KG, 3rd Duke; was Lord Lieut of the Tower Hamlets and Constable of the Tower of London; *d* 1754; *s* by his brother **(9)** HARRY, 4th Duke; *d* 1759; *s* by his son **(10)** CHARLES, KB, 5th Duke; was Lieut of Tower of London, and Lord-Lieut of Hants; *d* unmarried 1765; *s* by his brother **(11)** HARRY, 6th Duke; was and Adm of the White; *d* 1794, when the dukedom expired, and the barony, earldom, and marquessate devolved upon his kinsman **(12)** GEORGE, 12th Marquess, descendant of Lord Henry, 3rd son of 4th Marquess; *d* 1800; *s* by his son **(13)** CHARLES INGOLDSBY, 13th Marquess; *b* 1765; assumed in 1839 the additional surname of Burroughs: *m* 1800, Anne da of John Andrews, Esq, of Shotney Hall, co Northumberland; *d* 1843; *s* by his son *b* **(14)** JOHN, 14th Marquess, *b* 1801: *m* 1855, the Hon Mary Montagu, who *d* 1868, el da of 6th Baron Rokeby *(ext)*; *d* 1887; *s* by his son **(15)** AUGUSTUS JOHN HENRY BEAUMONT, 15th Marquess; *b* 1858; Major Coldstream Guards; killed at battle of Magersfontein in S Africa 1899; *s* by his brother **(16)** HENRY WILLIAM MONTAGU, 16th Marquess, *b* 1862; Lord-Lieut of Hants 1904-17; Chm of Hants Co Council 1905-9; Major Rifle Bde in France 1914-17: *m* 1st, 1892, Dame Charlotte Josephine, GBE, who *d* 1924, da of late Col John Stanley Howard, of Ballina Park, co Wicklow, and widow of Samuel Garnett; 2ndly, 1925, Caroline, who *d* 1949, da of Abraham Hoffnung, and widow of Major Claude Marks, DSO; 3rdly, 1952, Bapsy, MA, da of Most Rev Khurshedi Pavry; *d* 1962, *s* by his kinsman **(17)** RICHARD CHARLES (only son of late Major Charles Standish Paulet, MVO, grandson of late Rev Lord Charles Paulet, 2nd son of 13th Marquess), 17th Marquess, *b* 1905, *d* 1968; *s* by his kinsman **(18)** NIGEL GEORGE (el son of George Cecil Paulet, el son of Cecil Henry Paulet, uncle of 17th Marquess), 18th Marquess and present peer; also Earl of Wiltshire, and Baron St John of Basing.

WINCHILSEA AND NOTTINGHAM, EARL OF (Finch Hatton) (Earl E 1628 and 1681, Bt E 1611 and 1660)

CHRISTOPHER DENYS STORMONT FINCH HATTON, 16th Earl of Winchilsea, 11th Earl of Nottingham, 17th Baronet of Eastwell, and 11th Baronet of Raunston; *b* 17 Nov 1936; *s* 1950; *ed* Eton, and Gordonstoun; Hereditary Lord of Roy Manor of Wye: *m* 1962, Shirley, el da of late Bernard Hatfield, of Wylde Green, Sutton Coldfield, and has issue.

Arms – Argent, a chevron between three griffins passant sable. **Crest** – A pegasus courant argent, wings expanded or. **Supporters** – *Dexter*, a pegasus wings elevated argent, ducally gorged or; *sinister*, a griffin wings elevated sable, gorged as the dexter. *Residence* – South Cadbury House, nr Yeovil, Somerset.

SON LIVING

DANIEL JAMES HATFIELD (*Viscount Maidstone*), *b* 7 Oct 1967.

DAUGHTER LIVING

Lady Alice Nan Christiane, *b* 1970.

BROTHER LIVING

Conscious of no guilt

Hon Robin Heneage (Town House Farm House, Clemsfold, Horsham, W Sussex RH12 3PP), *b* 1939; *ed* Gordonstoun: *m* 1962, Molly Iona, yr da of Col Palgrave Dawson Turner Powell, of Damson Hill Cottage, Swanmore, Hants, and has had issue, Christopher Benjamyn *b* 1966, — Rupert Stormont, *b* 1968, — Nicola Jane, *b* 1964, *d* 1967, — Louisa Henrietta Mari (Mariska), *b* 1971.

AUNT LIVING (*Daughter of 14th Earl*)

Lady Daphne Margarita, *b* 1913: *m* 1935, Air-Commodore Whitney Willard Straight, CBE, MC, DFC, Auxiliary Air Force, who *d* 1979, and has issue living, Camilla Caroline *b* 1937: *m* 1960, Maj Michael Ian Vansittart Bowater, Scots Guards, son of late Lt-Col Sir Ian Frank Bowater, DSO, TD (*see* Bowater, Bt, *cr* 1939), — Amanda Betsy, *b* 1952. *Residence* – 3 Aubrey Road, W8.

COLLATERAL BRANCHES LIVING

Granddaughters of late Rev William Robert Finch Hatton, son of late Rev Hon Daniel Heneage Finch Hatton, brother of 10th Earl of Winchilsea and Nottingham:—
    Issue of late Brig-Gen Edward Heneage Finch Hatton, CMG, DSO, late the Buffs, *b* 1868, *d* 1940: *m* 1912, Dagmar Gladys, who *d* 1975, da of late Col Francis George Archibald Wiehe, formerly 68th Durham LI:—
Ann Zephine, *b* 1912: *m* 1943, Group-Capt Maurice Ashdown Newnham, OBE, DFC, RAF, VR, and has issue living, Nicola Ann, *b* 1946. *Residence* – Briar Cottage, Duckmead Lane, Liss, Petersfield, Hants. —— Essex Dagmar FINCH HATTON, *b* 1916.

Descendants of late Hon Heneage Finch (2nd son of 1st Earl of Nottingham), who was *cr Earl of Aylesford* 1714 (see that title).

PREDECESSORS – (1) *Sir* MOYLE Finch, Knt, was *cr a Baronet* 1611 (of Eastwell): *m* Elizabeth, only da of Sir Thomas Heneage, Knt, of Copt Hall, Essex, which Lady was *cr Viscountess Maidstone* (peerage of England) 1623 and Countess of Winchilsea (peerage of England) 1628; Sir Moyle *d* 1614; *s* by his son (2) *Sir* THEOPHILUS, 2nd Bt; *dsp*; *s* by his brother (3) *Sir* THOMAS, 3rd Bt, who in 1633 *s* his mother as 2nd Earl; *d* 1634; *s* by his son (4)Heneage, 3rd Earl; an earnest royalist; having rendered efficient aid in restoring the monarchy was in 1600 *cr* by Charles II *Baron FitzHerbert of Eastwell*, co Kent (peerage of England); was Lord-Lieut of co Kent; *d* 1689; *s* by his grandson (5) CHARLES, 4th Earl; *d* 1712; *s* by his uncle (6) HENEAGE, 5th Earl; *dsp* 1726; *s* by his half-brother (7) JOHN, 6th Earl; *dsp* 1729, when the Barony of FitzHerbert of Eastwell became extinct, and the baronetcy, viscountcy and earldom reverted to his kinsman (8) DANIEL, PC, 7th Earl, who in 1682 has *s* his father as 2nd Earl of Nottingham (see * infra); was Sec of State 1689-94 and 1702-4, Lord Pres of the Council 1714-16, and Lord-Lieut of Kent; *d* 1730; *s* by his son (9) DANIEL, 8th Earl; *dsp* 1760; *s* by his nephew (10) GEORGE, KG, 9th Earl, son of Rt Hon William Finch, MP, 2nd son of 7th Earl; was Lord Lieut of co Rutland; *d* unmarried 1826; *s* by his cousin (11) GEORGE WILLIAM Finch Hatton 10th Earl, grandson of Hon Edward, MP (5th son of 7th Earl), who assumed without Roy Licence the additional surname of Hatton; *b* 1791, *m* 1st, 1814, Lady Georgiana Charlotte, da of 3rd Duke of Montrose; 2ndly, 1837, Emily Georgina, da of Rt Hon Sir Charles Bagot, GCB; 3rdly, 1849, Fanny Margaret, who *d* 1909, da of Edward Royd Rice, of Dane Court, Kent; *d* 1858; *s* by his son (12) GEORGE JAMES, 11th Earl, *b* 1815; sat as MP for Northamptonshire (C) 1837-41: *m* 1st, 1846, Lady Constance Henrietta Paget, who *d* 1878, da of 2nd Marquess of Anglesey; 2ndly, 1882, Lady Elizabeth Georgiana, who *d* 1904, widow of George Leopold Bryan, MP, and da of 2nd Marquess of Conyngham; *d* 1887; *s* by his half-brother (13) MURRAY EDWARD GORDON, 12th Earl, *b* 1851; MP for Lincolnshire S (C) 1884, and for Lincolnshire, Holland, or Spalding, Div 1885-7; largely interested in agricultural questions: *m* 1875, Edith, who *d* 1944, da of late Edward William Harcourt; *d* 1898; *s* by his brother (14) HENRY STORMONT, 13th Earl, *b* 1852: *m* 1882, Anne, who *d* 1924, da of late Adm of the Fleet Sir Henry John Codrington, KCB; *d* 1927; *s* by his son (15) GUY MONTAGU GEORGE, OBE, DSC, 14th Earl, *b* 1885; European War 1915-18 (DSC, OBE): *m* 1910, Margaretta Armstrong, who *d* 1952, da of Anthony Joseph Drexel, of Philadelphia, USA; *d* 1939; *s* by his son (16) CHRISTOPHER GUY HENEAGE, 15th Earl, *b* 1911; Lieut RNVR: *m* 1st, 1935 (*m diss* 1946), Countess Gladys, who *d* 1978, third da of Count László Széchényi, Hungarian Min in London; 2ndly, 1946, Agnes Mary, who *d* 1964, da of late Patrick Joseph Conroy, JP, of Malvern House, Wigan; *d* 1950; *s* by his son (17) CHRISTOPHER DENYS STORMONT, 16th Earl and present peer; also Viscount Maidstone, and Baron Finch.

*(1) *Sir* HENEAGE Finch, Knt, PC, son of Hon Sir Heneage Finch, Speaker of the House of Commons (3rd son of Sir Moyle Finch and Elizabeth, Countess of Winchilsea), sat successively as MP for Canterbury, St Michael's, and Oxford; in 1660 was appointed Solicitor-Gen, knighted, and *cr a Baronet* (of Raunston) 1660; in 1670 became Attorney-Gen; in 1673 was made Keeper of the Great Seal, and *cr Baron Finch*, of Daventry, co Northampton (peerage of England); in 1675 was promoted to be Lord High Chancellor of England and *cr Earl of Nottingham* (peerage of England); was nominated 1677 Lord High Steward of England; *d* 1682; *s* by his son (2) DANIEL, 2nd Earl, who in 1729 *s* as 7th Earl of Winchilsea (ante).

WINDLESHAM, BARON (Hennessy) (Baron UK 1937 Bt UK 1927)

I live by force and arms

DAVID JAMES GEORGE HENNESSY, CVO, PC, 3rd Baron, and 3rd Baronet; *b* 28 Jan 1932; *s* 1962; *ed* Ampleforth, and Trin Coll Oxford (MA, Hon Fellow); late Lt Gren Gds; Managing Dir of Grampian Television 1967-70; Chm of Bow Group 1959-60 and 1962-63, and a Member of Westminster City Council 1958-62; Min of State Home Office 1970-72, Min of State, N Ireland 1972-73; Lord Privy Seal, and Leader of House of Lords 1973-74, and Leader of the Opposition, House of Lords March to Oct 1974; Man Dir of ATV Network 1975-81 (Joint Man Dir from 1974), Chm 1981; Dir of "The Observer" 1981-89, Dir of W. H. Smith since 1986, and Vice-Pres of Roy TV Soc 1977-82; Chm of Oxford Preservn Tst 1979-89, Oxford Soc 1985-88, and Parole Bd 1982-88; Joint Dep Chm The Queen's Silver Jubilee Appeal 1977; Dep Chm Roy Jubilee Trusts 1977-80; a Trustee, The Royal Collection since 1993, Charities Aid Foundation 1977-81, the British Museum since 1981 and Community Service Volunteers since 1981; a Member Museums and Galleries Commn 1984-86; Chm of Trustees of British Museum since 1986, Visiting Fellow All Souls Coll, Oxford 1986; Prin Brasenose Coll, Oxford since 1989; *cr* PC 1973: *m* 1965, Prudence, who *d* 1986, yr da of Lt-Col Rupert T. W. Glynn, MC, of Harlesford House, Tetsworth, Oxon, and has issue.

𝔄rms – Gules, a boar passant proper, on a chief or a trefoil slipped vert between two roses of the field, barbed and seeded also proper. 𝔠rest – In front of a dexter arm embowed in armour, the hand grasping a battle-axe, a trefoil slipped and a red rose stalked and leaved saltire-wise, all proper. 𝔖upporters – On either side an Officer of the Irish Brigade in the service of the King of France in the eighteenth century proper, the dexter supporting with the exterior hand a gold mounted and tasselled staff proper.
Address – c/o House of Lords, SW1A 0PW. *Club* – Brooks's.

SON LIVING

Hon JAMES RUPERT, *b* 9 Nov 1968; *ed* Eton, and Bristol Univ.

DAUGHTER LIVING

Hon Victoria Jane, *b* 1966; *ed* London Univ (BA).

SISTERS LIVING

Hon Marie-Louise (*Hon Lady de Zulueta*), *b* 1930: *m* 1955, Sir Philip Francis de Zulueta, who *d* 1989, and has issue living, Francis Philip Harold (39 Lyford Rd, SW18 3LU), *b* 1959: *m* 1st, 1981, Miranda Jane, da of late Philip Alexander Howden, of Worminghall, Bucks; 2ndly, 1987, Pandora, formerly wife of Hon Edward Abdy Wodehouse (*see* E Kimberley), and eldest da of Mrs W. J. Germing, of Mortlake, and has issue living (by 2nd *m*), Sebastian Philip William *b* 1990, Gala Marie-Louise Philomena *b* 1988, — Louise Angela Mary, *b* 1956: *m* 1982, Mark Donald Seligman, son of Spencer Walter Oscar Seligman, of 64 Bedford Gdns, W8, and has issue living, Jocelyn David *b* 1983, Lucinda Marie Joanne *b* 1985, Iona Louise *b* 1990. *Residence* – Flat 5, 7 Prince's Gate, SW7 1QL.
Hon Rosalie Ann, *b* 1934: *m* 1960, Peter John Gervase Elwes, of 75 Murray Rd, Wimbledon, SW19 (B Rennell), and has issue living, Luke Andrew Cary, *b* 1961: *m* 1987, Anneke Lucille, only da of Hans du Moulin, of Farnham, Surrey, and has issue living, Jake Peter *b* 1993, — Benedict James, *b* 1963: *m* 1991, Georgina Claire, only da of Michael Rapinet, of Northend, Henley-on-Thames, Oxon, — Marcus David, *b* 1964, — Harriet Clare, *b* 1968.
Hon Annabel Jane, *b* 1937: *m* 1963, Ian Duncan Chisholm, MRCP, of The Manor House, Stratton on the Fosse, Bath, Avon BA3 4QU, and has issue living, Roderick Bryan Duncan, *b* 1964, — Daniel Hugh, *b* 1966, — Alexander James, *b* 1968: *m* 1993, Eliza, yr da of Thomas Frank Dermot Pakenham (*see* E Longford), — John Malcolm, *b* 1970.

AUNTS LIVING (*Daughters of 1st Baron*)

Hon Noreen Madeleine, *b* 1910: *m* 1931 (*m diss* 1948), Michael Bull, and has issue living, Michael Matthew, MBE, *b* 1932; *ed* Ampleforth; late Maj Coldstream Guards; MBE 1969: *m* 1962, Jane, only da of Harry Inglis, of Lane Lodge, Stoke Green, Slough, Bucks, and has issue living, Richard Matthew Charles *b* 1963, Philip Henry *b* 1969, Emma Jane, *b* 1964, — George Jeffrey (The Old Vicarage, Arkesden, Saffron Walden), *b* 1936; *ed* Ampleforth: *m* 1960, Fleur-Thérèse, only da of Patrick Freeland, of Zimbabwe, and has issue living, George Sebastian Matthew *b* 1960, Rupert Frederick Alain *b* 1963, Justin Bartholomew Peter *b* 1964, Cassian Michael Thomas *b* 1968, Tamsin Emily Mary *b* 1972. *Residence* – Belgravia Court, 33 Ebury St, SW1.
Hon Kathleen Irene Mary, *b* 1914: *m* 1947, Wilfred Ernest Barnett, who *d* 1992, of Pullington Cottage, Benenden, Cranbrook, Kent, and has issue living, Robin George (Ponds House, Hurst Green, E Sussex), *b* 1951; *ed* Worth Abbey Sch: *m* 1973, Carolyn Seward, el da of Ronald E. Plummer, of Rowley, Wadhurst, Sussex, and has issue living, Max Robin Nicholas *b* 1983, Annabel Penelope *b* 1978, Julia Seward *b* 1980, Stephanie Lucinda *b* 1987, — Nicholas James, *b* 1955; *ed* Worth Abbey Sch.

WIDOW LIVING OF SECOND BARON

PAMELA (DINAN) (58 Eaton Sq, SW1W 9BG), da of Francis Kennedy: *m* 2ndly, 1957, as his 2nd wife, the 2nd Baron, who *d* 1962; 3rdly, 1966, William Marsden Elverston-Trickett.

COLLATERAL BRANCH LIVING

Issue of late Maj Hon Frederick Francis George Hennessy, MBE, yr son of 1st Baron; *b* 1906, *d* 1969: *m* 1932, Merritt Jean, who *d* 1976, da of late Alfred A. Longsdon:—

Peter Grant Auguste (Cradle House Farm, Wigginton, Banbury, Oxon) *b* 1944: *m* 1968, Sally Ann, yst da of Dr Clarence Laverne Johnson (*see* Royden, Bt, 1980 Edn), and has issue living, James George, *b* 1970, — Benedict John, *b* 1978, — Katherine Ann, *b* 1973, — Sophie Elizabeth, *b* 1981. ——— Maunagh Jean (Blacksmiths Cottage, Idbury, Oxon), *b* 1933: *m* 1953, Timothy William Jacques Leopold Koch de Gooreynd (*see* M Queensberry, colls, 1985 Edn), who *d* 1987, and has issue living, Peter Frederick Leopold, *b* 1958: *m* 1990, Carolyn Antonia N., yr da of Ambrose Parker, of Hereford Sq, SW7, and has issue living, Tamara Manuela *b* 1992, — Alexander Francis William, *b* 1969, — Stella Antoinette Jeanne, *b* 1954: *m* 1976, Kenneth Mannering, and has issue living, William *b* 1977, Olivia *b* 1981, Alexia *b* 1983, Miranda *b* 1986, — Manuela Enriqueta Maria, *b* 1957, — Annabel Maria Therese, *b* 1963: *m* 1990, Christopher Alexander. ——— Susan Jane (16 Paradise Walk, SW3 4JL), *b* 1938: *m* 1963, Charles Edward Morley-Fletcher, who *d* 19—, and has issue living, Michael Francis, *b* 1964: *m* 1991, Elisabeth Anne, elder da of David Quintin Gurney, of Bawdeswell Hall, Norfolk (*see* Boughey, Bt, colls, 1985 Edn), and has issue living, Oliver Charles *b* 1994, — Patrick Edward, *b* 1966, — Frederick Maurice, *b* 1969, — Caroline Angela Elisabeth, *b* 1971.

PREDECESSORS – **(1)** George Richard James Hennessy, OBE, son of late Richard Hennessy, of Bagnolet, Cognac, France; *b* 1877; High Sheriff of Hants 1910-11; European War 1915-18 as major King's Roy Rifle Corps and on Staff of 8th Div; was Parliamentary Private Sec (unpaid) to Min of Labour 1921-22, a Junior of the Treasury 1922-24, and 1924-25, Vice-Chamberlain of HM's Household 1925-28, Treasurer of HM's Household 1928-29 and (in National Govt) Sept to Nov 1931, and Vice-Chm Conservative and Unionist Party 1931-41; sat as MP for Winchester Div of Hampshire (*U*) 1918-31; *cr* a *Baronet* 1927, and *Baron Windlesham*, co Surrey (peerage of United Kingdom) 1937: *m* 1898, Ethel Mary, who *d* 1951, da of late Charles Reginald Wynter; *d* 1953; *s* by his el son **(2)** James Bryan George, 2nd Baron; *b* 1903; Brig late Grenadier Guards: *m* 1st, 1929, Angela Mary, who *d* 1956, da of late Julian Duggan; 2ndly, 1957, Pamela, formerly wife Dermot A. Dinan, who *m* 3rdly 1966, William Marsden Elverston-Trickett, da of Francis Kennedy; *d* 1962; *s* by his son **(3)** David James George, 3rd Baron and present peer.

WINDSOR, FAMILY AND HOUSE NAME OF THE ROYAL FAMILY.

Windsor, Viscount; son of Earl of Plymouth.

WINSTANLEY, BARONY OF (Winstanley) (Extinct 1993)

SONS LIVING OF LIFE BARON (*By 1st marriage*)

Hon Nicholas Clayton Platt, *b* 1945.

(By 2nd marriage)

Hon Stephen Woodhouse, *b* 1957.

DAUGHTER LIVING OF LIFE BARON (*By 1st marriage*)

Hon Diana Christine, *b* 1960.

WIDOW LIVING OF LIFE BARON

Joyce Mary (*Baroness Winstanley*), da of late Arthur Woodhouse: *m* 1955, as his 2nd wife, Baron Winstanley, MRCS, LRCP (Life Baron), who *d* 1993. *Residence* – Hare Hall, Dunnerdale, Broughton-in-Furness, Cumbria.

WINTERBOTTOM, BARONY OF (Winterbottom) (Extinct 1992)

SONS LIVING OF LIFE BARON (by 1st marriage)

Hon John (20 Pantile Rd, Oatlands Village, Weybridge, Surrey KT13 9PY), *b* 1940; *ed* Charterhouse, and Clare Coll, Camb: *m* 1980, Sheila Marie, da of Arthur Evershed, of 2 Beehive Close, Ferring, nr Worthing, W Sussex, and has issue living, Robert Ian, *b* 1981.

(by 2nd marriage)

Hon Dudley Walter Gordon (27 Coleherne Court, SW5 0DL), *b* 1946; *ed* Charterhouse, Kent Univ, and Wolfson Coll, Oxford; Sec Chelsea Arts Club: *m* 1st, 1978 (*m diss* 1991), Mirjana Bukvić; 2ndly, 19—, Lauren, da of Dr Brian Creighton Sproule, of Kincoppa, Elizabeth Bay Rd, Elizabeth Bay, Sydney, Australia, and has issue living (by 1st *m*), Thomas, *b* 1989, — Olga, *b* 1987.

Hon Graham Anthony, *b* 1948; *ed* Charterhouse, and RNC Dartmouth: *m* 1984 (*m diss* 19—), Caroline Joy, only da of Guy Bodgard Webster, of Cranbrook, Toddington, Beds.

DAUGHTER LIVING OF LIFE BARON (*By 2nd marriage*)

Hon Caroline Margaret Alyson, *b* 1950; *ed* Oxford Polytechnic.

WIDOW LIVING OF LIFE BARON

IRENE EVA (IRA) (*Baroness Winterbottom*), da of late Dr Walter Munk, of Berlin, and of Mount Carmel, Haifa: *m* 1944, as his 2nd wife, Baron Winterbotton (Life Baron), who *d* 1992. *Residence* – 9 Bisham Gdns, Highgate, N6 6DJ.

WINTERTON, EARL (Turnour) (Earl I 1766)
(Name pronounced "Turner")

(DONALD) DAVID TURNOUR, 8th Earl (has not yet established his right to the Peerages); *b* 13 Oct 1943; *s* 1991; *ed* Waterloo Lutheran Univ, Ont (BA): *m* 1968, Jill Pauline, da of late John Geddes Esplen, of Bala, Ont, and has issue.

Arms – Ermines, on a cross quarterly, pierced argent, four fers de moline sable. **Crest** – A lion passant guardant argent, holding in the dexter forepaw a fer de moline, sable. **Supporters** – Two lions argent, semée of fers de moline, sable. *Residence* – 6672 Mockingbird Lanes, Mississauga, Ont L5N 5K1.

DAUGHTERS LIVING

(*Lady*) Michele Susan, *b* 1973.
(*Lady*) Amy Elizabeth, *b* 1976.

BROTHERS LIVING

ROBERT CHARLES, *b* 30 Jan 1950: *m* 1st, 1974 (*m diss* 1976), Sheila, da of Garth H. Stocking, of Brampton, Ont; 2ndly, 1983, Patricia Ann, da of William Avery, of Cambridge, Ont, and has issue living (by 2nd *m*), Sarah Elizabeth, *b* 1983, — Meagan Ann, *b* 1985. *Residence* – 553 Duke St, Cambridge, Ont N3H 3T2, Canada.
Murray John, *b* 6 Feb 1951; *ed* Univ of Waterloo, Ont (OD 1975, MSc 1979): *m* 1980, Brenda Jill, da of late Dr James Alexander Tremayne Behan, of Orillia, Ont, and has issue living, Jonathan Winterton Behan, *b* 18 April 1985. *Residence* – 4 Lansdowne Rd South, Cambridge, Ont N1S 2T3, Canada.

To be, rather than seem to be

SISTER LIVING OF SEVENTH EARL

Margaret Ethel, *b* 1917: *m* 1939, Donald S. McGeary, of 514-2511 Lakeshore Rd W, Oakville, Ont, Canada, L6L 6L9, and has issue living, Donald Garth, *b* 1941: *m* 1975, Irene Claire, da of George Woodruff, of Niagara Falls, Ont, Canada, — Robert Wayne, *b* 1944: *m* 1974, Karen Louise, da of Walter Warms, of 56 Thatcher Drive, Winnipeg, Canada, and has issue living, Whitney Anne *b* 1987, Kaitlin Diane *b* 1990, — Hugh Gordon, *b* 1951: — James Douglas, *b* 1954: *m* 1976, Elaine Leslie, da of Gilbert Aulis, of 853 Cathedral Av, Winnipeg, Manitoba, Canada, and has issue living, Matthew James *b* 1980, Jordon Garth *b* 1983, Devon Elaine *b* 1985, — Wendy Louise, *b* 1948: *m* 1st, 1968 (*m diss* 1977), Miles Stanton Cullum; 2ndly, 1978, Walter Orawski, (RR4 Wingham, Ont, Canada), and has issue living, (by 2nd *m*) Timon Andrew *b* 1981, Nadia Katherine *b* 1978, Lara Jackolynn *b* 1986.

MOTHER LIVING

Evelyn Isabel, da of late Dr Charles Albert Oulton, of Saskatoon, Sask: *m* 1941, (Cecil) Noel Turnour, DFM, CD, RO, FAAO (yr brother of 7th Earl), who *d* 1987. *Residence* – 47 Kenmore Av, Cambridge, Ont N1S 3H4, Canada.

WIDOW LIVING OF SEVENTH EARL

MARION ELEANOR (*Marion, Countess Winterton*), da of late Arthur Phillips, of Stirling, Ont: *m* 1971, as his 2nd wife, the 7th Earl, who *d* 1991. *Residence* – 1326 55th St, Delta, BC, Canada.

COLLATERAL BRANCHES LIVING

Grandchildren of late John Horatio Turnour, 5th son of late Rev Hon Adolphus Augustus Turnour, 3rd son of 2nd Earl:—
Issue of late Keppel Arthur Turnour, *b* 1856, *d* 1930: *m* 1878, Margaret, who *d* 1901, da of late C. C. Wallace, Greenbank, Isle of Bute:—
Donald Winterton, *b* 1883. —— James Owen, *b* 1884. —— Keppel Ernest, *b* 1885. —— Alice, *b* 1881: *m* 1910, Cecil Henry Henty. —— Sybil Ruth, *b* 1890. *Residence* –
Issue of late Edward Edmund Hewitt Turnour, *b* 1864, *d* 1915: *m* 1900, Mary Ann, da of Duncan C. Milne, of Adelaide, S. Australia:—
Marjorie Balman Winterton, *b* 1906.

PREDECESSORS – (1) EDWARD TURNOUR Garth, assumed in 1744 by Roy licence the surname of Turnour; *cr Baron Winterton*, of Gort, co Galway (peerage of Ireland) 1761, and *Viscount Turnour* and *Earl Winterton* (peerage of Ireland) 1766; *d* 1788; *s* by his son (2) EDWARD TURNOUR, 2nd Earl; *d* 1831; *s* by his son (3) EDWARD, 3rd Earl; *d* 1833; *s* by his son (4) EDWARD, 4th Earl; *b* 1810: *m* 1832, Maria, who *d* 1904, da of Sir Peter Pole, 2nd Bt; *d* 1879; *s* by his son (5) EDWARD, 5th Earl, *b* 1837: *m* 1882, Lady Georgiana Susan Hamilton, who *d* 1913, da of 1st Duke of Abercorn, KG; *d* 1907; *s* by his only son (6) EDWARD, TD, PC, 6th Earl, *b* 1883; Major TA Reserve, Sussex Yeo; Under-Sec of State for India 1922-4, and 1924-29, Chancellor of Duchy of Lancaster 1937-9, Dep Sec of State for Air and Vice-Pres of Air Council 1938, Assist to Home Sec 1938-9, and Paymaster Gen 1939; MP for Horsham Div of Sussex (C) 1904-18, for Horsham and Worthing Div 1918-45, and for W Sussex 1945-51; *cr Baron Turnour* (peerage of UK) 1952: *m* 1924, Hon Cecilia Monica Wilson, who *d* 1974, da of 2nd Baron Nunburnholme; *d* 1962, when the UK Barony (*cr* 1952) became ext; *s* by his kinsman (7) ROBERT CHAD (el son of Cecil Turnour, grandson of Charles Chad Turnour, el son of Rev Hon Adolphus Augustus Turnour, 3rd son of 2nd Earl), 7th Earl, *b* 1915; Flight-Sergeant RCAF, with Canadian NATO Force Sqdn, Sardinia 1957-58, served 1939-45 War: *m* 1st, 1941,

Kathleen Ella, who *d* 1969, da of D. B. Whyte, of Saskatoon, Sask; 2ndly, 1971, Marion Eleanor, da of late Arthur Phillips, of Stirling, Ont; *d* 1991; *s* by his nephew **(8)** DONALD DAVID (eldest son of late (Cecil) Noel Turnour, DFM, CD, RO, FAAO, yr brother of 7th Earl), 8th Earl and present peer; also Viscount Turnour and Baron Winterton.

Winton, Earl of; title borne by Earl of Eglinton.

WISE, BARON (Wise) (Baron UK 1951)

JOHN CLAYTON WISE, 2nd Baron; *b* 11 June 1923; *s* 1968; a Farmer: *m* 1946, Margaret Annie, da of Frederick Victor Snead, of Banbury, and has issue.
Residence – Lynn Cottage, Castle Hill, Hemyock, Devon EX15 3RU. *Club* – Farmers'.

SONS LIVING

Hon CHRISTOPHER JOHN CLAYTON, *b* 19 March 1949; *ed* Norwich Sch and Southampton Univ (BSc); PhD. *Residence* – Demeter, Woodmancote, Cirencester, Glos.
Hon Martin Highfield, *b* 1950; *ed* Norwich Sch and Bristol Univ (MB, ChB, MD); FRCS. *Residence* – 3 Rosedale Close, Titchfield, Fareham, Hants.

SISTERS LIVING

Hon Joan Mary, *b* 1912: *m* 1938, John Reginald Wood, of Small Acre, Hewish, Weston-super-Mare, Somerset, and has issue living, Michael George, *b* 1939, — David Clayton, *b* 1946, — Mary Janet, *b* 1947.
Hon Jean Phyllis, *b* 1914: *m* 1939, Lieut-Col John Patrick Turrill, OBE, TD, RA, and has issue living, John Ewen, *b* 1948, — Judith Elizabeth, *b* 1946, — Ruth Eleanor, *b* 1947. *Residence* – 12 Woburn Close, Caversham, Reading.
Hon Eileen Ellen, *b* 1916: *m* 1940, Sq Ldr Gerald Edmund Hastings, RAF, and has issue living, Eileen Mary, *b* 1948, — Bridget Talmine, *b* 1950. *Residence* – Bridge Cottage, Rousden, Lyme Regis, Dorset.

PREDECESSORS – **(1)** FREDERICK JOHN Wise, son of Edward Wise, of Bury St Edmunds; *b* 1887; MP for King's Lynn (*Lab*) 1945-51; *cr Baron Wise*, of King's Lynn, co Norfolk (peerage of UK); 1951: *m* 1911, Kate Elizabeth, da of John Michael Sturgeon, of Horringer, Bury St Edmunds; *d* 1968; *s* by his son **(2)** JOHN CLAYTON, 2nd Baron, and present peer.

Wodehouse, Baron; son of Earl of Kimberley.

WOLFENDEN, BARONY OF (Wolfenden) (Extinct 1985)

SON LIVING OF LIFE BARON

Hon Daniel Mark, *b* 1942: *m* 1972, Sally Frankel, and has issue, two sons.

DAUGHTERS LIVING OF LIFE BARON

Hon Priscilla, *b* 1937: *m* 1959, Lt-Col F. L. Dainty, of Thump Head Cottage, 22 Boobery, Sampford Peverell, Devon.
Hon Deborah, *b* 1943: *m* 1966, Francis Eveleigh, of Boehill, Uplowman, nr Tiverton, Devon EX16 7DZ, and has issue, one son and one da.

WIDOW LIVING OF LIFE BARON

EILEEN LE MESSURIER (*Baroness Wolfenden*), 2nd da of A. J. Spilsbury: *m* 1932, Baron Wolfenden, CBE (Life Peer), who *d* 1985. *Residence* – The White House, Westcott, nr Dorking, Surrey.

WOLFSON, BARON (Wolfson) (Life Baron 1985, Bt (UK) 1962, of St Marylebone, co London)

LEONARD GORDON WOLFSON, *Life Baron* and 2nd *Baronet*, son of Sir Isaac Wolfson, 1st Bt; *b* 11 Nov 1927; *s* his father in his baronetcy, 1991; *ed* King's Sch, Worcester; Hon Fellow St Catherine's Coll, Oxford, Wolfson Coll, Camb, Wolfson Coll, Oxford, Worcester Coll, Oxford, Univ Coll, London, and London Sch of Hygiene and Tropical Medicine; Member of Court of Benefactors R Soc of Medicine; Trustee Imperial War Museum since 1988; Hon FRCP 1977, Hon PhD Tel Aviv 1971, Hebrew Univ 1978, DCL Oxon 1972, Hon LLD Strathclyde 1972, Dundee 1979, Cantab 1982, London 1982, Hon DSc Hull 1977, Wales 1984, Hon DHL Bar Ilan Univ 1983; Patron R Coll of Surgeons; Chm and a Founder Trustee Wolfson Foundation; Chm Great Universal Stores, and Burberrys Ltd; *cr* Kt 1977, and *Baron Wolfson*, of Marylebone in the City of Westminster (Life Baron) 1985: *m* 1st, 1949 (*m diss* 1991), Ruth, da of Ernest A. Sterling, of London; 2ndly, 1991, Mrs Estelle Jackson widow of Michael Jackson, and has issue by 1st *m*.

Arms – Per pale dovetailed vert and or, on a chevron counterchanged between in chief two roses, also or and gules respectively, and in base an ancient hand bell proper, two pears sable and gold. **Crest** – In front of two rods of Æsculapius in saltire proper, a touch inflamed also proper. *Address* – 18-22 Haymarket, SW1Y 4DQ.

DAUGHTERS LIVING *(By 1st marriage)*

Hon Janet Frances, *b* 1952: *m* 1st, 1972 (*m diss* 1989), Michael Philip Green; 2ndly, 1990, Gilbert de Botton, and has issue living (by 1st *m*), Rebecca Sarah Wolfson, *b* 1974, — Catherine Victoria Wolfson, *b* 1976. *Address* – c/o GAM, 12 St James's Place, SW1A 1NX.

Hon Laura, *b* 1954: *m* 1975, Barry Stephen Townsley, and has issue living, Charles Ralph Wolfson, *b* 1984, — Alexandra Jane Wolfson, *b* 1977, — Georgina Kate Wolfson, *b* 1979, — Isabella Edith wolfson, *b* 1994. *Address* – c/o Townsley & Co, 44 Worship St, EC2A 2JT.

Hon Deborah, *b* 1959: *m* 19—, G— Davis. *Residence* –

Hon Elizabeth, *b* 1966: *m* 1991, Daniel Peltz, son of Dr Sam Pletz, of W1, and has issue living, Max, *b* 19—, — Francesca Edith, *b* 1992. *Residence* –

WOLFSON OF SUNNINGDALE, BARON (Wolfson) (Life Baron 1991)

DAVID WOLFSON, son of Charles Wolfson; *b* 9 Nov 1935; *ed* Clifton, Trin Coll, Camb (MA), and Stanford Univ, California (MBA); Hon Fell Hugh's Hall, Camb 1989, Hon FRCR 1978, Hon FRCOG 1989; Great Universal Stores 1960-78 and since 1993 (Dir 1973-78 and since 1993); Sec to Shadow Cabinet 1978-79, Chief of Staff, Political Office, 10 Downing St 1979-85; Chm Alexon Group plc (formerly Steinberg Group plc) 1982-86, and Next plc since 1990; non-Exec Dir Stewart Wrightson Holdings plc 1985-87, and Next since 1989; *cr* Knt 1984, and *Baron Wolfson of Sunningdale*, of Trevose, co Cornwall (Life Baron) 1991: *m* 1st, 1962 (*m diss* 1967), Patricia Elizabeth, da of late Louis Rawlings; 2ndly, 1967, Susan E., da of Hugh Davis, and has issue by 2nd *m*.

Address – c/o House of Lords, SW1A 0PW.

SONS LIVING *(By 2nd marriage)*

Hon Simon Adam, *b* 1967.
Hon Andrew Daniel, *b* 1969.

DAUGHTER LIVING *(By 2nd marriage)*

Hon Deborah Sarah, *b* 1973.

Wolmer, Viscount; grandson of Earl of Selborne.

WOLVERTON, BARON (Glyn) (Baron UK 1869)

CHRISTOPHER RICHARD GLYN, 7th Baron; *b* 5 Oct 1938; *s* 1988; *ed* Eton; FRICS: *m* 1st, 1961 (*m diss* 1967), Carolyn Jane, yr da of late Antony Noel Hunter, of 33 Brompton Sq, SW3; 2ndly, 1975 (*m diss* 1989), Mrs Frances Sarah Elisabeth Stuart Black, eldest da of Robert Worboys Skene, of 12 Kensington Gate, W8; 3rdly, 1990, Gillian Konig, and has issue by 1st *m*.

Arms – Argent, an eagle displayed with two heads sable, guttée d'or. **Crest** – An eagle's head, erased sable, guttée d'or; in the beak an escallop argent. **Supporters** – On either side an eagle with wings elevated sable, guttée d'or, gorged with a collar gemel or, and holding in the beak an escallop argent. *Residence* – 97 Hurlingham Rd, SW6.

Firm to my trust

DAUGHTERS LIVING (By 1st marriage)

Hon Sara-Jane, *b* 1963: *m* 1993, John Francis O'Callaghan, yr son of James O'Callaghan, of co Clare.
Hon Amanda Camilla, *b* 1966.

BROTHER LIVING

Hon ANDREW JOHN, *b* 30 June 1943; *ed* Eton, and New Coll, Oxford (MA), Fellow of Corpus Christi Coll, Oxford: *m* 1st, 1965 (*m diss* 1986), Celia Laws; 2ndly, 1986, Wendy Carlin, and has issue living (by 1st *m*), Miles John, *b* 1966, — Lucy Abigail, *b* 1968, — (by 2nd *m*) Jonathan, *b* 1990, — Tessa, *b* 1987. *Residence* – 167 Divinity Rd, Oxford.

SISTERS LIVING

Hon Susan, *b* 1940: *m* 1962, Nicholas Greenaway Mills, yr son of Lt-Col Robert Breynton Yarnton Mills, OBE, MC, of Barrington Grove, Burford, Oxon, and has issue living, Charlotte Sophia, *b* 1964: *m* 1991, Capt James D. T. Bainbridge, 16th/5th Royal Lancers, yr son of late David Bainbridge, of Hurworth Hall, W Darlington, and has issue living, Charlotte Isabelle Greenaway *b* 1993, — Maria Louise Greenaway, *b* 1967. *Residence* – Lower Upton Farm, Burford, Oxon.
Hon Joanna Caroline, *b* 1955.

UNCLE LIVING (brother of 6th Baron)

Hilary Beaujolais, *b* 1916; *ed* Eton; Capt RASC; Man Dir Gallaher Ltd (ret 1976): *m* 1938, Caroline, yst da of late William Perkins Bull, QC, of Lorne Hall, Rosedale, Toronto, Canada, and has issue living, James Hilary, *b* 1939; *ed* Eton; Man Dir N Borneo Timbers; *m* 1964 (*m diss* 1983), Lucinda March, da of W/Cmdr Gordon Stanley Keith Haywood, RAF (ret) (*see* E Darnley), and has issue living Caspar Hilary Gordon *b* 1969, Marina Jane *b* 1966: *m* 1991, Robert P. Furniss-Roe (14 rue des Renaudes, Paris 75017, France), son of late Henry Furniss-Roe, of Bishopsteignton, Devon (and has issue living, Olivia Sophie *b* 1993), — (Caroline) Ann, *b* 1941: *m* 1st, 1968 (*m diss* 1979), Padmanabh Vijai Pillai, yr son of Dr P. P. Pillai, of New Delhi, 2ndly, 1980, Gowri Shankar, of Castle Hill Cottage, Boothby Graffoe, Lincoln, — Sarah, *b* 1948: *m* 1st, 1967 (*m diss* 1971), Richard Patrick King, only son of late Richard Francis King, of Assam India; 2ndly, 1979 (*m diss* 1982), Nicholas John Turner, son of John Turner; 3rdly, 1984, Robert Gino Henson, of Ermine House, Boothby Graffoe, Lincoln LN5 0LD, son of late John Gordon (Gino) Henson, of Ermine House, Boothby Graffoe, and has issue living (by 2nd *m*), James William Hilary *b* 1980, (by 3rd *m*) Jessica Ann Frances *b* 1985, Cecilia Sarah *b* 1990.

WIDOW LIVING OF SIXTH BARON

AUDREY MARGARET (*prefers to be known as Mrs Audrey Glyn*), da of late Richard Stubbs, of Haseley Manor, Oxford: *m* 1937, Maj the 6th Baron, CBE, who *d* 1988. *Residence* – Fennels, Long Crendon, Aylesbury, Bucks.

COLLATERAL BRANCHES LIVING

Granddaughter of late Sir Francis Maurice Grosvenor Glyn, KCMG, 2nd son of Maurice George Carr Glyn, yr son of Hon Pascoe Charles Glyn, 6th son of 1st Baron:—
Issue of late Jeremy Christopher Glyn, *b* 1930, *d* 1984: *m* 1956, Robina Elspeth (Upton Farm House, Upton, Andover, Hants), da of Sir George Arthur Harford, 2nd Bt:—
Lucinda Mary, *b* 1958.

Granddaughter of late Maurice George Carr Glyn (ante):—
Issue of late Pascoe Anthony George Glyn, *b* 1911, *d* 1935: *m* 1934, Katharine Florita Rosehill, Lawrenny, Kilgetty, Dyfed (who *m* 2ndly, 1936, Patrick Lort-Phillips, Lieut Grenadier Guards, who *d* 1979), da of late Lieut-Col Arthur Morton Grenfell, DSO (V Cobham, colls):—
Mary Georgiana, *b* 1935: *m* 1954 (*m diss* 1963), Lt-Cdr John William Talbot Lewes, RN, and *d* 1992, leaving issue (*see* E Shrewsbury, colls).

PREDECESSORS – (1) GEORGE CARR GLYN, 4th son of Sir Richard Carr Glyn, 1st Bt; *b* 1797; was a partner in the banking house of Glyn, Mills, Currie and Co, and Chairman of the London and North Western Railway; *cr Baron Wolverton*, of Wolverton, co Bucks (peerage of United Kingdom) 1869: *m* 1823, Marianne, da of late Pascoe Grenfell, of Taplow Court, Bucks; *d* 1873; *s* by his son (2) GEORGE GRENFELL, PC, 2nd Baron, *b* 1824; sat as MP for Shaftesbury (*L*) 1857-73, and was successively Joint Sec to Treasury, Paymaster-Gen, and Postmaster-Gen: *m* 1848, Georgiana Maria, who *d* 1894, da of Rev George Tufnell, of Uffington, Berks; *d* 1887; *s* by his nephew (3) HENRY RICHARD, 3rd Baron, *b* 1861; *dsp* 1888; *s* by his brother (4) FREDERICK, 4th Baron, *b* 1864; a Partner in the Metropolitan banking firm of Glyn, Mills and Co; a Lord-in-Waiting to Queen Victoria 1891-3, and Vice-Chamberlain of the Household to King Edward VII 1902-5: *m* 1895, Lady Edith Amelia Ward, CBE, who *d* 1956, da of 1st Earl of Dudley; *d* 1932; *s* by his son (5) NIGEL REGINALD VICTOR, 5th Baron, *b* 1904; Capt RA (TA); *d* 1986; *s* by his kinsman (6) JOHN PATRICK RIVERSDALE, CBE, 6th Baron, *b* 1913; Maj Gren Gds, served 1939-45 War (wounded); Dir Glyn, Mills & Co; Chm Yorkshire Bank Ltd: *m* 1937, Audrey Margaret, da of late Richard Stubbs, of Haseley Manor, Oxford; *d* 1988; *s* by his elder son (7) CHRISTOPHER RICHARD, 7th Baron and present peer.

Woodstock, Viscount; son of Earl of Portland

WOOLF, BARON (Woolf) (Life Baron 1992)

HARRY KENNETH WOOLF, PC, son of late Alexander Woolf; *b* 2 May 1933; *ed* Fettes, and Univ Coll, London (LLB, Fellow 1981); Hon LLD Buckingham, Bristol and London Univs, Hon Fellow Leeds Polytechnic (now Univ); commn'd 15/19th Royal Hussars 1954, Capt Army Legal Ser 1955; Bar Inner Temple 1954, Recorder Crown Court 1972-79, Junior Counsel Inland Revenue 1973-74, First Treasury Junior Counsel in Common Law 1974-79, Judge of High Court of Justice (Queen's Bench Div) 1979-86, Presiding Judge SE Circuit 1981-84, Lord Justice of Appeal 1986-92, since when a Lord of Appeal in Ordinary; Member Senate of Bar and Bench 1981-85; Chm Lord Chancellor's Advisory Cttee on Legal Educn 1987-90, Middx Justice's Advsy Cttee 1987-90, and Board of Management Inst of Advanced Legal Studies 1986-94; Chm Butler Trust since 1992; Pres Law Teachers' Assocn 1985-90, Central Council for Jewish Social Services since 1988, and W London Magistrates' Assocn 1987-92 Chm St Mary's Hosp Special Trustees since 1993; Gov Oxford Centre for Hebrew Studies since 1988; *cr* Knt 1979, PC 1986, and *Baron Woolf*, of Barnes, London Borough of Richmond (Life Baron) 1992: *m* 1961, Marguerite, da of George Sassoon, and has issue.
Address – House of Lords, SW1A 0PW. *Club* – Garrick.

SONS LIVING

Hon Jeremy Richard George, *b* 1962; *ed* Clifton, Sussex Univ, and Trinity Hall, Camb.
Hon Andrew James David, *b* 1965; *ed* Clifton, St Paul's, Southampton Univ, and Woolfson Coll, Camb.
Hon Eliot Charles Anthony, *b* 1967; *ed* Eton, and Robinson Coll, Camb.

WOOLLEY, BARONY OF (Woolley) (Extinct 1986)

SONS LIVING OF LIFE BARON (*By 1st marriage*)

Hon William Graham (Hatton Hall, Hatton Heath, Cheshire), *b* 1927: *m* 1955, Joan, who *d* 1974, da of Ralph Thomas Rowlands, of Connah's Quay, Flintshire; 2ndly, 1984, Shirley Ann, da of Thomas Lega, of Bulolo, Papua, New Guinea, and has issue.
Hon Harold Ewart (1350, Laurier Av, Vancouver, BC, Canada), *b* 1929; MD, FRCS(C): *m* 1954, Margaret, yr da of Alderman T. S. Bennett, JP, of Worcester, and has issue.
Hon David Jeffs (Fernhill Farm, 4222 216th St, RR14 Langley, BC, Canada V3A 7R2), *b* 1934; Capt, Air Canada: *m* 1958, Freda Constance, da of Alfred W. S. Walker, of Barrow-in-Furness, and has issue.
Hon Peter Jeffs (2660 Queens Av, W Vancouver, BC, Canada), *b* (twin) 1934: MA, CA: *m* 1960, Lois, da of Edward Chanter, of Tiverton, Devon, and has issue.

DAUGHTERS LIVING OF LIFE BARON (*By 2nd marriage*)

Hon Hazel Eleanor, *b* 1938; JP: *m* 1961, William David Harper, MA, MB, BChir, of Clogwyn y Gwin, Rhyd Ddu, Beddgelert, Gwynedd, and has issue.
Hon Christine Maralyn, *b* 1946: *m* 1st, 1970 (*m diss* 1980), Barrie Scott Morgan, BSc, PhD; 2ndly, 1984, Lt-Cdr David Rodwell, MIEE, CEng, RN, of 35 Northumberland Av, Wanstead, E12.

WOOLTON, EARL OF (Marquis) (Earl UK 1956)

By fortitude and courage it shall be given

SIMON FREDERICK MARQUIS, 3rd Earl, *b* 24 May 1958; *s* 1969: *m* 1987, Hon Sophie Frederika, only child of 3rd Baron Birdwood, and has issue.

Arms – Sable, on a bend engrailed between two garbs or a rose gules barbed and seeded proper between two lions rampant of the field. Crest – Suspended from and between the antlers of a stag proper, a stirrup and leather. Supporters – On either side a lion rampant or, gorged with a riband azure, pendent therefrom by a chain also or, an escutcheon azure charged with a liver bird argent.
Residences – Auchnacree House, Glenogil, by Forfar, Angus DD8 3SX; 18 Lower Addison Gdns, W14 8BQ.

DAUGHTERS LIVING

Lady Olivia Alice, *b* 1990.
Lady Constance Elizabeth, *b* 1991.

SISTER LIVING

Lady Alexandra Susan, *b* 1961: *m* 1984, Philip Roger Chandos Elletson, of The Old Rectory, Huish, nr Marlborough, Wilts, son of Roger Elletson, of The Grey House, Forton, Lancs, and has issue living, Edward Roger Chandos, *b* 1990, — Laura Katherine Elizabeth, *b* 1985, — Sophia Josephine Rose, *b* 1986.

WIDOW LIVING OF SECOND EARL

CECILY JOSEPHINE (*Countess Lloyd-George of Dwyfor*) (Ffynone, Boncath, Pembrokeshire; 47 Burton Court, SW3), elder da of Maj Sir Alexander Penrose Gordon-Cumming, MC, 5th Bt: *m* 1st, 1957, as his 2nd wife, 2nd Earl of Woolton, who *d* 1969; 2ndly, 1969 (*m diss* 1974), 3rd Baron Forres, who *d* 1978; 3rdly, 1982, as his 2nd wife, 3rd Earl Lloyd-George of Dwyfor.

PREDECESSORS – (1) Sir FREDERICK JAMES Marquis, CH, PC, DL, son of Thomas Robert Marquis, of Kirkham, Lancs; b 1883; ed Manchester Gram Sch, and Manchester Univ; Managing Dir and Chm of Lewis's Investment Trust and Asso Cos 1926-39 and 1945-51 and Hon Pres 1951-64; Min of Food 1940-43; Min of Reconstruction, and Member of War Cabinet 1943-45, Lord Pres of Council May to July 1945, and 1951-52, and Chancellor of Duchy of Lancaster 1952-55 (and Min of Materials 1953-54); Chm of Conservative Party 1946-55; Chancellor of Manchester Univ 1944-64; cr Baron Woolton, of Liverpool, co Lancaster (peerage of UK) 1939, Viscount Woolton, of Liverpool, co Lancaster (peerage of UK) 1953, and Earl of Woolton, and Viscount Walberton, of Walberton, co Sussex (peerage of UK) 1956: m 1st, 1912, Maud, who d 1961, da of Thomas Smith, of Manchester; 2ndly, 1962, Margaret Eluned, MB, ChB, who d 1983, only da of Richard Thomas; d 1964; s by his only son **(2)** ROGER DAVID, 2nd Earl, b 1922: m 1st, 1946 (m diss 1953), Hon Lucia Edith Lawson, only da of 4th Baron Burnham; 2ndly, 1957, (Cecily) Josephine (who m 2ndly, 1969 (m diss 1974), 3rd Baron Forres, and 3rdly, 1982, as his 2nd wife, 3rd Earl Lloyd-George of Dwyfor), elder da of Maj Sir Alexander Penrose Gordon-Cumming, MC, 5th Bt; d 1969; s by his only son **(3)** SIMON FREDERICK, 3rd Earl and present Peer; also Viscount Woolton, Viscount Walberton, and Baron Woolton.

Worlingham, Baron, title of Earl of Gosford of Roll of HL.

Worsley, Baron; son of Earl of Yarborough.

WRAXALL, BARON (Gibbs) (Baron UK 1928)

GEORGE RICHARD LAWLEY GIBBS, 2nd Baron; b 16 May 1928: s 1931; ed Eton, and RMA; late Maj N Somerset and Bristol Yeo, and late Lt Coldstream Guards.

Arms – Argent, three battle-axes erect sable within a bordure nebuly of the last. **Crest** – A dexter arm embowed in armour, the hand in a gauntlet proper bearing a battle-axe bendwise sinister sable. **Supporters** – On either side a St Kilda sheep proper, each charged on the shoulder with a portcullis chained or. **Seat** – Tyntesfield, Wraxall, Bristol BS19 1NU. **Clubs** – Royal Automobile, Cavalry and Guards'.

Tenacious of purpose

BROTHER LIVING

Hon Sir EUSTACE HUBERT BEILBY, KCVO, CMG (Coddenham House, Coddenham, nr Ipswich; Pratt's and Beefsteak Clubs), b 3 July 1929; ed Eton, and Ch Ch, Oxford; HM Diplomatic Serv 1954-85; CMG 1982, KCVO 1986: m 1957, Evelyn Veronica, only da of late Sydney K. Scott, of Reydon Grove Farm, Southwold, Suffolk, and has issue living, Antony Hubert, b 1958: m 1988, Caroline Jane, da of late Arthur Gould, — Andrew Christopher, b 1965, — Jonathan Charles William, b 1969, — Miranda Caroline, b 1961: m 1993, Andrew David Fox Jolliffe, only son of B. R. Jolliffe, of Bedford, — Alexandra Mary Henrietta, b 1971.

HALF-SISTER LIVING

Hon Doreen Albinia de Burgh, b 1913: m 1937, Charles Bathurst Norman, Bar-at-Law, and has issue living, George Alfred Bathurst (14 Orchard Rise, Richmond, Surrey), b 1939; Bar Inner Temple 1961; Metropolitan Stipendiary Magistrate 1981, Circuit Judge 1986: m 1st, 1967 (m diss 1967), Prudence Veronica, da of F. H. Keenlyside, of Salisbury, Rhodesia; 2ndly, 1973, Susan Elizabeth, da of James Ball, of 46 Park Av, Bromley, Kent, and has issue living (by 2nd m), Charles Canning Bathurst b 1979, Harriet Anstice Bathurst b 1977. — Victoria Mary Bathurst, b 1940: m 1st, 1961 (m diss 1967), Raymond Edward Barthop, late Capt Northamptonshire Regt: 2ndly, 1977, Patrick Giles Andrew Eyre, of 8 Cheyne Gdns, SW3 (see B Acton), and has issue living (by 1st m), Nicola Vivien b 1964, (by 2nd m) Toby Charles Peter b 1983. Residence – Villa Villetri, Vallée de Vaux, Jersey.

PREDECESSORS – (1) Rt Hon GEORGE ABRAHAM Gibbs, el son of late Antony Gibbs, of Tyntesfield, Bristol, and 16 Hyde Park Gardens, W; b 1873; was Parliamentary Private Sec to Sec of State for the Colonies (Rt Hon W. H. Long, MP) and Govt Whip in House of Commons 1917-21, and Treasurer of HM's Household April 1921 to Jan 1924 and Nov 1924 to Jan 1928; MP for W Div of Bristol (U) Jan 1906 to Jan 1928; cr PC 1923 and Baron Wraxall, of Clyst St George, co Devon (peerage of United Kingdom) 1928: m 1st, 1901, Victoria Florence de Burgh Long, CBE, who d 1920, el da of Rt Hon Walter Hume Long, MP (afterwards 1st Viscount Long of Wraxall); 2ndly, 1927, Hon Ursula Mary Lawley, OBE, RRC, who d 1979, da of 6th Baron Wenlock; d 1931; s by his son **(2)** GEORGE RICHARD LAWLEY, 2nd Baron and present peer.

WRENBURY, BARON (Buckley) (Baron UK 1915)

JOHN BURTON BUCKLEY, 3rd Baron; *b* 18 June 1927; *s* 1940; *ed* Eton, and Kings Coll, Camb (MA); Solicitor 1952; a partner in the legal firm of Freshfields, of Grindall House, 25 Newgate St, EC1 1956-74, since when of Thomson Snell & Passmore, of 3 Lonsdale Gdns, Tunbridge Wells; Dep Legal Adviser to National Trust 1955-56: *m* 1st, 1956 (*m diss* 1961), Carolyn Joan Maule, da of Col Ian Burn-Murdoch, OBE, of Gartincaber, Doune, Perthshire; 2ndly, 1961, Penelope Sara Frances, da of Edward Fort, of The White House, Sixpenny Handley, Dorset, and has issue by 2nd *m*.

Arms – Azure, a chevron cottised between two stags' heads cabossed in chief and a garb in base all or, on a chief engrailed ermine a buckle between two crosses patée fitchée gules. **Crest** – On a mount vert a demi-stag at gaze gules, attired and gorged with a collar, a chain attached reflexed over the back or, supporting a garb of the last. **Supporters** – On either side a buck at gaze gules, collared, attired, and chained or.
Residence – Oldcastle, Dallington, near Heathfield, Sussex. *Club* – Oriental.

SON LIVING (By 2nd marriage)

Hon WILLIAM EDWARD, *b* 19 June 1966.

DAUGHTERS LIVING (By 2nd marriage)

Hon Elizabeth Margaret, *b* 1964; resumed her maiden name 1991: *m* 1st, 1988 (*m diss* 1991), Capt Andrew Murray Macnaughton, Argyll and Sutherland Highers, elder son of R. M. Macnaughton, of Edinburgh; 2ndly, 1993, Dr Timothy Grey Morgan, son of Prof Colyn Grey Morgan, of Mayals, Swansea.

Hon Katherine Lucy, *b* 1968.

SISTER LIVING

Hon Mary Graham, *b* 1929: *m* 1961, John Richard Seymour Homan, CBE, of 30 High St, Ticehurst, Sussex, and has issue living, Robert Seymour, *b* 1964, — Frances Mary, *b* 1967, — Rosalind Clare *b* 1969.

UNCLES LIVING (Sons of 1st Baron)

Rt Hon Sir Denys Burton, MBE, *b* 1906; *ed* Eton, and Trin Coll, Oxford (MA, Hon Fellow); Bar Lincoln's Inn 1928, and a Bencher 1949; Pro-Treasurer Lincoln's Inn 1967, and Treasurer 1969; Master, Merchant Taylors' Co 1972; a CStJ; Junior Treasury Counsel 1949-60, a Judge of High Court of Justice (Chancery Div) 1960-70, and a Lord Justice of Appeal 1970-81; a Judge of Restrictive Practices Court 1962-70 (Pres 1968-70), a Member of Law Reform Cttee 1963-73, and Pres of Senate of four Inns of Court 1970-72; has American Medal of Freedom; 1939-45 War a Maj RAOC; MBE (Mil) 1945; Knt 1960; PC 1970: *m* 1932, Gwendolen Jane, who *d* 1985, da of late Sir Robert Armstrong-Jones, CBE, MD, FRCP, FRCS, DSc, of Plas Dinas, Caerns, and has issue living, Jane Gwenllian Armstrong (*Lady Slade*), *b* 1936: *m* 1958, Rt Hon Sir Christopher John Slade, of 16 Elthiron Rd, SW6, and has issue living, Richard Penkivil *b* 1963: *m* 1994, Lucy Jane, da of George Cacanas, of Upper Swainswick, Bath, Lucinda Jane *b* 1959: *m* 1985, Christopher Charles Tite, son of Leslie J. Tite, of Wandsworth, SW18 (and has issue living, William Christopher James *b* 1990, Oliver Henry Charles *b* 1992, Serena Catherine Lucinda *b* 1994), Victoria Albinia *b* 1962: *m* 1988, Hugh J. Henderson-Cleland, son of J. G. W. Henderson-Cleland, of Clapham, SW4 (and has issue living Archibald Hugh *b* 1994, Georgia *b* 1989, Charlotte May *b* 1991), Amelia Caroline *b* 1966: *m* 1992, Capt Matthew Jackson, RE, son of Cdr M. F. Jackson, RN, of Old Portsmouth, Hants, — Catherine Elizabeth Armstrong, *b* 1938: *m* 1961, Charles Kenneth Roylance Nunneley, of 19 Rosaville Rd, SW6 7BN, and of Fyfield House, Pewsey, Wilts, and has issue living, Luke James Charles (40 Kilmaine Rd, SW6) *b* 1963: *m* 1990, Katerine Ruth, 2nd da of B. F. Panter, of Walton-on-Thames, Surrey (and has issue living, Rebecca *b* 1992), Alice Georgina *b* 1964: *m* 1989, Nicholas Bruce Chapple, of 6 Green Lane Cottages, Churt, Surrey (and has issue living, Ben *b* 1994), Clare Sabina *b* 1967, Frances Mary *b* 1969, — Marion Miranda Armstrong, *b* 1945. *Residences* – Flat 6, 105 Onslow Sq, SW7; Stream Farm, Dallington, Sussex. *Clubs* – Brooks's, Beefsteak.

COLLATERAL BRANCH LIVING

Issue of late Hon Colin Burton Buckley, MB, BCh, *b* 1899, *d* 1981: *m* 1925, Evelyn Joyce, who *d* 1987, da of Hugh C. Webster, of Lea House, Harpenden, Herts:—

Martin Christopher Burton (Crouchers, Rudgwick, Sussex RH12 3DD), *b* 1936; Bar Lincoln's Inn 1961, Registrar in Bankruptcy, Companies Court, since 1988: *m* 1964, Victoria Gay, da of Dr Stanhope Furber, of Oak Cottage, Bracknell, Berks, and 14 Wimpole St, W1, and has issue living, Arthur Burton, *b* 1967: *m* 1992, Amanda Jane Ridley, — Samuel Burton, *b* 1973, — Hannah Kate, *b* 1965, — Amanda Victoria, *b* 1968: *m* 1991, Anthony Clarke, — Jessica Beth, *b* 1971. —— Bridget Elizabeth, *b* 1929. —— Jessica Margaret, *b* 1932: *m* 1957, Michael John Knott. —— Alison Rachel, *b* 1933: *m* 1959, Benjamin Fisher. —— Hazel Charlotte, *b* 1934.

PREDECESSORS – (1) *Rt Hon* HENRY BURTON Buckley, son of late Rev John Wall Buckley, V of St Mary's, Paddington, W; *b* 1845; was a Member of the Bar Committee and of Bar Council 1882-98, a Judge of High Court of Justice 1900-1906, and a Lord Justice of Appeal 1906-15; *cr Baron Wrenbury*, of Old Castle, Sussex (peerage of United Kingdom) 1915; *m* 1887, Bertha Margaretta, who *d* 1935, da of Charles Edward Jones, of 20 Cornwall Gardens, SW; *d* 1935; *s* by his son (2) BRYAN BURTON, 2nd Baron, *b* 1890: *m* 1925, Helen Malise, who *d* 1981, da of His Honour John Cameron Graham, of Ballewan, Blanfield, Stirlingshire; *d* 1940; *s* by his son (3) JOHN BURTON, 3rd Baron and present peer.

WRIGHT OF ASHTON UNDER LYNE, BARONY OF (Wright) (Extinct 1974)

SONS LIVING OF LIFE BARON

Hon Owen Mortimor (Wingthorne, Slade Rd, Newton, Swansea), *b* 1934: *m* 1960, Barbara, da of Arthur Hudson, and has issue.
Hon Glyn David (12 Brookfield Grove, Ashton under Lyne, Lancs), *b* 1940: *m* 1965, May Elizabeth, da of George Frederick Alldridge, and has issue.

WRIGHT OF RICHMOND, BARON (Wright) (Life Baron 1994)

PATRICK RICHARD HENRY WRIGHT, GCMG, son of late Herbert Wright, of The Hermitage, Chetwode, Buckingham; b 28 June 1931; ed Marlborough, and Merton Coll, Oxford; National Service Lieut RA; entered Foreign Service 1955 and served in Beirut, Washington, Cairo, and Bahrain; Priv Sec (overseas affairs) to the Prime Minister 1974-744; Ambassador to Luxembourg 1977-79, and Syria 1979-81; Dep Under-Sec FCO 1982-84; Ambassador to Saudi Arabia 1984-86; Permanent Under-Sec FCO and Head of Diplomatic Service 1986-91; Dir of Barclays Bank, Unilever, British Petroleum, De La Rue, and BAA; Member of Security Commn since 1993; Member of Council of Royal Institute of Internat Affairs, Royal College of Music, Order of St John, and United World Coll of the Atlantic; Vice-Pres of Home-Start; Governor of Wellington Coll, Ditchley; Hon Fell of Merton Coll, Oxford 1987; KStJ 1990; CMG 1978, KCMG 1974, GCMG 1989; cr Baron Wright of Richmond, of Richmond-upon-Thames, in the London Borough of Richmond-upon-Thames (Life Baron) 1994: m 1958, Virginia Anne, step da of late Col Samuel John Hannaford, of Hove, and has issue.

𝕬rms – Per fess gules and or, on a pale counterchanged between in chief two oak leaves or each charged with a quaver azure and in base as many oak leaves gules each charged with a quaver gold a doric column proper and overall a chevron per pale azure and gules. 𝕮rest – Beneath a palm tree a pelican in its piety with its young all proper. 𝕾upporters – Dexter, a bichon frisé rampant and in trim aspect proper; sinister, a stag guardant gold. Address – c/o House of Lords, SW1A 0PW.

SONS LIVING

Hon Marcus, b 1959.
Hon Angus, b 1964.

DAUGHTER LIVING

Hon Olivia, b 1963.

WROTTESLEY, BARON (Wrottesley) (Baron UK 1838, Bt E 1642)

CLIFTON HUGH LANCELOT DE VERDON WROTTESLEY, 6th Baron and 14th Baronet, b 10 Aug 1968; s 1977; ed Eton, Edinburgh Univ, and RMA Sandhurst; 2nd Lieut Gren Gds 1992; patron of three livings.

𝕬rms – Or, three piles sable and a canton ermine. 𝕮rest – Out of a ducal coronet or a boar's head ermine, crined and tusked gold. 𝕾upporters – On either side a unicorn argent, armed, maned, tufted, unguled, gorged with a ducal coronet, and chain reflexed over the back or pendent from the coronet an escutcheon, charged with the arms of Wrottesley.
Residence – 57 Rostrevor Rd, SW6 5AR. Clubs – Carlton, Lansdowne, Cavalry and Guards'.

Strength is increased by union

HALF-UNCLES LIVING (sons of 5th Baron by 3rd marriage)

Hon STEPHEN JOHN, b 21 Dec 1955; ed Harrow; journalist: m 1982, Mrs Rosamund Clare Fletcher (neé Taylor), and has issue living, Alexandra Wynne Marie, b 1985, — Stephanie Victoria, b 1988. Residence – 5 Montrose Av, Orangezicht, Cape Town 8001.
Hon Nicholas Charles, b 1963; ed Harrow, and Cape Town Univ (BA 1985, LLB 1987, LLM 1992): m 1991, Denny Marian Welman. Residence – 5 Derby Mews, Derby Rd, Kenilworth, Cape Town 7700.

GRANDMOTHER LIVING

Roshanara Barbara WINGFIELD-STRATFORD-JOHNSTONE, da of Esmé Cecil Wingfield-Stratford, DSc (see V Powerscourt, colls) assumed by deed poll 1970 the surnames of Wingfield-Stratford-Johnstone, m 1st, 1941 (m diss 1949), Maj Richard John Wrottesley, MC (later 5th Baron Wrottesley), who d 1977; 2ndly, 1950, Lt-Col Norman David Melville Johnstone, MBE, Gren Gds, of Park House, Gaddesby, Leics, LE7 8WH.

MOTHER LIVING

Georgina Anne, el da of Lt-Col Peter Thomas Clifton, CVO, DSO (see Bruce, Bt, cr 1804, colls): m 1st, 1967 (Nevada), Hon Richard Francis Gerard Wrottesley, who dvp 1970; 2ndly, 1982, Lt-Col Jonathan Lovett Seddon-Brown, Scots Gds, and has issue by 1st m (ante). Residence – 57 Rostrevor Rd, SW6 5AR.

WIDOW LIVING OF SON OF FIFTH BARON

Judy, da of — Matthews: *m* 1981, as his 2nd wife, Hon Mark Wrottesley, son of 5th Baron, who *d* 1986.

WIDOW LIVING OF FIFTH BARON

MARY ADA VAN ECHTEN (*Baroness Wrottesley*) (18 Sonnehoogte, Thomas Rd, Kenilworth, Cape Province 7700, S Africa), only da of late Edgar Dryden Tudhope, of Kenilworth, CP, S Africa: *m* 1955, as his 3rd wife, the 5th Baron, who *d* 1977.

COLLATERAL BRANCHES LIVING

Issue of late Hon Mark Wrottesley, only son by 2nd *m* of 5th Baron, *b* 1951, *d* 1986: *m* 1st, 1974 (*m diss* 1978), Marie Louise du Plooy; 2ndly, 1981, Judy (*née* Matthews), formerly wife of —:—
(By 1st *m*) Caroline May, *b* 19—. —— Veronica, *b* 19—.

(In remainder to Baronetcy)

Grandson of late Rev Francis John Wrottesley, son of late Rev Edward John Wrottesley, son of late Capt Edward Wrottesley, RN, 5th son of 8th Baronet:—
Issue of late Edward Algernon Wrottesley, *b* 1879, *d* 1957: *m* 1906, Mabel Letitia, who *d* 1955, da of late Francis Clowes, JP, of Sutton Hall, Stalham, Norfolk:—
(Arthur) John Francis, *b* 1908; *ed* Wellington Coll, and Univ Coll, Oxford (BA 1929, MA 1933); Bar Inner Temple 1932; European War 1939-45 as Capt Roy Norfolk Regt: *m* 1936, Marjorie Mary, MBE (1973), only da of late Frank Wilde, of Moorland Road, Edgbaston, and has issue living, David John (29 Twentywell Rd, Bradway, Sheffield), *b* 1940: *m* 1969, Christine Ann, only da of Henry Smith, of Sheffield, and has issue living, Angela Jane *b* 1977, — Michael Francis (17 Ordnance Hill, NW8 6PR), *b* 1945: *m* 1973, Francesca Jacqueline, only da of late Jack Miller, and has issue living, Alexander Francis *b* 1976, Maxim George *b* 1980, — Elizabeth Mavis, *b* 1938: *m* 1st, 1962, Capt John Michael Parr, RAEC; 2ndly, 1982, I. Breac C. MacLeod, of Anvil House, Hook Norton, Oxon OX15 5NH, and has issue living (by 1st *m*), Richard John *b* 1964: *m* 1988, Alison Jane, yr da of Graham Massey, of Moore, Cheshire (and has issue living, James Richard *b* 1992, Sophie Rebecca *b* 1993), Sarah Anne Elizabeth, *b* 1965: *m* 1992, Stephen John Ross, of 10 Canynge Rd, Clifton, Bristol BS8 3JX, Rosalind Mary *b* 1975, (twin) 1945: *m* 1968, Graeme Allan Lythe, of 38 Vicarage Rd, East Sheen SW14 8RU, and has issue living, Edward Graeme *b* 1970; 2nd Lieut Queen's Own Hussars 1992, Lieut 1994, James Edgar *b* 1972, Henry Frederick *b* 1975. *Residence* – 54 Warrington Cres, W9 1EP.

PREDECESSORS – **(1)** Sir WALTER Wrottesley, Knt, son of Sir Hugh Wrottesley (High Sheriff of co Stafford), descended in the male line from Sir Hugh de Wrottesley, KG (temp 1348), a zealous royalist, was *cr* a *Baronet* 1642; *d* 1659; *s* by his son **(2)** Sir WALTER, 2nd Bt; *d* 1686; *s* by his son **(3)** Sir WALTER, 3rd Bt; *d* 1712; *s* by his son **(4)** Sir JOHN, MP, 4th Bt; *d* 1726; *s* by his el son **(5)** Sir HUGH, 5th Bt; *d* 1729; *s* by his brother **(6)** Sir WALTER, 6th Bt; *d* 1731; *s* by his brother **(7)** Sir RICHARD, 7th Bt; was sometime MP for Tavistock, and a Principal Clerk of the Board of Green Cloth; subsequently took Holy Orders, and having been a Royal Chaplain was appointed Dean of Worcester; *d* 1769; *s* by his son **(8)** Sir JOHN, 8th Bt; was Maj-Gen in the Army, sometime MP for Staffordshire and Equerry to HRH the Duke of York; *d* 1787; *s* by his son **(9)** Sir JOHN, 9th Bt; having been successively MP for Staffordshire and Lichfield, was *cr* Baron Wrottesley, of Wrottesley, co Stafford (peerage of United Kingdom) 1838; *d* 1841; *s* by his son **(10)** JOHN, DCL, FRS, 2nd Baron; *b* 1798; was Pres of the Royal So, and one of the founders of the Astronomical So: *m* 1821, Sophia Elizabeth, da of late Thomas Giffard of Chillington, Staffordshire, *d* 1867; *s* by his son **(11)** ARTHUR, 3rd Baron; *b* 1824; a Lord-in-Waiting to Queen Victoria 1869-74 and 1880-85, and Lord-Lieut of Staffordshire 1871-87: *m* 1861, Hon Augusta Elizabeth Denison, who *d* 1887, da of 1st Baron Londesborough; *d* 1910; *s* by his el son **(12)** VICTOR ALEXANDER, 4th Baron; *b* 1873; *d* 1962; *s* by his nephew **(13)** RICHARD JOHN, MC, (only son of late Hon Walter Bennet Wrottesley, yst son of 3rd Baron), 5th Baron, *b* 1918, Maj (Reserve); OStJ; 1935-49 War: *m* 1st, 1941 (*m diss* 1949), Roshanara Barbara, da of Esmé Cecil Wingfield-Stratford, DSC (V Powerscourt, colls); 2ndly, 1949 (*m diss* 1953), (Joyce) Marion, da of late Frederick Alexander Wallace, and formerly wife of Maj Sean Rainey; 3rdly, 1955, Mary Ada Van Echten, only da of Edgar Dryden Tudhope, of Rondebosch, CP, S Africa; *d* 1977; *s* by his grandson **(14)** CLIFTON HUGH LANCELOT DE VERDON (only son of late Hon Richard Francis Gerard Wrottesley, 2nd son of 5th Baron), 6th Baron and present peer.

WYATT OF WEEFORD, BARON (Wyatt) (Life Baron 1987)

WOODROW LYLE WYATT, yr son of late Robert Harvey Lyle Wyatt, of Esher, Surrey, by his wife, Ethel, da of David Morgan, of Pontypridd, Glam; *b* 4 July 1918; *ed* Eastbourne, and Worcester Coll, Oxford (MA); served as Maj World War II (despatches); MP for Aston Div of Birmingham (*Lab*) 1945-55, and for Bosworth Div of Leics (*Lab*) 1959-70, Parl Under-Sec of State and Fin Sec War Office May-Oct 1951; journalist, jt founder *Panorama* (with Richard Dimbleby) 1955; Chm Horserace Totalisator Bd since 1976; author of *The Jews at Home, Southwards From China, Into the Dangerous World, The Peril in Our Midst, Distinguished for Talent, Turn Again, Westminster, The Exploits of Mr Saucy Squirrel, The Further Exploits of Mr Saucy Squirrel, What's Left of the Labour Party?, To the Point, Confessions of an Optimist,* (ed with introduction) *The Way We Lived Then: the English story in the 1940s, High Profiles* (play); *cr* Kt 1983, and *Baron Wyatt of Weeford,* of Weeford, co Staffs (Life Baron) 1987: *m* 1st 1939 (*m diss* 1944), Susan Cox; 2ndly, 1948 (*m diss* 1956), Nora Robbins; 3rdly, 1957 (*m diss* 1966), Lady Moorea Hastings, eldest da of 15th Earl of Huntingdon; 4thly 1966, Veronica (Verushka), widow of Baron Dr Laszlo Banzsky von Ambroz, and da of Jeno Racz, and has issue by 3rd and 4th *m.*

ᴀrms – Gu, on a fesse or, between three boars' heads erased arg, two lions passant sa. Ꮯrest – Out of a mural coronet arg, a demi-lion rampant sa, charged on the shoulder with an estoile of the first, and holding an arrow proper. Ꮪupporters – *Dexter,* a boar argent bristled hooved and tusked or gorged with a collar dancetty gules; *sinister,* a lion sable gorged with a collar dancetty gold. ᴍotto – Vi attamen honore (with strength but nevertheless with honour).
Residence – 19 Cavendish Av, NW8 9JD.

SON LIVING (*by 3rd marriage*)

Hon Pericles Plantagenet James Casati, *b* 1963.

DAUGHTER LIVING (*by 4th marriage*)

Hon Petronella Aspasia, *b* 1968.

WYFOLD, BARON (Hermon-Hodge) (Baron UK 1919, Bt UK 1902)

HERMON ROBERT FLEMING HERMON-HODGE, 3rd Baron, and 3rd Baronet; *b* 26 June 1915; *s* 1942; *ed* Eton and Le Rosey, Switzerland; is Capt Gren Gds (Res), formerly a Dir of Robert Fleming Holdings, Ltd.

ᴀrms – Sable, a lion couchant erminois holding between the paws a bale of cotton proper. Ꮯrest – An eagle, wings addorsed and inverted or, supporting with the dexter claw an increscent argent, and looking at the rays of the sun issuant from clouds proper. Ꮪupporters – On either side a trooper of the Oxfordshire Yeomanry (Queen's Own Oxfordshire Hussars).
Residences – Sarsden House, Churchill, Oxon; Les Trois Couronnes, Vevey, Switzerland. *Address* – 25 Copthall Av, EC2R 7DR. *Clubs* – Carlton, Pratts, Metropolitan (New York).

SISTERS LIVING

Hon Lorna Frances, *b* 1911: *m* 1941, John Barkley Schuster, TD (Parker of Waddington, By), who *d* 1984, and has issue living, Peter Jonathan (Nether Worton Cottage, Nether Worton, Oxon; The Lodge, 41 Wandle Rd, SW17), *b* 1952: *m* 1984, Emma M., elder da of Christopher Codrington, of Manor Farm House, Petersham, Surrey, and has issue living, George Barkley *b* 1989, Hannah Frances *b* 1986, — Richard Douglas (The Grange, Over Worton, Oxon), *b* 1953: *m* 1986, Jennifer C., da of David G. W. Barham, of Hole Park, Rolvenden, and formerly wife of Simon Francis Mann (*see* Mann, Bt, colls), — Joanna Valentine (Nether Worton House, Middle Barton, Chipping Norton, Oxford OX7 7AT; 63 Bourne St, SW1), *b* 1950: *m* 1971 (*m diss* 1989), Orme Roosevelt Clarke, who *d* 1992, and has issue (*see* Clarke, Bt, *cr* 1831). *Residence* – The Manor Farm, Nether Worton, Middle Barton, Oxon OX5 4AS.

Glory is the reward of valour

Hon Dorothy Charmian, *b* 1913: *m* 1938, Maj Richard Evelyn Fleming, MC, TD, late Lovat Scouts, who *d* 1977 (Rose, Bt, *cr* 1874, colls), and has issue living, James Roland (Blanche House, Northleach, Glos), *b* 1944: *m* 1975, Kathryn Alice, da of late D. A. Rooksby, and has issue living, Christian Peter *b* 1977, Thomas Roland, *b* 1980, — Adam Richard (P.O. Box 4197, Rivonia 2128, Republic of South Africa), *b* 1948: *m* 1979, Caroline Jane, 2nd da of Sir Hereward Wake, 14th Bt, MC, and has issue living, Hector Adam *b* 1982, Angus Richard *b* 1988, Eleanor Kate *b* 1985, — George Andrew (York Cottage, Churchill, Oxon), *b* 1950: *m* 1979, Elaine, da of Peter Owen, of The Old Rectory, Mixbury, Oxon, and has issue living, Frederick Richard *b* 1981, — Roderick John (The Dower House, Sarsgrove, Churchill, Oxon), *b* 1953: *m* 1979, Diana Julia, eldest da of Sir Hereward Wake, 14th Bt, MC, and has issue living, Chloe Dorothy *b* 1989. Hermione Kisty *b* (twin) 1989, — Fergus

Hermon Robert, *b* 1959, — Kathleen Alexandra (Sydenham Farm, Broadwell, Moreton-in-Marsh, Glos, GL56 0YE), *b* 1941: *m* 1962 (*m diss* 1979), Capt Simon John Loder, late Gren Gds (*see* Loder, Bt, colls), — Mary Fern, *b* 1942: *m* 1971, Jeremy Donnithorne Taylor, of Cold Harbour Farm, North Aston, Oxford, and has issue living, James Fionn *b* 1971, Katherine Clare Romayne *b* 1973, — Dorothy Frances, *b* 1955. *Residence* – Inverliver Farm, Taynuilt, Argyll.

COLLATERAL BRANCH LIVING

Issue of late Rear-Adm Hon Claude Preston Hermon-Hodge, DSC, 5th son of 1st Baron, *b* 1888, *d* 1952: *m* 1918, Gwendoline Rose, who *d* 1949, da of J. Goulding Davis, Public Works Depart, India:—
Pauline Frances Gwendoline, *b* 1921: *m* 1947, Major Meyrick James Magrath, DFC, RA, and has issue living, Carol Rose, *b* 1949. —— Stella Riette, *b* 1925: *m* 1949, David Ashley Courtenay, who *d* 1983, of Woodcutters, Ambersham Common, Midhurst, and has issue living, David Anthony Orin, *b* 1958, — Geraldine, *b* 1953: *m* 1977, Rev Douglas John Dales, and has issue living, Christopher St John Douglas *b* 1981, Basil Michael Dunstan *b* 1987, Gwendoline Clare Courtenay *b* 1984.

PREDECESSORS
PREDECESSORS – (1) Robert Trotter Hermon-Hodge, TD, el son of late George William Hodge, of Newcastle-upon-Tyne; *b* 1851; sat as MP for Accrington Div of N-E Lancashire (C) 1886-92, for S, or Henley, Div of Oxfordshire 1895-1906 and 1917-18, and for Croydon 1909-10; sometime Lieut-Col and Hon Col Comdg Queen's Own Oxfordshire Hussars Yeo; assumed by Roy licence the additional surname of Hermon 1903; *cr* a *Baronet* 1902, and *Baron Wyfold*, of Accrington, co Lancaster (peerage of United Kingdom) 1919: *m* 1877, Frances Caroline, who *d* 1929, only da of Edward Hermon, of Wyfold Court, Oxon; *d* 1937, *s* by his son (2) Roland Hermon, DSO, MVO, 2nd Baron; *b* 1880; Major and Brevet Lieut-Col late Reserve of Officers; S Africa 1899-1902, European War 1914-18 (DSO): *m* 1906, Dorothy, who *d* 1976, el da of Robert Fleming, of Joyce Grove, Oxfordshire, and 27, Grosvenor Square, W1; *d* 1942; *s* by his son (3) Hermon Robert Fleming, 3rd Baron and present Peer.

WYNFORD, BARON (Best) (Baron UK 1829)

Liberty in the laws

Robert Samuel Best, MBE, 8th Baron; *b* 5 Jan 1917; *s* 1943; *ed* Eton; Lieut-Col (ret) RWF, Croix de Guerre 1943; a DL of Dorset; MBE (Mil) 1952: *m* 1941, Anne Daphne Mametz, da of late Maj-Gen John Randle Minshull-Ford, CB, DSO, MC (Harmood-Banner, Bt), and has issue.

Arms – Sable, a cinquefoil within an orle of cross crosslets or; on a canton of the last, a portcullis of the first. **Crest** – Out of a ducal coronet or, a demi-ostrich rising argent, in its beak a cross crosslet fitchée gold, gorged with a plain collar, and pendent therefrom a portcullis sable. **Supporters** – Two eagles reguardant, wings elevated, each standing on a Roman fasces, all proper.
Seat – Wynford House, Wynford Eagle, Dorchester, Dorset.

SON LIVING

Hon John Philip Robert (The Manor, Wynford Eagle, Dorchester, Dorset DT2 0ER), *b* 23 Nov 1950; *ed* Radley, Keele Univ and RAC Cirencester: *m* 1981, Fenella Christian Mary, only da of Arthur Reginald Danks (*see* B Gifford), and has issue living, Harry Robert Francis, *b* 9 May 1987, — Sophie Hannah Elizabeth, *b* 1985.

DAUGHTERS LIVING

Hon Caroline Anne Sabina, *b* 1942: *m* 1964, Edward Patrick Gundry, of 15 Genoa Av, SW15 (*see* Williams, Bt, *cr* 1915, 1980 Edn) and has issue living, David Patrick Edward, *b* 1976, — Rachel Anne, *b* 1965, — Alexandra Clare, *b* 1967.
Hon Jacqueline Dorothy Mametz, *b* 1946: *m* 1969, Jeremy James Richard Pope, OBE, FRSA, of Field Cottage, Compton Abbas West, Maiden Newton, Dorset, — Rory Christian Robert, *b* 1970, — Rupert Philip, *b* 1973, — Toby Francis, *b* 1977.

BROTHER LIVING

Hon Patrick George Matthew (Monk's House, Durford Wood, Petersfield, Hants, Boodle's Club), *b* 1923; *ed* Wellington Coll; Lt RNVR 1941-46; Chm/Man Dir Wiggins Teape Group; Dir BAT Industries, Ranks Hovis McDougal; Past Master of Ironmongers' Co; FRSA; Offr Order of Crown of Belgium 1980; *m* 1947, Heather, da of Hamilton Gardner, and has issue living, Christopher John Patrick (27 Warwick Rd, N11 2SB), *b* 1948: *m* 1st, 1973 (*m diss* 1977), Anna Marion Richmond Rowe, only da of David Rowe Mitchell; 2ndly, 1977, Margherita Antonietta, da of Alberto Pietro Toninato, and has issue living (by 2nd *m*), Francesca Victoria *b* 1984, — David Robert, *b* 1953, — Philip Edward Fraser, *b* 1960, — Clare Phyllis, *b* 1955: *m* 1992, Philip A. Willatt, yst son of Ian Duncan Willatt, MD, of Lavant, Chichester, Sussex.

DAUGHTERS LIVING OF SIXTH BARON

Hon Grace Janet Mary, *b* 1907: *m* 1930, Edward Kenneth Macleod Hilleary, MVO, of Nettlebed House, Droxford, Hants, and has issue living, Shena Sarah, *b* 1931: *m* 1954, Lt-Cdr Harry R. Cornell, RN (ret), of Garden House, Droxford, Hants, — Wendy Jemima, *b* 1933: *m* 1954, Ian Hedderwick, of Lot 35, Robinson Rd, Albany, Western Australia 6330, Australia, — Gillian Marianne, *b* 1936: *m* 1975, Maj J. D. Bengough, The Black Watch (Royal Highland Regt) (ret) of White Lodge, Sidbury, Sidmouth, Devon.
Hon Eva Constance Edith, *b* 1909: *m* 1932, Philip Valentine Mackinnon, son of late Rt Hon Sir Frank Douglas Mackinnon, Lord Justice of Appeal, and has had issue. *Residence* – Toller Fratrum, Dorset.
Hon Mary Jemima, *b* 1912: *m* 1944, Jack Hendy, and has issue living, John Giles, *b* 1948, — Peter Gerard, *b* 1953. *Residence* – 1 Portherras Cross, Pendeen, Penzance, Cornwall TR19 7DY.

COLLATERAL BRANCHES LIVING

Grandchildren of late Adm Hon Sir Matthew Robert Best, KCB, DSO, MVO (infra):—
Issue of late Capt George Frederic Matthew Best, OBE, RN, *b* (Dec) 1908, *d* 1994: *m* 1940, Rosemary Elizabeth
(Wallhayes, Nettlecombe, Bridport, Dorset DT6 3SX), da of Maj J. Chadwick-Brooks, OBE, of Bedford Park, W14:—
John Vincent Matthew (29 Folkestone Rd, Walthamstow, E17), *b* 1948; *ed* Sussex Univ (BSc): *m* 1970, Penelope Ann, da of
John H. Williams, of Washington, DC, USA, and Isle of Arran, and has issue living, Tobias Graham, *b* 1974, — Crispin Alex
Sebastian, *b* 1983, — Philippa Hannah, *b* 1972. —— Annis Rosemary Georgina, *b* 1944: *m* 1971, Col Richard M.
Connaughton, late RCT, and has issue living, Michael Thomas George, *b* 1972, — Emma Caroline Jane, *b* 1974.

Issue of late Adm Hon Sir Matthew Robert Best, KCB, DSO, MVO, 3rd son of 5th Baron, *b* 1878, *d* 1940:
m (Jan) 1908, Annis, who *d* 1971, da of C. F. Wood, of Lee Priory, Littlebourne, Canterbury:—
Margaret Annis, *b* 1913: *m* 1st, 1937, Com Alexander Pollock Gibson, RN (*ka* 1940); 2ndly, 1941, as his second wife, Capt
Godfrey Alexander French, CBE, RN, who *d* 1988, and has issue living, (by 2nd *m*) Matthew (Beechfield Farm, Curry Rivel,
Langport, Som TA10 0NP), *b* 1945; Lt-Cdr RN: *m* 1983, Nicola Mary, da of Eustace Arthur McNaught, and has issue living,
Annis Evelyn *b* 1984, Eleanor Winifred *b* 1986, Charlotte Imogen *b* 1990, — David (21 Prospect Rd, St Albans, Herts AL1
2AT), *b* 1947; Dir Relate (Nat Marriage Guidance) since 1987: *m* 1974, Sarah Anne, da of Rt Rev Henry David Halsey,
Bishop of Carlisle, and has issue living, Thomas Weatherhead *b* 1978, Alexander Matthew *b* 1980, William Sholto *b* 1983,
Henry Kenneth Robert *b* 1993, — Jenny Margaret *b* 1950: *m* 1982, Peter Bigham Crossley, of The Old Vicarage, Henton, nr
Wells, Somerset BA5 1PD, son of late T. Crossley, OBE, ICS, and has issue living, Giles Bigham *b* 1983, James Bigham *b*
1988, Hannah Margaret *b* 1986. *Residence* – Molly Bawn, Stoke Abbott, Beaminster, Dorset DT8 3JT.

Grandchildren of late Capt Hon James William Best, OBE, VD (infra):—
Issue of late Rear Adm Thomas William Best, CB, *b* 1915, *d* 1984: *m* 1942, Brenda Joan (Hincknowle, Melplash,
Bridport, Dorset DT6 3UG), da of late F. A. Hellaby MC, LLD, of Auckland, NZ:—
Rupert Thomas (39 Beach Rd, Emsworth, Hants PO10 7HR), *b* 1943; Cdr RN: *m* 1971, Margaret Ludgate, da of late Maj
Alan Murray, 3rd Carabiniers (Prince of Wales's Drag Gds), and has issue living, Thomas Matthew, *b* 1973, — William
Rupert, *b* 1982, — Sarah Margaret, *b* 1976. —— James Frederick, *b* 1948; BA Oxon: *m* 1980, Sara Victoria, da of Brian
Cole, of 49 Milverton Rd, NW6, and has issue living, Harry James, *b* 1983, — Tom, *b* 1987, — Mary-Rose Victoria, *b* 1981.
—— Joanna Mavis, *b* 1945; *ed* Durham Univ (BA): *m* 1970, Maj Thomas James Knott, RE, son of Lt-Gen Sir Harold Edwin
Knott, KCB, OBE, MD, and has issue living, Felicity Anne, *b* 1971, — Alison Joanna, *b* 1973, — Amelia Mary, *b* 1982.
Issue of late Samuel James Best, *b* 1927, *d* 1974: *m* 1954, Jennifer Elspeth Mary (Kings House, Powerstock,
Dorset), el da of Max H. Heilbut:—
Crispin John, *b* 1955. —— Jane Mary, *b* 1957. —— Susannah Catherine, *b* 1962. —— Deborah Gabriel, *b* 1966.

Issue of late Capt Hon James William Best, OBE, VD, yst son of 5th Baron, *b* 1882, *d* 1960: *m* 1914,
Florence Mary Bernarda, who *d* 1961, da of Sir Elliott Lees, 1st Bt, DSO:—
His Honour Judge Giles Bernard (Pitcombe, Little Bredy, Dorchester, Dorset), *b* 1925; *ed* Wellington and Jesus Coll, Oxford;
Bar Inner Temple 1951; Dep Chm Dorset Quarter Sessions 1967-71, and Recorder of Crown Court 1972-75, since when
Circuit Judge. —— Henry Nicholas, *b* 1930; *ed* Wellington Coll; former Man Dir Anglo Blackwells Ltd, and SKW Metals UK
Ltd: *m* 1963, Elisabeth Rose Ursula, el da of Hans Joachim Druckenbrodt, of Marburg, W Germany, and Rittergut
Minsleben, Wernigerode, E Germany, and has issue living, Frederick Henry Achim, *b* 1964, — Thomas Bernard Nicholas, *b*
1968, — Isabel Florence Christina, *b* 1972. *Residence* – Whitelackington House, Ilminster, Somerset TA19 9EF. —— Alice
Mary, *b* 1919: *m* 1939, Christopher Wentworth Dilke, late Lt-Col RA (*see* Dilke, Bt). *Residence* – Valehouse Farm, Whitchurch
Canonicorum, Bridport, Dorset. —— Helen Margaret, *b* 1923.

Grandchildren of late Capt Hon John Charles Best, 2nd son of late Rev Hon Samuel Best, 3rd son of 1st
Baron:—
Issue of late Capt William Best, Roy Welch Fusiliers, *b* 1874, *d* 1950: *m* 1903, Constance Adela, who *d* 1963, da of
late Col Charles Wingfield, of Onslow, Shrewsbury:—
John William, MBE (Lawton Hall, Leominster, Herefordshire), *b* 1912; formerly Fl-Lt RAF; 1939-45 War (prisoner); MBE
(Mil) 1964: *m* 1st, 1938 (*m diss* 1959), Mary Constance, da of Robert Charles Otter, of Royston Manor, Clayworth; 2ndly,
1959, Mary Elisabeth (CORBIN), da of late Dr Edward Lancelot Bunting, of Hardwicke Manor, Worcs, and has issue living,
(by 1st *m*) Robert John (Vivod, Llangollen, Clwyd), *b* 1946: *m* 1976, Juliet, da of Peter John Owen, of The Old Rectory, Mix-
bury, Brackley, Northants, and has issue living, William *b* 1981, Lucinda Emma *b* 1977, Candida Mary *b* 1979, — Antonia
Mary, *b* 1948: *m* 1970, Christopher Duncan Steuart Wilson-Clarke, of Greenbanks, Coptiviney, Ellesmere, Shropshire, and
has issue living, Alpha Georgia *b* 1978, Laura Alice *b* 1979. —— Hilda Mary, *b* 1909: *m* 1935, Ranald Macdonald Brodie
Macalister, who *d* 1980, formerly Capt Roy Indian Army Ser Corps and has issue living, Angus Charles, *b* 1937; *ed*
Gordonstoun: *m* 1st, 1963 (*m diss* 1981), Gustava, da of Ulrich Liebing, of Eckernforde, Germany; 2ndly, 1986, Jeanne
CUMMINGS, da of late Clinton Barclay-Allardice, of Providence, RI, USA and has issue living (by 1st *m*), Duncan Joachim *b*
1964, Kai-Donald *b* 1970, Elke Maree *b* 1966, — Fiona Anne MACALISTER, *b* 1947: *m* 1973 (*m diss* 1981), William Lorimer, son
of Robert Lorimer, of Edinburgh, and has issue living, Siubhan Macalister *b* 1976, Ciaran Sorcha *b* 1978. *Residence* –
Glenbarr Abbey, Glenbarr, Tarbert, Argyll.

Grandchildren of late Hon Thomas William Best, 3rd son of late Rev the Hon Samuel Best, 3rd son of 1st
Baron:—
Issue of late Capt Humphrey Willie Best, CBE, DSO, RN, *b* 1884, *d* 1959: *m* 1914, Helen Grace, who *d* 1975, da of
late Mrs James Meakin, of Weeford, Ashby de-la-Zouch:—
Walter John, *b* 1917: *m* 1941, Elizabeth, yst da of Kenneth M. Simpson, of Trinidad, and Forres, and has issue living, Anne
Mackintosh, *b* 1944: *m* 1966, Robert Brian Massey of 8 Gilwell Rd, Valsayn Park, Trinidad, and has issue living, Stewart
John *b* 1967, Ian James *b* 1972, Catherine Anne *b* 1975, — Fiona Elizabeth Wynford, *b* 1949: *m* 1972, Anthony John Cotter,
of 2 Crabtree Gdns, Headley, Bordon, Hants GU35 8LN, and has issue living, Andrew John *b* 1976, Heather Jane, *b* 1979.
Residence – 10 Cronk Drean, 2nd Avenue, Douglas, Isle of Man. —— Peter Anthony (White House, Trevilson, St Newlyn
East, Newquay, Cornwall TR8 5JF), *b* 1922; Flight-Lieut RAF (ret); 1939-45 War (prisoner): *m* 1st, 1948, Sheelah Gillian
Vernon St John, who *d* 1979, only da of late Lt-Col D. St J. Baxter, of Chichester, Sussex; 2ndly, 1979, B. Smyth, and has
issue living (by 1st *m*), Peter Kimble (Iona Cottage, 6 Main St, Cranswick, Driffield, N Humberside), *b* 1952; F/Lt RAF: *m*
1974, Georgina Alison Gibson, and has issue living, Oliver Giles *b* 1977, Timothy Tristan *b* 1978, Gemma Lucy Gillian *b* 1982,
— Jeremy Dean (Brambles, Mitchell Fruit Garden, Mitchell, Newquay, Cornwall), *b* 1954; horticulturalist: *m* 1978, Claudia
Anhalies Roost, and has issue living, Timothy Peter *b* 1985, Christine Sara *b* 1984, Miriam Anna *b* 1987, — Hilary Jane *b*
1949: *m* 1971, Robert Dale Johnson, of 17 Glenwood Drive, Washington, Penn 15301, USA, and has issue living, Dale
Anthony *b* 1974, Jeremy Ross *b* 1976. —— Pamela Grey, *b* 1920: *m* 1947, Philip H. Hawkins, of Veryan, Sheafe Drive,
Cranbrook, Kent, and has issue living, Jonathan Edward Spencer (Smokepenny, Lunedale Rd, Dibden Purlieu, Hants), *b*
1953: *m* 1978, Sarah Sants Smith, and has issue living, Catherine Sarah *b* 1980, Emily Elizabeth *b* 1982, — Caroline Tessa *b*
1948: *m* 1971, James Harvey Bradnock, of Russets, 8 Shuteleigh, Wellington, Som TA21 8PG, and has issue living, Thomas
Philip *b* 1975; *ed* Exeter Coll, Oxford, Edward James Peter *b* 1978.

PREDECESSORS – (1) *Rt Hon Sir* WILLIAM DRAPER Best, DCL, 3rd son of late Thomas Best, of Haselbury Plucknett, Somerset; *b* 1767; appointed Solicitor to the Prince of Wales 1813, and Attorney-Gen 1816; sat successively as MP for Petersfield and Bridport; was a Judge of the Common Pleas 1819-24, and Chief Justice of that Court 1824-9; sometime Dep Speaker of House of Lords; *cr Baron Wynford*, of Wynford Eagle, co Dorset (peerage of United Kingdom) 1829: *m* 1794, Mary Anne, who *d* 1840, da of late Jerome Knapp; *d* 1845; *s* by his son **(2)** WILLIAM SAMUEL, 2nd Baron; *b* 1798: *m* 1821, Jane, who *d* 1895, da of William Thoyts, of Sulhampstead, Berks; *d* 1869; *s* by his son **(3)** WILLIAM DRAPER MORTIMER, 3rd Baron, *b* 1826: *m* 1857, Caroline Eliza Montague, who *d* 1913, el da of Evan Baillie, of Dochfour; *d* 1899; *s* by his brother **(4)** HENRY MOLYNEUX, 4th Baron, *b* 1829; *d* 1903; *s* by his cousin **(5)** GEORGE (son of late Rev Hon Samuel Best, 3rd son of 1st Baron), 5th Baron, *b* 1838: *m* 1870, Edith Anne, who *d* 1924, da of Matthew Henry Marsh, of Ramridge House, Andover; *d* 1904; *s* by his son **(6)** PHILIP GEORGE, DSO, 6th Baron; *b* 1871; Major (ret) RHA; European War 1914-19 (DSO): *m* 1906, Hon Eva Lilian Napier, who *d* 1974, da of 2nd Baron Napier of Magdala; *d* 1940; *s* by his brother **(7)** SAMUEL JOHN, 7th Baron, *b* 1874: *m* 1st, 1914, Evelyn Mary Aylmer, who *d* 1929, da of Maj-Gen Sir Edward Sinclair May, KCB, CMG; 2ndly, 1933, Marguerite, who *d* 1966, da of Charles Pratt, and widow of William Kenneth Allies; *d* 1943; *s* by his el son **(8)** ROBERT SAMUEL, 8th Baron and present peer.

<h2 style="text-align:center">WYNNE-JONES, BARONY OF (Wynne-Jones) (Extinct 1982)</h2>

<h3 style="text-align:center">DAUGHTERS LIVING OF LIFE BARON (By 1st m)</h3>

Hon Kristin, *b* 1931: *m* 1956, Dr Charles Joseph Gallagher, who *d* 1964, and has issue.
Hon Sigrid, *b* 1935: *m* 1962, Dr Marvin Goldiner, of Oakland, Cal, USA, and has issue.

<h3 style="text-align:center">WIDOW LIVING OF LIFE BARON</h3>

RUSHEEN (*Baroness Wynne-Jones*) (16 Chelsea Embankment, SW3), da of Neville Preston: *m* 1972, as his second wife, Baron Wynne-Jones (Life Baron), who *d* 1982.

<h2 style="text-align:center">YARBOROUGH, EARL OF (Pelham) (Earl UK 1837)</h2>

The love of country prevails

CHARLES JOHN PELHAM, 8th Earl; *b* 5 Nov 1963; *s* 1991; *ed* Eton, and Bristol Univ: *m* 1990, Anna-Karin, da of George Zecevic, of 1 Swan Walk, SW3, and has issue.

Arms – The two coats of *Pelham* quarterly, viz, 1st and 4th azure, three pelicans argent vulning themselves proper; 2nd and 3rd gules, two pieces of belt erect argent decorated with buckles and studs or. **Crest** – A peacock in his pride argent. **Supporters** – *Dexter*, a bay horse reguardant, charged on the body with three ancient buckles gold; *sinister*, a water spaniel dog reguardant or, charged on the body with three crosses flory sable.
Seat – Brocklesby Park, Habrough, Lincolnshire.

<h3 style="text-align:center">SONS LIVING</h3>

GEORGE JOHN SACKVILLE (*Lord Worsley*), *b* 9 Aug 1990.
Hon William Charles John Walter, *b* 1991.
Hon James Marcus, *b* 1994.

<h3 style="text-align:center">SISTERS LIVING</h3>

Lady Sophia, *b* 1958: *m* 1983, (Patrick William) John Kinmont, son of Dr Patrick David Clifford Kinmont, of Carlton Ashes House, Hough-on-the-Hill, Grantham, Lincs. *Residence* – 45 Lynette Av, SW4 9HF.
Lady Arabella, *b* 1960: *m* 1984, Christopher Casey, only son of late Ronald Casey, of Pecklands Farm, Stansted, Kent, and has issue living, a son, *b* 1993, — Laura Alexandra, *b* 1986, — Emma Olivia, *b* 1988.
Lady Vanessa Petronel, *b* 1961: *m* 1987, Timothy Colin Brown, ony son of Peter Brindley Brown, of 27 Isles Court, Ramsbury, Wilts. *Residence* – 56 Hugh St, SW1V 4ER.

Residence – Dunsford House, Uffcott, Swindon, Wilts SN4 9NB.

<h3 style="text-align:center">AUNT LIVING (daughter of 6th Earl)</h3>

Lady Janet Marcia Rose DOUGLAS PENNANT, *b* 1923: *m* 1948, John Charles Harper, who assumed by Royal Licence 1950 the surname and arms of Douglas Pennant in lieu of his patronymic, son of late Sir Charles Henry Harper, KBE, CMG, and has issue living, Richard Charles, *b* 1955; *ed* Stanbridge Earls Sch: *m* 1978, Georgia, yst da of late Theodorus Giorgiou, of Limassol, Cyprus, and has issue living, — Edmond Hugh, *b* 1960. *Residence* – Penrhyn, Bangor, Gwynedd.

<h3 style="text-align:center">DAUGHTERS LIVING OF FIFTH EARL</h3>

(co-heiresses to the Baronies of Fauconberg and Conyers)

Lady Diana Mary, *b* 1920; SRN 1945: *m* 1952, Robert Miller, who *d* 1990, as the result of a motor accident in Harare, and has issue living, Marcia Anne, *b* 1954; adopted by Maj Michael H. L. Lycett, and renamed Anthea Theresa LYCETT (retains right of succession to the baronies), — Beatrix Diana, *b* 1955: *m* 1991, Simon William Jones Armstrong (Box 49, Gilgil, Kenya), only son of late Christopher Wyborne Armstrong, OBE, of Kwetu Farm, Gilgil, Kenya. *Address* – c/o Zimbank, Box 2270, Harare, Zimbabwe.
Lady (June) Wendy, *b* 1924; late 3rd Officer WRNS; Joint Master Tynedale Hunt 1974-77: *m* 1959, as his 2nd wife, Maj Michael Hildesley Lycett Lycett, CBE, late Royal Scots Greys, of West Grange, Scots Gap, Morpeth, Northumberland NE61 4EQ.

WIDOW LIVING OF SEVENTH EARL

FLORENCE ANN PETRONEL (*Ann, Countess of Yarborough*), da of late John Herbert Upton, of Ingmire Hall, Yorks, and formerly wife of Lieut Charles John Riddell Duffin, Scots Guards: *m* 1957, the 7th Earl, who *d* 1991. *Residence* – Flat 6, St Albans Mansions, Kensington Court Place, W8 5QH.

COLLATERAL BRANCH LIVING

Issue of late Hon Henry Cornwallis Pelham, 3rd son of 3rd Earl, *b* 1868, *d* 1924 (having assumed by Roy licence 1905 the surname and arms of Pelham only): *m* 1892, Edith Katherine, who *d* 1966, da of late Col William Arthur Roberts, formerly RHA, and subsequently Ch Constable of Metropolitan Police:—
Marjorie Edith, *b* 1897: *m* 1919, Henry George Dacres Dixon, who *d* 1947, and has issue living, Michael George Dacres (Diamond Mountain Rd, Calistoga, Calif, USA), *b* 1922; formerly Capt King's Roy Rifle Corps; 1939-45 War (wounded, invalided out): *m* 1st, 1946 (*m diss* 1960), Evelyn Nancy, da of Maj (William) Bertram Bell, 12th Lancers (By Barrymore); 2ndly, 1960, Azneve, da of late Martin Takakjian, of Long Island, New York, USA; 3rdly, 1983, Trudy, da of Irving Stern, of Cleveland, Ohio, USA, and has issue living, (by 1st *m*), Henry George *b* 1948, Annabel Jane *b* 1954, — Robin Charles Dacres (Goudhurst, Kent), *b* 1926; late Lt King's Roy Rifle Corps: *m* 1956, Sarah Manners Baron, and has issue living, Charles Richard *b* 1960: *m* 1985, Angela Dickinson, Anna Mary *b* 1957: *m* 1980, Mark Lilly, Sophie *b* (twin) 1957: *m* 1988, Richard T. Maylam, son of Thomas Maylam, of Tonbridge, Kent.

PREDECESSORS – (1) CHARLES Anderson-Pelham, MP for Beverley 1768-74, and for Lincolnshire 1774-94, was *cr Baron Yarborough*, of Yarborough, co Lincoln (peerage of Great Britain) 1794; *d* 1823; *s* by his son (2) CHARLES, DCL, FRS, 2nd Baron; sat as MP for Great Grimsby 1803-7, and for Lincolnshire 1807-23; *cr Baron Worsley*, of Appuldurcombe, Isle of Wight, and *Earl of Yarborough* (peerage of United Kingdom) 1837; *d* 1846; *s* by his son (3) CHARLES ANDERSON WORSLEY, 2nd Earl; sat as MP for Newport, Isle of Wight 1830-1, and for N Lincolnshire 1832-47; was Lord-Lieut of co Lincoln; *d* 1862; *s* by his son (4) CHARLES ANDERSON PELHAM, 3rd Earl; *b* 1835; sat as MP for Grimsby 1857-62: *m* 1858, Lady Victoria Alexandrina, who *d* 1927, da of 4th Earl of Listowel; *d* 1875; *s* by his son (5) Rt Hon CHARLES ALFRED WORSLEY, KG, 4th Earl; *b* 1859; Vice-Adm and Lord-Lieut for Lincolnshire; Capt of HM's Hon Corps of Gentlemen-at-Arms 1890-92, and Lieut-Col Comdg Lincolnshire Imperial Yeo 1901-7; assumed for himself and issue by Roy licence 1905 the surname and arms of Pelham only: *m* 1886, Hon Marcia Amelia Mary Lane-Fox (*Baroness Fauconberg and Conyers* in her own right), OBE, who *d* 1926, el da of 12th Baron Conyers; *d* 1936; *s* by his son (6) SACKVILLE GEORGE, MC, 5th Earl; *b* 1888; Lieut-Col Comdg Notts Yeo (Sherwood Rangers); European War 1914-19 (MC) European War 1939-45: *m* 1919, Nancye, who *d* 1977, da of late Alfred Brocklehurst; *d* 1948, when the Baronies of Fauconberg and Conyers fell into abeyance between his two daughters, and he was *s* in the Earldom and the Baronies of Yarborough and Worsley by his brother (7) MARCUS HERBERT, 6th Earl, *b* 1893; a DL for Lincs, 1950-66: *m* 1919, Hon Pamela Douglas-Pennant, who *d* 1968, da of 3rd Baron Penrhyn; *d* 1966; *s* by his son (8) JOHN EDWARD, 7th Earl, *b* 1920; Maj Grenadier Guards, Lord Lieut Lincs, High Sheriff 1964: *m* 1957, (Florence) Ann Petronel, da of late John Herbert Upton, of Ingmire Hall, Yorks, and formerly wife of Lieut Charles John Riddell Duffin, Scots Guards; *d* 1991; *s* by his only son (9) CHARLES JOHN, 8th Earl and present peer; also Baron Yarborough, and Baron Worsley.

Yarmouth, Earl of; son of Marquess of Hertford.

YORK, DUKE OF, SEE ROYAL FAMILY

YOUNG, BARONESS (Young) (Life Baroness 1971)

JANET MARY YOUNG, da of John Norman Leonard Baker; *b* 23 Oct 1926; *ed* Headington Sch, Oxford, Prospect Hill Sch, New Haven, Conn, USA, Mt Holyoke Coll, USA, and St Annes Coll, Oxford (MA); Hon Fell of St Anne's Coll, Oxford: DL Oxon 1990; a Member of Oxford City Council 1957-72 (Alderman 1967-72, Leader Conservative Group Oxford City Council 1967-72); a Baroness-in-Waiting to HM 1972-73; Parl Under-Sec of State Dept of Environment 1973-74; Vice Chm Conservative Party Organization 1975-83; (Dep Chm 1977-79, Co-Chm Women's Nat Cttee 1979-83); Min of State, Dept of Educ and Science 1979-81; Chancellor of Duchy of Lancaster 1981-82 and Leader of House of Lords 1981-82; Lord Privy Seal 1982-83; Min of State, Foreign and Commonwealth Office 1983-87; Dir Nat Westminster Bank plc since 1987, and Marks & Spencer plc since 1987; Trustee Lucy Cavendish Coll, Camb; a Vice-Pres The West India Cttee since 1988; Chancellor of Greenwich Univ since 1993, Member of Court of Cranfield Univ since 1992; *cr Baroness Young*, of Farnworth, co Palatine of Lancaster (Life Baroness) 1971: *m* 1950, Dr Geoffrey Tyndale Young, and has issue.
Residence – 23 Northmoor Rd, Oxford.

DAUGHTERS LIVING

Hon Alexandra Janet, *b* 1951: *m* 1974, John Douglas Slater, of 12 Edgar Rd, Winchester, Hants, and has issue living, one son and one da.
Hon Rosalind Ann, *b* 1954: *m* 1977, Stephen McIntyre, of 48 Taleworth Rd, Ashtead, Surrey, and has issue living, Peter James, *b* 1981, — David Edward, *b* 1984.
Hon Juliet Marguerite, *b* 1962: *m* 1986, Stephen Paul Brown, elder son of Dr Stanley Brown, of Harborne, Birmingham, and has issue living, Simon Richard, *b* 1989.

YOUNG OF DARTINGTON, BARON (Young) (Life Baron 1978)

MICHAEL YOUNG, son of Gibson Young, a musician; *b* 9 Aug 1915; *ed* Dartington Hall Sch, and London Univ (MA, PhD), Hon LittD Sheffield 1965, Hon Dr Open Univ 1973, Hon DLitt Adelaide 1974; Bar Gray's Inn 1939; Dir of Political and Economic Planning 1941-45, and Sec Research Dept, Labour Party 1945-51; Dir, Inst of Community Studies since 1953, and Trustee, Dartington Hall since 1942 (Dep Chm since 1980); memb NEDC 1975; Pres of Consumers Assocn 1965, Nat Extension Coll 1971, ACE 1976; Chm Mutual Aid Centre, the Tawney Soc 1982; Author; *cr Baron Young of Dartington*, of Dartington, co Devon (Life Baron) 1978: *m* 1st, 1945, Joan Lawson; 2ndly, 1960, Sasha, broadcaster and novelist, who *d* 1993, da of Raisley Stewart Moorsom, and has issue by 1st and 2nd *m*.
Residence – 18 Victoria Park Sq, E2.

SONS LIVING *(By 1st marriage)*

Hon Christopher Ivan *b* 1946.
Hon David Justin (18 Camden Rd, NW1), *b* 1949.

(By 2nd marriage)

Hon Toby Daniel Moorsom (67 Gibson Sq, N1), *b* 1963.

DAUGHTER LIVING *(By 1st marriage)*

Hon Emma Dorothy *b* 1956.

(By 2nd marriage)

Hon Sophie Ann *b* 1961.

YOUNG OF GRAFFHAM, BARON (Young) (Life Baron 1984)

DAVID IVOR YOUNG, PC, son of Joseph Young, by his wife, Rebecca; *b* 27 Feb 1932; *ed* Christ's Coll, Finchley, and Univ Coll, London (LLB); solicitor 1956; Chm Eldonwall Ltd 1961-75, and Manufacturers Hanover Property Services 1974-84; Dir Town & City Properties Ltd 1972-75; Chm British Organisation for Rehabilitation by Training 1975-80 (Pres 1980-82); Member Admin Cttee World Organisation for Rehabilitation by Training Union 1980-84; Chm Internat Council of Jewish Social and Welfare since 1981; Dir Centre for Policy Studies 1979-82 (Member Management Bd 1977); Member English Industrial Estates Corpn 1980-82; Chm Manpower Services Commn 1982-84; Dept of Industry Industrial Adviser 1979-80, and Special Adviser 1980-82; Member Nat Economic Development Council since 1982; Min without Portfolio 1984-85, Sec of State for Employment 1985-87, for Trade and Industry 1987-89; Pres Inst of Directors since 1993, of Jewish Care since 1990, and of Central Council for Jewish Community Services since 1993; Exec Chm Cable & Wireless plc since 1990; Dir Salomon Inc 1990-94; Trustee Royal Opera House Trust; Hon FRPS; *cr PC 1984, and Baron Young of Graffham*, of Graffham, co W Sussex 1984 (Life Baron): *m* 1956, Lita Marianne, da of Jonas Shaw, and has issue.
Address – 124 Theobalds Rd, WC1X 8RX. *Club* – Savile.

DAUGHTERS LIVING

Hon Karen Debra (*Hon Lady Rix*), *b* 1957: *m* 1983, Sir Bernard Anthony Rix (Hon Mr Justice Rix), son of late Otto Rix, of London, and has issue living, Jacob, *b* 19—, — Gideon, *b* 19—, — Jonathan, *b* 19—, — Hannah, *b* 19—, — Rachel Elsie, *b* 1994.
Hon Judith A., *b* 1960, *m* 1989, Jeremy A. Amias, yr son of Alan Amias, of London.

YOUNGER OF LECKIE, VISCOUNT (Younger) (Viscount UK 1923, Bt 1911)

Swift and bold

Younger as the years go by

EDWARD GEORGE YOUNGER, OBE, TD, 3rd Viscount, and 3rd Baronet; *b* 21 Nov 1906; *s* 1946; *ed* Winchester, and at New Coll, Oxford (BA 1928); Lt-Col (ret) Argyll and Sutherland Highlanders (TA); Lord Lt of Stirlingshire and Falkirk 1964-79; 1939-45 War as Col Gen Staff (OBE); OBE (Mil) 1940: *m* 1930, Evelyn Margaret, MBE, who *d* 1983, da of late Alexander Logan McClure, KC (Sheriff of Aberdeen, Kincardine, and Banff), of 16 Heriot Row, Edinburgh, and has issue.

Arms – Parted per saltire or and gules, a rose counterchanged, in base a martlet sable, on a chief azure three covered cups or. **Crest** – An armed leg couped at the thigh proper, garnished and spurred or. **Supporters** – *Dexter*, a lion rampant sable; *sinster*, a wolf argent; both armed and langued gules.
Seat – Leckie House, Gargunnock, Stirlingshire FK8 3BN. *Clubs* – New Club, Edinburgh.

SONS LIVING

Hon GEORGE KENNETH HOTSON, TD, PC (*Baron Younger of Prestwick*), *b* 22 Sept 1931; *cr Baron Younger of Prestwick* (Life Baron) 1992 (see that title).
Hon Alexander James, *b* 1933; *ed* Winchester, and Worcester Coll, Oxford (BA 1956); late Capt Argyll and Sutherland Highlanders (TA); Dir of Sir Joseph Causton & Sons, Ltd 1963-68; Managing Dir of Robt Maclehose & Co Ltd 1968-77; Dir of Simpson Label Co Ltd, Dalkeith; served Korea 1952: *m* 1959, Annabelle Christine, da of late Gerald Furnivall, of Middle Brook, Bishop's Waltham, Hants, and has issue living, Nicholas Gerald Gilmour, *b* 1963, — Rupert Edward Alexander, *b* 1966; *ed* Winchester, and King's Coll, Aberdeen, — Amanda Charlotte Frances, *b* 1961: *m* 1st, 1981 (*m diss* 1986), Simon John Miller Richard; 2ndly, 1989, William Alexander Clark, of 18 Coates Cres, Edinburgh, elder son of Dr Alister Clark, of Hurlingham Sq, W6, and has issue living, Ruari Alexander *b* 1991, Harry Edward *b* 1992, — Araminta Lucy, *b* 1967. *Residence* – Wester Leckie, Kippen, Stirlingshire. *Club* – Highland Brigade.
Hon Robert Edward Gilmour, *b* 1940; *ed* Winchester, and New Coll, Oxford (BA), Edinburgh Univ and Glasgow Univ; Sheriff of Glasgow and Strathkelvin 1979-82 Sheriff of Tayside Central and Fife at Stirling and Falkirk 1982-87 and at Stirling and Alloa 1987-92, since when Sheriff of Stirling: *m* 1972, Helen Jane, da of late Eric Gerald Hayes, of Craigdhu, Barbreck, Lochgilphead, Argyll (*see* Muir, Bt), and has issue living, Fergus Robert, *b* 1975, — Meriel Charlotte, *b* 1973. *Residence* – Old Leckie, Gargunnock, Stirling.

DAUGHTER LIVING

Hon Rosalind Evelyn, *b* 1937 *m* 1960, Thomas Ross Charles Cropper, JP, and has issue living, Charles Thomas Howe, *b* 1962: *m* 1994, Sophia, da of Antony de Mestre, — Robert Douglas, *b* 1969, — Jill Marion, *b* 1961: *m* 1984, Michael John Hawker, and has issue living, William Thomas George *b* 1990, Annabel Kate *b* 1988, Emma Louise *b* 1993, — Annabel Rosalind, *b* 1966. *Residence* – Greenhills, Willow Tree, NSW.

WIDOW LIVING OF SON OF SECOND VISCOUNT

Elizabeth Kirsteen (*Hon Lady Younger*) (3 New Buildings, Shore Rd, Old Bosham, W Sussex PO18 8JD), only da of late William Duncan Stewart, JP, of Achara, Duror, Argyll: *m* 1934, Rt Hon Sir Kenneth Gilmour Younger, KBE, who *d* 1976, and has issue (see colls infra).

COLLATERAL BRANCH LIVING

Issue of late Rt Hon Sir Kenneth Gilmour Younger, KBE, yr son of 2nd Viscount, *b* 1908, *d* 1976; MP (*L*) Grimsby 1945-59; Min of State for Foreign Affrs 1950-51: *m* 1934, Elizabeth Kirsteen (ante), only da of late William Duncan Stewart, JP, of Achara, Duror, Argyll:—
James Samuel, *b* 1951; *ed* Westminster, and New Coll, Oxford: *m* 1984, Katharine Anne, da of C. K. Spencer, of Abergavenny, Gwent, and has issue living, Edward Kenneth Spencer, *b* 1986. *Residence* – 28 Rylett Cres, W12 9RL. —— Susannah Mary, *b* 1936; *ed* Somerville Coll, Oxford (MA). —— Christina Lucy, *b* 1950; *ed* St Hilda's Coll, Oxford.

PREDECESSORS – (1) GEORGE Younger, el son of late James Younger, brewer, of Alloa, by Janet, who *d* 1912, da of late John McEwan, of Alloa; *b* 1851; was Chm of George Younger & Son, Ltd, of Alloa, and a Director of National Bank of Scotland, and of Lloyds Bank, Ltd; Lord-Lieut for Stirlingshire 1926-9; MP for Ayr (*C*) Jan 1906 to Oct 1922; *cr* a Baronet 1911, and *Viscount Younger of Leckie*, of Alloa, Clackmannanshire (peerage of United Kingdom) 1923: *m* 1879, Lucy, who *d* 1921, da of Edward Smith, MD, FRS, of Heanor Fall, Derbyshire, and Harley Street, W; *d* 1929; *s* by his son (2) JAMES, 2nd Viscount, *b* 1880; Lieut-Col (ret) Fife and Forfar Yeo, Vice-Lieut for Clackmannanshire, a Director of George Younger & Son, Ltd, of Alloa, and Ensign of Roy Co of Archers (King's Body Guard for Scotland); European War 1914-19 (DSO): *m* 1906, Maud, who *d* 1957, da of Sir John Gilmour, 1st Bt; *d* 1946; *s* by his son (3) EDWARD GEORGE, 3rd Viscount and present peer.

YOUNGER OF PRESTWICK, BARON (Younger) (Life Baron 1992)

GEORGE KENNETH HOTSON YOUNGER, KCVO, TD, PC, eldest son of 3rd Viscount Younger of Leckie, OBE, TD; *b* 22 Sept 1931; *ed* Winchester (Fellow 1992), and New Coll, Oxford (MA); Hon LLD Glasgow 1992, Hon DLitt Napier Univ 1992, Hon D Univ Edinburgh 1992; late Major Argyll and Sutherland Highlanders (TA), served BAOR and Korea 1951, Hon Col 154 Regt RCT (V) 1977-85, Brig HM Body Guard for Scotland (Royal Company of Archers); DL Stirlingshire 1968; Gov Royal Scottish Academy of Music 1962-70, Dir Royal Bank of Scotland since 1989 (Chm since 1991), Murray Johnstone Investment Trusts since 1989, Scottish Equitable Life Assurance Soc since 1990, SPEED Ltd since 1991, and Chm Siemens Plessey (UK) Ltd since 1991, and Ayrshire Community Airport Project (now PIK Ltd) since 1991; Scottish Conservative Whip 1965-67, Dep-Chm Scottish Conservative & Unionist Assocn 1967-70, Joint Parl Under Sec of State for Scotland for Development 1970-74, Min of State for Defence Jan-March 1974, Chm Conservative Party in Scotland 1974-76, Sec of State for Scotland 1979-Jan 1986, Sec of State for Defence 1986-89; MP Ayr Div of Ayrshire and Bute (C) 1964-92; Chancellor of Napier Univ since 1993; *cr* PC 1979, *Baron Younger of Prestwick*, of Ayr in the District of Kyle and Carrick (Life Baron) 1992, and KCVO 1993: *m* 1954, Diana Rhona, eldest da of late Capt Gerald Seymour Tuck, DSO, RN (ret), of Little London, Chichester, Sussex, and has issue.

Arms – The arms of Viscount Younger of Leckie with shield, crest and supporters each debruised of a three point label or. *Residence* – Easter Leckie, Gargunnock, Stirlingshire. *Clubs* – Caledonian (London), Highland Brigade.

SONS LIVING

Hon James Edward George, *b* 11 Nov 1955; *ed* Winchester, and St Andrews Univ (MA); MBA, MCIM; Personnel Mangr Coats Patons plc 1979-84; Consultant Angela Mortimer Ltd 1984-86; Asst Dir Stephens Consultancies 1986-92; Dir MacInnes Younger since 1993: *m* 1988, Jennie Veronica, da of William Wootton, of Chanters House, Pilton, Som, and has issue living, Alexander William George, *b* 13 Nov 1993, — Emily Evelyn, *b* 1990, — Alice Elizabeth, *b* 1992. *Residence* – 34 Elmfield Rd, SW17. *Club* – New (Edinburgh).
Hon Charles Gerald Alexander, *b* 1959; *ed* Winchester: *m* 1986, Sally Elizabeth, elder da of late Kenneth Mackenzie Neil Fergusson, of Blinkbonny House, Haddington, E Lothian, and has had issue, Arabella Emily, *b* 1987, — Katrina Louise, *b* 1990, — Georgina Harriet, *b* and *d* 1993.
Hon Andrew Seymour Robert, *b* 1962; *ed* Winchester: *m* 1989, Hilary Margaret, yst da of Philip Alexander Forbes Chalk, of The Barn House, Hurstbourne Priors, Whitchurch, Hants, and has issue living, Rosanna Lucy *b* 1994. *Residence* – Esk Bank House, Cradley, Malvern, Worcs.

DAUGHTER LIVING

Hon Joanna Rosalind, *b* 1958; has resumed her maiden name: *m* 1986 (*m diss* 1989), Gregory William Rossiter Cooper, son of late Brian Cooper, of Ealing, W5. *Residence* – 38 Haverhill Rd, SW12 0HA.

YPRES, EARLDOM OF (French) (Extinct 1988)

DAUGHTERS LIVING OF THIRD EARL

(By 1st marriage)

Lady Charlene Mary Olivia, *b* 1946: *m* 1965, Charles Mordaunt Milner (*see* Milner, Bt). *Address* – PO Box 41, Klatmuts, Cape, S Africa.
Lady Sarah Mary Essex, *b* 1953.
Lady Emma Mary Helena, *b* 1958: *m* 1st, 1980 (*m diss* 1989), Charles Geoffrey Humfrey, only son of Charles Michael Humfrey, of Alderney, CI; 2ndly, 1991, Christopher Francis Wolferstan Chanter, son of David Wolferstan Chanter, of The Vine House, Abbots Leigh, Bristol, and has issue living (by 1st *m*), Charles Hamish Lowndes French, *b* 1986, — (by 2nd *m*) Thomas Fulco French Wolferstan, *b* 1992.

(By 2nd marriage)

Lady Lucy Kathleen, *b* 1975.

SISTER LIVING OF THIRD EARL

Lady Patricia Mary Charlemont, *b* 1919: *m* 1942, Henry Edmund Roland Kingsbury (E Bradford, colls), who *d* 1980, and has issue living, Philip Charles Orlando (The Old Farm House, Stoke Row, Henley-on-Thames, Oxon), *b* 1944; *ed* Winchester; late 2nd Lt 15th/19th King's R Hussars: *m* 1971, Huberta Maria Daly, da of late Maj Jobst Heinrich von Reinhard, and has issue living, Julian Henry Orlando *b* 1972, Francis Alexander Lowndes *b* 1973, Oliver Philip Lambart *b* 1976, Mariella Charlotte Pauline *b* 1982, — Gerald Richard Charlemont (Dadbrook House, Cuddington, Berks), *b* 1945; *ed* Winchester: *m* 1975, Clico, only da of Capt Bernard MacIntyre, DSC, RN (ret), of Birdham, Sussex, and has issue living, Thomas Jake Essex Charlemont *b* 1977, Toby Bernard Richard Henry *b* 1979, Gemma Alice Olivia Charlotte *b* 1984. *Address* – c/o Lloyds Bank plc, 6 Pall Mall, SW1 Y5H.

WIDOW LIVING OF THIRD EARL

DEBORAH (*Countess of Ypres*), da of R. Roberts, of Liverpool: *m* 1972, as his 2nd wife, the 3rd Earl, who *d* 1988. *Residence* – 2 Southwood Court, Northway, Hampstead Garden Suburb, NW11.

COLLATERAL BRANCH LIVING

Issue of late Lt-Col Hon (Edward) Gerald Fleming French, DSO, 2nd son of 1st Earl; *b* 1883, *d* 1970: *m* 1906, Leila, who *d* 1959, da of Robert King, JP, formerly of Natal, S Africa:—
Essex Leila Hilary (*Viscountess Monsell*), *b* 1907: *m* 1st, 1929 (*m diss* 1935), Vyvyan Drury; 2ndly, 1950, 1st Viscount Monsell, and has issue living, (by 1st *m*) Romayne, *b* 1930. —— Violet Valerie (*Hon Mrs Philip L. Kindersley*), *b* 1909: *m* 1st, 1931 (*m diss* 1934), 4th Baron Brougham and Vaux, who *d* 1967; 2ndly, 1936, Hon Philip Leyland Kindersley (*see* B Kindersley). *Residence* – The Coach House, Northwick Park, Blockley, Glos.

ZETLAND, MARQUESS OF (Dundas) (Marquess UK 1892, Bt GB 1762)

Try

LAWRENCE MARK DUNDAS, 4th Marquess, 6th Earl of Zetland, 7th Baron Dundas and 8th Baronet; *b* 28 Dec 1937; *s* 1989; *ed* Harrow, and Christ's Coll, Camb; late 2nd Lieut Grenadier Guards; patron of one living; Steward Jockey Club since 1992, Dir British Horseracing Board since 1993: *m* 1964, Susan Rose, 2nd da of late Guy Richard Chamberlin, of Shefford House, Great Shefford, Newbury, Berks, and has issue.

Arms – Argent, a lion rampant gules, within a double tressure flory counterflory, all within a bordure azure. **Crest** – A lion's head affrontée gules, encircled by an oak bush proper. **Supporters** – Two lions proper, each crowned with an antique crown or, and gorged with a chaplet of oak leaves vert; pendant from each chaplet an escutcheon, that on the *dexter* charged with the arms of *Bruce*, viz argent, a saltire and chief gules, and on a canton argent, a lion rampant azure; that on the *sinister* with the arms of *Fitzwilliam*, viz lozengy or and gules.
Seat – Aske, Richmond, N Yorks. *Town Residence* – 44 Bramerton St, SW3. *Clubs* – All England Lawn Tennis; Jockey.

SONS LIVING

ROBIN LAWRENCE (*Earl of Ronaldshay*), *b* 5 March 1965; *ed* Harrow, and RAC Cirencester.
Lord James Edward, *b* 1967; *ed* Harrow, and RAC Cirencester: *m* 1991, Melanie C., eldest da of Robert Henry Whitefield, of The Old Rectory, Stocking Pelham, Herts, and has issue living, Poppy Alice, *b* 1993.

DAUGHTERS LIVING

Lady Henrietta Kate, *b* 1970.
Lady Victoria Clare, *b* 1973.

BROTHERS LIVING

Lord David Paul Nicholas, *b* 1945; *ed* Harrow, and Central Sch of Speech and Drama; song writer: *m* 1971, Corinna, da of Denys Scott, of 11 Glebe Place, SW3, and has issue living, Harry Thomas Jeingo, *b* 1981, — Daisy Star, *b* 1975. *Residence* – 17 Mandeville Courtyard, 142 Battersea Park Rd, SW11 4NB.
Lord (Richard) Bruce, *b* 1951; *ed* Harrow: *m* 1st, 1974 (*m diss* 1981), Jane Melanie, yst da of Ernest Frederick Wright, of 47 Montrose Place, SW1; 2ndly, 1983, Sophie Caroline, only da of Henry Giles Francis Lascelles (*see* E Harewood, colls), and has issue living (by 1st *m*), Max, *b* 1978, — Emily Louisa, *b* 1980, — (by 2nd *m*) Flora, *b* 1986, — Tallulah, *b* 1988. *Residence* – 49 Stephendale Rd, SW6.

SISTER LIVING

Lady Serena Jane, *b* 1940: *m* 1964, Capt Nigel Ion Charles Kettlewell, JP, RN, and has issue living, Robert James, *b* 1965; *ed* Sherborne, — Melissa Jane, *b* 1968: *m* 1992, John S. Nicholson, yr son of C. J. Nicholson, of E Lambrook, Som, — Charlotte Rose, *b* 1970. *Residence* – The Old Rectory, Newton Toney, Salisbury, Wilts SP4 0HA.

AUNTS LIVING (*daughters of 2nd Marquess*)

Lady Viola Mary, *b* 1910.
Lady Jean Agatha, *b* 1916: *m* 1939, Capt Hector Lorenzo Christie, who *d* 1969, and has issue living, William Lawrence, *b* 1948; *ed* Eton: *m* 1st, 1976 (*m diss* 1979), Pamela Rosalind Grace (Grace Coddington), da of late William Reginald Dudley Coddington, and formerly wife of Michael Chow; 2ndly, 1991, Mrs Amanda Kate Victoria Howard, only da of Derek Nimmo, actor, of Kensington, and formerly wife of Hon Nicholas Paul Geoffrey Howard (*see* E Carlisle colls), and has issue living (by 2nd *m*), Charles Hector Lorenzo *b* 1994, Florence Ella Kate *b* 1991, — Carolyn Anne, *b* 1946: *m* 1st, 1966 (*m diss* 1970), John Julian Reynolds (*see* Reynolds, Bt); 2ndly, 1974 (*m diss* 1981), Robert Scully, of San Francisco, USA; 3rdly, 1986 (George) Roger Waters, of 1 Fife Rd, SW14, and has issue living (by 2nd *m*), Harry William *b* 1976, India Rose *b* 1978. *Residence* – Seven Springs, Upper Lambourn, Newbury, Berks.

WIDOW LIVING OF THIRD MARQUESS

PENELOPE (*Penelope, Marchioness of Zetland*), da of late Col Ebenezer John Lecky Pike, CBE, MC, of Little Glebe, Fontwell, Sussex: *m* 1936, the 3rd Marquess, who *d* 1989. *Residences* – Hartforth Hill, nr Richmond, N Yorks; 59 Cadogan Place, SW1.

COLLATERAL BRANCHES LIVING (*In remainder to the Earldoms, Barony and Baronetcy*)

Grandchildren of late Hon John Charles Dundas, brother of 1st Marquess:—
Issue of late Frederick James Dundas, *b* 1877, *d* 1950: *m* 1913, Sylvia Mary, who *d* 1976, el da of Hugh March Phillips, of Chapel Court, Kenn, near Exeter:—
Sir Hugh Spencer Lisle, CBE, DSO, DFC (Schoolroom, Dockenfield, Farnham, Surrey, and 55 Iverna Court, W8. White's Club) *b* 1920; *ed* Stowe; Group Capt (ret) RAF; DL Surrey 1969, and High Sheriff 1989; 1940-45 War (despatches); DFC 1941; DSO 1944 (Bar 1945); Kt 1987: *m* 1950, Hon (Enid) Rosamond Lawrence, da of 3rd Baron Trevethin and 1st Baron Oaksey, and has issue living, James Frederick Trevor (16 Norland Sq, W11 4PX), *b* (Nov) 1950: *m* 1979, Jennifer A., da of Lt-Col John Daukes, of Chaucers, Seale, nr Farnham, Surrey, and has issue living, a son *b* 1989, Clare Jessica *b* 1984, Lucy Rose *b* 1986, — Sarah Jane, *b* 1953: *m* 1977, Terence McGlade, of 190 Crawford St, Toronto, Ont M6J 2V6, Canada, and has issue living, Victoria Rose Clare *b* 1983, Charlotte Amanda *b* 1984, — Amanda Rose, *b* 1956: *m* 1986, Thomas Nicholas McKinlay Service, of 30 Baskerville Rd, SW18 3RS, yr son of late Ian McKinlay Service, and has issue living, George *b* 1992, Katherine Mary Rose *b* 1987, Louisa Amy *b* 1989. —— Elizabeth Mary (*Dowager Lady Muir*), *b* 1914: *m* 1936, Sir John Harling Muir, 3rd Bt, who *d* 1994. *Residence* – Bankhead, Blair Drummond, Perthshire. —— Charmian, *b* 1931: *m* 1955, Maurice R. Snowden, of Manor Cottage, Milton, Banbury, Oxon, and has issue living, John Frederick Hugh, *b* 1955, — Mark Lawrence, *b* 1957.

Grandchildren of late Hon William Fitzwilliam James Dundas (infra):—
Issue of late Robert Bruce Dundas, *b* 1900; *d* 1980: *m* 1934, Enid Mary, da of late Cdr Francis William Roberts, RN:—

David Lawrence, *b* 1936; *ed* Shrewsbury, and Balliol Coll, Oxford (Domus Exhibitioner): *m* 1968, Faith Dorine, da of Harold Scott, of Friendship, Jamaica, WI. —— Jennifer Elizabeth Mary *b* 1942: *m* 1963, John Warren Williams, of 6 Swinton Close, Ipswich, Suffolk, and has issue living, Patricia Helen, *b* 1965.

Issue of late Hon William Fitzwilliam James Dundas, brother of 1st Marquess, *b* 1860, *d* 1945: *m* 1892, Mary Maud, who *d* 1945, da of late Lieut-Col H. A. Prinsep:—
Janet Elizabeth, *b* 1911.

Grandchildren of late Hon Cospatrick Thomas Dundas, brother of 1st Marquess:—
Issue of late Vice-Adm John George Lawrence Dundas, CB, CBE, *b* 1893, *d* 1952: *m* 1928, Ruth (255 Buckingham Way, San Francisco, Cal 94132, USA), da of Archibald Coleman:—

John Archibald Lawrence (151 Concord St, Apt 13, Newton Lower Falls, Mass 02162, USA), *b* 1942: MD; *ed* Groton, and Harvard Univ: *m* 1967 (*m diss* 1985), Dorothy Polk, da of H. Bradford Washburn, of Boston, Mass, and has issue living, Michael Henry Lawrence, *b* 1969, — Patrick George Bradford, *b* 1973, — Matthew Colgate, *b* 1976, — Jennifer Deirdre, *b* 1971. —— Elgiva Ruth, *b* 1929; PhD: *m* 1951, Penn Thomas Watson, of 4408 Pamlico Drive, Raleigh, N Carolina, USA, and has issue living, Rom Purefoy (378 Central St, Newton, Mass 02166, USA), *b* 1955: *m* 1981, Susan Bazett, — Ruth Coleman, *b* 1952: *m* 1st, 1974 (*m diss* 1978), Jack Barry Tanenbaum; 2ndly, 1982, Jeffrey Scheuer, of 56 West 10th St, New York, NY 10011, USA, — Clare Thomas, *b* 1958: *m* 1st, 1982 (*m diss* 1992), James Acker, MD; 2ndly, 1993, Louis Gallo, of 544 Riverside Drive, Ormond Beach, Florida 32176, USA. —— Rosemary Maud, *b* 1933; MA: *m* 1954, Dr Robert Gray Patton, of 85 Parker Av, San Francisco, Cal 94118, USA, and has issue living, Mary Gray, *b* 1956: *m* 1986, Roger T. Phelps, — Sarah Dundas, *b* 1959: *m* 1991, Peter Feichtmeir, — Susannah MacRae, *b* 1964. —— Deirdre Clare, *b* 1935; MA: *m* 1st, 1958 (*m diss* 1960), Clifford Enright; 2ndly, 1961, Dr Walter Munro Newton, of 406A Cocos Pl, Honolulu, Hawaii 96818, USA, and has issue living, (by 1st *m*) Iva Margaret, *b* 1959, — (by 2nd *m*) Walter Monroe, *b* 1962, — Elisabeth Dundas, *b* 1970. —— Alexandra Mary, *b* 1946; PhD: *m* 1st, 1965 (*m diss* 1973), John Andrew Todd; 2ndly, 1988, Stephen Russell Fox, PhD, of 13 Campbell Park, Somerville, Mass 02144, USA, and has issue living (by 1st *m*), John Andrew, *b* 1970.

(In special remainder to Baronetcy only)

Grandson of late Thomas George Dundas (infra):—
Issue of late Thomas Archibald Dundas, *b* 1880, *d* 19—: *m* 1903, Sybil Katherine, da of late F. R. Hampshire:—
Thomas Archibald David, *b* 1904.

Grandson of late Joseph Dundas, son of late Lt-Col Thomas Dundas, son of late Thomas Dundas, MP, brother of 1st Bt:—
Issue of late Thomas George Dundas, *b* 1853, *d* 1929: *m* 1879, Mary, who *d* 1923, da of late Lieut-Col Duncan Henry Caithness Reay Davidson, of Tulloch (Mackenzie, Bt, *cr* 1703 (of Gairloch), colls):—
Ronald George, *b* 1885: *m* 1912, Olive Mary, da of Robert Scott-Day, and has issue living, Eleanor Mary, *b* 1914. *Residence –* Los Angeles, California, USA.

PREDECESSORS – **(1)** LAWRENCE Dundas, Comy-Gen and Contractor to the Army 1747-59; *cr* a *Baronet* 1762 with remainder to his brother Thomas; MP for Edinburgh 1768-81; *d* 1781; *s* by his son **(2)** Sir THOMAS, 2nd Bt; MP for co Stirling 1768-9; Lord-Lieut and Vice-Adm of Orkney and Shetland; *cr Baron Dundas*, of Aske, co York (peerage of Great Britain) 1794; *d* 1820; *s* by his son **(3)** LAWRENCE, 2nd Baron; successively MP for Richmond and York. Lord-Lieut and Vice-Adm of Orkney and Shetland; *cr Earl of Zetland* (peerage of United Kingdom) 1838; *d* 1839; *s* by his son **(4)** THOMAS, KG, 2nd Earl; MP for Richmond 1818-30 and 1835-9, and York 1830-32 and 1833-5; Lord-Lieut of N Riding of York, and Grand Master of Freemasons of England 1843-69; *d* 1873; *s* by his nephew **(5)** Rt Hon LAWRENCE, KT (el son of Hon John Charles Dundas, MP, 4th son of 1st. Earl, by Margaret Matilda, who *d* 1907, da of James Talbot, of Mary Ville, co Wexford), 3rd Earl, *b* 1844; MP for Richmond (*L*) 1872-3; Lord-in-Waiting to Queen Victoria 1880, and Lord-Lieut of Ireland 1889-92; *cr* KT 1900, and *Marquess of Zetland* and *Earl of Ronaldshay*, in co of Orkney and Shetland (peerage of United Kingdom) 1892: *m* 1871, Lady Lilian Selina Elizabeth Lumley, who *d* 1943, da of 9th Earl of Scarbrough; *d* 1929; *s* by his el son **(6)** LAWRENCE JOHN LUMLEY, KG, GCSI, GCIE, PC, 2nd Marquess, *b* 1876; formerly Capt 1st N Riding of Yorkshire Artillery, W Div RA, Major 4th Batn Green Howards, and Hon Col 62nd (Northumbrian) Anti-Aircraft Brig RA (TA); sat as MP for Hornsey Div of Middlesex 1907-16; appointed a Member of Roy Commn on Indian Public Ser 1912, Gov of Bengal 1916, and Pres of Roy Geographical So 1922 (a Trustee thereof 1925-47, and of Roy India So 1923-50; Sec of State for India 1935-40 (also for Burma 1937-40); Chm of Executive Committee of National Trust 1931-45, and Lord Lieut of N Riding of Yorkshire 1945-51; bore Sword of State at Coronation of King George VI: *m* 1907, Cicely, who *d* 1973, da of Col Mervyn Archdale, formerly 12th Lancers; *d* 1961; *s* by his el son **(7)** LAWRENCE ALDRED MERVYN, 3rd Marquess, *b* 1908; DL N Yorks, Treasurer Royal Masonic Institution for Girls, temp Maj Yorkshire Yeo, served 1939-45 War in Middle East (despatches): *m* 1936, Penelope, da of late Col Ebenezer John Lecky Pike, CBE, MC, of Little Glebe, Fontwell, Sussex; *d* 1989; *s* by his eldest son **(8)** LAWRENCE MARK, 4th Marquess and present peer; also Earl of Zetland, Earl of Ronaldshay, and Baron Dundas.

ZOUCHE, BARON (Frankland) (Baron E 1308, Bt (E) 1660)
(Title pronounced "Zooch")

JAMES ASSHETON FRANKLAND, 18th Baron and 12th Baronet; *b* 23 Feb 1943; *s* to Baronetcy 1944, and to Barony 1965; Capt 15th/19th King's R Hussars: *m* 1978, Sally Olivia, yr da of Roderic M. Barton, of Brook House, Pulham, St Mary, Norfolk, and has issue.

Arms – Azure, a dolphin naiant embowed or, on a chief of the second two saltires gules. **Crest** – A dolphin hauriant argent and entwined round an anchor erect proper.
Residence – 7 St Vincent Place, Albert Park, Vic 3206, Australia.

SON LIVING

Hon WILLIAM THOMAS ASSHETON, *b* 23 July 1984.

DAUGHTER LIVING

Hon Lucy Victoria, *b* 1982.

AUNT LIVING (*Daughter of Mary Cecil, Baroness Zouche*)

Hon Barbara Mary FRANKLAND, *b* 1906; resumed by deed poll 1958 her maiden surname of Frankland in lieu of that of Lucas: *m* 1st, 1926 (*m diss* 1937), Brig Otho Leslie Prior-Palmer, 9th Lancers (DSO 1945, Knt 1959), who *d* 1986; 2ndly, 1937 (*m diss* 1943), 5th Earl of Normanton, who *d* 1967; 3rdly, 1943 (*m diss* 1962), Peter Lucas, and has issue living, (by 1st *m*) Diana Mary Leslie, *b* 1929: *m* 1974, Bruno de Marco. *Residence* – Ridge House, Stockland, Honiton, Devon.

COLLATERAL BRANCHES LIVING

Issue of late W/Cmdr Hon Roger Nathaniel Frankland, RAuxAF (Res), yr son of Mary Cecil, Baroness Zouche, *b* 1909, *d* 1989: *m* 1st, 1931 (*m diss* 1947), Elizabeth Cecil, who *d* 1968, da of Arthur Cecil Sanday, of 41 Evelyn Gdns, SW7; 2ndly, 1947, Olivia, who *d* 1987, da of late Rev Hon Nigel Campbell (*see* E Cawdor), and widow of Maj Samuel John Rennie Bucknill, Irish Gds:—
(By 1st *m*) Timothy Cecil (c/o Hill Samuel Co Ltd, 100 Wood St, EC2), *b* 1931; *ed* Charterhouse; Lieut 15th/19th Hussars; Dir Hill Samuel Co Ltd since 1967: *m* 1957 (*m diss* 1968), Lynette, yr da of Lt-Cmdr Ian Hope Dundas, RNVR, and has issue living, Nicholas Charles (East Park House, Handcross, W Sussex RH17 6BD), *b* 1958: *m* 1991, Suzanne H., only da of Michael Race, of Tole House, Keymer, Sussex, and has issue living, Tallulah Cecily *b* 1992, Camellia Tatjana *b* 1994, — Mathew Curzon, *b* 1962, — Adam Christian *b* 1965. —— Frederick Mark, *b* 1934; *ed* Charterhouse, and Pembroke Coll, Camb (BA).

(In remainder to the Barony only)

Grandchildren of late Emily Anne Curzon (da of late Hon Edward Cecil Curzon, 2nd son of Harriet Anne, Baroness de la Zouche), who *m* 1861, Augustus Frederick Wentworth Gore, formerly 7th Hussars:—
Issue of late Francis Southwell Cecil Charles Gore, Lieut Middlesex Regt, *b* 1879, *ka* 1917: *m* 1904, Frances Rose Mary, who *d* 1974, only da of C. Maybrook:—
Francis Norton Wentworth, CBE, *b* 1906; Brigadier (ret) late RA; OBE (Mil) 1947, CBE (Mil) 1960: *m* 1939, Else Gurli Astrid, da of late Evald Christensen, of Copenhagen, Denmark and has issue living, Peter Wentworth (Saddlers, Mark Cross, Crowborough, Kent), *b* 1946; Capt Queen's Own Hussars: *m* 1975, Joanna Penelope, da of late John Guy Bedford, and has issue living, Emily-Jane Wentworth *b* 1977, Robert Edward Wentworth *b* 1979, — Frances Jane Wentworth, *b* 1947: *m* 1970, Maj Colijn Thomson-Moore, Irish Gds (ret), of 14 Clareville Court, Clareville Grove, SW7, and Barne, Clonmel, co Tipperary, and has issue living, Richard Charles Randal *b* 1978, Alexandra Louise *b* 1977. *Residence* – Vine Cottage, Point Hill, Rye, Sussex TN31 7NP.

PREDECESSORS – (1) WILLIAM la Zouche, Lord of Haryngworth, was summoned to Parliament of England as a Baron 1308-14; *d* 1352; *s* by his grandson (2) WILLIAM, 2nd Baron; summoned to Parliament during his grandfather's lifetime 1348-51, and after his grandfather's decease 1352-82; *d* 1382; *s* by his son (3) WILLIAM, 3rd Baron; summoned to Parliament 1383-94; *d* 1396; *s* by his son (4) WILLIAM, KG, 4th Baron; summoned to Parliament 1396-1414; *d* 1415; *s* by his son (5) WILLIAM, 5th Baron; summoned to Parliament 1426-63; *d* 1463; *s* by his son (6) WILLIAM, 6th Baron, who in 1466 was summoned to Parliament in right of his mother as *Baron St Maur*; *d* 1468; *s* by his son (7) JOHN, 7th Baron; was summoned to Parliament 1482-3; attainted 1485, and attainder reversed 1495; again summoned to Parliament 1509-15; *d* 1526; *s* by his son (8) JOHN, 8th Baron; summoned to Parliament 1529-48; *d* 1550; *s* by his son (9) RICHARD, 9th Baron; was summoned to Parliament 1552; *d* 1552; *s* by his son (10) GEORGE, 10th Baron; summoned to Parliament 1553-66; *d* 1569; *s* by his son (11) EDWARD, 11th Baron; was summoned to Parliament 1571-1625; was Lieut of N and S Wales, and Constable of Dover and Warden of the Cinque Ports; *d* 1625, when the Baronies of Zouche and St Maur became abeyant between his two daus, Elizabeth and Mary, and remained so until 1815, when the abeyance of the Barony of Zouche was terminated in favour of (12) Sir CECIL Bisshopp, 8th Bt, who became 12th Baron in right of his mother, she being the descendant in the 6th generation of Elizabeth, el da of 11th Baron (ante); *d* 1828, when the baronetcy devolved upon his cousin, and the barony became abeyant between his two daus, Harriet Anne Curzon (infra), and Katherine Annabella, wife of Sir George Richard Brooke-Pechell, 4th Bt; in 1829 the abeyance was terminated in favour of his el da (13) HARRIET ANNE, known as Baroness de la Zouche: *m* 1808, Hon Robert Curzon, MP, son of 1st Viscount Curzon (*see* E Howe); *d* 1870; *s* by her son (14) ROBERT Curzon, 14th Baron; *b* 1810; was MP for Clitheroe: *m* 1850, Emily Julia, da of the Rt Hon Sir Robert Wilmot-Horton, 3rd Bt; *d* 1873; *s* by his son (15) ROBERT NATHANIEL CECIL GEORGE, 15th Baron; *b* 1851: *m* 1875 (*m diss* 1876), Hon Annie Mary Eleanor Fraser, who *d* 1895, 2nd da of 17th Baron Saltoun; *d* 1914; *s* by his sister (16) DAREA, *b* 1860; *d* 1917; *s* by her cousin (17) MARY CECIL (da of late Col George Augustus Curzon, grandson of late Harriet Anne, Baroness de la Zouche), *b* 1875: *m* 1901, Sir Frederick William Francis George Frankland, 10th Bt, who *d* 1937 (see * infra); *d* 1965; *s* by her grandson (18) Sir JAMES ASSHETON Frankland (only son of Hon Sir Thomas William Assheton Frankland, 11th Bt), who *s* as 12th Bt 1944 (infra); 18th Baron and present peer.
*(1) WILLIAM, son of *Sir* Henry Frankland of Thirkelby, Yorks, *b c* 1640; MP for Thirsk, *cr* a Baronet of England 1660: *m* 1662, Arabella, who *d* 1687, da of Hon Henry Belasyse, *d* 1697, *s* by his son (2) Sir THOMAS, 2nd Bt, *b c* 1665; PMG 1690-1715 and MP for Thirsk, *m* 1683, Elizabeth, who *d* 1733, da of Sir John Russell, 4th Bt (*cr* 1629) by Frances, da of Oliver Cromwell, Lord Protector; *d* 1726; *s* by his el son (3) Sir THOMAS, 3rd Bt; a Lord of Admiralty 1730-41 and MP for Harwich and Thirsk: *m* 1st, Dinah, who *d* 1741, da of Francis Topham; 2ndly, 1743, Sarah Moseley, who *d* 1783; *d* 1747; *s* by his nephew (4) Sir CHARLES HENRY, 4th Bt (el son of Henry Frankland, 4th son of 2nd Bt) *b* 1716; Collector at Boston,

Mass, 1741-57 and Consul-Gen at Lisbon 1757-67: *m* 1756, Agnes (who *m* 2ndly, 1781, John Drew, banker, and *d* 1783) da of Edward Surriage, of Marblehead, New England; *d* 1768; *s* by his brother **(5)** *Sir* Thomas, 5th Bt, *b* 1718; Admiral of the White and MP for Thirsk: *m* 1743, Sarah Rhett, of S Carolina, who *d* 1808; *d* 1784; *s* by his el surv son **(6)** *Sir* Thomas, FRS, 6th Bt, *b* 1750; MP for Thirsk: *m* 1773, Dorothy, who *d* 1820, da of William Smelt; *d* 1831; *s* by his only surv son **(7)** *Sir* Robert, 7th Bt; *b* 1784; MP for Thirsk; assumed by Roy Lic 1837 the surname of Russell after Frankland on inheriting Chequers Court, Bucks, from Sir Robert Greenhill Russell, Bt: *m* 1815, Louisa Anne, who *d* 1871, da of Lord George Murray (D Atholl); *d* 1849; *s* by his cousin in the Baronetcy but not the estates **(8)** *Sir* Frederick William, 8th Bt (el son of Rev Canon Roger Frankland, yst son of 5th Bt), *b* 1793; served at Waterloo and Peninsula: *m* 1821, Katherine Margaret, who *d* 1871, da of Capt Isaac Scarth; *d* 1878; *s* by his el surv son **(9)** *Sir* William Adolphus, 9th Bt *b* 1837; Lt-Col RE: *m* 1864, Lucy Ducarel, who *d* 1928, da of Francis Adams, of Clifton, Glos; *d* 1883; *s* by his el son **(10)** *Sir* Frederick William Francis George, 10th Bt, *b* 1868; Maj Beds Regt Matabele and S African Wars: *m* 1st, 1890, Charlotte, who *d* 1892, da of John Augustus di Zerega, of New York; 2ndly, 1901, Mary Cecil Curzon, *Baroness Zouche*, who *d* 1965 (ante); *d* 1937; *s* by his el son **(11)** *Hon Sir* Thomas William Assheton, 11th Bt, *b* 1902; Maj 15th/19th Hussars: *m* 1st, 1931 (*m diss* 1941), Edna Maud, da of Frederick Hynde Fox; 2ndly, 1942, Pamela Catherine Mabell (Rous), da of Capt Hon Edward James Kay-Shuttleworth (B Shuttleworth), and who *d* 1972, having *m* 3rdly, 1946 (*m diss* 1968), as his 2nd wife, Henry Michael Barclay; 4thly, 1970, Robert Hugh Pardoe; *d* 1944; *s* by his only son **(12)** *Sir* James Assheton, 12th and present Bt, who *s* as 18th Baron Zouche (ante) 1965.

ZUCKERMAN, BARONY OF (Zuckerman) (Extinct 1993)

SON LIVING OF LIFE BARON

Hon Paul Sebastian, *b* 1945; *ed* Rugby, Trin Coll, Camb (MA), and Reading Univ (PhD): *m* 1972 (*m diss* 1987), Mrs Janette Hampel, da of R. R. Mather, of Stoke-by-Clare, Suffolk. *Residence* – The Old Rectory, Grosvenor Rd, SW1. *Club* – Brooks's.

DAUGHTER DECEASED OF LIFE BARON

Hon Stella Maria, *b* 1947: *ed* Cranborne Chase Sch, E Anglia Univ (BA) and London Univ (PhD): *m* 1977, Dr Andrew R. Norman, and *d* 1992, leaving issue, Sebastian Henry Andrew, *b* 1982, — Hester Joanna Rachel, *b* 1978.

WIDOW LIVING OF LIFE BARON

Lady Joan Alice Rufus Isaacs (*Baroness Zuckerman*); JP Birmingham 1961, Norfolk 1967, da of 2nd Marquess of Reading: *m* 1939, Prof Rt Hon Baron Zuckerman, OM, KCB, FRS (Life Baron), who *d* 1993. *Residence* – The Shooting Box, Burnham Thorpe, King's Lynn, Norfolk.

LORDS SPIRITUAL

(Archbishops and Bishops of the Church of England)
(See also page 56)

ARCHBISHOPS

Canterbury (103rd), George Leonard Carey, *b* 1935 apptd 1991.
York (95th), John Stapylton Habgood, *b* 1927 apptd 1983.

BISHOPS

London (131st), David Michael Hope, *b* 1940, apptd 1991.
Durham (93rd), (Anthony) Michael Arnold Turnbull, *b* 1935, apptd 1994.
Winchester (95th), Colin Clement Walter James, *b* 1926, apptd 1985.
Bath and Wells (76th), James Lawton Thompson, *b* 1936, apptd 1991.
Birmingham (7th), Mark Santer, *b* 1936, apptd 1987.
Blackburn (7th), Alan David Chesters, *b* 1937, apptd 1989.
Bradford (8th), David James Smith, *b* 1935, apptd 1992.
Bristol (54th), Barry Rogerson, *b* 1936, apptd 1985.
Carlisle (65th), Ian Harland, *b* 1932, apptd 1989.
Chelmsford (7th), John Waine, *b* 1930, apptd 1986.
Chester (39th), Michael Alfred Baughen, *b* 1930, apptd 1982.
Chichester (99th), Eric Waldron Kemp, *b* 1915, apptd 1974.
Coventry (7th), Simon Barrington-Ward, *b* 1930, apptd 1985.
Derby (5th), Peter Spencer Dawes, *b* 1928, apptd 1988.
Ely (67th), Stephen Whitefield Sykes, *b* 1939, apptd 1990.
Exeter (69th), (Geoffrey) Hewlett Thompson, *b* 1929, apptd 1985.
Gloucester (39th), David Edward Bentley, *b* 1935, apptd 1993.
Guildford (7th), Michael Edgar Adie, *b* 1929, apptd 1983.
Hereford (103rd), John Keith Oliver, *b* 1935, apptd 1990.
Leicester (5th), Thomas Frederick Butler, *b* 1940, apptd 1991.
Lichfield (97th), Keith Norman Sutton, *b* 1934, apptd 1983.
Lincoln (70th), Robert Maynard Hardy, *b* 1936, apptd 1986.

Liverpool (6th), David Stuart Sheppard, *b* 1929, apptd 1975.
Manchester (10th), Christopher John Mayfield, *b* 1935, apptd 1993.
Newcastle (10th), Andrew Alexander Kenny Graham, *b* 1929, apptd 1991.
Norwich (70th), Peter John Nott, *b* 1933, apptd 1985.
Oxford (41st), Richard Douglas Harries, *b* 1936, apptd 1987.
Peterborough (36th), William John Westwood, *b* 1925, apptd 1984.
Portsmouth (7th), Timothy John Bavin, *b* 1935, apptd 1985.
Ripon (11th), David Nigel de Lorentz Young, *b* 1931, apptd 1977.
Rochester (vacant).
St. Albans (8th), John Bernard Taylor, *b* 1929, apptd 1980.
St. Edmundsbury & Ipswich (8th), John Dennis, *b* 1931, apptd 1986.
Salisbury (77th), David Staffurth Stancliffe, *b* 1942, apptd 1993.
Sheffield (5th), David Ramsay Lunn, *b* 1930, apptd 1980.
Sodor & Man (79th), Noel Debroy Jones, *b* 1932, apptd 1989.
Southwark (8th), Robert Kerr Williamson, *b* 1926, apptd 1991.
Southwell (9th), Patrick Burnet Harris, *b* 1934, apptd 1988.
Truro (12th), Michael Thomas Ball, *b* 1932, apptd 1990.
Wakefield (11th), Nigel Simeon McCulloch, *b* 1942, apptd 1992.
Worcester (111th), Philip Harold Ernest Goodrich, *b* 1929, apptd 1982.

PEERS' SONS, DAUGHTERS, BROTHERS AND SISTERS; WIDOWS OF SONS OF PEERS; ALSO GRANDCHILDREN OF DUKES, MARQUESSES AND EARLS
(Bearing Courtesy Titles)

Abbott, Hon Mary M. *Lindsay of Birker, B.*
Acheson, Hon Patrick B. V. M. *Gosford, E.*
Ackner, Hon Martin S. *Ackner, B.*
Acloque, Hon Camilla *Howard de Walden, B.*
A'Court, Hon James Holmes *Heytesbury, B.*
Acton, Rev Hon J. Charles Lyon-Dalberg- *Acton, B.*
Acton, Hon Edward D. J. Lyon-Dalberg- *Acton, B.*
Acton, Hon Joan H. J. M. C. Lyon-Dalberg- *Acton, B.*
Acton, Hon John C. F. H. Lyon-Dalberg- *Acton, B.*
Acton, Hon Margaret M. T. Lyon-Dalberg- *Acton, B.*
Acton, Hon Peter H. Lyon-Dalberg- *Acton, B.*
Acton, Hon Robert P. Lyon-Dalberg- *Acton, B.*
Adam, Hon Vivien E. Forbes *Ravensdale, B.*
Adam, Hon Irene C. Forbes *Wenlock, By.*
Adams, Hon Annabella J. *Palumbo, B.*
Adams, Lady Celia A. *Fortescue, E.*
Adams, Hon Eileen E. *Castlemaine, B.*
Adams, Hon M. Elizabeth *Trevethin and Oaksey, B.*
Adams, Hon Marjorie H. *Darwen, B.*
Adamson, Hon Alison M. Campbell *Elliott of Morpeth, B.*
Adderley, Hon Edward J.A. *Norton, B.*
Adderley, Hon Nigel J. *Norton, B.*
Adderley, Hon Olivia F.E. *Norton, B.*
Addington, Hon Elizabeth C. *Sidmouth, V.*
Addington, Hon Gurth L. F. *Sidmouth, V.*
Addington, Hon Hiley W. D. *Sidmouth, V.*
Addington, Hon Jeremy F. *Sidmouth, V.*
Addington, Hon Leslie R. B. *Sidmouth, V.*
Addington, Hon Thomas R. C. *Sidmouth, V.*
Addison, Hon Jacqueline F. *Addison, V.*
Addison, Hon William M. W. *Addison, V.*
Adeane, Hon G. Edward *Adeane, By.*
Adler, Hon Aviva *Jakobovits, B.*
Adorian, Hon Ruth I. *Wakefield of Kendal, B.*
Agar, Lady Marisa C. *Normanton, E.*
Agar, Hon Mark S. A. *Normanton, E.*
Agar, Lady Portia C. *Normanton, E.*
Agnew, Hon A. Joanna M. *Campbell of Eskan, B.*
Agnew, Hon Clare R. *Glentoran, B.*
Agnew, Hon (Doreen M.) Lady *Jessel, B.*
Agnew, Hon Joyce V. *Godber, By.*
Aird, Lady Priscilla *Willoughby de Eresby, Bs.*
Aird, Lady Margaret D. Stirling- *Glasgow, E.*
Aitken, Hon A. Rory *Beaverbrook, B.*
Aitken, Hon Charlotte S. *Beaverbrook, B.*
Aitken, Hon Maxwell F. *Beaverbrook, B.*
Aitken, Hon Sophia V. A. *Beaverbrook, B.*
Aitken, Hon (Penelope L.) Lady *Rugby, B.*
Alchin, Hon Juliet A. *Hankey, B.*
Alexander, Hon Ada K. *Bellew B.*
Alexander, Hon Brian J. *Alexander of Tunis, E.*
Alexander, Hon David R. J. *Alexander of Weedon, B.*
Alexander, Lady Leonora J. *Caledon, E.*
Alexander, Lady Lucy C. *Alexander of Tunis, E.*
Alexander, Hon Mary F. A. *Alexander of Weedon, B.*
Alexander, Lady Rose M. *Alexander of Tunis, E.*
Alexander, Hon Thomas B. *Alexander of Potterhill, B.*
Alexander, Hon William R. S. *Alexander of Weedon, B.*
Allan, Hon Alexander C. S. *Allan of Kilmahew, B.*
Allan, Hon Jane M. *Allan of Kilmahew, B.*
Allbutt, Hon Gail *Macfarlane of Bearsden, B.*
Allen, Hon Fiona M. *Lovat, L.*
Allen, Hon Francesca N. *Plurenden, B.*
Allen, Hon Joan C. C. *Allen of Hurtwood, By.*
Allen, Hon Joan E. *Platt, B.*
Allen, Hon John D. *Croham, B.*
Allen, Hon Lionel P. *Allen of Fallowfield, B.*
Allen, Hon Richard A. *Croham, B.*
Allenby, Hon Mrs Claude W. H. *Allenby, V.*
Allenby, Hon Henry J. H. *Allenby, V.*
Allfrey, Hon Jocelyne *Daventry, V.*
Allhusen, Hon Claudia V. *Rushcliffe, By.*
Allsopp, Hon Elizabeth T. *Hindlip, B.*
Allsopp, Hon Henry W. *Hindlip, B.*
Allsopp, Hon John P. *Hindlip, B.*
Allsopp, Hon Kirstie M. *Hindlip, B.*
Allsopp, Hon Natasha F. *Hindlip, B.*

Allsopp, Hon Norah H. *Hatherton, B.*
Allsopp, Hon Sophia A. *Hindlip, B.*
Alport, Hon Arthur E. B. *Alport, B.*
Ambrose, Hon Angela F. H. *Blanch, B.*
Amery, Hon C. Louise M. *Amery of Lustleigh, B.*
Amery, Hon Leopold H. H. J. *Amery of Lustleigh, B.*
Amias, Hon Judith A. *Young of Graffham, B.*
Amory, Hon Margaret I. G. Heathcote- *Howard de Walden, B.*
Anderson, Hon Cecilia C. *Waterpark, B.*
Anderson, Hon Emily M. *Astor, V.*
Anderson, Lady Flavia J. L. *Halsbury, E.*
Anderson, Lady Gillian M. *Perth, E.*
Anderson, Hon Paulette A. *Sainsbury, B.*
Andrew, Hon Gwyneth M. *Aberdare, B.*
Andrews, Hon Katharine A. *Douglas of Kirtleside, By.*
Andrews, Lady Patricia A. *Clancarty, E.*
Anggard, Hon Adele B. A. *Hankey, B.*
Annesley, Lady Frances E. *Annesley, E.*
Annesley, Hon Francis W. D. *Valentia, V.*
Annesley, Hon Haidée *Rawlinson, B.*
Annesley, Hon Michael R. *Annesley, E.*
Annesley, Hon Peter J. *Valentia, V.*
Annesley, Hon Philip H. *Annesley, E.*
Anson, Lady Eloise A. E. *Lichfield, E.*
Anson, Lady Rose M. M. *Lichfield, E.*
Arbuthnott, Hon Hugh S. *Arbuthnott, V.*
Arbuthnott, Hon J. Keith O. *Arbuthnott, V.*
Arbuthnott, Hon Louisa N. *St Helens, B.*
Arbuthnott, Hon William D. *Arbuthnott, V.*
Archer, Hon James H. *Archer of Weston-super-Mare, B.*
Archer, Hon Sonia G. O. *Birdwood, B.*
Archer, Hon William H. *Archer of Weston-super-Mare, B.*
Armit, Hon Serena H. C. *Caldecote, V.*
Armstrong, Hon Jane O. *Armstrong of Ilminster, B.*
Armstrong, Hon M. Kathleen *Napier of Magdala, B.*
Armstrong, Hon Peter W. *Armstrong of Sanderstead, By.*
Armstrong, Hon Teresa B. *Armstrong of Ilminster, B.*
Armstrong, Lady C. Caroline C. Burnett *Stradbroke, E.*
Arthur, Hon Edward A. *Glenarthur, B.*
Arthur, Hon Emily V. *Glenarthur, B.*
Arthur, Hon Janet S. *Brain, B.*
Arthur, Hon Matthew R. *Glenarthur, B.*
Arthurton, Hon Phillipa S. *Mills, V.*
Arundell, Hon Caroline R. T. *Talbot of Malahide, B.*
Arundell, Hon Catherine M. T. *Talbot of Malahide, B.*
Arundell, Hon Edward R. *Talbot of Malahide, B.*
Arundell, Hon Richard J. T. *Talbot of Malahide, B.*
Arwyn, Hon Arwyn H. D. *Arwyn, B.*
Ashby, Hon Michael F. *Ashby, B.*
Ashby, Hon Peter N. *Ashby, B.*
Ashford, Lady W. Anne G. *Dundonald, E.*
Ashton, Hon John E. *Ashton of Hyde, B.*
Ashton, Hon T. Henry *Ashton of Hyde, B.*
Askew, Hon Lucy J. *Henderson of Brompton, B.*
Askew, Lady Susan A. *Sutherland, D.*
Aspden, Hon Judith A. *Harmar-Nicholls, B.*
Aspinall, Hon Judith M. *Mackenzie-Stuart, B.*
Aspinall, Lady Sarah M. *Howe, E.*
Asquith, Hon Celia R. *Oxford and Asquith, E.*
Asquith, Lady Clare P. F *Oxford and Asquith, E.*
Asquith, Hon Dominic A. G. *Oxford and Asquith, E.*
Asquith, Hon Frances S. *Oxford and Asquith, E.*
Asquith, Lady Helen F. *Oxford and Asquith, E.*
Asquith, Hon Isabel A. *Oxford and Asquith, E.*
Asquith, Hon Luke *Asquith of Bishopstone, By.*
Asquith, Hon Magdalen *Oxford and Asquith, E.*
Asquith, Hon Mark J. *Oxford and Asquith, E.*
Asquith, Lady M. Annunziata *Oxford and Asquith, E.*
Asquith, Hon Mrs Paul *Asquith of Bishopstone, By.*
Assheton, Hon Nicholas *Clitheroe, B.*
Assheton, Hon Ralph J. *Clitheroe, B.*
Astley, Hon Delaval T. H. *Hastings, B.*

Brown, Hon Sally B. *Gray of Contin, B.*
Brown, Lady Vanessa P. *Yarborough, E.*
Brown, Hon Christina L. Darell- *Huntingfield, B.*
Brown, Lady Kenya E. Tatton- *Kitchener of Khartoum, E.*
Brown, Hon Alice *Kilmaine, B.*
Browne, Lady Alannah G. *Sligo, M.*
Browne, Lady Clare R. *Sligo, M.*
Browne, Hon Dominick G. T. *Oranmore and Browne, B.*
Browne, Hon Garech D. *Oranmore and Browne, B.*
Browne, Hon Geoffrey C. M. *Oranmore and Browne, B.*
Browne, Hon John F. S. *Kilmaine, B.*
Browne, Lady Karen L. *Sligo, M.*
Browne, Lady Lucinda J. *Sligo, M.*
Browne, Hon Martin M. D. *Oranmore and Browne, B.*
Browne, Lady Moyra B. M. *Bessborough, E.*
Browne, Lady Sheelyn F. *Sligo, M.*
Browne, Hon Mrs Tara *Oranmore and Browne, B.*
Browne, Lady Ulick *Sligo, M.*
Bruce, Hon Adam R. *Elgin, E.*
Bruce, Hon George B. T. *Elgin, E.*
Bruce, Hon Alastair J. L. *Aberdare, B.*
Bruce, Hon Alexander V. *Elgin, E.*
Bruce, Hon Mrs Bernard *Elgin, E.*
Bruce, Hon Charles B. *Aberdare, B.*
Bruce, Hon E. David *Elgin, E.*
Bruce, Hon George J. D. *Balfour of Burleigh, L.*
Bruce, Lady Georgiana M. *Elgin, E.*
Bruce, Hon Henry A. F. *Aberdare, B.*
Bruce, Hon Ishbel *Balfour of Burleigh, B.*
Bruce, Hon James H. M. *Aberdare, B.*
Bruce, Hon James M. E. *Elgin, E.*
Bruce, Hon M. Jean D. *Glentanar, By.*
Bruce, (Hon) Katherine G. *Balfour of Burleigh, L.*
Bruce, Lady Martha V. *Elgin, E.*
Bruce, Hon Michael G. *Bruce of Donington, B.*
Bruce, Hon Nigel H. C. *Aberdare, B.*
Bruce, Hon Mrs Robert *Elgin, E.*
Bruce, Hon Mrs Victor A. *Aberdare, B.*
Bruce, Hon Victoria *Balfour of Burleigh, L.*
Bruce, Lady Carina D. Brudenell- *Ailesbury, M.*
Bruce, Lady Catherine A. Brudenell- *Ailesbury, M.*
Bruce, Lord Charles A. Brudenell- *Ailesbury, M.*
Bruce, Lady Kathryn J. Brudenell- *Ailesbury, M.*
Bruce, Lady Louise Brudenell- *Ailesbury, M.*
Bruce, Lady Piers Brudenell- *Ailesbury, M.*
Bruce, Lady Sylvia D. Brudenell- *Ailesbury, M.*
Bruce, Hon Alexander P. Hovell-Thurlow-Cumming-*Thurlow, B.*
Bruce, Hon Sir J. Roualeyn Hovell-Thurlow-Cumming- *Thurlow, B.*
Bruce, Hon Roualeyn R. Hovell-Thurlow-Cumming- *Thurlow, B.*
Brudenell, Hon Marian C. *Dilhorne, V.*
Bryden, Hon M. Deborah *Killanin, B.*
Buchan, Hon Mrs Alastair F. *Tweedsmuir, B.*
Buchan, Lady Evelyn R. *Normanby, M.*
Buchan of Auchmacoy, Hon B. Susan F. *Howard de Walden and Seaford, B.*
Buchan, Hon William de l'A *Tweedsmuir, B.*
Buckley, Hon Sir Denys B. *Wrenbury, B.*
Buckley, Hon Katherine L. *Wrenbury, B.*
Buckley, Hon William E. *Wrenbury, B.*
Buckley, Hon Giancarla Alen- *Forte, B.*
Buckman, Hon Griselda R. *Henley, B.*
Buckmaster, Hon Colin J. *Buckmaster, V.*
Buckmaster, Hon Grace L. *Ashfield, By.*
Budgen, Hon Patricia R. *Newborough, B.*
Bull, Hon Judith F. *Cranworth, B.*
Bull, Hon Noreen M. *Windlesham, B.*
Buller, Hon Elizabeth L. Manningham- *Dilhorne, V.*
Buller, Hon James E. Manningham- *Dilhorne, V.*
Buller, Hon Mervyn R. Manningham- *Dilhorne, V.*
Buller, Hon Benjamin F. A. Yarde- *Churston, B.*
Buller, Hon Francesca E. Yarde- *Churston, B.*
Buller, Hon Mrs John R. H. Yarde- *Churston, B.*
Buller, Hon Katherine M. Yarde- *Churston, B.*
Bulloch, Hon Katrina Y. *Soulsby, B.*
Bullock, Hon Adrian C. S. *Bullock, B.*
Bullock, Hon Matthew P. D. *Bullock, B.*
Bullock, Hon O. Nicholas A. *Bullock, B.*
Bulmer, Lady Marcia Rose *Granville, E.*
Bunbury, Hon George A. K. McClintock-*Rathdonnell, B.*
Bunbury, Hon James A. H. McClintock *Rathdonnell, B.*

Bunbury, Hon Pamela R. McClintock- *Rathdonnell, B.*
Bunbury, Hon Sasha A. McClintock *Rathdonnell, B.*
Bunbury, Hon William L. McClintock- *Rathdonnell, B.*
Bune, Hon Sarah J. *Bruntisfield, B.*
Bungay, Hon Atalanta A. *Beaumont of Whitley, B.*
Burbury, Hon Sarah D. *Caradon, B.*
Burden, Hon Adrienne G. *Burden, B.*
Burden, Hon Andrew P. *Burden, B.*
Burden, Hon Carol M. *Burden, B.*
Burden, Hon Fraser W. *Burden, B.*
Burden, Hon Ian S. *Burden, B.*
Burley, Hon Laura B. *Butterworth, B.*
Burn, Hon Anne C. *Wilberforce, B.*
Burness, Hon Marie L. *Forte, B.*
Burnett, Hon Nicola *Cross, V.*
Burnier, Hon Kamala *Sinha, B.*
Burns, Hon Mary M. *Sidmouth, V.*
Burvill, Hon Victoria A. *Marshall of Goring, B.*
Burt, Hon Vanessa M. L. *Ampthill, B.*
Bury, Lady Mairi *Londonderry, M.*
Busse, Hon Susan A. *Trevelyan, B.*
Buswell, Hon Barbara *Fisher, B.*
Butler, Hon Sir Adam C. *Butler of Saffron Walden, B.*
Butler, Hon Betty Q. *Dunboyne, B.*
Butler, Hon Edmund H. R. *Mountgarret, V.*
Butler, Hon Elizabeth O. *Erskine of Rerrick, B.*
Butler, Hon Godfrey C. S. P. *Carrick, E.*
Butler, Hon John F. *Dunboyne, B.*
Butler, Lady Juliana M. P. *Carrick, E.*
Butler, Hon Lindsay S. T. S. *Carrick, E.*
Butler, Hon Mary S. *Dunboyne, B.*
Butler, Hon Mrs P. A. Somerset D. *Carrick, E.*
Butler, Hon Penelope C. *Forteviot, B.*
Butler, Hon Piers E. T. L. *Carrick, E.*
Butler, Hon Piers J. R. *Mountgarret, V.*
Butler, Hon Sir Richard C. *Butler of Saffron Walden, B.*
Butler, Hon S. James *Butler of Saffron Walden, B.*
Butterfield, Hon Jeremy J. *Butterfield, B.*
Butterfield, Hon Jonathan W. S. *Butterfield, B.*
Butterfield, Hon Toby M. J. *Butterfield, B.*
Butterworth, Hon John W. B. *Butterworth, B.*
Buxton, Hon A. James F. *Buxton of Alsa, B.*
Buxton, Hon Jane E. *Noel-Buxton, B.*
Buxton, Hon Lucinda C. *Buxton of Alsa, B.*
Buxton, Hon Margaret E. *Bridges, B.*
Buxton, Hon Richard C. *Noel-Buxton, B.*
Buxton, Hon Simon C. *Noel-Buxton, B.*
Buxton, Hon Timothy L. *Buxton of Alsa, B.*
Buxton, Hon Victoria J. *Buxton of Alsa, B.*
Buxton, Hon Antonia H. Noel- *Noel-Buxton, B.*
Buxton, Hon Charles C. Noel- *Noel-Buxton, B.*
Buxton, Hon Lucy M. Noel- *Noel-Buxton, B.*
Buxton, Hon Michael B. N. Noel- *Noel-Buxton, B.*
Byers, Hon Charles W. *Byers, B.*
Byford, Hon Elizabeth-Anne S. *Ventry, B.*
Byng, Hon Georgina I. *Torrington, V.*
Byng, Hon Henrietta R. *Torrington, V.*
Byng, Hon James E. *Strafford, E.*
Byng, Hon Julian F. *Strafford, E.*
Byng, Hon Malaika A. *Torrington, V.*
Byng, Hon William R. *Strafford, E.*
Byrne, Hon Nona G. *Lawrence, B.*
Byron, Hon Caroline A. V. *Byron, B.*
Byron, Hon Charles R. G. *Byron, B.*
Byron, Hon Emily C. *Byron, B.*
Byron, Hon Sophie G. *Byron, B.*
Cabot, Hon Ann S. M. *Whitfield, B.*
Caccia, Hon Antonia C. *Caccia, B.*
Cadman, Hon Arthur D. *Cadman, B.*
Cadman, Hon Giles O. R. *Cadman, B.*
Cadman, Hon James R. *Cadman, B.*
Cadman, Hon Nicholas A. J. *Cadman, B.*
Cadman, Hon Sybil M. *Cadman, B.*
Cadogan, Hon Edward C. *Cadogan, E.*
Cadogan, Lady Mary V. *Cavan, E.*
Cadogan, Hon William J. *Cadogan, E.*
Cain, Hon Alexander. C. C. Nall- *Brocket, B.*
Cain, Hon Antalya S. L. Nall- *Brocket, B.*
Cain, Hon David L. R. Nall- *Brocket, B.*
Cain, Hon David M. A. Nall- *Brocket, B.*
Cain, Lady Katherine E. Nall- *Selborne, E.*
Cain, Hon Richard P. C. Nall- *Brocket, B.*
Cain, Hon William T. A. Nall- *Brocket, B.*
Cairns, Hon Alistair *Cairns, E.*
Cairns, Hon D. Patrick *Cairns, E.*

Colville, Hon R. James I. *Colville of Culross, V.*
Colville, Hon Rupert G. S. *Colville of Culross, V.*
Colvin, Hon Nichola *Cayzer, B.*
Combe, Lady Mary E. C. *Kilmorey, E.*
Combe, Lady Silvia B. *Leicester, E.*
Compton, Lady Emily R. *Northampton, M.*
Compton, Lady Lara K. *Northampton, M.*
Compton, Lady Louisa *Northampton, M.*
Compton, Lady Tania F. *Clanwilliam, E.*
Compton, Lord William J. B. *Northampton, M.*
Connell, Lady Alexandra V. C. A. *Erroll, E.*
Connell, Lady Susan L. *Northesk, E.*
Constantine, Hon Roy *Constantine of Stanmore, B.*
Conwy, Hon Charlotte S. G. Rowley- *Langford, B.*
Conwy, Hon Christopher G. H. Rowley- *Langford, B.*
Conwy, Hon John S. Rowley- *Langford, B.*
Conwy, Hon Owen G. Rowley- *Langford, B.*
Conwy, Hon Peter A. Rowley- *Langford, B.*
Conyngham, Lord F. W. Patrick *Conyngham, M.*
Conyngham, Lady Henrietta T. J. *Conyngham, M.*
Conyngham, Lady John *Conyngham, M.*
Conyngham, Lord Simon C. E. W. *Conyngham, M.*
Conyngham, Lady Tamara J. *Conyngham, M.*
Cook, Hon Sarah I. *Murray of Epping Forest, B.*
Cooke, Hon James V. F. *Cooke of Islandreagh, B.*
Cooke, Hon Michael J. A. *Cook of Islandreagh, B.*
Cooke, Hon Sarah M. M. *Kenyon, B.*
Cooke, Hon Victoria S. *Cooke of Islandreagh, B.*
Cookson, Hon Angela M. M. *Hemphill, B.*
Cooper, Hon Jason C. D. B. *Norwich, V.*
Cooper, Hon Joanna R. *Younger of Prestwick, B.*
Cooper, Lady Maureen I. *Clancarty, E.*
Cooper, Hon Mrs A. John P. H. Ashley-
    Shaftesbury, E.
Cooper, Lady Frances M. E. Ashley- *Shaftesbury, E.*
Cooper, Hon Nicholas E. A. Ashley- *Shaftesbury, E.*
Copley, Hon Thomas D. Bewicke *Cromwell, B.*
Copsey, Hon Jenifer C. *Healey, B.*
Corbett, Hon Catherine *Acton, B.*
Corbett, Hon John P. C. *Rowallan, B.*
Corbett, Hon Joseph M. *Rowallan, B.*
Corbett, Hon Melanie I. *Moynihan, B.*
Corbett, Hon Robert C. *Rowallan, B.*
Corcuera, Lady Mary V. S. *Gosford, E.*
Cordingley, Hon Emma G. A. *Portsmouth, E.*
Corke, Hon Shirley F. *Bridges, B.*
Cormack, Hon G. R. Jean *Davies, B.*
Cormack, Lady Miranda M. *Kilmuir, E.*
Cornwallis, Hon F. W. Jeremy *Cornwallis, B.*
Cornwallis, Hon P. W. David *Cornwallis, B.*
Cornwallis, Hon Vanessa R. *Cornwallis, B.*
Corrall, Hon Sheila M. *Lowry, B.*
Corran, Hon Miranda A. *Chaplin, Vy.*
Corry, Lady Martha C. Lowry- *Belmore, E.*
Corry, Hon Montagu G. G. Lowry- *Belmore, E.*
Corry, Hon Rosemary D. L. Lowry- *Plumer, V.*
Corry, Hon Juliet E. Steuart- *Milverton, B.*
Corsar, Hon Dame Mary D. *Balerno, B.*
Cosgrave, Lady Louisa *Cathcart, E.*
Cotterell, Hon Harriet P. S. *Camoys, B.*
Cotterell, Hon (Molly P. B.) Lady *Camrose, V.*
Cotton, Hon David P. D. Stapleton- *Combermere, V.*
Cotton, Hon Sophia M. Stapleton- *Combermere, V.*
Cotton, Hon Thomas R. W. Stapleton- *Combermere, V.*
Cottrell, Hon Fiona C. M. *Manton, B.*
Coulson, Hon Elizabeth A. *Crowther-Hunt, B.*
Courtenay, Lady Camilla G. *Devon, E.*
Courtenay, Hon Camilla M. *Devon, E.*
Courtenay, Hon Charles P. *Devon, E.*
Courtenay, Hon Eleonora V. *Devon, E.*
Courtenay, Lady Mary E. *Devon, E.*
Courtenay, Hon Rebecca E. *Devon, E.*
Coutanche, Hon John A. G. *Coutanche, By.*
Coutts, Hon Crispin J. A. N. Money- *Latymer, B.*
Coutts, Hon Fanny C. M. Money- *Latymer, B.*
Coutts, Hon Giles T. N. Money- *Latymer, B.*
Coutts, Hon Henry E. Money- *Latymer, B.*
Coutts, Hon Hugo N. Money- *Latymer, B.*
Coutts, Hon Lucy R. Money- *Deedes, B.*
Coutts, Hon Penelope A. C. Money- *Emmet of Amberley, By.*
Coutts, Hon Vera C. M. Money- *Latymer, B.*
Coventry, Lady Anne D. *Coventry, E.*
Coventry, Lady Maria A. *Coventry, E.*
Cowan, Hon Mary L. *Dilhorne, V.*
Cowen, Hon Shelagh M. *Rank, B.*
Cowdy, Hon Haidée *Rawlinson of Ewell, B.*
Cox, Hon Christopher W. Roxbee *Kings Norton, B.*

Cox, Hon Jeremy W. Roxbee *Kings Norton, B.*
Craig, Hon Christopher C. B. *Craig of Radley, B.*
Craig, Hon Susan E. *Craig of Radley, B.*
Craig, Hon Roxane Laird *Balfour of Inchrye, B.*
Craigie, Hon Emma B. *Rees-Mogg, B.*
Cram, Lady Jeanne L. *Argyll, D.*
Craufurd, Hon Caroline H. Houison *Kemsley, V.*
Crawford, Lady Susanna *Eglinton, E.*
Creagh, Hon Daphne A. Brazier- *Lurgan, B.*
Cresswell, Hon Alexandra *Lane of Horsell, B.*
Cretton, Hon Catherine A. *de Vesci, B.*
Crewdson, Hon L. Clare *Grimthorpe, B.*
Crews, Hon Anne P. *Boston, B.*
Croft, Hon Bernard W. H. P. *Croft, B.*
Crofton, Hon Mrs A. Marcus L. *Crofton, B.*
Crofton, Hon C. Marus G. *Crofton, B.*
Crofton, Hon E. Harry P. *Crofton, B.*
Crofton, Hon Freya C. *Crofton, B.*
Crofton, Hon Georgiana A. *Crofton, B.*
Crolla, Hon S. P. Rose *Cornwallis, B.*
Cronin, Hon Jane *Elton, B.*
Cronshaw, Lady Miranda *Lonsdale, E.*
Crook, Hon Catherine H. *Crook, B.*
Crook, Hon Robert D. *Crook, B.*
Crookenden, Hon (Patricia N.) Lady *Kindersley, E.*
Cropper, Hon Rosalind E. *Younger of Leckie, V.*
Cross, Hon L. G. Kilorn *Ebury, B.*
Cross, Hon R. S. Frances *Torrington, V.*
Cross, Hon Susan M. *Milverton, B.*
Crossley, Hon Alicia P. B. *Somerleyton, B.*
Crossley, Hon Hugh F. S. *Somerleyton, B.*
Crossley, Hon Louisa B. V. *Somerleyton, B.*
Crossley, Hon R. Nicholas *Somerleyton, B.*
Crossman, Lady Rose M. *Alexander of Tunis, E.*
Crosthwait, Hon Cynthia D. *Jenkins of Hillhead, B.*
Crowder, Hon Patricia W. M. *Mowbray, B.*
Crowther, Hon Charles, W. *Crowther, By.*
Crowther, Hon David R. G. *Crowther, By.*
Crowther, Hon Nicola M. *Crowther, By.*
Cruickshank, Hon Victoria E. *Hillingdon, By.*
Crutchley, Hon Penelope A. *O'Neill of the Maine, B.*
Cubitt, Hon Mrs Roland *Ashcombe, B.*
Cullen, Hon Harriet H. H. *Hartwell, B.*
Cullinan, Hon Dorothea J. *Horder, B.*
Cumberlege, Hon C. Mark *Cumberlege, Bs.*
Cumberlege, Hon Justin F. *Cumberlege, Bs.*
Cumberlege, Hon Oliver R. *Cumberlege, Bs.*
Cuming, Hon Christine V. H. *Robertson of Oakridge, B.*
Cumming, Hon Mary S. *Henderson of Brompton, B.*
Cuninghame, Lady M. Joan M. *Fitzwilliam, E.*
Cunliffe, Hon Henry *Cunliffe, B.*
Cunliffe, Hon Luke *Cunliffe, B.*
Cunliffe, Hon Merlin *Cunliffe, B.*
Cunnack, Hon Alice E. M. *Wester Wemyss, By.*
Cunningham, Hon Edith L. *MacDermott, B.*
Curling, Hon Melissa *Llewlyn-Davies, B.*
Currey, Hon Heather M. *Strange, By.*
Curry, Hon Helen F. A. Towneley-
    O'Hagan, O'Hagan, B.
Curzon, Hon C. Avril *Scarsdale, V.*
Curzon, Lady Anna E. *Howe, E.*
Curzon, Hon David J. N. *Scarsdale, V.*
Curzon, Hon Diana G. *Scarsdale, V.*
Curzon, Lady Emma C. *Howe, E.*
Curzon, Lady Flora G. *Howe, E.*
Curzon, Hon James F. N. *Scarsdale, V.*
Curzon, Lady Lucinda R. *Howe, E.*
Curzon, Lady Mary Gaye *Howe, E.*
Curzon, Hon Peter G. N. *Scarsdale, V.*
Curzon, Hon Richard F. N. *Scarsdale, V.*
Curzon, Hon Benjamin A. Roper- *Teynham, B.*
Curzon, Hon David J. H. Roper- *Teynham, B.*
Curzon, Hon Henrietta M. F. Roper- *Teynham, B.*
Curzon, Hon Hermione M. H. E. Roper- *Teynham, B.*
Curzon, Hon Holly A-M. Roper- *Teynham, B.*
Curzon, Hon Jonathan C. J. Roper- *Teynham, B.*
Curzon, Hon Michael H. Roper- *Teynham, B.*
Curzon, Hon Peter M. Roper- *Teynham, B.*
Curzon, Hon William T. Roper- *Teynham, B.*
Curzon, Hon Sophie P. Roper- *Teynham, B.*
Cust, Hon Peregrine E. Q. *Brownlow, B.*
Cuthbert, Lady Victoria L. D. *Northumberland, D.*
Czernin, Hon M. Hazel C. *Howard de Walden, B.*
d'Abo, Lady Ursula *Rutland, D.*
Dainty, Hon Priscilla *Wolfenden, B.*
Dale, Hon Natasha D. Capstick- *Rayne, B.*
Dalgety, Hon Hilda L. L. *Tayside, By.*

Daliot, Hon Judith *Samuel, V.*
Dallmeyer, Hon Ursula N. *Kinross, B.*
Dalrymple, Lady Antonia M. A. I. *Galloway, E.*
Dalrymple, Hon Colin J. *Stair, E.*
Dalrymple, Hon David H. *Stair, E.*
Dalrymple, Hon Hew N. *Stair, E.*
Dalrymple, Hon Michael C. *Stair, E.*
Dalrymple, Lady Anne-Louise M.
  Hamilton *Albemarle E.*
Dalyell of The Binns, Hon (Kathleen M.
  A.) *Wheatley, B.*
Dalzell, Lady Muriel M. *Carnwath, E.*
Damer, Hon Edward L. S. Dawson- *Portarlington,
  E.*
Damer, Hon Henry L. S. Dawson- *Portarlington, E.*
Damer, Hon Lionel J. C. S. Dawson- *Portarlington,
  E.*
Damer, Lady Marina D. Dawson- *Portarlington, E.*
Damerell, Lady Mary B. *Northesk, E.*
Daniel, Hon Sarah *Rothschild, B.*
Daniel, Hon Lucy V. T. *Talbot of Malahide, B.*
Daniel, Lady Valerie D. *Lloyd George of Dwyfor, E.*
Daniell, Hon Mary E.J. *Rennell, B.*
Danilovich, Hon Irene *Forte, B.*
Danks, Hon Serena M. *Gifford, B.*
Darby, Hon Meriel K. *Home of the Hirsel, B.*
Dare, Hon Phyllida A. *Benson, B.*
Darling, Hon Isabel *Darling of Hillsborough, B.*
Darling, Hon Peter G. *Darling of Hillsborough, B.*
Darling, Hon R. Julian *Darling, B.*
das Neves, Hon Amanda M. A. *Grey of Naunton, B.*
Davey, Hon Heather M. *Morris of Grasmere, B.*
Davey, Hon Margaret W. *Helsby, B.*
David, Hon Nicholas C. *David, B.*
David, Hon R. Sebastian D. *David, B.*
Davidson, Hon Camilla B. *Davidson, V.*
Davidson, Hon Kristina L. *Davidson, V.*
Davidson, Hon Malcolm W. M. *Davidson, V.*
Davidson, Hon Sheila A. *Greenhill, B.*
Davies, Hon Ann P. Prys *Prys-Davies, B.*
Davies, Hon Arwyn H. *Arwyn, B.*
Davies, Hon Benjamin *Darwen, B.*
Davies, Hon Benjamin M. G. *Davies, B.*
Davies, Hon David D. *Davies of Penrhys, B.*
Davies, Hon David D. *Davies, B.*
Davies, Hon Edward D. G. *Davies, B.*
Davies, Hon Eldrydd J. *Davies, B.*
Davies, Hon Elin P. Prys *Prys-Davies, B.*
Davies, Hon F. Ronald *Darwen, B.*
Davies, Hon Gwynfor *Davies of Penrhys, B.*
Davies, Hon Jonathan H. *Davies, B.*
Davies, Hon Islwyn E. E. *Davies, B.*
Davies, Hon Katharine A. D. S. *Swinfen, B.*
Davies, Hon Lucy *Davies, B.*
Davies, Hon Mary *Darwen, B.*
Davies, Hon Naomi *Darwen, B.*
Davies, Hon Paul *Darwen, B.*
Davies, Hon Philip C. M. *Davies, B.*
Davies, Hon Sarah *Darwen, B.*
Davies, Hon Stephen H. *Darwen, B.*
Davies, Hon Theresa K. *David, Bs.*
Davies, Hon Thomas B. *Darwen, B.*
Davies, Lady Venetia C. K. *Kinnoull, E.*
Davies, Hon Victoria C. *Platt of Writtle, Bs.*
Davies, Hon Harriet L. R. Llewelyn *Llewelyn-
  Davies, B.*
Davies, Hon Rachel M. Lloyd *Clifden, Vy.*
Davies, Hon Caroline M. E. Twiston *Suffield, B.*
Davis, Lady Alison E. *Attlee, E.*
Davis, Hon Beatrice M. *Mills, V.*
Davis, Hon Deborah *Wolfson, B.*
Davis, Hon Henry Clinton- *Clinton-Davis, B.*
Davis, Hon Melissa Clinton- *Clinton-Davis, B.*
Davis, Hon Catherine R. Lovell- *Lovell-Davis, B.*
Davis, Hon Stephen L. Lovell- *Lovell-Davis, B.*
Davison, Hon Mrs Alexander *Broughshane, B.*
Davison, Hon Elizabeth *Slater, B.*
Davison, Hon W. Kensington *Broughshane, B.*
Dawkins, Hon Sarah *Bangor, V.*
Dawnay, Lady Angela C. R. *Buccleuch, D.*
Dawnay, Hon Iris I. A. *Ingleby, V.*
Dawnay, Hon Mrs James R. *Downe, V.*
Dawnay, Hon Richard H. *Downe, V.*
Dawnay, Hon Sarah F. *Downe, V.*
Dawson, Hon Ivy M. *Auckland, B.*
Dawson, Hon Katherine J. Crosbie *Joicey, B.*
Deacon, Hon Elizabeth A. *Barnard, B.*
Deakin, Hon Rose A. *Donaldson of Kingsbridge, B.*
Dean, Hon Catherine *Muskerry, B.*

Dean, Hon Jenefer C. *Hillingdon, By.*
Dean, Hon Jonathan F. *Muskerry, B.*
Dean, Hon Nicola *Muskerry, B.*
Dean, Hon Thalia M. *Craigmyle, B.*
Debarge, Hon Robina J. *Rotherwick, B.*
Debenham, Hon Daphne J. *Godber, By.*
de Botton, Hon Janet F. *Wolfson, B.*
de Bunsen, Hon Alexandra *Carrington, B.*
de Cabarrus, Lady Caroline M. *Northumberland, D.*
de Caicedo, Hon Camilla E. M. E. *Jessel, B.*
de Castellane, Lady Charlotte-Anne *Buccleuch, D.*
de Chair, Lady A. Juliet D. M. *Fitzwilliam, E.*
de Courcy, Hon Diana R. *Kingsale, B.*
Deedes, Hon Jeremy W. *Deedes, B.*
de Grey, Hon Amanda L. *Annan, B.*
de Grey, Hon Elizabeth A. *Walsingham, B.*
de Grey, Hon Robert *Walsingham, B.*
de Kermaignant, Hon Fanny L. *Vernon, B.*
Delap, Hon Anastasia D. *Glenkinglas, By.*
de Laszlo, Hon Sandra D. *Hacking, B.*
Delevingne, Hon Angela M. H. *Greenwood, V.*
Delfont, Hon David *Delfont, B.*
de Lisle, Hon Aubyn C. *Thurlow, B.*
de Lisle, Hon Mary R. *Ingleby, V.*
della Grazia, (Lady Hermione G. Palli),
  Duchessa *Powis, E, and Darcy de Knayth, Bs.*
de Marffy, Hon Pelline M. *Acton, B.*
de Meyer (Lady Susan A.), Countess
  Carlisle, E.
de Moleyns, Hon Brigitte C. Daubeny *Ventry, B.*
de Moleyns, Hon Francis W. Daubeny *Ventry, B.*
de Moleyns, Hon Lisa Daubeny *Ventry, B.*
Dempster, Lady Camilla M. E. *Leeds, D.*
Denham, Lady Mary Anne *Moray, E.*
Denison, Hon James F. *Londesborough, B.*
Denison, Hon Laura R. *Londesborough, B.*
Denman, Hon C. John *Denman, B.*
Denman, Lady Frances E. *Howe, E.*
Denman, Hon James S. *Denman, B.*
Denman, Hon Richard T. S. *Denman, B.*
Denning, Hon Robert G. *Denning, B.*
Dennys, Hon Lavinia M. Y. *Cobham V.*
Dent, Hon (Ann C.) Lady *Pender, B.*
Dent, Hon Diana Mary *Ingrow, B.*
Dent, Hon Anne Elizabeth *Ingrow, B.*
Dent, Lady Elizabeth B. M. *Kinnoull, E.*
Dent, Lady Katherine A. *Townshend, M.*
Dent, Hon Rosamond *Furnivall, By.*
Dent, Lady Rosanagh E. A. M. *Headfort, M.*
Dent, Hon Sarah *Dacre, Bs.*
Dent, Hon Tatiana *Nunburnholme, B.*
d'Erlanger, Lady Caroline M. *Cholmondeley, M.*
d'Erlanger, Hon M. Elizabeth J. *Exmouth, V.*
de Rosnay (Hon Stella C.) Baroness Joël *Gladwyn,
  B.*
Desai, Hon Nuala *Desai, B.*
Desai, Hon Sven *Desai, B.*
Desai, Hon Tanvi *Desai, B.*
de Santana, Hon Susan M. Ribeiro *Wedgwood, B.*
Devereux, Hon Charles R. de B. *Hereford, V.*
Devereux, Hon Edward M. de B. *Hereford, V.*
de Villiers, Hon Alexander C. *de Villiers, B.*
de Villiers, Hon Mrs John M. *de Villiers, B.*
Devlin, Hon Dominick *Devlin, B.*
Devlin, Hon Gilpatrick *Devlin, B.*
Devlin, Hon Matthew *Devlin, B.*
Devlin, Hon Timothy *Devlin, B.*
Devonald, Hon Charlotte E. A. *Croft, B.*
Dewar, Hon Alexander J. E. *Forteviot, B.*
Dewar, Hon Henrietta C. *Forteviot, B.*
Dewar, Hon Miranda P. *Forteviot, B.*
Dewar, Hon Simon T. *Forteviot, B.*
Dewdney, Hon Caroline *Ashley of Stoke, B.*
de Wichfeld, Lady A. A. Maryel *Perth, E.*
de Zulueta, Hon (Marie-Louise) Lady *Windlesham,
  B.*
d'Hauteville, (Hon Joanna P.) Comtesse de
  Renusson *Rennell, B.*
Diamond, Hon Derek *Diamond, B.*
Diamond, Hon Joan *Diamond, B.*
Diamond, Hon Martin *Diamond, B.*
Diamond, Hon Nigella L. *Lawson of Blaby, B.*
Diamond, Hon Ruth *Diamond, B.*
di Cáraci, Lady Charlotte *Dartmouth, E.*
Dickinson, Hon Andrew *Dickinson, B.*
Dickinson, Hon David C. *Dickinson, B.*
Dickinson, Hon Hugh G. *Dickinson, B.*
Dickinson, Hon Jessica R. *Mancroft, B.*
Dickinson, Hon Martin H. *Dickinson, B.*

Grimshaw, Hon Shelagh M. M. *Milner of Leeds, B.*
Grimston, Hon C. Antony S. *Grimston of Westbury, B.*
Grimston, Hon G. Charles W. *Grimston of Westbury, B.*
Grimston, Lady Flora H. *Verulam, E.*
Grimston, Lady Hermione F. *Verulam, E.*
Grimston, Hon Hugo G. S. *Verulam, E.*
Grimston, Hon Michael J. H. *Grimston of Westbury, B.*
Grimston, Hon Robert J. S. *Grimston of Westbury, B.*
Grimston, Hon Sam G. *Verulam, E.*
Grimston, Hon Janet E. G. *Grantchester, B.*
Grose, Hon R. Juliana *Brookeborough, V.*
Grosvenor, Hon Georgina L. *Ebury, B.*
Grosvenor, Hon Hugh R. *Ebury, B.*
Grosvenor, Lady Jane M. *Westminster, D.*
Grosvenor, Hon Julian F. M. *Ebury, B.*
Grosvenor, Lady Mary C. *Westminster, D.*
Grosvenor, Hon Richard A. *Ebury, B.*
Grosvenor, Hon Mrs R. Victor *Ebury, B.*
Grosvenor, Lady Edwina L. *Westminster, D.*
Grosvenor, Lady Tamara K. *Westminster, D.*
Grosvenor, Lady Viola G. *Westminster, D.*
Grosvenor, Hon William W. *Ebury, B.*
Groves, Hon Julia C. *Cullen of Ashbourne, B.*
Guerrico, Lady Moira B. *Granard, E.*
Guest, Hon Andrew B. G. *Guest, B.*
Guest, Hon Charles J. *Wimborne, V.*
Guest, Hon Christopher J. G. *Guest, B.*
Guest, Hon David W. G. *Guest, B.*
Guest, Hon Ilona C. *Wimborne, V.*
Guest, Hon Julian J. *Wimborne, V.*
Guest, Hon Simon E. G. *Guest, B.*
Guest, Hon Anthony Haden- *Haden-Guest, B.*
Guest, Hon Christopher Haden- *Haden-Guest, B.*
Guest, Hon Elissa Haden- *Haden-Guest, B.*
Guest, Hon Hadley Haden- *Haden-Guest, B.*
Guest, Hon Nicholas Haden *Haden-Guest, B.*
Gueterbock, Hon Philippa L. *Berkeley, B.*
Gueterbock, Hon Robert W. *Berkeley, B.*
Guerterbock, Hon Thomas F. *Berkeley, B.*
Guinness, Hon Catriona R. *Moyne, B.*
Guinness, Hon Desmond W. *Moyne, B.*
Guinness, Hon Mrs Diarmid E. *Moyne, B.*
Guinness, Lady Emma L. *Iveagh, E.*
Guinness, Hon Erskine S. R. *Moyne, B.*
Guinness, Hon Finn B. *Moyne, B.*
Guinness, Hon Fiona E. *Moyne, B.*
Guinness, Hon Jasper J. R. *Moyne, B.*
Guinness, Hon Kieran A. *Moyne, B.*
Guinness, Lady Louisa J. *Iveagh, E.*
Guinness, Hon Murtogh D. *Moyne, B.*
Guinness, Hon Rory M. B. *Iveagh, E.*
Guinness, Hon Sebastian W. D. *Moyne, B.*
Guinness, Hon Thomasin M. *Moyne, B.*
Guinness, Hon Valentine G. B. *Moyne, B.*
Gully, Hon Catherine M. A. *Selby, V.*
Gully, Hon Edward T. W. *Selby, V.*
Gully, Hon James E. H. Y. *Selby, V.*
Gundry, Hon Caroline A. S. *Wynford, B.*
Gunston, Lady Doris G. *Dufferin, M.*
Gurdon, Hon B. Charles *Cranworth, B.*
Gurdon, Hon Louisa-Jane *Cranworth, B.*
Gurdon, Hon S. W. Robin *Cranworth, B.*
Gurney, Hon D. Miranda *Thurlow, B.*
Gwinn, Lady Alice A. J. *Antrim, E.*
Gwinnett, Lady Doreen S. *Belmore, E.*
Gwyn, Hon Clare *Devlin, B.*
Hacking, Hon Belinda A. *Hacking, B.*
Hacking, Hon Christian E. G. *Hacking, B.*
Hacking, Hon Daniel R. *Hacking, B.*
Hacking, Hon Douglas F. *Hacking, B.*
Hacking, Hon Edgar B. *Hacking, B.*
Hacking, Hon Fiona M. *Ferrier, B.*
Hacking, Hon L. Bruce *Hacking, B.*
Hacking, Hon M. D. Leo *Hacking, B.*
Haddon, Hon Teresa M. *Head, V.*
Hadfield, Hon Maureen *Segal, B.*
Hadley, Lady Paulina M. L. *Cottenham, E.*
Haguenauer, Hon Elizabeth C. J. *Cottesloe, E.*
Haig, Lady A. Rainà *Haig, E.*
Haig, Lady E. Vivienne T. *Haig, E.*
Haines, Hon Emma C. *Bancroft, B.*
Haire, Hon Christopher P. *Haire of Whiteabbey, B.*
Haire, Hon Michael J. K. *Haire of Whiteabbey, B.*
Hale, Hon Dorothy L. *Hale, B.*
Hale, Hon Ian W. P. *Hale, B.*

Hales, Lady Celestria M. M. *Gainsborough, E.*
Hall, Hon Alison E. *Gridley, B.*
Hall, Hon (Diana J.) Lady *Sackville, B.*
Hall, Hon Georgina A. *Hall, V.*
Hall, Hon Jane O. *Braintree, By.*
Hall, Hon Lena M. *Hall, V.*
Hall, Hon Ann King- *King-Hall, By.*
Hall, Hon Jane King- *King-Hall, By.*
Hall, Hon Susan King- *King-Hall, By.*
Hallman, Hon Anne S. McCririe- *Walston, B.*
Hambro, Hon Charlotte C. *Soames, B.*
Hamilton, Hon Alexandra M. *Belhaven, L.*
Hamilton, Hon Archibald G. *Hamilton of Dalzell, B.*
Hamilton, Hon Benjamin J. *Hamilton of Dalzell, B.*
Hamilton, Lord C. Anthony *Abercorn, D.*
Hamilton, Hon Evelyn W. J. *HolmPatrick, B.*
Hamilton, Hon Frederick C. A. *Belhaven, L.*
Hamilton, Hon Gavin G. *Hamilton of Dalzell, B.*
Hamilton, Hon Ion H. J. *HolmPatrick, B.*
Hamilton, Hon James H. S. *HolmPatrick, B.*
Hamilton, Hon John D. *Hamilton of Dalzell, B.*
Hamilton, Hon Julia E. H. *Belhaven, L.*
Hamilton, Lord Nicholas E. C. *Abercorn D.*
Hamilton, Hon Robert P. *Hamilton of Dalzell, B.*
Hamilton, Lady Sophia A. *Abercorn, D.*
Hamilton, Lady Isobel J. Baillie- *Haddington, E.*
Hamilton, Lady Susan M. Baillie- *Haddington, E.*
Hamilton, Lady Anne Douglas- *Hamilton, D.*
Hamilton, Lady David Douglas- *Hamilton, D.*
Hamilton, Lord David S. Douglas- *Hamilton, D.*
Hamilton, Lady Eleanor Douglas- *Hamilton, D.*
Hamilton, Lord Hugh M. Douglas- *Hamilton, D.*
Hamilton, Lord James A. Douglas- *Hamilton, D.*
Hamilton, Lady James A. Douglas- *Tweedsmuir, B.*
Hamilton, Lord John W. Douglas- *Hamilton, D.*
Hamilton, Lady Malcolm Douglas- *Hamilton, D.*
Hamilton, Lord Patrick G. Douglas- *Hamilton, D.*
Hamond, Hon Charity P. Harbord- *Suffield, B.*
Hamond, Hon Charles A. A. Harbord- *Suffield, B.*
Hamond, Hon John E. R. Harbord- *Suffield, B.*
Hamond, Hon Robert P. M. Harbord- *Suffield, B.*
Handcock, Hon Ronan M. E. *Castlemaine, B.*
Hankey, Hon Alexander M. A. *Hankey, B.*
Hankey, Hon Christopher A. *Hankey, B.*
Hankey, Hon Donald R. A. *Hankey, B.*
Hankey, Hon Henry A. A. *Hankey, B.*
Hanley, Hon (Lorna M. D.)Lady *Hollenden, B.*
Hanlon, Lady Colleen *Cowley, E.*
Hanmer, Lady Frances J. *Enniskillen, E.*
Hannon, Lady Fiona M. *Montrose, D.*
Hanscomb, Hon Elinor R. *McNair, B.*
Hansen, Hon Elizabeth J. *Bradbury, B.*
Hanson, Hon Robert W. *Hanson, B.*
Hardesty, Hon Rachel H. *Cunliffe, B.*
Harding, Hon David R. J. *Harding of Petherton, B.*
Harding, Hon Diana (Dido) M. *Harding of Petherton, B.*
Harding, Hon Francis W. H. *Harding-Davies, Bs.*
Harding, Hon William R. J. *Harding of Petherton, B.*
Hardinge, Hon Andrew H. *Hardinge, V.*
Hardinge, Hon Charles A. *Hardinge of Penshurst, B.*
Hardinge, Hon Edward F. *Hardinge of Penshurst, B.*
Hardinge, Hon Emilie C. *Hardinge, V.*
Hardinge, Hon Hugh F. *Hardinge of Penshurst, B.*
Hardinge, Hon Julian A. *Hardinge of Penshurst, B.*
Hardinge, Hon Maximillian E. *Hardinge, V.*
Hardinge, Hon Olivia M. *Hardinge, V.*
Hardy, Hon (Diana J.) Lady *Hindlip, B.*
Hardy, Hon Joanna M. *Porritt, B.*
Hardy, Hon Beryl G. Cozens- *Cozens-Hardy, By.*
Hardy, Hon Mrs Antony G. Gathorne- *Cranbrook, E.*
Hardy, Hon Argus E. Gathorne- *Cranbrook, E.*
Hardy, Lady Flora Gathorne- *Cranbrook, E.*
Hardy, Hon Hugh Gathorne- *Cranbrook, E.*
Hare, Hon Alan V. *Listowel, E.*
Hare, Hon Caspar J. *Blakenham, V.*
Hare, Hon Cressida *Blakenham, V.*
Hare, Lady Diana *Listowel, E.*
Hare, Hon A. Elizabeth C. *Amery of Lustleigh, B.*
Hare, Hon Emily *Blakenham, V.*
Hare, Lady Rose A. *Darnley, E.*
Hare, Hon Timothy P. *Listowel, E.*
Harmsworth, Hon Abigail P. T. *Harmsworth, B.*
Harmsworth, Hon Dominic M. E. *Harmsworth, B.*
Harmsworth, Hon Mrs Eric B. N. *Harmsworth, B.*
Harmsworth, Hon Esmond V. *Rothermere, V.*
Harmsworth, Hon H. Jonathan E. V. *Rothermere, V.*
Harmsworth, Lady Jessamine C. M. *Aberdeen, M.*

Harmsworth, Hon Philomena H. O. *Harmsworth, B.*
Harmsworth, Hon Pollyanna M. C. *Harmsworth, B.*
Harmsworth, Hon Timothy T. J. *Harmsworth, B.*
Harper, Hon Hazel E. *Woolley, B.*
Harries, Hon Anne M. *De L'Isle, V.*
Harriman, Hon Pamela B. *Digby, B.*
Harris, Hon Charles E. *Malmesbury, E.*
Harris, Hon Daisy C. *Malmesbury, E.*
Harris, Hon Deborah J. A. *Harris of Greenwich, B.*
Harris, Hon J. Elizabeth *Ogmore, B.*
Harris, Hon Frances M. *Malmesbury, E.*
Harris, Hon Francis O. A. *Harris of Greenwich, B.*
Harris, Hon George R. J. *Harris, B.*
Harris, Hon Guy R. *Malmesbury, E.*
Harris, Hon James H. C. *Malmesbury, E.*
Harris, Hon Linda C. *Bellwin, B.*
Harris, Hon Thelma E. *Airedale, B.*
Harris, Hon Henrietta M. J. Reader- *Wakehurst, B.*
Harrison, Lady Isabella B. R. *Jersey, E.*
Hart, Hon Richard O. *Hart of South Lanark, Bs.*
Hart, Hon Stephen C. *Hart of South Lanark, Bs.*
Hartig, Hon Linda *Glendyne, B.*
Harvey, Hon Guy A. V. *Harvey of Prestbury, B.*
Harvey, Hon Mrs John W. *Harvey of Tasburgh, B.*
Harvey, Hon Juliet A. C. *Harvey of Tasburgh, B.*
Harvey, Hon Philip W. V. *Harvey of Prestbury, B.*
Harvey, Hon Vivienne N. *Gridley, B.*
Harvey, Lady Julia H. Craig- *Northumberland, D.*
Harwood, Hon Elizabeth M. *Leonard, B.*
Harwood, Lady Felicity A. *Attlee, E.*
Haslam, Hon Judith *Oranmore and Browne, B.*
Hastings, Hon Eileen E. *Wise, B.*
Hastings, Hon (Elizabeth A. M.) Lady *Fitzalan of Derwent, Vy.*
Hastings, Lady Selina S. *Huntingdon, E.*
Hastings, Hon Amanda L. Abney- *Loudoun, Cs.*
Hastings, Lady Clare L. Abney- *Loudoun, Cs.*
Hastings, Hon Frederick J. Abney- *Loudoun, Cs.*
Hastings, Hon Lisa Abney- *Loudoun, Cs.*
Hastings, Hon Rebecca Abney- *Loudoun, Cs.*
Hastings, Hon Simon Abney- *Loudoun, Cs.*
Hathorn, Hon Jean R. *Evans, By.*
Hatton, Lady Alice N. C. Finch *Winchilsea, E.*
Hatton, Hon Robin H. Finch *Winchilsea, E.*
Havers, Hon Nigel *Havers, B.*
Havers, Hon Philip *Havers, B.*
Haw, Hon Helen E. D. *Hastings, B.*
Hawke, Hon Edward G. *Hawke, B.*
Hawke, Hon Julia G. *Hawke, B.*
Hawks, Lady Kara V. L. Conroy *Kingston, E.*
Hay, Lord Alistair J. M. *Tweeddale, M.*
Hay, Hon Amanda J. *Mackenzie-Stuart, B.*
Hay, Lady Amelia D. J. *Erroll, E.*
Hay, Lord Andrew A. G. *Tweeddale, M.*
Hay, Lady Atalanta R. *Kinnoull, E.*
Hay, Lord Charles D. M. *Tweeddale, M.*
Hay, Lord Hamish D. M. *Tweeddale, M.*
Hay, Lady H. Olga *Lauderdale, E.*
Hay, Lady Iona C. *Kinnoull, E.*
Hay, Lady Laline L. C. *Erroll, E.*
Hay, Lady Marioth C. *Tweeddale, M.*
Hay, Lady Melissa A. *Kinnoull, E.*
Hay, Hon Richard M. I. *Erroll, E.*
Hay, Lady Bettina M. Drummond- *Crawford, E.*
Haydon, Hon Kathleen M. *Mottistone, B.*
Hayes, Hon (Rosalind M.) Lady *Finlay V.*
Hayes, Hon Sarah *Maclay, B.*
Hayhoe, Hon Crispin B. G. *Hayhoe, B.*
Hayhoe, Hon Dominic A. S. *Hayhoe, B.*
Hayhoe, Hon Sarah A. S. *Hayhoe, B.*
Haynes, Hon Penelope M. *Vaux of Harrowden, B.*
Hayter, Hon Deborah G. *Maude of Stratford-upon-Avon, B.*
Hayward, Lady Patricia M. *Courtown, E.*
Hazlerigg, Hon Arthur G. *Hazlerigg, B.*
Hazlerigg, Hon Robert M. *Hazlerigg, B.*
Hazlerigg, Hon Thomas M. *Hazlerigg, B.*
Head, Hon George R. *Head, V.*
Head, Hon Sarah G. *Head, V.*
Head, Hon Simon A. *Head, V.*
Healey, Hon Cressida *Healey, B.*
Healey, Hon Timothy B. *Healey, B.*
Healing, Hon Elizabeth M. L. M. *Petre, B.*
Hearn, Hon Kathleen G. *Guillamore, V.*
Heaton, Hon Charles J. C. Henniker- *Henniker, B.*
Heaton, Hon Mark I. P. C. Henniker- *Henniker, B.*
Heckendorn, Hon Roselle S. *Bruce-Gardyne, Bs.*
Heffler, Lady Tara F. *Munster, E.*
Heimann, Hon Diana H. *MacLeod of Borve, Bs.*

Helberg, Hon Sarah A. *Rendlesham, B.*
Helme, Hon Mirabel J. *Moyne, B.*
Helsby, Hon Nigel C. *Helsby, B.*
Hemphill, Hon Pamela *Rhodes, B.*
Hemphill, Hon Angela M. Martyn- *Hemphill, B.*
Hemphill, Hon Charles A. Martyn- *Hemphill, B.*
Hemphill, Hon Mary A. Martyn- *Hemphill, B.*
Hemsley, Hon Gwenllian E. *Northbourne, B.*
Henderson, Hon Angus G. *Faringdon, B.*
Henderson, Hon Corinne D. *Lloyd of Hampstead, B.*
Henderson, Hon Diana C. *Fairhaven, B.*
Henderson, Hon Elizabeth F. *May, B.*
Henderson, Hon Flora E. *Lifford, V.*
Henderson, Hon James H. *Faringdon, B.*
Henderson, Hon Launcelot D. J. *Henderson of Brompton, B.*
Henderson, Hon Richard C. A. *Henderson of Brompton, B.*
Henderson, Hon Roderic H. D. *Faringdon, B.*
Henderson, Hon Susannah J. *Faringdon, B.*
Henderson, Hon Thomas A. G. *Faringdon, B.*
Hendry, Hon Elspeth M. *Ironside, B.*
Hendy, Hon Mary J. *Wynford, B.*
Henghes, Hon Penelope K. T. *Balogh, By.*
Hennessy, Hon James R. *Windlesham, B.*
Hennessy, Hon Victoria J. *Windlesham, B.*
Henry, Hon Christian A. *Hughes, B.*
Henry, Hon Helen J. *Somers, B.*
Hensman, Hon Mary S. *Wakefield of Kendal, B.*
Herbert, Lady Alice M. *Pembroke, E.*
Herbert, Hon Andrew C. *Powis, E.*
Herbert, Hon Caroline M. L. *Hemingford, B.*
Herbert, Hon Carolyn P. *Carnarvon, E.*
Herbert, Hon Christopher D. L. *Hemingford, B.*
Herbert, Hon David A. R. *Pembroke, E.*
Herbert, Hon David M. *Powis, E.*
Herbert, Lady Diana M. *Pembroke, E.*
Herbert, Hon Edward D. *Powis, E.*
Herbert, Lady Emma L. *Pembroke, E.*
Herbert, Lady Flora K. *Pembroke, E.*
Herbert, Hon George R. O. M. *Carnarvon, E.*
Herbert, Hon Henry M. *Carnarvon, E.*
Herbert, Lady Jemima J. *Pembroke, E.*
Herbert, Hon Mrs Mervyn R. H. M. *Carnarvon, E.*
Herbert, Hon Michael C. *Powis, E.*
Herbert, Hon Oliver H. D. *Hemingford, B.*
Herbert, Hon Peter J. *Powis, E.*
Herbert, Hon Peter M. *Tangley, By.*
Herbert, Lady Samantha J. E. *Powis, E.*
Herbert, Hon Saoirse *Carnarvon, E.*
Herbert, Lady Sophia E. *Pembroke, E.*
Herbert, Lady Stephanie M. C. *Powis, E.*
Herd, Hon Sheelagh M. *Galway, V.*
Herring, Hon E. Louise *Astor of Hever, B.*
Herschell, Hon Arabella J. *Herschell, B.*
Hersey, Hon Katherine V. *Northbourne, B.*
Hervey, Lord Frederick W. A. *Bristol, M.*
Hervey, Lord F. W. C. Nicholas W. *Bristol, M.*
Hervey, Lady Isabella F. L. *Bristol, M.*
Hervey, Lady Victoria F. I. *Bristol, M.*
Hesketh, Hon Catherine I. *Moyne, B.*
Hesketh, Lady Mary C. *Scarbrough, E.*
Hesketh, Hon Flora Fermor- *Hesketh, B.*
Hesketh, Hon Frederick H. Fermor- *Hesketh, B.*
Hesketh, Hon John Fermor- *Hesketh, B.*
Hesketh, Hon Robert Fermor- *Hesketh, B.*
Hesketh, Hon Sophia C. Fermor- *Hesketh, B.*
Hesse, Hon (Margaret C.), Princess of *Geddes, B.*
Hewitt, Hon Alice M. *Lifford, V.*
Hewitt, Hon Annabel L. *Lifford, V.*
Hewitt, Hon James T. W. *Lifford, V.*
Hewlett, Hon J. Richard *Hewlett, B.*
Hewlett, Hon T. Anthony *Hewlett, B.*
Heycock, Hon Clayton R. *Heycock, B.*
Heyman, Hon Isobel Cooper- *Pargiter, B.*
Heywood, Hon Rosalind L. B. *Aberdare, B.*
Heywood, Lady Sophia H. *Clanwilliam, E.*
Hibbert, Hon Henry T. Holland- *Knutsford, V.*
Hibbert, Hon James E. Holland- *Knutsford, V.*
Hicks, Lady Pamela C. L. *Mountbatten of Burma, Cs.*
Hicks, Hon Amy G. Joynson- *Brentford, V.*
Hicks, Hon Emma R. Joynson- *Brentford, V.*
Hicks, Hon Paul W. Joynson- *Brentford, V.*
Higham, Hon Barbara C. *Hampden, V.*
Highett, Hon Jean M. *Swaythling, B.*
Hildyard, Hon Aislinn M. K. *Morris, B.*
Hill, Lady Anne C. D. *Cranbrooke, E.*
Hill, Lord Anthony I. *Downshire, M.*

Llewellyn, Lady Honor M. M. *Lisburne, E.*
Llewellyn, Lady Delia M. Dillwyn-Venables- *St Alldwyn, E.*
Lloyd, Hon Davina M. *Lloyd, B.*
Lloyd, Hon Joanna E. *Selwyn-Lloyd, B.*
Lloyd, Hon Laura B. B. *Lloyd, B.*
Lloyd, Hon Thelma M. *Leighton of St Mellons, B.*
Lloyd, Hon Victoria M. *Harlech, B.*
Loch, Hon Allegra H. *Loch, B.*
Loch, Hon Sara N. *Loch, B.*
Loder, Hon James D. G. *Wakehurst, B.*
Loder, Hon Robert B. *Wakehurst, B.*
Loder, Hon Timothy W. *Wakehurst, B.*
Loizeau, Hon Eliza *Hutchinson of Lullington, B.*
Lolley, Hon Elizabeth H. *Keith of Avonholm, By.*
Lomax, Hon Elizabeth M. *Hampden, V.*
Long, Hon A. Cathrine *Congleton, B.*
Long, Hon Charlotte H. *Long, V.*
Long, Hon James R. *Long, V.*
Long, Hon Jean *Douglass of Cleveland, B.*
Long, Hon John H. *Long, V.*
Long, Hon Meriel D. *Kensington, B.*
Longman, Lady Elizabeth M. *Cavan, E.*
Longmore, Lady Felicity A. *Wavell, E.*
Longmore, Hon Jean M. *Forres, B.*
Lonsdale, Hon Jean H. Heywood- *Rollo, L.*
Lopes, Hon Andrew J. *Roborough, B.*
Lopes, Hon Emily J. *Roborough, B.*
Lopes, Hon George E. *Roborough, B.*
Lopes, Hon Katie V. *Roborough, B.*
Lopes, Hon Louisa *Roborough, B.*
Lopes, Hon Massey J. H. *Roborough, B.*
Lopes, Hon Melinda C. *Roborough, B.*
Lopes, Hon Sarah, V. *Astor of Hever, B.*
Lorban, Hon Kirsten V. M. *Grantchester, B.*
Loudon, Lady Prudence K. P. *Jellicoe, E.*
Louloudis, Hon Madeleine M. *Dillon, V.*
Love, Hon Robin M. Cox McNeill *Cox, Bs.*
Lovell, Hon Virginia *Weatherill, B.*
Low, Hon Charles H. S. *Aldington, B.*
Lowe, Lady Elisabeth O. *Cairns, E.*
Lowe, Hon Sally J. *Plummer of St Marylebone, B.*
Lowell, Lady Caroline M. *Dufferin, M.*
Lowry, Hon Anne L. *Lowry, B.*
Lowry, Hon Margaret I. *Lowry, B.*
Lowson, Hon (A. Patricia) Lady *Strathcarron, B.*
Lowther, Hon Amanda U. G. *Swansea, B.*
Lowther, Hon Mrs Anthony G. *Lonsdale, E.*
Lowther, Hon Benjamin J. *Ullswater, V.*
Lowther, Hon Charles A. J. *Lonsdale, E.*
Lowther, Hon Clare P. *Ullswater, V.*
Lowther, Hon Edward J. *Ullswater, V.*
Lowther, Hon Emma M. *Ullswater, V.*
Lowther, Hon James N. *Lonsdale, E.*
Lowther, Hon Jennifer *Ullswater, V.*
Lowther, Lady Marie-Louisa K. *Lonsdale, E.*
Lowther, Hon Mrs Timothy L. E. *Lonsdale, E.*
Lowther, Hon William J. *Lonsdale, E.*
Loyd, Lady Tara G. *Erne, E.*
Luard, Hon Philippa M. A. J. *Chetwynd, V.*
Lubbock, Hon Helen A. B. *Boyd-Orr, By.*
Lubbock, Hon Lyulph A. J. *Avebury, B.*
Lubbock, Hon Maurice P. G. *Avebury, B.*
Lubbock, Hon Victoria S. M. *Avebury, B.*
Lucas, Hon Ivor T. M. *Lucas of Chilworth, B.*
Lucas, Hon Simon W. *Lucas of Chilworth, B.*
Lucas, Hon Timothy M. *Lucas of Chilworth, B.*
Ludlow, Lady Margaret M. *Loudoun, Cs*
Luke, Hon Œ. Clarissa *Chaplin, Vy.*
Luke, Hon Felicity M. *Crowther, By.*
Lumley, Lady Rose F. L. *Scarbrough, E.*
Lumley, Hon Thomas H. *Scarbrough, E.*
Luttrell, Lady Elizabeth H. *Ferrers, B.*
Lycett, Lady J. Wendy *Yarborough, E., and Fauconberg and Conyers By.*
Lyell, Hon (Katharine) Lady *Runciman of Doxford, V.*
Lygon, Lady Dorothy *Beauchamp, E.*
Lygon, Hon Mrs Richard E. *Beauchamp, E.*
Lyle, Hon Teresa R. *Mayhew, B.*
Lyon, Lady Diana E. Bowes- *Strathmore, E.*
Lyon, Hon George N. Bowes- *Strathmore, E.*
Lyon, Hon John F. Bowes- *Strathmore, E.*
Lyon, Hon (Rachel P.) Lady Bowes- *Strathmore, E.*
Lyons, Hon Deborah *Lyons of Brighton, B.*
Lyons, Hon Rodney *Lyons of Brighton, B.*
Lyons, Hon William *Lyons of Brighton, B.*
Lyttelton, Hon Benedict *Chandos, V.*

Lyttelton, Hon Christopher C. *Cobham, V.*
Lyttelton, Hon Deborah C. *Chandos, V.*
Lyttelton, Hon Laura K. *Chandos, V.*
Lyttelton, Hon Matthew P. A. *Chandos, V.*
Lyttelton, Hon N. Adrian O. *Chandos, V.*
Lyttelton, Hon Nicholas M. *Cobham, V.*
Lyttelton, Hon Oliver A. *Chandos, V.*
Lyttelton, Hon Richard C. *Cobham, V.*
Lyttelton, Hon Rosanna M. *Chandos, V.*
Lytton, Lady Caroline M. N. *Lytton, E.*
Lytton, Lady Katrina M. N. *Lytton, E.*
Lytton, Lady Lucy M. F. *Lytton, E.*
Lytton, Lady Madeleine E. *Lytton, E.*
Lytton, Lady Sarah T. M. *Lytton, E.*
Lytton, Hon T. Ronald C. L. *Lytton, E.*
Lytton, Hon Wilfrid *Lytton, E.*
McAlpine, Hon David M. *McAlpine of Moffat, B.*
Macalpine, Hon Dorothy F. *Bethell, B.*
McAlpine, Hon John J. *McAlpine of Preston Candover, B.*
McAlpine, Hon Mark L. *McAlpine of Preston Candover, B.*
McAlpine, Hon Skye *McAlpine of West Green, B.*
McAlpine, Hon Sir William H. *McAlpine of Moffat, By.*
MacAndrew, Hon Diana S. *MacAndrew, B.*
MacAndrew, Hon Nicholas *MacAndrew, B.*
MacAndrew, Hon Oliver C.J. *MacAndrew, B.*
MacAndrew, Hon Tessa D. *MacAndrew, B.*
McAulay, Hon Rita L. *Kadoorie, B.*
Macauley, Hon Diana P. *Camrose, V.*
McBeath, Hon Janet M. *Ebbisham, B.*
McCall, Hon Gillian P. *Denman, B.*
McCallum, Lady Charlotte M. *Cathcart, E.*
McCarraher, Hon Belinda J. *Kenilworth, B.*
MacCarthy, Hon Christina A. *Wakehurst, B.*
McCausland, Lady Margaret L. *Mount Edgcumbe, E.*
McCluskey, Hon Catherine M. *McCluskey, B.*
McCluskey, Hon David F. *McCluskey, B.*
McCluskey, Hon John M. *McCluskey, B.*
McConnell, Hon Elizabeth M. *Selby, V.*
McCorquodale, Lady E. Sarah L. *Spencer, E.*
McCowen, Hon Philippa U. M. *Burton, B.*
McCraith, Hon Philippa M. E. *Robins, B.*
McCulloch, Hon Cecily M. C. *Cornwallis, B.*
MacCullum, Hon Celia Y. L. *de Villiers, B.*
MacDermott, Hon John C. *MacDermott, B.*
MacDermott, Hon Robert W. J. *MacDermott, B.*
Macdiarmid, Hon Lucinda M. J. *Darling, B.*
Macdonald, Hon Alexander D. A. *Macdonald, B.*
Macdonald, Hon Alexandra L. *Macdonald, B.*
Macdonald, Hon Elspeth R. *Craigmyle, B.*
Macdonald, Hon Isabella C. *Macdonald, B.*
MacDonald, Hon Jacaranda F. *Craigavon, V.*
MacDonald, Hon Janet A. *MacDonald, B.*
Macdonald, Hon Joan M. *Lambury, By.*
Macdonald, Hon Mrs Kenneth *Macdonald of Gwaenysgor, B.*
Macdonald, Hon Margaret A. *Trent, By.*
McDonald, Hon Margaret J. *Fraser of Lonsdale, B.*
Macdonald, Hon Meriel I. *Macdonald, B.*
Macdonald, Hon Patricia J. K. *Tryon, B.*
Macdonald, Hon Rosemary *Alanbrooke, V.*
Macdonald of Macdonald, Hon G. E. Hugo T. *Macdonald, B.*
McDonnell, Lady Flora M. *Antrim, E.*
McDonnell, Hon Hector J. *Antrim, E.*
McDonnell, Hon James A. G. *Antrim, E.*
McDonnell, Lady Rachel *Antrim, E.*
McDonnell, Hon Randal A. St J. *Antrim, E.*
McDougall, Hon Carolyn J. *Griffiths, B.*
MacDowel, Hon Angela C. *Hazlerigg, B.*
McFadzean, Hon Gordon B. *McFadzean, B.*
Macfarlane, Hon Hamish *Macfarlane of Bearsden, B.*
Macfarlane, Hon Marguerite *Macfarlane of Bearsden, B.*
McGowan, Hon A. Charlotte *Eden of Winton, B.*
McGowan, Hon Catriona C. H. *McGowan, B.*
McGowan, Hon Dominic J. W. *McGowan, B.*
McGowan, Hon Harry J. C. *McGowan, B.*
Macgowan, Hon Jane A. *Casey, By.*
McGowan, Hon Mungo A. C. *McGowan, B.*
McGrath, Hon Virginia M. *Carew, B.*
MacGreevy, Hon Catriona M. *Craigmyle, B.*
McGregor, Hon Alistair J. *McGregor of Durris, B.*
McGregor, Hon Gregor W. *McGregor of Durris, B.*
McGregor, Hon William R. *McGregor of Durris, B.*

McIlroy, Hon Elizabeth N.   *Rochester, B.*
McIndoe, Lady Felicity A. A.   *Courtown, E.*
MacInnes, Hon Janitha S.   *Craigavon, V.*
McIntosh, Hon Francis R.   *McIntosh of Haringey, B.*
McIntosh, Hon Philip H. S.   *McIntosh of Haringey, B.*
Mackay, Hon Æneas S.   *Reay, L.*
Mackay, Hon Asia B.   *Tanlaw, B.*
Mackay, Lady Ailsa F.   *Inchcape, E.*
Mackay, Hon Alan J. F.   *Inchcape, E.*
Mackay, Baron (and Hon) Alexander W. R.   *Reay, L.*
Mackay, Hon Antonia   *Reay, L.*
Mackay, Hon Brooke   *Tanlaw, B.*
Mackay, Hon Colin J.   *Mackay of Ardbrecknish, B.*
Mackay, Hon Cynthia   *Vansittart, B.*
Mackay, Hon David F.   *Mackay of Ardbrecknish, B.*
Mackay, Hon Edward A.   *Reay, L.*
Mackay, Lady Elspeth   *Inchcape, E.*
Mackay, Hon Fiona J.   *Mackay of Ardbrecknish, B.*
Mackay, Hon Isabel V.   *Reay, L.*
Mackay, Hon Iona H.   *Tanlaw, B.*
Mackay, Hon Ivan C.   *Inchcape, E.*
Mackay, Hon James   *Mackay of Clashfern, B.*
Mackay, Hon James B.   *Tanlaw, B.*
Mackay, Hon James J. T.   *Inchcape, E.*
Mackay, Hon Laura E.   *Reay, L.*
Mackay, Lady Lucinda L.   *Inchcape, E.*
Mackay, Hon Rebecca A.   *Tanlaw, B.*
Mackay, Hon Shane L.   *Inchcape, E.*
Mackay, Hon Shona R.   *Mackay of Clashfern, B.*
McKenna, Lady Cecilia E.   *Albemarle, E.*
Mackenzie, Hon Alasdair   *Cromartie, E.*
Mackenzie, Lady Anne M. I.   *Grafton, D.*
Mackenzie, Lady Jean   *Rothes, E.*
Mackenzie, Hon S. A. Julia   *Cromartie, E.*
Mackeson, Hon (Camilla) Lady   *Keith of Castleacre, B.*
Mackie, Hon George Y.   *John-Mackie, B.*
Mackie, Hon James A.   *John-Mackie, B.*
Mackie, Hon John M.   *John-Mackie, B.*
Mackie, Hon Mary Y.   *John-Mackie, B.*
Mackinnon, Hon Eva C. E.   *Wynford, B.*
Mackinnon, Hon Patricia A.   *Audley, B.*
Mackinnon, Hon Patricia C.   *Glentoran, B.*
Mackintosh, Hon Diana M.   *Mackintosh of Halifax, V.*
Mackintosh, Hon Fiona E. A.   *Listowel, E.*
Mackintosh, Hon George J. F.   *Mackintosh of Halifax, V.*
Mackintosh, Hon Graham C.   *Mackintosh of Halifax, V.*
Mackintosh, Hon Thomas H. G.   *Mackintosh of Halifax, V.*
McLaren, (Hon Dame) Anne L. D.   *Aberconway, B.*
McLaren, Hon Christopher   *Aberconway, B.*
Maclaren, Lady Edith H.   *Loudoun, Cs.*
McLaren, H. Charles   *Aberconway, B.*
McLaren, Hon Michael D.   *Aberconway, B.*
McLaren, Lady Rose M. P.   *Anglesey, M.*
Maclay, Hon Angus G.   *Maclay, B.*
Maclay, Hon David M.   *Maclay, B.*
Maclay, Hon Joseph P.   *Maclay, B.*
Maclay, Hon Rebecca D.   *Maclay, B.*
Maclay, Hon Thomas M.   *Maclay, B.*
Maclay, Hon Mrs Walter S.   *Maclay, B.*
Maclean, Hon Sir Lachlan H. C.   *Maclean, Bt (cr 1631).*
Maclean, Hon Sarah E. C.   *Rowallan, B.*
Maclean, Lady Sarah E. J.   *Aylesford, E.*
Maclean, Hon (Veronica N.) Lady   *Lovat, L.*
McLeavy, Hon Mrs Douglas J.   *McLeavy, By.*
McLeavy, Hon Frank W.   *McLeavy, By.*
McLeod, Hon Eva M. E.   *MacLeod, Bt (cr 1924).*
Macleod, Hon Hermione J.   *Rathdonnell, B.*
MacLeod, Hon Sir John M. N.   *MacLeod, Bt (cr 1924).*
MacLeod, Hon Neil D.   *MacLeod, Bt (cr 1924).*
MacLeod, Hon Torquil A. R.   *MacLeod of Borve, Bs.*
McLintock, Hon Carla A.   *Hill-Norton, B.*
McManus, Hon Alice C. E.   *Hemingford, B.*
McMeekan, Hon Sarah A. V. de la P.   *Decies, B.*
McMichael, Hon Paquita M. J.   *Florey, B.*
Macmillan, Hon Adam J. R.   *Stockton, E.*
Macmillan, Hon Daniel M. A.   *Stockton, E.*
Macmillan, Hon David M. B.   *Stockton, E.*
Macmillan, Lady Louisa A.   *Stockton, E.*
Macmillan, Lady Rebecca E.   *Stockton, E.*
Macnab, Hon Diana M.   *Kilmany, B.*
Macnab, Hon Elisabeth J.   *Arwyn, B.*

Macnab, Hon Sarah M.   *Polwarth, L.*
Macnaghten, Hon (Beatrice) Lady   *Macnaghten, B.*
McNair, Hon Duncan J.   *McNair, B.*
McNair, Hon Josephine M.   *McNair, B.*
McNair, Hon W. Samuel A.   *McNair, B.*
McNaught, Hon Fiona   *Macfarlane of Bearsden, B.*
MacNaughton, Hon Liza J.   *Cowdray, V.*
McNeal, Hon Julia   *Gaitskell, Bs.*
McNeile, Hon Henrietta C. L.   *Ingleby, V.*
McNulty, Lady Sarah L.   *Belmore, E.*
Macpherson, Hon Alexandra G.   *Northbrook, B.*
Macpherson, Hon Andrew C. J.   *Strathcarron, B.*
Macpherson, Hon Anne A.   *Macpherson of Drumochter, B.*
Macpherson, Hon Ian D. P.   *Strathcarron, B.*
Macpherson, Hon James A.   *Macpherson of Drumochter, B.*
Macpherson, Hon Jennifer M.   *Macpherson of Drumochter, B.*
Macpherson, Hon Laura A.   *Northbrook, B.*
Macpherson, Hon Mary S.   *Drumalbyn, B.*
Macpherson, Hon Sarah C.   *Carew, B.*
McQuiston, Lady Silvy C.   *Bath, M.*
MacRae, Hon Susan M.   *Southwell, V.*
McWatters, Hon Veronica   *Stamp, B.*
Maffey, Hon Christopher A.   *Rugby, B.*
Maffey, Hon Mark A.   *Rugby, B.*
Maffey, Hon Robert C.   *Rugby, B.*
Maffey, Hon Selina P.   *Rugby, B.*
Maffey, Hon Simon C. L.   *Rugby, B.*
Maher, Hon Sarah J.   *Burnham, B.*
Mais, Hon Jonathan R. N.   *Mais, B.*
Mais, Hon Richard J. I.   *Mais, B.*
Maitland, Lady Caroline C. M.   *Lauderdale, E.*
Maitland, Lady Elizabeth S.   *Lauderdale, E.*
Maitland, Hon John D.   *Lauderdale, E.*
Maitland, Hon Rosemary C.   *Abertay, By.*
Maitland, Hon Sydney M. P.   *Lauderdale, E.*
Major, Hon Charles J. G. Henniker-   *Henniker, B.*
Major, Hon Mark I. P. C. Henniker-   *Henniker, B.*
Major, Hon Richard A. O. Henniker-   *Henniker, B.*
Makgill, Hon Diana M. R.   *Oxfuird, V.*
Makgill, Hon Edward A. D.   *Oxfuird, V.*
Makgill, Hon Hamish M. A.   *Oxfuird, V.*
Makgill, Hon Ian A. A.   *Oxfuird, V.*
Makgill, Hon Robert E. G.   *Oxfuird, V.*
Makins, Hon Christopher J.   *Sherfield, B.*
Makins, Hon Dwight W.   *Sherfield, B.*
Malcolm, Hon Annabel M. A.   *Norrie, B.*
Maldura, Lady Arabella A. D. Emo Capodilista   *De La Warr, E.*
Malet, Hon M. Cherry   *Wigram, B.*
Malpas, Hon Venetia J. Colborne-   *Manners, B.*
Maltby, Lady Sylvia V. A.   *Malmesbury, E.*
Mancroft, Hon Georgia E.   *Mancroft, B.*
Mandelson, Hon Mary J.   *Morrison of Lambeth, B.*
Manners, Lady Charlotte L.   *Rutland, D.*
Manners, Lord Edward J. F.   *Rutland, D.*
Manners, Lady H. Teresa   *Rutland, D.*
Manners, Lord John   *Rutland, D.*
Manners, Hon John H. R.   *Manners, B.*
Manners, Hon Richard N.   *Manners, B.*
Manners, Lord Roger D.   *Rutland, D.*
Manners, Hon Thomas J.   *Manners, B.*
Manners, Lady Violet D. L.   *Rutland, D.*
Mansfield, Hon Guy R. J.   *Sandhurst, B.*
Mansfield, Hon Mrs Ralph G. K.   *Sandhurst, B.*
Mar, Lady Janet H. of   *Mar, Cs.*
Mar, Lady Susan H. of   *Mar, Cs.*
Marckus, Hon Rachel M. F.   *King of Wartnaby, B.*
Marcow, Hon Hannah O.   *Marks of Broughton, B.*
Marffy, Hon Pelline M.   *Acton, B.*
Margesson, Hon Jane H.   *Margesson, V.*
Margesson, Hon Rhoda F.   *Margesson, V.*
Margesson, Hon Richard F. D.   *Margesson, V.*
Margesson, Hon Sarah H.   *Margesson, V.*
Marks, Hon Adrianne B. E.   *Stone, B.*
Marks, Hon Simon R.   *Marks of Broughton, B.*
Marlar, Hon Gillian D.   *Taylor of Hadfield, B.*
Marlow, Hon Teresa   *Sackville, B.*
Marquis, Lady Constance E.   *Woolton, E.*
Marquis, Lady Olivia A.   *Woolton, E.*
Marr, Hon Jacqueline   *Ashley of Stoke, B.*
Marrian, Lady Emma C.   *Cawdor, E.*
Marriott, Hon Dinah L.   *Dacre, Bs.*
Marsh, Hon Andrew   *Marsh, B.*
Marsh, Hon Christopher   *Marsh, B.*
Marsh, Hon (Felicity C. F.) Lady   *McFadzean of*

Montgomerie, Hon Robert S.　*Eglinton, E.*
Montgomerie, Hon Roger H.　*Eglinton, E.*
Montgomerie, Hon William J.　*Eglinton, E.*
Montgomery, Hon Bridget A.　*Fisher, B.*
Montgomery, Hon Henry D.　*Montgomery of Alamein, V.*
Moore, Hon Astraea J. D.　*Barnetson, B.*
Moore, Hon C. Sheila　*Digby, B.*
Moore, Hon Garrett A.　*Drogheda, E.*
Moore, Hon Janie St. G.　*Charlemont, V.*
Moore, Lady Marina A.　*Drogheda, E.*
Moore, Hon Martin　*Moore of Lower Marsh, B.*
Moore, Hon Richard　*Moore of Lower Marsh, B.*
Moore, Hon Stephanie　*Moore of Lower Marsh, B.*
Moorehead, Hon Kerena A.　*Melchett, B.*
Moorhouse, Lady Diana M.　*Leicester, E.*
Morehead, Lady Patricia C.　*Annesley, E.*
Moreton, Hon Claire A.　*Ducie, E.*
Moreton, Hon Douglas H.　*Ducie, E.*
Moreton, Hon James B.　*Ducie, E.*
Moreton, Hon Robert M.　*Ducie, E.*
Morgan, Hon Fionn F. B.　*O'Neill, B.*
Morgan, Hon Owain　*Elystan-Morgan, B.*
Morgan, Hon Elizabeth M. Grey　*Wrenbury, B.*
Morley, Hon Andrew J. S. Hope-　*Hollenden, B.*
Morley, Hon Ian H. Hope-　*Hollenden, B.*
Morley, Hon Robin G. Hope-　*Hollenden, B.*
Moro, Hon Anne M. T.　*Huntingfield, B.*
Morris, Hon Carolie M. W.　*Mountmorres, V.*
Morris, Hon Caroline H.　*Morris of Kenwood, B.*
Morris, Hon C. Christopher　*Morris of Grasmere, B.*
Morris, Hon Christopher J. R.　*Morris of Castle Morris, B.*
Morris, Hon E. Patrick　*Morris, B.*
Morris, Hon Elizabeth　*Hill of Luton, B.*
Morris, Hon George R. F.　*Killanin, B.*
Morris, Hon James　*Morris, B.*
Morris, Hon John M.　*Killanin, B.*
Morris, Hon Jonathan D.　*Morris of Kenwood, B.*
Morris, Hon Lucy　*Morris, B.*
Morris, Hon Michael F. L.　*Killanin, B.*
Morris, Hon Michaela M.　*Morris, B.*
Morris, Hon Patricia M.　*Nolan, B.*
Morris, Hon Thomas A. S.　*Morris, B.*
Morris, Lady V. Audrey B.　*Shrewsbury, E.*
Morrish, Hon Rosalind B.　*Wade, B.*
Morrison, Hon A. Sara F. S.　*Long, V.*
Morrison, Hon Alasdair V. O.　*Dunrossil, V.*
Morrison, Hon Alasdair G.　*Dunrossil, V.*
Morrison, Hon Andrew W. R.　*Dunrossil, V.*
Morrison, Hon Catriona M.　*Dunrossil, V.*
Morrison, Hon Sir Charles A.　*Margadale, B.*
Morrison, Hon Charlotte A.　*Galway, V.*
Morrison, Hon Helena G.　*Garner, B.*
Morrison, Hon James I.　*Margadale, B.*
Morrison, Hon Joanna C.　*Dunrossil, V.*
Morrison, Hon Louisa M. C.　*Napier and Ettrick, L.*
Morrison, Hon Mary A.　*Dunrossil, V.*
Morrison, Hon Dame Mary A.　*Margadale, B.*
Morrison, Hon Mrs Nial R.　*Dunrossil, V.*
Morrison, Hon Sir Peter H.　*Margadale, B.*
Morrison, Hon Philippa A.　*Hives, B.*
Morrison, Hon Ranald J.　*Dunrossil, V.*
Morrison, Lady Sophia L. S.　*Devonshire, D.*
Morrissey, Lady Joanna A.　*Townshend, M.*
Morse, Hon Jennifer　*Delfont, B.*
Morton, Hon Alicia D.　*Rugby, B.*
Morton, Hon Alistair C. R.　*Morton of Shuna, B.*
Morton, Hon Douglas W.　*Morton of Shuna, B.*
Morton, Hon Kenneth J.　*Morton of Shuna, B.*
Mosley, Hon Clare I.　*Ravensdale, B.*
Mosley, Hon (Diana) Lady　*Redesdale, B.*
Mosley, Hon Ivo A. R.　*Ravensdale, B.*
Mosley, Hon Marius　*Ravensdale, B.*
Mosley, Hon Michael　*Ravensdale, B.*
Mosley, Hon Robert　*Ravensdale, B.*
Mosley, Hon Shaun N.　*Ravensdale, B.*
Moss, Hon Susannah E.　*Alvingham, B.*
Mosselmans, Hon Prudence　*McCorquodale of Newton, B.*
Mostyn, Hon Llewellyn R. L. Lloyd-　*Mostyn, B.*
Motion, Hon Penelope M.　*Harcourt, V.*
Motl, Hon Marion A.　*Molloy, B.*
Mountbatten, Lord Ivar A. M.　*Milford Haven, M.*
Mountbatten, Lady Tatiana H. G.　*Milford Haven, M.*
Moyle, Hon Roland D.　*Moyle, By.*
Moynihan, Hon Antonita M. C. F.　*Moynihan, B.*
Moynihan, Hon Aurora L. M.　*Moynihan, B.*

Moynihan, Hon Colin B.　*Moynihan, B.*
Moynihan, Hon Kathleen M. H. I. J.　*Moynihan, B.*
Moynihan, Hon Miranda, D. I.　*Moynihan, B.*
Mudge, Hon Maureen A.　*Wigg, B.*
Muff, Hon Andrew R.　*Calverley, B.*
Muff, Hon Jonathan E.　*Calverley, B.*
Muff, Hon Peter R.　*Calverley, B.*
Muggeridge, Hon Sarah　*Walsingham, B.*
Muir, Lady Linda M.　*Enniskillen, E.*
Muir, Lady Rosemary, M.　*Marlborough, D.*
Mulholland, Hon Brian H.　*Dunleath, B.*
Mulji, Hon Rosaleen E.　*Moyne, B.*
Mullins, Hon Sarah, V.　*Bearsted, V.*
Mumford, Lady Mary, K.　*Norfolk, D.*
Mummery, Hon E. Rosamund Lockhart-　*Elles, Bs.*
Mundy, Lady Bridget Miller　*Minto, E.*
Munro, Hon Diana M.　*Clydesmuir, B.*
Munro, Hon Marjorie A. Walker-　*Biddulph, B.*
Murphy, Hon Emma E.　*Teynham, B.*
Murray, Hon Amanda M. M.　*Braybrooke, B.*
Murray, Hon Catherine A.　*Murray of Gravesend, B.*
Murray, Hon David P.　*Murray of Epping Forest, B.*
Murray, Hon Dinah K. C.　*Greenwood of Rossendale, B.*
Murray, Hon Geoffrey C.　*Dunmore, E.*
Murray, Lady Georgina D. M.　*Mansfield, E.*
Murray, Hon Iona M. S.　*Mansfield, E.*
Murray, Hon Isabella M. A.　*Mansfield, E.*
Murray, Hon James W.　*Mansfield, E.*
Murray, Hon Jill　*Constantine of Stanmore, B.*
Murray, Lady Kate R.　*Dunmore, E.*
Murray, Hon Nicola R.　*Murray of Epping Forest, B.*
Murray, Lady Rebecca　*Dunmore, E.*
Murray, Hon Sally A. H.　*Willis, B.*
Murray, Hon Stephen W.　*Murray of Epping Forest, B.*
Murray, Hon Timothy J.　*Murray of Gravesend, B.*
Murray, Hon Virginia　*Bowden, B.*
Murray, Hon (Winifred M.) Lady　*Hardinge of Penshurst, B.*
Murray, Hon Barbara M. Drummond-　*Rankeillour, B.*
Murray, Hon Robert F. A. Erskine-　*Elibank, B.*
Murray, Hon Timothy A. E. Erskine-　*Elibank, B.*
Murray, Hon Diana Wolfe　*Home of the Hirsel, B.*
Murrell, Hon L. G. Kiloran　*Ebury, B.*
Murton, Hon H. Peter J. C.　*Murton of Lindisfarne, B.*
Musgrave, Hon Rosemary J.　*Watkinson, V.*
Musker, Lady Rose D.　*Durham, E.*
Mussell, Hon M. Jean　*Craigmyle, B.*
Musson, Hon (Elspeth L.) Lady　*Glanusk, B.*
Musters, Hon Mary V. Chaworth-　*Galway, V.*
Myddelton, Lady M. Margaret　*Lansdowne, M.*
Myddelton, Hon Sarah C.　*Hindlip, B.*
Naggar, Hon Marion　*Samuel of Wych Cross, B.*
Nairac, Lady Jane F. M.　*Airlie, E.*
Nairne, Lord Robert H. Mercer-　*Lansdowne, M.*
Nandy, Hon A. Luise　*Byers, B.*
Napier, Hon Andrew P.　*Napier of Magdala, B.*
Napier, Hon C. Malcolm　*Napier and Ettrick, L.*
Napier, Hon Ermine M.　*Napier of Magdala, B.*
Napier, Hon Francis D. C.　*Napier and Ettrick, L.*
Napier, Hon Georgina H. K.　*Napier and Ettrick, L.*
Napier, Hon H. Lenox　*Napier and Ettrick, L.*
Napier, Hon James R.　*Napier of Magdala, B.*
Napier, Hon Jean　*Hastings, B.*
Napier, Hon Mrs J. Greville　*Napier and Ettrick, L.*
Napier, Lady Mariota C.　*Mansfield, E.*
Napier, Hon Michael E.　*Napier of Magdala, B.*
Napier, Hon Mrs Neville A. J. W. E.　*Napier and Ettrick, L.*
Napier, Hon Nicholas A. J.　*Napier and Ettrick, L.*
Nathan, Hon Jennifer R.　*Nathan, B.*
Nathan, Hon Nicola J. E.　*Nathan, B.*
Nathan, Hon Rupert H. B.　*Nathan, B.*
Nathanson, Hon Victoria E. A.　*Thorneycroft, B.*
Neave, Hon R. Patrick S.　*Airey of Abingdon, Bs.*
Neave, Hon Victoria A.　*McAlpine of West Green, B.*
Neave, Hon William R. S.　*Airey of Abingdon, Bs.*
Needham, Hon Mrs A. E. Peter　*Kilmorey, E.*
Needham, Hon Andrew F.　*Kilmorey E.*
Needham, Lady Christina C.　*Kilmorey, E.*
Needham, Hon Christopher D.　*Kilmorey, E.*
Needham, Hon Patrick J.　*Kilmorey, E.*
Nelson, Hon (Elizabeth Ann B.) Lady　*Falkland, V.*
Nelson, Hon Henry R. G.　*Nelson of Stafford, B.*
Nelson, Hon James J.　*Nelson of Stafford, B.*
Nelson, Hon Mrs John M. J. H.　*Nelson, E.*

Ramsay, Hon Anthony *Dalhousie, E.*
Ramsay, Hon John P. *Dalhousie, E.*
Ramsay, Hon Lorna T. *Dalhousie, E.*
Ramsay, Hon Mary M. H. *MacAndrew, B.*
Ramsay, Hon Sir Patrick W. M. *Dalhousie, E.*
Ramsay, Hon Simon *Dalhousie, E.*
Ramsay of Mar, Hon Elizabeth A. M. *Saltoun, Bs.*
Ramsbotham, Hon Sir Peter E. *Soulbury, V.*
Ramsey, Hon Alice E. M. *Saltoun, Bs.*
Rank, Hon Moira *Southborough, B.*
Rankin, Lady Jean M. F. *Stair, E.*
Rasch, Lady E. Anne *Beaufort, D.*
Rawlins, Hon Rachel E. C. *Boston, B.*
Rawlinson, Hon Anthony R. *Rawlinson of Ewell, B.*
Rawlinson, Hon Catharine *Trend, B.*
Rawlinson, Hon Michael V. *Rawlinson of Ewell, B.*
Raynar, Hon Sarah E. A. *Mountgarret, V.*
Rayne, Hon Alexander P. *Rayne, B.*
Rayne, Hon Nicholas A. *Rayne, B.*
Rayne, Hon Robert A. *Rayne, B.*
Rayne, Hon Tamara A. *Rayne, B.*
Rayner, Hon Madeleine B. *Rayne, B.*
Raynes, Lady F. Rozelle B. *Manvers, E.*
Raynsford, Hon Joan R. *Wakefield of Kendal, B.*
Rea, Hon Daniel W. *Rea, B.*
Rea, Hon Mrs Findlay R. *Rea, B.*
Rea, Hon C. Julian *Rea, B.*
Rea, Hon Matthew J. *Rea, B.*
Rea, Hon Quentin T. *Rea, B.*
Rea, Hon Rebecca *Llewelyn-Davies, B.*
Read, Hon Diana M. W. Crewe- *Robins, B.*
Recordon, Hon Dinah *Baker, B.*
Redmayne, Hon Sir Nicholas J. *Redmayne, By.*
Rees, Hon Colyn R. *Merlyn-Rees, B.*
Rees, Hon Gareth D. *Merlyn-Rees, B.*
Rees, Hon Patrick M. *Merlyn-Rees, B.*
Reid, Hon Angela M. A. *Amherst of Hackney, B.*
Reid, Lady Laura L. *Clanwilliam, E.*
Reilly, Hon Brigid M. *Glenavy, By.*
Reith, Hon James H. J. *Reith, By.*
Reith, Hon Julie K. *Reith, By.*
Remnant, Hon Hugo C. *Remnant, B.*
Remnant, Hon Philip John *Remnant, B.*
Remnant, Hon Robert James *Remnant, B.*
Rendall, Hon Sarah E. *Sackville, B.*
Renfrew, Hon Alban *Renfrew of Kaimsthorn, B.*
Renfrew, Hon Helena *Renfrew of Kaimsthorn, B.*
Renfrew, Hon Magnus *Renfrew of Kaimsthorn, B.*
Renny, Hon Nicola G. *Moncreiff, B.*
Renton, Hon Davina K. *Renton, B.*
Renwick, Hon Michael D. *Renwick, B.*
Renwick, Hon Robert J. *Renwick, B.*
Repard, Hon Peggy *Denham, B.*
Reynolds, Hon Joan M. *Kenilworth, B.*
Reynolds, Lady Kathleen M. G. *Newcastle, D.*
Rhodes, Hon Margaret *Elphinstone, L.*
Rhys, Lady Anne M. *Wellington, D.*
Rhys, Hon Mrs David S. *Dynevor, B.*
Rhys, Hon Mrs Elwyn V. *Dynevor, B.*
Rhys, Hon Hugo G. U. *Dynevor, B.*
Rhys, Hon Susanna M. E. *Dynevor, B.*
Ricardo, Lady Barbara M. *Wharncliffe, E.*
Rice, Hon Charles J. Spring *Monteagle of Brandon, B.*
Rice, Hon Michael Spring *Monteagle of Brandon, B.*
Richard, Hon Alun S. *Richard, B.*
Richard, Hon David S. *Richard, B.*
Richard, Hon Isobel M. K. *Richard, B.*
Richard, Hon William J. *Richard, B.*
Richards, Hon Irene M. *Leatherland, B.*
Richards, Hon Joyce *Taylor of Gryfe, B.*
Richards, Hon Michael H. *Milverton, B.*
Richardson, Hon Averil D. *Rushcliffe, By.*
Richardson, Hon Sarah A. *Clifford of Chudleigh, B.*
Richardson, Hon Simon B. S. *Richardson of Duntisbourne, B.*
Richardson, Hon Valentine E. M. *Braintree, By.*
Rickards, Hon Gillian M. *Hunt of Fawley B.*
Rickett, Hon Susanna *Ridley of Liddesdale, B.*
Riddell, Hon (Sarah) Lady *Richardson of Duntisbourne, B.*
Ridgely, Hon Janetta *Raglan, B.*
Ridley, Hon Annabel *Hawke, B.*
Ridley, (Hon) Helen L. C. *Asquith of Yarnbury, By.*
Ridley, Hon Julia H. *Aberconway, B.*
Ridley, Hon Matthew W. *Ridley, V.*
Ridley, Hon Nicholas *Ridley, V.*
Riley, Hon F. Georgina *Sanderson of Bowden, B.*
Riley, Hon Ruth M. *Hives, B.*

Ringsell, Hon Cassandra P. A. *St Vincent, V.*
Rippon, Hon Anthony S. Y. *Rippon of Hexham, B.*
Rippon, Hon Fiona C. *Rippon of Hexham, B.*
Ritchie, Hon Charles R. R. *Ritchie of Dundee, B.*
Ritchie, Hon Jean D. *Stuart of Findhorn, V.*
Ritchie, Hon Philippa J. *Ritchie of Dundee, B.*
Rix, Hon (Karen D.) Lady *Young of Graffham, B.*
Robb, Lady Violet C. L. *Ormonde, M.*
Robbins, Hon Richard *Robbins, B.*
Roberts, Hon Ann E. *Goronwy-Roberts, B.*
Roberts, Hon Mrs David S. *Clwyd, B.*
Roberts, Hon Hugh G. A. *Clwyd, B.*
Roberts, Hon Jane E. S. *Roskill, B.*
Roberts, Hon Jeremy T. *Clwyd, B.*
Roberts, Hon Joan M. *Royle, By.*
Roberts, Hon John M. *Clwyd, B.*
Roberts, Hon Juliana E. *Scarsdale, V.*
Roberts, Hon Marjorie *Macfarlane of Bearsden, B.*
Roberts, Hon Owen D. *Goronwy-Roberts, B.*
Roberts, Hon P. Jane S. *Aldington, B.*
Roberts, Hon Mrs W. H. Mervyn *Clwyd, B.*
Robertson, Hon Christopher J. *Wharton, Bs.*
Robertson, Hon Elizabeth A. *Bourne, B.*
Robertson, Lady Joan P. Q. *Wavell, E.*
Robertson, Hon Myles C. D. *Wharton, Bs.*
Robertson, Hon Nicholas C. *Wharton, Bs.*
Robertson, Hon Patricia L. *Wharton, Bs.*
Robertson, Hon William B. E. *Robertson of Oakridge, B.*
Robins, Hon Elizabeth M. G. *Lloyd of Kilgerran, B.*
Robinson, Hon Claire E. *Portman, V.*
Robinson, Hon Gai Rencie *Salmon, B.*
Robinson, Hon Mrs Richard A. G. *Martonmere, B.*
Robinson, Hon Stella H. *Hollenden, B.*
Robinson, Hon Susannah J. Maitland- *Faringdon, B.*
Robson, Hon Elizabeth *Atkin, B.*
Robson, Hon Erik M. W. *Robson of Kiddington, Bs.*
Robson, Lady J. Penelope J. *Ferrers, E.*
Roche, Hon E. Hugh B. *Fermoy, B.*
Roche, Hon (H. Alexandra B.) Lady *Selby, V.*
Roche, Hon Mrs John F. A. *Roche, By.*
Roche, Hon Mary C. B. *Fermoy, B.*
Roche, Hon P. Maurice B. *Fermoy, B.*
Roche, Hon Thomas G. *Roche, B.*
Rodd, Hon James R. D. T. *Rennell, B.*
Rodd, Hon Lilias *Rennell, B.*
Rodd, Hon Rachel *Rennell, B.*
Rodd, Hon Sophie M. J. *Rennell, B.*
Rodney, Hon Diana R. *Rodney, B.*
Rodney, Hon Mrs Michael G. *Rodney, B.*
Rodwell, Hon Christine M. *Woolley, B.*
Roe, Hon Susan *Lewin, B.*
Rogers, Hon Loretta A. *Martonmere, B.*
Rolfe, Hon Louise J. D. *Barnetson, B.*
Roll, Hon Elizabeth *Roll of Ipsden, B.*
Roll, Hon Joanna *Roll of Ipsden, B.*
Rollo, Hon David E. H. *Rollo, L.*
Rollo, Hon Mrs David I. *Rollo, L.*
Rollo, Hon James M. *Rollo, L.*
Rollo, Hon John D. *Rollo, L.*
Rollo, Hon Simon D. P. *Rollo, L.*
Rollo, Hon Mrs William H. C. *Rollo, L.*
Rolnick, Hon Julia R. *Joseph, B.*
Rootes, Hon Mrs Brian G. *Rootes, B.*
Rootes, Hon Nicholas G. L. *Rootes, B.*
Roper, Hon Sarah-Jane L. *Prior, B.*
Ropner, Hon Charlotte M. *Piercy, B.*
Rose, Hon Irene P. *Hirst, By.*
Rose, Lady Jean M. *Dalhousie, E.*
Rose, Hon (Phœbe M. D.) Lady *Phillimore, B.*
Rose, Hon Susan J. *Northbourne, B.*
Rose, Lady Katherine P. Townsend- *Erne, E.*
Rosen, Hon June A. *Lever, B.*
Rosenbaum, Hon Jane E. *Ashley of Stoke, B.*
Roskill, Hon Julian W. *Roskill, B.*
Rospigliosi, Hon Helen M. G. *Acton, B.*
Ross, Hon Huw W. *Ross of Newport, B.*
Ross, Hon James G. *Ross of Newport, B.*
Ross, Hon Roxana R. C. N. *Killearn, B.*
Rothenberg, Hon Mary *Pentland, By.*
Rothschild, Hon Amschel M. J. *Rothschild, B.*
Rothschild, Hon Emily M. *Rothschild, B.*
Rothschild, Hon Emma G. *Rothschild, B.*
Rothschild, Hon Hannah M. *Rothschild, B.*
Rothschild, Hon Miranda *Rothschild, B.*
Rothschild, Hon Nathaniel P. V. J. *Rothschild, B.*
Rothschild, Hon Victoria K. *Rothschild, B.*
Roubanis, Lady Sarah C. *Marlborough, D.*
Rous, Lady Brigitte A. *Stradbroke, E.*

Rous, Lady Heidi S. *Stradbroke, E.*
Rous, Hon Henham M. *Stradbroke, E.*
Rous, Lady Henrietta E. *Stradbroke, E.*
Rous, Hon Hektor F. *Stradbroke, E.*
Rous, Lady Ingrid A. *Stradbroke, E.*
Rous, Hon John *Stradbroke, E.*
Rous, Lady Marye V. I. *Stradbroke, E.*
Rous, Lady Minsmere M. *Stradbroke, E.*
Rous, Hon Maximilian O. *Stradbroke, E.*
Rous, Lady Pamela K. *Stradbroke, E.*
Rous, Hon Peter J. M. *Stradbroke, E.*
Rous, Hon Ramsar F. *Stradbroke, E.*
Rous, Lady S. Rayner *Stradbroke, E.*
Rous, Hon Sir William E. *Stradbroke, E.*
Rous, Hon Mrs W. Keith *Stradbroke, E.*
Rous, Hon Wesley A. *Stradbroke, E.*
Rous, Hon Winston W. *Stradbroke, E.*
Rous, Hon Yoxford U. U. *Stradbroke, E.*
Rous, Lady Zea K. *Stradbroke, E.*
Rowcliffe, Hon Una M. *Slim, V.*
Rowlandson, Hon Antonia J. H. *Caldecote, V.*
Rowley, Hon (Celia E. V.) Lady *Galway, V.*
Rowley, Lady Sibell *Beauchamp, E.*
Rowse, Hon Mrs Rosemary S. V. *Grimston of Westbury, B.*
Royle, Hon Lucinda K. F. *Fanshawe of Richmond, B.*
Rubie, Hon Jane A. *Ravensworth, B.*
Rubin, Hon Susan A. *Rayne, B.*
Ruck, Hon Catherine D. *Braybrooke, B.*
Rudd, Hon Fiona C. R. *Ritchie-Calder, B.*
Rudd, Hon Hilary A. *Peddie, B.*
Rule, Hon Miranda J. C. *Dynevor, B.*
Runcie, Hon James *Runcie, B.*
Runciman, Hon Anne E. *Cromwell, B.*
Runciman, Hon Catherine *Runciman of Doxford, V.*
Runciman, Hon David W. *Runciman of Doxford, V.*
Runciman, Hon Lisa *Runciman of Doxford, V.*
Runciman, Hon Sir Steven (J. C. S.) *Runciman of Doxford, V.*
Rundall, Lady Rosalthé F. *Harrowby, E.*
Runge, Hon (Fiona) Lady *Strathcarron, B.*
Rusbridger, Hon Lindsay M. *Mackie of Benshie, B.*
Rush, Lady Tracy A. *Mount Edgcumbe, E.*
Russell, Hon Adam M. H. *Russell of Liverpool, B.*
Russell, Hon Ann B. *Congleton, B.*
Russell, Hon Anthony J. M. *Ampthill, B.*
Russell, Hon Catherine V. *Ponsonby of Shulbrede, B.*
Russell, Hon Daniel C. E. *Russell of Liverpool, B.*
Russell, Hon David W. E. *Ampthill, B.*
Russell, Hon Easter D. *Kennet, B.*
Russell, Hon Edward C. S. *Russell of Liverpool, B.*
Russell, Hon Mrs Edward W. C. *Ampthill, B.*
Russell, Hon Elizabeth M. G. L. *Mostyn, B.*
Russell, Hon Emma K. *Russell of Liverpool, B.*
Russell, Hon F. Damian *Russell of Killowen, B.*
Russell, Hon Frances M. *Sempill, L.*
Russell, Lord Francis H. *Bedford, D.*
Russell, Hon (H. Elizabeth) Lady *Ebbisham, B.*
Russell, Lord Hugh H. *Bedford, D.*
Russell, Lord James E. H. *Bedford, D.*
Russell, Hon John F. *Russell, E.*
Russell, Hon John H. T. *Ampthill, B.*
Russell, Hon Kathleen M. *Ashbourne, B.*
Russell, Hon Mrs Langley G. H. *Russell of Liverpool, B.*
Russell, Hon Leonora M. K. *Russell of Liverpool, B.*
Russell, Hon Lucy L. C. *Russell of Liverpool, B.*
Russell, Lady Mary *Haddington, E.*
Russell, Hon Nicole *Churston, B.*
Russell, Lord Robin L. H. *Bedford, D.*
Russell, Lord Rudolf *Bedford, D.*
Russell, Lady Sarah E. *Russell, E.*
Russell, Hon Valentine F. X. M. *Russell of Killowen, B.*
Russell, Hon William F. L. *Russell of Liverpool, B.*
Russell, Hon William S. *de Clifford, B.*
Russell, Hon Gustavus M. S. Hamilton- *Boyne, V.*
Russell, Hon Richard G. Hamilton- *Boyne, V.*
Rutland, Hon Joan C. F. *Milne, B.*
Ryde, Hon Mary T. *Robinson, By.*
Ryder, Hon D. A. Hugo C. *Harrowby, E.*
Ryder, Hon Emily G. H. *Harrowby, E.*
Ryder, Hon Frederick W. D. *Harrowby, E.*
Ryder, Hon Henry M. D. *Harrowby, E.*
Ryder, Hon Jill P. *Ryder of Eaton Hastings, B.*
Ryder, Hon John S. T. D. *Harrowby, E.*
Ryder, Hon Michael J. *Ryder of Eaton Hastings, B.*

Ryecart, Lady Marcia M. J. *Norfolk, D.*
Ryland, Hon (Jeryl M. S.) Lady Smith- *Cranworth, B.*
Ryman, Hon Shirley *Summerskill, Bs.*
Sacher, Hon Rosalind E. C. *Rowallan, B.*
Sachs, Hon (Janet M.) Lady *Goddard, By.*
Sackville, Lady Arabella A. D. *De La Warr, E.*
Sackville, Hon Edward G. R. *De La Warr, E.*
Sackville, Hon Thomas G. *De La Warr, E.*
Sackville, Hon M. Teresa Stopford *Cowdray, V.*
Sagan, Hon Patricia *Sherfield, B.*
Saggers, Lady Kirstie A. *Montrose, D.*
Saglio, Hon Tara C. *Combermere, V.*
Sain, Hon Harriet M. *Burnham, B.*
Sainsbury, Hon John J. *Sainsbury of Preston Candover, B.*
Sainsbury, Hon Mark L. *Sainsbury of Preston Candover, B.*
Sainsbury, Hon Paulette A. *Sainsbury, B.*
Sainsbury, Hon Sarah J. *Sainsbury of Preston Candover, B.*
Sainsbury, Hon Simon D. D. *Sainsbury, B.*
Sainsbury, Hon Timothy A. D. *Sainsbury, B.*
Saint, Lady J. S. Rose *Shrewsbury, E.*
St. Aubyn, Hon C. Gwendolen C. *Carnock, B.*
St. Aubyn, Hon Giles R. *St. Levan, B.*
St. Aubyn, Hon O. Piers *St. Levan, B.*
St. Clair, Hon Annabel R. *Sinclair, L.*
St. Clair, Hon Laura A. *Sinclair, L.*
St. Clair, Hon Matthew M. K. *Sinclair, L.*
St. George, Lady Henrietta F. D. *Grafton, D.*
St. John, Hon Anthony T. *St. John of Bletso, B.*
St. John, Hon Helen E. *St. John of Bletso, B.*
St. John, Hon Henry F. *Bolingbroke and St. John, V.*
St. John, Hon Nicholas A. *Bolingbroke and St. John, V.*
St. John, Hon Oliver J. *Bolingbroke and St. John, V.*
St. John, Hon Sally H. *Rootes, B.*
St. John, Hon Vanessa M. *Palmer, B.*
St. Leger, Hon David H. *Doneraile, V.*
St. Leger, Hon Edward H. *Doneraile, V.*
St. Leger, Hon Elizabeth A. *Doneraile, V.*
St. Leger, Hon Karen J. *Doneraile, V.*
St. Leger, Hon Maeve I. M. *Doneraile, V.*
St. Leger, Hon Nathaniel W. R. St. J. *Doneraile, V.*
Salaman, Hon Nancy A. *Samuel, V.*
Sale, Hon Ismay H. M. *Southampton, By.*
Sales, Hon Isobel C. *Boston, B.*
Salmon, Hon David N. C. *Salmon, B.*
Salvesen, Lady Arabella F. *Buchan, E.*
Samuel, Hon Anthony G. *Bearsted, V.*
Samuel, Hon Dan J. *Samuel, V.*
Samuel, Hon Michael J. *Bearsted, V.*
Samuel, Hon Nicholas A. *Bearsted, V.*
Samuel, Hon Philip E. H. *Samuel, V.*
Samuels, Hon Ann *Bruce of Donington, B.*
Sandeman, Hon Phyllis E. *Newton, B.*
Sandeman, Hon Sylvia M. *Maclehose of Beoch, B.*
Sanders, Hon Rowena M. *Hawke, B.*
Sanderson, Hon Andrea *Sanderson of Ayot, By.*
Sanderson, Hon C. David R. *Sanderson of Bowden, B.*
Sanderson, Hon Evelyn *Sanderson of Ayot, By.*
Sanderson, Hon Frances *Sanderson of Ayot, By.*
Sanderson, Hon Michael *Sanderson of Ayot, By.*
Sanderson, Hon Murray L. *Sanderson of Ayot, By.*
Sanderson, Hon Stephanie *Sanderson of Ayot, By.*
Sandilands, Hon Margaret E. G. *Torphichen, L.*
Sandilands, Hon Mary C. S. *Torphichen, L.*
Sanson, Hon Camilla J. *Thurso, V.*
Sarson, Hon Gillian I. J. *Hanworth, V.*
Saumarez, Hon Claire *de Saumarez, B.*
Saumarez, Hon Emily *de Saumarez, B.*
Saumarez, Hon Victor T. *De Saumarez, B.*
Savile, Lady Alethea F. C. *Mexborough, E.*
Savile, Hon C. Anthony *Mexborough, E.*
Savile, Hon James H. H. J. *Mexborough, E.*
Savile, Lady Lucinda S. C. *Mexborough, E.*
Savile, Hon Henry L. T. Lumley- *Savile, B.*
Savile, Hon Yvonne C. *Schon, B.*
Scarlett, Hon James H. *Abinger, B.*
Scarlett, Hon John L. C. *Abinger, B.*
Scarlett, Hon Peter R. *Abinger, B.*
Scarr, Lady Davina J. *Erne, E.*
Schilizzi, Lady G. Sophia A. *Waldegrave, E.*
Schreiber, Hon Nicola C. *Marlesford, B.*
Schreiber, Hon Sophie L. *Marlesford, B.*

Stoddart, Hon Howard D. *Stoddart of Swindon, B.*
Stoddart, Hon Mathwyn H. *Stoddart of Swindon, B.*
Stokes, Hon Michael D. G. *Stokes, B.*
Stone, Hon Catherine M. *Dormer, B.*
Stone, Hon Jane T. *O'Hagan, B.*
Stone, Hon Richard M. E. *Stone, B.*
Stonor, Hon Emily M. J. *Camoys, B.*
Stonor, Hon Georgina M. H. *Camoys, B.*
Stonor, Hon Julia M. C. M. *Camoys, B.*
Stonor, Hon Ralph W. R. T. *Camoys, B.*
Stopford, Hon Mrs Edward R. B. *Courtown, E.*
Stopford, Hon Jeremy N. *Courtown, E.*
Stopford, Lady Marjorie G. *Courtown, E.*
Stopford, Lady Rosanna E. A. *Courtown, E.*
Stopford, Hon Terence V. *Courtown, E.*
Stopford, Hon Thomas *Stopford of Fallowfield, By.*
Storey, Hon Sir Richard *Buckton, By.*
Stotten, Lady Irmengarde *Ducie, E.*
Stourton, Hon Charlotte M. *Mowbray, B.*
Stourton, Hon Edward W. S. *Mowbray, B.*
Stourton, Hon James A. *Mowbray, B.*
Stourton, Lady Joanna *Cavan, E.*
Stourton, Hon Sophia U. *Camoys, B.*
Stourton, Hon Mrs Edward P. J. Corbally *Mowbray, B.*
Stowasser, Hon Helen M. *Platt, B.*
Strachey, Hon Antonia P. M. *O'Hagan, B.*
Strachey, Hon Nino N. O. *O'Hagan, B.*
Strachey, Hon Richard T. *O'Hagan, B.*
Straight, Lady Daphne M. *Winchilsea, E.*
Straker, Hon Ann G. *Milne, B.*
Strangways, Hon Raymond G. Fox- *Ilchester, E.*
Stratford, Hon Oriel A. D. *Massereene, V.*
Strauss, Hon Brian T. *Strauss, B.*
Strauss, Hon Hilary J. *Strauss, B.*
Strauss, Hon Roger A. *Strauss, B.*
Streatfield, Lady Moyra C. *Courtown, E.*
Street, Hon Jane E. *Bridge of Harwich.*
Stride, Hon Susan *Macdonald of Gwaenysgor, B.*
Strutt, Hon Mrs Charles R. *Rayleigh, B.*
Strutt, Hon Guy R. *Rayleigh, B.*
Strutt, Hon Hedley V. *Rayleigh, B.*
Strutt, Hon Jean E. *Davidson, V.*
Strutt, Hon John F. *Rayleigh, B.*
Strutt, Hon Peter A. *Belper, B.*
Strutt, Hon Richard H. *Belper, B.*
Stuart, Hon Alicia St G. *Charlemont, V.*
Stuart, Hon Andrew M. *Stuart of Findhorn, V.*
Stuart, Lady Arabella *Moray, E.*
Stuart, Hon Celia E. *Castle Stewart, E.*
Stuart, Hon Charles R. S. *Moray, E.*
Stuart, Hon Chloe A-M *Stuart of Findhorn, V.*
Stuart, Hon J. Dominic *Stuart of Findhorn, V.*
Stuart, Hon James, W. W. *Moray, E.*
Stuart, Lady Louisa M. *Moray, E.*
Stuart, Hon Rosalie J. *Stuart of Findhorn, V.*
Stuart, Lady Sarah G. *Moray, E.*
Stuart, Hon Simon W. E. *Castle Stewart, E.*
Stuart, Hon Vanessa M. *Stuart of Findhorn, V.*
Stuart, Lord Anthony Crichton- *Bute, M.*
Stuart, Lady David O. Crichton- *Bute, M.*
Stuart, Lady Caroline Crichton- *Bute, M.*
Stuart, Lady Janet E. Crichton- *Eglinton, E.*
Stuart, Lady Cathleen Crichton- *Bute, M.*
Stuart, Lady Rhidian Crichton- *Bute, M.*
Stuart, Lady Rowena K. Crichton- *Clanwilliam, E.*
Stuart, Hon Katherine A. Mackenzie *Mackenzie-Stuart, B.*
Stuart, Hon Laura M. Mackenzie *Mackenzie-Stuart, B.*
Stubber, Hon Susanna C. Hamilton *Brookeborough, V.*
Stucley, Hon (Sheila M. W.) Lady *Poltimore, B.*
Sulyak, Hon Rosamond S. *Croham, B.*
Summerskill, Hon Michael B. *Summerskill, By.*
Surrell, Hon Maureen D. *Lyveden, B.*
Sutcliffe, Hon D. Valerie P. *Garvagh, B.*
Sutcliffe, Hon Helen *Rhodes, B.*
Sutherland, Hon Alexander C. R. *Sutherland, Cs.*
Sutherland, Hon Elizabeth *Sutherland, Cs.*
Sutherland, Hon Rachel E. *Sutherland, Cs.*
Sutherland, Hon Rosemary M. *Sutherland, Cs.*
Svenningson, Hon Daphne R. *Garvagh, B.*
Swann, Lady Hilda S. M. *Iddesleigh, E.*
Swann, Hon G. M. Peter *Swann, B.*
Swann, Hon Lydia M. *Lifford, V.*
Swann, Hon Richard M. *Swann, B.*
Swire, Lady Judith *Northampton, M.*
Sykes, Hon Betty C. Dugdale *Muskerry, B.*

Sykes, Hon Laura C. *St Brides, B.*
Sykes, Hon Nicola M. C. *Buxton of Alsa, B.*
Tabor, Hon Pamela R. *Glendyne, B.*
Tabor, Hon Rebecca *Runcie, B.*
Tahany, Lady Caroline A. *Cadogan, E.*
Tait, Lady Katharine J. *Russell, E.*
Talbot, Hon Cynthia E. *Wimborne, V.*
Talbot, Hon Rose M. *Talbot of Malahide, B.*
Talbot, Hon Edward W. H. A. Chetwynd-*Shrewsbury, E.*
Talbot, Hon Paul A. A. B. Chetwynd- *Shrewsbury, E.*
Talbot, Lady Victoria J. Chetwynd- *Shrewsbury, E.*
Tangye, Lady Marguerite R. *Darnley, E.*
Tarassenko, Lady Ann M. E. *Craven, E.*
Taylor, Hon Bernard A. *Taylor of Mansfield, B.*
Taylor, Hon Catherine V. *Elliott of Morpeth, B.*
Taylor, Hon Charles R. H. *Taylor, B.*
Taylor, Hon David L. *Taylor of Gosforth, B.*
Taylor, Hon Frances R. *Bellwin, B.*
Taylor, Lady Helen M. L. *Kent, D.*
Taylor, Hon M. Jane *McAlpine of West Green, B.*
Taylor, Hon Jeremy S. *Taylor, B.*
Taylor, Hon L. L. Carole *Alport, B.*
Taylor, Hon Marilyn R. *Fisher of Camden, B.*
Taylor, Hon Melinda C. *Brookeborough, V.*
Taylor, Hon Pamela M. *Geddes of Epsom, B.*
Taylor, Hon Paul N. *Taylor of Blackburn, B.*
Taylor, Hon Priscilla J. *Piercy, B.*
Taylor, Hon Rosanna *Cowdray, V.*
Taylor, Hon Ruth D. *Taylor of Gosforth, B.*
Taylor, Hon Sarah L. *Rippon of Hexham, B.*
Taylor, Hon Sylvia A. *Joicey, B.*
Taylor, Lady Ursula D. *Ailesbury, M.*
Taylor, Hon Susan R. Haden- *Daresbury, B.*
Taylor, Hon Christopher J. Suenson- *Grantchester, B.*
Taylor, Hon James G. Suenson- *Grantchester, B.*
Taylor, Hon Jeremy K. Suenson- *Grantchester, B.*
Taylour, Hon Henry *Headfort, M.*
Teakle, Hon Juliet A. *Talbot of Malahide, B.*
Tebbit, Hon John B. *Tebbit, B.*
Tebbit, Hon William M. *Tebbit, B.*
Tedder, Hon Andrew J. *Tedder, B.*
Tedder, Hon Mina U. M. *Tedder, B.*
Tedder, Hon Richard D. *Tedder, B.*
Tedder, Hon Robin J. *Tedder, B.*
Telfer, Hon Lætitia M. *Balfour of Burleigh, L.*
Tellwright, Hon Caroline F. *Stafford, B.*
Templeman, Hon Michael R. *Templeman, B.*
Templeman, Hon Peter M. *Templeman, B.*
Tenison, Lady Maria L. King- *Kingston, E.*
Tennant, Hon Amy J. E. *Glenconner, B.*
Tennant, Hon Charles E. P. *Glenconner, B.*
Tennant, Hon Christopher C. Tennant *Glenconner, B.*
Tennant, Hon Mrs David P. *Glenconner, B.*
Tennant, Lady Emma *Devonshire, D.*
Tennant, Hon F. May P. *Glenconner, B.*
Tennant, Lady Harriot *Radnor, E.*
Tennant, Hon Mrs Henry L. *Glenconner, B.*
Tennant, Hon Mrs James G. H. *Glenconner, B.*
Tennant, Lady Margaret H. I. M. *Airlie, E.*
Tennant, Hon Tobias W. *Glenconner, B.*
Tennyson, Hon Mark A. *Tennyson, B.*
Tetley, Lady Patricia M. *Strathmore, E.*
Teverson, Hon Joanna R. G. *Gore-Booth, B.*
Thatcher, Hon Carol *Thatcher, Bs.*
Thatcher, Hon Mark *Thatcher, Bs.*
Thellusson, Hon Charles W. B. *Rendlesham, B.*
Thellusson, Hon Mrs Hugh E. *Rendlesham, B.*
Thellusson, Hon Peter R. *Rendlesham, B.*
Thesiger, Hon Dawn L. *Chelmsford, V.*
Thesiger, Hon Frederick C. P. *Chelmsford, V.*
Thesiger, Hon Philippa M. *Chelmsford, V.*
Thesiger, Hon Tiffany G. *Chelmsford, V.*
Thomas, Hon Carolyn M. *Whitelaw, V.*
Thomas, Hon Charles I. G. *Thomas of Swynnerton, B.*
Thomas, Hon David N. M. *Thomas of Gwydir, B.*
Thomas, Hon H. Isambard T. *Thomas of Swynnerton, B.*
Thomas, Hon Hew B. M. *Thomas of Gwydir, B.*
Thomas, Hon Isabella P. *Thomas of Swynnerton, B.*
Thomas, Hon Jacqueline *Cooper of Stockton Heath, B.*
Thomas, Hon Jane *Ridley of Liddesdale, B.*
Thomas, Hon Ursula *Henley, B.*
Thomas, Hon W. Michael W. *Thomas, B.*

Thomas, Hon Moyra Freeman- *Tweedmouth, By.*
Thompson, Hon Tessa, M. Ogilvie *Dacre, Bs.*
Thomson, Hon Anna-Karina *Cadogan, E.*
Thomson, Hon David K. R. *Thomson of Fleet, B.*
Thomson, Hon Elizabeth F. *Francis-Williams, By.*
Thomson, Lady Jacqueline R. M. R. *Reading, M.*
Thomson, Hon Lesley L. *Thomson of Fleet, B.*
Thomson, Hon Peter J. *Thomson, of Fleet, B.*
Thomson, Hon Callum M. M. Mitchell- *Selsdon, B.*
Thorne, Lady Anne P. *Limerick, E.*
Thorneycroft, Hon John H. *Thorneycroft, B.*
Thornton, Hon Caroline *Howe of Aberavon, B.*
Thorold, Hon Phyllis M. *Ampthill, B.*
Throckmorton, Lady Isabel V. K. *Rutland, D.*
Thwaites, Hon Flora M. *Jenkin of Roding, B.*
Thynne, Hon Christopher J. *Bath, M.*
Thynne, Lady Lenka A. *Bath, M.*
Thynne, Lady Valentine C. *Bath, M.*
Tidborough, Hon Christine G. *Addison, V.*
Timpson, Lady Selina C. *Clanwilliam, E.*
Tipping, Hon Catherine J. *Darwen, B.*
Tirard, Lady Nesta *Leinster, D.*
Todd, Hon Alexander H. *Todd,B.*
Todd, Hon Hilary A. *Todd, B.*
Todd, Lady Patricia M. Graham- *Norbury, E.*
Tollemache, Hon Edward *Tollemache, B.*
Tollemache, Hon Hugh J. H. *Tollemache, B.*
Tollemache, Hon James H. T. *Tollemache, B.*
Tollemache, Hon John N. L. *Tollemache, B.*
Tollemache, Hon Michael D. D. *Tollemache, B.*
Tollemache, Hon Timothy J. E. *Tollemache, B.*
Tomassini, Hon Beth M. *Rothschild, B.*
Tombs, Hon Catherine B. *Tombs, B.*
Tombs, Hon Elisabeth J. *Tombs, B.*
Tombs, Hon Margaret C. *Tombs, B.*
Tomlins, Hon Angela M. *Carbery, B.*
Tonge, Hon Judith F. *Allen of Fallowfield, B.*
Tooth, Hon Caroline Lucas- *Poole, B.*
Tordoff, Hon Frances J. *Tordoff, B.*
Tordoff, Hon Mark E. *Tordoff, B.*
Tordoff, Hon Mary C. *Tordoff, B.*
Tordoff, Hon Nicholas G. *Tordoff, B.*
Tottenham, Lady Ann E. *Ely, M.*
Tottenham, Lady George R. *Ely, M.*
Tottenham, Lord Richard J. *Ely, M.*
Tottenham, Lord Timothy C. *Ely, M.*
Tower, Hon Victoria M. A. *Leverhulme, V.*
Townend, Hon Katherine P. *Hambleden, V.*
Townsend, Lady Juliet *Birkenhead, E.*
Townshend, Lady Carolyn E. A. *Townshend, M.*
Townshend, Lady Joanna A. *Townshend, M.*
Townshend, Lord John P. *Townshend, M.*
Townshend, Hon Thomas C. *Townshend, M.*
Townsley, Hon Laura *Wolfson, B.*
Trafford, Hon Audrey E. *Taylor of Hadfield, B.*
Trafford, Hon Mark R. *Trafford, B.*
Trafford, Hon Tanya H. *Trafford, B.*
Tree, Lady Anne E. B. *Devonshire, D.*
Trefgarne, Hon George G. *Trefgarne, B.*
Trefgarne, Hon Gwion G. *Trefgarne, B.*
Trefgarne, Hon Justin P. G. *Trefgarne, B.*
Trefgarne, Hon Mary E. *Trefgarne, B.*
Trefgarne, Hon Rebecca *Trefgarne, B.*
Trefgarne, Trevor G. *Trefgarne, B.*
Trefusis, Hon Caroline H. Fane *Clinton, B.*
Trefusis, Hon Charles P. R. Fane *Clinton, B.*
Trefusis, Hon Henrietta J. Fane *Clinton, B.*
Treherne, Lady Sheelah A. *Sligo, M.*
Trench, Hon Roderick N. G. *Ashtown, B.*
Trench, Lady Caragh S. Le Poer *Clancarty, E.*
Trenchard, Hon Alexander W. *Trenchard, V.*
Trenchard, Hon John *Trenchard, V.*
Trenchard, Hon Katherine C. *Trenchard, V.*
Trenchard, Hon Laura M. *Trenchard, V.*
Trenchard, Hon Thomas H. *Trenchard, V.*
Trenchard, Hon William J. *Trenchard, V.*
Trend, Hon Michael St. J. *Trend, B.*
Trend, Hon Patrick St J. *Trend, B.*
Treuhaft, Hon Jessica L. *Redesdale, B.*
Trevor, Hon Iain R. Hill- *Trevor, B.*
Trevor, Hon Marke C. Hill- *Trevor, B.*
Trevor, Hon Nevill E. Hill- *Trevor, B.*
Tribe, Hon Winifred *Waterpark, B.*
Tritton, Hon Georgina A. *Ward of Witley, V.*
Tritton, Hon Sally L. *Nelson of Strafford, B.*
Troubridge, Hon Rosemary *Penrhyn, B.*
Troubridge, Hon (Venetia D.) Lady *Weeks, B.*
Trowbridge, Hon D. Frances L. St. G. *Charlemont, V.*

Tryon, Hon Anthony G. M. *Tryon, B.*
Tryon, Hon Aylmer D. *Tryon, B.*
Tryon, Hon Charles G. B. *Tryon, B.*
Tryon, Hon Edward H. *Tryon. B.*
Tryon, Hon Victoria C. *Tryon, B.*
Tryon, Hon Zoë E. *Tryon, E.*
Tufnell, Hon Georgina M. *Chesham, B.*
Tufnell, Hon Victoria E. *Belhaven, L.*
Tufton, Hon Emma *Hothfield, B.*
Tufton, Hon Nicholas W. S. *Hothfield, B.*
Tufton, Hon William S. *Hothfield, B.*
Tulloch, Hon Marion H. *Dulverton, B.*
Turnbull, Hon Janet, E. *Armstrong of Sanderstead, By.*
Turnbull, Hon Mary E. *Congleton, B.*
Turner, Hon Andrew J. E. *Netherthorpe, E.*
Turner, Hon Anna E. *Netherthorpe, B.*
Turner, Hon Anne M. C. *Rowallan, B.*
Turner, Hon D. Joan *Alvingham, B.*
Turner, Hon Edward N. *Netherthorpe, B.*
Turner, Hon Elizabeth A. *Schuster, By.*
Turner, Hon Jeanette *Jacobovits, B.*
Turner, Hon Joanna E. *Piercy, B.*
Turner, Hon Patrick A. *Netherthorpe, B.*
Turner, Hon P. N. Nigel *Netherthorpe, B.*
Turner, Lady Rose M. S. *Hardwicke, E.*
Turrill, Hon Jean P. *Wise, B.*
Turton, Hon Gerald C. *Tranmire, B.*
Turton, Hon Michael A. *Tranmire, B.*
Tweedie, Hon Prudence M. *Sidmouth, V.*
Twelvetrees, Hon Catherine S. *du Parcq, By.*
Twining, Hon John P. *Twining, B.*
Twining, Hon William L. *Twining, B.*
Tyrrell, Lady Caroline S. E. *Tweeddale, M.*
Tyser, Hon Susan F. *Remnant, B.*
Uhlman, Hon Nancy D. J. *Croft, B.*
Ulyate, Hon Katharine, H. *Borwick, B.*
Ulyatt, Hon Frances M. *Douglas of Barloch, B.*
Underhill, Hon Robert *Underhill, B.*
Underhill, Hon Terry L. *Underhill, B.*
Unwin, Lady Arabella H. M. *Lansdowne, M.*
Urquhart, Hon Anne S. *Griffiths, B.*
Urquhart, Hon Ronald D. J. *Tayside, By.*
Urquhart, Hon William J. L. *Tayside, By.*
Uttley, Hon Katherine B. *St. John of Bletso, B.*
Vaizey, Hon Edward *Vaizey, B.*
Vaizey, Hon Polly *Vaizey, B.*
Vaizey, Hon Thomas *Vaizey, B.*
Valentine, Hon Janet S. *Weir, V.*
Valerè, Hon Gloria *Constantine, B.*
Van der Noot, Hon Barbara M. *Cullen of Ashbourne, B.*
Van Koetsveld, Hon Margaret R. *Geddes, B.*
Van Moyland, Hon Cecily Steengracht *Raglan, B.*
Van Raalte, Hon Mary A. *Kemsley, V.*
Vance, Hon Imogen A. I. *Moynihan, B.*
van der Woude, Hon Esme M. G. *Rothermere, B.*
Vane, Hon Carolyn M. *Barnard, B.*
Vane, Hon Henry F. C. *Barnard, B.*
Vane, Hon Louise C. *Barnard, B.*
Vane, Hon Sophia R. *Barnard, B.*
Vane, Hon Christopher J. Fletcher- *Inglewood, B.*
Vane, Hon Henry W. F. Fletcher- *Inglewood, B.*
Vane, Hon Miranda M. Fletcher- *Inglewood, B.*
Vane, Hon Rosa K. Fletcher- *Inglewood, B.*
Vanneck, Hon Mrs Andrew N. A. *Huntingfield, B.*
Vanneck, Hon David G. *Huntingfield, B.*
Vanneck, Hon Gerard C. A. *Huntingfield, B.*
Vanneck, Hon John E. *Huntingfield, B.*
Vanneck, Hon Sir Peter B. R. *Huntingfield, B.*
Vanneck, Hon Richard F. *Huntingfield, B.*
Vanneck, Hon Vanessa C. *Huntingfield, B.*
Vanstone, Hon Mary R. *Brock, By.*
Varley, Hon Elizabeth S. *Montagu of Beaulieu, B.*
Varney, Lady Mary B. *Lindsay, E.*
Vaughan, Lady Auriel R. M. *Lisburne, E.*
Vaughan, Hon Digby D. *Lisburne, E.*
Vaughan, Hon John E. M. *Lisburne, E.*
Vaughan, Hon Lucinda M. L. *Ashburton, B.*
Vaughan, Hon Lucy B. *Lisburne, E.*
Vaughan, Hon Mary P. *Monck, V.*
Vaughan, Hon Michael J. W. M. *Lisburne, E.*
Velissaropoulos, Hon Penelope J. *Hindlip, B.*
Verdon, Lady Diana H. *Hertford, M.*
Vereker, Hon Foley R. S. P. *Gort, V.*
Vereker, Hon Nicholas L. P. *Gort, V.*
Verney, Hon Dorothy C. *Tollemache, B.*
Verney, Hon John M. *Willoughby de Broke, B.*
Verney, Hon Mary K. *Falmouth, V.*

SURNAMES OF PEERS AND PEERESSES,
WHERE THESE DIFFER FROM
PEERAGE TITLES, ARRANGED UNDER LAST SURNAME

Where the final part of a compound surname is identical with the peerage title, it has not been included.

SURNAME *Peerage*

ACHESON *Gosford, E.*
A'COURT, HOLMES *Heytesbury, B.*
ADDERLEY *Norton, B.*
ADDINGTON *Sidmouth, V.*
AGAR *Normanton, E.*
ALEXANDER *Caledon, E.*
ALLEN *Croham, B.*
ALLSOPP *Hindlip, B.*
AMAN *Marley, B.*
ANDERSON *Waverley, V.*
ANNESLEY *Valentia, V.*
ANSON *Lichfield, E.*
ARTHUR *Glenarthur, B.*
ARUNDEL, MONCKTON- *Galway, V.*
ARUNDELL *Talbot of Malahide, B.*
ASQUITH *Oxford & Asquith, E.*
ASSHETON *Clitheroe, B.*
ASTLEY *Hastings, B.*
BAILEY *Glanusk, B.*
BAILLIE *Burton, B.*
BALFOUR *Kinross, B.*
BALFOUR *Riverdale, B.*
BAMPFYLDE *Poltimore, B.*
BARING *Ashburton, B.*
BARING *Cromer, E.*
BARING *Howick of Glendale, B.*
BARING *Northbrook, B.*
BARING *Revelstoke, B.*
BARKER *Trumpington, Bs.*
BARNES *Gorell, B.*
BARNEWALL *Trimlestown, B.*
BARRIE *Abertay, By.*
BASS, HASTINGS- *Huntingdon, M.*
BATESON, DE YARBURGH-
Deramore, B.
BATHURST *Bledisloe, V.*
BEACH, HICKS- *St. Aldwyn, E.*
BEAUCLERK *St. Albans, D.*
BEAUMONT *Allendale, V.*
BECKETT *Grimthorpe, B.*
BELLOW *Bellwin, B.*
BENNET *Tankerville, E.*
BENTINCK *Portland, E.*
BERESFORD *Decies, B.*
BERESFORD *Waterford, M.*
BERRY *Camrose, V.*
BERRY *Hartwell, B.*
BERRY *Kemsley, V.*
BERTIE *Lindsey & Abingdon, E.*
BEST *Wynford, B.*
BETHELL *Westbury, B.*
BETHUNE, LINDSAY- *Lindsay, E.*
BIGHAM *Mersey, V.*
BIGHAM *Nairne, L.*
BINGHAM *Clanmorris, B.*
BINGHAM *Lucan, E.*
BIRCH *Rhyl, B.*
BISHOP *O'Cathain, Bs.*
BLACKWOOD *Dufferin and*
Clandeboye, B.
BLIGH *Darnley, E.*
BOOTH, SCLATER- *Basing, B.*
BOSCAWEN *Falmouth, V.*
BOURKE *Mayo, E.*
BOUVERIE, PLEYDELL- *Radnor, E.*
BOWDEN *Aylestone, B.*
BOWYER *Denham, B.*
BOYD *Kilmarnock, B.*
BOYLE *Cork, E.*
BOYLE *Glasgow, E.*
BOYLE *Shannon, E.*
BRABAZON *Meath, E.*
BRAND *Hampden, B.*
BRETT *Esher, V.*
BRIDGEMAN *Bradford, E.*
BRODRICK *Midleton, V.*
BROOKE *Alanbrooke, V.*
BROOKE *Brookeborough, V.*
BROOKS *Crawshaw, B.*
BROUGHTON *Fairhaven, B.*
BROWNE *Kilmaine, B.*
BROWNE *Oranmore & Browne, B.*
BROWNE *Sligo, M.*
BROWNLOW *Lurgan, B.*
BRUCE, HOVELL-THURLOW-
CUMMING- *Thurlow, B.*

BUCHAN *Tweedsmuir, B.*
BUCKLEY *Wrenbury, B.*
BULLER, MANNINGHAM-
Dilhorne, V.
BULLER, YARDE- *Churston, B.*
BUNBURY, McCLINTOCK-
Rathdonnell, B.
BUTLER *Carrick, E.*
BUTLER *Dunboyne, B.*
BUTLER *Lanesborough, E.*
BUTLER *Mountgarret, V.*
BUTLER *Ormonde, M.*
BUXTON *Noel-Buxton, B.*
BRUCE, BRUDENELL- *Ailesbury, M.*
BRUCE *Aberdare, B.*
BRUCE *Balfour of Burleigh, L.*
BRUCE *Elgin, E.*
BYNG *Strafford, E.*
BYNG *Torrington, V.*
CAIN, NALL- *Brocket, B.*
CALDER *Ritchie-Calder, B.*
CAMPBELL *Argyll, D.*
CAMPBELL *Breadalbane, E.*
CAMPBELL *Cawdor, E.*
CAMPBELL *Colgrain, B.*
CAMPBELL *Stratheden, B.*
CANNING *Garvagh, B.*
CAPELL *Essex, E.*
CARINGTON *Carrington, B.*
CARNEGIE *Fife, D.*
CARNEGIE *Northesk, E.*
CARNEGIE *Southesk, E.*
CARY *Falkland, V.*
CAULFEILD *Charlemont, V.*
CAVENDISH *Chesham, B.*
CAVENDISH *Devonshire, D.*
CAVENDISH *Waterpark, B.*
CAYZER *Rotherwick, B.*
CECIL *Amherst of Hackney, B.*
CECIL *Exeter, M.*
CECIL *Rockley, B.*
CECIL, GASCOYNE- *Salisbury, M.*
CHALONER *Gisborough, B.*
CHAPMAN *Northfield, B.*
CHARTERIS *Wemyss, E.*
CHESHIRE *Ryder of Warsaw, Bs.*
CHICHESTER *Donegall, M.*
CHOLMONDELEY *Delamere, B.*
CHUBB *Hayter, B.*
CHURCHILL, SPENCER-
Marlborough, D.
CLARK, CHICHESTER- *Moyola, B.*
CLINTON, FIENNES- *Lincoln, E.*
CLIVE, WINDSOR- *Plymouth, E.*
COCHRANE *Dundonald, E.*
COCKS *Somers, B.*
COKAYNE *Cullen of Ashbourne, B.*
COKE *Leicester, E.*
COLE *Enniskillen, E.*
COLLINS *Stonham, B.*
COLVILLE *Clydesmuir, B.*
COMPTON *Northampton, M.*
CONWY, ROWLEY- *Langford, B.*
COOPER *Norwich, V.*
COOPER, ASHLEY- *Shaftesbury, E.*
COPLEY, BEWICKE- *Cromwell, B.*
CORBETT *Rowallan, B.*
CORRY, LOWRY- *Belmore, E.*
COTTON, STAPLETON-
Combermere, V.
COURTENAY *Devon, E.*
COUTTS, MONEY- *Latymer, B.*
COWDREY *Herries of Terregles, Ly.*
COX, ROXBEE *Kings Norton, B.*
CRAIG *Craigavon, V.*
CRICHTON *Erne, E.*
CRIPPS *Parmoor, B.*
CROSSLEY *Somerleyton, B.*
CUBITT *Ashcombe, B.*
CURZON *Howe, E.*
CURZON *Scarsdale, V.*
CURZON, ROPER- *Teynham, B.*
CUST *Brownlow, B.*
DALRYMPLE *Stair, E.*
DAMER, DAWSON- *Portarlington, E.*
DAVIES *Darwen, B.*

DAVISON *Broughshane, B.*
DAWNAY *Downe, V.*
DEANE *Muskerry, B.*
DE COURCY *Kingsale, B.*
DE GREY *Walsingham, B.*
DE MOLEYNS, DAUBENY *Ventry, B.*
DENISON *Londesborough, B.*
DEVEREUX *Hereford, V.*
DEWAR *Forteviot, B.*
DIXON *Glentoran, B.*
DODSON *Monk Bretton, B.*
DOUGLAS *Morton, E.*
DOUGLAS *Queensberry, M.*
DOUGLAS, AKERS- *Chilston, V.*
DRUMMOND *Perth, E.*
DRUMMOND OF
MEGGINCH, Strange, Bs.
DUGDALE *Crathorne, B.*
DUKE *Merrivale, B.*
DUNCOMBE *Feversham, B.*
DUNDAS *Melville, V.*
DUNDAS *Zetland, M.*
EADY *Swinfen, B.*
EDEN *Auckland, B.*
EDEN *Avon, E.*
EDEN *Henley, B.*
EDGCUMBE *Mount Edgcumbe, E.*
EDMONDSON *Sandford, B.*
EDWARDES *Kensington, B.*
EDWARDS *Chelmer, B.*
EDWARDS *Crickhowell, B.*
EGERTON *Sutherland, D.*
EGERTON *Wilton, E.*
ELIOT *St. Germans, E.*
ELLIS, SCOTT- *Howard de Walden,*
B.
ERSKINE *Buchan, E.*
ERSKINE *Mar & Kellie, E.*
ERSKINE, ST. CLAIR- *Rosslyn, E.*
EVANS *Energlyn, B.*
EVANS *Mountevans, B.*
EVE *Silsoe, B.*
FANE *Westmorland, E.*
FEILDING *Denbigh, E.*
FELLOWES *Ailwyn, B.*
FELLOWES *De Ramsey, B.*
FERRIS, GRANT *Harvington, B.*
FIENNES *Saye & Sele, B.*
FITZ-CLARENCE *Munster, E.*
FITZGERALD *Leinster, D.*
FITZHERBERT *Stafford, B.*
FITZ-MAURICE *Orkney, E.*
FITZMAURICE, MERCER NAIRNE
PETTY- Lansdowne, M.
FITZROY *Grafton, D.*
FLETCHER, AUBREY- *Braye, Bs.*
FLOWER *Ashbrook, V.*
FOLJAMBE *Liverpool, E.*
FORBES *Granard, E.*
FRANKLAND *Zouche, B.*
FRASER *Lovat, L.*
FRASER *Saltoun, Ly.*
FRASER *Strathalmond, B.*
FREKE, EVANS- *Carbery, B.*
FREMANTLE *Cottesloe, B.*
FRENCH *de Freyne, B.*
GALBRAITH *Strathclyde, B.*
GANZONI *Belstead, B.*
GEORGE, LLOYD *Tenby, V.*
GIBBS *Aldenham, B.*
GIBBS *Wraxall, B.*
GIBSON *Ashbourne, B.*
GIFFARD *Halsbury, E.*
GILBEY *Vaux of Harrowden, B.*
GLYN *Wolverton, B.*
GODLEY *Kilbracken, B.*
GORDON *Aberdeen, M.*
GORDON *Huntly, M.*
GORE *Arran, E.*
GORE, ORMSBY *Harlech, B.*
GOWER, LEVESON- *Granville, E.*
GRAHAM *Montrose, D.*
GRANT OF GRANT *Strathspey, B.*
GRANT, OGILVIE- *Seafield, E.*
GRAY, ANSTRUTHER- *Kilmany, B.*
GREAVES *Dysart, Cs.*

GREENALL *Daresbury, B.*
GRENFELL *St. Just, B.*
GRENVILLE, FREEMAN- *Kinloss, L.*
GREVILLE *Warwick, E.*
GRIMSTON *Verulam, E.*
GROSVENOR *Ebury, B.*
GROSVENOR *Westminster, D.*
GUEST *Wimborne, V.*
GUETERBOCK *Berkeley, B.*
GUINNESS *Iveagh, E.*
GUINNESS *Moyne, B.*
GULLY *Selby, V.*
GURDON *Cranworth, B.*
HALL *Lockwood, B.*
HAMILTON *Abercorn, D.*
HAMILTON *Belhaven, L.*
HAMILTON *Dudley, Bs.*
HAMILTON *Holm Patrick, B.*
HAMILTON, BAILLIE-
  Haddington, E.
HAMILTON, DOUGLAS- *Selkirk, E.*
HAMOND, HARBORD- *Suffield, B.*
HAMPDEN, HOBART-
  Buckinghamshire, E.
HANDCOCK *Castlemaine, B.*
HARDY, GATHORNE- *Cranbrook, E.*
HARE *Blakenham, V.*
HARE *Listowel, E.*
HARMSWORTH *Rothermere, V.*
HARRIS *Malmesbury, E.*
HASTINGS, ABNEY *Loudoun, Cs.*
HATTON, FINCH *Winchilsea, E.*
HAY *Erroll, E.*
HAY *Kinnoull, E.*
HAY *Tweeddale, M.*
HENDERSON *Faringdon, B.*
HENDERSON *Rowley, B.*
HENNESSY *Windlesham, B.*
HERBERT *Carnarvon, E.*
HERBERT *Hemingford, B.*
HERBERT *Pembroke, E.*
HERBERT *Powis, E.*
HERBERT *Tangley, By.*
HERVEY *Bristol, M.*
HEWITT *Lifford, V.*
HIBBERT, HOLLAND- *Knutsford, V.*
HICKS, JOYNSON- *Brentford, V.*
HILL *Downshire, M.*
HILL, CLEGG- *Hill, V.*
HODGE, HERMON- *Wyfold, B.*
HOGG *Hailsham of St Marylebone, B.*
HOME, DOUGLAS *Dacre, Bs.*
HOOD *Bridport, V.*
HOPE *Glendevon, B.*
HOPE *Linlithgow, M.*
HOPE *Rankeillour, B.*
HOPKINSON *Colyton, B.*
HOPWOOD *Southborough, B.*
HOWARD *Carlisle, E.*
HOWARD *Effingham, E.*
HOWARD *Strathcona, B.*
HOWARD *Suffolk, E.*
HOWARD, FITZALAN *Norfolk, D.*
HOWELLS *Geraint, B.*
HUBBARD *Addington, B.*
HUGGINS *Malvern, V.*
HUGHES *Cledwyn of Penrhos, B.*
HUTCHINSON, HELY-
  Donoughmore, E.
INGRAMS *Darcy de Knayth, Bs.*
INSKIP *Caldecote, V.*
IRBY *Boston, B.*
ISAACS, RUFUS- *Reading, M.*
JACKSON *Allerton, B.*
JAMES *Northbourne, B.*
JEBB *Gladwyn, B.*
JERVIS *St. Vincent, V.*
JOCELYN *Roden, E.*
JOHNSTON, LAWSON *Luke, B.*
JOHNSTONE, HOPE *Annandale &
  Hartfell, E.*
JOHNSTONE, VANDEN-BEMPDE-
  Derwent, B.
JOLLIFFE *Hylton, B.*
JONES *Maelor, B.*
JONES, ARMSTRONG- *Snowdon, E.*
JONES, GWYNNE *Chalfont, B.*
KEARLEY *Devonport, V.*
KEITH *Kintore, E.*
KEMP *Rochdale, B.*
KENNEDY *Ailsa, M.*
KENWORTHY *Strabolgi, B.*
KEPPEL *Albemarle, E.*
KER INNES *Roxburghe, D.*
KERR *Lothian, M.*
KERR *Teviot, B.*
KING *Lovelace, E.*

KITSON *Airedale, B.*
KNATCHBULL *Brabourne, B.*
KNIGHTLEY, FINCH- *Aylesford, E.*
KNOX *Ranfurly, E.*
KYNYNMOUND, ELLIOT-
  MURRAY- *Minto, E.*
LADE, MILLES- *Sondes, E.*
LAMB *Rochester, B.*
LAMBART *Cavan, E.*
LAMPSON *Killearn, B.*
LANGTON, TEMPLE-GORE-
  Temple, E.
LASCELLES *Harewood, E.*
LAW *Coleraine, B.*
LAW *Ellenborough, B.*
LAWRENCE *Oaksey, B.*
LAWSON *Burnham, B.*
LEGGE *Dartmouth, E.*
LEGH *Newton, B.*
LEGH, CORNWALL- *Grey of Codnor,
  B.*
LEITH *Burgh, B.*
LENNOX, GORDON *Richmond, D.*
LESLIE *Rothes, E.*
LEVER *Leverhulme, V.*
LIDDELL *Ravensworth, B.*
LINDSAY *Crawford, E.*
LISTER, CUNLIFFE- *Swinton, E.*
LITTLETON *Hatherton, B.*
LODER *Wakehurst, B.*
LOPES *Roborough, B.*
LOW *Aldington, B.*
LOWTHER *Lonsdale, E.*
LOWTHER *Ullswater, V.*
LUBBOCK *Avebury, B.*
LUMLEY *Scarbrough, E.*
LYON, BOWES *Strathmore, E.*
LYSAGHT *Lisle, B.*
LYTTELTON *Chandos, V.*
LYTTELTON *Cobham, V.*
McDONNELL *Antrim E.*
MACKAY *Inchcape, E.*
MACKAY *Reay, L.*
MACKAY *Tanlaw, B.*
MACKENZIE *Cromartie, E.*
McLAREN *Aberconway, B.*
MACMILLAN *Stockton, E.*
MACPHERSON *Strathcarron, B.*
MAFFEY *Rugby, B.*
MAITLAND *Lauderdale, E.*
MAJOR, HENNIKER- *Henniker, B.*
MAKGILL *Oxfuird, V.*
MAKINS *Sherfield, B.*
MANNERS *Rutland, D.*
MANSFIELD *Sandhurst, B.*
MARQUIS *Woolton, E.*
MARSHAM *Romney, E.*
MASON *Blackford, B.*
MAUDE *Hawarden, V.*
MAXWELL *Farnham, B.*
MAXWELL *de Ros, Bs.*
MEADE *Clanwilliam, E.*
MELVILLE, LESLIE *Leven, E.*
MILLAR *Inchyra, B.*
MILLS *Hillingdon, B.*
MITFORD *Redesdale, B.*
MOLYNEUX *Sefton, E.*
MOND *Melchett, B.*
MONTAGU *Manchester, D.*
MONTAGU *Swaythling, B.*
MONTAGU *Amwell, B.*
MONTGOMERIE *Eglinton, E.*
MOORE *Drogheda, E.*
MORETON *Ducie, E.*
MORGAN, VAUGHAN *Reigate, B.*
MORLEY, HOPE- *Hollenden, B.*
MORRIS *Killanin, B.*
MORRISON *Dunrossil, V.*
MORRISON *Margadale, B.*
MOSLEY *Ravensdale, B.*
MOUNTBATTEN *Edinburgh, D.*
MOUNTBATTEN *Milford Haven, M.*
MUFF *Calverley, B.*
MULHOLLLAND *Dunleath, B.*
MURRAY *Atholl, D.*
MURRAY *Dunmore, E.*
MURRAY *Mansfield, E.*
MURRAY, ERSKINE- *Elibank, L.*
NEEDHAM *Kilmorey, E.*
NEVILL *Abergavenny, M.*
NEVILLE *Braybrooke, B.*
NEWDEGATE, FITZROY *Daventry,
  V.*
NEWTON *Eltisley, By.*
NICOLSON *Carnock, B.*
NIVISON *Glendyne, B.*
NOEL *Gainsborough, E.*

NORTH *Guilford, E.*
NORTHCOTE *Iddesleigh, E.*
NORTON *Grantley, B.*
NORTON *Rathcreedan, B.*
NUGENT *Westmeath, E.*
O'BRIEN *Inchiquin, B.*
OF MAR *Mar, C.*
OGILVY *Airlie, E.*
O'NEIL *Rathcavan, B.*
ORR *Boyd-Orr, B.*
PAGE *Whaddon, B.*
PAGET *Anglesey, M.*
PAKENHAM *Longford, E.*
PAKINGTON *Hampton, B.*
PALMER *Lucas of Crudwell, Bs.*
PALMER *Selborne, E.*
PARKER *Macclesfield, E.*
PARKER *Morley, E.*
PARNELL *Congleton, B.*
PARSONS *Rosse, E.*
PATON, NOEL- *Ferrier, B.*
PAULET *Winchester, M.*
PEAKE *Ingleby, V.*
PEARSON *Cowdray, V.*
PEASE *Gainford, B.*
PEASE *Wardington, B.*
PELHAM *Chichester, E.*
PELHAM *Yarborough, E.*
PELLEW *Exmouth, V.*
PEMBERTON, LEIGH- *Kingsdown,
  B.*
PENNANT, DOUGLAS- *Penrhyn, B.*
PENNY *Marchwood, V.*
PEPYS *Cottenham, E.*
PERCEVAL *Egmont, E.*
PERCY *Northumberland, D.*
PERY *Limerick, E.*
PHILIPPS *Milford, B.*
PHILIPPS *St. Davids, V.*
PHILIPPS *Strange of Knokin, Bs.*
PHIPPS *Normanby, M.*
PLUMPTRE *FitzWalter, B.*
PLUNKETT *Dunsany, B.*
PLUNKETT *Louth, B.*
POLLOCK *Hanworth, V.*
POMEROY *Harberton, V.*
PONSONBY *Bessborough, E.*
PONSONBY *de Mauley, B.*
PONSONBY *Sysonby, B.*
POWLETT, ORDE- *Bolton, B.*
POWYS *Lilford, B.*
PRATT *Camden, M.*
PRESTON *Gormanston, V.*
PRIMROSE *Rosebery, E.*
PRITTIE *Dunalley, B.*
QUIN, WYNDHAM- *Dunraven, E.*
RAMSAY *Dalhousie, E.*
RAMSBOTHAM *Soulbury, V.*
RHYS *Dynevor, B.*
RICE, SPRING *Monteagle of
  Brandon, B.*
RICHARDS *Milverton, B.*
ROBERTS *Clwyd, B.*
ROBERTSON *Wharton, Bs.*
ROBINSON *Martonmere, B.*
ROCHE *Fermoy, B.*
RODD *Rennell, B.*
ROPER, TREVOR- *Dacre of Glanton,
  B.*
ROSPIGLIOSI *Newburgh, E.*
ROUS *Stradbroke, E.*
ROYLE *Fanshawe of Richmond, B.*
RUSSELL *Ampthill, B.*
RUSSELL *Bedford, D.*
RUSSELL *de Clifford, B.*
RUSSELL, HAMILTON- *Boyne, E.*
RUTHVEN, HORE- *Gowrie, E.*
RYDER *Harrowby, E.*
SACKVILLE *De La Warr, E.*
ST. AUBYN *St. Levan, B.*
ST. CLAIR *Sinclair, L.*
ST. JOHN *Bolingbroke, V.*
ST. LEGER *Doneraile, V.*
SAMUEL *Bearsted, V.*
SANDERS *Bayford, By.*
SANDILANDS *Torphichen, L.*
SAUMAREZ *de Saumarez, B.*
SAVILE *Mexborough, E.*
SCARLETT *Abinger, B.*
SCHREIBER *Marlesford, B.*
SCOTT *Eldon, E.*
SCOTT, HEPBURNE- *Polwarth, L.*
SCOTT, MONTAGU DOUGLAS
  Buccleuch, D.
SCRYMGEOUR *Dundee, E.*
SEAGER *Leighton of St. Mellons, B.*
SEELY *Mottistone, B.*

SEYMOUR Somerset, D.
SEYMOUR Hertford, M.
SHAW Craigmyle, B.
SHAW Kilbrandon, B.
SHIRLEY Ferrers, E.
SHORE Teignmouth, B.
SHORT Glenamara, B.
SIDDELEY Kenilworth, B.
SIDNEY De L'Isle, V.
SINCLAIR Caithness, E.
SINCLAIR Pentland, B.
SINCLAIR Thurso, V.
SKEFFINGTON Massereene, V.
SMITH Bicester, B.
SMITH Colwyn, B.
SMITH Hambleden, V.
SMITH Kirkhill, B.
SMITH, BUCHANAN- Balerno, B.
SMITH, WALKER- Broxbourne, B.
SNOW Burntwood, B.
SOMERSET Beaufort, D.
SOMERSET Raglan, B.
SOSKICE Stow Hill, By.
SOUTER Audley, B.
SPENCER Churchill, V.
STANHOPE Harrington, E.
STANLEY Derby, E.
STERN Michelham, B.
STEVAS, ST JOHN- St John of
   Fawsley, B.
STEWART Galloway, E.
STEWART Stewartby, B.
STEWART, VANE-TEMPEST-
   Londonderry, M.
STONOR Camoys, B.
STOPFORD Courtown, E.
STOURTON Mowbray, B.
STRACHEY O'Hagan, B.
STRACHEY Strachie, B.
STRANGWAYS, FOX- Ilchester, E.
STRUTT Belper, B.
STRUTT Rayleigh, B.

STUART Castle Stewart, E.
STUART Moray, E.
STUART, CRICHTON- Bute, M.
SWAN Sharples, Bs.
TALBOT, CHETWYND-
   Shrewsbury, E.
TAYLOR Ingrow, B.
TAYLOR, SUENSON- Grantchester,
   B.
TAYLOUR Headfort, M.
TENISON, KING- Kingston, E.
TENNANT Glenconner, B.
THELLUSSON Rendlesham, B.
THESIGER Chelmsford, V.
THOMAS Tonypandy, V.
THOMSON Tweedsmuir of Belhevie,
   BS.
THOMSON, MITCHELL- Selsdon, B.
THYNN Bath, M.
TOLER, GRAHAM- Norbury, E.
TOTTENHAM Ely, M.
TRACEY, HANBURY- Sudeley, B.
TREFUSIS, FANE- Clinton, B.
TRENCH Ashtown, B.
TRENCH, LE POER Clancarty, E.
TUFTON Hothfield, B.
TURNER Netherthorpe, B.
TURNOUR Winterton, E.
TURTON Tranmire, B.
UPTON Templetown, V.
URQUHART Tayside, B.
VANE Barnard, B.
VANE, FLETCHER- Inglewood, B.
VANNECK Huntingfield, B.
VAUGHAN Lisburne, E.
VEREKER Gort, V.
VERNEY Willoughby de Broke, B.
VERNON Lyveden, B.
VESEY de Vesci, V.
VILLIERS Clarendon, E.
VILLIERS, CHILD- Jersey, E.
VIVIAN Swansea, B.

WALLOP Portsmouth, E.
WALROND Waleran, B.
WALSH Ormathwaite, B.
WARD Bangor, V.
WARD Dudley, E.
WARRENDER Bruntisfield, B.
WATSON Manton, B.
WEIR Inverforth, B.
WELLESLEY Cowley, E.
WELLESLEY Wellington, D.
WEST, SACKVILLE- Sackville, B.
WESTENRA Rossmore, B.
WHITE Annaly, B.
WHITE James of Holland Park, Bs.
WHITELEY Marchamley, B.
WHITFIELD Kenswood, B.
WILBRAHAM, BOOTLE-
   Skelmersdale, B.
WILLEY Barnby, B.
WILLIAMS Berners, Bs.
WILLIAMS, REES- Ogmore, B.
WILLIAMSON Forres, B.
WILLOUGHBY Middleton, B.
WILLS Dulverton, B.
WILSON Moran, B.
WILSON Nunburnholme, B.
WINGFIELD Powerscourt, V.
WINN St. Oswald, B.
WODEHOUSE Kimberley, E.
WOOD Halifax, E.
WOOD Holderness, B.
WOODALL Uvedale of North End, B.
WOODHOUSE Terrington, B.
WORTLEY, MONTAGU
   STUART Wharncliffe, E.
WRIGHT Wootton of Abinger, Bs.
WYNDHAM Egremont, B.
WYNN Newborough, B.
YERBURGH Alvingham, B.
YORKE Hardwicke, E.
YOUNG Kennet, B.
YOUNG, HUGHES- St. Helens, B.

THE BARONETAGE

THE RANDIDATE

THE BARONETAGE

The ALPHABETICAL ARRANGEMENT includes (*i*) the names of Baronets, and (*ii*) the names of extinct baronetcies that are represented in the female line.
Compound surnames are arranged under the last and principal surname,
   e.g. Havelock-Allan will be found under the letter A.

The scope of EACH ARTICLE IN THE BARONETAGE is designed to include information concerning every *living* male descended in the male line from the first Baronet, and of all *living* females being issue of males so descended. For remainders to Baronetcies see article on Baronets in Preliminary Section.

DECEASED FEMALE COLLATERALS and their issue are not as a rule referred to in this work.

ISSUE of the members of two families mentioned in the work, who happen to have intermarried, are usually referred to under the father's name.

CHRISTIAN NAMES OF THE HEIR apparent or presumptive are given in capital letters.

CREATIONS:— E= England (22 May 1611 to 30 April 1707).
             NS= Nova Scotia or Scotland (28 May 1625 to 30 April 1707).
             I= Ireland (30 Sept 1619 to 31 Dec 1800).
             GB= Great Britain (1 May 1707 to 31 Dec 1800).
             UK= United Kingdom (1 Jan 1801 to present time).

Since 1929, Baronets of England, Ireland, Great Britain, and the United Kingdom have been permitted to depict their respective Badges suspended by the ribbon below the shield of arms, as was already the case in respect of Baronets of Nova Scotia.

ABDY (UK) 1850, of Albyns, Essex

Firm and faithful

Sir VALENTINE ROBERT DUFF ABDY, 6th *Baronet*; *b* 11 Sept 1937; *s* his father, *Sir* ROBERT HENRY EDWARD, 1976; *ed* Eton: *m* 1971 (*m diss* 1982), Mathilde, da of Etienne Coche de la Ferté, and has issue.

𝔄rms – Or, two chevronels between three trefoils slipped sable. ℭrest – An eagle's head couped proper, beaked azure.
Residences – Clos du Petit Bois, St Martin's, Guernsey, CI; Newton Ferrers, Callington, Cornwall; 13 Villa Molitor, 75016 Paris, France.

SON LIVING

ROBERT ETIENNE ERIC, *b* 22 Feb 1978.

Sir Thomas Neville Abdy, 1st Bt, of Albyns, Essex, was MP for Lyme Regis 1847-52, and High Sheriff of Essex 1875.

ABERCROMBY (NS) 1636, of Birkenbog, Banffshire

He aims at high things

Sir IAN GEORGE ABERCROMBY, 10th *Baronet*, only son of Robert Ogilvie Abercromby, el son of David James Abecromby, 4th son of 5th Bt; *b* 30 June 1925; *s* his kinsman, *Maj Sir* ROBERT ALEXANDER, MC, DL, 1972; *ed* Lancing, and Bloxham Sch, Banbury: *m* 1st, 1950 (*m diss* 1957), Joyce Beryl, da of Leonard Griffiths, of Spencer's Wood, Berks; 2ndly, 1959, Fanny Mary Udale (Mollie), only da of Dr Graham Udale-Smith, of Sitio Litre, Puerto de la Cruz, Tenerife; 3rdly, 1976, Diana Marjorie, da of Horace Geoffrey Cockell, of Ditton House, Oxhey Woods, Herts, and widow of Capt Ian Charles Palliser Galloway, Seaforth Highlanders, of Blervie, Forres, Morayshire, and has issue by 2nd *m*.

Arms – Quarterly: 1st and 4th argent, a chevron gules between three boars' heads, erased azure, langued of the second; 2nd and 3rd grand quarters: 1st and 4th argent, a lion passant guardant gules, crowned with an imperial crown: 2nd and 3rd argent, three popinjays vert, beaked and membered gules. **Crest** – A falcon rising belled proper. **Supporters** – Two greyhounds argent, collared gules. **Motto** – Vive ut vivas (*Live, that thou mayest live*).
Residence – Sitio Litre, Puerto de la Cruz, Tenerife, Canaries.
Clubs – Ski Club of Great Britain, Kandahar, Real Nautico (Tenerife).

DAUGHTER LIVING *(By 2nd marriage)*

Maria Amelia, *b* 1960: *m* 1988, Wellesley Theodore Octavius Wallace, son of late Dr Caleb Paul Wallace, of W Clandon, Surrey, and has issue living, James Abercromby Octavius *b* 1989, — Lucy Maria Diana, *b* 1991. *Residence* – Whitecroft, W Clandon, Surrey.

COLLATERAL BRANCH LIVING

Granddaughter of Douglas Charles Abercromby, 4th son of 6th baronet:—
Issue of late Keith Douglas Abercromby, *b* 1887 *d* 1968: *m* 1st, 1913, Eva Winifred, who *d* 1930, only da of late Harry Millward Wright; 2ndly, 1939, Mrs Hilda Brocket Lemon, who *d* 1985, da of Alan Sandys, Bar-at-Law:—
(By 1st *m*) Joan Eileen (36 Marlborough Pl, NW8 0PD), *b* 1919: *m* 1st, 1939 (*m diss* 1948), Alan James Butler Aldridge; 2ndly, 1948, Richard Lloyd Joseph Wills, CBE, MC, who *d* 1969; 3rdly, 1972, Maj-Gen James Alexander Rowland Robertson, CB, CBE, DSO, DL, and has issue living, (by 1st *m*) Gail Susan Eva, *b* 1946: *m* 1974, Raymond Henry Cornish, and has issue living, Belinda Mary Eva *b* 1975, Peta Eleanor *b* 1986.
Sir Alexander Abercromby, of Birkenbog, MP for Banffshire, 7th in descent from George Abercrombie, whose lands were erected into the Barony of Pitmedden 1513, was created a Bt of Nova Scotia 1636 with remainder to his heirs male. The 2nd baronet sat as MP for co Banff in Scottish Parliament 1694, and the 5th baronet sat at MP for the same co 1812-18. Sir George William Abercromby, DSO, 8th Bt, was convener of Banff Co Council 1929-61, and Lord-Lieut of Banffsire 1946-64. Sir Robert Alexander Abercromby, MC, 9th Bt, was Vice-Lieut of Banffshire 1965-71.

ACKROYD (UK) 1956, of Dewsbury, West Riding of Yorkshire

Sir JOHN ROBERT WHYTE ACKROYD, 2nd *Baronet*; *b* 2 March 1932; *s* his father, *Sir* CUTHBERT LOWELL, 1973; *ed* Bradfield, and Worcester Coll, Oxford (MA); an Underwriting Member of Lloyd's, a Member of the Council of the Zoological Soc of London since 1987, a Member of Central Council, Victoria League for Commonwealth Friendship 1973-75, Hon Sec of the Royal Coll of Music since 1981, Vice-Pres of Bromley Symphony Orchestra and a Churchwarden of St Mary-le-Bow, Cheapside, Patron of London and International Sch of Acting (LISA) since 1984, Hon Sec Pilgrims of Great Britain 1966: *m* 1956, Jennifer Eileen McLeod, da of late Henry George Stokes Bishop, of Stow-on-the Wold, and has issue.

Arms – Azure on a pale between two oak leaves or a sword erect gules. **Crest** – A goat's head erased azure armed or charged on the neck with a rose argent barbed and seeded proper.
Residence – Flat 1, 65 Ladbroke Grove, Holland Park, W11 2PD.

SONS LIVING

TIMOTHY ROBERT WHYTE, *b* 7 Oct 1958; *ed* Bradfield, and LAMDA; actor. *Residence* – Flat 4, 33 Chepstow Rd, W2 5BP. *Club* – MCC. —— Andrew John, *b* 1961; painter.

DAUGHTERS LIVING

Jane Victoria McLeod, *b* 1957; sculptor: *m* 1992, as his 2nd wife, David Robert Ewart Annesley, of 77 Park Av North, N8, and has issue (*see* E Annesley, colls). —— Kate Georgina McBride, *b* 1963: *m* 1986, Fabrice Gilles Marion, of 35-41 rue de l'Oasis, 92800 Puteaux, France, eldest son of Roger Marion, of 80 rue de Grennelles, Paris 7e, and has issue living, Oscar, *b* 1991, — Oriane, *b* 1987, — Tiphaine Jennifer, *b* 1989, — Héloïse, *b* 1994.

BROTHER LIVING

Christopher Lowell, *b* 1934; *ed* Bradfield, and Magdalene Coll, Camb (BA 1957, MA 1961): *m* 1961, Caroline Rachael, only da of Eric Lewis, of Upper Bridlemere, Woodhall Spa, Lincs, and has issue living, Marcus Lowell, *b* 1964, — Vivyan Katy, *b* 1962, *m* 1987, David Clive Whittaker, 2nd son of Kenneth Whittaker, of Overdale, Dunblane, Perthshire, and has issue living, Giles *b* 1988. *Residence* – Nutfield, Wickhurst Rd, Weald, Kent.

Sir Cuthbert Lowell Ackroyd, 1st Bt, son of Benjamin Batley Ackroyd, of Dewsbury, Yorks, was Lord Mayor of London 1955-56.

ACLAND (E) 1678, with precedence from 1644, of Columb-John, Devon

Unshaken

Sir JOHN DYKE ACLAND, 16th *Baronet*; *b* 13 May 1939; *s* his father, Sir RICHARD THOMAS DYKE, 1990; *ed* Clifton, Magdalene Coll, Camb (MA), and Univ of W Indies (MSc): *m* 1961, Virginia, yr da of Roland Forge, of The Grange, Barnoldby-le-Beck, Lincs, and has issue.

Arms – Checky argent and sable, a fesse gules. **Crest** – A man's hand apaumée couped at the wrist in a glove lying fessewise to the sinister, thereon a falcon perched all proper, jessed and belled or.
Seat – Killerton, Broadclyst, Devon. *Residence* – Sprydon, Broadclyst, Exeter, Devon EX5 3JN.

SONS LIVING

DOMINIC DYKE, *b* 19 Nov 1962; *ed* Edinburgh Univ (MA): *m* 1990, Sarah Anne, 3rd da of Ven Kenneth Unwin, formerly Archdeacon of Pontefract, and has issue living, Patrick, *b* 18 Nov 1993, — Florence, *b* (twin) 1993. —— Piers Dyke, *b* 1964; *ed* Univ Coll, London (BSc, PhD); Bar Lincoln's Inn 1992: *m* 1993, Lucinda M., da of Dr John Draper Raiman, of Highans Park, E4.

DAUGHTER LIVING

Holly, *b* 1972.

BROTHERS LIVING

Robert Dyke, *b* 1941; *ed* Bryanston, and London Univ (MB BS); FRCS England, LRCP London: *m* 1st, 1963 (*m diss* 1983), (Susan Maureen) Sarah, da of Cmdr James Wood, RN, of Liss, Hants; 2ndly, 1983 (*m diss* 1990), Susan Ann, da of Thomas L. Bishop of Crestwood, Kentucky, USA, and has issue living (by 1st *m*), Daniel James, *b* 1969; has discontinued use of forename Dyke; *ed* Berkely Univ, Calif, — Beatrice Maud, *b* 1966; has discontinued use of forename Dyke; *ed* Duke Univ, Calif, — (by 2nd *m*) Benjamin Thomas, *b* 1984, — Emily Grace, *b* 1986. *Residence* – 2020 Winston Av, Louisville, Kentucky, USA. —— Henry Dyke, *b* 1943; *ed* Clifton, and Magdalene Coll, Camb (BA); DPhil Oxon: *m* 1967 (*m diss* 1977), (Irene) Norma, da of Percy Norman Gatley, of 28 Cherry Tree Av, Runcorn, Ches. *Residence* – 1339 Talmadge St, Los Angeles, Calif, USA.

COLLATERAL BRANCHES LIVING

Issue of late Arthur Geoffrey Dyke Acland, 2nd son of 14th Bt, *b* 1908, *d* 1964: *m* 1932 (Winifred) Julian Dorothy, da of Lt-Col Sydney Roden Fothergill, JP, DL, of Lowbridge House, Kendal:—
Oliver Geoffrey Dyke, *b* 1934; 2nd Lt Border Regt: *m* 1959, Judith Veronica, 2nd da of late Peter Willans, of 18 Canonbury Park North, N1, and has issue living, Peter Geoffrey Dyke, *b* 1961, — Francis Oliver Dyke, *b* 1963, — Christopher John Dyke, *b* 1966. *Residence* – Barnsdale, Burneside, nr Kendal, Cumbria. —— Robin Julian Dyke, *b* 1937. —— Edward Francis Dyke, *b* 1942.

Grandchildren of late Capt John Edward ACLAND (infra):—
Issue of late Capt Henry Vivian Acland, *b* 1883, *d* 1968: *m* 1st, 1910, Jeanne, who *d* 1950, only da of M. Vander Nest, formerly Min for Belgium in USA; 2ndly, 1951, Mrs Inez Sweetwood (c/o Toronto-Dominion Bank, Queen and Kent St, Charlottetown, Prince Edward Island), da of Robert Everett Mutch, of Charlottetown, Prince Edward Island:—
(By 1st *m*) Patricia Evelyn, *b* 1920: *m* 1945, Robert Browne-Clayton, late Lt, Princess Patricia's Canadian LI, of 4534 Gordon Drive, Kelowna, BC, Canada, and has issue living, Patrick Robert (385 5th St, Campbell River, BC, Canada V9W 3X4), *b* 1947; *ed* Nôtre Dame Univ, Nelson, BC (BSc), — Peter Shane (1444 Lawrence Av, Kelowna, BC, Canada V1Y 6M8), *b* 1949; *ed* BC Univ (BSc): *m* 1972, Mary Elizabeth, da of W. C. Law, of Vancouver, BC, and has issue living, Nicole Ann *b* 1975, Celia Jeanne *b* 1977, — Jeanne Madeline (104 1585 West 11th Av, Vancouver, BC, Canada V6J 2B5), *b* 1953; *ed* BC Univ (BSc).

Grandsons of late Capt Henry Vivian Acland (ante):—
Issue of late Capt John Ernest Vivian Acland, R Westminster Regt, Canadian Army, *b* 1911, *d* 1982: *m* 1st, 1935, Edith Eleanor, who *d* 1953, da of late John Waterman of Vancouver, BC; 2ndly, 1954, Joan Wilmot:—
(By 2nd *m*) Peter Vivian, *b* 1955. —— Anthony Robert, *b* 1957.

Grandchildren of late Lt-Gen Arthur Nugent FLOYER-ACLAND, CB, DSO, MC, 2nd son of late Capt John Edward ACLAND (infra):—
Issue of late Brig Stafford Nugent Floyer-Acland, CBE, *b* 1916, *d* 1994: *m* 1950, Patricia Egidia Hastings (The Dairy House, W Stafford, Dorchester), da of late Lt-Col Richard St Barbe Emmott, IA (ret) (*see* Cts Loudoun, colls):—
Richard Stafford (Mill House, Harley, nr Shrewsbury, Shropshire SY6 6NE), *b* 1952; *ed* Marlborough; Maj LI: *m* 1983, Sarah Margaret, da of Henry Millington Synge, of Nesscliffe, Shropshire, and has issue living, Charles Stafford, *b* 1987, — Olivia Joy, *b* 1985, — Beatrice Rose, *b* 1990. —— Andrew Arthur (5 Foxcote, Andoversford, nr Cheltenham, Glos), *b* 1955; *ed* Marlborough, and Durham Univ (BA): *m* 1987, (Penelope) Lucy Priscilla, elder da of Julian Gerard Wathen (*see* Starkey, Bt,

1985 Edn), and has issue living, Toby Julian, *b* 1989. ——— Victoria Egidia, *b* 1962; *ed* Bristol Univ (BA): *m* 1992, Nagi El-Bay, of Sisams Cottage, Nightingale Lane, Cleeve Prior, Worcs, eldest son of Saad El-Bay, of Heliopolis, Egypt, and has issue living, Noorah Egidia, *b* 1993.

Granddaughter of late Col Charles Arthur Williams Troyte, eldest son of late Arthur Henry Dyke TROYTE, 2nd son of 10th baronet:—
Issue of late Capt John Edward ACLAND, 4th King's Own Regt, *b* 1848, *d* 1932 (having discontinued the use of the surname Troyte): *m* 1882, Norah Letitia Nugent, who *d* 1938, da of late Henry Hyde Nugent Bankes, of Studland Manor, Dorset:—
Victoria Letitia Troyte, *b* 1897: *m* 1928, Maj-Gen Nigel William Duncan, CB, CBE, DSO, DL, late RTR, who *d* 1987, and has issue living, Elizabeth Letitia, *b* 1929: *m* 1954, Maj John Christopher Byron Deverell, RHA (ret), of Upton Noble Manor, Somerset, and has issue living, John Duncan *b* 1955; *ed* Eton, RMA Sandhurst, and Christ's Coll, Camb; Lt-Col Royal Scots Dragoon Gds: *m* 1993, Susanne Christiana Kampert, of Dortmund, Germany (and has issue living, John Conrad Christopher *b* 1993), Virginia Letitia *b* 1957, — Janet Lyndsay Norah, *b* 1932: *m* 1956, Maj Malcolm Vincent Chichester Firth, RA (ret), of Eastcott Manor, Easterton, Devizes, Wilts SN10 4PL, and has issue living, Richard Lyndsay Martin *b* 1957; *ed* Downside, and RMA Sandhurst; Capt 4th/7th Royal Dragoon Gds: *m* 1987, Georgina Clare, da of Capt Frederick Henry Beresford Mainwaring-Burton, DSC, RM, of Tarrant Keynston, Dorset, Andrew William Mallaby *b* 1960; *ed* Downside, and Reading Univ (BSc): *m* 1989, Amanda, da of Christopher Marriott, of Whitchurch, Berks (and has issue living, Edward Peter William *b* 1993), Patrick Nigel Vincent *b* 1961; *ed* Downside: *m* 1986, Susan, da of late Gerald Grehan, of Naas, co Kildare (and has issue living, Robert William Gerald *b* 1988, Ian James Duncan *b* 1991, James Andrew Donald *b* 1994), David Malcolm Angus *b* 1964; *ed* Dauntsey's Sch, Exeter Univ (BA), and Durham Univ (MA), — Christina Lalage, *b* 1935: *m* 1959, Lt-Col Roger Halliburton Young, RA, of Creek End, Keyhaven, Lymington, Hants, and has issue living, James Lindsay *b* 1967: *m* 1993, Helen, da of Neville Wood, of Spofforth, Yorks, Anthony Halliburton *b* 1968; Capt the Light Dragoons. *Residence* – Marley House, Winfrith Newburgh, Dorchester, Dorset.

Granddaughter of late Capt John Edward ACLAND (ante):—
Issue of late Capt John Bevill Acland, *b* 1890, *d* 1966: *m* 1914, Marjorie, who *d* 1977, da of H. Guernsey:—
Ione Vivienne (161 Acland Rd, Ganges, Salt Spring Is, BC), *b* 1915; Headmistress of Strathcona Lodge Sch, Shawnigan Lake, BC 1959-69: *m* 1936, Charles Clement Guthrie, who *d* 1966, and has issue living, Barnaby Fairbairn, *b* 1937; *ed* Univ of Victoria (BA), — Nicholas Bruce, *b* 1938; *ed* Univ of BC (BSc, BEd): *m* 1966, Anna Scott, and has issue living, Russell Sean *b* 1967, Ross Cameron *b* 1968, Ian Benjamin *b* 1970, Ryan David *b* 1981, Jennifer Sarah *b* 1974.

Descendants of late Sir Henry Wentworth Dyke Acland, KCB (4th son of 10th baronet), who was *cr* a *Baronet* 1890:—
See Acland, Bt, *cr* 1890.

Grandchildren of late Lt-Col Baldwyn John Dyke Acland, eldest son of late Cdr Benjamin Dyke Acland (infra):—
Issue of late John Ben Dyke Acland, *b* 1916, *d* 1991: *m* 1st, 1941 (*m diss* 1950), Beatrice Margaret, who *d* 1957, da of William Willes, of Newbold Comyd, Leamington Spa; 2ndly, 1950, Lorna May Woodthorpe (1 East St, Uffculme, Devon EX15 3AL), da of late Capt Harry Woodthorpe Graham, MC, of Uitenhague, S Africa:—
(By 1st *m*) John William Brian Dyke (6 St John's Terr, Devoran, Cornwall), *b* 1942; *ed* Bradfield, and Cambourne Sch of Mines: *m* 1968, Georgina Scarborough, and has issue living, Peter, *b* 1978, — Samantha Louise, *b* 1969: *m* 1994, Wensley Grosvenor Haydon-Baillie, of Wentworth Woodhouse, Yorks, son of late Malcolm Haydon-Baillie, and of late Mrs Peter Murray-Lee, — Carina, *b* 1972. ——— (By 2nd *m*) Thomas Jeremy Dyke (86 Hurstbourne Rd, Forest Hill, SE23), *b* 1952; *ed* Plymouth Coll; has issue living (by Pat England), Joseph Peter Reynolds, *b* 1988, — Polly Jane Reynolds, *b* 1993. ——— Diana Jane Dyke, *b* 1954: *m* 1975, Leonardo Martinez, of Plaza San Francisco 3, Mahon, Menorca, and has issue living, Maria-Carmen, *b* 1977.

Grandchildren of late Cdr Benjamin Dyke Acland, 2nd son of Rev Peter Leopold Dyke Acland, 5th son of 10th baronet:—
Issue of late Capt Hubert Edward Peter Dyke Acland, *b* 1884, *d* 1953: *m* 1912, Dorothy Marion, who *d* 1958, da of Sir John Henry Thorold, 12th Bt:—
Anne Dyke, *b* 1915; formerly Subaltern ATS: *m* 1948, Ian Graham Gordon, who *d* 1993. *Residence* – The Old Laundry, Syston, nr Grantham, Lincolnshire.
Issue of late Capt Lauchlan Henry Dyke Acland, MC, *b* 1889, *d* 1969: *m* 1923, Doris Dar, who *d* 1980, da of Hugh Davidson, of 12 Queensbury Pl, SW:—
Julian Dyke (11 Dunton Close, Four Oaks, Sutton Coldfield, Warwicks), *b* 1924; *ed* St Paul's Sch, Magdalen Coll, Oxford (MA, BSc), and Sheffield Univ (PhD), BM, BCh: *m* 1964, Alison, da of Arthur William Chapman, CBE, of 53 Ranmor Cres, Sheffield, and has issue living, Ann Sarah, *b* 1965.

Grandson of late Capt Hubert Edward Peter Dyke Acland (ante):—
Issue of late Roger Dyke Acland, *b* 1920, *d* 1984: *m* 1st, 1945 (*m diss* 1951), Sylvia, only child of late Nicholas Galperin, of St John's Wood, NW; 2ndly, 1951, Molly, da of David McLurg, of Washington, USA:—
(By 2nd *m*) Simon Nicholas Dyke, *b* 1953: *m* 1981, Kathleen Spellman, and has issue living, Rosemary Anjelica, *b* 1983. *Residence* – Avalon, Camphill Devon Community, Hampstead Village, Buckfastleigh, Devon.

Granddaughter of late Rev Henry Dyke Acland, 3rd son of Rev Peter Leopold Dyke Acland (ante):—
Issue of late Eng-Rear-Adm Edward Leopold Dyke Acland, CB, MVO, DL, *b* 1878, *d* 1968: *m* 1910, Phyllis, who *d* 1973, da of late Connell Whipple:—
Adria Margaret (37 Church St, Henley-on-Thames, Oxon RG9 1SE), *b* 1914: *m* 1st, 1935, Arthur Francis Procter, who *d* 1970, son of late Sir Henry Edward Edleston Procter, CBE; 2ndly, 1971, Lt-Col James Hawke Dennis, TD, Chevalier of Legion of Honour, who *d* 1985, and has issue living (by 1st *m*) Susan Caroline, *b* 1939: *m* 1969, Timothy Gordon Keown, of Cockslease Farm House, Fawley, Henley-on-Thames, and has issue living, David Nigel *b* 1971, Alice Belinda *b* 1972.

Grandchildren of late Col Sir Hugh Thomas Dyke Acland, CMG, CBE, FRCS (infra):—
Issue of late Sir (Hugh) John Dyke Acland, KBE, *b* 1904, *d* 1981: *m* 1935, Katherine Wilder (Mount Peel, Canterbury, NZ), da of John Davies Ormond, of Hawkes Bay, NZ:—
John Barton Ormond (Mount Peel, Canterbury, NZ), *b* 1936: *m* 1961, Dorothy Rosemary, da of Allan Albert Hobson, of Fielding, NZ, and has issue living, John Barton, *b* 1964, — Paul Hobson, *b* 1965, — Henry Dyke, *b* 1975, — Jessica Emily, *b* 1963: *m* 1989, Richard Jeffrey Staniland, of 27 Winchendon Rd, SW6 5DR, and has issue living, George Richard Acland *b* 1993, Lucinda Katherine Acland *b* 1991, — Georgina Katharine, *b* 1969, — Alexandra Evelyn, *b* 1970. ——— Mark Arundel (Mount Somers Stn, Canterbury, NZ), *b* 1939: *m* 19—, Joanna, da of John Quaife, of Mount Albert Stn, Wanaka, and has issue living, David Quaife, *b* 19—, — Benjamin Napier, *b* 19—, — Hamish Ormond *b* 19—. ——— *Rev* Simon Henry Harper (27B Tite St, SW3 4JR), *b* 1941: *m* 1970 (*m diss* 1983), his cousin, Nicola Hornby, da of John Pavey (infra), and has issue living, Michael Bernard Pavey, *b* 1971, — Luke Simon Burgoyne, *b* 1980, — Kim Lin Ovans, *b* 1973, — Anna Katherine Hornby, *b* 1975. ——— Audrey Ann, *b* 1937: *m* 1960, Hamish McHardy, of Tauroa, Havelock N, NZ, and has issue living, Jonathan Forbes, *b* 1962, — Kate Acland, *b* 1961, — Rebecca Thornley, *b* 1965, — Sarah Ormond, *b* 1966, — Emma

Elizabeth, *b* 1968. —— Evelyn Wilder, *b* 1947: *m* 1973, James Leybourne Wallace, LLB (*see* Jackson, Bt, *cr* 1915, colls), of Sundrum, Woodbury, NZ, and has issue. —— Sarah Burgoyne, *b* 1951.

Grandchildren of late Hon John Barton Arundel Acland, 6th son of 10th baronet:—
Issue of late John Dyke Acland, *b* 1863, *d* 1944: *m* 1902, Mary Eveline, who *d* 1961, el da of late Rev Canon Harry Woodford St Hill:—
Thomas St Hill (c/o ANZ Bank, Geraldine, S Canterbury, NZ), *b* 1910; 1939-45 War with NZEF: *m* 1963, Margaret Ellen, da of late John Musgrove, and widow of Cdr John Swift Sharp, OBE, RD, RNR. —— Emily Mary Dyke, *b* 1905; is a JP for Somerset; 1939-45 War in ATS. *Residence* – Middle Croft, Bossington Lane, Porlock, Som.
Issue of late Henry Dyke Acland, *b* 1867, *d* 1942: *m* 1906, Elizabeth Grace, who *d* 1942, da of the Hon James Watson, MLC, of Sydney, NS Wales:—
Philippa Mabel, *b* 1914. *Residence* – 8 Dublin Street, Christchurch, New Zealand.
Issue of late Col Sir Hugh Thomas Dyke Acland, CMG, CBE, FRCS, *b* 1874, *d* 1956: *m* 1903, Evelyn Mary, who *d* 1964, da of late J. L. Ovans:—
Colin Dyke (Woodbourne, Main Rd, N Paraparaumu, NZ), *b* 1906; 1939-45 War with S Africa Forces: *m* 1936, Sybil Marjorie, da of T.A. Warner, of Durban, Natal, and has issue living, Hugh Thomas Dyke (17 Onehuka Rd, Melling, Lower Hutt, Wellington, NZ), *b* 1940: *m* 1965, Fredericka Scott, da of G. A. Hutton, of Bangor, Darfield, N Canterbury, NZ, and has issue living, Thomas Dyke *b* 1972, Susannah Scott *b* 1967, Annabel Emily *b* 1970, — Mary Ann Warner, *b* 1936: *m* 1st, 1964 (*m diss* 1968), Josef Maria Baukes; 2ndly, 1970, Christopher John Hindmarsh, and has issue living (by 2nd *m*), John Marcos Acland *b* 1973, Brigid Acland *b* 1971, Nicola Acland *b* 1974. —— Michael Dyke, *b* 1911; 1939-45 War as Lt NZ Artillery: *m* 1946, Elizabeth Vibaert, da of H. de C.McArthur, of Dunedin, NZ, and has issue living, Peter McArthur, *b* 1947, — Alastair Michael, *b* 1950, — Richard, *b* 19—. *Residence* – Christchurch, NZ. —— Elizabeth Evelyn Dyke, *b* 1913; sometime Lt S African Women's Auxiliary Army Ser: *m* 1944, John Pavey, who *d* 1952, and has issue living, Timothy John *b* 1945, — Phillida Ann, *b* 1946, — Nicola Hornby, *b* 1948: *m* 1970 (*m diss* 1983), her cousin, Rev Simon Henry Harper Acland, and has issue (ante), — Miranda Jane, *b* 1950. *Residence* –

The 1st baronet, Sir John Acland, in the service of Charles I, impaired his fortune by raising and supporting a troop to garrison his house at Columb-John. He was created a baronet, but in the confusion of the civil war the letters patent were destroyed, and on the fall of the royal party he was fined £1,800. After the Restoration, new letters patent were granted, but not till the year 1677, on account of a long minority in the family, in consideration of which the patent specially granted precedency from 1644. The 10th baronet sat as MP for Devon 1812-18, and 1820-32, and for N Devon (C) 1837-57. The 11th baronet sat as MP for W Somerset, Wellington Div 1837-46 and 1865-86. John, grandson of 6th baronet, was also *cr* a baronet, 1818 (ext 1871) and assumed the additional surname of Palmer. The 12th baronet, Sir (Charles) Thomas Dyke, was Dep Warden of the Stannaries, and sat as MP for E Cornwall (L) 1882-5, and for E, or Launceston, Div of Cornwall 1885-92. The 13th baronet, Rt Hon Sir Arthur Herbert Dyke, was Vice-Pres of Committee of Council on Education (with a seat in the Cabinet) Aug 1892 to June 1895, a Member of Privy Council, Committee on Industrial Research, and MP for Rotherham Div of S Part of W Riding of York (L) 1885-98. The 14th baronet, Rt Hon Sir Francis Dyke, sat as MP for Yorkshire, N Riding, Richmond Div (L) 1906-10, for Cornwall, Camborne Div 1910-22, for Devonshire, Tiverton Div 1923-4, and for Cornwall, N Div 1932-9, and was Financial Sec to War Depart 1908-10 and 1911, Under-Sec of State for Foreign Affairs 1911-15, Financial Sec to Treasury 1915, and Parliamentary Sec to Board of Agriculture and Fisheries 1915-16. The 15th baronet, Sir Richard Thomas Dyke, was MP for Barnstaple Div of Devon (L and subsequently *Common Wealth*) 1935-45, and for Gravesend Div of Kent (Lab) 1947-55.

ACLAND (UK) 1890, of St Mary Magdalen, Oxford

Unshaken

Sir (CHRISTOPHER) GUY (DYKE) ACLAND, MVO, 6th *Baronet*, *b* 24 March 1946; *s* his father, *Maj Sir* ANTONY GUY, RA, 1983; *ed* Allhallows Sch, and RMA Sandhurst; Lt-Col RA (ret); Equerry to HRH The Duke of Edinburgh 1988-90; Equerry to HM and Deputy Master of HM's Household since (Aug) 1994; MVO 1990: *m* 1971, Christine Mary Carden, yst da of John William Brodie Waring, MB BS, of Waterdip, Totland Bay, Isle of Wight, and has issue.

Arms – Checky argent and sable, a fesse gules. **Crest** – A man's hand apaumée couped at the wrist in glove lying fessewise to the sinister, thereon a falcon perched all proper, jessed and belled or.
Club – Royal Yacht Sqdn.

SONS LIVING

ALEXANDER JOHN DYKE, *b* 29 May 1973. —— Hugh Antony Waring Dyke, *b* 1976.

HALF-SISTER LIVING

Gail Alison Jane, *b* 1942: *m* 1968, Anthony James Rayment, of 30 Lyall Av, Toronto, Ont M4E IV9, Canada.

SISTER LIVING

Caroline Barbara Margaret, *b* 1947; SRN, SCM: *m* 1972, Peter Desmond George Sleigh, of Waimate, NZ, and has issue living, David Ralph, *b* 1972, — John Antony, *b* 1973, — Catherine Joan, *b* 1976, — Margaret Gail *b* 1980, — Susan Mary, *b* 1980 (twin).

DAUGHTERS LIVING OF THIRD BARONET

Elizabeth Margaret, *b* 1919: *m* 1943 (*m diss* 1968), Maj Edward Cecil O'Brien, OBE, Parachute Regt (*see* B Inchiquin colls). *Residence* – Barnaderg, Letterfrack, co Galway. —— (Emily) Patricia, *b* 1931: *m* 1953, Kenneth John Coles, and has issue living, Elizabeth Anne, *b* 1954. *Residence* – The Old Rectory, Newtimber, Hassocks, W Sussex.

WIDOW LIVING OF FIFTH BARONET

MARGARET JOAN (*Margaret, Lady Acland*), el da of late Maj Nelson Rooke, HLI, of Markham House, Badminton: *m* 1944, as his second wife, Maj Sir Antony Guy Acland, RA, 5th Bt, who *d* 1983.

COLLATERAL BRANCHES LIVING

Issue of late Lt-Col James Alison Acland, DSO, younger son of 4th baronet, *b* 1919, *d* 1993: *m* 1942, Diana Marcia, only da of late James Edward Briggs, of The Elms, Troy, Monmouth:—
David James Dyke, *b* 1947; *ed* Nautical Coll, Pangbourne, RNC Dartmouth; Cdr RN (Fleet Air Arm): *m* 1975, Amanda Joy, SRN, el da of John Alan Norman, of Floods, Curland, Taunton, Som, and has issue living, Thomas Alison Dyke, *b* 1977, — Timothy John Dyke, *b* 1978. —— Ion Andrew Dyke, *b* 1949; *ed* Nautical Coll, Pangbourne; Lt-Cdr RNR (ret 1989), Master Mariner; Capt in Cmnd BT (Marine) Ltd Cableship: *m* 1976, Susan Jean, SRN, SCM, da of John Jervis Chapman, of Lake Rd, Poole, Dorset. —— Angela Marcia Dyke, *b* 1946: *m* 1981, Maurice FitzGibbon, of 14 Burcote Rd, SW18, el son of Maurice FitzGibbon, FRIC, FCS, MInstPI, of Haverbreaks, Lancaster.

Granddaughters of late Sir Reginald Brodie Dyke Acland, KC, 5th son of 1st baronet, *b* 1856, *d* 1924: *m* 1885, Helen Emma, who *d* 1943, da of late Rev Thomas Fox, R of Temple Combe, Wincanton, Som:—
Issue of late Edward Fox Dyke Acland, *b* 1891, *d* 1978: *m* 1924, Beatrice, who *d* 1972, da of late Dr J. W. Laver, of Grimston, Norfolk:—
Barbara Elizabeth, *b* 1929; FRSA, FSA: *m* 1949, Richard George Adams, Hon FRSL, author, of Benwells, 26 Church St, Whitchurch, Hants, and has issue living, Juliet Vera Lucy, *b* 1958; MA (Stanford, USA), AM (Stanford USA): *m* 1981, Peter Johnson, FRSA, and has issue living, Robert Alasdair Edward *b* 1994, Lucy Charlotte Acland *b* 1986, Miranda Sylvia Louise *b* 1991, — Rosamond Beatrice Elizabeth, *b* 1960: *m* 1983, Michael Mahony, and has issue living, Sarah Elizabeth Louise *b* 1989, Grace Anna Kathryn *b* 1991. —— Phillis Penelope Jane, *b* 1932; SRN: *m* 1958, Glynn Meirion Owen, MBE, of 17 St Isan Rd, Heath, Cardiff, and has issue living, William Edward, *b* 1959: *m* 1992, Rebecca Barnacle, — Eleri Jane, *b* 1961; SRN, Registered Sick Children's Nurse: *m* 1983, Patrick Dodge, and has issue living, Thomas Patrick *b* 1986, Alan James *b* 1989, Emma Jane *b* 1992, — Alys Mair, *b* 1964: *m* 1990 (*m diss* 1992), David Marles. —— Judith Sarah, *b* 1942.
Issue of late Wing-Cdr Wilfrid Reginald Dyke Acland, DFC, AFC, *b* 1894, *d* 1937: *m* 1921, Mary Strange who *d* 1991, having *m* 2ndly, 1939 Air Commodore Thomas Edward Barham Howe, CBE, AFC, who *d* 1970, da of late Thomas Marshall, of Lee-on-Solent:—
Joan Mary Louise, *b* 1923; European War 1941-5 as 3rd Officer WRNS: *m* 1946, Lt-Cdr Peter Allen Ridd Gould, RN, of Hambledon, 35 Stoke Rd, Cobham, Surrey KT11 3BG, and has issue living, Timothy Acland Ridd, *b* 1948: *m* 1976 (*m diss* 1994), Veronica Ruth Franklin, and has issue living, James Acland Ridd *b* 1979, Lucinda Jane Louise *b* 1977, — Angela Mary, *b* 1950: *m* 1970, Nicholas David Gooda, and has issue living, Edward Anthony *b* 1970, Anita Helen *b* 1973. —— Cynthia Helen, *b* 1928: *m* 1953, Robert Coston Taylor, of The Farm House, Enton Green, Godalming, Surrey, and has issue living, Frederick Robert Acland, *b* 1961; BSc, LRPS, — Pamela Harriet, *b* 1957: *m* 1983, George Goldsbrough, only son of E. Goldsbrough, of Johannesburg, S Africa.

Granddaughters of late Capt Francis Edward Dyke Acland, 6th son of 1st baronet:—
Issue of late Herbert Arthur Dyke Acland, *b* 1886, *d* 1968: *m* 1914, Maud Kathleen, who *d* 1986, da of late Col G. E. Branson, of Broomgrove, Sheffield:—
Gwyneth Sybil (*Lady Carden*) (Moongrove, East Woodhay, Newbury, Berks), *b* 1918; FCA: *m* 1st, 1942, Fl-Lt Roderick Stanley Emerson, RAFVR, of Argentina, who was *ka* 1944; 2ndly, 1962, Lt-Col Sir Henry Christopher Carden, 4th Bt, OBE, and has issue living, (by 1st *m*) George Anthony Dyke (Culverthorpe Hall, Grantham, Lincs), *b* 1943: *m* 1972, Jillian Graham, da of late F. Graham Roberts, OBE, and has issue living, George Mark *b* 1974, Edward Anthony *b* 1976, William Robert *b* 1982. —— Stephanie Jane, *b* 1924: *m* 1947, Reginald Chase, LDSRCS Eng, who *d* 1981, of Blue Hills, Finchampstead Ridges, Berks, and has issue living, Phillip Reginald (Warwick Court, Winchester, Hants), *b* 1949: *m* 1st, 1984 (*m diss* 1985), Josephine Marian, da of W. J. Whiting, of Cheadle Hume, Cheshire; 2ndly, 1988, Josephine Eleanor Weeks, — Douglas Martyn (17 Darlaston Rd, Wimbledon, SW19), *b* 1955: *m* 1983, Noëlle Mary Rose, da of Mrs Barbara Thompson of West Broyle, Chichester, and has issue living, Guy William Thompson *b* 1989, Verity Jane *b* 1986.

Grandchildren of late Col Alfred Dyke Acland, CBE, 7th son of 1st baronet:—
Issue of late Lt-Col Arthur William Acland, OBE, MC, TD, *b* 1897, *d* 1992: *m* 1926, Violet Gwendolen, who *d* 1984, yr da of late Rev Canon Hon Robert Grimston (*see* E Verulam, colls, 1985 Edn):—
David Alfred (The Manor, Notgrove, Cheltenham, Glos; *Club* – Royal Yacht Sqdn), *b* 1929; *ed* Eton, and ChCh Oxford (MA): *m* 1960, Serena Elizabeth, da of late Sir Cyril Hugh Kleinwort (*see* Kleinwort, Bt, colls), and has issue living, Harry Alexander (Wheatsheaf House, Shrewton, Wilts SP3 4EQ), *b* 1963: *m* 1991, Catherine Juliet, MB BS, who *d* 1992, as the result of a yachting accident, da of Cmdr Richard Masterman, RNR, of Thuborough House, Sutcombe, Holsworthy, Devon, — Lucy Henrietta, *b* 1962: *m* 1988, Nicholas C. Morris, yst son of C.P. Morris, of Radnor Walk, SW3, and has issue living, Leo *b* 1991, Pandora *b* 1989. —— Martin Edward (Standon Green End, Ware, Herts; *Club* – Royal Yacht Sqdn), *b* 1932; *ed* Eton; JP Herts, High Sheriff 1978: *m* 1956, Anne Maureen, OBE, DStJ, da of late Stanley Ryder Runton, of Ilkley, Yorks, and has issue living, Michael Christopher Dyke (*Club* – Royal Yacht Sqdn), *b* 1958; *ed* Eton, and RNC Dartmouth; Capt RM; ADC to Lt-Gen Wilkins, Commandant-Gen RM: *m* 1988, Miranda Jane Elisabeth, eldest da of John Bradshaw, of 11 Cheyne Place, SW3, and has issue living, Tara Katherine Elisabeth *b* 1990, Susanna Rose Juliet *b* 1993. — Richard Arthur Dyke (*Club* Royal Yacht Sqdn), *b* 1962; *ed* Eton, Wye Agric Coll, and London Univ: *m* 1990, Alison Jane, da of Dr Bruce Osborne, of Westacott House, Goodleigh, Barnstaple, N Devon, and has issue living, Thomas Alexander *b* 1994, Charlotte Emma Victoria *b* 1992. — Peter Edward Dyke, *b* 1964. —— Charles Robert, *b* 1937; *ed* Eton, and RMA Sandhurst; Capt Grenadier Guards.

Issue of late Brig Peter Bevil Edward Acland, OBE, MC, TD, JP, *b* 1902, *d* 1993: *m* 1927, Bridget Susan (Little Court, Feniton, Honiton, Devon), da of late Rev Herbert Barnett (Hon Canon Ch Ch Oxford), of Farley Moor, Binfield, Bracknell, Bucks (Lethbridge, Bt, Colls):—
Sir John Hugh Bevil, KCB, CBE (Feniton Court, Honiton, Devon), *b* 1928; *ed* Eton; Maj-Gen Scots Guards, and Equerry to HRH late Duke of Gloucester 1957-59; Malaya 1950-51; Cyprus 1951-52; Egypt 1952-53; Kenya 1960-62; Zanzibar 1962-63; Libya 1968-69; CO, 2nd Scots Gds 1968-71; Comd Land Forces Cyprus 1976-78; GOC SW Dist 1978-81; Comd Commonwealth Force, Rhodesia 1979-80; Hon Col Exeter Univ OTC 1981, R Devon Yeo 1983; R Wessex Yeo 1989; DL Devon 1984; CBE (Mil) 1978; *cr* KCB 1980: *m* 1953, Myrtle Christian Euing, da of Brig Alastair Wardrop Euing Crawford, of Auchentroig, Stirlingshire, and has issue living, Peter John, *b* 1954: *m* 1979, Amanda, da of Brian Ryrie, of Nairobi, Kenya, and has issue living, Katharine Elisabeth *b* 1981, Elizabeth Caroline *b* 1983, — Victoria Susan, *b* 1958: *m* 1986, Thomas J. Goddard, yst son of Maj David Goddard, of The Mill, Lympstone, Devon, and has issue living, Luke *b* 1992, Rosanna *b* 1990. —— Sir Antony Arthur, GCMG, GCVO (The Provost's Lodge, Eton College, Windsor, Berks SL4 6DH), *b* 1930; *ed* Eton, and Ch Ch Oxford; Hon LLD Exeter 1988, William & Mary Coll, Virginia 1990, and Reading 1992; entered Foreign Ser 1953; Prin Private Sec to Sec of State for Foreign Affairs 1972, Ambassador to Luxembourg 1975-77, and to Spain 1977-79; Permanent Under-Sec of State FCO, and Head of HM Diplomatic Service 1982-86; Ambassador to Washington 1986-91, since when Provost of Eton Coll; *cr* CMG, 1976, KCVO 1976, KCMG 1982, GCMG 1986, and GCVO 1991: *m* 1st, 1956, (Clare) Anne, who *d* 1984, el da of late Francis Reynolds Verdon, of Littlefields, Sidbury, Devon; 2ndly, 1987, Mrs Jennifer McGougan (*nee* Dyke), of Bicton, Devon, and has issue living (by 1st *m*), Simon Hugh Verdon, *b* 1958: *m* 1988, Josephine, elder da of Michael Valentine, and has issue living, two das, — Nicholas Antony Bevil, *b* 1960: *m* 1984, Sophia Caroline Annabel, only da of David John Yorke, of Hall Foot, Worston, Clitheroe, Lancs (*see* B Clitheroe), and has issue living, Thomas *b* 1989, Hugh *b* 1994, Olivia *b* 1990, — Katharine Mary, *b* 1965.

The 1st Baronet, Sir Henry Wentworth Acland, KCB, MD, LLD, DCL, FRS (4th son of 10th baronet of creation 1678, *see* ante), a well-known scientist, was Regius Professor of Medicine at Oxford, Hon Physician to HM King Edward VII when

Prince of Wales, and Member and Pres of Medical Council of United Kingdom. Adm Sir William Alison Dyke Acland, CVO, 2nd Bt, was Naval ADC to Queen Victoria 1896-9, second in command of Channel Squadron 1901-2, and Adm Sup of Gibraltar Dockyard 1902-04. Lt-Col Sir William Henry Dyke Acland, MC, AFC, TD, 3rd Bt, was Maj RFC and RAF in European War 1914-18 (wounded, despatches, MC, 4th class Order of St George (Russia), AFC) and cmd'd Royal Devon Yeo RA (TA). His brother, Capt Sir Hubert Guy Dyke Acland, DSO, RN, 4th Bt, served in European War 1914-18 (despatches, DSO), cmd'd HMAS Australia 1937-38 and HMAS and HMS Albatross 1938, and served 1939-45 War. He *m* Lalage Mary Kathleen, eldest da of Capt John Edward Acland (Acland, Bt, *cr* 1678, colls). Maj Sir Antony Guy Acland, 5th Bt, served RA 1937-58, specialising in Anti-Aircraft, Instructor Fire Control, Instructor in Gunnery, Development and Trials 1958, ret 1958 and joined Saunders-Roe on rocket development and trials projects.

Acland (Fuller-Acland-Hood), see Hood.

ADAIR (UK) 1838, of Flixton Hall, Suffolk (Extinct 1988)

Maj-Gen Sir ALLAN HENRY SHAFTO ADAIR, GCVO, CB, DSO, MC, 6th and last *Baronet.*

DAUGHTERS LIVING OF SIXTH BARONET

Bridget Mary (*Lady Darell*), *b* 1928: *m* 1953, Brig Sir Jeffrey Lionel Darell, MC, 8th Bt, Coldm Gds. *Residence* – Denton Lodge, Harleston, Norfolk. —— Annabel Violet, *b* 1937.

ADAM (UK) 1917, of Hankelow Court, co Chester

The cross gives me welcome rest

Sir CHRISTOPHER ERIC FORBES ADAM, 3rd *Baronet*, *b* 12 Feb 1920; *s* his uncle, *Gen Sir* RONALD FORBES, GCB, DSO, OBE, 1982; *ed* Abinger Hill Sch, Surrey, and privately: *m* 1957, Patricia Anne Wreford, yr da of late John Neville Wreford Brown, of Maltings, Abberton, Colchester, Essex.

Arms – Argent, a mullet pierced between three cross-crosslets fitchée gules, a chief of the last thereon a pale or, charged with a rose of the second, barbed and seeded proper. **Crest** – A cubit arm argent holding in the hand a cross-crosslet fitchée in bend sinister, and charged on the wrist with a rose, both as in the arms.
Residence – 46 Rawlings St, SW3.

ADOPTED DAUGHTER LIVING

Sarah Anne, *b* 1960: *m* 1986, Andrew J. Allen (assumed the surname of Allen by deed poll 1964), son of Prof Alec Eden, of Torquay, Devon, and has issue living, Edward Christopher, *b* 1989, —— Alicia Elizabeth, *b* 1991.

DAUGHTERS LIVING OF SECOND BARONET

Barbara Forbes (*Lady Proctor*), *b* 1917: *m* 1953, as his 2nd wife, Sir (Philip) Dennis Proctor, KCB, who *d* 1983. *Residence* – 102 High St, Lewes, E Sussex, BN7 1XH. ——• Bridget Islay Forbes, MBE, *b* 1927; Col WRAC (ret); MBE (Mil) 1960. *Residence* – Ardmore, Netherhampton, Salisbury, Wilts SP2 8PU. —— Isobel Forbes, *b* (twin) 1927. *Residence* – 4 Alderville Rd, SW6 3RJ.

COLLATERAL BRANCHES LIVING

Issue of late Colin Gurdon Forbes Adam, CSI, 3rd son of 1st baronet, *b* 1889; *d* 1982: *m* 1920, Hon Irene Constance Lawley, who *d* 1976, da of 3rd Baron Wenlock:—
Rev (STEPHEN) TIMOTHY BEILBY FORBES (Woodhouse Farm, Escrick, York Y04 6HT), *b* 19 Nov 1923; *ed* Eton, and Balliol Coll, Oxford; Rifle Bde 1942-47 in France and Far East; ordained 1962; Rector of Barton-in-Fabis with Thrumpton, Southwell, Notts 1964-70; priest-in-charge of Southstoke, Bath and Wells 1974-84: *m* 1954, Penelope, da of George Campbell Munday, MC, of Leverington Hall, Wisbech, Cambs, and has issue living, Anna Victoria, *b* 1955, —— Catherine Mary, *b* 1956: *m* 1991, Kristan David Stone, 2nd son of Stanley Stone. —— Lucy, *b* 1960, —— Sonia Clare, *b* 1963. —— Nigel Colin (Skipwith Hall, Selby, Yorks), *b* 1930; JP, High Sheriff N Yorks 1976, DL 1991; *ed* Eton, and King's Coll, Camb: *m* 1st, 1954, Teresa Hermione Idena, only da of Cdr David Robertson, RN; 2ndly, 1987, (Mildred) Malise Hare, formerly wife of William Guy David Ropner (see Ropner, Bt, *cr* 1904, colls), and da of late Col George Armitage, MC, TD, of Newburgh House, Coxwold, Yorks, and has issue living (by 1st *m*), Charles David (Charity Farm, Skipwith, Selby, N Yorks), *b* 1957: *m* 1982, Rosalind Cecilia, da of Geoffrey Colvile, of Ivy House Farm, East Malling, Kent, and has issue living, (Crispin) Bielby *b* 1987, Hal *b* 1989, Charlotte Irene *b* 1992, —— Titus Desmond, *b* 1960, —— Julian Nigel Peregrine, *b* 1961: *m* 1986, Christina Maria, da of Colin Woodiwiss, of 55 Connaught St, W2, and has issue living, Luke George Nigel *b* 1987, —— Harry Crispin, *b* 1962. —— Virginia Mary (The Elms, Bubwith, Selby, Yorks), *b* 1922: *m* 1948, Capt Hugo Francis Guy Charteris, MC, Scots Gds, who *d* 1970 (see E Wemyss, colls).

Grandchildren of late Colin Gurdon Forbes Adam, CSI (ante):—
Issue of late Desmond Francis Forbes Adam, *b* 1926, *d* 1958: *m* 1949, Hon Vivien Elisabeth (11 Mulberry Walk, SW3), da of Sir Oswald Ernald Mosley, 6th Bt (see B Ravensdale):—
Rupert Colin (Richardsons, Skipwith, nr Selby, N Yorks), *b* 1957: *m* 1981, Mrs Anya B. Hillman, da of Richard Cadbury Butler. —— Cynthia Rebecca, *b* 1950: *m* 1978, H. Clive Chaddock, of The Manse, Harray, Orkney, only son of H.

Chaddock, of 2 Mornington Av, Crosby, Liverpool, and has issue living, Jack Colin, *b* 1981, — Harry Desmond, *b* 1984, — Benjamin Gabriel, *b* 1987. ——— Arabella Irene, *b* 1952; has issue living, Archie Desmond Hugo, *b* 1980, — Wilfrid Peter Jamie, *b* 1983, — Alfy Sholto, *b* 1988.

The 1st baronet, Sir Frank Forbes Adam, CB, CIE, was Pres of Bombay Chamber of Commerce 1884-9, and Manchester Chamber of Commerce 1893, 1894, and 1903-5. The 2nd baronet, Gen Sir Ronald Forbes Adam, GCB, DSO, OBE, late RA, served in European Wars 1914-18 in France and Italy (despatches thrice), and 1939-45 in France and Belgium (despatches), was Gen Officer Comdg-in-Ch N Command June 1940 and A-G to the Forces June 1941-May 1946; Chm to British Council 1946-54, Pres Library Ass 1949, and Chm of Exec Board of UN Educn, Scientific and Cultural Organisation 1952-54.

AGNEW (NS) 1629, of Lochnaw, Wigtownshire

By counsel not by rashness

Sir CRISPIN HAMLYN AGNEW OF LOCHNAW, 11th *Baronet*; *b* 13 May 1944; *s* his father, Sir FULQUE MELVILLE GERALD NOEL, 1975; *ed* Uppingham, and RMA; Maj RHF (ret 1981); Advocate 1982; Rothesay Herald since 1986; a Member of Queen's Body Guard for Scotland (Roy Co of Archers); Chief of the Name of Agnew; Representor of the baronial house of Agnew of Lochnaw; Hereditary Sheriff of Wigton; a Member of Expeditions to Greenland 1966, Antarctica 1970, Nuptse Himal 1975, and Everest 1976; Leader of Expeditions to Greenland 1968, Patagonia 1972, and Api Himal 1980: *m* 1980, Susan Rachel Strang, journalist and broadcaster, yr da of late Jock Wykeham Strang Steel (*see* Steel of Philiphaugh, Bt), and has issue.

Arms – Argent, a chevron between two cinquefoils in chief gules, and a saltire couped in base azure. **Crest** – An eagle issuant and reguardant proper. **Motto** – Consilio Non Impetu. **Supporters** – Two heraldic tigers proper collared and chained or.

Residence – 6 Palmerston Rd, Edinburgh, EH9 1TN. **Clubs** – Army and Navy.

SON LIVING

MARK DOUGLAS NOEL, yr of Lochnaw, *b* 24 April 1991.

DAUGHTERS LIVING

Isabel Sevilla Wilhelmina, *b* 1984. ——— Emma Rachel Elizabeth, *b* 1986. ——— Roseanna Celia Nancy, *b* 1989.

WIDOW LIVING OF TENTH BARONET

SWANZIE (*Swanzie, Lady Agnew of Lochnaw*) (3 Lonsdale Terr, Edinburgh, EH3 9HN), da of late Maj Esme Nourse Erskine, CMG, MC (*see* E Buchan, colls): *m* 1937, Sir Fulque Melville Gerald Noel Agnew of Lochnaw, 10th Bt, who *d* 1975.

COLLATERAL BRANCHES LIVING

Grandsons of late Col Quentin Graham Kinnaird Agnew, DSO, MVO, 4th son of 8th baronet:—
Issue of late Col David Quentin Hope Agnew, *b* 1900, *d* 1975: *m* 1928, Janet May Dilkes, who *d* 1980, da of late Rev Charles Herbert Malden, R of Little Gransden, Beds:—
Andrew David Quentin (Garth House, Furnace, Machynlleth, Powys), *b* 1929; *ed* Trin Coll, Glenalmond and Edinburgh Univ (BSc); PhD Bangor: *m* 1957, Shirley, da of late James Arnold Smithson, of Woodstock, Simonstone, Lancs, and has issue living, David James, *b* 1960, — Peter Jonathan, *b* 1963, — Robin Andrew *b* 1966. ——— Jonathan Herbert (11 Ulting Lane, Langford, Maldon, Essex CM9 6QB), *b* 1933: *m* 1958, Mary Kathleen, who *d* 1982, da of late Brig Stannus Grant Gordon Fraser, MC, Indian Army (ret), and has issue living, George Archibald Quentin, *b* 1962, — Michael Stannus, *b* 1965, — Susan Louise, *b* 1963.
Issue of late Cdr John Andrew Agnew, RN, *b* 1903, *d* 1977: *m* 1934, Ysabel Augusta Aurelia, who *d* 1979, da of Don Ernesto Larios, of Algeciras, Spain:—
Fulke Quentin Ernesto (Monte de la Torre, Los Barrios, Provincia de Cadiz, Spain), *b* 1938; Maj RHF (ret): *m* 1970, Susan Georgina, el da of late Group Capt Frank Hastings Tyson RAF (ret), of Diss, Norfolk, and has issue living, Tomas Quentin, *b* 1972, — John Benedict, *b* 1976, — Luisa Beatriz, *b* 1973.

Grandchildren of late Col Quentin Graham Kinnaird Agnew, DSO, MVO, (ante):—
Issue of late Capt Patrick Alexander Agnew, Seaforth Highlanders, *b* 1908, *ka* 1943: *m* 1936, Baroness Johanna Elizabeth (who *m* 2ndly, 1944, Lt-Col William Stanley Baird), da of Baron Barthold MacKay (*see* L Reay, colls):—
Robin Andrew Patrick Mackay (MS 897, Ravensbourne, Queensland 4352, Australia), *b* 1940: *m* 1965, Diana Clyde, da of Humphrey Dinsdale Phillips and formerly wife of David Allan Bennett, and has issue living, Gordon Alexander Mackay *b* 1967. ——— Rosemary Joanna Evelyn, *b* 1938: *m* 1960, Arthur Struan Hannay Robertson, and has issue living, Duncan Struan Alexander, *b* 1961, — Jonathan Dougal, *b* 1962, — Alastair James, *b* 1967, — Patrick Hamish, *b* 1970. *Address* – Box 70245, Bryanston 2021, RSA.

Granddaughter of late Rev David Carnegie Andrew Agnew, 3rd son of 7th baronet:—
Issue of late Andrew David Carnegie Agnew, *b* 1856, *d* 1927: *m* 1882, Minnie Dale, who *d* 1928, da of David Dale Buchanan:—
Ivy Diamond Dale, *b* 1895.

Grandchildren of late Sir Stair Andrew Agnew, KCB, 5th son of 7th baronet:—
Issue of late Stair Carnegie Agnew, *b* 1872, *d* 1940: *m* 1913, Sylvia Bellville, who *d* 1974, da of late Alexander Martin Bremner, Bar-at-Law, of 1 St Petersburgh Place, W, and 3 Paper Buildings, Temple, EC:—
Lesley Stair, *b* 1919; Sister Mary Magdalene; has been Canoness Regular of Order of St Augustine since 1945.
Issue of late Col Herbert Charles Agnew, OBE, late RE, *b* 1880, *d* 1949: *m* 1919, Enys, who *d* 1985, da of late James Wason, of Merton Hall, Wigtownshire:—

John Nevin, *b* 1922; *ed* Rugby, and Ch Ch Oxford (MA); Lt-Col (ret) Coldstream Guards: *m* 1951, Margaret Scott, da of late Moffat Thomson, of Lambden, Berwickshire, and has issue living, Andrew Robert (Springfield, Lasswade, Midlothian), *b* 1956: *m* 1981, Patricia, da of Sir Russell Fairgrieve, CBE, TD, of Pankalan, Boleside, Galashiels, Selkirk, and has issue living, Roy Duncan *b* 1984, Jonathan Michael *b* 1986, Christina Margaret *b* 1982, — James Douglas (52 The Chase, SW4), *b* 1959: *m* 1984, Elizabeth Mary, da of Dr John Atherton Cameron, of The Old Vicarage, Marystowe, Lifton, Devon, and has issue living, Charlotte Elizabeth *b* 1987, Georgina Catherine *b* 1990, Alexandra Isobel *b* 1992, — Jean Catherine, *b* 1953: *m* 1979, Richard Swan, son of late Lt-Col Sir William B. Swan, KCVO, CBE, TD, JP, of Blackhouse, Eyemouth, Berwickshire, and has issue living, Peter Allan *b* 1982, Nicola Anne *b* 1981, Alice Margaret *b* 1984. *Residence* – Bonjedward House, Jedburgh, Scotland. —— Patrick William, *b* 1927; *ed* Rugby, and Trin Coll, Camb (BA 1947, MA 1963): *m* 1958, Anne Meryl Turner, and has had issue, David Martin, *b* 1959; Capt RHF; *k* in a helicopter crash 1984, while serving with Frontier Force, Oman, — Stephen William, *b* 1963, — Hazel Patricia, *b* 1963.

Grandson of late Capt Douglas Agnew, RN, only son of late Thomas Frederick Agnew, 6th son of 7th Bt:—

Issue of late Maj (Frederick) Douglas Agnew, TD, *b* 1909, *d* 198-: *m* 1st, 1938 (*m diss* 1950), Barbara, da of R. T. B. Glasspool, of Calday Grange School, W Kirby; 2ndly, 1951, Vivien Elizabeth Willoughby, da of Harold Willoughby Bartlett, of Vine House, Well End, Bourne End, Bucks:—

(By 1st *m*) Jocelyn, *b* 1940: *m* 1965, Raymond Graham Jenner, of 1c Park Hill Close, Carshalton Beeches, Surrey, and has issue living, Angus Donald Agnew, *b* 1966, — Bruce Roderick, *b* 1969.

Granddaughters of late Thomas Frederick Andrew Agnew, 6th son of 7th baronet:—

Issue of late Percy Reginald Agnew, *b* 1878, *d* 1952: *m* 1909, Ethel Adelaide Susan Wakefield, who *d* 1962:—

Maud Susan Rosemary: *m* 1941, Jarvis H. Campbell, and has issue living, John Agnew, *b* 1949: *m* 1974, Kathleen Mary, yr da of Alexander Shaw Ferguson Wilson, of The Orchard, Kilbride, Doagh, co Antrim, — Adelaide Elizabeth, *b* 1943, — Eily Jane, *b* 1945, — Dinah Mary, *b* 1953. *Residence* – The Moat Inn, Donegore, Dunadry, co Antrim. —— Poppy Eily, *b* 1915. —— Denise Frances, *b* 1917. —— Nancy Marion, *b* 1919: *m* 1939, Philip Humphrey Vellacott, and has issue living, Giles Wakefield, *b* 1949, — Julia Clare, *b* 1943, — Teresa, *b* 1944. *Residence* – Tan y Bryn, Franksbridge, Llandrindod Wells.

This family descends from Andrew Agnew, who was granted the lands of Lochnaw, made Hereditary Constable of Lochnaw 1426 and subsequently granted the Hereditary Sheriffdom of Wigton 1451. Sir Andrew, 7th of Lochnaw (ktd 1595), *d* after 1616; his eldest son, Sir Patrick, 8th of Lochnaw, MP for Wigtonshire 1628-33, was granted 16,000 acres of land in Nova Scotia, erected into the Barony of New Agnew and *cr* a Baronet of Nova Scotia with remainder to his heirs male whatsoever: *m* Margaret, da of Sir Thomas Kennedy of Culzean; *d* 1661; *s* by his eldest son, Sir Andrew, 9th of Lochnaw, 2nd Bt, ktd in his father's lifetime, MP for Wigtonshire 1644-49 and 1665-71: *m* Lady Anne Stewart, da of 1st Earl of Galloway; *d* 1671; *s* by his eldest son, Sir Andrew, 10th of Lochnaw, 3rd Bt, MP for Wigtonshire 1685 and 1689-1702: *m* Jean, da of Sir Thomas Hay of Park; *d* 1702; *s* by his eldest son, Sir James, 11th of Lochnaw, 4th Bt: *m* Lady Mary Montgomerie, da of 8th Earl of Eglinton; *d* 1735; *s* by his eldest son, Sir Andrew, 12th of Lochnaw 5th Bt, Commanded 21st Royal North British Fusiliers (late RSF), Lt Gen in the Army and Gov of Carlisle Castle; received £4,000 for the abolition of the jurisdiction of the Sheriff of Wigtonshire: *m* Eleanor, da of Thomas Agnew, by whom he had 21 children; *d* 1771; *s* by his 5th son, Sir Stair, 13th of Lochnaw, 6th Bt; cotton and tobacco merchant in Glasgow: *m* 1st, Mary, da of Thomas Baillie of Polkemmet; 2ndly, Margaret, da of Thomas Naesmyth of Dunblair; *d* 1809; *s* by his grandson (eldest son of Andrew, yr of Lochnaw: *m* Hon Martha da of 26th Lord Kinsale), Sir Andrew, 14th of Lochnaw, 7th Bt, MP for Wigtonshire 1830-37, added to Lochnaw Castle in 1822, involved with the Sabbath Day Observance movement: *m* Madeline, da of Sir David Carnegie of Southesk, Bt (but for the attainder 7th Earl of Southesk); *d* 1849; *s* by his eldest son, Sir Andrew, 15th of Lochnaw, 8th Bt, Capt 93rd Highlanders and later 4th Light Dragoons, MP for Wigtonshire 1856-68: *m* Louisa, da of 1st Earl of Gainsborough; *d* 1892; *s* by his eldest son, Sir (Andrew) Noel, 16th of Lochnaw, 9th Bt, Barrister, MP for Edinburgh South 1900-06: *m* Gertrude, da of Hon Gowran Vernon; *d* 1928; *s* by his nephew (son of Charles Hamlyn Agnew, 3rd son of 8th Bt), (Sir) Fulque Melville Gerald Noel, 17th of Lochnaw, 10th Bt (did not use the title), Registrar at Fort Hare Univ, S Africa 1952-60 (dismissed for anti-apartheid activities): *m* Swanzie, da of Major Esme Erskine, CMG, MC (*see* E Buchan, colls); *d* 1975; *s* by his son, the 11th and present Bt.

AGNEW (UK) 1895, of Great Stanhope Street, St George, Hanover Square, co London.

Sir JOHN KEITH AGNEW, 6th *Baronet*; *b* 19 Dec 1950; *s* his father *Major Sir* (GEORGE) KEITH, 1994; *ed* Gresham's Sch, Holt, and RAC, Cirencester.

Arms – Per saltire argent and gules, in pale two cinquefoils and in fesse as many saltires couped, all counterchanged. **Crest** – An eagle reguardant, wings expanded proper, each wing charged with a pale or, holding in its mouth a sword pointed upwards also proper, and resting the dexter claw on a saltire couped gules.
Seat – Rougham Hall, Bury St Edmunds. *Residence* – Lawney's Farm, Rougham, Bury St Edmunds, Suffolk IP30 9JG.

BROTHER LIVING

GEORGE ANTHONY, *b* 18 Aug 1953; *ed* Gresham's Sch, Holt, and Univ of East Anglia. *Residence* – Freewood Cottage, Bradfield St George, Bury St Edmunds, Suffolk.

UNCLE LIVING (*son of 3rd baronet*)

Consilio et impetu

By wisdom and vigour

Stephen William (4a Prince Alfred Parade, Newport, NSW 2106, Australia), *b* 1921; *ed* Rugby, and Trin Coll, Camb; late Lt 7th Hussars; 1939-45 War (wounded): *m* 1st, 1947 (*m diss* 1966), Elizabeth, da of late James Brooks Close, of Aldeburgh, Suffolk; 2ndly, 1967, Mrs Adene Leona Cookson, yr da of Vincent John Brady, of Sydney, and has issue living, (by 1st *m*) John Stuart (Fincham Farm, Rougham, Kings Lynn), *b* 1949; *ed* Gordonstoun, and RAC, Cirencester: *m* 1982, Diana Margaret Zoë, el da of Cmdr Christopher Ellis Baker, RN, of Cley, Norfolk, and has issue living, Jethro Luke *b* 1988, Edgar Christopher *b* 1990, Garth Stephen *b* 1992, — Bolton (Oulton Hall, Norwich, Norfolk), *b* 1950; *ed* Gordonstoun: *m* 1989, Clare Elizabeth, da of late Henry Everet Tinsley, of Langrick Grange, Boston, Lincs, and has issue living, William Henry Bolton *b* 1991, Rosemary Brooks *b* 1989, — James Brooks Close (Church Farm, Oulton, Norwich), *b* 1953; *ed* Gordonstoun, and RAC, Cirencester: *m* 1984, Judith Dianne, da of Edward Gilbert, of 5 Todman Av, Pymble, Sydney, Australia, and has issue living, Catherine Penelope *b* 1986, Louise Frances Elizabeth *b* 1988, — Stephen Hardcastle (The Old Rectory, West Acre, Kings Lynn, Norfolk), *b* 1954; *ed* Gordonstoun: *m* 1993, Amanda, only da of E.W. Trafford, of Wroxham, Norfolk, — Theodore Thomas More (The Little Manor, Thorndon, Suffolk), *b* 1961; *ed* Rugby: *m* 1993, Clare Margaret, yr da of John Joseph Buxton, of Horsey Hall, Gt Yarmouth (*see* Buxton, Bt, colls), — St John Kenneth (4 The Wheatcroft, Harborne, Birmingham), *b* 1964; *ed*

Rugby, and Sheffield Univ: *m* 1992, Jenny R., elder da of Gerald W. Youngs, of Sankence Lodge, Aylsham, Norfolk, — Margaret Elizabeth Diana, *b* 1952: *m* 1977, Richard Eustace Thomas Gurney, of Heggatt Hall, Horstead, Norfolk (*see* M Hertford, colls).

WIDOW LIVING OF FIFTH BARONET

Baroness ANNE MERETE LOUISE (*Lady Agnew*), yr da of Baron Johan Schaffalitzky de Muckadell, of Rødkilde, Fyn, Denmark: *m* 1948, Maj Sir (George) Keith Agnew, TD, 5th Bt, who *d* 1994.

COLLATERAL BRANCHES LIVING

Grandchildren of late Charles Gerald Agnew (infra):—
Issue of late Sir Geoffrey William Gerald Agnew, *b* 1908, *d* 1986: *m* 1934, Hon Doreen Maud Jessel, who *d* 1990, da of 1st Baron Jessel:—
Jonathan Geoffrey William, *b* 1941; *ed* Eton, and Trin Coll, Camb (MA); Chm J.G.W. Agnew & Co Ltd, and London Insurance Market Investment Trust plc: *m* 1st, 1966 (*m diss* 1985), Hon (Agneta) Joanna (Middleton) Campbell, yr da of Baron Campbell of Eskan (Life Baron); 2ndly, 1990, Marie-Claire, elder da of Bernard Dreesmann, and has issue living (by 1st *m*), Caspar Jonathan William, *b* 1967: *m* 1991, Annabel J., elder da of Tim Summers, of Godalming, Surrey, and has issue living, Hector Jonathan Timothy *b* 1993, — Lara Joanna, *b* 1969, — Katherine Agneta, *b* 1971, — (by 2nd *m*) Clarissa Virginia, *b* 1992. —— (Morland Herbert) Julian, *b* 1943; *ed* Eton, and Trin Coll, Camb (MA): *m* 1st, 1973, Elizabeth Margaret, yst da of William B. Mitchell, of Gateside, Blanefield, Stirlingshire; 2ndly, 1993, Victoria, 2nd da of Maj Henry Ronald Burn Callander, MC (*see* Crossley, Bt, colls), and has issue living (by 1st *m*), Thomas Julian Noel, *b* 1975, — Amelia Elizabeth, *b* 1979. —— Jennifer Maud, *b* 1937: *m* 1962, Paul Lazell, of 55 St James's Gdns, W11, and The Manor House, Wighton, Norfolk, only son of Henry George Leslie Lazell, of Reigate, Surrey, and has issue living, Sebastian Henry, *b* 1963: *m* 1989, Belinda Mary, elder da of Peter Beck, of Wimbledon, and has issue living, Frederick Henry *b* 1990, Hamish William *b* 1992, — Dominic Geoffrey Paul, *b* 1972, — Natasha Jennifer, *b* 1967: *m* 1991, Duncan James Bell, yst son of late Harold Bell, of Devon, and has issue living, Joshua James *b* 1994.

Grandchildren of late Charles Morland Agnew, OBE, 2nd son of 1st baronet:—
Issue of late Charles Gerald Agnew, *b* 1882, *d* 1954: *m* 1906, Olive Mary, who *d* 1946, da of late Ven William Danks, Canon of Canterbury:—
(Denys) Martin (4 Grosvenor Court, 22 Grove Rd, East Cliff, Bournemouth BH1 3DB), *b* 1919; *ed* Eton, and Trin Coll, Camb (BA); Maj RA (Emergency Reserve); 1939-45 War (Special Forces); former Vice-Pres American Express Internat UK and Ireland: *m* 1st, 1943, Monica (BA (1981) MA Psych (1983), DPsych (1989), PhD (1992) Univ of Colorado), da of Rev S. Foskett, MD, of Killinghall, Harrogate; 2ndly, 1949, Josephine Ann, da of Alan Ross, of Natal, S Africa; 3rdly, 1974, Rosetta Mary, da of Mrs Ethel Benjamin, of Johannesburg, S Africa; 4thly, 1988, Mrs Doreen Rosemary Wylde, of Amsterdam, Florence and London, and has issue living, (by 1st *m*) Jeremy Andrew Derrick (3912 Linden Place, Colorado Springs, Colorado, USA), *b* 1943; *ed* Eton, and Colorado Coll, USA (BA), and Univ of Colorado (BS, PhD): *m* 1968, Mary Sylvia Perkins, and has issue living, Tracy Marie *b* 1974, Christine *b* 1977, — (by 2nd *m*) William George Morland, *b* 1955: *m* 1984, Antonia Jane, yr da of Capt Richard Lawrence Garnons-Williams, of the Manor House, Gate Helmsley, York, — (Emma Christianne) Annabel (*Marchioness Conyngham*), *b* 1951: *m* 1987, as his 4th wife, 7th Marquess Conyngham.
Issue of late Lieut-Col Kenneth Morland Agnew, DSO, OBE, MC, RA (ret), *b* 1886, *d* 1951: *m* 1st, 1910, Edith, who *d* 1950, da of late Dr A. H. Laver, of Sheffield; 2ndly, 1921, Louise, da of David Harris, of Leeds; 3rdly, 1942, Lilian, who *d* 1951, da of George Matmerson, of Johannesburg, S Africa:—
(By 1st *m*) Joyce, *b* 1913: *m* 1940, Maj Edwin Peter Holness, RA (ret). *Residence* – 34 Roehampton Close, Roehampton Lane SW15 5LU.
Issue of late Major Alan Graeme Agnew, *b* 1887, *d* 1962: *m* 1913, Dorothy Cecil, who *d* 1959, da of late William Winstanley Strode, of Pole House, King's Langley:—
Peter Graeme, MBE; *b* 1914; Wing Com RAF Vol Reserve; MBE (Mil) 1946: *m* 1937, Mary Diana, only da of late James Philip Hervey, of Knutsford, Cheshire, and has issue living, Ian Hervey (Oak Lodge, Ifield Wood, Crawley, Sussex), *b* 1941: *m* 1964, Amanda Barbara, da of late Maj A. Wyndham-Read, and has issue living, Mark Wyndham *b* 1966, Jonathan Graeme *b* 1968, — James Philip (Trenarth Cottage, Constantine, Falmouth, Cornwall TR11 5JN), *b* 1947: *m* 1972, Carol Ann, only da of late Edward Garfield Williams, of Constantine, Cornwall, and has issue living, William Edward Philip *b* 1976, Emma Victoria *b* 1972, — Penelope Mary, *b* 1939: *m* 1961, Col Norman Thomas Davies, MBE, JP, of Lowfields Cottage, London Rd, Hartley Wintney, Hants RG27 8HY, and has issue living, Edward Peter *b* 1962; Maj LI: *m* 1992, Susan Mary, yr da of Joseph Goble, of Harare, Zimbabwe, Clare Mary *b* 1964, — Diana Nicola, *b* 1945: *m* 1st, 1966 (*m diss* 1978), Anthony David Mayhew; 2ndly, 1983, Maj Antony Michael Tippett, of 14E Paveley Drive, SW11 3TP, and has issue living (by 1st *m*), Anthony James *b* 1969, Gavin Mark *b* 1971, Louisa Clare *b* 1973. *Residence* – The Old House, Manaccan, nr Helston, Cornwall TR12 6HR. —— Jacquelin, *b* 1916: *m* 1937, Joseph Stanley Desmond Whitaker, and has issue living, Graeme Stanley (Crowland, Ancaster, nr Grantham), *b* 1938: *m* 1959, Penelope Ann, da of late Group Capt E. H. Walker, and has issue living, Charles Allan *b* 1962, Anthony John *b* 1964, Bridget Ann *b* 1960, — Nigel Glynne (Broomfield House, Yatton, Keynell, nr Chippenham), *b* 1940: *m* 1964, Patricia Caroline, da of Ian F. Stewart, of Mollstone Wood, Red Lane, Limpsfield, Surrey, and has issue living, Jeremy Stewart *b* 1967, Patricia Frances *b* 1967, — David Alan (Menzion, by Biggar, Lanarkshire), *b* 1941: *m* 1963, Madeline, da of late M. Paux, of Koniz, Switzerland, and has issue living, Jean-François *b* 1965, Patrique *b* 1969, Marie-Claude *b* 1964, — Jonathan Milnes, *b* 1947: *m* 1974, Christine, da of William Turner, of Menzion, Tweedsmuir.

Grandchildren of late Victor Charles Walter Agnew (infra):—
Issue of late Lt-Col (Charles) David Agnew, 15th/19th Hussars, *b* 1916, *d* 1987: *m* 1949, Mary Lorna (c/o National Westminster Bank, 1 Market St, York), da of late Rt Rev Henry St John Stirling Woollcombe, Bishop of Selby:—
(David) Richard Charles, *b* 1953; *ed* Harrow: *m* 1978, Charlotte Anne, yr da of John Calkim Whately-Smith (*see* B Hotham, colls), and has issue living, Dickon James, *b* 1981. — Joanna Woollcombe, *b* 1981. — Susan Lorna, *b* 1950: *m* 1976, Alastair Philip Hunter Smart, who *d* 1992, of Yeoman's Cottage, Great Ouseburn, York, and has issue living, Angus David Alastair, *b* 1978, — Harriet Bridget *b* 1981. —— Vanda Jane, *b* 1959: *m* 1986, Julian Edward Lambton, of Pennybridge House, Pennybridge, Ulverston, Cumbria, and has issue (*see* E Durham, colls).

Grandchildren of late Walter Agnew 3rd son of 1st baronet:—
Issue of late Victor Charles Walter Agnew, *b* 1887, *d* 1929: *m* 1913, Phyllis May Claude (who *d* 1981, having *m* 2ndly, 1932, Air Commodore Andrew George Board, CMG, DSO, DL, RAF, who *d* 1973), da of late Claude Baggallay, KC, of 32 Draycott Place, SW:—
Elizabeth Moran, *b* 1914: *m* 1938, Brig Brian Kingzett, CBE, MC, of Long Hill House, Castle Hill Lane, Mere, Warminster, Wilts, and has issue living, Charles David Brian, *b* 1942, — Sarah Elizabeth, *b* 1945.
Issue of late Lt-Col Richard Leslie Agnew, 15th/19th King's Roy Hussars, *b* 1900, *d* 1987: *m* 1st, 1927 (*m diss* 1946), Leila May, da of Brig-Gen Anthony Courage, DSO, MC; 2ndly, 1953, Hilda Dorothy, who *d* 1993, da of late Thomas Henry Spinks:—
(By 1st *m*) (Richard) Mark Walter (The Curate's House, Melbury Osmond, Dorchester, Dorset), *b* 1930; Lieut (ret) RN: *m* 1st, 1955 (*m diss* 1963), Edwina Ottilie Jane, eldest da of late Maj-Gen Sir Robert Edward Laycock, KCMG, CB, DSO (*see* E Dudley, colls); 2ndly, 1972, Lady Teresa Jane Fox-Strangways, who *d* 1989, da of 7th Earl of Ilchester; 3rdly, 1992, Elspeth, da of late Lt-Col A.I. Macpherson, of Lochgilphead, Argyll, and widow of Capt William Richard Dalrymple Gerard-Pearse,

CBE, LVO, RN, of Dinder, Som, and widow of 9th Viscount Galway, and has issue living (by 1st *m*), Leonie, *b* 1956: *m* 1979, Daniel Davis, of New York, and has issue living, Benjamin Daniel *b* 1985, Sarah Jane *b* 1983. —— (Leila) Rosemary, *b* 1928: *m* 1st, 1948 (*m diss* 1959), Kenneth Malcolm Ritchie, only son of late Kenneth Leslie Ritchie; 2ndly, 1962, Robert John Lyle, of Glan Wysc, Sennybridge, Brecon LD3 8PS, eldest son of late Capt Robert Charles Lyle, MC, of Weston Grange, Thames Ditton, Surrey, and has issue living (by 1st *m*), Linda Rosemary Anne, *b* 1951: *m* 1st, 1973, Fl Lt Nigel Corbishley, who *d* 1984; 2ndly, 1988, Fl Lt Michael Pichel-Juan, of The Woodhouse Arms, Corby Glen, Grantham, Lincs NG33 ANJ, and has issue living (by 1st *m*), Benjamin James *b* 1977, Jonathan Piers *b* 1979, Rupert Charles *b* 1982, — Venetia Claire, *b* 1953: *m* 1972, Robert Christopher Springett Sanders, and has issue living, Philip Malcolm *b* 1982, Katherine Joan *b* 1974, Josephine Rosemary *b* 1980, Sally-Anne Madeleine *b* 1984, — (by 2nd *m*), Richard Charles Cecil (3 Glycena Rd, SW11 5TP), *b* 1965: *m* 1993, Joanna Mary Smith, — Lucinda, *b* 1963: *m* 1989, John Julian Peter Johnson, of Rockstone, La Rue des Vaux de l'Eglise, St Martin, Jersey JE3 6BF, CI, and has issue living, William Charles Eric *b* 1994, Elizabeth Daisy *b* 1992. —— Lavinia Mary, *b* 1933: *m* 1st, 1952 (*m diss* 1956), Geoffrey Arnold Ellert, son of John Arnold Ellert, of Oreham House, Henfield, Sussex (*see* Havelock-Allan, Bt, 1937 Edn); 2ndly, 1956, Jonathan Rashleigh, of Dumbledore, Warren Row, nr Wargrave, Berks, only son of late Vernon Leslie William Rashleigh, and has had issue (by 1st *m*), Sallyann Barbara, *b* 1954; assumed surname of Rashleigh by deed poll 1977: *m* 1st, 1973, Anthony Phillips; 2ndly, 1992, Philip M. Boreham, and has issue living (by 1st *m*), Melissa Mary *b* 1976, Victoria Claire *b* 1978, Antonia Melanie *b* 1981, — Serena, *b* 1956; assumed surname of Rashleigh by deed poll 1970: *m* 1977, Roderick Baird, and has issue living, Thomas Roderick *b* 1982, Rosemary Alice *b* 1984, Holly Madeleine *b* 1986, — (by 2nd *m*) Julian Philip, *b* 1957; *d* 1993, — Elizabeth Jane, *b* 1961.

The 1st baronet Sir William (many years senior partner in the firm of Thos Agnew and Sons, of Manchester, Liverpool, and London, and Chm of Bradbury, Agnew, and Co (Limited), proprietors and publishers of *Punch*), sat as MP for SE Lancashire (*L*) 1880-85, and for Lancashire (SE), Stretford Div 1885-6, and the 2nd baronet sat as MP for Salford, W Div (*L*) 1906-18.

Agnew-Somerville, see Somerville

AINSWORTH (UK) 1916, of Ardanaiseig, co Argyll

Sir (THOMAS) DAVID AINSWORTH, 4th *Baronet*; *b* 22 Aug 1926; *s* his half-brother, Sir JOHN FRANCIS, 1981; *ed* Eton; late Lieut 11th Hussars; merchant banker: *m* 1957, Sarah Mary, da of late Lt-Col Hugh Carr Walford, 17th/21st Lancers, and has issue.

Arms – Gules three Battleaxes two and one and as many Buckles tongues to the dexter one and two Argent; **Crest** – Between two Battleaxes blades outwards Argent a Falcon wings displayed and inverted Or beaked and legged Gules belled and jessed Gold.
Residences – Ashley House, Wootton, Woodstock, Oxon; 80 Elm Park Gdns, SW10.

SONS LIVING

ANTHONY THOMAS HUGH, *b* 30 March 1962; *ed* Harrow. —— Charles David, *b* 1966; *ed* Harrow; late Lieut 11th Hussars.

DAUGHTERS LIVING

Serena Mary, *b* 1958: *m* 1987, Stelios Peratinos, of Brokini No 4, Corfu 49100, Greece, and has issue living, Nicholas David, *b* 1987, — George Stamatis, *b* 1988. —— Tessa Jane, *b* 1959: *m* 1986, Nicholas Cecil John Fortescue, and has issue (*see* E Fortescue, colls), of 80 Langthorne St, SW6 6JX.

WIDOW LIVING OF THIRD BARONET

ANITA MARGARET ANN (*Anita, Lady Ainsworth*), el da of late Harold Arthur Lett, of Kilgibbon and Ballynadara, Enniscorthy, co Wexford: *m* 1946, as his 2nd wife, Sir John Francis Ainsworth, 3rd Bt, who *d* 1981. *Residence* - 6 Aubury Park, Shankill, co Dublin.

The 1st baronet, Sir John Stirling Ainsworth, was a mine-owner, and sat as MP for Argyllshire (*L*) Aug 1903 to Nov 1918.

AIRD (UK) 1901, of Hyde Park Terrace, Paddington, co London

Sir (GEORGE) JOHN AIRD, 4th *Baronet*; *b* 30 Jan 1940; *s* his father, *Col Sir* JOHN RENTON, MVO, MC, 1973; *ed* Eton, Ch Ch, Oxford (MA), and Harvard Univ (MBA); a Page of Honour to HM 1955-57: *m* 1968, Margaret Elizabeth, yr da of Sir John Harling Muir, 3rd Bt, TD, and has issue.

Arms – Gules, on a chevron between in chief two wolves' heads erased, and in base a mullet of six points within an increscent all argent, two falcons' heads erased sable. **Crest** – On a bull-headed rail fessewise, a lion rampant holding erect between the paws a spike point downwards all proper.
Residence – Grange Farm, Evenlode, Moreton-in-Marsh, Glos.

SON LIVING

JAMES JOHN, *b* 12 June 1978.

DAUGHTERS LIVING

Vigilantia
By vigilance

Rebecca, *b* 1970. —— Belinda Elizabeth, *b* 1972.

SISTERS LIVING

Susan Priscilla, *b* 1942. —— Petra Daphne (*Baroness Willoughby de Broke*), *b* 1944: *m* 1965, 21st Baron Willoughby de Broke. —— Amanda Alecia, *b* 1946.

WIDOW LIVING OF THIRD BARONET

Lady PRISCILLA Heathcote-Drummond-Willoughby (*Lady Priscilla Aird*) (Wingrove House, Chipping Campden Glos), da of 2nd Earl of Ancaster: *m* 1939, Col Sir John Renton Aird, 3rd Bt, MVO, MC, who *d* 1973.

COLLATERAL BRANCHES LIVING

Grandchildren of late Malcolm Rucker Aird (infra):—
Issue of late Malcolm Henry Aird, OBE, *b* 1899, *d* 1965: *m* 1922, Joan Meredith, who *d* 1986, da of Henry Sturgis:—
Malcolm Robin Meredith, *b* 1923; *ed* Canford; 1939-45 War as Capt Irish Guards (wounded): *m* 1955, Barbara, da of J. Addison Wilson, and has issue living, Julian Malcolm, *b* 1955, —— Zandra Theresa Jane, *b* 1960: *m* 1989, Michael Alistair Patrick Mercer, of 13 Potley, Corsham, Wilts SN13 9RY, son of Maj P. Mercer, of Cotes, Leics, and of Mrs J. Davis, of Bradford-on-Avon, Avon. —— *Sir* Alastair Sturgis, KCVO (31 St James's Palace, SW1), *b* 1931; *ed* Eton, and RMC; late Capt 9th Lancers; Equerry to HM Queen Elizabeth The Queen Mother 1960-64, Asst Private Sec and Extra Equerry 1964-73, Comptroller of the Household to HM Queen Elizabeth the Queen Mother 1964-73, since when Private Sec, Comptroller and Equerry; LVO 1969, CVO 1976, KCVO 1984: *m* 1963, Fiona Violet, LVO, da of late Lt Col Ririd Myddleton, LVO, Coldstream Gds (*see* M Lansdowne), and has issue living, Caroline Margaret Violet, *b* 1964: *m* 1989, Capt Charles John Allfrey, The Royal Hussars (PWO) (*see* V Daventry), —— Henrietta Idina, *b* 1966. —— Jeremy John (Quarry Wood Cottage, Burghclere, Newbury, Berks), *b* 1936; *ed* Eton: *m* 1967, Mary Elizabeth, da of late Lt-Col Sir William Richard De Bacquencourt Des Voeux, 9th Bt, and has issue living, David William, *b* 1968, —— Catherine Rosemary Jean, *b* 1972.
Issue of late Maj Ronald Aird, MC, TD, *b* 1902, *d* 1986: *m* 1925, Viola Mary, who *d* 1965, da of Sir Godfrey Baring, 1st Bt, KBE:—
Gillian Viola, *b* 1930: *m* 1st, 1951 (*m diss* 1961), Robert Ian MacDonald; 2ndly, 1962, Christopher Michael Maude, of Feildings, Hoe Lane, Flansham, Bognor Regis, Sussex, and has issue living (by 1st *m*), Ian, *b* 1955, —— Zara, *b* 1953: *m* 1980, Daniel E. Harris, —— (by 2nd *m*) Victoria Viola, *b* 1968.

Issue of late Malcolm Rucker Aird, 2nd son of 1st baronet, *b* 1872, *d* 1934: *m* 1898, Nellie Margaret, who *d* 1954, da of Jeremiah Dummett, formerly of 54 Porchester Terrace, W:—
Ruth Sarah, *b* 1909: *m* 1940, Robert Ross Buchanan Brown, CBE, and has issue living, Ian Robert Aird, *b* 1946: *m* 1969 (*m diss* 1982), Tessa Elizabeth, da of Desmond Pertwee, and has issue living, Katherine *b* 1972, Emily *b* 1974, Rebecca Rose *b* 1984, —— Sarah Elizabeth, *b* 1944, —— Margaret Jane, *b* 1947. *Residence* – 14 Spring Walk, Wargrave, Berks.
The 1st baronet, Sir John, was a partner in the firm of John Aird and Co, contractors (who carried out the Assuan Dam and Assiut Barrage in Egypt), and sat as MP for Paddington, N Div (*C*) 1887-1906.

AITCHISON (UK) 1938, Lemmington, co Northumberland

Sir CHARLES WALTER DE LANCEY AITCHISON, 4th *Baronet*; *b* 27 May 1951; *s* his father, *Major Sir* STEPHEN CHARLES DE LANCEY, 1958; *ed* Gordonstoun; Dir Walter Willson Ltd and de Lancey Lands Ltd; ARICS; late Lt 15th/19th KRH: *m* 1984, Susan, yr da of late Edward Ellis, of Hest Bank, Lancs, and has issue.
Residence – Middle Bank House, Barbon, Kirkby Lonsdale, Cumbria LA6 2LG. *Club* – Northern Counties.

SON LIVING

RORY EDWARD DE LANCEY, *b* 7 March 1986.

DAUGHTER LIVING

Tessa Charlotte, *b* 1982.

BROTHER LIVING

(Stephen) Edward (Howden Dene Farm House, Corbridge, Northumberland), *b* 1954; *ed* Fettes; Chm and Man Dir Walter Willson Ltd and Sealand Properties: *m* 1978 (*m diss* 19—), Mrs Harriet N. Thomson, yr da of late Dr Henry Miller, and has issue living, Stephen Henry, *b* 1981, —— Amanda Jo, *b* 1983.

UNCLE LIVING (Son of 2nd baronet)

David Lachlan, *b* 1928: *m* 1955, Dorothy Hazel, da of late S. K. Walton, of Wanwood Hill, Alston, Cumberland, and has issue living, Jeremy David, *b* 1959, — Dawn Elizabeth, *b* 1956. *Residence* – The Red House, Apperley Rd, Stocksfield, Northumberland.

AUNT LIVING (Daughter of 2nd baronet)

Shena Diana, *b* 1927. *Residence* – Spindle Lodge, Spindlestone, Belford, Northumberland.

WIDOW LIVING OF THIRD BARONET

ELIZABETH ANNE MILBURN, MB, BS, el da of late Lt-Col Edward Reed, of Ghyllheugh, Longhorsley, Northumberland: *m* 1st, 1950, Maj Sir Stephen Charles de Lancey Aitchison, 3rd baronet, who *d* 1958; 2ndly, 1974, Roland Antony Cookson, CBE, DCL, who *d* 1991, of The Brow, Wylam, Northumberland.

The 1st baronet, Sir Stephen Harry Aitchison (son of John Gordon Aitchison), was a JP for City and Co of Newcastle-upon-Tyne and for Northumberland. The 2nd baronet, Sir Walter de Lancey Aitchison, FSA (Scot), was Chm and Managing Director of Walter Willson, Ltd, and of de Lancey Lands Ltd. The 3rd baronet, Major Sir Stephen Charles de Lancey Aitchison, late 13th/18th Roy Hussars, was Managing Director of Walter Willson Ltd, and of de Lancey Lands Ltd.

ALBU (UK) 1912, of Grosvenor Place, City of Westminster, and Johannesburg, Province of Transvaal, Union of South Africa.

All turns out well

Sir GEORGE ALBU, 3rd *Baronet*; *b* 5 June 1944; *s* his father, *Sir* GEORGE WERNER, 1963; *ed* Michael House, and Cedara Agric Coll, S Africa: *m* 1969, Joan Valerie, da of late Malcolm Millar, and has issue.

Arms – Per chevron raguly or and vert, in the dexter chief an acorn, in the sinister a flower of a sugar bush, both slipped and leaved, and in base a bear sejant proper. **Crest** – The battlements of a tower or, issuant therefrom a demi-bear proper, holding in the dexter paw a flower of the sugar plant as in the arms.
Residence – Glen Hamish Farm, Richmond, Natal, S Africa.

DAUGHTERS LIVING

Camilla Jane, *b* 1972. ——— Victoria Mary, *b* 1976.

SISTERS LIVING

Susan Nomakepu (*Hon Mrs David Stapleton-Cotton*), *b* 1932: *m* 1955, Hon David Peter Dudley Stapleton-Cotton, and has issue (*see* V Combermere). *Residence* – The Old Buffers, Station Rd, Darling, Cape, S Africa. ——— Julia Mary ALBU, *b* 1937; has resumed her maiden name: *m* 1957 (*m diss* 1978), Hon Michael John Harbottle Grimston, and has issue (*see* B Grimston of Westbury). *Address* – PO Box 67250, Bryanston, S Africa. ——— Caroline, *b* 1943: *m* 1969, Philip G. Lorentz, and has issue living, William George, *b* 1971, — Charles Gordon, *b* 1975, — Marie Louise Caroline Rosie, *b* 1978. *Residence* – 21 Ridge Rd, La Lucia, Durban 4051, S Africa.

The 1st baronet, Sir George Albu (son of Simon Albu, of Berlin), was naturalized as a British subject in Transvaal 1887 and in England 1911, and was Chm and Managing Director of General Mining and Finance Corporation, Ltd. The 2nd baronet, Sir George Werner Albu, was Chm of General Mining and Finance Corporation, Ltd.

ALEXANDER (UK) 1921, of Edgehill, Stamford, Connecticut, U.S.A.

Sir DOUGLAS ALEXANDER II, 3rd *Baronet*; *b* 9 Sept 1936; elder son of late Lt-Cdr Archibald Gillespie Alexander, US Coast Guard, yr son of 1st baronet; *s* his uncle, *Sir* DOUGLAS HAMILTON, 1983: *ed* Rice Univ, Houston, Texas (MA 1961); PhD (1967) Univ of N Carolina; Pres Edgehill Investment Co: *m* 1958, Marylon, da of Leonidas Collins Scatterday, of Worthington, Ohio, USA, and has issue.

꿈rms – Azure, on a chevron between three lymphads, sails furled, oars in action or, as many grenades fired proper. Crest – In front of a talbot's head erased sable, gorged with a collar gemelle gules, two crescents or.
Residence – 2499 Windsor Way Court, Wellington, Florida 33414, USA.

SONS LIVING

DOUGLAS GILLESPIE, *b* 24 July 1962; *ed* Reed Coll, Portland, Oregon (BA 1984). —— Andrew Llewellyn, *b* 1967, *ed* Bowdoin Coll, Brunswick, Maine (BA 1989).

BROTHER LIVING

Archibald Bonsall (6540 Cholla Drive, Scottsdale, Arizona 85253, USA), *b* 1940: *m* 1967, Catherine Clair, da of John Cyril Biggins, of Montclair, New Jersey, USA, and has issue living, Sean Hamilton, *b* 1970, — Cristina Cripps, *b* 1969.

Vita perit labor non moritur
Life perishes, labour never dies

SISTER LIVING

Margery Griffith, *b* 1945: *m* 1st, 1969 (*m diss* 1971), Richard Danch Cleland; 2ndly, 1972, Frederic James Ramsey III, of 68 Florence Rd, Riverside, Connecticut 06878, USA.

The 1st baronet, Sir Douglas Alexander (son of Andrew Alexander, of Errol, Perthshire and Hamilton, Canada), was for many years Pres of The Singer Manufacturing Co, of New York.

ALEXANDER (UK) 1945, of Sundridge Park, co Kent

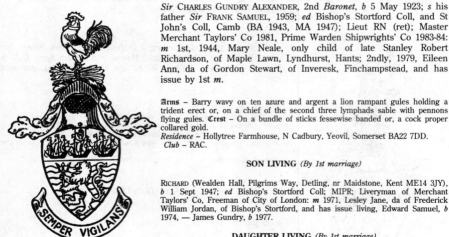

Sir CHARLES GUNDRY ALEXANDER, 2nd *Baronet*, *b* 5 May 1923; *s* his father *Sir* FRANK SAMUEL, 1959; *ed* Bishop's Stortford Coll, and St John's Coll, Camb (BA 1943, MA 1947); Lieut RN (ret); Master Merchant Taylors' Co 1981, Prime Warden Shipwrights' Co 1983-84: *m* 1st, 1944, Mary Neale, only child of late Stanley Robert Richardson, of Maple Lawn, Lyndhurst, Hants; 2ndly, 1979, Eileen Ann, da of Gordon Stewart, of Inveresk, Finchampstead, and has issue by 1st *m*.

꿈rms – Barry wavy on ten azure and argent a lion rampant gules holding a trident erect or, on a chief of the second three lymphads sable with pennons flying gules. Crest – On a bundle of sticks fessewise banded or, a cock proper collared gold.
Residence – Hollytree Farmhouse, N Cadbury, Yeovil, Somerset BA22 7DD.
Club – RAC.

SON LIVING (*By 1st marriage*)

RICHARD (Wealden Hall, Pilgrims Way, Detling, nr Maidstone, Kent ME14 3JY), *b* 1 Sept 1947; *ed* Bishop's Stortford Coll; MIPR; Liveryman of Merchant Taylors' Co, Freeman of City of London: *m* 1971, Lesley Jane, da of Frederick William Jordan, of Bishop's Stortford, and has issue living, Edward Samuel, *b* 1974, — James Gundry, *b* 1977.

DAUGHTER LIVING (*By 1st marriage*)

Always watchful

Jennifer, *b* 1949.

BROTHER LIVING

John Edward, *b* 1924; late Lieut RNVR: *m* 1953, Maureen Dickson, and has issue living, Jonathan Charles, *b* 1957, — Catherine, *b* 1954. *Residence* – Dene Court, Oldfield Drive, Heswall, Wirral, Cheshire.

SISTERS LIVING

Elizabeth Jane, *b* 1927: *m* 1949, Lieut-Col Peter Walter Swinton Boult, TD, and has issue living, Geoffrey Pattisson, *b* 1957, — Rosanne Margaret, *b* 1950, — Alison Judith, *b* 1955. *Residence* – Wellwood, Watts Lane, Chislehurst, Kent. —— Margaret Mary, *b* 1929: *m* 1951, Neville Manwaring Wells and has issue living, Michael Edward Alexander, *b* 1956, — Martin Charles Stanley, *b* 1959, — Frances Mary, *b* 1954. *Residence* – Wood End, Kent Hatch, Edenbridge, Kent.

The 1st baronet, Sir Frank Samuel Alexander (son of Edward Alexander, of Highgate, N) was a shipowner and shipbroker, and was Lord Mayor of London 1944-5.

CABLE-ALEXANDER (UK) 1809, of the City of Dublin.

Per mare, per terras
By sea and land

Sir PATRICK DESMOND WILLIAM CABLE-ALEXANDER, 8th *Baronet*; *b* 19 April 1936; *s* his father, *Sir* DESMOND WILLIAM LIONEL, 1988; *ed* Downside, and RMA Sandhurst; late Lt-Col Royal Scots Drag Gds (Carabiniers and Greys); Bursar and Clerk to the Council Lancing Coll since 1984: *m* 1st, 1961 (*m diss* 1976), Diana Frances, eldest da of late Col Paul Heberden Rogers, of Bushey, Herts; 2ndly, 1976, Jane Mary, da of Anthony Arthur Gough Lewis, MD, FRCP, of Oxford, and has issue by 1st and 2nd *m*.

Arms – Per pale argent and sable a chevron, and in base a crescent counterchanged; on a canton azure a harp or, in the sinister chief point a mullet of the last. **Crest** – An armed arm embowed holding a sword proper, charged on the wrist with a mullet or. *Address* – Windrush House, Hoe Court, Lancing, W Sussex BN15 0QX.

SON LIVING *(By 2nd marriage)*

FERGUS WILLIAM ANTONY *b* 19 June 1981.

DAUGHTERS LIVING *(By 1st marriage)*

Melanie Jane, *b* 1963. —— Louise Fenella, *b* 1967.

HALF-SISTERS LIVING

Jacqueline, *b* 1942: *m* 1962, Dillon Godfrey Welchman, of 11 Holmbush Rd, Putney, SW15 3LE, and has issue living, James Dillon, *b* 1969; *ed* Sherborne, and Reading Univ, — Sara Dawn, *b* 1964: *m* 1990, Gregory Sebastian Porter, and has issue living, William Edward *b* 1992. —— Susan, *b* 1948: *m* 1970, Richard Humphrey Hardwicke (c/o Lloyds Bank, 72 Fenchurch St, EC3), and has issue living, Humphrey Richard *b* 1978, — Caroline Amelia, *b* 1977.

HALF-UNCLE LIVING *(son of 6th baronet by 2nd marriage)*

Nigel William ALEXANDER, *b* 1925; *ed* Haileybury; Maj (ret) Grenadier Guards; 1939-45 War: *m* 1964, Anne, da of Bernard Ambrose Wheatley, of Stolford, Somerset, and has issue living, Hugh William, *b* 1967; *ed* Haileybury, — Charlotte Anne, *b* 1971. *Residence* – Rose Cottage, Underhill Lane, Lower Bourne, Farnham, Surrey GU10 3NF.

MOTHER LIVING

Mary Jane, da of James O'Brien, JP, of Enniskillen, co Fermanagh: *m* 1935 (*m diss* 1941), Desmond William Lionel Cable-Alexander, later 7th Bt, who *d* 1988.

WIDOW LIVING OF SEVENTH BARONET

MARGARET MABEL (*Margaret, Lady Cable-Alexander*), da of late John Leopold Burnett, of Dublin: *m* 1942, as his 2nd wife, Sir Desmond William Lionel Cable-Alexander, 7th Bt, who *d* 1988. *Address* – 1 Denne Park House, Horsham, W Sussex.

COLLATERAL BRANCHES LIVING

Grandchildren of late Richard Alexander-Shaw, son of late William John Alexander-Shaw (who had assumed the additional surname of Shaw 1846), 2nd son of 1st baronet:—
  Issue of late Godfrey William ALEXANDER, *b* 1861, *d* 1903, having discontinued the surname of Shaw: *m* 1890, Alice Maude, da of James Priestley, of Bankfield, Taylor Hill, Huddersfield:—
Kathleen, *b* 1892. *Residence* –
  Issue of late Charles Henry ALEXANDER, *b* 1866, *d* 1898: *m* 1890, Susie Macauly, da of Robert Alexander, of Harwich, Kent, Canada:—
Robert Godfrey, *b* 1894. *Residence* –

Of this family the Earls of Caledon are a branch. John Alexander (el son of Capt Andrew Alexander, of Ballyclose, who was attainted in 1689) had three sons (1) John, ancestor of the Alexanders of Milford, co Carlow, (2) Nathaniel, ancestor of the Earls of Caledon and Earls Alexander of Tunis, (3) William, ancestor of William Alexander, 1st baronet, who was Lord Mayor of Dublin. The 2nd baronet was a Director of the Bank of Ireland, and the 3rd baronet was Attorney-General to HM King Edward VII, when Prince of Wales, and a Member of the Council of HRH. Sir Desmond William Lionel Cable-Alexander, 7th Bt, assumed by deed poll 1931 the additional surname of Cable-Alexander in lieu of his patronymic.

HAGART-ALEXANDER (UK) 1886, of Ballochmyle, co Ayr

Perseverance conquers. Without fear

Sir CLAUD HAGART-ALEXANDER, 3rd *Baronet*, son of late Wilfred Archibald Alexander, 2nd son of 2nd Baronet; *b* 6 Jan 1927; *s* his grandfather *Sir* CLAUD, 1945; *ed* Sherborne, and Corpus Christi Coll, Camb (BA); Vice-Lord-Lieut Ayrshire and Arran (Strathclyde) 1983; JP; additional surname of Hagart recognized by decree of Lord Lyon 1948; a DL for Ayr: *m* 1959, Hilda Etain, yr da of late Miles Malcolm Acheson, late Chinese Maritime Customs Ser (D St Albans, colls), and has issue.

Arms – Quarterly: 1st and 4th, per pale argent and sable, a chevron between a fleur-de-lys in chief and a crescent in base all counterchanged, within a bordure parted per pale gules and or, *Alexander*; 2nd, per bend azure and argent, in chief a star of sixteen points or, and in base another star of as many points of the first, on a bend sable a lion passant of the second between two crosses moline of the third, *Hagart*; 3rd, gules, two straight swords in saltire, points downwards, proper, hilted and pommelled or, between two fleur-de-lys in chief and base of the second and two mullets in the flanks argent, *McCaul*. **Crest** – 1st, an elephant passant proper, *Alexander*; 2nd, a lion rampant, proper, *Hagart*.
Seat – Kingencleuch House, Mauchline, Ayrshire KA5 5JL. *Club* – New (Edinburgh).

SONS LIVING

CLAUD, *b* 5 Nov 1963; *ed* Trin Coll, Glenalmond, and Glasgow Univ (BSc): *m* 1994, Elaine Susan, only da of Vincent Park, of Winnipeg, Manitoba, Canada. *Residence* – 3820 West 17th Av, Vancouver, BC, Canada V6S IA4. —— Boyd John, *b* 1966; *ed* Trin Coll, Glenalmond, and Liverpool Univ.

DAUGHTERS LIVING

Helenora Etain, *b* 1960: *m* 1983, Carl C. Smith, and has issue living, Christon Claud William, *b* 1987, — Aidan Boyd Angus, *b* 1988. —— Anna Joanna Elizabeth, *b* 1961: *m* 1984, Michael C. L. Adam, son of C. L. Adam, of Somerset House, Somerset Rd, Wimbledon, and has issue living, James Robert, *b* 1991, — Charlotte Etain, *b* 1989.

SISTER LIVING

Penelope Marion Acheson (*Lady Head*) *b* 1924: *m* 1967, as his second wife, Sir Francis David Somerville Head, 5th Bt, of 10 Fairway, Merrow, Surrey.

COLLATERAL BRANCH LIVING

Issue of late Claud Alexander, 3rd son of 2nd baronet, *b* 1897; *d* 1976: *m* 1st 1928, Maude, who *d* 1936, da of Lt-Col J. Oswald Clazey, of Lamorva, Falmouth; 2ndly 1949, Peggy, formerly wife of late Bernard Lawrence Silley, and da of Ewart Raby le Mare, of Birchington, Kent:—
(By 1st *m*) John Oswald Claud, CB, OBE, *b* 1936; Maj-Gen R Signals; OBE (Mil) 1974, CB (Mil) 1991: *m* 1962, Mary, el da of Col Derek Grant Birkett, OBE, RA, and has issue living, Liza Jane, *b* 1964, — Sharon Louise, *b* 1968.
The 1st baronet, Maj-Gen Sir Claud Alexander (son of Boyd Alexander, of Ballochmyle and Southbar, co Ayr), served in Crimea 1854-5 and was MP for S Ayrshire (*C*) 1874-85.

ALISON (UK) 1852 (Extinct 1970)

Sir FREDERICK BLACK ALISON, 5th and last *Baronet*.

DAUGHTER LIVING OF FIFTH BARONET

Phoebe Ann, *b* 1926: *m* 1947, Leslie Thomas Allen, of Down Cottage, Lamberhurst Down, Lamberhurst, Kent, and has issue living, Richard Thomas, *b* 1948, — Bruce Harry, *b* 1950, — David Frederick, *b* 1953, — Peter Robert, *b* 1961.

HAVELOCK-ALLAN (UK) 1858, of Lucknow

Faithfully

He bears the cross bravely

Sir ANTHONY JAMES ALLAN HAVELOCK-ALLAN, 4th *Baronet; b* 28 Feb 1904; *s* his brother, *Sir* HENRY RALPH MORETON, 1975; *ed* Charterhouse, and in Switzerland; a Film Producer: *m* 1st, 1939 (*m diss* 1952), Valerie Louise (the film actress Valerie Hobson), da of late Cdr Robert Gordon Hobson, RN; 2ndly, 1979, Maria Theresa Consuela (Sara), da of late Carlos Ruiz de Villafranca, formerly Spanish Ambassador to Chile and to Brazil, and has had issue by 1st *m*.

Arms – Quarterly, 1st and 4th sable, a cross potent quarter pierced or, charged with four guttes de sang; in chief two lions heads erased of the second, all within a bordure engrailed erminois; a canton ermine, *Allan;* 2nd and 3rd, vert, a castle double-turreted argent between two fleurs-de-lys in chief, and a crosscrosslet fitchée in base or, *Havelock.* **Crest** – 1st, a demi-lion rampant argent, ducally crowned gules, charged on the shoulder with a cross-crosslet fitchée sable, holding in the dexter paw a cross potent or, supporting in the sinister a rudder of the second; 2nd, a lion rampant gules, semée of ermine spots, charged on the shoulder with a castle argent, sustaining a Danish battleaxe proper.
Address – c/o Lloyds Bank Ltd, 14 Berkeley Sq, W1. *Clubs* – Boodle's, and RAC.

SONS LIVING AND DECEASED (*By 1st marriage*)

Simon Anthony Henry, *b* 1944; *d* 1991. —— (ANTHONY) MARK DAVID, *b* 4 April 1951; *ed* Eton, Durham Univ (BA), and Trin Coll, Camb (LLB); Bar Inner Temple 1974, QC 1993, since when an Assistant Recorder: *m* 1st, 1976 (*m diss* 1984), Lucy Clare, da of late Alexander Plantagenet Mitchell-Innes, of Kitchers, Albury, Herts; 2ndly, 1986, Alison Lee Caroline, da of late Leslie Francis Foster, and has issue living (by 2nd *m*), Miranda Antonia Lousie, *b* 1993. *Residence* – 38 West Sq, SE11 4SP.

HALF-BROTHER LIVING

Gervaise George Michael, *b* 1921: *m* 1946, Rhoda, da of Thomas Beard, of Swansea, and has issue living, Thomas Allan Spencer, *b* 1949, — Louise Charlotte, *b* 1954. *Residence* –

HALF-SISTERS LIVING

Diana Constance (The Nest, Robin Hatch, Pembury Rd, Tunbridge Wells, Kent TN2 4NA): *m* 1939, Evelyn Francis Scott, who *d* 1981, and has issue living, Angus Allan Lindsay, *b* 1940, — Julian Peter Francis, *b* 1946, — David Nigel, *b* 1947, — Mark Michael, *b* 1950, — Ralph Neil Allan, *b* 1958, — Nina Alison Margaret, *b* 1941, — Elaine Ruth, *b* 1953. —— Nancy Stella: *m* 1947, Maj Patrick Thorvald Auchmuty Musters, RA, of 4 Spring Close, Market Overton, Oakham, Leics LE15 7PT, and has issue living, Patrick Havelock Auchmuty, *b* 1952, — Fiona Havelock Auchmuty, *b* 1948, — Gillian Havelock Auchmuty, *b* (twin) 1952, — Nicola Havelock Auchmuty, *b* 1954.

COLLATERAL BRANCHES LIVING

Granddaughter of George Eric Havelock, yr son of Capt Joshua HAVELOCK, next brother of 1st Bt (who was in special remainder to the Baronetcy):—
Issue of late Eric Henry Edwardes Havelock, CB, CBE, *b* 1891, *d* 1974: *m* 1st, 1919, Christina Ramsay Scott, who *d* 1958, da of late Alexander Moodie, of Edinburgh; 2ndly, 1962, Eileen, who *d* 1972, da of late Col John W. H. Potts, RHA, and widow of Maj-Gen Walter Reginald Paul, CBE:—
(By 1st *m*) Elizabeth Kerr, *b* 1920: *m* 1946, Konstanty Kosciuszko, of Apart 2C, 1196 Eastern Parkway, Brooklyn 11213, New York, USA, and has issue living, Stefan Henry, *b* 1959.

Granddaughters of late George Broadfoot HAVELOCK, yst brother of 1st baronet:—
Issue of late Major Beresford Arthur Jardine Havelock (only son), 2nd Batn attached 7th Ser Batn Prince of Wales's (N Staffordshire Regt), *b* 1889, *ka* at Baku Sept 1918 (despatches): *m* (March) 1916, Kathleen Margaret (who *m* 2ndly, 1921, Major Daniel Frederick Bartlett, MBE, Indian Army), da of Sydney Smith, formerly Dep Inspector-Gen of Police, Punjab:—
Patricia Margaret Helen, *b* (Dec) 1916. —— Beres Aileen, *b* (*posthumous*) Feb 1919.

Maj-Gen Sir Henry Havelock, KCB, father of the 1st baronet, distinguished himself by his unparalleled march from Allahabad to Cawnpore and Lucknow, which latter place he held with astonishing bravery against the rebels for two months. A patent of baronetcy in his favour was granted 26 Nov 1857, but as he died two days prior to the date thereof, the honour was extended to his son, Henry Marshman, with special remainder, in default of his issue male, to his father's issue. Lieut-Gen Sir Henry Marshman Havelock, VC, GCB, 1st baronet, Col-in-Ch Roy Irish Regt, who also served with distinction during the Indian Mutiny, assumed by Roy licence 1880 the additional surname of Allan, and sat as MP for Sunderland (*L*) 1874-81, and for Durham, S-E Div (LU) 1885-92 and 1895-97, when he was murdered by Afridis in the Khyber Pass having *m* 1865, Lady Alice Moreton, who *d* 1922, 2nd da of 2nd Earl of Ducie. Sir Henry Spencer Moreton Havelock-Allan, 2nd baronet, was Parliamentary Private Sec to Under-Sec of State for India (Hon E. S. Montagu, MP) 1910-14, and sat as MP for Durham Co, Bishop Auckland Div (*L*) 1910-18. He served during European War 1916-18 as Major 17th Lancashire Fusiliers (wounded).

ALLEN (UK) 1933, of Marlow, co Buckingham (Extinct 1939)

Sir FRANCIS RAYMOND ALLEN, 2nd and last *Baronet.*

DAUGHTER LIVING OF FIRST BARONET

Violet Parkinson, *b* 1903: *m* 1st, 1924, Alfred Francis Hope Baldry; 2ndly, 1942, William Fisher-Luttrelle, and has issue living, (by 1st *m*) Felicia, *b* 1927, — Ann, *b* 1931. *Residence* – 6 Medallion Place, Thames Reach, Maidenhead, Berks.

WIDOW LIVING OF SECOND BARONET

ALTHEA JOAN (BLACK), da of Owen Leonard Hanks, of Wallasey Bay, Essex: *m* 2ndly, 1935, Sir Francis Raymond Allen, 2nd baronet, who *d* 1939, when the title became ext; 3rdly, 1941, Capt Dennis L. Bennett, Staffordshire Yeo, who was *ka* 1942; 4thly, 1945, Lieut-Col Oliver Charles Berger, Roy Scots Greys, of 19 Warwick Sq, SW1, and has issue living (by 4th *m*), one son and one da.

ALLEYNE (GB) 1769, of Four Hills, Barbados
(Name pronounced "Alleen")

Rev Sir JOHN OLPHERTS CAMPBELL ALLEYNE, 5th *Baronet*; *b* 18 Jan 1928; *s* his father, *Capt Sir* JOHN MEYNELL, DSO, DSC, RN, 1983; *ed* Eton, and Jesus Coll, Camb (MA); ordained 1955, Rector of Weeke, Winchester, 1975-93 (ret): *m* 1968, Honor Emily Margaret, el da of late William Albert Irwin, of Linkview Park, Upper Malone, Belfast, and has issue.

Arms – Per chevron gules and ermine in chief two lions heads erased or. **Crest** – Out of a ducal coronet a horse's head argent.
Residence – 2 Ash Grove, Guildford, Surrey GU2 5UT.

SON LIVING

RICHARD MEYNELL, *b* 23 June 1972.

DAUGHTER LIVING

Clare Emma Gila, *b* 1969.

SISTERS LIVING

Non tua te moveant sed publica voti

Let not your own interests move you but rather the wishes of the public

Eileen Violet, *b* 1923. —— Rosemary, *b* 1925: *m* (6 Dec) 1954, John Perry, who *d* (10 Dec) 1954. *Residence* – Greenacres, Minstead, Lyndhurst, Hants.
Sir John Gay, the 1st baronet, represented St Andrew's in the Barbados House of Assembly 1757-67, and was Speaker of the House 1767-97; he had two sisters, one married the 1st Earl of Radnor, and the other, Sir Charles Knowles, 1st baronet.

HEATHCOAT-AMORY (UK) 1874, of Knightshayes Court, Tiverton, Devon

Sir IAN HEATHCOAT-AMORY, 6th *Baronet*; *b* 3 Feb 1942; *s* his father, *Lt-Col Sir* WILLIAM, DSO, 1982; *ed* Eton, a DL and JP for Devon: *m* 1972, (Frances) Louise, da of late (Jocelyn Francis) Brian Pomeroy (*see* V Harberton, colls), and has issue.

Arms – Quarterly: 1st and 4th argent, two bars gules; on a bend engrailed with plain cottises sable, two annulets of the field, *Amory*; 2nd and 3rd, vert, three piles, one reversed in base between the others issuant from the chief, each charged with a pomme, thereon a cross of the second, *Heathcoat*. **Crest** – 1st, the battlements of a tower or, therefrom issuant a talbot's head azure charged with two annulets fessewise, and interlaced gold, *Amory*; 2nd, upon a mount vert, between two roses springing from the same gules, stalked and leaved proper, a pomme charged with a cross or, *Heathcoat*.
Residence – Calverleigh Court, Tiverton, Devon EX16 8BB.

SONS LIVING

WILLIAM FRANCIS, *b* 19 July 1975. —— Harry James, *b* 1977. —— Patrick Thomas, *b* 1979. —— Benjamin David, *b* 1983.

BROTHER LIVING

Charles William, *b* 1945; *ed* Eton; Capt R Green Jackets: *m* 1st, 1977, Harmony Joanna, yr da of Malcolm Charles Alastair Lyell; 2ndly, 1988 (*m diss* 1991), Hon Angela Jane, eldest da of 4th Baron Borwick, MC; 3rdly, 1991, Mrs Diana Elizabeth Mann, and has issue living (by 1st *m*), Simon Charles, *b* 1982, — Toby Derick, *b* 1985. *Residence* – Meethe Barton, S Molton, N Devon EX36 4JA.

SISTERS LIVING

Diana Chrystel, *b* 1938: *m* 1962, Peter Allan Sichel, of Château d'Angludet 33460, Cantanac, France, and has issue living, Allan Gordon, *b* 1962, — James William, *b* 1963, — Charles Edward, *b* 1963 (twin), — Benjamin Pierre, *b* 1966, — David Mark, *b* 1968, — Rebecca, *b* 1978. —— Catherine Elizabeth, *b* 1945 (twin): *m* 1st, 1967 (*m diss* 1975), Michael Godfrey Melvin Groves; 2ndly, 1977, David Alan Drummond Cavender, of The Manor House, Dowlish Wake, Ilminster, Som, and has issue living (by 1st *m*), Alistair Michael William, *b* 1968, — Henry Grenville Havelock, *b* 1971.

UNCLE LIVING *(Son of 2nd baronet)*

Roderick, MC (Allington Grange, nr Chippenham, Wilts), *b* 1907; *ed* Eton; Brig late Royals; High Sheriff of Yorks 1971-72; 1939-45 War in Middle East, Italy and France (MC): *m* 1947, Sonia Myrtle, da of late Commodore Edward Conyngham Denison, MVO, RN (*see* B Londesborough, colls), and widow of Maj Edgar Fitzgerald Heathcoat-Amory, R Devon Yeo (infra), and has issue living, David Philip, MP (12 Lower Addison Gdns, W14), *b* 1949; *ed* Eton, and Ch Ch, Oxford; Treas HM Household (Dep Chief Whip) 1992-93, since when Min of State for Foreign and Commonwealth Affairs; MP (*C*) Wells since 1983: *m* 1978, Linda Margaret Legh, yr da of Alec Desmond Adams, of The Old Rectory, Winchfield, Hants, and has issue living, John *b* 1980, Matthew *b* 1982, Florence *b* 1988, — Bridget Alexandra (*Lady Beck*), *b* 1952: *m* 1st, 1984, Michael R.L. Cockerell, eldest son of Prof Hugh A.L. Cockerell; 2ndly, 1991, as his 2nd wife, Sir (Edgar) Philip Beck, of Pylle Manor, Shepton Mallet, Som, and has issue living (by 1st *m*), Eliza *b* 1985, Alice Fanny *b* 1987.

WIDOW LIVING OF THIRD BARONET

Joyce (*Joyce, Lady Heathcoat-Amory*) (Knightshayes House, Tiverton, Devon), only da of Newton Wethered, of Brook Corner, Brook, Surrey: *m* 1937, Capt Sir John Heathcoat-Amory, 3rd Bt, who *d* 1972.

WIDOW LIVING OF FIFTH BARONET

Margaret Isabella Dorothy Evelyn (*Margaret, Lady Heathcoat-Amory*) (14 Pomeroy Rd, Tiverton, Devon), yr da of Col Sir Arthur Havelock James Doyle, 4th Bt: *m* 1933, Lt-Col Sir William Heathcoat-Amory, 5th Bt, DSO, who *d* 1982.

COLLATERAL BRANCHES LIVING

Grandchildren of late Lieut-Col Harry William Ludovic Heathcoat Heathcoat-Amory (infra):—
Issue of late Richard Frank Heathcoat-Amory, *b* 1903 *d* 1957: *m* 1938, Hon Margaret Irene Gaenor Scott-Ellis (Hele Manor, Exebridge, Dulverton, Som TA22 9RN), da of 8th Baron Howard de Walden:—
(Ian) Mark (Hele Manor, Dulverton, Somerset), *b* 1941; *ed* Eton, and Ch Ch, Oxford: *m* 1982, Charlotte Elizabeth, da of (Doulrish) Evelyn Louis Joll, of 7 Pelham Place, SW7, and has issue living, Evelyn Caroline, *b* 1985, — Olivia Rachel, *b* 1988, — Katharine Eleanor, *b* 1991. —— Evelyn Helen (*Lady Jacomb*), *b* 1939: *m* 1960, Sir Martin Wakefield Jacomb, and has issue living, Matthew Barnabas Wakefield, *b* 1963, — Thomas Richard (The Malt House, Chilton, Oxon), *b* 1964: *m* 1988, Philippa A., yst da of Frederick Thomas Winter, CBE, of Uplands, Lambourn, Berks, and has issue living, Tara *b* 1989, Saffron *b* 1992, — Emma Félise, *b* 1961: *m* 1988, Simon Jock Bruce, of 17 Wendell Rd, W12, and has issue (*see* E Elgin and Kincardine, colls). —— Rachel Belinda (Saddlers, Croscombe, Wells, Somerset), *b* 1946: *m* 1973 (*m diss* 1986), Christopher Joseph Ryan, and has issue living, Jessica Siobhan Elizabeth, *b* 1976, — Margherita, *b* 1978.

Issue of late Lieut-Col Harry William Ludovic Heathcoat Heathcoat-Amory, 3rd son of 1st baronet, *b* 1870; *d* 1945: *m* 1st, 1898, Evelyn Mary, who *d* 1929, da of late Edward James Stanley (E Derby, colls); 2ndly, 1931, Marjorie Una, who *d* 1973, da of Rev Edgar Astley Milne, R of Compton Valence, Dorset, and widow of E. P. Gundry, of Chilfrome, Dorchester:—
(By 1st *m*) Mary Millicent, *b* 1907: *m* 1930, Capt Adam Trevor Smail, 11th Hussars, and has issue living, Simon Trevor (Melcombe Newton Farm, Melcombe Bingham, Dorchester), *b* 1934; *ed* Eton; late Major 11th Hussars: *m* 1960, Margaret, da of late Maj Hon Arthur Bernard John Grenfell (*see* B Grenfell, colls), and has issue living, Tom Patrick *b* 1964, Lucy Jane *b* 1962. *Residence* – Melcombe Newton Farm, Melcombe Bingham, Dorchester, Dorset.

Grandchildren of late Major Ludovic Heathcoat-Amory, 5th son of 1st baronet:—
Issue of late Major Edgar Fitzgerald Heathcoat-Amory, Roy Devon Yeo, *b* 1917, *ka* in Normandy 1944: *m* 1940, Sonia Myrtle (who *m* 2ndly, 1947, Brigadier Roderick Heathcoat-Amory, MC, The Royals (ante)), only da of Commodore Edward Conyngham Denison, MVO, RN (*see* B Londesborough, colls):—
Michael FitzGerald (Chevithorne Barton, Tiverton, Devon), *b* 1941; *ed* Eton, and Ch Ch, Oxford; High Sheriff Devon 1985-86: *m* 1st, 1965 (*m diss* 1970), Harriet Mary Sheila, da of late Lt-Gen Sir Archibald Edward Nye, GSCI, GCMG, GCIE, KCB, KBE, MC (*see* E Ranfurly, colls, 1985 Edn); 2ndly, 1975, (Sarah) Arabella Marjorie, da of late Raimund von Hofmannsthal (*see* M Anglesey, 1980 Edn), and formerly wife of Piers von Westenholz, and has issue living, (by 1st *m*) Edward Fitzgerald, *b* 1967; *ed* Eton, and Bristol Univ: *m* 1994, Alice M.R., elder da of David Paget Thomson, of Little Stoke House, Wallingford, Oxon, — (by 2nd *m*) Lucy Sonia Elizabeth, *b* 1977, — Jessica Diana Mary, *b* 1979. —— Amanda Mary (*Countess Cairns*) (Bolehyde Manor, Allington, Chippenham, Wilts), *b* (*posthumous*) 1944: *m* 1964, 6th Earl Cairns.

The 1st baronet, Sir John, maternal grandson of John Heathcoat, MP, of Bolham, Devon, was partner J. Heathcoat & Co, Lace Manufacturers; MP for Tiverton (*Lib*) 1868-85; assumed by Roy Licence the additional surname and arms of Heathcoat, and was *cr* a *Baronet* 1874. The 4th baronet, *Sir* Derick, KG, GCMG, TD, PC, Chancellor of the Exchequer 1958-60, British High Commr in Canada 1961-63, was *cr* Viscount Amory, of Tiverton, co Devon; *dunm* 1981, when the Peerage became *ext*.

ANSON (UK) 1831, of Birch Hall, Lancashire

Never despair

Sir PETER ANSON, CB, 7th *Baronet*, *b* 31 July 1924; *s* his father, *Sir* EDWARD REYNELL, 1951; *ed* RNC Dartmouth; CEng, FIEE; High Sheriff Surrey 1993, DL 1993; Rear Adm (ret); Comdg Officer, HMS *Alert* 1957-58, on Staff of RN Tactical Sch 1959-61, Comdg Officer, HMS *Broadsword* 1961-62, Dep Dir, Weapons Radio (Naval), Min of Defence 1963-65, and Dir 1965-66, Comdg HMS *Naiad* and Capt (D) Londonderry Sqdn 1966-68, and Comdg HMS *Mercury*, and Capt HM Signal Sch 1968-70, Cdr Naval Forces Gulf 1970-72 and Assist Ch Defence Staff (Sigs) 1972-74; SW Pacific 1941-45 (prisoner); Chm Marconi Space Systems Ltd 1985-; Man Dir Marconi Space Systems Ltd 1984; Divisional Man Satellites Marconi Space and Defence Systems Ltd 1977; Assist Marketing Dir Marconi Space and Defence Systems Ltd 1975; Chm UK Industrial Space Cttee 1980-82; CB (Mil) 1974: *m* 1955, Elizabeth Audrey, da of late Rear Adm Sir (Charles) Philip Clarke, KBE, CB, DSO, and has issue.

Arms – Argent, three bendlets engrailed gules, a crescent for difference. **Crest** – Out of a ducal coronet or, a spear's head proper.
Residence – Rosefield, 81 Boundstone Rd, Rowledge, Farnham, Surrey GU10 4AT.

SONS LIVING

PHILIP ROLAND (34 Martello Rd, Eastbourne, E Sussex BN22 7SS), *b* 4 Oct 1957; *ed* Charterhouse, and Chelsea Coll, London (BPharm). —— Hugo William, *b* 1962: *m* 1986, Sharon E., da of L. J. Gardner, of Palmers Green, London.

DAUGHTERS LIVING

Louisa Frances, *b* 1956: *m* 1st, 1978 (*m diss* 1985), Robert W. A. Cuthill; 2ndly, 1994, Dr Michael Barnsley. —— Sarah Elizabeth, *b* 1966: *m* 1992, Robert A. van Lieshout, only son of J.A. van Lieshout, of Helmond, The Netherlands.

BROTHER LIVING

Sir John, KCB (18 Church Rd, Barnes, SW13 9HN), *b* 1930; *ed* Winchester, and Magdalene Coll, Camb (MA); 2nd Permanent Sec HM Treasury 1987-90; CB (Civil) 1980, KCB (Civil) 1990: *m* 1957, Myrica, da of late Dr H. Fergie-Woods, and has issue living, Christopher Edward, *b* 1958; MA, PhD: *m* 1986, Susan Melanie, PhD, da of R. Robinson, of Cleveleys, Lancs, and has issue living, Thomas Anthony *b* 1987, Matthew David *b* 1990, Joshua Daniel *b* 1993, — Timothy John, *b* 1967, — Rachel Mary, *b* 1961; BA: *m* 1984, Michael John Snelson, son of D. L. Snelson, of Handforth, Cheshire, and has issue living, William Lawrence *b* 1991, Katherine Louise *b* 1989, — Elizabeth Margaret, *b* 1968.

WIDOW LIVING OF SIXTH BARONET

FRANCES ALISON (*Dowager Lady Anson*), da of late Hugh Pollock (see Montagu-Pollock, Bt, colls): *m* 1923, Sir Edward Reynell Anson, 6th baronet, who *d* 1951. *Residence* – 85 Boundstone Rd, Rowledge, Farnham, Surrey GU10 4AT.

The 1st baronet, a younger brother of the 1st Viscount Anson, and uncle of the 1st Earl of Lichfield, greatly distinguished himself during the Peninsular War. The 2nd baronet was killed in a railway accident at Wigan, 2 August 1873. The 3rd baronet, Rt Hon Sir William Reynell, PC, was Warden of All Souls' Coll, Oxford 1881-1914, Vice-Chancellor, Oxford Univ 1898-9, Parliamentary Sec to Board of Education 1902-5, MP for Oxford Univ (LU) 1899-1914, and a Trustee of National Portrait Gallery and of British Museum. The 4th baronet, Sir Denis George William, was drowned in the Thames July 1914, shortly after his succession to the Baronetcy. The 5th baronet, Sir John Henry Algernon, Lieut RN; *d* on active service 1918. The 6th baronet, Sir Edward Reynell served in RN during European War 1915-19, and as Lieut-Col RA during European War 1939-45.

ANSTRUTHER OF THAT ILK (NS) 1694, of Balcaskie, and (NS) 1700 of Anstruther, Fife

Sir RALPH HUGO ANSTRUTHER, GCVO, MC, 7th *Baronet* of 1st and 12th of 2nd creation, son of late Capt Robert Edward Anstruther, MC, only son of 6th Baronet; *b* 13 June 1921; *s* his grandfather, *Col Sir* RALPH WILLIAM, 1934, and his cousin, *Sir* WINDHAM ERIC FRANCIS CARMICHAEL-ANSTRUTHER OF CARMICHAEL AND OF ANSTRUTHER, 1980; *ed* Eton, and at Magdalene Coll, Camb (BA 1940); is a Member of the Queen's Body Guard for Scotland (Roy Co of Archers), a DL of Fife and Caithness, and formerly Major Coldstream Guards; Equerry to HM Queen Elizabeth The Queen Mother since 1959 and Treasurer since 1961; Assist Private Sec 1959-64; Hereditary Carver to the Sovereign, and a Master of the Royal Household in Scotland; 1939-45 War (wounded, MC), Malaya 1948-50 (despatches); CVO 1967, KCVO 1976, GCVO 1992.

Arms – Argent, three piles sable, above the shield, from which is pendent by an orange-tawny ribbon the appropriate badge of a Baronet of Nova Scotia, is placed a chapeau gulse furred ermine thereon a helmet with mantling sable doubled argent and issuant from a crest-coronet of four strawberry leaves (three visible) or is set for crest two arms in armour holding a pole-axe with both hands gauntleted proper. **Motto** – Periissem ni Periissem. **Supporters** – Two falcons with wings expanded proper, beaked and membered gules, belled and jessed or.

Seats – Balcaskie, Pittenweem, Fife; Watten, Caithness.

COLLATERAL BRANCHES LIVING

Grandchildren of late Henry Torrens Anstruther, 2nd son of 5th baronet:—
Issue of late Douglas Tollemache Anstruther, *b* 1893, *d* 1956: *m* 1st, 1914 (*m diss* 1924), Enid who *d* 1964, da of late Lord George Granville Campbell (D Argyll, colls); 2ndly, 1925, Evelyn Mabel, who *d* 1981, da of Sir John Wormald, KBE:—
(By 1st *m*) IAN FIFE CAMPBELL (Estate Office, Barlavington, Petworth, Sussex GU28 0LG; Brooks's Club), *b* 11 May 1922; *ed* Eton and New Coll, Oxford; an author; Capt late R Corps of Signals; a Member of the Queen's Body Guard for Scotland (Roy Co of Archers); 1939-45 War with Argyll and Sutherland Highlanders, Signals and Intelligence Corps: *m* 1st, 1951 (*m diss* 1963), Honor, el da of late Capt Gerald Blake; 2ndly, 1963, Susan Margaret Walker, da of H. St. J. B. Paten, and has issue living, (by 1st *m*) Emily Kate Campbell, *b* 1953, — (by 2nd *m*) Sebastian Paten Campbell, *b* 1962, — Tobias Alexander Campbell, *b* 1968, — Rachel Whittome Campbell, *b* 1965, — Harriet Joan Campbell, *b* 1967: *m* 1991, Hamish H. A. Summers, of 14 Onslow Mews W, S Kensington, SW7 3AF, eldest son of Tony Summers, of Adelaide, Australia, and has issue living, Celestia Nell Campbell *b* 1993, — Eleanor Thurloe Campbell, *b* 1971. —— (Janet) Finetta Campbell (Westwood, Bucklebury Alley, Cold Ash, Newbury, Berks RG16 9NN), *b* 1920: *m* 1st, 1945 (*m diss* 1959), Rev William Pritchard Cole, Chap to Forces; 2ndly, 1968 (*m diss* 1983), Clive Ernest Baker, and has issue living, (by 1st *m*) Michael Henry Campbell, *b* 1945, — Janet Barbara Campbell, *b* 1947.

Grandchildren of late Adm Robert Hamilton Anstruther, CMG, 3rd son of 5th baronet:—
Issue of late Col Philip Noel Anstruther, DSO, MC, *b* 1891, *d* 1960: *m* 1st, 1920 (*m diss* 1931), Mary Hope who *d* 1963, da of Harold Chaloner Lewin, of Birchdale, Bromley, Kent; 2ndly, 1937, Mary Were, of New Zealand; 3rdly, 1952, Mrs Marion Secretan, da of late Capt I. Gregor MacGregor, RNR:—
(By 1st *m*) Robert Lewin, *b* 1924; *ed* Eastbourne Coll; is a FRICS: *m* 1950, Rosemary Nathalie, only da of Com (E.) Guy Ernest Williamson, MBE, RN, and has issue living, Peter Robert, *b* 1955: *m* 1981 (*m diss* 1984), Joanna Mary, da of Ken Herring, OBE, and has issue living, Charlotte Daisy *b* 1982, — Catherine Jane, *b* 1951: *m* 1981, Robert Adrian Emerson, and has issue living, Nicolas *b* 1980, Joseph *b* 1983, — Sally Elizabeth, *b* 1958: *m* 1st, 1978, James Trevor Reader; 2ndly, 1984, John Michael Smith, and has issue living (by 1st *m*), Mark Richard James *b* 1981, Rebecca Claire *b* 1979, (by 2nd *m*) Victoria Wendy *b* 1984. *Residence* – Windy Ridge, Peartree Lane, Dymchurch, Romney Marsh, Kent. —— Jean Mary (The Little House, 2E Southlands Grove, Bromley, Kent BR1 2DQ), *b* 1921: *m* 1951, Fl-Lt Robert (Robin) Owen Blackall, RAF, who *d* 1952.

Grandchildren of late Lieut-Col Robert Hamilton Lloyd-Anstruther, son of late Col James Hamilton Lloyd-Anstruther, son of late Brig-Gen Robert Anstruther, el son of 3rd baronet:—
Issue of late Sir Fitzroy Hamilton ANSTRUTHER-GOUGH-CALTHORPE, Bt, *b* 1872, *d* 1957, who was *cr* a *Baronet* 1929 (see that title).

Granddaughters of late Lt-Col William Anstruther-Gray, of Kilmany, Cupar, Fife, and of Carntyne, Lanarks, 3rd son of Col John Anstruther-Thomson, of Charleton, co Fife, elder son of John Anstruther-Thomson, of Charleton, co Fife, eldest son of Col John Anstruther, 3rd son of 2nd baronet:—
Issue of late William John St Clair ANSTRUTHER-GRAY, MC, PC (*Baron Kilmany*), *b* 1905, *d* 1985; *cr* a *Baronet* 1956, and *Baron Kilmany* (Life Baron) 1966: *m* 1934, Monica Helen, OBE, who *d* 1985, da of late Geoffrey Lambton (*see* E Durham, colls, 1985 Edn):—
Hon Diana Mary, *b* 1936; DL Fife 1992: *m* 1959, James Charles Macnab of Macnab (The Macnab), of Leuchars Castle Farmhouse, Luechars, St Andrews, Fife KY16 0EY, and has issue living, James William Archibald (Macnab of Macnab, yr), *b* 1963: *m* 1994, Dr Jane Louise, da of late Dr David Mackintosh, of Exmouth, Devon, — Geoffrey Charles, *b* 1965, — Virginia Mary, *b* 1960: *m* 1986, Richard Laurence Oliphant Fyffe, elder son of Laurence Fyffe, MC, JP, DL, of Corsindae, Sauchen, Aberdeenshire, and has issue living Alice Catherine *b* 1989, Emma Cicely *b* 1992, — Katharine Monica, *b* 1968. —— *Hon* Jane Caroline, *b* 1943: *m* 1st 1962 (*m diss* 1992), Hon George Anthony Weir; 2ndly, 1992, F. Graham Gillies, who *d* 1992, and has issue (by 1st *m*) (*see* V Weir). *Residence* – Kilmany, Cupar, Fife KY15 4QW.

The 1st baronet of Balcaskie, Sir Robert Anstruther (third son of Sir Philip Anstruther) purchased Balcaskie in 1698. The 5th Baronet was Lord-Lieut of co Fife and sat as MP for co Fife (*L*) 1864-80, and for St Andrews District of Burghs 1885-6. The 6th Baronet was also Lord-Lieut of co Fife. The 1st baronet of Anstruther, Sir John Anstruther, son of Sir William Anstruther, eldest son of Sir Philip Anstruther (ante), was MP for county of Fife, and was created a baronet with remainder to heirs male 6 Jan 1700.

Anstruther-Gough-Calthorpe, see Calthorpe.

ANTROBUS (UK) 1815, of Antrobus, Cheshire

Sir PHILIP COUTTS ANTROBUS, 7th *Baronet*, son of late Geoffrey Edward Antrobus, grandson of Gibbs Crawfurd Antrobus, brother of 2nd Bt; *b* 10 April 1908; *s* 1968; 1939-45 War (prisoner): *m* 1st, 1937, Dorothy Margaret Mary, who *d* 1973, da of late Rev William George Davis; 2ndly, 1975, Doris Primrose, who *d* 1986, da of late Harry George Watts, and widow of Thomas Ralph Dawkins; 3rdly, 1991, Esmé Florence Bayes, da of Dudley Charles Windsor, and widow of Frank Herbert Mawer, and has issue by 1st *m*.

Mindful of God, grateful to friends

Arms – Lozengy or and azure, on a pale gules three estoiles of the first. Crest – Issuing out of rays proper an unicorn's head couped argent, horned and maned or, gorged with a leaf of laurel proper. Supporters – Two horses proper.
Residence – West Amesbury House, Amesbury, Wilts.

SONS LIVING (By 1st marriage)

EDWARD PHILIP (PO Box 695, Rivonia 2128, S Africa), *b* 28 Sept 1938; *ed* Witwatersrand Univ (BSc (Min Eng)) and Magdalene Coll, Camb (MA): *m* 1966, Janet Sarah Elizabeth, who *d* 1990, da of Philip Walter Sceales, of Johannesburg, and has issue living, Francis Edward Sceales, *b* 1972, — Barbara Joanna, *b* 1968, — Sarah Diana, *b* 1970. —— Michael Ronald (PO Box 433, Cradock 5880, S Africa), *b* 1939; Dip of Agric (S Africa): *m* 1968, Sandra, da of J. H. Moolman, of Middleton, Cape Prov, and has issue living, Philip Michael, *b* 1973, — Cherie Joann, *b* 1969, — Elizabeth Ruth, *b* 1971.

DAUGHTER LIVING (By 1st marriage)

Patricia Jennifer, *b* 1948: *m* 1971, Maj Michael George Rodgers Montgomery, RE (c/o Lloyds Bank, Gentlemans Walk, Norwich), and has issue living, Charles George Philip, *b* 1979, — Geraldine Claire Margaret, *b* 1977.

BROTHER LIVING

Crawfurd Ralph (P.O. Box 390, Grahamstown, 6140, S Africa), *b* 1915; 1939-45 War (wounded): *m* 1943, Sheila, da of late Ven Archdeacon A. E. McKenzie, and has issue living, Prof Geoffrey Gordon (5 South St, Grahamstown, CP 6140, S Africa), *b* 1944; *ed* Natal Univ (MSc Agric), and Rhodes Univ (PhD); Registrar (Academic) to Univ of Fort Hare 1988-90, Prof of Economics Rhodes Univ, Grahamstown, since 1991: *m* 1973, Margaret Elizabeth, da of late Roy Nettleton Gordon, and has issue living, Charles Crawfurd *b* 1982, Richard Roy *b* (twin) 1982, Helen Catherine *b* 1976, Shirley Jean *b* 1977, — Margaret Jean (Jacques House, Kingswood Coll, Grahamstown, S Africa), *b* 1947: *m* 1969 (*m diss* 1984), John Rodney Baker, and has issue living, John Andrew *b* 1971, Bruce Stephen *b* 1975, Carol Lynne *b* 1973.

SISTERS LIVING

Ida Dorothy, *b* 1909; 1939-45 War in S African Mil Nursing Ser: *m* 1st, 1937, Frank Thomas Hayes, of Cathcart, Cape Province, S Africa; 2ndly, 1944, Cyril Embleton Hilton Barber, and has issue living (by 1st *m*), Heather Ann, *b* 1938, — (by 2nd *m*) Valerie May Hilton, *b* 1948: *m* 1974, William Gerald Sieberhagen, of 16 Bay View Rd, Wynberg, Cape Prov, S Africa, and has issue living, Hilton John, *b* 1978. *Residence* - 20 Cornwall Rd, Kenton-on-Sea, Cape Prov, S Africa. —— Mary Shakerley, *b* 1913: *m* 1937, Edward Mounsey Gilfillan, JP, and has issue living, Edward Crawford, *b* 1940: *m* 1968, Ruth-Mary MacJannet, and has issue living, Edward Hugh *b* 1970, Ross Mounsey *b* 1974, Claire Mary *b* 1972, — Philip Mounsey, *b* 1950, Dr Vet Sc, Camilla Mary, *b* 1938: *m* 1968, Henry Guerney Gush, and has issue living, Giles Joseph Guerney *b* 1968, — Andrew *b* 1970, — Jocelyn May, *b* 1948: *m* 1978, Christiaan Visser, and has issue living, Richard *b* 1982, Christine *b* 1982. *Residence* - Conway Farm, PO Conway Station, Cape Province, S Africa.

COLLATERAL BRANCHES LIVING

Granddaughters of late Ralph Edmund Antrobus (infra):—
Issue of late Geoffrey John Antrobus, *b* 1904, *d* 1990: *m* 1st, (Jan) 1938, Mary Dorothea Van der Byl, who *d* 1950; 2ndly, 1953, Antonia Marie (BLEW) (2a 5th Av, Parktown North, Johannesburg, S Africa), da of late William H. Carlin, of Johannesburg, S Africa:—
(By 1st *m*) Prunella Mary, *b* (Oct) 1938: *m* 1961, David Burt, of Silton, Peaslake, Surrey, and has issue living, Lyndon Oliver Antrobus, *b* 1965, — Nicola Katherine, *b* 1962. —— Chloe Louise, *b* 1943: *m* 1969, Alan Douglas Saunders, of Gordon Heights, Constantia, Cape Town, S Africa, and has issue living, Thandi Antonia, *b* 1973, — Lucy, *b* 1975.

Grandsons of John Coutts Antrobus (nephew of 2nd baronet):—
Issue of late Ralph Edmund Antrobus, *b* 1871, *d* 1927: *m* 1901, Millicent, who *d* 1937, da of late Edward Lindsey De Morgan:—
Edmund Shakerley Alexander (20A Sherwood Rd, Forest Town, Johannesburg 2193, S Africa), *b* 1919; *ed* Magdalene Coll, Camb (BA 1946), and at McGill Univ, Montreal (MSc 1949, PhD 1955); 1939-45 War as Capt RA: *m* 1947, Shelagh Elizabeth Rich, and has issue living, Edmund Bayard, *b* 1949: *m* 1978, Gillian Van Hasselt, and has issue living, Sara Kate *b* 1988, Lucy *b* 1989, Olivia *b* 1991, — Bryan Ralph, *b* 1951. — Christopher Adrian, *b* 1952. — Robin Clive (28 Broadbent Loop, Leeming, Perth, W Australia 6155), *b* 1954: *m* 1982, Theresa Susan, da of Arthur Allenby Noble, and has issue living, Courtney Lynne *b* 1990.
Issue of late Rev Jocelyn James Antrobus, *b* 1876, *d* 1953: *m* 1915, Justine Mary Louisa, who *d* 1964, da of late Maj William Affleck King (Duckworth-King, Bt, colls):—
Mary Elizabeth (16 Prospect Place, Camden Rd, Bath), *b* 1918.

Grandson of Walter Guy Antrobus (infra):—
Issue of late Robert Michael Antrobus, *b* 1910, *d* 1961: *m* 1st, 1938 (*m diss* 1948), Janet Lyle Holmes, da of late Neil Mackay, of Seapoint, Cape Town, S Africa; 2ndly, 1959, Peggy, da of Douglas Graham, and widow of Donald Halley:—
(By 1st *m*) Norman Hugh (17 Plover St, Horizon, Extension, 1 Roodeport, Transvaal), *b* 1940: *m* 1963, Barbara Gwen, da of E. J. M. Gravitt, of Pietermaritzburg, and has issue living, Stephen Craig, *b* 1965, — Liane Mary, *b* 1966.

Grandchildren of late John Coutts Antrobus (ante):—
Issue of late Walter Guy Antrobus, *b* 1879, *d* 1963: *m* 1907, Kathleen Frances, da of late Brig-Gen Arthur Broadwood, CVO (E Clanwilliam, colls):—
Henry Lindsay (PO Box 428 Umtentweni, Natal 4235), *b* 1916; *ed* Witwatersrand Univ; an AMICE: *m* 1943, Mary Lammie, da of Thomas Howie, of Wankie, Zimbabwe and has issue living, Ronald James, *b* 1950, — Rosemary Lindsay, *b* 1947, — Helen Kathleen, *b* 1951. ⸺ Dennis Ronald, *b* 1920; *ed* Witwatersrand Univ (BSc 1949): *m* 1950, Audrey Eleanor, da of William James McGill, of Rustenberg, and has issue living, Dennis Mark, *b* 1956, Sally Elizabeth, *b* 1952.
Issue of late Lt-Col Ronald Henry Antrobus, MC, DL, *b* 1891, *d* 1980: *m* 1921, Muriel Kathleen, who *d* 1980, da of late Richard Henry Gosling, of Hawthorn Hill, Bracknell, Berks (Dyer, Bt), and widow of Capt Henry Miles Chetwynd-Stapylton (*see* V Chetwynd, colls, 1916 Edn):—
John Ronald Lindsay (The School House, 18 School Lane, Eaton, Congleton, Cheshire CW12 2NG), *b* 1926; *ed* Eton, Magdalene Coll, Camb (MA), and Trin Coll, Oxford; late Lt Duke of Wellington's Regt, and 8th R Irish Hussars; Palestine 1947-48 as Lt 17th/21st Lancers: *m* 1st, 1952 (*m diss* 1960), Ann, el da of late Cdr Denys Royds Brocklebank, RN, of Longbridge House, Warminster, Wilts (*see* E Crawford and Balcarres, colls, 1985 Edn); 2ndly, 1961 (*m diss* 1966), Margaret Jane, only child of late Dr J. H. Penman, of Eskbank, Midlothian; 3rdly, 1966, Rochelle Christine, yr da of late Theodore William Candee, of Pasadena, Cal, USA, and has issue living, (by 1st *m*) Nigel John Lindsay (Grey Wall, Ship St, East Grinstead, W Sussex), *b* 1953; *ed* Michael Hall Sch, Forest Row, — James Hugh Lindsay, *b* 1954; *ed* London Univ (Charing Cross Hosp Med Sch); BSc, MB BS, FRCA: *m* 1983, Elisabeth Anne, yr da of Bryan Jarman Wright, of Norwich, Norfolk, and has issue living, Philip Edward *b* 1987, Lucy Elizabeth *b* 1989, — (by 3rd *m*) Richard Henry Lindsay, *b* 1967; *ed* Keele Univ (BA), — Charles Edward Lindsay, *b* 1968, — Rosemary Caroline Lindsay, *b* 1969, — Jane Elizabeth Lindsay, *b* 1972, — Catherine Mary Lindsay, *b* 1975.
This Baronetcy was conferred upon Edmund Antrobus, of Antrobus Hall, Antrobus Village, Cheshire, with special remainder to his nephews Edmund (who *s* as 2nd Bt) and Gibbs Crawfurd (ancestor of 7th Bt).

ARBUTHNOT (UK) 1823, of Edinburgh

Sir KEITH ROBERT CHARLES ARBUTHNOT, 8th *Baronet*; *b* 23 Sept 1951; *s* his father, *Capt Sir* HUGH FITZGERALD, 1983, *ed* Wellington, and Edinburgh Univ: *m* 1982, Anne R., yr da of late Brig Peter Moore, of Hastings Hill House, Churchill, Oxon, and has issue.

Arms – Azure, a crescent between three mullets, two and one, argent; the whole within a bordure or, charged with three boars' heads, couped gules. **Crest** – A peacock's head proper. **Supporters** – *Dexter*, a wyvern vert vomiting flames proper; *sinister*, a greyhound argent, collared and line reflexed over the back gules.
Seat – Mount Ulston, Jedburgh, Roxburghshire. *Residence* – Whitebridge, Peebles, Peebleshire.

SONS LIVING

ROBERT HUGH PETER, *b* 2 March 1986. ⸺ Patrick William Martin, *b* 1987.

DAUGHTER LIVING

Alice Elizabeth Mary, *b* 1990.

BROTHER LIVING

David William Patrick, *b* 1953; *ed* Wellington: *m* 1988, Diane, only da of John Yeomans, of Hill House, Baughurst, Hants, and has issue living, Phoebe Elizabeth, *b* 1988, — Rosanna Mary, *b* 1989.

SISTER LIVING

Christian Aline, *b* 1950: *m* 1973, (Geoffrey) John Morley (*see* V Hood, colls), and has issue living, William Everard Hugh, *b* 1980, — Aline Elizabeth Georgina, *b* 1974, — Emily Alice, *b* 1977. *Residence* – Mount Ulston, Jedburgh, Roxburghshire.

WIDOW LIVING OF SEVENTH BARONET

JULIA GRACE (*Julia, Lady Arbuthnot*), only da of late Lt-Col Frederick Gerard Peake, CMG, CBE, of Hawkslee, St Boswells, Roxburghshire, and formerly wife of — Grant: *m* 1977, as his 2nd wife, Capt Sir Hugh Fitzgerald Arbuthnot, 7th Bt, who *d* 1983. *Residence* – East Border Farm, Brundeanslaws, Jedburgh, Roxburghshire.

COLLATERAL BRANCHES LIVING

Grandchildren of late Henry FitzGerald Arbuthnot (infra):—
Issue of late Hugh FitzGerald Arbuthnot, *b* 1903, *d* 1990: *m* 1928, Kathleen Phyllis (Peggy), who *d* 1982, da of late Reginald Walter Sheppard, of Looe:—
Robert Ian FitzGerald (Robin), *b* 1933; *ed* Haileybury; 2nd Lieut Royal Warwicks Regt; *d* of gunshot wounds while serving in Korea, 1953. ⸺ Patrick Stephen FitzGerald (The Litten, Grimsdells Lane, Amersham, Bucks), *b* 1936; *ed* Haileybury: *m* 1967, Jennifer Anne, da of late Sidney George Roe, and has issue living, Simon Charles FitzGerald, *b* 1969. ⸺ Rosemary Elizabeth FitzGerald, *b* 1930; *ed* Headington Sch, Oxford, and Bristol Univ (BA): *m* 1957, William Allen Humpherson, FRCO,

BDS, LRAM, of The White Cottage, Somerset Rd, Reigate, Surrey, and has issue living, Robert William, *b* 1958, — Michael Hugh, *b* 1962, — Edward Allen, *b* 1970, — Susan Linley, *b* 1960.

Granddaughter of late Rev Robert Keith Arbuthnot, 3rd son of 2nd baronet:—
Issue of late Henry FitzGerald Arbuthnot, *b* 1873, *d* 1917: *m* 1900, Ivy, who *d* 1959, da of late John W. Minchin, of Ootacamund, Madras:—
Madeline Ivy, *b* 1908: *m* 1928, Geoffrey Wilmot Teed, who *d* 1989, and has issue living, Christopher Litherland (80 Linden Av, Herne Bay, Kent), *b* 1933: *m* 1978, Mary Rose, da of late Alan Edward Hearn, of Harold Wood, Essex, and widow of Arthur Tilbrook, — Hugh Arbuthnot (65 Fisherton St, Salisbury) *b* 1936: *m* 1966, Marjorie Gillian, BA, da of late Charles Theodore Law-Green, Notary Public, of Bradford, and has issue living, Jane Arbuthnot *b* 1970, Caroline Green *b* 1972, — Ruth Sinclair, *b* 1930: *m* 1954, Derek Hale, of Glade House, 28a London Rd, Great Glen, Leics, and has issue living, Jonathan Wilmot *b* 1964: *m* 1993, Gaynor, da of E.R. Astin, of Budleigh Salterton, Christine Morley *b* 1956: *m* 1984, Michael Andrew Hollis, of 36 Fleckney Rd, Kibworth Beauchamp, Leics (and has issue living, Nicholas Elkin *b* 1987, Matthew Jonathan *b* 1990, Sarah Morley *b* 1986), Deborah Sinclair *b* 1959 (has issue living, by John Martin Stew, Edward Christopher *b* 1992), — Aurea Wilmot *b* 1943: *m* 1968, Christopher James Collier Hart, of 38 High St, Marshfield, Chippenham, and has issue living, Barnaby Teed *b* 1975, Alexandra Prinz *b* 1972. *Residence* – The Halt, 2 Lowercroft, Fairford, Glos.

Granddaughters of late Maj John Bernard Arbuthnot, MVO (infra):—
Issue of late David George Arbuthnot, *b* 1905, *d* 1985: *m* 1st, 1933 (*m diss* 1946), Hon Elizabeth Dorothy Kemeys-Tynte, later Baroness Wharton, who *d* 1974; 2ndly, 1946, Barbara Margherita, who *d* 1974, da of Francis Chiappini, JP, of Wynberg, Cape Province, S Africa, and widow of Percy Seymour Douglas-Hamilton (*see* D Hamilton, colls):—
(By 1st *m*) (*See* Bs Wharton).

Grandchildren of late Col George Arbuthnot, son of late John Alves Arbuthnot, 2nd son of 1st baronet:—
Issue of late Major John Bernard Arbuthnot, MVO, *b* 1875, *d* 1950: *m* 1903, Olive, who *d* 1953, only da of late Sir Henry Arthur Blake, GCMG:—
Terence John (6 Sheridan Court, Barkston Gdns, SW5 0ET), *b* 1906, *ed* Eton; Group-Capt RAF (ret), and an OStJ; Mohmand Operations 1935 (despatches), 1939-45 War in France (despatches, Order of Leopold of Belgium, Croix de Guerre): *m* 1937, Karin Gunborg, who *d* 1983, da of Carl Adolph Sundgren, of Hudiksvall, Sweden, and has issue living, (John Sten) Robert (Flat 6, 86 Redcliffe Gdns, SW10), *b* 1941; *ed* Sherborne: *m* 1st, 1971 (*m diss* 1982), Elizabeth Marjorie, da of Sir (Charles) Henry Plumb (later Baron Plumb); 2ndly, 1983, Swee Lien Ong, da of Boon Bah Ong, of Petaling Jaya, W Malaysia, and has issue living (by 2nd *m*), James Robert Yu-Ming *b* 1984, Jennifer Mei-Chen *b* 1987, — Susan Christine, *b* 1939: *m* 1970, B. John Minchin, who *d* 1987, and has issue living, Karen Christine *b* 1972, Joanna Lesley *b* 1975, — Diana Karin, *b* 1942: *m* 1963, Geert Holger Sonderhoff, of 316 Stevens Drive, W Vancouver, BC, Canada, and has issue living, Terence Sven *b* 1965, Stefan Andrew *b* 1967. —— Irene Joan Grace, *b* 1904

Granddaughters of late Maj John Bernard Arbuthnot, MVO (ante):—
Issue of late Cdr Bernard Kieran Charles Arbuthnot, DSC, *b* 1909; *d* 1975: *m* 1939, Rosemary Harold, who *d* 1978, da of late Lt-Col Harold Thompson, DSO:—
Shirley, *b* 1949: *m* 1970, Nigel Murray, of Myrtle Grove, Youghal, co Cork, and has issue living, Simon Peregrine Gauvain, *b* 1974, — Iona Louise Arbuthnot, *b* 1972. —— Penelope Anne, *b* 1953: *m* 1983, Michael Drake Stewart, of Stokestown, New Ross, co Wexford, and has issue living, Kerry Blake (a da), *b* 1987.

Grandson of late Adm Sir Geoffrey Schomberg Arbuthnot, KCB, DSO (infra):—
Issue of late Michael Geoffrey Henderson Arbuthnot, *b* 1919; *d* 1948, (Nicole) Patricia (5 Egerton Place, SW3 2EF), da of late Lt-Col Richard Leslie Halliburton Collins, of Thurston House, Bury St Edmunds:—
Peter Geoffrey (52 Lawrence St, Glasgow G11 5HD), *b* 1950; *ed* Stowe, and Trin Coll, Camb: *m* 1979, Belinda, el da of Herbert Terry-Engell, of Guernsey, CI, and has issue living, James Nicholas, *b* 1982, — Harriet Emily *b* 1984.

Granddaughter of late Adm Charles Ramsay Arbuthnot, 2nd son of late George Clerk Arbuthnot, 3rd son of 1st baronet:—
Issue of late Adm Sir Geoffrey Schomberg Arbuthnot, KCB, DSO, *b* 1885, *d* 1957: *m* 1913, Jessie Marguerite, who *d* 1947, 2nd da of late William Henderson, of Berkley House, Frome:—
Mary Marguerite, *b* 1914: *m* 1934, Lt-Col Walter Stuart Augustus Clough-Taylor, late RWF (E Castle Stewart), who *d* 1988, and has issue living, Juliet Mary, *b* 1935: *m* 1st, 1961 (*m diss* 19—), Timothy Charles Austin Horn; 2ndly, 1978, Colin Malcolm Paul, of Yew Tree Cottage, Halland, Lewes, Sussex BN8 6PW, and has issue living (by 1st *m*), Francis William Austin *b* 1962, Charlotte Mary *b* 1965.

Grandchildren of late James Arbuthnot, 3rd son of late George Clerk Arbuthnot (ante):—
Issue of late (George) Ramsay Arbuthnot, *b* 1880, *d* 1932: *m* 1910, Rose Anna Branson, who *d* 1973:—
George Ramsay (56 Wimborne Close, Bransholme, Hull), *b* 1930: *m* 1950, Sheelah Margaret Inchbold, and has issue living, Graham Stewart, *b* 1952; *ed* Salthouse High Sch, — Glynis Kathleen, *b* 1954: *m* 1977 (*m diss* 1988), John Campbell, and has issue living, Jamie John *b* 1980, Zoe *b* 1978, — Colleen, *b* 1964: *m* 1984, Philip Dolan, and has issue living, Kelly Arbuthnot *b* 1986, Lynsey Caroline Arbuthnot *b* 1988, — Alison Georgina, *b* 1968. —— Ruby Molly, *b* 1912: *m* 1941, Reginald Mullet, of 17 Pitman Av, Barton-on-Humber, Lincs. —— Ivy, *b* 1913: *m* 1931, (William Charles) Norman Chilvers, who *d* 1986, of 52 Graham Av, Hull, and has had issue, Raymond Dennis, *b* 1932; *d* 1994, — David, *b* 1937, — Michael Charles, *b* 1949, — Malcolm Roy, *b* 1954, — Betty Doreen, *b* 1934, — Joyce, *b* 1936, — Joan Mary, *b* 1944, — Audrey Lyn, *b* 1952. —— Queenie Steward, *b* 1923: *m* 1941, Lesley Fox, of 7 Snowhill Close, Bransholme, Hull, and has issue living, Norman, *b* 1942, — Raymond, *b* 1948, — Sylvia, *b* 1953.

Grandchildren of late Lt-Col Archibald Hugh Arbuthnot (infra):—
Issue of late Lt-Cdr Archibald Hugh Gough Arbuthnot, RN, *b* 1900; *d* 1959: *m* 1st, 1935 (*m diss* 1954), Molly Irene Frances Weeks; 2ndly, 1955, (Emma) Mary (4 Jesmond Rd, Hove), da of late Rev Gilbert Ambrose Bell, MA:—
(By 2nd *m*) Viola Jane, *b* 1957.
Issue of late Maj Patrick Charles Arbuthnot, *b* 1902, *d* 1988: *m* 1952, Evelyn Margaret (Quay Head, Sampford Peverell, Tiverton, Devon EX16 7BS), da of late George Robert Crawford, of Leamington:—
Patrick Hugh Alexander (Chorley Cottage, 1 Haddon Road, Chorleywood, Herts), *b* 1954; *ed* Blundell's, and Sidney Sussex Coll, Camb: *m* 1988, Susan Elizabeth, da of John Frederick Shaw, of Auckland, NZ, and has issue living, Charles Alexander, *b* 1990, — Robert Hugh, *b* 1991. —— Colin Hugh David, *b* 1957; *ed* Blundell's, and Sidney Sussex Coll, Camb.
Issue of late Ernest Douglas Arbuthnot, *b* 1905, *d* 1984: *m* 1939, (Eveline) Mary (10 Vicar St, Wymondham, Norfolk), da of late Harold Morgan, of Worksop, Notts:—
Antony Hugh Gough (Runham, Norfolk), *b* 1948; *ed* Blundell's: *m* 1974, Frances, da of S/Ldr F. W. Williamson, of Garveston, Norfolk, and has issue living, Rupert, *b* 1981, — Emily Kate, *b* 1974. —— Robin Douglas, *b* 1951: *ed* Blundell's: *m* 1979, Elizabeth Ann, da of F. C. Palmer, of Yarmouth, Norfolk, and has issue living, Kitty Ann, *b* 1980, — Amy Elizabeth, *b* 1984. —— Ann Faith, *b* 1941; JP, BA, MB, BS, MRC (Psych): *m* 1966, Raymond Barker, and has issue living, Kate Abigail, *b* 1973, — Lucy Grace, *b* 1975.

Grandchildren of late Maj Archibald Ernest Arbuthnot, 3rd son of Archibald Francis Arbuthnot, 4th son of 1st baronet:—

Issue of late Lieut-Col Archibald Hugh Arbuthnot, *b* 1874, *d* 1957: *m* 1st, 1900, Gertrude, who *d* 1918, da of late Rev Frederick Charles Green, V of Denmead, Hants; 2ndly 1920, Marjory, who *d* 1975, da of late Rev Howard Beech, formerly R of Barlavington and Burton-with-Coates, Sussex:—

(By 1st *m*) Sheila Gertrude Tollemache, *b* 1917; 1939-45 War as Subaltern, ATS: *m* 1942, Maj Roy Dunlop, MBE, Derbyshire Yeo, of Meadow Cottage, Aldingbourne, nr Chichester, W Sussex, and has issue living, Robert Andrew (Chilgrove Cottage, Chilgrove, Chichester, Sussex), *b* 1948: *m* 1985, Catherine Jennifer Ewart, and has issue living, Robert James *b* 1987, Letitia Annabel *b* 1989, — Caroline Jane, *b* 1944: *m* 1973, James Lawrence Monro, MB, BS, FRCS, of Rolle House, East Tytherley, nr Salisbury, Wilts, and has issue living, Charles Reed *b* 1975, Andrew James *b* 1981, Rosanne Elspeth *b* 1978, — Elspeth Marilyn (44 Tivoli St, Cheltenham, Glos), *b* 1951: MB, BS, DA, DRCOG. —— (By 2nd *m*) Faith Deborah Etrenne, *b* 1921; 1939-45 War as Subaltern, ATS: *m* 1948, Edmund O'Donnel Colley Grattan, FRCS, of Quoins, Pound Place, Petworth, W Sussex, late Colonial Med Ser, Kenya, who *d* 1985, and has issue living, Howard Colley Arnout Hugh, *b* 1949; *ed* Wellington Coll, — Clive Edmund Hume, *b* 1953; *ed* Wellington Coll, and King's Coll, Camb; MRCP: *m* 1980, Diana Mary, da of late Lt-Cdr William John Prowse, RN, and has issue living, Amanda Mary Winifred *b* 1983, Harriet Lucy *b* 1988, Abigail Frances *b* 1991, Claudia Etrenne *b* 1994, — Sarah Faith Madalyn, *b* 1950: *m* 1981, Iain Charles Mackie, ARICS, and has had issue, Alistair Graham *b* 1983, Neil Edmund *b* 1986, Ewan James Stuart *b* and *d* 1988, Edward James Stephen *b* 1991, — Clare Winifred Melissa, *b* 1956.

Issue of late Capt Ernest Kennaway Arbuthnot, DSO, RN (ret), *b* 1876 *d* 1945: *m* 1st, 1910, Edith Elizabeth (the actress Miss Evie Greene), who *d* 1917, da of Richard Bentley Greene, formerly of Parnholt, Laburnum Grove, Portsmouth; 2ndly, 1920, Gladys who *d* 1946, da of late William Butland Mann, of Downe, Broadhampton, S Devon:—

(By 2nd *m*) John Keith, OBE, RN (23 Bowfell Rd, W6 9HE; 11 Ivry St, Ipswich, Suffolk IP1 3QP; Naval and Military Club), *b* 1927; Lt-Cdr RN (ret); 1939-45 War; Korea 1951 and 1954; OBE (Mil) 1967: *m* 1949, Susan Philippa, only da of Kenneth Petrie Letts, of Tickerage Mill, Blackboys, Sussex, and has had issue, Richard Keith (87 Haverhill Rd, SW12), *b* 1950: *m* 1st, 1978 (*m diss* 1980), Jacqueline Hazel, da of George William White; 2ndly, 1984, Anne L. Pitman, — Charles Petrie *b* 1959: *m* 1991, Penelope Jane, only da of J.F.J. Dickinson, of Kirby-le-Soken, Essex, — Sally Anne, *b* 1954: *m* 1st, 1972 (*m diss* 1978), Richard Dumbrell-Howie; 2ndly, 1983, Brian Bovie, of Flat 3, Arndale, Anglesea Rd, Kingston, Surrey, — (Philippa) Jane, *b* 1961; WPC Chelsea Police Station; *k* in IRA bomb attack nr Harrods, 1983. —— Peter Kennaway (Winstons, Fieldgate Close, Monks Gate, Horsham, Sussex), *b* 1930; Lt RN (ret); Korea 1952: *m* 1957, Mia, el da of late Maj Percy Montagu Nevile, of Skelbrooke, Yorks, and has issue living, Matthew Kennaway, *b* 1959, — Mr and Mrs Peter K. Arbuthnot also have two adopted das, Katherine Jane, *b* 1964: *m* 1987, Keith Robert Howe, of 12 Rushwood Close, Haywards Heath, W Sussex, yst son of F. J. Howe, of Newcastle-upon-Tyne, — Emma Mary, *b* 1966: *m* 1992, Nigel S. Dent, of 25 Monks Walk, Beeding, Steyning, W Sussex, son of late C. R. Dent, of Steyning, W Sussex.

Grandchildren of late Robert George Arbuthnot, 4th son of late Archibald Francis Arbuthnot (ante):—

Issue of late Capt Robert Wemyss Muir Arbuthnot, MC, *b* 1889, *d* 1962: *m* 1915, Mary, who *d* 1986, elder da of Norman Coghill, of Almington Hall, Market Drayton:—

Rev Andrew Robert Coghill, *b* 1926; *ed* Eton; 1939-45 War as Capt Scots Guards (wounded), Chm Arbuthnot Latham Holdings Ltd 1974-81; Dir Sun Alliance and Lon Insurance 1970-91; ordained a Priest 1975, Lon Healing Mission: *m* 1952, Mrs Audrey Eileen Dutton-Barker, da of Denys Billinghurst Johnson, MC, of Midhurst, Sussex, and has issue living, Charles Robert Denys (17 Frewin Rd, SW18 3LR), *b* 1956; *ed* Eton, and Camb Univ (MA): *m* 1985, Jennifer Rosemary, da of C. T. Arden-White, of Wormley, Surrey, and has issue living, Alexander Barnabas David *b* 1993, Kezia Louise *b* 1987, Johanna Rachel *b* 1989, — Caroline Rose, *b* 1954: *m* 1st, 1977 (*m diss* 1988), Paul J. Francis Clusker; 2ndly, 1988, Andrew Gueter, and has issue living (by 1st *m*), Rowan *b* 1978, Jade *b* 1980, Sacha *b* 1984, Christian *b* 1986, (by 2nd *m*) Samuel *b* 1990. *Residence* – Monksfield House, Tilford, nr Farnham, Surrey. —— Juliet Mary Gough, *b* 1917: *m* 1939, Guy Marsden Halsey, TD, who *d* 1990 (*see* Halsey, Bt, colls). *Residence* – Whitehouse Farm, Gaddesden Row, nr Hemel Hempstead, Herts HP2 6HG.

This family is a branch of the Lairds of Arbuthnot, who have held lands in Kincardineshire from about 1160. The 1st baronet, Sir William, Lord Provost of Edinburgh in 1822, entertained George IV to a public banquet in that city, and was created a baronet by the King in person, the patent, however bearing date 1823. The 4th baronet, Rear-Adm Sir Robert Keith Arbuthnot, KCB, MVO, was *ka* at the battle of Jutland 1916 (despatches, posthumous KCB). The 5th baronet, Brig-Gen Sir Dalrymple Arbuthnot, CMG, DSO, served in S Africa 1900-1901, and in European War 1914-18 (CMG, DSO). The 6th baronet, Major Sir Robert Dalrymple, 24th Lancers, was *ka* in Normandy 1944.

ARBUTHNOT (UK) 1964, of Kittybrewster, Aberdeen

Praising God

Sir WILLIAM REIERSON ARBUTHNOT, 2nd *Baronet*; *b* 2 Sept 1950; *s* his father, *Sir* JOHN SINCLAIR-WEMYSS, MBE, TD, 1992; *ed* Eton; employed with Arbuthnot Latham Holdings Ltd 1970-76; Joynson-Hicks & Co, Solicitors 1978-81; Underwriting Member of Lloyd's; Liveryman of Worshipful Co of Grocers.

Arms – Azure, a crescent between three mullets argent, a bordure gules charged with two escallops in chief and a buck's head cabossed or in base, and in centre chief (overlapping bordure) an inescutcheon argent. **Crest** – A peacock's head and neck proper, accompanied on either side by a spray of strawberry leaves vert, each flowered of a cinquefoil Argent.
Residence – 14 Ashburn Gdns, SW7 4DG.

BROTHER LIVING

JAMES NORWICH, MP, *b* 4 Aug 1952; *ed* Eton, and Trin Coll, Camb (MA); Bar Inner Temple 1975 and Lincoln's Inn 1977; MP (C) for Wanstead and Woodford since 1987: *m* 1984, Emma Louise, da of (John) Michael Broadbent, of 87 Rosebank, Holyport Rd, SW6, and has issue living, Alexander Broadbent, *b* 1986, — Katherine Rose Joste, *b* 1989, — Eleanor Sophie Duff, *b* 1992.

SISTERS LIVING

Elizabeth Mary, *b* 1947; *ed* St Mary's Sch, Calne, and Kent Univ (BA). —— Louise Victoria, *b* 1954; *ed* St Mary's Sch, Calne, and Exeter Univ (LLB); Solicitor: *m* 1984, David Bernard Lancaster, Solicitor, of Beech House, Ramsdell, Basingstoke RG26 5PR, only son of late Maj Bernard Thomas Lancaster, of Salisbury, Wilts, and has issue living, Rachel Alice, *b* 1985, —

Rebecca Saskia, *b* 1987, — Tamara Louise, *b* 1988. —— Alison Jane, *b* 1957; *ed* Benenden, and New Hall, Camb (MA); Solicitor.

WIDOW LIVING OF FIRST BARONET

(MARGARET) JEAN (*Lady Arbuthnot*), yr da of late (Alexander) Gordon Duff: *m* 1943, Sir John Sinclair-Wemyss Arbuthnot, 1st Bt, MBE, TD, who *d* 1992. *Residence* – 7 Fairholt St, SW7 1EG.

The 1st baronet, Sir John Sinclair-Wemyss Arbuthnot, MBE, TD (el son of Maj Kenneth Wyndham Arbuthnot, Seaforth Highlanders, and grandson of William Reierson Arbuthnot, 5th son of George Arbuthnot of Elderslie, brother of Sir William Arbuthnot, 1st Bt (*cr* 1823)), was MP (C) for Dover Div of Kent 1950-64, a Church Commr for England 1962-77, and a Member of Church Assembly and Gen Synod of Church of England 1955-75.

ARCHDALE (UK) 1928, of Riversdale, co Fermanagh

Follow the destiny allotted

Sir EDWARD FOLMER ARCHDALE, DSC, RN, 3rd *Baronet*; *b* 8 Sept 1921; *s* his father, *Vice Adm Sir* (NICHOLAS) EDWARD, CBE, 1955; *ed* Copthorne Sch, and RNC Dartmouth; served WW II; Capt RN (ret); 1939-45 War (despatches, DSC): *m* 1954 (*m diss* 1978), Elizabeth Ann Stewart, da of late Maj-Gen William Boyd Fellowes Lukis, CBE, RM, and has issue.

Arms – Quarterly 1st and 4th, azure, a chevron ermine between three talbots passant or, *Archdale*; 2nd, or, a chevron sable, *Mervyn*; 3rd quarterly, 1st and 4th azure, three fleurs-de-lis or; 2nd and 3rd gules, three gem rings gold, all within a bordure or, charged with a tressure flory, gules, in the centre point an inescutcheon argent charged with a tilting spear and sword saltireways, points upwards proper, *Montgomery*. **Crest** – Out of a ducal crest coronet or, an heraldic tiger's head argent, maned, tufted and armed sable. **Motto** – Data Fata Secuta.
Residence – 19 Dermott Rd, Comber, co Down BT23 5LG.

SON LIVING

NICHOLAS EDWARD, *b* 2 Dec 1965.

DAUGHTERS LIVING

Annabel Frances, *b* 1956. —— Lucinda Grace, *b* 1958: *m* 1991, Targino Luedy Kalid Filho, and has issue living, Sibylla Archdale, *b* 1993.

COLLATERAL BRANCHES LIVING

Issue of late William Porter Palgrave Archdale, CBE, 2nd son of 1st baronet, *b* 1883, *d* 1956: *m* 1918, Alice Edith Palgrave, who *d* 1963, da of late Capt Charles Alexander Price Chetwynd-Talbot (E Shrewsbury, colls):—
Mervyn Talbot, *b* 1924; DL Tyrone 1974, High Sheriff Tyrone 1985: *m* 1951, Aureole Helen, da of late Rev Canon Robert Hamilton Whelan, and has issue living, Peter Mervyn, Lt Cmdr RN; *b* 1953: *m* 1976, Caroline Anne, da of N. R. C. Griffin, and has issue living, Jonathan Talbot *b* 1982, Kathryn Emma *b* 1984, — Geraldine Angel, *b* 1952. *Residence* – The Cottage Farm, Knockmoyle, Omagh, co Tyrone.

Issue of late Lt-Col Audley Quintin Archdale, RHA, 3rd son of 1st baronet, *b* 1886, *d* 1978: *m* 1922, Mary Edith Haigh, who *d* 1987, da of Oliver Bury, MICE, JP, of 7 Vale Av, Chelsea, SW3:—
Rosemary, *b* 1923: *m* 1949, William Anthony Twiston Davies, who *d* 1989, of The Mynde, Much Dewchurch, Hereford, and has issue living, Audley William (43 Chester Sq, SW1), *b* 1950; *ed* Radley: *m* 1985, Hon Caroline Mary Elaine Harbord-Hamond, da of 11th Baron Suffield, MC, and has issue living, Antonia Rose *b* 1987, Sophie Louise *b* 1990, Zoë Caroline *b* 1992, — Nigel Anthony (Grange Hill Farm, Naunton, Cheltenham, Glos), *b* 1957; *ed* Radley: *m* 1st 1981 (*m diss* 1987), Hon Sara Emma Hamilton-Russell, who *d* 1989, da of 10th Viscount Boyne; 2ndly, 1988, Catherine B., yst da of John Farey, of Bredon's Norton, nr Tewkesbury, and has issue living (by 2nd *m*), Sam *b* 1992, — Alexandra Rosemary, *b* 1954: *m* 1986, Robin L.F. Burgess, of Hall Flatt, Scaleby, Carlisle, Cumbria, elder son of late Sir John Lawie Burgess, OBE, TD, JP, DL, of The Limes, Cavendish Terrace, Carlisle, and has issue living, James *b* 1994, Rose Charlotte *b* 1987, Catherine *b* 1989, Rachel *b* 1992, — Penelope Auriol, *b* 1959: *m* 1982, Giles H. Mounsey-Heysham, of Castletown House, Rockcliffe, Carlisle, Cumbria, son of late Maj R. H. G. Mounsey-Heysham, and has issue living, Toby *b* 1984, Benjamin *b* 1986, Rory *b* 1989, Anna *b* 1991. —— Judith Penelope, *b* 1924. —— Anne Alicia, MBE, *b* 1928; MBE (Civil) 1973.

Issue of late Capt Humphrys Archdale, DSC, RN, yst son of 1st baronet; *b* 1896; *d* 1972: *m* 1944, Mary Katherine, who *d* 1975, da of late Robert Leslie Gilbert:—
Gilbert Humphrys, *b* 1947; *ed* Tonbridge: *m* 1984, Susan Anne, elder da of Dennis John Boyles, of Enton, Surrey, and has issue living, Thomas Robert Humphrys, *b* 1988, — Peter Charles Alexander, *b* 1991. *Residence* – Shaftesbury, Dorset.

The 1st baronet, the Rt Hon Sir Edward Mervyn Archdale (el son of Nicholas Montgomery Archdale, of Crock na Crieve, co Fermanagh), was MP for N Div of Fermanagh (*U*) 1898-1903 and 1916-22, and a Member of House of Commons of N Ireland 1921-37. He was first Min of Agriculture, N Ireland 1921-33, and of Commerce 1921-5. The 2nd baronet, Vice-Adm Sir Nicholas Edward Archdale, CBE, served during European War 1914-18 Comdg Submarine Flotillas, and was Senior Naval Officer, Copenhagen 1920.

ARMSTRONG (UK) 1841 of Gallen Priory, King's County

I am still unconquered

Sir ANDREW CLARENCE FRANCIS ARMSTRONG, CMG, 6th *Baronet*, elder son of late Edmund Clarence Richard Armstrong (Bluemantle Pursuivant of Arms), only son of late Andrew Charles Armstrong, 3rd son of 1st baronet; *b* 1 May 1907; *s* his cousin, *Sir* ANDREW ST CLARE, 1987; *ed* St Edmund's Ware, and Christ's Coll, Camb (BA 1928); Permanent Sec, Min of Mines and Power, Federation of Nigeria, ret 1961; CMG 1959: *m* 1st 1930, Phyllis, who *d* 1930, da of late Lt-Col Roland Henry Waithman, DSO; 2ndly, 1932, Laurel May, who *d* 1988, elder da of late Alfred Wellington Stuart, of New Zealand, and has issue by 2nd *m*.

Arms – Quarterly: 1st and 4th argent, issuing from the sinister a dexter arm embowed habited gules grasping the trunk of an oak-tree eradicated and broken at the top proper (Armstrong); 2nd and 3rd argent, two ravens hanging paleways sable suspended from an arrow gules headed and feathered proper piercing both their heads fessways (Murdoch). Crests – 1 (Armstrong), an arm in armour embowed the hand grasping the broken trunk of an oak-tree, all proper; 2 (Murdoch), a raven rising sable pierced through the breast by an arrow as in the arms. Mottoes – Invictus maneo (below), Omnia pro bono (over 2nd crest).
Residence – Thamesfield Court, Henley-on-Thames, Oxon RG9 2LX.

SON LIVING *(By 2nd marriage)*

CHRISTOPHER JOHN EDMUND STUART, MBE (c/o National Westminster Bank, Marlow, Bucks), *b* 15 Jan 1940; *ed* Ampleforth, and RMA; Lt-Col RLC; MBE 1979: *m* 1972, Georgina Elizabeth Carey, 2nd da of Lt-Col W. G. Lewis, of Hayling Island, Hants, and has issue living, Charles Andrew, *b* 1973, — James Hugo, *b* 1974, — Sam Edward, *b* 1986, — Victoria Jane, *b* 1980.

BROTHER LIVING

Edmund Charles Mark, *b* 1914; *ed* St Edmund's Ware, and St John's Coll, Camb (BA 1935); 1939-45 War as Lt (S) RNR; civil servant MoD (ret 1977); assumed by deed poll 1945 the christian names of Edmund Charles Mark in lieu of Edmund Clarence Charles: *m* 1st, 1939 (*m diss* 1949), Patricia Phyllis Vassall, da of late Edward Robert Vassall Adams, of Horn's Cross, Devon; 2ndly, 1951, Dorice, who *d* 1983, da of late William Harold Austin, of White Cottage, Marlow, Bucks, and has issue living (by 2nd *m*), Mark Simon Warneford (20 Boulevard Princesse Charlotte, MC 98000, Monte Carlo), *b* 1954; *ed* The Royal Naval Sch, Tal Handaq, Malta, Univ of Kent at Canterbury, and Sorbonne (BA 1977); with Sotheby's, Monaco: *m* 1992, Roselyne Jeanne Thérèse, da of Roberto Moro, of Cavalaire-sur-Mer, Var, France, and has issue living, Anne-Victoire Emily *b* 1993, — Sean Andrew (Free Hill House, Westbury-sub-Mendip, Wells, Som), *b* (triplet) 1954; *ed* The Royal Naval Sch, Tal Handaq, Malta, and Bristol Univ (BSc 1976, MBA 1992); Co Dir, — Patrick Austin, *b* (triplet) 1954; *ed* The Royal Naval Sch, Tal Handaq, Malta, and Merrist Wood Agric Coll., Surrey; horticulturalist. *Residence* – Free Hill House, Westbury-sub-Mendip, Somerset BA5 1HJ.

SISTER LIVING

Katherine Mary, *b* 1909: *m* 1937, Jerrold Vassall Adams, who *d* 1989, eldest son of late Edmund Robert Vassall Adams (ante), and has had issue, Paul Rory, *b* 1941; MD, PhD; Surg Lt-Cdr RN: *m* 1967, Nicola (High Hedges, Brookthorpe, Glos GL4 0US), elder da of Dr R. Lissau, of Wynstones, Brookthorpe, Glos, and *d* 1983, leaving issue, Guy Luke *b* 1969, Daniel Francis *b* 1971, — Augusta Frances, *b* 1938: *m* 1st, 1958 (*m diss* 1972), Alastair Ian Hamish Valentine; 2ndly, 1972 (*m diss* 1984), Christopher K. Keele; 3rdly, 1984, Michael John Carr Regester, of 4 Abbey Cottages, Medmenham, Bucks SL7 2HB, and has issue living (by 1st *m*), Hamish Guy *b* 1958: *m* 1981 (*m diss* 19—), Sarah Alexandra MacDermott, formerly of Perth, W Australia, Ranald Andrew *b* 1962, Katherine Ann *b* 1959: *m* 1984, Michael Das Gupta, of Perth, W Australia (and has issue living, Nathan Lee *b* 1987, Jessica Dawn *b* 1983, Hannah *b* 1993), (by 2nd *m*), Stephanie Jane *b* 1974, — Sarah Catherine, *b* 1945: *m* 1971, Richard Thomas Holland, of 29 Victoria Park Av, Toronto M4E 351, Canada, and has issue living, Derek Simon *b* 1977, Toby Michael *b* 1984, Camilla Juliet *b* 1973. *Residence* – Granny's Cottage, Whittington Green, nr Marlow, Bucks SL7 2ES.

SISTER LIVING OF FIFTH BARONET

Edith Fisher, *b* 1910: *m* 1933, Clarence Cliff, who *d* 1981, and has issue living, Frances, *b* 1938: *m* 1962, Julius Dienes de Mezökövesd, and has issue living, Katherine *b* 1970. *Residence* – 33 Freyberg Rd, Lyall Bay, Wellington, New Zealand.

COLLATERAL BRANCHES LIVING

Grandchildren of late Andrew Charles Armstrong, 3rd son of 1st baronet:—
Issue of late John Andrew Armstrong, *b* 1892, *d* 1974: *m* 1935, Pauline who *d* 1983, da of late Maj C. O. N. Williams, of Pulborough, Sussex:—
Jill Sara, *b* 1937: *m* 1958, Capt Alexander Bayly Maxwell-Hyslop, 17th/21st Lancers (ret) of The Manor House, Toller Whelme, Beaminster, Dorset DT8 3NN, and has issue living, Lucinda Frances, *b* 1959: *m* 1985, Charles John Moubray, of 22 Narbonne Av, SW4, son of Michael Moubray, of Ridlington House, Rutland, and has issue living, James *b* 1987, — Zara Belinda, *b* 1962: *m* 1988, Maj James Pollock, Irish Gds, son of Brig J. P. O'H. Pollock, of Upper Froyle, Hants.

Granddaughters of late Montagu Fullerton Armstrong, 5th son of 1st baronet:—
Issue of late Jack Proby Armstrong, *b* 1878, *d* 1953: *m* 1912, Maria Dominga Alvarenga (Guatemala City, Guatemala), da of John Molina:—
Martha Florence, *b* 1921: *m* 1st, 1944 (*m diss* 1956), Elmer Page Madsen; 2ndly, 1958, James W. Thornton, of Coventry Estates, Bealeton, Virginia 22712, USA, son of late Sir Henry Worth Thornton, KBE.
Issue of late Frederick Edmund John Armstrong, *b* 1889, *ka* 1919: *m* 1915, Stella, who *d* 1966, el da of J. R. Morgan, late of Portmore, Weymouth:—
Beatrice, *b* 1916: *m* 1937, Com Edric Guy Philip Bromfield Knapton, DSC, RN, and has issue living, Guy Augustus Bromfield, *b* 1940: *m* 1966, Catherine Margaret Ffoulkes, da of Francis Herbert Walker, — Julian Richard Anthony, *b* 1954, — Vanessa Josephine Stella, *b* 1944, — Marie Victoria Gwendolyn, *b* 1947, — Louise Elizabeth Teresa, *b* 1956.
—— Madeline, *b* 1917: *m* 1942 (*m diss* 1967), Bernard Michael Edmund O'Mahoney, and has issue living, Kevin Edmund, *b*

1943, *d* 1983, — Hugh Frederick Michael, *b* 1948, — Stephen Lawrence Thomas, *b* 1956, — Philippa Katherine, *b* 1944, — Deirdre Lillian Mary, *b* 1958.

Granddaughter of late Charles Nesbitt Frederic Armstrong, 6th son of 1st baronet:—
Issue of late George Nesbitt Armstrong, *b* 1883, *d* 1971: *m* 1st, 1906 (*m diss* 1908), Phoebe Georgina Frances Ruby, who *d* 1939, only da of Col Jocelyn Otway; 2ndly, 1913, Evelyn Mary, who *d* 1973, da of late Michael Doyle, of Brisbane:—
(By 2nd *m*) Helen Pamela Fullerton (Melba) (*Pamela, Baroness Vestey*) (Coombe Cottage, Coldstream, Vic, Aust), *b* 1918; raised to the rank of a Baron's widow 1955: *m* 1939, Capt Hon William Howarth Vestey, Scots Gds, who was *ka* in Italy 1944, only son of 2nd Baron Vestey.
This family was anciently settled on the Scottish Border, and John Armstrong, Laird of Gilnockie Hall, Eskdale, the most famous leader of the warlike clans that made frequent inroads into the northern counties of England, was, with many of his retainers, executed on the orders of King James V of Scotland about 1530. Andrew Armstrong, his descendant, and ancestor of the present family, migrated to Ireland early in the 17th century, and settled in co Fermanagh; he greatly distinguished himself in the army of Charles I. Capt Sir Andrew H. Armstrong, 3rd Bt, was High Sheriff of King's co 1914.

ARMSTRONG (UK) 1892, of London (Extinct 1944)

Sir FRANCIS PHILIP ARMSTRONG, OBE, 3rd and last *Baronet*

WIDOW LIVING OF SECOND BARONET

MILLICENT (*Lady Armstrong*), da of late Adolph Leopold Ortlepp, of Graaff Reinert, Cape Province, S Africa: *m* 1925, as his second wife, Sir George Elliot Armstrong, CMG, 2nd baronet, who *d* 1940.

ARMYTAGE (GB) 1738, of Kirklees, Yorkshire

Always ready

Sir (JOHN) MARTIN ARMYTAGE, 9th *Baronet*; *b* 26 Feb 1933; *s* his father, Capt Sir JOHN LIONEL, 1983; *ed* Eton, and Worcester Coll, Oxford.

𝕬rms – Gules, a lion's head erased between three cross-crosslets argent. 𝕮rest – A dexter arm embowed couped at the shoulder habited or, the cuff argent, holding in the hand proper a staff gules, headed and pointed or.
Seat – Kirklees Park, Brighouse, Yorks. *Residence* – Halewell, Withington, Cheltenham GL54 4BN.

SISTER LIVING

Ann, *b* 1928: *m* 1st, 1948 (*m diss* 1960), Francis Richard Anson, who *d* 1989 (*see* E Lichfield, colls): 2ndly, 1962 (*m diss* 1971), Philip John Warburton-Lee, of Broad Oak, Whitchurch, Salop; 3rdly, 1972, as his 2nd wife, Maj David Henry Fetherstonhaugh, of Plas Kinmel, Abergele, Clwyd, and has issue living, (by 1st *m*) (*see* E Lichfield, colls), — (by 2nd *m*), John Henry Bernard, *b* 1965.

HALF-SISTER LIVING (*Daughter of 8th baronet by 2nd marriage*)

Christina Mary, *b* 1952: *m* 1980, Richard Cornish, of 12 Market St, Bradford on Avon, Wilts.

MOTHER LIVING

Evelyn Mary Jessamine, da of late Edward Herbert Fox (Arbuthnot, Bt, *cr* 1823, colls), of Adbury Park, Hants : *m* 1st, 1927 (*m diss* 1946), Capt John Lionel Armytage (later Sir John Armytage, 8th Bt), who *d* 1983; 2ndly, 1946 (*m diss* 1950), Capt John Samuel Pontifex Cooper; 3rdly, 1950, Lt-Col John Warwick Tainton Wooldridge, who *d* 1973; 4thly, 1980, her 2nd husband, Capt John Samuel Pontifex Cooper. *Residence* – Thompson's Hill, Sherston, Malmesbury, Wilts.

AUNT LIVING (*Daughter of 7th baronet*)

Barbara Ellen, *b* 1906: *m* 1930 (*m diss* 1949), Col Henry David Makgill-Crichton-Maitland, OBE, REME (ret), who *d* 1970 (*see* E Lauderdale, colls). *Residence* – 24 Hope St, Weymouth, Dorset.

WIDOW LIVING OF EIGHTH BARONET

(MARIA) MARGARETE (*Lady Armytage*), da of Paul Hugo Tenhaeff, of Bruenen, Niederhein: *m* 1949, as his second wife, Capt Sir John Lionel Armytage, 8th Bt, who *d* 1983. *Residence* – Kirklees Park, Brighouse, York.

COLLATERAL BRANCHES LIVING

Issue of late Rear-Adm Reginald William Armytage, GC, CBE, yr son of 7th baronet, *b* 1903, *d* 1984: *m* 1928, Sylvia Beatrice (The Malt House, Downton, Wilts), da of Lt-Col Charles Russell Staveley-Staveley, of Pamflete, Holbeton, Plymouth:—
DAVID GEORGE, CBE (Sharcott Manor, Pewsey, Wilts), *b* 4 Sept 1929; Capt RN; comdg HMS *Minerva* 1968-70, Defence Policy Staff 1970-72, and Naval Assistant to First Sea Lord 1972-74, commanded 7th Frigate Sqdn 1976-77, commanded Standing Naval Force Atlantic 1980-81; ADC 1981; CBE (Mil) 1981: *m* 1954, Countess Antonia Cosima, el da of Count Cosimo Diodono de Bosdari (*see* Walker-Okeover, Bt, 1985 Edn), and has issue living, Hugh Anthony, *b* 6 Aug 1955, — Charles David (26 Cicada Rd, SW18), *b* 1962: *m* 1987, Katharine Alexandra, yr da of Dr Anthony Cooper Sudell Bloomer, of London W2, and has issue living, Harry Charles George *b* 1992, — Davina Jane, *b* 1956: *m* 1977, Lt-Col David Martin Chappel, 4th/

7th R Dragoon Guards, who *d* 1990, and has issue living, William David George *b* 1987, Rupert Henry Edward *b* 1989, Jeremy David Hugh *b* 1990. —— Maurice John Reginald (Maplehurst, Staplehurst, Tonbridge, Kent), *b* 1932: *m* 1956, Brioni Katharine, da of Gerald Wellington Williams (*see* D Northumberland, colls, 1985 Edn), and has issue living, Lucinda Jane Brioni, *b* 1959: *m* 1983, Maj Mark Andrew Tilden Hibbert-Hingston, Coldstream Guards, elder son of Andrew Donovan Huntly Hibbert-Hingston (*see* E Denbigh and Desmond, colls, 1976, Edn) and has issue living, Jonathan *b* 1985, Nicholas *b* 1988, James *b* 1989, Edwina *b* 1986, Joy *b* 1991, — Nicola Susan Katharine, *b* (twin) 1959: *m* 1981, Maj Richard Bowen Woosnam, 15th/19th King's R Hus, of Cefnllysgwynne, Builth Wells, Powys, elder son of Charles Woosnam, and has issue living, David Ralph William *b* 1983, Katharine Patricia Mary *b* 1985, — Jane Annette, *b* 1962. —— Roderick Charles (Nelson House, East Ilsely, Berks), *b* 1934: *m* 1961, Susan, da of Maj Reginald T. Whitehead, of Abergavenny, and has issue living, Marcus David, *b* 1964, — Gaye, *b* 1965.

    Grandchildren of late John Hawksworth Armytage (infra):—
  Issue of late Walter John Armytage, *b* 1913, *d* 1980: *m* 1st, 1947 (*m diss* 1958), Daphne Frances Mary, only da of late Thomas Grant Fletcher, of Ardmulchan, Navan, co Meath, and formerly wife of Philip Alwyn Lucas; 2ndly, 1959, Marion Elizabeth, who *d* 1986, only child of late Maj David Mitchell Anderson, DL, LLD, of Creevy Rocks, Saintfield, co Down, and widow of Edward John Wakefield d'Arcy;—
(By 1st *m*) Julian Ralph Fitzroy (18 Lowndes Sq, SW1), *b* 1948; *ed* Milton Abbey: *m* 1st, 1973 (*m diss* 1982), Laura, da of late Capt Ian Galloway; 2ndly, 1983, Julia, da of Lawrence George Buchanan, and has issue living (by 2nd *m*), Georgina Caroline, *b* 1986, — Edwina Frederica, *b* 1992. —— Clare Frances Elizabeth ARMYTAGE, *b* 1950: *m* 1973 (*m diss* 1983), Jonathan E. Clarke. —— (By 2nd *m*) Diana Marion, *b* 1960.

    Issue of late John Hawksworth Armytage, 2nd son of 6th baronet, *b* 1873, *d* 1944: *m* 1912, Everilda Frances (who assumed by deed poll 1938 the additional surname of Creyke), da of late Ralph Creyke (Bacon, Bt):—
Ellen Elizabeth, *b* 1915: *m* 1st, 1940 (*m diss* 1945), John Antony de Berniere Hallows; 2ndly, 1945, (Henry) Duncan Crow. *Residence* – Little Bendrose, Finch Lane, Amersham Common, Bucks.
This family is descended (according to a pedigree attested by Sir Henry St George, Norroy King of Arms) from John Army-tage, of Wrigbowls, Lincolnshire, *temp* King Stephen. Two branches of the family at different times have been created baronets. Brig-Gen Sir George Ayscough Armytage, CMG, DSO, 7th baronet, served in European War 1914-18 as Brig-Gen Comdg an Inf Brig, DSO, CMG.

ARNOTT (UK) 1896, of Woodlands, St Anne, Shandon, co Cork

Sir ALEXANDER JOHN MAXWELL ARNOTT, 6th *Baronet; b* 18 Sept 1975; *s* his father, *Sir* JOHN ROBERT ALEXANDER, 1981.

Arms – Per chevron argent and azure, in chief two mullets and in base a crescent, all counterchanged, on a chief of the second three mullets of the first. **Crest** – On a rock a tower proper, therefrom a pennant of one point flying to the sinister azure. *Residence* – 11 Palmerston Rd, Dublin.

Speratum et completum
Hoped for and realized

BROTHER LIVING

ANDREW JOHN ERIC, *b* 20 June 1978.

UNCLE LIVING (Son of 4th baronet)

Eric John (Trottsford Farm, Headley, Hants; 11 Milford House, 7 Queen Anne St, W1; Kildare St and Garrick Clubs), *b* 1929; *ed* Harrow, and Trin Coll, Dublin (MB and BCh, FRCS): *m* 1960, Veronica Mary, only da of late Capt Arvid Langué Querfeld von der Seedeck, of West Green Cottage, Hartley Wintney, Hants, and has issue living, Stephen John, *b* 1962: *m* 1989, Katherine Jane Keep, eldest da of Colin Thompson, of The Old House, Sutton Veny, Wilts, and has issue living, Oliver Timothy John *b* 1990, Lara Georgina Emma *b* 1992, — Robert Lauriston John, *b* 1971, — Tatiana Amelia, *b* 1963: *m* 1986, Nicholas Paul Whishaw, eldest son of Michael Whishaw, of Anaheim Hills, California, USA, and has issue living, Timothy Alexander *b* 1988.

WIDOW LIVING OF FIFTH BARONET

ANN MARGARET (*Lady Arnott*) (11 Palmerston Rd, Dublin), da of late Terence Alphonsus Farrelly, of Kilcar, co Cavan: *m* 1974, Sir John Robert Alexander Arnott, 5th Baronet, who *d* 1981.

COLLATERAL BRANCHES LIVING

    Grandchildren of late John Frederic Arnott, MC (infra):—
  Issue of late Lt-Cdr (John) Anthony Arnott, RNVR, FRICS, *b* 1921, *d* 1980: *m* 1944, Jean Barbara (Devon Cottage, Bourton, Dorset), da of late Charles Lovett Gill, of Odiham, Hants:—
John David (Pauwhof 170, 2289 B.M., Rijswijk, Netherlands), *b* 1947; *ed* Cheltenham Coll, Birmingham Univ and Liverpool Univ (BA): *m* 1971, Jennifer Mary Dooley, and has issue living, John Andrew, *b* 1974, — Myles Anthony, *b* 1980. —— (Ann Margaret) Amabel, *b* 1945: *m* 1st, 1969, Robert Hughes; 2ndly, 1981, Peter Bolton, of 7 Silver St, Wells, Som BA5 1UN and has issue living (by 2nd *m*), Gabriel Peter, *b* 1982, — Mary Christabel, *b* 1985.

    Granddaughter of late David Taylor Arnott, 2nd son of 1st baronet:—
  Issue of late John Frederic Arnott, MC, *b* 1892, *d* 1967: *m* 1919, Phyllis, who *d* 1967, da of James Cundell:—
Patricia Ruth (3 Uigshadder, by Portree, I of Skye), *b* 1920: *m* 1961, Evrard Burke (formerly Bourque), who *d* 1964.

    Grandchildren of Sir John Alexander Arnott, 2nd Bt, JP, DL:—
  Issue of late Maj Thomas John Arnott, *b* 1899, *d* 1979: *m* 1927, Lettice Mary, who *d* 1986, da of late Lt-Col Charles Montagu Crompton-Roberts, of Drybridge, Monmouth (Greenwell, Bt):—
Peter John (38 Braemar, Kersfield Rd, SW15; *Club* – Army and Navy), *b* 1929; late Lt 15th/19th Hussars. —— Guy (12/500 Marine Parade, Biggera Waters, Queensland 4216, Australia; *Club* – United Service, Brisbane), *b* 1932; late Lt 15th/19th Hussars: *m* 1963, Diana, who *d* 1982, da of D. Staines, of Wahroonga, Queensland. —— Caroline, *b* 1934.

The 1st baronet, Sir John Arnott (son of John Arnott, of Auchtermuchty, Fifeshire), was a noted philanthropist and largely connected with many Irish industries, and sat as MP for Kinsale (*L*) 1859-63.

ARTHUR (UK) 1841, of Upper Canada

Sir STEPHEN JOHN ARTHUR, 6th *Baronet*; *b* 1 July 1953; *s* his father, *Sir* BASIL MALCOLM, 1985: *ed* Timaru Boys' High Sch, *m* 1978 (*m diss* 19—), Carolyn Margaret, da of Burnie Lawrence Diamond, of Cairns, Queensland, Australia, and has issue

𝕬rms – Or, on a chevron azure between two clarions in chief gules and a kangaroo sejant in base proper, two swords the points upwards also proper, points and hilts of the first; on a chief of the third a horse courant argent. 𝕮rest – In front of two swords in saltire proper, pommels and hilts or, a pelican in her piety sable, the nest or. *Residence* – Grene Gables, Seadown, No 3 RD, Timaru, New Zealand.

SON LIVING

BENJAMIN NATHAN, *b* 27 March 1979.

Stet fortuna domûs
May the fortune of the house stand

DAUGHTERS LIVING

Amanda, *b* 1975. —— Melanie, *b* 1976.

SISTERS LIVING

Marylin Jane, *b* 1950: *m* 1972, W.B.M. Keeman, of Pohutukawa Drive, Howick, Auckland, NZ, and has issue living, Zane Basil Cornelius, *b* 1974, — Kris William Reginald, *b* 1981, — Lauriely Elizabeth Wanda, *b* 1976. —— Cheryl Dawn, *b* 1951: *m* 1971, G.L. Blanchard, of 1RD Springbrook, Timaru, NZ.

AUNTS LIVING (*Daughters of 4th baronet*)

Helen Fay, *b* 1931: *m* 1st, 1949 (*m diss* 1981), Morton King; 2ndly, 1982, Peter William Caird, of 8RD Waimate, S Canterbury, NZ, and has issue living (by 1st *m*), Donald Malcolm, *b* 1950, — Peter Morton, *b* 1955, — Yvonne Jane, *b* 1951, — Maree Fay, *b* 1960. —— Maureen Beatrice, *b* 1933: *m* 1st, 1953 (*m diss* 1972), James Warren Patterson; 2ndly, 1976, James Wright McLauchlan, of Nydia Bay, Private Bag, Havelock, Marlborough, NZ, and has issue living (by 1st *m*), Warren John, *b* 1954, — James Bartley, *b* 1956, — Desmond Bruce, *b* 1965, — Moira Fay, *b* 1957, — Rosana Mae, *b* 1961. —— Elizabeth Adele, *b* 1948: *m* 1972, Lindsay Gerald Dawkins, of 129 Wellington St, Picton, Marlborough, NZ, and has issue living, Hayden Gerald, *b* 1977, — Leah Janette, *b* 1973.

WIDOWS LIVING OF FOURTH AND FIFTH BARONETS

DORIS FAY (*Dowager Lady Arthur*), da of Joseph Wooding, JP, of Woodland Grange, Woodbury, and Geraldine, S Canterbury, New Zealand: *m* 1928, Sir George Malcolm Arthur, 4th Bt, who *d* 1949. *Residence* – 421 Waimea Rd, Wakatu, Nelson, New Zealand.
SANDRA COLLEEN (*Lady Arthur*), da of William Boaz, of Whangarei, New Zealand: *m* 1983, as his 2nd wife, Sir Basil Malcolm Arthur, 5th Bt, who *d* 1985. *Residence* – 6 Ellerton Way, Wellington, New Zealand.

MOTHER LIVING

Elizabeth Rita, da of Alan Mervyn Wells, of Wakefield, Nelson, New Zealand: *m* (Jan) 1950 (*m diss* 1983), as his 1st wife, Sir Basil Malcolm Arthur, 5th Bt, who *d* 1985.

COLLATERAL BRANCHES LIVING

Grandsons of late George Arthur, son of late Col Edward Penfold Arthur, Bombay CS, 4th son of 1st baronet:—
Issue of late George Frederick Neale Arthur; *b* 1878, *d* 1939: *m* 1905, Edith Lavender, da of late J. H. Taylor:—
George Leonard, *b* 1908; Maj (ret) S African Staff Corps; W Desert 1941-42, Dep Assist Adjt-Gen British Forces in Palestine 1943-44, Inniskilling Fus in Italy 1944, and a Member of British Mil Mission to Greece 1945; DAAG Natal 1949-57; a Member of Provincial Council, Natal (United Party), and Cabinet Min Natal Exec Cttee 1966-70: *m* 1936, Gladys Raina, da of George Percy Farr, JP, of Bedford, Cape Province, S Africa, and has issue living, Gavyn Farr, *b* 1951; *ed* Harrow, and Ch Ch, Oxford (MA), Bar Middle Temple 1975. *Residence* – 24 Lowndes St, SW1. —— Archibald John, *b* 1909. *Residence* –

Grandchildren of late Rev John Sigismund Arthur, MC (*infra*):—
Issue of late Capt Leonard John Henry Arthur, RAMC (TA), *b* 1926, *d* 1983: *m* 1954, Hon Janet Stella Brain (Royal Oak Cottage, Church Broughton, Derby), da of 1st Baron Brain:—
Robert Leonard Sigismund, *b* 1955. —— Linet Stella, *b* 1956. —— Tansy Amy Anne, *b* 1959. —— Elaine Fay, *b* 1961. —— Hazel Jane, *b* 1964. —— Ruth Gilly, *b* 1966.

Grandchildren of late Sigismund Raynor Arthur, eldest son of late John Raynor Arthur (*infra*):—
Issue of late Rev John Sigismund Arthur, MC, *b* 1894, *d* 1974: *m* 1925, Constance Amy Farquhar, who *d* 1980, da of Joseph Sladen, late ICS:—
Flora Jessamine Mary, *b* 1928; MA Oxon: *m* 1954, Charles Edward Elliott, BM, BCh, of 35 Cook St, Northgate, Brisbane, Qld, and has issue living, Charles John Peter (Lot 4, Arthy's Road, Cooran, Qld 4569; PO Box 161, Pomona, Qld), *b* 1955: *m* 1982, Elizabeth Mary, da of Denley Keeling, and has issue living, Charles Leonard George *b* 1983, James Edward *b* 1984, Henry Robert *b* 1988, Georgina Mary-Jane *b* 1990, — John Michael (104 Cavendish St, Nundah, Brisbane, Qld 4012), *b* 1956: *m* 1986, Barbara Jane, da of Bernard Russell Arthur Stuart, and has issue living, Conor Stuart *b* 1992, Caitlin Elaine *b* 1988, Sally Brenda *b* 1990, — Thomas George (3791 West 3rd Av, Vancouver, BC, Canada), *b* 1958: *m* 1982, Gwenneth Mary, da of John Stanley Shaw, and has issue living, Tristan *b* 1989, Reece *b* 1991, Tyne Rebecca *b* 1993, — Mary Jessamine, *b* 1960: *m* 1990, Lee Cameron Thompson, and has issue living, Eliot George *b* 1991, Rachel Rebecca *b* 1993, — Lucy Jane, *b* 1972. —— Rose Eleanor, *b* 1931; MA Oxon: *m* 1961, Rev Canon Edward Longman, of 16 Coleshill St, Sutton Coldfield, W

Midlands B72 1SH, and has issue living, Harold John, *b* 1962; MA Cantab: *m* 1989, Alison Louise, da of Col William E.I. Armstrong, and has issue living, Margaret Amy Armstrong *b* 1994, — Peter George, *b* 1965: *m* 1994, Melanie Joy, da of late Terry James Pitcher, — George Roland, *b* 1969; BSc, — Anna Frances, *b* 1963; MA (Oxon). —— Cecil Lucy Sylvia, *b* 1939: *m* 1980, Richard Denis Vooght, of 14 Kingsdown Parade, Bristol 6, and has issue living, Jenny Madeleine Rose, *b* 1981, — Abigail Katharine Amy, *b* 1983.

       Issue of late Sir (Oswald) Raynor Arthur, KCMG, CVO, *b* 1905, *d* 1973: *m* 1935, Mary Elizabeth, MBE, who *d* 1994, da of late Rt Hon Sir Cecil Arthur Spring Rice, GCMG, GCVO (*see* B Monteagle of Brandon, colls):—

Thomas Sigismund Raynor (Burwash Glebe, Etchingham, Sussex), *b* 1940; *ed* Eton, and Oriel Coll, Oxford (MA): *m* 1966, Angela Susan Clare, da of late Lt-Col Roland T. W. MacLeod, of Weston, Dunsyre, Lanark, and has issue living, George Raynor Macleod, *b* 1969, — Juliet Caroline, *b* 1966. —— Valentine Bridget, *b* 1968: *m* 1991, J. Hugo S. Akerman, of Ragnall Farm, Carswell Marsh, Faringdon, Oxon, eldest son of John Akerman, of SW12, and has issue living, Valentine Cosima *b* 1994, — Alexandra Maxine, *b* 1973. —— Caroline Anne Florence, *b* 1937: *m* 1972, Courtney Kenny, of Ballinrobe, co Mayo, Ireland; 14 Grange Grove, N1, and has issue living, Courtney Arthur Francis, *b* 1983.

       Grandson of late John Raynor Arthur, 6th son of 1st baronet:—
       Issue of late Major Edmond John Arthur, *b* 1873, *d* 1953: *m* 1921, Kathleen Emily Isabel Ada, who *d* 1987, da of George Penn Simkins:—

George Henry Edmond (RD5, Papakura, Auckland, NZ), *b* 1927: *m* 1950, Kathleen, da of Frederick Joseph Bow, of Sea Mills, Bristol, and has issue living, Robert George, *b* 1950: *m* 1969, Janice Margaret, da of Gerald Poolman, of 266 Tavy House, Plymouth, and has issue living, Niel Robert *b* 1970, Kieron Gerald *b* 1970.

This family migrated from Cornwall to Plymouth early in the 18th century. The 1st baronet, Lieut-Gen Right Hon Sir George Arthur, KCH, DCL, Col of the 50th Foot, was knighted in 1837. He was successively Governor of Honduras, Van Diemen's Land, Upper Canada, and Bombay and Provisional Gov-Gen of India 1846. The 3rd baronet, Capt Sir George Compton Archibald Arthur, MVO, was Private Sec of State for War. The 5th baronet, Sir Basil Malcolm Arthur, who served as MP for Timaru, NZ for 23 years, was Min of Transport and Min in Charge of State Insurance Office, NZ, and Speaker of New Zealand House of Representatives 1984-85.

ASHBURNHAM (E) 1661, of Broomham, Sussex

Will God, and I shall

Sir DENNY REGINALD ASHBURNHAM, 12th *Baronet*: *b* 24 March 1916; *s* his father, *Sir* FLEETWOOD, 1953; is Capt S Staffordshire Regt, and a co-heir to Barony of Grandison: *m* 1946, Mary Frances, da of Major Robert Pascoe Mair, of Wick, Udimore, Sussex, and has had issue.

𝕬rms – Gules, a fesse between six mullets argent. 𝕮rest – Out of a ducal coronet or an ash-tree proper.
Residence – Little Broomham, Church Lane, Guestling, Hastings, E Sussex TN35 4HS.

GRANDCHILDREN LIVING

       Issue of late John Anchitel Fleetwood Ashburnham, *b* 1951, *d* 1981: *m* 1975, Corinne A. (who *m* 2ndly, 1982, John Philip Merricks, of The Manor, Icklesham, Winchelsea, E Sussex), da of D. W. J. O'Brien, of The Grey House, Hooe Common, Battle, E Sussex:—

JAMES FLEETWOOD, *b* 17 Dec 1979. —— Henrietta Mary, *b* 1981.

DAUGHTERS LIVING

Frances, *b* 1947: *m* 1973, Robert Charles Taylor, of Summerhayes, Pett, Hastings, E Sussex, and has issue living, Robert Denny, *b* 1982, — Ellen Frances, *b* 1979. —— Honor Rosemary, *b* 1949: *m* 1981, Frank Cooke, of Broomhill Farm, Camber, Rye, E Sussex, and has issue living, Matthew John, *b* 1983, — Lucy Frances, *b* 1981, — Alice Mary, *b* 1985.

SISTER LIVING

Honor Elfrida, *b* 1920: *m* 1951, Ernest James Boorman.

This family, which takes its name from Ashburnham (originally written Esseburnham), in Sussex, is of great antiquity. This line derives from Richard of Broomham, 2nd son of Thomas Ashburnham, *temp* Henry VI. The el son John was ancestor of the Earls of Ashburnham (ext 1924). Sir Denny Ashburnham, 1st baronet, was MP for Hastings, and Victualler of the Navy. The 2nd baronet was Chamberlain of the Exchequer and MP for Hastings; the 4th baronet was Bishop of Chichester: and the 7th baronet was Chancellor and Prebendary of Chichester. Sir Anchitel Piers, 9th baronet, assumed by Roy licence 1899 the additional surname of Clement.

ASKE (UK) 1922, of Aughton, East Riding of Yorkshire.

Rev Sir CONAN ASKE, 2nd *Baronet*; *b* 22 April 1912; *s* his father *Sir* ROBERT WILLIAM, LLD QC, 1954; *ed* Rugby, and Balliol Coll, Oxford (MA): *m* 1st, 1948, Vera, who *d* 1960, yr da of late George Rowbotham, of Iffley, Oxford, and formerly wife of Roland Faulkner; 2ndly, 1965, Rebecca, yr da of late Hugh Fraser Grant, of Wick, Caithness.

Arms – Argent, a martlet sable between two bars azure, each charged with as many cross-crosslets of the first. Crest – In front of a Saracen's head proper wreathed around the temples argent and azure, two roses argent.
Residence – 167 Malvern Rd, Worcester, WR2 4NN.

BROTHER LIVING

ROBERT EDWARD (45 Holland Rd, W14), *b* 21 March 1915: *m* 1940, Joan Bingham, only da of Capt Bingham Ackerley, of White Lodge, Cobham, and has issue living, Robert John Bingham, *b* 1941.

SISTER LIVING

Margaret, *b* 1910: *m* 1936, Richard Adolphe Charles Du Vivier, CBE, of 45 Chatsworth Rd, Ealing, W5, and has had issue, (Charles) Richard, *b* 1938; *ed* Malvern, and King's Coll, Camb; *d* 1992, — Hugh Michael (43 Britannia Rd, SW6 2HJ), *b* 1945; *ed* Malvern, and Trin Coll, Dublin: *m* 1969, Jacqueline Sarah, da of Harry Reginald Albert de Belleroche, of 38 De Vere Gdns, W8, and has issue living, Juliet Amy *b* 1979, Katherine Lucy Sarah *b* 1984, — Carol Anne, *b* 1941: *m* 1st, 1963 (*m diss* 1969), Bearnard O'Riain, of Dun Laoghaire, co Dublin; 2ndly, 1978, Cmdt Allan Joseph Shaw, of 28 La Roche Drive, Humewood, 6001 Port Elizabeth, S Africa, and has issue living (by 1st *m*), Manus Justin *b* 1966, Natasha Celina *b* 1963, (by 2nd *m*) Nicholas Simon Dominic *b* 1978, Simon Philip Benedict *b* 1984, — Nicola Jill, *b* 1953: *m* 1975, Gordon Walter Prosser, of 7 Hooley Range, Heaton Moor Rd, Stockport, Cheshire SK4 4HU, and has issue living, Alexander Marcos *b* 1978, Hugh Angus *b* 1980, Giles Henry James *b* 1983, Edward Hamish Neal *b* 1987.

The 1st baronet, Sir Robert William Aske, TD, LLD, QC (son of late Edward Aske, of Hull), was Dep Sheriff of Hull 1906-8, and sat as MP for Newcastle-upon-Tyne E Div (*Lib*) 1923-24, and 1929-45.

Assheton-Smith (Duff-Assheton-Smith), see Duff.

ASTLEY (UK) 1821, of Everleigh, Wiltshire (Extinct 1994)

Sir FRANCIS JACOB DUGDALE ASTLEY, 6th and last *Baronet*.

DAUGHTER LIVING OF SIXTH BARONET

Bridget Mary, *b* 1939: *m* 1960, Capt John Pollock Maxwell, R Tank Regt, of Brook Lodge, Brook Lane, Hambledon, Hants PO7 4TF, and has issue living, Robert Astley Kennedy, *b* 1962, — Simon Harrison, *b* 1965.

SISTER LIVING OF FIFTH BARONET

Pamela Irene ASTLEY-CORBETT, *b* 1919: *m* 1951, Archibald Thomas Dunn, who *d* 1977, and has issue living, Thomas Astley, *b* 1952: *m* 1984, Jane Margaret Dudley, da of late John Guy Dudley Parsons, and has issue living, Archibald Guy Astley *b* 1985, Frederick William Francis *b* 1986, Henry Thomas George *b* 1988, Augustin *b* 1993, — Archibald John Hugh (Moat Hall, Layham, nr Ipswich, Suffolk), *b* 1955: *m* 1987, Allison Adams, da of Morton Hutchinson Clark, of 608 Linkhorn Drive, Virginia Beach, Virginia, USA, and has issue living, William Francis Corbett *b* 1990, Anna *b* 1992, — Marcia Mary, *b* 1953: *m* 1975, Justin Francis Quintus Fenwick, and has issue (*see* B Lilford, colls), — Susannah Madeline Sara, *b* 1956, — Katherine Elizabeth Corisande, *b* 1962.

WIDOW LIVING OF SIXTH BARONET

BRITA MARGARETA JOSEFINA (*Lady Astley*), da of late Karl and Signe Nyström, of Stockholm: *m* 1934, Capt Sir Francis Jacob Dugdale Astley, 6th Bt, who *d* 1994. *Residence* – Heath Mount, Rake, Liss, Hants GU33 7PG.

Aubrey-Fletcher, see Fletcher.

AUSTIN (UK) 1894, of Red Hill, Castleford, West Riding of York.

Trust in God and He will give strength

Sir MICHAEL TRESCAWEN AUSTIN, 5th *Baronet, b* 27 Aug 1927; *s* his father, *Sir* William Ronald, 1989: *ed* Downside; 1939-45 War with RNVR; sometime Master of Braes of Derwent: *m* 1951, Bridget Dorothea Patricia, da of late Francis Farrell, of Miltown, Clonmellon, co Meath, and has issue.

𝔄rms – Gules, eight mullets three, three and two argent, within a border dovetailed or, charged with four thistles slipped and leaved proper. 𝔆rest – A dexter arm embowed in fesse, couped at the shoulder, vested or, cuff indented ermine, the hand proper grasping a cross botony fitchée gules, resting on the arm a mullet of the last. *Residence* – Goldburn, Okehampton, Devon EX20 3BD.

DAUGHTERS LIVING

Mary, *b* 1951: *m* 1981, John Orchard, of Mill-Roy, Budleigh Salterton, Devon. —— Jane (Goldburn, Okehampton, Devon EX20 3BD), *b* 1954. —— Susan, *b* 1956: *m* 1978, Antony Farrell, of Station House, Ballivor, co Meath, and has issue living, Sean Patrick, *b* 1982, — Bridget, *b* 1980.

BROTHER LIVING

ANTHONY LEONARD (Court Barton, Crediton, Devon), *b* 30 Sept 1930; *ed* Downside: *m* 1st, 1956 (*m diss* 1966), Mary Annette, da of Richard Kelly, of Greenogue, Kilsallaghan, co Dublin; 2ndly, 1967, Aileen Morrison Hall, da of William Hall Stewart, and has issue living (by 1st *m*), Peter John, *b* 29 July 1958, — Nicholas Michael James, *b* 1960, — Caroline Dorothy, *b* 1957, — (by 2nd *m*), Rebecca Dorothy Mary, *b* 1968.

WIDOWS LIVING OF THIRD AND FOURTH BARONET

RHODA NOREEN (*Mrs John B. F. Austin,* preferred style), da of late Herbert Lloyd Pinches, of Eastbourne, and widow of Col Charles Vincent Douglas Rose: *m* 1960, as his 2nd wife, Sir John Byron Fraser Austin, 3rd Bt, who *d* 1981.

MARY HELEN (*Mrs M. H. Austin,* preferred style), da of Francis Henry Arthur Joseph Farrell, of Miltown House, co Meath: *m* 1958, as his 2nd wife, Sir William Ronald Austin, 4th Bt, who *d* 1989.

COLLATERAL BRANCHES LIVING

Issue of late John Standish Thomas Joseph Austin, 2nd son of 1st baronet, *b* 1875, *d* 1941: *m* 1908, Gwendolyne Aubrey Beverley, who *d* 1959, da of late Capt Beverley Robinson, of Hyde Lodge Winchester:—
John Standish Beverley, *b* 1909; *ed* Ampleforth, and Downside. *Residence* – 33 Muncaster Gate, Malton Rd, York. —— Janetta Agnes Gwendolyne, *b* 1912.

Issue of late Joseph Edward Austin, 4th son of 1st baronet; *b* 1881, *d* 1938: *m* 1914, Katherine Matilda, who *d* 1968, da of late John Ryan, MD, FRCSI, of Castleconnell, co Limerick:—
Richard Joseph Byron, *b* 1926; *ed* Ampleforth. —— Joan Agnes Mary, *b* 1917: *m* 1949, Michael Laurence Bexon, MC, and has issue living, Julian Michael Adrian, *b* 1950, — Dominic Edmund Christian, *b* 1954.

The 1st baronet, Sir John Austin, sat as MP for Osgoldcross Div of E Part of W Riding of Yorkshire (*L*) 1886-1906.

AYKROYD (UK) 1920, of Lightcliffe, West Riding of co of York

Victory in truth

Sir WILLIAM MILES AYKROYD, MC, 3rd *Baronet*; *b* 24 Aug 1923; *s* his father, *Sir* ALFRED HAMMOND, 1965.

Arms – Azure, on a chevron ermine between three stags' heads erased or, as many crosses couped sable. **Crest** – In front of a stag's head erased and gorged with a wreath of oak proper, two crosses as in the arms.
Residence – Buckland Newton Place, Dorchester, Dorset.

COLLATERAL BRANCHES LIVING

Issue of late Col Harold Hammond Aykroyd, OBE, MC, TD, DL, 2nd son of 1st baronet; *b* 1896, *d* 1974: *m* 1st, 1926 (*m diss* 1938), Nina Marguerite, da of late Edward J. Hulse, of Oakdene Duffield Rd, Derby; 2ndly, 1941, Kathleen Ellen (The Glebe House, Aldborough, Boroughbridge, N Yorks), el da of late Harry Tyrrell-Gray, FRCS:—
(By 1st *m*) Susan, *b* 1931: *m* 1st, 1951 (*m diss* 1958), John Kenneth Benney, RE; 2ndly, 1968, Christopher John Day, and has issue living, (by 1st *m*) Cecilia Anne, *b* 1952. —— Sally Mary (The Old Cottage, High St, Whixley, York), *b* 1934: *m* 1960, Christopher Boyd Stoddart, who *d* 1984, and has issue living, Mark Harold Boyd, *b* 1966: *m* 1990, Suzanna Baynard, and has issue living, Tom Lawrence Boyd *b* 1993, — Margaret Jane, *b* 1962: *m* 1987, Steven Bentley, and has issue living, Christopher Alan *b* 1990, Tobias Frank *b* 1993. —— (By 2nd *m*) Harriet Louisa, *b* 1951: *m* 1977, John Flinders Highley, of Lawrence House, Studley Roger, Ripon, N Yorks, and has issue living, Samuel Thomas George, *b* 1981, — Henry William Charles, *b* 1985.

Issue of late Col George Hammond Aykroyd, TD, yst son of 1st baronet, *b* 1900, *d* 1972: *m* 1924, Margaret Roberts, who *d* 1981, da of Sir Frederic Alfred Aykroyd, 1st Bt, *cr* 1929:—
MICHAEL DAVID (The Homestead, Killinghall, Harrogate, Yorks), *b* 14 June 1928: *m* 1952, Oenone Gillian Diana, da of Donald George Cowling, MBE, of Leeds, and has issue living, Henry Robert George (Cushnie, Auchterless, Turriff, Aberdeen), *b* 1954: *m* 1975, Lucy Merlin, da of late Col Jack Houghton Brown, and has issue living, George Jack *b* 1977, Bertie Thomas *b* 1983, Emma Rachel *b* 1978, Kate *b* 1989, Rose *b* (tw͏in) 1989, — Annabel Mary Diana, *b* 1956: *m* 1979, Robin Guy Graham, and has issue (*see* Graham, Bt, *cr* 1662), — Sarah Jane, *b* 1960: *m* 1985, Guy Matthew Davis, of The Caretaker's Flat, Shardeloes Park, Bucks, son of James Davis, of The Garden Flat, Shardeloes Park, Bucks, — Susannah Margaret, *b* 1964. —— (John) Richard (Molino del Cancon, Casares, Malaga, Spain), *b* 1934: *m* 1st, 1963 (*m diss* 1974), Catherine Marthe, el da of George Vettier, of La Hulottière, Yvré, L'Evéque (Sarthe), France; 2ndly, 1974, Lavinia Mary, da of late Patrick Thomas Beasley (*see* E Wilton, 1990 Edn), and formerly wife of Confrey A. Phillips, and has issue living (by 1st *m*) Bettina Dominique, *b* (Nov) 1963, — (by 2nd *m*), Serena Mary *b* 1976, — Clare Lavinia, *b* 1978. —— David Peter (The Priory, Nun Monkton, York), *b* 1937: *m* 1958, (Lydia) Huldine, yr da of Richard Beamish, of Castlelyons, co Cork, and has had issue, Nicholas William, *b* 1962; *d* 1989, as a result of a motor accident in Ireland, — Amanda Huldine, *b* 1960, — Emily Sorrell, *b* 1970, — Matilda Rose, *b* 1978. —— Patricia Jean, *b* 1925.
The 1st baronet, Sir William Henry Aykroyd (son of Alfred Aykroyd, of Oakwood, Manningham, Yorkshire), was a Director of T. F. Firth & Sons, Ltd, of Brighouse, and High Sheriff for W Riding of Yorkshire 1926.

AYKROYD (UK) 1929, of Birstwith Hall, Hampsthwaite, co York

Victory in truth

Sir JAMES ALEXANDER FREDERIC AYKROYD, 3rd *Baronet*; *b* 6 Sept 1943; *s* his uncle, *Sir* CECIL WILLIAM, 1993; *ed* Eton, Aix-en-Provence Univ, and Madrid Univ; is patron of the living of Hampsthwaite: *m* 1973, Jennifer, da of late Frederick William Marshall, MB, BS, DA (Eng), of 3 Penylan Av, Porthcawl, Glam, and has issue.

Arms – Azure, on a chevron ermine between three stags' heads erased or, as many crosses patonce sable. **Crest** – In front of a stag's head erased and gorged with a chaplet of oak proper, two crosses as in the arms.
Seat – Birstwith Hall, near Harrogate. *Residence* – 5 Highbury Terrace, N5 1UP.

DAUGHTERS LIVING

Gemma Jane, *b* 1976. —— Victoria Louise, *b* 1977.

HALF-BROTHERS LIVING AND DECEASED

Jeremy Charles, *b* 1950; *d* 1982. —— TOBY NIGEL BERTRAM, *b* 13 Nov 1955; *ed* Eton, and St Catharine's Coll, Camb (MA). *Residence* – 37 Pembridge Villas, W11 3EP.

SISTER LIVING

Jean Margaret Elizabeth (The Old Vicarage, Moreton Pinkney, Daventry, Northants NN11 6SJ), *b* 1940: *m* 1st, 1962 (*m diss* 1972), Michael Frederick David Morley; 2ndly, 1984, Col Timothy John Seymour Eastwood, RA, and has issue living (by 1st *m*), Harry Michael Charles, *b* 1965, — Edward James Cecil, *b* 1967.

HALF-SISTER LIVING

Rachel, *b* 1952: *m* 1981, Charles Patrick Helmore, of Wyndham Cottage, Rogate, nr Petersfield, Hants GU31 5BL, and has issue living, Max David Charles, *b* 1984, — Caspar William, *b* 1987.

MOTHER LIVING

Margot, DBE (*Dame Margot Smith*), da of late Leonard Graham-Brown, MC, FRCS, of 82 Portland Place, W1: *m* 1st, 1938 (*m diss* 1947), as his 1st wife, Bertram Aykroyd, who *d* 1983, yst son of 1st baronet; 2ndly, 1947, Roy Smith MC, TD, who *d* 1983. *Residence* – Howden Lodge, Spennithorne, Leyburn, N Yorkshire DL8 5PR.

STEPMOTHER LIVING

Catalina, da of late Henry Marchington, of Hope Green, Adlington, Cheshire: *m* 1949, as his 2nd wife, Bertram Aykroyd, who *d* 1983, yst son of 1st baronet. *Residence* – Houghtons, East Harting, Petersfield, Hants GU31 5LU.

COLLATERAL BRANCH LIVING

Issue of late Frederic Howard Aykroyd, 2nd son of 1st baronet, *b* 1907, *d* 1978: *m* 1932, (Ruth) Joan, who *d* 1992, da of Carlton Oldfield, of Moor Hall, Harewood, Yorks:—
Mary Elisabeth Wendy Carlton, *b* 1934: *m* 1st, 1955 (*m diss* 1980), Nigel David Sykes Porter; 2ndly, 1989, William Richard Whitwell, of The Old Vicarage, Whorlton, Barnard Castle, co Durham. —— Joanna Jane, *b* 1937: *m* 1960, Christopher Jonathan Pumphrey, TD, DL, of Bolam West Houses, Middleton, Morpeth, Northumberland, and has issue living, Edward Jonathan Lawrence, *b* 1963, — Andrew Charles, *b* 1965: *m* 1991, Juliet Evelyn, yr da of John Harold Booth Blackett (*see* Blackett, Bt, colls), — (Sara) Rose, *b* 1962: *m* 1987, Nicholas Walter Alexander, eldest son of Cyril Alexander, of Woodside, Dollar, Clackmannanshire, and has issue living, Christopher James Turnbull *b* 1991, Lucy Kate *b* 1990. —— Victoria Margaret, *b* 1939: *m* 1962, Robin Fleming, of Barton Abbey, Steeple Aston, Oxon, and has issue living, Philip, *b* 1965, — Rory David, *b* 1968, — Joanna Kate, *b* 1963.
The 1st baronet, Sir Frederic Alfred Aykroyd (son of William Edward Aykroyd, of Ashdown, Apperley Bridge, Yorks, uncle of Sir William Henry Aykroyd 1st baronet (*cr* 1920)), was a Merchant and High Sheriff of Yorkshire 1941-42.

AYLMER (I) 1622, of Donadea, co Kildare

Sir RICHARD JOHN AYLMER, 16th *Baronet*; *b* 23 April 1937; *s* his father, *Sir* FENTON GERALD, 1987: *m* 1962, Lise, da of Paul Emile Demers, of Montreal, and has issue.

Arms – Argent, a cross sable between four Cornish choughs proper. **Crest** – A Cornish chough proper rising out of a ducal coronet or.
Residence – 3573 Lorne Av, Montreal, Quebec H2X 2A4, Canada.

SON LIVING

FENTON PAUL, *b* 31 Oct 1965; *ed* Selwin House Sch, and Concordia Univ: *m* 19—, Pina, da of Mrs Velia Mastromonaco.

DAUGHTER LIVING

Genevieve, *b* 1963.

SISTER LIVING

Rosalind Alice, *b* 1941: *m* 1st 1965 (*m diss* 1973), Michael Neal Dennis White, of Victoria, BC; 2ndly 1977, Milton Cameron, of 2197 Queen's Av, W Vancouver, BC V7V 2Y1, Canada, and has two adopted children, Michael Aylmer CAMERON, *b* 1968, — Anna Rosalind CAMERON, *b* 1970.

COLLATERAL BRANCHES LIVING

Grandson of late Capt John Evans-Freke Aylmer, 2nd son of 11th baronet:—
Issue of late Rear-Adm Henry Evans-Freke Aylmer, CBE, *b* 1878, *d* 1933: *m* 1910, Edith Winifred, who *d* 1952, da of late Vet-Col Sir Francis Duck, KCB, FRCVS:—
John Francis, *b* 1910; late RAF. *Residence* –

Granddaughters of late Rev William Josiah Aylmer, 3rd son of 7th baronet:—
Issue of late William Henry Aylmer, *b* 1833, *d* 1882: *m* 1st, 1861, Henrietta, who *d* 18-, da of Dr Martin; 2ndly, 1874, Elizabeth, who *d* 1936, da of late Dr Gordon, of Sydney, N S Wales:—
(By 2nd *m*) Blanche Emily. —— Ida Mildred. —— Madge Irene. —— Muriel Lilian.

Granddaughters of late William Henry Aylmer (ante):—
Issue of late Percy Gordon Aylmer, *b* 1865, *d* 1923: *m* 1888, Eliza Anne, who *d* 1951, da of late William Haddon:—
Inez Amy (c/o Holy Spirit Convent, Brisbane, Qld, Aust), *b* 1895: *m* 1921, Cyril Frederick Mullins, who *d* 1965. —— Muriel Eileen (75 Wyralla Av, Epping, NSW), *b* 1907.

Grandchildren of late Percy Gordon Aylmer (ante):—
Issue of late Arthur William Aylmer, *b* 1899, *d* 1964: *m* 1924, Daisy, da of William Goodall of Firthcliffe, NY:—
Constance Elizabeth, *b* 1931: *m* 1953, Charles T. Brown, and has issue living.
Issue of late Justin Kenneth William Aylmer, *b* 1893, *d* 1951: *m* 1918, Winifred Clare Mullins:—
Francis Gordon, *b* 1919: *m* 19-, Dura Marion Onus, of Inverell, NS Wales, and has issue living, Michael, *b* 19-, — Peter, *b* 19-, — Anthony, *b* 19-, — Marion Dura, *b* 19-. —— Ernest Austin (Clement Terr, Christie's Beach, St Lawrence, Australia), *b* 1921: *m* 1943, Jean Elsie, da of late James Alfred Walker, of Earlwood, NS Wales, and has issue living, David Ernest, *b* 1945, — Philip Kenneth Raymond, *b* 1952, — James Raymond, *b* 1953, — Margaret Jean, *b* 1944, — Irene Clare, *b* 1950.

—— Kenneth Richard, *b* 1922: *m* 1952, Trudy, da of W. Everingham. —— Bruce William, *b* 1927: *m* 19-, Elizabeth Law, and has issue living, Robert, *b* 19-, — Barbara, *b* 19-. —— Marjorie Irene, *b* 1924: *m* 1946, John Michael McGann, and has issue living, Beverley Gay, *b* 1948, — Lynette Joy, *b* 1951, — Jeanette Ellen, *b* 1953.

    Issue of late Frederick Gordon Aylmer, *b* 1900, *d* 1954: *m* 1940, Alma Elton (48 Maxim St, West Ryde, Sydney, NSW 2114):—
Carolyn Ann, *b* 1946; BSc, BA: *m* 1970, Ronald Bucholtz. —— Margaret Susan, *b* 1948: *m* 1969, Alan Robert Underwood (3 James Rd, Brooklyn), and has issue living, Julie, *b* 1975, — Fiona, *b* 1978.
The Aylmers are found in the cos of Dublin and Kildare in the 13th century, and John Aylmer got the Manor of Lyons, co Kildare, about 1400 by *m* with Helen Tyrrell. The present representative of the Lyons, or Elder Branch, is Gerald Valentine Aylmer. Sir Gerald Aylmer, Knt, *cr* a Baronet 1621-2 (founder of the Donadea branch of the family), was third son of Richard Aylmer, of Lyons, co Kildare (temp 1509-1559). The 13th baronet, Sir Fenton John Aylmer, VC, KCB, was a Lieut-Gen in the Army.

BACKHOUSE (UK) 1901, of Uplands, Darlington, co Durham, and The Rookery, Middleton Tyas, North Riding of Yorkshire.

Confido in Deo

I trust in God

Sir JONATHAN ROGER BACKHOUSE, 4th *Baronet*, *b* 30 Dec 1939; *s* his father, *Major Sir* JOHN EDMUND, MC, 1944; *ed* Ampleforth, and Brasenose Coll, Oxford; formerly a Dir of W. H. Freeman and Co, Ltd, publishers.

Arms – Per saltire or and azure, a saltire engrailed ermine between two roses in pale gules barbed and seeded proper, and as many passion crosses in fesse of the first. **Crest** – In front of a rock proper thereon an eagle displayed vert holding in each claw a passion cross or, a serpent on its back, the tail nowed, also proper.

BROTHER LIVING

OLIVER RICHARD, FCA, Member Securities Inst, *b* 18 July 1941; *ed* Ampleforth, and RMA Sandhurst: *m* 1970, Gillian Irene, only da of L. W. Lincoln, of Northwood, Middx, and has an adopted son and an adopted da. *Residence* – Highcroft, 141 Quickley Lane, Chorleywood, Rickmansworth, Herts WD3 5PD.

SISTERS LIVING

Jenifer Ann, *b* 1938: *m* 1959, Arthur Wreford Reed, who *d* 1989, and has issue living, Dominic Wreford, *b* 1962, — Rupert Wreford, *b* 1964, — Catherine Anna, *b* 1960, — Suzanne Belinda, *b* 1961. *Residence* – Flat 4, 69 Charlwood St, SW1V 4PG. —— Judith Mary, *b* (*posthumous*) 1945: *m* 1st, 1967 (*m diss* 1971), Garth Bentley Gibson; 2ndly, 1973, Filippo Lo Giudice, of Via di S Eufemia II, 00187 Rome, Italy, and has issue living (by 2nd *m*), Barbaro, *b* 1982, — Barbara, *b* 1975, — Francesca, *b* 1987.

AUNT LIVING

Joan Margaret, *b* 1920: *m* 1944, Lt Archibald Norman Macpherson, RN (ret), and has issue living, Allan Alisdair (53 Culmstock Rd, SW11 6LY), *b* 1951, — Angus John (44 Kyrle Rd, SW11 6BA), *b* 1953: *m* 1982, Anne Louise Felicity Barford, and has issue living, William Archibald *b* 1988, Eloise Isobel *b* 1985, Myrtle Maud *b* 1991, — Susan Margaret, *b* 1947: *m* 1973, Maj Harry Alexander Desmond Buchanan, MC, late Gren Gds, of Keepers, Totford, nr Alresford, Hants SO24 9TJ, and has issue living, Harry Alexander *b* 1980. *Residence* – Commonwood, Bearsted, Kent.

WIDOW LIVING OF THIRD BARONET

JEAN MARIE FRANCES, only child of late Lt-Col Gavin Robert Vernon Hume-Gore, MC: *m* 1st, 1937, Major Sir John Edmund Backhouse, 3rd Bt, MC, RA, who was *ka* 1944; 2ndly, 1953 (*m diss* 1966), (William) Nicol Gray, CMG, DSO, KPM, who *d* 1988; 3rdly, 1970, Norman Renshaw Sharpe, of Twinpines Orchard, Ohaeawai RD 2, Kaikohe, Bay of Islands, NZ.

COLLATERAL BRANCHES LIVING

    Issue of late Richard Miles Backhouse, brother of 3rd baronet, *b* 1911, *d* 1969: *m* 1st, 1948 (*m diss* 1951), Angela Mary, da of late Peter Haig-Thomas (*see* E Normanton, 1971 Edn), and widow of Capt Richard Dudley Melchior Gurowski, Scots Guards; 2ndly, 1951, Edeltraud Margaretha (73 Divinity Rd, Oxford OX4 1LH), da of Hofrat Dr Hans Perz of Vienna:—
(By 2nd *m*) Louise Maria Theodora, *b* 1955: *m* 1984, Maj Jonathan Arthur Francis Howard, Royal Hus (PWO), and has issue (*see* E Carlisle, colls). —— Julia Maria Florence, *b* 1956: *m* 1990, Paul Cameron Taylor, of 41 Hambalt Rd, SW4 9EQ, son of late J. A. Taylor, of Westbourne, Bournemouth, and has issue living, Maximilian John, *b* 1993, — Marie-Louise Florence May, *b* 1992.

    Grandchildren of late Lt-Col Miles Roland Charles Backhouse, DSO, TD, yst son of 1st baronet:—
    Issue of late Major Roger Trelawny Backhouse, RRC, *b* 1905, *d* 1977: *m* 1938, Beatrice Ada Janet (Penny Cottage, Crakehall, Bedale, N Yorks), da of late Capt Hedleigh St George Bond, R Canadian Engineers, of Toronto, Canada:—
Jane Trelawny, *b* 1939: *m* 1st, 1962 (*m diss* 1982), Michael Lake Coghlan; 2ndly, 1982, Duncan Irwin Eyre, of Silvester Cottage, Hudswell, Richmond, N Yorkshire, and has issue living (by 1st *m*), Henry Trelawny Lake, *b* 1964: *m* 1994, Stevan Caldwell, of NSW, Australia, — Benjamin Patrick Lake, *b* 1970, — Jane Louise Lake, *b* 1962, — Serena Mary Lake, *b* 1969. —— Avery St George, *b* 1941: *m* 1st 1963 (*m diss* 1973), Colin Frohawk Burrell; 2ndly 1978, Jeremy James Fraser, of Stutton Vale Farm, Tattingstone, Ipswich, Suffolk, and has issue living (by 1st *m*), Oliver Roy St George BACKHOUSE, *b* 1966: assumed surname of Backhouse in lieu of his patronymic by deed pool 1990, — Katharine Victoria, *b* 1964: *m* 1989, Peter John Bowring, and has issue living, Oscar Peter James *b* 1989, — (by 2nd *m*) Juliet Avery Virginia, *b* 1980. —— Elizabeth Esté, *b* 1943: *m* 1969, Angus Hugh Fraser, of Hornton Hall, Banbury, Oxon, and has issue living, Sophie Lavinia, *b* 1971, — Camilla Elizabeth, *b* 1973, — Emma Caroline, *b* 1977.

Issue of late Jonathan Backhouse, *b* 1907, *d* 1993: *m* 1934, Alice Joan, who *d* 1984, da of Brig Gen Charles Richard Woodroffe, CMG, CVO, CBE:—

David Miles (South Farm, Fairford, Glos GL7 3PN), *b* 1939; *ed* Eton: *m* 1969, Sophia Ann, da of late Col C.H.S. Townsend, and has issue living, Benjamin Jonathan, *b* 1974, — Cilla Gael, *b* 1972. —— William (Layer Marney Wick, Colchester, Essex CO5 9UT), *b* 1942; *ed* Eton: *m* 1971, Deborah Jane, da of late Lt-Col Hon David Edward Hely-Hutchinson (*see* E Donoughmore), and has issue living, Timothy James, *b* 1981, — Harriet Diana, *b* 1975, — Tessa Louise, *b* 1977. —— Joanna (Hawkins Farm, Monk, Eleigh Tye, Ipswich, Suffolk IP7 7JW), *b* 1936: *m* 1956, Jeremy James Norris Wyatt, who *d* 1988, only son of late Sir Myles Dermot Norris Wyatt, CBE, and has issue living, Thomas, *b* 1967, — Sarah, *b* 1957, — Nell Victoria, *b* 1959, — Carina Mary, *b* 1963.

Issue of late Maj Wilfred Jasper Backhouse, MBE, *b* 1913, *d* 1980: *m* 1946, Nancy Catherine (Horsey Island, Kirbyle-Soken, Essex), da of Lindsay Edward Bury, CBE, and widow of David Haig-Thomas:—

Joseph Lindsay, *b* 1953. —— Mary, *b* 1947: *m* 1973, Angus Bancroft, of Water Farm, Raydon, Hadleigh, Suffolk, and has issue living, William Harry, *b* 1978, — Anna Charlotte, *b* 1975. —— Hannah Margaret, *b* 1948: *m* 1968, Robert Braeme Skepper, of Ferry Farm, Sudbourne, Woodbridge, Suffolk, and has issue living, Jonathan *b* 19—, — Jane, *b* 19—, — Georgina, *b* 19—, — Poppy, *b* 19—.

The 1st baronet, Sir Jonathan Edmund Backhouse (el son of late Edmund Backhouse, JP, of Trebah, Falmouth), was a DL and JP for N Riding of Yorkshire and co Durham. The 2nd baronet, Sir Edmund Trelawny, was Professor, Peking Univ 1902-13, and subsequently Professor of Chinese, King's Coll, London. The 3rd baronet, Maj Sir John Edmund Backhouse, MC, RA, was *ka* 1944.

BACON, First (E) 1611, of Redgrave, Suffolk; Second (E) 1627, of Mildenhall, Suffolk

Moderation is stable

Sir NICHOLAS HICKMAN PONSONBY BACON (*Premier Baronet of England*), 14th Baronet of Redgrave, and 15th Baronet of Mildenhall; *b* 17 May 1953; *s* his father, *Lt-Col Sir* EDMUND CASTELL, KG, KBE, TD, 1982; *ed* Eton, and Dundee Univ (MA); a Page of Honour to HM 1966-69; Barrister-at-law (Gray's Inn 1978): *m* 1981, Susan Henrietta, da of Raymond Dinnis, of Delaware Farm, Edenbridge, Kent, and has issue.

Arms – Gules, on a chief argent, two mullets pierced sable. **Crest** – A boar passant ermine.
Residence – Raveningham Hall, Norwich.

SONS LIVING

HENRY HICKMAN, *b* 23 April 1984. —— Edmund, *b* 1986. —— Nathaniel, *b* 1989. —— Thomas Castell, *b* 1992.

SISTERS LIVING

Lavinia Winifred, *b* 1939; a Trustee of Nat Galleries of Scotland since 1986: *m* 1972, Stephen Cokayne Gibbs, of Dougarie, Isle of Arran (*see* B Aldenham and Hunsdon of Hunsdon, colls). —— Elizabeth Albinia, *b* 1944: *m* 1971, Ronald James Bremner Hoare, of Roydon Hall, Diss, Norfolk IP22 3XL, and has issue living, Jocelyn Charles Stewart, *b* 1974, — Selina Albinia, *b* 1976, — Nicola Clare, *b* 1977. —— Sarah (*Lady Nicholson*), *b* 1947: *m* 1970, Sir Paul Douglas Nicholson, of Quarry Hill, Brancepeth, co Durham, and has issue (*see* Lawson Tancred, Bt).

AUNTS LIVING (*Daughters of 12th baronet*)

Albinia Joane (244 Cranmer Court, SW3), *b* 1897: *m* 1924, Brig Wilson Theodore Oliver Crewdson, CBE, late RA, who *d* 1961, and has issue living, Wilson Peregrine Nicholas, *b* 1926: *m* 1957, Hon Lucy Clare Clare Beckett, only da of 3rd Baron Grimthorpe, and has issue (*see* B Grimthorpe), — Christopher John, *b* 1930: *m* 19—, Eileen Jones, — Sarah Albinia (*Lady Dowson*), *b* 1929: *m* 1950, Sir Philip Manning Dowson, CBE, PRA, of 1 Pembroke Studios, Pembroke Gdns, W8, and has issue living, one son and two das, of whom Aurea Katharine (*Hon Mrs James Colville*) *b* 1962; *ed* Royal Coll of Art (MA): *m* 1993, Dr the Hon (Richmond) James Innys Colville, 2nd son of 4th Viscount Colville of Culross. —— Katharine Mary, *b* 1906: *m* 1930, John Fowell Buxton, who *d* 1970 (*see* Buxton, Bt colls). *Residence* – Newhouse Farm, Wareside, Ware, Herts.

WIDOW LIVING OF THIRTEENTH BARONET

PRISCILLA DORA (*Priscilla, Lady Bacon*), DL (Orchards, Raveningham, Norwich NR14 6NS), da of Col Sir Charles Edward Ponsonby, 1st Bt TD: *m* 1936, Lt-Col Sir Edmund Castell Bacon, 13th Bt, KG, KBE, TD, who *d* 1982.

COLLATERAL BRANCHES LIVING

Issue of late Thomas Walter Bacon, 4th son of 10th baronet of Redgrave and 11th baronet of Mildenhall, *b* 1863, *d* 1950: *m* 1901, Edith Mary, who *d* 1950, da of late Alexander Samuel Leslie Melville (E Leven and Melville, colls):—

Anthony Walter, *b* 1902; *ed* Eton, and Trin Coll, Camb (BA 1923); formerly Flight-Lieut Auxiliary Air Force: *m* 1941, Lola Mary, da of late Charles Stanley Martin, of Dowlais, Glamorgan, and has issue living, Christopher Nicholas (Boundary Farm, Framsden, Stowmarket, Suffolk), *b* 1945; *ed* Eton: *m* 1977, Margaret Anne, yst da of late John Walker Craig, of Terrace House, Earl Soham, Woodbridge, Suffolk, and has issue living, Nathaniel John *b* 1978, Catharine Anne *b* 1979. *Residence* – Crag Pit House, Aldeburgh, Suffolk.

Grandchildren of late Thomas Walter Bacon (ante):—

Issue of late Francis Thomas Bacon, OBE, FRS, *b* 1904, *d* 1992: *m* 1934, Barbara Winifred (Trees, 34 High St, Little Shelford, Cambridge CB2 5ES), da of late Godfrey Papillon, of Barrasford, Northumberland:—

Edward Thomas Godfrey (17 Abingdon Court, Abingdon Villas, W8), *b* 1939; *ed* Eton, and Fitzwilliam House, Camb (MA): *m* 1980, Angelina Mary, da of late Alphonse Morhange, and has issue living, Francis Edward Alphonse, *b* 1982, — Veronica

Elizabeth, *b* 1984. —— (Elizabeth) Daphne, *b* 1935: *m* 1958, Giles Arthur Vivian-Neal, of Welbeck House, Brooke, Norfolk, and has issue living, Henry Arthur, *b* 1963, — James Francis, *b* 1968, — Gina Rosemary, *b* 1960, — Marianne Clare, *b* 1961.
Issue of late Christopher Henry Bacon, *b* 1906, *d* 1956: *m* 1940, Diana Sybil Richmond (Ramsden Farm, Ebony, Tenterden, Kent), da of late Frederick Richmond Brown (*see* Brown, Bt):—
Richard Anthony (Devondale, Beh's Lane, Uralba Rd, Alstonville, NSW 2477, Australia) *b* 1943: *m* 1973, Doreen Nan, da of John Keillar, and has issue living, Georgina Louise, *b* 1974, — Philippa Jane, *b* 1977. —— Timothy Roger (67 Britannia Rd, SW6) *b* 1947: *m* 1985, Marylyn Rowan Ogilvie, twin da of late Arthur Grant, of Trecarrell, St Just in Roseland, Cornwall, and has issue living, Rosalind Sarah, *b* 1987, — Laura Charlotte, *b* 1988. —— Elizabeth Anne, *b* 1942: *m* 1971, Pierre Bartlett (Leeswood Hall, Mold, Clwyd), and has issue living, Nicholas Michael, *b* 1972, — Andrew Christopher, *b* 1977, — Suzannah Louise, *b* 1973.

Grandsons of late Rev Reginald Cazalet Bacon, son of late Rev Francis Bacon, son of late Nicholas Bacon, 2nd son of 8th baronet of Redgrave and 9th baronet of Mildenhall, *b* 1861:—
Issue of late Capt Francis Rimington Bacon, *b* 1891, *d* 1947: *m* 1919, Winifred Marie, who *d* 1973, da of late Col George Henry Brook Coats, CB, of 5 Powis Sq, Brighton:—
Roger David Coats, *b* 1922; *ed* Downside, and Trin Coll, Camb; late Capt Irish Gds: *m* 1947, Phyllis Eleanor Claire, da of late Roland Oliver, of Hong Kong, and has issue living, Sarah, *b* 1948, — Fiona Jane, *b* 1950, — Veronica Claire, *b* 1953, — Diana Mary, *b* 1958, — Jennifer, *b* 1963. *Residence* – Bonaventure, 2 Caledon Rd, Poole, Dorset, BH14 9NN. —— Anthony Peter Coats (10 Buccleuch Rd, Branksome Park, Poole, Dorset BH13 6LE), *b* 1924; *ed* Downside, and Trin Coll, Camb; MB, BChir, MD, FRCP: *m* 1947, Helen, da of Harold Jaques, of Legram's Lane, Bradford, and has issue living, Hugh Francis, *b* 1952, — Peter Jaques (76 Pencisely Rd, Llandaff, Cardiff CF5 1DQ), *b* 1953; *ed* Downside, and St Thomas's Hosp Med Sch (MB, BS, MRCP, FRCS): *m* 1977, Susan, da of David Montague Rowse, of Clapper Hill, Ramsdell, Basingstoke, Hants, and has issue living, Nicholas *b* 1980, George Anthony Hugh *b* 1986, Diana Mary Louise *b* 1982, Annabel Jane Elizabeth *b* 1984, — Annette Susan, *b* 1959, — Patricia Margaret, *b* 1962.
This family is descended from Sir Nicholas Bacon (Lord Keeper of the Great Seal to Queen Elizabeth I), who was father of that great luminary of science Sir Francis Bacon, born 1561. Sir Nicholas' el son Sir Nicholas was the first person to receive a Baronetcy. Sir Hickman Beckett, 12th Bt, was a JP and DL for Lincolnshire (High Sheriff 1887), and a County Alderman for Lindsey Div of Lincolnshire (Chm 1914-24). Sir Edmund Castell, 13th Bt, KG, KBE, TD, was Lord Lieut for Norfolk 1949-78, a Dir Lloyds Bank Ltd 1949-73, Pro-Chancellor of Univ of E Anglia 1969-73, High Steward of Norwich Cathedral 1956-79, and of Gt Yarmouth 1968-82, a Church Commr 1955-63, Chm British Sugar Corpn 1957-68, and Chm Economic Development Cttee of Agric 1966-71; served NW Europe 1944 (despatches OBE).

BADDELEY (UK) 1922, of Lakefield, Parish of St Mary Stoke Newington, co London

In thee, O Lord, I trust

Sir JOHN WOLSEY BERESFORD BADDELEY, 4th *Baronet*; *b* 27 Jan 1938; *s* his father Sir JOHN BERESFORD 1979; *ed* Bradfield: *m* 1962, Sara Rosalind, da of late Colin Crofts, of Scarborough, and has issue.

Arms – Argent, a sword erect between two crosses couped gules, on a chief of the last a hind trippant between two garbs or. **Crest** – An arm couped and erect, vested azure, cuff argent, the hand holding an open book buckled and clasped proper between two crosses as in the arms.
Residence – 41 School Hill, Storrington, W Sussex.

DAUGHTERS LIVING

Sara Alexandra, *b* 1964: *m* 1989, Andrew C. E. Turner, elder son of D. E. Turner, of W Chiltington, Sussex; has issue living, Peter Andrew John *b* 1982. —— Anna Victoria, *b* 1965: *m* 1992, Brian A. Chambers, eldest son of D. B. Chambers, of Rutherglen, Victoria, Australia. —— Emma Elisabeth, *b* 1972.

SISTERS LIVING

Susan Catherine, *b* 1932: *m* 1956, Anthony Philip Harris, of Corner Cottage, Middle St, Petworth, W Sussex, and has issue living, Ian Robert Beresford, *b* 1958: *m* 1988, Rosie, da of Rotin Tebaki, of Gizo, Solomon Is, and has issue living, William Atoia Beresford *b* 1992, Emily Kirika *b* 1989, Lucy Teromita *b* 1993, — Michael Anthony, *b* 1959: *m* 1988, Joanna Mary, da of Rear Adm Peter Nicholas Marsden, of Lucerne, Niton, IoW, and has issue lving, Thomas Wolsey *b* 1991, Henry Beresford *b* 1993, — David John Tindall, *b* 1961: *m* 1989, Deborah L. M., da of late R. H. Green, of Ludlow, Shropshire, and has issue living, Robert Anthony *b* 1991, Isabelle Margaret *b* 1990, — Peter Wolsey, *b* 1964: *m* 1989, Amelia Angela, da of Nigel Azis, of Cokes Barn, West Burton, Pulborough, W Sussex, and has issue living, Jack Wolsey *b* 1991, Nicholas Peter *b* 1993, — Andrew Charles, *b* 1966, — Lucinda Jane, *b* 1963: *m* 1991, Andre Jon Neumann, son of R. Neumann, of Wellington, NZ, and has issue living, Benjamin Charles *b* 1993. —— Shirley Anne, *b* 1934: *m* 1956, Alan Richard Anthony Grout-Smith, and has issue living, John Alan Beresford, *b* 1962, — Nicola Susan, *b* 1958, — Sally Caroline, *b* 1960. *Residence* – Saddlers, Church Lane, Bury, W Sussex.

AUNT LIVING (*Daughter of 2nd baronet*)

Betty Mary, *b* 1909: late JP for Wilts: *m* 1938, Donald George Matthews Blanchard, and has issue living, Peter Donald (Manor Farm, Burbage, Marlborough, Wilts), *b* 1945; *ed* Marlborough, and Wye Agric Coll (BSc): *m* 1982, Pamela Anne, da of Basil Constanduros, and has issue living, Thomas Peter *b* 1984, — Diana Mary, *b* 1939: *m* 1964, Simon John Vaisey Faux, of Culleys Farm, Clench Common, Marlborough, Wilts, and has issue living, James Edward Vaisey *b* 1969, Jenny Anne *b* 1966, Susan Jane *b* 1967, — Anne Catherine, *b* 1942: *m* 1973, Timothy David Holgate, of The Hermitage, Marlborough College, Wilts, and has issue living, Mark Edward *b* 1975, Clare Susannah *b* 1977, Amy Louisa *b* 1979, — Mary Patricia, *b* 1950: *m* 1978, Peter James Henley Stibbard, of The Old House, Preston, Ramsbury, Wilts, and has issue living, Andrew George *b* 1983. *Residence* – Littlefield, Burbage, Marlborough, Wilts.

WIDOW LIVING OF THIRD BARONET

NANCY WINIFRED (*Nancy, Lady Baddeley*) (Bury House, Bury, Sussex), da of late Thomas Wolsey, of Smallburgh Hall, Norfolk: *m* 1929, Sir John Beresford Baddeley, 3rd Bt, who *d* 1979.

COLLATERAL BRANCHES LIVING

Issue of late Mark Baddeley, 2nd son of 1st baronet, *b* 1871, *d* 1930: *m* 1918, Mabel Annie, da of John Frederick Trigg:—

MARK DAVID, *b* 12 May 1921; *ed* Cliftonville Coll. —— Mabel Joyce.

Issue of late Bernard Beresford Baddeley, 3rd son of 1st baronet, *b* 1876, *d* 1956: *m* 1900, Ethel Emily, who *d* 1955, da of Sir David Burnett, 1st Bt:—

Allan Beresford, *b* 1909; *ed* Christ's Coll, Camb (BA 1931, MA 1936); formerly Capt RE: *m* 1945, Dorothy Ronwen, da of late H. J. Head, of Highlands, Wych Cross, Sussex, and has issue living, Paul Allan, *b* 1948: *m* 1977, Lesley, da of R. G. Springett, and has issue living, Thomas Sands *b* 1978, Samuel Joseph *b* 1980, — John Burnett, *b* 1951, — Rozanne Mary, *b* 1946: *m* 1973, Ashley Beeby, and has issue living, Morgan Douglas *b* 1978, Joshua John *b* 1981. *Residence* – Hawkins's, Tytherington, Wotton-under-Edge, Glos.

The 1st baronet, Sir John James, head of the firm of Baddeley Bros, wholesale stationers, etc, of 19 and 20, Moor Lane, EC2, was Sheriff of City of London 1908-09 and Lord Mayor 1921-22. The 2nd baronet, Sir (John) William Baddeley, was Managing Director of the firm of Baddeley Bros, Ltd, and Alderman (Cripplegate Ward) for City of London, and Master of Stationers' and Newspapermakers' Co 1937. The 3rd baronet, Sir John Beresford Baddeley, was Managing Director of Baddeley Bros, Ltd.

BAGGE (UK) 1867, of Stradsett Hall, Norfolk

Sir (JOHN) JEREMY PICTON BAGGE, 7th *Baronet*; *b* 21 June 1945; *s* by his father, *Maj Sir* JOHN ALFRED PICTON, ED, 1990; *ed* Eton; FCA; Councillor King's Lynn and W Norfolk Borough Council since 1981; Freeman City of London: *m* 1979, Sarah Margaret Phipps, da of late Maj James Shelley Phipps Armstrong (*see* Smith, Bt, *cr* 1947, 1990 Edn), and has issue.

Arms – Lozengy paly bendy, argent and gules, two flaunches or, on a chief of the last an annulet between two cinquefoils of the second. **Crest** – A pair of wings addorsed or, semée of annulets gules.
Seat – Stradsett Hall, King's Lynn, Norfolk PE33 9HA. *Club* – Boodle's.

SONS LIVING

ALFRED JAMES JOHN, *b* 1 July 1980. —— Albert Daniel Bracewell, *b* 1985.

DAUGHTER LIVING

Alexandra Mary Pleasance, *b* 1982.

BROTHERS LIVING

(Alfred) James Stephen (28 Luttrell Av, SW15), *b* 1952; *ed* Eton; Blues & Royals; ADC to Gov S Australia 1975-77; Bar-at-law Lincoln's Inn 1979-93, since when Partner, Norton Rose, Solicitors: *m* 1981, Victoria Imogen, elder da of Michael Andrew Lyndon Skeggs, of Oakhall, Cornhill-on-Tweed, Northumberland, and has issue living, Edwina Rose, *b* 1985. —— Thomas Philip (Hall Farm, Irnham, Grantham, Lincs NG33 4JD), *b* 1955; *ed* Eton, RMA Sandhurst, and RAC Cirencester; ARICS; Capt Blues & Royals; ADC to GOC 4 Armd Div 1977-78; ptnr Strutt & Parker 1987.

SISTERS LIVING

My hope is in God

Christabel Rosamund (Windlesham Park, Windlesham, Surrey), *b* 1940; High Sheriff Greater London 1990: *m* 1st, 1963, James Hinton Scott (*see* V Downe, 1962 Edn), who *d* 1988; 2ndly, 1990, as his 2nd wife, Peter Dimmock, CVO, OBE, and has issue living (by 1st *m*), Anthony Craufurd, *b* 1964; *ed* Charterhouse, and RMA Sandhurst, Capt The Blues and Royals, — Lucinda Ruth, *b* 1966, — Sara Rosamund, *b* 1968. —— Rosaleen Pleasance, *b* 1947: *m* 1972, Maj Jonathan James Buxton, of 62 Endlesham Rd, SW12, and has issue (*see* Buxton, Bt, colls). —— Elizabeth Mary Frances, *b* 1949: *m* 1981, Dean Rasheed, of Arkaba Station, Hawker, S Australia 5434, and has issue living, Edward James, *b* 1985, — Lucy Elizabeth, *b* 1983.

WIDOW LIVING OF SIXTH BARONET

ELIZABETH HELENA (*Dowager Lady Bagge*), da of late Daniel James Davies, CBE, Commr for Newfoundland in London: *m* 1939, Maj Sir John Alfred Picton Bagge, 6th Bt, ED, who *d* 1990. *Residence* – Stradsett Hall, King's Lynn, Norfolk PE33 9HA.

COLLATERAL BRANCH LIVING

Issue of late Major Henry Percy Bagge, MC, yst son of 3rd baronet, *b* 1879, *d* 1942: *m* 1928, Marjorie Aubrey, who *d* 1951, da of late Com Alexander Young Crawshay Mainwaring Spearman (Spearman, Bt, colls):—

Mary Pleasance (7 Stack House, Cundy St, SW1), *b* 1929; *ed* Newnham Coll, Camb (BA): *m* 1952 (*m diss* 1973), Amir Feridun Garakani.

The 1st baronet, Sir William Bagge (son of late Thomas Philip Bagge, JP, DL, of Stradsett, and Islington, Norfolk), sat as MP for West Norfolk (*C*) 1837-57 and 1865-80. The 6th baronet, Sir John Alfred Picton Bagge, ED, Maj Inns of Court Regt, was High Sheriff and DL Norfolk, and Chm W Norfolk Dist Council.

BAILEY (UK) 1919, of Cradock, Province of Cape of Good Hope, Union of South Africa

Virtue is my fortress

Sir DERRICK THOMAS LOUIS BAILEY, DFC, 3rd *Baronet*; *b* 15 Aug 1918; *s* his half-brother, Sir JOHN MILNER, 1946; *ed* Winchester, and Ch Ch, Oxford; Capt S African Air Force; formerly 2nd Lieut S African Irish; European War 1939-45 (DFC): *m* 1st, 1946 (*m diss* 19—), (Katherine) Nancy, da of Robin Stormonth Darling, of Rosebank, Kelso, Scotland; 2ndly, 1980 (*m diss* 1990), Mrs Jean Roscoe, and has issue by 1st *m*.

Arms – Argent, on a fesse between three martlets gules a bezant between two sprigs of mimosa proper. Crest – A demi-female figure with arms extended proper habited azure, round the neck a ruff, and trimmed at the collar, cuffs and shoulders argent, holding in the dexter hand a castle or, and in the sinister a sprig of mimosa also proper.
Seat – Bluestones, Alderney, CI.

SONS LIVING *(By 1st marriage)*

JOHN RICHARD (67 Darley Rd, Randwick, NSW 2031, Australia), *b* 11 June 1947; *ed* Winchester, and Christ's Coll: *m* 1977, Philippa Jane, only da of John Sherwin Mervyn Pearson Gregory, of Monnington House, Monnington-on-Wye, Hereford, and has issue living, James Edward, *b* 7 Sept 1983, — Michael Abe, *b* 1987, — Anna, *b* 1980. —— Thomas Noel (Lower Brinsop Court Farm, Hereford HR4 7AZ), *b* 1948; *ed* Bradfield: *m* 1987, Penelope Jane, da of F. B. Aggas, of Kibworth, Leics, and has issue living, Peter Robert, *b* 1988, — Charles Richard, *b* 1990, — Jack Frederick, *b* 1994. —— William Abe (Poortje Stud, PO Box 83, Colesberg 5980, Cape Prov, S Africa), *b* 1950; *ed* Winchester: *m* 1982, Nikki, formerly wife of — Riley, and da of late Vernon Langerman, of Cape Town, and has issue living, David Moir, *b* 1983, — Camilla, *b* 1985. —— Patrick James (Upton Court, Upton Bishop, Ross-on-Wye, Hereford HR9 7UN), *b* 1959; *ed* Bradfield: *m* 1st, 1983 (*m diss* 1986), Hon Lucy Jane Hamilton-Russell, yst da of 10th Viscount Boyne; 2ndly, 1990, Sarah E., yr da of Brian J. Hammond, of White Leas, Sopworth, Chippenham, Wilts.

DAUGHTER LIVING *(By 1st marriage)*

Patricia Rosemary, *b* 1951: *m* 1986, Anthony Howard Collins, of Llantellen, Skenfrith, Gwent, son of Michael Collins, of W Grinstead, Sussex, and has issue living, Edward, *b* 1989, — Sam, *b* 1991, — Tara, *b* 1987.

BROTHER LIVING

James Richard Abe, DFC, *b* 1919 *ed* Winchester, and Ch Ch, Oxford, formerly Squadron Leader RAF, Vol Reserve; European War 1939-45 (DFC): *m* 1st, 1958 (*m diss* 1963), Gillian Mary, who *d* 19—, da of John Kilgour Parker, of Cape Town, S Africa; 2ndly, 1964, Barbara (TAYLOR), da of Harry Epstein, of Johannesburg, and has had issue, (by 1st *m*) Jonathan Alcuin Abe, *b* 1959, — (by 2nd *m*) Alaric James Abe, *b* 1965, *d* 1986, — Prospero James Thomas, *b* 1969. *Address* – PO 226, Bryanston, Transvaal.

SISTER LIVING

Noreen Helen Rosemary, *b* 1921: *m* 1st, 1941, W/Cdr Peter Anker-Simmons, DFC, RAF, who *d* 1947; 2ndly, 1947 (*m diss* 1951), Count Peter Christian Raben-Levetzau, who *d* 1969, and has had issue, (by 1st *m*) Richard James (Manutsa Farm, PO Box 84, Hoedspruit, Eastern Transvaal), *b* 1944: *m* 1981 (*m diss* 1982), — , and has issue living, Justin Rorke James *b* 1982, — (Noreen) Starr, *b* 1941: *m* 1st, 1967 (*m diss* 1975), as his 2nd wife, Sir Vivyan Edward Naylor-Leyland, 3rd Bt, who *d* 1987; 2ndly, 1986, Philip Thomas Harper, of Tebula, PO Box 2442, Tzaneen, S Africa, — (by 2nd *m*) Paul Michael (*Count Raben-Levetzau*), *b* 1949, — Alexandra Louise, *b* 1948; *d* 1984. *Residences* – L'Ermitage, rue de Soeurs, Vineuil, St Firmin, 60500 Chantilly, France; 94 Pretoria Av, Atholl, Johannesburg, S Africa.

The 1st baronet, Sir Abe Bailey, KCMG (son of Hon Thomas Bailey, of Queenstown, S Africa), was engaged in Farming in Cape Colony, and a Company Director; implicated in Jameson Raid (sentenced to two years' imprisonment and fined £2,000); S African War 1899-1902 as an Intelligence Officer, and Major Gorringe's Flying Column; S-W Africa 1914-15 as Major and DAQMG Union Forces; in 1908 raised and equipped at own expense 200 Inf and 100 Mounted Inf to quell Zululand Rebellion in Natal; had Corps of Sharpshooters in Flanders during European War 1914-18; a Member of House of Assembly, Union of S Africa 1910-24; a MLA of Cape Colony and of Transvaal (Whip in both Parliaments).

BAILLIE (UK) 1823, of Polkemmet, Linlithgowshire

It shines in the dark

Sir GAWAINE GEORGE HOPE BAILLIE, 7th *Baronet*; *b* 8 March 1934; *s* his father, *Sir* ADRIAN WILLIAM MAXWELL, 1947; *ed* Eton, and Camb Univ: *m* 1966, Mrs Lucile Margot Gardner, da of Senator Louis P. Beaubien, and has issue.

Arms – Azure, nine mullets, three, three, two, and one or within a bordure counter-nebulée argent and sable. **Crest** – Issuant out of clouds proper an estoile or. **Supporters** – Two lions guardant argent. *Residence* – Freechase, Warninglid, Sussex RH17 5SZ.

SON LIVING

ADRIAN LOUIS, *b* 26 March 1973.

DAUGHTER LIVING

Liza Katharine, *b* 1969.

COLLATERAL BRANCH LIVING

Granddaughter of late Thomas Baillie, 4th son of 1st baronet:—
Issue of late William Baillie, *b* 1861, *d* 1928: *m* 1892, Mary, who *d* 1946, el da of late Rev Walter Fellows, Incumbent of St John's, Toorak, Melbourne:—
Julia Mary (Alexandra), *b* 1905: *m* 1943, Leonhard Adam, LLD, D Phil, who *d* 1960, and *d* 1993, leaving issue, Mary Clare, *b* 1945: *m* 1st, 1964 (*m diss* 1969), Gabriel A. Michaelides; 2ndly, 1981, Moshe Murvitz (c/o Israel Philharmonic Orchestra, Tel Aviv), and has issue living (by 2nd *m*), Batia Leonora *b* 1982.

The father of the 1st baronet was a Lord of Session (Lord Polkemmet). Sir William, 2nd baronet, sat as MP for Linlithgowshire (*C*) 1845-7. The 5th baronet, Sir Gawaine George Stuart Baillie, Lieut 2nd Dragoons, was *ka* 1914. The 6th baronet, Sir Adrian William Maxwell Baillie, sat as MP for Linlithgowshire (*C*) 1931-5, and for Tonbridge Div of Kent 1937-45.

BAIRD (NS) 1695, of Saughton Hall, Edinburghshire

By strength and valour

Sir JAMES RICHARD GARDINER BAIRD, MC, 10th *Baronet*; son of late Capt William Frank Gardiner Baird, 2nd son of 8th baronet; *b* 12 July 1913; *s* his uncle, *Maj Sir* JAMES HOZIER GARDINER, MC, 1966; *ed* Eton, and University Coll, Oxford; formerly Capt Kent Yeo; 1939-45 War (MC): *m* 1941, Mabel Ann (Gay) Tempest, da of Algernon Gill, and has issue.

Arms – Gules, a sanglier passant or; on a canton ermine a sword pale-wise proper. **Crest** – A boar's head erased or. *Residence* – Church Farm House, Guist, Norfolk NR20 5AJ. *Club* – Naval and Military.

SONS LIVING

(JAMES) ANDREW GARDINER, *b* 2 May 1946; *ed* Eton: *m* 1984 (*m diss* 198-), Jean Margaret, da of late Brig Sir Ian Liddell Jardine, 4th Bt, OBE, MC, and has issue living, Alexander, *b* 28 May 1986. —— William Julian Gardiner (7 Bettridge Rd, SW6), *b* 1947; *ed* Milton Abbey: *m* 1984, Nichola Bridget Halsall, da of Lt-Col Cecil West, OBE, of Hythe, Kent.

DAUGHTER LIVING

Lavinia Mary Arabella (25 Broadhinton Rd, SW4 0LT), *b* 1951.

COLLATERAL BRANCHES LIVING

Issue of late William Henry Gardiner Baird, yr brother of 10th baronet, *b* 1914, *d* 1989: *m* 1st, 1946 (*m diss* 1966), Helen Mary, eldest da of late Rev Canon Edward Charles Rich, of 31 Yeoman's Row, SW3; 2ndly, 1966, C. Gwendolyn (Cleeve Court Cottage, Streatley-on-Thames, Berks), da of late James Smart, OBE, of Ottawa:—
(By 1st *m*) Mervyn Edward Hozier (22 The Terrace, Sunninghill, nr Ascot, Berks SL5 9NH), *b* 1947; *ed* Milton Abbey: *m* 1970, Isobel Frances, only da of late Stewart Winzor, of Adelaide, S Australia, and has issue living, James Edward Hozier, *b* 1976, — Mirella Frances Hozier, *b* 1973. —— Roderick Frank Gardiner (161 Craighleith Rd, Edinburgh EH4 2EB), *b* 1955; *ed* The Elliot Sch, Putney: *m* 1985, Julia Mary, elder da of Gerald Barry, WS, of Humbie, E Lothian, and has issue living, Arabella Elizabeth Gardiner, *b* 1987. —— Judith Mary Gardiner, *b* 1951: *m* 1974, David Ashworth Sydney Phillips Cosby, of Ballycrew House, Aughrim, co Wicklow, 3rd and yst son of late Maj Errold Ashworth Sydney Cosby, of Straddbally Hall, co Leix, and has issue.

Descendants of late William Baird (el son of late William Baird, 2nd surviving son of 1st baronet), whose 2nd son David was *cr* a *Baronet* 1809 with special remainder to his el brother Robert:—

See Baird, Bt, *cr* 1809.

King Charles I issued a warrant creating James Baird, of Newbyth, co Haddington, Baron Devern, but he died before the patent passed the great seal. His el son, Sir John Baird, was a Lord of Session under the style of Lord Newbyth, and his son Sir William of Newbyth was *cr* a baronet (NS 1680, ext 1745). The 2nd son of James Baird of Newbyth, Robert of Saughton Hall, Midlothian, an Edinburgh merchant, was *cr* a baronet with remainder to heirs male of the body. Sir William Baird, 5th baronet, *m* 1750, Frances, da of the celebrated Col James Gardiner, of Bankton, who was *k* at the battle of Prestonpans 1745.

BAIRD (UK) 1809, of Newbyth, Haddingtonshire

By strength and valour

Sir DAVID CHARLES BAIRD, 5th *Baronet,* son of late William Arthur Baird, 2nd son of 3rd baronet; *b* 6 July 1912; *s* his uncle, *Sir* DAVID, MVO, 1941; *ed* Eton, and Cambridge Univ.

𝔄rms – Gules, in chief within an increscent an estoile of eight points argent; in base a boar passant or; on a canton ermine a sword erect proper, pommel and hilt gold. ℭrest – 1st, a Mameluke mounted on a horse, and holding in his dexter hand a scimitar all proper; 2nd, a boar's head erased or.
Residence – 52 High St, Kirkcudbright DG6 4JX.

SISTERS LIVING

Margaret Stuart, *b* 1910: *m* 1938, Marcus Humphrey Ure Spurway, and has issue living, Humphrey John (Linhouse, Livingstone, W Lothian), *b* 1942: *m* 1968, Rosaline Avril Orr Walker, and has issue living, Charles *b* 1972, Mark *b* 1973, Guy *b* 1974, Kalitza *b* 1977, — George Henry, *b* 1945, — Kalitza Mary Stuart, *b* 1939: *m* 1961, Patrick Alexander Campbell Fraser, of Borthwickshiels, Hawick, Roxburghshire, and has issue living, Fiona Margaret *b* 1963, Lucinda Caroline *b* 1964, Theresa Elizabeth *b* 1967, — Theresa Frances, *b* 1941: *m* 1966, Richard Dawnay Innes, of Playford Hall, Ipswich (*see* V Downe, colls, 1985 Edn), and has issue living, Antonia *b* 1967, Sara *b* 1969, Johanna *b* 1970, Katherine *b* 1973. *Residence* – Harburn, W Calder, W Lothian. ——— Hersey Ellen, *b* 1916: *m* 1939 (*m diss* 1959), Maj Lachlan Gordon-Duff, Gordon Highlanders, and has issue living, Simon Lachlan (Lodge Farm, Stowood, nr Beckley, Oxon OX3 9SR), *b* 1942: Maj Scots Gds: *m* 1990, Mrs Caroline Edith Mary Craig, elder da of late Col Charles Neil Howard, MC late Black Watch (*see* E Denbigh, colls), — Robert Andrew (Glebe House, Stobo, Peebleshire), *b* 1945: *m* 1973, Mrs Caroline Orby Robarts, da of Maj Robert Clifton Gascoigne (*see* Munro, Bt, *cr* 1634, colls), and has issue living, Hersey Diana *b* 1973, Philippa Sophie *b* 1976. *Residence* – Spring Cottage, Hardgate, Castle Douglas, Kirkcudbrightshire.

COLLATERAL BRANCHES LIVING

Issue of late Robert Walter Stuart Baird, yr brother of 5th baronet, *b* 1914, *d* 1989: *m* 1st, 1938 (*m diss* 1960), Maxine Christine, only da of Rupert Darrell, of New York, USA; 2ndly, 1960, Maria Florine Viscart (16 rue des Granges, Geneva 1204, Switzerland):—
(By 1st *m*) CHARLES WILLIAM STUART (12 Falstaff St, Sunnybank Hills, Brisbane, Qld 4109, Australia), *b* 8 June 1939; *ed* in Switzerland: *m* 1965, Jane Joanna, da of late Brig A. Darley Bridge, and has issue living, Tara Francesca Stuart, *b* 1970, — Senta Louise Stuart, *b* 1973, — Petra Helen Stuart, *b* 1975. ——— (By 2nd *m*) Frances, *b* 1960.

Grandchildren of late Robert George Baird, son of late Robert Henry Baird, son of late Capt Wynne Baird, RN, brother of 2nd baronet:—
Issue of late Maj Robert Douglas Baird, MC, *b* 1893, *d* 1969: *m* 1926 Alice Patience (Bright Haven, Sandford Mill Rd, Cheltenham, Glos GL53 7QH), da of late Cecil Gordon Crawley, CBE, of 19 Cranley Pl, SW7:—
Dawn, *b* 1927: *m* 1968, Geoffrey Haig Loyd, of Remenham House, Ocle Pychard, Hereford (*see* Oakeley, Bt).
Issue of late Maj George Henry William Baird, *b* 1903, *d* 1992: *m* (Jan) 1931, Catherine Augusta, who *d* 1986, da of late Capt Francis William Forester (Milbank, Bt):—
Angus George David (Hartsfield House, Westland Green, Little Hadham, Ware, Herts SG11 2AJ), *b* 1934; *ed* Eton: *m* 1961, Fiona Elizabeth Hildred, da of John Sholto Fitzpatrick Cooke, CBE, and has issue living, Andrew James, *b* 1970, — Nicola Laura, *b* 1964, — Eliza Caroline *b* 1967. ——— Diana Catherine, *b* (Dec) 1931: *m* 1953, Julian Charles Lewis Jenkinson, of Folly Faunts House, Goldhanger, Maldon, Essex, and has issue (*see* Jenkinson, Bt, colls).
The 1st baronet, Rt Hon Sir David Baird, GCB, PC (2nd son of late William Baird, el son of late William Baird, 2nd surviving son of Sir Robert Baird, 1st Bt (*cr* 1695)), was a distinguished military commander, and was *cr* a baronet with special remainder to the heirs male of his brother, Robert. At the capture of Seringapatam he headed the storming party, and as Commander-in-Chief he captured the Cape of Good Hope. In the battle of Corunna he lost an arm. On his death without issue in 1847, he was succeeded under the special remainder by his nephew, David. This family is a junior branch of Baird, baronet of Saughton Hall, to whose title the present Baronet of Newbyth is in remainder. The 3rd baronet, Sir David, served in the Crimea, and in the Indian Mutiny.

BAKER (UK) 1802, of Wembley (Extinct 1959)

Sir RANDOLF LITTLEHALES BAKER, DSO, 4th and last *Baronet.*

DAUGHTER LIVING OF FOURTH BARONET

Selina Littlehales (Ranston, Blandford, Dorset), *b* 1925: *m* 1955, Major William Harry Gibson Fleming, JP, DL, RA (ret), who *d* 1981, and has issue living, James Randolf (Smugglers Mead, Stepleton, Blandford, Dorset), *b* 1958: *m* 1986, Fiona Lucy, da of Robert Don, of Elmham House, Dereham, Norfolk, and has issue living, Hector *b* 1987, William Robert *b* 1989, Olivia Rose *b* 1992, — Anthea Margaret, *b* 1956.

SHERSTON-BAKER (GB) 1796, of Dunstable House, Richmond, Surrey.

Sir ROBERT GEORGE HUMPHREY SHERSTON-BAKER, 7th *Baronet*; *b* 3 April 1951; *s* his father, *Sir* HUMPHREY DODINGTON BENEDICT SHERSTON, 1990: *m* 1991, Vanessa R. A., yst da of C. E. A. Baird, of Grouville, Jersey, CI, and has issue.

𝔞rms – Argent, a saltire sable charged with five escallops erminois, on a chief azure a lion passant of the third, armed and langued gules. 𝔠rest – A demi-lion rampant per fesse indented, erminois and pean, holding in the paws an escallop argent charged with an ermine spot.
Residence – Wealden House, North Elham, Kent CT4 6UY.

Fidei coticula crux

The cross is the test of faith

SON LIVING

DAVID ARBUTHNOT GEORGE, *b* 24 Nov 1992.

DAUGHTER LIVING

Amy Margaret, *b* 1994.

SISTERS LIVING

Margaret Elizabeth, *b* 1939: *m* 1969, Peter Leggatt, son late Harry Leggatt, and of Mrs Gerald Cobb, of Meonstoke, Hants. *Residence* – —. ——— Sarah Loraine, *b* 1940: *m* 1963, Christopher Charles Jervis Johnson-Ferguson, 2nd son of Lt-Col Sir Neil Edward Johnson-Ferguson, 3rd Bt, TD, and has issue. *Residence* – . ——— Jane Magdalen, *b* 1948. *Residence* – .

COLLATERAL BRANCHES LIVING

Issue of late John Dunstan Sherston BAKER, 2nd son of 4th baronet, *b* 1882, *d* 1940: *m* 1915, Anna Josephine, who *d* 1952, da of late Alexander Wood, FSA:—
Peter SHERSTON-BAKER, MC (3D Sheen Gate Gdns, SW14), *b* 1918: *ed* Downside; Maj (ret) RA; a Queen's Messenger 1964-77; 1939-45 War (despatches, MC): *m* 1947, Elizabeth, da of late Mrs Walter Hugh Barham, of 1 Camden Park, Tunbridge Wells, and has issue living, Veronica (243 Waldegrave Rd, Strawberry Hill Twickenham, Middx TW1 4SY), *b* 1948: *m* 1969 (*m diss* 1989), Christopher Carlton Fulton, son of late F. J. A. Fulton, of Nelson, NZ, and has issue living, Guy Charles Jeffreys *b* 1970, Robyn Frances Jeffreys *b* 1973, — Josephine *b* 1950: *m* 1975, John Gordon Chambers, of 26 Shalstone Rd, SW14, son of late Norman Henry Chambers, of 24 Liverpool Rd, St Albans, Herts, and has issue living, Oliver Henry Sherston *b* 1979, — Gabrielle, *b* 1954: *m* 1977, Geoffrey Tuff of 74 Little Meadow, Writtle, Essex, son of late Col Charles Reginald Tuff, and has issue living, Rebecca *b* 1981, Alice *b* 1983. ——— Loraine Josephine: *m* 1938, Count Alexandre Gaston Pierre du Bouzet, who *d* 1989, and has had issue, Jean Pierre, *b* 1938, — Patrick Peter (10 Cité Rougemont, 75009 Paris), *b* 1939: *m* 1968, Susan, da of Ake Böhn, of Stockholm, and has issue living, Alexandre *b* 1971, Mikaël *b* 1974, — Christian Xavier, *b* 1942, — Jean François, *b* 1950, — Marguerite Loraine, *b* 1940: *m* 1964, (Andrew) Ivan Bruce, of Beechwood Main St, Shawell, Leics LE17 6AG, son of William Douglas Bruce, and *d* 1991, leaving issue, Douglas Ivan *b* 1967, Christina Loraine *b* 1970, Marina Yolanda *b* 1978, — Anne France, *b* 1943: *m* 1966, Peter Meakin, of 4 Violet Rd, Claremont 7700, S Africa, — Chantal, *b* 1946: *m* 1967, Jean François David, of 21 Avenue de Parc St James, 92200 Neuilly-sur-Seine, Paris, son of Jean David, and has issue living, Olivier Charles *b* 1968, Christophe Pierre André *b* 1970, Ingrid Antoinette Loraine *b* 1973, — Béatrice Marie Madeleine, *b* 1958: *m* 1988, Gilles Bouhours, of 43 rue d'Alma, 92400 Courbevoie, France, son of Louis Bouhours, and *d* 1993, leaving issue, Amoury *b* 1988, Cèdric *b* 1990. *Residence* – 21 Avenue de Parc St James, 92200 Neuilly-sur-Seine, Paris, France.
This family was settled in the west of England several centuries before the creation of the baronetcy. The 1st baronet received a baronetcy for raising and maintaining for King George III a troop of 500 horse styled "The Richmond Rangers", and the 4th Bt was many years Recorder of Barnstaple and Bideford and a County Court Judge. The 5th Baronet, Sir Dodington George Richard Sherston, Lieut-Col (ret) IMS, assumed by deed poll 1923 (recorded at Heralds' College) the additional surname of Sherston.

Baker-Wilbraham, see Wilbraham.

BALFOUR (UK) 1911, of Albury Lodge, Albury, Hertfordshire (Extinct 1929)

Sir ROBERT BALFOUR, 1st and last *Baronet*.

GRANDDAUGHTERS LIVING OF FIRST BARONET

(Issue of late Alexander Balfour, el son of 1st baronet, *b* 1882, *d* 1923: *m* 1910, Ruth Frances, who *d* 1940, da of late John D. Macfarland, banker, of Lincoln, Nebraska, USA) — Nancy, OBE (36E Eaton Sq, SW1), *b* 1911; OBE (Civil) 1965. ——— Margaret, *b* 1917: *m* 1948, John B. Ashbrook, and has issue living, Susan Margaret, *b* 1950: *m* 1973, F. V. Casselman, of Mass, USA, — Katherine Jessie, *b* 1955. *Residence* – Wrango Hall, Denham Village, Bucks.

BALL (UK) 1911, of Merrion Square, City of Dublin, and Killybegs, co Donegal

Sir CHARLES IRWIN BALL, 4th *Baronet; b* 12 Jan 1924; *s* his father, *Sir* NIGEL GRESLEY, 1978; *ed* Sherborne; a Chartered Accountant: *m* 1st, 1950 (*m diss* 1983), Alison Mary, da of late Lt-Col Percy Holman Bentley, MBE, MC, of Farnham, Surrey; 2ndly, 1994, Christine Trilby Knowles and has issue by 1st *m.*

Arms – Argent, on a chevron gules between three fireballs proper a galley with one mast, sail furled, pennant flottant in stern of the first. **Crest** – An arm vambraced embowed argent, charged with two ogresses, the hand proper grasping a fireball as in the arms.
Residence – Killybegs, Eddystone Rd, Thurlestone, Kingsbridge, Devon TQ7 3NU

SONS LIVING *(By 1st marriage)*

RICHARD BENTLEY (Evenshade, Sandowa Rd, Esher, Surrey KT10 9TT), *b* 29 Jan 1953; *ed* Sherborne, and Leicester Univ; ACA: *m* 1991, Beverley Ann, da of Bertram Joffre Wright.

DAUGHTER LIVING *(By 1st marriage)*

Diana Margaret (56 Barrons Way, Comberton, Cambridge), *b* 1955.

BROTHER LIVING

Ronald Herbert (31 Waterlip Cottage, Cranmore, Shepton Mallet, Som BA4 4RN), *b* 1925: *m* 1st, 1950, Pamela Mary, who *d* 1969, da of late John Morton, of Hunningham Grange, Warwicks; 2ndly, 1970 (*m diss* 1980), Mrs Diana Joy Maitland, da of late Lt-Col James Pridham, of 54 Elm Park House, Fulham Rd, SW10, and has issue living (by 1st *m*), Christopher Nigel Morton (31 Waterlip Cottage, Cranmore, Shepton Mallet, Som BA4 4RN), *b* 1951: *m* 1974, Melanie, da of Col David James Fenner, of 1 Riverside Cottage, Lyme Regis, Dorset, and has issue living, Peter Jonathan *b* 1981, Amelia Kate *b* 1983, — Jonathan Gresley (The Headlands, Luntley, nr Pembridge, Hereford HR6 9EJ), *b* 1956: *m* 1981, Molly, da of late Christopher Major, and has issue living, Christopher James *b* 1984, Katherine Elizabeth *b* 1987, Joanna Rachel *b* (twin) 1987, — Rupert Valentine (Smugglers Bar, Parque Don José, Costa del Silencio, Arona, Tenerife, Spain), *b* 1958: *m* 1981, Christine, da of Cliff Hampson, of 46 Hereford Rd, Blackburn, Lancs, and has issue living, James Irwin Hampson *b* 1992, Emma Frances *b* 1983, — Susan Mary (9 Peter St, S Golden Beach, NSW 2483, Australia), *b* 1953: *m* 1979 (*m diss* 1981), Steven Rhead Allen.

SISTER LIVING

Valerie Margaret, *b* 1929: *m* 1953, Christopher Elliott Winn, and has issue living, David Elliott (219 Hempstead Rd, Hempstead, nr Gillingham, Kent), *b* 1958: *m* 1988, Esther Maria Lewis, and has issue living, Catherine Elizabeth *b* 1988, Stephanie Fay *b* 1991, — Joanna Margaret, *b* 1955: *m* 1979, Anthony Oliver Bay Green, of Oak Cottage, Hill House Hill, Liphook, Hants, and has issue living, Barnaby Oliver Bay *b* 1983, Samantha Margaret Bay *b* 1981, Susannah Katharine Bay *b* 1986, — Fiona Anne, *b* 1957: *m* 1985, Charles Christopher Carter Brett, of St Swithin's Gate, Kingsgate Rd, Winchester, Hants, and has issue living, Luisa Annabel Carter *b* 1987, Claudia Alessandra Isabel *b* 1990. *Residence* – 8 Broadlands Court, Kew Gardens Rd, Richmond, Surrey.

COLLATERAL BRANCH LIVING

Issue of late Ivan Hellicar Ball, 4th son of 1st baronet, *b* 1894, *d* 1963: *m* 1929, Dorothy, who *d* 1992, da of late Charles E. Gill:—
Ursula Pamela Joyce, *b* 1930: *m* 1959, Herbert John Lewis, of Strath Isla, Wothorpe Drift, Stamford, Lincs, and has issue living, Peter John, *b* 1961, — Joanna Mary, *b* 1964, — Sarah Catherine, *b* 1966. —— Dorothy Lucia Anne (2 Abbots Way, Neston, S Wirral, Cheshire L64 3SU), *b* 1933.
The 1st baronet, Sir Charles Bent Ball, MD, FRCSI, was Hon Surg to King Edward VII in Ireland 1904-10 and to King George V 1910-16. The 2nd baronet, Sir (Charles) Arthur Kinahan Ball, MD, was appointed Regius Professor of Surgery, Dublin Univ 1933.

HARMOOD-BANNER (UK) 1924, of Liverpool, co Lancaster (Extinct 1990)

Sir GEORGE KNOWLES HARMOOD-BANNER, 3rd and last *Baronet.*

DAUGHTERS LIVING OF THIRD BARONET

Susan, *b* 1951. —— Gillian, *b* 1953: *m* 1981, John Richard Taylor-Medhurst, and has issue living, (John) Tim Banner, *b* 1982, — James Richard Banner, *b* 1984, — Henry Bruce Banner, *b* 1987, — Peter George Banner, *b* 1989. *Residence* – Greenbanks, Cranbrook Rd, Hawkhurst, Kent TN18 5EF.

SISTERS LIVING OF THIRD BARONET

Elizabeth, *b* 1908: *m* 1931, Ronald Percy Crawshaw, and has issue living, James, *b* 1947, — Joanna, *b* 1934, — Cordelia Anne, *b* 1937. *Residence* – Chestnut Cottage, Beckley, nr Rye, E Sussex. —— Frances Cordelia (3 Castle Sq, Tenby, Pembs), *b* 1913: *m* 1941 (*m diss* 1948), Capt James Jardine-Hunter-Paterson, King's Own Scottish Borderers.

WIDOW LIVING OF THIRD BARONET

ROSEMARY JANE (*Lady Harmood-Banner*), da of Col Maurice Lawrence Treston, CBE: *m* 1947, Sir George Knowles Harmood-Banner, 3rd Bt, who *d* 1990, when the title became ext. *Address* – c/o National Westminster Bank, Sloane Square Branch, 14 Sloane Sq, SW1 8EQ.

BANNERMAN (NS) 1682, of Elsick, Kincardineshire

For my country

Sir DAVID GORDON BANNERMAN, OBE, 15th *Baronet*; *b* 18 Aug 1935; *s* his brother, *Sir* ALEXANDER PATRICK, 1989; *ed* Gordonstoun, and New Coll, Oxford (MA); late 2nd Lieut Queen's Own Cameron Highlanders; Min of Defence; OBE 1976: *m* 1960, Mary Prudence, elder da of Rev Philip Frank Ardagh-Walter, V of Woolton Hill, Hants, and has issue.

𝔄rms – Gules, a banner displayed argent, thereon a canton azure charged with St Andrew's cross of the second, as the badge of Scotland. 𝔠rest – A demiman in armour holding in his right hand a sword proper. 𝔖upporters – Two armed men proper.
Address – c/o Drummonds Bank, 49 Charing Cross Rd, SW1.

DAUGHTERS LIVING

Clare Naomi, *b* 1961: *m* 1991, Michael Angus O'Neill, only son of Shane O'Neill, of Betchton, Cheshire. —— Margot Charlotte, *b* 1962. —— Arabella Rose, *b* 1965. —— Clodagh Isobel Rose, *b* 1975.

SISTERS LIVING

Ruth Mary Charlotte, *b* 1937: *m* 1958, Michael Joseph Orgill Massey, MA, MB, BChir, MFOM, who *d* 1989, of Upwood, Shepley Rd, Barnt Green, Worcs, and has issue living, Jonathan David, *b* 1962; BEng (Hons), — William Michael, *b* 1964, — James Richard, *b* 1966, — Alexander Mary, *b* 1959; MB BS, — Charlotte Elizabeth, *b* 1960; MB BS. —— Janet Elizabeth Naomi, *b* (twin) 1937; ARCM 1959: *m* 1966, Warren Jackson, MA, of 7 Gildridge Rd, Manchester 16, and has issue living, Catherine Elizabeth, *b* 1967; BA 1989, — Ruth Helen Isobel, *b* 1969.

DAUGHTER LIVING OF ELEVENTH BARONET

Eve Mary, *b* 1921: *m* 1951, (Thomas) Cecil (Leyburn) Symmes, who *d* 1991, of 39 Karu Crescent, Waikanae, NZ 6454, and has issue living, Howard Alexander (5 Connaught Terrace, Wellington, NZ), *b* 1954: *m* 1989, Jane Williams, and has issue living, Kirk Thomas *b* 1992, — George Weymouth, *b* 1956: *m* 1989, Veronica Anne Challies.

WIDOW LIVING OF THIRTEENTH BARONET

BARBARA CHARLOTTE (*Dowager Lady Bannerman*), da of late Lt-Col Alec Cameron, OBE, IMS, of Southwold, Suffolk: *m* 1932, Lt-Col Sir Donald Arthur Gordon Bannerman, 13th Bt, who *d* (16 Sept) 1989. *Residence* – Cecil Court, 2 Priory Rd, Kew, Richmond, Surrey TW9 3DG.

WIDOW LIVING OF FOURTEENTH BARONET

JOAN MARY (*Joan, Lady Bannerman*), da of late John Henry Wilcox, of Tadcaster, Yorks: *m* 1977, Sir Alexander Patrick Bannerman, 14th Bt, who *d* (21 Nov) 1989. *Residence* – 73 New Causeway, Reigate, Surrey.

COLLATERAL BRANCHES LIVING

Granddaughters of late Edward Mordaunt Bannerman (infra):—
Issue of late D'Arcy Bannerman, *b* 1875, *d* 1952: *m* 1896, Mary, who *d* 1962, da of Rev Richard Dennett, DCL, formerly R of Ashton, Chudleigh, Devon:—
Thora DARSIE (c/o British Embassy Consular Section, Lima, 1 Peru), *b* 1903; has assumed her forename DARSIE as her surname: *m* 1931, Raymond Frederick Budden, late of Meteorological Office, Air Min, who *d* 1972.
Issue of late Com Bertrand Bannerman, DSO, *b* 1883, *d* 1954: *m* (April) 1909, Vera, who *d* 1976, da of Edward Stuart:—
Sheila Christina (*Lady Walsham*), *b* (Dec) 1909: *m* 1936, Rear-Adm Sir John Scarlett Warren Walsham, 4th Bt, CB, OBE, who *d* 1992. *Residence* – 19 Beckford Close, Tisbury, Wilts.

Granddaughter of late Mordaunt Francis Bannerman, 8th son of late Edward Mordaunt Bannerman, 6th son of Patrick Wilson Bannerman, 2nd son of Charles Bannerman, 2nd brother of 6th baronet:—
Issue of late Nigel Mordaunt Bannerman, *b* 1943, *d* 1975: *m* 1971, Jane Alison (18 Pilgrims Close, Farnham, Surrey), el da of Paul Taylor, of Milford, Godalming, Surrey:—
Henrietta Jane, *b* 1973.

The ancestors of this family were hereditary banner-bearers to the kings of Scotland. The baronetcy was conferred by Charles II upon Sir Alexander Bannerman for "his constant loyalty during the Rebellion, and the heavy calamities he had suffered on that account." The 3rd baronet raised a regiment, and was with it at the battle of Culloden. His son, the 4th baronet, sold the Elsick estate for a nominal price, having been threatened with forfeiture on account of his father's and his own alleged participation in the rebellion of 1745. A portion of the Elsick estate was repurchased by 9th baronet, and passed on his death to his da, the wife of the 10th Earl of Southesk. Sir Arthur D'Arcy Gordon Bannerman, KCVO, CIE, 12th Bt, was Resident, Kashmir 1917-21, and Gentleman-Usher to HM King George V 1928-36. Lt-Col Sir Donald Arthur Gordon Bannerman, 13th Bt, Queen's Own Cameron Highlanders 1918-48, wrote *A Short Family Family History* and *Random Recollections*, and was a Housemaster at Gordonstoun 1948-52 and Fettes 1952-69.

BARBER (UK) 1960, of Greasley, co Nottingham

Col Sir WILLIAM (FRANCIS) BARBER, TD, 2nd *Baronet, b* 20 Nov 1905; *s* his father, *Col Sir* (THOMAS) PHILIP, DSO, TD, 1961; Hon Col 1961-66; a JP for Notts 1952, and High Sheriff 1964-65; 1939-45 War as Maj S Notts Hussars Yeo RHA in Palestine, Egypt, N Africa and NW Europe: *m* 1st, 1936 (*m diss* 1978), Diana Constance, who *d* 1984, da of late Lt-Col Thomas Owen Lloyd, CMG; 2ndly, 1978, Jean Marie, widow of Dr Harry Carew Nott, of Adelaide, S Aust, and has issue by 1st *m.*

Arms – Ermine, two chevronels, between three fleurs-de-lys gules a bordure embattled also gules. **Crest** – In front of two swords in saltire points upward proper hilts and pomels or, a bull's head erased also proper.
Residence – Lamb Close House, Eastwood, Notts, NG16 3QX.

SON LIVING *(By 1st marriage)*

(THOMAS) DAVID (Windrush House, Inkpen, Berks), *b* 18 Nov 1937; *ed* Eton, and Trin Coll, Camb (MA); late 2nd Lt RA 1957-58: *m* 1st, 1972 (*m diss* 1975), Amanda Mary, da of Frank Rabone, of Beacon Barn Farm, Coton, Milwich, Staffs, and widow of Maj Michael Healing, Gren Gds; 2ndly, 1978, Jeannine Mary, formerly wife of John Richard Boyle (*see* E Cork and Orrery, colls), and da of Capt Timothy John Gurney, Coldm Gds, of The White House, Hare St, Buntingford, Herts (*see* De Bathe, Bt, ext), and has issue living (by 1st *m*), Thomas Edward, *b* 1973; *ed* Eton, — (by 2nd *m*) William Samuel Timothy, *b* 1982, — Sarah Emily, *b* 1981.

DAUGHTER LIVING *(By 1st marriage)*

Diana Mary, *b* 1939: *m* 1965, Nicholas Bache Barlow Davie-Thornhill, Hinderclay Hall, Diss, Norfolk (Barlow, Bt, *cr* 1907), and has issue living, John Philip Bache, *b* 1966, — Adrian George Barber, *b* 1968.

SISTERS LIVING

Joan (The Old Stables, Lamb Close, Eastwood, Notts), *b* 1907: *m* 1934, Rev Canon Sydney John Galloway, who *d* 1969. —— Beatrice Naomi (The Manse, Moor Green, Newthorpe, Notts), *b* 1911: *m* 1939, Flight Lieut Charles David Stewart, RAF, who was *ka* 1940. —— Honor (Limehurst, Halam Rd, Southwell, Notts), *b* 1914: *m* 1947, Cdr Noel Hunt, RNVR (ret), who *d* 1974.

COLLATERAL BRANCH LIVING

Issue of late Thomas Cecil Barber, el son of 1st baronet, *b* 1903, *d* 1930: *m* 1928, Joyce Mary (who *m* 2ndly, 1933 (*m diss* 1948), Col John Sydney North FitzGerald, CVO, MBE, MC, who *d* 1976 (*see* By North, colls); 3rdly, 1948, Lt-Col Arthur Frederick Reginald Wiggins, who *d* 1961), da of late Dr Edward Williams Hedley, MBE, of The Cottage, Thursley, Surrey:—
Susan, *b* 1930: *m* 1st, 1951 (*m diss* 1965), Ian Hope Johnstone; 2ndly, 1968, David Day, who *d* 1970, and has issue living, (by 1st *m*), Robin, *b* 1956, — Rosanna, *b* 1958: *m* 1982, Andrew Hugh Hope, and has issue living, Clara Harriet *b* 1984.
The 1st baronet, Col Sir (Thomas) Philip Barber, DSO, TD (son of late Thomas Barber, of Lamb Close, Greasley, Notts), was Hon Col S Notts Hussars Yeo, High Sheriff of Notts 1907, a Councillor of Notts Co Council 1898-1925, and Alderman 1925-61 (Chm 1931-45), and Pro-Chancellor of Nottingham Univ 1955-61.

BARBOUR (UK) 1943, of Hilden, co Antrim (Extinct 1951)

Right Hon Sir JOHN MILNE BARBOUR, 1st and last *Baronet.*

DAUGHTER LIVING OF FIRST BARONET

Elizabeth Law Milne, *b* 1910: *m* 1st, 1941, Hugh Chapman MacLean, who *d* 1945; 2ndly, 1954, Robin Young Paton, MB, FRCS, who *d* 1974. *Residences* – Gorse Hill Manor, Gorse Hill Road, Virginia Water, Surrey; 9 Astell St, SW3.

BARCLAY (NS) 1668, of Pierston, Ayrshire

The cross of Christ is our crown

Sir COLVILLE HERBERT SANFORD BARCLAY, 14th *Baronet*, el son of late Rt Hon Sir Colville Adrian de Rune Barclay, KCMG, 3rd son of 11th baronet; *b* 7 May 1913; *s* his uncle, *Sir* ROBERT CECIL DE BELZIM, 1930; *ed* Eton, and Trin Coll, Oxford (BA 1935, MA 1946); was a 3rd Sec in Diplo Ser 1938-41; European War 1939-45 as Lieut-Com RNVR: *m* 1949, Rosamond Grant Renton, da of late Dr Walter Armstrong Elliott, of Chandler's Ford, Hants, and has issue.

Arms – Azure, a chevron between three crosses patée or. **Crest** – A sword erect proper, hilted and pommelled or.
Residence – Pitshill, Petworth, Sussex.

SONS LIVING

ROBERT COLRAINE (Rua Irlanda 94, Jardim Europa, 01450-050 Sao Paulo, Brazil), *b* 12 Feb 1950; *ed* Eton, and E Anglia Univ: *m* 1980, Lucilia, da of Carlos Saboia de Albuquerque, of Ipanema, Rio de Janeiro, Brazil and has issue living Henry William Saboia, *b* 16 Jan 1982, — Caroline Saboia, *b* 1983. —— Alistair James Elliott, *b* 1952. —— (Colville) Edwin Ward (Little Hilliers, Stopham, Pulborough, Sussex), *b* 1956; *ed* Charterhouse, and Aberdeen Univ: *m* 1992, Fiona M., da of late Robin Bell, of Coopers Green, Uckfield, Sussex, and has issue living, Frederick Colville Beresford *b* 1993.

BROTHERS LIVING

Cecil Edward Sanford (Oakley House, Oakley, nr Diss, Norfolk) *b* 1914: *ed* Eton, and Magdalen Coll, Oxford (BA): *m* 1st, 1939 (*m diss* 1957), Yvonne Eleanor Mutch, da of Sir William Edward Leonard Shenton; 2ndly 1958, Marcia Isobel Mary, da of late John Horatio Macoun, and has issue living, (by 2nd *m*) Melanie Sarita, *b* 1958: *m* 1985, Roger William Stephen Hale, and has issue living, John William Sanford *b* 1988, Harriet Sarita *b* 1989. —— Robert Charles Sanford (Green Bank South, Grundisburgh, nr Woodbridge, Suffolk IP13 6TD), *b* 1918; *ed* Eton, and Magdalen Coll, Oxford, formerly Maj Intelligence Corps; a JP, and a Chevalier of Legion of Honour; Croix de Guerre: *m* 1st, 1941 (*m diss* 1964), Camilla, da of Sir George Menteth Boughey, 9th Bt, CBE; 2ndly, 1964, Alice Molly, who *d* 1985, da of late Sydney Blackman, and has issue living (by 1st *m*) Peter John (8 Broomhill Rd, SW18), *b* 1941: *m* 1964 (*m diss* 1973), Angela Mary, da of Harold Francis Blackborow, and has issue living, Alasdair James *b* 1968, Piers David *b* 1972, — Michael George (Frostland Farm, Newchurch, Romney Marsh, Kent), *b* 1945: *m* 1973, Susan, da of James Thompson, and has issue living, Philippa *b* 1973, Sacha *b* 1976, — Jonathan Robert (The Old Vicarage, Stoke Holy Cross, Norwich, NR14 8AB), *b* 1947: *m* 1969, Clare Amabel, da of late Capt Philip Cecil Langdon Yorke, OBE, RN (*see* E Hardwicke, colls), and has issue living, Timothy Robert *b* 1984, Emily Rose *b* 1976, — Christopher Richard (29 Bicester Rd, Richmond, Surrey), *b* 1949: *m* 1986, Linda Anne, da of Joseph Redshaw, and has issue living, Leonora Sophie *b* 1989, Chloe Imogen *b* 1989.

COLLATERAL BRANCHES LIVING

Granddaughter of late William Malo de Rune Barclay (*b* 1871, *d* 1917), 3rd son of William Malo de Rune Barclay (infra):—
Issue of late Leslie William Hamilton de Rune Barclay, MBE, *b* 1899, *d* 1983: *m* 1927, Mabel Dobson Freene:—
Beverley Lesley Lorraine (2 Danmark Court, Buderim, Queensland 4556, Australia), *b* 1936; *ed* Sydney Church of England Gram Sch for Girls.

Granddaughter of late William Malo de Rune Barclay, 3rd son of 10th baronet:—
Issue of late Aubrey Henri de Rune Barclay, *b* 1880, *d* 1950: *m* 1903, Alice Anne, who *d* 1969, el da of Sir Edward Osborne Gibbes, 3rd Bt:—
Betty Theodosia: *m* 1936, Russell Gellatly, of 3 Harbour St, Wollongong 2500, NSW, and has issue living, Peter Russell, *b* 1947: *m* 1967, Marilyn Fay, el da of Peter Fletcher, of Dural, NSW, — Susan Alice (50 Grace Av, French's Forest, NSW), *b* 1939: *m* 1961, Roy Lancaster Lucena, who *d* 1975, and has issue living, Peter Blair Lancaster *b* 1964, Karen Jane *b* 1962, Belinda Maree *b* 1969.

Grandchildren of Frederick Arthur d'Epinay Barclay, 4th son of late William Malo de Rune Barclay (ante):—
Issue of late William Cradock de Rune Barclay, NZ Forces, *b* 1906, *d* 1992: *m* 1943, Frances Berenice Aplin:—
Elizabeth Beauchamp, *b* 1945: *m* 1967, Anthony Leatherbarrow, of 14B Stephen St, Upper Hutt, NZ, and has issue living, Clifford Beau, *b* 1975, — Catherine Anne, *b* 1972.
Issue of late Capt Beauchamp d'Epinay Barclay, RAMC, *b* 1911; *ka* Hong Kong 1941: *m* 1935, Margaret Katharine (who *m* 2ndly, 1945, Ian Rutherford, of 38 Michie Street, Roslyn, Dunedin, New Zealand), da of late James Begg, of Dunedin, New Zealand:—
James Fergus (Cruachan, RD1 Miller's Flat, Central Otago, NZ), *b* 1940: *m* 1964, Sally Elizabeth, da of Hugh Stuart Fleming, MB, ChB, of Hove, Sussex, and has issue living, Andrew James, *b* 1967, — Hamish Beauchamp, *b* 1969, — Fiona Jane, *b* 1972. —— Margaret Elizabeth, *b* 1936: *m* 1958, John Michael Gibbs, MB, ChB, FFARCS, FFARACS, of 150 Hackthorne Rd, Christchurch 2, NZ, and has issue living, David Douglas, *b* 1966, — Margaret Jennifer, *b* 1959, — Hilary Eva, *b* 1961, — Helen Dorothy, *b* 1970. —— Frances Beauchamp, *b* 1938: *m* 1966, Robert Campbell, MICE, MIStructE, of 3 Over Place, Knutsford, Ches WA16 8NN, and has issue living, James Robert, *b* 1968, — Alastair John, *b* 1969, — Margaret Elizabeth, *b* 1966.

Issue of late Capt Leslie George de Rune Barclay, son of late Henry Torrens de Rune Barclay, 4th son of 10th baronet, *b* 1870, *d* 1965: *m* 1926, Dorothea, who *d* 1971, el da of Rev Charles Herbert Griffith:—
Ninian de Rune (111 St Helens Rd, Hastings, E Sussex), *b* 1927: *m* 1971, Aileen Margaret, el da of late Maj Hayes, and has issue living, Robert David, *b* 1972, — Anna Marie, *b* 1974. —— Michael George (27611 Santa Clarita Rd, Saugus, Cal 91350, USA), *b* 1932, late RAF: *m* 1953, Agnes Joy, yr da of A. Batehup, of Northiam, Sussex, and has issue living, Wendy Margaret, *b* 1954, — Beverley Ann, *b* 1959.

The ancestors of this family were of distinction in Ayrshire in the 12th century. The 8th baronet, who had been officially employed on the Continent, fell into the hands of the French, 1798. He was closely confined in the Temple, and twice tried by a Military Commission on account of a mission he was supposed to have filled at the Hague 1796-8. He was each time acquitted, and in November 1799 was released and sent by cartel to England by the special order of Bonaparte.

BARING (UK) 1911, of Nubia House, Northwood, Isle of Wight

By uprightness and labour

Sir JOHN FRANCIS BARING, 3rd *Baronet*; *b* 21 May 1947; *s* his uncle, *Maj Sir* CHARLES CHRISTIAN, 1990; *ed* Eton, RAC Cirencester, and LSE: *m* 1971, Elizabeth, yr da of late Robert David Henle Pillitz, of Juramento 3437, Buenos Aires, Argentina, and has issue.

ᴀrms – Azure, a fesse or, in chief a bear's head couped proper, muzzled and ringed of the second. Crest – A mullet erminois, two of the points resting on the pinions of a pair of wings conjoined and elevated argent. *Residence* – 17 East 96th St, New York, NY 10138, USA.

SONS LIVING

JULIAN ALEXANDER DAVID, *b* 10 Feb 1975. ⸺ James Francis, *b* 1984.

DAUGHTER LIVING

Andrea Hermione, *b* 1977.

BROTHER LIVING

(Andrew) Michael (Godfrey) (Ravenscourt House, Ravenscourt Park, W6), *b* 1949; *ed* Eton, and — Coll, Oxford: *m* 1976, Anstice Mary Blanche, da of late Alfred George Cardale, of Newbury, Berks, and has issue living, Alexander Francis, *b* 1978, ⸺ Edward George, *b* 1980, ⸺ Andrew Thomas, *b* 1983, ⸺ Rosalind Mary Blanche, *b* 1986.

SISTER LIVING

Ann Hermione, *b* 1941; *ed* Southampton Univ (PhD 1990), Fellow St Hilda's Coll, Oxford 1994: *m* 1963, Alistair John Buchanan, of Hill Barn, Gt Bedwyn, Marlborough, Wilts, son of John James Buchanan, of 67 Chester Sq, SW3, and has issue living, Catherine Anne Louise, *b* 1965, ⸺ Teresa Margaret, *b* 1967, ⸺ Helen Hermione, *b* 1973.

MOTHER LIVING

Margaret Fleetwood (*Countess of Malmesbury*), OBE, JP, DL, yst da of late Col Robert William Pigott Clarke Campbell-Preston, of Ardchattan Priory, Argyllshire: *m* 1st, 1938, Capt Raymond Alexander Baring, who *d* 1967; 2ndly, 1991, as his 2nd wife, 6th Earl of Malmesbury, of Greywell Hill, Basingstoke, Hants.

COLLATERAL BRANCH LIVING

Granddaughters of late Capt Raymond Alexander Baring, yr son of 1st baronet:—
Issue of late Charles Peter Baring, *b* 1939, *d* 1987: *m* 1st, 1964 (*m diss* 1974), Sarah, yr da of late Lt-Col William Gill Withycombe, of Providence House, Sutton, Thirsk, N Yorks; 2ndly, 1976, Susannah Jane (31 Grantley St, Shelton, Shrewsbury SY3 5LA), da of Dr William Ezra Smith, of Bashaw, Alberta, Canada:—
(By 1st *m*) Arabella, *b* 1965. ⸺ Henrietta, *b* 1966. ⸺ (By 2nd *m*) Gabriella Louise, *b* 1977. ⸺ Olivia, *b* 1980.

Sir Godfrey Baring, KBE, 1st Bt, son of late Lieut-Gen Charles Baring (*see* B Northbrook, colls), was Chm of co Council for Isle of Wight, an Alderman of London co Council 1920-22, Parliamentary Private Sec (unpaid) to Under-Sec of State for the Colonies 1908, and to Pres of Board of Education 1911, and sat as MP for Isle of Wight (*L*) 1906-1910, and N-W or Barnstaple Div of Devonshire 1911-18. Major Sir Charles Christian, 2nd Bt, JP, DL, was a Member of Cttee of Management of Board of Visitors, HM Prison, Parkhurst.

BARLOW (UK) 1803, of Fort William, Bengal

Love peace

First of all things be thou pious

Sir CHRISTOPHER HILARO BARLOW, 7th *Baronet*; *b* 1 Dec 1929; *s* his father, *Wing-Com Sir* RICHARD HUGH, AFC, RAF, 1946; *ed* Eton, and McGill Univ, Montreal (BArch): *m* 1952, Jacqueline Claire de Marigny, el da of John Edmund Audley, of Chester, and has issue.

𝕬rms – Argent, on a chevron engrailed gules between three cross-crosslets fitchée azure, two lions passant counter-passant supporting an eastern crown or, in chief between the two cross-crosslets a branch of olive and another of palm in saltire proper. 𝕮rest – Out of an eastern crown or a demi-lion argent, the paws supporting a cross-crosslet as in the arms, issuing from the crown on the dexter side of the lion a branch of olive and on the sinister another of palm both proper. 𝕾upporters – On either side an angel proper, vested argent, zoned and on the head an eastern crown or; the dexter holding in the exterior hand a balance or, and in the other a book proper, the sinister bearing in the exterior hand an olive branch, and in the other an escroll proper.
Residence – 18 Winter Av, St John's, Newfoundland.

SON LIVING

CRISPIAN JOHN EDMUND AUDLEY, *b* 20 April 1958; sometime Inspector R Hong Kong Police: *m* 1981, Anne Wai Ching Siu, and has issue living, Jennifer Claire Audley, *b* 1990. *Residence* – 22 Milford Rd, Plumstead, Cape Town 7800, S Africa.

DAUGHTERS LIVING

Persephone Claire, *b* 1953: *m* 1975, Robert Eric Booth, of The Timbers, Church Rd, Kettleburgh, Woodbridge, Suffolk IP13 7LE, and has issue living, Katherine Claire, *b* 1982, — Sophie Elizabeth Barlow, *b* 1986. —— Caroline Claire, *b* 1960: *m* 1986, James Cass Jordan, of 11813 Silent Valley Lane, Gaithersburg, Maryland, USA.

BROTHERS LIVING

David Peter, *b* 1931; *ed* Eton, and Peterhouse, Camb: *m* 1958, Mary June Emmerton, of Victoria, British Columbia, and has issue living, Peter Stephen, *b* 1961, — Richard Owen, *b* 1963, — Rosemary Sylvia Mary, *b* 1968. *Residence* – 1335 Franklin Terr, Victoria, BC, V8S 1C8. —— Anthony Donald (No 4 The Grange, Evesham Rd, Cheltenham, Glos GL52 3AE), *b* 1935; *ed* Stowe: *m* 1st, 1962 (*m diss* 19—), Ginette Burki, of Courrendlin, Switzerland; 2ndly, 19—, Patricia Jennifer Bond, of Geneva, Switzerland, and has issue living (by 2nd wife), Nicholas Hugh, *b* 1973.

SISTER LIVING

Lucinda Mary, *b* 1941: *m* 1962, Edward James Chubb, of Blackbird Cottage, Woodside Lane, King's Stanley, Stonehouse, Glos, and has issue living, Richard John, *b* 1963, — William Maurice, *b* 1969.

WIDOW LIVING OF SIXTH BARONET

Rosamund Sylvia de la Fontain, da of late Francis Swithin Braithwaite Anderton: *m* 1st, 1928, Wing-Com Sir Richard Hugh Barlow, 6th Bt, AFC, RAF, who *d* 1946; 2ndly, 1950, Rev Leonard Haslett Morrison, MA, Bar-at-law, who *d* 1985. *Residence* – Laurel Cottage, Parracombe, Barnstaple, N Devon EX31 4QQ.

Sir George Hilaro Barlow, GCB, the 1st baronet, was a Member of the Council of Bengal, Provisional Governor-General of India 1805-7, and Governor of Madras 1807-13. The 2nd baronet was a Judge of the Supreme Court of Calcutta. Sir Morison, the 3rd baronet, who was in the 7th Hussars and 9th Lancers, served during the Indian Mutiny (medal with clasp for Lucknow). The 4th baronet, Sir Richard, was a Member of the Legislative Council of Madras and Chm of Madras Harbour Trust. The 5th baronet, Col Sir Hilaro William Wellesley, CB, CMG, was 11 years Sup of Roy Laboratory, Woolwich, SE, and was subsequently in Min of Munitions. The 6th baronet, Wing-Com Sir Richard Hugh, AFC, served in European War 1939-45 (AFC).

BARLOW (UK) 1902, of Wimpole Street, St Marylebone, co London

I will renew my youth like the eagle

Sir THOMAS ERASMUS BARLOW, DSC, RN, 3rd *Baronet*; *b* 23 Jan 1914; *s* his father, *Sir* (JAMES) ALAN (NOEL), GCB, KBE, 1968; *ed* Winchester; Capt RN (ret); 1939-45 War (DSC); DL of Bucks 1976: *m* 1955, Isabel, da of late Thomas Munn Body, MRCS, LRCP, of Middlesbrough, and has issue.

Arms – Argent, on a pile sable between two torches erect in base fired proper, an eagle displayed with two heads of the field. **Crest** – In front of a staff erect entwined by a serpent proper, an eagle's neck erased with two heads argent, thereon a rose gules.
Residence – 45 Shepherds Hill, N6 5QJ. *Clubs* – Athenaeum, Savile.

SONS LIVING

JAMES ALAN (Galgorm Manor, Ballymena, co Antrim BT42 1EA) *b* 10 July, 1956, *ed* Highgate, and Manchester Univ (BSc); metallurgist; ptnr Glassdrumman House, Annalong 1984-93, since when Maître d'Hotel Galgorm Manor. —— Philip Thomas, *b* 1960.

DAUGHTERS LIVING

Monica Ann *b* 1958. —— Teresa Mary, *b* 1963.

BROTHERS LIVING

Erasmus Darwin (Elbrook House, Ashwell, Baldock, Herts), *b* 1915; *ed* Marlborough, and Trin Coll, Camb (MA, MB, BChir); MRCS England, LRCP London; DPM; FRC Psych; late Sen Lecturer and Consultant in Psychiatry, St Thomas's Hosp; a Dir of Group Investors, Ltd; Dir CIC Investment Holdings Ltd; Chm Bath Inst of Medical Engineering from 1975: *m* 1938, Brigit Ursula Hope, da of late Ladbroke Black, and has issue living, Thomas Jeremy Erasmus (20 Leverton St, NW5 2PJ), *b* 1939; MA, ARCM: *m* 1962 (*m diss* 1994), Jane, da of Bernard Hollowood, and has issue living, Josiah Bernard *b* 1973, and three adopted children, Mark Thomas Duncan *b* 1967, Thomas Daniel *b* 1972, Deborah Marian Susan *b* 1970, — Camilla Ruth, *b* 1942: *m* 1st, 1965 (*m diss* 1973), Martin Christopher Mitcheson, MB, BChir, DPM; 2ndly, 1974, Stuart Anthony Whitworth-Jones, and has issue living, (by 1st *m*) Luke Thomas *b* 1966, Amy Brigit *b* 1967, (by 2nd *m*) Eleanor Gwen *b* 1975, — Gillian Phyllida, *b* 1944: *m* 1966, Fabian Peake, of 1 Woodstock Rd, NW, son of late Mervyn Peake, the writer, and has issue living, Edward *b* 1981, Lewis *b* 1981 (twin), Florence *b* 1973, Clover *b* 1975, Tabitha *b* 1978. —— Andrew Dalmahoy, *b* 1916; *ed* Eastbourne Coll, and Trin Coll, Camb (MA, MB and BChir); MRCP, London: *m* 1951, Yvonne Tanner, and has issue living, Martin Thomas, *b* 1953, — Claire, *b* 1954. *Residence* – 10 Wimpole St, W1M 7AB. —— Horace Basil, FRS (Trin Coll, Camb), *b* 1921; *ed* Winchester, Trin Coll, Camb (MB and BCir) and Harvard Univ, USA (MD); Fellow of Trin Coll, Camb, 1950-54, of King's Coll, Camb 1954-64, and Prof of Physiology, Berkeley Univ, Calif, USA 1964-73, since when Prof of Physiology, Camb Univ: *m* 1st, 1954 (*m diss* 1970), Ruth Chattie, da of Dr Myer Salaman; 2ndly, 1980, Elisabeth Miranda, da of J. Weston Smith, of Hampstead, and has issue living, (by 1st *m*) Rebecca Nora, *b* 1956, — Natasha Helen, *b* 1958, — Naomi Jane, *b* 1962, — Emily Anne, *b* 1967, — (by 2nd *m*) Oscar Hugh, *b* 1986, — Ida Lucy, *b* 1988, — Pepita Elisabeth, *b* 1990.

SISTER LIVING

Hilda Horatia, *b* 1919: *m* 1944, John Hunter Padel, BA, MB, BS, DPM, and has issue living, Oliver James, *b* 1948, — Felix John, *b* 1955, — Adam Frederick, *b* 1958, — Ruth Sophia, *b* 1946, — Nicola Mary, *b* 1951. *Residence* - Manor Farm House, Hinton Waldrist, Faringdon, Oxon SN7 8RN.

COLLATERAL BRANCHES LIVING

Granchildren of late Sir Thomas Dalmahoy Barlow, GBE (infra):—
Issue of late Basil Stephen Barlow, *b* 1918, *d* 1991: *m* 1st, 1940 (*m diss* 1950), Harriette Alice, da of late His Honour Judge (Robert) Peel, OBE, KC (*see* Worsley-Taylor, Bt (ext) 1959 Edn); 2ndly, 1950, Gerda Theresa Zaar Ferrari da Grado (Stancombe Park, Dursley, Glos), da of late Prof Dr Zaar, of Graz, Austria:—
(By 2nd *m*) Nicholas Dalmahoy, *b* 1951; *ed* Eton. —— Maria-Theresa, *b* 1953: *m* 1977, Martin William Llewellyn. —— (Esther) Alexandra, *b* 1956.

Issue of late Sir Thomas Dalmahoy Barlow, GBE, 2nd son of 1st baronet, *b* 1883, *d* 1964: *m* 1911, Esther Sophia, JP, who *d* 1956, da of Henry Gaselee:—
Theodora Gertrude (Flat 76, Hurlingham Court, Ranelagh Gdns, SW6), *b* 1912: *m* 1936 (*m diss* 1951), Carl Winter, who *d* 1966, and has issue living, Robert Stephen, *b* 1939, — John Barlow, *b* 1944, — Caroline Helen, *b* 1942.

The 1st baronet, Sir Thomas Barlow, KCVO, MD, FRCP, FRS (son of late James Barlow, JP, of Greenthorne, Edgworth), Physician Extraor to Victoria 1899-1901, Edward VII and George V, Physician to the Households of Queen Victoria 1897-1901 and King Edward VII, 1901-10 and George V 1910-36. The 2nd Bt Sir (James) Alan Noel Barlow, GCB, KBE, was 2nd Sec to Treasury 1942, and Chm of Nat Gallery 1948-55. He donated his collections of Persian pottery to the Ashmolean 1953, and Chinese porcelain to Univ of Sussex 1967.

BARLOW (UK) 1907, of Bradwall Hall, Sandbach, co Chester

Sir JOHN KEMP BARLOW, 3rd *Baronet*; *b* 22 April 1934; *s* his father, Sir JOHN DENMAN, 1986; *ed* Winchester, and Trin Coll, Camb (BA 1956); Chm Thomas Barlow & Bro Ltd, and Majedie Investment plc: *m* 1962, Susan, elder da of late Col Sir Andrew Marshal Horsbrugh-Porter, 3rd Bt, DSO, and has issue.

Arms – Per pale ermine and gules, three chevrons counter-changed, over all two lions combatant or. **Crest** – A lion sejant affrontée or holding erect in the forepaws a cross-crosslet fitchee gules.
Residence – Bulkeley Grange, Malpas, Cheshire SY14 8BT.
Clubs – Brooks's, Jockey.

SONS LIVING

(JOHN) WILLIAM MARSHAL (4 Wharfedale St, SW10), *b* 12 March 1964; *ed* Eton, and Liverpool Univ: *m* 1991, Sarah Hilary, da of John Nobes, of Windsor, Berks, and has issue living, John William Oakley, *b* 4 April 1993. —— Thomas David Bradwall, *b* (Jan) 1966; *ed* Eton: *m* 1993, Melissa Emily, only da of Anthony Andrew Ward Kimpton, of Tarrington, Herefords (*see* B Hazlerigg, 1990 Edn). —— Andrew Michael Kemp, *b* (Dec) 1966; *ed* Harrow. —— Charles James Bulkeley, *b* 1970.

BROTHERS LIVING

George Bradwall (Robin's Cob, Henbury, Macclesfield, Ches), *b* 1938; *ed* Radley: *m* 1967, Daphne Anne, da of Henry R. Birtwistle, of Gt Dudland, Sawley, Clitheroe, Lancs, and has issue living, Jeremy George Read, *b* 1968, — Edward Bradwall, *b* 1972, — Deborah Jane Kemp, *b* 1970. —— Mark Henry Denman (Waldridge Manor, Stockwell Lane, Meadle, Aylesbury) *b* (twin) 1938; *ed* Radley: *m* 1968, Rosemary Alexandra, da of late J. Alan Bell, of Anglesey, and has issue living, Andrew Mark Egerton, *b* 1972, — Camilla Frances, *b* 1970.

SISTER LIVING

Jennifer Beatrice, *b* 1932; has issue living, Sacha Jane Anna, *b* 1971; *ed* Yehudi Menuhin Sch, and USC Los Angeles. *Residence* – Flat 3, 9 Kensington Park Gdns, W11.

COLLATERAL BRANCH LIVING

Issue of late Thomas Bradwall Barlow, yr son of 1st baronet, *b* 1900, *d* 1988: *m* 1943, Elizabeth Margaret, who *d* 1988, da of late Hon Bertrand Sackville-West (*see* B Sackville):—
Henry Sackville, OBE (PO Box 10139, 50704 Kuala Lumpur, Malaysia), *b* 1944; *ed* Eton, and Trin Coll, Camb (MA); FCA; OBE 1989. —— Anna Elizabeth (Thornby House, Northampton), *b* 1949.

The first baronet, Sir John Emmott, was senior partner in the firms of Thomas Barlow and Brother of London and Manchester, and Barlow and Co of Calcutta, Shanghai, Singapore, and Kuala Lumpur (Federated Malay States), and sat as MP for Frome Div of Somerset (*L*) 1892-5, and 1896 to 1918.

MONTAGUE-BARLOW (UK) 1924, of Westminster, co London (Extinct 1951)

Rt Hon Sir (CLEMENT) ANDERSON MONTAGUE-BARLOW, KBE, 1st and last *Baronet*.

WIDOW LIVING OF FIRST BARONET

(DORIS) LOUISE (*Lady Montague-Barlow*), da of H. Edward Reed, of Sandwich, Kent: *m* 1934, Rt Hon Sir (Clement) Anderson Montague-Barlow, KBE, 1st Baronet, who *d* 1951, when the title became ext.

BARNEWALL (I) 1623, of Crickstown Castle, Meath

I had rather die than be disgraced

Sir REGINALD ROBERT BARNEWALL, 13th *Baronet*; *b* 1 Oct 1924; *s* his father, *Sir* REGINALD JOHN, 1961 *ed* Xavier Coll, Melbourne; 1939-45 War with AIF in S-W Pacific: *m* 1st, 1946, Elsie Muriel, who *d* 1962, da of Thomas Matthews Frederick, of Brisbane, Queensland; 2ndly, 1962, Maureen Ellen, da of William Daly, of S Caulfield, Victoria, and has issue by 1st and 2nd *m*.

Ærms – Ermine, a bordure engrailed gules. Crest – From a plume of five ostrich feathers, or, gules, azure, vert, and argent, a falcon rising of the last.
Residence – Innisfree, Normandie Court, Mount Tamborine, Queensland 4272, Australia.

SON LIVING *(By 2nd marriage)*

PETER JOSEPH, *b* 26 Oct 1963; *ed* St Joseph's Coll, Nudgee, and Queensland Univ (B Agric Sc Econ); Lieut 2nd/14th Light Horse QMI, Royal Australian Armoured Corps, since 1982: *m* 1988, Kathryn Jane, da of Hugh Carroll, of Brisbane, Queensland, and has issue living, Jessica Rose, *b* 1992. *Residence* – 26 Tirrabella St, Carina Heights, Queensland 4152, Australia.

DAUGHTERS LIVING *(By 1st marriage)*

Mary Catherine, *b* 1947: *m* 1979, Peter Lynch, of Toowoomba, Queensland. —— Frances Patricia, *b* 1948: *m* 1969, Michael Curley, of Brisbane, Queensland. —— Margaret Anne, *b* 1952.

COLLATERAL BRANCHES LIVING

Granchildren of late Arthur Walter Aylmer Barnewall (infra):—
Issue of late Alfred Reginald Barnewall, *b* 1921, *d* 1979: *m* 1950, Daisy Mabel, da of late Charles Newman:—
Graeme David, *b* 1957: *m* 1987, Lindy Jean, da of James Donaldson, and has issue living, Samantha Kate, *b* 1994. *Residence* – 20 Lachlan Court, Sunbury, Victoria 3429, Australia. —— Ronald William, *b* 1960: *m* 1986, Susan Jennifer, da of Raymond Welsford. *Residence* – 1 Wootton Court, Melton South, Victoria 3338, Australia. —— Michael James, *b* 1962: *m* 1988, Glenda Michelle, da of Michael Condon. *Residence* – 2 Bishop Place, W Melton, Victoria 3337, Australia, and has issue living, Jessica Kate, *b* 1990, — Sarah Jane, *b* 1992. —— Kaye Lorraine, *b* 1951. —— Margaret Anne, *b* 1953. —— Sandra Maree, *b* 1970.

Issue of late Arthur Walter Aylmer Barnewall, 2nd son of 11th baronet, *b* 1890, *d* 1961: *m* 1921, Hilda, da of Thomas Triffit:—
John Robert (50 Anderson St, Euroa, Victoria 3666, Australia), *b* 1922: *m* 1950, Joan Catherine, da of late Shadrack Allen, and has issue living, John Robert, *b* 1952: *m* 1981, Jennifer Hooper, and has issue living, Ann Louise *b* 1986, Laura Mary *b* 1989, — Kieran Gerard, *b* 1958, — Anthony Brian, *b* 1960, — Mark Raymond, *b* 1961, — Eileen Mary, *b* 1951, — Catherine Frances, *b* 1955, — Clare Therese, *b* 1970. —— Henry Marcus Joseph (56 Elizabeth Drive, Rosebud, Victoria 3939, Australia), *b* 1924: *m* 1976, Barbara Ruth Mary, da of late Reginald Lindsley, and widow of John Douglas Bayes. —— Kevin Arthur (3 Rosamond Cres, Doncaster E. Victoria 3109, Australia) , *b* 1925: *m* 1949, Marjorie Joyce, da of Charles Body, and has had issue, Ross David, *b* 1950: *m* 1973, Dianne Robyn (17 Landale Av, Croydon, Vic 3136), da of Victor Jordan (formerly Vitto Giordano), and *d* 1989, leaving issue, David Mathew *b* 1973, Daniel Leigh *b* 1976, Benjamin Scott *b* 1978, — Murray Charles (Hennessy St, Port Campbell, Vic 3269), *b* 1954: *m* 1976, Lesley Christine, da of Ronald O'Brien, and has issue living, Brooke *b* 1978, Lisa *b* 1979, — Kevin Bruce, *b* 1956, — Dianne Maree, *b* 1952: *m* 1970, Michael John Primmer, of 4 Morrison St, Colac, Vic 3250, son of Roy Charles Primmer, and has issue living, Michael John *b* 1976, Matthew Scott *b* (twin) 1976, Leanne Maree *b* 1971 Jacqueline Louise *b* 1972, — Debra Michelle, *b* 1962: *m* 1984, Robert James Phibbs, of 15 Olympus Drive, Croydon, Vic 3136, son of Mervyn John Phibbs, and has issue living, Cody James *b* 1990, Loran Michelle *b* 1988. —— Patrick Thomas (74 Yuille St, Frankston, Victoria 3199, Australia), *b* 1928: *m* 1947, Mavis Leone, da of Charles Cooper, and has had issue, Dennis John, *b* 1948; RAN, served Vietnam War with HMAS *Brisbane*; *d* 1971, — Suzanne Elizabeth, *b* and *d* 1952, — Annette Lynne, *b* 1954: *m* 1973, Wayne Peterson, and has issue living, Dennis Norman *b* 1980, Amanda Patricia *b* 1976.

Granddaughter of late Alfred George Barnewall (infra):—
Issue of late Patrick Joseph Barnewall, JP, *b* 1915, *d* 1980: *m* 1949, Daphne Mavis (c/o Postmaster, Tootool, NSW, Australia), da of Charles Turner Lockhart:—
Naomi Patricia, *b* 1955.

Issue of late Alfred George Barnewall, half-brother of 11th baronet, *b* 1880, *d* 1952: *m* 1915, Sarah, da of J. Footter, of Violet Town, Victoria, Australia:—
John Robert, *b* 1917: *m* 1946, Marietza Elizabeth, da of Henry James O'Rourke, of Tullamore, NSW, and has issue living, John Jeffrey, *b* 1951: *m* 1976, Frances Erica, da of Eric Ernest Virieux, of Glen Garry, Tasmania, and has issue living, Tammie Elizabeth *b* 1980, Alison Louise *b* 1983, — Marietza Anne, *b* 1947, — Linda Mary, *b* 1955, — Dorothea Laree, *b* 1959. *Residence* – Eloora, Whitemark, Flinders Island, Tasmania. —— Francis Richard, *b* 1922; 1939-45 War with AIF in SW Pacific: *m* 1951, Margaret Mary, da of L. Lyons, of Euchuca, Victoria, Australia, and has issue living, Brian Francis, *b* 1956: *m* 1981, Judith Diane, da of late Thomas Bowland, of Whitemark, Flinders Island, Tasmania, and has issue living, Holly Renae *b* 1985, Rhianna Kate *b* 1987, — Kerry Teresa, *b* 1952, — Dianne Margaret, *b* 1953. *Residence* – Whitemark, Flinders Island, Tasmania. —— George Raymond, *b* 1923. —— Terrence James (53 Seignior St, Junee, NSW 2663, Australia), *b* 1935: *m* 1st, 1957, Jannete, da of Robert Smith, of Junee; 2ndly, 1978, Marie Patricia, da of Fredric Davies, of Sydney, and formerly wife of John Layton, and has issue living, (by 1st *m*) Judith Margaret, *b* 1959: *m* 1979, Warren Wright, and has issue living, Daniel Leigh *b* 1981, Nathan Warren *b* 1983, — Teena Merrie, *b* 1965; Nurse, Canberra ACT. —— Kathleen Joyce, *b* 1919. *Residence* – Tootool, NSW, Australia.

Descendants of Robert Barnewall, who settled in America 1840, and Benjamin, who went to Australia (uncles of 11th baronet), and Samuel Barnewall and William Barnewall (great-uncles of 11th baronet), who both emigrated to America.

This family, the name of which was originally de Berneval, is of great antiquity. Sir Michael de Berneval, who landed on the coast of Cork before 1170, was the first of the family who settled in Ireland. The 2nd baronet suffered severely during the Cromwellian usurpation; and of the extensive possessions then wrested from him, he obtained, after the re-establishment of the monarchy, only his castle and 2000 acres of land. The 3rd baronet was MP for Meath 1689-90. Sir George, 4th Bt (a descendant of the 2nd son of the 1st Bt), established his right to this title in 1744; his cousin, Thomas, however, did not assume it, and it remained dormant from 1790 until 1821, when the succession of Sir Robert, 8th Bt, was registered at the Ulster Office, Dublin.

BARRAN (UK) 1895, of Chapel Allerton Hall, Chapel Allerton, West Riding of co York, and of Queen's Gate, St Mary Abbots, Kensington, co London

The love of country

Sir JOHN NAPOLEON RUTHVEN BARRAN, 4th *Baronet: b* 14 Feb 1934; *s his father, Sir* JOHN LEIGHTON, 1974; in remainder to Lordship of Ruthven of Freeland; *ed* Winchester; late Lt 5th R Inniskilling Dragoon Gds; served British High Commission Ottawa 1964-67; Head of Videotex Services, COI: *m* 1965, Jane Margaret, da of late Sir Stanley George Hooker, CBE, of Orchard Hill, Milbury Heath, Wotton-under-Edge (*see* B Bradbury, 1985 Edn), and has issue.

Arms – Per saltire gules and sable, a bear passant or, muzzled of the second, between two mascles palewise of the third. **Crest** – In front of a tower gules charged with three mascles intertwined palewise, a lion's jamb fessewise erased or.
Residences – 17 St Leonard's Terr, SW3; The Hermitage, East Bergholt, Suffolk.

SON LIVING

JOHN RUTHVEN, *b* 10 Nov 1971.

DAUGHTER LIVING

Susannah Margaret, *b* 1981.

UNCLES LIVING (*Sons of 2nd baronet*)

Edward Nicholson (Ackworth Grange, Pontefract, W Yorkshire), *b* 1910; *ed* Winchester, and Trin Coll, Camb (BA 1931, MA 1935); formerly Capt 5th R Inniskilling Dragoon Gds: *m* 1st, 1940, Daphne Margaret, da of Herbert William Bird, of Norther, Cranleigh, Surrey; 2ndly, 1955, Patricia Helen, el da of A. G. Blake, and has issue living, (by 1st *m*) Nicholas Dudley Edward, *b* 1942: *m* 1964, Feliksa, da of Feliks Pabilionis, of Omaha, Nebraska, and late of Kaunas, Lithuania, and has issue living, Antony Nicholas *b* 1967, Daniel Nicholas *b* 1968, — (by 2nd *m*) Charles Patrick Edward, *b* 1955, — (by 1st *m*) Alice Daphne Margarita, *b* 1946: *m* 1975, Giovanni Battista Luigi Dalle Nogare, of Bulleen, Victoria, Australia, and has issue, — (by 2nd *m*) Frances Margarita, *b* 1958: *m* 1979, John de Moraville, of Frethorne House, Wantage, Oxon. ——— *Sir* David Haven, *b* 1912; *ed* Winchester, and Trin Coll, Camb (BA); Pres, Asiatic Petroleum Corpn (NY) 1958-61; Chm of Shell Transport and Trading Co Ltd 1966-72, Midland and International Banks, Midland Bank 1980-82, *cr* Knt 1971: *m* 1944, Jane Lechmere, da of late Nicholas Lechmere Cunningham Macaskie, QC, and has had issue, †Tristram Cosmo, *b* 1945: *m* 1973, Miranda Clare (The 'Oldall, Brent Eleigh, Sudbury, Suffolk CO10 9NP), yst da of Maj Sir Robert Crichton Mitchell Cotts, 3rd Bt, and *d* 1992 in a motor accident, leaving issue, Ferdinand Roc *b* 1974, Giuseppe Maria *b* 1978, Petra Sely *b* 1975, — Julian Mark Lechmere (Welham Farm, Shepton Montague, Castle Cary, Som), *b* 1947: *m* 1st, 1970, Mary, da of Sir Edward Wilder Playfair, KCB; 2ndly, 1986, Diana, da of late Cosmo de Bosdari, and has issue living (by 1st *m*), Leo David *b* 1973, Laurence Edward *b* 1977, Tabitha Jane *b* 1972, (by 2nd *m*) Cosmo Ralph *b* 1990, Emily Dolores *b* 1988, — Marius Peregrine Lechmere (64 St Marks Rd, W10 6NN), *b* 1949: *m* 1972, Veronica Teresa, da of Prof Alphonsus Ligouri d'Abreu, CBE, of Ford House, Coughton, Alcester, Warwicks (Throckmorton, Bt), and has issue living, Perdita Elizabeth *b* 1972, Lorna Marina *b* 1974, Phoebe Alice *b* 1981, Amy Louise *b* 1984, — Adrian Stuart Lechmere, *b* 1959, — Jane Francesca, *b* 1950: *m* 1980, Philip Anthony Francis Scoones, of 199 Goldhawk Rd, W12, only son of Dr Francis Scoones, of Abbotsbury Rd, W14, and has issue living, Benedict Boniface Nicholas *b* 1983, Eleanor Jane *b* 1981, — Lalage Margarita, *b* 1957, — Calista Maria Lechmere, *b* 1960: *m* 1986, William Walrond Lucy, of 10 Grace's Rd, SE5, only son of Maj D.P.V. Lucy, of The Chantry, Ilminster, Som, and has issue living, Tancred Edmund Walrond *b* 1992, Laetitia Alice Haven *b* 1989. *Residences* – 36 Kensington Sq, W8 5HP; Brent Eleigh Hall, Sudbury, Suffolk CO10 9NP. *Club* – River (New York).

COLLATERAL BRANCHES LIVING

Grandchildren of late Philip Austyn Barran (*infra*):—
Issue of late Arthur Haworth Barran, *b* 1911, *d* 1991: *m* 1945, Rosa (42 Oregon Drive, Taupo, NZ), da of late John Russell Greenwood, of The Oval, Tranmere Park, Guiseley, Yorks:—
Jonathan Haworth (13 Tumene Drive, Owhata, Rotorua, NZ), *b* 1946; *ed* Badingham Coll: *m* 1973, Lindsey Margaret, da of late Clifford Bruce Ward, and has issue living, Alastair Haworth, *b* 1973, — Rachael Louise, *b* 1976. ——— Helen Margaret, *b* 1949, *d* 1953. ——— Elizabeth Claire, *b* 1954: *m* 1977, David George Glendinning, of Woodbrook, Omatane, RD2, Taihape, NZ, and has issue living, Richard David Peter, *b* 1981, — Hamish Donald, *b* 1986, — Thomas John, *b* 1990, — Sophie Rosa, *b* 1984.

Issue of late Philip Austyn Barran, yr brother of 2nd baronet, *b* 1876, *d* 1953: *m* 1908, Dorothy Currer, who *d* 1956, only da of late Arthur Currer Briggs, of Leeds:—
Donald Austyn Nicholson, MB, BChir, MRCS, LRCP, FRSM, *b* 1922; *ed* Repton, and Trin Coll, Camb (MB and BChir, MA); FFARCS and FRSM. *Residence* - 3 Gt Western Terr, Glasgow, W2. ——— Dorothy Stella Margaret, *b* 1919: *m* 1943, Joseph William Sloan Allison, CA, and has issue living, Joseph Philip Sloan (4 Raeburn St, Edinburgh 4), *b* 1944: *m* 1976, Caroline Margaret, da of late James Roxburgh Paton, of Gullane, and has issue living, James Austyn Sloan *b* 1978, Gerard Joseph Roxburgh *b* 1982, Peter William Donald *b* 1987, Catherine Margaret Elaine *b* 1980, — Judith Stella Elaine, *b* 1948: *m* 1968, Cdr Simon Hugh Stone, RN, of 120 Divinity Rd, Oxford, and has issue living, Charlotte Anne *b* 1972, Harriet Jane *b* 1974, — Dorothy Lucy Louise, *b* 1951. *Residence* - The Cottage, Longbarn, Cardross, Dunbartonshire.

Grandchildren of late Alfred Barran, 4th son of 1st baronet:—

Issue of late Claude Roulston Barran, *b* 1885, *d* 1942: *m* 1911, Edith, who *d* 1973, da of late Arthur Gaunt, of Stanningley Hall, Leeds:—
Lilian Joan (Littlecroft, Burton Leonard, Harrogate, HG3 3RW) *b* 1912. —— Katharine Muriel, *b* 1913; MB and ChB Leeds 1940. *Residence* – Prospect House, Scotton, Knaresborough.

Issue of late Richard Wharton Barran, *b* 1905, *d* 1961: *m* 1936, Marie Eileen (34 Homepark House, South St, Farnham, Surrey GU9 7RU), da of late George Crabbe, of Ceylon:—
Valerie Anne Heather, *b* 1941: *m* 1977, Malcolm Gordon Chase, FCA (Byways, 12 Kent Rd, Fleet, Hants GU13 9AH), and has issue living, Jennifer Marianne Alison, *b* 1978, — Sarah Elizabeth Lucy, *b* 1979.

Issue of late George Fletcher Barran, MD, BCh, *b* 1908, *d* 1983: *m* 1936, Clare Mary Elizabeth (The Cottage, Flinterghyll, Dent, Sedbergh, Cumbria LA10 5QR), da of Albert Dudley, of London:—
George Wharton (Rose Farm, East Ruston, Norfolk), *b* 1939: *m* 1st, 1967, Sue Russell; 2ndly, 1984, Sally Elizabeth, da of David Charles Jeffcott Mansfield, of Suffolk, and has issue living, (by 1st *m*) Nicholas George, *b* 1968, — (by 2nd *m*) George Arthur Mansfield, *b* 1985, — Elizabeth Margery, *b* 1986. —— Richard Martin, *b* 1941. —— Hugh Paull (1 Church Walk, N Petherton, Som TA6 6SE), *b* 1943: *m* 1973, Anthea Janet, da of late Rowland W. Baker-Beall, of Beer, Devon, and has issue living, Rowland Paull, *b* 1974, — Alice Matilda, *b* 1978. —— Rosemary Clare, *b* 1947: *m* 1974, Capt Rae Tugwell, RA, and has issue living, David Alexander Barran, *b* 1978, — Laura Clare, *b* 1976.

Granddaughters of late Henry Barran, 5th son of 1st baronet:—

Issue of late Henry Vernon Flower Barran, *b* 1894, *d* 1943: *m* 1921, Cicely, who *d* 1985, da of late Vice-Adm Francis Wade Caulfeild, CBE (*see* V Charlemont, colls):—
Mary Rosalie, *b* 1922: *m* 1963, Antony Giles Heron, of Bank House, Glaisdale, Whitby, Yorks. —— Elfrida Cicely, *b* 1929: *m* 1957, Martin Bennett Cordeaux, of 15 Lee Rd, Lincoln LN2 4BJ, and has issue living, Charles Nicholas (136 Victoria Av, Kingston-upon-Hull), *b* 1958: *m* 1987, Margaret Elizabeth, da of William M. A. Davidson, of Hopeman, Elgin, Moray, and has issue living, Michael Robert *b* 1992, Heather Claire *b* 1988, — Elizabeth Katharine, *b* 1961, — Cicely Jane, *b* 1964. —— Selina Elizabeth, *b* 1934: *m* 1960, Michael Stanley Makower, of Gogar House, Blairlogie, by Stirling (*see* V Chetwynd, colls). —— Christabel Lucy, *b* 1939.

Grandchildren of late Sir Rowland (Hirst) Barran, 6th son of 1st baronet:—

Issue of late Capt Hugh Bradley Barran, MC, *b* 1889, *d* 1975: *m* 1917, Estelle, da of late Frank Lockhart Cox, of 85 Cadogan Gdns, SW3:—
Hugh Rowland Murray (Robin) (Hildenley, Malton, Yorks), *b* 1929: *m* 1957, Diana Buttercup, da of late Eric Geoffrey Dawnay (*see* V Downe, colls), and has issue living, Patrick Robin, *b* 1959: *m* 1989, Miranda Jane, da of Christopher John Spence, of Chieveley Manor, Newbury, Berks (*see* Ropner, Bt, *cr* 1952), and has issue living, Hugo Jeremy *b* 1993, Daisy Charlotte *b* 1991, — Nicholas Eric Hugh (Lodge Cottage, Barton-le-Willows, York YO6 7PD), *b* 1964: *m* 1990, Emma Louise Moya, only da of Robert George Gee (*see* E Shrewsbury, colls), and has issue living, Hebe Elisabeth Blair *b* 1993, — Annabelle Clare, *b* 1960: *m* 1989, Edward B. McMullan, of 34 Southolm St, SW11 5EZ, son of Alan McMullan, of Fixby, Huddersfield, W Yorks, and has issue living, Alexander *b* 1991, Poppy Victoria Ines *b* 1992, — Verena April, *b* 1968: *m* 1993, William A. Ritson, son of Capt Tim W. Ritson, of Ebnal Grange, Malpas, Cheshire. —— Jean Lockhart, *b* 1919. —— Elspeth Estelle, *b* 1921. —— Ann Lockhart, *b* 1930: *m* 1950, Maj John Francis Leetham Robinson, MC, 12th R Lancers, of The Normans, Bilbrough, York, and has issue living, Hugh Andrew Leetham (Sandwith Lodge, Bilbrough, York), *b* 1955: *m* 1980, Amanda Jane Menage, and has issue living, Oliver Leetham *b* 1981, Georgina *b* 198-, — Marion Lockhart (*Hon Mrs Michael Bourne*), *b* 1951: *m* 1985, Hon Michael Kemp Bourne, of 50 Bradbourne St, Fulham, SW6, son of late Baron Bourne, GCB, KBE, CMG (Life Baron), — Caroline Mary, *b* 1957: *m* 1987, John Edwards, of 26 Summerfield Av, Queens Park, NW6, and has issue living, Thomas *b* 1991, Kate *b* 1990, — Joanna Susan, *b* 1961: *m* 1982, Capt Martin James Butterfield Drake, Duke of Wellington's Regt, of 98 The Mount, York, and has issue living, James *b* 1988, Lucie *b* 1985.

The 1st baronet, Sir John Barran, who was founder of the firm of John Barran and Sons merchants, of Leeds, sat as MP for Leeds (*L*) 1876-85, and for Yorkshire, W Riding, E Part Otley Div 1886-95. The 2nd baronet, Sir John Nicholson Barran, was Parliamentary Private Sec to Rt Hon H. H. Asquith MP, and sat as MP for Hawick Dist (*L*) 1909-18.

Barrett-Lennard, see Lennard.

BARRINGTON (UK) 1831, of Limerick.

The same while I live

Sir ALEXANDER FITZWILLIAM CROKER BARRINGTON, 7th *Baronet*; *b* 19 Nov 1909; *s* his brother, *Sir* CHARLES BACON, 1980; *ed* Shrewsbury and Ch Ch Oxford; served 1939-45 War as Capt (POW); Publisher.

Arms – Argent, three chevronels gules and a label of three points vert, on a canton of the second, a trefoil slipped or. **Crest** – Out of a crown vallery or a hermit's bust with a cowl vested paly argent and gules.
Residence – 11 Tedworth Sq, SW1 4DU.

DAUGHTERS LIVING OF SIXTH BARONET

Victoria Elizabeth Josephine (Barrihurst Bungalow, Cranleigh, Surrey), *b* 1940. —— Diana Mary Rose, *b* 1946: *m* 1968, Thomas Manuel, of Serridge Lodge, Trafalgar, Cinderford, Glos, and has issue living, Jessica Barrington, *b* 1977.

COLLATERAL BRANCHES LIVING

Grandsons of late Col Joseph Thomas Barrington, el son of Daniel Barrington, 2nd son of 1st baronet:—
Issue of late John Frederick Barrington, DSO, *b* 1881, *d* 1961: *m* 1916, Christine Mary Stella, who *d* 1962, da of late C. Kuhling, of North Ferriby, E Yorkshire:—
JOHN WILLIAM (PO Box 894, Invermere, BC VOA 1K0, Canada), *b* 28 Oct 1917; *ed* Stowe; Maj (ret) Roy Irish Fusiliers; Palestine 1939 (medal with two clasps), European War 1939-45 in Italy (1939-45 star, Italy star, two medals), GHQ Middle East 1947-48: *m* 1st, 1949, Annie, who *d* 1985, da of Florian Wetten, of Coire, Switzerland; 2ndly, 1986, Evelyn Carol Paterson, da of late Oscar Broten, of Oslo, Norway, and has issue living (by 1st *m*), Benjamin, *b* 1950: *m* 1980, Carola Christel Mogck, and has issue living, Patrick Benjamin *b* 1988, Marisa Christel *b* 1982, — Reto, *b* 1953: *m* 1976, Shelley Ann Lapham, and has issue living, Lauren Anne, *b* 1984, Amy *b* 1986, — Annette, *b* 1951: *m* 1984, David Clinckett, and has issue living, Nicole *b* 1985, Claire *b* 1987. —— Peter Malet, MC, TD, *b* 1920; *ed* Wellington Coll; admitted a Solicitor 1947; European War 1939-45 as Maj RA and RHA (despatches thrice, MC and Bar, 1939-45 Star, Africa Star, N-W Europe Star, two medals): *m* 1945, Joan Warren, da of Col Guy Warren Meade, DSO, MC, and formerly wife of Christopher John Spence, and has issue living (by 1st *m*), Charles Peter (The Lodge, Great Bealings, nr Woodbridge, Suffolk IP13 6NW), *b* 1946; *ed* Wellington Coll; ACA 1970: *m* 1969, Ann Elizabeth, da of H. B. Foster, and has issue living, Elizabeth Ann *b* 1973, — Michael, *b* 1951. *Residence* – The Lodge, Grayswood Beeches, Highercombe Rd, Haslemere, Surrey GU27 2LH.

Grandson of late Capt Richard Williams Barrington, HEICS, yr son of Daniel Barrington (ante):—
Issue of late Richard Irving Williams Barrington, *b* 1892, *d* (Nov) 1928: *m* 1922, Constance Elizabeth Mary (who *m* 2ndly, 1930, Major Alan Murdoch), only child of late Harry Manders:—
Laurence Hew Williams, *b* (June) 1928; *ed* Eton; Maj Roy Wiltshire Yeo; formerly Capt Coldstream Gds, Malaya, 1950 (despatches): *m* 1st, 1950 (*m diss* 1968), (Patricia) Anne Isabella, da of Ralph Whitson; 2ndly, 1968, Merle Aurelia, da of Sir Leonard Ropner, MC, TD, 1st Bt (*cr* 1952), and formerly wife of Christopher John Spence, and has issue living (by 1st *m*), Rupert Hew Williams, *b* 1963: *m* 1991, (Ann) Olivia, elder da of Nicholas Ronald Nutting (*see* Nutting, Bt, colls) and has issue living, Dominic Hew Williams *b* 1994, — Serena Henrietta Williams, *b* 1956: *m* 1977, Adrian Michael Campbell Underwood, of 757 Wandsworth Rd, SW8, — (by 2nd *m*), Shaun Richard Williams, *b* 1969. *Residence* – Oddington Lodge, Moreton-in-Marsh, Glos.

This family claims to be descended from Odo du Barentin, who came to England with the Conqueror. Fifteenth in descent from Odo, who received grants of land in Essex, and became custodian of Hatfield forest, was Sir Francis Barrington, of Barrington Hall, Essex, created a baronet, 1611. This title became extinct, upon the death of the 10th baronet, in 1833; but prior thereto (1831) a baronetcy had been conferred upon a yr branch, Sir Joseph Barrington, of Limerick, who, with his sons, founded the Limerick Hospital and Infirmary, an institution incorporated by Act of Parliament.

BARROW (UK) 1835, of Ulverstone, Lancashire

Little suffices

Sir RICHARD JOHN UNIACKE BARROW, 6th *Baronet*; *b* 2 Aug 1933; *s* his father, *Major Sir* WILFRID JOHN WILSON CROKER, 1960; *ed* Beaumont; Capt (ret) Irish Gds; joined Internat Computers and Tabulators, Ltd 1960: *m* 1961 (*m diss* 1974), Alison Kate, yr da of late Capt Russell Grenfell, RN (ret), and has issue.

Arms – Sable, two swords in saltire points upwards argent, pommels and hilts or between three fleurs-de-lis, one in chief and two in flanche, an anchor erect in base of the last. **Crest** – On a mount vert a squirrel sejant cracking a nut all proper, charged on the shoulder with an anchor.

SON LIVING

ANTHONY JOHN GRENFELL, *b* 24 May 1962; *ed* Dulwich, and Edinburgh Univ (MA): *m* 1990, Rebecca Mary, da of — Long, of —. *Residence* – 551A Garratt Lane, SW18 4SR.

DAUGHTERS LIVING

Nony Mary Louise, *b* 1963: *m* 1992, Simon Alastair Hugh Kerr-Smiley (*see* Smiley, Bt, colls). —— Frances Teresa Catherine, *b* 1971.

SISTERS LIVING

Rosamond Mary Geraldine, *b* 1927: *m* 1956, George Myles Sterling, and has issue living, Myles Patrick, *b* 1958, — Andrew David, *b* 1963, — Natalie Rosamond *b* 1960. *Residence* – Castletown, Coolbawn, Nenagh, co Tipperary. —— Ann Patricia, *b* 1928: *m* 1951 (*m diss* 1960), Maj Anthony Richard Carr, and has issue living, Julian Anthony Robie, *b* 1955. *Residence* – Fellover, St Breward, nr Bodmin, Cornwall. —— Angela Mary Philippa, *b* 1940: *m* 1968, Geoffrey Swaine, of 9 Oaktree Close, Ealing, W5, and has issue living, Jonathon David, *b* 1971, — Mary Angela, *b* 1972.

AUNT LIVING (*Daughter of 4th baronet*)

Mildred Mary Winifred, *b* 1901: *m* 1st, 1922, Edward Stanhope Benbow Rowe, who *d* 1941; 2ndly, 1949, Gerard Dun, and has issue living, (by 1st *m*) John, *b* 1930, — Anthony, *b* 1934, — Ursula, *b* 1923, — Joscelyn, *b* 1925. *Residence* – Canada.

COLLATERAL BRANCHES LIVING

Issue of late Alfred Francis Lendon Barrow, 3rd son of 4th baronet, *b* 1904, *d* 1989: *m* 1933, Ruth (13 The Lindens, Gt Austins, Farnham, Surrey GU9 8LA), only da of William Sydney Milsum:—
John Lendon (31 Lingfield Av, Torkington Park, Hazel Grove, Cheshire), *b* 1934: *m* 1961, Maureen Ann, da of Alfred Stanley Gover, and has issue living, Paul Lendon, *b* 1966, — Nicola Mary, *b* 1963, — Anthony Francis (Street Farm, Tilford, Surrey), *b* 1937: *m* 1962, Alexa, da of Raleigh Ashlin Skelton, and has issue living, Kevin Mark, *b* 1963, — Katharine Laura, *b* 1965. —— Simon William (Oratory School, Woodcote, Reading, Berks), *b* 1942: *m* 1977, Brenda Cora, da of Dermot Ernest Kelly, and has issue living, Julian Alexander Dermot, *b* 1981, — Jennifer Ann, *b* 1979. —— Susanne Mary, *b* 1946: *m* 1st, 1972 (*m diss* 1983), Patrick Hugh Walker-Taylor; 2ndly, 1987, Charles D'Arcy, of Norreys, Heath Lane, Crondall, Farnham, Surrey, and has issue living, (by 1st *m*) Timothy Patrick, *b* 1974, — Alice Mary, *b* 1976, — Sally Anne, *b* 1981. —— Catherine Ruth, *b* 1950: *m* 1976, Christopher John Price, of 9 Tilney Close, Alton, Hants, and has issue living, Robert Christopher, *b* 1981, — Sarah Kate, *b* 1978.

Issue of late Edward Joseph Merriman Barrow, 4th son of 4th baronet, *b* 1912, *d* 1988: *m* 1938, Mary Ellen (12 West Hermitage, Belle View, Shrewsbury, Shropshire), da of John William Allen, of Shrewsbury:—
Timothy John, *b* 1946; BVSC; MRCVS: *m* 1969, Fiona, da of Eric Lord, of Croydon, Surrey. —— Diana Margaret, *b* 1938: *m* 1st, 1963 (*m diss* 1979), Peter McConnell; 2ndly, 1980, Geoffrey Lindsay Clarke, ACIOB, of 5 Thurston Close, Grestun Manor, Abingdon, Oxon OX14 5RD, and has issue living (by 1st *m*), Simon John, *b* 1969, — Julie Mary, *b* 1967: *m* 1987, William Alexander Humphries, of 51 St Amand Drive, Abingdon, Oxon OX14 5RG, and has issue living, Edward Simon Alexander *b* 1992, Emma Diana Lindsay *b* 1988, — Sarah Frances, *b* 1971. —— Marylin Elizabeth Emily, *b* 1944: *m* 1970, John Richard Butler, FSVA, of Rope Walk Cottage, Lyth Hill, Shrewsbury, and has issue living, Jane Mary, *b* 1972.

The 1st baronet, Sir John Barrow, for many years Secretary to the Admiralty, and Founder of the Royal Geographical Society, was highly distinguished as an author, a traveller, and a meritorious public servant, to whose memory a monumental tower, 100 feet high, was erected by public subscription on the Hoad Hill, Ulverston, his birthplace. The 2nd baronet was Chief Clerk at the Colonial Office and Secretary and Registrar of the Order of St Michael and St George, of which he was a Companion. The 3rd baronet, Sir John Croker Barrow, was a Bar-at-Law of Lincoln's Inn, and a JP for Kent. The 4th baronet, Sir Francis Laurence John Barrow, was an architect and ornithologist

BARRY (UK) 1899, of St Leonard's Hill, Clewer, Berks, and Keiss Castle Wick, Caithness-shire

Sir (LAURENCE) EDWARD ANTHONY TRESS BARRY, 5th *Baronet*; *b* 1 Nov 1939; *s* his father, *Maj Sir* Rupert Rodney Francis Tress, MBE, 1977; *ed* Haileybury; Capt Grenadier Guards 1958-64; Lord of the Manors of Ockwells and Lillibrooke, Berks, and Baron de Barry of Portugal: *m* 1st 1968 (*m diss* 1991), Fenella, da of Mrs Hilda Hoult of Knutsford, Cheshire; 2ndly, 1992, Elizabeth Jill, da of Geoffery Bradley, of Fishtoft, Boston, and has issue by 1st *m*.

ᚼᚱᛗᛋ – Azure, two lions passant guardant or.
Residence – 4 The Gables, Argos Hill, Rotherfield, E Sussex TN6 3QJ.

SON LIVING *(By 1st marriage)*

WILLIAM RUPERT PHILIP TRESS, *b* 13 Dec 1973.

DAUGHTER LIVING *(By 1st marriage)*

Alexandra Diana Frances Louise, *b* 1977.

HALF-BROTHERS LIVING

Timothy Rupert Francis Tress (Le Carroi de Bonchamp, 37240 Ligueil, Indre et Loire, France), *b* 1952, late Capt RMP: *m* 1977, Valerie, yst da of Mrs M. D. M. Reid, of Otterburn, Northumberland, and has issue living, Victoria Louise Frances Tress, *b* 1982, — Georgina Alicia Frances Tress, *b* 1985, — Henrietta Elizabeth Frances Tress, *b* 1990. —— Nicholas Mark Francis Tress (The Kennels, Lenacre St, Eastwell, Ashford, Kent), *b* 1957: *m* 1985, Fiona Mary, yr da of late John Rankin, QC, of Prospect House, Boughton, Faversham, Kent, and has issue living, Lucy Arabella Francis Tress, *b* 1987, — Katharine Rose Francis Tress, *b* 1989. —— Jonathan Rodney Francis Tress, *b* 1960.

SISTER LIVING

Amorel Madeleine Frances Tress, *b* 1936: *m* 1959, Maj Peter Miles Lambert, Gren Gds (*see* D Wellington, colls).

HALF-SISTERS LIVING

Tara Caroline Frances Tress, *b* 1954: *m* 1977, (Fokko) Peter Anthony Kortlang, of The Duck Farm Cottage, Sandy Hurst Lane, Ashford, Kent, and has issue living, Piers Anthony Fokko Tress, *b* 1978, — Christian Rupert Fokko Tress, *b* 1988, — Lavinia Cordelia Frances Tress, *b* 1982, — Venetia Sophia Frances Tress, *b* 1984. —— Xandra Georgina Frances Tress, *b* 1962.

AUNT LIVING *(Daughter of 3rd baronet)*

Sheila Yvonne Elizabeth Doris, *b* 1915: *m* 1941, Col John Loftus Carter, RM (M Ely, colls), of 56 The High St, Charing, nr Ashford, Kent, and has issue living, Brian Loftus, OBE, *b* 1945; Col RM; OBE 1989: *m* 1st, 1969 (*m diss* 1971), Caroline Jane Halsey; 2ndly, 1973, Eva Jorunn Berglund, of Horten, Norway, and has issue living, (by 1st *m*) Andrew Charles Loftus *b* 1971, (by 2nd *m*) Anneli Victoria Solveig *b* 1980, — Sally Elizabeth, *b* 1943: *m* 1970, David William Mearns Gow (The Oak House, Church Lane, Aldington, Kent), and has issue living, William Hugh Mearns *b* 1971, Amanda Elizabeth Mearns *b* 1973.

GREAT-AUNT LIVING *(Daughter of 2nd baronet)*

Margaret Colquhoun (Abbey Mews, Amesbury, Wilts), *b* 1894; 1914-18 War in VAD Jan 1917 to Dec 1918 (two medals): *m* 1919, Capt James Clifton Colquhoun, MBE, formerly Highland LI, and has issue living, James Barry, *b* 1931, — William Baliol, *b* 1934, — Elizabeth, *b* 1924, — Margaret, *b* 1927.

WIDOW LIVING OF FOURTH BARONET

SHEILA GEORGINA VERONICA (*Sheila, Lady Barry*) (Brisley Rise, Willesborough Lees, Ashford, Kent), da of late Maj George Joseph Francis White, MBE, of Ashford, Kent: *m* 1951, as his 2nd wife, Maj Sir Rupert Rodney Francis Tress Barry, 4th Bt, MBE, who *d* 1977.

COLLATERAL BRANCHES LIVING

Grandchildren of late William James Barry (*infra*):—
Issue of late Lt-Col Gerald Barry, MC, *b* 1896, *d* 1977: *m* 1923, Lady Margaret Pleydell-Bouverie, da of 6th Earl of Radnor:—
Richard John (Hampton Fields, nr Cirencester, Glos), *b* 1938: *m* 1965, Jillian Frances, da of Lt-Col A. L. Novis, MC, of Fryern House, Storrington, Sussex, and has issue living, James Tress, *b* 1967, — Anthony Gerald, *b* 1969, — Bridget Margaret, *b* 1973. —— Anne (*Marchioness of Aberdeen and Temair*), *b* 1924: *m* 1950, 6th Marquess of Aberdeen and Temair. —— Diana, *b* 1927: *m* 1st, 1951 (*m diss* 1959), Kenneth Robert Motion; 2ndly, 1959 (*m diss* 1984), Nathaniel Edward Sherwood, and has issue living, (by 1st *m*) Richard Peter, *b* 1954, — Sarah, *b* 1955, — (by 2nd *m*) David Gerald, *b* 1960. —— Patricia Helen, *b* 1932: *m* 1958, Peregrine Michael Hungerford Pollen (*see* Pollen Bt colls). —— Pamela Rosemary, *b* (twin) 1938: *m* 1966, Colin Vyvyan Peterson, of Balldown Farmhouse, Sparsholt, Hants, son of late Sir Maurice Drummond Peterson, GCMG, and has issue living, Andrew Drummond, *b* 1967, — Thomas Richard, *b* 1970, — Helen Margaret, *b* 1969, — Alice Diana, *b* 1974.
Issue of late Cmdr Hubert Wyndham Barry, RN (ret), *b* 1898, *d* 1992: *m* 1936, Violet Agatha (Sutton Manor Nursing Home, Sutton Scotney, Winchester, Hants S021 3JX), da of Sir Edward Archibald Ruggles-Brise, 1st Bt, Mᗷᗡ, TD, MP:—
William Edward (12 Kensington Park Mews, W11; The Malt House, Manningford Abbots, Pewsey, Wilts), *b* 1938; *ed* Eton, and Trin Coll, Camb: *m* 1965, Juliet Alexandra Sarah, da of James Herbert Lonsdale Musker (*see* E Lauderdale, colls), and has issue living, Catherine Jane, *b* 1968; *ed* St Paul's Girls' Sch, and Durham Univ (MSc). —— James Hubert, *b* 1947; *ed* Eton. —— Rosemary, *b* 1939: *m* 1963, Alastair Pinckard Leslie, TD, late Capt RSF (*see* E Rothes). —— Susan (*Baroness Glenarthur*), *b* 1945: *m* 1969, 4th Baron Glenarthur.

Issue of late William James Barry, 4th son of 1st baronet, *b* 1864, *d* 1952, *m* 1896, Lady Grace Murray, MBE, who *d* 1960, da of 7th Earl of Dunmore:—

Nancy Elizabeth, *b* 1910: *m* 1935, George Nigel Capel Cure, TD, DL, JP, and has issue living, George Ronald (Blake Hall, Ongar, Essex), *b* 1936: *m* 1968, Caroline, who *d* 1986, only da of Giles Yarnton Mills, of Puys sur Dieppe, France, and has issue living, three sons, — Michael, *b* 1947, — Sarah Virginia (*Hon Mrs Thomas R. Lindsay*), *b* 1938: *m* 1961, Hon Thomas Richard Lindsay, of The Old Rectory, Ashmore, Salisbury, Wilts SP5 5AG (*see* E Crawford). *Residence* – Ashlings, Moreton Rd, Ongar, Essex.

Issue of late Col Stanley Leonard Barry, CMG, CBE, DSO, MVO, late 10th Hussars, 5th son of 1st baronet, *b* 1873, *d* 1943: *m* 1st, 1906, Hannah Mary, who *d* 1924, el da of James Hainsworth, of 34 Phillimore Gardens, W8, and formerly wife of Col W. MacGeorge, 6th Dragoon Guards; 2ndly, 1927, Laline Annette, who *d* 1969, da of late William Harvey Astell, JP, DL (sometime Lt Grenadier Guards), of Woodbury Hall, Sandy, Beds, and widow of Lt-Col Arthur Preston Hohler, DSO (V Gort):—

(By 1st *m*) Jeanne Irene (*Hon Mrs James A. G. McDonnell*), *b* 1915: *m* 1939, Hon James Angus Grey McDonnell (*see* E Antrim). *Residences* – Hoebridge Cottage, Balls Cross, Petworth, Sussex; 36 Farley Court, Melbury Rd, W14.

The 1st baronet, Sir Francis Tress Barry, was descended from Richard Barry, of Eynsham, Oxon, temp 1476, and the family arms were recorded by Lawrence Barry, of Hampton Gay Manor, Oxon, at the Visitations of Oxfordshire in 1566 and 1574, identical with those recorded for Sir Robert Barry, of Stanton Barry, Bucks, temp Edward I; Sir Francis was *cr* Baron de Barry in Portugal 1876, sat as MP for Windsor (*C*) 1890-1906, and was Consul-Gen in Great Britain for Ecuador. The 2nd baronet, Sir Edward Arthur Barry, was High Sheriff of Berks in 1907, and Lieut-Col Berks Yeo.

BARTLETT (UK) 1913, of Hardington-Mandeville, Somerset

Sir JOHN HARDINGTON DAVID BARTLETT, 4th *Baronet*; *b* 11 March 1938; *s* his father, *Lt-Col Sir* (HENRY) DAVID HARDINGTON, MBE, 1989; *ed* St Peter's, Guildford; Freeman Pattenmakers' Co, and Freeman City of London: *m* 1st, 1966, Susan Elizabeth, who *d* 1970, da of Norman Waldock, of Gt Bookham, Surrey; 2ndly, 1971, Elizabeth Joyce, da of George Thomas Raine, of Norbiton Rd, Kingston-upon-Thames, Surrey, and has issue by 1st and 2nd *m*.

Arms – Argent, two barrulets dancettée between in chief two cinquefoils and in base a crescent issuant therefrom a cross formée fitchée, all azure. **Crest** – A demi eagle displayed azure, winged or, supporting with the beak a pennon of the first, charged with the arms.
Residence – Hardington House, Ermyn Way, Leatherhead, Surrey KT22 8TW.

SONS LIVING (By 2nd marriage)

ANDREW ALAN, *b* 26 May 1973. —— Stephen, *b* 1975.

DAUGHTER LIVING (By 1st marriage)

Nicola Jane, *b* 1969.

BROTHERS LIVING

Simon Hardington (Cobweb Cottage, 23 Lower Town, Sampford Peverell, Devon EX16 7BJ), *b* 1940; *ed* St Peter's, Guildford: *m* 1967 (*m diss* 1972), Antoinette Lois, da of Gaston Charpentier, and has issue living, Rebecca Rosamund, *b* 1969. —— Christopher Mandeville (1 Redlands Bank Cottages, Mid Holmwood, Dorking, Surrey RH5 4ES), *b* 1942; *ed* St Peter's, Guildford: *m* 1966, Brenda June, da of Eric Thorne, of Beech Cottage, Coneyhurst Lane, Ewhurst, Surrey, and has issue living, Paul David *b* 1968; *ed* —, — Sarah Jane, *b* 1972.

With fortitude and fidelity

AUNT LIVING (sister of 2nd and 3rd baronets)

Irene Theodora, *b* 1908. *Residence* – Garden Flat, 9 Holland Park Av, W11 3RH.

DAUGHTERS LIVING OF SECOND BARONET

Julia Jane, *b* 1937: *m* 1966, John Atkinson, and has issue living, Thomasina Kate, *b* 1967, — Teresa Mary, *b* 1968, — Cressida Jane Elizabeth, *b* 1971. *Residence* – 12 Brookside, Cambridge CB2 1JE. —— Lucy Mary le Breton, *b* 1941: *m* 1969, as his 2nd wife, Adrian Alexander Bridgewater (*see* B Vivian, 1985 Edn), and has issue living, Benjamin Hardington, *b* 1979, — Nancy le Breton, *b* 1971, — Daisy Maud, *b* 1973. *Residence* – Manor Farm, Gt Eversden, Cambs. —— Annabel Kate, *b* 1945: *m* 1988, as his 2nd wife, Anthony David McCall, and has issue living, Hardington Alexander William, *b* 1988. *Residence* – 214 West 17th St, Apt PHC, New York, NY 10011-5347, USA.

WIDOW LIVING OF THIRD BARONET

JEANNE MARGARET ESTHER (*Jeanne, Lady Bartlett*), da of Charles William Brewer, of St John's Wood: *m* 1982, as his 3rd wife, Lt-Col Sir (Henry) David Hardington Bartlett, 3rd Bt, who *d* 1989. *Residence* – Brockley Place, Brockley, Bury St Edmunds, Suffolk IP29 4AG.

COLLATERAL BRANCHES LIVING

Issue of late Eric Oscar Bartlett, 4th son of 1st baronet, *b* 1882, *d* 1968: *m* 1907, Irene, who *d* 19—, da of late Lawrence Alport, of 100 Lexham Gdns, W.:—

Betty Frances, *b* 1908: *m* 1933, Gordon Bushell Hedley, late Bengal Pilot Ser, and has issue living, Richard, *b* 1940, — Anne Wilhelmina Betty, *b* 1934. —— Mary Augusta, *b* 1911: *m* 1st, 1934, Fl-Lt Roy James Oliphant Bartlett, RAF, who *d* 1936; 2ndly, 1941, Group Capt James Douglas Ferrier Bruce, RAF, and has issue living, (by 1st *m*) Peter Howard Oliphant *(posthumous)*, *b* 1937, — Jill Rose Alyne Charlotte, *b* (Dec) 1934: *m* 1955, Stuart Bollam, and has issue living, Miles Stuart *b* 1957, Kim Pauline, *b* 1956, — (by 2nd *m*) Mhairi Christina Deborah *b* 1945.

Issue of late Maj Norman Edwin Bartlett, yst son of 1st baronet, *b* 1888, *d* 1972: *m* 1st, 1917 (*m diss* 1928), Mary Adelaide Leslie, who *d* 1981, da of Norman R. Foster, of 47 Murray Rd, Wimbledon SW; 2ndly, 1928, Sheila Barton, who *d* 1993, da of Mrs Hill, of 11 Bentinck Terr, SW8:—
(By 1st *m*) Norman Alaric, RN (Lonesome Pine, Bickenhall, Taunton, Som), *b* 1920; Lt-Cdr and Pilot, Flying Branch, RN (ret); 1939-45 War (despatches): *m* 1945, Mary Paterson Waugh, and has issue living, Michael Alaric, *b* 1946: *m* 1st, 1967, Sheila Taylor, 2ndly, 1983, Linda Ireson, and has issue living (by 1st *m*), Colin *b* 1967, Glen *b* 1971, (by 2nd *m*) Andrew *b* 1984, Gary *b* 1986, — Carol Anne, *b* 1948: *m* 1985, Harry Page. —— Hazel Leslie (21 Garstons, Bathford, Avon BA1 7TE), *b* 1922: *m* 1st, 1947, George Edward Short, who *d* 1962; 2ndly, 1966, Philip John Elwood, who *d* 1979, and has had issue (by 1st *m*), Edward Louis, *b* 1949; *d* 1967, — Jennifer Anne, *b* 1947: *m* 1st 1964 (*m diss* 19—), James William Price; 2ndly, 1978, Vivian Leslie Stuart Stokes, and has issue living (by 1st *m*), Hamish Dudley *b* 1965, — Angela Jill, *b* 1948: *m* 1970 (*m diss* 19—), Brian K. Rogers, and has issue living, Thomas Edward George *b* 1977, Jamie Alexander Francis Forgan *b* 1988, Tiffany Roberta Kate *b* 1974, — Catherine Leslie, *b* 1952: *m* 1st, 1977 (*m diss* 19—), Mark Hoy; 2ndly, 1987, Alan Jones, and has issue living (by 2nd *m*), Nicola Suzanne *b* 1988, Elizabeth Leslie *b* 1991. —— (By 2nd *m*) Derek (Fiveways, Warfield, Bracknell, Berks), *b* 1930; late Maj LG: *m* 1956, Joan Patricia, da of R. J. Breyfogle, and has issue living, Peter Mandeville, *b* 1960, — Robert Hardington, *b* 1965, — Jonica Mary, *b* 1958. —— Edwina, *b* 1933: *m* 1956, Esmond Dunn Boldero, late Capt LG, of Gyles Croft, Bellingdon, Chesham, Bucks, and has issue living, Jonathan Dunn, *b* 1958; Capt LG, — Alexandra, *b* 1964: *m* 1988, Nicholas Rory Tapner, of 13 Woodstock Rd, W4 1D5, — Louisa, *b* 1966.

Sir Herbert Henry Bartlett, 1st Bt, was many years Chm of Perry and Co (Bow) Limited, contractors, and was one of the principal contractors involved in the construction of Tower Bridge, Bakerloo Underground, Waterloo Station, and other notable buildings. He founded the Bartlett Sch of Architecture, part of Univ Coll London, was a Freeman of the City of London, and a Member Pattenmakers' Co (Master three times).

BARTTELOT (UK) 1875, of Stopham, Sussex
(Name pronounced "Bartlot")

In good time

Sir BRIAN WALTER DE STOPHAM BARTTELOT, OBE, 5th *Baronet*; *b* 17 July 1941; *s* his father, *Brigadier Sir* WALTER DE STOPHAM, DSO 1944; *ed* Eton; Col Coldstream Gds (ret 1992); is patron of two livings; Equerry to HM 1970-72; OBE (Mil) 1983; Mil Sec to Maj-Gen Commanding London District and Household Divn 1978-80; Commanding officer 1st Bn Coldstream Guards 1982-85; Regt Lt-Col commanding Coldstream Guards 1987-92; Col Foot Guards 1989-92; Member HM Body Guard of The Hon Corps of Gentlemen at Arms since 1993; DL West Sussex 1988; Liveryman of Gunmakers' Co 1980: *m* 1969, Hon (Mary Angela) Fiona Weld Forester, yst da of late 7th Baron Forester, and has issue.

Arms – Quarterly, 1st and 4th sable, three sinister gloves pendent argent, tasselled or, *Barttelot*; 2nd and 3rd quarterly, per fesse argent and gules, four crescents countercharged, *Stopham*. **Crest** – 1st, a swan couchant wings endorsed argent, *Barttelot*; 2nd, a castle with three turrents sable, *Stopham*.
Seat – Stopham House, Pulborough, Sussex. **Residence** – Stopham Park, Pulborough, Sussex RH20 1EB. **Clubs** – Cavalry and Guards', Pratt's, Farmers'.

DAUGHTERS LIVING

Isabel Emily, *b* 1971. —— Sophie Rosalind, *b* 1973. —— Ursulina May, *b* 1978. —— Emma Amelia, *b* 1981.

BROTHER LIVING

ROBIN RAVENSCROFT (Targrove, Fittleworth, Sussex), *b* 15 Dec 1943; *ed* Seaford Coll, and Perth Univ, W Aust: *m* 1987, Teresa, elder da of late Kenneth Greenlees, and has issue living, Hugo Ravenscroft, *b* 7 April 1990, — Emily Rose, *b* 1988.

UNCLE LIVING (*Son of 3rd baronet*)

William Frederick Geoffrey Nelson (Flat 5, Stopham House, Pulborough, Sussex), *b* 1905; *ed* Wellington Coll; formerly Lieut-Col RE: *m* 1930, Jane Elizabeth, who *d* 1990, da of late D. Stirling, of Santiago, Chile, and has issue living, Richard James Walter Stuart, *b* 1932, — Elizabeth Georgiana Margaret, *b* 1933: *m* 1st, 1955 (*m diss* 1973), James Drury Edward Kelly, Essex Regt; 2ndly, 1973, Nigel John Petrie Mermagen, of Richmond House, Chard, Som, and has issue living (by 1st *m*), Thomas James Barttelot *b* 1956: *m* 1981 (*m diss* 1986), Sarah Jane St Clair Weir (and has issue living, Louis Frederick Charles *b* 1986), Rose Jane Elizabeth *b* 1958: *m* 1984, John Charles Harding (and has issue living, Minnie Apphia Rose *b* 1990, Patience Elizabeth Ann *b* 1992).

WIDOW LIVING OF FOURTH BARONET

SARA PATRICIA, da of late Lt-Col Herbert Valentine Ravenscroft, JP, of The Abbey, Storrington, Sussex: *m* 1st, 1938, Brig Sir Walter de Stopham Barttelot, 4th Bt, DSO, who was *ka* 1944; 2ndly, 1965, Cdr James Nigel Walter Barttelot, RN (ret) (*infra*).

COLLATERAL BRANCH LIVING

Issue of late Lieut-Com Nigel Kenneth Walter Barttelot, RN, 2nd son of 2nd baronet, *b* 1883, *ka* 1914: *m* 1906, Dorothy Maud (who *d* 1961, having *m* 2ndly, 1923, as his 2nd wife, Vice-Adm Sir Frank Forrester Rose, KCB, DSO, who *d* 1955), el da of late Frederick Aldcroft Kay:—

James Nigel Walter, *b* 1911; Cdr RN (ret): *m* 1st, 1936, Rachel Mildred, who *d* 1964, da of Raymond Courage, of Edgcote, Banbury; 2ndly, 1965, Sara Patricia, da of late Lt-Col Herbert Valentine Ravenscroft, and widow of Brig Sir Walter de Stopham Barttelot, 4th Bt, DSO (ante) and has issue living, (by 1st *m*) Nigel Michael Anthony (80 Windsor Rd, Cambridge), *b* 1941: *m* 1971, Serena, da of F. W. Brett, of The Little Cottage, Hurst, Twyford, Berks, and has issue living, Piers Nigel Edward *b* 1976, Sasha Rachel *b* 1972, Olivia Henrietta *b* 1974, Hannah *b* 1981, — David James Raymond (49 Grandison Rd, SW11), *b* 1946; Liveryman Armourers' and Brasiers' Co 1980: *m* 1st, 1973 (*m diss* 1980), Lucinda Jane, da of late Cdr G. R. Callingham, RN (ret); 2ndly, 1983, Charmian, elder da of late Cdr John S. Kerans, DSO, RN (ret), of 44 Gordons Way, Oxted, Surrey, — Carol Rachel Mildred (Altyre House, Gt Horkesley, Colchester, Essex CO6 4AB), *b* 1938: *m* 1961 (*m diss* 1988), Torquil Robin Armour Macmillan, and has issue living, James Armour *b* 1965: *m* 1986, Susan Margaret Falle (and has issue living, Joshua *b* 1990, Benedict *b* 1993, Sophie Charlotte *b* 1987), Andrew Giles *b* 1968, Timothy Iain *b* 1969, Lucinda Jane Carol *b* 1963: *m* 1989, John Brezak (and has issue living, Tiffany *b* 1992). *Residence* – Crowpits, Stopham, Pulborough, Sussex RH20 1ED.

John Barttelot, who *d* 1428, acquired Stopham in the right of his wife Joan, da and co-heir of William de Stopham. The Rt Hon Sir Walter Barttelot, CB, PC, 1st baronet, sat as MP for W Sussex (*C*) 1860-85, and for Sussex, NW, or Horsham, Div 1885-93. Capt Sir Walter Barttelot, 2nd baronet, was *ka* 1900, while Comdg 2nd Vol Batn Roy Sussex Regt. The 3rd baronet, Sir Walter Balfour Barttelot, DSO, Major and Brevet Lieut-Col Coldstream Guards, was *k* during European War while Mil Attaché at Teheran (Croix de Guerre). The 4th baronet, Brigadier Sir Walter de Stopham Barttelot, DSO, late Coldstream Guards, was *ka* in France 1944.

BARWICK (UK) 1912, of Ashbrooke Grange, Borough of Sunderland (Extinct 1979)

Sir RICHARD LLEWELLYN BARWICK, 3rd, and last *Baronet*.

DAUGHTERS LIVING OF THIRD BARONET *(by 1st wife Valerie Maud, who d 1989, da of Robert Jeremiah Skelton, of Nairobi, Kenya)*

Rozanne Valerie, *b* 1950: *m* 1970, Alan Michael Bulmer, of Coombe Cross House, East Meon, Petersfield, Hants, and has issue living, Caroline Valerie, *b* 1974, — Rozalind Margot, *b* 1978. —— Sandra-Anne (The New Inn, Coln St Aldwyns, nr Cirencester, Glos GL7 5AN), *b* 1952; MD 1986: *m* 1st 1971 (*m diss* 1986), Timothy George Wheaton Heycock; 2ndly, 1989, Brian Antony Evans, son of late Evan Stanley Evans, CBE, FRCS, and has issue living (by 1st *m*) Tobias George Francis, *b* 1974, — Nathalie Louise Katharine, *b* 1976. —— Victoria Maud Lorraine, *b* 1961: *m* 1994, Andrew Kenneth Wallis, of Cockrupp Farm, Coln St Aldwyns, nr Cirencester, Glos, son of Francis Wallis.

COLLATERAL BRANCH LIVING

Issue of late George Short Barwick, 2nd son of 1st baronet, *b* 1879, *d* 1937: *m* 1913, Marianne, who *d* 1975, da of late William Marshall, of Davenham, Ches:—

Diana Marianne, *b* 1917: *m* 1st, 1945 (*m diss* 1955), Lieut John Louis Arnott Bowles, RN; 2ndly, 1959, Gerald Leopold Wiener, OBE, of 45 Edwardes Sq, W8, and has issue living, (by 1st *m*) (George) Anthony John (Holmhead, Corsock, Castle Douglas, Kirkcudbrightshire DG7 3DT), *b* 1946: *m* 1979, (Joan) Miranda Mary, 2nd da of Maj Julius Arthur Sheffield Neave, CBE (*see* Neave, Bt, colls), and has issue living, Richard Anthony Julius *b* 1981, Humphrey John Edward *b* 1984, Georgina Helen Diana *b* 1987, — Sarah Margaret Diana, *b* 1949: *m* 1991, Henry Christopher Bennett, of The Shrubbery, Linton, Cambs (*see* Bazley, Bt), and has issue living, Jonathan Ronald Sebastian *b* 1991.

BATES (UK) 1880, of Bellefield, co Lancaster

Sir GEOFFREY VOLTELIN BATES, MC, 5th *Baronet*, son of late Major Cecil Robert Bates, DSO, MC, 3rd son of 2nd baronet; *b* 2 Oct 1921; *s* his uncle *Sir* PERCY ELLY, GBE, 1946; *ed* Radley; Capt (ret) 8th Hussars, and Maj (ret) Cheshire Yeo; High Sheriff of Flintshire 1969; 1939-45 War (MC): *m* 1st, 1945, Kitty, who *d* 1956, da of Ernest Kendall-Lane, of Saskatchewan, Canada; 2ndly, 1957, Hon Olivia Gwyneth Zoë Fitz Roy, who *d* 1969, da of 2nd Viscount Daventry; 3rdly, 1971, Juliet Eleanor Hugolyn Whitelocke-Winter, widow of Edward Colin Winter, and da of late Cdr G Whitelocke, RN, and has issue by 1st and 2nd *m*.

Arms – Argent, on a fesse azure a quatrefoil between two fleurs-de-lys argent, between in chief two quatrefoils azure, and in base a fleur-de-lys of the same. **Crest** – A stag's head erased azure, attired or, transfixed by two arrows crosswise of the second, and charged on the neck with two quatrefoils in pale or. *Residence* – Gyrn Castle, Llanasa, Holywell, Clwyd CH8 9BG.

Labore et virtue
By labour and virtue

SONS LIVING *(By 1st marriage)*

EDWARD ROBERT, *b* 4 July 1946; *ed* Gordonstoun. —— Richard Geoffrey, *b* 1948: *m* 1971, Diana Margaret Ronkin, who *d* 1990, and has issue living, James Geoffrey, *b* 14 March 1985, — Margot Zoe, *b* 1976, — Nichola Sarah, *b* 1979. *Residence* – Pirates House, Bowen Bay, Bowen Island, BC, Canada V0N 1G0.

DAUGHTER LIVING *(By 2nd marriage)*

Celina Zoë, *b* 1958: *m* 19—, Timothy M. Radcliffe, only son of R. J. Radliffe, of Bodedern, Anglesey, and has issue living, Olivia Philppa Zoë, *b* 1993.

COLLATERAL BRANCHES LIVING

Issue of late Col Denis Haughton Bates, MC, TD, 5th son of 2nd baronet, *b* 1886, *d* 1959: *m* 1922, Aline Mary, who *d* 1974, da of Edward T. Crook, of Woodlands Hall, Bridgnorth:—

Philip Edward, VRD (2 Squirrels Cottages, Poles Lane, Woodside, Lymington, Hants SO41 8AD) *b* 1925; *ed* Shrewsbury; Maj (ret) RM Force VR; 1943-45 War: *m* 1952, Mary Patricia Carol, da of Lt-Col Clive Vincent Moberly-Bell, OBE, and has issue living, Hugh Percy (Hathaway House, Lower Pennington Lane, Lymington, Hants), *b* 1953: *m* 1977, Angela Roberta Wall, and has issue living, James Edward *b* 1984, Kathryn Ann *b* 1981, — Denis Moberly (Wisteria Cottage, Minstead, Lyndhurst, Hants SO4 7FX), *b* 1954: *m* 1979, Hilary Mackay, and has issue living, Alastair Martin *b* 1987, Jennifer Jane *b* 1985, — Patricia Mary, *b* 1956: *m* 1978, Dr Anthony Yates, of Yate's Place, Lot 5 Minsterly Rd, Denmark 6333, W, Australia, and has issue living, Colin Robert *b* 1979, Robert Mark *b* 1981, Christopher John *b* 1983, William Anthony *b* 1987, — Carol Elisabeth, *b* 1957: *m* 1981, Brian Hedley Thomas, of Bracken Dene, 17 Clifton Rd, Parkstone, Poole, Dorset, and has issue living, Sophie Patricia *b* 1983, Nicola Hedley *b* 1985. —— Denise Elisabeth, *b* 1928: *m* 1958, Rev Canon Thomas Michael Rylands, and has issue living, Thomas Gordon, *b* 1959; *ed* Shrewsbury, and Univ of Birmingham (BSc): *m* 1985, Jane Lesley, da of Alan Goode, and has issue living, Thomas Christopher *b* 1987, Peter Michael *b* 1993, Louise Victoria *b* 1989, — *Rev* Mark James, *b* 1961; *ed* St Hild and St Bede Coll, Durham (BA): *m* 1986, Rev Amanda, da of Peter Craig Byrom, OBE, and has issue living, Samuel George Ambrose *b* 1990, Frances Elisabeth *b* 1988, — Alison Joane *b* 1963; *ed* Moreton Hall, and City and Guilds Coll of Art. *Residence* – Haughton Thorn, nr Tarporley, Cheshire CW6 9RN.

Issue of late Lieut-Col Austin Graves Bates, DSO, MC, 6th son of 2nd baronet, *b* 1891, *d* 1961: *m* 1920, Jean Christian Marguerite, who *d* 1982, da of Col James Hunter, of Anton's Hill, Coldstream, Berwickshire:—

Jeremy Dickson (Anton's Hill, Coldstream, Berwickshire), *b* 1932; *ed* London Univ (BSc 1955): *m* 1978, Elizabeth Marjorie, da of late H. W. Rudd, of High Pines, Woodend Drive, Sunninghill, Ascot, Berks, and has issue living, Thomas James Dickson, *b* 1980, — Sarah Marjorie, *b* 1981. —— Martin Graves (17 Queen's Gate Place, SW7 5NY), *b* 1935; *ed* St Edmund Hall, Oxford (BA); late Queen's Own Cameron Highlanders: *m* 1965, Susan Myfanwy Prudence, da of Capt Robert Edward Dudley Ryder, VC, RN (*see* E Harrowby, colls), and has issue living, Oliver Robert Hunter, *b* 1969, — Susannah Hilaré Myfanwy, *b* 1970.

Issue of late Maurice Halifax Bates, Lt RA, 7th son of 2nd baronet, *b* 1898, *d* 1925: *m* 1922, May Frances (who *d* 1969, having *m* 2ndly, 1927, Brig Ralph Emerson Pickering, CBE, late Queen's Roy Regt, who *d* 1962), da of late Sir Edward Arthur Henry Blunt, KCIE, OBE (Blunt, Bt colls):—

Ann Maurice, *b* (posthumous) 1925. *Residence* – Little Hatchett, Hatchett Lane, Beaulieu, Brockenhurst, Hants SO42 7WA.

Granddaughter of late Sydney Eggers Bates, 3rd son of 1st baronet:—
Issue of late Col Arthur Sydney Bates, DSO, TD, *b* 1879, *d* 1958: *m* 1905, Mary da Costa, who *d* 1962, da of late Lieut-Col Charles Robert Crosse, CMG, MVO, formerly Roy W Kent Regt:—

Anne Mary (Beech House, Wootton St Lawrence, Basingstoke, Hants), *b* 1915: *m* 1939, Lt-Col John Oliver-Bellasis, DSO, JP, DL, Royal Fusiliers, who *d* 1979, and has issue living, Charles Arthur John (The Old Rectory, Boxford, nr Newbury, Berks), *b* 1940; *ed* Winchester, and Royal Agric Coll, Cirencester; FRICS; MRAC: *m* 1972, Julia Elizabeth, da of Lt Cdr John Errol Manners, DSC, RN (ret), of Laurel House, Great Cheverell, Devizes, Wilts, and has issue living, John Edward *b* 1976, Richard Charles *b* 1977, Clare Elizabeth *b* 1974, — Hugh Richard, *b* 1945; *ed* Winchester, and RMA; Maj WG (ret 1977); FRAgS: *m* 1971, Daphne Phoebe, yr da of Arthur Christopher Parsons (*see* E Rosse, colls), and has issue living, Joanna Gwenda *b* 1975, Nicola Mary *b* 1978. *Residence* – Wootton House, Wootton St Lawrence, Basingstoke, Hants.

The 1st baronet, Sir Edward, was MP for Plymouth (C) 1871-80 and 1885-92. The 4th baronet Sir Percy Elly, GBE, was Chm of Cunard Steamship Co, Ltd, and of Cunard-White Star Ltd.

BATES (UK) 1937, of Magherabuoy, co Londonderry

Sir (JOHN) DAWSON BATES, MC, 2nd *Baronet*; *b* 21 Sept 1921; *s* his father, *Rt Hon Sir* (Richard) Dawson, OBE, 1949; *ed* Winchester, and Balliol Coll Oxford; formerly Major Rifle Brig; Middle East, CMF, NW Europe 1939-45 (MC): *m* 1953, Mary Murray, da of late Lt-Col Joseph Murray Hoult, RA, of Norton Place, Lincoln, and has issue.
Residence – Butleigh House, Glastonbury, Som BA6 8SU.

SONS LIVING

RICHARD DAWSON HOULT, *b* 12 May 1956. —— Charles Joseph Dill, *b* 1959: *m* 1984, Suzanne C., yr da of David Beaumont, of Much Hadham, Hertfordshire, and has issue living, Patrick Charles Beaumont, *b* 1990, — Oliver James Beaumont, *b* 1993, — Claudia, *b* 1988.

DAUGHTER LIVING

Drusilla Mary Cynthia, *b* 1954: *m* 1983, Gervase Belfield, eldest son of late Eversley Belfield, of Beauchamp, Sark, CI, and has issue living, Laura Daisy, *b* 1987, — Matilda May, *b* 1992.

The 1st baronet, Rt Hon Sir (Richard) Dawson Bates, OBE (son of late Richard Dawson Bates, solicitor, of Belfast), was Min for Home Affairs, N Ireland 1921-43.

BATHO (UK) 1928, of Frinton, Essex

Sir PETER GHISLAIN BATHO, 3rd *Baronet*; *b* 9 Dec 1939; *s* his father, Lt-Col *Sir* MAURICE BENJAMIN, 1990; *ed* Ampleforth; Co Councillor Suffolk 1989-93: *m* 1966, Lucille Mary, da of late Wilfrid Francis Williamson, of The White House, Saxmundham, Suffolk, and has issue.

Arms – Gules, on a fess argent two castles of the first, over all a sword in pale point upwards proper. **Crest** – A dragon sejant or gorged with a mural crown gules, and holding in the dexter claw a sword as in the arms.
Residence – Park Farm, Saxmundham, Suffolk IP17 1DQ.

SONS LIVING

RUPERT SEBASTIAN GHISLAIN, *b* 26 Oct 1967. —— Alexander Francis Ghislain, *b* 1970. —— Hugh Charles Ghislain, *b* 1973.

BROTHER LIVING

Richard Ghislain (Carlton, Marden, Hereford HR1 3ES), *b* 1941; *ed* Ampleforth and Wye Coll, London Univ (BSc): *m* 1970, Georgina Catherine Ann Gwynne, da of late William Reginald Gwynne Chadwick, of The Croft, Abergavenny, Gwent, and has issue living, Charles William Ghislain, *b* 1971; *ed* Belmont Abbey, — Sarah Catherine Ghislaine, *b* 1974.

Neither do I hesitate at trifles

SISTERS LIVING

Anne Madelaine Bessie Ghislaine, *b* 1938: *m* 1964, Stephen Robert Morgan Oliver, of St Briavels, Wetherden, Stowmarket, Suffolk, and has issue living, Felix Benjamin Morgan, *b* 1966, — Alban Geoffrey Morgan, *b* 1968, — Damian Paul Morgan, *b* 1970, — Justin Edmund Morgan, *b* 1978. —— Jacqueline Ghislaine, *b* 1947: *m* 1987, Ian David Bruce-Jones, of Little Garth, The Street, Walberswick, Southwold, Suffolk IP18 6UH, son of late Douglas Bruce-Jones, of Warlingham, Surrey.

The 1st baronet, Sir Charles Albert Batho (son of late William Smith Batho, of Highgate, N), was an Alderman of City of London (Aldgate Ward) 1921-38, Sheriff 1925-6, and Lord Mayor 1927-8. The 2nd baronet, Lt-Col Sir Maurice Benjamin Batho, was Regional Advisor on Cereals Collection to Min of Finance, Iran, 1944, and Dept Dir of Rice Procurement, Bengal, 1945.

HERVEY-BATHURST (UK) 1818, of Lainston, Hants
(Name pronounced "Harvy-Bathurst")

Sir FREDERICK PETER METHUEN HERVEY-BATHURST, 6th *Baronet*; *b* 26 Jan 1903; *s* his father, *Major Sir* FREDERICK EDWARD WILLIAM, DSO, 1956; *ed* Eton; Capt late Grenadier Guards: *m* 1st, 1933 (*m diss* 1956), Maureen Gladys Diana, el da of late Charles Gordon, of Boveridge Park, Salisbury; 2ndly, 1958, Cornelia, da of late Frederic White Shepard, of New York, USA, and widow of Dr John Lawrence Riker, of Rumson, New Jersey, USA, and has issue by 1st *m*.

Arms – Quarterly, 1st and 4th, sable, two bars ermine, and in chief three crosses-patée or, a crescent for difference, *Bathurst*; 2nd and 3rd, gules, on a bend argent three trefoils vert, a martlet for difference, *Hervey*. **Crest** – 1st, a dexter arm embowed in armour proper, grasping a spiked club or, *Bathurst*; 2nd, an ounce passant sable, bezantee ducally gorged and chained or, in the paw a trefoil slipped vert, *Hervey*.
Seat – Somborne Park, King's Somborne, Hants. *Residence* – Bellevue Av, Rumson, New Jersey, USA.

SON LIVING *(By 1st marriage)*

Hold thy faith

(FREDERICK) JOHN CHARLES GORDON, *b* 23 April 1934; *ed* Eton, and Trin Coll, Camb (BA 1957); is Lieut Grenadier Guards (Reserve): *m* 1957, Caroline Myrtle, da of Sir William Randle Starkey, 2nd Bt, and has issue living, Frederick William John, *b* 1965: *m* 1991, Annabel P., yr da of Donald Warburg, of Zurich, — Louisa Caroline (*Lady Portal*), *b* 1959: *m* 1982, Sir Jonathan Francis Portal, 6th Bt, — Sophia Selina Irene, *b* 1961: *m* 1982, Henry Nicholas Almroth Colthurst, of 1 Wandle Rd, SW17 7DL, yst son of Sir Richard La Touche Colthurst, 9th Bt. *Residence* – Somborne Park, King's Somborne, Hants.

DAUGHTER LIVING *(By 1st marriage)*

Selina Anthea Maureen, *b* 1936: *m* 1st, 1959 (*m diss* 1989), Brig Peter Gerald Sandeman Tower, CBE, Coldstream Guards (Butler Bt, *cr* 1628); 2ndly, 1990, (Oswald) Henry Chaldecott (*see* Worsley-Taylor, Bt, 1959 Edn), and has issue living (by 1st *m*), William John, *b* 1963, — Nicola Jane, *b* 1961: *m* 1987, Richard D. Crosthwaite, yr son of late Tudor Derek Crosthwaite, of 4 Soudan Rd, SW11 4HH. *Residence* – Lauristina Cottage, Lower Inkpen, Newbury, Berks RG15 0DP.

HALF-BROTHER LIVING

Benjamin Alexander Frederick, OBE, *b* 1920; *ed* Eton and Trin Coll Camb (BA); Maj late Grenadier Guards and Special Forces; a DL of Herefordshire; 1939-45 War (wounded, despatches twice); OBE (Civil) 1985: *m* 1st, 1947, Hon Elizabeth Violet Virginia Somers Cocks, who *d* 1986, only child of 6th Baron Somers; 2ndly, 1992, Mrs Anne Pollak, only da of late Rev Thomas Vernon Garnier, OBE, and formerly wife of Robert Pollak, of Burtons Farm, Ledbury, Herefords, and has issue living (by 1st *m*), James Felton Somers, *b* 1949: *m* 1982, Hon Sarah Rachel Peake, 2nd da of 2nd Viscount Ingleby, and has issue living, Imogen Elizabeth Somers *b* 1986, Isabella Katherine Somers *b* 1990, — George Arthur Somers, *b* 1952.
Seat – Eastnor Castle, Ledbury, Herefordshire. *Residence* – Hillend House, Eastnor, Ledbury, Herefordshire.

COLLATERAL BRANCH LIVING

Grandchildren of late Capt Sidney Lionel Paston-Cooper, son of Lt-Col Lionel Paston-Cooper (who assumed the name of Paston-Cooper by R Licence 1905), 2nd son of 3rd baronet, *b* 1887, *d* 1934: *m* 1927, Ermyntrude Mary, who *d* 1936, da of Henry Caley, of Hovingham, Yorks:—
    Issue of late Astley Cecil Hervey PASTON-COOPER, *b* 1929; *d* 1978: *m* 1950, Jean Louise, da of Lawrence Dickinson, of 8 Dorset Avenue, Welling, Kent:—
Lionel Lawrence Hervey, *b* 1951: *m* 1987, Edwina Jane, da of F. Ward Smith, of Wave Crest, Whitstable, Kent, and has issue living, Thomas Astley Ward, *b* 1993. *Residence* – 33 St Mark's Rd, Teddington, Middx. —— Sally Anne, *b* 1953.

The 1st baronet, Sir Felton Elwell Hervey, was a grandson of late Hon Felton Hervey, 7th son of 1st Earl of Bristol (*see* M Bristol), and was ADC to the Duke of Wellington after Waterloo. He assumed in 1801 the additional surname and arms of Bathurst, and on his death without issue in 1819, he was succeeded, under special remainder, by his next brother, Sir Frederick Anne Hervey-Bathurst, 2nd Bt. Lt-Col Sir Frederick, 4th baronet, sat as MP for S Wilts (*C*) 1861-5. Major Sir Frederick Edward William, 5th Bt, DSO, Grenadier Guards, served in Egyptian Campaign 1898, S Africa 1900, and European War 1914-18 (DSO).

BAYNES (UK) 1801, of Harefield Place, Middlesex

Rage supplies arms

Sir JOHN CHRISTOPHER MALCOLM BAYNES, 7th *Baronet*; *b* 24 April 1928; *s* his father, *Sir* RORY MALCOLM STUART, 1979; *ed* Sedbergh Sch, RMA Sandhurst, and Edinburgh Univ (MSc); late Lt-Col Queen's Own Highlanders, served in The Cameronians (Scottish Rifles) 1948 until disbandment 1968; Malaya 1950-53 (despatches): *m* 1955, Shirley Maxwell, only da of late Robert Allan Dodds, of Foxbury, Lesbury, Alnwick, and has issue.

Arms – Sable, a shin-bone in fesse surmounted of another in pale argent; on a canton of the last, a vulture proper. **Crest** – A cubit arm vested, azure, cuffed erminois, the hand holding a jaw-bone argent. **Supporters** – Two savages wreathed with holly about the head and waist, carrying clubs over their exterior shoulders all proper.
Residence – Talwrn Bach, Llanfyllin, Powys SY22 5LQ. *Club* – Army & Navy.

SONS LIVING

CHRISTOPHER RORY, *b* 11 May 1956: *m* 1992, Sandra Merriman, and has issue living, Alasdair William Merriman, *b* 1993. *Residence* – Greywalls, Findon, Sussex. —— Timothy Peter (Bagend, Steeple Aston, Oxford OX5 3RU), *b* 1957: *m* 1986, Estelle Anne Gabrielle, elder da of late Nicholas John Dennys Parry de Winton, of Llangattock House, Penpergwm, Abergavenny, Gwent, and has issue living, Rory Nicholas Aimery, *b* 1992. —— Simon Robert Maurice, *b* 1960: *m* 1992, Margaret Anne Mary, yr da of Sydney Boag, of Boar's Hill, Oxford. —— William John Walter, *b* 1966.

COLLATERAL BRANCH LIVING

Grandson of late Edward Neil Baynes, yst son of 3rd baronet:—
    Issue of late Edward Stuart Augustus Baynes, OBE, *b* 1889, *d* 1972: *m* 1918, Helen Mary (32 Avondale Cres, Killiney, co Dublin), da of G. Meredith, of Epsom, and widow of J. S. White:—
Anthony Edward George (School Hill, Little Minster, Minster Lovell, Oxon), *b* 1921; Artist; 1939-45 War as Sub-Lt RNVR.

The 1st baronet, Sir Christopher, was the son of William Baynes (a Gentleman of the Privy Chamber to George II and George III), of Harefield Place, Middlesex, and Kilburn Hall, Yorkshire, descended from the old Yorkshire family of Bayne, originally de Bayeux; Sir Christopher served in Royal Horse Guards 1781-8, and in 1796 was Major-Commandant of the Uxbridge Gentlemen and Yeomanry Cavalry, which corps he helped to raise; he was also a DL for Middlesex.

BAZLEY (UK) 1869, of Hatherop, co Gloucester

Consider the end

Sir THOMAS STAFFORD BAZLEY, 3rd *Baronet*, son of the late Gardner Sebastian Bazley, only son of 2nd baronet; *b* 5 Oct 1907; *s* his grandfather, *Sir* THOMAS SEBASTIAN, 1919; *ed* Harrow, and Magdalen Coll, Oxford: *m* 1945, Carmen, only da of James Tulla, of 11 Stanley Gardens, W11, and has issue.

𝔄rms – Per pale azure and sable, a bee volant or between three fleurs-de-lis argent. 𝔠rest – A cubit arm erect proper charged with a bee volant or, the hand holding a chapeau gules, turned up gold; the whole between two branches of oak vert.
Residence – Eastleach Downs Farm, Eastleach Turville, Cirencester, Gloucestershire GL7 3PX.

SONS LIVING

THOMAS JOHN SEBASTIAN, *b* 31 Aug 1948. —— Anthony Martin Christopher, *b* 1958. —— John Francis Alexander, *b* 1961.

DAUGHTERS LIVING

Catherine, *b* 1950. —— Virginia, *b* 1953.

SISTER LIVING

Rachel Constance, *b* 1909: *m* 1939, Edward John Ronald Bennett, and has issue living, John Sebastian (Colbourne House, Ufton, nr Leamington Spa, Warwicks CV33 9PE), *b* 1942: *m* 1971, Sara Hermione, da of Maj John Alfred Inglis Jones, of Saddlewood, Camberley, and has issue living, William James Alexander *b* 1978, Alexander Thomas Edward *b* 1985, Jemima Charlotte *b* 1974, Camilla Sophie *b* 1976, — Henry Christopher (The Shrubbery, Linton, Cambs), *b* 1946: *m* 1991, Sarah Margaret Diana, da of John Louis Arnott Bowles (*see* Barwick, Bt, colls), and has issue living, Jonathan Ronald Sebastian *b* 1991, — Edward Alexander, *b* 1948: *m* 1993, Tarja Hannele, da of Kapteeni Evp Tenho Taavetti Reponen, of Kaijala, Finland, — Charles Michael (twin), *b* 1948: *m* 1975, Barbara Joyce, da of George Hammond, of NY, USA, and has issue living, George Christopher *b* 1976, Henry Arthur *b* 1985, Emma Reese *b* 1983, — Victoria, *b* 1940: *m* 1964, Henry Alexander Fowell Buxton, and has issue (*see* Buxton, Bt, colls).

COLLATERAL BRANCH LIVING

Granddaughter of late Gardner Sebastian Bazley, only son of 2nd baronet (ante):—
Issue of late Anthony Gardner Bazley, *b* 1911, *d* 1937: *m* 1934, Anne (*Baroness Howard of Penrith*) (who *m* 2ndly, 1944, 2nd Baron Howard of Penrith), da of late John Beaumont Hotham (*see* B Hotham, colls):—
Susan Antonia (Dean Farm, Coln St Aldwyn, Cirencester, Glos GL7 5AX), *b* 1937: *m* 1st, 1958 (*m diss* 1970), Peter Humphrey Alexander Van Oss (*see* E Waldegrave, 1947 Edn); 2ndly, 1970 (*m diss* 1984), William John Vicary, and has issue living (by 1st *m*), Mark Peter Anthony *b* 1959: *m* 1985, Caroline Elizabeth, da of Ian Maxwell Scoggins, of High Thicket, Dockenfield, nr Farnham, Surrey, and has issue living, Emily Atalanta *b* 1988, Francesca Camilla *b* 1989, Octavia Rose *b* 1994, — Anthony Tom Francis, *b* 1961, — Juliet Anne Favell (twin), *b* 1961: *m* 1991, Robert Gwyn Palmer, only child of late J. Gwyn Palmer, of Treboeth, W Glam, — Katharine Susanna, *b* 1964, — (by 2nd *m*) William Sebastian, *b* 1973.
The 1st baronet sat as MP for Manchester (*L*) 1858-80, and the 2nd baronet was High Sheriff of Gloucestershire 1874.

BEAUCHAMP (UK) 1911, of Grosvenor Place, City of Westminister (Extinct 1976)
(Name pronounced "Beecham")

Sir BROGRAVE CAMPBELL BEAUCHAMP, 2nd and last *Baronet*.

DAUGHTER LIVING OF SECOND BARONET

Patricia Evelyn, *b* 1925: *m* 1949, Maj Michael William Thomas Leatham, who *d* 1992, and has issue living, Simon Anthony Michael, *b* 1951: *m* 1973, Cristiana Elisabeth, da of Dr Carl Uvo Stein, of Hindenburgstrasse 31, Oldenburg, Germany, and has issue living, Anthony Michael *b* 1977, Nicholas James Edward *b* 1981, — Edward Arthur Martyn (19 Inner Park Rd, Wimbledon SW19), *b* 1953: *m* 1975, Elizabeth Scarlet, da of Charles Hardwick, of Hampshire Hunt Cottage, Ropley, and has issue living, Alexander Charles Edward *b* 1982, Evelyn Elizabeth *b* 1980. *Residence* – King's Moor, Sunningdale, Berks.

BEAUCHAMP (UK) 1918, of Woodborough, co Somerset (Extinct 1983)
(Name pronounced "Beecham")

Sir PETER (DOUGLAS CLIFFORD) BEAUCHAMP, 2nd and last *Baronet*.

DAUGHTER LIVING OF FIRST BARONET

Dorothy Joan, *b* 1901: *m* 1st, 1931, Maj Claude Darcy Stratton de Lisle Bush, who *d* on active ser 1941; 2ndly, 1946, as his 2nd wife, Brig Keith Frederick William Dunn, CBE, DL, RA, who *d* 1985, and has issue living (by 1st *m*), Michael Peter Tobin (The Granary, Oare, Hermitage, Newbury, Berks), *b* 1938; *ed* Eton; Royal Dragoons 1957-61: *m* 1st, 1964 (*m diss*

1971), Jane Anne, only da of late Edward Bower, of Biniaraix, Soller de Mallorca; 2ndly, 1971, Carolyn Ann, elder da of Trevor Stanley Passmore, of Pilot's View, Alderney, CI, and formerly wife of David Bruce Douglas Lowe, and has issue living (by 1st *m*), Angus Claude Beauchamp *b* 1965. *Residence* – Willow Cottage, The Green, Uley, Gloucestershire.

PROCTOR-BEAUCHAMP (GB) 1745, of Langley Park, Norfolk
(Name pronounced "Proctor-Beecham")

Always faithful

Sir CHRISTOPHER RADSTOCK PROCTOR-BEAUCHAMP, 9th *Baronet*; *b* 30 Jan 1935; *s* his father, *Rev Sir* IVOR CUTHBERT, MB, BCh, 1971; *ed* Rugby, and Trin Coll, Camb (MA): *m* 1965, Rosalind Emily Margot, da of Gerald Percival Wainwright, of 135 Marina, St Leonard's-on-Sea, and has issue.

Arms – Argent, a chevron between three martlets sable **Crest** – On a mount vert, a greyhound sejant argent, spotted brown, collared or.
Residence – The White House, Harpford, nr Sidmouth, Devon EX10 0NJ.

SONS LIVING

CHARLES BARCLAY, *b* 7 July 1969. —— Robert Ivor, *b* 1971.

DAUGHTER LIVING

Rosalind Caroline, *b* 1967.

BROTHER LIVING

Rev Anthony Hazlerigg (The Rectory, 18 Thorpe Rd, Kirby Cross, Frinton-on-Sea, Essex CO13 0LT), *b* 1940; *ed* Monkton Combe Sch and Trin Coll, Camb (MA); ordained 1975: *m* 1965, Anne Elise, da of late Rev Thomas Hewitt, V of St George's, Worthing, and has issue living, Guy James (97 Avenue Rd, Portswood, Southampton, Hants SO14 6BD), *b* 1967: *m* 1992, Hilda Catherine, da of R. H. Craig, of Campbeltown, Argyll, — Julian Thomas, *b* 1968, — Claire Alexandra, *b* 1970.

SISTER LIVING

Rosemary Jean, *b* 1936: *m* 1964, Thomas Henry Geake, MA, AMIMechE, and has issue living, William Beauchamp, *b* 1968, — Elisabeth Marjorie, *b* 1965, — Helen Mary, *b* 1967.

UNCLE LIVING (*Son of 7th baronet*)

Basil Ralph, *b* 1906; *ed* Marlborough, and Toronto Univ (Diploma in Agriculture 1932): *m* 1st, 1932 (*m diss* 1957), Joan, da of Tom Storey; 2ndly, 1957, Diana, da of late Lt-Col Bernard H Elliott, RA, of Goring House, North Woodchester, nr Stroud, Gloucestershire, and has issue living, (by 1st *m*) Nicholas (26 Howard St, Thatto Heath, St Helens, Lancs WA10 3RG), *b* 1935; FRHS, FPWI: *m* 1964, Pauline, da of Jacob de Mos, of Hook of Holland, and has issue living, Alison de Mos *b* 1965, Sarah Jane *b* 1966, Victoria Isobel *b* 1967, — Carol Margot, *b* 1933: *m* 1958, Claude de Pina D. Swain, of 29 Springhead, Tunbridge Wells, Kent TN2 3NY, and has issue living, Charles de Pina Beauchamp *b* 1959: *m* 1984, Caroline Kerr, da of Alexander Alfred Stuart, of Holly House, Manor Lane, Gerrards Cross SL9 7NJ (and has issue living, Charles Douglas Stuart *b* 1988, Victoria Caroline *b* 1989), Claudia Fenella *b* 1961: *m* 1983, Richard William Pettifer, son of W/Cdr John Kenyon Pettifer, RAF, of Paddock House, Little London, Whitchurch, Aylesbury, Bucks HP22 4LE (and has issue living, Julian Richard *b* 1987, William Gregory *b* 1989, Felix George *b* 1991), — Elisabeth Waldegrave (Flat 3, Croft Rd, Willesborough, Ashford, Kent TN24 8AZ), *b* 1934, — (by 2nd *m*) Sophie Joy (43 Richmond Av, Islington N1 0MB), *b* 1958. *Residence* – Penhwyr, Dinas Cross, Newport, Dyfed SA42 0UQ.

COLLATERAL BRANCHES LIVING

Granddaughter of late Sir Edward Beauchamp (2nd son of late Rev William Henry Beauchamp, 2nd son of 3rd baronet), who was *cr* a *Baronet* 1911.
See Beauchamp, Bt, *cr* 1911. Ext 1976.

Grandchildren of Reginald Percy Beauchamp (infra):—
Issue of late Percy Tremayne Beauchamp, *b* 1908, *d* 1959: *m* 1935, Eileen Alice, who *d* 1964, da of Arthur Edward Croft:—
Anthony Tremayne, *b* 1937: *m* 1961, Nancy Ann, da of Mark Vincent Jones, of Muddy Creek, Tas, and has issue living, Christopher Tremayne, *b* 1964, — Mark Andrew, *b* 1972, — Wendy Ann, *b* 1965: *m* 1984, Allan Gregory Mason. —— Suzanne Elizabeth, *b* 1946.

Grandchildren of late Robert Beauchamp, 3rd son of 3rd baronet:—
Issue of late Reginald Percy Beauchamp, *b* 1873, *d* 1944: *m* 1904, Malvina Blanche Natalie, who *d* 1967, da of Jonathan Purdy Plummer:—
Geoffrey Frank (El-Retiro, Rosevears, W Tamar, Tasmania), *b* 1914: *m* 1950, Dorothy Vernon, who *d* 1970, da of Vernon Thomas Lewis, of 9 Hilda Cres, Hawthorne, Vic, and has issue living, Pamela Nerida, *b* 1952. —— Nerida Nadine (El-Retiro, Rosevears, W Tamar, Tasmania) *b* 1916: *m* 1935 (*m diss* 1943), Ronald Breadalbane Postle.

Grandchildren of late Edward Hayes Beauchamp, eldest son of late Capt Edward Halhed Beauchamp, RN, 3rd son of George Edward Beauchamp (infra):—
Issue of late Edward Guy Beauchamp, *b* 1885, *d* 1966: *m* 1918, Louise France Caroline, da of late A. T. Haultain, of Napier, NZ:—

Trevor Haultain, *b* 1919; Capt 2nd NZEF; 1939-45 War in S-W Pacific and Italy: *m* 1952 Beryl Irene, da of Herbert Maxwell, of Otorahanga, King Country, NZ, and has issue living, Robin Max, *b* 1953, — Christine, *b* 1960.
  Issue of late Herbert Rolf Haultain Beauchamp, DCM, *b* 1890, *d* 1968: *m* 1st 1918 Ida, who *d* 1952, da of late John Stevenson, of Naumai, Wanganui, NZ; 2ndly 1955, Mary Joyce, who *d* 1979, da of late Capt James Stevenson Hempton, of Dunedin, NZ.
(By 1st *m*) John Proctor (91 Deep Creek Rd, Torbay, Auckland 10, NZ), *b* 1923; 1939-45 War with New Zealand Forces: *m* 1947, Barbara, da of Oliver Coupland, of 18 Grey St, Wanganui, NZ, and has issue living, Warwick Rolf, *b* 1952: *m* 1974, Jan, da of Lester Wintere, of Parr Terr, Milford, NZ, — Michael Douglas, *b* 1957: *m* 1978, Laura Ann, da of Rev Campbell Nicol, of Milton, South Otago, NZ, and has issue living, Christopher David *b* 1979, Robin Anthony Nicol *b* 1985, — Bruce Proctor *b* 1963, — Margaret Anne, *b* 1947: *m* 1st, 1966, Colin Daniel Mayes; 2ndly, 1974, Stewart Rankin, and has issue living (by 2nd *m*), Douglas John *b* 1978, — Jane Allison, *b* 1950: *m* 1974, Alan Stewart Davis, — Elizabeth Claire, *b* 1956: *m* 1974, Peter David Anderson. —— Jill, *b* 1926: *m* 1949, Ronald Parkin, of 2 Webster St, Westown, New Plymouth, NZ, and has issue living, Jan, *b* 1952, — Carolyn, *b* 1950, — Andrea, *b* 1954.

     Grandchildren of late Herbert Lloyd Beauchamp, 2nd son of Capt Edward Halhed Beauchamp, RN, 3rd
     son of George Edward Beauchamp, 2nd son of 2nd baronet:—
  Issue of late Hugh Edward Beauchamp, *b* 1886, *d* 1962: *m* 1st, 1907, Grace Ethel, da of F. Quistorf, of Santa Cruz, California, USA; 2ndly, 19—, Tekla, who *d* 19—, da of Carl Viborg, of Stockholm, Sweden:—
(By 1st *m*) Dorothy Margaret, *b* 1909: *m* 1931, Harry Eugene Lennon.
  Issue of late Herbert Cecil Beauchamp, *b* 1888, *d* 1969: *m* 1913, Dora, who *d* 1968, da of H. Dohrmann, of Reinbeck, Iowa:—
David Dohrmann (830 Overhill Drive, Redding, Cal, USA 96001), *b* 1916; F/O Air Transport Command, US Army Air Corps: *m* 1941, Jean Anita, da of Wade Greening Moores, of Redding, Cal, USA, and has issue living, Mark David Beauchamp, *b* 1952: *m* 1st, 1980 (*m diss* 1987), Carla Jenoyce Norton, of Redding, Cal, USA; 2ndly, 1988, Ellen Paris, of Santa Monica, Cal, USA, — Sarah Caroline, *b* 1954: *m* 1988, Harry Holverson, of Arcata, Cal, USA, and has issue living, Elizabeth Jean *b* 1989.

     Granddaughter of late Henry Champion Beauchamp, yst son of late George Edward Beauchamp (ante):—
  Issue of late James Lloyd Hobart Beauchamp, *b* 1862, *d* 1927: *m* 1891, Maria Radford Knight, da of late Augustus George Stead:—
Maria Georgiana, *b* 1892: *m* 1928, Robert Desmond Carruthers, and has issue living, Marie Lucy Beauchamp, *b* 1930.

     Grandchildren of late Capt Willoughby George Beauchamp, eldest son of Willoughby James Beauchamp,
     4th son of Henry William Johnson Beauchamp, el son of William Henry Beauchamp, 3rd son of 1st
     baronet:—
  Issue of late Capt Willoughby Greaves Beauchamp, CBE, VRD, Ceylon, RNVR, *b* 1890, *d* 1960: *m* 1912, Kathleen Alice, who *d* 1983, da of late Dr W. B. Benison, of King's Heath, Worcestershire:—
(Kathleen) Patricia (Rooftops, 19 Church St, Wiveliscombe, Taunton, Som TA4 2LR), *b* 1913; formerly Junior Com ATS: *m* 1947, Alfred Thomas Morant, who *d* 1987, and has issue living, Willoughby Vivian Paul (5 Villa Thoreton, 75015 Paris), *b* 1950: *m* 1975, Monica Oates, — Julian Philip, *b* 1953: *m* 1977, Jane Peppard, and has issue living, Timothy Charles *b* 1982, Donna Kathleen *b* 1979, — Auriol Ann Melicent, *b* 1948: *m* 1975, Ottavio Croze, of 592B Dorsoduro, 30123 Venice, Italy, who *d* 1993, and has issue living, Ottavio Alfred *b* 1976, Cristina *b* 1979. —— Elaine Joyce, *b* 1916: *m* 1st, 1936 (*m diss* 1954), Edward Gordon Windus; 2ndly, 1955, Anthony Edward Davy Windus, of Flat 2, 7 Elwyn Rd, Exmouth, S Devon EX8 2EL, and has issue living, (by 1st *m*) Michael Edward Beauchamp, *b* 1937: *m* 1st, 1965 (*m diss* 1971), Evelyn Vera Pugh; 2ndly, 1990, Paola Elaine Ozkizil, and has issue living (by 1st *m*), Dirk Edward Beauchamp *b* 1966: *m* 1993, Isobel Mary Chisholm, Fiona Elaine Beauchamp *b* 1968: *m* 1992, James David McAllister (and has issue living, Hamish James *b* 1994), — Stefanie Gail Elaine, *b* 1940: *m* 1959, Robin Outram, of PO Box 24, Kilifi, Kenya, and has issue living, Stephen Jeremy *b* 1960: *m* 1992, Colleen Carr-Hartley (and has issue living, Ryan Stephen *b* 1993), Christopher James *b* 1961: *m* 1989, Helen Lewis (and has issue living, Joshua Martin *b* 1990, Anthony James *b* 1992), Suzanne Nicola Gail *b* 1963: *m* 1988, Gordon Russell St Amond Millar (and has issue living, Craig Russell St Amond *b* 1990, Kaila Gail Belinda *b* 1991). —— Barbara Meredith, *b* 1923: *m* 1943, Ronald Arthur Lushington, late Maj Indian Army, of Box 1091, Fourways 2055, Transvaal, S Africa, and has issue living, Christopher Saxton, *b* 1947: *m* 1982, Maria Gabriella Quatrochchi, and has issue living, Shaun Robert *b* 1983, Kaley Nicola *b* 1986, — Madeleine Dawn, *b* 1945: *m* 1972, Raynes Lloyd Sherewell, of Meadowend, Bryanston, S Africa, and has issue living, Francis Lloyd *b* 1975, Isla Madeleine *b* 1977.
  Issue of late Com Harold Charles Beauchamp, Roy Indian Navy, *b* 1891, *d* 1942: *m* 1918, Olive, who *d* 1983, da of Maurice Smelt Duke, MRCS, of 272 Kennington Park Rd, SE:—
Peter Clare (31 Langham Gdns, W13 8PY), *b* 1928; *ed* Cheltenham. —— Betty (Elisabeth), *b* 1922: *m* 1946, James Paten Cooper, late Maj King's African Rifles, and has issue living, Charles James Beauchamp Douglas, *b* 1954: *m* 1985, Anne Nicholson, — Caroline Elisabeth Beauchamp Paten, *b* 1949: *m* 1977, Richard Barton, and has issue living, Ashley Douglas *b* 1982, Hannah Olive *b* 1979, — Rosemary Deborah Beauchamp, *b* 1951: *m* 1991, Philip Ashbourn, and has issue living, Rose Emily *b* 1992. *Residence* - 18 Clarence Hill, Dartmouth, Devon.
  Issue of late Cdr Lawrence King Beauchamp, RN, *b* 1900, *d* 1966: *m* 1924, Helen Mary Victoria, da of late Robert Edward Stuart, solicitor, of Gannicox, Stroud, Glos:—
Julian Lawrence Stuart (Keepers Cottage, Whatley Combe, Frome, Som BA11 3JX) *b* 1928; MNI, Assoc RINA; Cdr RN; *ed* Kelly Coll: *m* 1st, 1951 (*m diss* 1966), Jennifer, who *d* 1978, da of late Harry George Parkes, of Wolverhampton; 2ndly, 1968, Isobel Mary, who *d* 1992, da of late Thomas Layfield, of Beckenham, and widow of Cdr Peter Angus Fickling, RN, and has issue living (by 1st *m*), Timothy Christopher Julian, *b* 1952; *ed* Kelly Coll, Birmingham Univ, and London Univ; BSocS, MA: *m* 1977, Anna Maria Magdalena, da of Henryk Zukowski, of Warsaw, Poland, and has issue living, John Christopher Michael *b* 1981, — Caroline Susan *b* 1954: *m* 1st, 1977, Graeme Stanley Thomson Gibson, who *d* 1978; 2ndly, 1979, G. Stephen W. Woods, of Greystones, Le Mont de Rozel, St Martin, Jersey CI, and has issue living (by 2nd *m*), (Gerald) Alexander William *b* 1981, Georgina Rozelle *b* 1982, — (by 2nd *m*) Fenella Jane Isobel, *b* 1970. —— Daphne Helen Stuart, *b* 1932.

     Grandson of late Henry King Beauchamp, 2nd son of late Willoughby James Beauchamp (ante):—
  Issue of late Brig Henry Rex Beauchamp, OBE, late RAPC, and Royal Leicestershire Regt, *b* 1906, *d* 1991: *m* 1st, 1937 (*m diss* 1947), Moira Helen, da of late G. H. Normand, of Edinburgh; 2ndly, 1954, Mrs Elizabeth Margaret Dobson (Oakfields, 20 Buckstone Close, Everton, Lymington, Hants), da of A. H. Ford-Moore, of Salisbury:—
(By 1st *m*) David Fitzgerald, *b* 1940; *ed* Uppingham, and Trin Coll, Oxford: *m* 1971, Victoria-Mary, da of James Clark, of Conn, USA, and has issue living, Gillian Alexandra, *b* 1973, — Catriona Clare, *b* 1974, — Tanya Catherine, *b* 1976.

     Grandsons of late Willoughby James Beauchamp (ante):—
  Issue of late Vernon Francis Beauchamp, *b* 1869, *d* 1949: *m* 1897, Amy, who *d* 1948, da of late William Henry Herbert, of Great Missenden, Bucks:—
Lucien Willoughby, *b* 1903: *m* 1937, Nancy Knight, da of Bradford Richards, and has issue living, Peter Willoughby, *b* 1943: *m* 1970, Stacy Ann, da of Joseph Maurice Scanlon, of Middleboro', Mass, — Sandra, *b* 1945. *Residence* - 9 Sunset Drive, South Easton, Mass 02375, USA.

     Grandson of late Vernon Francis Beauchamp (ante):—
  Issue of late Alan Charles Douglas Beauchamp, *b* 1901, *d* 1976: *m* 1944, Olga, da of W. K. Rhodes:—
Hugh Alan Vernon, *b* 1945.

Sir William Beauchamp-Proctor, 1st Bt (grandson of Ephraim Beauchamp of White Hall, Tottenham, Middx, citizen and mason of London); was MP for Middlesex 1747-68 which latter name he added by Act of Parliament in compliance with the terms of the will of his maternal uncle, George Proctor of Langley Park, Norfolk. The 4th Bt assumed by Roy licence 1852 the surname of Proctor-Beauchamp in lieu of Beauchamp-Proctor. The 6th Bt, Col Sir Horace George, CB Norfolk Regt, was *ka* 1915. The Rev Sir Montagu Harry Proctor-Beauchamp, 7th Bt, was a Missionary in China 1885-1936.

BEAUMONT (E) 1661, of Stoughton Grange, Leicestershire.

Exalted, not elated

Sir GEORGE HOWLAND FRANCIS BEAUMONT, 12th *Baronet; b 24 Sept 1924; s his father, Sir* GEORGE ARTHUR HAMILTON, 1933; *ed* Stowe; formerly Warrant Officer Australian Army; is patron of one living; N-W Europe 1944-45 with Coldstream Guards, and as Lieut 60th Rifles: *m* 1st, 1949 (*m diss* 1951), Barbara, da of William Singleton; 2ndly, 1963 (*m diss* 1986), Henrietta Anne, da of late Dr Arthur Weymouth, and has issue by 2nd *m*.

Arms – Azure, semée of fleurs-de-lis, a lion rampant or. Crest – On a chapeau azure, semée of fleurs-de-lis amd turned up ermine, a lion passant or.
Residence – Stretton House, Manor Court, Stretton-on-Fosse, nr Moreton-in-Marsh, Glos GL56 9SB.

DAUGHTERS LIVING *(By 2nd marriage)*

Georgina Brienne Arabella, *b* 1967. —— Francesca Renée Henrietta, *b* (twin) 1967.

COLLATERAL BRANCH LIVING

Granddaughter of late Francis Henry Beaumont, son of late William Francis Bertie Beaumont, brother of 8th baronet:—
Issue of late Major Francis Montagu Beaumont, *b* 1857, *d* 1936: *m* 1904, Sybil Anne, who *d* 1949, da of Higford Higford, formerly of Hartsfield, Betchworth:—
Crystal Katherine (Henspark Cottage, Dulverton, Som), *b* 1908: *m* 1930, Leslie James Earl, who *d* 1988, and has issue living, Diana, *b* 1931: *m* 1st, 1952 (*m diss* 1959) R. E. Williams; 2ndly, 1959, David Bassett, of West Woodburn, East Anstey, Tiverton, Devon, and has issue living, (by 1st *m*) Janice *b* 1953, (by 2nd *m*) Earl Jonathan *b* 1960, Gwenda Margaret *b* 1962, — Rosemary Margaret, *b* 1934: *m* 1953, Vernon Hammett, of West Anstey, S Molton, Devon, and has issue living, Peter *b* 1962, Joanna *b* 1960: *m* 1982 (*m diss* 1989), Graham Howard, of Molland PO, S Molton, Devon (and has issue living, Samuel John *b* 1985, Jemma Grace Louise *b* 1984), — Lesley Anne, *b* 1950: *m* 1975, Philip Veysey, of Venford Farm, Dulverton, Somerset, and has issue living, James William Philip *b* 1979, Benjamin Stewart *b* 1980, Rachel Ruth *b* 1982.

This family is descended in a direct paternal line from John de Brienne, King of Jerusalem and Emperor of Constantinople, and his 2nd son, Louis, *m* Agnes, heiress of Beaumont, in France, whose sons took the name of Beaumont. Henry, the 4th son of Louis and 2nd Lord Beaumont, married Eleanor, 5th daughter of Henry Plantagenet, Earl of Lancaster, grandson of King Henry III. On the death of William, 2nd Viscount Beaumont, the el branch became extinct in the male line (*see* D Norfolk). A younger branch (descended from Thomas Beaumont, second son of 4th Baron Beaumont) settled at Cole Orton, *temp* Edward IV, of which was Nicholas Beaumont, who died 1585, leaving, besides other issue, two sons: (1) Sir Henry, whose son, Sir Thomas, was created a baronet in 1619, and Viscount Beaumont, of Swords, Dublin, in 1622, which titles became extinct on the death of the 3rd viscount, in 1702; (2) Sir Thomas, of Stoughton, grandfather of Sir Thomas, the 1st baronet, from whom is descended the present baronet. Sir Thomas, 1st Bt, was MP for Leicestershire, and Sir Henry, 2nd Bt, was also MP for Leicestershire 1679-87. Sir George, 4th Bt, represented Leicester in Parliament 1702-37, and the 7th Bt, Sir George Howland, sat for Beeralston 1790-96.

WRIXON-BECHER (UK) 1831, of Ballygiblin, Cork

Sir WILLIAM FANE WRIXON-BECHER, MC, 5th *Baronet*; *b* 7 Sept 1915; *s* his father, *Sir* EUSTACE WILLIAM WINDHAM, 1934; *ed* Harrow, and Magdalene Coll, Camb (BA); is Lieut and temporary Major Rifle Brig (Supplementary Reserve); European War 1939-45 in Middle East and Italy (twice wounded, MC); *m* 1st, 1946 (*m diss* 1960), Hon (Ursula) Vanda Maud (BRIDGEWATER), who *d* 1984, 2nd da of 4th Baron Vivian; 2ndly, 1960, Yvonne Margaret (MOSTYN), yst da of Arthur Stuart Johnson, JP, of Henshall Hall, Congleton, Cheshire, and has issue by 1st *m*.

Arms – Vair, argent and gules, on a cantoon or a stag's head couped sable. **Crest** – Out of a ducal coronet or, a demi-lion ermine gorged with a plain collar vair. *Residence* – 37 Clabon Mews, SW1. *Clubs* – MCC, Royal Green Jackets, I Zingari (Secretary 1952-92).

SON LIVING (By 1st marriage)

JOHN WILLIAM MICHAEL (28 Atherton St, SW11; *Clubs* – White's, MCC, I Zingari), *b* 29 Sept 1950; *ed* Harrow, and Univ of Neuchâtel; Lloyds 1971-87, Wise Speke Financial Services 1987-93, since when Holmwoods Group.

He lives twice who lives well

DAUGHTER LIVING (By 1st marriage)

Susannah Elizabeth, *b* 1948: *m* 1st, 1970, Gordon M. A. P. Whitson, who *d* 1974; 2ndly 1975, Timothy William Jackson (Forth Lodge, Hill Rd, Gullane, East Lothian), and has had issue (by 1st *m*) James Alexander, *b* 1973 — (by 2nd *m*), William Harry, *b* 1978, — Lucy Alexandra Esther, *b* 1983, *d* 1984.

SISTERS LIVING

Sheila, *b* 1913. ——— Rosemary, *b* 1914: *m* 1938 (*m diss* 1948), Cyril Jeremy Taylor Watson, who *d* 1974. *Residence* – Ashways, Stogumber, Taunton, Som.

The 1st baronet, Sir William Wrixon, MP for Mallow, assumed by Roy licence in 1831, his mother's maiden name of Becher. She was Mary, da of John Townsend Becher of Annisgrove, co Cork, and sister and heir of Henry Becher of Creagh. Their ancestor, Fane Becher, was granted lands in co Cork 1588.

BECKETT (UK) 1921, of Kirkdale Manor, Nawton, N Riding of Yorkshire

Sir MARTYN GERVASE BECKETT, MC, 2nd *Baronet*; *b* 6 Nov 1918; *s* his father, *Hon Sir* (WILLIAM) GERVASE, 1937; *ed* Eton and Trin Coll, Camb (BA); RIBA; Capt Welsh Guards; 1939-45 War (MC): *m* 1941, Hon Priscilla Léonie Helen Brett, da of 3rd Viscount Esher, and has issue.

Arms – Gules, a fesse between three boars' heads couped erminois, a crescent for difference. **Crest** – A boar's head couped or, pierced by a cross patée fitchée erect gules. *Residences* – 3 St Alban's Grove, W8 5PN; Kirkdale Farm, Nawton, Yorks.

SONS LIVING

RICHARD GERVASE (33 Groveway, SW9), *b* 27 March 1944; *ed* Eton; QC 1988: *m* 1976, Elizabeth Ann, da of Maj (Charles) Hugo Waterhouse (*see* D Marlborough, 1990 Edn), and has issue living, Walter Gervase, *b* 16 Jan 1987, — Willa Marjorie, *b* 1977, — Molly Rachel, *b* 1979, — Catherine Rose, *b* 1983. ——— Jeremy Rupert (Kirkdale Manor Farm, Nawton, Kirkbymoorside, Yorks), *b* 1952: *m* 1978, Perdita Rosemary, yst da of late Capt Hugo Francis Guy Charteris, MC (*see* E Wemyss, colls), and has had issue, Joseph Hugo, *b* 1980, — Matthew Martyn, *b* 1984, *d* 1985, — William Slingsby, *b* 1987, — Lorna Elizabeth, *b* 1982.

To benefit the State

DAUGHTER LIVING

Lucy Caroline, *b* 1942: *m* 1st, 1962 (*m diss* 1969), Adrian Whitfield; 2ndly, 1970, John Warrack, of Beck House, Rievaulx, nr Helmsley, York, and has issue living (by 1st *m*) Teresa, *b* 1963, — Emily, *b* 1965, — (by 2nd *m*), Benedict John, *b* 1971, — Christopher Martyn, *b* 1974.

HALF-SISTER LIVING

Ann Prunella (Flat 21, 27 Onslow Sq, SW7), *b* 1907: *m* 1936, Harry Bathurst Norman, GM, MD, who *d* 1966, and has issue living, Paul Bathurst (Brundon Hall, Sudbury, Suffolk), *b* 1937: *m* 1960, Susan Mary, yr da of Charles Orbell, of The Hermitage, Clare, Suffolk, and has issue living, Hal Charles *b* 1969, Arabella Harriet Bathurst *b* 1961, Teresa Prunella *b* 1963, Deborah Mary *b* 1966, — Harriet Rose, *b* 1939, — Deirdre Nell, *b* 1946: *m* 1st, 1964 (*m diss* 1970), Luciano Billi, of Florence; 2ndly, 1971, Nicholas Paul Beresford-Jones, of The Sett, Leavenheath, Colchester, Essex, and has issue (by 1st *m*) Selina Elizabeth *b* 1964: *m* 1987, Timothy Charles Kleingeld (and has issue living, Oliver Max *b* 1992, Lydia Mary *b* 1994), (by 2nd *m*), Alexandra Juliet *b* 1973.

The 1st baronet, Hon Sir (William) Gervase Beckett (2nd son of late William Beckett-Denison, and brother of 2nd Baron Grimthorpe), was Principal Proprietor and Editor-in-Ch of *Saturday Review*, and MP for Whitby Div of N Riding of Yorkshire (*C*) 1906-18, for Scarborough and Whitby Div thereof 1918-22, and for N Div of Leeds 1923-9.

PASTON-BEDINGFELD (E) 1661, of Oxburgh, Norfolk

Despising earthly things I look
only towards the sun

Sir EDMUND GEORGE FELIX PASTON-BEDINGFELD, 9th *Baronet*; *b* 2 June 1915; *s* his father, *Sir* HENRY EDWARD, 1941; *ed* Oratory Sch, and New Coll, Oxford; is a co-heir to Barony of Grandison, and Major Welsh Guards; European War 1939-45 (wounded, despatches); Freeman City of London, and Liveryman of the Bowyers' Company; Pres Suffolk Heraldry Soc 1993: *m* 1st, 1942 (*m diss* 1953), Joan Lynette, who *d* 1965, da of Edgar G. Rees, of Llwyneithin, Llanelly; 2ndly, 1957, Agnes Kathleen Susan Anne Danos, who *d* 1974, da of late Miklos Gluck, of Budapest, Hungary; 3rdly, 1975, Mrs Peggy Hannaford-Hill, who *d* 1991, of Fort Victoria, Zimbabwe; 4thly, 1992, Mrs Sheila Riddell, eldest da of late John Douglas, of Edinburgh, and has issue by 1st *m*.

Arms – Quarterly, 1st and 4th, ermine, an eagle displayed gules, *Bedingfeld*; 2nd and 3rd, argent, six fleurs-de-lis, three, two, and one azure, a chief indented or, *Paston*. **Crests** – 1st, an eagle displayed or, *Bedingfeld*; 2nd, a griffin sejant wings elevated or gorged with a collar gules, therefrom a line held in the beak and terminating in a ring of the last, *Paston*. **Badges** – A fetter the thong gules edged and studded and with buckles at both ends chained together gold, *Bedingfeld*; a loop of chain or, *Paston*.
Seat – Oxburgh Hall, King's Lynn, Norfolk. *Residence* – The Old Stables, Great Barton, Bury St Edmunds, Suffolk IP31 3RZ.

SON LIVING *(By 1st marriage)*

HENRY EDGAR (Oxburgh Hall, King's Lynn, Norfolk PE33 9PS; College of Arms, Queen Victoria St, EC4V 4BT; *Club* – Boodle's), *b* 7 Dec 1943; *ed* Ampleforth; Chartered Surveyor; Rouge Croix Pursuivant of Arms 1983, York Herald of Arms 1993; Kt of Sovereign Mil Order of Malta; Freeman City of London and Liveryman of the Scriveners' and Bowyers' Cos; Vice-Pres of the Norfolk Heraldry Soc and of the Cambridge Univ Heraldic and Genealogical Soc: *m* 1968, Mary da of late Brig Robert Denis Ambrose, CIE, OBE, MC, and has issue living, Richard Edmund Ambrose, *b* 8 Feb 1975; *ed* Ampleforth, — Thomas Henry, *b* 1976; *ed* Ampleforth, — Katherine Mary, *b* 1969; *ed* St Mary's, Camb, and Bath Univ (BSc), — Charlotte Alexandra, *b* 1971; *ed* St Mary's, Camb.

DAUGHTER LIVING *(By 1st marriage)*

Alexandra Winifred Mary, *b* 1947: *m* 1970 (*m diss* 1977), J. Michael Yearsley; *m* 2ndly, 1978, Jack Pemberton, and has issue living (by 1st *m*), Simon, *b* 1973, — Nicola, *b* 1971, — Jennifer, *b* 1976, — (by 2nd *m*) Benjamin, *b* 1981, — Joseph, *b* 1983, — Grace, *b* 1985.

SISTER LIVING

Frances Mary Teresa, *b* 1919: *m* 1st, 1949, Frank Douglas Playford, who *d* 1956; 2ndly, 1957, Maitland Maitland-Nimmo, who *d* 1977; 3rdly, 1978, Philip James Greathead, and has issue living (by 2nd *m*), Adam Peter, *b* 1960: *m* 1989, Sandra Cavalieri, and has issue living, one son and one da, — Mariella, *b* 1958: *m* 1981, Rodney Vincent Norman, and has issue living, Natasha Felicity *b* 1982, Sarah Frances *b* 1984. *Residence* – PO Box 14, Kalk Bay 7990, Cape Province, S Africa.

COLLATERAL BRANCH LIVING

Issue of late Francis Augustus Bedingfeld, 6th son of 7th baronet, *b* 1874, *d* 1950: *m* 1926, Dorothy Mary Hooker, who *d* 1932:—
Rev Richard Francis (Padre Pio Mission, P.O. Harding 4680, Natal, S Africa), *b* 1930; consecrated Bishop in irregular orders 1987. —— Elizabeth Mary Teresa, *b* 1928; a nun of Convent of Loreto, PO Box 135, Strand 7140, Cape Province, S Africa.

This family took its name from Bedingfield, Suffolk, where they settled in 11th cent. Edmund Bedingfeld (*d* 1451) acquired the lordship of Oxburgh on marriage with Margaret, sister and co-heir of Sir Thomas Tuddenham. During the civil wars Sir Henry Bedingfeld, Knt, besides being imprisoned in the Tower, lost £47,194 18s 18d in the King's cause. His son claimed this amount of Charles II, but that monarch, being unable to pay the money, created him a baronet. The 6th baronet assumed, in 1830, by Royal Licence, the additional surname and arms of Paston, having married Margaret Anne, da and heir of Edward Paston of Appleton, Norfolk, and Horton, Glos.

BEECHAM (UK) 1914, of Ewanville, Huyton, co Palatine of Lancaster

Nil sine labore

Nothing without labour

(*Sir*) JOHN STRATFORD ROLAND BEECHAM, 4th *Baronet* (does not use title); *b* 21 April 1940; *s* his father, *Sir* ADRIAN, 1982; *ed* Winchester, and Queen's Coll, Oxford.

Arms – Per fesse gules and sable, a fesse nebuly plain cotised, in chief an escallop between two martlets and the like in base all or. **Crest** – A swan's head erased argent, beaked gules, holding an escallop and between two escallops or.

BROTHER LIVING

ROBERT ADRIAN *b* 6 Jan 1942; *ed* Winchester, and Clare Coll, Camb: *m* 1969, Daphne Mattinson, and has issue living, Michael John, *b* 1972, — Judith Mary, *b* 1970.

SISTER LIVING

Jane (Longdon Manor, Shipston-on-Stour), *b* 1945: *m* 1969, Frederick Charles Brabyn, and has issue living, Adrian Alexander Benjamin, *b* 1972, — Lowdy (a da), *b* 1978.

WIDOW LIVING OF SECOND BARONET

SHIRLEY JEAN (*Shirley, Lady Beecham*) (Denton House, Denton, Harleston, Norfolk IP20 0AA), da of Albert George Hudson, of 69 Oakwood Pk Rd, N14: *m* 1959, as his 3rd wife, Sir Thomas Beecham, 2nd Bt, CH, who *d* 1961.

COLLATERAL BRANCHES LIVING

Issue of late Thomas Welles Beecham, yr son of 2nd baronet, *b* 1909, *d* 1988: *m* 1937, Mozelle, who *d* 1988, da of Edward Cairn:—
Thomas Richard, *b* 1944. —— Henry John (Tidmington Lodge, Tidmington, Shipston-on-Stour, Warwicks), *b* 1947; *ed* Winchester: *m* 1978, Carola Fiona, da of Charles Ring, of The Green, Puddletown, Dorset. —— Ann Margaret, *b* 1949: *m* 1978, Charles Hoste Hetherington, of Yew Tree, Donhead St Mary, nr Shaftesbury, Dorset, and has issue living, Peter Hoste, *b* 1980, — John Gabriel, *b* 1982, — Rebecca Claire, *b* 1984, — Emma Sarah Elizabeth, *b* 1992. —— Elizabeth Marion, *b* (twin) 1949: *m* 1st, 1969 (*m diss* 1977), Andrew George Birtwell; 2ndly, 1987, Christopher Hall, of Hundalee Cottars Farm, by Jedburgh, Roxburghshire TD8 6PA, and has issue living, (by 1st *m*) Emily Jane, *b* 1970, — (by 2nd *m*) Madeline Thomasina, *b* 1988.

Granddaughter of late Henry Beecham, 2nd son of 1st baronet:—
Issue of late Maj Joseph Michael Beecham, MBA, RA, *b* 1917, *d* 1994: *m* 1939, Sylvia (C7 Shirley Towers, Vane Hill Rd, Torquay, Devon TQ1 2BY), only child of late Frank B. Nathan, of 14 Charleville Mansions, W14:—
Valerie Anne, *b* 1941: *m* 1st, 1960, John Keenan, MB, BChir, son of late James Keenan; 2ndly, 1978, Julian Allan, of 22 Westgate Terrace, SW10 9BJ, son of late Maj Alexander William Allan, and has issue living (by 1st *m*), Lucinda Jane, *b* 1964, — Katharine Victoria, *b* 1968.

Issue of late (Henry Robert) Derrick Beecham, 2nd son of late Henry Beecham (ante), *b* 1921, *d* 1988: *m* 1st, 1943, (*m diss* 1949), Annie Ellen, da of late Thomas John King; 2ndly, 1951, Sheila (28 Grove Park Gardens, W4), da of Bertram John Martin, of Bushey Heath, Herts:—
(By 1st *m*) Jasmine Heather, *b* 1944: *m* 1963, David George Heaps, of Benington Bury, Walkern Rd, Benington, Herts SG2 7LN, and has issue living, Daniel Blue, *b* 1974, — Judith Ann, *b* 1971. —— Priscilla Rosamunde, *b* 1947: *m* 1982, Wilfred Staples. —— Susan Jane *b* 1949; adopted 1950 by W. A. Whithear, whose surname she assumed: *m* 1969 (*m diss* 1985), Roland Vaughan, and has issue living, Rhianon Jane, *b* 1969.

Issue of late Paul Beecham, 3rd son of Henry Beecham (ante), *b* 1923, *d* 1986: *m* 1952, Mary, who *d* 1990, da of William Arthur, of Pill Lawn, Barnstaple, Devon:—
William Henry Mark, *b* 1954, *d* 1990. —— Hugh Joseph, *b* 1957: *m* 1990, Rachel Nelson, and has issue living, Celia Mary, *b* 1992. —— Matthew Arthur, *b* 1965. —— Sarah Caroline, *b* 1953: *m* 1st, 1971, Kevin Pigott, who *d* 1974; 2ndly, 1981, Graham Jonathan Howard, of Wonston Barn, Wonston, nr Winchester, Hants, and has issue living, (by 1st *m*) Dominic Kingsley, *b* 1972, — (by 2nd *m*) Freya Helewise, *b* 1982. —— Hannah Charlotte, *b* 1956: *m* 1989, John O'Mahony, of 8 Wolstonbury Rd, Hove, E Sussex BN3 6EJ, son of late Joseph O'Mahony, and has issue living, Callum Paul Joseph, *b* 1993, — Catherine Holly Amber, *b* 1990. —— Emma Ruth BEECHAM (Y Wern, Llanfairfechan, Gwynedd), *b* 1960; has resumed her maiden name: *m* 1977 (*m diss* 1992), Peter Lloyd Edmondson, and has issue living, Richard Thomas Lloyd, *b* 1980, — Josephine Alice Mary, *b* 1978.

Issue of late Christopher Beecham, 4th son of Henry Beecham (ante) *b* 1925, *d* 1970: *m* 1951, Kathleen Elizabeth, da of Maj Bertie Orme Collis, of Pinner, Middx:—
Philip Henry Orme, *b* 1962: *m* 1983 (*m diss* 1988), Suzanne, da of William Wright, of London. —— Diana Mary, *b* 1953: *m* 1974, John Heap, of Southampton, Hants, and has issue living, Jessica Amy, *b* 1989. —— Honor June, *b* 1955: *m* 1984, Michael William Johnson, of Lichfield, Staffs. —— Jennifer Kate, *b* 1957: *m* 1986, Peter Cook, of Faversham, Kent. —— Penelope Carol, *b* 1960: *m* 1984 (*m diss* 1994), Philip William Gray. —— Sally Helen, *b* 1965.

The 1st baronet, Sir Joseph Beecham, was the well-known pill manufacturer, of St Helens, a Director of A. and F. Pears (Limited), and Mayor of St Helens 1899-1900, and 1910-11-12. The 2nd baronet, *Sir* Thomas Beecham, CH, the well-known Musical Conductor, was knighted in 1916.

BEEVOR (GB) 1784, of Hethel, Norfolk

Gentle in manner, but vigorous in deed

Sir Thomas Agnew Beevor, 7th *Baronet; b* 6 Jan 1929; *s* his father, Com *Sir* Thomas Lubbock, RN, 1943; *ed* Eton, and Magdalene Coll, Camb: *m* 1st 1957 (*m diss* 1965), Barbara Clare, yst da of Capt Robert Lionel Brooke Cunliffe, CBE, RN (ret) (*see* Cunliffe Bt, colls); 2ndly, 1966 (*m diss* 1975), Carola, da of His Honour Judge Jesse Basil Herbert, MC, QC (*see* B Rea, 1985 Edn); 3rdly, 1976, Mrs Sally Elisabeth Bouwens, only da of Edward Madoc, of White Hall, Saham Toney, Thetford, Norfolk, and has issue by 1st *m*.

Arms – Per pale or and argent, on a chief indented sable, three lions rampant of the first. **Crest** – A beaver passant proper.
Residence – Hargham Hall, Norwich.

SON LIVING (By 1st marriage)

(Thomas) Hugh Cunliffe, *b* 1 Oct 1962; *ed* Radley, Pembroke Coll, Camb, and RAC Cirencester: *m* 1988, Charlotte Louise, eldest da of Keith Ernest Harvey, of Nuthall, Nottingham, and has issue living, Thomas William Harvey, *b* 15 April 1990, — Joshua Peter Hugh, *b* 1992.

DAUGHTERS LIVING (By 1st marriage)

Bridget Anastasia, *b* 1958: *m* 1984, Matthew J. LeF. Porteous, FRCS, eldest son of John Porteous, of London W11, and has issue living, Samuel Thomas Le Fanu, *b* 1986, — Tancred John Octavian, *b* 1988, — Anastasia Catherine Lucie, *b* 1991, — Elizabeth Clare Mary, *b* 1993. —— Juliana Clare, *b* 1960: *m* 1988, Dr Roderick Peter Ross Marrs, son of Alan Ross Marrs, of Watchet, Somerset, and has issue living, Adam, *b* 1990.

SISTERS LIVING

Ina Margaret Anastasia, *b* 1920: *m* 1942, Capt John Lewis, RA, and has issue living, Peter John Elliott, *b* 1943, — William Beevor, *b* 1948, — Judith Margaret Anne, *b* 1946. —— Jocelyn Mary (*Lady Warner*), *b* 1927: *m* 1949, Sir (Edward Courtenay) Henry Warner, 3rd Bt. *Residence* – The Grove, Great Baddow, Essex. —— Christian Chevallier, *b* 1934: *m* 1959, George Habib Homsi, of 3401, Slade Run Drive, Falls Church, Virginia 22042, USA.

COLLATERAL BRANCHES LIVING

Granddaughter of late Ralph Jermy Beevor, 3rd son of 4th baronet:—
Issue of late Ralph Branthwayt Beevor, *b* 1895, *d* 1970: *m* 1921, Phyllis Margaret Ashburner, who *d* 1972, da of Henry Oliver Minty:—
Ruth Margaret, *b* 1929: *m* 1956, Dennis Frederick Outwin, of Curacao, Ray Park Rd, Maidenhead, Berks SL6 8NN, and has issue living, Christopher Dennis, *b* 1960, — Daphne Margaret, *b* 1958: *m* 1984 (*m diss* 1994), John Albert Benford, and has issue living, Abigail Jane *b* 1987, — Wendy Ruth, *b* 1964: *m* 1991, Dr David John Ekbery.

Granddaughter of late Rowland Beevor (*infra*):—
Issue of late Lt-Col Cecil Thomas Ashworth Beevor, OBE, TD, *b* 1898, *d* 1989: *m* 1925, Violet Babington, who *d* 1985, da of Edward Babington Lenton, of Ivy House, Fritton, Gt Yarmouth, Norfolk:—
Elizabeth Bridget Babington, *b* 1928: *m* 1952, John Clifford Painter, of Myrobalan, Upton, Norfolk, and has issue living, Stephen Langman, *b* 1956, — Hilary Joanna, *b* 1953, — Philippa Jane, *b* 1961.

Issue of late Rowland Beevor, 6th son of 4th baronet, *b* 1866, *d* 1942: *m* 1893, Margaret Frances, who *d* 1954, da of George Evans:—
Miles (Badger Farmhouse, Badger, Wolverhampton WV6 7JS), *b* 1900; *ed* Winchester and New Coll Oxford (BA 1921); admitted a Solicitor 1925; is a JP for Herts, 1939-45 War as Flight-Lt RAF Vol Reserve: *m* 1st, 1924, Margaret Florence, who *d* 1934, da of late Algernon John Frederick Platt, of Barnby Manor, Newark-on-Trent; 2ndly, 1935, Sybil, who *d* 1991, only da of Lt-Col John Babington Gilliat, DSO, of The Manor House, Welwyn, Herts, and has issue living, (by 1st *m*) John Rowland (104 Defoe House, Barbican, EC2), *b* 1930; *ed* Winchester, and Ch Ch, Oxford (BA; FCA): *m* 1955, Fenella Sybil, da of Brig John Gordon Bedford-Roberts, CBE, and has issue living, Timothy James *b* 1957, Justin Miles *b* 1961: *m* 1990, Isobel Rose, of Cambridge, Catrina Margaret *b* 1958: *m* 1989, Robert MacLean Mull, only son of Arthur Mull, of Whitwell House, Huntingdon (and has issue living, Ishbel Mary *b* 1990, Olivia *b* 1992), — (by 2nd *m*) Antony Romer (20 Radipole Rd, SW6 5DL), *b* 1940; *ed* Winchester, and New Coll, Oxford (BA): *m* 1970, Cecilia, da of late John G Hopton, and has issue living, Mark Andrew Antony *b* 1975, Karen Louise *b* 1974, — Ronald Hugh (35 Fairfax Rd, Bellevue Hill, NSW 2023, Australia), *b* 1947; *ed* Winchester, and Worcester Coll, Oxford (BA): *m* 1st, 1972 (*m diss* 1977), Sabina Margaret Anne, da of Harman Joseph Gerard Grisewood, CBE; 2ndly, 1981, Fiona Mary, da of John Francis Partridge, of Toragay, Sollas, N Uist, and has issue living, (by 2nd *m*) Harriet Clare *b* 1984, — Helen *b* 1943: *m* 1966, Norman Jonathon Dudley Foster, of Badger Farmhouse, Badger, Wolverhampton WV6 7JS, and has issue living, Peter *b* 1972, Charlotte Anne *b* 1967, Caroline Jane *b* 1968, Elizabeth Amy *b* 1970.
Sir Thomas Beevor, 1st Baronet (son of Thomas Beevor, of Norwich), was a great agriculturalist. The 6th Baronet, Cdr Sir Thomas Lubbock, RN, was *ka* 1943.

BEIT (UK) 1924, of Tewin Water, Tewin, co Hertford (Extinct 1994)

Sir Alfred Lane Beit, 2nd and last *Baronet*.

WIDOW LIVING OF SECOND BARONET

Clementine Mabell Kitty (*Lady Beit*), da of late Maj Hon Clement Bertram Ogilvy Mitford, DSO (*see* B Redesdale, colls): *m* 1939, Sir Alfred Lane Beit, 2nd Bt, who *d* 1994. *Residences* – Russborough, Blessington, co Wicklow; 2 The Little Boltons, SW10.

BELL (UK) 1885, of Rounton Grange, co York, and of Washington Hall, co Durham

Perseverance

Sir John Lowthian Bell, 5th *Baronet; b* 14 June 1960; *s* his father, *Sir* Hugh Francis, 1970; *ed* Glenalmond, and Royal Agric Coll, Cirencester: *m* 1985, Venetia Mary Frances, 2nd da of J.A. Perry, of Llanstefan, Taunton, Som, and has issue.

Arms – Argent on a fesse azure, between three hawks' lures of the second, as many hawks' bells of the first. **Crest** – A hawk or, holding in its beak a hawk's lure azure, and resting its dexter claw on a sun in splendour or.
Seat – Arncliffe Hall, Ingleby Cross, Northallerton, Yorks.

SON LIVING

John Hugh, *b* 29 July 1988.

DAUGHTER LIVING

Sophia Amelia Bridget, *b* 1990.

BROTHERS LIVING

David Hugh, *b* 1961. —— Andrew Mark, *b* 1963. —— Thomas Hugh, *b* 1964.

WIDOW LIVING OF FOURTH BARONET

Mary, MB, ChB (The Hollins, E Rounton, Northallerton, Yorks DL6 2LG); D Obst RCOG; a JP for Yorks, da of late George Howson, MC, of The Hyde, Hambleden, Bucks: *m* 1st, 1959, as his 2nd wife, Sir Hugh Francis Bell, 4th Bt, who *d* 1970; 2ndly, 1991, as his 2nd wife, Prof Dominick Stuart Graham, MC, late Maj RA (*see* Graham, Bt, *cr* 1629, colls).
The 1st baronet, Sir Lowthian Bell, an Ironmaster and Coal-owner, sat as MP for Hartlepool (*L*) 1875-80. The 2nd baronet, Sir (Thomas) Hugh, was Lord-Lieut for N Riding of York 1906-31, and Pres Iron and Steel Institute 1907-10. The 3rd baronet, Sir Maurice Hugh Lowthian Bell, CMG, TD, was Col Yorkshire Regt, and served in S Africa 1900-1901, and in European War 1914-19 (CMG).

MORRISON-BELL (UK) 1905, of Otterburn Hall, Elsdon, Northumberland

Perseverance

Sir William Hollin Dayrell Morrison-Bell, 4th *Baronet; b* 21 June 1956; *s* his father, *Capt Sir* Charles Reginald Francis 1967; *ed* Eton, and St Edmund Hall, Oxford: *m* 1984, Cynthia Hélène Marie, yr da of Teddy White, of 41 Iverna Gdns, W8, and has issue.

Arms – Quarterly, 1st and 4th, sable, on a fesse ermine between three bells argent, a falcon close between two crescents of the field; 2nd and 3rd, argent, on a fesse azure between three Moors' heads couped at the neck proper, the turbans vert turned up argent, three roses or. **Crest** – 1st, a falcon close proper, belled and jessed or, holding in the beak a bell argent; 2nd, in front of a Moor's head couped at the shoulders as in the arms three roses gules.
Seat – Highgreen, Tarset, Northumberland. *Residence* – 106 Bishop's Rd, SW6 7AR.

SON LIVING

Thomas Charles Edward, *b* 13 Feb 1985.

BROTHER LIVING

Julian Francis Tarret, *b* 1959: *m* 1st, 1984, Penelope Josephine, da of late Lt-Col Richard Ian Griffith Taylor, DSO, MC, JF, DL, of Chipchase Castle, Wark-on-Tyne, Northumberland (*see* By Buckland, 1973-74 Edn), and formerly wife of Robert John Elkington (*see* B Wolverton, 1970 Edn); 2ndly, 1991, Karenina A., da of Nigel O'Flaherty, of Glenlion, Cabinteely, Dublin 18, and has issue living (by 1st *m*), Charles Richard Francis, *b* 17 Nov 1986, —— (by 2nd *m*) Alice Ursula Grace, *b* 1992.

AUNTS LIVING (*Daughters of 2nd baronet*)

Kathleen Frances, TD *b* 1906; a JP and an Hon Alderman for Northumberland (formerly Alderman); formerly Senior Com ATS. *Residence* – Charlton, Tarset, Northumberland. —— Veronica Frances, *b* 1911: *m* 1942, John Jerome Stonborough, formerly Maj Canadian Army, and has issue living, Jerome Claude, *b* 1943; *ed* Stowe, —— John Tarret Christian, *b* 1948; *ed* Gordonstoun: *m* 1987, Jane, only da of Louis Berger, and widow of Charles Tallents, and has issue living, Eloise Charlotte India *b* 1988, —— Margaret Isabella, *b* 1944; *ed* Benenden. *Residence* – Glendon, Corfe Mullen, Wimborne, Dorset BH21 3HB.

WIDOW LIVING OF THIRD BARONET

Prudence Caroline (70 Doneraile St, SW6), only da of late Lt-Col Wyndham Dayrell Davies, 60th Rifles (ret): *m* 1st, 1955, Sir Charles Reginald Francis Morrison-Bell, 3rd Bt, who *d* 1967; 2ndly, 1969, Peter Gillbanks.

COLLATERAL BRANCHES LIVING

Issue of late (Arthur) Clive Morrison-Bell (2nd son of 1st baronet), who was *cr* a *Baronet* 1923:—
See Morrison-Bell, Bt, *cr* 1923 (ext).

Issue of late Ernest Fitzroy Morrison-Bell, OBE, 3rd son of 1st baronet, *b* 1871, *d* 1960: *m* 1902, Maud Evelyn, who *d* 1960, da of late Lieut-Col Frank Henry, JP, formerly 9th Lancers, of Elmestree, Tetbury, Gloucestershire:—

Louise Monica (Long Cottage, Davis St, Hurst, Berks), *b* 1903: *m* 1929, Col Cecil Everard Montague Grenville-Grey, CBE, late KRRC, who *d* 1973, and has issue living, Wilfrid Ernest, *b* 1930: *m* 1963, Edith Dlamini, and has issue living, Wilfrid Jonathan *b* 1964, Peter Thulani *b* 1967, Susan Thandi (twin) *b* 1964, — Susan Monica (*Duchess of Richmond and Gordon*), *b* 1932: *m* 1951, 10th Duke of Richmond and Gordon. —— Claire Wilhelmina Maud, *b* 1907: *m* 1928, Maj Robert Moubray, formerly 16th Lancers, who *d* 1961, and has issue living, John Robert Fitzroy (Maxton Westend, St Boswells, Melrose, Roxburghshire), *b* 1945: *m* 1972, Patricia Maeve MacLeod, and has issue living, Belinda Mary Claire *b* 1973, — Evelyn Mary (*Duchess of Sutherland*), *b* 1929: *m* 1979, 6th Duke of Sutherland, — Anne Catherine Wilhelmina, *b* 1931, — Gillian Claire (*Lady Boughey*), *b* 1933: *m* 1976, Sir Richard James Boughey, 10th Bt, who *d* 1978. *Residence* – The Glebe House, Maxton, St Boswells, Roxburghshire. —— Mary Ernestine, *b* 1910; formerly Sen Com ATS: *m* 1946, Brig Geoffrey William Goschen, DSO, MC, late RHA, who *d* 1988, and has issue living, John Henry, *b* 1949, — Mary (10B Downfield Rd, Clifton, Bristol BS8 2JT), *b* 1948: *m* 1973, David Robson Moore, who *d* 1987, and has issue living, Nathaniel James William *b* 1974, Roxanne Diana *b* 1977. *Residence* – 2 Close Gdns, Tetbury, Glos GL8 8DO.

Issue of late Lieut-Col Eustace Widdrington Morrison-Bell, 4th son of 1st baronet, *b* 1874, *d* 1947: *m* 1914, Hon Harriet Margaret Hepburn-Stuart-Forbes-Trefusis, who *d* 1975, da of 20th Baron Clinton:—

Pamela Elizabeth, *b* 1918. —— Sylvia Morwenna, *b* 1922: *m* 1941, Maj Arthur Thomas Chamberlayne, R Fusiliers, and has issue living, Michael Thomas (Lower Hearn, Headley, Hants), *b* 1943; *ed* Wellington Coll; FCA. *Residence* – Clouds Garden Lodge, East Knoyle, Salisbury, Wilts.

The 1st baronet, Sir Charles William Bell, assumed by Roy Licence 1905 the additional surname and arms of Morrison. The 2nd baronet, Sir Claude William Hedley Morrison-Bell, sometime Capt Argyll and Sutherland Highlanders, served on N-W Frontier of India 1897-8 and during European War 1914-18.

MORRISON-BELL (UK) 1923, of Harpford, co Devon (Extinct 1956)

Sir (ARTHUR) CLIVE MORRISON-BELL, 1st and last *Baronet*.

DAUGHTERS LIVING OF FIRST BARONET

Shelagh Jocelyn (*Lady Campbell*), *b* 1913: *m* 1st, 1943 (*m diss* 1951), William Cooper Moore; 2ndly, 1968, as his 2nd wife, Sir Ralph Abercromby Campbell, who *d* 1989, of Lomans Hill, Hartley Wintney, Hants, and has issue living (by 1st *m*), David Anson Clive (373 Marion St, Denver, Colorado 80218, USA), *b* 1944: *m* 1978, Christiane Hyde, da of Casper Citron, of New York, NY, USA, and has issue living, Cornelia Wingfield *b* 1986. —— Patricia Louisa *b* 1919: *m* 1st, 1941 (*m diss* 1956), Maj John Nevile Wake Gwynne, RA, who *d* 1981 (Wake, Bt); 2ndly, 1968, Henry Michael Barclay, of Hanworth Hall, Norfolk, and has issue living (by 1st *m*), Nevile Martin (7 Campden Hill Mansions, Edge St, W8), *b* 1941; *ed* Eton, and Trin Coll, Oxford: *m* 1st, 1972, Charlotte, da of late Sir Cyril Hugh Kleinwort (*see* Kleinwort Bt, colls) and formerly wife of Richard Lawrence Baillieu; 2ndly, 1983, Frederica Rosana Gale Lennox, and has issue living (by 1st *m*), Chloe Patricia *b* 1973, — Jessica Violet, *b* 1944: *m* 1st, 1966, Charles Cospatrick Douglas-Home, who *d* 1985 (*see* B Home of the Hirsel, colls); 2ndly, 1993, Rodney Leach.

GRATTAN-BELLEW (UK) 1838, of Mount Bellew, co Galway

Sir HENRY CHARLES GRATTAN-BELLEW, 5th *Baronet*; *b* 12 May 1933; *s* his father, *Lieut-Col Sir* CHARLES CHRISTOPHER, MC, 1948; *ed* Ampleforth; was Assist Dist Commr Kenya Police Reserve 1953-4, and Dist Officer, Kenya Administration 1954-55; journalist, radio and TV broadcaster, publisher; Dir of several Cos: *m* 1st, 1956 (*m diss* 1966), Naomi, formerly wife of Herbert Ellis, and da of late Dr Charles Cyril Morgan, of Chester; 2ndly, 1967 (*m diss* 1974), Gillian Hulley; 3rdly, 1978, Elzabe Amy, only da of Henry Gilbert Body, of Utrecht, Natal, and widow of J. B. Westerveld, of Pretoria, and has issue by 2nd *m*.

Arms – Quarterly, 1st and 4th sable, fretty or, a crescent argent or difference, *Bellew*; 2nd and 3rd, per saltire sable and ermine over all a lion rampant or, *Grattan*. **Crests** – 1st, an arm embowed in armour proper, charged with a crescent for difference, grasping in the hand a sword proper, pommel and hilt or, *Bellew*; 2nd, a dove proper, holding in its dexter claw a sceptre and standing on a barrel or, *Grattan*.
Residence – Sandford Park, PO Box 7, Bergville, Natal 3350, S Africa.

Tout d'en haut. *All from above*

SON LIVING (*By 2nd marriage*)

PATRICK CHARLES, *b* 7 Dec 1971.

DAUGHTER LIVING (*By 2nd marriage*)

Deirdre Sophia, *b* 1967.

SISTER LIVING

Deirdre Maureen, *b* 1924: *m* 1946, Gerard Kiernan, and has issue living, Charles Dominick, *b* 1947, — Henry Gerard, *b* 1952, — Valerie Maureen, *b* 1946, — Maureen Gabriel, *b* 1949, — Dawn Vivien, *b* 1956. *Residence* – 35 Priory Grove, Stillorgan, Dublin.

COLLATERAL BRANCHES LIVING

Issue of late Thomas Henry Grattan-Bellew, 4th son of 3rd baronet, *b* 1901, *d* 1967: *m* 1933, Bettina Idrone Dorothy (Mount Loftus, Goresbridge, co Kilkenny), el da of late Maj John Edward Blake Loftus, of Mount Loftus, co Kilkenny:—

Patrick Edward (Mount Loftus, Goresbridge, co Kilkenny; 472 Edison Av, Ottawa, Ontario, Canada K2A 1T9), *b* 1934; *ed* Univ Coll, Dublin (BSc), and McGill Univ, Canada (MSc); PhD Camb; a mineralogist: *m* 1980, Elly Bollegraaf-Dwinger, da of late Nathan Gruner, and step-da of late Ernst Bollegraaf. —— Idrone Pauline Mary, *b* 1936: *m* 1964, Roger William Brittain, of 90 Broxash Rd, SW11 DAB, and has issue living, William Henry Grattan, *b* 1965, — Charles Francis, *b* 1966, — James Nicholas, *b* 1971, — Georgina Mary Idrone, *b* 1968.

Issue of late Sir Arthur John Grattan-Bellew, CMG, QC, 5th and yst son of 3rd baronet, *b* 1903, *d* 1985: *m* 1931, Winifred Mary, who *d* 1979, da of Edmond R. Mahony, of Kilinan, Kilchreest, co Galway:—

(Arthur Henry) Bertram (Hole Farm, Gt Waldingfield, nr Sudbury, Suffolk), *b* 1937; *ed* Downside; 2nd Lieut late 8th Hussars; Jt Master of the Galway Blazers: *m* 1961, Georgina Madeleine Mary, da of Sir George Edward Mordaunt Milner, 9th Bt, and has issue living, Charles Henry Mordaunt, *b* 1964, — Sophie Rose, *b* 1962. —— Gillian Barbara, *b* 1934: *m* 1967, Peter Haggard Lyster, of Little Chishill Manor, Cambs, and has issue living, Thomas Henry, *b* 1971, — Grania Mary, *b* 1968, — Anna Gillian, *b* 1969.

The 1st baronet was fourth in descent from Michael Bellew of Mount Bellew, a descendant of Christopher Bellew, brother of Sir Patrick Bellew, 1st baronet (*cr* 1688) (*see* B Bellew). The father of the 3rd baronet assumed by Roy licence the additional surname and arms of Grattan. The 4th baronet, Sir Charles Christopher, MC, was Lieut-Col King's Roy Rifle Corps (Reserve).

BELLINGHAM (GB) 1796, of Castle Bellingham, co Louth
(Name pronounced "Bellinjum")

So it is

Aihsi · il · est

Amicus · Amico

A friend to a friend

Sir NOEL PETER ROGER BELLINGHAM, 7th *Baronet* (of 2nd creation), *b* 4 Sept 1943; *s* his father, *Sir* ROGER CARROLL PATRICK STEPHEN, MB, ChB, DA, 1973; *ed* Lindisfarne Coll: *m* 1977, Jane, da of Edwin William Taylor, of Willow Close, White Hall Rd, Sale, Cheshire.

Arms – Argent, three bugle horns sable, stringed gules and garnished or. **Crest** – A buck's head couped or.
Seat – Castle Bellingham, co Louth. *Residence* – 20 Davenport Park Rd, Davenport, Stockport, Cheshire SK2 6JS.

BROTHER LIVING

ANTHONY EDWARD NORMAN, *b* 24 March 1947; *ed* Rossall.

WIDOW LIVING OF SIXTH BARONET

MARY (*Mary, Lady Bellingham*) (Castle Bellingham, co Louth), da of late William Norman: *m* 1941, Sir Roger Carroll Patrick Stephen Bellingham, 6th Bt, MB, ChB, DA, who *d* 1973.

COLLATERAL BRANCHES LIVING

Grandchildren of late Maj Sydney Edwin Bellingham, el son of late Lt-Col William Johnston Bellingham, 5th son of 2nd baronet:—

Issue of late Major Alan Mure Bellingham, MC, *b* 1881; *d* 1946: *m* 1st, 1914 (*m diss* 1930) Beatrix Laura, who *d* 1962, da of late John Henry Harrison, ICS; 2ndly, 1930, Mabel Theodora Lucy, who *d* 1981, da of Theodore Seton Dury, Ch Master, Supreme Court, and formerly wife of Nestor Seppings Tirard:—

(By 1st *m*) Beatrix Pamela BELLINGHAM-KIGGELL, *b* 1918; assumed the surname of Bellingham-Kiggell by deed poll 1970: *m* 1st, 1938 (*m diss* 1945), Ronald Arthur Cleave; 2ndly, 1947 (*m diss* 1962), John Chatterton Coysgarne Sim, and has issue living, (by 1st *m*) Zenia Sophia SIM, *b* 1938; assumed by deed poll 1948 the name of Sim in lieu of her patronymic, — (by 2nd *m*) Carol Ann, *b* 1950. —— (By 2nd *m*) Patrick Alan Sydney (22 Willow View, Straightway Head, Whimple, Devon), *b* 1936; *ed* Christ's Hosp: *m* 1st, 1958 (*m diss* 1981), Elizabeth Mary, da of late Harold Hall Bagnall, of Westerham, Kent; 2ndly, 1981 (*m diss* 1990), Elizabeth Mary, da of Maj Stanislas Lis, Polish Army, and widow of Arnold Derrick Workman; 3rdly, 1991, Brenda Mary Nixon, formerly wife of Jack Hal Nixon, and has issue living (by 1st *m*), Alan Hall (96 Ross St, Cambridge CB1 3BU), *b* 1960; *ed* Christ's Hosp, and St Catharine's Coll, Camb: *m* 1984 (*m diss* 1991), Anne Crick, — Dorcas Elizabeth (157 Simpson Village, Milton Keynes, Bucks), *b* 1962: *m* 1984 (*m diss* 1994), Richard Puczynski, — Isobel Marie, *b* (twin) 1962: *m* 1982, Philip Morgan, and has issue living, Charles Henry *b* 1986, Purdey Ashley *b* 1988, — (by 2nd *m*) Jasper Guy Patrick, *b* 1981, — Katharine Lucy Rose, *b* 1985. —— Brigid Alaine, *b* 1933: *m* 1st, 1954 (*m diss* 1969), Brian Deakin; 2ndly, 1970 (*m diss* 1978), Richard Barham; 3rdly, 1978, Dr Gene Don Smith, who *d* 1985, of 2795 Teller St, Lakewood, Colorado 80215, USA, and has issue living (by 1st *m*), Charles Rupert Deakin BARHAM (14 Drury St, Hill End, Qld 4101, Australia), *b* 1956; legally adopted by stepfather 1972 and assumed surname of Barham; patronymic retained as a forename: *m* 1985, Cheryl Robyn Pearce, and has issue living, Courtney Rebecca *b* 1993, — Timothy Graham DEAKIN (14 Nearco St, Fig Tree Pocket, Qld 4068, Australia), *b* 1959: *m* 1985, Leith Perkins, and has issue living, Kiera Adele *b* 1991, — Helena Judith DEAKIN (19599 E Belleview Place, Aurora, Colorado 80015, USA), *b* 1958; has issue living, Jessica Renee *b* 1990.

Grandchildren of late Thomas Eudo Bellingham (infra):—
Issue of late William Eudo Bellingham, *b* (Dec) 1882, *d* 1954: *m* 1906, Louisa Bertha, who *d* 1935, da of William Arthur Krick, of Chicago, USA:—
William Arthur Eudo (2810 Merrimac Blvd, Toledo, Ohio 43606, USA), *b* 1909: *m* 1932, Myrna Arlene, da of Edwin T. Netser, and has issue living, William Edwin (4506 Shadow Glen Drive, Colorado Springs, CO 80909, USA), *b* 1938: *m* 1959, Renee Anne, da of Wayne McGrew, and has issue living, William Keith (2915 Haystack Drive, Colorado Springs, CO 80922, USA), *b* 1967: *m* 1990, Clara Margi Hutchinson (and has issue living, William Clifton *b* 1992), Catherine Anne *b* 1971, — Kay Arlene, *b* 1934: *m* 1st, 1959 (*m diss* 1989), Thomas Huntington Taylor; 2ndly, 1993, Lewis Saxby, of 5565 Citation Rd, Toledo, Ohio 43606, USA, and has had issue, Thomas Huntington *b* 1959: *d* 1993, Jane Arlene *b* 1961: *m* 1994, Peter Elfers, of 777 N Macqueston Pky, Mt Vernon, NY 10552, USA, — Jean Carolyn, *b* 1941: *m* 1967, Patrick James Johnson, of 3534, Edgevale, Toledo, Ohio 43606, USA, and has two adopted children, Jonathan Patrick *b* 1971, Jodi Jean *b* 1973, — Linda Anne, *b* 1944: *m* 1970, Richard Henry Allardyce, of 11606 Helmont Drive, Oakton, VA 22124, USA, and has issue living, Kristin Lynn *b* 1976, Julie Anne *b* 1979, — Gwen Francis, *b* 1946: *m* 1970, Richard Osenbaugh, of 3543 Robin, Toledo, Ohio 43623, USA. —— †Frederick Richard, *b* 1923: *m* 1st, 1944 (*m diss* 1947), Mary Winifred, da of Cary C. Winans; 2ndly, 1951, Elizabeth Hayes; 3rdly, 1958, Geraldine Helen Hermanson (140 N Hilltop Drive, Titusville, Florida 32796-2529, USA), and *d* 1990, leaving, (by 1st *m*) Patricia, *b* 1945, — Kathleen, *b* 1947, — (by 2nd *m*) Michelle, *b* 1952, — (by 3rd *m*) Timothy Shane, *b* 1959: *m* 1985, Leslie Anne Fritz, and has issue living, Shane Patrick *b* 1989, Brian Lewis *b* 1992. —— Louise Hazel, *b* 1913: *m* 1932, Conrad Edward Nelson, and has issue living, Constance Paulette, *b* 1944: *m* (March) 1963, Thomas Neil Nelson, of 2711 East First St, Marina Terrace, Ft Myers, FL 33901, USA, and has issue living, Rodney Kirk *b* (Nov) 1963, — Ryan Jay, *b* 1973.

Issue of late John Stuart Bellingham, *b* 1889, *d* 1965: *m* 1937, Doreen, who *d* 1974, da of late Edward O'Brien, of Ambleside, Westmorland:—
Roger Graham (13 Ridgeway Close, Lightwater, Surrey GU18 5XU) *b* 1939: *m* 1965, Pauline, da of David Rankine, and has issue living, Alan Graham, *b* 1966, — John Terrance, *b* 1969.

Grandchildren of late William Stewart Bellingham, son of late John Bellingham, brother of 2nd baronet:—
Issue of late Thomas Eudo Bellingham, *b* 1849, *d* 1923: *m* (March) 1882, Grace, who *d* 1905, da of late Rev W. Harkness, MA, of Athea, co Limerick:—
Thomas Francis Gordon, *b* 1885: *m* 1918, Iva Abigail, da of A. E. Bridge, and has issue living Stewart (Bawlf, Alberta, Canada), *b* 1921: *m* 19—, and has issue living, Roger *b* 19—, a da *b* 19—, — William Milton, *b* 1922, — Stephen Ramsay (Calgary, Alberta, Canada), *b* 1924: *m* 19—, and has issue living. *Residence* – Bawlf, Alberta, Canada. —— Hazel, *b* 1887: *m* 1915, Charles Wundabaldt Christen, who *d* 1961, and has issue living, Charles Patrick Harkness *b* 1918: *m* 1946, Virginia Beane, and has issue living, Charles Patrick *b* 1947, Julia Hazel *b* 1949, Christina Helen *b* 1953, — John Wundabaldt, *b* 1923: *m* 1943, Theresa Lucille Lovich, and has issue living, John Charles *b* 1946, Steven William *b* 1948, Daniel Thomas *b* 1952, David Paul *b* 1953, Patricia Terese *b* 1944, — Hazel Mary *b* 1924: *m* 1st, 1943, Albert Jackson; 2ndly, 1946, Lawrence Robert Hanstein, of Staunton, Illinois, USA, and has issue living, (by 1st *m*) Anthony Lee *b* 1945, (by 2nd *m*) Laurence Robert *b* 1948, David *b* 1953, Mary Lynn *b* 1951.

Grandson of late Arthur D'Arcy Bellingham, 5th son of William Stewart Bellingham (ante):—
Issue of late Lt-Col Arthur Stuart Bellingham, *b* 1893, *d* 1969: *m* 1923, Jean (Glencara, Rathconrath, Mullingar, co Westmeath; Salar Lodge, Leenane, co Galway; The Cliffs, Howth, co Dublin), da of Andrew Arthur, of Rosemount, Ayrshire:—
John Stuart (5 rue Paul-Louis-Courier, Paris VII), *b* 1929; *ed* Eton, and Magdalene Coll, Camb (BA).

Grandchildren of late Lt-Col Arthur Stuart Bellingham (ante):—
Issue of late (Arthur) Henry Bellingham, Lieut, Leicestershire Yeo, *b* 1926, *d* 1959: *m* 1953, June Marion Cloudesley, of Congham Lodge, Hillington, King's Lynn, who *m* 2ndly, 1962, Col Ian Bruce Baillie, Life Gds, who *d* 1978 (*see* B Burton, colls), da of Arthur Cloudesley Smith, FRCS:—
Henry Campbell, MP, *b* 1955; *ed* Eton, and Magdalene Coll, Cambridge (BA 1977); Barrister-at-Law, Middle Temple 1978; MP for Norfolk North West (C) since 1983: *m* 1993, Emma Louise, da of Peter John Henry Whiteley (*see* E Guilford). —— Elizabeth Alison, *b* 1956: *m* 1989, Richard Charles Rowley, only son of Sir Charles Robert Rowley, 7th Bt.

This ancient family derives its name from Bellingham-in-Tyndale, Northumberland. William de Bellingham was Sheriff of Tyndale 1279. Robert of Bellingham, temp Henry V, *m* Elizabeth, da of Sir Richard Tunstall, KG. His el son, Sir Henry was *cr* Knt Banneret at Battle of Wakefield 1460, whose son, Sir Robert, was similarly honoured at Battle of Stoke 1487. The present family descend from Alan of Levens, Westmorland, 8th son of Robert (ante). Alan's gt-grandson, Robert, settled in Ireland and was father of (i) Sir Daniel of Dubber, co Dublin, Lord Mayor of Dublin, who was *cr* a Bt of Ireland 1687 (title ext 1699), and (ii) Henry of Gernonstown (later called Castle Bellingham) co Louth. Henry served as Cornet in a Regt of Cavalry raised in the north for suppressing the Irish rebellion. By his wife, Lucy Sibthorpe, he was father of Col Thomas who raised a Regt of Cavalry and served with William III, where he acted as his guide during the march from Dundalk to the Boyne. After that battle he accompanied the King to Duleek. In consequence, James II's army destroyed Castle Bellingham by fire. His grandson, Alan of Castle Bellingham, *m* 1738, Alice, da of co-heir of the Rev Hans Montgomery of Grey Abbey, co Down. Alan's 4th son, Sir William, was in 1796 *cr* a Bt of GB with remainder to the heirs male of the body of his father, and was MP for Reigate and Private Sec to Pitt. He was *s* by his nephew, Sir Alan (el son of Alan, el brother of 1st Bt) 1826. Sir (Alan) Henry, 4th Bt was MP for co Louth and Private Chamberlain to Popes Pius IX, Leo XIII and Pius X. Brig-Gen Sir Edward Henry Charles Patrick, CMG, DSO, late R Scots, was a Senator of the Irish Free State 1925-56.

BENN (UK) 1914, of The Old Knoll, Metropolitan Borough of Lewisham

By God's favour

Sir (JAMES) JONATHAN BENN, 4th *Baronet*, *b* 27 July 1933; *s* his father, *Sir* JOHN ANDREWS, 1984; *ed* Harrow, and Clare Coll, Camb (BA 1957, MA 1961); Dir Reedpack Ltd, Chm and Chief exec, Reed Paper and Board (UK) Ltd, Chm J. & J. Maybank Ltd, and Chm Reed Transport Ltd, Pres, British Paper and Board Industries Federation 1985-87: *m* 1960, Jennifer Mary, eldest da of late Dr Wilfred Vivian Howells, OBE, of The Ferns, Clun, Shropshire, and has issue.

Arms – Argent, two barrulets indented gules, between in chief as many dragons' heads erased and in base a pencil and a pen in saltire proper, tied with a lace azure, pendent therefrom a torteau, charged with a figure "1914" or. **Crest** – On a rock a spear erect proper, flowing therefrom a pennon azure, charged with the word "Onward", letters or.
Residence – Fielden Lodge, Tonbridge Rd, Ightham, nr Sevenoaks, Kent TN15 9AN.

SON LIVING

ROBERT ERNEST (ROBIN) (Fielden Lodge, Tonbridge Rd, Ightham, nr Sevenoaks, Kent TN15 9AN), *b* 17 Oct 1963; *ed* Judd Sch, Tonbridge, and Corpus Christi Coll, Camb (BA 1985, MA 1989); ACA 1989; Manager Deloitte & Touche, Luxembourg: *m* 1985, Sheila Margaret, 2nd da of Dr Alastair Macleod Blain, of Braco Lodge, Elgin, Moray.

DAUGHTER LIVING

Juliet Clare, *b* 1966: *m* 1993, Simon M. Erridge, yr son of Francis Erridge, of Goldhanger, Essex.

BROTHER LIVING

Timothy John, *b* 1936; *ed* Harrow, Princeton Univ, and Clare Coll, Camb (MA); Lt Scots Guards; formerly Chm and Man Dir of Benn Bros Ltd; Chm Timothy Benn Publishing Ltd, Bouverie Publishing Co Ltd, South Eastern Magazines Ltd, Buckley Press Ltd, Henry Greenwood & Co Ltd, Stone & Cox (Publications) Ltd, Dalesman Publishing Co Ltd: *m* 1st, 1959 (*m diss* 1973), Valerie Hamlyn, yr da of late Capt P.H.W. Davie; 2ndly, 1973, Mrs Susan Elizabeth Hardingham, only da of George Hodges; 3rdly, 1982, Christina Grace Townsend, da of late W. R. Hughes, and has issue living (by 1st *m*), Peter Quentin, *b* 1961, — William Justin, *b* 1964, — Thomas Hamlyn, *b* 1967: *m* 1988, Yvette, yr da of G. B. Wilson, of Buckfastleigh, Devon, and has issue living, Louella *b* 1986, Charlotte *b* 1989, Jemima Jaye *b* 1993.

SISTERS LIVING

Susan Paschal, *b* 1930: *m* 1952, Michael Graeme Compton, of Michaelmas Lodge, Limpsfield, Surrey, and has issue living, Josephine, *b* 1953, — Ann, *b* 1956. —— Christina Frances, *b* 1948: *m* 1976, J. Andrew R. Wilton, and has issue living, Henry, *b* 1979. —— Marigold Margaret, *b* 1950.

UNCLE LIVING

Edward Glanvill, *b* 1905; *ed* Harrow, and Clare Coll, Camb; Pres of Benn Bros Ltd; Major E Surrey Regt: *m* 1931, Beatrice Catherine, MBE, da of late Claude Newbald, of Lyndhurst, Wallington, Surrey, and has issue living, James Glanvill, *b* 1944: *m* 1st, 1967, Judith, da of late W. H. McMinn, of 15 Ingram House, Hampton Wick, Surrey; 2ndly, 1973, Susan May, da of late Vivian G. Beardsell, of Yellow Flat, Borde Hill, Haywards Heath, W Sussex; 3rdly, 1990, Claire Stephanie, da of Eric Baverstock, of 4 Bealings Close, Southampton Hants, and has issue living (by 2nd *m*) Peter Glanvill *b* 1974, Alistair James *b* 1975, Suzanna Victoria *b* 1979, — Elizabeth, *b* 1936: *m* 1961, Kenneth Charles Stewart Young, of Old Rectory, Buckland, nr Aylesbury, Bucks, and has had issue, Catherine Ann *b* 1962, Miranda *b* 1964, *d* 1988. *Residence* – Crescent Cottage, Aldeburgh, Suffolk IP15 5HW.

AUNTS LIVING

Elizabeth, *b* 1907: *m* 1935, Paul Alfred Shinkman, who *d* 1975, and has issue living, Paul Glanvill (617 Shady Lawn Rd, Chapel Hill, NC 27514, USA), *b* 1936; *ed* Landon Sch, Harvard Coll (BA), Univ of Michigan (MA, PhD): *m* 1969, Judith Kay, da of F. E. Barnett, of Charlotte, NC, USA, — Christopher Joseph (2448 Emerson St, Palo Alto, Cal 94301, USA) *b* 1940; *ed* St Albans Sch, Thiel Coll (BA), Westminster Coll (MA), Univ of Pittsburgh (PhD): *m* 1965, Marsha Ann, el da of Marshall Axel Friberg, of Jamestown, NY, and has issue living, Matthew Christopher *b* 1972, Elizabeth Ann *b* 1975, — Bernard Francis (5600 Wood Way, Sumner, Bethesda, Maryland 20816, USA), *b* 1943; *ed* St Mark's Sch, Dartmouth Coll (BA): *m* 1974, Gillian Claire, yr da of Daniel Crawley, of London, SE, and has issue living, Paul Daniel *b* 1983, Claire Amelia *b* 1980. *Residence* – 3040, Dent Pl, NW, Georgetown, Wash, DC 20007, USA. —— Julia Wedgwood, *b* 1916: *m* 1945, Albert Edward Louis Mash, OBE, who *d* 1991, and has issue living, John Martin, *b* 1948; BA, PGCE: *m* 1973, Ann Patricia Sweeney, and has issue living, Julian John *b* 1980, Holly Louisa *b* 1977, — Jennifer Dorothy *b* 1946: *m* 1973, Geoffrey Wade, who *d* 1993, and has issue living, George William *b* 1974, Gwendolen Jane *b* 1976, Elizabeth Julia *b* 1978. *Residence* – 5 Oakleigh Court, Church Lane, Oxted, Surrey RH8 9PT.

WIDOW LIVING OF THIRD BARONET

Hon URSULA HELEN ALERS HANKEY (*Hon Lady Benn*), da of 1st Baron Hankey: *m* 1929, Sir John Andrews Benn, 3rd Bt, who *d* 1984. *Residence* – 15 The Waldrons, Oast Rd, Hurst Green, Oxted, Surrey RH8 9DY.

COLLATERAL BRANCHES LIVING

Issue of late Capt Frederick Christopher Benn, 3rd son of 2nd baronet, *b* 1912, *ka* 1941: *m* 1937, Phyllis, who *d* 1990, da of late E. M. Preston, of Slaugham Park, Sussex:—
Oliver Preston (Hackhurst Stud, Lower Dicker, Hailsham, Sussex), *b* 1938; *ed* Eton, and Clare Coll, Camb; 2nd Lieut Intelligence Corps; Bar Middle Temple 1970: *m* 1970, Clarissa Dorothy Jeannette, da of Guillermo Sergio Santa Cruz y

Zerrano, of Weybridge, Surrey, and has issue living, Belinda Alice Irene, *b* 1970: *m* 1993, Timothy Francis Farnfield (*see* Wigram, Bt, colls).

Issue living of late Rt Hon (William) Wedgwood Benn, DSO, DFC, PC (2nd son of 1st baronet), who was *cr Viscount Stansgate* 1942 (*see* that title).

The 1st baronet, Sir John Williams Benn, Chm of Benn Brothers (Limited), publishers, was a Member of London County Council 1889-1922 (Chm 1904-5), and sat as MP for St George's Div of Tower Hamlets (*L*) 1892-95, and for Devonport 1904-10. The 2nd baronet, Sir Ernest John Pickstone Benn, CBE, was a Director (sometime Chm) of Benn Bros Ltd, of Ernest Benn Ltd, and of United Kingdom Provident Institution, Pres of So of Individualists, and High Sheriff of co London 1932. The 3rd baronet, Sir John Andrews Benn, was Chm United Kingdom Provident Inst 1951-69, and Chm of English-Speaking Union of the Commonwealth 1969-72.

BENNETT (UK) 1929, of Kirklington, co Nottingham

To serve the King

Sir RONALD WILFRID MURDOCH BENNETT, 3rd *Baronet*, *b* 25 March 1930; *s* his father, *Sir* (CHARLES) WILFRID, TD, 1952; *ed* Wellington, and Trin Coll, Oxford: *m* 1st, 1953, Audrey Rose-Marie Patricia, only da of Maj A. L. J. H. Aubépin, of co Mayo; 2ndly, 1968, Anne, da of late Leslie George Tooker, and has issue by 1st *m*.

Arms – Gules, a cross moline between three demi-lions rampant or. **Crest** – In front of a lion rampant gules charged on the shoulder with a cross moline argent, a scaling ladder fessewise or.
Residence – 23 rue de Rive, 1260 Nyon, Switzerland.

DAUGHTERS LIVING *(By 1st marriage)*

Anne-Marie Julia, *b* 1954: *m* 1973, Stephen Hickman. —— Georgina Marion, *b* 1956.

SISTER LIVING

Anne, *b* 1928: *m* 1st, 1961, Gerald Norman Fox-Edwards; 2ndly, 1974, Conrad Lyddon Voss-Bark, of Lyd Cottage, Leat Rd, Lifton, Devon, and has issue living (by 1st *m*), Adam, *b* 1962, — Jane, *b* 1964.

HALF-UNCLE LIVING *(Son of 1st baronet by 2nd marriage)*

Peter, *b* 1938; *ed* Charterhouse, and Pembroke Coll, Camb: *m* 1966, Monique Christine, el da of Amade Monsempès, of St Maur, Des Fossès, Seine, France.

AUNT LIVING *(Daughter of 1st baronet by 1st marriage)*

Audrey, *b* 1904: *m* 1928, Douglas Haultain Phillips, son of Hon Sir William Watkin Phillips, and has issue living, Susan, *b* 1929: *m* 1954, Timothy Ernle Gilpin (By Ernle), and has issue living, Joanna Clare *b* 1955, Henrietta Haultain *b* 1957, — Caroline Louise, *b* 1931.

WIDOW LIVING OF FIRST BARONET

LEOPOLDINE (*Dowager Lady Bennett*), da of Leopold Armata, of Vienna: *m* 1938, as his 2nd wife, Sir Albert James Bennett, 1st Bt, who *d* 1945.

COLLATERAL BRANCHES LIVING

Grandchildren of late Frank Carlton Bennett, 2nd son of 1st baronet:—
Issue of late Michael Bennett, *b* 1924, *d* 1987: *m* 1952, Janet Hazel Margaret (Flat 70, Albert Hall Mansions, SW7), da of Brig Edward Joseph Todhunter, TD, JP, of The Glebe House, Great Bedwyn, nr Marlborough, Wilts:—
MARK EDWARD FRANCIS, *b* 5 April 1960. —— Caroline Mariella Carleton, *b* 1954. —— Victoria Serena, *b* 1957.
Issue of late David Bennett, *b* 1927, *d* 1988: *m* 1959, Hilary Sheridan (The Gate House, Wing, Leighton Buzzard, Beds), da of Bernard F. Clarke:—
Algernon James, *b* 1962. —— Sarah Elizabeth, *b* 1967.
Sir Albert James Bennett, 1st baronet (son of late Edward Bennett), sat as MP for Mansfield Div of Notts (*L*) 1922-3, and for Central Div of Nottingham (*U*) 1924-30. Sir (Charles) Wilfrid Bennett, TD, 2nd baronet, was Lieut-Col Notts Yeo (Sherwood Rangers), and a Metropolitan Magistrate 1946-52.

Beresford-Peirse, see Peirse.

BERNARD (UK) 1954, of Snakemoor, co Southampton

Sir DALLAS EDMUND BERNARD, 2nd *Baronet*; *b* 14 Dec 1926; *s* his father, Sir DALLAS GERALD MERCER, 1975; *ed* Eton, and Corpus Christi Coll, Oxford (MA); Chm Thames Trust Ltd 1983-86, Nat & Foreign Securities Trust Ltd 1982-86; Dir Italian Internat Bank plc; Dir Morgan Grenfell & Co Ltd 1964-79; Member Monopolies and Mergers Commn 1973-79: *m* 1st, 1959 (*m diss* 1979), Sheila Mary, el da of Arthur Gordon Robey; 2ndly, 1979, Mrs Monica J. Montford, da of late James Edward Hudson, and has issue by 1st and 2nd *m*.

Arms – Sable, two greyhounds rampant and addorsed argent in chief as many stags' heads caboshed or. **Crest** – Issuant from a circlet of bezants, a demi bear sable, muzzled or.
Residence – 8 Eaton Pl, SW1X 8AD.

DAUGHTERS LIVING *(By 1st marriage)*

Juliet Mary, *b* 1961. —— Alicia Elizabeth, *b* 1964. —— Sarah Jane, *b* 1968.

(By 2nd marriage)

Olivia Louise, *b* 1981.

SISTER LIVING

Margaret Anne, *b* 1929; *ed* Southover Manor, Lewes; has resumed the surname of Cleverly: *m* 1st, 1952 (*m diss* 1974), William Geoffrey Cleverly, MB, BS; 2ndly, 1975 (*m diss* 1980), Charles Bevan Meeres.
Sir Dallas Gerald Mercer Bernard, 1st Bt, son of Edmund Bowen Bernard, JP, of Snakemoor, Botley, Hants, was Man Dir of Jardine Matheson & Co, Ltd, 1922-28, Dep Gov of Bank of England 1949-54 and Chm of Courtaulds Ltd, 1962-64.

BERNEY (E) 1620, of Parkehall in Redham, Norfolk

Nothing rashly nor with fear

Sir JULIAN REEDHAM STUART BERNEY, 11th *Baronet*, only son of late John Reedham Erskine Berney, Lieut R Norfolk Regt, only son of 10th baronet; *b* (posthumous) 26 Sept 1952; *s* his grandfather, Sir THOMAS REEDHAM, MC, 1975; *ed* Wellington, and NE London Polytechnic; ARICS: *m* 1976, Sheena Mary, yr da of Ralph Day, of Driftwood, Elm Green Lane, Danbury, Essex, and has issue.

Arms – Quarterly gules and azure, a cross engrailed ermine. **Crest** – A garb argent.
Residence – Reeds House, 40 London Rd, Maldon, Essex CM9 6HE.

SONS LIVING

WILLIAM REEDHAM JOHN, *b* 29 June 1980. —— Hugo Ralph, *b* 1987.

DAUGHTER LIVING

Jessica Mary, *b* 1982.

AUNTS LIVING

Estelle Elaine, *b* 1922: *m* 1st, 1940, Maj Kenneth William Bols, Indian Army, who was *ka* in Italy 1944 (Strickland-Constable, Bt, colls); 2ndly, 1946, Lt-Col Mark Frederic Strutt, MC, RHA (TA) (*see* B Rayleigh, colls), and has issue living, (by 1st *m*) Andrew Nevile David, *b* 1943; Maj The Blues and Royals: *m* 1st, 19—, Sally Jane, only da of ACM Sir John Alexander Carlisle Aiken, KCB; 2ndly, 1980, Mrs Anne Hard, yst da of J. A. Meade, of London, — Erica Sarah *b* 1941: *m* 1966, Nigel Frederick Burch, — (by 2nd *m*) (*see* B Rayleigh, colls). *Residence* – Crix, Hatfield Peverel, Essex. —— Elizabeth Ann (Claydon House, Clare Rd, Hundon, Suffolk CO10 8DL), *b* 1927: *m* 1952 (*m diss* 1960), Allan E Shepherd. —— Claire, *b* 1933: *m* 1st, 1956 (*m diss* 19—), Lt Jeremy Michael Lynch, RN; 2ndly, 1992, Prof Richard Christie, of 11 Akademie St, Franschhoek, 7690 Cape Town, S Africa, and has issue living (by 1st *m*), Lewis Reedham, *b* 1967, — Nicole, *b* 1958, — Tania, *b* 1962.

MOTHER LIVING

Hon Jean Davina Stuart (*Hon Mrs Ritchie*) (Tannachie, Findhorn, Forres, Moray 1V36 0YJ), da of 1st Viscount Stuart of Findhorn: *m* 1st, 1951, John Reedham Erskine Berney, Lieut R Norfolk Regt, who was *ka* Korea 1952; 2ndly, 1954, Percy William Jesson; 3rdly, 1985, Michael D. Ritchie.

COLLATERAL BRANCHES LIVING

Granddaughters of late John Hanson Berney (infra):—
Issue of late Hugh Barton Berney, MB, ChB, *b* 1902, *d* 1977: *m* 1931, Lillian Irene, who *d* 1977, da of Robert William Grigor, of Blenheim, NZ:—
Helen, *b* (Nov) 1931: *m* 1955 Rev Edward Maurice Dashfield, of 53 Miro St, Masterton, NZ, and has issue living, Philip Berney, *b* 1958, — James Gilbert, *b* 1961, — Prudence Ann, *b* 1956. —— Janet Douglas, *b* 1935; BA (1955): *m* 1960, Terence Daniel O'Leary, CMG, and has issue living, John Terence, *b* 1960, — Daniel Hugh (twin), *b* 1960, — Helen Fiona, *b* 1964.

Issue of late Sinclair Henry Hanson Berney *b* 1906, *d* 1967: *m* 1936, Barbara May (39A Opaki Rd, Lansdowne, Masterton, NZ), da of late Andrew Roby Bloxam, of Christchurch, NZ:—
Jenifer May, *b* 1938: *m* 1965, David Kennedy Logan, of 94 Titoki St, Lansdowne, Masterton, NZ, and has issue living, John Berney Kennedy, *b* 1968, — Helen Margaret, *b* 1966, — Robyn Elizabeth, *b* 1971. —— Diana Margaret (21 Lincoln Av, Tawa, Wellington, NZ), *b* (twin) 1938: *m* 1962 (*m diss* 1983), John Allan D. Burnett, and has issue living, Andrew John Hanson, *b* 1971, — Margaret Jane, *b* 1967: *m* 1994, Stephen David Daltrey, of Croydon, Surrey.

Issue of late John Hanson Berney, 3rd son of 9th baronet, *b* 1868, *d* 1959: *m* 1900, Margaret, who *d* 1948, da of Sinclair George, of New Zealand:—
John Reedham (PO Box 25, Rawene, Northland, NZ), *b* 1911: *m* 1937, Joyce, da of Donald Bennett, and has issue living, John Reedham Donald, *b* 1944: *m* 1975, Noralyne Maxine, da of G. Reid, of Hawaii, and has issue living, Gareth Elijah *b* 1977, Nalani Kalua *b* 1976, Juana Marguerite *b* 1979, — Richard Warwick, *b* 1946, — Jocelyn Margaret, *b* 1938: *m* 1960, Thomas William Burgess, of Sydney, Australia, and has issue living, Matthew Sinclair *b* 1966, Janette Joyce *b* 1961, — Juliet Alice, *b* 1953. —— Margaret Lorraine, *b* 1914: *m* 1937, Harold Arthur Roland Dunderdale, of Edinburgh, and has issue living, Francis John Berney, *b* 1939, — David Bruce, *b* 1942, — Antonia Margaret, *b* 1944. —— Barbara Dorothy, *b* (twin with Richard Bruce, AFC, AmDFC, DFM, RAF 1939-45 War (despatches); *k* in flying accident 1948) 1916: *m* 1942, Melvin Cooper Armstrong, of 15 College Av, Christchurch 5, S Island, NZ, and has issue living, David Warwick, *b* 1946, — Richard Thomas, *b* 1948, — Philippa Jane, *b* 1943.

Issue of late Alexander David Berney, 7th son of 9th baronet, *b* 1877, *d* 1942: *m* 1924, Alice, who *d* 1939, da of A. J. Moore, of Lowestoft:—
Olive Maud, *b* 1925: *m* 1st, 19—, Paul Rafoth, of USA; 2ndly, 19—, Rolf Merton, of Fiddler's Roost, Knapton Estate, Smith-Parish 3-06, Bermuda.

The Berneys, claiming to be of Norse origin, were seated at Berney, near Walsingham, Norfolk, at the time of the Norman Conquest. It is further claimed that they are one of the three families who settled in England before the Conquest and have never wanted a male heir. The 1st baronet, Sir Richard Berney, was Sheriff of Norfolk 1622, and the 4th baronet was Sheriff of Norwich 1762.

BETHUNE (NS) 1683, of Scotscraig, co Fife

Kind or gracious. A Crown for a mitre

Sir ALEXANDER MAITLAND SHARP BETHUNE, 10th *Baronet*; *b* 28 March 1909; *s* his father, Sir ALEXANDER SHARP, 1917; *ed* Eton, and Magdalene Coll, Camb; formerly Capt Intelligence Corps; ret Co Director: *m* 1955, (Ruth) Mary, da of James Hurst Hayes, of Marden House, East Harting, Sussex, and has issue.

Arms – Quarterly, 1st, azure, a fesse chequy or and gules between three lozenges of the second, *Bethune*; 2nd, azure, on a St Andrew's Cross argent, a bleeding heart transpierced with two swords disposed in saltire, points downwards proper, hilted and pommelled or, the heart having over it a mitre of gold placed on the field and tasselled gules surrounded with a bordure or, charged with the Royal Tressure, flowered and counter-flowered of the fourth (the coat of augmentation granted by King Charles II); 3rd, argent, a fesse azure between two cross crosslets fitchée in chief, and in base a mullet sable, *Sharp*; 4th, argent, on a chevron sable an otter's head erased of the first, *Balfour*. **Crests** – 1st, a demi-otter sable; 2nd, a celestial crown or. *Residence* – 21 Victoria Grove, W8 5RW.

DAUGHTER LIVING

Lucy Elizabeth, *b* 1959.

COLLATERAL BRANCH LIVING

Granddaughter of late Major Robert Bethune, son of late Lieut-Gen Alexander Sharp (afterwards Bethune), JP, DL, de jure 7th baronet:—
Issue of late Lt-Col Henry Alexander Bethune, *b* 1866, *d* 1946; *m* 1902, Elinor Mary, who *d* 1955, da of John Brown Watt, of Sydney, NS Wales:—
Mary Sharp, *b* 1903: *m* 1929, Lieut-Col Harry Francis Keir Wedderburn, Black Watch (Roy Highland Regt), who was *ka* 1943 (*see* Ogilvy-Wedderburn, Bt, colls). *Residence* – Mountquhanie, Cupar, Fife KY15 4QJ.

Sir William Sharp, Knt, of Scotscraig, co Fife, was created a baronet 1683. On the death in 1780 of the 6th baronet, Sir William Sharp, who *m* Margaret, da of John Bethune, of Blebo, co Fife, and sister and eventual heir of Henry Bethune, of Blebo, the Baronetcy became dormant and so remained until 1916, when Alexander Bethune (formerly of Blebo) assumed the additional name of Sharp, having established his right to the title as 9th Baronet before the Baronetage Committee of the Privy Council, as son of late Capt Alexander Bethune, JP, DL, of Blebo, co Fife, de jure 8th baronet, grandson of late Lt-Gen Alexander Sharp, de jure 7th baronet (who on succession to Blebo in 1815 assumed by Roy Licence the surname of Bethune in lieu of his patronymic), only son of 6th baronet.

EVANS-BEVAN (UK) 1958, of Cadoxton-juxta, Neath, co Glamorgan

Sir MARTYN EVAN EVANS-BEVAN, 2nd Baronet; *b* 1 April 1932; *s* his father, *Sir* DAVID MARTYN, 1973; *ed* Uppingham; High Sheriff of Breconshire 1967-68; Freeman of City of London; Liveryman of Worshipful Co of Farmers: *m* 1957, Jennifer Jane Marion, da of Robert Hugh Stevens, of Lady Arbour, Eardisley, Herefordshire, and has issue.

Arms – Argent, three boars' heads couped sable on a chief gules a demi lion rampant erased or between two castles of the field. **Crest** – Issuing from the battlements of a tower argent a demi lion rampant or gorged with a collar gules holding between the paws a boar's head as in the Arms.
Residence – Felin-Newydd, Llande Falle, Brecon, Powys. *Club* – Carlton.

SONS LIVING

DAVID GAWAIN, *b* 16 Sept 1961: *m* 1987, Philippa Alice, yst da of Patrick Sweeney, of East Moors, Helmsley, N. Yorks, and has issue living, Patric David, *b* 9 Feb 1994, — Alice Laura, *b* 1989. —— Richard Martyn, *b* 1963. —— Thomas Rhydian, *b* 1966. —— Huw Evan, *b* 1971.

SISTER LIVING

Marigold Evans (*Countess of Rothes*), *b* 1934: *m* 1955, 21st Earl of Rothes. *Residence* – Tanglewood, West Tytherley, Salisbury.

WIDOW LIVING OF FIRST BARONET

EIRA WINIFRED (*Eira, Lady Evans-Bevan*) (Spring Valley, St Ouen, Jersey), el da of late Sidney Archibald Glanley, 2nd son of late Rev David Lloyd Glanley, MA: *m* 1929, Sir David Martyn Evans-Bevan, 1st Bt, who *d* 1973.

BIBBY (UK) 1959, of Tarporley, co Palatine of Chester

Sir DEREK JAMES BIBBY, MC, 2nd *Baronet*, *b* 29 June 1922; *s* his father, *Sir* (ARTHUR) HAROLD, 1986; *ed* Rugby, and Trin Coll, Oxford (MA 1941); DL for Cheshire 1987; Pres Bibby Line Group Ltd; 1939-45 War as Capt RA (wounded, MC): *m* 1961, Christine Maud, da of late Rt Rev Frank Jackson Okell, Bishop of Stockport, and has issue.

Arms – Azure a saltire parted and fretty argent surmounted in fesse pointby a lion rampant pean between two escallops in pale and as many mullets of six points in fesse of the second. **Crest** – Upon a plate a cubit arm erect holding a sword in bend sinister proper pomel and hilt or.
Residence – Willaston Grange, Hadlow Rd, Willaston, S Wirral, Cheshire L64 2UN.

SONS LIVING

MICHAEL JAMES, *b* 2 Aug 1963; *ed* Rugby, and Oxford Univ; CA.. —— Geoffrey Frank Harold, *b* 1965; *ed* Rugby, and Exeter Univ: *m* 1994, Sarah, eldest da of Frederick Robinson, of Huntington, Cheshire. —— Peter John, *b* 1969; *ed* Rugby, and Manchester Univ. —— David Richard, *b* 1970; *ed* Rugby, and Bath Univ.

DAUGHTER LIVING

Jennifer Margaret, *b* 1962; *ed* Howells, and Oxford Univ; CA.

SISTERS LIVING

Patricia Mary, *b* 1921; *m* 1st, 1944 (*m diss* 1956), Ronald Stuart Kinsey; 2ndly, 1962, Iain Hall Brookes Macdonald, who *d* 1990, and has issue living (by 1st *m*), Anne Quenelda Stuart, *b* 1947; *m* 1972, Julian Ralph Avery, of Bardown, Stonegate, Wadhurst, E Sussex TN5 7EL, — Hilary Jane Stuart, *b* 1951: *m* 1983, Simon Francis Reed, of 62 Streathbourne Rd, SW17. *Residence* – 100 Old Church St, SW3 6EP. —— Joan Elizabeth, *b* 1926; *m* 1st, 1951, Major Reginald Francis Foster, Indian Army, who *d* 1974; 2ndly, 1985 (*m diss* 1987), Clifford Haines, and has issue living (by 1st *m*), Rachel Frances, *b* 1955; *m* 1977 (*m diss* 1990), Gp-Capt Ian Thomas Nicoll, RAF. *Residence* – Meonside, Workhouse Lane, East Meon, Hants GU32 1PD. —— Anne Marjorie, *b* 1928: *m* 1st, 1951, Lt-Col John Hamilton Palairet, who *d* 1969; 2ndly, 1976 (*m diss* 1980), Denis Justin Beattie, and has issue living (by 1st *m*), Sarah Lillias, *b* 1953: *m* 1977, Christopher Neston Ord Capper, of Chedglow Manor, Crudwell, Malmesbury, Wilts SN16 9EZ, — Joanna Vivian, *b* 1955: *m* 1979, Jeremy Hicks, of Gaskells Farmhouse, Winstone, nr Cirencester, Glos GL7 7JZ, — Ailsa Jane, *b* 1957; *m* 1980, Stephen John Duyland Bush, of The Old Farm, Latchley, nr Gunnislake, Cornwall PL18 9AX *Residence* – 102 Walton St, SW3 2JJ.

The 1st baronet, Sir (Arthur) Harold Bibby, DSO, who was Snr Partner in the firm of Bibby Bros & Co 1935-73 and Chm of Bibby Line Ltd 1935-69, was a DL for Cheshire and High Sheriff 1934-35.

BIDDULPH (E) 1664, of Westcombe, Kent

Sir Ian D'Olier Biddulph, 11th *Baronet*; *b* 28 Feb 1940; *s* his father, *Sir* Stuart Royden, 1986: *m* 1967, Margaret Eleanor, only da of late John Gablonski, of Oxley, Brisbane, and has issue.

𝕬rms – Vert, an eagle displayed argent. 𝕮rest – A wolf rampant argent, wounded on the shoulder proper.
Address – Fernway Pty Ltd, Mail Service 23, Mt Walker, via Rosewood, Queensland 4340, Australia.

SON LIVING

Paul William, *b* 30 Oct 1967.

DAUGHTERS LIVING

Julie Denise, *b* 1969. —— Roslyn Mary, *b* 1971.

SISTERS LIVING

Wendy Margaret, *b* 1946: *m* 1966, Huan Donald John Fraser, of 10 El Rancho St, Daisy Hill, Qld 4127, and has issue living, Stuart Donald John, *b* 1974, — Gina Margaret, *b* 1969, — Jodie Maree, *b* 1972. —— Mary Estelle, *b* 1947: *m* 1968, Ian Sutherland, of Edward St, Tambo, Qld 4478, and has issue living, Timothy Andrew, *b* 1969, — Lee-Anne, *b* 1970.

WIDOW LIVING OF TENTH BARONET

Muriel Margaret (*Muriel, Lady Biddulph*), 3rd da of Angus Harkness, of Hamly Bridge, S Australia: *m* 1939, Sir Stuart Royden Biddulph, 10th Bt, who *d* 1986. *Residence* – 129 Dennis Rd, Springwood, Queensland 4127, Australia.

COLLATERAL BRANCHES LIVING

Issue of late Malcolm Francis Biddulph, son of 9th baronet, *b* 1910, *d* 1983: *m* 1936, Inez Margaret, who *d* 1978, da of James Donnelly, of Longreach, Qld, Australia:—
Peter Michael (Blackall St, Dingo, Qld 4702, Australia), *b* 1939: *m* 1963, Beverley Marie, who *d* 1987, only da of late Wilson Story, of St George's Heights, Sydney, NSW, and has issue living, Michael Andrew, *b* 1964: *m* 1989, Tamara, yst da of Thomas Kelly, of Charleville, Qld, — Sean Gregory, *b* 1970, — Craig, *b* 1973, — Mark Sterling, *b* 1975, — Anne Marie, *b* 1971. —— David Francis (Blackall Motel, Blackall, Qld, Australia), *b* 1942: *m* 1968, Doreen Power, and has issue living, Dennis, *b* 1980, — Sally, *b* 1973. —— Janice Claire, *b* 1937: *m* 1958 (*m diss* 1978), Lionel Garth Moody, and has issue living, Peter, *b* 1969, — Alison Marie, *b* 1959: *m* 1980, Michael Stally, — Tanya Claire, *b* 1962, — Fiona Margaret, *b* 1963.

Descendants, if any, of late Francis Henry Biddulph (who was *b* 1839, and left issue a son), uncle of 9th baronet.

Descendants, if any, of late Charles Biddulph (who left issue, one son), 2nd son of late John Burnet Biddulph (*b* 1796), 5th son of late Simon Biddulph (infra), and great-uncle of 9th baronet.

Grandchildren of late William Burnett Biddulph (infra):—
Issue of late Ernest William Biddulph, *b* 1889, *d* 1963: *m* 1939, Anna Brando:—
William Burnett (Moria, 158 Heerenstraat, Vryheid 3100, Natal, S Africa), *b* 1930: *m* 1955, Helena Hendrina Naude, and has issue living, Erlo William Burnett, *b* 1965, — Zelda, *b* 1956: *m* 1979, Manus Andreas Louw, and has issue living, Hermanus Andreas *b* 1984, — Janène, *b* 1962: *m* 1981, Wilm Kempden Smalberger, and has issue living, Chantel *b* 1983, — Bernadine, *b* 1974. —— Magdalena Suzanna *b* 1944: *m* 1964, Raymond Fraser Morris, of 109 South St, Vryheid, Natal, and has issue living, Wayne William, *b* 1966, — Delainie Anne, *b* 1970, — Rochell *b* 1979.

Grandchildren of late Ernest Walstrand Biddulph, 3rd son of late John Burnet Biddulph (*b* 1796), 5th son of late Simon Biddulph, great-grandfather of the 9th baronet:—
Issue of late William Burnett Biddulph, *b* 1859, *d* 1946: *m* 18—, Florentia Magdalena, who *d* 1947, da of late James Brookes, of Farm, Welgelegen, Van Reenen, Orange Free State:—
Joseph Gilbert, *b* 1891: *m* 1921, Anna Struwig, and has issue living, William Burnett, *b* 1925: *m* 1951, Hester Botha, and has issue living, Joseph Gilbert *b* 1955, Wilma *b* 1953, Annalise *b* 1955, Brenda *b* 1956, — Catherina, *b* 1922: *m* 1943, Hans Jurie Vosloo, Box 36, Sandspruit, Transvaal, and has issue living, George Sebastiaan *b* 1944, Joseph Gilbert *b* 1950, Anna Margaretta *b* 1955, — Florentina, *b* 1923: *m* 1944, Willem Pieter Van Breda, of Sandspruit, Transvaal, and has issue living, Frederic Charles *b* 1946, Joseph Gilbert *b* 1948, Willem Pieter *b* 1952, Burnett *b* 1956, — Anna, *b* 1930: *m* 1950, Desmond Stokes, and has issue living, William *b* 1951, Joseph *b* 1954, Ann *b* 1952, Nellie *b* 1958, Margaret *b* 1959, Desiree *b* 1962, — Josephine, *b* 1936: *m* 1955, Hilbert Austin Glad, of 14 Marais St, Heidelberg, Transvaal, and has issue living. Hilbert Pierre *b* 1958, Joseph Alfred *b* 1959. —— Alphonso Charles, *b* 1896. —— Henry William, *b* 1898: *m* 1925, Johanna Elizabeth Francisca Struwig, and has issue living, William Burnett (PO 160, Volksrust, Transvaal), *b* 1927: *m* 1955, Maria Susanna Johanna Swanepoel, of Estcourt, Natal, and has issue living, Henry William, *b* 1956, Eleanor Burnett *b* 1959. —— Jacobus Cornelius, *b* 1899: *m* 1930, Miemie Van Reenen, and has issue living, William Burnett, *b* 1939: *m* 1960, Gesina Van Aswegen, and has issue living, Reenen Jacobus *b* 1961, — Elizabeth Susanna, *b* 1932: *m* 1954, Hendrick Van Zyl, of 30a, Dan Piernaar Rd, Volksrust, Transvaal, and has issue living, Susan Mari *b* 1959. —— Simon Thomas, *b* 1911: *m* 1947, Mrs Jacoba Wilhelmina Dannhauser, da of Matheus Willemse. —— Catherine Maude, *b* 1903. —— Maria Elizabeth, *b* 1909: *m* 1929, Tiberius Neser, and has issue living, Florentina Magdalena, *b* 1930: *m* 1953, Roy Goldhill, of 18 St David's Road, East London, Cape Prov, S Africa, and has issue living, David Roy *b* 1958. —— Violet Maud, *b* 1915: *m* 1939, Hendrik Sebastiaan Kriek, and has issue living, Sebastian William, *b* 1949.
Issue of late Alphonso Biddulph, *b* 1860, *d* 19—: *m* 1887, Catharina Magdalene Hendrica, da of late Joseph Brookes (ante):—
Ernest Walstrand, *b* 1888. —— Joseph Cornelis, *b* 1889: *m* 1924, Anna Maria Grobler, and has issue living, Anna Maria, *b* 1927. —— Henry Stephen, *b* 1892. —— Bertie William, *b* 1893. —— Edward Charles, *b* 1897. —— Alphonso Gilbert, *b* 1904. —— Violet Catherine, *b* 1895. —— Florence Emma Roselin, *b* 1907.

Granddaughters of late John Burnet Biddulph (ante):—

Issue of late Edward John Biddulph, *b* 1829, *d* 1909: *m* 18—, Fanny, da of Edward Tunbridge, of Sundays River, Cape Province, S Africa:—
Ina, *b* 1879. —— Freda, *b* 1886: *m* 1912, and has issue living.

Descendants, if any, of late Thomas Burnet Biddulph, 5th son of late John Burnet Biddulph (*b* 1796) (ante).

SELBY-BIGGE (UK) 1919, of King's Sutton, co Northampton (Extinct 1973)

Sir JOHN AMHERST SELBY-BIGGE, OBE, 2nd and last *Baronet*.

DAUGHTERS LIVING OF SECOND BARONET

Lydia Jane, *b* 1920: *m* 1941 (*m diss* 1946), Gabriel Morand. —— Cornelia Diana, *b* 1922: *m* 1947, Hugh Max Bowden, of Port Douglas, N Queensland, and has issue living, Anna Melissa Radclyffe, *b* 1954, — Joanna Katherine Radclyffe, *b* 1963. —— Mary Elizabeth, *b* 1924: *m* 1st, 1951, John Sheals Pratt, MD, who *d* 1956; 2ndly, 1967, Group Capt Richard Irwin Knight Edwards, DFC, AFC, RAF (ret), who *d* 1967.

BIRD (UK) 1922, of Solihull, co Warwick

Sir RICHARD GEOFFREY CHAPMAN BIRD, 4th *Baronet*; *b* 3 Nov 1935; *s* his father *Sir* DONALD GEOFFREY, 1963; *ed* Beaumont: *m* 1st, 1957, Gillian Frances, who *d* 1966, da of Bernard Haggett, of Solihull; 2ndly, 1968, Helen Patricia, only da of Frank Beaumont, of Pontefract, and has issue by 1st and 2nd *m*.

Arms – Vert, on a pale or two popinjays of the field, on a chief ermine three garbs of the second. **Crest** – A garb as in the arms between two roses per pale gules and argent, leaved and slipped proper.
Residence – 39 Ashleigh Rd, Solihull, W Midlands B91 1AF.

SONS LIVING (By 1st marriage)

JOHN ANDREW, *b* 19 Jan 1964. —— Mark Richard, *b* 1965.

DAUGHTERS LIVING (By 1st marriage)

Cecilia Mary, *b* 1957. —— Frances Bernadette, *b* 1959. —— Brigitte Ann, *b* 1960. —— Rowena Clare, *b* 1962.

(by 2nd marriage)

Catherine Veronica, *b* 1970. —— Denise Helen, *b* 1972.

BROTHER LIVING

Success is the reward of endeavour

Peter Donald Chapman, *b* 1938; *ed* Beaumont: *m* 1962, Vera Mary, da of Albert Seymour, of Northfield, and has issue living, Anthony Donald, *b* 1964, — Christopher Robert, *b* 1967. *Residence* – The Gables, Whitecroft Rd, Bream, nr Lydney, Glos.

SISTER LIVING

Elizabeth Anne, *b* 1931: *m* 1955, John Rodney Wilford Brigg, and has had issue, David Lockwood John *b* 1956: *m* 1982, Carolyn Froy, and *d* 1989, leaving issue, Joanna Louise *b* 1986, — Michael James, *b* 1957; B Chir 1982, MB 1983: *m* 1991, Fiona Anne Wheatcroft, and has issue living, Emma Charlotte *b* 1992, — Peter Donald, *b* (twin) 1957; MB BS 1980: *m* 1986, Lynne Goulden, and has issue living, William James *b* 1987, Thomas David *b* 1989, Aimée Eleanore Beatrice *b* 1992. *Residence* – The Soundings, Bosham Hoe, Chichester PO18 8ET.

AUNT LIVING

Eleanore Marshall: *m* 1932, Vernon Harms-Cooke, who *d* 1987, and has issue living, Sylvia HARMS-COOKE (Monks Meadow, Iveley, Winchcombe, Glos), *b* 1934; has resumed her maiden name: *m* 1959, Peter John Smith, and has issue living, Nigel Peter *b* 1961, Charles Francis *b* 1963, Christabel *b* 1964, — Annalova (Monks Meadow, Iveley, Winchcombe, Glos), *b* 1936: *m* 1953, David Stanley Faber, who *d* 1981, and has issue living, Geoffrey David *b* 1961, Rosanne *b* 1955, Colleen *b* 1957, Anita *b* 1959, — Geoffrena *b* 1938: *m* 1959, Lt-Col James William Beachus (ret), HQ Rhine Garrison BFPO 140, and has issue living, Timothy James *b* 1962, Simon Jeremy *b* 1964, Justin *b* 1968, Lucinda *b* 1961, Tanya *b* 1966, — Eleanore, *b* 1940: *m* 1964, James Thomas Askew, of 34 Verran Rd, Camberley, Surrey GU15 2ND, — Carol, *b* 1941: *m* 1st, 1962, John Edmund Davies; 2ndly, 1990, Kenneth Rose, of 6 Bibsworth Av, Broadway, Worcs, and has issue living (by 1st *m*), Anthony William Gordon *b* 1968, Tracey Anne *b* 1971. *Residence* – Monks Meadow, Iveley, Winchcombe, Glos.

DAUGHTER LIVING OF SECOND BARONET

Pamela Stephanie Helen EVANS, *b* 1909; assumed by deed poll 1974 the surname of Evans: *m* 1st, 1934 (*m diss* 1946), Reginald William Bell; 2ndly, 1952 (*m diss* 1973), Vicomte Alain de Mauduit de Kervern, and has issue living, (by 1st *m*) Robert Reginald, *b* 1935, — Thomas Randal, *b* 1937, — William Andrew, *b* 1940, — (by 2nd *m*) Françoise Hélène, *b* 1952. *Residence* – Mille Fiori, 20217 St Florent, France.
Sir Alfred Frederic Bird, 1st Bt (*cr* a Knt 1920, nominated a Baronet 1 Jan 1922, *d* Feb 1922), was Chm of Alfred Bird and Sons (Limited), Manufacturing Chemists, and sat as MP for W Div of Wolverhampton (*CoU*) Jan 1910 to Feb 1922. Sir

Robert Bland Bird, KBE, 2nd baronet, was Chm of Alfred Bird & Sons, and sat as MP for W Div of Wolverhampton (*C*) 1922-29, and 1931-45.

BIRKIN (UK) 1905, of Ruddington Grange, Ruddington, Notts

Prepared for peace and war

Sir JOHN CHRISTIAN WILLIAM BIRKIN, 6th *Baronet*, *b* 1 July 1953; *s* his father, *Sir* CHARLES LLOYD, 1985; *ed* Eton, Trin Coll, Dublin, and at London Film Sch; Freelance TV Producer and Director: *m* 1994, Emma Louise, da of Roger Leonard Gage, of Chantry House, Aveton Gifford, nr Kingsbridge, Devon.

𝕬rms – Argent, a cross raguly couped vert between in the 1st and 4th quarters, a bee volant, and in the 2nd and 3rd a birch tree eradicated proper. 𝕮rest – A scorpion erect proper.
Residence – 23 St Luke's St, SW3 3RP.

SISTERS LIVING

Jennifer Claire Eleanor, *b* 1941: *m* 1971, Charles de Clermont, and has issue living, Araminta, *b* 19—. —— Amanda Jane Averill, *b* 1943; has issue living, Luke TOYNE, *b* 19—.

COLLATERAL BRANCHES LIVING

Issue of late Major Philip Austen Birkin, OBE, 5th son of 1st baronet, *b* 1869, *d* 1951: *m* 1900, Frances Emily who *d* 1953, 2nd da of Joseph Littlewood, JP, of the Park, Nottingham:—
Frances Marjorie, *b* 1905: *m* 1st, 1928, Duncan William Grant, who *d* 1933; 2ndly, 1938, Douglas Charles Lockwood. *Residence* – La Adela, Vivorata, Argentina.

Grandchildren of late Maj Harry Laurence Birkin, TD, 6th and yst son of 1st baronet:—
Issue of late Hon Air Commodore (James) Michael Birkin, CB, DSO, OBE, DFC, AFC, *b* 1912, *d* 1985; *m* 1st, 1956 (*m diss* 1977), Antonia, da of late Lt-Col A.F. Stanley-Clarke; 2ndly, 1980, Susan (The Boathouse, Ashlake, Fishbourne, I of Wight), da of late Edward Mitchell, of Wellington, Shropshire:—
(By 1st *m*) JAMES FRANCIS RICHARD, *b* 27 Feb 1957. —— Abigail Victoria Ann, *b* 1959.
Issue of late Lt-Cdr David Leslie Birkin, DSC, *b* 1914, *d* 1991: *m* 1943, Judy Mary (Judy Campbell, the actress) (21 Old Church St, SW3), da of late John Arthur Gamble, OBE (J. A. Campbell):—
Andrew Timothy, *b* 1945; *ed* Harrow; author of *The Lost Boys*; has recognised issue living, David Tristan BIRKIN, *b* 1977, —— Alexander Kingdom BIRKIN, *b* 1980, — Edmund (Ned) Xavier BIRKIN, *b* 1985. —— Jane Mallory, *b* 1946; actress: *m* 1965 (*m diss* 1968), John Barry, composer, and has issue living, Kate, *b* 1967; has issue living (by Pascal de Kermadec), Roman *b* 1987, — (by Serge Gainsbourg, who *d* 1991), Charlotte GAINSBOURG, *b* 1971; actress, — (by Jacques Doillon), Lou DOILLON, *b* 1982. —— Linda Mary Deborah, *b* 1950: *m* 1978, Michael Charles William Norreys Jephson, of Hawthorn Lodge, Bushy Park, Teddington, Middx, and has issue living, Henry Denham Robert Arthur, *b* 1983, — George Mounteney David Aubrey, *b* 1984, — Jack Norreys William Orlando, *b* 1988.

The 1st baronet, Sir Thomas Isaac Birkin (son of Richard Birkin, JP, of Aspley Hall, Nottingham), was a Director of Great Northern Railway Co, and of Mercantile Steamship Co, and High Sheriff of Notts 1892. The 2nd baronet, Sir Thomas Stanley Birkin, was High Sheriff for Notts 1915. The 3rd baronet, Sir Henry Ralph Birkin, was a well-known Racing Motorist, and holder of several records.

BIRKMYRE (UK) 1921, of Dalmunzie, co Perth

Advance

Sir ARCHIBALD BIRKMYRE, 3rd *Baronet*; *b* 12 Feb 1923; *s* his father, Sir HENRY, 1992; *ed* Radley; Burma 1942-45 as Capt RA; Memb London Stock Exchange 1960-88: *m* 1953, Gillian Mary, only da of late Eric Mytton Downes, OBE, of Dordon House, Hurst, Berks and has issue.

Arms – Per chevron argent and sable, in chief two eagles heads erased and in base a thistle leaved and slipped all proper. **Crest** – In front of a rising sun proper an eagle displayed sable.
Residence – The Old Presbytery, Buckland, Faringdon, Oxon SN7 8QW. *Clubs* – Boodle's, Huntercombe Golf, M.C.C.

SON LIVING

JAMES, *b* 29 Feb 1956; *ed* Radley: *m* 1990, Leslie Amanda, elder da of Dr Richard Lyon, of Seal Beach, California, USA, and has issue living, Alexander, *b* 24 May 1991. *Residence* – Ashmore Green Cottage, Ashmore Green, Berks RG16 9EY.

DAUGHTERS LIVING

Alison Mary (*Baroness De Ramsey*), *b* 1954: *m* 1984, as his 2nd wife, 4th Baron De Ramsey, and has issue (*see* B De Ramsey). *Residence* – Abbots Ripton Hall, Huntingdon, Cambs. —— Serena Jane, *b* 1960: *m* 1988, Hugo Edward Stainton Jackson, yr son of Sir (John) Edward Jackson, KCMG, of 17 Paulton's Sq, SW3, and has issue living, George Edward Stainton, *b* 1990, — Thomas Archie Stainton, *b* 1994. *Address* – c/o Sir Edward Jackson, KCMG, 17 Paulton's Sq, SW3.

SISTER LIVING

Jane Henrietta, *b* 1929: *m* 1952, Major Robert Evelyn Russell Smallwood, of Finches, Pembury, Kent TN2 4BA, and has issue living, Rosemary Jane, *b* 1954: *m* 1977, Andrew Peter Geoffrey Holmes, of 51 Doneraile St, SW6 6EW, — Susan Caroline, *b* 1957: *m* 1979, Peter Richard Vivian Houston (*see* B Swansea), of Fair Dawn, Packhorse Lane, South Stoke, Bath BA2 7DJ.

COLLATERAL BRANCH LIVING

Issue of late Archy Birkmyre, yr son of 1st baronet, *b* 1904, *d* 1992: *m* 1940, Doreen (Dalchonzie Lower Cottage, by Comrie, Perthshire PH6 2LB), only child of late Robert Barclay, of Kilbirnie, Ayrshire:—
David, *b* 1941; *ed* Trinity Coll, Glenalmond: *m* 1976, Mrs Margot Rogerson, da of late William Rogerson, of Rothesay, Isle of Bute, and has issue living, Rebecca, *b* 1978. —— Adelaide (*Hon Mrs John Borthwick of Borthwick*), *b* 1945: *m* 1974, Hon John Hugh Borthwick of Borthwick, of The Neuk, Heriot, Midlothian, and has issue (*see* L Borthwick).
The 1st baronet, Sir Archibald Birkmyre, CBE (son of late Henry Birkmyre, of Port Glasgow), was knighted 1917, and was senior partner in the firm of Birkmyre Bros, merchants, of Calcutta.

BLACK (UK) 1922, of Midgham, co Berks

Not the cross, but the light

Sir ROBERT DAVID BLACK, 3rd *Baronet*, *b* 29 March 1929; *s* his father Sir ROBERT ANDREW STRANSHAM, 1979; *ed* Eton; Maj (ret) R Horse Guards; late Maj Berks and Westminster Dragoons (TA), and Berks Territorials (TAVR III); Vice-Chm (Berkshire) Eastern Wessex TAVRA 1985-92; Hon Col 94 (Berkshire Yeomanry) Signal Sqdn (V) since 1988; DL Caithness 1991; High Sheriff Oxfordshire 1993; Joint MFH Garth and S Berks Hunt: *m* 1st, 1953 (*m diss* 1972), Rosemary Diana, da of Sir Rupert John Hardy, 4th Bt; 2ndly, 1973 (Dorothy) Maureen, yst da of Maj Charles Robert Eustace Radclyffe, and widow of Alan Roger Douglas Pilkington, and has had issue by 1st *m*.

Arms – Argent, a saltire sable between two crescents in pale and as many mullets in fesse gules, on a chief of the second three trefoils slipped of the field. **Crest** – Issuant out of a cloud a demi-lion rampant proper, charged on the shoulder with a trefoil vert and holding in the paws a fylfot sable.
Residences – Elvendon Priory, Goring, Reading, Berks; Shurrery Lodge, Shebster, Thurso, Caithness. *Clubs* – Cavalry and Guards', Fly Fishers'.

DAUGHTERS LIVING AND DECEASED (By 1st marriage)

Diana Sarah, *b* 1955: *m* 1979, Mark Robert Newton, of The Old Rectory, Church Langton, Leics, and has issue living, William David Rupert, *b* 1989, — James Robert George, *b* 1993. —— Fiona Caroline, *b* 1957: *m* (May) 1982, Christopher E. J. Jerram, only son of Col Edward Jenner Jerram, MC, of Poplars Farm, Evenlode, nr Moreton-in-Marsh, Glos, and *d* (Dec) 1982. —— Joanna Rosemary Violet, *b* 1966: *m* 1991, Christopher Robert Caspar Wild, yr son of Robert Wild, of Slade Farm, Ockham, Surrey.
The 1st baronet, Sir Robert James Black, was Chm of Mercantile Bank of India, and a Director of Shell Transport Co (Limited).

BLACKETT (E) 1673, of Newcastle, Northumberland

We will labour in hope

Sir FRANCIS HUGH BLACKETT, 11th *Baronet*; *b* 16 Oct 1907; *s* his brother, *Sir* GEORGE WILLIAM, 1994; *ed* Eton; Maj The Royal Dragoons (ret), 1939-45 War: *m* 1st, 1950, Mrs Elizabeth Eily Barrie, who *d* 1982, 2nd da of late Howard Dennison, of Valparaiso, Chile; 2ndly, 1985, Mrs Joan Chowdry, and has issue by 1st *m*.

Arms – Argent, on a chevron between three mullets pierced sable three escallops of the field.
Residence – Brewhouse, Halton Castle, Corbridge, Northumberland *Club* – Cavalry and Guards'.

SONS LIVING *(By 1st marriage)*

HUGH FRANCIS, *b* 11 Feb 1955; *ed* Eton: *m* 1982, Anna M., yr da of J. St G. Coldwell, of Somerton, Oxon, and has issue living, Henry Douglas, *b* 2 Feb 1992, — Amelia, *b* 1984, — Isabella, *b* 1986, — Flora, *b* 1988. *Residence* – Halton Castle, Corbridge, Northumberland. —— Marcus Henry, *b* 1961. *Residence* – 11 Waverley Rd, Liverpool L17 8TY.

DAUGHTERS LIVING *(By 1st marriage)*

Angela Frances, *b* 1951: *m* 1979, Ewan Follett Bell (*see* B Wyfold, 1980 Edn), and has issue living, Archibald, *b* 1981, — Caspar Francis, *b* 1989, — Georgia Elizabeth, *b* 1983. *Residence* – Easter Coul, Auchterarder, Perthshire. —— Charlotte Elizabeth, *b* 1952; has issue living, Theophania Eve BLACKETT OGRAM, *b* 1990. *Residence* – 30A Mount Ephraim Rd, SW16.

DAUGHTERS LIVING OF NINTH BARONET

Caroline Ann, *b* 1936: *m* 1957, Capt (Geoffrey Thomas) Warren Fenwicke-Clennell, late 11th Hussars, of Kirk Hammerton House, York, and 8 Donne Place, SW3, and has issue living, Nicholas (Deans Hall, Little Maplestead, Halstead, Essex C09 2RT), *b* 1959: *m* 1984, Susan Elizabeth, da of Peter Roy Herbert Gould, of Little Barn, Gt Chesterford, Saffron Walden, Essex, and has issue living, Oliver Edward *b* 1986, Toby *b* 1988, Antonia Ursula *b* 1991, — Luke Thomas, *b* 1961, — Katharine Mary, *b* 1963: *m* 1989, James Richard Boughey, yr son of late Sir Richard James Boughey, 10th Bt. —— Lucinda Mary (*Lady Peto*), *b* 1940: *m* 1st, 1964 (*m diss* 1971), Ewan Iain Macleod Hilleary; 2ndly, 1971, Sir Michael Henry Basil Peto, 4th Bt, of Lower Church Cottage, Cliddesden, Basingstoke, and has issue living (by 1st *m*), Iain Douglas, *b* 1965, — (by 2nd *m*) (*see* Peto, Bt, *cr* 1927).

WIDOW LIVING OF TENTH BARONET

DAPHNE LAING (*Dowager Lady Blackett*), da of late Maj Guy Laing Bradley, of Bridge End House, Hexham: *m* 1964, as his 2nd wife, Sir George William Blackett, 10th Bt, who *d* 1994. *Residence* – Colwyn, Corbridge on Tyne, Northumberland.

COLLATERAL BRANCHES LIVING

Issue of late Maj Rupert Henry Blackett, DLI (ret), yst son of 8th baronet, *b* 1911, *d* 1992: *m* 1941, Mrs Felicity Mary Audley Clapton (Errington Hill Head, Hexham, Northumberland), da of late Lt-Col William Alfred Scudamore Smith:—
Piers Rupert, *b* 1941; *ed* Univ of Cape Town Med Sch (MB, ChB). *Residence* – —. —— (Rose) Miranda, *b* 1944: *m* 1975 (*m diss* 19—), Merlin Pearson-Rogers, and has issue living, Jack Rupert, *b* 1977. *Residence* – —

Grandson of late Harold Blackett, el son of late John Charles Blackett, RN, 4th son of 5th baronet:—
Issue of late Henry Beaumont Blackett, *b* 1886, *d* 1964: *m* 1916, Evelyn Nora Mary, who *d* 1966, da of J. Booth Lazenby, of Newcastle-on-Tyne:—
John Harold Booth (Seven Stars House, Whalton, Morpeth, Northumberland NE61 3XA. *Club* – Cavalry and Guards'), *b* 1923; *ed* Radley; 1939-45 War as Lieut 15th/19th King's Roy Hussars: *m* 1953, Veronica Heath Stuart, da of Henry Tegner, of Whalton, Northumberland, and has issue living, (John) Simon (Clunie Cottage, Braemar, Aberdeenshire AB35 5XQ), *b* 1954; *ed* Radley: *m* 1987, Hon Geva Charlotte Caroline Winn, only da of 5th Baron St Oswald, and has issue living, (Helena) Charlotte Rose *b* 1988, (Camilla Harriet) Eve *b* 1989, Letitia *b* 1991, Annabel *b* 1993, — Rupert Beaumont (Merle Cottage, 89 High St, Westerham, Kent), *b* 1957; *ed* Radley: *m* 1984, Hendrika Theresa, da of Wilhelmus Marinus Bouwman, of Utrecht, Netherlands, and has issue living, James Henry *b* 1988, William Luke *b* 1994, Rebecca Anne *b* 1985, Kate Elizabeth *b* 1990, Lucy Georgia *b* (twin) 1994, — Caroline Rose, *b* 1960: *m* 1987, Robert Murray-Brown, yst son of late Lt-Col C. R. Murray-Brown, DSO, and of Lady Loyd, of Aldeburgh, Suffolk, and has issue living, Francis William *b* 1994, — Juliet Evelyn, *b* 1965: *m* 1991, Andrew Charles Pumphrey (*see* Aykroyd, Bt, *cr* 1929, colls).

Granddaughter of John Charles Blackett, RN (ante):—
Issue of late Adm Henry Blackett, CBE, *b* 1867, *d* 1952: *m* 1906, Hon Pamela Mary Fisher, who *d* 1949, yst da of 1st Baron Fisher:—
Pamela, *b* 1911: *m* 1957, Clifford Henry Bray, who *d* 1980. *Residence* – 8 Homedrive House, 95/97 The Drive, Hove, Sussex BN3 6GE.

The 1st baronet, Sir William Blackett (son of William Blackett, of Hoppyland, co Durham), was MP for Newcastle-upon-Tyne 1673-80. The 2nd baronet, Sir Edward, was MP for Newcastle-upon-Tyne, and an Alderman and sometime Mayor of that borough. Sir Hugh Douglas Blackett, 8th baronet, was High Sheriff of Northumberland 1914; Sir Charles Douglas Blackett, 9th baronet, was High Sheriff of Northumberland 1953.

BLAIR (UK) 1945, of Harrow Weald, co Middlesex (Extinct 1962)

Sir REGINALD BLAIR, 1st and last *Baronet*.

GRANDDAUGHTER LIVING OF FIRST BARONET

(Issue of late Capt Malcolm Reginald Blair, Roy Fusiliers, el son of 1st baronet, *b* 1906, *ka* in France 1940: *m* 1936, Sheila Pasmore), Jenny Mabel, *b* 1937: *m* 1st, 1957 (*m diss* 19—), Robert Alan Cumming Greenleas; 2ndly, 19—, Peter Trier, of Alderwood House, Greenham Common, Newbury, Berks.

ADOPTIVE GRANDSON OF FIRST BARONET

Adopted son of late Walter MacLellan Blair, 2nd Lieut Royal Fusiliers, 3rd and yst son of 1st baronet, *b* 1913, *d* on active service 1941: *m* 1937, Mrs Margaret (Madge) Assheton Smith (who *d* 1966, having *m* 3rdly, 1949, Douglas Patrick Motion), da of late Cyril Assheton Luckman, and formerly wife of Hugh Ernest Assheton Smith:—
Michael Cyril Assheton Blair (4 The Almshouses, Church Hill, Hurst, nr Reading, Berks RG10 0SL), *b* 1936; *ed* Harrow: *m* 1st, 1962 (*m diss* 1976), Tessa Annette, da of John Derek Fowler; 2ndly, 1992, Anna Mary Louise, da of John Gordon Fraser, of 2 Ash Lane, Winsford, Som, and has issue living (by 1st *m*), Nicholas Derek Assheton, *b* 1963, — Timothy Michael Assheton, *b* 1964, — Christopher John Assheton, *b* 1964.

DAUGHTER LIVING OF FIRST BARONET

Mary Lile Wieland, *b* 1910: *m* 1937, Lieut-Com G. Vernon W. Harrison, RN, who was *ka* 1941, and has issue living, Peter Reginald Wallace, *b* 1939.

HUNTER BLAIR (GB) 1786, of Dunskey

Vigilance, strength, pleasure

Sir EDWARD THOMAS HUNTER BLAIR, 8th *Baronet*, *b* 15 Dec 1920; *s* his father, *Sir* JAMES 1985; *ed* Eton, and Balliol Coll, Oxford; 1939-45 War with KOYLI; Member of Kirkcudbrightshire Co Council 1970-71; *m* 1956, Norma, who *d* 1972, el da of late Walter Sidney Harris, and has an adopted son and da.

Arms – Quarterly: 1st, argent, a chevron gules between three bugles vert, vested and stringed of the second, *Hunter*; 2nd, argent, on a chevron gules between three cross-crosslets fitchée sable a fleur-de-lis or, within a double tressure flory counterflory of the second, *Kennedy* of Culzean; 3rd, argent, on a saltire sable eight mascles of the field, in chief a star sable eight mascles of the field, in chief a star gules, *Blair*; 4th argent, a shake-fork sable, and in chief a rose gules, surmounted of a mullet of the field, *Cunninghame of Brownhill*. **Crest** – A stag's head cabossed proper. **Supporters** – *Dexter*, a dog of chase salient argent; *Sinister*, an antelope springing proper, gorged with an open crown and a chain hanging thereat or.
Residence – Parton House, Castle Douglas, Kirkcudbrightshire DG7 3NB.

ADOPTED SON LIVING

Alan Walter, *b* 1961.

ADOPTED DAUGHTER LIVING

Helen Cecilia, *b* 1963: *m* 1985, L.B. (James) Watson, 2nd son of Peter Watson, of 17 Adams Rd, Cambridge, and has issue living, Emily Ann, *b* 1989, — Natasha Jean, *b* 1991.

BROTHER LIVING

JAMES, *b* 18 March 1926; *ed* Eton, and Balliol Coll, Oxford; formerly Lt Scots Guards; a DL for Ayrshire. *Residence* – Blairquhan Castle, Maybole, Ayrshire.

COLLATERAL BRANCHES LIVING

Issue of late Com Gaspard Patrick Hunter Blair, RN, 2nd son of 6th baronet, *b* 1895, *ka* 1941; *m* 1929, Sophie (who *d* 1968, having *m* 2ndly, 1945, as his 2nd wife, Rear Adm Robert Cathcart Kemble Lambert, DSO, who *d* 1950), el da of late Prince Alexis Koudacheff:—
Francis, *b* 1930; formerly Sub-Lieut RNVR: *m* 1957, Joyce, da of Cdr James Graham, OBE, RN, and has issue living, Patrick David, *b* 1958, — Michael Francis, *b* 1959, — Peter James, *b* 1961, — Alexander John, *b* 1974, — Caroline Mary, *b* 1963. *Residence* – Marbrack, Carsphairn, Castle Douglas, Kirkcudbrightsire. —— Katherine Isabel, *b* 1933; *ed* Oxford Univ (MA); BA London 1958 *m* 1960, Michael R. Stidworthy, of The Old Rectory, Caldecote, Cambridge, and has issue living, John Damian, *b* 1967, — Alexander Luke, *b* 1969, — Xenia Mary Gabriel, *b* 1961, — Imogen Theresa, *b* 1963.

Grandchildren of late Major Reginald Stanley Hunter Blair, MBE, 7th son of 4th baronet:—
Issue of late Lt-Col David Walter Hunter Blair, *b* 1894, *d* 1961: *m* 1st, 1919 (*m diss* 1941), Barbara, who *d* 1965, da of late George Cameron Norman: 2ndly, 1941, Hughe Thelma, who *d* 1972, da of late Capt H. E. Reid, R. Scots, and widow of Maj J. W. Williams, 2nd Punjab Regt; she *m* 3rdly, 1965, Adm Sir Walter Thomas Couchman, KCB, CVO, DSO, OBE, of Tandymead, Bromeswell, nr Woodbridge, Suffolk:—
(By 1st *m*) John David (34 Orange Grove Drive, Box 269, Harare, Zimbabwe), *b* 1925; *ed* Eton: *m* 1st, 1952 (*m diss* 1978), Jennifer Mary, only da of Leslie Hamilton Gault; 2ndly, 1988, Edwina Margaret, da of late James Done, of Harare, Zimbabwe, and has issue living (by 1st *m*), Thomas, *b* 1957: *m* 1986, Caroline (Pol), only da of D. Unwin, of Coventry, Warwicks, and of Mrs D. M. Bee, of St John, Jersey, and has issue living, Jack David Hamilton *b* 1989, Sophie *b* 1991, — Jane, *b* 1956: *m* 1982, William Scott Hutton; 2ndly, 19—, Max Wolf, and has issue living (by 1st *m*), Oliver David *b* 1982, Louis Philip *b* 1985, (by 2nd *m*) Gabriella Ilse *b* 1990, Cordelia Iris *b* 1992, — Sophie, *b* 1960: *m* 1984, Philip John McCann, el son of Ian

Col David Theodor Dobie, DSO, formerly Parachute Regt; 2ndly, 1949 (*m diss* 1965), as his 2nd wife, Maj Hugh Cam Hobhouse, N Somerset Yeo (*see* Hobhouse, Bt); 3rdly, 1965, John Alastair Livingston Timpson, MC, late Scots Gds, of Preedy's Cottage, Castle Combe, Wilts.

   Issue of late Cdr Ronald Hunter Blair, DSC, RN, *b* 1898, *d* 1968: *m* 1929, Nancye (Fiddlers Hall, Charlestown, Fife), da of late W. B. Colbeck, of Auckland, NZ:—

Alister (Gilder Lodge, Althorne, Chelmsford, Essex), *b* 1930; *ed* Wellington; Lt-Cdr RN, (ret); Korea 1952-53, Jennifer Shirley, el da of Rev Basil William Greenup, of Rock, Cornwall, and has issue living, Nicholas Patrick Alister, *b* 1959. ——— Reginald Stuart, *b* 1942; late Lt Gordon Highlanders: *m* 1968, Jennifer Marjorie, el da of Jack Paley Yorke, and has issue living, Camilla Louise, *b* 1970, — Antonia Claire, *b* 1972. ——— Ronald Patrick, *b* 1944: *m* 1972, Mary Fitzhugh, da of William T. Stewart, Jr, of Far Hills, New Jersey, USA, and has issue living, James Stewart, *b* 1974, — a son, *b* 1977. ——— Julia, *b* 1932: *m* 1st, 1958, Charles Maitland Zane; 2ndly, 1966, Arnold J. Bauer, and has issue living, (by 1st *m*) Lucy Sarah Mackenzie, *b* 1960, — (by 2nd *m*) Rebecca, *b* 1968. ——— Elizabeth Mary (twin), *b* 1944.

Sir James Hunter Blair, 1st baronet was MP and Lord Provost of Edinburgh, and a partner in the banking house of Sir William Forbes and Co. He was 2nd son of John Hunter of Mainholm and Brownhill, Ayrshire, yr son of James Hunter of Abbotshill, Ayrshire, an estate granted to his ancestor James Hunter by charter 1569. The 1st Bt added the name of Blair about 1774, having *m* 1770, Jean, sister and heir of David Blair, and only da of John Blair of Dunskey, Wigtownshire by Anne Kennedy, sister and co-heir of 10th Earl of Cassillis. The 5th baronet, Rt Rev Sir David Oswald, was Abbot of Dunfermline and Private Chamberlain to Pope Leo XIII.

BLAKE (I) 1622, of Menlough, Galway

Virtus sola nobilitas

Virtue alone ennobles

Sir (THOMAS) RICHARD VALENTINE BLAKE, 17th *Baronet; b* 7 Jan 1942; *s* his father, *Sir* ULICK TEMPLE, 1963; *ed* Bradfield: *m* 1st, 1976, Jacqueline, da of late Desmond E. Daroux, and formerly wife of Peter Alers Hankey; 2ndly, 1982 (*m diss* 1986), Bertice Reading, singer, who *d* 1991, formerly wife of Eddie Meyer.

Arms – Argent, a fret gules. **Crest** – A tiger-cat passant guardant proper. *Residence* – 74 Petersfield Rd, Midhurst, W Sussex GU29 9JR.

COLLATERAL BRANCHES LIVING

   Grandchildren of late Major Cecil Bruce Blake (infra):—
  Issue of late Major Charles Anthony Howell Bruce Blake, Roy Ulster Rifles, *b* 1911, *ka* in Korea 1951: *m* 1948, Elspeth (who *m* 2ndly, 1961, Patrick Michael Gardner, MBE, who *d* 1980), da of late Lt-Col A. M. Arnott:—
ANTHONY TEILO BRUCE, *b* (*posthumous*) 5 May 1951; *ed* Wellington: *m* 1988, Geraldine, da of Cecil Shnaps, of Cape Town, S Africa, and has issue living, Sarah Elizabeth Bruce, *b* 1990, — Rachael Louise Bruce *b* 1991. ——— Caroline Bruce, *b* 1949.
  Issue of late Valentine John Bruce Blake, *b* 1914, *d* 1993: *m* 1950, Carla Maria Aida Wrinch-Schulz (Carnival, Spikle, Conna, co Cork), of Gardens, Cape Town, S Africa:—
Jonathan Luttrell (53 Sellick Drive, Croydon, Victoria 3136, Australia), *b* 1953: *m* 1977, Eleanora Mostert, of Holland, and has issue living, Suzanne May, *b* 1978, — Tonya Carla, *b* 1982, — Rachel Marie, *b* 1984. ——— Kerry Valentine (Kolumbus Strasse 19, 8000 Munich 90, Germany), *b* 1963. ——— Rosalie Julianne, *b* 1951: *m* 1977, Kevin Byrne, of Tollgate, Church St, Milnthorpe, Cumbria, and has issue living, Anna Louise, *b* 1981, — Philippa Elizabeth, *b* 1984. ——— Noelle Claire Louise, *b* 1959.

   Granddaughters of late Surg-Maj Walter Blake, 2nd son of late Walter Blake, grandson of 10th baronet:—
  Issue of late Maj Cecil Bruce Blake, *b* 1880, *d* 1937: *m* 1909, Effie, who *d* 1969, da of S. Earnshaw Howell, JP:—
Elinor Joyce, *b* 1910: *m* 1933, Cyril Hall Green, and has issue living, Jeremy Dominic Blake (Ballyvolane House, Castlelyons, co Cork) *b* 1934: *m* 1965, Gabriel Meredith Benson, and has issue, — Celia Elinor Vadyn, *b* 1936: *m* 1958, Edward John Mansel Hugh Frampton Child-Villiers, and has issue (*see* E Jersey, colls). ——— Patricia Honora, *b* 1919: *m* 1st 1942 (*m diss* 1951), Samuel Francis Hewitt Haughton, MB, BCh; 2ndly, 1957, Joseph Gerald Caulfield Kirby-Turner, who *d* 1961 (B Kilmaine, colls), and has issue living, (by 2nd *m*) Belinda Shiralee Anne, *b* 1959: *m* 1990, Jehanbaz Ali Khan, — Sharon Briar Rose, *b* 1960: *m* 1987, David Andrew Wallace, of Springfield House, Ballacolla, Abbeyleix, co Laois, 2nd son of Bruce Wallace, of Fruitlawn, Abbeyleix, and has issue living, Timothy Caulfield Daniel *b* 1991, Victoria Kirby *b* 1989.

   Descendants of late John Blake, 4th son of 3rd baronet:—

   Grandchildren of late Valentine Joseph Blake (infra):—
  Issue of late Lt-Col Arthur Maurice Joseph Blake, MC, LRCP, LRCS, *b* 1884, *d* 1974: *m* 1938, Barbara (Moret, Edmondstown Park, Dublin 16), only da of Raymond Stephenson, of Cranford, Stillorgan Rd, Dublin:—
Martin Joseph (Castlewood House, Durrow, Co Leix), *b* 1952. ——— Anne Meriel Josephine, *b* 1939: *m* 1964, Patrick Leonard, of Edmondstown Park, Dublin 16, and has issue living, John Arthur (Sean), *b* 1967, — Jeremy Charles *b* 1973, — Dominic Stephen *b* 1975, — Natasha Veronica, *b* 1965. ——— Erica Mary Josephine, *b* 1940: *m* 1966, Bernard H. C. Corbally, of Gilspear, Kilmacanogue, co Wicklow, and has issue living, Simon Herbert Arthur, *b* 1967, — Colin George Eric *b* 1968, — Ruth Ida Mary, *b* 1974, — Linda Clare Cecilia, *b* 1977.

   Grandson of late Valentine O'Connor Blake, son of late Maurice Blake, grandson of late Maurice Blake (*d* 1789), grandson of late John Blake (ante):—
  Issue of late Valentine Joseph Blake, *b* 1843, *d* 1912: *m* 1880, Hon Mary French, who *d* 1919, da of 3rd Baron de Freyne:—
Gerald, *b* 1896: *m* 1943, Ann Deegan, and has issue living, Valentine, *b* 1945: *m* 1971, Madelene only da of J. Andrews, of Perivale, Middx, — Gerald, *b* 1947: *m* 1968, Elaine Thomas, of Baglan, Glam, and has issue living, Gervase *b* 1969, Emma Josephine *b* 1972, — Arthur, *b* 1950. *Residence* –

The founder of this family is said to have accompanied King John to Ireland in 1185. The 1st baronet, Sir Valentine Blake, was Mayor of Galway borough 1611 and 1630. The 6th baronet, Sir Walter, was the first Catholic gentleman of any distinction who joined William III; he maintained and clothed a regiment at his own expense.

BLAKE (GB) 1772, of Langham, Suffolk (Extinct 1975)

Cdr Sir CUTHBERT PATRICK BLAKE, DSO, RN, 6th and last *Baronet*.

DAUGHTER LIVING OF SIXTH BARONET

Veronica Anstace, *b* 1919; late 2nd Officer WRNS: *m* 1942, Maj Hugh Gilson-Taylor, Suffolk Regt, who *d* 1984, and has issue living, Christopher Gilson, *b* 1943: *m* 1st, 1969 (*m diss* 1981), Patricia Anne, da of Ismay Emanuel, of London, W6; 2ndly, 1987, Luise Daemen, of Zürich, Switzerland, and has issue living (by 1st *m*), Andrew Blake *b* 1972, David Patrick *b* 1975, — Anstace Felicity, *b* 1949: *m* 1971, Gilbert William Peter Wright, and has issue living, Jonathan William Blake *b* 1972, James Robert *b* 1974. *Residence* – 3 Harefield, Long Melford, Sudbury, Suffolk CO10 9DE.

BLAKE (UK) 1907, of Tillmouth Park, Cornhill, co Northumberland

I shall rise again

Sir (FRANCIS) MICHAEL BLAKE, 3rd *Baronet*; *b* 11 July 1943; *s* his father, *Sir* (FRANCIS) EDWARD COLQUHOUN, 1950; *ed* Rugby: *m* 1968, Joan Ashbridge, only da of Frederic Cecil Ashbridge Miller, of Ramsay Lodge, Kelso, and has issue.

Arms – Per chevron argent and sable, a chevron per chevron in chief two garbs and in base a frette all countercharged. **Crest** – A morion proper, thereon a martlet argent, holding in the beak a sprig of barley sable.
Residence – The Dower House, Tillmouth Park, Cornhill-on-Tweed, Northumberland TD12 4UR.

SONS LIVING

FRANCIS JULIAN, *b* 17 Feb 1971. —— Nicholas Winston, *b* 1974.

HALF-SISTER LIVING

Caroline Anne Honey, *b* 1948: *m* 1975, Adam Henville Simonds, who *d* 1989, of 31 Lauder Rd, Edinburgh EH9 2JG, and has issue living, Alasdair David Henville, *b* 1977, — Kim Shona, *b* 1980.

WIDOW LIVING OF SECOND BARONET

DOREEN MAUD, da of late James Bertram Sample, of Stoneleigh, Hexham-on-Tyne, Northumberland: *m* 1st, 1947, as his 2nd wife, Sir (Francis) Edward Colquhoun Blake, 2nd Bt, who *d* 1950; 2ndly, 1961, Wing Cmdr John Francis Grey, DSO, DFC, RAF, who *d* 1964. *Residence* – Oxendean Burn, Cornhill-on-Tweed, Northumberland TD12 4UW.

COLLATERAL BRANCH LIVING

Issue of late Patrick Delaval Blake, yr son of 1st baronet, *b* 1904, *d* 1961: *m* 1st, 1927 (*m diss* 1944), Phyllis, da of W. Lee Ellison, of Chester; 2ndly, 1944, Mrs Ruby Holdsworth, who *m* 3rdly, 1973, W. E. Sweet, and *d ca* 1983:—
(By 1st *m*) Ian Francis (Nibelungengasse 1, A-1010 Vienna, Austria), *b* 1929; Lt-Cdr RN: *m* 1st, 1954 (*m diss* 1977), Frances Jillian, da of W. T. Barton of Shepherd's Hurst, Outwood, Surrey; 2ndly, 1979, Elisabeth Maria Aloisia Theresia, da of Univ Prof Dr Gustav Ortner, of Vienna, Austria, and has issue living, (by 1st *m*) Philip Ian, *b* 1955: *m* 1986, Rebecca, da of Rev Bernard Marshall, — Carol Patricia, *b* 1957: *m* 1st, 1980 (*m diss* 1982), Clive Richardson; 2ndly, 19—, Hugh Campbell, and has issue living (by 2nd *m*), Emma Mary Scott *b* 1987, Charlotte Fiona *b* 1989, Sarah Victoria *b* 1992. —— Mary Douglas, *b* 1931: *m* 1965, Dr Peter Branson, Oaklands Cottage, Wray Common, Reigate, Surrey, and has an adopted son and da, Adam Robert, *b* 1969, — Sara Jane, *b* 1972.

The 1st baronet, Sir Francis Douglas Blake, CB (son of late Francis Blake, of Tillmouth Park, Northumberland) sat as MP for Berwick-on-Tweed Div of Northumberland (*Co L*) 1916-22. The 2nd Baronet, Sir Francis Edward Colquhoun Blake, was Capt RA (TA Reserve), and served in European War 1914-18 and European War 1939-45.

BLAKER (UK) 1919, of Brighton, Sussex.

Sir JOHN BLAKER, 3rd *Baronet*; *b* 22 March 1935; *s* his father, *Maj Sir* REGINALD TD, 1975: *m* 1st, 1960 (*m diss* 1965), Catherine Ann, da of late Francis John Anselon Thorold (*see* Thorold, Bt, colls); 2ndly, 1968, Elizabeth Katharine, da of Col John Tinsley Russell, DSO.

ᚷrms – Ermine three chevronelles, in chief two towers sable. ᚳrest – A horse's head sable, charged with three chevronelles argent.
Residence – Stantons Farm, East Chiltington, nr Lewes, Sussex.

SISTER LIVING

Anne, *b* 1932: *m* 1953, Edmund Crosby Cockburn, and has issue living, Crosby Bay, *b* 1956, — Crosby Kim, *b* 1958, — Georgina Gay, *b* 1954. *Residence* – Glebe Farm, Shuckburgh, Daventry, Northants.

WIDOW LIVING OF SECOND BARONET

SHEILA KELLAS (*Sheila, Lady Blaker*) (5 Oak Bank, Lindfield, Sussex), da of Alexander Cran, MB, of Little Court, Merrow, nr Guildford: *m* 1930, Maj Sir Reginald Blaker, 2nd Bt, TD, who *d* 1975.
The 1st baronet, Sir John George Blaker, OBE, was Mayor of Brighton 1895-9.

BLAKISTON (GB) 1763, of the City of London
(Name usually pronounced "Blackiston")

Sir FERGUSON ARTHUR JAMES BLAKISTON, 9th *Baronet*; *s* his father, *Sir* (ARTHUR) NORMAN HUNTER, 1977; *b* 19 Feb 1963; *ed* Lincoln Coll NZ (Dip Ag): *m* 1993, Linda Jane, da of late Robert John Key, farmer, of Queenstown, NZ.

ᚷrms – Argent, two barsgules, in chief three cocks of the last. ᚳrest – A cock gules.
Residence – 28 McKenzie St, Geraldine, S Canterbury, NZ.

BROTHER LIVING

NORMAN JOHN BALFOUR, *b* 7 April 1964.

WIDOW LIVING OF SEVENTH BARONET

ANN HOPE PERCIVAL (*Ann, Lady Blakiston*) (42A Corton, Warminster, Wilts), da of late Purcell Cooke Jeans, of Cortington Grange, Warminster, Wilts: *m* 1954, as his 2nd wife, Sir Arthur Frederick Blakiston, 7th Bt, MC, who *d* 1974.

COLLATERAL BRANCHES LIVING

Grandchildren of late Charles Robert Blakiston, 5th son of 3rd baronet, *b* 1825, *d* 1898: *m* 1858, Mary Anna, who *d* 1924, da of late Most Rev Henry John Chitty Harper, DD, sometime Bishop of Christchurch, and Primate of New Zealand:—
Issue of late Charles Douglas Blakiston, *b* 1868 *d* 1950: *m* 1908, Ethel Anne, who *d* 1967, da of late John Henley Whishaw, of Featherston, NZ:—
Charles Michael Hardy, *b* 1919: *m* 1945, Nancy, da of Charles E. Holmes, of Wellington, New Zealand, and has issue living, David Holmes (Bruce Rd, PO Box 1039, Levin, NZ), *b* 1946: *m* 1982, Sara Margaret, da of Maj-Gen Robin Hugh Ferguson Holloway, CB, CBE, of Waikanae, NZ, and has issue living, Matthew Robin *b* 1983, — Roger Charles (BP 2649, Noumea, New Caledonia, NZ), *b* 1948: *m* 1st, 1975 (*m diss* 1991), Victoria Jane, da of Peter L. Marshall, of Taoroa, Taihape, NZ; 2ndly, 1993, Francoise Vallino, and has issue living (by 1st *m*), Charles Rupert Hardy *b* 1976, Samuel James *b* 1980, Alice *b* 1977, (by 2nd *m*) Isaura *b* 1993, — Simon Michael (Bruce Rd, Levin, NZ), *b* 1952: *m* 1981, Nell, da of Michael Pouajen, of Bipi Island, Papua New Guinea, and has issue living, Manu Sangak *b* 1983. *Residence* – 7 Lighthouse Rd, Napier, NZ.
—— Barbara Helen Joan: *m* 1st, 1940, Henry Frank Seymour, who was *ka* 1941; 2ndly, 1945, Allan Frederick Palairet, who *d* 1990, of 7/107 Walker Rd, Point Chevalier, Auckland, NZ, and has issue living (by 1st *m*) Nicholas Charles (Wensleydale Station, Private Bag, Gisborne, NZ), *b* 1941: *m* 1966, Patricia Anne Ingram, of Auckland, and has issue living, Howard Frank *b* 1970, Patrick James *b* 1974, Andrea June *b* 1972, — (by 2nd *m*) Anthea Gay, *b* 1949: *m* 1973, Noel Morris Kershaw, of Koeko, Moutere, Nelson, NZ, — Penelope Sue, *b* 1955: *m* 1974, Lindsay Graeme Everingham, of Lot 1, Meryla St, Couridjah, NSW 2571, Australia, and has issue living, Nicholas James *b* 1975, Malika *b* 1978.

Grandchildren of late John Rochfort Blakiston, son of Maj John Blakiston, 27th Regt, 2nd son of 2nd baronet:—
Issue of late John Francis Blakiston, CIE, *b* 1882, *d* 1965: *m* 1st, 1918 (*m diss* 1930), Paula, da of late E. Allen Howard, Bar-at-law; 2ndly, 1937, Margaret Dora, who *d* 1991, el da of Rev G. A. Ward-Jackson, R of Rousham, with Lower Heyford, Oxford:—
(By 2nd *m*) John Alan Cubitt (Grove House, Lydiard Millicent, nr Swindon, Wilts SN5 9LP), *b* 1938: Lt-Col 13th/18th R Hus: *m* 1975, Sally Anne, da of Lt-Col John David Logan Dickson, MC, RHA (*see* E Westmorland, colls), and has issue living, John William Matthew, *b* 1982, — Caroline Mary, *b* 1979, — Emma Elizabeth, *b* 1981. —— Susan Anne Margaret, *b* 1940.

—— Jane Mary Dora Helen, *b* 1944: *m* 1st, 1968 (*m diss* 1978), Richard Parker; 2ndly, 1991, Edward Peter Jonathan Darmady, and has issue living (by 1st *m*), Nycolas Sebastian Robert Blakiston, *b* 1970, — Venetia Clare Rosalind, *b* 1969.

Grandchildren of late Capt Richard Blakiston-Houston, son of late Capt John Blakiston-Houston, eldest son of late Richard Bayly Blakiston-Houston (who assumed by Royal Licence 1843 the additional surname of Houston), 5th son of 2nd baronet:—
Issue of late Col John Matthew Blakiston-Houston, DL, *b* 1898, *d* 1984: *m* 1931, Lettice Arden, who *d* 1982, da of Henry Gervas Stobart, of Thornton Hall, Thornton-le-Dale, Yorkshire:—

Richard Patrick (Beltrim Castle, Gortin, co Tyrone; Roddens, Ballywater, co Down), *b* 1948; *ed* Eton, and RAC, Cirencester; ARICS 1972; JP and DL co Down and High Sheriff 1989: *m* 1988, Lucinda Mary Lavinia, da of Lt Cdr Theodore Bernard Peregrine Hubbard, RN (ret), of Thurston Croft, Thurston, Bury St Edmunds, Suffolk (*see* Norfolk, D), and has issue living, Jack Peregrine, *b* 1989, — Christopher George, *b* 1991, — Leticia Sadhbh Miriam, *b* 1993. —— Mary Bridget, *b* 1932: *m* 1956, Gavin Rowan Hamilton, of The Horse Mill, Stenton, Dunbar, E Lothian, and has issue living, James (Hamish) John, *b* 1961: *m* 1990, Venetia E., da of John Carter, of High Holms, Steel, Hexham, Northumberland, and has issue living, Frederick John *b* 1993, — Patrick Gawaine, *b* 1964, — Catherine Nicola Blanche, *b* 1957: *m* 1987, Bartholomew Evan Eric Smith, and has issue (*see* E Northesk, colls). —— Anne (*Lady Hallifax*), *b* 1934: *m* 1962, Adm Sir David John Hallifax, KCB, KCVO, KBE, RN (*see* Hughes, Bt, *cr* 1773 1972-73 Edn), who *d* 1992, of The Brew House, Englefield, Reading, Berks RG7 5EN, and has had issue, Thomas Ronald, *b* 1965, — Matthew William Hughes, *b* 1967; *ed* Edinburgh Univ; drowned in a boating accident 1989, — Louisa Kate, *b* 1964: *m* 1993, Hugo Roderick Charles Burnand, son of Peter Vere Burnand. —— Prudence, *b* 1936: *m* 1964, John Archibald Douglas-Menzies, of Mounteagle, Fearn, Ross-shire, and has issue living, John William, *b* 1966, — Andrew Edward, *b* 1968, — James, *b* 1970. —— Elizabeth, *b* 1939: *m* 1973, Michael Geoffrey Minton Haines, of 82A Mortimer Rd, N1, and has issue living, Francis Christopher Minton, *b* 1975, — Richard Walter Minton, *b* 1977, — Rosaline Marion Minton, *b* 1979. —— Patience Victoria, *b* 1944: *m* 1979, Ron Long, of Twiglees, Boreland, Dumfriesshire, and has issue living, Joshua, *b* 1975, — Daniel, *b* 1977.

Grandsons of late Ralph Blakiston, eldest son of late John Richard Blakiston, son of late Rev Peyton Blakiston, MD, FRS, 6th son of 2nd baronet:—
Issue of late Rev Robert Ralph Christian Blakiston, *b* 1890, *d* 1983: *m* 1929, Winifred Muriel, who *d* 1988, yr da of late John Frost, of Ripley, Derbys:—

John Robert, *b* 1931; *ed* Haileybury: *m* 1960, Carol Helen, yst da of John C. Durham, of Anniswood, Warninglid, Sussex, and has issue living, Michèle Anne, *b* 1964, — Rachel Jane, *b* 1966. *Residence* – Wood Sorrel Cottage, Nutley, Sussex.
Issue of late John Horace Blakiston, *b* 1897, *d* 1982: *m* 1928, Winifred Kathleen Maybank, who *d* 1988, da of Archie William Webb, of Banstead, Surrey:—

David, *b* 1934; *ed* Haileybury, and Loughborough Coll (BSc, MIMechE, CEng): *m* 1962, Joanna Averil, da of Cecil Green, of Kingsthorpe, Northampton, and has issue living, John, *b* 1967; BCom, ACMA, — Anne, *b* 1970; BA , — Carol Clare, *b* 1972. *Residence* – Tara, 65 Curley Hill Rd, Lightwater, Surrey GU18 5YH.

Grandchildren of late Matthew Folliott Blakiston, son of late Rev Peyton Blakiston, MD, FRS (ante):—
Issue of late Rochfort Folliott Blakiston, *b* 1860, *d* 1949: *m* 1st, 1907, Ellen Kate, who *d* 1929, only da of late George Greenleaf, of Great George Street, Westminster, SW; 2ndly, 1930, Elizabeth Lilian Diana, who *d* 1976, el da of Rev David Jones, V of Goodwick, Pembrokeshire:—

(By 2nd *m*) Digby Rochfort David (Yet y Gors, Seleddau, Fishguard, Dyfed), *b* 1931: late Lt RN: *m* 1959, Dorothea Irene Louise Walser, and has issue living, Matthew Simon Rochfort, *b* 1964, — Louise, *b* 1961: *m* 198-, Andrew P. M. Jenkins, of Gelliwernfawr, Felindre, nr Swansea, yr son of Dr John Richard Everett Jenkins, of Michaelston-le-Pit, S Glamorgan, — Caroline, *b* 1962. —— Michael Peyton Folliott (90 York Mansions, Prince of Wales Drive, SW11) *b* 1933; *ed* Trin Coll, Oxford (MA); *m* 1973, Mrs Fanny Marie Francis, el da of Henri Roquette, of Lille, France.

This is a branch of the family of Blakiston, of Blakiston, co Durham, in which two baronetcies were conferred in 1615 and 1642, expiring respectively in 1619 and 1713. The 1st baronet of the present creation was Sheriff of London 1753, and Lord Mayor 1760.

BLANE (UK) 1812, of Blanefield, Ayrshire (Extinct 1916)

Com Sir CHARLES RODNEY BLANE, RN, 4th and last *Baronet*.

DAUGHTER LIVING OF FOURTH BARONET

Helen Mary, *b* 1913: *m* 1940, William Robert Tomkinson, TD, late Capt Middx Regt, who *d* 1980, and has issue living, Robert Charles (Home Farm, Wappenham, nr Towcester, Northants), *b* 1941: *m* 1968, Joanna Sally Hastings, and has issue living, James Robert *b* 1970, Simon William *b* 1972, — David Edward (Stonecrop, Rectory Lane, Buckland, Betchworth, Surrey RH3 7BL), *b* 1945: *m* 1976 (*m diss* 1993), Catherine Jane Monica Austen, da of late Lt-Col Austen Bertram Knight, MC, of Pamber End, Basingstoke, Hants, and has issue living, Elizabeth Helen Beatrice *b* 1978, Catherine Amy Mary *b* 1980, — Virginia Susan, *b* 1943: *m* 1964, Maj-Gen Andrew Evans, late 5th R Inniskilling Dragoon Gds, and has issue living, Lucinda Emma Katherine *b* 1967, Alexandra Louise Harriet *b* 1969, — Diana Helena (twin), *b* 1943: *m* 1969, David Rainald Lewthwaite, and has issue living (*see* Lewthwaite, Bt). *Residence* – Stonecrop, Rectory Lane, Buckland, Betchworth, Surrey.

BLENNERHASSETT (UK) 1809, of Blennerville, co Kerry

Sir (MARMADUKE) ADRIAN FRANCIS WILLIAM BLENNERHASSETT, 7th *Baronet*; *b* 25 May 1940; *s* his father, *Lieut Sir* MARMADUKE CHARLES HENRY JOSEPH CASIMIR, RNVR, 1940; *ed* McGill Univ, Imperial Coll, London (MSc) and Cranfield Business Sch (MBA): *m* 1972, Carolyn Margaret, da of late Gilbert Brown, and has issue.

Arms – Gules, a chevron ermine between three dolphins embowed argent. **Crest** – A wolf sejant proper.
Residence – 54 Staveley Rd, Chiswick, W4 3ES.

SON LIVING

CHARLES HENRY MARMADUKE, *b* 18 July 1975.

DAUGHTER LIVING

Celina Mary Charlotte, *b* 1973.

COLLATERAL BRANCHES LIVING

Grandchildren of late Capt William Lewis Rowland Paul Sebastian Blennerhassett, DSO, OBE, yst son of 4th baronet:—
Issue of late Maj (Casimir Paul Francis) Rowland Blennerhassett, *b* 1911, *d* 1993: *m* 1945, Elizabeth Charlotte Josephine (10 Cavendish Court, 38 St George's Rd, Paston Place, Kemptown, Brighton, Sussex BN3 1FU), da of late Com Gregory Stapleton, RN (*see* D Norfolk, colls), and widow of Maj Francis John Angus Skeet:—

Fortune helps the brave

John Rowland, *b* 1952. —— Rosanna Frances, *b* 1946.

Granddaughter of late Rowland Ponsonby Blennerhassett, son of late Richard Francis Blennerhassett, son of late Rowland Blennerhassett, 4th son of 1st baronet:—
Issue of late Richard Francis Ponsonby Blennerhassett, *b* 1879, *d* 1938: *m* 1914, Silvia, who *d* 1957, only da of late Frederic W. H. Myers, of Leckhampton, Cambridge:—
Diana Mary Ponsonby, *b* 1916: *m* 1939, Richard John Moreton Goold-Adams CBE, only son of late Maj Sir Hamilton Goold-Adams, GCMG, CB. *Residence* – 33 Great Pulteney St, Bath, Avon BA2 4BX.
The ancestors of this family were long seated in Cumberland, and took their name from the township of Blennerhassett in that co. Members of the family represented Carlisle in nearly every Parliament from Richard II to James I, and later frequently represented either Kerry co or the borough of Tralee. Robert Blennerhassett settled in co Kerry in the reign of James I. The 4th baronet, Rt Hon Sir Rowland, sat as MP for Galway (L) 1865-74, and for co Kerry 1880-85. The 5th baronet, Sir Arthur Charles Francis Bernard, held various positions in the Indian Civil Service ending as JP for the Central Provinces. He *d* 1915. The 6th baronet, Lieut Sir Marmaduke Charles Henry Joseph Casimir was *ka* 25 May 1940 serving in HMS *Greyhound* at Dunkirk.

BLOIS (E) 1686, of Grundisburgh Hall, Suffolk
(Name pronounced "Bloyss")

Sir CHARLES NICHOLAS GERVASE BLOIS, 11th *Baronet*: *b* 25 Dec 1939; *s* his father, *Capt Sir* GERVASE RALPH EDMUND, MC, 1968; *ed* Harrow and Trin Coll, Dublin: *m* 1967, Celia Helen Mary, only da of late Cyril George Francis Pritchett, CBE, of Mayfield, and has issue.

Arms – Gules, a bend vair between two fleurs-de-lis argent. **Crest** – A gauntlet proper holding a fleur-de-lis argent.
Residence – Red House, Westleton, Saxmundham, Suffolk.

SON LIVING

ANDREW CHARLES DAVID, *b* 7 Feb 1971.

DAUGHTER LIVING

Helen Janet, *b* 1974.

Je me fie en Dieu
I trust in God

BROTHER LIVING

Rodney John Derek (Cockfield Hall, Yoxford, Suffolk), *b* 1941; *ed* Harrow; High Sheriff Suffolk 1989: *m* 1968 (*m diss* 1992), Lady (Elizabeth) Caroline (Elinor Evelyn) Giffard, da of 3rd Earl of Halsbury, and has issue living, Camilla Frances Elizabeth, *b* 1970, — Susanna Gillian Caroline, *b* 1972.

SISTER LIVING

Gillian Frances Audrey (Foxcote Grange, Andoversford, Cheltenham, Glos), *b* 1943: *m* 1st, 1965 (*m diss* 1970), Hugh Christopher Riddle; 2ndly, 1975, Gilbert John Chalk, of Rickmansworth, Herts (*see* E Shrewsbury, colls), and has issue living, (by 2nd *m*) Alexander John Gervase, *b* 1976, — Christopher Harry Gilbert, *b* 1985, — Nicola Elizabeth, *b* 1978.

AUNT LIVING (*Daughter of 9th baronet*)

Christian Frances, *b* 1902: *m* 1st, 1928 (*m diss* 1940), Edward Archibald Fraser Harding; 2ndly, 1940, Geoffrey Henry Cecil Bing, QC, of Stanhope, Yoxford, Suffolk, and has issue living, (by 2nd *m*) Inigo Geoffrey, *b* 1944, — Richard, *b* 1946.

MOTHER LIVING

Audrey Winifred, only da of late Col Harry Johnson, DSO, of Boden Hall, Ches: *m* 1938 (*m diss* 1948), Capt Sir Gervase Ralph Edmund Blois, MC (later Sir Gervase Blois, 10th Bt), who *d* 1968. *Residence* – Foxcote Cottage, Andoversford, Glos.

COLLATERAL BRANCHES LIVING

Grandchildren of late Maj Eardley Steuart BROOKE, TD (infra):—
    Issue of late Thomas Eardley Blois BROOKE, *b* 1918, *d* 1986: *m* 1948, Joy Mary (Cresborough, Rhos, Haverfordwest, Pembrokeshire), only da of Maj-Gen Robert Stedman Lewis, CB, OBE:—
Thomas Robin Eardley BLOIS-BROOKE (Orchard Cottage, Orchard Lane, Stewkley, Leighton Buzzard, Beds LU7 0HS), *b* 1951; *ed* Wellington: *m* 1978, Philippa de Courcy, da of John Fryer, and has issue living, Thomas Eardley, *b* 1982, — Edward Charles, *b* 1984. —— Jennifer Mary, *b* 1949: *m* 1980, Guy William Meakin Farmiloe, of Heatherbank, Sheepsetting Lane, Heathfield, E Sussex TN21 0UY, yr son of Leslie Farmiloe, of Saint Maximin, 30700 Uzes, France, and has issue living, Toby Nicholas, *b* 1987. —— Elizabeth Anne, *b* 1953: *m* 1986, Michael John Read, of 91 Camberwell Gr, SE5 8JH, elder son of T. H. Read, of Northlands, Fishbourne, Chichester, Sussex, and has issue living, Harry Thomas, *b* 1987, — Alice Louise, *b* 1990.

Issue of late Major Eardley Steuart BROOKE, TD, 3rd son of 8th baronet, *b* 1869, *d* 1955, who assumed by Roy licence 1931 for himself and issue the surname and arms of Brooke in lieu of his patronymic: *m* 1916, Violet Mary Magdalene, who *d* 1945, da of Thomas Sproat, of Port Mary, Kirkcudbright, and Valparaiso:—
Michael Steuart BLOIS-BROOKE, RD, *b* 1919; is Lieut-Com RNR; re-assumed by deed poll 1953, the surname of Blois in addition to and before that of Brooke: *m* 1949, Mary, yr da of Cecil Harvey Mead, of Oak House, Crawley Down, Sussex, and has issue living, Mark Harvey, *b* 1954, — Susan Penelope, *b* 1950: *m* 1973, Nigel Robert Clifford (PO Box 190, George Town, Grand Cayman, Cayman Is), and has issue living, Joanna Mary *b* 1976, Louise Rosemary *b* 1979, — Diana Mary, *b* 1959. *Residence* – St Austin's House, Curtis Lane, Sheringham, Norfolk.

Grandchildren of late Maj Eardley Steuart Brooke, TD (ante):—
    Issue of late Robert John Brooke, BL, *b* 1923, *d* 1963: *m* 1949, Ann Hamerton Gordon (St Aidan's, Morebattle, Kelso), el da of late Capt Francis Gordon Troup, of Dunbennan:—
Alastair John BLOIS-BROOKE (Pen Hay, Bevington, nr Berkeley, Glos), *b* 1950: *m* 1989, Julia, da of J. A. Burgess, of Bristol, and has issue living, Alexander David, *b* 1991, — Christopher John *b* 1993. —— Ian Steuart BLOIS, *b* 1953: *m* 1991, Clare, da of late Peter Champkin, of Sussex, and has issue living, Katharine Ann, *b* 1993. —— (Katharine) Margaret, *b* 1961: *m* 1989, Ian W. Thomson, 2nd son of late Lewis Thomson, of Canberra, Australia, and has issue living, Robert Lewis, *b* 1994, — Amy Blois *b* 1991.

Granddaughters of late Lieut-Col Dudley George Blois, DSO, RFA (infra):—
    Issue of late Wing Com John Dudley Blois, RAF Regt (late Major Irish Guards), *b* 1915, *d* 1954: *m* 1948, Elizabeth Catharine, who *d* 1993, da of Rear-Adm Sir Wellwood George Courtenay Maxwell, KBE, CMG (B Chesham):—
(Elizabeth) Frances Moyra (6 St Augustine's Mansions, Bloomburg St, SW1V 2RG), *b* 1949. —— Sarah Jane, *b* 1951: *m* 1982, Miles Tobias (Toby) Ward, of Rye House, Silchester, nr Reading, Berks, yr son of late P. T. Ward, and of Mrs Mark Chaytor, of Aston Towers, Coal Aston, Derby's, and has issue living, Lomax Blois, *b* 1984, — Sam Philip, *b* 1986, — Thomas Dudley, *b* 1990.

Issue of late Lieut-Col Dudley George Blois, DSO, RFA, 5th son of 8th baronet, *b* 1875, *ka* 1916: *m* 1914, Georgiana Isabella Frances, who *d* 1967, da of late Adm Sir Compton Edward Domvile, GCB, GCVO (Peel, Bt, *cr* 1800, colls):—
Jane Elizabeth Georgiana Joan (26 Manchester St, WIM 5PG), *b* 1916; formerly 3rd Officer WRNS.

Issue of late Rev Gervase Vanneck Blois, yst son of 8th baronet, *b* 1881, *d* 1961: *m* 1914, Hon Hester Murray Pakington, who *d* 1973, da of 3rd Baron Hampton:—
Anthony Gervase, DFC, *b* 1918; *ed* Wellington Coll, and Phillips Acad, Andover, Mass, USA; formerly Flight-Lieut, RAF Vol Reserve: *m* 1957, Ivy Tucker, who *d* 1983, da of William Charles Bell. *Residence* – 19 Bilton Road, Rugby. —— David Pakington, *b* 1923; Capt MN: *m* 1951, Joan, da of late Capt L. R. Brock, and has issue living, Michael David Stuart (PO Box 595, 2149 Riverclub, Republic of South Africa), *b* 1955: *m* 1983, Heather, da of James W. Davidson, of Buccleuch, nr Johannesburg, S Africa, and has issue living, Stuart Murray *b* 1992, Fiona Claire *b* 1994, — Angela Claire, *b* 1958: *m* 1982, Steven Russell Tuhey, of 2 River Lane, Randalls Road, Leatherhead, Surrey. *Residence* – 34 Strawberry Vale, Twickenham, Middx, TW1 4RU. —— Evelyn Hester (*Baroness MacLeod of Borve*), *b* 1915; *cr Baroness MacLeod of Borve* (Life Baroness) 1971 (see that title). —— Elizabeth Mary, *b* 1921; formerly Subaltern ATS: *m* 1953, Francis George Smith, of 8681, Shepherd Way, Delta, British Columbia, Canada, and has issue living, Fiona Elizabeth, *b* 1956, — Gillian Hester, *b* 1958, — Jennifer Margaret, *b* 1962.

Issue of late Lieut-Col William Thornhill Blois, brother of 8th baronet, *b* 1841, *d* 1889, *m* 1874, Fanny Elizabeth, who *d* 1912, el da of late William Arkwright, of Sutton Scarsdale, Chesterfield:—
Ernest Pierrepoint, *b* 1880: *m* 1900, Lilian Emily, who *d* 1918, da of J. W. Moore, and has issue living, Trevor Galfridus, *b* 1904, — Esmé Ernestine, *b* 1901, — Agnes Mary, *b* 1903, — Fanny Elizabeth, *b* 1911, — Nancy Avril, *b* 1918. —— Basil Frederic, *b* 1881; *ed* Wellington Coll; formerly Capt RFA (TF): *m* 19—, Kathleen, who *d* 1922, da of late Robert Overell. —— Geoffrey Stephen, *b* 1884.

Galfridus de Blois held lands in Walpole, Suffolk, *temp* Richard I. The family resided at Norton, Suffolk, till *temp* King Henry VII, and at Grundisburgh Hall, Suffolk. They removed in 1693 to Cockfield Hall, which is still in possession of a member of the Blois family.

BLOMEFIELD (UK) 1807, of Attleborough, co Norfolk

Sir (THOMAS) CHARLES (PEREGRINE) BLOMEFIELD 6th *Baronet, b* 24 July 1948; *s* his father, *Lt-Cdr Sir* THOMAS EDWARD PEREGRINE, 1984; *ed* Wellington, and Mansfield Coll, Oxon; is a Co Dir: *m* 1975, Georgina Geraldine, da of late Cdr Charles Over, RN, of Lugger End, Portscatho, Cornwall, and has issue.

Arms – Sable, on a chevron argent a branch of laurel between two bomb shells fired proper; and on a canton or, a spear's head imbrued proper. **Crest** – Issuant from a mural crown argent a demi-heraldic tiger azure, armed and tufted or, collared argent, and holding a sword broken in the middle proper.
Address – c/o Bank of Scotland, 38 Threadneedle St, EC3.

SON LIVING

THOMAS WILLIAM PEREGRINE, *b* 16 July 1983.

DAUGHTERS LIVING

Emma Georgina, *b* 1980. ——— Harriet Elizabeth, *b* 1986.

WIDOW LIVING OF FIFTH BARONET

GINETTE (*Ginette, Lady Blomefield*), formerly wife of George Harting, and da of late Dr Raphael Massart, of 15 Boulevard des Invalides, Paris: *m* 1947, Lt-Cdr Sir Thomas Edward Peregrine Blomefield, 5th Bt, RNVR, who *d* 1984.

COLLATERAL BRANCHES LIVING

Grandson of late Lt-Col Wilmot Blomefield, OBE, RE (infra):—
Issue of late His Honour Judge Peregrine Maitland Blomefield, *b* 1917, *d* 1988: *m* 1941, Angela Catherine, yst da of late Maj Geoffrey Hugh Shenley Crofton:—
Adam Peregrine Horatio, *b* 1946; *ed* Repton, and Trin Coll, Oxford: *m* 1st, 1970 (*m diss* 1976), Esther Margaret, da of Vaughan Lewis, of Swansea; 2ndly, 1981, Gertraud Elisabeth, da of Heinrich Tophinke, of Mörnsheim, and has issue living, (by 1st wife) Anna Claudia, *b* 1972, — (by 2nd wife) Georges Peregrine, *b* 1982, — Nora Katharina, *b* 1976. *Residence* – Chaussée de Namur 73, B-1315 Incourt, Belgium.

Issue of late Lieut-Col Wilmot Blomefield, OBE, RE, yst son of 4th baronet, *b* 1878, *d* 1926: *m* 1907, Jessie Leila, who *d* 1976, only da of late William A. Hodges, JP, of East Bridgeford, Notts:—
Rosemary Eardley (*Lady Hayman*), *b* 1914: *m* 1942, Sir Peter Telford Hayman, KCMG, CVO, MBE, who *d* 1992, of Uxmore House, Checkendon, Oxon, and has issue living, Christopher Wilmot Arden, *b* 1947: *m* 1979, Joanna, da of James O'Reilly, of Ballyfaskin, Ballylanders, co Limerick, and has issue living, Daniel Peter James *b* 1980, — Virginia Rosemary, *b* 1944: *m* 1974, Michael Jerrold Philipson, and has issue living, Stephen Ralph Peter *b* 1977, Claire Leila *b* 1980.

Grandson of late Edward Hugh Blomefield, MVO, son of Rev Samuel Edward Blomefield, 3rd son of 2nd baronet:—
Issue of late Allan Herbert Blomefield, *b* 1891; *d* 1978: *m* 1935, Olive Nesfield Cookson, who *d* 1980:—
Roger Stanley (41 Forresters Rd, Burbage, Hinckley), *b* 1937; LBIPP, AMPA: *m* 1959, Eve Kathleen Bartlett, and has issue living Adrian Paul, *b* 1964: *m* 1994, Roseann Kane, — Dawn Lesley, *b* 1960.

Granddaughters of late Lawrence Woodyeare Blomefield (infra):—
Issue of late John Woodyeare Blomefield, *b* 1903, *d* 1967: *m* 1927, Dorothea Mae, who *d* 1981, da of A. Farr:—
Anne Shirley (5 Loerie Mews, Loerie Lane, Beacon Bay, E London 5241, S Africa), *b* 1927: *m* 1st, 1947 (*m diss* 1966), Pieter Barendse Botha Van Gend; 2ndly, 1969, Cecil James Meyers, who *d* 1992, and has issue living, (by 1st *m*) Nardi Anne, *b* 1949: *m* 1971, William Henry Raubenheimer, — Cornelia Mae, *b* 1952: *m* 1983, Terence Anthony Carroll, and has issue living, Byron Terence Anthony *b* 1986, — (by 2nd *m*) Donovan James, *b* 1972. ——— Elizabeth Jill (31 Leadwood Place, Beacon Bay, E London 5241, S Africa), *b* 1931: *m* 1st, 1954, John Charsley Meyer, who *d* 1979; 2ndly, 1989 (*m diss* 1990), David Edward Hugh Davies, and has issue living (by 1st *m*), Mark William, *b* 1955: *m* 1977, Noël Lynn Cotton, and has issue living, Lindi Elaine *b* 1979, Julie Elizabeth *b* 1981, Kristy Lynn *b* 1983, — Bruce Woodyeare, *b* 1957, — Colin John, *b* 1959: *m* 1982, Rosemary Anne Seeney, and has issue living, Ross John *b* 1984, James Colin *b* 1987.

Granddaughter of late Rev John Blomefield, 4th son of 2nd baronet:—
Issue of late Lawrence Woodyeare Blomefield, *b* 1870, *d* 1956: *m* 1899, Celia Nora, who *d* 1961, da of late A. B. Caldwell:—
Frances Celia, *b* 1901: *m* 1922, Dr Arnold Klosser van Niekerk, dental surgeon (S Africa), who *d* 1976, and has issue living, Olive Joan (PO Box 14174, West Bank, E London 5218, S Africa), *b* 1926: *m* 1947, Kenneth Louis Clur, and has issue living, Robert Louis *b* 1955: *m* 1978, Cheryl Lynn Randall (and has issue living, Greggory Louis *b* 1981, Tarryn Lynn *b* 1985), Linda Anne *b* 1947: *m* 1967, Christian John Flemmer (and has issue living, Wendy Ann *b* 1970, Caryn *b* 1976, Angela *b* 1978), Beverley Louise *b* 1952: *m* 1978, Richard Charles Bishop (and has issue living, Russell Allan *b* 1984, Kristi-Lee *b* 1983) Linda Ann *b* 1948, Beverley Louise *b* 1952, — Valerie Ellen (17 Greenfields, Pinewood Rd, Rondebosch, Cape 7700, S Africa), *b* 1928: *m* 1948, Garth Cox Latimer, who *d* 1966, and has issue living, Dean Andrew *b* 1949: *m* 1979 (*m diss* 1987), Susan Coetzee (and has issue living, Tamara Anne *b* 1980, Caralyn Grace *b* 1982), Michael Garth *b* 1951: *m* 1977, Jacqueline Barbara Forbes (and has issue living, Gareth Ross *b* 1982, Kerry-Anne *b* 1984), Alan John *b* 1953: *m* 1977, Anne Muriel Sabberton (and has had issue, Gregg *b* 1983 *d* 1986, Brennan John *b* 1987, Peta Anne *b* 1981).

Granddaughter of late Rev Robert Allan Blomefield, 5th son of 2nd baronet:—
Issue (by 2nd *m*) of late Rev George Pinchin Allan Blomefield, *b* 1843: *m* 1st, 1879, Madeleine Amelia, who *d* 1896, da of late Rev Alfred Bligh Hill, Vicar of St Paul's, Tiverton; 2ndly, 1898, Kathleen Ruth, who *d* 1926, da of late Lewis Stephen Woodthorpe, of Glazenwood, Braintree, Essex:—
May Dorothy Wilmot, *b* 1901. *Residence* – St Mary's Home, Stone, Staffs.

Grandson of late Rev Charles David Blomefield, 6th son of 2nd baronet:—
Issue of late Charles Allan Blomefield, *b* 1871, *d* 1940: *m* 1902, Minnie, who *d* 1964, el da of Loftus Otway Burrowes:—

Allan Arthur, *b* 1903; *ed* Witwatersrand Univ (BSc 1925); is Principal of English Med Sch, Lichtenburg, Transvaal: *m* 1930, Dorothy Jane, da of A. T. Adams, and has issue living, Justine, *b* 1931, — Jennifer, *b* 1934.

 Grandsons of late Charles Allan Blomefield (ante):—
 Issue of late Loftus Charles Blomefield, *b* 1905, *d* 1981: *m* 1937, Una Innes (214 Zwartkop Rd, Pietermaritzburg, Natal 3201, S Africa), da of J. A. Munro:—
John Alan (214 Zwartkop Rd, Pietermaritzburg, Natal, S Africa), *b* 1942: *m* 1967, Norma Ann, el da of B. A. R. Schefermann, and has issue living, Peter Annand, *b* 1970, — Monica Ann, *b* 1968. —— Thomas Loftus (24 Harewood Av, Helderberg Estate, Somerset West, Cape Province, S Africa), *b* 1944; *ed* Univ of Natal (MSc Agric 1980): *m* 1980, Pamela Anne, 2nd da of Dr J. T. Sonnenberg, and has issue living, Stephen Lyle, *b* 1989, — Jessica Rosanne, *b* 1986. —— Margaret Otway, *b* 1938: *m* 1962, Allan John Nicol, of Nottingham Rd, Natal, S Africa, and has issue living, Deborah Margaret, *b* 1968, — Jacqueline Jennifer, *b* 1970.
The 1st baronet, Maj-Gen Sir Thomas, commanded the Artillery in the expedition to Copenhagen 1807. The 4th Baronet, Sir Thomas Wilmot Peregrine, acted as Private Sec to Successive Pres of Board of Trade (Baron Stanley of Preston, and Sir Michael Hicks-Beach, Bt), and was Assist Sec to Board of Trade (Finance Depart) 1901-8.

LYNCH-BLOSSE (I) 1622, of Galway

Sir RICHARD HELY LYNCH-BLOSSE, 17th *Baronet*, *b* 26 Aug 1953: *s* his father, *Sir* DAVID EDWARD, 1971; *ed* Welwyn Garden City, and R Free Hosp (Univ of London); MRCS, LRCP 1978; MB, BS 1979; DRCOG 1983; MRCGP 1984; Capt RAMC: *m* 1976, Cara Lynne, only da of George Longmore Sutherland, of St Ives, Cambs, and has issue.

Arms – Azure, a chevron between three trefoils slipped or. **Crest** – A lynx passant coward argent.
Residence – The Surgery, Clifton Hampden, Oxfordshire OX14 3EL.

DAUGHTERS LIVING

Katherine Helen, *b* 1983. —— Hannah Victoria, *b* 1985.

SISTERS LIVING

Caroline Susan, *b* 1951: *m* 1st, 1978 (*m diss* 1984), Christopher Elliot Stuart, only son of late Anthony Stuart, of Birstall, Leics; 2ndly, 1987, Steven Rollnick, of 67 Conway Rd, Cardiff and has issue living, (by 1st *m*) Josephine Rachel Blosse, *b* 1979, — (by 2nd *m*) Jacob Julian, *b* 1987. —— Bridget Ruth, *b* 1958.

AUNT LIVING (*Sister of 16th baronet*)

Sylvia Diana, *b* (*posthumous*) 1928: *m* 1958, Maj Robert Basil Sullivan-Tailyour, late Worcestershire & Sherwood Foresters Regt, of The Curate's Egg, Dymocks Lane, Sutton Veny, Warminster, Wilts, and has issue living, James Robert, *b* 1960, — Sarah Jane, *b* 1963.

Neither rashly nor timidly

DAUGHTER LIVING OF FIFTEENTH BARONET

Susan Frances, *b* 1917; 1939-45 War with WAAF: *m* 1942, Wing-Cdr Brian Noble, RAF (ret), of Old Inn Cottage, Inwardleigh, Okehampton, Devon, and has issue living, Nigel Brian, *b* 1947; Lt-Col RAPC: *m* 1974, Diana Mary Fogg, and has issue living, James Colin *b* 1975, Charles Christopher *b* 1977, — Elizabeth Hilary, *b* 1945: *m* 1974, Richard Charles Perry, and has issue living, Charles Edward Bruce *b* 1978, Katherine Jane Susannah *b* 1979.

DAUGHTER LIVING OF THIRTEENTH BARONET (*By 2nd marriage*)

Frances Clodagh, *b* 1936: *m* 1960, Paul Richard Nevell, and has issue living, Christopher Paul *b* 1965, — James Robert, *b* 1968.

WIDOW LIVING OF SIXTEENTH BARONET

ELIZABETH (*Elizabeth, Lady Lynch-Blosse*), da of late Thomas Harold Payne, of Welwyn Garden City: *m* 1950, Sir David Edward Lynch-Blosse, 16th Bt, who *d* 1971.

COLLATERAL BRANCHES LIVING

 Grandson of late Capt Edward Falconer Lynch-Blosse, uncle of 13th baronet, and son of late Very Rev Henry Lynch-Blosse, Dean of Llandaff, 2nd son of 8th baronet:—
 Issue of late Maj Cecil Eagles Lynch-Blosse, *b* 1890; *d* 1966: *m* 1st, 1915 (*m diss* 1940), Dorothy Delahaize, who *d* 1962, da of late Rev John Delahaize Ouvry R of Haydon, Sherborne; 2ndly, 1943, his cousin, Violet Emily, who *d* 1976, da of late Francis Traherne Lynch-Blosse:—
(By 1st *m*) (ERIC) HUGH, OBE (17 Queens Acre, Newnham, Glos GL14 1DJ); *b* 30 July 1917; *ed* Blundell's, and RAF Coll; Group Capt RAF (ret); OBE (Mil) 1952: *m* 1946, Jean Evelyn, da of late Cdr Andrew Robertson Hair, RD, RNR, of Edinburgh, and has issue living, David Ian, *b* 14 Jan 1950; *ed* Blundells: *m* 1st, 1984, Mrs Barbara Susan McLaughlin, who *d* 1985; 2ndly, 1989, Nadine, da of J. Baddeley, and has issue living (by 2nd *m*) Oliver Daniel *b* 12 Nov 1989, Jessica Hannah *b* 1992, — Valerie Jean, *b* 1947: *m* 1974, Irvine Cormack, of Fieldridge, Broombarn Lane, Great Missenden, Bucks.

 Grandchildren of late Maj Cecil Eagles Lynch-Blosse (ante):—
 Issue of late Anthony Cecil Lynch-Blosse, *b* 1919, *d* 1991: *m* 1st, 1942 (*m diss* 1946), Margaret, da of late Maj-Gen David Graeme Ridgeway, CB, DSO, of Kenya; 2ndly, 1948, Marjorie Elizabeth (PO Box 1602, Lunenburg, Nova Scotia B0J 2CO, Canada), da of late James Joseph William Morris, of Portland, Maine, USA:—

(By 2nd *m*) Michael Anthony (2111 Redbud Court, Edmond, Oklahoma 73013, USA), *b* 1950: *m* 1977, Barbara Lorraine, da of late Jack Haberthur, of St Augustine, Florida, USA, and has issue living, Danielle Bryann, *b* 1981, — Shannon Elizabeth, *b* 1983, — Heather Michelle, *b* 1985, — Brittany Noel, *b* 1989. —— Sean James (178 Amesbury Line Rd, Haverhill, Massachusetts 01830, USA), *b* 1960; has issue living, Sean James SANTIAGO, *b* 1984. —— Sharon Delahaize (Mountain Club, Bldg 12-4B, Morris Plains, NJ 07950, USA), *b* (twin) 1960.

Issue of late George Robert Lynch-Blosse, *b* 1895, *d* 1976: *m* 1929, Lucy Myra, who *d* 1988, da of Bertram Adams, of Auckland, NZ:—

Robert Edward (8 Cassandra Grove, Sunnynook, Auckland, NZ), *b* 1932: *m* 1954, Alannah Marie, da of John Donald Graham Drought, and has issue living, Robert Mark, *b* 1955, — Brendon Scott, *b* 1960, — Jennifer Sue, *b* 1957. —— Gerald Bertram (Rotorua, NZ), *b* 1936: *m* 1966, Moira Jean, da of R. B. Johns, of Auckland, NZ, and has issue living, Craig Allan, *b* 1967, — Blair Robert, *b* 1974, — Catharine Mary, *b* 1970, — Joanne Maree, *b* 1972. —— Timothy Richard (31A Coldham Crescent, St Johns Park, Auckland, NZ), *b* 1939; Snr Police Sgt (ret): *m* 1962, Joan, da of Richard Wittington, of Auckland, and has issue living, Stephen John, *b* 1964, — David Paul, *b* 1966. —— Andrew John (7 Catherine St, Onehunga, Auckland, NZ), *b* 1946: *m* 1968, Janice Marie, da of E Swinburne, and has issue living, Christopher Andrew, *b* 1972, — Timothy Nigel, *b* 1974.

The family of Lynch is of great antiquity in Connaught, being among the earliest settlers who were denominated the "Tribes of Galway". Sir Henry Lynch, 1st Bt, and Sir Robuck (Robert) Lynch, 2nd Bt, successively sat as MP for Galway. The 2nd Baronet was Mayor of Galway 1638. Sir Henry Lynch, 3rd Bt, was a Baron of the Exchequer in Ireland 1686. Sir Robert, 6th Bt, assumed the additional surname of Blosse, having *m* 1749, Elizabeth, da and heir of Francis Barker, and heir of Tobias Blosse, of Little Belstead, Suffolk.

BLOUNT (E) 1642, of Sodington, Worcestershire
(Name pronounced "Blunt")

Lux tua via mea

Thy light, my path

Sir WALTER EDWARD ALPIN (JASPER) BLOUNT, DSC, 12th *Baronet*; *b* 31 Oct 1917; *s* his father *Sir* EDWARD ROBERT, 1978; *ed* Beaumont Coll, and Sidney Sussex Coll, Camb (MA 1943); solicitor; farmer; Lt RNVR; 1939-45 War (DSC and two Bars): *m* 1954, Eileen Audrey, only da of late Hugh Blasson Carritt, and has issue.

Arms – Barry nebulée of six or and sable. **Crest** – An armed foot in the sun.
Residences – 19 St Ann's Terrace, St John's Wood, NW8 EPH; Tilkhurst, Imberhorne Lane, E Grinstead, Sussex RH19 1TY.

DAUGHTER LIVING

Nicola Jane Eileen, *b* 1955: *m* 1990, Charles Foster Glanville, son of John Foster Glanville, DSC, of Emsworth, Hants, and has issue living, Edward Foster Blount, *b* 1992, — Robert, *b* 1993.

SISTER LIVING

Diana Apollonia, *b* 1916. *Residence* – South Heathercombe, nr Manaton, Newton Abbot, Devon TQ13 9XE.

The 1st baronet suffered for his loyalty during the civil war, and was long imprisoned, first at Oxford, and afterwards in the Tower. Sir Walter Kirkham Blount, 3rd Bt, was Sheriff of Worcestershire 1687-8, and Sir Edward, 8th Bt, was High Sheriff of the same county in 1835.

BLUNDEN (I) 1766, of Castle Blunden, Kilkenny

We must yield to love

Sir PHILIP OVERINGTON BLUNDEN, 7th *Baronet*, *b* 27 Jan 1922; *s* his brother, *Lt-Cdr Sir* WILLIAM, RN, 1985; *ed* Repton; World War II 1942-45 with RN: *m* 1945, Jeanette Francesca Alexandra (WRNS), eldest da of Capt D. Macdonald, RNR, of Portree, Isle of Skye, and has issue.

Arms – Quarterly: 1st and 4th argent, ten billets four, three, two, and one, sable; 2nd and 3rd, or a lion passant-guardant per pale gules and sable. **Crests** – 1st, a demi-lion rampant per fesse sable and argent, armed and langued gules; 2nd, a griffin sergeant vert, armed, winged and beaked or.
Residence – 60 The Drive, Castletown, Celbridge, co Kildare.

SONS LIVING

HUBERT CHISHOLM, *b* 9 Aug 1948; *ed* Avoca Sch, Blackrock; 1st Bn Irish Guards: *m* 1975, Allish O'Brien, and has issue living, Edmond, *b* 31 July 1982, — Amelia, *b* 1977. —— John Maurice Patrick, *b* 1955.

DAUGHTER LIVING

Marguerite Eugenie, *b* 1967.

DAUGHTERS LIVING OF SIXTH BARONET

Sarah Vanessa, *b* 1946: *m* 1970, John Edward Spencer Perceval Maxwell, of Moore Hill, Tallow, co Waterford, son of Edward Perceval Maxwell, of Ballyclement, Tallow, co Waterford. —— Grizelda Jane, *b* 1948. —— Caroline Susan (twin), *b* 1948. —— Rowena Mary Phillida, *b* 1952: *m* 1985, Andrew Gillies Macbain, of

Cranagh Castle, Templemore, co Tipperary. —— Elizabeth Anne, *b* 1955: *m* 1985, Nicholas Bryan Marshall, of 47 Smith St, Cairns, Queensland, Australia, elder son of Bryan Marshall, of Compton House, Compton, Berks. —— Fiona Christine, *b* 1958.

WIDOW LIVING OF SIXTH BARONET

PAMELA MARY (*Pamela, Lady Blunden*), da of late John Purser, of Merton House, Dublin 6; formerly 2nd Officer WRNS: *m* 1945, Lt-Cdr Sir William Blunden, 6th Bt, RN, who *d* 1985. *Residence* – Castle Blunden, Kilkenny.

COLLATERAL BRANCH LIVING

Issue of late Eric Overington Blunden, yr son of 4th baronet, *b* 1892, *d* 1969: *m* 1918, Bridget Constable, who *d* 1980, da of late Henry George Constable Curtis:—
Josephine Bridget Annette, *b* 1926: *m* 1947, Col George Vicary Kenyon, CBE, TD, DL, who *d* 1990, of Highfields Lodge, Ware, Herts, and Pier View, Dunmore East, co Waterford, and has issue living, Robin George Blunden, *b* 1950; *ed* Charterhouse: *m* 1984, Marcia Joan, da of Hon Mr Justice John T. Ludeke, of Sydney, NSW, Australia, — Crispin Simon Vicary, *b* 1955; *ed* Charterhouse: *m* 1983, Carolyn Isabel, da of Collingwood Peter Drinkwater, of Sacombe, Ware, Herts, and Bradden, Isle of Man, — Rowena Josette Caroline, *b* 1953.
The 1st baronet was MP for Kilkenny and a distinguished member of the Irish Bar. Sir William Blunden, MB, 4th Bt, was High Sheriff of co Kilkenny 1904, and *d* 25 Oct 1923, only three days prior to his son and successor, Sir John, 5th Bt.

BLUNT (GB) 1720, of London

Sir DAVID RICHARD REGINALD HARVEY BLUNT, 12th *Baronet*; *b* 8 Nov 1938; *s* his father, *Sir* RICHARD DAVID HARVEY, 1975: *m* 1969, Sonia Tudor Rosemary, da of late Albert Edward Day, and has issue.

Arms – Per pale or and sable, barry nebuly of six counterchanged. **Crest** – Issuing out of clouds a sun in splendour charged with an eye issuing tears, all proper.
Residence – 74 Kirkstall Rd, SW2 4HF.

DAUGHTER LIVING

Davina Angela Rosemary, *b* 1972.

HALF-SISTERS LIVING

Georgina Lavinia, *b* 1945: *m* 1981, Martin Frederick Trotter, yr son of late Maj Frederick Liddell Trotter, JP, of Mells Park, Frome, Somerset. *Residence* – Winterwell Farm, Northleach, Glos. —— Caroline Margaret *b* 1947.

AUNTS LIVING

Cecily Maud Helen, *b* 1910: *m* 1934, Robin Whitworth, of 9 Richmond Rd, Oxford OX1 2JJ, son of late Geoffrey Arundel Whitworth, CBE, FRSL, and has issue living, Anna Maureen Cecily, *b* 1945. —— Doris Julia Sybil (Old Barn, Beech Farm Rd, Sedlescombe, E Sussex TN33 0QS), *b* 1916: *m* 1945, Maj Frederick William Kennedy, Indian Army, who *d* 1972, and has issue living, Amber Julia, *b* 1946: *m* 1st, 1972 (*m diss* 1984), Rodger A. Brooks; 2ndly, 1985, David Sinclair, of Le Village, 66300 Camélas, France, — Susan Anne, *b* 1948: *m* 1976, Patrick McSwiney, of 12 Macaulay Rd, SW4, and has issue living, Luke

Thy light is my life

Frederick Patrick *b* 1984, Zoe Julia *b* 1980.

WIDOW LIVING OF ELEVENTH BARONET

MARGARET (*Margaret, Lady Blunt*), da of John H. Dean, of Duntisbourne Leer, Cirencester: *m* 1943, as his 2nd wife, Sir Richard David Harvey Blunt, 11th Bt, who *d* 1975.

COLLATERAL BRANCHES LIVING

Issue of late Charles William Lockhart Blunt, 3rd son of 8th baronet, *b* 1882, *d* 1958: *m* 1913, Lilian, who *d* 1958, da of late C. Calcutt, of Goudhurst, Kent:—
ROBIN ANTHONY (15 York House, Turk's Row, SW3; 14 Allée du Château, 31770 Colomiers, France) *b* 23 Nov 1926; *ed* Wellington Coll, CEng, MIMechE: *m* 1st, 1949 (*m diss* 1962), Sheila Stuart, da of C. Stuart Brindley; 2ndly, 1962, June Elizabeth, da of Charles Wigginton, of The Park, Duffield, and has issue living (by 1st *m*) Jonathan Stuart, *b* 1955, — (by 2nd *m*) Mark Charles, *b* 1963.

Issue of late Henry Wilfrid Blunt, yst son of 8th baronet, *b* 1887, *d* 1957, *m* 1915, Maud Etta, da of late J. Hyde:—
Gabrielle Hilda, *b* 1919: *m* 1st, 1941 (*m diss* 1950), Capt Tony Thawnton, 3rd King's Own Hussars; 2ndly, 1955 (*m diss* 1972), Julian Bond, and has issue living, (by 1st *m*) Paul John Anthony BOND, *b* 1946, adopted 1955 by his stepfather, Julian Bond, whose surname he assumed; has issue living (by Jenny Desmond), Laurence Jack *b* 1983, Alice Pearl Sweetpea *b* 1981, — Nicholas Peter BOND, *b* 1947; adopted 1955 by his stepfather, whose surname he assumed; W/Cdr RAF & RNZAF (ret 1994): *m* 1970, Diane Christine Edwards, and has issue living, Karen Kirsten *b* 1972, Alexis Alison *b* 1977, — (by 2nd *m*) Stella Mary, *b* 1956. *Residence* – 3 Gingerbread Lane, Hawkhurst, Kent.

Grandson of late Sir Edward Arthur Henry Blunt, KCIE, OBE, elder son of late Capt Francis Theophilus Blunt (infra):—
Issue of late Lt-Col John Edward Chicheley Blunt, RA, *b* 1907, *d* 1988: *m* 1936, Margaret (Appletree Cottage, North Carr Farm, Terrington, York YO6 4PN), da of R. Whiteley, of Heath, Wakefield:—

John Michael Chicheley (Birdforth, Terrington, York YO6 4PX), *b* 1937; *ed* Canford, and RMA Sandhurst; Major RA: *m* 1964, Pauline Susan, da of M. Oliver, of Market Harborough, and has issue living, James William, *b* 1969; *ed* Canford, and Portsmouth (BA), — Richard Michael, *b* 1971; *ed* Canford, and RMA Sandhurst.

Grandchildren of late Capt Francis Theophilus Blunt, 2nd son of the Rev Edward Powlett Blunt, yr son of late James Blunt, el son of Walter Blunt, 5th son of 2nd baronet:—
Issue of late Right Rev Bishop Alfred Walter Frank Blunt, DD, formerly Bishop of Bradford, *b* 1879, *d* 1957: *m* 1909, Margaret Catherine, who *d* 1963, el da of Lieut-Col Joshua Duke, formerly Indian Med Ser:—
David Alfred Chicheley, *b* 1915: *m* 1940, Dorothy Brailsford Booth, and has issue living, Peter Robin Chicheley (Home Farm, Newburgh, Coxwold, York), *b* 1946: *m* 1st, 1969, Angela Shirley, who *d* 1992, da of late Arthur Benjamin Drane, MA, of 33 Simbalk Lane, Bishopthorpe, York; 2ndly, 1993, Jane Clough, and has issue living (by 1st *m*), Michael Peter Chicheley *b* 1975, Jenny Elizabeth *b* 1972, — Patricia Anne Brailsford *b* 1941: *m* 1967, Timothy Steuart Hallam Piper, of St Anselm's, Bakewell, Derbyshire, son of late Donald Piper, and has issue living, Richard David Steuart *b* 1969, Nicholas James Steuart *b* 1970, James William Steuart *b* 1976, Sarah Catherine Brailsford *b* 1982. *Residence* – 21 Simbalk Lane, Bishopthorpe, York.
—— Helen Amy, *b* 1911: *m* 1st, 1934 (*m diss* 1941), Christopher Hodgson; 2ndly 1942 (*m diss* 1948), Geoffrey Dawson; 3rdly, 1962, Richard Marshall Bond, of Flat 214, Audley Court, Audley Rd, Saffron Walden, Essex CB11 3SD, and has issue living, (by 2nd *m*) Jane, *b* 1943: *m* 1st, 1965 (*m diss* 1983), Nigel Hartley Dryden Butterworth (*see* Dryden, Bt, 1990 Edn); 2ndly, 1984, Dr John Glennie, of Thatched Cottage, Widdington, Saffron Walden, Essex, and has issue living, (by 1st *m*), Julian Richard Nigel *b* 1970, Fiona Catherine *b* 1967: *m* 1992, Christopher Gregory Crace, of Molens Cottage, White Colne, Colchester, Essex (and has issue living, Sasha Amy *b* 1994). —— Margaret Dorothy, *b* 1913: *m* 1936, Rudolf Paul Gerard Kirchem, and has issue living, Michael Hans Edward (36 Southview Court, Guildford Rd, Woking), *b* 1937: *m* 1965 (*m diss* 1976), Jean Miriam McKenna, and has issue living, Michael John Geoffrey *b* 1966, Catherine Marina *b* 1967, — Elisabeth Jane, *b* 1940: *m* 1971, David George Cross, of 25 Cité Joseph Bech, Gonderange, Luxembourg, and has issue living, Andrew David Jonathan *b* 1973, Geoffrey Mark Timothy *b* 1974, Nicholas Edward Benjamin *b* 1976, — Anthony Peter Francis, *b* 1953. *Residence* – Adlington Lodge, Albury Rd, Burwood Park, Walton on Thames, Surrey.

Grandchildren of late Maj-Gen Grant Blunt, RE, yst son of Rev Edward Powlett Blunt (ante):—
Issue of late Col Conrad Edward Grant Blunt, CBE, DSO, *b* 1868, *d* 1948: *m* 1st, 1900, Aimée, who *d* 1918, da of Col Abel Straghan, CB; 2ndly, 1920, Beatrice, who *d* 1946, widow of Frank Fullagar:—
(By 1st *m*) †Hugh Clavell, *b* 1908: *m* 1939, Elizabeth Marjorie, who *d* (Sept) 1986, only da of W. S. Campbell, and has *d* (May) 1986, leaving issue, Susan Pamela, *b* 1940; uses her maiden name: *m* 1992, Brian James Clayden, of 751 Eden Place, W Vancouver, BC, Canada BCV 7T, and has issue living, Kay Meredith BLUNT-CLAYDEN (son) *b* 1981. —— Marjorie Nina, *b* 1903: *m* 1930, George Douglas Laurie Pile, CBE, who *d* 1965, and *d* 1982, leaving issue, Richard Edward Laurie (Ampney Knowle, nr Cirencester, Glos), *b* 1934: *ed* Stowe, and Trin Coll, Camb (MA): *m* 1962, Elizabeth-Ann, yr da of Charles Henry Lewis Bubb, of Brook House, Cricklade Wilts, and has issue living, Edward George Laurie *b* 1965; *ed* Radley, Hugo Richard Laurie *b* 1967; *ed* Eton, and Edinburgh Univ (MA), — Celia Aimée Lorna Laurie, *b* 1937: *m* 1959, Prince Andrei Vladimirovitch Drutskoy-Sokolinsky, of 36 Av Des Statuaires, 1180 Brussels, Belgium, and has issue living, Alexander *b* 1963, Nicolai *b* 1966, Ilyena *b* 1961.
Issue of late Arthur Powlett Blunt, CMG, *b* 1883; *d* 1946: *m* 1919 (*m diss* 1937), Winifred Grace, who *d* 1988, da of Dr W. H. Fawcett, of Bournemouth:—
Grant Anthony Clavell (12 Warwick Drive, SW15), *b* 1920; *ed* Bradfield; ACIS; Capt RM (ret); 1939-45 War: *m* 1942, June Dorothy, da of J. C. Liddle, and has issue living, Alistair Clavell, *b* 1946; *ed* Bradfield, Essex Univ (BA), and Heriot Watt Univ, Edinburgh (MSc): *m* 1st, 1973 (*m diss* 1980), Elizabeth Harden; 2ndly, 19—, Ida, da of Col Estioko, of Quezon City, Philippines, and has issue living (by 2nd *m*), Joachim Estioko Grant *b* 1982, Thomas Paul *b* 1985, — Gene Carol, *b* 1943; *ed* Cheltenham Ladies' Coll and Bedford Coll, London (BSc): *m* 1967, Bertrand Edouard Doger de Speville, of 55, The Avenue, Richmond, Surrey, and has issue living, Guy Rollo *b* 1971; *ed* Ampleforth, and R Holloway & Bedford New Coll, London (BSc), Claire Anne Maude *b* 1974. —— Evelyn Powlett Clavell, RD (45 Uplands Court, Tallai, Queensland 4213, Australia) *b* 1924; Lt-Cdr RNR, 1939-45 War with RNVR: *m* 1956, Patricia, da of Col William Joseph Gaunt Beach, MBE, and has issue living, Jonathan Andrew Clavell, *b* 1959, — Sarah Virginia Clavell, *b* 1957, — Philippa Mary Clavell, *b* 1960: *m* 1987, —, and has issue living, Rachel, *b* 19—, Rebecca, *b* 19—.

Descendants of late Lt-Col Edward Walter MACKENZIE (who assumed the additional surname of Mackenzie 1905, but subsequently discontinued the use of the surname Blunt), el son of Maj-Gen Charles Harris Blunt, CB, 4th son of Edward Walter Blunt, 3rd son of Walter Blunt (ante): *m* 1899, Sibell Lilian, Countess of Cromartie, who *d* 1962 (*see* E Cromartie).
Grandson of late Hugh Roper Blunt (infra):—
Issue of late Michael Hugh Blunt, *b* 1920, *d* 1983: *m* 1958, Susanne Mary, who *d* 1983, da of Lawson Field, of Gisborne, NZ:—
Gerald Hugh Lawson, *b* 1959: *m* 1990, Emma Tamsin Harcourt, da of Phillip Armes, of Hurstpierpoint, W Sussex, and has issue living, Isabella Rose Henrietta, *b* 1992. *Residence* – 63 Barnard St, Wadestown, Wellington, NZ.

Grandchildren of late Col Arthur Blunt, 6th son of late Edward Walter Blunt (ante):—
Issue of late Arthur Wharton Blunt, *b* 1866, *d* 1939: *m* 1906, Mary, who *d* 1936, da of Col Arthur Edward Ward, formerly Roy Welch Fusiliers:—
Joyce Cautley, *b* 1921: *m* 1946, Peter J. Presnail, of 210 Coromandel Parade, Coromandel Valley, S Aust 5051, and has issue living, Richard, *b* 1947: *m* 1975, Marilyn Rowan, and has issue living, Catharine Louise *b* 1980, Elizabeth Anne *b* 1982, — Shirley, *b* 1951: *m* 1972, Jeremy Cuthbertson, and has issue living, Dayle Deanne Shirley *b* 1986, — Hazel, *b* 1954: *m* 1990, Leon Marshall.
Issue of late Hugh Roper Blunt, *b* 1874, *d* 1931: *m* 1915, Agnes Sara, who *d* 1948, da of Charles Gray, of Waiohika, Gisborne, New Zealand:—
Richard Mark (9 Highbridge Way, Karrinyup, Western Australia 6018), *b* 1924; late Lt RN: *m* 1st, 1952 (*m diss* 1963), Adrien Seldon Truss; 2ndly, 1965, Patricia Eileen, da of Walter Stanley Lee, of Perth, W Aust, and has issue living, (by 1st *m*), Teresa June, *b* 1953, — (by 2nd *m*) David Mark, *b* 1967, — Georgia Alison, *b* 1969.
Issue of late Lieut-Col Allan St John Blunt, DSO, *b* 1880, *d* 1931: *m* 1914, Doris Elizabeth, who *d* 1948, da of late John G. Stephen, of Douglas, Isle of Man:—
Elizabeth Shirley, *b* 1923: *m* 1944, Harry Batten Poustie, DSC, RD, and has issue living, John David, *b* 1948: *m* 1981, Sandra Mason, — Michael Ian, *b* 1954: *m* 1977, Coral Purton, and has issue living, Simon Ian William *b* 1978, James Michael *b* 1981, Elizabeth Claire *b* 1979, Rosemary *b* 1984, — Richard Hugh, *b* 1965: *m* 1989, Sandra Cording, — Charles Christopher (twin), *b* 1965: *m* 1993, Heather Pinner, — Vivienne Mary *b* 1951: *m* 1974, Leslie Keast, and has issue living, Christopher John *b* 1978, Deborah Jane *b* 1977, Katherine Louise *b* 1983, — Louise Caroline, *b* 1964: *m* 1991, Gary Castleton, and has issue living, Joshua Allan *b* 1993. *Residence* – Little Fairstowe, Ashburton Rd, Bovey Tracey, Devon.

According to the pedigree on record at the College of Arms, Sir John, 1st baronet, was the fourth child of Thomas Blunt, of Rochester, Kent. Thomas, "shoemaker and baptist", was baptized at St Nicholas, Rochester, 24 July 1665, and was buried at St Nicholas, Rochester, 28 March 1703, his father having been John Blunt, of St Sepulchre's, London, "upholder." In 1732 the Court of Chivalry summoned and fined the 1st Bt for using without right the arms of Sir Charles Blount, Lord Mountjoy, Earl of Devonshire: he appealed from the sentence, and a day was appointed for hearing his appeal, but he died before any further proceedings took place, and the officially recorded arms of the family are as described above. The 4th baronet sat as MP for Lewes (L) 1832-7, and Capt Sir John Harvey Blunt, 8th Bt, Roy Dublin Fusiliers, served throughout the Indian Mutiny.

CRAWLEY-BOEVEY (GB) 1784, of Highgrove, Gloucestershire
(Name pronounced "Crawley-Boovey")

To be, rather than seem to be

Sir THOMAS MICHAEL BLAKE CRAWLEY-BOEVEY, 8th *Baronet*; *b* 29 Sept 1928; *s* his father, *Sir* LAUNCELOT VALENTINE HYDE, 1968; *ed* Wellington Coll, and St John's Coll, Camb (MA); late 2nd Lt Durham LI; Editor of *Which?* 1976-81: *m* 1957, Laura, who *d* 1979, el da of late Jan Pouwels Coelingh, of The Hague, Holland, and has issue.

Arms – Erminois, on a fesse azure between three cranes proper a saltire couped between two cross-crosslets fitchée or, on a chief ermine a bend gules, charged with three guttes-d'or between two martlets sable. **Crest** – A mount vert thereon a crane proper gorged with a collar or, holding in his dexter claw a saltire couped on the last.
Residence – Trebanau, Cilycwm, Llandovery, Dyfed SA20 0HP.

SONS LIVING

THOMAS HYDE, *b* 26 June 1958. —— William Walstan, *b* 1960.

BROTHER LIVING

Anthony Francis d'Auvergne (4 Station Rd, Lydney, Glos), *b* 1932; *ed* RNC Dartmouth: *m* 1968 (*m diss* 1976), Gertrud, da of late Dr Johannes Felix Potrykus, of Soerabaya, Java.

COLLATERAL BRANCHES LIVING

Grandson of late Capt Edward Martin Crawley-Boevey, 2nd son of 5th baronet:—
Issue of late Richard Martin Crawley-Boevey, *b* 1908; *d* 1977: *m* 1945, Gladys Frances Farrer Young, who *d* 1955:—
Timothy Martin, *b* 1949: *m* 1975, Agnes Avelene Peché, and has issue living, Richard Martin, *b* 1979, —— Karin, *b* 1976.
Residence – 38 Balfour Rd, Pinetown, Natal 3610, S Africa 3610.

Issue of late Rev Canon Arthur Curtis Crawley-Boevey, 3rd son of 5th baronet, *b* 1874, *d* 1965: *m* 1906, Evelyn Rosalie, who *d* 1962, da of late Robert Carnegie, of Terenure, co Dublin:—
Rev Robert Arthur (3 St Michaels Close, Urchfont, Devizes, Wilts), *b* 1912; *ed* Hertford Coll, Oxford (MA): *m* 1947, Josephine, da of late Joseph Howard, of Evenlode House, Moreton-in-Marsh, Glos, and has issue living, David Alexander (Lewins, Shurlock Row, nr Reading, Berks RG10 0PR), *b* 1948: *m* 1977, Isabelle Frances Lee, da of late Donald Eyre, of Torquay, and has issue living, Catherine Rosanna *b* 1979, Sarah Frances *b* 1982, Julia Alexandra *b* 1985, —— Peter Robert (25 Elizabeth St, Mentone 3194, Victoria, Australia), *b* 1957: *m* 1991, Joanne Margaret, da of Ian Kurrle, of Somers, Australia, and has issue living, Robert Ian, *b* 1993, —— Juliet Ann, *b* 1950: *m* 1975, Andrew Dean, of St Margarets, Willand Rd, Cullompton, Devon EX15 1AP, and has issue living, Kelvin John *b* 1985, Jamie Lee *b* 1986. —— Nancy Albinia (Sceapea, Sheepy Magna, Atherstone, Warwickshire), *b* 1910. —— Marjorie Evelyn, *b* 1916. —— Elizabeth Jocosa, *b* 1918; *ed* Girton Coll, Camb.

Grandson of late Arthur William Crawley-Boevey, 6th son of 4th baronet:—
Issue of late Major Martin Crawley-Boevey, DSO, MC, Duke of Cornwall's LI, *b* 1883, *d* 1954: *m* 1919, Elizabeth Adela, who *d* 1972, da of late Capt Roger Hall, DL, of Narrow Water, co Down, and widow of Lieut-Col Neville Reay Daniell, DSO (E Clanwilliam, colls):—
Antony, MBE, *b* 1921; Maj (ret) 17th/21st Lancers; 1939-45 War with 7th Hussars; MBE (Mil) 1964: *m* 1st, 1950 (*m diss* 1957), Cynthia Louise, who *d* 1988, da of late William Hugh Neville Bagot, of Haut du Mont, La Haule, Jersey; 2ndly, 1960, Josephine Beryl, da of Lt-Col N. H. Kindersley, of Sunny Cottage, Piddletrenthide, Dorset, and has issue living, (by 1st *m*) Susan Elizabeth Mary, *b* 1951: *m* 1980, Dr Peter Laurence Stanley Hard, of Upper Street House, Pulborough, W Sussex RH20 1AF, and has issue living, Georgina Susan *b* 1981, Emily Alice *b* 1984, — (by 2nd *m*) Martin Henry, *b* 1963, —— Simon Antony, *b* 1967, —— Katherine Lucy, *b* 1964: *m* 1991, Nicholas J. Walters, of 5 Winsham Grove, Clapham Common, SW11 6NB, elder son of Dr P. J. R. Walters, of Clifden, co Galway. *Residence* – Sunny Cottage, Piddletrenthide, Dorchester, Dorset DT2 7QX.

Grandchildren of late Octavius Charles Crawley-Boevey (infra):—
Issue of late Santiago Carlos Crawley-Boevey, *b* 1872, *d* 1913: *m* 18—, a da of Alamos Cuadra, of Valparaiso, Chile:—
Charles, *b* 1897. —— Marie, *b* 1899.

Issue of late Octavius Charles Crawley-Boevey, 7th son of 4th baronet, *b* 1846, *d* 1897: *m* 1871, Maria Francisca, da of Bernardino Murga, Judge of the Corte Superior, Arequipa, Peru:—
Edward Maximo, *b* 1875. —— Mary Isabel, *b* 1878: *m* 1904, Frederico de la Fuenta, and has issue living, Frederico Francisco, *b* 1906, — Hilda Carmela, *b* 1911. —— Rose Agnes, *b* 1880. —— Lilian Maude Antonia, *b* 1882. —— Leonor Octavia, *b* 1884. —— Blanche Josephine, *b* 1889: *m* 1910, Gerald Bingham (M Sligo, colls, 1912 Edn), and has issue living, Norah Frances, *b* 1912, — Dorothy Blanche, *b* 1913, — Eileen Gertrude, *b* 1915, — Elizabeth Hilda, *b* 1918. —— Ella Margaret, *b* 1894. —— Hilda Ines, *b* 1896.

Grandchildren of late Thomas William Crawley, el son of late Rev Thomas William Crawley (infra):—
Issue of late Thomas Charles Rochfort Crawley, *b* 1882, *d* 1963: *m* 1914, Margaret (71 Duke St, Dryden, Ontario, Canada), da of Charles McKerrow, MB of Workington, Cumberland:—
Thomas Bryson (PO Box 546, Mount Albert, Ontario, Canada, LOG 1MO), *b* 1918: *m* 1947, Christina, only da of H. Vollweiter, of Toronto, Canada, and has issue living, Thomas Henry, *b* 1958, —— Christopher John, *b* 1963, —— Gilda Carolyn,

b 1951, — Carla Susan, *b* 1953, — Lisa Marlene, *b* 1956. —— James Bryan (139 Kingston Row, Winnipeg, Manitoba R2M 0S7, Canada), *b* 1921: *m* 1964, Edith Janice Doreen, da of Charles Player Halls, of Regina, Sask, Canada, and has issue living, Devin Charles Bryan, *b* 1968: *m* 1993, Heather Cullen. —— Margery, *b* 1915.

Issue of late Rev Canon John Lloyd Crawley, *b* 1884, *d* 1951: *m* 1921, Marion, who *d* 1961, da of Charles McKerrow, MB:—

Rev John Lloyd Rochfort (Cove, Tarbert, Argyll PA29 6SX), *b* 1922; V of St Anthony's, Newcastle 1953-59, V of Longhoughton and R of Howick 1959-69, and Master of St Thomas the Martyr, Newcastle, and Chap Newcastle Univ 1969-74, R of Cockermouth 1974-86, Kt: *m* 1947, Isabell, da of late William Robson, of Reaveley Powburn, Alnwick, and has issue living, Michael John (Imperial Coll, Silwood Park, Ascot, Berks), *b* 1949; PhD; DIC: *m* 1971, Greer Anne, only da of George Williams, of New London, Conn, USA. —— Margaret, *b* 1924: *m* 1946, Maj William Vivian Dickinson, MBE, RA, who *d* 1994, and has issue living, John (16 Conduit Rd, Sheffield), *b* 1948: *m* 1st, 1970 (*m diss* 1973), Dianne Warby; 2ndly, 1981, Christine Gregory, — Michael (16a Horsebrook Park, Calne, Wilts SN11 8EY), *b* 1955: *m* 1982, Rachel Garson, — Richard, *b* 1960, — Rev Susan (Brightside Vicarage, 24 Beacon Rd, Brightside, Sheffield S9 1AD) *b* 1949; ordained priest 1994; priest in charge St Margaret & St Thomas, Brightside: *m* 1971 (*m diss* 1974), Kenneth Hope.

Grandchildren of Rev Thomas William Crawley, son of late Rev John Lloyd Crawley, 2nd son of 2nd baronet:—

Issue of late Lt-Col George Burridge Crawley, *b* 1858, *d* 1932: *m* 1st, 1882 (*m diss* 1887), Kate Ouseley, da of late Surg-Maj Henry Sherlock; 2ndly, 1892, Adelaide, who *d* 1946, da of late Charles Bell Syer:—

(By 1st *m*) George Ouseley, *b* 1883.

Issue of late Charles Purrier Crawley, *b* 1859, *d* 1896: *m* 18—, Emily Kent, da of late — Hooper:—

Charles Robert Thomas Edmund, *b* 1880. —— Noel George, *b* 1888. —— Albinia, *b* 19—. —— Hannah Dorothy, *b* 1887.

Grandsons of late Charles James Crawley, only son of late Rev Charles Yonge Crawley, son of late Rev Charles Crawley, 3rd son of 2nd baronet:—

Issue of late (Charles) Alan Crawley, *b* 1887, *d* 1975: *m* 1915, Jean Nairn (830 Sayward Rd, Vic, BC, Canada), only child of David Horn, of Winnipeg:—

(Charles) David (1757 N Stanley Av, Los Angeles, Calif 90046, USA), *b* 1916; *ed* BC Univ (BA); 1939-45 War as F/O RCAF: *m* 1st, 1942 (*m diss* 1960), Lois Kathleen, only da of Francis Ritchie, of Vancouver, BC; 2ndly, 1965, Dorothy Fern Fried, of Los Angeles, Calif, and has issue living (by 1st *m*) (Charles) Peter (c/o 830 Sayward Rd, Victoria, BC, Canada V8Y 1R4), *b* 1943: *m* 1st, 1963 (*m diss* 1971), Carole Cavalier, of Los Angeles, Calif; 2ndly, 1987, Janet Lesley King, of Vic, BC, Canada, and has issue living (by 1st *m*), Theresa Lynn *b* 1963, Brandi Michelle *b* 1969, Trista *b* 1971, — (Christopher) David (1051 Hampshire Rd, Victoria, BC, Canada V8S 4S8), *b* 1947: *m* 1st, 1972 (*m diss* 1977), Erin McMartin, of Sidney, BC, Canada; 2ndly, 1980 Victoria Jean Miller, of Ottawa, Canada, and has issue living (by 1st *m*), Aleta *b* 1974 (by 2nd *m*) Jennifer Michelle *b* 1982, — (by 2nd *m*) Andrew, *b* 1973. —— Michael (830, Sayward Rd, Victoria, BC, Canada V8Y 1R4), *b* 1919; *ed* Ravenscourt Sch, Winnipeg; 1939-45 War with RCASC.

Grandson of late William Savage Crawley, son of late Rev William Crawley, 5th son of 2nd baronet:—

Issue of late William Evelyn Maddock Crawley, *b* 1859, *d* 1926: *m* 1st, 1894, Fanny Gertrude, who *d* 1911, da of late Arthur Wellesley Critchley; 2ndly, 1913, Harriet Gladys, da of late Robert Chambres Chambres:—

(By 2nd *m*) Evelyn Myres Chambres, *b* 1914.

The 1st baronet, Sir Charles Barrow, sat as MP for Gloucester 1751-89; his patent of baronetcy was made with remainder to his kinsman, Thomas Crawley-Boevey, grandson of Thomas Crawley, who, on inheriting Flaxley Abbey 1726, took the additional surname of Boevey; the 6th baronet, Sir Francis Hyde, and the 7th baronet, Sir Launcelot Valentine Hyde, were Verderers of the Forest of Dean.

BOILEAU (UK) 1838, of Tacolnestone Hall, Norfolk

With all my heart

Sir GUY FRANCIS BOILEAU, 8th *Baronet*; *b* 23 Feb 1935; *s* his father, Sir EDMOND CHARLES, 1980; *ed* Xavier Coll, Melbourne, and RMC Duntroon, Aust; Lt-Col; Observer, UN Mil Observer Gp in India and Pakistan 1959-60; Instructor, Aust Army Training Team, Vietnam 1963-64, attached US Dept of Defence, Washington, DC 1966-68; Security Adviser, Dept of the Administrator, Territory of Papua - New Guinea 1970-71; Comdg Officer, Army Intelligence Centre 1972-74; Directing Staff (Instructor), Aust Staff Coll 1975-76: *m* 1962, Judith Frances, da of Senator George Conrad Hannan, of Glen Iris, and Canberra, and has issue.

Arms – Azure, a castle triple towered or, masoned sable, and in base a crescent of the second. **Crest** – A pelican in her piety proper charged on the breast with a saltire couped gules.
Residence – 14, Faircroft Av, Glen Iris, Victoria 3146, Australia.

SONS LIVING

NICHOLAS EDMOND GEORGE, *b* 17 Nov 1964. —— Christopher Guy, *b* 1969.

DAUGHTERS LIVING

Simone Teresa, *b* 1963. —— Caroline Virginia, *b* 1968. —— Antonia Josephine, *b* 1975.

BROTHER LIVING

Peter Linden (Seaton St, Glen Iris, Vic, Aust), *b* 1937: *m* 1967, Claudia, da of Alan Edward Mills, of Wanganui, NZ, and has issue living, Dominic Peter, *b* 1968, — James Edward, *b* 1971, — Simon Charles, *b* 1975.

UNCLE LIVING (Son of 5th baronet)

Patrick Etienne, b 1912; m 1940, Je Frances, da of late John Jordan Moore, and has issue living, Michael Donald, b 1949, — Patricia Ann, b 1943.

DAUGHTERS LIVING OF SIXTH BARONET (By 1st marriage)

Prudence Despréaux, b 1925: m 1954, Anthony Harvey, of 138 Napoleon St, Eltham, Victoria, Australia, and has issue living, Georgia, b 1955, — Tracey, b 1958. —— Angela Mary, b 1927: m 1949, John Stewart Milne, of Caserne, Croydon, Victoria, Australia, and has issue living, Anthony Stewart, b 1950, — Virginia, b 1951, — Sarah, b 1952, — Jane, b 1954, — Lisa, b 1956, — Elizabeth, b 1967, — Melanie, b 1967.

(By 2nd marriage)

Madelon Mary, b 1945: m 1970, Geoffrey George Foletta, of Broadford, Victoria 3658, Aust, and has issue living, Gregory George, b 1972, — Samuel Geoffrey, b 1976, — Hamish, b 1978, — Monique Louise, b 1974. —— Elizabeth Ann, b 1948: m 1974, Simon John File, of Inverell, NSW, Aust, and has issue living, Simon Charles, b 1977, — Trinity, b 1975, — Melody, b 1976. —— Mary Anne, b 1953: m 1976, John Yeager Pye, of 11 Towner Place, Gowrie, ACT, Australia, and has issue living, Benjamin, b 1977, — Angus, b 1978, — William James Boileau, b 1984, — Elizabeth Catherine, b 1987.

WIDOW LIVING OF SIXTH BARONET

MARY CATHERINE (Mary, Lady Boileau) (146 Power St, Hawthorn, Vic, Aust), da of late Lawrence Riordan, of Cradock, S Australia: m 1941, as his 2nd wife, Maj Sir Gilbert George Benson Boileau, 6th Bt, who d 1978.

WIDOW LIVING OF SEVENTH BARONET

MARJORIE LYLE (Marjorie, Lady Boileau) (61 Erica Av, Glen Iris, Vic, Aust), da of late Claude Monteath D'Arcy, of Launceston, Tasmania: m 1934, Sir Edmond Charles Boileau, 7th Bt, who d 1980.

COLLATERAL BRANCH LIVING

Grandchildren of late Edmund William Pollen Boileau, 3rd son of 1st baronet:—
Issue of late Edmond Charles Boileau, b 1877, d 1940: m 1902, Jean Ballantyne, who d 19—:—
Maurice, b 1904. —— Catherine, b 1908. Residence –

This baronet is descended in an unbroken line from Etienne Boileau, Baron de Castelnau and St Croix (Province of Languedoc), who, in 1250, on the departure of Louis IX for the Holy Land, was appointed during his absence, Governor of Paris, and 1st Grand Provost of France. He drew up the first Municipal Code, which is still used. His descendant, Charles Boileau, Baron of Castelnau and St Croix, fled to England at the Revocation of the Edict of Nantes. Descendants of the same family own the original French property.

BOLES (UK) 1922, of Bishop's Lydeard, Somerset

Sir JEREMY JOHN FORTESCUE BOLES, 3rd Baronet; b 9 Jan 1932; s his father, Capt Sir GERALD FORTESCUE, 1945; ed Stowe: m 1st, 1955 (m diss 1970), Dorothy Jane, yr da of James Alexander Worswick, of Enmore, Som; 2ndly, 1970 (m diss 1981), Elisabeth Gildroy, yr da of Edward Phillip Shaw, of Englefield Green, Surrey, and widow of Oliver Simon Willis Fleming; 3rdly, 1982, Marigold, eldest da of Donald Frank Seckington, of Clevedon, Avon, and widow of Laurence Frederick Aspey, and has issue by 1st and 2nd m.

Arms – Azure, on a fesse ermine, between three standing bowls argent, out of each a boar's head or, a portcullis also or. Crest – In front of a rising sun or a demi-boar azure, pierced in the left shoulder by an arrow proper.

SONS LIVING (By 1st marriage)

RICHARD FORTESCUE (1 Oldbrook, Holbrook Rd, Lydbrook, Glos GL17 9PY), b 12 Dec 1958: m 1990, Allison Beverley, da of Brian MacDonald, and has issue living, James Alexander Fortescue, b 25 May 1993. —— David Hastings Fortescue, b 1967.

DAUGHTERS LIVING (By 1st marriage)

Sarah Jane, b 1956: m 1986, Paul Bird, and has issue living, Simon Callum, b 1990, — Georgina Jane, b 1988. —— (By 2nd marriage) Jessica Blanche Mary, b 1971.

As I do to thee so will I do to others

The 1st baronet, Lieut-Col Sir Dennis Fortescue Boles, CBE (son of late Rev James Thomas Boles, of Ryll Court, Exmouth, and Moyge, co Cork), was MP for W, or Wellington, Div of Somerset (C) 1911-18, and for Taunton Div of Somerset 1918-21. The 2nd baronet, Capt Sir Gerald Fortescue, 17th/21st Lancers, d on active ser 1945.

BONHAM (UK) 1852

To be, rather than to seem to be

Sir ANTONY LIONEL THOMAS BONHAM, 4th *Baronet; b* 21 Oct 1916; *s* his father, *Major Sir* ERIC HENRY, CVO, 1937; *ed* Eton, and RMC Sandhurst; Major (ret) Royal Scots Greys; a DL of Glos: *m* 1944, Felicity, only da of late Col Frank Lionel Pardoe, DSO, of Barton-bury, Cirencester, and has issue.

Arms – Sable, a chevron nebulée between three crosses patée fitchée at the foot argent; on a canton of the last a squirrel sejant gules. **Crest** – A mermaid holding in the dexter hand a wreath of coral and in the sinister a mirror proper. *Residence* – Ash House, Ampney Crucis, Cirencester, Glos GL7 5RY.

SONS LIVING

(GEORGE) MARTIN ANTONY (15 St James St, Castle Hedingham, Essex CO9 3EN; RAC Club), *b* 18 Feb 1945; *ed* Eton, and Aston Univ, Birmingham: *m* 1979 (*m diss* 1992), Nenon Baillieu, el da of Robert Ruttan Wilson, of Durford Knoll, Petersfield, Hants (*see* Bs Berners, colls), and has issue living, Michael Francis, *b* 24 May 1980, — Lucie Nenon, *b* 1982, — Camilla Felicity, *b* 1984, — Sarah Yvette, *b* 1987. —— Simon Philip (Rectory House, Ogbourne St George, nr Marlborough, Wilts), *b* 1947: *m* 1977, Elizabeth Ann, yr da of late Robert Ducas, of Saratoga Springs, NY, and has issue living, Zoe Virginia, *b* 1979, — Sophie Jean, *b* 1982. —— Timothy Eric, *b* 1952: *m* 1978, Hester Suzette, yst da of Sir James Arnold Stacey Cleminson, MC, DL, of Loddon Hall, Hales, Norfolk, and has issue living, Emma Claire *b* 1981, — Georgina Sarah *b* 1983.

The 1st baronet, Sir Samuel George Bonham, KCB (son of Capt George Bonham, HEICS, a descendant of Sir John Bonham, of Stanway Hall, Essex), was Gov of Straits Settlements 1837-47, and Gov and Com-in-Ch of British Trade in China 1847-53. The 2nd baronet, Sir George Francis, was Envoy Extraor and Min Plen to Serbia 1900-1903, and to Swiss Confederation 1905-9. The 3rd baronet, Sir Eric Henry, CVO, was Comptroller of the Household to HRH Prince Arthur of Connaught 1913-26.

BONSOR (UK) 1925, of Kingswood, Epsom, Surrey

Every good thing is the gift of God

Sir NICHOLAS COSMO BONSOR, MP, 4th *Baronet; b* 9 Dec 1942; *s* his father, *Maj Sir* BRYAN COSMO, MC, TD, 1977; *ed* Eton, and Keble Coll, Oxford (MA); Bar Inner Temple 1967; late R Bucks Yeo; MP for Nantwich 1979-83, and for Upminster since 1983: *m* 1969, Hon Nadine Marisa Lampson, da of 2nd Baron Killearn, and has issue.

Arms – Per fesse azure and argent, a pale counterchanged, three lions' heads erased or, on a chief also or three roses gules, barbed and seeded proper. **Crest** – A wolf passant sable, collared and chained gold, resting the dexter fore-paw on a rose as in the arms. *Residence* – 2 Waldegrave Court, Upminster, Essex.

SONS LIVING

(ALEXANDER) COSMO, *b* 8 Sept 1976. —— James Charles, *b* 1983.

DAUGHTERS LIVING

Sacha Henrietta, *b* 1974. —— Elizabeth Nadine, *b* 1987. —— Mary Catherine, *b* (twin) 1987.

BROTHER LIVING

Richard Angus, *b* 1947; *ed* Eton, and Keble Coll, Oxford (BA): *m* 1971, Susan Anne, da of Flight-Lieut David Henry Lewis Wigan, RAFVR (*see* By Tweed-mouth), and has issue living, — Rupert James, *b* 1974, — Edward Richard, *b* 1976, — Clare Lucinda, *b* 1981. *Residences* – 61 Hartington Rd, W4; Cliddesden Down House, Basingstoke, Hants RG25 2JD.

UNCLE LIVING (Son of 2nd baronet)

David Victor, MC, *b* 1918; *ed* Eton; Major late Grenadier Guards; European War 1939-45 (MC): *m* 1945, Sheila, da of Maj-Gen Sir Miles William Arthur Peel Graham, KBE, CB, MC (E Lovelace, colls), and has issue living, Anthony Miles (16 Pembroke Rd, W8), *b* 1948: *m* 1980, Frances Elizabeth, only da of David Lindsay Bankes, of 32 Holroyd Rd, SW15 6LN, and has issue living, Miles *b* 1984, Sophie *b* 1982, Laura *b* 1988, — Neil Reginald David (9 Second Av, SW14 8QF), *b* 1950: *m* 1992, Sophie B., da of Col Frederick Walter James, TD, DL, of Hopstone, Claverley, nr Wolverhampton, — Caroline Sheila, *b* 1946: *m* 1974, Bruce Hodges, of Fell Yard, Slapton, Towcester, Northants, and has issue living, a da *b* 1978, a da *b* 1980. *Residence* – Little Stocks, Aldbury, near Tring, Herts HP23 5RX.

AUNT LIVING (Daughter of 2nd baronet)

Daphne Marion, *b* 1924: *m* 1st, 1944, Clyde Euan Miles Graham, Flying Officer RAF, who was *ka* 1944 (*see* E Peel, colls), 1956 Edn); 2ndly, 1948, Alexander David Stewart, MBE, TD, who *d* 1985 (*see* E Galloway, colls). *Residence* – North Green, Kelsale, Saxmundham, Suffolk.

WIDOW LIVING OF THIRD BARONET

ELIZABETH, (*Elizabeth, Lady Bonsor*), (Ascot Lodge, Ascot, Berks), da of Capt Angus Valdimar Hambro, of Milton Abbas, Dorset: *m* 1942, Maj Sir Bryan Cosmo Bonsor, 3rd Bt, MC, TD, who *d* 1977.

COLLATERAL BRANCH LIVING

Issue of late Robert Cecil Bonsor, MC, 3rd son of 1st baronet, *b* 1880, *d* 1932: *m* 1922, Enid, da of S. Lawrence:—
Michael Cosmo (Broadfield House, Yattendon, Berks), *b* 1926; *ed* Eton; Lieut Gren Gds 1944-47: *m* 1951, Ann Marie, da of Marcus Wallenberg, and has issue living, Robert Angus Cosmo (3923 Green Look Court, Fairfax, Virginia 23033, USA), *b* 1963: *m* 1989, Kasandra Noel, yst da of Dr Joseph Patton, of Great Falls, Virginia, USA, — Celia Jane, *b* 1954: *m* 1983, Nigel Douglas Pilkington, of 11 Chester Sq, SW1 yst son of Maj Thomas Douglas Pilkington, JP, of Hyde Mill, Stow-on-the-Wold, Glos, and has issue living, Emma Douglas *b* 1985, Tessa Douglas *b* 1987, — Charlotte Serena *b* 1956: *m* 1980, Christopher J. Milln, of Kelvedon Hall, Kelvedon, Colchester, Essex, elder son of John Milln, of Froglane Farm, Rotherwick, Hants, and has issue living, Frederick John *b* 1985, Louise Emma *b* 1983, — Camilla Ann (22 Queen's Gate Terrace, SW7), *b* 1961. —— Ann Elizabeth, *b* 1923.

The 1st baronet, Sir (Henry) Cosmo Orme Bonsor, sat as MP for Surrey, NE, or Wimbledon, SW, Div (*C*) 1885-1900, and was sometime a Director of the Bank of England. The 2nd baronet, Sir Reginald, was Major Surrey Yeo, Chm of John Dickinson & Co, Ltd, of Apsley Mills, Hemel Hempstead, and High Sheriff of Bucks, 1940-41.

BOORD (UK) 1896, of Wakehurst Place, Ardingly, Sussex
(Name pronounced "Board")

By integrity and industry

Sir NICOLAS JOHN CHARLES BOORD, 4th *Baronet*, *b* 10 June 1936; *s* his father, *Sqdn-Ldr Sir* RICHARD WILLIAM, 1975; *ed* Eton, Sorbonne, Societa Dante Alighieri (Italy), and Univ of Santander (Spain): *m* 1st, 1960 (*m diss* 1965), Francoise, da of Giuseppe Tempra; 2ndly, 1965, Françoise Renée, da of Marcel Clovis Mouret, of 69, Traverse de Carthage, 13 Marseilles 8.

𝖆rms – Per fesse azure and gules, a goat's head erased within an orle of eight martlets argent. 𝕮rest – A goat argent, guttee de poix, resting the dexter leg on an escutcheon gules, charged with a martlet of the first.
Residence – 61 Traverse le Mée, 13009-Marseilles, France.

BROTHER LIVING

ANTONY ANDREW (Darch House, Stogursey, Bridgwater, Som), *b* 21 May 1938; *ed* Charterhouse: *m* 1960, Anna Christina von Krogh, and has issue living, Andrew Richard, *b* 1962, — Tamsin Katrina, *b* 1961.

MOTHER LIVING

Yvonne Swingler, only da of late Joseph Arthur Hubert Bird: *m* 1933, (*m diss* 1944), Sqdn-Ldr Sir Richard William Boord, 3rd Bt, who *d* 1975.

The 1st baronet, Sir (Thomas) William Boord (el son of Joseph Boord, JP, of Harefield Grove, Uxbridge), was a partner in the firm of Boord and Son, distillers, and a Director of London and Provincial Bank Limited, and sat as MP for Greenwich (*C*) 1873-95.

BOOTH (UK) 1916, of Allerton Beeches, City of Liverpool

Neither rashly nor timidly

Sir DOUGLAS ALLEN BOOTH, 3rd *Baronet*; *b* 2 Dec 1949; *s* his father, Sir PHILIP, 1960; television and film writer; *ed* Beverley Hill High Sch, and Harvard Univ (BA): *m* 1991, Yolanda Marcela Scantlebury, and has issue.

Arms – Per pale and per chevron argent, ermine, and sable, in chief two boars' heads erased and erect of the last and in base a like boar's head of the first. **Crest** – A rose gules, barbed, seeded and encircled by two olive branches proper, thereon a lion passant argent.
Residence – 1626 Sycamore Drive, Topanga, CA 90290, USA.

DAUGHTER LIVING

Zahra Jessica, *b* 1993.

BROTHER LIVING

DEREK BLAKE, *b* 7 April 1953; *ed* Hampshire Coll, and Univ of California (BA).

UNCLE LIVING (*Son of 1st baronet*)

Edmund, *b* 1908: *m* 1933, Henrietta Mary, who *d* 1987, da of late Sir Charles (Stewart) Addis, KCMG, and has issue living, Anthony Edmund, *b* 1934; *ed* Gordonstoun, and King's Coll, Camb (MB, BCh); FRCS, FRCSE: *m* 1st, 1957, Margaret Helen Elizabeth, da of late Maj A. B. Miller; 2ndly, 1969, Susan Ailsa Letitia, da of late Lt R. O'Neill Roe, RN, and has issue living (by 1st *m*), Edmund Stuart *b* 1960, Sam Andrew *b* 1962, Adam Piper *b* 1963, (by 2nd *m*) Harriet Ailsa *b* 1971, Emily Charlotte *b* 1973, — Martin Butler (60 Elmbridge, Churchgate St, Old Harlow, Essex), *b* 1936; *ed* Gordonstoun, and King's Coll, Camb (MA): *m* 1968, Margaret Hilary, da of Clifford Birch, of York, — Philip Addis, *b* 1946, — Edmund, *b* 1948, — (Mary) Rachel, *b* 1939; *ed* Cranborne Chase Sch: *m* 1967, James William Bruce Douglas, BM, BCh.

WIDOW LIVING OF SECOND BARONET

ETHEL, da of Joseph Greenfield, of New York, USA; has resumed surname of Booth: *m* 1st, 1948, as his 2nd wife, Sir Philip Booth, 2nd baronet, who *d* 1960; 2ndly, 1962 (*m diss* 1965), Prof Winston R. Weisman, PhD. *Residence* – 1255, Daniels Drive, Los Angeles, Calif 90035, USA.

The 1st baronet, Sir Alfred Allen (son of late Alfred Booth, JP, of Liverpool) was a director of Alfred Booth & Co, Ltd, and sometime chairman of Cunard Steamship Co, Ltd.

GORE-BOOTH (I) 1760, of Artarman, Sligo

Genti aequus utrique
Just to either line

Sir ANGUS JOSSLYN GORE-BOOTH, 8th *Baronet*; *b* 25 June 1920; *s* his brother, Sir MICHAEL SAVILE, 1987; *ed* Radley, and Worcester Coll, Oxford (BA); formerly Capt IG, served N-W Europe 1945: *m* 1948 (*m diss* 1954), Hon Rosemary Myra Vane, only da of 10th Baron Barnard, CMG, OBE, MC, TD, and has issue.

Arms – Quarterly of six: 1st quarterly, 1st and 4th, argent three boars heads couped and erect sable; 2nd and 3rd, gules, a fesse between three cross-crosslets or; 2nd, argent, on a fesse sable three bezants; 3rd, argent a lion's head erased between three crescents gules; 4th, gules three cinquefoils argent; 5th, gules on a bend or, three martlets; 6th, checky azure and argent a fesse gules. **Crest** – 1st, a lion passant pean, the dexter forepaw resting on a chaplet of roses proper, *Booth*; 2nd, a wolf rampant argent ducally gorged or, *Gore*. **Mottoes** – **over First Crest** – "Quod ero spero" (*I hope for what I shall be*); **over Second Crest** – "In hoc signo vinces" (*Under this sign thou shalt conquer*).
Seat – Lissadell, co Sligo.

SON LIVING

JOSSLYN HENRY ROBERT, *b* 5 Oct 1950; *ed* Eton, Balliol Coll, Oxford (BA) and INSEAD (MBA): *m* 1980, Jane Mary, only da of Hon Sir Roualeyn Hovell-Thurlow-Cumming-Bruce (*see* B Thurlow), and has issue living, Mary Georgina, *b* 1985, — Caroline Sarah, *b* 1987. *Residence* – Hartforth, Richmond, Yorks DL10 5JR.

DAUGHTER LIVING

Georgina Clara Rosaleen Eirenice, *b* 1949: *m* 1970 (*m diss* 1981), Clive Abercromby Blomfield-Smith, only son of Brig D. C. Blomfield-Smith, MBE, and has issue living, Edward Abercromby, *b* 1973; *ed* Wellington Coll, — Olivia Rosemary, *b* 1976. *Residence* – Zetland House, Staindrop, Darlington, co Durham.

COLLATERAL BRANCHES LIVING

Grandchildren of late Mordaunt Gore-Booth, yr son of 5th baronet:—
Issue of late Paul Henry Gore-Booth, GCMG, KCVO (*Baron Gore-Booth*), *b* 1909, *d* 1984 (*cr* a Life Baron 1969): *m* 1940, Patricia Mary (*Baroness Gore-Booth*) (152 Rivermead Court, Ranelagh Gdns, SW6 3SF), da of late Montague Ellerton, of Yokohama, Japan:—
Hon David Alwyn, CMG (c/o FCO, SW1A 2AH; 27 Wetherby Mansions, SW5 9BH), *b* 1943; *ed* Eton, and Ch Ch, Oxford (MA); HM Amb to Saudi Arabia since 1993; CMG 1990: *m* 1st, 1964 (*m diss* 1970), Jillian Sarah, yr da of James Wyatt Valpy;

2ndly, 1977, Mrs Mary Elizabeth Janet Gambetta, only da of Sir David Francis Muirhead, KCMG, CVO (*see* Hollenden, B, 1990 Edn), and has issue living (by 1st *m*), Paul Wyatt Julian, *b* 1968. —— *Hon* Christopher Hugh, *b* (twin) 1943; *ed* Eton, and Durham Univ: *m* 1st, 1979 (*m diss* 1988), Mrs Jolanta Maria Nicholls, only da of late Dr L. S. Bernacinski; 2ndly, 1993, Mrs Annette Sheila Melli, da of late Joseph Rose, and has issue living (by 1st *m*), Oliver Lucian Ralph, *b* 1980. —— *Hon* Celia Mary, *b* 1946; *ed* Downe House, and London Acad of Music and Dramatic Art: *m* 1983, Douglas George Gill, of 15a Pemberton Gdns, N19 5RR, and *d* 1992, leaving issue, Fionn Paul, *b* 1984. —— *Hon* Joanna Rosamond Georgina, *b* 1954; *ed* Sherborne Sch, and New Hall, Camb (MA): *m* 1978, Paul Richard Teverson, and has issue living, Richard Hugh, *b* 1984, — Peter Henry, *b* 1991, — Cathryn Frances, *b* 1986.

    Issue of late Colum Robert Gore-Booth, *b* 1913, *d* 1959: *m* 1st, 1939, Joan Yvonne Ballard, adopted da of Rev C. W. Chastel de Boinville; 2ndly, 1947, Mary (who *m* 2ndly, 1971, Michael William McLean Barker, who *d* 1982), da of late Edward Paget Scholfield, JP, of Sandhall, Howden, York (D Northumberland, colls):—
(By 2nd *m*) Francis Peter, *b* 1948. —— (Nicholas) Justin, *b* 1952: *m* 1982, (Patricia) Roberts, and has issue living, Jane, *b* 1984, — Helen, *b* 1986, — Sarah, *b* 1988. —— Susan Caroline, *b* 1950: *m* 1973, Ashley Casie-Chitty, who *d* 1982.
This family has a common origin with the Earl of Arran, Earl Temple of Stowe, Baron Harlech, and Gore Bt (*cr* 1622). Nathaniel Gore, father of Sir Booth Gore, 1st baronet, *m* 1711, Lettice, da and heir of Humphrey Booth, of Dublin. Sir Robert Newcomen Gore, 3rd baronet, assumed by Roy licence 1804, the additional surname and arms of Booth.

BOOTHBY (E) 1660, of Broadlow Ash, Derbyshire

Sir BROOKE CHARLES BOOTHBY, 16th *Baronet*; *b* 6 April 1949; *s* his father, *Sir* HUGO ROBERT BROOKE, 1986; *ed* Eton, and Trin Coll, Camb: *m* 1976, Georgiana Alexandra, da of late Sir John Wriothesley Russell, GCVO, CMG (*see* D Bedford, colls), and has issue.

Arms – Argent, on a canton sable a lion's jamb erased erect or. **Crest** – A lion's jamb as in the arms.
Residence – Fonmon Castle, Barry, South Glamorgan, CF62 3ZN.

DAUGHTERS LIVING

Aliki Ann Charlotte, *b* 1977. —— Francesca Rafela Marina, *b* 1983.

SISTERS LIVING

Penelope Ann, *b* 1939: *m* 1959 (*m diss* 1965), Cdr Timothy Hale, RN, and has issue living, Veronica Ann Leslie, *b* 1960. —— Caroline Serena, *b* 1941: *m* 1st 1962 (*m diss* 1972), Ifor Lewis; 2ndly 1977, Richard Hugh Parry, of Manton Weir Farm, Manton, Marlborough, and has issue living (by 1st *m*), Vivienne Serena, *b* 1966, — Carina Cecilia, *b* 1969, — (by 2nd *m*) James Hugo, *b* 1981.

AUNT LIVING (*Daughter of 14th Baronet*)

The death of Christ is to me the death of death

Serena Margaret, *b* 1914: *m* 1958, Herbert Charles Richards Homfray, who *d* 1960. *Residence* – Church House, Penllyn, Cowbridge, Glamorgan.

COLLATERAL BRANCHES LIVING

    Grandsons of late George Boothby (*infra*):—
    Issue of late George William Bernard Boothby, *b* 1917, *d* 1972: *m* 1942, Avril Alice, who *d* 1993, da of John Edward Innell:—
GEORGE WILLIAM (Ivy Wall House, Back Lane, Batcombe, Shepton Mallet, Somerset), *b* 18 June 1948; Capt Merchant Navy: *m* 1977, Sally Louisa Thomas, and has issue living, Jane Penelope, *b* 1979, — Fenella Susan, *b* 1981, — Imogen Roberta, *b* 1982. —— Richard Charles Brooke (83 St Quintin's Av, N Kensington W10 6PB), *b* 16 Dec 1955; *ed* Barry Boys' Comprehensive Sch, Manchester Univ (MusB), and Salzburg Mozarteum; musician: *m* 1992, Fiona Clare, da of Peter Padfield.

    Granddaughter of late Com George William Boothby, son of late Rev Brooke Boothby, 2nd son of 7th baronet:—
    Issue of late George Boothby, *b* 1867, *d* 1921: *m* 1904, Mabel Gertrude, who *d* 1961, da of Bernard Flanagan:—
Violet Dora, *b* 1908: *m* 1935, Ernest Victor Evans, of 11 Birch Grove, Barry, S Glam CF6 8SX, and has issue living, Geoffrey Boothby (44 Greenfield Rd, Brunton Park, Gosforth, Newcastle-upon-Tyne), *b* 1937; MSc, PhD: *m* 1964, Elizabeth Jane Furneaux Friend, and has issue living, Michael Meredith *b* 1965, Susan Sian *b* 1967. —— Edna Frances, *b* 1910: *m* 1940, Ronald George Henry Steele, and has issue living, Elizabeth Penelope *b* 1944. *Residence* – Rangeworthy, 3 West Town Drive, Brislington, Bristol.

    Granddaughters of late Capt William Osbert Boothby, CVO, CB, RN (*infra*):—
    Issue of late Maj Christopher Evelyn Boothby, RM, *b* 1912, *d* 1991: *m* 1940, Pamela Gertrude (26 Cwrt Deri, Heol-y-Felin, Rhiwbina, Cardiff CF4 6JB), da of late Frederick Lewis Heriot-Maitland (*see* E Lauderdale, colls):—
Marilyn Susan, *b* 1944: *m* 1967, Stanley LeBlanc, of 2301 Oakwood Drive, Carrollton, Texas 75006, USA, and has issue living, James Boothby, *b* 1971, — Sarah Maria, *b* 1968. —— Diana Mary, *b* 1948: *m* 1969, John Michael Spiller, of 3 Clos Brynderi, Rhiwbina, Cardiff, S Wales, and has issue living, Nicholas Michael, *b* 1979, — Christina Ruth, *b* 1976.

    Grandchildren of late Basil Tanfield Beridge Boothby (*infra*):—
    Issue of late (Evelyn) Basil Boothby, CMG, *b* 1910, *d* 1990: *m* 1946, Susan Penelope (23 Holland Park Av, W11), da of late Brig Gen Hon Arthur Melland Asquith, DSO (*see* E Oxford and Asquith, colls):—
John Joseph (19 Frithville Gdns, W12), *b* 1947; *ed* St Lawrence Coll, Ramsgate, and London Univ: *m* 1982, Isabel Rose, eldest da of John Paget Chancellor (*see* Paget, Bt, *cr* 1886), and has issue living, Roland Arthur, *b* 1984, — Francis George, *b* 1987, — Dolores Ann, *b* 1992. —— †Philip Sebastian, *b* 1952; *d* 1974. —— Henry Alexander (459 Latimer Rd, W10 6RD), *b* 1955 *ed* Trin Coll, Dublin, MB BS 19—: *m* 1992, Laura Frances Albinia, elder da of Richard St Clair de la Mare (*see* M Normanby, colls). —— Emily Albertine, *b* 1948: *m* 1967, Piers Paul Read, writer, of 50 Portland Rd, W11 4LG, son of late Sir Herbert Edward Read, DSO, MC, and has issue living, Albert Nathaniel, *b* 1970, — William Edward, *b* 1978, — Martha Mariana, *b* 1972, — Beatrice Mary, *b* 1981.

Granddaughters of late Rev Evelyn Boothby, 2nd son of Rev Charles Boothby, 3rd son of 7th baronet:—
Issue of late Capt William Osbert Boothby, CVO, CB, RN, *b* 1866, *d* 1913: *m* 1907, Hilda Lambert, who *d* 1960, da of late Capt Henry Stephen Swiney, 69th Regt:—
Margaretta Laura, *b* 1908. *Residence* – 22 Providence Place, Abbey St, Farnham, Surrey.
Issue of late Basil Tanfield Beridge Boothby, *b* 1873, *d* 1948: *m* 1909, Katharine Georgina, who *d* 1938, only surviving da of late Major F. B. Knox, RA:—
(Katharine) Anne, *b* 1915: *m* 1939, Col Hubert Layard Chesshyre, RE, who *d* 1981, and has issue living, (David) Hubert Boothby, LVO, FSA, *b* 1940; Rouge Croix Pursuivant of Arms 1970-78, since when Chester Herald of Arms; Registrar College of Arms since 1992; Secretary, Order of the Garter; LVO 1988, — William John, *b* 1943; Col late RE, Defence Attaché, Prague: *m* 1975, Capt Bimala Bangdel, QARANC, of Kalimpong, W Bengal, — Matthew Henry (1 Grasmere Rd, Muswell Hill, N10 2DH), *b* 1944; MA, MB, BChir, MRCGP, FFARCS: *m* 1976, Jennifer Diana, da of Maj John Christopher Clapham Maude, MC, Croix de Guerre, and has issue living, Emily Laura Diana *b* 1977, Lydia Katharine *b* 1979, Mary Elizabeth *b* 1983, — John Francis, *b* 1948: *m* 1982, Mary Rebecca, el da of late Maj J. F. J. Worth, of The Mount, Salisbury, and has issue living, Joseph Hugo *b* 1984, Thomas Francis *b* 1985, Sarah Margaret *b* 1990, Rebecca Katharine *b* 1992, — Katharine Mildred, *b* 1947: *m* 1969, Thomas Peregrine Stansfeld Bryant, MA, DipArch, of 24 Exeter House, Putney Heath, SW15 3SX, and has issue living, William Hugh Chesshyre *b* 1974, Charlotte Rosemary Chesshyre *b* (twin) 1974, Jessica Katharine Chesshyre *b* 1980, — Alice Jane, *b* 1956: *m* 1st, 1984 (*m diss* 1989), Marc Mucha; 2ndly, 1992, Mark Timothy Swanston Sutton, Prof Guildhall Sch of Music & Drama. *Residence* – Don Jon House, Canterbury.

Grandson of late Rev Walter Ralph Jebb Boothby, 3rd son of Col Basil Charles Boothby (infra):—
Issue of late Basil Frederick Boothby, MBE, *b* 1904, *d* 1984: *m* 1934, Dorothy Marian, who *d* 1990, da of Frank Gould, of Ryde, I of Wight, and Calcutta:—
Christopher Brooke (St Nicholas, Hollow Rd, Bury St Edmunds, Suffolk), *b* 1938; *ed* Lancing; MRCP London, MRCS, FRCP England; Consultant Paediatrician, W Suffolk Hosp; Hon Clinical Assist, Hosp for Sick Children, Gt Ormond St; Mem of Gen Nursing Council for England and Wales since 1978: *m* 1969, Anne Barrow Dalston, of Torcross, Devon, and has issue living, Hugo Thomas Brooke, *b* 1972, — William Jebb Dalston, *b* (twin) 1972, — Margaret Elizabeth Prescott, *b* 1974.

Grandchildren of late Col Basil Charles Boothby, 4th son of late Rev Charles Boothby (ante):—
Issue of late Capt Evelyn Leonard Beridge Boothby, DSO, RN, *b* 1876; *d* 1937: *m* 1st, 1905, Esmé Frances Nevill Augusta, who *d* 1913, da of Sir Edward Beauchamp, 1st Bt, MP; 2ndly, 1924, Lucy Margaret Amy, who *d* 1948, widow of Capt F. T. Gardiner, Highland LI:—
(By 2nd *m*) Walter Evelyn Brooke (40 Calmore Gdns, Totton, Southampton), *b* 1927: *m* 1st, 1951 (*m diss* 1974), Yvonne, da of J. S. Capewell, of Harlesden, NW; 2ndly, 1974, Catharine Jane, da of Ralph Forrester Stobart, of Newton Farm, Tregony, Cornwall, and has issue living (by 1st *m*), Martin William (Owl Lodge, 14 Kings North Gdns, Folkestone, Kent CT20 2QW), *b* 1953: *m* 1982, Stephanie Anne, da of H. G. Mills, of Portstuart, co Londonderry, and has issue living, Bryn *b* 1982, Tara *b* 1980, — Bruce Michael (123 Walnut Tree Rd, Charlton Village, Shepperton, Middx TW17 0RR), *b* 1959: *m* 1984, Trudy Frith, da of Kenneth Frith Williams, of Sunbury, Middlesex.
A baronetcy was conferred, in 1644, upon Henry Boothby, of Claytor Close; but, though the creation received the sign-manual of Charles I, it did not pass the Great Seal, by reason of the confusion of the civil wars. At the Restoration his only son, William Boothby, of Broadlow Ash, Derbyshire, was *cr* a Baronet *de novo* by Charles II, with the date of 1660. Ashbourne Hall, Derbyshire, the seat of the family for 200 years, was sold in 1846, in accordance with the will of the 9th baronet. The 10th baronet, Sir Brooke, was in Diplo Ser, and the 11th, Sir Charles Francis, was Lieut N Mayo Mil.

BOREEL (E) 1645, of Amsterdam, Holland
(Name pronounced "Borale")

Jonkheer Sir FRANCIS DAVID BOREEL, 13th *Baronet*; *b* 14 June 1926; *s* his father *Jonkheer Sir* ALFRED, 1964, *ed* Univ of Utrecht: *m* 1964, Suzanne, da of Willy Campagne, of Paris, and has issue.

𝔄rms – Argent, on a chevron between three bugle horns sable, two whips thonged proper, on a chief gules a lion passant guardant or. 𝔖upporters – On clouds two angels proper, vested argent.
Residence – Kapellstraat 25, 4351 AL Veere, Netherlands.

DAUGHTERS LIVING

Reiniera Adriana, *b* 1965. —— Christina Wilhelmina, *b* 1966. —— Titia Florence, *b* 1973.

COLLATERAL BRANCHES LIVING

Granddaughters of late Jonkheer William Walter Astor Boreel, son of late Jonkheer Francis Robert Boreel, son of Lt-Gen William Francis Boreel, 3rd son of 7th baronet:—
Issue of late Jonkheer Robert John Ralph Boreel, *b* 1867, *d* 1904: *m* 1891, Edith Margaret, who *d* 1933 (having *m* 2ndly, 1905, Jacob Pieter Crommelin), da of Philo Ives, of Hartford, Connecticut, USA:—
Helen Barbara Isabella (c/o Nat Westminster Bank, 96-97 Strand, WC2), *b* 1894: *m* 1921 (*m diss* 1944), Ralph Clarmont Skrine Stevenson, CMG (*cr* KCMG 1946 and GCMG 1949), who *d* 1977, and has issue living, Mark Boreel *b* 1924. —— (Edith) Wendela Dorothy, *b* 1896; Asso R Soc Painter Etchers: *m* 1924, Leslie George Wylde, late Lt Canterbury Regt (NZ Forces), who *d* 1935, and has issue living, James Paxton de Eglesfield, *b* 1927. *Residence* –

Grandchildren of late Jonkheer James Lucas Boreel (infra):—
Issue of late Jonkheer Gerard Lucas Cornelis Boreel, *b* 1913, *d* 1970: *m* 1943, Virginia Rae who *d* 1972, da of Frank Gervin Bright, of New York:—
STEPHAN GERARD (Elzenoord 30, 8172 AZ Vaassen, Netherlands), *b* 9 Feb 1945: *m* Francien P. Kooijman, and has issue living, Jacob Lucas Cornelis, *b* 29 Sept 1974. —— Maurits (Wieselseweg 102, 7345 CC Apeldoorn, Netherlands), *b* 1946: *m* 1971, Tilde Anna Eisma, and has issue living, Gerard Lucas, *b* 1973, — Joris Siebrand, *b* 1975, — Maurits Willem, *b* 1981. —— Joan (Grentelsweg 70, 7345 CR Wenum Wiesel, Netherlands) *b* 1949.

Grandchildren of late Jonkheer Gerard Salomon Boreel, 2nd son of Jonkheer Jacob Otto Bernard Boreel, yr son of Jonkheer Lucas Boreel, 4th son of 7th baronet:—
Issue of late Jonkheer James Lucas Boreel, b 1883, d 1939: m 1911, Baroness Adriana Sophia, who d 1958, da of Baron Maurits van Randwijck:—
Maurits (Oude Kleefsebaan 217, 6572 AM Bergen Dal, Netherlands), b 1914: m 1942 (m diss 1980), Antoinette Crommelin, and has issue living, Lucas Jacob (Beekmansdalseweg 9 6522 KC, Nijmegen, Netherlands), b 1945: m 1st 1966 (m diss 1975), Henriette van Teunenbroek; 2ndly 1978, Angeline Marie Sassen, and has issue living (by 1st m), Elsa-Bertha b 1967: m 1992, Emile R. Lemoine, of USA, Esther Nanette b 1970, (by 2nd m) Sophie Mechteld b 1980, Maeke Willemijn b 1982, — Paul Marinus (Rembrandtlaan 22, 3941 CH Doorn, Netherlands), b 1949: 19—, Simone C. Bouwman, and has issue living, David Gustaaf b 1979, Thomas Arthur b 1982, — Willem (Beerse 112, 3961 HE Wijk bij Duurstende, Netherlands), b 1952: m 1978 (m diss 1983), Louis G. Peizel, and has issue living, Robert Jan b 1981, — Jacoba Francina, b 1943: m 1968, Arnold Hendrick Tieleman. —— Henriette, b 1917: m 1947, Dirk J. G. Buurman, of Hulkesteinflat, Utrechtseweg 145/101, 6812 AB Arnhem, Netherlands.
Issue of late Jonkheer Hugo Boreel, b 1884, d 1962: m 1930, Baroness Emilie Henriette Adele, who d 1970, da of Baron Cornelis Jan van Tuyll van Serooskerken:—
Lucas Gerard (Eikenhorstlaan, 19, 2245 BC Wassenaar, Netherlands), b 1931: m 1960, Marie Louise, da of Pierre van Son. —— Cornelis Jan (Pieter de Hooghlaan 23, 3723 GR Bilthoven, Netherlands) b 1932; Sec Boreel Foundation: m 1959, Claudine Wilhelmina Woltera, da of Willem Jan Royaards, and has issue living, Robert Jan Willem, b 1960: m 1993, Sigrid, da of S. Karsten, — Lucas Wolter, b 1966: m 1994, Jacqueline Nelly, da of H.A.G. Hofman, — Claudine Emilie Amarante, b 1963: m 1992, H.M. Hinloopen. —— Geert Frans (Bruggenbosch, Blikkenweg 15, 7391 NA Twello, Netherlands) b 1934: m 1958, Henriette Nancy Leopoldine, da of Jonkheer B W. F. van Riemsdijk, and has issue living, Hugo Geert (Ohrobecka 420, 1400 Praag Libus, Czech Republic), b 1959: m 1986, Alice Marie, da of William Schwartz, — Barthold Willem Lucas (Kloveniersburgwal 103 II, 1011 KB Amsterdam, Netherlands), b 1960: m 1992, Petra Martine, da of Pieter Arie de Ruiter, and has issue living, Daan Floris b 1993, — Pauline Danielle, b 1964.

Granddaughter of late Jonkheer Jacob Otto Bernard Boreel, 5th son of late Jonkheer Jacob Otto Bernard Boreel (ante):—
Issue of late Jonkheer Marius Willem Boreel, b 1856, d 1905: m 1886, Cornelia, who d 1939, da of late Jonkheer Theodor Prins van Westdorpe, of Haarlem, Netherlands:—
Catharina Margaretha, b 1891: m 1918, Henri Louis van Eeghen, who d 1977. Residence – Noordhout, Driebergen, Netherlands.

Grandson of late Jonkheer Paulus James Boreel, 5th son of late Jonkheer Jacob Otto Bernard Boreel (ante):—
Issue of late Marie Boreel, b 1893, d 1971: m 1925, James Skinner Mackenzie Eddison, OBE, who d 1965.
John Michael (Suite N° 102 FNP, GF Cosmopolitan Tower Condo, 134 Valero St, Makati, Metro Manila, Philippines), b 1930; BSc, FICE, FASCE, MIStructE, MEIC: m 1956, Marjorie Joyce Halley.

Grandchildren of late Jonkheer Hendrik Etienne Gustave Boreel (infra):—
Issue of late Jonkheer Jacob Gerard Joseph Boreel, b 1891, d 1945: m 1914, Charlotte Susanna (Hanenburglaan 198, The Hague), da of Eduard Manuel:—
Henri Etienne Gustave (Pyrolalaan 80, 2554 HG, The Hague, Netherlands), b 1915: m 1949, Hendrika Catharina Allegonda, da of Ferdinand Karel August Luder, and has issue living, Henri Etienne Gustave (Pr Beatrixlaan 104, 2741 DJ Waddixveen, Netherlands), b 1952: m 1990, Janneke van der Gaag, — Jacqueline Marguérite Charlotte, b 1950, — Margot Jeanne Françoise, b 1955, — Jacqueline Louise, b 1918: m 1943, Jan Arbouw, of Sportlaan 466, The Hague, Netherlands.
Issue of late Jonkheer Willem Boreel, b 1893, d 1973: m 1915, Clasine Justine Cornelie, da of Willem Anton Van Andel:—
Robert Hugo, b 1919; Maj-Gen Dutch Army: m 1939, Marie Louise Colette, da of Wilhelmus Jacobus Antonius Van der Valk, and has issue living, Paul, b 1947: m 1968, Martha Deirdre de Graaf, and has issue living, Daphne Cherette b 1968, Cynthia Jasmine b 1970, — Ernst Boudewijn, b 1948, — Maud, b 1941: m 1964, Frederik Racke. —— Paul René, b 1922: m 1946, Audrey, da of Arthur James Ritchie, and has issue living, Robert Willem, b 1947, — Helen Elisabeth, b 1948: m 1970, Wayne McKell. —— Jeanne Marie Josephine, b 1916: m 1939, Hendrik Dirk Buurman, who d 1989, of Brussels, Belgium.

Grandchildren of late Jonkheer Theodoor Gustaaf Victor Boreel, son of late Jacob Boreel (b 1777), son of late Jacob Boreel (b 1746), next brother of 7th baronet:—
Issue of late Jonkheer Hendrick Etienne Gustave Boreel, b 1866, d 1908: m 1889, Jeanne Josephine, who d 1944, da of Jacob Gerard Joseph Breyman:—
Alfred, b 1894: m 1st, 1920 (m diss 1953), Marie Francoise, da of Frederik Hendrik de Bruine; 2ndly, 1955, Raden Dalia Mingsih, and has issue living (by 1st wife), Jacob Alfred, MD (Korte Parkweg 4, Bloemendaal, Netherlands), b 1932: m 1st, 1959 (m diss 1982), Albertine, da of Jan Willem Cornelis De Vletter; 2ndly, 1984, Martine van Leeuwen, and has issue living (by 1st m), Jacob Jan b 1960, David Tibor b 1962, Michiel (van Dalenlaan 10, 2082 VG Santpoer-Ouid, Netherlands) b 1963: m 1988, Carla Louise van Gorselan, — Eleonore, b 1920: m 1951, Cornelis Ian Reindert Phaff, — Ilse Anetta Jacoba, b 1924: m 1951, Gustaaf Adolf Cordesius, of Vlierboomstraat 614, The Hague, Netherlands, — (by 2nd wife), David Dradjat, b 1959, — Yvonne Annette, b 1953. —— Jacoba, b 1895: m 1917, Rene Johny Kerdijk, of Djkarta, Indonesia, who d 1968.

Granddaughters of late Jonkheer Johan Jacob Boreel, 2nd son of Jonkheer Theodoor Gustaaf Victor Boreel (ante):—
Issue of late Jonkheer Willem Boreel, CBE, Capt R Netherlands Navy, b 1895; d 1977: m 1923, Ernestina Augusta Maria (Dennenlaan 101, 6711 RB Ede, Netherlands), da of Prof Dr Hajo Brugmans:—
Maria Augusta, b 1924: m 1953, Cornelis Christiaan van Saarloos, MD (Helomapark 10, 9244 BT Beetsterzwaag, Friesland, Netherlands). —— Sophia Fredrika, b 1927: m 1958, Dr Mario Mancosu (Piedimonte 35, Terni, Umbria, Italy).

Grandchildren of late Jonkheer Victor Eduard Anthon Boreel, 3rd son of Jonkheer Theodoor Gustaaf Victor Boreel (ante):—
Issue of late Jonkheer Willem Boreel, b 1898, d 1981: m 1926, Elizabeth Johanna MAria Peman (96 Paulinastraat, The Hague, Netherlands), da of Dr Adriaan Marinus Kakebeeke:—
†Victor Eduard, b 1928: m 1955, Gijsberta, da of Dirk Nicolaas Verschoor, and d 1992, leaving issue, Willem Hendrik Dirk, b 1956, — Victor Cornelis, b 1959, — Barbara Saskia, b 1961: m 1992, Pieter van der Meulen.
Issue of late Jonkheer Eduard Boreel, b 1901, d 1967: m 1st (m diss 1946), Karin Elisabeth, who d 1992, da of Jonkheer Maximiliaan Jacob Theodor van de Poll; 2nd, 1950, Maria Luisa Marques (Rua Ribeiro Sanches 21-3, Lisbon, Portugal), da of Dr José Santos Gouveia:—
(By 1st m) Victor Charles (Vaartstraat 55, Brugge, Belgium), b 1932: m 1957, Béatrice Marie Louise Andrée, da of Jonkheer Paul Marie Camille Frédéric de Kerckhove dit van der Varent and has issue living, Frederik Eduard Paul, b 1958: m 1991, Reinira M., da of Baron van Pallandt, — Christine Ghislaine Béatrice Karin b 1957. —— Maximiliaan Willem Felix (Brouillaud, 24300 Nontron, France), b 1935: m 1962, Meta Dorothea Ludmilla, da of René André Rost Onnes, and has issue living, Ghislaine Cornélie Carine, b 1963: m 1988, Thoomas Crema, of Georgetown, Washington, DC, USA, — Eugénie Renée b 1965: m 1990, Willem Bos, of Cologny, Geneva, Switzerland. —— Karin Ghislaine Johanna (21 Av Herbert Hoover, Brussels) b 1940.

The 1st baronet, an envoy to England, was knighted by King James I in 1619, and it is related that he received from King Charles II on 28 June 1653, a Royal Warrant as a Baron of England. The 9th baronet was a Member of the Upper House of Representatives in the Netherlands, and was several times President of the Second Chamber of the States-General, and Gov of North Holland. The 10th Baronet, was Gentleman of the Privy Chamber to the King of the Netherlands and subsequently Chamberlain to the Queen of the Netherlands.

BORTHWICK (UK) 1908, of Whitburgh, Humbie, Co Haddington

Sir JOHN THOMAS BORTHWICK, MBE, 3rd *Baronet*; only son of late Hon James Alexander Borthwick, 2nd son of 1st Bt; *b* 5 Dec 1917, *s* to baronetcy on death of his uncle, 1st and last Baron Whitburgh, 1967; *ed* Eton, and Trin Coll, Oxford; late Maj Rifle Brig (TA); MBE (Mil) 1945: *m* 1st, 1939 (*m diss* 1961), Irene, who *d* 1978, only child of Joseph Heller, of 2 Buckingham Place, SW1; 2ndly, 1962, Irene, da of late Leo Fink, of 26 Rue Franqueville, Paris XVI, and has issue living by 1st and 2nd *m*.

Arms – Argent, a cinque foil sable, on a chief invected of the last two cinquefoils of the first. **Crest** – A staff raguly fessewise sable, thereon a blackamoor's head in profile couped proper.
Residence – 41 Mizzentop, Warwick, Bermuda.

SONS LIVING *(By 1st marriage)*

ANTONY THOMAS (1 Arundel Gdns, W11 2LN), *b* 12 Feb 1941; *ed* Eton: *m* 1st, 1966, Gillian Deirdre Broke, twin da of Nigel Vere Broke Thurston, RN; 2ndly, 1985, Jenny, eldest da of George Lanning, and has issue living (by 1st *m*), Matthew Thomas Thurston, *b* 1968, — Suzanna Claire Irene, *b* 1970, — Camilla Fay Broke, *b* 1973. —— Peter Richard John, *b* 1943: *m* 1970, Helen, yr da of T. C. Vogel, of Cudgewa, Vic, Aust, and has issue living, Linton, *b* 1977, — Maya Irene, *b* 1975, — Iona Christine, *b* 1980. —— Patrick James Joseph (10 Llanvair Close, South Ascot, Berks) *b* 1945: *m* 1st, 1969, Amanda Rosemary, yr da of R. G. A. Wells, of Lines End, Winchelsea, Sussex; 2ndly 1978, Sally A., da of Geoffrey Chase Gardner, and has issue living, (by 1st *m*) Alexander, *b* 1971, — (by 2nd *m*) Edward, *b* 1978, — Timothy, *b* 1983, — Sophie, *b* 1977, — Annabel, *b* 1981.

(By 2nd marriage)

Mark George Alexander, *b* 1962: *m* 1988, Maria Cornejo. —— John Kelly Leo, *b* 1965.

COLLATERAL BRANCHES LIVING

Issue of late Hon William Borthwick, 3rd son of 1st baronet, and brother of 1st Baron Whitburgh, *b* 1879, *d* 1956: *m* 1909, Ruth Margery, who *d* 1971, only da of late Jason Rigby, MICE, of Wimbledon, SW:— William Jason Maxwell, DSC (North House, Brancaster Staithe, King's Lynn, Norfolk) *b* 1910; *ed* Winchester and Trin Coll, Camb; Bar Inner Temple 1933; late Com RNVR; 1939-45 War (DSC): *m* 1937, Elizabeth Cleveland, who *d* 1978, da of late Herbert Elworthy, of Timaru, NZ, and has issue living, Alister Jason (Deepdale Farm, Burnham Deepdale, King's Lynn, Norfolk), *b* 1945: *m* 1970, Verily Anne, da of Albert Augur East, and has issue living, Jason Matthew *b* 1971, Fiona Anne *b* 1974, Anna Elizabeth *b* 1981, — Josephine Cleveland, *b* 1939: *m* 1960, John James Luddington (Millhouse, Brancaster, King's Lynn, Norfolk), and has issue living, Peter William *b* 1966, Julia Ruth *b* 1961: *m* 1983, Mark Eustace Landon, Mary Elizabeth *b* 1965, — Rosalind Cleveland, *b* 1942: *m* 1968, Robert Andrew Spedding, of The Manor, Sampford Spiney, Horrabridge, Devon, and has issue living, Harry George William *b* 1973, Joanne Elizabeth *b* 1970, — Celia Cleveland, *b* 1947. *Clubs* – United University, Royal Thames Yacht. —— (Elinor) Valerie, *b* 1915: *m* 1940, Maj Robert William Augustus Fane, MBE, RA, who *d* 1989, and has issue (*see* E Westmorland, colls). *Residence* – Hoo Lodge, Hoo, Woodbridge, Suffolk. —— Margaret Ruth, *b* 1926: *m* 1949, Henry Neville Hemsley, and has issue living, John Neville, *b* 1956: *m* 1984, Nicole Irene, da of Rudolph Hans Walter, of Zürich, and has issue living, Ralph Neville *b* 1985, Colette Irene *b* 1987, — Oliver Charles, *b* 1960, — Clare Margaret, *b* 1953: *m* 1980, Charles Edward Spencer Atkins, and has issue living, Edward Oliver *b* 1982, Nicholas Charles *b* 1985, Matthew Spencer *b* 1988, — Patricia Mary, *b* 1964. *Residence* – Langham Lodge, Oakham, Rutland.

Grandchildren of late Hon William Borthwick (ante):—
Issue of late Brian Thomas Borthwick, *b* 1920, *d* 1989: *m* 1946, Jennifer Ruth, JP (Manor Farm Lodge, Brancaster, King's Lynn, Norfolk PE31 8AU), da of Maj Evelyn Ronald Moncrieff Fryer, MC, Gren Gds, of Selborne, Hants (*see* E Peel, colls, 1985 Edn):—
Simon William Frederick (36 Kenilworth Rd, W5), *b* 1950: *m* 1974, Bozena, da of Alfons Edward Podwojski, of Poland, and has issue living, Michael Edward Waclaw, *b* 1977, — Ian Philip Miroslaw, *b* 1979, — William Martin Stanislaw, *b* 1981, — Alexander Thomas Zdzilaw, *b* 1983. —— Nicholas James, *b* 1953: *m* 1981, Peng-Chin, da of Lával Li Kwong In, of Mauritius, and has issue living, Anthony Timothy William, *b* 1984. —— Charles Thomas, *b* 1955: *m* 1984, Jayne Alexandra, only da of Donald Cooke, of Warmington, Peterborough, and has issue living, Maximilian Thomas *b* 1985, — Anna Georgina, *b* 1987. —— Timothy Michael (10 St Ann's Villas, W11), *b* 1958: *m* 1987, Justin, yr da of Jerry Rosenholtz, of Chicago, USA. —— Sara Marjorie, *b* 1951.

Grandchildren of late Hon Malcolm Algernon Borthwick (infra):—
Issue of late Lt-Col Algernon Malcolm Borthwick, MC, TD, *b* 1907, *d* 1975: *m* 1935, Edith Wylde, who *d* 1975, da of James Stanley Addison, of Wethersfield Place, Essex:—
Malcolm (Heriot, Midlothian), *b* 1938: *m* 1966, Dorothy Mary Prudence, 2nd da of Alan M. Barker, of Salisbury, and has issue living, Benedict, *b* 1971, — Sophie Alexander, *b* 1967, — Kate Cecile, *b* 1969. —— Winifred Letitia, OBE, *b* 1936; Trustee Nat Portrait Gallery since 1992; OBE (Civil) 1992: *m* 1962, His Honour Judge (Stephen) Tumim, HM Ch Inspector of Prisons and has issue living, Matilda Edith, *b* 1963, — Emma Renée, *b* 1964, — Olivia, *b* 1968. —— Lucilla Blanche, *b* 1942: *m* 1960 (*m diss* 1977), Hon Samuel James Butler (*see* B Butler of Saffron Walden).

Issue of late Hon Malcolm Algernon Borthwick, yst son of 1st baronet, and brother of 1st Baron Whitburgh, *b* 1881, *d* 1941: *m* 1905, Blanche Buckland, who *d* 1965, da of Henry Thomson Gorrie, of Auckland, NZ:—

Patrick John (Te Whanga, Masterton, NZ), *b* 1908; *ed* Harrow: *m* 1931, Nancy Hope, who *d* 1984, da of Guy C. Williams, of Te Parae, Masterton, NZ, and has issue living, Thomas Malcolm (Rocklands, Redesdale, Vic 3444, Australia), *b* 1933; *ed* Harrow: *m* 1957, Wendy Alison, da of late Linden Wood, of N Adelaide, and has issue living, Thomas Linden *b* 1958; *ed* MGS Melbourne: *m* 19—, Margaret Mary, da of late Edward Ferncliffe Bartley (and has issue living, Lachlan Thomas *b* 1991, Charles Patrick *b* 1993), Angus Patrick *b* 1959; *ed* Geelong Gram Sch: *m* 1985, Jane Amanda Louise, da of late Robin Ninian Paisley (and has issue living, Williamm James *b* 1988, Harry Robert *b* 1991), Nigel *b* 1963; *ed* Scotch Coll: *m* 1994, Susan Valentia, da of Christopher James Stafford Morris, — Robin John (Waitui, Masterton, NZ), *b* 1938: *m* 19—, Robin Gay McGregor, and has issue living, Patrick John *b* 1967, Shamus James *b* 1969, Belinda Hope *b* 1965, — Hamish Charles (Dakabin, McDonalds Rd, Palmwoods, Qld 4555, Australia), *b* 1940; *ed* Christ's Coll, NZ: *m* 1965, Anne Florence, eldest da of Edward Dixon Cameron, of Teebah, Hannaford, Qld, and has issue living, Geoffrey Robert *b* 1966, Andrew Hamish *b* 1968: *m* 1991, Cindy-Anne, yst da of James Lawson Storey, of Mooloolaba, Qld, James Patrick *b* 1971: *m* 1994, Karen Maree, eldest da of Noel Garth Hooper, of Buderim, Qld, Fiona Anne Jeane *b* 1969, — Patricia Mary, *b* 1936: *m* 1956, Michael Dillon Bell, of Ngaiana, Masterton, NZ, and has issue living, Henry Dillon (Ngaiana, Masterton, NZ) *b* 1957; *ed* Christ's Coll, NZ: *m* 19—, Rebecca Anne Lawrence (and has issue living, Amelia *b* 1988, Emma *b* 1990), Johnathan Dillon *b* 1960: *m* 1990, Lady Lilias Catriona Maighearad Graham, da of 7th Duke of Montrose (and has issue living, Charles *b* 1993), Sarah *b* 1959: *m* 1982, Roger Broughton, of Pohatu, Masterton, NZ (and has issue living, Thomas *b* 1986, Belinda *b* 1985, Rosie *b* 1989), Nicola Mary *b* 1962: *m* 1989, Marcus Yardley Wilkins, of 131 Grace Rd, Tauranga, NZ (and has issue living, Marcus George *b* 1991, Patrick James *b* 1993). —— Letitia Blanche, *b* 1913: *m* 1st, 1934, Capt Michael Valentine Paul Fleming, who *d* of wounds while a pow 1940 (Rose, Bt, *cr* 1874, colls); 2ndly, 1945, James Currie Thomson, MBE, TD, JP, DL, late Lt-Col Queen's Own Cameron Highlanders, and has had issue (by 1st *m*), Valentine Patrick (Stonewall Park, Edenbridge, Kent), *b* 1935: *m* 1963, Elizabeth Helen, only da of late Hon Sir Geoffrey Cokayne Gibbs, KCMG (*see* B Aldenham, colls), and has issue living, Matthew Valentine (Great Woodland Farm, Lyminge, Kent) *b* 1964: *m* 1989, Caroline Mary, yst da of John Joseph Buxton, of Horsey Hall, Gt Yarmouth, Norfolk (*see* Buxton, Bt, colls) (and has issue living, Hannah Elizabeth *b* 1992), Harry Geoffrey *b* 1966, Rupert Michael *b* 1969, Thomas Mungo *b* 1971, — Christopher Michael (Briff Farm, Bucklebury Common, nr Reading, Berks) *b* 1937: *m* 1975, Judy, da of Lt-Col Godfrey Jeans, of Broadchalke, Wilts, and has issue living, Lucy *b* 1976, Nicola *b* 1977, — David Algernon, *b* 1938: *m* 1967, Jocelyn Ishabel Ann (who *m* 2ndly, 1978, as his 2nd wife, John Edmund Kincaid Floyd *see* Floyd, Bt), da of late Sir John MacLeod, TD, late Queen's Own Highlanders, and *d* 1975, leaving issue (*see* B Dulverton, colls), — Gillian *b* 1940: *m* 1966, Nigel Colin Newbery, of Barbon, Kirkby Lonsdale, via Carnforth, Cumbria, and has issue living, Alexander Douglas *b* 1970, Georgina Blanche *b* 1967, Beatrice Laura *b* 1968, — (by 2nd *m*) James Borthwick (Mains of Cairnies, Glenalmond, Perthshire), *b* 1946: *m* 1970, Maureen Angela, yr da of W. G. Scott, of Forres, and has issue living, James Angus Wilfred *b* 1972, Tanya Hilda *b* 1974, — Clare Nell (*Hon Mrs Robin C. Denison-Pender*) *b* 1946: *m* 1966, Hon Robin Charles Denison-Pender, of Jessups, Mark Beech, Edenbridge, Kent (*see* B Pender). —— Racrel Sybil, *b* 1914; is a JP for Wilts: *m* 1937, Maj Peter Sturgis, who *d* 1986, and has issue living, Julian Russell, (Dauntsey Park, Chippenham, Wilts), *b* 1938: *m* 1981, Mrs Christine Sutherland, elder da of late Patrick Butler-Henderson, RAFVR (*see* B Faringdon, colls), and has issue living, Hugh Russell *b* 1983, — Toby Russell (Brook Farm, Gt Somerford, Chippenham, Wilts SN15 5JA), *b* 1947: *m* 1972, Gail Virginia, elder da of Brian Cole, and has issue living, Robert Tobias *b* 1974, Victoria *b* 1977, Nicola *b* 1982, — Ann Elisabeth (24 South Eaton Place, SW1; Garden Cottage, Dauntsey Park, Chippenham, Wilts), *b* 1945. *Residence* – Dauntsey Park, Chippenham, Wilts.

Sir Thomas Borthwick, 1st Bt, *b* 1835, son of Thomas Borthwick of Edinburgh; was Chm and Snr partner of Thos Borthwick & Sons (Ltd), Colonial Merchants; was nominated a peer June 1912, but *d* July 1912, before the patent passed the Great Seal. His widow Letitia Mary, da of Thomas Banks, received Roy licence Feb 1913 to use the title of *Baroness Whitburgh* Dec 1912; she *d* 1935. Their son Sir Thomas Banks, 2nd Bt, was *cr Baron Whitburgh* Dec 1912; he *d* 1967, when the Barony became ext, and the Baronetcy passed to his nephew, Sir John Thomas, 3rd Bt.

BOSSOM (UK) 1953, of Maidstone, Kent

Hon Sir CLIVE BOSSOM, 2nd *Baronet*; *b* 4 Feb 1918; *s* his father ALFRED CHARLES, Baron Bossom (Life Baron), in his baronetcy 1965; *ed* Eton; Maj (ret) The Buffs; Master of Grocers' Co 1979; FRSA; a Co Councillor for Kent 1949-52; Internat Pres of Internat Social Service (ISS); Pres BARC and Anglo-Netherlands Soc; Vice-Pres Anglo-Belgian Soc, Iran Soc, and Vice-Pres d'honneur Federation International de l'Automobile (FIA); Almoner Order of St John; Chm of Europ Assistance, Ltd 1971-88, of Ex-Ser War Disabled Help Dept 1973-88, of RAC 1975-78, of RAC Motor Sports Council 1975-82; Council of R Geographical Soc 1971-77; Council of Royal Soc of Arts 1969-72; PPS to Joint Parl Secs to Min of Pensions and Nat Insurance 1960-62, to Sec of State for Air 1962-64, and to Home Sec 1970-72; MP for Leominster (*C*) 1959-74; KStJ; Kt Cdr Order of Orange Nassau (Netherlands); Cdr Order of Crown of Belgium; Cdr of Order of Leopold II of Belgium; Order of Homayoun (Iran): *m* 1951, Lady Barbara Joan North, el sister of 9th Earl of Guilford, and has issue.

Arms – Gules a representation of a steel building column and three floor girders with wind bracing projecting therefrom to the sinister or, on a chief of the second an antique lamp inflamed sable between on the dexter a rose gules barbed proper, and on the sinister a thistle leaved and slipped also proper. Crest – Upon a mount vert an oak tree fructed charged with an eye irradiated proper.
Residence – 97 Cadogan Lane, SW1X 9DU. *Clubs* – Carlton, RAC.

SONS LIVING

BRUCE CHARLES (Overbury Court, nr Tewkesbury, Glos GL20 7NP), *b* 22 Aug 1952; *ed* Eton, Coll of Estate Management, and Harvard Business Sch; FRICS: *m* 1985, Penelope Jane, only child of late Edward (Ruby) Holland-Martin, of Overbury Court, nr Tewkesbury, Glos, and has issue living, George Edward Martin, *b* 21 Feb 1992, — Rosanna Emily, *b* 1986, — Amanda Lucy, *b* 1988. —— Andrew Clive, *b* 1954. —— James Edward, *b* 1962.

DAUGHTER LIVING

Arabella Emily, *b* 1968.

COLLATERAL BRANCH LIVING

Issue of late Doric Bossom, yr son of Life Baron and 1st Baronet, *b* 1922, *d* 1959: *m* 1949, June (Flat 6, 89 Cadogan Gdns, SW3 2RE) (who *m* 2ndly, 1967, Maj Kenneth Arnold Gibbs Crawley, TD, who *d* 1988, *see* Crawley-Boevey, Bt, colls, 1968 Edn), el da of V. B. Longworth, of Port Elizabeth, S Africa:—

Doric Alfred Howard, *b* (*posthumous*) 1960: *m* 1986, Sara J., only da of Lt-Col Derek Vaughan, and has issue living, Theo Doric Alfred, *b* 1988, — Caspar Luke Sebastian, *b* 1991. *Residence* – 9 Rumbold Rd, SW6 2JA.

Alfred Charles Bossom, son of Alfred Henry Bossom, of Holloway, London, was MP for Maidstone (*C*) 1931-59, and was *cr* a baronet 1953, and *Baron Bossom*, of Maidstone, co Kent (Life Baron) 1960.

Bosville Macdonald, see Macdonald.

HOUSTOUN-BOSWALL (UK) 1836
(Name pronounced "Hoostun-Boswall")

Sir (THOMAS) ALFORD HOUSTOUN-BOSWALL, 8th *Baronet*, *b* 23 May 1947; *s* his father, *Sir* THOMAS, 1982: *m* 1971, Eliana Michele, da of Dr John Pearse, of New York, and has issue.

Arms – Not recorded at Lyon Office.
Residences – 18 rue Basse, Biot 06410, France; 11 East 73rd St, New York, NY10021, USA.

SON LIVING

ALEXANDER ALFORD, *b* 16 Sept 1972.

DAUGHTER LIVING

Julia Glencora, *b* 1979.

SISTER LIVING

Amber Georgina, *b* 1946: *m* 1969, Alan Moore, of 14 Stafford Terrace, W8, and has issue living, Thomas James, *b* 1980, — Georgina, *b* 1972, — Chloe, *b* 1977.

HALF-SISTER LIVING

Sophie, *b* 1973.

UNCLE LIVING (*Son of 6th baronet*)

Alistair, *b* 1931. *Residence* –

DAUGHTERS LIVING OF FIFTH BARONET

Pamela Nanine, *b* 1916: *m* 1938, William Oliver Calvert, who *d* 1959, and has issue living, Ian Arbuckle, *b* 1939, — George William, *b* 1951, — Susan Arbuckle, *b* 1942. —— Patricia Mary, *b* 1917: *m* 1939, Maj Leslie Le Mottee, late RA, and has issue living, Judith Christina, *b* 1942, — Pamela Mary, *b* 1947. *Residence* – 34 Kingsway, Ewell, Surrey. —— Elizabeth Flora, *b* 1923: *m* 1941, Anthony Hawker, MC, formerly Maj RA, and has issue living, Nicholas George James, *b* 1942, — Victoria Jane, *b* 1956. *Residence* –

DAUGHTER LIVING OF FOURTH BARONET

Elizabeth Phœbe, *b* 1915: *m* 1940 (*m diss* 1956), Major John Alastair Livingston Timpson, MC, Scots Guards, and has issue living, Nicholas George Lawrence (Ardington Croft, Wantage, Oxon), *b* 1941: *m* 1972, Lady Selina Catherine Meade, el da of 6th Earl of Clanwilliam, and has issue living, Lawrence Rupert John *b* 1974, Catherine Selina Alexandra *b* 1979, — Rupert Alastair Hugh, *b* 1945: *m* 1980, Anne, eldest da of H. Meigh, of Ash House, Cheltenham, — Gerard Brian Sebastian, *b* 1946: *m* 1972, Siobhan Anne Southwell, da of Maurice Fitzgerald, of Hill Place, Haywards Heath, Sussex, — Veronica Naomi Livingston (*Veronica, Countess Peel*), *b* 1950: *m* 1973 (*m diss* 1987), 3rd Earl Peel.

MOTHER LIVING

Margaret (*Margaret, Lady Houstoun-Boswall*), da of George Bullen-Smith, of Squirrels, Arlington, Sussex: *m* 1945 (*m diss* 1970), Sir Thomas Houstoun-Boswall, 7th Bt, who *d* 1982. *Residence* – 8 College Rd, Eastbourne.

WIDOW LIVING OF SEVENTH BARONET

ANNE-LUCIE (*Anne-Lucie, Lady Houstoun-Boswall*), da of Pierre Naquet: *m* 1971, as his 2nd wife, Sir Thomas Houstoun-Boswall, 7th Bt, who *d* 1982.

COLLATERAL BRANCH LIVING

Granddaughter of late Alfred Houstoun Boswall, 5th son of 2nd baronet:—
Issue of late Capt Charles Houstoun-Boswall, R Scots Greys, *b* 1894; *d* 1946: *m* 1935, Marguerite Yvonne Savage, da of Herbert Pritchard, of Toronto, Canada, and Nassau, Bahamas:—
Jane Carolyn, *b* 1936: *m* 1957, John Clyfford Trevor, and has issue living, Mark Clyfford Houstoun, *b* 1961: *m* 1985, Elise Thayer, eldest da of David Green, of West Hayes, Rockbourne, Hants, and has issue living, Alexander John Houstoun *b*

1990, Natasha Thayer Houstoun *b* 1992, — Richard Charles Houstoun, *b* 1969, — Carolyn Elizabeth, *b* 1959: *m* 1989, Patrick Lahiff, and has issue living, Max Alexander Patrick *b* 1989, Jack Willia;m Oliver *b* 1991, — Emma Cecil, *b* 1963: *m* 1991, David Blake, and has issue living, Rory Dominic David *b* 1993. *Residence* – Northborough Manor, Peterborough, Cambs PE6 9BJ.

This baronet is male heir and representative of the ancient family of the Houstouns of Cotrioch hereditary baillees and justiciaries of the Barony of Busbie, Wigtownshire, and of Calderhall, Midlothian. Gen Sir William Houstoun, GCB, 1st Baronet, was a Gen in the Army. The 2nd baronet, Col in Grenadier Guards, assumed in 1847 the additional surname of Boswall on his marriage with Euphemia, daughter of Thomas Boswall, of Blackadder. The 3rd baronet was Capt Grenadier Guards and Convener of Berwickshire. The 4th baronet, Capt Sir George Reginald, Grenadier Guards, was killed in action 1915. The 5th Baronet, Capt Sir (Thomas) Randolph Houstoun-Boswall served in Royal Scots, and *d* 1953. His son and heir, George Cleeton Houstoun-Boswall, Lt Royal Scots, was killed on active ser at Hong Kong, 1941. The 6th baronet, Maj Sir Gordon Houstoun-Boswall, 1st Life Guards (whose father, Col Thomas Alford Houstoun-Boswall-Preston, assumed by Roy licence in 1886 the additional surname of Preston) discontinued the surname of Preston 1953.

BOUGHEY (GB) 1798, of Newcastle-under-Lyme, Staffordshire
(Name pronounced "Boey")

Neither to seek nor to despise distinction

Sir JOHN GEORGE FLETCHER BOUGHEY, 11th *Baronet*; *b* 12 Aug 1959; *s* his father Sir RICHARD JAMES, 1978; *ed* Eton, and Univ of Zimbabwe.

Arms – Quarterly: 1st and 4th, sable, a cross wavy erminois between four plates, each charged with an arrow in bend sable of the first, *Fletcher*; 2nd and 3rd, argent, three bucks' heads erased and affrontée ermine, *Boughey*. **Crests** – 1st, a plate charged with a pheon per pale ermine and sable; 2nd, out of an eastern crown gold the points alternate or and argent, a buck's head ermine, attired and collared of the first.
Residence – Bratton House, Westbury, Wilts BA13 4RN.

BROTHER LIVING

JAMES RICHARD, *b* 29 Aug 1960; *ed* Eton, and RAC Cirencester: *m* 1989, Katherine Mary, only da of Capt (Geoffrey Thomas) Warren Fenwicke-Clennell (*see* Blackett, Bt), and has issue living, George Richard Douglas, *b* 27 March 1992, — Victoria Rose, *b* 1990.

SISTERS LIVING

Julia Mary, *b* 1952: *m* 1973, Peregrine James Chadwyck-Healey, of Vern Leaze, Calne, Wilts (*see* Chadwyck-Healey, Bt). —— Rosalind Jane, *b* 1954: *m* 1978, Richard Herbert Dennis Steele, of Hazeldene, Highgate Rd, Forest Row, Sussex. —— Clare Anne (Chestnut Cottage, Stubhampton, Blandford, Dorset), *b* 1957.

AUNTS LIVING (*Daughters of 9th baronet*)

(Mary) Hermia, *b* 1914: *m* 1935, Robert Hugh Priestley, of Oakley Manor, Basingstoke. —— Camilla (Saxlingham Hall Nursing Home, The Green, Saxlingham Nethergate, Norwich, Norfolk NR15 1TH), *b* 1916: *m* 1941 (*m diss* 1964), Robert Charles Sanford Barclay (*see* Barclay, Bt). —— Anne, *b* 1922: *m* 1946, (James) Roddy Huff, Lieut US Army, and has issue living, James David (88 Whitehead Rd, Buford, Georgia, USA), *b* 1947, — Elizabeth Anne (109 Winsome Lane, Chapel Hill, N Carolina 27516, USA), *b* 1949: *m* 1971, David M. Rooks III, and has issue living, Kathryn Elizabeth *b* 1979, Adrienne Emily *b* 1982, — Celia, *b* 1958: *m* 1983, Michael Mark Mattingly, of 304 Strasburg Pike, Lancaster, Pennsylvania 17602, USA, and has issue living, Emma Caitlin *b* 1986, Chloë Elizabeth *b* 1989.

MOTHER LIVING

Davina Julia (*Baroness Loch*), da of late FitzHerbert Wright (*see* V Powerscourt, 1990 Edn): *m* 1st, 1950 (*m diss* 1975), Sir Richard James Boughey, 10th Bt, DL, JP, who *d* 1978; 2ndly, 1979, as his 2nd wife, 4th Baron Loch, MC, who *d* 1991, of Bratton House, Westbury, Wilts, and Lochluichart, by Garve, Ross-shire.

WIDOW LIVING OF TENTH BARONET

GILLIAN CLAIRE (*Lady Boughey*) (Alebank House, Ancrum, Jedburgh, Roxburghshire TD8 6XH), yst da of late Maj Robert Moubray, DL, late 16th Lancers (*see* Morrison-Bell, Bt): *m* 1976, as his 2nd wife, Sir Richard James Boughey, 10th Bt, JP, DL, who *d* 1978.

COLLATERAL BRANCHES LIVING

Granddaughter of late Maj-Gen John Boughey, 2nd son of late Lt-Col George Fenton Fletcher Boughey, 3rd son of 2nd baronet:—
Issue of late Rev Anchitel Harry Fletcher Boughey, *b* 1849, *d* 1936: *m* 1883, Katharine Annie, who *d* 1935 da of late I. S. Lovell, of Thornby, Rugby:—

Katharine Clare (Beda): *m* 1st, 1915, Robert Mervyn Powys Druce, who *d* 1949; 2ndly, 1950, Lionel John Treleaven Polgreen, MC, who *d* 1980, and *d* 1990, leaving issue (by 1st *m*), Pamela Matilda, *b* 1918: *m* 1943, Richard Stratton, of the Manor House, Kingston Deverill, Wilts, and has issue living, David (Manor Farm, Kingston Deverill, Warminster, Wilts BA12 7HB) *b* 1944: *m* 1976, Frances Alice, da of Harry Hardwill, of Hurst Farm, Blackdown, Beaminster, Dorset (and has issue living, Richard William *b* 1977, Henry Robert *b* 1978, Alice Louise *b* 1980), Peter William (160 Castelnau, SW13 9ET) *b* 1947: *m* 1973, Caroline Claire, da of George Michael Sparkes, of Paddock Wood, E Knoyle, Salisbury, Wilts (and has issue living, Edward Alexander Boughey *b* 1981, George William Boughey *b* 1984, Jack Richard Michael *b* 1988, Emily Caroline

McKechnie *b* 1979), Rosemary *b* 1949: *m* 1976, Anthony John Livesey Boardman, of Nenstone House, Westbury, Brackley, Northants (and has issue living, Andrew Nicholas Livesey *b* 1977, Tom Christopher William *b* 1979, Simon David Richard *b* 1982), Hilary *b* 1951: *m* 19—, — Welsummer, of Adstock Manor Stud, Buckingham MK18 2HT, — Evelyn Patricia (Manor Barn, Binham, Fakenham, Norfolk), *b* 1922: *m* 1st, 1942 (*m diss* 1949), Lieut Richard D. Deuchar, RNVR; 2ndly 1960 (*m diss* 1974), Philip Wayre, and has issue living, (by 1st *m*) Carol *b* 1943: *m* 1967, William Alexander, of The Old School House, Frampton-on-Severn, Glos (and has issue living, Juliet Patricia *b* 1968: *m* 1993, Paul Atherton, Fiona Catherine *b* 1969), Rosalind *b* 1945: *m* 1972, Michael Banks, of Manor Farm, Waresley, Beds (and has issue living, Melanie Catharine *b* 1974, Nicola *b* 1977), Juliet *b* 1948: *m* 1969, Adrian John Taunton, of The Old Barn House, Kelling, Holt, Norfolk (and has issue living, Dominic *b* 1976, Harriet Lovell *b* 1979). *Residence* – 156 Sloane St, SW1.

Grandson of late William Fenton Fletcher Boughey, 4th son of 2nd baronet:—
Issue of late Com Alfred Fletcher COPLESTONE-BOUGHEY, RN, *b* 1883, *ka* during battle of Jutland 1916, having assumed by deed poll 1910 the surname of Coplestone before that of Boughey: *m* 1910, Mary Cliffe, who *d* 1955, da of late Frederick Coplestone, CBE, JP, of Richmond Hill, Chester:—
John Fenton, *b* 1912; *ed* Shrewsbury, and Brasenose Coll, Oxford (BA 1934); Bar Inner Temple 1935; Judge of Co Courts 1969: *m* 1944, Gilian Beatrice, da of late Hugh Alfred Counsell, of Appleby, Westmorland, and has issue living, William Fenton (Ebworthy, Manaton, Devon TQ13 9UL), *b* 1947; *ed* Winchester, Brasenose Coll, Oxford (MA), and Kings Coll, London (LLM): *m* 1978, Clare Louise, only da of late Lester B. Wilson, and has issue living, Robert Fenton *b* 1984, Katharine Elizabeth *b* 1987, — Mary, *b* 1946. *Residence* – 82 Oakley St, SW3. *Club* – Athenæum.
Sir Thomas Fletcher, 1st Bt, was High Sheriff of Staffordshire 1783 and 1789. The 2nd baronet (MP for Staffordshire 1820-22) assumed by sign-manual 1805 the surname of Boughey, in lieu of his patronymic. The 3rd baronet, Sir Thomas Fletcher Fenton, was High Sheriff of Staffordshire 1832, and the 4th baronet, Sir Thomas Fletcher, was also High Sheriff of that county 1898. The 5th baronet, Sir George, was R of Forton 1863-1908, and the 7th, Sir Robert, V of Betley. Sir George Menteth, CBE, 9th baronet, was Under-Sec to Govt of Punjab 1912-13, and sometime Principal Clerk, Med Ser Div, Min of Pensions.

ROUSE-BOUGHTON, First (E) 1641, of Lawford Parva, Warwickshire; Second (GB) 1791, of Rouse Lench, Worcestershire (Extinct 1963)

Sir EDWARD HOTHAM ROUSE-BOUGHTON, 13th and last *Baronet* of Lawford, and 5th and last of Rouse Lench.

WIDOW LIVING OF THIRTEENTH BARONET

ELIZABETH (*Lady Rouse-Boughton*) (Dickens Cottage, Seagrove Bay, Seaview, Isle of Wight), da of late E. W. Hathaway Hunter, and widow of Geoffrey Swaffer: *m* 1948, as his 2nd wife, Maj Sir Edward Hotham Rouse-Boughton, 13th baronet, who *d* 1963, when the title became ext.

COLLATERAL BRANCH LIVING

Granddaughter of late Andrew Johnes ROUSE-BOUGHTON-KNIGHT, 2nd son of 10th baronet, *b* 1869, *d* 1928: *m* 1891, Isabel Harriet, who *d* 1955, da of late Algernon Charles Heber-Percy (D Northumberland, colls):—
Dorothea Emily, *b* 1892.

BOULTON (UK) 1905, of Copped Hall, Totteridge, Herts

I · WILL · NEVER · QUIT

Sir (HAROLD HUGH) CHRISTIAN BOULTON, 4th *Baronet*; *b* 29 Oct 1918; *s* his father, *Sir* (DENIS DUNCAN) HAROLD (OWEN), 1968; *ed* Ampleforth Coll; late Capt Irish Guards (Sup Reserve); 1939-45 War: *m* 1944, Patricia Mary OBE (who reassumed by deed poll 1951 her maiden name of Maxwell-Scott), da of late Maj-Gen Sir Walter Joseph Constable Maxwell-Scott, CB, DSO, 1st Bt.

Arms – Argent, on a bend gules two leopards' faces of the field a chief arched of the second thereon two falcons close proper. *Crest* – Upon a hollybush a falcon rising, holding in the dexter claw a bird-bolt in pale, head downwards, and in the beak a sprig of holly all proper. *Supporters* – *Dexter*, a Knight of St John in armour, robed proper; *sinister*, a female figure representing Charity vested argent, with mantle gules, round the head a fillet argent inscribed "Caritas", and holding in the exterior hand a heart or, inflamed proper.
Residence – 37 Jay Av, Nepean, Ontario, Canada K2G 0C1.

SISTER LIVING

Marie Louise, *b* 1921: *m* 1948, James Russell Smith, and has issue living, Carlton Michael, *b* 1949, — Duncan Rumsey, *b* (twin) 1949, — Marie Louise, *b* 1952. *Residence* – 83 Bryant St, Buffalo, New York 14209, USA.
Sir Samuel Bagster Boulton, 1st baronet, JP, DL, AICE (Telford Medallist), was Chm of Burt, Boulton and Haywood (Limited), of London and Paris, Chm London Labour Conciliation Board, and a pioneer in many industrial and philanthropic movements. The 2nd baronet, Sir Harold Edwin, CVO, CBE, was Vice-Pres The Queen's Institute of Dist Nursing, Founder and Hon Manager of the House of Shelter, Chm of Mendicity Soc, and Founder and Joint Chm People's Palace Horticultural Soc.

BOULTON (UK) 1944, of Braxted Park, co Essex

Sir WILLIAM WHYTEHEAD BOULTON, CBE, TD, 3rd *Baronet*; *b* 21 June 1912; *s* his brother, *Maj Sir* EDWARD JOHN, 1982; *ed* Eton, and Trin Coll, Camb (BA honours 1934); Bar Inner Temple 1936; served 1939-45 War in Middle East 1939-44, Staff Coll Camberley 1944, served with Allied Command in Germany 1945-50; Hon Lt-Col RHA Essex Yeo (TA); Sec to General Council of the Bar 1950-74, and to the Senate of the Inns of Court and the Bar 1974-75; CBE (Civil) 1958, Knt 1975: *m* 1944, (Margaret) Elizabeth, only da of late Brig Henry Noel Alexander Hunter, DSO, and has issue.

𝕬rms – Argent on a bend engrailed couped gules three leopards' faces or. 𝕮rest – Upon a holly bush fructed a falcon rising proper, belled or.
Residences – The Quarters House, Alresford, Colchester, Essex; 37 Rutland Gate, SW7.

SON LIVING

JOHN GIBSON, *b* 18 Dec 1946; *ed* Stowe.

DAUGHTERS LIVING

Julia Rosalind, *b* 1945: *m* 1965, Anthony John Nevill Russell, of Elm House, Elmdon, Saffron Walden, Essex, and has issue living, William Jonathan, *b* 1968, — Jennifer Rosalind, *b* 1969. —— Susan Elizabeth, *b* 1949: *m* 1985, Roger Donald Harrison, of The Pink House, Hedgerley Close, Cambridge CB3 0EW, yr son of Robert Harrison, of Stratford-upon-Avon, and has issue living, Alexander Barnaby, *b* 1986, — Rupert Michael, *b* 1988.

BROTHER LIVING

Christopher Carmichael, *b* 1919; *ed* Eton, and Trin Coll, Camb; 1939-45 War in France, Middle East, Italy, and Austria as Capt Intelligence Corps and with Allied Commn in Austria. *Address* – Flat 1, Les Arches, Mont Felard St Lawrence, Jersey, CI.
Sir William Whytehead Boulton, 1st Bt (son of William Whytehead Boulton, JP, of Beverley, Yorkshire), was Govt Whip, and a Junior Lord of the Treasury 1940-42, and Vice-Chamberlain of HM's Household 1942-4, and sat as MP for Central Div of Sheffield (C) 1931-45.

BOWATER (UK) 1914, of Hill Crest, Borough of Croydon

Sir JOHN VANSITTART BOWATER, 4th *Baronet*; *b* 6 April 1918, son of late Capt Victor Spencer Bowater, 3rd son of 1st baronet; *s* his uncle, *Sir* (THOMAS) DUDLEY (BLENNERHASSETT), 1972: *m* 1943, Joan Kathleen, who *d* 1982, da of late Wilfrid Ernest Henry Scullard, of Boscombe, and has issue.

𝕬rms – Argent, on an inescutcheon sable between eight martlets in orle gules a crescent of the field.
Residence – 214 Runnymede Av, Bearwood, Bournemouth, BH11 9SP.

SON LIVING

MICHAEL PATRICK (The Anchorage, Quay West, Minehead, Som), *b* 18 July 1949: *m* 1968, Alison, da of Edward Wall, of Knowle, and has issue living, Suzanne, *b* 1969, — Juliette, *b* 1972, — Jennifer, *b* 1973, — Katherine, *b* 1980.

DAUGHTER LIVING

Penelope Ann, *b* 1954: *m* 1973, Martin Doughty, son of Geoffrey Doughty, of 16 Victoria Rd, Acocks Green, Birmingham B27 7YA, and has issue living, Samantha, *b* 1976, — Hannah, *b* 1978, — Laura, *b* 1982.

DAUGHTERS LIVING OF SECOND BARONET

Daphne Audrey, *b* 1919. —— Rowena Maud, *b* 1926.
Sir (Thomas) Vansittart Bowater, 1st Bt (son of William Vansittart Bowater, of Bury Hall, Lower Edmonton, N), was an Alderman of the City of London 1907-38, Lord Mayor 1913-14, and MP 1924-38.

BOWATER (UK) 1939, of Friston, Suffolk

Sir EUAN DAVID VANSITTART BOWATER, 3rd *Baronet*; *b* 9 Sept 1935; *s* his father, *Sir* NOEL VANSITTART, GBE, MC, 1984; *ed* Eton, and Trin Coll, Camb: *m* 1964, Susan Mary Humphrey, da of A. R. O. Slater, FCA, and has issue.

Arms – Argent, an orle of eight martlets gules on an inescutcheon sable a crescent of the field. Crest – A rainbow issuant from water proper.

SONS LIVING

MORAY VANSITTART, *b* 24 April 1967. —— Lucien Ross Thomas, *b* 1973.

DAUGHTERS LIVING

Jackie, *b* 1965. —— Alexis, *b* 1969.

SISTERS LIVING

Anne Patricia, *b* 1925: *m* 1954, Group Capt Randolph Stuart Mills, DFC, RAF, and has issue living, Philip Stuart, *b* 1956, — William Stuart, *b* 1957. —— Jane Gillian, *b* 1930: *m* 1953, Christopher William Restarick Beeson, and has issue living, Mark, *b* 1954, — Peter, *b* 1956, — David, *b* 1957, — Oona, *b* 1960. *Residence* – Ford Farm, Manaton, Devon.

COLLATERAL BRANCH LIVING

Issue of late Lt-Col Sir Ian Frank Bowater, GBE, DSO, TD, Lord Mayor of London 1969-70, yr son of 1st baronet, *b* 1904; *d* 1982: *m* 1927, Hon Ursula Margaret Dawson (38 Burton Court, Franklin's Row, SW3 4SZ), da of 1st Viscount Dawson of Penn:—
Michael Ian Vansittart (16 Rocky Point Rd, Rowayton, Conn 06853, USA), *b* 1934; *ed* Eton; Maj (ret) Scots Gds; Head of Communications Bowater Corpn: *m* 1960, Camilla Caroline, el da of Air Commodore Whitney Willard Straight, CBE, MC, DFC (*see* E Winchilsea), and has issue living, Arabella Charlotte, *b* 1961: *m* 1990, Carl W. Wend, jr, son of Carl Wend, of White Plains, New York, — Katherine Elizabeth, *b* 1963: *m* 1988, Mark Beaumont, son of Michael Beaumont, and has issue living, James *b* 1990, Emma Camilla *b* 1992, — Caroline Mary, *b* 1964, — Sophie Melissa, *b* 1970. —— Susan Vansittart, *b* 1929: *m* 1956, George Crofton Addison Doughty, of 60 Clonmel Rd, SW6 5BJ, son of late Sir Charles Doughty, QC, and has issue living, Caroline Susan, *b* 1958, and an adopted son, John Addison, *b* 1961. —— Charlotte Mary, *b* 1937: *m* 1st, 1961, (Denis) Anthony Russell, who *d* 1966 (*see* Russell, Bt, colls, *cr* 1916); 2ndly, 1970, J. Watcyn Lewis, of 66 Clifton Hill, NW8 0JT, and has issue living (by 1st *m*) (*see* Russell, Bt, colls, *cr* 1916) (by 2nd *m*), Damian Watcyn, *b* 1971, — Gareth Hugh Bowater, *b* 1973.
The 1st baronet, Major Sir Frank Henry Bowater, TD (son of William Vansittart Bowater, of Bury Hall, Lower Edmonton, N, and brother of Sir (Thomas) Vansittart Bowater, 1st Bt (*cr* 1914)), sometime Major RFA, was a Paper Maker and a Lieut and Alderman of the City of London (Sheriff 1929-30, Lord Mayor 1938-9). Sir Noël Vansittart Bowater, GBE, MC, 2nd Bt, was Alderman of the City of London 1944-70, and Lord Mayor 1953-54.

BOWDEN (UK) 1915, of City of Nottingham

With faith and hope

Sir FRANK HOUSTON BOWDEN, 3rd *Baronet*; *b* 10 Aug 1909; *s* his father, *Sir* HAROLD, GBE, 1960; *ed* Rugby, and Merton Coll, Oxford (BA 1931, MA 1953); assumed the additional forename of Houston 1960; formerly Lieut (S) RNVR; 1939-45 War: *m* 1st, 1934 (*m diss* 1936), Marie José Stiénon de Messey, only da of Charles Stiénon, of Paris, and Comtesse Laure de Messey; 2ndly, 1937, Lydia Eveline, who *d* 1981, da of Jean Manolovici, of Bucharest, Roumania; 3rdly, 1989, Oriol Annette Mary, only da of Charles Hooper Bath, of London, and has issue by 1st and 2nd *m*.

Arms – Quarterly, sable and or, over all a bow in bend of the second, between two cycle wheels charged in the centre with a winged foot, couped at the ankle, all proper. Crest – A heron's head erased at the neck proper, gorged with a mural crown gold.
Residence – The Old Vicarage, Winkfield, Windsor, Berks SL4 4SE. *Clubs* – White's, Royal Thames Yacht.

SONS LIVING (*By 1st marriage*)

NICHOLAS RICHARD (4 Hensting Farm Cottages, Hensting Lane, Fishers Pond, Eastleigh, Hants S05 7HH), *b* 13 Aug 1935; *ed* Millfield.

(*By 2nd marriage*)

Adrian Harold Houston (33 Grosvenor Sq, W1; Carlton, White's, Royal Thames Yacht, and Knickerbocker (New York) Clubs), *b* 1938; *ed* Radley, and Merton Coll, Oxford (MA); assumed the additional forename of Houston 1960: *m* 1968, Marjorie Walter, da of John Dozier Gordan, of New York City, USA, and has issue living, Alexander Gordan, *b* 1972, — Richard Waring Baylor, *b* 1979, — Stephanie Florence, *b* 1975. —— Aubrey Francis Houston (The Old Vicarage, Winkfield, Windsor, Berks; Brooks's Club), *b* 1940; *ed* Eton, and Merton Coll, Oxford (MA); assumed the additional forename of Houston 1960: *m* 1969, Mary Julia, da of David

Richard Colville (*see* V Colville of Culross, colls), and has issue living, James Edward Houston, *b* 1975, — Victoria Houston, *b* 1973. —— Gregory Andrew Houston (Bucknell Manor, Bicester, Oxfordshire; White's Club), *b* 1948; *ed* Eton, and Mansfield Coll, Oxford (MA); assumed the additional forename of Houston 1960: *m* 1978, Michaela, da of Sir John Figgess, KBE, CMG, and has issue living, Charles John Houston, *b* 1986, — Alexandra Frances Houston, *b* 1981, — Georgina Houston, *b* 1983.

SISTER LIVING

Ruth, *b* 1911: *m* 1st, 1932 (*m diss* 1947), Christopher Bourchier Wrey, who *d* 1976 (*see* Wrey, Bt, colls); 2ndly, 1947, Ernest Wittmann. *Residence* – Flat 3, Hale House, 34 de Vere Gdns, W8.

Sir Frank Bowden, 1st Bt, was Founder, Chm, Managing Director, and Principal Owner of Sturmey-Archer Gears (Limited), and of Raleigh Cycle Co (Limited). Sir Harold Bowden, GBE, 2nd Bt was Pres of Raleigh Industries Ltd, and High Sheriff of Notts 1933.

BOWEN (UK) 1921, of Colworth, co Bedford

Audaces·fortuna·juvat

Fortune favours the brave

Sir MARK EDWARD MORTIMER BOWEN, 5th *Baronet*; *b* 17 Oct 1958; *s* his father, Sir THOMAS FREDERIC CHARLES, 1989; *ed* Wellington Coll: *m* 1983, Kerry Tessa, da of Michael John Moriarty, of The Grey House, Links Rd, Worthing, Sussex, and has issue.

Arms – Azure, a lion rampant within an orle, all within four roses or and as many bezants alternately. **Crest** – A lion sejant proper holding in the dexter paw a Bowen knot argent.
Residence – 14 Pendarves Rd, West Wimbledon, SW20 8TS.

SON LIVING

GEORGE EDWARD MICHAEL, *b* 27 Dec 1987.

DAUGHTER LIVING

Grace Francesca *b* 1989.

SISTERS LIVING

Julia Rosemary (13 Barnet Close, Yeovil, Som), *b* 1950: *m* 1970 (*m diss* 1983), Lt-Cdr Robert Andrew Fewings, RN, and has had issue, Paul Stuart, *b* 1973; *d* 1993, — James Andrew Murray, *b* 1977. —— Margot Claire, *b* 1952: *m* 1974, Malcolm Ivison Kirkpatrick, of 70 Netherby Park, Weybridge, Surrey, and has issue living, Joanna Claire, *b* 1978, — Verity Juliet Elizabeth, *b* 1986.

WIDOW LIVING OF FOURTH BARONET

JILL CLAUDE MURRAY (*Jill, Lady Bowen*), da of Cyril Lloyd Evans, of Prestea, Ghana, W Africa: *m* 1947, Sir Thomas Frederic Charles Bowen, 4th Bt, who *d* 1989. *Residence* – 1 Barford Close, Fleet, Hants.

COLLATERAL BRANCH LIVING

Issue of late Harold Cedric Bowen, yr son of 1st baronet, *b* 1896, *d* 1959: *m* 1921, Vera Donnet, who *d* 1967:—
Nicholas Edward (Gregers Grams vei 18, Oslo 3, Norway), *b* 1923; *ed* Harrow; is Wing-Cdr RAF (ret); served in World War II; Mil and Air Attaché at Oslo 1968-71: *m* 1944, Evelyn, da of late Edward Batty, and has issue living, Michael Edward (Phoenix House, Beadlam, York), *b* 1944; *ed* Harrow: *m* 1968, Gillian Margaret, da of Col B. R. D. Garside, MC, and has issue living, Nicola Emma *b* 1969, Victoria Margaret *b* 1972, Anabel Elizabeth *b* 1974, — Christopher Anthony Richard (71 Bolingbroke Grove, SW11), *b* 1947; *ed* Harrow: *m* 1975, Mary Olivia, da of Alexander Walcot Stewart, and has issue living, Robert Alexander Edward *b* 1978, Katherine Olivia *b* 1976, Clare Rowena *b* 1982. —— Clarissa, *b* 1929: *m* 1954, Mervyn Heald, QC, of Colhook Lodge, Ebernoe, Petworth, Sussex, son of Rt Hon Sir Lionel Frederick Heald, QC, MP, and has issue living, Robert Lionel, *b* 1974, — Henrietta Sara, *b* 1955: *m* 1981, Adam Curtis, and has issue living, James Nathaniel *b* 1990, Sophie Clarissa *b* 1986, — Annabel Clare, *b* 1957: *m* 1989, Timothy Peter Smith, and has issue living, Harrison Oscar *b* 1990, Ottoline Amelia *b* 1994, — Julia Elizabeth, *b* 1959: *m* 1979, Charles Stewart Prescot, and has issue living, Nicholas Hugh *b* 1980, Rupert James *b* 1985, Alexandra Constance *b* 1990.

Sir Albert Edward Bowen, 1st Bt (son of Edward Bowen, of Hanley), was Pres of Buenos Aires Great Southern Railway Co, and of many Cos in City of London. Major Sir Edward Crowther Bowen, 2nd Bt, 6th Inniskilling Dragoons, served during European War 1914-18 (MC). Sir John Edward Mortimer Bowen, 3rd Bt, was *k* in a motor racing accident 1939.

BOWLBY (UK) 1923, of Manchester Square, Borough of St Marylebone

ne·cede·malis

Yield not to adversity

Sir RICHARD PEREGRINE LONGSTAFF BOWLBY, 3rd *Baronet*; *b* 11 Aug 1941; *s* his uncle, *Sir* ANTHONY HUGH MOSTYN, 1993; *ed* Dauntsey's Sch: *m* 1963, Xenia, only da of late Roderick Paul Agnew Garrett, of 28 Southwood Lane, N6, and has issue.

Arms – Per fesse sable and argent, a pale with three hinds' heads erased two and one, and as many annulets one and two all counterchanged. **Crest** – Three annulets interlaced one and two or, between two thorn branches proper. *Residence* – Boundary House, Wyldes Close, NW11 7JB.

SON LIVING

BENJAMIN, *b* 2 Nov 1966; *ed* King Alfred Sch: *m* 1992, Mylanna Sophia, elder da of Michael Case Colyer, of Harlech, Gwynedd. *Residence* – 15 Highwood Av, N12 8QL.

DAUGHTER LIVING

Sophia, *b* 1969.

BROTHER LIVING

Robert John Mostyn, *b* 1948; *ed* Grenville Coll. *Residence* – Wyldes Close Corner, Wyldes Close, Hampstead Way, NW11 7JB.

SISTERS LIVING

Mary Hamilton Victoria Ignatia, *b* 1939: *m* 1st, 1964 (*m diss* 1980), Capt Timothy Richard Holbrook Dawson, RE; 2ndly, 1980, Anthony Gatling, of White Lodge, Berwick St James, Salisbury, Wilts, and has issue living (by 1st *m*), Guy Philip Richard, *b* 1965; *ed* John Masefield Gram Sch, and City Univ, — Patrick Timothy John, *b* 1969; *ed* Solihull Sch, and Univ Coll London: *m* 1993, Anna, da of Rev Canon Richard Kingsbury, of The Rectory, Church Lane, Caversham, Reading. —— Pia Rose Whitworth, *b* 1945: *m* 1968, Carlos Duran, of 70 Northway, NW11, and has issue living, Xohan, *b* 1968; *ed* Oak Lodge, — Xavier, *b* 1973; *ed* King Alfred Sch, — Xulia Tareixa, *b* 1978.

DAUGHTERS LIVING OF SECOND BARONET

Anthea, *b* 1930: *m* 1956, Jolyon Dromgoole, of 13 Gladstone St, SE1 6EY, and has issue living, Emma, *b* 1957, — Julia, *b* 1961, — Rose, *b* 1964, — Susanna, *b* (triplet) 1964, — Belinda, *b* (triplet) 1964. —— Sophia, *b* 1945.

DAUGHTERS LIVING OF FIRST BARONET

Dorothy Evelyn Mostyn (*Lady Phelps Brown*), *b* 1910: *m* 1932, Sir Ernest Henry Phelps Brown, MBE, FBA, Professor of Economics, London Univ, and sometime Fellow of New Coll, Oxford, and has issue living, Nicholas Anthony Phelps, *b* 1936; *ed* Trinity Hall, Cambridge, — Thomas Henry Phelps, *b* 1948; *ed* New College, Oxford, — Juliet Virginia Phelps, *b* 1934; *ed* Newnham College, Cambridge: *m* 1964, Keith Hopkins, Professor of Ancient History, University of Cambridge. *Residence* – 16 Bradmore Rd, Oxford.

MOTHER LIVING

Ursula, 3rd da of Tom George Longstaff, MD: *m* 1938, Lt-Col (Edward) John Mostyn Bowlby, CBE, MD, 2nd son of 1st baronet, who *d* 1990. *Residence* – Wyldes Close Corner, Hampstead Way, NW11.

WIDOW LIVING OF SECOND BARONET

DORA EVELYN (*Dowager Lady Bowlby*), da of late John Charles Allen, of York: *m* 1930, Sir Anthony Hugh Mostyn Bowlby, 2nd Bt, who *d* 1993. *Residence* – The Old Rectory, Ozleworth, Wotton-under-Edge, Glos GL12 7QA.

The 1st baronet, Sir Anthony Alfred Bowlby, KCB, KCMG, KCVO, FRCS (Pres Coll of Surgs 1920-23), was Surg to Royal Household 1904-10, and an Hon Surg to HM 1910-29, and served in S African War 1899-1900 in charge of Portland Hospital (despatches, medal, CMG), and during European War 1914-19 as Maj-Gen Army Med Ser, and as Advisory Consulting Surg to British Forces in France (American DSM).

BOWMAN (UK) 1884, of Holmbury St Mary, co Surrey

We conquered formerly with these arms

Sir JOHN PAGET BOWMAN, 4th *Baronet*; *b* 12 Feb 1904; *s* his father, the *Rev Sir* PAGET MERVYN, 1955; *ed* Eton; formerly 2nd Lieut 98th (Surrey and Sussex Yeo, Queen Mary's) Army Field Brig, RA (TA): *m* 1st, 1931, Countess Cajetana Hoyos, who *d* 1948, da of Count Edgar Hoyos, of Schloss Soos, Lower Austria; 2ndly, 1948, Frances Edith Marian, who *d* 1992, da of late Sir (James) Beethom Whitehead, KCMG (E Midleton); 3rdly, 1993, Christian, yst da of Col Sir Arthur Grant of Monymusk, 10th Bt, CBE, DSO, and widow of John Gordon Ogston Miller, and has had issue by 1st *m*. Sir John Bowman *d* 16 Aug 1994.

𝕬rms – Or, on a chevron between three bows stringed palewise gules, two lions combatant of the first between as many escallops argent. ℭrest – Upon a mount vert the stump of a tree proper, around the upper part a belt sable, and pendant therefrom, on the dexter side, a quiver gules filled with arrows argent. *Residence* – The Walled Garden, Chamberlain St, Wells, Somerset BA5 2PE.

SON DECEASED (*By 1st marriage*)

David Anthony Paget *b* 16 Oct 1935: *m* 1968, Valerie Winifred (Sherwood, Boar's Hill, Oxford), da of Reginald Cyril Tatham, FRCS, of Spinney Croft, N Ferriby, E Yorks, and *d* 9 April 1985.

DAUGHTER LIVING (*By 1st marriage*)

Rachel Elinor, *b* 1938; SRN; *m* 1967, Gerald William Wensley Clarkson, of Crouch Lane Farm, Crouch Lane, Winkfield, Berks, and has issue (*see* Lane, Bt).

COLLATERAL BRANCHES LIVING

Grandchildren of late John Frederick Bowman, 2nd son of 1st baronet:—
Issue of late Maj Humphrey Ernest Bowman, CMG, CBE, *b* 1879, *d* 1965: *m* 1st 1916, Frances Guinevere, who *d* 1923, da of late Lt-Col Arthur Henry Armytage (Armytage, Bt); 2ndly, 1925, Elinor Marion, who *d* 1957, da of Rev Charles Conybeare, and widow of Arthur William Bowman (infra):—
(By 1st *m*) PAUL HUMPHREY ARMYTAGE (24 Albert Edgecliff Rd, Sydney, NSW 2027, Australia; White's, Royal Corinthian Yacht, and The Brook (New York) Clubs) *b* 10 Aug 1921; *ed* Eton; sometime Maj Coldstream Guards; Dir Hill Samuel & Co Ltd 1962-78: *m* 1st, 1943 (*m diss* 1947), Felicité Anne Araminta, da of Sir Harold Alfred MacMichael, GCMG, DSO (*see* E Leven and Melville, colls, 1946 Edn); 2ndly, 1947 (*m diss* 1974), Gabrielle May, formerly wife of Lt-Col Walter Currie, US Army; 3rdly, 1974, Elizabeth Deirdre, yr da of late Bruce R. Campbell, of Goorianawa, NSW, and formerly wife of Maj-Gen Thomas Bell Lindsay Churchill, CB, CBE, MC, and has issue living, (by 2nd *m*) Amanda Caroline, *b* 1947. — Cynthia Pamela Mary (*Lady Macdonald*) *b* 1918: *m* 1st, 1943 (*m diss* 1969), Rear Adm Josef Czeslaw Bartosik, CB, DSC, RN, son of Thomas Bartosik, of Warsaw; 2ndly, 1980, Vice Adm Sir Roderick Douglas Macdonald, KBE, of Ollach, Braes, Isle of Skye, and has issue living, (by 1st *m*) Jan Josef (11 Morpeth Mansions, SW1), *b* 1946: *m* 1978, Lesley Anne, da of Dr J. Meehan, of Forest Mere, Liphook, Hants, and has issue living, James *b* 1980, Lucy Olivia *b* 1983, — Conrad Josef (Sam) (4 Beauclerc Rd, W6), *b* 1948: *m* 1978, Claudia, da of Maj T. Pitman, of Cliffe Lodge, Leyburn, Yorks, and has issue living, Luke *b* 1982, Daniel *b* 1985, Humphrey *b* 1989, — Matthew Timothy (9 Lansdown Crescent, Cheltenham, Glos), *b* 1954: *m* 1980, Catherine, da of late J. McDonnell, of Dundalk, Ireland, and has issue living, Robert *b* 1982, — Kristina Cynthia (2 Hill Close, Pershore, Worcs), *b* 1945: *m* 1969, Christopher Thomasson, of Somerton Castle, nr Lincoln, and has issue living, Thomas *b* 1970, Charles *b* 1976, Sophy *b* 1969, Clare *b* 1977.
Issue of late Clive Frederick Bowman, MC, *b* 1884, *d* 1972: *m* 1920, Erica Violet, who *d* 1972, da of late Col Robert George Wardlaw-Ramsay, DL (B Magheramorne, colls):—
Martin Ramsay (The Boat House, Camusdarach, Arisaig, Inverness-shire), *b* 1928; *ed* Ampleforth, and Ch Ch, Oxford (MA); Bar Inner Temple 1953; formerly 2nd Lt The King's Regt; CC Inverness-shire 1973-75. — Erica Rosemary, *b* 1921: *m* 1948, Douglas Burch Law, formerly Maj Seaforth Highlanders, of Redfriars, E Linton, E Lothian EH40 3DS, and has issue living, Nicholas Simon, *b* 1954; *ed* Wellington Coll: *m* 1979, Virginia Halliday, and has issue living, Hamish *b* 1982, Sarah Catherine *b* 1980, — James Christopher, *b* 1956; *ed* Wellington Coll. —— Heather Mary, *b* 1922: *m* 1956, Trevor Cairns, of 4 Ashmore Terrace, Sunderland SR2 7DE and has issue living, Conrad Thomas, *b* 1957; *ed* Dublin Univ, Edinburgh Univ, — Edmund Frederick, *b* 1960; *ed* Peterhouse, Cambridge: *m* 1987, Alison Margery Anna Court. —— Dorothea Vivien, *b* 1924; a Nun of Order of the Sacred Heart.

Granddaughter of late Rev Arthur Gerald Bowman, 3rd son of 1st baronet:—
Issue of late Arthur William Bowman, London Regt, *b* 1887, *ka* 1918: *m* 1911, Elinor Marion (who *d* 1957, having *m* 2ndly, 1925, Humphrey Ernest Bowman, CMG, CBE (ante)), da of late Rev Charles Conybeare, R of Tichborne, Hants:—
Barbara Paget, *b* 1912: *m* 1932, Wing-Com Douglas Sender, RAF (ret), who *d* 1987, and has issue living, Michael Conybeare (4 Rivermount Gdns, Portsmouth Rd, Guildford, Surrey), *b* 1933; *ed* Wellington Coll: *m* 1962 (*m diss* 1984), Judith Olivia Hedley, and has issue living, Richard Paget *b* 1964, — Katherine Elizabeth *b* 1966, — Penelope Markland, *b* 1936: *m* 1959, Lt-Col Anthony John Carter Wells, RA (ret), RAA (ret), of Wirrabara, Devon Rd, Exeter, NSW 2579, Australia, and has issue living, Pandora Markland *b* 1965: *m* 1991, Gregory John Bailey (and has issue living, Samantha Markland JOBBINS WELLS *b* 1986, Jasmine BAILEY *b* 1993), — Joanna Paget, *b* 1953: *m* 1982, Christopher John Askham, of 10 Frogmore Village, St Albans, Herts, and has issue living, Jonathan Piers *b* 1986. *Residence* – L'Espine, Millbrook, Jersey.
The 1st baronet was an eminent ophthalmic surgeon. Sir W. Paget Bowman, 2nd Bt, was many years Registrar of the Corporation of the Sons of the Clergy. The Rev Sir Paget Mervyn Bowman, 3rd Bt, was R of Shere, Rural Dean of Cranleigh and Surrogate 1919-50.

BOWMAN (UK) 1961, of Killingworth, co Northumberland (Extinct 1990)

Sir GEORGE BOWMAN, 2nd and last *Baronet*.

DAUGHTERS LIVING OF SECOND BARONET

Julie Victoria, *b* 1961. —— Louise Janet, *b* 1963. —— Claire Elizabeth, *b* 1965.

SISTER LIVING OF SECOND BARONET

Mary, *b* 1925: *m* 1950, John Robert Rayne, and has issue living, Susan, *b* 1952.

WIDOW LIVING OF FIRST BARONET

JEAN (*Jean, Lady Bowman*) (Woodlands, Killingworth Station, Forest Hall, Newcastle-upon-Tyne), da of Henry Brooks, of Ashington, Northumberland: *m* 1922, Sir James Bowman, KBE, 1st baronet, who *d* 1978.

WIDOW LIVING OF SECOND BARONET

OLIVE (*Lady Bowman*), da of — Case, of South Shields: *m* 1960, Sir George Bowman, 2nd Bt, who *d* 1990. *Residence* – Parkside, Killingworth Drive, Killingworth Station, Newcastle 12.

Bowyer (Bowyer-Smyth), see Smyth.

BOYCE (UK) 1952, of Badgeworth, co Gloucester

Sir ROBERT (CHARLES) LESLIE BOYCE, 3rd *Baronet*, *b* 2 May 1962; *s* his father, *Sir* RICHARD (LESLIE), 1968: *m* 1985, Fiona Margaret, 2nd da of John Savage, of Whitmore Park, Coventry.

𝔄rms – Or on a chevron gules an open book proper edges and clasps of the first on a chief of the second a portcullis chained also of the first between two swords erect also proper pomels and hilts gold. ℭrest – A demi lion gules grasping in the dexter paw a pen or.
Residence – The Barn House, Ascott Earl, Ascott-under-Wychwood, Oxon OX7 6AG.

SISTER LIVING

Sarah Jane Leslie, *b* 1960

UNCLE LIVING (*Son of 1st baronet*)

JOHN LESLIE (182 Huntingdale Rd, Mt Waverley, Victoria 3149, Aust), *b* 16 Nov 1934: *m* 1st, 1957 (*m diss* 1975), Finola Mary, da of late James Patrick Maxwell, of Bansha, co Tipperary; 2ndly, 1980, Fusako, da of Yonesaku Ishibashi, of Sinagawa-ku, Tokyo, Japan, and has issue living, (by 1st *m*) Richard Alan, *b* 1968, — Elizabeth Jane Leslie, *b* 1958, — Evelyn Mary, *b* 1961, — Suzanne Caroline, *b* 1963, — (by 2nd *m*) Miyo Maybery, *b* 1981, — Kyoko Jacqueline, *b* 1983.

WIDOW LIVING OF SECOND BARONET

JACQUELINE ANNE, only da of Roland A. Hill, of Ascott-under-Wychwood, Oxon: *m* 1st, 1958, Sir Richard (Leslie) Boyce, 2nd Bt, who *d* 1968; 2ndly, 1974, Christopher Richard Boyce-Dennis, of The Barn House, Ascott Earl, Ascott-under-Wychwood, Oxon.

COLLATERAL BRANCH LIVING

Issue of late Charles Francis Leslie Boyce, late Maj 5th Bn Glos Regt (TA), yst son of 1st baronet, *b* 1936, *d* 1985: *m* 1963, Elizabeth (1 Upton Grove Cottages, Tetbury Upton, Tetbury, Glos), only da of William Todd, of 130 Meadoway, Bishop's Cleeve, Cheltenham:—
Edward Neal Leslie, *b* 1965. —— Philip William James, *b* 1971. —— Kathryn Maybery, *b* 1966: *m* 1990, Alistair Cone, and has issue living, Megan Louise, *b* 1993, — Victoria Claire Alexandra, *b* 1973.
The 1st baronet Sir (Harold) Leslie Boyce, KBE (son of Charles Macleay Boyce, of Sydney, NSW), was Sheriff of Gloucester 1941-2, and Lord Mayor of London 1951-2, and sat as MP for Gloucester (C) 1929-45.

BOYD (UK) 1916, of Howth House, Howth, co Dublin

I trust

Sir ALEXANDER WALTER BOYD, 3rd *Baronet,* son of late Major Cecil Anderson Boyd, MC, MD, late RAMC, 2nd son of 1st baronet; *b* 16 June 1934; *s* his uncle, *Sir* WALTER HERBERT, 1948: *m* 1958, Molly Madeline, da of late Ernest Arthur Rendell, of RR3 Vernon, British Columbia, and has issue.

Arms – Azure, a fesse chequy argent and gules between three estoiles or. Crest – Out of a crest coronet or charged, with three ermine spots, a dexter hand erect having the two last fingers turned in and the rest pointing upwards proper.
Residence – Box 261, Whistler, BC V0N 1B0, Canada.

SONS LIVING

IAN WALTER RENDELL, *b* 14 March 1964: *m* 1986, Lee-Ann Dillon, and has issue living, Kyle Robert Rendell *b* 1987, — Cameron Rendell Ian, *b* 1991, — Dawson Alexander Cecil, *b* 1992. —— Robert Alexander Rendell, *b* 1966.

DAUGHTERS LIVING

Heather Lynn, *b* 1959: *m* 1st, 1986 (*m diss* 1992), Francis J. McAnally; 2ndly, 19—, Peter E. McLennan, and has issue living (by 1st *m*), Matthew Alexander, *b* 1986, — Erin Christine, *b* 1989. —— Susan Christine, *b* 1961: *m* 1985 (*m diss* 1990), Paul H. Saarinen, and has issue living, Tory (son), *b* 1988, — Melissa Jenna, *b* 1990. —— Sandra Molly, *b* 1967: *m* 1992, Eric A. Bay.

HALF-SISTERS LIVING

Deirdre Anna, *b* 1925: *m* 1944, Walter V. Dunham, of 532 11th St, New Westminster, BC, Canada, and has issue living, David, *b* 1964, — Ruth Aideen, *b* 1946, — Patricia Ann, *b* 1948, — Beverley Jean, *b* 1951, — Mary Elizabeth, *b* 1953. —— Aideen Gwendolyn, *b* 1926: *m* 1947, Robert Laird Russell, of 3022 S 253rd St, Kent, Washington, USA, and has issue living, Heather Joanne, *b* 1959. —— Ruth Mary, *b* 1927: *m* 1951, Anthony Weisgarber, and has issue living, Kathleen Mary *b* 1957, — Tracy Ann *b* 1962. *Residence* – 1154, Tolmie Av, Victoria, BC.

COLLATERAL BRANCHES LIVING

Grandson of late Lieut-Col Henry Alexander Boyd (infra):—
Issue of late Major Ronald Walter Boyd MC, Roy Ulster Rifles, *b* 1914, *ka* 1944; *m* 1939, Virginia (Courthay, 47 Gatton Rd, Reigate, Surrey RH2 0HJ) (who *m* 2ndly 1949), Humphrey Allen Walter, ERD who *d* 1979, da of late John Freeman, of Bexleyheath, Kent:—
Nigel Cecil John, *b* 1943; *ed* Seaford.

Issue of late Lieut-Col Henry Alexander Boyd, CMG, DSO, 3rd son of 1st baronet, *b* 1877, *d* 1943: *m* 1908, Moya, who *d* 1959, da of late John Shaw Exham, JP, of Worlington, Suffolk:—
Heather, *b* 1910. *Residence* – 82 Foster Av, Mount Merrion, co Dublin.

Issue of late Robert Reginald Boyd, yst son of 1st baronet, *b* 1880, *d* 1959: *m* 1922, Agnes Maria Dorothea, who *d* 1964, da of late Lt-Col Charles Harrison, of Ross, Herefordshire:—
Walter Michael Stewart (3 Glenarm Court, Flagstaff Hill 5159, S Australia) *b* 1924: *m* 1951, Janet Brown, and has issue living, Nicholas Michael (20 Kenny Drive, Duncraig, W Australia 6023), *b* 1954: *m* (and has issue), — Jonathan Peter, *b* 1956, — Emma Jane, *b* 1960. —— Robert Stanley, CB (Great Beere, North Tawton, Devon EX20 2BR), *b* 1927; *ed* Wellington Coll, and Trin Coll, Dublin (BA, LLB); Bar-at-law, Inner Temple, 1954; Solicitor of Inland Revenue 1979-86; CB 1982: *m* 1965, Ann, da of late Daniel Hopkin, MC, MP.

The 1st baronet, the Rt Hon Sir Walter Boyd, PC, LLD, was successively Receiver Judge for Ireland, a Judge of the Court of Bankruptcy in Ireland, and one of the Justices of the High Court of Justice in Ireland. The 2nd baronet, Sir Walter Herbert Boyd, KC, was Ch Registrar of Bankruptcy (Ireland) 1912-37.

BOYLE (UK) 1904, of Ockham, Salehurst, Sussex

Sir STEPHEN GURNEY BOYLE, 5th *Baronet*; *b* 15 Jan 1962; *s* his father, *Sir* RICHARD GURNEY, 1983.

Arms – Per bend raguly gules and argent, two staves raguly in bend counter-changed. **Crest** – In front of a lion's head couped argent, a staff fessewise gules. *Address* – 28 The Lawn, Harlow, Essex CM20 2JX.

BROTHERS LIVING

MICHAEL DESMOND, *b* 16 Sept 1963. —— Roger Edward Bartholemew, *b* 1966.

AUNT LIVING (*Daughter of 2nd baronet*)

Ann Constance Beatrice, *b* 1926: *m* 1948, Jack Brunner Gold (Brunner, Bt), and has issue living, Jason, *b* 1950; *ed* St Paul's: *m* 1972, Ann Elizabeth Stewart, and has issue living, Matthew Guy *b* 1981, James Alexander *b* 1991, — Georgina Beatrice, *b* 1952: *m* 1981, Kenneth Neil Burney Dunlop, and has issue living, Kenneth Edward George *b* 1984, Richard Nicholas *b* 1985. *Residence* – 123 St George's Rd, SE1.

MOTHER LIVING

Elizabeth Ann, yr da of Norman Dennes, of Middle Green, Poulshot, Devizes, Wilts: *m* 1961 (*m diss* 1974), Richard Gurney Boyle (later Sir Richard Boyle, 4th Bt), who *d* 1983.

The 1st baronet, Sir Edward, KC, a Dir of London and India Docks and the Imperial Life Office, sat as MP for Taunton (C) 1906-9. The 2nd baronet, Sir Edward, was a JP for Sussex (High Sheriff 1927), acting British High Commr for Serbia 1915, and Chm Balkan Cttee 1924-45. He *d* 1945. The 3rd baronet, Sir Edward, CH, PC, was Min of Educ 1962-64, and Min of State Educ and Science April-Oct 1964, MP for Handsworth Div of Birmingham (C) 1950-70, Vice-Chancellor of Leeds Univ 1970-81, Chm Top Salaries Review Body 1971-81, and was *cr Baron Boyle of Handsworth*, of Salehurst, co Sussex (Life Baron) 1970. He *d* 1981.

BRADFORD (UK) 1902, of South Audley Street, City of Westminster, co London

Sir EDWARD ALEXANDER SLADE BRADFORD, 5th *Baronet*; *b* (*posthumous*) 18 June 1952; *s* his half-brother, *Sir* JOHN RIDLEY EVELYN, 1954.

Arms – Argent, on a fesse embattled counter-embattled between three mural crowns sable, as many stags' heads erased or. **Crest** – A stag's head erased or, charged on the neck with a mural crown, and suspended from the mouth a bugle horn stringed sable. *Residence* –

HALF-SISTER LIVING

Alison Rose, *b* 1939: *m* 1957, James Ronald Creighton Adams, and has issue living, John Evelyn Creighton, *b* 1959, — Bradford Michael, *b* 1965. *Residence* – Riverside House, N Manchester, Indiana, USA.

UNCLE LIVING (*Son of 2nd baronet*)

DONALD CLIFTON, *b* 22 May 1914; formerly Capt Seaforth Highlanders: *m* 1949, Constance Mary, da of late C. J. Morgan, of Glyncorrwg, S Wales, and has issue living, Susan Jane, *b* 1950, — Joanna Mary, *b* 1957. *Residence* – The Barns, Tapnell, Yarmouth, IoW PO41 0YJ.

Humani nihil alienum
Nothing concerning man
is indifferent to me

MOTHER LIVING OF FOURTH BARONET

Alison (Marylands Farm, Chislehampton, Oxford), da of John Lawson of Borrobol, Sutherland: *m* 1st, 1937 (*m diss* 1947), Maj Sir Edward Montagu Andrew Bradford, 3rd Bt, who *d* 1952; 2ndly, 1951, John Owen Fisher Davies, CBE, MD, MRCP, who *d* 1978.

WIDOW LIVING OF THIRD BARONET

MARJORIE (CHAPMAN) (*Lady Bradford*), da of Samuel Bere of Addiscombe, Surrey: *m* 1950, as his second wife, Major Sir Edward Montagu Andrew Bradford, 3rd Bt, who *d* 1952. *Residence* – Faith Cottage, Pett, Sussex.

COLLATERAL BRANCH LIVING

Issue of late Lt-Col Edward Austen Bradford, DSO, yst son of 1st baronet, *b* 1879, *d* 1958: *m* 1908, Margaret Louisa, who *d* 1972, da of late Herbert Carey Hardy, of Danehurst, Sussex:—
Berenger Colborne, DSO, MBE, MC, *b* 1912; *ed* Eton; is Brigadier, late Black Watch (commanded 5th and 2nd Batns), and a Member of Queen's Body Guard for Scotland (Royal Company of Archers); European War, 1939-45 (wounded, despatches, MBE, MC, DSO and Bar); MBE (Mil) 1942, DSO 1944 (Bar 1945): *m* 1951, Susan, da of late Col Arthur Hanning Vaughan-Lee, of Dillington Park, Ilminster, Somerset, and has issue living, Robert Berenger Pickering (Holestone Lodge, Pool O'Muckart, Clackmannanshire), *b* 1952, — Andrew Edward Hanning (Kincardine, Kincardine O'Neil, Aberdeenshire), *b* 1955; *ed* Eton, and Aberdeen Univ (BSc); Member Queen's Body Guard for Scotland (Royal Company of Archers): *m* 1978, Nicola Barbara, da of late David Philip Smythe, and has issue living, a son *b* 1980, a son *b* 1988, a da *b* 1982, — Ronald James Knight, *b* 1958; *ed* Aberdeen Univ (BSc) Maj The Black Watch (Royal Highland Regt); served NI (despatches): *m* 1986,

Katherine Ferguson, yr da of Sir Ian Denholm, CBE, of Newton of Belltrees, Lochwinnoch, Renfrewshire, and has issue living, Victoria Jane Ferguson *b* 1989, Kirstin Elizabeth Hardy *b* 1992, — Margaret Jane, *b* 1953: *m* 1982, Robert Hamilton Gladstone of Capenoch, of Capenoch, Thornhill, Dumfries-shire, and has issue living, a son *b* 1983, a son *b* (twin) 1983, a da *b* 1986. *Residence* – Kincardine, Kincardine O'Neil, Aberdeenshire. —— Diana Elizabeth, *b* 1919: *m* 1941, Rupert P. Shervington, late Capt RE, and has issue living, Evelyn Arthur, *b* 1942; BA, Trin Coll, Dublin, — Diana Clare, *b* 1943, — Caroline Faith, *b* 1954. *Residence* – The Villa Ware, Ware Lane, Lyme Regis, Dorset DT7 3EJ.

The 1st baronet, Col Sir Edward Ridley Colborne, was Commr of Police of the Metropolis 1890-1903. The 2nd baronet, Col Sir Evelyn Ridley Bradford, Comdg 2nd Batn Seaforth Highlanders (Ross-shire Buffs, Duke of Albany's), was *ka* 1914. The 3rd baronet, Sir Edward Montagu Andrew, was Major The Cameronians.

BRADY (UK) 1869, of Hazelbrook, co Dublin, Ireland (Extinct 1927)

Sir WILLIAM LONGFIELD BRADY, 4th and last *Baronet.*

DAUGHTER LIVING OF FOURTH BARONET

Ethne Florence, *b* 1902.

DAUGHTER LIVING OF THIRD BARONET

Jessie Elizabeth Maziere *b* 1901.

BRICKWOOD (UK) 1927, of Portsmouth

Nothing arduous

Sir BASIL GREAME BRICKWOOD, 3rd *Baronet*; *b* 21 May 1923; *s* his half-brother, *Sir* RUPERT REDVERS, 1974; *ed* King Edward's Gram Sch, Stratford, and Clifton; served with RAF 1940-46: *m* 1st, 1947, Betty Cooper; 2ndly, 1956, Shirley Anne, da of Richard Wallace Brown, and has issue by 2nd *m*.

Arms – Argent a pale checky azure and or between two oak trees couped vert on a chief gules three ears of barley slipped and leaved of the third and a sprig of hop slipped and leaved proper in saltire between two billets gold. **Crest** – A demi savage wreathed about the temples with a chaplet of oak holding in the dexter hand a sprig of hop slipped and leaved proper and resting the sinister hand upon a billet or.
Club – RAF.

DAUGHTERS LIVING (By 2nd marriage)

Tessa Anne, *b* 1959. —— Gail Anne BRICKWOOD, *b* 1963; has resumed her maiden name: *m* 1984 (*m diss* 19—), Michael Horsnell, elder son of R.N. Horsnell, of Thorvington, Essex.

DAUGHTERS LIVING OF SECOND BARONET

Sally (Neale), *b* 1933: *m* 1956, Nigel William Seville Yonge, of Homefields, Bulls Lane, Cowfold, Sussex, and has issue living, William Jonathan Michael, *b* 1961, — Andrew James Neale, *b* 1964, — Susannah Mary, *b* 1957, — Annabel Mary, *b* 1959. —— Ann Neale, *b* 1934: *m* 1st, 1959, John Colin Caldecott Bauer; 2ndly, 1986, Peter A. Van den Bergh, and has issue living (by 1st *m*), John William, *b* 1960, — Nicola Anne, *b* 1962: *m* 19—, Jonathan Glover, and has issue living, Hugo James Malcolm *b* 1992.

The 1st baronet, Sir John Brickwood, was Chm and Managing Director of Brickwood & Co Ltd, brewers, of Portsmouth, and sometime Chm of Portsmouth Chamber of Commerce.

BRINCKMAN (UK) 1831, of Burton or Monk Bretton, Yorkshire

By persevering

Sir THEODORE GEORGE RODERICK BRINCKMAN, 6th *Baronet*; *b* 20 March 1932; *s* his father, *Sir* RODERICK NAPOLEON, DSO, MC, 1985; *ed* Millfield, Trin Coll Sch, Port Hope, Ontario, Ch Ch, Oxford, and Trin Coll, Toronto Univ; publisher and antiquarian bookseller: *m* 1st, 1958 (*m diss* 1983), Helen Mary Anne, da of late Arnold Elliot Cook, of Toronto, Canada; 2ndly, 1983, Hon Greta Sheira Bernadette Grant-Ferris, da of Baron Harvington (Life Baron), and formerly wife of (i) John Frederick Edward Trehearne, and (ii) Christopher Mark Henry Murray, and has issue by 1st *m*.

Arms – Quarterly: 1st and 4th, argent, three hills azure, for Brinckman; 2nd and 3rd, ermine, two eagles displayed in chief gules, and a lion rampant in base proper collared and a chain therefrom reflexed over the back or, for Broadhead.
Crest – A pair of wings quarterly argent and azure.
Residence – Hazleton Manor, Cirencester, Glos GL7 6PG. *Club* – White's, University (Toronto)

SONS LIVING *(By 1st marriage)*

THEODORE JONATHAN, *b* 19 Feb 1960; *ed* Lakefield College Sch, Ontario, Yale Univ (BA), and Columbia Graduate Sch of Journalism (MSc) (93 Roxborough St W, Toronto, Ontario M5R 1T9, Canada). —— (Roderick) Nicholas, *b* 1964; *ed* Lakefield College Sch, Ontario, Univ of Toronto (BA), and Univ of Victoria Law Sch (LLB) (54 Astley Av, Toronto, Ontario, Canada).

DAUGHTER LIVING *(By 1st marriage)*

Sophia Theresa (74 Abdale Rd, W12 7EU), *b* 1963; *ed* Bishop's College Sch, Quebec.

BROTHER LIVING

John Francis (191 St George St, Toronto, Ontario, Canada M5R 2M6), *b* 1933: *m* 1st, 1963 (*m diss* 1973), Susan Jennefer, da of Peter Woodburn Blaylock, of Toad's Tooting, Ile Bizard, Quebec, Canada; 2ndly, 1983 (*m diss* 1988), Eve Napier, da of Clifford Murray, of Huntington, Quebec, Canada, and has issue living, (by 1st *m*) Adam Blaylock, *b* 1965, — Theodora Southam, *b* 1966, — (by 2nd *m*) John Christian Napoleon, *b* 1985, — and further issue (by Kerry, da of Thomas Bingham, of Victoria, BC), Nigel Thomas Bingham, *b* 1988.

HALF SISTER LIVING

Theadora Elizabeth, *b* 1944: *m* 1st, 1964 (*m diss* 1976), Gerard Francis Campbell (*see* B Harlech); 2ndly, 1978, Dennis Cordell Lavarack, and has issue living, (by 1st *m*) (*see* B Harlech), — (by 2nd *m*) Milo Napoleon, *b* 1978, — Emerald Clare, *b* 1981. *Residence* – 491 Fulham Rd, SW6.

COLLATERAL BRANCHES LIVING

Granddaughter of late William Henry Brinckman, son of William Edward Brinckman, RN, 3rd son of 1st baronet:—
    Issue of late William Brian Brinckman, *b* 1904, *d* 1975: *m* 1937, Marjorie, da of late John Ashbrook Hughes:—
Hilary Anne, *b* 1937.

Granddaughter of late William Edward Brinckman, RN (ante):—
    Issue of late Major Rowland Brinckman, OBE, *b* 1861, *d* 1948; *m* 1st, 1891, Anna Alexander, who *d* 1910, da of late Professor J. E. Cairnes; 2ndly, 1911, Marian, who *d* 1941, da of late Richard Baxter:—
(By 1st *m*) Christine Phyllida (*Lady Marshall*), *b* 1907: *m* 1931, Sir Hugo Frank Marshall, KBE, CMG, who *d* 1986, and has issue living, Robert Rowland (194 Richmond Rd, Kingston-on-Thames, Surrey), *b* 1942: *m* 1966, Joan Monica Theresa, da of Rev Canon H. Leach, of Johannesburg, — David William, *b* 1945: *m* 1969, Lorraine June, da of C. W. Robbins, of Miami Beach, Florida, and has issue living, William Denys *b* 1970, Reuben Grey *b* 1972, Henry Balfour *b* 1977, Alexander Rowland *b* 1988, Danae Gwyneth *b* 1980, — Janet Mary, *b* 1937: *m* 1960, David B. Cunliffe-Jones, of 9 Elson Rd, Formby, Lancs, and has issue living, Andrew Robert *b* 1962, Peter David *b* 1964, Judith Elizabeth *b* 1961, Rosemary Janet Helen *b* 1968. *Residence* – Murhill House, Limpley Stoke, nr Bath.

The 1st baronet whose patronymic was Broadhead, in 1842 resumed for himself and issue by Roy licence, the family name of Brinckman. He sat as MP for Yarmouth 1820-26. Sir Theodore, 2nd Baronet, sat as MP for Canterbury (*L*) 1868-74. Sir Theodore Francis, CB, 3rd Baronet, was Hon Col The Buffs and sometime Lieut-Col London Regt. Sir Theodore Ernest Warren, 4th baronet, was Major 1st Life Guards. The 5th baronet, Sir Roderick Napoleon, DSO, MC, was Col Grenadier Guards and ADC to Gov-Gen and C-in-C, Canada, and to Gov of Victoria, and was Ch of Staff, Mil Mission to Moscow 1944-45 and Head of Liaison Mission to Netherlands 1945.

BRISCO (GB) 1782, of Crofton Place, Cumberland

Take with a grateful hand

Sir DONALD GILFRID BRISCO, 8th *Baronet*; *b* 15 Sept 1920; *s* his father, *Sir* HYLTON MUSGRAVE CAMPBELL, 1968; *ed* Wairapa Coll, NZ; a Sheep Farmer; a JP; 1939-45 War, as a Pilot with RNZAF and RAF in Europe and Mediterranean (prisoner): *m* 1945, Irene, only da of Henry John Gage, of Ermine Park, Brockworth, Glos, and has issue.

Arms – Argent, three greyhounds courant in pale sable. **Crest** – A greyhound courant sable seizing a hare proper.
Address – 27a Chambers St, PO Box 8165, Havelock North, Hawke's Bay, NZ.

DAUGHTERS LIVING

Barbara Ann, *b* 1946: *m* 1983, William Ian Wilson, of Lot 56 Melaleuca Drive, Lamb Island, Queensland 4184, Australia. —— Penny Christine (1/448 Marine Parade, Biggera Waters, Qld 4216, Australia), *b* 1949. —— Jill Kathleen, *b* 1952: *m* 1974, Wayne George Brunton, of 97 Awanui St, New Plymouth, NZ.

SISTERS LIVING

Joan Elsie, *b* 1923: *m* 1952, F. J. A. McTague, of 33 Kennedy Rd, Napier, Hawke's Bay, New Zealand, and has issue living, Robert Howard, *b* 1953, — Richard Patrick, *b* 1957, — Steven Francis, *b* 1965. —— Oriel Patricia, *b* 1926: *m* 1st, 1950 (*m diss* 1974), James C Waldren; 2ndly, 1975, Lt-Col Reginald Henry Spicer, MC, who *d* 19—, and has issue living, (by 1st *m*) Murray David, *b* 1951, — Christine Lesley, *b* 1953. *Residence* – 2/211 Windsor Av, Hastings, Hawke's Bay, NZ.

COLLATERAL BRANCH LIVING

Issue of late Gilfred Rimington Brisco, uncle of 8th Bt, *b* 1895, *d* 1981: *m* 1941, Constance Freda, who *d* 1980, 2nd da of Charles John Polson, of Masterton, NZ:—
CAMPBELL HOWARD (Kawariri, Hokonui, No 2 RD, Winton, Southland, NZ), *b* 1944: *m* 1969, Kay Janette, da of Ewan W. McFadzien, of Gt North Rd, Winton, Southland, NZ, and has issue living, Kent Rimington, *b* 1972, — Shannon Gregory, *b* 1974, — Rebecca Kaye, *b* 1978. —— Rosemary Robyn, *b* 1943: *m* 1966, Peter Colin Neale, of 24 Newcastle St, Rose Bay, Sydney 2029, Australia, and has issue living, Adam Hylton, *b* 1968.
Sir John Brisco, 1st Bt of Crofton, was grandson of John Brisco of Crofton, descended from Isold Brisco of Brisco, who acquired the Manors of Crofton, Whinnow, and Dundraw, in right of his wife, Margaret, da of Sir John Crofton, and was great-grandson of Robert Brisco, of Brisco, Cumberland. The 5th baronet Sir Hylton Ralph Brisco, was drowned as sea on a voyage to Bombay 1922: he *m* 1st, 1904 (*m diss* 1915), Lilian Mabel, da of late James King; 2ndly, 1916, Grace *m diss* 1921, da of late Henry Vaughan.

BRISCOE (UK) 1910, of Bourn Hall, Bourn, co Cambridge (Abeyant 1994)

I perform and persevere

†*Sir* (JOHN) JAMES BRISCOE, 5th *Baronet*; *b* 15 July 1951; *s* his father, *Sir* JOHN LEIGH CHARLTON, DFC, 1993; *ed* Oratory Sch, and Univ Coll, London: *m* 1985, Felicity Mary, eldest da of David Melville Watkinson, of Gowthorpe Manor, Swardeston, Norwich, and has issue. Sir James Briscoe *d* as the result of a motor accident 2 July 1994, when the baronetcy fell into abeyance pending the birth of his posthumous child.

Arms – Argent, two greyhounds courant sable, on a chief arched of the last two roses of the first, barbed and seeded proper. **Crest** – Upon a mount of heather proper a greyhound courant paly of twelve argent and sable.
Residence – Hall Barn, Swainsthorpe, Norwich, Norfolk NR14 8QA.

DAUGHTER LIVING

Amanda Mary Louise *b* 1993.

BROTHER LIVING

EDWARD HOME (Bank End Lodge, Forty Green Rd, Beaconsfield, Bucks HP9 1XL), *b* 27 March 1955; *ed* Ampleforth: *m* 1st 1979 (*m diss* 1987), Anne Mary, da of Peter Vincent Lister, of Southside, Kingsash, The Lee, Great Missenden, Bucks; 2ndly, 1994, Sandy Elizabeth King, 2nd da of Victor Lloyd, of 1a Orchard Mews, Seer Green, Bucks, and has issue living (by 1st *m*), Guy Home Sebastian, *b* 1983, — Fay D'Arcy, *b* 1981.

SISTER LIVING

Diana Clare, *b* 1949.

UNCLE LIVING (*son of 3rd baronet*)

Richard Kynaston, *b* 1914; *ed* Charterhouse, and Balliol Coll, Oxford (BA 1936, MA 1947); ACA 1940; FCA 1960; European War 1940-45 as Capt RA: *m* 1951, Margaret Hamilton, da of Sir Hugh Mallinson Rigby, 1st Bt, KCVO, FRCS. *Residence* – Maple House, Higher Combe Road, Haslemere, Surrey GU27 2LQ.

WIDOW LIVING OF FOURTH BARONET

TERESA MARY VIOLET, OBE (*Teresa, Lady Briscoe*), da of Brig-Gen Sir Archibald Fraser Home, KCVO, CB, CMG, DSO: *m* 1948, Sir John Leigh Charlton Briscoe, 4th Bt, DFC, who *d* 1993. *Residence* – 9 St Michael's Green, Beaconsfield, Bucks HP9 2BN.

COLLATERAL BRANCHES LIVING

Grandchildren of late Hugh Kynaston Briscoe, CSI, CIE (infra):—
Issue of late John Arthur Briscoe, *b* 1925, *d* 1983: *m* 1955, Hilary Mary (who *m* 2ndly, 1990, John Willis, of Wressle House, nr Brigg, S Humberside DN20 0RU), da of late S. K. Shaw, of Lynbank, Mill Gap Rd, Eastbourne:—
Neil David, *b* 1956: *m* 1981, Bryony Virginia Jane, da of Sqdn Ldr Clifford Basil Warwick-Spaul, of St Vincents, Tilstock, Shropshire, and has issue living, Peter, *b* 19—, — Jenny Louise, *b* 19—. —— Andrew Mark, *b* 1960: *m* 1990, Clare —. —— Lindsay Ann, *b* 1958: *m* 1983, Timothy Fell.

Issue of late Hugh Kynaston Briscoe, CSI, CIE, yst son of 1st baronet, *b* 1879, *d* 1956: *m* 1919, Noel, who *d* 1971, da of late John E. Worrall, of Langstones, 39 Bidston Rd, Oxton, Birkenhead:—
Ellen Kathleen, *b* 1920: *m* 1945, Maj Anthony Stanley Purcell Jeans, TD, Wilts Regt, and has issue living, Michael Anthony Purcell, *b* 1947: *m* 1975, Christine Anne Woodley, — Jennifer Rosemary Ellen, *b* 1950: *m* 1982, Maj Peter McComas, RA. *Residence* – Testaway, Chilbolton, nr Stockbridge, Hants. —— Nancy Charlton (Yew Box, Penton Mewsey, Andover, Hants), *b* 1921. —— Mary Clare, *b* 1928: *m* 1954, James Anthony Farrer-Halls, and has issue living, Alan Anthony, *b* 1961: *m* 1983, Linda Sturgess, — Barbara Mary, *b* 1955: *m* 1983, Gary William Taylor, — Gillian Clare, *b* 1958. *Residence* – 4 Framers Court, Ellis Way, Lane End, High Wycombe, Bucks HP14 3LL.
Sir John James Briscoe, 1st baronet, was High Sheriff of Cambridgeshire 1888. Sir (John) Charlton Briscoe, MD, FRCP, 3rd baronet, was a Consulting Physician to King's Coll Hospital and to Evelina Hospital for Sick Children.

RUGGLES-BRISE (UK) 1935, of Spains Hall, Finchingfield, Essex

Sir JOHN ARCHIBALD RUGGLES-BRISE, CB, OBE, TD, 2nd *Baronet; b* 13 June 1908; *s* his father, *Col Sir* EDWARD ARCHIBALD, MC, TD, MP, 1942; *ed* Eton; is a JP for Essex, a Freeman of Chelmsford, a former Gov of Felsted and Chigwell Schs, a KStJ, an Underwriting Member of Lloyd's, appointed Lord-Lt of Essex 1958, and Pro Chancellor of Essex Univ 1963-74; Pres Country Landowners Assocn 1958-59, and Game Fair; Chm of Standing Council of the Baronetage 1958-63 and a Church Commr 1959-65; formerly Hon Col 459th Mixed Heavy Anti-Aircraft Regt RA (TA); 1939-45 War (OBE); OBE (Mil) 1945, CB (Civil) 1958.

Arms – Quarterly, 1st and 4th, gules, a cross between four mascles argent, all within a bordure sable, charged with eight quatrefoils of the second, *Brise*; 2nd and 3rd, argent, on a chevron gules, between three roses of the second, barbed, seeded, leaved and slipped proper, as many estoiles or, *Ruggles*. **Crest** – 1st, a demi-crocodile sable, *Brise*; 2nd, in front of twelve arrows in saltire proper, heads outwards, a tower or, inflamed proper, *Ruggles*.
Seat – Spains Hall, Finchingfield, Braintree, Essex CM7 4PF. *Club* – Carlton.

BROTHER LIVING

GUY EDWARD, TD, *b* 15 June 1914; *ed* Eton; late Capt Essex Yeo; a DL of Essex; High Sheriff 1967-68; a Member of London Stock Exchange; Consultant of Brewin Dolphin & Co (Stockbrokers) and Vice-Chm Riding for the Disabled Trust; 1939-45 War in N Africa (prisoner (Italy), escaped): *m* 1st, 1940, Elizabeth, who *d* 1988, only da of late James Knox, of Smithstone House, Kilwinning, Ayrshire; 2ndly, 1944, Christine Margaret Fothergill-Spencer, only da of late Lt John A. Fothergill, and has issue living (by 1st *m*), Timothy Edward, *b* 1945; *ed* Eton: *m* 1975, Rosemary E., yr da of J. S. Craig, of 1 Buckland Court, 37 Belsize Park, NW3 4EB, and has issue living, Archibald Edward *b* 1979, Charles Evelyn *b* 1983, Iain *b* 1989, Olivia Agnes *b* 1977, Felicity Rose *b* 1984, — James Rupert, *b* 1947; *ed* Eton, — Samuel Guy (Mill House, Little Bardfield, Essex), *b* 1956: *m* 1979, Katharine Margaret, only da of late Brig Richard John Bishop, MBE, MC, RA (ret) (*see* V Thurso, colls), and has issue living, Edward James *b* 1985, Camilla Jane *b* 1983. *Residences* – Housham Tye Manor, Harlow, Essex CM17 0QL; Ledgowan Lodge, Achnasheen, Wester Ross. *Club* – City of London.

SISTER LIVING

Violet Agatha, *b* 1907: *m* 1936, Com Hubert Wyndham Barry, RN (ret) (*see* Barry, Bt, colls). *Residence* – Flat 5, Sutton Manor Mews, Sutton Scotney, Winchester, Hants SO21 3JX.

The 1st baronet, Col Sir Edward Archibald Ruggles-Brise, MC, TD (son of Archibald Weyland Ruggles-Brise, JP, DL, of Spains Hall, Finchingfield, Essex), was Lieut-Col and Brevet Col late 104th (Essex Yeo) Brig, RA (TA), Vice-Lieut for Essex, and MP for Maldon Div of Essex (C) 1922-3 and 1924-42.

BROADBENT (UK) 1893, of Brook Street, co London, and Longwood, Yorkshire

Sir ANDREW GEORGE BROADBENT, 5th *Baronet*; *b* 26 Jan 1963; *s* his father, Sir GEORGE WALTER, AFC, 1992; *ed* Monkton Combe; late Capt The Prince of Wales's Own Regt of Yorkshire.

Arms – Per pale ermine and azure, a fesse nebulée counter-changed, in the dexter chief quarter a caduceus erect proper. **Crest** – In front of a pheon the staff rompée, a serpent nowed, all proper.
Resides in York.

SISTER LIVING

Ione Charlotte Elizabeth, *b* 1967.

UNCLE LIVING (*brother of 4th baronet*)

αιεν αριετευειν

To excel always

ROBERT JOHN DENDY, *b* 4 Nov 1938; *ed* Stamford Sch; FRICS. *Residence* – 19 Aplin Way, Lightwater, Surrey GU18 5TT.

WIDOWS LIVING OF THIRD AND FOURTH BARONETS

MIRANDA (*Miranda, Lady Broadbent*), 2nd da of late Donald George Pilcher-Clark, of Port St Mary, IoM: *m* 1982, as his second wife, Sir William Francis Broadbent, 3rd Bt, who *d* 1987. *Residence* –
VALERIE ANNE (*Lady Broadbent*), only da of (Cecil) Frank Ward, of York: *m* 1962, Sir George Walter Broadbent, AFC, 4th Bt, who *d* 1992. *Address* – c/o Lloyd's Bank, 2 Pavement, York YO1 2NE.

COLLATERAL BRANCH LIVING

Grandchildren of late Maj Walter Broadbent, MD, FRCP, 3rd son of 1st baronet:—
Issue of late Hubert William Lonsdale Broadbent, MB, *b* 1908, *d* 1988: *m* 1934, Marjorie, da of late Sir Arthur Kirwan Agar, Ch Justice of British Honduras:—
Graham Agar (17 Heathgate, Hampstead Garden Suburb, NW11 7AR), *b* 1938; *ed* Charterhouse, and Pembroke Coll, Camb (BA): *m* 1964, (Valerie) Suzanne, elder da of Charles Edward Henry Wytton, of Hampstead Garden Suburb, NW11, and has issue living, Charles Richard, *b* 1968. — Philip David, *b* 1972. — Juliet Fiona, *b* 1977. —— Judith Anne, *b* 1935: *m* 1960, Robin Scoones, of Bessells Cottage, Iwerne Courtenay, Blandford Forum, Dorset, and has issue living, Ian Christopher, *b* 1962, — Simon Richard, *b* 1964, — Timothy Graham, *b* 1967.
Sir William H. Broadbent, KCVO, MD, FRCP, hon LLD, FRS, 1st Bt, son of John Broadbent, was an eminent consulting Physician and Physician-in-Ord to Queen Victoria, King Edward VII and the Prince of Wales. Sir John Francis Harpin Broadbent, MD, FRCP, MRCS, 2nd Bt, was Consulting Physician to St Mary's Hospital, London Fever Hospital, and King Edward VII Sanatorium, Midhurst.

BROCKLEBANK (UK) 1885, of Greenlands, co Cumberland and Springwood, co Lancaster

Sir AUBREY THOMAS BROCKLEBANK, 6th *Baronet*; *b* 29 Jan 1952; *s* his father, *Maj Sir* JOHN MONTAGUE, TD, 1974; *ed* Eton, and Univ Coll, Durham (BSc): *m* 1979 (*m diss* 1990), Anna-Marie, da of Dr William Dunnet, of Heroncroft, Woldingham, Surrey, and has issue.

Arms – Argent, three brocks proper, each on a mount vert; on a chief azure as many escallops of the first. **Crest** – On an anchor fessewise sable, a cock argent, combed and wattled gules, and charged on the shoulder with an escallop of the first.
Residence – 120 Gloucester Terrace, W2 6HP. *Club* – Brooks's.

SONS LIVING

AUBREY WILLIAM THOMAS, *b* 15 Dec 1980. —— Hamish John, *b* 1987.

WIDOW LIVING OF FIFTH BARONET

PAMELA SUE (*Lady Brocklebank*), da of late William Harold Pierce, OBE, of Bidston, Cheshire, and formerly wife of Maj Leslie Forshaw-Wilson: *m* 1950, Maj Sir John Montague Brocklebank, TD, 5th Bt, who *d* 1974.

COLLATERAL BRANCHES LIVING

God send grace

Grandson of late Major John Jasper Brocklebank, DSO (infra):—
Issue of late Lt-Cdr John Maurice Brocklebank, RNVR, *b* 1917, *ka* 1945: *m* 1944, Evelyn Margaret, who *d* 1985, da of Gordon Pyper, and widow of T. L. Stephenson, 2nd Lieut:—
John Daniel (8 Grange Rd, Barnes, SW13 9RE), *b* (*posthumous*) 1945; *ed* Eton, and Keble Coll, Oxford: *m* 1971, Donna Jean, da of Maj Clixby Fitzwilliams, of Hazeldene, Healing, nr Grimsby, and has issue living, Daniel Maurice, *b* 1975, — Edward John, *b* 1982.

Issue of late Maj John Jasper Brocklebank, DSO, 2nd son of 2nd baronet, *b* 1875, *d* 1942: *m* 1914, Constance Mary, who *d* 1965, da of late Sir Robert Leonard Powell, JP, of Flowers Hill, Pangbourne:—
Thomas Gordon (PO Box 75, Breyten, Transvaal 2330, S Africa), *b* 1921; *ed* Eton; formerly Lt RNVR (Fleet Air Arm): *m* 1st, 1952, Gillian Chester, who *d* 1966, da of late William Francis Cardew; 2ndly, 1970, Edith Josephine, da of late William Geoffry Ward, and widow of Neville Wells Abbott, and has issue living, (by 1st *m*) Robin John, *b* 1954, — Geoffrey Cardew, *b* 1959, — Christopher Philip, *b* 1963, — Anne Frances, *b* 1962.

Issue of late Robert Allport Brocklebank, 3rd son of 2nd baronet, *b* 1878, *d* 1946: *m* 1903, Frances, yst da of late John H. Walker, JP for cos Fife and Forfar:—
Oliver, RN, *b* 1908; became Lt-Com 1939: *m* 1st, 1931, Diana, who *d* 1994, da of late Col Wilford Boteler, DSO, RA; 2ndly, 1947, Marjorie Joan Snowling, and has issue living, (by 2nd *m*) Alison Philippa, *b* 1948, — Elizabeth Joanna, *b* 1950, — Edwina Jane, *b* 1952. *Residence* – Redbourne, Lowestoft Rd, Gorleston-on-Sea, Norfolk.

Grandchildren of late Rev Charles Henry Brocklebank, 4th son of 1st baronet:—
Issue of late Charles Gerald Brocklebank, MC, *b* 1893, *d* 1940: *m* 1925, Beatrice Gresley, who *d* 1992, da of late Falconer Madan:—
Charles William (Giffords Hall, Stoke-by-Nayland, Suffolk; 17 Grosvenor Sq, W1), *b* 1930; *ed* Eton, and Ch Ch Oxford: *m* 1965, Marcia Andrea, da of late Arthur Early, of Kalamazoo, Michigan, USA, and has issue living, James Gerald, *b* 1970, — William Falconer, *b* 1976, — Diana Lasswell, *b* 1968. ——— Mary, *b* 1926: *m* 1948, Michael Guy Molesworth Bevan, who *d* 1992 (*see* V Molesworth, 1931 Edn), and has issue living, Roger Anthony Briscoe (3 Albion St, W2), *b* 1951; *ed* Eton: *m* 1st, 1980 (*m diss* 198-), Marion Casey, da of Theodore Donahue, of Litchfield, Connecticut, USA; 2ndly, 1994, Beverly D. Anastopolis, — William George Briscoe (Longstowe Hall, Longstowe, nr Cambridge), *b* 1958: *m* 1985, Annabel Jane, da of William Bertram Weatherall, of Shorndown, Mursley, Bucks (*see* Russell, Bt, *cr* 1916, colls), and has issue living, George Michael Briscoe *b* 1988, Lucy Clare *b* 1990, Victoria Mary *b* 1993, — James Edward Briscoe (Bulby Hall, Bulby, Lincs), *b* 1960: *m* 1986, Susan Fiona, da of Victor Parker, of Appleton, Cheshire, — Penelope Anne, *b* 1955: *m* 1982, Geoffrey Thomas Carwardine Probert, of Grounds Farm, Hook Norton, Banbury, Oxon, son of Lt-Col Richard Harlackenden Probert, OBE, DL, of Bevills, Bures, Suffolk, and has issue living, Thomas Henry Carwardine *b* 1985, Jack Michael Harlackenden *b* 1993, Rebecca Mary *b* 1988, Isobel Loveday *b* 1991. *Residence* – Longstowe Hall, Longstowe, nr Cambridge CB3 7UH. ——— Ann, *b* 1928.

The 1st baronet, Sir Thomas, was son of Wilson Fisher, of Keekle, Whitehaven; assumed in 1845, by Roy licence the surname of Brocklebank, on succeeding to the estate of his maternal uncle Thomas Brocklebank, of Greenlands, Cumberland, and was High Sheriff of Cumberland 1864. The 2nd baronet was High Sheriff of Lancashire 1908, and the 3rd baronet, Sir Aubrey (Chm of Thomas and John Brocklebank (Limited), and a Director of Suez Canal Co, Cunard Steamship Co (Limited), and other cos), was High Sheriff of Cumberland 1921.

BRODIE (UK) 1834, of Boxford, Suffolk

Sir BENJAMIN DAVID ROSS BRODIE, 5th *Baronet*; *b* 29 May 1925; *s* his father, *Sir* BENJAMIN COLLINS, MC, 1971; *ed* Eton; late R Signals: *m* , and has issue.

Arms – Azure, on a chevron between three mullets argent, three civic wreaths vert. **Crest** – A dexter cubit arm erect, holding a civic wreath as in the arms with three arrows, one in fesse and two in saltire points towards the dexter argent.

SON LIVING

ALAN, *b* — 19—.

DAUGHTER LIVING

—, *b* — 19—.

BROTHER LIVING

Colin Alexander, *b* 19 April 1929; *ed* Eton and Magdalen Coll, Oxford; Bar Middle Temple 1953; QC 1980; Bencher Lincoln's Inn 1988; late 8th (King's Irish) Hussars: *m* 1955, Julia Anne Irene, da of late Norman E. Wates, of Elmore, Chipstead, Surrey, and has issue living, Christian Norman, *b* 1957, — Alexander Colin, *b* 1959. *Residence* – 24 Old Buildings, Lincolns Inn, WC2.

SISTER LIVING

Angela Mary, *b* 1933; *ed* St Andrews Univ (MA, Hons Econ). *Residence* – Betchworth Lodge, Betchworth, Surrey.

COLLATERAL BRANCH LIVING

Grandson of late Capt Edgar Waldegrave Brodie, 3rd son of late Rev William Brodie, 2nd son of 1st baronet:—
Issue of late Capt Malcolm William O'Callaghan Brodie, *b* 1887, *d* 1966: *m* 1st, 1922, Phyllis Gwavas, who *d* 1940, da of Henry Tredenham Fitzherbert Carlyon; 2ndly, 1948, Sybil Barbara, da of late Henry Shearburn Clark, of Fenhill, Hawke's Bay, NZ:—
(By 1st *m*) Mark Donald Carlyon William (Ballinahinch, RD2, Napier, NZ), *b* 1928: *m* 1955, Patricia, da of Judge A. A. Whitehead, of NZ, and has issue living, Malcolm Robert, *b* 1956, — Douglas William, *b* 1958, — Christopher Mark, *b* 1961, — Philip John Edgar, *b* 1964.

The 1st baronet, Sir Benjamin Collins Brodie, DCL, FRS, a distinguished surgeon, was Pres of Roy Soc, Serjeant-Surgeon to King William IV, and to Queen Victoria, and first Surgeon-in-Ordinary to late Prince Consort: the 2nd baronet was Waynflete Professor of Chemistry, Oxford Univ, and the 3rd baronet was High Sheriff for Surrey 1912.

BROMHEAD (UK) 1806, of Thurlby, Lincolnshire
(Name pronounced "Brumhead")

By concord property is increased

Sir JOHN DESMOND GONVILLE BROMHEAD, 6th *Baronet*; *b* 21 Dec 1943; *s* his father, *Col Sir* BENJAMIN DENIS GONVILLE, OBE, 1981; *ed* Wellington Coll, and privately.

Arms – Azure, on a bend argent, between two leopards' faces or, a mural crown gules, between two fleurs-de-lis sable. **Crest** – Out of a mural crown gules, an unicorn's head argent, armed or, in the mouth a rose gules, slipped and leaved proper.

SISTERS LIVING

Diana Jane Gonville, *b* 1940: *m* 1966, Dr Paul Sherwood, of 2 Devonshire Place, W1, and has issue living, Robin Paul Austen, *b* 1969, — Julian George, *b* 1974. —— Anne Kathleen Gonville, *b* 1942: *m* 1965, Robin James German, of Thurlby Hall, Lincoln, and has issue living, Patrick Benjamin James, *b* 1967, — Robin Piers Gonville, *b* 1969, — Alexander Henry Bromhead, *b* 1971.

WIDOW LIVING OF FIFTH BARONET

NANCY MARY (*Lady Bromhead*) (Thurlby Hall, Lincoln), da of late Thomas Seon Lough, of Buenos Aires, Argentina: *m* 1938, Col Sir Benjamin Denis Gonville Bromhead, 5th Bt, OBE, who *d* 1981.

COLLATERAL BRANCHES LIVING

Grandchildren of late Maj Edward Gonville Bromhead, el son of 4th baronet:—
Issue of late Lt-Col Edmund de Gonville Hosking Bromhead, *b* 1903, *d* 1976: *m* 1938, Joan (12 Market Sq, Bicester, Oxon OX6 7AW), da of late Brig Sir Henry Lawrence Scott, CB, DSO, MC:—
JOHN EDMUND DE GONVILLE (Duiker House, Fencott, Islip, Oxford), *b* 10 Oct 1939; *ed* St Andrew's Coll, Grahamstown, S Africa, and RAF Coll, Cranwell; Capt British Airways: *m* 1965, Janet Frances, da of Henry Brotherton, of Moreton-in-Marsh, Glos, and has issue living, Alistair John de Gonville, *b* 1969, — Amanda-Jane de Gonville, *b* 1965. —— David de Gonville, CBE, LVO, *b* 1944; *ed* St Andrew's, S Africa, and RMA; Lt-Col R Regt of Wales, Brig 1991; Gen Ser Medal (Clasps), S Arabia and NI; Equerry to HRH The Prince of Wales 1982-84; Freeman of the Bezirk of Wilmersdorf 1993; LVO 1984, OBE (Mil) 1988, CBE (Mil) 1994: *m* 1970, Susan, da of Cdr Richard Furley Fyson, DSC, JP, RN, and has issue living, James Henry de Gonville, *b* 1974, — Annabel Suzanne de Gonville, *b* 1973, — Antonia Diana de Gonville, *b* 1978. —— Jacqueline Anne Gonville, *b* 1942: *m* 1971, James Boonzaier (7 Ngaio Rd, Kelburn, Wellington 5, NZ), and has issue living, Ann Maria Gonville, *b* 1977, — Julia Gonville, *b* 1979.

Issue of late Major Benjamin Gonville Bromhead, 2nd son of 4th baronet, *b* 1876, *d* 1939: *m* 1912, Edith Maud, who *d* 1975, da of late Lt-Col R. C. Andrews, Indian Army:—
Robert Benjamin Gonville, CBE (Brownshill Court, Wick St, Stroud, Glos GL6 7QN), *b* 1913; *ed* Dover Coll; Col (ret) late Roy Berkshire (Duke of Edinburgh's R Regt); Burma 1943 (MBE), Cyprus 1958 (despatches, OBE); Ser Adviser to British High Commr in Nigeria 1960-63; Col the Duke of Edinburgh's R Regt (Berks and Wilts) 1965-70; MBE (Mil) 1943, OBE (Mil) 1958, CBE (Mil) 1966: *m* 1947, Mary Traill, da of late Harold McMeekin, of Bearsden, Dunbartonshire. —— Kathleen Constance, *b* 1915: *m* 1941, Lt-Col Cyril Frederick Hembrough Walter, Indian Army, of 5 St Mary's Close, Chitterne, Warminster, Wilts, and has issue living, Jonathan, *b* 1944.
Anthony Bromhead of Wheatley, Notts, supported Charles I and was killed at Newark. His el son Benjamin purchased Thurlby and Bassingham manors, Lincs and *d* 1702. Bordman Bromhead of Thurlby *m* 1756, Frances, da and heir of William Gonville, last male heir of family whose ancestor, Edmund de Gonville founded Gonville Hall (now Gonville and Caius Coll), Camb, 1348. Their son, Lt-Gen Sir Gonville Bromhead, was the 1st baronet.

BROMLEY (GB) 1757, of East Stoke, Nottinghamshire

Think firmly

Sir RUPERT CHARLES BROMLEY, 10th *Baronet*; *b* 2 April 1936; *s* his father, *Maj Sir* RUPERT HOWE, MC, 1966; *ed* Michaelhouse, Natal, Rhodes Univ, and Ch Ch, Oxford; Bar Inner Temple 1959: *m* 1962, Priscilla Hazel, da of late Maj Howard Bourne, HAC, and has issue.

𝕬rms – Quarterly, per fesse indented gules and or. 𝕮rest – a pheasant sitting proper.
Residence – PO Box 249, Rivonia 2128, Transvaal, S Africa.

SONS LIVING

CHARLES HOWARD, *b* 31 July 1963. —— Philip Anthony, *b* 1964: *m* 1994, Carole Frances, yr da of Gerard Damp, of Malmesbury, CP, S Africa. —— Henry Walford, *b* 1970.

BROTHER LIVING

Maurice David (50/1 Tambon Sanna Maeng, Amphur Sansai, Chiangmai 50200, Thailand), *b* 1941: *m* 1st, 1965 (*m diss* 1984), Heather Mary Estcourt-Cutter; 2ndly, 1985, Renita Lopez Amador, and has issue living (by 1st *m*), Michael, *b* 1982, — Caroline Margaret, *b* 1966: *m* 19—, G. Ramierz (and has issue), — Jennifer Mary, *b* 1968: *m* 19—, R. Aguirre (and has issue), — (by 2nd *m*) Robert Howe, *b* 1986.

DAUGHTERS LIVING OF EIGHTH BARONET

Anne, *b* 1915: *m* 1939, Thomas Henry Perceval Lloyd, who *d* 1992, of 42 Freshfield Bank, Forest Row, E Sussex, and has issue living, David Anthony Henry (21 Trinity Sq, Margate, Kent), *b* 1945; has issue living, Emma Louise *b* 1979, — Mary-Anne (21 Trinity Sq, Margate, Kent), *b* 1941: *m* 1962, William Dennis Hurn, who *d* 1989, and has issue living, Michael John *b* 1966, Belinda Ann *b* 1963, Tania Brigitta *b* 1968, Chantal Anne *b* 1978, — Arabella Patricia (42 Freshfield Bank, Forest Row, E Sussex), *b* 1954: *m* 1972 (*m diss* 1989), — Andrup, and has issue living, Daniel Lloyd *b* 1973, Georgina Kirsten *b* 1978. —— Elizabeth Mary (*Lady Collins*), *b* 1919: *m* 1st, 1940, 6th Baron Sudeley who was *ka* 1941; 2ndly, 1965, Maj Sir Arthur James Robert Collins, KCVO, of 38 Clarence Terr, Regent's Park, NW1 4RD, and Kirkman Bank, Knaresborough, Yorks.

DAUGHTER LIVING OF SIXTH BARONET

Esther Lilian, *b* 1905: *m* 1st, 1927 (*m diss* 1943), Major Sir John Donald Alexander Arthur Makgill, 12th Bt (later 12th Viscount of Oxfuird), who *d* 1985; 2ndly, 1946, James J. A. Murray, LLB, Capt 1/10th Ghurkha Rifles, who *d* 1964. *Residence* – Coney Island, Ardglass, co Down.

COLLATERAL BRANCH LIVING

Granddaughter of late Thomas Bromley, 5th son of 3rd baronet:—
Issue of late Rupert Fitzroy Bromley, *b* 1862, *d* 1933: *m* 1902, Emilye, who *d* 1936, da of late Capt Rennie, CB:—
Rosemary Sylvia, *b* 1906: *m* 1939, Alfred John Owston, who *d* 1961, and has had issue, Anthony John Wyndham, *b* 1940; *ed* Eton; Bar Inner Temple 1965: *m* 1967, Vivien Patricia, da of late Brig Robert Hugh Bellamy, CBE, DSO (*see* E Harewood, colls), and *d* 1992, leaving issue (*see* E Harewood, colls), — Nicholas Adrian Fenton, *b* 1947; *ed* Stowe. *Residence* – 4 Coniger Rd, SW6.

The 1st baronet, Sir George Smith, married Mary Howe, great-granddaughter of Prince Rupert. Lord Carrington is descended from a yr brother of the first baronet. Sir George Bromley, 2nd Bt, assumed by sign-manual in 1778, the name of Bromley in lieu of his patronymic. Sir Robert Bromley, 6th Bt, was Administrator of St Kitts and Nevis. Sir Maurice Bromley-Wilson, 7th Bt was High Sheriff of Westmorland 1901, and assumed by Roy licence 1897 the additional surname and arms of Wilson. Rear-Adm Sir Arthur Bromley, KCMG, KCVO, 8th baronet, was a Gentleman Usher to HM 1927-61, and Ceremonial and Reception Sec, Dominion and Colonial Office 1931-53.

BROOKE (E) 1662, of Norton Priory, Cheshire

FASTE WITHOUT FRAUDE

Sir RICHARD NEVILLE BROOKE, 10th Baronet; *b* 1 May 1915; *s* his father, *Sir* RICHARD CHRISTOPHER, 1981; *ed* Eton; formerly Lt Scots Gds; 1939-45 War (prisoner, escaped); FCA; Snr Partner, Price Waterhouse & Co European Firms 1969-75: *m* 1st, 1937 (*m diss* 1959), Lady Mabel Kathleen Jocelyn, who *d* 1985, da of 8th Earl of Roden; 2ndly, 1960, Jean Evison, da of late Lt-Col Arthur Cecil Corfe, DSO, and formerly wife of Sir Nicolas John Cheetham, KCMG, and has issue by 1st *m*.

Arms – Or, a cross engrailed per pale gules and sable. **Crest** – A brock, or badger, passant proper.
Residence – Pond Cottage, Crawley, nr Winchester, Hants. *Club* – Boodle's.

SONS LIVING *(By 1st marriage)*

(RICHARD) DAVID CHRISTOPHER (The Manor House, Cholderton, Wilts), *b* 23 Oct 1938; *ed* Eton: *m* 1st, 1963 (*m diss* 1978), Carola Marion, el da of Sir Robert Erskine Hill, 2nd Bt; 2ndly, 1979, Lucinda, only da of John Frederick Voelcker, of Happy Hill, Lidgetton, Natal, and formerly wife of William Barlow, and has issue living (by 1st *m*), Richard Christopher, *b* 10 July 1966, — Edward Marcus, *b* 1970. —— Piers Leighton (37 Yeomans Row, SW3), *b* 1940; *ed* Eton: *m* 1967, Susan, da of John Davenport, of New York City, and has issue living, Sebastian Piers, *b* 1974, — Arabella Elinor, *b* 1973.

SISTER LIVING

Audley Marian (45 Hartäckerstrasse, 1190 Vienna, Austria), *b* 1913: *m* 1937, Kurt Adolf Seebohm, who *d* 1981, and has issue living, Kurt Florian, *b* 1939: *m* 1967, Karin Schaeffer, of Salzburg, and has issue living, Katja *b* 1972, — Andrea Gabrielle, *b* 1941.

WIDOW LIVING OF NINTH BARONET

KATHLEEN ENDA (*Kathleen, Lady Brooke*) (Dublin), da of late Francis John Gildea, of Dun Laoghaire, Dublin; *m* 1967, as his 2nd wife, Sir Richard Christopher Brooke, 9th Baronet, who *d* 1981.

COLLATERAL BRANCHES LIVING

Grandchildren of late Victor Alexander Brooke, 4th son of 7th baronet:—
Issue of late Victor James Brooke, *b* 1899, *d* 1976: *m* 1927, Doris Isabella, who *d* 1971, da of late John Bull Ware:—
Bladen James (107 Hillvue Rd, Tamworth, NSW 2340, Australia), *b* 1928; a JP; Alderman, Tamworth City Council 1987-: *m* 1958, Adeline Ruth, da of Kenneth Field Clemson, JP, of Wyndella, Collarenebri, NSW, and has issue living, Daron James Clemson, *b* 1964: *m* 1993, Cherelle Kay, da of Phillip Corbett, of Sydney, — Kim Anabel, *b* 1959: *m* 1979, John Francis Mannion, JP, of 7 Mataro Av, Muswellbrook, NSW 2333, Australia, eldest son of William Mannion, of Tamworth, NSW, and has issue living, Elissa Jane *b* 1982, Rebekah Anne *b* 1983, — Anthea Kay, *b* 1960: *m* 1989, Scott Robert Hamilton, of 1/347A Livingstone Rd, Marrickville, Cammiray, NSW 2204, Australia, only son of William Robert Hamilton, of Melbourne, and has issue living, Luke Bladen William *b* 1994, Samantha Nichole Brooke *b* 1991.
Issue of late Reginald Marcus Brooke, *b* 1905, *d* 1980: *m* 1st, 1927, Beth Allender, who *d* 1957, da of Andrew John Telfer; 2ndly, 19—, Dulcie Louise (11 Hill St, Port Macquarie, NSW, Australia), da of late Joseph Arnold, of George St, Inverell, NSW:—
(By 1st *m*) Peter Brabazon (40 Sullaroop St, Duffy, ACT 2611, Australia), *b* 1929; is a JP: *m* 1954, Beverley Elizabeth, only da of Francis William George Vincent, of 14 Virginia St, N Wollongong, NSW, and has issue living, Victor Garry, *b* 1956. —— David John (Brisbane, Queensland, Australia), *b* 1933: *m* 1st, 1956 (*m diss* 1960), Wendy Vida, only da of late David Arthur Kenneth Miller, of 84 Midson Rd, Epping; 2ndly, 196-, Eileen Adele, da of William Henry Humphreys, of 5 Linda St, Sherwood, Queensland, and has issue living, (by 2nd *m*) Stephen Mark, *b* 1963, — Lynda Kay, *b* 1961, *m* 19—, Stephen Williams, and has issue living, Danielle Anita Virginia *b* 1981, — Stacey Ann, *b* (twin) 1963. —— Richard Michael, *b* 1937. —— Pamela Elizabeth, *b* 1935: *m* 1st, 1953 (*m diss* 19—), Anthony John Glasgow; 2ndly, 1962, Grahame Vance Baillie, of 24 Kennedy St, Appin, NSW, Australia, and has issue living, (by 1st *m*) Peter John, *b* 1954, — Denise Beth, *b* 1957.

The 1st baronet, Sir Henry Brooke, was four times appointed Sheriff of Cheshire by the Parliamentarians. The 2nd baronet, Sir Richard, was Sheriff of the same co 1667. The 3rd baronet, Sir Thomas, was Gov of Chester Castle during the greater part of Queen Anne's reign.

BROOKE (UK) 1903, of Summerton, Castleknock, co Dublin

Sir FRANCIS GEORGE WINDHAM BROOKE, 4th *Baronet*; *b* 15 Oct 1963; *s* his father, *Maj Sir* GEORGE CECIL FRANCIS, MBE, 1982; *ed* Eton, and Edinburgh Univ (MA): *m* 1989, Katharine Elizabeth, only da of Marmaduke James Hussey (*see* E Waldegrave), and has issue.

Arms – Or, a cross engrailed per pale gules and sable, in dexter canton a crescent of the second, and in sinister canton a martlet of the third, for difference. **Crest** – A badger passant proper, charged with a crescent and a martlet gules. *Residence* – 49 Masbro Rd, W14 0LU.

SON LIVING

GEORGE FRANCIS GEOFFREY, *b* 10 Sept 1991.

DAUGHTER LIVING

Olivia Nancy, *b* 1994.

SISTER LIVING

Glory, the end

Emma Nancy, *b* 1965: *m* 1993, Charles C. Thompson, only son of S/Ldr James Thompson, of Mijas, Spain. *Residence* – 28 Irene Rd, SW6 4AP.

WIDOW LIVING OF THIRD BARONET

Lady MELISSA EVA CAROLINE WYNDHAM-QUIN (*Lady Melissa Brooke*), el da of 6th Earl of Dunraven and Mount-Earl: *m* 1959, Maj Sir George Cecil Francis Brooke, MBE, 3rd Bt, who *d* 1982. *Residence* – Glenbevan, Croom, co Limerick.

COLLATERAL BRANCHES LIVING

Issue of late George Brooke, Lt Irish Gds, el son of 1st baronet, *b* 1877, *ka* 1914: *m* 1907, Nina, who *d* 1970, da of late Rt Hon Lord Arthur William Hill (M Downshire, colls):—
Nancy Myra, *b* 1911: *m* 1st, 1931 (*m diss* 1934), John Hollingworth Roberts; 2ndly, 1941, Capt Charles Michael Stratton, who *d* 1991, of Moss Cottage, 48 High St, Croughton, Brackley, Northants, and has issue living, (by 2nd *m*) Patrick Michael (23 Elm Rd, Winchester, Hants SO22 5AG), *b* 1945: *m* 1992, Miriam, da of David Anderson, of 3 Pine Walk, Liss Forest, Liss, Hants, and has issue living, Luke Nicholas *b* 1994, — Juliet Nina, *b* 1942: *m* 1973, John William Clark-Maxwell, of Speddoch, Dumfries-shire, and has issue living, James Michael Gilchrist *b* 1975; assumed the addl forename of Gilchrist by deed poll 1990, Alice Louise *b* 1979.

Issue of late Capt John Brooke, DSC, RN (ret), 6th son of 1st baronet, *b* 1887, *d* 1974: *m* 1918, Margaret Winifred, MBE, only da of late Col Francis Tothill, RA, of Roseneath, Fareham:—
Geoffrey Arthur George, DSC, (Beech House, Balcombe, Sussex RH17 6PS), *b* 1920; *ed* RNC, Dartmouth; Lt-Cdr RN (ret); 1939-45 War in Europe and Far East (DSC, Atlantic Star, Mediterranean star, Pacific star): *m* 1956, Venetia Mabel, only da of late Capt Hon Oswald Wykeham Cornwallis, OBE, RN (ret) (*see* B Cornwallis, colls), and has issue living, Caroline Jane, *b* 1957: *m* 1989 (*m diss* 1992), Barry Rudolf, of Santa Fé, New Mexico, — Venetia Anne Margaret, *b* 1959, — Georgina Emily Rose, *b* 1963: *m* 1st, 1986, Lanto Millington Synge, eldest son of late John Samuel Synge, of Mill Grange, Ballinglen, co Wicklow; 2ndly, 1993, Michael Paul Boulter Bochmann, of Roebuck Cottage, Burford, Oxon, son of late Martin Paul Bochmann.

Issue of late Basil Gerald Brooke, 7th son of 1st baronet, *b* 1894, *d* 1969: *m* 1919, Essex Vere (23 Halsey St, SW3), da of Sir Charles Vere Gunning, CB, CMG, 7th Bt:—
Henry Arthur Gunning, MC (23 Halsey St, SW3; Cavalry and Guards' Club), *b* 1923; *ed* Winchester; Col 16th/5th The Queens R Lancers 1980-85; Lt-Col Comdg 16th/5th The Queens R Lancers 1966-69; 1939-45 War in Tunisia and Italy (MC).

This family is a branch of the family of Viscount Brookeborough (of Colebrooke, co Fermanagh). The 1st baronet, Sir George Frederick was a Director (sometime Gov) of the Bank of Ireland, over 50 years head of the late firm of George F. Brooke and Son, wine merchants, of Dublin, and High Sheriff for co Wexford 1882, and for co Dublin 1898.

BROOKE (UK) 1919, of Almondbury, West Riding of Yorkshire

EST·NEC·ASTU

Nor is it by craft

Sir ALISTAIR WESTON BROOKE, 4th *Baronet*; *b* 12 Sept 1947; *s* his father, *Maj Sir* JOHN WESTON, 1983; *ed* Repton, and RAC Cirencester: *m* 1982, Susan Mary, only da of Barry Griffiths, of Church House, Norton, Powys, and has issue.

Arms – Argent, a cross nebulée per pale gules and sable, in the first and fourth quarters a boar's head erased of the last. **Crest** – In front of a sword erect, the blade entwined by two serpents respecting each other proper, a boar's head erased sable.
Seat – Fearn Lodge, Ardgay, Ross-shire.
Residence – Wootton Farm, Pencombe, Hereford.

DAUGHTER LIVING

Lorna Rosemary Weston, *b* 1983.

BROTHER LIVING

CHARLES WESTON (Midfearn, Ardgay, Ross-shire IV24 3DL) *b* 27 Jan 1951; *ed* Repton: *m* 1984, Tanya Elizabeth, da of Antony Thelwell Maurice, of Lloran, Robertson, NSW, Australia, and has issue living, John Weston, *b* 23 Feb 1992, — Nicola Margery, *b* 1985, — Emily Grace, *b* 1988.

AUNTS LIVING (*Daughters of 2nd baronet*)

Elizabeth Jean, *b* 1910: *m* 1939, Lt-Cdr Malcolm Buist, RN, who *d* 1965, and has issue living, Elizabeth Mary, *b* 1944: *m* 19—, — Jane Christine, *b* 1947.
—— Hazel Mary, *b* 1918: *m* 1942, Maj John Alexander Lochore, Seaforth Highlanders, who was *ka* 1944, son of Sir James Lochore, and has issue living, Hamish John (Burgie House, Forres, Moray), *b* 1943; late Capt R Scots Greys; DL Moray 19—: *m* 1970, Pollyann Elise, da of Lt-Col Hon David Edward Hely-Hutchinson (*see* E Donoughmore), and has issue living, Alexander David *b* 1971, Hugh Mark *b* 1974, Clare Hermione *b* 1977, — Fiona Margery, *b* 1945: *m* 1971, Lt-Cdr Ian Patrick Forbes Meiklejohn, RN, of Forres, Moray, and has issue living, James Forbes *b* 1976, Clodagh Kirsteen *b* 1974. *Residence* – Burgie Mains, Forres, Moray.
Sir John Arthur Brooke, 1st baronet, was a Director of John Brooke and Sons (Limited), of Armitage Bridge, Huddersfield, a JP, and Chm York House of Laymen, Maj Sir John Weston Brooke, 3rd Bt, was a JP and DL for Ross-shire.

BROOKSBANK (UK) 1919, of Healaugh Manor, Healaugh, West Riding of Yorkshire

Sir (EDWARD) NICHOLAS BROOKSBANK, 3rd *Baronet*; *b* 4 Oct 1944; *s* his father, *Lt-Col Sir* (EDWARD) WILLIAM, TD, JP, DL 1983; *ed* Eton; Capt The Blues and Royals: *m* 1970, Hon Emma Myrtle Mary Anne Wood, only da of Baron Holderness, PC (Life Baron), and has issue.

Arms – Azure, two bars wavy argent within a bordure or. **Crest** – A white hart's head couped proper, attired or, accolled with two bars wavy azure.
Seat – Ryton Grange, Malton, N Yorks.

SON LIVING

FLORIAN TOM CHARLES, *b* 9 Aug 1982.

DAUGHTER LIVING

Victoria Mary Grania, *b* 1985.

WIDOW LIVING OF SECOND BARONET

ANN (*Ann, Lady Brooksbank*), da of Lt-Col Thomas Claud Clitherow, DSO, of Hotham Hall, Brough, Yorks: *m* 1943, Lt-Col Sir Edward William Brooksbank, 2nd Bt, who *d* 1983. *Residence* – Menetborpe Hall, Malton, N Yorkshire.

COLLATERAL BRANCH LIVING

Issue of late Lt-Col Edward York Brooksbank, 2nd son of 1st baronet, *b* 1888; *d* 1935: *m* 1912, Hazel, who *d* 1968, da of late Henry Brockholes Thomas, of Scaftworth Hall, Yorks:—
Stamp Godfrey (45 Cedar Lodge, Lythe Hill Park, Haslemere, Surrey), *b* 1922; *ed* Eton; 1939-45 War with Coldstream Gds: *m* 1942, Celia Dorothy, da of late Maj Hon Sir John Spencer Coke, KCVO (*see* E Leicester, colls), and has issue living, David William, *b* 1946; *ed* Eton: *m* 1972, Vanessa, el da of late Kenneth A. Whittome, and has issue living, Scott William *b* 1976, Charles Henry *b* 1979, Anna Louise *b* 1984, — George Edward Hugh, *b* 1949; *ed* Eton: *m* 1985, Nicola, yr da of Michael Newton, of Balcombe, Sussex, and has issue living, Jack *b* 1986, Thomas *b* 1988. —— Diana Hazel, *b* 1914: *m* 1st, 1936, Robert Froude Norton, who *d* 1967; 2ndly, G. Milford-Cottam. —— Crystal Elizabeth, *b* 1924: *m* 1st, 1946 (*m diss* 1960), Henry Desmond Verner Pakenham, CBE (*see* E Longford, colls); 2ndly, 1960, Ivor George Salmond, OBE, who *d* 1981; 3rdly, Vere Tweedie, and has issue living (by 1st *m*) (*see* E Longford, colls), — (by 2nd *m*), Felicity Diana, *b* 1962.
The 1st baronet, Sir Edward Clitherow Brooksbank (son of late Edward Brooksbank of Healaugh Manor, Tadcaster, and Newton House, Whitby), was Chm of Barkston Ash Conservative Assoc for over 40 years.

BROUGHTON (E) 1660, of Broughton, Staffordshire
(Name pronounced "Brawton")

Sir DAVID DELVES BROUGHTON, 13th *Baronet*; *b* 7 May 1942; son of late Lt Cdr Peter John Delves Broughton, RN (by his 1st wife, Nancy Rosemary, who *d* 1960, da of late J. E. Paterson), only son of late Lt-Col Geoffrey Delves Broughton, OBE, yr son of late Lt-Col Delves Broughton, only son of late Rev Delves Broughton, 2nd son of 8th baronet; *s* his kinsman, *Sir* EVELYN DELVES, 1993; craftsman: *m* 1969, Diane, da of Ronald Lindsay Nicol, of 29 Grange Rd, Kew, Victoria 3101, Australia.

Arms – Argent, two bars gules, on a canton of the second a cross of the field. **Crest** – A sea-dog's head couped gules, finned argent.
Residence – 6 Engayne Av, Sandy, Beds SG19 1BM.

DAUGHTER LIVING (*by Hildegard Weitzel*)

Jennifer Zoë WEITZEL, *b* 1977.

HALF-BROTHER LIVING

GEOFFREY DELVES (140 Claremont Av, Scarborough, Ontario, Canada M1N 3S4), *b* 1962: *m* 1986, Karen Louise, da of Thomas Wright, of Toronto, Ontario, and has issue living, Peter Thomas Delves, *b* 16 Aug 1991, — Kathryn Louise Delves, *b* 1988, — Jennifer Anne Delves, *b* 1989.

HALF-SISTERS LIVING

Susan Delves, *b* 1950: *m* 1970, Clyde Charles Victor Dimmell, of 60 Manning Cres, Newmarket, Ontario, Canada. —— Patricia Delves, *b* 1953: *m* 1982, William Henry Mair. —— Shelagh Delves, *b* 1959.

DAUGHTERS LIVING OF TWELFTH BARONET

Isabella Delves, *b* 1958; *ed* Heathfield, and Columbia Univ, New York; Assist Features Ed British *Vogue* since 1991; Memb Rare Breeds Soc, and Farming Wildlife Advisory Group (Glos Branch): *m* 1st, 1981 (*m diss* 1983), Nicholas Taylor, of USA; 2ndly, 1989, Detmar Hamilton Lorenz Arthur Blow (*see* B Tollemache, colls), of Hilles, Edge, Stroud, Glos GL6 6NW. —— Julia Helen Delves, *b* 1961. —— Lavinia Mary Delves, *b* 1965: *m* 1st, 1985, Douglas Gerald Dawes, who *d* 1989, yst son of Cdr Michael Dawes, RN; 2ndly, 1992, as his 2nd wife, Harry George Vivian Verney (*see* Verney, Bt, *cr* 1818, colls), of The Old Forge, Ewen, Cirencester, Glos, and has issue living (by 1st *m*), Frederick Evelyn, *b* 1988, — Rosamond Esmé, *b* 1985, — (by 2nd *m*) (*see* Verney, Bt, *cr* 1818, colls).

DAUGHTER LIVING OF ELEVENTH BARONET

Rosamond (*Lady Lovat*), *b* 1917: *m* 1938, 15th Lord Lovat. *Residence* – Balblair House, Beauly, Inverness-shire.

STEPMOTHER LIVING

Evelyn Gunn (6061 Yonge St, Suite 1504, Willowdale, Ontario, Canada), da of late J. G. Sutherland: *m* 1948, as his 2nd wife, Lt Cdr Peter John Delves Broughton, RN, who *d* 1963.

WIDOW LIVING OF TWELFTH BARONET

RONA (*Dowager Lady Delves Broughton*), da of Ernest Clifford Johns, of Wargrave, and formerly wife of Donald Ian Crammond: *m* 1974, as his 3rd wife, Sir Evelyn Delves Broughton, 12th Bt, who *d* 1993. *Residences* – 37 Kensington Square, W8; Doddington Park, Nantwich, Cheshire.

COLLATERAL BRANCHES LIVING

Grandsons of late Vernon Delves Broughton, eldest son of late Rev Thomas Delves Broughton, elder son of late Thomas Delves Broughton, 3rd son of 6th baronet:—
Issue of late Vernon Warburton Delves Broughton, *b* 1864, *d* 1936: *m* 1899, Frangiski, who *d* 1957, da of late Epamenondas da Ponte, of Cephalonia, Greece:—
John Francis, *b* 1901. —— James Epamenondas, *b* 1916; BScEng: *m* 1st, 1945, Iris Evelyn Grace, who *d* 1959, da of late Joseph Jameson, of Wembley; 2ndly, 1962, Jean Margaret, da of late Arthur Williams, of Caerleon, Wales, and has issue living (by 1st *m*), Roger Vernon (Plas Cottage, Llanarmon-yn-Ial, Mold, Clwyd), *b* 1949, — Evelyn Rosemary, *b* 1947: *m* 1975, Anthony Dacres Symes, of 10 Hanover St, Bath, Avon, and has issue living, David Matthew Trenchard *b* 1976, Anna Louisa Trenchard *b* 1979, — (by 2nd *m*) Nicolas Charles, *b* 1969, — Sonia Francesca, *b* 1967: *m* 1992, Alistair McLay, and has issue living, Fiona Margaret *b* 1989, Shona Catherine *b* 1992. *Residence* – Moynes Court, Mathern, Chepstow, Gwent NP6 6HZ. —— Paul Nicholas, *b* 1916 (twin): *m* 1948, Joyce, who *d* 1984, da of late Eric Francis Duckham, and has issue living, Jonathan (The Dairy House, Ryme Intrinseca, Yetminster, Dorset DT9 6JX), *b* 1949: *m* 1972, Susan Elizabeth, da of Donald Marston, of 12 Donstan Rd, Highbridge, Som, and has issue living, Alexander Paul *b* 1981, Kathryne Alice *b* 1978, Anne Elizabeth *b* 1984. *Residence* – 1 College View, Fore St, Kingswear, Devon. —— Rachael da Ponte, *b* 1907: *m* 1942, James Thomas Currie, who *d* 1985, and *d* 1993, having had issue, Lyn Maria da Ponte, *b* 1942: *m* 1964, Alan Roylance Storey, of Manston Rd, Remuera, Auckland, NZ, and has issue living, Peter Douglas *b* 1976, Rachael Christina da Ponte *b* 1967, Alana Maria da Ponte *b* 1968, — Janetta Patricia da Ponte, *b* 1945: *m* 1970, John Hemus Griffiths, of Auckland, NZ, and *d* 1982, having had issue, Mark James Hemus *b* and *d* 1975, Athena Elizabeth da Ponte *b* 1971, Maria Francesca da Ponte *b* 1973, — Lynda Yvonne da Ponte, *b* 1947: *m* 19—, Nicholas Dimitri Benveniste, who *d* 1992.

Grandchildren of late Brig Theodore Delves Broughton (*infra*):—
Issue of late Brian Charles Delves Broughton, *b* 1903, *d* 1976: *m* 1931, Margaret Gwenda, who *d* 1991, da of late Edmund Law:—
Rev Simon Brian Hugo (Christ Church Vicarage, 3 Christ Church Rd, Northampton), *b* 1933; *ed* Marlborough, and Exeter Coll, Oxford (MA): *m* 1971, Tin Tin Mar Marcia Patricia, da of U Ni, of Burma, and has issue living, Philip Andrew, *b* 1972; 2nd Queen's Chorister of St George's Chapel, Windsor, 1981, Head Chorister 1985; *ed* Eton (scholar), and New Coll, Oxford.

Granddaughter of late Cdr Cecil Delves Broughton, RN, 3rd son of late Rev Thomas Delves Broughton (ante):—
Issue of late Brigadier Theodore Delves Broughton, *b* 1872, *d* 1944: *m* 1st, 1897, Marion Julia, who *d* 1905, da of late Charles Augustus Theodore Bouwens; 2ndly, 1908, Eva Joanna, who *d* 1959, el da of Col John Warre Sill (Sutton, Bt colls):—
(By 1st *m*) Diana Sill, *b* 1920.

Granddaughters of late Col John Delves Broughton, son of late Gen William Edward Delves Broughton, yr son of late Thomas Delves Broughton (ante):—
Issue of late Brian Delves Broughton, *b* 1879, *d* 1926: *m* 1912, Elizabeth Annie, da of H. K. Osborn, of Ladysmith, Natal:—
Cecilia Dorothy, *b* 1913: *m* 1938, Major Guise Montgomery Foxton Beaumont, ED, and has issue living, Michael Foxton (9 Leicester St, Grahamstown, Cape, S Africa), *b* 1939: *m* 1966, Marion Egerton, da of B. E. B. White, of Glen Cliff, Bedford, Cape, S Africa, and has issue living, Warrick Foxton *b* 1967, Bruce Egerton *b* 1969, — Keith Alan (PO Box 152, Alice 5700, S Africa), *b* 1945: *m* 1969, Lynda Jean, yst da of C. W. Giles, of Pietermaritzburg, Natal, and has issue living, Gavin Guise *b* 1970, Stephen John *b* 1972. *Address* – Brushwood, Box 93, Grahamstown, Cape, S Africa. —— Joan Christine (Bryanson, PO Winters Klooff, Natal, S Africa), *b* 1916: *m* 1942, Leonard Newnham Malyon, who *d* 1983, and has issue living, Rodney Charles, *b* 1956, — Sandra Ellen, *b* 1944: *m* 1st, 1969, Sinclair Stanley Blunden, who *d* (April) 1980; 2ndly, (Oct) 1980, Herbert Graham Roslyn Smith, and has issue living, (by 1st *m*) Merle Iris *b* 1970, Fiona Joan *b* 1973, Lynda Joy *b* 1975.

Grandson of late Edward Walthall Delves WALTHALL, son of late Edward Delves Broughton, son of late Edward Delves Broughton, 5th son of 6th baronet:—
Issue of late Capt Henry Douglas Delves WALTHALL, OBE, *b* 1880, *d* 1931: *m* 1911, Hilda Maud, who *d* 19—, da of late Frederick Leigh Hancock (JP for Flintshire and High Sheriff 1910), of The Warren, Broughton, near Chester:—
Leigh Edward Delves WALTHALL, CBE, DSC, RN, *b* 1914; became Capt 1952; was Director of Air Equipment Admiralty 1959-61; European War 1939-45 as Fleet Air Arm Pilot (DSC); *m* 1951, Dorothy Margaret, el da of late Hugh Robert Leonard, of Ladywalk, Heronsgate, Hertfordshire, and has issue living, Fiona Ann, *b* 1953, — Louisa Delves, *b* 1956: *m* 1977, Lt-Col Rodney Crisp, OBE, Intelligence Corps, and has issue living, Dominic John *b* 1981, Charles Edward Delves *b* 1986, Joanna Margaret Delves *b* 1984, — Theodora Serena Delves, *b* 1959: *m* 1990, David Ian Jones. *Residence* – Hillhouse Farm, Sapperton, Cirencester. *Club* – Army and Navy.
The annals of this old Staffordshire family extend to *temp* Henry VI. Sir Brian Broughton 3rd Bt, was MP for Newcastle 1715-24. He *m* 1710, Elizabeth, only da and sole heir of Sir Thomas Delves, 3rd Bt, of Doddington, co Chester. The 4th baronet, their son, who *s* also to the Doddington Estates in Cheshire, assumed the additional name of Delves, in compliance with the terms of his grandfather's will. The 6th Bt was High Sheriff of Staffordshire in 1740, and the 9th in 1859.

BROUN (NS) 1686, of Colstoun, Haddingtonshire.

Let majesty flourish

Sir LIONEL JOHN LAW BROUN, 12th *Baronet*; *b* 25 April 1927; *s* his father, Sir (JAMES) LIONEL, 1962.

𝕬rms – Gules, a chevron between three fleurs-de-lis or. 𝕮rest – A lion rampant gules, holding in the dexter forepaw a fleur-de-lis and in the sinister a rose both or.
Address – c/o 23 Clanalpine St, Mosman, NSW, Australia 2088.

COLLATERAL BRANCHES LIVING

Issue of late William Arthur Broun, 2nd son of 10th baronet, *b* 1876, *d* 1925: *m* 1916, Marie Victoria, who *d* 1964, da of W McIntyre, of N Sydney:—
WILLIAM WINDSOR (23 Clanalpine St, Mosman, NSW 2088, Australia), *b* 1917; FCA (Australia); 1939-45 War as Lieut AIF: *m* 1952, D'Hrie, da of Frank R. King, of Bingara, NSW, and has issue living, D'Hrie Sheree, *b* 1956; *ed* Univ of NSW (B Com): *m* 1988, Rev Zachary Veron, and has issue living, Désirée D'Hrie Marie *b* 1991, Anne Grace *b* 1993, — Rani Beverley, *b* 1959; *ed* Sydney Univ (LLB): *m* 1985, Richard Patrick Morrison, and has issue living, Silas Patrick Broun *b* 1987, Jasper William *b* 1989, Isaac Richard *b* 1991, Savannah Rose *b* 1994.. —— Hulance Haddington (462 Pittwater Rd, N Manly 2100, NSW), *b* 1919; 1939-45 War as Sergeant Pilot RAAF, Middle East 1940-42: *m* 1947, Joy Maud, da of A. L. Stack, of Mosman, NSW, and has issue living, Wayne Hercules (7 Hafey (or Hasey?) Rd, Kenthurst, NSW 2154, Australia), *b* 1952; *ed* Sydney Gram Sch; formerly Lieut 5 Bn RAR: *m* 1976, Anna Marie Paolucci, and has issue living, Richard Haddington *b* 1984, Samantha Louise *b* 1981, — Robyn Joy, *b* 1948: *m* 1974, Cedric Hoare, and has issue living, Timothy James *b* 1976, Jeremy Lachlan *b* 1981, Nicole Suzanne *b* 1978, — Julie Christine, *b* 1955: *m* 1978, William Lyons, and has issue living, Tamara Suzanne *b* 1982, Eleanor Amy *b* 1985, Georgia Anne *b* 1988. —— †Lionel McIntyre, *b* 1921; 1939-45 War with RAAF: *m* 1955, Shirley, who *d* 1990, da of A. L. Stack (ante) and *d* 1990, leaving issue, Walter Leslie, *b* 1961; *ed* New England Univ. — Steven McIntyre, *b* 1963; *ed* New England Univ: *m* 1992, Helen McRae-Smith, — Lucinda Maree, *b* 1957; *ed* Sydney Univ (LLB): *m* 1981, Russell Anthony Aboud, MB, and has issue living, Angus Alfred McIntyre *b* 1985, Annabelle Louise *b* 1988, Jacqueline Lucinda *b* 1994. —— John Hercules August (13 Kilroy St, Gunnedah, NSW), *b* 1923: *m* 1st, 1953, Patricia Johnson; 2ndly, 1962, Margaret, da of Reginald Chapman, of Dubbo, NSW, and has issue living, (by 1st *m*) Richard, *b* 1954, — (by 2nd *m*) Tracy Lee, *b* 1963, — Phoebe Margaret, *b* 1968: *m* 1992, Andrew Beniac.

Issue of late Reginald Augustus Broun, 3rd son of 10th baronet, *b* 1878, *d* 1948: *m* 1910, Alice Maude, who *d* 1983, da of W. B. Wilkinson, of Mosman, NSW:—
Reginald William Wilkinson, *b* 1912. *Residence* – Dalblair, Gunnedah, NSW. —— Noël Marian, *b* 1918: *m* 1944, Charles Edward Robinson, of Southernwood, 15 Cambridge St, Mooroolbark, Victoria, Aust 3138, and has issue living, Bernard James, *b* 1946: *m* 1968, Annie Kernihan, and has issue living, Nicole Marie *b* 1973, Emma Jane *b* 1975.

Grandchildren of late David Limond Broun (infra):—
Issue of late William James Broun, *b* 1882, *d* 1963: *m* 1st, 1914, Miriam Rheta, da of Sidney T. Peryman, of Mosman, Sydney, NSW; 2ndly, 1947, Dorothea Esther, who *d* 1968, da of David A. Strahley, of Sandy Knowe, Inverell, NSW:—

(By 1st *m*) William James Peryman (24a Gladstone Parade, Lindfield, NSW), *b* 1922; *ed* Sydney Univ (BE); formerly Lt RAN: *m* 1956, Penelope Jane, da of late W. T. H. Horn, of Canberra, and has issue living, William James Harvey *b* 1958: *m* 1980, Margaret Anne, da of late A. W. Quinn, of Roseville, NSW, and has issue living, William James Christopher *b* 1983, Jacqueline Ann *b* 1986, — Anthony Fraser Cameron, *b* 1960. —— Malcolm David (61 Greenwich Rd, Greenwich, NSW 2065), *b* 1935; *ed* Sydney Univ (BA, LLB); Bar NSW 1959, QC 1982; accorded the honour of Cyfaill y Celtaidd, Celtic Council of Australia: *m* 1st, 1962 (*m diss* 1971), Janet Patricia, da of late Allan Douglas Edwards; 2ndly, 1972, Wendy Sue, da of W. J. Hannelly, and has issue living, (by 1st *m*) Alexander Alan Hercules, *b* 1965, — Charlotte Doriam, *b* 1963: *m* 1989, Olivier Jean Jacques Eugene dit Rochesson, son of Jacques Eugene dit Rochesson, of Clamecy, France, — Sophie Amelia, *b* 1969, — (by 2nd *m*) Nicholas Malcolm, *b* 1975, Virginia Barbara *b* 1976. —— Wilga Joan, *b* 1917: *m* 1937, Ian Cecil de Courcy Dutton, of 59 Barraba St, Manilla, NSW 2346, and has issue living, Ian Herbert, *b* 1941: *m* 1963, Irene Elizabeth Mary Archer, and has issue living, Anthony Ian de Courcy *b* 1970, Michael Leslie de Courcy *b* 1974, Jennifer de Courcy *b* 1966, — Peter James, *b* 1952: *m* 1975, Judith Margaret Atherton, and has issue living, Grant Peter de Courcy *b* 1977, Peter Jaye de Courcy *b* 1979, Thomas Arthur de Courcy *b* 1984, Lee Jane de Courcy *b* 1976, — Christopher Cecil, *b* 1955: *m* 1978, Vicki Janelle Beard, and has issue living, Casey John de Courcy *b* 1980, Rachael Maree de Courcy *b* 1982, Melanie Louise de Courcy *b* 1984, — Anne Wilga, *b* 1938: *m* 1957, William Arthur Jones, and has issue living, Wayne William Dutton *b* 1958: *m* 1980, Kerry Therese Weaver (and has issue living, Scott Jeremy *b* 1983), Robert Hugh Dutton *b* 1967, Debra Anne Dutton *b* 1959: *m* 1979, David John Oliphant (and has issue living, Joshua Luke *b* 1983, Zoe Aleesha *b* 1981), Rebekah Letitia Dutton *b* 1970, — Melissa Judith, *b* 1945: *m* 1969, Kenneth Beresford Abberfield, and has issue living, Derk Beresford *b* 1973, Natalie Terese *b* 1969, Stephanie Maree *b* 1971, — Pauline, *b* 1946: *m* 1st, 1967 (*m diss* 1974), David Ross Medway; 2ndly, 1974, John Allan Phoo, and has issue living, (by 1st *m*) Shayne David *b* 1968, Allyn Ross *b* 1969, Jarrod Barrington *b* 1971, (by 2nd *m*) Jayson John *b* 1975, Matthew James *b* 1983, Suzanne Lillian *b* 1976, — Miriam Lillian, *b* 1953: *m* 1975 (*m diss* 1983), Paul Christopher Thomas, and has issue living, Darren Paul de Courcy Dutton *b* 19—. —— Mario Rheta, OAM (Orroroo, RMB 266, Moore Creek, Tamworth, NSW, Australia), *b* 1918: OAM 1986: *m* 1st, 1943 (*m diss* 1970), Capt Maxwell Charles Halliday, AIF, DDS, MDS; 2ndly, 1970, Hon Mr Justice (Martin Francis) Hardie, who *d* 1974, and has issue living, (by 1st *m*) Miriam Victoria, *b* 1948: *m* 1973, Adam Cowper Hudson, BE, BSc, of 14 McRae Place, Turramurra, NSW 2074, Australia, and has issue living, David Adam Halliday *b* 1976, Emma Victoria Gillett *b* 1978, Alice Rheta Broun *b* 1980, — Catherine Eleanor Broun, *b* 1952: *m* 1973, Philip MacArthur Brown, of Subiaco, Walcha, NSW 2354, Australia, and has issue living, Hamish Ross MacArthur *b* 1980. —— Dorothy Lenglen (Orroroo, RMB 266, Moore Creek, Tamworth, NSW 2340), *b* 1919: *m* 1947 (*m diss* 1975), Walter Woods, NSW, and has issue living, Michael William Frank (Tregarthen, Dunoon Rd, Tamworth, NSW, Australia), *b* 1954: *m* 1983, Helen Lynette Trythall, and has issue living, Timothy Michael *b* 1989, Jessica Margaret *b* 1992, — Adam Lindsay Broun, *b* 1956, — Justin Thomas, *b* 1957; has issue living (by Nicola Griffin), Ashlea GRIFFIN WOODS *b* 1986, — Margarita Henry, *b* 1959, — Sara Dorothy Broun, *b* 1962; has issue living (by Glenn Atkinson), Caitlin Hayley *b* 1993. —— June Joy, *b* 1921; *ed* NSW Univ (BA): *m* 1949, Ross Abbott Hayes, MB, BS, FRCPA, FRCPath, JP, of 15A Kulgoa Rd, Bellevue Hill, NSW, and has had issue, Clive Broun Abbott (1 Genders Av, Burwood, NSW), *b* 1950: *m* 1985, Jennifer Anne McLean, and has issue living, Rebecca McLean *b* 1987, Michaela McLean *b* 1990, — Jamie Abbott Broun (2 Royal St, Chatswood, NSW), *b* 1953: *m* 1986, Ellen Armstrong, and has issue living, Ryan Armstrong *b* 1987, Taylor Broun *b* 1991, Dakoda *b* 1992, — David Broun Abbott (17 Kaboda St, Dover Heights, NSW), *b* 1954: *m* 1981, Jackie Ann Ryba, and has issue living, Kobe Ryba *b* 1984, Billi Ryba *b* 1987, Zoe Ryba *b* 1992, — Matthew George Broun, *b* 1964; *d* 1987.

Descendants, if any, of late Peter Nicholas Broun, Colonial Sec, of Swan River, son of late William Broun, 2nd son of 6th baronet, *b* 1797, *d* 1846: *m* 1824, Caroline, da of James Simpson, by whom he had issue, M'Bride, James, Charles, and five daughters.

Granddaughter of late Richard M'Bryde Broun, son of late William Broun (ante):—
Issue of late Capt William Luke Broun (P & O Co's Ser), *b* 1850, *d* 1935: *m* 1st, 1886, Harriet Louisa, who *d* 1906, da of late William Boodle, solicitor, of Cheltenham; 2ndly, 1909, Alice Glen, who *d* 1959, widow of Charles Wilson, of Melbourne, Australia:—
(By 2nd *m*) Edith Elizabeth McBryde, *b* 1911: *m* 1940, Douglas Matthew Duder Raper, who *d* 1981, and has issue living, Rosemary Elizabeth Broun, *b* 1949: *m* 1972, George Antony Alexander Johnson, and has issue living, Matthew Alexander *b* 1979, Antony Christopher *b* 1983, Elizabeth Alice *b* 1977, — Sarah Christian Broun, *b* 1952: *m* 1983, Keith Raphael Briffa, and has issue living, Amy Katherine Raper *b* 1984, Kirsten Fay Broun *b* 1986.

This family claims descent from Walter le Brun, a warrior who came to Scotland from France about 1073, supported the cause of King Malcolm III and obtained the baronies of Colstoun in Haddingtonshire and Gamilshiels in Berwickshire. In 1116 he was a witness to an inquisition of the possessions of the Church of Glasgow. In 1248 Philip le Brun witnessed a charter by Sir Roger de Mowbray to Matthew, ancestor of the Lairds of Moncrief. Prior to 1267, Sir David Broun, Baron of Colstoun, knighted by King Alexander III, married the daughter of Sir Hugo de Gifford, Baron of Yester, the wizard warrior described in Sir Walter Scott's "Marmion". As they were proceeding to the church, Sir Hugo stopped the bridal procession beneath a pear tree and, plucking one of the pears, gave it to his daughter, saying that so long as the gift was preserved, good fortune would never desert her or her descendants, but if harm should come to it misfortune would surely follow. It became renowned as the "Colstoun Pear". In about 1513, George Broun, 12th Laird of Colstoun, married Marion Hay, daughter of John, 2nd Lord Hay of Yester, ancestor of the Marquess of Tweeddale. Sir Patrick Broun of Colstoun, Sheriff-Depute of Edinburgh 1670-1681, Commissioner of Supply, was created a Baronet of Nova Scotia 16 Feb 1686. Sir George Broun, the 2nd Baronet, married Lady Elizabeth Mackenzie (daughter of George, 1st Earl of Cromartie) who, succumbing to temptation, bit a piece out of the Colstoun Pear. In accordance with the wizard's warning, misfortunes gathered. Sir George suffered losses and was obliged to sell Colstoun to his brother Robert, who subsequently was drowned with his two sons when their coach overturned while crossing a swollen river. His estates were inherited by his eldest daughter Jean, who married a cousin Charles Broun of Cleghornie. On Sir George's death in 1718 without issue the baronetcy was assumed by his cousin George Broun as 3rd Baronet. The pear minus the bite is still preserved in a silver box at Colstoun and even when shorn of its superstitious surroundings is, nevertheless, a wonderful vegetable curiosity.

BROWN (UK) 1863, of Richmond Hill

There is unity among brothers

Sir CHARLES FREDERICK RICHMOND BROWN, TD, 4th *Baronet*, son of late Frederick Richmond Brown, 2nd son of 2nd baronet; *b* 6 Dec 1902; *s* his uncle, Sir MELVILLE RICHMOND, 1944; *ed* Eton; is Capt (ret) Welsh Guards, and Lieut-Col Comdg 7th Batn Green Howards (TA) and a DL of N Riding of Yorks: *m* 1st, 1933 (*m diss* 1948), Audrey, da of late Brig-Gen Hon Everard Baring, CVO, CBE (*see* B Revelstoke, colls); 2ndly, 1951 (*m diss* 1968), Hon Gwendolin Carlis Meysey-Thompson, who *d* 1989, yst da of 1st Baron Knaresborough; 3rdly, 1969, Pauline Emily Gwyneth Mansel, who *d* 1994, da of late Arden Henry William Llewelyn Morgan, and widow of Edward John Westgarth Hildyard, FSA, FRES, of Middleton Hall, Pickering, Yorks, and has issue by 1st *m*.

ᚼrms – Quarterly; 1st and 4th, gules, a chevron or between two bears' paws erased in chief argent, and, four hands conjoined in saltire of the second in base; on a chief engrailed gold, an eagle displayed sable, *Brown*; 2nd and 3rd, argent a chevron nebuly sable between two moorhens close in chief proper and a fleur-de-lys in base azure, *Luxmoore*. ᚼrest – A bear's paw erased argent, issuant out of a wreath of oak vert, holding a sinister hand proper.
Residence – Middleton, Pickering, N Yorks. *Clubs* – Cavalry and Guards', Pratt's.

SON LIVING (By 1st marriage)

GEORGE FRANCIS RICHMOND, *b* 3 Feb 1938; Maj Welsh Guards ret; Extra Equerry to HRH the Duke of Edinburgh 1961-63, and ADC to Gov of Queensland 1963-65: *m* 1978, Philippa Jane, da of late Capt Edward Joseph W. Willcox, and has issue living, Sam George Richmond, *b* 1979, — Harry Richmond, *b* 1982, — Edward Richmond, *b* 1987.

Residence – Mas de Sudre, 81600 Gaillac, France.

DAUGHTERS LIVING (By 1st marriage)

Jennifer Richmond, *b* 1934. ——— Elizabeth Maud Richmond *b* 1943: *m* 1970, Guy M. A. Crawford, of St Blanes, Dunblane, Perthshire, and has issue living, George, *b* 1974, — Alice, *b* 1975.

SISTER LIVING

Diana Sybil Richmond, *b* 1913: *m* 1940, Christopher Henry Bacon, who *d* 1956 (*see* Bacon, Bt, colls). *Residence* – Ramsden Farm, Ebony, Tenterden, Kent.

COLLATERAL BRANCHES LIVING

Granddaughters of late Col James Clifton Brown (*infra*):—
Issue of late Brig-Gen Howard Clifton Brown, *b* 1868; *d* 1946: *m* 1903, Mary Eirene, who *d* 1951, da of late Hon Sir Henry Edward Agincourt Hodges, a Puisne Judge of Supreme Court, Melbourne:—
Elizabeth Clifton, *b* 1914; formerly Co Assist ATS: *m* 1944, Major Edmund Archibald Calvert, DL, late Roy Dragoons (Cholmeley, Bt), and has issue living, Henry Clifton (Holmbush, Faygate, Horsham), *b* 1948: *m* 1976, Ruth Margaret, da of Col Geoffrey Russell Armstrong, DSO, MC, TD (*see* E Enniskillen, colls), and has issue living, Piers Henry *b* 1977, Henrietta Amelia *b* 1980, — Jennifer Clifton, *b* 1947: *m* 1970, Josceline Grove, of 34 Stevenage Rd, SW6, and of Fasnakyle, Inverness-shire, and has issue living, Miranda Clifton *b* 1974, Venetia Mary *b* 1976. *Residence* – Rose Cottage Farm House, Faygate, Horsham, Sussex RH12 4SE. ——— Katharine Clifton, *b* 1917: *m* 1946, Ion Hunter Touchet Garnett-Orme, CBE, who *d* 1991. *Residence* – Cheriton Cottage, Cheriton, Alresford, Hants. ——— Margaret Eirene Clifton (*Margaret, Baroness Amherst of Hackney*), *b* 1921: *m* 1939, 3rd Baron Amherst of Hackney, CBE, who *d* 1980. *Residence* – 138 Cranmer Court, Sloane Av, SW3.
Issue of late Edward Clifton CLIFTON-BROWN, *b* 1870, *d* 1944 (having assumed by deed poll 1923 (enrolled at College of Arms) the additional surname of Clifton): *m* 1897, Dora Winifred, who *d* 1962, yst da of late George Hanbury, of Blythewood, Maidenhead:—
Rhona (*Lady Cracroft-Amcotts*), *b* 1901: *m* 1927, Lt-Col Sir Weston Cracroft-Amcotts, MC, late RE, who *d* 1975, and has issue living, Rosemary Grace, *b* 1928: *m* 1952, Lt-Cdr Gervis Hugh Frere Frere-Cook, RN (ret), who *d* 1974, and has issue living, Simon Aubrey Cracroft *b* 1955: *m* 1981, Jennifer Jane Greenwood (and has issue living, Joanna Christine *b* 1984, Sarah Jane *b* 1986), David Bartle Cracroft *b* 1957: *m* 1986, Christine Margaret Strong (and has issue living, Hugh Leonard *b* 1987, Guy Weston *b* 1989, Piers Gervis *b* 1993), Jane Elizabeth Cracroft *b* 1954: *m* 1979, Charles Richard Ekin Pepys, and has issue (*see* E Cottenham), — Marian Cicely, *b* 1931: *m* 1957, Thomas Charles Weguelin Micklem, of Foxbridge Farm, Kirdford, Billingshurst, Sussex RH14 0LB, and has issue living, Jeremy Charles Cracroft *b* 1961, Philippa Rhona *b* 1958: *m* 1986 (*m diss* 1992), Gary Maxwell Weiley, Sylvia Diana *b* 1964: *m* 1986, Andrew Alistair Gavin Gow (and has issue living, Simeon Nathaniel Benjamin *b* 1990), — Bridget Katharine, *b* 1933: *m* 1959, Robert Peel Charles Cracroft-Eley, of Hackthorn Hall, Lincoln, and has issue living, Charles William Amcotts (Yew Tree Farm, Hackthorn, Lincoln) *b* 1963: *m* 1991, Margaret E., only da of Roger Lole, of Hermitage Farm, Wadborough, Worcs, Annabel Louise Cracroft *b* 1961: *m* 1987, (Andrew Stewart) Ross Jones, of 153 Portland Rd, W11, eldest son of late R. H. Jones, of London (and has issue living, Felix Maxwell *b* 1990, Imogen Margaux *b* 1993), — Penelope Sylvia, *b* 1938. *Residence* – Hackthorn Hall, Lincoln.
Issue of late Douglas Clifton Brown, *b* 1879, *d* 1958 *cr Viscount Ruffside* 1951 (see that title):—

Grandsons of late Edward Clifton Clifton-Brown (*ante*):—
Issue of late Lt-Col Geoffrey Benedict Clifton-Brown, *b* 1899, *d* 1983: *m* 1927, Robina Margaret Hill, who *d* 1978, da of late Rowland Sutton (*see* Sutton, Bt, colls):—
Edward Geoffrey (14 St James Gdns, W11; W Bradley House, Glastonbury, Som), *b* 1928: *m* 1st, 1953 (*m diss* 1958), Jillian Mary, da of David Walkinshaw, of Bishopton, Half Moon Hall, Haslemere; 2ndly, 1960, Sarah Simonetta, yr da of Roger Herbert Frances, OBE, of 7 Clarendon Close, W2, and has issue living (by 1st *m*), James Benedict, *b* 1956: *m* 1980, Priscilla Sarah, da of Sir John Valentine Jardine Paterson, of North Bavant, Warminster, Wilts, and has issue living, a son *b* 1985,

Laura *b* 1987, — Margaret Joanna, *b* 1957, — (by 2nd *m*), Louisa, *b* 1961: *m* 1991, Alexander Penrose Gordon Cumming, son of Sir William Gordon Gordon Cumming, 6th Bt, — Sarah, *b* 1964. —— Robert Lawrence (Little Bradley House, nr Haverhill, Suffolk), *b* 1929: *m* 1952, Florence Elizabeth Lindsay, el da of Ronald Arthur Vestey (*see* Vestey, Bt), and has issue living, Geoffrey Robert, *b* 1953: *m* 1979, Alexandra Mary, yr da of W/Cdr Denis Peto-Shepherd, of Great Durnford, Wilts, and has issue living, Jacqueline Florence *b* 1983, — Ronald Colin, *b* 1963: *m* 1987, Emily Joan, yr da of Laver John Morgan Oliver, of Bury St Edmunds, Suffolk, and has issue living, George *b* 1992, a da *b* 1993, — Jane Elizabeth, *b* 1954: *m* 1978, Mark Corner Bailey, son of Leonard Corner Bailey, of Brinkley, Cambs, and has issue living, Peter Robert Corner *b* 1983, a son *b* 1993, Rosemary Catherine *b* 1980, Florence *b* 1989, — Angela Florence, *b* 1956: *m* 1984, Timothy Sills, of Whites Farm, Helions Bumpstead, Haverhill, Suffolk, and has issue living, James *b* 1987, Robert Marett *b* 1990, Michael *b* 1993.

Issue of late Maj Anthony George Clifton-Brown, TD, *b* 1903, *d* 1984: *m* 1st, 1930, Delia Charlotte Gordon, who *d* 1947, da of late George Edward Wade, sculptor; 2ndly, 1949, Phyllis Adrienne (Bridget), who *d* 1977, da of late Francis Harvey, of Kyle, co Wexford, and formerly wife of late Capt Alexander McGowan McCulloch, RN:—

(By 1st *m*) Georgiana Elmira, *b* 1934: *m* 1962, Prof Anthony Charles Bailey, LLM, Barrister-at-law, of 2 Coleridge St, Elwood, Victoria 3184, Australia, son of Hugh Somerville Bailey, of Hampstead, NW, and has issue living, Edward Hugh Clifton, *b* 1966, — Jane Delia, *b* 1964: *m* 1990, Robin Arthur Wellesley Redgrave, of 32 Cambridge Mansions, Battersea, SW11 4RU, yr son of Maj-Gen Sir Roy Redgrave, KBE, MC, of Chelsea, SW, and has issue living, Thomas Roy Philip *b* 1993, — Felicity Caroline, *b* 1970: *m* 1994, Mark Julian Lewis, of 106 Burke Rd, Malvern, Vic 3145, son of Hywel Lewis, of Bribie Is, Queensland. —— Mora Delia, *b* 1936: *m* 1957, John Norman Abell, of Whittonditch House, Ramsbury, nr Marlborough, Wilts SN8 2PZ, son of late Sir George Edmond Brackenbury Abell, KCIE, OBE, and has issue living, Martin George, *b* 1962, — Antony Philip Norman, *b* 1964, — Sarah Elizabeth, *b* 1959: *m* 1984, William Mark Evans, of 60 Portland Rd, W11, and has issue living, Matthew George *b* 1987, Michael Timothy *b* 1990, Stephanie Susan *b* 1988. —— Julia Mary, *b* 1942: *m* 1985, Brian Edward Leaver, of 44 Ardross St, Applecross, WA 6153, Australia.

Grandchildren of late Col James Clifton Brown, second son of late Alexander Brown, el son of 1st baronet:—

Issue of late Capt Cedric Clifton Brown, *b* 1887, *d* 1968: *m* 1938, Mary Aymee Lilian, OBE, who *d* 1980, da of late Rev John A. Labouchere:—

Peter Cedric Clifton (Ballinamona, Cashel, co Tipperary), *b* 1939: *m* 1968, Petronelle, yr da of S. L. Grubb, of Beechmount, Fethard, co Tipperary, and has issue living, John Cedric Clifton, *b* 1970, — Louis Peter, *b* 1971, — Henry Samuel Clifton, *b* 1974. —— Anthony John Clifton (Perces, Greenstead Green, Halstead, Essex CO9 1RB), *b* 1942; *m* 1st, 1967 (*m diss* 1988), Françoise, da of M. Mooser, of Neuchâtel, Switzerland; 2ndly, 1989, Veronica Jane, eldest da of Reginald Eric Stevens, of 1 The Orchard, Church St, Willingdon, Eastbourne, E Sussex, and has issue living (by 1st *m*), Douglas Alexandre Clifton *b* 1968, — Philippe Anthony Clifton, *b* 1975. —— Ursula Mary Clifton, *b* 1941.

Descendants of late Alexander Hargreaves Brown (3rd son of late Alexander Brown, el son of 1st baronet), who was *cr* a *Baronet* 1903:—

See Pigott-Brown, Bt.

Sir William Brown, 1st baronet, an eminent merchant in Liverpool and New York, sat as MP for South Lancashire 1846-59, and was High Sheriff of Lancashire 1863. He established the mercantile firm of Brown, Shipley, and Co, Liverpool, and founded, in 1860, the Public Library and Museum in William Brown Street, Liverpool, at a cost of £42,000, and for that and other services to Liverpool he was created a baronet. The 2nd baronet was High Sheriff of Northamptonshire 1873.

PIGOTT-BROWN (UK) 1903, of Broome Hall, Capel, Surrey

There is unity among brothers

Sir William Brian Pigott-Brown, 3rd *Baronet*, *b* 20 Jan 1941; *s* his father, *Sir* John Hargreaves, 1942; *ed* Eton.

Arms – Quarterly, 1st and 4th gules, a chevron or between two bears' paws erased in chief argent, and four hands conjoined in saltire of the second in base; a chief engrailed of the last thereon an eagle displayed sable (for distinction), in the honour point a cross-crosslet of the third, *Brown*; 2nd and 3rd ermine, three fusils conjoined in fesse sable, *Pigott*. **Crest** – Issuant out of a wreath of oak vert a bear's paw erect argent, holding a sinister hand couped at the wrist proper.
Residence – 47 Eaton Mews North, SW1X 8LL.

AUNT LIVING (*daughter of 1st baronet*)

Joan Terrell Hargreaves (*Lady Prideaux*), *b* 1911: *m* 1934, Col Sir John Francis Prideaux, OBE, DL, who *d* 1993, and has issue living, Christopher John (Doddershall Park, Aylesbury; Brooks's Club), *b* 1936; *ed* Eton: *m* 1959, Celia, da of Sir Peter Averell Daniell, TD, DL, of Glebe House, Buckland, Surrey, and has issue living, David John *b* 1962: *m* 1989, Sally M., da of Ian Liddell, of Sheering, Essex, and of Mrs Colin Carter, of Ousden, Suffolk (and has issue living, Thomas *b* 1992), Charles *b* 1966, Lavinia Marion *b* 1961: *m* 1st, 1981, Barry J. Cameron, of Western Australia; 2ndly, 1992, Allan Gilfillan (Sam) Mainds and has issue, Polly *b* 1994, — Michael Charles Terrell (Selehurst, Lower Beeding, Horsham, Sussex), *b* 1950; *ed* Eton, and Trin Coll, Camb: *m* 1975, Mrs Susan H. Monsarrat, da of late Peto Bennett, of La Haute, Fliquet, Jersey, and has issue living, John Peto *b* 1979, Laura Hargreaves *b* 1976, — Editha Anne, *b* 1940: *m* 1968, Alaster Templeton of The Old Rectory, Whatfield, nr Ipswich, Suffolk, and has issue living, Katherine Elizabeth *b* 1968, Jane Celia *b* 1970. *Residence* – Rallywood, Ockley, Surrey.

WIDOW LIVING OF SECOND BARONET

Helen Viola Egerton, only da of late Maj Gilbert Francis Egerton-Cotton (*see* V Combermere, colls): *m* 1st, 1940, Capt Sir John Hargreaves Pigott-Brown, Coldstream Guards, 2nd Baronet, who was *ka* 1942; 2ndly, 1948, Capt Charles Raymond Radclyffe, late Roy Scots Greys. *Residence* – Lew, Oxfordshire.

COLLATERAL BRANCH LIVING

Issue of late Walter Hargreaves BROWN, 2nd son of 1st baronet, *b* 1881, *d* 1936: *m* 1913, Alberta Laura who *m* 2ndly, 1937, Alexander Innes, MC (Innes, Bt, *cr* 1628, colls), da of late Capt Guy Mainwaring, RN:—
Susan Henrietta Hargreaves, *b* 1914: *m* 1935, Curtis Delmar-Morgan, DSC, RNVR, who *d* 1987, of Eadens Wedge, East Meon, Petersfield, Hants, and has issue living, Michael Walter (Swaynes, Rudgwick, Sussex), *b* 1936: *m* 1962, Marjorie, da of John Kennedy Logan, and has issue living, Benjamin John *b* 1966, Katharine Susan *b* 1968, Alexandra Jane *b* 1971, — Jeremy Hugh, *b* 1941: *m* 1st, 1966, Nicolie Jane, da of Howard Eden Smith; 2ndly, 1978, Mary E., da of R. J. Hope, of Cookham Dean, Berks, and has issue living, (by 1st *m*) Piers Jonathan *b* 1974, Frances Jane *b* 1971, (by 2nd *m*) Alexander Curtis *b* 1981, Alice Clodagh *b* 1984, — (Dorothy) Sarah, *b* 1956: *m* 1979, Peter S. Cooper, and has issue living, Robert James *b* 1989, Elizabeth Anne *b* 1987. ——— Margaret Hargreaves, *b* 1917: *m* 1st, 1938, Robert Graham Fletcher, who *d* 1960; 2ndly, 1961, Alexander Ronan Nelson, and has issue living, (by 1st *m*) Alastair Robert Leslie, *b* 1941; *ed* Eton: *m* 1965, Maria Lucia Simoes, and has issue living, Robin Simoes *b* 1972, Monica Simoes *b* 1966, Katia Simoes *b* 1967, — Charles Hugh (Ardlussa, Isle of Jura, Argyll), *b* 1946; *ed* Eton: *m* 1970, Rose Noreen Nugent Sherlock, and has issue living, Andrew Charles *b* 1972, Catriona Rose *b* 1973, Elizabeth Noreen *b* 1976, — Ronald James (Easter Lennieston, Thornhill, by Stirling FK8 3QP), *b* 1948; *ed* Eton: *m* 1974, Damaris Hunneman, and has issue living, Ewan James *b* 1978, Robert Gordon *b* 1980, — Fiona Margaret, *b* 1939, — Katharine Hargreaves, *b* 1953: *m* 1977, Douglas Johnson, and has issue living, Fiona Mary *b* 1977, Helen Margaret *b* 1979. *Residence* – Muckairn, Taynuilt, Argyll.

The 1st baronet, Sir Alexander Hargreaves Brown (*see* Brown, Bt, *cr* 1863, colls), sat as MP for Wenlock (8) 1868-85, and for Mid or Wellington, Div of Shropshire (LU) 1885-1906. His el son Capt Gordon Hargreaves Brown was *ka* 1914. He *m* 1910, Edith Ivy, el da and co-heir of Adm William Harvey Pigott of Doddershall Park, Bucks who in 1925 assumed the additional surname and arms of Pigott for herself and her issue. Their son, Capt Sir John Hargreaves Pigott-Brown, 2nd Bt Coldstream Guards, was *ka* 1942.

Browne (Cave-Browne-Cave), see Cave.

BROWNRIGG (UK) 1816

Sir NICHOLAS GAWEN BROWNRIGG, 5th *Baronet*, son of late Gawen Egremont Brownrigg, 2nd and only surviving son of 4th Baronet; *b* 22 Dec 1932; *s* his grandfather, *Rear-Adm Sir* DOUGLAS EGREMONT ROBERT, CB, 1939: *m* 1st, 1959 (*m diss* 1965), Linda Louise, da of Jonathan B. Lovelace, of Beverly Hills, California, USA; 2ndly, 1971, Valerie Ann, da of Julian A. Arden, of Livonia, Michigan, USA, and has issue by 1st *m*.

Arms – Argent, between three crescents gules, a lion rampant-guardant sable holding in the dexter fore-paw a sword proper, hilt or, thereon a serpent entwined vert; and for augmentation, on a chief embattled of the last, a representation of the sceptre of the King of Kandy or, and of the banner of the said King, being gules within a bordure with a ray of the sun issuing from each angle a lion passant holding a sword in saltire, the whole ensigned with a representation of the crown of Kandy. **Crests** – 1st, augmentation, a demi-Kandian proper holding in the dexter hand a sword and in the sinister the crown of Kandy; 2nd, out of a mural crown or, a sword erect in pale proper, hilt or, thereon a serpent entwined vert.
Address – PO Box 548, Ukiah, Calif 95482, USA.

Virescat vulnere virtus
Valour strengthens from a wound

SON LIVING *(By 1st marriage)*

MICHAEL GAWEN (c/o US Dept of State, 2100 C St NW, Washington, DC 20520, USA), *b* 11 Oct 1961; US Foreign Service 1985—: *m* 19—, (Dr) Margaret Dillon, da of Dr Clay Burchell, and has issue living, Nicholas James, *b* 7 July 1993.

DAUGHTER LIVING *(By 1st marriage)*

Sylvia Alderyn, *b* 1964.

MOTHER LIVING

Baroness Lucia, da of late Baron Victor von Borosini, of 1270, Mesa Rd, San Marino 9, California, USA: *m* 1st, 1931 (*m diss* 1936), Gawen Egremont Brownrigg (ante); who *d* 1938; 2ndly, 1936 (*m diss* 1941), John Burnham; 3rdly, 1941 (*m diss* 1957), Com Edmund Lyford Engel, US Naval Reserve; 4thly, 19—, Harry Albert Batten, who *d* 1966. *Residence* – 207 Griegos Rd, NE, Albuquerque, New Mexico 87107-4002, USA.

The 1st baronet, Sir Robert Brownrigg, GCB (son of Henry Brownrigg, of Rockingham, co Wicklow), was a Gen in the Army, and Col 9th Foot. The 4th baronet, Sir Douglas Egremont Robert, CB, was a Rear-Adm RN.

BRUCE (NS) 1628, of Stenhouse, Stirlingshire

We have been

Sir (FRANCIS) MICHAEL IAN BRUCE, 12th *Baronet*; *b* 3 April 1926; *s* his father, *Sir* MICHAEL WILLIAM SELBY, 1957; discontinued use of his Christian name of Francis; US Marine Corps, Amphibious Forces, and Fleet Marines Force 1943-46 (Solomons, Bismarck Archipeligo, and Philippines Campaigns); Member of Sqdn A, 7th Regt NY 1948 (ret); Master's Ticket 1968; Pres Newport Sailing Club and Academy of Sail, Newport Beach since 1978, Pres American Maritime Co since 1981: *m* 1st, 1947 (*m diss* 1957), Barbara Stevens, da of Francis J. Lynch; 2ndly, 1961 (*m diss* 1963), Frances Keegan; 3rdly, 1966 (*m diss* 1975), Marilyn Anne, da of Carter Mullaly; 4thly, Patricia Gail, da of Frederich Root, and has issue by 1st *m*.

ᴀᴙᴍꜱ – Or, a saltire and chief gules, in the dexter canton an escutcheon argent charged with a chief sable. ᴄᴙᴇꜱᴛ – On a cap of dignity an arm from the shoulder couped fessewise holding a sceptre ensigned on the point with an open crown as that worn by Robert I of Scotland. ꜱᴜᴘᴘᴏᴙᴛᴇᴙꜱ – *Dexter*, a knight in armour the vizor open and a plume of feathers in his helmet holding a sceptre in his right hand all proper; sinister, a lion rampant azure armed and langued gules, crowned with the crown of Robert I, and gorged with that of David II, chained with an antique chain or.
Address – 34 Cormorant Circle, Newport Beach, California 92663, USA; *Clubs* – Balboa Bay, Newport Beach, and The Vikings of Orange, Newport Beach.

SONS LIVING *(By 1st marriage)*

MICHAEL IAN RICHARD *b* 10 Dec 1950. —— Robert Dudley, *b* 1952.

HALF-BROTHER LIVING

Michael David Lennon, *b* 1948.

HALF-SISTER LIVING

Corinna Mary Constance, *b* 1940.

WIDOW LIVING OF ELEVENTH BARONET

MARGARET HELEN (*Margaret, Lady Bruce*), da of late Sir Arthur Lennon Binns, CBE, MC; late Section Officer, WAAF: *m* 1946, as his fourth wife, Sir Michael William Selby Bruce, 11th Bt, who *d* 1957. *Residence* – —

COLLATERAL BRANCHES LIVING

Issue of late William Nigel Ernle Bruce, yr son of 10th baronet, *b* 1895, *d* 1953: *m* 1921, Violet Pauline, who *d* 1970, da of Col Willington Shelton, of Bruree, co Limerick:—
Pauline Margaret, *b* 1922: *m* 1946, Wing-Com Geoffrey Page, DSO, DFC, RAF (ret), and has issue living, Nigel Geoffrey, *b* 1953, — Jamie Douglas, *b* 1958, — Pauline Shelley, *b* 1948.

Grandchildren of late Capt Arthur Neil Bruce, son of late William Cuningham Bruce, 2nd son of 7th baronet:—
Issue of late William Cuningham Bruce, *b* 1866, *d* 1924: *m* 1897, Ellen, da of John Scott:—
Robert Neil, *b* 1904. —— William Cuningham, *b* 1907. —— Colin Cadell, *b* 1914. —— Corinna Joan, *b* 1916. —— Lornas Dorothy, *b* 1910.

Granddaughter of late Robert Cathcart Bruce, MD, 3rd son of late Maj-Gen Alexander James Bruce, el son of late Alexander Fairlie Bruce (*b* 1799), 3rd son of 7th baronet:—
Issue of late Robert Cathcart Bruce, *b* 1898, *d* 1966: *m* 1927, Christian Adeline, who *d* 1990, da of late William Henderson, of Berkley House, Frome:—
Fairlie Cathcart, *b* 1928: *m* 1951, Charles William Hutton, BArch FRICS, of Brook House, Sampford Brett, Taunton, Som TA4 4LE, and has issue living, Fairlie Elizabeth, *b* 1952: *m* 1977, Philip Julian Moore, ARICS, of 35 Stilehall Gdns, W4, and has issue living, Alastair Philip *b* 1980, Dominic William *b* 1983, — Julia Frances (The Old Mill, Eynsford, Kent), *b* 1954; has issue by Darrell Martin Whittaker, Luke Hutton WHITTAKER *b* 1981, Tom Hutton WHITTAKER *b* 1983, — Anina Mary (37 St James's Square, Bath, Avon), *b* 1955; has issue by Martin Bruce Robertson, Walter Douglas HUTTON *b* 1982, Zoë Bruce HUTTON *b* 1979, Rose Matilda HUTTON *b* 1986.

Grandchildren of late Alexander Fairlie Bruce, *b* 1857, son of George Cadell Bruce, 2nd son of Alexander Fairlie Bruce, *b* 1799 (ante):—
Issue of late Lt-Cdr Alan Cathcart Fairlie Bruce, RN, *b* 1894, *d* 1927: *m* 1919, Barbara Clarributt, who *d* 1992, da of E. Clarributt Skinner:—
Colin Michael Fairlie (Airth House, South Drive, Littleton, Winchester, Hants SO22 6PY), *b* 1925; *ed* Christ's Hospital, and Oxford (MA) and Edinburgh Univs; World Bank, Washington DC 1965-84; part-time economic development consultant; Far East, 1943-45 as Sub-Lt RNVR: *m* 1st, 1946, Patricia Mary Platt; 2ndly, 1963, Georgina Morrison Baker, and has issue living, (by 1st *m*) Timothy Michael Fairlie (400 Knecht Drive, Dayton, Ohio 45405, USA), *b* 1948: *m* 1978, Kate Ella Armpriester, — Alan Simon Fairlie (HC Box 41, Elm Rd, Bolinas, Cal 94924, USA), *b* 1950; *ed* Kingston Polytechnic (Dip Arch); RIBA; Vice-Pres Stone Marraccinni and Patterson, San Francisco: *m* 19—, Mary Jan Alzado, and has issue living, Abigail Emily Fairlie *b* 1969, Sarah Alison Fairlie *b* 1981, — Jonathan Neil Fairlie (33 Henley Rd, Iffley, Oxford), *b* 1958: *m* 19—, Carrie Marie Gomm, and has issue living, Joshua Thomas Fairlie *b* 1983, Lauren Fairlie *b* 1980, Sian Katie Fairlie *b* 1981, Jessica Fairlie *b* 19—, — Lindsay Madeleine Fairlie, *b* 1953: *m* 1970, Barry Shapland, of Dene Cliff, Palace House Rd, Hebden Bridge, W Yorks, and has issue living, Fionn *b* 19—, Ruari *b* 19—, Megan *b* 19—, — Jenny Catriona Fairlie, *b* 1960; *ed* Nottingham

Univ: *m* 19—, Andrew Harker, and has issue living, Thomas *b* 19—, Grace Catriona *b* 1993, — (by 2nd *m*) Fiona Elspeth, *b* 1965. —— John Alan Fairlie (Beechbrook, 16 ½ Colebrook St, Winchester, Hants SO23 9LH), *b* 1926; *ed* Christ's Hosp, and Oxford Univ; Personnel Mgr, R Dutch Shell Group of Cos 1948-84; Far East 1945-47 as Lieut, RA: *m* 1950, Joyce Edna Soffe, and has issue living, Iain Alasdair Fairlie (45 Albemarle St, Harwich, Essex), *b* 1954; *ed* Camb Univ (BA), and R Coll of Art (Dip in Film Making); has issue living, David Malcolm BRUCE *b* 1993, Hannah Eileen Jones BRUCE *b* 1987, Alexandra Kathleen Jones BRUCE *b* 1991, — Andrew Stuart Cathcart (14 Hastings Close, Polegate, E Sussex), *b* (twin) 1954; *ed* Manchester Polytechnic (BA), and Bristol Polytechnic (Dip in Personnel Admin): *m* 1988, Maureen Hull, — Alison Jean, *b* 1951: *m* 1977, Paul Richard Moore, of Triffeny, 13a Stoney Lane, Winchester, Hants, and has issue living, Jonathan Paul Bruce *b* 1980, Nicola Jane Bruce *b* 1982. —— Barbara Jean, *b* 1921: *m* 1941, Col Robert John Augustine Hornby, OBE (ret), E Surrey Regt, of Meadowbank Barn House, Ascott-under-Wychwood, Oxon, and has issue living, Vivien Sheena (*Deaconess Hon Mrs Edward F. Northcote*) (96 Otho Ct, Augustus Close, Brentford Dock, Middx), *b* 1942: *m* 1963 (*m diss* 1980), Hon Edward Frederic Northcote, TD (*see* E Iddesleigh), — Louise Panette, *b* 1947: *m* 1967, Kenneth Dudley Johns Bootes-Johns, of 11 Sherborne House Stables, Sherborne, Glos.

    Grandchildren of late Col Elliott Armstrong Bruce, 7th son of late Alexander Fairlie Bruce, *b* 1799 (ante):—
    Issue of late Lieut-Col Malcolm Edward Lloyd Bruce, Indian Army, *b* 1872, *d* 1952: *m* 1903, Clementina Blyth, who *d* 1958, yst da of late W. F. B. Dalzel, MD, Surg-Major Bengal Army:—
Elizabeth Mary Dalzel (twin), *b* 1910: *m* 1933, Neville Eugene Govett, who *d* 1972, and has issue living, Bryan, *b* 1934; *ed* St Paul's Sch, — Richard, *b* 1937; *ed* St Paul's Sch, — Robert John, *b* 1944. *Residence* – 13 Clydesdale Gdns, Richmond, Surrey.
    Issue of late Elliott Henry Rochfort Bruce, *b* 1874, *d* 1933: *m* 1905, Frances Maude, who *d* 1949, da of A. McDonald:—
Elliott McDonald, *b* 1906; *m* 1932, Kathleen, da of G. Clarke, and has issue living, Michael, *b* 1939, — Josephine, *b* 1945, — Heather, *b* 1949. *Residence* – Launceston, Tasmania. —— Malcolm Alexander, *b* 1913: *m* 1942 (*m diss* 19—), Doris Gwynnith, and has issue living, Donald Malcolm, *b* 1944, — Geoffrey, *b* 1946, — Richard, *b* (twin) 1946. —— Beryl Brenda *b* 1919: *m* 1947, Herbert Winston Eaton, and has issue living, Geoffrey Winston, *b* 1949, — Linda Christine, *b* 1952.

    Grandchildren of late Michael McCubbin Bruce, 8th son of Alexander Fairlie Bruce, *b* 1799 (ante):—
    Issue of late Robert Cathcart Bruce, *b* 1880, *d* 1968: *m* 1916, Emma Dolores, who *d* 1983, da of late John Croce:—
Vivian Richard, MB, FRCGP (Lindavanally, 25A George Douglas Drive, Ryedale, Dumfries DG2 7EP), *b* 1919: *m* 1st, 1942, Norah Maeve Yates, who *d* 1960; 2ndly, 1962 (*m diss* 1983), Bernadette Yates; 3rdly, 1983, Valerie Florence May Bruce, da of late Nelson Fitzroy Baylis, and has issue living, (by 1st *m*) Robert James, OBE (The Red House, Salperton, Northleach, Cheltenham, Glos GL54 4EE), *b* 1946; Maj RM (ret): *m* 1969, Elizabeth Jane Moira, da of late David Clement Burgess, and has issue living, Robert David Cathcart *b* 1977, James Hubert William *b* 1985, (Elizabeth) Maeve *b* 1970: *m* 19—, Adrian Bruce-Purchase (formerly Purchase), of 244 High St, Bath Easton, Bath, Avon BA1 7RA (and has issue living, Jake Hamilton *b* 1993), (Laura) Christian *b* 1971, — Michael Alexander, *b* 1949; FCA; Chief Accountant and Administrator Hall-Houston Malaysia Ltd, Kuala Lumpur, Malaysia: *m* 1983, Patricia Sheila, da of Col Peter Johnson, and has issue living, Alexander Peter *b* 1987, David *b* 1990, Natasha *b* 1985, Diana *b* (twin) 1990, — Richard Hubert (61 Heathcote Drive, Sileby, Loughborough, Leics), *b* 1956, — (by 2nd *m*) Paul Cathcart (18 Ouseley Close, Marston, Oxford), *b* 1963; BSc: *m* 1989, Louise, da of late Hari Ratan Ker (and has issue living, Hannah Amy *b* 1992), — Angus Peter, *b* 1964: *m* 1990 (*m diss* 1993), Jennifer Tatum, — Joseph Douglas, *b* 1970.
    Issue of late Charles Kerr Bruce, *b* 1880, *d* 1955: *m* 1928, Lily, who *d* 1959, da of Charles Leonard:—
Ian Robert (Three Firs Cottage, Bramshott Chase, Hindhead, Surrey GU26 6DG), *b* 1931: *m* 1st, 1956 (*m diss* 1980), Dorothy Evelyn Knight; 2ndly, 1994, Elisabeth Joan, da of late Col Harry Lacy, and widow of Richard Swanwick, and has issue living (by 1st *m*), Anne, *b* 1960, — Caroline Jane, *b* 1963. —— Margaret, *b* 1930: *m* 1956, Norman Terence Whight, of The Cherries, 15 Fairfield Way, Hildenborough, Kent, and has had issue, Charles Bruce, *b* 1963; *d* 1980, — Fiona Margaret, *b* 1960. —— Audrey Mary, *b* 1935: *m* 1958, George David James Morgan, of 16 Heslop Rd, SW12 8EG, and has issue living, Christopher David, *b* 1962, — Felicity Claire, *b* 1960.

    Grandchildren of late Robert Perry Bruce (infra):—
    Issue of late Michael Macaulay Bruce, *b* 1904, *d* 1964: *m* 1937, Louise Françoise (62 Bolton Rd, Windsor, Berks), da of Prof Van der Pot, of the Netherlands:—
Robert William (Highbury, Tedgness Rd, Grindleford, nr Sheffield), *b* 1940: *m* 1964, Jennifer Patricia Guilfoyle Brown, and has issue living, Michael Gregory Macaulay, *b* 1968, — Rosalind Ellen Macaulay, *b* 1966, — Miranda Jane Macaulay, *b* 1970. —— Michael Zachary (62 Bolton Rd, Windsor, Berks), *b* 1951: *m* 1981, Ellen, da of Sigbert Leuchthold, of Switzerland, and has issue living, Edgar, *b* 1989, — Catherine, *b* 1984, — Leanne, *b* 1986. —— Mary Louise, *b* 1938: *m* 1961, Colin Hugh Prince, of 19 Alexandra Rd, Kingston upon Thames, and has issue living, Hamish Robin John, *b* 1966, — Anna Louise, *b* 1964. —— Vanessa Bertha Jane, *b* 1942: *m* 1968, Christopher Ryle, of Upland Cottage, Holt Hill, Holt End, Bealey, Worcs, and has issue living, Deborah Louise, *b* 1968, — Xanthe, *b* 1969, — Octavia Georgina, *b* 1979. —— Barbara Lucy, *b* 1945: *m* 1969, Paul Lewis Henderson, of The Beeches, Boston Spa, W Yorkshire, and has issue living, James *b* 1974, Barnaby *b* 1981, Juliet *b* 1972.

    Grandchildren of late Alexander Fairlie Bruce, *b* 1799 (ante):—
    Issue (by 2nd *m*) of late Robert Perry Bruce, *b* 1861, *d* 1914: *m* 1st, 1886 (*m diss* 1899), Ethel Blanche, who *d* 1911, da of late John Russell, of Merthyr Tydfil; 2ndly, 1903, Olive Maud, who *d* 1968, 2nd da of late Joseph Babington Macaulay, formerly of Rosebush, Pembrokeshire and Paignton, S Devon:—
Nigel Macaulay, *b* (twin) 1906; India and Burma 1942-45 as Maj RA, ADC to GOC-in-C 14th Army, Burma: *m* 1940, Helen Woodhall. *Residence* – Little Grange, Hollesley, nr Woodbridge, Suffolk. *Club* – Army and Navy.

    Grandchildren of late Robert Perry Bruce (ante):—
    Issue of late Edward Macaulay Bruce, *b* 1908, *d* 1986: *m* 1939, Nancy Elinor (Horseshoe Cottage, Arlington, Bibury, Glos), yr da of late Lt-Col F.G.C. Humfrey, late 12th Bengal Cav:—
David Nigel Macaulay (15 St Helena Rd, Bristol BS6 7NR), *b* 1947; *ed* Gresham's Sch, St Andrew's Univ (MA), and Edinburgh Univ (MPhil); Lecturer at Bristol Polytechnic: *m* 1972, Diana, da of Cluny Dale, and has issue living, James, *b* 1974, — Rebecca, *b* 1977. —— Elizabeth Mary, *b* 1942: *m* 1966 (*m diss* 1978), Dirk Detert, PhD, and has issue living, Niels Bruce, *b* 1970, — Jan Bruce, *b* 1974.

    Grandchildren of late Eric Henry Stuart Bruce, only son of late Gen Michael Bruce, grandson of late Patrick Craufurd Bruce, 5th son of 6th baronet:—
    Issue of late Brigadier Ian Robert Craufurd George Mary Bruce, DSO, MBE, *b* 1890, *d* 1956: *m* 1926, Joan Mary, who *d* 1991, da of late Lt-Col Rowland Charles Feilding, DSO (*see* E Denbigh, colls):—
Anne Mary, *b* 1927: *m* 1953, Nicholas Patrick Reyntiens, and has issue living, Dominick Percival Ian (5 Craster Rd, SW2), *b* 1957; dancer and actor: *m* 1988, Caroline Sophie, yr da of William Adrian Liddell (*see* B Ravensworth, colls), — John Patrick Martin, *b* 1964, — Edith Mary Isabel, *b* 1954, — Lucy Mary Anne, *b* 1959: *m* 1982, Nicholas Durnan, of Compton Farmhouse, Compton Durville, S Petherton, Som TA13 5ET, and has issue living, Sophie Belle *b* 1984, Grace Louise *b* 1987. *Residences* – Ilford Bridges Farm, Close Stocklinch, Ilminster, Som. —— Janet Mary, *b* 1928: *m* 1950, Peter Michaeljohn Ward, and has issue living, Jonathan Francis Bruce (2 Olive Hill, Wyck Rissington, Cheltenham, Glos GL54 2PW), *b* 1954: *m* 1979, Sarah Elizabeth Sophia, da of Maj Mark Winton Slane Fleming, 10th R Hus (*see* By Emmet of Amberley), and has

issue living, Christopher Luke *b* 1980, Hugh Basil *b* 1982, — Robert Richard Craufurd, *b* 1959, — Edmund Giles William (115 Exchange Rd, W Bridgford, Nottingham NG2 6BX), *b* 1962: *m* 1991, Gillian Elizabeth McCord, — Damian Peter Michael, *b* 1966, — Clare Dorothy, *b* 1951: *m* 1976, Christopher James Thomson, of 28 Gordonbrock Rd, SE4, and has issue living, Edmund Christopher *b* 1985, Lucy Stephanie *b* 1981, — Catharine Joan, *b* 1952: *m* 1983, Henry Swift Thompson, Jr, of 11 Douglas Crescent, Edinburgh, and has issue living, James Edwin Jerome *b* 1987, Emma Joan Douglas *b* 1985, Joanna Janet Henrietta *b* 1991, — Magdalen Mary, *b* 1955: *m* 1989, Axel Howarth Goodbody, of 2 First Av, Bath BA2 3NW, and has issue living, Brendan Christian *b* 1987, Rowland Benedict *b* 1993, Laura Brigid *b* 1990, — Hester Janet Teresa *b* 1964: *m* 1992, James Alastair Innes, of 7 Wardie Crescent, Trinity, Edinburgh EH5 1AF. *Residence* – Waterdell House, Croxley Green, Herts WD3 3JH. —— Helen Mary, *b* 1929: *m* 1st, 1956 (*m diss* 1980), Stephen Edward Francis Bally, who *d* 198—; 2ndly, 1983, Edward Todd, of 55 Tallia Rd, Mudgeeraba, Queensland 4213, Australia, and has issue living, (by 1st *m*) Ian Stephen Edward (25 Denis St, Ayr 4807, Australia), *b* 1959: *m* 1983, Mrs Kay Louise Moffitt (née Lewis), and has issue living, Sarah Ann Frances *b* 1992, and has adopted his stepchildren, Mark William *b* 1976, Tabitha Louise *b* 1978, and Jodie Marie *b* (twin) 1978, — Alexander St John (43 Millen Crescent, Healy, Mount Isa, Qld 4825, Australia), *b* 1963: *m* 1993, Kay Therese Halley, — David Anthony, *b* 1968, — Louise Frances Joan (Maleny, Australia), *b* 1957: *m* 1977 (*m diss* 1987), David Bain, and has issue living, Aaron Ian *b* 1987, Madonna *b* 1976, Michelle *b* 1978. —— Eynor Mary (Hidden Waters, Avon Castle Drive, Ringwood), *b* 1933: *m* 1957, Alfred Edwin Bell, who *d* 1987, and has issue living, Christopher Michael Ian, *b* 1958, — Julian Sebastian, *b* 1962: *m* 1989, Justin Chappell Day, — Theodore Richard John, *b* 1972. —— Philena Mary Edith (Flat 4, 36 Russell Rd, W14), *b* 1949.

This family is a cadet branch of the Bruces of Clackmannan, from whom the Earls of Elgin also derive their descent. Sir William Bruce, who was created a baronet with remainder to his heirs male whatsoever, was a yr son of William son and heir of Sir Alexander Bruce of Airth, 6th in descent from Sir Edward Bruce of Airth, yr son of the second Sir Robert Bruce of Clackmannan, who *d* before 1406.

BRUCE (UK) 1804, of Downhill, Londonderry

We have been

Sir HERVEY JAMES HUGH BRUCE, 7th *Baronet; b* 4 Sept 1952; *s* his father, *Sir* HERVEY JOHN WILLIAM, 1971; *ed* Eton; Maj Gren Gds: *m* 1st, 1979, Charlotte Sara Jane, el da of John Temple Gore, of Bridgefoot, Spedham, Midhurst, W Sussex (*see* E Eglinton, 1990 Edn); 2ndly, 1992, J. M. (Anna), yst da of Frank Pope, of Tavistock, Devon, and has issue (by 1st *m*).

Arms – Or, on a saltire gules a harp of the field, stringed argent, on a chief of the second a canton argent, charged with a lion rampant azure. **Crest** – A lion passant azure holding in his dexter paw a trefoil slipped proper. *Residence* – 23 Cranbury Rd, SW6. *Club* – Cavalry and Guards'.

SON LIVING *(By 1st marriage)*

HERVEY HAMISH PETER, *b* 20 Nov 1986.

DAUGHTER LIVING *(By 1st marriage)*

Laura Crista, *b* 1984.

SISTER LIVING

Lauretta Chinty, *b* 1950: *m* 1st, 1971, David Ralph Foster Harbord, Capt 15th/19th King's Royal Hussars, who *d* 1974 (*see* B Suffield, colls); 2ndly, 1978, Nicholas Charles Wetherill Ridley, of 150 Walton St, SW3 elder son of Harold Ridley, of 53 Harley St, W1.

UNCLE LIVING *(Son of 5th baronet)*

Ronald Cecil Juckes (24 Fairfax Rd, Teddington, Middx), *b* 1921: *m* 1960, Jean, da of Lewis James William Murfitt, and has issue living, Alan James, *b* 1964.

COLLATERAL BRANCHES LIVING

Issue of late Lt-Col Percy Robert CLIFTON, CMG, DSO, TD, JP, DL, 2nd son of 4th baronet, *b* (twin) 1872, *d* 1944 (having assumed by Roy licence 1919 the surname and arms of Clifton only in lieu of his patronymic): *m* 1st, 1898, Aletheia Georgina, who *d* 1904, da of Rt Hon Sir Richard Horner Paget, 1st Bt (*cr* 1886); 2ndly, 1909, Evelyn Mary Amelia, da of late Major Thomas Leith (E Carnwath):—
(By 2nd *m*) Peter Thomas CLIFTON, CVO, DSO, *b* 1911; Lt-Col (ret) Gren Gds; mem HM Body Guard of Hon Corps of Gentlemen at Arms since 1960, Clerk of the Cheque and Adjutant 1973-79, Standard Bearer 1979-81, ret; Italy 1943-45 (DSO); a JP for Hants and a DL for Notts; DSO 1945: *m* 1934 (*m diss* 1936), Ursula Sybil, da of Sir Edward Hussey Packe, KBE (B Colebrooke, ext); 2ndly, 1948, Patricia Mary Adela, DStJ, da of late Maj J. M. Gibson-Watt, of Doldowlod, co Radnor, and widow of Maj Robert Nevill Cobbold, Welsh Gds (M Abergavenny, colls), and has issue living, (by 2nd *m*) Georgina Anne, *b* 1949: *m* 1st, 1967, Hon Richard Francis Gerard Wrottesley, who *d* 1970, 2nd son of 5th Baron Wrottesley; 2ndly, 1982, Lt-Col Jonathan Lovett Seddon-Brown, Scots Gds, of 57 Rostrevor Rd, SW6, — Rose Amelia (*Hon Mrs Mark W. Vestey*), *b* 1952: *m* 1975, Hon Mark William Vestey (*see* B Vestey). *Residence* – Dummer House, Dummer, Basingstoke, Hants.

Issue of late Henry James Bruce, CMG, MVO, 4th son of 4th baronet, *b* 1880, *d* 1951: *m* 1915, Tamara Karsavina (the ballerina), who *d* 1978, da of M. Karsavin, of Petrograd, Russia:—
Nikita, *b* 1916: *m* 1st (*m diss* 1946), Kay (Kay Bannerman, actress and dramatic author), who *d* 1991, da of Capt Robert G. Bannerman; 2ndly, 1957, Dorothy Mary Norah Mostyn, da of William Mostyn Bell, and has issue living (by 2nd *m*), Nicholas Henry William, *b* 1960, — Caroline Mary Tamara, *b* 1958: *m* 1984, Keith Douglas Crampton, son of Douglas Crampton. *Residence* – 38 Longfield Drive, Amersham, Bucks.

Grandson of late Rev Canon Lloyd Stewart Bruce, 4th son of 2nd baronet:—
Issue of late Rev Robert Douglas Bruce, *b* 1867, *d* 1944: *m* 1894, Alice Margaret who *d* 1955, da of late Henry William Lord, Bar-at-Law:—

Nigel Patrick, BM, BCh, *b* 1905; *ed* Keble Coll, Oxford (BA); Hosp of the Epiphany, Kamdara, Bihar, India 1934-40; 1939-45 War as Capt RAMC: *m* 1934, Audrey Patricia Villiers, only child of late Rev Owen Samuel Edward Clarendon, V of Iffley, Oxford, and has issue living, Clare, *b* 1935: *m* 1956 (*m diss* 1972), Peter Colpoys Paley Johnson, only son of Lt-Col Sir John Paley Johnson, 6th Bt (*cr* 1755).

Grandchildren of the Rev Robert Douglas Bruce (ante):—
Issue of late Rev Michael Bruce, *b* 1908, *d* 1968: *m* 1935, Jean Stuart (29 Grange Rd, Edinburgh, EH9 1UQ), da of late Ian Campbell, LRCP, LRCS, of 11 Herford Rd, Harrogate:—
Robert John (19 Grange Rd, Edinburgh, EH9 1UQ), *b* 1936. —— Elspeth Mary, *b* 1942: *m* 1965, Stuart Semple, MB, ChB, of Mounthooly, Winchburgh, Broxburn, W Lothian, EH52 6PY, and has issue living, Jean, *b* 1968, — Sheila, *b* 1970, — Mairi, *b* 1971, Elspeth, *b* 1975.

Grandchildren of late Rev Canon Lloyd Stewart Bruce (ante):—
Issue of late Rev Francis Rosslyn Courtenay Bruce, DD, *b* 1871, *d* 1956: *m* 1908, Rachel, who *d* 1971, el da of late Richard Hanbury Joseph Gurney, JP, DL (Buxton, Bt):—
Merlin, OBE, *b* 1909; Cdr RN (ret); 1939-45 War; Korea 1950-52 (despatches); Councillor Hemel Hempstead RDC 1961-70; OBE (Mil) 1959: *m* 1933, Marjorie Joan, who *d* 1991, only da of late William Hitchcock, of Kettlewells Farm, St Albans, and has issue living, Euslin (37 Clinton Cres, St Leonards on Sea, Sussex, TN38 0RN), *b* 1933; late Sub-Lt RN: *m* 1957, Enid Pedley, and has issue living, Quinton Rosslyn *b* 1959, Roderick Hulme *b* 1962, Damian Trispen *b* 1970, Jeremy Larick *b* 1974, Nicola Jane *b* 1958, Caroline Fiona *b* 1964, — Rollo (28 West End Grove, Horsforth, Leeds), *b* 1939; *ed* St Catharine's Coll, Camb (BA): *m* 1965, Katharine Margaret, da of Ronald Hill, of Princethorpe, Warwicks, and has issue living, Rory James *b* 1968 (has issue living, Jack Merlin *b* 1993), Lucy Helen *b* 1966. *Residence* – 50 Tumbling Bay Court, Henry Rd, Oxford OX2 0PE. —— Erroll, *b* 1913; Cdr RN (ret): *m* 1939, Silvia Daphne, only da of late Col C. R. Sylvester Bradley, and has issue living, Peregrine (Pilgrims, Broadmead, Sway, Lymington, Hants), *b* 1940; late Capt R Signals: *m* 1974, Fiona Anne, da of Gp Capt Reginald Bryson Wardman, OBE, AFC, and has issue living, Rachel *b* 1974, Anna *b* 1976, — Peter (Kestrel Cottage, Shirley Holmes, Lymington, Hants; *Club* – Royal Yacht Sqdn), *b* 1941, Cdr RN, — Rosamund, *b* 1943: *m* 1st, 1962, Terence Patrick Griffin; 2ndly, 1978, Jeremy Alan Holmes, MA, MB, BCh, MRCP, FRCPsych, of The Old Rectory, Stoke Rivers, Devon, and has issue living, (by 1st *m*) Benedict James *b* 1963, Polly Bridget *b* 1966 (has issue living, Marcus *b* 1991, Rosy *b* 1986, Zenta Esther *b* 1987), Matilda Victoria *b* 1968, Flora Rhalou *b* 1972, (by 2nd *m*) Joshua Thomas Cecil *b* 1983, — Errollyn, *b* 1950: *m* 19—, Richard Charles Lindley, MA, DPhil, of Hainworth, Keighley, W Yorkshire, and has issue living, Samuel James *b* 1977, Joseph Galen *b* 1983, Emma Rosamund *b* 1978, — Chloe Siola, *b* 1965. *Residence* – Lofts, Lower Pennington, Lymington, Hants. —— Verily, *b* 1915: *m* 1st, 1940, Capt Donald Clive Anderson, late Indian Army, who *d* 1957; 2ndly, 1971, Paul Edward Paget, CVO, FSA, FRIBA, of Templewood, Northrepps, Cromer, Norfolk (see Paget, Bt, colls, *cr* 1871), and has issue living, (by 1st *m*) Edward (Templewood, Northrepps, Cromer, Norfolk) *b* 1948: *m* 1973, Mrs Christina Bolt, yr da of F. G. Raymond, and has issue living, Evelyn *b* 1973, Beatrice *b* 1978, — Marian, *b* 1941: *m* 1964, James Haldane O'Hare, of 35 Waldeck Rd, Norwich, and of 33 Frogshall, Northrepps, Cromer, Norfolk NR27 0LJ, and has issue living, Justin *b* 1966: *m* 1991, Janet Robb, of Whale Beach, Sydney, Australia, Christina *b* 1965: *m* 1989, Simon Gerredd Evans, of Sally Beans House, Northrepps, Norfolk (and has issue living, Botticelli Verily Boadicea *b* 1990, Piranesi Vita Lolita *b* 1992), Eloise *b* 1970, — Rachel, *b* 1943: *m* 1965, Prof David Henry Bradby, MA, PhD, of Lower Damsels, Northrepps, Norfolk, and has issue living, Lawrence *b* 1968, Donald *b* 1973, Hannah *b* 1966, and an adopted son, Nguyen Thanh Sang *b* 1970 (adopted 1980), — Janie, *b* 1952: *m* 1971, Charles Hampton, of 118 Hurst St, Cowley St John, Oxford, and has issue living, Orlando *b* 1975, Joseph *b* 1978, Daisy Maya *b* 1973, — Alexandra (21 Humberstone Rd, Cambridge), *b* 1953; MA (Cantab): *m* 1st, 1972 (*m diss* 1989), Michael Holgreaves Allerhand; 2ndly, 1993, Gray Innis Walker, yr son of Rev Colin Walker, and has issue living (by 1st *m*), Taffeta Annie *b* 1976, Rhalou Gladys *b* 1979. —— Lorema, *b* 1920: *m* 1942, Alan Wilfrid Gough Goolden, MB, BS, MRCP, FRCR, and has issue living, Adrian French, *b* 1945: *m* 1st, 1971 (*m diss* 1979), Penelope, da of John Godber; 2ndly, 19—, Sally, da of Malcolm Lower, MB, and has issue living (by 1st *m*), Jack Malago *b* 1973, Amy Apple Louise *b* 1976, Rosemary Alice *b* 1978, (by 2nd *m*) Leo Samson *b* 1989, — Robin Massey, *b* 1948: *m* 1976, Mrs Madelaine Mulholland, da of George Nation, and has issue living, Oliver Nation *b* 1978, Rachel Bruce *b* 1980. *Residence* – 31 West St, Osney Island, Oxford.
Issue of late Capt Wilfred Montagu Bruce, CBE, RD, RNR, *b* 1874, *d* 1953: *m* 1913, Hon Dorothy Florence Boot, who *d* 1980, da of 1st Baron Trent:—
Nancy Jessica, *b* 1915: *m* 1940, Adriano Guarnieri, who *d* 1983, and has issue living, Giovanni Bruce, *b* 1947: *m* 1973, Cristina Ongania, and has issue living, Gaia *b* 1973, Valentina *b* 1978, Isotta *b* 1982, — Antonio Wilfrid, *b* 1949: *m* 1981, Anna Lisa Sacerdoti, and has issue living, Matteo *b* 1981, Ambra *b* 1983, — Andrea, *b* 1953: *m* 1981, Luisa Gamba, and has issue living, Lorenzo *b* 1983, Matilde *b* 1981, — Francesca Flora, *b* 1941: *m* 1968, Giuliano Ferrari Bravo, PhD (Cantab), and has issue living, Nicolo *b* 1968, Jacopo *b* 1970, Martino *b* 1974. *Residences* – via Principe 71, Ronca de Treviso, Italy; Les Pommiers, Millbrook, Jersey, CI.

Grandchildren of late Arthur Bonnycastle Dalrymple Bruce (infra):—
Issue of late Arthur Blair Dalrymple Bruce, *b* 1924, *d* 1985, having assumed the name of Arthur in lieu of his first christian name of Frederick: *m* 1951, Patricia (258 S Taylor Mills Drive, Richmond Hill, Ontario, Canada), da of late Richard Raymond Jarvis, of Ottawa:—
Richard Neale Dalrymple, *b* 1954. —— Susan Elizabeth, *b* 1955: *m* 1984, Jefferson Scott Reade, and has issue living, Shannon Kathleen, *b* 1986, — Kirstin Alexandra, *b* 1988.

Granddaughter of late Henry Barnard Dalrymple Bruce, el son of late Lt-Col Henry Stewart Beresford Bruce (infra):—
Issue of late Arthur Bonnycastle Dalrymple Bruce, *b* 1890, *d* 1934: *m* 1916, Marguerite Heloise, who *d* 1976, da of Frederick Edward Neale, of Chatham, New Brunswick:—
Heloise Patricia, *b* 1918: *m* 1945, Capt Robert John McLaughlin, Toronto Scottish Regt, who *d* 1949, and has issue living, Robert Bruce *b* (posthumous) 1949. *Residence* – 85 Clifton Rd, Toronto, Canada.

Granddaughters of late Arthur James Henry Bruce (infra):—
Issue of late Arthur Michael Edward Bruce, *b* 1938, *d* 1993: *m* 1st, 1962 (*m diss* 19—), Holly, da of Carl Cunningham, of Toronto; 2ndly, 1993, (Dorothy) Ferne Lancaster (2003-415 Greenview Av, Ottawa, Ont, Canada):—
(By 1st *m*) Wendy Raina, *b* 1968. —— Susan Ann, *b* 1969.

Grandchildren of late Arthur Hill Nunn Bruce, 2nd son of late Lt-Col Henry Stewart Beresford Bruce, eldest son of late Adm Sir Henry William Bruce, 3rd son of 1st baronet:—
Issue of late Arthur James Henry Bruce, *b* 1901, *d* 1992: *m* 1931, Gladys, da of Edward Bearinger, of Waterloo, Ont:—
Patricia Mary Jane, *b* 1934: *m* 1956, Robert Arthur Davey, of 64 Lockhart Rd, Collingwood, Ont, Canada L9Y 2L3, and has issue living, Robert Bruce, *b* 1958 (has issue living, Ryan *b* 1992), — Steven Michael, *b* 1967: *m* 1990, Linda Diane Godwin, — Susan Patricia, *b* 1960, — Karen Elizabeth, *b* 1962: *m* 1993, Gregory Willison, and has issue living, Brendan Gregory Bruce *b* 1993.
Issue of late Reginald Alexander Steen Bruce, *b* 1904, *d* 1993: *m* 1933, Marie, da of George Albert Blouin, of Ottawa, Ont:—

Robert Arthur Stewart, b 1936: m 1963, Karen, da of James Dunn, of Old Chelsea, Quebec, and has issue living, Reginald Arthur Spencer, b 1964, — Alexander James Robert, b 1967, — D'Arcy Stewart Anthony, b 1968, — Justin Martin Maynard, b 1971. —— Marie Elizabeth Claire, b 1934: m 1956, Frederick Reginald Anfossie, of 2771 Salina St, Ottawa, Ont, Canada K2B 6P8, and has issue living, Frederick Bruce, b 1957: m 19—, Maryann Helen, da of Andrew Stasko, of Odessa, Ont, and has issue living, Frederick Andrew b 1985, Matthew Alexander b 1990, Mackenzie Elizabeth Irene b 1992, — Christine Elodie, b 1959, — Janet Marie, b 1961: m 1988, Michael Ernest Peiffer, and has issue living, Emily Claire b 1989, Katherine Marie b 1991, — Heather Claire, b 1963, — Margo Elizabeth, b 1968. —— Sandra Margo Ann, b 1938: m 1960, Grant Pereigo McDonald, of RR2 Tadoussac Drive, Aylmer East, PQ, Canada, and has issue living, Reginald Albert Stroud, b 1962, — Robert Bruce Reid, b 1963, — Adam Alfred Grant, b 1964, — John Arthur Steen, b 1968.

   Issue of late Stewart Frederick Dundonald Bruce, b 1905; d 1982: m 1940, Kathleen Edna (513 Westminster Av, Ottawa, Ontario, Canada), da of Charles Cooke, of Ottawa:—

Nona Frances Evelyn, b 1944: m 1970, John Douglas Argue, of 19 Maplehill Way, Nepean, Canada, and has issue living, Bruce Dugan, b 1975, — Sally, b 1973. —— Joan Kathleen Susan BRUCE-NIBOGIE, b 1946: m 1972, Walter William Nibogie, of PO Box 69, Victoria St, Metcalfe, Ontario K0A 2PO, and has issue living, Jeremy Ryan Bruce, b 1977, — Krista Kathleen Andra, b 1975. —— Nancy Elizabeth Ann, b 1949: m 1975, Myles Julien Kowalyshen, and has issue living, Bryan Mikael, b 1977, — Kara Anne, b 1979.

   Issue of late Allan Ernest Hill Bruce, b 1907, d 1973: m 1930 (m diss 1946), Maria Ann, da of Elidore Sauvé, of Ottawa, Canada:—

Allan Alexander Dundonald (18 Lynhar Rd, Nepean, Ontario K2H 6L9), b 1931: m 1956, Patricia Anne Leeks, and has issue living, Stewart Allan Robert, b 1957, — Steven Christopher David, b 1961, — Donald Andrew James, b 1964: m 1988, Deborah Lynn Boright, and has issue living, Jessica Dawn b 1989. —— Hervey William Beresford (5 Ashford Drive, Ottawa, Ont, Canada), b 1932: m 1966, Molly Margaret MacLaurin, and has issue living, Cameron Allan Beresford, b 1972, and two adopted sons, Todd Roy, b 1961, — Scott Rodrick, b 1962. —— Marie Lorraine Caroline, b 1934: m 1957, Patrick Francis Timlin, of 78 Harris Place, Ottawa, Ont, K2G 2P8, Canada, and has issue living, Michael Allan, b 1961, — Robert Patrick, b 1966, — Brenda Marion, b 1958.

   Granddaughter of late Lt-Col Henry Stewart Beresford Bruce (ante):—
   Issue of late Col Stewart Armit Macdonald Bruce, b 1858, d 1937: m 1891, Helen, da of late John McGregor, of Balmenach, Cromdale, Morayshire:—
Jean Mariette Isabel Otway, b 1892: m 1916 (m diss 1932), Cyril Gordon Taylor.

   Granddaughter of late Reginald Archibald Kenneth Bruce, 7th son of late Lt-Col Henry Stewart Beresford Bruce (ante):—
   Issue of late Capt William Reginald Richard Stewart Bruce, Irish Guards, b 1910, ka 1944: m 1934, Mirabel Melville Gray (who m 2ndly 1946, J. M. Hawkes), da of J. D. Walker, of Balgownie Lodge, Aberdeenshire:—
Mirabel Hermione, b 1941: m 1st, 1964 (m diss 1972), Alan Hamill, MN; 2ndly, 197-, James G Simpson, and has issue living (by 2nd m), James Alexander Bruce, b 1976.

   Granddaughter of late Rear-Adm James Minchin Bruce, son of late Adm Sir Henry William Bruce, KCB, 3rd son of 1st baronet:—
   Issue of late James Minchin Bruce, b 1859, d 19—: m 1888, Ethelwynne, da of the Rev James Powell:—
Minnie, b 1889. Residence –

   Granddaughter of late Major Stewart Hervey Bruce, son of late Lieut-Col Stewart Craufurd Bruce, 4th son of 1st baronet:—
   Issue of late Rev Stewart Alexander Bruce, b 1870, d 1956: m 1911, Ada Frances who d 1945, da of late Dr R. E. MacDowell:—
Maire Frances Patricia, b 1913: m 1939, Sqdn-Ldr Reginald Maurice Cracknell, MBE, late RAFVR, who d 1970, and has issue living, Andrew Alexander Leon, b 1943, — Peter Bruce, b 1947. Residence – 4 Ashcroft, Cedar Drive, Hatch End, Middx.

The Bruces of Downhill, Londonderry, descend from Patrick Bruce of Newton, yr brother of Sir William Bruce of Stenhouse, 1st baronet (cr 1628). Sir Henry Harvey Bruce, 1st baronet, was 5th in descent from him. The only brother of the 1st baronet of this creation, Sir Stewart Bruce, also received a patent of baronetcy in 1812 (extinct 1841). The Rt Hon Sir Henry Hervey Bruce, PC, 3rd Bt, was Lieut and Custos Rotulorum for Londonderry (High Sheriff 1846), and sat as MP for Coleraine (C) 1862-74 and 1880-85. The 4th baronet was High Sheriff of co Londonderry 1903.

Bruce-Gardner, see Gardner.

BRUNNER (UK) 1895, of Druids Cross, Little Woolton, Lancashire; Winnington Old Hall, Winnington, Cheshire; and Ennismore Gardens, Westminster, co London

If thou art wise, drink

Sir JOHN HENRY KILIAN BRUNNER, 4th *Baronet; b* 1 June 1927; *s* his father, *Sir* FELIX JOHN MORGAN, 1982; *ed* Eton, and Trin Coll, Oxford; formerly Lieut RA: *m* 1955, Jasmine Cicely, da of late John Wardrop-Moore (Erskine, Bt, *cr* 1821, colls), and has issue.

Arms – Gules, a fountain playing proper, charged on the basin with a rose gules, in chief two mullets of six points or. **Crest** – In front of a wing erect gules, a fountain as in the arms.
Residence – 138 Victoria Av, Dalkeith, W Australia 6009.

SONS LIVING

NICHOLAS FELIX MINTURN, *b* 16 Jan 1960. —— (Mark) Jonathan Irving, *b* 1962.

DAUGHTER LIVING

Claire Eliza, *b* 1958.

BROTHERS LIVING

(Timothy) Barnabas Hans, *b* 1932; *ed* Eton, and Trin Coll, Oxford; formerly Lt Irish Gds: *m* 1960, Helen Ursula, da of Norris Marshall, of 17 Oxford Rd, Teddington, Middx, and has issue living, Jacob Sebastian, *b* 1961, — Conrad Orlando, *b* 1966, — Francesca Laura, *b* 1963, — Imogen Charlotte, *b* 1965. *Residence* – 24 Bedford Gdns, W8. —— Hugo Laurence Joseph, *b* 1935; *ed* Eton, and Trin Coll, Oxford; High Sheriff Oxfordshire 1988, DL: *m* 1967, Mary Rose Catherine, da of late Arthur Joseph Lawrence Pollen (*see* Pollen, Bt, colls), and has issue living, Joseph Gabriel, *b* 1967, — Samuel Felix, *b* 1972, — Magnus Gregory Nathaniel, *b* 1974, — Philip James Daniel, *b* 1977, — Francis John Michael, *b* 1982, — Isabel Mary, *b* 1969. *Residence* – 26 Norham Rd, Oxford OX2 6SF.

WIDOW LIVING OF THIRD BARONET

DOROTHEA ELIZABETH (*Elizabeth, Lady Brunner*), OBE, JP, da of late Henry Brodribb Irving: *m* 1926, Sir Felix John Morgan Brunner, 3rd Bt, who *d* 1982. *Residence* – Greys Court, Henley-on-Thames, Oxon RG9 4PG.

COLLATERAL BRANCHES LIVING

Issue of late Daniel Felix Brodribb Brunner, 3rd son of 3rd baronet, *b* 1933, *d* 1976: *m* 1959, Helen Elizabeth, of Clayhill, Stoke Row, Henley-on-Thames, Oxon (who *m* 2ndly, 1981, Douglas Mitchell), only da of James Alan Price, FRCP, of Heaton, Bradford:—
Rupert James Brodribb, *b* 1961. —— Piers Daniel Carlyle, *b* 1967. —— Rachel Elizabeth, *b* 1962: *m* 1983, Raymond Talbot, of Malvern, Worcs. —— Lucy Charlotte, *b* 1964: *m* 1992, James R. Anderson, of 42 Clifton Gdns, Maida Vale, W9 1AU, son of Robin Anderson, of Quainton, Bucks.

Grandchildren of late Harold Roscoe Brunner, 3rd son of 1st baronet:—
Issue of late Anthony Brunner, *b* 1901; assumed by deed poll 1919 the christian name of Anthony in lieu of his baptismal names of Egbert Sidney Houston; *d* 1970: *m* 1934, Amy Phyllis Ivy (Felicity) Whittaker (The Weavers Cottage, Gorwell, Watlington, Oxford):—
John Kilian Houston (The Square House, Palmer St, South Petherton, Som TA13 5DB) *b* 1934; *ed* Cheltenham; author and poet: *m* 1st, 1958, Marjorie Rosamond, who *d* 1986, only da of late Edwin Charles Sauer; 2ndly, 1991, Tan Li Yi, 3rd da of late Tan Quan, of Guangzhou, Guangdong, China. —— Verena Hilda May, *b* 1937; MA, and Dip Ed Edinburgh: *m* 1967, Arthur Edward William Thornton, of 24 Mannerston Holdings, Linlithgow, W Lothian, and has issue living, Amabel Celia, *b* 1976, — Felicity May, *b* 1977.
Issue of late Wing-Cdr Oswald Patrick O'Brien Brunner, RAF, *b* 1908, *d* 1966: *m* 1933, Elaine (Wotton House, Wotton Underwood, nr Aylesbury, Bucks), da of late Richard Howlett, of Ambassadors' Court, St James's Palace, SW1:—
Mary Elizabeth April, *b* 1936: *m* 1961, David Arthur Steuart Gladstone, CMG, of 2 Mountfort Terr, Barnsbury, N1 1JJ, and has issue living, Patrick, *b* 1969, — Perdita *b* 1965: *m* 198-, Mark Williams, of 21A Barnsbury Terrace, N1, and has issue living, Christopher James *b* 1989.

The 1st baronet, Rt Hon Sir John Tomlinson Brunner, PC, was second son of Rev John Brunner, a native of Zurich, and proprietor of Mere Bank Sch, Everton, Liverpool; he founded Brunner Mond and Co (Limited), alkali manufacturers, of Northwich, Cheshire, and gave new building and land for the Witton Gram Sch, Northwich; subscribed liberally to Liverpool Univ (besides endowing Chairs of Economic Science, Physical Chemistry and Egyptology); also donated to the Nantwich, Winsford, and Middlewich Public Libraries, and in July, 1885, presented to the town of Northwich a Public Library (rebuilt in 1909); gave Village Halls to several villages, and "Guildhalls" to Runcorn and Winsford; sat as MP for Cheshire, Northwich Div (*L*) 1885-6, when he was defeated; re-elected 1887, and sat until 1910. The 2nd baronet, Sir John Fowler Brunner (who discontinued by deed poll a third christian name of Leece), was a Director of Brunner, Mond and Co (Limited), and of Madeley Collieries (Limited), and sat as MP for Lancashire (SW), Leigh Div (*L*) Jan 1906 to Jan 1910, for Cheshire, Northwich Div Jan 1910 to Nov 1918, and for Southport Dec 1923 to Oct 1924.

BRUNTON (UK) 1908, of Stratford Place, St Marylebone.

The incitement of glory is the torch of the mind

God is our refuge and strength

Sir (EDWARD FRANCIS) LAUDER BRUNTON, 3rd *Baronet*; *b* 10 Nov 1916; *s* his father, *Sir* (JAMES) STOPFORD (LAUDER), 1943; *ed* Trin Coll Sch, Port Hope, at Bryanston Sch, and McGill Univ (BSc MD and CM); Hon Attending Physician, R Victoria Hosp Montreal, a Fellow of International Soc of Hematology, and of American Coll of Physicians; 1940-45 War as Capt R Canadian Army Med Corps: *m* 1946, Marjorie Grant, only da of David Sclater Lewis, MSc, MD, FRCP (Canada), of Montreal, and has issue.

Arms – Or, a caduceus sable on a chief azure three pallets argent. **Crest** – On a mount vert, a beacon fired between two sprigs of laurel proper.
Address – PO Box 140, Guysborough, Nova Scotia, Canada BOH 1N0.

SON LIVING

JAMES LAUDER, *b* 24 Sept 1947; *ed* Bishops Coll Sch, Montreal and McGill Univ (BSc 1968, MDCM 1972); MD, FRCP (Canada); Prof of Medicine Toronto Univ, Head Divn of Infectious Diseases, Dept of Medicine, Univ of Toronto, Microbiologist in Chief, The Toronto Hosp, Toronto: *m* 1st, 1967 (*m diss* 1983), Susan Elizabeth, da of Charles Hons; 2ndly, 1984, Beverly Anne Freedman, and has issue living (by 1st *m*), Douglas Lauder, *b* 1968, — Jennifer Anne, *b* 1971, — (by 2nd *m*) Robert James, *b* 1987. *Residence* – 7 Blaine Drive, Don Mills, Ont M3B 2G3, Canada.

DAUGHTER LIVING

Nancy Elizabeth, *b* 1949: *m* 1977, Ian Willson.

SISTER LIVING

Ethel Alice Bonsall (1765 Vernon St, Halifax, Nova Scotia, Canada), *b* 1918: *m* 1942, Ralph Hoskins.

The 1st baronet, Sir (Thomas) Lauder Brunton, MD, DSc, FRS, FRCP, LLD, was an eminent Consulting Physician. The 2nd baronet, Sir (James) Stopford (Lauder) Brunton, was a Mining Geologist.

Buchan-Hepburn, see Hepburn.

BUCHANAN (UK) 1878, of Dunburgh, Stirlingshire.

Never conquered

Sir ANDREW GEORGE BUCHANAN, 5th *Baronet*; *b* 21 July 1937; *s* his father, *Sir* CHARLES JAMES, 1984; *ed* Eton, Trin Coll, Camb, and Wye Coll, London Univ; late 2nd Lieut Coldstream Gds; farmer, Chartered Surveyor and Co Dir; High Sheriff Notts 1976, DL 1985, and Lord Lieut 1991; Chm Bd of Visitors, HM Prison, Ranby 1983: *m* 1966, Belinda Jane Virginia (JP Notts), da of Donald Colquhoun Maclean, of Thurloe Sq, SW7, and widow of Gresham N. Vaughan, and has issue.

Arms – Or, a lion rampant sable between two otters' heads erased in chief proper and a cinque-foil in base of the second, all within a double tressure flory counter flory of the last. **Crest** – An armed dexter hand holding a cap of dignity purpure, the facings ermine. **Supporters** – *Dexter*, a falcon wings elevated and addorsed proper, belled and beaked or; *sinister*, a gryphon sable; each charged on the breast with two branches of laurel conjoined or.
Residence – Hodsock Priory, Blyth, Worksop, Notts S81 0TY.

SON LIVING

GEORGE CHARLES MELLISH, *b* 27 Jan 1975.

DAUGHTER LIVING

Laura Evelyn, *b* 1967: *m* 1992, A. James Mayes, yr son of Brig Andrew Mayes, of Kensington, W8.

BROTHER LIVING

Hugh Charles Stanley (The Manor House, Little Milton, Oxon), *b* 1942; *ed* Eton, and McGill Univ, Canada; solicitor; Member of Oxfordshire CC 1985-89: *m* 1969, Nony Caroline Vatcher, da of Lt-Col John Johnston Dingwall, DSO, of Lyford Grange, Lyford, Oxon (*see* V Galway, colls, 1985 Edn), and has issue living, James Iain Stanley, *b* 1974, — Clarissa Victoria Rosamund, *b* 1972, — Arabella Patricia Dingwall, *b* 1981.

SISTERS LIVING

Georgina Mary Gabrielle, *b* (Dec) 1932: *m* 1966, Michael Denzil Grierson Clayton, of 6 Cobden Cres, Edinburgh, who *d* 1991, and has issue living, Roger Lancelot, *b* 1969, — Harriet Beatrix Evelyn, *b* 1971. —— Constance Carolyn, *b* 1934: *m* 1961, Hugh John Alexander Lindsay, of The Old Rectory, Litton Cheney, nr Dorchester, Dorset DT2 9AH (*see* E Crawford). This family descends from Archibald Buchanan of Auchintorlie, Dunbartonshire (a cadet of Buchanan of Leny), whose yst son Andrew was grandfather of the 1st baronet, Rt Hon Sir Andrew Buchanan, successively Ambassador at Berlin, St Petersburg and Vienna. The 4th baronet, Sir Charles James, was High Sheriff of Notts 1962 and County Commr for Notts of Boy Scouts Assocn 1949-62.

Buchanan-Jardine, see Jardine.

LEITH-BUCHANAN (GB) 1775, of Burgh St Peter, Norfolk

Sir CHARLES ALEXANDER JAMES LEITH-BUCHANAN, 7th *Baronet*; only son of late John Wellesley Macdonald Leith-Buchanan, el son of James Macdonald Buchanan Leith-Buchanan, 3rd son of 4th baronet, *b* 1 Sept 1939; *s* his kinsman, Sir GEORGE HECTOR MACDONALD, 1973; Pres United Business Machines Inc since 1978: *m* 1962 (*m diss* 1987), Marianne, da of Col Earle Wellington Kelly, and has issue.

Arms – Quarterly: 1st and 4th or, a cross-crosslet fitchée sable, between three crescents in chief and as many fusils in base gules; 2nd, or, a lion rampant sable, in the dexter forepaw a heart gules within a double tressure flory counterflory of the second, all within, a bordure compony argent and azure; 3rd, counterquartered, 1st argent, a lion rampant gules, 2nd or, a hand couped at the wrist holding a cross crosslet fitchée gules, 3rd, per fesse or and vert in chief a lymphad sable and in base a salmon naiant argent; 4th argent an oak tree eradicated proper charged with an eagle displayed or, all within a bordure invected gules. **Crest** – 1st, a cross-crosslet as in the arms, and, a dexter hand erect proper couped below the wrist, holding a dagger of the last, hilt and pommel or.
Residence – 7510 Clifton Rd, Clifton, Va 22024, USA.

SON LIVING

GORDON KELLY McNICOL, *b* 18 Oct 1974.

DAUGHTER LIVING

Mary Elizabeth, *b* 1964.

AUNT LIVING

Jean Isobel Barbara (645 Chelsea Cloisters, SW3), *b* 1911.

STEPMOTHER LIVING

Isabel Sim (Floyd, Scargil, Berwick, Vic, Aust), da of late A. W. Fraser, of Birchwood, Inverness; *m* 1948, as his 2nd wife, John Wellesley Macdonald Leith-Buchanan (ante), who *d* 1956.

WIDOW LIVING OF SIXTH BARONET

BARBARA (*Barbara, Lady Leith-Buchanan*), da of Willard Phelps Leshure, of Springfield, Mass, USA: *m* 1933, Sir George Hector Macdonald Leith-Buchanan, 6th Bt, who *d* 1973.

COLLATERAL BRANCHES LIVING

Granddaughter of late Charles John Leith-Buchanan (infra):—
Issue of late Thomas Wellesley Macdonald Leith-Buchanan, *b* 1907, *d* 1967: *m* 1932, Mary C. (100 Sulphur Springs Rd, Ancaster, Ont, Canada), da of late Allan J. Cameron, Bar-at-law, of Halifax, Nova Scotia:—
Eleanor Clare, *b* 1935: *m* 1955, William Hugh Shaw, and has issue living.

Issue of late Charles John Leith-Buchanan, 4th son of 4th baronet, *b* 1875, *d* 1948: *m* 1905, Mary Eleanor, who *d* 1946, da of William Farmer, of Ancaster, Ontario, Canada:—
Mary Elizabeth Warburton, *b* 1911. *Residence* – —
The family, of considerable antiquity in Scotland, is in direct descent from William Leith, Provost of Aberdeen 1350. The 1st baronet, Sir Alexander Leith, was Lieut-Col 88th Foot; his father was killed while commanding artillery at siege of Havannah, 1763. The 3rd baronet, Sir Alexander Wellesley William Leith, *m* Jemima, da of Hector Macdonald Buchanan, and their son, Sir George Hector, 4th baronet assumed the additional surname of Buchanan 1877.

Buckworth-Herne-Soame, see Soame.

WILLIAMS-BULKELEY (E) 1661, of Penrhyn, Caernarvonshire

Sir RICHARD THOMAS WILLIAMS-BULKELEY, 14th *Baronet*, *b* 25 May 1939; *s* his father, *Lt-Col Sir* RICHARD HARRY DAVID, 1992; *ed* Eton; Capt Welsh Gds 1963; High Sheriff Gwynedd 1993; FRICS: *m* 1964, Sarah Susan, eldest da of late Rt Hon Lord Justice (Sir Henry Josceline) Phillimore, OBE, and has issue.

𝔄rms – Quarterly: 1st and 4th, sable a chevron between three bulls' heads cabossed argent; a canton ermine, *Bulkeley*; 2nd and 3rd, gules, a chevron ermine between three men's heads couped in profile proper, *Williams*. Crest – 1st, out of a ducal coronet a bull's head argent, horned or, charged with a cheron sable; 2nd, a stag's head cabossed argent.
Seat – Baron Hill, Beaumaris, Anglesey. *Residence* – Red Hill, Beaumaris, Anglesey LL58 8YS.

SONS LIVING

RICHARD HUGH, *b* 8 July 1968; *ed* Eton, and Reading Univ (BSc). —— Harry David, *b* (twin) 1968; *ed* Eton, and Manchester Univ (BA).

DAUGHTER LIVING

Victoria Mary, *b* 1973; *ed* St Mary's, Wantage.

BROTHER LIVING

Michael (Pigeon Hill, Lilley Bottom, nr Luton, Beds LU2 8NH), *b* 1943; *ed* Eton; Lt Welsh Gds; insurance broker: *m* 1968, Ellen-Marie, eldest da of late L— Falkum-Hansen, of Oslo, Norway, and has issue living, James, *b* 1970; *ed* Rugby, and Reading Univ (BSc), — David Haakon, *b* 1973; *ed* Eton.

COLLATERAL BRANCH LIVING

Granddaughter of late Maj Arthur Wellesley Williams, 3rd son of 9th baronet:—
Issue of late Rupert Owain Glendwr Williams, *b* 1886, *d* 1939: *m* 1899, Marion Winkworth, who *d* 1937, only child of late Henry Hammond, of Duncton, Sussex:—
Sylvia Mary *b* 1905.
This family descends in the male line, as did the House of Tudor, from Ednyfed Vychan, Chief Minister of Llywelyn the Great. William ap Griffith, of Cochwillan, Caernarvonshire, 10th in descent, assisted Henry VII at Bosworth. His son William Williams was the first to adopt that surname. His great-great-grandson, Sir Griffith Williams, of Penrhyn (nephew of John Williams, Archbishop of York), was *cr* a baronet by Cromwell 1658 and by Charles II 1661. Sir Richard Bulkeley Williams, 10th Bt, assumed the additional surname of Bulkeley in 1826 on succeeding to the estates of Viscount Bulkeley.

BULL (UK) 1922, of Hammersmith, co London

Sir SIMEON GEORGE BULL, 4th *Baronet*; *b* 1 Aug 1934; *s* his father, *Sir* GEORGE, 1986; *ed* Eton, Innsbruck, and Paris; admitted a solicitor 1959; sr partner in the legal firm of Bull & Bull, 199 Piccadilly, W1; Hon Solicitor to Standing Council of the Baronetage: *m* 1961, Annick Elisabeth Renee Genevieve, yr da of late Louis Bresson, of Chateau des Masselins, Chandai, Orne, France, and has issue.

𝔄rms – Sable, three astronomical signs of Taurus or. Crest – A bull's head cabossed sable, charged on the forehead with the sign of the Taurus as in the arms.
Residences – Oakwood, Island Rd, Sturry, Kent; Pen Enez, Tremeoc, Finistère, France. *Club* – Royal Thames Yacht, MCC.

SON LIVING

STEPHEN LOUIS, *b* 5 April 1966; *ed* Downside, and Slough Coll of Computer Technology.

DAUGHTERS LIVING

Jacqueline-Hester, *b* 1964. —— Sophia Ann, *b* 1971.

SISTER LIVING

Charlotte Sophia, *b* 1938; *ed* Roedean, and at Emma Willard Sch, New York: *m* 1964, Christopher Adney Walter Gibbons, of 4 Hammersmith Terr, W6, son of late Adney Walter Gibbons, and has issue living, Sybil Jemima, *b* 1965, — Georgina Loveday, *b* 1967.

UNCLE LIVING (*son of 1st baronet*)

Anthony, CBE, *b* 1908; *ed* Gresham Sch, Holt, and Magdalene Coll, Camb (MA); Col late RE; Transport Consultant; Vice-Chm of London Transport Exec 1965-71 (Pres of Inst of Transport 1960-70), and a CStJ; Transport Div Control Commr for Germany (British Element), Berlin 1945-46; 1939-45 War (American Bronze Star); OBE (Mil) 1944, CBE (Civil) 1968: *m* 1946, Barbara, who *d* 1947, da of Peter Donovan, of Great Banks, Rye, Sussex, and has issue living, Caroline (*Lady Chichester-Clark*), *b* 1947: *m* 1974, as his 2nd wife, Sir Robert Chichester-Clark (M Donegall, colls), and has issue living,

Adam Tamniarn *b* 1975, Thomas Finn *b* 1976. *Residence* – 35 Clareville Grove, SW7 5AU. *Club* – United Oxford and Cambridge Univ.

The 1st baronet, Rt Hon Sir William (James) Bull, FSA, was senior partner in the firm of Bull & Bull, solicitors, of 3 Stone Buildings, Lincoln's Inn, WC, and King Street, Hammersmith, W, a Director of Equity and Law Life Assurance Co, and of Siemens, Ltd, Pres of Council of Roy Albert Hall, Hon Solicitor to League of Mercy, and to Roy So of St George, first Hon Freeman of Hammersmith, and Maltravers Herald of Arms Extraor; sat as MP for Hammersmith (C) 1900-1918, and for S Div thereof 1918-29, and was Parliamentary Private Sec to Rt Hon W. H. Long, MP (afterwards Viscount Long of Wraxall) 1902-21. The 2nd baronet, Flight-Lieut Sir Stephen John, RAF Vol Reserve, partner in the firm of Bull & Bull was *ka* in Java 1942.

BULLOCK (UK) 1954, of Crosby, co Palatine of Lancaster (Extinct 1966)

Sir (HAROLD) MALCOLM BULLOCK, MBE, 1st and last *Baronet*.

DAUGHTER LIVING OF FIRST BARONET

Priscilla Victoria; Dir of Newbury racecourse; *b* 1920: *m* 1947, Peter Robin Hood Hastings Bass, who *d* 1964 (*see* E Huntingdon, colls). *Residence* – Well's Head House, Kingsclere, nr Newbury, Berks. *Club* – Jockey.

BUNBURY (E) 1681, of Stanney Hall, Cheshire

To be rather than to seem

Sir MICHAEL WILLIAM BUNBURY, 13th *Baronet*, *b* 29 Dec 1946; *s* his father, *Sir* (JOHN) WILLIAM NAPIER, 1985; *ed* Eton, and Trin Coll, Camb (MA); appointed to the Council of the Duchy of Lancaster 1993: *m* 1976, Caroline Anne, da of Col Anthony Derek Swift Mangnall, OBE, of The Old Vicarage, Little Bedwyn, Marlborough, Wilts, and has issue.

Arms – Argent, on a bend sable three chess-rooks of the field. Crest – Two swords saltire-wise through the mouth of a leopard's face or, the blades proper, hilted and pommelled gold.
Residence – Naunton Hall, Rendlesham, Woodbridge, Suffolk IP12 2RD.

SONS LIVING

HENRY MICHAEL NAPIER, *b* 4 March 1980. —— Edward Peter, *b* 1986.

DAUGHTER LIVING

Katherine Rosemary, *b* 1978.

BROTHERS LIVING

Charles Thomas (22 Balham Park Rd, SW12 8DU), *b* 1950; *ed* Radley, and RAC, Cirencester: *m* 1st, 1971 (*m diss* 1985), Sarah Elizabeth, eldest da of William D. Hancock, of Sherborne Hall, King's Lynn, Norfolk; 2ndly, 1986, Amanda Carol, yr da of John Richard Daniel Green (*see* B Bicester), and has issue living (by 1st *m*), Emma Sarah, *b* 1973, — Rebecca Louise, *b* 1974, — Venetia Alice, *b* 1978, — (by 2nd *m*) James William Rufus, *b* 1989, — Dominic John Frederick, *b* 1990, — Augusta Jane, *b* 1991. —— Christopher Henry, *b* (twin) 1950; *ed* Radley: *m* 1988, Mrs Amanda M. B. Greenwell, elder da of H. E. R. Stewart, MC, of Paulton's Sq, SW3, and formerly wife of Timothy Smallwood. *Residence* – 5 The Benthills, Thorpness, Suffolk.

AUNT LIVING (*Daughter of 11th baronet*)

Margaret Elinor, *b* 1918: *m* 1945, Lt-Col James Michael Heigham Royce Tomkin, MC, DL, 5th R Inniskilling Dragoon Gds, of Red House, Wissett, Halesworth, Suffolk, and has issue living, Alastair Peter Royce, *b* 1949, — Richard James Royce, *b* 1951, — Caroline Susan (*Hon Mrs David Brougham*), *b* 1947: *m* 1st, 1967 (*m diss* 1976), Julian Dixon, of Grantham, Lincs; 2ndly, 1977, Hon David Peter Brougham (*see* B Brougham and Vaux).

WIDOW LIVING OF TWELFTH BARONET

MARGARET PAMELA (*Pamela, Lady Bunbury*), da of late Thomas Alexander Sutton (*see* Sutton, Bt, colls): *m* 1940, Sir (John) William Napier Bunbury, 12th Bt, who *d* 1985. *Residence* – 9 Lee Rd, Aldeburgh, Suffolk IP15 5HG.

COLLATERAL BRANCHES LIVING

Grandchildren of late Lt-Col Gerald Bruce St Pierre Bunbury, IA, eldest son of Lt-Col William St Pierre Bunbury, 3rd and yst son of late Col Henry William St Pierre Bunbury, CB, 3rd son of 7th baronet:—
Issue of late Brig Francis Ramsay St Pierre Bunbury, CBE, DSO, *b* 1910, *d* 1990: *m* 1933, Elizabeth Pamela Somers, who *d* 1969, da of late Francis Reginald Liscombe, of Lansoar House, Lansoar, Monmouthshire:—
Charles Napier St Pierre, MBE (HQ Berlin and Signals Regt, BFPO 45), *b* 1941; *ed* Rugby; Maj Duke of Wellington's Regt, N Ireland 1974; MBE (Mil) 1974: *m* 1977, Veronica Evelyn, only da of Capt Peter Evelyn Fanshawe, CBE, DSC, RN (*see* E Lindsay and Abingdon, colls), and has issue living, William Francis St Pierre, *b* 1982, — Victoria Elizabeth St Pierre, *b* 1979. —— Ann Geraldine St Pierre, *b* 1934: *m* 1978, Roland Ernest Bird, CBE, of 22 Coneydale, Welwyn Garden City, Herts.

Grandson of late Lt-Col William St Pierre Bunbury (ante):—

Issue of late Brig Noel Louis St Pierre Bunbury, DSO, *b* 1890, *d* 1971: *m* 1923, Iris Graham, who *d* 1965, da of James Baird Whitelaw, of N Berwick:—
David St Pierre (1 Hazelwood Rd, Hale, Cheshire), *b* 1926; *ed* Imperial Coll of Science and Tech, London (PhD, BSc).

This family traces its origin to a yr branch of the Norman house of St Pierre. From Hugh Lupus, second Norman Earl of Chester, the family obtained the manor of Bunbury in Cheshire. David de Bunbury, 7th in descent from St Pierre, acquired by marriage, *temp* Edward III, the lordship of Stanney, which the family possessed until 1859. 11th in descent from David de Bunbury was Sir Thomas, the 1st baronet. The 6th baronet, Sir Thomas Charles, was forty-three years MP for Suffolk. The 7th baronet, Lieut-Gen Sir Henry Edward, KCB, sat as MP for Suffolk, and was Under-Sec of State for War 1809-16. Sir Edward Herbert Bunbury, 9th baronet, was MP for Bury St Edmunds (*L*) 1847-52.

RICHARDSON-BUNBURY (I) 1787, of Augher, co Tyrone

Lt Cmdr *Sir* (RICHARD DAVID) MICHAEL RICHARDSON-BUNBURY, RN, 5th *Baronet*, el son of late Richard Richardson-Bunbury, 2nd son of late Moutray Frederic Richardson-Bunbury, 2nd son of late William Richardson-Bunbury, 2nd son of 2nd Baronet; *b* 27 Oct 1927; *ed* RNC, Dartmouth; *s* his kinsman, *Sir* MERVYN WILLIAM, 1953: *m* 1961, Jane Louise, da of late Col Alfred William Pulverman, IA, and has issue.

Arms – Quarterly: 1st and 4th, ermine, a chess-rook between two leopards' faces in bend between two bendlets sable, *Bunbury*; 2nd and 3rd, azure, on a fesse argent between an ancient ship the sails furled in chief, and in base a bull's head couped or, a saltire gules, *Richardson*. **Crests** – 1st, in front of a tree proper on a mount vert a leopard's face, paly of six argent and sable, transfixed by two arrows in saltire also proper; 2nd, a lion rampant ermine, in the mouth a trefoil slipped vert, between the fore-paws a torteaux charged with a cross-crosslet or.
Residence – Upper House, Crowcombe, Som TA4 4AG.

Virtue appears like an oak

SONS LIVING

ROGER MICHAEL, *b* 2 Nov 1962; *ed* Sherborne, and Manchester Univ (BA).
—— Thomas William, *b* 1965; *ed* Millfield, and Durham Univ (BA).

BROTHER LIVING

Roger Hugh Moutray (Fonthill Cottage, Lewannick, Launceston, Cornwall), *b* 1934; Capt RN: *m* 1965, Carol Irene, da of F. J. H. Arnold, of 10 The Beeches, Bramley, Guildford, and has issue living, Robert Moutray, *b* 1968, — David, *b* 1972, — Judith Mervyn, *b* 1967, — Elizabeth (twin), *b* 1972.

SISTERS LIVING

Margaret Delves, *b* 1931; SRN: *m* 1966, James Harvey Woolliams, of Wick Farm Lodge, West Kington, Chippenham, Wilts, and has issue living, Richard Frank, *b* 1968. —— Angela Mervyn, *b* 1946; BA.

COLLATERAL BRANCHES LIVING

Grandsons of late Moutray Frederic Richardson-Bunbury (infra):—
Issue of late James Richardson-Bunbury, *b* 1901, *d* 1970: *m* 1938, Betty Winifred, who *d* 1984, da of Col Roger Gordon Thomson, CMG, DSO (Broughton, Bt, colls, 1976 Edn):—
Patrick James (Unit 33, Habitat, Great Eastern Highway, Riverdale, W Australia 6103) *b* 1939; *ed* Millfield. —— William Hedley (77 Talbot Av, S Como, W Aust 6152), *b* 1940; *ed* King's Sch, Bruton, and Durham Univ (BA); MACE; DipEd: *m* 1964, Jennifer Anne, da of L. D. Syer, of Folkestone, and has issue living, Alison Claire, *b* 1969, — Katherine Anne, *b* 1971. —— Andrew (104 Hydethorpe Rd, SW12 0JB), *b* 1943; *ed* Millfield, and Keble Coll, Oxford (MA), DipEd (Makerere Univ, Uganda), CQSW: *m* 1976, Christine, da of late J. A. Halley, of Workington, Cumberland, and has issue living, Daniel Christian, *b* 1981, — Rebecca, *b* 1980.

Grandchildren of late William Richardson-Bunbury, 2nd son of 2nd baronet:—
Issue of late Moutray Frederic Richardson-Bunbury, *b* 1865, *d* 1917: *m* 1896, Mary Capel Vines, who *d* 1949:—
Kathleen (15 Kershaw St, Subiaco, Perth, W Australia 6008), *b* 1903: *m* 1926, Guy Waterman Elkington, MB, MRCP, who *d* 1967, and has issue living, Edward James, *b* 1927: *m* 1958, Margaret Joan Kent, and has issue living, Timothy Kent *b* 1962, Christopher John *b* 1964, David James *b* 1966, Joanna *b* 1960, — Arthur Guy (Broad-Acres, 12 High St, Wick, Bristol BS15 5QJ), *b* 1929: *m* 1954, Rosemary, da of Seymour Willoughby Anketell-Jones, and has issue living, Richard Seymour *b* 1957: *m* 1980, Alison Goodall (and has issue living, Edwin Guy Goodall *b* 1987, Rew Seymour Goodall *b* 1990), Jane *b* 1955, Margaret *b* 1959: *m* 1981, Stephen Govan (and has issue living, Peter Alexander *b* 1985, Christopher Alan *b* 1987), Susan *b* 1962, Elizabeth Anne *b* 1970, — Christopher Richard (90 Stafford Rd, Kenwick, W Australia 6107), *b* 1933: *m* 1967, Jane Elizabeth, da of H. H. Bale, of Kidderminster, and has issue living, Timothy James *b* 1970: *m* 1994, Carolie Ruth, da of R. Burton, of Carlisle, WA, Peter Garry *b* 1971, — John Henry (45 Herreshoff Ramble, Ocean Reef, W Australia 6027), *b* 1939: *m* 1969, Norma Joan Darcey, and has issue living, Derek John *b* 1971, Jeffrey Steven *b* 1975, — Mary Violet, *b* 1930: *m* 1961, John Lawrence Atkinson, of 106 Arkana Rd, Balga, W Australia 6061, and has issue living, Guy Lawrence *b* 1962, Thomas Geoffrey *b* 1964, Garth Piers (26 Cedric St, Stirling, W Australia 6027), *b* 1966: *m* 1990, Maria Dicristofaro (and has issue living, Rebecca *b* 1993).
Issue of late Archibald Edward Richardson-Bunbury, *b* 1868, *d* 1937: *m* 1909, Vida Muriel, who *d* 1967, da of late Arthur Heppingstone:—
†Archibald Vernon, *b* 1916: *m* 1939, Iris Jensen, and *d* 1993, leaving issue, Edward Vernon, *b* 1941, — Richard Archibald, *b* 1943, — Dorothy Margaret, *b* 1940, — Wendy Muriel, *b* 1944, — Patricia Iris, *b* 1948, — Doreen Jennifer, *b* 1948. *Residence* – Marybrook House, Busselton, W Australia. —— Dorothy Emelie, *b* 1911: *m* 1st, 1932, Robert Edward Drake Brockman; 2ndly, 1940, Wilfrid Gordon Johnston, and has issue living (by 1st *m*), Mervyn Molloy JOHNSTON (Chapman Hill, via Busselton, W Australia 6280), *b* 1935; has assumed the surname of Johnston in lieu of his patronymic, — (by 2nd *m*) Elizabeth Margaret (Busselton, W Australia 6280), *b* 1941: *m* 19—, — Copeland, — Judith Bunbury, *b* 1942: *m* 1966, Hubert

van Helden, of 62 Stanley St, Nedlands, W Australia 6009, and has issue living, Nicholas *b* 1966, Vincent *b* 1971, and an adopted da, Caroline *b* 1970. — Margaret Bunbury, *b* 1944: *m* 19—, Peter Shugg, of 88 Florence St, Nedlands, W Australia 6009, — Vida Bunbury (Augusta, W Australia 6290), *b* 1948: *m* 19—, — Harp, — Robin Bunbury (Nedlands, W Australia 6009), *b* 19—: *m* 19—, — Kane. *Residence* – 49 Clifton St, Nedlands 6009, W Australia. —— Marjorie Vida (The Sundowner Centre, 416 Stirling Highway, Claremont, W Australia 6010), *b* 1918: *m* 1940, Norman William Malcolm, who *d* 1972, and has issue living, Miles William Eric Bunbury (Unit 2, 17 Airlie St, Claremont, W Australia 6010), *b* 1944: *m* 1972, Joan Elizabeth Bragg, and has issue living, Marie-Louise Bunbury *b* 1981; also has issue, Lisa Joy BROOKES *b* 1970, — Anthony Bunbury (61 Hobbs Av, Dalkeith, W Australia 6009), *b* 1953: *m* 1975, Sally Bovell, and has issue living, Angus Peter Bunbury *b* 1983, Dugald Anthony Bunbury *b* 1987, Daisy Amelia Bunbury *b* 1979, — Sabina Bunbury, *b* 1947: *m* 1969, Peter John Dempster, of Grass Valley, via Northam, W Australia 6401, and has had issue, Anthony Peter *b* 1973, Amanda *b* 1970: *d* 1993, Amy *b* 1976, Amelia *b* 1981.

This family was originally Scottish; they became possessed of the Castle of Augher, in Tyrone by the marriage of Archibald Richardson with the da of Sir James Erskine. Sir James, the 2nd baronet in 1822, assumed his aunt's name of Bunbury.

BURBIDGE (UK) 1916, of Littleton Park, co Middlesex

Labour conquers all things

Sir HERBERT DUDLEY BURBIDGE, 5th *Baronet*, only son of Herbert Edward Burbidge, 2nd son of 1st baronet; *b* 13 Nov 1904; *s* his kinsman, Sir JOHN RICHARD WOODMAN, 1974; *ed* Univ Sch, Victoria, BC, Canada: *m* 1933, Ruby, who *d* 1994, da of Charles Ethelbert Taylor, of The Willows, Comox, Vancouver 1, BC, and has issue.

ᴀrms – Argent, a chevron sable between in chief two gads proper and in base an unicorn of the second. ℭrest – A stag's scalp, between the attires a boar's head erased and erect, all proper.
Residence – 3809 W 24th Av, Vancouver, BC V65 1LD, Canada.

SON LIVING

PETER DUDLEY (3809 West 24th Av, Vancouver, BC, Canada), *b* 20 June 1942: *m* 1967, Peggy Marilyn, da of Kenneth Anderson, of Ladner, BC, and has issue living, John Peter, *b* 1975, — Kathleen Jean, *b* 1973.

ADOPTED DAUGHTER LIVING OF FOURTH BARONET

Alexandra Louise, *b* 1970.

DAUGHTER LIVING OF THIRD BARONET

Susan Woodman, *b* 1927: *m* 1949, Michael Deric Lloyd Pearson, and has issue living, Robert Lloyd, *b* 1954, — Teresa Ann, *b* 1951, — Kate Alexandra, *b* 1959. *Residence* – Broughton, 104 Coombe Lane West, Kingston upon Thames, Surrey.

DAUGHTER LIVING OF SECOND BARONET

Alva Grace Woodman, *b* 1913: *m* 1935, Gerald Rudall Holman, who *d* 1969, and has had issue, Rodney Woodman, *b* 1942: *m* 1973, Jill Andrew, and *d* 1976, — Carol Woodman, *b* 1938: *m* 1961, John Humphrey Beattie, of Willow House, Blundel Lane, Stoke D'Abernon, Surrey, and has issue living, Fiona Ann *b* 1962: *m* 1987, Philip Blood, — Nicola Jane *b* 1966. *Residence* – White Lodge, Elmstead Rd, W Byfleet, Surrey.

WIDOW LIVING OF THIRD BARONET

JOAN ELIZABETH (HAMILTON) (*Joan, Lady Burbidge*) (7 Willows Court, Pangbourne, Reading), da of Ernest Reginald Moxey, of London, formerly wife of late Leslie Montagu (Jack) Hamilton: *m* 1946, as his 2nd wife, Sir Richard Grant Woodman Burbidge, 3rd baronet, who *d* 1966.

WIDOW LIVING OF FOURTH BARONET

BENITA ROXANE (*Benita, Lady Burbidge*) (Albury Farmhouse, Draycot, Tiddington, Oxon OX9 2LY), da of late Adrian Willem Mosselmans, of Ascot, Berks: *m* 1956, Sir John Richard Woodman Burbidge, 4th baronet, who *d* 1974.

The 1st baronet, Sir Richard Burbidge, was Managing Director of Harrods (Limited), of Knightsbridge, SW, Joint Managing Director of Harrods (Buenos Aires) Limited, Chm of Dickins and Jones (Limited), a Director of Hudson's Bay Co, and a Member of Advisory Board of Ministry of Munitions.

BURDETT (E) 1665, of Burthwaite, Yorkshire

Sir SAVILE AYLMER BURDETT, 11th *Baronet*; *b* 24 Sept 1931; *s* his father, *Sir* HENRY AYLMER, MC, 1943; *ed* Wellington Coll, and at Imperial Coll, London; late temporary Sub-Lieut (E) RNVR: *m* 1962, June Elizabeth Campbell, only da of late Dr James Mackay Rutherford, of Westside, Knowl Hill, Woking, Surrey, and has issue.

Arms – Paly of six argent and sable, on a bend gules three martlets or. **Crest** – On a tower argent a martlet with wings displayed or.
Residence – Farthings, 35 Park Av, Solihull, W Midlands B91 3EJ.

SON LIVING

CRISPIN PETER, *b* 8 Feb 1967: *m* 1988, Julia Winifred Gresham, yr da of John Gresham Copeland, of Church Lawton, Cheshire.

DAUGHTER LIVING

Felicity Susan, *b* 1963.

SISTER LIVING

Jennifer Joyce, *b* 1934: *m* 1st, 1952, Marian Stachowiak; 2ndly, 1970, Gordon Skinner; 3rdly, 19—, Donald Wise, and has issue living (by 1st *m*), Nicholas John, *b* 1959, — Martin Allen, *b* 1961, Sarah Margaret, *b* 1957. *Residence* – 304 Bexhill Rd, St Leonards-on-Sea, Sussex.

DAUGHTER LIVING OF EIGHTH BARONET

Constance Hay BURDETT (7 Kensington Heights, Campden Hill Rd, W8 7BA), *b* 1908; resumed her maiden name of Burdett for herself and her issue 1953: *m* 1938 (*m diss* 1952), Albert Charles Blau, Swiss Diplo Ser, and has issue living, Charles Albert BURDETT (Roncal 7, 28002 Madrid, Spain) *b* 1942: *m* 1977, Christina L, da of Jost E. von Kursell, and has issue living, Charles Nicholas Wentworth *b* 1978, Andrew James Hay *b* 1983, Alexandra Christina Coutts *b* 1981, — John Coventry BURDETT (11 Lawn Crescent, Kew, Surrey), *b* 1945: *m* 1970, Judith Lisle Folkes, and has issue living, Edward Charles Coventry *b* 1974, Camilla Rose Sanderson *b* 1984.

COLLATERAL BRANCH LIVING

Issue living of late Lt-Col Ernest Wyndham Burdett, DSO, MC, yst son of late Rev William Jerome Burdett, yr son of 6th Bt, *b* 1887, *d* 1962: *m* 1919, Hebe Etheldreda Ellen Curwen, who *d* 1967, da of late Lt-Col Gilbert R. H. Collis, of 24 Ovington Sq, SW:—
Arlingham Jerome D'Arcy (Birch Piece, Milland, Liphook, Hants GU30 7NA), *b* 1922; Lt-Cdr, RN (ret): *m* 1948, Elizabeth Alix, el da of late Sir Charles Holditch Bristow, CIE, and has issue living, Jeremy Francis D'Arcy, *b* 1951: *m* 1976, Jacqueline Elizabeth Mary, da of late Ian Corner, and has issue living, Daniel Ian Jerome *b* 1977, Lucy Joanna *b* 1979, Jenny Alix *b* 1983, — Richard Wyndham *b* 1962, — Susan Priscilla, *b* 1949: *m* 1973, John Patrick Manley, of The Beeches, Bunny, Nottingham NG11 6QA, and has had issue, Robert George *b* and *d* 1980, Edward John *b* 1981, Anna Louise *b* 1976, Katherine Elizabeth *b* 1984, — Marion Elizabeth, *b* 1953.
Sir Francis, 1st Bt, was son of Francis Burdett, of Burthwaite, co York.

BURKE (I) 1797, of Marble Hill, Galway

One king, one faith, one law

Sir JAMES STANLEY GILBERT BURKE, 9th *Baronet*: *b* 1 July 1956; *s* his father, *Sir* THOMAS STANLEY, 1989: *m* 1980, Laura, da of Domingo Branzuela, of Catmon, Cebu, Philippines, and has issue.

Arms – Erminois, a cross gules; in the first quarter a lion rampant sable. **Crest** – A cat-a-mountain sejeant-guardant proper, collared and chained or.
Residence – Lindenbergstrasse 231, CH-5618 Bettwil, Switzerland.

SON LIVING

MARTIN JAMES, *b* 22 July 1980.

DAUGHTER LIVING

Catherine Elisabeth, *b* 1982.

SISTER LIVING

Caroline Elizabeth, *b* 1959.

COLLATERAL BRANCHES LIVING

Grandson of late Henry Ulick Burke (infra):—
Issue of late Lt-Col Ulick Richard Samuel Burke, *b* 1907, *d* 1963: *m* 1930, Cynthia (132, Marine Court, St Leonards, Sussex), da of H. Darling:—
Jeremy Ulick (Woodleigh, 15 Daltry Rd, Stevenage, Herts), *b* 1931; *ed* Univ Coll, NW; CEng, FICE, FIArb: *m* 1st, 1954 (*m diss* 1962), Anne, el da of J. E. Chinneck, of Berkhamsted, Herts; 2ndly, 1963, Prudence Mary, da of H. P. Stride, of

Milbury Heath, Glos, and has issue living (by 1st *m*), Ulick Simon, *b* 1957, — (by 2nd *m*) Ulick Jacquelyn, *b* 1964, — Ulick Karen, *b* 1966.

Granddaughter of late Ulick Ralph Burke, son of late Charles Granby Burke, 2nd son of 2nd baronet:—
Issue of late Henry Ulick Burke, *b* 1874, *d* 1960: *m* 1st, 1902, Rose Uvedale, who *d* 1931, da of late Lt-Col Parry Okeden, of Turnworth, Dorset; 2ndly, 1934, Eva Mary (STRIDE), who *d* 1964, da of late Thomas Foster:—
(By 1st *m*) Katrina Marian, *b* 1904: *m* 1st, 1927 (*m diss* 1949), Guy Louis Beachim Beauchamp, who *d* 1969, of Norton Hall, Stratton-on-the-Fosse, nr Bath; 2ndly, 1950, Surg-Com Francis William Armytage Fosbery, RN who *d* 1973, and has issue living (by 1st *m*), John Louis, *b* 1930. *Residence* – Easthill, Upper Westwood, nr Bradford-on-Avon, Wilts.

Grandson of late Capt James Henry Thomas Burke, CB, RN, son of Maj Gen James Henry Burke, 3rd son of 2nd Baronet:—
Issue of late James Howe Campbell Ulick Burke, *b* 1880, *d* 1946: *m* 1st, 1912 (*m diss* 1928), Lilian Maud, da of William John Whenmouth; 2ndly, 1930, Annie Amelia Granville, of 6, Churchfield Road, Ealing, W13:—
(By 2nd *m*) James Ulick Hubert, *b* 1932. *Residence* – 6 Churchfield Road, Ealing, W13.

Sir Thomas, 1st Bt, raised a Regt of Foot at his own expense during the Napoleonic Wars. The 2nd baronet was Vice-Lieut for co Galway (High Sheriff 1838), and sat as MP therefor 1830-32. The 3rd baronet was also MP for co Galway 1847-65.

BURNETT (NS) 1626, of Leys, Kincardineshire (Dormant 1959)

Sir ALEXANDER EDWIN BURNETT OF LEYS, OBE, 14th *Baronet*, *d* 9 May 1959.

COLLATERAL BRANCH LIVING

Descendants of late Alexander Burnett (2nd son of 6th baronet), who assumed the surname and arms of Ramsay by Roy licence, and was *cr* a *Baronet* 1806:—
Of whom *Sir* ALEXANDER WILLIAM BURNETT RAMSAY, 7th *Baronet*, *b* 4 Aug 1938, is presumed heir to this Baronetcy.

The lands of Leys are held under a charter from Robert Bruce, dated 1324. The 1st baronet, Sir Thomas Burnett, though a Covenanter, was much trusted by Charles I, and was a friend of the great Marquess of Montrose. He was uncle of the famous Dr Gilbert Burnet, Bishop of Salisbury. The son of the 6th baronet, who assumed the name of Ramsay, was created a baronet 1806. The 12th baronet, Col Sir Thomas Burnett, RA, was Lord-Lieut and Convener for co of Kincardine. The 13th baronet, Maj-Gen Sir Thomas Lauderdale Gilbert Burnett, CB, CMG, DSO, was Brigadier of Queen's Body Guard for Scotland (Roy Co of Archers), Vice-Lieut of Kincardineshire, and Col of the Gordon Highlanders, and commanded the 14th, 153rd and 8th Inf Brigs and 51st (Highland) Div (TA).

BURNETT (UK) 1913, of Selborne House, County Borough of Croydon

In arduis fortitudo

Firmness in dangers

DAVID HUMPHERY BURNETT, MBE, TD, 3rd *Baronet*; *b* 27 Jan 1918; *s* his father, *Col Sir* LESLIE TREW, CBE, TD, 1955; *ed* Harrow, and St John's Coll, Camb (MA): FRICS, FLS; a Lt of City of London, Dir of The Proprietors of Hay's Wharf Ltd 1950-80 (Chm 1965-80), Guardian Royal Exchange Assurance 1967-88, a Member of Port of London Authority 1962-75 and Chm of S London Botanical Inst 1964-80; Chm of The London Wharfingers Assocn 1964-71; Master of Co of Watermen and Lightermen 1964, and of Girdlers' Co 1970; late Maj RA (TA) 1939-45 War in France, Africa, Sicily, and Italy (despatches, MBE); MBE (Mil) 1945: *m* 1948 Geraldine Elizabeth Mortimer, da of late Sir Godfrey Arthur Fisher, KCMG, and has issue.

Arms – Per chevron or and sable, two holly leaves in chief vert, in base a hunting horn of the first, stringed argent. *Crest* – Issuing from flames a branch of holly erect proper.
Residences – Tandridge Hall, nr Oxted, Surrey RH8 9NJ; Tillmouth Park, Cornhill-on-Tweed, Northumberland. *Club* – Turf.

SONS LIVING

CHARLES DAVID (1 Queen's Gate Place, SW7), *b* 18 May 1951; *ed* Harrow, and Lincoln Coll, Oxford: *m* 1989, Victoria Joan, elder da of James Simpson, of Rye, Sussex, and has issue living, Roberta Elizabeth, *b* 1992. —— John Godfrey, *b* 1954; *ed* Harrow.

BROTHER LIVING

Richard Leslie, *b* 1932; *ed* Eton, and King's Coll, Camb; LRAM 1952, ARCM 1952; formerly 2nd Lt R Leicester Regt: *m* 1969, Katrina Eveline, only da of W. Graeme Hendrey, of Snatts Hill, Bletchingley, Surrey. *Residences* – 3 Macaulay Rd, SW4; Finchcocks, Goudhurst, Kent.

SISTERS LIVING

Joan Dorothy, *b* 1920: *m* 1953, John Clement Herbert Taylor, and has had issue, Geoffrey, *b* 1958, *d* 1980, — Thomas, *b* 1960, — Marian Joan, *b* 1956. *Residence* – Braydells, Haywards Heath, Sussex. —— Nancy, *b* 1926: *m* 1st, 1948 (*m diss* 1960), Ian Alastair Sinclair; 2ndly, 1972, Prof A. H. Gerrard, of Leyswood, Groombridge, Sussex, and has issue living, (by 1st *m*), Guy, *b* 1951, — Josephine Anne, *b* 1949, — Karen Lesley, *b* 1954.

Sir David, 1st baronet, was Lord Mayor of London 1912-13. Sir Leslie Trew, CBE, TD, 2nd baronet, was Hon Col 460th Heavy Anti-Aircraft Regt RA (TA), and Master of Coopers Co 1947.

BURNEY (UK) 1921, of Preston House, Preston Candover, co Southampton.

Sir CECIL DENNISTOUN BURNEY, 3rd *Baronet*; *b* 8 Jan 1923; *s* his father, *Cdr Sir* (CHARLES) DENNISTOUN, CMG, 1968; *ed* Eton, and Trin Coll, Camb; Chm Hampton Trust plc 1975-87; Chm JMD Group plc 1986-92; a MLC, N Rhodesia 1959-64, and an MP for Zambia 1964-68; RNVR 1942-45: *m* 1957, Hazel Marguerite, yr da of late Thurman Coleman, of Weymouth, and formerly wife of Trevor de Hamel, and has issue.

Arms – Azure, a pale argent two bars counter-embattled counterchanged between in chief and in base a fountain proper. **Crest** – Out of a naval crown gold a bull's head azure, armed or.
Addresses – PO Box 32037, Lusaka, Zambia; 5 Lyall St, SW1X 8DW.

SONS LIVING

NIGEL DENNISTOUN, *b* 6 Sept 1959; *ed* Eton, and Trinity Coll, Cambridge. —— Philip Julian Gerard, *b* 1961.

The 1st baronet, Adm of the Fleet Sir Cecil Burney, GCB, GCMG, was 2nd in Command of Grand Fleet at battle of Jutland 1916 and 2nd Sea Lord 1916-1917. The 2nd baronet, Cdr Sir (Charles) Dennistoun Burney, CMG, RN, was inventor of Explosive Paravane and Protector Paravane during the 1914-18 War.

What is done honourably is right

BURRARD (GB) 1769, of Walhampton, Hampshire (Extinct 1965)

DAUGHTER LIVING OF EIGHTH BARONET

Elizabeth Geraldine (Colwin, Rouge Huis Av, St Peter Port, Guernsey, CI), *b* 1927.

BURRELL (GB) 1774, of Valentine House, Essex.

Sir (JOHN) RAYMOND BURRELL, 9th *Baronet*; *b* 20 Feb 1934; *s* his father, *Lt-Col Sir* WALTER RAYMOND, CBE, TD, DL, 1985; *ed* Eton: *m* 1st, 1959 (*m diss* 1971), Rowena Frances, da of late Michael H. Pearce; 2ndly, 1971, Margot Lucy, da of F.E. Thatcher, of Sydney, NSW, and has issue by 1st and 2nd *m*.

Arms – Vert, three plain shields argent, each having a bordure engrailed or.
Seat – Knepp Castle, Horsham, West Sussex. *Residence* – 14 Rosemont Av, Woollahra, Sydney, NSW 2025, Australia.

SON LIVING *(By 1st marriage)*

Per fluctus ad oram
Through the waves to the shore

CHARLES RAYMOND, *b* 27 Aug 1962; *ed* Millfield, and RAC Cirencester: *m* 1993, Isabella Elizabeth Nancy, elder adopted da of Michael Lambert Tree (*see* D Devonshire). *Residence* – Knepp Castle, Horsham, W Sussex RH13 8LJ.

(by 2nd marriage)

Andrew John, *b* 1974.

DAUGHTER LIVING *(By 2nd marriage)*

Catherine Anne Lucy, *b* 1977.

BROTHER LIVING

Mark William (Bakers Farm, Shipley, West Sussex RH13 7JJ; 43A Reeves Mews, W1Y 3PA), *b* 1937; *ed* Eton, and Pembroke Coll, Camb (BA): *m* 1966, Mrs Margot Rosemary Munro, yr da of Westray Pearce, of Killara, NSW, and has issue living, William Westray, *b* 1967; *ed* Eton: *m* 1994, Celia Ann, only da of late Peter Shelmerdine, of Toorak, Melbourne, Australia, —— Anthony Merrik, *b* 1969; *ed* Eton, — Sophia Judith, *b* 1974.

SISTERS LIVING

Penelope Anne, *b* 1932: *m* 1953, John Richard Greenwood, DL, of Stone Hall, Balcombe, W Sussex RH17 6QN, and has issue living, John Simon, *b* 1955; *ed* Eton, — James Anthony, *b* 1959; *ed* Millfield: *m* 1985, (Julia) Anne, yr da of late Edward Maynard Denny, and has issue living, Jennifer Adelaide *b* 1987, — Anne Lucinda, *b* 1957, — Fiona Mary, *b* 1962: *m* 1987, Charles John Martin, 3rd son of Cyril Patrick John Martin, and has issue living, Michael George *b* 1990, Charlotte Emma *b* 1988, Susanna Tara *b* 1993. —— Julia Mary Rona, *b* (twin) 1934: *m* 1953, Jeremy Fox Eric Smith, DL, of The Old Rectory, Slaugham, Handcross, W Sussex, and has issue living, Julian Raymond Eric (Balcombe House, W Sussex RH17 6PB), *b*

1956; *ed* Eton, and New Coll, Oxford: *m* 1982, Caroline Fiona, elder da of W/Cdr Gordon Leonard Sinclair, DFC (*see* E Fortescue), and has issue living, Oliver George Eric *b* 1983, Henry Thomas Eric *b* 1986, Lucy Alexandra *b* 1984, — Hugo Jeremy Eric (Ley Farm House, Dullingham, Newmarket, Suffolk CB8 9XG), *b* 1957; *ed* Eton, and Exeter Univ: *m* 1992, Sophie Diana, da of Jeffrey Hernu, — Dione Angela (*Countess of Verulam*), *b* 1954: *m* 1976, 7th Earl of Verulam, and has issue (*see* E Verulam), — Sarah Helen, *b* 1962: *m* 1987, Ashley Charles Preston, of The Mill House, Gibbons Mill, The Haven, Billingshurst, W Sussex, and has issue living, Frederick Charles Fox *b* 1989, Rupert Merrik Arthur *b* 1993.

UNCLE LIVING (*son of 7th baronet by 1st marriage*)

Peter Eustace, CBE (Long Hill, Moulton Rd, Newmarket, Suffolk CB8 8QQ), *b* 1905; *ed* Eton; formerly Squdn Ldr, RAF; Dir of National Stud 1937-71; 1940-44 War Sqdn Ldr RAF; CBE (Civil) 1957: *m* 1st, 1929 (*m diss* 1940), Margaret Edith Pamela, da of late Lt-Col Stephen Hungerford Pollen, CMG (*see* Pollen, Bt, colls); 2ndly, 1971, Mrs Constance P. Mellon, of Ligonier, Pa, USA, and has issue living (by 1st *m*), Harrow; *m* 1st, 1960 (*m diss* 1968), Julian Sarah, el da of David Hugo Burr; 2ndly, 1968, Molli Cecily Lalla, da of late Stanley Cooke, of Knysna, Cape, South Africa, and has issue living (by 1st *m*), Peter *b* 1963.

HALF-AUNT LIVING (*daughter of 7th baronet by 2nd marriage*)

Etheldreda Josephine (*Dreda, Baroness Tryon*), *b* 1909: *m* 1939, 2nd Baron Tryon, who *d* 1976. *Residence* – Church Farm, Great Durnford, Salisbury.

COLLATERAL BRANCH LIVING

Issue of late Peter Timothy Burrell, late Lieut RN, el son of Peter Eustace Burrell, CBE (*ante*), *b* 1930, *d* 1975: *m* 1955, Patricia Clarice Marion (The Dower House, Tacolneston, Norfolk), da of Capt Arthur Thomas Thompson, of Morcott, Rutland, and formerly wife of Ralph John Hamilton Pollock (*see* Pollock Bt, colls):—
Nicola Pamela Jane, *b* 1957: *m* 1989, James Donald McGregor Reevely, yr son of Desmond Reevely, of Mill Corner, W Chiltington, Sussex, and has issue living, Lucy Elizabeth Constance, *b* 1991.

The first baronet was Sir Charles Raymond, who was created with remainder to his son-in-law, William Burrell, who succeeded as 2nd baronet. The 3rd baronet sat as MP for Shoreham (*C*) 1806-62, and at the time of his death was "father" of the House of Commons. The 4th baronet was also MP for Shoreham (*C*) 1862-76, and the 5th baronet sat as MP for New Shoreham (*C*) 1876-85, Lieut-Col Sir Merrik Raymond Burrell, CBE, 7th Bt, was High Sheriff of Sussex 1918, and Pres of Roy Agricultural Soc of England 1936, and served in S Africa 1900-01, and during European War 1914-19 as Lieut-Col (CBE). Lt-Col Sir Walter Raymond Burrell, CBE, TD, 8th Bt, was Chm CLA, Pres Royal Agric Soc of England, an Alderman W Sussex CC, and DL W Sussex, served 1939-45 War with Surrey & Sussex Yeo.

BUTCHER (UK) 1960, of Holland, co Lincoln (Extinct 1966)

Sir HERBERT WALTER BUTCHER, MP, 1st and last *Baronet*.

DAUGHTERS LIVING OF FIRST BARONET

Joy Daphne, *b* 1936: *m* 1956, Jonathan Payn Fellows-Smith, of 30 Tandridge Drive, Orpington, Kent BR6 8BZ, and has issue living, Richard Jonathan, *b* 1957: *m* 1983, Collette Middleton, — Charles Herbert, *b* (twin) 1957, — James William, *b* 1958. —— Pauline Mary, *b* 1938: *m* 1960, John Embleton Cardwell, of 12 Woodcote Park Av, Purley, Surrey, and has issue living, David Anthony, *b* 1963, — William John, *b* 1966, — Caroline Mary, *b* 1961: *m* 1988, Richard Charles Geary, — Jane Elizabeth, *b* 1967. —— Elisabeth Clare, *b* 1944: *m* 1966, John Alun Kelvin-Davies, of 133 Fishpool St, St Albans, Herts, AL3 4RY, and has issue living, Claire Elisabeth, *b* 1967, — Holly Ann *b* 1969.

BUTLER (I) 1628, of Cloughgrenan, co Carlow, Ireland.

As I find

Sir RICHARD PIERCE BUTLER, 13th *Baronet*; *b* 22 July 1940; *s* his father, *Col Sir* THOMAS PIERCE, CVO, DSO, OBE, 1994; *ed* Eton, New York Univ, and Inst of Chartered Accountants in England and Wales; MBA, FCA: *m* 1965, Diana, da of Col Stephen John Borg of The Palms, St Julians, Malta, and has issue.

𝕬rms – Or, a chief indented azure, a bordure indented ermine. 𝕮rest – Out of a ducal coronet or, a plume of five ostrich feathers therefrom a falcon rising argent.
Seat – Ballin Temple, Ardattin, co Carlow. *Residence* – 18 Chapel St, SW1X 7BY.

SONS LIVING

THOMAS PIERCE, *b* 9 Oct 1966; *ed* Eton, and Univs of Pennsylvania and Lausanne; MBA, Bsc: *m* 1993, Lucinda Pamela, eldest da of Edward Joseph Murphy, of Ste Foy, Quebec, Canada. *Address* – 60 Conduit St, Hong Kong. —— Stephen Patrick, *b* 1968; *ed* Eton, and Univ of E Anglia (BSc). —— Rupert Dudley, *b* 1971.

SISTERS LIVING

Caroline Rosemary, *b* 1939: *m* 1958, Maj-Gen Richard Charles Keightley, CB, 5th Roy Inskilling Dragoon Guards, of Kennels Cottage, Tarrant Gunville, Dorset, el son of late Gen Sir Charles Frederic Keightley, GCB, GBE, DSO, and has issue living, Charlotte Joan, *b* 1961: *m* 1985, Howard Stephen Buchanan Jenkinson, of The Rectory, Willey, Broseley, Shropshire TF12 5JJ, elder son of Barry Jenkinson, of Chetton Grange, Bridgnorth, Shropshire, and has issue living, Alistair Charles Buchanan *b* 1988, William Howard Thomas *b* 1990, Benjamin Christopher Patrick *b* 1994, Sophia Elizabeth Rosemary *b* 1992, — Arabella Caroline, *b* 1962: *m* 1989, Peter J. O'Connell, eldest son of T. O'Connell, of Dorset, — Victoria Rosemary, *b* 1965. —— Virginia Pamela Liège, *b* 1949: *m* 1970, Capt Michael Cunningham, The Queen's Own Hussars, of Dolhyfryd, Denbigh, Clwyd, and has issue living, Charles Alexander Clunie, *b* 1978, — Rupert Jasper Clunie, *b* 1984, — Sophia Louisa Caroline, *b* 1973, — Henrietta Maria Charlotte, *b* 1975.

AUNT LIVING *(Daughter of 11th baronet)*

Joan, *b* 1908: *m* 1943, Robert Nigel Bright Brunt, CBE, who *d* 1982, and has issue living, Nicholas John Pierce (118 Elm Grove Rd, Barnes, SW13 0BS), *b* 1946; *ed* Marlborough; Lt-Col Royal Fusiliers, — Nigel Richard Pierce (Mildmay House, Twyford, Winchester, Hants SO21 1NT), *b* 1948; *ed* Harrow, — Rosemary Helen, *b* 1944; *ed* Lady Eleanor Holles Sch, and King's Coll, London Univ (BA): *m* 1971, Rev Anthony Broughton Hawley, MA, of The Rectory, Mill Lane, Kirkby, Liverpool L32 2AX. *Residence* – Oak Cottage, Knowle Lane, Cranleigh, Surrey.

WIDOW LIVING OF TWELFTH BARONET

ROSEMARY LIÈGE WOODGATE (*Dowager Lady Butler*), da of late Maj James Hamilton Davidson-Houston, of Pembury Hall, Kent: *m* 1937, Sir Thomas Pierce Butler, CVO, DSO, OBE, 12th Bt, who *d* 1994. *Residence* – 6 Thurloe Sq, Kensington, SW7 2SX.

COLLATERAL BRANCHES LIVING

Grandchildren of late Hans Pierce Butler (infra):—
Issue of late Richard Pierce Butler, *b* 1911, *d* 1976: *m* 1st, 1933, Vida McDonald, who *d* 1968; 2ndly, 1970, Elsa Butler (now Lee) (196 Plainsview, Regina, Sask, Canada SR3 6LZ):—
(By 1st *m*) Arthur Hans Pierce (Erickson, Manitoba, Canada), *b* 1934: *m* 1955, Elsie Elaine Laycock, and has issue living, Walter Richard Pierce, *b* 1989, Leah Jane Findlater, — Kerrie Lee, *b* 1966. —— Kathleen Enid Selena, *b* 1935: *m* 1956, John Francis Lochhead, of Basswood, Manitoba, Canada, and has issue living, Richard Francis, *b* 1959: *m* 1982, Judy Loucks, and has issue living, Andrew Francis *b* 1990, Catherine Jean *b* 1985, — George Walter, *b* 1967, — Phyllis Marie, *b* 1961: *m* 1986, John Adam Land, and has issue living, Dylan Adam *b* 1993, Nicole Marie *b* 1989. —— Sheila Margaret Eva, *b* 1939: *m* 1958, John Richard Fawcett (Box 515, Swan River, Manitoba, Canada) and *d* 1984, leaving issue, Cherylyn Sheila, *b* 1961: *m* 1980, Dennis Watts, and has issue living, Jeremy Steven *b* 1983, Amanda Marie *b* 1981, — Kimberly Dawn, *b* 1963: *m* 1983, Dennis Napady, and has issue living, Stephanie Eva Rose *b* 1984, Lynette Dennisa *b* 1986, Raylene Johnelle *b* 1991, Tamara *b* 1993, — Lorilee Faye, *b* 1967: *m* 1988, Curtiss Barrett, and has issue living, Tyler Richard Joseph *b* 1991, Taran John *b* 1993.

Grandchildren of late Richard Pierce Butler, 2nd son of 9th baronet:—
Issue of late Hans Pierce Butler, *b* 1880, *d* 1940: *m* 1st, 1908, Agnes Lenore, who *d* 1931, da of late William Edward Spurstow Moulson, of Solsgirth, Manitoba; 2ndly, 1932, Maude Addison, who *d* 1973:—
(By 1st *m*) John Edward (Youngstown, Alberta), *b* 1916: *m* 1940, Kathleen Wilson, and has issue living, Walter, *b* 1941: *m* 1968, Elaine Prowse, and has issue living, Karen *b* 1974, Susan *b* 1977, — Melvin *b* 1943: *m* 1970, Patricia Bolduc, and has issue living, Val *b* 1970, Melvin *b* 1973, — Donald, *b* 1945: *m* 19—, —, and has issue living, Ryan *b* 1981, Lynn *b* 1966, Tami *b* 1973, and an adopted da, Mandy *b* 1972, — Gordon, *b* 1949: *m* 1st, 19—, — ; 2ndly, 1985, Lee Ann Johnston, and has issue living (by 1st *m*), Curt *b* 1976, Kim *b* 1974, (by 2nd *m*) Matthew *b* 1986, Timothy *b* 1988. —— Arthur Cecil (Box 26D, RR2 Winnipeg, Manitoba, R3C 2E6), *b* 1919: *m* 1st, 1942, Joan Goodings, who *d* 1951; 2ndly, 1956, Isabelle Panting, and has issue living, (by 1st *m*) Leslie Grant, *b* 1947, — Barbara, *b* 1944: *m* 1964, Gary McRindle, and has issue living, Joan Louise *b* 1965, Judy Lynn *b* 1970, — (by 2nd *m*) James Arthur George, *b* 1957, — Thomas David, *b* 1964, — Valerie Louise, *b* 1960: *m* 1981, James Roger Merkl, and has issue living, James Roger *b* 1983, Ashley Dawn Valene *b* 1987, Selina Alynn *b* 1993. —— William Hans (Foxwarren, Manitoba), *b* 1922: *m* 1943, Betty Atwell, and has issue living, Alan David *b* 1944: *m* 1965, Linda Stewart, and has issue living, David Pearce *b* 1969: *m* 1992, Kirstine Miller, Mark *b* 1978, Tanis Dawn *b* 1975, — Garth Charles, *b* 1946: *m* 1966, Gwenyth Dodge, and has issue living, William Neal *b* 1969: *m* 1992, Bonnie Allen (and has issue living, Brendan 1989, Nicole Randi *b* 1992), Kathleen Audrey *b* 1967, — William Grant, *b* 1957: *m* 1978, Mary Dalton, and has issue living, Jeremy Hans *b* 1987, Cory Grant *b* 1990. —— Charles Edwin (Solsgirth, Manitoba), *b* 1926: *m* 1948, Marian McKay, and has issue living, Morley, *b* 1951: *m* 1973, Lexie Hodgson, and has issue living, Jared Chane *b* 1977, Mandie Leigh *b* 1975, Shanda *b* 1984, — Barry, *b* 1953: *m* 1974, Karen Pizzey, and has issue living, Jack Heath *b* 1976, Vicki Lynn *b* 1978, Charla Ann *b* 1979, Kari Dayle *b* 1981. —— Sidney Clarence (Dugald, Manitoba), *b* 1928: *m* 1952, Joan Murray. —— (By 2nd *m*) Home Pierce (Box 1, Site 25, RR8, Calgary, Alberta, Canada T2J 2T9), *b* 1939: *m* 1962, Robin Carol Boaden, and has issue living, Robert Pierce, *b* 1967, — Katy-Jo, *b* 1964. —— (By 1st *m*) Agnes Gertrude, *b* 1913: *m* 1932, Walter Taylor, of 3262, Clive Av, Vancouver, BC, and has issue living, William, *b* 1942, — Constance Lena, *b* 1934: *m*

1952, Mike Rooney. —— Eva Constance, *b* 1915: *m* 1936, Walter McTavish, and has issue living, Walter Lloyd, *b* 1936, —— Corinne Gertrude, *b* 1938: *m* 1957, Edward James Perrin, — Selina Elsie, *b* 1944, — Wynona May, *b* 1952. —— (By 2nd *m*) France Kathleen Marina, *b* 1935: *m* 1956, Garry Neil Chaloner, of 15479-93rd Av, Surrey, BC, Canada V3R 9B6, and has issue living, Neil Garry, *b* 1962, — Susan Leslee Anne, *b* 1960. —— Brenwyn Maude, *b* 1937: *m* 19—, — Klassen, of 414, 7 Av NW, Calgary, Alberta T2N 0Y7, Canada.

Grandchildren of late Frederick Francis Baron Butler (infra):—
Issue of late Reginald Percy BUTLER-FITZGERALD, *b* 1896, *d* 1983, having assumed by authority of Ch Herald of Ireland 1946, the additional surname and arms of FitzGerald, and discontinued by deed poll 1946 the christian name of FitzGerald: *m* 1930, Muriel, who *d* 1971, yst da of F. J. B. Martin, of New Farm, Brisbane, Queensland:—
Frederick FitzGerald (PO Box 6054, Gold Coast Mail Centre, Queensland 4217, Australia), *b* 1933. —— Geraldine BUTLER-FITZGERALD (17 Enderley Av, Clayfield, Brisbane, Queensland 4011, Australia), *b* 1946; resumed her maiden name 1990: *m* 1972 (*m diss* 1988), John Conoplia, and has issue living, Rebecca Frances, *b* 1973, — Jessica Jane, *b* 1976.

Grandchildren of late Capt Henry William Paget Butler, 4th son of 8th baronet:—
Issue of late Frederick Francis Baron Butler, *b* 1861, *d* 1926: *m* 1891, Bertha Florence, who *d* 1928, da of late P. J. Dunne, of Rockhampton, Queensland:—
Mabel Florence, *b* 1905. *Residence* – Adelaide, S Australia.
Issue of late Thomas Percy Butler, *b* 1862, *d* 1933: *m* 1st 1905, Harriette Gwendoline, who *d* 1931, da of late Col John Henry Graham Smyth, CMG (E Mount Cashell, ext); 2ndly, 1932, Rosabel May, who *d* 1954, only da of Capt Charles Walker, 21st Fusiliers, and widow of Sir George Beresford Butler, of Island View, Clifden, co Galway:—
(By 1st *m*) Tyssen Desmond, *b* 1906; Major (retired) Roy Welch Fusiliers: *m* 1940, Dorothy, da of George Saltonstall West, of Chestnut Hill, Massachusetts, USA, and has issue living, George Tyssen, *b* 1943, — Richard Percy, *b* 1944.
Address – c/o National and Grindlays Bank, 54 Parliament St, SW1.

Granddaughter of late James Butler, 4th son of 7th baronet:—
Issue of late Beauchamp Charles Butler, *b* 1865, *d* 1919: *m* 1896, Elizabeth (who *m* 2ndly, 19—, — Hamilton), da of late T. Findlay Muirhead, of Durban, Natal:—
Eileen Doris, *b* 1901: *m* 19—, — Jones, and has issue living, a son, *b* 19—. *Residence* – Repson Road, Durban, Natal.

Grandchildren of late Capt John Bayford Butler, RN, el son of Capt Charles George Butler, RN, 5th son of 7th baronet:—
Issue of late Francis Algernon Butler, *b* 1878, *d* 1935: *m* 1909, Dorothy Jean, da of late Douglas James Chester, of Bedford:—
Doreen Marjorie, *b* 1912: *m* 1st, 1932, Frank Clear, of Victoria, BC, who *d* 1989; 2ndly, 1945, Charles Emil Burgess, of Victoria, BC, who *d* 1971; 3rdly, 1955, Lawrence George Alexander, of Victoria, BC, who *d* 1990, and *d* 1976, leaving issue (by 1st *m*), Donald Lloyd Francis (Maple Ridge, BC, Canada), *b* 1937: *m* 1956, Anne Dolores Barne, and has issue living, Raymond Lloyd *b* 1957, Charles Patrick *b* 1958, Sharon Ann *b* 1966, — Marjorie Butler, *b* 1932: *m* 1951, Raymond Marquette, RCAF, of Fourth St, Nanaimo, BC, Canada, and has issue living, Gregory Dean *b* 1953, Matthew Perry *b* 1958, Kevin Anthony *b* 1960, Christopher Adam *b* 1964, — Barbara Joan, *b* 1934: *m* 1957, Denis Joseph Beaulac, of Fernie, BC, Canada, and has issue living, Michael Brian *b* 1951, Joseph Denis *b* 1958, Daniel Mark *b* 1962, Delvina Marie *b* 1959, Doreen Marie *b* (twin) 1959, Jacqueline Marie *b* 1960, Joni Marie *b* 19—, — Frances Rhoda, *b* 1935: *m* 1954, Kenneth Roy Suddaby, of Brentwood Bay, BC, Canada, and has issue living, Michelle Lynn *b* 1962, Liana Marie *b* 1965, — (by 2nd *m*) Helaine Charlotte, *b* 1944: *m* 1st, 19—, Kenneth Donald Charters; 2ndly, 1987, Lisle Darwin Frank, of Westholme, BC, Canada, and has issue living (by 1st *m*) Wayne Kenneth *b* 1964, Douglas Allan *b* 1962, Debra Lynn *b* 1962. —— Eileen Mary Paget, *b* 1914; 1939-45 War with CWAC in UK, Holland and France 1940-44; *dunm* 1979. —— Vivienne Frances, *b* 1920: *m* 1939, Sidney Bryan Beswick, of 411-1433 Faircliff Lane, Victoria, BC, Canada V8S 3J6, and has issue living, Kenneth Bryan (216 Linden Av, Victoria, BC), *b* 1941: *m* 19—, Sonja Georgette, da of George Yakimovich, of Victoria, BC, and has issue living, Gary Bryan *b* 1966, Laura Sonja *b* 1970, — Gary Chester (24 Fairway Drive, Spruce Grove, Alberta), *b* 1954: *m* 1976, Laura Rose, da of Gordon Barne, of Port Alberni, BC, and has issue living, Bryan Samuel Butler *b* 1981.
Issue of late Humphrey Charles Butler, *b* 1880, *d* 1969: *m* 1st 1904, Emily Laura, who *d* 1916, da of late Alexander J. Baxter; 2ndly, 1918, Helen Howard, who *d* 1919; 3rdly, 1920, Sheila Gertrude Edith, da of late William Bernard Blackwell:—
(By 1st *m*) †Humphrey de Bohun Bayford, *b* 1904; *ed* Haileybury, and Stanford Univ (AB 1928): *m* 1930, Mildred, who *d* 1986, da of late William Erskine Duncan, of Oroville, Cal, USA, and *d* 1991, leaving issue, Bayford Duncan (6350 Butler Circle, Penryn, CA 95663, USA), *b* 1938, *ed* Stanford Univ (AB); MS Agric Econ of Univ of California at Davis 1962: *m* 1964 (*m diss* 1986), Nancy, da of James F. Grandin, and has issue living, Bayford Duncan *b* 1965, James Devereux *b* 1969, Cortlandt Pierce *b* 1974. —— (by 3rd *m*) †Greville Humphrey, *b* 1921; *ka* 1945. —— Anthony Bernard, *b* 1929; Maj RTR (ret): *m* 1st, 1969 (*m diss* 1972), Amanda McBlain, da of Lt-Col W McBlain Stephen; 2ndly, 1973, Mrs Harriet Eileen Harland.

Grandchildren of late Lt-Col Charles Walter Butler, OBE, son of late William Charles Butler, 2nd son of Capt Charles George Butler, RN (ante):—
Issue of late Maj Richard Shirley Butler, Gloucestershire Regt, *b* 1907, *d* 1988: *m* 1940, Auriol Lilian Evelyn (Long Ham House, Cornwood, S Devon), da of late Rev A. R. Biddle, of Temple Hill, East Budleigh, Devon:—
Patrick James Richard, *b* 1944; *ed* Wellington, and Auckland Univ, NZ. —— Penelope Eve BUTLER BROOKE (Southwood Hayes, Chilmark, Salisbury, Wilts), *b* 1942; *ed* Ruskin Sch of Drawing and Fine Art: *m* 1968 (*m diss* 1988), Lt-Col Thomas Christopher Peter Brooke, IG, and has issue living, James Richard Henry Ormonde, *b* 1972; *ed* Eton, and Newcastle Univ.
Issue of late Brig Walter George Ormonde Butler, DSO, MC, *b* 1917, *d* 1967: *m* 1945, Pamela Winsome Muriel (who *m* 2ndly, 1970, Brig Cuthbert Grafton Moore, OBE, of Patches, On the Green, Amport, Andover) da of Dr Sidney Owen, of Isleworth, Middlesex:—
David Simon Ormonde (Britty Hill Cottage, Britty Hill, Elstead, Surrey), *b* 1947: *m* 1971, Vivienne Claire, el da of Cdr R. P. FitzGerald, RN, of Petworth, Sussex, and has issue living, Toby George Ormonde, *b* 1974, — Alice Chia, *b* 1979.

Grandchildren of late James Thomas Butler, grandson of William Paul Butler, 4th son of 5th baronet:—
Issue of late Somerset Edward Molyneux Butler, LRCSI, LRCPI, *b* 1867, *d* 1914: *m* 1902, Elise Jessie, who *d* 1942, only child of Reginald Bearcroft:—
Margaret Elise, *b* 1902: *m* 1928, Maj Philip Anderson, A & SH, who *d* 1968, and has issue living, Oliver George Bearcroft (Orchard Farm, Kirkmichael, Ayrshire), *b* 1943; Reserve A & SH: *m* 1969, Phillipa Kate, da of late Maj C. L. Stephenson, and has issue living, Philip George *b* 1970, Emily Mary *b* 1971, Nancy Rose *b* 1983. *Residence* – Orchard Farm, Maybole, Ayrshire.

Grandchildren of late Charles Richard Butler, eldest son of late James Thomas Butler (ante):—
Issue of late Group-Capt James Humphrey Butler, RAF, *b* 1897, *d* 1979: *m* 1st, 1925, Marguerite Kathleen Louise, who *d* 1938, da of John Hale, of Donaghcloney House, Donaghcloney, co Down; 2ndly, 1939, Freda, who *d* 1993, da of F. E. Peto, of Pietermaritzburg, S Africa:—
(By 1st *m*) Charles Humphrey John (11210 Thomlar Drive, Fairfax Station, VA 22039, USA), *b* 1927; *ed* Wellington, and Univ of Virginia (AB); Lt-Col US Army Reserve: *m* 1957, Elizabeth Ann, who *d* 1990, da of Harry F. Mett, of Schenectady, NY,

and has issue living, Bradford Frederick, *b* 1962; *ed* Univ of Oregon (BS 1984); 2nd Lieut US Army: *m* 1992, Kyong-Oh, of S Korea. —— (By 2nd *m*) Barbara Ann Somerset, *b* 1941; late 2nd Officer WRNS: *m* 1971, Godwin Scerri, of Malta, and has issue living, Fiona Somerset Paula, *b* 1973, — Eleanor Margaret Louise, *b* 1978. —— Isobel Louise (13 Northcote Rd, St Margaret's, Twickenham, Middx), *b* 1945.

Issue of late Edward Walter Charles Butler, *b* 1900, *d* 1988: *m* 1939, Iris Courtenay, da of late Rev G. Moriarty, R of Erganagh, co Tyrone:—

Walter Richard Courtenay (160 Drum Rd, Cookstown, co Tyrone), *b* 1944; late 3rd Officer, Blue Funnel Line: *m* 19—, Alexandra McQueen, and has issue living, Gavin, *b* 1980, — Corrin, *b* 1982, — Ewan, *b* 1984. —— Maeve Geraldine Audley, *b* 1940: *m* 1964, Rt Rev Brian Desmond Anthony Hannon, Bishop of Clogher since 1986, of The See House, Fivemiletown, co Tyrone, and has issue living, Desmond Pierce O'Brian, *b* 1965, — Brendan Gerald, *b* 1968, — Edward Neil Anthony, *b* 1970.

Issue of late Lieut-Col Beauchamp Henry Butler, DSO, Roy Inniskilling Fusiliers, *b* 1902, *ka* 1943: *m* 1938, Vera May (who *m* 2ndly 1946, Major Charles Patrick Fitzgerald, of Turlough Park, Castlebar, co Mayo, and *d* 1986), da of the late Maj W. Stewart, MC, JP, of Daisy Hill, Clogher, co Tyrone:—

Michael Henry, *b* 1939; formerly in Roy Signals. —— Patrick Beauchamp Rupert (Turlough Park, Castlebar, co Mayo), *b* 1943: *m* 1982, Deirdre Anne, da of late Very Rev John Ernest Leeman, Dean of Killala, and has issue living, Andrew John Beauchamp, *b* 1990, — Nicola Ann Leeman, *b* 1985, — Susannah May Frances, *b* 1987.

The 1st baronet, Sir Thomas Butler, High Sheriff and MP for co Carlow, was the natural son of Hon Sir Edmund Butler, 2nd son of 9th Earl of Ormonde. Lieut-Col Sir Richard Pierce Butler, OBE, 11th baronet, was High Sheriff of co Carlow 1905, and served in S African War 1901-2, and in European War 1914-19 (despatches twice, OBE).

BUTLER (UK) 1922, of Old Park, Devizes, Wilts.

Sir (REGINALD) MICHAEL THOMAS BUTLER, QC, 3rd *Baronet*; *b* 22 April 1928; *s* his father, *Sir* (REGINALD) THOMAS, 1959; *ed* Brentwood Coll, Victoria, BC, Univ of BC (BA), and Osgoode Hall Sch of Law, Toronto; Bar and Solicitor Ontario 1954 and BC 1967; QC 1967: *m* 1st, 1952 (*m diss* 1967), Marja Margaret Elizabeth, only da of late Ewen H. McLean, of Toronto; 2ndly, 1968 (*m diss* 1974), Mrs Barbara Anne Hogan, da of late Kevin Cahill, of Dublin; 3rdly, 1980, Judith Ann, da of late Harold Blackwell, of London, Ontario, and has issue by 1st *m*.

Arms – Azure, three covered cups in pale between two flaunches or, each charged with a cross-crosslet sable. Crest – A demi-horse sable, charged on the shoulder with a covered cup and resting the sinister hoof upon a cross-crosslet or.
Residences – Old Park Cottage, 634 Avalon Rd, Victoria, BC V8V 1N7, Canada.

SONS LIVING *(By 1st marriage)*

(REGINALD) RICHARD MICHAEL, *b* 3 Oct 1953: *m* 1982, Dale Karen, only da of Frederick William Piner, of Vancouver, BC, and has issue living, (Reginald) Paul, *b* 26 June 1988, — Andrew, *b* 1991, — Nicholas, *b* 1993. —— Geoffrey MacLean, *b* 1956. —— Thomas David, *b* 1960.

ADOPTED SON LIVING *(son of Sir Michael's second wife by her previous marriage)*

Patrick Colman, *b* 1958 (adopted 1971).

BROTHER LIVING

Peter Woods, *b* 1933; QC: *m* 1959, Lucia Harris, and has issue living, Hugh, *b* 1960, — James, *b* 1965, — Thomas, *b* 1963, Andrea, *b* 1961, — Theresa, *b* 1967. *Residence* – Vancouver, British Columbia.

BUTLER (UK) 1926, of Edgbaston co Warwick (Extinct 1939)

Sir WILLIAM WATERS BUTLER, 1st and last *Baronet*.

COLLATERAL BRANCH LIVING

Issue of late William Owen Butler, only son of 1st baronet, *b* 1898, *d* 1935: *m* 1922, Beatrice Eileen (who *d* 1970, having *m* 2ndly, 1939 (*m diss* 1950), Lt-Com Clive Gordon Trencham, RN (ret), who *d* 1982), da of Thomas Charles Byrne:—

Patricia Ann, *b* 1924: *m* 1947, Peter Henry Murray Yeo, and has issue living, Christopher David, *b* 1948, — Sally Ann, *b* 1950, — Murray Clare, *b* 1953. —— Teresa Jill, *b* 1928: *m* 1951 (*m diss* 1974), Robert Arthur Young, who *d* 1977, and has issue living, Robert Mark, *b* 1951, — Sarah Caroline, *b* 1954. —— Genevieve Owen, *b* (*posthumous*) 1935: *m* 1970 (*m diss* 1972), William McQueen. *Residence* – 27261 Sunset Blvd East, Lathrup Village, Michigan 48076, USA.

BUTT (UK) 1929, of Westminster, co London

I am what I am

Sir (ALFRED) KENNETH DUDLEY BUTT, 2nd *Baronet*; *b* 7 July 1908; *s* his father, *Sir* ALFRED 1962; *ed* Rugby, and Brasenose Coll, Oxford; 1939-45 War as Major RA; an Underwriting Member of Lloyd's 1931-74; Managing Dir of Brook Stud Co 1962-81: *m* 1st, 1938 (*m diss* 1948), Kathleen Breen, da of late E. Farmer, of Shanklin, Isle of Wight; 2ndly, 1948, Marie Josephine, da of late John Bain, of Wadhurst, and widow of Lt-Col Ivor Watkins Birts.

Arms – Argent, on a chevron engrailed gules between in chief two torteaux and in base a trefoil slipped vert, with a portcullis chained or. **Crest** – A lion sejant proper gorged with a collar gemelle or, and supporting with the dexter fore paw a spear, the head fracted and dependent also proper.
Residence – Wheat Hill, Sandon, Buntingford, Herts SG9 0RB. *Club* – Carlton.

WIDOW LIVING OF FIRST BARONET

WILHELMINE (Vilma) (*Viscountess Harberton*) (2 Brock Terrace, St Peter Port, Guernsey), da of late Heinrich Wahl: *m* 1st, 1960, as his second wife, Sir Alfred Butt, 1st Bt, who *d* 1962; 2ndly, 1978, 10th Viscount Harberton.
Sir Alfred Butt, 1st Bt, son of F. Butt, of Hampshire, was Director of Rationing, Min of Food 1917-18, Chm and Managing Dir, Theatre Royal, Drury Lane 1925-31, and MP for Wandsworth (Balham and Tooting Div) (*U*) 1922-36.

BUXTON (UK) 1840, of Belfield, Dorset

Sir THOMAS FOWELL VICTOR BUXTON, 6th *Baronet*; *b* 18 Aug 1925; *s* his father, *Sir* THOMAS FOWELL, 1945; *ed* Eton, and Trin Coll, Camb; Scots Guards 1943-1948: *m* 1955, Mrs Doris Mary Chisenhale-Marsh, who *d* 1965, da of Peter Randall Johnson.

Arms – Argent, a lion rampant tail elevated and turned over the head sable, between two mullets of the second. **Crest** – A buck's head couped gules, attired or, gorged with a collar of the last, therefrom pendent an escutcheon argent, charged with an African's head sable. **Supporters** – *Dexter*, an African sable, wreathed about the head and loins vert; *sinister*, a buck gules, attired or.
Residence – c/o Marinero Circle, Tiburon, Cal, USA.

SISTER LIVING

Montagu Lucy, *b* 1927: *m* 1965, John Harold Rose, of Evelegh's, Long Wittenham, Abingdon, Oxon.

COLLATERAL BRANCHES LIVING

Branch from 2nd son of 4th Baronet:—

Issue of late Capt Roden Henry Victor Buxton, CBE, RN, 2nd son of 4th baronet, *b* 1890, *d* 1970: *m* 1st, 1917, Dorothy Alina, who *d* 1956, da of late Col Charles William Robert St John, RE; 2ndly, 1957, Hilda, MBE (Rodwell Cottage, Loddon, Norwich), da of late Charles Alfred Meadows, of Rainham, Kent:—
(By 1st *m*) JOCELYN CHARLES RODEN, VRD (Rodwell House, Loddon, Norfolk), *b* 8 Aug 1924; Lt-Cdr RNVR; 1939-45 War (despatches), Korea 1953: *m* 1960, Ann Frances, da of Frank Smitherman, MBE, HM Foreign Ser, and has issue living, Frances Dorothy, *b* 1960: *m* 1st, 1981 (*m diss* 1989), Oliver P. St John, eldest son of Lt-Col Charles A. R. L. St John, of Glebe Manor, Havant; 2ndly, 1989, Henry Ellis Jones-Davies, son of Col T. E. Jones-Davies, JP, DL, of Erwlon, Nantgaredig, Carmarthen, and has issue living (by 2nd *m*) Edward Owain Ellis *b* 1991, Thomas Llywelyn Ellis *b* 1993, — Harriet Lucy (*Hon Mrs Michael Dalrymple*), *b* 1962: *m* 1991, Hon Michael Colin Dalrymple, yst son of 13th Earl of Stair, KCVO, MBE, — Caroline Sarah, *b* 1964: *m* 1987, Nicholas M. Jarrett, son of Lt-Col Michael Jarrett, of Wellow, Hants. —— Gerard St John Roden (Pitteadie House, Kirkcaldy, Fife KY2 5UN; Osborne House, Trunch, nr N Walsham, Norfolk NR28 0PX; Naval and Military Club, and Puffins (Edinburgh)), *b* 1927; Lt Cdr RN; 1944-45 War: *m* 1954, Judith Averil, da of late Hon Angus Dudley Campbell, CBE (*see* B Colgrain) and has issue living, Crispin Charles Gerard (*Clubs* - Naval and Military, Puffins (Edinburgh)), *b* 1958, — Charlotte Anne Gerard, *b* 1955: *m* 1981, Sardar Mandhir Singh Sethi, son of Sardar Mehar Singh Sethi, of Chandigarh, India, and has two das, Selina Sangeeta Kaur *b* 1984, Hermione Sukjeevan Kaur *b* 1988, — Laura Joan Gerard, *b* 1961. —— Anne Frances Roden (*Hon Mrs Thomas H. Hazlerigg*), *b* 1922: *m* 1951, Maj Thomas Arnett Hughes-Ross, MBE, RCT, who *d* 1981, and has issue living (*Hon Mrs Thomas Heron Hazlerigg* (*see* Hazlerigg, B), and has issue living (by 1st *m*), Nicola Henrietta St John (Stable Cottage, Bolwick Hall, Marsham, Norfolk), *b* 1946: *m* 1st, 1965 (*m diss* 1969), Charles Rupert Raw; 2ndly, 1975, John Latimer Smith, and has issue living (by 2nd *m*), Richenda Anne Latimer *b* 1976, Dalila Nerissa Claire *b* 1982, — Richenda Antoinette de Winterstein (10 Thurloe Close, SW7), *b* 1949. —— Elisabeth Lucy Roden (38 Spottiswoode St, Edinburgh EH9 1DG), *b* 1922: *m* 1945, Thomas Arnett Hughes-Ross, MBE, RCT, who *d* 1981, and has issue living, Timothy Arnett Ross, *b* 1954: *m* 1985, Sally Anne Roe, and has issue living, Thomas Ashley James *b* 1987, Hannah May *b* 1990, — Joanna Elisabeth Ross, *b* 1952: *m* 1973, Anver Jamal Rizvi, and has issue living, Tamara Elisabeth Shamsa *b* 1982, Carina Lucy Parveen *b* 1985, — Penelope Jane Ross, *b* 1956. —— Phyllida Dorothy Roden, *b* 1932: *m* 1959, Ronald Carlile Buxton (infra).

Branch from 3rd son of 4th Baronet—

Issue of late Maj Clarence Edward Victor Buxton, MC, 3rd son of 4th baronet, *b* 1892, *d* 1967: *m* 1st, 1917 (*m diss* 19—) Mary Aline, MBE, who *d* 1954, da of Lt-Col Frederic Ewart Bradshaw, DSO; 2ndly, 1945, Mrs Mavis Jean Fox (Kinuni, Vipingo, Kenya Coast), da of Walter Bromhead:—

(By 1st *m*) Maurice (4 Westmoreland Place, SW1V 4AD), *b* 1919; Capt Coldm Gds; 1939-45 War: *m* 1st, 1941 (*m diss* 1978), Alison Mary, da of L. L. Savill, of Comenden Manor, Cranbrook; 2ndly, 1979, Susan Whiteway, da of A. H. Alexander, of Halifax, Nova Scotia, Canada. —— †Rupert (PO Box 950, Mutari, Zimbabwe), *b* 1923; 1939-45 War as Lt RNVR: *m* 1st, 1949 (*m diss* 1968), Ann, da of Prof Frank Debenham, OBE, of Cambridge; 2ndly, 1972, Betty Webb, of S Africa, and *d* 1994, leaving issue, (by 1st *m*), Jonathan, *b* 1950, — Paul Stephen, *b* 1954, — Colin, *b* 1957, — (by 2nd *m*) Sarah Jane, *b* 1976. —— Gwendolen, *b* 1921: *m* 1960, Terence Leland Bowes, and has issue living, Katherine, *b* 1963. —— Rosemary, *b* 1927: *m* 1955, Francis Henry Alastair Julian Lochrane, of The Corner House, Mapleton, nr Ashbourne, Derbys. —— (By 2nd *m*) Rowena Clarence, *b* 1945: *m* 1st, 1970 (*m diss* 1978), Colin Woods; 2ndly, 1984, Fredrik Louis Tauber, of 125 Cheryl Drive, Hendersonville, TN 37075, USA. —— Carissa Clarence, *b* 1946: *m* 1974, Peter Ray Nightingale (c/o GPO Box 1, Hong Kong), and has issue living, Edward Clarence, *b* 1976, — Rosalind Lucy, *b* 1978, — Eva Helen Charis, *b* 1980, — Rosemary Victoria Catherine, *b* 1983, — Rowena Nell, *b* 1989.

Branches from yr sons of 3rd baronet:—

Issue of late Rt Hon Noel Edward NOEL-BUXTON (2nd son of 3rd baronet), who was *cr Baron Noel-Buxton* 1930 (*see* that title).

Issue of late Charles Roden Buxton, 3rd son of 3rd baronet, *b* 1875, *d* 1942: *m* 1904, Dorothy Frances, who *d* 1963, da of late Arthur Trevor Jebb, of Ellesmere, Salop:—
David Roden (Old Ellwoods, 55 Bridleway, Grantchester, Cambs CB3 9NY), *b* 1910; *ed* Trin Coll, Camb (MA): *m* 1st, 1939 (*m diss* 1948), Annelore, who *d* 1988, da of H. Albers; 2ndly, 1950, Mary Violet, da of late Denis Alfred Jex Buxton (*infra*), and has had issue (by 1st *m*) Roden Arnold (15 Henleaze Gdns, Bristol BS9 4HH) *b* 1942; *ed* St Christopher Sch, and Trin Coll, Camb (MA); DArch; RIBA: *m* 1971, Linda Jane, da of Richard Miller MVO, of Bromley, Kent, and has issue living, Samuel Roden *b* 1972, Oliver Silas *b* 1976, — (by 2nd *m*) Charles Benedict, *b* 1958: *m* 1985, Caroline Mavis Beadle, and has issue living, Toby Finbarr *b* 1990, Richard Ronan *b* 1992, Martin Patrick Mingulay *b* 1994, — James Andrew Denis, *b* 1964, — Elizabeth Eglantyne, *b* 1951, *d* 1985: *m* 1976, John Waterfield, — Richenda Mary, *b* 1953: *m* 1987, Michael Desmond Tennyson Barley, Walnut Tree Cottage, 61 Fowlmere Rd, Heydon, nr Royston, Herts SG8 8PZ, 2nd son of late J. H. T. Barley, of Tunbridge Wells, Kent, and has issue living, Max John Roden *b* 1989, Orlando Hugh Buxton *b* (twin) 1989, Joshua Bernard Tennyson *b* 1990, — Francesca, *b* 1956.

Issue of late Leland William Wilberforce Buxton, yst son of 3rd baronet, *b* 1884, *d* 1967: *m* 1912, Ada Mary, who *d* 1979, el da of the Rev Thomas Henry Royal Oakes, BD, formerly R of Thurgarton, Norwich:—
Aubrey Leland Oakes, MC, *b* 1918; *cr Baron Buxton of Alsa* 1977 (see that title). —— Diana Elizabeth, *b* 1915: *m* 1939, Cdr Adrian James Dent, RN, of Quarr Acre, Brighton Rd, Sway, Hants, son of Sir Francis Henry Dent, CVO, and has issue living, Simon Adrian (Am Steinberg 59, 8031 Steinebach, Germany), *b* 1949: *m* 1972 (*m diss* 1985), Brigitte Englehart, and has issue living, Clara *b* 1973, — Jeremy Francis (2 Keble House, Putney SW15 3LS), *b* 1952: *m* 1971 (*m diss* 1988), Penelope Linton, and has issue living, Simon Timothy *b* 1971, Jason Paul *b* 1973, — Gladys Henrietta (Meadow Thatch, Mount Pleasant, Sway, Hants SO41 8LS), *b* 1940: *m* 1963 (*m diss* 1989), Simon Aidan Reynolds, and has issue living, Augustine Francis *b* 1964, Thomas Becket *b* 1968, Sophie Elizabeth *b* 1965, — Janet Sylvia, *b* 1947: *m* 1976, Maj Michael Robjohn, MBE, R Irish Rangers, of Ramley Cottage, Ramley Rd, Pennington, Lymington, Hants SO41 8LH, and has issue living, Benjamin James *b* 1983, Molly Fionnuala *b* 1987, Diana Bryony *b* 1979. —— Mary Judith, *b* 1922; formerly in ATS: *m* 1st, 1942, Philip Arthur Leo Gompertz, Lt RA, who was *ka* 1942; 2ndly, 1945, Maj Clement Wynter Lister, RA (ret), of Walnut Corner, Orford, Woodbridge, Suffolk, and has had issue, (by 2nd *m*) Patrick Thomas Buxton, *b* 1948, *d* 1989, — Philippa Judith (22 Belitha Villas, N1 1PD), *b* 1946; MA (RCA): *m* 1971 (*m diss* 1980), David John Lloyd Watkins, MA.

Branches from 2nd son of 2nd Baronet:—

Grandchildren of late Edward Gurney Buxton (*infra*):—
Issue of late Lt-Col Desmond Gurney Buxton, *b* 1898, *d* 1987: *m* 1930, Rachel Mary who *d* 1994, da of late Lt-Col Arthur Francis Morse, of Coltishall Mead, Norwich:—
Andrew Edward (36 Burnsall St, SW3), *b* 1935; *ed* Eton, and Magdalene Coll, Camb (MA): *m* 1967, Barbara Anne, da of late Cyril Gascoigne Lloyd (*see* Preston, Bt, 1980 Edn), and has issue living, Harry Desmond Gascoigne, *b* 1972, — Laura Catherine, *b* 1968, — Nicola Rachel Anne, *b* 1971. —— James Desmond (23 Murrayfield Rd, Edinburgh EH12 6EP), *b* 1947; *ed* Eton, and Magdalene Coll, Camb (MA): *m* 1975, Annabella, yst da of late Douglas Collins, of Gt Missenden, Bucks (*see* Backhouse, Bt, colls, 1980 Edn), and has issue living, Jasper Francis, *b* 1979, — Oliver Desmond, *b* 1980. —— Annabel Audrey, *b* 1938: *m* 1979, Iain Francis Wauchope Buchan, of 144 Bronsart Rd, SW6 6AB, yr son of late H. F. W. W. Buchan. —— Rosalinde Rachel, *b* 1939: *m* 1965, John Raoul Wilmot Stansfeld, JP, DL, of Dunninald, Montrose, Angus, and has issue (*see* Eardley-Wilmot, Bt, colls). —— Elizabeth Laura, *b* 1941: *m* 1962, Rev William Lister Archibald Pryor, of Elm Tree Cottage, Summer Fields, Oxford, 2nd son of late Rev Archibald Selwyn Pryor, of The Rectory, Upper Broughton, Leics, and has issue living, Alexander Timothy William, *b* 1968, — Hugh William Arthur, *b* 1974, — Victoria Elizabeth, *b* 1965.

Granddaughters of late Samuel Gurney Buxton, 2nd son of 2nd baronet:—
Issue of late Edward Gurney Buxton, *b* 1865, *d* 1929: *m* 1895, Laura, MBE, who *d* 1957, da of late John Gurney:—
Daphne, MBE, *b* 1905; MBE (Civil) 1974: *m* 1929, Capt Russell Thomas Harmer, formerly RE, who *d* 1940, son of late Sir Sidney Frederic Harmer, KBE, FRS, and has issue living, Thomas Edward (The Grange, Rackheath, Norwich), *b* 1932: *m* 1960, Ruth MacMillan, da of David L. Walker, of Old Bank House, Aylsham, Norfolk, and has issue living, Charles Russell *b* 1962, Edward David *b* 1967, Nicholas John *b* 1974, Mary Elizabeth *b* 1963: *m* 1989, Neil Fraser Robertson, Ann Catherine *b* 1965, — Daniel Sidney (1106-6369 Coburg Rd, Halifax, Nova Scotia), *b* 1936: *m* 1962 (*m diss* 1980), Jacqueline Erwin, da of R. J. Moore, of Halifax, Nova Scotia, and has issue living, Stephen Russell *b* 1963, Colin John *b* 1966, — Jean Laura, *b* 1930: *m* 1953, David Ian Hird, of Thornbury, Sheethanger Lane, Hemel Hempstead, Herts, HP3 0BG, and has issue living, Alison Daphne *b* 1954: *m* 1980, Edward Evans, Claire Laura *b* 1955: *m* 1978, Peter Pearson, Isobel Rosalie *b* 1957: *m* 1981, Nigel Cooper, Vivien Anne *b* 1959: *m* 1984, Ian Plummer, Penelope *b* 1961: *m* 1982, John White. *Residence* – West Grange, Rackheath, Norwich. —— Monica, *b* 1916: *m* 1937, Maj Robert Henry Calvert, Middx Yeo, of Picts House, Horsham, Sussex (Cholmeley, Bt), who *d* 1987, and has issue living, Monica Julia (*Lady Blewitt*), *b* 1939: *m* 1st, 1964, Maj John Dominic Morrogh Bernard, Irish Gds, who *d* 1968; 2ndly, 1969, Maj Sir Shane Gabriel Basil Blewitt, KCVO, IG, of South Corner, Duncton, Petworth, Sussex, and has issue living, (by 1st *m*) Alexander Dominic Calvert *b* 1966, Katherine Mary *b* 1965: *m* 1994, Keith Bryant, son of Keith Bryant, of Borden, Kent, (by 2nd *m*) Piers Shane Basil Calvert *b* 1972, Davina Henrietta *b* 1970, — Diana *b* 1941: *m* 1981, Richard Makepeace Martineau, of The Lawn, Walsham-le-Willows, Bury St Edmunds, Suffolk, — Patricia Rohays, *b* 1943: *m* 1968, Michael Charles Richardson, of St Vincents, Addington, W Malling, Kent, and has issue living, Mark Jonathan *b* 1969, Lucinda Patricia *b* 1971, Anna Monica *b* 1973, — Georgina Sophia, *b* 1949: *m* 1973, John Richard Hull Moore, of Woodlands Farm, Nuthurst, Horsham, Sussex, and has issue living, Alexander John Calvert *b* 1975, Mariamne Sophia *b* 1978, Sophie Diana *b* 1980.

Grandchildren of late Edward Gurney Buxton (*ante*):—
Issue of late Hubert Edward Buxton, *b* 1901, *d* 1973: *m* 1932 (*m diss* 1948), Anne Hawise Colleton, da of of late Col Arthur Hautayne Bowring, RFA (*see* Colleton Bt, ext, 1980 Edn):—

Robert Hugh (60a Ladbroke Grove, W11 2PB), *b* 1933; *ed* Eton: *m* 1st, 1963 (*m diss* 1972), Helen Loveday, el da of D. M. R. Piesse, of St Helena; 2ndly, 1973 (*m diss* 1991), Mrs Judith Serena Lourenço, da of John Richard Rumsey; 3rdly, 1992, Mrs Anne Gamble, da of late Antony McCormick, of Sunning House, Sunningdale, Berks, and has issue living (by 1st *m*), David Colleton, *b* 1964, — Henry Gurney, *b* 1966, — (by 2nd *m*), Jonathan Hugh, *b* 1978. —— Sara Carolyn Colleton *b* 1937: *m* 1964, Peter James Foot (RMB 1073, Porongurup Rd, Mount Barker, W Aust 6324), and has issue living, Lorna Alice, *b* 1965, — Elizabeth Angela, *b* 1967.
    Issue of late Mervyn Buxton, Lieut RAPC, *b* 1903, *d* (on active service) 1944: *m* 1932, Carmela Mary Beatrice, who *d* 1989, da of George Herbert Lyon:—
Simon Lyon (104 Cameron St, Edgecliff, NSW), *b* 1935; *ed* Wellington Coll, and at Magdalene Coll, Camb (BA): *m* 1971, Janet Susan, da of Haille Paine, of Bowral, NSW, and has issue living, Thomas Lyon, *b* 1973, — Bennington Haille, *b* 1975. —— Ian Lyon (12 Grand Parade, Tynemouth, Tyne & Wear, NE30 4JS), *b* 1937; *ed* Wellington Coll, and Glasgow Univ (BSc, PhD); CEng; Reader in Marine Transport, Newcastle Univ; author of *Big Gun Monitors*, *Cargo Access Equipment for Merchant Ships*, and *Metal Industries*: *m* 1966 Jean Mary, da of late William Cochrane, of E Lothian, and has issue living, Keith Mervyn Lyon, *b* 1974, — Fiona Anne, *b* 1969; *ed* Sheffield Hallam Univ (BSc).
    Issue of late Mark Buxton, *b* 1909, *d* 1972: *m* 1949, Cynthia Anne Cecil (8 Walker Av, W Perth, W Aust), da of Edmund C. Clifton, of Perth, W Aust, and widow of P/O O. K. Fisher, RAF:—
Jeremy Clifton Gurney, *b* 1952; *ed* Ch Ch Gram Sch, Perth, and Univ of W Aust (BA 1974, MA 1977).

            Granddaughters of late Samuel Gurney Buxton, 2nd son of 2nd baronet:—
        Issue of late Capt Richard Gurney Buxton, *b* 1887, *d* 1972: *m* 1914, Mary Primrose, who *d* 1972, da of late Maj Anthony Stephen Ralli, 12th Lancers:—
Pamela Chloe (Wiveton Hall, Holt, Norfolk, and 25 Wellington Sq, SW3), *b* 1915: *m* 1948, Michael Desmond MacCarthy, who *d* 1973, and has issue living, Desmond James, *b* 1956: *m* 1993, Hon Christina Anne Loder, da of 3rd Baron Wakehurst, — Mary Lisa, *b* 1950. —— Marian Camilla, *b* 1919: *m* 1947, Maj Richard Peyton, late RHA, and has issue living, Robin Derek, *b* 1950, — Nigel Richard, *b* 1951.

Branches from 3rd son of 2nd Baronet:—

            Grandchildren of late Gerald Buxton, el son of Edward North Buxton, 3rd son of 2nd Baronet:—
        Issue of late Lieut-Col Edward North Buxton, MC, *b* 1894, *d* 1957: *m* 1st, 1924, Hon Sibyl O'Neill, MBE, who *d* 1946, sister of 3rd Baron O'Neill; 2ndly, 1951, Daphne Rosemary (St Clements, Rushall, Diss, Norfolk), da of late Lieut H. N. Munro, RNVR, of Rushall, Diss:—
(By 1st *m*) Mark Gerald Edward North (Coffyns, Spreyton, Crediton, Devon), *b* 1929; *ed* Harrow, and Trin Coll, Camb (BA 1952): *m* 1962, Leucha Daphne Mary, yr da of late Col Sir Edward Courtney Thomas Warner, DSO, MC, 2nd Bt, and has issue living, Edward North, *b* 1963; *ed* Harrow, and Edinburgh Univ (BSc 1985): *m* 1992, Fiona Helen, elder da of E. Nicholas Shaw, of Sheriffston, Elgin, Moray, — Terence Mark *b* 1965. —— Morna Annabel, *b* 1926: *m* 1951, Clive Ernest Arkle, MB, ChB, who *d* 1991, and has issue living, Alexander Edward Buxton, *b* 1953, — Alwyn Gerald Buxton, *b* 1957, — Bridget Ayliffe Buxton, *b* 1955, — Ann Daphne Buxton, *b* 1959: *m* 1988, Stephen Derek Pitts. *Residence* – Bryn-y-Pin, Ty'n-y-Groes, Conwy, Gwynedd.

            Grandchildren of late Edward North Buxton (ante):—
        Issue of late Maj Anthony Buxton, DSO, *b* 1881, *d* 1970: *m* 1926, Mary Philomena, who *d* 1953, da of late Hon Bernard Constable-Maxwell (D Norfolk, colls):—
John Joseph (Horsey Hall, Gt Yarmouth) *b* 1927; *ed* Ampleforth, and Trin Coll, Camb (BA); DL Norfolk 1989: *m* 1958, Bridget, only da of Charles de Bunsen (*see* Buxton, Bt, 1953 Edn), and has issue living, Robin Anthony, *b* 1963, — Jane Mary, *b* 1959: *m* 1986, Timothy James Sheldon, of 9 Gap Rd, Wimbledon, SW19 8JG, yst son of Rev J. G. Sheldon, of Cowden Rectory, Kent, and has issue living, Bridget *b* 19—, Minna *b* 19—, Louisa Margaret *b* 1992, — Clare Margaret, *b* 1960: *m* 1993, Theodore Thomas More Agnew, 5th son of Stephen William Agnew, of Oulton, Norfolk (*see* Agnew, Bt (*cr* 1895)), — Caroline Mary, *b* 1965: *m* 1989, Matthew Valentine Fleming, and has issue (*see* Borthwick, Bt, colls). —— Elizabeth Mary, *b* 1926: *m* 1951, Michael Walter Bonn, of Oaklands, St Peters, Jersey, and has issue living, Simon Michael Joseph, *b* 1953: *m* 1981, Melissa Ann, da of Lt-Col Daniel Patrick Cadoux-Hudson, of Brighton, and has issue living, Edward Simon Daniel *b* 1982, Hugh Michael Leo *b* 1984, Harry Joseph Anthony *b* 1986, Laura *b* 1988, — Sara Mary Philomena, *b* 1952: *m* 1978, Charles George Lacy Hulbert-Powell (*see* E St Leven), — Mary Elizabeth, *b* 1956, — Theresa Mary, *b* 1959. —— Jean Mary, *b* 1930: *m* 1956, Christopher Richard Miles, of Court Lodge Farm, Bletchingly, Surrey (*see* Greenwell, Bt). —— Judith Mary (Sister Mary Pia, IBVM) (47 Fitzjohns Av, NW3 6PG), *b* 1932; is a Nun.

Branch from 7th son of 2nd Baronet:—

            Grandson of late Hugh Forster Buxton (2nd son of Francis William Buxton, 7th and yst son of 2nd baronet):—
        Issue of late Philip Olaf Buxton, JP, *b* 1906, *d* 1978: *m* 1934, Ruth Christian, JP, who *d* 1976, da of late Aubrey Trevor Lawrence, MBE, KC (Lawrence Bt, *cr* 1867, colls):—
Hugh Lawrence (Widford Manor, Widford, Burford, Oxon, OX18 4DU); *b* 1936; *ed* Eton, and Ch Ch Oxford; JP: *m* 1965, Elizabeth Caroline Tilden Whitelocke, da of late D. A. Abernethy, MA, BM, BCh, FRCS, MRCOG, of Bampton, Oxon, and has issue living, Guy Lawrence, *b* 1969, — Belinda Ruth, *b* 1967, — Anne Caroline, *b* 1975.

Branches from eldest son of 2nd son of 1st baronet:—

            Grandchildren of late Henry Fowell Buxton, eldest son of late John Henry Buxton, eldest son of late Thomas Fowell Buxton, 2nd son of 1st baronet:—
        Issue of late John Fowell Buxton, *b* 1902, *d* 1970: *m* 1930, Katharine Mary (Newhouse Farm, Wareside, Ware, Herts), da of Sir Nicholas Henry Bacon, 13th Bt:—
Henry Alexander Fowell (Mardocks Mill, Wareside, Ware, Herts SG12 7QN), *b* 1937; *ed* Eton; High Sheriff Herts 1992, DL 1993: *m* 1964, Victoria, only da of (Edward John) Ronald Bennett, of Hartwell Farm, Cirencester (*see* Bazley, Bt), and has issue living, Nicholas Fowell, *b* 1966: *m* 1994, Henrietta Louise, eldest da of Richard Wilson Jewson, of Dades Farm, Barnham Broom, Norfolk, — Anthony John, *b* 1968, — Katharine Louise, *b* 1971. —— Bridget Jane (*Hon Mrs Reuben Pleydell-Bouverie*) *b* 1931: *m* 1956, Hon Reuben Pleydell-Bouverie (*see* E Radnor). —— Anna Katharine, *b* 1934: *m* 1966, George Watkin Myrddin-Evans, of Church House, Llandefalle, Llyswen, Powys, and has issue living, David Guildhaume, *b* 1967. —— Penelope Mary Albinia, *b* 1939; JP: *m* 1966, Richard Christopher Naylor (*see* Holt, Bt, *cr* 1935, 1985 Edn), and has issue living, Thomas Murray, *b* 1967, — Harriet Albinia, *b* 1970. —— Elizabeth Priscilla, *b* 1947: *m* 1976, Maj Thomas Tudor Riversdale Lort-Phillips, Gren Gds, and has issue living, Hugh Thomas, *b* 1981, — Frances Katharine, *b* 1977, — Anna Elizabeth, *b* (twin) 1977. —— Teresa Constance, *b* (twin) 1947.
        Issue of late Maj Robert James Buxton, MB BChir, MRCS, LRCP, DOMS, *b* 1908, *d* 1968: *m* 1935, Lilla Mary Alyson, who *d* 1979, da of C. E. Pumphrey, of W Bitchfield, Belsay, Northumberland:—
James Anthony Fowell (Galhampton Manor, Yeovil, Som), *b* 1948; *ed* Harrow, and Trin Coll, Camb (BA); Bar Inner Temple 1971, disbarred at own request 1983; admitted a solicitor of the supreme court 1984: *m* 1975, Margaret Elizabeth, only da of late Adm Hon Sir Guy Herbrand Edward Russell, GBE, KCB, DSO (*see* B Ampthill, colls), and has issue living, Edward Guy Fowell, *b* 1978, — Charles Robert James, *b* 1986, — Harriet Faith Alyson, *b* 1976, — Meriel Lavinia Margaret, *b* 1980.

—— Richard Moberly (40 Clarendon St, Cambridge CB1 1JX), *b* 1953; *ed* Harrow, Trin Coll, Camb (BA, MA), and Yale Univ (Master of Environmental Studies); Solicitor 1978: *m* 1979, Julia Grace, da of Commodore Frank Dudley Elcock RCN (ret), of Ottawa, Ontario Canada, and has issue living, David Mark Reford, *b* 1983, — Simon Cosmo Robert, *b* 1985, — Elinor Grace Alyson, *b* 1988. —— Victoria Mary Rose, *b* 1937: *m* 1958, David James Faulkner, Maj Irish Gds, who *d* 1993 (*see* D Buccleuch, colls). —— Lavinia Hermione (*Lady Thorpe*) (Brooklands, Wheal Butson, St Agnes, Cornwall), *b* 1938: *m* 1966 (*m diss* 1989), Hon Mr Justice (Sir Mathew Alexander) Thorpe, and has issue living, Gervase James Doncaster, *b* 1967, — Alexander Lambert, *b* 1969, — Marcus Somerled, *b* 1971. —— Lettice Katharine, *b* 1941. —— Rosamond Mary Alyson, *b* (twin) 1948: *m* 1977, Ven Anthony C. Foottit, of Ivy House, Whitwell St, Reepham,. Norwich, Norfolk, and has issue living, James Hugh Percival, *b* 1978, — Caroline Mary Alyson, *b* 1980, — Georgina Rose *b* 1983.

    Issue of late Capt Joseph Gurney Fowell Buxton, Grenadier Guards, *b* 1913, *ka* 1943: *m* 1938, Elizabeth Langley (who *m* 2ndly, 1946, Alexander Ludovic Grant, who *d* 1986, of Marbury Hall, Whitchurch, Shropshire), da of late Major Robert Barbour, of Bolesworth Castle, Tattenhall, Chester.
Andrew Robert Fowell (Bentley Park, Ipswich, Suffolk), *b* 1939; *ed* Winchester, and Pembroke Coll, Oxford (BA); late 2nd Lt Grenadier Guards: *m* 1965, Jane Margery, only da of late Lt-Col John Peter Grant of Rothiemurchus, MBE (*see* Cs of Dysart), and has issue living, Tessa Rose, *b* 1966, — Veronica Mary, *b* 1970. —— Joseph William Henry (Rockstowes Hill, Uley, Dursley, Glos GL11 5AS), *b* 1943; *ed* Harrow; Capt Gren Gds: *m* 1st, 1972, Sarah Louise, who *d* 1974, el da of Lt-Col Richard Patrick Pilkington Smyly, MC, of Eaton Garden House, Eccleston, Chester; 2ndly, 1981, Ann, da of Paul Boggis-Rolfe, of Martens House, Willow Lane, Wargrave-on-Thames, Berks, and has issue living (by 2nd *m*), William Paul, *b* 1983, — Robert, *b* 1984, — Laura Elizabeth Verena, *b* 1990. —— Meriel Rose, *b* 1940; Extra Lady in Waiting to HRH Princess Alexandra, the Hon Lady Ogilvy: *m* 1st, 1964, Robert Ivan Kenyon-Slaney, who *d* 1984, and has issue (*see* B Kenyon, colls); 2ndly, 1985, Peter Maurice Afia, of 14 Douro Place, W8 5PH.

    Issue of late Lt-Cdr Michael Auriol Buxton, RNVR, *b* 1914, *d* 1990: *m* 1938, Elizabeth Edith Millicent (Rose Cottage, Gayton, King's Lynn, Norfolk), yr da of late Capt Robert Hamond Arthur Elwes, RASC, of Congham House, King's Lynn:—
Gervase Michael (22 Chipstead St, SW3), *b* 1939; *ed* Harrow, and Trin Coll, Camb; late 2nd Lieut Royal Scots Greys: *m* 1965, Susan Margaret, da of late Malcolm McKenzie, of 40 Hans Place, SW1, and has issue living, Matthew Thomas Gervase, *b* 1967, — Jocelyn David, *b* 1972, — Lucy Jane, *b* 1966, — Caragh Susan, *b* 1969. —— Christopher Robert (Mulberry House, Little Wilbraham, Cambridge CB1 5LE), *b* 1940; *ed* Harrow; FRICS: *m* 1st, 1965 (*m diss* 1970), Judy Frances, eldest da of Gordon Hollingsworth Dixon, of Somerton House, Winkfield Row, Berks; 2ndly, 1973, Priscilla, da of Maj John Gardner, and has issue living (by 1st *m*), Timothy James, *b* 1967, — Richard Anthony, *b* (twin) 1967, — (by 2nd *m*) Edward Robert, *b* 1977, — Thomas Michael, *b* 1980, — Alexandra Mary, *b* 1975. —— Jonathan James (62 Endlesham Rd, SW12), *b* 1943; *ed* Harrow; Maj late 17th/21st Lancers: *m* 1972, Rosaleen Pleasance, da of late Sir John Alfred Picton Bagge, 6th Bt, and has issue living, Georgina Elizabeth, *b* 1973, — Victoria Rose, *b* 1975, — Rosaleen Poppy, *b* 1979. —— Charles Joseph, *b* 1951; *ed* Harrow; Lt-Col 17th/21st Lancers: *m* 1978, Veronica Juliet Mary, yr da of Francis David Paterson-Morgan, of Hospital of St Cross, Winchester, Hants, and has issue living, Leonie Carinna Rose, *b* 1979, — Katriona Topaz Mary, *b* 1985, — Sophie, *b* 1990.

    Grandchildren of late John Henry Buxton, el son of late Thomas Fowell Buxton (ante):—
    Issue of late Rev Leonard Buxton, *b* 1877, *d* 1946; *m* 1903, Kathleen, who *d* 1958, da of late Capt John Digby Wingfield-Digby, of Coleshill Park, Warwickshire, and Sherborne Castle, Dorset:—
Rev Edmund Digby (Pilgrims, 10 Pound Hill, Alresford, Hants, SO24 9BW), *b* 1908; *ed* Charterhouse, and Trinity Coll, Camb (MA): *m* 1940, Katharine Monsarrat, el da of late John Arthur Hargreaves, of Neston, Cheshire, and has issue living, *Rev* Edmund Francis (The Vicarage, Short Heath, Willenhall, West Midlands), *b* 1942; *ed* Sherborne, Trin Coll, Camb, (MA), Birmingham Univ (DPS), and Sheffield Univ (Master of Min in Theology): *m* 1969, Jane Mary, only da of Rev Arthur Leslie Jones, of Upwey Rectory, Weymouth, and has issue living, Nicholas Andrew *b* 1972, Thomas Mark *b* 1974, Asha Theresa *b* 1976 (adopted 1979), — Antony Leonard, *b* 1950; *ed* Sherborne, and Trin Coll, Camb: *m* 1977, Heather Morwenna Marie, da of Surg Rear-Adm Leslie Bartlett Osborne, and has issue living, Laura Ethel *b* 1978, — Mary Ethel, *b* 1944: *m* 1972, David James Grundy, MB, BS, FRCS (The Old Post Office, Besomers Drove, Lover Redlynch, Salisbury, Wilts SP5 2PN), and has issue living, Katharine Mary *b* 1973, Joanna Lucy *b* 1976, — Lucy Jane, *b* 1947. —— Kenneth Leonard, FRCS, LRCP (19 Swallowfield Park, nr Reading, Berks RG7 1TG), 1909; *ed* Charterhouse, and at Trin Coll, Camb (Exhibitioner, BA 1930 MA 1935): *m* 1935, Agnes Josephine, da of late Rev Dr Tom Bragg, V of Christ Church, Lowestoft, and has issue living, Paul Kenneth (Old Inzievar House, by Dunfermline, Fife KY12 8HA), *b* 1936; *ed* Trin Coll, Camb (MA, MB, BChir, FRCP Ed): *m* 1962, Heather Clive, da of Lt-Col J. C. Edlmann, of Tattenhall, Chester, and has issue living, Jonathan Charles Fowell (43 Thorparch Rd, SW8) *b* 1965; *ed* Shrewsbury, and Pembroke Coll, Oxford: *m* 1990, Victoria J. H., da of late Seth Bottom, of Killuney, Armagh, Joanna Rachel, *b* 1967, — Andrew Wakefield, *b* 1939, — Angela Josephine, *b* 1944: *m* 1974, Simon Christopher Edward Kendall, of Cumbers, Liss, Hants, GU33 7LL, and has issue living, Benjamin Edward Buxton *b* 1976, Matthew Simon Digby *b* 1979, Andrew Christopher Barclay *b* 1984, — Susanna Rachel, *b* 1945: *m* 1969, Terry William Walter Hookway, of Oakleigh House, 4, Wallingford Rd, Goring-on-Thames RG8 0AH, and has issue living, John Leonard Walter *b* 1973, Timothy Kenneth Walter *b* 1983, Peter Francis Walter *b* 1984, Rachel Lucy *b* 1975. —— Daniel Richard (Waratah Rd, RD3, Tauranga, NZ), *b* 1913; *ed* Bryanston, and Trin Coll, Camb; *m* 1940, Josephine Burdekin, and has issue living, Timothy Richard Blake (308 Fencourt Rd, RD1, Cambridge, NZ), *b* 1942: *m* 1964, Juliette Gaye, da of late C. W. L. Jex-Blake, of RD2, Whitianga, NZ, and has issue living, Darren Richard Blake *b* 1966, Shane Laurence Blake *b* 1968, — David Adrian Leonard (Culzean, 19 Lanark St, Mosgiel, NZ), *b* 1945; *ed* Massey Univ, NZ (BSc Ag): *m* 1970, Lynley Anne, da of J. O'Connor, of 10 Mere Mere St, Timaru, NZ, and has issue living, Adrian David *b* 1973, Bruce John *b* 1975, Greig Daniel *b* 1978. —— *Rev* Digby Hugh (Rosemary Holt, Edward Rd, St Cross, Winchester, Hants SO23 9RB), *b* 1916; *ed* Stowe Sch, and Trin Coll, Camb (MA). —— Kathleen Hannah, *b* 1905. —— Ruth Lydia, *b* 1906: *m* 1941, John Willoughby Harris, of Deepback, Fairfield Rd, North Levin, NZ, and has issue living, Patrick John (17 Paruru Av, Nortcote, Auckland, NZ), *b* 1946; *ed* Wanganui Collegiate Sch, and at Canterbury Univ (BE): *m* 1972, Diana, da of Ian McW Harkness, of Fendleton, Christchurch, NZ, and has issue living, Michael Patrick *b* 1978, Lucy Elizabeth *b* 1981, — Elizabeth Hannah, *b* 1943: *m* 1st, 1963, Alfred Rudolf Bernd Ehrdhardt; 2ndly, 1980, Frank Marlow, of Kawiu Rd, Levin, NZ, and has issue living, (by 1st *m*) Richard Brent *b* 1972, (by 2nd *m*) Clare Margaret *b* 1980.

    Grandchildren of late John Henry Buxton (ante):—
    Issue of late Rev Arthur Buxton, *b* 1882, *d* 1958: *m* 1908, Esmé Caroline, who *d* 1971, da of late Col Francis William Pixley, VD, DL, JP, FSA, of Wooburn House, Wooburn, Bucks:—
Nigel Arthur, MB, BChir, MRCS, LRCP (Eagle Lake Rd, South River, Ontario, Canada POA 1XO), *b* 1909; *ed* Harrow, and Trin Coll, Camb (BA), LMCC; 1939-45 War as Capt RAMC: *m* 1948, Elmira, MD, da of late William Richli, MD, of Mariposa, Cal, USA, and has issue living, David Edson (32201 Ne Dial Rd, Camas, Wash 98607, USA), *b* 1949: *m* 1974, Terri, da of Gerald Snyder, of Oregon, USA, and has issue living, Daniel Elliot *b* 1976, Douglas Edward *b* 1979, — John Arthur, *b* 1950; MD, FACS (Fellow American Coll of Surgs): *m* 1983, Susan, da of Paul Smith, of Pennsylvania, USA, and has issue living, Ashley *b* 1987, Sara *b* 1985, — Louise Elizabeth, *b* 1952; Dr of Health Science: *m* 1978, Kimber Schneider, MD, Certified Ophthalmologist, and has issue living, Jonathan *b* 1982, Richard *b* 1985. —— Mary, *b* 1913.

Branches from 3rd son of 2nd son of 1st Baronet

    Grandchildren of late Major Geoffrey Charles Buxton, TD, el son of late Geoffrey Fowell Buxton, CB, 3rd son of Thomas Fowell Buxton, 2nd son of 1st baronet:—

Issue of late Major Peter Stapleton Buxton, Leicestershire Yeo, *b* 1904, *ka* 1944: *m* 1934, Julia Victoria (Mansion House, Gainford, Darlington, co Durham), da of late Claude Edward Pease:—

James Geoffrey Pease (Manor Farm House, Lubenham, Market Harborough, Leics LE16 9TD), *b* 1939; *ed* Eton, and Trin Coll, Camb: *m* 1970, Meriel Jessica, da of late Maj Denis Cowen, of E Farndon Manor, Market Harborough, and has issue living, Hugh David, *b* 1975, — Rose Emma, *b* 1973. —— Anne Victoria, *b* 1936: *m* 1959, Robin Slingsby Pease, of Hill House, Gainford, co Durham, and has issue living, Peter Charles Gordon, *b* 1965, — Victoria Julia Diana, *b* 1962, — Annabel Primrose Robin, *b* 1971.

Granddaughters of Geoffrey Fowell Buxton, CB (ante):—
Issue of late Maj Ivor Buxton, DSO, TD, *b* 1884, *d* 1969: *m* 1918, Phyllis Dorothy, who *d* 1976, da of late Col Hugh Gurney Barclay, CVO, of Colney Hall, Norwich, and widow of Henry Cecil Johnson, DSO:—

Nancy, *b* 1919; *m* 1st, 1940, Lt-Col John Noel Ronald Loveday, 16th/5th Lancers, who was *ka* 1944; 2ndly, 1947, Maj John Hallifax Weller Poley, MC, of Boxted Hall, Bury St Edmunds, who *d* 1976, and has issue living, (by 1st *m*) Tessa, *b* 1942: *m* 1972, Andrew Henry Scott, and has issue living, Archie John *b* 1973, Daniel Ian *b* 1974, Tobina Fiona *b* 1977, Laura Nancy *b* 1979, — (by 2nd *m*) Richard Hallifax (Keeper's Cottage, Boxted, Bury St Edmunds, Suffolk IP29 4LN), *b* 1949: *m* 1st, 1970 (*m diss* 1991), Sarah Francesca, el da of John Valentine Gosling, of The Claw, Brushford, Dulverton, Som; 2ndly, 1992, Isobel Muriel, da of Maj Douglas Wade Reader, of Halvergate House, Halvergate, Norfolk, and has issue living (by 1st *m*), Guy Hallifax *b* 1975, Katherine Francesca *b* 1973, Annabelle Rose *b* 1980, (by 2nd *m*) Hugh Thomas *b* 1994, — Nicholas Toby, *b* 1950: *m* 1992, P. Sue Bond. —— Felicity Mary (*Lady Blacker*), *b* 1921: *m* 1st, 1942, Maj John Rew, who was *ka* 1943; 2ndly, 1947, Gen Sir Cecil Hugh Blacker, GCB, OBE, MC, of Cowpasture Farm, Hook Norton, Banbury, and has issue living (by 2nd *m*), Terence, *b* 1948; *ed* Wellington Coll, and Trin Coll, Camb; author: *m* 1975, Hon Caroline Susan Dean Soper, da of Baron Soper (Life Baron), and has issue living, Alexander *b* 1977, Alice *b* 1979, — Philip, *b* 1949; Sculptor, and former Nat Hunt Jockey: *m* 1979, Susan, da of Colin Davies, of Oakgrove, Chepstow, and has issue living, Daniel *b* 1982, Stephanie *b* 1984.

Granddaughters of late Com Bernard Buxton, DSO, 2nd son of Geoffrey Fowell Buxton, CB (ante):—
Issue of late Group-Capt Geoffrey Mungo Buxton, OBE, RAF, *b* 1906, *d* 1979: *m* 1929, Horatia Mary (Wiveton Green, Holt, Norfolk), da of late Adm Sir William Wordsworth Fisher, GCB, GCVO:—

Carolyn Viola, *b* 1934. —— Juliet Horatia, *b* 1937. —— Rose Vivian, *b* 1951.

Granddaughter of late Com Bernard Buxton, DSO (ante):—
Issue of late Major Samuel Luckyn Buxton, MC, 17th/21st Lancers, *b* 1914, *ka* Italy 1944: *m* 1941, Pamela Mary (who *m* 2ndly, 1946, Baron Buxton of Alsa, MC (Life Baron) (ante), and *d* 1983), da of Sir Henry Ralph Stanley Birkin, 3rd Bt:—

Christina Hermione, *b* 1944: *m* 1967, John David Millard Barnes, of 28 Bramham Gdns, SW5, and has issue living, Amanda Mary, *b* 1968, — Sarah Hermione, *b* 1970.

Branches from 4th son of 2nd son of 1st Baronet:—

Grandchildren of late Patrick Alfred Buxton, CMG, FRS, MRCS, LRCP, el son of Alfred Fowell Buxton, 4th son of Thomas Fowell Buxton (ante):—
Issue of late Martin Patrick Buxton, *b* 1920, *d* 1966: *m* 1949, Jacqueline Marcelle, who *d* 1968, da of Percival James Stokes:—

James Patrick, *b* 1957: *m* 1970, Liane Frances Jones, and has issue living, Angharad Grace Jones, *b* 1993. —— Eleanor Ruth *b* 1950: *m* 1970, Paul Hudson Stanford. —— Rachel Phyllida, *b* 1952: *m* 1973, Leslie William Huson, and has issue living, Thomas Patrick, *b* 1977, — Ruth Huson *b* 1980. —— Alice Richenda, *b* 1954: *m* 1974, Charles Walsh, and has issue living, Patrick, *b* 1982, — Brendan, *b* 1990, — Katherine, *b* 1987.

Issue of late Fl-Lt Andrew Patrick Buxton, DFC, late RAF, *b* 1923, *d* 1952: *m* 1949, Kathleen Audrey (who *m* 2ndly, 1955, Martin Francis Wood, of The Manor House, Little Wittenham, Oxon), da of late Rev J. H. Stanfield, of Seaton, Devon:—

Robin David, *b* 1950: *m* 1986, Elizabeth Holmes, and has issue living, Andrew, *b* 1986, — Christopher, *b* 1992. —— Sarah Margaret, *b* 1951.

Issue of late Alfred Fowell Buxton (ante):—
Issue of late Patrick Alfred Buxton, CMG, FRS, MRCS, LRCP, *b* 1892, *d* 1955: *m* 1917, Muryell Gladys, who *d* 1989, da of late Rev Hon William Talbot Rice (*see* B Dynevor, coll):—

Helen Muryell, *b* 1925; *ed* Camb Univ (BA 1948): *m* 1948, Arthur Robert Donald Wright, OBE, and has issue living, Simon Nicholas, *b* 1949, — Patrick Stephen, *b* 1951: has issue living, Edward Fenton *b* 1985, Nicholas Patrick *b* 1987, Richard *b* 1990, — Hannah Elizabeth, *b* 1953, — Charlotte Helen, *b* 1956: *m* 1979, George Reynolds Cannon, who *d* 1992, of Denver, Colorado, USA, and has issue living, Patrick George *b* 1984, Samuel Claude *b* 1986, — Lesley Rachel, *b* 1961: *m* 1993, Nicholas Knight, who *d* 1993. *Residence* – Mill Barn, Coulston, Westbury, Wilts. —— Rachel Katharine, *b* 1930; *ed* Camb Univ (BA 1951): *m* 1952, Christopher Herzig, CBE, who *d* 1993, and has issue living, Stephen Christopher, *b* 1954: *m* 1977, Anita, da of Johan Mostert, of Pretoria, S Africa, and has issue living, Austin Jarred *b* 19—, Richenda Grace *b* 1986, — Francis Patrick, *b* 1955: *m* 1980, Petra, da of Prof Ambrose Rogers, of Univ Coll, London, and has issue living, Anthony *b* 1990, Robert *b* 1992, — Edmund Martin, *b* 1958: *m* 1990, Ana Novaković, and has issue living, Thomas Dusan *b* 1990, Katherine Novaković *b* 1993, — Hugh John *b* 1961: *m* 1992, Isobel Oriane Clare, eldest da of Maj Count Charles John de Salis, DL, and has issue (*see* Ly Herries of Terregles, colls), — Harriet Elizabeth, *b* 1963. *Residence* – 13A The Causeway, Horsham, W Sussex. —— Lucy Bertha (*Lady Chandler*), *b* 1932; *ed* Camb Univ (BA 1954): *m* 1955, Sir Geoffrey Chandler, CBE, and has issue living, Hilary Jane, *b* 1957: *m* 1981, James A. Otter, son of John Otter, of Pilton, Northants, and has issue living, Thomas Geoffrey *b* 1983, Nicholas *b* 1990, — Sarah Elizabeth, *b* 1959: *m* 1991, Richard A. Armstrong, of 51 Sefton St, SW15 1NA, eldest son of Dr Alan Armstrong, of Bladon, Oxon, — Clare Marjorie, *b* 1961: *m* 1991, John Walker, of Ranfold Barn, Slinfold, W Sussex RH13 7RL, — Susan Ann (9 Maude Rd, Camberwell, SE5 8NY), *b* 1964. *Residence* – 46 Hyde Vale, Greenwich, SE10 8HP.

Issue of late Denis Alfred Jex Buxton, *b* 1895, *d* 1964: *m* 1923, Emily Mary, who *d* 1970, da of late William Hollins (B Sherwood):—

Paul William Jex (Castle House, Chipping Ongar, Essex; *Club* – Brooks's), *b* 1925; *ed* Rugby, and Balliol Coll, Oxford (MA); formerly Capt Coldm Gds; Diplo Ser 1950-71; banking 1972-74; NI Office since 1974, Assist Under-Sec of State 1981-85; NW Europe 1945 (wounded): *m* 1st, 1950 (*m diss* 1971), Katharine, who *d* 1977, da of Sir Hubert Hull, CBE; 2ndly, 1971, Hon Margaret Evelyn Bridges, da of 1st Baron Bridges, and formerly wife of Trevor Henry Aston, and has issue living (by 1st *m*), Charles Hubert Jex *b* 1951: *m* 1976, Cecile Moss, and has issue living, Sam *b* 1977, Amy *b* 1980, — Tobias Richard Valentine, *b* 1953; has issue living, Oliver *b* 1982, Xavier *b* 1990, Yvo *b* (twin) 1990, — Mary Katharine, *b* 1956; has issue living, Joe GRACE *b* 1993, — (by 2nd *m*) Sophia Frances, *b* 1972, — Hero Elizabeth, *b* 1974. —— Mary Violet, *b* 1924: *m* 1950, as his second wife, David Roden Buxton (ante). —— Cecilia Rachel (3 Linton Rd, Oxford) *b* 1927; *ed* Lady Margaret Hall, Oxford (MA); a Fellow of Wolfson Coll, Oxford: *m* 1951 (*m diss* 1968), Marcus Dick, who *d* 1971, and has issue living, Jasper Henry, *b* 1956: *m* 1988, Louise Blum, — Catherine Sophia, *b* 1953, — Cressida Rose, *b* 1960. —— Elizabeth Rosalind (89 Brian Av, Norwich NR1 2PD), *b* 1929: *m* 1953 (*m diss* 1964), Tristram Yelin, who *d* 1982, and has issue living, Francis North Hunter Buxton, *b* 1957, — Cecilia Mary, *b* 1954, — Natasha Vera *b* 1959.

Branches from youngest son of 2nd son of 1st Baronet:—

Granddaughter of late Thomas Fowell Buxton (infra):—
Issue of late Rev Barclay Fowell Buxton, *b* 1860, *d* 1946: *m* 1886, Margaret Maria Amelia, who *d* 1947, da of late William Railton, of 65, Onslow Square, SW:—
Rachel Jane, *b* 1905. *Residence* – Wayside, Stanway, Colchester Essex.

Grandchildren of late Rev Barclay Fowell Buxton, 5th son of late Thomas Fowell Buxton, 2nd son of 1st baronet:—
Issue of late Capt Murray Barclay Buxton, MC, *b* 1889, *ka* 1940: *m* 1920, Janet Mary Muriel, who *d* 1942, da of Sir (Edward) Hildred Carlile, CBE, 1st Bt:—
Ronald Carlile, *b* 1923; *ed* Eton, and Trin Coll, Camb (MA); formerly Capt REME, is a Co Dir; MP for Leyton (*C*) 1965-66: *m* 1959, Phyllida Dorothy Roden, yr da of late Capt Roden Henry Victor Buxton, CBE, RN (ante), and has issue living, Peter Hildred, *b* 1960: *m* 1987, Eleanor Charlotte, da of Richard Anthony Brooke Winch, of Swannington Manor, Norfolk, and has issue living, Laura Juliet *b* 1990, — Robert Victor, *b* 1964, — Camilla Janet St John *b* (twin) 1960: *m* 1992, Edward Thomas Baxter, of Gilston, Leven, Fife, son of late Alan G. L. Baxter, WS, of Gilston, Fife, — Vanessa Anne Carlile, *b* 1962.
Residences – 67 Ashley Gdns, SW1; Kimberley Hall, Wymondham, Norfolk.
Issue of late Alfred Barclay Buxton, *b* 1891, *ka* 1940: *m* 1916, Edith Mary Crossley, who *d* 1977, da of C. T. Studd, formerly of 17 Highland Rd, Upper Norwood, SE:—
Susan Studd (*Lady Wood*), MBE, *b* 1918; MBE (Civil) 1990: *m* 1943, Sir (Arthur) Michael Wood, CBE, MB, BS, FRCS, who *d* 1987, Founder and Dir Gen AMREF ("The Flying Doctor"), and has issue living, Mark Lionel, *b* 1945, — Hugo Charles, *b* 1948, — Janet Mary, *b* 1946, — Katrina Susan, *b* 1951. *Address* – Box 24277, Nairobi, Kenya.
Issue of late Barclay Godfrey Buxton, MBE, MC, *b* 1895, *d* 1986: *m* 1922, Dorothea Reader, who *d* 1967, yr da of late Reader Harris, KC, of Clapham, SW:—
Christopher Godfrey Reader, OBE, *b* 1929; *ed* Charterhouse, and Trin Coll, Camb (MA); Master of Business Admin Dartmouth Coll, USA, 1955; OBE (Civil) 1982: *m* 1964 (*m diss* 1969), Margaret Isabel, yr da of Lt-Col H. B. Watkins, of Knighton, Radnorshire. *Residences* – Kirtlington Park, Oxon; 61 Harcourt Terr, SW10 9JP. —— Joanna Margaret Reader, MBE, *b* 1927; *ed* Sherborne Sch for Girls, and Edinburgh Univ; Market Research Consultant; MBE (Civil) 1993. *Residence* – 21A Porchester Terr, W2.
The family of Buxton were seated for nearly three centuries at Coggeshall, Essex. The 1st baronet, Sir Thomas Fowell Buxton, MP for Weymouth (*L*) 1820-36, was distinguished for his exertions for the abolition of slavery and reform of the penal code. The 3rd baronet, Sir Thomas Fowell, GCMG, sometime a partner in the firm of Truman, Hanbury and Co, sat as MP for Lyme Regis (*L*) 1865-8, and was Gov of S Australia 1895-8. The 4th baronet was High Sheriff of Essex 1905. The 5th baronet was High Sheriff of Essex 1928.

BUZZARD (UK) 1929, of Munstead Grange, Godalming, co Surrey

Be what you seem to be

Sir ANTHONY FARQUHAR BUZZARD, 3rd *Baronet*; *b* 28 June 1935; *s* his father *Rear-Adm Sir* ANTHONY WASS, CB, DSO, OBE, 1972; *ed* Charterhouse, Ch Ch, Oxford (MA), Ambassador Coll, Pasadena, Cal (BA), and Bethany Theological Coll (MA Th); ARCM; freelance educational Consultant and Tutor; Lecturer, Atlanta Bible Coll, Georgia, USA: *m* 1970, Barbara Jean, da of Gordon Earl Arnold, of Mendon, Michigan, USA, and has issue.

Arms – Per chevron azure and argent, in chief two covered cups of the second and in base a rod of Æsculapius proper. **Crest** – Rising from clouds an eagle proper, gorged with an Eastern crown or.
Address – 185 Summerville Drive, Brooks, Georgia 30205, USA.

DAUGHTERS LIVING

Sarah Jane *b* 1971. —— Claire Judith *b* 1974. —— Heather Elizabeth, *b* 1988.

BROTHER LIVING

TIMOTHY MACDONNELL (Kennel Cottage, Lindfield, Haywards Heath, Sussex, RH16 2QN), *b* 28 Jan 1939; a LRAM and a Graduate of Roy Schs of Music: *m* 1970, Jennifer Mary, da of late Peter Patching, and has issue living, Jonathan Mark, *b* 1977, — Rachel Mary, *b* 1974.

SISTER LIVING

Gillian Margaret, *b* 1944; BSc: *m* 1979, William John Oates Blenkinsop, of 46 Melrose Rd, SW18 1LY.

AUNT LIVING (*Daughter of 1st baronet*)

Isabel May, *b* 1910: *m* 1933, Cdr Herbert William Acworth, RN, who *d* 1987, and has issue living, William Farquhar, *b* 1934: *m* 1964, Susan Henrietta, yr da of late Capt Roddie Casement, OBE, RN, (*see* Greenwell, Bt), and has issue living, William Bernard *b* 1965: *m* 1993, Julia Beale, James Michael *b* 1966, Anna Claire *b* 1970, — Adam Buzzard, *b* 1943, — Susan Esmé, *b* 1936, — Jane Marion, *b* 1941.

COLLATERAL BRANCH LIVING

Issue of late Surg-Lt-Cdr Edward Miller Buzzard, FRCP, RNVR, yr son of 1st baronet, *b* 1909, *d* 1976: *m* 1937, Sylvia Bevan (The Barn, Oakley Park, Frilford Heath, Abingdon, Oxon), da of late John William Fordham of Hughenden, Loughborough Rd, Leicester:—
†David, *b* 1950; *d* 1985. —— Sarah Bevan, *b* 1941: *m* 1962, Michael William Leishman Gear, of Samscotts, Sheepscombe, nr Stroud, Glos, and has issue living, Susan Anne Buzzard, *b* 1965, — Nicola Leishman, *b* 1967. —— Judith Miller, *b* 1944: *m* 1968, Sydney Guy Anthony Scammell, of 5 Courtfield, 1 Castlebar Hill, W5, and has issue living, Anthony Charles Miller, *b*

1974, — Louise Jane, *b* 1975. ——— Sylvia Anne, *b* 1947: *m* 1973, Rupert Grenside Bowen, of 83 Montholme Rd, Battersea, SW11, and has issue living, Miranda Juanita, *b* 1975, — Henrietta Alice, *b* 1977.
The 1st baronet, Sir (Edward) Farquhar Buzzard (son of late Thomas Buzzard, MD, FRCP, of 74 Grosvenor St, W1), was Physician Extraor, to HM 1924-32, Physician-in-Ord 1932-6, and an Extra Physician 1937-45.

BYASS (UK) 1926, of Port Talbot, co Glamorgan (extinct 1976)

Sir GEOFFREY ROBERT SIDNEY BYASS, TD, 2nd and last *Baronet*.

DAUGHTERS LIVING OF SECOND BARONET

Gillian Mary, *b* 1921: *m* 1948, Kenneth Mackenzie Knight, of 33 Jemmett Rd, Ashford, Kent, and has issue living, Nigel Geoffrey Roy, *b* 1950, — Simon Gerald, *b* 1953. ——— Daphne Caroline, *b* 1925: *m* 1st, 1949, Capt Ian Guy Mathews, Duke of Cornwall's LI; 2ndly, 1962, Lt-Col William Roland Lawson, of Court Mews, Newnham Bridge, Tenbury Wells, Worcs, and has issue living, (by 1st *m*) Caroline, *b* 1951: *m* 1972, — Belinda, *b* 1952: *m* 1973. ——— Pamela Julia, *b* 1926: *m* 1953, Arthur David Veall, of Merry Hall, Newbridge on Wye, Powys, and has issue living, Robert John, *b* 1955, — Christopher Toby, *b* 1956, — Ivan, *b* 1964, — Julia Diana, *b* 1958. ——— Rosemary Valentine (Sydney, NSW, Australia), *b* 1933: *m* 1959, Kenneth Michael Bond Wright, who *d* 1982, and has issue living, Sarah Caroline, *b* 1960, — Charlotte Mary, *b* 1962. ——— Ursula Marian, *b* 1940: *m* 1963, John Patrick Dornton, of Stonewall House, Duck St, Churchill Green, Bristol, and has issue living, Charles Geoffrey, *b* 1964, — Elizabeth Henrietta, *b* 1967, — Susannah Marian, *b* 1971.

Cable-Alexander, see Alexander.

CAHN (UK) 1934, of Stanford-upon-Soar, co Nottingham

Sir ALBERT JONAS CAHN, 2nd *Baronet*; *b* 27 June 1924; *s* his father, *Sir* JULIEN, 1944; *ed* Harrow: *m* 1948, Malka, da of late Reuben Bluestone, and has issue.

Arms – Gules, a cross raguly ermine between in the second and third quarters a fleur-de-lis or. **Crest** – In front of a fox's head erased two branches of willow in saltire proper.
Seat – Stanford Hall, Loughborough. *Residence* – 10 Edgecoombe Close, Warren Rd, Kingston upon Thames, Surrey KT2 7HP.

SONS LIVING

JULIEN MICHAEL (1 Court Hope Villas, Wimbledon, SW19), *b* 15 Jan 1951; *ed* Harrow: *m* 1987, Marilynne Janelle, da of Frank Owen Blyth, and has issue living, Benjamin Albert, *b* 28 Feb 1988, — Jessie Laura, *b* 1976. ——— Edward John (13 Windsor Court, SW1Z), *b* 1959.

DAUGHTERS LIVING

Madeleine Jane (52 Cascade Rd, N10), *b* 1949: *m* 1979 (*m diss* 1987), Richard Albert Smith, and has issue living, Charles Joseph, *b* 19—, — Mariza Joanna Phyllis, *b* 19—. ——— Valerie Janet, *b* 1954: *m* 1982, Peregrine Kenneth Oughton Crosthwaite, of 30 Larpent Av, SW15 6UU, and has issue living, Nicholas Anthony, *b* 1985, — Thomas William, *b* 1986, — Sally-Anne Claire, *b* 1989.

BROTHER LIVING

Richard Ian (Crispa, Bashurst Copse, Itchingfield, Horsham, Sussex), *b* 1927: *m* 1964, Marietta da of Joseph Seidler.
The 1st baronet, Sir Julien Cahn (son of Albert Cahn), was Master of Burton Hunt 1926-35; of Woodland Pytchley Foxhounds 1935-7, and of Fernie's Foxhounds 1937-9, and sponsored and captained many cricket teams on tours abroad.

POSSVNT·QVIA·POSSE·VIDENTVR

They are able who believe they can

CAIN (UK) 1920, of Wargrave Manor, co Berkshire (Extinct 1969)

Sir ERNEST CAIN, 2nd and last *Baronet*.

DAUGHTERS LIVING OF SECOND BARONET

Ann, *b* 1925. ——— Joan, *b* (twin) 1925: *m* 1952, Ian Merrick Cuthbertson Hill, OBE, and has issue living, Christopher Michael Ian, *b* 1957, — Susan Elizabeth, *b* 1955: *m* 1979, Norman Allen Bradley. *Residence* – Windsor House, Gotham, Cranborne, Wimborne, Dorset BH21 5QY. ——— Vivien Elizabeth WILSON, *b* 1932; has reverted to her former married name: *m* 1st, 1954 (*m diss* 1959), Charles William Munro Wilson; 2ndly, 1961 (*m diss* 1966), Baron Pierre Cervello, and has issue living, (by 1st *m*) Amanda Louise, *b* 1956. *Residence* – Mais de Pan, Les Stes Maries de la Mer, 13460 Camargue, France.

ANSTRUTHER-GOUGH-CALTHORPE (UK) 1929, of Elvetham Hall, Elvetham, co Southampton

The same way but by different steps

Sir EUAN HAMILTON ANSTRUTHER-GOUGH-CALTHORPE, 3rd *Baronet, b* 22 June 1966, son of late Niall Hamilton Anstruther-Gough-Calthorpe; *s* his grandfather, *Brig Sir* RICHARD HAMILTON, CBE, 1985; *ed* Harrow, and RAC, Cirencester.

Arms – Quarterly: 1st and 4th checky or and azure, a fesse ermine, and (for distinction) a canton ermine, *Calthorpe*; 2nd, gules, on a fesse argent, between three boars' heads couped or, a lion passant azure, and (for distinction) a canton ermine, *Gough*; 3rd, argent, three piles issuing from the chief sable, *Anstruther*. Crests – 1st, a boar's head couped erect argent, charged (for distinction) with an ermine spot azure, *Calthorpe*; 2nd, a boar's head couped argent, pierced through the check with a broken spear gules, and charged (for distinction) with an ermine spot azure, *Gough*; 3rd, two arms in armour holding in the gauntlet a battle-axe all proper, *Anstruther*.

SISTER LIVING

Lara Nancy Don, *b* 1968.

UNCLE LIVING (*Son of 2nd baronet*)

JOHN AUSTEN (Shroner Wood, Martyr Worthy, Winchester, Hants), *b* 14 July 1947; *ed* Harrow: *m* 1st, 1977 (*m diss* 1986), Lady Mary Gaye Georgiana Lorna Curzon, da of 5th Earl Howe, and formerly wife of late (Kevin) Esmond (Peter) Cooper-Key (*see* V Rothermere); 2ndly, 1987, Vanessa Mary Theresa, yst da of Lt Cdr Theodore Bernard Peregrine Hubbard, RN (*see* D Norfolk), and formerly wife of David St Vincent Llewellyn (*see* Llewellyn, Bt, *cr* 1922), and has issue living (by 1st *m*), Jacobi Richard Penn, *b* 1983, — Georgiana Moireach Gay, *b* 1978, — Isabella Amaryllis Charlotte, *b* 1980, — (by 2nd *m*) Gabriella Zanna Vanessa, *b* 1989, — Octavia Elsa, *b* 1991.

GREAT-AUNTS LIVING (*Daughters of 1st baronet*)

Frances Jean, *b* 1910: *m* 1942, His Honour Judge (Frank Alleyne) Stockdale, el son of late Sir Frank Arthur Stockdale, GCMG, CBE, and has had issue, James Arthur FitzRoy (Moons Mill, Tinkers Lane, Hadlow Down, E Sussex), *b* 1948; *ed* Eton, and Southampton Univ (LLB); Bar Gray's Inn 1972: *m* 1974, Jane Mary Gabriel, el da of William Hazzard, and has issue living, John Francis *b* 1978, Kathryn Jane *b* 1980, Philippa Rachel *b* 1982, Elinor Victoria *b* 1985, — Sarah Victoria, *b* 1943: *m* 1965, Christopher N. A. Castleman, and *d* 1979, leaving issue, Jonathan William *b* 1971, Amanda Lucy *b* 1967, — Frances Jane, *b* 1946: *m* 1967, Charles J. Deacon, of 9 Dinorbin, 79/81 Woodcote Rd, Wallington, Surrey, and has issue living, Julian Mark *b* 1972, Rebecca *b* 1970. *Residence* – Victoria Place, Monmouth, Gwent NP5 3BR. —— Barbara (*Baroness Luke*), *b* 1911: *m* 1932, 2nd Baron Luke. *Residence* – Odell Castle, Bedfordshire, MK43 7BB.

MOTHER LIVING

Martha Rodman (*Lady Nicholson*), da of Col Stuart Warren Don, of 5 Orchard Court, Portman Sq, W2: *m* 1st, 1964, Niall Hamilton Anstruther-Gough-Calthorpe, who *d* 1970, eldest son of 2nd baronet; 2ndly, 1975, Sir Charles Christian Nicholson, 3rd Bt (*cr* 1912).

Sir FitzRoy Hamilton Anstruther-Gough-Calthorpe, 1st Bt (el son of late Lieut-Col Robert Hamilton Lloyd-Anstruther (Anstruther, Bt, colls)), assumed by Roy Licence 1910, the surname and arms of Anstruther only; also later by Roy Licence 1910, for himself and issue the surnames of Gough-Calthorpe in addition to, and after that of Anstruther, and the Arms of Gough and Calthorpe quartered with those of Anstruther, having *m* 1898, Hon Rachel Gough-Calthorpe, who *d* 1951, el da and co-heir of 6th Baron Calthorpe.

CAMERON (UK) 1893, of Balclutha, Greenock (Extinct 1968)

Sir JOHN CAMERON, 2nd and last *Baronet*.

DAUGHTER LIVING OF FIRST BARONET

Margaret Lilian (Half Acre House, 14 Northcroft Rd, Englefield Green, Surrey TW20 0DU), *b* 1901.

CAMPBELL (NS) 1628, of Auchinbreck

Sir ROBIN AUCHINBRECK CAMPBELL, 15th *Baronet*, *b* 7 June 1922; *s* his father, *Sir* LOUIS HAMILTON, 1970; *ed* Eton; late Lt (A) RNVR; sheep farmer: *m* 1st, 1948, Rosemary (Sally), who *d* 1978, da of Ashley Dean, of Christchurch, NZ; 2ndly, 1978, Elizabeth Mary, da of Sir Arthur Colegate, MP (Worsley, Bt), and formerly wife of Richard Wellesley Gunston (*see* Gunston, Bt), and has issue by 1st *m*.

Arms – Gyronny of eight or and sable, and a bordure checky ermine and purpure. **Crest** – A dexter hand proper holding a spur or.
Residence – 287A Waikawa Rd, Picton, NZ. *Clubs* – Christchurch (NZ), and Bembridge Sailing.

SON LIVING *(By 1st marriage)*

LOUIS AUCHINBRECK, *b* 17 Jan 1953: *m* 1976, Fiona Mary St Clair, da of Gordon King, of Middlehill, Marlborough, NZ, and has issue living, Lucinda Louise, *b* 1982, — Charlotte Virginia, *b* 1985.

DAUGHTERS LIVING *(By 1st marriage)*

Rosemary Fiona, *b* 1955. —— Sophia Louise, *b* 1960: *m* 1984, Philip Michael Darcey Pinniger, son of late T. K. Pinniger, of Hunters, Lincoln's Inn, and has issue living, Rhiannon Louise, *b* 19—.

DAUGHTER LIVING OF TWELFTH BARONET

Mary Sara (*Lady Fitzpatrick*), TD, *b* 1917; a CStJ: *m* 1944, Gen Sir (Geoffrey Richard) Desmond Fitzpatrick, GCB, DSO, MBE, MC, Col The Blues and Royals, and has issue living Brian Richard Charles (11 Warwick Sq, SW1), *b* 1950; *ed* Eton, — Sara Georgina, *b* 1948: *m* 1976, R. Stewart Whittington, of 109 Beaufort St, SW3. *Residence* – Belmont, Otley, Ipswich, Suffolk IP6 9PF.

COLLATERAL BRANCH LIVING

Descendants of late Patrick Campbell, of Stuck, co Bute, brother of late Rev Duncan Campbell, V of Kilfinnan, great-great-great-grandfather of 8th baronet:—

Grandchildren of late Sir Archibald Young Gipps Campbell, KCIE, CSI, CBE, VD (infra):—
Issue of late Lt-Col Archibald Hugh Campbell, R Sigs, *b* 1914, *d* 1981: *m* 1940, Mary Alison (24 Langside Drive, Comrie, Perthshire PH6 2HR), da of late Lt-Col Herbert Nugent Young, DSO, R Inniskilling Fus:—
Archibald James (25 Greville Park Rd, Ashtead, Surrey KT21 2QU), *b* 1943: *m* 1976, Lorna Isobel, da of John Scott, of Elderslie, Renfrewshire, and has issue living, Archibald Malcolm Scott, *b* 1979, — Ewan Anton Hugh, *b* 1983, — Iona Lanor, *b* 1980, — Isla Rowena, *b* 1985. —— Alison Margaret, *b* 1941: *m* 1966, Robert John Michael, and has issue living, Anthony Richard, *b* 1967, — Geraint Philip, *b* 1977, — Isobel Margaret, *b* 1969. —— Christian Jean Mary, *b* 1948.

Grandsons of late Archibald Samuels Campbell, great-great-great-grandson and heir male of late Rev Patrick Campbell, of Torblaren, and grandson and heir male of late Patrick Campbell, of Stuck, co Bute (ante):—
Issue of late Sir Archibald Young Gipps Campbell, KCIE, CSI, CBE, VD, *b* 1872, *d* 1957: *m* 1910, Frances Irene, who *d* 1967, da of late Rev Henry Savill Young, of Mallard's Court, Stokenchurch, Oxfordshire (Young, Bt, *cr* 1769, colls):—
Colin Alan George (The Old Manse, Lochgair, by Lochgilphead, Argyll PA31 8SB), *b* 1917; Capt (ret) Black Watch, late Foreign Ser: *m* 1st, 1945 (*m diss* 1961), Mary Cosser, da of late Ramsay Young; 2ndly, 1966, Joanna Frances, da of late George Falconer Ball, MC, and has issue living, (by 1st *m*) Mary Irene Young, *b* 1946: *m* 1973, Patrick Barwise, of No 6 Grange House, Highbury Grange, N5 2QD, and has issue living, Alexander Mark Colin *b* 1976, Katharine Mary *b* 1979, — Claire Elizabeth, *b* 1949: *m* 1983, Michael Anthony Bastian, of 10 Riverside, Swallowfields, Totnes, Devon TQ9 5JB, — Fiona Penelope, *b* 1955: *m* 1980, Lt-Cdr Peter Langford Rice, RN, of Oak Lodge, Laverstock, Salisbury, Wilts SP1 1QJ, and has issue living, Eleanor Young Rowley Campbell *b* 1985, Alice Camilla Campbell *b* 1987. —— †Niall Patrick, *b* 1925; Lt (ret) RE: *m* 1st, 1953 (*m diss* 1965), Gillian Margaret Elizabeth, da of Arthur John Morris; 2ndly, 1967, Peta Caroline (Westbrook, 5 Leadhall Crescent, Harrogate HG2 9NG), da of William Kelso Paul, and *d* 1988, leaving issue, (by 1st *m*) Sarah Caroline, *b* 1954: *m* 1985, David Thomas Woodward, of Rookery Cottage, Clay Lane, Marton-over-Winsford, Cheshire, and has issue living, Lucy Elizabeth Campbell *b* 1988, Stephanie Jane Campbell *b* 1990, — Julia Anne, *b* 1956: *m* 1980 (*m diss* 1995), David Jon Slym, and has issue living, Jessica Elizabeth *b* 1982, Katherine Margaret *b* 1985, — (by 2nd *m*) James William Patrick, *b* 1968, — Malcolm Niall Kelso *b* 1978, — Rebecca Louise, *b* 1971.

This baronetcy was conferred upon Sir Dugald Campbell, Knight, with remainder to his heirs male whatsoever. Upon the death of the 6th baronet in 1812, Dugald Campbell, of Kildalloig, Day-Keeper of the Great Seal in Ireland, is said to have become *de jure* 7th baronet, but not to have assumed the title, and the baronetcy remained dormant until 1841, when it was claimed by Dugald Campbell's heir, John Eyton Campbell, of Killdalloig, who proved himself heir to the title, and was subsequently recognized as 8th baronet *de facto*.

CAMPBELL (NS) 1668 (about), of Aberuchill, Perthshire

Victory follows the brave

Sir COLIN MOFFAT CAMPBELL, MC, 8th *Baronet*; *b* 4 Aug 1925; *s* his father, *Capt Sir* JOHN ALEXANDER COLDSTREAM, 1960; *ed* Stowe; Chm James Finlay & Co, Ltd; European War 1944-5 with Scots Guards (wounded, MC): *m* 1952, Mary Anne Chichester, da of late Brigadier George Alexander Bain, OBE (*see* M Donegall, colls, 1990 Edn), and has had issue.

Arms – Quarterly: 1st and 4th, gyronny of eight or and sable; 2nd, argent, a lymphad with her oars in action sable; 3rd, or a fesse checky argent and azure; all within a bordure ermine. **Crest** – A lion guardant gules crowned with laurel and holding in his dexter paw a sword proper, hilted and pommelled or, and in the sinister a dag, or Highland pistol. **Supporters** – Two bloodhounds guardant, proper, collared and leashed or.
Residence – Kilbryde Castle, Dunblane, Perthshire FK15 9NF. *Clubs* – Boodle's, Royal Calcutta Turf, Nairobi and Muthaiga (Kenya), Western (Glasgow).

SONS LIVING

JAMES ALEXANDER MOFFAT BAIN, *b* 23 Sept 1956; *ed* Stowe; Capt Scots Gds: *m* 1993, Carola Jane, yr da of George Denman (*see* B Denman). —— John Alistair Chichester, *b* 1960; *ed* Fettes: *m* 1987, Carole Lesley, yr da of Geoffrey Knowles, of Cornton, Stirling.

DAUGHTER DECEASED

Janet Mary Bain, *b* 1953: *m* 1975, Nicholas John Muir (*see* Muir Bt), and *d* 1978.

BROTHER LIVING

Alistair Bromley, OBE, *b* 1927; *ed* Tonbridge; Vice-Chm Countryside Commn for Scotland 1972-81, since when Member of Scottish Land Court; OBE (Civil) 1976: *m* 1952, Rosemary, da of late J. Lindsay Pullar of Glenfarg House, by Perth, and has issue living, Christopher John, *b* 1954, —— Caroline Margaret, *b* 1956: *m* 1980, Andrew J. Fraser, son of late John C. Fraser, and has issue living, John Campbell *b* 1987, Alice Margaret *b* 1986, Rosamund Mary *b* 1990, —— Colina Mary, *b* 1964: *m* 1989, Jonathan Humphrey, son of David Humphrey. *Residence* – Grainston Farm, Kilbryde, Dunblane, Perthshire, FK15 9NF.

COLLATERAL BRANCHES LIVING

Granddaughter of late Alexander Bulwer Campbell (infra):—
Issue of late Alexander Colin le Grand Campbell, *b* 1898, *d* 1980: *m* 1922, Mavis Macdonald, who *d* 1937:—
Janet Glenn, *b* 1926: *m* 1953, Neil Lester, of 551 South Titirangi Rd, Auckland 7, NZ, and has issue living, Mark Robert Alexander, *b* 1954.

Grandson of late Alexander le Grand Campbell, 2nd son of 4th baronet:—
Issue of late Alexander Bulwer Campbell, *b* 1855, *d* 1938: *m* 1894, Maude, da of J. Knight:—
Clyde Coldstream, *b* 1904; Solicitor, Auckland, NZ: *m* 1st, 1936, Mary Fisher; 2ndly, Eleanor Laura Curnow, of Auckland, who *d* 1982 and has issue living, (by 2nd *m*) Alexander Edward Lindsay, *b* 1948: *m* 1977, Mary Lesley Griffin, and has issue living, Elizabeth Mary *b* 1978, Joanna Margaret *b* 1980, Kathryn Laura *b* 1982, —— Margaret Alison, *b* 1945.

Grandsons of late Col George Frederick Colin Campbell, CMG, VD, 2nd son of late Alexander le Grand Campbell (ante):—
Issue of late Capt Alan le Grand Campbell, *b* 1896, *d* 1960: *m* 1928, Barbara Alison, da of late James Marchbanks of Wellington, NZ:—
John Graham Colin, *b* 1929: *m* 1957, Anna Margaret, da of late Bertram Kay, of Fulham, London, and has issue, Alexander James le Grand, *b* 1958, —— Robert Neil, *b* 1960. —— Donald James (Campbell St, Karori, Wellington, NZ), *b* 1930; ANZIA: *m* 1963, Barbara Mary, da of Frank Grear, of Nelson, NZ.

Grandchildren of late William Hunter Campbell, yr son of late Robert Stuart Campbell (*b* 1815), yst son of William Campbell, WS, 4th son of 3rd baronet:—
Issue of late Robert Stuart Campbell, *b* 1873, *d* 1903, Annie, who *d* 1960, da of John Holloway:—
†Stuart William Ivor, *b* 1910, *d* 1992. —— †Herbert John Shelley *b* (twin) 1910, *d* 1992. —— Annie Elizabeth, *b* 1906: *m* 1928, Andrew B. Straughan, who *d* 1987, of 126 Park St, Goderich, Ont N7A 1K8, Canada, and has issue living, Benson Robert James, *b* 1929: *m* 1950, Catherine La Verdiere, and has issue living, Stephen Benson *b* 1960, Heather Victoria *b* 1970, —— Martin Kalmor, *b* 1931: *m* 1952, Noreen Fuller, and has issue living, Martin Wayne *b* 1953: *m* 1991, Nancy Ann Walters (and has issue living, Justin Kaleb *b* 1992), Michael James *b* 1955: *m* 1986, Heather de Penier (and has issue living, Alexander John *b* 1988, Scott James *b* (twin) 1988, Nicholas *b* 1992), Brian Alexander *b* 1960: *m* 1986, Grechten Ball (and has issue living, Sarah Nicole *b* 1991), Martha Noreen *b* 1962: *m* 1987, Robert Marcel Girard (and has issue living, Laura Alexandra Noreen *b* 1992), —— Donald Ivan, *b* 1934: *m* 1951, Lois Freeman, and has issue living, Donald Kenneth *b* 1957: *m* 1977, Anita Bourdeau (and has issue living, Jefferey *b* 1980, Lori Ann *b* 1978), Linda Elizabeth *b* 1951: *m* 1973, Donald Johnston (and has issue living, Mark *b* 1978, Alecia *b* 1980), Barbara Louise *b* 1959: *m* 1978, Philip Petre (and has issue living, Michael *b* 1980), —— William Stuart, *b* 1936: *m* 1960, Victoria La Verdiere, and has issue living, William Glenn *b* 1967, Cynthia Catherine *b* 1962, Nancy Carol *b* 1963, —— Clayton Lyal, *b* 1936: *m* 1st, 1963, — ; 2ndly, 1982, Donna Gibson, and has issue living, (by 1st *m*) Clayton Lyal *b* 1964, Sean Andrew *b* 1966, (by 2nd *m* adopted) James *b* 1986, —— Roy Campbell, *b* 1940: *m* 1966, Irene Phillips, and has issue living, Cameron Alexander *b* 1967, Allyson Elizabeth *b* 1970, Christine Lydia *b* 1972, —— John Arnold Clark, *b* 1944: *m* 1964, Marion Sutherland, and has issue living, David Joseph *b* 1965, Susan Anne *b* 1967, —— David Glenn, *b* 1946: *m* 1969, Katharine Huff, and has issue living, John Andrew *b* 1973, Jeffrey David *b* 1975, Sarah Katharine *b* 1977.

Grandchildren of late Robert Stuart Campbell (ante):—
Issue of late Robert Edmund Hunter Campbell, *b* 1904, *d* 1980 (matriculated arms as Campbell of Bellsyde, Ont, with Lyon Court 1964): *m* 1st, 1930, Minerva, who *d* 1955, da of W. J. Finlay; 2ndly, 1964, Marjorie (Josephine St, Wingham, Ont, Canada), da of Frank Preston:—
(By 1st *m*) Charles Robert (Seaforth, Ont, Canada), *b* 1943: *m* 1964, Margaret Jane, da of late Charles E. Campbell, and has issue living, James Robert, *b* 1965: *m* 1989, Catherine T. Kelly, —— Barry Charles, *b* 1966, —— Christine, *b* 1969. —— Grace Anne Pauline, *b* 1933: *m* 1952, Frederick McGee, of Box 154, Wingham, Ontario, Canada, and has issue living, Robert

William John, *b* 1953: *m* 1975, Brenda Joanne Maize, and has issue living, Jonathan Robert *b* 1983, David James *b* 1984, Heather Joanne *b* 1978, — Ronald Frederick, *b* 1958: *m* 1979, Susan Mae Harrison, and has issue living, Christopher Ronald *b* 1986, Candace Mae *b* 1981, — Janet Grace *b* 1955: *m* 1977, Kenneth Russell MacAdams, and has issue living, Darryl Kenneth *b* 1978, Kevin Robert *b* 1981.

Issue of late William John Campbell, *b* 1875, *d* 1963: *m* 1901, Mary Hutton, who *d* 1933—
John, *b* 1916: *m* 1946, Muriel Mackay, and has issue living, Robert, *b* 1956, — Linda M., *b* 1951. —— Jean B., *b* 1905, *d* 1987.

Issue of late George Alexander Campbell, *b* 1882, *d* 1967: *m* 1st, 1906, Jennie Hutton; 2ndly, 1925 Flossie Saunders, who *d* 1960:—
(By 1st *m*) John Hunter (Blyth, Ontario, Canada) *b* 1914: *m* 1st, 1935, Margaret Gillies; 2ndly, 1945, Frances Rosetta Gillies, and has issue living (by 1st *m*) Harold John Linklater, *b* 1935: *m* 1957, Rose-Marie Whitfield, and has issue living, John Lewis *b* 1957, Scott Harold *b* 1970, Sherri Lou *b* 1959, — Ronald Keith, *b* 1939: *m* 19—, Elizabeth Mary Oliver, and has issue living, Ronald Thomas *b* 1970, William Paul *b* 1972, — Gail, *b* 1941: *m* 1959, Kenneth Nekon Paterson, and has issue living, (by 2nd *m*) Danny, *b* 1948, Mary Barbara, *b* 1946: *m* 1967, Douglas Ross Howson, and has issue living, Douglas Jeffrey, *b* 1969, Sherri Lynn, *b* 1972. —— Harold Alexander (Blyth, Ontario, Canada), *b* 1919: *m* 1939, Adeline Isabel Cardiff, and has issue living, William John, *b* 1939: *m* 1958, Diana Teresa Wozniak, and has issue living, Curtis William *b* 1961: *m* 1978, Tammy Kerr and has issue living, Daniel William *b* 1986, Lisa Marie *b* 1985), Randall Steven Harold *b* 1962: *m* 1986, Elizabeth Heath, Lorie Diana Catherine *b* 1959: *m* 1st, 1979, Kevin Faber; 2ndly, 1988, Mark Fischer (and has issue living, (by 1st *m*) Kristopher Kevin *b* 1981, Jacqueline Lorie *b* 1983, (by 2nd *m*) Natasha Danielle *b* 1988), Suzanne Adeline *b* 1969, — Dwight Alexander, *b* 1941: *m* 1960, Lyla Joan Marie Johnston, and has issue living, Grant Dwight *b* 1961: *m* 1985, Elaine Jobe, Charlene Marie *b* 1960: *m* 1987, Gary Carpenter (and has issue living, Matthew Garrison Campbell *b* 1987), — Sharon Rebecca Jane *b* 1967, — Nancy Lee, *b* 1942: *m* 1965, John Michael Pawitch, and has issue living, Michael Alexander, *b* 1972, Mark Andrew, *b* 1975, — Frances Elizabeth, *b* 1961: *m* 1984, Steven Roy Bearss, and has issue living, Candice Elizabeth *b* 1985, Amanda Jane *b* 1987. —— Mary Haugh, *b* 1909: *m* 1928, Edgar McMichael, who *d* 1978, and has issue living, Alice Isobel, *b* 1933: *m* 1956, Robert Morrison, who *d* 1966, and has issue living, Bruce Edward *b* 1963. —— (By 2nd *m*) Stuart Edgar, *b* 1934: *m* 1963, Shirley Lee, who *d* 1988, and has issue living, Denise, *b* 1964, Karen Ann, *b* 1967. —— Margaret Lillian Christine, *b* 1927: *m* 1954, John Toth, and has issue living, James John, *b* 1954. —— Ina May, *b* 1929: *m* 1962, Herbert Stephen. —— Florence Alexandra, *b* 1930: *m* 1965, Ronald Dolmage.

The 1st baronet, a Lord of Justiciary in Scotland, under the title of Lord Aberuchill, was a Privy Councillor, and sat as MP for Perthshire 1690-1702. He lost £17,201 (Scots), from the Highland army under Lord Dundee, and though an Act of Parliament granting him compensation was passed, he did not receive the money. The original patent or baronetcy is lost, and the actual date when it was conferred is not known.

CAMPBELL (UK) 1808, of Succoth, Dunbartonshire

Labour overcomes everything

LABOR·OMNIA·SVPERAT

Sir ILAY MARK CAMPBELL OF SUCCOTH, 7th *Baronet*; *b* 29 May 1927; *s* his father, *Capt Sir* GEORGE ILAY, 1967; *ed* Eton, and Ch Ch, Oxford (MA); Joint Scottish Agent for Christie, Manson & Woods since 1973 (Scottish Agent 1968-73); Chm Christie's & Edmistons Ltd (Christie's, Scotland) since 1978; Pres of Assocn for Protection of Rural Scotland; Member of Gardens Cttee, National Trust for Scotland since 1993; Convener Church of Scotland Cttee for Artistic Matters since 1987; Hon Vice Pres Scotlands Garden Scheme since 1983; Dir High Craigton Farming Co, Trustee Crarae Gardens Charitable Trust: *m* 1961, Margaret Minette Rohais, only da of James Alasdair Anderson (*see* E Halsbury), and has issue.

Arms – Quarterly; 1st and 4th, gyronny of eight engrailed or and sable; 2nd and 3rd azure, a lion rampant argent, within a bordure counter-compony argent and azure. *Wallace of Elderslie.* **Crest** – A camel's head couped proper; **Supporters** – *Dexter*, a lion rampant guardant proper; *sinister*, a savage wreathed about the temples and loins with oak leaves, all proper.
Residence – Crarae Lodge, by Inveraray, Argyll PA32 8YA. *Club* – Turf.

DAUGHTERS LIVING

Cecilia Margaret Lucy, *b* 1963: *m* 1988, Capt Malcolm Gregor Charles MacGregor, yr of MacGregor, elder son of Brig Sir Gregor MacGregor of MacGregor, 6th Bt. —— Candida Harriett Rohais, *b* 1964: *m* 1991, Gerard Joseph Rafferty, elder son of Richard Byrne Rafferty, of Bellshill, Lanarks, and has issue living, Ruaraidh Ilay Byrne, *b* 1993.

Sir Ilay Campbell, 1st baronet, was Lord President of Court of Session, with the title of Lord Succoth; and the 2nd baronet Sir Archibald was a Lord of Session 1809-24, with the same designation. The 1st baronet's mother, Helen, who *d* 1767, was the only da and heir of John Wallace of Elderslie.

CAMPBELL (UK) 1815

Sir LACHLAN PHILIP KEMEYS CAMPBELL, 6th *Baronet*; *b* 9 Oct 1958; *s* his father, *Col Sir* GUY THEOPHILUS HALSWELL, OBE, MC, 1993; *ed* Lyceé Français, Temple Grove, Eton, and RMA Sandhurst; late RGJ, served N Ireland, Queen Victoria's Rifles (TA): *m* 1986, Harriet Jane Sarah, only da of Frank Edward Jex Girling, of West Malvern, Worcs, and has issue.

Arms – Quarterly: 1st and 4th, gyronny of eight or and sable; 2nd, argent, a lymphad, sails furled and oars in action sable, with a flag and pennants flying gules; 3rd, or, a fesse checky azure and argent, all within a bordure embattled ermine. Crest – A boar's head arrachée or.
Residence – 20 Rush Hill Rd, SW11.

SON LIVING

ARCHIBALD EDWARD FITZGERALD, *b* 13 June 1990.

BROTHER LIVING

Rory Charles FitzGerald (Flat C, 103 Gloucester Rd, SW7 4SF), *b* 1961; *ed* Lycée Français, Temple Grove, Amersham Art Coll, and Royal Coll of Music; actor: *m* 1985 (*m diss* 1991), Angela Victoria, da of late Victor Orman Phillis, of Pacific Highway, Killara, NSW, Australia.

WIDOWS LIVING OF FOURTH AND FIFTH BARONETS

ALIDA VIRGINIA (ALLAN) (*Alida, Lady Campbell*), only child of Augustus Peeters van Nieuwenrode, of Belgium: *m* 1955, as his second wife, Major Sir Guy Colin Campbell, 4th Bt, who *d* 1960. *Residence* – St. Andrews, Fife.
ELIZABETH WILLS-WEBBER (*Elizabeth, Lady Campbell*), formerly wife of D. H. Parker; actress as Lizbeth Webb: *m* 1956, Col Sir Guy Theophilus Halswell Campbell, 5th Bt, OBE, MC, who *d* 1993. *Residence* – 18 Lansdown Terrace, Malvern Rd, Cheltenham, Glos GL50 2JT.

COLLATERAL BRANCHES LIVING

Issue of late Col John Archibald Campbell, yst son of 3rd baronet, *b* 1898, *d* 1974: *m* 1st, 1925 (*m diss* 1940), Dorothy, da of late John Field, of Perthi, Ruthin; 2ndly, 1944 (*m diss* 1963), Elizabeth, da of Renard Pearth, of Pittsburgh, USA:—
(By 1st *m*) Colin Guy Napier (23 Lansdowne Gdns, SW8; White's and Puffins Clubs), *b* 1930; Capt late KRRC: *m* 1st, 1965, Mrs Lucy Barnett Smith, da of James A. Barnett, of Bel Air, Cal, USA, and formerly wife of Clifford Smith, Jr; *m* 2ndly, 1987, Charmian Rachel, formerly wife of Archibald Hugh Stirling, yr of Keir (*see* Stirling-Maxwell, Bt), and yr da of Col Lord George Francis John Montagu Douglas Scott (*see* D Buccleuch), and has issue living (by 1st *m*), Georgina Dorothy, *b* 1969, — Tessa Sylvia, *b* 1971. ——— (By 2nd *m*) (Henrietta) Nina Sylvia, *b* 1945: *m* 1971, Andrew Guy Louis de Chappuis Konig, of 6 Molyneux St, W1, and has issue living.

Grandchildren of late Charles James Napier Campbell, 3rd son of 2nd baronet:—
Issue of late Major Edward Fitzgerald Campbell, *b* 1890, *d* 1950: *m* 1915, Agnes Catherine, who *d* 1977, da of late Henry Templer Prior, Master of Supreme Court:—
Charles Colin (Woolpit Farm, Ewhurst, Cranleigh, Surrey), *b* 1923; *ed* Loretto, and Pembroke Coll, Camb (Foundation Scholar) (MA); 1939-45 War as Lt RE: *m* 1970, Julia Margaret Rachel, da of Anthony Smithson Russell, and has issue living, James Charles Anthony, *b* 1971, — Lucy Catherine Isabel, *b* 1974. ——— Geraldine Mary (11 Culverwell Gdns, Winchester, Hants), *b* 1917: *m* 1941, Maj Neville Glyn Williams, MC, Indian Army, who was *ka* in Burma 1945, and has issue living, Fiona Glyn, *b* 1944: *m* 1963, Julian John Hamling Smith, of Bishopsway, Twyford, nr Winchester, and has issue living, Colin Nigel Neville *b* 1965; *ed* Winchester, Emma Mary Glyn *b* 1968. ——— Frances Margaret, *b* 1919: *m* 1954, Denys Newell Pitts Squarey, who *d* 1983. *Residence* – Brigge House, Broughton, Stockbridge, Hants.

Granddaughter of late Percy Fitzgerald Campbell, 7th son of 2nd baronet:—
Issue of late Capt Ian Percy FitzGerald Campbell, OBE, *b* 1890, *d* 1963: *m* 1923, Gwladys Mary, MBE, who *d* 1989, da of late Lewis Pugh, KC:—
Graeme Diana, *b* 1929: *m* 1954, Louis Paul Humphrey ffrench-Constant, BM, BCh, who *d* 1990, of Silozwe, Pill Creek, St Feock, Truro, Cornwall TR3 6SE, and has issue living, Edward Paul Simon (Tregew, Grenna Lane, Perranwell Station, Truro, Cornwall), *b* 1958; BM, BCh: *m* 1987, Elizabeth Frances Maitland, da of Malcolm Sydney Maitland Adams, MB, ChB, and has issue living, Matthew Paul *b* 1994, Katherine Anne Louise *b* 1987, Anna Elizabeth *b* 1989, Sophie Isabel *b* 1992, — Rosamund Sally, *b* 1956: *m* 1981, Justin Wynn, and has issue living, Kieran *b* 1986, Melissa *b* 1989, — Tanya Mary Louise, *b* 1963, — Juliet Patricia, *b* 1967.

Grandson of late Major Ion Edward FitzGerald Campbell, Duke of Cornwall's LI, *b* 1897, *d* (April) 1936: *m* 1933, Evelyn Julia (who *d* 1992, having *m* 2ndly, 1952, as his second wife, the 11th Earl of Southesk, KCVO, who *d* 1992), da of Lieut-Col Arthur Peere Williams-Freeman, DSO, OBE:—
Ion Edward FitzGerald (Feathercombe, Hambledon, Godalming, Surrey GU8 4DP), *b* (*posthumous*), (May) 1936: *m* 1963, Muriel Elisabeth, da of late Brig Leslie Frederick Ethelbert Wieler, CB, CBE, and has issue living, John Edward FitzGerald, *b* 1964: *m* 1990, Patricia, da of James O'Brien, and has issue living, Laura *b* 1992, — Leslie James FitzGerald, *b* 1965, — Robert Christopher FitzGerald, *b* 1967, — Peter Michael FitzGerald, *b* 1972.

Issue of late Ion Douglas FitzGerald Campbell, 8th son of 2nd baronet, *b* 1868, *d* 1915: *m* 1891, Mabel Unsworth, who *d* 1931, da of late Capt Unsworth Quin, of Dublin:—
Pamela Georgina Theophila, *b* 1899: *m* 1919, Rudolph Agnew, and has had issue, Peter Douglas, *b* 1922: *m* 1946, Margaret Tawse, — Rudolph Ion Joseph (White's, and Cavalry and Guards' Clubs), *b* 1934: *m* 1st, 1957 (*m diss* 1964), Tessa, da of Sqdn-Leader John Molony Longley; 2ndly, 1965 (*m diss* 1980), Hon Clare Rosalind Dixon, da of 2nd Baron Glentoran; 3rdly, 1980, Whitney, da of Chester Ingersoll Warren, and has issue living, (by 2nd *m*) James Ion Daniel *b* 1968: *m* 1992, Sarah K., only da of Peter Newman, of Frensham, Surrey, Charlotte Diana Pamela Geraldine *b* 1970, — Pamela Joan, *b* 1923: *m* 1941, Lt-Cdr Peter Piggford, and has issue living, Andrew Donovan *b* 1956, Sybil Jane *b* 1941.

Issue of late George Theophilus Campbell, 9th son of 2nd baronet, *b* 1872, *d* 1924: *m* 1917, Winifred Edna
    Boyd, da of late James FitzGibbon Black, *b* Montreal:—
Elspeth Griselda Theophila, *b* 1919: *m* 1946, Robin John Patrick Flynn, MC, DFC, and has issue living, Michael George
Alexander Robin Fitzgerald Campbell, *b* 1949, — Reidy Georgina Campbell, *b* 1948.

Granddaughters of late Capt Frederic Augustus Campbell, 4th son of 1st baronet:—
Issue of late John St Clair CAMPBELL-BRABAZON, OBE, *b* 1865, *d* 1942, having assumed by Roy licence 1923 the
    additional surname of Brabazon: *m* 1900, Caroline Leavett, of Mayford Lodge, Mayford, Woking:—
Pamela Francis, *b* 1903: *m* 1st, 1921 (*m diss* 1930), Francis Baer; 2ndly, 1931, Flight-Lieut Herbert Geoffrey Brookman, RAF
(ret) who *d* 1936; 3rdly, 1937 (*m diss* 1956), Robert Walter Guy Grindlay. *Residence* – Shore House, The Quay, Burnham-on-
Crouch, Essex. ——— Geraldine, *b* 1904: *m* 1928, Brigadier Edward Hamilton Grant, late Argyll and Sutherland Highlanders,
and has issue living, Rosemary Ann, *b* 1930. *Residence* – Warner's Hall, Burnham-on-Crouch, Essex.
The 1st baronet, Sir Guy Campbell, CB (el son of late Lieut-Gen Colin Campbell, Lieut-Gov of Gibraltar 1809-14), was a Maj-
Gen in the Army, and Col of the 3rd West India Regiment; served with distinction throughout the Peninsular war and at
Waterloo. The 2nd baronet, Sir Edward FitzGerald, Col 60th Rifles, served with distinction in the Punjab campaign 1848 and
through the Indian Mutiny campaign 1857-8. The 3rd baronet, Sir Guy Theophilus, was Lieut-Col 60th Rifles and served in
Afghan War 1878-80. The 4th baronet, Sir Guy Colin, was Major 60th Rifles, and served in European Wars 1914-19 and
1941-45.

CAMPBELL (UK) 1831, of Barcaldine and Glenure, Argyllshire

I am prepared

PARATUS SUM

Sir NIALL ALEXANDER HAMILTON CAMPBELL, 8th *Baronet*; *b* 7 Jan
1925; *s* his father *Sir* IAN VINCENT HAMILTON, CB 1978; *ed*
Cheltenham, and Corpus Christi Coll, Oxford; Hereditary Keeper of
Barcaldine Castle; Bar Inner Temple 1951; 1939-45 War as Lt RM;
Assist Sec, St Mary's Hosp, Paddington 1955-60, Sec W Middx Hosp,
Isleworth 1960, and Dep House Gov, London Clinic 1960-68, since
when Sec to Board of Management, Royal Home and Hosp for
Incurables, Putney: *m* 1st, 1949 (*m diss* 1956), Patricia Mary, da of
R. Turner; 2ndly, 1957, Norma Joyce, da of W. N. Wiggin, of
Albrighton, and has issue by 2nd *m*.

Arms – Quarterly: 1st, gyronny of eight or and sable, *Campbell*; on a canton
argent a bend sable, between a unicorn's head in chief and a cross-crosslet
fitchée in base gules, *Dennistoun*; 2nd, or, a fesse checky azure and argent,
Stewart of Lorn; 3rd argent, a lymphad, sails furled and oars in action sable,
Lorne; 4th gyronny of eight or and sable, *Campbell*; on a canton gules two bars,
or *Cameron of Lochiel*; the whole within a bordure quarterly or and sable. **Crest**
– A Highlander fully armed and equipped, having a claymore in the dexter hand
and on the sinister arm a target or. **Supporters** – *Dexter*, a leopard; *sinister*, a
stag — all proper.
Seat – Barcaldine Castle, Ledaig, Argyllshire. *Residence* – The Old Mill, Milltown, Muddiford, Barnstaple EX31 1DX.

SONS LIVING (By 2nd marriage)

RODERICK DUNCAN HAMILTON (East Almer Farmhouse, Almer, Blandford, Dorset DT11 9EL), *b* 24 Feb 1961: *m* 1989, Jean
Caroline, da of Laurence Bicknell, of Tom's Hill, Lobb, Braunton, Devon, and has issue living, Kate Emily Dennistoun, *b*
1990, — Anna Iona Hamilton, *b* 1993. ——— Angus Charles Dundas, *b* 1967.

DAUGHTERS LIVING (By 2nd marriage)

Fiona Madeline Hamilton, *b* 1958. ——— Lucy Catriona Margaret, *b* (twin) 1967.

COLLATERAL BRANCH LIVING

Issue of late Richard Henry Dennistoun Campbell, yr brother of 7th baronet, *b* 1901, *d* 1978: *m* 1936,
    Kathleen Adair, yst da of late Richard Fallowes Dunn, of Wolverhampton:—
Lorne Mary Dennistoun, *b* 1939. ——— Elizabeth Gay Adair, *b* 1942.

Granddaughter of late Maj-Gen John Peter William Campbell, 3rd son of 1st baronet:—
Issue of late Gerald Edward Lyon Campbell, *b* 1863, *d* 1902: *m* 1886, Sybil (who *d* 1958, having *m* 2ndly, 1911, Com
    Wentworth Vernon Cole, formerly RN), da of Maj-Gen Thomas Ross Church, CIE:—
Mary Hamilton, *b* 1888: *m* 1915, Alfred Thomas Duncan Anderson, who *d* 1949, and has issue living, Ian Duncan Hamilton, *b*
1916, — Alec Vernon *b* 1921.
This family is descended from Patrick Campbell, of Innerzeldies, legitimated son of Sir Duncan Campbell, 1st baronet of
Glenorchy, ancestor of the Earls of Breadalbane (a branch of the Ducal House of Argyll). Sir Duncan Campbell of
Barcaldine, 1st Bt, was Capt Scots Fusilier Guards, and served at Copenhagen, Walcheren, and the Peninsula. He *m* 1815,
Elizabeth Dreghorn, da of John Dennistoun of Dennistoun, Dunbartonshire. Sir Alexander, 2nd Bt, was Sergeant-at-Arms in
Queen Victoria's Household. The 3rd Bt, Sir Duncan Alexander Dundas, CVO, was Gentleman Usher of the Green Rod
1884-95, and Sec to Order of the Thistle 1895-1926. The 4th baronet, Sir Alexander William Dennistoun Campbell, was Col
Indian Army. The 5th baronet, Sir Duncan John Alfred Campbell, was sometime a Dist Judge in Central India, and Acting
Commr in Burma and Central Provinces, India. The 6th baronet, Sir (Francis) Eric Dennistoun Campbell was Capt S Lancs
Regt and served in 1914-18 War Afghan War 1919. The 7th baronet, Sir Ian Vincent Hamilton Campbell, CB, was Private Sec
to Ch of Air Staff 1926-27 and to Permanent Sec of Air Min 1927-30, and Assist Private Sec to successive Secs of State for
Air 1930-34, Prin Air Min 1939, and Assist Under-Sec of State 1945-55.

CAMPBELL (UK) 1913, with precedence of 1804, of Ardnamurchan, Argyllshire

Sir BRUCE COLIN PATRICK CAMPBELL, 3rd *Baronet* (*cr* 1913) (but his name does not, at the time of going to press, appear on the Official Roll of Baronets); *b* 2 July 1904; *s* his father, *Lieut-Col Sir* JOHN BRUCE STUART, DSO, 1943; *ed* Edinburgh Acad; no information concerning this baronet has been received since 1943.

𝕬rms – Not recorded in Lyon Register.

SISTERS LIVING AND DECEASED

Noelle Eva Mabel, *b* 1909: *m* 1st, 1929 (*m diss* 1946), Noel Rees; 2ndly, 1946, Maxwell C. Elliot, and *d* 1993, leaving issue (by 1st *m*), John David Campbell (Ferry Cottage, 5 Thetis Terr, Westerley Ware, Kew, Surrey TW9 3AU), *b* 1932; *ed* Clifton Coll; a Tea Broker: *m* 1st 1963, Christine Phyllis Wadsworth; 2ndly, 19—, Mrs Diana Peters, and has issue living, (by 1st *m*) Oliver David Campbell *b* 1965: *m* 1993, Jennifer Andersen, and has issue living, Benjamin Michael David Campbell *b* 1993, — Jeremy Stephen Campbell (31 Athlone Towers, Lower Bridge Rd, Durban North, 4016, S Africa), *b* 1933; *ed* Clifton Coll: *m* 1956, Laura Kathleen Riddle, and has issue living, Lincoln Noel Campbell *b* 1958, Simon Colin Campbell *b* 1960, David Jason Campbell *b* 1969, — (by 2nd *m*) Colin Maxwell Campbell (124 Willis St, Westminster, Maryland 21157, USA) *b* 1947: *m* 1st, 1968 (*m diss* 19—), Robina Dogger, of Briars Court, Limpsfield Chart, Oxted, Surrey; 2ndly, 19—, Gloria Patterson, — (by 1st *m*), Jennifer Campbell, *b* 1936: *m* 1st, 1958, John Bowie; 2ndly, 1980, James Douglas Robertson, of 18 Millers Court, Chiswick Mall, W4, and has issue living (by 1st *m*), Robin Maxwell John *b* 1961, Claire Alexandra *b* 1959: *m* 1985, Peter V. Allen (and has issue living, Thomas V. *b* 1987, James A. *b* 1989). —— Marjorie Ethelle (Flat E2, Queen Alexandra's Court, St Mary's Rd, Wimbledon, SW19), *b* 1911: *m* 1938, Malcolm Melville, who *d* 1942, and has issue living, Pamela Elaine Marguerite, *b* 1940: *m* 1959, Richard Crockett Knox, of Flat 3b, Great Eastern Court, Taman Nakhoda, off Holland Rd, Singapore 10, and has issue living, Andrew Melville *b* 1961, Fiona Heather *b* 1964, — Heather Jacqueline Malcom *b* 1942: *m* 1971, Richard Norton Orlando Kingsbury, of Hamsell Farm, Eridge, Sussex (*see* B Brabourne, colls, 1980 Edn), and has issue living, Nicholas James Melville *b* 1971, Benjamin Francis Knatchbull *b* 1978.

Donald Campbell was created a Baronet of Nova Scotia 1628, and resigned his dignity into the King's hands on 28 Aug 1643, for a new enfeoffment of it and the lands annexed, in favour of his nephew and heirs male. Upon the decease of Donald, his nephew (George) did not, however, claim the title, neither did the three next succeeding heirs, but about 1790 John Campbell, great-great-grandson of George Campbell (ante) resumed the title as 6th baronet, being followed in turn by his son John, Lieut-Gov of St Vincent's 1845-53, and his grandson, Maj-Gen John William Campbell, CB (who served in Crimean Campaign 1855, in China Campaign 1860 and in Afghan War 1879-80), whose claim, however, to be placed on the Roll of Baronets in right of the 1628 creation was not recognized, but upon whom a new Baronetcy of the United Kingdom was conferred in Nov 1913, with special precedence as above-mentioned. The 2nd baronet *d* (whilst a prisoner in Palembang Camp, Sumatra) 1943.

CAMPBELL (UK) 1939, of Airds Bay, co Argyll, and Bromley, co Kent (Extinct 1954)

Sir CHARLES DUNCAN MACNAIR CAMPBELL, 2nd and last *Baronet*.

DAUGHTERS LIVING OF FIRST BARONET

Frances Henriette, *b* 1904; FSA (Scot): *m* 1930, Rear-Adm Keith McNeil Campbell-Walter, CB, US Legion of Merit who *d* 1976, having assumed by deed poll and Letters Patent recorded at College of Arms 1952, the additional surname of Campbell before that of his patronymic, and has issue living, Richard Keith (9 Passmore St, SW1W 8HR), *b* 1941; *ed* Milton Abbey: *m* 1st, 1963 (*m diss* 1973), Marion Clare, only da of F. G. Minter, MBE, of Knock Manor, Wilts; 2ndly, 1973, Dorothy Ann, yst da of late T. W. Oliver, of Old Bewick Farm, Alnwick, and has issue living (by 1st *m*), Lavinia Jane *b* 1964, Petrina Jean *b* 1967, (by 2nd *m*) Jamie Oliver *b* 1972, — Michael McNeil CAMPBELL OF AIRDS BAY (Font Hill, Trinity Hill, St Helier, Jersey; Cavalry and Guards', and Puffins Clubs), *b* (twin) 1941; *ed* Wellington; Maj Scots Gds (ret); recognized by Lord Lyon as representative of family of Campbell of Airds Bay and discontinued the use of the surname of Campbell-Walter 1954: *m* 1963, Anne Catriona, da of late Capt Ian Andrew Tait, Queen's Own Cameron Highlanders, and has issue living, Gillean Lorne Frederick McNeil *b* 1967, Theresa Anne Henrietta *b* 1964, Henrietta Constance *b* 1969, — Fiona Frances Elaine (*Fiona, Baroness Thyssen-Bornemisza de Kaszon*), *b* 1932: *m* 1956 (*m diss* 1965), Baron Hans-Heinrich Thyssen-Bornemisza de Kaszon, and has issue living, *Baron* Lorne Johannes *b* 1963, *Baroness* Francesca Anne Dolores (*HI&RH Archduchess Karl Thomas of Austria*) *b* 1958: *m* 1993, HI&RH Archduke Karl Thomas Robert Maria Franziskus Georg Bahnam of Austria, elder son of HI&RH Archduke Otto of Austria (Dr Otto von Habsburg), formerly Crown Prince of Austria and Hungary (and has issue HI&RH Archduchess Eleonore Jelena Maria del Pilar Christina Iona *b* 1994), — Sheila Elspeth, *b* 1934; JP: *m* 1957, John William Henry Pretty, MB, BS, late Flt-Lt RAF Med Ser, of Ducks Court, High Halstow, Rochester, Kent, and has issue living, Michael John *b* 1962: *m* 1993, Lianne Patricia, elder da of Ross Goulding, of Auckland, NZ, Nicola Sheila *b* 1958: *m* 1985, Nicholas Hugh Bruce Jones, of Hololio Farm, Clevedon, Auckland, NZ (and has issue living, Bruce Nicholas *b* 1988, Henry Frederick *b* 1991, Camilla Jean *b* 1986), Susan Frances *b* 1961: *m* 1987, James Douglas Napier, of 3 Merlewood Av, Cashmere, Christchurch, NZ, Jane Rebecca *b* 1968. *Residences* – 19A Princes Gate Mews, SW7 2PS; 10 Ellenabeich, Isle of Seil, by Oban, Argyll PA34 4RQ. —— Elspeth Ada *b* 1919: *m* 1940, Laurence William Orchard, of 8 Templars Place, St Peter St, Marlow, Bucks SL7 1NU, and has issue living, William Henslow (Hesscot, Rutland Rd, Maidenhead, Berks), *b* 1947: *m* 1st, 1973 (*m diss* 1988), Susan Jane Field; 2ndly, 19—, Mrs Susan Davidson, and has issue living (by 1st *m*), Dominic Henslow *b* 1976, Edward William *b* 1978, Alexander Peter *b* 1980, — Laurence Augustine, *b* 1950: *m* 1986, Lucinda Mary Emrys-Roberts, and has issue living, Peter Augustine *b* 1990, Rosalind Ann *b* 1988, — Anthony Edward, *b* 1962, — Gillian Mary, *b* 1941, — Sarah Elspeth, *b* 1942: *m* 1967, Norman Hampel, of Two Oaks, Slade Oak lane, Denham, Bucks, and has issue living, Simon Mark, *b* 1968, John Laurence *b* 1969, Angus James *b* 1973, Nicola Jane *b* 1971, — Wendy Frances, *b* 1944.

Sir Edward Taswell Campbell of Airds Bay, 1st Bt, was MP for Camberwell NW Div 1924-29, and for Bromley, Kent 1930-45; PPS to Lord Privy Seal 1940-43. His eldest son, Sir (Charles) Duncan McNair Campbell of Airds Bay, 2nd Bt, *dsp* 1954 (when the baronetcy became ext), and his only remaining son, Gillian Lorne Campbell, DFC, Fl Lieut RAFVR, was *ka* 1942. Sir Edward's eldest da, Frances Henriette (ante) *s* her brother as Representor of the family of Campbell of Airds Bay, and her yr son, Michael McNeil Campbell of Airds Bay, was officially recognised by the Lord Lyon as her Representor 1954, when he matriculated the arms.

COCKBURN-CAMPBELL (UK) 1821, of Gartsford, Ross-shire
(Name pronounced "Coburn-Campbell")

Watchful

Sir THOMAS COCKBURN-CAMPBELL, 6th *Baronet*; *b* 8 Dec 1918; *s* his father, *Sir* ALEXANDER THOMAS, 1935; *ed* Church of England Gram Sch, Melbourne, Australia; author of *Land of Lots of Time*: *m* 1st, 1944 (*m diss* 1981), Josephine Zoi, el da of Harold Douglas Forward, of Cunjardine, W Australia; 2ndly, 1982 (*m diss* 1990), Janice Laraine, yst da of William John Pascoe, of Bundoora, Victoria, and has issue by 1st *m*.

Arms – Quarterly 1st and 4th: quarterly, i and iv gyronny of eight or and sable, *Campbell*; ii, argent, a galley or lymphad sails furled, oars in action sable; iii, or, a fesse checky azure and argent, over all a chief argent charged with a rock proper superscribed "Gibraltar," between two medals for Seringapatam and Talavera; 2nd and 3rd, quarterly, i and iv, argent, an ostrich feather ensigned with an Imperial crown proper, between three cocks, two and one, gules; ii and iii, six mascles three two and one or, *Cockburn*. **Crest** – 1st, a dexter hand holding a scimitar all proper, *Campbell*. *Residence* – 14 Lincoln St, York, 6302 W Australia.

SON LIVING *(By 1st marriage)*

ALEXANDER THOMAS (11 Templetonia Retreat, Livingston Estate, Canning Vale 6155, W Australia), *b* 16 March 1945: *m* 1969, Kerry Anne, el da of late Sgt K. Johnson, of Mt Hawthorne, W Aust, and has issue living, Thomas Justin, *b* 10 Feb 1974, — Felicity Ann, *b* 1981.

BROTHER LIVING

Alexander Bruce (90 Evans St, Shenton Park, W Australia), *b* 1923; Leading Aircraftman, Roy Australian Air Force; S-W Pacific 1944-45: *m* 1951, Beryl, da of William Elder, of Shenton Park, W Australia, and has issue living, Susan Peta, *b* 1954, — Nola Gay, *b* 1957, — Judith Ann, *b* 1961, — Alison Lee, *b* 1964.

Lieut-Gen Sir Alexander Campbell, 1st Bt, Col of 80th Regiment, greatly distinguished himself at Seringapatam, also in the Peninsula, 1809-11, where he commanded a division of the British Army. He was created a baronet 1815, and in 1821 obtained a new patent, which extended the limitation to the male issue of his daughter Olympia (Mrs Cockburn), and afterwards to the male issue of his daughter Isabella Charlotte (Lady Malcolm), which is now extinct. The 2nd baronet assumed in 1824 the additional surname of Campbell. Sir Thomas, 4th baronet, was Pres of Legislative Council of W Australia.

HOME-PURVES-HUME-CAMPBELL (NS) 1665, of Purves Hall, Berwickshire (Dormant or Extinct 1960)
(Name pronounced "Hume-Purves-Hume-Campbell")

Sir JOHN HOME-PURVES-HUME-CAMPBELL, 8th and last *Baronet*.

DAUGHTERS LIVING OF EIGHTH BARONET

Mabel Jane (L'Olivier, Route de Mons, Tourrettes-Fayence, France 83), *b* 1905. —— Elsie Barbara *b* 1907: *m* 1st, 1928 (*m diss* 1940), Donovan Storr Allom; 2ndly, 1954, George Moxon Cook, and has issue living (by 1st *m*), Michael Donovan, *b* 1930; *ed* Wellington Coll, and Trin Coll, Camb, — Bridget Barbara, *b* 1935, — Sheila Ann, *b* 1938.

Campbell-Orde, see Orde.

CARDEN (I) 1787, of Templemore, Tipperary

Sir JOHN CRAVEN CARDEN, 7th Baronet; *b* 11 March 1926; *s* his father, *Sir* JOHN VALENTINE, MBE, 1935; *ed* Eton: *m* 1947, Isabel Georgette, yst da of late Robert de Hart, and has issue.

Arms – Argent, a mascle gules between three pheons sable. **Crest** – A pheon sable.
Clubs – White's.

DAUGHTER LIVING

Isabel Mary, *b* 1952.

COLLATERAL BRANCH LIVING

Grandsons of late Major Henry Charles Carden, DSO, 2nd son of 4th baronet:—
Issue of late Rev Canon Henry Craven Carden, *b* 1882, *d* 1964: *m* 1913, Olive, who *d* 1966, da of late Rev Canon C. V. Gorton:—
DERRICK CHARLES, CMG (38 Headbourne Worthy House, Winchester, Hants SO23 7JG), *b* 31 Oct 1921; *ed* Marlborough and Ch Ch, Oxford, in Sudan Political Ser 1942-54; entered HM's Dip Ser 1954; HM Political Agent, Qatar, Persian Gulf 1955-58, Oriental Sec, British Embassy, Tripoli, Libya 1958-62, at Foreign Office, 1962-64 Head of Chancery, Cairo 1964-65, Consul-Gen, Muscat 1965-69, and Dir Middle East Centre of Arab Studies 1969-73, since when Ambassador to Yemen Arab Republic 1973-76; Visiting Fellow Inst of Development Studies Sussex Univ 1977, since when Ambassador to Sudan; a JP; CMG 1974: *m* 1952, Elizabeth Anne, da of late Capt Alfred Spalding Russell, DSO, RN, and has issue living, John Craven (7 Cleveland Rd, Chichester), *b* 1953: *m* 1983, Celia Howitt, and has issue living, Patrick John Cameron *b* 1988, — Peter James Charles, *b* 1958, — Elisabeth Louise, *b* 1956, — Clare Margaret, *b* 1961.

With faith and love

Issue of late John Humphrey Carden, *b* 1886, *d* 1957: *m* 1923, Eileen Winifred Bourke (2 Alexandra Road, Brecon), da of late Lieut-Col Thomas Patrick Shannon, RASC:—
Patrick Henry, *b* 1928; in Trin House Pilotage Ser: *m* 1951, Rosalie Alice, da of late Rev Canon S. W. Groom, formerly V of Holy Trinity, Lamorbey, Sidcup, and has issue living, Derek Edward Trevor, *b* 1952: *m* 1977, Amanda Mary Smyllie, and has issue living Toby James *b* 1980, Philip Paul *b* 1983, Oliver Mark *b* 1987, — Nigel John Patrick, *b* 1954, — Roger Michael Colin, *b* 1956: *m* 1989, Helena Louise Davis, and has issue living, Katy Louise *b* 1993. *Residence* – The Old Rectory, 91 Windmill St, Gravesend, Kent. —— Michael Humphrey *b* 1929; late Capt Worcestershire Regt. *Residence* – 2 Alexandra Rd, Brecon.

Issue of late Frederick Richard Carden, 3rd son of 4th baronet, *b* 1856, *d* 1935: *m* 1885, Miriam, da of — Beale:—
Richard Craven, *b* 1893. —— Selwyn, *b* 18—. —— Rodney, *b* 18—. —— Geoffrey, *b* 18—. —— Helen Mary: *m* 1912, Herbert Roger. —— Pattie: *m* 1915, D. A. Morrell.

Issue of late Capt Coldstream James Carden, 4th son of 4th baronet, *b* 1857, *d* 1925: *m* 1891, Rose Margaret Ponton, yst da of late David Johnstone, of Croy Shandon, Dunbartonshire:—
Eileen Margaret, *b* 1893: *m* 1919, Brig Thomas Dix Perkin, DL, KSLI, who *d* 1961, and *d* 1984.

Grandson of late Lieut-Col Henry Westenra Carden (infra):—
Issue of late Bernard Westenra Carden, *b* 1887, *d* 1951: *m* 1923, Gwendoline, who *d* 1980, da of Joseph Price, of Leamington:—
Patrick Westenra, *b* 1928; *ed* Univ of Wales (BSc 1951): *m* 1955, Janet Hilda, da of William Stickland, of Cambridge, and has issue living, David Westenra, *b* 1957: *m* 1984, Jane Leslie Clough, and has issue living, Benjamin Westenra *b* 1989, Timothy Peter *b* 1992, — Trevor Courtenay *b* 1959, — Angela, *b* 1961: *m* 1985, Keith West, and has issue living, Christopher William *b* 1990, Heather Carol *b* 1992, — Carol Mary, *b* 1967. *Residence* – Sandy Top, 174 Station Rd, Fordingbridge, Hants SP6 1DS.

Granddaughters of late Rev Arthur Carden, 3rd son of 3rd baronet:—
Issue of late Lieut-Col Henry Westenra Carden, *b* 1857, *d* 1928: *m* 1st, 1886, Emily Elphinstone, who *d* 1918, da of late Rev William Courtenay Clack, R of Moretonhampstead, Devon; 2ndly, 1919, Beatrice, who *d* 1944, da of Peter Sharp, formerly of Cannock, Stafford:—
Muriel Elphinstone, *b* 1899: *m* 1924, Charles Pelham Thursby, who *d* 1977, and has issue living, Hugh James, *b* 1931. *Residence* – The Bungalow, Clive, Salop. —— Christina Annette (205, 7720-108th St, Edmonton, Alberta, Canada), *b* 1900: *m* 1924, John Elliot Weir, who *d* 1976, and has issue living, Charles Henry (14003-75th Av, Edmonton, Alberta, Canada T5R 2Y5), *b* 1925; MSc, DLS, PEng: *m* 1949, Kathleen McLellan, and has issue living, Douglas Charles *b* 1953, Wendy Kathleen *b* 1954, Sandra Christina *b* 1957, — Carden Fraser (14 Atlanta Cres, Calgary, Alberta, Canada), *b* 1927: *m* 1950, Freda Irene McCoy, and has issue living, Carlene Ann *b* 1951: *m* 1972, Ronald Joseph Bourassa (and has issue living, Jeffery Alexander *b* 1976, Ronalee Jo-Ann *b* 1974, Danielle Lynn Patricia *b* 1975), Marion *b* 1954: *m* 1973, Carmon Marshall Woodworth (and has issue living, Collin Matthew *b* 1976, Carl Alexander *b* 1978), Patti *b* 1961: *m* 1984, David Mitchell Dennis.
This family, originally of Lincolnshire, settled at Templemore, co Tipperary, about 1650.

CARDEN (UK) 1887, of Wimpole Street, Middlesex, and of Molesey, Surrey

Sir CHRISTOPHER ROBERT CARDEN, 5th *Baronet, b* 24 Nov 1946; *s* his father, *Sir* HENRY CRISTOPHER, OBE, 1993; *ed* Eton, and Aberdeen Univ (BSc Forestry): *m* 1st, 1972 (*m diss* 1979), Sainimere Rokotuibau, of Suva, Fiji; 2ndly, 1981, Clarita Peralta, of Manila, Philippines.

Arms – Per pale sable and gules, a staff sling in bend between four pheons saltirewise, all argent. **Crest** – On a fasces fessewise or, a wolf's head erased sable, pierced in the neck with an arrow bendwise or, point downwards gold, embrued proper.
Address – Casilla 1341, Santa Cruz, Bolivia.

SISTER LIVING

Melinda Jane, *b* 1950: *m* 1975, Andrew James Wilson, of Glenfall Stables, Ham, Charlton Kings, Cheltenham, Glos, son of Capt G. A. J. Wilson, of Ballyburn, Castledermot, co Kildare, and has issue living, Fiona Jane, *b* 1981, — Sarah Bobby, *b* 1984.

MOTHER LIVING

Jane St Clare, da of late Lt-Col Thomas Edward St Clare Daniell, OBE, MC: *m* 1st, 1943 (*m diss* 1961), as his 1st wife, Sir Henry Christopher Carden, 4th Bt, OBE, who *d* 1993; 2ndly, 1962, Maj Thomas Douglas Pilkington of Reay, of Hyde Mill, Stow-on-the-Wold, Cheltenham, Glos.

WIDOW LIVING OF FOURTH BARONET

With faith and love

GWYNETH SYBIL, FCA (*Gwyneth, Lady Carden*), da of late Herbert Arthur Dyke Acland, and widow of Fl-Lt Roderick Stanley Emerson (*see* Acland, Bt (*cr* 1980), colls): *m* 1962, as his 2nd wife, Sir Henry Christopher Carden, 4th Bt, OBE, who *d* 1993. *Residence* – Moongrove, East Woodhay, Newbury, Berks.

COLLATERAL BRANCH LIVING

Granddaughter of late Alexander James Carden, 3rd son of 1st baronet:—
Issue of late Henry Carden, *b* 1872, *d* 1948: *m* 1st, 1894, Martha Vinnineda, who *d* 1918, da of Ernst Tronson of Romsdalen, Norway; 2ndly, 1919, Mildred Kedge, who *d* 1946:—
(By 1st *m*) Florence Lillian, *b* 1895: *m* 1924, Brigadier Francisco Rabia Muñoz, Mexican Army. *Residence* – Antonio Maura, 181 Col Moderna, Mexico, DF.
The 1st baronet, Sir Robert Walter Carden (sometime MP for Barnstaple) was Lord Mayor of London 1857, and an Alderman 1849-88. The 2nd baronet was High Sheriff of Hants 1891. The 3rd baronet was High Sheriff of Hants, 1922.

CAREW (E) 1661, of Haccombe, Devonshire

Sir RIVERS VERAIN CAREW, 11th *Baronet*; *b* 17 Oct 1935; *s* his father, *Sir* THOMAS PALK, 1976; *ed* St Columba's Coll, co Dublin, and Dublin Univ (BAgric(Hort), MA); author of *Figures out of Mist*: *m* 1st, 1968 (*m diss* 1991), Susan Babington, da of late Harold Babington Hill, of London; 2ndly, 1992, Siobhán, 2nd da of late Críostoir Seán Mac Cárthaigh, of Cork, and has issue by 1st *m*.

Arms – Or, three lions passant in pale sable. **Crest** – A main-mast, the round top set off with palisadoes or, a demi-lion issuant thereout sable.
Address – Undercliffe Cottage, Clarence St, Dartmouth, Devon TQ6 9NW.

SON LIVING *(By 1st marriage)*

GERALD DE REDVERS, *b* 24 May 1975.

Nil conscire sibi

Conscious of no guilt

DAUGHTERS LIVING *(By 1st marriage)*

Marcella Tamsin, *b* 1970. —— Marina Lys, *b* 1972. —— Miranda Rose, *b* (twin) 1973.

SISTER LIVING

Oenone Venetia, *b* 1929: *m* 1957, John O'Sullivan, of 17 Brighton Av, Rathgar, Dublin 6, and has issue living, Rowan John Amadeus, *b* 19—, — Kilda Mary Venetia *b* 19—, — Marney Darrell Owen, *b* 19—.

HALF-SISTER LIVING

Zia (23 Hill Lands, Wargrave, Berks), *b* 1914; 1939-42 War with WAAF: *m* 1939, Maj Hugh Richard Stirling, RA, who *d* on active service 1944, and has issue living, Anthony Carew (High Wood, Green Lane, Ellisfield, nr Basingstoke, Hants), *b* 1942; *ed* Pangbourne Nautical Coll: *m* 1968, Geraldine Erica, yst da of Fl Lt Walter Frank Barker, of Wargrave, — Valerie Frances, *b* 1943: *m* 1969, Jeremy Hamilton Lightly, and has issue living, Yvonne Susan *b* 1970, Nicola Jane *b* 1973.

COLLATERAL BRANCHES LIVING

Grandson of late Col Peter Fitzwilliam Carew, late Suffolk Regt, elder son of Rev Henry William Carew, eldest son of Thomas Carew, of Rattery, Devon, 3rd son of 7th baronet:—
Issue of late Capt John Mohun Carew, MC, 3rd Gurkha Rifles, *b* 1921, *d* 1980: *m* 1950, Barbara Joan Stewart, who *d* 1993, da of Maj Arthur Neil Stewart Roberts, OBE, and widow of Maj Richard Henry Baird Shakespear:—
Nicolas John Stewart, *b* 1952. *Residence* – 20 Famian Place, Binfield, Berks RG12 5BX.

Grandchildren of late Com Alfred Curtis Carew, RN, 2nd son of Thomas Carew, of Rattery, Devon (ante):—
Issue of late Thomas Alfred Curtis Carew, *b* 1895, *d* 1970: *m* 1921, Christina, da of John Hanna:—
Patrick Henry Curtis, CD (1070 Sunnyside Rd, Kelowna, BC, Canada VIZ ZN8), *b* 1931; *ed* Trafalgar Sch, Nelson, and Kelowna Senior High Sch; Brig-Gen late R Canadian Dragoons; Korea 1952-53 (two medals); NW Europe 1959-63; Cyprus 1966; NW Europe 1970-72: *m* 1954, Norma Diane, da of Claude Rupert Methune Willcox, of Vancouver, BC, and has issue living, Janice Lynn, *b* 1956, — Suzanne Marie, *b* 1961. —— Verona Lorraine, *b* 1922: *m* 1945, Allan Cameron Barton, of Boucherie Rd, Westbank, BC, Canada, and has issue living, Thomas Allan, *b* 1946, — Gerald Patrick, *b* 1948, — Allan Bruce, *b* 1956. —— Dorothy Joan, *b* 1925: *m* 1948, Charles Henry Pfyffer von Altishofen (Box 40, East Kelowna, BC, Canada, VOH 160), and has issue living, Charles Russell, *b* 1950, — Richard Louis, *b* 1956, — Christine Marie, *b* 1951, — Alice Jerryl, *b* 1955.
Issue of late Nicholas John Carew, *b* 1904, *d* 1974: *m* 1930, Miken Viola, da of late George Borg:—
Nicholas Darrell (3405 27th St, Vernon, BC, Canada), *b* 1932; *ed* Vernon Senior High Sch, and Univ of BC. —— Shirley Elizabeth Diane, *b* 1931: *m* 1953, —.

Granddaughter of late Thomas Carew, of Rattery, Devon, 3rd son of 7th baronet:—
Issue of late Com Alfred Curtis Carew, RN, *b* 1847, *d* 1927: *m* 1893, Susannah, who *d* 1939, da of late Edmund Grantham:—
Dorothy Susannah, *b* 1894: *m* 1932, Hugh Fraser Cunningham.

Granddaughter of late Charles Robert Sydenham Carew (infra):—
Issue of late Capt Peter Gawen Carew, *b* 1894, *d* 1966: *m* 1927, Ruth, who *d* 1983, da of Arthur Chamberlain, JP, of Rackenford Manor, Tiverton:—
Nicola CAREW (*Lady Kennard*), *b* 1930; resumed in 1968 the surname of Carew: *m* 1st, 1950 (*m diss* 1968), Charles Louis Breitmeyer, solicitor; 2ndly, 1985, Lt-Col Sir George Arnold Ford Kennard, 3rd Bt, and has issue living (by 1st *m*), Hugo Charles BREITMEYER (The Stables, Warnicombe, Tiverton, Devon EX16 4PP), *b* 1951: *m* 1986, Diana Margaret, elder da of Michael Harold Wrigley, OBE, of Ganton, Yorks, and has issue living, Alice Holway *b* 1988, Eleanor Audrey *b* 1991, — Peter Alan CAREW, *b* 1953; assumed 1970 the surname of Carew: *m* 1984, Laura L., da of Esmond Gerahty, of West Farm, Owermoigne, Dorest, and has issue living, a son *b* 1985, a son *b* 1989, a da *b* 1987, — Henry John CAREW (4 Gowan Av, SW6; Overlands, Tiverton, Devon), *b* 1957; assumed 1970 the surname of Carew: *m* 1976, Louise Star, yr da of Roger Francis Mortimer, by his wife, Cynthia Sydney, yst da of late Maj Henry Denison Pender, DSO, OBE, MC (yr brother of 1st Baron Pender), and has issue living, Benjamin Charles Henry *b* 1985, Rebecca Louise *b* 1978, — Geoffrey Nicholas CAREW, *b* 1962; assumed 1970 the surname of Carew: *m* 1987, Maxine, da of Douglas Robson, of Cote, Eskdalemuir, nr Langton, Dumfriesshire, and has issue living, Thomas Mohun *b* 1990, Sophy Bloodaxe *b* 1992. *Residence* – Gogwell, Tiverton, Devon EX16 4PP.

Granddaughter of late Rev Robert Baker Carew, son of late Rev Thomas Carew, 3rd son of 6th baronet:—
Issue of late Charles Robert Sydenham Carew, *b* 1853; *d* 1939: *m* 1891, Muriel Mary Heathcoat, who *d* 1939, da of Sir John Heathcoat Heathcoat-Amory, 1st Bt:—
Nancy, *b* 1899.

The family of Carew is of great antiquity in Devon and Cornwall, and claims a common descent with the Dukes of Leinster and Earls of Plymouth from Walter Fitz-Other, who was Castellan of Windsor 1078. For several generations the heads of the family are described as Barons of Carew and Idrone, but none of them sat in Parliament with the exception of Nicholas de Carew, who subscribed to the celebrated Barons' letter to the Pope in 1300, and from his second son the present family is descended in a direct line.

Carew Pole, see Pole.

CARLILE (UK) 1917, of Ponsbourne, co Hertford (Extinct 1942)

Sir (EDWARD) HILDRED CARLILE, CBE, TD, 1st and last *Baronet*.

DAUGHTER LIVING OF FIRST BARONET

Eleanor Cicely: *m* 1927, Rev Thomas Vyner Southey, who *d* 1928, V of Ponsbourne.

CARLILE (UK) 1928, of Gayhurst, co Buckingham (Extinct 1950)

Sir (WILLIAM) WALTER CARLILE, OBE, 1st and last *Baronet*.

WIDOW LIVING OF FIRST BARONET

KATHARINE ELIZABETH MARY (*Lady Carlile*) (15 Oak Tree Court, Portland Drive, Willen, Milton Keynes, Bucks MK15 9LP), only da of late Rev G. H. Field, of Gayhurst, Newport Pagnell, Bucks; JP Bucks 1948-78; has resumed her former style: *m* 1st, 1940, as his 2nd wife, Sir (William) Walter Carlile, OBE, 1st Bt, who *d* 1950, when the title became ext; 2ndly, 1973, as his 2nd wife, Geoffry Dover, who *d* 1984.

GIBSON-CRAIG-CARMICHAEL (NS) 1702, of Keirhill, co Edinburgh, and (UK) 1831, of Riccarton, Midlothian

Live to God, and you shall live

Sir DAVID PETER WILLIAM GIBSON-CRAIG-CARMICHAEL, 15th *Baronet* of Keirhill, and 8th *Baronet* of Riccarton; *b* 21 July 1946; *s* his father Sir (ARCHIBALD HENRY) WILLIAM, 1969; *ed* Queen's Univ, Kingston, Canada (BSc): *m* 1973, Patricia, da of Marcos Skarnic, of Santiago, Chile, and has issue living.

ᴁrms – Quarterly: 1st and 4th, ermine, on a fesse sable three crescents argent, *Craig*; 2nd and 3rd, gules, three keys fesseways in pale, wards downwards or, *Gibson*. ᴄrest – A knight on horseback in full armour, his right hand grasping a broken tilting spear shivered all proper. ᴋupporters – Dexter, a man in armour holding in exterior hand a spear all proper; sinister, a war-horse argent, saddled and bridled proper. *Residence* – Quintas, Nova Lima, Brazil. *Address* – Casilla 2461, Santiago, Chile.

SON LIVING

PETER WILLIAM, *b* 29 Dec 1975.

DAUGHTER LIVING

Margaret Anne, *b* 1977.

BROTHERS LIVING

Alasdair John, *b* 1948: *m* 1973, Irene, da of Bruno Haverbeck, of Santiago, Chile. —— Andrew Charles, *b* 1952.

SISTER LIVING

Susan Ann, *b* 1949: *m* 1970, Richard John Darling, and has issue living, Christopher John, *b* 1971, — Nicholas Patrick, *b* 1973.

AUNTS LIVING (*Daughters of 13th baronet*)

Emily Edith, *b* 1915. —— Kathleen Joan, *b* 1919: *m* 1940, Charles Taylor Darling, of Universidad Nacional de Tucuman, Argentina, and has issue living, Anthony Robin, *b* 1941, — Richard John, *b* 1944, — Judith Ann, *b* 1946.

COLLATERAL BRANCHES LIVING (*In remainder to the Nova Scotia (cr 1702) Baronetcy only*)

Issue (by 1st *m*) of late John Murray Gibson-Carmichael, 3rd son of 10th baronet (*cr* 1702), *b* 1860, *d* 1923: *m* 1st, 1892, Amy Katherine, who *d* 1899, da of Frederick Archdale; 2ndly, 1921, Beatrice Mary, who *d* 1964, da of James Donoghue, of co Westmeath:—
Violet Penelope, *b* 1899: *m* 1929, Dennis Wheeler-Carmichael (who assumed by deed poll 1929 the additional and final surname of Carmichael and *d* 1980), and has had issue, Thomas Montague *b* 1932: *m* 1957, Jane (The Woodlands, The Street, Chilcompton, nr Bath, Avon BA3 4HB), da of late Noel Cross, and *d* 1993, leaving issue, George Alexander *b* 1959: *m* 1986, Marianne Jean, 2nd da of Hon Cecil Towry Henry Law (*see* B Ellenborough) (and has issue living, James Henry *b* 1990, Guy Thomas *b* 1992), Charles Edward *b* 1961, — Margaret Mary (78 Ray Lea Rd, Maidenhead, Berks), *b* 1930: *m* 1949, Archibald Colville, who *d* 1970, and has issue living, Thomas David (Oudenakker Str 46, Weert, The Netherlands) *b* 1952: *m* 1979, Ellen, da of Col Leendert Cornelis Schreuders (ret), of Weert, Holland (and has issue living, Andrew David *b* 1981, Mark Robert *b* 1983, Daniel John *b* 1985), William Henry Archibald *b* 1955: *m* 1981, Sally-Anne, yst da of Capt J. R. D. Sears, of The Actrees, Berkeley, Glos (and has issue living, Archie *b* 1991, Diana *b* 1985), Rosemary Elizabeth *b* 1950: *m* 1974, Neil Robert Colquhoun (*see* Greenwell, Bt).

Grandson of late James Whitaker Gibson, son of late William Charles Gibson, CMG, a descendant of Alexander Gibson of Durie, brother of 1st baronet:—
Issue of late William James Carmichael Gibson, *b* 1883, *d* 1955: *m* 1918, Maude, da of Roger Buston:—
John Carmichael, *b* 1919. *Residence* – 10 Clanricarde Gardens, W2.

Sir James, 1st Bt (*cr* 1831), was second son of William Gibson (B Carmichael, colls), and assumed the additional surname of Craig 1818. The 2nd baronet, Rt Hon Sir William, PC, sat as MP for Edinburghshire (*L*) 1837-41, and for Edinburgh city 1841-52, and was Lord Clerk Register and Keeper of the Signet of Scotland 1862-78. Sir James, 3rd Bt, was Brigadier Roy Co of Archers (King's Body Guard for Scotland). The 4th Bt, Sir Archibald Charles Gibson-Craig, Lieut Highland LI, was *ka* 1914 (despatches). The Nova Scotia Baronetcy (*cr* 1702) was conferred upon Thomas Gibson, son of Sir John Gibson of Pentland and Addistone, with remainder to his heirs male whatsoever, and the 6th baronet (John) of this creation assumed the additional surname of Carmichael succeeding under the entail of Skirling, Peebles-shire, while Sir Thomas David 11th Bt, was *cr* Baron Carmichael 1912. In 1914, Capt Henry Thomas Gibson-Craig *s* his brother as 5th Bt of Riccarton, and in Jan 1926, his kinsman, the 1st Baron Carmichael, in the NS Baronetcy (*cr* 1702) of Keirhill; *d* 1926, having assumed the additional surname of Carmichael.

Carmichael-Anstruther, see Anstruther.

RIVETT-CARNAC (UK) 1836, of Derby

Thus they go to Heaven

Rev Sir (THOMAS) NICHOLAS RIVETT-CARNAC, 8th *Baronet*, son of late Vice-Adm James William Rivett-Carnac, CB, CBE, DSC, 2nd son of 6th baronet; *b* 3 June 1927: *s* his uncle, *Sir* HENRY GEORGE CRABBE, 1972; *ed* Marlborough; late Maj Scots Gds; Malaya 1950 (despatches); V of St Mark's, Kennington Oval, SE11 1972-89, Rural Dean of Lambeth (Southwark) 1978-82, Hon Canon of Southwark Cathedral since 1980: *m* 1977, Susan Marigold MacTier, yr da of late C. Harold Copeland.

Arms – Quarterly, argent and azure, two swords in saltire proper between three mullets, one in chief and two in fesse, and a crescent in base counterchanged. **Crest** – a sword erect pommel and hilt or, issuing from a crescent ermine, the internal part gules.
Address – 1 The Stable, Ashburnham Place, Battle, E Sussex TN33 9NF.

BROTHER LIVING

MILES JAMES (The Manor House, Martyr Worthy, Winchester SO21 1DY), *b* 7 Feb 1933; *ed* RNC Dartmouth; Cdr RN; Far East Fleet Patrols and Borneo Territories 1964-65 (despatches); Man Dir Baring Bros & Co Ltd: *m* 1958, April Sally, da of late Maj Arthur Andrew Sidney Villar, of 48 Lowndes Sq, SW1, and has issue living, Jonathan James, *b* 1962, — Simon Miles, *b* 1966, — Lucinda Jane (*Hon Mrs Valentine Guinness*), *b* 1960: *m* 1986, Hon Valentine Guy Bryan Guinness, 2nd son of 3rd Baron Moyne.

SISTER LIVING

Isla Carolyn (*Baroness Abinger*), *b* 1925: *m* 1957, 8th Baron Abinger, of Sheepcote House, Castle Hedingham, Essex CO9 3HA, and has issue.

AUNT LIVING (*daughter of 6th baronet*)

Aileen Mary (15A Kensington Mansions, Trebovir Rd, Earls Court, SW5), *b* 1908: *m* 1945, Edward F. Wakeford, who *d* 1973.

COLLATERAL BRANCHES LIVING

Issue of late Maj John Temple Rivett-Carnac, late The Duke of Wellington's Regt, yst son of 6th baronet, *b* 1906, *d* 1991/2: *m* 1st, 1941 (*m diss* 1951), Sarah Winifred (7 Main Rd, Farrarmere, Benoni 1500, S Africa) (who *m* 2ndly, 1978, Capt Lancelot Charles Henry Hope, who *d* 1978), only da of Wilfred Herbert Eglin, of Trimmingham, Halifax, W Yorks; 2ndly, 1951, Vivienne Mary Fairchild, who *d* 1979:—
(By 1st *m*) (John) Clive (49 Dalbini Drive, Mulbarton, Johannesburg 2091, S Africa), *b* 1944. —— Rosemary Jane, *b* 1943: *m* 1972, John Drysdale Gilchrist, of 4b Bright St, Western Extension, Benoni, S Africa, and has issue living, David Matthew, *b* 1976, — George Robert, *b* 1979.

Grandson of late William John Rivett-Carnac, 2nd son of 1st baronet:—
Issue of late Col Percy Temple Rivett-Carnac (brother of 6th baronet), *b* 1852, *d* 1932: *m* 1898, Alice, who *d* 1928, da of late Maj Sidney Herbert, of Pietermaritzburg, S Africa:—
Percival Sydney (763 Wharncliffe Rd, Duncan, BC, Canada V9L 2K2), *b* 1904: *m* 1950, Joan, da of late Jeffery Waddington, and has issue living, Jeremy Charles Percy (4400 Telegraph Rd, Cowichan Bay, BC, Canada), *b* 1954: *m* 1981, Monique Madeleine Marie Faivre, and has issue living, Paul Fabien Alexander *b* 1981, Gabriel Gérard Faivre *b* 1984, — Sahlaa, *b* 1952: *m* 1973, Robert Morris, of 42 Dunham Cres, Aurora, Ontario, Canada L4G 2V4, and has issue living, Jeffery Luke *b* 1981, Jay Matthew *b* 1985, — Gai (adopted da), *b* 1957: *m* 1979 (*m diss* 1984), Ian James.

Granddaughter of late Wilfred Theodore Rivett-Carnac, yst brother of 6th baronet, *b* 1864, *d* 1929: *m* 18—— (*m diss* 19——), Alice, da of late John Southam, and widow of —— Wells:—
Issue of late Peter Rivett-Carnac, *b* 1900, *d* 1948: *m* 1944, Grace Kilgore, who *d* 1979, of Traynor, Saskatchewan, Canada:—
Eleanor Grace, *b* 1946: *m* 1968, Peter Johnston, of RR1 Barrie, Ontario, Canada L4M 4Y8, and has issue living, Christina, *b* 1969, — Cheri Lyn (adopted da), *b* 1976.

Granddaughters of late Vernon Charles Rivett-Carnac, son (by 1st *m*) of late Charles James Rivett-Carnac (infra):—
Issue of late Nelson Charles Rivett-Carnac, *b* 1906, *d* 1979: *m* 1932, Bertha Ella Inez Litt, who *d* 1978:—
Cleone Patricia (Finistere, 254 Te Awa Av, Napier, New Zealand), *b* 1933. —— Lynette Marion (66 Glengarry Rd, Glen Eden, Auckland, New Zealand), *b* 1934: *m* 1956 (*m diss* 1979), John Lathom Croft, and has issue living, Michelle Lathom, *b* 1957. —— Robin Genevieve, *b* 1939: *m* 1st, 1957 (*m diss* 1986), Alfred Edward Symon; 2ndly, 1986, John Miller Mercer, who *d* 1988, and has issue living, (by 1st *m*) Christopher Robin St Clair, *b* 1957, — Caroline Jane Fitzalan, *b* 1962, — Sarah Diana Fitzalan, *b* 1963.
Issue of late Maurice Vernon Rivett-Carnac, *b* 1910, *d* 1964: *m* 1934, Merlene Clare Crosby (24 Churchill St, Whangarei, New Zealand):—
Paul Charles (152 Flower St, Northgate 4013, Brisbane, Queensland, Australia), *b* 1945: *m* 1965, Valerie Kay Anderson, and has issue living, Natalie Eve, *b* 1969, — Lisa Marie, *b* 1971. —— Marie Anne, *b* 1938: *m* 1957, Clive Palmer, of Hikurangi, North Island, New Zealand, and has issue living, Michael Brett, *b* 1959, — Gregory John, *b* 1960, — Victoria Ann, *b* (twin) 1960, — Jacqueline Ellen, *b* 1965. —— Dianne Adele, *b* 1943: *m* 19——, David Lambdin, of 852B Birch Cir, Ft Devens, Mass 01433, USA, and has issue living, Shayne, *b* 1963. —— Christine Verna, *b* 1941: *m* 1972, Wayne Wilson Ridgley, of New Zealand, and has issue living, Cory, *b* 1975, — Dionne, *b* 1973, — Vicky, *b* 1978.

Grandchildren (by 2nd *m*) of late Charles James Rivett-Carnac, eldest son of late Charles Forbes Rivett-Carnac, 3rd son of 1st baronet:—
Issue of late Douglas Charles Mahisra Rivett-Carnac, OBE, *b* 1907, *d* 1989: *m* 1946, Barbara Joyce (The Chilterns, Woodgreen, Fordingbridge, Hants), da of late A. R. Pratt:—
Christopher Charles (Heathermoor, Hale Purlieu, Fordingbridge, Hants), *b* 1947: *m* 1974, Sara Catherine, da of late Dr R. J. C. Hutchinson, and has issue living, Thomas Charles, *b* 1977, — Alexander John, *b* 1980, — Michael James, *b* 1983, —

Louise Claire, *b* 1976. —— John Benedict (Lion House, 23 Onslow Rd, Richmond, Surrey), *b* 1949: *m* 1975, Mary Rose, da of Col K. A. P. Fergusson, and has issue living, Charles John Fergus, *b* 1991, — Sophie Caroline, *b* 1979, — Francesca Jane, *b* 1982, — Alice Josephine, *b* 1984. —— Michael Francis, *b* 1950: *m* 1984, Robert Grace, only da of W/Cdr R. O. Mearns Jones, of 22 Parkview Close, Charlton Hill, Andover, Hants, and has issue living, Philippa Jane Mearns, *b* 1988.

Issue of late Charles Francis Rivett-Carnac, Indian Army, *b* 1909, *d* 1958: *m* 1936, Lorna, Evelyn Pemberton, who *d* 1993, da of late B. Darling:—
Jacqueline Anne, *b* 1957: *m* 1957, David Lindsay Millar, OBE, of Bepton Lodge, Bepton, nr Midhurst, W Sussex, and has issue living, Guy McIntyre, *b* 1959: *m* 1983, Kim Lorraine, da of Philip Birch, and has issue living, Katherine Forbes *b* 1981, — Mark Charles Forbes, *b* 1961: *m* 1987, Anna Jo, da of W/Cdr A. MacKinnon, and has issue living, Rory James McIntyre *b* 1989, — Nicholas Lindsay (35 Tunley Rd, SW17 7QH) *b* 1962: *m* 1989, Karen Elizabeth, da of Dr Hugh McLean (and has issue living, Henry James Forbes *b* 1993).

Issue of late Louis Charles Wykeham Rivett-Carnac, *b* 1912, *d* 1985: *m* 1939, Alice, who *d* 1976, da of late J. Docherty:—
Clive Anthony Charles (1 Sandford Gdns, Knights Templar Way, High Wycombe, Bucks), *b* 1940: *m* 1971, Marilyn, da of H. C. Wilkes, and has issue living, James, *b* 1976. —— John Daniel, *b* 1979. —— Louis Charles James (Anchor Cottage, The Holway, Winterton-on-Sea, Gt Yarmouth, Norfolk), *b* 1942: *m* 1968 (*m diss* 1983), Ann Elsey, and has issue living, Paul Antony, *b* 1969, — Andrew Justin, *b* 1970. —— Timothy Charles (1 Julian Rd, Folkestone, Kent), *b* 1949: *ed* Aston Univ (BSc hons): *m* 1st, 1977 (*m diss* 1983), Virginia Trust; 2ndly, 1984, Michelle Jefferies, and has issue living (by 1st *m*), Tristan, *b* 1978, — James Michael, *b* 1980, — Charlotte Louise, *b* 1977, — (by 2nd *m*) Sebastian Louis, *b* 1984, — Nicholas, *b* 1987. —— Nichola Frances, *b* 1947: *m* 1st, 1967 (*m diss* 1981), Robin Wentworth Mason; 2ndly, 1983, Ernest Dare, of 19 Ashby Drive, Rushden, Northants, and has issue living (by 1st *m*), Toby Wentworth, *b* 1970, — Christopher Wentworth, *b* 1971.

Grandchildren of late John Thurlow Rivett-Carnac, 2nd son of Charles Forbes Rivett-Carnac (ante):—
Issue of late Lt-Col John Claude Thurlow Rivett-Carnac, MC, KPM, *b* 1888, *d* 1975: *m* 1st, 1923, Ola Jane, who *d* 1953, da of S. Wilson, of Maine, USA; 2ndly, 1953, Hon Evelyn Hope Balfour, who *d* 1967, da of 1st Baron Riverdale, and widow of Gp Capt Eustace Jack Linton Hope, AFC, RAF:—
(By 1st *m*) Sheila Veronica Mary (Gladstone Rd, RD4 Hadlow, Timaru, New Zealand), *b* 1927: *m* 1st, 1954 (*m diss* 1969), John Coleman Averill; 2ndly, 1969, Alfred Edwin Valentine, who *d* 1981, and has issue living (by 1st *m*), John Miles Rochford, *b* 1958 *m* 1984, Torill Peele, — Andrew Clive Rochford, *b* 1960, — Catherine Veronica, *b* 1955: *m* 1979, George Braoudakis, and has issue living, Emmanuel John *b* 1985, Georgina Virginia *b* 1982, Elizabeth Lucy *b* (twin) 1985, — Elizabeth Jane Rochford, *b* 1957: *m* 1980, Andrew Barrett, and has issue living, two das. —— (By 2nd *m*) John Charles Malcolm (27 Pilgrims Lane, Bugbrooke, Northants), *b* 1955: *m* 1984, Carol Ann Hedley, and has issue living, Amanda *b* 1986, Tamara *b* 1989.

Issue of late Lt-Col Herbert Gordon Rivett-Carnac, Indian Army, *b* 1892, *d* 1962: *m* 1925, Cushla Margarette, who *d* 1974, da of Lt-Col Robert Southey Pottinger:—
Eric Gordon, *b* 1926. —— John Southey, *b* 1929.

Issue of late Edward Charles Rivett-Carnac, *b* 1901, *d* 1980: *m* 1st, 1932, Mary Dillon, who *d* 1970, da of Col Francis Bethel Ware, DSO, VD, of London, Ontario; 2ndly, 1975, Ora-Lee, who *m* 3rdly, 1984, Dan Eckley, of 3290 Plumas St, Apt 317, Reno, Nevada 89509, USA, and 206-1035 Belmont Av, Victoria, BC, Canada V8S 3TS, da of late Harry Edward Tharsing, of Berkeley, Cal, USA, and widow of Capt R. A. Pennington, OBE, RCNVR:—
(By 1st *m*) Beverley Ann (1746 Garnet Rd, Victoria, BC, Canada V8P 3E1), *b* 1933: *m* 1954 (*m diss* 1968), A. F. Griffin, and has issue living, Brenda Gayle, *b* 1956.

Grandson of late Harry Morland Rivett-Carnac, 3rd son of late Charles Forbes Rivett-Carnac (ante):—
Issue of late Charles Walter Rivett-Carnac, *b* 1893, *d* 19—: *m* 1920, Freda Gertrude, who *d* 1959, da of late Frederick Hean Roger, of Melbourne, Australia:—
Gordon Seymour (200 Lawrence Rd, Mt Waverley, Victoria 3149, Australia), *b* 1925: *m* 1949, Marian Propert, da of Robert Newman Scott, of Melbourne, and has issue living, Susan Marian, *b* 1956: *m* 1980, John Gardiner Manning, of 18 Mayfield Dr, Mt Waverley, Victoria 3149, Australia, and has issue living, Benjamin John Garry *b* 1982, Andrew Stephen *b* 1987, Emma *b* 1985, — Penelope Berril, *b* 1961.

Grandson of Gordon Seymour Rivett-Carnac (ante):—
Issue of late Garry Seymour Rivett-Carnac, *b* 1950, *d* 1979: *m* 1974, Jane Baker (Victoria, Australia):—
Scott Harry, *b* 1978.

Grandchildren of late Charles Walter Rivett-Carnac (ante):—
Issue of late Roger Arnott James Rivett-Carnac, *b* 1927, *d* 1967: *m* 1947, Lorna Isabel (who *m* 2ndly, 19—, Raymond Ernest Merrett, of 10 Cunliffe Rd, Killara, NSW 2071, Australia), da of late John Hamilton-Dee:—
Peter William (8 Oxford St, Newtown, NSW 2042, Australia), *b* 1955; BAppSc. —— Lana Kay, *b* 1949: *m* 1968, Ronald John Ernest Russell, of 34 Porlock Way, Karrinyup, W Australia 6018, and has issue living, Glenn John, *b* 1971, — Joanne Jeanette, *b* 1973, — Sharon Jane, *b* 1974. —— Jeanette Anne, *b* 1953: *m* 1978, David Keith Gordon Milne, of 13 Daintrey St, Fairlight, NSW 2094, Australia, and has issue living, Lisa, *b* 1980, — Tanya Judith Kay, *b* 1983.

Granddaughter of late Charles Forbes Rivett-Carnac, 3rd son of 1st baronet:—
Issue of late Col Seymour Gordon Rivett-Carnac, RE, *b* 1868, *d* 1931: *m* 1st, 1893, Martha Ella Maude, who *d* 1920, da of John Latch; 2ndly, 1925, Marian Frances, who *d* 1982, da of H. W. Rowland, formerly of The Bryn, Wyesham, Monmouth:—
(By 2nd *m*) Ann, *b* 1928; *ed* Newnham Coll, Camb (BA honours 1950, MA honours 1954): *m* 1956, Alan Mitchell Burgess, CEng, MIEE, MInstMC, of 6 Pegman Close, Guisborough, Cleveland, and has issue living, Martin Frank, *b* 1960, — Janet Rachel, *b* 1958, — Sarah Kathleen, *b* 1962.

The 1st baronet was Chairman of the East India Co 1836-37 and 1837-38; MP for Sandwich, 1938-39 and Governor of Bombay 1839-41. His father, James Rivett, of HEICS (Bombay), assumed by Royal Warrant in 1801 the additional surname of Carnac. The 2nd baronet sat as MP for Lymington (*C*) 1852-60. The 4th baronet, Sir Claud James, having been missing for many years, an order was issued in the Chancery Div of 11 March 1924, presuming his death as having occurred 31 Dec 1909. Sir William Percival, 5th Bt, *d* 21 March 1924. The 6th baronet, the Rev Sir George Clennell (sometime R of Woldingham), was son of William John Rivett-Carnac, 2nd son of 1st Bt.

CARY (UK) 1955, of Withington, co Lancaster

Sir ROGER HUGH CARY, 2nd *Baronet*; *b* 8 Jan 1926; *s* his father, *Sir* ROBERT ARCHIBALD, 1979; *ed* Eton, and New Coll, Oxford (BA Modern History 1949); Lt Grenadier Gds (Reserve), and an Asso of Roy Historical Soc; was Documentary Producer BBC 1950-56 and Talks Assist, European Ser, 1956-58, Dep Editor *The Listener* 1958-61, Management Training Organiser, BBC 1961-66, Snr Assist Secretariat BBC 1966-74, Special Assist Public Affairs BBC 1974-77, Special Assist to Man Dir BBC TV 1977-83, Chief Assist to the Secretary, BBC 1982-83, Chief Assist to Dir of Programmes TV 1983-86, since when a Consultant to Dir Gen; Sec Central Music Advisory Cttee BBC 1966-77 and 1983; a Trustee of Kedleston since 1988: *m* 1st, 1948 (*m diss* 1951), Marilda, da of late Maj Philip Pearson-Gregory, MC; 2ndly, 1953, Ann Helen Katharine, el da of Hugh Blair Brenan, OBE, former Assist Sec Roy Hosp, SW1, and has issue by 1st and 2nd marriages.

Arms – Argent, on a bend cotised sable three roses of the field barbed and seeded proper in-sinister chief a cinquefoil gules. **Crest** – A swan, wings elevated and addorsed proper between two cinquefoils gules.
Residence – 23 Bath Rd, Chiswick, W4 1LJ. *Clubs* – Pratt's, First Guards.

SONS LIVING (By 2nd marriage)

NICOLAS ROBERT HUGH (266 Priest's Lane, Shenfield, Brentwood, Essex), *b* 7 April 1955; *ed* St Paul's, and London Univ (BA): *m* 1979, Pauline Jean, da of Dr Thomas Ian Boyd, MB, ChB, and has issue living, Alexander Robert, *b* 27 Nov 1981, — Nathaniel Ian, *b* 1983, — Peter, *b* 1988. —— (Roger) Nathaniel Blair, *b* 1957: *m* 1978, Tesney Vera, da of Jasper Partington, and has issue living, Jonathan Nicolas Partington, *b* 1985.

DAUGHTERS LIVING (By 1st marriage)

(By 1st *m*) Marcia Susan, *b* 1949; BA; landscape painter: *m* 1971, Hon Robin Gibson-Watt, of Gelligarn, Llandrindod Wells, Powys LD1 6EY, and has issue living (*see* B Gibson-Watt).

(By 2nd marriage)

Charlotte Rhoda Rosamond, *b* 1960: *m* 1982, David Mayou, son of Simeon Mayou, and has issue living, George, *b* 1984, — Jack, *b* 1986, — Joseph Edward, *b* 1987, — Joshua, *b* 1989.

CASSEL (UK) 1920, of Lincoln's Inn, City of London

Sir HAROLD FELIX CASSEL, TD, QC (*His Honour Sir Harold Cassel, Bt, TD, QC*) 3rd *Baronet*, *b* 8 Nov 1916; *s* his brother, *Sir* FRANCIS EDWARD, 1969; *ed* Stowe, and Corpus Christi Coll Oxford; Bar Lincoln's Inn 1946; QC 1970; Recorder of Gt Yarmouth 1968-72; Recorder of Crown Court 1972-76, Circuit Judge 1976-88; 1939-45 War, as Capt RA: *m* 1st, 1940 (*m diss* 1963) Ione Jean, da of late Capt Evelyn Hugh Barclay (B Somerleyton); 2ndly, 1963, Mrs Eileen Elfrida Smedley, da of James Rider Faulkner, and has issue by 1st *m*.

Arms – Per fesse embattled azure and gules, in chief a pair of scales or between two swords points upwards, pommels and hilts of the third and in base a portcullis also of the third. **Crest** – A lion rampant gules, resting the dexter paw on a mill-rind gold.
Residence – 49 Lennox Gdns, SW1.

Let justice be done

SONS LIVING (By 1st marriage)

TIMOTHY FELIX HAROLD (Studdridge Farm, Stokenchurch, Bucks), *b* 30 April 1942; *ed* Eton; Bar Lincoln's Inn 1965; QC 1988: *m* 1st, 1971 (*m diss* 1977), Mrs Jenifer Samuel, da of Kenneth Bridge Puckle; 2ndly, 1979, Ann (*Baroness Mallalieu*) (Life Baroness), only da of late Sir (Joseph Percival) William Mallalieu and has issue living (by 1st *m*) Alexander James Felix, *b* 25 May 1974, — Natalia Hermione, *b* 1972, — (by 2nd *m*) *Hon* Bathsheba Anna, *b* 1981, — *Hon* Cosima Ione Harriet, *b* 1984. —— Jeremy James, *b* 1950: *m* 1982, Vivien Helen, da of John David Hayter, of Kingham Farm, Hollington, Highclere, Berks, and has issue living, Hugo Timothy, *b* 1982, — Felix, *b* 1988, — Chloë Sieglinda, *b* 1984. —— Evelyn Martin, *b* 1952.

DAUGHTER LIVING (By 1st marriage)

Miranda Phyllis, *b* 1946: *m* 1980, Ronald Ryer, of USA, and has issue living, Sarah Elizabeth Jean, *b* 1986.

SISTER LIVING

Josephine Helen, *b* (twin) 1916: *m* 1939, Griffith Cresswell Evans Pugh, BM, BCh, and has issue living, David Sheridan Griffith (Hatching Green House, Harpenden, Herts), *b* 1940, — Simon Francis (10 Coniger Rd, SW6), *b* 1945, — Oliver Lewis Evans (28 Redan St, W14), *b* 1955, — Harriet Veronica, *b* 1946: *m* 1974, James Tuckey, of 95 Elgin Cres, W11 2JF and has issue living, Venetia *b* 1978, Elizabeth *b* 1980, Rose *b* 1981. *Residence* – Hatching Green House, Hatching Green, Harpenden, Herts.

The Rt Hon Sir Felix Cassel, QC, 1st Bt (son of M. S. Cassel, of 2 Orme Sq, W), was Pres of Management Cttee of Cassel Hosp for Functional Nervous Disorders, a Member of Council of King Edward VII Sanatorium, Midhurst, and Chm of Trustees of Cassel Education Trust, Judge Advocate-Gen 1916-34, and MP for St Pancras, W (*C*) 1910-16.

CAVE (UK) 1896 of Cleve Hill, Mangotsfield, co Gloucester: Sidbury Manor, Sidbury, co Devon; and Stoneleigh House, Clifton, Bristol

Cave
Beware

Sir CHARLES EDWARD COLERIDGE CAVE, 4th *Baronet*; *b* 28 Feb 1927; *s* his father, *Sir* EDWARD CHARLES, 1946; *ed* Eton; formerly Lieut Devonshire Regt; High Sheriff of Devon 1969; DL of Devon; *m* 1957, Mary Elizabeth, da of late John Francis Gore, CVO, TD (*see* E Arran, colls), and has issue.

Arms – Azure, fretty argent, on a fesse or a greyhound courant sable, collared of the second, a bordure of the third pelletée. **Crest** – A daisy-flower slipped proper, a greyhound's head issuant therefrom per pale argent and sable, guttée counterchanged.
Seat – Sidbury Manor, Sidmouth, Devon.

SONS LIVING

JOHN CHARLES (Buckley, Sidbury, Sidmouth, Devon), *b* 8 Sept 1958; *ed* Eton: *m* 1984, Carey Diana elder da of John Lloyd, of Coombeland, Cadeleigh, Tiverton, Devon, and has issue living, George Charles, *b* 8 Sept 1987, — William Alexander, *b* 1992, — Alice Elizabeth, *b* 1989. —— Nicholas Stephen (Mouseplatt, Sidbury, Sidmouth, Devon EX10 0QE), *b* 1961: *m* 1991, A. Frances E. eldest da of Simon Hicks, of Battersea, SW11, and of late Mrs Patty Gordon. —— Thomas Henry, *b* 1964. —— Richard Hugh, *b* 1967.

SISTER LIVING

Daphne Frances, *b* 1930. *Residence* – Greenhead, Sidbury, Devon.

COLLATERAL BRANCH LIVING

Granddaughters of late Maj Arthur Stephen Cave, 4th son of 1st baronet:—
Issue of late Ronald Arthur Cave, *b* 1910, *d* 1964: *m* 1936, Audrey Oenone (Ramblers, Holford, Somerset), da of Dr Francis Child, formerly of Penlee, Weybridge:—
Diana Ann, *b* 1938: *m* 1957, Charles Thoburn Maxwell II, and has issue living, Bruce Maxwell, *b* 1959, — Steven Maxwell, *b* 1961, — Brandon Maxwell, *b* 1964. —— Sylvia Margaret, *b* 1944: *m* 1992, Richard Antony Hackney.

This family is probably a branch of the Caves of Yorkshire and Leicestershire, but their recorded pedigree commences with John Cave of Leigh Sinton, co Worcester, *temp* 15th century, who was ancestor of Sir Richard Cave, Kt, a distinguished General *k* at Naseby, and also of John Cave (great-grandfather of 1st baronet), founder of the Cave bank at Bristol. The arms, which have been confirmed three times by the Heralds' College, were originally granted in the reign of Henry VII. The 1st baronet, Sir Charles Daniel, was a Director of Union of London and Smith's Bank (Limited), and the 2nd baronet, Sir Charles Henry, was High Sheriff of Devon 1926.

CAVE-BROWNE-CAVE (E)1641, of Stanford, Northamptonshire

Beware

Sir ROBERT CAVE-BROWNE-CAVE, 16th *Baronet*; *b* 8 June 1929; *s* his father, *Sir* CLEMENT CHARLES, 1945; *ed* St George's Sch, Vancouver, Univ Sch, Victoria, and British Columbia Univ: is Pres of Cave & Co Ltd: *m* 1st, 1954 (*m diss* 1975), Lois Shirley, da of John Chalmers Huggard, of Winnipeg, Canada; 2ndly, 1977, Joan Shirley, da of Dr Kenneth Ashe Peacock, of W Vancouver, BC, and has issue by 1st *m*.

Arms – Quarterly: 1st and 4th, azure, fretty argent, *Cave*; 2nd and 3rd, azure, a chevron between three escallops or, a bordure engrailed gules, *Browne*. **Crest** – 1st, a greyhound courant sable, collared argent; 2nd, a stork, proper, winged and gorged with a ducal crown or, beaked and membered gules.
Residence – 20901-83 Av, RR11, Langley, British Columbia V3A 6Y3, Canada.

SON LIVING (*By 1st marriage*)

JOHN ROBERT CHARLES, *b* 22 June 1957,

DAUGHTER LIVING (*By 1st marriage*)

Lisé Irene, *b* 1955.

WIDOW LIVING OF FIFTEENTH BARONET

DOROTHEA PLEWMAN (*Dorothea, Lady Cave-Browne-Cave*), da of Robert Greene Dwen, of Chicago, USA: *m* 1923, Sir Clement Charles Cave-Browne-Cave, 15th Bt, who *d* 1945.

COLLATERAL BRANCHES LIVING

Grandchildren of late Rev Fitzherbert Astley Cave-Browne-Cave, son of late Rev William Astley Cave-Browne-Cave, 2nd son of 9th baronet:—

Issue of late Cecil Beckwith Cave-Browne-Cave, *b* 1871, *d* 1953: *m* 1st, 1896, Sara Eleanor, who *d* 1928, da of late John W. Nicholson, of St John, New Brunswick; 2ndly, 1929, Edith Beatrice, who *d* 1948, da of Alfred Evans, JP formerly of Chesham Bois, Bucks:—

(By 2nd *m*) Penelope Margaret Cecil (c/o Barclays Bank Ltd, 31 Avenue de la Costa, Monaco 98000), *b* 1931: *m* 1965, Timothy Fitzgerald ffrench-Mullen, who *d* 1982, and has issue living, Candetta Lydia Cecil, *b* 1966, — Tara Eve Siobhan, *b* 1970. —— Catherine Priscilla Astley, *b* 1937: *m* 1958, David Bates, and has issue living, Joanna Catherine, *b* 1959. *Residence* – Villa Jilguero, la Candia Alta, La Orotava, Tenerife, Canary Islands.

Issue of late Courtney Priestly Edwards Cave-Browne-Cave, *b* 1890, *d* 1961: *m* 1915, Helen Freda, who *d* 1955, only da of A. J. Cable, of Epping, Essex:—

Paul Astley *b* 1917; Printer and Publisher; formerly Capt Gen List; a JP for Southampton: *m* 1940, Joan Myfanwy, da of late Thomas Norman Jones, JP, of Rhyl, N Wales, and has issue living, Paul, *b* 1954; *ed* Manchester Univ (BA): *m* 1979, Jane, da of late Maj J. Reeves, of St Austell, Cornwall, — Jane, *b* 1943; *ed* Birmingham Univ (BSc): *m* 1980, Eugene Versluysen, of 1539 T St NW, Washington DC, USA, — Adrienne, *b* 1947; BA (Cantab), — Sarah, *b* 1959: *m* 1983, James Chiriankandath. —— Lyndon Fraser, *b* 1923; *ed* Liverpool Univ; Dip Arch (Liverpool), M Phil (Warwick), FSA: *m* 1952, Betty, only da of Walter Rush, of Dinnington, Yorks, and has issue living, Anthony John (9 Preseli Close, Meadow Vale, Risca, Gwent NP1 6RQ), *b* 1952; LLB, London: *m* 1980, Susan Margaret, da of K. G. L. Chalk, of Leamington Spa, Warwickshire, and has issue living, Edmund Jonathan *b* 1981, Melissa Betty *b* 1983, — *Rev* Bernard James William (97 Barton Rd, Lancaster) *b* 1954; MA (Cantab); Chap Lancaster Univ: *m* 1977, Rosalind, GRNCM, LRAM, only da of Col Oliver Robert Corbett, ERD, and has issue living, James William *b* 1979, Lucy Marie *b* 1983. *Residence* – 24 Portland St, Leamington Spa, CV32 5EY. —— Anthony, DSO (Cheney Longville, Craven Arms, Shropshire SY7 8DR), *b* 1925; *ed* Birmingham Sch of Architecture; an ARIBA; Burma 1945 as Capt S Wales Borderers (DSO), Sumatra 1945-46 as Intelligence Officer, 4th Indian Inf Bde, 26th Indian Div; DSO 1945: *m* 1957, Dinah Ann, da of J. W. Mitchell, of Longville, Much Wenlock, Salop, and has had issue, Genille Anthony, *b* 1959, *d* 1977, — Courtney Peter, *b* 1961: *m* 1988, Rachel Sarah, da of Brian Fish, of Ettington, Warwicks, and has issue living, Jack Priestley *b* 1994, — Jonathan Lyndon, *b* 1962, — William Astley, *b* 1967: *m* 1988, Lorraine Katharine, da of Philip Wood, of Leamington Spa, Warwicks, and has issue living, Alexandra Grace *b* 1990. —— Bernard Adrian *b* 1926; 1939-45 War as Lt, Middx Regt, Palestine 1946-47: *m* 1961 (*m diss* 1975), Ann, da of late Richard George William Pritchard, JP, of Roddis House, Wellesbourne, Warwick, and has issue living, Richard Ambrose, *b* 1962, — Rowland Fraser (P.O. Box 2224, Niagara Falls, Ontario, Canada L2E 6Z3), *b* 1966, — Helen Ann, *b* 1963: *m* 1991, Rui Manual Martins, of 114 Ellerslie, Willowdale, Ontario, Canada M2N 1X8, and has issue living, Kyle Anthony *b* 1992. *Address* – 49 Sunvale Crescent S.E., Calgary, Alberta, Canada T2X 2S7.

Grandsons of late Edward Johnson Cave-Browne-Cave (infra):—

Issue of late Edward Jordayne Cave-Browne-Cave, *b* 1885, *d* 1970: *m* 1910, Jane Ella, who *d* 1968, da of late Joseph Hilton Cant, of Appleby:—

Genille Hilton Jordayne (3480 Simpson St, Apt 901, Montreal, Quebec, Canada H3G 2N7), *b* 1912; *ed* BC Univ (MA), and Massachusetts Inst. of Tech (PhD); Prof of Chemistry, McGill Univ, Montreal: *m* 1944, Mary Margaret Elizabeth, da of Lt-Col Robert Henry Palmer, DSO (*see* Palmer, Bt, *cr* 1660, colls). —— Wilmot Wyamarus, *b* 1915: *m* 1969, Janet Kyle, da of late Thomas Peddie, MA.

Grandsons of late William Cave-Browne-Cave, 2nd son of late Thomas Cave-Browne-Cave, 3rd son of 9th baronet:—

Issue of late Stretton Cave-Browne-Cave, *b* 1878, *d* 1961: *m* 1907, Ethel Milbro, who *d* 1943, da of late W. H. B. Higgin-Birket, of Birket Houses, Lancashire:—

Glen Myles LEVERING, *b* 1910; *ed* Winchester; is an Aeronautical Engineer; assumed the name of Glen Myles Levering in lieu of Myles Verney Cave-Browne-Cave 1944: *m* 1936 (*m diss* 1943), Christina Elizabeth, da of late Wilfred Bentley, of Inglewood, Huddersfield, and Westward Ho!, Windermere. —— Stretton Patrick, *b* 1911; *ed* Sedbergh; formerly in Warwickshire Yeo: *m* 1954, Pamela, da of Col H. S. Cole, of Stonebank, Ilkley, Yorkshire. *Residence* – Topham's Farm, Conistone-with-Kilnsey, nr Skipton, Yorks.

Grandchildren of late Stretton Cave-Browne-Cave (ante):—

Issue of late Bryan William Cave-Browne-Cave, OBE, *b* 1915, *d* 1980: *m* 1947, Margaret Royston, MBE, who *d* 1978, da of late Alfred Cooke, of Gorse Hill, Linton, Wetherby, Yorks:—

Myles Alfred (c/o Denton Hall, 5 Chancery Lane, EC4), *b* 1949; *ed* Rugby, and St Edmund Hall, Oxford (MA); Solicitor 1974: *m* 1986, Sally Jayne, da of Geoffrey Lilley, of 15 King's Av, Higham Ferrers, Northants, and has issue living, Sam, *b* 1980, — 1990. —— Claire Birket, *b* 1948: *m* 1970, Stuart William Brown, and has issue living, Matthew Myles Antony, *b* 1980, — Laura Zoë, *b* 1977. —— Elise Margaret, *b* 1952: *m* 1972, Franz Friedrich Nadenau, and has issue living, Stephan, *b* 1974.

Grandchildren of late Sir Thomas Cave-Browne-Cave, CB, 3rd son of late Thomas Cave-Browne-Cave (ante):—

Issue of late Wing-Cdr Thomas Reginald Cave-Browne-Cave, CBE, RAF, *b* 1885, *d* 1969: *m* 1st, 1918, Marjorie Gwynne, who *d* 1969, da of late Albert Wright; 2ndly, 1969, Elsie May, who *d* 1991, da of late James Ricks:—

(By 1st *m*) Thomas Milton (The Old Rectory, Clatworthy, Wiveliscombe, Taunton TA4 2EQ), *b* 1926: *m* 1964, Anne, da of Ralph P. Symons, of Truro, and has issue living, Thomas Edward, *b* 1968, — Janet Mary *b* 1965; BSc Manchester and London. —— Gillian Mary, *b* 1923; BSc London.

Grandchildren of late Frank Wyamarus Cave-Browne-Cave (*b* 1844), 6th son of late Thomas Cave-Browne-Cave (ante):—

Issue of late Frank Wyamarus Cave-Browne-Cave, *b* 1886, *d* 1942: *m* 1926, Kathleen, who *d* 1983, da of late John Douglas de Fenzi:—

Norman John, *b* 1927: *m* 1st, 1952 (*m diss* 1957), Eveline Fay, who *d* 1989, yr da of late John Stanley Hill; 2ndly, 1957, Margaret Dobbs, da of late John Stanley Maw, and has issue living, (by 1st *m*) Peter Stanley, *b* 1955: *m* 1987, Caroline Anne, eldest da of Gerald Smith, of Alfriston, Sussex, and has issue living, Thomas Edward *b* 1991, Lucy Fay *b* 1989, — and two adopted das Helen, *b* 1966, — Joanna *b* 1967: *m* 1992, Andrew J. Pearce, of 83, Ryeworth Rd, Charlton Kings, Cheltenham, Glos, son of J. Pearce, of Prestbury, Cheltenham. *Residence* – Trefeddian Hotel, Aberdovey, Gwynedd. —— Anne Molly, *b* 1929: *m* 1952, Selwyn W. Hill, and has issue living, Anthony Wootton, *b* 1966, — Frances Anne, *b* 1954, — Judith Wootton, *b* 1955, — Stacey Wootton (da), *b* 1961. *Residence* – Farcroft, Balkan Hill, Aberdovey, Gwynedd.

Granddaughter of late Rev John Cave-Browne, el son of Lt-Col Edward Cave-Browne, 4th brother of 9th baronet:—

Issue of late William Charles Cave-Browne, b 1867, d 1916: m 1895, Maude Alice, who d 1949, da of late Maj-Gen W. J. Jones, MSC:—
Selina Verney Cleveland (10409-98 St, Grande Prairie, Alberta, Canada), b 1899: m 1923, Alan Kingsford Watts, who d 1957, and has issue living, Patricia Sela, b 1927: m 1947, Harold Keith Gerow (33-151-8 Av S.W., Salmon Arm, BC, Canada), and has issue living, Rodney Dale b 1948, Donald Keith b 1952: m 1978, Carol Newnes (and has issue living, Brock Alan b 1978), Terry Francis b 1954, Randall Kingsford b 1958: m 1980, Debbie Scott (and has issue living, Darcy Lee Kingsford b 1980, Scott Keith b 1982), Cameron Lee b 1962: m 1984, Diane Kinnear (and has issue living, Darin Cameron b 1987, Jennifer Kathleen b 1990), — Joan Genille, b 1931: m 1st, 1949, Iain Blair MacAlister, who d 1970; 2ndly, 1973, George Wilfred Yates, Box 33, Site 9, RR1, Sexsmith, Alberta, Canada, and has issue living (by 1st m), Laurence Blair b 1950: m 1974, Janice Hodges (and has issue living, Kathy-Jo Marie b 1975, Chanelle Rae b 1979), Robert Kingsford b 1951: m 1974, Patricia Murphy (and has issue living, Daniel Robert b 1979, Jennifer Anne b 1977), Vickie Joan b 1952: m 1972, Sheldon Winston Hotte (and has issue living, Iain Edward b 1976, Laine Blair b 1978, Naomi Selaclair b 1980).

Granddaughters of late Maj-Gen William Cave-Browne, CBE, DSO, MC (infra):—
Issue of late Brig John Raban Cave-Browne, MC, b 1917, d 1989: m 1940, Ulrica Ellen (The Walled Garden, Wonersh, Guilford, Surrey), da of late Maj Frank Paget-Hoblyn:—
Susan Margaret, b 1942: m 1969, Richard Laybourne Perry, of The Walled Garden, Wonersh, Guilford, Surrey GU5 0PB, and has issue living, Nicholas Charles Laybourne, b 1972, — Camilla Margaret, b 1970. — Ulrica Sarah, b 1946: m 1969, Patrick Lawrence Gargrave Coventon, and has issue living, Natasha Louise, b 1973, — Charlotte Sophia, b 1975.

Grandchildren of Edward Raban Cave-Browne, CSI, yst son of Lt-Col Edward Cave-Browne (ante):—
Issue of late Maj-Gen William Cave-Browne, CBE, DSO, MC, b 1884, d 1967: m 1916, Muriel, who d 1971, da of J. W. Wainwright, AMICE:—
Caroline Jane, b 1926: m 1948, Derek Marten Brightman, DSC, of Keepers, Dunsfold, Surrey, and has issue living, Christopher Marten, b 1949, — Jeremy Richard, b 1951, — Elizabeth Jane, b 1953, — Nicola Anne, b 1959.
Issue of late Major Horace Cave-Browne, Indian Army, b 1886, d 1960: m 1920, Alice Rose, who d 1972, da of late Col P. A. Weir, Indian Med Serv:—
Patrick Norman Rose (150 Greenbank Rd, Edinburgh, EH10 5RN), b 1926; ed Charterhouse; Maj late N Rhodesia Regt and late Seaforth Highlanders; Orientation and Mobility Instructor, Roy Blind Sch, Edinburgh: m 1956, Mary Davy, da of late Lt-Col M. F. D. Cobbold, Indian Army, and has issue living, Margaret Alison, b 1959: m 1981, Alan McLellan Millar, of 37 Bankton Park West, Murieston, Livingston, W Lothian EH54 9BP, — Ann Mary, b 1961. — Alison Barbara Rose b 1932; ed R Sch for Daughters of Officers of the Army, Bath; served WRNS: m 1954, Maj Robin John Ronald Campbell, Queen's Own Highlanders (Seaforth and Camerons) (see E Cawdor, colls). Residence – Kinrara, Aviemore, Inverness-shire PH22 1QA.

According to a pedigree collected and certified by the Garter King of Arms, 1632, this family is derived from Jordan de Cave, who inherited the Lordships of North and South Cave, co York, 1068. Sir Thomas Cave, 1st baronet, was, during the civil war, a strenuous supporter of his sovereign. The 2nd baronet was MP for Coventry, and the 3rd and 7th baronets each sat as MP for Leicestershire. The 3rd baronet, Sir Thomas Cave, of Stanford Hall, m Hon Margaret Verney, a descendant of the 1st Baron Braye. Sarah Otway-Cave, of Stanford Hall, only da of Sir Thomas, 6th Bt, became Baroness Braye on the termination of the abeyance in 1839, and was great great great grandmother of the present peeress. John, father of the 9th baronet, assumed the name of Browne by Act of Parliament 1752, his mother having been an heiress of that name, and Sir William 9th baronet assumed the additional surname of Cave by Roy licence 1839. The 12th baronet, Rev Sir Genille, sometime engaged in ranching, and served in Boxer Expedition, in Spanish-American War 1898-99 and during 1914-18 War; afterwards a Min in Wesleyan Methodist Church in America; took Holy Orders in Church of England 1920, and became R of Londesborough, Yorkshire. The 13th baronet, Sir Reginald Ambrose, was Capt RN, and served at Bombardment of Alexandria 1882.

CAYLEY (E) 1661, of Brompton, Yorkshire

Sir DIGBY WILLIAM DAVID CAYLEY, 11th *Baronet*; son of late Lt-Cdr William Arthur Seton Cayley, 2nd son of late Digby Leonard Arthur Cayley (infra); b 3 June 1944; s his kinsman, Maj Sir KENELM HENRY ERNEST, 1967; ed Malvern, and Downing Coll, Camb (MA): m 1969 (m diss 1987), Christine Mary, only da of late Derek Francis Gaunt, of Ilkley, Yorks, and has issue.

Arms – Quarterly argent and sable, a bend gules charged with three mullets of the first. Crest – A demi-lion rampant or charged with a bend gules, thereon three mullets argent, in the paws a battleaxe argent, helved gules.
Residence – Heylyns, 70A Bath St, Abingdon, Oxon OX14 1EB.

DAUGHTERS LIVING

Emma Jane, b 1974. —— Catherine Mary, b 1975.

Callide sed honeste

With skill but with honour

SISTER LIVING

Josephine Beatrice Seton, b (twin) 1944: m 1968, Giacomo Bertolini, of Via Bergognone 27, Milan, Italy.

DAUGHTERS LIVING OF TENTH BARONET

Angela Elizabeth (Brompton, Scarborough, Yorks), b 1930, m 1950 (m diss 1959), as his 1st wife, Sir Robert John Frank, 3rd Bt, who d 1987. —— Susan Dorothy Marie Gabrielle (Lady Lawson-Tancred), b 1934: m 1st, 1955 (m diss 1977), Maldwin Andrew Cyril Drummond (see E Perth colls); 2ndly, 1978, Sir Henry Lawson-Tancred, 10th Bt. Residence – Aldborough Manor, Boroughbridge, Yorks. —— Virginia Anne (Hon Lady Storey), b 1936: m 1961, Hon Sir Richard Storey, 2nd Bt, of Settrington House, Malton, Yorks, and 7 Douro Pl, W8. —— Belinda Jane, b 1940: m 1962, Mark Singleton Evans, of Manor House, Brompton-by-Sawdon, Scarborough, Yorks, and has issue living, Arthur Nicolas Singleton Cayley, b 1963, — Alexander Kenelm Singleton Cayley, b 1970, — Amanda Elizabeth Singleton Cayley, b 1966: m 1990, Damien Peter Adam Doyle McCrystal, son of Cal C. McCrystal, of Totteridge Lane, N20. —— April Mary, b 1945: m 1969, Thomas Vernon Partridge, of 40 Princedale Rd, W11, and has issue living, William Kenelm Thomas, b 1972, — Annabel Elizabeth Diana b 1974. —— Alison Rose, b (twin) 1945: m 1972, Patrick Dermot Maloney, of The Green, Brompton-by-Sawdon, Scarborough, Yorks, and has issue living, Elizabeth Mary, b 1974, — Caroline Rose, b 1979, — Katharine Olivia, b 1976. —— Joanna

Storm (*Hon Mrs Richard H. Cornwall-Legh*), *b* 1947: *m* 1974, Hon Richard Henry Cornwall-Legh, of Dairy Farm, High Legh, Knutsford, Cheshire WA16 0QS, only son of 5th Baron Grey of Codnor, CBE, and has issue (*see* B Grey of Codnor).

MOTHER LIVING

Natalie Maud (Drake House, 1 Water Lane, Little Welnetham, Bury St Edmunds, Suffolk), yr da of late Ernest Grey, of North Beacons, Conway: *m* 1937, Lt-Cdr William Arthur Seton Cayley (ante), who *d* 1964.

COLLATERAL BRANCHES LIVING

Granddaughter of late Digby Leonard Arthur Cayley (grandfather of 11th baronet), el son of Digby Cayley (*b* 1834), 2nd son of 7th baronet:—
Issue of late Maj Digby Coddington Cayley, *b* 1895, *d* 1965: *m* 1924, Beatrice Elizabeth Eleanora (Coolmore House, Thomastown, co Kilkenny), da of Robert Charles Campbell-Renton, of Lamberton, and Mordington, Berwick-on-Tweed:—
Katherine Sonia (*Sonia, Baroness ffrench*), *b* 1926: *m* 1954, 7th Baron ffrench, who *d* 1986. —— Amanda Beatrice, *b* 1938.

Grandchildren of late Adm George Cuthbert Cayley, CB, 2nd son of Digby Cayley (*b* 1834) (ante):—
Issue of late Capt Charles Paul Cuthbert Cayley, RE, *b* 1906, *d* on active service 1945: *m* 1939, Cassandra Rosamond Elaine (who *d* 1989, having *m* 2ndly, 1946, John Sarginson, who *d* 1972), da of Sir Digby Algernon Hall Legard, 13th Bt:—
GEORGE PAUL (Applegarth, Brewers Green, Roydon, Diss, Norfolk IP22 3SD), *b* 23 May 1940; *ed* Felsted: *m* 1967, Shirley Southwell, da of Frank Woodward Petford, of Kirby Cane, Norfolk, and has issue living, Paul Alistair, *b* 1971, — Kevin George, *b* 1974. —— Sarah Philadelphia, *b* 1943.

Granddaughter of late Digby Cayley (*b* 1834) (ante):—
Issue of late Capt Harry Francis Cayley, DSO, RN, *b* 1873, *d* 1954: *m* 1900, Margery, who *d* 1901, da of Sir Thomas George Freake, 2nd Bt:—
Alexandra Margery Eileen, *b* 1901: *m* 1928, Lt-Cdr Arthur Frank Armitage, RN (ret), and has issue living, Mark Cecil Christopher, *b* 1937, — Diana Eileen, *b* 1932: *m* 1956, John Trevor Lewis, of Gosport House, Laugharne, Carmarthenshire.

Granddaughter of late Rev Reginald Arthur Cayley, 3rd son of 7th baronet:—
Issue of late Capt Edmund Henry George Cayley, *b* 1870, *d* 1945: *m* 1st, 1898, Marie Olga, who *d* 1910, da of Otto Martin, of Valparaiso, Chile; 2ndly, 1914, Laura Eugénie Beatrice, who *d* 1949, da of late George Fox:—
Evelyn Olga Vivienne, *b* 1899: *m* 1923, Wilhelm Wilkendorf, of Quilpue, and has issue living, Heinz Ferdinand Otto (of Quilpue, Chile), *b* 1927: *m* 1958, Ursula Wilckens, of Valparaiso, Chile, and has issue living, Richard *b* 1959, Astrid *b* 1960, — Harold Christian (Casilla 3070, Santiago, Chile), *b* 1934: *m* 1966, Senta Schwarzenberg, of Santiago, and has issue living, Robert Christian *b* 1970, Stephan Alfred (twin) *b* 1970, Helga Veronica *b* 1968.

Granddaughters of late Capt Edmund Henry George Cayley (ante):—
Issue of late Squadron Leader Damyon Edmund Martin Cayley, *b* 1909, *d* 1957: *m* 1944, Mary Ann, who *d* 1973, da of Stephen Taylor, of Sheffield:—
Barbara Ann, *b* 1945: *m* 1962, Victor Mason, and has issue living, Michael Shaun, *b* 1965, — Deborah Anne, *b* 1963. —— Patricia Janis, *b* 1948: *m* 19—.

Grandsons of late Rev Edward Cartwright Cayley, DD (infra):—
Issue of late Arthur Bowen Cayley, *b* 1898, *d* 1973: *m* 1921, Katherine Vanderwerken, who *d* 1973, da of Peleg Howland, of Toronto:—
Edward Cartwright (44 Jackes Av, Apt 1713, Toronto, Ontario, Canada M4T 1E5), *b* 1922: *ed* Trin Coll Sch, Port Hope, and Toronto Univ (BA); MA Columbia Univ; Lt-Cdr RCNVR; late Assist Headmaster of Holderness Sch; 1939-45 War: *m* 1st, 1944 (*m diss* 1956), Margaret Noble, of Mansfield, Notts; 2ndly, 1956, Catherine Norma, da of late Alexander Stuart, of Eganville, Ont, and has issue living (by 1st *m*), David Cartwright, *b* 1946, — Susan Margaret, *b* 1948, — Catherine Jane, *b* 1952. —— Peleg Howland (Glen Lea, High Pitfold, Hindhead, Surrey), *b* 1924; *ed* The Grove, Lakefield, Ont; Capt RCN (ret): *m* 1st, 1945 (*m diss* 1953), Freda Rosemary, da of Alfred Cotter, of 8 Cherryhill, Beechlands, Belfast; 2ndly, 1955, Patricia Challinor, da of Dr John C. Poole, of Craig Allen, Lettermore, Argyll, and has issue living, (by 1st *m*) Jennifer Margaret, *b* 1947, — (by 2nd *m*) John Howland, *b* 1956, — Richard Arthur, *b* 1960, — Christopher Peter, *b* 1966.
Issue of late Hugh Cartwright Cayley, *b* 1901, *d* 1967: *m* 1st, 1928, Ethel Ann Farquharson, who *d* 1934, da of Wilmot L. Matthews; 2ndly, 1940, Gladys, da of J. T. Large:—
(By 1st *m*), Hugh Cartwright *b* 1932.

Granddaughters of late Rev John D'Arcy Cayley, el son of William Cayley, MP, 2nd son of John Cayley, *b* 1761, el son of John Cayley, *b* 1730, 2nd son of Cornelius Cayley, *b* 1692, 5th son of Cornelius Cayley, 4th son of 1st baronet:—
Issue of late Rev Edward Cartwright Cayley, DD, *b* 1864, *d* 1921: *m* 1895, Alice, who *d* 1951, da of late Rev A. J. Broughall, formerly R of St Stephen's, Toronto:—
Sylvia, *b* 1909: *m* 1937, Ven Terence Patrick Crosthwait, Archdeacon of York. *Residence* – 44 Jackes Av, Apt 1713, Toronto, Ontario, Canada M4T 1E5. —— Ray D'Arcy, *b* 1912: *m* 1947, William Ramsay Osler of RR2, Saanichton Vosimo, BC, Canada.

Grandchildren of late William Cayley, MP (ante):—
Issue of late Francis Cayley, *b* 1845, *d* 1909: *m* 1874, Jane Isabel, who *d* 1920, da of late Henry Easton, Collector of Customs, of Cobourg, Ontario:—
William Henry, *b* 1881. —— Emma Robinson, *b* 1876. —— Adelaide Mary, *b* 1877: *m* 19—, R. H. Strickland. —— Muriel Isabel, *b* 1879: *m* 19—, Jay Scholefield. *Residence* –

Grandchildren of late Claud Thornton Cayley, son of late John Cayley (*b* 1816) (infra):—
Issue of late Claud D'Arcy Cayley, *b* 1882, *d* 1948: *m* 1917, Lilian Gertrude, who *d* 1943, da of R. Hall of Retford, Notts:—
Robert Edward Digby, *b* 1918: *m* 1942, Mary Robson. *Residence* –
Issue of late Capt Edward St Quenton Cayley, *b* 1887, *d* 1941: *m* 1916, Sybil Frances, who *d* 1975, da of late Rev Joseph Alfred Halloran, of The Old Parsonage, Ospringe, Faversham:—
Patricia St Quentin, *b* 1922: *m* 1948, Anthony Bruce Askew, who *d* 1980, and has issue living, Rory Anthony Rank, *b* 1949: *m* 1978, Susan Mary Mawson, and has issue living, Henrietta Charlotte Rank *b* 1980, Georgina Anne *b* 1982, — Cleone St Quentin, *b* 1952: *m* 1977, Maxim Hastings Pengelley, of Lywood House, Ardingly, W Sussex, and has issue living, Tristan Anthony Hastings *b* 1979, Venetia St Quentin *b* 1982. *Residence* – Birches Farm, Isfield, Uckfield, E Sussex.
Issue of late Charles Knightley Cayley, *b* 1888, *d* 1916: *m* 1915, Alice Leach, of S Africa, who *d* 1956:—

Alice Knightley, b 1916: m 1940, Christian John Rosslee, SAAF 1939-45 War, Capt SA Airways (ret), of Walton Rd, St Francis Bay, S Africa and has issue living, Jean Knightley, b 1944: m 1966 (m diss 1974), Edmund Nixon, and has issue living, Vanessa Jane b 1970, Andrea Knightley b 1973, — Gael Iris, b 1946: m 1971 (m diss 1981), Uwe Neke, and has issue living, Kirsten Sima b 1972, Justine Cayley b 1973.

Granddaughter of late John Cayley (b 1816), 4th son of late John Cayley (b 1761) (ante):—
Issue of late Francis Osmund Cayley, b 1856, d 1921: m 1882, Marion Louisa, who d 1943, da of Sir James Lukin Robinson, 2nd Bt:—
Marjorie Gordon, b 1897: m 1925, John William Gamble Boyd, and has issue living, John William Gamble b 1929; RCAF — Philip Cayley, b 1932: RCAF, — Peter Beverley, b 1935. Residence – Toronto, Canada.

Grandchildren of late Hugh Charles Cayley, only son of late Sir Richard Cayley, 3rd son of late Edward Cayley (b 1782) (infra):—
Issue of late Capt Richard Wilkins Cayley, late REME, b 1902, d 1991: m 1935, Joan Harvey, who d 1990, da of late Dr E. Harvey Sutcliff, of Torrington, N Devon:—
William Richard (2 Meadow Rd, Corn Meadow Lane, Claines, Worcs), b 1944; ed Taunton Sch: m 1972, Mary Elizabeth, da of George Arthur Baillie, of The Riggs, Midlem, Selkirk, and has issue living, Alexander Richard, b 1973, — Arthur Edward, b (twin) 1973, — Lucy Claire Christina, b 1984. —— Mary Catherine, b 1938: m 1963, Richard John Wood, of Chapel Hill, Wellington Coll, Crowthorne, Berks, and Ashlar, Hilton, Blandford, Dorset, and has issue living, James Julian, b 1965: m 1992, Samantha, da of Stuart Schofield, of Cove, Farnborough, Hants, — Jonathan Mark, b 1968. —— Janet Rose, b 1940: m 1965, Barry Keith Palmer, of The Poppies, 20 Queen's Drive, Great Malvern, Worcs, and has issue living, Daniel Barry, b 1970, — Louise Jane, b 1967: m 1992, — Eleanor Mary, b 1969.

Grandchildren of late Cyril Henry Cayley, MD, son of late Dep-Surg-Gen Henry Cayley, CMG, FRCS, 4th son of late Edward Cayley (b 1782), only son of Edward Cayley (b 1733), 3rd son of Cornelius Cayley (b 1692) (ante):—
Issue of late Henry Douglas Cayley, OBE, b 1904, d 1991: m 1940, Nora Innes (63 Beluga St, Mount Eliza, Victoria, Australia), da of late Maj Nigel Paton, of Covehithe, Wrentham, Suffolk:—
Neil Henry (7 Cooleena Rd, Elanora Heights, Sydney, NSW, Australia), b 1943; ARICS, FVLE; Dir Cayleys Pty Ltd, Property Consultants: m 1970, Julie, da of A. L. Bowen, of Melbourne, Australia, and has issue living, Henry James, b 1972, — Victoria Anne, b 1971: m 1993, Patrick Andrew Dare. —— Innes Margaret, b 1941: m 1971, Terence John Benson, and has issue living, Andrew Douglas, b 1973, — Mark David, b 1975. —— Lindsay Mary, b 1948: m 1970, Ian Leslie James, and has issue living, Alison Mary, b 1980, — Kirsty Innes, b 1982.

Granddaughter of Maj-Gen Douglas Edward Cayley, CB, CMG, 3rd son of late Dep-Surg-Gen Henry Cayley, CMG, FRCS, (ante):—
Issue of late Com Richard Douglas Cayley, DSO, RN, b 1907, d on active ser 1943: m 1933, Nancy (who m 2ndly, 1943, Herbert Samuel Gild, FRCS), yr da of Edward Coutts, of Sweffling, Fleet, Hants:—
Jennifer Jane, b 1934: m 1956, Sqdn-Ldr Arthur Christopher Doggett, RAF (see B Horder, 1968 Edn), and has issue living, Antonia Clare, b 1958, — Jessia, b 1963.

Grandson of late Bernard Cayley (infra):—
Issue of late William Bernard Cayley, b 1907, d 1963: m 1935, Bronwen, who d 1976, da of R. C. Young, of Yanco, NS Wales:—
John William Douglas (56 Rippon Rd, Hamilton, Victoria 3300, Aust), b 1938; ed Geelong Gram Sch, Victoria, and Melbourne Univ (BSc agriculture): m 1964, Glenys Robertson, da of W. R. Wilson, of Newcastle-upon-Tyne, and has issue living, Ross Andrew, b 1965; ed Hamilton Coll, Victoria, and Melbourne Univ (BSc), — Fiona Bronwen Robertson, b 1968; ed Hamilton Coll, Victoria, Melbourne Univ (BA), New Hall, Camb (M Phil), and Jesus Coll, Camb (PhD).

Granddaugter of late Dep-Surg-Gen Henry Cayley, CMG, FRCS (ante):—
Issue of late Bernard Cayley, b 1871, d 1914: m 1904, Gertrude Mary, who d 1942, da of J. C. Large:—
Agnes Mary (53 Cobham Rd, Fetcham, Leatherhead, Surrey), b 1906: m 1926, Maj Charles Fraser Raper, late Indian Army, 3rd Madras Regt, 6th Rajputana Rifles, who d 1965, and has issue living, John James, b 1927, — Charles Richard, b 1929.

Grandchildren of late Rear Adm Henry Priaulx Cayley, R Australian Navy, 6th and yst son of Dep-Surg-Gen Henry Cayley, CMG, FRCS (ante):—
Issue of late Henry Francis Cayley, b 1910, d 1981: m 1940, Marea (44A Shirley Rd, Wollstoncraft, Sydney, NSW), da of Colin Borthwick, of Sydney:—
Charles Francis, b 1943. —— Susan Aneva Mary, b 1947. —— Mary Lorraine, b 1950.

Grandchildren of late Arthur Cayley, 6th son of late Edward Cayley, b 1782 (ante):—
Issue of late Osbert Arthur Cayley, b 1869, d 1947: m 1910, Dorothy, who d 1942, da of late Rev George Herbert Lewis (Indian Ecclesiastical Establishment, ret), of Allandale, Burnham, Somerset:—
Forde Everard de Wend, MBE, MD, FRCP, b 1915; formerly Capt RAMC; 1939-45 War in Far East (prisoner, MBE); MBE (Mil) 1946: m 1941, Eileen Lilian, da of late Arthur C. Dalton, and has issue living (Arthur) Charles Digby (17 Conolly Rd, W7), b 1946; ed Brighton Coll, and Middx Hosp; MB, BS, MRCP: m 1969, Jeanette Ann, MSc, MB, BS, MFFP, da of late G. Avery, of Plymouth, and has issue living, George Cornelius Forde b 1971; LLB, Adam Charles Francis b 1975, Seth Marcus Hugo b 1980, — Michael Forde (13 Grove Rd, East Molesey, Surrey) b 1950; ed Brighton Coll, and St John's Coll, Oxford (MA): m 1987, Jennifer, MA, MB, BS, da of late Patrick Lytle, of Southsea. —— Frances Dorothy, b 1912: m 1941, S. A. Yates, who d 1977. Residence – 33 Kenilworth Rd, Ealing, W5.

The Sire de Cailly (or Cayley), from Cailly in Normandy, was one of the followers of William the Conqueror, and is celebrated in the Roman de Rou. His descendants were settled in Norfolk for three centuries, when the chief representative of the family removed to Yorkshire, where his descendants have since remained. The 1st baronet, Sir William Cayley, was knighted by Charles I, and created a baronet by Charles II, for his services in the Civil War. He m Dorothy, daughter of Sir William St Quintin, of Harpham, a lineal descendant of Joan, daughter of Edward I. The 6th baronet, Sir George, was a pioneer of aviation. In 1804 he made a successful model glider, and in 1809 a full sized glider which he flew with ballast in lieu of a pilot. In 1852 he launched the first man-carrying glider. The 9th baronet, Sir George Everard Arthur, Capt Roy Defence Corps, d on active service 1917.

CAYZER (UK)1904, of Gartmore, co Perth

Cautiously but fearlessly

Sir JAMES ARTHUR CAYZER, 5th Baronet; *b* 15 Nov 1931; *s* his brother, *Sir* NIGEL JOHN, 1943; *ed* Eton.

Arms – Party per chevron azure and argent, in chief two fleurs-de-lis or, and in base an ancient ship with three masts, sails furled sable, colours flying gules; a chief invected of the third thereon three estoiles of the first. **Crest** – A sea-lion erect proper, holding in the dexter paw a fleur-de-lis, and supporting with the sinister an estoile, both or.
Seat – Kinpurnie Castle, Newtyle, Angus PH12 8TW. *Club* – Carlton.

SISTERS LIVING

Deva, *b* 1923: *m* 1946, Lieut-Com John Studholme Brownrigg, DSC, RN, who *d* 1971, only son of late Adm Sir (Henry John) Studholme Brownrigg, KBE, CB, DSO, and has issue living, Henry John Studholme, *b* 1961: *m* 1985, Sally Anne, da of late Barry Jepson, and has issue living, Jonathan Studholme *b* 1990, a da *b* 1988. *Residence* – 2 The Court, Ridgeway Lane, Lymington, Hants SO41 9NR.. —— Angela, *b* 1926: *m* 1950, Anthony Malcolm Galliers-Pratt, CBE, and has issue living, Rupert Anthony, *b* 1951: *m* 1973, Alexandra Mary, da of Maj Hugh Rose, of Buriton House, Buriton, nr Petersfield, and has issue living, George Anthony *b* 1979, Frederick Hugh *b* 1981, Isabella Eileen *b* 1985, Alexandra Georgina Angela *b* 1988, —— Nigel Kenneth CAYZER (Thriepley House, Lundie, Angus), *b* 1954; assumed surname of Cayzer by deed poll 1982: *m* 1986, Henrietta Caroline Rose, yr da of late Sir Richard Tatton-Sykes, 7th Bt, and has issue living, Arthur James Richard *b* 1988, Virginia Angela *b* 1990, Angelica Eileen Rose *b* 1992, —— Anthony Charles (61 Rutland Gate, SW7 1PT), *b* 1958. *Residence* – Mawley Hall, Cleobury Mortimer, Worcs DY14 8PN.

AUNT LIVING *(daughter of 2nd baronet)*

Iris Cecilie (14 Victoria Court, Grand Av, Hove), *b* 1905: *m* 1938 (*m diss* 1968), Duncan Alistair McKellar, and has issue living, Heather Joy, *b* 1943: *m* 1965, Kenneth Leonard Hyman, of Flat 1, Little Silver, Marsham Way, Gerrard's Cross, Bucks, and has issue living, Jeanne Cecile *b* 1966, Tara Penelope *b* 1968.

COLLATERAL BRANCHES LIVING

Issue of late August Bernard Tellefsen Cayzer, 3rd son of 1st baronet, who was *cr* a *Baronet* 1921:—
Of whom *Sir* (WILLIAM) NICHOLAS, 2nd Bt (*cr Baron Cayzer* (Life Baron) 1981), *b* 21 Jan 1910: is *hp* to this baronetcy.

Issue of late Arthur Edward Bryant Cayzer, 4th son of 1st baronet, *b* 1878, *d* 1909: *m* 1905, Louise Margaret, who *d* 1966, da of John Birkett, of Kendal:—
Nancy Avis Louise, *b* 1909: *m* 1936, Alister Curtis Leeson, who *d* 1991, and has issue living, Ian Arthur (Eaton House, Eaton Park, Cobham, Surrey), *b* 1937: *m* 1965, Eileen Margaret Tennent, and has issue living, Sally Louise *b* 1968, Patricia Anne *b* 1971. *Residence* – Heathfield, Chilworth, Hants.

Issue of late Sir Herbert Robin Cayzer, 5th son of 1st baronet, who was *cr Baron Rotherwick* 1939 (see that title).

Issue of late Major Harold Stanley Cayzer, 6th son of 1st baronet, *b* 1882 *d* 1948: *m* 1908, Mary Kate, who *d* 1946, el da of Joseph Hume Dudgeon, of Merville, Booterstown, co Dublin:—
Harold Stanley, *b* 1910; *ed* Eton; Major 11th Hussars (Reserve); 1939-45 War (wounded): *m* 1st, 1943 (*m diss* 1956), Doussa, da of Fahmy Bey Wissa, of Ramleh, Egypt; 2ndly, 1959 (*m diss* 1967), Pamela da of Geoffrey Myers, of Christchurch, NZ; 3rdly, 1971, Beatrice Fairbanks Murray, yst da of former US Amb at Large. *Residences* – Mont Plaisant House, Rue de la Generotte Castel, Guernsey CI; 190 South County Rd, Palm Beach, Fla 33480, USA. *Clubs* – Buck's, Lansdowne, White's, Cavalry and Guards', Portland, The Old Guard, Bath and Tennis (Florida).

The 1st baronet, Sir Charles Cayzer, was head of the firm of Cayzer, Irvine and Co (Limited), steamship owners, of London, Liverpool, Manchester, and Glasgow, and sat as MP for Barrow-in-Furness (*C*) 1892 to 1906. The 3rd baronet, Sir Charles William Cayzer, was MP for Cheshire, City of Chester Div (*C*) 1922-40, and a Member of Roy Co of Archers (King's Body Guard for Scotland): *m* 1919, Beatrice Eileen, OBE, who *d* 1981, elder da of late James Meakin, of Westwood Manor, Staffs, by his wife, late Emma Beatrice (Countess Sondes), da of Percy Hale Wallace, of Muckamore Abbey, co Antrim. The 4th baronet, Sir Nigel John Cayzer, Lieut Scots Guards, was *ka* in Italy 1943.

CHADWICK (UK) 1935, of Bidston, co Palatine of Chester

Sir JOSHUA KENNETH BURTON CHADWICK, 3rd *Baronet*; *b* 1 Feb 1954; *s* his father, *Sir* ROBERT PETER, 1983.

Arms – Azure, on water in base barry wavy argent and vert an ancient ship or sail set and banner flying at the stern of the second, each charged with a martlet of the first, at the masthead a pennon gules fimbriated argent, in chief a lion passant between two mullets of the last. **Crest** – Or and azure a demi-sea horse proper gorged with a naval crown and holding between the fins a portcullis chained or.
Residence – 3/1933 Gold Coast, Highway, Burleigh Heads, Qld 4220, Australia.

IN CANDORE DECUS

Honour is purity

SISTER LIVING

Wendy Lorraine, *b* 1951: *m* 1978, Andrew Haig Palmer, of 4 Douglas St, Kensington, Whangarei, NZ.

HALF-SISTERS LIVING

Diana, *b* 1938: *m* 1965, Andrew William Neilson Gemmill, of 18 Lyndhurst St, Richmond, Melbourne, Victoria 3121, Australia, and has issue living, Tristan John, *b* 1967, — Giles William, *b* 1968, — Lucinda Harriet, *b* 1972. —— Sally Virginia, *b* 1940, *m* 1961, Grahame Robert Hadwen, of 21-145 Moray St, New Farm, Brisbane, Queensland 4005, Australia, and has issue living, Michael Robert, *b* 1970, — Debbie Anne, *b* 1963, — Susan Jane, *b* 1965.

AUNT LIVING (*Daughter of 1st baronet*)

Gwynfa Burton, *b* 1906: *m* 1935 (*m diss* 1955), George D'Arcy Edmondson, CMG, CVO, OBE. *Residence* – 40 Ovington Street, SW3.

WIDOW LIVING OF SECOND BARONET

(BERYL) JOAN (*Lady Chadwick*), da of Stanley Frederick James Brailsford: *m* 1950, as his second wife, Sir Robert Peter Burton Chadwick, 2nd Bt, who *d* 1983. *Address* – PO Box 98, Post Office, Tokomaru Bay, New Zealand.
The 1st baronet, Sir Robert Burton Burton-Chadwick (el son of Joseph Chadwick, of Liverpool), assumed by deed poll 1936, the additional surname of Burton; was head of the firm of Chadwick & Askew, shipowners, of Liverpool and London, and Parliamentary Sec to the Board of Trade 1924-28. He sat as MP for Barrow-in-Furness (C) 1918-22 and for Wallasey 1922-31.

Chadwyck-Healey, see Healey.

CHAMBERLAIN (UK) 1828 of London (Extinct 1980)

Sir HENRY WILMOT CHAMBERLAIN, 5th and last *Baronet*.

COLLATERAL BRANCH LIVING

Granddaughter of late Lt-Cdr Henry Chamberlain, RN, 2nd son of late Rear-Adm William Charles Chamberlain, 3rd son of 1st baronet:—
Issue of late Capt Neville Grahame Chamberlain, *b* 1896, *d* 1945: *m* 1927, Edna Claire, who *d* 1951, da of John Spence-Nicol, of Wellington, New Zealand:—
Pamela Barbara, *b* 1928: *m* 1950, Peter James Pound, and has issue living, William Grahame, *b* 1951, — Toby James, *b* 1954, — Hugo Giles Barclay *b* 1957. *Residence* – 7 Broughton Rd, Ipswich, Suffolk IP1 3QR.

Champion de Crespigny, see de Crespigny.

DALRYMPLE-CHAMPNEYS (UK) 1910, of Littlemead, Nutley, Sussex (Extinct 1980)

Sir WELDON DALRYMPLE-CHAMPNEYS, CB, DM, 2nd and last *Baronet*.

WIDOW LIVING OF SECOND BARONET

NORMA HULL (*Lady Dalrymple-Champneys*) (40 Ritchie Court, 380 Banbury Rd, Oxford), da of late Col Richard Hull Lewis, of co Cork, and widow of A. S. Russell, DSc, MC, of Ch Ch, Oxford; Hon Research Fell, Somerville Coll, Oxford; ed *Complete Poetical Works of George Crabbe*, 1988 (Rose Mary Crawshay Prize, British Academy): *m* 1974, as his 2nd wife, Sir Weldon Dalrymple-Champneys, 2nd Bt, CB, DM, FRCP (Hon Fell Oriel Coll, Oxford), Hon Physician to King George VI, who *d* 1980.

CHANCE (UK) 1900, of Grand Avenue, Hove, co Sussex

Deo non fortuna
Through God, not by chance

Sir (GEORGE) JEREMY FFOLLIOTT CHANCE, 4th *Baronet*, *b* 24 Feb 1926; *s* his father, Sir ROGER JAMES FERGUSON, 1987; *ed* Gordonstoun, and Ch Ch, Oxford (MA); late RNVR; formerly a Dir of Massey-Ferguson Ltd, Coventry: *m* 1950, his cousin, Cecilia Mary Elizabeth, da of late Sir (William) Hugh Stobart Chance, CBE (infra), and has issue.

Arms – Gules, a saltire vair between two fleurs-de-lis in pale and as many towers in fesse argent. **Crest** – A demi-lion rampant gules, semée of annulets or, holding between the paws a sword erect entwined by a wreath of oak all proper.
Residence – Rhosgyll Fawr, Chwilog, Pwllheli, Gwynedd LL53 6TQ.

SONS LIVING

(JOHN) SEBASTIAN, *b* 2 Oct 1954; *ed* Dartington Hall, and Stourbridge Coll of Art (BA): *m* 1977, Victoria Mary, da of Denis McClean, of Newcastle-upon-Tyne, and has issue living, Thomas Hugh Jeremy, *b* 14 May 1983, — Michael John Ferguson, *b* 1987, — Madeleine Katharine Eustacia, *b* 1981. —— Roger William Tobias (Toby), *b* 1960; *ed* Eton, and Fitzwilliam Coll, Camb (BA).

DAUGHTERS LIVING

Victoria Katherine Elizabeth, *b* 1952. —— Helena Mary ffolliott, *b* 1957: *m* 1979, John Christopher (Toby) Beaufoy, elder son of Harold Beaufoy, of 76 High St, Kenilworth, Warwicks, and has issue living, William Tobias Roland, *b* 1986, — Joanna Mary Constance, *b* 1988.

SISTER LIVING

Teresa Margaret, *b* 1930: *m* 1955, George Gilbert Kennedy, DFC, of Cashelnagor, Gortahork, co Donegal, and has issue living, Seamus Michael ffolliott, *b* 1963, — Miles Thomas Pitt, *b* 1965.

COLLATERAL BRANCH LIVING

Grandchildren of late George Ferguson Chance, 2nd son of 1st Baronet:—
Issue of late Sir (William) Hugh Stobart Chance, CBE, *b* 1896; *d* 1981: *m* 1st, 1926 (*m diss* 1961), Cynthia May, da of late Maj Addison Francis Baker Cresswell, of Cresswell and Harehope, Northumberland; 2ndly, 1961, Rachel, who *m* 3rdly, 1983, Lt-Col Thomas Argyll Robertson, who *d* 1994, of Box Farmhouse, Birlingham, Pershore, Worcs, da of late Lt Cyril Henry Cameron, RHA, of Tasmania, and formerly wife of James W. Carr:—
(By 1st *m*) (William) John Ferguson (15 Monteith Place, Durban North 4051, Natal, S Africa), *b* 1929: *m* 1st, 1951, Elizabeth Kathleen, da of Victor J. S. Crookes, of Chartwell, Umzinto, Natal; 2ndly, 1989 (*m diss* 1992), Mrs Ingrid Bonnet, *née* von Christierson, and has issue living (by 1st *m*), Christopher John Hugh, *b* 1952: *m* 1976, Merilyn Koller, and has issue living, Justin William Timmins *b* 1988, Lara *b* 1978, Sarah *b* 1982, — James William Frederick, *b* 1952: *m* 1978, Tessa Stretton-Barry, and has issue living, David *b* 1981, Philippa *b* 1979, Camilla *b* 1985, — Richard George Ferguson, *b* 1956: *m* 1987, Nicola Anne Butcher, and has issue living, Michael John William *b* 1989, Natasha Anne *b* 1991, — Sarah Elizabeth, *b* 1960. —— Hugh Nicholas, *b* 1940: *m* 1st 1963 (*m diss* 1977), Caroline Susan, da of Patrick Edward Michael Holmes, of Stourton House, Stourbridge, Worcs; 2ndly, 1990, Mrs Rose E. Baldwin, elder da of — Heft, of Winsconsin, USA, and has issue living (by 1st *m*), Timothy William Holmes, *b* 1966, — Henry Charles Hugh, *b* 1969, — Lucy Emma, *b* 1971. —— (Kathleen) Idonea Cresswell, *b* 1927: *m* 1st 1948 (*m diss* 1956), William Henry Dunamace Heaton-Armstrong, son of Sir John Dunamace Heaton-Armstrong, MVO; 2ndly, 1956 (*m diss* 1965), Lt-Cdr John Timothy Fetherston-Dilke, CBE, RN (ret); 3rdly, 1965 (*m diss* 1975), Colin Frederick Rogers, LDS, RCS; 4thly, 1992, Martin Joseph Crossley, and has issue living (by 1st *m*), Anthony Eustace John, *b* 1950; *ed* Ampleforth, and Bristol Univ; Bar-at-law, Grays Inn 1973: *m* 1st, 1973, Susan Margaret, da of Ian Peter Allnut, of Karen Cottage Boulters Lane, Maidenhead, Berks; 2ndly, 1982, Anne Frances, da of Mrs E. E. M. Robigo, and formerly wife of Marcus Hugh Lecky, and has issue living (by 2nd *m*), John William *b* 1983, Eleanor Katharine *b* 1985, Celestine Anne *b* 1988, — Mary Suzanne Bertha, *b* 1949: *m* 1977, John Beresford-Iles, of Melbourne, Australia, — Bridget Cynthia, *b* 1952 (has issue, Morgan Lei, a da, *b* 1973): *m* 1982 (*m diss* 1991), Michael Roger David Dansey, of Auckland, NZ, and has further issue, Katherine Marie Bridget *b* 1984, Georgina Michaela Celestine *b* 1986, — Rachel Catherine, *b* 1954, — (by 2nd *m*), Timothy Hugh, *b* 1958, — Miranda Catherine, *b* 1956: *m* 1985, William Murray Lindsay (*see* E Mansfield, colls, 1990 Edn), and has issue living, Alicia Flora *b* 1987, Harriet Idonea *b* (twin) 1987. —— Cecilia Mary Elizabeth (*Lady Chance*), *b* 1928: *m* 1950, her cousin, Sir (George) Jeremy ffolliott Chance, 4th Bt (ante). —— Bridget Nicola (Willow Cottage, Kingsland, Herefordshire, HR6 9RU), *b* 1931: *m* 1963, Rt Rev John Richard Gordon Eastaugh, sometime Bishop of Hereford, who *d* 1990, and has issue living, James Gordon Mark, *b* 1964, — Edward John Hugh, *b* 1970, — Katharine Elizabeth Sophia, *b* 1967.

The 1st baronet was for many years head of the firm of Chance Bros and Co (manufacturers of dioptric illuminating apparatus for lighthouses, etc) of Smethwick and Oldbury, near Birmingham.

CHAPMAN (UK) 1958, of Cleadon, co Durham

Mildly but firmly

Sir DAVID ROBERT MACGOWAN CHAPMAN, 3rd *Baronet*; *b* 16 Dec 1941; *s* his father *Col Sir* ROBERT (ROBIN) MACGOWAN, CBE, TD, 1987; *ed* Marlborough, Grenoble Univ, and McGill Univ, Montreal (BCom); High Sheriff Tyne and Wear 1993; a Dir North of England Building Soc, Northern Rock Building Soc since 1994, and Wise Speke Ltd, Stock and Share Brokers, Newcastle-upon-Tyne; Chm Northern Unit of Stock Exchange 1988-91: *m* 1965, Maria Elizabeth de Gosztonyi-Zsolnay, da of Dr Nicholas de Mattyasovszky-Zsolnay, of Pecs, Hungary, and has issue.

Arms – Per chevron argent and gules a crescent counterchanged in dexter chief a portcullis chained sable over all in pale a sword point downwards proper pommel and hilt or. Crest – Issuant from a wreath of oak proper a dexter arm embowed vested gules cuffed argent grasping in the hand a harpoon also proper.
Residence – Westmount, 14 West Park Rd, Cleadon, Sunderland, Tyne and Wear SR6 7RR. *Club* – Northern Counties.

SON LIVING

MICHAEL NICHOLAS, *b* 21 May 1969.

DAUGHTER LIVING

Christina Elisabeth, *b* 1970.

BROTHER LIVING

Peter Stuart (62 Lansdowne Rd, W11 2LR) *b* 1944; *ed* Marlborough, the Sorbonne, and Trin Coll, Camb (MA), and LSE (MSc); Dir Chapman Hendy Associates: *m* 1972, Joan, da of R. S. V. Hewitt, of Middle Barton, Oxon, and has issue living, Christopher Edward, *b* 1974, — Victoria Rose, *b* 1977, — Katherine Rebecca, *b* 1980, — Rachel Emily, *b* 1981.

SISTER LIVING

Elizabeth Mary, *b* 1946; *ed* Benenden, St Aidan's Coll, Durham, and Columbia Univ, New York (Phi Beta Kappa): *m* 1967, Dr Mark Ivan Levy, of 126 Corte Madera Av, Mill Valley, Cal 94941, USA, and has issue living, Noah, *b* 1970, — Gabriel, *b* 1972.

UNCLE DECEASED (*son of 1st baronet*)

Henry James Nicholas (Jerards, Sandford Orcas, Sherborne, Dorset DT9 4SE), *b* 1914; *ed* Marlborough, and Corpus Christi Coll, Camb (Scholar, MA); in Colonial Admin Ser 1937-57; Member of Dorset Co Council 1962-74 (Alderman 1970), and 1977-81; Member of Dorset Area Health Authority 1974-82; a Gov of Sherborne Sch 1967-80; Member of Council of Sherborne Sch for Girls 1965-84: *m* 1950, Anne Barbara, da of Sir David Wilson Croft, KCB, KBE, CIE, CVO, and *d* 1991, leaving issue, Caroline Anne, *b* 1955: *m* 1985, Christopher John Steane, and has issue living, Sebastian James David *b* 1986, Isobel Sarah *b* 1988.

WIDOW LIVING OF SECOND BARONET

BARBARA MAY (*Barbara Lady Chapman*), da of Hubert Tonks, of Ceylon: *m* 1941, Col Sir Robert (Robin) Macgowan Chapman, 2nd Bt, CBE, TD, who *d* 1987. *Residence* – Pinfold House, Cleadon, Sunderland, Tyne and Wear SR6 7RR.

Sir Robert Chapman, CB, CMG, CBE, DSO, TD, son of Henry Chapman, JP of Westoe, S Shields, was a Chartered Accountant, MP for Houghton-le-Spring Div of co Durham (C) 1931-35, and High Sheriff of co Durham 1940-41. Sir Robin Chapman, 2nd Bt, was a ptnr Chapman, Hilton and Dunford, of S Shields, a consultant with Spicer and Pegler, Chm James Hogg & Sons (N Shields) Ltd, etc; Vice Lord Lieut for Co Tyne and Wear 1974-84.

CHARLES (UK) 1928, of The Abbey Grange, Waltham Abbey, co Essex and of Manchester Square, Parish of St Marylebone, co London (Extinct 1975)

Sir NOEL HUGHES HAVELOCK CHARLES, KCMG, MC, 3rd and last *Baronet*.

WIDOW LIVING OF THIRD BARONET

GIPSY JOAN (*Lady Charles*) (36 Sloane Court West, SW3), da of late Sir Walter Lawrence, of Hyde Hall, Sawbridgeworth, Herts: *m* 1957, as his 2nd wife, Sir Noel Hughes Havelock Charles, KCMG, MC, who *d* 1975, when the title became ext.

CHAYTOR (UK) 1831, of Croft, Yorkshire, and Witton Castle, Durham

Fortune wills it

Sir GEORGE REGINALD CHAYTOR, 8th *Baronet*; *b* 28 Oct 1912, son of late William Richard Carter Chaytor, el son of Reginald Clervaux Chaytor, yr son of 2nd baronet; *s* his kinsman, *Sir* WILLIAM HENRY CLERVAUX, 1976; patron (alternatively) of Witton-le-Wear V: *m* 1970, Mrs Elsie Magdeline Rogers.

Arms – Per bend dancettée argent and azure, four quartrefoils two and two bendwise counter-changed. Crest – A buck's head couped lozengy argent and sable, attired or, in the mouth a trefoil slipped vert.
Residence – 103-9372 Fletcher Av, Chilliwack, BC, Canada.

SISTERS LIVING

Florine May, *b* 1920: *m* 1951, Edwin John Dauncey, of 7596 Lougheed Highway, N Burnaby, BC, Canada, and has issue living, Darwin Ross, *b* 1953, — Dale Allen, *b* 1956, — Douglas Edwin, *b* 1960. — Doreen Isabelle, *b* (twin) 1920: *m* 1941, Herbert William Scott, of 157 Westview Drive, Penticton, BC, V2A 7V9, Canada, and has issue living, Edward William (6896 Winnifred Place, Saanichton, BC, Canada V05 1M0), *b* 1946, — Beverley Ann (B6520 Bella Vista Drive, Victoria, BC, Canada V8Z 6Y4), *b* 1949.

DAUGHTER LIVING OF SEVENTH BARONET

(Carol) Miranda (24 Cruden St, N1), *b* 1948.

WIDOW LIVING OF SEVENTH BARONET

PATRICIA NORA (*Patricia, Lady Chaytor*) (43 Abbey Rd, Knaresborough, N Yorks HG5 8HY), da of Loftus Joseph McCaffry, and formerly wife of George Walkley Alderman: *m* 1947, Sir William Henry Clervaux Chaytor, 7th Bt, who *d* 1976.

COLLATERAL BRANCHES LIVING

Grandchildren of late Reginald Clervaux Chaytor, yst son of 2nd baronet:—
Issue of late Herbert Archibald Chaytor, *b* 1884, *d* 1979: *m* 1911, Effie Bell, who *d* 1976, da of William Smith:—
(HERBERT) GORDON (1899 Deborah Drive, Duncan, BC, Canada V9L 5A5), *b* 15 June 1922: *m* 1947, Mary Alice, da of Thomas Craven, and has issue living, Bruce Gordon (2785 Sooke Rd, Victoria, BC, Canada V9C 2P7), *b* 31 July 1949: *m* 1969, Rosemary Lea, da of Reid Stephen, of Lake Cowichan, and has issue living, John Gordon *b* 17 Jan 1973, Sharon Kathleen *b* 1969, — Kenneth Reginald, *b* 1952: *m* 1973, Susan Shroetter, of Toronto, Ont, and has issue living, Wisteria Willow *b* 1974, Naomi Sage *b* 1976, — Robert David, *b* 1958. — Dorothy May (406-1010 MacKenzie Av, Victoria, BC, V8X 4B2, Canada), *b* 1912: *m* 1936, George Walter Blewett, who *d* 19—.
Issue of late Perley Edgar Chaytor, *b* 1886, *d* 1939: *m* 1907, Dora May Lodge:—
Jean Pearl, *b* 1908: *m* 19—, John H. Sutherland, of 665 Twawwassen Beach, Delta, BC, Canada V4M 2J2. — Rita Alberta, *b* 1909: *m* 1936, Donald S. Cowan, of 1368 Duncan Dr, Delta, BC, Canada V4L 1R4, and has issue living, Donald R., *b* 1943: *m* 1966, Louise, da of late Robert Coltart, and has issue living, Steven M. *b* 1971, Michael L. *b* 1975, Andrea E. *b* 1973, — Barbara L., *b* 1941: *m* 1963, Ken Matsuzaki, son of I. Matsuzaki, of Delta, BC, and has issue living, Dean Scott *b* 1972, Dana Jane *b* 1970. — Audrey, *b* 1913: *m* 19—, George S. Laing, of 1657, East 62nd Ave, Vancouver, BC, Canada V5P 2K8.

Grandchildren of late Alfred Henry Chaytor, KC, 2nd son of late John Clervaux Chaytor, *b* 1836, eldest son of late John Chaytor, 2nd son of 1st baronet:—
Issue of late (Alfred) Drewett Chaytor, *b* 1901, *d* 1977: *m* 1929, Rachel Elizabeth, of Spennithorne Hall, Leyburn, Yorks, da of late Rev Canon William Hartley Carnegie, Sub-Dean of Westminster Abbey, and Chap to Speaker of House of Commons:—
William Drewett (The Hall, Croft, Darlington), *b* 1937: *m* 1964, Susan Philippa, el da of James Lawrence Bunting Ansell, MRCS, LRCP, and has issue living, Clervaux James, *b* 1967, — Nicholas John Drewett, *b* 1976, — Katharine Elizabeth, *b* 1970. — Elizabeth, *b* 1934, *m* 1959, Lt David Henry Ashwin, of Hill Farm, Dedham, Colchester, and has issue living, Philip David, *b* 1960, — Henry William, *b* 1962, — Rachel Elizabeth, *b* 1964. — Jane, *b* 1935: *m* 1st, 1966, John Richard Evelyn Atkinson, who *d* 1973; 2ndly, 1976, John A. C. Watherston, of 39 Sutherland St, SW1, and has issue living (by 1st *m*), Richard Matthew Clervaux, *b* 1968, — Harriet Rachel *b* 1972, (by 2nd *m*), Charles Crispin *b* 1977. — Susannah Albina (*Hon Mrs Edward L. Jackson*) (Cottisford, Brackley, Northants, NN13 5SW), *b* 1939: *m* 1971, Hon Edward Lawies Jackson, who *d* 1982, son of 3rd Baron Allerton.

Issue of late Alfred Henry Chaytor, KC (ante), *b* 1869, *d* 1931: *m* 1899, Dorothy Elizabeth, who *d* 1960, eldest da of Harry Percy Burrell:—
Edward Drewett, MC (6 Bridle Path, Cherry Cross, Totnes, Devon), *b* 1913; *ed* Eton; Lt-Col (ret) West Yorks Regt: Burma 1944-45 (MC): *m* 1938, Mary Monica, only da of Rev Canon Thomas John Woodall, of The Close, Salisbury, and has issue living, Richard Clervaux, *b* 1939: *m* 1983, Janet, da of Irving D. Miller, of Malboro, USA, — Michael Clervaux, *b* 1944. — Dorothy Anne, *b* 1912: *m* 1937, George Egerton Lambert Manley, and has issue living, Robert John Lambert, *b* 1938, — Christopher Michael, *b* 1948, — Peter George, *b* 1949: *m* 1975, Elaine Mary, only da of John Bernard Dancer, MRCS, LRCP, — Jessica Helen, *b* 1940: *m* 1968, Charles James Mansfield, of PO Box 127, Roma, Qld, son of Hon Sir Alan James Mansfield, KCMG, KCVO, and has issue living, Anthony Roderick *b* 1969, David William *b* 1970. *Residence* – 126 Ebury St, SW1.

Grandchildren of late Col Lawrence Clervaux Chaytor, MC, VD (infra):—
Issue of late John Lawrence Clervaux Chaytor, *b* 1926; *d* 1976: *m* Susan Ruth (Marshlands, Marlborough, NZ), da of G. M. Turrell, of Banks Peninsula, Canterbury, NZ:—
Sarah Frances Clervaux, *b* 1956. — Miranda Jane Clervaux, *b* 1958. — Frances Alexandra Clervaux, *b* 1961.

Grandchildren of late John Clervaux Chaytor (*b* 1836) (ante):—
Issue of late Col Lawrence Clervaux Chaytor, MC, VD, New Zealand Mounted Rifles, *b* 1892, *d* 1954: *m* 1920, Dorothy Mary Bullen (of Marshlands, Marlborough, New Zealand), da of late John Robert Bullen Tripe:—
Anthony David Clervaux, *b* 1934. — Jocelyn Dorothy Clervaux, *b* 1921: *m* 1947, Michael Fearon Hall, and has issue living, Michael Timothy Chaytor, *b* 1949, — Annabel Rose, *b* 1954, — Georgina Miranda Mary, *b* 1959. *Residence* – Pendeen Hororata, Canterbury, New Zealand. — Frances Anne Clervaux, *b* 1922: *m* 1956, Michael Kenneth Macdonald, of Gallovie, Hastings, NZ, and has issue living, Fiona Anne, *b* 1958, — Caroline, *b* 1959.

Issue of late Col John Clervaux Chaytor, RA, *b* 1896, *d* 1957: *m* 1930, Olive Mary, who *d* 1957, da of Col Reginald
Brittan, DSO, OBE, of Failand Hill, Failand, Somerset:—
Pamela June, *b* 1934: *m* 1959, Capt Henry Raymond Harvey Fooks, son of Sir Raymond Hatherell Fooks, CBE, of Reves Hall
Farm, Eyke, Suffolk, and has issue living, Caroline Mary, *b* 1961, — Serena Alice, *b* 1963, — Sarah Clervaux, *b* 1965.
—— Jennifer Margaret (Oak Farm, Gwehelog, Usk, Gwent) *b* 1936: *m* 1st, 1959 (*m diss* 1985), Thomas Barrington Cubitt, of
Forbury House, Kintbury, Berks; 2ndly, 1985, (Edward) Martin Dean, who *d* 1985, son of Col Frank Longueville Dean, and
has issue living, (by 1st *m*) Anabelle Jane, *b* 1964, — Alicia Mary, *b* 1965: *m* 1992, Christopher Edward Howard Guinness,
elder son of Lt-Cdr Sir Howard Christian Sheldon Guinness, VRD, RNR, — Miranda Louise, *b* 1967, — Sophia Henrietta, *b*
1968, — Natasha Isabelle, *b* 1976.

Grandchildren of late Arthur Chaytor, 2nd son of John Clervaux Chaytor, *b* 1806 (ante):—
Issue of late Arthur Cuthbert Chaytor, *b* 1873, *d* 1948: *m* 1908, Linda, who *d* 1971, da of Charles Martin, of Stoke,
Nelson, New Zealand:—
Jack Martin (20A Homestead Rd, Whangaparaoa, Auckland, New Zealand), *b* 1913: *m* 1937, Ida Kathleen da of E. A. Russell,
and has two children, Warren John, *b* 19—: *m* 19—, Susan Mary Rohl, and has issue living, Melanie Elizabeth *b* 19—,
Kathryn Alanna *b* 19—, — Lynne Marie, *b* 19—: *m* 19—, Clifton Hallam, and has issue living, Richard Wayne *b* 19—, Donna
Adele *b* 19—, Kathryn Marie *b* 19—. —— Jose Melva (22B Evelyn Rd, Howick, Auckland, New Zealand), *b* 1909.
Issue of late Capt Frank Clervaux Chaytor, *b* 1884, *d* 1962: *m* 1922, Alice, who *d* 1983, da of John Hill, of
Winslow:—
Joan Clervaux, *b* 1925: *m* 1952, Ian McKelvie Bull, and has issue living, Mary Clare, *b* 1953, — Susan Alice, *b* 1958.

The 1st baronet of the *cr* 1831 was descended from Henry Chaytor, brother of Sir William Chaytor (*cr* 1671). He and the
2nd baronet sat in Parliament for Sunderland and Durham respectively. Christopher Chaytor, Surveyor-Gen to Queen
Elizabeth I, obtained a grant of arms in 1571. He married Elizabeth, sole heiress of the Clervaux family, which had owned
estates at Croft since 1246. William Chaytor, grandson of Christopher Chaytor, was *cr* a Baronet 1671 (title ext 1721). The
4th baronet was High Sheriff of co Durham 1902.

CHETWYND (GB) 1795, of Brocton Hall, Staffordshire

What God wills, let it be done

Sir ARTHUR RALPH TALBOT CHETWYND, 8th *Baronet*, son of late
William Ralph Talbot Chetwynd, MC, brother of 7th baronet; *s* his
uncle, *Sir* (ARTHUR HENRY) TALBOT, OBE, MC, 1972; *b* 28 Oct 1913;
ed Vernon Prep Sch, Vernon, BC, and Provincial Normal Sch; Dir
Remedial Gymnastics BC Workman's Compensation Board 1942; Ch
Instructor Med Reconditioning RCAF 1943-45; Associate in Physical
and Health Ed, Univ of Toronto, and Publicity Officer Univ of
Toronto Athletic Assocn 1946-52; Chm Chetwynd Films Ltd, Toronto,
Canada since 1977; Pres Brocton Hall Communications Ltd, Toronto,
Canada: *m* 1940, Marjory May MacDonald, el da of late Robert
Bruce Lang, of Vancouver, BC, and has issue.

Arms – Quarterly, 1st and 4th, azure a chevron between three mullets or; 2nd
and 3rd argent, two gules.
Residences – 117 King St East, Apt 3, Coburg, Ontario K9A 1L2; The Carib,
Holetown, St James, Barbados, WI. *Clubs* – Naval and Military, Empire (Canada;
Past Pres), Royal Canadian Yacht.

SONS LIVING

ROBIN JOHN TALBOT, *b* 21 Aug 1941: *m* 1967, Heather Helen, el da of George Lothian, of Baie D'Urfe, Quebec, and has issue
living, Peter James Talbot, *b* 1973, — Kimberly Anne, *b* 1971. —— (William) Richard Talbot (1090 Sycamore Cres, Oshawa,
Ont L1G 6S7, Canada), *b* 1946: *m* 1971, Patricia Anne, da of late Geoffrey Senior, of Manchester, and has issue living, Hugh
Geoffrey Talbot, *b* 1973, — Brian William Talbot, *b* 1977.

COLLATERAL BRANCHES LIVING

Granddaughters of late Charles Chetwynd, 3rd and yst son of late Maj William Fawkener Chetwynd, 2nd
son of 1st baronet:—
Issue of late Charles William George Chetwynd, *b* 1894, *d* 1975: *m* 1st, 1914 (*m diss* 1932), Olive Mary, yr da of J.
Hall, of Huntingdon; 2ndly, 19—, — 3rdly, 19—, Mary Elizabeth (The Brook, Evesbatch, Bishop's Frome,
Worcester WR6 5BE), da of Arthur Griffiths, JP, of Worcester:—
(By 1st *m*) Rhona Mary, *b* 1916: *m* 1940, Philip Graham Stacey Brinson, and has issue living, John, *b* 1948. —— (By 3rd
m), Valerie Elizabeth, *b* 1940: *m* 1st, 1961, Rupert Carrington; 2ndly, 1978, Lt-Col Mark F. Murray, RM, of The Brook,
Evesbatch, Bishops Frome, Hereford and Worcester WR6 5BE.

Grandsons of late Charles William George Chetwynd (ante):—
Issue of late Basil Charles Fawkener Chetwynd, *b* 1915, *d* 1980: *m* 1944, Margaret Joan, who *d* 1992, da of late
George Ernest Welch:—
Paul Ernest Fawkener (Greenacres, Charlton Rd, Creech Heathfield, Taunton, Somerset), *b* 1945: *m* 1972, Shirley Evelyn, el
da of Raymond Godfrey Manuel, of Creech Heathfield, and has issue living, Karen Lynne, *b* 1975, — Wendy Caroline, *b*
1977. —— Raymond Charles Fawkener (Westlake, Cockpit Rd, Great Kings Hill, nr High Wycombe, Bucks), *b* 1950: *m*
1974, Susan Jane, el da of John Kershaw, of Taunton, Som, and has issue living, Joanne Louise, *b* 1978, — Rebecca Claire, *b*
1978 (twin), — Sarah Jane, *b* 1982.
Sir Philip Chetwynd, 2nd son of Sir John Chetwynd of Chetwynd, Salop (*d c* 1240), whose family was of great antiquity in
that co, obtained Ingestre, Staffs, by marriage with Isabella, da and heir of Sir Adam de Mytton. Their descendant, Sir
William Chetwynd of Ingestre (*d* 1547), had issue, Thomas of Ingestre (*d* 1555) and Anthony of Ridge, Staffs, grandfather of
the 1st, 2nd and 3rd Viscounts Chetwynd, who inherited Ingestre. Thomas of Ingestre (*d* 1555) was grandfather of John
Chetwynd of Ingestre (*d* 1592), whose 4th son, Thomas of Rugeley, Staffs (*d* 1633), was ancestor of the Chetwynds of
Brocton in that co. Sir George Chetwynd 1st Bt, was 5th in descent from Thomas (*d* 1633). The 1st baronet, many years
Clerk to the Privy Council, received knighthood in 1787, and the 2nd sat as MP for Stafford. Sir George Chetwynd 4th Bt,
was High Sheriff of Warwickshire 1875.

CHEYNE (UK) 1908, of Leagarth, Fetlar, and North Yell, co Zetland
(Name pronounced "Chain")

He conquers by patience

Sir JOSEPH LISTER WATSON CHEYNE, OBE, 3rd *Baronet*; *b* 10 Oct 1914; *s* his father, *Col* Sir JOSEPH LISTER, MC, 1957; *ed* Stowe, and Corpus Christi Coll, Camb; 2nd Sec (Information) British Embassy, Rome 1968-70, 1st Sec 1970-73, 1st Sec (Information) 1973-76; curator, Keats-Shelley Memorial House, Rome 1976-90; European War 1939-45 as Major, Queen's Westminsters, KRRC; OBE (Civil) 1976: *m* 1st, 1938 (*m diss* 1955), Mary Mort, who *d* 1959, da of Vice-Adm John Derwent Allen, CB; 2ndly, 1955, Cicely, da of Thomas Metcalfe, of Padiham, Lancashire, and has issue by 1st and 2nd marriages.

Arms – Azure, on a bend between six crosses patée fitchée argent an oak tree eradicated proper, fructed or. **Crest** – A cross patée fitchée argent.
Residences – Leagarth, Fetlar, Shetland; Po' di Serse, via Po' del Vento 19A, Paciano (PG) 06060, Italy.

SONS LIVING *(By 1st marriage)*

PATRICK JOHN LISTER (37 Chapel Lane, Hale Barns, Altrincham, Cheshire WA15 0AG), *b* 2 July 1941: *ed* Lancing: *m* 1968, Helen Louise Trevor, yr da of Louis Smith, of Marine Lodge, 25 Driftwood Gardens, Southsea, Hants PO4 9ND, and has issue living, Louis Richard Patrick Lister, *b* 25 March 1971, — Elizabeth Henrietta Louise, *b* 1969, — Mary Catherine Fleur, *b* 1974, — Caroline Victoria Alice, *b* 1979.

(By 2nd marriage)

John Joseph Peter (La Vignaccia, Via Del Bandino 6, Pergine Val D'Arno, Arezzo, Italy), *b* 1956: *m* 1980, Emma, 2nd da of late Luciano Sestini, of Arezzo, Italy, and has issue living, Edward William Watson, *b* 1980. —— James Andrew Watson (20 Via Calabria, Roma, Italy), *b* 1957; *ed* Stowe: *m* 1984, Frederica Elda Cristina, yr da of Paolo Napolitani, of Rome, and has issue living, William Giovanni Joseph Watson, *b* 1986.

DAUGHTERS LIVING *(By 1st marriage)*

Ann Caroline Lister, *b* 1939: *m* 1961, Lt-Col Ronald Eric Croll Adam, Queen's Own Highlanders. *Residence* – Coombe House, Sharnden, Mayfield, E Sussex TN20 6QA.

(By 2nd marriage)

Helen Margaret Watson, *b* 1959: *m* 1989, Rinaldo G M Rinaldi (Piazza San Salvatore in Lauro 13, Roma, Italy), elder son of late Avv Francesco Rinaldi.

BROTHER LIVING

Andrew Watson, *b* 1921; *ed* Stowe, and Loughborough Coll, Leicester; late Capt RE, and a FICE; Burma 1941-45, NW Europe 1945 (despatches): *m* 1946, Joyce, da of Conway Stanton, of Kensington, SW10. *Residence* – 49 Hurlingham Court, Ranelagh Gdns, SW6.

COLLATERAL BRANCHES LIVING

Issue of late Brig William Watson Cheyne, DSO, OBE, 2nd son of 2nd baronet, *b* 1920, *d* 1970: *m* 1946, Laurel Audrey (12 Crondace Rd, SW6), da of late Lt-Gen Sir Balfour Oliphant Hutchison, KBE, CB (*see* Jervis-White-Jervis, Bt (ext), colls, 1990 Edn):—
Julian Lister Hutchison, *b* 1947. —— David Watson (19 Ladbroke Gdns, W11 2PT), *b* 1948; *ed* Stowe and Trin Coll, Camb (BA): *m* 1978, (Judith) Gay McAuslane, el da of David Anstruther Passey, of The Hall, Kirkby Fleetham, Northallerton, Yorks, and has issue living, Alexander William David, *b* 1980, — Rory Alistair Watson, *b* 1984, — Rupert Valentine Hutchinson, *b* 1989. —— (William) Gerald (32 Ringmer Av, SW6), *b* 1950; *ed* Stowe, and Trin Coll, Camb (BA): *m* 1978 (*m diss* 1984), Clare Rosdew, da of Stamford Robert Francis Vanderstegen-Drake, of The Old Tannery, Ecchinswell, Newbury, Berks (*see* Mowbray, Bt), and has issue living, Katherine Clare, *b* 1980. —— Bridget Nelita, *b* 1955: *m* 1984, Richard Patrick Lanyon, of 16 Dryburgh Rd, SW15, eldest son of Major Patrick Lanyon, of The Great House, Timberscombe, Minehead, Somerset, and has issue living, William Patrick, *b* 1988, — Frances Alice, *b* 1986, — Alexandra Polly, *b* 1990.

Issue of late William Hunter Watson Cheyne, MB, MRCS, LRCP, 2nd son of 1st baronet, *b* 1889, *d* 1957: *m* 1923, Grizel, who *d* 1975, da of I. F. Bayley, formerly of Halls, East Lothian:—
George Watson, *b* 1929; *ed* Sherborne, and Corpus Christi Coll, Camb (MA, LLM); Bar Gray's Inn 1955: *m* 1964, (Alison) Diana Muir, da of C. Muir Jones, of Hawarden, Chester, and has issue living, Piers William Watson, *b* 1965; *ed* Radley, and Bristol Univ (BA): *m* 1994, Anne, eldest da of Jean-Louis Richard, of St Germain-en-Laye, France, — Phyllida Alison, *b* 1968; MA, MPhil Cantab; Inner Temple 1992, — Catriona Helen, *b* 1971. *Residence* – The Priory, Monk Sherborne, Basingstoke, Hants. —— Janet Mary Watson (*Baroness Cochrane of Cults*), *b* 1931: *m* 1956, 4th Baron Cochrane of Cults. *Residence* – Cults, Cupar, Fife.

The 1st baronet, Sir (William) Watson Cheyne, KCMG, CB, FRCS, FRS, an eminent surgeon, and Pres of Roy Coll of Surgs, was Lord-Lieut of Orkney and Shetland 1919-30, and sat as MP for Edinburgh and St Andrews Univ (C) 1917-18 and for Edinburgh St Andrews, Glasgow, and Aberdeen Univs (Co U) 1918-22. The 2nd baronet, Sir Joseph Lister Cheyne, MC, was Col Comdg 16/5th Lancers.

CHICHESTER (E) 1641, of Raleigh, Devonshire

Ferme en foy

Firm in faith.

Sir (EDWARD) JOHN CHICHESTER, 11th *Baronet; b* 14 April 1916; *s* his father, *Com Sir*EDWARD GEORGE, RN (ret), 1940; *ed* Radley, and RMC Sandhurst; late Capt Roy Scots Fusiliers; is patron of one living; was King's Foreign Service Messenger 1947-50, and with Imperial Chemical Industries Ltd 1950-60; European War 1939-45 with Roy Scots Fusiliers, and as Lieut RNVR: *m* 1950, Hon Anne Rachel Pearl Douglas-Scott-Montagu, da of 2nd Baron Montagu of Beaulieu, and widow of Major Howel Joseph Moore-Gwyn, Welsh Guards, and has had issue.

Arms – Checky or and gules, a chief vair. **Crest** – A heron rising with an eel in its beak proper.
Address – Battramsley Lodge, Boldre, Lymington, Hants SO41 8PT.

SONS LIVING

JAMES HENRY EDWARD, *b* 15 Oct 1951; *ed* Eton: *m* 1990, (Margaret) Anne, only da of Maj John Walkelyne Chandos-Pole, JP, DL, of Radbourne Hall, Derbys, and has issue living, Edward John Chandos-Pole, *b* 27 July 1991, — Charles James, *b* 1992. —— Julian John Raleigh, *b* 1963.

DAUGHTERS LIVING AND DECEASED

Coral Anne, *b* 1954: *m* 1977, Christopher Angus McEwen, MICE, of Aldhams, Bromley Rd, Lawford, Manningtree, Essex CO11 2NE, and has issue living, Rosanna Clare, *b* 1981, — Alexia Catherine, *b* 1982, — Sabrina Caroline, *b* 1988. —— Georgina Caroline, *b* 1955: *m* 1985, Christopher J. Leyland, of Greymare Farm, Belford, Northumberland NE70 7PG, son of late John Christopher Michael Leyland (*see* Cotterell, Bt, 1944 Edn), and has issue living, Benjamin John, *b* 1994, — Emma Rose, *b* 1989. —— Mary Rose, *b* 1957: *m* 1978, as his 2nd wife, Greville Patrick Charles Howard (*see* E Suffolk and Berkshire, colls), and *d* 1980.

SISTER LIVING

Mary, *b* 1917: *m* 1941, Cdr John Blakeley Russell, DSC, RN (ret), and has issue living, Christopher John, *b* 1954, — Hermione Anne, *b* 1942: *m* 1962, Robin Labron Johnson, and has issue living, Nicolas Patrick Amyas Labron *b* 1963, Tristan Alexander Labron *b* 1965, — Cherry Rose, *b* 1952: *m* 1977, Fl Lt Andrew Renshaw, and has issue living (*see* Renshaw, Bt).

COLLATERAL BRANCHES LIVING

Issue of late Marcus Beresford Chichester, yst son of 9th baronet, *b* 1896, *d* 1985: *m* 1925, Myra Brownrigg, who *d* 1985, yst da of late Maj Harvey Brownrigg Jay:—
Imogen Ann (Crawley Lodge, Yarcombe, Honiton, Devon), *b* 1926: *m* 1948, Maj Arthur John Digby Hamilton, Scots Gds, who *d* 1980 (*see* Fairlie-Cunninghame, Bt, 1964 Edn), and has issue living, Philip Arthur Marcus, *b* 1949, — Edward Digby Hamilton, *b* 1953, — James John, *b* 1959, — Thomas Patrick, *b* (twin) 1959, — Kate Antonia, *b* 1950: *m* 1st, 1972 (*m diss* 1979), Robin Salt; 2ndly, 1981, Simon Peter Dewhurst, of Sicily Oak, Cholmondeley, Malpas, Cheshire, and has issue living (by 1st *m*), Thomas Bertram *b* 1972, Antonia Jane *b* 1974 (by 2nd *m*), Patrick Digby *b* 1983, Frederick Olivier *b* 1989. —— Jane Catherine, *b* 1929: *m* 1957, Roger Longrigg, of Orchard House, Crookham, Hants, and has issue living, Laura Jane, *b* 1958, — Frances Angelica, *b* 1961, — Clare Selina, *b* 1963.

Grandchildren of late George Chichester, 6th son of 8th baronet:—
Issue of late Group Capt Patrick George Chichester, OBE, RAF, *b* 1901, *d* 1983: *m* 1931, Gladys Evelyn Vesta Clemency, who *d* 1977, da of William Carnegie Barnes, of Hayne Manor, Lewdown, Devon:—
Jeremy Patrick (Hawthorn Cottage, Congresbury, Som BS19 5BE), *b* 1932: *m* 1956, Kathleen Anne, only da of William George Lloyd, of Nashley House, Weston-super-Mare, Som, and has issue living, Mark Arlington Raleigh (The Lodge, Hayne Manor, Lewdown, nr Okehampton, Devon), *b* 1957; Lieut RN: *m* 1984, Adrienne Valmai, yr da of Douglas Henry Cook, of Sutherland Drive, Hutton, Avon, and has issue living, Amelia *b* 1989, Alicia Vesta Anne *b* 1991, — Matthew Patrick Lloyd, *b* 1966, — Miranda Frances Louise, *b* 1962: *m* 1987, Trevor D. Jones, son of K. H. Jones, of Tenterden, Kent. —— Patricia Gladys Clemency, *b* 1939: *m* 1963, Anthony Arthur Greves Quinton, MD, and has issue living, Lucinda Clemency, *b* 1965. —— Caroline Sandra Pietre Katrina, *b* 1944: *m* 1970, Capt Michael George Temple Harris, RN, of The White House, Seven Stars Lane, Tamerton Foliot, Plymouth (*see* B Harris, colls). —— Clarissa Evelyn Georgette, *b* 1948: *m* 1972, Keith James Keating, of Cloncurry, W Qld, Aust, and has issue living, Simon Keith, *b* 1979, — Melissa Evelyn, *b* 1973, — Georgina Naomi, *b* 1974.

Grandson of late Rev Charles Chichester (*infra*):—
Issue of late Sir Francis Charles Chichester, KBE, *b* 1901, *d* 1972: *m* 1st, 1923, Muriel Eileen, who *d* 1929, da of late M. F. Blakiston; 2ndly, 1937, Sheila Mary, who *d* 1989, da of late Gerald Craven, of Belle Eau Park, Notts:—
(By 2nd *m*) Giles Bryan (9 St James's Pl, SW1), *b* 1946; *ed* Ch Ch, Oxford: *m* 1979, Virginia, yst da of late Edwin Ansell, and has issue living, George Arthur Francis, *b* 1981, — Charles Edward Orlando, *b* 1990, — Jessica Mary, *b* 1984.

Issue of late Rev Charles Chichester, 7th son of 8th baronet, *b* 1868, *d* 1938: *m* 1896, Emily Annie, who *d* 1962, da of late Samuel Page, of Chitt's Hill, Wood Green, N:—
Barbara (Longridge, West Hill, Ottery St Mary, Devon), *b* 1907: *m* 1951, John Charles Fanshawe Royle, JP, who *d* 1973. —— Cicely (6A Marlborough Rd, Exeter) *b* 1913.

This family took its name from Chichester Sussex. On the marriage of Thomasine Raleigh with John Chichester in 1384 this family settled at Raleigh, Devon. Sir Roger Chichester was knighted by the king at the siege of Calais, and afterwards served at Poitiers. The 9th baronet, Rear-Adm Sir Edward Chichester, was a Naval ADC to HM Queen Victoria and HM King Edward VII 1899-1902.

CHILD (UK) 1868, of Newfield, and of Stallington Hall, Staffordshire and of Glen Losset, co Argyll
(Extinct 1958)

Sir (SMITH) HILL CHILD, GCVO, CB, CMG, DSO, 2nd and last *Baronet*.

DAUGHTER LIVING OF SECOND BARONET

Mary Cornelia, *b* 1933: *m* 1959, Henry Charles Whitbread, who *d* 1993, and has issue living, Caroline Mary, *b* 1960: *m* 1986, Major (Jonathan) Peter Wikeley, RA, of Hill View Farm, Brickyard Lane, Corfe Mullen, Dorset BH21 3RJ, 3rd son of Sqdn/Ldr J. D. Wikeley, of Gillingham, Dorset, and has issue living, Rosalyn Elizabeth *b* 1990, — Flora Joscelyne, *b* 1962, — Angela Helen, *b* 1965. *Residence* – Haymans Farm, Plaistow, Billingshurst, W Sussex RH14 0PQ.

CHILD (UK) 1919, of Bromley Palace, Bromley, Kent

To imitate rather than to envy

Sir (COLES JOHN) JEREMY CHILD, 3rd *Baronet*; *b* 20 Sept 1944: *s* his father, *Sir* (COLES) JOHN, 1971; *ed* Eton, and Poitiers Univ; actor: *m* 1st, 1971 (*m diss* 1976), Deborah Jane, da of Henry Percival Snelling; 2ndly, 1978 (*m diss* 1987), Jan, yst da of Bernard Todd, of Kingston upon Thames; 3rdly, 1987, Elizabeth (Libby), yst da of Rev Grenville Morgan, of Canterbury, Kent, and has issue (by 1st, 2nd and 3rd *m*).

Arms – Per chevron azure and gules, on a chevron engrailed ermine between three eagles close argent a fylfot sable. **Crest** – An eagle, wings expanded argent charged on the breast with a fylfot sable, holding in the beak by its neck a serpent entwined round the body vert.
Residence – The Old Mill House, Mill Lane, Benson, Oxford.

SONS LIVING *(By 2nd marriage)*

(COLES JOHN) ALEXANDER, *b* 10 May 1982.

(by 3rd marriage)

Patrick Grenville, *b* 1991.

DAUGHTERS LIVING *(By 1st marriage)*

(Honor) Melissa, *b* 1973.

(by 2nd marriage)

Leonora, *b* 1980.

(by 3rd marriage)

Eliza Caroline, *b* 1989.

SISTERS LIVING

Deirdre Kathleen, *b* 1934: *m* 1959, Antony Edward Woodall, of The Old Rectory, Wyddial, Buntingford, Herts (Crawley-Boevey, Bt, colls), and has issue living, James Henry, *b* 1960, — Andrew Hugh, *b* 1963: *m* 1990, Jane Mary Ashton, and has issue living, Gabriel Sanderson *b* 1992, Constance Rose *b* 1991, — Edward Antony John, *b* 1967. —— Honor Diana, *b* 1936: *m* 1st, 1959, Capt Noel Hardwick Matterson, late R Dragoons, who *d* 1982; 2ndly, 1985, Robin Patrick Fremantle (*see* E Cottesloe, colls), and has issue living (by 1st *m*), Charles John Hardwick *b* 1960: *m* 1987, Elizabeth Caroline McGregor Moffat, — Justin George Hardwick, *b* 1962, — Nicholas Noel Hardwick, *b* 1963: *m* 1992, Georgia Cadwaladr, — Dominic Graham Hardwick, *b* 1965: *m* 1992, Camilla Mary Roche.

Sir Coles Child, 1st Bt, was son of Coles William John Child, JP, DL, of Bromley, Kent. The latter's great-great-grandfather John Child, of Yaxley, Hunts (*d* 1743): *m* Isabella, da of William Coles, of London.

CHITTY (UK) 1924, of The Temple

Sir THOMAS WILLES CHITTY, 3rd *Baronet*; *b* 2 March 1926; *s* his father, *Sir* (THOMAS) HENRY WILLES, 1955; *ed* Winchester, and Univ Coll, Oxford: *m* 1951, Susan Elspeth Russel, da of late Rudolph Glossop, and has issue.
Residence – Bow Cottage, West Hoathly, Sussex RH19 4QF.

SON LIVING

ANDREW EDWARD WILLES, *b* 20 Nov 1953.

DAUGHTERS LIVING

Cordelia Anne, *b* 1955. —— Miranda Jane, *b* 1967. —— Jessica Susan, *b* 1971.

BROTHERS LIVING

Michael Willes, *b* 1929: *m* 1954, Janet Leonora, da of W. A. Messenger, of Forest Down, Pyrford, Woking, and has issue living, Sebastian William, *b* 1958, — Anne-Marie, *b* 1966. *Residence* – Leonora Cottage, Mithian, St Agnes, Cornwall. —— John Henry Willes (31 Church Way, Sanderstead, Surrey), *b* 1932; late Lt RA: *m* 1968, Diana Mary, da of G. D. B. Dear, of Coulsdon, Surrey, and has issue living, Antonia Mary Willes, *b* 1970, — Louise Elizabeth Willes, *b* 1973.

COLLATERAL BRANCH LIVING

Issue of late Robert Michael Willes Chitty, 2nd son of 1st baronet, *b* 1893, *d* 1970: *m* 1922, Norah A., da of W. Cooke, of Toronto:—
Thomas Michael Willes, *b* 1930: *m* 1952, Edith Jeremy Weir, of Toronto, and has issue living, Robert Arthur, *b* 1953, — Diana, *b* 1956, — Susan Elizabeth *b* 1957. —— Norah Elizabeth, *b* 1926: *m* 1958, Ross Alexander Wilson and has issue living, Lesley, *b* 1959.
The 1st baronet, Sir Thomas Willes Chitty, KC (son of Thomas Edward Chitty), was a Master of Supreme Court 1901-20, and Senior Master of Supreme Court and King's Remembrancer 1920-26. The 2nd baronet, Sir (Thomas) Henry Willes Chitty, wsa a Bar-at-law of Inner Temple.

CHOLMELEY (UK) 1806, of Easton, Lincolnshire
(Name pronounced "Chumly")

Sir Montague John Chomeley, 6th *Baronet; b* 27 March 1935; *s* his father, *Lt-Col Sir* Hugh John Francis Sibthorp, CB, DSO, 1964; *ed* Eton; Capt Grenadier Guards: *m* 1960, Juliet Auriol Sally, yst da of Maj-Gen Sir (Eustace) John Blois Nelson, KCVO, CB, DSO, OBE, MC (*see* D Grafton), and has issue.

𝕬rms – Gules, two helmets in chief proper, and a garb in base or; a mullet for difference Crest – A garb or.
Seat – Easton Hall, Grantham. *Residence* – Church Farm, Burton le Coggles, Grantham, Lincs. *Clubs* – Cavalry and Guards', White's.

SON LIVING

(Hugh John) Frederick (Sebastian), *b* 3 Jan 1968: *m* 1993, Ursula Ann, eldest da of Hugh Peter Derwyn Bennett, QC, of Highbrook, Ardingly, Sussex.

DAUGHTERS LIVING

Camilla, *b* 1962: *m* 1982, William Murdoch, eldest son of Andrew Murdoch, of Parsonage Farm, Hurstbourne Tarrant, Andover, Hants, and has issue living, Andrew William, *b* 1991, — John Oliver, *b* 1994. —— Davina, *b* 1964: *m* 1985, Nicholas Morgan, and has issue living, Peter, *b* 1987, — James, *b* 1990.
This family is a younger branch of the noble house of Cholmondeley. Henry Cholmeley, of Burton Coggles, settled in Lincolnshire in the 16th century, and from him the present baronet is descended in a direct line. The 1st baronet was MP for Grantham 1820-26, and the 2nd baronet sat for many years successively as MP for Grantham and Lincolnshire North (*L*). The 4th baronet, Capt Sir Montague Aubrey Rowley Cholmeley, Grenadier Guards, was *ka* Dec 1914.

CHRISTISON (UK) 1871, of Moray Place, Edinburgh (Extinct 1993)

Sir (Alexander Frank) Philip Christison, GBE, CB, DSO, MC, 4th and last *Baronet*, who *d* 21 Dec 1993, aged 100.

DAUGHTERS LIVING OF FOURTH BARONET (By 1st marriage)

Alison Ann, *b* 1924; formerly Junior Com WAC (India): *m* 1945, Capt Denis Clode James, Roy Indian Army Ser Corps, of 83 Branksome Gdns, City Beach, Perth, W Aust, and has issue living, Michael Christison, *b* 1947, — Philip Christison, *b* 1949, — Jane Alison, *b* 1946, — Kandy Ann, *b* 1953. —— Fiona Christison, *b* 1932: *m* 1954 (*m diss* 1977), Peter Thomson McLintock (*see* McLintock, Bt).

SISTER LIVING OF FOURTH BARONET

Alison Florence Alexandra, *b* 1901: *m* 1925, Paymaster-Capt Philip Skelton Graham, RN, who *d* 1965, and has issue living, Philip Colin Christison (26 Pilgrims Way, Canterbury, Kent), *b* 1926: *m* 1955, Dorothy, da of Frederic W. Ireland, and has issue living, Michael (29 Jacob's Wells Rd, Clifton, Bristol) *b* 1957: *m* 1988 (*m diss* 1992), Kaz, da of — Williams-Harms, Eleanor *b* 1959: *m* 1983, David Bittleston (and has issue living, Maximilian *b* 1990), — Alison Monica (*Baroness Jenkin of Roding*), *b* 1928: *m* 1952, Baron Jenkin of Roding, PC (Life Baron), of Home Farm, Matching Rd, Hatfield Heath, Bishops Stortford, Herts, — Marion Dorothea, *b* 1930: *m* 1960, Michael Richards, of 65 Brunstane Rd, Portobello, Edinburgh, EH15 2QS, and has issue living, Hugh *b* 1961: *m* —, Daniel *b* 1967, Alison *b* 1962, Clare *b* 1964: *m* 1987, Dr MacLean Ransom, — Penelope Jean, *b* 1934: *m* 1975, William Charles Jackson, of 36A Devonshire Rd, Chorley, Lancs. *Residence* – St Anne's House, Windsor Gdns, Musselburgh, Midlothian.

CHURCH (UK) 1901, of Harley Street, co London, and Woodside, Hatfield, Herts (Extinct 1979)

Sir GEOFFREY SELBY CHURCH, CBE, MC, TD, 2nd and last *Baronet.*

COLLATERAL BRANCH LIVING

Issue of late John William Church, Lt Hertfordshire Regt, el son of 1st baronet, *b* 1878, *ka* 1918: *m* 1908, Brenda, who *d* 1951, da of late Hugh Lee Pattinson, of 85 Linden Gardens, Bayswater, W:—
Lesbia Mary, *b* 1916: *m* 1941, Sergei G. Kadleigh, ARIBA, of 12B Miles Rd, Clifton, Bristol BS8 2NN, Avon.

CLARK (UK) 1883, of Cavendish Square, co Middlesex (Extinct 1979)

Sir ANDREW EDMUND JAMES CLARK, MBE, MC, QC, 3rd and last *Baronet.*

DAUGHTERS LIVING OF THIRD BARONET *(By 2nd marriage)*

Jennifer Jane, *b* 1934; Bar Inner Temple 1955: *m* 1956, John Bertrand Worsley, of Furlong House, Hurstpierpoint, Sussex BN6 9QA (*see* B Napier of Magdala, colls, 1980 Edn), and has issue living, James Jonathan, *b* 1957: *m* 1987, Marion Coratte, and has issue living, Arthur Richard Jacques *b* 1988, Edward Andrew Stanimir *b* 1989, — Harriet Laura, *b* 1960: *m* 1986, Mark Thornycroft Vernon, and has issue (*see* Vernon, Bt, colls), — Alison Margaret, *b* 1963: *m* 1992, Christian Holstein, and has issue living, Jacob Sebastian *b* 1993, — Victoria Mary, *b* 1966. —— Susan Mary, *b* 1936; Bar Inner Temple 1957: *m* 1958, Ian Malcolm Maxwell-Scott, who *d* 1993, and has issue (*see* Constable-Maxwell-Scott, Bt, *cr* 1642).

CLARK (UK) 1886, of Melville Crescent, Edinburgh

In God I trust

Sir FRANCIS DRAKE CLARK, 5th *Baronet*; *b* 16 July 1924; *s* his brother, *Sir* JOHN DOUGLAS, 1991; *ed* Edinburgh Academy; served 1939-45 War with RN: *m* 1968, Mary, yr da of late John Alban Andrews, MC, FRCS, and has issue.

Arms – Azure, a fesse or between a castle triple towered argent masoned sable in chief, and a crescent of the second in base. **Crest** – A demi-lion rampant azure, holding in his dexter paw a battleaxe proper.
Residence – Woodend Cottages, Burgh-next-Aylsham, Norfolk NR11 6TS.

SON LIVING

EDWARD DRAKE, *b* 27 April 1966; *ed* Westminster, and St Andrews Univ.

SISTER LIVING

Laura Moubray, *b* 1916: *m* 1940, Maj Hugh Mackinlay Renwick, RAC (ret), who *d* 1991, of Greenacres, 49 Gogarbank, Edinburgh 12, and has issue living, William Norman Hugh, *b* 1950; *ed* Melville Coll, Edinburgh: *m* 1970 (*m diss* 1982), Patricia Jamieson, and has issue living, George Martin *b* 1970, Paul William *b* 1974, — Diana Elizabeth, *b* 1942: *m* 1st, 1967 (*m diss* 1972), Allan Miller Duthie; 2ndly, 1972, David Richardson, of Carlesgill, Langholm, Dumfriesshire, and has issue living (by 2nd *m*), Susan Carolyn, *b* 1975, — Cynthia Caroline, *b* 1947.

UNCLE LIVING *(Son of 2nd baronet)*

John Maurice, MBE, *b* 1903; *ed* Edinburgh Academy, and The Leys Sch, Cambridge, Hon Maj (ret) RE (Movement Control); MBE (Mil) 1944: *m* 1933, Winnie Stratton, da of late Dr Campbell Highet, and has issue living, Hugh Lothian (Belstone Cottage, Blackford, Queen Camel, nr Yeovil, Som), *b* 1939; Lt-Col (sometime comdg) Argyll and Sutherland Highlanders (ret): *m* 1967, Deborah Mary Ann, da of Col William Innes Moberly, CBE, and has issue living, Hugo Ian Moberly *b* 1970; Capt Argyll and Sutherland Highlanders, Harry James Lothian *b* 1972, Benedict John Innes *b* 1975, Luke Edward Campbell *b* 1979, — Hamish Douglas, *b* 1945; Maj Argyll and Sutherland Highlanders (ret); despatches Aden 1967: *m* 1969, Wendy Ann Macdonald, only da of Ian M. Harper, of Redlairdston, Buchlyvie, Stirlingshire, and has issue living, Ian Nicholas Harper *b* 1971, Mark James Macdonald *b* 1974. *Residence* – Little Thornbank, Long Street, Sherborne, Dorset DT9 3BS.

WIDOW LIVING OF FOURTH BARONET

ANNE (*Dowager Lady Clark*), da of late Angus Gordon, of Beauly, Inverness-shire, and widow of William Swan, of Edinburgh: *m* 1969, Sir John Douglas Clark, 4th Bt, who *d* 1991. *Residence* – 52 Ormidale Terrace, Edinburgh 12.

COLLATERAL BRANCHES LIVING

Issue of late Brig Henry James Douglas Clark, MC, 2nd son of 2nd Bt, *b* 1888, *d* 1978: *m* 1915, Isobel, who *d* 1969, da of Lt-Col Wentworth Forbes, of Glebe House, Brackley:—
Wentworth Douglas (Jesus Hospital, High St, Bray, Bucks), *b* 1916; Lt-Col Argyll and Sutherland Highlanders (ret); 1939-45 War (wounded): *m* 1948, Florence Mary, who *d* 1987, da of late Duncan Richard Ricketts, and formerly wife of Alexander Addis Leslie, and has issue living, (Wentworth Mary) Carolyn, *b* 1949: *m* 1st, 1972 (*m diss*), Gp/Capt Peter Butt, RAF; 2ndly, 1992, Richard Northcote, and has issue living (by 1st *m*), Susannah Jane *b* 1974, Annabel Laura Mary *b* 1988.

Grandson of Maj John Maurice Clark, MBE (ante):—
Issue of late Lt Ian Campbell Clark, RM, *b* 1937, *ka* Sarawak (despatches) 1966: *m* 1962, Melita, of 15 Springfield

Rd, Guildford, Surrey (who *m* 2ndly, 1971 (*m diss* 1979), Anthony Hurst), only da of late Ivor G. Powell, of Woking, Surrey:—
Timothy Ian Hugh, *b* (*posthumous*) 1966.

Grandchildren of late Lt-Col Thomas George Clark, TD, 2nd son of 1st baronet:—
Issue of late Capt Thomas George Clark, *b* 1895, *d* 1986: *m* 1921, Mary Hall, who *d* 1987, da of late Thomas Aldcorn, of Johannesburg, S Africa:—
Thomas George Ramsay Davidson (Tyneford House, Ford, Midlothian), *b* 1922; a Chartered Accountant, and former Dir T & T Clark, publishers; 1939-45 War with RAF: *m* 1956, Sheila Campbell, da of Herbert Campbell Brown, of Littleacre, Strathkinnes Rd, St Andrews, Fife, and has issue living, Thomas George Nigel, *b* 1965, — Sheena Campbell, *b* 1959, — Karen Ramsay, *b* (twin) 1959: *m* 1985, Christopher John Heaton-Armstrong, eldest son of Capt Thomas Michael Robert Heaton-Armstrong, of Couligarton, Aberfoyle, Perth, and has issue living, Gabrielle Louise *b* 1991, — Gillian Davidson, *b* 1962. —— Wendy Margaret, *b* 1935: *m* 1968, George Gordon Brown, Maj (ret) 9/12th R Lancers; Barrister, of Kingshot, Edward Rd, St Cross, Winchester, Hants, and has issue living, Richard Gordon, *b* 1973, — Melanie Ann, *b* 1969.
Sir Thomas Clark, 1st baronet (many years senior partner in the publishing firm of T and T Clark of Edinburgh), was Lord Provost of Edinburgh 1885-8. Sir John Maurice Clark, 2nd Bt, MBE, VD, DL (sometime senior partner in the publishing firm of T and T Clark), was Chm Scottish Life Assurance Co (Limited), and Col (sometime Comdg) 7th Batn, Roy Scots. Sir Thomas Clark, 3rd Bt, DL, was sometime snr ptnr in publishing firm T. & T. Clark, Hon Col The Forth Heavy Regt, RA, and Chm TAAVA Scotland 1955-65.

CLARK (UK) 1917, of Dunlambert, City of Belfast

FREE·FOR·A·BLAST

Sir COLIN DOUGLAS CLARK, MC, 4th *Baronet; b* 20 July 1918; *s* his brother, *Capt Sir* GEORGE ANTHONY, 1991; *ed* Eton, and Trin Coll, Camb (BA 1939, MA 1944); European War 1939-45 as Maj RE (despatches, MC): *m* 1946, Margaret Coleman, yst da of Maj-Gen Sir Charlton Watson Spinks, KBE, DSO, and widow of Maj Guy William Going Threlfall, MC, 8th Hus, and has issue.

Arms – Barry wavy of four argent and azure, a galley with sail set and flags flying all or, on a chief of the second a thistle slipped with two leaves, between two roses of the third. **Crest** – A demi huntsman proper, vested azure, blowing a horn or.
Residence – Flaxpool House, Crowcombe, Taunton, Somerset TA4 4AW.

SON LIVING

JONATHAN GEORGE, *b* 9 Oct 1947; *ed* Eton; late Capt Royal Green Jackets: *m* 1971, Susan Joy, da of Brig Thomas Ian Gordon Gray, and has issue living, George Simon Gray, *b* 3 Oct 1975; *ed* Shrewsbury, — Polly Caroline, *b* 1973, — Tessa Louise, *b* 1978. *Residence* – Somerset House, Threapwood, Malpas, Cheshire.

DAUGHTERS LIVING

Sarah Louise, *b* 1949: *m* 1975, Michael Alan de Cheveley Kohler, of 16a Marlborough Rd, Richmond, Surrey, TW10 6JR, and has issue living, Rosalie de Cheveley, *b* 1979, — Mirabel Margaret Macadam, *b* 1982, — Katharine Isobel Lesoipa, *b* 1985. —— Gillian Margaret Ann, *b* 1957: *m* 1987, Roger Dixon Spain, of The Old Hall, Whitecross Lane, Tilney All Saints, King's Lynn, Norfolk PE34 4SR.

BROTHER LIVING

Peter Aubrey, *b* 1927; *ed* Campbell Coll, Belfast: *m* 1951, Rosemary Frazer, da of T. Frazer Mackie, of Guincho, Helen's Bay, co Down, and has issue living, Richard Henry Frazer (Ardvarragh, Archway, Mold, Clwyd CH7 1JX), *b* 1952: *m* 1977, Hazel Yvonne Elizabeth, da of Edmund Irvine Smith, of Ellenvine, Craigavad, co Down, and has issue living, Linda Helen *b* 1978, Fiona Elizabeth *b* 1980, — Michael Peter George (4 Chaple Acres, East Abercromby St, Helensburgh, Dunbartonshire), *b* 1955: *m* 1976, Sandra Muriel Jane Foster, da of Martin Reid-Foster, of Flagpoint, Campbell St, Helensburgh, and has issue living, Paul Michael Frazer *b* 1978, Jamie Stewart *b* 1979, Garry Martin *b* 1982, Katie Jane *b* 1984. *Residence* – Cillenamara, Ringhaddy, Killinchy, co Down.

SISTER LIVING

Beatrice Norah, *b* 1911: *m* 1st, 1931 (*m diss* 1946), Major Theodore Bertram Doxford, RASC; 2ndly, 1953, Col William Buckley Nicholl Roderick, OBE, who *d* 1957; 3rdly, 1961, John Wrench, who *d* 1981, and has issue living, (by 1st *m*) Angela Beatrice, *b* 1935: *m* 1st, 1958 (*m diss* 1968), Martin W. R. Heinzl; 2ndly, 1968, Ernest Edward Giles Beeson, of Le Courtillet, Saumarez Rd, St Martins, Guernsey, CI, and has issue living, (by 1st *m*) Philip Carlos Martin (Fairfield, Mill Lane, S Chailey, E Sussex) *b* 1960: *m* 1986, Yvonne Clemence, Robert Peter Douglas *b* 1962, Martina Georgina Angela *b* 1959: *m* 1981, David Angus Stewart White, of 26 Lloyde Rd, Hove, Sussex (and has issue living, Alexander Martin Stewart *b* 1982, George Robert David *b* 1984, Jolyon Ronald *b* 1989, Dominic Antony *b* 1991), (by 2nd *m*) Julia Mary *b* 1969: *m* 1991, Robert Alder, of Lea Crest, Le Foulon, St Peter Port, Guernsey (and has issue living, Sophie Julia *b* 1992), Sarah Elizabeth *b* 1970. *Residence* – La Ronde, Coin Colin, St Martins, Guernsey GY4 6AH.

DAUGHTER LIVING OF THIRD BARONET

Elizabeth Frances Catherine, *b* 1960: *m* 1981, Nicholas James Reid, late Royal Green Jackets, and has issue living, Henry George Donald, *b* 1984, — Georgina Charlotte Elizabeth, *b* 1987. *Residence* – Scotland House, Stoke by Nayland, Colchester, Suffolk C06 4QG.

WIDOW LIVING OF THIRD BARONET

NANCY CATHERINE (*Dowager Lady Clark*), da of George Wallis Newport Clark, of Upperlands, co Londonderry: *m* 1949, Sir George Anthony Clark, 3rd Bt, who *d* 1991. *Residence* – Tullygirvan House, Ballygowan, co Down.
The 1st baronet, Sir George Smith Clark (son of James Clark, of Paisley), was MP for N Div of Belfast (C) 1907-10, and a Member of Senate of N Ireland 1925-34.The 2nd baronet, Sir George Ernest Clark, was High Sheriff of co Antrim 1940, and

of co Down 1941. The 3rd baronet, Sir George Anthony Clark, was High Sheriff of co Antrim 1954, a Senator N Ireland 1951-69, a DL Belfast, Grand Master of Grand Orange Lodge of Ireland 1957-68, and Imperial Grand Master of Imperial Grand Orange Council of the World 1961-63; MP for Dock Div of Belfast (U) in Parliament of N Ireland 1938-45.

STEWART-CLARK (UK) 1918, of Dundas, West Lothian

Sir JOHN (JACK) STEWART-CLARK, 3rd *Baronet*; *b* 17 Sept 1929; *s* his father, *Sir* STEWART, 1971; *ed* Eton, and Balliol Coll, Oxford; AMP Harvard Business Sch; late Lt Coldm Gds; Member of Queen's Body Guard for Scotland (Roy Co of Archers); Man Dir of J & P Coats, Pakistan, Ltd 1961-67, of J A Carp's Garenfabrieken, Helmond, Holland, 1967-70, and Philips Electrical, Ltd, London 1971-75, and Pye of Cambridge, Ltd 1974-79; Dir Low & Bonar plc, and Oppenheimer Internat; elected rep to European Parliament 1979: *m* 1958, Lydia Frederika, da of Jonkheer James William Loudon, of Valkenswaard, Netherlands, and has issue.

𝕬rms – Sable, a fesse chequy argent and azure, between a crescent or in chief, a boar's head couped of the last, armed and langued of the third in base, a bordure ermine for difference. 𝕮rest – An anchor cabled gules.
Seat – Dundas Castle, South Queensferry, W Lothian.
Residence – Puckstye House, Holtye Common, nr Cowden, Kent TN8 7EL. *Club* – White's.

SON LIVING

ALEXANDER DUDLEY (28 Fairfield St, SW18 1DW), *b* 21 Nov 1960; *ed* Worth Abbey.

DAUGHTERS LIVING

Daphne Beatrix Felicia, *b* 1959; has issue living, Chiara Stephenson *b* 1986. —— Nadia Marie Anne, *b* 1963: *m* 1990, Patrick J Waterfield, yr son of Jolyon Waterfield, of Edge Grove, Aldenham, Herts, and has issue living, Natasha Sophie, *b* 1993, — Elena Grace, *b* (twin) 1993. —— Zarina Gabrielle, *b* 1965. —— Natalie Frederika Louise, *b* 1969.

SISTER LIVING

(Sara) Norina Marie, *b* 1932: *m* 1961, Col Patrick Thomas Salvin Bowlby, TD, of Caythorpe Hall, Caythorpe, Grantham, Lincs, and has issue living, Anthony Adrian Francis Salvin, *b* 1962: *m* 1988, Camilla Victoria, only da of James Cookson, of Sticklepark, Yarlington, Wincanton, Som, and has issue living, James *b* 1993, — Michael Stewart Salvin, *b* 1964: *m* 1987, Amanda Jane Harvey, and has issue living, Thomas Edward Salvin *b* 1988, — Karina Jane Maria Minette Salvin, *b* 1968.

AUNT LIVING (*Daughter of 1st baronet*)

Elizabeth Morna, *b* 1914.

The 1st baronet, Sir John, was a Director of Clark and Co (Limited), and assumed the additional surname of Stewart 1909.

CLARKE (UK) 1831, of Dunham Lodge, Norfolk

Sir (CHARLES MANSFIELD) TOBIAS CLARKE, 6th *Baronet*; *b* 8 Sept 1939; *s* his father, *Sir* HUMPHREY ORME, 1973; adopted the additional christian name of Tobias 1962; *ed* Eton, Ch Ch Oxford (MA), Sorbonne, and NY Univ, Graduate Business Sch; Vice-Pres London Branch of Bankers Trust Co, New York: *m* 1st, 1971 (*m diss* 1979), Charlotte, el da of Roderick Walter, of 12 Stanford Court, Cornwall Gdns, SW7; 2ndly, 1984, Teresa Lorraine Aphrodite, da of Somerset Struben de Chair, of St Osyth's Priory, St Osyth, Essex, and has issue by 2nd *m*.

Arms – Ermine, on a bend cotised gules, three swans argent between three annulets sable. Crest – A mount vert, thereon a lark wings elevated or, in the beak an ear of wheat proper, the dexter claw resting on an annulet as in the arms.
Residences – 80 Campden Hill Rd, W8 7AA; The Church House, Bibury, Glos.
Clubs – Boodle's, Pratt's, Jockey (Paris), The Brook (New York), Racquet and Tennis (New York), Pilgrims.

SON LIVING *(By 2nd marriage)*

LAWRENCE, *b* 12 March 1990.

DAUGHTERS LIVING *(By 2nd marriage)*

Theodora Roosevelt, *b* 1985. —— Augusta Elfrida, *b* 1987.

UNCLE LIVING *(Son of 4th baronet)*

Charles Frederick Orme, *b* (twin) 1909; *ed* Eton, and Ch Ch, Oxford: *m* 1942, Sylvia Vera, da of late Leo Kaelin, of Einsiedeln, Switzerland, and has issue living, William Oliver, *b* 1943: *m* 1981, Elizabeth, da of John Ivimy, and has issue living, Frederick William Michael *b* 1982, Percival John Theodore *b* 1983, Maximilian Tobias Ivimy *b* 1986, — Katharine Sybil CLARKE, *b* 1950; resumed her maiden name: *m* 1981 (*m diss* 1991), Michael Pearl. *Residence* – Hohbühlstrasse 16, 9400 Rorschach, Switzerland.

COLLATERAL BRANCHES LIVING

Issue of late Orme Roosevelt Clarke, yr son of 5th baronet, *b* 1947, *d* 1992: *m* 1st, 1971 (*m diss* 1989), Joanna Valentine, da of John Barkley Schuster, TD (*see* B Wyfold); 2ndly, 1991, Christine V. (41 Kensington Place, W8), da of J. G. O'Flaherty, of Melbourne, Australia:—
(By 1st *m*) Nicholas Orme, *b* 1976. —— (By 2nd *m*) Alexander, *b* 1992.

Grandsons of late William Peter Dunham Clarke, OBE, el son of late William Alexander Clarke (infra):—
Issue of late Peter Ethelston Clarke, *b* 1916, *d* 1975: *m* 1940, Isabel Helen, da of Philip Elton Longmore, CBE:—
Peter Alexander, *b* 1941; *ed* Eton, and Trin Coll, Camb: *m* 1967, Lilah Victoria Mary, da of John Forrester, of Ardnacross, Isle of Mull, and has issue living, Paul Sebastian, *b* 1971, — Timothy Forrester, *b* 1975, — Robert Theodore, *b* 1983.
—— John Elton, *b* 1948; *ed* Eton, and Kent Univ: *m* 1979, Caroline Anne Bannatyne, da of Edward Michael Courage, and has issue living, Edward Peter, *b* 1985, — Helena Margaret, *b* 1981.

Grandchildren of late William Alexander Clarke (3rd son of 2nd baronet):—
Issue of late Paul Humphrey Clarke, MC, *b* 1891, *d* 1946: *m* 1927, Joyce Chicheley, who *d* 1934, da of late Richard Chicheley Plowden:—
Humphrey (124 Off Lane, Gladstone, Queensland, Australia), *b* 1929. —— Barbara (46 Hargreaves Av, Chelmer, Brisbane, Queensland 4068, Australia), *b* 1928: *m* 1951 (*m diss* 1973), Anthony Lucien Noon Arlaud, and has issue living, Anthony Stephen, *b* 1953, — David Paul, *b* 1955: *m* 1981, Hilary Dawn, da of John Goldsworthy Palmer, and has issue living, Kimberly Rose *b* 1992, — Christopher John *b* 1961; *ed* Queensland Inst of Technology (BB Comn): *m* 1984 (*m diss* 1990) Mette Slej, da of Villy Bertelsen.

Granddaughers of late Paul Humphrey Clarke, MC (ante):—
Issue of late Paul Ivor Clarke, *b* 1931; *d* 1977: *m* 1963, Angela Mary (Elgon, Tilsmore Rd, Heathfield, E Sussex), da of late Thomas George Cleaver:—
Fiona Mary, *b* 1964. —— Rosemary Ann, *b* 1965.

The 1st baronet, Sir Charles Mansfield Clarke, was Physician to Queen Adelaide. The 3rd baronet, Gen Sir Charles Mansfield Clarke, GCB, GCVO, served on Taptee River with 57th Regt 1858, in New Zealand Wars 1861 and 1863-6, in Zulu Campaign 1879 (despatches, medal with clasp, CB), and in Basutoland 1880-81 (medal with two clasps), and was Gov of Malta and in command of troops there 1903-7.

CLARKE (UK) 1882, of Rupertswood, Colony of Victoria

Signum·quærens·in·vellere

Seeking the sign in the wool

Sir RUPERT WILLIAM JOHN CLARKE, MBE, 3rd *Baronet; b* 5 Nov 1919; *s* his father, *Sir* RUPERT TURNER HAVELOCK, 1926; *ed* Eton, and Magdalen Coll, Oxford (MA), Hon Fellow Trinity Coll, Melbourne; FAIM; Maj Irish Guards, Consul-Gen for Monaco in Melbourne, Chm P & O Australia Ltd until 1992; Pres Royal Humane Soc of Australasia Inc; Member Board of Howard Florey Inst (Melbourne); ADC (later PA) to Com-in-Ch, Middle East 1942-43; N Africa 1942-43 (MBE), Italy 1943-45 (despatches); MBE (Mil) 1943, Chev Légion d'Honneur (France), Offr Order of Léopold (Belgium), Order of the Grimaldi (Monaco): *m* 1947, Kathleen Grant, da of Peter Grant Hay, of Toorak, Victoria, Aust, and has issue.

Arms – Or, two bars azure between four escallops, three in chief and one in base gules; two flaunches of the second. **Crest** – In front of a dexter arm embowed in armour, the hand in a gauntlet proper holding an arrow in bend sinister or, flighted argent, three escallops also or.
Residences – Richmond House, 56 Avoca St, S Yarra, Australia 3141; Bolinda Vale, Clarkefield, 3430 Victoria, Australia. *Clubs* – Cavalry and Guards', Lansdowne, Australian, Athenæum, Melbourne (Victoria), Union (Sydney), Queensland (Brisbane).

SONS LIVING

RUPERT GRANT ALEXANDER, *b* 12 Dec 1947; *ed* Melbourne Univ (LLB): *m* 1978, Susannah, da of Sir (Richard) Robert Law-Smith, and has issue living, Rupert Robert William, *b* 24 June 1981, — Samantha Kathleen, *b* 1980, — Joanna Georgina, *b* 1983. ——— Peter Robert Justin John, *b* 1955: *m* 1983, Andrea Wilkes, da of Joshua Pitt, and has issue living, William Peter Norman Grant, *b* 1986, — Alexandra Kathleen, *b* 1984.

DAUGHTER LIVING

Vanessa Margaret, *b* 1952: *m* 1975, Roden David Cutler, son of Sir Arthur Roden Cutler, VC, AK, KCMG, KCVO, KStJ, CBE, and has issue living, Jonathan Roden Rupert David, *b* 1981, — Richard William Grant Clarke, *b* 1983, — James Robert Oliver David, *b* 1986, — Christina Annabelle Kate, *b* 1988.

SISTER LIVING

Elizabeth Elsie Faith, *b* 1924: *m* 1952, Willoughby Alfred Lake, who *d* 1986, and has issue (*see* Lake, Bt). *Residence* – Ashleigh, Much Hadham, Herts.

COLLATERAL BRANCHES LIVING

Issue of late Hon William Lionel Russell Clarke, 3rd son of 1st baronet, *b* 1876, *d* 1954: *m* 1908, Florence Douglas, who *d* 1961, da of late Col Henry Douglas Mackenzie (Mackenzie, Bt, *cr* 1673, colls):—
(*Hon*) Michael Alastair, *b* 1915; *ed* Harrow, and New Coll, Oxford (BCL, MA); 1939-45 War as Lieut Australian Imperial Force; a MLC, Victoria: *m* 1948, Helen Rosalind, da of Essington Lewis, CH, and has issue living, Andrea Rosalind, *b* 1950, — Louise Merilyn, *b* 1953, — Rosemary Janet, *b* 1956. *Residence* – 82 Mathoura Rd, Toorak, Victoria, Australia. ——— Janet Marjorie Nina, *b* 1911: *m* 1941, Capt Henry Armstrong Hammond, 5th Light Horse, AIF, of Swift St, Murrumburrah, NSW, and has issue living, Russell Rupert, *b* 1945: *m* 1973, Cheryl Gay, da of W. R. Harvey.

Grandchildren of late Hon Sir Francis Grenville Clark (infra):—
Issue of late William Antony Francis Clarke, *b* 1908, *d* 1953: *m* 1939, Jessie Deakin, da of Herbert Robinson Brookes:—
Francis Brookes, *b* 1940: *m* 1st, 1969 (*m diss* 1976), Jacqueline, da of Graham Crossley; 2ndly, Vivica Spens, and has issue living, Antony Graham, *b* 1970. ——— William Severn, *b* 1945; BA, BSc, MBA. ——— Janet Deakin, *b* 1942; *ed* Melbourne Univ (Dip OT): *m* 1970, Robert Stirling Hogarth-Scott, of 6 Selbourne Rd, Toorak, Victoria, Aust, and has issue living. ——— Barbary Cotton, *b* 1950; *ed* Melbourne Univ (BA).
Issue of late Colin Grenville Clarke, *b* 1914, *d* 1962: *m* 1943, Elizabeth Lennox, da of Norman Lennox Speirs:—
Jason William, *b* 1952. ——— Sally Miranda, *b* 1949.

Issue of late Hon Sir Francis Grenville Clarke, KBE, 5th son of 1st baronet, *b* 1879, *d* 1955: *m* 1901, Nina Ellis, who *d* 1948, da of Thomas Cotton, banker, of Melbourne:—
Patricia Kathleen, *b* 1906: *m* 1939, Sqdn Ldr Raymond Vincent O'Byrne, who *d* 1973.

Grandchildren of late Lt-Col Reginald Hastings Clarke, 6th son of 1st baronet:—
Issue of late Reginald Clive Nevil Clarke, *b* 1910, *d* 1964: *m* 1935, Elizabeth Macpherson, who *d* 1965:—
Robin, *b* 1935: *m* 1958, Prunella, da of Wilfred Weigall, of Cobden, Vic, Australia, and has issue living, Anthony Clive, *b* 1963, — Sara Elizabeth, *b* 1965. ——— Lucilla (Ernestine), *b* 1937.
This family was settled at Weston Zoyland, Somerset since the beginning of the 18th century. The Hon William John Turner Clarke, father of 1st baronet, settled in Australia in 1829. The 1st baronet, Hon Sir William John Clarke, was many years engaged in pastoral pursuits in Victoria and was a MLC there.

Clarke-Jervoise, see Jervoise.

CLAY (UK) 1841, of Fulwell Lodge, Middlesex

Sir RICHARD HENRY CLAY, 7th *Baronet, b* 2 June 1940; *s* his father, *Sir*
HENRY FELIX, 1985; *ed* Eton; *m* 1963. Alison Mary, only da of Dr James
Gordon Fife, of Summer Hill, Alde House Drive, Aldeburgh, Suffolk, and
has issue.

Arms – Argent, a chevron engrailed paly of eight sable and or between three trefoils
of the second. Crest – Two wings argent each charged with a chevron engrailed
between three trefoils slipped sable.
Residence – The Copse, Shiplate Rd, Bleadon, Avon BS24 0NX.

Per orbem
Throughout the world

SONS LIVING

CHARLES RICHARD, *b* 18 Dec 1965; *ed* Manor Sch, Cambridge, and Univ of E Anglia
(BA). —— Thomas Henry, *b* 1967; *ed* Manor Sch, Cambridge. —— James Felix, *b*
1969; *ed* Manor Sch, Cambridge, and York Univ (BA).

DAUGHTERS LIVING

Virginia Rachel, *b* 1964: *m* 1988, Robin P. Taylor, of Anchor Farm, Anchor, Shropshire
SY7 8PR, yst son of late Richard Taylor, of Grange Farm, Bourn, Cambs, and has
issue living, Richard James, *b* 1993, — Megan Catherine, *b* 1992. —— Catherine Victoria, *b* 1971; *ed* Bath Univ (BA).

SISTERS LIVING

Jenny Elizabeth (31 The Terrace, Aldeburgh, Suffolk), *b* 1936: *m* 1959 (*m diss* 1975), Oswyn Murray, MA, only surv son of
late (Malcolm) Patrick Murray, CB, and has issue living, James Augustus Henry, *b* 1961, — Octavia, *b* 1965. —— Sarah
Richenda, *b* 1938: *m* 1979, Frederic Henry Wise, of 9 Market Cross Place, Aldeburgh, Suffolk.

UNCLE LIVING (*son of 5th baronet*)

Anthony George Hobhouse, MB, BCh (8 Springfield Crescent, Sherborne, Dorset) *b* 1914; *ed* Camb Univ (MA, MB, BCh);
late Maj RAMC; 1939-45 War: *m* 1st, 1938 (*m diss* 1959), Elizabeth Alice, da of Sir Gilbert Charles Upcott, KCB; 2ndly, 1960,
Patricia Barbara, who *d* 1967, da of late Archibald Foulcher, of West Wickham, Kent; 3rdly, 1971, Pamela Joan, da of Edward
Farley Oaten, of Walton-on-Thames, and has issue living, (by 1st *m*) Christopher George Anthony (6 Berkeley Rd, Bristol,
6), *b* 1940: *m* 1973, Diana, da of Edward Hippolyte Joseph Burbidge, and has issue living, Felix Temple *b* 1974, Francis
Benjamin *b* 1976, Caroline Emily *b* 1978, — (by 2nd *m*) Timothy Paul, *b* 1961.

AUNTS LIVING (*Daughters of 5th baronet*)

Janet, *b* 1907: *m* 1948, Humphrey Seymour Outterson Wood, who *d* 1971. *Residence* – 29 Fore St, Evershot, Dorset.
—— Theresa Rachel, *b* 1911; DSc 1955: *m* 1974, Rodney G. Searight, of 129 Oakwood Court W14.

WIDOW LIVING OF SIXTH BARONET

PHYLLIS MARY (*Dowager Lady Clay*), yr da of Richard Horace Paramore, MD, FRCS, of 4 Bilton Rd, Rugby: *m* 1933, Sir
Henry Felix Clay, 6th Bt, who *d* 1985. *Residence* – Wheelwrights, Cocking, Midhurst, Sussex, GU29 0HJ.

This family descends from the Clays of Crich, co Derby. George Clay, of Cambridge, who married Elizabeth, daughter of
Felix Calvert, of Ferneaux Pelham, in 1670, was great-grandfather of George Clay, born 1757, who for upwards of half a
century was extensively engaged in London as a merchant and shipowner, and his son, William, created a baronet, was MP
for the Tower Hamlets 1832-57, Secretary of the Board of Control 1839-41, and author of numerous works on Joint Stock
Banking, Banks of Issue, the Currency, etc.

CLAYTON (GB) 1732, of Marden Park, Surrey

QUID LEONE FORTIUS

What is braver than the lion

Sir DAVID ROBERT CLAYTON, 12th *Baronet*; *b* 12 Dec 1936; *s* his father, *Sir* ARTHUR HAROLD, DSC, 1985; *ed* HMS Conway, and Sir John Cass Coll, London; Capt MN; Dir Oceanic Liners (UK) Ltd since 1989: *m* 1971, Julia Louise, da of late Charles Henry Redfearn, and has issue.

Arms – Argent, a cross sable between four pellets. **Crest** – A leopard's paw erased and erect argent, grasping a pellet. **Second Motto** – Virtus in actione consistit (*Virtue consists in action*).
Residence – Rock House, Kingswear, Devon TQ6 0BX.

SONS LIVING

ROBERT PHILIP, *b* 8 July 1975. —— John Richard, *b* 1978.

SISTER LIVING

Ann, *b* 1933: *m* 1st, 1951 (*m diss* 1977), Alfred Plews; 2ndly, 1978, John Hawksely Martin.

DAUGHTER LIVING OF EIGHTH BARONET

Cynthia Anne, *b* 1914; 1939-45 War as Section Officer WAAF: *m* 1949, as his second wife, Walter Gerald Cloete Graham, CBE, and has two adopted children, Alan Richard, *b* 1956, — Harriet Jane, *b* 1954: *m* 1986, Fulvio Richetto. *Residence* – Knabbs Farmhouse, Fletching, Uckfield, Sussex TN22 3SX.

WIDOW LIVING OF ELEVENTH BARONET

DIANA KATHERINE MARY (*Diana, Lady Clayton*), only child of late Capt Charles Alverey Grazebrook, 60th Rifles, and formerly wife of (i) Peter Neve, and (ii) — Bircham: *m* 1965, as his 4th wife, Sir Arthur Harold Clayton, 11th Bt, DSC, who *d* 1985. *Residence* – Colonsay, Kingswear, Devon.

COLLATERAL BRANCHES LIVING

Issue of late FitzRoy Richard Henry Clayton, yr son of 10th baronet, *b* 1907, *d* 1989: *m* 1st, 1930, Morwen, who *d* 1941, da of Judge Fedor Andrew Satow (V Chilston); 2ndly, 1944, Moira Consuelo, who *d* 1971, da of Philip Fidelis Ryan, of Ceylon; 3rdly, 1973, (Phyllis) Margaret (Partridge Cottage, Chilmark, Salisbury, Wilts SP3 5AQ), da of late Reginald James Tindal, of Wirral, Cheshire, and widow of Sydney James Pullan, of Lillington Manor, Leamington Spa:—
(By 1st *m*) Barry Drew Satow, *b* 1935. —— Ailsa, *b* 1932: *m* 1952, William Findlay Key, and has issue living, Richard William, *b* 1960, — Philippa Margaret, *b* 1954: *m* 1974, Anthony Victor Lithgow, — Gail Morwen, *b* 1956.

Grandson (by 2nd *m*) of late FitzRoy Richard Henry Clayton (ante):—
Issue of late Roderick John Clayton, *b* 1945, *d* 1980: *m* 1968, Diana Melissa (24 Duke's Ave, Chiswick, W4 2AE), yr da of late late Sir (Horace) Alan Walker, of Eaton Pl, SW1:—
Patrick Justin FitzRoy, *b* 1970. —— Louisa Jane, *b* 1972.

Grandson of late Lieut-Col Sir FitzRoy Augustus Talbot Clayton, KCVO, son of late Rev Augustus Philip Clayton, 5th son of 4th baronet:—
Issue of late Capt Cecil Fraser Talbot Clayton, *b* 1880, *d* 1940: *m* 1st, 1909 (*m diss* 1918), Kathleen Agnes, da of late Lieut-Col William E. Bradish-Ellames, of Manor House, Little Marlow; 2ndly, 1918, Alice, who *d* 1957, da of late John T. Hatton, JP:—
(By 2nd *m*) Gilbert Talbot Hatton, *b* 1920; European War 1943-5 in RAF Vol Reserve. *Residence* – Cobbles, Broadstone, Dorset.

Grandsons of Col Emilius Clayton (*b* 1841), eldest son of Capt Emilius Clayton (*b* 1803), eldest son of Lt-Col George Clayton, 2nd son (by 2nd *m*) of William Clayton, 2nd son of 1st baronet:—
Issue of late Lt-Col Emilius Clayton, OBE, *b* 1884, *d* 1967: *m* 1915, Irene Dorothy Constance, who *d* 1971, da of late Col T. E. Strong, Indian Army:—
Michael Thomas Emilius, CB, OBE (Hillside Cottage, Marshwood, Bridport, Dorset DT6 5QF), *b* 1917; attached Min of Defence 1939-1977; OBE (Civil) 1958, CB (Civil) 1976: *m* 1942, Mary Margery, el da of late Dr J. Roberts Pate, of Oxford, and has issue living, Amanda Rosemary, *b* 1949; *ed* Reading Univ (BA, PhD): *m* 1976, Peter Hobson, MA, of The Headmaster's House, Charterhouse, Godalming, Surrey GU7 2DE. —— Anthony Hugh Le Quesne, TD (April Cottage, 43 Ford Lane, Lower Bourne, Farnham, Surrey GU10 4SF), *b* 1928; MA and PhD, St Andrews Univ; FSA, Scot; Lt-Col Intelligence Corps (TAVR); Kenya Civil Ser 1952-65, since when Sen Lect, RMA, Sandhurst: *m* 1973, Judith Mary, da of P. L. Blackstone, of Rhu, Dunbarton, and has issue living, Robert Anthony Emilius, *b* 1975, — Penelope Fleur, *b* 1977.

Grandchildren of late Lieut-Col Henry Edward Gilbert Clayton (infra):—
Issue of late Henry Hubert Clayton, *b* 1906, *d* 1989: *m* 1944, Isobel May, who *d* 1990, da of W. G. Winters, of Pembroke, Ontario, Canada:—
William Edward (5595 Wallace Av, Delta, BC V4M 3Z3, Canada), *b* 1945: *m* 1967, Sharon Joan, da of Kenneth Campbell, of Edmonton, Alberta, and has issue living, Stacey Anna, *b* 1972, — Susan Amanda, *b* 1975. —— Florence Nancy Thackray, *b* 1947: *m* 1971, Erik van Veenen, and has issue living, Hendrick Hubert Clayton, *b* 1982, — Vanessa *b* 1977, — Erica Maegan, *b* 1979.

Grandchildren of late Major Sir Edward Gilbert Clayton, CB, el son of late Maj-Gen Henry Clayton, 2nd son of Lt-Col George Clayton (ante):—
Issue of late Lieut-Col Henry Edward Gilbert Clayton, *b* 1867, *d* 1947: *m* 1900, Huberta, da of Capt Hubert Grenfell, RN, formerly of Alverstoke, Hants:—
Grace Cynthia Maude, *b* 1909: *m* 1934, Philip Hennell Amsden, formerly RN, of Headquarters Rd, RR4, Courtenay, BC V9N 7J3, USA, and has issue living, Michael Phillip, *b* 1935: *m* 1959, Lorna Ryder, and has issue living, Brian *b* 1964, Lisa *b* 1959: *m* 1989, Robert Mallony (and has issue living, Erin *b* 1990), Sherri *b* 1961: *m* 19—, John McCall (and has issue living, Kyle *b* 1988, Thomas *b* 1990), Maureen *b* 1962, Juli *b* 1966, — Harry Linton, *b* 1938: *m* 1965, Josephine Venebles, and has issue

living, Sarah b 1974, — Stephen Oliver, b 1944: m 1968, Janet Ives, and has issue living, Jessica b 1975, Jacquline b 1978, — Robin Petite, b 1941: m 1966 (m diss 1972), Allen Cripps, and has issue living, Cynthia b 1968.

Sir William Clayton, MP, the 1st baronet (cr 1732), was a nephew of Sir Robert Clayton, Knight, Lord Mayor of London 1679. The 2nd, 3rd and 4th baronets were also Members of Parliament, and the 5th baronet, Gen Sir William Robert, KCB, a distinguished Waterloo officer, sat as MP for Great Marlow (L) 1831-42. The 6th Baronet was High Sheriff for co Bucks 1876, and at his death the title devolved upon his kinsman Sir Gilbert Augustus Clayton-East, 3rd Baronet of Hall Place, whose immediate ancestor was William East, of Hall Place, Berks, created a baronet in 1766, which title became extinct 1828. His nephew, the 1st baronet of the 2nd creation (1838), of Hall Place, Sir East George Clayton-East, was 2nd son of Sir William Clayton, 4th baronet (cr 1838), and nephew of Sir Gilbert East, the last baronet of the 1st creation. The 2nd baronet took the surnames of Gilbert-East and the arms of East for his life only by Roy licence 1839. The 7th baronet, Sir Gilbert Augustus Clayton-East, s his father 1866 in the Baronetcy cr 1838 as 3rd Bt, and his kinsman, Sir William Robert Clayton 1914 in the Baronetcy cr 1732 as 7th Bt, having resumed in 1870 the name and arms of Clayton-East in lieu of Gilbert-East. Sir Robert Alan Clayton-East-Clayton, 9th Bt of Marden and 5th Bt of Hall Place, assumed by deed poll 1932 the surnames of Clayton-East-Clayton in lieu of Clayton-East, and d Sept 1932, when the Baronetcy of Hall Place became ext, and the baronetcy of Marden Park devolved on his kinsman, Sir Harold Philip Dudley Clayton, 10th Bt.

CLERK (NS) 1679, of Penicuik, Edinburgh
(Name pronounced "Clark")

Victory loves care

Sir JOHN DUTTON CLERK, CBE, VRD, 10th Baronet: b 30 Jan 1917; s his father, Sir GEORGE JAMES ROBERT, 1943; ed Stowe; Commodore RNR (ret); FRSE; a JP for Midlothian since 1955, Vice-Lieut 1965-72, Lord-Lieut 1972-92; Ensign Queen's Body Guard for Scotland (Royal Company of Archers); CBE (Mil) 1966: m 1944, Evelyn Elizabeth, da of late W. Robertson, and has issue.

Arms – Or, a fesse checky azure and argent between two crescents in chief gules, and a boar's head couped in base sable. Crest – A demi-huntsman winding a horn proper. Supporters – Dexter, a naked man wreathed about the middle with oak, in the dexter hand a bow, over his shoulder a quiver of arrows, and the skin of a wild beast hanging behind his back all proper; sinister, A druid priest with flowing beard proper, vested and hooded argent, holding in the sinister hand an oak-branch acorned vert.
Seat – Penicuik House, Penicuik, Midlothian EH26 9LA.

SONS LIVING

ROBERT MAXWELL (Penicuik House, Penicuik, Midlothian EH26 9LA), b 3 April 1945; ed Winchester, and London Univ (BSc Agric); FRICS; Member Queen's Body Guard for Scotland (Royal Company of Archers): m 1970, Felicity Faye, yr da of George Collins, of Grayshott House, Bampton, Oxford, and has issue living, George Napier, b 1975, — Edward James, b 1986, — Julia Elizabeth, b 1973. —— Piers Edward John (Newport House, Weston-under-Lizard, Shifnal, Shropshire TF11 8JT), b 1955; ed Winchester, and Aberdeen Univ (BLE); ARICS: m 1983, Lucy Ann, only da of Michael Hewens, of Crookham Manor, Thatcham, Berks, and has issue living, William James, b 1987, — Iona Mary, b 1985.

DAUGHTERS LIVING

Aymée Lavinia, b 1947: m 1969, George Robin Paget Ferguson, of 5 Windsor Terr, Clifton, Bristol, and has issue living, John Spencer Guy b 1974, — Alice Rose, b 1971, — Corinna May, b 1979. —— Honor Elizabeth, b 1957.

SISTERS LIVING

Susan Rosemary Dacre, b 1905: m 1928, Col Hugh Francis d'Assisi Stuart Law, DSO, OBE, MC, TD, DL, late Irish Guards and Border Regt (TA), who d 1984, and has issue living, Hugh Francis Stephen John, b 1931; late Capt 9th Lancers, — Francis Robin Luke Alexander, b 1946, — Rosemary Bridget Honor Stuart, b 1930. Residence – Barony House, Lasswade, Midlothian. —— Aymée Lavender, b 1907; radionic therapist: m 1928, Col Alan Vincent Gandar Dower, TD, DL, 2nd Dragoon Guards, who d 1980, and has issue living, Natalie Gay Stuart, b 1931. Residence – Swinbrook Cottage, Swinbrook, Oxon.

COLLATERAL BRANCHES LIVING

Grandsons of late George Edward Clerk, b 1850, el son of late George Edward Clerk (b 1815), 2nd son of 6th baronet:—
Issue of late George Edward Clerk, MD, CM, b 1877, d 1938: m 1903, Annie, da of Eugene Manny:—
Sydney Percy, b 1912: m 1938, Thérèse, da of Louis St Laurent, and has issue living, Michelle Marie Madeleine, b 1940, — Hélène, b 1943. —— Joseph Harry, b 1914: m 1950, Alberta Therese, da of Armand Drouin, and has issue living, Irene Gail, b 1952.
Issue of late Abel Clerk, b 1897, d 1964: m 1927, Cecile, da of R. Poisson:—
André Arthur (10430, Meunier St, Ahuntsic, Montreal, Canada), b 1929: m 1955, Claire, da of Armand Charbonneau, and has issue living, Georges, b 1958, — Benoit, b 1962, — Bruno, b 1964, — Micheline, b 1956.

Grandchildren of late Edmund Antoine Clerk (infra):—
Issue of late Walter Charles Clerk, b 1891, d 1937: m 1st, 1915, Jeanne Beauchamp, who d 1920; 2ndly, 1922, Gabrielle Beauchamp:—
(By 1st m) Françoise, b 1917: m 1943, Pierre R. Gendron, DSC, Sub-Lieut Roy Canadian Naval Vol Reserve, who d 1983. —— Marguerite, b 1919: m 1943, Jacques de Tonnancour. —— (By 2nd m) George b 1925: m 1950, Lucette C. Barbeau,

and has issue living, Patrice, *b* 1964, — Philippe, *b* 1959, — Josée, *b* 1952, — Michelle, *b* 1953, — Danie, *b* 1957. *Residence* – —— Robert, *b* 1926. —— Suzanne, *b* 1924.

Grandchildren of late George Edward Clerk (ante):—
Issue of late Edmund Antoine Clerk, *b* 1858, *d* 1921: *m* 1886, Malvina Tourville, who *d* 1900:—
Guy, *b* 1893; late Customs Officer: *m* 1916, Jeanne Mongeau. —— Henry, *b* 1896: *m* 1918, Liliane Payette, and has issue living, Gérard (265 Beverley Av, Mount Royal, 304, Quebec, Canada) *b* 1919; Capt Canadian Army: *m* 1949, Lucille McCaughan, and has issue living, Joanne, *b* 1955, — Jacques, *b* 1922; P/O RCAF: *m* 19—, Rejane Gauvin, — Raymonde, *b* 1918: *m* 1940, Paul Fortin, and has issue living, Micheline *b* 1941, Monique *b* 1943. —— Aline, *b* 1894: *m* 1916, C. Henri Rouleau.
Issue of late Alexander Marie Joseph Clerk, *b* 1861, *d* 1932: *m* 1888, Blanche Gelinas, who *d* 1942:—
Bernard, *b* 1902. —— Marie, *b* 1894. —— Pauline, *b* 1896. —— Yvette, *b* 1912: *m* 1937, Jacques Trépanier, LLD, Journalist, and has issue living, François *b* 1938, — Maurice, *b* 1942, — Hélène, *b* 1943, — Josette, *b* 1946, Micheline, *b* 1947. *Residence* – 211, Walnut Av, St Lambert, Quebec, Canada.
Issue of late Jean Pio Robert Clerk, *b* 1870, *d* 1932: *m* 1898, Marie Alma, da of late Hon Senator L. O. David:—
Jacques Donald, *b* 1904: *m* 19—, Elizabeth Labrecque, and has issue living, Robert, *b* 1929, — Gilles, *b* 1931, — Jacques, *b* 1935, — Lise, *b* 1928, — Janine, *b* 1933. —— Louis Phillippe Duncan, *b* 1907: *m* 1936, Gabrielle, da of the Hon G. C. Simond, and has issue living, Henri, *b* 1941, — Michelle, *b* 1937. —— Jean Elton, *b* 1919. —— Jeanne Isabella, *b* 1899: *m* 19—, Theodore Fauteux, and has issue living, Pierre, *b* 1928, — Louise, *b* 1927. —— Camille Gertrude, *b* 1902.

Grandchildren of late Alexander Marie Joseph Clerk (ante):—
Issue of late Maurice Clerk, *b* 1893, *d* 1926: *m* 1926, Marguerite Lajoie:—
Louise, *b* 1926: *m* 1948, Léopold Brégent.
Issue of late Edouard Clerk, *b* 1889, *d* 1982: *m* 1917, Fernande, who *d* 1969, da of Hon Dr Ernest Choquette, MLC, of Quebec:—
Michel (Chemin des Patriotes, Saint-Hilaire, Quebec, Canada), *b* 1920; M Com 1943: *m* 1952, Monique Martineau, and has had issue, Philippe, *b* 1953, — Cyril, *b* 1954, — Emmanuel, *b* 1960, — Catherine, *b* 1957, *d* 1987, — Sophie, *b* 1964, *d* 1987. —— Marc, *b* 1923: *m* 1949, Gabrielle Brunet, PhD, and has issue living, David, *b* 1952, — Nathalie, *b* 1950. —— Stephen, *b* 1926; QC: *m* 1954, Thérèse Saint-Jacques, and *d* 1989, having had issue, Eric Fraser, *b* 1955: *m* 1982, Ileana Balladares Diez, and has issue living, Christina *b* 1993, — Nicolas, *b* 1957, *d* 1976, — Jean, *b* (twin) 1957. —— Pierre, *b* 1928; painter: *m* 1953, Adriana Bertolini, and has issue living, Jessica, *b* 1954.
Issue of late Paul Clerk, *b* 1890, *d* 1960: *m* 1927, Alice Gascon, who *d* 1947:—
Paul, *b* 1930: *m* 1975, Vivian Winsor. —— Françoise, *b* 1928: *m* 1952, Léon O. Des Lauriers, SBStJ, of 1105 Deguire St, Saint-Laurent, Quebec, Canada H41 1MI, and has issue living, François, *b* 1959, — Nathalie, *b* 1962: *m* 1989, Alain Barrette, and has issue living, Nicolas *b* 1990, Amélie *b* 1993. —— Andrée, *b* 1933: *m* 1955, René Beaucage, who *d* 1991, and has issue living, Michel, *b* 1956, — Dominique, *b* 1959, — Edith, *b* 1962.

Grandchildren of late Major Edward Clerk, 7th son of 6th baronet:—
Issue of late William Henry Clerk, *b* 1867, *d* 1915: *m* 1906, Sarah Cecilia Reeves, who *d* 1954:—
Edward, *b* 1907: *m* 1940, Dora Appleby, and has issue living, Edward Peter, *b* 1941. —— William Robert, *b* (twin) 1907.
Issue of late Herbert Edward Clerk, *b* 1871, *d* 1931: *m* 1908, Helen, who *d* 1946, da of late Jules A. Heuer:—
Mary Helen, *b* 1915: *m* 1939, Michael George Russell Adams, who *d* 1989, and has issue living, Nicholas Henry Harvey (Hollies Farm, Postland, Crowland, Peterborough PE6 0LS), *b* 1943, Lt-Col Light Div (R Green Jackets) (ret): *m* 1964, Leila, da of Maj G. M. King, and has issue living, Mark Henry Leo *b* 1966, Claire Laura Catherine *b* 1971, — George Miles Bramston (131 Percy Rd, W12), *b* 1956: *m* 1987, Christine Martin, and has issue living, Abigail *b* 1988, — Daffodil Jane Florence, *b* 1946: *m* 1971, Charles Brian Marriage, of Netherhill Cottage, Botley, Southampton, and has issue living, Thomas Charles *b* 1976, Louise Caroline *b* 1974, Ellen Elizabeth *b* 1980. *Residence* – Hazelhurst, Dymock, Glos.

Grandchildren of late Arthur Stanley Clerk (infra):—
Issue of late Charles Beverley Clerk, *b* 1904, *d* 1983: *m* 1925, Angela Herbin, who *d* 1969:—
Alexander Simpson (Oakdeen Place, Kentville, Nova Scotia, Canada), *b* 1930: *m* 1953, Shirley Evangeline, da of Robert S. Cook, of Kentville, Nova Scotia, and has issue living, Charles Alexander (Truro, Nova Scotia, Canada), *b* 1954: *m* 1987, Friedel Moser, — Thomas Richard, *b* 1956: *m* 1980, Kimberley Denhartog, and has issue living, Courtney Ruth *b* 1980, Kendra Ann *b* 1983, — Katharine Lois, *b* 1958: *m* 1980, Peter Charles Cooper, of Kentville, Nova Scotia, and has issue living, Christopher Allan *b* 1984, Jason Alexander *b* 1986, Elizabeth Katherine *b* 1988, — Susan Bernice, *b* 1961: *m* 1986, Mark Stuart Hersey, and has issue living, Justin Robert *b* 1986, Benjamin Stuart *b* 1988, Angela Faye *b* 1985, — Faye Marie, *b* 1965. —— Mary Beverley (Nichols Rd, Kentville, Nova Scotia, Canada) *b* 1929: *m* 1954, William Stevens, who *d* 1979, and has issue living, William Charles, *b* 1954, — Marylynne Margaret, *b* 1958: *m* 1980, Michael Carl Middelkoop, of Halifax, Nova Scotia, and has issue living, Adam Jason *b* 1986, Stephanie Anne *b* 1983.

Granddaughter of late Col Alexander Clerk, 8th son of 6th baronet:—
Issue of late Arthur Stanley Clerk, *b* 1864, *d* 1948: *m* 1897, Edith Maud, who *d* 1955, da of late C. E. Sheffield, of Nova Scotia:—
Dorothy Evangeline, *b* 1902: *m* 1926, Arthur Merlin, who *d* 1983, of 82 Broadway Av, Apt 1, Toronto, M4P 1T7, Ont, and has issue living, Marilyn, *b* 1928: *m* 1st, 19— (*m diss* 1967), Kenneth Arthur Wynne; 2ndly, 1967, Richard Arthur Kirby, of 244 Armour Blvd, N York, Ontario M3H 1N2, Canada, and has issue living, (by 1st *m*) Kenneth Arthur *b* 1955: *m* 1983, Barbara Anne Jame, Derrick Andrew *b* 1957: *m* 1988, Brenda Lee Crack.

The family is descended from John Clerk, distinguished for his loyalty and attachment to the party of Mary Stuart. His great-grandson, John was created a baronet by Charles II. The 2nd baronet was a Baron of the Exchequer of Scotland 1707-55. The 6th baronet, a Privy Councillor, was MP for Edinburghshire (C) 1818-32 and 1835-7, for Stamford 1838-47, and for Dover 1847-52, and during his political career, held office in several administrations. Sir George Douglas, 8th Bt, was Lieut-Col in the Army, and a Commr of Supply for cos Midlothian and Peebles.

CLERKE (E) 1660, of Hitcham, Buckinghamshire
(Name pronounced "Clark")

Sir JOHN EDWARD LONGUEVILLE CLERKE, 12th *Baronet*, son of late Francis William Talbot Clerke, Lieut Coldstream Guards (*ka* 1916), el son of 11th baronet; *b* 29 Oct 1913; *s* his grandfather, *Sir* WILLIAM FRANCIS, 1930; *ed* Eton, and Magdalene Coll, Camb (BA 1934); is Capt Reserve of Officers Roy Wilts Yeo (TA); FCA (1948) (ret): *m* 1948 (*m diss* 1986), Mary, da of late Lieut-Col Ivor Reginald Beviss Bond, OBE, MC, of Prosperity, Natal, S Africa, and has issue.

Arms – Argent, on a bend gules between three pellets as many swans of the field; on a sinister canton azure a demi-ram salient of the first, and in chief two fleurs-de-lis or, over all a baton trunked. **Crest** – A ram's head couped proper. *Residence* – 48 Savernake Av, Melksham, Wilts SN12 7HD.

SON LIVING

FRANCIS LUDLOW LONGUEVILLE, *b* 25 Jan 1953; *ed* Diocesan Coll, Cape Town, Stellenbosch Univ (BA), and Witwatersrand Univ (LLB): *m* 1982, Vanessa Anne, only da of late Charles Cosman Citron, of 506 Fortuna Beach Rd, Mouille Point, Cape Town, S Africa, and has issue living, William Francis Talbot, *b* 1987, — Camilla Frances, *b* 1984.

DAUGHTERS LIVING

Albinia Jennifer, *b* 1949. —— Teresa Mary, *b* 1951: *m* 1982, Michael Cyprian Waller-Bridge, of 101 Barrowgate Rd, W4 4QS (*see* Grayson, Bt, 1980 Edn), and has issue living, Jasper Cyprian, *b* 1987, — Isobel Noeline, *b* 1984, — Phoebe Mary, *b* 1985.

COLLATERAL BRANCH LIVING

Grandchildren of late Francis William Talbot Clerke, elder son of 11th baronet:—
Issue of late G/Capt Rupert Francis Henry Clerke, DFC, RAF *b* 1916, *d* 1988: *m* 1st, 1945 (*m diss* 1972), Ann Jocelyn, da of late M. J. Tosswill; 2ndly, 1975, Pamela Emily (3 Havelock Court, Warsash, Hants), da of late F. H. Bayliss:—
(By 1st *m*) Robert William, *b* 1952. —— Nicola Frances, *b* 1950.
The first person named in the pedigree of this family (some members of which were benefactors to Magdalen College, Oxford) is Richard Clerke, of Willoughby, *temp* Henry VI. From him is descended in the 4th generation, Sir John Clerke, who, at the battle of Spurs, 1513, took the Duke of Longueville prisoner, and for that signal service received from Henry VIII a grant of the canton of honourable augmentation, still borne in the family arms. The 9th baronet served in the 52nd Regt at Waterloo.

CLIFFORD (UK) 1887, of Flaxbourne, Marlborough, New Zealand

Sir ROGER JOSEPH GERRARD CLIFFORD, 7th *Baronet*; *b* 5 June 1936; *s* his father, *Sir* ROGER CHARLES JOSEPH GERRARD, 1982; *ed* Beaumont: *m* 1968, Joanna Theresa, da of Cyril James Ward (*see* Ward, Bt, *cr* 1911), and has issue.

Arms – Checky or and azure, a fesse gules. **Crest** – Out of a ducal coronet or, a wyvern rising gules.
Address – 135 Totara St, Christchurch 4, NZ.

DAUGHTERS LIVING

Angela Mary Jane, *b* 1971. —— Annabel Mary Louise *b* 1973.

BROTHER LIVING

Semper paratus
Always ready

CHARLES JOSEPH, of 44 Ngaio Road, Waikanae, New Zealand, *b* (twin) 5 June 1936: *m* 1983, Sally Madeline, da of William Hartgill Pennefather Green.

SISTER LIVING

Elizabeth Mary Jane, *b* 1938: *m* 1972, Godfrey Matthew Goodson, of 4 Golf Rd, Heretaunga, Wellington, NZ, and has issue living, Charles Godfrey, *b* 1974, — Catherine Cecilia Mary, *b* 1973.

COLLATERAL BRANCH LIVING

Granddaughter of late Charles William Clifford JP, 3rd son of 1st baronet:—
Issue of late Capt George Gilbert Joseph Clifford, *b* 1893, *ka* 1940: *m* 1925, Alcie Mary (*Alcie Mary, Lady Clifford*) (52 Onslow Sq, SW7 3NX); granted 1958, the same style, title, place, and precedence as if her late husband had survived and succeeded to the title, da of J. J. Calder, of Ardargie, Perthshire:—
Anne Caroline, *b* 1926. *Residence* – 52 Onslow Sq, SW7 3NX.
The 1st Baronet, Sir Charles, el son of George Lambert Clifford (5th son of the Hon Thomas Clifford, 2nd son of 3rd Baron Clifford of Chudleigh), was Speaker of the House of Representatives NZ 1853-60.

COATES (UK) 1921, of Haypark, City of Belfast

Sir DAVID CHARLTON FREDERICK COATES, 3rd *Baronet*; *b* 16 Feb 1948; *s* his father, *Brig Sir* FREDERICK GREGORY LINDSAY, 1994; *ed* Millfield: *m* 1973, Christine Helen, da of Lewis F. Marshall, of Ely, Cambs, and has issue.

Arms – Gules, a chevron cotised argent, on a chief ermine two bells or; on an escutcheon of pretence, quarterly, 1st and 4th argent, a fir tree growing out of a mount in base vert surmounted by a sword in bend supporting a crown in the dexter canton proper, and in chief and base, a lion's head erased armed and langued gules; 2nd and 3rd gules, three bears' heads couped argent, muzzled sable. **Crest** – A cock statant, wings closed, gules.
Residence – 30 Hauxton Rd, Little Shelford, Cambs CB2 5HJ.

SONS LIVING

JAMES GREGORY DAVID, *b* 12 March 1977. —— Robert Lewis Edward, *b* 1980.

SISTERS LIVING

Elizabeth Sara Ann, *b* 1941: *m* 1964, Maj Carol James Hay Gurney, 2nd Green Jackets (ret) (High Sheriff Suffolk 1993), of Higham Lodge, Higham, Stratford St Mary, Suffolk, and has issue living, Christopher Hay *b* 1968, — Sara Catherine, *b* 1965: *m* 1990, Rupert Lyle Charles Eley, son of Oliver John Maxwell Eley. —— Moira Louise, *b* 1945: *m* 1967, Anthony Hunt, of 74 Lynn St, Swaffham, Norfolk, and has issue living, Nigel David Anthony Howard, *b* 1968, — Michael William Richard, *b* 1971, — Jonathan Andrew Frederick *b* 1974.

AUNT LIVING (*daughter of 1st baronet*)

Jean Ann Dorothy (610 Bridlespur Lane, Earlysville, VA 22936, USA), *b* 1919: *m* 1938, Thomas Roland Lecky Sinclair, who *d* 1991, son of late Capt Sir Kenneth Duncan Lecky Sinclair, DL, RNR, and has issue living, Francis David Nicholas (RTI, Box 196, Earlysville, VA 22936, USA), *b* 1940: *m* 1st, 1963 (*m diss* 1966), Peggy Elizabeth Biller; *m* 2ndly, 1984, Mary Virginia Otto, and has issue living, (by 2nd *m*) Thomas William Patrick *b* 1985, Frederick Duncan Andrew *b* 1990, — Kenneth Richard Coates (1204 Colonial Way, Charleston, W Va, USA) *b* 1946: *m* 1972, Marion Evans Jefferds, of W VA, USA, and has issue living, Joseph Jefferds *b* 1975, Elizabeth Young *b* 1973, Catherine Coates *b* 1978, — Eleanor Margaret, *b* 1943: *m* 1st, 1962 (*m diss* 1981), Walter Roger Shope, Lt-Col US Army; 2ndly, 1986, James Edwin Lewis, of 635 Chatas Court, Lake Mary, Florida 32746, USA, and has issue living, (by 1st *m*) Thomas Roger *b* 1968: *m* 1992, Lisa Ann Crandall, Jean Marie *b* 1964.

WIDOW LIVING OF SECOND BARONET

JOAN NUGENT (*Joan, Lady Coates*), da of late Maj-Gen Sir Charlton Watson Spinks, KBE, DSO: *m* 1940, Brig Sir Frederick Gregory Lindsay Coates, 2nd Bt, who *d* 1994. *Residence* – Launchfield House, Bryantspuddle, Dorset DT2 7HN.
The 1st baronet, Sir William Frederick Coates, JP, DL (son of David Lindsay Coates, JP, of Clonallon, Belfast), was senior partner in William F. Coates & Co., stockbrokers, of Belfast, High Sheriff of Belfast 1906, Lord Mayor of Belfast 1920, 1921, 1922, 1929, and 1930, High Sheriff of co Antrim 1931, a Freeman of City of Belfast, and first Member of the Senate of N Ireland. The 2nd baronet, Brig Sir Frederick Gregory Lindsay, was with Min of Supply 1947-53, Col Gen Staff, War Office and Min of Defence 1961-66, and Dir Munitions, Defence Research and Development Staff, Assist Mil Attaché, Washington, USA 1966-69.

MILNES COATES (UK) 1911, of Helperby Hall, Helperby, North Riding of Yorkshire

While I breathe I will struggle

Professor Sir ANTHONY ROBERT MILNES COATES, 4th *Baronet; b* 8 Dec 1948; *s* his father, *Lt-Col Sir* ROBERT EDWARD JAMES CLIVE, DSO, 1982; *ed* Eton, and St Thomas's Hosp; BSc, MBBS, MRCS, MRCP, MD; Professor and Chm Dept of Medical Microbiology, St George's Hospital Medical Sch, London: *m* 1978, Harriet Ann, yr da of Raymond Burton, of The Old Rectory, Slingsby, York, and has issue.

Arms – Per fesse or and argent, three pallets sable, two flaunches gules, the dexter charged with a rose of the second, barbed and seeded proper, and the sinister with a lion passant also of the second. Crest – Upon a rock proper, a cock or, charged on the breast with a quatrefoil gules, and resting the dexter leg on an escarbuncle argent.
Residences – Helperby Hall, Helperby, York; Hereford Cottage, 135 Gloucester Rd, SW7 4TH.

SON LIVING

THOMAS, *b* 19 Nov 1986.

DAUGHTERS LIVING

Sara, *b* 1981. —— Sophie, *b* 1984.

SISTER LIVING

Mary Freda, *b* 1947: *ed* St Mary's, Wantage, Univ Hall, Buckland, and Sheffield Univ (BA, CQSW); a JP: *m* 1977, Peter Gordon Brodrick, of 25 Wandle Rd, SW17 7DL, and has issue living, Robert Cumberland, *b* 1983, — Frances Celia, *b* 1979, — Emma Charlotte, *b* 1981.

AUNTS LIVING (*Daughters of 2nd baronet*)

Bridget Sibyl, *b* 1910; Lady-in-Waiting to HRH The Princess Royal 1953-63: *m* 1st, 1931 (*m diss* 1944), Harold David Cuthbert, Scots Gds, who *d* 1959; 2ndly, 1962, Seton Hedley Dearden, MBE, of Hill House, W Witton, Leyburn, N Yorks, and has issue living, (by 1st *m*) (John) Aidan (Beaufront Castle, Hexham), *b* 1934: *m* 1975, Lady Victoria Lucy Diana Percy, 2nd da of 10th Duke of Northumberland, KG, TD, PC, and has issue living, David Hugh *b* 1987, Alice Rose *b* 1978, Lucy Caroline *b* 1982, Mary Belinda *b* 1984, — Belinda Jane Elizabeth (*Hon Mrs Matthew Beaumont*), *b* 1932: *m* 1973, as his 2nd wife, Hon Matthew Henry Beaumont, of Bearl House, Stocksfield, Northumberland NE43 7AJ (*see* V Allendale), — Caroline Alice Celia (43 Eland Rd, SW11), *b* 1940: *m* 1985 (*m diss* 1992), Jonathan Mark Hamilton Priaulx Raban. —— Elizabeth Hermione, *b* 1914: *m* 1937, William Barclay Harris, QC, of Moatlands, E Grinstead, Sussex, and 29 Barkston Gdns, SW5, and has issue living, Jonathan William (9 Lower Addison Gdns, W14), *b* 1940: *m* 1966, Nabila, da of Fares Sarofim Bey, OBE, of Minia and Cairo, — Jessica Elizabeth, *b* 1938: *m* 1973, Peter Tcherepnine, of 1192 Park Av, New York, NY, USA, — Hermione Mary, *b* 1942: *m* 1982, Marc Karlin, of 80 Highbury Hill, N5.

WIDOW LIVING OF THIRD BARONET

Lady (ETHEL) PATRICIA HARE (*Lady Patricia Milnes Coates*), da of 4th Earl of Listowel, and widow of Lt-Col Charles Thomas Milnes Gaskell, Coldm Gds (E Ranfurly): *m* 1945, Lt-Col Sir Robert Edward James Clive Milnes Coates, DSO, 3rd Bt, who *d* 1982.
The 1st baronet, Sir Edward Feetham Coates (a member of the firm of Coates, Son and Co, stockbrokers, of Gresham St, EC), MP for Lewisham (C) 1903-18, and W Lewisham 1918-21. Sir Edward Clive Coates, 2nd Bt, who *m* 1906, Lady Celia Hermione Crewe-Milnes, da of 1st and last Marquess of Crewe, assumed by deed poll 1946 the surname of Milnes-Coates.

COATS (UK) 1905, of Auchendrane, Maybole, co Ayr

With a faithful heart

COEUR·FIDÈLE

Sir ALASTAIR FRANCIS STUART COATS, 4th *Baronet*; *b* 18 Nov 1921; *s* his father, *Lt-Col Sir* JAMES STUART, MC, 1966; *ed* Eton; Capt late Coldstream Guards: *m* 1947, Lukyn, da of Capt Charles Gordon, and has issue.

Arms – Or, three mascles sable, a chief engrailed azure, semée-de-lis of the field. **Crest** – A stag's head erased proper, charged on the neck with an escarbuncle or.
Residence – Birchwood House, Durford Wood, Petersfield, Hants GU31 5AW.

SON LIVING

ALEXANDER JAMES, *b* 6 July 1951; *ed* Eton. *Residence* – 5 Bina Gdns, SW5 0LD.

DAUGHTER LIVING

Sarah Mary, *b* 1948: *m* 1st, 1972 (*m diss* 1976), William Humble David Jeremy, Viscount Ednam, el son of 4th Earl of Dudley; 2ndly, 1976, Archibald David Sampson Lloyd, of 49 Kenilworth Av, SW19 (Keane, Bt), and has issue living (by 2nd *m*), Katherine Mary, *b* 1978, — Amy Constance, *b* 1981.

BROTHERS LIVING

Ivor Paul, *b* 1923; late Lieut 12th Lancers: *m* 1959, Gay, da of Dr Charles Pinckney, and has issue living, Dominic Peter, *b* 1962, — James Charles, *b* 1964, — Emma Lucinda, *b* 1960, — Sophie Louise, *b* 1966. *Residence* – 25 Narbonne Av, SW4 9JR. —— James Raymond, *b* 1928.

COLLATERAL BRANCH LIVING

Issue of late Alfred Mainwaring Coats, 2nd son of 1st baronet, *b* 1869, *d* 1942: *m* 1895, Elizabeth, who *d* 1940, da of late Morris Barnewall, of Flushing, Long Island, USA:—
Elizabeth Barnewall, *b* 1902: *m* 19— (*m diss* 1938), Kenneth McCall, and has issue living.

The first baronet, Sir James Coats (a Director J. and P. Coats (Limited), sewing cotton manufacturers of Ferguslie Thread Works, Paisley), was el son of Sir Peter Coats, of Auchendrane, Ayrshire, who was el surviving son of late James Coats, of Paisley, and el brother of late Thomas Coats, of Ferguslie and Maxwellton (*see* B Glentanar and Glen-Coats, Bt). The second baronet, Sir Stuart Auchincloss Coats, was Private Chamberlain of Sword and Cape to Popes Pius X, Benedict XV, Pius XI and Pius XII, and sat as MP for Wimbledon (*C*) 1916-18, and for E Div of Surrey 1918-22.

GLEN-COATS (UK) 1894, of Ferguslie Park, Paisley, co Renfrew (Extinct 1954)

Sir THOMAS COATS GLEN GLEN-COATS, 2nd and last *Baronet*.

COLLATERAL BRANCH LIVING

Issue of late Alexander Harold Glen-Coats, 2nd son of 1st Baronet, *b* 1883, *d* 1933: *m* 1924, Elizabeth Millar, who *d* 1969, da of late Thomas Greenlees, of Newark, Paisley:—
(Margaret) Elizabeth (Home Farm, Hindon, Salisbury), *b* 1928. —— (Winifred) Lettice (Clouds Park, E Knoyle, Salisbury), *b* 1929; a JP of Wilts.

COCHRANE (UK) 1903, of Woodbrook, Old Connaught, Bray, co Wicklow, Lisgar Castle, Bailieborough, co Cavan, and Kildare Street, City of Dublin

By virtue and labour

Sir (HENRY) MARC SURSOCK COCHRANE, 4th Baronet, *b* 23 Oct 1946; *s* his father, *Maj Sir* DESMOND ORIEL ALASTAIR GEORGE WESTON, 1979; *ed* Eton, and Trin Coll, Dublin (MA); Hon Irish Consul General in Lebanon 1979-84; Dir Hambros Bank Ltd 1979-85, Dir GT Management plc since 1986: Trustee Chester Beatty Library and Gallery of Oriental Art, Dublin: *m* 1969, Hala, 2nd da of Fouad Mahmoud Bey es-Said, of Beirut, Lebanon, and has issue.

Arms – Azure, on chevron engrailed argent, between in chief two boars' heads erased or, and in base a sun in splendour of the last, a thistle proper between two trefoils slipped vert. **Crest** – In front of two tilting-spears in saltire a bay horse passant all proper.

SONS LIVING

ALEXANDER DESMOND SURSOCK, *b* 7 May 1973. —— Patrick Talal, *b* 1976.

DAUGHTER LIVING

Faiza Maria Rosebud, *b* 1971.

BROTHERS LIVING

Alfred Marie Stanislas Sursock, *b* 1948: *ed* Eton, and Univ of Rome (DrArch, MSDI). —— Roderick Inigo Marie Sursock, *b* 1952; *ed* Le Rosay, and American Univ of Beirut.

SISTER LIVING

Isabelle Maria Elsa Sursock, *b* 1962: *m* 1987, Count Gregorio Riccardi, son of late Count Roberto Riccardi, and Sra Giulio Pascucci-Righi.

AUNT LIVING (*Daughter of 2nd baronet*)

Elizabeth Margaret, *b* 1915: *m* 1939, Robert Elsworth Steen, MD, FRCPI, who *d* 1981, and has issue living, David Michael Cochrane Elsworth, *b* 1945; *ed* Eton, and Oriel Coll, Oxford (MA); FCA: *m* 1971, Rosemary Florence, el da of Maj William Bellingham Denis Dobbs, R Ulster Rifles (ret), (*see* B Vestey, colls), and has issue living, Peter Robert Denis Elsworth, *b* 1977, Jane Elizabeth Norah *b* 1973, Lucy Alannah Rosemary *b* 1975, Rosalie Frances Elsworth (twin) *b* 1977, — Sarah Fiola Elsworth, *b* 1942: *m* 1975, Capt Lewis Dixon-Brown, RM (ret), only son of late Brig Cecil Thomas Dixon-Brown, OBE, RM (*k* on active ser 1942), and has issue living, Elizabeth-Olga Cochrane *b* 1977, Cecily Anne Cochrane *b* 1979, Nicola Frances Cochrane *b* 1982. *Residence* – Elstow, Foxrock, co Dublin.

HALF-AUNT LIVING (*Daughter of 2nd baronet*)

Jan Asa Helen Grahame, *b* 1939.

WIDOW LIVING OF THIRD BARONET

YVONNE (*Yvonne, Lady Cochrane*) (Palais Sursock, Rue Sursock, Beirut, Lebanon), only child of late Alfred Bey Sursock, of Beirut, Lebanon: *m* 1946, Maj Sir Desmond Oriel Alastair George Weston Cochrane, 3rd Bt, who *d* 1979.

The 1st baronet, Sir Henry Cochrane, was Governing Director of Cantrell and Cochrane (Limited) mineral water manufacturers, of Dublin, and an Alderman of that City for over 25 years. Sir Ernest Cecil, 2nd Bt, was an Hon Gentleman-in-Waiting to the Lord-Lieut of Ireland 1908-09, and a dramatist (author of *A Matter of Fact* and *Monica*).

COCKBURN (NS) 1671, of That Ilk
(Name pronounced "Coburn")

He arises with a song

ACCENDIT CANTU

VIGILANS ET AUDAX

Watchful and bold

Sir JOHN ELLIOT COCKBURN, 12th *Baronet*; *b* 7 Dec 1925; *s* his father, *Lieut-Col Sir* JOHN BRYDGES, DSO, 1949; *ed* RNC Dartmouth, and RAC Cirencester: *m* 1949, Glory Patricia, el da of late Nigel Tudway Mullings, of Snitterfield, Stratford-on-Avon, and has issue.

Arms – Quarterly: 1st and 4th argent, three cocks gules, *Cockburn*: 2nd and 3rd, gules, six mascles or, three, two and one, *Weapont*; all within a bordure vert. Crest – A cock crowing proper.
Residence – 48 Frewin Rd, SW18 3LP. *Club* – Naval and Military.

SONS LIVING

CHARLES CHRISTOPHER, *b* 19 Nov 1950; *ed* Emanuel Sch, City of London Poly (BA) and Garnett Coll: *m* 1st, 1978, Beverly J., only da of B. Stangroom, of Richmond, Surrey; 2ndly, 1985, Margaret Ruth, da of Samuel Esmond Bell, of 18 Portland Dr, Bury Green, Cheshunt, Herts, and has issue living (by 2nd *m*), Christopher Samuel Alexander, *b* 24 March 1986, — Charlotte Elspeth Catherine, *b* (twin) 1986. *Residence* – 4 Connaught Rd, Teddington, Middlesex TW11 0PS. —— James Chandos, *b* 1952. —— Jonathan McQueen, *b* 1956.

DAUGHTERS LIVING

Julia Georgina, *b* 1954. —— Catherine Isabel, *b* (twin) 1956: *m* 1982, Stephen Edward Keal.

SISTER LIVING

Frances Isabel, *b* 1921.

COLLATERAL BRANCHES LIVING

Granddaughters of late Col George William Cockburn, 4th son of 7th baronet:—
Issue of late Charles Edward Stuart Cockburn, *b* 1867, *d* 1917: *m* 1894, Lilian, who *d* 1943, da of Sir Morton Edward Manningham-Buller, 2nd Bt:—
Rosalind, MBE; MBE (Civil) 1962: *m* 1921, Cdr Guy Darracott Millar, RN (ret), who *d* 1940. *Residence* –
Issue of late Donald Graham Cockburn (twin), *b* 1872, *d* 1938: *m* 1st, 1915, Dorothy Agnes, who *d* 1916, da of Lewis Evans; 2ndly, 1922, Nora, who *d* 1947, el da of G. Walton, and widow of H. D. Douglas:—
(By 1st *m*) Edith Penelope, *b* 1916.
Alexander de Cockburn, ancestor of this family, was Heritable Usher of the White Rod 1373 and later Keeper of the Great Seal of Scotland. Sir James Cockburn of that Ilk, 1st Bt, purchased from his cousin Sir Archibald Cockburn, 4th Bt (whose title became dormant 1880) the lands of Langton, Berwickshire, and office of Usher.

Cockburn-Campbell, see Campbell.

CODRINGTON (GB) 1721, of Dodington, Gloucestershire

VULTUS·IN·HOSTEM

Face to the enemy

Sir WILLIAM ALEXANDER CODRINGTON, 8th *Baronet*; *b* 5 July 1934; *s* his father, *Lieut-Com Sir* WILLIAM RICHARD 1961; *ed* St Andrew Coll, S Africa, and S African Naval Coll; Dir World-Wide Shipping Agency Ltd, Hong Kong.

Arms – Argent, a fesse embattled counter-embattled sable fretty gules between three lions passant of the third. Crest – Not recorded at College of Arms.
Residence – Flat A 1st Floor, 31 Cloudview Rd, Hong Kong.

BROTHERS LIVING

GILES PETER (Villa Félipe, Avenue Fernand Martin, Villefranche-sur-Mer, France), *b* 28 Oct 1943: *m* 1989, Shirley Linda Duke, and has issue living, Christopher Harry, *b* 1988, — Daniel Peter, *b* 1993, — Michele Anne, *b* 1990. —— Andrew Richard (5 Cambridge News, Kingsley, Perth, Western Australia 6026, Australia), *b* 1947; Capt: *m* 1975, Claire Marie Agnes Frichot, of Mahé, Seychelles, and has issue living, Adrian Richard, *b* 1981, — Estelle Louise, *b* 1985.

SISTER LIVING

Sally Ann, *b* 1939: *m* 1962, Philip John Francis Collingwood, of 51 Longcroft Lane, Welwyn Garden City, Herts, and has issue living, Richard Francis, *b* 1964, — Sophia Catherine Mary, *b* 1963: *m* 1989, Julian Thomas Rowe, — Charlotte Mary, *b* 1966.

MOTHER LIVING

Joan Kathleen Birelli, el da of Percy E. Nicholas: *m* 1933 (*m diss* 1952), Lieut-Com Sir William Richard Codrington, 7th Bt, who *d* 1961.

COLLATERAL BRANCHES LIVING

Issue of late Frank Christopher Codrington, yr son of 6th baronet, *b* 1908, *d* 1992: *m* 1933, Monica Bawn, who *d* 1983, eldest da of Sir James Philip Reynolds, 1st Bt, DSO, MP:—
Christopher Michael, *b* 1937; *ed* St Andrew's Coll, Grahamstown, S Africa: *m* 1972, Christine Beatrice, eldest da of Lt-Col Max Emil Bürki, of Château Surpierre, Switzerland, and has issue living, Rosalind Bawn, *b* 1974, — Emily Jane, *b* 1977.

Issue of late Gerald William Henry Codrington (son of late Christopher William Codrington, MP, grandson of late Edward Codrington (*infra*)), who was *cr* a *Baronet* 1876:—
See Codrington, Bt, *cr* 1876.

Grandchildren of late Lt-Gen Sir Alfred Edward Codrington, GCVO, KCB, yr son of late Gen Sir William John Codrington, GCB, MP, 2nd son of late Adm Sir Edward Codrington, GCB, 3rd son of late Edward Codrington, 4th son of 1st baronet:—
Issue of late Col Sir Geoffrey Ronald Codrington, KCVO, CB, CMG, DSO, OBE, TD, *b* 1888, *d* 1973: *m* 1923, Cecilia Mary, who *d* 1979, da of late Ernest James Wythes, CBE (Thorold, Bt):—
Michael Christopher Alfred (Beech Cottage, Farm Lane, Gt Bedwyn, Marlborough, Wilts), *b* 1926; late Maj 16th/5th Lancers: *m* 1st, 1953 (*m diss* 1986), Irene Margaret, who *d* 1994, da of late Col Mark Edward Makgill-Crichton-Maitland, CVO, DSO (*see* E Lauderdale, colls); 2ndly, 1986, Alma Patricia, widow of Norman G. Batcheller, and da of late Patrick Sheridan, and has issue living (by 1st *m*), Camilla Anne, *b* 1957, — Bridget Margaret (116 Portland Rd, W11), *b* 1958: *m* 1st 1979, George Daniel Rossiter, who *d* 1984; 2ndly, 1990, Ross O'N. Witherow, and has issue living, (by 1st *m*) Peter Goodman *b* 1983, (by 2nd *m*), Thomas Edward *b* 1991, — Katherine Alice, *b* 1965. —— James Geoffrey (Lyde Barn, Lower Lyde, Herefordshire), *b* 1935: *m* 1961, Lorraine, el da of R. G. A. Wells, of Stable Cottage, Winchelsea, E Sussex, and has issue living, Richard Melville, *b* 1962, — Charles Sebastian, *b* 1964, — Annabelle Cecilia, *b* 1967: *m* 1991, Graham P. Sylvester, only son of Dr Derek Sylvester, of Almondsbury Field, Lower Almondsbury, Bristol. —— Mary Alice (*Hon Mrs Robert T. Boscawen*), *b* 1924; a JP of co London: *m* 1949, Rt Hon Robert Thomas Boscawen, MC, MP (*see* V Falmouth). —— Emma Cecilia (West Lodge, Wilton, Salisbury), *b* 1930.
Issue of late Capt William Melville Codrington, CMG, MC, *b* 1892, *d* 1963: *m* 1935, Katharine Theodosia (The Cottage, Hambleton, Oakham, Rutland) (who *m* 2ndly, 1968, Edward Kirkpatrick, who *d* 1972), da of John Houston Sinclair, CMG, CBE (Cockburn, Bt, colls):—
Jane Evelyn, *b* 1937: *m* 1961, Richard Miles Micklethwait, of Preston Hall, Oakham (*see* D Norfolk, colls). —— Teresa Anne, *b* 1944: *m* 1979, John Stuart Wheeler (*see* Gibbons, Bt), of 73 The Chase, SW4 0NP, and has issue living, Sarah Rose, *b* 1980, — Jacquetta Lydia, *b* 1981, — Charlotte Mary, *b* 1985.
The 2nd baronet, who died 1792, disinherited his son, Sir William, 3rd Bt, and bequeathed his estates to his nephew, Christopher Bethell-Codrington, whose grandson was *cr* a baronet 1876.

CODRINGTON (UK) 1876, of Dodington, Gloucestershire

True virtue is imperishable

Sir SIMON FRANCIS BETHELL CODRINGTON, 3rd *Baronet*; *b* 14 Aug 1923; *s* his father *Sir* CHRISTOPHER WILLIAM GERALD HENRY, 1979; *ed* Eton; formerly Major Coldstream Guards; European War 1942-5 in Italy: *m* 1st, 1947 (*m diss* 1959), Joanne, da of John William Molineaux, of Rock Castle, Kilmacsimon, co Cork, and widow of William Humphrey Austin Thompson; 2ndly, 1959 (*m diss* 1979), Pamela Joy Halliday, da of Major George Walter Bentley Wise, MBE; 3rdly, 1980 (*m diss* 1987), Mrs Sarah Gwynne Gaze (*née* Pennell); 4thly, 1989, Shirley Ann, da of Percival Lionel Davis, and has issue living by 2nd *m*.

Arms – Argent, a fesse embattled counter-embattled sable fretty gules between three lions passant of the third. **Crest** – Issuant from a coronet composed of four roses set upon a rim or a dragon's head gules between two dragon's wings per fesse or and azure.
Seat – Dodington Park, Chipping Sodbury, Gloucestershire. **Residence** – Bean Cottage, Dodington, Chipping Sodbury, Bristol BS17 6SF.
Club – Cavalry and Guards'.

SONS LIVING *(By 2nd marriage)*

CHRISTOPHER GEORGE WAYNE (The Old Hundred, Tormarton, Badminton, Avon), *b* 20 Feb 1960; *ed* Millfield, and RAC Cirencester : *m* 1991, Noelle Lynn, da of Dale Wilford Leverson, of Texas, USA, and of Mrs Genell Benner, of Ohio, and has issue living, Alexander Edward Kristoffer, *b* 9 Nov 1993. —— Bethell, *b* 1961. —— Hugo John, *b* 1964: *m* 1992, Antonia Hannah Beaufort, eldest da of Andrew McCullough, of Windsor, Berks.

This family is a younger branch of the Codringtons, baronets, of Dodington, creation 1721. The Codringtons have been established in Gloucestershire since *temp* Henry IV. The 1st Bt was Sir Gerald William Henry Codrington, son of late Christopher William Henry Codrington, MP (*see* Codrington, Bt, *cr* 1721, colls).

COGHILL (GB) 1778, of Coghill, Yorkshire

He does not sleep who keeps guard

Sir EGERTON JAMES NEVILL TOBIAS (TOBY) COGHILL, 8th *Baronet*; *b* 26 March 1930; *s* his father, *Sir* JOSCELYN AMBROSE CRAMER, RNVR, 1983; *ed* Gordonstoun, and Pembroke Coll, Camb (MA): *m* 1958, Gabriel Nancy, da of late Maj Dudley Claud Douglas Ryder (*see* E Harrowby, colls), and has issue.

Arms – Quarterly: 1st and 4th ermine a chevron between three cocks gules, *Coghill*: 2nd and 3rd, gules, on a chevron argent three pellets, a chief indented of the second. Crest – On a mount vert a cock gules charged on the breast with a bezant.
Residence – Sourden, Rothes, Morayshire AB38 7AE.

SON LIVING

PATRICK KENDAL FARLEY (26 Gowrie Rd, SW11), *b* 3 Nov 1960.

DAUGHTER LIVING

Elizabeth Louisa Gay, *b* 1962.

SISTER LIVING

Faith Patricia Elizabeth, *b* 1928: *m* 1955, James Leslie Garson, of Hill Farm, Elsfield, Oxford OX3 9SW, and has issue living, Jeremy James, *b* 1961, — Elizabeth Lucy, *b* 1956, — Rachel Margaret, *b* 1958: *m* 1982, Michael Dickinson, and has issue living, Samuel Caradoc *b* 1985, Hannah Beatrice *b* 1987, Phoebe Rose *b* 1990, Eleanor Grace, *b* (twin) 1990, — Isobel Laura, *b* 1968: *m* 1992, Tobias Andrew Baxter.

HALF-SISTERS LIVING AND DECEASED

Bridget Olivia Françoise, *b* 1949. —— Jocelyn Edith Louise, *b* 1952, *d* 1983: *m* 1972, Stephen George Thomas, of 135 Sommerville Rd, Ashley Down, Bristol. —— Deborah Katharine Hildegarde, *b* 1954: *m* 1987, Alan Nye, of 35 Nevil Rd, Bishopston, Bristol, and has issue living, Alistair William James, *b* 1989, — Lucy Elizabeth Katherine, *b* 1991.

COLLATERAL BRANCHES LIVING

Grandchildren of late Claude Plunket Coghill, 4th son of 4th baronet:—
Issue of late Joscelyn Kendal Bushe Coghill, *b* 1893 *d* 1959: *m* 1925, Maud Evelyn, da of late Leslie Phillips Filder, of Crawley, Sussex:—
John Kendal Plunket, OBE, *b* 1929; *ed* Sherborne, late Lt-Col RAOC; OBE (Civil) 1990: *m* 1951, Diana Mary, da of late Frederick Charles Callen, of Tanganyika, and has issue living, Michèle Mary, *b* 1957: *m* 1988, Julian David Sinclair Lyon, of 4 East Meads, Onslow Village, Guildford, Surrey GU2 5SP, 2nd son of Stewart Lyon, of Guildford, and has issue living, Georgina Mary Coghill *b* 1991, — Amanda Patricia, *b* 1960: *m* 1985, Stephen John Lowcock Downing, of 22, Bowood Rd, SW11, and has issue living, Thomas Peter *b* 1989, Katherine Louise *b* 1991, — Samantha Jane, *b* 1967: *m* 1990, Peter James Wilken. *Address* – 8 East Meads, Onslow Village, Guildford, Surrey GU2 5SP. —— Sheila Mary, *b* 1926: *m* 1952, David Polwhele Cooper, and has issue living, Shaun David Coghill, *b* 1956, — Sally Muara Coghill, *b* 1954, — Julie Rosalyn Coghill, *b* 1965, — Lucinda Jane Coghill, *b* 1966. *Residence* – Pine Trees, 3 Ferguson Av, Greendale, Harare, Zimbabwe.

The 1st baronet, Sir John Cramer, LLD, of Coghill Hall, Knaresborough (grandson of Oliver Cramer, of Ballyfoile, co Kilkenny, and his wife Hester, sister of Rt Hon Marmaduke Coghill, Chancellor of the Exchequer, Ireland), succeeded to the family estates of his cousin Hester, da and heiress of James Coghill, LLD, and widow of 1st Earl of Charleville, and assumed by roy licence the additional surname of Coghill 1774/5. His successor Sir John Thomas Coghill, 2nd Bt, and his brother and successor, Sir Josiah Coghill Coghill, 3rd Bt, assumed by Roy licence the surname of Coghill only in 1807 and 1817 respectively. The 4th baronet was High Sheriff of co Dublin in 1859, and was *s* by his second son as 5th Bt, the el, Nevill Josiah Aylmer Coghill, VC, Lieut 24th Regt, having been killed while saving the Colours of his regt at the battle of Isandhlwana 22 Jan 1879. Sir Egerton Coghill, 5th Bt, *s* 1905; landscape painter (studied Barbizon School, Paris); DL co Cork. His eldest son, Sir Patrick Coghill, 6th Bt, *s* 1921, served in both European Wars with distinction, the Arab Legion, in Turkey and Iraq; DL Hertfordshire. His brother, Sir Joscelyn Coghill, 7th Bt, *s* 1981, *d* 1983.

WALEY-COHEN (UK) 1961, of Honeymead, co Somerset

Sir STEPHEN HARRY WALEY-COHEN, 2nd *Baronet; b* 22 June 1946; *s* his father, *Sir* BERNARD NATHANIEL, 1991; *ed* Eton, and Magdalene Coll, Camb (MA); Financial journalist *Daily Mail* 1968-73, Editor *Money Mail Handbook* 1973 and 1974; Dir Euromoney Publications Ltd 1969-77, Publisher Euromoney 1977-83; Chief Executive Maybox Group plc 1984-89; Gov of Wellesley House Sch; Man Dir Victoria Palace, Dir S. M. Theatre Ltd, Society of London Theatre, and Exeter Preferred Capital Investment Trust plc; Chm Policy Portfolio plc, Willis Faber and Dumas (Agencies) Ltd; Chm Jewish Colonisation Assocn; Chm UK Executive Cttee, British American Project for the Successor Generation: *m* 1st, 1972 (*m diss* 1986), Pamela Elizabeth, yr da of J. E. Doniger, of Knutsford, Cheshire; 2ndly, 1986, Josephine Burnett, yr da of late Duncan M. Spencer, of Bedford, New York, and has issue by 1st and 2nd *m.*

Arms – Quarterly, 1st and 4th argent, on a chevron gules cottised azure, between in chief two roses of the second barbed and seeded proper, and in base a buck's head couped also proper, three annulets or, *Cohen;* 2nd and 3rd, argent a chevron azure cottised sable between in chief two eagles displayed of the last and in base on a mount vert a hind trippant proper, *Waley.* **Crest** – 1st, a buck's head couped argent, attired or, holding in the mouth a rose slipped gules, the neck encircled by a wreath of oak proper between four barrulets gules, *Cohen;* 2nd, out of a bush of fern a hind's head proper in the mouth a rose argent stalked and leaved also proper, *Waley.*
Residence – 1 Wallingford Ave, W10 6QA. *Club* – Garrick.

SONS LIVING *(By 1st marriage)*

LIONEL ROBERT, *b* 7 Aug 1974; *ed* Eton, and Bath Univ.. —— Jack David, *b* 1979.

DAUGHTERS LIVING *(By 1st marriage)*

Harriet Ann, *b* 1976.

(By 2nd marriage)

Tamsin Alice, *b* 1986. —— Freya Charlotte, *b* 1989.

BROTHER LIVING

Robert Bernard (18 Gilston Rd, SW10 9SR; *Clubs* – Boodle's, Jockey and Queen's), *b* 1948; *ed* Eton; Exec at Christie, Manson & Woods Ltd 1969-81, Gen man in USA 1970-73; Chm Alliance Medical Ltd, Dir Samuel Properties Ltd since 1977; sec of Amateur Riders Assoc 1978-84 and founder member of Horseracing Advisory Council since 1979; Steward at Cheltenham 1980, Plumpton 1978, Warwick 1983, Epsom 1982, and Sandown 1983; elected Jockey Club 1983: *m* 1975, Hon Felicity Ann Samuel, da of 3rd Viscount Bearsted, and has issue living, Marcus Richard, *b* 1977, — Sam Bernard, *b* 1982, — Thomas Andrew, *b* 1984, — Jessica Suzanna, *b* 1979.

SISTERS LIVING

Rosalind Alice, *b* 1945; *ed* Cranborne Chase Sch: *m* 1966, Philip Ralph Burdon, of 140 Straven Rd, Christchurch, NZ, and has issue living, Miranda Ruth, *b* 1970, — Rebecca Joyce, *b* 1972, — Josephine Virginia, *b* 1975. —— (Eleanor) Joanna, *b* 1952; *ed* Cranborne Chase Sch, and Girton Coll, Camb (MA): *m* 1977, Keith Bradoc Gallant, of Branford, Conn, USA, and has issue living, Christopher Edward Bernard (Kit), *b* 1988, — Isobel Claire, *b* 1993.

WIDOW LIVING OF FIRST BARONET

Hon JOYCE CONSTANCE INA NATHAN, MA, JP (*Hon Lady Waley-Cohen*), only da of 1st Baron Nathan: *m* 1943, Sir Bernard Nathaniel Waley-Cohen, 1st Bt, who *d* 1991.

The 1st baronet, Sir Bernard Nathaniel Waley-Cohen (el son of Sir Robert Waley Cohen, KBE, who *d* 1952, of Caen Wood Towers, Highgate, N6, and Honeymead, Simonsbath, Somerset) assumed by deed poll 1950 his final forename as an additional surname. An Underwriting Member of Lloyd's he served as Alderman of City of London 1949-84, Sheriff of City of London 1955-56, and Lord Mayor of London 1960-61.

COLFOX (UK) 1939, of Symondsbury, co Dorset

Light, Law, Liberty

Sir (WILLIAM) JOHN COLFOX, 2nd *Baronet*; *b* 25 April 1924; *s* his father, *Sir* (WILLIAM) PHILIP, MC, 1966; *ed* Eton; a JP for Dorset; High Sheriff 1969; DL 1977; 1939-45 War as Lt RNVR: *m* 1962, Frederica Loveday, da of Adm Sir Victor Alexander Charles Crutchley, VC, KCB, DSC, DL, of Mappercombe Manor, Bridport, Dorset, and has issue.

Arms – Sable, three spinning-cogs erect and in fesse or, on chief argent, as many fox-heads couped at the neck gules. **Crest** – A fox proper, charged on the body with two fleurs-de-lys in fesse sable, and resting the sinister paw on a fleur-de-lys gules. *Residence* – Symondsbury House, Bridport, Dorset.

SONS LIVING

PHILIP JOHN (117 Eccleston Mews SW1X 8AQ), *b* 27 Dec 1962; *ed* Eton: *m* 19—, Julia R., yr da of Geoffrey St George Schomberg, of Durfort, France, and Mrs H. D. Lyon, of Dallington, Sussex, and has issue living, Alice *b* 1993, — Lilly, *b* (twin) 1993. —— Edward Timothy, *b* 1969.

DAUGHTERS LIVING

Victoria Mary, *b* 1964. —— Charlotte Ismay Joan, *b* 1966: *m* 1987, Capt James William Harwood Daniel, WG, eldest son of Col John Daniel, and has issue living, Olivia Mary Frederica, *b* 1988. —— Constance Ruth, *b* 1971.

SISTERS LIVING

Susan Helen Frances, *b* 1929: *m* 1950, William Henry Batten, and has issue living, David Henry Cary, *b* 1952: *m* 1981, Sarah Bagnell, — Michael John, *b* 1960: *m* 1984, Joanna Winslade, and has issue living, two sons and one da, — Tessa Mary, *b* 1954: *m* 1976, John Mackenzie-Green, and has issue two sons and one da, — Bridget Caroline, *b* 1955: *m* 1978, Angus Handasyde Dick, and has issue two sons and one da. *Residence* – Church Farm, Ryme Intrinsica, Dorset. —— Bridget Alice, *b* 1931: *m* 1st, 1958, Lt-Col Peter Amyand Brenton Wickham, late RA, who *d* 1967; 2ndly, 1968, Alexander David Evelyn Mure, JP, of Pevington Farm, Pluckley, Kent, and has issue living (by 1st *m*), Anthony John Macarthur, *b* 1960: *m* 1994, Georgina Dimity Cumberland-Brown, — Mark Andrew, *b* 1962: *m* 1991, Corinne Lynne Barker, and has issue living, William Peter Mure *b* 1993, — Tania Catherine, *b* 1959.

COLLETT (UK) 1934, of Bridge Ward in the City of London

Sir IAN SEYMOUR COLLETT, 3rd *Baronet*; *b* 5 Oct 1953; *s* his grandfather, *Sir* HENRY SEYMOUR, 1971; *ed* Lancing Coll; a Freeman of City of London: *m* 1982, Philippa J., only da of James R. I. Hawkins, of Preston St Mary, Suffolk.

Arms – Azure, on a chevron couped or between three hinds trippant proper, collared of the second, an arch sable, between two open books, also proper. **Crest** – A demi-hind proper, collared or, resting the sinister foot on an escutcheon gold, charged with a maul sable. *Residence* – Pound Farm, Gt Glemham, Suffolk. *Clubs* – MCC, Aldeburgh Golf, Aldeburgh Yacht.

SON LIVING

ANTHONY SEYMOUR, *b* 1984.

DAUGHTER LIVING

Georgina, *b* 1986.

SISTER LIVING

Joanna Ruth, *b* 1956; a Freeman of City of London: *m* 1984, Nigel E. Wicks, eldest son of Malcolm E. Wicks, of Peterborough, and has issue living, Jennifer Ruth, *b* 1989. *Club* – Hurlingham.

UNCLE LIVING (Son of 2nd baronet)

Sir Christopher, GBE, *b* 1931; *ed* Harrow and Emmanuel Coll, Camb (MA); Capt RA (TA); a FCA, a Freeman of City of London, a Liveryman of Glovers' Co (Master 1981-82), a Liveryman of Chartered Accountants' Co, and a Liveryman of Haberdashers' Co; Common Councilman 1973-79; Alderman 1979, Sheriff 1985, Lord Mayor of City of London 1988; *cr* GBE 1988: *m* 1959, Christine Anne, da of late Oswald Hardy Griffiths, of Nunthorpe, Yorks, and has issue living, Alastair John Calvert (77 Faraday Rd, Wimbledon, SW19), *b* 1961: *m* 1992, Tiana J., only da of Anthony Peck, of Kingston upon Thames, Surrey, — Angus Christopher Calvert, *b* 1964, — Alexandra Louise Calvert, *b* 1972. *Residence* – Flat 13, Somerset House, Somerset Rd, Wimbledon, SW19. *Club* – City Livery and City of London.

AUNT LIVING (Daughter of 2nd baronet)

Margaret Ruth, MBE, *b* 1922; AIMA, JP, a Freeman of City of London: *m* 1950, Col George Victor Nudd Chadd, OBE, TD, JP, DL, of Mardle House, Wangford, nr Beccles, Suffolk, and has issue living, Richard Jonathan (Ditchingham Cottage, Ditchingham, nr Bungay, Suffolk), *b* 1953; (BA Oxon); Notary Public: *m* 1977, Jane, da of Dr William Ayles, of Edinburgh, and has issue living, Hugo George William *b* 1987, Emma Louise Mary *b* 1981, Caroline Lavinia Rose *b* 1983, — Nicholas Martyn Philip (Thatched Cottage, Rushmere, nr Lowestoft, Suffolk), *b* 1958; Freeman City of London; Liveryman Farriers'

Co: *m* 1987, Amelia Catherine, da of Timothy Sallitt, of France, and has issue living, Edward George Alexander *b* 1991, Eleanor Alice *b* 1993.

GREAT UNCLE LIVING (*Son of 1st baronet*)

David Brooke (3 Buckenham Court, Southwold, Suffolk), *b* 1907; a Freeman of City of London, a Fellow of The Plastics and Rubber Inst, a Dir of Dunlop Co Ltd 1952-67; Hon Member and Past Pres of Rubber & Plastics Research Assocn of Great Britain; former Member of London Electricity Board, and Senior Pro-Chancellor of Loughborough Univ of Technology 1966-80; DTech (Hons): *m* 1933, Mary Cecily Beatrice, FCA, da of late Hugh C. Aston, and has issue living, Anthony Hugh (7 Drayton Close, Fetcham Park, Leatherhead, Surrey KT22 9EZ), *b* 1936; MA Camb; CEng; FICE; a Freeman of City of London: *m* 1962, Christine Ann Little, and has issue living, Gail Christine *b* 1964, Clare Elizabeth *b* 1967, June Alison *b* 1969, — Elizabeth Anne, *b* 1934; Freeman of City of London: *m* 1957, David Luard Boult, of Mariners, Southwold, Suffolk and has issue living, David Mark *b* 1960, Edward William *b* 1963, Nicola Anne Louise, *b* 1958, — Bridget Mary, *b* 1945: *m* 1981, James David Blackburn, of Railroad Mills Rd, Pittsford, NY, USA, and has issue living, David Peter *b* 1986, Barbara Ann (adopted) *b* 1972.

MOTHER LIVING

Sheila Joan (*Lady Miskin*), only da of late Harold Scott, of Inverleith Gdns, Edinburgh; a Freeman of City of London: *m* 1st, 1951, David Seymour Collett, who *d* 1962, el son of 2nd baronet; 2ndly, 1980, as his 2nd wife, Sir James William Miskin, QC, who *d* 1993, late Recorder of London.

WIDOW LIVING OF SECOND BARONET

RUTH MILDRED (*Ruth, Lady Collett*) (Sunset House, Southwold, Suffolk), el da of late William Thomas Hatch, MICE, MIEE: *m* 1920, Sir Henry Seymour Collett, 2nd Bt, who *d* 1971.

COLLATERAL BRANCHES LIVING

Issue of late Richard Ionn Collett, 4th son of 1st baronet, *b* 1901, *d* 1993: *m* 1926, Helen Alice, who *d* 1992, da of late Harry Hayns:—
Norman Ionn (78 Warren Rd, Donaghadee, co Down), *b* 1927; *ed* Ipswich Sch, Perse Sch, Cambridge, and HMS Conway: *m* 1954, Ethne Maureen, da of Samuel Chadwick, and has issue living, Kevin Samuel Richard, *b* 1955, — Norman Michael, *b* 1959, — Helen Margaret, *b* 1962. —— James Masterman (Owl's Hoot, 23 Bramley Av, Coulsdon, Surrey CR3 2DS), *b* 1930; *ed* Ipswich Sch, Perse Sch, Cambridge, and Bishop's Stortford Coll: *m* 1962, Rosalind Mary, da of John Humphrey Lane, of Meldreth, Woodcote Av, Wallington, Surrey, and has issue living, Lucinda Mary, *b* 1963. —— †Richard Patrick, *b* 1932; *ed* Ipswich Sch, Perse Sch, Cambridge, and Bishop's Stortford Coll; Capt RE (TA): *m* 1958, Gillian Anne (Thatches, Hall Lane, Witnesham, nr Ipswich, Suffolk), da of Alfred James Remes, and *d* 1982, leaving issue, Jane Louise, *b* 1960, — Johanna Mary, *b* 1962. —— Henry Alexander, *b* 1944; *ed* Bishop's Stortford Coll; ACA; a Freeman of City of London; a Liveryman of Distillers' Co: *m* 1969, Joy Eileen, da of Rev Ross McPherson Heard, of Hatch Beauchamp Rectory, Taunton, Somerset, and has issue living, Christian Tom, *b* 1972, — Ross Tobias, *b* 1973.

Issue of late John Collison Collett, 5th son of 1st baronet, *b* 1903, *d* 1956: *m* 1928, Ethel Ruth (Stable End, Windhill, Bishop's Stortford, Herts), da of late Benjamin A. Glanvill:—
John Brian Glanvill, *b* 1929: *m* 1959, Phyllis Ivy Sybil Kiddy, and has issue living, Robert Glanvill, *b* 1961, — John Charles, *b* 1969, — Helen Mary, *b* 1960. *Residence* – Countess Wells Farm, Framlingham, Suffolk. —— Peter Glanvill, *b* 1933: *m* 1st, 1959, Cecilia Judith, who *d* 1966, da of Gerald Eliot Meysey Bromley-Martin; 2ndly, 1973, Mary Jean, da of Leonard George Truelove, and has issue living, (by 1st *m*) Gerard Henry Glanvill (11 Clarence Rd, Stansted, Essex), *b* 1961: *m* 1989, Nicola May Marie, da of William Robson, and has issue living, Charles Henry *b* 1992, Sally Elizabeth *b* 1990, — Thomas John Eliot, *b* 1962, — Alexander Peter Glanvill, *b* 1965, — Nicola Mary, *b* 1959, — (by 2nd *m*) Rebecca Mary, *b* 1974, — Anna Catherine, *b* 1976. *Residence* – Stable End, Windhill, Bishop's Stortford, Herts CM23 2ND. —— Sheila Mary *b* 1931: *m* 1955, John Donald Sewell, and has issue living, David John Elliott, *b* 1956, — Andrew William, *b* 1961, — Michael James, *b* 1967, — Jean Mary, *b* 1958 *Residence* – Brettenham Park, nr Ipswich, Suffolk. —— Diana, *b* 1940: *m* 1st, 1959 (*m diss* 1969), Thomas Joseph Henighan; 2ndly, 1971, Robert Hugh MacDonald (Box 204, N Gower, Ontario, Canada), and has issue living (by 1st *m*), Stephen Patrick Glanvill, *b* 1960, — Phoebe Clare, *b* 1964.

Issue of late Roger Collett, yst son of 1st baronet, *b* 1909, *d* 1972: *m* 1934 (*m diss* 19—), Doreen Frances Alvie, da of late Sydney Platt:—
Roger James (8 Vanbrugh Fields, Blackheath, SE3 7TZ), *b* 1942; *ed* Ellesmere Coll: *m* 1966 Valerie Doreen, da of late Prof Cyril George Beasley, and has issue living, Christopher James, *b* 1973, — Nicola Valerie, *b* 1971. —— Susan Marjory, *b* 1939: *m* 1960, James Stafford Coombe, of Glenmore, Church Lane, Chipstead, Surrey, and has issue living, Andrew James Grant, *b* 1964, — John Edward, *b* 1979, — Caroline Jane, *b* 1961, — Edwina Gay, *b* 1963, — Georgina Susan, *b* 1974, — Genevieve Frances, *b* 1983.

The 1st baronet, Sir Charles Henry Collett (son of Henry John Richard Collett, JP of The Hall, Peasenhall, Suffolk), was a Common Councilman of the City of London 1912-27, an Alderman 1927-38, Sheriff 1932-3, and Lord Mayor 1933-4.

COLMAN (UK) 1907, of Gatton Park, Gatton, Surrey

Quick enough if well enough

Sir MICHAEL JEREMIAH COLMAN, 3rd *Baronet*; *b* 7 July 1928; *s* his father, Sir JEREMIAH 1961; *ed* Eton; Capt Queen's Own Yorks Yeo (RARO); Chm of Reckitt & Colman plc since 1986; 1st Church Estates Commissioner 1993; Dir of Reckitt & Colman Ltd and Foreign & Colonial Private Equity Trust plc; Pres R Warrant Holders Assocn 1984; Associate of Trin House and Member of Lighthouse Board since 1985, Younger Brother 1994; Member of the Court of Skinners' Co since 1985; Member of Gen Council and Finance Cttee of King Edward's Hospital Fund for London; Special Trustee, St Mary's Hospital, Paddington: *m* 1955, Judith Jean Wallop, da of late Vice Adm Sir Peveril Barton Reibey Wallop William-Powlett, KCB, KCMG, CBE, DSO (*see* E Portsmouth, colls), and has issue.

Arms – Ermine, on a pale rayonée or, between two crosses flory sable, a lion rampant gules. Crest – In front of two wings argent, each charged with an estoile azure, a rock proper, thereon a caltrap or. Badge – Issuant through an antique crown or, a greyhound's head proper.
Residence – Malshanger, Basingstoke, Hants RG23 7EY.

SONS LIVING

JEREMIAH MICHAEL POWLETT, *b* 23 Jan 1958; *ed* Eton, and Univ of Leicester (LLB): *m* 1981, Susan Elizabeth, yr da of John Henry Britland, of 15 Straylands Grove, York, and has issue living, Joseph Jeremiah, *b* 31 Oct 1988, — Nathaniel James, *b* 1990, — Eleanor Mary, *b* 1985. —— John Powlett, *b* 1962.

DAUGHTERS LIVING

Olivia Helena Judith, *b* 1956: *m* 1979, Rev Patrick J. Whitworth, yr son of Maj-Gen Reginald Henry Whitworth, CB, CBE, of Abbey House Farm, Goosey, Wantage, Oxon, and has issue living, David John William, *b* 1990, — Emma Rachel, *b* 1982, — Louisa Judith, *b* 1984, — Sophia Rose, *b* 1987. —— Victoria Rose, *b* 1960: *m* 1988, Rev Matthew S. Persson, of 41 Marloes Rd, W8 6LA, elder son of Rt Rev William Michael Dermot Persson, Bishop of Doncaster, and has issue living, Augustus William, *b* 1990, — Bartholomew Jo, *b* 1993. —— Alice Mary *b* 1965: *m* 1994, Timothy A. C. Page, eldest son of Col (John Patrick) Anthony Page, of Croft House, Brackley.

BROTHER LIVING

Oliver James, *b* 1933: *m* 1967, Hon Cynthia Makins, twin da of 1st Baron Sherfield, and has issue living, Thomas James, *b* 1969, — Camilla Mary, *b* 1972. *Residence* – 7 Tor Gardens, W8 7AB.

SISTER LIVING

Gillian Veronica, *b* 1926.

The 1st baronet, Sir Jeremiah Colman (son of Jeremiah Colman, of Carshalton Park, Surrey), was Chm of J. & J. Colman Ltd, manufacturers, of Norwich and London, and a Lieut for City of London.

COLQUHOUN (GB) 1786, of Luss, Dumbarton
(Name pronounced "Cohoon")

If I can

Sir IVAR IAIN COLQUHOUN OF LUSS, 8th *Baronet*; *b* 4 Jan 1916; *s* his father, *Lt-Col Sir* IAIN, KT, DSO, LLD, 1948; *ed* Eton; is Chief of the Clan Colquhoun, and Capt Gren Gds, DL and JP of Dunbartonshire and Hon Sheriff Substitute: *m* 1943, Kathleen, 2nd da of late Walter Atholl Duncan, of 53 Cadogan Sq, SW1, and has issue.

Arms – Argent, a saltire engrailed sable. **Crest** – A hart's head couped gules, attired argent. **Supporters** – Two ratch-hounds argent, collared sable.
Seat – Camstraddan, Luss, Dunbartonshire G83 8NX. *Clubs* – White's, Puffin's, Royal Ocean Racing.

SON LIVING

MALCOLM RORY (74 Nightingale Lane, SW12 8NR; White's and Turf Clubs), *b* 20 Dec 1947; *ed* Eton, and London Univ: *m* 1st, 1978 (*m diss* 1983), Susan, el da of Stewart W. Timmerman, of Harrisburg, Penn, USA; 2ndly, 1989, Katharine A. H., eldest da of A. C. Mears, of Canberra, Australia, and has issue living (by 1st *m*), Patrick John, *b* 17 Dec 1980, — (by 2nd *m*) Fergus Alexander Mears, *b* 1991, — Georgina Iona Helena, *b* 1993.

DAUGHTER LIVING

Iona Mary (*Duchess of Argyll*), *b* 1945: *m* 1964, 12th Duke of Argyll. *Residence* – Inveraray Castle, Argyll.

SISTERS LIVING

Fiona Bryde (*Fiona, Countess of Arran*), *b* 1918: *m* 1937, 8th Earl of Arran, who *d* 1983. *Residence* – Pimlico House, Hemel Hempstead, Herts. —— Robina, *b* 1923; sometime in WRNS: *m* 1950, Capt Alan Lewis Wigan, King's Roy Rifle Corps (Reserve) (*see* Wigan, Bt). —— Frances Mary, *b* 1925.

COLLATERAL BRANCH LIVING

Issue of late Donald Colquhoun, yr son of 7th baronet, *b* 1920, *d* 1992: *m* 1946, Josephine Griselda (Marminiac, France), only da of late Charles Wilfrid Janson, of 16 Wilton Crescent, SW1:—
James, *b* 1947; *ed* Gordonstoun. —— Iain, *b* 1949; *ed* Gordonstoun. —— Catherine, *b* 1958.

The earliest surname under which the family of Colquhoun is traced is that of Kilpatrick. Sir John Colquhoun of Luss, 14th in descent from Umphridus de Kilpatrick (*temp* Alexander II), was created a baronet of Nova Scotia by Charles I. Sir Humphrey Colquhoun, 3rd Bt, in 1704 resigned his Baronetcy to the Crown, and obtained a new patent with the old precedency, but with the remainder to his son-in-law James Grant, (who on succeeding to the Baronetcy assumed the surname of Colquhoun, but resumed that of Grant in 1719) and the heirs male of his marriage with Sir Humphrey's da (*see* E Seafield). In 1786 James, 4th son of the above mentioned James Grant, was *cr* a Baronet of Great Britain. The 3rd baronet (*cr* 1786), sat as MP for Dunbartonshire in 1802; and Sir James, the 4th baronet (who *m* 1843, Jane, 2nd da of Sir Robert Abercromby, 5th Bt, of Birkenbog, co Banff), was Lord-Lieut of Dunbartonshire, and MP (*L*) therefor 1837-41. Sir James, 5th Bt, was also Lord-Lieut of Dunbartonshire 1887-1907. Lieut-Col Sir Iain Colquhoun, KT, DSO, LLD, Scots Guards, was Lord-Lieut of Dunbartonshire, Lord High Commr for Church of Scotland 1932, 1940, and 1941, and Lord Rector of Glasgow Univ 1934.

COLT (E) 1694, of St James's-in-the-Fields Liberty of Westminster, Middlesex

He conquers who endures

Sir EDWARD WILLIAM DUTTON COLT, 10th *Baronet*, son of late Major John Rochfort Colt, North Staffordshire Regt, half-brother of 9th baronet; *b* 22 Sept 1936; *s* his uncle *Sir* HENRY ARCHER, DSO, MC 1951; *ed* Douai; MB BS, London: FRCP; FACP; Associate Clinical Prof of Medicine, Columbia Univ, and Associate Attending Physician St. Luke's Hosp, New York, NY 10025: *m* 1st, 1966 (*m diss* 1972), Jane Caroline, da of James Histed Lewis, of 12 Pont Céard, Versoix, Geneva, and Washington, DC; 2ndly, 1979, Suzanne Nelson (*née* Knickerbocker), and has had issue by 2nd *m*.

Arms – Argent, a fesse between three colts courant sable. **Crest** – A colt passant or.
Residence – 12 E 88th St, New York, NY 10128, USA.

SON DECEASED (*By 2nd marriage*)

Tristan Charles Edward, *b* 27 June 1983; *d* 19 May 1992.

DAUGHTER LIVING (*By 2nd marriage*)

Angela Cecily, *b* 1979.

SISTER LIVING

Joan Margaret Roper, *b* 1932.

The pedigree of this family commences with Thomas Colt, of Carlisle; his son, Thomas Colt, of Essex and Suffolk (Keeper of the Rolls of Chancery in Ireland, and a Privy Councillor to King Edward IV), was father of John Colt, whose da Joan (or Jane) was 1st wife of Sir Thomas More, Lord Chancellor of England. From him descended George Colt (son of Sir Henry Colt, Knt, who was son of George Colt, High Sheriff of Suffolk 1587, and great-grandson of Sir George Colt, Knt); he was father of the 1st baronet, Sir Henry Dutton Colt, Adj to Prince Rupert, Ensign of the Yeoman of the Guard, and MP for Westminster *temp* William III and Anne. His brother, John Dutton Colt, was MP for Leominster, and his brother, Sir William Dutton Colt, Knt, was Master of the Horse to Prince Rupert, and Envoy at the Courts of Hanover and Dresden.

COLTHURST (I) 1744, of Ardrum, co Cork

Justum et tenacem

Just and firm of purpose

Sir RICHARD LA TOUCHE COLTHURST, 9th *Baronet*; *b* 14 Aug 1928; *s* his father, *Sir* RICHARD ST JOHN JEFFERYES, 1955; *ed* Harrow, and Peterhouse, Camb (MA); Member Dendrology Society; Organiser of Blarney Castle International Three Day Event, 1992, 1993 and 1994; a Liveryman of Grocers' Co: *m* 1953, Janet Georgina, da of late Leonard Almroth Wilson-Wright, of Coolcarrigan, co Kildare, and has issue.

Arms – Argent, on a fesse azure between three colts courant sable, as many trefoils slipped or. **Crest** – A colt statant sable.
Seats – Blarney Castle, co Cork; Ardrum, Inniscarra, co Cork. *Clubs* – MCC, Pitt (Camb), Hawks' (Camb), 1 Zingari.

SONS LIVING

CHARLES ST JOHN (Turret Farm, Blarney, co Cork; MCC, RIAC (Dublin) and City University Clubs), *b* 21 May 1955; *ed* Eton, Magdalene Coll, Camb (MA), and Univ Coll, Dublin; Solicitor, Cork: *m* 1987, Nora Mary, da of Mortimer Kelleher, of Dooniskey, Lissarda, co Cork, and has issue living, John Conway La Touche, *b* 13 Oct 1988, — Charlotte Louisa Margaret, *b* 1990, — Isabel Janet Denys *b* 1991. —— James Richard (Westholme Farm Cottage, Collins End, Goring Heath, Reading, Berks RG8 7RH; Leander, MCC); *b* 1957; *ed* Eton, and St Thomas's Med Sch, London Univ (BSc MB BS) 1982, FRCS (Edin) 1985; MBA (Brunel) 1992; inventor, medical business consultant: *m* 1990, Dominique G., elder da of Gale Coles, of Little Streele, Framfield, E Sussex. —— Henry Nicholas Almroth (1 Wandle Rd, SW17 7DL; MCC, Pitt (Camb)), *b* 1959; *ed* Eton, and Ch Coll, Camb (MA): *m* 1982, Sophia Selina Irene, yr da of (Frederick) John Charles Gordon Hervey-Bathurst, of Somborne Park, King's Somborne, Hants (*see* Hervey-Bathurst, Bt), and has issue living, Edward Henry John, *b* 1986, — Harriet Sophia, *b* 1984, — Caroline Georgina, *b* 1991.

DAUGHTER LIVING

Georgina Margaret, *b* 1961; Underwriting Member of Lloyd's; Organiser of Blarney Castle International Three Day Event, 1992, 1993 and 1994; author of *Fighting Back* (1990).

BROTHER LIVING

George Silver Oliver Annesley, *b* 1931; *ed* Harrow and Trin Coll, Camb (MA); late 2nd Lt Life Gds; Member of London Stock Exchange, Partner de Zoete and Bevan 1961-81, Liveryman Goldsmiths' Co, Member of Court of Common Council (Broad St Ward) 1976-80: *m* 1st, 1959 (*m diss* 1966), Hon Elizabeth Sophia Sidney, el da of 1st Viscount De L'Isle, VC, KG, GCMG, GCVO; 2ndly, 1968, Caroline Romaine, da of late Cdr Anthony Boyce Combe (*see* Farquhar, Bt, colls, 1990 Edn), and has issue living, (by 1st *m*) Shaunagh Anne Henrietta *b* 1961: *m* 1980, Thomas Peter William Heneage (*see* E Morton, colls), — (by 2nd *m*) Romaine Louisa, *b* 1969, — Rowena Barbara, *b* 1971. *Residences* – The South Lodge, Pitchford, nr Condover, Shropshire SY5 7DN; Le Bourg, 16450 Beaulieu-sur-Sonnette, St Claud, Charente, France. *Clubs* – Turf, Pratt's and MCC.

HALF-SISTER LIVING (Daughter of 8th Baronet by 1st marriage)

Shournagh Dorothy, b 1914: m 1937, Robert Tristram Combe, Lt Coldm Gds, who d of wounds received in action at Dunkirk 1940, and has issue living, Richard Tristram (Earnshill, Hambridge, Langport, Som), b 1938; ed Eton; Capt Coldm Gds; Underwriting Member of Lloyds; a JP: m 1985, Mrs Bridgett Anne Glide, da of late Charles Fleetwood Crombie, of South Hillside, Strete, Dartmouth, Devon, — Henry Cecil (1st Floor, 15 Tai Yuen Village, Yung Shue Wan, Lamma Island, Hong Kong), b 1940: m 1st, 1968, Gillian Margaret, who d 1973, da of late Ralph Hancock, of Port Elizabeth, S Africa; 2ndly, 1975 (m diss 1992), Ingerise Andersen, and has issue living, (by 1st m) Nicholas Hamilton b 1969; Dip Eng; Leighton Engineering Ltd, Tsing Yi Island, Hong Kong, (by 2nd m) Kirstina Louise b 1977, Andrea Shournagh Margrethe b 1979. Residence – Hundry Lodge, Hambridge, nr Langport, Som.

The 1st baronet, Sir John Colthurst (el son of John Colthurst, of Ardrum and Ballyandy) was MP for Doneraile 1751-60, for Youghal 1761-8, and for Castle Martyr 1769-75. Sir John Conway Colthurst, 2nd Bt, d of wounds received in a duel 1787. Sir Nicholas Colthurst, 3rd Bt, was MP for Johnstown, Longford 1783-90, and for Castle Martyr 1791-5, and High Sheriff, co Cork 1788. Sir Nicholas Conway Colthurst, 4th Bt, was MP for the City of Cork 1812-29. Sir George Conway Colthurst, 5th Bt, was MP for Kinsale (L) 1863-74 and High Sheriff, co Cork 1850. Sir George St John Colthurst, 6th Bt, was High Sheriff, co Cork 1884; ADC to Lord Lieut of Ireland. Sir George Oliver Colthurst, 7th Bt, served in 1914-19 War as Capt Special Cav, South Irish Horse (Croix de Guerre). Sir Richard St John Jefferyes Colthurst, 8th Bt, was High Sheriff of co Dublin 1920-21.

Colyer-Fergusson, see Fergusson.

CONANT (UK) 1954, of Lyndon, co Leics.

It shall be given to him who tries

Sir JOHN ERNEST MICHAEL CONANT, 2nd *Baronet*; b 24 April 1923; s his father Sir ROGER JOHN EDWARD, CVO, 1973; ed Eton, and Corpus Christi Coll, Camb (BA); High Sheriff of Rutland 1960: m 1st, 1950, Periwinkle Elizabeth, who d 1985, elder da of late Dudley Thorp, of Brothers House, Kimbolton, Hunts; 2ndly, 1992, Mrs Mary Clare Attwater, yr da of William E. Madden, of Petersfield, Hants, and has issue by 1st m.

Arms – Per saltire gules and azure billetée or. **Crest** – A stag proper the dexter foreleg resting on a shield gules billetée or.
Residence – Periwinkle Cottage, Lyndon, Oakham, Rutland.

SONS LIVING (By 1st marriage)

(SIMON) EDWARD CHRISTOPHER, b 13 Oct 1958; ed Eton, and RAC Cirencester. —— William John Nathaniel, b 1970.

DAUGHTERS LIVING (By 1st marriage)

Fiona Elizabeth, b 1955: m 1987, Jonathan P. N. Driver, elder son of R. M. Driver, of Warren Bay, Watchet, Somerset, and has issue living, Alexander Edward, b 1990. —— Melanie Lucinda, b 1961: m 1986, Richard Alastair Firmston-Williams, son of late Gordon Firmston-Williams, and has issue living, Hamish Alastair, b 1991, —— Jessica Alice, b 1989, —— Emily Periwinkle, b 1994.

BROTHERS LIVING

Guy Timothy Geoffrey, b 1924; ed Stowe; formerly Fl Lt RAF; JP and DL Northants, High Sheriff 1969: m 1st, 1953 (m diss 19—), Elizabeth, da of late A. T. Handley, I of Wight; 2ndly, 1981, Davina Huntley, el da of Sir Guy Hope Holland, 3rd Bt, and has issue living (by 1st m), Rupert Edward Geoffrey, b 1964: m 1993, Kathryn Jean, 4th da of Harold Miller, of Bridgend, Glam, — Sheena Lorraine, b 1954, — Elizabeth Jane, b 1955, — Diana Juliet, b 1960: m 1985, Peter S. McMahon, 2nd son of R. F. McMahon, of NZ, — (by 2nd m) Melissa Sothern, b 1984. Residence – Bulwick Park, nr Corby, Northants. —— Charles Richard, b 1929; ed Eton: m 1958, Katherine Anne Ross, da of Hubert George Anthony Ross-Wilson, of Gaddesby, Leics, and has issue living, Caroline-Rose, b 1959: m 1988, Timothy John Hawkins, of 35 Nansen Rd, SW11, yr son of late Lt-Col Tony Hawkins, OBE, of Chelsea, SW10, and has issue living, William Anthony Charles Horatio b 1992, Charlotte Lucy b 1990, — Francesca Louise, b 1962: m 1986, Philip Henry Kendall, of 7 Cheltenham Terr, SW3, and has issue living, Josephine Louise b 1988, — Claudia Daphne, b 1991. Residence – Rose Cottage, Gaddesby, Leics LE7 4WD.

CONGREVE (UK) 1927, of Congreve, co Stafford (Extinct 1941)

Com Sir GEOFFREY CECIL CONGREVE, DSO, RN, 1st and last *Baronet*; ka 1941.

DAUGHTERS LIVING OF FIRST BARONET

Anne Henrietta, b 1923: m 1944, Richard M. T. Tyler, formerly Capt RE, and has issue living, (John) Christian Congreve, b 1945: m 1st, 1968 (m diss 1984), Kathryn Cornelia, da of late George Rader, of Old Red Hill Rd, Dauphin, Penn, USA; 2ndly, 1987, Ciaran Anne Magdalene (the actress Ciaran Madden), da of late James George Madden, of Glebe House, Tollesbury, Essex, and has issue living (by 1st m), Frederick Christian Townsend b 1975, Elisabeth Helen Madeleine b 1977, Madeleine Amelia Congreve b 1981, — (Richard Henry) Felix (12 Brandlehow Rd, SW15 2ED), b 1954, — Camilla Madeleine Mary, b 1946: m 1969, John Michael Antony Dinkel, who d 1991, of 14 Victoria Rd, Brighton, Sussex BN1 3FS, and has issue living, Cosima Lucy b 1971, Sophie Alexandra b 1975, — Amelia Henrietta Rose (10 Albany Rd, Montpelier, Bristol BS6 5LH), b 1950: m 1968 (m diss 1981), Mark Walter Fletcher, and has issue living, Benjamin Charles b 1971, Ellen Maisie Madeleine b 1973, Rose Athalie RANDLES b 1981. Residence – Brachamfield House, Burstock, Beaminster, Dorset. —— Marygold

Elizabeth, *b* 1926: *m* 1953, Maj Ian Stafford Alexander, Roy Irish Fusiliers (ret), and has issue living, Maria Congreve, *b* 1959; resumed her maiden name 1987: *m* 1983 1st, (*m diss* 1985), James Richard Anthony Bamford; 2ndly, 1989, as his 3rd wife, Maj Raymond Alexander Carnegie (*see* D Fife, colls). *Residence* – Castle Bank, Stowe by Chartley, Stafford. —— Carola, *b* 1929: *m* 1948 (*m diss* 1959), John Horatio Gordon Shephard, formerly Capt Gren Gds, who *d* 1993, and has issue living, Thomas Horatio Congreve (Claigan Farmhouse, Dunvegan, Isle of Skye), *b* 1949: *m* 1971, Hon Mary Anna Shaw, 2nd da of late Baron Kilbrandon, PC (Life Baron), and has issue living, Samuel *b* 1973, Edward Congreve *b* 1975, Francis *b* 1977, Christian *b* 1985, Josephine *b* 1981, —— Henry John (20 Lots Rd, SW10 0QF), *b* 1955. *Residence* – 20 Lots Rd, SW10.

STRICKLAND-CONSTABLE (E) 1641, of Boynton, Yorkshire

To the will of God

Sir ROBERT FREDERICK STRICKLAND-CONSTABLE, 11th *Baronet*; *b* 22 Oct 1903; *s* his brother, *Sir* HENRY MARMADUKE, 1975; *ed* Magdalen Coll, Oxford (MA DPhil); Lt-Cdr RNVR: *m* 1st, 1929 (*m diss* 1931), Rosalind Mary, da of Arthur Webster; 2ndly, 1936, Lettice, yst da of late Maj Frederick Strickland (infra), and has issue by 2nd *m*.

Arms – Quarterly: 1st and 4th, gules and vair a bend or, *Constable*; 2nd and 3rd, gules a chevron or, between three crosses-pattée argent on a canton ermine a buck's head erased and attired sable, *Strickland*. **Crest** – 1st, a ship, sails furled, all or.*Constable*; 2nd, a turkey cock in his pride proper, *Strickland*. *Residence* – 3 Chart Lane, Brasted, Westerham, Kent.

SONS LIVING (By 2nd marriage)

FREDERIC (Field House Farm, Flaxton, York), *b* 21 Oct 1944; *ed* Westminster, Corpus Christi Coll, Camb (BA), and London Business Sch (MSc): *m* 1982, Pauline Margaret, da of — Harding, and has issue living, Charles, *b* 1985, — Rose, *b* 1983. —— John Robert Francis (Combe Wood, Brasted, Westerham, Kent), *b* 1949; *ed* Bryanston, Slade Sch of Fine Art, and London Univ (Higher Dip in Fine Art): *m* 1971, Christine, da of D. W. Roberts, of St Paul's Cray, Kent, and has issue living, Thomas Robert, *b* 1976, — Louisa Emma, *b* 1979.

DAUGHTERS LIVING (By 2nd marriage)

Miranda, *b* 1938; *ed* London Univ (BA). —— Elizabeth Diana, *b* 1940; *ed* Roy Coll of Music (ARCM), and Staatliche Hochschüle für Musik, Cologne: *m* 1972, John Maxwell Fairley, BSc, and has issue living, Lucy Fiona, *b* 1974, — Alice Susannah, *b* 1977.

WIDOW LIVING OF TENTH BARONET

Countess (ERNESTINE) EDINA (*Edina, Lady Strickland-Constable*) (Wassand Hall, nr Hull), da of late Rudolf, Count von Rex, formerly Saxon Min in Vienna: *m* 1929, Sir Henry Marmaduke Strickland-Constable, 10th Bt, who *d* 1975.

COLLATERAL BRANCHES LIVING

Issue of late Major Frederick Strickland, 2nd son of 8th baronet, *b* 1867, *d* 1934: *m* 1903, Mary Beatrix, who *d* 1965, da of late Sir John Isaac Thornycroft, LLD, FRS:—

Lettice (*Lady Strickland-Constable*), *b* 1913: *m* 1936, as his 2nd wife, Sir Robert Frederick Strickland-Constable, 11th Bt (ante).

Issue of late Capt Henry Strickland, OBE, RN, 4th son of 8th baronet, *b* 1873, *d* 1934: *m* 1910, Hon Ida Mary Hazel Willoughby, who *d* 1965, da of 10th Baron Middleton:—

Monica Lucy Ann, BSc, *b* 1916; BSc London Univ 1938. *Residence* – Barton Hill House, Whitwell, York, YO6 7JY.

Grandsons of late Walter Richard Strickland (who assumed by deed poll 1886 the surname of Cholmley, but continued to use the surname of Strickland), son of Rev Nathaniel Constantine Strickland, 6th son of 6th baronet:—

Issue of late Gerald Constantine Strickland, MM, *b* 1888, *d* 1962: *m* 1st, 1910 (*m diss* 1921), Mary, da of John Hampton, of Pretoria; 2ndly, 1922, Magdalene, da of Peter Hünten, of Pretoria, S Africa:—

(By 1st *m*) †Gerald John, *b* 1911; *ed* Rand Univ: *m* 1940, Patricia, who *d* 1988, da of Archibald Edward Benson, of Pretoria, and *d* 1993, leaving issue, John (Sunray Apartments 502, 7600 Blanco, San Antonio, Texas 78216, USA), *b* 1950, — Margaret Julia Patricia, *b* 1942: *m* 1978, Hubert Henri Malherbe, of 12105 S Hidden Valley, Club Drive, Sandy, Utah 84092, USA.

Issue of late Arthur William Strickland, *b* 1890, *d* 1970: *m* 1918, Violet May, who *d* 1956, da of Edward S. Margerum, of Merrylands, W Aust:—

Stanley Arthur (28 Cavendish Rd, New Malden, Surrey), *b* 1920: *m* 1952, Eileen Mary, da of late Patrick Henry Keeley, of Surbiton and has issue living, Janet Frances, *b* 1960. —— John Edward (56 Chertsey Drive, N Cheam, Surrey) *b* 1923: *m* 1953, Rose Ena, da of late George Thomas William Greenfield, of N Cheam, Surrey, and has issue living, Christopher Graham, *b* 1962: *m* 1986, Tracey Susan, da of Charles Alec Lang, of Abbey Wood, London, and has issue living, Charlie *b* 1990, Lauren *b* 1986, — Susan Carol, *b* 1960: *m* 1977, Trevor Fisher, of Carshalton, Surrey, and has issue living, Alan David *b* 1977, Liam Steven *b* 1991, Natalie Alison *b* 1979, — Alison Ruth, *b* 1966: *m* 1989, Frederick Charles Wakelin, of Shepperton, Middx, and has issue living, Charlotte Rose *b* 1990, Rachel Louise *b* 1992.

Granddaughters of late Hugh Strickland, 2nd son of late Rev Nathaniel Constantine Strickland, 6th son of 6th baronet:—

Issue of late Nathaniel Lewis Hugh Strickland, *b* 1899, *d* 1954: *m* 1923, Unity Margaret, who *d* 1975, da of late Arthur Birch:—

Mavis Rae, *b* 1929: *m* 1952, Eric Richard Earl, of 7 Lombardy Drive, Berkhamsted. —— Mary Joy, *b* (twin) 1929: *m* 1952, George Arthur Jones, of Hayley House, Main St, Brancaster, N Norfolk. —— Margaret Anne, *b* 1932: *m* 1st, 1953 (*m diss* 1977), Lionel Wood; 2ndly, 1977, Dr Israel Kessel, who *d* 1985, of The Stables, Little Common, Stanmore, Middx.

Grandchildren of late Robert Strickland, elder son of Walter Strickland, eldest son of George Strickland, 2nd son of 5th baronet:—
Issue of late Claude Francis Strickland, CIE, b 1881, d 1962: m 1915, Dorothy Lisa, who d 1972, da of late G. A. Branson, MD, of Dandaraga, Riddell, Victoria, Australia:—
Patricia Elizabeth Mary, b 1916: m 1941, Col Arthur Vyvyan Denton, Loyal Regt, of The Dial House, Lower Bourne, Farnham, Surrey, and has issue living, Amanda Elizabeth Ann Vyvyan, b 1943: m 1968, David Frederick James Leathers (see V Leathers), — Joanna Mary Vyvyan, b 1946: m 1974, Martyn Laurence. —— Frances Pamela Ann, b 1919: m 1st, 1942, Anthony William Vivian, RAF Vol Reserve, who was ka in Mediterranean 1942; 2ndly, 1946, Capt Anthony James Parr, of Old Dove House, Kingbourne Green, Harpenden, Herts, and has issue living, (by 2nd m) Francis Nicholas, b 1949: m 1974, Sakiko Fukuda, — Laetitia Mary, b 1948: m 1970, William Logan Jack, of Huntingdon Court, Kington, Herefords, and has issue living, Robert Logan b 1977, Rosemary Ann b 1979.
Issue of late Cecil Eustace Strickland, BSc, b 1889, d 1981: m 1st, 1923 (m diss 1942), Dorothy Enid, 2nd da of Edward Stocker, of Blackheath, SW; 2ndly, 1949, Galatea, da of Costas Patzatzis, of Cairo:—
(By 1st m) Martin Robert Cecil (4 Irene Rd, Rondesbosch, Cape, S Africa), b 1927; BSc, MIEE: m 1953, Judith Melvia, da of Cecil Kerr, and has issue living, Walter Robert Cecil, b 1954: m 1980, Christine Clark, and has issue living, James Robert b 1984, Natalie Judith b 1982, Kyle Rhoana b 1989, — Hugh Edward, b 1955: m 1984, Bridget Newmarch, and has issue living, Charles Robert b 1987, Evelyn Judith b 1985, — Kenneth William, b 1959, — Alexander David, b 1965. —— Walter Nicholas (4293 South Deer Run Court, Cross Plains, WI 53528, USA), b 1930; PhD: m 1st, 1956 (m diss 1964), Margaret Brown, of Dunoon, Argyll; 2ndly, 1968, Marie, da of Lynn Shields, of Salt Lake City, and has issue living, (by 1st m) Gina Elizabeth, b 1963, — (by 2nd m) Robert Nicholas, b 1971. —— Jessica Helen, b 1951: m 19—, Philip Lissaman, of Marlborough, NZ, and has issue living, Bridget, b 1979, — Claire, b 1982, — Sandra, b 1983.
Issue of late Clement Cyprian Strickland, b 1892, d 1943: m 1920, Violet Isobel, who d 1983, da of late Meyrick Edward Selby-Lowndes, JP, of Mursley Grange, Winslow, Bucks:—
Rev Paul Clement Lowndes, b 1921: m 1950, Emily Hartley, of Pontefract, and has had issue, Walter Francis Lowndes, b 1953; ed St John's, Leatherhead; d 1970, — Janet Elizabeth, b 1951: m 1979, Allan James Miller, of Carthona, 209 Woodbridge Rd, Ipswich, Suffolk, — Mary Isobel, b 1961.

Granddaughters of late Walter Kennedy Strickland, son of late Charles Strickland, son of late George Strickland (ante):—
Issue of late Com Charles Walter Campbell Strickland, RN, b 1873, d 1918: m 1909, Constance Margaret Lorn Campbell (who d 1959, having m 2ndly, 1928, Benjamin Charles Apps), da of late Major F. W. Campbell, RHA:—
Katarin Jarrard Campbell, b 1914: m 1938, John Evan Privett, of Priory Cottage, Naish, East Coker, Yeovil, Som, and has issue living, John Hugh Charles, b 1939: m 1971, Jane Dilys Rowland Macqueen, and has issue living, Jonathan Edward Macqueen b 1972, Rowland Alexander Charles b 1978, Guy Frederick Andrew b 1981, Philada Jane b 1974, — Robin Jarrard Campbell, b 1940: m 1964, Penelope Lisbeth Bate, and has issue living, James Jarrard Campbell b 1966, Edward Tobias b 1970, Kathryn Louise b 1968, — Alan Frederick, b 1943: m 1st, 1975 (m diss 19—), Carolin Graham Fawcett; 2ndly, 1981, Jenny Maria Miller, and has issue living (by 2nd m), Imogen Frances b 1981, Alice Rose b 1987, — Christina Katarin b 1946: m 1984, Cedric Thomas Sandford, and has issue living, Anna Elizabeth b 1990.

Granddaughters of late Algernon Henry Peter Strickland, son of late Algernon Augustine de Lille Strickland (infra):—
Issue of late Algernon Walter Strickland, b 1891, d 1938: m 1915, Lady Mary Charteris, who d 1991, having m 2ndly, 1943, Major John George Lyon, RA, da of 11th Earl of Wemyss:—
Pamela Sabina, b 1921: m 1947, Maj Henry Benjamin Van Der Gucht, MC, late R Northumberland Fusiliers, and has issue living, Guy Tristam, b 1951, — Hugo Charles, b 1956, — Juliet Clare, b 1948. Residence – Apperley Court, Gloucester. —— Sara Ann Mary (Lady Carr), b 1926: m 1950, Prof Sir (Albert) Raymond Maillard Carr, late Warden of St Anthony's Coll, Oxford, of Burch, N Molton, N Devon, and has issue living, Adam Henry Maillard, b 1951, — Matthew Xavier Maillard (4 Perham Rd, W14), b 1953; Portrait Painter: m 1988, Lady Anne Mary Somerset, only da of 11th Duke of Beaufort, and has issue living, Eleanor b 1992, — Alexander Rallion Charles, b 1958, — Laura Selina Madeline, b 1954: m 1978, Richard Edmond Barrowclough, of Burch, N Molton, N Devon, and has issue (see E Limerick, colls). Residence – Pyncombe Farm, Wiveliscombe, Som.

Grandchildren of late Claud Hugh Strickland, 4th and yst son of Algernon Augustine de Lille Strickland, elder son of Augustine Edmund Christopher Strickland (infra):—
Issue of late Walter Claud Strickland, b 1896; d 1982: m 1st, 1932 (m diss 1946), Charmian Louise, only child of Lt-Col Harold Cazenove Hessey, of Bethersden, Kent; 2ndly, 1954, Mary Julianne, el da of late Wilfred Henry Kellam-Harris, of Putney, SW:—
(By 2nd m) Walter Hugh Jeremy, b 1960.
Issue of late Hugh Baring Strickland, b 1899, d 1972: m 1954, Pauline (Ventonvaise, Callestick, Truro), da of P. Wood, of Shaldon, Devon:—
Christopher Claud Hugh, b 1955. —— Sarah Janet, b 1962.

Grandchildren of late Walter Cecil Strickland, son of late Augustine Edmund Christopher Strickland, 4th son of late George Strickland, 2nd son of 5th baronet:—
Issue of late Dudley Herbert Cecil Strickland, b 1860, d 1953: m 1901, Margaret, who d 19—, da of Edwin J. Gilbert, of San Bernardino, California, USA:—
Arthur Cecil, b 1902. —— Violet St Leger: m 19—, — Frederick Segrist.
Issue of late Cecil St Leger Strickland, b 1876, d 1929: m 1903, Lucy Estes, who d 1968, da of late Henry Edward Smithes, of Mount Pleasant, Kansas, USA:—
Joan, b 1908: m 1933, Maj George Vilett Rolleston, Worcestershire Regt (Supplementary Reserve), and has issue living, George Lancelot St Leger, MBE, b 1939; Capt Coldstream Guards; MBE (Mil) 1969: m 1976, Claude-Annie, da of N. J. Cointet, of Paris and Beirut, and has issue living, James Andrew St Leger b 1981, Natalia Lucy b 1980. Residence – Holetown House, Sampford Spiney, Yelverton, S Devon.
The 1st baronet, Sir William Strickland, was summoned to Cromwell's House of Peers as Lord Strickland. The 3rd baronet was a distinguished MP during the reigns of William III, Anne and George I, and the 4th baronet was a Lord of the Treasury and Secretary for War temp George II. The 7th baronet assumed, in 1865, by royal permission, the surname of Cholmley for himself and those of his heirs male who may succeed to the Cholmley estates. He m 1818, Mary, da and heir of Rev Charles Constable of Wassand, Yorks. Sir Walter William Strickland, 9th Bt, became a Czechoslovakian citizen and did not use the title.

Constable-Maxwell-Scott, see Scott.

COOK (UK) 1886, of Richmond, Surrey

Esse quam videri

To be rather than to seem

Sir CHRISTOPHER WYMONDHAM RAYNER HERBERT COOK, 5th *Baronet*; *b* 24 March 1938; *ed* King's Sch, Canterbury; late RAF; *s* his father, *Sir* FRANCIS FERDINAND MAURICE, 1978; Co Dir since 1979; Dir Diamond Guarantees Ltd 1980-91: *m* 1st, 1958 (*m diss* 1975), Malina, da of Aster Gunasekera, and formerly wife of Cyril Wettasinghe, of Ceylon; 2ndly, 1975, Margaret, da of late John Murray, and formerly wife of Ronald Miller, and has issue living by 1st and 2nd *m*.

Arms – Gules, a rose argent barbed and seeded proper between three crescents of the second, a chief vaire. **Crest** – Issuant from a chaplet of roses gules a dexter arm embowed proper, holding in the hand a mullet of six points or between two branches of oak vert.
Residence – La Fontenelle, Ville au Roi, St Peter Port, Guernsey, CI, GY1 1NZ.

SONS LIVING *(By 1st marriage)*

RICHARD HERBERT ASTER MAURICE, *b* 30 June 1959.

(By 2nd marriage)

Alexander James Frederick, *b* 1980.

DAUGHTERS LIVING *(By 1st marriage)*

Priscilla Melina, *b* 1968.

(By 2nd marriage)

Caroline Emma, *b* 1978.

HALF-SISTER LIVING *(Daughter of 4th Bt by 6th marriage)*

Cleone Willa Johanne Vera Rosemary (25 Ampthill St, Norwich, Norfolk), *b* 1952: *m* 1970 (*m diss* 1983), Peter Wilson, and has issue living, Stuart Francis James, *b* 1971, — Catherine Jane Brenda Rachael, *b* 1972.

MOTHER LIVING

Joan Loraine, da of John Aloysius Ashton-Case: *m* 1937 (*m diss* 1942), as his 3rd wife, Sir Francis Cook, 4th Bt, who *d* 1978. *Residence* – 22 Springfield Av, Hartley Wintney, Hants.

WIDOW LIVING OF FOURTH BARONET

BRIDGET BRENDA (*Dowager Lady Cook*), da of late Thomas David Lynch, and formerly wife of late Capt John Barclay Polland, RNVR: *m* 1956, as his 7th wife, Sir Francis Ferdinand Maurice Cook, 4th Bt, FRSA, who *d* 1978. *Residence* – Le Coin, La Haule, St Aubin, Jersey, CI.

COLLATERAL BRANCHES LIVING

Grandson of late Wyndham Francis Cook (infra):—
Issue of late Humphrey Wyndham Cook, *b* 1893, *d* 1978: *m* 1st, 1926 (*m diss* 1934), Gillian, da of late Frederick William Hedderley, of Oxford; 2ndly, 1941, Anne Beattie Blakeley, who *d* 197-, da of late John Moffett, of Ballynnhinch, N Ireland:—
(By 1st *m*) William Wyndham Humphrey, *b* 1928.

Issue of late Wyndham Francis Cook, 2nd son of 1st baronet, *b* 1860, *d* 1905: *m* 1887, Frederica Evelyn Stilwell, who *d* 1925, da of late F. J. Freeland, of Chichester:—
Ursula Maud Wyndham, *b* 1900: *m* 1st, 1921 (*m diss* 1924), Highat Cecil Harcourt Smith, son of Sir Cecil Harcourt Smith, CVO; 2ndly, 1924, Cecil Walter Lazenby.

The 1st baronet, Sir Francis Cook (son of late William Cook, of Roydon Hall, Kent), was *cr Visconde de Monserrate*, of Cintra, Portugal, and was founder and donor of Queen Alexandra's House (an institution for lady art students), Kensington Gore, and a well-known collector of works of art. Sir Frederick Lucas, 2nd Bt, was head of the firm of Cook, Son and Co, warehousemen and Shippers, of St Paul's Churchyard, EC, and SAT as MP for Lambeth, Kennington Div (C) 1895 to 1906. Sir Herbert Frederick, 3rd Bt, Bar-at-law, was a Trustee of National Gallery 1923-30, and National Portrait Gallery 1916-30, and author of Giorgione, and Reviews & Appreciations and other publications.

COOKE (E) 1661, of Wheatley Hall, Yorkshire

Sir DAVID WILLIAM PERCEVAL COOKE, 12th *Baronet*, *b* 28 April 1935; *s* his father, *Sir* CHARLES ARTHUR JOHN, 1978; *ed* Wellington, RMA Sandhurst, and Open Univ (BA 1983); Lt-Col RCT; FCIT, FBIM, AMInstTA, AssocRAeS: *m* 1959, Margaret Frances, da of late Herbert Skinner, of Knutsford, Ches, and has issue.

𝕬rms – Or, a chevron gules between two lions passant-guardant sable. 𝕮rest – Out of a mural crown argent, a demi-lion guardant issuant as in the arms gorged with a ducal coronet or.
Residence – Flat 5, Rolph Court, Fosseway Av, Moreton-in-Marsh, Glos.

DAUGHTERS LIVING

Sara Elisabeth Mary, *b* 1960: *m* 1984, Darren P. Grosvenor, and has issue living.
—— Louise Diana Margaret, *b* 1962: *m* 1986 (*m diss* 1988), Michael Moriarty.
—— Catherine Faith Maria, *b* 1968.

SISTER LIVING

Amanda Norah Mildred, FRES, *b* 1939: *m* 1st, 1964 (*m diss* 1970), David Old; 2ndly 1975, Robert W. Watson, FAIA, FCIS, FFAA, FBAA, FCommA, FRES, who *d* 1982, and has issue living (by 1st *m*), Amanda Mary Perceval, *b* 1966. *Residence* – 15 Bilton Grove Av, Harrogate, N Yorks.

AUNT LIVING

Elizabeth Hera, *b* 1928: *m* 1968, Group Capt Cecil Edgar Arthur Garton, OBE, RAF (ret), of Quinta da Boa Vista, Funchal, Madeira, and has issue living, Patrick William, *b* 1969, —— Dorothy Margaret, *b* 1970.

COLLATERAL BRANCHES LIVING

Issue of late William Francis Henry Cooke, el son of 10th baronet, *b* 1903, *d* 1950: *m* 1946, Irene Mary, widow of Capt O. Belingham Smith:—
Patricia Irene Mildred, *b* 1949.

Granddaughter of late Arthur Gordon Wyatt Cooke, yr son of 9th baronet:—
Issue of late William Bryan Cooke, *b* 1909, *d* 1974: *m* 1959, Marion June, yr da of late Maj Mervyn Hampden Corsellis:—
Marion Nathalie COOKE, *b* 1960; MA 1983, MA 1987, PhD 1990; Assist Prof, English Dept, McGill Univ; retained surname of Cooke after marriage: *m* 1984, Samuel Altman, LLB, MBA, of Toronto, Ontario, Canada, and has issue living Jordan Saul Cooke ALTMAN, *b* 1988, —— Bryan Jeremy ALTMAN, *b* 1990, —— Simon Zev ALTMAN, *b* 1993.

Grandchildren of late George Bryan Cooke-Yarborough, son of George Cooke-Yarborough (*b* 1794), son of John Cooke-Yarborough (*b* 1765), grandson of George Cooke, 2nd son of 3rd baronet:—
Issue of late George Eustace Cooke-Yarborough, *b* 1876, *d* 1938: *m* 1914, Daphne Isabel (who *m* 2ndly, 1950, Capt Tadeusz Mincer, who *d* 1969, and *d* 1984), yr da of Henry Cordy Wrinch of Ipswich:—
EDMUND HARRY, *b* 25 Dec 1918; *ed* Canford Sch, Ch Ch Oxford (BA 1944, MA 1944); FEng; formerly Dep Ch Scientist UK Atomic Energy Authority (ret): *m* 1952, Anthea Katharine, da of John Alexander Dixon, of King Charles Cottage, Colden Common, nr Winchester, and has issue living, Anthony Edmund (73 Ravenscourt Rd, W6 0UJ), *b* 1956; *ed* Eton, and Gonville and Caius Coll, Camb (MA): *m* 1990, Joanna S., da of Anthony Northrop, of Felgate Farm, Ashfield-cum-Thorpe, Stowmarket, Suffolk, and has issue living, George Edmund *b* 1991, Eliza Flora *b* 1993, —— Jane Anthea, *b* 1958: *m* 1986, Giles Vicat, of Woodbine Cottage, Bucknell, Bicester, Oxon OX6 9RS, elder son of Alan Vicat, of Shoreham-by-Sea, Sussex, and has issue living, Felix *b* 1989, Theodore *b* 1993. *Residence* – Lincoln Lodge, Longworth, nr Abingdon, Oxon OX13 5DU.

Grandchildren of late Capt Orfeur Frederick Cooke-Yarborough (*infra*):—
Issue of late Bryan Orfeur Eustace Cooke-Yarborough, *b* 1907, *d* 1987: *m* 1938, Ellen (Nellie) Martha, who *d* 1974, da of late John Myers, of Mount Silinda, Zimbabwe:—
Edmund Orfeur (160 Marimba Rd, Matsheumhlope, Bulawayo), *b* 1940: *m* 1966, Jennifer Anne, da of Lt-Col John Winterton Scott, and has issue living, David Jon Orfeur, *b* 1970, —— Nichola Joan, *b* 1966: *m* 1987, Roderick Young. —— Rosemary Anne, *b* 1945: *m* 1966, Rodney Franklin Buckley, of 60A Padfield Rd, Pinetown 3600, Natal, and has issue living, Craige Franklin, *b* 1970, —— Samantha Anne, *b* 1974. —— Susan Mary, *b* 1951: *m* 1973, Jacobus Petrus van Lelyveld, of 13 Moubray Cres, Triangle, Zimbabwe, and has issue living, Darren Richard, *b* 1974, —— Tracy Lee, *b* 1977, —— Sherryl Lyn, *b* 1979.
Issue of late Thomas Nicholas Cooke-Yarborough, *b* 1910, *d* 1991: *m* 1940, Elizabeth Thomson (6 Westbury Court, Hedge End, Southampton), da of late William Gilmore, of Edinburgh:—
Nicholas Michael, *b* 1941: *m* 1967, Sheila, da of R. Symonds, of Southampton, and has issue living, Sarah Louise, *b* 1969, —— Claire Elizabeth, *b* 1972.

Grandchildren of late George Bryan Cooke-Yarborough (*ante*):—
Issue of late Capt Orfeur Frederick Cooke-Yarborough, *b* 1878, *d* 1965: *m* 1906, Anne (Nancy) Henrietta Lucy, who *d* 1965, el da of late Rev William Wyatt, R of Broughton Brigg, Lincs:—
Nancy Penelope Mary (Spicers, Newtown, Heytesbury, Warminster, Wilts BA12 0HN), *b* 1912: *m* 1939, Lt-Col George Michael Donaldson Wingate, RA, who *d* 1970, and has issue living, Elizabeth Anne, *b* 1940, —— Sarah Penelope, *b* 1944: *m* 1964, Lt Michael R. R. Peever, RN, who *d* 1982, and has issue living, Richard Charles *b* 1971. —— Orfeur Henrietta Rosemary, *b* 1918; formerly in ATS: *m* 1944, Maj William Victor Smith, Lancs Yeo, of March Wall, King's Drive North, Caldy, Wirral, Ches L48 1LL, and has issue living, Richard Orfeur Bateson (12 Thurstaston Rd, Irby, Wirral), *b* 1949: *m* 1984, Vivien Dovey, —— Rosemary Julia, *b* 1945: *m* 1972, John Brian Cheshire, of 14 Maes-y-Llan, Llanfairtalhaiarn, Clwyd, and has issue living, Melissa Rosemary Jean *b* 1972, Alkana Susan *b* 1978.
Issue of late Humfrey Charles Cooke-Yarborough, *b* 1880, *d* 1955: *m* 1911, Honor Lake, who *d* 1977, da of late Col Henry Lake Wells, CIE, RE:—
Michael Humfrey (33 Alde Lane, Aldeburgh, Suffolk), *b* 1915; is an architect: *m* 1942, Pamela, da of late Sir John Baldwin, KCMG, CB, and has issue living, Ann, *b* 1944: *m* 1967, Alain Paul René Nérot, of 14 Allées des Acacias, 137170 Chambray-les-Tours, France, and has issue living, Alex *b* 1975, Lucie *b* 1974, —— Penelope *b* 1946: *m* 1974, George Roger Frank Wall-bridge, of The Chapel, Roe Green, Sandon, Buntingford, Herts SG9 0QJ. —— Steven Sandford, *b* 1919; an Engineer; formerly Capt RE: *m* 1941, Evelyn, da of late Charles Buccleuch Scott, of Trinidad, and has issue living, Christopher (6802 SW 64th Av S, Miami, FL 33143, USA), *b* 1949, —— Nicholas (701 SE 51st Av, Ocala, FL, USA), *b* 1952: *m* 1983, Tina, da of

Marco Sierra, of Miami, Florida, and has issue living, Michael Charles *b* 1988, Stephanie Marie *b* 1986. *Residence* – 3555 Crystal Court, Miami, Florida 33133, USA. —— Eustace, *b* 1921; an Industrial Designer: *m* 1981, Patricia Marion Gardiner. *Residence* – Spring House, Priors Way, Aldeburgh, Suffolk.

Granddaughter of late Alfred Cooke-Yarborough, 2nd son of George Cooke-Yarborough (*b* 1794) (ante):—
    Issue of late Randall Francis Cooke-Yarborough, *b* 1883, *d* 1980: *m* 1917, Norma, who *d* 1970, da of George Downes, of Opara, Hokianga, NZ:—
Pauline, *b* 1923: *m* 1947, Raymond Leslie Gerrard Rogers, of Nilgrid, S India, and has issue living, Sandra Frances, *b* 1946, — Diana Leslie, *b* 1948.

Grandchildren of late Richard Cooke-Yarborough (*b* 1851), son of Richard Cooke-Yarborough (*b* 1805), son of John Cooke-Yarborough (ante):—
    Issue of late Francis Michael Cooke-Yarborough, *b* 1904, *d* 1970: *m* 1933, Mary, who *d* 1965, da of late Everett L. Hudson, of Newcastle-upon-Tyne:—
Richard Everett (2 Ramsay Av, W Pymble, NSW), *b* 1935; BSc (Honours) 1961, FAIAS 1983: *m* 1960, Sheila Margaret, da of late John Hugill, of Strathnaver, Walton, Brampton, Cumberland, and has issue living, Helena Margaret, *b* 1960; BSc (Hons): *m* 1983, John Robert Croker, of 17 Constitution Rd, Dulwich Hill, NSW, — Claire Mary, *b* 1963, — Ruth Meryl *b* 1967. —— Jean Christine, *b* 1937: *m* 1960, Alan Keith Martin, BSc, PhD, of Dalmore, Greenhead, Mauchline, Ayrshire, and has issue living, Colin Seath, *b* 1962, — Patricia Anne, *b* 1964, — Christine Fiona, *b* 1966, — Mary Kay, *b* 1967. —— Mary Elizabeth *b* 1942: *m* 1965, Robert Alexander Porteous, of 65 Lyncroft Gdns, Hounslow, Middx, and has issue living, Alexander Michael, *b* 1967 — Robert James, *b* 1968.

Grandchildren of Richard Cooke-Yarborough (*b* 1805) (ante):—
    Issue of late Rev Canon John James Cooke-Yarborough, *b* 1855, *d* 1941: *m* 1890 Emily, who *d* 1947, da of late Richard Foster, of Homewood, Chislehurst:—
Margaret Hope (22 Dean Hill Ct, E Sheen, SW14), *b* 1891: *m* 1915, Herbert Prior Ingram, of Trinidad, who *d* 1943, and has issue living, Margaret Jane, *b* 1916: *m* 1945, Peter Hallett Fraser, and has issue living, Richard Thomas Yarborough *b* 1951, Robert Peter *b* 1954, Judy Rosemary *b* 1947, — Rosamond Marion, *b* 1918: *m* 1944, Alan Robson, and has issue living, Anthony Prior *b* 1946, Alicia Ann *b* 1950., — Elizabeth Serena, *b* 1904: *m* 1927 (*m diss* 1941), Sqd-Ldr Philip Jackson-Taylor, RAF, who was *k* on active ser 1945.

Grandson of late Charles Edward Cooke, son of late Capt Bryan William Darwin Cooke, 2nd son of late William Darwin Cooke (*b* 1764), only son of late Bryan Cooke, 2nd son of late John Cooke, 7th son of 3rd baronet:—
    Issue of late Capt Arthur Charles Darwin Cooke, *b* 1876, *d* 1963: *m* 1913, Muriel, who *d* 1958, el da of late Leonard Brownlow Horrocks:—
David Charles Darwin (175 Victoria Av, Remuera, Auckland, New Zealand), *b* 1917; Lt, New Zealand Forces; 1939-45 War: *m* 1944, Phyllis Edith, da of late Capt Arthur Henry Prosser, OBE, and has issue living, Richard Charles Darwin, *b* 1947: *m* 1972, Dorothy Jane, da of late Eric George Woollams, — Elizabeth Angela Darwin, *b* 1948: *m* 1970, Martin John Beattie, LLB, of 184 Popes Rd, Manurewa, Auckland, NZ, and has issue living, James Brian David *b* 1976, Rosemary Ann *b* 1971, Amanda Jane *b* 1973.
    Issue of late Philip Bryan Cooke, *b* 1886, *d* 1968: *m* 1st, 1909, Florence Alma, who *d* 1950, da of James Leamy, of Vancouver, BC; 2ndly, 1951, Katharine, who *d* 1963, da of David Walter Price, of Westerley, Rhode Island, USA:—
(By 1st *m*) Bryan Edward (Glenorie, Galah Drive, Hahndore 5245, S Australia), *b* 1910: Maj AIF (Reserve); 1939-45 War/ prisoner: *m* 1st, 1933 (*m diss* 1945), Margaret Ida, who *d* 1965, da of late Walter Hiskens, of Melbourne; 2ndly, 1946, June Mary, da of late Arthur Tregea, of Sydney, and has issue living (by 1st *m*) Robin May (Ganamead, Rocks Crossing, via Mt George, 2424 NSW, Australia), *b* 1936: *m* 1st, 1956 (*m diss* 1960), Michael Threlfall; 2ndly, 1961 (*m diss* 1983), Bruce Arthur Rickard, and has issue living (by 1st *m*) Philip *b* 1957, (by 2nd *m*) Samuel Bruce *b* 1962, James Arthur *b* 1963, Nicholas Lancelot *b* 1965, — (by 2nd *m*), Elizabeth Alice, *b* 1948: *m* 1st 1966 (*m diss* 1979), John Curley; 2ndly, 1980, Robert Michael Drury, of 5 Crampton Court, West Lakes, Adelaide 5021, S Aust, and has issue living (by 1st *m*), Louise Alice *b* 1967, Amanda June *b* 1970, Penelope Anne *b* 1971, (by 2nd *m*) Kathleen Bethal *b* 1981.

Grandson of late Lancelot Darwin Cooke (infra):—
    Issue of late Charles Bryan Cooke, *b* 1925, *d* 1975: *m* 1952, Vajira Wijesinghe Kannangara (Ramanathan Hall, Peradeniya, Sri Lanka):—
Arjuna Bryan, *b* 1953; BSc (Eng) (Sri Lanka), AMIEE (Lond): *m* 1990, Ramyamala Dhana Lakshmie Gunawardane. *Residence* – 21/9 Polhengoda Gdns, Colombo 5, Sri Lanka.

Granddaughter of late Rev Charles Herbert Cooke (infra):—
    Issue of late Lancelot Darwin Cooke, *b* 1891, *d* 1975: *m* 1922, Edith Euphemia Catherine, assumed the forename of Halimah in lieu of Edith Euphemia Catherine by deed poll 19—, da of late Maj Allan Ewen Grant, IMS:—
Sheila Beatrice (6630 Linda Vista Rd, Apt 3, San Diego, Ca 92111, USA), *b* 1923: *m* 1943, Lt-Col John A Nelson, Med Corp, US Army, who *d* 1963, and has issue living, James Darwin, *b* 1946, — Lance Edward, *b* 1947, — Richard Crosby, *b* 1949: *m* 1973, Nancy Mack, and has issue living, Colin Douglas *b* 1981, Dael Byrony *b* 1978.

Granddaughters of late Rev Charles Cooke, 4th son of late Bryan Darwin Cooke (*b* 1764) (ante):—
    Issue of late Rev Charles Herbert Cooke, *b* 1862, *d* 1946: *m* 1890, Ida Beatrice, who *d* 1941, da of late Rev G. F. A. Armstrong, R of Lorum, co Carlow:—
Marjorie Sheila (PO Box 86, Triangle, Zimbabwe): *m* 19—, Thomas Murray MacDougal, OBE, MC. —— Betty Mary (The Lodge, Bonmahon, co Waterford): *m* 1929, Louis Dennis Martin, and has issue living, Patrick Graeme, *b* 1930.

Grandchildren of late Maj Philip Tatton Davies-Cooke, OBE, el son of late Maj Philip Bryan Davies-Cooke, el son of late Philip Davies-Cooke, great grandson of late Henry Cooke 2nd son of 2nd baronet:—
    Issue of late Col Philip Ralph Davies-Cooke, CB, TD, *b* 1896, *d* 1974: *m* 1924, Kathleen Mabel, OBE, who *d* 1994, da of late William Hugh Davies-Cooke (infra):—
(Philip) Peter (Gwysaney Hall, Mold, Clwyd CH7 6PA), *b* 1925; late Capt 1st R Dragoons: *m* 1st, 1957, Jane, who *d* 1981, da of Edmund George Coryton (Carew, Bt, colls); 2ndly, 1985, Mrs Zinnia Mary Arfwedson (CHARLTON), elder da of late Col Reggie Hodgkinson, of Shennington House, Stratford upon Avon, and has issue living (by 1st *m*), Richard Piers, *b* 1960: *m* 1986, Sarah Jane, eldest da of John Latham, of Caldecott Hall, Farndon, nr Chester, and has issue living, James Portland *b* 1988, Sophie Jane *b* 1989, — Paul Bryan, *b* 1962, — Michael Anthony, *b* 1965: *m* 1993, Helen Marie, da of Eric Roberts, of Nercwys, Clwyd. —— David Ralph (25 Barkston Gdns, SW5), *b* 1930; late Capt R Welch Fus: *m* 1955, Henrietta Sarah Angénis, da of Edward Jan Hoos (see B Brownlow, 1990 Edn), and has issue living, Philip Rupert Hugh, *b* 1960, — Nicola Sarah Angénis, *b* 1958: *m* 1988, Ian William Reed, of Colpa, Gilgandra, NSW 2827, Australia, yr son of D. C. Reed, of Wirral, Molong, NSW, and has issue living, Emma Sarah Annabel *b* 1989, Alice Bronwyn Diana *b* 1991. —— Philippa Marjorie, *b* 1938: *m* 1961, William George Antony Warde-Norbury, late Coldm Gds, of Hooton Pagnell Hall, Doncaster, S Yorks, son of Harold George Warde-Norbury, and has issue living, Mark William Antony, *b* 1962, — Alistair George, *b* 1966.
    Issue of late Capt Richard Anthony Davies-Cooke *b* 1909, *d* 1962: *m* 1934, Berys who *d* 1966, da of late T. Fanning-Evans, of Plas Cadnant, Menai Bridge, Anglesey:—

Doris Caroline, *b* 1935: *m* 1971, Arthur Henry Grant, and has issue living, Arthur Paul, *b* 1972.

Grandson of late Bryan Davies POOLE; assumed by R Lic 1907 the surname of Poole in lieu of Cooke; eldest son of Col Bryan George Davies-Cooke, 2nd son of Philip Davies-Cooke (ante):—
Issue of late Capt Bryan Cudworth Halsted Poole, RWF, *b* 1892, *d* 1971; *m* 1925, Eleanor Margaret Lawson, who *d* 1948, da of Rt Hon Sir Adrian Knox, KCMG, KC, LLB.
Adrian Bryan (Dellawong, Box 279, Wellington 2820, NSW, Australia; *Clubs* – Union Sydney, Royal Sydney Golf), *b* 1927: *m* 1957, Philippa, da of Judge Adrian Herbert Curlewis, CVO, CBE and has issue living, Adrian Peter, *b* 1958, — Bryan David Edward, *b* 1964, — Belinda Margaret, *b* 1960, — Susan Philippa, *b* 1962.

Granddaughters of late Col Bryan George Davies-Cooke (ante):—
Issue of late William Hugh Davies-Cooke, *b* 1862, *d* 1941: *m* 1900, Mabel Louisa, who *d* 1956, da of late Capt E. W. Philips, of Rhûal Mold—
Sybil Gwynydd (Longcroft, Leeds Close, PO Highlands, Harare, Zimbabwe), *b* 1901. —— Kathleen Mabel, OBE, *b* 1903; Chm of Executive Committee of Girl Guides' Assoc of Great Britain 1948-51; OBE (Civil) 1964: *m* 1924, Col Philip Ralph Davies-Cooke, CB, TD, who *d* 1974 (ante).
This family was settled in the vicinity of Doncaster. Laurence Cooke, Prior of Doncaster 1536-38, was executed at Tyburn 1540 for denying the King's Supremacy. Sir George Cooke of Wheatley, Yorks, 1st Bt, was great-grandson of the prior's brother William. He received his baronetcy for his father's and his services for the Royal cause in the Civil War, with remainder to his next brother, Henry, who *s* as 2nd Bt 1683, and rebuilt Wheatley Hall.

COOPER (UK) 1821, of Gadebridge, Hertfordshire

Sir PATRICK GRAHAM ASTLEY COOPER, 6th *Baronet*, el son of late Col Clifton Graham Astley Cooper, DSO, RA, 3rd son of late Major Loftus Lewis Astley Cooper, 8th son of 2nd baronet; *b* 4 Aug 1918; *s* his kinsman, *Sir* HENRY LOVICK, 1959; *ed* Marlborough; formerly Senior Assist Land Commr, Min of Agriculture and Fisheries: *m* 1942, Audrey Anne, yr da of late Major Jervoise Collas, Mil Knight of Windsor, and has issue.

𝖆rms – Vert, a fesse embattled or between two pheons in chief, and as many thighbones saltirewise in base argent. Crest – Out of a mural crown argent, a demi-sphere erect proper, fringed or, pointed argent, and surmounted by two palm-branches in saltire vert.
Residence – The White Cottage, 3 Townside, Haddenham, Aylesbury, Bucks HP7 8BG.

Nothing is great that is not good

SON LIVING

ALEXANDER PASTON ASTLEY (8 Berkshire Close, Leight-on-Sea, Essex SS9 4RJ), *b* 1 Feb 1943: *m* 1974, Minnie Margaret, da of late Charles Harrison.

DAUGHTERS LIVING

Patricia Ann, *b* 1950; *ed* Malvern Girls' Coll, and E Anglia Univ: *m* 1979, Michael Robert Snodin, of 58 Leyborne Park, Kew, Richmond, Surrey, and has issue living, Oliver Karl Astley, *b* 1985. —— Helena Rosalind Collette, *b* 1958: *m* 1982, Jonathan David Holford, of 76 King St, Maryport, Cumbria, and has issue living, Graham Richard Desmond, *b* 1984, — Diana Sophia, *b* 1986.

COLLATERAL BRANCHES LIVING

Grandchildren of late Capt Albert Beauchamp Astley Cooper, 9th son of 2nd baronet:—
Issue of late Lieut-Col Geoffrey Beauchamp Astley Cooper, OBE, *b* 1884, *d* 1948: *m* 1st, 1911, Gladys Mary, who *d* 1912, da of Lieut-Col Orbell Henry Oakes of Nowton Court, Bury St Edmunds; 2ndly, 1914, Louisa Maude, who *d* 1972, da of late I. W. H. White, of West Lea, Meanwood, Leeds:—
(By 2nd *m*) Gerald Nigel Astley, *b* 1916; *ed* Wellington Coll; Maj (ret) 1st R Green Jackets: *m* 1st, 1941 (*m diss* 1945), Mary Constance, da of late Capt Basil Hamilton Piercy, RN (ret) (B Fortevoit); 2ndly, 1951, Joan Ryland, da of Dr Bernard Wall, of Coleshill, Warwickshire, and has issue living, (by 1st *m*) Juliet Jane, *b* 1942: *m* 1964, Peter Robert Bellfield, of The Old Rectory, Clopton, Woodbridge, Suffolk IP13 6QB, and has issue living, Robert James Astley *b* 1965; *ed* Framlingham Coll; Lieut RN: *m* 1994, Zoë, da of Capt Thomas Le Marchand, RN, of Hasketon, Woodbridge, Suffolk, Charles Peter *b* 1969; *ed* Uppingham, Edward Jonathan *b* 1972; *ed* Uppingham, — (by 2nd *m*) Desmond Beauchamp, *b* 1955; *ed* Wellington Coll (Scholar), and St Peters Coll, Oxford; with Algo Saibi of Bahrain: *m* 1984, Randa, da of Dr Joseph Yammine, and has issue living, Kimball *b* 1986, Joseph *b* (twin) 1986, — Felicity Ann, *b* 1954; *ed* Royal Sch, Bath, and Durham Univ: *m* 1981, Maj-Gen Anthony David Pigott, CBE, of Hessett, Bury St Edmunds, Suffolk, twin son of Lt-Col P. J. Pigott, of Bexhill-on-Sea, and has issue living, James Anthony Alexander *b* 1991, Matthew Thomas Michael *b* 1992, Anna Louisa *b* 1984. *Residence* – Five Bells Cottage, Hessett, nr Bury St Edmunds. —— Rosemary Anne, *b* 1920: *m* 1946, Lt-Col Peter Jarrett Lewis, The Buffs, who *d* 1983, and has issue living, Virginia Rosemary, *b* 1949: *m* 1974, Maj-Gen Roderick Alexander Cordy-Simpson, CB, OBE, Light Dragoons, and has issue living, Angus John *b* 1978, Zoë Finovola *b* 1976. *Residence* – Thedwastre, Thurston, nr Bury St Edmunds.

Granddaughters of late Clement Astley Paston Cooper, 10th son of 2nd baronet:—
Issue of late Stephen Clement Paston Cooper, *b* 1885, *d* 1935: *m* 1915, Florence Gertrude Taylor, who *d* 1966:—
Diana Susan, *b* 1919: *m* 1st, 1939 (*m diss* 1967), Com Cecil John Grenfell, RN (ret) (E Cavan, colls); 2ndly, 1969, Clive Walter Edwin Windsor-Richards, of Golf Lodge, Steepways, Hindhead, Surrey, GU26 6PQ, and has issue living (by 1st *m*), John Stephen (58 Heath Rd, Petersfield, Hants) *b* 1940; Capt RN: *m* 1967, Stephanie Ann, da of Capt James Marigold, RN, and has issue living, James Christopher *b* 1969, Nicholas Ian *b* (twin) 1969, Alastair Mark *b* 1974, — Richard Francis (12 Grindlestone Court, Whittinghame Lane, Goosnargh, Lancs PR3 2AU), *b* 1944: *m* 19—, Jennifer, da of —, — Michael Gerrard *b* 1947, — Sally Angela *b* (twin) 1947: *m* 1980, Francis Robert Gugen, of 24 Cheniston Gardens, W8 6TH, and has issue living, Lucy Francesca *b* 1981. —— Pamela Jane (Cheyne Lodge, Brook Rd, Wormley, Godalming, Surrey), *b* 1921: *m* 1966 (*m diss* 1974), Lt-Cdr John Woolven Anderton, VRD, RNVR (ret).

The 1st baronet, Sir Astley Paston Cooper (5th son of late Rev Samuel Cooper, DD, R of Great Yarmouth, Yelverton, and Morley), and was an eminent Surg. He was created a Baronet with special remainder, in default of male issue, to his nephew, Astley Paston Cooper (3rd son of his el brother, the Rev Samuel Lovick Cooper, R of Ingoldsthorpe and Barton, Norfolk), by whom he was *s*.

COOPER (UK) 1863, of Woollahra, New South Wales

Sir WILLIAM DANIEL CHARLES COOPER, 6th *Baronet*; *b* 5 March 1955; *s* his father, *Maj Sir* CHARLES ERIC DANIEL, 1984: *m* 1988, Julia Nicholson.

Arms – Azure, a chevron engrailed between two lions passant in chief and a star of eight points in base or. **Crest** – A lion sejant or, collared azure, supporting with the dexter paw a lance erect proper, and suspended therefrom by a chain or an escutcheon also azure charged with a star as in the arms.
Residence – 1 Victoria Cottages, Andover Rd, Micheldever Station, Winchester, Hants SO21 3AX.

BROTHER LIVING

GEORGE JOHN (21 The Little Boltons, SW10 9LJ; Hinton House, Ablington, Bibury, Cirencester, Glos), *b* 28 June 1956; *ed* Harrow.

WIDOW LIVING OF FIFTH BARONET

Perseverantia omnia vincit

Perseverance conquers all things

(MARY) ELISABETH (*Elisabeth, Lady Cooper*) (Pudley Cottage, Castle St, Aldbourne, Wilts SN8 2DA), da of late Capt John Eagles Henry Graham-Clarke, JP, of Frocester Manor, Stonehouse, Glos, and formerly wife of Robert Erland Nicolai d'Abo: *m* 1953, as his 2nd wife, Maj Sir Charles Eric Daniel Cooper, 5th Bt, The Royals, who *d* 1984.

COLLATERAL BRANCHES LIVING

Granddaughter of late Arthur Hamilton Cooper (infra):—
Issue of late Geoffrey Mervyn Cooper, *b* 1916, *d* 1984: *m* 1st, 1941 (*m diss* 1956), Elise Marie, da of late George McGregor Richmond, of Balnacraig, Perthshire; 2ndly, 1957 (*m diss* 19—), Jean Margaret, da of William Ross-Brown, of Durban, Natal; 3rdly, 19— (*m diss* 19—), Jean —:—
(By 1st *m*) Marie Frances Richmond (*Hon Mrs Robert Eliot*), *b* 1942; a JP of Cornwall: *m* 1st, 1979, A.R. Lusk, of Comrie, Perthshire, who *d* 1981; 2ndly, 1983, Hon (Montagu) Robert (Vere) Eliot (*see* E St Germans), who *d* 1994.

Issue of late Arthur Hamilton Cooper, 2nd son of 3rd baronet, *b* 1881, *d* 1973: *m* 1910, Mabel Alice, who *d* 1973, da of Sir William Henry Smith-Marriott, 5th Bt:—
Robert Henry (The Down House, Blandford St Mary, Dorset; Carlton Club), *b* 1922; *ed* RN Coll, Dartmouth; a JP of Dorset; 1939-45 War as Lt RN (wounded): *m* 1946, Teri, elder da of Emin Agolli Doshishti, by his wife HH Princess Adilé Zogu, sister of HM late King Zog of Albania, and has issue living, William Jeremy Daniel (Middle Farm House, Down House Estate, Blandford Forum, Dorset DT11 0HG), *b* 1951: *m* 1975, Teresa Margaret, da of late Ralph Ernest Bamford, of Frogmore, Winterbourne Whitchurch, Blandford Forum, Dorset, and has issue living, Daniel Alexander Westrow *b* 1982, Richard Gregory Christopher *b* 1984, Samuel Robert Paul *b* 1988, — Westrow Gerald Alan, *b* 1956: *m* 1986, Helen Margaret, da of George William Stokes, of 25 Greencourt Gdns, Croydon, and has issue living, Katherine Teri Helen *b* 1988.

The 1st baronet, Sir Daniel, GCMG, was the first Speaker of Legislative Assembly of NS Wales 1856-60.

COOPER (UK) 1905, of Shenstone Court, Shenstone, co Stafford

Sir RICHARD POWELL COOPER, 5th *Baronet*; *b* 13 April 1934; *s* his father, *Sir* FRANCIS ASHMOLE, 1987; *ed* Marlborough: *m* 1957, Angela Marjorie, elder da of Eric Wilson, of Norton-on-Tees, Durham, and has issue.

Arms – Ermine, on a pile argent three martlets sable, and on a chief gules two boars' heads couped or. **Crest** – Between two sprigs of holly erect a lion's jamb grasping in the paw a like sprig in bend sinister, all proper.
Residence – Lower Farm, Chedington, Beaminster, Dorset DT8 3HY. *Clubs* – Bucks and Carlton.

SON LIVING

RICHARD ADRIAN, *b* 21 Aug 1960; *ed* Millfield

DAUGHTERS LIVING

Jane Alice, *b* 1958. —— Belinda Gay, *b* 1963.

SISTERS LIVING

Jacqueline Margaret, *b* 1939: *m* 1962, Peter Desmond Flaherty, of Glen Cottage, Butlers Dene Rd, Woldingham, Surrey, and has issue living, Andrew Niall *b* 1970, — Sally Clodagh, *b* 1963, — Sheena Mary, *b* 1964, — Julia Siobhan, *b* 1966. —— Dione Frances, *b* 1944: *m* 1970, Christopher Bruce Jones, of Ashmole, RD Manurewa, Auckland, NZ.

Complete things attempted

WIDOW LIVING OF FOURTH BARONET

DOROTHY FRANCES HENDRIKA (*Dowager Lady Cooper*), da of late Emile Deen, of Berkhamsted Hill, Herts: *m* 1933, Sir Francis Ashmole Cooper, 4th Bt, who *d* 1987. *Residence* – Mas Folie, 320 Route de la Madeleine, 06140 Tourrettes S/Loup, France. The 1st baronet, Sir Richard Powell, was Vice-Pres of Council of Royal Agricultural Soc, and High Sheriff of Staffordshire 1901, and the 2nd baronet was a JP for Herts, and sat as MP for Walsall (*C*) 1910-22.

COOTE (I) 1621, of Castle Cuffe, Queen's County, Ireland

Cost what it may

Sir CHRISTOPHER JOHN COOTE, 15th *Baronet*; *b* 22 Sept 1928; *s* his father *Rear Adm Sir* JOHN RALPH, CB, CBE, DSC, 1978; *ed* Winchester, and Ch Ch Oxford (MA); late Lieut 17th/21st Lancers; Coffee and Tea Merchant: *m* 1952, Anne Georgiana, yr da of late Lt-Col Donald James Handford, RA (Bs D'Arcy de Knayth, colls), and has issue.

Arms – Argent, a chevron sable between three coots close proper. **Crest** – A coot proper.
Residence – Monkton House, Broughton Gifford, Melksham, Wilts SN12 8PA.

SON LIVING

NICHOLAS PATRICK, *b* 28 July 1953; *ed* Winchester: *m* 1980, Mona Rebecca, da of late Moushegh Bedelian, and has issue living, Rory Alasdair, *b* 3 April 1987, — Eleanor Marianne, *b* 1984.

DAUGHTER LIVING

Vanessa Jean, *b* 1955; *ed* Southampton Univ (BSc), and Camborne Sch of Mines (MSc); AMIGeol, AMIMM, FGS.

BROTHER LIVING

Terence Eyre (Rushmoor, The Warren, Radlett, Herts WD7 7DU), *b* 1933; *ed* Winchester: *m* 1976, Jennifer, only da of late H. B. Cumming, of Duncal Farm, Bulawayo, Zimbabwe, and has issue living, Jonathan Eyre, *b* 1977, — Sarah Jane *b* 1980.

Truth conquers

WIDOW LIVING OF FOURTEENTH BARONET

NOREEN UNA (*Dowager Lady Coote*) (Firlawn House, The Street, Holt, Wilts BA14 6QH), da of late Wilfred Tighe of Rossanagh, co Wicklow: *m* 1927 Rear-Adm Sir John Ralph Coote, CB, CBE, DSC, who *d* 1978.

COLLATERAL BRANCHES LIVING

Issue of late John Methuen Coote, OBE, 2nd son of 12th baronet, *b* 1878, *d* 1967: *m* 1912, Leonora Wray who *d* 1969, da of late John Townsend Trench, of Kenmare (B Ashtown, colls):—
Joanna Frances (Gins, Beaulieu, Hants) *b* 1913; 1939-45 War 1st Officer WRNS; HM Diplo Ser 1948-73. —— Diana Jean, MBE, *b* 1914; N-W Europe 1944-45 as Senior Cdr ATS; MBE (Mil) 1946: *m* 1946, Edmund Luxmoore, of Glenspean, Inverness-shire, and Staindrop Hall, Staindrop, co Durham DL2 3NH, and has issue living, Michael John, *b* 1948: *m* 1st, 1973 (*m diss* 19—), Margaret Rosemary, da of Surg-Cdr John Graham More-Nisbett RN, of The Drum, Gilmerton, Edinburgh; 2ndly, 1988, Ann Dalrymple-Smith, and has issue living (by 1st *m*), Andrew Aylmer *b* 1976, James *b* 1979, — Richard

Aylmer, *b* 1955, — Elizabeth Jean, *b* 1950: *m* 1st, 1976, Geoffrey Wells Abbott, of Harare, Zimbabwe; 2ndly 1987, Alexander Lindsay Macdonald, of Ardgour, Fort William PH33 7AB, and has issue living, (by 1st *m*) Jessica *b* 1980, Lucy *b* 1983.

Issue of late Com Bernard Trotter Coote, OBE, 3rd son of 12th baronet, *b* 1880, *d* 1955: *m* 1907, Grace Harriet, who *d* 1958, el da of late Very Rev John Joseph Robinson, DD (B Avebury):—
Michael Henry (13 Laurelton, Bushy Park Rd, Rathgar, Dublin 6), *b* 1913; *ed* Woking Gram Sch: *m* 1st, 1939, Barbara Netterville, who *d* 1987, da of late Richard Netterville Eaton, of Roslyn Churchtown, Dundrum, co Dublin; 2ndly, 1987, Joan May, da of late W. W. G. Stevenson, of Cowper Drive, Dublin 6, and has issue living, (by 1st *m*) David Brian (Slieve Thoul, Brittas, co Dublin), *b* 1942: *m* 1968, Elizabeth Joy, da of late A. P. Brooks, of Dublin, and has issue living, Susan Barbara *b* 1972, Linda Elizabeth *b* 1975, — Deirdre Joan, *b* 1940: *m* 1973, Sean Rowsome, of Ballintober, Hollywood, co Wicklow, — Sheila Anne (2 Wellhead Lane, Westbury, Wilts), *b* 1946: *m* 1968, Maj Patrick Brian Hemming Robeson, 6th Queen Elizabeth's Own Gurkha Rifles, and has issue living, Simon Michael Hemming *b* 1970, Nicholas Andrew Hemming *b* 1973, Philippa Charlotte Hemming *b* 1969, — Jennifer Hazel, *b* 1949: *m* 1969, Peter Stuart Todd, of Monastery, Enniskerry, co Wicklow, and has issue living, Sam Stuart *b* 1981, Sarah Stuart *b* 1972, Jane Stuart *b* 1974, and an adopted da, Cathy *b* 1976. —— Rt Rev Roderic Norman, DD (Friday Woods, Stoke Rd, Cobham, Surrey KT11 3AS), *b* 1915; *ed* Woking Gram Sch, and Trin Coll, Dublin (MA, DD); Bishop of Gambia and the Rio Pongas 1951-57, Bishop of Fulham 1957-66, Bishop of Colchester 1966-87; Archdeacon of Colchester 1969-72: *m* 1964, Erica Lynette, da of late Rev Eric G. Shrubbs, MBE, R of Lawshall, Suffolk, and has issue living, Patrick Shrubbs, *b* 1972, — Antoinette Alexandra, *b* 1965, — Bernadette Sophie, *b* 1966. —— Brian Philip, MC (The Hollies, Church St, Rudgwick, Horsham, W Sussex), *b* 1919; *ed* Woking Gram Sch, and Coll of St Columba, Dublin; Wing-Cdr (ret) RAF Regt; Prin of Queen Elizabeth's Training Coll, Leatherhead 1972-79; Dep Dir Queen Elizabeth's Foundation for the Disabled 1979-84; 1939-45 War as Capt Recce Corps (MC): *m* 1949, Elizabeth Helen, da of late W. J. Rutt, of Trimley St Mary, Suffolk, and has issue living, Grace Elizabeth, *b* 1956: *m* 1984, Ian Arthur Bagster, of Furneaux Pelham, Herts.

Granddaughters of late Com Bernard Trotter Coote, OBE, RN (ante):—
Issue of late G/Capt Rev Denis Ivor Coote, CBE, *b* 1908, *d* 1985: *m* 1st, 1933, Olive Sheelagh (late Fl Officer WAAF), who *d* 1978, only da of late Hugh Crompton Bishoff, of Woodhayes, Woodlands, Southampton; 2ndly, 1979, Mary (12 Belle Vue Rd, Parkstone, Dorset BH14 8TW), da of William McDonough, of Newcastle upon Tyne:—
(By 1st *m*) Caragh Mary (42 Orchardstown Drive, Rathfarnham, Dublin), *b* 1949: *m* 1973 (*m diss* 1983), Patrick O'Fáoláin, and has issue living, Tamsin Emilie, *b* 1973.
Issue of late Wing-Com Patric Bernard Coote, RAF, *b* 1910, *d* (presumed *ka*) 1941: *m* 1935, Muriel (Culver Haye, Motcombe, Shaftesbury, Dorset), da of late Maj-Gen Alexander Montagu Spears Elsmie, CB, CMG:—
Ann Patricia, *b* 1937. —— Susan Brigid, *b* 1939: *m* 1970, Geoffrey Maurice Young, of 78 Harpenden Rd, St Albans, Herts AL3 6DA, and has issue living, Michael Patrick, *b* 1971, — Catherine Ann, *b* 1974.

Grandson of late Charles Chenevix Coote, OBE (infra):—
Issue of late Maj Mervyn Charles Coote, RE, *b* 1913, *d* 1985: *m* 1949, Inger Dahl (30 Ettrick Lodge, The Grove, Gosforth, Newcastle-upon-Tyne), da of Dahl Sorensen, of Copenhagen, Denmark:—
Peter Mervyn Dahl (332 Maple Avenue, Oakville, Ontario, Canada), *b* 1950; BA, BArch (Hons), ARIBA: *m* 1976, Ann Patricia, da of William John Taylor, and has issue living, Joanna Louise, *b* 1980, — Sophie Alexandra, *b* 1984, — Charlotte, *b* 1993.

Issue of late Charles Chenevix Coote, OBE, 4th son of 12th baronet, *b* 1884, *d* 1944: *m* 1908, Alice Maud, who *d* 1948, only da of late Most Rev John Baptist Crozier, DD, Archbishop of Armagh, and Primate of All Ireland:—
Dermot Chenevix, OBE, RN (28 North Rd, Wells, Som BA5 2TL), *b* 1915; Cdr (ret) 1939-45 War, Operations in Madagascar (despatches); OBE (Mil) 1967: *m* 1945, Dorothy Oliver, 2nd Officer, WRNS, and has issue living, Christopher Chenevix, *b* 1946; Lt-Cdr RN (ret): *m* 1971, Cheryl, da of William Bridge, and has issue living, James Chenevix *b* 1971, Timothy Charles *b* 1973, — Richard Anthony, *b* 1950; BSc: *m* 1974, Lynne, da of Sydney Matthews, and has issue living, Christopher Neil *b* 1977, William Richard *b* 1987, Emma Louise *b* 1980. —— Cecilia Maud, *b* 1911; FLA: *m* 1st, 1935 (*m diss* 1945), Benjamin Thomas Bowman; 2ndly, 1950 (*m diss* 1952), Mortimer Wilmot Bennitt, Under-Sec of Min of Works; 3rdly, 1962, John Ainsworth Gordon, of 4 Chapel Lane, Alnwick, Northumberland NE66 1XT, and has issue living, (by 1st *m*) Charles Christopher Benjamin (Mariners, Anglesea Rd, Wivenhoe, Colchester, CO7 9JR), *b* 1939: *m* 1961, June Vivian Murray, and has issue living, Timothy Charles *b* 1968, Sarah Louise *b* 1962, Emma Lucy, *b* 1966, — James Thomas, *b* 1941; BA, Dip Ed. —— Patricia Aileen, *b* 1919; formerly Section Officer WAAF, and attached RAF Delegation, Washington; USA: *m* 1943, Air Commodore Nelles Woods Timmerman, DSO, DFC, RCAF, and has issue living, Mark, *b* 1945, — Peter, *b* 1950, — Nicola Mary, *b* 1952: *m* 1979, Eric Jean Pierre Maillé, and has issue living, Victor Alfred *b* 1993, Dominique Patricia *b* 1986. *Address* – House 407, 55 Waterford Drive, Weston, Ont M9R 2N7, Canada.

Issue of late Arthur Philip Coote, JP, 5th son of 12th baronet, *b* 1887, *d* 1954: *m* 1918, Margaretta, who *d* 1977, da of late Albert Leslie Wright (B Fitzwalter, colls):—
Stephen Arthur (Home Farm, Ashford Carbonell, Ludlow, Salop), *b* 1925; *ed* Repton, Selwyn Coll Camb, and Roy Agric Coll Cirencester; formerly Lt Rifle Bde: *m* 1951, Sheila Mary Healey, and has issue living, Michael Philip John, *b* 1952, — Nicholas Anthony, *b* 1955, — Peter Richard, *b* 1965. —— Bridget (Lentune Ford, Walhampton, Lymington, Hants SO41 5RB), *b* 1924: *m* 1959, Capt Reginald Fife Whinney, DSC, RN, who *d* 1992, Walhampton Hill, Lymington, Hants, and has issue living, Alison Bridget, *b* 1963: *m* 1991, Jonathan West, of Petersfield, Hants GU32 3NE, and has issue living, Bede Robert Fife *b* 1992.

Grandchildren of late Com John Pemberton Plumptre Coote, 3rd son of 11th baronet:
Issue of late Lieut-Col Mervyn Chidley Coote, *b* 1885; *d* 1950: *m* 1915 Cecil Maud Vera, who *d* 1989, da of late Maj-Gen Cecil William Park, CB:—
Chidley (Emano St, Nelson, New Zealand), *b* 1918: *m* 1954, Mavis Ellen Thompson. —— Eleanor Patricia, *b* 1916: *m* 1940, James Chilton Francis Hayter, of Rocklands, Golden Bay, Nelson, NZ, and has had issue, Stephen James, *b* 1945, *d* 1987. —— Maureen Joyce, *b* 1923: *m* 1963, Samuel Nicholson, of 93 Coronation Rd, Morrinsville, Waikato, NZ, and has issue living, Ian Andrew, *b* 1964. —— Rosemary Cecilia, *b* 1929: *m* 1951, Joseph Trevor Clark, of Kakenga Rd, Stoke, Nelson, NZ, and has issue living, Anthony Joseph, *b* 1952: *m* 1979, Cushla Kerr, and has issue living, Benjamin Joseph *b* 1981, Anna Louise *b* 1984, — Peter Andrew, *b* 1954, — Geoffrey Robert, *b* 1956, — Jeremy John, *b* 1961.

Grandchildren of late Cecil Henry Coote, 5th son of 11th baronet:—
Issue of late John Cecil Coote, M.M. *b* 1889, *d* 1937: *m* 1915, Edith Blechynden, who *d* 1976:—
John Robin, *b* 1916; European War 1939-45 as Major 20th New Zealand Armoured Regt: *m* 1947, Anna May McDonald, and has had issue, John McDonald (Damian Grove, Lower Hutt, NZ), *b* 1949; Lieut RNZAC: *m* 1976, Stephanie Buchanan, and has issue living, Jack Buchanan *b* 1980, Evan Blechynden *b* 1985, Anna Doloughan *b* 1982, — Isobel Anne, *b* 1950: *m* 1978, Mark Rodger Taylor, of Havelock N, NZ, — Alison May, *b* 1954, *d* 1975, — Ann Cecile, *b* 1956: *m* 1979, Dr Duncan Bull, of Erin, Ontario, Canada, and has issue living, Alexandra Alison *b* 1981, Ainsley Frances *b* 1984. *Residence* – 88 Valley, Wakefield, New Zealand. —— †Peter Chidley, *b* 1921; formerly Flying Officer Roy New Zealand Air Force: *m* 1942, Nancy Bower Playter (Waingaro, Takaka, NZ), and *d* 1990, leaving living, Robin Maxwell (Clifton, Takaka, NZ), *b* 1943: *m* 1st, 1968 (*m diss* 1987), Jacqueline Phillippa Elliott; 2ndly, 1991, Glennis Susan Hinch. —— Richard Eyre, *b* 1929; Korea 1950-52 as Lt New Zealand Forces: *m* 1953, Janet Patricia Armatage Holmes, and has issue living, Stephen Richard, *b* 1955: *m* 1978, Judith

Goff, and has issue living, Logan Eyre *b* 1981, Tyler Lesley *b* 1982, — David Eyre, *b* 1959; Warrant Officer US Army: *m* 1979, Jody Susan Bishop, — Jonathan Robert, *b* 1966, — Sarah Patricia, *b* 1965. *Residence* – Ballyfin, Enner Glynn Rd, Nelson, NZ. —— Edith Jane, *b* 1919: *m* 1953, Ralph Armatage Holmes, and has issue living, Marion Jane, *b* 1954. *Residence* – Armatage, Wakapuaka Rd, RD1, Nelson, NZ.

   Issue of late Frederick Stanley Coote, OBE, *b* 1896; *d* 1967: *m* 1920, Edith Farquarharson Crowe, who *d* 1985:—
John Oldham (47 Caversham St, SW3) *b* 1921; Capt RN (ret); 1939-45 War: *m* 1944, Sylvia, el da of late Rear-Adm J. L. Syson, and has issue living, Judith Sylvia, *b* 1945: *m* 19—, — Angela Mary, *b* 1947, — Belinda Jane, *b* 1953.

   Issue of late Eric Royds Methuen Coote, *b* 1902, *d* 1974: *m* 1932, Patricia Vercoe, who *d* 1993 :—
Philip Arthur Cecil (Mountrath, 26 Mount St, Nelson, NZ), *b* 1935: *m* 1957, Gabrielle Alice Goodman, and has issue living, John Anthony Royds (St Arnaud, Nelson, NZ), *b* 1959: *m* 1992, Kris Vollebrght, and has issue living, Jack Eric *b* 19—, — Richard Philip, *b* 1964, — Timothy Philip (twin), *b* 1964, — Thomas Stanley Eyre, *b* 1967, — Catherine Alice, *b* 1958, — Bridget Ann, *b* 1961: *m* 1990, Lloyd James Harwood, and has issue living, George Sebastian *b* 1994, Amelia Alice *b* 1993. —— Robert Malcolm (Mountrath, 23 Browallia Cres, Loftus 2232, Sydney, NSW), *b* 1947: *m* 1971, Rhondda Beverly Kenny, of Sydney, NSW, and has issue living, Justin Russell Royds, *b* 1977, — Deborah Michelle, *b* 1974. —— Jennifer Margaret, *b* 1933: *m* 1959, Arthur Edward Maskill, and has issue living, Patricia Ann, *b* 1960, — Margaret Kaye, *b* 1961, — Virginia Robyn, *b* 1964, — Diana Mary, *b* 1965.

   Grandchildren of late Charles Purdon Coote, son of late Charles Purdon Coote, son of late Capt Robert Carr Coote, brother of 9th baronet:—
   Issue of late Major Charles Robert Purdon Coote, *b* 1875, *d* 1954: *m* 1933, Noel Margaret Jephson (Durham House, Balsham, Cambs CB1 6EZ), da of late Lt-Col Ernest Henry Denne Stracey (*see* Stracey, Bt colls):—
Nicola Harriette (*Baroness Clinton*), *b* 1937: *m* 1959, 22nd Baron Clinton. —— Margaret Lydia Faith, *b* 1939: *m* 1966, Colin Patrick Annesley Martin Hill (*see* E Annesley, colls), of 104 Bayard Lane, Princeton, New Jersey 08540, USA. —— Caroline Anne, *b* 1940: *m* 1963, Baron Lambert Frederick Casijn van Till, Royal Netherlands Navy (ret), of Fortlaan 1, Bussum, Holland, and has issue living, Rupert Maurice Casijn, *b* 1967, — Edward Nicholaas Frederick, *b* 1972, — Lydia Julie, *b* 1964, — Vanessa Caroline, *b* 1976. —— Rosamond Aileen, *b* 1943: *m* 1965, Timothy Hetherington Earle Bulwer-Long, 15th/19th King's R Hussars (ret), of Balsham House, Balsham, Cambs, and has issue living, Lucy Wiggett, *b* 1966, — Charlotte Louise, *b* 1968, — Harriet Elizabeth, *b* 1977, — Laura Rose, *b* 1980. —— Mary Patricia, *b* 1945.

Sir Charles Coote, 1st Bt, Provost-Marshal and Vice-President of the Province of Connaught, greatly distinguished himself at the relief of Birr, 1642. The 2nd baronet was created in 1661, Earl of Mountrath, in the peerage of Ireland, when the baronetcy merged in the peerage. The 7th earl and 8th baronet, having no heir, obtained in 1800 a new creation, that of Baron Castle Coote, with special remainder, which title became extinct in 1827, when the baronetcy reverted to the great-great-grandson of the 2nd son of 1st baronet. Rear Adm Sir John Ralph Coote, CB, CBE, DSC, 14th Bt, was Dept Dir of Naval Ordnance (Material) and Ch Ordnance Engineer Officer 1955-8.

COPE (E) 1611, of Hanwell, Oxfordshire (Dormant or Extinct 1972)

Sir MORDAUNT LECKONBY COPE, 16th and last *Baronet.*

WIDOWS LIVING OF FIFTEENTH AND SIXTEENTH BARONETS

ANGELA ROSE ELIZABETH (*Lady Thomas*), da of James A. S. Wright, AFC, FDS, RCS: *m* 1st, 1956, Sir Anthony Mohun Leckonby Cope, 15th Bt, who *d* 1966; 2ndly, 1967, Hon Mr Justice Swinton Thomas, of 36 Sheffield Terr, W8. —— EVELINE (*Lady Cope*) (Clare Park, Crondall, nr Farnham, Surrey GU10 5DT), da of late Alfred Bishop, of Tuffley, Gloucester: *m* 1936, as his 2nd wife, Sir Mordaunt Leckonby Cope, MC, 16th Bt, who *d* 1972, when the title became dormant or ext.

CORBET (UK) 1808, of Moreton Corbet, Shropshire

Deeds are
the praise
of valour

While
I breathe
I hope

God feeds the raven

Sir JOHN VINCENT CORBET, MBE, 7th *Baronet*, son of late Archer Henry Corbet, grandson of late Richard Corbet, 2nd son of 1st baronet; *b* 27 Feb 1911; *s* his kinsman, *Sir* GERALD VINCENT, 1955; *ed* Shrewsbury Sch, RMA, Woolwich, and at Magdalene Coll, Camb (MA); Lt-Col (ret) RE, a JP, a DL, and a Co Councillor for Shropshire (High Sheriff 1966); an OStJ; a member of Ch Assembly and Gen Synod 1960-76; NW Frontier of India 1935; India, Burma and Malaya 1939-45 (despatches, MBE); MBE (Mil) 1946: *m* 1st, 1937 (*m diss* 1948), Elfrida Isobel eldest da of A. G. Francis, of Trowbridge, Wilts; 2ndly, 1948, Doreen Elizabeth Stewart (GRAY), who *d* 1964, da of late Arthur William Gibbon Ritchie, of Enniskillen; 3rdly, 1965, Annie Elizabeth, MBE, da of late James Lorimer, of Christchurch, NZ.

Arms – Or, a raven sable. **Crests** – 1st, An elephant statant argent, tusked or, the trappings sable, fimbriated or, on his back a castle triple-towered of the last; 2nd, a squirrel sejant cracking a nut or.
Residence – Acton Reynald, Shrewsbury SY4 4DS. *Club* – Royal Thames Yacht.

SISTER LIVING

Helen Anne Evelyn, *b* 1913: *m* 1946, John Dennis Russell, who *d* 1973, and has issue living, Christopher Corbet, *b* 1949: *m* 1979, Leila Elizabeth, el da of Maj Charles John Richard Errington, of The Old Rectory, Ubbeston, Halesworth, Suffolk, and has issue living, Richard Corbet *b* 1981, Catriona Corbet *b* 1980, Alice Ella *b* 1983, — Georgina Anne (*Lady Craufurd*), *b* 1947: *m* 1987, as his 2nd wife, Sir Robert James Craufurd, 9th Bt. *Residence* – East Grove, Lymington, Hants.

This family is descended in an unbroken male line from Hugh Corbeau (or Corbet), a noble Norman, who with two sons came over with William the Conqueror. One of these sons, Roger Fitz-Corbet, was father of William de Corbet, who settled at Wattlesborough, Shropshire, and was the common ancestor of the present baronet, and of Peter Corbet, of Caus Castle, who was summoned to Parliament as a baron *temp* Edward I, which title became ext 1347. Moreton Corbet Castle, the ancient family seat, was destroyed by fire during the Civil Wars, and is a beautiful ruin. The present baronet descends from Richard Corbet, yr brother of Sir Vincent Corbet, MP, who was created a baronet 1642 (title ext 1688), and whose widow was created Viscountess Corbet, of Linslade, for life. The 5th baronet, Sir Roland James, Lieut Coldstream Guards, was *ka* 1915, together with three other possible heirs of his generation.

CORNWALL (UK) 1918, of Holcombe Burnell, co Devon (Extinct 1962)

Sir REGINALD EDWIN CORNWALL, 2nd and last *Baronet*.

DAUGHTER LIVING OF FIRST BARONET

Laura Ellen.

CORRY (UK) 1885, of Dunraven, co Antrim

Vigilans et audax
Watchful and bold

Sir WILLIAM JAMES CORRY, 4th *Baronet*; *b* 1 Aug 1924; *s* his father, *Sir* JAMES PEROWNE IVO MYLES, 1987; *ed* RNC Dartmouth; Lt Cdr RN (ret): *m* 1945, Diana Pamela Mary, only da of late Lt-Col James Burne Lapsley, MC, IMS, and has issue.

Arms – Gules, a saltire engrailed argent, between in chief, a rose of the last, in fesse two thistles slipped proper, and in base a trefoil slipped or. **Crest** – A cock combed and wattled proper, and charged on the breast with a trefoil slipped vert.
Residence – East Hillerton House, Hillerton Cross, Bow, Crediton, Devon EX17 5AD

SONS LIVING

JAMES MICHAEL, *b* 3 Oct 1946; *ed* Downside: *m* 1973, Sheridan Lorraine, da of Arthur Peter Ashbourne, of Crowland, Peterborough, and has issue living, William James Alexander, *b* 7 Dec 1981, — Robert Philip John, *b* 1984, — Christopher Myles Anthony, *b* 1987. *Residence* – 24 Ligo Av, Stoke Mandeville, Aylesbury, Bucks HP22 5TX. —— Timothy William, *b* 1948; *ed* Downside; Lt-Col RGJ: *m* 1971, Bridget Isabella, da of Sydney Litherland, of Tenerife, Canary Is, and has issue living, Edward Charles, *b* 1976, — Georgina Katharine, *b* 1974, — Charlotte Louise, *b* 1981. —— Nicholas John, *b* 1958; *ed* Downside. —— Simon Miles, *b* 1961; *ed* Downside; Lt Cdr RN.

DAUGHTERS LIVING

Jane Susannah, *b* 1949: *m* 1976, John Anthony Redman, of 32 Glenmore Rd, Minehead, Som, only son of late Henry Gordon Redman, OBE, of Brockenhurst, Hants, and has issue living, Angus Richard William, *b* 1986. —— Patricia Diana, *b* 1956: *m* 1987, Mark Hassell, of 40 Avern Rd, E Molesey, Surrey, only son of M. Hassell, of Woodbank House, Teddesley Rd, Penkridge, Staffs 5TG 5RH, and has issue living, Oliver James Bowen, *b* 1990, — Rebecca Holly, *b* (twin) 1990.

SISTER LIVING (*daughter of 3rd baronet by 1st marriage*)

Susan (Knottfield, Ballagale Av, Surby, IoM), *b* 1926.

HALF-SISTER LIVING (*daughter of 3rd baronet by 2nd marriage*)

Amanda Jane, *b* 1947: *m* 1972, Hamlyn Gordon Jones, MA, PhD, FIHort, of 13 Mill St, Warwick CV34 4HB, and has issue living, Katherine Myleta Gordon, *b* 1974, — Julia Patricia Gordon, *b* 1976.

MOTHER LIVING

Molly Irene, yst da of late Maj Otto Joseph Bell: *m* 1st, 1921 (*m diss* 1937), as his 1st wife, Sir James Perowne Ivo Myles Corry, 3rd Bt, who *d* 1987; 2ndly, 1938, Capt John Forster Cochrane, DSC, RN, who *d* 1970. *Residence* – Knottfield, Ballagate Av, Port Erin, IoM.

WIDOW LIVING OF THIRD BARONET

Cynthia Marjorie Patricia (*Dowager Lady Corry*), widow of Capt David Alexander Polson, Seaforth Highlanders, and da of late Capt Frederick Henry Mahony, The Cheshire Regt, and of late Mrs Francis Bliss, of Santa Barbara, Calif, USA: *m* 1946, as his 2nd wife, Sir James Perowne Ivo Myles Corry, 3rd Bt, who *d* 1987. *Residence* – Dunraven, Fauvic, Jersey, CI.

This family emigrated from Dumfriess-shire to co Down early in the 17th century. The 1st baronet sat as MP for Belfast (*C*) 1874-85, and for Mid Armagh Div 1886-91 Armagh co. The 2nd baronet, Sir William, was a Director of Cunard Steamship Co, Ltd. The 3rd baronet, Sir James Perowne Ivo Myles, was Secretary and a Director of Port Line Ltd, and Vice-President of King George's Fund for Sailors, The Royal Alfred Merchant Seamen's Society and the Royal Merchant Navy School.

CORY (UK) 1919, of Coryton, Whitchurch, co Glamorgan

One heart, one way

Sir (CLINTON CHARLES) DONALD CORY, 5th *Baronet*; *b* 13 Sept 1937; *s* his father, *Sqdn-Ldr Sir* CLINTON JAMES DONALD, 1991; *ed* Brighton Coll, and abroad.

𝔄rms – Argent, a saltire between two quatrefoils in pale sable, on a chief azure a griffin's head erased between two quatrefoils or. 𝕮rest – In front of a griffin's head erased or between two wings per pale of the last and gules three quatrefoils sable.
Residence – 18 Cloisters Rd, Letchworth, Herts SG6 3JS.

UNCLE LIVING (*son of 2nd baronet*)

Philip Cecil Donald, *b* 20 Feb 1913. *Residence* – Dawneys Corner, Pirbright, Woking, Surrey, GU24 0JB.

AUNTS LIVING (*daughters of 2nd baronet*)

Valerie (*Lady Gane*), *b* 1905: *m* 1st, 1928 (*m diss* 1948), Walter Pidcock Woolland, who *d* 1949; 2ndly, 1954, as his 2nd wife, Sir Irving Blanchard Gane, KCVO, who *d* 1972, and has issue living, (by 1st *m*), David Anthony Walter (Baydon Manor Cottage, Marlborough, Wilts SN8 2HG), *b* 1929, — Peter Donald Cory, *b* 1931. *Residence* – Sandaig, Knoydart, Inverness-shire. —— Diana Ethel Muriel, *b* 1918: *m* 1943, Maj Andrew Lyell, DFC, RA, late Dorset Yeo, and has issue living, Vivien Diana, *b* 1944, — Clementina Lindsay, *b* 1949. *Residence* – Wester Auchleuchrie, Forfar, Angus DD8 3TU.

GREAT AUNT LIVING (*Daughter of 1st baronet*)

Carmen (*Dowager Baroness McGowan*), *b* 1914: *m* 1937, 2nd Baron McGowan, who *d* 1966. *Residence* – Bragborough Hall, Daventry, Northants.

WIDOW LIVING OF FOURTH BARONET

Mary (*Lady Cory*), only da of Arthur Douglas Hunt, MD, ChB, of Park Grange, Duffield Rd, Derby: *m* 1935, Sqdn-Ldr Sir Clinton James Donald Cory, 4th Bt, RAFVR, who *d* 1991. *Residence* – 18 Cloisters Rd, Letchworth, Herts SG6 3JS.

The 1st baronet, Sir (James) Herbert Cory (a Director of John Cory & Sons, Ltd, shipowners), was High Sheriff for Glamorgan 1913, and MP for Cardiff Dist (*C*) Nov 1915 to Nov 1918, and S Div thereof Dec 1918 to Nov 1923.

Cory-Wright, see Wright.

COTTER (I) 1763, of Rockforest, Cork

While I breathe I hope

Sir DELAVAL JAMES ALFRED COTTER, DSO, 6th *Baronet*; *b* 29 April 1911; *s* his father, *Sir* JAMES LAURENCE, 1924; *ed* Malvern, and RMC Sandhurst; Lieut-Col (ret) 13th/18th Roy Hussars; N-W Europe 1944-45 (DSO); DSO 1944: *m* 1st, 1943 (*m diss* 1949), Roma, only da of Adrian Rome, of Dalswinton Lodge, Salisbury, S Rhodesia, and widow of Squadron-Leader Kenneth A. Kerr MacEwen, RAF; 2ndly, 1952, Eveline Mary, who *d* 1991, da of late Evelyn John Mardon, of Halsway Manor, Crowcombe, Somerset, and widow of Lieut-Col John Frederick Paterson, OBE, RHA, and has issue by 1st *m*.

Arms – Quarterly: 1st and 4th, argent a chevron gules between three serpents proper, *Cotter*; 2nd and 3rd, azure, a fesse dancettée a fleur-de-lis in chief and a mullet in base or, *Rogerson*. **Crest** – A dexter arm embowed, armed and grasping a dart, all proper.
Residence – Greenlines, Iwerne Courtney, Blandford, Dorset DT11 8QR. *Club* – Army and Navy.

DAUGHTERS LIVING (By 1st marriage)

Sarah Gay Lisette, *b* 1944: *m* 1976, Michel Vigneron, of 4 Villa DuFresne, 75016, Paris. —— Charnisay Ann, *b* 1946: *m* 1971, Capt Charles A. H. Gwyn, Scots Gds, of Humbie House, Humbie, E Lothian, and has issue living, Simon, *b* 1979, — Victoria, *b* 1972, — Rebecca, *b* 1975, — Jessica, *b* 1977.

COLLATERAL BRANCHES LIVING

Issue of late Laurence Stopford Llewelyn Cotter, 2nd son of 5th baronet, *b* 1912, *ka* 1943: *m* 1935, Grace Mary (The Barn, Bovey Tracey, nr Newton Abbot, Devon) (who *m* 2ndly, 1945, Lt-Col Geoffrey Rittson-Thomas, late Manchester Regt, who *d* 1975), da of late Ivor Downing, of Beverley, Llanishen, Cardiff:—
PATRICK LAURENCE DELAVAL (Lower Winsham Farm, Knowle, Braunton, N Devon), *b* 21 Nov 1941; *ed* Blundell's, and Roy Agric Coll, Cirencester: *m* 1967, Janet, da of late George Potter, of Goldthorne, Barnstaple, and has issue living, Julius Laurence George, *b* 1968, — Jemima Grace Mary, *b* 1970, — Jessica Lucy Kathleen, *b* 1972. —— Peta Natalie (Collaton St Mary, Paignton, Devon) *b* 1935: *m* 1963 (*m diss* 1972), George Derek Wilson, and has issue living, Paul Sean, *b* 1964, — William Robin, *b* 1966, — Adam Edward, *b* 1969, — Charlotte Emma, *b* 1971. —— Primrose Anne, *b* 1939: *m* 1st, 1960 (*m diss* 1967), Richard Hugh Nicholas Creswell, 2ndly, 1968 (*m diss* 1969), Henry George Herbert, Viscount Throwley, son of 4th Earl Sondes (now 5th Earl Sondes); 3rdly, 1976, Charles Denys Burnett-Hitchcock, of 2 Southdean Gdns, SW19, and has issue living, (by 1st *m*) Belinda Jane, *b* 1960: *m* 1986, James Roger Glinn Eaton, — Robin Amanda, *b* 1962, — (by 3rd *m*) Jacob Nicholas, *b* 1978.

Issue of late Thomas Lombard Cotter, brother of 5th baronet, *b* 1888, *d* 1923, *m* 1912, Victoria Jean Robertson, who *d* 1923:—
Bettine, *b* 1920: *m* 1st, 1943, J. Harrison Owen, RAAF, who was *ka* 1943; 2ndly, 1946 (*m diss* 1956), Wing-Com Richard C. Cresswell, DFC, RAAF; 3rdly, 1956, Group-Capt Alan Graham Douglas, CBE, MC, RAF Regt.

Grandchildren of late Col George Sackville Cotter, CB, son of late Rev James Laurence Cotter, LLD (infra):—
Issue of late James Laurence Cotter, *b* 1839, *d* 1889: *m* 1868, Frances, da of Capt Ironside:—
George Sackville, *b* 1870. —— Wemyss M'Kenzie Osborne, *b* 1872. —— Henry Martin Stuart, *b* 1873. —— Oliver Wendell Holmes, *b* 1879. —— Agnes Mary. —— Evadne Kilgour. —— Ada Margaret. —— Katherine. —— Anne Winifred.

Grandchildren of late James Laurence Cotter (ante):—
Issue of late Arthur Douglas Cotter, *b* 1878, *d* 1918: *m* 1904, Marion Church Solmes:—
James Guthrie Sackville, *b* 1906: *m* 19—, and has issue living. —— George Clinton Solmes, *b* 1905: *m* 19—, and has issue living. —— Frances Marion Louise, *b* 1908: *m* 1926, Alexander Nicholson Salisbury, who *d* 19—, and has issue living, Virginia Puella, *b* 1927: *m* 19— Lloyd Fieley, and has issue living, a son, *b* 19—, a da, *b* 19—, a da *b* 19—.

Granddaughter of the Rev William Henry Cotter, LLD (infra):—
Issue of late Capt George Edmund Sackville Cotter, *b* 1882, *d* on active ser 1917: *m* 1914, Beatrice Mary Grove (who *m* 2ndly, 1921, Brig John Keily Gordon, DSO, RHA, and *d* 1981), da of Com Hans Thomas Fell White, JP, of Springfort Hall, Mallow, co Cork:—
Benita May, *b* 1915: *m* 1st, 1936, Major Arthur William Granville Dobbie, RE, who was *ka* 1944, el son of Lt-Gen Sir William George Shedden Dobbie, GCMG, KCB, DSO; 2ndly, 1950, Major Derek Wrey Savile, RA, who *d* 1992, and has issue living, (by 1st *m*) William Ian Cotter, *b* 1939; Brig RE, — (by 2nd *m*) George Keith Wrey, *b* 1951: *m* 1987, Philippa Mary, elder da of Brian Dudgeon, of Broadfield, Guildford, and has issue living, Joshua Andrew Keith *b* 1990, Samuel Christopher *b* 1992, Hannah Elizabeth *b* 1989. *Residence* – Cross Ways, Middle Gordon Rd, Camberley, Surrey.

Granddaughter of late Rev James Laurence Cotter, LLD, el son of late Rev George Sackville Cotter, 4th son of 1st baronet;—
Issue of late Rev William Henry Cotter, LLD, *b* 1844, *d* 1931: *m* 1st, 1878, Catherine Letitia, who *d* 1894, da of late George Stawell, of Crobeg, co Cork; 2ndly, 1896, Eva, who *d* 1903, da of J. T. Sikes, of Elmvale, co Cork, and Kincora, Ceylon:—
(By 2nd *m*) Eva Maude (Little Kenbank, Dalry, Castle Douglas, Kirkcudbrightshire), *b* 1901: *m* 1921, Lt-Col Alexander Patrick Cathcart Hannay, OBE, MC, Queen's Own Cameron Highlanders (also Sqdn-Ldr RAF), who *d* 1977, and has issue living, Patrick Victor Cathcart (16 via Privata Cieli, La Spezia, Italy), *b* 1923; MA, PhD: *m* 1st, 1943, Maria Benita Rosalia Greco, who *d* 1944; 2ndly, 1948, Elvira Teodora Facchetti, who *d* 1964; 3rdly, 1965, Mrs Iride Giuseppina Antonietta Ercolini, who *d* 1986, — Timothy John (Hope Cottage, Dalry, Castle Douglas, Kirkcudbrightshire), *b* 1929, Fl-Lt RAF: *m* 1st, 1956 (*m diss* 1974), Judith Butler; 2ndly, 1974, Linda Jess Elizabeth Callan, of Edinburgh, and has issue living, (by 1st *m*) Patrick George *b* 1958: *m* 1988, Urasa, da of Aim Sanasen, of Bangkok, Thailand (and has issue living, Pimon *b* 1991, Tim *b* 1993), William Victor Bladworth *b* 1963, (by 2nd *m*) Neil Lennox Cotter *b* 1976, Timothy Alexander *b* 1977.

Grandson of late James Laurence Sackville Cotter, 3rd son of late George Sackville Cotter (*b* 1829), eldest son of Col George Sackville Cotter (*b* 1783), 2nd son of Rev George Sackville Cotter (ante):—
Issue of late James Laurence Cotter, *b* 1900, *d* 1960: *m* 1924, Anna, da of R. Harris, of Penna, USA:—

James Laurence, *b* 1925; Lt-Cdr US Navy (ret): *m* 1st, 1950 (*m diss* 1972), G. Cerra; 2ndly, 1972, Mariruth Reed, and has issue living (by 1st *m*), Thomas J., *b* 1954: *m* 1977, Karen Jones, and has issue living, Thomas J. *b* 1979, Matthew R. *b* 1981, — Gwendolyn A., *b* 1957. *Residence* – 5562 Zieger Rd, Verona, PA 15147, USA.

Grandsons of late William Crofts Cotter, 2nd son of late Col George Sackville Cotter (*b* 1783) (ante):—
    Issue of late James Laurence Cotter, *b* 18—, *d* 1943: *m* 1916, Jane, who *d* 19—, da of William Blyth, of Edinburgh:—
Laurence Meldrum, *b* 1917. *Residence* – Meadow Creek, Alberta, Canada. —— James Lawrence *b* 1919; European War 1942-5 with Roy Canadian Army Ser Corps: *m* 1948, Phyllis, da of Frank Peters, of Claresholm, Alberta, Canada, and has issue living, Garry Laurence, *b* 1953, — Marlane Phyllis, *b* 1957, — Karen Jean, *b* 1959. *Address* – Box 473, Claresholm, Alberta, Canada. —— Blyth Sackville, *b* 1921.

Grandchildren of late Joseph Henry Cotter (infra):—
    Issue of late Charles Henry Cotter, *b* 1898, *d* 1976: *m* 1924, Louise da of late John Wesley Ray, of Miami, Manitoba, Canada:—
Charles Roy Henry (584 Victoria Av, Belleville, Ont), *b* 1927: *m* 1953, Gertrude Elizabeth, da of Hugh V. McCann, of Ottawa, and has issue living, Joseph Henry, *b* 1957, — Patricia Ann, *b* 1954, — Mary Elizabeth, *b* 1960, — Barbara Jane, *b* 1963, — Catherine Louise, *b* 1965. —— John Raymond (338 Hartviksen St, Port Arthur, Ont), *b* 1929: *m* 1957, Vivienne Margaret, da of Henry A. Patton, of 4 Cotesbach Rd, Clapton, E5, and has issue living, Stephen Henry, *b* 1960, — Karen Louise, *b* 1959, — Susan Margaret, *b* 1961. —— Marjorie Ethel, *b* 1930: *m* 1954, John Durward Johnson, of RR No 5, Truro, Nova Scotia, and has issue living, David Robert, *b* 1955, — Eric Charles, *b* 1957, — Bruce Allan, *b* 1958, — John Andrew, *b* 1965, — Susan Elizabeth, *b* 1961.
    Issue of late Walter Richard Cotter, *b* 1902, *d* 1971: *m* 1923, Lois, da of George Benton King, of Camas, Washington, USA:—
Eugene Richard (210E 8th South, Springville, Utah, USA), *b* 1924: *m* 1947, Mary Agnes, da of Robert Ramsey, of Tempe, Arizona, USA, and has issue living, Charles Eugene, *b* 1952, — Neil Edward, *b* 1957, — Jennifer Marie, *b* 1954. —— George Henry, *b* 1926: *m* 1st, 1949 (*m diss* 19—), Barbara Gene, da of Glenn Maxwell, of Richmond, Cal, USA; 2ndly, 1971, Judith Kay, da of Rex Clark, of Indianapolis, Indiana, USA, and has issue living, (by 1st *m*) Walter Richard, *b* 1953, — Kevin George, *b* 1966.

Granddaughters of late Rev Richard Henry Cotter, 5th son of late Rev Joseph Rogerson Cotter (*b* 1790) (ante):—
    Issue of late Rev Joseph Henry Cotter, *b* 1867, *d* 1937: *m* 1896, Ethel Mary, who *d* 1960, da of late Surg-Maj Samuel Kyle Cotter, MD (infra):—
Adelaide Beatrice Ethel, *b* 1903: *m* 1931, Wilfred Joseph Gagnon, who *d* 1977, and has issue living, Wilfred Joseph, *b* 1934: *m* 1st, 1954 (*m diss* 19—), Glenda Mae Johnston; 2ndly, 19—, — Diane Dean, and has issue living (by 1st *m*), Garry John *b* 1962, Robert Allan *b* 1966, — Paul Martin (59 Coleridge Crescent NW, Calgary, Alberta T2K 1X8, Canada), *b* 1937; (BE Geology): *m* 1961, Maureen Walsh, and has issue living, Paul James *b* 1964, Deanna Louise *b* 1962, Yvonne Michele *b* 1963, Jennifer *b* 1966, Lisa Marie *b* 1990, — Winnifred Alice, *b* 1932: *m* 1st, 1953, Stephen Ivan Berkes, who *d* 1990; 2ndly, 1992, George Frank Istace, of Box 190, Whitewood, Saskatchewan SOG 5CO, Canada, and has issue living (by 1st *m*), Stephen Michael *b* 1958, Linda Ann *b* 1954 : *m* 1974, Edward Istace (and has issue living, Craig Stephen *b* 1978, Drew *b* 1983, Dana *b* (twin) 1983), Nancy Lynn *b* 1956: *m* 1979, Garth Simms (and has issue living, Kelly James *b* 1979, Kirk Michael *b* 1982, Michele Leslie *b* 1983). —— Lilian Muriel Edith, *b* 1910.

Grandchildren of late Rev Richard Henry Cotter (ante):—
    Issue of late Alexander McCaul Cotter, *b* 1871, *d* 1929: *m* 1896, Mildred Bertha Eveline, who *d* 1925, da of George Edwards:—
Felix Alexander, *b* 1900: *m* 1929, Ella Elenor Christopherson, of Brock, Sask, and has issue living, William Leroy, *b* 1935, — Bernice Eveline, *b* 1930. *Residence* – 5994, Dumfries St, Van, BC. —— Louis Stephen (RR2, Mannville, Alberta, T0B 2WO, Canada), *b* 1913; 1939-45 War with Canadian Army: *m* 1941, Elizabeth Ellen, da of Harry Thomas, of Mannville, Alberta, Canada, and has issue living, Gavin Bryson (98 Larose Dr, St Albert, Alberta, Canada T8N 2TZ), *b* 1947: *m* 1972 (*m diss* 1988), Rita Maureen, da of Allan McDonell, of St Albert, Alberta, Canada, and has issue living, Tyler Bryce *b* 1975, Kelly Shannon *b* 1978, — Arlene Berna, *b* 1942: *m* 1968, Dr Richard Ellis Danziger, Capt USN, of 3211 Erie St, San Diego, California 92117, USA, and has issue living, Derek Scott *b* 1972, Kathryn Erin *b* 1975. —— Florence Mildred, *b* 1906: *m* 1929, William James Shury, of 1751 97th St, N Battleford, Sask, Canada, and has issue living, David William (1371-100th St, N Battleford, Sask, Canada), *b* 1930; *ed* Sask Univ (LLB): *m* 1956, Jane Miller, and has issue living, William Brent Cotter *b* 1963, Debra Elizabeth *b* 1956, — Garry Clair, *b* 1938: *m* 1960, Claudia Fradette, and has issue living, Brian Keith *b* 1963, Todd Kevin *b* 1964, — Harold Lloyd, *b* 1942: *m* 1961, Alice Hartman, and has issue living, Dale Lloyd *b* 1962, Kyle Damon *b* 1971, — Terrance James, *b* 1944: *m* 1965, Mary, da of Doyle Edwards, of Saskatoon, and has issue living, Gregory Doyle *b* 1970, Sandra Lynn *b* 1966, Laurie Ann *b* 1971, — Donalaine Elizabeth *b* 1932: *m* 1955, Harold Jones, and has issue living, Glenn Harold *b* 1960, — Evelyn Mildred, *b* 1933, is a Sch Teacher: *m* 1955, Donald MacKenzie, of 959 Herbert Rd, Richmond, BC, Canada, and has issue living, Janice *b* 1957, Valerie *b* 1958, Wendy *b* 1963.

Grandchildren of late Alexander McCaul Cotter (ante):—
    Issue of late Lloyd George Cotter, *b* 1916, *d* 1968: *m* 1945, Iris May Webb, who *m* 2ndly, 1970, Charles Rogerson Cotter, who *d* 1983 (*see* Cotter, Bt, colls, 1980 Edn):—
Burney Thomas, *b* 1946: *m* 1969, Rosemarie, da of Michael Koroluk, Geraldton, Ont, Canada, and has issue living, Kevin Michael, *b* 1980, — Christine Michelle, *b* 1975, — Shari Diane, *b* 1977, — Bonnie Mildred, *b* (twin) 1946: *m* 1972, Paul Halagaza, and has issue living, Mark Leonard, *b* 1975.

Grandchildren of late Rev Richard Henry Cotter (ante):—
    Issue of late Gerald de Purcell Cotter, *b* 1881, *d* 1941: *m* 1917, Rosalind, who *d* 1961, da of James Billington Coughtrie, formerly of Hong Kong:—
Hilary James Coughtrie (38 Jill's Court, Barrie, Ontario L4M 4L7, Canada), *b* 1918; *ed* Westminster, and at Pembroke Coll, Oxford (MA): Lt (ret) RN; late ADC to Gov-Gen of British Somaliland: *m* 1957, Patricia Kathleen Angela Mary Esther, only da of late James Doyne, of Castlerickard, co Meath, and has issue living, Godwin Arthur, *b* (Jan) 1959; *ed* Univ of Toronto (BSc), — Hilary Patrick, *b* (Dec) 1959; *ed* Univ of Toronto (BSc), — Marcian Gerald, *b* 1962, — Rosalind Catherine, *b* 1958; *ed* Magdalen Coll, New Hampshire, USA (BA): *m* 1983, Brian David Pouliot, and has issue living, Dominic John Pio *b* 1984, Thomas Aquinas *b* 1986, Benedict Joseph-Marie *b* 1988, Francis Joseph-Marie *b* 1990, Jerome Joseph-Marie *b* 1994, Monique Marie *b* 1992, — Rebecca Claire, *b* 1961; *ed* Univ of Toronto, and Toronto York Univ (BA, BSc); SRN, — Mary Jane Frances, *b* 1963; SRN: *m* 1993, Ogden Michael Forbes, — Rowena Josephine, *b* 1964; SRN, — Rachel Anne Monica, *b* 1967; SRN. —— Arthur Gerald Purcell, MB, *b* 1924; *ed* Westminster, Oxford Univ, and Trin Coll, Dublin; late Capt RE: *m* 1959, Isabel Adams, of Gortin, co Tyrone, and has issue living, Colin Arthur, *b* 1961, — Lynda Marie, *b* 1962. —— Angela Mary Purcell, *b* 1921: *m* 1st, 1951, Ulick O'Connor Milborne-Swinnerton-Pilkington, who *d* 1979 (*see* Milborne-Swinnerton-Pilkington, Bt); 2ndly, 1981, Cdr Edward Alfred Eborall, RNVR, FIEE, of Tally Ho House, Castletownshend, co Cork.
    Issue of late Joseph Rogerson Cotter, *b* 1869, *d* 1957: *m* 1913, Ellen Harriet, who *d* 1948, da of late Surg-Maj Samuel Kyle Cotter, MD:—

Joan Jamieson, *b* 1916; *ed* Trin Coll, Dublin (BA); late Subaltern ATS: *m* 1944, Henry Haskins Ferrell, Junior, MD, late Capt US Army Med Corps, and has issue living, Henry Haskins (III), MD, *b* 1951: *m* 1984 (*m diss* 1987), Anne Elizabeth Edmunds, — Leslie Cotter (a da), *b* 1949: *m* 1974, José Manuel Kauffmann, and has issue living, Alejandro José *b* 1980, Ana Elena *b* 1982, — Joan Pinson, *b* 1954. *Residence* – 511 Cathedral Drive, Alexandria, Virginia, 22314, USA.

Grandchildren of late Duncan Donald Darrock Cotter, 6th Regt, 8th son of late Rev Joseph Rogerson Cotter (*b* 1790) (ante):—
Issue of late Major Arundel John Plunkett Cotter, US Army, *b* 1883, *d* 1952: *m* 1911, Emma Stothard, da of William Robert Carter:—
Arundel, *b* 1912; Lieut-Col US Army; European War 1939-45: *m* 1st, 1942 (*m diss* 1952), Madelyn, da of Forest Mitchell; 2ndly, 19—, Gabrielle Pauline, da of Harry Tarter, of Washington, DC, and has issue living, (by 1st *m*) Arundel, *b* 1944, — (by 2nd *m*) Harry Bruce, *b* 1955, — Robert Darrock, *b* 1956. —— Joyce, *b* 1914; *ed* Connecticut Coll for Women (BS 19—): *m* 1948, Lieut-Col George Kern, US Army.
Issue of late Harry Norman Cotter, DDS, *b* 1885, *d* 1960: *m* 1912, Rose Isabel, who *d* 1975, da of Henri Malabre, of Kingston, Jamaica:—
Harry Norman Rogerson (533 Driftwood Rd, North Palm Beach, Florida, 33403, USA), *b* 1922; *ed* Cornell Univ (ME 1948): Lt, US Marine Corps (Reserve); 1939-45 War: *m* 1950, Beverly Jane, da of Alfred Edmund Hayes, and has issue living, Thomas Joseph, *b* 1952, — Anthony John, *b* 1962, — Patrick Hayes, *b* 1963, — Lark Ellen, *b* 1951, — Noreen Ann, *b* 1954, — Andrea Jane, *b* 1955. —— Margaret Charlotte, *b* 1917: *m* 1942, Cæsar Leopold Pitassy, LLB, of 11 Hidden Green Lane, Larchmont, New York, USA, and has issue living, Richard Norman *b* 1943.

Grandchildren of late Harry Norman Cotter DDS (ante):—
Issue of late Richard Duncan Rogerson, *b* 1922, *d* 1976: *m* 1949, Mary Theresa (5333 Ravensworth Rd, N Springfield, Virginia, USA), da of late James J. Kellcher:—
Richard Duncan, *b* 1950. —— Michael Patrick, *b* 1952. —— Peter James, *b* 1953. —— David Henry, *b* 1955. —— Matthew, *b* 1961. —— Eileen Mary, *b* 1956. —— Elizabeth Ann, *b* 1960.

Grandchildren of late Surg-Major Samuel Kyle Cotter, MD, yst son of late Rev Joseph Rogerson Cotter (*b* 1790) (ante):—
Issue of late Major Raymond Kyle Cotter, MC, Indian Army (ret); *b* 1889, *d* 1948: *m* 1914, Beryl Jessie Macdonald, who *d* 1972, da of late Charles Macdonald Wintle, Sup Frontier Police, India:—
Derek Raymond Kyle (18 Castleton Close, Mannamead, Plymouth, Devon PLE 5AE), *b* 1916: *m* 1st, 1938, Daphne Cushion who *d* 19—; 2ndly, 19—, —, and has issue living, (by 1st *m*) Anthony Derek, *b* 1941, — Merril Victoria, *b* 1942, — Carolyn, *b* 1948, — (by 2nd *m*) Nicholas Paul, *b* 19—. —— Kathleen Beryl Kyle (Susan),˙ (87 Dartford Rd, Sevenoaks, Kent), *b* 1915: *m* 1st, 1933 (*m diss* 1942), Reginald Barnes Elwin, ICS; 2ndly, 1942, Major Denis Erskine Ward, Roy Tank Regt (V Bangor, colls), who was *ka* 1945; 3rdly, 1946, her former husband, Reginald Barnes Elwin, ICS, who *d* 1961; 4thly, 1978, Stanley Chapman, and has issue living, (by 3rd *m*) David Michael Harrison, *b* 1948, — Peter John Ashton, *b* 1950, — (by 1st *m*) Verity Anne, *b* 1934: *m* 1959, Terry Nicholas Blows, of 58 Channel View Rd, Campbells Bay, Auckland 10, NZ, and has issue.
This family was seated in co Cork prior to the fifteenth century. Sir James Cotter of Anngrove, co Cork, was C-in-C of James II's forces in Cos Cork, Limerick and Kerry. His son, James Cotter, executed in 1720, was father of Sir James Cotter of Rockforest, Co Cork, 1st Bt, who was MP for Askeaton in the Irish Parliament. In 1874, Ludlow Cotter, son and heir of 4th Bt, was the last to receive a knighthood as a privilege of the Order under the second Letters Patent. He *dvp* 1882.

COTTERELL (UK) 1805, of Garnons, Herefordshire

I did not seize it, I recovered it

Sir JOHN HENRY GEERS COTTERELL, 6th *Baronet*; *b* 8 May 1935; *s* his father, Lt-Col *Sir* RICHARD CHARLES GEERS, CBE, TD, 1978; *ed* Eton, and RMC Sandhurst; Capt Roy Horse Guards: *m* 1959, (Vanda) Alexandra (Clare) (High Sheriff Hereford and Worcester 1992), da of Maj Philip Alexander Clement Bridgewater (*see* B Vivian, 1985 Edn), and has issue.

Arms – Quarterly or and argent, a cross engrailed per pale sable and gules, in the second quarter two escallops, and in the third one, all of the third; over all a bend also sable. **Crest** – An arm in armour embowed proper, garnished or, the hand gauntleted also proper, resting on an escutcheon argent, charged with a talbot's head erased sable, collared and lined or.
Residence – Garnons, Hereford HR4 7JU. *Club* – White's.

SONS LIVING

HENRY RICHARD GEERS, *b* 22 Aug 1961: *m* 1986, Carolyn Suzanne, Extra Lady in Waiting to HRH The Duchess of York since 1989, elder da of John Moore Beckwith-Smith, of Maybanks Manor, Rudgwick, Sussex, and has issue living, Richard John Geers, *b* 1 May 1990, — George Dominic Geers, *b* 1994, — Poppy, *b* 1988. —— James Alexander Geers, *b* 1964: *m* 1991, Maria C. B., da of W. F. McManus, of Bryngwyn Close, Hereford, and has issue living, William John Geers, *b* 1992. —— David George Geers, *b* 1968.

DAUGHTER LIVING

Camilla Jane, *b* 1963: *m* 1993, Mark James Kenneth Houldsworth (*see* E Morton, colls, 1963 Edn).

BROTHER LIVING

Thomas Richard Geers, *b* 1939; *ed* Eton: *m* 1966, Caroline Wan-Cheng, who *d* 1991, elder da of Foong Chong.

SISTERS LIVING

Rose Evelyn, *b* 1932: *m* 1954 (*m diss* 1976), Charles Eric Alexander Hambro (*cr* a Life Baron 1994), son of Col Sir Charles Jocelyn Hambro, KBE, MC, and has issue living, Charles Edward, *b* 1959: *m* 1986, Nicole J., only da of Dr James A. Nicholas, of 22 Cayuga Rd, Westchester, New York, and has issue living, Charles James *b* 1991, Christiana *b* 1988, Alissa Katherine *b* 1989, — Alexander Robert, *b* 1962, — Clare Evelyn, *b* 1957: *m* 1989, Eivind Rabben, only son of Knut Rabben, of Oslo, Norway, and has issue living, Edward Olav *b* 1992, Alexander Haakon *b* 1994. *Residence* – Barton House, Guiting Power, nr Cheltenham, Glos. —— Anne Lettice (*Lady Sinclair*), *b* 1933: *m* 1968, 17th Lord Sinclair. *Residence* – Knocknalling, Dalry, Kircudbrightshire.

WIDOW LIVING OF FIFTH BARONET

Hon MOLLY PATRICIA (*Hon Lady Cotterell*) (Flat 1, 4 Eaton Place, SW1) da of 1st Viscount Camrose, formerly wife of 1st Baron Sherwood, and widow of Capt Roger Charles George Chetwode (*see* B Chetwode): *m* 1958, as his 2nd wife, Lt-Col Sir Richard Charles Geers Cotterell, CBE, TD, 5th Bt, who *d* 1978.

Col Sir John Geers, 1st Baronet, sat as MP for Herefordshire 1804-31; his grandfather, John Brooks, of Broadway, assumed the surname and arms of Cotterell, by Roy licence. The 3rd baronet was MP for Herefordshire 1857-9, and the 4th baronet was Lord-Lieut of Herefordshire 1904-33 (High Sheriff 1897).

COTTS (UK) 1921, of Coldharbour Wood, Rogate, Sussex

Forward trusting in God

Sir (ROBERT) CRICHTON MITCHELL COTTS, 3rd *Baronet*; *b* 20 Oct 1903; *s* his brother, Sir (WILLIAM) CAMPBELL MITCHELL-COTTS, 1964; *ed* Harrow, and Balliol Coll, Oxford; Maj (ret) Irish Guards: *m* 1942, Barbara Mary Winefride, who *d* 1982, da of late Capt Herbert John Throckmorton, RN (*see* Throckmorton, Bt, colls), and has had issue.

Arms – Azure, on a chevron between in chief two lions rampant and in base a representation of the Southern Cross, three lymphads sable. **Crest** – A quadriga or. *Residence* – 16 High St, Needham Market, Suffolk IP6 8AP.

SONS LIVING

RICHARD CRICHTON MITCHELL, *b* 26 July 1946; *ed* Oratory Sch. —— Hamish William Anthony Mitchell, *b* 1951; *ed* Ampleforth.

DAUGHTERS LIVING AND DECEASED

Lucinda Mary Agnes Mitchell, *b* 1944: *m* 19—, Christopher Kerrison, and *d* 1987. —— Susannah Marie-Josephe Mitchell, *b* 1945: *m* 1971, John Davies, of Cheshire, and has issue living, Justin, *b* 1981. —— Miranda Clare Mitchell (The 'Oldall, Brent Eleigh, Sudbury, Suffolk CO10 9NP), *b* 1948: *m* 1973, Tristram Cosmo Barran, who *d* 1992 in a motor accident, son of Sir David Haven Barran, and has issue (*see* Barran, Bt).

The name of this family was originally spelt Coutts. The 1st baronet, Sir William Dingwall Mitchell Cotts, KBE (son of late William Cotts, of Sanquhar, Dumfries-shire), was head of the firm of Mitchell Cotts and Co, of London, and of allied firms in S Africa and elsewhere (merchants, colliery proprietors, and steamship owners), and sat as MP for Western Isles (NL) 1922-23. Sir (William) Campbell Mitchell-Cotts, 2nd baronet, an actor, assumed by deed poll 1932 the additional surname of Mitchell.

COUPER (UK) 1841
(Name pronounced "Cooper")

Sir (ROBERT) NICHOLAS OLIVER COUPER, 6th *Baronet*; *b* 9 Oct 1945; *s* his father, *Maj Sir* GEORGE ROBERT CECIL, 1975; *ed* Eton, and RMA Sandhurst; late Capt Blues and Royals: *m* 1st, 1972 (*m diss* 1986), Kirsten Henrietta, da of late Maj George Burrell MacKean, JP, DL, of Loughanmore, Dunadry, co Antrim (*see* E Donoughmore, colls); 2ndly, 1991, Katrina Frances, da of Sir (Charles) Michael Walker, GCMG, of W Chiltington, W Sussex, and has issue by 1st *m*.

Arms – Or, a chevron gules charged with another ermine, between three laurel-leaves slipped vert. **Crest** – Out of a mural coronet argent, a hand holding a garland proper. *Residences* – Annery Barton, Monkleigh, Bideford, N Devon; 79 Devonshire Rd, W4 2HU. *Club* – Cavalry and Guards'.

SON LIVING *(By 1st marriage)*

JAMES GEORGE, *b* 27 Oct 1977.

DAUGHTER LIVING *(By 1st marriage)*

Caroline Doune, *b* 1979.

SISTER LIVING

By valour

Jennifer Susan Amanda, *b* (twin) 1945.

COLLATERAL BRANCHES LIVING

Grandchildren of late James Robert Couper, 4th son of 2nd Bt:—
Issue of late Maj John Every Couper, MBE, *b* 1900, *d* 1966: *m* 1928, Katherine Audrey Mary, who *d* 1987, da of late William Ross Alexander, of Cupar, Fife:—
Jonathan Every, *b* 1931; *ed* Douai.
Issue of late Capt Jem Ramsay Couper, 27th Lancers, *b* 1904, *d* 1979: *m* 1940, Aileen Jessie (Los Amigos, Santa Eleadora, FCNGSM, Argentina), da of late Thomas Robert Lamb Abbott:—
Francis Jem, *b* 1946; *ed* Marlborough. —— Caroline, *b* 1941: *m* 1968, Enrique Avendano, of 6405 30 De Agosto, FCNDFS, Prov de Buenos Aires, Argentina, and has issue living, Diego, *b* 1970, — Enrique Maria, *b* 1977, — Cecilia Maria, *b* 1969.

Granddaughter of late Gen James Kempt Couper, 2nd son of 1st baronet:—
Issue of late William Lemprière Couper, *b* 1874, *d* 1926: *m* 1919, Isabel Hodgson, who *d* 1968, having *m* 2ndly, 1952, Arthur Alfred Hitch, who *d* 1965:—
Cara Jocelyn Mary (45540 Spruce Drive, Sardis, British Columbia), *b* 1921: *m* 1952, Verne Barrett Dickey, who *d* 1984, and has issue living, William Miles, *b* 1955: *m* 1992, Tulia Carranza, and has issue living, Matthew Verne *b* 1993, — Roy Couper, *b* 1957, — Alan Verne, *b* 1960, — Mary Isabel, *b* 1953: *m* 1974, M. Borden, and has issue living, Jeffrey Wayne *b* 1975, Lisa Marie *b* 1977.
Col Sir George, CB, KH, 1st Bt, Capt 92nd Regt at Copenhagen; served throughout Peninsular War (medal with five clasps); was Mil Sec to Sir James Kempt in Canada, and subsequently to Lord Durham; afterwards Comptroller of Household and Equerry to HRH the Duchess of Kent. The 2nd baronet, Sir George Ebenezer Wilson Couper, KCSI, CB, CIE, of the HEICS, was present at the siege of Lucknow as ADC to Sir Henry Lawrence and Sir John Inglis, subsequently becoming Gov of N-W Provinces, India. Sir Guy Couper, 4th Bt, *d* 1975, when the baronetcy passed to Maj Sir George Robert Cecil Couper, 5th Bt, el son of James Robert Couper, 4th son of 2nd Bt.

COWAN (UK) 1921, of the Baltic, and Bilton, co Warwick (Extinct 1956)

Adm Sir WALTER HENRY COWAN, KCB, DSO, MVO, 1st and last *Baronet*.

DAUGHTER LIVING OF FIRST BARONET

Martha Gillian Rosemary, *b* 1905. *Residence* – Merle Cottage, Scampston, Malton, Yorks.

Cowell-Stepney, see Stepney.

COXEN (UK) 1941, of Seal, co Kent (Extinct 1946)

Major Sir WILLIAM GEORGE COXEN, 1st and last *Baronet*.

WIDOW LIVING OF FIRST BARONET

KATHLEEN ALICE (*Lady Coxen*), da of late Edward Doncaster, of Snettisham, Norfolk: *m* 1912, Maj Sir William George Coxen, 1st Bt (Lord Mayor of London 1939-40), who *d* 1946, when the title became ext. *Residence* – 8a Wellswood Park, Torquay.

Cradock-Hartopp, see Hartopp.

Craig (Gibson-Craig-Carmichael), see Carmichael.

CRAUFURD (GB) 1781, of Kilbirney, North Britain

Distinction without a stain

Sir ROBERT JAMES CRAUFURD, 9th *Baronet*; *b* 18 March 1937; *s* his father, *Sir* JAMES GREGAN, 1970; *ed* Harrow, and Univ Coll, Oxford (MA); Member of London Stock Exchange: *m* 1st, 1964 (*m diss* 1987), Catherine Penelope, yr da of late Capt Horatio Westmacott, RN; 2ndly, 1987, Georgina Anne, da of late John Dennis Russell (*see* Corbet Bt), and has issue (by 1st *m*).

Arms – Argent, two tilting spears in saltire proper between four ermine spots sable, a bordure chequy gules and of the field. Crest – An ermine proper.
Residence – 7 Waldemar Avenue, SW6 5LB.

DAUGHTERS LIVING (By 1st marriage)

Caroline Anne, *b* 1965. ——— Penelope Jane, *b* 1967. ——— Veronica Mary, *b* 1969.

SISTERS LIVING

Jane Elizabeth, *b* 1932: *m* 1st, 1960 (*m diss* 1979), Maj Michael Cumby Spurrier, late DLI; 2ndly, 1979, John Robson Hoyle, of 12 Linkfield, E Molesey, Surrey. ——— Margaret Ruth, *b* 1934: *m* 1962 (*m diss* 1989), John Peter Hudson, and has issue living, Alexander Matthew HUDSON CRAUFURD, *b* 1965; *ed* Edinburgh Univ (BA); assumed the surname of Craufurd in addition to that of Hudson by Deed Poll, — Emma Caroline, *b* 1963, — Erica, *b* 1968.

DAUGHTERS LIVING OF SEVENTH BARONET

Isolda Vereker (21 Glendale Drive, SW19), *b* 1912: *m* 1945, Maj James Clement, and has issue living, James Robert Alexander, *b* 1949, — Helen Alexa Caroline, *b* 1950. ——— Cynthia (6 Etloe House, Church Rd, Leyton E10 7DE) *b* 1917: *m* 1st, 1944, Jacques Pinkasfeld, who *d* 1963; 2ndly, 1972, Lt-Col Albert Francis Lamb, who *d* 1981, and has issue living (by 1st *m*), Peter Charles, *b* 1950, — Rosemary, *b* 1952.

WIDOW LIVING OF EIGHTH BARONET

RUTH MARJORIE (*Dowager Lady Craufurd*), (Brightwood, Aldbury, Tring, Herts), da of Frederic Corder, of Ipswich: *m* 1931, Sir James Gregan Craufurd, 8th baronet, who *d* 1970.

COLLATERAL BRANCH LIVING

Granddaughters of late Capt Henry Robert Craufurd, grandson of Maj-Gen Robert Craufurd, 3rd son of 1st baronet:—
Issue of late Col Robert Quentin Craufurd, DSO, *b* 1880, *d* 1943: *m* 1st, 1909, Mildred Mary, who *d* 1929, da of late Rt Hon William Kenny, a Judge of High Court in Ireland, of Marlfield, Cabinteely, co Dublin; 2ndly, 1931, Muriel Frances, who *d* 1969, da of late George Edward Darroch, of 40 Stanhope Gdns, SW, and Braidley, Canford Cliffs, Dorset:—
(By 1st *m*) Dorothy Mary, *b* 1910; a Nun. ——— Mildred Heather Mary (61 Finborough Rd, SW10), *b* 1916.
This family descends from John who possessed the Northern part of the Barony of Crawford 1153. His son, Sir Reginald de Craufurd, *m* Margaret, da and heir of James de Loudoun, and his descendants inherited the lands of Loudoun which passed to Susan, da and heir of Sir Reginald Craufurd executed by the English at Carlisle 1307. She *m* Sir Duncan Campbell of Reidcastle, from whom descend the Earls of Loudoun. Sir Alexander Craufurd, 1st Bt, was 11th in descent from Archibald Craufurd of Previck and Thirdpart, living 1401, 2nd son of Thomas of Auchenames, great-grandson of Hugh, yr brother of Sir Reginald.

CRAVEN (UK) 1942, of Crowhurst, co Surrey (Extinct 1946)

Sir DEREK WORTHINGTON CLUNES CRAVEN, 2nd and last *Baronet*.

DAUGHTER LIVING OF SECOND BARONET

Jennifer Anne, *b* (*posthumous*) 1946.

WIDOW LIVING OF SECOND BARONET

MARJORIE KATHLEEN WALLIS (*Lady Craven*), da of late Alfred Henry Hopkins: *m* Dec 1945, as his second wife, Sir Derek Worthington Clunes Craven, 2nd Bt, who *d* 1946, when the title became ext. *Residence* – Aberfeldie, Peckon's Hill, Ludwell, Shaftesbury, Dorset.

Crawley-Boevey, see Boevey.

Crespigny, see de Crespigny.

CRISP (UK) 1913, of Bungay, Suffolk

Sir (JOHN) PETER CRISP, 4th *Baronet*; *b* 19 May 1925; *s* his father, *Sir* JOHN WILSON, 1950; *ed* Westminster: *m* 1954, Judith Mary, yst da of late Herbert Edward Gillett, FRICS, of Marlborough, Wilts, and niece of Sir Harold Gillett, 1st Bt, MC, and has issue.

Arms – Paly of four ermine and gules, on a chevron or five horseshoes sable. **Crest** – A camelopard sejant or, gorged with a collar with chain reflexed over the back gules, supporting with the dexter foreleg an oar of the Royal State Barge proper.
Residence – Crabtree Cottage, Drungewick Lane, Loxwood, Billingshurst, W Sussex RH14 0RP.

SONS LIVING

JOHN CHARLES, *b* 10 Dec 1955: *m* 1992, Mary Jo, eldest da of Dr Daniel J. MacAuley, of Belfast, and has issue living, George Peter Daniel, *b* 17 Sept 1993. —— Michael Peter, *b* 1957: *m* 1988, Pauline Sarah, only da of Sydney Gold, of Pinner, Middx, and has issue living, Alexander Samuel, *b* 1990, — Joshua Peter, *b* 1993. —— Charles Frank, *b* 1960: *m* 1992, Susan Jennifer, elder da of Deryck Scrase, of Rudgwick, W Sussex, and has issue living, Frederick, *b* 1993.

DAUGHTER LIVING

Catherine Mary, *b* 1962.

COLLATERAL BRANCH LIVING

Res·non·verba

Deeds not words

Issue of late Bernard Woodward Crisp, 3rd son of 1st baronet; *b* 1875; *d* 1963 *m* 1901, Elsa Florence, who *d* 1938, da of Robert Schwarz:—
Joan Veronica (4 Sprimont Place, SW3), *b* 1904; *m* 1st, 1927 (*m* diss 1951), Trevor Gayer Fetherstonaugh, MC, MB, ChM; 2ndly, 1953, Capt John Egerton Broome, DSC, RN (ret), who *d* 19—.
The 1st baronet, Sir Frank Crisp (son of John Shalders Crisp, of Bramfield, Suffolk), was senior partner in the legal firm of Ashurst, Morris, Crisp & Co, of 17 Throgmorton Avenue, EC.

CRITCHETT (UK) 1908, of Harley Street, Borough of St Marylebone

Sir IAN GEORGE LORRAINE CRITCHETT, 3rd *Baronet*; *b* 9 Dec 1920; *s* his father, *Sir* (GEORGE) MONTAGUE, MVO, 1941; *ed* Harrow, and Clare Coll, Camb (BA 1942); formerly Flight-Lieut RAF Vol Reserve; entered Foreign Office 1948; was 3rd Sec (Commercial) in Vienna 1950-51, 2nd Sec (Commercial) in Bucharest 1951-53, 2nd Sec in Cairo 1956; 1st Sec, later Counsellor, FCO 1962 (ret 1980): *m* 1st, 1948, Paulette Mary Lorraine, who *d* 1962, da of late Col Henry Brabazon Humfrey, formerly Indian Army; 2ndly, 1964, Jocelyn Daphne Margret, el da of late Cdr Christopher Mildmay Hall, of Higher Boswarva, Penzance (*see* Broughton, Bt, 1980 Edn), and has issue by 2nd *m*.

Arms – Azure, a fire chest argent, flames proper, between three crickets or. **Crest** – A starling in front of an iris flowered proper.
Residence – Uplands Lodge, Pains Hill, Limpsfield, Surrey RH8 0RF.

SON LIVING (By 2nd marriage)

CHARLES GEORGE MONTAGUE, *b* 2 April 1965.

DAUGHTER LIVING (By 2nd marriage)

SUIVEZ RAISON

Follow right

Xanthe Clare Lorraine, *b* 1968.
The 1st baronet, Sir (George) Anderson Critchett, KCVO, was a KGStJ, Pres of Ophthalmological Soc 1899-1900, and Surg-Oculist to King Edward VII 1901-10, and to King George V 1910-18, and Surg-Oculist-in-Ord to King George V 1918-25, and the 2nd baronet, Sir (George) Montague Critchett, MVO, was in Lord Chamberlain's Office, St James's Palace 1912-41.

CROFT (E) 1671, of Croft Castle, Herefordshire

To be rather than to seem

Sir OWEN GLENDOWER CROFT, 14th *Baronet*; *b* 26 April 1932; *s* his father, *Sir* BERNARD HUGH DENMAN, 1984: *m* 1959, Sally Patricia, da of Dr Thomas Montagu Mansfield, of Brisbane, Qld, and has issue.

Arms – Quarterly per fesse indented azure and argent; in the 1st quarter a lion passant guardant or. Crests – 1st, a lion passant guardant argent; 2nd, a wyvern sable vulned in the side gules.
Residence – Salisbury Court, Uralla 2358, NSW, Australia.

SON LIVING

THOMAS JASPER (51 Park St, Uralla, NSW 2358, Australia), *b* 3 Nov 1962; *ed* The Armidale Sch, Armidale, and Darling Downs Inst (Assoc Dip Mech Eng): *m* 1989, Catherine Fiona, da of Graham William White.

DAUGHTERS LIVING

Patricia Alice, *b* 1960: *m* 1993, Peter James Rasmussen. —— Georgiana, *b* 1964.

BROTHERS LIVING

Hugh Fiennes Denman (Callemondah, Duri, NSW 2344, Aust), *b* 1942: *m* 1972, June Alison Cairnes, da of late John Wauch Johnston, of Straban, Walcha, NSW, and has issue living, Edwina Alexandra Cairnes, *b* 1974, — Katrina Alison Cairnes, *b* 1976, — Philippa Ann Cairnes, *b* 1977, — Lucinda Anna Cairnes, *b* 1983. —— Bernard John (Westview, PO Box 253, Guyra, NSW 2365, Australia), *b* 1943: *m* 1977, Janet Madeleine, da of Lloyd Alfred Streader, of Melbourne, Vic, and has issue living, David William, *b* 1977, — Ian Archer, *b* 1981, — Briony Elizabeth, *b* 1979, — Alice Madeleine, *b* 1985.

SISTERS LIVING

Margaret, *b* 1935: *m* 1960, David Arundel Wright, and has issue living, Phillip Arundel, *b* 1963, — David Andrew, *b* 1965, — Charlotte May, *b* 1961, — Catherine Arundel, *b* 1969. *Residence* – Wallamumbi, Armidale, 2350, NSW. —— Camilla, *b* 1947.

UNCLE LIVING (Son of 12th baronet)

Herbert Frederick, *b* 1906: *m* 1932, Marjorie Valmai, who *d* 1990, da of R. Evans, and has issue living, Peter Herbert (Wongalee, Uralla, NSW), *b* 1933: *m* 1965, Ann, da of late L. G. Carpenter, of Toll-Bar, Cooma, NSW, and has issue living, Guy Herbert *b* 1966, — Andrew Peter *b* 1968, — Robert Ryland (P.O. Box 1586, Armidale, NSW 2350, Australia), *b* 1937: *m* 1966, Helen, da of late D. J. Fraser, and has issue living, Quentin Stewart, *b* 1967, Carlisle Robert *b* 1974, Sinclair Fraser *b* 1976, — James Philip (Weebaree, Uralla 2358, NSW), *b* 1950: *m* 1972, Elaine, da of late S. K. Wall, of Cowra, and has issue living, Michael James *b* 1977, Rowena Jane *b* 1974, — Shirley Anne *b* 1934: *m* 1954, David Gill, of 3 Buckingham Drive, Pottsville Beach, NSW 2489, Australia, and has issue living, Michael David *b* 1957: *m* 1982, Kim Elizabeth, da of late R. R. Crutcher, of Wee Waa, NSW (and has issue living, Nichole May *b* 1986, Samantha Jane *b* 1992), Philippa Shirley *b* 1955: *m* 1975, James Douglas Page, of Boolneringbar, Copmanhurst, NSW, Australia (and has issue living, Robert James *b* 1975, Rachelle Philippa *b* 1978, Jacqueline Frances *b* 1982), Katrina Anne *b* 1958: *m* 1988, John Douglas Kerrison, of 16 Victoria St, Tamworth, NSW, Australia (and has issue living, Dean Andrew *b* 1993, Anna Maree *b* 1991). *Residence* – Bareena, Uralla, NSW.

AUNTS LIVING (Daughters of 12th baronet)

Phyllis Lucy, *b* 1901: *m* 1923, George Stuart Robertson Park, and has issue living, Walter Stuart (Wongabindi, New Winton Rd, Tamworth, NSW 2340, Australia), *b* 1925: *m* 1950, June Coates, and has issue living, Elizabeth *b* 1951: *m* 1973, Robert John Nicoll, of 29 Curzon St, Toowoomba, Queensland 4350, Australia (and has issue living, Brett Robert *b* 1975, Sharon Elizabeth *b* 1977), Wendy *b* 1954: *m* 1985, John Stephen Dobis (and has issue living, John Steven Walter *b* 1990, Jessica June Katalin *b* 1993), Deborah *b* 1957: *m* 1979, Gary Craig, of Baronia, Duri, NSW 2416, — Ian Croft (Mirrabooka, Roma 4455, Queensland, Australia), *b* 1936: *m* 1960, Kay, only da of A. Shaw, of Lammermoor, Wee Woa, NSW, and has issue living, Kenneth Ian *b* 1963, Geoffrey Steven *b* 1964, Nicholas David *b* 1970, Janine Maree *b* 1968, — Phyllis Joan, *b* 1924: *m* 1949, Roger L'Estrange Rankine, Capt AIF, who *d* 1982, of 100 Upper St, Tamworth, NSW, and has issue living, Timothy Roger *b* 1951: *m* 1975, Leticia, elder da of late G. Forté (and has issue living, Dean Roger Forté *b* 1978, David Forté *b* 1979, Alexandra Forté *b* 1987), Andrew Stuart *b* 1954: *m* 1981, Mary-Alice, eldest da of John Lloyd, of Delungra, NSW (and has issue living, Roger Angus *b* 1984, Maxim John *b* 1989, Prudence Lucy *b* 1986), Steven John *b* 1960: *m* 198-, Belinda Jan, elder da of Richard Boden, of Mount Ousley, NSW (and has issue living, Thomas *b* 1987, Sophie Catherine *b* 1990, Eloise Claire Alice *b* 1992), — Mary Isabel, *b* 1928: *m* 1949, John Mervyn Wilshire, of 41 Hyman St, Tamworth 2340, NSW, and has issue living, Malcolm John *b* 1958: *m* 1984, Fiona Anne Slattery (and has issue living, Julie Kathryn *b* 1986), Marilyn Mary *b* 1950: *m* 1973, Timothy John O'Keefe, of 13 Napier St, Tamworth, NSW (and has issue living, George Alexander *b* 1974, Adam Timothy *b* 1975), Christine Linda *b* 1953: *m* 1972, Lowell Reardon, of 156 Green Point Dr, Green Point, via Forster, NSW 2428 (and has issue living, Melissa Louise *b* 1973, Rebeccca Gai *b* 1976). *Residence* – 8 Daruka Rd, Tamworth 2340, NSW.

WIDOW LIVING OF THIRTEENTH BARONET

HELEN MARGARET (*Helen, Lady Croft*), da of Harry Weaver, of Armidale, NSW: *m* 1931, Sir Bernard Hugh Denman Croft, 13th Bt, who *d* 1984. *Residence* – 133 Dangar St, Armidale, NSW 2350, Australia.

COLLATERAL BRANCHES LIVING

Issue of late Frederick James Croft, 3rd son of 12th baronet, *b* 1909, *d* 1993: *m* 1943, Barbara (Lugwardine, Barraba, NSW 2347, Australia), da of Howard Carter, of Barraba, NSW:—
Edward Hugh Wynford, *b* 1944: *m* 1969, Jennifer Mary, da of Thomas James Stirton, of Armoobilla, Cheepie, Qld, and has issue living, Edward James Wynford, *b* 1971, — Andrew John Wynford *b* 1974, — Amanda Jane, *b* 1978, — Lucinda Jennifer, *b* 1981.

Issue of late Archer John Croft, yst son of 12th baronet, *b* 1913, *d* 1971: *m* 1939, Marcie Issell Heathfield, who *d* 1976, da of late Clifton Hazlewood Eliott (*see* Eliott, Bt, colls).
Antony John (Vale St, Tamworth, NSW 2340, Australia), *b* 1940: *m* 1966 (*m diss* 1978), Kathleen Francis, yr da of R. F. Kelsall, and has issue living, Michael John, *b* 1967, — Tania Jane, *b* 1968. ⸺ David Archer (12 Hambledon Hill Rd, Singleton, NSW, Australia), *b* 1946: *m* 1971, Violeta, only child of V. Deikus, of 6 Albert St, Cabramatta, NSW, and has issue living, Justin Damian, *b* 1973, — Nathan David, *b* 1975, — Rebecca Lee *b* 1978. ⸺ Stephen Hugh, *b* 1953.

Grandson of late Brig-Gen William Denman Croft, CB, CMG, DSO (infra):—
Issue of late Capt William Owen Glendower Croft, Indian Army, *b* 1913, *d* 1946: *m* 1944, Margaret, da of late Major Tobin, Indian Army:—
Richard Owen Glendower (Barnesfield, South St, Boughton, Faversham, Kent), *b* 1944; *ed* Kent Univ; Lt 1st Bn Cameronians (Scottish Rifles): *m* 1967, Elizabeth Jillian Allen, and has issue living, James Owen, *b* 1972, — Emma Kate, *b* 1974.

Issue of late Brig-Gen William Denman Croft, CB, CMG, DSO, 4th son of 9th baronet, *b* 1879, *d* 1968: *m* 1912, Esmé, who *d* 1977, da of Sir Arthur Edwin Sutton, 7th Bt:—
Rev John Armentieres, MC (Vine House, The Common, Wincanton, Som; Army and Navy Club), *b* 1915; *ed* Stowe; Maj (ret) RA; late Indian Army; V of Gwinear 1960-70; NW Frontier 1935 (despatches), Burma 1944 (wounded, MC): *m* 1948, Sheila Kathleen, da of late Maj J. A. Ford, of Pengreep, Cornwall, and has issue living, Edmund Hugh Glendower, *b* 1954, — Patricia Lucy, *b* 1951: *m* 1973, Maj Robert Rowe, R Irish Rangers, and has issue living, Victoria Lucy *b* 1977, Harriet Alice *b* 1979. ⸺ Violet Lorna, *b* 1917: *m* 1942, Lt-Cdr Thomas Charteris Black, RNVR, and has issue living, Peter Michael, *b* 1952, — Jane Margaret, *b* 1943, — Susan Mary, *b* 1945. ⸺ Angela Desiree, *b* 1923: *m* 1st, 1955, Roland Grievson, who *d* 1974; 2ndly, 1984, Walter Carlson, of 14A Upper Glenburn Rd, Bearsden, Glasgow G61.

Issue of late Jasper Brodie Croft, 7th son of 9th baronet; *b* 1884; *d* 1950: *m* 1907, Catherine Harriett, who *d* 1975, da of F. G. Taylor, of Terrible Vale, NSW:—
Jasper Thomas (50 Sandstone Crescent, Lennox Head 2478, NSW, Australia), *b* 1924; Fl Lt RAAF; JP: *m* 1948, Editha Deirdre, da of late George Mansfield Westgarth, of Scone, NSW and has issue living, Jasper David (c/o NSW Agriculture & Fisheries, Wagga Wagga, NSW, Australia); *b* 1949; BA, MSc; JP: *m* 1977, Frances Ellen, da of Francis Hamilton, of Condobolin, and has issue living, Jasper Brett Frank *b* 1983, Amanda Kate *b* 1980, — Bettina Kay, *b* 1951: *m* 1973, David Peter Leslie, of Beverley, Nevertire, NSW, and has issue living, Andrew David *b* 1978, Karina Jodi *b* 1976, Kristy Peta *b* 1987, — Kerrie Leigh (a da) *b* 1954. ⸺ Kitty McLeod (Unit 49/45 Cook St, St David's Retirement Village, Forestville, NSW), *b* 1908: *m* 1938, Peter Assheton, who *d* 1970, and has had issue, Pedir Raif Orme, *b* 1941: *m* 1972, Nancy Shaw, of Sydney, NSW, and *d* 1992, leaving issue, Olwen Annaliese *b* 1975, — Rowena Tydwr, *b* 1939: *m* 1966, Zbyszek Lisak, of Lorne House, Kingsland, Herefordshire HR6 9RU, and has issue living, Tamara *b* 1967, Nadya *b* 1968. ⸺ Isabel McLeod, *b* 1911: *m* 1945, Bassett Fredrick Care, of 16 Beaumetz St, Sandgate 4017, Qld, and has issue living, Frederick McLeod, *b* 1948: *m* 1969, Jennifer Dianne, da of late Arthur Silas Faulk, and has issue living, Thomas Lachlan *b* 1986, Amanda *b* 1970, Sally *b* 1972. ⸺ Marjorie McLeod, *b* 1912: *m* 1943, Cecil Gordon Lowe, RAAF, of 32 North Rd, Woodridge, Qld, and has issue living, Benjamin John, *b* 1944: *m* 1st, 1962 (*m diss* 1975), Gloria Daphne, da of W. Williams, of W Aust; 2ndly, 1979, Patricia Lee Florian, and has issue living, (by 1st *m*) Dallas Gordon *b* 1969, (by 2nd *m*) Jason McLeod *b* 1979, — William James, *b* 1951: *m* 1974, Caroline, da of Kenneth Watson, and has issue living, Daniel William *b* 1975, Drummond Murray *b* 1978, Benjamin Gordon *b* 1979, — Catherine Jane, *b* 1947: *m* 1969, Brian Finnigan, of 65 Ashton St, Kingston, Qld, and has issue living, Matthew Brian *b* 1977, David Joseph *b* 1980, Joanne Maree *b* 1973, Anna *b* 1987, — Susanne Barbara, *b* 1950: *m* 1971, Kenneth Murray, of Tieri, Qld, and has issue living, Rachel Susanne *b* 1977, Deanne Gai *b* 1978, Alaina Alexandrea *b* 1981, — Elizabeth, *b* 1953: *m* 1975, Peter Anthony Ware, of Qld, and has issue living, Jodie Alisha *b* 1980, Melissa Jane *b* 1983, — Mary-Anne *b* 1955: *m* 1977, Denis Townsend, of Qld, and has issue living, Shane Andrew *b* 1980, Timothy Neil *b* 1983. ⸺ Enid Barbara McLeod, *b* 1915: *m* 1959, Maj George Hyde, AIF, who *d* 1975. ⸺ Nancy Perena McLeod, *b* 1921: *m* 1950, Eric W. Adams, of Balnabeen, Silver Leigh Rd, Kingsthorpe, Qld 4400, Australia.

Grandchildren of late Richard Benyon Croft, son of late Rev Richard Croft 3rd son of 6th baronet:—
Issue of late Lieut-Col Richard Page Croft, *b* 1872, *d* 1961: *m* 1908, Eva Pansy Millicent Philippa Stanhope, who *d* 1940, da of William Sharp Waithman, JP, DL (E Harrington):—
Richard Arthur FitzRoy Page, *b* 1910; late Major RASC; 1939-45 War (despatches): *m* 1st, 1939 (*m diss* 1956), Felice Amy (Peggy) McClymont; 2ndly, 1956, Daphne Frye, who *d* 1978; 3rdly, 1981, Maria Isabel (*née* De Eguidazu), and formerly wife of Count Aymon de Roussy de Sales, and has issue living, (by 1st *m*) Richard Nicholas Page, *b* 1941: *m* 1st, 1967, Teresa Mary, who *d* 1971, da of late Donald Jewell, of Burry Port, Carmarthenshire, and formerly wife of Sverré Wilberg, of Frederikstadt, Norway; 2ndly, 1973, Bruna Campesato, — Hugo Douglas Page, *b* 1944: *m* 1969, Dawn Pryde, and has issue living, Richard Page *b* 1973, Edward Page *b* 1976, James Craggs Page *b* 1979, Arabella *b* 1971, — Miriam Anne Page, *b* 1948: *m* 1974, Piers Rogers, of Castlebury, Ware, Herts, and has issue living, Samuel Bennett *b* 1978, Scarlett Alice *b* 1980. *Residence* – The Round House, Ware, Herts SG12 7PR.
Issue of late Rt Hon Sir Henry Page Croft, CMG, TD, 1st Bt, who was *cr Baron Croft* 1940 (see that title).

Jasper de Croft came from Normandy 1066. Croft Castle, built 1200, was sold about 1765, having descended from father to son for more than 700 years (but was bought back by the Trustees for the 11th Bt in 1924, and is now the property of the National Trust). Members of the family represented Herefordshire in sixteen Parliaments between 1297 and 1874. Sir John Croft of Croft Castle *m* Janet, da of Owen Glendower. The father of the first baronet was Bishop of Hereford. The 10th baronet, Sir Herbert Archer Croft, Capt Herefordshire Regt, was *ka* 1915. The 11th baronet, Sir James Herbert Croft, Capt No 1 Commando Special Ser Batn, was *k* on active ser 1941.

CROFT (UK) 1818, of Cowling Hall, Yorkshire

Sir THOMAS STEPHEN HUTTON CROFT, 6th *Baronet*; *b* 12 June 1959; *s* his father, *Maj Sir* JOHN ARCHIBALD RADCLIFFE, 1990; *ed* King's Sch, Canterbury, Univ Coll, London (BSc), and Royal Coll of Art (MA); Architect.

Arms – Quarterly per fesse indented or and gules, in the first quarter a lion passant-guardant of the second. **Crest** – A lion passant guardant per pale, indented gules and erminois, the dexter fore paw resting on a shield argent charged with a star of the Order of the Tower and Sword. **Supporters** – Dexter, a lion guardant or, gorged with a wreath of laurel vert, therefrom pendent an escutcheon gules, charged with a tower or; sinister, a bull sable, horned crined hoofed and gorged with a wreath of laurel or, therefrom pendent an escutcheon argent, charged with the star of the Order of the Tower and Sword. *Residence* – 53 Leinster Sq, W2 4PV.

ESSE QUAM VIDERI

To be rather than to seem

UNCLE LIVING (*brother of 5th baronet*)

CYRIL BERNARD, *b* 6 June 1918; late Lieut The Buffs: *m* 1st, 1957, Sheila Maisie, who *d* 1979, da of Henry Clark Cox, of Whitstable, Kent; 2ndly, 1980, Anne Heather Newbatt, da of Howard Cormack Bessant, and has issue living (by 1st *m*), Diana Louise, *b* 1959: *m* 19—, Neil Frederick Crumbie, — Wendy Jane, *b* 1961. *Residence* – Rayham Meadow, Rayham Rd, Whitstable, Kent CT5 3DZ.

WIDOW LIVING OF FIFTH BARONET

LUCY ELIZABETH (*Lady Croft*), Lieut ATS, Hon Col WRAC (TA), da of late Maj William Dallas Loney Jupp, OBE, of Stafford: *m* 1953, Maj Sir John Archibald Radcliffe Croft, 5th Bt, who *d* 1990. *Residence* – The Barn House, Rayham Rd, Whitstable, Kent CT5 3DZ.

This family is of common origin with the Crofts of Herefordshire, and the Crofts of Stillington Hall, Yorks. Sir John Croft, 1st Bt, a Portuguese Commr, Knt of the Portuguese Order of the Tower and Sword, and Baron da Serra da Estrella in Portugal, did considerable service in the Peninsular war by risking his life to obtain information for the Duke of Wellington, and in distributing the British Parliamentary grant of £100,000 for relieving the Portuguese, and was Hon Chargé d'Affaires at Lisbon 1815.

CROFTON (UK) 1801, of Mohill, Leitrim

(*Sir*) HUGH DENIS CROFTON, 8th *Baronet*; *b* 10 April 1937; *s* his half-nephew, *Sir* (HUGH) PATRICK SIMON, 1987, but does not use the title; *ed* Eton, Worcester Coll, Oxford (BA), and Bristol Univ (BA).

Arms – Per pale indented or and azure, a lion passant-guardant counterchanged, a crescent for difference. **Crest** – Seven ears of wheat, on one stalk proper.

BROTHER LIVING

EDWARD MORGAN, *b* 26 July 1945; *ed* Eton, and RMA; Maj Coldstream Gds (ret 1986): *m* 1977, Emma Victoria Mildred, only da of Sir Henry George Massy Dashwood, 8th Bt (*cr* 1684), and has issue living, Henry Morgan, *b* 1979, — George Edward, *b* 1981. *Residence* – Long Durford, Upper Durford Wood, Petersfield, Hants.

DAUGHTER LIVING OF SEVENTH BARONET

Atalanta Chloe Majken, *b* 1969.

WIDOW LIVING OF SIXTH BARONET

MARGARET AMELIA (*Margaret, Lady Crofton*), da of late Judge Morris Dallett, of Philadelphia, USA: *m* 1933, as his 3rd wife, Lt-Col Sir Morgan George Crofton, DSO, 6th Bt, who *d* 1958. *Residence* – 34 Rhinefield Close, Brockenhurst, Hants SO42 7SU.

DAT·DEUS·INCREMENTUM

God gives the increase

WIDOW LIVING OF SEVENTH BARONET

LENE (*Lady Crofton*), da of Kai Augustinus, of Copenhagen, and of Mrs R. Tonnesen, of Port Elizabeth, S Africa, and formerly wife of Michael Eddowes: *m* 1967, Sir (Hugh) Patrick Simon Crofton, 7th Bt, who *d* 1987. *Residence* – Foxleys Farm, Holyport, nr Maidenhead, Berks.

MOTHER LIVING OF SEVENTH BARONET

Rosalie, da of late John Lever Tillotson, of Bidston Court, Cheshire: *m* 1st, 1934 (*m diss* 1941), Maj Morgan George Crofton, who *d* 1947; 2ndly, 1947, Lt-Col George St Vigor J. Vigor, OBE, late Welsh Gds, who *d* 1979. *Residence* – 27 Park St, Windsor, Berks.

COLLATERAL BRANCHES LIVING

Granddaughters of late Lt-Gen James Crofton, 3rd son of Capt Morgan Crofton, RN, el son of Morgan Crofton, 3rd son of 1st baronet:—

Issue of late Charles D'Arcy Crofton, b 1879, d 1955: m 1910, Mary Helen Elizabeth, who d 1960, da of H. G. Gearing, formerly of Tea Hill, Coonoor, Nilgris, S India:—

Patience D'Arcy, b 1911: m 1936, Lieut-Col Joseph Richard Waters, OBE, RA, and has issue living, Prudence D'Arcy, b 1937: m 1969, Harry Waugh, of 14 Camden Sq, NW1, and has issue living, Jamie Horsburgh b 1973, Harriet D'Arcy b (twin) 1973, — Ann Gillian, b 1938: m 1961, Peter Llewellyn Sheldon, and has issue living, Valentine D'Arcy b 1969, Clare Helen b 1966. *Residence* – Down Cottage, Frant, Tunbridge Wells. ——— Beatrice Barrett, b 1915: m 1938, Brig Anthony John le Grand Jacob, MBE, late RE, of The Rose Cottage, St James's Green, Southwold, Suffolk, and has issue living, John, b 1940, — Rupert, b 1948, — Rosemary, b 1944, — Alice, b 1950.

Issue of late John Hutchinson Crofton, MB, MRCS, b 1883, d 1953: m 1914, Aice, who d 1943, da of late Arthur Charles Humphreys-Owen, MP, of Glansevern, Montgomeryshire:—

Anne Dorothy, b 1915. *Address* – c/o Westminster Bank Ltd, Maidenhead, Berks.

Grandchildren of late Rev Henry Woodward Crofton, 2nd son of Rev William Morgan Crofton, 2nd son of Morgan Crofton, 3rd son of 1st baronet:—

Issue of late Maj Geoffrey Hugh Schenley Crofton, late Suffolk Regt, b 1881, d 1955: m 1908, Monica, who d 1977, da of late A. W. Hall, of Barton Abbey, Steeple Aston:—

Henry Horatio, b 1910; Capt W Yorks Regt. ——— Monica Melesina Nem, b 1915. ——— Angela Catherine, b 1917.

Grandson of late Maj Charles Woodward Crofton, yr son of late Rev Henry Woodward Crofton (ante):—

Issue of late Maj Hugh Charles Henry Crofton, RA, b 1915, d 1986: m 1949, Margery (Kirklington, N Yorks), da of late T. Summerson, of Sunderland:—

John Hugh (Arkengarthdale, N Yorks), b 1954; ed Giggleswick Sch: m 1981, Martha June, da of William Thomas Holbert, of 435 Bluebird Lane, Delray Beach, Fla 33445, USA, and has issue living, Emma Zoe, b 1983, — Chloe Alexandra, b 1986.

Grandchildren of late Francis Blake Crofton, 5th son of Rev William Crofton (ante):—

Issue of late Algernon Francis Blake, b 1873, d 19—: m 1893, Edith, da of James Hall of Peterborough, Ontario:—

Katherine CEBRIAN; resumed her former surname of Cebrian 19—: m 1st, 1919, Louis de Laveaga Cebrian, who d 1937; 2ndly, 1938, Douglas Lindsay Pringle, who d 1960, and has issue living, (by 1st m) Luis Enrique, b 1933, — José Maria de Laveaga, b 1934: m 1958, Celia King McNeare, and has issue living, José Algernon Crofton b 1959, Luis Miguel Crofton b 1962.

Issue of late Arthur Molesworth Crofton, b 1874, d 1945: m 1897, Gwendolin Forrest, who d 1950, of Quebec, Canada:—

Brian Forrest (409 Kent St, Whitby, Ontario, Canada), b 1905: m 1930, Violet, da of Thomas Janes, R Canadian Mounted Police (Marine Section), and has issue living, Ralph Janes, b 1931: m 1954, Marcella, da of James Billard, and has issue living, Ralph Kevin b 1958, Heather Cavelle b 1956: m 1979, Jeffery Mitchell (and has issue living, Alicia Violet b 1982), — Ross Blake, b 1935: m 1961, Claire, da of Frederick Burke, and has issue living, Sandra Jane b 1962, Karen Eileen b 1964, — Brian Eric, b 1944: m 1970, Helen, da of James Seto, and has issue living, Brian James b 1971, David Andrew b 1973, — Gwendolyn Patricia, b 1939: m 1965, Harvey Thompson, and has issue living, Paul Gregory b 1970, David Harvey b 1975. ——— Edith Jane, b 1941: m 1966, Gary Carman Jones, and has issue living, Jeffery Carman Blake b 1973, — Brenda Faye, b 1943: m 1965, Clive Orville Gabour Denyke, and has issue living, Sean Forrest b 1968, Arthur Anslem b 1972. ——— Henry Desmond, b 1907: m 1st, 1937, Frances Veron Borgeest, who d 1942; 2ndly, 1951, Marie Jeanne, da of Joseph Muloin, and widow of Sqn-Ldr Oliver J. Gaboury, RCAF. ——— Charles Patrick, b 1913: m 1943, Catherine Kennedy, and has issue living, David Ian, b 1944, — Arthur Blake, b 1946, — Alan, b 1953, — Terence, b (twin) 1953, — Catherine Patricia, b 1948, — Joan, b 1949. ——— Francis Terence, b 1915; is an organist.

Sir Morgan Crofton, 1st Bt of Mohill, co Leitrim, was 5th in descent from Henry Crofton of Mohill, yst son of Henry Crofton of Ballymurry (d 1643), el son of Edward Crofton of Ballymurry (d 1627). The father of the 4th baronet Col Hugh Denis Crofton (who commanded 20th Regt at Alma and was wounded at Inkerman) was accidentally shot by a soldier of the 32nd Foot, at Preston, September 15th, 1861, while commanding the Depôt Battalion; and it is a singular circumstance that the same bullet killed the Adjutant of the Battalion (Capt J. Hanham), who was also heir to a baronetcy. Lieut-Col Sir Morgan George Crofton, DSO, 2nd Life Guards, 6th Bt, served in S Africa 1899-1902 (severely wounded at relief of Ladysmith), 1914-18 War (DSO), and in 1939-45 War. The 6th baronet's eldest son, Maj Morgan George Crofton, dvp 1947, having m 1st, 1934 (m diss 1940), Rosalie (who m 2ndly, 1947, Lt-Col George St Vigor J. Vigor, OBE, Welch Gds, who d 1979), da of late John Lever Tillotson, of Bidston Court, Cheshire, and had issue an only child, Sir Hugh Patrick Simon Crofton, 7th Bt, who d in a motor accident 1987.

CROFTON (UK) 1838, of Longford House, Sligo

God gives the increase

Sir MALBY STURGES CROFTON, 5th *Baronet* (but his name does not, at time of going to press, appear on the Official Roll of Baronets); *b* 11 Jan 1923; *s* his father, *Major Sir* (MALBY RICHARD) HENRY, DSO, 1962; *ed* Eton and Trin Coll, Camb; Member of London Stock Exchange since 1957; member of Kensington Borough Council since 1962 (Leader since 1968); GLC 1970-73 and since 1977; 1941-45 War as Capt Life Gds in Middle East and Italy: *m* 1961 (*m diss* 1966), Elizabeth Madeline Nina, el da of late Maj Rhys Clavel Mansel (*see* Mansel, Bt, colls).

ℛrms – Per pale indented or and azure, a lion passant-guardant counterchanged. ℭrest – Seven ears of wheat on one stalk proper. *Seat* – Longford House, co Sligo, *Residence* – 17 Launceston Place, W8.

SISTER LIVING

Beatrix Katharine, *b* 1921; formerly Junior Com ATS. *Residence* – 2 Caithness Rd, W14.

AUNT LIVING (*Daughter of 3rd baronet*)

Dorothy. *Address* – Arva, Upper Glenageary Rd, Glenageary, co Dublin.

COLLATERAL BRANCHES LIVING

Grandchildren of late Col Malby Edward Crofton, 3rd son of 2nd baronet:—
Issue of late Col Malby Crofton, DSO, *b* 1881; *d* 1948: *m* 1911, Sarah Dorothy Beatrice, JP, who *d* 1976, da of late Col William Frederick Noel Noel, formerly RE (E Gainsborough, colls):—
(Ursula) Doryne (Elizabeth), *b* 1921; European War 1939-45 in Middle East (Africa Star); Section Officer WAAF: *m* 1951, William Robert Castle Cleary, RIBA, son of late Sir William Castle Cleary, KBE, CB. *Residence* – 64 Pelham Court, Fulham Rd, SW3.
Issue of late Brig Roger Crofton, CIE, MC, *b* 1888, *d* 1972: *m* 1st, 1914, Stella Clifton, who *d* 1916, da of late Judge Thomas Gilbert Carver, KC; 2ndly, 1921, Dorothy Frances, who *d* 1953, da of Col Henry Melville Hatchell, DSO, formerly R Irish Regt; 3rdly, 1954, Agnes Marjorie, who *d* 1982, aged 100, da of Samuel Osborn, and widow of (1) Capt Cyril Oswald Denman-Jubb, Duke of Wellington's Regt, and (2) John Johnston May:—
(By 2nd *m*) (HENRY EDWARD) MELVILLE, MBE (Haldon, St Giles Hill, Winchester, SO23 8JH), *b* 15 Aug 1931; *ed* Hilton Coll, Natal, and Trin Coll, Camb (BA Eng); formerly Prin Admin Officer, HM Overseas Civil Ser, MBE (Civil) 1970: *m* 1955, Mary Brigid, twin da of late Gerald K. Riddle, of Buttercombe, Newton Abbot, and has issue living, Julian Malby, *b* 1958: *m* 1989, Hilary, da of Thomas James Twort, of 35 Sompting Av, Worthing, Sussex, and has issue living, Harriet Sophie *b* 1992, — Nigel Melville, *b* 1964, — Nicola Dorothy, *b* 1961: *m* 1990, Julian D. P. George, elder son of John George, of Bridge House, Castle Eaton, Wilts, and has issue living, Henry Dacre Malby *b* 1994.
In 1661 a baronetcy was conferred upon Sir Edward Crofton of the Mote, co Roscommon (*d* 1675), grandson of Edward Crofton of Ballymurry, co Roscommon (*d* 1627); it became extinct on the death of the 5th baronet in 1780, and a new baronetcy was granted in 1838 to Sir James Crofton of Longford House, co Sligo, descended from Thomas Crofton, uncle of 1st Bt, and subsequent to 1780 the senior male line of Croftons in Ireland.

CROSS (UK) 1941, of Bolton-le-Moors, co Lancaster (Extinct 1968)

Rt Hon Sir RONALD HIBBERT CROSS, KCMG, KCVO, 1st and last *Baronet*.

DAUGHTERS LIVING OF FIRST BARONET

Angela Louise Vereker (*Hon Mrs Neil D. Campbell*), *b* 1925: *m* 1951, Hon Neil Donald Campbell, DSC, son of 2nd Baron Colgrain. *Residence* – Yorks Hill Farm, Ide Hill, Sevenoaks, Kent. —— Diana Marion Hibbert (*Marchioness of Downshire*), *b* 1927: *m* 1st, 1955 (*m diss* 1986), James Richard Emery Taylor; 2ndly, 1989, as his 2nd wife, 8th Marquess of Downshire. *Residence* – Clifton Castle, Ripon, N Yorks HG4 4AB. —— Susanna Carolyn, *b* 1938: *m* 1966, Francis Trajan Sacheverell Sitwell (*see* Sitwell, Bt). *Residence* – Weston Hall, Towcester, Northants.. —— Karina Mary, *b* 1942: *m* 1965, Maj Sean Michael Barton, 22nd Cheshire Regt. *Residence* – Goldsborough House, Sutton Montis, Yeovil, Som.

CROSSLEY (UK) 1909, of Glenfield, Dunham Massey, co Chester

I believe and love.

Sir NICHOLAS JOHN CROSSLEY, 4th *Baronet*; *b* 10 Dec 1962; *s* his father, *Sir* CHRISTOPHER JOHN, 1989.

𝕬rms – Azure, a chevron between in chief two Tau crosses and in base a hind statant. 𝕮rest – A hind's head couped or, holding in the mouth a Tau cross azure.
Residence –

BROTHER LIVING

JULIAN CHARLES, *b* 11 Dec 1964.

WIDOWS LIVING OF SECOND AND THIRD BARONETS

ELIZABETH JOYCE (*Elizabeth, Lady Crossley*), da of late Enoch Shenton, of Boxmoor, Herts: *m* 1954, as his second wife, Sir Kenneth Irwin Crossley, 2nd Bt, who *d* 1957. *Residence* – The Old Bakery, Milton Lilbourne, Pewsey, Wilts SN9 5LQ.
LESLEY A. (*Lady Crossley*), el da of late Dr K. A. J. Chamberlain: *m* 1977, as his second wife, Sir Christopher John Crossley, 3rd Bt, who *d* 1989. *Residence* – 6B Laverton Mews, SW6.

STEP-GRANDMOTHER LIVING

Marjorie (WINTERBOTTOM), da of late John Gilley: *m* 2ndly, 1932, as his second wife, Lieut-Com Nigel John Crossley, RN who was *ka* 1939; 3rdly, 1957, as his second wife, Capt Richard William Ravenhill, CBE, DSC, RN.

MOTHER LIVING

Carolyne Louise (*Carolyne, Lady Crossley*), da of late Leslie Grey Sykes, of Sandbanks, Dorset: *m* 1959 (*m diss* 1969), as his first wife, Sir Christopher John Crossley, 3rd Bt, who *d* 1989.

COLLATERAL BRANCHES LIVING

Issue of late Anthony Crommelin Crossley, MP, only son of 2nd baronet, *b* 1903, *d* 1939: *m* 1927, Clare (12a Selwood Place, SW7; Brankelow Folly, Whitchurch, Shropshire), da of late Brig Alan Fortescue Thomson, DSO:—
Penelope Georgina (*Penelope, Countess of Lindsay*) *b* 1928: *m* 1st, 1951 (*m diss* 1969), Maj Henry Ronald Burn Callander, MC; 2ndly, 1969, 15th Earl of Lindsay, who *d* 1989, and has issue living (by 1st *m*), Sarah Alexandra Mary, *b* 1952: *m* 1993, Peter Thomas Beckett, eldest son of late Thomas Beckett, and of Mrs John Armitage, of Hall O'Coole, Cheshire, — Victoria, *b* 1954: *m* 1993, as his 2nd wife, (Morland Herbert) Julian Agnew (*see* Agnew, Bt, *cr* 1895, colls), — Emma Georgina (Gigi), *b* 1959: *m* 1992, William Henry Salomon, only son of Sir Walter Hans Salomon and has issue living, a da *b* 1994. *Residences* – Stewards Cottage, Combermere, Whitchurch, Shropshire SY13 4AY. —— (Virginia Charlotte) Theresa, *b* 1936: *m* 1st, 1956 (*m diss* 1973), Alain R. E. Camu, of Brussels; 2ndly, 1973, Marchese Francesco d'Ayala Valva, and has had issue (by 1st *m*), Adrien Bonaventure, *b* 1957: *m* 1989, Melanie J., eldest da of Roger Worboys, of Putney, and has issue living, Helena Claire *b* 1991, — Francois Henri, *b* 1958: *d* 1990, — Nicholas Pascal (65 Finlay St, SW6), *b* 1961: *m* 1991, Mrs Rebecca Compton, only da of Sir Alan Lewis Wigan, 5th Bt, and has issue living, Marguérite *b* 1993, — Virginie Charlotte, *b* 1959: *m* 1986, Napier Anthony Sturt Marten, and has issue (*see* By Alington), — (by 2nd *m*) Tancredi Simone, *b* 1975, — Sebastino Vittorio, *b* 1978. *Residences* – 12 Selwood Place, SW7; Camporempoli, Pietrafitta, Castellina in Chianti, Tuscany, Italy.

Grandchildren of late Eric Crossley, 2nd son of 1st baronet:—
Issue of late Michael Nicholson Crossley, *b* 1912, *d* 1987: *m* 1st, 1940 (*m diss* 1945) Doreen Maud, only da of George Tibbitt; 2ndly, 1957, Sylvia, who *d* 1975, only da of late Cdr P. A. Heyder, RN; 3rdly, 1977, Moyra Louisa Margaret (*née* Hewitt) (Loughrigg, Box 379, White River, E Transvaal, SA), widow of Maj-Gen Theodore Henry Birkbeck:—
(By 2nd *m*) Sloan Nicholas, *b* 1958. —— Claudia Bettine, *b* 1959. —— Alison Michele, *b* 1964.
The 1st baronet, Sir William John Crossley (son of Major Francis Crossley, of Glenburn, co Antrim, descended from the Crossleys of Scaitcliffe, Todmorden), a Director of Manchester Ship Canal, and Chm of Crossley Bros (Limited), of Manchester, sat as MP for Altrincham Div of Cheshire (*L*) 1906-10. The 2nd baronet, Sir Kenneth Irwin Crossley, JP, was High Sheriff of Cheshire 1919.

Culme-Seymour, see Seymour.

GORDON CUMMING (UK) 1804, of Altyre, Forres

Sir WILLIAM GORDON GORDON CUMMING, 6th *Baronet*; *b* 19 June 1928; *s* his father, *Major Sir* ALEXANDER PENROSE, MC, 1939; *ed* Eton; late Lieut Roy Scots Greys: *m* 1st, 1953 (*m diss* 1972), Elisabeth, da of late Maj-Gen Sir (William) Robert Norris Hinde, KBE, CB, DSO; 2ndly, 1972 (*m diss* 1976), Lady Pauline Anne Illingworth, sister of 13th Earl of Seafield, and formerly wife of James Henry Harcourt Illingworth; 3rdly, 1989, Sheila Bates, and has issue by 1st *m*.

Arms – Quarterly, 1st and 4th azure three garbs or; 2nd and 3rd argent three bendlets sable, each charged with as many roses of the field; on an escutcheon of pretence argent, the following achievement: quarterly, 1st and 4th grand quarters counterquartered, 1st, azure three boars' heads couped or, armed and langued gules, *Gordon*; 2nd, three lions' heads erased gules, *Badenoch*; 3rd, or three crescents between the Royal tressure gules, *Seton*; 4th, azure, three fraziers argent, *Frazer*; 2nd and 3rd grand quarters, gules, three stars or, *Sutherland*, all within a bordure of the last. **Crest** – A cat salient proper armed azure. **Mottoes** – (*for Cumming*) — "Courage"; (*for Gordon*), — "Sans crainte" (*Without fear*). **Supporters** – *Dexter*, a greyhound proper, gorged with a collar gules charged with two buckles or; *sinister*, a savage proper wreathed about the head and middle with laurel vert, brandishing a club proper; the whole within a bordure or, *Cumming*. **Crest** – A lion rampant or, in the dexter paw a dagger proper. *Cumming*. **Supporters** – Two horses argent.

Seat – Altyre, nr Forres, Morayshire.

SON LIVING (*By 1st marriage*)

ALEXANDER PENROSE (ALASTAIR), *b* 15 April 1954: *m* 1991, Louisa, elder da of Edward Geoffrey Clifton Brown (*see* Brown, Bt, colls), and has issue living, William, *b* 4 April 1993. *Residence* – Wardend House, Altyre, nr Forres, Morayshire.

DAUGHTERS LIVING (*By 1st marriage*)

Sarah, *b* 1955: *m* 1990, Dominic W. Langlands Pearse, of Holwell Downs Farm, Busford, Oxon, yst son of Cmdr Ian Langlands Pearse, and has issue living, Ned, *b* 1993. —— Charlotte, *b* 1958: *m* 1984, Michael Edwards, son of John Edwards, of Darnaconnar, Barrhill, Girvan, Ayrshire. —— Henrietta, *b* 1959: *m* 1988, Donald Statham, son of D. E. S. Statham.

SISTERS LIVING

Cecily Josephine (*Countess Lloyd George of Dwyfor*) (Glenogil, by Forfar, Angus; The Hall, Freshford, Bath; 47 Burton Court, SW3), *b* 1925: *m* 1st, 1957, as his 2nd wife, 2nd Earl of Woolton, who *d* 1969; 2ndly, 1969 (*m diss* 1974), 3rd Baron Forres, who *d* 1978; 3rdly, 1982, as his 2nd wife, 3rd Earl Lloyd George of Dwyfor. —— Philippa, *b* 1933: *m* 1955, David Archibald Innes (*see* V Downe, colls, 1985 Edn), and has issue living, Guy Archibald, *b* 1956. —— John Hugh, *b* 1959: *m* 1988, Deborah Jane, da of Rev W. A. G. Buxton (and has issue). — Davina Evelyn, *b* 1957: *m* 1989, Wojciech Markiewicz, and has issue living, William David *b* 1991. *Residences* – Hensill House, Hawkhurst, Kent; Titsey Place, Oxted, Surrey.

COLLATERAL BRANCHES LIVING

Issue of late Michael Willoughby Gordon Cumming, 3rd son of 4th baronet, *b* 1901, *d* 1979: *m* 1st, 1923 (*m diss* 1943), Rachel Jean, who *d* 1968, da of late Col John Anstruther Thomson (Anstruther, Bt, colls); 2ndly, 1943, (Shirley) Barbara (98 Southmoor Rd, Oxford), da of late Torben Laub, of Rush Court, Wallingford, Berks:—
(By 2nd *m*) (Priscilla) Jane, *b* 1950: *m* 1991, Edwin F. Osborn, son of Rev Reginald Osborn, of Freeland, Oxford. *Residence* – 98 Southmoor Rd, Oxford. —— Catherine Rose, *b* 1952: *m* 1972, Desmond Fforde, of High Croft, Church Place, Redborough, nr Stroud, Glos.

Issue of late Lt Cdr Roualeyn Geoffrey Gordon Cumming, RN, 2nd son of 4th baronet, *b* 1895, *d* 1928: *m* 1923, Mary Violet Katharine (who *m* 2ndly, 1929 (*m diss* 1939), John S Newall; 3rdly, 1941 (*m diss* 1948), Geoffrey Hugh Wilkinson, and *d* 1984), da of late Capt W. M. Marter:—
Alexander Roualeyn, CMG, CVO (Woodstock, West Way, Chichester, Sussex), *b* 1924; Group Capt (ret) RAF; Assist Sec, Dept of Trade and Industry; *cr* CVO 1970, CMG 1977: *m* 1st, 1965, Beryl Joyce MacNaughton, who *d* 1973, da of late Naughton Dunn; 2ndly, 1974, Elizabeth Patricia, who *d* 1983, da of Travers Robert Blackley, CMG, CBE, of Gurrane, Fermoy, co Cork, and has issue living, (by 1st *m*) Ann Penrose, *b* 1968, — (by 2nd *m*) Mary Elizabeth, *b* 1975.

Grandson of late Henry William Grant Gordon Cumming, elder son of late Henry Gordon Cumming, 3rd son of 2nd baronet:—
Issue of late Cdr Henry Ronald Gordon Cumming, OBE, RN, *b* 1893, *d* 1971: *m* 1927, Lorna Isabelle, who *d* 1974, da of Ernest W. Morey, of Johannesburg:—
Rev Henry Ian (Bay Cottage, Brookside, Runcton, Chichester, Sussex PO20 6PX), *b* 1928: *m* 1955, Janet Elizabeth Latimer Cleave, and has issue living, Jane Evelyn, *b* 1957; *m* 1994, Guy Hadland, — Joanna Mary, *b* 1959: *m* 1988, Christopher Morris, and has issue living, James *b* 1993, Julia *b* 1990, — Lucille Clare, *b* 1962: *m* 1988, Charles Thellusson, and has issue living, Amy Elizabeth *b* 1993, — Deborah Diana, *b* 1965: *m* 1991, Andrew Woodward.

Granddaughters of late Maj Francis Hastings Toone Gordon Cumming, 6th son of 2nd baronet:—
Issue of late William Ian Gordon Cumming, *b* 1864, *d* 1949: *m* 1891, Rose, who *d* 1934, da of A. White, of New Zealand:—
Constance Alexa, *b* 1892: *m* 1925, Guy D'Eresby Goyder. —— Mary Adela Rose, *b* 1895: *m* 1915, George Berners Kynvett, and has issue living, Henry Berners, *b* 1915, — Mark Alastair, *b* 1918: *m* 1941, Ola B., da of G. F. Peters, of Dannevirke, NZ. —— Ethel Fredereka, *b* 1899: *m* 1926, Harold Sedcole Malcolm. *Residence* –
Issue of late Charles Lennox Gordon Cumming, *b* 1865, *d* 1948: *m* 1901, Mary Elizabeth, da of W. E. Thomas, of Dallas, Texas, USA:—
Constance Alexa: *m* 1st, 1922, Clarence Ray Herrington, who *d* 1946; 2ndly, 1949, Q. B. Workman, and has issue living, (by 1st *m*) Phyllis Rae, *b* 1930: *m* 1954, John Snead Billups, and has issue living, Patti Jon *b* 1956, Molli Elizabeth *b* 1958. *Residence* – 1st and Floyd Streets, Tulia, Texas, USA. —— Marjorie Mary: *m* 1927, Randle James Culwell, and has issue living, Gordon James *b* 1929: *m* 1948, Grace Elaine, da of Dr Bascom MacIntosh Puckett, and has issue living, Michael

James *b* 1950, Grace Victoria *b* 1951. *Residence* – 1121 Broadmoor, Amarillo, Texas, USA. —— Kathleen Elizabeth, *b* 1909: *m* 1932, Jerome Maurice Baker. *Residence* – 1306 West 6th Street, Plainview, Texas, USA.

The Cumyn or Cumming family settled in Scotland in the reign of David I. Richard Comyn, of Northallerton received grants of lands in Roxburghshire. John Comyn, of Badenoch, chief of this family, married Eleanor, sister of King John Balliol, by which marriage Sir John of Badenoch "Red Cumyn" was a competitor for the kingdom of Scotland. Robert Cumming, 13th of Altyre, Forres, chief of the family, who bore undifferenced arms, married Lucy, da of Sir Ludovic Gordon of Gordonstoun, and his great-grandson Sir Alexander Cumming, 1st Bt, took the name of Gordon Cumming on *s* to the estates of Gordon of Gordonstoun.

CUNARD (UK) 1859, of Bush Hill, Middlesex (Extinct 1989)

Capt Sir GUY ALICK CUNARD, 7th and last *Baronet*.

COLLATERAL BRANCH LIVING

Granddaughters of late William Cunard, 2nd son of 1st baronet:—
Issue of late Cyril Grant Cunard, *b* 1867, *d* 1914: *m* 1896, Beatrice Rhoda, who *d* 1945 (having *m* 2ndly, 1918, Capt Walter H. Curran, Canadian Mil Forces, who *d* 1931), da of late George Louis Monck Gibbs (Elton, Bt):—
Penelope Elton, *b* 1909: *m* 1st, 1934, Brig Nigel Dugdale, CBE, 17th/21st Lancers, who *d* 1955; 2ndly, 1967, George Arthur Loveday, TD, who *d* 1981, and has issue living, (by 1st *m*) Sam William, *b* 1948: *m* 1973, Phyllis Waldock (and has issue), — Antonia Rosetta, *b* 1939: *m* 1969, Nicholas Young, who *d* 1992, of 7 Hamilton Terr, NW8 (*see* Young, Bt, *cr* 1813, colls), — Teresa Beatrice, *b* 1946: *m* 1973, — (and has issue). *Residence* – Bushton Manor, Wootton Bassett, Wilts. —— Virginia Beatrice, OBE (Flat 12 River House, The Terrace, Barnes, SW13), *b* 1912; is a CStJ; MBE (Civil) 1946, OBE (Civil) 1956: *m* 1963, Judge John Harcourt Barrington, TD, who *d* 1973.

CUNINGHAME (NS) 1672, of Corsehill, Ayrshire

Sir JOHN CHRISTOPHER FOGGO MONTGOMERY CUNINGHAME, 12th *Baronet*; *b* 24 July 1935; *s* his brother, *Sir* WILLIAM ANDREW MALCOLM MARTIN OLIPHANT, 1959; *ed* Fettes Coll, and Worcester Coll, Oxford; late Lieut Rifle Brig; Dir Ryobi Lawn & Garden Ltd, Purolite International Ltd, Bedford Capital Financial Corp, and other companies: *m* 1964, Laura Violet, da of Sir Godfrey Nicholson, 1st Bt (*cr* 1958), and has issue.

Arms – Argent, a shake-fork sable, a crescent for difference. **Crest** – A unicorn's head erased, proper.
Residence – The Old Rectory, Brightwalton, Newbury, Berks RG16 0BL. *Clubs* – Boodle's, Pratt's.

DAUGHTERS LIVING

Christian Elizabeth, *b* 1967. —— Georgiana Rose, *b* 1969. —— Elizabeth Clara, 1971.

WIDOW LIVING OF ELEVENTH BARONET

SARA CAROLYN (*Lady Fergusson*), da of late Brig-Gen Lord Esmé Charles Gordon Lennox, KCVO, CMG, DSO (*see* D Richmond and Gordon, colls): *m* 1st, 1956, Sir William Andrew Malcolm Martin Oliphant Montgomery Cuninghame, 11th Bt, who *d* 1959: 2ndly, 1959, Sir Ewen Alastair John Fergusson, GCMG, GCVO, son of Sir Ewen Macgregor Field Fergusson. *Address* – c/o Coutts & Co, 440 Strand, WC2R 0QS.

This family descends from Andrew Cuninghame, 1st of Corsehill, 2nd son of 4th Earl of Glencairn (dormant 1796), to whom the baronet is probably next in line.

FAIRLIE-CUNINGHAME (NS) 1630, of Robertland, Ayrshire

By fortitude   *I am prepared*

Sir WILLIAM HENRY FAIRLIE-CUNINGHAME, 16th *Baronet*; *b* 1 Oct 1930; *s* his father, Sir WILLIAM ALAN, 1981: *m* 1972, Janet Menzies, da of late Roy Menzies Saddington, and has issue.

Arms – Quarterly, 1st and 4th argent, a shake-fork between a bugle-horn in chief and two castles in base sable, *Cuninghame*; 2nd and 3rd, or, a lion rampant and in chief three stars gules, *Fairlie*. **Crests** – 1st, a unicorn's head proper, armed or, *Cuninghame*; 2nd, a lion's head or, *Fairlie*. **Supporters** – Two knights in complete armour, holding in their exterior hands batons or.
Residence – 29A Orinoco Street, Pymble, NSW 2073, Australia.

SON LIVING

(WILLIAM) ROBERT HENRY, *b* 11 July 1974.

UNCLE LIVING (*Son of 13th baronet*)

John Hastings, *b* 1899; Bachelor of Architecture, Sydney Univ; Lt (ret) Austn Forces: *m* 1934, Margaret, da of Charles Woodhill, of NSW, and has issue living, David Hastings (47 Cremorne Rd, Cremorne, Sydney, NSW), *b* 1937: *m* 1963, Susan Gai, da of Henry White, of Coolah, NSW, and has issue living, Charles Hastings *b* 1966, Annabel *b* 1964, — Peter (9 Austinmer St, Austinmer, NSW), *b* 1939: *m* 1972 (*m diss* 1992), Felicity Helen, da of Douglas Service, of Sydney, and has issue living, Samuel John *b* 1976, Georgina Mary *b* 1979. — Elisabeth, *b* 1941: *m* 1st, 1962 (*m diss* 1972), William Leslie Murray Robson; 2ndly, 1974, Peter Thomas Glanville, who *d* 1975, and has issue living, (by 1st *m*) Andrew Fairlie Murray *b* 1963, Hamish Hastings Murray *b* 1965, — Georgina Jane, *b* 1947: *m* 1972, Christopher Harrold Martin, of Norfolk, Cassilis, NSW, and has issue living, Jonathan Hastings *b* 1977, Toby *b* 1980, Amber *b* 1979. *Residence* – 279 Morrison Rd, Ryde, NSW, Australia.

AUNT LIVING (*Daughter of 13th baronet*)

Amabel Marguerite, *b* 1901: *m* 1933, Alick Scott Osborne, who *d* 1957, and has issue living, William Fairlie Cuninghame, *b* 1934: *m* 1964, Janet Stewart Stevenson, and has issue living, Alick Stevenson, *b* 1968, Stewart William *b* 1970, Susan Margaret *b* 1967, — Andrew Hastings, *b* 1937: *m* 1st, 1966, Barbara Constance Heron, who *d* 1973; 2ndly, 1974, Judith Nancy Pope, and has issue living, (by 1st *m*) Phillip Scott *b* 1967, Eleanor Marguerite *b* 1969, — Mary Macartney, *b* 1933: *m* 1959, John William Laurie, of 40 Kenthurst Rd, St Ives, NSW, and has issue living, William Alick Osborne *b* 1963, Margaret Kathleen *b* 1961, Sarah Elisabeth (twin) *b* 1963, Georgina Mary *b* 1969. *Residence* – 695 Pacific Highway, Gordon 2072, NSW.

DAUGHTERS LIVING OF FOURTEENTH BARONET

Margaret Alice (43 Honeyton St, Seaton, S Australia): *m* 1946, Stanley C. Wood, who *d* 1971, and has issue living, Harold Anthony, *b* 1948, — Norma Margaret, *b* 1947: *m* 1968, George Millar Knight, of 23 Fairfax Av, Millswood, S Australia, and has issue living, Peter Stanley *b* 1972, Robert Reginald *b* 1981, Helen Margaret *b* 1973, Elizabeth Georgie *b* 1983, — Janice Alice, *b* 1952: *m* 1970, Edward James, of 17 Tereva Cres, Mulgrave, Victoria, Australia, and has issue living, Simon Stanley *b* 1976, David Matthew *b* 1979, Julie Alice *b* 1971, Karen Linda *b* 1973. — Ann (26 Cranbrook Av, Cremorne, Sydney, NSW), *b* 19—: *m* 1955, Arlie William Vout, who *d* 1985. — Patricia: *m* 19—, Peter Goddard Sheldon, of 31 Stanton Rd, Mosman, Sydney, NSW, and has issue living, Robert Stewart *b* 1961: *m* 1992, Sharon Susan Armstrong, — Antony Stewart, *b* 1966, — Jane Stewart, *b* 1963.

COLLATERAL BRANCHES LIVING

Granddaughters of late Charles Rawdon Cuningham (infra):—
Issue of late Eric de Burgh Cuningham, *b* 1900, *d* 1946: *m* 1934, Betty Maurice (Closeburn, 197 Walker St, N Sydney, NSW 2060) (she *m* 2ndly, 1952, Henry William Hardess Waller, who *d* 1961; 3rdly, 1969, Michael Alexander Addison Kirkpatrick, who *d* 1991) da of late Mrs M. Barton, of Leura, NSW:—
Anthea, *b* 1936: *m* 1959, Michael Havelock Marchbank, and has issue living, Jonathan Havelock, *b* 1964. — Joanna Cuningham, *b* 1960, — Katharine Jane, *b* 1962. — Rhonwen CUNINGHAM, *b* 1943; has resumed her maiden name: *m* 1971 (*m diss* 1981), Jack Aylward Mooney, and has issue living, Sean Aylward Michael, *b* 1972.
Issue of late Archibald Loudoun Cuningham, Australian Imperial Force, *b* 1905, *ka* Malayan Campaign 1942: *m* 1936, Nancy Maurice (who *d* 1994, having *m* 2ndly, 1946, Robin Ellison Cuningham (infra)), da of late Mrs M. Barton, of Leura, NS Wales:—
Nancy Robin, *b* 1939: *m* 1964, Peter Edwin Bell (285a Durham St, Bathurst, NSW 2795, Australia), and has issue living, Alastair Christian Loudoun, *b* 1967: *m* 1992, Anastasia Louise Lord, — Belinda Jane, *b* 1965: *m* 1994, Terrence John Betts, — Fairlie Louise, *b* 1972.
Issue of late Robin Ellison Cuningham, *b* (twin) 1905, *d* 1984: *m* 1946, Nancy Maurice, who *d* 1994, widow of his twin brother Archibald Loudoun Cuninghame (ante):—
Georgine Ellison, *b* 1951: *m* 1975, Robert Ranald Mackay, of Tinagroo, Scone, NSW, Australia, and has issue living, Robert Gordon, *b* 1983.

Issue of late Charles Rawdon Cuningham, brother of 13th baronet, *b* 18—, *d* 1909: *m* 1894, Harriet Maria, who *d* 1953, da of late Edward Hardman Macartney (Macartney, Bt, colls):—
Alister Gordon (8 Park Lane, Albury, NSW 2640) *b* 1902: *m* 1948, Catherine Ida, da of late Hugh Rule, of Rockhampton, and has issue living, Robert Gordon, *b* 1953: *m* 1983, Christine Anne, da of Dr William Godwin Gray, of Markdale, Ontario, Canada, and has issue living, Emily Marguerite *b* 1985, Joanna Christine Mary *b* 1986, Jane Fairlie *b* 1988.

Grandson of late John Fairlie Cuningham (infra):—
Issue of late John Henry Cuningham, *b* 1898, *d* 1969: *m* 1924, Kathleen, MB, MS da of late Prof T. E. Clouston, DD:—
James Fairlie Boyd, *b* 1932.

Grandchildren of late Surg-Gen James Macnabb Cuningham, CSI, MD, son of late Major William Cuningham (infra):—
Issue of late Arthur Mactier Cuningham, *b* 18—, *d* 1940: *m* 1888, Agnes Murray, of Newby, Williams Road, Toorak, Victoria, Australia:—

Mary Mactier. —— Nora: *m* 1920, Leslie Albert Austin, Lieut Australian Forces (Reserve of Officers), and has issue living, Derek Leslie *b* 1921. *Residence –*
Issue of late John Fairlie Cuningham, *b* 1862, *d* 1935: *m* 1894, Margaret Campbell:—
Donald Macrae, *b* 1905: *m* 1929, Rose Eleanor, da of late Samuel Wilde Wills, and has issue living, John Fairlie, *b* 1943, — Florence Ann, *b* 1933: *m* 1957, David Jones, BVSc, Sydney Univ. —— Mary Stewart.

Grandchildren of late William Glencairn Cuninghame, only son of Francis George Glencairn Cuningham (infra):—
Issue of late Anthony Glencairn Cuninghame, *b* 1935, *d* 1982: *m* 1961, Pamela Rosemary (Stones, Uffcott, Broad Hinton, Swindon, Wilts SN4 9NB), da of late Robert Horton, of The Manor, Broad Hinton, Wilts:—
Andrew Glencairn, *b* 1965. —— Sally Helen, *b* 1962. —— Clair Elizabeth, *b* 1964: *m* 1991, Martin Brian Anstice, son of Malcolm Anstice, of Huish Episcopi, Somerset.

Granddaughter of late Francis Goode Cuningham (infra):—.
Issue of late Lieut-Col Francis George Glencairn Cuningham (who adopted the spelling of Cuninghame 19—), *b* 1880, *d* 1956: *m* 1912, Violet Jessie, who *d* 1957, da of Capt Phipps Hornby, Rifle Brig (Prince Consort's Own):—
Carol Jean, *b* 1915: *m* 1950, John Douglas Philip Watney, of 5 Grove Mount, Ramsey, Isle of Man, and has issue living, Guy Charles Glencairn, *b* 1954: *m* 1980, Mary Jane, el da of Sqdn Ldr John Sands, RAF, of Ramsey, Isle of Man.

Grandson of late Major William Cuningham, son of late Alexander Cuningham, 2nd son of 5th baronet:—
Issue of late Francis Goode Cuningham, *b* 1836, *d* 1911: *m* 1st, 1864, Anne Colquhoun, who *d* 1877, da of Boyd Alexander Cuninghame; 2ndly, 1879, Jean Elizabeth, who *d* 1939, da of Col William Forbes Hutton, HEICS:—
(By 2nd *m*) John Loudoun, *b* 1887.
This family is descended from the Hon William Cunningham (1st of Craigends), 2nd son of the 1st Earl of Glencairn, by the Hon William's 2nd *m* in 1499 with Dame Marion Auchinleck. The 1st baronet, Master of the Works to James VI of Scotland, was created a baronet, with remainder to heirs male whatsoever. At the death of his nephew, Sir David Cuningham, 4th baronet, the title remained dormant until assumed by William Cuningham, on being served heir in 1778, to his great-great-grandfather, Sir David Cuninghame, of Robertland, who was grandfather of the 1st baronet. The 5th baronet *m* Margaret, da of William Fairlie of Fairlie, co Ayr, to whose estate he succeeded. The 6th baronet assumed the additional surname of Fairlie, and the 8th received a grant of supporters to himself and his heirs male succeeding him in the baronetcy. The 13th baronet, Sir William Edward, assumed by deed poll 1912, the surname of Fairlie-Cuninghame in lieu of his patronymic Cuningham.

CUNLIFFE (GB) 1759, of Liverpool, Lancashire

Faithfully

Sir DAVID ELLIS CUNLIFFE, 9th *Baronet*, *b* 29 Oct 1957: *s* his father, *Sir* CYRIL HENLEY, 1969; *ed* St Alban's Gram Sch: *m* 1983, Linda Carol, da of John Sidney Batchelor, of 12 Marquis Lane, Harpenden, Herts.

Arms – Sable, three conies courant argent, two and one. **Crest** – A greyhound sejant argent, collared sable.
Residence – Sunnyside, Burnthouse Lane, Needham, Harleston, Norfolk IP20 9LN.

DAUGHTERS LIVING

Emma Mary, *b* 1986. —— Katherine Alice, *b* 1990. —— Bridget Carol, *b* 1991.

BROTHER LIVING

ANDREW MARK *b* 17 April 1959: *m* 1980, Janice Elizabeth, da of Ronald William Kyle, and has issue living, Mark Ellis, *b* 1982, — Sarah Nicolette, *b* 1984, — Danielle Juliette *b* 1989, — Rachael Eileen Margaret *b* 1992.

SISTER LIVING

Susan Nicolette, *b* (twin) 1959.

WIDOW LIVING OF EIGHTH BARONET

EILEEN M. (17 Gurney Court Rd, St Albans), da of Frederick William Parkins, and widow of Charles Clifford, of Walton-on-Thames: *m* 2ndly, 1956, Sir Cyril Henley Cunliffe, 8th Bt, who *d* 1969; 3rdly, 1970, Frederick Henry Moore, who *d* 1987.

COLLATERAL BRANCHES LIVING

Grandchildren of late William Lockhart Cunliffe (infra):—
Issue of late Lt-Col Bruce Fergusson Cunliffe, *b* 1925, *d* 1989: *m* 1947, Joanne (481 State St, Portsmouth, NH, USA), da of Richard Holbrook, of Keene, NH, USA:—
Taylor Fergusson, *b* 1950. —— Orinda, *b* 1949: *m* 1970, Edward Andrew Jerue, of 53 Western Av, Westfield, MA 01085, USA, late Capt US Marine Corps, and has issue living, Tristan Aubrey, *b* 1975, — Brook Kai, *b* 1977, — Seth Orion, *b* 1979, — Summer Alia, *b* 1974. —— Catherine Suthers, *b* 1956: *m* 1978, Lawrence Samuel Muller, of Tallahassee, Florida, USA, and has issue living, Randi Michelle *b* 1981.

Grandchildren of late Col Ernest William Cunliffe, son of late David Cunliffe, BCS, 3rd son of 4th baronet:—
Issue of late William Lockhart Cunliffe, *b* 1902, *d* 1982: *m* 1923, Maude Ethel, who *d* 1983, da of Henry Suthers, of New York, USA:—
Stuart Owen (17 Squassick Rd, West Springfield, Mass, USA), *b* 1931; *ed* Kimball Union Acad, Meriden, New Hampshire; sometime in US Marine Corps: *m* 1957, Mary, da of David Beglund, of Albany, New York, USA, and has issue living, Fred

Owen *b* 1958, David William *b* 1960, — Lorna Margaret, *b* 1929: *m* 1949, Amos Webster Gile, of Wyeth Rd Circle, W Lebanon, NH, USA, and has issue living, John Lockhart *b* 1952, Joanne Lorna *b* 1951: *m* 1972, Svein Michaelsen, of Bergen, Norway, Pamela Jean *b* 1954. —— Colin Fergusson (Torlundy, 71 Windermere Rd, SW16) *b* 1909; 1939-45 War with Gren Gds and as Maj N Staffordshire Regt: *m* 1st, 1934, Muriel Constance Gore, who *d* 1953; 2ndly, 1954, Sally Marion Mackay. —— Sonia, *b* 1911: *m* 1st, 1935 (*m diss* 1948), Frank Shaw; 2ndly, 1948, Eric Skead, of 60 Victoria St, Orillia, Ont, Canada, and has issue living, (by 1st *m*) Sandra, *b* 1936, — (by 2nd *m*) Howard, *b* 1949.

      Granddaughter of late Capt Ellis Brooke Cunliffe, el son of Ellis Watkin Cunliffe, 3rd son of 3rd baronet:—
      Issue of late William Noel Cunliffe, *b* 1877, *d* 1933: *m* 1910, Nellie Phyllis, who *d* 1976, da of Sir John Aird, 2nd Bt:—
Gundred, *b* 1913: *m* 1937, Mervyn Cunliffe-Fraser, 3 West Halkin St, SW1, and has issue living, Valerie, *b* 1942: *m* 1972, Mark Trenor Thomasin-Foster, of Moulsham Hall, Great Leighs, Essex, and has issue living, Nicholai Charles *b* 1975, Christopher William *b* 1976, David *b* 1979.

      Grandchildren of late Brooke Stewart Cunliffe, only son of Brooke Cunliffe (*b* 1815), elder son (by 1st *m*) of Brooke Cunliffe (*b* 1790) (infra):—
      Issue of late Capt Brooke Foster Gordon Cunliffe, Scottish Horse Yeo, *b* 1889, *d* 1981: *m* 1921, Catherine Hay, who *d* 1962, da of Col H. R. Peake:—
Brooke Malcolm, *b* 1928; Supt, Rhodesian Police (ret). —— Diana Hay (50 Corstorphine Hill Gdns, Edinburgh), *b* 1923.

      Grandchildren of late Col Foster Lionel Cunliffe, son of late Brooke Cunliffe (*b* 1790), 4th son of 3rd baronet:—
      Issue of late Capt Robert Lionel Brooke Cunliffe, CBE, RN, *b* 1895, *d* 1990: *m* 1st, 1926, Barbara Eleanor, who *d* 1970, da of Col Harry Cooper, of Pakenham Lodge, Pakenham, Suffolk; 2ndly, 1971, Christina, who *d* 1989, da of Rev Canon Sydney Cooper:—
(By 1st *m*) Bridget Eleanor, *b* 1927: *m* 1957, Hugh Rosslyn Inigo Sackville-West, MC, of Knole, Sevenoaks, Kent (*see* B Sackville). —— Nicolette Anne, *b* 1929: *m* 1954, Robert Charles Cotton (*see* V Combermere, colls). —— Barbara Clare (The Garden House, Pakenham, Bury St Edmunds, Suffolk), *b* 1936: *m* 1957 (*m diss* 1965), Sir Thomas Agnew Beevor, 7th Bt.

Sir Ellis Cunliffe 1st Bt, MP for Liverpool (*d* 1767), descended from a yr branch of the Cunliffes of Hollins, Lancs. Sir Robert Henry Cunliffe, 4th baronet, a General in the Bengal Army received the honour of knighthood. The 6th baronet, Major Sir Foster Hugh Egerton Cunliffe, Rifle Brig (Prince Consort's Own), was *ka* 1916.

Cunliffe-Owen, see Owen.

CUNNINGHAM (UK) 1963, of Crookedstone, Killead, co Antrim (Extinct 1976)

Sir (SAMUEL) KNOX CUNNINGHAM, QC, 1st and last *Baronet*.

WIDOW LIVING OF FIRST BARONET

DOROTHY ENID (*Lady Cunningham*), a JP; da of late Edwin Riley, of Bilston, Staffs: *m* 1935, Sir (Samuel) Knox Cunningham, QC, 1st Bt, who *d* 1976, when the title became ext.

DICK-CUNYNGHAM, First (NS) 1669, Cunyngham of Lambrughtoun, co Ayr; Second (NS) 1707, Dick, of Prestonfield, Edinburgh (Extinct 1941)

Major Sir (COLIN) KEITH DICK-CUNYNGHAM, 9th of 1st and 11th of 2nd creation and last *Baronet*; (*ka* 1941).

COLLATERAL BRANCH LIVING

      Issue of late Maj-Gen James Keith Dick-Cunyngham, CB, CMG, DSO, 3rd son of 7th and 9th baronet, *b* 1877, *d* 1935: *m* 1905, Alice Daisy, who *d* 1963, da of late Lieut-Col Sir Harold Arthur Deane, KCSI:—
Janet Mary DICK-CUNYNGHAM, *b* 1917, resumed her maiden surname 1963: *m* 1940 (*m diss* 1960), Capt Roderick Francis Oliver, Roy Horse Guards, (Grant-Suttie, Bt, colls), and has issue living, Caroline Stephanie, MBE *b* 1944; MBE (Civil) 1975: *m* 1st, 1965 (*m diss* 1967), Nicholas Kilmaine de Courcy-Ireland; 2ndly, 1987, Charles Cousins, — Georgina Mary *b* 1946: *m* 1977, Robert Kilgore, of Sunnyvale, California. *Residence* – Huerta las Palomas, Coín, Provincia de Malaga, Spain.

CUNYNGHAME (NS) 1702, of Milncraig, Ayrshire

Sir ANDREW DAVID FRANCIS CUNYNGHAME, 12th *Baronet*; *b* 25 Dec 1942; *s* his father, *Sir* (HENRY) DAVID ST LEGER BROOKE SELWYN, 1978; *ed* Eton; FCA: *m* 1st, 1972, Harriet Ann, da of Charles Thomas Dupont, of Montreal, Canada; 2ndly, 1989, Isabella, da of late Edward Everett Watts, Jr, and has issue by 1st *m*.

𝔄rms – Argent, a shake-fork sable between three fleurs-de-lis azure. ℭrest – A unicorn argent, unguled maned and armed or, lying on a mount vert. 𝔖upporters – *Dexter*, a knight in armour holding in his exterior hand a spear; *sinister*, a knight in the disguise of a countryman with a bonnet habited azure his thighs armed proper, and in his sinister hand a corn fork in pale of the last.
Residences – 17 Vicarage Gdns, W8 4AH; The School House, Williamscot, Banbury, Oxon. *Club* – Brooks's.

DAUGHTERS LIVING *(By 1st marriage)*

Ann Marie Albinia, *b* 1978. —— Tania Albinia Pamela Jean, *b* 1983.

BROTHERS LIVING

JOHN PHILIP HENRY MICHAEL SELWYN, (26D Belgrave Rd, SW1V 1RG), *b* 9 Sept 1944; *ed* Eton: *m* 1981, Marjatta, 2nd da of Martti Markus, of Muhos, Finland, and has issue living, Alexander David Martti, *b* 1985, — Niina Kaarina, *b* 1983. —— Arthur James Augustus (Grange Farm, Grange Lane, Alvechurch, Worcs B48 7DJ), *b* 1951; *ed* Westminster: *m* 1977, Rachel-Claire, el da of Guy Baines, FRCS, of Cattespoole, Tardebigge, Worcs, and has issue living, Richard George Arthur Selwyn, *b* 1980, — Edward David Lyulph, *b* 1983.

COLLATERAL BRANCHES LIVING

Issue of late Ian Francis Rowland Selwyn Cunynghame, yr son of 10th baronet, *b* 1910, *d* 1988: *m* 1st, 1938, Cicely Mary, who *d* 1945, elder da of late Francis Chaytor Starkey; 2ndly, 1947, Eugénie Beatrice Gwendolen, who *d* 1962, da of late James Howard Allport, and widow of Rear Adm John Uniacke Penrose-Fitzgerald, CB:—
(By 1st *m*) Michael Ian Francis Starkey (Dury Stores, N Nesting, Shetland), *b* 1945; *ed* Chilton Cantelo House, Yeovil: *m* 1970, Penelope Mary, yr da of Allan Mortimer, of Ballinger, Bucks, and has issue living, Ian Michael, *b* 1979, — Daisy Albinia, *b* 1981. —— Sarah Albinia Starkey, *b* 1940: *m* 1964, Feico Jan Leemhuis, of 429 Lansdowne Av, Westmount, Quebec Prov, Canada, and has issue living, Adrian Samuel, *b* 1969, — Ian, *b* 1971 (adopted son), — Cicely Toosje, *b* 1974. —— Caroline Mary Albinia Starkey, *b* 1943: *m* 1968, Barry John Lloyd, of 31 Ridgemount, Guildford, Surrey, and has issue living, Hannah Cicely, *b* 1973, — Leila Kate, *b* 1975. —— (By 2nd *m*) Moira Janet Albinia Allport, *b* 1947: *m* 1969, Konstantin Andreevich Stramentov, of Gurrington House, Woodland, nr Ashburton, Devon, and of Rhicarn, Lochinver, Sutherland, and has issue living, Bruce Sergei Cunynghame, *b* 1977, — Andrew Nikita Cunynghame, *b* 1979, — Alexandra Jane Cunynghame, *b* 1973, — Darya Esme Cunynghame, *b* 1983.

Issue of late Stuart Cunynghame, yr son of 9th baronet; *b* 1874, *d* 1962: *m* 1915, Helen Dorothy, who *d* 1944, da of late Rev A. Holland Taylor, DD:—
Colin Kenneth, *b* 1918; Maj late Indian Army. —— David Francis (British Airways, PO Box 4756, Durban, S Africa), *b* 1920; Capt late Indian Army; Airline Sales Representative, BOAC: *m* 1st, 1947 (*m diss* 1957), Ruth Armitage, da of late Walter Patrick Murray; 2ndly, 1964 (*m diss* 1975), Renate Maria Dietrich; 3rdly, 1984, Leslie Stokoe (*née* Anderson), and has issue living, (by 1st *m*) Diana Patricia, *b* 1950, — (by 2nd *m*) Christopher Daniel, *b* 1966, — Deborah Avril, *b* 1968.

Grandson of late James Robertson Thurlow Cunynghame, 4th son of 8th baronet:—
Issue of late Francis Thurlow Hardinge Cunynghame, *b* 1880, *d* 1940: *m* 1909, Frances Anne, who *d* 1954, da of Nicholas Murnane, of Brisbane:—
Frank Vincent, *b* 1910: *m* 1949, Mary Hennessy, and has issue living, Helen Anne, *b* 1949, — Diane Frances, *b* 1952, — Jennifer Anne, *b* 1955, Frances Mary, *b* 1957. *Residence* – 18 Serpentine Parade, Vaucluse, Sydney, NS Wales.

Grandson of late Arthur Hardinge David Cunynghame, son of late Gen Sir Arthur Augustus Thurlow Cunynghame, GCB, 5th son of 5th baronet:—
Issue of late Maj David Hardinge Cunynghame, *b* 1897, *d* 1986: *m* 1934, Ruth Ilon Ismay Mary (Minster Lovell, nr Oxford), da of Rev A.E. Phillips:—
Francis Arthur David Anthony, *b* 1935.

This family is a yr branch of the Earls of Glencairn (dormant since 1796), claiming descent from 2nd son of 1st Earl (*d* 1488). The 1st baronet, Sir David Cunynghame of Milncraig, co Ayr, a distinguished lawyer, and an eloquent member of the Scottish Parliament, was *cr* a Baronet with remainder to his "heirs male in perpetuum." The 10th baronet, Sir Percy Francis, OBE, in Sarawak Civil Ser 1886-1909, was Lieut-Col Middlesex Regt, and served in European War 1914-18 (despatches).

CURRIE (UK) 1847

Sir DONALD SCOTT CURRIE, 7th *Baronet*, *b* 16 Jan 1930; *s* his uncle, *Sir* ALICK BRADLEY, 1987: *m* 1st, 1948 (*m diss* 1951), Charlotte, da of Charles Johnston, of Mesa, Arizona, USA; 2ndly, 1952, Barbara Lee, da of A. P. Garnier, of Calif, USA, and has issue by 1st and 2nd *m*.

𝕬rms – Gules, a saltire couped argent, in the centre chief point a rose of the last barbed and seeded proper. 𝕮rest – A cock proper, resting its foot upon a rose argent, barbed and seeded proper.
Residence – 9061 WCR 34, Platteville, Colorado 80651, USA.

Largs

SONS LIVING *(By 1st marriage)*

DONALD MARK, *b* 1949: *m* 1st, 1969 (*m diss* 1969), Gloria, da of A. Price, of Calif, USA; 2ndly, 1969 (*m diss* 1971), Inga Mae, da of — Rouse, of —, and has issue living (by 2nd *m*), Mark Donald, *b* 1970. *Residence* –

(by 2nd marriage)

Gary Dwayne (Box 116, Vona, Colorado, USA), *b* 1953: *m* 1970, Wilma Kathleen, da of Tom Wyatt, of Colorado, USA, and has issue living, Bradley Wayne, *b* 1973, — Brandy Sue, *b* 1971.

DAUGHTERS LIVING *(By 1st marriage)*

Julia Ann, *b* 1950: *m* 1969, Eugene R. Gangaware, USAF, and has issue living, Elizabeth Ann, *b* 1970, — Tiffany Sue, *b* 1974, — Wendy Opal, *b* 1976, — Jeanette Mae, *b* 1978. *Residence* – . —— Janet Sue, *b* (twin) 1950: *m* 1st, 1970 (*m diss* 1970), Jack D. Hawkins, of Idaho, USA; 2ndly, 1973, Robert Eugene Buck, of Nebraska, USA, and has issue living (by 2nd *m*), Todd Allen, *b* 1973, — Terry Lee, *b* 1975. *Residence* –

(by 2nd marriage)

Tina Marie, *b* 1955: *m* 1974 (*m diss* 1992), Ricky Lee Linneman, of Gillette, Wyoming, USA, and has issue living, Shawn Michael, *b* 1976, — Tye Rae (a son), *b* 1985, — and an adopted da, Shayne Michelle, *b* 1973. *Residence* – 19750 8th Av, Fort Morgan, Colorado 80701, USA. —— Kathren Evelyn, *b* 1959: *m* 1973, Earl Avara, and has issue living, Scott William, *b* 1979, — Jennifer Marie, *b* 1981. *Residence* – Star Route, Box 89-2, Byers, Colorado 80103, USA.

BROTHERS LIVING

James Davidson (15603 Espola Rd, Poway, Calif 92604, USA), *b* 1932: *m* 1956, Olga Mary, da of Miguel Otero, of Tampa, Flar, USA, and has issue living, Lila Jane, *b* 1957: *m* 1979, Justin Chase Estep, and has issue living, Crystal Lila, *b* 1980. —— George Robert, *b* 1943: *m* 1st, 1962 (*m diss* 1972), Lucy Lavonne, da of S. A. Gilliam, of Charlotte, N Carolina, USA; 2ndly, 19—, Judith, da of — Hoffman, of —, and has issue living (by 1st *m*), Michael Todd, *b* 1963, — Richard Eric, *b* 1967. *Residence* – 3631 Columbia Av, Palmdale, Calif 93550, USA.

SISTER LIVING OF SIXTH BARONET

Annie Flora, *b* 1897: *m* 1920, Clinton B. Fiske Harsh, who *d* 1974, and has issue living, George Clinton (Box 134, Cliff, New Mexico, USA), *b* 1920: *m* 1948, Julia Cecelia, da of Mathew John Retmiller, of Utica, Michigan, and has issue living, Rhett Mathew *b* 1954: *m* 1980, Cinde Lu Ball, of Mesa, Arizona (and has issue living, Mathew Clinton *b* 1980, Joshua Lee *b* 1983, Jason Earl *b* 1985), Diane Elizabeth *b* 1949: *m* 1st, 1968 (*m diss* 1971), Charles D. Mannino; 2ndly, 1971 (*m diss* 1983), Tamás Elemér Belá Kokovay (and has issue living, (by 1st *m*) Meridee Francis *b* 1968, (by 2nd *m*) Stephen Tamás *b* 1981, Estike *b* 1975, Erzsebet *b* (twin) 1975, Julia Etelka *b* 1979, (and further issue) Clinton George *b* 1991), — Robert Currie (1916, Yucca Drive, Silver City, New Mexico, 88061, USA), *b* 1922: *m* 1948, Majorie Ruth, da of James E. Shean, of Silver City, New Mexico, and has issue living, Mathis Brayton *b* 1955: *m* 1975, Leona Rae, da of James Dudley Messer, of New Mexico (and has issue living, Brayton Bradley *b* 1978, Robert Cole *b* 1981), Alice Anne Thadia *b* 1949, June Margil *b* 1950: *m* 1975, James Monroe Foster, of New Mexico, USA, Alexis Mary *b* 1958, Cecily Louise *b* 1960: *m* 1984, Lt-Cdr Julio Jesus Gutierrez, US Navy, — Glenn Ray, *b* 1925: *m* 1949, Jeanne, da of Theophilus M. Prator, of New Orleans, Louisiana, USA, and has issue living, Glenn Ray *b* 1958: *m* 1982, Cheryl Ann Harty, Sandra *b* 1951: *m* 1977, Davis Carea Dixon, of New Orleans, Louisiana, USA (and has issue living, Katherine Jean *b* 1982), Christine Elizabeth *b* 1954, Nancy Jeanne *b* 1956.

MOTHER LIVING

Janet, da of late James Scott, of Bayfield, Las Animas, Colorado, USA: *m* 1928, George Donald Currie, who *d* 1980. *Residence* – 105 Sixth St, Las Animas, Colorado, USA.

COLLATERAL BRANCHES LIVING

Issue of late Percy George Colin Currie, 3rd son of 2nd baronet, *b* 1857, *d* 1932: *m* 1885, Agnes Grace Johnstone, da of late Charles Paterson, of Dumfries:—
Muriel Helen, *b* 1887: *m* 1911, Edgar Green, formerly Indian Telegraph Depart, and has issue living, Richard Colin, *b* 1914, — Agnes Muriel Rachel, *b* 1915, — Margaret Suzanne, *b* 1919. —— Ethel Lilian Adelaide, *b* 1893.

Granddaughters of late Maj-Gen Fendall Currie, 6th son of 1st baronet:—
Issue of late Fendall James Pears Currie, *b* 1867, *d* 1946: *m* 1890, Christina, da of David Anderson:—
Veda Mary Fendall, *b* 1891: *m* 1922, Thomas Scott MacMillan of 83 Creyke Rd, Ilaen, Christchurch 4, NZ, and has issue living, Mary Christina, *b* 1924, — Elizabeth Scott, *b* 1925.
Issue of late Lieut-Col Ivor Bertram Fendall Currie, DSO, *b* 1872, *d* 1924: *m* 1906, May Constance, who *d* 1937, da of late F.-M. Sir George Stuart White, VC, GCB, OM, GCSI, GCMG, GCIE, GCVO, LLD:—
Sylvia Constance, *b* 1910: *m* 1937, Nigel George Kingsford Burgess, and has issue living, Anthony Malcolm Kingsford, *b* 1941, — Simon George Fendall, *b* 1945. *Residence* – 52 Cornwall Gdns, SW7.

Grandson of late Rivers Grenfell Currie, 8th son of 1st baronet:—
Issue of late Maj Disney Rivers Currie, MC, *b* 1894, *d* 1964: *m* 1919, Ethel Jeanette Bryce, who *d* 1981, da of Arnold Bryce Smith:—

Frederick Disney Rivers (Whitehayes, 93 Church St, Willingdon, Eastbourne), *b* 1921; Burma, 1943 as Capt Roy Scots (wounded): *m* 1949, Jean Alison, da of Lionel Westropp Jardine, CIE (*see* Jardine, Bt, *cr* 1916), and has issue living, Peter Frederick Rivers (85 Bouverie Rd, N16) *b* 1950: *m* 1973, Mary Rose Veronica, da of E. J. Goodman, and has had issue, Philip Simon Rivers, *b* 1977, Francis William Mordaunt *b* and *d* 1980, Morag Claire Rowan *b* 1981, — Jennifer Jean, *b* 1953: *m* 1st, 1972 (*m diss* 19—), Alan Sayers; 2ndly, 19—, Jeffrey R. Smith, of 3 Ridge Rd, Falmer, E Sussex, and has issue living (by 1st *m*), Jonathan Alan *b* 1974, — Daniel William *b* 1976, — Fiona Alexandra (134 Wannock Lane, Lower Willingdon, E Sussex), *b* 1958.

This family came from Duns, Berwickshire. William Currie, who *d* 1781, became a London banker. His grandson, Sir Frederick Currie, 1st Bt, was successively Foreign Secretary to the Indian Governmnent, a Member of the Supreme Council in India, a member of the Court of Directors of the HEICS, and one of the Home Council in London.

CURTIS (UK) 1802, of Cullands Grove, Middlesex

We conquer step by step

Sir WILLIAM PETER CURTIS, 7th *Baronet*, *b* 9 April 1935; *s* his father, *Sir* PETER, 1976; *ed* Winchester, Trin Coll, Oxford (MA) and R Agric Coll, Cirencester; late 16/5th Lancers.

Arms – Paly of six or and azure, a fesse checky argent and sable, on a canton gules a dragon's wing erect of the third, in base a sword proper, pommel and hilt of the first, surmounting a key in saltire of the second. **Crest** – A ram's head couped argent, surmounted by two branches of oak in saltire proper. *Residence* – Oak Lodge, Bank St, Bishop's Waltham, Hants S03 1AN.

SISTERS LIVING

Rosemary Antonia Joan, *b* 1943: *m* 1966, John Clarkson Spink, of Poplars Farm, Rotherwick, Basingstoke, Hants RG27 9BH, and has issue living, Jonathan Peter Charles *b* 1976, — Timothy Mark Christopher, *b* 1981, — Annabel Louise, *b* 1970. —— Fiona Mary, *b* 1946: *m* 1968, Anthony David Findon Littlejohn, of Lythe Farm, Steep, Petersfield, Hants, and has issue living, — Patrick David, *b* 1979, — Ruth Hermione, *b* 1971, — Georgina Clare, *b* 1973.

DAUGHTER LIVING OF FIFTH BARONET

Winifred Lotus, *b* 1904: *m* 1927, Capt Alan Walter Dolby, who *d* 1943, sometime R Berks Regt, and has issue living, John Horace Curtis (Highway Cottage, Whitchurch, Pangbourne, Berks RG8 7DD), *b* 1928; *ed* St Paul's Sch; *m* 1959, Anthea Louise Whitamore, and has issue living, Timothy William Curtis *b* 1964, Caroline Lurleen Curtis, *b* 1960, — Robert Francis (11 Oldfield Rd, Bath BA2 3ND), *b* 1933; *ed* Christ's Hosp Sch; is Master Mariner Merchant Navy: *m* 1st, 1960 (*m diss* 1967), Jean Patricia, da of Sidney Clark; 2ndly, 1981, Priscilla Jane, da of late Percy Ridley, OBE, DSC, Bengal Pilot Ser, and has issue living, (by 1st *m*) Simon Francis Curtis (520 Athlone Av, Ottawa, Canada) *b* 1962: *m* 1989, Faye Tough (and has issue living, Alan Curtis *b* 1989), Louise Wynett *b* 1964: *m* 1985, Richard Kracher, of 2208-133A Av, Edmonton, Alberta T5A HJ9, Canada (and has issue living, James Richard *b* 1992, Holly Louise *b* 1989, Christina Ellen *b* 1990). *Address* – Rush Court, Shillingford Rd, Wallingford, Oxon.

WIDOW LIVING OF SIXTH BARONET

JOAN MARGARET (*Lady Curtis*), (Little Manor, Bishop's Waltham, Hants), da of late Reginald Nicholson (E Waldegrave): *m* 1934, Sir Peter Curtis, 6th Bt, who *d* 1976.

COLLATERAL BRANCHES LIVING

    Grandchildren of late Edward Beaumont Cotton Curtis, 2nd son of late William Cotton Curtis (infra):—
    Issue of late Gerald Edward Curtis, *b* 1909, *d* 1975: *m* 1939, Philippa, who *d* 1975, da of late Capt Philip Clayton Alcock, JP, DL, of Overton Lodge, Ludlow:—
EDWARD PHILIP (Lower Court, Bitterley, Ludlow, Shropshire SY8 3HP), *b* 25 June 1940; *ed* Bradfield, and RMA; Maj 16/5th Lancers (ret); stockbroker: *m* 1978, Catherine Mary, da of Henry J. Armstrong, of Christchurch, NZ, and has issue living, George Edward, *b* 31 Oct 1980, — Patrick James, *b* 1986, — Henrietta Rose, *b* 1979, — Clementine Zita, *b* 1983. —— Sonia Mary, *b* 1944: *m* 1971 (*m diss* 1976), Charles Hamilton Ewart, of Sydney, Australia, and has issue living, Gabrielle Alice Anne, *b* 1972.

    Grandchildren of late William Cotton Curtis, el son of late George Lear Curtis, 2nd son of 2nd baronet:—
    Issue of late Lieut-Col Hubert Montagu Cotton Curtis, DSO, *b* 1876, *d* 1948: *m* 1st, 1915 (*m diss* 1929), Lilian, who *d* 1931, da of late Louis Watson, of Brighton, and widow of Alfred Broadwood; 2ndly, 1929, Marcella Olive Penrose Robinson, who *d* 1969:—
(By 2nd *m*) William Richard (White Wold, Mill Hill, Weston Colville, nr Cambridge CB1 5NY), *b* 1933; *ed* Eton: *m* 1961, Janice Clare, da of William Yates Duckworth, of Garstang, Lancs, and has issue living, William Giles, *b* 1962; *ed* Ampleforth, and RMA Sandhurst; commn'd 13th/18th Hussars 1985, — Mark Edward, *b* 1964, — Timothy David, *b* 1968, — Anna Clare, *b* 1963. —— Hilda Lucy Penrose (7 Lyston Lane, Long Melford, Suffolk), *b* 1930: *m* 1955 (*m diss* 1968), Charles Henry Anderson, Capt R Inniskilling Fus, and has issue living, Lucie Rose, *b* 1956, — Arabella Joan Louisa, *b* 1960, — Caroline Rebecca, *b* 1961.

    Grandchildren of late Rear-Adm Arthur Cecil Curtis, 2nd son of late George Lear Curtis (ante):—
    Issue of late Brig Arthur Drury Curtis, *b* 1888, *d* 1950: *m* 1st, 1915, Margery May, who *d* 1943, el da of Robert Barlow, of Bombay; 2ndly, 1946, Evelyn Muriel, who *d* 1951, da of Murray Simmons, of Whitton, Middlesex:—
(By 1st *m*) (Arthur) Derek Edward, MC, *b* 1917; *ed* ISC, RMA Woolwich, and St Catharine's Coll, Camb (BA 1939, MA 1960); Lt-Col RE (ret); European War 1939-45 in France (MC): *m* 1943, Katherine Mary, da of late Thomas Hadfield, of Sheffield, and has issue living, (Arthur) Richard Edward (Stable House, 10 Sambourne Rd, Warminster, Wilts BA12 8LJ; Army and Navy Club), *b* 1947; Capt RA (ret); *ed* Haileybury, and RMA Sandhurst: *m* 1983, Georgina Carolyn, da of James Michael Arnott, of Woodmylne, of Bailey Cottage, Old Bursledon, Hants, and has issue living, Harriet Arabella *b* 1986, Imogen Elizabeth *b* 1988, Florence Helena *b* 1990, — Katherine Margaret, *b* 1944: *m* 1969, Lt-Col M. A. Langdon, RM, of

Worth Cottage, Worth, Wookey, Wells, Som BA5 1LW, and has issue living, Julian Charles Anthony *b* 1972, Mathilda Mary *b* 1974, Eliza Katherine *b* 1979. *Residence* – Oak Covert, Kingsley Av, Camberley, Surrey, GU15 2NA. *Club* – Royal Commonwealth Society. —— Joan Mary Lavie, *b* 1916: *m* 1940, Col Edward Raymond Lewis, CBE, of Worcester Cottage, Beaufort West, Bath, and has issue living, — Robert Edward Curtis, *b* 1941, — Penelope Alison, *b* 1947.

Granddaughter of late Brig Arthur Drury Curtis (ante):—
 Issue of late Lt-Col Robert Cecil Curtis, *b* 1922, *d* 1992: *m* 1952, Pamela Margaret (Yew Tree, Little Coxwell, Faringdon, Oxon SN7 7LP), da of late Oliver S. Sedgwick, of Chislehurst, Kent:—
Carol Frances Margaret, *b* 1956: *m* 1979, Maj Rowland Charles John Woollven, BSc, FRGS, RE, and has issue living, Virginia Alexandra Frances, *b* 1989.

Grandchildren of late Rear-Adm Arthur Cecil Curtis (ante):—
 Issue of late Capt Cecil Montagu Drury Curtis, OBE, *b* 1889, *d* 1966: *m* 1933, Rosa Marion (3 Church Close, Evercreech, Somerset), da of late R. H. Woodley:—
Christopher Francis, *b* 1939; BA, Oxford; PhD, Edinburgh: *m* 1970, Jill Pickup, PhD. —— Hazel Rosemary, *b* 1934: *m* 1960, Sidney Edward Smith, of 8 Blunts Wood Rd, Haywards Heath, Sussex, and *d* 1993, leaving David Edward, *b* 1965, — Rosalind Margaret, *b* 1961, — Alison Claire, *b* 1963, — Stephanie Jane, 1968.
 Issue of late Francis Augustus Drury Curtis, *b* 1891, *d* 1927: *m* 1916, Gwendolen Angelo Taylour, who *d* 1961, da of late Edwin Taylour English, of Toronto, Canada:—
Ada Harriette Drury, *b* 1918: *m* 1958, John Bernard Scowcroft, Ch Engineer, Merchant Navy, who *d* 1989, and has issue living, Sarah Jane, *b* 1960. *Residence* – Roseland, Cubert, Newquay, Cornwall.

Descendants, if any, of late Augustus John Curtis, 4th son of 2nd baronet (whose son Maj Augustus Frederick Curtis *b* 1840, left issue three sons).

Granddaughter of late Lieut-Gen William Frederick Curtis, el son of late Timothy Abraham Curtis, 3rd son of 1st baronet:—
 Issue of late Col William Frederick de Hubbenet Curtis, *b* 1842, *d* 1906: *m* 1880, Mary Owen, who *d* 1934, da of late John Ward Nicholls, Sec of Greenwich Hospital:—
Joceline Sophia Lilian: *m* 1925, Paul Stutfield. *Residence* –

Grandchildren of late Capt George Arthur Hamilton Curtis, RAN, el son of late Col James Charles Curtis (infra):—
 Issue of late Cecil Arthur Hamilton Curtis, *b* 1895, *d* 1970: *m* 1929, Constance May, who *d* 1968, da of Aubrey E. Webb, of Melbourne, Aust:—
Geoffrey Cecil Hamilton (Tigh-na-Ceard, Mt Cotton Rd, Capalaba, Qld), *b* 1932: *m* 1960, Barbara Ellen, da of Peter Angus, of Newmarket, Brisbane, Qld, and has issue living, Fiona Madeline Hamilton, *b* 1962, — Helen Mary Hamilton, *b* 1964. —— Anne Eleanor Hamilton, *b* 1935.

Grandchildren of late Col James Charles Curtis, son of late Timothy Abraham Curtis (ante):—
 Issue of late Alfred William Hamilton Curtis, *b* 1864, *d* 1918: *m* 1901, Euphemia Hilda McClung, da of William A. C. Reynolds, and widow of Henry Cooperthwaite:—
James Alfred Percy Hamilton, *b* 1907; Lt 2nd Bn Rocky Mountain Rangers (ret): *m* 1939, Barbara Milsom, da of Frank Weldon Russell, of Dartmouth, Nova Scotia, and has issue living, James Russell Hamilton (650 Beachview Drive, N Vancouver, BC, Canada, VFG 1R1), *b* 1941; B Com (UBC), MBA (SFU): *m* 1966, Marion Eileen, BEd, da of George B. Moore, of Vancouver, BC, and has issue living, James David Hamilton, *b* 1974, Russell Andrew Hamilton *b* 1975, — Alfred William Hamilton *b* 1945: *m* 1971, Barbara Joan, da of Benjamin Earl Tompkins, of Terrace, BC, and has issue living, James William Hamilton *b* 1973. —— Grace Anna Delicia Florence Hamilton, *b* 1903: *m* 1923, Laurie E. Wiren, and has issue living, John *b* 1930, — James, *b* 1934, — Margaret, *b* 1926, — Leonore, *b* 1928. —— Margaret Euphemia Cecilia Hamilton *b* 1909: *m* 1940, Lloyd E. Kindleysides.

Grandchildren of late Col Charles Herbert Curtis, el son of late Charles William Curtis, el son of Charles Berwick Curtis, 4th son of 1st baronet:—
 Issue of late Maj Timothy Herbert William Curtis, *b* 1882, *d* 1966: *m* (Jan) 1913, Edith Marjorie, who *d* 1968, da of late F. Aldcroft Kay:—
Pamela Kay, *b* (Oct) 1913; sometime Junior Com ATS: *m* 1943, Maj John Howard Nickson, RA, of South Well, Marnhull, Dorset, and has issue living, Simon John Curtis, *b* 1945, — Jeremy David, *b* 1947, — Cecelia Anne, *b* 1953. —— Mary Kay, *b* 1917: *m* 1939, Col Alexander George Jeffrey Readman, DSO, R Scots Greys, of 15 Victoria Sq, SW1, and has issue living, Timothy Christopher George, *b* 1944, — Teresa Mary (*Hon Mrs Christopher C. Lyttelton*), *b* 1947: *m* 1973, Hon Christopher Charles Lyttelton (*see* V Cobham).
 Issue of late Maj Philip Pinckney Curtis, MC, late 15th The King's Royal Hussars: *m* 1st, 1925 (*m diss* 1933), Hélène Ellinor Clare, da of late Capt Glen Kidston, 3rd Bn Black Watch; 2ndly, 1941, Marion (Thatched Cottage, Blackwater, Lyndhurst, Hants SO43 7FJ), da of late George Berkeley Wilson, of Long Barn, Ringwood:—
(By 1st *m*) Cherry April Ellinor, *b* 1926: *m* 1949, Maj Terence Leslie Gossage, MBE, late KOYLI, of Flexford House, Sway, Lymington SO41 6DP, and has issue living, Philip Leslie, *b* 1951: *m* 1st, 1983 (*m diss* 1986), Deborah Ann Darrell; 2ndly, 1991, Nicola Jane, da of Sir Nigel Frederick Althaus, of Swallowcliffe, Wilts, and has issue living (by 2nd *m*), James Peter *b* 1993, — Andrew Alexander, *b* 1963: *m* 1988, Jessica Lucy, da of late Cdr Gresham Vaughan, RN, and has issue living, Henrietta Ellinor *b* 1993, — Julia April Ellinor, *b* 1954: *m* 1982, Christopher Jenkin, and has issue living, Annabel Louise *b* 1985, Camilla Rose *b* 1988. — Alison Audrey Primrose, *b* 1928: *m* 1956, William Ashe Dymoke Windham, of Parc Gwynne, Glasbury-on-Wye, via Hereford HR3 5LL (*see* Bowyer Smyth, Bt, colls). —— (By 2nd *m*) Timothy Malise (Street Farmhouse, Vernham St, nr Andover, Hants SP11 0EL), *b* 1942; *ed* Eton, Trin Coll, Camb (BA), and Harvard Business Sch, USA (MBA): *m* 1st, 1968 (*m diss* 1982), Sally Elizabeth, da of Ambrose Stevens Higgins, of Bangor, Maine, USA; 2ndly, 1986, Cecilia Leueen, da of Maj Peter Brown, of Longworth, Oxon, and has issue living (by 1st *m*), Timothy George, *b* 1972, — Edward Ambrose, *b* (twin) 1972, — Katherine Pinckney, *b* 1970. —— Giles Philip (Walnut Tree Cottage, Upper Wootton, Basingstoke, Hants), *b* 1945; *ed* Eton, and St Andrews Univ (BSc): *m* 1971, Sarah Anne, el da of late Lt-Col Walter George Finney (*see* E Perth, colls), and has issue living, Rowena Mary, *b* 1972, — Arabella Jean, *b* 1975, — Camilla Sarah, *b* 1979, — Lavinia Frances, *b* 1982.

Granddaughters of late Thomas Reginald Curtis, 3rd son of late Charles William Curtis (ante):—
 Issue of late Col William Patrick Stewart Curtis, OBE, *b* 1899, *d* 1965: *m* 1929, Margaret Pamela Adderley, who *d* 1979, da of Lt-Col H. Adderley Cradock:—
Jill Elizabeth, *b* 1930: *m* 1952, Frederick Michael Pelly (*see* Pelly, Bt). —— Dorcas Sara, *b* 1932: *m* 1965, Robin Ross, RM, of 15 York and Albany Close, Walmer, Deal. —— Jocelyn Patricia, *b* 1936: *m* 1960, Mark Tress (19 Finlay Street, SW6 6HE), and has issue living, Oliver James Mark, *b* 1967, — Amanda, *b* 1961, — Camilla, *b* 1963. —— Victoria Anne Dorothea Adderley *b* 1939: *m* 1965, Denis Gamberoni, of 43 Chepstow Pl, W2, and has issue living, Tobias Felix, *b* 1970, — Justine Louise, *b* 1964. —— Tessa Cecilia Evelyn, *b* 1943.

Grandchildren of late Charles William Curtis (ante):—
Issue of late Eustace Henry Curtis, *b* 1863, *d* 1948: *m* 1904, Laura, da of Alfred Ibbotson, of 45 Hill Street, Berkeley Square, W1:—
John Eustace, *b* 1910. —— Corina Laurel Mary, *b* 1908.

Granddaughter of Charles Berwick Curtis (ante):—
Issue of late James Falconer Curtis, *b* 1827, *d* 1879: *m* 1st, 1861, Josephine Adelaide, who *d* 1868, da of late Col Mangin; 2ndly, 1872, Mary Helen, who *d* 1919, da of late Rev J. Brown of Langford, Notts;—
Gertrude Madeline (Redhill Nursing Home, Annandale, 28 Warwick Rd, Redhill, Surrey) *b* 1875: *m* 1913, Imre Knopp, who *d* 1946.

Grandchildren of late Col Edward George Curtis, CMG, 3rd son of late Maj-Gen Reginald Curtis, 3rd son of Charles Berwick Curtis (ante):—
Issue of late Lt-Col David Sacheverell Curtis, *b* 1913, *d* 1990: *m* 1st, 1935 (*m diss* 1945), Annora Beatrice, da of late Maj Frederick Rowland Williams-Wynn, CB (*see* Williams-Wynn, Bt, colls); 2ndly, 1948 (*m diss* 1957), Pamela Ruth, da of late Reginald Walter Preston; 3rdly, 1957, Monica Sarah (20 Pembridge Crescent, W11), da of late Mrs Nina Payne, of Athens:—
(By 1st *m*) Edward Peregrine Sacheverell (Oak House, The Green, Richmond, Surrey; *Club* – -White's), *b* 1937; *ed* Stowe; late Lieut 8th Hussars: *m* 1970, Marie-Adèle, da of late Francis Le Baron Smoot, of Georgetown, Washington DC, and has issue living, Charles Edward Peregrine, *b* 1971, — William Francis Peregrine, *b* 1974, — Robert Frederick Peregrine, *b* 1978, — Caroline Annora Adèle, *b* 1980. —— Hugh Frederick (58 The Vineyard, Richmond, Surrey. *Clubs* – White's, RTYC), *b* 1941; *ed* Stowe: *m* 1970, Maija Kaarina, da of Aulis Samuli Pyy, of Helsinki, and has issue living, Victoria Ann, *b* 1971; *ed* Westonbirt, St Paul's Girls' Sch, and Somerville Coll, Oxford (BA), — Natasha Kaarina Helena, *b* 1973; *ed* Godolphin Latymer Sch, and Univ of Manchester, — Annabel Mary, *b* 1981. —— (By 3rd *m*), Isabella Alexandra Nina, *b* 1959: *m* 1984 (*m diss* 1992), Goulven Courtaigne, of 9 rue de l'Amiral Mouchez, Paris, son of Pierre Courtaigne, of Versailles, and has issue living, Emma Louise Marie, *b* 1985.

Granddaughter of late Spencer Henry Curtis, 5th son of Charles Berwick Curtis (ante):—
Issue of late Major Spencer Carey Curtis, TD, *b* 1865; *d* 1945: *m* 1902, Edith Mabel, who *d* 1931, da of late T. J. Eaton, of Malmesbury, Cape Colony:—
Sylvia Rosamond D'Urban Carey (Little Orchard, Buckham Thorns, Westerham, Kent), *b* 1908: *m* 1932, Thomas Musgrave Pyke, OBE, TD, HM's Inspector of Schs (ret), who *d* 1992 and has issue living, Susan Musgrave, *b* 1935: *m* 1966, John Leo Monaghan (10 Wilton Close, Street, Somerset), and has issue living, David John *b* 1968, Benjamin Musgrave *b* 1970, — Anne Curtis, *b* 1939; MB, BS: *m* 1962, Dr John Ferens Turner, of The Old Vicarage, Church Rd, Combe Down, Bath, and has issue living, Edward Thomas *b* 1966, Sophia Jane *b* 1964, Jessica Charlotte *b* 1968.

Granddaughters of late Wilfred Henry Curtis, 2nd son of late Spencer Henry Curtis (ante):—
Issue of late Anthony Edmund Spencer Curtis, *b* 1906 *d* 1962: *m* 1931, M. Nancy, who *d* 1986, (who *m* 2ndly 1969, John Ormsby Chapple) only child of late R. Nesbit Taylor, of Meadow Bank,Epsom:—
Jean Anna, *b* 1933: *m* 1st, 1960 (*m diss* 1978), John Richard Aley; 2ndly, 1980, Brian James Humphreys, of Jalna, St Johns Rd, Crowborough, E Sussex TN6 1RT. —— Brenda Carey, *b* 1936: *m* 1st, 1960, William John Stickland Budd; 2ndly, 1979, Malcolm Cecil Upstone, of Hermitage End, Treblers Rd, Crowborough, E Sussex, and has issue living (by 1st *m*), Duncan Spencer, *b* 1962, — Roger Alastair, *b* 1964, — Caroline Carey, *b* 1965.

Granddaughter of late Henry Downing Curtis, yst son of Charles Berwick Curtis (ante):—
Issue of late Vice-Adm Berwick Curtis, CB, CMG, DSO, *b* 1876, *d* 1965: *m* 1st, 1907, his cousin Mildred Henrietta Constable, who *d* 1927, da of Frank John Constable Curtis; 2ndly, 1929, Violet Penelope Munro, who *d* 1973, da of late Robert J. B. Thomson, and widow of Lt-Cdr George Francis Cholmley, of Thorpe Bassett, Malton, Yorks:—
(By 1st *m*) Janet Henrietta (Marrett Cottage, Hoarwithy, Hereford), *b* 1908: *m* 1st, 1927 (*m diss* 1936), Com William Kenneth Ramsden Cross, RN, who was *ka* 1941; 2ndly, 1940 (*m diss* 1950), Major Arthur Christopher John Congreve, who *d* 1992; 3rdly, 1951, A. Russell Cowell, who *d* 1964, and has issue living, (by 1st *m*) Giles Berwick (Halfpenny House, Common Hill, Fownhope, Hereford), *b* 1928; Lt-Cdr RN (ret): *m* 1st, 1953 (*m diss* 1971), Sonia, da of E. Welsby Williams; 2ndly, 1971, Lavinia, da of Gp Capt P. C. Thomson, and has issue living (by 1st *m*), Piers William *b* 1955, Belinda Jane *b* 1954, — Henrietta Caroline, *b* 1931: *m* 1957, Christopher Jermyn Pratt, of The Clergy House, Marlston, Newbury (*see* M Bath, colls, 1969 Edn), and has issue living, Roderick Jermyn *b* 1959, James Berwick, *b* 1963.
The 1st baronet was Lord Mayor of London 1794-5, and sat as MP for the City of London 1790-1820. He was offered a peerage, but declined the honour.

Cusack-Smith, see Smith.

DALRYMPLE (UK) 1887, of Newhailes, Midlothian (Extinct 1971)

Sir (Charles) Mark Dalrymple, 3rd and last *Baronet*.

WIDOW LIVING OF THIRD BARONET

Lady Antonia Marian Amy Isabel Stewart (*Lady Antonia Dalrymple*) (Newhailes, Musselburgh, Midlothian), only da of 12th Earl of Galloway: *m* 1946, Sir (Charles) Mark Dalrymple, 3rd Bt, who *d* 1971, when the title became ext.

Dalrymple-Champneys, see Champneys.

Dalrymple-Hay, see Hay.

Dalrymple-White, see White.

ELPHINSTONE-DALRYMPLE (UK) 1828, of Horn, and Logie Elphinstone, Aberdeenshire
(Dormant or Extinct 1956)

Sir FRANCIS NAPIER ELPHINSTONE-DALRYMPLE, CBE, DSO, 7th *Baronet*; *d* 18 Dec 1956, and concerning the next heir, his kinsman, HEW DRUMMOND ELPHINSTONE-DALRYMPLE, no information is available. At the time of going to press no name appears on the Official Roll of Baronets in respect of this title.

DAUGHTERS LIVING OF SEVENTH BARONET

Penelope Eleanore, *b* 1911: *m* 1st, 1939, James Peter Henry Balston, Flying Officer, Auxiliary Air Force, who was *ka* 1940; 2ndly, 1954, Russell Alexander Lovell, of 9 Jonathan Lane, Sandwich, Cape Cod, Mass 02563, USA. ——— Daphne Jean, *b* 1916: *m* 1938, Brig David Meynell, CBE, late Roy Irish Fusiliers, who *d* 1986, and has issue living, Timothy, *b* 1940, — Peter David, *b* 1945. *Residence* – 6 Elm Rd, Gt Stukeley, Huntingdon, Cambs, PE17 5AU

This family is descended from Hon Sir Hew Dalrymple, 3rd son of James, 1st Viscount Stair, sometime Lord President of the Court of Session, and also MP for North Berwick, who was created a baronet 1698 (*see* E Stair, colls). Francis Anstruther Elphinstone Dalrymple, 5th son of 1st baronet, left issue, Hew Drummond *b* 1857, and Francis Herbert, *b* 1862. If they left male issue, the senior in line would be heir to this Baronetcy.

HAMILTON-DALRYMPLE (NS) 1698, of North Berwick, Haddingtonshire

Sir HEW FLEETWOOD HAMILTON-DALRYMPLE, KCVO, 10th *Baronet*; *b* 9 April 1926; *s* his father, *Sir* HEW CLIFFORD, 1959; *ed* Ampleforth; Maj (ret) Gren Guards; Capt Queen's Body Guard for Scotland (Roy Co of Archers), Adjt 1964-85, President of the Council since 1988; a DL E Lothian 1964, Vice-Lieut 1973, Lord Lieut 1986; Dir of Scottish & Newcastle Breweries 1967-86, Vice-Chm 1983-86, Chm Scottish American Investment Co 1985-93 (Dir since 1967-93), CVO 1974, KCVO 1985: *m* 1954, Lady Anne-Louise Mary Keppel, da of 9th Earl of Albemarle, MC, and has issue.

Arms – Quarterly: 1st and 4th grand quarters or on a saltire azure between two water-bougets in flank sable, nine lozenges of the first, *Dalrymple*; 2nd and 3rd grand quarters, quarterly 1st and 4th gules, three cinquefoils, ermine; 2nd and 3rd, argent, a lymphad with sails furled sable, all within a bordure componée argent and azure, the first charged with hearts gules and the second with mullets argent, *Hamilton*. **Crest** – A rock proper. **Supporters** – *Dexter*, a lion guardant gules; *sinister*, a falcon proper.
Residence – Leuchie, North Berwick, East Lothian. *Club* – Cavalry and Guards'.

SONS LIVING

HEW RICHARD, *b* 3 Sept 1955; *ed* Ampleforth, Corpus Christi Coll, Oxford (MA), Clare Hall, Camb (M Phil), and Lond Univ (MSc): *m* 1987, Jane Elizabeth, yr da of Lt-Col John Morris, of Leighterton, Glos, and has issue living, Hew John Lucian, *b* 28 Aug 1990, — Hero Cecilia, *b* 1989, — Fania Mary Anne, *b* 1992. *Residence* – Blackdykes, North Berwick, E Lothian. ——— *Rev* John James, *b* 1957; *ed* Ampleforth, and Queen's Coll, Oxford; RC Priest. ——— Robert George, *b* 1959; *ed* Ampleforth: *m* 1984, Anna Mary, only da of Maj David Gibson, of Bishopswood Grange, nr Ross-on-Wye, Herefordshire, and has issue living, David Fleetwood, *b* 1993, — Effie Charlotte, *b* 1986, — Sophia Louise, *b* 1988, — Honor Rose, *b* 1991. *Residence* – Bolton Old Manse, by Haddington, E Lothian. ——— William Benedict, *b* 1965; *ed* Ampleforth, and Trin Coll, Camb: *m* 1991, Olivia Mary Juliet, 3rd da of Simon Joseph Fraser (*see* L Lovat, colls). *Residence* – 80 Cardcross St, W6.

SISTER LIVING

Elsie Margaret Mary, *b* 1922: *m* 1947, Major Martin Antony Gibbs, Coldstream Gds, and has issue living, Antony William Hew (The Home Farm, Barrow Gurney, Bristol), *b* 1947; *ed* Eton and Worcs Coll, Oxford: *m* 1974, Lady Virginia Rous, da of 5th Earl of Stradbroke, and has issue living, Abram *b* 1976, William Martin *b* 1986, Mary *b* 1975, Emily-Anna *b* 1978, Elizabeth Rose *b* 1979, Margaret Blanche *b* 1988, — Mary Blanche, *b* 1949; *ed* London Univ (BA): *m* 1971, Rupert Leander Pattle Ridge, son of late Maj Robert Vaughan Ridge, of Brockley, Som, and has issue living, Thomas Leander *b* 1972, Edward Francis *b* 1976, Marian Sophia *b* 1973, Adeline Dyce Albinia Rose *b* 1979, — Anstice Bridget, *b* 1951: *m* 1978, Antony Richard Howard, and has two children (*see* B Howard of Penrith), — Cecily Ann Albinia, *b* 1952: *m* 1975, Robert Mathers, who was *k* in a traffic accident 1992, and has issue living, John Alexander Joseph *b* 1978, Simon Martin *b* 1984, Ralph Michael *b* 1987, Alice Mary Albinia *b* 1976, Imogen Blanche *b* 1982, — Katharine Rose, *b* 1955, — Julian Margaret, *b* 1957: *m* 1986, Julian Alexander Stanley, son of Oliver Duncan Stanley, of 5 The Park, NW11, and has issue living, Isaac Martin *b* 1990, Madeline Leah *b* 1988, Elinor Katherine Eve *b* 1992. *Residence* – Sheldon Manor, Chippenham, Wilts.

COLLATERAL BRANCH LIVING

　　　　Descendants (if any) of Robert Dalrymple-Horn-Elphinstone (2nd son of Robert Dalrymple-Horn-Elphinstone, 3rd son of Hew Elphinstone, 2nd son of 1st baronet), who was *cr* a *Baronet* 1828:—
See Elphinstone-Dalrymple, Bt (dormant or ext).

The 1st baronet, Hon Sir Hew Dalrymple, 3rd son of 1st Viscount Stair, sat as MP for North Berwick in the Scotch Parliament, and was subsequently Lord President of Session, and one of the Commissioners appointed to arrange the Articles of Union. Sir Hew, the 2nd baronet, was MP for co Haddington, and King's Remembrancer in the Exchequer for Scotland. The 3rd baronet, Sir Hew, MP for Midlothian, assumed the additional surname of Hamilton, and the 4th baronet assumed the surname of Hamilton after Dalrymple (*see* E Stair, colls), while the 8th baronet assumed it before that of Dalrymple.

DALYELL (NS) 1685, of the Binns

(*Sir*) THOMAS (TAM) DALYELL OF THE BINNS, MP, 11th Baronet (established his claim in 1973, but does not use title); son of late Lt-Col Gordon Loch, CIE, DL, JP; *b* 9 Aug 1932; *s* his mother, (*Dame*) ELEANOR ISABEL (*de jure Baroness*), who *d* 1972 (da of Sir James Bruce Wilkie-Dalyell, 9th Bt), who, with her husband, assumed the surname and arms of Dalyell of The Binns (officially recognized that year by Lord Lyon King of Arms); *ed* Eton, and King's Coll, Camb; Dep Dir of Studies, Ship-School, Dunera, 1961-62, Sec of Labour Standing Conference on the Sciences 1962-64, PPS to Min of Housing of Local Govt 1964-66; PPS to Leader of House of Commons 1967-68, and to Sec of State for Social Security 1968-70; a Member of Public Accounts Cttee, House of Commons 1962-65, and of House of Commons Select Cttee on Science and Tech 1966-68; Chm of Parl Labour Party Foreign Affairs Group 1973, Vice-Chm of Parl Labour Party 1974; Member of European Parliament 1975-78, Vice-Chm of Sub-Cttee on Public Accounts of Budget Cttee 1975-78; a Member of Select Cttee of Scrutiny on European Legislation 1979-83; a Member of National Executive Committee, Labour Party 1986-87; Political Columnist of *New Scientist* since 1968, author of *Devolution: the End of Britain*; *The Case for Ship Schools* 1960; *Ship School Dunera* 1962; *One Man's Falklands* 1982; *Thatcher's Torpedo* 1983; *A Science Policy for Britain* 1983; *Misrule: How Mrs Thatcher deceived Parliament* 1987; *Dick Crossman: A Portrait* 1989; MP for W Lothian (*Lab*) since 1962: *m* 1963, Hon Kathleen Mary Agnes Wheatley, only da of Baron Wheatley (Life Baron), and has issue.

Arms – Quarterly, 1st and 4th, sable a naked man with his arms extended proper on a canton argent a sword and pistol disposed in saltire also proper for *Dalyell of the Binns*; 2nd, or a saltire engrailed sable between two swans proper naiant in lochs undy azure and argent and in chief point a mullet gules for difference for *Loch*; 3rd, or a bend chequy sable and argent betwixt three buckles azure for *Menteith of Auldcathie*. Over all an intra-escutcheonal additament of a Baronet of Nova Scotia. **Crest** – A dexter arm issuant from the wreath the hand grasping a scimitar proper hilted and pommelled or. **Supporters** – Two lions sejant guardant gukes armed and langued azure each supporting with its inferior forepaw a pavilion pole sable with rosette and pennon spike garnished or, the pennon argent with forks of the same and sable is charged with a sword and pistol in saltire proper.
Residence – The Binns, Linlithgow EH49 7NA.

SON LIVING

GORDON WHEATLEY, *b* 26 Sept 1965.

DAUGHTER LIVING

Moira Eleanor, *b* 1968.

COLLATERAL BRANCHES LIVING (*Males and Females in remainder*)

Descendants of George Falconar of Carlowrie, W Lothian, el son of Jane Stewart (who *m* David Falconar of Carlowrie and *d* 1837), da and heir of Magdalen (who *m* Robert Stewart of Binny, W Lothian), da of 3rd Bt:—

Granddaughter of late George Mercer Falconer-Stewart, 2nd son of George Falconar of Carlowrie (ante) (*see* L Falconer of Halkerton).

Grandchildren of late Helen Jane (who *m* John Monsey Collyer of Gimingham, Norfolk, and *d* 1919), yr da of George Falconar of Carlowrie (ante):—
Issue of late Brig-Gen John Johnston Collyer, CB, CMG, DSO, *b* 1870, *d* 1941: *m* 1903, Hilda Rochford, da of Michael Henry Quinn:—
†Freda Falconar, *b* 1906: *m* 1938, Donald Stewart, of 4 Chequers, Drama Street, Somerset West, Cape 7130, S Africa, and *d* 1989, leaving issue, Ian Patrick Collyer (Matepe Estate, Marandellas, Zimbabwe): *m* and has issue, two sons, — Neil D. Collyer (Kooringa Estate, PO Box Fingal, Tasmania, Australia): *m* and has issue, two das.
Issue of late Roger Messenger Monsey Collyer, *b* 1874, *d* 19—: *m* 1909, Maud Winifred, da of late Byron Noel:—
Helen Nova, *b* 1911. —— Elizabeth Maud, *b* 1913. —— Ruth Amy, *b* 1914. —— Winifred Noel, *b* 1918. —— Judith, *b* 1921.
This Baronetcy was created with a special remainder "to heirs male and of tailzie." The right of the 9th baronet, Sir James Bruce Wilkie-Dalyell of the Binns, to be placed on the Official Roll of the Baronetage was admitted by the Baronetage Committee of the Privy Council on 1 July 1914.

DARELL (GB) 1795, of Richmond Hill, Surrey

Sir JEFFREY LIONEL DARELL, MC, 8th *Baronet*, only son of late Col Guy Marsland Darell, MC, 3rd son of 5th Baronet; *b* 2 Oct 1919; *s* his cousin, Sir WILLIAM OSWALD, 1959; *ed* Eton, and RMC Sandhurst; High Sheriff of Norfolk 1985-86, Brig (ret) Coldstream Guards, and patron of one living commanded 1st Batn Coldstream Guards 1957-9, AAG, War Office 1959-61, Coll Comd, RMA Sandhurst 1961-64, Regimental Lt-Col Comdg Coldstream Guards 1964, and Comdg 56th (London) Inf Bde (TA) 1965-67; Vice-Pres of Regular Commns Board 1968-70, Comdt Mons Officer Cadet Sch 1970-72; ADC to HM 1973-74; Trustee and Memb of London Law Trust since 1981; 1939-45 War (MC): *m* 1953, Bridget Mary, da of Maj Gen Sir Allan Henry Shafto Adair, 6th Bt, GCVO, CB, DSO, MC, and has issue.

ᴀrms – Azure, a lion rampant or ducally crowned argent. Crest – Out of a ducal coronet or a Saracen's head couped at the shoulders proper, bearded sable, wreathed about the temples or and azure, on his head a cap of the last fretty argent tasselled or, turned up ermine.
Residence – Denton Lodge, Harleston, Norfolk IP20 0AD. *Club* – Army and Navy

SON LIVING

GUY JEFFREY ADAIR, *b* 8 June 1961; *ed* Eton, and RMA Sandhurst; Coldm Gds 1981-84; Dir Fenchurch Group Ltd since 1993; *m* 1988, (Justine) Samantha, da of Mr Justice T. Reynolds, of Quambi Place, Edgecliff, Sydney, Australia, and has issue living, Sophia Elizabeth Alexandra, *b* 1989, — Amelia Flora Frances, *b* 1993. *Residence* – 10 Rigault Rd, SW6.

DAUGHTERS LIVING

Katherine Mary, *b* 1954: *m* 1977, (John) Richard Astor, and has issue (*see* B Astor of Hever, colls). —— Camilla Viola, *b* 1956: *m* 1983, Henry Robert Thomas Adeane, of Babraham, Cambridge, only son of late Charles Raymond Wyndham Adeane, and has issue living, Anthony Charles, *b* 1991, — Madeline Bridget, *b* 1987. *Residence* – 44 Sterndale Rd, W14.

SISTER LIVING

Cynthia Mary, *b* 1916: *m* 1940, Michael Webster Harrap, and has issue living, Simon Richard (Perryland, Bentley, Farnham, Surrey; 16 Kelso Place, W8 5QD), *b* 1941; *ed* Harrow: *m* 1969, Diana, yr da of late Capt Ian Stanley Akers-Douglas (*see* V Chilston, colls), and has issue living, Nicholas Guy *b* 1975, Louise Jane *b* 1971, Lara Sophie *b* 1979, — John Michael Darell (35 Kenway Rd, SW5 0RE), *b* 1943; *ed* Harrow: *m* 1973, Elizabeth Helen Rodica, yr da of Radu Tilea (*see* E Carnarvon, colls), and has issue living, Peter Mark *b* 1975, Edward Michael *b* 1983, — Giles Thresher (Hill Farm, Bentley, Farnham, Surrey GU10 5HB), *b* 1948; *ed* Harrow: *m* 1981, Sona Sophia, elder da of late John Gladstone, TD, of Capenoch, Thornhill, Dumfriesshire, and has issue living, Richard Thresher *b* 1984, Gilbert William Frederick *b* 1987, Isla Marie *b* 1990. *Residence* – Marsh House, Bentley, nr Farnham, Surrey GU10 5JF.

DAUGHTER LIVING OF SIXTH BARONET

Margaret Eleanor Phyllis: *m* 1930, Baron Helmut William Bruno Schröder, who *d* 1969, and has issue living, *Baron* Bruno Lionel (42 Lansdowne Rd, London W11 4LU), *b* 1933; *ed* Eton, Univ Coll Oxford (MA), and Harvard Business Sch (MBA): *m* 1969, Patricia Leonie Mary (Piffa), da of late Maj Adrian Holt, and has issue living, Leonie *b* 1974, — *Baroness* Charmaine Brenda, *b* 1935: *m* 1958, Georg Wilhelm von Mallinckrodt, of 64 Chelsea Sq, SW3 6LE, and has issue living, Philip Stephan Arnold *b* 1962, Edward Gustav Paul *b* 1965, Claire Louise *b* 1960: *m* 1987, Henry Julian Nicholas Fitzalan Howard, of 103 Abingdon Rd, W8 6QU (and has issue: *see* D Norfolk), Nina Sophie *b* 1967.

The 1st baronet, Sir Lionel Darell, sat as MP for Lyme Regis 1780-84, and for Heydon 1784-1802. The 2nd baronet, Sir Harry Verelst Darell, was extensively engaged in commerce in Bengal. Sir Lionel Darell, 5th Baronet, was High Sheriff of Gloucestershire 1887. The 6th baronet, Col Sir Lionel Edward Darell, DSO, 1st Life Guards, was a Co Councillor, Co Alderman, and High Sheriff of Gloucestershire 1924, and Hon Col 5th Batn Gloucestershire Regt 1936.

DASHWOOD (E) 1684, of Kirtlington Park, Oxfordshire

Nothing is inaccessible to virtue

Sir RICHARD JAMES DASHWOOD, 9th *Baronet*; *b* 14 Feb 1950; *s* his father, Sir HENRY GEORGE MASSY, 1972; *ed* Eton; Lt 14th/20th Kings Hussars; T & AVR 1973: *m* 1984 (*m diss* 1993), Kathryn Ann, elder da of Frank Mahon, of Barretts Farm, Eastbury, Newbury, Berks, and has issue

ᴀrms – Argent, on a fesse double cotised gules three gryphous' heads erased or. Crest – A griffin's head erminois, erased gules. ᴤupporters – On either side a male gryphon argent, gorged with a collar flory counterflory gules.
Residence – Ledwell Cottage, Sandford St Martin, Oxon, OX7 7AN. *Club* – Boodle's.

SON LIVING

FREDERICK GEORGE MAHON, *b* 29 Jan 1988.

SISTER LIVING

Emma Victoria Mildred, *b* 1955: *m* 1977, Maj Edward Morgan Crofton (*see* Crofton, Bt, *cr* 1801). *Residence* – Long Durford, Upper Durford Wood, Petersfield, Hants GU31 5AW.

COLLATERAL BRANCHES LIVING

Issue of late Arthur Paul Dashwood, OBE, 3rd son of 6th baronet, *b* 1882, *d* 1964: *m* 1919, Edmeé Elizabeth Monica (E. M. Delafield, novelist), who *d* 1943, da of late Count Henry Philip Ducarel de la Pasture:—

Rosamund Margaret, *b* 1923: *m* 1948, Leslie Harold Truelove, MRCP, late RNZAF, and has issue living, Paul Alexander, *b* 1948, — Leslie Simon, *b* 1950, — Patrick, *b* 1955, — Michael Andrew, *b* 1961.

Grandchildren of late Alexander Thomas Dashwood, elder son of Alexander John Dashwood, eldest son of Lt-Col Alexander Wilton Dashwood, yr son of Thomas Dashwood, EICS, yr son of 2nd baronet:—

Issue of late Alexander John Dashwood, *b* 1905, *d* 1979: *m* 1947, Mary Whitburn (3 Ladwill Sq, Ashburton, nr Newton Abbot, Devon), da of late Reginald Frank Thorne, of Southborough, nr Tunbridge Wells:—

Alexander Thomas Whitburn (9 Bradley Rd, Mannamead, Plymouth, Devon), *b* 1950: *m* 1977, Christine Ellen, da of Walter Lewis Badge, of 20 Ocean View Rd, Bude, Cornwall, and has issue living, Benjamin Alexander John, *b* 1979. —— Jeremy Charles Whitburn, *b* 1957. —— Sophia Ann Whitburn, *b* 1954.

Grandchildren of late George Lionel Dashwood, yst son of Lt-Col Alexander Wilton Dashwood (ante):—

Issue of late Sir Henry Thomas Alexander Dashwood, *b* 1878, *d* 1959: *m* 1909, Norah Creina Bruce, who *d* 1948, da of Henry Arthur Whately, of Midford Castle, Bath:—

Robert Henry Nevile, *b* 1921; *ed* Harrow, and Magdalene Coll, Camb (BA 1942, MA 1946); formerly Capt RA; is a JP, DL and High Sheriff (1980) for Northants: *m* 1959, Ruth Mary, da of Dr W. B. R. Monteith, of Purston Manor, Brackley, Northants, and has issue living, David Henry William, *b* 1960, — Ian Bruce Robert, *b* 1962. *Residence* – Farthinghoe Lodge Farm, Farthinghoe, Brackley, Northants. —— Norah Creina Frances, *b* 1910: *m* 1958, William Nell. *Residence* – Farthinghoe Lodge Farm, Farthinghoe, Brackley, Northants.

Grandchildren of late Maj Claude Burrard Lewes Dashwood, 2nd son of late Rev Robert Lewes Dashwood, grandson of late Samuel Francis Dashwood, great-grandson of Richard Dashwood, of Ledwell, co Oxon, 3rd son of 1st baronet:—

Issue of late Capt Robert Armand Lewes Dashwood, *b* 1916, *d* 1986: *m* 1938, Peggy Violet, who *d* 1963, only da of Herbert Reeves, of Bournmouth:—

Ian Burrard Lewes (Camelot, 1 Groeneveld Rd, Rondebosch 7700, Cape, S Africa), *b* 1947: *m* 1968, Marlene Dolores, el da of Pieter Kruger, of Sea Point, Cape, and has issue living, Paul Burrard Lewes, *b* 1972, — Annemarie, *b* 1969. —— Anne, *b* 1956.

Issue of late Capt Sidney Lewes Dashwood, MBE, *b* 1882, *d* 1966: *m* 1922, Joan, who *d* 1963, da of Sir Sidney Gerald Burrard, 7th Bt, KCSI:—

Mary Edith Burrard, *b* 1923: *m* 1946, John Harry Walrond Simmons, MBE, who *d* 1994, of Selva, Lincombe Lane, Boar's Hill, Oxford, and has issue living, Geoffrey Philip, *b* 1952: *m* 1976, Wendy Jean, da of Maurice Aylen, of Barton-on-Sea, and has issue living, Heather Julie *b* 1988, — Roland Paul, *b* 1957, — Rosemary Jane, *b* 1949, — Pamela Anne, *b* 1959.

Descendants of Richard Dashwood, of Cockley Cley, Norfolk, 2nd son of Alderman George Dashwood, of Hackney, Middlesex, and brother of 1st Bt, who are in special remainder to the Baronetcy:—

Grandchildren of late Charles Horace Pettus Dashwood, el son of Rev Charles John Dashwood, R. of Billingford, Norfolk (*d* 1890), 4th in descent from Richard Dashwood, of Cockley Cley (ante):—

Issue of late Horace Raikes Dashwood, of Caldecott Hall, Fritton, Suffolk, *b* 1885, *d* 1967: *m* 1912, Jessie Nina, who *d* 1978, da of late Walter Cassels, of Buenos Aires, Argentina:—

John Horace Cassels (Chestnut Cottage, Weyside Close, Milford-on-Sea, Hants), *b* 1913; Maj (ret) RASC: *m* 1941, Christina FitzGibbon, and has issue living, Elizabeth Patricia, *b* 1942, — Annette Diana, *b* 1947, MB BS: *m* 1975, Peter Anthony Goulden (Beechings, Water St, Hampstead Norreys, Newbury, Berks, RG16 0SB), and has issue living, Michael John Toby *b* 1979, Nicholas James *b* 1981, — Rosemarie, *b* 1950. —— Donald Cassels (Long Acre, Cley, Holt, Norfolk), *b* 1914: *m* 1941, Rachel, da of Rev James Mortimer La Fontaine McAnally, formerly R of Hethersett, Norfolk, and has issue living, Timothy James (43 Wood Lane, Fleet, Hants), *b* 1947; *ed* Marlborough, King's Coll, Camb (scholar), and Trin Coll, Oxford: *m* 1983, Katherine Ruth, da of late John Oliver Harris, of Epsom, Auckland, NZ, and has issue living, Peter James Oliver *b* 1985, Anne Jennifer Raven *b* 1987, — Margaret Jessie, *b* 1942: *m* 1983, Neil Douglas Sconce, of 11 Cromer Villas Rd, SW18 1PH, only son of late Maj Douglas Sconce, and has issue living, Francisca Barbara *b* 1985. —— Elizabeth Cassels, *b* 1916: *m* 1st, 1941, Antony Josiah Boek Gimson, who was *ka* 1942; 2ndly, 1944, Owen Lloyd Davies, of Shepperd's Hill, Toowoomba, Qld 4350, Australia, and has issue living (by 1st *m*), Josiah Jeremy Dashwood Boek, *b* 1942, — (by 2nd *m*), Elizabeth Anne, *b* 19—.

Issue of late Richard Raikes Dashwood, *b* 1890, *d* 1967: *m* 1918, Rachel Mary Windham, da of late Rev Alfred Charles Lowth, R. of Colden Common, Winchester:—

Roland Pettus (Los Sauces, General Villegas, Argentina; 110 Tourist Rd, Toowoomba, Qld 4350, Australia), *b* 1922: *m* 1946, Helen Theresa, da of Leslie Armitage, of La Mimosa, Buena Esperanza, Argentina, and has issue living, John Richard, *b* 1959, — Alan Roland, *b* 1960, — Paul Charles, *b* 1962, — Ray James, *b* 1964. —— Jean Mary, *b* 1919: *m* 1941, her cousin, John Stuart Michael Dashwood (infra). —— Edith Rachel, *b* 1920: *m* 1949, Ian McCulloch, of La Totora, Villa Valeria, Argentina, who *d* 1971. —— Molly Frances, *b* 1925: *m* 1946, George Locke Smiles, of Beta Gamma, Ombu, Argentina, and has issue living, Dorothy June, *b* 1957.

Grandchildren of late Edmund Samuel Dashwood, surg, 2nd son of Rev Charles John Dashwood, R. of Billingford, Norfolk (*d* 1890) (ante):—

Issue of late John Rawdon Dashwood, *b* 1889, *d* 1961: *m* 1918, Marian, who *d* 1965, da of Robert Kohlhoff Clark, tea-planter, of Ceylon:—

John Stuart Michael (10 Curtis St, Toowoomba, Qld, 4350, Australia), *b* 1917: *m* 1941, his cousin, Jean Mary, da of late Richard Raikes Dashwood (ante), and has issue living, Geoffrey Richard (27 rue de l'Etang de la Tour, 78120 Rambouillet, France), *b* 1942: *m* 1966, Eliane Michèle, da of Kleber Barrassé, of Colombes, Seine, France, and has issue living, Sophie Michèle *b* 1968, Valerie Mary *b* 1971, Annabel Anne *b* 1973, — Oliver Michael, *b* 1947; schoolmaster at Toowoomba Gram Sch: *m* 1983, Ann, da of Joseph Waxman, of Merricks North, Vic, Australia, and has issue living, Robert Michael *b* 1983, Timothy Kester Paul *b* 1985. —— Mary Elizabeth Anne (18 Crofton Lane, Hill Head, Fareham, Hants, PO14 3LP), *b* 1921: *m* 1942, Lt-Cdr Patrick Hugh Moss, RN, who *d* 1989, and has issue living, Nigel Patrick Stringer (Henhurst Lodge, Beare Green Road, Ockley, Dorking, Surrey), *b* 1946: *m* 1971, Linda, da of Reginald Alfred Baillie, of 26 Green Lane, Copnor, Portsmouth, and has issue living, James Robert *b* 1975, Jonathan Mark *b* 1977, — Jane Elizabeth Moss (14 Maizemore Walk, Lee-on-Solent, Hants), *b* 1943: *m* 1st, 1969 (*m diss* 1974), Roger Sowerby; 2ndly, 1976 (*m diss* 1980), Brian James Maby.

Descendants of late Henry Dashwood, MP, grandson of Lt-Col George Dashwood (who assumed the surname and arms of Peyton, and was *cr* a *Baronet* 1776), brother of 1st baronet (The male line, now ext, was in special remainder to the Baronetcy.)

See Peyton, Bt, (ext).

Alderman George Dashwood, of London, undertook, with others, to farm the whole revenue of the kingdom of Ireland *temp* Charles II. He afterwards, with others, farmed the whole revenues of excise and hearth money in England, and was a commissioner of Revenue till his death in 1682. A patent of baronetcy was granted to him, but as he did not take it out, his widow was given the precedence of a baronet's widow, while a new patent of baronetcy was granted to his son with special remainder, in default of male issue, to the male descendants of his father. The 1st baronet of this creation was MP for Banbury, the 2nd was MP for Oxfordshire, and the 3rd MP for Woodstock. Alderman Francis Dashwood, of London, elder brother of Alderman George Dashwood (ante), was father of Sir Francis Dashwood, 1st baronet, of West Wycombe.

DASHWOOD (GB) 1707, of West Wycombe, Buckinghamshire

PRO·MAGNÂ CHARTÂ

For the Great Charter

Sir FRANCIS JOHN VERNON HEREWARD DASHWOOD, 11th *Baronet*, and Premier Baronet of Great Britain; *b* 7 Aug 1925; *s* his father, *Sir* JOHN LINDSAY, CVO, 1966; *ed* Eton, Ch Ch, Oxford (MA) and Henry Fellow at Harvard Business Sch; a Member of Lloyd's; a Co Councillor of Bucks 1951-52; High Sheriff of Bucks 1976; author of *The Dashwoods of West Wycombe* 1987: *m* 1st, 1957, Victoria Ann Elizabeth Gwynne, who *d* 1976, only da of late Maj John Frederick Foley, Baron de Rutzen, Welsh Guards (Foley-Philipps, Bt); 2ndly, 1977, Marcella Teresa Guglielmina Maria, da of Marcellino Scarafina, formerly wife of Giuseppe Sportoletti Baduel, and widow of Jack Frye, CBE, and has issue by 1st *m*.

Arms – Argent, on a fesse double cotised gules, three griffins' heads erased or.
Crest – A griffin's head erased per fesse, erminois and gules.
Residence – West Wycombe Park, Bucks. *Club* – White's.

SON LIVING (By 1st marriage)

EDWARD JOHN FRANCIS, *b* 25 Sept 1964; *ed* Eton, and Reading Univ (BSc); ARICS: *m* 1989, Lucinda Nell, only da of Gerrard Herman Francis Miesegaes, of 14 Queen's Elm Sq, SW3, and has issue living, George Francis, *b* 17 June 1992, — Robert Edward, *b* 1993, — Victoria Lucinda, *b* 1991.

DAUGHTERS LIVING (By 1st marriage)

Emily Jane, *b* 1958: *m* 1981, Charles William Lennox Naper (*see* Valentia colls, 1973/4 Edn), and has issue living, Nicholas, *b* 1984, — Edward, *b* 1986, — John, *b* 1990. —— Georgina Helen, *b* 1960: *m* 1991, Charles Humphrey Joseph Weld, and has issue (*see* L Lovat, colls), of Chideock Manor, Dorset. —— Caroline Sarah, *b* 1962.

BROTHER LIVING

John (27 Matham Rd, East Molesey, Surrey), *b* 1929; *ed* Eton, and Ch Ch, Oxford: *m* 1st, 1959 (*m diss* 1964), Susan Boyter Duncombe, el da of Maj Ernest Duncombe Shafto, of Little Beamishe, Aldeburgh, Suffolk; 2ndly, 1965, Harriet Louise, el da of J. P. Spencer, of Norbury Park, Mickleham, Surrey, and has issue living (by 2nd *m*), Thomas *b* 1973, — Rebecca Louise, *b* 1971.

SISTER LIVING

Maud Helen Sarah (*Baroness Aberdare*), *b* 1924: *m* 1946, 4th Baron Aberdare, of 32 Elthiron Rd, SW6.

The Dashwoods were established in NE Dorset in early Tudor times, and Henry Dashwode is named in the Subsidy for Tarrant Gunville 1524/5 and the muster 1539. In the person of Robert Dashwood, son of Thomas Dashwood of Tarrant Monkton next Tarrant Gunville, the senior line of the family moved after 1575 to Stogumber in Somerset where the said Robert Dashwood (*d* 1610) was the ancestor of the Baronets line. The 1st baronet was knighted 1702, and sat as MP for Winchilsea. The 2nd baronet became 8th Baron LeDespencer in right of his mother, and was successively head of the War Office, Chancellor of the Exchequer, and Postmaster-General. He died without male issue, and the barony fell in abeyance. The 3rd baronet — who was half-brother to the 2nd baronet — assumed the additional surname of King. Sir John Dashwood, 4th Bt, who *d* 1849, was fifth in descent from Ann Agar, sister of John Milton, the poet, and sat as MP for Wycombe 1796-31. The 5th baronet sat as MP for Bucks (*L*) 1832-7, and for Wycombe 1837-62.

DAVID (UK) 1911, of Bombay (Extinct 1964)

Sir PERCIVAL VICTOR DAVID EZEKIEL DAVID, 2nd and last *Baronet*.

DAUGHTER LIVING OF SECOND BARONET

Katherine Viola Monica, *b* 1914: *m* 1952, William Frederick Taylor. *Residence* – 35 Monkridge, Haslemere Rd, Crouch End Hill, N8.

WIDOW LIVING OF SECOND BARONET

SHEILA JANE YORKE (*Lady David*), da of late Arthur Yorke Hardy: *m* 1st, 1953, as his 2nd wife, Sir Percival Victor David Ezekiel David, 2nd baronet, who *d* 1964, when the title became ext; 2ndly, 1968, Dr John D. Riddell, who *d* 1976, whereupon she resumed her former style.

FERGUSON DAVIE (UK) 1847, of Creedy, Devonshire

Under the auspices of Christ

Sir ANTONY FRANCIS FERGUSON DAVIE, 6th *Baronet, b* 23 March 1952; *s* his father, *Rev Sir* (ARTHUR) PATRICK, TD, 1988; *ed* Stanbridge Earls and Birkbeck Coll, London Univ.

Arms – Quarterly; 1st and 4th, argent, a chevron sable between three mullets pierced gules; 2nd and 3rd, azure, three cinquefoils or, upon a chief of the last a lion passant, gules. **Crests** – 1st, a pascal lamb reguardant argent; 2nd, a kingfisher wings elevated proper, in the beak a branch of olive vert fructed or. *Residence* – 37A Barkston Gdns, SW5 0ER.

COLLATERAL BRANCHES LIVING

Issue of late Edward Cruger Ferguson Davie, 4th son of 3rd baronet, *b* 1868, *d* 1948: *m* 1905, Blanche Evelyn, who *d* 1959, da of late William Wyndham Hasler, of Aldingbourne House, Sussex:—

JOHN, *b* 1 May 1906; *ed* Winchester: *m* 1942, (Joan) Zoë, who *d* 1987, da of late Raymond Hoole, of Vancouver, BC, and has issue living, Michael (63 Hillgate Pl, Balham Hill, SW12 9ES), *b* 1944: *m* 1968 (*m diss* 1993), (Margaret) Jean, da of late Douglas John Macbeth, of Bowdon, Ches, and has had issue, James Michael *b* 1970; *d* 1988, — Julian Anthony (c/o Lloyds Bank, Witton, Birmingham 17), *b* 1950: *m* 1976, Louise, da of John Marsden, of Huttons Ambo, York, and has issue living, Charles John *b* 1978, John Robert *b* 1981, William Edward *b* 1986. *Residence* – 7/9 Rue de Matilly, 1338 Lasne, Belgium.

Grandchildren of late Henry Herrick Ferguson Davie (*b* 1869) (infra):—
Issue of late Henry Herrick Ferguson Davie, *b* 1894, *d* 1952: *m* 1919, Julia Victoria, da of John Stokes, of London:—
Henry Herrick (1420, Washington Avenue, Severn, Baltimore, Maryland, USA), *b* 1920: *m* 1st, 1941 (*m diss* 1943), Joyce Sanders, of Brooklyn, Baltimore, USA; 2ndly, 1951, Anna Marie, da of Bender Clarke, of Gambrillo, Maryland, USA, and has issue living, (by 1st *m*) Henry Herrick, *b* 194—, — (by 2nd *m*) Anna Louise, *b* 1952.
Issue of late Charles Francis Ferguson Davie, *b* 1898, *d* 1967: *m* 1924, Alice Clarke, who *d* 1968, da of Henry Newman, of Potterne, Wilts:—
Muriel Frances, *b* 1926: *m* 1st, 1948 (*m diss* 1952), Basil Anthony King; 2ndly, 1952, Bernard, William Pearce, of 1003 Harbour View, Victoria Embankment, Durban, S Africa, and has issue living (by 2nd *m*), Michael Stephen, *b* 1953: *m* 1st, 1975 (*m diss* 1977), Judith Melanie McClelland; 2ndly, 1979, Carol Ann Ebelthite, and has issue living (by 2nd *m*), Clinton Noel *b* 1990, Megan Bernardine *b* 1980, Mandy *b* 1985, Tamsin *b* 1988, — Geoffrey Mark, *b* 1956: *m* 1981, Belinda Ryall, of Natal, and has issue living, Raymond *b* 1984, Bronwyn Muriel *b* 1983, — Robert Andrew, *b* 1959: *m* 1st, 1980 (*m diss* 1988), Odette Jean-Jacques; 2ndly, 1992, Beverley Ann Smith, and has issue living (by 1st *m*), Dylan Bradley *b* 1983, Lloyd *b* 1985.

Grandchildren of late Capt William Carey Ferguson Davie (infra):—
Issue of late William George Michael Ferguson Davie, *b* 1923, *d* 1973: *m* 1953, Margaret Mary (Wendy) (700, East 15th St, North Vancouver, BC, V7L 2S4, Canada), da of late Capt William J. Fowler:—
Christopher Mark, *b* 1956: *m* 1st, 1976 (*m diss* 1982), Wendy K., da of John McGillivray, of Castlegar, BC, Canada; 2ndly, 1984, Joanne Elma, da of David James Thomas, QC. —— Deirdre Ann, *b* 1955: *m* 1977 (*m diss* 1988), Herbert J. Markgraf, of Kelowna, BC, Canada. —— Jean Elizabeth, *b* 1961: *m* 1986, Gordon Richard Boothe, of Summerland, BC.

Granddaughter of late Henry Herrick Ferguson Davie (*b* 1869), 2nd son of late Rev Charles Robert Ferguson Davie, 4th son of 1st baronet:—
Issue of late Capt William Carey Ferguson Davie, *b* 1900, *d* 1974: *m* 1922, Katherine, who *d* 1986, da of late William Robertson Kay, of Sutton, co Dublin:—
Jean Anne, *b* 1932: *m* 1956, George Hellyer-Crawford, of Anglesea, Killiney Rd, Killiney, co Dublin, and has issue living, Anne Katherine, *b* 1959: *m* 1984, Thomas P. O'Reilly, of Tullamore, Co Offaly, and has issue living, Nanci Jean *b* 1994, — Alison Jane, *b* 1963.
Frances Juliana Davie (only surviving sister of Sir John Davie, 9th baronet (*cr* 1641), and niece and heiress of Sir Humphrey Phineas Davie, 10th and last baronet, who *d* 1846): *m* 1823, Gen Henry Robert Ferguson. In the following year the baronetcy was revived in favour of Gen Ferguson, who had assumed by Roy licence 1846 the additional surname and arms of Davie after his patronymic.

d'Avigdor-Goldsmid, see Goldsmid.

DAVIS (UK) 1946, of Barrington Hall, co Cambridge

Sir JOHN GILBERT DAVIS, 3rd *Baronet*; *b* 17 Aug 1936; *s* his father, *Sir* GILBERT, 1973; *ed* Oundle, and RNC Dartmouth: *m* 1960, Elizabeth Margaret, el da of Robert Smith Turnbull, of Falkirk, and has issue.

𝕬rms – Quarterly; 1st and 4th, per saltire sable and argent, two pierced mullets or in pale and a dexter and sinister dragon's wing in fesse gules, *Davis*; 2nd and 3rd, per fesse embattled gules and argent in chief three castles or, *Terrett*. 𝕮rest – In front of a spear erect the shaft couped argent, and in front of a vol of dragon's wings three pierced mullets as in the arms.
Residence – 5 York Ridge Rd, Willowdale, Ontario M2P 1R8, Canada.

SON LIVING

RICHARD CHARLES, *b* 11 April 1970.

DAUGHTERS LIVING

Wendy Elizabeth, *b* 1962. —— Linda Mary, *b* 1964.

SISTER LIVING

Ann, *b* 1931: *m* 1956 (*m diss* 1976), John Robert Whatley, and has issue living, Alison Jane, *b* 1959. *Residence* – Chestnut Tree, Wildcroft Wood, Gasden Lane, Witley, Surrey.

AUNT LIVING (*Daughter of 1st baronet*)

Margaret, *b* 1904: *m* 1935, Col Ernest O. A. Singer, RAMC, who *d* 1957. *Residence* – 119 Barkston Gardens, SW5.

The 1st baronet, Sir (Arthur) Charles Davis (son of George John Davis), formerly of Stone Castle, Greenhithe, Kent, was an Underwriting Member of Lloyd's, High Sheriff of Kent 1934-5, and Lord Mayor of London 1945-46.

Davis-Goff, see Goff.

Davson, see Glyn (cr 1927).

DAWSON (UK) 1920, of Edgwarebury, co Middlesex

Deeds not words

Sir HUGH MICHAEL TREVOR DAWSON, 4th *Baronet*; *b* 28 March 1956; *s* his father, *Maj Sir* (HUGH HALLIDAY) TREVOR, 1983.

𝕬rms – Azure, on a chevron ermine between three bird bolts argent a rose gules, slipped and leaved between two daws respectant proper. 𝕮rest – Out of a naval crown or a daw proper.
Residence – 11 Burton Court, Franklin's Row, SW3.

BROTHER LIVING

NICHOLAS ANTONY TREVOR, *b* 17 Aug 1957.

AUNTS LIVING (*Daughters of 2nd baronet*)

Ursula Anne Trevor, *b* 1919. —— Avice Louise Trevor *b* 1923: *m* 1942 (*m diss* 1964), Maj Edwyn Inigo Lloyd Mostyn, MC, Scots Guards (*see* B Mostyn, colls). —— Patricia Elinor Trevor, *b* (twin) 1923: *m* 1st, 1943 (*m diss* 1953), Maj Raymond Alexander Carnegie, late Scots Guards (*see* E Southesk); 2ndly, 1953, John Maxwell Menzies, and has issue living, (by 1st *m*) (*see* E Southesk), —— (by 2nd *m*) Miranda Jane, *b* 1954: *m* 1979, Dermot Julian Jenkinson (*see* Jenkinson Bt, colls), —— Sarah Jane, *b* 1955: *m* 1980 (*m diss* 19——), Nigel Rawlence, —— Cynthia Emma, *b* 1958: *m* 1986, Ian C.L. Harrison, son of J.T.C. Harrison, of Little Stream, Ascot, Berks, —— Katherine Patricia, *b* 1960. *Residence* – Kames, Duns, Berwickshire.

WIDOW LIVING OF THIRD BARONET

CAROLINE JANE (*Lady Dawson*) (11 Burton Court, Franklin's Row, SW3), only da of William Antony Acton (*see* V Cowdray, colls): *m* 1955, Maj Sir (Hugh Halliday) Trevor Dawson, 3rd Bt, who *d* 1983.

The 1st baronet, Com Sir (Arthur) Trevor Dawson, RN (son of late Hugh Dawson, Bar-at-law), was a Director and Sup of Ordnance of Vickers, Ltd, Chm of their Armament and Shipbuilding Management Board, and Vice-Principal of Council of Imperial Soc of Knights Bachelor.

DAWSON (UK) 1929, of Appleton Roebuck, co York (Extinct 1974)

Sir LAWRENCE SAVILLE DAWSON, 2nd and last *Baronet*.

DAUGHTER LIVING OF SECOND BARONET

Barbara Jane, *b* 1940.

WIDOW LIVING OF SECOND BARONET

RUTH M., da of late John Smith Baxter, of Harrogate; *m* 1971, as his 2nd wife, Sir Lawrence Saville Dawson, 2nd baronet (but did not use title), who *d* 1974, when the title became ext. *Residence* – Oldholme, Gorey Hill, Jersey, CI.

DE BATHE (UK) 1801, of Kingstown Cashel, co Meath (Extinct 1941)

Sir CHRISTOPHER ALBERT DE BATHE, RAF Vol Reserve, 6th and last *Baronet*; *ka* 1941.

DAUGHTER LIVING OF SIXTH BARONET

Charlotte Louise, *b* 1934: *m* 1967, Arthur Cyril Bryan, of 16, Drayton Gdns, SW10.

HALF-SISTER LIVING OF SIXTH BARONET

Bridget, *b* 1922: *m* 1942, Capt Timothy John Gurney, Coldstream Guards, and has issue living, Christopher, *b* 1950: *m* 1986, Linda Harvey, — Jeannine Mary, *b* 1943: *m* 1st, 1964 (*m diss* 1978), John Richard Boyle (*see* E Cork, colls); *m* 2ndly, 1978, as his 2nd wife, Thomas David Barber, of Windrush House, Inkpen, Berks (*see* Barber, Bt), — Lucinda Marjorie (*Baroness Hothfield*) *b* 1946: *m* 1st, 1965 (*m diss* 1972), Capt Graham Morison Vere Nicoll, Welsh Guards (*see* Madden, Bt), 2ndly, 1975, 6th Baron Hothfield, of Drybeck Hall, Appleby-in-Westmorland, Cumbria. *Residence* – Maidshot, Great Hormead, Buntingford, Herts.

DEBENHAM (UK) 1931, of Bladen, co Dorset

Sir GILBERT RIDLEY DEBENHAM, 3rd *Baronet*, *b* 28 June 1906; *s* his brother, *Sir* PIERS KENRICK, 1964; *ed* Eton, and Trin Coll, Camb (BChir): *m* 1935, Violet Mary (Mollie), who *d* 1994, el da of late His Honour Judge (George Herbert) Higgins, and has had issue.

𝔄rms – Sable, a bend cottised between two crescents or. 𝔠rest – In front of a garb or, a sickle erect proper, the blade pointing to the sinister. *Residence* – Tonerspuddle Farm, Dorchester, Dorset.

GRANDCHILDREN LIVING

Issue of late George Andrew Debenham, *b* 1938, *d* 1991: *m* 1969, Penelope Jane, da of John David Armishaw Carter:—
THOMAS ADAM, *b* 28 Feb 1971. —— (Anna) Rose, *b* 1972.

SONS LIVING

William Michael, *b* 1940; *ed* Bryanston, and Trin Coll, Camb (BA); MSC: *m* 1974, Gunnel Birgitta, da of Holger Elis Valfrid Holmgren, and has issue living, Oliver William, *b* 1976, — Martin Ellis, *b* 1980. —— Paul Edward, *b* 1942; *ed* Bryanston, and Trin Coll, Camb (BA, MB, BChir); MRCP: *m* 1968, Jennifer Mary, MB, ChB, da of late G. W. Rees, and has issue living, Edward James, *b* 1970, — Michael John, *b* 1973, — Clare Elizabeth, *b* 1977.

DAUGHTER LIVING

Virginia Mary, *b* 1936: *m* 1st, 1960 (*m diss* 19—), Graham Leslie Nicol, of 53 Upper Park Rd, NW3; 2ndly, 1982, Nigel Denison Purchon, FLS, of 54 Gondar Gdns, NW6, and has issue living (by 1st *m*), Stephen Leslie, *b* 1961, — Alan Leslie, *b* 1966, — Lucy Jean, *b* 1963.

DAUGHTERS LIVING OF SECOND BARONET

Caroline Susan (*Lady Neill*), *b* 1930: *m* 1954, Sir Francis Patrick Neill, QC, son of late Sir Thomas Neill, and has had issue, Timothy Piers Patrick, *b* 1955, — Robin Charles Richard, *b* 1956, — Jonathan Francis Kenrick, *b* 1960: *m* 1991, Lucy, yr da of Frank Mullens, of McMahon's Point, Sydney, Australia, — Matthew Piers Thomas, *b* 1965: *m* 1990, Kirstin R., da of Ian Tegner, of 44 Norland Sq, W11, and *d* 1993, leaving issue, Cecilia *b* 199—, — Harriet Susan Anne, *b* 1962: *m* 1987, Douglas Michael Free, son of Thomas Free, of Metheringham, Lincs, — Emma Charlotte Angela, *b* 1967. *Residence* – 8 Milborne Grove, SW10. —— Anne Charlotte, *b* 1932: *m* 1962, Peter Muir Horsfield, QC, of 24 Liverpool Rd, Kingston Hill, Surrey, and has issue living, Andrew Piers, *b* 1963: *m* 1991 Gigi, yr da of Dr Yvon Carignan, of Basking Ridge, NJ, USA, — Charles Peter, *b* 1964, — Thomas Martin, *b* 1966.

SISTER LIVING

Cecil Audrey, *b* 1906: *m* 1953, Charles Robert Bielby, who *d* 1967.

COLLATERAL BRANCH LIVING

Issue of late Martin Ridley Debenham, yst son of 1st Bt, *b* 1909, *d* 1977: *m* 1937, Beatrice Sydney (Dairy House, Affpuddle, Dorset), da of late Ven Harry Sydney Radcliffe:—

James Martin Robert (East Farm, Affpuddle, Dorchester, Dorset, DT2 7HH), *b* 1951: *m* 1982, Jean Veronica, da of late Maj Royston Eric Acres, MBE, and has issue living, Bosworth Ridley Oriole Acres, *b* 1982, — Branwell George Kenrick Acres, *b* 1985, — Bathsheba Alice Maisie, *b* 1989, — and has also adopted stepchildren, Circe Alexandra Acres, *b* 1970, — Salome Gabriella Pilkington Acres, *b* 1975. —— Susanna Elizabeth, *b* 1943: *m* 1964, Alexander Surtees Chancellor, and has issue (*see* Paget Bt, *cr* 1886).

The 1st baronet, Sir Ernest Ridley Debenham (son of late Frank Debenham, of Fitzjohns Avenue, Hampstead, NW3), was Chm of Debenhams, Ltd.

DE BUNSEN (UK) 1919, of Abbey Lodge, Hanover Gate, Metropolitan Borough of St Marylebone (Extinct 1932)

Rt Hon Sir MAURICE WILLIAM ERNEST DE BUNSEN, GCMG, GCVO, CB, 1st and last *Baronet.*

DAUGHTER LIVING OF FIRST BARONET

Hilda Violet Helena (*Lady Salisbury-Jones*), *b* 1900: *m* 1st, 1921, Major Richard Guy Cecil Yerburgh, OBE, Irish Guards, who *d* 1926; 2ndly, 1931, Maj-Gen Sir (Arthur) Guy Salisbury-Jones, GCVO, CMG, CBE, MC, late Coldstream Guards, who *d* 1985, and has issue living, (by 1st *m*) John Maurice Armstrong (Barwhillanty, Parton, Castle Douglas), *b* 1923; late Capt IG: *m* 1973, Ann Jean Mary, da of Peter Maclaren, of Brooklands, Crocketford, Kirkcudbrightshire, — Oscar Guy de Bunsen (Chemin du Grammont 9, 1806 Saint-Légier, Vaud, Switzerland), *b* 1925: *m* 1953 (*m diss* 1970), Alicia, da of late Horace Marshall, of Grimston Lodge, Tadcaster, — (by 2nd *m*) Raymond Arthur, *b* 1933; late 2nd Lt Coldm Gds, — Mariette Helena (*Baroness Saye and Sele*), *b* 1936: *m* 1958, 21st Baron Saye and Sele. *Residence* – Broughton Castle, Banbury, Oxon OX15 5EB

de Capel Brooke, see Brooke.

CHAMPION DE CRESPIGNY (UK) 1805, of Champion Lodge, Essex (Extinct 1952)
(Name pronounced "Champion de Crepiny")

Sir VIVIAN TYRELL CHAMPION DE CRESPIGNY, OBE, 8th and last *Baronet.*

DAUGHTER LIVING OF EIGHTH BARONET

FLEUR CHAMPION DE CRESPIGNY (Mount Pleasant Farm, Bexhill-on-Sea, Sussex), *b* 1937; resumed the surname of Champion de Crespigny by deed poll: *m* 1967 (*m diss* 1975), John William Gordon-Harris, and has issue living, William, *b* 1970, — Victoria Fleur, *b* 1972.

MALLABY-DEELEY (UK) 1922, of Mitcham Court, co Surrey (Extinct 1962)

Sir ANTHONY MEYRICK MALLABY-DEELEY, 3rd and last *Baronet.*

DAUGHTER LIVING OF SECOND BARONET

Valerie Constance, *b* 1928: *m* 1947, Michael Peter Heaslett, and has issue living, Ingrid Ursula, *b* 1952, — Ilsa Kirsten, *b* 1954, — Helga Karen, *b* 1955, — Sigrid Anna, *b* 1959: *m* 1980, Stephen John Cull, of 7 Ghyll Rd, Heathfield, E Sussex.

DE HOGHTON (E) 1611, of Hoghton Tower, Lancashire
(Name pronounced "de Horton")

In spite of wrong

Sir (RICHARD) BERNARD (CUTHBERT) DE HOGHTON, 14th *Baronet*; *b* 26 Jan 1945; *s* his half-brother, *Sir* (HENRY PHILIP) ANTHONY MARY, 1978; *ed* Ampleforth, McGill Univ, Montreal (BA) and Birmingham Univ (MA): *m* 1974, Rosanna Stella Virginia, da of Terzo Buratti, of Florence, Italy, and has issue.

Arms – Sable, three bars argent. Crest – A bull passant, argent, ears, tips of the horns, mane, hoofs, and points of tail, sable. Supporters – Two bulls argent.
Seat – Hoghton Tower, Hoghton, Preston, Lancashire PR5 0SH.

SON LIVING

THOMAS JAMES DANIEL ADAM, *b* 11 April 1980.

DAUGHTER LIVING

Elena Susannah Isabella *b* 1976.

WIDOW LIVING OF TWELFTH BARONET

PHILOMENA, da of late Herbert Simmons, of Walton-le-Dale, Lancashire: *m* 1st, 1944, as his 2nd wife, Sir Cuthbert de Hoghton, 12th baronet, who *d* 1958; 2ndly, 1960, Richard Grahame Adams, JP, formerly of HM Colonial Admin Ser, N Nigeria, who *d* 1985.
Residence – Dower House, Bourton on the Water, Cheltenham, Glos.

COLLATERAL BRANCH LIVING

Issue of late Major Vere de Hoghton, 2nd son of 11th baronet, *b* 1882, *ka* 1915: *m* 1911, Alice Dorothy Patience (who *d* 1968, having *m* 2ndly, 1921, Joseph Eccles, who *d* 1944), da of Sir Frank Hollins, 1st Bt:—
Diana, *b* 1913: *m* 1937, Major Brian Pierson Doughty-Wylie, MC, Roy Welch Fusiliers, who *d* 1982 (*see* V Chelmsford, colls).
This baronetcy is 5th in precedence of the Roll of the Baronets, but as the 2nd, 3rd, and 4th creations are borne by Earls, it ranks immediately after the Premier baronetcy of Bacon. The property of Hoghton has been in the family since *temp* King Stephen. Members of the family were sheriffs of the county from the 13th century and knights of the shire representing Lancashire from the 14th century. Sir Richard de Hoghton held the office of Chief Steward 1399-1422. Following the Earls of Derby, they are the second oldest Freemen of Preston. The 1st baronet, Sir Richard Hoghton, MP for Lancs, entertained King James I for several days at Hoghton Tower. The 2nd baronet, Sir Gilbert, MP for Lancs, was Gentleman of the Bedchamber to King Charles I, and a Royalist leader. The 3rd and 4th baronets represented Lancs in Parliament, and the 5th, 6th and 7th baronets each sat as MP for Preston. The 8th baronet assumed the additional surname of Bold, and the 9th baronet resumed in 1862 by Roy licence the ancient surname of de Hoghton.

DE LA BÈRE (UK) 1953, of Crowborough, co Sussex

Sir CAMERON DE LA BÈRE, 2nd *Baronet*; *s* his father, *Sir* RUPERT 1978; *b* 12 Feb 1933; *ed* Tonbridge and abroad: *m* 1964, Clairemonde, only da of late Casimir Kaufmann, of 26 Avenue William Favre, Geneva, Switzerland, and has issue.

Arms – Argent on a fesse between three crescents sable a lizard of the field. Crest – Issuant from an ancient crown or, a plume of five ostrich feathers argent charged with a ladybird proper.
Residence – 1 Avenue Theodore Flournoy, 1207 Geneva, Switzerland.

DAUGHTER LIVING

Réjane, *b* 1965.

BROTHER LIVING

ADRIAN, *b* 17 Sept 1939.

SISTERS LIVING

Valerie, *b* 1923. —— Camilla (6 Quarry Hill, Sevenoaks, Kent), *b* 1926, *m* 1953 (*m diss* 1959), Louis Georges Bourcier, and has issue living, Andrew Charles, *b* 1954, —— Yolande (twin), *b* 1954.
Sir Rupert De la Bère, KCVO, 1st Bt, son of Reginald De la Bère, was Lord Mayor of London 1952-53, *m* 1919, Marguerite, who *d* 1969, da of Lt-Col Sir John Humphery; *d* 1978.

DE LA RUE (UK) 1898, of Cadogan Square, Chelsea, co London
(Name pronounced "Dellarue")

Seek the truth

Sir ANDREW GEORGE ILAY DE LA RUE, 4th *Baronet*; *b* 3 Feb 1946; *s* his father, *Sir* ERIC VINCENT, 1989; *ed* Millfield: *m* 1984, Tessa Ann, elder da of David Dobson, of Stragglethorpe Grange, Lincoln, and has issue.

Arms – Or, three bars gules each charged with as many estoiles of the first, in chief an increscent and a decrescent of the second. **Crest** – Between two olive branches vert a cauldron gules, fired and issuant therefrom a snake nowed proper.
Residences – Stragglethorpe Grange, Brant Broughton, Lincs; 27 Kersley St, SW11.

SONS LIVING

EDWARD WALTER HENRY, *b* 25 Nov 1986. —— Harry William, *b* 1989.

BROTHER LIVING

John Vincent Francis, *b* 1953; *ed* Eton. *Residence* – PO Box 485, Elizabethtown, NY 12932, USA.

HALF-BROTHER LIVING

Vincent St George, *b* 1965; *ed* Stowe.

AUNT LIVING (*daughter of 2nd baronet*)

Diana Beryl, *b* 1914. *Residence* – Longfield, Rusper, Horsham, Sussex.

WIDOW LIVING OF THIRD BARONET

CHRISTINE (*Christine, Lady de la Rue*), da of Kurt Schellin, MD, of Greenwich, Conn, USA: *m* 1964, as his 2nd wife, Sir Eric Vincent de la Rue, 3rd Bt, who *d* 1989. *Residence* – Ayton Castle, Eymouth, Berwickshire TD14 5RD.

COLLATERAL BRANCHES LIVING

Issue of late Ian Hector de la Rue, 3rd son of 2nd baronet, *b* 1910, *d* 1991: *m* 1936, Violet Bertha, who *d* 1983, da of Thomas Despard Bridges:—
Anthony St Vincent (Chichindwe, 322 Ard-na-Lea Close, Glen Lorne, Harare, Zimbabwe), *b* 1947; *ed* Peterhouse: *m* 1st, 1971 (*m diss* 1985), Ann Wyndham, da of Frederic Roberts Blair, of Lloyds Neck, Long Island, NY; 2ndly, 1986, Merry, da of Lt-Col Sir Edward Hugh Dudley Thompson, MBE, TD, of Culland Hall, Brailsford, Derby, and has issue living (by 1st *m*) Thomas Edward, *b* 1973; *ed* Peterhouse, — Michael Alexander, *b* 1975; *ed* Peterhouse, — Diana Alexandra, *b* 1982, — (by 2nd *m*) Justine Andrea, *b* 1987.

Issue of late Stuart Andros de la Rue, 3rd son of 1st baronet, *b* 1883, *d* 1927: *m* 1912, Margaret Griselda, who *d* 1987, having *m* 2ndly, 1928, Air-Marshal Sir Bertine Entwisle Sutton, KBE, CB, DSO, MC, who *d* 1946, da of late Alexander Dundas Ogilvy Wedderburn, KC (*see* Ogilvy-Wedderburn, Bt, colls):—
Wedderburn Anthony, *b* 1914: *m* 1st, 1937, Jean Roberts; 2ndly, 1948, Marjorie Holland (MARSH), da of William Holland Harris. —— Ann Griselda, *b* 1918: *m* 1938, Group Capt John Norwood, RAF, who *d* 1978, and has issue living, Janet, *b* 1939, — Jill, *b* 1941. *Residence* – Old Coach House, Cannon St, Lymington, Hants.
Sir Thomas, 1st Bt, was many years Chm of Thomas de la Rue and Co, Limited.

de MONTMORENCY (I) 1631, of Knockagh, co Tipperary

Sir ARNOLD GEOFFROY DE MONTMORENCY, 19th *Baronet*; *b* 27 July 1908; *s* his cousin, *Sir* REGINALD D'ALTON LODGE, 1979; *ed* Westminster, and Peterhouse, Camb (LLB, MA); Bar Middle Temple 1932; 1939-45 War as Maj RASC: *m* 1949 (*m diss* 1953) and re-married 1972, Nettie Hay, da of late William Anderson, of Morayshire.

𝕬rms – Or, a cross gules, between four eaglets displayed azure. 𝕮rest – A peacock in his pride, proper.
Residence – 2 Garden Court, Temple, EC4Y MBY. *Chambers* – Francis Taylor Building, Temple, EC4Y GBL.

COLLATERAL BRANCH LIVING

Granddaughter of late Major Reymond Hervey de Montmorency, el son of late Major Reymond Henry de Montmorency, son of Lieut-Col Reymond Hervey de Montmorency, MP (who had resumed this ancient name by Roy licence in lieu of Morres 1815), son of late Rev Reymond Morres, nephew of 1st Viscount Mountmorres, and great-great-grandson of 2nd baronet:—
Issue of late Reymond Hervey de Montmorency, *b* 1871, *d* 1938: *m* 1905, Gwynedd Maud, who *d* 1936, da of Lieut-Col G. T. Thomas, MRCS, LRCP, DPH, IMS:—

Ann Marion, *b* 1911: *m* 1st, 1935, George Henry Carbutt, who *d* 1956; 2ndly, 1958, Ernest William Swanton and has issue living, (by 1st *m*) Francis (Billy) (The White House, Langham, Colchester), *b* 1936: *m* 1958, Sally Fenella, da of James Cole Harris, and has issue living, George Henry de Montmorency (28 Nansen Rd, SW11 5NT) *b* 1963: *m* 1991, Camilla Lucy, da of Hon Mr Justice (Sir Peter Edlin) Webster, of Bratton, Wilts, and of Mrs Susan Murray, of Fulham, SW6, (and has issue living, a son *b* 1994), Emma Louise *b* 1961: *m* 1987, Alexander Harold Swinton, son of Maj-Gen Sir John Swinton, KCVO, OBE, DL, of Kimmerghame, Duns, Berwickshire, — Edward Reymond (Mount Hall, Gt Horkesley, Colchester) *b* 1940: *m* 1966, Susan Elizabeth, twin da of Robert Peter Healing (*see* B Petre), and has issue living, James Michael Edward *b* 1972, Laura Frances Victoria *b* 1981. *Residence* – Delf House, Sandwich, Kent.
This baronetcy was granted to John Morres, of Knockagh, in 1631, and on the death of Sir Nicholas, 8th Bt, in 1796, the title devolved upon the 2nd Viscount Mountmorres. In 1815 the 3rd Viscount, and Lt-Col Reymond Hervey Morres, ancestor of the present baronet, resumed by Roy licence the surname of de Montmorency. In 1951, on the death of the 7th Viscount Mountmorres (also 7th Baron), the Viscountcy and the Barony became ext and the Baronetcy passed to his kinsman, Sir (Hervey) Angus de Montmorency, OBE, who *s* as 16th baronet. The 17th Baronet, Sir Miles, was a member of R Soc of British Artists, painter of portraits for National War Records.

DENNY (I) 1782, of Castle Moyle, Kerry

Sir ANTHONY CONINGHAM DE WALTHAM DENNY, 8th *Baronet*; *b* 22 April 1925; *s* his father, *Rev Sir* HENRY LYTTELTON LYSTER, 1953; *ed* Clayesmore, Anglo French Art Centre, and Regent St Polytechnic School of Architecture; FRSA, MCSD; a Designer, Partner in firm of Verity and Beverley, Architects and Designers; an Hereditary Freeman of Cork; 1943-45 War with RAF in Middle East: *m* 1949, Anne Catherine, elder da of late Samuel Beverley, FRIBA, and has issue.

𝕬rms – Gules, a saltire argent between twelve cross-crosslets or. 𝕮rest – A cubit arm vested azure, turned up argent, holding in the hand proper five wheat-ears or.
Residence – The Priest's House, Muchelney, Langport, Somerset TA10 0DQ.

SONS LIVING

PIERS ANTHONY DE WALTHAM, *b* 14 March 1954; *ed* King Alfred Sch, and Westfield Coll, Lond Univ: *m* 1987, Ella Jane, only da of Peter P. Huhne, of SW5, and has issue living, Matilda Ann, *b* 1988, — Isabel Margaret, *b* 1990. *Residence* – Chapel Cottage, Court Mill, Merriott, Crewkerne, Somerset. —— Thomas Francis Coningham, *b* 1956; *ed* King Alfred Sch, and Edinburgh Coll of Art: *m* 1985, Benita Jane, yr da of late Sq-Ldr Simon Hugh Kevill-Davies, RAF (*see* Lees, Bt, *cr* 1897), and has issue living, Madeline Anne, *b* 1987. *Residence* – Lower Cross Cottage, Hinton St Mary, Sturminster Newton, Dorest.

The harvest also shall be mine

ADOPTED DAUGHTER LIVING

Sophy Elinor Sisophanh, *b* 1974; *ed* Univ of West of England.

BROTHERS LIVING

Barry Francis Lyttelton, LVO (Tudor House, Broadwindsor, Dorest DT8 3QP), *b* 1928; *ed* Clayesmore, and RMA Sandhurst; Maj RA (ret); formerly in Queen's Royal Regt, and Cadet Indian Army; FCO 1962-89, Counsellor (ret); LVO, 1979; Commander Order of St Olav (Norway) 1981: *m* 1st, 1951 (*m diss* 1968), Mrs Gertrude Tamara Crofton, da of late Henry Carnet Jex, of Hong Kong; 2ndly, 1969, Anne Rosemary Jordon, da of Col James Frederick White, MC, late Warwicks Fus, of Claypit Hall, Foxearth, Suffolk, and has issue living (by 1st *m*), James Barry Lyster, *b* 1958: *m* 19—, Susan Elizabeth, da of Derek Scholfield, of Dummer, Hants, and has issue living, Thomas James Lyttelton *b* 1988, — Shelagh Joan Lyttelton, *b* 1959: *m* 1989, Paul Nigel Wickman, son of Guy Wickman, of Reigate, Surrey, and has issue living, Edward Guy Denny *b* 1991, Eleanor Katherine Denny *b* 1994, — (by 2nd *m*) Emma Harriet Lyttelton, *b* 1970. —— Edward Maurice FitzGerald (Robyn), *b* 1930; *ed* Clayesmore, and Royal Coll of Art; ARCA 1957: *m* 1953, Anna Rose Frances, da of G. Teesdale and has issue living, Dominic Charles Fitzgerald, *b* 1963, — Edward Drouet Coningham, *b* 1975, — Lucy Anna Dando, *b* 1966.

—— Richard William Geoffrey (Court Hill, Potterne, Devizes, Wilts), *b* 1940: *m* 1st, 1961 (*m diss* 1978), Andrée Suzanne Louise, el da of Marcel Louis Parrot, of 210 Rue de Rivoli, Paris; 2ndly, 1984, Linda May, da of Maximillian Magnun, of Calcutta, India, and formerly wife of William Jones, and has issue living, Lyster Richard Henry, *b* 1961, —— Walter Victor Marcel, *b* 1963: *m* 1990, Lorna Caroline, elder da of Maurice Statham, of Aylesbury, Bucks, —— Giles Anthony William, *b* 1964, —— Julius André Geoffrey, *b* 1966.

COLLATERAL BRANCHES LIVING

Granddaughters of late Lt-Col Richard Denny, 7th son of Rev Henry Denny (infra):—
Issue of late Maj (Richard) Brougham Denny, *b* 1889, *d* 1967: *m* 1st, 1928 (*m diss* 1963), Sybil Nina, who *d* 1977, da of late Francis N. Evans-Freke; 2ndly, 1967, Edith Winifred, da of late G. F. Winstone, of Worcester:—
Diana Brougham, *b* 1930: *m* 1960, Ronald Herbert Macintosh, CEng, AMIME, MRINA, of 77 Oriel Av, Tawa, Wellington, NZ, and has two adopted das, Claire Diana, *b* 1965: *m* 1st, 1985 (*m diss* 1988), Steven Charles Marshall; 2ndly, 1988, Peter John Ball, of 17 Lake Apex Drive, Gatton, Queensland, Australia, and has issue living (by 1st *m*), Kylie Deanna *b* 1987, (by 2nd *m*) Benjamin Peter *b* 1989. —— Fiona Juliet, *b* 1966: *m* 1993, Nyoman Putra Abriawan, of Bali, Indonesia. —— Juliet Oldfield, *b* 1932: *m* 1952, Peter Walter Taylor, ARSM, PhD, FGS, of The Chipping Croft, Tetbury, Glos GL8 8EY and has issue living, Christopher Richard de Courcy, *b* 1957, —— Caroline Mary Louise, *b* 1954: *m* 1988, Douglas Wagstaff, MA, and has issue living, James Douglas *b* 1989, Adam *b* 1990, —— Catherine Jane, *b* 1961: *m* 1988, Anthony Nicholas Dickinson, and has issue living, Piers Anthony Brougham *b* 1993.

Granddaughters of late Edmund Barry Denny, 9th son of late Rev Henry Denny, 3rd son of 3rd baronet:—
Issue of Henry Allen Maynard Denny, *b* 1887, *d* 19—: *m* 1st, 1926, Kathleen Mary, da of late W. W. Goddard, of Stroud, Gloucestershire; 2ndly, 1950, Elsi Margaret, da of late R. O. Williams, and widow of J. Ryall:—
(By 1st *m*) Norah Peta, *b* 1928: *m* 1949, Robert Addison King, and has issue living, Keith Allan (Banff, Alta), *b* 1951: *m* 1974, Heather Ann, da of late William Farquharson, —— Kathy Diane *b* 1953, —— Rachel Ann *b* 1955. —— Kathleen Wendy Elizabeth, *b* 1930: *m* 1st, 1952 (*m diss* 1963), James Palmer Lee; 2ndly, 1964, William Ernest Smith, and has issue living (by 1st *m*), Randall *b* 1953, —— Teresa *b* 1955: *m* 1975, Michael Farup, of Salt Spring Island, BC and has issue living, Jodie Lee *b* 1975.
Issue of late Capt Thomas Hamilton Denny, MBE, Indian Army, *b* 1893, *d* 1959: *m* 1920, Muriel Mary, who *d* 1974, da of late Edward Doncaster, of Silk Willoughby, Sleaford:—
Pamela Diana, *b* 1924: *m* 1952 (*m diss* 1969), Anthony Miles Denny, and has issue living, Patrick Jonathan Hamilton, *b* 1956: *m* 1981, Bridget Anne Meneer, and has issue living, Samuel Patrick *b* 1988, Lucy Anne *b* 1982, Kate Joanna *b* 1985, —— Caroline Peta, *b* 1955: *m* 1st, 1982 (*m diss* 1983), Errol Currie; 2ndly, 1986, Kevin Clive Arthur Hollyoak, and has issue living (by 2nd *m*), Rory Clive Anthony *b* 1987, Liam *b* 1992. *Residence* – Daphne Cottage, 55 High Street, Aldeburgh, Suffolk IP15 5AU.

Grandson of late Arthur de Courcy MacGillycuddy Denny, 4th son of late Edmund Barry Denny (ante):—
Issue of late Maynard de Courcy Barry Denny, *b* 1927, *d* 1993: *m* 1966, Christine Mary, da of Walters S. Browne, of Ipswich:—
Anthony de Courcy Edmund, *b* 1973.

Grandchildren of late Ven Anthony Denny, 4th son of 3rd baronet:—
Issue of late George Herbert Denny, *b* 1851, *d* 1937: *m* 1876, Ellen, who *d* 1937, da of N. Jarvis:—
Edward Jarvis, *b* 1879: *m* 1903, Clara Elizabeth, da of August Will, and has issue living, Ellen Elizabeth, *b* 19—, —— Catharine Antoinette, *b* 19—. —— Anthony George, *b* 1882: *m* 1910, Mathilda Henrietta, da of C. Dargeloh. —— Catharine Magill: *m* 1900, Curtis L. Sleeper. *Residence* –

Granddaughters of late Edward Coningsby Denny (infra):—
Issue of late William Coningsby Denny, *b* 1867, *d* 1935: *m* 1892, Rose Elizabeth, who *d* 1947, da of late Joseph Ingram, of Wellington Square, Hastings:—
Marjorie Ethel, *b* 1896. *Residence* – Tralee, 54 Privett Road, Alverstoke, Gosport, Hants.
Issue of late Charles Edward Denny, *b* 1875, *d* 1946: *m* 1902, Alice, who *d* 1965, da of Samuel Grantham Baker, of Brighton:—
Letitia Ivy Coningsby, *b* 1904: *m* 1940, Woolmore Stewart Duncan. *Residence* – Bowersbury, Bowers Heath, Harpenden, Herts. —— Ethel Mildred Coningsby, *b* 1907: *m* 1933, Sydney Walter Stubbs, and has issue living, Brian Maurice Denny, *b* 1936, —— Colin Anthony, *b* 1939. —— Richard Ivan, *b* 1949. —— Kathleen Mary Coningsby, *b* 1910: *m* 1936, Joseph Harry Smith, and has issue living, Peter Nigel Coningsby (19 Redding Drive, Amersham, Bucks), *b* 1948: *m* 1978, Susan Spriggs, and has issue living, Oliver James Coningsby *b* 1980, Victoria Clare Coningsby *b* 1982, —— Kathleen Hazel Coningsby, *b* 1940: *m* 1964 (*m diss* 1979), Peter James Guile, and has issue living, Christopher James *b* 1968, Moyra Elizabeth *b* 1970, —— Yvonne Coningsby, *b* 1944: *m* 1965, Stanley Ritter, of Tophams, Brays Lane, Hyde Heath, Bucks, and has issue living, Martin Neill *b* 1976, Michelle Clare *b* 1973. *Residence* – Inchkeith, 54 Swakeleys Drive, Ickenham, Middlesex. —— Geraldine Coningsby, *b* 1917: *m* 1939, Stanley Robson Clarke, and has issue living, Barry Ian Charles, *b* 1946, —— Diana Susan, *b* 1948. *Residence* – 44 Swakeleys Drive, Ickenham, Middlesex.

Grandsons of late William Denny, 5th son of 3rd baronet:—
Issue of late Edward Coningsby Denny *b* 1839, *d* 1888: *m* 1863, Louisa Mary, who *d* 1916, da of late Augustus Callaway, of Rogate, Sussex:—
Horace, *b* 1877: *m* 1904, Mabel, da of Adm Arthur de Bellin, late Roy Italian Navy, and has issue living, John, *b* 19—, —— a da, *b* 19—, —— a da, *b* 19—. *Residence* –
Issue of late Henry Arthur Denny, Lieut RFA, *b* 1841, *d* 1888: *m* 1870, Emma Florence, who *d* 1886, da of late A. Denny, JP of Rockfield, Tramore:—
Frederick Wootton, *b* 1881; formerly Lieut Duke of Edinburgh's (Wiltshire Regt): *m* 1913, Rose, da of Charles T. G. Bright, of Toronto, and widow of —— Cramp, and has issue living, Shirley Geraldine, *b* 1915. *Residence* –

Granddaughter of late Lieut Alfred Edward Denny, RN, son of late William Denny (ante):—
Issue of late Major William Alfred Charles Denny, OBE, *b* 1871, *d* 1934: *m* 1st, 1896, Lucy Florence, who *d* 1931, only da of late Maj-Gen Herbert Coningham, of 32 Vernon Terrace, Brighton; 2ndly, 1933, Beatrice Mary Louisa, who *d* 1942, only child of late Alfred Boydell Golborne, of Chester, and widow of his cousin, Edmund Henry Denny:—
(By 1st *m*) Eileen Mary Diana, *b* 1903: *m* 1933, William Samuel Sandes Boxwell, who *d* 1961.
Sir Robert Denny, Knt, was MP for Cambridgeshire 1391-3, and Lieut of the Duke of Bedford, Constable of England, at the time of the siege of Rouen. His descendant, Sir Edmond Denny (son of William Denny, of Cheshunt —— High Sheriff of Herts 1480), King's Remembrancer to Henry VII, and a Baron of the Exchequer, was father of Rt Hon Sir Anthony Denny, PC, MP, Chief Gentleman of the Privy Chamber and Groom of the Stole to Henry VIII, the only Gentleman who dared to inform the King of his approaching end, and received from him a pair of gloves (which still exists) worked with pearls; he was constituted an Executor of Henry VIII, and one of the Guardians of Edward VI. His grandson, Sir Edward Denny, was created Lord Denny de Waltham 1604, and Earl of Norwich 1626. The present family is descended from Sir Edward Denny, Knight Banneret, MP (a yr son of Rt Hon Sir Anthony Denny), who, being Governor of Kerry and Desmond, Gentleman of the Privy Chamber to Queen Elizabeth, and Com under Adm Howard, etc, received a grant of the Seignory of Dennyvale

and Castlemore, co Kerry, with the Desmonds' chief castle of Tralee, in 1587, as a reward for his naval and military services. For successive generations the family provided representatives for Tralee and co Kerry in Parliament. Sir Barry, 2nd Bt, was about to be raised to the peerage when he was killed in a duel 1794. Sir Cecil Edward Denny, 6th Bt (sometime Archivist and Keeper of Records of Govt of Alberta, and historian of that Province), founded Calgary (Alberta). There is no such place as "Castle Moyle," which is an error in the patent of Baronetcy for Castle More, ie "the great castle" of Tralee. The Rev Sir Henry Lyttelton Lyster Denny, 7th Bt, was V of Winslow-cum-Shipton 1916-18, R of Horsted Keynes 1918-20, V of St Mark's, Myddelton Square, EC, and Fellow of Sion Coll 1920-25, R of Wickham 1925-30, R of Abinger, Surrey 1930-36, and R and V of Burwash 1938-52.

DENNY (UK) 1913, of Dumbarton, co Dunbarton

Brave and kind

Sir ALISTAIR MAURICE ARCHIBALD DENNY, 3rd *Baronet*; *b* 11 Sept 1922; *s* his father, Sir MAURICE EDWARD, KBE, 1955; *ed* Marlborough; European War 1939-45 with Fleet Air Arm: *m* 1949, Elizabeth Hunt, da of Major Sir (Ernest) Guy Richard Lloyd, DSO, 1st Bt (*cr* 1960), and has had issue.

ᚪrms – Azure, three suns in their splendour in chief or, and in the honour point a martlet of the last for difference. **Crest** – A dexter hand erect, pointing with two fingers at a sun in his splendour, all proper.
Residence – Crombie Cottage, Abercrombie, Anstruther, Fife KY10 2DE. *Club* – Royal and Ancient Golf.

SONS LIVING AND DECEASED

CHARLES ALISTAIR MAURICE, *b* 7 Oct 1950; *ed* Wellington Coll, and Edinburgh Univ: *m* 1981, Belinda M. J., yr da of J. P. McDonald, of Dublin, and has issue living, Patrick Charles Alistair *b* 2 Jan 1985, — Georgina Mary, *b* 1989. —— †Nigel Peter, *b* 1952; *ed* Wellington Coll; *d* 1977. —— Mark Richard Leslie, *b* 1955; *ed* Wellington Coll: *m* 1983, Junemary, 2nd da of R. E. Jameson, of Durban, S Africa, and has issue living, James William Leslie, *b* 1986, — Michael, *b* 1991, — Suzannnah Caroline, *b* 1988.

BROTHER LIVING

Graham Royse (Ash Cottage, Balfron Rd, Killearn, Glasgow G63 9NJ), *b* 1927; *ed* Marlborough, and King's Coll, Camb.

SISTERS LIVING

Rosamund Margaret, *b* 1917: *m* 1941, Lieut Col John Malcolm Thorpe Churchill, DSO, MC, Seaforth Highlanders, and has issue living, Malcolm John Leslie, *b* 1942, — Rodney Alistair Gladstone, *b* 1947. *Residence* – Sunhill House, Mayford, near Woking, Surrey. —— Patricia Leslie, *b* 1931: *m* 1952, Thomas Dunlop Bruce Jones, MC, of House on the Hill, Dunblane, Perthshire (Dunlop Bt), and has issue living, Veronica Margaret, *b* 1953, — Victoria Leslie, *b* 1956, — Claire Patricia, *b* 1958, — Juliet Mary, *b* 1966.
The 1st baronet, Sir Archibald Denny, LLD (son of Peter Denny, of Helenslee, Dumbarton), was a Naval Architect and a Director of William Denny & Bros Ltd, shipbuilders and engineers, of Dumbarton. The 2nd baronet, Sir Maurice Edward Denny, KBE, was Pres of William Denny & Bros, Ltd, Chm of Air Registration Board, and Pres of Institute of Marine Engineers 1935-6, and of Junior Institution of Engineers 1943-4.

DERING (E) 1627, of Surrenden Dering, Kent (Extinct 1975)

Sir RUPERT ANTHONY YEA DERING, 12th and last *Baronet*.

DAUGHTER LIVING OF TWELFTH BARONET

Susan Helen, *b* 1941: *m* 1967, Henry John Fredman, and has issue living, Jenny Annabelle, *b* 1968.

WIDOW LIVING OF TWELFTH BARONET

BETTY BRIDGETT (*Lady Dering*) (Bellings, Midhurst, Sussex), only da of late Lt-Col Vere Powys Druce, of Rose Cottage, Charminster, Dorset: *m* 1940, Lt-Col Sir Rupert Anthony Yea Dering, 12th Bt, who *d* 1975, when the title become ext.

COLLATERAL BRANCHES LIVING

Granddaughters of late Lt-Col Edgar William Wallace Dering, son of late Cholmeley Charles William Dering, 2nd son of 7th baronet:—
Issue of late Cdr Claud Lacy Yea Dering, DSO, RN, *b* 1885, *d* 1943: *m* 1915, Winifred, who *d* 1941, da of Edmund Gellibrand, of Petrograd:—
Enid Deborah Claud (11 Welbeck Court, Addison Bridge Place, W14), *b* 1922: *m* 1942 (*m diss* 1965), Robin Craig Guthrie, portrait painter, and has issue living, Linnet Marion, *b* 1946.
Issue of late Anthony Lionel Yea Dering, *b* 1890, *d* 1953: *m* 1916, Gertrude Frances Cordelia, who *d* 1969, only da of Archibald Henry Boyd, Bar-at-Law, of Bellevue, Westward Ho! (Denny, Bt):—
Joan Rosalind Cordelia, *b* 1917. *Residence* – 2 Thellusson Lodge, Aldeburgh, Suffolk.
John Dering, who *d* 1425, acquired the manor of Surrenden (later Surrenden Dering), Kent, on marriage to Christian, da and heir of John Hawte by Joan, da and heir of John Surrenden. The 1st baronet was Lieut of Dover Castle, and his five immediate successors represented Kent in Parliament, while the 8th baronet sat as MP for Wexford 1830, Romney 1831-2,

and E Kent 1852-7 and 1863-68. The 9th baronet was Min to Mexico 1894-1900, and to Brazil 1900-1906. The 10th baronet, Sir Henry Edward Dering, sold Surrenden Dering in 1928.

DES VŒUX (I) 1787, of Indiaville, Queen's County (Extinct 1944)

Lieut-Col Sir WILLIAM RICHARD DE BACQUENCOURT DES VŒUX, 9th and last *Baronet*; *ka* in Holland 1944.

DAUGHTERS LIVING OF NINTH BARONET

Mary Elizabeth, *b* 1940: *m* 1967, Jeremy John Aird, of Quarry Wood Cottage, Burghclere, Newbury, Berks, and has issue (*see* Aird, Bt, colls). —— (Patricia) Jane, *b* 1941: *m* 1965, Penrhyn Charles Benjamin Pockney, of West Court, Inkpen, Newbury, Berks, and has issue living, Richard Penrhyn, *b* 1968, — James Charles, *b* 1969. —— Dorothy Susan, *b* 1944: *m* 1973, Lt-Cdr John David Caldecott, RN, of Ladle Hill House, Old Burghclere, Newbury, Berks, and has issue living, Edward Randolph, *b* 1976, — Jane Cynthia, *b* 1974, — Laura Cicely, *b* 1978, — Alice Selina, *b* 1978 (twin).

DE TRAFFORD (UK) 1841, of Trafford Park, Lancashire

Sir DERMOT HUMPHREY DE TRAFFORD, VRD, 6th *Baronet*; *b* 19 Jan 1925; *s* his father, *Sir* RUDOLPH EDGAR FRANCIS, OBE, 1983; *ed* Harrow, and Ch Ch, Oxford (MA): *m* 1st, 1948 (*m diss* 1973), Patricia Mary, only da of late Francis Mycroft Beeley, of Long Crumples, nr Alton, Hants; 2ndly, 1974, Xandra Carandini, only da of Lt-Col Geoffrey Trollope Lee, and formerly wife of Roderick Walter, and has issue by 1st *m*.

Arms – Argent, a griffin segreant gules. **Crest** – A thrasher proper, his hat and coat per pale argent and gules, sleeves counterchanged, breeches and stockings of the 2nd and 3rd, his flail of the 1st.
Residences – The Old Vicarage, Appleshaw, Hants; 1 Roper's Orchard, SW3 5AX.
Clubs – White's, Roy Ocean Racing.

SONS LIVING (By 1st marriage)

JOHN HUMPHREY (30 Norland Sq, W11 4PU; Royal Ocean Racing Club), *b* 12 Sept 1950; *ed* Ampleforth, and Bristol Univ (BSc): *m* 1975, Anne, da of Jacques Faure de Pebeyre, and has issue living, Alexander Humphrey, *b* 28 June 1978, — Isabel June, *b* 1980. —— Edmund Francis, *b* 1952; *ed* Worth, and Ch Ch, Oxford. —— Gerard Thomas Joseph, *b* 1968; *ed* Harrow, and Ch Ch, Oxford.

DAUGHTERS LIVING (By 1st marriage)

Mary Annette, *b* 1949. —— Elizabeth Eugenie, *b* 1951: *m* 1975, John Augustin Langdon, of 50 Chepstow Rd, W2, and has issue living, Tobias Hector, *b* 1985, — Frederick George, *b* 1989. —— Patricia Clare, *b* 1955: *m* 1975, (Patrick) William Uvedale Corbett, of 31 Sydney St, SW3, and has issue living, Edmund Uvedale, *b* 1983, — Laura, *b* 1985. —— Victoria Mary, *b* 1958: *m* 1983, Andrew Roberts, and has issue living, Mark Lonsdale, *b* 1985, — Katherine, *b* 1987. —— (Cynthia) June Bernadette, *b* 1959: *m* 1990, Nicholas C. Kirkman, eldest son of Maj Charles Kirkman, of Lymington, Hants, and has issue living, Christopher Chevalier, *b* 1991. —— (Antonia) Lucy Octavia, *b* 1966.

DAUGHTERS LIVING OF FOURTH BARONET

Mary (*Lady Bowes-Lyon*) (Beltingham House, Bardon Mill, Hexham, Northumberland), *b* 1920: *m* 1941, Maj-Gen Sir Francis James Cecil Bowes-Lyon, KCVO, CB, OBE, MC, who *d* 1977 (*see* E Strathmore, colls). —— Violet (*Lady Aitken*), *b* 1926: *m* 1951, as his 3rd wife, Group Capt Sir (John William) Maxwell Aitken, DSO, DFC, 2nd Bt (who *s* as 2nd Baron Beaverbrook 1964, but disclaimed this peerage for life), who *d* 1985. *Residence* – Mickleham Downs House, Dorking, Surrey. —— Catherine, *b* 1928: *m* 1952, Fulke Thomas Tyndall Walwyn, CVO, who *d* 1991, and has issue living, Jane, *b* 1957. *Residence* – Saxon House Stables, Lambourn, Berks.

COLLATERAL BRANCHES LIVING

Grandchildren of late Charles Edmund de Trafford, 2nd son of 2nd baronet:—
Issue of late Capt Hubert Edmund Francis de Trafford, *b* 1893, *d* 1974: *m* 1927, Hon Cecilia, who *d* 1982, da of 1st Baron Strickland (ext), and 6th Count Della Catena (Maltese Nobility):—
Gerald Edmund Hubert (Villa Bologna, Attard, Malta, GC), *b* 1929; *ed* McGill Univ (BA), and Oxford Univ; a Knt of Sovereign Mil Order of Malta: *m* 1971, (Helena Catherina) Charlotte, only da of Herman Sybrand Hallo, former Ambassador of the Netherlands, of 27 Verdala St George's Dragonara, Malta, and has issue living, Jasper Peter Paul Sybrand, *b* 1975, — Aloisia Cecilia Mary, *b* 1973. —— Anthony Charles Everard (The Wain House, Home Farm, Upper Slaughter, Cheltenham, Gos GL54 2JJ), *b* 1935: *m* 1966, Gabrielle Frances, da of Maj Ronald Edward Boone, of Rockcliffe House, Upper Slaughter, Glos. —— †Hubert George Joseph, *b* 1937: *m* 1st, 1966 (*m diss* 1973), Christine Elizabeth, only da of Lt-Cdr Maurice Sydney Adams, RN (ret); 2ndly 1975, Mary Kate Willis (Ta Majsiet, Tal Balal, B'Kara, Malta), da of late Lt-Col Edward C. A. Willis Fleming, and *d* 1993, leaving issue (by 1st *m*), Rachel Samantha, *b* 1967: *m* 1991, Bengt G. Sjöberg, of Tjurgränd 4, 175 45 Järfälla, Stockholm, Sweden, and has issue living Rebecca Linnéa Christine *b* 1993, — Martha Christine Joanna, *b* 1969, — (by 2nd *m*) John Oliver George, *b* 1976, — George Jonathon Augustus, *b* 1980, — Fleur Cecilia Kate, *b* 1978. —— Margaret Annette, *b* 1928: *m* 1952, Cdr William John Macnamara Faulkner, RN, of Falconswood, Petersfield, Hants, and has issue living, Hugh Edmund Brooke (3 Birley Rd, N20 0HB), *b* 1953: *m* 1992, Hon Mrs Sarah Louise Walsh, elder da of Baron Wedderburn of Charlton (Life Baron), and has issue living, Lucy Grace *b* 1993, — Mark William Bingham (Hollintree House, Newsham, Thirsk, N Yorkshire YO7 4DH), *b* 1955; Lt-Col 5th Royal Dragoon Gds: *m* 1979, Hon Deborah Jane

MacAndrew, only da of 2nd Baron MacAndrew, and has issue living, James William MacAndrew *b* 1983, Alexander Charles MacAndrew *b* 1987, Patrick Mark MacAndrew *b* 1992, — Rosalinda Mary *b* 1958: *m* 1986, Francis Michael Willis, and has issue living, Francis Edmund Hugh *b* 1989, Robert William Peter *b* 1991, Matthew Henry Michael *b* 1993, — Catharine Frances, *b* 1961: *m* 1984, Andrew Templer Scott, of 49 Telford Av, Streatham Hill, SW2 4XL (*see* B Camoys, colls), and has issue living, Rory David Templer *b* 1993, Alice Emily Cecilia *b* 1989. ―――― Elizabeth Clare Hilda Melita (*Lady Turner*), *b* 1932: *m* 1963, Adm Sir Arthur Francis Turner, KCB, DSC, who *d* 1991, of Plantation House, East Horsley, Surrey, and has issue living, Francis Christopher Neale, *b* 1966: *m* 1992 Rebecca Jane Thompson, — Michael Paul Charles, *b* 1969.

Granddaughter of late John Randolphus de Trafford, 3rd son of 1st baronet:—
Issue of late Galfrid Aloysius Cathcart de Trafford, *b* 1856, *d* 1924: *m* 1887, Cecile Elizabeth Margaret, who *d* 1945, da of late Comte Hubert de Stacpoole:—
Daphne Ruth Elizabeth Adelaide Mary, *b* 1903. *Residence* – 40 Pagoda Av, Richmond, Surrey.
The knightly family of Trafford of Trafford, Lancs can be traced in the male line to the 12th century. Sir Thomas Joseph Trafford, 1st Bt in 1842 received a Roy licence to resume the original name of de Trafford. Sir Humphrey, 4th Bt owner and breeder of racehorses, and was a snr steward of the Jockey Club 1936 and 1942-53. Sir Rudolph, 5th Bt, was Chm Atlas Assurance and Philip Hill Higginson and Elliott-Automation.

DEVITT (UK) 1916, of Chelsea, co London

Sir THOMAS GORDON DEVITT, 2nd *Baronet*, son of late Arthur Devitt, el son of 1st Baronet; *b* 27 Dec 1902; *s* his grandfather, *Sir* THOMAS LANE, 1923; *ed* Sherborne, and Corpus Christi Coll, Camb (MA), Senior Partner in the firm of Devitt and Moore; late Chm of National Service for Seafarers, and a Gov of Sherborne Sch; 1940-45 War as Lt-Col Seaforth Highlanders and Officer Comdg Raiding Support Regt; has Roy Order of Phoenix of Greece with swords: *m* 1st, 1930 (*m diss* 1936), Joan Mary, da of late Charles Reginald Freemantle, of Hayes Barton, Pyrford, Surrey; 2ndly, 1937 (*m diss* 1953), Lydia Mary, da of late Edward Milligen Beloe, of King's Lynn, Norfolk; 3rdly, 1953, Janet Lilian, only da of late Col Hugh Sidney Ellis, CBE, MC, and has issue by 2nd and 3rd *m*.

𝕬rms – Per pale gules and azure a bascule argent, chained or, in chief a fountain. 𝕮rest – A merman azure, pointing with the index finger of the dexter hand and holding in the sinister hand a rudder gold.
Residences – 49 Lexden Rd, Colchester, Essex, CO3 3PY; 5 Rembrandt Close, SW1.

SON LIVING (*By 3rd marriage*)

JAMES HUGH THOMAS, *b* 18 Sept 1956; *ed* Sherborne, and Corpus Christi Coll, Camb (MA): *m* 1985, Susan Carol, elder da of Dr (Adrian) Michael Campbell Duffus, of Woodhouse Farm, Thelbridge, Crediton, Devon, and has issue living, Jack Thomas Michael, *b* 29 July 1988, — William James Alexander, *b* 1990, — Gemma Florence, *b* 1987.

DAUGHTERS LIVING (*By 2nd marriage*)

Georgina Jane (*Hon Mrs Nigel G. Parker*), *b* 1937: *m* 1965, Hon Nigel Geoffrey Parker, of Combe Lane Farm, Wormley, Godalming, Surrey (*see* E Morley). ―――― Stephanie Gordon, *b* 1942: *m* 1966, Col J. N. Dudley Lucas, late The Royal Scots (The Royal Regt), of Becketts, Chilmark, Salisbury, Wilts, and has issue living, Timothy James Stephen, *b* 1968, — Chloe Henrietta, *b* 1967.

(*By 3rd marriage*)

Angela Susan, *b* 1954: *m* 1979, Iain Cardean Spottiswoode Morpeth, of 9 Polworth Rd, Streatham, SW16 2ET, elder son of Sir Douglas Spottiswoode Morpeth, of Shamley Green, Surrey, and has issue living, Richard Douglas Gordon, *b* 1985, — Duncan Hugh Sinclair, *b* 1987, — James Rutherford Thomas, *b* 1992, — Catherine Louise Nicholl, *b* 1990.

COLLATERAL BRANCHES LIVING

Issue of late Howson Foulger Devitt, 2nd son of 1st baronet, *b* 1869, *d* 1949: *m* 1908, Winifred Lina, who *d* 1972, el da of late Richard Woollcombe, of Starmead, Wokingham, Berks:—
Howson Charles, OBE (Gat-e-Whing, Andreas, I of Man), *b* 1909; *ed* Sherborne, and Trin Hall, Camb; an Underwriting Member of Lloyds; 1939-45 War as Wing Com RAF (OBE); OBE (Mil) 1941: *m* 1939, Elisabeth Carola, da of Edward Fairholme, of Burke's Corner, Beaconsfield, and has issue living, Richard Howson, *b* 1940, — Carola Waveney, *b* 1942: *m* 1962, Peter John Laidlaw Jenkins, of Pages, Shalford, Braintree, Essex, and has issue living, Mark Alan Laidlaw *b* 1964, Carola Rosemary *b* 1965, Tamsin Elisabeth *b* 1970. ―――― Peter Kenneth (Upper Sherbrook, Sherbrook Hill, Budleigh Salterton, E Devon EX9 6DA), *b* 1911; *ed* Sherborne; Wing-Cdr Roy AuxAF, and a DL for Surrey; 1939-45 War (despatches): *m* 1st, 1935, Eunice Stephanie, yst da of late Sir Charles Sheriton Swan; 2ndly, 1950, Joan Elizabeth, da of late T. Forbes Robertson, of Santa Barbara, Cal, USA; 3rdly, 1953 (*m diss* 1965), remarried his 1st wife, Eunice Stephanie (ante), and has issue living, (by 1st *m*) Jeremy Peter (2 Chelfham Barton Cottages, Chelfham, Barnstaple, N Devon EX31 4RP), *b* 1937; Cdr RN (ret): *m* 1961, Elspeth, el da of Brig William Edward Guest, MBE, of The Cottage, Lizard, Cornwall, and has issue living, Mark Edward Peter *b* 1962, Simon Charles Guest *b* 1964, Nicholas Jeremy James *b* 1968, Timothy William Guy (twin) *b* 1968, — Lorna Stephanie, *b* 1942: *m* 1963, Geoffrey Glynn-Jones, and has issue living, Timothy Patrick, *b* 1965, Lavinia Mary, *b* 1969, — Jacquetta Anne, *b* 1946: *m* 1st, 1968 (*m diss* 1974), Christopher David Legge; 2ndly, 1976, Robert Patrick Pease, of 12 Elm Grove Rd, Barnes, SW13 0BT, and has issue living (by 2nd *m*), Tanya Jacquetta *b* 1977, Sophie Claire *b* 1980, — Vivien Gay, *b* 1948. ―――― Ursula Helen, *b* 1912: *m* 1935, Maj Michael Alastair Spencer-Nairn, Fife and Forfar Yeo (TA) (*see* Spencer-Nairn, Bt). ―――― Sheila Winifred (twin), *b* 1912: *m* 1936, Edward Michael Harrison, of Barn House, Otterton, Budleigh Salterton, Devon, and has issue living, Hugh Michael James (Ringcombe Farm, West Anstey, S Molton, Devon), *b* 1942: *m* 1st, 1968 (*m diss* 1974), Joanna Mary, da of late Col W. R. Healing, of Budleigh Salterton; 2ndly, 1974, Stephanie Christine, el da

of the Rev Peter Haslewood Shaw, of Greatworth, Northants, Cheshire, and has issue living, (by 1st *m*) James Edward *b* 1969, (by 2nd *m*) Camilla Rose *b* 1975, Zoë Grace *b* 1977, — Juliet Mary, *b* 1937: *m* 1964, Tuckerman Moss, PhD, of 67 Alta Vista, Orinda, Ca, USA, and has issue living, Michael Duval *b* 1965 Jeremy Gilbert *b* 1968, Rebecca Alice (twin) *b* 1968, — Lucy Clare, *b* 1950: *m* 1971, Paul Robert Hulme, of Tarr Steps Hotel, Hawkridge, Dulverton, Som, and has issue living, Richard Jeremy *b* 1973, Emma Catherine *b* 1971.

       Grandchildren of late Herbert Pye-Smith Devitt, MRCS, LRCP (infra):—
       Issue of late (Herbert) Lionel Devitt, *b* 1910; *d* 1964: *m* 1st, 1939 (*m diss* 1948), (Myfanwy Rina) Doreen, da of late Alwyn H. Holman; 2ndly, 1949 (*m diss* 1954), Sheila Mary da of Edmond Ironside Bremner; 3rdly, 1954, Fleur Traherne Thomas (11B Bina Gdns, SW6):—
(By 1st *m*) Michael Wyn (Farmhill Manor, Braddan, I of Man), *b* 1943: *m* 1967, Susan Gundreda de Warrenne, only child of Walter Kingsley Brett, and has issue living, Roland, *b* 1972, — Madeleine, *b* 1969. —— Judith Anne Mary, *b* 1940: *m* 1963, Edward David Beresford Tebbs, of Coombe End Cottage, Golf Club Drive, Coombe, Kingston upon Thames, and has issue living, Andrew, *b* 1971, — Lucy, *b* 1965, — Amanda, *b* 1967.

       Issue of late Herbert Pye-Smith Devitt, MRCS, LRCP, 3rd son of 1st baronet, *b* 1873, *d* 1958: *m* 1st, 1903, Roberta Mary Cornelia, who *d* 1934, el da of late Major James George Anderson, Roy Irish Fusiliers; 2ndly, 1935, Muriel, who *d* 1951, da of late Reginald M. Snow, of Bideford, Devon, and widow of Flight-Lieut G. E. Blake, RAF; 3rdly, 1952, Carola Evelyn, who *d* 1984, da of late E. Howard May, and widow of William Walter Brownlee:—
(By 1st *m*) Dorothea *b* 1904: *m* 1930, Harry Martin Ward Clarke, who *d* 1963, and has had issue, Rosemary *b* 1932: *m* 1958, Michael Herzig, of 56 Farnham Rd, Guildford, Surrey, and *d* 1978, leaving issue, Andrew Michael *b* 1960, Peter John *b* 1962, Martin Robert *b* 1966, Catherine Jane *b* 1969, — Jenifer Jane, *b* 1935. —— Margaret Mary, *b* 1915: *m* 1944, Cedric Herbert Bramley, and has issue living, Roberta, *b* 1949: *m* 1981, Jean-Louis René Daniel Joly, of 114 Elphinstone Rd, Hastings, E Sussex, and has issue living, Claire Margaret *b* 1981, Kathryn Mary *b* 1982. *Residence* – Windrush, 30 Wealden Way, Little Common, Bexhill-on-Sea.

       Grandsons of late Herbert Pye-Smith Devitt, MRCS, LRCP (ante):—
       Issue of late Philip Eyre Devitt, *b* 1907, *d* 1992: *m* 1947, Patricia Melicent (Whydown Lodge, Little Common, Bexhill-on-Sea, Sussex), el da of late Walter Edward Leslie, of Tarbert, co Kerry:—
Desmond Philip, *b* 1950. —— Ann Patricia, *b* 1954.
       Issue of late John Desmond Devitt, MRCS, LRCP, *b* 1917, *d* 1973: *m* 1957, Pamela Ruth da of late L. B. Foot, of Egbury, Hants:—
Timothy John Herbert (Ground Floor Flat, 5 Carden Rd, SE15), *b* 1958. —— Jonathan Stephen (31 Ryedale, SE22), *b* 1960: *m* 1992 Maria Soledad Fidalgo Suarez, and has issue living, Calum John, *b* 1993. —— (Andrew) James (25 Milford Ct, Huddersfield, W Yorks), *b* 1962.
       Issue of late Philip Henry Devitt (yst son of 1st baronet (*cr* 1916)), who was *cr* a *Baronet* 1931:—
See Devitt, Bt, *cr* 1931 (ext).

Sir Thomas Lane Devitt, 1st Bt (sometime senior partner in the firm of Devitt and Moore, and Pres of Chamber of Shipping of the United Kingdom 1890, and of Institute of Marine Engineers 1913-14), was one of the Managers of the Orient Line from its foundation, Pres of the Shipping Federation 1890 to 1923 (also Chm 1890-1914), Chm of Lloyd's Register of Shipping 1911-22, and Founder of the Nautical Coll, Pangbourne.

DEVITT (UK) 1931, of Pangbourne, Berks (Extinct 1947)

Sir PHILIP HENRY DEVITT, 1st and last *Baronet*.

DAUGHTERS LIVING OF FIRST BARONET

Theodora Joan, *b* 1919. —— Elizabeth Anne (*Lady Koelle*). *b* 1921: *m* 1948, as his 2nd wife, Vice-Adm Sir Harry Philpot Koelle, KCB, who *d* 1980, and has issue living, Victoria Anne, *b* 1949: *m* 1980, Andrew James Carter, and has issue living, Philip Harry *b* 1976, Jack Edward *b* 1981, Timothy Robert *b* 1985, — Philippa June, *b* 1951: *m* 1979, Hugo C. Woolley and has issue living, Giles Thomas *b* 1984, Emily Anne *b* 1981. *Residence* – Ascham, Molyneux Park Rd, Tonbridge Wells, Kent. —— Jennifer Margaret, *b* 1923. —— Bridget Helen (twin), *b* 1931: *m* 1952, Oliver Michael Robin Greenwood, who *d* 1992, late Capt Coldstream Guards, and has issue living, Simon Nelson, *b* 1954: *m* 1984, Sara A. Johnston, — Christopher Philip, *b* 1957: *m* 1988, Tara Simonis, — James William Dickon, *b* 1974, — Nicola Jane, *b* 1954: *m* 1979, Robert C. Atkinson. *Residence* – Tyn y Waen, Glasfryn, Corwen, Clwyd.

DEWEY (UK) 1917, of South Hill Wood, Bromley, Kent

The wise man is strong

VIR SAPIENS FORTIS EST

Sir ANTHONY HUGH DEWEY, 3rd *Baronet,* el son of late Major Hugh Grahame Dewey, MC, el son of 2nd Baronet; *b* 31 July 1921; *s* his grandfather, *Rev Sir* STANLEY DAWS, 1948; *ed* Wellington Coll, and Roy Agric Coll Cirencester, is a JP for Somerset; European War 1940-45 as Capt RA and Major N Somerset Yeo: *m* 1949, Sylvia Jacqueline Rosamund, da of late John Ross MacMahon, MB, CM, of Branksome Manor, Bournemouth, and has issue.

Arms – 1st and 4th per fesse sable and, or, three cinquefoils between two barrulets between three dragons' heads erased counterchanged, in each of their mouths a sword in bend proper, pommels and hilts of the second, *Dewey*; 2nd and 3rd sable, a griffin segreant ermine, armed or, the wings erminois, a bordure compony argent and gules, *Ballard.* **Crest** – A dragon's head erased sable, holding in the mouth, a sword in bend proper, pommel and hilt or, betwee two dragons' wings of the last, on each a bend of the first, charged with a cinquefoil of the third.
Residence – The Rag, Galhampton, Yeovil, Somerset BA22 7AH. *Club* – Army and Navy.

SONS LIVING

RUPERT GRAHAME, *b* 29 March 1953; solicitor: *m* 1978, Suzanne Rosemary, da of late Andrew Lusk, of Fordie, Comrie, Perthshire, and has issue living, Thomas Andrew, *b* 27 Jan 1982, — Oliver Nicholas, *b* 1984, — Laura Kate, *b* 1988. *Residence* – Church Farm House, Wellow, Bath, Avon BA2 8QS. —— Charles Ross, *b* 1960: *m* 19—, Melinda R., da of late Peter Marriott, and has issue living, Fabian Peter Christopher, *b* 1993. *Residence* – Manor Cottage, Egford, Frome, Som BA11 3JQ.

DAUGHTERS LIVING

Delia Mary, *b* 1951: *m* 1977, Nicholas John Wingfield-Digby, 2nd son of Rev Canon Stephen Basil Wingfield-Digby, MBE, of The Vicarage, Sherborne, Dorset, and has issue living, James, *b* 1988, — Emily Clare, *b* 1981, — Julia Mary, *b* 1985. —— Carola Jane, *b* 1955: *m* 1981, Robert Hiles Sutton, son of John Ormerod Sutton, of The Old Schoolhouse, Tichborne, Hants, and has issue living, Patrick William, *b* 1984, — Jonathan David Ormerod, *b* 1990, — Joanna Kate, *b* 1987. —— Angela Rosamund, *b* 1957: *m* 1992, Ivan Hicks, and has issue living, Miles Anthony, *b* 1992, — Alice Rosamund, *b* 1986, — Lydia Jane, *b* 1987.

SISTER LIVING

Hilary Mary, *b* 1923; BSc London 1944, MSc 1947: *m* 1953, Paul Faulconer Morgan, and has issue living, Hugh Faulconer, *b* 1960: *m* 1988, Rebecca Susan Kate, da of Dr John Alfred Humphrey Waterhouse, of Birmingham, and has issue living, Elsa Charlotte *b* 1990, Sophia Myfanwy *b* 1992, — Clare Anne, *b* 1954: *m* 1980, Derek Crosby Coleman, and has issue living, Ben Richard *b* 1987, Catherine Helen *b* 1984, — Stella Margaret, *b* 1956, — Patricia Hilary, *b* 1957: *m* 1992, Mark Andrew Wood, son of Richard Kenneth Wood, of Hetherley, Glos. *Residence* – Hollin Old Hall, East Bollington, Macclesfield, Cheshire, SK10 5LY.

COLLATERAL BRANCHES LIVING

Grandchildren of late Maj Hugh Grahame Dewey, MC, el son of 2nd baronet:—
Issue of late Maj Michael Grahame Dewey, *b* 1928, *d* 1973: *m* 1954, Anne Cecilia (Warden Grange, Chipping Warden, Banbury, Oxon), da of late Brig Edward Thomas Arthur George Boylan, CBE, DSO, MC (*see* O'Brien, Bt, 1980 Edn):—
Philippa Mary, *b* 1955: *m* 1980, Stephen William George Neel, of Langleys Farm, Charlton, Malmesbury, Wiltshire, and has issue living, George, *b* 1983, — Henry William, *b* 1988, — Jessica Anais, *b* 1985. —— Amanda Julia, *b* 1957: *m* 1978, Col Richard Neville Brayley Quicke, Light Dragoons, and has issue living, Edward James, *b* 1983, — Michael Charles, *b* 1985, — Thomas William, *b* 1987, — Jonathan Alexander, *b* 1992.

Issue of late Norman Strafford Dewey, MC, 2nd son of 2nd baronet, *b* 1896, *d* 1985: *m* 1925, Ursula Marguerite (5 Kings Court, Kelsey Park Av, Beckenham, Kent, BR3 2TT), da of late H.D.D. Barman, of Helensburgh:—
Thomas Norman (4 Beadon Rd, Bromley, Kent BR2 9AT), *b* 1926; *ed* Radley, Pembroke Coll, Camb (MA), and Brunel Univ (MTech); CEng; MIEE, MIMechE: *m* 1964, Janet Mary, da of late B.C. Baxter, of Enfield, Middlesex, and has issue living, Stephen Thomas, *b* 1965; *ed* Brighton Coll, and Sheffield Univ (B Eng, PhD): *m* 1992, Elizabeth Ann, da of J. Cartledge, of Sheffield, — Claire Margaret, *b* 1966; *ed* Bromley High Sch, and City of London Univ (BA): *m* 1994, Timothy Michael Corum. —— David Lewis (Happs Edge, 60 Box Lane, Bovingdon, Herts), *b* 1927; *ed* Radley, and Pembroke Coll, Camb (MA); PhD London 1953: *m* 1960, Jacqueline Anne, da of late L.F. Curtis, of Dartford, Kent, and has issue living, Nigel Lewis, *b* 1967, — Fiona Jane, *b* 1961: *m* 1989, Andre Mook, of Douw van der Kraplaan 23, 2252 Bt Voorschoten, Netherlands, and has issue living, Christopher Benjamin *b* 1992, — Helen Gay, *b* 1964: *m* 1988, Ross Andrew Heath, of 6 Berry Court, Maddington 6109, Perth, Australia, and has issue living, David Russell *b* 1993. —— Martin Ross (Terra Cotta, Llandevaud, nr Newport, Gwent, NP6 2AE), *b* 1933; *ed* Radley: *m* 1964, Barbara, who *d* 1990, da of late David Sharp, of Wokingham, and has issue living, Ross Meredith, *b* 1966. —— Olive Rosemary, *b* 1931: BSc London 1955: *m* 1962, Peter Gordon Hiam Wilson, of Holywater House, Rembrandt House, Bury St Edmunds, Suffolk IP33 2LR, and has two children, Alan Richard Hiam, *b* 1964, — Carol Tania, *b* 1966: *m* 1987, Adam Edward Grainger Simpson, of Quinta do Montinho, Monthinos De Luz, 8600 Lagos, Portugal.

Issue of late Thomas Lewis Dewey, 3rd son of 2nd baronet, *b* 1900, *d* 1951: *m* 1936, Josephine Mary Sadler (who *m* 2ndly, 1957, Andrew Mackenzie Ross, MD, DLO, of Cherry Tree Cottage, Nether Compton, Sherborne, Dorset), da of Joseph Sadler Stockton, of Whitely Woods, Sheffield:—
Peter Lewis, *b* 1938; *ed* Lancing: *m* 19—, Hilary —. —— Jennifer Ann, *b* 1937: *m* 1966, Lt-Col David Younger, Queen's Own Hussars, of Ravenswood, Melrose, Roxburghshire, and has issue living, William Grahame Ralph, *b* 1970, — James David, *b* 1972, — Catherine Belinda, *b* 1967.

Issue of late Dr Theodore Stanley Dewey, 4th son of 2nd baronet, *b* 1902, *d* 1978: *m* 1929, Monica, da of Vincent Daniel, of Coppings, Leigh, Kent:—

Terence Charles, *b* 1933; *ed* Ampleforth, and Pembroke Coll, Camb (MA 1961); commissioned RNVR 1954. —— Timothy Hugh (The Cottage, Kelston, Bath), *b* 1935; *ed* Ampleforth: *m* 1962, Margaret Mia, da of late Dr T. R. D. Aubrey, of Bitton, Glos, and has issue living, Adrian Charles, *b* 1963, — Annabel Mary, *b* 1965: *m* 1987, Peter Vernon Mosse, of 115 Park Av, Barking, Essex IG11 8QY, only son of late Richard Kemble Mosse, of Bromyard, Herefords, — Laura Rose, *b* 1967, — Jessica Mia, *b* 1968. —— Amanda Jane, *b* 1931: *m* 1st, 1956 (*m diss* 1966), John Robin Millner; 2ndly, 1966, Peter Michael Lloyd Wenham, and has issue living (by 1st *m*) Julian John, *b* 1958, — Piers Theodore, *b* 1960, — Giles William, *b* 1961, — (by 2nd *m*) Susanna Jane, *b* 1964, — Arabella Monica, *b* 1966. —— Caroline Mary, *b* 1938: *m* 1961, Julian Reginald Brinton Clist, MBE, and has issue living, Sophia Anne Brinton, *b* 1963, — Samantha Gebrielle Brinton, *b* 1964: *m* 1992, Andrew M. Coates, — Imogen Cecilia Brinton, *b* 1969. —— Corinne Rose (twin), *b* 1938: *m* 1960, Stanley Keith Knowles, and has issue living, Tobias Sebastian, *b* 1961, — Hugh Stanley Keith, *b* 1962, — Benedict Caradoc, *b* 1968, — Miranda Vivian, *b* 1964.

Grandson of late Marshall Dewey, yr son of 1st baronet (infra):—
Issue of late Sidney Maurice Dewey, *b* 1902, *d* 1968: *m* 1931, Dorothy Catherine Holt, who *d* 1968:—
Anthony Guy, *b* 1932; *ed* Repton: *m* 1968, Mrs Caroline Rose Hardie, da of late L. M. Hanbury-Bateman, and has issue living, Martin Guy, *b* 1969, — Nicholas George, *b* 1971.
Sir Charles Dewey, 1st Bt, was Pres of Prudential Assurance Co. The Rev Sir Stanley Daws Dewey, 2nd Bt, was Preb of Exeter Cathedral 1935-43, and High Sheriff of Devon 1945.

TENNYSON-d'EYNCOURT (UK) 1930, of Carter's Corner Farm, Parish of Herstmonceux, co Sussex

Nothing rashly

Sir MARK GERVAIS TENNYSON-D'EYNCOURT, 5th *Baronet*; *b* 12 March 1967; *s* his father, *Sir* GILES GERVAIS, 1989; *ed* Charterhouse, and Kingston Polytechnic (BA); fashion designer; Freeman City of London 1989.

Arms – Quarterly: 1st and 4th, azure, a fesse dancettée between ten billets, four and six or, *d'Eyncourt*; 2nd and 3rd, gules, three leopards' faces or, jessant-de-lis azure, over all a bend of the last, *Tennyson*. **Crests** – 1st, a lion passant guardant argent, on the head a crown of fleur-de-lis or, the dexter fore-paw supporting a shield charged with the arms of *d'Eyncourt*; 2nd, a dexter arm in armour, the hand in a gauntlet or, grasping a broken tilting spear, enfiled with a garland of laurel proper, *Tennyson*.

WIDOW LIVING OF SECOND BARONET

VINNIE LORRAINE (*Vinnie, Lady Tennyson-d'Eyncourt*) (Catalino Pueblo, 2556 Avenida Maria, Tucson, Arizona 85718, USA), da of late Andrew Pearson, of Minneapolis, USA, and widow of Robert J. O'Donnell: *m* 1964, as his 2nd wife, Sir (Eustace) Gervais Tennyson-d'Eyncourt, 2nd Bt, who *d* 1971.

WIDOW LIVING OF THIRD BARONET

Forward

NORAH (*Norah, Lady Tennyson-d'Eyncourt*), da of late Thomas Gill, of Sheffield, Yorks: *m* 1977, as his 3rd wife, Sir (John) Jeremy Eustace Tennyson-d'Eyncourt, 3rd Bt, who *d* 1988. *Residence* – Bayons House, Hinton St George, Somerset TA17 8RX.

WIDOW LIVING OF FOURTH BARONET

JUANITA (*Lady Tennyson d'Eyncourt*), da of late Fortunato Borromeo: *m* 1966, Sir Giles Gervais Tennyson d'Eyncourt, 4th Bt, who *d* 1989. *Address* – c/o Hyde Mahon Bridges, 52 Bedford Row, WC1R 4UH.

The 1st baronet, Sir Eustace Henry William Tennyson-d'Eyncourt, KCB, FRS, DSc, LLD (son of late Louis Charles Tennyson-d'Eyncourt, of Bayons Manor, Market Rasen), was a Naval Architect, Director of Naval Construction, Admiralty, and Principal Technical Adviser 1912-23, and Head of the Landships Committee which designed and produced the first tanks.

Dick-Cunyngham, see Cunyngham.

Dick-Lauder, see Lauder.

DILKE (UK) 1862, of Sloane Street, Chelsea

Leo inimicis amicis
columba

Sir JOHN FISHER WENTWORTH DILKE, 5th *Baronet*; *b* 8 May 1906; *s* his father, *Sir* FISHER WENTWORTH, 1944; *ed* Winchester, and New Coll, Oxford; in HM's Foreign Ser 1929-32; head of British official wireless news 1942-5; late staff of *The Times* Foreign Depart and BBC External Ser: *m* 1st, 1934 (*m diss* 1949), Sheila, only da of late Sir William Seeds, KCMG; 2ndly, 1951, Iris Evelyn, only da of late Ernest Clark, and has issue by 1st *m*.

Arms – Quarterly of nine: 1st, gules, a lion rampant per pale argent and or; 2nd, argent, a mullet gules; 3rd, sable a chevron between three leopards' faces or; 4th, argent, a cross grady throughout sable; 5th, paly or six argent and gules a bend counterchanged; 6th, gules, on a bend argent three escallops azure; 7th, paly of six argent and sable on a bend gules, three mullets argent; 8th, quarterly: or and gules on a bend sable, between two fretts or, three escallops of the first; 9th, ermine two chevrons sable. **Crest** – A dove proper.
Residence – Ludpits, Etchingham, E Sussex TN19 7DB.

SONS LIVING *(By 1st marriage)*

CHARLES JOHN WENTWORTH, *b* 21 Feb 1937; *ed* Winchester, and King's Coll, Camb (BA); Provost, Brompton Oratory SW7. —— Timothy Fisher Wentworth (15 Wemyss Rd, SE3), *b* 1938; *ed* Winchester and New Coll, Oxford (MA); BM, BCh; FRCP London: *m* 1965, his cousin, Caroline Sophia, da of late Christopher Wentworth Dilke (infra), and has issue living, Felix Wentworth, *b* 1967, — Rosemary Frances, *b* 1970.

COLLATERAL BRANCHES LIVING

Issue of late Michael Clifford Wentworth Dilke, 2nd son of 4th baronet, *b* 1909, *d* 1944: *m* 1940, Rosemary Blanche, who *d* 1974, da of Capt Sir Thomas Herbert Cochrane Troubridge, 4th Bt, and widow of Capt Roderick Kilgour Mackenzie, yr, of Kincraig:—
Lucilla Rose *b* 1941: *m* 1970, Gareth Ulric van den Bogaerde, of 42 Bennerley Rd, Wandsworth, SW11, and has issue living, Ulric Michael Amadeus Landrover, *b* 1970, — Alice Rosemary Patience Lucilla, *b* 1973.

Issue of late Christopher Wentworth Dilke, novelist, 3rd son of 4th baronet, *b* 1913, *d* 1987: *m* 1939, Alice Mary (Valehouse Farm, Whitchurch Canonicorum, Bridport, Dorset DT6 6RP), da of late Hon James William Best (*see* B Wynford, colls):—
Fisher William Wentworth (142 Iffley Rd, W6), *b* 1948; *ed* Westminster, Sussex Univ and Camb Univ (PhD): *m* 1985, Diana Madelaine, da of Dr Raymond John Adie, and has issue living, Thomas Wentworth, *b* 1991, — Stella Maye, *b* 1987, — Athene Elizabeth, *b* 1988. —— Caroline Sophia, *b* 1940: *m* 1965, her cousin, Timothy Fisher Wentworth Dilke, and has issue (ante). —— Annabel Mary (23 Lynette Av, SW4), *b* 1942: *m* 1975, Georgi Markov, who was assassinated 1978, and has issue living, Alexandra Raina, *b* 1976. —— Lucy Catherine, *b* 1952; *ed* York Univ (MA): *m* 1975, Anthony Charles Pinney (*see* B Norton, 1960 Edn), of Egremont Farm, Payhembury, Devon, and has issue living, Samuel Charles, *b* 1980, — Katharine Elizabeth, *b* 1979.
The 1st baronet took a prominent part in the International Exhibitions of 1851 and 1862, and sat as MP for Wallingford (*L*) 1865-8. The 2nd baronet, Rt Hon Sir Charles Wentworth Dilke, was Under-Sec for Foreign Affairs 1880-82, and Pres of Local Govt Board 1882-5, and sat as MP for Chelsea (*L*) 1868-86, and for Forest of Dean Div of Gloucestershire 1892-1911.

DILLON (UK) 1801, of Lismullen, Meath (Extinct 1982)

WIDOW LIVING OF EIGHTH BARONET

(ELIA) SYNOLDA AUGUSTA (*Lady Dillon*), only da of late Cecil Butler Cholmondeley Clarke, of The Hermitage, Holycross, co Tipperary (*see* B Hemphill, 1925 Edn): *m* 1947, Sir Robert William Charlier Dillon, 8th Bt (a Baron of the Holy Roman Empire, *cr* 1782), who *d* 1982, when the title became *ext*.

Dillwyn-Venables-Llewelyn, see Llewelyn.

DIXIE (E) 1660, of Market Bosworth, Leicestershire (Dormant or Extinct 1975)

Sir (ALEXANDER ARCHIBALD DOUGLAS) WOLSTAN DIXIE, 13th *Baronet*, *d* 1975. A possible heir to the baronetcy may exist among the descendants (if any) of Capt Richard Thomas Dixie, brother of the 6th, 7th and 9th baronets, or of Beaumont or John Dixie, brothers of the 3rd baronet, or of Henry Dixie, yr son of the 1st baronet.

DAUGHTERS LIVING OF THIRTEENTH BARONET *(By 2nd marriage)*

Eleanor Barbara Lindsay (Bosworth Park, Leics); *b* 1952: *m* 1983, (*m diss* 1986) Scott M. Mellor, of USA; has issue living (by William H. Wood, of USA), Emma Louise Olivia DIXIE-WOOD, *b* 1988. —— Caroline Mary Jane, *b* 1960: *m* 1989, Andrew Davies; has issue living, Charles Wolstan Christopher PHIZACKLEA DIXIE, *b* 1983, — Abigail Charlotte, *b* 1990.

DAUGHTER LIVING OF TWELFTH BARONET

Frances Dorothy Madeleine Barbara da la Motte (Room 6, Visitation Convent, Bridport, Dorset DT6 3AP), *b* 1912: *m* 1st, 1944, Ernest Thomas Riley Kirby, who *d* 1966; 2ndly, 1974, Cdr John Weddall Pontifex, RN, who *d* 1977.

WIDOW LIVING OF THIRTEENTH BARONET

Dorothy Penelope (*Lady Dixie*) (Market Bosworth, Leics), da of E. King-Kirkman: *m* 1950, as his 2nd wife, Sir (Alexander Archibald Douglas) Wolstan Dixie, 13th Bt, who *d* 1975, when the title became dormant or ext.

This family was settled at Bosworth *temp* Queen Elizabeth I. Sir Wolstan Dixie, 1st baronet, received his warrant of baronetcy from Charles I, for his activity and zealousness in the royal cause, however, through the confusion of the times, the patent was not taken out until 1660, in which year Sir Wolstan was Sheriff of Leicestershire.

DIXON (UK) 1919, of Astle, Chelford, co Palatine of Chester

Manners maketh man

Sir Jonathan Mark Dixon, 4th *Baronet*, son of late Capt Nigel Dixon, OBE, RN, yr son of 2nd baronet; *b* 1 Sept 1949; *s* his uncle, *Capt Sir* John George, 1990; *ed* Winchester, and University Coll, Oxford (BA 1972, MA 1987): *m* 1978, Patricia Margaret, da of James Baird Smith, and has issue.

Arms – Gules, a fleur-de-lis or, on a chief argent three ermine spots sable. Crest – A demi-lion rampant gules-holding between the paws a fylfot or.
Residence – 19 Clyde Rd, Redland, Bristol BS6 6RJ.

SONS LIVING

Mark Edward, *b* 29 June 1982. —— Timothy Nigel, *b* 1987.

DAUGHTER LIVING

Katherine Anne, *b* 1980.

DAUGHTER LIVING OF THIRD BARONET

Mary Jane, *b* 1951: *m* 1976, Olav Alexander Ek. *Residence* – Blijdensteinlaan 11, 1217 PD, Hilversum, The Netherlands.

AUNT LIVING (*daughter of second baronet*)

Beryl, *b* 1916. *Residence* – 96 East St, Corfe Castle, Dorset.

MOTHER LIVING

Margaret Josephine, da of late Maurice John Collett, of Aston Lodge, Malvern Wells, Worcs: *m* 1948, Capt Nigel Dixon, RN, who *d* 1978. *Residence* – 1 Abbots Quay, Wareham, Dorset.

WIDOW LIVING OF THIRD BARONET

Caroline (*Dowager Lady Dixon*), elder da of late Charles Theodore Hiltermann, of 31 Melbury Court, W8: *m* 1947, Capt Sir John George Dixon, 3rd Bt, late 4th Hus SR of Officers, who *d* 1990. *Residence* – Avenue Ed Muller 3, 1814 La Tour de Peilz, Vaud, Switzerland.

Sir George Dixon, 1st Bt, was High Sheriff for Cheshire 1881.

DODDS (UK) 1964, of West Chiltington, co Sussex.

Sir RALPH JORDAN DODDS, 2nd *Baronet*; *b* 25 March 1928, *s* his father, *Sir* (EDWARD) CHARLES, MVO, 1973; *ed* Winchester, and RMA Sandhurst; late Capt 13/18th Hussars; an Underwriting Member of Lloyd's since 1964: *m* 1954, Marion, da of late Sir Daniel Thomas Davies, KCVO, and has issue.

Arms – Azure issuant from a chief argent and out of a sunburst a dexter hand proper between two crabs heads downward argent each transfixed by a sword or on the chief a steer's head and caboshed sable armed gold between two capons proper. **Crest** – A demi woman affronty proper vested azure holding an open book proper inscribed with the chemical formula for stilboestrol sable.
Residence – 49 Sussex Square, W.2. *Clubs* – Cavalry and Guards', and Hurlingham.

DAUGHTERS LIVING

Caroline, *b* 1956: *m* 1st, 1981, James George Ball; 2ndly, 1987, David Pegg. —— Arabella, *b* 1961: *m* 1982, Maj Philip Henry Marmion Dymoke, WG (*see* E Westmorland, colls).
The 1st baronet, Sir (Edward) Charles Dodds, MVO, son of Ralph Edward Dodds, of Darlington, and London, was Pres Roy Coll of Physicians 1962-66.

SMITH-DODSWORTH (GB) 1784, of Newland Park and Thornton Watlass, Yorkshire

Sir JOHN CHRISTOPHER SMITH-DODSWORTH, 8th *Baronet*; *b* 4 March 1935; *s* his father, *Sir* CLAUDE MATTHEW, 1940; *ed* Ampleforth: *m* 1st, 1961 (*m diss* 1971), Margaret Anne, da of Alfred Jones, of Pludds, Gloucestershire; 2ndly, 1972, Margaret Theresa, who *d* 1990, da of Henry Grey, of Auckland, NZ; 3rdly, 1991, Lolita, da of Romeo Pulante, of Laur, Nueva Ecija, Philippines, and has issue by 1st, 2nd and 3rd *m*.

Arms – Quarterly: 1st and 4th, argent, a bend engrailed sable between three annulets gules, *Dodsworth*; 2nd and 3rd, per saltire argent and sable two trefoils slipped in pale gules, *Smith*. **Crest** – 1st, a dexter cubic arm in chain mail or, the hand proper grasping a broken tilting spear or, embrued gules, *Dodsworth*; 2nd, out of a ducal coronet or, a boar's head couped at the neck azure, crined and tusked or, *Smith*.
Seat – Thornton Watlass Hall, Ripon, Yorkshire. *Residence* – Driving Creek, Coromandel, NZ.

Pro lege senatu que rege
*Govern in accordance
with law and parliament*

SONS LIVING *(By 1st marriage)*

DAVID JOHN, *b* 23 Oct 1963; *ed* Ampleforth.

(By 2nd marriage)

Daniel Leui'i, *b* 1974.

DAUGHTERS LIVING *(By 1st marriage)*

Cyrilla Denise, *b* 1962.

(By 3rd marriage)

Joanna Marie, *b* 1993.

SISTERS LIVING

Mary Cyrilla, *b* 1933: *m* 1978 (*m diss* 1993), Gresham Clacy, of Arizona, USA. —— Julia Agnes, *b* 1938: *m* 1963, Brian Maccelari, of Johannesburg, S Africa, and has issue living, Douglas Charles Dodsworth, *b* 1965, — Jeremy Christopher Dodsworth (twin), *b* 1965, — Mary Frances Dodsworth, *b* 1963, — Angela Josephine Dodsworth, *b* 1969.

The 1st baronet, Sir John Silvester Smith (son of John Smith, of Newland Hall, Yorkshire), married the sister and heiress of Frederick Dodsworth, of Thornton Watlass, whose surname their children assumed. Thomas Dodsworth, of Dodworth, W Riding, co York, Receiver to Henry, 3rd Lord Fitzhugh, KG, acquired the Thornton Watlass estate in 1415 by marriage with Agnes, da and heiress of Hugh Thoresby, Ch Capt of Richmondshire, and niece of John Thoresby, Cardinal St Praxis, Archbishop of York, and Chancellor of England, who built the Choir of York Cathedral. Of this family was Sir Edward Dodsworth, Comy-Gen to the Army of the Parliament, and Roger Dodsworth, the famous Yorkshire antiquary. Besides the families of Silvester, Dodsworth and Thoresby the Smiths of Newland represent Howarth of Howarth, co Lancashire, founded by Osbert Howarth, Master of the Buckhounds to Henry II, and Blayney, Barons Blayney, of Monaghan, which peerage *cr* 1621, became extinct in 1874. This family is lineally descended from Lionel, Duke of Clarence, third son of Edward III, through Mortimer, Percy, Clifford, Conyers, D'Arcy, Stapylton and Dodsworth.

DOMVILLE (UK) 1814, of St Albans, Hertfordshire (Extinct 1981)

Lieut-Com Sir (Gerald) Guy Domville, RN, 7th and last *Baronet*; *d* 1981.

DAUGHTERS LIVING OF SIXTH BARONET

Anne Juliet, *b* 1923; sometime Section Officer WAAF: *m* 1943 (*m diss* 1959), Walter Siner, 1st Lieut USA Air Force, and has issue living, Guy Domville, *b* 1947, — Anne Catherine, *b* 1945. *Residence* – The Bothy, Compton, near Guildford, Surrey. —— Rosemary Gervaise, *b* 1924: *m* 1955 (*m diss* 1979), Rev Wolfgang Müller, and has issue living, Harald Martin Domville, *b* 1956, — Mark Bernhard Domville, *b* (twin) 1956, — Steven Rufus Domville, *b* 1959.

Don-Wauchope, see Wauchope.

DORMAN (UK) 1923, of Nunthorpe, co York

Sir CHARLES GEOFFREY DORMAN, MC, 3rd *Baronet*; *b* 18 Sept 1920; *s* his father, *Sir* BEDFORD LOCKWOOD, CBE, 1956; *ed* Rugby, and at Brasenose Coll, Oxford (BA 1941, MA 1947); Lt-Col (ret) 13th/18th Hussars; 1939-44 War in Middle East and Italy (MC): *m* 1954 (*m diss* 1972), Elizabeth Ann (a CStJ), who *d* 1993, only da of late George Gilmour Gilmour-White, OBE, JP, of North Cerney, Cirencester, and has issue.

Arms – Argent, two bars azure, each charged with as many roses of the field, barbed and seeded proper, over all a lozenge sable charged with a lion's head erased or. **Crest** – Upon a rock proper, a lion's paw erased sable, grasping a spear in bend sinister proper.
Residence – Hutton Grange Cottage, Gt Rollright, Chipping Norton, Oxon, OX7 5SQ.

DAUGHTER LIVING

Eve Constance, *b* 1962.

COLLATERAL BRANCHES LIVING

Vir·tus·in·ar·duis

Valour in difficulties

Grandchildren of late Arthur John Dorman (infra):—
Issue of late Richard Dorman, *b* 1918, *d* 1976: *m* 1947, Diana Keppel, da of late Dr Henry Edward Barrett, of 33 Holland Park, W11:—
PHILIP HENRY KEPPEL (10A Grand Av, Hassocks, W Sussex BN6 8DA), *b* 19 May 1954; *ed* Marlborough, and Univ of St Andrews: *m* 1982 (*m diss* 1992), Myriam Jeanne Georgette, da of late René Bay, of Royan, France, and has issue living, Megan Bay Keppel, *b* 1984. —— Jane Elizabeth Keppel, *b* 1950: *m* 1977, Michael Orr.

The 1st baronet, Sir Arthur John Dorman, KBE, was Founder and Chm of Dorman, Long & Co Ltd, of Middlesbrough. The 2nd, Sir Bedford Lockwood Dorman, CBE, was Dep Chm of N Riding of Yorkshire Quarter Sessions, and Chm of N Riding of Yorkshire War Agricultural Executive Committee.

Doughty-Tichborne, see Tichborne.

DOUGLAS (UK) 1831, of Glenbervie, Kincardine

Sir SHOLTO COURTENAY MACKENZIE DOUGLAS, MC, 5th and last *Baronet*: *d* 1986 (his name never having appeared on the Official Roll of Baronets).

DAUGHTERS LIVING OF FIFTH BARONET

Jean Mackenzie, *b* 1930: *m* 1956 (*m diss* 1968), Capt Brian Joseph Craig, late R Signals, and has issue living, Alastair James Mackenzie, *b* 1960, — Duncan Quinnell Mackenzie *b* 1963. *Residence* – 18 Portland Av, Hove 3. —— Lorna Inga Mackenzie, *b* 1932: *m* 1st, 1955 (*m diss* 1972), James Neil Maclay; 2ndly, 1973, Capt John Edward Homewood, of Trees, Higher Broad Oak Rd, West Hill, Devon EX11 1XJ, and has issue living (by 1st *m*), Mary Christine, *b* 1955.

DOYLE (UK) 1828 (Extinct 1987)

Sir JOHN FRANCIS REGINALD WILLIAM HASTINGS DOYLE, 5th and last *Baronet*; *d* 1987.

DAUGHTER LIVING OF FIFTH BARONET

Sylvia Yolande, *b* 1948. *Residence* – Burnt House Cottage, Bargains Lane, Little Markle, Ledbury, Hereford and Worcester.

SISTER LIVING OF FIFTH BARONET

Margaret Isabella Dorothy Evelyn (*Margaret, Lady Heathcoat-Amory*) *b* 1907: *m* 1933, Col Sir William Heathcoat-Amory, 5th Bt, DSO, KRRC, who *d* 1982. *Residence* – 14 Pomeroy Rd, Tiverton, Devon.

D'OYLY (E) 1663, of Shottisham, Norfolk

Do no ill, quoth Doyle

Sir NIGEL HADLEY MILLER D'OYLY, *b* 6 July 1914; *s* his half-brother, Sir JOHN ROCHFORT, 1986; *ed* Radley, and RMC Sandhurst; formerly Maj R Scots; served 1939-45 War in Hong Kong, France, War Office: *m* 1939, Dolores, who *d* 1971, da of Robert H. Gregory, of New Lodge, Crowhurst, Sussex, and has issue.

Arms – Gules, three bucks' heads cabossed argent. **Crest** – Out of a ducal coronet or, two wings, erect sable bezantée, between which and resting on the strawberry leaf of the coronet an estoile of six points argent.
Residence – New Lodge, Crowhurst, nr Battle, E Sussex TN33 9AB.

SON LIVING

HADLEY GREGORY, *b* 29 May 1956; *ed* Milton Abbey: *m* 1st, 1978 (*m diss* 1982), Margaret Mary Dent; 2ndly, 1991, Annette Frances Elizabeth, yst da of Maj Michael White, of Farnham Royal, Bucks, and has issue living (by 2nd *m*), India Dolores, *b* 1992. *Residence* – Flat B, 37 New North Rd, Islington, N1 6JB.

DAUGHTERS LIVING

Carol Dolores, *b* 1942: *m* 1st, 1961 (*m diss* 1966), Robert Macvarish; 2ndly, 1968, Charles Pearce, and has issue living (by 1st *m*), Simon, *b* 1962, — Robyn, *b* 1964, — (by 2nd *m*) Carl, *b* 1970. *Residence* – New Lodge, Crowhurst, nr Battle, Sussex. —— Sherry Angela (Woodcote, Crowhurst, nr Battle, Sussex), *b* 1946: *m* 1969 (*m diss* 1981), Charles Coxsedge, and has issue living, Benjamin John, *b* 1975, — Hannah Ruth, *b* 1974.

DAUGHTERS LIVING OF THIRTEENTH BARONET

Jill Rochfort, *b* 1931: *m* 1952, George Creighton, of 31 Jalan Kampong Chantek, Singapore, 2158, and has issue living, Glen John, *b* 1953: *m* 1976 (*m diss* 1990), Catherine Heffernan and has issue living, Chay George *b* 1982, Keir James (twin) *b* 1982, Maxine Leah *b* 1979, — Ian Robert, *b* 1960: *m* 1988 (*m diss* 1991), Alexandra Mary Poxon, — Linden Gay, *b* 1954: *m* 1974, Rolf Evans, and has issue living, Scott Jamie *b* 1977, Jacey Samantha *b* 1979. —— Ann Hastings, *b* 1936: *m* 1959, Thomas Hepburn James, of Lambs Farm, Tanyard Lane, Danehill, East Sussex, RH17 7JN, and has issue living, Shona Ann, *b* 1960: *m* 1986 (*m diss* 1994), Simon James Robert Thomas, — Karen Hepburn, *b* 1964: *m* 1987, David Leslie Ashby, — Tiffany Carterette, *b* 1965: *m* 1991, Shaun Dudley Sizen.

COLLATERAL BRANCH LIVING

Issue of late Edward Halliday D'Oyly, son of 10th baronet, *b* 1865, *d* 1957: *m* 1891, Laura, who *d* 19—, da of Herbert George Yatman, formerly of Studley, Wimborne Rd, Bournemouth:—
Mary Edith, *b* 1892. —— Mildred Dorothea, *b* 1893.

Robert d'Ouilly, who came over with William the Conqueror, and was Baron of Hocknorton, in Oxfordshire, in 1071-2, built and fortified Oxford Castle, and was made Constable of Oxford. The 3rd Baron of Hocknorton founded the Abbey of Oseney on an island in the Isis. This family descends from Sir Henry D'Oyly of Pondhall, Sheriff of Suffolk, who *d* 1564. The 1st baronet, Sir William D'Oyly, MP for Norfolk and Yarmouth, a partisan of the royal cause, was knighted, and subsequently created a baronet. Sir William D'Oyly, 2nd baronet, a Teller of the Exchequer, was knighted during the lifetime of his father. Sir John Hadley D'Oyly, 6th baronet, Collector of Calcutta and of the twenty-four Pergunnahs, sat as MP for Ipswich during the trial of his friend Warren Hastings. Sir Charles D'Oyly, 7th Baronet, HEICS, was a distinguished amateur artist. Maj-Gen Sir Charles Walters D'Oyly, 9th baronet, Bengal Army, served in Gwallor Campaign and Indian Campaign 1857.

DRUGHORN (UK) 1922, of Ifield Hall, Ifield, Sussex (Extinct 1943)

Sir JOHN FREDERICK DRUGHORN, 1st and last *Baronet*.

DAUGHTERS LIVING OF FIRST BARONET

Lucienne Frederique, *b* 1893: *m* 1914, Dacre de Jersey Croudace, AIMM, CE, who *d* 1977, and has issue living, John Michael Dacre (Dacredale, Borrowdale, Harare, Zimbabwe) *b* 1928: *m* 1952, Heather Margaret Gilmour, and has issue living, Alistair Michael Dacre *b* 1965, Rosmairi Heather *b* 1954, Caroline Jean *b* 1958, Janette Alison *b* 1962, — William Ian *b* 1931: *m* 1956, Marilyn Patricia Jones, and has issue living, Peter George *b* 1965, Mark Andrew *b* 1969, Deborah Lucienne *b* 1961, — David Brian *b* 1932: *m* 1972, Grace Lily Logan, — Elizabeth Lucienne *b* 1915: *m* 1945, Robert Cherer Smith, of End of Kingsmead Rd, PO Borrowdale, Harare, Zimbabwe, and has issue living, Gareth *b* 1953, Deryn *b* 1946: *m* 1966, Michael James Read, Beulah Joy *b* 1949: *m* 1971, Graham McGuiness, — Margaret Frederique, *b* 1916: *m* 1939, Gerald Alfred O'Reilly, and has issue living, Gerald James *b* 1940: *m* 1966, Marie Fitzgibben, Kevin *b* 1945: *m* 1966, Wendy Bailey, Patrick *b* 1948: *m* 1972, Jennifer Barnard, Anne Bernice *b* 1942: *m* 1970, Manuel Tavares, — Eileen Mary, *b* 1917: *m* 1940, Keith Alistaire Forbes, and has issue living, Brian Alistaire *b* 1942: *m* 1966, Shaughn Watson, Nigel *b* 1950, Jacqueline *b* 1953, — Pamela Denise, *b* 1919: *m* 1942, Lawrence Stanley Rix, and has issue living, Jeremy *b* 1952, Graham *b* 1954, Allan *b* 1957, Molly *b* 1947: *m* 1967, Robin Booth, Patricia *b* 1950: *m* 19—, Michael Toronyi. *Residence* – Dacredale, Borrowdale, Harare, Zimbabwe. —— Maud Frederica, *b* 1897: *m* 1926, Lionel James Berry, BSc,ARIC, and has issue living, Joyce Ann, *b* 1928: *m* 1951, Ronald Lynch, and has issue living, Michael *b* 1953, James *b* 1956, Susan *b* 1958, — Susan Elizabeth Wendy, *b* 1932; ARCM, LRAM.

COLLATERAL BRANCH LIVING

Issue of late John Frederic Drughorn, son of 1st baronet, *b* 1887, *d* 1919: *m* 1914, Marie Elizabeth, who *d* 1943, da of George Newport:—

Marie Frederica Elizabeth, *b* 1915: *m* 1945, Charles F. Hudson. *Residence* – 18 Alexandra Rd, Uckfield, Sussex.

DRYDEN (GB) 1733, of Ambrosden, Oxfordshire; and 1795, of Canons Ashby, Northamptonshire

Sir JOHN STEPHEN GYLES DRYDEN, 11th *Baronet* of 1st and 8th of 2nd creation; *b* 26 Sept 1943; *s* his father, *Sir* NOEL PERCY HUGH, 1970; *ed* The Oratory Sch: *m* 1970, Diana Constance, da of Cyril Tomlinson, of Highland Park, Wellington, NZ, and has issue.

Arms – Azure, a lion rampant, and in chief a sphere between two estoiles or. **Crest** – A demi-lion sustaining in his right paw a sphere as in the arms. *Address* – Spinners, Fairwarp, Uckfield, East Sussex TN22 3BE.

SON LIVING

JOHN FREDERICK SIMON, *b* 26 May 1976.

DAUGHTER LIVING

Caroline Diana Rosamund, *b* 1980.

AUNT LIVING

Evelyn Kate Mary, *b* 1909: *m* 1931, Brig Gerald Ernest Thubron, DSO, OBE, N Stafford Regt, who *d* 1992, and has issue living, Colin Gerald Dryden, *b* 1939; *ed* Eton; FRSL; writer (won Hawthornden Prize for Literature 1987), — Carol Sheena, *b* 1937, *d* 1959, — and an adopted da, Sarah Elizabeth, *b* 1963. *Residence* – Pheasant's Hatch, Piltdown, Sussex.

WIDOW LIVING OF TENTH BARONET

ROSAMUND MARY (*Rosamund, Lady Dryden*) (Spinners Cottage, Fairwarp, Uckfield, Sussex), da of late Stephen Francis Eustace Scrope: *m* 1941, Sir Noel Percy Hugh Dryden, 10th baronet, who *d* 1970.

Sir Erasmus Dryden, Sheriff of Northamptonshire, was created a baronet 1619. One of his grandsons was John Dryden, the celebrated poet. The title became extinct at the death of the 7th baronet in 1770, when the estates devolved upon his niece, who married John Turner, 2nd son of Sir Edward Turner, 2nd baronet of Ambrosden. Mr Turner in 1791 assumed by sign-manual the surname and arms of Dryden only, was knighted 1793, and created a baronet 1795. The 4th baronet, of creation 1795, in 1874 succeeded, as 7th baronet, to the Turner baronetcy, creation 1733.

DUCKWORTH (UK) 1909, of Grosvenor Place, City of Westminster

Perseverance

Sir RICHARD DYCE DUCKWORTH, 3rd *Baronet*; *b* 30 Sept 1918; *s* his father, *Sir* EDWARD DYCE, 1945; *ed* Marlborough Coll; formerly Major RA: *m* 1942, Violet Alison, da of late Lieut-Col George Boothby Wauhope, DSO, of The Mount House, Highclere, Newbury, and has issue.

Arms – Argent: on a chevron engrailed azure, between two leopards' faces in chief and a garb in base sable, three crosses patée or. **Crest** – Upon a mount between two palm branches vert, a garb fesseways or charged with two crosses patée in fesse, and surmounted by a duck sable.
Residence – Dunwood Cottage, Shootash, Romsey, Hants.

SONS LIVING

EDWARD RICHARD DYCE (Holly Cottage, Moreton Paddox, Warwick CV35 9BU), *b* 13 July 1943; *ed* Marlborough, and Cranfield: *m* 1976, Patricia, only da of Thomas Cahill, of 3 Beaulieu Close, Datchet, Berks, and has issue living, James Dyce, *b* 1984, — Helen Dyce, *b* 1987. —— Anthony George Dyce, *b* 1946: *m* 1974, Geraldine, da of Kevin Broderick, of 118 Mount Merrion Ave, Blackrock, co Dublin, and has issue living, Nathaniel James Dyce, *b* 1977.

COLLATERAL BRANCH LIVING

Issue of late Capt Arthur Dyce Duckworth, RN, 3rd son of 1st Bt, *b* 1896, *d* 1973: *m* 1927, Grace Ella Mary, who *d* 1993, da of late Edmund Lionel Pontifex, of Bishopscourt, Broadwater Down, Tunbridge Wells:—

Geoffrey Loraine Dyce, CBE (Weir Cottage, Bickton, Fordingbridge, Hants SP6 2HA), *b* 1930; *ed* Stowe; Brig late RTR; ADC to HM 1982-85, CBE (Mil) 1977: *m* 1961, Philippa Ann, da of Sir (Edward) Percy Rugg, and has issue living, Jeremy Dyce, *b* 1963, — Juliet Ann, *b* 1964: *m* 1992 Christopher Brian Davidson Smith. —— Rosemary Margaret Dyce, *b* 1931: *m* 1957, Brig Athelwold Colin Devereux Watts, late Army Air Corps, of Shearings, Rockbourne, Fordingbridge, Hants, SP6 3NA, and has issue living, Andrew Colin Iremonger, *b* 1960: *m* 1987, Katherine Gooch, and has issue living, Jonathon *b* 1991, Jessica *b* 1990, — Nigel John Iremonger, *b* 1962: *m* 1988, Helen Debney, and has issue living, Matthew *b* 1991, Daniel *b* 1993, — Caroline Susan Devereux, *b* 1958: *m* 1979, Gordon Montgomery, and has issue living, Duncan *b* 1982, Alistair *b* 1989, Jenna *b* 1984, — Kay Rosemary Devereux, *b* 1963: *m* 1988, Hugh Fox, of Wakes Colne, Essex, and has issue living, Jamie *b* 1991, Jonathan *b* 1992, Toby *b* 1994.
The 1st baronet, Sir Dyce Duckworth, MD, LLD, was an eminent physician, Treasurer, Roy Coll of Physicians 1884-1923, Pres of Clinical Soc of London 1891-3, and Hon Physician to King Edward VII, when Prince of Wales 1890-1901. The 2nd baronet, Sir Edward Dyce was a Puisne Judge of High Court of Burma 1924-27.

Duckworth-King, see King.

DU CROS (UK) 1916, of Canons, Middlesex

Sir CLAUDE PHILIP ARTHUR MALLET DU CROS, 3rd *Baronet*; *b* 27 Dec 1922; *s* his father, *Capt Sir* PHILIP HARVEY, 1975, formerly Capt WG: *m* 1st, 1953 (*m diss* 1974), Christine Nancy, who *d* 1968, da of late F. E. Bennett, of Spilsby, Lincs, and formerly wife of George Tordoff; 2ndly, 1974 (*m diss* 1982), Margaret Roy, da of late Roland James Frater, of Gosforth, Northumberland, and has issue by 1st *m*.

Arms – Quarterly; 1st vert, a greyhound courant argent in chief a crescent or; 2nd azure, an eastern crown or; 3rd azure, within the horns of a crescent a heart in chief argent; 4th azure, a saltire or, and on an escutcheon argent, a rose gules, stalked and leaved vert. **Crest** – Out of an eastern crown or, a demi greyhound sable.
Residence – Longmeadow, Ballaugh Glen, Ramsey, I of Man. *Clubs* – Carlton, Guards'.

SON LIVING (By 1st marriage)

JULIAN CLAUDE ARTHUR MALLET, *b* 23 April 1955; *ed* Eton: *m* 1984, Patricia M., only da of Gerald A. Wyatt, of Littlefield School, Liphook, Hants, and has issue living, Alexander Julian Mallet, *b* 25 Aug 1990, — Henrietta Mary, *b* 1988.

SISTERS LIVING

Edome Dita Mallet (Quita Pena, Hinton St George, Somerset), *b* 1924. —— Primrose Millicent Elaine Mallet, *b* 1938; assumed by deed poll the surname MALLET-HARRIS upon marriage; FLS, the botanical artist: *m* 1978, James Gordon Shute Harris, of Mallet Court, Curry Mallet Somerset (*see* B Airedale).
The 1st baronet, Sir Arthur du Cros (son of late (William) Harvey du Cros, JP, formerly MP for Hastings), was Founder and sometime Chm and Pres of Dunlop Rubber Co Ltd, and Founder, with his father, of Pneumatic Tyre Industry, a Pioneer of Rubber Growing Industry, and a Founder of Junior Imperial League, and first Chm of its Committee. He initiated Motor

Ambulance Movement during European War 1914-19, and sat as MP for Hastings (C) 1908-18, and for Clapham Div of Wandsworth 1918-22.

Dudley-Williams, see Williams.

Duff-Gordon, see Gordon.

DUGDALE (UK) 1936, of Merevale and Blyth, co Warwick

Sloth is the plague of one's country.

Sir WILLIAM STRATFORD DUGDALE, CBE, MC, 2nd *Baronet*; *b* 29 March 1922; *s* his father, *Sir* WILLIAM FRANCIS STRATFORD, 1965; *ed* Eton, and Balliol Coll, Oxford; a JP and DL of Warwicks (High Sheriff 1971-72); Solicitor 1949; 1939-45 War as Capt Grenadier Gds in N Africa and Italy (despatches, MC); Chm Nat Water Council 1982-83; CBE (1982): *m* 1st, 1952, Lady Belinda Pleydell-Bouverie, who *d* 1961, da of 7th Earl of Radnor; 2ndly, 1967, Cecilia Mary, da of Sir William Malcolm Mount, 2nd Bt, and has issue by 1st and 2nd *m*.

Arms – Quarterly; 1st and 4th argent a cross moline gules, charged in the centre with a Garter King of Arms, coronet or, and in the 1st quarter a torteau; 2nd and 3rd, barry of ten argent and azure, over all a lion rampant gules. **Crest** – A Griffin's head, wings endorsed or, gorged with a coronet as in the arms.
Seat – Merevale Hall, Atherstone, Warwickshire.
Residences – Blyth Hall, Coleshill, Birmingham; 24 Bryanston Mews West, W1H 7FR. *Clubs* – White's, Brooks's, Jockey.

SONS LIVING *(By 1st marriage)*

(WILLIAM) MATTHEW (STRATFORD), *b* 22 Feb 1959: *m* 1990, Paige Sullivan, da of late Thomas Haines Dudley Perkins, and has issue living, William Stratford, *b* 15 Aug 1992, — Clementine Alexandra Louise, *b* 1991, — Fernanda Elizabeth Grace, *b* 1994. *Residence* – The Gatehouse, Merevale Lane, Atherstone, Warwicks CV9 2LA.

(By 2nd marriage)

Thomas Joshua Stratford, *b* 1974.

DAUGHTERS LIVING *(By 1st marriage)*

Laura (*Hon Mrs Arthur Hazlerigg*), *b* 1953: *m* 1986, Hon Arthur Grey Hazlerigg, only son of 2nd Baron Hazlerigg. — Matilda, *b* 1955: *m* 1989, Marcus May, son of Col R. K. May, of Cairn House, Warwick Bridge, Carlisle, Cumbria. — Charlotte (*Hon Mrs Gerard Noel*), *b* (twin) 1955: *m* 1985, Hon Gerard Edward Joseph Noel, 2nd son of 5th Earl of Gainsborough.

(By 2nd marriage)

Adelaide Margaret Victoria Jane, *b* 1970.

BROTHER LIVING

Sir John Robert Stratford, KCVO (Tickwood Hall, Much Wenlock, Shropshire TF13 6NZ; Brooks's, and White's Clubs), *b* 1923; *ed* Eton, and Ch Ch, Oxford; Lord-Lieut of Shropshire 1975-94; *cr* KCVO 1994: *m* 1956, Kathryn Edith Helen, DCVO, da of late Rt Hon Oliver Frederick George Stanley, MC, MP (*see* E Derby, colls), and has issue living, Edward Stratford, *b* 1959, — Henry Stratford (122 St Stephen's Av, W12), *b* 1963: *m* 1991, Adi Litia Cakobau Mara, da of the President of Fiji and Paramount Chief of Lau, and Adi Lady Lala Mara, Paramount Chief of Rewa, and has issue living, a son *b* 1993, — Elizabeth Alice, *b* 1957, — Mary, *b* 1961.

SISTERS LIVING

Susan: *m* 1950, Timothy Neil Hughes-Onslow, of 32 Godfrey St, SW3 (*see* E Onslow, colls). — Judith Margaret: *m* 1952, Maj John Evelyn Shirley, KRRC (ret), of Ettington Park, Stratford-on-Avon (*see* E Ferrers, colls).
The present baronet is descended from Sir William Dugdale, Garter King of Arms 1677-86, and author of *Monasticon Anglicanum* and *Baronage of England*, who *d* 1686. Richard Geast, maternal nephew of John Dugdale of Blyth, Mowbray Herald Extraordinary, having inherited Blyth Hall, assumed by Royal Licence 1799 the surname and arms of Dugdale. His wife, Penelope Bate, was the el da of co-heir of Francis Stratford of Merevale Hall, Warwicks, which was inherited by their son, Dugdale Stratford Dugdale, great-grandfather of 1st baronet.

DUNBAR (NS) 1694, of Mochrum, Wigtownshire

Sir JEAN IVOR DUNBAR, 13th *Baronet*; *b* 4 April 1918; *s* his father, *Sir* ADRIAN IVOR, 1977; late Sgt Mountain Engineers, USA Army: *m* 1st, 1944 (*m diss* 1979), Rose Jeanne, da of Henry William Hertsch; 2ndly, 1987 (*m diss* 1988), Mrs Vivianna Patricia Arrow de Blonville, da of Ernest Bloomfield, and formerly wife of (i) Francesco Enea, and Herman Arrow, and has issue by 1st *m*. Sir Jean Dunbar *d* Aug 1993.

Arms – Gules, a lion rampant argent, armed and langued azure, within a bordure of the second charged with eight roses of the first, barbed and seeded vert, in a dexter canton argent a saltire azure, surmounted of an inescutcheon charged with a lion rampant gules within a double tressure flory counterflory gules. Crest – A horse's head argent, bridled and reined gules. Supporters – Two white doves imperially crowned proper.
Seat – Mochrum Park, Kirkcowan, Wigtownshire. *Residence* – .

SONS LIVING *(By 1st marriage)*

JAMES MICHAEL, *b* 17 Jan 1950; Capt USAF: *m* 1978, Margaret Jacobs and has issue living, Michael Joseph, *b* 5 July 1980,, — David Scott, *b* 1983,, — Stacy Beth, *b* 1985,, — Cassandra Talbot, *b* 1991,. —— Dennis William, *b* 1952.

DAUGHTER LIVING *(By 1st marriage)*

Anne Marie, *b* 1946: *m* 19—,. —— Bickauskas.

HALF-BROTHERS LIVING

Rowland Adrian (1 Sandhurst Av, Cullercoats, Tyne and Wear), *b* 1934; late US Med Corps: *m* 1957, Janet Lockhart, da of George Heron, of Newton Stewart, Wigtownshire, and has issue living, Mary Naomi, *b* 1958: *m* 1983, Edward Thomas Lisle, and has issue living, Scott *b* 1988, Sarah Elizabeth *b* 1985, Joanna Marie *b* 1986, — Sylvia Katharine, *b* 1960: *m* 1984, Derek Graham, and has issue living, Ross Christopher *b* 1985, David Adrian *b* 1989, Laura Marie *b* 1987, — Shonna Janet, *b* 1962. —— Donald Robert (51 Judith Av, Knodishall, Saxmundham, Suffolk), *b* 1936; formerly Senior Master Sgt US AF, and US Army Med Corps: *m* 1st, 1957, Marie F., da of Douglas Allen, of Newtown Stewart, Wigtownshire; 2ndly, 1963, Susan Elizabeth May, da of William Radden Gates, and has issue living (by 1st *m*), Allan William, *b* 1958, — Roseanne, *b* 1960, — (by 2nd *m*), David Wayne, *b* 1966, — Linda Carol, *b* 1969.

DAUGHTERS LIVING OF ELEVENTH BARONET

Joyce Marguerite, *b* 1912. —— Vida Mary, *b* 1916. *Residence* – 69 Grandison Road, Battersea, SW11.

COLLATERAL BRANCHES LIVING

Issue of late William Uthred Dunbar, brother of 12th baronet, *b* 1902, *d* 19—: *m* 1924, Theresa Rose Della, who *d* 19—, da of Jerome Cole:—
William Thomas, *b* 1925: *m* 19—.

Grandsons of late Richard Taylor Dunbar, el son of Lt-Col Thomas Clement Dunbar, 4th son of James Dunbar, yr son of 5th baronet:—
Issue of late Lt-Col William Henry George Dunbar of Kilconzie, OBE, TD, *b* 1893 (legitimated in terms of Legitimation (Scotland) Act 1968, and in remainder to baronetcy); unsuccessfully petitioned Lord Lyon to *s* to baronetcy 1984; author of *Dunbars' 1000 Years*; *d* 1987: *m* 1st, 1917, Stella Kathleen, who *d* 1941 as the result of enemy action, da of Henry Underdown, of Dover; 2ndly, 1941, Joan Marguerite, who *d* 1966, da of Capt Sydney Church Leopard, TD, RAMC, of Eastbourne, Midhurst, Sussex; 3rdly 1967, Irene Mary (Greenways, Oxenden Sq, Herne Bay, Kent CT6 8TW), da of Charles Edwin Frith, of Weeley, Essex:—
(By 1st *m*) Graham William DUNBAR OF KILCONZIE, *b* 1920: *m* 1955, Alice Louise, da of Joseph Lollee, of Stolzenberg, Uzwill, St Gall, Switzerland, and has issue living, Andrew William, Younger of Kilconzie (Doorfstrasse 19, 4222 Zwingen, Basel, Switzerland), *b* 1961; BSc, — Janet Marjorie (Moosmühle Strasse 20, 9112 Schachen, Herisau, Switzerland), *b* 1964. *Residence* – 4 Gibbs Close, Cheshunt, Herts EN8 9RX.
Issue of late Richard John Victor Michael Dunbar, *b* 1897 (legitimated in terms of Legitimation (Scotland) Act 1968, and in remainder to baronetcy), *d* 1983: *m* 1932, Daffodil Helen (14 Voltaire Court, Ennerdale Rd, Richmond, Surrey TW9 3PQ), only da of late Rev Eardley Wilmot Michell, V of Bolney, Sussex:—
Gavin Cospatric Michell, RD (Summer Place, Loddon Drive, Wargrave, Berks) *b* 1936; *ed* St Catharine's Coll, Camb (MA); Cdr RNR: *m* 1960, Jean, only da of Dr Roy Kemball Price, of Hove, Sussex, and has issue living, Emma Claire, *b* 1961, — Katrina Michelle, *b* 1964, — Lisa Carol, *b* 1966. —— David Randolph Michell, FCA, (The Hermitage, 193 Lower Road, Great Bookham, Surrey), *b* 1938: *m* 1965, Brenda, yr da of Maurice W. Mitchell, of Ashstead, Surrey, and has issue living, James Stuart Michell, *b* 1967, — Struan Gordon David, *b* 1970.
The present baronet is descended from the Dunbars, the ancient Earls of March and Moray, and is the lineal male representative of the heritable Sheriffs of Elgin and Forres, and chief of that name. Alexander Dunbar, Younger of Conzie, obtained Mochrum by marriage in 1564. The 1st Baronet had a Charter, under the great seal, of the lands and barony of Mochrum in 1677, and was *cr* a Baronet with a grant of supporters on his coat of arms. The 3rd baronet was Judge-Advocate for Scotland. Sir William, 7th baronet, sat as MP for Wigton Burghs (*L*) 1857-65, was successively a Lord of the Treasury, Keeper of the Privy Seal to HRH the Prince of Wales, Keeper of the Great Seal to HRH in Scotland, one of the Council to HRH, and Comptroller-Gen of the Exchequer, and Auditor-Gen of Public Accounts. The 9th baronet, Sir William Cospatrick Dunbar, CB, was Assist Under-Sec for Scotland 1885-1902, and Registrar-Gen for England and Wales 1902-9. The 10th baronet, Sir James George Hawker Rowland, *d* 23 Jan 1953, and the 11th baronet, Sir Richard Sutherland, *d* 25 Jan 1953.

DUNBAR (NS) 1698, of Durn, Banffshire

SPES DABIC AUXILIUM

Hope will give aid

Sir DRUMMOND COSPATRICK NINIAN DUNBAR, MC, 9th *Baronet*; *b* 9 May 1917; *s* his father, *Sir* GEORGE ALEXANDER DRUMMOND, 1949; *ed* Radley, and Worcester Coll, Oxford (BA 1938); Major (ret) Black Watch; European War 1939-45 in Middle East, N Africa, Sicily, and Normandy (twice wounded, MC): *m* 1957, Sheila Barbara Mary, da of John Berkeley de Fonblanque, and has issue.

Arms – Quarterly; 1st and 4th, gules, a lion rampant within a bordure argent, charged with eight roses of the first barbed and seeded vert; 2nd and 3rd, or, three cushions within the royal tressure gules, all within a bordure nebuly, quartered azure and gules. **Crest** – Two sprigs of laurel in saltire proper. *Residence* – Town Hill, Westmount, Jersey, CI. *Club* – Naval and Military.

SON LIVING

ROBERT DRUMMOND COSPATRICK, Younger of Durn, *b* 17 June 1958; *ed* Harrow, and Ch Ch, Oxford: *m* 1994, Sarah, da of Robert Brooks, of Hattingley, Hants.

COLLATERAL BRANCHES LIVING

Grandchildren of late Hugh Stephen Dunbar, 3rd son of 7th baronet:—
Issue of late Uthred Ninian Vere Dunbar, *b* 1910, *d* 1977: *m* 1942, Susan Kathleen, da of Arthur George Thompson:—
Stephen Bruce, *b* 1949. —— Eleanor Lynne, *b* 1947.
Issue of late William Hancorn Vere Dunbar *b* 1912, *d* 1984: *m* 1936, Dorothy Christobel, da of James Smith Gow:—
Coral Lisette, *b* 1939: *m* 1964, Henry William Walker, and has issue living, Gordon Henry *b* 1965.
Issue of late Aldred Cospatrick Dunbar, *b* 1916, *d* 1971: *m* 1940, Isidoris Elliott, who *d* 1986, da of Maj William Harrison:—
Raymond Robert, *b* 1943.
Issue of late Robert Fyfe Dunbar, *b* 1920, *d* 1991: *m* 1941, Eileen May (33 Julia Rd, Overport, Durban, Natal, S Africa), da of Frederick Locke:—
George Drummond, *b* 1957: *m* 1990, Lydia, da of Gawie Grobbelaar, and has issue living, Merissa Anne, *b* 1992. —— Beverley Anne, *b* 1946: *m* 1974, John Derek Walters, who *d* 1992. —— Gail Elizabeth, *b* 1953: *m* 1976, Patrick Murphy. —— Dianne Roberta, *b* 1959: *m* 1991, Peter Riddle, of Oxon, and has issue living, Robert Adam, *b* 1992.

Issue of late Patrick Martin Borlase Dunbar, 4th son of 7th baronet, *b* 1884, *d* 1925: *m* 1924, Mary who *d* 1983, el da of late Claude F. Shoolbred, of Greenstead Hall, Halstead, Essex:—
Patricia Martin *b* (*posthumous*) 1926: *m* 1951, William Harold Groves, and has issue living, Martin Westley, *b* 1960, — James Arthur, *b* 1967. *Residence* – 2 Cumberland Av, Vandia Grove, Randburg, Johannesburg, Transvaal, S Africa.
This family is lineally descended from James, 4th Earl of Moray, by Isabel Innes, and so from John, 1st Earl of Moray (3rd creation 1371-3), who *m* Marjorie, da of Robert II, King of Scots (first of the Stewart Kings), and was brother of George, 10th Earl of Dunbar and uncle of 11th and last of the ancient Earls of Dunbar, whose line was founded by Gospatric, Earl of Northumberland (see following article), grandson of Elgitha, da of Ethelred II, King of England. The Baronetcy was created with remainder to the heirs male of the body of the grantee and their heirs male for ever.

DUNBAR (NS) 1700, of Northfield, Moray

Vigilance strengthens hope

VIGILANTIA ROBORAT

Sir ARCHIBALD RANULPH DUNBAR, 11th *Baronet*; *b* 8 Aug 1927; *s* his father, *Maj Sir* (ARCHIBALD) EDWARD, MC, 1969; *ed* Wellington, Pembroke Coll, Camb, and Imp Coll of Tropical Agric, Trinidad; late Agric Officer, Uganda Civil Ser, and HMOCS: *m* 1974, Amelia Millar Sommerville, da of late Horace Campbell Davidson, of 10 Forth View Cres, Currie, Midlothian, and has issue.

Arms – Quarterly: 1st and 4th, gules, a lion rampant argent within a bordure of the last charged with eight roses of the field, *Dunbar*; 2nd and 3rd, or three cushions within the royal tressure gules, *Ranulph*; all within a bordure quartered azure and of the first. **Crest** – A dexter hand apaumée reaching at an astral crown proper. *Residence* – The Old Manse, Duffus, Elgin IV30 2QD.

SON LIVING

EDWARD HORACE, *b* 18 March 1977.

DAUGHTERS LIVING

Harriet Sophie, *b* 1974. —— Stephanie Clare, *b* 1975.

BROTHER LIVING

Alexander Arbuthnott (Pitgaveny, Elgin, Moray), *b* 1929; *ed* Wellington Coll, and Pembroke Coll, Camb; Bar, Inner Temple, 1953: *m* 1965, Elizabeth Susannah, da of Rev Edward Denzil Chetwood Wright, of Brattleby House, Brattleby, Lincs (see Strickland-Constable, Bt, colls, 1985 Edn), and has issue living, Crinan James, *b* 1965, — Clodagh Rebecca Helen, *b* 1968.

This family is paternally descended in direct male line (through John Dunbar, Earl of Moray, by his wife, Marjorie, da of Robert II) from Gospatric, Earl of Northumberland (see preceding article) in right of his mother Ealdgyth, grandda of Ethelred II, King of England. He had from his cousin, Malcolm III, son of Duncan I, a grant of Dunbar in 1072. Earl Gospatric's father, Maldred, King of Cumbria, was younger brother of Duncan I, who became King of Scots in right of his mother, Bethoc, wife of Crinan the Thane (married *circa* 1000), el da and heir of Malcolm II, King of Scots. The 1st baronet, 4th Laird of Hempriggs, died without male issue, when the baronetcy (with remainder to his heirs male whatsoever) devolved upon his brother. The 3rd baronet *d* in 1763, and his cousin Alexander Dunbar of Northfield (descendant of the 2nd Laird of Hempriggs), was served heir-male, 1776 by the Lord Lyon, who directed him to continue the designation of Northfield.

DUNBAR (NS) 1706, of Hempriggs, Caithness-shire

Dame MAUREEN DAISY HELEN DUNBAR OF HEMPRIGGS (*Lady Dunbar of Hempriggs*), *Baroness*, da of late Courtenay Edward Moore, el son of late Jessie Mona Duff (who *m* Rev Canon Courtenay Moore), da of *de jure* 5th baronet; *b* 19 Aug 1906; *s* her kinsman, *Sir* GEORGE COSPATRICK Duff-Sutherland-Dunbar, 1963 (succession recognized by Lyon Court 1965); assumed the name of Dunbar 1963, and recognized in the name of Dunbar of Hempriggs by Lyon Court 1965: *m* 1940, Leonard James Blake, who *d* 1989, former Dir of Music, Malvern Coll, and has issue.

Arms – Quarterly: 1st gules, a lion rampant within a bordure argent, charged with eight roses of the field, *Dunbar*; 2nd, gules, three mullets or, a crescent of the last for difference, *Sutherland*; 3rd vert, on a fesse dancettée ermine between a buck's head cabossed in chief and two escallops in base or, a mullet of the first for difference, *Duff*; 4th, or, three cushions within a double tressure flory counter-flory gules. *Randolph*; all within a bordure vairy or and gules. **Crest** – A key and sword in saltire proper. **Supporters** – *Dexter*, a lion rampant argent; *sinister*, a savage man holding a baton over his shoulder proper. *Residences* – 51 Gloucester St, Winchcombe, Cheltenham; Ackergill, Wick, Caithness.

SON LIVING

RICHARD FRANCIS Dunbar of Hempriggs, younger (712 Crossway Rd, Burlingame, Cal 94101, USA), *b* 8 Jan 1945: *m* 1969, (Elizabeth Margaret) Jane, only da of George Lister, of Gloucester, and has issue living, Emma Katherine, *b* 1977, — Fiona Blake, *b* 1981.

DAUGHTER LIVING

Eleanor Margaret DUNBAR, *b* 1949: *m* 1st, 1973 (*m diss* 1987), David C. Eldridge; 2ndly, 1989, Michael Constable, and has issue living, (by 1st husband) Hannah Louise, *b* 1980, — (by 2nd husband) Thomas Matthew Dunbar, *b* 1987.

COLLATERAL BRANCHES LIVING   (*Males and females in remainder*)

Grandchildren of Jessie Mona Duff (who *m* 1869, Rev Canon Courtenay Moore), da of *de jure* 5th Bt:—
Issue of late Harriet Emma Moore, *b* 1874, *d* 1957: *m* 1909, Lieut-Col Hubert Bernard Tonson Rye, DSO, who *d* 1950, formerly Roy Munster Fusiliers (Dancer, Bt):—
Eudo John *b* 1910; formerly Maj Duke of Cornwall's LI: *m* 1940, Rosemary Hilda, da of late Maj Guy Hughes, XIIth Bengal Cav, and has issue living, Rohaise Harriet Julia, *b* 1942: *m* 1966, Christopher Thomas-Everard, of Broford Farm, Dulverton, Som, and has issue living, Guy Richard *b* 1969, Lucilla Damaris Mary *b* 1966, Adella Jessie Bridget *b* 1974, — Caroline Mary Georgina, *b* 1947, — Amarylde Louise, *b* 1950: *m* 1972, Richard Peter Eliot.
Issue of late Jessie Louisa Rickard (who resumed that surname 1916), *b* 1876, *d* 1963: *m* 1st, 1901, Robert Dudley Innes Ackland, of Boulston, Pembrokeshire; 2ndly, 1908, Lieut-Col Victor George Howard Rickard, Roy Munster Fusiliers, who was *ka* 1915; 3rdly, 1916 (*m diss* 1935), Lieut-Col Tudor Fitzjohn, DSO (formerly Worcestershire Regt):—
(By 2nd marriage) Justin Victor (Swiftsden Farm, Hurst Green, Sussex), *b* 1913: *m* 1939, Joan, da of late Alexander William Haig, of Henley-on-Thames, and has issue living, Alexander, *b* 1944, — Catherine, *b* 1949, — Patricia, *b* 1955.

Granddaughter of Gen Sir Beauchamp Duff, GCB, GCSI, KCVO, CIE, son of Garden William Duff, next brother of *de jure* 5th Bt:—
Issue of late Douglas Garden Duff, OBE, *b* 1886, *d* 1968: *m* 1914, Margaret Crawley, who *d* 1970, da of late J. E. Vincent:—
Margaret Jean, *b* 1919: *m* 1st, 1943 (*m diss* 1947), René Dorval, of Montreal, Canada; 2ndly, 1957, Percy Mansfield Scaddan, of Flat 6, Priory Walk, 73-75 Staines Rd East, Sunbury, Middx, and has issue living, (by 1st *m*) Marie Margaret Diane, *b* 1943: *m* 1964, Henry Robert Denholm Hallam, of Dunblane, 284 Staines Rd East, Sunbury on Thames, Middx, and has two adopted children, Alison Jeanette *b* 1966, Paul Ian Douglas *b* 1969.

Descendants of Louisa Alice Duff, da of Robert George Duff, brother of *de jure* 5th Bt, *b* 1853 *d* 1926: *m* 1876, 3rd Baron Vivian, who *d* 1893:—
See B Vivian.

Granddaughters of late Col James Duff of Knockleith, yst brother of *de jure* 5th Bt:—
Issue of the late Rev Canon Garden Llanoe Duff, *b* 1858, *d* 1938: *m* 1885, Elizabeth, who *d* 1944, da of Andrew Anderson Dunlop, younger of Keppoch:—
Kathleen Jane (St Katharine's Convent, Parmoor, Henley-on-Thames), *b* 1891. —— Helen Mary (St Katharine's Convent, Parmoor, Henley-on-Thames), *b* 1894.

Grandchildren of late James Duff Duff (infra):—
Issue of late Maj-Gen Alan Colquhoun Duff, CB, OBE, MC, *b* 1896, *d* 1973: *m* 1935, Diana Frances (Rider's Croft, Little Chesterford, Essex), el da of late Col Richard Parry Crawley, DSO, OBE, MVO:—

James Richard Valentine (1 Tan y Berllan, Deganwy, Gwynedd LL31 9RD), *b* 1941: *m* 1973, Helen Jolliffe, and has issue living, James Lindsey Alan, *b* 1975. —— Lindsay Margaret, *b* 1937: *m* 1st, 1959 (*m diss* 1972), Stephen Francis Robertson; 2ndly, 1972, Colin M. Carden, of 21 Pinewood Drive, Horning, Norfolk NR12 8L2, and has issue living, (by 1st *m*) Patrick John, *b* 1962, — Penelope Ann *b* 1964, — (by 2nd *m*) Charles Anthony, *b* 1973, — David Henry, *b* 1976. —— Christian Frances (12 Pine Tree Grove, Middleton St George, Darlington DL2 1AG), *b* 1942.

       Grandchildren of late Col James Duff of Knockleith (ante):—
         Issue of late James Duff Duff, *b* 1860, *d* 1940: *m* 1895, Laura Eleanor, da of Sir William Fitzwilliam Lenox-
           Conyngham, KCB:—
Mary Geraldine (The Hope Nursing Home, Brooklands Av, Cambridge), *b* 1904. —— Hester Laura Elisabeth, *b* 1912. *Residence* – 12 Pine Tree Grove, Middleton St George, Darlington DL2 1AG.

       Grandson of late Adm Sir Alexander Ludovic Duff, GCB, GBE, KCVO, 4th son of Col James Duff of
         Knockleith (ante):—
         Issue of late Helen Douglas, *b* 1887, *d* 1978: *m* 1923, Lt-Cdr Edgar Dolphin, DSO, RN:—
Peter Western (Stable Cottage, Speen Lane, Newbury, Berks RG13 1RJ), *b* 1924; Lt-Cdr RN (ret): *m* 1st, 1948 (*m diss* 1953), Anne Marion Galbraith; 2ndly, 1955, Margaret Sally, da of Cdr Patrick Rycroft Maurice, OBE, RN (ret), and has issue living (by 2nd *m*), Mark Patrick, *b* 1958: *m* 19—, Kirstie Leyland-Naylor, and has issue living, Tristan Ross *b* 1985, Kylie *b* 1987, — Jane Douglas, *b* 1957: *m* 1988, Anthony Julian Bellmont, and has issue living, Jack Robert *b* 1990, Thomas Patrick *b* 1992, — Sarah Katherine, *b* 1962: *m* 1986, Peter James McLaverty, and had issue living, Christopher *b* 1988.

       Grandsons of late Dorothy Alexandra Duff (*Lady James*), OBE, da of late Adm Sir Alexander Ludovic Duff,
         GCB, GBE, KCVO, (ante):—
         Issue of late Capt Christopher Alexander James, RN, *b* 1916, *d* 1969: *m* 1938, Cynthia, who *d* 1971, da of late
           Douglas Swire (E Glasgow, colls):—
Julian Alexander Ludovic (The Lodge, St Aubyns, Rottingdean, Brighton, BN2 7GA), *b* 1939: *m* 1965, Hilary, da of Thomas Browne, of Puddletown, Dorset, and has issue living, Christopher Mark William, *b* 1967, — David Hugh Geoffrey, *b* 1969, — Andrew Michael Richard, *b* 1976. —— David Robin Millais JAMES-DUFF (Hatton Castle, Turriff, Aberdeenshire), *b* 1945; assumed by deed poll, 1963, the additional surname of Duff after his patronymic: *m* 1st, 1970, Monica, da of Thomas Browne, of Puddletown, Dorset; 2ndly, 19—, Jayne, da of James Bryce, of Coupar Angus, Perthshire, and has issue living, (by 1st *m*) Rory Thomas, *b* 1978, — Fiona Louise, *b* 1971, — Tania Robin, *b* 1973, — Nicola Mary, *b* 1980, — (by 2nd *m*) Gardie William Beauchamp, *b* 1993. —— Simon Christopher (20 Delvino Rd, SW6), *b* 1946: *m* 1975, Anna Catherine, da of late Col William Burleigh Shine, of Englemere Lodge, Ascot, Berks.

       Grandsons of late Rev Charles Edmund Duff son of late Col James Duff of Knockleith (ante):—
         Issue of late Capt Ian Archibald James Duff, MC, *b* 1895, *d* 1949: *m* 1916, Kathleen Frances, who *d* 1932, da of
           Patrick Vernon Chinnery Haldane:—
Patrick Charles, *b* 1920. —— Alexander Ian, *b* 1922.

       Granddaughters of late Col James Duff of Knockleith (ante):—
         Issue of late John Duff, *b* 1864, *d* 1936: *m* 1st, 1897, Constance Evelina Pratt, who *d* 1898; 2ndly, 1904, Lily Clough,
           who *d* 1905:—
(By 1st *m*) Evelina Frances Helen (1048, Ripple Av, Pacific Grove, Cal 93950, USA), *b* 1898. —— (By 2nd *m*) Lily Katharine, *b* 1905. *Residence* – 26 Matham Rd, East Molesey, Surrey.
This Nova Scotia Baronetcy was conferred with remainder to *heirs whatsoever*, ie, it can be and has been inherited through or by a female representative of the family. The 1st Bt, Hon James Sutherland, advocate, 2nd son of 2nd Lord Duffus *m* Elizabeth, da and ultimate heiress of Sir William Dunbar of Hempriggs, 1st Bt (*cr* 1700) (Dunbar, Bt, of Northfield) whose surname and arms he assumed. The 3rd Baronet assumed the title of Lord Duffus as heir male of the body and *d* 1843, leaving an only son, the 4th Baronet, who did not claim the Peerage title. After the death in 1875 of Sir George Dunbar, 4th Bt the male issue of the 1st Bt became ext, and the Baronetcy devolved on Capt (Sir) Benjamin Duff, *de jure* 5th Bt (son of his sister Louisa, who married, 1805, Garden Duff of Hatton, Aberdeenshire), but he did not prove his right to the title. Sir George Duff-Sutherland-Dunbar, grandson of the *de jure* 5th Bt, who assumed the additional surnames of Sutherland-Dunbar on succeeding to the Hempriggs and Ackergill estate, established his right as 6th Bt at Lyon Court 1899. His son Sir George Cospatrick Duff-Sutherland-Dunbar, 7th Bt, *d* 1963, and was *s* by Dame Maureen Daisy Helen Dunbar, granddaughter of Jessie Mona (who *m* 1869 Rev Canon Courtenay Moore), da of *de jure* 5th Bt and established her right as Baronetess at Lyon Court 1965.

HOPE-DUNBAR (NS) 1664, of Baldoon

The more prepared, the more powerful

Sir DAVID HOPE-DUNBAR, 8th *Baronet, b* 13 July 1941; *s* his father, *Major Sir* BASIL DOUGLAS, 1961; *ed* Eton, and Roy Agric Coll, Cirencester; ARICS: *m* 1971, Kathleen Ruth, yr da of late J. Timothy Kenrick, of Birmingham, and has issue.

Arms – Quarterly, 1st, gules, a lion rampant argent, armed and langued azure, a bordure of the second charged with ten roses, of the field, barbed and seeded vert, *Dunbar*; 2nd, azure, on a chevron or betwen three bezants a bay leaf slipped veret, a mullet of the second in chief for difference, *Hope*; 3rd, argent, a man's heart imperially crowned proper, on a chief azure three mullets of the field, *Douglas*; 4th counter-quartered, 1st and 4th gules, three cinquefoils ermine, 2nd and 3rd, argent, a lymphad sails furled, sable, flagged gules, *Hamilton*. **Crest** – A horse's head couped argent, bridled gules. **Supporters** – Two lions rampant guardant argent, armed and langued gules, each holding in one of the forepaws a rose slipped proper. *Residence* – Banks House, Kirkcudbright.

SON LIVING

CHARLES, *b* 11 March 1975.

DAUGHTERS LIVING

Philippa, *b* 1973. —— Juliet Antonia, *b* 1976.

COLLATERAL BRANCHES LIVING (*Males and females in remainder*)

Grandchildren of late Helen Jacqueline Hope (Mrs Alan Burns), MBE, sister of 6th baronet:—

Issue of late Lt-Col John Alan Burns, *b* 1905, *d* 1987: *m* 1944, Joyce Margaret (Fairfield, 9 Cole Rd, Bruton, Som), da of G.A.B. August, of Bedford:—

Felicity Margaret, *b* 1945: *m* 1974, Francis Michael Morton Peto, of Cowdenknowes Mains, Earlston, Berwickshire (*see* Peto, Bt, *cr* 1855). —— Marion Jacqueline, *b* 1948: *m* 1968, Lt-Col Peter Guy Chamberlin, R Green Jackets, of Coldharbour House, St Mary Bourne, nr Andover, Hants, and has issue living, Edward Alan, *b* 1974, — Lucinda Geraldine, *b* 1970, — Vanessa Louise, *b* 1977.

Issue of late Charles Hope Burns, *b* 1912, *d* 1958: *m* 1949, Barbara Delscey (16 Sinclair St, Milngavie, Glasgow), da of late Dr E. Macmillan, of Pretoria, S Africa:—

Geoffrey Douglas Charles, *b* 1954: *m* 1980, Celia, da of Guy Kynaston of Croxdalewood, Co Durham, and has issue living, Kirstin, *b* 1981, — Phebe, *b* 1985, — Shiona, *b* 1988. —— Delscey Hope, *b* 1951.

This baronetcy was granted to David Dunbar, of Baldoon, co Wigtown, in 1664, with remainder "provydit to his heirs male and tailzie." On the death of the grantee the baronetcy became dormant, and so remained until 1916, when Major Charles Dunbar Hope-Dunbar (*see* M Linlithgow, colls), grandson of Lady Isabella Ellen Hope, da of 5th Earl of Selkirk, and a descendant of Mary (who *m* Lord Basil Hamilton) grandda and sole heiress of the 1st Bt, in 1916, successfully proved his claim before the Baronetage Committee of the Privy Council to be placed on the Official Roll of Baronets as the 6th Baronet.

DUNCAN (UK) 1905, of Horsforth Hall, Guiseley, West Riding of Yorkshire (Extinct 1964)

Sir (CHARLES EDGAR) OLIVER DUNCAN, 3rd and last *Baronet*.

WIDOW LIVING OF THIRD BARONET

ETELKA DE VANGEL (*Lady Duncan*): *m* 1958, Sir (Charles Edgar) Oliver Duncan, 3rd baronet, who *d* 1964, when the title became ext.

DUNCAN (UK) 1957, of Jordanstone, co Perth (Extinct 1974)

Sir JAMES ALEXANDER LAWSON DUNCAN, 1st and last *Baronet*.

WIDOW LIVING OF FIRST BARONET

BEATRICE MARY MOORE (*Lady Duncan*) (Jordanston, by Alyth, Perthshire), da of Thomas Laurence O'Carroll, of Ballinvullen, co Cork, and widow of Maj Philip James Kington Blair-Oliphant, of Ardblair Castle, Perthshire: *m* 1966, as his 2nd wife, Sir James Alexander Lawson Duncan, 1st baronet, who *d* 1974, when the title became ext.

PAUNCEFORT-DUNCOMBE (UK) 1859, of Great Brickhill, Buckinghamshire

Non fecimus ipsi
*We have not done it
ourselves*

Sir PHILIP DIGBY PAUNCEFORT-DUNCOMBE, 4th *Baronet*; *b* 18 May 1927; *s* his father, *Maj Sir* EVERARD PHILIP DIGBY, DSO, 1971; *ed* Stowe; Maj (ret) late Gren Gds; DL of Bucks; Harbinger HM Body Guard of the Hon Corps of Gentlemen at Arms 1993: *m* 1951, Rachel Moyra, da of Maj Henry Gerald Aylmer (*see* B Aylmer, colls), and has issue.

ꌗrms – Quarterly: 1st and 4th per chevron engrailed gules and argent three talbots' head erased counterchanged, a chief ermine, *Duncombe*; 2nd, gules, three lions rampant argent, *Pauncefort*; 3rd azure. ꌓrest – 1st, out of a ducal coronet or a horse's leg sable, the shoe argent, charged with a cross-crosslet gold, *Duncombe*; 2nd, a lion rampant argent ducally crowned or, and charged on the shoulder with an escallop sable, *Pauncefort*.
Residence – Great Brickhill Manor, Milton Keynes, Bucks. *Club* – Cavalry and Guards'.

SON LIVING

DAVID PHILIP HENRY, *b* 21 May 1956; *ed* Gordonstoun, and RAC Cirencester: *m* 1987, Sarah Ann, elder da of late Reginald T. G. Battrum, and has issue living, Henry Digby, *b* 16 Dec 1988, — Laura Mary, *b* 1991. *Residence* – Westfield Farm, Gt Brickhill, Bletchley, Bucks MK17 9BG.

DAUGHTERS LIVING

Diana (The Grange, Gt Horwood, Milton Keynes, Bucks) *b* 1953: *m* 1974, Jeremy David Trevor West (B Graves, colls), and has issue living, Edward, *b* 1984, — Katrina, *b* 1981. —— Charlotte, *b* 1967.

SISTER LIVING

Sophia, *b* 1925: *m* 1957, Archibald Evariste Yuill, JP, of 32 Eresby House, Rutland Gate, SW7 1BG, and has issue living, William George Henry, *b* 1961.
The father of the 1st baronet, Philip Pauncefort, assumed by Roy licence, in 1804, the additional surname of Duncombe and *m* Lady Alicia Lambart, da of 7th Earl of Cavan.

DUNDAS (UK) 1898, of Arniston, Borthwick, Midlothian (Extinct 1970)

Sir THOMAS CALDERWOOD DUNDAS, MBE, 7th and last *Baronet*.

DAUGHTERS LIVING OF SEVENTH BARONET

Alice Kirsty (*Lady Pilkington*), *b* 1937: *m* 1960, Sir Antony Richard Pilkington, of Crofton, Lodge, Kingsley, Ches, and has issue living, Jerome Antony Simon, *b* 1961, — David Christopher, *b* 1963, — Simon Benedict, *b* 1972, — Miranda Kirsty *b* 1966. —— Davina Margaret, *b* 1939: *m* 1966, Martin Charles Findlay, of Ledburn Manor, Leighton Buzzard, Beds (*see* E Dartmouth).

DAUGHTERS LIVING OF FOURTH BARONET

Althea Enid Philippa, *b* 1939: *m* 1972, Aedrian Bekker, of Arniston, Gorebridge, Midlothian, who *d* 1990, and has issue living, Kirsty Jean, *b* 1973, — Henrietta May, *b* 1975. —— Myfanwy Elizabeth Jean, *b* 1946; BA: *m* 1977, Mark Walker Baldwin, MSc, PhD, of 24 High St, Cleobury Mortimer, Kidderminster, Worcs, and has issue living, Samuel Philip Telford *b* 1978, — Patrick Charles Jeremy, *b* 1980, — Alexander Dundas Lancey, *b* 1983. —— Joanne Montgomerie, *b* 1949: *m* 1974, Richard Henry James Kerr-Wilson, MB, BChir, of 26 Moorend Rd, Leckhampton, Cheltenham, Glos, and has issue living, Alice Dundas, *b* 1977, — Héloïse Lucy, *b* 1979, — Catriona Olivia, *b* 1986.

WIDOWS LIVING OF FOURTH AND SEVENTH BARONETS

JEAN MARIAN, da of James A. Hood, of Midfield, Lasswade, Midlothian: *m* 1st, 1936, Sir Philip Dundas, 4th Bt, who *d* 1952; 2ndly, 1953, Alastair Stewart, of Chemin Davel 24, 1009 Pully, Vaud, Switzerland. —— ISABEL (*Lady Dundas*) (6 The Green, Slaugham, Handcross, Sussex), da of late Charles Goring (*see* Goring, Bt, colls): *m* 1933, Maj Sir Thomas Calderwood Dundas, 7th Bt, MBE, who *d* 1970, when the title became ext.

DUNLOP (UK) 1916, of Woodbourne, co Renfrew

Deservedly

Sir THOMAS DUNLOP, 3rd *Baronet; b* 11 April 1912; *s* his father, *Sir* THOMAS, 1963; *ed* Shrewsbury, and St John's Coll, Camb; Chartered Accountant, a partner in the firm of Thomas Dunlop & Sons, ship and insurance brokers, of 50 Wellington St, Glasgow, until firm ceased trading 1986; late Chm of Savings Bank of Glasgow; an OStJ; 1939-45 War as Maj Roy Signals: *m* 1947, (Adda Mary) Alison, da of late Thomas Arthur Smith, of Lindsaylands, Biggar, and has issue.

Arms – Argent, a double-headed eagle displayed gules, armed and membered azure; on a chief of the last, a three-masted galley under full sail proper, flagged of the second, at her stern the banner of Scotland, all between two garbs or. **Crest** – A dexter hand couped at the wrist, grasping a dagger all proper. *Residence* – The Corrie, Kilmacolm, Renfrewshire PA13 4NY.

SON LIVING

THOMAS (Bredon Croft, Bredons Norton, Tewkesbury, Glos GL20 7HB), *b* 22 April 1951; *ed* Rugby, and Aberdeen Univ (BSc): *m* 1984, Eileen, elder da of late Alexander Henry Stevenson, of Hurlford, Ayrshire, and has issue living, Thomas, *b* 11 March 1990, — Nicola Mary, *b* 1987.

DAUGHTER LIVING

Jennifer Margaret, *b* 1948: *m* 1st, 1978 (*m diss* 1983), Rupert V. Bruce; 2ndly, 1983, David Johnson of High Gables, Thelwall, Warrington, and has issue (by 2nd *m*), James David, *b* 1992, — Charlotte Mary, 1991.

SISTER LIVING

Dorothy Frances, *b* 1921: *m* 1948, Ernest Forrester Fortune, MBE, TD, who *d* 1993, of Allanton, Elie, Fife, and has issue living, George Dunlop (PO Box 707, 07080 Palma, Mallorca, Spain), *b* 1953: *m* 1977, Patricia Elise, da of Eric Moore, of Cheadle, Lancs, — Susan Elizabeth, *b* 1949.

COLLATERAL BRANCHES LIVING

Issue of late Capt William Beckett Dunlop, RHA, yr son of 2nd baronet, *b* 1915, *d* 1970: *m* 1947, Charmian Katherine Chauncy (66 Novar Drive, Glasgow, G12), da of late Col Gavin Charteris Towers Speirs, of Hume, Bearsden, Dunbartonshire:—
Anthony Charles Beckett, *b* 1948; *ed* Rossall. —— Michael William Beckett, *b* 1951; *ed* Rugby. —— Simon Speirs Beckett, *b* 1955; *ed* Millfield.

Issue of late Peter Mitchell Dunlop, 2nd son of 1st baronet, *b* 1883, *d* 1962: *m* 1915, Florence Leathard, who *d* 1983, da of John Gardner Brewis:—
Mary Mitchell, *b* 1924: *m* 1963, Walter A. Bishop, who *d* 1983, of Larchfield, Old Rd, Buckland, Betchworth, Surrey.

Issue of late Robert Jack Dunlop, youngest son of 1st baronet, *b* 1891, *d* 1952: *m* 1918, Maude Rowena, who *d* 1988, da of late William C. Teacher, of Bellcairn, Cove, Dunbartonshire:—
†George Teacher, *b* 1923: *m* 1950, Margaret Jane Schoelles, and *d* 1992, leaving issue, Nicholas George Teacher, *b* 1956, — Rosalie Anne, *b* 1951, — Carolyn Jane, *b* 1954, — Philippa Christine, *b* 1961, — Sally Margaret, *b* 1963. *Residence* – Torwood, Rhu, Dunbartonshire. —— Robert Jack, *b* 1927: *m* 1950, Dorothy Shirley Dixon, and has issue living, Robert Alastair, *b* 1951: *m* 1975, Jane Christian Rankin, — Timothy Dixon, *b* 1953: *m* 1979, Pauline Anne Paisley, — Andrew James, *b* 1959: *m* 1991, Lucia Elizabeth Mary Campbell Murfitt, — Gillian Elizabeth, *b* 1956: *m* 1983, David James Conway. *Residence* – Glaiceriska Cottage, Appin, Argyll. —— Audrey Dorothy, *b* 1932: *m* 1952, Antony Leonard Cullen, MC, TD, and has issue living, Michael Robert Antony, *b* 1955: *m* 1991, Julie Cox, — Roderick Leonard Dunlop, *b* 1958: *m* 1983, Marianne Carlsen and has issue living, three sons, — John Hamish Charles, *b* 1965: *m* 1989, Susan Flowers, and has issue living, one son, and two das, — David Alastair Thomas, *b* 1971, — Rowena Gay, *b* 1959, — Audrey Hilary, *b* 1963: *m* 1989, John Grigg, and has issue living, two sons. *Residence* – Leighon, Manaton, Newton Abbot, S Devon.
The 1st baronet, Sir Thomas Dunlop, GBE (son of Thomas Dunlop, of Glasgow), was head of the firm of Thomas Dunlop & Sons, shipowners and grain merchants, of Glasgow, and Lord Provost of Glasgow and Lord-Lieut of co of City of Glasgow 1914-17.

DUNN (UK) 1921, of Bathurst, Province of New Brunswick, Dominion of Canada (Extinct 1976)

Sir PHILIP GORDON DUNN, 2nd and last *Baronet.*

DAUGHTERS LIVING OF SECOND BARONET

Serena Mary (*Baroness Rothschild*), *b* 1934: *m* 1961, 4th Baron Rothschild, of 28 Warwick Av, W9, and Stowell Park, Marlborough, Wilts, and has issue. —— Nell Mary, *b* 1936; author of *Up The Junction, Poor Cow, Grandmothers*, etc: *m* 1957 (*m diss* 1979), Jeremy Christopher Sandford, and has issue living, Roc (1 Brewer St, W1A 4RZ), *b* 1957; has issue living (by Cassia Sarah Jacoba, da of Michael Kidron, of 221 Portobello Rd, W11), Cato Philip SANDFORD *b* 1989, — Reuben (3 White Horse St, W1Y 7LA), *b* 1964, — Jem (3 White Horse St, W1Y 7LA), *b* 1967.

FOURTH AND FIFTH DAUGHTERS OF FIRST BARONET (*By 1st marriage*)

(Leila) Brigid, *b* 1919: *m* 1st, 1939, Count Peter Wolff-Metternich, who was *ka* 1941; 2ndly, 1944, Joseph Bromovsky, of Dub, Czechoslovakia, and *d* 1991, leaving issue (by 1st *m*) *Count* Tassilo Peter Franziskus Paul Maria (Nuffield, The Close, Doyle Rd, St Peter Port, Guernsey, CI), *b* 1940: *m* 1968 (*m diss* 19—), Cecilia Mary Elsworthy, da of late Basil Gray, CB, CBE, Keeper of Oriental Antiquities British Museum, and has issue living, *Count* Boris Peter Basil *b* 1973, *Count* Edwin Sebastian

Gleb *b* (twin) 1973, *Countess* Josephine Leila Helen *b* 1969; BSc, *Countess* Mopsa Eliza Lucy *b* 1970, — (by 2nd *m*) Anthony (30 Rossetti Gardens Mansions, St Looe Av, SW3), *b* 1948: *m* 1989, Fabia A., da of Dr Jerome Francis Sturridge, of 2 Upper Harley St, W1, and of Mrs Michael Bowman-Vaughan, of Mardon House, Northumberland, — Francis Philip (17 The Little Boltons, SW10), *b* 1958: *m* 1990, Helen Jane, yst da of Peter Cooper, of Tideford, Devon, and has issue living, Anastazia Brigid *b* 1992, a da *b* 1994, — Josette (*Hon Mrs Robert Loder*), *b* 1945: *m* 1973, Hon Robert Beauclerk Loder, CBE, of 14 Ladbroke Grove, W11 3BQ, yst son of 2nd Baron Wakehurst, KG, KCMG, and has issue. *Residence* – Ottmanach, Pisheldorf, Kärnten, Austria.

(By 2nd marriage)

Anne, *b* 1929; painter: *m* 1st, 1951 (*m diss* 1960), Michael Wishart, painter and writer; 2ndly, 1960 (*m diss* 1987), as his 2nd wife, Rodrigo Moynihan, CBE, the portrait painter, who *d* 1990, and has issue living (by 1st *m*), Francis Dominic (Lambesc, Aix-en-Provence, France), *b* 1951; *ed* Bryanston, and Slade Sch of Art; painter, and founder Co-ordination Associative Regional pour la Défense de l'Environment (CARDE) 1990: *m* 1982, Catherine, da of Jean Vormus, and has issue living, James Derek *b* 1982, Antonin Michael *b* 1988, — (by 2nd *m*) Daniel Henry, *b* 1959. *Residence* – 40 Avenue du Leman, Lausanne, Switzerland.

WIDOW LIVING OF FIRST BARONET

MARCIA ANASTASIA (*Baroness Beaverbrook*), da of John Christoforides, of Leyswood, Groombridge, Sussex; Hon L. L. D. Dalhousie; Chancellor of Dalhousie Univ since 1968: *m* 1st, 1942, as his 3rd wife, Sir James Hamet Dunn, QC, 1st baronet, who *d* 1956; 2ndly, 1963, as his 2nd wife, 1st Baron Beaverbrook, who *d* 1964. *Residence* – Saint Andrews, New Brunswick, Canada.

DUNNING (UK) 1930, of Beedinglee, Lower Beeding, Sussex

Sir SIMON WILLIAM PATRICK DUNNING, 3rd *Baronet*; *b* 14 Dec 1939; *s* his father, Sir WILLIAM LEONARD, 1961; *ed* Eton: *m* 1975, Frances Deirdre Morton, da of Maj Patrick William Morton Lancaster, of Wapsbourne Manor, Sheffield Park, Sussex, and formerly wife of Capt Nigel Edward Corbally Stourton (*see* B Mowbray, colls), and has issue.
Residence – Low Auchengillan, Blanefield, Glasgow, G63 9AU.

DAUGHTER LIVING

Mariota Kathleen Masika, *b* 1976.
The 1st baronet, Sir Leonard Dunning (son of late Simon Dunning, of Warwick Square, SW), was an Inspector of Constabulary at Home Office 1912-30.

Dunnington-Jefferson, see Jefferson.

DUNTZE (GB) 1774, of Tiverton, co Devon

Sir DANIEL EVANS DUNTZE, 8th *Baronet*; *b* 4 April 1926; son of late George Douglas Duntze, son of late John Alexander Duntze, son of late Adm John Alexander Duntze, grandson of 1st baronet; *s* his kinsman, Sir JOHN ALEXANDER, 1987; *ed* Washington Univ Sch of Fine Arts, St Louis, Mo; commercial artist; served in 1939-45 War in USAAF: *m* 1954, Marietta, da of Ferdinand Welsh, of St Louis, Mo, USA, and has issue.
Residence – 8049 Gannon, St Louis, Missouri 63130, USA.

SON LIVING

DANIEL EVANS, *b* 11 August 1960; *ed* Univ of Missouri, St Louis, Mo, USA.

DAUGHTERS LIVING

Jill Alison, *b* 1957: *m* 1988, Eugene Pfeiffer, and has issue living, William Thomas, *b* 1988, — Benjamin Carl, *b* 1991. *Residence* – 7827 Greensfelder Lane, University City, Mo, USA 63130. —— Dr Robin Evans, *b* 1959: *m* 1987, Dr Mark Wright, and has issue living, Thomas Walker, *b* 1991. *Residence* – 8944 Powell, Brentwood, MO, USA 63144.

SISTER LIVING

Dorothy Jane, *b* 1923: *m* 1950, Hal Roach, and has issue living, Michael Todd (21322 Wilderness Drive, Mountain Brook, Alabama 35213, USA) *b* 1952: *m* 19— (*m diss* 19—), and has issue living, Chauncey Blane *b* 1979, — Scott Evans (3814 Old Leeds Rd, Mountain Brook, Alabama 35213, USA), *b* 1953: *m* 1978, Leigh Anne Sellers, and has issue living, Katie Elizabeth *b* 1979, Hillary Anne *b* 1981, — Brooke Normile (204 Fairmont Drive, Mountain Brook, Alabama 35213, USA), *b* 1955: *m* 1983, Susan Lynn Alford, and has issue living, Keegan Wade *b* 1984, Sarah Savannah *b* 1986, — Todd Douglas (1454 Linkwood Lane, Decatur, Georgia 30033, USA), *b* 1957: *m* 1986, Daisy Cleveland, and has issue living, Zachary Cleveland *b* 1987. *Residence* – 9 Woodhill Rd, Birmingham, Alabama 35213, USA.

DAUGHTER LIVING OF SIXTH BARONET

Elizabeth Joan, *b* 1944: *m* 1966, Nicholas Lowther James Grove, of Cliffe House, Forge Hill, Aldington, Ashford, Kent, and has issue living, Richard Nicholas Dougal, *b* 1970, — Iain Anthony Douglas, *b* 1973.

WIDOW LIVING OF SIXTH BARONET

NESTA (*Dowager Lady Duntze*), da of late Thomas Richard Pendrell Herbert, of Newport, Mon, and formerly wife of late Lt-Col Godfrey Ariel Evill: *m* 1966, as his 2nd wife, Sir George Edwin Douglas Duntze, 6th Bt, CMG, who *d* 1985. *Residence –* Flat 9, 55 Elm Park Gdns, SW10.

WIDOW LIVING OF SEVENTH BARONET

EMILY ELLSWORTH (*Emily, Lady Duntze*), da of Elmer Ellsworth Harlow, of New Bedford, Mass: *m* 1935, Sir John Alexander Duntze, 7th Bt, who *d* 1987. *Address –* c/o Linda F. Greiner, PO Box 457, Washington, NJ 07882, USA.

The 1st baronet, an eminent merchant of Exeter, was sometime MP for Tiverton. The 2nd baronet was Receiver-General of the taxes of the co of Devon. The 6th baronet, Sir George Edwin Douglas Duntze, CMG, was a Provincial Commr, Uganda.

DUPREE (UK) 1921, of Craneswater, Portsmouth, co Southampton

The world is my field.

Sir PETER DUPREE, 5th *Baronet*; *b* 20 Feb 1924; *s* his father, *Capt Sir* VICTOR, 1976: *m* 1947, Joan, da of late Capt James Desborough Hunt.

Arms – Vert, on a bend between two calves passant or three mullets of the field. **Crest** – A lion sejant proper supporting with the dexter forepaw a flagstaff proper, flowing therefrom a banner vert, charged with a mullet or.
Residence – 15 Hayes Close, Chelmsford, Essex, CM2 0RN.

SISTER LIVING

Mary, *b* 1926: *m* 1948, George Dutton Gibb, CB, FDS, RCS, of Yenda, Haw Lane, Bledlow Ridge, High Wycombe, Bucks, and has issue living, Elizabeth, *b* 1951: *m* 1983, Peter Glen, of 10 Paddocks, Wendover, Aylesbury, Bucks.

HALF-UNCLE LIVING (*Son of 1st baronet by 2nd marriage*)

Thomas William (Paradis Roc, Bloc D, Chemin de St Christophe, 06130 Grasse, France; White's and Household Brigade Yacht Clubs), *b* 1913; *ed* Harrow; late Lt Gren Gds; sometime Private Sec to HM's Ambassador, Paris; Hon Attaché at HM's Embassy, Madrid 1936-8, in News Depart, Foreign Office 1938-43, Dept Assist to British Resident Min, Allied Force Headquarters, Algiers 1943-44, Press Attaché (local rank of 1st Sec), HM's Embassy, Paris 1944-46, Foreign Office Observer (Press Relations) at Trials of Major War Criminals, Nuremberg 1946 and again in News Depart Foreign Office April to Oct 1946: *m* 1st, 1938 (*m diss* 1953), Anne, da of Sir Henry Getty Chilton, GCMG; 2ndly, 1953, Mrs Jacqueline Harari, da of Commendatore Leo Goldschmied, and has issue living, (by 1st *m*) Delia, *b* 1939: *m* 1962, Peter Guy, and has issue living, Dominic William *b* 1963, Susannah *b* 1965, — Sarah Anne, *b* 1942: *m* 1977, Michael Wilkins, of 47 St Johns Av, SW15 6AL, and has issue living, William Michael *b* 1978, Sarah Jeanne *b* 1979.

HALF-AUNT LIVING (*Daughter of 1st baronet by 2nd marriage*)

Irene Amy Marion: *m* 1936, John Gerrard Brendan O'Hagan, Squadron-Leader RAF, of Upperton Cottage, Petworth, W Sussex, and has issue living, Timothy David Brendan, *b* 1945; *ed* Oxford Univ (DPhil) *m* 1970, Jennifer Kaue, and has issue living, Gabrielle *b* 1973, Rachel *b* 1974, — Elizabeth Mary Marion, *b* 1936: *m* 19—, (*m diss* 1961), John Bevington, and has issue living, Mark *b* 1963, Amanda *b* 1967, Catherine *b* 1968, — Jennifer Ann, *b* 1938: *m* 1962, Guy Liardet, Capt RN, and has issue, Patrick *b* 1965, Frances *b* 1962, Sophie *b* 1969.

DAUGHTER LIVING OF THIRD BARONET

Mary Marcella Lucy: *m* 1941, Terence Patrick Lawrence, of Fawley Vicarage, Wantage, son of late Sir Walter Lawrence, JP, of Hyde Hall, Sawbridgeworth, and has issue.

COLLATERAL BRANCHES LIVING

Issue of late Eric Dupree, 4th son of 1st baronet, *b* 1895, *d* 1932: *m* 1928, Gwendoline Violet, who *d* 1993, da of Henry Harvey:—
Monica Mary (43b York Street, Broadstairs, Kent), *b* 1930: *m* 1954 (*m diss* 1974), Robin Gordon Hazlitt Morris, and has issue living, Anthony John David, *b* 1955, — John Richard Hazlitt, *b* 1958, — Andrew Quentin Dupree, *b* 1963. —— Barbara Jane (51 High Street, Broadstairs, Kent), *b* 1931: *m* 1st, 1954, Lt John Richard Haward, RN, who *d* 1956; 2ndly, 1957 (*m diss* 1967), Ronald Mitchell, and has issue living, (by 2nd *m*), Terence Roger Anstey, *b* 1957, — Robert Killian, *b* 1959, — Simon Paul Adam, *b* 1966.

Issue of late Lt-Cdr James Dupree, RNVR, 5th son of 1st baronet, *b* 1899, *d* 1972: *m* 1928, Mary Ethel Gillott, who *d* 1949, da of late T. W. Reid, and widow of A. Stuart Elsworth:—
(THOMAS WILLIAM JAMES) DAVID (Little Fircliff, Whitworth Rd, Darley Dale, nr Matlock), *b* 5 Feb 1930. —— Jennifer Rosemary Gillott, *b* 1933: *m* 1962, Roberto Lorenzo Mercadaz, and has issue living, a son, *b* 19—, — a son, *b* 19—, — Maria-Victoria, *b* 1964, — a da, *b* 1975.

Issue of late Capt John Rupert Dupree, 7th son of 1st baronet, *b* 1915, *d* 1965: *m* 1946, Ann Margaret Frances (who *m* 3rdly, 1965, Roger Thornycroft, DSC, who *d* 1983, son of late Sir John Edward Thornycroft, KBE; and 4thly, 1984, Stuart Warren Don, of 113 Dovehouse St, SW3), only da of late Lt-Col Robert George Barlow, Seaforth Highlanders (ret), and formerly wife of late Hon William Gladstone Bethell (*see* B Bethell):—
Michael John, *b* 1947: *m* 1982, Alexandra Columbia, da of Michael Anthony Telfer Smollett, and has issue living, Tamara, *b* 1985.

The 1st baronet Col Sir William Thomas Dupree, VD, TD (son of late William Dupree) was Mayor of Portsmouth 1901-3 and 1909-10 and Hon Col RFA. The 2nd baronet, Sir William was Chm and Managing Director of the Portsmouth and Brighton United Breweries, Ltd.

DURAND (UK) 1892, of Ruckley Grange, Salop
(Name pronounced "Du-rand")

Esperance en Dieu
Hope in God

Sir EDWARD ALAN CHRISTOPHER DAVID PERCY DURAND, 5th *Baronet*; *b* 21 Feb 1974; *s* his father, *Rev Sir* (HENRY MORTIMER) DICKON MARION ST GEORGE DURAND, 1992; *ed* St Columba's Coll, Dublin, Summerhill Coll, Sligo, and Milltown Inst of Theology and Philosophy.

Arms – Azure, five fusils conjoined in fesse within a bordure or; on a chief embattled of the last, a pair of manacles of the first. **Crest** – Over a rock proper, a crescent argent between two laurel branches or.
Residence – Lisnalurg House, Sligo.

BROTHER LIVING

DAVID MICHAEL DICKON PERCY *b* 6 June 1978; *ed* St Columba's Coll, Dublin.

SISTERS LIVING

Rachel Elizabeth Marion, *b* 1972; *ed* St Columba's Coll, Dublin, Heatherley Sch of Fine Art, London, and Nat Coll of Art and Design, Dublin. —— Madeleine Eleanor Marion, *b* 1980.

AUNT LIVING (*sister of 4th baronet*)

Elizabeth Pamela Marion, *b* 1932: *m* 1957, Maj George Naismith Bowden, Loyal Regt (ret), of Higher Shute Farm, Huish Champflower, Taunton, Somerset, and has two adopted children, Alexander Dickon Naismith, *b* 1971, — Veronica Mary Patricia, *b* 1968.

DAUGHTER LIVING OF THIRD BARONET

Patricia Marion, *b* 1925: *m* 1st, 1960, Wing-Cdr Howard Rex English Rumsey, who *d* 1964; 2ndly, 1969, Kenneth Alec James Booth, MBE, FILA, who *d* 1981, of Fletching Cottage, Fletching St, Mayfield, E Sussex TN20 6TN, and has issue living (by 1st *m*), Alan, *b* 1962, — Fiona Marion, *b* 1964.

WIDOW LIVING OF FOURTH BARONET

STELLA EVELYN (*Lady Durand*), el da of late Capt Christopher Carleton L'Estrange, of Lisnalurg, co Sligo: *m* 1971, Rev Sir (Henry Mortimer) Dickon Marion St George Durand, 4th Bt, who *d* 1992. *Residence* – Lisnalurg House, Sligo, Republic of Ireland.

Sir Edward Law Durand, 1st Bt, Resident in Nepal 1888-91 was el son of Maj-Gen Sir Henry Marion Durand, KCSI, CB, Lt-Gov of Punjab 1870, *m* 1880, Maude Ellen, who *d* 1953, da of Algernon Charles Heber-Percy (D Northumberland).

DURRANT (GB) 1784, of Scottow, Norfolk

Sir WILLIAM HENRY ESTRIDGE DURRANT, 7th *Baronet*; *b* 1 April 1901: *s* his father, *Sir* WILLIAM HENRY ESTRIDGE, 1953; is a JP; S-W Pacific 1939-45 (three medals): *m* 1927, Georgina Beryl Gwendoline, who *d* 1968, da of Alexander Purse, of Kircubbin, co Down, and has issue.

Arms – Or, a cross-crosslet ermines between four ermine spots sable. **Crest** – A boar passant per fesse wavy argents and gules, bristled and tusked azure, and pierced through the body with a broken lance bendwise sable, point downwards, gold.
Residence – 1634 Pacific Highway, Wahroonga, NSW 2076, Australia.

SON LIVING

WILLIAM ALEXANDER ESTRIDGE, *b* 26 Nov 1929; is Capt 12th/16th Hunter River Lancers, and a JP: *m* 1953, Dorothy, BA, da of Ronal Croker, of Quirindi, NS Wales, and has issue living, David Alexander, *b* 1960, — Susan Elizabeth, *b* 1962. *Residence* – Spring Park, Gaspard, via Quirindi, NS Wales.

DAUGHTER LIVING

Beryl Elizabeth Wildbredt, *b* 1928: *m* 1952, Douglas James Weaving (9 Darling Ct, Shepparton, Vic 3630, Australia), and has issue living, John Laurence, *b* 1956, — Peter Douglas, *b* 1958, — Elizabeth Anne, *b* 1953.

COLLATERAL BRANCH LIVING

A dishonouring stain is worse than death

Issue of late Reginald Walter Estridge Durrant, yr son of 6th baronet, *b* 1905, *d* 1986: *m* 1937, Joy Minnie (42 Hayle St, St Ives, NSW 2075, Australia), da of William George Smith, of Manly, NSW, Australia:—
Beverley Joy, *b* 1938: *m* 1957, Stanley Ross Ackers, of 17 Apps Av, Turramurra, NSW, Australia, and has had issue, Geoffrey Ross, *b* 1965, *d* 1991, — Annette Ruth, *b* 1959, — Margaret Lynne, *b* 1963. —— Kaye Lorraine, *b* 1944: *m* 1966, Malcolm Harvey Bird, of 384 Bobbin Head Rd, Turramurra, NSW, Australia, and has issue living, Murray Scott, *b* 1969, — Julie Anne, *b* 1968.

This family was established in Rutland and Derbyshire. William Durrant, from whom the present baronet is in direct descent, migrated to Scottow, Norfolk, and *d* 1700. Sir Thomas, 1st baronet, was High Sheriff of Norfolk 1784.

DYER (E) 1678, of Tottenham, Middlesex

Sir (HENRY) PETER FRANCIS SWINNERTON DYER, KBE, FRS, 16th *Baronet*; *b* 2 Aug 1927; *s* his father, *Sir* LEONARD SCHROEDER SWINNERTON, 1975; *ed* Eton (Fellow 1981) and Trin Coll, Camb (Fellow 1955, Dean 1963-73); FRS (1967); Master of St Catharine's Coll, Camb 1973-83, Prof Maths Camb Univ 1971-88, lect 1960-71, Univ Lectr Camb Mathematical Lab 1960-67; Vice-Cllr 1979-81; Chm Cttee on Academic Organisation (Lond Univ) 1980-82; Visiting Prof, Harvard Univ 1971; Commonwealth Fund Fellow, Univ of Chicago 1954-55 and Research Fellow Trin Coll Camb 1950-54; Chm Univ Grants Cmmn 1983-89; Chief Executive, Univ Funding Council 1989-92; Chm Sec of State for National Heritage's Advisory Cttee, the Library and Information Sers Council since 1992; KBE (1987): *m* 1983, Dr Harriet Crawford, er da of Rt Hon Sir Patrick Reginald Evelyn Browne, OBE, TD.

Arms – Or, a chief indented gules. **Crest** – Out of a ducal coronet or a goat's head argent, horned gold.
Residence – The Dower House, Thriplow, Cambs.

Unwilling to frighten, unacquainted with fear

SISTER LIVING

Anne Winifred Swinnerton, *b* 1932.

DAUGHTER LIVING OF TWELFTH BARONET

Jacqueline Christine Swinnerton, *b* (*posthumous*) 1918; late Asst Section Officer WAAF: *m* 1st, 1943 (*m diss* 1949), Colin E. C. Campbell; 2ndly, 1949, Col Vincent Paravicini, TD, who *d* 1989, and has issue living (by 1st and 2nd *m*). *Residence* – Nutley Manor, Basingstoke, Hants, RG25 2HL.

COLLATERAL BRANCHES LIVING

Granddaughters of late Maj Richard Stewart Dyer-Bennet (infra):—
Issue of late Richard Dyer-Bennet, folk singer, *b* 1913, *d* 1991: *m* 1st, 1936 (*m diss* 1941), Elizabeth Hoar Pepper; 2ndly, 1942, Melvene Ipcar (Star Route 62 Box 29, Great Barrington, MA 01230, USA):—
(By 1st *m*) Ellen WOOD (7921 Millvale Rd, Chesterfield, VA 23832, USA), *b* 1937; has assumed her stepfather's surname. —— Eunice, *b* 1939: *m* 1962, Hilary Roche Davis, of 11030 SW 42 Court, Davie, FL 33328, USA, and has issue living, Robert

Hilary, *b* 1967, — Lance Bradshaw, *b* 1971, — Mary Ellen, *b* 1965: *m* 19—, Scott Vincent Smith. ——— (By 2nd *m*) Bonnie, *b* 1943. ——— Brooke (a da), *b* 1946.

Grandchildren of late Frederick Stewart Hotham DYER-BENNET (assumed additional surname of Bennet 1894), only son of late Maj Frederick Carr Swinnerton Dyer, 3rd son of 9th baronet:—
Issue of late Maj Richard Stewart Dyer-Bennet, *b* 1886, *d* 1983: *m* 1st, 1912 (*m diss* 1955), Miriam Wolcott, who *d* 1973, da of late Prof Edward Bull Clapp, of California Univ, USA: 2ndly, 1956, Christina (98 Mayplace Rd, E Barnehurst, Kent DA7 6EH), da of late John Colbert, of Newcastle-upon-Tyne:—
(By 1st *m*) JOHN (907 Winona St, Northfield, Minn 55057, USA), *b* 17 April 1915; Emeritus Prof of Mathematics at Carleton Coll, Northfield, Minn: *m* 1951, Mary Abby, da of late George B. Randall, and has issue living, David, *b* 1954, — Barbara, *b* 1965. ——— Miriam (10 Ross St, Toronto, Ont, Canada M5T 1Z9), *b* 1922: *m* 1st, 1945 (*m diss* 1962), Thomas Timothy Crocker; 2ndly, 1963, Kenneth O. May, who *d* 1977, and has issue living (by 1st *m*), Steven, *b* 1949, — Thomas, *b* 1952, — Cedric, *b* 1954, — Edith, *b* 1947.

Grandchildren of late Maj Richard Stewart Dyer-Benet (ante):—
Issue of late Frederick Dyer-Benet, architect, *b* 1918, *d* 1991: *m* 1941, Patricia Esther Arndt (154 Hillcroft Way, Walnut Creek, CA 94596, USA):—
Oliver (5847 Sharpe Rd, Calistoga, CA 94515, USA), *b* 1945: *m* 1984, Linda Helen Specht, and has issue living, Colin Wesley, *b* 1988, Katherine Elise, *b* 1985. ——— John (425 42nd Ave, Oakland, CA 94609, USA), *b* 1947. ——— Cynthia (634 King St, Santa Rosa, CA, USA), *b* 1949: *m* 1983, David Karl Peoples.
Issue of late Christopher Dyer-Bennet, *b* 1920, *d* 1985: *m* 1st, 1945, Peggy Friedman; 2ndly, 1973, Mrs Anna Louise Erben Baumhoff:—
(By 1st *m*) Christopher, *b* 1946. ——— Matthew, *b* 1948. ——— Anne, *b* 1952.

Grandson of late Capt Stewart John Dyer, 4th son of 9th baronet, *b* 1842, *d* 1925: *m* 1873, Emily Mary Elizabeth, who *d* 1912, only child and heir of late Henry Edmund Bythesea, of Nettleton, Wilts.
Issue of late Major Stewart Barton Bythesea Dyer, DSO, 2nd Life Guards, *b* 1917: *m* 1906, Mai (she *m* 2ndly, 1921), Baron A. Pontenani, who *d* 1937, da of late Capt S. L. Osborne, RN, of Shankling, Isle of Wight:—
Thomas Musgrave Swinnerton, *b* 1907; *ed* Oratory Sch, and St Catharine's Coll Camb, formerly Lieut The Buffs; European War 1939-44 in Middle East: *m* 1936 (*m diss* 1948), Violet Elizabeth, da of Ebenezer Cunningham.

Grandchildren of late Thomas Richard Dyer, son of late Capt Edward Dyer, son of late Edward Dyer, brother of 8th baronet:—
Issue of late Frederick Thomas Swinnerton Dyer, *b* 1898, *d* 1982: *m* 1927, Beatrice Henrietta, who *d* 1978, da of Charles John Davies:—
John Frederick (Holdens, Shipton Green, Itchenor, Chichester), *b* 1928; late Fl-Lt RAF: Sen Training Capt British Airways (ret): *m* 1950, Linda Mary, da of Thomas Rees James, and has issue living, Martin John Swinnerton, *b* 1955; *ed* Worcester Coll, Oxford (MA, DPhil) and King's Coll, Camb (M^B, BChir); MRCP; Mere's Student, St. John's Coll, Camb, since 1987-90: *m* 1982, Sally Ann, da of John Woodward of Torquay, and has issue living, Samuel John Swinnerton *b* 1987, Rebecca Ann Swinnerton *b* 1984, — Richard Kenneth Swinnerton, *b* 1960; *ed* Hadlow Coll. ——— Julian Swinnerton (The Mews, Rystwood, Forest Row, East Sussex) *b* 1936; late PO RAF; Co Sec, Vickers Group of Cos; Assist Sec Vickers Ltd, 1973-94: *m* 1961, Patricia Newman, and has issue living, Jeremy Swinnerton, *b* 1964; *ed* Sheffield Hallam Univ (BA Hons), — Ann-Louise, *b* 1966. ——— Jean Anne, *b* 1931: *m* 1952, A.W. Gransden, of 23 Mavis Close, Ewell, Surrey, and has issue living, Jonathan Kim, *b* 1953: *m* 1980, Janice Ruth, da of William Smith of Beddington, Surrey, — Joanna Debra, *b* 1957.
Issue of late Hugh Swinnerton Dyer, ED, *b* 1902, *d* 1981: *m* 1933, Barbara Eileen Homewood:—
David Swinnerton (Apt 417, 371, S Ellesmere Av, Burnaby, BC), *b* 1934; with Dept of Attorney-Gen (Sheriff Office): *m* 1971, Beverley, da of Robert W. Steep. ——— Patrick Swinnerton, *b* 1937; *ed* Haileybury: *m* 1st, 1960 (*m diss* 1970), Elizabeth Rule, da of late Air Marshal Sir Thomas Arthur Warne-Brown, KBE, CB, DSC; 2ndly, 1971, Angela Evelyn Caldicott, and has issue living, (by 1st *m*), Thaila Elisabeth Swinnerton *b* 1962, — Lucinda Jane Swinnerton *b* 1963, — Susannah (Zanna) K. Swinnerton, *b* 1966: *m* 1991, Stuart D. R. Bell, of 130 Fawe Park Rd, Putney, SW15, elder son of John Sydney Bell, of The Manor House, Overthorpe, Banbury, Oxfordshire.

Grandchildren of late Thomas Harry Dyer (infra):—
Issue of late John Arnold Swinnerton Dyer, *b* 1905, *d* 1971: *m* 1st, 1930, Theresa Sylvester, who *d* 1947, da of Henry Sylvester Stannard; 2ndly, 1949, Elizabeth Mahala, da of Edward Valentine Johnston, of Bedford:—
(By 1st *m*) Thomas John Swinnerton, *b* 1931. ——— (By 2nd *m*) Philip John, *b* 1952. ——— Linda Theresa, *b* 1950.

Grandchildren of late Frederick Campbell Spencer Dyer, 4th and yst son of late Capt Edward Dyer (ante):—
Issue of late Thomas Harry Dyer, *b* 1878, *d* 1937: *m* 1904, Kate, who *d* 1953, da of John Willis, of Harpenden, Herts:—
Nellie Jane Kathleen, *b* 1906; Proprietor of Nell Dyer's Hat Shop, William St, Dublin, for 21 years; emigrated to USA 1959; Private and Gen Hosp nurse (ret): *m* 1957, Francis Coyle, who *d* 1982, of Blackrock, co Dublin. *Residence* – 141 Healdsburg Av 13, Cloverdale, Calif 95425, USA. ——— Patricia Swinnerton, *b* 1912: *m* 1940, John Eric Mackenzie, Staff Sergeant, Roy Corps of Signals, and has issue living, Alan Ronald, *b* 1946, — Valerie Jean, *b* 1950. *Residence* – 2 Greenville Rd, Stradbrook Rd, Blackrock, co Dublin.
Issue of late Frank Stanley Dyer, *b* 1880, *d* 1961: *m* 1910, Ellen Knight (dec):—
†Benjamin Stanley, *b* 1914: *m* 1937, Lillian Averina, da of C. H. Gillan, and *d* 1993, leaving issue, Althea Dawn, *b* 1938: *m* 1956, Allan Francis Millin, of 939 Florimond St, Vancouver-Richmond, British Columbia, and has issue living, Montgomery Allan *b* 1956, Andrew Brian *b* 1961, Cynthia Dawn-Marie *b* 1958. ——— Frederick Douglas, *b* 1916: *m* 1941, Myrtle Winifred Foster, and has issue living, Barbara Louise (R 1926 Crescent Rd, Victoria, BC, Canada) *b* 1942: *m* 1965 (*m diss* 1966), Derry Allan McDonell, — Carol Ann, *b* 1947: *m* 1967, Ronald Douglas Robb (Mount Gardner Rd, General Delivery, Bowen Island, BC, Canada) — Nancy May, *b* 1957. *Residence* – 5287 Parker Av, Cordova Bay, Victoria, BC.
Sir William, 1st baronet, *m* Thomazine, only da and heir of Thomas Swinnerton, of Stanway Hall, Essex. Col Sir John Swinnerton, 6th baronet, was a Groom of the Bedchamber to the Prince of Wales (afterwards George IV). Lieut-Gen Sir Thomas Richard, 7th baronet, was Aide-de-Camp to Sir Ralph Abercromby in Egypt, and to Sir John Moore at Corunna. Com Sir Thomas Swinnerton, RN, 8th baronet, was present at numerous naval actions during the Peninsular war, and his brother, Lieut-Col Sir John, KCB, was present at Badajoz, Vittoria, St Sebastian, Pyreness, Nievelle, Nive, Orthes, and Toulousse. The 10th baronet served in Crimean war, and was present at Sebastopol, both assaults on the Redan and the bombardment and surrender of Kimburne. The 12th baronet, Sir John Swinnerton Dyer, MC, Capt Scots Guards, was *ka* 1917. The 15th baronet, Sir Leonard Schroeder Swinnerton Dyer, was Chm, Shropshire Co Council 1969-72.

DYKE (E) 1677, of Horeham, Sussex

Sir DAVID WILLIAM HART DYKE, 10th *Baronet*; *b* 5 Jan 1955; *s* his father, *Sir* DEREK WILLIAM HART, 1987; *ed* Ryerson Polytechnical Inst; BAA; Exec Dir Dixie Magazine

Arms – Or, three cinquefoils, sable. **Crest** – A cubit arm in armour, the hand in a gauntlet sable, garnished or, holding a cinquefoil slipped also sable. *Residence* – 28 King St West, Apt 14B, Stoney Creek, Ont, Canada L8G 1H4.

SISTER LIVING

Diana Lynn, *b* 1957: *m* 1986, John Costello McDonald. *Residence* – 52 Evelyn St, Brantford, Ontario, Canada.

UNCLE LIVING (*son of 8th baronet*)

(OLIVER) GUY HART, *b* 9 Feb 1928; *ed* Univ of British Columbia (BSc) *m* 1974, Sarah Alexander Hart, yr da of late Com the Rev Eric Hart Dyke, RN (see colls infra), and has issue living, Thomas Guy, *b* 1976, — Anya Elizabeth, *b* 1978. *Seat* – Lullingstone Castle, Eynsford, Kent.

AUNT LIVING (*daughter of 8th baronet*)

Rosemary June, *b* 1930: *m* 1st, 1952 (*m diss* 1969), Jack Farr; 2ndly, 1969, Michael Prince, and has issue living (by 1st *m*), Amanda Zoë Frances, *b* 1953. *Residence* – Edificio Anna Maria 2D, Camino Cala Mayor 13, Cala Mayor, Mallorca, Spain.

Prest a Faire
Ready to act

MOTHER LIVING

Dorothy, da of Thomas Ansley Moses, of Atlanta, Georgia, USA: *m* 1953 (*m diss* 1963), as his 1st wife, Sir Derek William Hart Dyke, 9th Bt, who *d* 1987.

COLLATERAL BRANCHES LIVING

Issue of late Percyvall Hart Dyke, el son of 7th baronet, *b* 1871, *d* 1922: *m* 1908, Edythe, who *d* 1937, da of late W. G. Harrison, QC:—
Edythe Frediswide (Marion, Connecticut, USA, 06444), *b* 1909: *m* 1st, 1935 (*m diss* 1949), Frederic Andrew Milward, late of Public Works Dept, Burma; 2ndly, 1950 (*m diss* 1956), Herbert Samuel Gallagher; 3rdly, 1956, Austin Edward Marsh, late Maj RASC, who *d* 1963.

Issue of late Reginald Charles Hart Dyke, 4th son of 6th baronet, *b* 1852, *d* 1943: *m* 1st, 1891, Guinevere Eva, who *d* 1894, da of late Gen Lord Alfred Paget, CB (M Anglesey, colls); 2ndly, 1897, Millicent Ada, who *d* 1946, da of late R. C. L. Bevan, of Trent Park, New Barnet:—
(By 2nd *m*) Ashley Francis Hart, *b* 1899; *ed* Eton: *m* 1940, Marie, da of Johan Voldengen, of Lier, Norway, and has issue living, Margaretha Millicent Hart, *b* 1946. *Residence* – .

Grandchildren of late Thomas Dyke, eldest son of late Rev Thomas Hart Dyke, 2nd son of 5th baronet:—
Issue of late Col Percyvall Hart Dyke DSO, Indian Army, *b* 1872, *d* 1952: *m* 1900, Louisa Catherine, who *d* 1961, da of Adm John Halliday Cave, CB:—
Trevor Hart, DSO (Clough House, Bamford, Debys; Army and Navy Club), *b* 1905: *ed* Marlborough; is Brig late Queen's R Regt; 1939-45 War in France and Burma (DS); a DL for Derbys since 1981; DSO 1944: *m* 1st, 1933 (*m diss* 1965), Eileen Joyce, da of late J. H. Niblock-Stuart; 2ndly, 1965, Mary Eliot, widow of Maj D. E. Lockwood, and has issue living, (by 1st *m*) Terence Percyvall Hart (Cavalry Club), *b* 1934; *ed* Marlborough; Capt The Royals: *m* 1963, Wanda Hermione Krystyna, only da of late Lt-Col Joseph Mostyn, of Barcliffe, Tamworth, Staffs (*see* Mostyn, Bt), and has issue living, Paul Percyvall Hart *b* 1965, James Terence Hart *b* 1966, — Jennifer Hart, *b* 1939: *m* 1967 (*m diss* 1979), Lt Oliver Nicholas Vaudrey, RN (ret), and has issue living, David Clough Percyvall *b* 1969, Annabel *b* 1972. —— Cicely Hart, *b* 1907: *m* 1936, Lt-Col John William Radclyffe Dugmore, KOYLI, who *d* 1992, and has issue living, William Radclyffe, *b* 1940: *m* 1974, Patricia Elizabeth, 2nd da of the late F. B. Jarvis, of Hen Ard, Morya Bychan, Gwynedd, and has issue living, Amy Tamsyn Elizabeth *b* 1976, Polly Louise *b* 1978, Daisy Catherine *b* 1983, — Janet Elvyn Catherine, *b* 1938: *m* 1964, John Peter Merrett, of Bank End, Plumgarth, Kendal, and has issue living, Peter William *b* 1965, Sophie Catherine *b* 1966, Nicola Mary *b* 1971. *Residence* – Storrs Hill, Windermere, Cumbria.

Grandchildren of late Col Percyvall Hart Dyke, DSO (ante):—
Issue of late Com the Rev Eric Hart Dyke, RN, *b* 1906, *d* 1971: *m* 1935, Mary, da of late Robert Alexander (Shaw-Stewart, Bt, colls):—
David, CBE, LVO (Hambledon House, Hambledon, Hants, PO7 6RU), *b* 1938; *ed* St Lawrence Coll, Ramsgate and Britannia RNC; Capt RN; ADC to HM 1988; LVO 1980, CBE (Mil) 1990: *m* 1967, Diana Margaret, da of Sir William Henry Tucker Luce, GBE, KCMG, and has issue living, Miranda Katharine, *b* 1972, — Alice Louisa, *b* 1975. —— Jane Hart, *b* 1936: *m* 1959, David Charles Holland, ERD, of Little Tye, Upper Hartfield, East Sussex and has issue living, Charles Thurstan, *b* 1962: *m* 1987, Rachel Margaret McCabe, and has issue living, Richard Oliver *b* 1994, Catherine Jane *b* 1992, — Caroline Mary, *b* 1960: *m* 1983, Dr Stephen Cox, and has issue living, James Robert *b* 1986, Jonathon Richard Andrew *b* 1992, Rachel Elizabeth *b* 1988, — Clare Lucinda, *b* 1966. —— Sarah Alexander Hart, *b* 1974: (Oliver) Guy Hart Dyke (ante).

Grandson of late Rev Percival Hart Dyke, 2nd son of late Rev Thomas Hart Dyke (ante):—
Issue of late Robert Percyvall Hart Dyke, *b* 1864, *d* 1954: *m* 1908, Mary Harriette Theodore, who *d* 1974, da of late Rev John Shephard (sometime V of Eton), Hon Canon of Ch Ch, Oxford, of 33 Craven Hill Gardens, W:—
Michael Percyvall Hart (10 Goldney Av, Clifton, Bristol BS8 4RA), *b* 1909; *ed* Marlborough; Middle East 1940-45 as Major RASC; *m* 1955, Jean MacGlashan, who *d* 1992, and has issue living, Timothy Percyvall Hart, *b* 1959: *m* 1992, Kate, only da of late C.H.G. Proctor, of Teignmouth, Devon, — Jeremy Percyvall Hart, *b* 1963, — Jennifer Mary Hart, *b* 1956: *m* 1984, Stephen Jeffrey Peacock, yst son of F. G. Peacock, of Hitchin, Herts, and has issue living, Thomas Michael *b* 1990, Alice Felicity *b* 1987.

Grandsons of late Col Edward Hart Dyke, 2nd son of late Lt-Col John Dixon Dyke (infra):—
Issue of late Percyvall Hart Dyke, *b* 1902; *d* 1982: *m* 1931, Helen Leonora, who *d* 1985, da of Dr Philip Henry Welch MacAdam, JP, Colonial Med Ser, of British Guiana:—
Michael Percyvall Hart (Mahaicony, 37 St John's Rd, Farnham, Surrey), *b* 1932. ——— Patrick Alan Hart (48 Abbots Ride, Farnham, Surrey), *b* 1938: *m* 1969, Elzbieta Izabella, da of Eugeniusz Lotocki, of Warsaw, and has issue living, James Paul, *b* 1972, — Stephen Peter, *b* 1975.

Granddaughters of late Lieut-Col John Dixon Dyke, 3rd son of 5th baronet:—
Issue of late Lieut-Col Frederick Hotham Dyke, *b* 1840, *d* 1934: *m* 1871, Emily, who *d* 1941, da of late Rev Charles Faunce Thorndike, of Villa Freeland, Trieste:—
Winifred Amy, *b* 1881: *m* 1911, Cyril Arthur Mileham, solicitor, and has issue living, Barbara Dera, *b* 1918: *m* 1936, Eric Adrian Milne, and has issue living, Adrian Edward *b* 1940, Ian Hugh Milne *b* 1950, Rosemary Faith *b* 1941: *m* 1966, Dr Christopher John Bretherton Hundleby, of 606 Forest Hills, Mowbray, Cape Town (and has issue living, Alison Mary *b* 1967). *Residence* – Bure Acre, Aylsham, Norfolk, NOR 07Y.
Issue of late Col George Hart Dyke, *b* 1847, *d* 1922: *m* 1895, Edith Louise, who *d* 1952, da of late Thomas William Kinder, Master of Mints of Hong Kong and Japan:—
Helen Sandra Millicent, *b* 1897: *m* 1920, Lieut-Col Esdaile Addison Burkitt Orr, MC, Roy Berkshire Regt, who *d* 1977, and has issue living, Elizabeth, *b* 1923: *m* 1947, William Edward Penlygon Moon, who *d* 1965, and has issue living, Sandra Anne *b* 1953. *Residence* – 2 St Peter St, Marlow, Bucks.
Sir Thomas Dyke, of Horeham, Sussex (whose father migrated from Cranbrook, Kent), *m* 1639, Catherine, da of Sir John Bramston, Lord Chief Justice of the King's Bench. His son Sir Thomas Dyke, 1st Bt was Commr of Public Accounts 1696. The 2nd baronet removed from Horeham to Lullingstone Castle, having married Anne, da and heir of Percival Hart of that place. Sir Percival Hart Dyke, 5th baronet, unsuccessfully claimed the Barony of Brayes, of which he was a co-heir through the Harts, 1836. The 7th baronet, Rt Hon Sir William Hart Dyke, sat as MP for W Kent (*C*) 1865-8 for Mid Kent 1868-85, and for Kent, Dartford Div 1885-1906, and was Sec to the Treasury 1874-80, Ch Sec for Ireland 1885-6, and Vice-Pres of Council on Education 1887-92.

Eardley-Wilmot, see Wilmot.

EARLE (UK) 1869, of Allerton Tower, Woolton, Lancashire

Preserve a medium

Sir (HARDMAN) GEORGE ALGERNON EARLE, 6th *Baronet*; *b* 4 Feb 1932; *s* his father, Sir HARDMAN ALEXANDER MORT, 1979; *ed* Eton: *m* 1967, Diana Gillian Bligh, da of late Col Frederick Ferris Bligh St George, CVO (*see* St George, Bt, colls), and has issue.

Arms – Argent, three pallets ermines. **Crest** – A lion's jamb erased sable, holding a harpoon argent.
Residence – Abington, Murroe, co Limerick. *Club* – Royal Yacht Sqdn.

SON LIVING

ROBERT GEORGE BLIGH, *b* 24 Jan 1970.

DAUGHTER LIVING

Katharine Susan, *b* 1968.

SISTER LIVING

Belinda Mary, *b* 1937: *m* 1st, 1959 (*m diss* 1968), Capt Patrick John Boteler Drury-Lowe, who *d* 1993 (*see* M Linlithgow, colls, 1990 Edn); 2ndly, 1973, Anthony David Arnold William Forbes, of Wakerley Manor, Oakham, Leics (*see* B Faringdon, colls, 1980 Edn), and has issue living (by 1st *m*), Lucy Belinda, *b* 1961: *m* 1989, David Charles Palmer, and has issue living (*see* V Churchill), — Candida Dorothy, *b* 1963: *m* 1990, G. Piers Bracher, only son of Peter Bracher, of The Old Rectory, Ashford, Kent, and has issue living, Barnaby Alexander Patrick, *b* 1993.

AUNTS LIVING (*Daughters of 4th baronet*)

Rosemary, *b* 1904. ——— Myrtle Valentine (Brackwood, Graffham, Petworth, W Sussex), *b* 1911: *m* 1st, 1933 (*m diss* 1947), Robert Owen Symon; 2ndly, 1948, Sydney Vernon, who *d* 1961; 3rdly, 1962, Brig Maurice Robert Lonsdale, DSO, OBE, who *d* 1989, and has issue living, (by 1st *m*) Mairi Edith, *b* 1935.

COLLATERAL BRANCHES LIVING

Issue of late Charles Frederic Earle, 6th son of 2nd baronet; *b* 1867, *d* 1939; *m* 1911, Alice Adelaide, who *d* 1942, da of Henry Cleveland, and widow of Patrick Cumin Scott, MB, of Blackheath, SE:—
Evelyn Alice, *b* 1912. *Residence* – 16 Rectory Green, Hayne Rd, Beckenham, Kent. ——— Josephine Noelle, *b* 1914: *m* 1941, Douglas Swinscow, DSc, MB, FLS, who *d* 1992, and has issue living. *Residence* – Everley, Monmouth St, Topsham, Exeter. ——— Rosamond Cleveland, *b* 1918: *m* 1939, Rev Canon Eric Albert Metcalfe, who *d* 1984, of 14 Burnhill Rd, Beckenham, Kent, and has issue living.

Grandchildren of late Cecil Arthur Earle, el son of late Arthur Earle (infra):—
Issue of late Capt Guy Fife Earle, *b* 1891, *d* 1966: *m* 1st 1918 (*m diss* 1922), Isabel Bridget, who *d* 1971, da of late Andrew Greville Rouse-Boughton-Knight (Rouse-Boughton, Bt); 2ndly, 1924 (*m diss* 1928), Helen Alice who *d* 1967, da of late Ninian Lowis Elliott (E Minto, colls); 3rdly, 1935, Bridget Joan, who *d* 1993, da of late Peter Sherston, of Hill House, Templecombe, Som:—

(By 1st *m*) Audrey Bridget (Arnolds, Burnham Market, Kings Lynn), *b* 1920. —— (By 3rd *m*) Michael Guy (Spring Creek, Bannockburn, Vic 3331, Aust), *b* 1942; *ed* Harrow, and Roy Agric Coll, Cirencester: *m* 1969, Morrell Francis Armytage, el da of Sqdn Ldr John Robert Nassau Molesworth, DFC (*see* V Molesworth, colls), and has issue living, Guy Robert, *b* 1973, — Nicholas Molesworth, *b* 1980, — Amanda Morrell, *b* 1971. —— Susan Mary (28A Hang Tau Village, New Territories, Hong Kong), *b* 1940: *m* 1978 (*m diss* 19—), Kenneth Searle, MBE, CMZS. —— Virginia Ida (Alma Cottage, North St, Beaminster, Dorset), *b* 1945: *m* 1971 (*m diss* 1977), Frederick Jackson, and has issue living, Conrad Guy Frederick, *b* 1973.

Issue of late Brig Eric Greville Earle, DSO, *b* 1893, *d* 1965: *m* 1st, 1918 (*m diss* 1931), Noel, who *d* 1975, da of Capt Edward Downes-Martin, formerly of Killoskehane Castle, co Tipperary; 2ndly, 1931, Diana Mary, who *d* 1964, da of late Dr Vaughan Harley, of Walton Hall, Bletchley:—

(By 1st *m*) David Eric Martin, OBE (Shipways, Church Lane, Kington Langley, Chippenham, Wilts), *b* 1921; *ed* Stowe, and Ch Ch, Oxford; Col RA; Burma 1945; Palestine 1947-48; Cyprus 1955-56; OBE (Mil) 1969: *m* 1947, Betty Isobel Shield, and has issue living, Charles Henry Diccon (Riseholme, Seven Hills Rd, Cobham, Surrey), *b* 1951: *m* 1984, (Margorie) Lucy, da of Dr William Mervyn Jones, of Waunfawr, Aberystwyth, Dyfed, and has issue living, Guy Charles William *b* 1985, James Edward David *b* 1987, — George David (15 Castello Av, Putney, SW15), *b* 1953: *m* 1985, Clare, da of late Graeme Campbell-Johnston, and has issue living, Graeme David Campbell *b* 1988, Andrew David Campbell *b* 1993, Rosemary Elizabeth Campbell *b* 1990, — Victoria Lilian Gay, *b* 1952: *m* 1977 (*m diss* 1989), Richard Walter Sutcliffe, and has issue living, Diccon Thomas George *b* 1983, Sophie Isobel Susan *b* 1980, — Charlotte Mary, *b* 1959: *m* 1991, Anthony N. A'Hern, of 34 Vicarage Rd, Maidenhead, Berks, only son of Maj T. A'Hern, of Sherborne, Dorset, and has issue living, William David Anthony *b* 1993. —— †Robin Denys Michael, OBE *b* 1922; *ed* Wellington Coll; formerly Lt Fleet Air Arm; SE Asia 1939-45, OBE 1942: *m* 1st, 1946 (*m diss* 1962), Rosemary, da of Maj F. A. Latter, of Birkdault, Lindfield; 2ndly, 1963 (*m diss* 19—), Anne da of late Capt Lawford; 3rdly, 1977, Ann — (El Palo, Malaga, Spain), and *d* 1990, leaving issue, (by 1st *m*) Toby Dick (Sunnyside, 54 Long Copse Lane, Emsworth, Hants PO10 7UR), *b* 1951: *m* 1981, Juliet Miranda, da of Basil Peredur Jones, of Constantine, Cornwall, and has had issue, Robin *b* 1982, *d* 1984, Joshua Robin *b* 1984, Barnaby Dicken *b* 1988, — Penelope Jane, *b* 1947: *m* 1977, Kenneth Brunton Ward, of 54 Langham Road, Teddington, Middx TW11 9HQ, son of James Alfred Ward, of Edinburgh, and has issue living, Gemma Kate *b* 1981, — Jemima Tamsin, *b* 1949: *m* 1st, 1970 (*m diss* 1985), Robert Arthur Meads, son of Arthur Meads; 2ndly, 1986, Roland Wooding, of 2 Little London, Silverstone, Northants NN12 8UP, son of George Clifford Wooding, and has had issue, (by 1st *m*) Nicholas John *b* 1972, Andrew David *b* 1975, *d* 1991, Caroline Elizabeth *b* 1977, (by 2nd *m*) David *b* 1986, — Lucy Noel, *b* 1954: *m* 1st, 19— (*m diss* 19—), son of —; 2ndly, 19—, Stuart Willson, of Brewer's Cottage, Plymtree, nr Cullompton, Devon, son of — Willson. —— Peter Noel Desmond, *b* 1923; *ed* Wellington Coll, and Ch Ch, Oxford (BA 1949, MA 1954); formerly Lt RNVR; Atlantic and S-E Asia 1939-45: *m* 1952, Shirley Hope, who *d* 1986, da of Wallace MacGregor, of Vancouver, British Columbia, and has issue living, Virginia Melanie, *b* 1963, and an adopted son and da, Robert Henry Matthew, *b* 1956, — Heather Anne, *b* 1958.

Grandsons of late Arthur Earle, 4th son of 1st baronet:—

Issue of late John Greville Earle, *b* 1869, *d* 1933: *m* 1920, Jacobina Reid, who *d* 1970, da of late James Clark, of Kilmarnock:—

John Arthur (21 via Udine, 34132 Trieste, Italy), *b* 1921; *ed* Winchester, and Trin Coll, Camb (BA 1948); European War 1939-45 in Middle East and Central Mediterranean as Capt Rifle Brig (wounded): *m* 1947, Anna Maria, da of late Maj-Gen Lorenzo Tiziani, Italian Army, of Trecenta, Italy, and has issue living, Lawrence Hardman (8 via Tor S Piero, Trieste, Italy), *b* 1948; *ed* Winchester, and Malta Univ (BA): *m* 1984, Rita Dougan, and has issue living, Mathew John *b* 1986, Martina Jacobina Paola *b* 1988, — Arabella Ida (14 via Machiavelli, Milan, Italy), *b* 1955. —— William Hardman, *b* 1924; *ed* Winchester, and Trin Coll, Camb (BA 1945, MA 1954); S-E Asia 1945 as Capt RE: *m* 1958, Vera Charteris, who *d* 1992, da of Colin Black, of Fryars, West Chiltington, Sussex, and has issue living, Rupert Langton, *b* 1960; *ed* Winchester, and Trin Coll, Camb (BA), — Greville Hoare, *b* 1963; *ed* Winchester, and Edinburgh Univ, — (Alice) Jacobina, *b* 1970; *ed* Edinburgh Univ. *Residence* – The Walnuts, Beanacre, Melksham, Wiltshire. *Club* – United Oxford and Cambridge. —— Richard Greville, *b* 1925; *ed* Winchester, and Trinity Coll, Camb (BA 1949, MA 1959); formerly Sub-Lt (A) RNVR, High Sheriff of Dorset 1983, DL Dorset 1984: *m* 1956, Joanna Mary, JP, da of Com H. K. B. Mitchell, CBE, JP, DL, RN (ret), of Folke Manor, Sherborne, Dorset, and has issue living, Elizabeth Mary, *b* 1957, — Susan Helen, *b* 1959: *m* 1993, Neil S. Ross, son of Leslie Ross, of Evesham, Worcs. *Residence* – Frankham Farm, Ryme Intrinseca, Sherborne, Dorset.

Issue of late Lawrence Mathew Earle, *b* 1881, *d* 1968: *m* 1916, Helen Elizabeth Dunkin, who *d* 1963, da of late Capt Frederic Street, of Dulverton:—

Nigel Lawrence (3 Belvedere Close, Dallington, Northampton, NN5 7DW), *b* 1926; *ed* Radley; 1944-45 War with R Armoured Corps: *m* 1951, Jean, da of late Dr Hugh McClintock, and has issue living, Brian Lawrence, *b* 1953, — Patrick Nigel, *b* 1958: *m* 1981, (Susan) Elizabeth, da of Capt David Kenneth Bawtree, RN, of Grant Rd, Farlington, Portsmouth, Hampshire, and has issue living, Guy *b* 1993, Amaryllis (Lily) Roxborough *b* 1991.

This family was settled at Warrington in the 16th century, and in 1709 died John Earle (son of Gregory Earle), a principal inhabitant of the place. His son John settled in Liverpool, and was Mayor thereof 1709. His grandson, Thomas, Mayor of Liverpool 1787, was father of William, also Mayor of Liverpool in 1836, as well as of Sir Hardman, 1st baronet. Sir Henry, DSO, 3rd baronet, was Lieut-Col King's Own Yorkshire LI. Sir (Thomas) Algernon, TD, 4th baronet, was Lieut-Col sometime Comdg Lancashire Hussars.

EBRAHIM (UK) 1910, of Bombay

God leading, nothing hurts

Sir (MAHOMED) CURRIMBHOY EBRAHIM, 4th *Baronet*; *b* 24 June 1935; *s* his father, *Sir* (HUSEINALI) CURRIMBHOY, 1952: *m* 1958, Dur-e-Mariam, da of Minuchehir Ahmed Nurudin Ahmed Ghulam Ally Nana, of Karachi, Sind, W Pakistan, and has issue.

Arms – Argent, in base on waves of the sea a Chinese junk sailing to the sinister, in chief also on waves two dhows sailing to the dexter all proper, and in chief per pale gules and or thereon a pale azure between a rose of the first and a lotus flower also proper, and charged with a mullet issuant from a crescent above five mullets in crescent also of the first. **Crest** – Above an Indian lily on water proper, a mullet radiated or.
Residence – Baitullah 33, Bait-ul-Amen Mirza Kalig Beg Rd, Jameshed Quarters, Karachi, Sind, W Pakistan.

SONS LIVING

ZULFIQAR ALI, *b* 5 Aug 1960; *ed* Habib Public Sch, and DJ Science Coll: *m* 1984, Adila, da of Akhtar Halipota, and has issue living, Mustafa, *b* 22 Sept 1985. —— Murtaza Ali, *b* 1963. —— Raza Ali, *b* 1964.

DAUGHTER LIVING

Durre Najaf, *b* 1969.

HALF-SISTERS LIVING

Mumtaz, *b* 1922: *m* 1941, Ahmed Rahim Valimahomed Peermahomed. —— Munira, *b* 1923: *m* 1941, Fazal Rahemtulla Maherali Chinoy.

GREAT-AUNTS LIVING (*Daughters of 1st baronet*)

Jenabai, *b* 1880: *m* 1896, Gulamhusein Ladhabhoy Ebrahim. —— Sherbanu, *b* 1882: *m* 1899, Gulamhusein Rehemtullah Khairaj. —— Labai, *b* 1883: *m* 1902, Abdullabhoy Gulamhusein Allana. —— Shireenbai, *b* 1888: *m* 1911, Rahin Vali Mahomed Pirmahomed. —— Khairubai (Khairunisha), *b* 1894: *m* 1916, Currimbhoy Nensey Khairaz. —— Mariumbai, *b* 1896: *m* 1916, Cassumali Subjeally. —— Sharifabai, *b* 1899: *m* 1921, Sulieman Rahimtulla Sayani. —— Khatijabai, *b* 1901: *m* 1923, Yusafali Moosabhoy Jaffer Pradham. *Residence* – Pabaney Villa, Warden Road, Bombay, India.

WIDOW LIVING OF THIRD BARONET

ALHAJA AMINA KHANUM (*Alhaja, Lady Ebrahim*), da of Al-Qassamally Jairazbhoy, of Gulshanabad, Peddar Rd, Bombay: *m* 1926, as his second wife (*m diss* 1944), Sir (Huseinali) Currimbhoy Ebrahim, 3rd baronet, who *d* 1952, and whom she re-married 1949. *Residence* – .

COLLATERAL BRANCHES LIVING

Issue of late Sir Fazulbhoy Currimbhoy Ebrahim, CBE, 4th son of 1st baronet, *b* 1873, *d* 1970: *m* 1889, Sakinabai, who *d* 1930, da of late Datoobhoy Ebrahim, of Cutch Mandvi:—
Ahmedbhoy Fazulbhoy, *b* 1902: *m* 1923, Zarina, da of late Ahmedbhoy Currimbhoy Ebrahim (infra), and has issue living, Ariff, *b* 1926, — Niamat, *b* 1928. —— Mohamedali, *b* 1904. —— Gulamali, *b* 1905: *m* 1928, Hamida, da of late Rehemtullah Currimbhoy Ebrahim (infra). —— Hoosein, *b* 1911. —— Amir Ali, *b* 1913.

Granddaughter of late Ebrahim CURRIMBHOY (infra):—
Issue of late Allen CURRIMBHOY, *b* 1924, *d* 1960: *m* 1958, Pritee Misra:—
Alia *b* 1961.

Grandchildren of late Gulamhusein Currimbhoy Ebrahim (infra):—
Issue of late Ebrahim CURRIMBHOY, *b* 1897, *d* 1969: *m* 1923, Zarina, da of Ahmed Curmally Janmahomed:—
Zinet, *b* 1925. —— Asif Currimbhoy (43 Bakhtawar, 22 N Dabholkar Rd, Bombay 400 006, India), *b* 1928: *m* 1951, Suraiya Ismail, da of Ismailbhoy Currimbhoy Ebrahim (ante), and has issue living, Tabrik, *b* 1952: *m* 1979, Nelofar Hussain, and has issue living, Sharik, *b* 1980, — Tarek, *b* 1954, — Nahed, *b* 1959: *m* 1982, Amit Moitra, and has issue living, Tahzeeb *b* 1983, Tahini *b* 1991.

Issue of late Gulamhusein Currimbhoy Ebrahim, 5th son of 1st baronet, *b* 1879, *d* 1918: *m* 1896, Khanoobai, da of Datoobhoy Ebrahim, of Cutch Mandvi (ante):—
Ali Mahomed, *b* 1902. —— Aziz, *b* 1915. —— Ammeena, *b* 1896: *m* 1916, A. O. Jamal, of Calcutta.

Grandchildren of late Ahmedbhoy Currimbhoy Ebrahim (infra):—
Issue of late Hosseinali Ebrahim, *b* 1908, *d* 1968: *m* 1928, Nazli, da of late Rehemtullah Currimbhoy Ebrahim (infra):—
Semine, *b* 1929. —— a da, *b* 1933.

Issue of late Ahmedbhoy Currimbhoy Ebrahim, 6th son of 1st baronet, *b* 1885, *d* 1925: *m* 1902, Shireen, da of Dost Mahomed Allana, of Bombay:—
Habibbhoy, *b* 1910. —— Zarina, *b* 1904: *m* 1923, Ahmedbhoy Fazulbhoy Ebrahim (ante). *Residence* –

Issue of late Rehemtullah Currimbhoy Ebrahim, 7th son of 1st baronet, *b* 1887, *d* 1928: *m* 1908, Sakinabai, da of Jafferbhoy Ratansey, formerly of Bombay:—
Nazli, *b* 1909: *m* 1928, Hooseinali Ebrahim, who *d* 1968, (ante). —— Hamida, *b* 1912: *m* 1928, Gulamali Ebrahim (ante).

Issue of late Habibbhoy Currimbhoy Ebrahim, 8th son of 1st baronet, *b* 1889, *d* 1949: *m* 1913, Khatijabai, da of Nensey Khairaj, of Bombay:—
Nazim, *b* 1915: *m* 1941, Zarina, da of Ahmed S. Moloobhoy, of Bombay, and has issue living, Reisa, *b* 1944. —— Sultan, *b*

1921: *m* 1949, Munira, da of late Sir Fazal Ibrahim Rahimtoola, CIE, and has issue living, Habib, *b* 1950. ——— Husem, *b* 1924. ——— Aziz, *b* 1927. ——— Munira, *b* 1926.

Issue of late Ismailbhoy Currimbhoy, 9th son of 1st baronet, *b* 1906, *d* 1975: *m* 1925, Zarina, da of Gulam Husain Sachedina Aziz *b* 1927, — Suraiya Ismail, *b* 1929: *m* 1951 Asif Currimbhoy Ebrahim (ante).

Sir Currimbhoy Ebrahim, 1st Bt, was a leading member of the Khoja Community, and an opium, yarn, cotton, silk, tea, sugar, and cloth merchant of Bombay, Hong Kong, Kobe, Shanghai, and Calcutta; owned the Currimbhoy, the Mahomedbhoy, the Ebrahimbhoy Pabaney, the Fazulbhoy, the Crescent, the Indore Malwa United Mills, the Pearl Mills, and many other factories (ginning and pressing), and the Indian Bleaching, Dyeing, and Printing Works; established a Girl's Sch, a Madressa at Mandvi, the Currimbhoy Ebrahim Khoja Orphanage in Bombay, and Dharmsalas at Mandvi and Bhuj; gave large donations to Bombay New Museum Fund, for the new Science Sch for Bombay, and for Scholarships for Mahomedans. The 2nd baronet, Sir (Mahomedbhoy) Currimbhoy Ebrahim, was a partner in the firm of Currimbhoy Ebrahim and Sons. Each Baronet on succession assumes the name of the 1st Bt.

ECHLIN (I) 1721, of Dublin
(Name pronounced "Ecklin")

Non sine praedâ

Not without prey

Sir NORMAN DAVID FENTON ECHLIN, 10th *Baronet*; *b* 1 Dec 1925; *s* his father, *Sir* JOHN FREDERICK, 1932; *ed* Masonic Boys' Sch, Clonskeagh, co Dublin; Capt (ret) Indian Army: *m* 1953, Mary Christine, only da of John Arthur, of Oswestry, Shropshire.

Arms – Quarterly, 1st and 4th or, an antique galley, sails furled sable, a forked pennon gules; 2nd and 3rd gules, a fesse chequey argent and azure, a chief of the last thereon a hound in full chase after a stag, both proper. **Crest** – A talbot passant proper. *Residence* – Nartopa, Marina Av, Appley, Ryde, I of Wight.

SISTER LIVING

Patricia Hazel, *b* 1928: *m* 1951, Fred Tiller, and has issue living, Fred, *b* 1966, — Hazel Jean, *b* 1952, — Heather Valerie, *b* 1956. *Residence* – Treemeadow, Lavender Rd, Hordle, Lymington, Hants.

AUNT LIVING

Aileen Alexandra: *m* 1919, John Atkinson, who *d* 1923.

The Echlin family is of ancient Scottish origin, and formerly possessed princely estates in Scotland, and also large domains in the counties of Kildare, Carlow, Dublin, Galway, and Mayo. Andrew Echlin, of Pittadro, Fifeshire, was Constable and Deputy-Gov of Edinburgh Castle during the siege of 1572. The Right Rev Dr Echlin, Bishop of Down and Connor, who *d* 1635, was great-grandfather of Sir Henry Echlin, Knight, a Baron of the Court of Exchequer in Ireland, who was created a baronet in 1721. The 2nd baronet sat as MP for Newry. The 3rd baronet dissipated the family estates. The 4th baronet was one of the gentlemen before whom Hamilton Ronan knelt in the Court of King's Bench to beg the King's pardon. The Kildare estates were dissipated by the 4th, 5th and 6th baronets. Sir Henry Frederick, 8th baronet, was sometime Landlord of The Cider House, Haddenham, Bucks, and Sir John Frederick, 9th baronet, was Sergeant in Roy Ulster Constabulary.

EDGE (UK) 1937 of Ribble Lodge, Lytham St Annes, co Lancaster

(*Sir*) WILLIAM EDGE, 3rd *Baronet*; does not use the title; *b* 5 Oct 1936; *s* his father, *Sir* KNOWLES, 1984; *ed* Shrewsbury, Trin Hall, Camb (MA), and Harvard Business Sch (MBA): *m* 1959, Avril Elizabeth, da of Harold Denson, and has issue.

Arms – Sable, an eagle displayed argent between four cinquefoils or. **Crest** – In front of a reindeer's head erased two rose sprigs in saltire proper flowered gules.
Residence – 66 Harrow Rd, Maidenhead, Berks.

SONS LIVING

EDWARD KNOWLES, *b* 6 June 1965. —— Martin William, *b* 1968.

DAUGHTERS LIVING

Christina Jane, *b* 1963. —— Susannah Clare, *b* 1971.

The 1st baronet, Sir William Edge (son of late Sir Knowles Edge, of Great Marld, Smithills, Bolton), sat as MP for Bolton-le-Moors (*L*) 1916-18 and 1918-23, and for Leicestershire, Bosworth Div 1927-45, and was knighted in 1922.

OFFICIO · EGERE · NOLO

I do not wish to fail in my duty

EDMONSTONE (GB) 1774, of Duntreath, Stirlingshire.

Sir ARCHIBALD BRUCE CHARLES EDMONSTONE, 7th *Baronet*; *b* 3 Aug 1934; *s* his father, *Sir* ARCHIBALD CHARLES, 1954; *ed* Stowe: *m* 1st, 1957 (*m diss* 1967), Jane, el da of Maj-Gen Edward Charles Colville, CB, DSO (*see* V Colville of Culross); 2ndly 1969, Juliet Elizabeth, da of Maj-Gen Cecil Martin Fothergill Deakin, CB, CBE (*see* Grant, Bt, *cr* 1705, 1980 Edn), and has issue by 1st and 2nd *m*.

Arms – Or, an annulet gules, stoned azure, between three crescents of the second within a double tressure flory-counter-flory of the second. **Crest** – Out of a crest-coronet of four strawberry leaves or, a swan's head and neck proper. **Supporters** – Two lions rampant gules.
Seat – Duntreath Castle, Blanefield, Stirlingshire G63 9AJ.

SONS LIVING (By 1st marriage)

ARCHIBALD EDWARD CHARLES, *b* 4 Feb 1961; *ed* Stowe, and RMA Sandhurst: *m* 1988, Ursula, eldest da of late Benjamin Worthington (*see* Howard-Lawson, Bt). *Residence* – 2A Rhodesia Rd, SW9 2EL. —— Nicholas William Mark, *b* 1964: *m* 1989, Mary M., da of Malcolm Hall, of Gibraltar Farm, Jersey, CI, and has issue living, Emily Cari, *b* 1990.

(By 2nd marriage)

Dru Benjamin Marshall, *b* 1971.

DAUGHTERS LIVING (By 1st marriage)

Philippa Carolyn, *b* 1958: *m* 1983 (*m diss* 1994), Peter William Huntington, and has issue (*see* Palmer, Bt, *cr* 1886).

(By 2nd marriage)

Elyssa Juliet, *b* 1973.

SISTERS LIVING

Mary Bettine (*Lady McGrigor*), *b* 1927: *m* 1948, Capt Sir Charles Edward McGrigor, 5th Bt, late Rifle Brig. *Residences* – Upper Sonachan, by Dalmally, Argyll; 18 Cranmer Court, SW3. —— Jane Fiona *b* 1931: *m* 1st, 1950 (*m diss* 1975), Maj Sir Andrew Rupert John Buchanan-Jardine, 4th Bt, MC, Horse Gds; 2ndly, 1976, Hugh Alastair Cameron-Rose, of 25c Kelso Place, W8; and Hoopers Farm, Kings Somborne, Hants SO20 6QG. —— Susan Morag, *b* 1941: *m* 1964, Robert Keith Erskine, of Cliftonwood, Newbridge, Midlothian (*see* E Buchan, colls).

COLLATERAL BRANCH LIVING

Issue of late Cdr Edward St John Edmonstone, RN, yst son of 5th Bt, *b* 1901, *d* 1983: *m* 1936, Hon Alicia Evelyn Browne, who *d* 1992, da of 5th Baron Kilmaine:—
(William Henry) Neil (Barcombe Old Rectory, nr Lewes, Sussex; 54 Warwick Square, SW1; *Club* – Pratt's), *b* 1942; *ed* Eton; FCA: *m* 1994, Mrs Selma Patricia Deidre Rees, da of late Sqdn-Ldr Finan O'Driscoll. —— (Helen) Antonia, *b* 1937: *m* 1960, Michael Edmund Hubert Gibbs, of 19 Caroline Place, W2 4AN (*see* Smith-Marriott, Bt, colls, 1973-74 Edn), and has issue living, Patrick Michael Evan (75 Arlington Rd, NW1 7ES), *b* 1962: *m* 1989, Catherine Barroll, and has issue living, Clemency *b* 1992, —— Edward Michael John, *b* 1964, —— Adrian Michael Philip, *b* 1967, —— Arabella Marina Clare, *b* 1969: *m* 1994, Quintin John Davies, of 36 Winfield House, Vicarage Crescent, SW11 3LN, son of late Thomas Davies.

This family is probably descended from an Edmundus of the powerful race of Seton, amid whose lands Edmonstone, the original family seat, is situated. Mary, da of King Robert III of Scotland, *m* (as her fourth husband) Sir William Edmonstone

VIRTUS · AUCET · HONOREM

Virtue adds to honour

of Culloden, and to her and her husband the lands of Duntreath were granted in 1445. The 1st baronet, Sir Archibald, was eldest son of Archibald Edmonstone of Duntreath, and Red Hall, co Antrim, and sat as MP for Dunbartonshire and the Ayr and Irvine Burghs 1761-95; the 2nd and 4th baronets (Sir Charles and Adm Sir William, CB) were MP for Stirlingshire 1812-21 and 1874-80 respectively. Sir Archibald Edmonstone, CVO, 5th baronet, was a Groom-in-Waiting to King Edward VII 1907-10 and d (April) 1954. Sir Archibald Charles, 6th baronet was sometime an ADC to Gov of Madras and d (June) 1954.

EDWARDS (UK) 1866, of Pye Nest, Yorkshire

Omne bonum Dei donum
Every good is the gift of God

Sir CHRISTOPHER JOHN CHURCHILL EDWARDS, 5th *Baronet*; *b* 16 Aug 1941; *s* his father, *Sir* HENRY CHARLES SERRELL PRIESTLEY, 1963; *ed* Frensham Heights Sch, and Loughborough Coll: *m* 1972, Gladys Irene Vogelgesang, and has issue.

Arms – Azure, on a bend nebulée argent, cotised or, a fleur-de-lis between two martlets of the field. Crest – Out of a crown vallery or, a talbot's head argent, a semée-de-lis azure.
Residence – 11637 County Club Drive, Westminster, Colorado 80234, USA.

SONS LIVING

DAVID CHARLES PRIESTLEY, *b* 22 Feb 1974. —— Ryan Matthew Churchill, *b* 1979.

BROTHER LIVING

Peter Henry, *b* 1944.

WIDOW LIVING OF FOURTH BARONET

DAPHNE MARJORY HILDA (*Daphne, Lady Edwards*) (24 Burntwood Grange Rd, Wandsworth Common, SW18), el da of William George Birt, of Kensington, W8; resumed her former married name of Edwards 1984: *m* 1st, 1935, as his 2nd wife, Sir Henry Charles Serrell Priestley Edwards, 4th baronet, who *d* 1963; 2ndly, 1972, Leonard Mallett.

The 1st baronet, Sir Henry Edwards, CB, Provincial Grand Master of Freemasons, W Riding, sat as MP for Halifax (*C*) 1847-52, and for Beverley 1857-68. The 3rd baronet, Sir John Henry Priestley Churchill Edwards, *d* on active ser 1942, whilst serving with Aust Forces.

EDWARDS (UK) 1921, of Treforis, co Glamorgan

Nothing without labour

Sir JOHN CLIVE LEIGHTON EDWARDS, 2nd *Baronet*; *b* 11 Oct 1916; *s* his father, *Sir* JOHN BRYN, 1922; *ed* Winchester; European War 1940-45 with RASC, and as Capt Roy Pioneer Corps.

Arms – Per chevron sable and argent, in chief two lions rampant, and in base a castle counterchanged. Crest – A stag's head erased proper, gorged with a coronet composted of eight roses set upon a rim or, between the attires an escarbuncle gold.
Residence – Milntown, Lezayre, Ramsey, Isle of Man.

Edwards-Moss, see Moss.

GREY EGERTON (E) 1617, of Egerton and Oulton, Cheshire

I trust not in arms, but in valour

Sir (PHILIP) JOHN CALEDON GREY EGERTON, 15th *Baronet*, *b* 19 Oct 1920; *s* his father, *Sir* PHILIP REGINALD LE BELWARD, 1962; *ed* Eton; late Capt Welsh Guards; European War 1939-45, in N Africa and Italy: *m* 1st, 1952, Margaret Voase, who *d* 1971, el da of late Rowland Rank, of Aldwick Place, Aldwick, W Sussex, and widow of Sqdn Leader Robert Alexander Ullman, RAF; 2ndly, 1986, Frances Mary, da of late Col Robert Maximilian Rainey-Robinson, of Broadmayne, Dorset, and widow of Sqdn Leader William Dudley Williams, DFC, RAF.

Arms – Quarterly, 1st and 4th, argent, a lion rampant gules between three pheons sable. *Egerton*; 2nd and 3rd, barry of six argent and azure, a label of five points gules, *Grey*. Crest – 1st, three arrows, two in saltire argent, and one in pale, pointed downwards or, barbed and feathered sable, banded with a ribbon gules; 2nd, on a dexter glove argent, a falcon rising or. Supporters –

Dexter, a lion argent ducally crowned or; *sinister*, a wyvern or; each gorged with a plain collar azure, and pendent therefrom an escutcheon gules charged with three pheons argent.
Address – Meadow House, W Stafford, Dorchester, Dorset DT2 8AQ. *Club* – Pratt's.

BROTHER LIVING

BRIAN BALGUY LE BELWARD EGERTON, *b* 5 Feb 1925; *ed* Repton. *Residence* – Regency Lodge, 56 Braidley Rd, Bournemouth, BH2 6JY.

COLLATERAL BRANCHES LIVING

Grandchildren of late F. M. Sir Charles Comyn Egerton, GCB, DSO, 3rd son of late Maj-Gen Caledon Richard Egerton, 5th son of 9th baronet:—
Issue of late Vice-Adm Wion de Malpas Egerton, DSO, *b* 1879, *ka* 1943: *m* 1913, Anita Adolphine, who *d* 1972, da of late A. R. David, of Eastfield, Grimsby:—
David Boswell, CB, OBE, MC, *b* 1914; Maj-Gen (ret); late RA; FIMechE; Dir-Gen of Artillery, Min of Defence, 1964-67, Vice-Pres, and Sen Army Member of Ordnance Board 1967-69, and Pres 1969-70; Col Comdt RA; 1939-45 War (MC); OBE (Mil) 1956, CB (Mil) 1968: *m* 1946, Margaret Gillian, da of late Rev Canon Charles Cuthbert Inge, of Streatley, Berks, and has issue living, William de Malpas (Northdown Farmhouse, Sutton Rd, Sutton Poyntz, Weymouth, Dorset), *b* 1949; *ed* Sherborne; MA Camb: *m* 1971, Ruth, only da of Rev George Watson, of St Albans Vicarage, Westcliff-on-Sea, and has issue living, Matthew Robert *b* 1977; *ed* Stanbridge Earls Sch, Richard John *b* 1980, — Charlotte Mary, *b* 1950; BA Oxford: *m* 1987, Stephen William Dixon, of 58 Abinger Av, Cheam, Surrey, son of Eric Dixon, of Windrush, Seaford, Sussex, and has issue living, John David William *b* 1988, Rose Margaret Elizabeth *b* 1991, — (Margaret) Caroline, *b* 1955; *ed* Oxford Univ (MA), and Lancaster Univ (MA): *m* 1984, Martin George White, BSc, FIA (2 Park Farm Rd, Kingston-upon-Thames, Surrey KT2 5TQ), son of late Alfred Walter White, of 66 Boxgrove Rd, Guildford, Surrey, and has issue living, Philip Martin *b* 1987, Robert Charles *b* 1989, Oliver Richard *b* 1992. *Residence* – Campion Cottage, Cheselbourne, Dorchester, Dorset; Army and Navy Club. — Penelope, *b* 1919; formerly 2nd Officer WRNS: *m* 1955 (*m diss* 1967), Maj John Michael de Burgh Ibberson, late 16th/5th Lancers, and has issue living, Erika Mary, *b* 1956: *m* 1985, — and has issue living, Owen Robert *b* 1986, Inigo John *b* 1987. *Residence* – 38A High St, Puddletown, Dorset. — Alison, *b* 1922; formerly 3rd Officer WRNS: *m* 1955, Lt-Col Richard Boutcher Gregory, RA (ret), and has issue living, Andrew Richard, *b* 1957; Lt-Col RA: *m* 1986, Sally Sheard, and has issue living, Rupert James *b* 1987, Charles Henry *b* 1990, — Jane Patricia, *b* 1960: *m* 1989, Capt David Christopher Wicks, RLC, and has issue living, Toby Edward *b* 1991. *Residence* – Rosslyn, Charmouth Rd, Lyme Regis, Dorset.

Grandson of late Sir Reginald Arthur Egerton, CB, 4th son of Maj-Gen Caledon Richard Egerton (ante):—
Issue of late Reginald Francis le Belward Egerton, *b* 1880, *d* 1927: *m* 1907, Elsie Lillian Rose Harris:—
Rowland le Belward (1165 Bay St, Apt 10, San Francisco, Calif 94123, USA) *b* 1914: *m* 1945, Denise, da of late Capt Denis Hayes, MBE.

Grandchildren of late John MARJORIBANKS-EGERTON, el son of late Philip Henry Egerton, ICS (infra):—
Issue of late Lt-Col John Louis Gerard Marjoribanks-Egerton, *b* 1901, *d* 1965: *m* 1936, (Cecilia Mary) Penelope, who *d* 1974, da of late Maj J. B. Barstow:—
John Caledon Richard, *b* 1940: *m* 1980, Helen Elizabeth, da of Frank Neville Hammond Dicks, of Amersham, Bucks, and has issue living, John Stephen, *b* 1981. *Residence* – Sneaton Hall, Sneaton, Whitby, Yorks. — Mary Penelope Jane, *b* 1938, MA, Oxford, MSc, Alberta: *m* 1963, John L. Bannister, of 7 Mann St, Cottesloe, W Australia 6011, and has issue living, William John Egerton, *b* 1967, — Katharine Penelope, *b* 1964, — Caroline Nancy, *b* 1968. — Sarah Cecilia Geraldine, *b* 1942; MA Oxon: *m* 1964, Charles B. Strouts, AMICE, of 32 Cleaver Sq, SE11, and has issue living, Henry Gerard Egerton, *b* 1966, — Emma Louise Penelope, *b* 1968. — Frances Mary Caroline, *b* 1948.
Issue of late Lt-Col Philip Morys Marjoribanks-Egerton, MBE, *b* 1903, *d* 1969: *m* 1933, Adeline Barbara, who *d* 1986, da of Maj Osborn Augustin Chambers (late R Warks Regt):—
Philippa Anne Mary (24 Wesley Av, Peverell, Plymouth PL3 4RA), *b* 1936: *m* 1st, 1959 (*m diss* 1976), Brian Edgar Ford; 2ndly, 1977, William Ernest Richards, who *d* 1978; 3rdly, 1979 (*m diss* 1984), Albin W. Piotr Szymusik, and has issue living (by 1st *m*), Philip Richard, *b* 1963, — Elizabeth Anne, *b* 1960: *m* 1980, Steven Hodgkinson (56 St Maurice View, Plympton, Plymouth), and has issue living, John *b* 1984, Laura *b* 1988, — Sarah Jane, *b* 1964, — Susan Lillian, *b* 1965.

Grandchildren of late Philip Henry Egerton, ICS, son of late William Egerton, 3rd son of late Philip Egerton, father of 8th and 9th baronets:—
Issue of late Graham Egerton, *b* 1861, *d* 1922: *m* 1886, Julia Donegan, da of T. Easley, of Dickson Co, Tennessee, USA:—
William Graham, *b* 1896; with USA Air Force: *m* 19-, Rebecca Crenshaw White, of Kentucky, and has issue living, William Graham, *b* 19-, — John, *b* 19-, — a da, *b* 19-, — a da, *b* 19-. — Philip Marjoribanks, *b* 1899; in US Dept of Agriculture; 1914-18 War with US Naval Air Force: *m* 19-, Susan Candler, of Corinth, Miss, USA.

Grandchildren of late William Egerton, ICS, son of late Philip Henry Egerton, ICS (ante):—
Issue of late William le Belward Egerton, ICS *b* 1901, *d* 1973, da of late Brig-Gen Edward Humphry Bland, CB, CMG, RE (ret):—
Sir Stephen Loftus, KCMG (Brooks's Club), *b* 1932; *ed* Eton and Trin Coll, Camb; formerly 2nd Lt KRRC; entered HM Foreign Ser 1956; Private Sec to Under Sec of State for Foreign Affairs 1961-62, Oriental Sec at Baghdad 1963-67; Counsellor at British Embassy, Tripoli, 1972, and Head of Energy Depart FO 1973-77, HM Consul-Gen Rio de Janeiro 1977-80, HM Ambassador to Iraq 1980-82; Assist Under Sec of State FCO 1982-86, HM Ambassador to Saudi Arabia 1986-89, to Italy 1989-92, and to Albania (non-resident) 1992; Consultant to Enterprise Oil plc; CMG 1978, KCMG 1988: *m* 1958, Caroline, da of Maj Eustace Thomas Edward Cary-Elwes, TD, late R Norfolk Regt, of Laurel House, Bergh Apton, Norfolk, and has issue living, William Luke le Belward, *b* 1966; *ed* Eton, and Trin Coll, Camb; entered Diplomatic Service 1988, 2nd Sec Moscow 1991-94, — Louisa Charlotte, *b* 1963; Associate Dir Lane Fox & Co, 35 Cadogan St, SW3. — Susan Kirsteen, *b* 1936; *ed* Reading Univ (BA 1959); entered Diplomatic Ser 1960: *m* 1962, Jeremy Sandford Cohen, of Wiston Mill, Nayland, nr Colchester, Essex CO6 4LX, and has issue living, Thomas William Otway *b* 1965; *ed* Leeds Univ (BA); Marketing Mangr Swise Pacific, Canton, China, — Lucy Jane, *b* 1968; *ed* Bath Univ (BA).

Grandchildren of late Sir Robert Eyles Egerton, KCSI, CIE, yst son of late William Egerton (ante):—
Issue of late Lieut-Gen Sir Raleigh Gilbert Egerton, KCB, KCIE, *b* 1860, *d* 1931: *m* 1st, 1894, Bridget Watson, who *d* 1894, el da of Watson Askew-Robertson (B Marjoribanks, *ext*); 2ndly, 1903, Maude Helen, who *d* 1935, only da of late Sir George Rendelsham Prescott, 4th Bt:—
Joanna Mary, MRCS, LRCP, *b* 1905: *m* 1934, Kenneth Hampden Pridie, MD, FRCS, and has issue living, Jonathan George Egerton, *b* 1939, — David Mark Hampden, *b* 1942, — Angus Kenneth, *b* 1945; MB, BS Bristol; FFRCS, — Diccon Charles, *b* 1947; BDS Bristol, — William Raleigh, *b* 1949; BEd Bristol; ACP, FCP, — Patricia Philippa (9 Church Steps, Minehead, Som), *b* 1935, — Judith Joanna (Totterdown Farm, Timberscombe, Som), *b* 1937. *Residence* – 58 St John's Road, Clifton, Bristol.

Issue of late Lieut-Col Charles Philip Egerton, *b* 1863, *d* 1943: *m* 1889, Lilian Isabel, who *d* 1950, da of Lieut-Gen Hugh Rose, Indian Army:—
Rowland Philip, *b* 1891: *m* 1918, Constance Alice, da of Edward Courtenay Pratt, of Montreal, and has issue living, Piers Brian Philip, *b* 1927: *m* 1948, Lorna, da of Lorne Green, of Ottawa, Canada, and has issue living, Brian Philip *b* 1949.

Grandchildren of late Lt-Col Philip Egerton (ante):—
Issue of late Robert Charles Egerton, MIEE, *b* 1903, *d* 1969: *m* 1929, Mary Elizabeth Shaw, da of the Rev Charles Morris Trownsell, R of Gidleigh, Devon:—
Julian Robert, (14 Gladsville Rd, Gladsville, Sydney, NSW), *b* 1940; MSc, PhD: *m* 1966, Kay Lewis, da of George M. Stewart, of Pennant Hills, Sydney, NSW. —— Una Mary, *b* 1939; MCSP: *m* 1963, Peter John Bayley Wassell, Hong Kong Police (c/o Police HQ, Arsenal St, Hong Kong), and has issue living, Mark Peter, *b* 1966, — Amanda Claire, *b* 1969, — Victoria Jane, *b* 1970.

Grandchildren of late Piers Egerton-Warburton, only son of Rowland Eyles Egerton-Warburton, el son of Rev Rowland Egerton-Warburton, 7th son of Philip Egerton, father of 8th and 9th baronets:—
Issue of late Capt John Egerton-Warburton, Scots Guards, *b* 1883, *d* of wounds received in action 1915: *m* 1908, Hon Lettice Legh, (who *d* 1968, having *m* 2ndly, 1919, Lt-Col John Dallas Waters, CB, DSO, who *d* 1967), da of 2nd Baron Newton:—
Elizabeth (*Viscountess Ashbrook*), *b* 1911: *m* 1934, 10th Viscount Ashbrook. *Residence* – Arley Hall, Northwich, Cheshire. —— Priscilla, *b* (*posthumous*) 1915: *m* 1st, 1936, Major (William Matthew) Viscount Wolmer, who *d* on active ser 1942, el son of 3rd Earl of Selborne; 2ndly, 1948, 4th Baron Newton, who *d* 1992; 3rdly, 1994, Frederick Charles Horace Fryer (*see* E Peel, colls, 1985 Edn). *Residence* – Vernon Hill House, Bishop's Waltham, Hants.
Issue of late Col Geoffrey Egerton-Warburton, DSO, TD, *b* 1888, *d* 1961: *m* 1927, Hon Georgiana Mary Dormer, MBE, who *d* 1955, da of 14th Baron Dormer:—
Peter (Mulberry House, Bentworth, Hants GU34 5RB; 54 Princes Gate Mews, SW7 2RB), *b* 1933; ed Eton, and RMA; late Capt Coldm Gds: *m* 1st, 1955 (*m diss* 1958), Belinda Vera, da of late James R. A. Young, of Cowdrays, East Hendred, Berks; 2ndly, 1960 (*m diss* 1967) Sarah Jessica Norman, el da of Maj Willoughby Rollo Norman, Gren Gds (*see* Norman, Bt); 3rdly, 1969, Hon Marya Anne Noble, da of Baron Glenkinglas, and has issue living, (by 2nd *m*) Charles Piers, *b* 1961: *m* 1989, Fiona Clare, only da of Robin Desmond Bonham-Carter, and has issue living, Piers *b* 1992, Marcus *b* 1994, — James Willoughby *b* 1963: *m* 1993, Elizabeth Boughton, eldest da of Vincent Riggio, of Long Island, NY, USA, — (by 3rd *m*), Christopher Geoffrey, *b* 1971, — Louisa Jane (twin), *b* 1971. —— Anne, *b* 1928: *m* 1954, His Hon Judge James Eccles Malise Irvine (School House, Caulcott, Bicester, Oxon OX6 3NE), and has issue living, David Peter Gerard, *b* 1963; ed Stowe, Oakham, Berks Coll of Agric, RMA Sandhurst, and RAC Cirencester; BSc Buckingham; Lieut Gren Gds 1987-91 (Gulf War Medal), Lieut Royal Wessex Yeo (Royal Glos Hussars), — Susan Caroline Jane, *b* 1961; ed St Mary's, Wantage, Oakham, and Aberdeen Univ (MA 1982). —— Jane, LVO (Crossways, Woodgreen, Fordingbridge, Hants), *b* 1931; Lady in Waiting to HRH Princess Alice, Duchess of Gloucester until 1984, since when an Extra Lady in Waiting; LVO 1983.

Granddaughter of late Rev James Francis Egerton-Warburton, 2nd son of late Rev Rowland Egerton-Warburton (ante):—
Issue of late Arthur Egerton-Warburton, *b* 1848, *d* 1927: *m* 1874, Edna, who *d* 1901, da of James Stowe:—
Ruth: *m* 1952, Edgar Hunt, who *d* 1959.

Grandchildren of late Rowland James Egerton-Warburton, 2nd son of Maj Peter Egerton-Warburton, CMG (infra):—
Issue of late John Egerton-Warburton, *b* 1873, *d* 1943: *m* 1913, Winifred Vaughan, of 131 Cambridge Terrace, Malvern, S Australia:—
Richard John, *b* 1916; Capt Australian Imperial Force (Reserve of Officers): *m* 1946, Audrey Doreen Roberts, of Melbourne, Victoria, Australia, and has issue living, Jill Rosalind, *b* 1948, — Elizabeth Jane, *b* 1952, — Bronwyn Grey, *b* 1954. *Residence* – 10 Palmer Avenue, Myrtle Bank, S Australia. —— Margaret (18 Superba Parada, Mosman, NSW), *b* 1919: *m* 1st, 1940, Lt Robert Paine, who was *ka* in New Guinea 1943; 2ndly, 1947, Maxwell Dunn, who *d* 1966, and has issue living, (by 1st *m*) Frances Margaret, *b* 1941.
Issue of late Peter Augustus Egerton-Warburton, *b* 1877, *d* 1944: *m* 1906, Ellen, who *d* 1949, da of W Fountain, of Saffron Walden:—
Elizabeth; is a Nursing Sister Australian Imperial Force: *m* 19-, Frank Mosey, of Anlaby, via Eudunda, S Australia 5374, Australia.
Issue of late Rowland Egerton-Warburton, *b* 1885, *d* 1963: *m* 1914, Isabel, who *d* 1957, da of W. F. Langdon, of Caulfield, Aust:—
Francis (42 Hortense St, Burwood, Vic, Aust), *b* 1917: *m* 1944, Joan, da of P. A. Ewing, of Bridgetown, W Aust, and has issue living, Anne, *b* 1945: *m* 1966, Herbert Timothy Lee-Steere, of Esperance, W Aust, and has issue living, Peter Timothy *b* 1968, Christopher Ian *b* 1969, Wendy Anne *b* 1972. —— Annie Isabel, *b* 1915: *m* 1939, Harold Vernon Bray, of 27 Clydesdale St, Como, W Aust, and has issue living, Robert Harold, *b* 1942: *m* 1968, Margaret Esme, da of T. W. Maxwell, of Como, W Aust, — Ian Michael, *b* 1943. — Marjorie Alison, *b* 1940: *m* 1963, William Francis Richardson, of Riverlea, Mardella, W Aust, and has issue living, Michael James *b* 1966, Felicity Jane *b* 1970, — Gillian Margaret, *b* 1948.

Granddaughter of late Maj Peter Egerton-Warburton, CMG, 4th son of late Rev Rowland Egerton-Warburton (ante):—
Issue of late William Egerton-Warburton, *b* 1847, *d* 1906: *m* 1877, Edith, da of W. M. Sandford:—
Mary, *b* 1885: *m* 1909, Herbert Wilfred Pownall, and has issue living, Robert Alfred, *b* 1913, — Elizabeth, *b* 1910, — Frances Mary, *b* 1917. *Residence* –

Grandchildren of late William Egerton-Warburton (ante):—
Issue of late Richard Sandford Egerton-Warburton, *b* 1880, *d* 1959: *m* 1908, Emily Meredith, who *d* 1965, da of Bayfield Moulden:—
Peter Bayfield (Unit 3, 7 North Parade, Kingswood, S Australia 5062), *b* 1909; served with 2nd AIF: *m* 1937, Roma Bailands Hosking, da of Frank Becker, of Adelaide, S Australia, and has issue living, Richard Francis (17A Macquarie Rd, Pymble, NSW 2073, Aust), *b* 1940: *m* 1966, Susan Elizabeth Chandler, of Perth, W Aust, and has issue living, Bayfield James *b* 1970, Matthew Robert *b* 1973, — Elizabeth Louise, *b* 1938: *m* 1962, Ian Wesley Giles, of 159 Gover St, N Adelaide, S Aust 5006, and has issue living, Benjamin-Peter Wesley *b* 1969, Anna Louise *b* 1963, Sally Elizabeth *b* 1964. —— Meredith, *b* 1913: *m* 1936, Donald Thomas Mitchell, of 15 Cudmore Av, Toorak, 5056, S Aust, and has issue living, Alan, *b* 1940, — Jean Meredith, *b* 1938, — Frances Egerton, *b* 1943. —— Alice Elizabeth Grey, *b* 1924: *m* 1947, Robert C. Bell, who *d* 1987, and has issue living, Hugh, *b* 1954, — Helen, *b* 1948, — Barbara, *b* 1950, — Judy, *b* 1952.

Grandchildren of late Richard Sandford Egerton-Warburton (ante):—
Issue of late Edward Howard Egerton-Warburton, *b* 1910, *d* 1974: *m* 1938, Margaret Newland (97 Gardner St, Como, W Australia 6152):—
Peter Ridgeway (Mt Burges Station, Coolgardie, W. Australia 6429), *b* 1941: *m* 1966, Vanda Sue, da of J. B. Wood, of Bunbury, W Aust, and has issue living, David Peter, *b* 1967: *m* 1990, Gena Huck, and has issue living, David William *b* 19—, —

Edward James, *b* 1976, — Deanna Sue, *b* 1969, — Rosa Margaret, *b* 1972. —— Ann, *b* 1946: *m* 1969, James William Clarke, and has issue living, Benjamin James, *b* 1970: *m* 1990, Tara Hotham Jenkins.
　　　　Issue of late William Arnold Egerton-Warburton, *b* 1918, *d* 1976: *m* 1940, Letty Dorian Parsons, who *d* 1977:—
Michael Philip, *b* 1948.

　　　　　　Grandchildren of late William Egerton-Warburton (ante):—
　　　　Issue of late Philip Egerton-Warburton, *b* 1882, *d* 1965: *m* 1912, Olive Rigarlsford, da of Alfred Palmer, late of Kapunda, S Australia:—
Patience Anne, *b* 1916. —— Cecily, *b* 1918.

　　　　　　Grandchildren of late George Grey Egerton-Warburton (infra):—
　　　　Issue of late Philip Grey Egerton-Warburton, *b* 1877, *d* 1954: *m* 1909, Verna Grace, who *d* 1939, da of S. J. Rowe, formerly of Perth, W Australia:—
Geoffrey Grey, *b* 1911: *m* (Jan) 1940, Marjorie Vere, da of late Nelson Hamilton-Taylor, of Mount Barker, W Australia, and has issue living, Arley Geoffrey, *b* (Dec) 1940, — Colin Yorke, *b* 1947, — Ione Vere, *b* 1942, — Vivien Gay, *b* 1944, — Caroline Marjorie, *b* 1952. *Residence* – Yeriminup, Cranbrook, W Australia. —— Ronald Grey, *b* 1914: *m* 1937, Edith Mabel, da of G. J. A. Swiney, of Albany, and has issue living, Philip Alexander, *b* 1938: *m* 1st, 1968 (*m diss* 1984), Sheila, da of Donald La Claire, of Vancouver, BC, Canada; 2ndly, 1986, Pauline Anne Maxwell, and has issue living (by 1st *m*), John Alexander *b* 1973, Brooke Elizabeth *b* 1971, — Michael George (Mirinup, Frankland River, W Aust), *b* 1941: *m* 1966, Lois Elizabeth, da of H. O. Grimbly, of Attadale, Perth, W Aust, and has issue living, Antony Michael Grey *b* 1967, Grey Edward *b* 1972, Roland George *b* 1977, — David Ronald, *b* 1945: *m* 1968, Margaret Elizabeth, da of A. E. Challenor, of Dandallup, W Aust, and has issue living, Joshua David *b* 1975, Blanche Elizabeth *b* 1971, Edwyna Margaret *b* 1974, — Jennifer Mary, *b* 1940: *m* 1964, John Mattiske, of Norla Kojonup, W Aust, and has issue living Peter Rex *b* 1972, Marie Louise *b* 1966, Philippa Jane *b* 1968, — Diana Margaret, *b* 1943: *m* 1972, Ivan Johnson, of Perth, W Aust, and has issue living, Daniel Slade *b* 1981, Joanna *b* 1974, Jennifer Lee *b* 1977. *Residence* – Lesmurdie, W Aust. —— Dorothy Antoinette, *b* 1909: *m* 1934, George Alexander Swiney, and has issue living, Wayne Haig Egerton, *b* 1935, — Graham Haig, *b* 1940. *Residence* – Franklands, Frankland River, W Aust.

　　　　　　Grandchildren of late Rowland Egerton-Warburton, son of late George Edward Egerton-Warbuton, yst son of Rev Rowland Egerton-Warburton (ante):—
　　　　Issue of late Philip Augustus Egerton-Warburton, *b* 1904, *d* 1981: *m* 1928 Alice Mary Price (RMB 228, W Pingelly, W Aust 6308):—
Rowland, *b* 1928: *m* 1953, Laurel Gloria Ferguson, and has issue living, Graeme, *b* 1954: *m* 1984, Raylene Holding, and has issue living, Peter *b* 1990, Emma *b* 1992, — Trevor, *b* 1958: *m* 19—(*m diss* 19—), Louise —, — Maxine, *b* 1955: *m* 1976, Gregory Beaton, and has issue living, Joseph Finlay *b* 1978, Donald Peter *b* 1980. —— Ross, *b* 1931: *m* 1954, Wilma Joan Smoker, and has issue living, Dean Ross, *b* 1961: *m* 1985, Diane Fay Roberts, and has issue living, Justin Roy *b* 1990, Troy Aron *b* 1994, Kristy Ann *b* 1992, — Evan Mark, *b* 1966: *m* 1992, Roslyn Gail Cowcill, — Alison Joy, *b* 1955: *m* 1st, 1974 (*m diss* 19—), Bruce Edward Dowsett; 2ndly, 1991, Robert Kevin Lee, and has issue living (by 1st *m*), Ashley Michael *b* 1977, Narelle Marie *b* 1974, — Robyn Lois, *b* 1957: *m* 1976, Arthur Raymond Lines, and has issue living, Craig Phillip *b* 1979, Maree Karen *b* 1981, — Coral Janet, *b* 1960: *m* 1986, Robert Martin Miles, and has issue living, Jackson Ross *b* 1990, Alex Stephen *b* 1992, Eric Gregory *b* 1993. —— Philip (RMB 512, Williams, W Aust 6391, Australia), *b* 1934: *m* 1959, Georgina May, da of H.F.J. Higginson, of Kanandah, Pingelly, W Aust, and has issue living, Michael Philip, *b* 1959: *m* 1982, Jillian Steer, and has issue living, Benjamin Michael *b* 1986, Nicholas Jeremy *b* 1990, Rebecca Therese *b* 1988, Rachael Holly *b* 1988, — Brett Francis, *b* 1970: *m* 1992, Candice —, — Debra Suzanne, *b* 1961: *m* 1990, Peter Evelyn-Liardet, and has issue living, Christopher Luke EGERTON-WARBURTON *b* 1982, Jennifer Kate *b* 1992. —— Peter, *b* (twin) 1934.

　　　　　　Grandchildren of late Horace Egerton-Warburton (infra):—
　　　　Issue of late John Le Belward Warburton, *b* 1882, *d* 1949: *m* 1913, Blanche Josephine van Zuilecom, of Yeenyellup, Kojonup, W Australia:—
John Egerton (Box 20, Kojonup, W Aust), *b* 1916: a farmer: *m* 1939, Celia Maltby, da of Allan Douglas Robinson, of Subiaco, Perth, W Aust, and has issue living, Quentin (Korellup, RMB 328, Kojonup 6395, W Aust), *b* 1942: *m* 1965, Mary Heath, da of J. W. Rowe, of Claremont, Perth, W Aust, and has issue living, David Grey *b* 1970, Robert John Quentin *b* 1972, Megan Ann *b* 1967: *m* 1993, Bruce Alexander McCracken, — Alan (Yeenyellup, Box 20, Kojonup, W Aust), *b* 1947: *m* 1971, Cynthia Margaret, da of C. D. Lee, of Royston Park, Kojonup, W Aust, and has issue living, George Thomas *b* 1988, Rachael Margaret *b* 1972, Emily Jane *b* 1974, Diana Elizabeth *b* 1986, — Celia Ruth, *b* 1940: *m* 1960, Anthony Randle Egerton-Warburton, (infra).
　　　　Issue of late Horace Grey Egerton-Warburton, *b* 1891, *d* 1956: *m* 1st, 1915, Ruth, who *d* 1918, da of Randle Egerton-Warburton (ante); 2ndly, 1920, Vera (St Werburgh's, Mount Barker, W Australia), da of Charles F. Lake, of Dandenong Road, Malvern, Melbourne, Australia:—
(By 1st *m*) Mary Ruth, *b* 1916: *m* 1st, 1941, Edward Henry Finch, Roy Australian Air Force, who was *ka* 1943; 2ndly, 1946, Vernon Wells, Roy Australian Air Force, and has issue living, (by 1st *m*) Penelope, *b* 1942, — (by 2nd *m*) Grey Egerton, *b* 1947, — Peter Randell Scott, *b* 1950, — Diana Ruth, *b* 1948. *Residence* - . —— Joan, *b* 1918: *m* 1941, Henry Graham Johnson, Australian Imperial Force, and has issue living, Richard Grey, *b* 1944, — Anthony Peter, *b* 1946. —— (By 2nd *m*) Edward Grey, *b* 1928: *m* 1960, Elizabeth, da of John Wade, of Perth, and has issue living, Grey Piers, *b* 1962: *m* 1992, Jennifer Anne, da of Dr P. Nash, of Mosman Park, Perth, W Aust, and has issue living, Angela Grace *b* 1993, — Robin, *b* 1967, — Rosemary, *b* 1961. —— Yexley Selina, *b* 1921: *m* 1946, Gordon Maitland-Roberts, Australian Imperial Force, and has issue living, Wade Maitland, *b* 1947, — Bruce Gordon, *b* 1950, — Helen Ena, *b* 1948. *Residence* – Chelsea, Moora, W Australia. —— Patricia Ann, *b* 1923: *m* (Jan) 1946, William Adolphus Chaffey, MLA, and has issue living, David Frank *b* 1957, Mary Ann *b* (Nov) 1946, — Elizabeth Patricia, *b* 1949. *Residence* – 119 Fitzroy Street, Tamworth, NS Wales. —— Ann Vera, *b* (twin) 1928: *m* 1952, Donald Charles Keir Collins, and has issue living, Bradford Keir, *b* 1958, — Scott Charles Egerton, *b* 1962, — Joanne Margaret, *b* 1953, — Jacqueline Anne, *b* 1955. *Residence* – 47 Martin Street, Mount Barker, W Australia. —— Helen Maud, *b* 1931: *m* 1957, John Halley Arnold, and has issue living, Richard John Halley, *b* 1960, — Brooke Egerton Halley, *b* 1962, — Amanda Jane, *b* 1958, — Michelle Tracey, *b* 1959. *Residence* – Selsley Downs, Kojonup, W Australia. —— Carlene Alice, *b* (twin) 1931: *m* 1957, John Ronald Penn, and has issue living, Fiona Carlene, *b* 1958, — Sally Louise, *b* 1960. *Residence* – Parsons St, Mount Barker, W Australia.

　　　　　　Grandchildren of late Augustus Egerton-Warburton, son of late George Edward Egerton-Warburton (ante):—
　　　　Issue of late Angus Egerton-Warburton, *b* 1889, *d* 1960: *m* 1925, Dorothy (RMB 406, Euretta, Kojonup, W Australia), da of John Weston, of Eastwood, Notts:—
Brian Wayne, *b* 1933. —— Ian Angus, *b* 1942: *m* 1965, Robin, da of Dr Robert Elphick, of Shenlon Park, and has issue living, Barney, *b* 1968, — Simone Elissa, *b* 1966. —— Joan Irma (South Parkfield, N Danalup, W Australia), *b* 1926: *m* 1st, 1950, Ross Bovell, who *d* 1950; 2ndly, 1955, John Griffin Money, who *d* 1962. —— Evelyn Isabel, *b* 1928: *m* 1953, Frank Devine, of Hillside, Frankland River, W Australia, and has issue living, Peter John, *b* 1954, — Christopher James, *b* 1956, Garry Matthew, *b* 1962, — Leonie Frances, *b* 1957. —— Margaret, *b* 1931. —— Dorothy June, *b* 1937: *m* 1961, John Kitto, and has issue living, Johnson Grey, *b* 1966, — Grantham Angus, *b* 1968.
　　　　Issue of late Reginald Hubert Egerton-Warburton, *b* 1894, *d* 1962: *m* 1925, Lena Mary Lambe (Woolareen, Konjonup, W Aust):—

Rex (Woolareen, Kojonup, W Aust), *b* 1928: *m* 1946, Muriel Faith Weise, and has issue living, Diane, *b* 1946: *m* 1968, John William Partridge, of Priory Park, Kojonup, W Aust, and has issue living, Craig John *b* 1969, Cindy Karen *b* 1968, — Denise, *b* 1947: *m* 1st, 1965, Kevin William Brown; 2ndly, 19—, — Hall, of Lower King Rd, Albany, W Aust 6330, Aust, and has issue living (by 1st *m*), Darrin Kevin *b* 1966, Gavin William *b* 1967, Byron Rex *b* 1971, — Maree, *b* 1953: *m* 1971, John James Matthews, and has issue living, Chad James *b* 1972, Damon John *b* 1974, Lisa Maree *b* 1979, — Dawn (Cherryton, Konjonup, W Aust), *b* 1926.

Grandchildren of late Randle Egerton-Warburton (infra):—
Issue of late Piers Edward Egerton-Warburton, *b* 1895, *d* 1961: *m* 1920, Winsome, who *d* 1971, da of John Ewing, MLC, of W Australia:—
Diana, *b* 1924: *m* 1945, Julian B. Goyder, and has issue living, Piers Bruce, *b* 1950, — Melody Anne, *b* 1946, — Elizabeth, *b* 1947. —— Pamela, *b* 1929: *m* 1953, Samuel Forster Clarkson, of 57 Irvine St, Peppermint Grove, Perth, W Aust, and has issue living, Simon Nicholas, *b* 1957, — Eve, *b* 1954. —— Jenefer, *b* 1933: *m* 1956, Ian P. Johnston, of Dardanup, W Australia, and has issue living, Ian Justin, *b* 1958, — Julia, *b* 1956, — Andrea, *b* 1963, — Diana, *b* 1965. —— Angela, *b* 1941: *m* 1964, John Charles Roberts, of 51 Saunders St, Mosman Park, W Aust, and has issue living, Andrew Timothy, *b* 1966, — Timothy Andrew, *b* 1970, — Denby Emma, *b* 1976.
Issue of late George Grey Egerton-Warburton, *b* 1899, *d* 1975: *m* 1929, Ethel Vernon, da of Edmund Vernon Drake-Brockman, JP:—
Anthony Randle (Brackenhurst, Bridgetown, W Aust), *b* 1935: *m* 1960, Celia Ruth, da of John Egerton-Warburton (ante), and has issue living, Randle, *b* 1963, — Nicholas, *b* 1966, — Belinda Jane, *b* 1961: *m* 1984, Andrew John Viner, of 15 Mimosa Av, Mount Claremont, W Australia, and has issue living, Jack Randle *b* 1986, Fleur Ruth *b* 1988, — Belinda Ruth, *b* 1967. —— Vernon Grey, *b* 1938: *m* 1970, Jeanny Vlahov, and has issue living, George, *b* 1971, — Anton, *b* 1972, — Virginia, *b* 1974. —— Dorothy Vernon, *b* 1929: *m* 1954, John Gordon Boyle, of 40 Tyrell St, Nedlands, 6009, W Aust, and has issue living, Angela Egerton, *b* 1955; *ed* Univ of Western Australia (BA, Dip Ed): *m* 1989, Anthony Francis Phillips, BA, M Phil, Dip Ed, and has issue living, Ariane Margaret Emerald *b* 1991, Genevieve Georgia Elizabeth *b* 1993, — Erica Egerton, *b* 1960; *ed* Univ of New South Wales (B L Arch): *m* 1987, Antony Luke Radunovich, B Mech Eng, and has issue living, Marcus John *b* 1989, Antony Michael *b* 1990, Miranda Adelaide *b* 1992. —— Fleur, *b* 1932: *m* 1956, John Aitken, of Hau-ora, Havelock North, Hawkes Bay, NZ, and has issue living, Timothy Murray, *b* 1957: *m* 1986, Susan Loffler, and has issue living, Richard George Murray *b* 1988, Andrew Robert *b* 1990, Michael Timothy *b* 1992, — Hamish Egerton, *b* 1960: *m* 1993, Susan Goodman, — Judith Jill, *b* 1962: *m* 1989, Bruce Thomas Wagg, and has issue living, Timothy Guy Thomas *b* 1991.

Granddaughters of late George Edward Egerton-Warburton (ante):—
Issue of late Randle Egerton-Warburton, *b* 1860, *d* 1938: *m* 1890, Eva, who *d* 1931, da of Edward Hester:—
Cecely Alice (Banyandah Farm, Esperance, W Aust), *b* 1892: *m* 1919, Maitland John Drake Brockman who *d* 1969, and has issue living, Egerton Charles (Laverton Downs, Laverton, W Aust), *b* 1927: *m* 1948, Daphne Anderson, and has issue living, John *b* 1949, Philip *b* 1950, Viki *b* 1954, Elizabeth *b* 1961, — Mollie Agatha *b* 1920: *m* 1949, Brig James Roy Anderson, CBE, late R Sussex Regt (United Service Club), and has issue living, Hamish Warburton Findlater *b* 1952, Sheena Fiona Egerton, *b* 1954, — Cecily Jean (Currajugg, Clyde Mountain, Braidwood, NSW), *b* 1921; reverted to surname of Drake-Brockman: *m* 1st, 1944 (*m diss* 1955), Richard Smallpiece Whitington; 2ndly, 1962 (*m diss* 1972), Maj-Gen Paul Alfred Cullen, CBE, DSO, ED, and has issue living, (by 1st *m*) Richard Mark *b* 1947, James Jerome *b* 1951, — Frances Margaret, *b* 1923: *m* 1951, John Fenwick, of Dempster St, Esperance, W Aust, and has issue living, Jane Deborrah *b* 1959. —— Margaret Augusta, *b* 1903: *m* 1st, 1932, Robert Willgress, BSc, who *d* 1956; 2ndly, 1956, William Francis Dudley Allison, of Protea Rd, George, Cape Province, S Africa.

The House of Egerton, one of the most ancient and distinguished in Cheshire, traces its descent to William le Belward, who was Baron of Malpas under the Norman Earl Palatine of that county. David, great-grandson of William le Belward, took the name of Egerton from the Lordship of Egerton, which he had inherited; and from him, in a direct line, is descended the present baronet. Sir Roland Egerton, 1st Bt, *m* Bridget, sister and co-heir of 15th Lord Grey de Wilton. The 7th Bt was created Earl of Wilton, with remainder to his maternal grandson, Hon Thomas Grosvenor. At his death in 1814 the baronetcy passed to his kinsman John Egerton of Oulton, descended from a yr son of 1st Bt. By Roy Warrant dated 30th June, 1825, King George IV granted to the Rev Sir Philip Egerton, 9th Bt, and all subsequent baronets on succeeding to the title the right to assume for themselves only the additional surname of Grey and the Arms and Supporters of Grey de Wilton. The 10th baronet sat as MP for Chester (C) 1830, for Cheshire West 1835-81. The 13th baronet, Rev Sir Brooke de Malpas Grey-Egerton, was R of Stoke-on-Terne, and Rural Dean of Hodnet 1901-13.

ELIOTT (NS) 1666, of Stobs, Roxburghshire

Be wise

Sir CHARLES JOSEPH ALEXANDER ELIOTT OF STOBS, 12th *Baronet*: *b* 9 Jan 1937, eldest son of late Charles Rawdon Heathfield Eliot, son of Alexander Boswell Vassal Eliott, half-brother of 9th baronet; *s* his kinsman, *Sir* ARTHUR FRANCIS AUGUSTUS BOSWELL, 1989; *ed* St Joseph's Christian Brothers, Rockhampton, nr Brisbane: *m* 1959, Wendy Judith, da of Henry John Bailey, of Toowoomba, Qld, and has issue.

Arms – Gules, on a bend or, a baton azure; in a dexter canton argent, a saltire azure surmounted of an inescutcheon or charged with a lion rampant within a double tressure flory counterflory gules, being the addition of Nova Scotia as a Baronet. **Crest** – A hand couped at the wrist in armour holding a cutlass in bend proper. **Supporters** – *Dexter*, a ram: *sinister*, a goat; both proper and gorged with a laurel branch vert, horned and hooved or. *Residence* – 27 Cohoe St, Toowoomba, Qld 4350, Australia.

SON LIVING

RODNEY GILBERT CHARLES, *b* 1966: *m* 1988, Andrea Therese Saunders, and has issue living, Steven Charles, *b* 1990, — Cassandra Jane, *b* 1989.

DAUGHTERS LIVING

Elizabeth Jane, *b* 1960: *m* — Armanasco, and has issue living, Daniel Charles, *b* 19—, — Lindsay Clare, *b* 19—, — Kimberley Jane, *b* 1991. —— Jenny, *b* 1961: *m* — Land. —— Josephine Mary Anne, *b* 1963: *m* — Grofski, and has issue living, Ethan Joseph, *b* 1990, — Brigitte Kate, *b* 1992. —— Clare Melinda, *b* 1973.

BROTHERS LIVING

Keith Robert Vincent (65 Bunya St, Grunslopes, Brisbane, Qld 4120, Australia), *b* 1942: *m* 1965, Annette Mary Kijrgaard, and has issue living, Brett Robert, *b* 1966. —— Raymond Francis, *b* 1946.

SISTERS LIVING

Irene Gertrude, *b* 1930: *m* 1950, Peter Brown (PO Box 4, Yeppon, Qld, Australia). —— Myrtle Davies, *b* 1935. —— Bella Loraine, *b* 1939.

AUNTS LIVING

Gertrude May, *b* 1893: *m* 1929, Henry Wilson Mercer, of Evanston, via Ilfracombe, Qld, Australia. —— Constance Elizabeth, *b* 1894: *m* 19—, Clarence Quinn. —— Annabella Carmichael, *b* 1897: *m* 1927, James Bryson, of Denham Terrace, Rockhampton, Qld, Australia.

DAUGHTER LIVING OF ELEVENTH BARONET

Margaret Frances Boswell ELIOTT, *b* 1948; resumed her maiden name: *m* 1974, Anthony E. B. Vaughan-Arbuckle, who *d* 1986; 2ndly, 19—, Christopher Powell Wilkins, and has issue living (by 1st *m*), Benjamin, *b* 1978, — Kate, *b* 1981. *Residence* – Redheugh, Newcastleton, Roxburghshire.

WIDOW LIVING OF ELEVENTH BARONET

FRANCES AILEEN (*Frances, Lady Eliott of Stobs*), eldest da of Sir Francis Kennedy McClean, AFC: *m* 1947, Sir Arthur Francis Augustus Boswell Eliot of Stobs, 11th Bt, who *d* 1989. *Residence* – Redheugh, Newcastleton, Roxburghshire.

MOTHER LIVING

Emma Elizabeth HARRIS: *m* 1925, Charles Rawdon Heathfield Eliott, who *d* 1972. *Residence* – 72 Derby St, Rockhampton, Qld, Australia.

COLLATERAL BRANCHES LIVING

Issue of late Clive John Eliott, *b* 1940, *d* 1971, brother of 12th baronet: *m* 1961, Estelle Maude Kelland:—
Bradley John, *b* 1962. —— Anthony Charles, *b* 1966. —— Dale Thomas, *b* 1969.

Grandson of late Gilbert William Henry Eliott, son of late Francis Willoughby Eliott (infra):—
Issue of late Gilbert William Eliott, *b* 1894, *d* 1961: *m* 1921, Lilian Mary, who *d* 1968, da of William Towle, of Nottingham, and widow of Neville Dalley:—
Gilbert Rowley Roxburgh (53 Epping Rd, Epping, NSW), *b* 1923; *ed* Sydney Univ (BDS); late F/Lt RAAF: *m* 1944, Helen Ross, yr da of A. H. Martin, MA, PhD, of Sydney, NSW, and has issue living, Gilbert William Heathfield, *b* 1961, — Christine, *b* 1945; *ed* Univ of New England, NSW (BSc), and Sydney Univ (Dip ED), — Virginia Ruth, *b* 1947.

Grandchildren of late Francis Willoughby Eliott, son of late Gilbert Eliott, CMG, 3rd son of 6th baronet:—
Issue of late Edward Percy Eliott, *b* 1860, *d* 1931: *m* 1890, Annie, who *d* 1944, el da of John Connolly, of Gayndah, Queensland:—
Gilbert, *b* 1891: *m* 1929, Barbara, second da of late Charles Saddlier, of Gayndah, Queensland. —— Marjorie, *b* 1892: *m* 1938, Robert Livingston Boyd.

Grandson of late Clifton Hazlewood Eliott (infra):—
 Issue of late Francis Heathfield Eliott, *b* 1908, *d* 1970: *m* 1939, Florence Nell (Congi, Woolbrook, NSW), da of late
O. B. Briggs:—
Graham Francis Heathfield (26 Kerferd St, Watson, ACT 2602), *b* 1941: *m* 1970, Karen Joyce, el da of Robert John Taylor, of
Mt Druitt, NSW, and has issue living, Miles Francis Heathfield, *b* 1977, — Martyn Graham Heathfield, *b* 1979, — Tristan
Robert Heathfield, *b* 1984, — Louise Karen Florence, *b* 1986. —— Geoffrey Osmer Heathfield (Congi, Woolbrook, NSW), *b*
1942: *m* 1974, Sally Green, of Moorabinda, Taroom, Qld, and has issue living, Mitchell Francis Heathfield, *b* 1978, — La-
chlan Edward Heathfield, *b* 1980.

Grandchildren of late Francis Willoughby Eliott (ante):—
 Issue of late Clifton Hazlewood Eliott, *b* 1872, *d* 1938: *m* 1905, Mary Isabel, who *d* 1960, el da of the Rev R. W.
Wilson, of Walcha, New England, NS Wales:—
Roger Clifton Heathfield (85 Oak St, Tamworth, 2340, NSW), *b* 1909; late AIF: *m* 1st, 1942 (*m diss* 1947), Winifred Maud,
only da of the Rev H. E. West, V of Tenterfield, NS Wales; 2ndly, 1948, Betty Muriel, el da of H. Williams, of Landsbrough,
Queensland, and has issue living, (by 2nd *m*) Roger John (Bective Station, Tamworth, NSW 2340, Australia), *b* 1955: *m* 1980,
Dianne Jennifer, yr da of William Henry Waugh, of Northbridge, NSW, and has issue living, Anika *b* 1982, — Robyn
Jeannette, *b* 1949: *m* 1st, 1974 (*m diss* 1979), Jeffrey Alan Anderson; 2ndly, 1986, Bruce Raymond Melville, and has issue
living, (by 1st *m*) Kris *b* 1975, (by 2nd *m*) James Raymond *b* 1988, Catherine Elizabet *b* 1990, — Wendy Sue, *b* 1954: *m*
1973, Alan John Hillier, of 54 Oak St, Tamworth, NSW 2340, and has issue living, Damian John *b* 1976, Brendan *b* 1978.
—— Lyndsay Raine Heathfield, *b* 1919; in Australian Imperial Force: *m* 1949, Rosemary Margaret, yr da of Gordon W.
Phillips, of 1 Carlos Rd, Artarmon, NS Wales, and has issue living, Andrew Clifton Heathfield, *b* 1954: *m* 1983, Melissa
Helen, only da of R. A. Lee, of 8 Bishop Crescent, Armidale, NSW, and has issue living, Dougal Heathfield *b* 1987, Stuart
Heathfield *b* 1988, — Gaeling Heathfield, *b* 1950, — Ruth Heathfield, *b* 1952, — Rosemary Ann Heathfield, *b* 1956. *Residence*
– Greenwells, Walcha, New England, NS Wales. —— Dorothy Mary Heathfield (Dickinson Court, 32 Dickinson St, Charles-
town, NSW 2290), *b* 1911: *m* 1933 (*m diss* 1957), Archibald John Kilpatrick, and has issue living, John Eliott, *b* 1936: *m* 1960,
Janice Ellen Stidolph, and has issue living, Andrew John *b* 1966, Peter Gordon *b* 1972, Leanne Jane *b* 1962, Donna Louise, *b*
1963, — Owen Heathfield, *b* 1942: *m* 1963, Marie Maynard, and has issue living, Russell Owen *b* 1964, Alison Lyn *b* 1966: *m*
1988, James Sidney Chappell, — Jillian Mary (26 Ker St, Charlestown, NSW 2290), *b* 1934: *m* 1956, Allan John Stuart, who *d*
1984, and has had issue, Paul Andrew *b* 1960, *d* 1983, Michael John *b* 1961, David Allan *b* 1963, Anthony Mark *b* 1970.

Grandsons of late Lt-Col Francis Augustus Heathfield Eliott, DSO, (infra):—
 Issue of late Heathfield George Henry Eliott, *b* 1897, *d* 1975: *m* 1922, Rhoda Isadora (Flat 206, Rosedale, Lower
Nursery Rd, Rosebank, Cape Town, S Africa), da of Frederick William Augustus Daly:—
Ian Cecil Heathfield (PO Box 41, Sunninghill 2157, Republic of S Africa), *b* 1923: *m* 1945, Berenice Louise, da of George
Joseph Washington, and has issue living, Anthony John, *b* 1949: *m* 1974, Sheila Kirkness, — Christopher Thomas, *b* 1953.
—— Ivor Keith Heathfield (300 Lister Rd, Rembrant Park, Johannesburg, S Africa), *b* 1926: *m* 1962, Edythe Gloria, da of
John Marshall Harrison, and has issue living, Graeme, *b* 1964, — Kevin John, *b* 1973, — Lynette, *b* 1963, — Louise, *b* 1967.

Granddaughter of late Lt-Col Francis Augustus Heathfield Eliott, DSO (infra):—
 Issue of late Lt-Col Hugh Herbert Heathfield Eliott, OBE, TD, *b* 1903, *d* 1976: *m* 1927, Barbara, who *d* 1983, da of
John Cullen Marsh, of Penge, SE:—
Ann Georgina Heathfield, *b* 1929: *m* 1954, William John Bullock, of The Mill Farm, Guarlford Rd, Malvern, Worcs WR14
3QP, son of William Edward Bullock, of The Mill Farm, Guarlford Rd, Malvern, and has issue living, Anthony John, *b* 1957:
m 1985, Catherine Sally Greville Fox, and has issue living, James William Basil *b* 1989, Edward Adam Hugh *b* 1993, — Nigel
Timothy, *b* 1960: *m* 1989, Susan Lindsay, da of Kenneth Ellis, of Tal-y-Bont, Gwynedd, N Wales.

Granddaughters of late Maj George Augustus Eliott, son of late Adm George Augustus Eliott, 5th son of
6th baronet:—
 Issue of late Lieut-Col Francis Augustus Heathfield Eliott, DSO, *b* 1867, *d* 1937: *m* 1896, Evelyn Georgina Stirling,
who *d* 1937, da of Richard William McDermott, of Dublin:—
Evelyn Heather, *b* 1898: *m* 1923, Horatio Wellesley Burgess, late Dragoon Gds, and has issue living, John Francis Wellesley
(Braces Leigh, Newland, Malvern, Worcs), *b* 1929: *m* 1953, Angela Mildren, and has issue living, Jonathan Nigel *b* 1955,
Grace Clare *b* 1958, — Margaret Jean, *b* 1924: *m* 1951, Richard Andrews, of 53 Middlebrook Rd, High Wycombe, Bucks, and
has issue living, Christopher John *b* 1952, Peter Richard *b* 1957, — Jennifer Evelyn, *b* 1938. *Residence* – 7 Wiltshire Gdns,
Bransgore, Dorset. —— Dymphna Helen Cynthia, *b* 1906: *m* 1930, John Richard Vernon, Nigerian Civil Ser (ret), who *d*
1984, and has issue living, Joanne Georgina Dymphna, *b* 1933: *m* 1953, Jorgen Lagoni, of Copenhagen, Denmark. *Residence* –
13 Rowans, Park, Lymington, Hants SO4 9GD.

The Eliotts or Elliots (then known as Elwalds or Ellots), are reputed to have come from Angus and settled as a clan in
Liddesdale under grant of lands from Robert the Bruce, whose purpose was to strengthen the Scottish defences of the
Middle March. Their chief built a tower on a bank overlooking Hermitage Water near its junction with the Liddel and was
therafter known as Robert Ellot of Redheugh. His successors for several generations were Captains of Hermitage Castle. The
Eliotts of Stobs are descended from Gilbert Ellot of Stobs, son of Robert Ellot, of Redheugh, and his wife, Jean Scott, known
as "Gibbie wi' the gowden gartins," who bought Stobs in 1607 from the heirs-portioners of his step-father, Gavin Ellot of
Stobs. The Elliots, Earls of Minto, are also descended from this first laird of Stobs. Gen George Augustus Eliott (Lord
Heathfield) the famous defender of Gibraltar, was yst son of the 3rd baronet. Sir William Francis Eliott, 7th baronet: *m* 1826,
Theresa, da of Sir Alexander Boswell, of Auchinleck, 1st Baronet, el son of James Boswell, biographer of Johnson, and sister
and heir of Sir James Boswell, 2nd Baronet, who *d* 1857.

ELLIOTT (UK) 1917, of Limpsfield, Surrey

CUM·ALLIS·PRO·ALLIS

With others, for others

Sir CLIVE CHRISTOPHER HUGH ELLIOTT, 4th *Baronet b* 12 Aug 1945; *s* his father, *Sir* HUGH FRANCIS IVO, OBE, 1989; *ed* Bryanston, Univ Coll, Oxford (BA), and Cape Town Univ (DPhil); Research Officer, Cape Town Univ 1968-75; FAO/UN Project Mangr Chad 1975-78, Tanzania 1978-86, Kenya 1986-89; Agricultural Operations Division, Rome since 1989: *m* 1975, Marie-Thérèse, da of Johann Rüttimann, of Hohenrain, Switzerland, and has issue.

🜨rms – Argent, on a chevron sable between three bunches of grapes proper as many bezants. Crest – A garb purpure charged with a fleur-de-lis or.
Address – AGO, FAO, via della terme di Caracalla, 00100 Rome, Italy.

SONS LIVING

IVO ANTONY MORITZ, *b* 9 May 1978. —— Nicolas Johann Clive, *b* 1980.

SISTERS LIVING

Susan Elspeth, *b* 1940: *m* 1969, Lt-Col Timothy James Tedder, Gren Gds (c/o Westminster Bank, 46 Terminus Rd, Eastbourne), and has issue living, Zara Elizabeth *b* 1971, — Laura, *b* 1974. —— Judith Margery, *b* 1942: *m* 1968, Erik Geissler, DPhil, and has issue living, — Stephen Francis, *b* 1975, — Beatrice Alison, *b* 1974, — Leonie Elizabeth Pauline, *b* 1978.

AUNTS LIVING (*Daughters of 2nd Baronet*)

Anne Carey *b* 1914; *ed* Lady Margaret Hall, Oxford (BA 1938): *m* 1939, John Thomson, late Capt RASC (The Knoll, Fulbrook, Burford, Oxon), and has issue living, Robert Hugh Gordon *b* 1947: *m* 1976, Rosalie Zoë Twitchin, and has issue living, Alix Rebecca *b* 1978, Camilla Rachel *b* 1981, — Andrew John, *b* 1949: *m* 1976 Alison Monica Berkley, and has issue living, Anna Marie *b* 1977, Pauline Clare *b* 1979, — Janet Carey, *b* 1941: *m* 1963, Keith Gilbert Robbins, and has issue living, Paul Gilbert John *b* 1965, Daniel Henry Keith *b* 1967, Adam Edward Ivo *b* 1972, Lucy Helen *b* 1970. —— Pauline Margery, *b* 1917; ARCM (Hon Fellow 1972).

WIDOW LIVING OF THIRD BARONET

ELIZABETH MARGARET (*Dowager Lady Elliott*), da of late Adolphus George Phillipson, of N Finchley, N12: *m* 1939, Sir Hugh Francis Ivo Elliott, 3rd Bt, OBE, who *d* 1989.

COLLATERAL BRANCH LIVING

Issue of late Thomas Anthony Keith Elliott, CMG, Ambassador to Israel, 2nd son of 2nd baronet, *b* 1921, *d* 1976: *m* 1951, Alethea Helen (1 Windrush, nr Burford, Oxon), el da of late Maj Alistair B. H. Richardson, King's Dragoon Gds (B Hotham, colls):—
Thomas Anthony William, *b* 1959: *m* 1986, Carolyn Smith, and has issue living, Anthony William Felix, *b* 1991, — Evelyn Alethea, *b* 1993. —— Victoria Carey, *b* 1952: *m* 1983, Frederick Dolan, and has issue living, Caitlin Emily, *b* 1987, — Alethea Cecilia, *b* 1990. —— Catherine Frances, *b* 1954: *m* 1982, George Cardona, and has issue living, Anthony, *b* 1985, — Alexander, *b* 1988, — Natalie, *b* 1987. —— Anne Louisa, *b* 1956: *m* 1981, Jurek Bielecki, and has issue living, Anton Andrej, *b* 1984, — Kazimir, *b* 1986, — Lukas, *b* 1989, — Roman, *b* 1990, — Darius, *b* 1993.

The 1st baronet, Sir Thomas Henry Elliott, KCB (son of late Thomas Henry Elliott, of Rue Ruhmkorff, Paris), was Sec to Board of Agriculture and Fisheries 1892-1913, Dep Master and Comptroller of the Mint, and *ex-officio* Engraver of HM's Seals 1913-17. The 2nd baronet, Sir Ivo D'Oyly Elliott, was Under-Sec, Depart of Commerce and Industry, Govt of India 1916-19, Sec to Govt United Provinces, India 1926-31, and Financial Commr Mauritius 1931. The 3rd baronet, Sir Hugh Francis Ivo Elliott, OBE, served with the Tanganyika Administration 1937-61, Permanent Sec Ministry of Natural Resources 1958-61, Administrator of Tristan da Cunha 1950-52, and with the International Union for Conservation of Nature 1962-80, as Sec Gen 1964-66.

Ellis-Griffith, see Griffith.

ELPHINSTON (NS) 1701, of Logie, co Aberdeen

Not by strength but by valour

Sir JOHN ELPHINSTON OF GLACK, 11th *Baronet*, son of late Thomas George ELPHINSTON, 2nd son of *de jure* 9th baronet; *b* 12 Aug 1924; *s* his uncle, *Maj Sir* ALEXANDER LOGIE ELPHINSTONE, 1970; *ed* Repton, and Emmanuel Coll, Camb (BA); late Lt RM; retired land agent; claimant to dormant Baronetcy of Elphinstone (*cr* 1628), and feudal Barony of New Glasgow, Nova Scotia: *m* 1953, Margaret Doreen, da of late Edric Tasker, of Cheltenham, and has issue.

Arms – Argent, on a chevron sable between three boar's heads erased gules, armed and langued azure, an episcopal mitre of the first. Crest – A dexter hand proper holding a garb or.
Residence – Pilgrims, Churchfields, Sandiway, Northwich, Cheshire CW8 2JS.

SONS LIVING

ALEXANDER (High Banks, Sandy Lane, Brampford Speke, Exeter, Devon EX5 5HW), *b* 6 June 1955; *ed* Repton and St John's Coll, Durham Univ; solicitor: *m* 1986, Ruth Mary, elder da of Rev Robert Curtis Dunnett, of Edgbaston, Warwickshire, and has issue living, Daniel John, *b* 24 Sept 1989, — Sarah Elisabeth, *b* 1992. —— Charles (West Water House, Edzell, Brechin, Angus), *b* 1958; *ed* Repton: *m* 1981, Lucy, da of Maj M. D. Reynolds, of Barnstaple, N Devon, and has issue living, William James, *b* 1986, — Thomas George, *b* 1988, — Mary Abigail, *b* 1984. —— Andrew James, *b* 1961. —— William Robert, *b* 1963.

SISTER LIVING

Marjorie Mary, *b* 1915: *m* 1939, Maj-Gen Reginald Carteret de Mussenden Leathes, CB, MVO, OBE, RM, who *d* 1987, of Furthur House, Highbrook, Ardingly, Sussex, and has issue living, Rupert de Mussenden (Dorset Business School, Bournemouth University, Bournemouth House, 17-19 Christchurch Rd, Bournemouth, Dorset BH1 3LG), *b* 1941: *m* 1967, Nicole Foucaud, and has issue living, Thomas de Mussenden *b* 1970, Isabelle de Mussenden *b* 1973, Francine de Mussenden *b* 1976, — Simon William de Mussenden, *b* 1948: *m* 1971, Belinda Haire, and has issue living, Timothy de Mussenden *b* 1978, Annabel de Mussenden *b* 1976, — Rev David Burlton de Mussenden, *b* 1949: *m* 1975, Mary Cross and has issue living, Benjamin John de Mussenden *b* 1979, Miriam Frances de Mussenden *b* 1982, — Rosemary Sarah de Mussenden, *b* 1944: *m* 1976, Arthur Horsley.

COLLATERAL BRANCH LIVING

Grandchildren of late John William Robert Elphinstone, 3rd son of *de jure* 9th Baronet, *b* 1884, *d* 1949: *m* 1st, 1912 (*m diss* 1924), Vera Mary, da of Lloyd W. Griffith; 2ndly, 1924 (*m diss* 1931), Bettine Ariana, who *d* 1969, da of Sir William Michael Curtis, 4th Bt (*cr* 1802); 3rdly, 1938, Edna M. Nethersole:—
Issue of late John Philip Elphinstone, *b* 1940, *d* 198-: *m* 1967, Beverley Madge Fischer:—
Colin Edward, *b* 1967. —— Angela, *b* 1974.

On 30 Nov 1927, Alexander Logie Elphinstone (ante) proved his right (as 10th Bt) to this Baronetcy (*cr* with remainder to heirs-male whatsoever) before the Baronetage Committee of the Privy Council, being a direct descendant of Nicholas Elphinstone of Glack, a grandson of Sir Henry Elphinstone of Pittendreich (who *s* to the Elphinstone estates in Stirlingshire 1435) (*see* B Elphinstone), and cousin of Sir John Elphinstone, 4th Bt of Logie, since whose death in 1743 the title had remained dormant.

ELPHINSTONE (UK) 1816, of Sowerby, Cumberland

Always ready

Sir (MAURICE) DOUGLAS WARBURTON ELPHINSTONE, TD, 5th *Baronet*, son of late Rev Canon Maurice Curteis Elphinstone, 4th son of 3rd Baronet; *b* 13 April 1909; *s* his cousin, *Sir* HOWARD GRAHAM, 1975; *ed* Loretto, and Jesus Coll, Camb (MA); Fellow Faculty of Actuaries, and FRSE; 1939-45 War as Maj London Scottish: *m* 1943, (Helen) Barbara, da of late George Ramsay Main, of Houghton, Kilmacolm, and has issue.

Arms – Argent guttée de sang, on a chevron embattled sable between three boars' heads erased gules, two swords proper, pommels and hilts or. **Crest** – Out of a mural crown gules a demi-woman affrontée habited, and in the dexter hand a sword erect proper, pommel and hilt or, in the sinister an olive-branch vert.
Residence – 11 Scotby Green Steading, Scotby, Carlisle, Cumbria CA4 8EH.

SON LIVING

JOHN HOWARD MAIN, *b* 25 Feb 1949; *ed* Loretto: *m* 1990, Diane Barbara Quilliam, da of late Dr Brian Quilliam Callow, of Johannesburg. *Residence* – Garden Cottage, 6 Amherst Rd, Sevenoaks, Kent TN13 3LS.

DAUGHTER LIVING

Janet Christine Helen, *b* 1953; BA Manchester: *m* 1983, Kevin Grant, and has issue living, Ruari Jack Elphinstone *b* 1991.

BROTHER LIVING

Rowland Henry (Windy Garth, Bolton, nr Appleby, Cumbria CA16 6AX), *b* 1915; *ed* Loretto, and Jesus Coll, Camb, MA, MB, BChir; formerly Surg-Lt RNVR: *m* 1954, Hester Bull, and has issue living, Henry Charles, *b* 1958, — Mary Georgiana, MBE *b* 1955; *ed* London Univ, MB BS, BSc; MBE (Civil) 1982, — Constance Hester, *b* 1957.

SISTER LIVING

Norah Christine (97 Rennies Mill Rd, St Johns, Newfoundland, A1B 2P1), MB BS, DCH, FRCP(C): *m* 1st, 1968, George Rex Renouf, who *d* 1971; 2ndly, 1973, William Joseph Browne, PC, QC, who *d* 1989.

DAUGHTERS LIVING OF FOURTH BARONET

Elizabeth Mary, *b* 1926: *m* 1952, Cdr Giles Anthony St George Poole, RN (ret), of Western House, Foston, Lincs, and has issue living, Philip Anthony Howard, *b* 1955, — Timothy Giles Elphinstone, *b* 1956, — Rosalind Kate Elizabeth, *b* 1961. —— Rosalind Constance, *b* 1930: *m* 1950, Robert William Atherstone, and has issue living, Howard Ian Damant, *b* 1954, — Anne Margaret Herschël, *b* 1950, — Rosemary Jane Herschël, *b* 1956, — Katherine Sarah Damant, *b* 1961, — Audrey Patricia Damant (twin), *b* 1961.

COLLATERAL BRANCH LIVING

Issue of late Rev Kenneth John Tristram Elphinstone, 3rd son of late Rev Canon Maurice Curteis Elphinstone (ante) (and brother of 5th baronet), *b* 1911, *d* 1980: *m* 1938, Felicity (who *m* 2ndly, Cmdr Eric Ford Schomberg Back, DSC, RN, of 46 St Ann Place, Salisbury, Wilts SP1 2SU), da of late Sir Gerald Berkeley Hurst, QC:—
Margaret Norah ELPHINSTONE, *b* 1948; BA Dunelm; has reverted to maiden name: *m* 1969 (*m diss* 1985), John David Button, BA, MPhil, and has issue living, Rosalind Margaret, *b* 1972, — Catherine Joanna, *b* 1974. *Residence* – 7/6 Ettrickdale Place, Edinburgh EH3 5JN.
This branch of the Elphinstones descends from Réné de Elphinstone, probably a descendant of Jock Elphinstone, a Member of Scots Guard in France 1494. Réné came to Scotland with Robert Stewart, Earl of Orkney, and *d* 1587. His yr son Robert was page to Prince Henry of Wales, son of James VI and I whose gt gt grandson, John Elphinstone, was Capt RN and Adm Russian Navy under Catherine *the Great*. His third and youngest son, Sir Howard, was the first baronet. He was a distinguished Peninsular veteran, and Col Comdt RE, and greatly distinguished himself at the capture of the Cape of Good Hope, in Egypt, and elsewhere. Sir Howard, 2nd baronet, sat as MP for Hastings (L) 1835-7, and for Lewes 1841-7.

Elphinstone-Dalrymple, see Dalrymple.

ELTON (GB) 1717, of Bristol

Sir CHARLES ABRAHAM GRIERSON ELTON, 11th *Baronet*; *b* 23 May 1953; *s* his father, *Sir* ARTHUR HALLAM RICE, 1973; *ed* Eton, and Reading Univ (BA 1976): *m* 1990, Lucy Lauris, da of late Lukas Heller and Mrs Caroline Garnham, and has issue.
Residences – Clevedon Court, Som BS21 6QU; 24 Maida Av, W2 1ST.

DAUGHTER LIVING

Lotte Caroline, *b* 1993.

SISTERS LIVING

Julia Margaret Hallam, *b* 1949. —— Rebecca Wiggin, *b* 1951: *m* 1984, L. Neal FitzSimons, of Kensington, Maryland, USA, son of late T.L. Fitz Simons and Mrs Wells N. Thompson.

WIDOW LIVING OF TENTH BARONET

MARGARET ANN (*Margaret, Lady Elton*) (Clevedon Court, Som); FSA, BA; da of Olafur Bjornson, MD, FRCS, of Winnipeg, Canada: *m* 1948, Sir Arthur Hallam Rice Elton, 10th Bt, who *d* 1973.

COLLATERAL BRANCHES LIVING

Grandchildren of late Rev Henry George Tierney Elton, 5th son of 6th baronet:—
Issue of late Charles Henry Elton, *b* 1857, *d* 1929: *m* 1st, 1879, Emily Grace, da of late Thomas Christmas, 8th Hussars; 2ndly, 1897 (*m diss* 1927), Edith May, da of J. F. Ward, of Hallam House, Walmer, Port Elizabeth, S Africa:—
(By 2nd *m*) CHARLES TIERNEY HALLAM, *b* 1898: *m* 1924, Helen, who *d* 1963, da of late Capt Frederick Patrick Waud, Mercantile Marine, and has issue living, Heather Agnes Campbell, *b* 1928. —— Arthur Hallam (25 Sunny Rd, Glenhazel, Johannesburg, S Africa), *b* 1901: *m* 1926, Georgina, who *d* 1963, da of late A. W. Hemming, and has issue living, Anthony Charles Hallam, *b* 1942, — Rosemary Patricia, *b* 1930, — June Margaret, *b* 1933. —— Kathleen Patricia Hallam ELTON, *b* 1908; has resumed the surname of Elton in lieu of that of Baker: *m* 1940 (*m diss* 1947), Frank Baker. *Residence* – 58 Hurd St, Newton Park, Port Elizabeth, S Africa.

Grandchildren of late Hallam Edmund Arthur Elton, only son of Edmund Hallam Elton (infra):—
Issue of late Timothy Hallam Elton, *b* 1933, *d* 1978: *m* 1964, Linda Susan (Thaba 'Nchu, Box 1, Cashel, Zimbabwe), el da of Maj George Richard Paton Pollitt, of Makalanga, Mazoe, Zimbabwe (*see* B Heytesbury, colls, 1985 Edn):—
Simon Marwood Hallam, *b* 1965. —— Anthony Hallam, *b* 1966. —— Sarah Katharine, *b* 1970.

Granddaughter of late Rev Henry George Tierney Elton (ante):—
Issue of late Edmund Hallam Elton, *b* 1860, *d* 1925: *m* 1887, Ada Constance, da of J. H. Webbe, of Crown Lands Depart, Cape Town:—
Lily Avice Hallam, *b* 1896: *m* 1st, 1934 (*m diss* 1946), L. J. Lake; 2ndly, 1968, Henry Adrian Harington, who *d* 1969. *Address* – Apple, PO Magoebas Kloof, via Pietersburg, Transvaal, S Africa.

Grandchildren of late Com Frederick Elton, RN (infra):—
Issue of late Frederick Ernest Bayard Elton, *b* 1895, *d* 1976: *m* 1st 1914 (*m diss* 1925), Dorothy, da of Adm Thomas Young Greet, of Horsham; 2ndly, 1925 (*m diss* 19—), Vera Ida, da of Hugh Goldie, of Osborne Grange, Bournemouth; 3rdly, 1930, Katherine Mary (32 The Close, Harpenden, Herts), da of Arthur Hamilton Hackett:—
(By 1st *m*) Daphne, *b* 1917: *m* 1936, Derek Maxwell Sanderson (*see* Sanderson, Bt), who *d* 1983. —— Stephanie, *b* 1920: *m* 1947, Eden James Hungerford Morgan. —— (By 3rd *m*) John Arthur Bayard *b* 1940: *m* 1971, Jennifer Elizabeth, el da of William George Thomson, of 25 Mill Lane, Shoreham-by-Sea, and has issue living, James Edmund Bayard, *b* 1972, — Katherine Elizabeth, *b* 1975, — Juliet, *b* 1977.

Grandson of late Frederick Bayard Elton, son of Isaac Elton (*b* 1771), 2nd son of Isaac Elton (*b* 1739), great-grandson of Jacob Elton, 3rd son of 1st baronet:—
Issue of late Com Frederick Elton, RN, *b* 1854, *d* 1922: *m* 1893, Ernestine, who *d* 1951, da of late Ernest White, JP, of Beaudesert Estates, Logan River, Queensland:—
Cedric Edward Bayard (Bucklebury Place, Woolhampton, Berks) *b* 1904; Capt Roy Fusiliers: *m* 1930, Barbara Mary Parrott, and has issue living, Nicholas Edward Bayard, *b* 1931: *m* 1960, Eileen Dorothy, da of Arthur Preece, of Ross-on-Wye, and has issue living, Patrick Edward Bayard *b* 1966, Nicola Jane *b* 1961.

Granddaughter of late Col Frederick Coulthurst Elton, CB, grandson of late Jacob Elton, 3rd son of late Isaac Elton (*b* 1739) ante:—
Issue of late Brig-Gen Frederick Algernon George Young Elton, late RA, *b* 1867, *d* 1921: *m* 1902, Katherine Elizabeth who *d* 1955, da of late Rev Nesfield Andrewes, V of Southwater, Sussex:—
Mary Katherine Gloria, *b* 1904: *m* 1926, Maj Stanley George Reeves Elton Barratt, 16th/5th Lancers (Reserve), who *d* 1973 (having assumed by Roy Licence 1970 the additional surname of Elton before that of Barratt), son of late Sir Sidney Barratt, JP, and has issue living, John Charles Stanley ELTON BARRATT (Millfield Cott, Bury Green, Little Hadham, Herts. *Club* – Special Forces), *b* 1930; *ed* Harrow; late 12th R Lancers; assumed by Roy Licence 1970 the additional surname of Elton before that of Barratt: *m* 1957, Olivia Golding Milward, only da of Lt-Col C. W. M. Rogers, TD, of Coopers Farm House, Lawshall, Suffolk, and has had issue, Thomas George Sinclair *b* 1964, *d* 1983, Katherine Joanna Milward *b* 1961; BSc: *m* 1986, John Geoffrey Singer, of 71 Abbey Rd, Chertsey, Surrey KT16 8NG, son of Dr Geoffrey Singer, of Spring Cottage, Amberley, Arundel, W Sussex (and has issue living, George Thomas *b* 1993, Rebecca Golding *b* 1990), — Frederick James Young ELTON BARRATT (Home Farm, Swalcliffe, Banbury, Oxon), *b* 1934; *ed* Millfield; late Roy Horse Gds; assumed by Roy Licence 1970 the additional surname of Elton before that of Barratt, — Gloria Anne Rosemary (Ballyrankin House, Bunclody, co Wexford), *b* 1928: *m* 1960, Cdr Charles John Skrine, RN, who *d* 1966, and has issue living, David Charles Sinclair *b* 1961: *m* 1988, Elizabeth Mary, da of James Kavanagh, of Kiltilly, Co Wexford (and has issue living, Tara Rosemary Kathleen *b* 1993), Susan Nesta Rosemary *b* 1963: *m* 1986, Stephen Geoffrey Clapham, of 73 Hazlebury Rd, SW6 2NA, eldest son of Col Derek Clapham, of Blue House Farm, Mattingley, Basingstoke, Hants (and has issue living, Christopher Derek Charles *b* 1987, Nicholas Walter Geoffrey *b* 1991). *Residence* – .

Grandson of late William Warry Elton, grandson of Edward Elton, brother of Isaac Elton (*b* 1739) (ante):—
Issue of late Lieut-Col William MARWOOD-ELTON, *b* 1865, *d* 1931 (having assumed by deed poll 1910, the additional surname of Marwood): *m* 1909, Juliet, who *d* 1964, only child of Robert Spelman Marriott:—
Nigel William David, DFC, *b* 1911; Group Capt (ret) RAF; European War 1939-45 (despatches twice, DFC, prisoner): *m* 1952, Daphne (LEE), da of Gordon Richards, of Chiltern Court, NW3. *Residence* – Higher Penpoll, St Veep, Lostwithiel, Cornwall. *Club* – Royal Ocean Racing.

The 1st and 2nd baronets were successively Mayors of Bristol, and each sat as MP for that City. The 7th baronet sat as MP for Bath (*L*) 1857-9, and the 8th was High Sheriff of Somerset 1895.

ERRINGTON (UK) 1963, of Ness, in co Palatine of Chester

Sir GEOFFREY FREDERICK ERRINGTON, 2nd *Baronet*; *b* 15 Feb 1926; *s* his father, Sir ERIC, 1973; *ed* Rugby, and New Coll, Oxford; Col late King's Regt (ret 1975), GSO3 (Int) HQ 11 Armd Div 1950-52, GSO3 (Int) M13 (b) War Office 1955-57, Bde Maj 146 Inf Bde 1959-61, Coy Comd RMAS 1963-65, Mil Assist to Adjt-Gen 1965-67, CO 1st Bn King's Regt 1967-69, GSO1, 1 (BR)Corps 1969-71, Col GS HQ NW Dist 1971-74, Asst Adjt-Gen M1 (MOD) 1974-75; Col The King's Regt 1975-86; Dir of Personnel Services, Brit Shipbuilders 1977-78; Bd Member Shipbuilding ITB 1977-78; Chm Man Cttee Kings and Manchester Regt's Assocn 1975-86, of Executive Appointments Ltd 1982-90; Member Kent Consumers Consultative Cttee, Southern Water Authority 1984-89; Chm Harefield Hosp NHS Trust since 1991; Vice-Chm Association for the Prevention of Addiction 1991-94, since when Chm; FRSA 1994; Liveryman, Coachmakers' and Coach Harness Makers' Co and Freeman (City of Lond) 1980: *m* 1955, Diana Kathleen Forbes, da of Edward Barry Davenport, of Edgbaston, and has issue.

Arms – Or an open book clasped on a chief azure a spur rowel upwards between two portcullises chained or. **Crest** – A liver bird supporting with the dexter claw an oak sapling proper.
Residences – Stone Hill Farm, Sellindge, nr Ashford, Kent TN25 6AJ; 203a Gloucester Place, NW1. *Clubs* – Boodle's; United Oxford and Cambridge.

SONS LIVING

ROBIN DAVENPORT (14 Nottingham Rd, SW17 7EA), *b* 1 July 1957; *ed* Eton. —— John Davenport (10 Dighton Rd, SW18), *b* 1959; *ed* Eton: *m* 1989, Prue, da of Brig Michael Lee, OBE, of Fulham, SW6, and has issue living, Isabel Jane Davenport, *b* 1993. —— Andrew Davenport (14 Nottingham Rd, SW17; Brooks's Club), *b* (twin) 1959; *ed* Eton; Commn'd Welsh Gds 1978-82: *m* 1983 (*m diss* 1989), Georgina Sophie, yr da of Lt-Gen Sir Derek Boorman, KCB, of Goodnestone, Kent.

BROTHER LIVING

Stuart Grant, CBE (Earleywood Lodge, Ascot, Berks SL5 9JP), *b* 1929; *ed* Rugby, and Trin Coll, Oxford (MA); JP of Berks; CBE 1994: *m* 1954, Anne, yr da of A. Eric Baedeker, of Edgbaston, and has issue living, David Grant (47 Southdean Gdns, SW19), *b* 1957; *ed* Rugby: *m* 1982, Catherine Ann, yr da of Kenneth Neville, of Sydney, Australia, and has issue, Timothy Grant *b* 1983, Nicholas David *b* 1985, Frederick Charles *b* 1988, — Charles Stuart, *b* 1961; *ed* Rugby: *m* 1992, Nicole Cauverien, — Elizabeth Anne, *b* 1958: *m* 1983, Jaimie Coltart Corke, of Burltons, Donhead St Mary, Wilts, son of David Corke, of Lyndhurst, Hants, and has issue living, Milo Jaimie *b* 1991, Daisy Elizabeth *b* 1985, Imogen Sally *b* 1986, Ella Clementine *b* 1994.

SISTER LIVING

Anne Jacqueline (1 Willow Tree Close, Wycombe Market, Suffolk), *b* 1935; *ed* Wycombe Abbey; Community Relations Officer, RAF Bentwaters 1964-85.

Sir Eric Errington, 1st Bt, was MP for Bootle (*C*) 1935-45 and Aldershot 1954-70.

ERSKINE (UK) 1821, of Cambo, Fife

Watchful and valiant

Sir (THOMAS) DAVID ERSKINE, 5th *Baronet*; *b* 31 July 1912; *s* his father, *Lieut-Col Sir* THOMAS WILFRID HARGREAVES JOHN, DSO, 1944; *ed* Eton, and Magdalene Coll, Camb (BA); Maj (ret) Indian Corps of Engineers; is a JP for co Fife; Vice-Lieut for co Fife 1982; Chm Fife CC 1970: *m* 1947, Ann, da of late Lieut-Col Neil Fraser-Tytler, DSO, TD, of Aldourie Castle, Inverness and has issue.

Arms – Quarterly, 1st and 4th, gules, an imperial crown within a double tressure flory counter-flory or; 2nd and 3rd argent, a pale sable; the whole within a bordure wavy ermine. **Crest** – On a garb fessewise or, banded azure, a cock wings elevated proper charged with a bendlet wavy sinister of the second. *Seat* – Cambo House, Kingsbarns, Fife. *Residence* – Westnewhall, Kingsbarns, St Andrews, Fife.

SONS LIVING

(THOMAS) PETER NEIL (Cambo House, nr St Andrews, Fife KY16 8QD), *b* 28 March 1950; *ed* Eton, Birmingham Univ, and Edinburgh Univ: *m* 1972, Catherine, da of Col G. H. K. Hewlett, and has issue living, Thomas Struan, *b* 6 Feb 1977, — James Dunbar, *b* 1979, — Gillian Christian, *b* 1983, — Mary Caroline, *b* 1986. —— William (c/o ICARDA, PO Box 5466, Aleppo, Syria), *b* 1952; PhD: *m* 1st, 1973, Sarah Jane McElroy, el da of Charles William McElroy Pratt, MD, of Orwell Grange, Orwell, Royston, Herts; 2ndly, 1982, Mireille, da of late Georges Abdelnour, of Aleppo, Syria, and has issue living, (by 2nd *m*) Thomas Georges, *b* 1989, — Philip Neil, *b* 1991.

SISTERS LIVING

Diana Mildred, *b* 1915: *m* 1st, 1941, Major N. R. M. Skene, DSC, RM, who *d* on active ser 1942; 2ndly, 1945, David Grant Buxton TD, late Maj Middlesex Regt, and has issue living (by 2nd *m*) Andrew Ralph, *b* 1947: *m* 1979 (*m diss* 19—), Sally Higginbottom, — Lucinda Dierdre, *b* 1945: *m* 1973, Tudor Venn, and has issue living, 2 sons and 1 da. *Residence* – Cedar Gables, 15 Frenze Rd, Diss, Norfolk. —— Victoria Margaret, *b* 1919; formerly 2nd Officer WRNS. *Residence* – 79 Bolingbroke Grove, SW11. —— Constance Gertrude, *b* 1921: *m* 1942, Maj Oliver Patch, DSO, DSC, RM, who *d* 1991, and has issue living, Janet Mary (58 Shelgate Rd, SW11), *b* 1945: *m* 1976 (*m diss* 1986), Simon Scott, — Olivia Cynthia (43 Cadogan Sq, SW1), *b* 1946: *m* 1st, 1972, Dimitri Tiomkin, who *d* 1979; 2ndly, 1988, James Alastair Sholto Douglas, son of Maj Henry James Sholto Douglas, late Scots Guards, of Hemingford Abbots, Huntingdon (*see* B Templemore, colls, 1959 Edn), — Emily Dorothea, *b* 1949: *m* 1st, 1980 (*m diss* 19—), Kenneth Page; 2ndly, 19—), Gavin Scott and has issue living (by 1st *m*) Harriet Constance Zenia *b* 1980, (by 2nd *m*) Tobias Oliver *b* 1986, — Diana Elizabeth (45 Tennyson St, SW8) *b* 1953: *m* 1974 (*m diss* 1981), Stephen Sullivan, — Penelope Margaret Christian, *b* 1957: *m* 1983, Gerald Olson, of 32 Compton Drive, Maidenhead, and has issue living, Nicholas Oliver *b* 1984, Natalie *b* 1986, Hannah *b* 1988. *Residence* – Orchard View, East Ling, Kent. —— Harriet Katherine Lucinda, *b* 1924: *m* 1945, Lt-Cdr Hugh Doheny, Roy Canadian Naval VR, and has issue living, Hugh Erskine, *b* 1946: *m* 1987, Margaret Collins, — Penelope Ann, *b* 1949: *m* 1st, 1972 (*m diss* 1982), Ronald Carter; 2ndly, 1986, Mario Bousquet, of Mount Orford, Quebec, — Kathleen Janet, *b* 1951: *m* 1972, Brian Hanna, of Grandmere, Quebec, — Mary Harriet, *b* 1952, — Lucinda Margaret Ruth, *b* 1956: has issue, Mira Harriet Kathleen *b* 1992, — Victoria Diana, *b* 1960: *m* 1982, Brian Herring, of Lennoxville, Quebec, and has issue living, Charles Thomas *b* 1983, Margaret Lucinda *b* 1985, Mary Grace *b* 1988. *Residence* – 95 Moulton Hill, RR1, Lennoxville, Quebec Province J1M 2A2, Canada.

COLLATERAL BRANCHES LIVING

Grandchildren of late Sir James Malcolm Monteith Erskine, 2nd son of late Capt David Holland Erskine, 2nd son of 1st baronet:—
Issue of late Denys Malcolm Erskine, *b* 1903, *d* 1966: *m* 1923, Aleda Julia, who *d* 1971, da of E. C. Brownfield:—
Margaret Lucile (44 Rosedale Ct, Newcastle-on-Tyne), *b* 1927: *m* 1stly 1960, Anthony Colin Radclyffe, who *d* 1976; 2ndly, 1978, Kenneth Warner.
Issue of late Maj Sir Derek Quicke Erskine, *b* 1905, *d* 1977: *m* 1927 Elisabeth Mary Stretton (Riverside Paddocks, PO Box 14968, Nairobi, Kenya), da of late Maj Reginald Stretton Spurrier, King's Dragoon Gds:—
Francis David Monteith, MC (Sanctuary Farm, PO Box 244, Naivasha, Kenya), *b* 1929: Kenya 1954 (MC): *m* 1958 (*m diss* 1963), Marie-Claude Irene, da of late Roland M. A. Mange, of Kenya, and has issue living, Clive Patrick Monteith *b* 1959: *m* 1985, Patrizia Pandora, da of Michele Loria, of Canino, Viterbo, Italy, and has issue living, Charlotte Irene *b* 1987, — Guy Francis, *b* 1961: *m* 1988, Juliet, da of John Dallas Amos, of Edinburgh, and has issue living, James Francis *b* 1989. —— Jane Petal, *b* 1928: *m* 1st, 1950 (*m diss* 1963), William Lee Harragin, son of late Sir Walter Harragin, CMG, QC; 2ndly, 1963 (*m diss* 1972), Robert William Young; 3rdly, 1973, David Wanric Allen (PO Box 14712, Nairobi, Kenya), and has issue living, (by 1st *m*) Mark Savile Austin, *b* 1956: *m* 1990, Patricia Walker, and has issue living, Daniel *b* 1992, Corinne Florence *b* 1994, — Vanessa Jane, *b* 1951: *m* 1977, Kirby McCaffrey, of Cedar Dr, Baltimore, Md, USA, and has issue living, James Flynn Cassius *b* 1980, — Robin Elisabeth, *b* 1953: *m* 1986, Peter Boone Hussey, and has issue living, Mary Victoria *b* 1988, Serwen *b* 1991, — Serena Claire, *b* 1959.
Issue of late Keith David Erskine, *b* 1907, *d* 1974: *m* 1st, 1936 (*m diss* 1940), Kathleen Diana, da of C. W. Kayser, of Eaton Hall, Retford; 2ndly, 1944, Audrey Skinner:—
(By 2nd *m*) Simon David, *b* 1953. —— Sarah Gay, *b* 1946: *m* 1967, Alex Ryan, and has issue living, Robert Keith, *b* 1973, — Audrey Mary, *b* 1970. —— Aleda Grace Elizabeth, *b* 1948. —— Fiona Margaret, *b* 1949: *m* 1971, Richard Mottram. —— Deborah Mary, *b* 1951: *m* 1974, David Langford Holt, of Pixie, Sandy Lane, Kingswood, Surrey, and has issue living, Benjamin, *b* 1976, — James (twin), *b* 1976, — Sara Maria, *b* 1978. —— Kathrina Jane, *b* 1956.
Issue of late James Monteith Erskine (twin), *b* 1907, *d* 1965: *m* 1931, Kathleen Brookes (2 Francis Court, Cranes Park Av, Surbiton, Surrey):—
David Monteith, *b* 1933; *ed* Camb Univ (MA); Solicitor 1960: *m* 1960, Tessa Victoria, da of Dr James Vernon, of Ascot, Berks, and has issue living, Dominic James Monteith, *b* 1962, — Malcolm David Vernon, *b* 1963, — Susan Eileen, *b* 1970. —— Shirley Monteith (twin), *b* 1933; *ed* Camb Univ (BA): *m* 1954, Barry Michael Clarke, of The Long House, Woodgreen, Hants, and has issue living, Thomas James Woodchurch, *b* 1958, — Eleanor Margaret, *b* 1962.
Sir David Erskine, 1st Bt, was a natural grandson of 9th Earl of Kellie. The 4th baronet, Sir Thomas Wilfred Hargreaves John Erskine, DSO, was Lieut-Col Queen's Own Cameron Highlanders, and served during European War 1914-16 (DSO).

Erskine-Hill, see Hill.

ESMONDE (I) 1629, of Ballynastragh, Wexford

JERUSALEM

Had rather die than be dishonoured

Sir Thomas Francis Grattan Esmonde, 17th Baronet , *b* 14 Oct 1960; *s* his father, *Sir* John Henry Grattan (*His Honour Judge Esmonde*), 1987; *ed* Sandford Park, and Trin Coll, Dublin; MB, BCh, BAO (1984), MRCPI, MRCP (UK): *m* 1986, Pauline Loretto, 2nd da of James Vincent Kearns, and has issue.

Arms – Ermine, on a chief gules three mullets argent. Crest – Out of a mural crown a Saracen's head all proper.
Seat – Ballynastragh, Gorey, co Wexford. *Residence* – 6 Nutley Av, Donnybrook, Dublin 4.

SON LIVING

Sean Vincent Grattan, *b* 8 Jan 1989.

DAUGHTER LIVING

Aisling Margaret Pamela Grattan, *b* 1991.

BROTHERS LIVING

Harold William Grattan, *b* 1964; *ed* Sandford Park, and Trin Coll, Dublin. —— Richard Anthony Grattan, *b* 1969; *ed* Sandford Park, and Trin Coll, Dublin.

SISTERS LIVING

Karen Maria Grattan, *b* 1965. —— Lisa Marion Grattan, *b* 1968; *ed* Nat Univ, Dublin.

UNCLES LIVING (*Sons of 15th baronet*)

Bartholomew Thomas Grattan, *b* 1937; *ed* Glenstal Abbey. *Residence* – Ballynastragh, Gorey, co Wexford. —— Anthony James Grattan, *b* 1943; *ed* Glenstal, and Univ Coll, Dublin. *Residence* – St Oliver's, Coolbawn, co Tipperary.

AUNTS LIVING (*Daughters of 15th baronet*)

Alice Mary Grattan, *b* 1929; *ed* National Univ of Ireland (BSc 1951). *Residence* – 8 Palmerston Park, Dublin 6. —— Eithne Marion Grattan, *b* 1931; is a LRAM. *Residence* – Ballynastragh, Gorey, co Wexford. —— Anne Caroline Grattan, *b* 1940. *Residence* – Ballynastragh, Gorey, co Wexford.

HALF-GREAT-UNCLES LIVING AND DECEASED (*Half-brothers of 15th baronet*)

†Owen James, *b* 1905; *ed* Downside: *m* 1938, Eira Margaret Antonia (Cloneen, Glendalough, co Wicklow, Republic of Ireland), da of late George Henry Louis Mackenzie (*see* Mackenzie, Bt, *cr* 1673, colls), and *d* 1993, leaving issue, Eugene Patrick Mackenzie, *b* 1942; *ed* MRC Duntroon, ACT, and Queensland Univ (BEcon), Lt-Col RAA (ret 1981); Man Dir Sharpe Gp of Companies since 1982: *m* 1972, Jennifer Ann, da of Sir Frank Victor Sharpe, CMG, OBE, of Brisbane, and has issue living, Godfrey Christian *b* 1980, Eugene James *b* 1983, Grania Adelaide *b* 1986, — Deborah Anne Barbara, *b* 1939: *m* 1968, Peter John Fraser Coutts, BEE, MSc, MA, PLD, — Gillian Mary Antonia, *b* 1940: *m* 1963, Colin Leslie Rosewarne, of Hardigreen Park, Mittagong, NSW, Aust, and has issue living, Andrew John *b* 1964, Liam Patrick *b* 1974, Allison Mary *b* 1966, Maria Patricia *b* 1969, — Vivienne Mary Patricia, *b* 1945: *m* 1970, Charles Timothy Cresswell, of Cilwych Farm, Bwlch, Powys, and has issue living, Dominie Sidney *b* 1975, Laragh Veronica Storm *b* 1973, — Rosemary Carolyn, *b* 1946: *m* 1966, Maj Robert Keith Peterswald, RAR, of 275A Nelson Rd, Mount Nelson, Hobart, Tasmania 7007, Australia, and has issue living, Charlotte Antonia *b* 1968, Georgina Ann *b* 1972. —— Patrick, MC (Ocklynge Manor, Mill Rd, Eastbourne BN21 2PG), *b* 1914; LRCP and LRCS Ireland; late Maj RAMC; Colonial Med Sers 1945-63; 1939-45 War (MC): *m* 1943, Norah Marcia, da of William Cooper, of Malton, Yorks, and has issue living, Margaret Shane, *b* 1944: *m* 1966, Col Peter Alexander Henderson, Cheshire Regt, of Court Farm, Corsley, Wilts, and has issue living, Dominic Patrick Alexander *b* 1968, Oliver Thomas Alexander *b* 1971, — Grania Mary, *b* 1947: *m* 1st, 1970 (*m diss* 1974), Denis Edward Chambers, 2ndly, 1975, (Ian Hugo) Loudon Greenlees, of Haymakers Farm, Waldron, E Sussex, and has issue living, (by 1st *m*) Laragh Victoria *b* 1971, (by 2nd *m*) Rupert Hugo Loudon *b* 1976, Thomas Ian Esmonde *b* 1985, Camilla Shane *b* 1978, Daisy Thomasina *b* 1987.

HALF-GREAT-AUNT LIVING (*Half-sister of 15th Baronet*)

Mary Carmel, *b* 1912: *m* 1935, Dermot St John Gogarty, Flying Officer RAF Vol Reserve, of Nairobi, Kenya, and has issue living, Michael Dermot St John, *b* 1936.

WIDOW LIVING OF SIXTEENTH BARONET

Pamela Mary (*Pamela, Lady Esmonde*), elder da of Dr Francis Stephen Bourke, FRCPI, MRIA: *m* 1957, Sir John Henry Grattan Esmonde, 17th Bt, who *d* 1987. *Residence* – 6 Nutley Av, Donnybrook, Dublin 4.

COLLATERAL BRANCH LIVING

Grandchildren of late Capt John Joseph Esmonde, LRCSI, RAMC, 2nd son of James Esmonde, JP, DL, son of Com James Esmonde, RN, grandson of 7th Bt:—
Issue of late Capt John Witham Esmonde, OBE, DSC, RN (half-brother of 15th Bt), *b* 1907; *d* 1983: *m* 1940, Aileen (Ballyellis, Buttevant, co Cork), da of late Harold Harold-Barry, of Ballyvonare, co Cork:—
Peter Witham, *b* 1945. —— Kevin Harold, *b* 1948. —— Helen Mary Karin, *b* 1950: *m* 1st, 1976, Paul Douglas Clark, of

Toronto, Canada; 2ndly, 1985, Lt-Col Robert Charles Couldrey, 7th DEO Gurkha Rifles, only son of C. J. Couldrey, of Limpsfield Common, Oxted, Surrey, and has issue living (by 2nd *m*), David Witham James *b* 1988, Annabel Mary, *b* 1986.

The Esmondes are descended from a family which was seated in co Wexford, and one of whose members was Bishop of Ferns in 1340, and another Bishop of Emly 1356. In the reign of Elizabeth I Sir Lawrence Esmond, abandoning the Roman Catholic faith, professed himself a Protestant, and was created Lord Esmonde. He married a Roman Catholic lady, one of the O'Flaherties, Dynasts of Iar of Connaught, by whom he had a son. The mother, fearing that her child would be reared a Protestant, ran off with the boy, whom she brought up as a strict Catholic. By the statute of Kilkenny, the marriage was voidable in law. The son subsequently gained possession of the Wexford estate, and would probably have gained the peerage, but for the confusion wrought by civil war. He raised a troop of horse for the service of Charles I, and commanded a Regt in the Duke of Buckingham's expedition to Rochelle, on his return from which he was created a baronet in his father's lifetime. The 2nd baronet *m* Lucia Butler, niece of 1st Duke of Ormonde; his seat, Huntington Castle, co Carlow, was built by Lord Esmonde 1625, and named after the ancient seat of his ancestors in England. The 9th baronet, Right Hon Sir Thomas, sat as MP for Wexford (*L*) 1841-7, and the 10th baronet sat as MP for Waterford (*L*) 1852-76. The 11th baronet Sir Thomas Henry Grattan (sometime a Chamberlain to Vatican Household), sat as MP for S Div of Dublin co (*N*) 1885-92, for W Kerry Div of co Kerry 1892-1900, and for N Wexford, Div of Wexford co 1900-18, and was a Senator of Irish Free State. The 12th baronet, Sir Osmond Thomas Grattan, was a Member of Parliament of Irish Free State 1923-7 and 1927-36. The 14th baronet, Sir John Lymbrick Esmonde, was a Bencher of King's Inns, Dublin, and Senior Counsel, and sat as MP for Tipperary, Co, N Tipperary Div (*N*) 1915-18. He was a Member of Dail Eireann 1937-44, and 1948-51. The 16th baronet, Sir John Henry Grattan Esmonde, bar King's Inn, Dublin 1950, who Senior Council 1971, and a Circuit Court Judge of W Circuit 1977-87.

ESPLEN (UK) 1921, of Hardres Court, Canterbury, Kent

(*Sir*) JOHN GRAHAM ESPLEN, 3rd *Baronet*; *b* 4 Aug 1932; *s* his father, *Sir* WILLIAM GRAHAM, 1989, but does not use the title; *ed* Harrow, and St Catharine's College, Cambridge (BA 1955): *m* 1956 (*m diss* 19—), Valerie Joan, yr da of Maj-Gen Albert Percy Lambooy, CB, OBE, and has issue.

Arms – Sable, on a pile between two mascles or, a lymphad of the field. **Crest** – In front of a demi-eagle displayed sable charged on each wing with a mascle as in the arms, an anchor fessewise or.

SON LIVING

WILLIAM JOHN HARRY, *b* 24 Feb 1967.

DAUGHTERS LIVING

Wendy Anne, *b* 1959. —— Fiona Mary, *b* 1960. —— Polly Caroline, *b* 1962.

The 1st baronet, Sir John Esplen, KBE (son of late William Esplen, of The Willows, Blundellsands), was sometime Senior Director of Esplen, Sons and Swainston (Limited), consulting engineers and naval architects, and Ch Technical Advisor to Min of Shipping during European War 1914-18.

Be faithful

EVANS (UK) 1920, of Wightwick, near Wolverhampton, co Stafford

Sir ANTHONY ADNEY EVANS, 2nd *Baronet*, *b* 5 Aug 1922; *s* his father, *Sir* WALTER HARRY, 1954; *ed* Shrewsbury, and Merton Coll Oxford: *m* 1st, 1948 (*m diss* 1957), Rita Beatrice, da of late Alfred David Kettle, of Souldern, Oxon, and formerly wife of Larry Rupert Kirsch; 2ndly, 1958, Sylvia Jean, and has issue by 1st *m*.

Arms – Gyronny of eight gules or, over all a lion passant, between two fleurs-de-lis in pale sable. **Crest** – In front of a wall embattled and masoned proper, a lion as in the arms.
Residence – Almer Manor, Blandford, Dorset, BT11 9EN.

SONS LIVING (*by 1st wife*)

—, *b* — 19—,
— —, *b* 19—.

DAUGHTER LIVING (*by 1st wife*)

—, *b* 19—.

With faith and virtue

SISTER LIVING

Diana Gillian Mary, *b* 1926: *m* 1st, 1948 (*m diss* 1954), Capt John Richard Pugh, RA; 2ndly, 1959, Alan Joseph Webber, who *d* 19—, and has issue living, (by 1st *m*) Vanessa Gillian WEBBER, *b* 1950; adopted 1959 by her step-father whose surname she assumed, — (by 2nd *m*) Daryl Adney, *b* 1960.

The 1st baronet Sir Walter Harry Evans (son of late Joseph Evans, JP, of The Lindens, Wolverhampton) was an hydraulic engineer, and a Co Councillor for Staffordshire.

EVANS (UK) 1963, of Rottingdean, co Sussex (Extinct 1983)

Sir (SIDNEY) HAROLD EVANS, CMG, OBE, 1st and last *Baronet*.

DAUGHTER LIVING OF FIRST AND LAST BARONET

Annabel Frances, *b* 1956.

WIDOW LIVING OF FIRST AND LAST BARONET

ELIZABETH (*Lady Evans*), da of William Jaffray, of Aberdeen: *m* 1945, Sir (Sidney) Harold Evans, CMG, OBE, 1st Bt, who *d* 1983. *Residence* – 1 Kipling Court, St Aubyns Mead, Rottingdean, Brighton, Sussex BN2 7JT.

Gwynne-Evans, see Evans-Tipping.

WORTHINGTON-EVANS (UK) 1916, of Colchester, Essex (Extinct 1971)

Sir (WILLIAM) SHIRLEY WORTHINGTON WORTHINGTON-EVANS, 2nd and last *Baronet*.

DAUGHTERS LIVING OF SECOND BARONET

Sarah MASON (17 The Gateways, Sprimont Place, SW3), *b* 1929: *m* 1st, 1957 (*m diss* 1971), Wing Cdr Hon Keith Alexander Henry Mason, DFC (later 3rd Baron Blackford), who *d* 1977; 2ndly, 1972, Eric Ivor Hopton; has resumed by deed poll her former married surname. —— Anne Louise (Annie-Lou), *b* 1934: *m* 1967 (*m diss* 1981), 2nd Baron Jeffreys. *Residence* – The Cottage, Willesley, Tetbury, Glos.

EVERARD (UK) 1911, of Randlestown, co Meath

Virtue consists in action

Sir ROBIN CHARLES EVERARD, 4th *Baronet*, *b* 5 Oct 1939; *s* his father, *Lt-Col Sir* NUGENT HENRY, 1984; *ed* Harrow, and Sandhurst; management consultant: *m* 1963, Ariel Ingrid, eldest da of late Col Peter Cleasby-Thompson, MBE, MC, of Blackhill House, The Arms, Little Cressingham, Thetford, Norfolk, and has issue.

Arms – Argent, a fesse wavy between three estoile gules. **Crest** – A pelican in her piety proper.
Residence – Church Farm, Shelton, Long Stratton, Norfolk NR15 2SB.

SON LIVING

HENRY PETER CHARLES, *b* 6 Aug 1970; *ed* Gresham's Sch, Holt.

DAUGHTERS LIVING

Catherine Mary, *b* 1964. —— Victoria Frances, *b* 1966.

SISTER LIVING

Susan Louise, *b* 1935: *m* 1957, Lieut Col Henry George Dormer, RA, only son of H.J. Dormer, of Chilton Court, Sudbury, Suffolk, and has issue living, Sara Louise, *b* 1958, — Charlotte Rose, *b* 1962. *Residence* – Downside, Shortheath Rd, Farnham, Surrey.

COLLATERAL BRANCH LIVING

Issue of late Matthias Richard Everard, 2nd son of 2nd baronet, *b* 1906, *d* 1949: *m* 1938, Maíghréad Mary, who *d* 1973, da of Michael Joseph Macardle, of Miltown Grange, Castlebellingham:—

Patrick Matthias (Marques de Zuya 2, Santa Maria de Guecho, Vizcaya, Spain; White Mills, Castlebellingham, co Louth), *b* 1943: *m* 1968, Felicity Anne Brigid, da of late Brig Ralph Nevill Thicknesse, and has issue living, Anthony Matthias, *b* 1980, — Michael Ralph, *b* 1988, — Patricia Karen, *b* 1973, — Katherine Sophie, *b* 1982.

Sir Nugent Talbot Everard, 1st Bt (appointed High Sheriff of co Meath 1883, and HM's Lieut 1906), was a Senator of the Irish Free State 1922-8, and *d* 11 July 1929. Major Sir Richard William Everard, 2nd Bt, *d* 22 July 1929.

EVERY (E) 1641, of Egginton, Derbyshire

Sir HENRY JOHN MICHAEL EVERY, 13th *Baronet*; *b* 6 April 1947; *s* his father *Sir* JOHN SIMON, 1988; *ed* Malvern; FCA; patron of one living: *m* 1974, Susan Mary, eldest da of Kenneth Beaton, JP, of Eastshotte, Hartford, Cambs, and has issue.

Arms – Erminois, two chevronels azure between two other gules. **Crest** – A demi-unicorn argent guttée-de-sang and crined or.
Seat – Egginton, Derby. *Residence* – Cothay, 26 Fishpond Lane, Egginton, Derbyshire DE65 6HJ.

SONS LIVING

EDWARD JAMES HENRY, *b* 3 July 1975. —— Jonathan Charles Hugo, *b* 1977. —— Nicholas John Simon, *b* 1981.

SISTERS LIVING

Celia Jane (Stovolds Hill Farm, nr Cranleigh, Surrey GU6 8LE), *b* 1944: *m* 1st, 1965, Nicholas Charles Harcourt Stephens, who *d* 1984; 2ndly, 19—, Robin Christopher Moore, and has issue living (by 1st *m*), Jasper Roland Every, *b* 1972, — Toby Oliver Every, *b* 1974, — Candida Imogen Every, *b* 1969. —— Juliet Frances, *b* 1945: *m* 1964, John Coltman McCullagh, of Bramleys, Alleyns Lane, Cookham Dean, Berks, and has issue living, Andrew John, *b* 1968, — Diana Mary, *b* 1965.

UNCLE LIVING (*son of 11th baronet*)

Charles Henry Sherard, *b* 1916; *ed* Harrow: *m* 1950 (*m diss* 1953), Deirdre Veronica, da of late Dr du Toit, of Johannesburg, S Africa, and has issue living, Vanessa Leila, *b* 1950: *m* 1974, Terrence William de Beer, of 17a Milton Rd, Westville N 3630, Natal, S Africa, and has issue living, Ryan Jeffery *b* 1979, Kelly Gillian *b* 1981. *Residence* – Casa Das Primas, Carvoeiro, Lagoa 8400, Algarve, Portugal.

Every man to his own

AUNT LIVING (*daughter of 11th baronet*)

Leila Penelope, *b* 1911: *m* 1935, Maj Vivian Horrocks Ward, TD, 5th Bn Sherwood Foresters (TA), and has issue living, Peter Every (Pinfold, Pin Mill Lane, Chelmondiston, nr Ipswich, Suffolk), *b* 1938: *m* 1962, Rosalind Brereton, yr da of Giffard Page, of St Anne's, King George Av, King's Lynn, Norfolk, and has issue living, Rupert *b* 1969, Edward *b* 1970, — Simon Charles Vivian (The Dower House, Bulmer, Sudbury, Suffolk), *b* 1942; *ed* Shrewsbury, and Trin Coll, Camb (MA); Memb Securities Institute: *m* 1965, Myrtle Jillian Eileen, only da of late Thomas Roycroft East, of Dublin, and has issue living, Victoria Penelope Jane *b* 1969, Antonia Lisa *b* 1971, Lucinda Fiona *b* 1971. *Residence* – Long Meadow House, Little Cornard, Sudbury, Suffolk.

WIDOW LIVING OF TWELFTH BARONET

JANET MARION (*Dowager Lady Every*), eldest da of late John Page, ARIBA, of Blakeney, Norfolk: *m* 1943, as his 2nd wife, Sir John Simon Every, 12th Bt, who *d* 1988. *Residence* – Egginton, Derby.

COLLATERAL BRANCHES LIVING

Grandsons (by 1st *m*) of late Capt Oswald Every, 75th Regt, brother of 10th baronet:—
Issue of late Edward Every, *b* 1865, *d* 19—: *m* 1902, Adeline, who *d* 1948, da of Ranson Smith:—
Edward Malcolm (102 Lincoln St, Brooklyn, Wisconsin, USA), *b* 1903: *m* 1934, Clarice Mildred, da of Elmer Doane, and has issue living, Thomas Owen, *b* 1938, — Barbara Ann, *b* 1942. —— Roderick Desmond, *b* 1904: *m* 1935, Carolyn Norma, da of Paul Tyler, and has issue living, Roderick Douglas, *b* 1936, — Lynn Gertrude, *b* 1943. —— Donovan Richmond (Evansville, Wisconsin, USA), *b* 1911: *m* 19—, Evelyn, da of Fred Rodd, and has issue living, Donovan Rodd, *b* 1941.

Grandson (by 2nd *m*) of late Capt Oswald Every (ante):—
Issue of late Francis William John Flower Every, *b* 1890, *d* 1979: *m* 1912, Mary Louisa, who *d* 1965, da of William John Murton:—
Christy Oswald (1 Combe Close, Axminster, Devon), *b* 1920: *m* 1948, Winifred Jessie, 2nd da of Luke Richards, and has issue living, Geoffrey Francis, *b* 1949: *m* 1971, Rosemarie, da of Otto Plec, of Borham Wood, — Stephen Victor (5 Loretto Rd, Axminster), *b* 1950: *m* 1975, Valerie Ena, da of late Peter Arthur Guest, of 25 Foxhill, Axminster, and has issue living, Caroline Amanda *b* 1980, Joanne Louise *b* 1982, Kathryn Frances *b* 1984, — Virginia Dawn, *b* 1953: *m* 1972, Alan Fry, of 2 Moor Fields, Colyton, Devon, — Katrina Mary, *b* 1957: *m* 1977, Michael Neale, of 35 Clive Rd, Colliers Wood, SW19, and has issue living, David Michael Ian *b* 1980, Laura Jane Alana *b* 1982.

Grandchildren of late Thomas Edward Every-Clayton, son of Lt-Col Edward Every-Clayton, 2nd son of 9th baronet:—
Issue of late Edward Every Every-Clayton, *b* 1867, *d* 1936: *m* 1st, 1892, Mary Fetherstonhaugh, who *d* 1905, da of Alexander Heylin, of Newcastle-upon-Tyne; 2ndly, 1907, Emily Mary, da of Arthur Edward Tooze, Bar-at-law:—
(By 1st *m*) Edith Margaret, *b* 1897. —— Ruth Fetherstonhaugh, *b* 1905.

Grandchildren of late Leopold Ernest Valentine Every-Clayton, MD, FRCS, son of late Thomas Edward Every-Clayton (ante):—
Issue of late Cecil Edward Every, *b* 1901; relinquished the surname of Clayton 1937; *d* 1974: *m* 1927, Viola, who *d* 1966, da of late Edward Ledger, of Hampstead, NW:—
Simon Flower (The White House, Crawley, Winchester), *b* 1929: *m* 1956, Diana Mary Jennifer, da of late Cdr L. J. F. Howard-Mercer, RN, and has issue living, James Edward (64 St John's Rd, Sevenoaks, Kent TN13 3NA), *b* 1961: *m* 1988, Caroline Anne, da of John Frederick Mallett, and has issue living, Elizabeth Joanna *b* 1993, Alexandra Margaret *b* 1993, — Jennifer Ann, *b* 1958, — Frances Elizabeth, *b* 1964: *m* 1990, William Thomas Pattisson, and has issue living, Frederick James *b* 1992. —— Ann, *b* 1933.

Grandchildren of late Thomas Edward Every-Clayton (ante):—

Issue of late George Frederick William Every-Clayton, *b* 1871, *d* 1928: *m* 1st 1892, Sarah, who *d* 1912, da of William Whittaker; 2ndly 1913, Evelyn May Yeates:—

Herbert Edward, *b* 1892: *m* 1913, Gwendolin Cox, who *d* 1931, and *d* 1961, leaving issue, Herbert Newbery, *b* 1917, — Andrita Valentine, *b* 1919: *m* 1938, William Kenneth Franklin, and has issue living, Daniel William *b* 1941: *m* 1965, Frances Yohradsky (and has issue living, William *b* 19—), Christine Louise *b* 1939: *m* 1961, Robert Toutant (and has issue living, Dianne Michelle *b* 1962, Jacqueline Marie *b* 1964). —— John Oswald, DSC, *b* 1898; *ed* Univ Sch, Victoria, British Columbia; is a Master Mariner; European War 1914-19 (torpedoed, two medals), European War 1939-45 as Lieut Canadian Navy Reserve and Capt Merchant Navy (DSC 1939-45 War Medal, Canadian Vol Medal, Africa Star, Italy Star, Atlantic Star, 1939-45 Star): *m* 1925, Marie, da of William Lloyd, of Liverpool, and *d* 1979, leaving issue, George William, *b* 1929; *ed* Canadian Public Schs, and British Columbia Univ: *m* 1950, Margot, da of William Forrest of Victoria, British Columbia. —— Thomas Edgar *b* 1899: *m* 1943, Ellen May Hill, and *d* 1986, leaving issue living, Wayne Thomas, *b* 1944: *m* 1974, Mary Hall, and has issue living, Patricia Mary, *b* 1975. —— Frederick Harris, *b* 1906: *m* 1937, Ann Brown Morrison, and has issue living, Barbara Ann Gail, *b* 1939: *m* 19—, Donald Anderson, of Campbell River, British Columbia, and has issue living, Nancy Janet *b* 1959, Cindy Donna *b* 1962. *Residence* – Campbell River, British Columbia. —— Arthur Eric Francis, *b* 1910: *m* 1948, Edna Beatrice Longley. —— Penelope Maud Valentine, *b* 1903: *m* 1934, George Anderson Churchill-Emery, who *d* 1941, and has issue living, Elizabeth Joy, *b* 1937: *m* 1955 (*m diss* 1978), Arthur Frederick Thompson, of Heriot Bay, British Columbia, and has issue living, Gordon Anthony *b* 1958: *m* 1984, Kelly Charlton (and has issue living, Justin Joseph *b* 1985), Michael Arthur George *b* 1959: *m* 1988, Monica Rambie (and has issue living, Mack Ramsay *b* 1989, Fairleigh Taylor *b* 1976). —— Edith Minnie, *b* 1912: *m* 1943, Norton Hopkins, who *d* 1961.

Grandchildren of late Reginald Arthur Eric Every-Clayton (infra):—

Issue of late John Arthur Every-Clayton, *b* 1903, *d* 1969: *m* 1937, Martha Parker, who *d* 1988:—

Margaret Lois, *b* 1940: *m* 1st, 1959 (*m diss* 1976), Terry Lee Williams, attorney for Bank of America; 2ndly, 1976, William Smutz. *Address* – RR2, Box 481, Heber Springs, ARK 72543, USA.

Issue of late William Wilding Every-Clayton, *b* 1905, *d* 1992: *m* 1940, Joan Adelaide (51 Church Hill, Honiton, Devon), da of late Ronald John Bennett, of Exeter, Devon:—

(Henry) John (3 Chestnut Way, Melton Mowbray, Leics LE13 0EB), *b* 1941: *m* 1963, Frances Anne Sangster, BA, of London, and has issue living, Catherine, *b* 1967, — Tessa, *b* 1969. —— Alan William (Beacon Down Cottage, Holcombe Burnell, Longdown, Exeter, Devon), *b* 1945: *m* 1968, Myra Wynn Arthur, of Axminster, Devon, and has issue living, Richard William, *b* 1971, — Anita Caroline, *b* 1973. —— Robert Edward (Ashton House, St Mary Church, Cowbridge, S Glam), *b* 1948; BA, FCA: *m* 1973, Karen Elizabeth Paine, BSc, of Sidbury, Devon, and has issue living, Andrew John, *b* 1979, — Katherine Lucy, *b* 1982, — Elizabeth Claire, *b* 1984. —— David Stuart, *b* 1955: *m* 1979, Angela Dauber, of Broadhembury, Devon, and has issue living, Christopher James, *b* 1985, — Helen Louise, *b* 1987. —— Pamela Nora Anne (Flat 1, 27 Stanley Rd, Teddington TW11 8TP), *b* (twin) 1955: *m* 1981 (*m diss* 1989), Jeremy Peter Leeds.

Issue of late Thomas Edward Every-Clayton, *b* 1906, *d* 1991: *m* 1938, Irmgard Adele, who *d* 1982, da of late Arthur Jaekel, of Tallinn, Estonia:—

Glenn Thomas (Seminario Congregacional, Rua Arealva 19, Tejipió, 50,000 Recife, Brazil), *b* 1941; *ed* Kingston Gram Sch, and Christ's Coll, Camb (BA); BD, ALBC: *m* 1971, Joyce Elizabeth Winifred, el da of Hugh McKee, of Randalstown, co Antrim. —— Clive William (14a E Aubinaustraat, 1932 St Stevens-Woluwe, Belgium), *b* 1942; *ed* Kingston Gram Sch, and London Bible Coll (BD, ALBC): *m* 1971, Dorothy, da of Archibald M.O. Dobbie, of Dalry, Ayrshire, and has issue living, Mark Brian, *b* 1975, — Paul David Christian, *b* 1979, — Grace Esther Josette, *b* 1973, — Joy Claire Joanna, *b* 1977.

Grandson of late Thomas Edward Every-Clayton (ante):—

Issue of late Reginald Arthur Eric Every-Clayton, *b* 1874, *d* 1965: *m* 1902, Fanny, who *d* 1958, 3rd da of William Wilding, of Bolton, Lancashire:—

George Herbert (617 SW 21st Circle, Boynton Beach, Florida 33426, USA), *b* 1907; *ed* Rutgers Univ, BSc: *m* 1931, Jane Cecelia Welsh, who *d* 1981, of New Brunswick, New Jersey, USA, and has issue living, Donald George (Paseo de los Halcones 202, Mayorazgos de los Gigantes, Antizapan de Zaragoza, Edo de Mexico, Mexico), *b* 1935: *m* 1957, Celia Yolanda Garcia, of Mexico City, and has issue living, Geoffrey *b* 1961: *m* 1988, Andrea Garcia Puente, of Mexico City, Lisa *b* 1959: *m* 1983, Angelo Ceciarelli, of Mexico City, Jennifer *b* 1963: *m* 1979, Eduardo Ezquerro, of Mexico City (and has issue living, Pamela *b* 1980, Priscilla *b* 1985), Noreen *b* 1969, — Jon Arthur (438 Old Trail, Baltimore, Maryland 21212, USA), *b* 1938; Lieut Col, US Army Reserve; Vietnam 1966-67 (101st Airborne Div) and 1970-71; Bronze Star for Valour and Purple Heart for Wounds: *m* 1968 (*m diss* 1982), Janet Theresa Sabo, of Lakewood, New Jersey, and has issue living, Jon Ernest *b* 1970; Private, US Army Res, Janina Theresa *b* 1973, Malinda Jane *b* 1978, — June Moonyeen, *b* 1940: *m* 1969, Daniel Herbert Young III, of 419 Dumbarton Rd, Baltimore, Maryland 21212, USA, and has issue living, Jonathan Herbert *b* 1970, Heather Jane *b* 1972.

Granddaughter (by 2nd *m*) of late Edward Every Every-Clayton (ante):—

Issue of late Major Charles Edward EVERY-HALSTED, *b* 1857, *d* 1935 (having assumed by Roy licence 1886 the name of Every-Halsted in lieu of Every-Clayton): *m* 1892, Lucy Clara (who *m* 2ndly, as his 2nd wife, Thomas FitzRoy Phillipps Fenwick, who *d* 1938) (Phillips, Bt, colls), da of late Lieut-Col G. F. Dallas:—

Mary Ruth, *b* 1898: *m* 1st, 1919 (*m diss* 1942), Capt Gerald Hargreave Mawson, MC, RE; 2ndly, 1951, Rev Henry William John Lancelot Reed Haywood, who *d* 1957, and has issue living (by 1st *m*) John Arthur Hargreave *b* 1923, — Charles Edward Hargreave, *b* 1926.

Sir Simon Every, 1st Bt, originally of Chardstock, Dorset (who *m* Anne, da and co-heir Sir Henry Leigh, of Egginton, Derbyshire, and removed to that place), was a loyal supporter Charles I. Sir John Every, 4th Bt, Capt RN, served in cause of William III with distinction.

EWART (UK) 1887, of Glenmachan, Strandtown, co Down, and of Glenbank, Belfast, co Antrim

In cruce spero

In the cross I hope

Sir (WILLIAM) IVAN CECIL EWART, DSC, 6th *Baronet*; son of late Maj William Basil Ewart, yst son of late Frederick William Ewart, 7th son of 1st baronet; *b* 18 July 1919; *s* his kinsman, *Sir* TALBOT, 1959; *ed* Radley; is a JP for Ards (County Court Div), and Chm of William Ewart & Son, Ltd, Linen' Manufacturers 1968-73, Chm Ewart New Northern Ltd, Belfast 1973-77; E Africa Representative of R Commonwealth Soc for the Blind in Uganda, Kenya and Tanzania 1977-84; Pres NI Chamber of Commerce and Industry 1974; High Sheriff co Antrim 1976; 1939-45 War Lt RNVR (prisoner, DSC): *m* 1948, Pauline Chevallier, who *d* 1964, da of late Wing-Cdr Raphael Chevallier Preston, OBE, AFC, of Derry Hill, Ballydugan, Downpatrick, co Down, and has issue.

𝕬rms – Or, three swords crossed, two in saltire and one in fesse, between in chief a cross-crosslet fitchée, and in base a dexter hand couped at the wrist gules. 𝕮rest – A hand erect gauntleted proper, holding a cross-crosslet fitchée gules.
Residence – Hill House, Hillsborough, co Down BT26 6AE. *Address* – PO Box 40870, Nairobi, Kenya. *Clubs* – Ulster (Belfast), Naval, and Nairobi.

SON LIVING

WILLIAM MICHAEL, *b* 10 June 1953; *ed* Radley.

DAUGHTERS LIVING

Susan Eveleen, *b* 1950: *m* 1973, Colin R. Cunningham. *Residence* – 17 Darragh, Whiterock, Killinchy, co Down BT23 6QD.
—— Patricia Rébé, *b* 1951: *m* 1971, Jeremy J.C. Browne. *Residence* – Claim Farm House, Manley, Frodsham, Cheshire WA6 6HT.

COLLATERAL BRANCHES LIVING

Issue of late George Herbert Ewart, 6th son of 1st baronet, *b* 1857, *d* 1924: *m* 1886, Alice Flora, who *d* 1945, yst da of late Richard Tipping Hamilton, of Willowbank, Kingstown, Dublin:—
Frances Madeline, *b* 1896: *m* 1917, Paymaster Lt-Com Philip Smiles, RN (ret), and has issue living, Alan, *b* 1924, — Roger Philip, *b* 1927, — Honor Madeleine, — Margaret. —— Helen Flora (3 Church Av, Newtownabbey, co Antrim), *b* 1898: *m* 1920, Lt-Col Louis Sydney Henshall, DSO, who *d* 1957, and has issue living, Herbert Ewart, *b* 1923, — James Arthur, *b* 1926, — Enid *b* 1921.

Granddaughter of late Frederick William Ewart, 7th son of 1st baronet:—
Issue of late Maj Gerald Valentine Ewart, OBE, DL, *b* 1884, *d* 1936: *m* 1911, Annie Ruth (Pearl) (Clontagh House, Crossgar, co Down), da of late Rev T. R. S. Collins, BD Chap to the Archbishop of Dublin:—
Eileen Geraldine: *m* 1939, Lieut-Com George Lennox Cotton, DSC, RNVR, and has issue living, Caroline Mourne Lennox, *b* 1942, — Elizabeth Grania Lennox, *b* 1944, — Kathleen Anne Lennox, *b* 1945. *Residence* – Clontagh House, Crossgar, co Down.

The 1st baronet, Sir William Ewart (son of late William Ewart, of Glenbank, near Belfast), was MP for Belfast (C) 1878-85, and for Belfast (N Div) 1885-89, and head of the firm of William Ewart & Son, Ltd, of Belfast. The 2nd Baronet, Sir William Quartus, was head of the firm of William Ewart & Son Ltd, of Belfast, and a KStJ. The 3rd baronet, Sir Robert Heard, was a Director of William Ewart & Son, Ltd, of Belfast.

ORR EWING (UK) 1886, of Ballikinrain, Stirlingshire, and Lennoxbank, co Dunbarton

Boldly

Sir RONALD ARCHIBALD ORR EWING, 5th *Baronet*; *b* 14 May 1912; *s* his father *Brig-Gen Sir* NORMAN ARCHIBALD ORR EWING, CB, DSO, 1960; *ed* Eton, and RMC Sandhurst; Maj (ret) Scots Guards; is a Member of Queen's Body Guard for Scotland (Roy Co of Archers), and a JP and a DL for Perthshire; 1939-45 War (prisoner): *m* 1938, Marion Hester, da of late Col Sir Donald Walter Cameron of Lochiel, KT, CMG (D Montrose), and has issue.

𝕬rms – Argent, a chevron gules, issuant therefrom a banner of the second thereon in the first quarter the arms of St Andrew - viz, azure a saltire argent; between in chief two mullets gules and in base the sun in its splendour, the whole within a bordure indented gules charged with three martlets argent, two in chief and one in base. 𝕮rest – A demi-lion rampant gules holding in its dexter paw a mullet as in the arms.
Seat – Cardross, Kippen, Stirling FK8 3JY. *Club* – New (Edinburgh).

SONS LIVING

ARCHIBALD DONALD (13 Warriston Crescent, Edinburgh EH3 5LA; New (Edinburgh) and Pratt's Clubs), *b* 20 Dec 1938; *ed* Gordonstoun, and Trin Coll, Dublin (BA); a Member of Queen's Body Guard for Scotland (Roy Co of Archers): *m* 1st, 1965 (*m diss* 1972), Venetia Elizabeth, da of Maj Richard Turner; 2ndly, 1972, Nicola Jean-Anne, da of Reginald Baron Black, of Brook House, Fovant, Salisbury, Wilts (*see* D Roxburghe, colls), and has issue living (by 2nd *m*), Alastair Frederick Archibald *b* 26 May 1982. —— Ronald James, *b* 1948; *ed* Gordonstoun, and Dundee Univ; LLB St Andrews.

DAUGHTERS LIVING

Janet Elizabeth, *b* 1940: *m* 1969, John Malcolm Wallace, of The Furnace, Ashburnham, Battle, Sussex, and has issue living, Jasper Simon, *b* 1973, — Jocelyn James *b* 1977, — Jemma Louise, *b* 1971. —— Fiona Marion, *b* 1946: *m* 1968, Adrian Peter Drewe, of Parsonage Farm House, Ticehurst, Wadhurst, E Sussex TN5 7DL, and has issue living, Jonathan James, *b* 1971, — Nicholas Robert Patrick, *b* 1982, — Anthony Adrian, *b* 1985.

BROTHER LIVING

Alan Lindsay, MC, *b* 1915; *ed* Eton, and Edinburgh Univ (BSc Forestry 1939); Master of Forestry, California Univ 1952; PhD British Columbia Univ 1956; late Forest Geneticist, British Columbia Forest Ser; formerly 2nd Lieut Argyll and Sutherland Highlanders; 1939-40 War in France (twice wounded, despatches, MC, prisoner): *m* 1945, Helen Isabelle, da of late William Evans, of Toronto, Canada, and has issue living, Alexander Evans (3500 Willow St, Vancouver, BC, Canada), *b* 1947: *m* 1973, Louise Cantin, of Montreal, Canada, and has issue living, Simon Alan *b* 1975, Etienne Alec *b* 1979, — Isobel Laura, *b* 1954: *m* 1975, Robert Wain Reid, and has issue living, James William *b* 1986, Jennifer Laura *b* 1987. *Residence* – 4712 Woodburn Court, West Vancouver, BC V7S 3B3, Canada.

SISTER LIVING

Jean Marjorie, *b* 1918: *m* 1941, Alexander Robert Webster, and has issue living, Robert Alexander, *b* 1942: *m* 1968, Margaret Elizabeth Mary, da of Gilbert Harrower, of Keith, Banffshire, and has issue living, Andrew Robert *b* 1970, Jill Margaret *b* 1973, — Yvonne Jean, *b* 1944: *m* 1st, 1965 (*m diss* 1969), Michael Montgomery; 2ndly, 1969, Leslie Murray, of Killinchy, Co Down, son of Morton Murray, and has issue living, (by 1st *m*) Alan Michael *b* 1966, Ian Aston *b* 1968, (by 2nd *m*) Laura Kay *b* 1972. *Residence* – 2A Leigh Court, Avonmore Rd, W Kensington, London W14 8RL.

COLLATERAL BRANCHES LIVING

Grandson of late Capt John Orr Ewing, 4th son of 1st baronet:—
Issue of late Archibald Ian Orr Ewing, *b* 1884, *d* 1942: *m* 1911, Gertrude Bertha, who *d* 1974, da of late Charles Herman Runge, of Chilworthy House, Chard, Somerset:—
(Charles) Ian (*Baron Orr-Ewing*), OBE, *b* 1912; *cr* a Baronet 1963 and Baron Orr-Ewing 1971.

Grandchildren of late Charles Lindsay Orr Ewing, MP, 5th son of 1st baronet:—
Issue of late Sir Ian Leslie Orr Ewing, MP, *b* 1893, *d* 1958: *m* 1917, Helen Bridget, MBE, who *d* 1978, da of late Hon Henry Lloyd Gibbs (B Aldenham, colls):—
Anthea Helen (Thorn Falcon House, Taunton, Som), *b* 1917: *m* 1st, 1938, Major Wilfrid Michael Fox, Coldstream Guards, who *d* 1975; 2ndly, 1977, Edward John Ninien Lowes, elder son of Edward Lowes, and has issue living (by 1st *m*), Charles St Vigor, *b* 1941: *m* 1st, 1964 (*m diss* 1992), Charlotte Certhia, da of Mervyn Jeffery Ingram, MB (*see* Ingram, Bt); 2ndly, 1994, Nicola Louise, da of Capt Edward de Lérisson Cazenove (*see* Kennedy, Bt), and formerly wife of Sir Charles Warren, 9th Bt, and has issue living (by 1st *m*), Laurence St Vigor *b* 1965, Nina Jane *b* 1970, — (Helen) Mary (*Lady Stewart-Wilson*), *b* 1939: *m* 1962, Lt-Col Sir Blair Aubyn Stewart-Wilson, KCVO, Scots Gds, of 3 Browning Close, Randolph Av, W9, and has issue living, Alice Helen *b* 1963: *m* 1985, Jonathan Cecil Ian Young, only son of Capt H. R. C. Young, RN, of Petersfield, Hants (and has issue living, Archibald Blair Cecil *b* 1991, India Mary Katharine *b* 1988), Sophia Mary *b* 1966: *m* 1991, A. Bruce McIntosh, eldest son of late Bob McIntosh, of Budleigh Salterton, Devon (and has issue living, Lily *b* 1993, Kitty *b* 1994), Belinda Anthea *b* 1970.
Issue of late Capt David Orr Ewing, DSO, RN, *b* 1900, *d* 1964: *m* 1930, Helen Mary Stuart, who *d* 1994, da of late Benjamin Noaks, of Bloemfontein, S Africa:—
Edward Stuart (Dunskey, Portpatrick, Stranraer, Wigtownshire), *b* 1931; Maj Black Watch (ret); a DL of Wigtownshire, and Lord Lieut since 1989: *m* 1st, 1958 (*m diss* 1981), Fiona Anne Bowman, yr da of Anthony Hobart Farquhar, of Hastingwood House, Harlow, Essex; 2ndly, 1981, Diana Mary, da of William Smith Waters, OBE, of Greenfoot House, Raughton Head, Cumbria, and has issue living (by 1st *m*), Alastair Lindsay, *b* 1964, — Jane Helen *b* 1961: *m* 1991, Patrick Giles Gauntlett Dear, of 201 E 86th St, Apt 32D, New York 10028, USA, yr son of M. A. G. Dear, of Algarve, Portugal, and has issue living, Frederick Edward Gauntlett *b* 1993, — Victoria Susan *b* 1962. —— Charles David (Torhousemuir, Wigtown, Wigtownshire), *b* 1936; Lt Cdr, RN: *m* 1962, Bridget Juliet, da of Sir Thomas Astley Woolaston White, 5th Bt (*cr* 1802), and has issue living, David Robert, *b* 1964; The Black Watch (Royal Highland Regt): *m* 1992, Sally Katrine, elder da of Col R. S. B. Watson, of Edinburgh, — Robert Charles, *b* 1966.

Sir Archibald Orr Ewing (7th son of late William Ewing, of Ardvullen House, Argyllshire, a merchant of Glasgow, and his wife Susan, da of John Orr, Provost of Paisley), 1st baronet, Dean of Faculties in Glasgow Univ, and an Ensign-Gen in Roy Co of Archers (HM's Body Guard for Scotland); MP for Dunbartonshire (C) 1868-92. Sir William, 2nd Bt, was a Member of Queen's Body Guard for Scotland (Roy Co of Archers). Brig-Gen Sir Norman Archibald Orr Ewing, 4th Bt, was a Lieut Queen's Body Guard for Scotland (Roy Co of Archers) and was Hon Col, 7th Bn Argyll and Sutherland Highlanders 1932-48.

FAGGE (E) 1660, of Wiston, Sussex

Sir JOHN WILLIAM FREDERICK FAGGE, 11th *Baronet*, son of late William Archibald Theodore Fagge, 4th son of 8th Baronet; *b* 25 Sept 1910; *s* his uncle, *Sir* JOHN HARRY LEE, 1940; is a farmer: *m* 1940, Ivy Gertrude, who *d* 1992, da of William Edward Frier, of 15 Church Lane, Newington, Kent, and has issue.

Arms – Gules, two bends vaire. **Crest** – An ostrich with wings expanded argent, beaked, legged and ducally gorged or holding in the beak a horseshoe proper. *Residence* – 11 Forbes Road, Faversham, Kent ME13 8QF.

SON LIVING

JOHN CHRISTOPHER, *b* 30 April 1942: *m* 1974, Evelyn Joy Golding.

DAUGHTER LIVING

Pauline Joy, *b* 1943.

SISTER LIVING

Gwendoline Beatrice May, *b* 1914.

DAUGHTER LIVING OF TENTH BARONET

Lucy Harriet Gertrude, *b* 1913. *Residence* – Boston, USA.

Safe if upright

COLLATERAL BRANCH LIVING

Granddaughter of late Rev John Frederick Fagge, 4th son of 6th baronet:—
Issue of late Sarah Elizabeth Fagge, *d* 1947: *m* 1889, George Goldie, JP, who *d* 1904:—
Ethelreda Marie Teresa, *b* 1899: *m* 1936, Lawrence Henry Shattock, FRIBA (Knight of St Gregory). *Residence* – Little Wiston, Crescent Rd, Wimbledon, SW20.

The 1st baronet, Sir John Fagge (son of late John Fagge, of Brensett, Kent), sat as MP for Rye 1645-53, for Sussex 1654-9 and 1681-5, and for Steyning 1660-81 and 1685-1701, and was a Col in Parliamentary Army. He purchased the estate of Wiston, Sussex, from Dr Thomas Shirley, which passed from Sir Robert Fagge, 4th Bt to his sister Elizabeth who *m* 1743, Sir Charles Goring, 5th Bt.

FAIRBAIRN (UK 1869), of Ardwick, Lancashire

Always the same

Sir (JAMES) BROOKE FAIRBAIRN, 6th *Baronet*; *b* 10 Dec 1930; *s* his father, *Sir* WILLIAM ALBERT, 1972; *ed* Stowe: *m* 1960, Mary Russell, who *d* 1992, only da of late William Russell Scott, MB, ChB, FFARCS, of 59 Wyke Rd, Weymouth, and has issue.

Arms – Argent, on a chevron between three boars' heads couped gules three bezants. **Crest** – The sun in his meridian splendour or. *Residence* – Barkway House, Bury Rd, Newmarket, Suffolk, CB8 7BT.

SONS LIVING

ROBERT WILLIAM, *b* 10 April 1965; *ed* King's Sch, Ely, and Durham Univ (BA): *m* 1990, Sarah Frances Colleypriest, elder da of Roger Griffin, of Malmesbury, Wilts, and has issue living, Imogen Mary Colleypriest, *b* 1993. —— George Edward, *b* 1969.

DAUGHTER LIVING

Fiona Mary, *b* 1967.

BROTHER LIVING

William Andrew (Midway Cottage, Norton, Chichester, W Sussex, PO20 6NJ), *b* 1934; *ed* Stowe; FCA, MSI: *m* 1961, Elspeth Alison, only da of late Robert Hally, of Brookfield, Barnham, W Sussex, and has issue living, James Andrew, *b* 1967: *m* 1994, Samantha Jane, only da of late David Harwicke, of The Paddocks, Hurst, Berks, — Nicola Christine, *b* 1962: *m* 1986, Dr Peter Gist, of 16 Oakwood Rd, Hampstead Garden Suburb, NW11 6QY, son of F. E. Gist, of Honiton, Devon, and has issue living, Duncan Edward *b* 1989, Rosemary Eleanor *b* 1988, Philippa Helen *b* 1992, — Katharine Alison, *b* 1964.

AUNTS LIVING (*Daughters of 4th baronet*)

Mildred Dorothy, *b* 1903. —— Constance Matilda, *b* 1908.

WIDOW LIVING OF FIFTH BARONET

CHRISTINE RENEE COTTON (*Lady Fairbairn*) (45 Williams Way, Radlett, Herts), da of late Rev Canon Robert William Croft, V of Kelvedon, Essex: *m* 1925, Sir William Albert Fairbairn, 5th Bt, who *d* 1972.

COLLATERAL BRANCHES LIVING

Issue of late Reginald Fairbairn, 3rd son of 2nd baronet, *b* 1856, *d* 1921: *m* 1880, May Elizabeth, da of J. F. Holt:—

Ada, *b* 1882.

Grandchildren of late Rev William Murray Fairbairn, son of late William Andrew Fairbairn (infra):—
Issue of late Vice-Adm Bernard William Murray Fairbairn, CBE, *b* 1880, *d* 1960, *m* 1905, Alice Mary, who *d* 1970, only da of late William Phillipps, of Leigham Villas, Plymouth:—
Alan Bernard Murray, MBE *b* 1906; *ed* Sherborne; Cdr RN (ret); 1939-45 War (despatches); MBE (1973): *m* 1943, Adeline Hilda, da of Lt-Col Edward Herbert Sweet, CMG, DSO, and has issue living, *Rev* John Alan, *b* 1946; *ed* Wellington Coll, and Trin Coll, Camb (MA): *m* 1982, Susan Patricia, da of late Dr Charles Sergel, of Milford-on-Sea, and has issue living, Timothy John Charles, *b* 1983, — Katharine Mary, *b* 1985. *Residence* – 22 Milford Court, Milford-on-Sea. —— David Patrick, *b* 1919; *ed* Sherborne; CEng, MIMechE, FIMarE; Lt-Cdr RN (ret): *m* 1950, Margaret Winifred Ferrers (formerly 2nd Officer WRNS), da of late Ronald Ernest Ferrers Courage, of Redcross Dulverton, and has issue living, William David Murray (Woodland View, Upton Noble, Shepton Mallet, Som BA4 6BB), *b* 1953; *ed* Radley, and Magdalene Coll, Camb (MA); Cdr RN: *m* 1983, Rowena Katherine, da of Walter Angus Murray, of West Hill Court, Ottery St Mary, Devon, and has issue living, Oliver James Murray *b* 1987, Fiona Nina Katherine *b* 1992, — Anne Mary, *b* 1951; formerly Sister of the Society of St Margaret, St Saviour's Priory, Haggerston: *m* 1993, Harry Fox, of 49 Walsingham, St John's Wood Park, NW8 6RJ. *Residence* – The Firs, Ryhall, Stamford, Lincolnshire PE9 4HF.
Issue of late Aubrey John Murray Fairbairn, *b* 1888, *d* 1961: *m* 1920, Adela, da of late Col T. A. Rawlins, of Clifton, Bristol, and Berrow, Somerset:—
Ian Aubrey, *b* 1927.

Grandsons of late William Andrew Fairbairn, 4th son of 1st baronet:—
Issue of late Edward Percy Fairbairn, *b* 1866, *d* 1931: *m* 1st, 1894, Mary, who *d* 1903, da of late John Sholto Douglas, of Tilquhillie, Kincardineshire; 2ndly, 1908, Constance, who *d* 1952, da of William Gaven Eden (B Henley, colls):—
(By 2nd *m*) George William, *b* 1911; formerly Capt RE; is an ARIBA: *m* 1940, Katharine Elizabeth, who *d* 1991, da of late Dr William Deane, of Waddington, Lincoln, and has issue living, Jacqueline Elizabeth, *b* 1948: *m* 1978, Luis Filipe Espadinha Fialho, of Casa Charrna, Albadeira, Lagos, Algarve, Portugal, son of late Pedro Manuel Fialho and Maria B. Espadinha, of Estoril, Portugal, and has issue living, Miguel Filipe *b* 1980, Andre Simon *b* 1984. *Residence* – Malt Kiln Lane, Brant Broughton, Lincoln. —— Patrick Yelverton (Annagh, The Warren, Mayfield, Sussex), *b* 1913; *ed* Charterhouse: *m* 1940, Dorothy Mary, who *d* 1986, da of late Lewis Henshaw, OBE, of Madras, and has issue living, Edward James (Applegarth, Bradfield, Berks), *b* 1950: *m* 1974, Fiona Catherine, da of Maj M. C. Gray, of Steep, Hants, and has issue living, Miranda Sarah *b* 1976, Rosalind Nesta *b* 1979, — Judith Constance, *b* 1946: *m* 1970, Keith Anthony Delgado Hornby, barrister, of 11 St Ann's Villas, W11, and has issue living, Jamie Alexander Fairbairn *b* 1976, Nicholas Thomas Fairbairn *b* 1980, Katya Eugenie *b* 1973.

Grandchildren of late William Fairbairn, son of late Rev Adam Henderson Fairbairn (infra):—
Issue of late Maj William Alan Thomas Fairbairn, TD, *b* 1908, *d* 1992: *m* 1944, Marian Ruth (Beauchamps, Milford-on-Sea, Hants), da of late Capt W. T. Wyllie:—
Stephen Alan (Borgarholtsbraut 57, Kopavogur, Iceland), *b* 1947; *ed* Radley; Dip AD Bath Academy of Art: *m* 1970, Margaret Joelsdottir, and has issue living, Hilda, *b* 1973, — Sandra, *b* 1979. —— Susan Mary (Robin Cottage, Pauls Lane, Sway, Lymington, Hants), *b* 1953; *ed* Stonar: *m* 1974, Richard Ivor Sommerin, and has issue living, James Adrian, *b* 1974.

Grandson of late Rev Adam Henderson Fairbairn, 7th son of 1st baronet:—
Issue of late Major David Alexander Fairbairn, OBE, Duke of Wellington's (W Riding) Regt, *b* 1882, *d* 1950: *m* 1920, Emmeline Mary, who *d* 1964, da of late Alfred Coxon, of Surbiton, and widow of Capt T. A. Abbott, RFA:—
Norman David Nigel (Whitmore Farm, Windlesham, Surrey), *b* 1921; *ed* Wellington Coll, and Cape Town Univ (BA); ARIBA, and a MIA; 1939-45 War with RA and 17th/21st Lancers: *m* 1951, Mary Josephine, da of Hector Hillaby, Bar-at law, and has issue living, Jonathan David, *b* 1952, — Mark Benson Hector, *b* 1960: *m* 1990, A. Fiona, elder da of Cmdr Graham P. Stock, of Thornford, Dorset, — Carol Evangeline Mary, *b* 1954, — Alexandra Josephine Margaret, *b* 1957.

Sir William Fairbairn, 1st Bt, el surviving son of Andrew Fairbairn of Smailholm, Roxburghshire, was a celebrated engineer who was associated with Stephenson in erecting the tubular bridge across the Menai Straits 1848. He was a founder of the British Assocn for the Advancement of Science.

Fairfax (Ramsay-Fairfax-Lucy), see Lucy.

Fairlie-Cuninghame, see Cuninghame.

FALKINER (I) 1778, of Annemount, Cork
(Name pronounced "Fawkner")

Sir EDMOND CHARLES FALKINER, 9th *Baronet*; *b* 24 June 1938; *s* his father, *Lieut-Col Sir* TERENCE EDMOND PATRICK, 1987; *ed* Downside: *m* 1960, Janet Iris, da of Arthur Edward Bruce Darby, of The Park, Stoke Lacey, Bromyard, Herefordshire, and has issue.

ⱥrms – Or, three falcons close proper, belled gules. ⱥrest – A falcon's lure proper, between two wings azure.
Residence – 111 Wood St, Barnet, Herts EN5 4BX.

SONS LIVING

BENJAMIN SIMON PATRICK, *b* 16 Jan 1962; *ed* Queen Elizabeth's, Barnet; has issue, Samuel James Matthew, *b* 1993. ⸺ Matthew Terence, *b* 1964; *ed* Queen Elizabeth's, Barnet.

BROTHER LIVING

Henry Leslie Basil, *b* 1940; *ed* Downside: *m* 1967, (Dorothea) Angela, only da of Peter Wolfe-Taylor, of Chimneys, Ockham, Surrey, and has issue living, Tobias Peter Riggs, *b* 1972; *ed* Millfield, ⸺ Max Henry Wolfe, *b* 1974; *ed* Millfield. *Residence* – Dormer Cottage, Frensham, Surrey.

SISTERS LIVING

Elizabeth Anne Thérèse, *b* 1929: *m* 1956, Michael David Hogg, and has issue (*see* Hogg, Bt colls). *Residence* – 19 Woodlands Road, SW13. ⸺ Mary Clare, *b* 1934: *m* 1st, 1956 (*m diss* 1980), Noel John Taylor, son of Charles Taylor, of Wylow, Mordiford, Hereford, 2ndly, 1991, Geoffrey Smith, and has issue living (by 1st *m*), Paul John, *b* 1957; *ed* Hereford Sch, ⸺ Mark Robert, *b* 1965, *ed* Hereford Sch; has issue living, Robert *b* 1990, Emma *b* 1992, ⸺ David James, *b* 1969; *ed* Hereford Sch; has issue living, Ashley *b* 1992, Thomas *b* 1993, ⸺ Jane Clare, *b* 1961, ⸺ Sarah Kate, *b* 1971; has issue living, Lucy Jane *b* 1988. *Residence* – 22 Penny Plock, Madley, Herefordshire. ⸺ Veronica Cicely, *b* 1935: *m* 1956, William David Brown, only son of William Moir Brown, MB, ChB, FRCS, of Cantilupe Cottage, Marden, Hereford, and has issue living, Adrian William, *b* 1958; *ed* Whitfriars Sch, Cheltenham, ⸺ Edward David, MBE (Mil), *b* 1960; *ed* Whitefriars Sch, Cheltenham: *m* 1993, Ruth Mary Sandy, ⸺ Rupert Duncan, *b* 1963; *ed* Whitefriars Sch, Cheltenham, ⸺ Dominic George Andrew, *b* 1966; *ed* Whitefriars Sch, Cheltenham. *Residence* – The Old Manse, Fownhope, Herefordshire.

COLLATERAL BRANCH LIVING

Issue of late Maj Gervase Leslie Falkiner, 3rd and yst son of 7th baronet, *b* 1909, *d* 1988: *m* 1934, Rosemary Hastings (15 Glebelands, Merriott, Som), elder da of Herbert Smith, of Tower, Mold, Flintshire:—

Richard Gervase, *b* 1936; *ed* Ampleforth: *m* 1959, Gabrielle Mary, only da of Frank Woodgate, of Ledley House, Ebrington, Chipping Campden, Glos, and has issue living, Sebastian, *b* 1963, ⸺ Sophia Mary, *b* 1962. *Residence* – 15 Yarell Mansions, Queen's Club Gdns, W14. ⸺ Michael George Patrick, *b* 1940; *ed* Ampleforth: *m* 1970, Joanna Rosamund, eldest da of late (Walter) Peter Baxter (*see* V Hawarden), and has issue living, Caroline Helen, *b* 1972, ⸺ Emily Rosemary, *b* 1974. *Residence* – Downclose Stud, North Perrott, nr Crewkerne, Som.

Sir Riggs Falkiner, MP, 1st Bt of Annemount, co Cork, was great-grandson of Michael Falkiner of Brigart, Leeds, who settled in Ireland about 1651. Sir Charles Leslie Falkiner, 4th Bt, was Capt RN, and as Lieut in 1810 headed the "Shannon" main deck boarders at capture of American ship "Chesapeake" (promoted Com). His brother, Lt-Col Sir Samuel Edmund Falkiner, 5th Bt, served throughout the Peninsular war, was present at Talavera, Busaco, Salamanca, Ciudad Rodrigo, Fuentes d'Onore, and was wounded three times.

FARQUHAR (GB) 1796, of Cadogan House, Middlesex
(Name pronounced "Farkwer")

By mind and hand

Sir MICHAEL FITZROY HENRY FARQUHAR, 7th *Baronet*; *b* 29 June 1938; *s* his father, *Sir* PETER WALTER, OBE, DSO, 1986; *ed* Eton, and RAC Cirencester: *m* 1963, Veronica Geraldine, elder da of Patrick Rowan Hornidge, of Helford Passage, Falmouth, Cornwall, and has issue.

Arms – Argent, a lion rampant sable between two sinister hands apaumée couped in chief gules, and a crescent in base azure. **Crest** – An eagle rising proper.
Residence – Manor Farm, West Kington, Chippenham, Wilts SN14 7JG. *Club* – White's.

SONS LIVING

CHARLES WALTER FITZROY, *b* 21 Feb 1964; *ed* Stowe. *Residence* – 3418B Empedrado, Tampa, Florida 33629, USA. —— Edward Peter Henry, *b* 1966; *ed* Stowe, and RMA Sandhurst. *Residence* – 109 Harbord St, SW6 6PS.

BROTHERS LIVING

Anthony Charles, *b* 1942; *ed* Eton: *m* 1969, Elizabeth Jane, da of late Col Timothy M. Braithwaite, of Honey Cottage, Limpley Stoke, Bath, and has issue living, Alexandra Elizabeth, *b* 1971, — Annabelle Jean, *b* 1973, — Antonia Katharine, *b* 1977. *Residence* – Glebe House, Turkdean, nr Cheltenham, Glos. —— Ian Walter, LVO, *b* 1945; *ed* Eton, and RMA Sandhurst; Capt Queen's Own Hussars; LVO 1972; Master Bicester & Warden Hill Hunt 1973, Jt Master, Beaufort Hunt 1985: *m* 1972, Pamela Jane, da of Charles L. Chafer, of Elleron Lodge, Pickering, Yorks, and has issue living, Emma Elizabeth, *b* 1977, — Victoria Rose, *b* 1979, — Rosanne Catherine, *b* 1983. *Residence* – Happylands, Doughton, Tetbury, Glos.

AUNT LIVING (*Daughter of 5th baronet*)

Ruth Violet Mary (*Ruth, Baroness Dulverton*), *b* 1910: *m* 1st, 1932 (*m diss* 1961), Major Richard Gennys Fanshawe, 16th/5th Lancers, who *d* 1988, son of Lieut-Gen Sir Edward Arthur Fanshawe, KCB; 2ndly, 1962, 2nd Baron Dulverton, who *d* 1992, and has issue living, (by 1st *m*) David Valentine (Chute Collis House, Upper Chute, Andover, Hants), *b* 1933; Col Gren Gds (ret): *m* 1963, Sheila Christine, el da of Maj-Gen John Malcolm McNeill, CB, CBE, and has issue living, Angus Edward *b* 1965, Robert Leighton *b* 1967; Capt Gren Gds: *m* 1992, Charlotte L. M. yr da of Hon Mr Justice (Sir Anthony Howell Meurig) Evans, RD, of Bucklers Hard, Hants, William David *b* 1971, — Brian Edward (Lady Wood, Knossington, Oakham, Leics), *b* 1936; Capt 9th/12th R Lancers: *m* 1960, Elizabeth, da of Geoffrey Pugh, of Temple Guiting House, Glos, and has issue living, James Robert (Pegasus Stables, Snailwell Rd, Newmarket, Suffolk) *b* 1961: *m* 1990, Jacqueline Mary Joan, da of late Geoffrey Cherry-Downes, Antony Geoffrey *b* 1964, Sarah Rose *b* 1967. *Residences* – Barnbrook Cottage, Milton Lilbourne, Pewsey, Wilts SN9 5LQ; Fassfern, Fort William, Inverness-shire.

COLLATERAL BRANCHES LIVING

Issue of late Lt-Col Charles Richard Farquhar, MC, 2nd son of 5th Baronet, *b* 1906 *d* 1980: *m* 1939, Dorothy Nancy (The Close, West Littleton, Chippenham, Wilts), da of Maj James Gerald Thewlis Johnson, DSO (Alleyne, Bt):—
Daphne Violet, *b* 1945: *m* 1973, Terence John Pardoe, of North Hazelrigg, Chatton, Alnwick, Northumberland, and has issue living, Robert Charles, *b* 1977, — Amanda Susan, *b* 1975. —— Angela Dorothy, *b* 1948: *m* 1977, Richard John Hassan Meade, OBE, and has issue living, James Richard, *b* 1981, — Harry Michael, *b* 1983, — Lucy Margaret *b* 1985.

Grandchildren of late Grenville Frederick Richard Farquhar, 4th son of 3rd baronet:—
Issue of late Guy William John Farquhar, *b* 1899, *d* 1962: *m* 1928 (*m diss* 1947), Daphne Mary Christian, da of late Lieut-Col Vivian Henry, CB (Millbank, Bt):—
Edward Vivian (37 Grange Av, Twickenham, Middx TW2 5TW), *b* 1929; *ed* Eton; late Capt 11th Hussars: *m* 1st, 1956 (*m diss* 1983), Polly, da of late Adm of the Fleet Sir Philip Louis Vian, GCB, KBE, DSO; 2ndly, 1985, Careena, only da of William Thomas, of Hebron, Dyfed, and has issue living, (by 1st *m*), Peter Christopher Edward, *b* 1959: *m* 1st, 1986, Susan Jane, only da of Michael Williams, of Fairfield House, Pedmore, Worcs; 2ndly, 1992, Victoria Susannah, elder da of Brig Peter Collins, of Threapwood, The Maultway, Camberley, Surrey, — Alastair Vian, *b* 1966, — Diana Susan, *b* 1961: *m* 1988, Nicholas David Morant, yst son of late Maj G. C. H. Morant, of Pigeon House Farm, Hatherden, Andover, Hants, and has issue living, Maximilian George Vian *b* 1991, Jack Edward Chearnley *b* 1993. —— Peter Guy Powlett (17 Netheravon Rd, W4 2NA), *b* 1936: *m* 1st, 1961 (*m diss* 1973), Rosemary Anne Eaton, only da of Eaton Hammond; 2ndly, 1974, Carolyn, el da of Graham Robertson, of E Lindfield, NSW, and has issue living (by 1st *m*), Richard Charles, *b* 1962: *m* 1988, Emma de Hoghton, elder da of Jonathan Reeves, of Tewkesbury, Glos (*see* V Chelmsford, colls), and has issue living, Araminta Claire *b* 1990, — James Edward, *b* 1963: *m* 1991, Victoria, da of late Michael Clinton, of Sedgehill, near Shaftesbury, Dorset, — (by 2nd *m*), a son, *b* 1980, — Hugh Graham, *b* 1984, — Jane, *b* 1982, — Alice Rose Jane, *b* 1987. —— Antonia Daphne Diana, *b* 1932: *m* 1956, Antony Noel Gordon Leaf (Cleeve House, Ampney St Peter, Cirencester), late Lieut 15/19th Hussars, and has issue living, Guy Edmond James, *b* 1962; *ed* Harrow, Hertford Coll, Oxford, and RMA Sandhurst; late Capt 15/19th Hussars: *m* 1993, Noelle Browning, of California, — Anna Georgina, *b* 1958: *m* 1988, George Francis Windsor-Clive, and has issue (*see* E Plymouth).

Issue of late FitzRoy James Wilberforce Farquhar, OBE, 5th son of 3rd baronet, *b* 1858, *d* 1941: *m* 1884, Ada Mary, who *d* 1944, da of Sir John William Cradock-Hartopp, 4th baronet:—
Arthur Ronald, DSC, *b* 1888; became Com 1924, and Capt (ret) 1934, served 1914-18 War (wounded), 1939-45 War.

Grandsons of late Ernest Farquhar, son of late Harvie Morton Farquhar, 2nd son of 2nd baronet:—
Issue of late Sir Harold Lister Farquhar, KCMG, MC, *b* 1894, *d* 1953: *m* 1917, Constance Audrey, who *d* 1963, da of late Hon Arthur Algernon Capell (E Essex, colls):—
Ian Rupert, *b* 1918; is Major Grenadier Guards: *m* 1944, Margarie Eugenie, da of late Francis John Gordon Borthwick, WS (*see* L Borthwick, colls), and has issue living, Francis Rupert, *b* 1952. *Residence* – Hamlyns, Chudleigh, S Devon. *Clubs* – White's, Pratt's.

Granddaughter of late Sir Harold Lister Farquhar, KCMG, MC (ante):—
Issue of late Adrian Farquhar, *b* 1924; *d* 1981: *m* 1955, Ann Elizabeth (Redlynch House, Salisbury), da of Edward John Johnston-Noad, of Paris:—
Annabel Cristina, *b* 1958: *m* 1983, Christopher Mark Yates, of 31 Lilyville Rd, SW6 5DP, son of T. Gordon Yates, of Covers, Lynchmere, W Sussex, and has issue living, Eden Mark Farquhar, *b* 1988, — Kieran Alexander Francis, *b* 1990.
Sir Robert Farquhar, Knt, of Munie, a yr son of the ancient family of Farquhar of Gilmilnscroft, was Deputy-Receiver of Scotland 1644, and Provost of Aberdeen 1646. His great-great-great nephew, Sir Walter, 1st baronet, was Physician to George IV when Prince Regent, and had a second son, Robert (first British Gov and Com-in-Ch of the Mauritius), who also was *cr* a Baronet in 1821 (*ext* 1924). The 5th baronet, Sir Walter Randolph Fitzroy Farquhar, Capt RFA, was *ka* 1918.

FARRAR (UK) 1911, of Bedford, Province of Transvaal, Union of South Africa (Extinct 1915)

Sir GEORGE HERBERT FARRAR, DSO, 1st and last *Baronet*.

DAUGHTER LIVING OF SECOND BARONET

Ella Marguerite (*Ella, Lady Watson*), *b* 1911: *m* 1935, Sir Thomas Aubrey Watson, 4th Bt, *cr* 1866, who *d* on active ser 1941.
Residence – Talton Lodge, Newbold-on-Stour, Stratford-on-Avon, Warwicks.

FARRINGTON (UK) 1818, of Blackheath, Kent

Sir HENRY FRANCIS COLDEN FARRINGTON, 7th *Baronet*; *b* 25 April 1914; *s* his father, *Sir* HENRY ANTHONY, 1944; *ed* Haileybury; Major (ret) late RA; Col (hon): *m* 1947, Anne, el da of late Major William Albert Gillam, DSO, Border Regt, and has issue.

Arms – Ermine, on a chevron gules between three leopard's faces sable as many bombs or, fired proper. **Crest** – A dragon wings elevated tail nowed vert bezanty, gorged with a mural crown argent and a chain reflexed over the back or, the body charged with two caltraps fessewise of the last.
Residence – Higher Ford, Wiveliscombe, Taunton, Som, TA4 2RL.

SON LIVING

HENRY WILLIAM (Castle, Wiveliscombe, Taunton, Somerset TA4 2TJ), *b* 27 March 1951; *ed* Haileybury, and RAC Cirencester; ARICS: *m* 1979, Diana Donne, ALI, yr da of Geoffrey Albert Broughton, of Impens, N Petherton, Som, and has issue living, Henry John Albert, *b* 4 Jan 1985, — Charles George Donne, *b* 1988.

Le bon temps viendra
There's a good time coming

DAUGHTER LIVING

Susan Maria (Tipnoller Cottage, Wiveliscombe, Taunton, Som, TA4 2RL), *b* 1949.

COLLATERAL BRANCHES LIVING

Grandchildren of late Alexander Farrington, 2nd son of 5th baronet:—
Issue of late Cmdr William Howard Farrington, RN, *b* 1907, *d* 1988: *m* 1934, Barbara, who *d* 1975, da of Herbert Smale, of 15 Harley St, W1:—
Andrew James (Bay Cottage, Wembury, Plymouth, Devon PL9 0HR), *b* 1942; *ed* Marlborough, and Birmingham Univ (BSc): *m* 1965, Susan Kathleen, BSc, da of Ronald Hugh Wylsher Britton, MRCS, LRCP, of 10 Lane Head Close, Croyde Bay, Braunton, N. Devon, and has issue living, William James, *b* 1967, — Eleanor Kathleen, *b* 1970, — Alice Joanna, *b* 1973. —— Susan FARRINGTON (3 Cedar Close, Wokingham, Berks RG11 1EA), *b* 1937; has resumed her maiden name: *m* 1980 (*m* diss 1987), Ieuan Davies Williams. —— Jenifer, *b* 1938: *m* 1965, Maj Martin Rothery Sheldon, Royal Scots Grays (ret), of The Old Vicarage, New Town, Wem, Shropshire SY4 5NU, and has issue living, Bryony Claire, *b* 1966, — Camilla Frances, *b* 1968, — Holly Samantha, *b* 1973. —— Angela, *b* 1941: *m* 1966, Andrew Arthur Rose, of Drimbuie, Kilchrenan, Taynuilt, Argyll PA35 1HF, and has issue living, David Andrew, *b* 1967, — Susannah Angela, *b* 1968, — Elizabeth Iona, *b* 1972

Issue of late John Marsden Farrington, yst son of 5th baronet, *b* 1874, *d* 1965: *m* 1917, Lynda May, who *d* 1981, da of George T. Simmonds, of Forest Hill, SE23:—
John Anthony (Moni Village, Limassol, Cyprus), *b* 1934; *ed* Eastbourne Coll: *m* 1958, Patricia Rose, da of John William Fowler, of Norwich, and has issue living, Charles Henry, *b* 1963; *ed* Shrewsbury: *m* 1990, Clair, el da of Francis Derek Rowland, and has issue living, Holly *b* 1992, — Richard John, *b* 1964; *ed* Shrewsbury: *m* 1993, Jasmine, da of Bill Pareira.

Granddaughter of late Anthony Charles Farrington, MRCS, LRCPE 4th son of 4th baronet:—
Issue of late Charles Anthony Beevor Farrington, *b* 1873, *d* 1939: *m* 1908, Mabel, who *d* 1970, da of late George Hastings Rust D'Eye:—
Marjorie Joan Cicely (8 Naish Rd, Barton-on-Sea, New Milton, Hants BH25 7PU), *b* 1910.

Grandchildren of late George Edward Marshall Farrington, eldest son of late Francis John Farrington, 4th son of Rev Edward Holmes Farrington, 2nd son of 3rd baronet:—
Issue of late Marshall Francis William, *b* 1912, *d* 1986: *m* 1939, Christina Johanna (Crystal), who *d* 1992, da of late William John MacSeveney, of Nsoko, Swaziland:—
Alastair Edward, *b* 1946: *m* 1964, Nesta Eureka Minnie, and has issue living, Craig Grant, *b* 1965, — Alastair Ian, *b* 1965: *m* 1990, Julie Rene van Lingen, and has issue living, Kirsty, *b* 1991, and adopted children, Kennedy *b* 1982, Slade Alastair *b* 1984, Jaydee *b* 1987, Shaylee *b* 1987, — Charlene Debra, *b* 1966: *m* 1992, Mark Philip Schroder, and has issue living, Alexander Mark, *b* 1992, — Desire Marshall, *b* 1968. —— Graham William, *b* 1947: *m* 1970 (*m* diss 1978), Persis Eleanor Tozer. —— Ian Fraser, *b* 1948: *m* 1972, Daphne Grace Colling, and has issue living, Bradley Graham, *b* 1974, — Wayne Lewis, *b* 1977. —— Jacqueline Valerie, *b* 1941: *m* 1962, Leopold William Kenneth Ferreira, and *d* 1981.

Sir Anthony Farrington, 1st Bt of this creation, was a Gen in the Army, Director-Gen of RA and Field Train, and an Hon DCL, Oxford, and *m* 1766, Elizabeth, da of Alexander Colden, Lieut-Gov of New York. Sir Henry Anthony, 6th Bt, was Ch Conservator of Forests, Central Provinces India 1923-7.

Faudel-Phillips, see Phillips.

FAYRER (UK) 1896, of Devonshire Street, St Marylebone, co London
(Name pronounced "Fairer")

Sir JOHN LANG MACPHERSON FAYRER, 4th *Baronet*; *b* 18 Oct 1944; *s* his father, *Lt-Cdr Sir* JOSEPH HERBERT SPENS, DSC, RNVR, 1976; *ed* Edinburgh Acad, and Univ of Strathclyde.

Arms – Argent, on a bend invected sable between in chief an Eastern crown gules and in base an esculapius proper enfiled with an Eastern crown of the third, three horse-shoes or. **Crest** – In front of a sword erect, point upward proper, pommel and hilt or, a horseshoe or between two wings erect gules.
Residences – Overhailes, Haddington, E Lothian EH41 3SB; 9 Westfield St, Edinburgh.

WIDOW LIVING OF THIRD BARONET

NOREEN CHRISTIAN MAY (*Lady Fayrer*), (Overhailes, Haddington, E Lothian), only da of late Rev John Yuill Walker, of Innerleithen: *m* 1964, as his 3rd wife, Lt-Cdr Sir Joseph Herbert Spens Fayrer, 3rd Bt, DSC, RNVR, who *d* 1976.

Ne tentes aut perfice
Do not attempt, or else
accomplish

COLLATERAL BRANCH LIVING

Granddaughters of late Lt-Col Frederick Durand Stirling Fayrer, 6th son of 1st baronet:—
Issue of late Colin Robert Fayrer, *b* 1907, *d* 1983: *m* 1946, Evelyn Elinor May (20 The Manor, Churchdown, Glos), da of late Thomas A. Carey, Ceylon Civil Ser:—

Anne Patricia (66 Lower Sloane St, SW1), *b* 1947: *m* 1991, Roderick John McKellar. —— Wendy Elizabeth, *b* 1949: *m* 1974, David L. Allworthy, of Forest House, 99 Blean Common, Blean, Canterbury, Kent, and has issue living, James Jonathan Fayrer, *b* 1977, — Anna Elizabeth, *b* 1979.
The 1st baronet, Sir Joseph, was a FRCS, FRCP, an Hon Physician to HM Queen Victoria, and an Hon Physician (Mil) and Physician Extraordinary to HM King Edward VII; Gov of Wellington Coll, and many years Surg-Gen and Pres of Med Board at India Office.

FEILDEN (UK) 1846, of Feniscowles, Lancashire

Sir HENRY WEMYSS FEILDEN, 6th *Baronet*; *b* 1 Dec 1916; *s* his cousin, Sir WILLIAM MORTON BULLER, MC, 1976; *ed* Canford, and King's Coll London; 1939-45 War with RE; Civil Servant (ret): *m* 1943, Ethel May, da of late John Atkinson, of Annfield Plain, co Durham, and has issue.

Arms – Argent, on a fesse cottised azure, between two martlets in chief and a rose in base gules, barbed and seeded proper, three lozenges or. **Crest** – A nuthatch perched upon a hazel-branch fructed, holding in its beak a rose gules, slipped proper. **Second Crest and Motto** – A palm-tree weighted proper. "Crescit sub pondere virtus" (*Virtue grows under its imposed weight*).
Seat – Feniscowles, Lancashire. *Residence* – Littledene, Heathfield Rd, Burwash, Etchingham, E Sussex, TN19 7HN. *Club* – MCC.

SON LIVING

Henry Rudyard, *b* 26 Sept 1951; *ed* Kent Coll, Canterbury, and Bristol Univ (BVSc); MRCVS: *m* 1982, Anne, da of late William Frank Bonner Shepperd, and has issue living, William Henry, *b* 5 April 1983. *Residence* – 30 Manor Close, Wickham, Fareham, Hants PO17 5BZ.

DAUGHTERS LIVING

Virtutis · Præmium · Honor
Honor is the reward of virtue

Jennifer May, *b* 1944: *m* 1st, 1972 (*m diss* 1981), Philip Andrew Cooper; 2ndly, 1981, Graham Alexander Donald, of 45D Seabird Lane, Discovery Bay, Lantau Island, Hong Kong, and has issue living (by 1st *m*), Harry Edward, *b* 1975, — Paul Andrew, *b* 1978. —— Anne Margaret, *b* 1947: *m* 1970, William Hugh Stokoe, of Chantry Down, Echopit Rd, Guildford, Surrey GU1 3TN, and has issue living, Rupert William, *b* 1980, — Joanna Mary, *b* 1976.

BROTHER LIVING

Randle Richard (Chartridge, West St, Mayfield, E Sussex TN20 6DS; MCC), *b* 1923; *ed* Marlborough, Corpus Christi Coll, Camb (MA), and Cuddesdon Theo Coll, Bar Lincoln's Inn 1949; Curate of St Andrew's Moulsecoomb 1955-57, and of Steyning 1957-58, Tutor-Organiser for Workers' Educational Assocn, for NE Lancs, 1958-63, and HM Inspector of Schs, 1963-66; Assist Editor (Political Affairs) *Keesing's Contemporary Archives* 1967-81, and a Member Gen Synod of Ch of England 1970-80: *m* 1957, Leonora Mary, who *d* 1991, da of John Laurence Marshall, of Leicester.

COLLATERAL BRANCHES LIVING

Issue of late Major Edward Leyland Cooke Feilden, OBE, 2nd son of 3rd baronet, *b* 1868, *d* 1921: *m* 1907, Hon Marjorie Graham Murray, who *d* 1967, da of 1st Viscount Dunedin:—

Esmè Mary Graham, *b* 1913: *m* 1935, George Richard Shaw, who *d* 1983, of Crossbank Hill, Hurworth-on-Tees, Darlington, and has issue living, Graham (West Bank, Kilmacolm, Renfrewshire PA13 4AY), *b* 1948: *m* 1972, Patricia Alexandra, da of William Veitch, and has issue living, William Graham *b* 1981, Katharine Alexandra *b* 1976, Philippa Jane *b* 1978, — Angela Mary Graham, *b* 1936: *m* 1955 (*m diss* 1990), Air Commodore Anthony Walkinshaw Fraser, RAF and has issue living, Robert Walkinshaw *b* 1963, Amanda Evelyn *b* 1956: *m* 1978 (*m diss* 1992), Mark Chaytor Dickinson (*see* Chaytor, Bt, 1990 Edn) (and has issue living, Maximillien *b* 1981, Olivia Esme *b* 1983, Georgia Eve *b* 1987), Antonia Esme *b* 1958: *m* 1983, Richard Heard, Alexandra *b* 1960: *m* 1987, Simon Reid-Kay, — Fiona Gilroy, *b* 1944: *m* 1962, Maj Fane Travers Gaffney, Welsh Guards (Guards' Club), of Crossbank Hill, Hurworth, co Durham, and has issue living, Bay Travers (2a Wyfold Rd, SW6 6SJ) *b* 1988, Helen, da of Henry Ernest Tugwell, of Farleigh Lane, Barming, Maidstone, Kent (and has issue living, Frederick *b* 1992), Richard Desmond *b* 1964, Adrian Tobias George Hannaford *b* 1972, Miranda *b* 1966: *m* 1987, Christopher John Charles Legard, elder son of Sir Charles Thomas Legard, 15th Bt, — Gelda Susan Marjorie Feilden, *b* 1947: *m* 1968, Robert Harding Churton, Maj 15th/19th King's R Hussars, of Greenside House, Greenside, Tyne & Wear NE40 4AA, and has issue living, Thomas Edward Harding *b* 1972, David Richard Harding *b* 1975.

Issue of late Lt-Col Randle Montague Feilden, CBE, 4th son of 3rd baronet, *b* 1871, *d* 1965: *m* 1924, Rachel Mary Gordon, who *d* 1933, da of late Horace Gordon Lowe, of Truro:—

John Randle, *b* 1931. —— Fay Adah Rachel (The Sail Loft, Mulberry Quay, Falmouth, Cornwall TR11 3HD), *b* 1925; BA, PhD London, Dip Psych; lecturer and research worker London Univ 1962-82, since when Emeritus Reader in Clinical Psychology, London Univ; Founder and Dir Centre for Personal Construct Psychology since 1982: *m* 1st, 1948 (*m diss* 1955), Anthony John Fransella, RAF; 2ndly, 1968, John Royden Cole Hodson.

This family has been settled near Blackburn, Lancashire, for more than four centuries. The 1st Baronet was MP for Blackburn (*C*) 1832-47.

Ferguson-Davie, see Davie.

JOHNSON-FERGUSON (UK) 1906, of Springkell, co Dumfries, Kenyon, Newchurch-in-Culcheth, co Palatine of Lancaster, and Wiston, co Lanark

Know thyself

Sir IAN EDWARD JOHNSON-FERGUSON, 4th *Baronet*: *b* 1 Feb 1932; *s* his father, Lt-Col Sir NEIL EDWARD, TD, 1992; *ed* Ampleforth, Trin Coll, Camb (BA), and Imperial Coll, London (DIC): *m* 1964, Rosemary Teresa, yr da of late Cecil John Whitehead, of The Old House, Crockham Hill, Edenbridge, and has issue.

Arms – Quarterly, 1st and 4th per fesse indented gules and or a pale counterchanged, in chief two boars' heads couped of the second and in base a thistle slipped proper; 2nd and 3rd azure, on a pile or a lion statant of the first, on a chief azure, between two sprigs of oak slipped, a pale or, thereon a like sprig of oak, all counter-changed. Crest – 1st, in front of a thistle erect thereon a bee volant proper, a boar's head couped or; 2nd, between two oak branches erect proper, a lion statant per pale azure and or, holding in the mouth a sprig of oak also proper.
Residence – Copthall Place, Upper Clatford, Andover, Hants SP11 7LR.

SONS LIVING

MARK EDWARD, *b* 14 Aug 1965; *ed* Ampleforth and Trin Coll, Camb (BA); Capt RE. —— Paul Duncan, *b* 1966; *ed* Ampleforth, and Keble Coll Oxford (MA); ACA: *m* 1990, Maria Barbara Antoinette, yst da of Prof Dr Karl-Heinz Menke, of Bonn, Germany, and has issue living, Cecilia Teresa Marie, *b* 1992. —— Simon Joseph, *b* 1967; *ed* Ampleforth, and Charing Cross Hosp, London; Capt RAMC.

BROTHERS LIVING

Christopher Charles Jervis, *b* 1933; *ed* Ampleforth, and RMC Sandhurst; Lieut The Greys: *m* 1963, Sarah Loraine, 2nd da of Sir Humphrey Dodington Benedict Sherston Sherston-Baker, 6th Bt, and has issue living, Charles Patrick, *b* 1972, — Victoria Margaret, *b* 1965, — Katharine Jane, *b* 1966: *m* 1992 Keith Thompson, — Lucy Mary, *b* 1974. —— Michael Herbert (Springkell, Eaglesfield, Dumfriess-shire), *b* 1934; *ed* Ampleforth; Capt Lowland Yeo; a JP for Dumfriess-shire: *m* 1963, Jennifer Mary, el da of Lt-Col Herbert Green, OBE, MC, of Manor House, Carlton Husthwaite, Thirsk, York, and has issue living, James Herbert, *b* 1965, — Robert Charles, *b* 1969, — Sarah Catherine, *b* 1965, — Fiona Marion, *b* 1966: *m* 1993 James Patrick Hodson (*see* Hodson, Bt), — Laura Rose, *b* 1967. —— Nicholas Swynfen (22 Rue Centrale, Hermance, Geneva, Switzerland), *b* 1938; *ed* Ampleforth: *m* 1st, 1963 (*m diss* 1975), Mabel, da of L— Dawson, of Plymouth; 2ndly, 1975 (*m diss* 1981), Maire, da of W— O'Reilly, of Dublin; 3rdly, 1984, Christina, da of Humberto Zambrano, of Ramos Arizpe, Mexico, and has issue living, (by 1st *m*) Alona Francesca, *b* 1964, — Karina Alicia, *b* 1966, — (by 2nd *m*) Ian Francis, *b*

1977, — Andrea Valerie, *b* 1975, — (by 3rd *m*) Alexander Edward, *b* 1985, — Christopher Andrew, *b* 1990, — Sophia Monica, *b* 1986.

UNCLE LIVING (*son of 2nd baronet*)

Raymond Patrick, TD, *b* 1912; *ed* Pembroke Coll, Oxford (BA 1934); is a DL for Cumbria; Lieut-Col late cmdg Westmorland and Cumberland Yeo, RA (TA); 1939-45 War (despatches): *m* 1987, Winifred Clare, elder da of Col Henry Edwards, of Oamaru, NZ. *Residence* – Westerkirk Mains, Langholm, Dumfries-shire.

COLLATERAL BRANCH LIVING

Issue of late Maj Brian Charles Johnson-Ferguson, TD, 2nd son of 2nd baronet, *b* 1908, *d* 1988: *m* 1947, Daphne Louie (Woodside, Canonbie, Dumfriesshire), elder da of Brig Walter Andrew Stirling, DSO, MC, RA, of Polstead, Suffolk:—
Torquil Charles, *b* 1949; *ed* Stanbridge Earls: *m* 1980, Margaret, yr da of L. D. Finlay, of Ashgrove House, Hepscott, Morpeth, Northumberland, and has issue living, Ninian Charles, *b* 1983, — Iona, *b* 1981, — Ailsa Finlay, *b* 1988. —— Denzil Crispin, *b* 1955; *ed* Charterhouse; *d* 1979. —— Merlin Louie, *b* 1950: *m* 1981, Peter James Dernie, son of late James Henry Dernie, of Preston, Lancs, and has issue living, Henry Crispin, *b* 1982, — Jemima Louie, *b* 1984, — Olivia Lucy, *b* 1986. —— Lorraine Giselle, *b* 1952: *m* 1975, Markus Luescher, and has issue living, Thomas, *b* 1978, — Callum, *b* 1982, — Ross, *b* 1987, — Kirsty, *b* 1980, — Nicola, *b* 1984.
The 1st baronet, Sir (Jabez) Edward (son of Jabez Johnson, JP, of Kenyon Hall, near Manchester), Chm of Jabez Johnson, Hodgkinson and Pearson (Limited), assumed by Roy licence 1881 the additional surname of Ferguson, and sat as MP for Mid, or Loughborough, Div of Leicestershire (*L*) 1885-6, and 1892-1900. The 2nd baronet, Sir Edward Alexander James Johnson-Ferguson, TD, was Lieut-Col and Brevet Col late Comdg Lanarkshire Yeo, and a Director of Tredegar Coal & Iron Co, Ltd.

FERGUSSON (NS) 1703, of Kilkerran, Ayrshire

Sweeter out of difficulties

That I may profit others

Sir CHARLES FERGUSSON, 9th *Baronet*; *b* 10 May 1931; *s* his father, Sir JAMES, FRSE, LLD, 1973; *ed* Eton: *m* 1961, Hon Amanda Mary Noel-Paton, da of Baron Ferrier (Life Baron), and has issue.

Arms – Azure, a buckle argent between three boars' heads couped or, in a dexter canton argent a saltire azure, surmounted of an inescutcheon or charged with a lion rampant within a double tressure flory counter-flory gules. **Crest** – A bee on a thistle proper. **Supporters** – Two gryphons or, armed and beaked gules.
Residence – Kilkerran, Maybole, Ayrshire KA19 7SJ.

SONS LIVING

ADAM, *b* 29 Dec 1962; Capt Army Air Corps: *m* 1989, Jenifer Kirsty, yr da of Adam Thomson, of Ormiston, E Lothian, and has issue living, Samantha Kirsty *b* 1992, — Lucy Alice, *b* 1993. —— Joseph Victor, *b* 1965: *m* 1990, Emma Sarah Louise, yr da of (William) Martin Cracknell, of Freuchie, Fife, and has issue living, Oliver William, *b* 1993.

BROTHER LIVING

Adam Dugdale, (15 Warwick Gdns, W14 8PH) *b* 1932; *ed* Eton, and Trin Coll, Camb; Member European Parliament for West Strathclyde, 1979-84, Special Advisor, FCO 1985-89: *m* 1965, (Elizabeth Catherine) Penelope, da of late (Thomas) Peter Hughes, of Furneaux Pelham Hall, Herts, and has issue living, James, *b* 1966, — Marcus Francis, *b* 1972, — Petra Christian, *b* 1968, — Lucy Josephine, *b* 1970.

SISTER LIVING

Alice Blanche Helen, *b* 1934: *m* 1960, Rt Hon (Ronald) Timothy Renton, MP, of Mount Harry House, Offham, Lewes, and has issue living, Alexander James Torre, *b* 1961, — Daniel Charles Antony, *b* 1965, — Christian Louise, *b* 1963: *m* 1993, Lloyd Michael Gudgeon, — Katherine Chelsea (twin), *b* 1965, — Penelope Sally Rosita, *b* 1970.

COLLATERAL BRANCHES LIVING

Issue of late Rev Simon Charles David Fergusson, *b* 1907, *d* 1982, Lt-Col Argyll and Sutherland Highlanders, 2nd son of 7th baronet: *m* 1945, Auriole Kathleen (Alton Albany, Barr, Girvan, Ayrshire), da of late Com Sir Geoffrey Henry Hughes-Onslow, KBE, DSC, RN (*see* E Onslow, colls):—
Alexander Charles Onslow, *b* 1949: *m* 1974, Jane Merryn, da of G/Capt Bertram Barthold, OBE, RAF, of Langarth, St Merryn, Cornwall, and has issue living, Iain Alexander Onslow, *b* 1975, — Dougal George Onslow, *b* 1977, — Christopher David Onslow, *b* 1986. —— John Geoffrey Onslow (Old Nisthouse, Harray, Orkney Isles KW17 2LQ), *b* 1954: *m* 1979, Ann Caroline, yst da of G/Capt Bertram Barthold, OBE, RAF (ante), and has issue living, Catherine Alice, *b* 1982, — Joannah Ruth, *b* 1989. —— Henrietta Charity Onslow, *b* 1952.

Issue of late Brig Bernard Edward Fergusson (*Baron Ballantrae*), KT, GCMG, GCVO, DSO, OBE, yst son of 7th baronet, *b* 1911; *cr* Baron Ballantrae (Life Baron) 1972; *d* 1980: *m* 1950, Laura Margaret, who *d* 1979, da of late Lt-Col Arthur Morton Grenfell, DSO, TD (V Cobham, colls):—
(Hon) George Duncan (does not use courtesy title), *b* 1955; *ed* Eton, and Magdalen Coll, Oxford: *m* 1981, Margaret Sheila, el da of Michael John Wookey, of Camberley, Surrey, and has issue living, Alexander Bernard Raukawa, *b* 1984, — Laura Margaret Huia, *b* 1982, — Alice Mary Marama, *b* 1986, — Elizabeth, *b* 1991. *Residences* – Ladyburn Lodge, Kilkerran, Maybole, Ayrshire; 32 Wilkinson St, SW8.

Issue of late Adm Sir James Andrew Fergusson, KCB, KCMG, 2nd son of 6th baronet, *b* 1871, *d* 1942: *m* 1901, Githa Enid, who *d* 1964, da of late Thomas C. Williams, of Wellington, New Zealand:—

Margaret Edith, *b* 1903: *m* 1961, Ralph Beckett Scholfield, who *d* 1976. *Residence* – Flat 8, 52 Onslow Gdns, SW7. —— Augusta Susan (Longwood, Bishop's Waltham, Hants), *b* 1904: *m* 1932, Capt George Francis Locke Marx, OBE, RN, who *d* 1965, and has issue living, Andrew John Locke, *b* 1933; Cdr RN: *m* 1963 (*m diss* 1982), Rosemary Evangeline, da of Christopher William Edward Collins, of The Old Rectory, Lackford, Bury St Edmunds, and has issue living, John William Francis *b* 1973, Caroline Elizabeth *b* 1964, Annabelle Mary *b* 1967, — David George Locke, *b* 1936; Managing Dir of John Rigby & Sons. —— Anne Mary, *b* 1919. *Residence* – 8 Palace Gardens Terr, W8.

Descendants of late Rt Hon Charles Dalrymple Fergusson (3rd son of 5th baronet), who assumed the surname and Arms of Dalrymple 1849, and was *cr* a *Baronet* 1887.
See Dalrymple, Bt.

Grandsons of late Robert Henry Duncan Fergusson (infra):—
Issue of late Robert Arthur George Fergusson, *b* 1878, *d* 1939: *m* 1912, Laura Gwendolen, who *d* 1962, da of late Arthur William English, of Wisbech, Cambridgeshire:—
Irwine Arthur (11 Ninda Rd, Shoalwater, W Australia 6169, Australia), *b* 1913; *ed* Fettes: *m* 1939, Pamela Vera, el da of Col P. R. Ayers, MC, of S Devon, and has issue living, Peter John Charles (Little Barn, 161 Oatlands Drive, Weybridge, Surrey), *b* 1943: *m* 1st, 1966, Angela Star, da of late Capt W. H. Behenna, of Bitterne, Southampton; 2ndly, 1981, Anne Marie Ghislaine, yr da of late Maj Tom Brown, OBE, MC, Croix de Guerre, and has issue living (by 1st *m*), Sean James *b* 1973, Fiona Star *b* 1978, — Christopher Simon Arthur (215 London Rd E, Batheaston, Bath, Avon), *b* 1949: *m* 1970, Susan Ann yst da of A. Probert, of Knowle, Bristol, and has issue living, Charlotte *b* 1972, Harriette *b* 1974, — Valerie Ann, *b* 1941, — Sheena *b* 1958. —— Donald Andrew (The Myrtles, Tarrington, Herefordshire), *b* 1920; *ed* Fettes: *m* 1958, Patricia Dorothy, da of D. K. Orton, of Entebbe, Uganda, and has issue living, Colin Ivan Paul, *b* 1960, — Martin Arthur, *b* 1963, — Heather Dorothy (twin), *b* 1963. —— Michael Ramsay (Box 959, Mutare, Zimbabwe), *b* 1922; *ed* Fettes, and Rhodes Univ, Grahamstown (BA 1948): *m* 1961, Joanna Rosalind, da of late H. Stratton, of Warminster, Wilts, and has issue living, Richard Anthony, *b* 1963.

Granddaughter of late Henry Duncan Fergusson, WS, 6th son of 4th baronet:—
Issue of late Robert Henry Duncan Fergusson *b* 1849, *d* 1904: *m* 1877, Mabel Frances, who *d* 1930, da of late Robert Balfour Wardlaw-Ramsay, of Whitehall:—
Irene Hilda: *m* 19—, Douglas Langhorne, and has issue living. *Residence* – 313 Petersham Road, Ham Common, Surrey.

Grandson of late Robert Dundas Octavius Fergusson, 8th son of 4th baronet:—
Issue of late Robert Dundas Arthur Graham Fergusson, *b* 1851, *d* 1896: *m* 1877, Mary Rachel, who *d* 1923, da of late Francis Whitworth Russell (Russell, Bt, *cr* 1812, colls):—
A son, *b* 1880.

The 1st baronet was an eminent advocate. The 2nd baronet, sometime MP for Sutherland, was afterwards a Lord of Session (Lord Kilkerran). The 3rd baronet sat as MP for Ayrshire 1774-84 and 1790-96 and for Edinburgh 1784-9. He claimed in 1796 the Earldom of Glencairn (created 1488); the Lords decided that he had proved himself to be heir-general to Alexander, Earl of Glencairn, who died 1670, but had not proved his right to the Earldom. The 6th baronet, Rt Hon Sir James, GCSI, KCMG, CIE, PC, LLD, Grenadier Guards (*k* in Jamaica earthquake 1907), served in Crimean War (wounded at battle of Inkerman), sat as MP for Ayrshire 1854-7 and 1859-68, and for N-E Div of Manchester 1885-1906, and was under-Sec of State for India 1886-7, Under-Sec at Home Office 1867-8, Gov and Com-in-Ch of S Australia 1868-73, Gov of New Zealand 1873-5, and of Bombay 1880-85, Under-Sec of State for Foreign Affairs 1886-91, and Postmaster-Gen 1891-2. Sir Charles, GCB, GCMG, DSO, MVO, LLD, 7th baronet, was Gen in Army, Gov-Gen and Com-in-Ch, New Zealand 1924-30, Chm W Indies Closer Union Commn 1933, and Lord-lieut of Ayrshire 1937-50. Sir James, 8th Bt, author and historian; Keeper of the Records of Scotland 1949-69, and Lord-Lieut of Ayrshire 1969-73.

COLYER-FERGUSSON (UK) 1866, of Spitalhaugh, Peeblesshire

By strength and skill

Sir JAMES HERBERT HAMILTON COLYER-FERGUSSON, 4th *Baronet*, son of late Max Christian Hamilton Colyer-Fergusson, Capt RASC (*k* on active ser at Ludgershall, 1940), el son of 3rd baronet; *b* 10 Jan 1917; *s* his grandfather, *Sir* THOMAS COLYER, 1951; *ed* Harrow and Balliol Coll, Oxford (BA 1939, MA 1945); formerly Capt The Buffs; 1939-45 War (prisoner); Officer BR (ret).

Arms – Argent, a lion rampant azure armed and langued gules, on a chief engrailed of the last a mullet between two cinquefoils of the first. **Crest** – A dexter hand grasping a broken spear in bend sinister all proper.
Residence – Flat 8, 61 Onslow Square, SW7 3LS. *Club* – Naval and Military.

COLLATERAL BRANCH LIVING

Issue of late Sir Louis Forbes FERGUSSON, KCVO, 2nd son of 2nd baronet, *b* 1878, *d* 1962: *m* 1922, Elizabeth Frances Ethel, who *d* 1986, da of Seth Lewis, of Gt Bookham, Surrey:—
Christine Forbes, *b* 1934: *m* 1966, Charles Raymond Evans, MA, of 6 Fabyc House, Cumberland Rd, Kew, Surrey TW9 3HH.

The 1st baronet, Sir William LLD, FRS, a distinguished surgeon, was many years Sergeant-Surgeon to HM Queen Victoria. Sir James Ranken Fergusson, 2nd Bt, was Vice-Lieut for Peebleshire, and a Member of Roy Co of Archers (King's Body Guard for Scotland). Sir Thomas Colyer, 3rd Bt, was High Sheriff of Kent 1906, and assumed the additional surname of Colyer 1890.

FFOLKES, (GB) 1774, of Hillington, Norfolk
(Name pronounced "Foaks")

Sir ROBERT FRANCIS ALEXANDER, FFOLKES, OBE, 7th *Baronet; b* 2 Dec 1943; *s* his father, *Sir* (EDWARD JOHN) PATRICK BOSCHETTI, 1960; *ed* Stowe, and Christchurch, Oxford; with Save The Children Fund 1974-; OBE (Civil) 1990.

Arms – Per pale vert and gules, a fleur-de-lis argent. **Crest** – A dexter arm embowed vested per pale vert and gules, cuff ermine, holding in the hand a spear proper.
Residence – 18 Chiddingstone St, SW6 3TG.

SISTER LIVING

Sara Elizabeth, *b* 1946: *m* 1968, Maj Jocelyn James Rhys Wingfield, LI, of 18 Chiddingstone St, SW6 3TG (*see* V Powerscourt, colls).

COLLATERAL BRANCH LIVING

Granddaughter of late Rev Henry Edward Browne ffolkes, 3rd son of 2nd baronet:—
Issue of late Robert Walling Everard ffolkes, *b* 1865, *d* 1931; *m* 1884, Ada, who *d* 1906, da of Col William Brierly:—
Evelyn Maud, *b* 1889.

What will happen, will happen

This family, in the person of Simon ffolkys, owned lands in Westley Waterless, Cambridgeshire, in 1486. Martin ffolkes, Pres of Roy and of Antiquarian Socs, inherited the Hovell estates in Norfolk through his mother, wife of Martin ffolkes, Attorney-Gen to Queen-Dowager of Charles II. The 5th baronet, the Rev Sir Francis Arthur Stanley, MVO, was an Hon Chap to Queen Victoria, a Chap-in-Ord to King Edward VII, and King George V, and a Chap to King Edward VIII and King George VI.

TWISLETON-WYKEHAM-FIENNES (UK) 1916, of Banbury, co Oxford

Sir RANULPH TWISLETON-WYKEHAM-FIENNES, OBE, 3rd *Baronet; b* (*posthumous*) 7 March 1944; *s* his father, *Lieut-Col Sir* RANULPH, DSO, 1944; *ed* Eton; late Capt R Scots Greys; attached 22nd SAS Regt 1966, seconded SAF 1968; White Nile Hovercraft Expedition 1969; British Jostedals Glacier Expedition 1970; Scots Greys Headless Valley Expedition 1971; Vice-Pres World Expeditionary Assocn since 1974; North Greenland Jebel Shams Trials 1976; British North Pole Expedition 1977; first man, with Charles Burton, to reach both N and S Poles overland, 1982; led archaeological expedition which rediscovered the lost city of Ubar in Oman, 1992; led the Pentland South Pole Expedition 1992-93, achieving the first crossing of Antarctica unsupported, the longest unsupported polar journey in history; a Liveryman of Vintners' Co; author of *Talent for Trouble* 1970, *Icefall in Norway* and *The Headless Valley* 1972, *Where Soldiers Fear to Tread* 1975, *Hell on Ice* 1978, *Bothie the Polar Dog* (with his wife) 1985, *Living Dangerously* 1988, *The Feather Men* 1990, *Atlantis of the Sands* 1991, and *Mind over Matter* 1993; won one of Man of The Year Awards 1982 and led the Transglobe Circumpolar Expedition of 1979-82; OBE 1993, Dhofar Campaign Medal 1968, Sultan's Bravery Medal 1970, Livingstones Gold Medal 1983, Gold Medal of the Explorers Club of New York 1983, Founders Medal R Geographical Soc 1984, Polar Medal 1987 (with bars for Arctic and Antarctica); Chm Offshore Abandonment Gp 1989: *m* 1970, Virginia Frances, Polar Medal 1987, da of late Thomas Pepper.

Look for a brave spirit

Arms – Quarterly, 1st and 4th azure, three lions rampant or, *Fiennes*; 2nd and 3rd argent, a chevron between three moles sable, *Twisleton*. **Crest** – 1st, a wolf sejant proper, gorged with a spiked collar, the line therefrom reflexed over the back or, *Fiennes*; 2nd, an arm embowed, vested sable, cuffed argent, holding in the hand proper a mole spade or, headed and armed of the second.
Residence – 10 Belgrave Rd, Barnes, SW13.

SISTERS LIVING

Susan Valerie, *b* 1933; *ed* Heathfield, Ascot and Cape Town Univ (BA 1951): *m* 1957, John Jervoise Fitzgerald Scott, Lt Col the Blues and Roys, and has issue living, Arabella Caroline, *b* 1959: *m* 1986, Francis D. Williams, — Venetia Lucy, *b* 1963. —— Celia Florence, *b* 1936; *ed* Trin Coll, Dublin (MB and BCh): *m* 1964, Dr Robert Savage Brown, of 1680 Rosehill Circle, St Paul, Minnesota, USA, and has issue living, Anthony Newson *b* 1966; MD: *m* 1993, Sarah Halcyon, da of William Frantzich, — Deirdre Ann, *b* 1965: *m* 1987, James Evans Brabenec, and has issue living, James Jordan *b* 1993, — Nicola Lois, *b* 1969: *m* 1991, Keith Eric Schlechte, and has issue living, Alexandra Rose, *b* 1993. —— Gillian Audrey *b* 1938: *m* 1960, Timothy George Hoult, of Lower Octon Grange, Foxholes, Driffield, N Humberside, and has issue living, Andrew George, *b* 1966, — Rosalind Elfrida, *b* 1961, — Rachel Celia, *b* 1963.

WIDOW LIVING OF SECOND BARONET

AUDREY JOAN (*Audrey, Lady Twisleton-Wykeham-Fiennes*), da of late Sir Percy Newson, 1st Bt, *ed* Heathfield, Ascot: *m* 1931, Lt-Col Sir Ranulph Twisleton-Wykeham-Fiennes, DSO, 2nd baronet, Roy Scots Greys, *d* of wounds received in action in Italy 1943. *Residence* – Robins, Church Lane, Lodsworth, Sussex.

The 1st baronet, Hon Sir Eustace Edward Twisleton-Wykeham-Fiennes, 2nd son of 17th Baron Saye and Sele, was MP for Oxfordshire N, and Banbury Div (*L*) 1906-10 and 1910-18, and Gov and Com-in-Ch of Seychelles 1918-21, and of Leeward Islands 1921-9. The 2nd baronet Sir Ranulph, DSO, Lieut-Col Roy Scots Greys, *d* of wounds received in action in Italy 1943.

FINDLAY (UK) 1925, of Aberlour, co Banff (Extinct 1979)

Lt-Col *Sir* ROLAND LEWIS FINDLAY, 3rd and last *Baronet*.

DAUGHTER LIVING OF THIRD BARONET (*By 1st marriage*)

Barbara Jane (*Jane, Countess of Westmorland*) (The Old Vicarage, Badminton, Avon), *b* 1928: *m* 1950, 15th Earl of Westmorland, GCVO, who *d* 1993.

DAUGHTERS LIVING OF SECOND BARONET

Moira Juliet, *b* 1927: *m* 1951 (*m diss* 1984), Meyrick Adam Ovens, and has issue living, Michael John (113 Narbonne Av, SW4 9LQ), *b* 1951; *ed* Sedbergh: *m* 1984 Sara Jane, elder da of John Robertson, and has issue living, John Henry Michael *b* 1989, — Charlotte Jean, *b* 1955. *Residence* – 15 Gayville Rd, SW11. —— Gillian, *b* 1930: *m* 1953, Maj-Gen John Myles (Robin) Brockbank, CBE, MC, DL, 9th/12th Royal Lancers, and has issue living, Henry John Findlay (30 Grafton Sq, SW4), *b* 1954; *ed* Eton, and Bristol Univ: *m* 1984, Serena, da of Capt John Macdonald-Buchanan, MC, of Cottesbrooke Hall, Northants (*see* By Woolavington, 1985 Edn), and has issue living, John *b* 1992, — Myles Robin (4 Burnley Rd, SW9 0SH), *b* 1958; *ed* Eton, and Ch Ch, Oxford: *m* 1989, Susanna J—, yr da of Sir John Drummond Milne, of Chilton House, Chilton Candover, Alresford, Hants, and has issue living, Harry John Myles *b* 1993, Sophie Elizabeth *b* 1991, — Anthony Lionel, *b* 1960; *ed* Eton, and Ch Ch, Oxford, — Harriet Jane, *b* 1954: *m* 1977, Michael Robert McCalmont, of Winton House, Hampstead Norreys, Newbury, Berks RG16 0TF, yst son of late Maj Dermot Hugh Bingham McCalmont, MC, of Mount Juliet, Thomastown, co Kilkenny, and has issue living, Arthur James *b* 1984, Katherine Rose *b* 1981. *Residence* – Manor House, Steeple Langford, Salisbury.

WIDOWS LIVING OF SECOND AND THIRD BARONETS

LAURA HAWLEY ELSOM (*Laura, Lady Findlay*), da of late Percival Hawley, of Hull: *m* 1947, as his 2nd wife Sir (John) Edmund Ritchie Findlay, 2nd baronet, who *d* 1962. —— MARJORY MARY (*Lady Findlay*) (Lyddington, Uppingham, Leics), only da of late Hon Claud William Biddulph (*see* B Biddulph, colls), and formerly wife of Maj Philip Wilfred Cripps (who *d* 1965) : *m* 1964, as his 2nd wife, Lt-Col Sir Roland Lewis Findlay, 3rd baronet, who *d* 1979, when the title became *ext*.

COLLATERAL BRANCH LIVING

Issue of late Peter Findlay, 3rd son of 1st baronet, *b* 1910, *d* 1967: *m* 1933, Helen, who *d* 1965, da of W. S. Brewer, of New York:—

Caroline Grace, *b* 1935: *m* 1st, 1956 (*m diss* 1962), Spencer William George Hooker; 2ndly, 1966, Wing-Cdr Lester Francis Humphries, AFC, AFM, RAF (ret), of Twyford, Hants, and has issue living, (by 1st *m*) Philip Anthony, *b* 1957, — Peter Neal Alan, *b* 1959, — (by 2nd *m*) Fiona Caroline, *b* 1968.

The 1st baronet, Sir John Ritchie Findlay, KBE, was proprietor of *The Scotsman*, Chm of Board of Trustees of National Galleries of Scotland, and of National Housing Co, and Lord-Lieut of co Banff. Sir (John) Edmund Ritchie Findlayd, 2nd Bt, was MP for Banffshire (*C*) 1935-45.

FINLAY (UK) 1964, of Epping, co Essex.

Sir DAVID RONALD JAMES BELL FINLAY, 2nd *Baronet*; *b* 16 Nov 1963; *s* his father, *Sir* GRAEME BELL, 1st Bt, ERD, 1987; *ed* Marlborough, Grenoble Univ and Bristol Univ.

Arms – Argent on a chevron azure between in chief two roses gules barbed and seeded proper, and in base an estoile of eight points gules within two wings conjoined and erect azure an ancient coronet or. **Crest** – In front of an oak tree fructed a whippet sejant proper gorged with an ancient coronet pendent therefrom by the chains a portcullis azure.
Residences – The Garden Flat, 106 Chesterton Rd, W10 6EP.

SISTERS LIVING

Fiona Daphne Margaret Bell, *b* 1956. *Residence* – 59 Bassett Rd, W10 6JR. —— Catrina Mary Bell, *b* 1959: *m* 1984, Robin Nigel Cleave Knight Bruce, elder son of Nigel Knight Bruce, of Crediton, Devon, and has issue living, Robert Evelyn Cleave, *b* 1993, — Siena-Rose, *b* 1990, — Vita June, *b* 1992. *Residence* – The Sanctuary, Shobrooke, Crediton, Devon EX17 1BG.

MOTHER LIVING

JUNE EVANGELINE (*Lady Finlay*), yr da of late Col Francis Collingwood Drake, OBE, MC, DL, 10th R Hussars, of Mill Hurst, Harlow, Essex: *m* 1953, Sir Graeme Bell Finlay, 1st Bt, ERD, who *d* 1987. *Residence* – 45 Artesian Rd, W2 5DB.

FISON (UK) 1905, of Greenholme, Burley-in-Wharfedale, West Riding of Yorkshire

Trust in God

Sir (RICHARD) GUY FISON, DSC, 4th *Baronet*, *b* 9 Jan 1917; *s* his father, *Capt Sir* (WILLIAM) GUY, MC 1964; *ed* Eton, and New Coll, Oxford; 1939-45 War with RNVR (DSC): *m* 1952, Elyn, who *d* 1987, da of Mogens Hartmann, of Bordeaux, and formerly wife of Count Renaud Doria, and has issue.

Arms – Per fesse azure and ermine, in chief three battle-axes argent, the staves or, and in base an heraldic tiger passant of the last. Crest – A demi-heraldic tiger or, collared gules, holding between the paws a shield argent, charged with a battle-axe sable.
Residence – Medwins, Odiham, Hants RG25 1NE.

SON LIVING

CHARLES WILLIAM, *b* 6 Feb 1954.

DAUGHTER LIVING

Isabelle Frances, *b* 1957.

BROTHER LIVING

John Michael, *b* 1920; *ed* Eton; 1939-45 War with RA. *Residence* – 9 de Walden St, W1.
The 1st baronet, Sir Frederick William, sat as MP for Doncaster Div, W Riding, Yorkshire (C) July 1895 to Jan 1906.

FITZGERALD (UK) 1880, of Valencia, co Kerry

My presence is victory

Sir GEORGE PETER MAURICE FITZGERALD, MC (*The 23rd Knight of Kerry*), 5th *Baronet*; *b* 27 Feb, 1917; *s* his father, *Capt Sir* ARTHUR HENRY BRINSLEY, 1967; *ed* Harrow and RMC; Maj (ret) IG; Palestine 1938 (despatches), 1939-45 War in Italy (MC) 2nd in Command 1st Bn IG 1944; 2nd in Command 2nd Bn IG 1946: *m* 1939, Angela Dora, da of late Capt James Rankin Mitchell, of 2 Mansfield St, W1, and has issue.

Arms – Ermine, a saltire gules; in centre point a cross pattée argent. Crest – A chevalier in complete armour on horseback at full speed, with his sword drawn and visor raised, proper; saddle gules, saddle-cloth or.
Residence – Colin's Farm House, 55 High St, Durrington, Salisbury, Wilts SP4 8AQ.

SON LIVING

ADRIAN JAMES ANDREW DENIS (16 Clareville St, SW7, and Lackaneask, Valentia Island, co Kerry; *Club* – Pratt's), *b* 24 June 1940; *ed* Harrow; a Councillor Roy Borough of Kensington and Chelsea 1974, and Mayor 1984-85.

DAUGHTER LIVING

Rosanna, *b* 1945: *m* 1964, Count Richard Beaumont Melchior Gurowski (8th Count, Prussia, *cr* 1787) of North End House, Damerham, Fordingbridge, Hants, and has issue living, Iona, *b* 1967, — Anya, *b* 1970.

COLLATERAL BRANCHES LIVING

Grandsons of Robert John FitzGerald, 2nd son of 1st baronet:—
Issue of Lt-Col Peter Francis FitzGerald, DSO, *b* 1879, *d* 1968: *m* 1909, Baroness Adrienne de Geer, who *d* 1973, da of late Baron Gustave de Geer, of Zeist, Holland:—
(Peter) Desmond (Querns House, Cirencester, Gloucestershire; *Club* – Army and Navy), *b* 1910; Capt late R Tank Regt; Kt of Malta: *m* 1945, Elizabeth J. C. Norman, and has issue living, Anthony Desmond (*Clubs* - Kildare St and University, and Lansdowne), *b* 1953; *ed* Ampleforth; a Sloane Fell of London Business Sch: *m* 1986, Janine Heather, eldest da of A. R. Miller, of Badgers Hollow, Godalming, Surrey, and has issue living, Peter Desmond Orlando *b* 1989, — Caroline Rosemary, *b* 1946: *m* 1970, Maj Philip Statham, RA, of Ridgeland, 177 Bassett Av, Southampton, and has issue living, Charles Reginald *b* 1971, Christopher Desmond *b* 1977, — Olivia Margaret GRAHAM (37 Cromwell Rd, SW7), *b* 1948, and has issue living, Alexandra Clare *b* 1974, — Louise Elizabeth, *b* 1951: *m* 1982, Richard John Burden, of 54 Emlyn Rd, W12 9TD, and has issue living, Jonathon Max Robert *b* 1986, Georgina Ann *b* 1983. —— Mervyn Robert Gustav (Pen Mill Cottage, Penselwood, Wincanton, Som), *b* 1911: *m* 1940, Hilary da of Percy Houghton Brown, LLD, and has issue living, Alastair Mervyn Malcolm (Rodmead, Maiden Bradley, Warminster, Wilts), *b* 1941: *m* 1964, Penelope Jane, el da of Lt-Col John Stewart Eyre, and has issue living, Colin John *b* 1970, Fiona Margaret *b* 1965, Katherine Lucy *b* 1967: *m* 19—, Richard Longbourne, — Peter Robin (Pen Mill Farm, Penselwood, Wincanton, Som, and 48 Queen's Gate Terrace, SW8; Travellers' Club), *b* 1943; *ed* Canford, and Trin Coll, Oxford: *m* 1976, Sarah, da of John Christopher Dykes, of 31 Pembroke Gdns, W8, and has issue living, Alanna Clare Juliet *b* 1978, Miranda Jessica *b* 1980, Harriet Sarah Isabel *b* 1986, — Elizabeth Ann, *b* 1945: *m* 1969, Francis Mark Dineley, of Aubrey House, Aubrey Walk, W8, and Woodlands, Berwick St John, Shaftesbury, Dorset, and has issue living, Alexander Perin *b* 1973, Maria Frances *b* 1971.

Grandson of late Peter David FitzGerald, 3rd son of 1st baronet:—

Issue of late Capt James Brinsley Peter FitzGerald, *b* 1894, *d* 1962: *m* 1924, Lady Moyra Marjorie Dawson-Damer, who *d* 1962, da of 5th Earl of Portarlington:—

Michael George Maurice (Gawcombe, Church Westcote, Oxford; South of Perth Yacht Club, and Farmers' Club), *b* 1925: *m* 1959, F. Ruth, da of Maj P. A. F. Spence, of Deddington Manor, Oxon, and has issue living, Peter Desmond Philip (Lansdowne Club) *b* 1961, — Sarah Moyra, *b* 1962, — Ann Rachel (twin), *b* 1962: *m* 1989 Maj Timothy David Edward Morris (7th Gurkha Rifles) and has issue living, Christopher *b* 1991, Guy *b* 1993.

The title of Knight of Kerry was conferred upon his son Maurice by John Fitz Thomas FitzGerald, Lord of Decies and Desmond, by virtue of his royal seigniory as a Count Palatine, and his descendants have ever since been so styled in Acts of Parliament, patents under the Great Seal, and other legal documents. The 1st baronet was the 19th Knight of Kerry. The 2nd baronet, Capt Sir Maurice FitzGerald, CVO, served in Ashanti 1873-4 (several times mentioned in despatches, medal with clasp), and was an Extra Equerry to HRH the Duke of Connaught.

FITZGERALD (UK) 1903, of Geraldine Place, St Finn Barr, co Cork

A sea of trees

Rev (*Sir*) DANIEL PATRICK FITZGERALD, 4th *Baronet*; *b* 28 June 1916; *s* his brother, Rev (*Sir*) EDWARD THOMAS, 1988, but does not use the title; a Roman Catholic Priest.

Arms – Ermine, on a saltire gules charged with two arrows saltirewise points downwards or, a chief arched of the second thereon a lymphan between two towers or. **Crest** – In front of three oak trees a knight mounted in full armour proper bearing on the sinister arm a shield argent charged with a civic crown gules.
Residence –

COLLATERAL BRANCH LIVING

Issue of late Andrew FitzGerald, 4th son of 1st baronet, *b* 1885, *d* 1969: *m* 1916, Elizabeth Barry-Murphy, who *d* 1952:—

JOHN FINNBARR (Meadowlands, Wilton Rd, Cork), *b* 1918: *m* 1949, Margaret Hogg, and has issue living, Andrew Peter, *b* 1950, — Geraldine, *b* 1953. —— Andrew Joseph (60 Glenbrook Park, Rathfarnham, Dublin, 14), *b* 1922: *m* 1953, Patrica Clark, and has issue living, Paul Andrew, *b* 1966, — Anne, *b* 1955, — Helen, *b* 1959. —— Margaret Mary, *b* 1920. —— Katherine, *b* 1925.

The 1st baronet, Sir Edward (son of Daniel FitzGerald, of Gurstmaurane, Iveleary, co Cork) was Lord Mayor of Cork, 1901, 1902 and 1903.

FITZHERBERT (GB) 1784, of Tissington, Derbyshire

One (only) will I serve

Sir RICHARD RANULPH FITZHERBERT, 9th *Baronet*; *b* 2 Nov 1963; *s* his uncle, Sir JOHN RICHARD FREDERICK, 1989; *ed* Eton: *m* 1993, Caroline Louise, da of Maj Patrick Shuter, of Grangefield House, Tetbury, Glos.

Arms – Gules, three lions rampant or. **Crest** – A cubit arm in armour erect, the hand appearing clenched within the gauntlet all proper.
Seat – Tissington Hall, Ashbourne, Derbyshire DE6 1RA.

SISTERS LIVING

Selina Helen, *b* 1965. —— (Juliet) Sarah, *b* (twin) 1965: *m* 1992, Anthony J. Clay, of Broome Hall, Chatwall, nr Church Stretton, Shropshire, eldest son of Glynne Clay, of Nantyderry, Gwent. —— Lucy Hyacinthe, *b* 1967.

AUNT LIVING (*Sister of 8th Baronet*)

Ann (10 Village Court, Duffield, Derbys), *b* 1916.

MOTHER LIVING

Charmian Hyacinthe, yr da of late Samuel Ranulph Allsopp (*see* B Hindlip, colls): *m* 1962, Rev David Henry FitzHerbert, MC, yr brother of 8th baronet, who *d* 1976. *Residence* – Sycamore House, Tissington, Ashbourne, Derbys.

COLLATERAL BRANCHES LIVING

Grandchildren of late Arthur Richard FitzHerbert, son of late Lt-Col Richard Henry FitzHerbert, 2nd son of 3rd baronet:—

Issue of late Arthur Geoffry Marshall FitzHerbert, *b* 1882, *d* 1974: *m* 1908, Hilda Eunice, who *d* 1966, da of late W. Gray, of Marton, NZ:—

ARTHUR WILLIAM (Tutaenui Rd, Marton, NZ), *b* 2 Sept 1922; 1939-45 War with RNZAF, and as Pilot Officer RAF: *m* 1952, Noeline Coral, da of Richard Kerkham, of Suva, Fiji, and has issue living, Arthur Gray, *b* 1954, — Madeline Grace, *b* 1953: *m* 1971 (*m diss* 1987), Barry Edward Fairburn, of Wanganui, NZ, and has issue living, Aaron Karl *b* 1972, Daniel Craig *b* 1974, Lisa Marie *b* 1975. —— Eileen Mildred, *b* 1919: *m* 1956, John Charles Shere, of Kahuterawa Rd, Palmerston North, NZ, and has an adopted son, Ian Geoffrey, *b* 1961: *m* 1984, Christine Gae Murcott, and has issue living, Caleb Charles David *b* 1992, Katie Elisabeth *b* 1985, Kelly Rose *b* 1989.

Issue of late Beresford Close FitzHerbert, b 1884, d 1969: m 1918, Gladys Ruby, who d 1985, da of John Owens, of Epsom, Auckland, NZ:—
Adeline Beryl (1/6 Speight Rd, Kohimarama, Auckland, NZ), b 1919: m 1946 (m diss 1961), Maxwell Robert Moore, F/O RNZAF, who d 1967, and has issue living, Beverley Robin, b 1955: m 1978, Barry James Anthony West of 2 Seascape Rd, Renuera, Auckland, NZ, and has issue living, Cameron James b 1988, Hannah Claire b 1984, Georgia Beryl b 1991, — Jennifer Beryl, b 1947: m 1973, John Charles Mortland, of Maungahau, Te Awanutu, NZ, and has issue living, Nicholas John b 1975, Hamish Alexander Maxwell b 1980, Katie Beryl b 1978, — Alison Anne, b 1951: m 1973, Philip Royce Allen, of 21 Lammermoor Dr, St Heliers Bay, Auckland, NZ, and has issue living, Scott Philip b 1978, Ainsley Alison b 1981. —— Dorothy Grace, b 1920: m 1945, Robert William Smith, F/O RNZAF, and has issue living, Robert Phillip Beresford, b 1951, — Dorothy Christine, b 1946, — Pauline Beresford, b 1947, — Barbara Anne, b 1954. —— Ngaire Beresford (2/88 Riddell Rd, Glendowie 5, Auckland, NZ), b 1923: m 1950 (m diss 1972), John McRobert Calder, F/O RNZAF, and has issue living, John Beresford (232 Cook Dr, Whitianga, NZ), b 1953: m 1975, Christine Doreen Orange, and has issue living, Jude Anthony b 1976, Casey Beresford b 1988, Philippa Chrystal b 1981, — Peter McRobert (68A Vale Rd, St Heliers, Auckland, NZ), b 1955: m 1st 1980 (m diss 1991), Rosalind Mary Webb; 2ndly, Sandra Joy Welsh.

Granddaughters of late Lt-Col Richard Henry FitzHerbert (ante):—
Issue of late Anthony Francis FitzHerbert, b 1863, d 1925: m 1893, Catherine Anne; who d 1954, da of late Charles Bull, of Aorangi, Fielding, New Zealand:—
Cicely Beresford, b 1900: m 1931, Henry William Petre (see B Petre, colls), who d 1983. Address – RD1 Motueka, S Island, New Zealand. —— Nellie, b 1905: m 1927, Strachan Agnew Goldingham, late Squadron Leader Roy New Zealand Air Force, who d 1980, and has had issue, Heather Linda, b 1929: m 1st, 1953 (m diss 1963), Lt-Cdr Michael Clinton Danby, RN; 2ndly, 1964, (Lionel) Peter Winterton Twiss, OBE, DSC, of Nettleworth, Titchfield, Hants, and d 1988, leaving issue, (by 1st m) Edward Strachan Clinton b 1960, Brigette Anne Rosemary b 1956: m 1984, Robin Buchanan, and has issue living, Angus Edward b 1985, Violet Victoria b 1987, a da b 1993.

Grandchildren of late Herbert Haffenden FitzHerbert, el son of late Rev Alleyne FitzHerbert, 3rd son of 3rd baronet:—
Issue of late Egbert FitzHerbert, b 1863, d 1944: m 1st, 1891, Florence Grace, who d 1905, da of late Edward Gregory, of Feilding, New Zealand; 2ndly, 1912, Margaret, da of late Benjamin John Holloway, of Thame, Oxon, and widow of Charles Joseph Little, of Eldon Road, Kensington, W:—
(By 1st m) John Alleyne, MC, b 1896; European War 1914-19 in France with 1st Australian Tunnelling Co (despatches, MC). —— Herbert Haffenden, b 1905: m 1934, Stella Marguerite, da of late W. F. Seymour, of Auckland, NZ. Residence – 101 Messines Road, Karori, Wellington, New Zealand.

Grandchildren of late Horace FitzHerbert, 3rd son of late Herbert Haffenden FitzHerbert (ante):—
Issue of late Herbert FitzHerbert, b 1887, d 1958: m (Jan) 1915, Winifred, who d 1932, da of William Walpole:—
†William Michael, b (Nov) 1915: m 1947, Elsie Lillian, da of Charles Ogle, and d 1994, leaving issue, William Anthony (RD3 Hunterville, NZ), b 1950: m 1980, Gaylene Patricia, da of Phillip John Dawson, of Marton, and has issue living, Timothy William b 1982, Peter b 1985, — Annette Margaret, b 1948: m 1968, Raymond Ernest Moss of RD7, Feilding, NZ, and has issue living, Helen Jane b 1970, Jo Ann, b 1972, Nicola Ann b 1978, — Jennifer Ann, b 1953: m 1st, 19— (m diss 19—), Gordon Bason; 2ndly, 19—, Nigel Basin, and has issue living, (by 1st m) Andrew Gordon b 1975, Anna Elise b 1970, (by 2nd m) Patrick b 1991, Elizabeth Francis b 1985, Emma (triplet) b 1991, Katie (triplet) b 1991. Residence – The Kestrels, Hunterville, New Zealand. —— Mary Winifred, b 1917: m 1941, Raymond Windelborn. —— Eleanor Margaret, b 1919. Residence – 66 Brunswick St, Lower Hutt, New Zealand.
Issue of late Norman FitzHerbert, b 1889, d 1961: m 1919, Evelyn (4 Anderson St, Putaruru, NZ), da of late Robert M. Pemberton, CE, of Waikare, NZ:—
John Anthony (31 Russell Terr, Putaruru, NZ), JP, ACA, b 1920: m 1st, 1942, Martha Betty, who d 1967, da of William George Hope; 2ndly, 1968, Gaynor Hudson, widow of Gordon Martin, of Hastings, NZ, and has issue living (by 1st m), David Anthony (PO Box 789, Manila, Philipinnes) b 1945; ACA: m 1969, Leith Alix Margaret, da of Clive A. Morton, of Auckland, NZ, and has issue living, Nicholas Anthony b 1975, Jochen Richard b 1978, Matthew David b 1981, — Timothy John (Martins Bay, RD 2, Warkworth, NZ), b 1951: m 1974, Prudence Mary, da of T. W. Bush, of Auckland, NZ, and has issue living, Stephen John b 1983, Anna Elizabeth b 1979, Jane Prudence b 1981, — Catherine Mary, b 1947: m 1969, Gary Victor Sigley, of 12 Bannockburn Pl, Auckland 5, NZ, and has issue living, Michael Ainsley b 1974, Christina Evelyn b 1971, Haidee Margaret b 1979, — Margaret Alison, b 1952: m 1973, Robert Stephen Wickman, of 35 Western St, Matamata, NZ, and has issue living, John Stephen b 1983, Chloe Jennifer b 1986. —— Richard Gurden (4 Anderson St, Putaruru, NZ), b 1922.
Issue of late Augustus FitzHerbert, b 1872, d 1908: m 1902, Ellen, da of late John Curd:—
James Bruce, b 1908: m 1940, Eileen Olson, of New Plymouth, New Zealand. Residence – Donnett Street, Opunake, New Zealand. —— Janet Ruth, b 1904: m 1939, Robert Steele Martin, MBE, JP, Engineer, and has issue living, Luke Steele (PO Box 878, Rotorua, New Zealand), b 1942; is a JP. Residence – Opunake, New Zealand. —— Maude Mount Cashel, b 1906. Residence –

Grandchildren of late Rev James FitzHerbert, 2nd son of late Rev Alleyne FitzHerbert (ante):—
Issue of late Humphrey Beresford FitzHerbert, b 1879, d 1951: m 1st, 1907, Kathleen, who d 1941, da of Charles Alexander, of Liverpool; 2ndly, 1941, Winifred Ivy Bing, who d 1962:—
(By 2nd m) Humphrey Bing Vivian (36 Westover Rd, Broadstairs, Kent), b 1942: m 1971, Pamela Joan, da of James Sidney Pitt, of 7 Streete Court Rd, Westgate on Sea, Kent. —— Susan Eirene Angelina, b 1945: m 1964, Robert Viggo Jensen (6 Balliol Rd, Broadstairs, Kent), and has issue living, Jetta Elva, b 1965.
Issue of late Capt Douglas Cecil FitzHerbert, b 1882, d 1933: m 1924, Daphne, who d 1979, da of late Henry Joseph Wigram (see Wigram, Bt, colls, 1980 Edn):—
(Alleyne) John, b 1931; ed Denstone; Capt Sherwood Rangers Yeo (TA) (ret): m 1959, Judith Mary, da of late Ernest T. Walker, and has issue living, (Amanda) Sara, b 1964; ed Oakham, and Swansea Univ (BSc). Residence – The Old Forge, Barkestone-le-Vale, Nottingham.

Grandsons of late Godfrey White FitzHerbert (infra):—
Issue of late Henry FitzHerbert, b 1908, d 1960: m 1940, Betty (who m 2ndly, 19—, Robert Fulton), da of Arthur W. Barnley, of Kiriga Estate, Thika, Kenya:—
Henry Nicholas (4 Swallow St, Flamingo Vlei, Cape Town 7405, S Africa) b 1952: m 1st, 1975 (m diss 1982), Karin Schweiger; 2ndly, 198—, — and has issue living, (by 1st m) Stuart, b 198—, — Liesel Tanya FitzHerbert, b 1979. —— Simon John, b 1953.

Granddaughter of late John Knight FitzHerbert, 5th son of 3rd baronet:—
Issue of late Godfrey White FitzHerbert, b 1864, d 1939: m 1900, Anna Rachel, who d 1961, da of late Henry Alleyne Pile (Alleyne, Bt, colls):—
Judith Agnes (c/o Emmanuel Grammar School, Derwen Fawr Rd, Swansea), b 1914.
The 1st baronet was 9th in male descent from Nicholas, 2nd son of John FitzHerbert, of Somersal Herbert, whose ancestors possessed it from the beginning of the 13th century. Nicholas, died 1472, having acquired Tissington by his marriage with

Margaret, da of Robert Fraunceys, of Foremark, and grand-da and co-heir of Sir Thomas Clinton (2nd son of 3rd Baron Clinton).

FLAVELLE (UK) 1917, of Toronto, Dominion of Canada (Extinct 1985)

Prepared for peace and war

Sir (JOSEPH) DAVID ELLSWORTH FLAVELLE, 3rd and last *Baronet.*

DAUGHTERS LIVING OF THIRD BARONET

Muriel Catherine, *b* 1944: *m* 1967, Rodger Henderson, of 242 Melrose Av, Toronto, Ontario M5M 1Z1, Canada, son of Peter Henderson, of Hamilton, Canada, and has issue living, Laura Katherine, *b* 1968, — Heather Anne, *b* 1971. —— Virginia Anne, *b* 1947: *m* 1970, Charles Arthur Millar, of 206 Arichat Rd, Oakville, Ontario, Canada, son of Charles Arthur Millar, of Mississauga, Ontario, and has issue living, Scott Arthur, *b* 1972, — Colin David, *b* 1976. —— Josephine Elizabeth, *b* 1950: *m* 1974, David Kenneth Martin, of 16 Meadowglade Crescent, Willowdale, Ontario, Canada, son of Dr Gordon Martin, of N York, Ontario, and has issue living, Christopher Flavelle, *b* 1979, — Andrew Flavelle, *b* 1983.

DAUGHTER LIVING OF SECOND BARONET

Clara Elizabeth, *b* 1918: *m* 1941, Gage Hayward Love, of West Winds, RR2, King, Ontario, Canada L0G 1K0, son of Harry Hayward Love, and has issue living, Gage Ellsworth, *b* 1942, — David Hayward, *b* 1946, — Peter Flavelle, *b* 1948, — William Geoffrey, *b* 1951.

WIDOW LIVING OF THIRD BARONET

MURIEL BARBARA (*Lady Flavelle*), da of David Reginald Morton: *m* 1942, Sir (Joseph) David Ellsworth Flavelle, 3rd Bt, who *d* 1985. *Residence* – 21490 Bay Village Dr, Fort Myers Beach, Florida 33931, USA.

AUBREY-FLETCHER (GB) 1782, of Clea Hall, Cumberland

Martis, non cupidinis

Of war, not of love

Sir HENRY EGERTON AUBREY-FLETCHER, 8th *Baronet*; *b* 27 Nov 1945; *s* his father, *Sir* JOHN HENRY LANCELOT, 1992; *ed* Eton: *m* 1976, (Sara) Roberta, da of late Maj Robert Buchanan, of Blackpark Cottage, Evanton, Ross-shire, and has issue.

𝔄rms – Quarterly: 1st and 4th, argent, a cross engrailed sable between four pellets each charged with a pheon argent, *Fletcher*; 2nd and 3rd azure, a chevron between three eagles' heads erased or, *Aubrey*. 𝔠rest – 1st, a horse's head argent, *Fletcher*; 2nd, an eagle's head erased or, *Aubrey*.
Address – Estate Office, Chilton, Aylesbury, Bucks HP18 9LR.

SONS LIVING

JOHN ROBERT, *b* 20 June 1977. —— Thomas Egerton, *b* 1980. —— Harry Buchanan, *b* 1982.

UNCLES LIVING (*sons of 6th baronet*)

Lancelot Philip, *b* 1919; *ed* Eton; Capt (ret) Grenadier Gds; 1939-45 War (wounded, prisoner): *m* 1952, Audrey Muriel, who *d* 1993, only da of (Frederick) Ronald Oliver (*see* B Hindlip, colls, 1990 Edn), and has issue living, Mark Lancelot, *b* 1964; *ed* Harrow, — Jane Elizabeth, *b* 1961: *m* 1988, Jonathan Mark Davies, of Jarves Farm, Whitewood Lane, S Godstone, Surrey RH9 8JR, only son of Frank Antony Davies, of Valewood Farm House, Haslemere, Surrey, and has issue living, James Robert *b* 1988, Katrina Elizabeth *b* 1991, Alexandra Sophie *b* 1993. *Residence* – Wychden, Chobham, Surrey. —— Edward Henry Lancelot (Stanford Hall, Lutterworth, Leics LE17 6DH), *b* 1930; *ed* Eton, and New Coll, Oxford; Lt-Col Gren Gds (ret); DL Northants: *m* 1st, 1953, Bridget Mary, who *d* 1977, el da of Brig Sir Henry Robert Kincaid Floyd, 5th Bt, CB, CBE; 2ndly, 1981, Hon Mary Penelope Verney-Cave (*Baroness Braye* in her own right), and has issue living (by 1st *m*), Richard Edward Henry, *b* 1954; *ed* Bradfield Coll, and RMA Sandhurst; Lt-Col Gren Gds (despatches 1988): *m* 1980, Caroline Margaret Jolley, step da of Maj Henry Charles Blosse-Lynch, Irish Gds, of Headley, Newbury, Berks, and has issue living, George Richard Edward *b* 1985, — Patrick John Kincaid (The Granary, Stratfield Saye Park, Stratfield Saye, Reading, Berks RG7 2BZ), *b* 1955; *ed* Bradfield Coll, and RAC Cirencester: *m* 1977, Elizabeth Ann, el da of late Victor Sheerman, and has issue living, Rebecca Louise *b* 1981, Victoria Mary *b* 1982, — Gillian Mary, *b* 1958: *m* 1991, Miles Courtenay Ambler, yr son of Capt Quintin Ambler, of Little Orchard, Chapmanslade, Wilts, and has issue living, Henry Richard Edward *b* 1994, Camilla Mary *b* 1992.

AUNT LIVING (*daughter of 6th baronet*)

Mary Elizabeth, *b* 1923: *m* 1951, Algernon Putland Devaynes Smyth, who *d* 1980, and has issue living, Charles Henry Devaynes, *b* 1955; *ed* Eton: *m* 1980, Virginia Anne, only da of Maj James Lionel d'Esterre Darby, of 25 Chatsworth Court, Pembroke Rd, W8, — Caroline Dorothy, *b* 1952: *m* 1981 (*m diss* 1992), Adrian Brandham Bishop Stroude. *Residence* – Rye Cottage, Silchester, Berks.

WIDOWS LIVING OF SIXTH AND SEVENTH BARONETS

NANCY CECIL (*Nancy, Lady Aubrey-Fletcher*), da of Joseph Cecil Bull, and widow of Maj Chas Reynolds: *m* 1965, as his 2nd wife, Maj Sir Henry Lancelot Aubrey-Fletcher, 6th Bt, CVO, DSO, who *d* 1969. *Residence* – Barnfield, Delly End, Hailey, Witney, Oxon.

DIANA MARY FYNVOLA (*Dowager Lady Aubrey-Fletcher*), only child of late Lt-Col Arthur George Edward Egerton, Coldm Gds: *m* 1939, Sir John Henry Lancelot Aubrey-Fletcher, 7th Bt, who *d* 1992. *Residence* – Chilton House, Chilton, Aylesbury, Bucks HP18 9LR.

COLLATERAL BRANCHES LIVING

Issue of late Nigel Chilton Aubrey-Fletcher, 2nd son of 6th baronet, *b* 1914, *d* 1980: *m* 1942, Areta Mae (4 Monmouth Court, Church Lane, Lymington, Hants SO41 3RB), da of Frederick Lees, of Hamilton, Ont, Canada:—

Philip Nigel (9 Kings Satern Rd, Lymington, Hants SO41 9QS), *b* 1944; *ed* Millfield: *m* 1969, Susan Anne, only da of Wing-Cdr M. L. Bathe, RAF (ret), and has issue living, Caroline Susan, *b* 1973, — Elizabeth Claire, *b* 1976. —— David Lancelot (Summer Lodge, 104 Western Rd, Tring, Herts H23 4BJ), *b* (twin) 1944; *ed* Millfield: *m* 1974, Carolyn Cochrane, only da of Kenneth F. Neale, of Beoley, Worcs, and has issue living, Sophie Rebecca, *b* 1976.

Issue of late John Lowther FLETCHER, 6th son of 3rd baronet, *b* 1851, *d* 1928: *m* 1893, Emily, who *d* 1937, da of late William Burkwood, and widow of Cecil H. Weston:—

Grace Vaughan, *b* 1891. —— Jacquetta May, *b* 1894: *m* 1919, Ronald G. Seaburne-May, Capt Sherwood Forresters, who *d* 1940, and has issue living, Daphne, *b* 1923, — Jacquetta Jane, *b* 1929.

Henry Fletcher, of Cockermouth, entertained Mary, Queen of Scots, on her journey from Workington to Carlisle, 1568, and presented her with robes of velvet, for which she returned him a letter of thanks. From him descended Sir Richard Fletcher, whose son, Henry, was created a baronet, 1640. He raised a regiment for Charles I, and was slain at Rawton Heath. The baronetcy expired with Sir Henry, 3rd baronet, who *d* a monk at Douay 1712. Sir Henry, 1st baronet of the present creation, was a Cdr in Navy of HEICS; a distinguished Director of the East India Co, and MP for Cumberland 1768-1802. The 4th baronet, Rt Hon Sir Henry Aubrey-Fletcher, CB, sat as MP for Horsham (*C*) 1880-85, and for Lewes, 1885-1910. He was Parliamentary Groom-in-Waiting to Queen Victoria 1885-86, and assumed by Roy licence 1903 the additional surname and arms of Aubrey. His brother Sir Lancelot, 5th baronet, also assumed by Roy licence 1910 this additional surname and arms. Maj Sir Henry Lancelot Aubrey-Fletcher, 6th baronet, was Lord Lieut of Bucks 1954-61, and HM Lieut of Body Guard of Hon Corps of Gentlemen-at-Arms 1956-57.

FLOYD (UK) 1816

Bearing patiently the dust and the sun

Sir GILES HENRY CHARLES FLOYD, 7th *Baronet*; *b* 27 Feb 1932; *s* his father, *Lt-Col Sir* JOHN DUCKETT, TD, 1975; *ed* Eton; High Sheriff of Rutland 1968; Chm Burghley Estate Farms Ltd: *m* 1st, 1954 (*m diss* 1978), Lady Gillian Moyra Katherine Cecil, da of 6th Marquess of Exeter; 2ndly, 1985, Judy Sophia, formerly wife of Thomas Ernest Lane, of Tickencote Hall, Stamford, and elder da of William Leonard Tregoning, CBE, of Landue, Launceston, Cornwall, and has issue by 1st *m*.

𝕬rms – Sable, a lion rampant-reguardant argent, on a chief embattled or a sword erect proper, pommel and hilt or, the blade passing through an eastern crown gules, between two tigers' faces also proper. 𝕮rest – A lion rampant-reguardant argent, murally crowned gules, bearing a flag (representing the standard of Tippoo Sultan) flowing to the sinister proper.
Residence – Tinwell Manor, Stamford, Lincs. *Clubs* – Turf, and Farmers'.

SONS LIVING (By 1st marriage)

DAVID HENRY CECIL, *b* 2 April 1956; *ed* Eton and RMA Sandhurst; late 15/19th Hussars; ACA 1983, FCA 1993; merchant banker: *m* 1981, Caroline Ann, da of John Henry Beckly, of Manor Farm, Bowerchalke, Salisbury, Wilts, and has issue living, Suzanna Mary Caroline, *b* 1983, — Claire, *b* 1986. —— Henry Edward Cecil, *b* 1958: *m* 1994, Leonor, da of late Sergio Castillo, of Santiago de Chile.

BROTHER LIVING

John Edmund Kincaid, *b* 1936; *ed* Canford; late Capt 15th/19th Hussars; Founder and Chm Floyd Oil Participations plc 1979-88: *m* 1st (*m diss* 1978), Victoria Jane, el da of late Richard N. Cannon, OBE, of Combe Place, Lewes; 2ndly, 1978, Jocelyn Ishabel Ann, widow of David Algernon Fleming (Borthwick, Bt, colls), and 2nd da of late Sir John MacLeod, TD, late Capt Queen's Own Cameron Highlanders, of Bunkers Hill, Farmington, Northleach, Glos (*see* B Dulverton, colls), and has issue living (by 1st *m*), Clare Victoria, *b* 1966: *m* 1993, David Simon Townshend Boscawen (*see* V Falmouth, Colls), — Nicola Anne, *b* 1967, — Marina Jocelin, *b* 1971. *Residence* – Turkdean Manor, Northleach, Glos.

COLLATERAL BRANCHES LIVING

Issue of late Lt-Col Charles Murray Floyd, OBE, RE, yst son of 4th baronet, *b* 1905, *d* 1971: *m* 1948, Mary Elizabeth, OBE, JP, DL (Broughton House, Broughton Gifford, Melksham, Wilts), only child of Robert Fleetwood Fuller, of Great Chalfield, Melksham, Wilts, and widow of Lt-Col Patrick John Salvin Boyle, RSF (*see* E Glasgow, colls):—

Robert Charles (Great Chalfield, Melksham, Wilts; Turf and Beefsteak Clubs), *b* 1949; *ed* Eton, Keble Coll, Oxford, and Pennsylvania Univ, USA: *m* 1977, Patricia Jan, yst da of Wing Cdr Timothy Ashmead Vigors, DFC, RAF, of Coolmore, Fethard, co Tipperary, and has issue living, Charles Oliver, *b* 1978, — James Robert, *b* 1981, — Alexander Edward, *b* 1987. —— Thomas Henry (Withey Place, Shalden, nr Alton, Hants), *b* 1951; *ed* Eton, and Univ Coll, Oxford: *m* 1977, (Penelope)

Sarah, el da of Sir James Cleminson, MC, DL, of Loddon Hall, nr Norwich, and has issue living, Henry James, *b* 1979, — John *b* 1981. —— William Duckett (71 rue Souveraine, 1050 Brussels, Belgium), *b* 1956; *ed* Eton, and New Coll, Oxford: *m* 1989, Principessa Donna Vittoria Valeria, elder da of late Prince Raimondo Alliata di Villafranca, of Palmermo, Italy, and has issue living, Priscilla, *b* 1992.

Grandson of late Rev Charles Greenwood Floyd, 4th son of 2nd baronet:—
Issue of late Lt-Col Arthur Bowen Floyd, DSO, OBE, *b* 1888, *d* 1965: *m* 1922, Iris Clare, who *d* 1975, da of D. Turner Belding, of East Dereham, and widow of Capt A. Stewart Ritchie, MC:—
John Anthony (Ecchinswell House, Newbury, Berks; Boodle's and White's Clubs, and MCC), *b* 1923; *ed* Eton; late KRRC; Chm Christie Manson & Woods Ltd, 1974-85, and Christie's Internat Ltd, 1976-88: *m* 1948, Margaret Louise, da of Maj H. Rosselli, of Worlington, Suffolk, and has issue living, Elizabeth Joanna, *b* 1951, — Caroline Philippa, *b* 1953: *m* 1984, Charles Henry Curzon Coaker, son of Maj-Gen Ronald Coaker, of Daleacre House, Lockington, Derby, and has issue living, Henry John Curzon *b* 1986, Thomas James Curzon *b* 1987, Molly Harriet *b* 1990.

Issue of late Charles Ashburnham Floyd, 6th son of 2nd baronet, *b* 1838, *d* 1920: *m* 1897, Mary, who *d* 1907, da of George Pomeroy, of Exeter:—
Julia Miranda Laura: *m* 1926, as his 2nd wife, Col John Spottiswoode Purvis, CBE, late RE, who *d* 1927. —— Gertrude Frederica Mary Ashburnham.
This family, of Welsh origin, was settled in Cheshire and Shrewsbury. Gen Sir John Floyd, 1st Bt, Col 8th Light Dragoons, distinguished himself in India as Col of 19th Light Dragoons, and was 2nd in command at the taking of Seringapatam, 1799, His daughter, Julia, *m* Sir Robert Peel the statesman. Brig Sir Henry Robert Kincaid Floyd, 5th Bt, CB, CBE, late 15th/19th Hussars (Col 1947-57) was Equerry to HRH the Duke of Gloucester 1927-28; BGS 8 Corps 1944, and Ch of Staff 8th Army 1944-45; Lord Lieut of Bucks 1961-68; HM Lieut of Body Guard of Hon Corps of Gentlemen-at-Arms 1966-68.

Foley-Philipps, see Philipps.

FORBES (NS) 1630, of Craigievar, Aberdeenshire

Sir JOHN ALEXANDER CUMNOCK FORBES OF CRAIGIEVAR, 12th *Baronet*, son (by 3rd *m*) of late Rear Adm Hon Arthur Lionel Ochoncar Forbes-Sempill, yst son of 17th Lord Sempill; *b* 29 Aug 1927; *s* his cousin, *Hon Sir* EWAN, 1991; *ed* Stowe; former Capt Seaforth Highlanders; JP Wigtown 1978: *m* 1st, 1956 (*m diss* 1963), Penelope Margaret Ann, only da of Arthur Gordon Grey-Pennington; 2ndly, 1966, Jane Carolyn, only da of Charles Gordon Evans, of Portpatrick, Wigtownshire.

Arms – Azure, a cross patée fitchee or between three bear's heads couped argent, muzzled gules. **Crest** – A cock proper. **Supporters** – *Dexter*. A knight in armour of the fifteenth century, armed at all points, raising the beaver of his helmet up and leaning on a shield or, charged with a lion rampant gules armed and langued azure—within a double tressure flowered and counterflowered with fleurs-de-lis of the second; *Sinister*, a bear argent, muzzled gules.
Residence – Auchendoon, Newton Stewart, Wigtownshire.

HALF-SISTER LIVING

Janet, *b* 1920; formerly Sergeant ATS: *m* 1958, Norman Walker, who assumed by deed poll 1958 the additional; surname of Forbes before his patronymic, and has issue living, Iain, *b* 1960. *Residence* – The Post House, Midlem, Selkirk TD7 4QB.

WIDOW LIVING OF ELEVENTH BARONET

ISABELLA (*Hon Lady Forbes of Craigievar*), da of late Alec Mitchell, of Glenrinnes, Banffshire: *m* 1953, Hon Sir Ewan Forbes of Craigievar, 11th Bt, who *d* 1991.

COLLATERAL BRANCHES LIVING

Grandchildren of late Lt-Col James Ochoncar Forbes, yr son of late James Ochoncar Forbes of Corse, Lumphanan, Aberdeen, brother of 17th Lord Sempill:—
Issue of late Lt-Col Patrick Walter Forbes, OBE, *b* 1914, *d* 1979: *m* 1939, Margaret Hawthorne (Gardener's Cottage, Breda, Alford, Aberdeenshire AB3 8NN), da of Charles Hawthorne Lydall, of Brightling, Sussex:—
ANDREW IAIN OCHONCAR, *b* 28 Nov 1945; *ed* Trin Coll, Glenalmond, RMA Sandhurst, and St Catherine's Coll, Oxford (MA); Maj (ret) Gordon Highlanders. *Residence* – 12 Denham Green Place, Edinburgh EH5 3PB. —— Mhairi Margaret, *b* 1942. —— Shelagh Anne, *b* 1948.

Descendants of Duncan Forbes (who *m* 1852, Hon Sarah Forbes, sister of 17th Lord Sempill), el son of Alexander Forbes, 5th son of Duncan Forbes-Mitchell, 2nd son of 4th Bt:—
See Ly Sempill.

Granddaughter of late Capt Arthur Newton Forbes-Gordon, el son of late Arthur Forbes-Gordon (infra):—
Issue of late Maj Arthur Dalrymple Forbes-Gordon of Langlee, Cameron Highlanders, *b* 1872, *d* 1931: *m* 1902, Dorothy Ione Helen, who *d* 1964, da of late Frederick Morton Eden (Eden, Bt, colls):—
Christian Dorothy ROYLE, *b* 1910; resumed the surname of Royle 1959: *m* 1st, 1934 (*m diss* 1938), Maj Frederick George Margaritus Grey, Highland LI; 2ndly, 1939, Maj John Popplewell Royle, Glider Pilot Regt, who was *ka* at Arnham 1944; 3rdly, 1950, Lt-Cdr John Charles Grattan, DSC, RN, and has issue living, (by 2nd *m*) Mark John Forbes, *b* 1941.

Grandson of late Capt William Balfour Forbes, AM, RN (infra):—
Issue of late Lt Arthur Walter Forbes, DSO, RN, *b* 1892, *d* lost at sea 1918: *m* 1917, Elizabeth (Eveline Betty), (who *d* 1961, having *m* 2ndly, 1919, Cdr John Gordon Aitchison, OBE, RN (Aitchison, Bt), who *d* 1964), da of late William Tudor Sutherland, of Skibo Castle, Sutherland:—
Arthur Michael Gerald Sutherland (*posthumous*) (11 Coxwell Ct, Cirencester, Glos GL7 2BQ), *b* 1918; Maj (ret) King's Own Scottish Borderers: *m* 1947, Phoebe Mabel, who *d* 1989, da of late Lt-Col Cyril Charles Johnson Barrett, CSI, CIE, and has issue living, Christine Helen, *b* 1949. — Lorna Betty May *b* 1952: *m* 1974, Martin John Guy Knights, MA, MB BS, MRCGP, DA, of Jenners Cottage, Poulton, Glos, and has issue living, Lucy Mary *b* 1980, Amelia May *b* 1981, Daisy Stella *b* 1987.

Grandson of late Arthur Forbes-Gordon, son of late Lt-Col Arthur Forbes, 5th son of 4th Bt:—
Issue of late Capt William Balfour Forbes, AM, RN, *b* 1845, *d* 1928: *m* 1889, Helen, who *d* 1958, da of late Capt Walter B. Persee, 90th Regt:—
William (Awosting, RD2 Hewitt, New Jersey 07421, USA), *b* 1905.
The Forbes of Craigievar, Aberdeenshire, descend from Patrick Forbes of Corse, 2nd son of 2nd Lord Forbes. Sir William Forbes of Craigievar, el son of William, 2nd son of William Forbes of Corse and nephew of Sir Arthur Forbes (*see* E Granard) was *cr* a *Baronet* of Nova Scotia with remainder to his heirs male 1630. He commanded a troop of horse in the Civil Wars, sat as MP for Aberdeen, and received a grant of 16,000 acres in New Brunswick. Sir William Forbes, 5th Bt, *m* 1780, the Hon Sarah Sempill, el da of the 12th Baron Sempill, and Sir William, 8th Bt (who *s* 1846), *s* as 17th Lord Sempill 1884, and assumed in 1885 the additional and principal surname of Sempill. On the death of 19th Lord Sempill 1965, the Lordship descended to his daughter (*see* Ly Sempill), and the baronetcy to his brother.

FORBES (UK) 1823, of Newe, Aberdeenshire.

Sir HAMISH STEWART FORBES, MBE, MC, 7th *Baronet*; *b* 15 Feb 1916; *s* his kinsman, *Col Sir* JOHN STEWART, DSO, 1984; *ed* Eton, Lawrenceville, USA, and SOAS London; Maj (ret) Welsh Gds; 1939-45 War (MC, prisoner after being captured at Dunkirk); MBE (Mil) 1945; KStJ: *m* 1st, 1945 (*m diss* 1981), Jacynthe Elizabeth Mary, da of late Eric Gordon Underwood; 2ndly, 1981, Mary Christine, MBE, da of late Ernest William Rigby, and has issue by 1st *m*.

Arms – Quarterly: 1st and 4th azure, three bears' heads couped argent, muzzled gules, *Forbes*; 2nd and 3rd, azure, three cinquefoils argent, *Fraser*. **Crest** – A falcon rising proper. **Supporters** – Two bears argent, muzzled gules.
Residence – Newe, Strathdon, Aberdeenshire AB36 8TY. *Clubs* – Chelsea Arts; Turf.

They will attain a higher point, who strive at things the most exalted

QUI AD SUMMA · NITUNTUR · ALTIUS IBUNT

SON LIVING *(By 1st marriage)*

JAMES THOMAS STEWART, *b* 28 May 1957; *ed* Eton, and Bristol Univ (BA): *m* 1986, Kerry Lynne, only da of Rev Lee Toms, of Sacramento, Calif, and has issue living, Theodora Christine, *b* 1989, — Katherine Elizabeth, *b* 1990. *Residence* – The Cottage, Hambleden, nr Henley, Oxon RG9 6RT.

DAUGHTERS LIVING *(By 1st marriage)*

(Caroline) Serena, *b* 1947: *m* 1984, E. Nicholas D. Herbert, only son of Ivor Herbert, of Bradenham, Bucks. — Jane Henrietta Mary, *b* 1950: *m* 1976, Tarka Richard Bourke Leslie-King (*see* Leslie, Bt, colls, *cr* 1876, 1985 Edn), and has issue living, William, *b* 1981, — Olivia, *b* 1985. — Christian Clare, *b* 1961: *m* 1988, Benjamin Victor Sheddon Scrimgeour, and has issue (*see* E Huntingdon, colls).

SISTERS LIVING

Mevagh (The Garage, 10A Edith Grove, SW10), *b* 1914: *m* 1948, Julius Joseph Alfred Horton, who *d* 1963. — Juanita Ann Stewart, *b* 1929: *m* 1st, 1949 (*m diss* 1954), Capt Anthony Maitland Steel, actor; 2ndly, 1961, Richard Currier Stickney, of Russet House, 22 Church St, W4, and has issue living (by 2nd *m*), Francis Robin Christopher, *b* 1962: *m* 1990, Lucy Anne, da of late Leonard H. R. Byng, of the Salutation, Sandwich, Kent (*see* E Moray).

DAUGHTERS LIVING OF SIXTH BARONET

Bridget Rosemary Zilla, *b* 1935; JP: *m* 1962, Col Francis Mitchell Kent Tuck, RE, of Allargue, Corgarff, Strathdon, Aberdeenshire, and has issue living, Rosemary Jean Winter, *b* 1963: *m* 1985, Adrian Jeremy Walker, of Upland House, Saxham St, Stowupland, nr Stowmarket, Suffolk, elder son of Sir Patrick Jeremy Walker, KCB, and has issue living, Thomas George Farquharson *b* 1987, Imogen Frances Katharine *b* 1989, Cecily Mary Elspeth *b* 1993, — Caroline Frances Stewart, *b* 1964: *m* 1993, Charles Denholm Ross Stewart, of 22c Sisters Av, SW11 5SR, yr son of David Ross Stewart, — Ellen Alexandra Farquharson, *b* 1968. — Elspeth Ann, *b* 1937; *ed* Aberdeen Univ (MA): *m* 1960, George Hardie, DA, of House of Newe, Strathdon, Aberdeenshire AB3 8TJ, and has issue living, Jonathan Forbes, *b* 1967, — Katharine Ann, *b* 1961, — Ruth Mary, *b* 1964. — Veronica Jean *b* 1938: *m* 1958, Edward Lancaster, DA, ARIBA, FRIAS, (31 McLeod Rd, Balloch, Inverness-shire), and has issue living, Alan Stewart, *b* 1961: *m* 1984 (*m diss* 1988), Sabine Wolniczak, and has issue living, Jonathan *b* 1984, Franziska *b* 1987, — Kevin Edward, *b* 1965: *m* 1991, Iona McGillivray, — Fiona Margaret, *b* 1958: *m* 1980, Robert Seymour, and has issue living, Duncan Robert *b* 1991, Hannah Frances *b* 1987. — Margaret Xanthe Patricia, *b* 1940, MB, ChB, Aberdeen: *m* 1964, Professor James Colquhoun Petrie, MB, ChB, FRCP Ed, FRCP (Lond), FFPM of 126 Desswood Place, Aberdeen, and has issue living, John Ross, *b* 1965, — Mark Colquhoun, *b* 1967, — Rachel Xanthe Ann, *b* 1967, — Paula Jane, *b* 1970. — Alison Stewart (99 Kinghorne St, Arbroath, Angus), *b* 1946: *m* 1968 (*m diss* 1981), T. Angus Ouchterlony, and has issue living, Peter Anthony Heathcote, *b* 1971, — James Angus Heathcote, *b* 1973, — Teresa Mary, *b* 1969.

SISTER LIVING OF SIXTH BARONET

Katharine Stewart (Newe, Aberdeenshire), *b* 1903.

COLLATERAL BRANCHES LIVING

Issue of late George Stewart Forbes, MRCVS, elder brother of 7th baronet, and eldest son (by 2nd *m*) of Lt-Col James Stewart Forbes, of Aslown, Aberdeenshire, only son of George Stewart, yr son of 3rd baronet, *b* 1911, *d* 1969: *m* 1st, 1938 (*m diss* 1949), Mrs Violet Mabel Doyle, da of Kenward Stuart Barker; 2ndly, 1949, Joan (Brindledown, Upper Lambourn, Berks), da of Frederick Turvey:—
(By 2nd *m*) Fiona Hay Lavens (Kingwood Stud, Lambourn, Newbury, Berks), *b* 1950: *m* 1970 (*m diss* 1992), Nicholas Ashmead Cliffe Vigors, and has issue living, Charles Stewart Cliffe, *b* 1973, — Sarah Louise Rosemary, *b* 1974. —— Alison Feridah, *b* 1952: *m* 1973, John Albert King, of Wheatlands Cottage, Finchampstead, Berks, and *d* 1983, leaving issue, James Stewart, *b* 1976, — Georgina Louise, *b* 1979. —— Teresa Frances Ida, *b* 1953: *m* 1978, Martin Gerard Byrne, of Mudgee, Australia, and has issue living, Simon Thomas, *b* 1988, — Clare Joan *b* 1986. —— Joanna Grace, *b* 1955: *m* 1983, Alan Gerard Clarke, of Sydney, NSW, Australia, and has issue living, Owen Taylor Stewart, *b* 1987. —— Sarah Georgina, *b* 1967. —— Nicola Jane Stewart, *b* 1969.

Issue of late Cdr Ian Dudley Stewart Forbes, DSC, RN, younger brother of 7th baronet, *b* 1919, *d* 1992: *m* 1st, 1950 (*m diss* 1960), Lady Penelope Anne Rous, da of 4th Earl of Stradbroke; 2ndly, 1961, Gunilla (Quhytewoollen House, Lockerbie, Dumfriesshire DG11 2NE), da of late Fritz Ryman:—
(By 1st *m*) Charles Stewart, *b* 1956; *ed* Westminster, and Trin Coll, Oxford (MA, MSc): *m* 1989, Alison, da of Maj E. R. Payne. —— Catriona, *b* 1951: *m* 1981, Michael Neville Charles Bradley, of 17 Worfield St, SW11 4RB, son of Malcolm Bradley, of Lymington, Hants, and has issue living, Edward Benjamin Michael, *b* 1982, — Belinda Daisy, *b* 1984, — Henrietta, *b* 1989. —— Caroline Ianthe FORBES (53 St Dunstan's Rd, W6), *b* 1952; *ed* York Univ (BA); photographer: *m* 1977 (*m diss* 1982), Katsuhisa Sakai, and has issue living, Tyler Christopher Forbes, *b* 1978; *ed* Latymer Upper Sch.
Sir Charles Forbes, 1st Bt, merchant of Bombay, was in 1833 served heir male to 3rd Lord Forbes of Pitsligo (peerage attainted 1745) when Lord Lyon allowed him the Pitsligo arms and supporters, being descended from William Forbes of Daach and Newe, yr brother of Sir Alexander Forbes of Pitsligo (*d* c 1496, from whom 1st Lord Forbes of Pitsligo was 5th in descent) and gt grandson of Sir William Forbes of Kynnaldy (*d* 1446), next brother of 1st Lord Forbes.

STUART-FORBES (NS) 1626, of Pitsligo, and Monymusk, Aberdeenshire

Neither timidly, nor rashly

Greater than adversity, a match for prosperity

Sir WILLIAM DANIEL STUART-FORBES, 13th *Baronet*; *b* 21 Aug 1935; *s* his uncle, *Sir* CHARLES EDWARD, 1985: *m* 1956, Jannette, da of late Hori Toki George MacDonald, of Marlborough, NZ, and has issue.

Arms – 1st and 4th, grand quarters, azure, on a chevron between three bears' heads couped argent, muzzled gules, a heart of the last; 2nd and 3rd, grand quarters, quarterly, 1st and 4th, azure, three bears' heads couped argent, muzzled gules; 2nd and 3rd, azure, three cinquefoils argent. **Crest** – Out of a baron's coronet a hand holding a scimitar all proper. **Supporters** – Two bears proper.
Residence – Macrocarpa Hall, Blenheim, Marlborough, New Zealand.

SONS LIVING

KENNETH CHARLES (Nukuhau, Taupo, NZ), *b* 26 Dec 1956: *m* 1981, Susan, da of Len Murray, of Taupo, NZ, and has issue living, Samuel Alexander Murray, *b* 21 Jan 1989, — Amy Dawn, *b* 1982, — Haylee Rachel, *b* 1985. —— Daniel Dawson, *b* 1962. —— Reginald MacDonald (26 Epping Place, Taupo, NZ), *b* 1964: *m* 1986, Heather, da of Phillip Jones, of Riverton, Invercargill, NZ.

DAUGHTERS LIVING

Catherine Florence, *b* 1958: *m* 1975, William Paraha, of 6a Arihia St, Taupo, NZ, and has issue living, William Bayden, *b* 1977, — Jayde Rebekah, *b* 1980. —— Eileen Jane, *b* 1960: *m* 1981, Neil Bertram Brown, of 57 North Rd, Kaitaia, NZ, and has issue living, Jessica Charlotte, *b* 1985, — Charlene Rachelle, *b* 1987.

SISTER LIVING

Avis Ilene, *b* 1932: *m* 1954, William Charles Russell, and has issue living, Stuart William, *b* 1961: *m* 1983, Laurette Dawn, da of John Cooper, of Newcastle, NSW, Australia, and has issue living, Gareth Stuart *b* 1986, Bryce Adrian *b* 1992, Lauren Renée *b* 1984, — Janice Kathyrn, *b* 1955: *m* 1981, Christopher Wayne Groube, of 20 St James Parade, Elsternwick, Vic, Australia, and has issue living, Nicolas James *b* 1986, Joshua Scott *b* 1989, — Diane Avis, *b* 1956: *m* 1987, (Norman) Allan Procter, of 5 Charlotte Close, Poole BH12 5HR, and has issue living, Daniel William *b* 1989, Michael Forbes *b* 1992, — Susan Margaret, *b* 1958: *m* 1981, Alberto Juan Gutierrez, of 149 West St, S Hurstville, NSW 2221, Australia, and has issue living, Andrew Ryan *b* 1983, Kameron Blair *b* 1991, Bryoni Kate *b* 1989. *Address* – c/o 149 West St, S Hurstville, NSW 2221, Australia.

AUNTS LIVING (*Daughters of 10th Baronet*)

Lilian May: *m* 1st, 19-, — Everett; 2ndly, 19—, E. Waddington, who *d* 1974. *Residence* – 110 Commercial Rd, Helensville, Auckland, NZ. —— Ilene Myrtle: *m* 1926, William Houslow, who *d* 1957, and has issue living, Kenneth Charles Patrick (Milton Terrace, Picton, NZ), *b* 1929. —— Gertrude Ellen: *m* 1939, Jack Jennings (*dec*), of 57 Ross St, Kilbernie, Wellington, NZ, and has issue living, John David, *b* 1944: *m* 1968, Beryl Margaret, yst da of Eric Weightman, of Notts, and has issue living, Richard David *b* 1968, Stuart Craig *b* 1970. —— Merlin (134a Muller Rd, Blenheim, Marlborough, NZ), *m* 1936, Ernest Edward Williams, who *d* 1974, and has issue living, Hugh Edward, *b* 1937: *m* 19—, Yvonne Carole, da of William Nott, of Marlborough, NZ, and has issue living, Daniel Isaac *b* 1965, Dale Lincoln *b* 1980, Carole Ann *b* 1965, — Lillian June, *b* 1963: *m* 1959, Anthony Laurence Roche Ryan, of Lochinvar, RD4, Blenheim, NZ, and has issue living, Christopher Michael *b* 1963, Edward Leo *b* 1965, Anthony John *b* 1974, Julia Felicia *b* 1960, Teresa Joan *b* 1961, Kathleen Patricia *b* 1962, Lucy Martha *b* 1969, Bernadette Maria *b* 1971, Michelle Joanne *b* 1972, — Barbara Joan (twin) (62 Howick Rd, Blenheim,

Marlborough, NZ), *b* 1938: *m* 1957, James Laurence William Adams, who *d* 1982, and has issue living, Michael James David *b* 1962, Cheralee Merlin *b* 1958, Rose June *b* 1960, Karen Anne, *b* 1957: *m* 1979, Philip Walter McNabb, (17 Fyfe St, Blenheim, NZ). ——— Gwendoline Rose (10 Rawhiti Village, 117 Bowhill Rd, N Beach, Christchurch, NZ): *m* 1952, Leonard Lowe, who *d* 1965, and has issue living, Peter Morris, *b* (Jan) 1956, — Barbara Theresa, *b* (Nov) 1956, — Yvonne Maria, *b* 1959.

GREAT AUNT LIVING (*Daughter of 9th baronet*)

Beatrice Fullarton: *m* 1914, James Royston Callender, and has issue living, William Stuart (42 Renfrew Av, Mount Albert, Auckland, New Zealand), *b* 1915: *m* 1952, Ella Jean Skuse, and has issue living, David Gordon *b* 1953, Robert Andrew *b* 1956, Linda Margaret *b* 1955, — Hugh Royston, *b* 1919: *m* 1949, Mary Lorna Elliot, of Artarmon, Sydney, NS Wales, and has issue living, Warwick Elliot *b* 1951, Vivien Elliot *b* 1953.

MOTHER LIVING

Marjory, da of late Daniel Gilchrist, of Mahakipawa, NZ: *m* 1st, 1932, William Kenneth Stuart-Forbes, 3rd son of 10th baronet, who *d* 1946; 2ndly, 1951, Rayner Clifford Connolly, of 60 Hutcheson St, Blenheim, Marlborough, NZ.

COLLATERAL BRANCHES LIVING

Issue of late Reginald Alexander Stuart-Forbes, yst son of 10th baronet, *b* 1909, *d* 1974: *m* 1940, Florence Annie (who *m* 2ndly, 1986, Ross Sharpe, of Riverdale, RD3, Blenheim, Marlborough, NZ), yr da of late Daniel Gilchrist, of Mahakipawa (ante):—
Dorothy Anne, *b* 1947: *m* 19— Rex Smith, of 38 Bridge St, S Brighton, Christchurch, NZ, and has issue, Todd, *b* 1974. ——— Marilyn, *b* 1951: *m* 1972, Alister James McAlpine, of Wairau Valley, RD1, Marlborough, NZ, and has issue living, Sarah, *b* 1978, — Emma, *b* 1981, — Katey, *b* 1985.

Issue of late William Forbes, 3rd son of 9th baronet, *b* 1876, *d* 1938: *m* 1906, Lillian Marian, who *d* 1959, da of late James Moore:—
Gwendoline Mary. *Residence* – 21 Elm Tree Ct, 123 Russell St, Palmerston North, New Zealand. ——— Moya: *m* 1942, Owen Alfred Wiley, who *d* 1989, and has issue living, Andrew Owen, *b* 1943, — Kevin Francis, *b* 1944, — Paul Royson *b* 1948, — Gordon John, *b* 1956. *Residence* – 9/18 Ada St, Palmerston North, New Zealand.

Grandchildren of late George Edward Forbes, son of George Forbes, 3rd son of 6th baronet:—
Issue of late Rev Canon Edward Archibald Forbes, *b* 1869, *d* 1929: *m* 1922, Enid Blackburn, who *d* 1971, da of late Rev Canon Garden Llanoe Duff (*see* Dunbar, Bt, *cr* 1706, colls):—
Andrew Garden Duff (Overskibo House, Dornoch, Sutherland), *b* 1925; *ed* Trin Coll, Glenalmond, at Wellington Coll, NZ, and Trin Coll, Camb (MA): *m* 1st, 1953 (*m diss* 1980), Alison, da of E. St Clair Wilson, of Wellington, New Zealand; 2ndly, 1989, Natalie Marion, da of late Lt-Col John Duguid Milne, OBE, of Ardmiddle, Turriff, Aberdeenshire, and has issue living (by 1st *m*), Alexander Duff (Druminnor Castle, Rhynie, Aberdeenshire), *b* 1955; *ed* Eton, and Trin Coll, Camb (MA), — Barbara Elizabeth (*Lady Grant*), *b* 1954: *m* 1982, Sir Archibald Grant, 13th Bt (*see* Grant, Bt, *cr* 1705), of House of Monymusk, Monymusk, Aberdeenshire, — Christian Margaret, *b* 1957: *m* 1985, Edward Maurice O'Morchoe, of Ashford, co Wicklow, yr son of late Maurice Gethin O'Morchoe, and has issue living, Frances Eileen *b* 1989, Patricia Christian *b* 1991, — Louisa Mary, *b* 1961: *m* 1985, Richard William Corbet Turnor, yr son of Maj Anthony Richard Turnor, CBE, of Foxley Manor, Malmesbury, Wilts (*see* Londesborough, B, 1980 Edn), and has issue living, William Michael Francis *b* 1988, Elizabeth *b* 1990, Rosalind Mary *b* 1993. ——— Elizabeth Helen (Underhill, Chideock, Bridport, Dorset), *b* 1923; BSc (Eng) London 1950: *m* 1951, Cdr Ralph Crichton Rupert Brooke, VRD, CEng, FIEE, RNR, who *d* 1985, and has issue living, John Ralph, *b* 1953, — Peter William, *b* 1957: *m* 1979, Jennifer Margaret, yst da of Walter Sidney Hobin and has issue living, Georgina Ellen Florence *b* 1990, — Jane Elizabeth, *b* 1955: *m* 1st, 1979 (*m diss* 1983), Graeme Tulley; 2ndly, 1990, Alistair Anderson Donald, and has issue living (by 2nd *m*), Benjamin Alexander Samuel *b* 1990, Rebekah Jane Deborah *b* 1992.
Issue of late Com Spencer Dundas Forbes, RN, *b* 1874, *ka* 1914: *m* 1913, Ethel yst da of late Lieut-Col J. S. Walker, Black Watch (Roy Highlanders), of Wilbury, Sunningdale, Berks:—
Spencer Malcolm Edward, *b* (*posthumous*), 1914: *m* 1st, 1940 (*m diss* 1947), Marie Teresa, da of Boleshaw Sulikowski, of Warsaw, Poland; 2ndly, 1954 (*m diss* 1980), Elizabeth Lechmere, da of late Sandys Stuart Macaskie, of Lustleigh, S Devon, and has issue living, (by 2nd *m*) James Fergus Spencer, *b* 1956, — Camilla Elizabeth, *b* 1958: *m* 1986, Ian E. Stewart, son of J. F. E. Stewart, of Whitehouse Farm, Warninglid, Sussex. *Residence* – 1 Coastguard Cottages, Lepe, Exbury, Hants. *Club* – Royal Yacht Squadron.

Grandchildren of late Capt Charles Hay Forbes, CBE (infra):—
Issue of late Lt-Cdr Reginald Arthur Forbes, RN (ret), *b* 1905, *d* 1975: *m* 1st, 1930 (*m diss* 1944), Margaret Evelyn, who *d* 1984, da of late Gideon Macpherson Rutherford (*see* Bs Willoughby de Eresby, colls); 2ndly, 1944, Joyce Charlotte Newton (Hammericks Rd, Blenheim, NZ):—
(By 1st *m*) James Hay (5708 Longfellow St, Riverdale, Maryland, USA), *b* 1931: *m* 1958, Helen Reddy, of Montreal, Canada, and has issue living, Peter Jonathan, *b* 1960, — Michael Todd, *b* 1963, — Susan Catherine, *b* 1959. ——— Margaret Christine, *b* 1933: *m* 1959, John Jervis Murray Bankes, solicitor, of Tempus House, Hinton Ampner, Alresford, Hants, and has issue living, Henry Francis John, *b* 1966, — Caroline Margaret, *b* 1964: *m* 1993, Jonathan Piers Young, only son of Peter Alan George Young, of Chudleigh, Devon, and has issue living, Henrietta Margaret Evelyn *b* 1994. ——— (By 2nd *m*) William Henry, *b* 1944.

Grandchildren of late Capt Charles Hay Forbes, CBE, son of late Capt James Arthur Forbes, RN, 4th son of George Forbes (ante):—
Issue of late Lieut-Com John Hay Forbes, DSO, RN, *b* 1906, *d* on active ser 1940: *m* 1930, Edith Sheilah (who *d* 1951, having *m* 2ndly, 1943, as his 2nd wife, Lt-Col Hon Richard Martin Peter Preston, DSO, who *d* 1965, 2nd son of 14th Viscount Gormanston), da of late Reginald de Crecy Steel, of Walton-on-Thames:—
Charles Hay (PO Box 71, Kericho, Kenya), *b* 1931; is a Tea Planter: *m* 1959, Juliet Rosalind Murray, and has issue living, John Hay, *b* 1960, — George Louis, *b* 1961, — Drostan Gerard, *b* 1962, — Sheila Emily, *b* 1963. ——— Angus John Reginald (*posthumous*) (2967 Routt Circle, Lakewood, Colorado 80215, USA), *b* 1941: *m* 1963, Victoria Seward, of California, USA, and has issue living, Richard Leland John, *b* 1965, — Caroline Lilah Jo, *b* 1963. ——— Fiona Eileen, *b* 1937: *m* 1st, 1961 (*m diss* 1976), Anthony Haig Morse; 2ndly, 1977, K. Anthony Ruddle, of Spring House, Ketton, Stamford, Lincs, and has issue living (by 1st *m*) Claire Emma, *b* 1962: *m* 1985, Martin George Wilson, of Chater Cottage, Aldgate, Ketton, Stamford, Lincs, son of Thomas Edward Wilson, of Beech House, Hambleton, Oakham, Rutland, Leics, and has issue living, George Anthony *b* 1986, Harriet Claire *b* 1988, Mariella Victoria *b* 1992, — Rachel Elizabeth, *b* 1965: *m* 1992 Nicholas John Curran, yr son of Peter Curran, of West Humble, Dorking.

Grandson of Capt James Arthur Forbes, CBE, RN (ante):—
Issue of late Air-Commodore James Louis Forbes, OBE, *b* 1880, *d* 1965: *m* 1919, Marjorie, da of Sir Thomas Putnam, and widow of Capt Philip Picot:—

James Alexander (Mill Cottage, Fulmer, Bucks), *b* 1919; 1939-45 War as Maj Gordon Highlanders: *m* 1946, Susan Elizabeth, da of Maj-Gen Alan Hugh Hornby, CB, CBE, MC, and has issue living, Michael James, *b* 1949, — Caroline Susan, *b* 1952.

Sir William Forbes, of Monymusk, Aberdeenshire (4th in descent from Duncan Forbes of Corsindae, 2nd son of 2nd Lord Forbes) was *cr* a Baronet with remainder to heirs male whatsoever. Sir Charles Hay Hepburn Stuart-Forbes, 10th baronet assumed the additional surname of Stuart. Sir Walter Scott, in his Notes to "Marmion", speaking of Sir William, the 6th baronet, an Edinburgh banker, says: "He was unequalled, perhaps, in the degree of individual affection entertained for him by his friends, as well as in the general esteem and respect of Scotland at large". Sir William Forbes, 7th baronet, *m* 1797, Williamina Wishart, only child and heir of Sir John Belshes-Wishart, afterwards Stuart, 4th Bt of Fettercairn, who was descended in the maternal line from Stuart of Castlemilk. Sir John Stuart Hepburn Forbes, 8th baronet assumed the additional surname and arms of Hepburn. He was heir general of the last Lord Forbes of Pitsligo (his ancestor, the 4th Bt, having *m* Mary, da of the 3rd son and sister of the 4th Lord). His only child *m* the 20th Baron Clinton, to whom the whole of the estates descended.

Forbes-Leith of Fyvie, see Leith of Fyvie.

FORD (UK) 1929, of Westerdunes, co of East Lothian

Sir ANDREW RUSSELL FORD, 3rd *Baronet*; *b* 29 June 1943; *s* his father, *Sir* HENRY RUSSELL, TD, JP, 1989; *ed* Winchester, New Coll, Oxford, Loughborough Coll of Education (DLC 1967) External BA London Univ, and External MA Birmingham Univ: *m* 1968, Penelope Anne, only da of Harold Edmund Relph, of 8 Grange Cross Close, West Kirby, Wirral, and has issue.

Arms – Vert, a chevron between a dexter and a sinister wing in chief and in base a pyramid all or. **Crest** – A sphinx wings elevated, the head ensigned with a plume and supporting between the fore-paws a papyrus stalk flowered and leaved or.
Residence – 20 Coniston Rd, Chippenham, Wilts SN14 0PX.

SONS LIVING

TOBY RUSSELL, *b* 11 Jan 1973. —— David Andrew, *b* 1984.

DAUGHTER LIVING

Julia Mary, *b* 1970.

SISTERS LIVING

Jill Dorothy, *b* 1937. —— Alison Patricia, *b* 1946: *m* 1970, Robert M. Cowe, of Fountain Hall, Pencaitland, E Lothian EH34 5EY, and has issue living, Peter Henry McNab *b* 1972, — Ian Duncan McNab, *b* 1974, — Anne Louise, *b* 1978. —— Belinda Christine, *b* 1951: *m* 1974, Graeme P. C. McWilliam, of Bridge End Cottage, Ulpha, Broughton-in-Furness, Cumbria, and has issue living, Ralph Andrew Campbell, *b* 1984, — Alastair James, *b* 1992, — Amelia Mary, *b* 1976, — Louise Sarah, *b* 1979, — Dorothy Helen, *b* 1987.

UNCLE LIVING (*son of 1st baronet*)

Harold Frank (Millhill, Meikleour, Perthshire PH2 6EF), *b* 1915; *ed* Winchester, and Univ Coll, Oxford; LLB (Edin) 1945; Lothians and Border Yeo Capt 1945 (pow); Sheriff substitute Forfar 1951-71; Sheriff-Perth 1971-80: *m* 1948, Lucy Mary, da of late J. R. Wardlaw Burnet, KC, of Edinburgh, and has issue living, Patrick John, *b* 1952, — Claire Lucy, *b* 1949: *m* 1975, John W. Blair, of Clint House, Stenton, E Lothian, and has issue living, Charles *b* 1980, Zepherine *b* 1978, Molly *b* 1985, — Harriet Mary, *b* 1955, — Katharine Anne, *b* 1958: *m* 1989, Timothy Paul Cullinan, MB, ChB, of 53 Mapledene Rd, Dalston, E8.

AUNT LIVING (*daughter of 1st baronet*)

Marjorie Elaine, *b* 1913: *m* 1941, Alan Murray, who *d* 1975, of 26 Gordon St, Mosman, NSW 2088, Australia, and has issue living, Peter Johnston (20 Dawson St, Naremburn, Sydney 2065, Australia), *b* 1943; *ed* Scots Coll, Sydney, and NSW Univ (BA Architecture); Master of Town and Country Planning, Sydney Univ: *m* 1967 (*m diss* 1987), Jennifer Lee, da of Harold Ambrose Terrey, of 5 Coolaroo Rd, Lane Cove, NSW, — Gillian Elaine (283 Green Point Drive, Green Point, via Forster, NSW 2428, Australia), *b* 1946: *m* 1967 (*m diss* 1978), Gary Richardson, and has issue living, Damien *b* 1971, Nathan *b* 1974, Heath *b* 1977, Kelly Ann *b* 1969.

WIDOW LIVING OF SECOND BARONET

MARY ELIZABETH (*Dowager Lady Ford*), da of late Godfrey F. Wright, of Whiddon, Bovey Tracey: *m* 1936, Sir Henry Russell Ford, 2nd Bt, TD, JP, who *d* 1989. *Residence* – 1 Broadgait Green, Gullane, East Lothian EH31 2DW.

The 1st baronet, Sir Patrick Johnston Ford (son of James Ford, of Edinburgh), sat as MP for Edinburgh, N Div (*U*) 1920-23, and 1924-35, and was a Junior Lord of the Treasury 1922-30.

ST CLAIR-FORD (GB) 1793, of Ember Court, Surrey

Sir JAMES ANSON ST CLAIR-FORD, 7th *Baronet*; *b* 16 March 1952; *s* his father, *Capt Sir* AUBREY, DSO, RN, 1991; *ed* Wellington, and Bristol Univ: *m* 1st, 1977 (*m diss* 1985), Jennifer Margaret, yr da of Commodore J. Robin Grindle, RN, of Drake House, Devonport; 2ndly, 1987, Mary Anne, elder da of His Honour late Judge (Nathaniel Robert) Blaker, QC, DL, of 2 Culver Rd, Winchester, Hants.

Arms – Per pale gules and or, two bends vaire; on a canton of the second a greyhound courant sable. **Crest** – A greyhound's head sable erased gules, muzzled or. *Residence* – 161 Sheen Lane, SW14.

Omnium rerum vicissitudo

All things are subject to change

SISTER LIVING

Julia Mary, *b* 1954: *m* 1977 (*m diss* 1983), John E. Kerr.

AUNT LIVING (*sister of 6th baronet*)

Daphne Jane Anson, OBE (Beck Cottage, Menethorpe, Malton, N Yorks), *b* 1914; OBE (Civil) 1972: *m* 1934, Col Geoffrey William Preston, RE, who *d* 1976, and has issue living, Roger St Clair, CBE (Whitegrounds, Thornthorpe, Malton, N Yorks), *b* 1935; Brig LI (late KOYLI); OBE (Mil) 1979, CBE (Mil) 1986: *m* 1964, Polly Mary, da of late Robin Marriott, and has issue living, Mark Robin *b* 1968, Hugh Geoffrey *b* 1970, Sarah Jane *b* 1966, — Judith Mary, *b* 1946: *m* 1967 (*m diss* 1992) Adrian C. Estcourt.

DAUGHTERS LIVING OF FIFTH BARONET

(Beryl) Cicely FORD, *b* 1921: *m* 1951, James Arthur Peter Peirce, MB, ChB, and has issue living, Martin Charles Arthur, *b* 1952, — Sarah Jane Charlotte, *b* 1955. *Residence* – St Annes, 4 Hill Rd, Swanage, Dorset. —— Janetta Olive FORD, *b* 1925: *m* 1964, David Ryland Pullinger, of 16 Hollow Oak Rd, Stoborough, Wareham, Dorset BH20 5AH.

WIDOW LIVING OF SIXTH BARONET

ANNE (*Dowager Lady St Clair-Ford*), da of Harold Cecil Christopherson, of Penerley Lodge, Beaulieu, Hants: *m* 1945, Capt Sir Aubrey St Clair-Ford, 6th Bt, DSO, RN, who *d* 1991. *Residence* – West Winds, Woodgreen, Fordingbridge, Hants.

COLLATERAL BRANCHES LIVING

Issue of late Lt-Cdr Drummond St Clair-Ford, RN, and brother of 6th baronet, *b* 1907, *ka* 1943: *m* 1933, Norah Elizabeth (who *m* 2ndly, 1945, Rear-Adm Peter Noel Buckley, CB, DSO, who *d* 1988, of Forest Cottage, Sway, Hants), da of Capt Charles James Astley Maberly, late 17th Lancers:—
COLIN ANSON (Inchmoy, Port of Menteith, Stirling FK8 3RA), *b* 19 April 1939: *m* 1964, Gillian Mary, da of Rear-Adm Peter Skelton, CB, and has issue living, Kate Mary, *b* 1967: *m* 1993, Jonathan Paul Weatherall, son of Ian Weatherall, of Purley, Surrey, — Fiona Elizabeth, *b* 1969. —— Robin Sam (21 Claremont Crescent, Edinburgh EH1 26L), *b* 1941: *m* 1980 Alison F, yr da of late William Dickson, of Corsham, Wilts, and has issue living, William Sam, *b* 1982, — Peter James, *b* 1984. —— Elizabeth Jane, *b* 1937: *m* 1961, John Nigel Courtenay James, and has issue living, Simon, *b* 1966, — Annabel Clare, *b* 1964.

Issue of late Cdr Vernon John St Clair-Ford, MBE, RN, yst brother of 6th baronet, *b* 1918, *d* 1952: *m* 1947, Patricia Mary (who *m* 2ndly, 1954, Lt-Cdr Michael Ainsworth, RN, who *d* 1978, and 3rdly, 1984, Richard Patrick Beeny, of Whitewater Lodge, Riseley Mill, nr Reading, Berks), da of late F. G. H. Bedford, of Petersfield, Hants:—
Timothy Bedford, *b* 1948: *m* 19—, Jennie Hemsley, and has issue living, Emma, *b* 1977, — Charlotte, *b* 1979. —— Gordon Sam, *b* 1950: *m* 1979, Hilary Jean, da of Maj H. Charlesworth, of Wokingham, Berks, and has issue living, Rufus, *b* 1980, — Joseph, *b* 1981, — Theresa, *b* 1984.

Grandchildren of late Rev Charles Primrose FORD, yst son of late Rev Charles Ford, 3rd son of 1st baronet:—
Issue of late Rev Roger Anson FORD, *b* 1878, *d* 1932: *m* 1916, Kathleen Orme, da of late Montague Torridge Morris, Colonial Civil Ser:—
Montague Patrick, *b* 1918; BSc, MRCVS; late Colonial Ser, N Nigeria: *m* 1st, 1951 (*m diss* 1967), Rosalind Elizabeth, da of Lt-Col Thomas Harold Barnes, of Castle Cary; 2ndly, 1969, Ivy Lillian Lowden, da of William Buckell, and has issue living (by 1st *m*), Sara Kathleen, *b* 1959. —— Charles Primrose (The Old Rectory, Skidbrooke, Louth, LN11 7DQ), *b* 1922, Fl Lt RAF (ret): *m* 1949, Margaret Watson, and has issue living, Victoria Primrose, *b* 1953. —— Dorothy Vernon, *b* 1930.
The 1st baronet was a Member of the Council in Barbados, and in 1790 sat as MP for Newcastle-under-Lyme. Capt St Clair Ford, yst son of 2nd Bt, and grandfather of the 6th Bt, assumed the additional surname of St Clair 1878.

Forestier-Walker, see Walker.

FORWOOD (UK) 1895, of The Priory, Gateacre, Childwall, co Palatine of Lancaster

Sir DUDLEY RICHARD FORWOOD, 3rd *Baronet*, *b* 6 June 1912; *s* his father, *Lieut-Col Sir* DUDLEY BAINES, CMG, 1961; *ed* Stowe; formerly Capt and temporary Major Scots Guards (Reserve); is an Underwriting Member of Lloyd's; Master of New Forest Buckhounds 1957-65; Hon Attaché British Legation, Vienna 1934-37, and Equerry to HRH the Duke of Windsor 1937-39; Chm New Forest Consultative Panel 1971-82, and Chm New Forest Agricultural Society 1964-82, Pres 1983; Chm of Crufts 1973-89, and Official Verderer of New Forest 1974-82; Trustee Kennel Club; Hon Dir Roy Agric Soc of England 1972-77, and Vice Pres since 1983: *m* 1952, Mary Gwendoline, formerly wife of (1) Inigo Brassey, Viscount Ratendone (later 2nd Marquess of Willingdon), (2) Frederick Robert Cullingford, and (3) Brig Donald Croft-Wilcock, and da of Basil S. Forster.

Fide virtute et labore

By faith, virtue and labour

Arms – Per fesse or and azure, in chief a cormorant sable, beaked and membered gules, between two fleurs-de-lis of the second, in base an ancient galley or, sail argent. **Crest** – Between two wings argent the battlements of a tower, thereon in front of a stag's head two hatchets in saltire all proper. **Residence** – Uppacott, Bagnum, nr Ringwood, Hants BH24 3BZ.

ADOPTED STEPSON LIVING

Rodney Simon Dudley FORWOOD, *b* 1940; *ed* Malvern; late Capt Irish Gds: *m* 1964, Jennifer Jane, da of Maj Gen Sir John Nelson, KCVO, CB, DSO, OBE, MC, and has issue (*see* D Grafton).

COLLATERAL BRANCHES LIVING

Issue of late Arthur Noel Forwood, 3rd son of 1st baronet *b* 1881, *d* 1960, *m* 1st, 1903 (*m diss* 1923), Evelyn Agnes, only da of W. Forrester Addie, JP; 2ndly, 1923, Hyacinth, da of late Henry Pollard, of Chester:—

(By 2nd *m*) PETER NOEL, *b* 15 Oct 1925; *ed* Radley; 1939-45 War with Welsh Guards: *m* 1950, Roy da of James Murphy, MBE, FRCS, LRCP, of Horsham, Sussex, and has issue living, Susan Noel, *b* 1951, — Diana Geraldine, *b* 1953: *m* 1980, Capt Edward Joshua Cooper, Irish Guards (ret), elder son of late Lt-Cmdr Edward Francis Patrick Cooper, RN, of Markree Castle, co Sligo (*see* B Castlemaine, colls, 1967 Edn), — Jane *b* 1954, — Joanna Baines, *b* 1956, — Caragh Vivien, *b* 1958, — Amanda Elizabeth, *b* 1963. *Residence* – Newhouse Farm, Shillinglee, Chiddingfold, Surrey. ——— Enid, *b* 1924: *m* 1950, Herbert J. Wale, of Glebe Farm, W Haddon, Northampton, and has issue living, Robert Noel Cattell, *b* 1957, — Gerald Richard, *b* 1959, — Angela Mary, *b* 1954. ——— Wendy Baines, *b* 1931.

The Rt Hon Sir Athur B. Forwood, 1st Bt, sat as MP for Lancashire (SW), Ormskirk Div (C) 1885-98, and was Sec to the Admirality 1886-92.

FOSTER (UK) 1838, of Norwich. (Extinct 1960)

Sir HENRY WILLIAM BERKELEY FOSTER, MC, 4th and last *Baronet*.

DAUGHTER LIVING OF FOURTH BARONET

Janet Elizabeth (56A Ladbroke Grove, W11), *b* 1930.

DAUGHTER LIVING OF THIRD BARONET

Georgina Patricia, *b* 1902. *Residence* – Flat 5, Woodridge House, Woodridge Close, Bracknell, Berks, RG12 2Q7.

FOSTER (UK) 1930, of Bloomsbury, co London

Sir JOHN (GREGORY) FOSTER, 3rd *Baronet*; *b* 26 Feb 1927; *s* his father, *Sir* THOMAS SAXBY GREGORY, 1957; *ed* Michaelhouse Coll, Natal, and Witwatersrand Univ (MB and BCh 1951); MRCP Edinburgh, FRCP, DIH London 1984; Physician; European War 1944-5 with S African Artillery: *m* 1956, Jean Millicent, da of late Elwin Watts, FRCSE, of Germiston, S Africa, and has issue.

Address – 7 Caledon St, PO Box 1325, George 6530, Cape Prov, S Africa. *Club* – Johannesburg Country.

SON LIVING

SAXBY GREGORY, *b* 3 Sept 1957: *m* 1989, Rowen Audrey, da of late Reginald Archibald Ford, of Durban, and has issue living, Thomas James Gregory, *b* 1 May 1991, — Robert John Gregory, *b* 1992.

DAUGHTERS LIVING

Deborah Jean Gregory, *b* 1959: *m* 19—, Steffen Zoutendijk, of 125 Wavecrest Av, Venice, Los Angeles, USA, and has issue living, Peter, *b* 1989. ——— Carolyn Gregory, *b* 1962. ——— Rosemary Gregory, *b* 1963.

COLLATERAL BRANCH LIVING

Issue of late Lewis Marshall Gregory Foster, yr son of 1st Baronet, *b* 1904, *d* 1970: *m* 1931, Margaret Amy (11 Vernon Close, Leamington Spa), da of Max Tillard, formerly of Johannesburg:—
Richard Tillard (PO Box 86, Southbroom, Natal, S Africa), *b* 1935: *m* 1st, 1964 (*m diss* 1973), Carola Margaret, da of Rev George Henry Talbot Roe, R of Wheathampstead, Herts; 2ndly, 1975, Mrs Winifred Moira Cameron, da of — Walker, and has issue living (by 1st *m*), Polly Tillard, *b* 1965, — Candy Tillard, *b* 1970. —— Eve Tillard, *b* 1932: *m* 1954, Donald Miller Croudace, of Woodcote Granary, Rouncil Lane, Kenilworth, Warwicks, and has issue living, Brigid Lucy, *b* 1959, — Charlotte Polly, *b* 1962.

The 1st baronet, Sir (Thomas) Gregory Foster (el son of late Thomas Gregory Foster, Bar-at-law), was Provost of Univ. Coll 1907-29, and Vice-Chancellor of Univ of London 1928-30.

FOULIS, (NS) 1634, of Colinton, Edinburgh
(Name pronounced "Fowls")

Ready with heart and hand

Sir IAN PRIMROSE LISTON FOULIS, 13th *Baronet*, son of late Lieut-Col James Alastair Liston-Foulis, son of late Lieut-Col Archibald Primrose Liston-Foulis, 4th son of 9th baronet; *b* 9 Aug 1937; *s* his kinsman *Sir* ARCHIBALD CHARLES, 1962; discontinued use of Liston as a surname, Lyon Court 1988.

Arms – Argent, three bay-leaves slipped vert. **Crest** – A dexter hand couped, holding a sword in pale, sustaining a wreath of laurel all proper.
Residence – Apdo de Correos 7, Portal 5-2-C, San Agustin de Guadalix, 28750 Madrid, Spain.

SISTERS LIVING

Simone Primrose, *b* 1934: *m* 1973, Geoffrey Richard Hall, of Flat 3, 10 Barton Terrace, Dawlish, Devon EX7 9QH. —— Susan Thérèse Olga (Calle Mayor 3, Berdun, Huesca, Spain), *b* 1941; painter and illustrator: *m* 1st, 1962 (*m diss* 1974), Peter John Lely; 2ndly, 1976, José Luis Larraz (Casasus), and has issue living (by 1st *m*), Edward James Mountenay, *b* 1965, — Josephine Anne, *b* 1963, — (by 2nd *m*), Mark, *b* 1977, — James *b* 1978, — Sophie Anne, *b* 1986.

AUNT LIVING

Avril Primrose, *b* 1915: *m* 1946, Major Desmond Allhusen, late KRRC, who *d* 1977. *Residence* – Court Cottage, 62 High West St, Dorchester, Dorset.

COLLATERAL BRANCHES LIVING

Granddaughter of late James Foulis, MD, FRCPE, son of late John Foulis, MD (infra):—
Issue of late Wilfrid Venour Foulis, *b* 1884, *d* 1951: *m* 1st 1909 (*m diss* 1923), Clara Millington, da of Alfred Dow, of King's Lynn; 2ndly, 1924, Ida (18 Osborne Villas, Hove, BN3 2RE), da of the Rev Joshua Brookes, Canon of Lahore:—
(By 2nd *m*) Ursula Patricia Carey, *b* 1926: *m* 1947 (*m diss* 1970), William Joseph Kiernan.

Granddaughter of late John Foulis, MD, 2nd son of 7th baronet:—
Issue living of late William Foulis, *b* 1848, *d* 1912: *m* 1874, Louisa May, who *d* 1939, da of late John Bell, of Sydney, NS Wales:—
Louisa May, *b* 1885. *Residence* – 92 Vaughan Street, Lidcombe, NS Wales.

Alexander Foulis of Colinton, co Edinburgh, was created a baronet with remainder to heirs male whatsoever. Sir James, the 2nd baronet, MP for Midlothian and a Privy Councillor, who was knighted during the lifetime of his father, was actively engaged in the wars in Scotland after the death of Charles I. He was, with his companions, the Earls of Leven, Crawford, and other gentlemen of rank, betrayed into the hands of the English, while attending a convention of Committee of Estates, at Alyth, in Angus. After the Restoration he was appointed Lord Justice Clerk, with the title of Lord Colinton. The 3rd baronet sat in the last Scottish Parliament 1706, and afterwards for Midlothian in the British Parliament. He was a Lord of Session and a Privy Councillor. On the death in 1825 of Sir James Foulis of Colinton, 6th Bt, the male line from the grantee and his father became ext, and the baronetcy passed to his 6th cousin and heir male, Sir James Foulis, 7th Bt, who was descended from George Foulis of Ravelston, uncle of the 1st Bt of Colinton. George's son, Sir John Foulis of Ravelston, was *cr* a Baronet in 1661, with remainder to heirs male of the body. The baronetcy of Ravelston was forfeited by Sir Archibald Primrose of Dunipace, 2nd Bt, for taking part in the rebellion of 1745, for which he was beheaded at Carlisle in 1746. The heir to this baronetcy, but for the attainder, is the Baronet of Colinton. Sir William Foulis of Colinton, 8th Bt (*cr* 1634), added the additional name of Liston, having *m* 1843, Henrietta Ramage Liston of Millburn Tower, great-niece and testamentary heir of Rt Hon Sir Robert Liston, GCB, HM Amb to USA.

FOWKE (UK) 1814, of Lowesby, Leicestershire.
(Name pronounced "Foke")

Arms are the guardians of peace

Sir DAVID FREDERICK GUSTAVUS FOWKE, 5th *Baronet*; *b* 28 Aug 1950; *s* his uncle, *Sir* FREDERICK WOOLLASTON RAWDON, 1987; *ed* Cranbrook Sch, Sydney, and Sydney Univ (BA).

Arms – Vert, a fleur-de-lis argent. **Crest** – 1st, a dexter arm embowed, vested and cuffed argent, the hand proper grasping an arrow in bend sinister or, barbed and flighted silver; 2nd, an Indian goat's head erased vert, armed and eared argent.
Residence – 1 Willyama Av, Medindie, S Australia 5081, Australia.

SISTER LIVING

(Louise) Caroline Daphne, *b* 1948: *m* 1970 (*m diss* 1994), Bruce Theodore Davies. *Residence* – 93 Ormond St, Kensington, Vic 3031, Australia.

DAUGHTERS LIVING OF FOURTH BARONET

Sarah Elizabeth (54 Orchard Av, Chichester, Sussex), *b* 1949: *m* 1989, Jon Robinson, and has issue living, Oliver, *b* 1980, — Kate, *b* 1981, — Alice, *b* 1990. —— Belinda Barbara, *b* 1955: *m* 1983, Richard Laban, of 53 Arcot Park, Sidmouth, Devon, and has issue living, Sam, *b* 1983, — Joe *b* 1985, — Lily, *b* 1986.

AUNT LIVING (*daughter of 3rd baronet*)

Betty Mirabelle, *b* 1912: *m* 1934, Major Charles Chichester, Roy Devon Yeo, and has issue living, Penelope Anne, *b* 1935: *m* 1959, Col Martin Frederick William Maxse, Coldm Gds, of Great Fisherton, Bishops Tawton, N Devon (*see* B Berkeley, colls), — Diana Margaret, *b* 1939: *m* 1967, (Edmond) Jerome Mahony, of Holly Park, Craughwell, co Galway, and has issue living, a son *b* 1972, Maria Lucia Mirabelle *b* 1969, a da *b* 1970, — Helena Elizabeth, *b* 1940. *Residence* – Hall, Barnstaple, N Devon.

MOTHER LIVING

Daphne, da of Aristos Monasteriotis, of Corfu: *m* 1946, Lt-Col Gerard George Fowke, 2nd son of 3rd baronet, who *d* 1969. *Residence* – 4 Queen's Park Rd, Bondi Junction, NSW 2022, Australia.
Sir Frederick Gustavus Fowke, 1st Bt, was son and heir of Lt-Gen Sir Thomas Fowke of Lowesby, Leics, Groom of the Bedchamber to the Duke of Cumberland.

FOWLER (UK) 1890, of Braemore, Ross-shire (Extinct 1933)

Rev Sir MONTAGUE FOWLER, 4th and last *Baronet*.

DAUGHTER LIVING OF FOURTH BARONET (*By 2nd marriage*)

Evelyn Denise (The Grange, Felcourt, East Grinstead, Sussex), *b* 1915: *m* 1st, 1936, Douglas Hamilton Watt, who *d* 1973; 2ndly, 1955, Lt-Col Alfred John Newling, CB, CBE, MVO, TD, who *d* 1957, and has issue living, (by 1st *m*) Donald George FOWLER-WATT (Brambletye, E Grinstead, Sussex), *b* 1937; assumed the additional surname of Fowler 1956: *m* 1960, Sheila Mary Beynon, and has issue living, Andrew James *b* 1961: *m* 1993, Vivienne Hedges, Duncan John *b* 1963: *m* 1992, Karen Monger, Susanna Jane *b* 1969.

FOX (UK) 1924, of Liverpool, co Palatine of Lancaster (Extinct 1959)

Sir GIFFORD WHEATON GREY FOX, 2nd and last *Baronet*.

DAUGHTER LIVING OF SECOND BARONET (*By 1st marriage*)

Georgina Myra Albinia, *b* 1930; OStJ: *m* 1951, Patrick Tobias Telfer Smollett of Bonhill, MC, DL, KJStJ Highland LI (ret), and has issue living, David Alexander Douglas Tobias, *b* 1953, — Gabrielle Georgiana, *b* 1960: *m* 1985, Robert Edmund John Boyle, eldest son of George Hamilton Boyle (*see* E Cork and Orrery, colls). *Residences* – Cameron, Alexandria, Dunbartonshire G83 8QZ; 9 Cleveland Row, SW1A 1DH.

DAUGHTER LIVING OF FIRST BARONET

Adeline Betty (*Lady Holman*): *m* 1st, 1929 (*m diss* 1939), Capt Basil Holmsdale Allfrey, late 9th Lancers, who *d* 1981; 2ndly, 1940, as his 2nd wife, Sir Adrian Holman, KBE, CMG, MC, who *d* 1974, and has issue living (by 1st *m*) Anthony Rodney (c/o John Murray (Publishers) Ltd, 50 Albemarle St, W1X 4BD) *b* 1930: *m* 1st, 1955 (*m diss* 1974), Hon Julian Mary, da of late Baron Russell of Killowen (Life Baron); 2ndly, 1978, France de Brito e Cunha, da of Visconde de Pereira Machado, and has issue living (by 1st *m*), Charles Sebastian Holmsdale, *b* 1959, Arabel Mary *b* 1956, Georgiana Rose, *b* 1957, — Peter (67 Park Walk, SW10) *b* 1932: *m* 1st, 1962 (*m diss* 1975), Susanna Gabrielle, da of late Capt George Wareing Drewry Ormerod, RA; 2ndly, 1978, Clare Elizabeth Carder, and has issue living (by 1st *m*), Richard James Nugent *b* 1963, Alexander Peter *b* 1965, Candida Elizabeth *b* 1970 (by 2nd *m*), Margaux *b* 1979, Constance *b* 1981. *Residence* – Green Farm, Chalvington, Sussex.

WIDOW LIVING OF SECOND BARONET

Lady MARIOTH CHRISTINA HAY (Forbes Lodge, Gifford, E Lothian), da of late Lt-Col Lord Edward Douglas John Hay, Gren Gds (*see* M Tweeddale), and formerly wife of Lt-Col George Richard Trotter, R Scots Greys (E Eglinton); resumed the surname of Hay 1971: *m* 2ndly, 1954, as his 2nd wife, Sq-Ldr Sir Gifford Wheaton Grey Fox, RAFVR, 2nd baronet, who *d* 1959, when the title became ext; 3rdly, 1963 (*m diss* 1971), Sir John Hastings James, KCVO, CB, who *d* 1980.

FRANK (UK) 1920, of Withyham, co Sussex

Sir (ROBERT) ANDREW FRANK, 4th *Baronet*; *b* 16 May 1964 *s* his father, *Sir* ROBERT JOHN, 1987; *ed* Eton; retailer: *m* 1990, Zoë Alia, elder da of late S. A. Hasan, of Windsor, Berks.
Residence – Periac, Forest Rd, Binfield, Berks RG12 5HD.

HALF-SISTERS LIVING (*Daughters of 3rd Bt by his 1st wife, Angela Elizabeth, eldest da of Sir Kenelm Henry Ernest Cayley, 10th Bt*)

Maria Elizabeth Jane, *b* 1952: *m* 1975, Vivian Murray Bairstow, and has issue living, George Robert, *b* 1987, — Katharine Selina, *b* 1982. *Residence* – Englewick, Englefield Green, Surrey. —— Katharine Lucy, *b* 1954: *m* 1976, Ian Forbes McCredie, OBE, son of John Henry McCredie, and has issue living, James Howard, *b* 1981, — Alexandra Elizabeth, *b* 1983. *Address* – c/o The Royal Bank of Scotland, 5-10 Great Tower St, EC3.

WIDOW LIVING OF THIRD BARONET

MARGARET JOYCE (*Joyce, Lady Frank*), only da of Herbert Victor Truesdale, of Heswall, Cheshire: *m* 1960, as his second wife, Sir Robert John Frank, 3rd Bt, who *d* 1987. *Residence* – Ruscombe End, Waltham St Lawrence, Reading, Berks.
The 1st baronet, Sir Howard George Frank, GBE, KCB, was senior partner in the firm of Knight, Frank, and Rutley, of 20 Hanover Square, W, 90 Princes Street, Edinburgh, and Ashford, Kent, a Director of Norwich Union Fire Insurance So, of Livett, Frank, and Son, of London and Southampton, and of Victoria and Albert Docks, and Director-Gen of Lands to War Office and Air Min and Min of Munitions 1917-22. The 2nd baronet, Sir Howard Frederick, Lieut Grenadier Guards, was *ka* 1944. The 3rd baronet, Sir Robert John, was F/O RAFVR and served in World War II.

Frankland-Payne-Gallwey, see Gallwey.

FRASER (UK) 1943, of Tain, co Ross

Deliverance and help

Sir JAMES DAVID FRASER, 2nd *Baronet*; *b* 19 July 1924; *s* his father, *Sir* JOHN, KCVO, MC, 1947; *ed* Edinburgh Acad, Magdalen Coll, Oxford (BA), and Edinburgh Univ (MB and ChB, ChM, FRCS Edinburgh); FRCS Eng, Hon FRCSI, Hon FRACS, FRCPE; Maj late RAMC, Prof of Clinical Science in Surgery, Southampton Univ, and Hon Consulting Surg, Southampton Group of Hosps 1969-81; formerly Sen Lect in Clinical Surgery, Edinburgh Univ Med Sch, Hon Consulting Surg Edinburgh Roy Infirmary, and Surg Colonial Med Ser; Postgrad Dean Edinburgh Univ Med Sch 1981-90; Pres, R Coll of Surgeons, Edinburgh 1982-85: *m* 1950, Edith Maureen, da of late Rev John Reay, MC, of Bingham Rectory, Notts, and has issue.

Arms – Azure, three cinque foils argent, on a chief of the last three bears' heads couped of the field muzzled of the second. **Crest** – A buck's head erased proper.
Residence – 2 Lennox St, Edinburgh EH4 1QA.

SONS LIVING

IAIN MICHAEL (213 Ocean Ave, Apt C, Seal Beach, Cal 90740, USA), *b* 27 June 1951; *ed* Trin Coll Glenalmond, and Edinburgh Univ (BSc); shipping company manager: *m* 1982 (*m diss* 1991), Sherylle Ann, da of Keith Gillespie, of Wellington, NZ, and has issue living, Benjamin, *b* 1986, — Joanna Karen, *b* 1983. —— Christopher John *b* 1954. *Residence* – 39A Devises Rd, Salisbury SP2 7AA.
The 1st baronet, Sir John Fraser, KCVO, MC (son of James Fraser, of Tain, Ross-shire), was Hon Surg to HM in Scotland, Regius Professor of Clinical Surgery, Edinburgh Univ, and Surg, Edinburgh Roy Infirmary 1925-47, and Principal and Vice-Chancellor of Edinburgh Univ 1944-47.

FREAKE (UK) 1882, of Cromwell House, Kensington, and Fulwell Park, co Middlesex (Extinct 1951)

Sir CHARLES ARLAND MAITLAND FREAKE, 4th and last *Baronet*.

DAUGHTER LIVING OF FOURTH BARONET

Sheila Winifred, *b* 1933: *m* 1957, John David O'Brien, who *d* 1980, son of Sir David Edmond O'Brien, 6th Bt.

FREDERICK (GB) 1723, of Burwood House, Surrey

Prudent simplicity blesses

Sir CHARLES BOSCAWEN FREDERICK, 10th *Baronet*; *b* 11 April 1919; *s* his father, *Lieut-Col Sir* EDWARD BOSCAWEN, CVO, 1956; *ed* Eton; Maj (ret) Gren Gds; a JP of Bucks; a Member Gen Commn of Income Tax since 1966, of Stock Exchange Council 1973-75 and Chm of Provincial Unit of Stock Exchange 1973-75; a Member of London Stock Exchange 1954-62; N Africa and Italy 1943-45 (despatches), Palestine 1946-47 (despatches), Malaya 1948-49, Egypt 1952-53: *m* 1949, Rosemary, el da of late Lt-Col Robert John Halkett Baddeley, MC, of Home Close, Donhead St Mary, Shaftesbury, and has issue.

Arms – Or, on a chief azure three doves argent. **Crest** – On a chapeau azure turned up ermine a dove as in the arms, holding in its beak an olive-branch proper.
Residence – Virginia Cottage, Stoke Trister, Wincanton, Somerset.

SONS LIVING

CHRISTOPHER ST JOHN, *b* 28 June 1950: *m* 1990, Camilla Elizabeth, only da of Sir (Walter) Derek Gilbey, 3rd Bt, and has issue living, Benjamin St John, *b* 29 Dec 1991, — Amy Rose, *b* 1994. *Residence* – Home Farm, Batcombe, Shepton Mallet, Somerset BA4 6HF. —— James Boscawen, *b* 1963.

DAUGHTERS LIVING

Anne Rosemary, *b* 1952: *m* 1st, 1976, François Maurice; 2ndly, 1991, Miles Arthur Maitland French (*see* E Lauderdale, colls), of 77 rue du Moulin de Saquet, 94800 Villejuif, France, and has issue living (by 1st *m*), Thomas James, *b* 1977, — Nicholas Charles Roger, *b* 1979, — (by 2nd *m*) Raphaël Maitland, *b* 1994, — Naomi Hilda, *b* 1992. —— Jill Elizabeth, *b* 1956: *m* 1986, Stephen Douglas, of Los Angeles, California.

COLLATERAL BRANCHES LIVING

Grandchildren of late Henry Penrice Frederick, 2nd son of late George Septimus Frederick, 7th son of late Lt-Col Thomas Frederick, elder son of late Maj-Gen Marescoe Frederick, brother of 4th baronet:—
Issue of late Roger Frederick, *b* 1900, *d* 1991: *m* 1928, Nora Mary, who *d* 1977, da of Col Herbert Mansfield Whitehead, OBE, of The Grange, Penkridge, Staffs:—
Roger Mansfield (16 Orchard Close, Yealmpton, Plymouth PL8 2JQ), *b* 1930: *m* 1959, Valerie Anne, da of late S. A. Watts, and has issue living, Alan Marescoe, *b* 1960: *m* 1991, Joanne Bennison, and has issue living, Benjamin John *b* 1993, Laura Anne *b* 1992, — Jonathan Denley, *b* 1962, — Thomas Russell, *b* 1965: *m* 1988, Rae Jervis, and has issue living, Annie Rae *b* 1993, — Catherine Mary, *b* 1967. —— Rowena Mary, *b* 1935: *m* 1957, Lt-Col Ralph Plant, Royal Signals, yr son of N. J. Plant, of Thurnscoe, Yorks, and has issue living, Naomi Elizabeth, *b* 1982, James Martin Ibbott, — Alison Mary, *b* 1959, — Stephanie Ann, *b* 1961, — Nicola Ruth, *b* 1964, — Vanessa Jane, *b* 1965. —— Briony Margaret, *b* 1941: *m* 1960, G/Capt John Hamilton, RAF, of 1 Kestrel Cottage, East Knoyle, Wilts SP3 6AD, and has issue living, John Roger, *b* 1961, — David Nicholas, *b* 1963.

Grandchildren of late Ernest Prescott Frederick, 3rd son of late George Septimus Frederick (ante):—
Issue of late Capt John Cromwell Frederick, RN, *b* 1920, *d* 1974: *m* 1st, 1942 (*m diss* 1965), Mary Oliveria, da of late Rev Wynyard Warner, MC; 2ndly, 1966, Margaret Lilian (Woodview, Meavy, Yelverton, Devon), da of Richard Henry Dalbiac (B Sherwood):—
(By 1st *m*) John Peter, *b* 1945: *m* 1972, Janie Mary, da of Scott Gundersen, of NZ. —— Sarah Ann, *b* 1943.

Granddaughter of late George Septimus Frederick (ante):—
Issue of late Arthur Marescoe Frederick, *b* 1869, *d* 1963: *m* 1900, Petrona Elena, who *d* 1965, da of late C. J. F. Davie, of Montevideo:—
Louisa Carmen (c/o H. Frederick, Esq, PO Box 18952, Montevideo, 11500 Uruguay), *b* 1905: *m* 1934, W. J. H. Van Wijngaarden, who *d* 1964.

Grandchildren of late Arthur Marescoe Frederick (ante):—
Issue of late Arthur Roland Frederick, *b* 1901, *d* 1988: *m* 1930, Maria Esther, who *d* 1985, da of late Francisco Costa, of Montevideo:—
Richard Frank (Montevideo, Uruguay), *b* 1935: *m* 1960, Gloria, da of late Carlos Gracía Arocena, and has issue living, Ricardo, *b* 1963: *m* 1994, Marina, da of late J. Ferrari, — Odile Maria, *b* 1962: *m* 1983 (*m diss* 1991), H. Pérez Noble, — Madelón María, *b* 1965: *m* 1992, Alvaro Piñeirúa. —— Lilian Susan, *b* 1932: *m* 1959, Hugo Sapelli Mendez, who *d* 1988, of Montevideo, Uruguay.
Issue of late John Davie Geoffrey Frederick, *b* 1903, *d* 1975: *m* 1st, 1929, Maria Mercedes, who *d* 1950, da of late Luis Labadie, of Montevideo; 2ndly, 1952, Elisa, da of late Juan Lotero:—
(By 1st *m*) John (Santa Rosa, Canelones, Uruguay), *b* 1930: *m* 1961, Marta Rosa, da of late Oscar Gulla, of Santa Rosa, Canelones, Uruguay, and has issue living, Carlos Alberto, *b* 1962: *m* 1985, Rosa, da of late F. Reggio, and has issue living, Carlos Nicolás *b* 1991, Fabiana Lorena *b* 1987, Lourdes Mercedes *b* 1993, — Rafael Daniel, *b* 1964: *m* 19—, Sonia, da of E. Baserga, and has issue living, Daniel *b* 1992, — Oscar Geoffrey, *b* 1966: *m* 19—, Melba, da of late J. Olivera, and has issue living, Luciana *b* 1992. —— Henry (PO Box 18952, Montevideo, Uruguay), *b* 1933: *m* 1958, Lia, da of Julio Arocena Capurro, of Buenos Aires, Argentina, and has issue living, Henry Martin, *b* 1959: *m* 1992, Aurora, da of Dr Jaime Polto, and has issue living, Henry José *b* 1993, María de los Milagros *b* 1994, — Diego José, *b* 1962: *m* 1990, María Claudia, da of late Claudino Miguez, — Jamie Luis, *b* 1966, — Mercedes Inés, *b* 1961: *m* 1985 Ing. Marcelo Pittamiglio.

Grandchildren of late Edward Gurdon Frederick, MRCS, LRCP, 8th son of George Septimus Frederick (ante):—
Issue of late Edward Vincent Frederick, *b* 1902, *d* 1969: *m* 1946, Joan Olive (80 Rodmell Av, Saltdean, Brighton, Sussex), da of late Albert Dunford, of Brighton:—
Christopher Hugh (c/o 80 Rodmell Ave, Saltdean, Brighton), *b* 1948; *ed* Embley Park, Romsey, Hants: *m* 1982 (*m diss* 1993), Mrs Diana Lesley Spiers, eldest da of late Leslie Kingham, of Coventry. —— Helen Mary, *b* 1947: *m* 1987, Brent Edwin Heath, of 441 Diehl Ave, San Leandro, CA 94577, USA, son of late Edwin C. Heath, of Phoenix, Arizona, USA. —— Auriol Rosalind (59B Camberwell Rd, SE5 0EZ), *b* 1952.

Granddaughter of late George Septimus Frederick (ante):—
Issue of late Herbert Frederick, *b* 1874, *d* 1949: *m* 1900, Alice Louisa, who *d* 1943, da of late W. H. Priest, of HM's Civil Ser:—
Edith Nora, *b* 1901. *Residence* – 40 Rousham Rd, Eastville, Bristol, BS5 6XJ.
Sir John Frederick, Knight, a wealthy merchant, Lord Mayor of London 1662, and MP for that city 1663, was a munificent benefactor of Christ's Hospital, and, after the great fire of 1666, rebuilt the hall at a cost of £5,000. Sir John, the 1st baronet, was his grandson. The 5th baronet was for several years MP for Surrey. The 8th baronet, Sir Charles Edward St John Frederick, OBE, was High Sheriff of Northants 1934. The 9th baronet, Lieut-Col Sir Edward Boscawen Frederick, CVO, Roy Fusiliers (ret), was an Exon of King's Body Guard of Yeoman of the Guard 1925-37, and Ensign 1937-50.

FREEMAN (UK) 1945, of Murtle, co Aberdeen

or Freedom through Work

Sir JAMES ROBIN FREEMAN, 3rd *Baronet*; *b* 21 July 1955; *s* his father, *Sir* (JOHN) KEITH NOEL, 1981.

Arms – Per fesse azure and vair ancient, three fusils in chief and a crescent in base or, a bordure engrailed gules. **Crest** – A fusil or between two wings displayed azure. *Address* – c/o Midland Bank, 192 Hoe St, Walthamstow, E17 3AN.

SISTER LIVING

Katharine Noël, *b* 1950.

AUNT LIVING (*Daughter of 1st baronet*)

Bridget Anne Elizabeth, *b* 1920: *m* 1st, 1942 (*m diss* 1946), John Vernon Rob; 2ndly, 1954, Godfrey Henry Beese, of Church House, East Grafton, Marlborough, Wilts, and has issue living, (by 1st *m*) Joanna Elizabeth, *b* 1943, — (by 2nd *m*) Christopher David, *b* 1955, — Thomas Jolyon, *b* 1957, — Deborah Helen, *b* 1956, — Philippa Lucy, *b* 1960.

HALF-AUNTS LIVING

Joan Margaret, *b* 1936: *m* 1955, John Richard Bine Morgan-Grenville (*see* Ly Kinloss). *Residence* – Upperton House, Petworth, Sussex. —— Susan Hilary Philippa, *b* 1939: *m* 1962, Robin Neill Lochnell Malcolm of Poltalloch, Chief of Clan Malcolm (MacCallum), of Duntrune Castle, Kilmartin, Argyll, and has issue living, Ian Rory, *b* 1963, — Andrew Neill, *b* 1965, — Kirsty Elizabeth, *b* 1964, — Josephine Clare, *b* 1969.

WIDOW LIVING OF SECOND BARONET

PATRICIA DENISON (*Lady Freeman*) (c/o Royal Bank of Scotland, 32 St Giles, Oxford OX1 3ND), da of late Charles W. Thomas: *m* 1946, Sir (John) Keith Noel Freeman, 2nd Bt, who *d* 1981.
The 1st baronet, Air Ch Marshal Sir Wilfrid Rhodes Freeman, GCB, DSO, MC (3rd son of William Robert Freeman), commanded Headquarters, Transjordan and Palestine 1930-34; was Comdt Roy Air Force Staff Coll 1934-36; appointed Air Member of Research and Development on Air Council 1936 (also for Production 1938-40), and Vice-Ch of Air Staff 1940; Ch Executive, Min of Aircraft Production 1942-45. Sir (John) Keith Noel Freeman, 2nd Bt, was Chm and Man Dir Garmantex Ltd.

FRY (UK) 1894, of Woodburn, Blackwell, co Durham

Sir FRANCIS WILFRID FRY, OBE, 5th and last *Baronet*.

Arms – Per fesse gules and sable, three horses courant in pale argent. **Crest** – A dexter arm embowed in armour proper, garnished or, charged on the upper arm with a horseshoe sable, the hand grasping a sword fesswise also proper, pommel and hilt gold.
Address – Cleveland Lodge, Gt Ayton, Middlesborough, Cleveland, TS9 6BT.

DAUGHTER LIVING OF FOURTH BARONET

Margaret Jane (c/o Lloyds Bank plc, Packhorse Rd, Gerrards Cross, Bucks SL9 8PF), *b* 1928: *m* 1956 (*m diss* 1978), Arthur Keith Redway, MSc, and has issue living, Jeremy Nicholas Fry, *b* 1958; *ed* Roedean, and in Canada.

WIDOW LIVING OF FIFTH BARONET

ANNE PEASE (*Lady Fry*), JP, eldest da of late Kenneth Henry Wilson, OBE, JP, of Park Hall, Kidderminster, Worcs: *m* 1943, Sir Francis Wilfrid Fry 5th Bt OBE who *d* 1987. *Residence* – Cleveland Lodge, Gt Ayton, N Yorkshire TS9 6BT.

COLLATERAL BRANCH LIVING

Issue of late Walter Raymond Fry, 3rd son of 1st baronet, *b* 1870, *d* 1944: *m* 1897, Lilian, who *d* 1956, da of late M. Vallauri, Ch Dragoman to Turkish Embassy at St Petersburg:—

Eleanor Priscilla, *b* 1898: *m* 1923, Frank Edwin Ransome, who *d* 1959, and has issue living, Frank Fellows (RD5, Box 381D, Kincaid Rd, Boonton, NJ 07005, USA), *b* 1924: *m* 1950, Lois Pape, and has issue living, Steven *b* 1951, Patricia *b* 1954, — John Fry, *b* 1927: *m* 1950, Marjorie Ann Fisher, and has issue living, Blair E. *b* 1951, Meredith *b* 1970, Barbara F. *b* 1955, Sara Jane *b* 1958.

The 1st baronet, Sir Theodore Fry, FSA, JP, DL (yr brother of late Francis James Fry, of Cricket St Thomas Chard, father of Sir Geoffrey Storrs Fry, KCB, CVO, 1st Bt, *cr* 1929, ext 1960), was a Dir of Iron, Coal and Shipping cos, and MP for Darlington (*L*) 1880-95.

FRY (UK) 1929, of Oare, co Wilts (Extinct 1960)

Sir GEOFFREY STORRS FRY, KCB, CVO, 1st and last *Baronet*.

DAUGHTER LIVING OF FIRST BARONET

Ann Jennifer Evelyn Elizabeth, *b* 1916: *m* 1st, 1942 (*m diss* 1947), Robert Vernon Heber-Percy (*see* D Northumberland, colls); 2ndly, 1949 (*m diss* 1985), Alan Ross, CBE, son of late John Brackenridge Ross, CBE, and has issue living (by 2nd *m*), Jonathan Timothy de Beaurepaire, *b* 1953.

FULLER (UK) 1910, of Neston Park, Corsham, Wiltshire

Maj Sir JOHN WILLIAM FLEETWOOD FULLER 3rd *Baronet*; *b* 18 Dec 1936; *s* his father *Maj Sir* (JOHN) GERARD HENRY FLEETWOOD, 1981; *ed* Bradfield, Maj (ret) The Life Guards: *m* 1968, Lorna Marian, only da of F. Richard Kemp-Potter, of Hillside, Findon, Sussex, and has issue.

Arms – Per pale nebuly azure and ermine two bars counterchanged, over all six martlets two, two, and two or. **Crest** – Issuant from a coronet flory or, a lion's head per pale nebuly azure and ermine. **Supporters** – *Dexter*, a lion reguardant proper; *sinister*, a wolf reguardant argent; each gorged with a collar or, pendant therefrom an escutcheon per pale nebuly azure and or, charged with six martlets counter-changed.
Seat – Neston Park, Corsham, Wilts SN13 9TG.

SONS LIVING

JAMES HENRY FLEETWOOD, *b* 1 Nov 1970. —— Andrew William Fleetwood, *b* 1972. —— Edward Richard Fleetwood, *b* 1977.

Deo Duce Confido.
I trust in God as my leader

BROTHER LIVING

Anthony Gerard Fleetwood, CBE (Little Chalfield Manor, Melksham, Wilts SN12 8NN; Bellvue House, Chiswick, W4) *b* 1940; *ed* Eton; late Lt The Life Guards; Lloyd's underwriter; Dir Fuller Smith and Turner plc since 1967 and Chm from 1982; Master of Brewers' Co 1986-87; Chm of Brewers' Society 1986-89; CBE 1990: *m* 1964, Julia Mary, el da of Lt-Col Eric Astley Cooper-Key, MBE, MC, of 25 Eaton Pl, SW1, and has issue living, William Gerard Fleetwood, *b* 1968, — Camilla Fleetwood, *b* 1966.

WIDOW LIVING OF SECOND BARONET

KATHERINE MARY (*Mary, Lady Fuller*) (Bay Tree Cottage, Chapel Lane, Neston, Corsham, Wilts SN13 9TD; Balmore, Cannich, Inverness), el da of late Douglas Leigh Spence, MC, BCh, MRCS, of Melksham, Wilts, and formerly wife of late E. H. Leventon: *m* 1966, as his 3rd wife Maj Sir (John) Gerard Henry Fleetwood Fuller, 2nd Bt, who *d* 1981.

COLLATERAL BRANCH LIVING

Issue of late Lt-Col Christopher Herbert Fleetwood Fuller, TD, yr son of 1st baronet, *b* 1908, *d* 1976: *m* 1939, Susan, who *d* 1977, da of late Maj-Gen Sir Percival Otway Hambro, KBE, CB, CMG:—

Charles Christopher Fleetwood, *b* 1945; *ed* Winchester. —— Penelope Susanne Fleetwood, *b* 1942: *m* 1966, George Oliver Worsley, and has issue (*see* Worsley, Bt). —— Victoria Henrietta Fleetwood (*Lady Starkey*), *b* 1944: *m* 1966, Sir John Philip Starkey, 3rd Bt, and has issue (*see* Starkey, Bt). —— Georgina Jacintha Fleetwood, *b* 1951: *m* 1978, Reuben Charles Harford, of Ashcroft House, Kingscote, Tetbury, Glos, only son of Lt-Col Charles Evelyn Harford, and has issue living, Hugh Scandrett, *b* 1980, — Christopher Evelyn, *b* 1985, — Beatrice Louise *b* 1982, — Henrietta Mary, *b* 1987.

The 1st baronet, Sir John Michael Fleetwood, KCMG, was a Junior Lord of the Treasury (unpaid) 1906-7, Vice-Chamberlain of HM's Household 1907-11, and sat as MP for W, or Westbury, Div of Wilts (*L*) 1900-1911, and Gov of Victoria 1911-14.

Fuller-Acland-Hood, see Hood.

FURNESS (UK) 1913, of Tunstall Grange, West Hartlepool

Sir STEPHEN ROBERTS FURNESS, 3rd *Baronet*; *b* 10 Oct 1933; *s* his father, *Sir* CHRISTOPHER 1974; *ed* Charterhouse; Lt RN (ret); sporting artist (as Robin Furness); jt MFH Bedale Foxhounds 1979-87: *m* 1961, Mary, elder da of Jack Fitzroy Cann, of Newland, Cullompton, S Devon, and has issue.

Arms – Per saltire argent and or, a talbot, sejant sable, on a chief wavy gules three plates. **Crest** – Issuant from a wreath of cinquefoils vert, a bear's paw erect argent, charged with a torteaux, grasping a javelin in bend sinister sable, pendent therefrom by the straps proper two spurs or.
Residence – Otterington Hall, Northallerton, N Yorks, DL7 9HW.

SON LIVING

MICHAEL FITZROY ROBERTS, *b* 12 Oct 1962; *ed* Sedbergh, and Askham Bryan Coll of Agric and Hort (HND); Farmer. *Residence* – Glebe Farm, S Otterington, Northallerton, N Yorks.

DAUGHTER LIVING

Serena Mary, *b* 1964: *m* 1991, Lieut Mark F. C. Searight, RM, yst son of late Maj M. P. C. Searight, of E Witton, N Yorks, and has issue living, Kate Isabella, *b* 1992.

BROTHERS LIVING

Simon John (The Garden House, Netherbyres, Eyemouth, Berwickshire TD14 5SE; Army and Navy Club), *b* 1936; Lt-Col, Hon Col 1993; The LI; Comdg 5th Bn the LI (ret 1978); Deputy Col (Durham) The LI since 1989-93; a DL of Berwickshire since 1983, Vice Lord Lieut since 1990; *ed* Charterhouse, and RMA Sandhurst; Chm Nat Trust for Scotland's Garden Cttee. —— Colin Gerard (Cockerdale Farm, Coxwold, York), *b* 1939: *m* 1958, Margaret Grace, only da of Alfred J. Haddock, and has issue living, Francis Christopher, *b* 1963, — Fiona Elizabeth, *b* 1959: *m* 1987, Peter Alan Cloke, only son of Roland Cloke and has issue living, Andrew Philip *b* 1994, — Julia Margaret, *b* 1960, — Nicola Jane, *b* 1964.

SISTER LIVING

Patricia Flower (Whitehall, Old Cleeve, Minehead, Somerset TA24 6HU), *b* 1931: *m* 1960, Maj Paul Ian Craven Payne, late The Royal Scots (despatches), and has issue living, Brian Wyndham *b* 1961; *ed* Winchester and Bristol Univ; BSc; Dip L; Capt The King's Troop RHA 1988-91; Bar, Inner Temple, 1993: *m* 1992, Sally Jane, da of Garnet Thomas, of Ferwig, Dyfed, — Paul Frederick Craven, *b* 1964; *ed* Millfield, BA; ceramist: *m* 1989, Jennifer Anne, yst da of James Donald Douglas, of Tenerife.

COLLATERAL BRANCH LIVING

Issue of late Frank Wilson Furness, MBE, JP, yst son of 1st baronet, *b* 1906, *d* 1993: *m* 1949, Georgeana Anne (Knowle House, Kirby Knowle, Thirsk, N Yorkshire Y07 2JB), only da of Col Victor Alexander Henry Daly, OBE, MC, and widow of Alan Guthrie, Flying Officer RAF:—
John Wilson, *b* 1952; *ed* Wellington: *m* 1983, Grania Patricia, el da of John Brabazon Booth, of Darver Castle, Dundalk, co Louth, and has issue living, Christopher, *b* 1990, — Virginia, *b* 1987.

The 1st baronet, Sir Stephen Wilson, was Chm of Furness, Withy and Co (Limited), and sat as MP for Hartlepool (*L*) 1910-14.

FRANKLAND-PAYNE-GALLWEY, (UK) 1812

I would rather die than be dishonoured

Sir PHILIP FRANKLAND-PAYNE-GALLWEY, 6th *Baronet*, only son of Lt-Col Lowry Philip Payne-Gallwey, OBE, MC, el son of Rev Francis Henry Payne-Gallwey, 4th son of Capt Philip Payne-Gallwey, yst son of 1st Bt; *b* 15 March 1935; *s* his kinsman *Sir* REGINALD FRANKLAND, 1964; *ed* Eton; late Lt 11th Hussars; Dir British Bloodstock Agency Ltd; assumed by Roy Licence 1966 the additional surname of Frankland before that of Payne and Gallwey.

Arms – Quarterly: 1st and 4th, per fesse or and gules, in chief an eagle displayed with two heads of the last, in base a bridge of three arches double towered argent, *Gallwey*; 2nd, gules, a fesse between two lions passant argent, *Payne*; 3rd, azure, a dolphin naiant or, on a chief of the last two saltires couped gules, *Frankland*. Crests – 1st, a cat-a-mountain passant guardant proper, gorged with a collar gemelle and charged on the body with a cross patée or, *Gallwey*; 2nd, a lion's jamb erased erect argent, holding the lower part of a tilting spear in bend sinister gules, *Payne*; 3rd, an anchor erect azure, stock or, the shank entwined by a dolphin hauriant argent, *Frankland*.
Residence – The Little House, Boxford, Newbury, Berks.

DAUGHTER LIVING OF FIFTH BARONET

Joan Flower, *b* 1914: *m* 1940, (Robert) Vincent Steven, and has issue living, Patricia Susan, *b* 1942: *m* 1968, Timothy John Charsley, BSc, and has issue living, Jonathan Robert *b* 1973, Andrew Vincent *b* 1976, — Margaret Sheila, *b* 1945: *m* 1st, 1969 (*m diss* 1986), Michael John Wigginton; 2ndly, 1988, Henry Michael Cunard Allen, RD, who *d* 1993, and has issue living, Alexander Steven *b* 1974, Julia Caroline *b* 1972. *Residence* – 227 Route St Maurice, 1814 La Tour de Peilz, Vaud, Switzerland.

MOTHER LIVING

Janet (The Little House, Boxford, Newbury, Berks), da of late Albert Philip Payne-Gallwey (infra): *m* 1933, her cousin, Lt-Col Lowry Philip Payne-Gallwey, OBE, MC (ante), who *d* 1958.

COLLATERAL BRANCHES LIVING

Granddaughter of late Albert Philip Payne-Gallwey (infra):—
Issue of late Lt-Col Peter Payne-Gallwey, DSO, *b* 1906, *d* 1971: *m* 1953, Ann Josephine who *d* 1988, da of Roger John Kinloch Barber-Starkey (Legard, Bt, colls):—
Nicola, *b* 1955: *m* 1978, Henry George Fetherstonhaugh, of Plas Llewellyn, Dolwen, Abergele, Clwyd (*see* V Galway).

Issue of late Albert Philip Payne-Gallwey, yst son of 1st baronet, *b* 1871, *d* 1931: *m* 1900, Katherine Mary, who *d* 1962, da of late Maj Vaughan Hanning Vaughan Lee, MP, of Dillington Park, Som:—
Janet, *b* 1903: *m* 1933, her cousin, Lt-Col Lowry Philip Payne-Gallwey, OBE, MC, 7th Queen's Own Hussars (ante), who *d* 1958.

The 1st baronet, Gen Sir William Payne, yr half-brother of Ralph Payne, Lord Lavington (ext 1807), Gov of Leeward Islands, assumed by Roy licence 1814 the additional surname of Gallwey in compliance with will of Tobias Wall Gallwey of St Kitts, his maternal uncle. The 2nd baronet, Sir William Payne-Gallwey, sat as MP for Thirsk (C) 1851-80. The 3rd Bt, Sir Ralph William assumed by Roy licence 1914 for himself and issue the additional surname Frankland. The 4th baronet, Sir John Frankland-Payne-Gallwey assumed by Roy licence 1919 the additional surname of Frankland.

GAMBLE (UK) 1897, of Windlehurst, St Helens, Co Palatine of Lancashire

Sir DAVID HUGH NORMAN GAMBLE, 6th *Baronet; b* 1 July 1966; *s* his father, *Sir* DAVID, 1984.

Arms – Or, on a pile gules between two trefoils slipped in base vert, a fleur-de-lis of the first, a chief ermine. **Crest** – On a mount between two trefoils slipped vert a stork argent, holding in the beak a rose gules, stalked, leaved, and slipped proper.
Residence – Keinton House, Keinton Mandeville, Somerton, Somerset TA11 4DX.

SISTERS LIVING

Caroline, *b* 1957. —— Elinor Josephine, *b* 1961.

WIDOWS LIVING OF FOURTH AND FIFTH BARONETS

OLGA EVELYN (Wood End, Tregony, Truro, Cornwall), da of Robin Arthur Norman Gamble (infra): *m* 1st, 1965, as his 2nd wife, her cousin, Sir David Arthur Josias Gamble, 4th Bt, who *d* 1982; 2ndly, 1989, Anthony Poole, son of Frank Poole, of Leicester.
DAWN ADRIENNE (*Lady Gamble*) (Keinton House, Keinton Mandeville, Somerton, Som), da of late David Hugh Gittins, Pilot Officer, RAF, of The Manor House, W Hagley, Worcs: *m* 1956, Sir David Gamble, 5th Bt, who *d* 1984.

Vix ea nostra voco

I scarce call these things ours

COLLATERAL BRANCHES LIVING

Issue of late Capt Robert Meredith Gamble, 2nd son of 3rd baronet, *b* 1909, *d* 1988: *m* 1st, 1931 (*m diss* 1940), Phyllis Mary, elder da of late Charles E. Bradbury; 2ndly, 1940, Diana Burnaby, who *d* 1977, da of late Walter Francis Drayson, AMICE, of Craven Hill, Lancaster Gate, W2:—
(By 2nd *m*) HUGH ROBERT GEORGE, *b* 3 March 1946: *m* 1989, Rebecca Jane, da of Lt Cdr David Odell, RN, of 11 Harbourside, Langstone, Havant, Hants. *Residence* – 34 Gallows Hill, Kings Langley, Watford, Herts WD4 8LU. —— Catherine Frances Dorothy, *b* 1940: *m* 1962, Anthony David Weguelin Bertram, of Windlehurst, 3 Surley Row, Caversham, Reading, Berks, and has issue living, Helen Diana Elizabeth, *b* 1965: *m* 1992, Stephen Thurgood, and has issue living, Alison Siân *b* 1994, — Isobel Catherine Joan, *b* 1966, — Laura Margaret Louise, *b* 1970, — Victoria Susannah Mary, *b* 1974. —— Sylvia Helen Jean (Cairnmore, Crianlarich, Perth FK20 8QS), *b* 1944: *m* 1967, John Alan Goodale, and has issue living, Benjamin John, *b* 1968, — Thomas, *b* 1971. —— Rosemary Diana Margaret, *b* 1948: *m* 1967, Nicholas Rooker Roberts, of Sheepwash Platt, Cooks Lane, Walderton, Sussex PO18 9EF, and has issue living, Andrew Arthur Rooker, *b* 1970, — Eleanor Burnaby Rooker, *b* 1972, — Hannah Margaret Rooker, *b* 1976.

Issue of late John Christopher Gamble, 3rd son of 3rd baronet, *b* 1910, *d* 1989: *m* 1939 (*m diss* 1965), Pamela Margaret Grace, da of Arthur Grayhurst Hewat (Aylmer, Bt).
Antony Aylmer (Evandale, Tasmania, Australia), *b* 1941: *m* 1961, Julie Leslie, and has issue living, David Antony, *b* 1962: *m* 1982, Louise Bott, and has issue living, Christopher David *b* 1984, Dylan John *b* 1992, Hollie Louise *b* 1993, — Christine, *b* 1964, — Kathleen Doris, *b* 1967, — Jeanne, *b* 1971: *m* 1993, Andrew Pennington. —— Ann, *b* 1943: *m* 1962, David J. F. Bailey, RAN, of Perth, Tasmania.

Granddaughters of late John Arthur Gamble, 4th son of 2nd baronet, *b* 1883; *d* 1947: *m* 1910, Lilian Jane Emily who *d* 1913, da of late Rev Arthur Raggett Cole, of Hurstbourne Priors, Hants:—
Issue of late Robin Arthur Norman Gamble, *b* 1912; *d* 1981: *m* 1st, 1939, Emily Goodall, who *d* 1944; 2ndly, 1947, Muriel Maud (Overcreek, St Just-in-Roseland, Truro, Cornwall), da of late John Hale, of Knowsley, Lancs:—
(By 1st *m*) Elaine Lilian (Heathside, Jackmans Lane, St Johns, Woking, Surrey), *b* 1941: *m* 1970, Malcolm Charles Gubbins, who *d* 1987, and has issue living, Fiona, *b* 1981. —— Olga Evelyn, *b* 1944: *m* 1st, 1965, as his 2nd wife, her cousin, Sir David Arthur Josias Gamble, 4th Bt, who *d* 1982; 2ndly, 1989, Anthony Poole, son of Frank Poole, of Leicester. *Residence* – Wood End, Tregony, Truro, Cornwall.

Granddaughter of Conrad Dorner Gamble, eldest son of late David Gamble, 3rd son of 1st baronet (infra):—
Issue of late Rodney Dorner Gamble, *b* 1911, *d* 1988: *m* 1st, 1937 (*m diss* 1946), Hester Vernon, who *d* 1969, 3rd da of William Vernon Judd, of Shrubbery, Sutton Scotney, Hants; 2ndly, 1948, Marjorie Maud (Claonadh, 11 Big Sand, Gairloch, Ross-shire), da of Jonathan Smithson:—
(By 1st *m*) Prudence Dorner, *b* 1941: *m* 1968, James Edward Stanley. *Residence* – Swallows, Owslebury, Winchester, Hants SO21 1LU.

Granddaughter (by 1st *m*) of David Gamble, 3rd son of 1st baronet (infra):—
Issue of late Lorentz Harry Gamble, *b* 1893, *d* 1968: *m* 1917, Annie Marian, who *d* 1972, da of F. T. Clarke, of Stony Stratford:—
Diana May (Bramble's Place, 6 Abbey Sq, Turvey, Beds), *b* 1920; formerly Jun Com ATS.

Grandchildren (by 2nd *m*) of David Gamble, 3rd son of 1st baronet (infra):—
Issue of late Graeme Neil, *b* 1904, *d* 1980: *m* 1936, Mary George (Coombe Cottage, Plainsfield, Over Stowey, Bridgwater, Som):—
Sheila Ann, *b* 1937: *m* 1959, James Bridley Douglas Bateman, of Lodmore Farm, E Harptree, Bristol, and has issue living, James Graeme Richard, *b* 1967, — William John Douglas, *b* 1974, — Angus Neil Cyril, *b* 1978, — Fiona Valerie, *b* 1964: *m* 1993, Mark Rule, — Sylvia Mary, *b* 1966, Rosalind Ann, *b* 1969. —— Judith Mary, *b* 1940: *m* 1962, Hagen Volken Dietrich Stöckl, and has issue living, Alexander Duncan Dietrich, *b* 1963, — Natasha Judith, *b* 1964. —— Jane Elizabeth, *b* 1943. —— Tessa Marion, *b* 1952: *m* 1976, Malcolm Paul Bennett of Summerstead House, Over Stowey, Bridgwater, Somerset TA5 1HA, and has issue living, Nicholas Paul, *b* 1984, — Jos Daniel Graeme, *b* 1986, — Fenella Heidi, *b* 1988.

Issue of late David Gamble, 3rd son of 1st baronet, *b* 1856, *d* 1933: *m* 1st, 1880, Josephine Henriette, who *d* 1899, da of Conrad von Dorner; 2ndly, 1901, Marion, who *d* 1955, da of Griffith Parsonage, of Australia:—
(By 2nd *m*) Alan Lionel, *b* 1905. *Residence* – 14 Lower Common South, Putney, SW15.

Grandchildren of late George Gamble, 4th son of 1st baronet:—
Issue, if any (by 2nd *m*) of late Charles Lancelot Gamble, *b* 1885, *d* 19—: *m* 1st, 1906 (*m diss* 1908), Zoë Armstrong; 2ndly, 1909.

Issue of late Henry Gamble, 6th son of 1st baronet, *b* 1868, *d* 1927: *m* 1895, Ethel, who *d* 1924, da of late Thomas Brewis:—
David Harry, *b* 1911: *m* 1949, May, who *d* 198-, only child of Olivier Swithenbank, JP, of Leeds. ——— Winifred Kathleen, *b* 1899: *m* 1927, Fred Russell Roberts, who *d* 1953. *Residence* – 14 First Cross Rd, Twickenham Green, Middlesex.
The 1st baronet, Sir David, KCB, was Mayor of St Helens 1868-70, 1882-3 and 1886-7, a pioneer of the Volunteer Movement, and first Hon Col (VD) 2nd Vol Batn Prince of Wales' Vols (S Lancashire Regt). The 2nd baronet, Sir Josias Christopher, was also Mayor of St Helens, 1888-9. The 3rd baronet, Sir David, was also Mayor of St Helens 1913-15. The 4th baronet, Sir David Arthur Josias, was Chm of Cirencester RDC, and served in Northern Province, Nigeria.

BRUCE-GARDNER (UK) 1945, of Frilford, co Berks

By work and strength

Sir DOUGLAS BRUCE BRUCE-GARDNER, 2nd *Baronet*; *b* 27 Jan 1917; *s* his father, *Sir* CHARLES, 1960; *ed* Uppingham, and Trin Coll, Camb; Chm GKN Steel Ltd 1965-67; Chm GKN Rolled & Bright Steel Ltd 1968-72; Dir GKN Ltd 1960-82; Dep Chm GKN Ltd 1974-77; Dir Iron Trades Employers Insurance Gp 1977-87 (Dep Chm 1984-87); Pres of Iron and Steel Inst 1966-67; Pres of British Independent Steel Producers' Assocn 1972; Prime Warden of the Worshipful Co of Blacksmiths 1983-84: *m* 1st, 1940 (*m diss* 1964), Monica Flumerfelt, da of late Professor Sir Geoffrey Jefferson, CBE, FRS; 2ndly, 1964, Sheila Jane, da of late Roger Stilliard, of Henley-on-Thames, Oxon, and has issue by 1st and 2nd *m*.

Arms – Or, a saltire couped gules, charged with five bezants, on a chief of the second a bee volant proper between two roses argent, barbed and seeded also proper. **Crest** – In front of a miner's pick and gad in saltire a thistle leaved and slipped all proper.
Residence – Stocklands, Lewstone, Ganarew, nr Monmouth NP5 3SS.

SONS LIVING *(By 1st marriage)*

ROBERT HENRY (121 Brackenbury Rd, London W6 0BQ; Travellers' Club), *b* 10 June 1943; *ed* Uppingham and Reading Univ; Dir Dept of Conservation and Technology, Courtauld hist of Art: *m* 1979, Veronica Ann HAND-OXBORROW, da of late Rev W. E. Hand, and has issue living, Thomas Edmund Peter, *b* 28 Jan 1982, — Richard Tyndall Jowett, *b* 1983.

(By 2nd marriage)

James Graham, *b* 1969.

DAUGHTERS LIVING *(By 1st marriage)*

Erica Judith, *b* 1941: *m* 1962, Paul H. Blackburn, of 4 Hilbrow Cottages, Old Horsham Rd, Beare Green, Dorking RH5 4RB, and has issue living, Richard Martin, *b* 1965, — Robert Paul, *b* 1967, — Katharine Mary *b* 1963: *m* 1986, Guy Mark Larkin, — Emma Louise (twin), *b* 1965: *m* 1984 (*m diss* 1988), Simon David Hamblin, and has issue living, Kirsty Alexandra *b* 1985. —— Sarah Tanis, *b* 1952: *m* 1987, Richard William Towse, son of John Towse, of London, and has issue living, Benjamin William, *b* 1988.

(By 2nd marriage)

Joanna Margaret, *b* 1966.

BROTHER LIVING

Bryan Charles, *b* 1924; *ed* Uppingham, and Trin Coll Camb (MA): *m* 1952, Helen Rosemary, da of late Digby B. Sowerby, of Kirmington House, nr Ulceby, Lincolnshire, and has issue living, Edwin Charles, *b* 1954, — Robin Digby (60 Cumberland St, SW1V 4LZ), *b* 1955: *m* 1987, Caroline Stuart, da of Peter S. Wright, of Thurlstone, Devon, — Stephen Bryan (Eaton Lodge, Pulford, Chester), *b* 1957: *m* 1990, Karen, yst da of Harry Spencer, of Mold, Clwyd, — Ian Douglas (Greenspot Farm, Oldmeldrum, Inverurie, Aberdeenshire AB51 0AG), *b* 1963: *m* 1990, Elisabeth (Beth) Mary, da of late R. D. White, and of Mrs D. H. McLellan, of Ollerton, Cheshire.
Sir Charles Bruce-Gardner, 1st Bt (son of late Henry Gardner, of Stanstead Lodge, SE23), was Industrial Advisor to the Gov of the Bank of England 1930-38, Chm Soc of British Aircraft Constructors 1938-43, Controller of Labour Allocation MAP 1943-44, Chief Executive for Industrial Conversion, Bd of Trade, 1944-46, Chm John Lysaght Ltd 1946-59, Dir GKN Ltd 1946-59, Dep Chm Steel Co of Wales 1946-60, Dir Consett Iron Co Ltd 1946-60, Vice-Chm Crompton Parkinson Ltd 1946-60, and Pres Iron and Steel Inst 1955-56.

GARTHWAITE (UK) 1919, of Durham

Sir (WILLIAM) MARK CHARLES GARTHWAITE, 3rd *Baronet*; *b* 4 Nov 1946; *s* his father *Sir* WILLIAM FRANCIS CUTHBERT, DSC, 1993; *ed* Gordonstoun, and Univ of Pennsylvania (BSc): *m* 1979, Victoria Lisette, da of Gen Sir Harry Tuzo, GCB, OBE, MC, of Heath Farm House, Fakenham, Norfolk, and formerly wife of Robert Henry Adolphus Hohler, and has issue.

Arms – Azure, a cross between in the first and fourth quarters five ears of wheat banded, and in the second and third quarters a greyhound rampant, all or. **Crest** – In front of a capstan sable, garnished gold, and fleur-de-lis also gold. *Residence* – 3 Hazlewell Rd, SW15 6LU.

Cuique suum

To each his own

SON LIVING

WILLIAM TUZO, *b* 14 May 1982.

DAUGHTERS LIVING

Rosie Francesca, *b* 1980. —— Jemima Victoria, *b* 1984.

HALF-BROTHERS LIVING

John William Philip (Burtons, Castle Hill, Brenchley, Kent), *b* 1958: *m* 1983, Sarah Elizabeth, da of Rev Charles Anthony Maclea March, of St Luke's Vicarage, Old Shoreham Rd, Brighton, Sussex, and has issue living, Joanna Rachel, *b* 1992. —— Andrew William David, *b* 1962. —— Simon William James (Ballingdon House, Gaddesdon Row, Herts HP2 6HX), *b* (twin) 1962: *m* 1989, Caroline Sally, elder da of John Pigott, of Thrales End, Harpenden, Herts, and has issue living, James William John, *b* 1991, —— George William Angus, *b* 1993.

HALF-UNCLE LIVING (*son of 1st baronet*)

Michael William Gladwin (c/o Barclays Bank, 160 Piccadilly, W1), *b* 1937; *ed* Trinity College Sch, Ontario.

MOTHER LIVING

Patricia Beatrice Eden, da of the late Cdr Charles Eden Neate, RN, and widow of Cdr Barry Leonard, RN: *m* 1945 (*m diss* 1952), as his 2nd wife, Sir William Francis Cuthbert Garthwaite, 2nd Bt, DSC, who *d* 1993. *Residence* – The Old Rectory, Hawling, Glos.

WIDOW LIVING OF SECOND BARONET

PATRICIA MERRIEL (*Patricia, Lady Garthwaite*), only da of late Sir Philip d'Ambrumenil: *m* 1957, as his 3rd wife, Sir William Francis Cuthbert Garthwaite, 2nd Bt, DSC, who *d* 1993.

COLLATERAL BRANCH LIVING

Issue of late Anthony William Garthwaite, 2nd son of 1st baronet, *b* 1917, *d* 1972: *m* 1950, Hon Waveney Mancroft Samuel, who *d* 1986, da of 1st Baron Mancroft:—
Nicholas Anthony William Mancroft, *b* 1952: *m* 1982, Caroline C., da of Thomas Willbourne, of Thorney, Peterborough, and has issue living, Oliver Julian, *b* 1986, — Felix Sebastian, *b* 1987, — Piers Marcus, *b* 1990.

The 1st baronet, Sir William Garthwaite (son of William Garthwaite, of Staindrop, Durham), was a shipowner and was engaged in sugar planting. He rendered services in developing relations between Canada and France, and inaugurating direct line of shipping between those countries, and Special Ser to Admiralty in European Wars 1914-18 and 1939-45.

Gervis (Tapps-Gervis-Meyrick), see Meyrick.

GETHIN (I) 1665, of Gethinsgrott, Cork

Sir RICHARD JOSEPH ST LAWRENCE GETHIN, 10th *Baronet*; *b* 29 Sept 1949; *s* his father, *Lt-Col Sir* RICHARD PATRICK ST LAWRENCE 1988; *ed* Oratory Sch, RMA Sandhurst, and RMC of Science, Shrivenham; BSc (Civil Engrg), MSc; Maj RCT: *m* 1974, Jacqueline Torfrida, da of Cdr David Cox, RN, and has issue.

Arms – Vert, a stag salient argent armed or. **Crest** – On a cap of dignity proper, a stag's head erased argent armed and ducally gorged or.
Residence – Trotts Ash, Sole Street, Cobham, Kent DA12 3AY.

DAUGHTERS LIVING

Katherine Torfrida, *b* 1976. —— Rosanna Clare, *b* 1979. —— Belinda Jacqueline, *b* 1981.

SISTERS LIVING

Helen Mary Elizabeth, *b* 1947: *m* 1975, David Strachan, of 20 Pollock Esplanade, Woolgoolga, NSW 2456, Aust, and has issue living, Rachael Fara, *b* 1977, — Roxanne Emma, *b* 1979. —— Fara Mary Nicola, *b* 1948: *m* 1969, Michael Smee, and has issue living, Oliver Leo, *b* 1971, — Milo Henry, *b* 1973, — Leo Joseph, *b* 1976. —— Georgina Jennifer Mary, *b* 1952: *m* 1979, Daniel Meadows, and has issue living, Harry Daniel *b* 1980, — Luke Roland, *b* 1982, — Jack Richard, *b* 1987. —— Mary Valentine Harriet, *b* 1954: *m* 1978, Martin Philip Runnacles, and has issue living, Elizabeth Jane Fara, *b* 1982, — Sarah Caroline, *b* 1988.

UNCLE LIVING (*son of 8th baronet*)

WILLIAM ALLAN TRISTRAM, MC (Carpenters, Chart Rd, Sutton Valence, Maidstone, Kent), *b* 13 Oct 1913; *ed* Oundle; Lt-Col (ret) RA; 1939-45 War in Mauritius, France and Germany (despatches, MC): *m* 1937, Nancy Ruth, only child of late Lieut-Col H. G. MacGeorge, late RE, of Paignton, and has issue living, Anthony Michael (Vale House, Loose, Maidstone), *b* 1939; *ed* Oundle, and Magdalene Coll, Camb (MA): *m* 1965, Vanse, da of late Col Cecil Disney Barlow, OBE, KSLI, and has issue living, Nicholas Richard Tristram *b* 1965, William Anthony David St Lawrence *b* 1970, Emma Kirstie *b* 1968, — Patricia Jane (Rose Cottage, Loose, Maidstone, Kent), *b* 1944: *m* 1967 (*m diss* 1981), Malcolm Pringle and has issue living, Richard Malcolm Andrew *b* 1974, Caroline Georgina *b* 1970.

AUNT LIVING (*daughter of 8th baronet*)

Norah Helen Catharine (2 Atwater Court, Lenham, Maidstone), *b* 1907: *m* 1938, James Andrew Paton Charles, who *d* 1979, and has issue living, Michael James Paton (85 Wylde Rd, Morley, Perth, W Australia), *b* 1939: *m* 1st, 1964 (*m diss* 1969), Barbara Elizabeth, da of A. M. Turner, of Strathfield, NSW; 2ndly, 1969, Maureen, da of J. Taylor, of Kiama, NSW, and has issue living, (by 2nd *m*) Julian Andrew Paton *b* 1973, Dominic *b* 1976, Timothy *b* 1979, — Edward William (Dacca, Bangladesh), *b* 1944: BSc Agric and Trop Dip Trinidad; MPhil: *m* 1973, Rosemarie, da of K. Kramer, of Winnipeg, Canada, and has issue living, Daniel *b* 1977, Andrew *b* 1980, Simon *b* 1984, Elizabeth Helen *b* 1975, — Elizabeth Ann, *b* (twin) 1944: *m* 1975 (*m diss* 1985), Clive Cromarty Bloom.

WIDOW LIVING OF NINTH BARONET

FARA (*Dowager Lady Gethin*); 2nd Officer WRNS, da of late Joseph Henry Bartlett: *m* 1946, Lt-Col Sir Richard Patrick St Lawrence Gethin, 9th Bt, who *d* 1988. *Residence* – Flat 28, The Maltings, Tewkesbury, Glos GL20 5NN.

COLLATERAL BRANCHES LIVING

Grandchildren of late Lt-Col Frederick Durrant Gethin (*infra*):—
Issue of late John Amory Forrest Gethin, *b* 1916, *d* 1965: *m* 1941, Barbara Damarel Cicely (Brae View, Wester Galcantray, Cawdor by Nairn), da of late Alan Robert Cecil Westlake, of Rowledge, Farnham, Surrey:—
Christopher John Forrest (Moorstone, Buckland-in-the-Moor, South Devon) *b* 1945; *ed* Stowe, Magdalene College Cambridge (MA), University of Sydney (MTCP), and Sch of Homoeopathy (Dip Hom): *m* 1983, Rebecca Mary, da of Benjamin Thomas Gibbins, of San Remo, Italy, and has issue living, Tobias John Forrest, *b* 1983. —— Nicholas Geoffrey Forrest (Shepherd's House, Chaldon Herring, Dorchester, Dorset), *b* 1950; *ed* Stowe, Ch Ch, Oxford (MA), R Academy of Music (LRAM), and Hochschule Für Musik, Vienna: *m* 1993, Catherine, da of John Nelson, of Cardiff. —— Stephen Amory Forrest (Peyzac le Moustier, Les Eyzies de Tayac, France), *b* (twin) 1950; *ed* Stowe, and Magdalene Coll, Camb (MA, Vet MB): *m* 1992, Christine, da of Hervé Fondecave, of Toulouse, France. —— Elizabeth Amoret, *b* 1942: *m* 1965, Nicholas John du Cane Wilkinson, Lt-Cdr RN (ret), of Birkwood Cottage, Wester Brae of Cantray, Croy, Inverness-shire, and has issue living, Piers Nicholas, *b* 1973, — Samantha Karen, *b* 1967, — Claire Felicity, *b* 1968.

Issue of late Lieut-Col Frederick Durrant Scott Gethin, 2nd son of 7th baronet, *b* 1879, *d* 1959: *m* 1915, Margaret Cecilia, who *d* 1955, da of L. R. W. Forrest, of Beech Holme, Wimbledon Common, SW:—
Margaret Joan, *b* 1920. *Residence* – 10 Bridge St, Saline, Dunfermline, Fife KY12 9TS.

Issue of late Percy Edward Lovell Gethin, yst son of 7th baronet, OBE, AFC, *b* 1884, *d* 1969: *m* 1918, Norah, who *d* 1960, da of James Norwood Stapledon:—
Robert Hugh (6 Montfort Fields, Kington, Herefords HR5 3AT), *b* 1918; *ed* Stowe, and Corpus Christi Coll, Camb (MA); 1939-45 War with Intelligence Corps, and 1st Airborne Div: *m* 1946, Marjorie Gertrude, da of B. E. Elliott, and has issue living, Rupert Mark Lovell, *b* 1957; *ed* Manchester Univ (BA, MA, PhD), — Damaris Alicia Honor, *b* 1952; *ed* E Anglia Univ (BA); and Manchester Univ (MBA): *m* 1985, José Guillermo Albarrán, who *d* 1988, and has issue living, Isabel Grace *b* 1987. —— Percy Amorey Beaufort (60 Scotland Rd, Cambridge), *b* 1925; *ed* King's Sch, Canterbury; BA London: *m* 1st, 1948 (*m diss* 1972), Sylva, da of B. Olters, of Gothenburg, Sweden; 2ndly, 1972, Mieko, da of late Choji Suzuki, of Tokyo, Japan, and has issue living, (by 1st *m*) Terence Bertil Amorey, *b* 1956; *ed* Imperial Coll, London Univ (BSc).

Grandchildren of late Percy Addison Hayward Gethin, el son of late William St Lawrence Gethin, 2nd son of late Capt Richard Gethin, son of 5th baronet:—

Issue of late Lieut-Col Percy St Lawrence Gethin, MBE, *b* 1889, *d* 1959: *m* 1913, Margery, who *d* 1968, da of late James J. Cleverly, of Walfish Bay, Cape Province, S Africa:—

Patrick St Lawrence Cleverly, *b* 1914; *ed* Cheltenham; Major (ret) Roy Inniskilling Fusiliers; European War 1939-42 (wounded): *m* 1940, Dagmar May, only child of late N. H. Daniell, of Race View, Coonoor, S India, and has issue living, Rowene Margaret, *b* 1944: *m* 1970, Salvador Rodriguez-Perez, of Namanga, Orchard Lane, E Hendred, Wantage, Oxon, OX12 8JW, and has issue living, Marcus Lawrence *b* 1974, — Elaine Patricia, *b* 1946: *m* 1968, Paul Disbury Marsh (319 Beechgrove Drive, Scarborough, Ont, Canada M1E 4A2), and has issue living, Jeremy Stephen *b* 1973, Nicola Clare *b* 1970. *Address* – 4 Orchard Close, Berry Lane, East Hanney, nr Wantage, Oxon OX12 0JD. —— Sheelagh Grace *b* 1923: *m* 1947, James Wilson Lindsay, CBE, of 22 Wellington Drive, Kingston 6, Jamaica, W1, and has issue living, Ian Gethin, *b* 1951: *m* 1978, Ann Bettany, and has issue living, Keri Gethin *b* 1986, Emma Alexandra *b* 1978.

Grandchildren of late Maj Randolph George Gethin, MBE (infra):—
Issue of late Maj Desmond Richard le Poer Gethin, *b* 1919, *d* 1984: *m* 1950, Susan Frances (who *m* 2ndly, 1988, Maj W. P. Mead, of 2 Harewood Green, Lymington, Hants SO41 0TZ), da of Brig F. Talbot Baines:—

Martin Anthony (Cnwc y Morfol, Letterston, Haverfordwest, Dyfed SA6Z 5XE), *b* 1952; *ed* St Columba's Coll, and Seale Hayne Coll: *m* 1978, Christine Ann, da of A.F. Bates, of Purley, Bognor Regis, Sussex, and has issue living, Robert Lawrence, *b* 1984, — Jared Desmond, *b* 1986. —— Deirdre Anne, *b* 1951.

Granddaughter of late Capt George Gethin, son of late Richard Gethin, grandson of late John Gethin, 2nd son of 3rd baronet:—
Issue of late Maj Randolph George Gethin, MBE, *b* 1871, *d* 1945: *m* 1911, Georgina Mary, who *d* 1956, da of late Rev George Beresford Power (Power, Bt, colls, *cr* 1836):—

Kathleen Beatrix (Rincurran, Ardbrack, Kinsale, co Cork), *b* 1912.

Grandsons of late Francis Reid Gethin, 2nd son of Richard Gethin (ante):—
Issue of late Capt Richard Gethin, *b* 1886, *d* 1976: *m* 1st, 1927 (*m diss* 1953), Mary Hunter, who *d* 1972, el da of Willoughby James Bond, of Farragh, co Longford; 2ndly, 1953, Winifred Louise (Registry Cottage, High St, Limpsfield, Surrey), da of Frank James Hall, of Edgbaston, Birmingham:—

(By 1st *m*) Richard Reid (6 Saxons Acre, Warminster, Wilts), *b* 1931: *m* 1980 (*m diss* 1994), Brenda Elizabeth, da of late Walter George Treadwell of Sidcup, Kent. —— Alexander Willoughby (Holly House, Orchehill Av, Gerrards Cross), *b* 1935; *ed* Jesus Coll, Camb (MA): *m* 1964, Patricia, yr da of Alfred Sweeney of Gerrards Cross, and has issue living, Alexandra Mary (33 Sterndale Rd, W14), *b* 1965; *ed* St John's Coll, Camb (MA), — Frances Sheilagh, *b* (twin) 1965; *ed* Downing Coll, Camb: *m* 1991, Quintus R. C. L. Travis. —— Elizabeth Alice, *b* 1970.

Richard Gethin of Mallow, co Cork, *b* about 1615, was MP for Clonmell 1639-66, and Newton Limavady 1661-66. He received large grants of land from Charles II, upon the understanding that he should establish an English colony and erect manufactories. He received letters patent by which the lands of Cariglemleary were erected into a manor by the name of Gethinsgrott. The 1st wife of the 2nd baronet, Grace Norton, was remarkable for her talent and piety, and a monument to her memory is erected in Westminster Abbey. The 8th baronet, Col Sir Richard Walter St Lawrence Gethin, CMG, DSO, late RA, served in S Africa 1899-1901, and in 1914-18 War.

OSBORNE-GIBBES (GB) 1774, of Springhead, Barbados (Extinct 1940)

Sir PHILIP ARTHUR OSBORNE-GIBBES, 4th and last *Baronet.*

COLLATERAL BRANCH LIVING

Issue of late Philip Ernest Osborne-Gibbes, 7th son of 2nd baronet, *b* 1862, *d* 1934: *m* 1904:
Dulcie, *b* 19—: *m* 1932, W. E. Bendrey, of Lakemba, Sydney, NSW, and has issue living, Michael, *b* 1938.

GIBBONS (GB) 1752, of Stanwell Place, Middlesex

It is more agreeable coming from
a pious king

Sir WILLIAM EDWARD DORAN GIBBONS, 9th *Baronet*; *b* 13 Jan 1948; *s* his father, *Sir* JOHN EDWARD, 1982; *ed* Pangbourne, RNC Dartmouth and Bristol Univ (BSc); JP Portsmouth 1990: *m* 1972, Patricia Geraldine Archer, LLB, da of Roland Archer Howse, and has issue.

𝔄rms – Gules, a lion rampant or debruised by a bend argent charged with a torteau between two crosses patée-fitchée sable. ℭrest – A lion's jamb erased and erect gules, charged with a bezant and holding a cross as in the arms. *Residence* – 5 Yarborough Rd, Southsea, Hants P05 3DZ.

SON LIVING

CHARLES WILLIAM EDWIN, *b* 28 Jan 1983.

DAUGHTER LIVING

Joan, *b* 1980.

SISTERS LIVING

Charlotte Anne Wentworth, *b* 1939; a JP Avon: *m* 1963, Hylton Henry Bayntun-Coward (High Sheriff Avon 1993), of Dunkerton Grange, nr Bath, Avon, and has issue living, Edward William George, *b* 1966, — Jonathan Henry Alexander, *b* 1972, — Emma Louise Wentworth, *b* 1964, — Polly Jane Constance, *b* 1970. —— Jane *b* 1942: *m* 1966, Neville James Henry Grant, of 13 Glenluce Rd, Blackheath, SE3 7SD, and has issue living, Thomas Paul Wentworth, *b* 1969, — Alexander Hugh Wentworth, *b* 1973.

AUNT LIVING (*Daughter of 7th baronet*)

Vera Gladys, *b* 1908; is a JP: *m* 1927, Geoffrey Fenwick Jocelyn Cumberlege, DSO, MC, who *d* 1979, and has issue living, Geoffrey Mark *b* 1930: *m* 1954, Shirley Lancaster, and has issue living, Belinda *b* 1956, Elizabeth *b* 1959, Sarah *b* 1960, Patricia *b* 1962, — Patrick Francis Howard (Vuggles Farm, Newick, Lewes, Sussex), *b* 1933: *m* 1961, Julia Frances, CBE, DL (*cr Baroness Cumberlege* (Life Baroness) 1990), da of Dr Lambert Ulrich Camm, of Appleton, Newick, Sussex, and has issue living, *Hon* Christopher Mark *b* 1962, *Hon* Justin Francis *b* 1964, *Hon* Oliver Richard *b* 1968, — *Rev* Francis Richard, *b* 1941: *m* 1983, Christine Browne, — Elizabeth Blanche, *b* 1928: *m* 1951 (*m diss* 1977), Patrick B. Brown, and has issue living, Stephen *b* 1952, Nigel *b* 1954, Geoffrey *b* 1959, Caroline *b* 1955, Jennifer Catherine *b* 1965. *Residence* – 7 Boxes Lane, Horsted Keyes, W Sussex RH17 7EJ.

MOTHER LIVING

Mersa Wentworth, da of late Maj Edward Bayntun Grove Foster, of Warmwell, Dorset: *m* 1937 (*m diss* 1951), Sir John Edward Gibbons, 8th Bt, who *d* 1982. *Residence* – 30 Cromwell Cresc, Clifton, Bristol 8.

COLLATERAL BRANCHES LIVING

Grandchildren of late Capt Frederick Gibbons, brother of 5th baronet:—
Issue of late Capt Frederick Kenrick Colquhoun Gibbons, RN, *b* 1865, *d* 1954: *m* 1895, Edith Kapiolani, who *d* 1959, da of late A. T. Atkinson, of Honolulu, Hawaii:—
Marjorie Kapiolani, *b* 1896: *m* 1925, Lieut-Col Pillans Scarth Whitehead, OBE, RA, and has issue living, Belinda Kapiolani, *b* 1929: *m* 1956, Archibald Peter Brown, and has issue living, Archibald Stephen *b* 1958, William Lambert *b* 1964, Isobel Clare *b* 1960, Judith Margaret *b* (twin) 1964. —— Nancy Alatau, *b* 1907: *m* 1939, Hugo Wilhelm Runfelt, and has issue living, Anne Marie, *b* 1941. *Residence* – Bastad, Sweden.

Grandchildren of late Robert Gibbons (*b* 1866), only son of late Rev Robert Gibbons, eldest son of late Robert Kenrick Gibbons (infra):—
Issue of late Com Robert Reginald Gibbons, OBE, RN, *b* 1894, *d* 1959: *m* 1st, 1922, Olive (*m diss* 1930), da of William Blane, CBE; 2ndly, 1930 (*m diss* 1939), Ellery, da of late Maj-Gen Sir Amyatt Hull, of Beacon Downe, nr Exeter; 3rdly, 1939, Joan Winifred, who *d* 1983, da of F. S. Paterson, of Southborough, Kent:—
(By 3rd *m*), Robert John (The Poplars, 32 First Av, Eastchurch, Isle of Sheppey, Kent ME12 4JN), *b* 1944: *m* 1st, 1966 (*m diss* 1971), Pauline Elizabeth, da of Stanley Charles March, of 41 Deerswood Rd, West Green, Crawley, Sussex; 2ndly, 1976 (*m diss* 1980), Anne Marie, da of Charles Lundberg, of 19 Jeymer Drive, Greenford, Middx; 3rdly, 1986, Elizabeth Jean, da of late W/Cdr Norman Henry Carrier, of 16 Russell Hill, Purley, Surrey, and has issue living (by 3rd *m*), Pippa Christine, *b* 1987. —— Susan, *b* 1941: *m* 1959, Dennis Gordon Pollard, of 27 School Lane, Ashurstwood, E Grinstead, Sussex RH19 3QW, and has issue living, Peter Dennis, *b* 1964, — Lesley Susan, *b* 1960: *m* 1978, Edward John Hart, of 30 Stanmore Grove, Kirkstall, Leeds LS4 2RG, and has issue living, Jennifer Susan *b* 1979, — Janet May, *b* 1969: *m* 1989, Andrew Paul Brander, of 5 Betchley Close, East Grinstead, W Sussex, son of Anthony Brander, of 10 Garden Close, East Grinstead, and has issue living, Christopher Iain *b* 1993, Emma Louise *b* 1990.

Grandchildren of late Sir William Gibbons, KCB, yst son of Robert Kenrick Gibbons, 2nd son of Robert Gibbons, 4th son of 2nd baronet:
Issue of late Sir William Kenrick Gibbons, CB, *b* 1876, *d* 1957: *m* 1915, Aileen Margaret Dale, who *d* 1969, da of George J. E. Trotter:—
Diana Maynard (Bernardene, The Green, Letchmore Heath, Watford, Herts), *b* 1916. —— Priscilla Doreen, *b* 1918. —— June Cecilia, *b* 1926.
Issue of late Lieut-Col Edward Stephen Gibbons, DSO, Duke of Cambridge's Own (Middlesex Regt), *b* 1883, *ka* 1918: *m* 1914, Annie Macgregor, who *d* 1968, da of late John Lyle, of Finnart House, Weybridge:—
Elisabeth Margaret, *b* 1915: *m* 1936, Lieut-Cdr John Edgar Burstall, RN, who *d* 1979, and has issue living, Mark Stephen, *b* 1945, — Elisabeth Ann, *b* 1937, — Gillian Margaret, *b* 1939. *Residence* – The Garden House, Orcheston, Salisbury, Wilts.

Grandson of late Lieut-Col Edward Stephen Gibbons, DSO (ante):—
Issue of late Lieut Cdr John William Gibbons, RN, *b* 1917, *d* 1993: *m* 1st, 1940 (*m diss* 1947), Alix, da of late Bertram Lenox-Simpson, of Forta Fayre, Havelet, Guernsey; 2ndly, 1964, Mrs Mary Lammin Stone (Flat 4, Lions Hall, St Swithun St, Winchester, Hants), yst da of late G. E. Woof:—

(By 1st *m*) Alan Clive, *b* 1941.

Grandchildren of late Lt-Col William Barton Gibbons, 3rd son of late Robert Gibbons (ante):—
Issue of late John Abel Gibbons, *b* 1854, *d* 1894: *m* 1884, Katharine Alice, who *d* 1937, da of Joseph Seymour Salaman, formerly of 143 Sutherland Avenue, W:—
Dorothy Margaret Maxwell: *m* 1914, John Brook (in Imperial Yeo during S African War, and as a Gunner in Canadian Field Artillery during European War), and has issue living, John Burbridge (1394 Mount Pleasant, Toronto, Canada), *b* 1914; is a Chemical Engineer: *m* 1940, Joanne Price, of Cleveland, Ohio, USA, and has issue living, David Jeremy *b* 1947, Calvin Price *b* 1955, Martha Lyn *b* 1944, — Philip Roy, DFC, *b* 1918; is Fl Lt Roy Canadian Air Force, and an Architect; 1939-45 War (DFC): *m* 1949, Sonia Dixon, of Bournemouth, and has issue living, Michael Brian *b* 1951, Gregory Laurence *b* 1953, Matthew Ian *b* 1959, Deborah Jane *b* 1955, Dinah Louise, *b* 1957, — June Rosemary, *b* 1920: *m* 1940, Charles H. Doty, of 49 Huntly St, Toronto, Canada, and has issue living, Stephen Charles *b* 1942, Susan Jane *b* 1944: *m* 19—,　　　　　Jacobsen, of St Anne de Sorel, Quebec, Barbara Jane *b* 1949.

Grandchildren of late John Crookenden de Courcy Gibbons (infra):—
Issue of late John Hayton Gibbons, *b* 1909, *d* 1963: *m* 1945, Phyllis (who *m* 2ndly, 19—, Donald Sheehan, of 24 Springdale Rd, Killara, NSW), da of　　　　:—
John William, *b* 1954. —— Victoria Hayton, *b* 1948. —— Elizabeth, *b* 1951.

Grandchildren of late Lieut-Col Frederick FitzRoy Gibbons, el son of late Lieut-Col William Barton Gibbons (ante):—
Issue of late John Crookenden de Courcy Gibbons, *b* 1874, *d* 1944: *m* 1907, Gladys Russell Jones, who *d* 1984:—
Marjorie Mary, *b* 1922: *m* 1944, Clive Stanley Willey, and has issue living, Lyn Gladys, *b* 1947, — Rae Marjorie, *b* (twin) 1947, — Sue Phillis, *b* 1951. *Residence* – 6 Maple Road, Melrose, Mass, USA, 02176.
Issue of late Charles Coulthurst Gibbons, *b* 1884, *d* (April) 1926: *m* 1st, 19— (*m diss* 1923), Muriel Tidswell, who *d* 1949; 2ndly, 1924, Constance Winifred, who *d* 1976, da of David George Edward Wilkinson:—
(By 2nd *m*) Peta Jane Coulthurst (*posthumous*), *b* (Nov) 1926: *m* 1957, James William Edward Brown. *Residence* – Broadacres, 2 St John's Rise, Woking, Surrey.

Granddaughter of late Charles Kenrick Gibbons, 3rd son of late Lt-Col William Barton Gibbons (ante); *b* 1856, *d* 1918: *m* 1890, Emily Hinds, who *d* 1958, da of late Charles F Corbin, of The Beacon, Surbiton:—
Issue of late Charles William Kenrick Gibbons, *b* 1893, *d* 1969: *m* 1922. Winifred Maud Ethel, who *d* 1966, da of late George Eccles, of Mayaro, Trinidad:—
Rose Margaret Emily (80 Surbiton Hill Park, Surbiton), *b* 1926; late Lt QARANC.

Granddaughter of late Charles Kenrick Gibbons (ante):—
Issue of late Edward John Kenrick, *b* 1900, *d* 1982; Town Clerk of Falmouth 1946-65: *m* 1938, Marguerite Leslie, who *d* 1977, da of late Nicholas Eyare Toke, of Penfillan House, Folkestone:—
Carol Leslie Kenrick (Hillside, Harlequin Lane, Crowborough, Sussex), *b* 1939.
The 1st baronet was Speaker of the House of Assembly, Barbados, and the 2nd baronet sat as MP for Wallingford. The 5th baronet was High Sheriff of Middlesex in 1891.

GIBSON (UK) 1926, of Great Warley, co Essex

Rev Fr Sir DAVID GIBSON, 4th *Baronet*; *b* 18 July 1922; *s* his father, *Sir* ACKROYD HERBERT, 1975.
Residence – St Therese's Court, 138 Raglan Rd, Devonport, S Devon PL1 4NQ.

SISTER LIVING

Joan Ingerid, *b* 1919: *m* 1942, Ronald Coad, of Trewhella, Cury, Helston, Cornwall.

DAUGHTER LIVING OF SECOND BARONET

Diana Lilian, *b* 1915: *m* 1943, Maj Anthony Peter Howorth Greenly, late R Berks Regt, of Dominion Beach 70, Ctra Cadiz KM 161, Estepona (Malaga), Spain, son of late Lt-Col Sir John Henry Maitland Greenly, KCMG, CBE, and has issue living, Richard Anthony Howorth (The Old Farmhouse, Vernham St, Vernham Dean, Andover, Hants SP11 0EL), *b* 1948: *m* 1981, Belinda Audrey, yst da of late (Richard) Rodney Lockett, MC, of Hall of Aberuthven, Auchterarder, Perthshire, and has issue living, Thomas Richard Howorth *b* 1983, Jack David Howorth *b* 1985, Sam James Howorth *b* 1988, — Sarah Mary, *b* 1947: *m* 1968, Capt Charles Edric Holdsworth Hunt, Coldstream Guards (*see* B Forester, colls), of Haworth House, Kintbury, nr Newbury, Berks RG15 0TP, — Dorian Isobel, *b* 1951: *m* 1976, Gerald Angus Campbell, of Oxenbridge Cottage, Readers Lane, Iden, E Sussex, and has issue (*see* Style, Bt, colls).
The 1st baronet, Sir Herbert Gibson, was a Solicitor, a member of the legal firm of Deacon & Co of 9 Great St Helens, EC, and Pres of Law So 1925 (Centenary year).

GIBSON (UK) 1931, of Linconia, and of Faccombe, co Southampton

Rev Sir CHRISTOPHER HERBERT GIBSON, CP, 4th *Baronet*; *b* 17 July 1948; *s* his father, *Sir* CHRISTOPHER HERBERT, 1994; ordained priest 1975.
Address – Holy Cross, Buenos Aires, Argentina.

SISTERS LIVING

Penelope Lake, *b* 1946. —— Pamela Dorothy Madeleine, *b* 1950; MD: *m* 1973, Julio Cesar Muzio, and has issue living, Paula, *b* 1976. —— Dawn, *b* 1953: *m* 1972, Daniel Carreras, of Apt 3-1026 Commercial Drive, Vancouver, BC V5L 3W9, Canada, and has issue living, Diego, *b* 1973, — Marie Noël, *b* 1975.

WIDOW LIVING OF THIRD BARONET

LILIAN LAKE (*Lady Gibson*), da of late Dr George Byron Young, of Colchester, Essex: *m* 1941, Sir Christopher Herbert Gibson, 3rd Bt, who *d* 1994.

COLLATERAL BRANCHES LIVING

Grandchildren of late Clement Herbert Gibson (infra):—
Issue of late Geoffrey Gibson, *b* 1934, *d* 1987: *m* 1964, Anne-Marie (Juncal 2174, ler peso "14", 1125, Buenos Aires, Argentina), da of late Martin de Selincourt:—
ROBERT HERBERT, *b* 21 Dec 1966: *m* 1992, Catherine Grace, da of Ernest William Pugh. —— Alexander Herbert, *b* 1973.
—— Clemency Rose, *b* 1968.

Issue of late Clement Herbert Gibson, 2nd son of 1st baronet, *b* 1900, *d* 1976: *m* 1933, Marjorie Julia who *ä* 1982, da of late Robert Anderson:—
Clement Herbert (Doucegrove Farm, Northiam, Sussex), *b* 1936: *m* 1966, Mrs Barbara Peel. —— Thomas (Westwell Manor, Westwell, Burford, Oxon), *b* 1943: *m* 1966, Anthea Fiona Catherine, da of late Lt-Col G. A. Palmer, RE, and has issue living, Miles Cosmo Archdale, *b* 1968, — Sebastian Thomas Maximilian, *b* 1972, — Benjamin Hugh George, *b* 1973.

Issue of late Gerald Herbert Gibson, 3rd son of 1st baronet, *b* 1902, *d* 1951: *m* 1924, Ursula Marion Wilson, of San Martin 296, Buenos Aires, Argentina, da of late W. Greenwell-Robson:—
Roy Herbert, *b* 1933: *m* 1970, Georgina Odette, da of Santiago Even, and has issue living, Valerie, *b* 1971. —— Diana Madeleine, *b* 1926.

Issue of late Cosmo Livingstone Herbert Gibson, yst son of 1st baronet, *b* 1904, *d* 1964: *m* 1937, Josephine Austin, da of James Austin Brown:—
Herbert, *b* 1938: *m* 1964, Margaret Jean, da of John Bruce Donald, and has issue living, James Bruce, *b* 1965, — Herbert Mark, *b* 1966, — Josephine Jean, *b* 1966, — Michel, *b* 1969, — Madeleine, *b* 1972. —— Cosmo David, *b* 1944. —— Noel Gerald *b* 1954. —— David Hope, *b* 1956: *m* 1989, Maria Pia Cullen, and has issue living, Michael, *b* 1992, — Jennifer *b* 1990. —— Yvonne, *b* 1939: *m* 1962, Baron Gaston Carlos Perkins Peers de Niewburgh, and has issue living, Thomas Gaston, *b* 1964: *m* 1993, Gianina, da of Nestor Koaper, and has issue living, Agustina *b* 1994, — Enrique Gaston, *b* 1968: *m* 1989, Soledad Bernal, and has issue living, Gaston Enrique *b* 1990, — Yvonne Cecilia, *b* 1967. —— Roxana, *b* 1943: *m* 1963, Eduardo Francisco Pampillo, and has issue living, Francisco Severiano, *b* 1980, — Veronica Roxana, *b* 1963: *m* 1990, Aaron Hodari, and has issue living, Juana *b* 1991, — Edwina Alexandra, *b* 1965, — Victoria Patricia, *b* 1968: *m* 1988, Pablo Barbieri, and has issue living, Martin *b* 1989, Agustina *b* 1993, — Silvina Gloria, *b* 1975.

Sir Herbert Gibson, KBE, 1st Bt (son of Thomas Gibson, of Edinburgh), was a landowner and merchant in the Argentine Republic and Chm of Inter-Allied Commission for Purchase of Cereals in Argentina and Uruguay 1917-19. Sir Christopher Herbert, 3rd Bt, was Manager of Leach's Argentine Estates 1946-51, later a Design Draughtsman, Tea Plantation Manager, and Poultry Farmer.

Gibson-Craig-Carmichael, see Carmichael.

GILBEY (UK) 1893, of Elsenham Hall, Essex

Sir (WALTER) GAVIN GILBEY, 4th *Baronet*; *b* 14 April 1949; *s* his father, *Sir* (WALTER) DEREK, 1991; *ed* Eton: *m* 1st, 1980 (*m diss* 1984), Mary, da of late William E. E. Pacetti, of Florida, USA; 2ndly, 1984, Anna, da of Edmund Prosser, of Birmingham.

Arms – Gules, a fesse nebulèe or, in chief a horse rampant between two estoiles, and the like in base, all of the last. **Crest** – In front of a tower proper, issuant from the battlements thereof a dragon's head gules, a fleur-de-lis or, all between two ostrich feathers argent.
Residence – 8201 SW 115 St, Miami, Florida 33156, USA.

SISTER LIVING

Camilla Elizabeth, *b* 1953: *m* 1990, Christopher St John Frederick, elder son of Maj Sir Charles Boscawen Frederick, 10th Bt.

HALF GREAT-UNCLE LIVING (*Son of 2nd baronet*)

WALTER ANTHONY, Member of the House of Keys (Ballacallin Mooar, Crosby, Marown, Isle of Man), *b* 26 Feb 1935; assumed by deed poll 1958 the name of Walter Anthony in lieu of that of Anthony Walter: *m* 1964, Jenifer Mary, da of James Timothy Noel Price, of Sunnyside House, Victoria Rd, Douglas, Isle of Man (O'Brien, Bt), and has issue living, Walter Anthony *b* 1966, — Caroline Anne, *b* 1967, — and an adopted da, Sarah Elizabeth, *b* 1969.

WIDOW LIVING OF THIRD BARONET

ELIZABETH MARY (*Dowager Lady Gilbey*), da of Col Keith Gordon Campbell, DSO, of Standen House, Newport, Isle of Wight: *m* 1948, Sir (Walter) Derek Gilbey, 3rd Bt, who *d* 1991. *Residence* – Grovelands, Wineham, nr Henfield, W Sussex BN5 9AW.

Issue of late Arthur Sebastian Gilbey, *b* 1919, *d* 1964: *m* 1947 Jennifer Beryl (GOULD), who *d* 1991, da of late William Nigel Ernle Bruce (*see* Bruce, Bt, *cr* 1628, colls, 1990 Edn):—
Christopher Sebastian Bruce (Rosewood, Hanging Langford, Salisbury, Wilts), *b* 1955: *m* 1980, Medina, da of Sir Reginald Bennett, of 30 Strand on the Green, W4 3PH, and has issue living, Jasper Sebastian Christopher, *b* 1981, — Sophie, *b* 1983. — Patricia, *b* 1949: *m* 1973, Andrew Michael Talbot Millar, of Woodlands Cottage, Brixton Hill, Benson, Oxon (Cockburn, Bt, colls), and has issue living, Alexander Darracot, *b* 1976, — Olivia Rosalind, *b* 1977. — Linda (*Hon Mrs Michael C. Gilbey*), *b* 1952: *m* 1971, Hon Michael Christopher Gilbey, of Pheasant's Ridge, Hambleden, Henley-on-Thames, Oxon RG9 6SD, and has issue living (*see* B Vaux of Harrowden).
Issue of late Capt Giles Milner Gilbey, MC, 12th R Lancers, *b* 1923, *d* 1983: *m* 1962, Diana Mary (RYERSON) (Flat 11, 53 Rutland Gate, SW7; Box 42, Colebrook, Conn 06021, USA), da of W. E. Melville-Cook, of Parkstone, Dorset:—
Lisa Maria, *b* 1965.

Issue of late Rupert Sydney Gilbey, yr son of late Arthur Nockolds Gilbey (ante), *b* 1900, *d* 1959: *m* 1927 Anne Penelope, who *d* 1970, da of late E. S. Prince:—
Simon Rupert, *b* 1929; *ed* Eton; formerly Capt 8th Hussars: *m* 1st, 1953 (*m diss* 1966), Chloë Rio, who *d* 1966, el da of late Col Christopher Rawlinson Cadge, of Ballygate House, Beccles, Suffolk; 2ndly, 1966, Mrs Sara Jane Twiston Davies, da of late Augustus Frederick Coryton, of Goleigh Farm House, Greatham, Hants, and has issue living, (by 1st *m*) Rupert John, *b* 1960, — Juliet Rio, *b* 1955: *m* 1979, John Michael Denison Bidwell, of Hackwood Farm, Robertsbridge, Sussex, and has issue living, James Denison *b* 1981, Patrick Simon *b* 1983, — Rachel Anne, *b* 1957: *m* 1981, Jonathan Dunn, of Hackwood Farm, Robertsbridge, Sussex, el son of A. Dunn, of 16 Pelham Place, SW7, and has issue, Thomas Alan *b* 1982, Imogen Chloë *b* 1985, Jessica Rose *b* 1988, — (by 2nd *m*) Lisa, *b* 1967. *Residence* – Mains of Soilzarie, Bridge of Cally, Blairgowrie, Perthshire. —— Sarah Anne *b* 1933: *m* 1953, Patrick Philip Bagshawe, and has issue living, Anthony William Newton, *b* 1956: *m* 1980, Alison Katrina, da of John Auld Macdonald, — Jasper Philip Adam, *b* 1960: *m* 1986, Chloë Mary Johnson, and has issue living, Samuel Oscar *b* 1986, Jessica Albinia *b* 1988, — Charlotte Anne, *b* 1954: *m* 1st, 1982 (*m diss* 1984), Stephen A. Buckle, son of late Lorne Buckle, of Ste Agathe des Monts, Quebec, Canada; 2ndly, 1989 (*m diss* 1991), Robert Bringhurst. *Residence* – Pond House, Meysey Hampton, Cirencester, Glos.
The 1st baronet, Sir Walter Gilbey, fifth son of late Henry Gilbey, of Bishop's Stortford, Herts, served in Pay Depart during Crimean War 1854-6; and was sometime Chm of W. & A. Gilbey, Ltd, wine merchants and distillers, of The Pantheon, Oxford Street, W; also a well-known Agriculturalist and Stock-breeder, and a Past Pres of Smithfield Club, of Hackney Horse So, of the Shire Horse So, Roy Agricultural So, and of Hunters' Improvement So. The 2nd baronet, Sir (Henry) Walter, was Chm of W. & A. Gilbey, Ltd, and a prominent figure in the horse-breeding and sporting worlds.

GILLETT (UK) 1959, of Bassishaw Ward, City of London

Truth conquers all things

Sir ROBIN DANVERS PENROSE GILLETT, GBE, RD, 2nd *Baronet*; *b* 9 Nov 1925; *s* his father, Sir (SYDNEY) HAROLD, MC, 1976; *ed* Nautical Coll, Pangbourne, and Hill Crest Sch; Hon DSc London 1976; 1943-45 Cadet with Canadian Pacific Steamships Ltd in Mediterranean and N Atlantic; Master Mariner 1951, Staff Comdr 1957; Elder Brother of Trinity House, Snr Warden of Hon Co of Master Mariners 1971 and Master 1979-80; Pres and FInstAM 1980-84, Vice-Pres 1985-94; Fellow and Founder Member of Nautical Inst; FInstD; KStJ; Common Councilman City of London 1965-69, Alderman 1969, Sheriff 1973-74, HM Lieut 1976, and Lord Mayor 1976-77; a Dir Wigham Poland Home Ltd, and Wigham Poland Management Sers Ltd 1965-86; Underwriting Member of Lloyd's; Dir St Katharine Haven Ltd 1979, Chm 1990-93; Pres National Waterways Transport Assocn 1979-83, RLSS UK Pres 1978-82, Dep Commonwealth Pres since 1982; Vice-Pres of City of London Red Cross, Vice-Chm Port of London Authority 1979-84, Chm of Lord Mayor's Flood Relief Fund, and of Princess Victoria's Distress Fund, Vice-Pres of City Centre St John's Ambulance, Trustee of Nat Maritime Museum, and of St Paul's Cathedral Trust; Lay Vice Patron Missions to Seamen; Chm and a Gov of Pangbourne Coll 1978-92; Council of Royal Coll of Music, FRCM 1991; Vice-Pres KGFS since 1993; Hon Comdr RNR (RD 1965); Gentleman Usher of the Purple Rod since 1985; Officer of the Order of Leopard of Zaire, Cdr of Order of Dannebrog of Denmark, Order of Johan Sedia Mahkota of Malaysia, Grand Cross of Municipal Order or Merit of Lima; Gold Medal of Administrative Management Soc (USA); GBE (Civil) 1976: *m* 1950, Elizabeth Marion Grace, el da of late John Findlay, JP, of Busby House, Lanarks, and has issue.

Arms – In front of a ship's helm proper, an early nineteenth century waistcoat azure semée de lys and purfled or on a chief of the second between two estoiles a balance of the first. **Crest** – A grey horse's head and neck erased proper gorged with a coronet composed of six fleur-de-lys affixed to a circlet and chained or.
Residence – 4 Fairholt St, Knightsbridge, SW7 1EQ. *Clubs* – City Livery, Royal Yacht Squadron, Royal London Yacht Club (Commodore 1984-85), City Livery Yacht Club (Admiral), St Katherine Yacht Club (Admiral).

SONS LIVING

NICHOLAS DANVERS PENROSE (44 Back St, Ashwell, Herts SG7 5PE), *b* 24 Sept 1955; *ed* Durlston Ct Sch, Pangbourne Coll, and Imperial Coll, London (BSc), ARCS, Project Manager, British Aerospace (Dynamics) Ltd; Liveryman Worshipful Co of Coachmakers 1982: *m* 1987, Haylie, elder da of Dennis Brooks, of Abertawe, W Glam. —— Christopher John (Charlton, North Rd, Chorleywood, Herts WD3 5LE) *b* 1958; *ed* Durlston Ct Sch, Pangbourne Coll, and King's Coll, Camb (MA), Roy Coll of Music, Nat Opera Studio 1982-83; Opera singer; Liveryman of Worshipful Co of Musicians 1981: *m* 1984, Julia A., yr da of late W. H. Holmes, of Tunbridge Wells, Kent, and has issue living, Adam Holmes, *b* 1989, — Tessa Holmes, *b* 1987.

Sir (Sydney) Harold Gillett, MC, 1st Bt, son of William Henry Gillett, of Highgate, N6, was Lord Mayor of London 1958-59.

GILMOUR (UK) 1897, of Lundin and Montrave, Parishes of Largo and Scoonie, co Fife

Not the pen, but custom

Sir JOHN EDWARD GILMOUR, DSO, TD, 3rd *Baronet*; *b* 24 Oct 1912; *s* his father, the *Rt Hon Sir* JOHN, GCVO, DSO, LLD, MP, 1940; *ed* Eton, and Trin Hall, Camb; Dundee Sch of Economics; Lt-Col Fife and Forfar Yeo 1947-51; Brevet Col 1952; Hon Col Highland Yeo RAC, TAVR 1971-75; JP and DL for Fife, Vice-Lieut 1979, and Lord-Lieut 1980-87; Lord High Commr to Gen Assembly of Church of Scotland 1982-83; Capt Queen's Body Guard for Scotland (R Co of Archers); NW Europe 1944-45 (wounded, DSO); MP for E Div of Fife (*C*) 1961-79, and Chm Conservative and Unionist Party in Scot 1965-67, DSO 1945: *m* 1941, Ursula Mabyn, da of late Frank Oliver Wills, of Cote Lodge, Westbury-on-Trym and has issue.

Arms – Argent, on a chevron between three trefoils slipped vert, as many bugle horns of the first. **Crest** – A hand fessewise couped at the wrist proper, holding a pen argent.
Seat – Montrave, Leven, Fife KY8 5NZ.

SONS LIVING

JOHN (Balcormo Mains, Leven, Fife KY8 5QF), *b* 15 July 1944; *ed* Eton, and North of Scotland Coll of Agriculture; Capt Fife and Forfar Yeo/Scottish Horse; MFH (Fife) since 1972; DL for Fife 1988: *m* 1967, Valerie Jardine, da of late George Walker Russell, and has issue living, (John) Nicholas, *b* 1970, — Patrick George William, *b* 1980, — Corinna Valerie, *b* 1972, — (Victoria) Juliet, *b* 1975. ——Andrew Frank (Pratis House, Leven, Fife), *b* 1947; *ed* Eton and West of Scotland Coll of Agric; Queens Body Guard for Scotland (Roy Co of Archers); Member of North East Fife District Council since 1984; JP 1984: *m* 1971, Mary Speirs, SSStJ, adopted da of late Sir Henry Campbell de la Poer Beresford-Peirse, CB, 5th Bt, and has issue living, Andrew Robert Campbell, *b* 1972, — David Edward, *b* 1974.

SISTER LIVING

Dame Anne Margaret, DBE, *b* 1909; Chm of Roy Free Hosp 1968-74; Vice-Chm of Exec Cttee BRCS (ret 1976), a Member Area Health Authority, Camden and Islington, of Council for Professions Supplementary to Medicine, and of Council of Florence Nightingale Hosp, Vice-Pres of Roy Coll of Nursing, and a DStJ; Dir and Commr for Middle East, British Red Cross and St John War Org 1943-45; CBE (Civil) 1945, DBE (Civil) 1957: *m* 1932, Lt-Cdr John Reginald Bryans, RN (ret), who *d* 1990, and has issue living, John Patrick Gilmour (Hatton, Leven, Fife), *b* 1933; late Lt-Cdr RN; FRGS: *m* 1st, 1959 (*m diss* 1970), Rosemary Ann, da of late Group Capt H. G. Wheeler, RAF; 2ndly, 1972, Patricia Mary, da of late W. A. MacPherson, and has issue living (by 1st *m*), Anthony James Gilmour *b* 1960, Edward John Gilmour *b* 1963, Robert Henry Charles *b* 1965, (by 2nd *m*) Lucy Anne *b* 1977. *Residence* – 57 Elm Park House, Elm Park Gdns, SW10.

HALF-SISTER LIVING

Daphne Mary, *b* 1922: *m* 1943, Group Cap Everett Large Baudoux, DSO, DFC, RCAF (ret), and has had issue, Michael Alfred, *b* 1951: *m* 1984, Carol Anne Hingley, and has issue living, Katherine Anne *b* 1986, — Patricia Mary, *b* 1944: *m* 1966, Raymond Wayne Docker, and *d* 1987, leaving issue, Thomas Everett *b* 1970, Philip Ian *b* 1972, — Sharon Jane, *b* 1948: *m* 1974, J. Lewis MacKay, and has issue living, James Jeffrey *b* 1978, Amy Kathleen *b* 1976. *Residence* – Big Island, Merigomish, Nova Scotia.

COLLATERAL BRANCH LIVING

Issue of late Douglas Gilmour, 5th son of 1st baronet, *b* 1889, *ka* 1916: *m* 1910, Doris Hyacinth, who *d* 1977, da of late Charles Paget Hooker, of Cirencester, son of late Sir Joseph Dalton Hooker, OM, GCSI, CB:—
Doris Pamela Yvonne, *b* 1914: *m* 1940, Maj Philip Donald Howitt Marshall, late Middlesex Regt, of Bowhayes, Chetnole, Sherborne, Dorset DT9 6PE, and has issue living, Nicholas Charles Gilmour (Glanhonddu House, Llandefaelog Fach, Brecon, Powys), *b* 1950: *m* 1st, 1974 (*m diss* 1983), Rosemary Anne, da of late Maj W. J. Kingdom, RA; *m* 2ndly, 1988, Fiona Anne, elder da of Christopher Anthony William Leng (*see* Ly Herries of Terregles), and has issue living (by 1st *m*), Emily Sarah *b* 1978, Harriet *b* 1980, (by 2nd *m*) Douglas James Gilmour *b* 1990, Scarlett Josephine *b* 1992, — Sarah Gilmour, *b* 1948: *m* 1976, Christopher David Legge, of The Old House, Kingsclere, Newbury, Berks, and has issue living, Louisa Rebecca *b* 1977, Octavia Christina, *b* 1980, Henrietta, *b* 1984, — Teresa Gilmour, *b* 1953: *m* 1987, Michael Denison Gale Way, of Upper Park House, Upper Park Rd, Kingston, Surrey KT2 5LD, and has issue living, Henry Charles *b* 1990. —— Myrtle (The Grange, Thornford, Sherborne, Dorset), *b* 1915: *m* 1st, 1938, John William Hathorn, Flying Officer, RAF (Reserve), who *d* (killed in a flying accident whilst on active ser) 1940; 2ndly, 1940 (*m diss* 1949), Capt Cecil Horace Power Bellwood, Gloucestershire Regt; 3rdly, 1949 (*m diss* 1952), Col Patrick Curran Perfect, late KOSB; 4thly, 1991, Lt-Col Henry Mesnard (Tim) Bromilow.
Sir John Gilmour, 1st Bt (el son of Allan Gilmour, of Lundin and Montrave, Fife, and South Walton, Renfrewshire), was a JP and DL for co Fife. The 2nd Bt, the Rt Hon Sir John, GCVO, DSO, PC, sat as MP for Renfrewshire, E Div (*C*) 1910-18, and for Glasgow, Pollok Div 1918-40, and was Junior Lord of the Treasury 1921-2, Sec for Scotland 1924-6, Sec of State for Scotland 1926-9, Min of Agriculture and Fisheries 1931-32, Sec of State for Home Depart 1932-5, and Min of Shipping 1939-40.

GLADSTONE (UK) 1846, of Fasque and Balfour, Kincardineshire

By fidelity and valour

Sir (ERSKINE) WILLIAM GLADSTONE, 7th *Baronet*; *b* 29 Oct 1925; *s* his father, (*Sir*) CHARLES ANDREW, 1968; *ed* Eton, and Ch Ch Oxford (MA); Lord Lieut of Clwyd since 1985; Assist Master at Eton Coll 1951-61, and Headmaster of Lancing Coll 1961-69; Chief Scout of the UK and Overseas Branches 1972-82; 1939-45 War as Sub-Lt RNVR: *m* 1962, Rosamund Anne, da of late Maj Robert Alexander Hambro, and has issue.

Arms – Argent, a savage's head affrontée, distilling drops of blood and wreathed about the temples with holly proper within an orle fleury gules, all within eight martlets in orle sable. **Crest** – Issuant from a wreath of holly proper, a demi-griffin sable, supporting between the claws a sword, the blade enfiled by a wreath of oak also proper.
Residences – Hawarden Castle, Clwyd CH5 3PB; Fasque, Laurencekirk, Kincardineshire.

SONS LIVING

CHARLES ANGUS (Glen Dye, nr Banchory, Kincardineshire), *b* 11 April 1964; *ed* Eton, and Worcester College, Oxford: *m* 1988, Caroline M., only da of Sir Derek Morison David Thomas, KCMG, HM Amb to Italy, and has issue living, Jack William, *b* 28 July 1989, — India Kate, *b* 1991, — Tara Rosamund, *b* 1992. —— Robert Nicolas, *b* 1968: *m* 1993, Nicola L., eldest da of Forbes Playfair, of Bale, Norfolk, and has issue living, Rosie Lindsay, *b* 1993.

DAUGHTER LIVING

Victoria Frances, *b* 1967: *m* 1991, Hugo C. Merison, son of Paul Merison, of Chiddingly, Sussex, and has issue living, Elinor Penelope, *b* 1994.

BROTHERS LIVING

Peter (Fasque, Fettercairn, Laurencekirk, Kincardineshire), *b* 1928; *ed* Eton, and Ch Ch Oxford (MA): *m* 1972, Jean Loveday, da of Allan Roy, of The Hawes, Ainsdale, Southport, and has issue living, Tom Xenophon, *b* 1973, — Allan Fergus, *b* 1978, — Cleodie Selina, *b* 1975. —— James Francis (West End, Hawarden Castle, Clwyd), *b* 1941; *ed* Eton, and Ch Ch, Oxford: *m* 1st, 1963, Janet Barbara, who *d* 1970, da of late Rudi Schumacher, of Kenya; 2ndly, 1972, Hon Josephine Jones, da of Baron Elwyn Jones (Life Baron), and has issue living (by 1st *m*), Melissa Janet, *b* 1970, — (by 2nd *m*) Andrew Elwyn, *b* 1974. —— Andrew Victor (Uphill House, Ponsworthy, Newton Abbot, Devon), *b* 1945; *ed* Eton; FRICS: *m* 1975, Nicola Anne, da of late Lt-Col M. L. D. Skewes-Cox, of Uphill House, Ponsworthy, Devon, and has had issue, Isla Sophie, *b* 1979, — Clova Felicity, *b* 1982.

SISTERS LIVING

Penelope Anne, *b* 1930. —— Sara Helen, *b* 1943: *m* 1970, Philip John Young, of East End Farm, Ringstead, Hunstanton, Norfolk, and has issue living, James Edward, *b* 1971, — John Anthony, *b* 1974.

COLLATERAL BRANCH LIVING

Issue of late Capt Stephen Deiniol Gladstone, MC, brother of 5th and 6th baronets, *b* 1891, *d* 1965: *m* 1923, Mary St Clair, who *d* 1976, da of Lt-Col Charles Davidson, of Aboyne:—
Stephen Charles (Florance House, Groombridge, Tunbridge Wells, Kent), *b* 1924; *ed* Eton; late Lt Welsh Guards: *m* 1952, Susan Valerie, da of John Lindsay Guise, of Woodhaie, Cross in Hand, Heathfield, Sussex, and has had issue, †Stephen James, *b* 1955, *d* 19—, — Clare Elizabeth, *b* 1953, — Catherine Mary, *b* 1959, — Juliet Anne (Pinewood Hill, Wormley, Godalming, Surrey), *b* 1960, — Victoria Jane, *b* 1963. —— John Neville (Old Buckhurst, Mark Beech, Kent), *b* 1932; *ed* Eton: *m* 1959, Jane Gordon, da of late Maj-Gen Robert Alexander Stephen, CB, CBE, MD, ChM, FRCS, QHS, and has issue living, David Gordon William, *b* 1960, — Peter Robert John, *b* 1963, — Claire Jane, *b* 1962. —— Mary Felicity, *b* 1926. —— Anne (Pinewood Hill, Wormley, Godalming, Surrey), *b* 1928: *m* 1957, Nigel John Robson, who *d* 1993, and has issue living, Andrew Stephen, *b* 1958: *m* 1982, Fiona, da of Jeremy Veasey, of Cinder Farm, N Chailey, Sussex, — William Nigel, *b* 1960, — Hugo John, *b* 1962.

The 1st baronet assumed, by Roy licence, the surname of Gladstone in lieu of his patronymic Gladstones. Sir Thomas, 2nd Bt, sat as MP for Queensborough (C) 1830, for Portarlington 1832-5, for Leicester 1835-7, and for Ipswich 1842, and was Lord-Lieut of Kincardineshire. Sir John Evelyn, 4th Bt, was a JP and DL for Wilts (High Sheriff 1897). Rt Hon William Ewart Gladstone, Prime Min 1868-74, 1880-85, 1886 and 1892-94, was yst son of 1st baronet, and grandfather of 5th and 6th baronets.

Glen-Coats, see Coats.

GLYN (GB) 1759, of Ewell, Surrey, and (GB) 1800, of Gaunt's House

Firm to my trust

Sir RICHARD LINDSAY GLYN, 10th *Baronet*, of Ewell, and 6th *Baronet*, of Gaunt's House; *b* 3 Aug 1943; *s* his father, *Col Sir* RICHARD HAMILTON, OBE, TD, 1980; *ed* Eton; late 2nd Lt 1st Bn R Hampshire Regt: *m* 1970 (*m diss* 1979), Carolyn Ann, da of late Roy Frank Williams, of Pasadena, Calif, USA, and has issue.

Arms – Argent, an eagle displayed with two heads sable guttée d'or, with a crescent for difference. **Crest** – An eagle's head erased sable, guttée d'or, holding in the beak an escallop argent.
Seat – Gaunt's House, Wimborne, Dorset.

SON LIVING

RICHARD RUFUS FRANCIS, *b* 8 Jan 1971.

DAUGHTER LIVING

Eliza Jane Rose, *b* 1975.

BROTHER LIVING

Jeremy George Trion (8 Guion Rd, SW6) *b* 1946; *ed* Eton.

SISTER LIVING

Amanda Jane, *b* 1940: *m* 1969, Lt-Col Charles John Holroyd, R Green Jackets (ret), of Providence Cottage, Chute Cadley, Andover, Hants and has issue (*see* E Cairns).

AUNTS LIVING (*Daughters of 8th baronet*)

Joanna May, *b* (Dec) 1909: *m* 1st, 1939, Major John Willmore Hume James, RHA, who was *ka* 1944; 2ndly, 1946, Col James Bernard Browne, late 16th Hussars, of The Dormers, Tarrant Keynston, Blandford, Dorset, and has issue living, (by 1st *m*) Charles, *b* 1940: *m* 1967, Virginia, da of Maj John Dennistoun, — (by 2nd *m*) Peter James, *b* 1951. —— Philippa Ann, *b* 1915; MB and ChB Edinburgh 1946: *m* 1949, Andrew B. Swan, MB, ChB, FRCPE, BSc, of The River House, Tarrant Rushton, Blandford, Dorset, and has issue living, Jeremy Michael, *b* 1952, — Jocelyn Ann, *b* 1956.

WIDOW LIVING OF NINTH BARONET

BARBARA (*Barbara, Lady Glyn*) (53 Belgravia Court, Ebury St, SW1), da of William Charles Ritchie Jardine, and formerly wife of Gp Capt Francis Henwood: *m* 1970, as his 2nd wife, Col Sir Richard Hamilton Glyn, 9th Bt, OBE, TD, who *d* 1980.

COLLATERAL BRANCHES LIVING

Issue of late Gerald Hugh Glyn, 2nd son of 8th baronet, *b* 1909, *d* 1981: *m* 1954, Philomena (West Dene House, Beech, Alton, Hants), da of Denis O'Leary, of Macroom, Co Cork:—
Charles Gerald, *b* 1959. —— Lesley Maye (83 Lyric Rd, SW13), *b* 1955.

Grandchildren of late Charles Robert Glyn, el son of Rev Charles Thomas Glyn (infra):—
Issue of late Charles Glyn, *b* 1878, *d* 1943: *m* 1912, Gwendolen, who *d* 1982, da of Charles Mills, of Riebeek House, Kenilworth, Cape Province, S Africa:—
Ronald St George, *b* 1913: *m* 1954, Marion Mevagh, da of Donald James Laing, of Kildrummy Farm, Rivonia, Johannesburg, and has issue living, Donald Charles St George, *b* 1954, — Patrick St George, *b* 1956, — Rowena May, *b* 1960, — Virginia Aitchison, *b* 1964. *Residence* – 10 St Andrew's St, Melrose, Johannesburg, S Africa. *Club* – Rand (Johannesburg). —— Kathleen Phillipa, *b* 1920: *m* 1st, 19—, Edward Charles Sawyer, who *d* 1946; 2ndly, 1962, Gordon George Booth, of 10 Roosevelt Rd, Gillitts 3603, Natal, S Africa, and has issue living, (by 1st *m*) Charles Garth, *b* 1946, — Bruce Gavin, *b* 1948, — Amanda May, *b* 1953.

Grandchildren of late Charles Glyn (ante):—
Issue of late John St George Glyn, *b* 1916, *d* 1985: *m* 1958, Norma Baillie (Ballyrock, 81 Highway, Fish Hoek, Cape Town, S Africa), da of Hugo Orlando Bean, of Nakwela Farms, Mazabuka, Zambia:—
Patricia Jane St George, *b* 1959; *ed* Capetown Univ (BA). —— Shirley Gwendoline St George, *b* 1962; *ed* Capetown Univ (BSc, LLB).

Grandchildren of late Charles Robert Glyn (ante):—
Issue of late Douglas John Glyn, *b* 1883, *d* 1952: *m* 1926, Dorothy Margaret, who *d* 1962, da of late Alexander Gordon of Wynberg, Cape, S Africa:—
William George Rutherford (PO Box 2310, Somerset W 7130, CP, S Africa), *b* 1927: *m* 1950, Lillamary, who *d* 1988, da of late I. W. Kretzen, and has issue living, Richard William Douglas (18 Moray Drive, Bryanston, Johannesburg, S Africa) *b* 1951; *ed* Natal Univ (BCom, LLB) and Trin Hall, Camb (LLB): *m* 1983, Mary Elizabeth, da of Robert Leonard Stanley, of 4 Moorside, Palmers Lane, Walberswick, Suffolk, — Brenda Margaret, *b* 1954; *ed* Natal Univ (BSc); CA (SA).
Issue of late Wilfrid Henry Glyn, *b* 1885, *d* 1967: *m* 1933, Petronella, who *d* 1975, da of late J. G. Strydom:—
Michael Robert Henry (The 49 Steps, 4 Gascoyne Street Observatory, Johannesburg, S Africa), *b* 1933: *m* 1960, Suzanne Ursula, da of late T. P. Lyons, and has issue living, Alister Michael, *b* 1965, — Jeremy Charles, *b* 1969, — Caroline Frances, *b* 1963.

Granddaughter of late Rev Charles Thomas Glyn, 2nd son of Thomas Christopher Glyn, 3rd son of 1st baronet (*cr* 1800):—
Issue of late Thomas Richard Glyn, *b* 1856, *d* 1937: *m* 1901, Florence Ann, who *d* 1928, da of late John Brownless, of Whorlton Grange, co Durham:—
Cicely May, *b* 1906: *m* 1931 (*m diss* 1947), John William Murray, MD, and has issue living, Caroline Glyn, *b* 1942.

Descendants of late George Carr Glyn (4th son of 1st baronet, *cr* 1800), who was *cr Baron Wolverton* 1869 (*see* that title).

(In remainder to the Baronetcy of Ewell only)

Grandchildren of late Capt Egerton John Glyn, son of late Clayton William Feake Glyn, son of late Rev Thomas Clayton Glyn (infra):—

Issue of late John Murray Egerton Glyn, *b* 1894, *d* 1936: *m* 1923, Iris Margaret, da of John P Lawton, of Mid Oaks, San Gabriel, Los Angeles, California, USA:—

John Murray Egerton, *b* 1926. —— Helena Margaret, *b* 1931.

Sir Richard, LLD, 1st baronet, a banker, was MP for London City, Lord Mayor of London 1758, and President of Bridewell and Bethlem Hospitals. His fourth son, Sir Richard Carr Glyn, Lord Mayor of London 1798, a banker in that City, and 2nd Pres of Bridewell and Bethlem Hospitals, was *cr* Baronet (GB), of Gaunt's House, Dorsetshire 1800. On the death of the 7th Baronet of Ewell in 1942, he was *s* by Sir Richard Fitzgerald Glyn, 4th Bt, DSO, of Gaunt's House, who was High Sheriff of Dorset 1927, and served in S Africa 1899-1902, and in European War 1914-18 (DSO).

GLYN (UK) 1927, of Berbice, British Guiana

Strength is counsel

Sir ANTHONY GEOFFREY LEO SIMON GLYN, 2nd *Baronet*; *b* 13 March 1922; *s* his father, Sir EDWARD RAE DAVSON, KCMG, 1937; assumed by deed poll 1957 the surname of Glyn in lieu of his patronymic and the additional forename of Anthony; *ed* Eton; European War 1941-45 as Capt Welsh Guards; novelist, biographer and travel-writer; Book Society Choice 1955 and 1959; Dollar Book-Club Choice 1957; ITV Play Prize 1961; Vermeil Medal of the City of Paris 1987: *m* 1946, Susan Eleanor (Bar-at-Law), da of Lieut-Col Sir Rhys Rhys Williams, DSO, QC, 1st Bt, and has had issue.

Arms – Argent, on a chevron sable between two stags lodged gules, attired of the second, and a representation of the sailing ship "Santa Maria" proper in base, three pheons inverted or. **Crest** – A dove proper, gorged with an antique crown or, standing upon a branch oak fructed proper.

Residence – Marina Baie des Anges, Ducal Apt U-03, 06270 Villeneuve-Loubet, Alpes Maritimes, France. *Club* – Pratt's.

DAUGHTERS LIVING AND DECEASED

Caroline Mary, *b* 1947; novelist; *d* 1981. —— Victoria Anne, *b* 1951; BA (Hon); Bar Inner Temple 1978.

BROTHER LIVING

CHRISTOPHER MICHAEL EDWARD DAVSON (4 Mermaid St, Rye, Sussex TN31 7ET), *b* 26 May 1927; *ed* Eton; late Capt Welsh Gds; FCA; Liveryman of Musicians' Co, and Freeman of City of London: *m* 1st, 1962 (*m diss* 1972), Evelyn Mary, only da of late James Wardrop; 2ndly, 1975, Kate, da of Ludo Foster, of Greatham Manor, Pulborough, Sussex, and has issue living, (by 1st *m*) George Trenchard Simon, *b* 1964.

The 1st baronet, Sir Edward Rae Davson, KCMG (son of late Sir Henry Katz Davson, a Member of Court of Policy, British Guiana), was a Past Chm of Federation of Chambers of Commerce of British Empire, and a Member of Imperial Economic Cttee, Colonial Development Advisory Cttee, and Empire Marketing Board. He *m* 1921, Margot Elinor, OBE, da of Clayton Louis Glyn and his wife Elinor Sutherland (the novelist Elinor Glyn).

GODFREY (I) 1785, of Bushfield, co Kerry, Ireland (Extinct 1971)

Sir WILLIAM MAURICE GODFREY, 7th and last *Baronet*.

DAUGHTERS LIVING OF SEVENTH BARONET

Susan Mary, *b* 1934: *m* 1st, 1959, Anthony Dale Jones; 2ndly, 1993, Robert James Olive, of Deerswood, Leith Hill, Dorking, Surrey, and has issue living (by 1st *m*), Timothy Simon, *b* 1965. — Petrina Claire, *b* 1961. — Annabel Mary, *b* 1963. —— Bridget Jane (*Lady Dervaird*), *b* 1937: *m* 1960, John Murray (a Lord of Session as Lord Dervaird), of 4 Moray Pl, Edinburgh, EH3 6DS, and has issue living, Alexander Godfrey, *b* 1964, — William John, *b* 1965: *m* 1988, Hazel Margaret, da of Dr Charles Glennie, of Edinburgh, and has issue living, Charles William *b* 1993, — David Gordon, *b* 1968. —— Iris Belinda, *b* 1939: *m* 1962, Robert Edward Jacob, of 36 Wellington Rd, Ballsbridge, Dublin 4, and has issue living, William Godfrey, *b* 1967, — Richard Thomas, *b* 1968, — Ann Caroline, *b* 1963, — Sarah Margaret, *b* 1965: *m* 1992, Finbar John Drennan, son of Frank Drennan, of Cork.

WIDOW LIVING OF SEVENTH BARONET

CAROLINE IRIS (*Lady Godfrey*) (Martins, The Forstal, Eridge, Tunbridge Wells, Kent), da of late Alban Robins, of Rusthall Grange, Tunbridge Wells: *m* 1933, Sir William Maurice Godfrey, 7th Bt, who *d* 1971, when the title became ext.

DAVIS-GOFF (UK) 1905, of Glenville, Parish of St Patrick's, co Waterford

Honesty is the best policy

Sir ROBERT WILLIAM DAVIS-GOFF, 4th *Baronet, b* 12 Sept 1955; *s* his father *Sir* ERNEST WILLIAM, 1980; *ed* Cheltenham Coll, *m* 1978, Nathalie Sheelagh, da of Terence Chadwick, of Lissen Hall, Swords, co Dublin.

Arms – Quarterly, 1st and 4th, azure, a chevron between two fleurs-de-lys in chief and a lion rampant in base or, a crescent for difference; 2nd and 3rd, per pale gules and argent, a chevron between three boars' heads couped, all counter-changed. **Crest** – A squirrel sejant argent.
Residence – Seafield, Donabate, Co Dublin, Republic of Ireland.

SONS LIVING

WILLIAM NATHANIEL, *b* 20 April 1980. —— Henry Terence Chadwick, *b* 1986. —— James Sammy Chadwick, *b* 1989.

DAUGHTER LIVING

Sarah Chadwick, *b* 1982.

SISTERS LIVING

Annabel Claire, *b* 1942: *m* 19— (*m diss* 19—), Mike Nichols, of Bridgewater, Conn, USA, and has issue living, Max *b* 1973, Jenny *b* 1976. —— Julia Christian, *b* 1943: *m* 1968 (*m diss* 19—), John G. Barker, and has issue living, Christian Charles, *b* 1970, — Andrea Mary, *b* 1971. —— Alice Maria, *b* 1948: *m* 1969, Christopher Quarry, of The Olde House, Oad St, Borden, Sittingbourne, Kent, and has issue living, Andrew Simon, *b* 1973, — Suzanne Nichola, *b* 1975.

UNCLE LIVING (*Son of 2nd baronet*)

Charles Herbert, *b* 1908; *ed* Repton and Trin Coll, Camb.

AUNT LIVING (*Daughter of 2nd baronet*)

Doreen Christian, *b* 1905: *m* 1935, Major Michael Wentworth Beaumont, TD, who *d* 1958 (*see* V Allendale, colls). *Residence* – Harristown House, Brannockstown, co Kildare.

Sir William G. Davis-Goff, 1st Bt, Sheriff of Waterford City 1869 and 1899, and High Sheriff of Waterford Co 1892, was a descendant of Rev Stephen Goffe, of Stanmer, Sussex (Fellow of Magdalen Coll, Oxford, *temp* 1595), whose son Stephen was Chaplain to Charles I. Sir Herbert, 2nd Bt, was High Sheriff of co Waterford 1914.

D'AVIGDOR-GOLDSMID (UK) 1934, of Somerhill, co Kent (Extinct 1987)

Maj-Gen Sir JAMES ARTHUR D'AVIGDOR-GOLDSMID, CB, OBE, MC, 3rd and last *Baronet.*

DAUGHTER LIVING OF SECOND BARONET

(Rosemary) Chloe, *b* 1945; High Sheriff Kent 1994: *m* 1969, (Anthony) James Moreton Teacher, of Hadlow Place, Kent TN11 0BW, and has issue (*see* Macnaghten, Bt, colls).

WIDOW LIVING OF SECOND BARONET

ROSEMARY MARGARET (*Lady d'Avigdor-Goldsmid*) (2 Eaton Mansions, SW1; The Old Laundry, Tudeley, Tonbridge, Kent), da of Lt-Col Charles Nicholl, of 52 Queen's Gate, SW, and formerly wife of Sir Peter James Cunliffe Horlick, 3rd Bt: *m* 1940, Maj Sir Henry Joseph d'Avigdor-Goldsmid, DSO MC, TD, 2nd Bt, who *d* 1976.

GOOCH (GB) 1746, of Benacre Hall, Suffolk.

Sir (RICHARD) JOHN SHERLOCK GOOCH, 12th *Baronet*; *b* 22 March 1930; *s* his father, *Col Sir* ROBERT ERIC SHERLOCK, KCVO, DSO, 1978; *ed* Eton; Capt (ret) The Life Gds; JP (Suffolk 1970).

Arms – Per pale argent and sable a chevron between three talbots statant counterchanged; on a chief gules three leopards' faces or. **Crest** – A talbot statant per pale argent and sable.
Seat – Benacre Hall, Beccles, Suffolk.

BROTHER LIVING

TIMOTHY ROBERT SHERLOCK, MBE (The Cedars, Covehithe, Wrentham, Beccles, Suffolk NR34 73W. *Clubs* – White's, Cavalry and Guards'); *b* 7 Dec 1934; *ed* Eton, and RMA Sandhurst; Maj The Life Gds (ret); MBE (Mil) 1970; Member of HM Bodyguard of Hon Corps of Gentlemen at Arms since 1986: *m* 1963, Susan Barbara Christie, only da of late Maj-Gen Kenneth Christie Cooper, CB, DSO, OBE, of Donhead St Andrew, Wilts, and has issue living, Lucinda, *b* 1970, — Victoria, *b* 1974.

Fide et virtute
By fidelity and valour

SISTER LIVING

Katharine Anne, *b* 1932: *m* 1967, Maj Andrew Patrick Forbes Napier, KStJ, DL, late Coldstream Gds, Member of HM Body Guard for Scotland (R Company of Archers), of Syleham Manor, nr Eye, Suffolk IP21 4LN (*see* B Essendon, 1970 Edn), and has issue living, James Frederick Brian, *b* 1968; *ed* Eton, and RMA Sandhurst; late Capt Coldstream Gds, — Katharine Louisa, *b* 1969.

COLLATERAL BRANCHES LIVING

Issue of late Col Brian Sherlock Gooch, DSO, TD, 2nd son of 10th baronet, *b* 1904, *d* 1968: *m* 1935, Monica Mary, who *d* 1975, only child of Nathaniel Arthur Heywood, of Glevering Park, Wickham Market, Suffolk:—
Arthur Brian Sherlock Heywood (Chitterne, Wilts), *b* 1937; *ed* Eton; Brig Staff, comdg The Life Gds 1978-81: *m* 1963, Sarah Diana Rowena, JP, da of late Lt-Col John Francis George Perceval, of Templehouse, co Sligo, and has issue living, Rowena Elizabeth, *b* 1965, — Katherine Sarah, *b* 1967: *m* 1992, Edward J. Hawkings, son of late Peter Hawkings, of Greywell, Hants. —— Thomas Sherlock Heywood (Chantry House, Greens Norton, Towcester, Northants NN12 8BL), *b* 1943: *m* 1971, Elizabeth, da of late Brig Guy Arthur Eliot Peyton, OBE, of Bengal Manor, Greens Norton, Towcester, Northants, and has issue living, Robert Brian Sherlock, *b* 1976, — Caroline Elisabeth, *b* 1973. —— (Mary) Elise (*Lady Quilter*), *b* 1940: *m* 1964, Sir Anthony Raymond Leopold Cuthbert Quilter, 4th Bt, of Sutton Hall, Woodbridge, Suffolk. —— Jennifer Isobel, *b* 1942: *m* 1965, Lt-Cdr John Marjoribanks Chevallier Guild, RN (who assumed the additional surname of CHEVALLIER before that of Guild by deed poll 1970), of Aspall Hall, Stowmarket, and has issue living, John Barrington Chevallier, *b* 1967, — Henry Chevallier, *b* 1968.

Issue of late Brig Richard Frank Sherlock Gooch, DSO, MC, yst son of 10th baronet, *b* 1906, *d* 1973: *m* 1939, Barbara Susan, who *d* 1981, da of late William Douro Hoare, CBE:—
Richard Edward Sherlock (Tigger Towers, Clare St, Cheltenham, Glos), *b* 1942: *m* 1stly 1967, Rosemary Hill; 2ndly 1981, Linda Kathleen, da of late John Caradus of Napier, NZ, and has issue living (by 1st *m*), Tobias Douro Sherlock, *b* 1969, — Theodore Frank Sherlock, *b* 1972.

Granddaughter of late Brig Richard Frank Sherlock Gooch, DSO, MC (ante):—
Issue of late William David Sherlock Gooch, *b* 1944, *d* 1978: *m* 1970, Anna Nicholls (30 Bridge St, Framlingham, Suffolk):—
Elisabeth Anne, *b* 1971.
The 1st baronet, Sir William, after serving gallantly in the wars of Queen Anne's reign, was appointed Lieut-Gov of Virginia. The 2nd baronet, Sir Thomas, was successively Bishop of Bristol, of Norwich, and of Ely. The 4th baronet, Sir Thomas, was High Sheriff of Suffolk 1785. The 5th and 6th baronets were each successively MP for that county.

GOOCH (UK) 1866, of Clewer Park, Berkshire.

Sir TREVOR SHERLOCK GOOCH, VRD, 5th *Baronet*, son of late Charles Trevor Gooch, 2nd son of Charles Fulthorpe Gooch, 2nd son of 1st baronet; *b* 15 June 1915; *s* his kinsman, *Sir* ROBERT DOUGLAS, 1989; *ed* Charterhouse; Fl-Lt RAFVR: *m* 1st, 1956, Denys Anne, who *d* 1976, only da of late Harold Victor Venables, of Edificio la Vileta, Camino Vecinal le Vileta 215, Palma de Mallorca, Baleares; 2ndly, 1978, Jean, da of late John Joseph Wright, and has issue by 1st *m*.

Arms – Per pale argent and sable, on a chevron between three talbots passant two escallops all counterchanged, on a chief engrailed gules a wheel between two leopards' faces or. **Crest** – A talbot per pale sable and argent gorged with a wreath of oak or, and resting the dexter foot on a gold wheel.
Residence – Jardin de la Rocqye, Mont de la Rocque, St Aubin, Jersey, CI.

Fide et virtute
By fidelity and valour

SON LIVING (*By 1st marriage*)

MILES PETER, *b* 3 Feb 1963; *ed* Victoria Coll, Jersey, and Preston Poly Lancs (B Eng).

DAUGHTERS LIVING *(By 1st marriage)*

Beverly Jacqueline, *b* 1957: *m* 1st, 1981 (*m diss* 1988), Laurence Andrew Wilde; 2ndly, 1988, Bernard Charles Amy, of St John's Villa, 68 St John's Rd, St Helier, Jersey, CI, and has issue living (by 1st *m*), Samantha Ria AMY, *b* 1983; legally adopted by her stepfather 1991. —— Vanda Madeleine, *b* 1958. —— Yvonne Daryl, *b* 1961. —— Rowan Claire, *b* 1971.

DAUGHTER LIVING OF FOURTH BARONET *(By 2nd marriage)*

Gillian Daphne (Trethewey Cottage, St Martin, nr Helston, Cornwall), *b* 1931: *m* 1st 1953 (*m diss* 1973), Guy Stephen Foster Wilkin; 2ndly, 1974, Kenneth George White, who *d* 1988, and has issue living, (by 1st *m*) Paul Guy Foster, *b* 1955: *m* 1978, Carolyn Noakes, and has issue living, Mathew Paul Foster *b* 1984, Samantha Ann Foster *b* 1982, — Mark Guy Foster, *b* 1957.

COLLATERAL BRANCHES LIVING

Granddaughter of late Charles Fulthorpe Gooch, 2nd son of 1st baronet:—
Issue of late Eric Daniel Astwood Gooch, *b* 1886, *d* 1937: *m* 1910, Gwynedd, who *d* 1964, da of late Col George Brooke Meares (M Townshend, colls):—
Pamela Vivian, *b* 1911: *m* 1934, Robert Herbert Smidt Van Gelder, and has issue living Jacqueline, *b* 1935, — Pamela Gwynedd Marie, *b* 1946: *m* 19—, David Lawrence Jamieson, of Westerland Stud, Graffham, Sussex, and has issue living, Antonia Alexandra *b* 1972, Melanie Pamela *b* 1976, — Margaret, *b* 1950. *Residence* - Rodlense House, Boldre, near Lymington, Hants.

Grandchildren of late George Daniel Gooch, son of Alfred William Gooch, 3rd son of 1st baronet:—
Issue of late Major George Ernest Gooch, MBE, TD, *b* 1905, *d* 1958: *m* 1933, Jennifer Eve, who *d* 1981, da of late Brig-Gen Philip Maud, CMG, CBE:—
John Daniel, VRD, SBStJ (The Schoolhouse, Oathlaw, Forfar, Angus), *b* 1935; *ed* Cheltenham Coll; FRICS: *m* 1972, Ann Patricia, da of David Miles Lubbock (*see* B Avebury, colls), and has issue living, Katherine Janita, *b* 1974, — Diana Veronica, *b* 1976. —— Peter David (1111 Skeena Place, Victoria, BC, Canada), *b* 1938; *ed* Cheltenham Coll; MSc: *m* 1965, Pamela Sarah, da of late Robert Hartley, and has had issue, Adam Daniel, *b* 1969, — Thomas Daniel, *b* 1970, — Fiona Louise, *b* 1972, *d* 1991. —— Belinda, *b* 1944: *m* 1984, Harry Merriman Ash, of The Forge, Burrowsfold, Castleton, Derbyshire, and has issue living, George Gooch *b* 1985.
The baronetcy was conferred upon Sir Daniel Gooch, who was Chm of the Great Western Railway 1865-89, for the services he rendered in promoting the successful submersion of the Atlantic Cables of 1865 and 1866.

GOODENOUGH (UK) 1943, of Broadwell and Filkins, co Oxford

Sir RICHARD EDMUND GOODENOUGH, 2nd *Baronet*; *b* 9 June 1925; *s* his father, *Sir* WILLIAM MACNAMARA, 1951; *ed* Eton, and Ch Ch, Oxford: *m* 1951, Jane Isobel, da of late Harry Stewart Parnell McLernon, of Gisborne, New Zealand, and has issue.

Arms – Or a chevron gules between three guttes de sang. **Crest** – A demi-wolf proper holding between his paws an escallop argent.

SON LIVING

WILLIAM McLERNON, *b* 5 Aug 1954; *ed* Stanbridge Earls: *m* 1982, Louise Elizabeth, da of Capt Michael Ortmans, LVO, RN, of 48 Bishops Rd, SW6, and has issue living, Samuel William Hector, *b* 11 June 1992, — Sophie Julia, *b* 1986, — Celia Isobel, *b* 1989.

DAUGHTERS LIVING

Rosemary Louise, *b* 1952: *m* 1st, 1977, Frederick Charles le Roux; 2ndly, 1993, Patrick George MacGregor Masson, son of late Dr George Aird Masson, MD, FRCPE, of Ballochneck, Buchlyvie, Stirlingshire, and has issue living (by 1st *m*), Amy Elizabeth, *b* 1978, — Nancy Jane, *b* 1983. —— Joanna Jane, *b* 1958.

BROTHER LIVING

(Frederick) Roger, *b* 1927; *ed* Eton, and Magdalene Coll, Camb (MA); MA Oxon; FRSA; FCIB 1968; Local Dir of Barclays Bank, Oxford 1969-87; a Dir of Barclays Bank UK Management plc 1979-87, of Barclays plc 1985-89, of Barclays Bank plc 1979-89, of Barclays Bank International Ltd 1977-87, and Advisory Dir Barclays Bank Thames Valley Region 1988-89, a Curator of Oxford Univ Chest 1974-93, a Trustee of Nuffield Medical Trust and Nuffield Dominions Trust (Chm since 1987) since 1968 and since 1981 Chm of Nuffield Orthopaedic Trust and of Oxford and Dist Hosps Improvement and Development Fund since 1982, a Gov of Shiplake Coll 1963-74 (Chm 1966-70), and of Wellington Coll 1968-74, and a Fellow of Linnean Soc (Member of Council 1968, Treas, 1970-75); High Sheriff of Oxfordshire 1987-88, DL Oxon since 1989; Supernumerary Fell of Wolfson Coll, Oxford since 1989; a patron of Anglo-Ghanaian Soc since 1991; Pres Oxfordshire Rural Community Council since 1993; Gov London Goodenough Trust for Overseas Graduates since 1985; RN 1946-48: *m* 1954, Marguerite June, only da of late David Forbes Mackintosh, of Bowling Green Cottage, Broadwell, nr Lechlade, Glos, and has issue living, David Frederick, *b* 1955; *ed* Clifton, and Grey Coll, Durham (BSc): *m* 1988, Nicola Dawn Foreman, and has issue living, Michael John Frederick *b* 1989, Mark William Anthony *b* 1991, — Annabel Margaret, *b* 1957; *ed* Lady Margaret Hall, Oxford (BA): *m* 1980, Lt-Col Paul Christopher Charles Molyneaux, RA, and has issue living, Harriet Frances Rose *b* 1986, Emma Flora Louise *b* 1989, — Victoria Frances, *b* 1961; *ed* Lady Margaret Hall, Oxford (BA): *m* 1989, David Richard Arden Bott, yr son of Dr Edward Bott, of Manor Fields, Moreton Morrell, Warwickshire, and has issue living, Patrick Edward Arden *b* 1991, Archie Frederick Arden *b* 1993. *Residence* - Broadwell Manor, Lechlade, Glos GL7 3QS. *Club* - Brooks's.

SISTER LIVING

Mary Dorothea, *b* 1940: *m* 1965, Capt John Alistair Ponsonby Forbes, late Coldstream Guards, of All Saints House, nr Axminster, Devonshire EX13 7LR, and has issue (*see* L Forbes, colls).

The 1st baronet, Sir William Macnamara Goodenough (son of late Frederick Craufurd Goodenough, of Filkins Hall, Lechlade), was Chm of Barclays Bank, of Nuffield Foundation, and of five other Nuffield Trusts, and Dep Steward of Oxford Univ.

GOODHART (UK) 1911, of Portland Place, St Marylebone, and Holtye, Sussex.

From God all things

Sir ROBERT ANTHONY GORDON GOODHART, 4th *Baronet*; *b* 15 Dec 1948; *s* his father, *Sir* JOHN GORDON, 1979; *ed* Rugby, and Lond Univ (Guy's Hosp) (MB, BS); MRCS, LRCP (1972), MRCGP (1976): *m* 1972, Kathleen Ellen, el da of late Rev Alexander Duncan MacRae, of 45 Laggan Rd, Inverness, and has issue.

𝔄rms – Gules, a buck trippant argent, in chief two bees volant or, on a chief nebulée of the third a Cross of Lorraine of the field, between two eagles displayed sable. ℭrest – A beehive or between two bees with a rainbow terminating in clouds proper.
Residence – The Old Rectory, Netherbury, Bridport, Dorset DT6 5NB.

SONS LIVING

MARTIN ANDREW, *b* 9 Sept 1974. —— Iain Michael, *b* 1980.

DAUGHTERS LIVING

Kim Elaine, *b* 1977. —— Rachel Alice, *b* 1987.

SISTER LIVING

Anne Rosemary, *b* 1945: *m* 1969, John Oliver Soul, Surg Capt RN, of Trevenevow, Crapstone Rd, Yelverton, Devon PL20 6BT, and has issue living, Nicholas John, *b* 1971, — Sarah Victoria, *b* 1974.

AUNTS LIVING

Dorothy Joyce, *b* 1921 (Bayfield, Copp Hill Lane, Budleigh Salterton, Devon EX9 6DT). —— Alice Mary, RD (Bayfield, Copp Hill Lane, Budleigh Salterton, Devon EX9 6DT); *b* 1926; DL.

WIDOW LIVING OF THIRD BARONET

(MARGARET MARY) EILEEN (*Eileen, Lady Goodhart*) (Venn House, Lamerton, Tavistock, Devon PL19 8RX), da of late Morgan Morgan, of Cray, Breconshire: *m* 1944, Sir John Gordon Goodhart, MB, FRCGP, 3rd Baronet, who *d* 1979.

The 1st baronet, Sir James Frederic Goodhart, MD, CM, FRCP (Hon LLD Aberdeen), was Consulting Physician to Guy's Hospital and to Evelina Hospital.

GOODSON (UK) 1922, of Waddeton Court, Parish Court, Parish of Stoke Gabriel, co Devon

Sir MARK WESTON LASSAM GOODSON, 3rd *Baronet*, son of late Maj Alan Richard Lassam Goodson, 2nd son of 1st baronet: *b* 12 Dec 1925; *s* his uncle, *Sir* ALFRED LASSAM, 1986; *ed* Radley, and Jesus Coll, Camb: *m* 1949, Barbara Mary Constantine, da of Surg-Capt Reginald Joseph McAuliffe Andrews, RN, of Crandel, Ferndown, Dorset, and has issue.

𝔄rms – Ermine, on a chevron between three quatrefoils gules, leaved and slipped vert, as many garbs or. ℭrest – A wolf's head erased gules, collared and charged on the neck with a spur or.
Residence – Kilham, Mindrum, Northumberland TD12 4QS.

SON LIVING

ALAN REGINALD, *b* 15 May 1960; *ed* Ampleforth.

DAUGHTERS LIVING

Phylida Mary, *b* 1950: *m* 1973, Dr Timothy Freeman Wright. —— Hilary Frances, *b* 1953. —— Christian Mary, *b* 1958: *m* 1983, Christopher Collins.

AUNT LIVING (*Daughter of first baronet*)

Kathleen Mary Lassam, *b* 1900; was Co Organizer WVS 1940-45; JP 1941-53: *m* 1920, Roy Neville Craig, MD, DPM, BS, MRCS, LRCP, and has issue living, David Neville, *b* 1924. *Residence* – The Old Parsonage, Wilmington, Honiton, Devon.

COLLATERAL BRANCH LIVING

Issue of late Hugh Lassam Goodson, OBE, 3rd and yst son of 1st baronet, *b* 1905, *d* 1985: *m* 1945, June Patricia (Waddeton Court, nr Brixham, S Devon TQ5 0EN), da of late Maj Joseph Charles Hunter, CBE, MC, DL, of Havikil Lodge, Scotton, Knaresborough:—

Alfred Lassam, *b* 1946: *m* 1st, 1970, Rosemary Anne Swales; 2ndly, 1989, Suzanne Harris, and has issue living, (by 1st *m*) Barnaby, *b* 1972, — Alfred, *b* 1974, — Amy, *b* 1977, — Polly, *b* 1979. —— Hugh Anthony Lassam (Waddeton Court, Brixham, S Devon TQ5 0EN; Royal Yacht Squadron, Royal Torbay Yacht Club, Royal Ocean Racing Club), *b* 1955; Chm of Devonshire Investment Estates; Rear Commodore of Royal Torbay Yacht Club 1988: *m* 1977, Jame Mary, da of Brian Kirley, of Southside, Cobham, Surrey, and has issue living, Hugo Matthew Lassam, *b* 1982. —— Sarah June, *b* 1947: *m* 1972, Guy Arthur Louis Cruwys, and has issue living, Robert, *b* 1976, — Emily, *b* 1974, — Mary, *b* 1978, — Belinda, *b* 1982. —— Penelope Jane, *b* 1948: *m* 1975, Capt Rhydian Peter Vaughan, and has issue living, Sholto, *b* 1977, — Orlando, *b* 1983, — Camilla, *b* 1980.

GOOLD (UK) 1801, of Old Court, Cork

Sir GEORGE LEONARD GOOLD, 7th *Baronet*; *b* 26 Aug 1923; *s* his father, *Sir* GEORGE IGNATIUS, 1967: *m* 1945, Joy Cecelia, da of late William Percival Cutler, of Melbourne, Victoria, and has issue.

Arms – Azure, on a fesse, or, between five goldfinches, three in chief and two in base proper, three mullets gules. **Crest** – A demi-lion rampant or.
Residence – 60 Canterbury Rd, Victor Harbour, S Aust, 5211.

SON LIVING

GEORGE WILLIAM (2 Ambleside Av, Mount Keira, NSW 2500), *b* 25 March 1950: *m* 1973, Julie Ann, da of late Leonard Powell Crack, of Whyalla, S Aust, and has issue living, George Leonard Powell, *b* 1 Dec 1975, — Jon, *b* 1977.

DAUGHTERS LIVING

Deus mihi providebit
God will provide for me

Dianne Joy, *b* 1946: *m* 1968, Gary Neville Button, of 28 Mary Penfold Drive, Rosslyn Park, Adelaide, S Australia 5072, and has issue living, Darren Scott, *b* 1970, — Kelly Lou, *b* 1972. —— Georgina Susan, *b* 1948: *m* 1969, Malcolm Kennedy Sard, of 12 First St, Napperby, S Aust, and has issue living, Stephen Kennedy, *b* 1970, — Michael Leonard, *b* 1974. —— Michelle Julie, *b* 1956: *m* 1979, John Joseph O'Dwyer, and has issue living, Stuart Goold, *b* 1981, — Rachel Louise, *b* 1985, — Sarah Kate, *b* 1988, — Hannah Charlotte, *b* 1990. —— Louise Mary GOOLD, *b* 1962; has retained her maiden name: *m* 1987, Paul James Christie, of 39 East Parkway, Colonel Light Gdns, Adelaide, S Australia 5041.

This family was settled for many centuries in the county and city of Cork. William Gould was Mayor of Cork *temp* Henry VII. George Gould, of Old Court, changed the spelling of his surname from Gould to Goold. His son Henry Michael, at a critical moment, rendered material political and pecuniary services to the Government of George III, and his son Francis was created a baronet with remainder to the heirs male of the body of his father.

GORDON (NS) 1631, of Embo, Sutherlandshire (Dormant 1956)

Sir HOME SETON CHARLES MONTAGU GORDON, 12th *Baronet*; *d* 1956, and at the time of going to press no name appears on the Official Roll of Baronets in respect of this title.

COLLATERAL BRANCHES LIVING

Granddaughters of late John Richard Colin Gordon (infra):—
Issue of late Colin Ernest Sutherland Gordon, *b* 1907, *d* 1940: *m* 1940, Patricia Hayward, da of Harold Newbigin, who *d* 1982, having *m* 2ndly, 1963, the Rev Kenneth Thomas Jenkins, of River Rd, Mylor, S Australia:—
Sarah Victoria, *b* 1944: *m* 1970, John Richard Bishop, and has issue living, Joseph Alexander Gordon, *b* 1978, — Andrew Gordon, *b* 1980. —— Dinah Jillian Hayward, *b* 1948: *m* 1970, Robert Neil Morrison, and has issue living, Colin Robert, *b* 1977, — Meagan Kate, *b* 1978, — Caroline Emma, *b* 1982.

Grandsons of late John Sutherland Gordon, son of Gilbert Gordon, of Woodlands, yr son of late Alexander Gordon in Dalcharn, great-grandson of late Hutcheon Gordon of Moy, yst brother of 1st baronet:—
Issue of late John Richard Colin Gordon, *b* 1868, *d* 1947: *m* 1906, Hilda, da of late Very Rev Ernest Sloman, Dean of St George's Cathedral, Georgetown, British Guiana:—
Michael Ian Newnham, *b* 1914; probable heir to Baronetcy; *ed* Charterhouse; formerly an Assist Commr of Police, Ghana: *m* 1944, Margaret Noreen, da of late Reginald Hubert Payne, and has issue living, Philip Michael Sutherland, *b* 1946, — Helen Elizabeth, *b* 1945: *m* 1982 (*m diss* 1986), Andrew John Tweedie, and has issue living, Alexandra Helen Rose *b* 1983, — Carol Margaret, *b* 1947: *m* 1980, Stuart Fraser Murray, and has issue living, William John Fraser *b* 1988, Holly Georgina Christian *b* 1981, Anna Florence Margaret *b* 1984. *Residence* – 11 Craven Rd, Reading.
Issue of late William James Sutherland Gordon, *b* 1870, *d* 1969: *m* 1906, Mabel N who *d* 1957, da of late J. J. Conner:—
Huntly Sutherland (825 Cleveland Av, Mount Vernon, Washington, USA), *b* 1911: *m* 1936, Ann Elizabeth, da of Charles A. Parker, and has issue living, Huntly Sutherland (1216 Patricia Lane, Burlington, WA 98233, USA), *b* 1937: *m* 1st, 1968 (*m diss* 1983), Nancy Aiken; 2ndly, 1989, Sandra Guantlett Rodgers, and has issue living, (by 1st *m*) Ann Elizabeth *b* 1971, — Charles Cooper (945-88th Av NE, Bellevue, Washington 98004, USA), *b* 1944: *m* 1968, Margaret Mellor Stull, and has issue living, Huntly S. *b* 1975, Parker Stull *b* 1981 Cori Ann *b* 1973, — Josephine Ann, *b* 1941: *m* 1964, William Irven McCaughey, of 9829 NE 21st, Bellevue, Washington, and has issue living, Susan Elizabeth *b* 1966: *m* 1992, Todd Christopher Meadows, of 6337 4th Av, NE, Seattle, WA 98115, USA, Sally Ann *b* 1968.

This family descends from Adam Gordon, Dean of Caithness, 3rd son of 1st Earl of Huntly. His great grandson, Sir John Gordon of Embo, was the 1st baronet, created with remainder to heirs male whatsoever.

GORDON (NS) 1706, of Afton and Earlston, Kirkcudbrightshire.

The Lord will Provide
Dominus providebit

Sir ROBERT JAMES GORDON, 10th *Baronet*; *b* 17 Aug 1932; *s* his father, *Sir* John Charles Gordon, 1982; probably next in remainder to the Viscountcy of Kenmure and Lordship of Lochinvar (Dormant since 1872): *m* 1976, Helen Julia Weston, da of late John Weston Perry, of Cammeray, NSW.

Arms – Azure, a bezant between three boars' heads erased or and in a dexter chief a canton of a Baronet of Nova Scotia. **Crest** – A dexter hand grasping a sabre proper. *Residence* – Earlstoun, Guyra, NSW 2365, Aust.

SISTER LIVING

Ann Gordon, *b* 1929: *m* 1953, Timothy Raymond Harry Savill, 183 Raglan St, Mosman, NSW, and has issue living, Joanna Mary Gordon, *b* 1956: *m* 1988, Giuliano Dambelli, son of Ilma Dambelli, of Brescia, Italy, — Lisbeth Jane Gordon, *b* 1958, — Camilla Ann Gordon, *b* 1961, — Katherine Helen Gordon, *b* 1963.

The family were distinguished loyalists during the Rebellion. The 1st baronet, Col Sir William, Governor of Fort William, led the descent on the west coast of Scotland at the time that the Duke of Monmouth landed in the south of England. Sir Alexander, the 2nd baronet, celebrated in Scottish history, escaped to Holland after the battle of Bothwell Bridge, but was afterwards captured; during his absence he was found guilty, and sentenced to death and forfeiture of estates. On his capture it was decreed that the sentence should be put in force, but, after six years' imprisonment in Edinburgh Castle, he was released in 1689.

DUFF GORDON (UK) 1813, of Halkin, Ayrshire.

Sir ANDREW COSMO LEWIS DUFF GORDON, 8th *Baronet*; *b* 17 Oct 1933; *s* his father, *Sir* DOUGLAS FREDERICK, 1964; late Worcestershire and Cheshire Regt; Suez 1953-54: *m* 1st, 1967 (*m diss* 1975), Grania Mary, da of Fitzgerald Villiers-Stuart, of Dromana, Villierstown, co Waterford; 2ndly, 1975, Eveline Virginia, yst da of Samuel Soames, of Boxford House, Newbury, and has issue by 1st and 2nd *m*.

Arms – Quarterly, 1st and 4th, azure, three boars' heads couped or, armed proper and langued gules, within a double tressure flory counterflory interchangeably with thistles, roses and fleurs-de-lis of the second, *Gordon*; 2nd and 3rd, vert, a fess dancettee ermine between a buck's head cabossed in chief and two escallops in base, or *Duff*. **Crest** – *Dexter*, two arms from the shoulder naked holding a bow, and ready to let fly an arrow all proper. *Sinister*, a demi-lion holding in the dexter paw a sword erect proper, hilted and pommelled or, charged on the shoulder with a mullet argent. **Supporters** – *Dexter*, a savage wreathed about the head and middle with laurel, holding in the dexter hand the branch of a tree all proper. *Sinister*, a stage proper unguled and attired or gorged with a ducal coronet of the last and pending therefrom an inescutcheon charged with the following arms, vert a fess dancettee ermine between a buck's head cabossed in chief and two escallops in base or, the fees charged of a mullet argent. *Residences* – Downton House, Walton, Presteigne, Radnorshire; 27 Cathcart Rd, SW10. *Club* – City University.

SONS LIVING *(By 1st marriage)*

COSMO HENRY VILLIERS, *b* 18 June 1968.

(By 2nd marriage)

William Andrew Lewis, *b* 1977. —— Thomas Francis Cornewall, *b* 1979. —— Frederick Samuel Douglas, *b* 1981.

AUNT LIVING *(Daughter of 6th baronet)*

Anne Maud, *b* 1903: *m* 1926, Richard S. de Q. Quincey, who *d* 1991. *Residence* – Blackaldern, Narberth, Pembrokeshire.

COLLATERAL BRANCH LIVING

Issue of late John Cornewall Duff-Gordon, MBE, 3rd son of Cosmo Lewis Cornewall, 2nd son of 3rd baronet, *b* 1869, *d* 1964: *m* 1920, Ruth Mary, who *d* 1977, da of C. F. Dodson:—
Cosmo John, *b* 1924. —— Alexander Mostyn, *b* 1927.
Sir James Duff, 1st Bt, of Hankin, Ayrshire, British Consul at Cadiz, was created a Bt with remainder to his maternal nephew. Sir William Duff-Gordon, 2nd Bt, was grandson of the 2nd Earl of Aberdeen (*see* M Aberdeen and Temair, colls).

SMITH-GORDON (UK) 1838.

*By courage,
not by craft*

*My hope is
in God*

SIR (LIONEL) ELDRED PETER SMITH-GORDON, 5th *Baronet; b* 7 May 1935; *s* his father, *Sir* LIONEL ELDRED POTTINGER, 1976; *ed* Eton and Trin Coll, Oxford: *m* 1962, Sandra Rosamund Ann, yr da of late Wing Cdr Walter Ronald Farley, DFC, and has issue.

Arms – Quarterly, 1st and 4th, per fesse azure and gules two barrulets engrailed ermine, between three boars' heads erased or, *Gordon*; 2nd and 3rd, argent on a bend cotissed between two unicorns' heads erased azure three lozenges or, a canton gules, thereon a sword erect proper, pommel and hilt gold the blade encircled by an eastern crown or, *Smith*. **Crest** – 1st, issuant from the battlements of a tower argent a stag's head affrontée proper, all between two palm-branches vert; 2nd (*for augmentation*), a representation of the ornamental centre-piece of the service of plate all proper presented to the 1st baronet by his European and native friends at Bombay; 3rd, issuant out of an eastern crown or, a dexter arm embowed in armour entwined with a branch of laurel proper, the hand grasping a sword also proper, pommel and hilt gold. *Residence* – 13 Shalcomb St, SW10.

SON LIVING

LIONEL GEORGE ELDRED, *b* 1 July 1964; *ed* Eton, Westfield Coll and King's Coll London: *m* 1993, Kumi, only da of Masashi Suzuki, of Urawa, Saitama, Japan. *Residence* – 424 West End Av #19K, New York, NY 10024, USA.

DAUGHTER LIVING

Isobel Charlotte Laura, *b* 1966.

The 1st baronet, Gen Sir Lionel Smith, GCB, GCH, received his baronetcy for distinguished military services in the West Indies, and for carrying out the emancipation of the slaves in Jamaica, of which island he was Gov-Gen. He was subsequently Gov of Mauritius, where he died, and where a column is erected to his memory. Sir Lionel Eldred Smith, 2nd Bt, assumed by Roy licence 1868, the additional surname and arms of Gordon, his mother, Isabella Curwen, having been a da of Eldred Curwen Pottinger of Mount Pottinger, co Down, by Anne, da of Robert Gordon of Florida Manor, co Down.

Gordon-Cumming, see Cumming.

GORE (I) 1622, of Magherabegg, co Donegal.

Sir NIGEL HUGH ST GEORGE GORE, 14th *Baronet; b* 23 Dec 1922; *s* his nephew, *Sir* RICHARD RALPH ST GEORGE, 1993: *m* 1952, Beth Allison, da of R. W. Hooper, of Allawah, Tambo, Qld, and has issue.

Arms – Gules, a fesse argent between three cross-crosslets fitchée or. **Crest** – A wolf rampant argent, collared gules.
Residence – Hillhaven, Preston Rd, Hodgson Vale, Toowoomba, Qld 4352, Australia.

DAUGHTER LIVING

Seonaid Beth, *b* 1955.

SISTERS LIVING

Sola salus servire Deo

*To serve God is the only
Salvation*

Phyllis Ruth St George (5 Chelsea Court, Toowoomba, Qld 4350, Australia), *b* 1912. —— Margaretta Leonie St George, *b* 1921: *m* 1958, John Henry Cory, of PO Box 607, Goondiwindi, Qld 4390, Australia, and has issue living, Alan Fitzroy, *b* 1961, — Janet Ruth, *b* 1959.

DAUGHTER LIVING OF ELEVENTH BARONET

Maxine Marjorie St George, *b* 1947: *m* 1968, Capt Timothy Basil Edward Eugster, Irish Gds, and has issue living, Maximilian Brian Michael, *b* 1969, — Alexandra Marcia Gabrielle, *b* 1971, — Julia Clare Elizabeth, *b* 1974.

DAUGHTERS LIVING OF TWELFTH BARONET

Annabel St George, *b* 1951: *m* 1989, Bruce Julian Knowles, of 18 Fairfax St, Red Hill, Qld 4059, Australia. —— Elizabeth St George, *b* 1952: *b* 1981, Patrick Hay Campbell, of RSD 385, Devonport, Tasmania 7310, Australia, and has issue living, Georgina Louise Gore, *b* 1989, — Claudia Jane Gore, *b* 1991. —— Juliet St George, *b* 1957: *m* 1982, David Sheridan Butler, of 31 Angus St, Goodwood, S Australia 5034, Australia.

WIDOW LIVING OF ELEVENTH BARONET

Irene Lamont, el da of Albert James Marshall, of Stranraer, Wigtownshire: *m* 1st, 1971, as his 3rd wife, Lt-Col Sir Ralph St George Brian Gore, 11th Bt, who *d* 1973; 2ndly, 1975, James Biggar, of Old House, Willards Hill, Etchingham, Surrey.

COLLATERAL BRANCHES LIVING

Grandchildren of late Frederick Dundas Corbet Gore, brother of 9th baronet:—
Issue of late Frederick Dundas Corbet Gore, *b* 1885, *d* 1964: *m* 1919, Ella Maud, who *d* 1967, da of Charles Sydney Jones, of Brisbane:—
DUNDAS CORBET, *b* 20 April 1921; *ed* Sydney Univ (BEng); 1939-45 War as Flt-Lt RAAF. —— Hugh Frederick Corbet (7 Romney Rd, St Ives, NSW) *b* 1934: *m* 1963, Jennifer Mary, el da of Milton Gordon Copp, of Rose Bay, NSW, and has issue living, Timothy Milton Corbet, *b* 1969, — Penelope Mary Corbet, *b* 1965, — Virginia Louise, *b* 1967. —— Rosemary Ella Corbet, *b* 1920; 1939-45 War with AIF: *m* 1957, Nicholas George Knox Adams, of 36 The Circle, Bilgola Plateau, Sydney, NSW 2107, Australia, and has an adopted son, David Alexander Ian, *b* 1963. —— Barbara Corbet, *b* 1926.

Grandchildren of late Francis Arthur Gore, el son of late Rev William Francis Gore, yst son of late Rev Thomas Gore, brother of 7th baronet:—
Issue of late Francis William Baldock Gore, *b* 1873, *d* 1937: *m* 1920, Mary Isabel Kirsteen, who *d* 1986, da of late Francis Corbet-Singleton, formerly of Finchampstead, Berks:—
(Francis) St John Corbet, CBE (Grove Farm, Stoke-by-Nayland, Colchester, Essex CO6 4SL), *b* 1921; *ed* Wellington Coll; Capt (ret) R Northumberland Fus; 1939-45 War: *m* 1st, 1951 (*m diss* 1975), Priscilla Margaret, da of Cecil Harmsworth King; 2ndly, 1981, Lady Mary Sophia, yst da of 3rd Earl of Selborne, and widow of Maj Hon (Thomas) Anthony Edward Towneley Strachey (*see* B O'Hagan), and has issue living, (by 1st *m*) William Ralph St John (Pencarrow Farm, Advent, Camelford, Cornwall), *b* 1956: *m* 1984, Mary Susan, yst da of late Edmund Arthur Collingridge, of Kentigern, Hunter's Hill, Sydney, Australia, and has issue living, Ralph St John Edmund *b* 1985, Alice Catharine Mary *b* 1988, — Catharine Harriet Cecilia, *b* 1954: *m* 1977, Richard Edward Geoffrey Gayner, and has issue living, John Robert Haydon *b* 1983, William Richard Francis *b* 1986. — Alan Charles Corbet, *b* 1926; *ed* Wellington Coll: *m* 1953, Ann Sabine, da of W. D. K. Thellusson, of Disley, Gloucestershire, and has issue living, Francis Charles Storar, *b* 1957, — Thomas Corbet, *b* 1960: *m* 1989, Skye Gyngell, and has issue living, Holly *b* 1989. *Residence* – Grandcourt Farm, East Winch, King's Lynn, Norfolk.
Issue of late Cyril Gerard Gore, *b* 1876, *d* 1954: *m* 1911, Gladys Marie Howard, who *d* 1974, da of Allan A. Spowers, Surveyor-Gen of Queensland:—
Leonie Frances, *b* 1918: *m* 1st, 1938, Hugh John Walsh; 2ndly, 1956, Shane Page, and has issue living, (by 1st *m*) Joanna Leonie, *b* 1939: *m* 1959, Mervyn Fitzhenry, and has issue living, William Hugh Shaun *b* 1961, Brendan Mervyn *b* 1964, Shamus Terence *b* 1968, Bridgit Madeline *b* 1963, — Emlyn Anna, *b* 1942: *m* 1960, John Thompson, and has issue living, Simon Patrick *b* 1963, Leonie Helen *b* 1961.

Grandchildren of late Cyril Gerard Gore (ante):—
Issue of late Francis Arthur Gore, *b* 1921, *d* 1987: *m* 1947, Lenore, da of Leonard Lee, of Queensland, Australia:—
Simon Gerard, *b* 1955: *m* 1979, Leone Christine, da of H. Beck, of Queensland, and has issue living, Richard Anthony, *b* 1984, — Adam William, *b* 1986, — Francis Arthur Douglas, *b* 1991. —— Leonie Christine, *b* 1948: *m* 1st, 1972, James Cruden; 2ndly, 1985, Jean-Marie Alain Simart, and has issue living, (by 2nd *m*) Thomas Elliot, *b* 1987, — Clélia Aurélia, *b* 1990. —— Amanda Lenore GORE, *b* 1954: *m* 1979 (*m diss* 1981), Robert John Lyttleton Turner, son of Roland Turner, of Tasmania.

Grandson of late William Wyndham Gore, eldest son of late Lieut Robert William Gore, RN (infra):—
Issue of late Lt-Col Thomas Gerard Gore, DSO, OBE, *b* 1907, *d* 1965: *m* 1933, Mrs Barbara Young:—
Gerard Anthony St George, *b* 1936; *ed* Radley; late Cyprus Police; Lieut 60th Rifles (KRRC) and Capt S African Infantry (Res): *m* 1st, 1957 (*m diss* 1973), Wendy, da of late Mrs C. V. Rippon, of Umkomaas, Natal; 2ndly, 1975 (*m diss* 1985), Velma, da of Capt McKinnon, of 4A Le Grand Rue, Grouville, Jersey, CI, and Baroness von Puttkamer; 3rdly, 1986, Felicity Ann, da of Kathleen Ferreira, of Sydenham, Johannesburg, and has issue living, (by 1st *m*) Sean Ralph St George, *b* 1961, — Nicole Holly St George, *b* 1965. *Address* – Private Bag X 20049, Empangeni 3880, S Africa.

Grandchildren of late Lieut Robert William Gore, RN, 3rd son of late Rev William Francis Gore (ante):—
Issue of late St George Arthur Gore, *b* 1886, *d* 1970: *m* 1st, 1914 (*m diss* 1954), Muriel Mary, da of John Brought-on, Surveyor-Gen of NSW; 2ndly, 1954, Mildred Prudence, who *d* 1979, da of late Charles James Vyner, MRCVS, of London:—
Thomas William St George (Cardross, Vic, Aust), *b* 1915: *m* 1945, Jane Nichols, who *d* 1968, only da of Samuel Bennett, of W Aust, and widow of Lt Donald Stewart Fletcher, RAA, and has issue living, Donald Stewart St George, *b* 1952. —— Patrick St George (Homeleigh, O'Connell, NSW), *b* 1921: *m* 1948, Coralie May, da of Mark Reuben Venn, of Tas, and has issue living, Robert Ralph St George (Box 157, Savage River, Tas), *b* 1949: *m* 1978, Prudence (DAVIS) da of Kenneth A. McKercher Burnie of Tas, and has issue living, William Robert Kenneth St George, *b* 1978, — Jonathan Ian St George, *b* 1953, — Peter Simon St George (3 Hasluck Place, Bathurst, NSW), *b* 1955: *m* 1979, Sylvia Joyce, da of Cyril Gardiner of Vittoria, NSW, and has issue living, Stephen Gregory St George *b* 1981.

Grandchildren of late Brig-Gen Robert Clement Gore, CB, CMG, only son of late Nathaniel Gore, 6th son of late Col William Gore, MP, son of late Rt Rev William Gore, Bishop of Limerick, eldest son of late Very Rev William Gore, Dean of Down, yr son of 3rd baronet:—
Issue of late Brig Adrian Clements Gore, DSO, *b* 1900, *d* 1990: *m* 1927, Enid Aimée (Horton Priory, Sellindge, Kent), da of late John Jameson Cairnes:—
Toby Clements (Monks Alley, Binfield, Bracknell, Berks; 94 Smith St, SW3), *b* (Dec) 1927; Maj Rifle Bde; High Sheriff Berks 1993: *m* 1959, (Isolde) Marian, yr da of late Edward H. Macintosh, of Rebeg, Kirkhill, Inverness-shire, and has had issue, Fiona Marian, *b* 1960: *m* 1987, Irvine J. Maccabe, 2nd son of Jeffrey J. Maccabe, of Dulwich Village, — Juliet Carolyn, *b* 1962, — Tessa Jane, *b* 1967; *d* 1994, in Thailand, — Stephanie Serena, *b* 1969. —— Dinah Priscilla, *b* 1930: *m* 1958, Lt-Col (John) Richard (Seymour) Besly, Gren Guards, and has issue living, Adrian Thomas, *b* 1963, — Michael John, *b* 1966, — Emma Belinda, *b* 1958: *m* 1984, Keith Warner, — Lucinda Mary, *b* 1960, — Sara-Jane Beatrice, *b* 1964. —— Belinda Beatrice (*Lady Milbank*), *b* 1940: *m* 1970, Sir Anthony Frederick Milbank, 5th Bt, and has issue.

Descendants of late Arthur Gore (2nd son of 1st baronet), who was *cr* a *Baronet* 1662 (*see* E Arran).
Sir Paul, or Poule, Gore, 1st Bt, Capt of Horse (brother of Sir John Gore, Lord Mayor of London 1624, ancestor of Earl Temple of Stowe), was granted lands in co Donegal in the reign of Elizabeth I which he designated Manor Gore. From his 2nd son Sir Arthur descended the Earls of Arran and from his 4th son Sir Francis, Gore of Lissadill baronets (now Gore-Booth). The 3rd baronet was a Privy Councillor and Custos Rotulorum of co Limerick. The 4th baronet, a Privy Councillor, was MP for co Donegal, Chancellor of the Exchequer, and afterwards Speaker of the House of Commons in Ireland. The 5th baronet sat as MP for co Donegal; and the 6th baronet, a distinguished military officer, was, after representing Donegal co in Parliament, created Baron Gore (1764), Viscount Belleisle (1768), and Earl of Ross (1771), and died without surviving male issue. Sir Ralph Gore, 10th Bt, was elected Commodore of Roy Yacht Squadron 1947, Pres of Yachting Assocn 1945, and of Roy Yachting Assocn 1953.

Gore-Booth, see Booth.

GORING (E) 1678 (with precedency of 1627), of Highden, Sussex.

Renascentur
They will rise again

Sir WILLIAM BURTON NIGEL GORING, 13th *Baronet*; son of late Major Frederick Yelverton Goring, 6th son of 11th baronet; *b* 21 June 1933; *s* his uncle, *Sir* FORSTER GURNEY, 1956; *ed* Wellington Coll; late Lieut 1st Roy Sussex Regt: *m* 1st, 1960 (*m diss* 1993), Hon Caroline Thellusson, el da of 8th Baron Rendlesham; 2ndly, 1993, Mrs Judith Rachel Walton Morison, da of Rev Raymond John Walton Morris, OBE, of Shaftesbury, and formerly wife of Thomas Richard Atkin Morison, QC (later Hon Mr Justice Morison).

𝕬rms – Argent, a chevron between three annulets gules. 𝕮rest – A lion rampant-guardant sable.
Residence – 16 Linver Rd, SW6 3RB.

COLLATERAL BRANCHES LIVING

Issue of late Lt-Cdr Edward Yelverton Combe Goring, RN, yr brother of 13th baronet, *b* 1936, *d* 1991: *m* 1969 (*m diss* 1990), Daphne Christine Seller: —
Elizabeth Christine, *b* 1970. —— Joanna Margaret, *b* 1972.

Issue of late Craven Charles Goring, 3rd son of 11th baronet, *b* 1881, *d* 1952: *m* 1908, Mary Elizabeth, da of John Conlon, of Roscommon:—
Beryl Elizabeth (Castle Farm, Bridgwater Rd, Bristol 3, Avon BS13 8AF), *b* 1909: *m* 1930, George Frederick Thawley, who *d* 1958, and has issue living, Peter Frederick (Castle Farm, Bridgwater Rd, Bristol 3, Avon BS13 8AF), *b* 1940: *m* 1966, Christine Mary, da of Charles Henry Jones Payne, and has issue living, Nicholas *b* 1971, Lisa *b* 1969.

Grandchildren of late Charles Goring (infra):—
Issue of late John Goring, CBE, TD, DL, *b* 1907, *d* 1990: *m* 1947, Lady Hersey Margaret, who *d* 1993, da of 8th Earl of Glasgow, and widow of Cdr Hon John Montagu Granville Waldegrave, DSC, RN (*see* By Radstock, ext):—
RICHARD HARRY (Findon Park House, Findon, W Sussex), *b* 10 Sept 1949; *ed* Eton; High Sheriff W Sussex 1993: *m* 1972, Penelope Ann, da of J. K. Broadbent, of Coppull Farm, Stanford, Cape, S Africa, and has issue living, Richard John, *b* 1978, — Charles, *b* 1980, — Dominic James David, *b* 1989, — Eloise Isabella, *b* 1974, — Catherine Clare, *b* 1975, — Gabrielle Mary, *b* 1991. —— John James (Upper Buncton, Wiston, Steyning, W Sussex), *b* 1953: *m* 1982, Maxine Jane, yr da of ACM Sir David Evans, GCB, CBE, CBIM, of Milton House, Little Milton, Oxon, and has issue living, Jasper David George, *b* 1986, — India Catherine, *b* 1984, — Elizabeth Iona, *b* 1989, — Francesca Mary Hyacinth, *b* 1992. —— Corinna Jane, *b* 1948: *m* 1969, Nigel Vere Nicoll, and has issue (*see* Madden, Bt). —— Anne Elizabeth (Linky Lea, Baro, by Haddington, East Lothian), *b* 1951.

Granddaughter of late Rev John Goring, son of late Charles Goring, 2nd son of 5th baronet:—
Issue of late Charles Goring, *b* 1863, *d* 1924: *m* 1906, Beatrice Gabrielle Mary, who *d* 1970, da of late Rev Arthur Osborne Alleyne, R of St Edmund's, Exeter:—
Isabel (*Lady Dundas*), *b* 1909: *m* 1933, Maj Sir Thomas Calderwood Dundas, MBE, 7th Bt (*cr* 1898), who *d* 1970, when the title became ext. *Residence* – 6 The Green, Slaugham, Handcross, Sussex.

Granddaughters of late Lt-Col Harold Goring, IA (infra):—
Issue of late Brian Hamilton Goring, MBE, *b* 1935, *d* 1989: *m* 1958, Prudence Mary (Lowerwood House, New Lane, Billingshurst, W Sussex RH14 9DS), da of George Baker, of Dickhurst, Lurgashall, Sussex:—
Alice Lucinda, *b* 1959: *m* 1984, Dominique Bouilliez, of Lille, France, and has issue living, Georges Brian Ferdinand Goring, *b* 1985, — William Philippe Xavier Goring, *b* 1987, — Esme Eleanor Joan Goring,4*b* 1983. —— Sya Charlotte, *b* 1964: *m* 1993, Marcus Henry Robert Elwes, of Elder Farm, Grimston, Norfolk, eldest son of Henry Arthur Elwes, of Congham, Norfolk, and has issue living, Millicent Lettice Susan Mary Primrose, *b* 1994. —— Lydia Mary, *b* 1965.

Grandson of late Maj Alan Goring, 3rd son of late Rev John Goring (ante):—
Issue of late Lt-Col Harold Goring, IA, *b* 1903, *d* 1990: *m* 1st, 1929, Mary Frances Eleanor (Kaisar-i-Hind medal), who *d* 1975, da of late Capt Hamilton Augustus Woodruffe, of Garsington, Oxon; 2ndly, 1975, (Joan) Henrietta Radcliffe, da of late Spencer Domett Secretan, of Swaynes, Rudgwick, Sussex:—
(By 1st *m*) George, (Holland House, Warnham, W Sussex), *b* 1937; *ed* Cheltenham, and Millfield; Maj The Queen's Regt (ret): *m* 1969 (*m diss* 1987), Nicola Jean, da of William Ian Gordon, of Rye, Sussex, and has issue living, Michael, *b* 1974, — Fiona Mary, *b* 1972.

Henry Goring, of Highden, Sussex, succeeded Feb 1679-80 as 2nd Bt (by virtue of the special remainder in the patent of 1678), Sir James Bowyer, 3rd Bt, of Leighthorne, Sussex (yr son of Sir Thomas Bowyer, *cr* a baronet 23 July 1627), surrendered by fine his patent and was granted a new patent dated 18 May 1678, for life with remainder after his death to Henry Goring, of Highden, Sussex (ante), and the heirs male of his body, with precedence of the former patent of 23 July 1627. The Goring family is of great antiquity in Sussex, and John Goring was MP for Sussex 1467. A member of the family was created Baron Goring 1628, and Earl of Norwich 1644, titles that became extinct on the death of the 2nd Earl (*cr* 1644) in March 1672. The 2nd baronet was MP for Sussex 1660, for Steyning 1661-79, and again for Sussex 1685-7; the 4th baronet, Col 31st Foot, was MP for Horsham 1707-8, Steyning 1708-15, and again for Horsham 1715, and the 6th baronet was MP for Shoreham 1790-6; the 7th baronet was High Sheriff of Sussex, 1827, and the 8th baronet sat as MP for Shoreham 1832-41. The 12th baronet, Sir Forster Gurney Goring, was appointed a Capt of Invalids, Roy Hospital, Chelsea 1912.

GOSCHEN (UK) 1916, of Beacon Lodge, Highcliffe, co Southampton.

For peace

Sir EDWARD CHRISTIAN GOSCHEN, DSO, 3rd *Baronet*;. *b* 2 Sept 1913; *s* his father, Sir EDWARD HENRY, 1933; *ed* Eton and Trin Coll, Oxford; dep Chm of Stock Exchange Cncl 1963-71, C with War Graves commissioner since 1977, European War 1939-45 in Italy as Major Tower Hamlets Rifles, Rifle Brig (TA) (DSO); DSO 1944: *m* 1946, Cynthia, JP, da of late Rt Hon Sir Alexander George Montagu Cadogan, OM, GCMG, KCB, PC (*see* E Cadogan, colls), and has issue.

Arms – Argent, a human heart gules flamant and transfixed by an arrow bendwise point upwards proper. **Crest** – Upon an arrow fessewise the point to the dexter a dove wings endorsed, all proper.
Residence – Lower Farmhouse, Hampstead Norreys, Berks.

SON LIVING

(EDWARD) ALEXANDER (Pixton Stables, Dulverton, Taunton, Somerset TA22 9HW) *b* 13 March 1949; *ed* Eton: *m* 1976, Louise Annette, da of Lt-Col Ronald Fulton Lucas Chance, MC, KRRC (*see* E Kintore), and has issue living, Charlotte Leila, *b* 1982.

DAUGHTER LIVING

Caroline Clare, *b* 1950: *m* 1989, Jonathan Mendham.

COLLATERAL BRANCHES LIVING

Grandchildren of late George Gerard Goschen (infra):—
Issue of late David Bernard Goschen, *b* 1931, *d* 1980: *m* 1954, Angela (Oakwood Cottages, High Routham, Bury St Edmunds, Suffolk), only da of James Macnabb:—
Sebastien Bernard, *b* 1959. —— Chrysoula Angela, *b* 1955. —— Mariora Vivienne, *b* 1957.

Issue of late George Gerard Goschen, yr son of 1st baronet, *b* 1887, *d* 1953: *m* 1930, Vivienne, who *d* 1957, da of late Bernard de Watteville:—
Tana Mary, *b* 1932: *m* 1962, John Alais Fletcher, and has issue living, Mark Alais, *b* 1963, — Miranda Clare, *b* 1964: *m* 1993, Toby Hawkins, — Katherine Alice, *b* 1966, — Alexandra Sophia, *b* 1970. *Residence* – Dolphin Cottage, Altwood Rd, Maidenhead.
The 1st baronet, Rt Hon Sir (William) Edward Goschen, GCB, GCMG, GCVO, was Envoy Extraor, and Min Plen at Belgrade and Copenhagen 1898-1905, Ambassador Extraor and Min Plen at Vienna and Berlin 1905-14, and Gentleman Usher to the Sword of State 1919-24. Sir Edward Henry Goschen, 2nd Bt, was sometime Controller of Secretariat, Egyptian Min of Finance.

Gough (Anstruther-Gough-Calthorpe), see Calthorpe.

GOULDING (UK) 1904, Millicent, Clane, co Kildare, and Roebuck Hill, Dundrum, co Dublin.
(Name pronounced "Goolding")

Sir (WILLIAM) LINGARD WALTER GOULDING, 4th *Baronet*; *b* 11 July 1940; *s* his father, Sir (WILLIAM) BASIL, 1982; *ed* Winchester, and Trin Coll, Dublin; Headmaster, Headfort Preparatory Sch, co Meath.

Arms – Per bend or and argent, a gryphon segreant within an orle of martlets sable. **Crest** – A dexter hand apaumée and couped at the wrist, encircled with a chaplet of oak leaves bendwise, and transfixed with an arrow bend sinisterwise, all proper.
Seat – Ballyrusheen, co Cork. *Address* – Dargle Cottage, Enniskerry, Co Wicklow, Eire.

BROTHERS LIVING

TIMOTHY ADAM, *b* 15 May 1945; *ed* Winchester: *m* 1971, Patricia Mohan, of Dublin. ——Hamilton Paddy, *b* 1947; *ed* Winchester, and Trin Coll, Dublin; First Officer, Aer Lingus: *m* 1970, Yvonne Denise, el da of S. V. Holmes Thompson, of Tir-Owen, Viewfort Park, Dunmurry, co Antrim.

BROTHER LIVING

Ossian, *b* 1913: *m* 1st, 1936 (*m diss* 1943), Felice Martell, of Montreal, Canada; 2ndly, 1943 (*m diss* 1962), Yasu Elisabeth Katherine, da of Lennart Tham, of Husqvarna, Sweden; 3rdly, 1962, Margaret Angela, who *d* 1988, da of late Frank Chadwick, of Eastbourne, Sussex, and has issue living, (by 1st *m*) Lynn *b* 1937: *m* 1st, 1958, Richard Edgeson Cathcart, Lt RN; 2ndly, 1966, Ken Irwin, — (by 2nd *m*) Richard George Michael, *b* 1951, — Carola Nesta Katherine, *b* 1946, — Sara Elizabeth Louise, *b* 1947. *Residence* – Etaples, France.

AUNT LIVING (*Daughter of 1st baronet*)

Kathleen: *m* 1912, Capt Maurice Falkine Dennis, formerly Seaforth Highlanders, who *d* 1960. *Residence* – Batlyngmede, Cannon Hill, Maidenhead.

WIDOW LIVING OF THIRD BARONET

Hon VALERIE HAMILTON MONCKTON (*Hon Lady Goulding*) (Dargle Cottage, Enniskerry, co Wicklow), only da of 1st Viscount Monckton of Brenchley: *m* 1939, Sir William Basil Goulding, 3rd Bt, who *d* 1982.

GRAAFF (UK) 1911, of Cape Town, Cape of Good Hope Province of Union of South Africa.

The Creator favours the just

Sir DE VILLIERS GRAAFF, MBE, 2nd *Baronet*: *b* 8 Dec 1913; *s* by his father, SIR DAVID PIETER DE VILLIERS, 1931; *ed* Cape Town Univ (BA 1932), and Magdalen Coll, Oxford (BA 1935, MA 1944); BCL 1936; Hon LLD Rhodes Univ 1969; Bar Inner Temple 1937; Advocate of Supreme Court of S Africa 1938; a Member of House of Assembly of Union of S Africa 1948-77; Leader of United Party 1956-77, since when Life Pres of New Republic Party; Dir of Graaffs' Trust; 1939-45 War with S African Defence Force (prisoner, MBE); MBE (Mil) 1947; DMS (South Africa 1978): *m* 1939, Helena le Roux, da of Frederick Carel Marthinus Voigt, of Claremont, Cape Province, S Africa, and has issue.

ֿrms – Argent, a Paschal Lamb proper, on a chief azure five stars of the first (representing the constellation of the Southern Cross). Crest – In front of three spades erect in pale, a dexter arm embowed in armour, the hand holding a scimitar, all proper. Supporters – *Dexter*, a Boer farmer supporting with the exterior hand a rifle *sinister*, a Cape miner supporting with the exterior hand a pickaxe, both proper.
Address – De Grendel, Private Bag GPO, Cape Town 8000, S Africa.

SONS LIVING

DAVID DE VILLIERS (Box 1, Hex River, Cape, South Africa), *b* 3 May 1940; *ed* Diocesan Coll, S Africa, Stellenbosch Univ (BSc Agric), Grenoble Univ, and Magdalen Coll, Oxford (BA); Dir of Graaffs' Trust; Fruit Farmer: *m* 1969, Sally, da of Robin Williams and has issue living, de Villiers, *b* 16 July 1970, — Robert, *b* 1974, — David John, *b* 1977, — Leeza, *b* 1973. —— Johann Frederick de Villiers, *b* 1948.

DAUGHTER LIVING

Genée de Villiers, *b* 1948.

BROTHER LIVING

Johannes de Villiers, *b* 1928; *ed* Cape Town Univ, and St John's Coll, Camb (Fellow 1951): *m* 1951, Lilian Clare, da of George Paget Thomson, and has issue living, Pieter Johannes, *b* 1958, — Janet Kathleen, *b* 1954, — Teresa Clare, *b* 1955, — Anna Louise, *b* (twin) 1955, — Monica Suzanne, *b* 1960, — Linda Elaine, *b* 1966. *Residence* – Morgenrood Rd, Kenilworth, Cape Province, S Africa.
The 1st baronet, Hon Sir David Pieter de Villiers Graaff, was Mayor of Cape Town 1892-2, Min without portfolio, Cape Colony 1908-10, Min of Public Works, Posts, and Telegraphs of Union of South Africa 1910-12, again Min without portfolio 1912-3, and Min of Finance 1915-6; acted as High Commr for S Africa in London 1914.

GRACE (GB) 1795, of Minchenden House, co Middlesex. (Extinct 1977)

Sir RAYMOND EUSTACE GRACE, 6th and last *Baronet*.

DAUGHTERS LIVING OF FIFTH BARONET

Aileen Mary Violet, *b* 1901: *m* 1st, 1933, William Bruce Hamilton, MB, BCh, Lt-Col RAMC, who *d* 1947; 2ndly, 1954, Louis Zeyfert, of Kalafat Corner, Rockfort Av, Dalkey, co Dublin, and has issue living, (by 1st *m*) Edward Bruce (Kalafat House, Sorrento Rd, Dalkey, co Dublin), *b* 1937; BA, BComm Dublin: *m* 1960, Daphne Theodora, BA, da of Judge Ian Rawdon Greene, of Pemba, Glenlucan Court, co Wicklow, and has issue living, Michael Raymond Maurice Bruce *b* 1960: *m* 1985, Miriam Ann, da of Desmond Fogarty, of Clifton House, Dalkey, co Dublin (and has issue living, Samantha Eileen *b* 1987, Robyn Caroline *b* 1991), David Edward Louis *b* 1964: *m* 1991, Nancy Brassil (and has issue living, Tristan David *b* 1993), Christopher Ian Bruce *b* 1967: *m* 1991, Joanne Moroney (and has issue living, Juliana Eibhlín *b* 1993), Venetia Eileen *b* 1963, Ciara Patricia *b* 1970, — Patricia Margaret Anna, *b* 1939: *m* 1960, Fl-Lt Rex Hamilton-Turley, RAF (ret), of 4 Collemore Rd, Dalkey, co Dublin, and has issue living, Myles Konrad *b* 1961, Simon Marcus *b* 1964, Hereward Christopher Rex *b* 1967, Lucy Grace *b* 1963, Ingrid Daphne Mary *b* 1966. —— Mary Lillian, *b* 1912: *m* 1st, 1940 (*m diss* 1969), Maj Paul McConnell, Ches Regt (ret); 2ndly, 1969, Lt-Col Clive O'Neill Wallis (ret) E Surreys, MC, JP, of 50 Bosman Drive, Windlesham, Berks.

COLLATERAL BRANCH LIVING

Granddaughter of late Col Sheffield Hamilton-Grace (nephew of 2nd baronet):—
Issue of late Major Raymond Sheffield Hamilton-Grace, *b* 1881, *ka* 1915: *m* 1912, Gladys, CBE, who *d* 1978 (having *m* 2ndly, 1919, Col Joseph Benskin, DSO, OBE, who *d* 1953), da of Michael Paul Grace, of 40 Belgrave Square, SW:—

Anne Veronica, *b* 1914; European War 1939-45 as Flight Officer WAAF (despatches): *m* 1948, Com William Frances Roderick Segrave, DSC, RN (ret), who *d* 1974, and has issue living, Roderick Alan Neil (21 Clarendon Gdns, Little Venice, W9 1AZ), *b* 1956; *ed* Ampleforth; has issue (by Hilary Greene), Alexander Nicholas *b* 1985, Laurence Francis *b* (twin) 1985, — Elisa Mary (47 Campden Hill Sq, W8 7JR), *b* 1949: *m* 1981, Andrew Barrow, and has issue living, Nicholas *b* 1983, Lauretta *b* 1981. *Residence* – Isfield Place, Isfield, nr Uckfield, Sussex.

GRAHAM (E) 1629, of Esk, Cumberland

Sir RALPH STUART GRAHAM, 14th *Baronet*; *b* 5 Nov 1950; *s* his father, Sir RALPH WOLFE, 1988; *ed* Hofstra Univ: *m* 1st, 1972, Roxanne, who *d* 1978, da of Mrs Lovette Gurzan, of Elmont, Long Island, New York; 2ndly, 1979, Deena Louise, da of William Robert Vandergrift, of 2963 Nemesis, Waukegan, Illinois, USA.

Arms – Quarterly: 1st and 4th, or, on a chief sable three escallops of the first, *Graham*; 2nd and 3rd, or, a fesse checky argent and azure in chief a chevron gules, *Stuart*. Crest – Two wings addorsed or.
Residence – 7441 Highway 705,#440, Nashville, Tennessee 37221, USA.

ADOPTED SON LIVING

Gabriel Lawrence, *b* 1974.

BROTHER LIVING

ROBERT BRUCE (325 Hubbs Av, Hauppauge, Long Island, NY 11788, USA), *b* 14 Nov 1953: *m* 1974, Denise, da of T. Juranich, of Floral Park, Long Island, NY, and has issue living, Brian Robert, *b* 19 March 1979, — Stephen Ralph, *b* 1981.

DAUGHTERS LIVING OF TWELFTH BARONET

Lynne Elizabeth, *b* 1937: *m* 1959, Robert Jager, of 110 Elward Av, West Islip, Long Island, New York, and has issue living, Marie Lynne, *b* 1960, — Cindy Kay, *b* 1961. —— Dana Stuart, *b* 1940: *m* 1961, Robert Brust, of 2501 Rutler St, Bellmore, Long Island, New York, and has issue living, Robert George, *b* 1961, — William Edward, *b* 1965, — Elizabeth Lynne, *b* 1971.

DAUGHTER LIVING OF ELEVENTH BARONET

Jessie Louise (Apt 12G, 9000, Shore Rd, West Brooklyn, NY 11209, USA), *b* 1907: *m* 1936, Robert S. Bolton, who *d* 1944.

WIDOWS LIVING OF TWELFTH AND THIRTEENTH BARONETS

ELIZABETH ANN (*Elizabeth, Lady Graham*) (45 Aster Av, North Merrick, Long Island, New York, USA), da of John Gerken, of St Albans, Long Island, USA: *m* 1932, Sir Montrose Stuart Graham, 12th Bt, who *d* 1975.
GERALDINE (*Geraldine, Lady Graham*) (904 Earps Court, Nashville, TN 37221, USA), da of Austin Velour, of Brooklyn, New York, USA: *m* 1949, as his 2nd wife, Sir Ralph Wolfe Graham, 13th Bt, who *d* 1988.

COLLATERAL BRANCHES LIVING

Issue of late Robert Vernon Graham, 3rd son of 10th baronet, *b* 1883, *d* 1943: *m* 1904, Charlotte Elizabeth, who *d* 1938, da of late Gilbert Baldwin Smith of Brooklyn, USA:—
Mildred Jane Elizabeth, *b* 1916: *m* 1st, 1942 (*m diss* 1953), William E. Young, RM; 2ndly, 1965 F. W. Rementer, of 829, Spruce St, Collingdale, Pa 19023, USA, and of St Petersburg, Fla, and has issue living, (by 1st *m*) William Ernest (Box 436, Millheim, Pa 16854, USA), *b* 1944; late US Navy, a doctor: *m* 1976, Marylou, da of Charles Matz, of Ohio, and has issue living, Jonathan *b* 1984, Gretchen *b* 1983.

Grandchildren of late Robert Vernon Graham (ante):—
Issue of late James Robert Stuart Graham, *b* 1907, *d* 1960: *m* 1929, Agnes, who *d* 1976, da of late Dennis Harvey, of Brooklyn, USA:—
Roberta Naomi, *b* 1930: *m* 1957, James Joseph Munson, of 226 Beach 119th St, Rockaway Park, New York, USA, and has issue living, James, *b* 1958, — John, *b* 1959, — Joseph, *b* 1964, — Marilyn, *b* 1963. —— Joan Charlotte, *b* 1933: *m* 1958, Herbert John Nichol, of Merrick, NY, USA, and has issue living, Robert, *b* 1959, — Stephen, *b* 1970, — Catherine, *b* 1962, — Linda, *b* 1967, — Susan, *b* 1972.
Issue of late Howard George William Graham, *b* 1910, *d* 1957: *m* 1938, Madelyn, da of Joseph Fitzsimmons, of Archbold, Pennsylvania, USA:—
Charlotte Elizabeth, *b* 1940: *m* 1960, Daniel Coradi, of 159 Chestnut St, Archbald, Pa 18403, USA, and has issue living, Robert, *b* 1961, — Kenneth, *b* 1963, — Andrew, *b* 1965, — Cregg, *b* 1973.
Issue of late Douglas Duncan Graham, *b* 1912, *d* 1984: *m* 1st, 1937 (*m diss* 1948), Harriet, da of Thomas Lloyd, of Brooklyn, USA; 2ndly, 1948, Sally (1428 Bellmore Av, Bellmore, New York, USA), da of Thomas Gale, of Southampton, Long Island, USA:—
(By 1st *m*) Harriet Mable, *b* 1938. —— (By 2nd *m*) James Robert, *b* 1952. —— Roland, *b* 1954. —— Brenda Gale, *b* 1949.

Issue of late George Edward Graham, yst son of 10th baronet, *b* 1890, *d* 1969: *m* 1912, Florence Ethel, who *d* 1979, da of late George Alfred Milne, of Brooklyn, New York:—

George Edward (329, Benton St, Orlando, Fla 32809, USA), *b* 1920; Lt-Col USAF (ret): *m* 1945, Jean Myra MacRury, and has issue living, Stuart George, *b* 1949, — Leslie Jean, *b* 1951. —— Dorothy, *b* 1917: *m* 1938, Ralph Alfred Hassler, and has issue living, Donald Evan, *b* 1950, — Laura Jean, *b* 1948, — Judith Ann, *b* 1953.

Granddaughter of late Lieut-Col Frederick Graham, el son of Maj-Gen Stuart Frederick Graham (infra):—
Issue of late Stuart Menteith Graham, *b* 1886, *d* 1957: *m* 1919, Leonore (Mollie) da of late Capt Morrish, Rifle
Brig:—
Marjorie Barbara Stuart, *b* 1921: *m* 1963, David Sherwin Walker.

Grandchildren of late Maj-Gen Stuart Frederick Graham, 5th son of 8th baronet:—
Issue of late Major William Bannatyne Graham, *b* 1858, *d* 1897: *m* 1884, Mary Beatrice, who *d* 1941, da of late Rev
E. H. Hansell, R of East Illsley, Berks:—
Edward William Harold, *b* 1888; formerly in Eastern Extension Telegraph Co, Cocos Keeling Islands; European War 1916-18
in Italy. —— Stuart Douglas, MC, *b* 1890; Brigadier (ret) late RA; is a Jurat of Roy Court Jersey; European War 1914-18 in
Salonica and France (despatches twice, MC), European War 1939-45 (wounded): *m* 1916, Marjorie Helen, el da of H. Le
Maistre. —— Mary Dorothy: *m* 1916, Wilfrid Saunders, formerly India Education Dept.
Issue of late Malcolm Macleod Graham, *b* 1872, *d* 19—: *m* 1896, Leopoldine (Buenos Aires, Argentine Republic), da
of Mark Gallacher, of Rosario, Argentine Republic:—
Richard Walter Malcolm, *b* 1903: *m* 19—. —— Oswald Charles, *b* 1906. —— Agnes Beatrice, *b* 1897: *m* 19—, Jack
Maclaughlin.

Descendants of late James Graham (2nd son of late Rev Robert Graham, DD, 2nd son of late
Very Rev William Graham, DD 3rd son of 2nd baronet), who was *cr* a *Baronet* 1783:—
See Graham, Bt *cr* 1783.

Grandchildren of late Major Fergus Graham, son of late Rev William Paley Graham, son of late Rev
Fergus Graham, LLD, 4th son of late Rev Robert Graham (ante):—
Issue of late Col Fergus Reginald Winsford Graham, DSO, MC, *b* 1884, *d* 1961: *m* 1915, Egeria Marion Spottiswood,
who *d* 1973, da of Vice-Adm Casper Joseph Baker, formerly of Oaklands, Petherton, Somerset:—
Dominick Stuart, MC (The Hollins, East Rounton, Northallerton, N Yorkshire), *b* 1920; Maj (ret) RA; PhD; Prof of History,
Univ of New Brunswick; 1939-45 War (wounded twice, despatches, MC): *m* 1st, 1947, Valerie Mary, da of late Farleigh H.
Greig, of Fleet, Hant; 2ndly, 1991, Mary, widow of Sir Hugh Francis Bell, 4th Bt, and da of late George Howson, MC, of
The Hyde, Hambledon, Bucks, and has issue living (by 1st *m*), Anita Caroline, *b* 1949, — Patricia Robin, *b* 1952.
—— Caroline Egeria Malise, *b* 1929: *m* 1952, Col Thomas Wemyss Muir, Queen's Dragoon Guards (ret), and has issue
living, James Fergus Wemyss, *b* 1963, — Elizabeth Anne, *b* 1955: *m* 1979, Lt-Col Sebastian John Lechmere Roberts, OBE,
Irish Gds, — Sarah Jane, *b* 1957: *m* 1986, Colin George Climie, — Alexandra Caroline, *b* 1959: *m* 1978, Nicholas Leese.
Residence – Torquhan, Stow, Midlothian.
The 1st baronet, Sir Richard Graham (son of Fergus Graham), was a Gentleman of the Horse to Charles I, and
distinguished himself at the battle of Edgehill. The 3rd baronet, Sir Richard, was *cr Viscount Preston* (peerage of Scotland)
1680, was British Ambassador to France and sometime a Sec of State to James II; after the Revolution he was condemned
for high treason, but was subsequently pardoned. The Baronetcy remained merged in the Viscountcy until the death of the
3rd Viscount in 1739, when it devolved upon his kinsman, Rev Sir William, 6th Bt.

GRAHAM 1662, of Norton Conyers, Yorkshire

Sir JAMES BELLINGHAM GRAHAM, 11th *Baronet*; *b* 8 Oct 1940; *s* his
father, *Wing-Com Sir* RICHARD BELLINGHAM, OBE, RAFVR, 1982; *ed*
Eton, and Ch Ch: *m* 1986, Halina, yr da of late Major Wiktor
Grubert, of Putney, London.

Arms – Quarterly: 1st and 4th or, of a chief sable three escallops of the field,
Graham; 2nd and 3rd, or, a fesse checky argent and azure in chief a chevronel
gules, *Stuart*; in the centre of the quarters a crescent of the third; all within a
border engrailed of the third. **Crest** – Two wings addorsed or.
Seat – Norton Conyers, Melmerby, nr Ripon. *Address* – 3 Glebe Rd, Bedford
MK40 2PL.

BROTHERS LIVING

WILLIAM REGINALD (Badger Bank, Norton Conyers, Ripon, Yorks), *b* 7 July 1942;
ed privately. —— Jeremy Richard (Badger Bank, Norton Conyers, Ripon, N
Yorks), *b* 1949; *ed* Eton: *m* 1976, Judith, da of Gerard McCann, of Castle House,
Aldborough, Boroughbridge, Yorks, and has issue living, Samuel Reginald, *b*
1979, — Edward Richard, *b* 1985, — Sophia Harriet, *b* 1977.

COLLATERAL BRANCHES LIVING

Issue of late Maj Alastair Graham, MC, 2nd son of 9th
baronet, *b* 1915, *d* 1975: *m* 1942, Gundreda Margaret
(Middleton Quernhow, Ripon, Yorks HG4 5HY), da of late J.
L. Graham Jones, MB, of Bockhampton House, Dorchester,
Dorset:—
Caroline Susan, *b* 1943: *m* 1990, Robert H. Richheimer, of 1596 Vista Claridad,
La Jolla, San Diego, California 92037, USA, only son of late Robert C.
Richheimer, of La Jolla, California. —— Priscilla Ann, *b* (twin) 1948: *m* 1968,
Maj Peter Norman Bingham Kennedy, TD, DL, of Doonholm, Ayr, and has
issue living, Sara Margaret, *b* 1971, — Annabel Deborah, *b* 1973, — Caroline
Anne, *b* 1980, — Rosanna Jane, *b* 1982.

Issue of late Jeremy Frank Graham, yst son of 9th baronet, *b* 1926, *d* 1992: *m* 1950, Susan May (Plaster
Pitts, Ripon, Yorks), 2nd da of late Col Sir Thomas Eustace-Smith, CBE, TD, of Barton Hall, Darlington:—
Robin Guy, *b* 1953: *m* 1979, Annabel Mary Diana, el da of Michael David Aykroyd (*see* Aykroyd, Bt *cr* 1920), and has issue
living, Andrew Guy Bellingham, *b* 1981, — Rory Michael, *b* 1984. —— Nigel Ronald, *b* 1957: *m* 1982, Henrietta Jane Fane,
da of Maj Jerome De Salis, of Bourne House, E Woodhay, Newbury, Berks (*see* B Monk Bretton). —— (Elizabeth) Jacoba,

b 1951: *m* 1971, Capt Christopher Russell Oldham, R Hussars (ret), of 78 Paxton Rd, W4 2QX, and has issue living, Justin Russell, *b* 1974. — Mark Russell, *b* 1977.

The 1st baronet of Norton Conyers, received his baronetcy from Charles II, 1662, for services rendered to the Restoration. He was the 2nd son of Sir Richard Graham, 1st Bt (*cr* 1629), of Esk, the distinguished Royalist and Gentleman of the Horse to King Charles I, and fought at Edgehill and Marston Moor. The 9th Bt, Major Sir (Reginald) Guy, DSO, served in S Africa 1899-1902 and in European War 1914-19 (DSO). The 10th Bt, Sir Richard was Chm of Yorkshire TV from 1968-82.

GRAHAM (GB 1783), of Netherby, Cumberland

Sir CHARLES SPENCER RICHARD GRAHAM, 6th *Baronet*; *b* 16 July 1919; *s* his father, *Lt-Col Sir* (FREDERICK) FERGUS, KBE, TD, 1978; *ed* Eton; formerly Maj Scots Gds; and DL of Cumbria (1970) (High Sheriff 1955-56), and Lord Lieut 1983-94; Pres of Country Land Owners Assocn 1971-73; Master of Farmers Co 1982-83 and Memb of Nat Water Council 1973-83; 1939-45 War (despatches), Malaya 1949-50; KStJ 1984: *m* 1944, (Isabel) Susan Anne, only da of Maj Robert Lambton Surtees, OBE, of Redworth Cottage, Littlestone, Kent, and has issue.

Arms – Quarterly: 1st and 4th or, on a chief sable three escallops of the field, *Graham*; 2nd and 3rd or, a fesse checky argent and azure in chief a chevronel gules, *Stuart*; in the centre of the quarters a crescent of the last; all within a bordure engrailed azure. **Crest** – Two wings addorsed or.
Seat – Crofthead, Longtown, Cumbria CA6 5PA. *Clubs* – Brooks's, Pratt's.

SONS LIVING

JAMES FERGUS SURTEES (The Tower, Kirkandrews-on-Esk, Longtown, Cumbria), *b* 29 July 1946; *ed* Milton Abbey: *m* 1975, Serena Jane, yr da of Maj Ronald Frank Kershaw (*see* E Lindsey and Abingdon, colls), and has issue living, Robert Charles Thomas, *b* 19 July 1985, — Catherine Mary, *b* 1978, — Iona Susan Alice, *b* 1980. ——— Malise Charles Richard (The Cottage, Sproxton, Melton Mowbray, Leics LE14 4QS), *b* 1948; *ed* Milton Abbey: *m* 1974, Hon Pamela Winifred, da of 1st Viscount Whitelaw, CH, MC, and has issue living, Arabella Mary Susan, *b* 1975, — Georgina Carol Cecilia, *b* 1977, — Laura Meliora Winifred *b* 1981, — Victoria Malise Samantha, *b* 1985.

DAUGHTER LIVING

Susanna Anne Mary, *b* 1951.

COLLATERAL BRANCHES LIVING

Grandson of late Rev Malise Reginald Graham, 2nd son of 2nd baronet:—
Issue of late Reginald Graham, *b* 1867, *d* 1908: *m* 1897, Helen Dacia, da of G. S. Herck, of St Petersburg:—
Ernest Reginald, *b* 1898.

Grandchildren of late (Richard) Preston Graham-Vivian, MVO, MC (infra):—
Issue of late Henry Richard Graham-Vivian, JP, DL, *b* 1923, *d* 1993: *m* 1955, Rosemary (Bosahan, Manaccan, Helston, Cornwall), only da of Col Giffard Loftus Tyringham:—
Richard John, *b* 1957. ——— Lavinia, *b* 1959.

Issue of late (Richard) Preston GRAHAM-VIVIAN, MVO, MC, 2nd son of 4th baronet (who assumed by Royal Licence 1929 the additional surname of Vivian), Windsor Herald 1947-66, Norroy and Ulster King of Arms 1966-72, *b* 1896, *d* 1979: *m* 1921, Audrey Emily (Wealden House, Warninglid, Sussex) da of late Maj Henry Wyndham Vivian (*see* B Swansea, colls):—
Catherine Maude (Ludgates, Nutbourne, Pulborough), *b* 1926: *m* 1947, Lt-Col John Peter Thomson-Glover, MC, 9th/12th Royal Lancers, who *d* 1968, and has issue living, Michael William (20 Crondace Rd, SW6), *b* 1948; *ed* Wellington, and Trin Coll, Camb (BA): *m* 1974, Katherine, da of John David Summers, and has issue living, James Antony *b* 1988, Peter David *b* (twin) 1988, Sarah Emily *b* 1977, Rebecca Evelyn *b* 1979, Rachel Caroline *b* 1981, — (Peter) James, *b* 1953; *ed* Wellington; FCA: *m* 1982, Veronica Harrison, and has issue living, Edward *b* 1984, Rosie Catherine *b* 1990, — Caroline Veronica, *b* 1950.

This family is descended from Very Rev William Graham, DD, 4th son of Sir George Graham, 2nd Bt, of Esk (*cr* 1629). The 2nd baronet of Netherby, Sir James, GBE, PC, an eminent statesman, sat as MP successively for Hull, East Cumberland, Carlisle, Pembroke, Dorchester, and Ripon, and filled various high offices of State.

GRAHAM 1906, of Larbert House, Larbert and Househill, Dunipace, co Stirling

Forget not

Sir JOHN ALEXANDER NOBLE GRAHAM, GCMG, 4th *Baronet*; *b* 15 July 1926; *s* his father, *Lt-Col Sir* JOHN REGINALD NOBLE, VC, OBE, 1980; *ed* Eton, and Trin Coll, Camb; Lt Gren Gds, Palestine 1946-47; 3rd Sec Bahrain 1951-52, Kuwait 1952-53, and Amman 1953-54, Assist Private Sec to Foreign Sec 1954-57, Second (later First) Sec Belgrade 1957-60, First Sec and Consul Benghazi 1960-61, FO 1961-66, Counsellor Kuwait 1966-69, Prin Private Sec to Foreign Sec 1969-72, Head of Chancery, Washington 1972-74, and Ambassador to Iraq 1974-77, Dep Under-Sec FCO 1977-78 and 1980-81; HM Amb to Iran 1979-80; UK Permanent Rep N Atlantic Council, Brussels 1982-86; Dir The Ditchley Foundation 1987-92; Registrar of the Most Distinguished Order of St Michael and St George since 1987; CMG 1972, KCMG 1979, GCMG 1985: *m* 1st, 1956, Marygold Ellinor Gabrielle, who *d* 1991, da of late Lt-Col Clive Grantham Austin, RHA, JP, DL (E Scarbrough); 2ndly, 1992, Jane, widow of Christopher Howells, and has issue living by 1st *m*.

Arms – Or, on a chief invected ermine three escallops of the first. **Crest** – A falcon proper, beaked and armed or, killing a stork argent armed gules.
Residence – Salisbury Place, Church St, Shipton under Wychwood, Chipping Norton, Oxon OX7 6BP. *Club* – Army and Navy.

SONS LIVING *(By 1st marriage)*

ANDREW JOHN NOBLE, MBE, *b* 21 Oct 1956; *ed* Eton, and Trin Coll Camb; Lt-Col Argyll and Sutherland Highlanders; MBE (Mil) 1993: *m* 1984, Susan Mary Bridget, da of Rear Adm John Patrick Bruce O'Riordan, CBE, RN (ret), of The Old Rectory, Whilton, Northants, and has issue living, James Patrick Noble, *b* 15 March 1990, — Katharine Rose, *b* 1986, — Louisa Christian, *b* 1988, — Isabella Alice, *b* 1993. *Clubs* – Army and Navy, MCC, RGS. —— George Reginald Clive, *b* 1958; *ed* Eton, and Trin Coll, Camb; journalist: *m* 1988, Carol A., da of Julian Madison, of Cleveland, Ohio, USA, and has issue living, John Reginald Austin, *b* 1992.

DAUGHTER LIVING *(By 1st marriage)*

Christian Rachel, *b* 1961: *m* 1985, Dr Matthew Scott Dryden, elder son of W.S. Dryden, of Great Gaddesden, Herts, and has issue living, Alexander William Scott, *b* 1988, — Thomas Andrew, *b* 1992, — Gabriella Josephine, *b* 1990.

SISTER LIVING

Lesley, *b* 1921: *m* 1945, Jock Wykeham Strang Steel, son of Sir Samuel Strang Steel, 1st Bt, and has issue (*see* Steel, Bt).
Residence – Haydean, Haddington, East Lothian EH41 4HN.

COLLATERAL BRANCH LIVING

Grandsons of late Sir (John) Frederick Noble Graham, 2nd Bt:—
Issue of late Maj-Gen Frederick Clarence Campbell Graham, CB, DSO, late Argyll and Sutherland Highlanders, *b* 1908, *d* 1988: *m* 1936, Phyllis Mary (The Gled, Mackeanston, Doune, Perthshire), da of late Maj-Gen Hugh Francis Edward MacMahon, CB, CSI, CBE, MC:—
Colin Hugh Campbell, TD (Mackeanston House, Doune, Perthshire. *Club* – New (Edinburgh)), *b* 1940; *ed* Eton; late Capt 51st Highland Volunteers (TAVR); Memb Queen's Body Guard for Scotland (Royal Co of Archers) since 1983; a Dir Grahams (Oporto) Ltd 1963-67, Export Exec Macdonald and Muir Ltd, Leith, 1978-91: *m* 1st, 1963 (*m diss* 1986), Joanna (Jan) Kathleen, da of late David Chancellor, of Pencaitland, E Lothian; 2ndly, 1986, Fiona Jacqueline Richmond, da of late John Michael Richmond Paton, of Hay Park, Stow, Borders, and has issue living, (by 1st *m*) William Frederick Chancellor, *b* 1963: *m* 1989, Victoria L., eldest da of John Beasley, of Shrewsbury, and has issue living, Frederick Sebastian Chancellor *b* 1994, Alice Elizabeth *b* 1991, — David Campbell, *b* 1969, — Suzanna Lucy, *b* 1967, — (by 2nd *m*) Rory Michael Alexander, *b* 1988, — Neil Alasdair Richmond, *b* 1991. —— Ewan Alastair MacMahon (c/o Lloyds Bank, Cox's & King's Branch, 6 Pall Mall, SW1), *b* 1944; *ed* Eton; Lt-Col Argyll and Sutherland Highlanders; Member Queen's Bodyguard for Scotland (Royal Company of Archers) since 1994: *m* 1st, 1967 (*m diss* 1982), Sara Diones, da of late Maj-Gen Reginald Geoffrey Stirling Hobbs, CB, DSO, OBE; 2ndly, 1982, Sarah Rose, da of late Cdr David Enderby Blunt, RN, and has issue living (by 1st *m*), Calum James MacMahon, *b* 1970, — Fergus Hugh Stirling, *b* 1973. —— (Kenneth) James (Gorsefield House, Newtown, nr Newbury, Berks RG15 9BE), *b* 1947; *ed* Eton, and Northwestern Univ, Chicago; late 2nd Lieut Argyll and Sutherland Highlanders; Exec Digital Equipment Corpn: *m* 1972, Victoria Margaret Anne, yst da of late Maj Andrew Stirling Home Drummond Moray, of Easter Ross, Comrie, Perthshire, and has issue living, Magnus James, *b* 1974, — Nina Louise, *b* 1976.
This family is a cadet branch of Graham of Tamrawer, descended from Graham of Auchincloich, nr Kilsyth, Stirlingshire, who derive from John, 3rd son of Sir David Graham (d c 1376), ancestor of Dukes of Montrose. The 1st baronet, Sir John Hatt Noble Graham was a member of the firm of William Graham and Co, merchants, of 400 Cathedral St, Glasgow, and of Grahams Co (London), East India merchants. The 2nd baronet was Chm of Glasgow Chamber of Commerce.

GRAHAM (UK) 1964, of Dromore, co Down

Sir JOHN MOODIE GRAHAM, 2nd *Baronet*; *b* 3rd April 1938; *s* his father, *Sir* CLARENCE JOHNSTON, 1966; *ed* Trin Coll, Glenalmond, and Queen's Univ, Belfast (BSc); Pres of N Ireland Leukaemia Research Fund: *m* 1970 (*m diss* 1982), Valerie Rosemary, da of late Frank Gill, of 5 Greenview Park, Belfast 9, and has issue.
Residences – Lista de Correos, 07819 Jesus, Ibiza, Baleares, Spain.

DAUGHTERS LIVING

Suzanne Margaret, *b* 1971. —— Alyson Rosemary, *b* 1974. —— Lucy Christina, *b* 1978.

Sir Clarence Johnston Graham, 1st Bt, was Chm of Standing Cttee, Ulster Unionist Council 1947-63, and a Dir of John Graham (Dromore) Ltd, Engineering Contractors.

GRANT (NS) 1688, of Dalvey

Te favente virebo

Under thy favour will I flourish

Sir PATRICK ALEXANDER BENEDICT GRANT, 14th *Baronet*; *b* 5 Feb 1953; *s* his father, *Sir* DUNCAN ALEXANDER, 1961; *ed* Abbey Sch, Fort Augustus and Glasgow Univ (LLB); Chm and Man Dir of Grants of Dalvey Ltd, Queen's Award for Exports 1992; Chieftain of Clan Donnachy: *m* 1981, Carolyn Elizabeth, MB, ChB, da of John Highet, MA, DPhil, of 319 Albert Drive, Glasgow, and has issue.

Arms – Gules, three antique crowns or within a bordure engrailed of the last with the Baronets' badge of Nova Scotia in the dexter canton. **Crest** – The trunk of an oak-tree sprouting out some leaves with the sun shining thereon all proper. **Supporters** – *Dexter*, a highlander; *sinister*, a negro proper. *Residence* – Tomintoul House, Flichity, Farr, Inverness-shire IV1 2XD.

SONS LIVING

DUNCAN ARCHIBALD LUDOVIC, *b* 19 April 1982. —— Neil Patrick, *b* 1983.

BROTHERS LIVING

Denzil Mohun Bede (Hubbards Corner, Gedding Rd, Bradfield St George Nr Bury St Edmunds, Suffolk), *b* 1955; *ed* Abbey Sch, Fort Augustus, and W Dean Coll, Chichester (BA); Man Dir of Suffolk Fine Arts Ltd: *m* 1977, Nicola, da of A. T. Savill, of Godalming, Surrey, and has issue living, Alexandra, *b* 1978, — Diana *b* 1983, — Charlotte *b* 1986. —— Drostan John (34 Morehampton Rd, Dublin 4), *b* 1956; BE, MBA: *m* 1986, Celia Gabriella, elder da of Gerald Mattei, and has issue living, Antonia Maria, *b* 1987, — Christina Andrea, *b* 1989.

SISTERS LIVING

Fiona Mary Julia, *b* 1950: *m* 1966, Christopher Kanthack St John Bird, of Cavendish Mill, Mill Lane, Cavendish, Sudbury, Suffolk, and has issue living, Christopher Kenelm Anthony, *b* 1967, — Theodore Denzil Drostan, *b* 1971, — Penelope Frances Julia, *b* 1968. —— Maria Teresa, *b* 1951: *m* 1968, Ramon Anthony Cooke, BE, CEng, MIEI, and has issue living, Jessica Fiona, *b* 1969.

AUNT LIVING (*Sister of 13th baronet*)

Diana Mary, *b* 1931; *ed* St Leonard's Sch, and London (BA 1954) Univ: *m* 1954, Jean-Pierre Dalcher, and has issue living, Claude Francis, *b* 1957, — Derrick Albert Alexander, *b* 1959: *m* 1987, Anne Parel, and has issue living, Samuel *b* 1991, Sarah *b* 1988, Rachel *b* 1993, — Anne, *b* 1956. *Residence* – Villa Fidelis, Chemin du Blessoney 18, 1092, Belmont-sur-Lausanne, Vaud, Switzerland.

GREAT-AUNT LIVING (*Daughter of 12th baronet*)

Guinevere (*Lady Tilney, DBE*), *b* 1916; formerly 2nd Officer WRNS; DL for Lancs; Member of BBC Gen Advisory Council since 1967, Pres Nat Council of Women of Gt Britain 1968-70, Chm Women's National Commn 1969-71, British Rep of UN Status of Women Commn 1970-73; Co-Chm Women Caring Trust since 1972; DBE (1983): *m* 1st, 1944, Capt K. Lionel Hunter, R Canadian Dragoons, who *d* 1947; 2ndly, 1954, Col Sir John Dudley Robert Tarleton Tilney, TD, JP, who *d* 1994, and has issue living, (by 1st *m*) Tony Lionel HUNTER-TILNEY, *b* 1947; *ed* Eton, and Magdalen Coll, Oxford (BA); assumed by deed poll 1954 the additional surname of Tilney: *m* 1970, Juliet Faller, and has issue living, Ludovic John Grant *b* 1971, Sophie Jessica Frances *b* 1975. *Residence* – 3 Victoria Sq, SW1.

COLLATERAL BRANCH LIVING

Issue of late Percy Frere Grant, MB, 4th son of 10th baronet, *b* 1869, *d* 1909: *m* (Feb) 1905, Theodora, who *d* 1938, da of J. H. Goodrich:—

Winifred Anne St John, *b* (Nov) 1905; *ed* Cape Town Univ (BA): *m* 1930, Gerard Anthony Thomson, of 55 Kings Way, Warner Beach S Coast, Natal 4125. —— Susan Ursula (10 Westerford Rd, Newlands, Cape, S Africa), *b* 1907: *m* 1930, Christian Arnold Wahl, who *d* 1967.

This baronetcy was conferred with remainder to heirs male whatsoever, and on the death of the 1st baronet without issue in 1695, the title remained unassumed until Patrick Grant, of Inverladinen, a distant relative, was served heir male general to the 1st baronet in 1752, *s* as 4th baronet and *d* in his 101st year in 1755. The 8th baronet, MP, for Cambridge, was Chairman of Committees in Parliament 1826-30, a member of the Board of Control 1835, and subsequently, a Commissioner for Auditing the Public Accounts. The 10th baronet was Principal and Vice-Chancellor of Edinburgh University 1868-84. The 11th baronet was Regius Professor of Public Law and of the Law of Nature and Nations in Edinburgh Univ 1890-1922. The 12th baronet was Foreign Sec to Gov of India 1914-19, and Ch Commr N-W Frontier Province 1919-21.

GRANT (NS) 1705, of Cullen, co Buchan

Sir ARCHIBALD GRANT, 13th *Baronet, b* 2 Sept 1954; *s* his father, *Capt Sir* FRANCIS CULLEN, 1966; *ed* Trinity Coll, Glenalmond, and RAC Cirencester (Dip Farm Mgmnt): *m* 1982, Barbara Elizabeth, el da of Andrew Garden Duff Forbes, of Overskibo House, Dornoch, Sutherland (*see* Stuart-Forbes, Bt, colls), and has issue.

Arms – Gules, three antique crowns or, within a border ermine. **Crest** – A Bible expanded proper. **Supporters** – Two Angels proper, wings or.
Seat – House of Monymusk, Monymusk, Aberdeenshire.

DAUGHTERS LIVING

Christian Mariot, *b* 1986. —— Catriona Elizabeth, *b* 1988.

BROTHERS LIVING

FRANCIS TOLLEMACHE, *b* 18 Dec 1955: *m* 1993, Virginia Elizabeth, da of R. Scott Russell, of E Hanney, Oxon. —— Duncan John Cullen, *b* 1957: *m* 1985, Maureen Cecilia, only da of Thomas Innes of Learney (*see* Innes, Bt, *cr* 1628), and has issue living, Robert Francis, *b* 1985, — Thomas William, *b* 1988, — Henry Douglas, *b* 1991.

SISTERS LIVING

Catriona Charmiane, *b* 1959. —— Sarah Jean, *b* 1961.

AUNTS LIVING (*Daughters of 10th baronet*)

Catherine Jean (*Lady Legge-Bourke*) (121 Dovehouse St, SW3 6JZ), *b* 1917: *m* 1938, Maj Sir Edward Alexander Henry Legge-Bourke, KBE, MP, DL, Royal Horse Gds, who *d* 1973, and has issue (*see* E Dartmouth, colls). —— Christian (*Lady Bowman*), *b* 1920: *m* 1st, 1942 (*m diss* 1951), Michael Fife William Angas, Gren Gds, who *d* 1983; 2ndly, 1953, John Gordon Ogston Miller, who *d* 1992; 3rdly, 1993, as his 3rd wife, Sir John Paget Bowman, 4th Bt, and has issue living, (by 1st *m*) Auburn Carolyn Catherine, *b* 1945, — Cherill Melmere, *b* 1947: *m* 1966 (*m diss* 1974), Charles Heckstall, of Virginia, USA, and has issue living, Cyprian Carolus *b* 1967.

DAUGHTERS LIVING OF ELEVENTH BARONET (*and Baroness Tweedsmuir of Belhelvie*)

Hon Joanna Catherine, *b* 1935: *m* 1954 (*m diss* 1966), Dominick Jones, son of Sir (George) Roderick Jones, KBE, and has issue living, Romily Arthur, *b* 1956. —— *Hon* Margaret Anne GRANT (24 Amity Grove, SW20 0LJ), *b* 1937; *ed* Lady Margaret Hall, Oxford (MA); has resumed her maiden name: *m* 1965 (*m diss* 1983), Nicholas Mangriotis, of Athens, Greece, and has issue living, Paraskevas, *b* 1971, — Arthuros, *b* 1974.

WIDOW LIVING OF TWELFTH BARONET

JEAN MARGHERITA (*Baroness Tweedsmuir*), da of late Capt Humphrey Douglas Tollemache, RN (*see* B Tollemache, colls): *m* 1st, 1953, Capt Sir Francis Cullen Grant, 12th Bt, who *d* 1966; 2ndly, 1980, as his 2nd wife, 2nd Baron Tweedsmuir, CBE, CD, of Kingston House, Kingston Bagpuize, Oxfordshire.

This family is a branch of the noble house of Grant (Earls of Seafield). Archibald Grant of Ballentomb, progenitor of this line was 4th son of James Grant, 3rd of Freuchie (now Castle Grant), who *d* 1553. The 1st baronet, Sir Francis (Lord Cullen, a Senator of the College of Justice and 4th in descent from Archibald) was created a baronet by Queen Anne. The 2nd baronet, Sir Archibald, carried out extensive agric reforms and tree planting. The 10th baronet, Col Sir Arthur Grant, CBE, DSO, served in S Africa 1899-1902, and during 1914-18 War (severely wounded). The 11th baronet, Maj Sir Arthur Lindsay Grant, Grenadier Guards, was *ka* 1944 (despatches). The 12th baronet, Capt Sir Francis Cullen Grant, RE served in Normandy campaign (despatches).

MACPHERSON-GRANT (UK) 1838, of Ballindalloch, Elgin (Extinct 1983)

Maj Sir EWAN GEORGE MACPHERSON-GRANT, 6th and last *Baronet*.

DAUGHTER LIVING OF SIXTH BARONET

Clare Nancy, *b* 1944; DL Banffshire: *m* 1967, Oliver Henry Russell, of Ballindalloch Castle, Banffshire, son of late Adm Hon Sir Guy Herbrand Edward Russell, GBE, KCB, DSO, and has issue (*see* B Ampthill, colls).

SISTER LIVING OF SIXTH BARONET

Mary, *b* 1905: *m* 1928, Col Andrew Hamilton Farquhar Fausset-Farquhar, DSO, TD, JP, Cameron and Gordon Highlanders, of Forest House, nr Dunkeld, Perthshire PH8 0JA, and has issue living, Angus Hamilton Macpherson, *b* 1934, — Hamish Bertram Mainwaring, *b* 1947, — Pamela Mary *b* 1929, — Daphne Primrose, *b* 1945: *m* 1982, Edmund Ralph Verney, only son of Maj Sir Ralph Bruce Verney, 5th Bt, KBE.

WIDOW LIVING OF SIXTH BARONET

(EVELYN) NANCY STOPFORD, da of late Maj Edward Spencer Dickin (E Courtown): *m* 1st, 1937, Maj Sir Ewan George Macpherson-Grant, 6th Bt, who *d* 1983, when the title became *ext*; 2ndly, 1986, James Dunbar Whatman, MC, late Gren Gds. *Residence* – Pitchroy Lodge, Blacksboat, Ballindalloch, Banffshire AB3 9BQ.

COLLATERAL BRANCH LIVING

Issue of late Alastair Macpherson-Grant, 3rd son of 3rd baronet, *b* 1874, *d* 1949: *m* 1904, Hester Charlotte, who *d* 1945, da of late Arthur C. Kennard, of 17 Eaton Place, SW:—

Anne Frances, *b* 1914: *m* 1939, Lt-Col William D. Keown-Boyd, OBE, 60th Rifles, and has issue living, Alexander, *b* 1949, — Jennifer, *b* 1942.

Grant-Suttie, see Suttie.

Grattan-Bellew, see Bellew

GRAY (UK) 1917, of Tunstall Manor, Hart, co Durham.

Sir WILLIAM HUME GRAY, 3rd *Baronet*, only son of late William Talbot Gray, el son of 2nd baronet; *b* 26 July 1955; *s* his grandfather, Sir WILLIAM, 1978; *ed* Eton, and Polytechnic of Central Lond: *m* 1984, Catherine, yst da of late John Naylor, of The Mill House, Bramley, Hants, and of Mrs Richard Jerram, of Trevanson, Wade-bridge, Cornwall, and has issue.

Arms – Barry of six argent and azure, a lion rampant gules, on a chief of the second two lymphads or. Crest – An anchor or in front of and supported by two lions jambs erased gules.
Seat – Eggleston Hall, Eggleston, Barnard Castle, co Durham.

SON LIVING

WILLIAM JOHN CRESSWELL, *b* 24 Aug 1986.

DAUGHTERS LIVING

Octavia, *b* 1987. —— Clementine, *b* 1990.

SISTERS LIVING

Victoria Eyre *b* 1958: *m* 1980, Nicholas David Barclay Straker, of Sough Hill, Caldwell, Darlington, co Durham, 2nd son of late Hugh Charles Straker, of Gaucin, Spain, and has issue living, Sam, *b* 1991, — Jacquetta, *b* 1984, — Chloë, *b* 1986. —— Emma, *b* 1962.

UNCLE LIVING (*Son of 2nd baronet*)

Nicholas Anthony, *b* 1934: *m* 1956, Amanda, only da of H. W. Edwards, of Ashmore Green, Newbury, Berks, and has issue living, Daisy, *b* 1970.

MOTHER LIVING

Rosemarie Hume (The Cottage, Eggleston Hall, Eggleston, Barnard Castle, co Durham), da of Air Commodore Charles Elliott-Smith: *m* 1954, William Talbot Gray, el son of 2nd Bt, who *d* 1971.

WIDOW LIVING OF SECOND BARONET

BERYL (*Beryl, Lady Gray*) (Bryanhaven, Eype, Dorset), da of Alfred Stott, of Crowborough, Sussex, formerly wife of Norman Scotson Henshaw: *m* 1947, as his 2nd wife, Sir William Gray, 2nd Bt, who *d* 1978.

The 1st baronet, Sir William Cresswell Gray, Chm of the firm of William Gray and Co Limited, and a Member of *Lloyds Register* Committee, founded the S Durham Steel and Iron Co Limited 1889.

GRAYSON (UK) 1922, of Ravenspoint, Co Anglesey

Virtue is the safest tower

Sir JEREMY BRIAN VINCENT GRAYSON, 5th *Baronet*; *b* 30 Jan 1933; *s* his uncle, *Sir* RUPERT STANLEY HARRINGTON, 1991; *ed* Downside: *m* 1958, Sara Mary, da of late C. F. Upton, of Monte Carlo, and has issue.

Arms – Sable, on a fesse between a portcullis in chief and a lymphad in base or, two ravens of the first. **Crest** – In front of a rising sun or, a tower proper, issuant therefrom a demi-lion sable resting between the paws a spur gold. *Residence* – 54 Bucharest Rd, SW18 3AR.

SONS LIVING

SIMON JEREMY, *b* 12 July 1959. —— Paul Francis, *b* 1965. —— Mark Christopher, *b* 1968.

DAUGHTERS LIVING AND DECEASED

Caroline Mary, *b* 1961. —— Anna Katherine, *b* 1962: *m* 1991, Christopher William Turner. —— Mary, *b* and *d* 1964. —— Lucy Kate, *b* 1970.

SISTER LIVING

Jane Angela (92 Talbot Rd, Highgate, N6 4RA), *b* 1931.

HALF-SISTER LIVING

Alicia Lorraine, *b* 1953: *m* 1973, Clive Trevor Thorne Rogers, of 70 Wattleton Rd, Beaconsfield, Bucks, and has issue living, Timothy Piers Thorne, *b* 1981, —— Sophie Claire Thorne, *b* 1977.

UNCLES LIVING (*sons of 1st baronet*)

Ambrose Desmond Harrington (La Jachère da la Grange, St Peter Port, Guernsey), *b* 1913; formerly a King's Foreign Ser Messenger: *m* 1966, Lilian, da of Gerald Westwood Potter, of Park Gates, Eastbourne and widow of Dr Lydiard Wilson. —— Godfrey Ramsay Harrington, *b* (twin) 1913; *ed* Downside: *m* 1939, Ida, da of late Sextus Hassing, of Frederica, Denmark, and has issue living, Simon Anthony *b* 1952, — Karen Grethe Maria, *b* 1940: *m* 1960, Colin Ross, and has issue living, Nicholas *b* 1962, — Lila Marianna, *b* 1945: *m* 1966, Colin Michael Creswell, son of late Sir Michael Justin Creswell, KCMG, — Lorna Theresa, *b* 1948: *m* 1972, Vicente Romero Ramirez, of Madrid, Spain, and has issue living, Miguel Romero Grayson *b* 1984. *Residence* – Soto de Viñuelas, Madrid, Spain.

AUNT LIVING (*daughter of 1st baronet*)

Meryl Lorraine Harrington, *b* 1909. *Residence* – 18 Barney St, Newport, Rhode Island 02840, USA.

MOTHER LIVING

SOFIA, 4th da of late George Buchanan, Commercial Counsellor at Chilean Embassy, London, of 7 Addison Rd, W14: *m* 1930 (*m diss* 1946), as his 1st wife, Brian Harrington Grayson, who *d* 1989, 3rd son of 1st baronet. *Residence* – —

STEPMOTHER LIVING

RUTH, da of late Oscar Louis Anders, of Littlethorpe Hall, Ripon, and formerly wife of Edwin Bernhard Gange: *m* 1949, as his 2nd wife, Brian Harrington Grayson, who *d* 1989, 3rd son of 1st baronet. *Residence* – Summerfield, 67 Lewes Rd, Ditchling, Hassocks, Sussex BN6 8TY.

WIDOWS LIVING OF THIRD AND FOURTH BARONETS

DOROTHY VERA (VICKI) HOARE (*Vicki, Lady Grayson*), da of Charles Serrell, of Hoylake, Cheshire: *m* 1946, as his 2nd wife, Sir Ronald Henry Rudyard Grayson, 3rd Bt, who *d* 1987. *Residence* – 5 Cheero Point Rd, Cheero Point, NSW, Australia.
VARI COLETTE (*Vari, Lady Grayson*), da of Maj Henry O'Shea, late IA and Royal Dublin Fus, of Cork: *m* 1950, as his 2nd wife, Sir Rupert Stanley Harrington Grayson, 4th Bt, who *d* 1991. *Residence* – PO Box 626, Indiantown, Florida 34956, USA.

COLLATERAL BRANCH LIVING

Issue of late Col Tristram Hugh Harrington Grayson, OBE, IG 4th son of 1st baronet, *b* 1902, *d* 1984: *m* 1928, Barbara, who *d* 1974, da of Morgan Ignatius Finucane, MRCS, JP, Bar-at-law, of 10 Ashley Pl, SW1:—
Patrick Tristram Finucane (38 Beaufort Mansions, Beaufort St, SW3 5AG; *Clubs* – Whites, Special Forces), *b* 1942; *ed* Downside, and RMA Sandhurst; Maj late IG; Dir Defence Systems Ltd; Dep Chm Kroll Associates: *m* 1965 (*m diss* 1989), Vivienne Mary, da of Hector Rowcliffe Munro, of Javea, Alicante, Spain, and has issue living, Mark Patrick Munro, *b* 1974, — Louise Mary Munro, *b* 1968, — Nikki Kathryn Munro, *b* 1970. —— Mary Dora Finucane (The White House, Gosmore, Hitchin, Herts), *b* 1931: *m* 1958, John Owen Blaksley, who *d* 1982, and has issue living, John Patrick, *b* 1959, — Richard Edmund, *b* 1961: *m* 1990, Sally-Anne, da of Dr John Deller, and has issue living, Thomas Percival *b* 1992, Alice Anastasia *b* 1993. —— Angela Mary Finucane, *b* 1934: *m* 1955, Michael John Drummond-Brady, Maj late The Queen's Regt, Member of HM Body Guard of Hon Corps Gentlemen at Arms, of Keepers Lodge, Great Chart, Ashford, Kent TN26 1JX, and has issue living, Simon Michael Grayson, *b* 1955: *m* 1988, Nicola, da of Peter Fletcher, — Mark Frederick Grayson, *b* 1957; BA: *m* 1984, Susie, da of Nicholas Fair, and has issue living, Frederick Mark *b* 1987, Lucy Elizabeth *b* 1989, — Emma Angela Grayson, *b* 1962.
The 1st baronet, Sir Henry Mulleneux Grayson, KBE (son of Henry Holdrege Grayson, JP, of Liverpool) was Lieut-Col RM, a Director of several Shipping and Shipbuilding Cos, and High Sheriff of Anglesey 1917-18, and sat as MP for W Div of Birkenhead (*Co U*) 1918-22.

GREEN (UK) 1886, of Wakefield, Yorkshire, and Ken Hill, Norfolk

Sir (EDWARD) STEPHEN LYCETT GREEN, CBE, 4th *Baronet*; *b* 18 April, 1910; *s* his father, *Sir* EDWARD ARTHUR LYCETT, 1941; *ed* Eton, and Magdalene Coll, Camb; Bar Lincoln's Inn 1933; a JP and DL and High Sheriff (1973-74) for Norfolk; Chm E Anglian Hosp Board 1959-74; Dep Chm Norfolk Quarter Sessions 1948-71; formerly Maj RA; a County Councillor for Norfolk 1946-9; 1939-45 War; CBE (Civil) 1964: *m* 1935, Constance Mary (Co Councillor for Norfolk 1958-77), da of late Ven Harry Sydney Radcliffe, Archdeacon of Lynn, and has issue.

Arms – Vert, guttee d'eau, three stags trippant or, in fesse two roses argent. **Crest** – In front of a mount vert thereon a stag trippant or, collared vert, three roses argent. *Residence* – Ken Hill, Snettisham, King's Lynn, PE31 7PG; *Clubs* – White's, Pratt's, Norfolk (Norwich).

Waste not

DAUGHTER LIVING

Livia Lycett, *b* 1937: *m* 1961, Robert Edmond Buscall, JP, DL (High Sheriff Norfolk 1993), and has living, Harry Charles, *b* 1963: *m* 1989, Kathryn Adrianna, da of Edward William Hill, of Farnham Royal, Bucks, and has issue living, Dominic *b* 1992, Nicholas Edmond *b* 1994, — Patrick Edward, *b* 1965. *Residence* – Carbrooke Hall, Thetford, Norfolk.

BROTHER LIVING

SIMON LYCETT, TD, *b* 11 July 1912; *ed* Eton, and Magdalene Coll Camb (BA); is a DL for W Riding of Yorkshire, and a JP for Wakefield; Lieut-Col Comdg Yorkshire Dragoons Yeo 1947-51; Chm Green's Economiser Group Ltd 1956-83; 1939-45 War: *m* 1st, 1935 (*m diss* 1971), Gladys, da of late Arthur Ranicar, JP, of Springfield, Wigan; 2ndly, 1971, Mary, da of late George Ramsden, of Dale House, Wakefield, and has issue living, (by 1st *m*) Diana Rose Francis, *b* 1935: *m* 1964, Capt Ronald Eden Wallace, of Mounsey Farm, Dulverton, Som (*see* Lindsay-Hogg, Bt, 1980 Edn), and has issue living, David Lycett *b* 1967: *m* 1991, Emma Lisa, elder da of S. R. Freegard, of Langbar, N Yorks (and has issue living, Miranda Ophelia Lycett *b* 1993). *Residence* – Cliff Bank, N Rigton, Leeds LS17 0BZ.

COLLATERAL BRANCHES LIVING

Grandchildren of late Cdr David Lycett Green, RN (infra):—
Issue of late Richard David Rafe Lycett Green, *b* 1925, *d* 1969: *m* 1st, 1948 (*m diss* 1956) (Marie) Patricia, da of Michael Maguire, of Melbourne, Aust, and widow of Capt Hon Peter Rudyard Aitken, R Fus (*see* B Beaverbrook); 2ndly, 1958, Margaret Alison, da of Maj Geoffrey Denis Lock, MBE, MC, of Rainbow Wood, Bath, and formerly wife of Yan Kai-Nielsen:—
(By 1st *m*) Edward Patrick Lycett, *b* 1950; *ed* Stowe: *m* 1st, 1971 (*m diss* 1975), Corden Sarah, da of C. B. Stretton Wilson, of Stratford-on-Avon; 2ndly, 1977, Annette Patricia Josephine, da of Oswald Patrick John Rochfort, of Broad Marston, Warwicks, and has issue living, (by 2nd *m*) Charlotte Rose, *b* 1979, — Alice Josephine, *b* 1983. —— Mary Angela, *b* 1949.

Issue of late Cdr David Cecil Lycett Green, RN, 2nd son of 2nd baronet, *b* 1892, *d* 1960: *m* 1st, 1923 (*m diss* 1944), Angela, who *d* 1992 yst da of late Edward Hubert Courage, of Kirkby-Fleetham Hall, Bedale; 2ndly, 1948, Margaret Dora Helen, who *d* 1988, having *m* 3rdly, 1970 (*m diss* 1978), Alec Pilkington, da of Lt-Col Henry Ross, CIE, OBE, and formerly wife of late Col Thomas Cromwell Williamson, DSO:—
(By 1st *m*) Rupert William Lycett (Manor Farm, Huish, Marlborough, Wilts), *b* 1938; late 2nd Lt Roy Armoured Corps: *m* 1963, Candida Rose, da of late Sir John Betjeman, CBE (*see* B Chetwode, 1985 Edn), and has issue living, David Lycett, *b* 1975, — John Peregrine Lycett, *b* 1978, — Lucy Rose Lycett, *b* 1964: *m* 1988, Alexander Evelyn Giles Ward (*see* E Bangor), — Imogen Rose, *b* 1966: *m* 1993, Augustus Jack Christie, 2nd son of Sir George William Langham Christie, DL, of Glyndebourne, E Sussex, — Endellion Rose, *b* 1969. —— Catherine Auriol Lycett, *b* 1935: *m* 1st, 1967, Raja Ranbir Singh; 2ndly, 1981, Patrick Field Till, and has issue living, (by 1st *m*) Xenia, *b* 1968, — Tamara, *b* 1970, — Alexia, *b* 1972.
Sir Edward Green, 1st Bt (el son of Edward Green, of Wakefield); Capt 1st W Yorkshire Yeo; sat as MP for Wakefield (C) 1874 (but was unseated) and July 1885 to July 1892 (when he resigned). Sir Edward Arthur Lycett Green, TD, 3rd Bt, was Lieut-Col and Brevet Col Yorkshire Dragoons, Yeo.

GREEN (UK) 1901, of Belsize Park Gardens, Hampstead, co London (Extinct 1959)

Sir GEORGE ARTHUR HAYDN GREEN, 4th and last *Baronet*.

DAUGHTER LIVING OF SECOND BARONET

Evelyn Kate, *b* 1905.

Green-Price, see Price.

GREENAWAY (UK) 1933, of Coombe, co Surrey

Either do not attempt, or complete

Sir Derek Burdick Greenaway, CBE, TD, 2nd *Baronet, b* 27 May 1910; *s* his father, *Sir* Percy Walter, 1956; *ed* Marlborough; Maj RA, a JP and a DL of Kent (High Sheriff 1971-72); Pres of Daniel Greenaway & Son, Ltd, printers; Joint Master of Old Surrey and Burstow Fox Hounds 1958-66, and Pres of Sevenoaks Div Conservative Assocn 1963-66 (Chm 1960-63); Assist Hon Treasurer of SE Area Conservative and Unionist Assocn 1966-69, Treasurer 1969-75, Chm 1975-79; Master, Stationers' & Newspaper Makers' Co 1974-75 (Silver Medal 1984); Hon Col 44 (HC) Signal Regt, (Cinque Ports) (TA) 1966-67 and Hon Col 36th (Eastern) Signal Regt (V) 1967-74; CBE (Civil) 1974: *m* 1937, Sheila Beatrice, only da of late Richard Cyril Lockett, of 58 Cadogan Place, SW1, and has issue.

Arms – Quarterly: 1 and 4, gules, a chevron between in chief two covered cups and in base a closed book clasps downwards or, *Greenaway*; 2 and 3, vert an ancient ship with three masts sails set or, between four seagulls close proper, *Burdick*. **Crest** – A griffin's head erased or, semée of roses gules, barbed and seeded proper, suspended from the beak an annulet gold.
Residence – Dunmore, Four Elms, Edenbridge, Kent TN8 6NE. *Clubs* – Carlton, City of London.

SON LIVING

John Michael Burdick (Lois Weedon House, Weedon Lois, Towcester, Northants NN12 8PJ), *b* 9 Aug 1944; *ed* Harrow; Lt Life Gds 1965-70; a Dir of Daniel Greenaway & Sons, Ltd 1970-79: *m* 1982, Susan Margaret, of Henry Birch, of Lion House, Tattenhall, Cheshire, and has issue living, Thomas Edward Burdick, *b* 3 April 1985, — Camilla Helen, *b* 1983.

DAUGHTER LIVING

Anne Jennifer: *m* 1969, Capt David Patrick Lewis Hewson, Blues and Royals, of 103 Abbotsbury Rd, W14, (B Merthyr), and has issue living, George Patrick David, *b* 1980, — Annabel Mary, *b* 1971, — Clare Louise, *b* 1973.

SISTER LIVING

Doreen Lydie, *b* 1908; a JP: *m* 1936, Harold Francis Ralph Sturge, who *d* 1993, and has issue living, Martin Greenaway (3 Lower Camden Place, Bath), *b* 1938, — Simon Harold (Lyndhurst, Woodhouse Lane, Holmbury St Mary, Surrey), *b* 1940: *m* 1st 1967, Hilary Barbara Highet; 2ndly, 1982, Sheila Anne Jean Longsdale, and has issue living (by 1st *m*), Charles Campbell *b* 1969, Alexander James *b* 1972.

COLLATERAL BRANCH LIVING

Issue of late Capt Alan Pearce Greenaway, JP, yr son of 1st baronet, *b* 1913, *d* 1994: *m* 1948, Patricia Frances, who *d* 1982, da of Sir Frederick Michael Wells, 1st Bt (*cr* 1948):—
Michael Philip (Criplands, Lindfield, W Sussex), *b* 1949; *ed* Harrow: *m* 1978, Alison Robya, da of Geoffrey Douglas Cohen, and has issue living, Daniel Pearce, *b* 1981, — Hannah Kate, *b* 1980, — Rebecca Lucy, *b* 1984. ——— Susan Mary, *b* 1952: *m* 1973, Alexander Andrew Campbell Cruickshank, of The Doone, Byfleet Rd, Cobham, Surrey, and has issue living, David Alexander, *b* 1976, — Benjamin Andrew, *b* 1982, — Sarah Frances Louise, *b* 1974.

The 1st baronet, Sir Percy Walter Greenaway (son of Daniel Greenaway, Dep of City of London), was Chm of Daniel Greenaway & Sons, Ltd, printers and stationers, and of other Cos, a Member of Court of Common Council of of City of London (Alderman 1923, Senior Sheriff 1931-2, and Lord Mayor 1932-3), and Master of Stationers' and Newspaper Makers' Co, 1932 (re-elected 1933), and Treasurer 1951.

GREENWELL (UK) 1906, of Marden Park, Godstone, co Surrey, and Greenwell, Wolsingham, co Durham

I become green

b 1973, — Rupert James, *b* 1977.

Sir EDWARD BERNARD GREENWELL, 4th *Baronet, b* 10 June 1948; *s* his father, *Capt Sir* PETER McCLINTOCK, TD, DL, 1978; *ed* Eton, Notts Univ (BSc), and Cranfield Inst of Technology (MBA), DL of Suffolk 1988: *m* 1974, Sarah Louise, yr da of late Lt-Col Philip Maitland Gore-Anley, of Sculthorpe House, Fakenham, Norfolk, and has issue.

𝕬rms – Or, two bars azure between three ducal coronets gules. ℭrest – A stork statant proper, beaked and legged gules, gorged with a wreath of laurel vert. *Seat* – Greenwell, co Durham. *Residence* – Gedgrave Hall, Woodbridge, Suffolk IP12 2BX. *Club* – Turf.

SON LIVING

ALEXANDER BERNARD PETER, *b* 11 May 1987.

DAUGHTERS LIVING

Belinda Clayre, *b* 1977. —— Lucy Rose, *b* 1979. —— Daisy Julia, *b* 1983.

BROTHER LIVING

James Peter (Boyton House, Boyton, Woodbridge, Suffolk IP12 3LH), *b* 1950; *ed* Eton; late Maj The Blues & Royals: *m* 1979, Serena Jane, yr da of Maj Hon Colin James Dalrymple (*see* E Stair), and has issue living, Andrew Peter, *b* 1983, — Davina Louise, *b* 1984.

SISTER LIVING

Julia Henrietta, *b* 1946: *m* 1970, Alexander Richard Trotter, DL, of Charterhall, Duns, Berwickshire, and has issue living, Henry Peter, *b* 1972, — Edward John,

AUNTS LIVING (Daughters of 2nd baronet)

Joyce Marjorie, *b* 1903: *m* 1927, Maj Walter Harold Miles, MBE, Dorsetshire Regt (ret), who *d* 1986, and has issue living, Christopher Richard (Court Lodge, Bletchingley, Surrey), *b* 1928: *m* 1956, Jean Mary, da of late Anthony Buxton, DSO (*see* Buxton, Bt colls), and has issue living, Robert John *b* 1957: *m* 1986, Juliet Caroline Frances, da of Brig John Rigby, of Hill House, Long Melford, Sudbury, Suffolk (and has issue living, David John *b* 1989, William Richard Christopher *b* 1992, Rebecca Rose *b* 1987), Hubert Christopher *b* 1959: *m* 1986, Madeleine, da of late Capt William Loftie (and has issue living, Robert William *b* 1988, Alastair James *b* 1990, Laura Caroline *b* 1992), Mary Anna Theresa *b* 1960, Sophia Mary *b* 1967, — Philip David (Hinton Hall, Lea Cross, Shrewsbury, Salop), *b* 1931: *m* 1st, 1960, Hon Julian Isabella Joan Chetwynd, who *d* 1981, da of 9th Viscount Chetwynd; 2ndly, 1985, Hon Christine Helena, eldest da of 7th Baron Forester, and formerly wife of 7th Baron Bolton, and has issue living (by 1st *m*), Charles Philip Chetwynd *b* 1962, Sara Isabella *b* 1961, — Rosemary Joyce, *b* 1935: *m* 1957, Michael Harper Gow, of Drummonie, Bridge of Earn, Perth, and has issue living, Christopher Michael Harper *b* 1961, Fergus Benjamin Harper *b* 1965, Lucinda Rosemary *b* 1959: *m* 1979, William Noel Collins (*see* E Donoughmore), of 19 Wingate Rd, W6 (and has issue living, Emily Lucinda Julian *b* 1981, Melissa Daisy *b* 1984), Amelia Jean *b* 1967. —— Barbara Patience (*Lady William-Powlett*), *b* 1906: *m* 1st, 1929, Capt Newton James Wallop William-Powlett, DSC, RN, who *d* 1963; 2ndly, 1966, her 1st husband's brother, Vice-Adm Sir Peveril Barton Reibey Wallop William-Powlett, KCB, KCMG, CBE, DSO, who *d* 1985 (*see* E Portsmouth, colls). —— Elisabeth Kathleen, *b* 1908: *m* 1931, Capt Roddie Casement, OBE, RN, who *d* 1987, and has issue living, Michael Bernard, OBE (Dene Cottage, West Harting, Petersfield, Hants), *b* 1933; *ed* Winchester; Cdr RN: *m* 1956, Christina Rose, 3rd da of Capt John Cassilis Maclean, RN, and has issue living, William Rory John *b* 1961: *m* 1989, Rachel, yst da of late John Berry (and has issue living, Daisy *b* 1992, Rosanna Isobel *b* 1994), Rachel Christina *b* 1957: *m* 1985, Charles James Middleton, of 6 Brandreth Rd, SW17 8ER, elder son of Brig R. C. Middleton, of Gannets, Tolleshunt D'Arcy, Essex (and has issue living, Jemima Louise Mary *b* 1988, Imogen Ayesha *b* 1991), Flora Susan (*Hon Mrs Henry L. A. Hood*) *b* 1959: *m* 1991, Hon Henry Lyttelton Alexander Hood, eldest son of 7th Viscount Hood (and has issue (*see* V Hood)), — Patrick John (122 Mansfield Rd, NW3 2JB), *b* 1935; *ed* Winchester and Trin Coll, Camb (MA): *m* 1966, Margaret Rose, da of Anthony George Lloyd, and formerly wife of Peter Jens McCowen, and has issue living, Hanna *b* 1968, Isabella *b* 1970, — Elisabeth Ann, *b* 1942: *m* 1963, Anthony John Howard, of Drove Cottage, Newbridge, Cadnam, Southampton, and has issue living, Tom Peter *b* 1967, Kate Elisabeth *b* 1965: *m* 1990, Stuart Judd (and has issue living, George William *b* 1992), Emma *b* (twin) 1967, — Susan Henrietta, *b* 1944: *m* 1964, William Farquhar Acworth, of Little Hidden Farm, Hungerford, Berks, and has issue (*see* Buzzard, Bt). —— Anna Margaret (60 Oxford Gdns, W10) *b* 1913: *m* 1st, 1940, Sir James Henderson-Stewart, MP, 1st Bt, who *d* 1961; 2ndly, 1965, Geoffrey Walford Wilks, CBE, TD, who *d* 1987. —— Ruth Veronica, *b* 1916: *m* 1st, 1936, William Reginald Colquhoun, TD, who *d* 1971; 2ndly, 1972, Peter Birchall, of Cotswold Farm, Cirencester, and has issue living (by 1st *m*) William Patrick (2 Thornton Close, Girton, Cambridge), *b* 1939: *m* 1971, Frances Elspeth, only da of late Archibald Cameron, and has issue living, Anna Elizabeth *b* 1973, Rhona Frances *b* 1978, — Alastair Peter, *b* 1941: *m* 1977, Elisabeth, el da of Capt Geoffrey Stanning, DSO, RN, of Mildenhall House, Mildenhall, Marlborough, and has issue living, Andrew John *b* 1983, Mary Louise *b* 1979, — John Humphrey (Brooke House, Frocester, nr Stonehouse, Glos), *b* 1943: *m* 1969, Susan Elizabeth, el da of Michael Ingram, of Driffield Manor, Cirencester, and has issue living, Mark Humphrey *b* 1973, James Arthur *b* 1975, Auriol Emma *b* 1982, — Neil Robert (Eton College, Windsor, Berks), *b* 1947: *m* 1974, Rosemary Elizabeth, da of late Archibald Colville (*see* Gibson-Craig-Carmichael, Bt), and has issue living, William Alexander *b* 1976, Nicholas Peter *b* 1978, Robert *b* 1983, Hamish Patrick *b* 1985, — Anna Margaret, *b* 1946: *m* 1968, Nigel Guthrie McNair Scott, of 1 Edwardes Sq, W8, and has issue (*see* V Camrose).

WIDOW LIVING OF THIRD BARONET

(JEAN) HENRIETTA ROSE, twin da of Peter Haig-Thomas (*see* E Normanton, 1970 Edn): *m* 1st, 1940, Capt Sir Peter McClintock Greenwell, 3rd Bt, who *d* 1978; 2ndly, 1985, Hugh Kenneth Haig, of Broomy Hall, Dalton, Newcastle-upon-Tyne.

COLLATERAL BRANCHES LIVING

Grandchildren of late Maj Aynsley Eyre Greenwell (*infra*):—
Issue of late Lt-Cdr Whitfield Ava Aynsley Greenwell RNVR, *b* 1907, *d* 1977: *m* 1935, Violet Rosemary Evelyn

(Shermanbury Place, Shermanbury, nr Horsham, Sussex), da of Frederick Charles Turner, CIE, of The Little Place, Lyme Regis, Dorset:—
William Maxwell Walpole, *b* 1942, *ed* Harrow. —— Eve Jennifer GREENWELL, *b* 1939; has resumed her maiden name: *m* 1974 (*m diss* 1981), Anthony Murly-Gotto, and has issue living, Antonia Mary Eve Alexandra, *b* 1975.
　　Issue of late Lt-Cdr Ivor Desmond Greenwell, RNVR, *b* 1911, *d* 1993: *m* 1939, Diana, who *d* 1991, da of Maj John Simeon Ward, The Rifle Bde:—
Jane Elizabeth, *b* 1954. —— Mary Claire, *b* (twin)1954.

　　　Grandchildren of late Maj Aynsley Eyre Greenwell, 2nd son of 1st baronet:—
　　Issue of late Basil Evelyn Greenwell, *b* 1915, *d* 1990: *m* 1st, 1948 (*m diss* 1952), Phyllis Joyce, da of late K. L. Weatherall Pepper, of Lewes, Sussex; 2ndly, 1955, Sarah (Tanners, River, Petworth, Sussex GU28 9AY), da of late Capt Hon Walter Seymour Carson, RN (By Carson, ext):—
(By 2nd *m*) Simon Lloyd (Tanners, River, Petworth, Sussex GU28 9AY), *b* 1956: *m* 1986, Caroline Posner, and has issue living, Thomas Basil, *b* 1990, — Louise, *b* 1986, — Emma, *b* 1989. —— †Giles Henry, *b* 1957, *d* 1990. —— Joanna Beatrice Taswell, *b* 1962: *m* 1986, Rupert Clevely. —— Virginia Annette, *b* 1965.
　　Issue of late Walpole Edward Greenwell, *b* 1920, *d* 1992: *m* 1963 (*m diss* 1972), Mrs Rosemary Heather Bunn, yr da of late John Pares-Wilson, of Little Shelford, and of Lady Daniels:—
Rupert John Walpole, *b* 1964.

　　　Issue of late Geoffrey Eyre Greenwell, yst son of 1st baronet, *b* 1894, *d* 1949: *m* 1922, Mildred (who *m* 2ndly, 1956), da of late J. Evans, of Norwood, SE:—
John Evelyn (East Field, Henfold Hill, Beare Green, Dorking, Surrey) *b* 1924; *ed* King's Sch, Canterbury; 1939-45 with RAFVR: *m* 1956, Frances Valerie Anne, da of late Marnix Cremer, of Lovelocks, Horley, and has issue living, Andrew John, *b* 1959, — Jane Frances, *b* 1963.

Sir Walpole Lloyd Greenwell, 1st Bt (2nd son of late Walpole Eyre Greenwell), was High Sheriff of Surrey 1903.
The Greenwell family was seated at Greenwell in the parish of Wolsingham, co Durham, from a very early period and Gulielmus Presbyter and his son James de Grenewelle are mentioned as holding land there in 1183 in the Bolden Book. A connected pedigree can be traced from John de Grenwell, of Park Yate in Wolsingham, who *d* before 13 Jan 1391.

GRESLEY (E) 1611, of Drakelowe, Derbyshire (Extinct 1976)

Sir WILLIAM FRANCIS GRESLEY, 13th, and last *Baronet.*

WIDOW LIVING OF THIRTEENTH BARONET

ADA MARY (*Lady Gresley*) (59A Grand Av, Southbourne, Bournemouth), da of late George Miller: *m* 1924, Sir William Francis Gresley, 13th Bt, who *d* 1976, when the title became ext.

COLLATERAL BRANCH LIVING

　　　Issue of late Nigel Morewood Gresley, el brother of 13th baronet, *b* 1892, *d* 1966: *m* 1921, Mary Mansfield, who *d* 1989, da of late R. M. Hobill:—
Mary Penelope (The Old Lodge, 92 Alumhurst Rd, Bournemouth, Dorset), *b* 1928: *m* 1959, Brian Stacy Warham Rigby-Hall, who *d* 1981, and has issue living, Robert Gresley, *b* 1965, — Frances Margaret, *b* 1968.

Grey (cr 1711), see Lambert (cr 1711).

GREY (UK) 1814, of Fallodon, Northumberland

Sir ANTHONY DYSART GREY, 7th *Baronet*; *b* 19 Oct 1949; *s* his grandfather, *Sir* ROBIN EDWARD DYSART, 1974; *ed* Guildford Grammar Sch Perth; Late Man, Fibre Glass Div Bel Art Corpn; Inspector Dept of Industrial Affairs, Govt W Aust: *m* 1970 (*m diss* 19—), Donna (Museum Curator), da of Donald Daniels, of 60 Park Lane, W1.

𝕬rms – Gules, a lion rampant within a bordure engrailed argent, a mullet for difference. ℭrest – A scaling ladder in bend sinister or, hooked and pointed sable.
Residence – —

MOTHER LIVING

Nancy (86 Kingsway Gdns, 38 King's Park Rd, Perth, W Aust 6005), da of late Francis John Meagher, of Winning Station, W Aust: *m* 1946, Edward Elton Grey, who *d* 1962, only son of 6th Bt.

The 1st baronet, Hon Sir George Grey, was third son of the 1st Earl Grey; the 2nd baronet, Rt Hon Sir George, GCB, PC, sat as MP for Devonport (*L*) 1832-47, for Northumberland North 1847-52, and for Morpeth 1853-74; was Sec of State for Home Department 1846-52, 1855-8 and 1861-6, Sec of State for the Colonies 1854-5, and Chancellor of the Duchy of Lancaster 1841 and 1859-61; the 3rd baronet, Rt Hon Sir Edward, KG, sat as MP, for Berwick-on-Tweed (*L*) 1885-1916, and was Under-Sec of State for Foreign Affairs 1892-95, and Sec of State for Foreign Affairs 1905-15, and Ambassador to USA (on special mission) 1919; *cr Viscount Grey of Fallodon*, co Northumberland 1916 (ext 1933).

To serve the king with good will

Grey Egerton, see Egerton.

GRIERSON (NS) 1685, of Lag, Dumfriesshire

Safer by this

Sir MICHAEL JOHN BEWES GRIERSON, 12th *Baronet*; *b* 24 July 1921; *s* his cousin, *Sir* RICHARD DOUGLAS, 1987; *ed* St Edmund's Sch, Canterbury: *m* 1971, Valerie Anne, da of late Russell Wright, of Gidea Park, Essex, and has issue.

𝕬rms – Gules, on a fesse or, between three fetterlocks argent a mullet azure. ℭrest – A lock as in the arms.
Residence – 40C Palace Rd, Streatham Hill, SW2 3NJ.

DAUGHTER LIVING

Sarah Anne, *b* 1973.

SISTER LIVING

Pamela Violet, *b* 1925: *m* 1955, Richard Wallace Vernon, and has issue (*see* Vernon, Bt, colls). *Residence* – Park Lodge, 46 Park Rd, Aldeburgh, Suffolk IP15 5EU.

COLLATERAL BRANCH LIVING

Issue of late Frederick Vedast Grierson, Lieut King's Own Scottish Borderers, yst son of 9th baronet, *b* 1888, *d* 1922: *m* 1909, Frederica, who *d* 1941, da of Arthur Frederick Skipp, of Cheltenham:—
Lorna Mary Sheila: *m* 1941 (*m diss* 1951), Carl Berger.

This family claim descent from Gilbert, yr son of Malcolm MacGregor of MacGregor (*d* 1374). Sir Robert Grierson, Knight, of Lag, who sat as MP for Dumfries 1678-86, was created a baronet with remainder to heirs male whatsoever. He was a great persecutor of the Covenantors, and presided at the trial and execution of two women known as the Wigtown Martyrs who refused to take the abjuration oath. He was "Sir Robert Redgauntlet" of Wandering Willie's tale in Sir Walter Scott's *Redgauntlet*. Sir Gilbert Grierson, 4th baronet, joined the Jacobite Rising 1715.

NORTON-GRIFFITHS (UK) 1922, of Wonham, Betchworth, co Surrey

For King and Empire

Sir JOHN NORTON-GRIFFITHS, 3rd *Baronet*; *b* 4 Oct 1938; *s* his father, *Maj Sir* PETER, 1983; *ed* Eton; late Sub-Lieut RN; ACA: *m* 1964, Marilyn Margaret, elder da of Norman Grimley, of S Blundellsands, Liverpool.

𝕬rms – 1st and 4th, sable, a flaming sword erect between two griffins combatant or, *Griffiths*; 2nd and 3rd argent, on a fesse raguly between two fleur-de-lis azure, a fleur-de-lis between two crescents or, *Norton*. 𝕮rest – 1st, a demi-lion rampant gules, grasping in the paws a flaming sword erect, *Griffiths*; 2ndly, a dexter gauntlet closed sable between two ostrich feathers argent, *Norton*. 𝕾upporters – *Dexter*, a Colonial soldier in the uniform of a trooper of the Second Regiment King Edward's Horse, resting the exterior hand upon a terrestrial globe in frame environed with a meridian; *sinister*, a labourer holding in the exterior hand a Jackhammer drill all proper.
Residence – 17 Royal Drive, Bricktown, NJ 08723, USA.

BROTHER LIVING

MICHAEL (Box 21791, Nairobi, Kenya), *b* 11 Jan 1941; *ed* Eton, and Keble Coll, Oxford (DPhil, Zoology); Ecologist, Serengeti Research Inst 1969-73; Man Dir of EcoSystems Ltd, Nairobi, Kenya 1977-87, Head Eastern Sahel Unit, World Conservation Union, 1988; Consultant to Global Environment Monitoring Programme of the United Nations Environment Programme since 1989: *m* 1965, Ann, only da of late Group Capt Blair Alexander Fraser, RAF, of 12 Mount Beacon, Lansdown, Bath (E Dundonald, colls), and has issue living, Alastair, *b* 23 Feb 1976.

SISTER LIVING

Anne, *b* 1936: *m* 1956, Richard Hathaway Morgan, and has issue living, Kathryn, *b* 1957, — Christina, *b* 1958, — Pascale, *b* 1960. *Residences* – 10 Multon Rd, SW18 5LH; Box 21791, Nairobi, Kenya.

COLLATERAL BRANCH LIVING

Issue of late Capt Michael Norton-Griffiths, RE, 2nd son of 1st baronet, *b* 1908, *ka* 1940: *m* 1936, Mrs Elizabeth Gertrude Colclough, who *d* 1988, having *m* 3rdly, 1946, George Paul Minchin Woodward, of New Jersey, USA, and 4thly, 1954, Ralph Arthur Hubbard, who *d* 1983 (*see* B Addington, colls), yr da of late Stephen Cozens, of Mackney Manor, Wallingford, Berks:—
Johanna, *b* 1936: *m* 1969, Keith Martin Butt, MA, Vet MB (Cantab), MRCVS, of Stonelands, Barn, Brize Norton, Oxon, and has issue living, Jason Martin, *b* 1972, — Ben Michael, *b* 1979, — Martha, *b* 1971.

The 1st Baronet, Lieut-Col Sir John Norton-Griffiths, KCB, DSO (son of late John Griffiths, of Brecon), assumed by deed poll 1917, the additional surname of Norton, and was Governing Director of Sir John Norton-Griffiths & Co, Ltd, public works contractors and engineers: served in S African War, first in Colonial Div, and afterwards as Capt and Adj Lord Roberts's Body Guard, Headquarter Staff, and in European War 1914-16 when he raised a Special Cav Regt, subsequently being on Staff of Engineer-in-Ch to organize and start Tunnelling Cos RE, and went on special mission to Roumania for destruction of oil wells and corn stores (despatches thrice, DSO): MP for Wednesbury (C) Jan 1910 to Nov 1918, and for Central Div of Wandsworth Dec 1918 to Oct 1924. Maj Sir Peter Norton-Griffiths, 2nd Bt, Bar Inner Temple, Mil Attaché Madrid 1941-42, was Man Dir Belgian Shell Co, SA 1953-60.

GROTRIAN (UK) 1934, of Leighton Buzzard, co Bedford

By courage and faith

Sir (PHILIP) CHRISTIAN BRENT GROTRIAN, 3rd *Baronet*; *b* 26 March 1935; *s* his uncle, *Sir* JOHN APPELBE BRENT, 1984; *ed* Eton, and Trin Coll, Toronto: *m* 1st, 1960, Anne Isabel, da of Robert Sieger Whyte, of Toronto; 2ndly, 1979, Sarah Frances, da of Reginald Harry Gale, of Montreal, and has issue.

𝕬rms – Gules, a wyvern or, in chief two roses argent, barbed and seeded proper. 𝕮rest – A wyvern or, resting the dexter leg upon a rose argent, barbed and seeded proper.
Residence – RR3, Mansfield, Ontario LON 1MO.

SONS LIVING *(By 1st marriage)*

(PHILIP) TIMOTHY ADAM BRENT, *b* 9 April 1962. *Residence* – 28 Bishop St, Toronto, Ontario, Canada M5R 1N2.

(By 2nd marriage)

John Hugh Brent, *b* 1982.

DAUGHTER LIVING *(By 2nd marriage)*

Frances Elizabeth, *b* 1980.

HALF-SISTER LIVING

Jane Felicity, *b* 1942: *m* 1964, Peter Lewis Andrews, of Old Timbers, Shere Rd, W Horsley, Surrey, and has issue living, Philip Kenneth, *b* 1964: *m* 1987, Caroline Jane, da of Raymond Woodcock, of Wivenhoe, Essex and has issue living, Lucy Jane *b* 1991, Emily Sarah *b* 1993, — Sarah Jane, *b* 1967: *m* 1993, Nicholas James Hughes, son of David Hughes, of Woldingham, Surrey.

DAUGHTERS LIVING OF FIRST BARONET

Lilian Désirée, *b* 1914. *Residence* – 10 New Yatt Rd, Witney, Oxon. ⸺ Mary Joizelle Elizabeth Pearl, *b* 1918: *m* 1947, John Gifford Ormerod, and has issue living, Elizabeth Mary, *b* 1949, — Caroline Anne, *b* 1955: *m* 1977, Michael James Blandford, of 6 Rochester Rd, Southsea, Hants, and has issue living, Alan James *b* 1979, Joanne Mary *b* 1982. *Residence* – 142 Tuffley Av, Gloucester.

STEPMOTHER LIVING

Margaret, da of late George Green, of Chapel Allerton, Leeds, formerly wife of late Roland Max Chaudoir, of Highgate, NW: *m* 2ndly, 1940, Sqdn Ldr Robert Philip Brent Grotrian (yst son of 1st Baronet), who *d* on active service in the Far East 1945; 3rdly, 1950, His Honour Judge (Richard Geraint) Rees, who *d* 1986. *Residence* – Sutton Lodge, 87 Oatlands Drive, Weybridge, Surrey.

MOTHER LIVING

Elizabeth Mary, only da of late Maj John Hardy-Wrigley: *m* 1st, 1931 (*m diss* 1940), Sqdn Ldr Robert Philip Brent (yst son of 1st Baronet), who *d* on active ser 1945; 2ndly, 1947, William Percy George, late US Foreign Service, who *d* 1955, and has further issue. *Residence* – 17 Hogarth Rd, Hove, Sussex BN3 5RH.

COLLATERAL BRANCH LIVING

Issue of late Major Charles Herbert Brent Grotrian, TD, BCL, JP, RA (TA), el son of 1st baronet, *b* 1902, *ka* Burma 1944: *m* 1936, Aileen Georgina, who *d* 1987, only da of late George Ernest Etlinger:—
Charlotte Elizabeth (17 Hogarth Rd, Hove, Sussex BN3 5RH), *b* 1941.
The 1st baronet, Sir Herbert Brent Grotrian, KC, DL, BCL (2nd son of Frederick Brent Grotrian, MP), was Recorder of Scarborough 1918-46, sat as MP for S-W Div of Kingston-upon-Hull (C) 1924-29, and was High Sheriff of Bedfordshire 1931.

GROVE (UK) 1874, of Ferne, Wiltshire

NY

DESSUX NY DESSOUX

Neither above nor below

Sir CHARLES GERALD GROVE, 5th *Baronet*; *b* 10 Dec 1929; *s* his brother, *Sir* WALTER FELIPE PHILIP, 1974.

Arms – Ermine, on a chevron engrailed gules; three scallops, the centre one or, the others argent. **Crest** – A talbot statant sable, collared argent. *Residence* – USA.

BROTHER LIVING

HAROLD THOMAS, *b* 6 Dec 1930.

MOTHER LIVING

Elena, da of late Felipe Crosthwaite: *m* 1926 (*m diss* Mexico 1933), Walter Peel Grove, who *d* 1944.

This family claims descent from John Grove, who settled in Wilts from Bucks. *temp* Henry VI. William Grove, MP for Shaftesbury, who died 1582, purchased Ferne in 1563 and Sedghill in 1582. Sir Thomas Fraser Grove, 1st Bt, was MP for S Wilts (*L*) 1865-74, and for Wilts S, or Wilton, Div 1885-92.

GUINNESS (UK) 1867, of Ashford, co Galway

SPES MEA IN DEO

My hope is in God

Sir KENELM ERNEST LEE GUINNESS, 4th *Baronet*, son of late Kenelm Edward Lee Guinness, MBE, RNVR, 2nd son of late Capt Benjamin Lee Guinness, 2nd son of 1st baronet; *b* 13 Dec 1928; *s* his uncle, *Sir* ALGERNON ARTHUR ST LAWRENCE LEE, 1954; *ed* Eton, and Mass Institute of Technology, USA; Engineer with International Bank for Reconstruction and Development (World Bank) 1954-75 and currently an indep Consulting Engineer, late 2nd Lieut Roy Horse Guards: *m* 1961, Mrs Jane Nevin Dickson, and has issue.

Arms – Quarterly: 1st and 4th per saltire gules and azure, a lion rampant or, on a chief ermine a dexter hand couped at the wrist of the first, *Guinness*: 2nd and 3rd argent, on a fesse between three crescents sable a trefoil slipped or, *Lee*. **Crests** – 1st, a boar passant, quarterly or and gules; 2nd, on a pillar argent, encircled by a ducal coronet or, an eagle preying on a bird's leg erased proper. **Supporters** – On either side a stag gules, attired and gorged with a collar gemmel or, pendant therefrom by a chain gold an escutcheon, the dexter charged with the arms of Guinness, and the sinister with those of Lee. (The supporters in the arms were granted to Sir Benjamin Lee Guinness, 1st baronet, and his heirs male, upon whom the dignity of a baronet may descend, as a special mark of favour for the public spirit and munificent liberality manifested by him in the restoration of St Patrick's Cathedral, Dublin).

Residence – Rich Neck, Claiborne, Maryland 21624, USA. *Clubs* – Cavalry and Guards', Household Division Yacht.

SONS LIVING

KENELM EDWARD LEE, *b* 30 Jan 1962. —— Sean St Lawrence Lee, *b* 1966.

SISTER LIVING

Geraldine St Lawrence, *b* 1930: *m* 1956, Mikhael Essayan, QC, and has issue living, Martin Sarkis, *b* 1959, — Joanna Consuelo, *b* 1958. *Residence* – 6 Chelsea Sq, SW3.

DAUGHTER LIVING OF THIRD BARONET

Susan (Shoonan) Rosemary Lee, *b* 1931: *m* 1st, 1953 (*m diss* 1956), Samuel Charles Gillchrest; 2ndly, 1958, Keith Rawlings Hall, and has issue living, (by 2nd *m*) Simon Patrick Rawlings, *b* 1959, — Timothy Mark Lee, *b* 1967, — Susan Felicity, *b* 1960, — Jennifer Margaret, *b* 1963.

Sir Benjamin Lee Guinness, MP, LLD, 1st Bt, sat as MP for Dublin City (*C*) 1865-8, and at his own cost restored the Cathedral of St Patrick, Dublin. His el son, Sir Edward, 2nd Bt, sat as MP for Dublin (*C*) 1868-9 and 1874-80, when he was *cr Baron Ardilaun*, of Ashford, co Galway (peerage of United Kingdom), which Barony became ext at his death in 1915.

GUISE (GB) 1783, of Highnam Court, Gloucestershire
(Name pronounced "Gyze")

The more honest, the more safe

Sir JOHN GRANT GUISE, 7th *Baronet; b* 15 Dec 1927; *s* his father, *Sir* ANSELM WILLIAM EDWARD, 1970; *ed* Winchester, and RMC Sandhurst; Capt (ret) Queen's Own Hussars; patron of one living: *m* 1992, Sally H. M., da of late Cmdr H. G. C. Stevens, RN.

Arms – Gules, seven lozenges conjoined vaire, three, three, and one, on a canton or a mullet of six points pierced sable. Crest – Out of a ducal coronet or a swan wings elevated argent, gorged with a ducal crown and chain over the back or. Supporters – (to descend with the baronetcy)—*Dexter*, a swan with wings endorsed argent crusilly and langued gules, beaked and membered sable, collared and chained or; *sinister*, a bear sable, billetty, collared and chained or, langued and armed gules.
Seat – Elmore Court, nr Gloucester GL2 6NT. *Club* – Turf.

BROTHER LIVING

CHRISTOPHER JAMES (Easton Town Farm, Sherston, Malmesbury, Wilts; 106 Claxton Grove, W6), *b* 10 July 1930; *m* 1969, Mrs Carole Hoskins Benson, elder da of Jack Hoskins Master, of The Dower House, Crawley, Winchester, Hants, and formerly wife of Charles Edward Riou Benson, and has issue living, Anselm Mark, *b* 1971, — Ruth Victoria Margaret, *b* 1972.

SISTER LIVING

Philippa Margaret, *b* 1926: *m* 1950, Maj Alastair Hugh Joseph Fraser, MC, Lovat Scouts (*see* L Lovat, colls), who *d* 1986. *Residence* – Moniack Castle, Kirkhill, Inverness-shire.

COLLATERAL BRANCHES LIVING

Issue of late Col Christopher Dering Guise, 3rd son of 4th baronet, *b* 1855, *d* 1926: *m* 1903, Ella Letitia, who *d* 1928, da of late Vice-Adm Gerard John Napier:—

Valérie Napier, *b* 1907.

Grandchildren of late Lt-Cdr Jack Francis Vernon Guise (infra):—
Issue of late John Nicholas Guise, *b* 1920, *d* 1981: *m* 1st, 1946 (*m diss* 196-), Valerie, da of Ronald Parker, of Warrie Station, W Aust; 2ndly 196-, Beverley, who *d* 1982, da of James Parker, of Maida Vale, W Aust:—
(By 1st *m*) Anthony John, *b* 1951. —— Nikki, *b* 1952. —— Judith Anne, *b* 1955. —— (By 2nd *m*) James Nicholas, *b* 1969.

Granddaughters of late Rivett Francis Guise, 2nd son of late Francis Edward Guise, 3rd son of 3rd baronet:—
Issue of late Lt-Cdr Jack Francis Vernon Guise, *b* 1882, *d* 1964: *m* 1917, Catherine Renée, who *d* 1970, da of late Gilbert Ireland-Blackburn, of Bristol:—
Marguerite Renee, *b* 1918: *m* 19—, Ralph James Lang, of 288 Summer Lakes Parade, Ballajura, WA 6066, Aust, and has issue living. —— Diana Mary, *b* 1925: *m* 19—, Graham Johnson, who *d* 1992, of 2 Gabor Rd, Wattle Grove 6107, W Aust, and has issue living. —— Tacy Avena, *b* 1927: *m* 1st, 19— (*m diss* 19—), Thomas Turbett; 2ndly, 19—, Bernard Kelly, of 23 Kooham Way, Balga 6061, W Aust, and has issue living, (by 1st *m*), —, (by 2nd *m*), —. —— Georgina Frances, *b* 1930: *m* 19—, Jack Pritchard, and has issue living.

Grandchildren of late Lt-Cdr Jack Francis Vernon Guise (ante):—
Issue of late Christopher Rivett Guise, *b* 1921, *d* 1991: *m* 1948, Marion Strang:—
Christopher John (8 Stevens St, High Wycombe, WA 6057, Australia), *b* 1949: *m* 1969, Daphne Jean, only da of Edgar Mackie, of Kalgoorlie, WA, and has issue living, David Johnathan, *b* 1977, — Diane Elizabeth, *b* 1974. —— Georgina Elizabeth, *b* 1951: *m* 1st, 1968 (*m diss* 19—), Peter Dowding; 2ndly, 1988, Marian Zupan, of Bassendean, WA, and has issue living (by 1st *m*). —— Penelope Jane, *b* 1955: *m* 1971, Ljubo Tolj, of 3 Salisbury Rd, Rivervale, WA 6103, Australia, and has issue living.
Issue of late Reginald Ireland Guise, *b* 1923, *d* 1978: *m* 1951, Gladys Constance (15 McLintock Way, Karrinyup, W Aust 6018), only da of late Robert Alexander Baxter, of Cunderdin, W Aust:—
Larry Steven, *b* 1958: *m* 1984, Susan, only da of Peter Gunning of 10 Bulimba Rd, Nedlands, W Aust 6009, and has issue living, Megan Isabella, *b* 1987, — Simone Renée, *b* 1989, — Caitlin Ruth, *b* 1992. —— Neil Reginald, *b* 1960: *m* 1984, Amanda Francis, el da of Michael Seabrooke, of 7 Boronia Ave, Wundowie, W Aust 6560, and has issue living, Holly Rebecca, *b* 1992. —— David Nigel, *b* 1970. —— Wendy Nola, *b* 1954.

Grandchildren of late Rivett Francis Guise (ante):—
Issue of late Capt Francis Edward Boissier Guise, *b* 1892, *d* 1970: *m* 1st, 1914, Ethel Mary, who *d* 1943, da of Edward Valentine Holme; 2ndly, 1944, Gertrude Joyce (10 Harrow Rd, Brislington, Bristol 4), da of E. F. Taylor, of Kingswood, Bristol:—
(By 2nd *m*) Christopher Francis (4 Blackthorn Close, Marford, nr Wrexham, Clwyd LL12 8LB), *b* 1945; late RN: *m* 1973, Gwynneth Hancock, of Bristol, and has issue living, Nicola, *b* 1974, — Rhian *b* (twin) 1974. —— Penelope Catherine, *b* 1946: *m* 1966, Nigel Wilkinson, of 2 Melford Gdns, Old Kempshott Lane, Basingstoke, Hants, and has issue living, Simon, *b* 1970, — Nicholas, *b* 1972. —— Elizabeth Anne, *b* 1950: *m* 1973, David Richard Fynn, of 50 Littledean, Yate, nr Bristol, and has issue living, Colin Richard, *b* 1980, — Deborah Caroline, *b* 1982. —— Rosemary Caroline, *b* 1954: *m* 1979, Michael Anthony Hills, of Cain Valley Hotel, High St, Llanfyllin, Powys SY22 5AQ, and has issue living, Jennifer Claire, *b* 1983.
Issue of late Lieut-Col John William Guise, *b* 1894, *d* 1963: *m* 1924 (*m diss* 1937), Dorothy Alma, da of Theodore Hewitt English:—
Patricia Frederica, *b* 1929.
Issue of late Christopher Probyn Guise, *b* 1899, *d* 1965: *m* 1st, 1931 (*m diss* 1956), Hope, who *d* 1983, da of late F. G. P. Neison, of Lahore; 2ndly, 1959 (*m diss* 1963), Catherine Elizabeth de Villiers:—
(By 1st *m*) Anselm Neison (Grays Rd, Pauatahanui, RD1, Porirua 6221, nr Wellington, New Zealand), *b* 1935: *m* 1959, Eileen Mary, da of Col Patrick Henry Cummins, IMS (ret) (*see* E Lauderdale, colls, 1985 Edn), and has issue living, Edward William, *b* 1962, — Christopher Patrick, *b* 1973, — Laura Joan, *b* 1960: *m* 1984, Wing Cmdr William John Sommer, RNZAF, of 45 Victory Crescent, Tawa, NZ, and has issue living, Michael Patrick *b* 1990, — Susan Mary, *b* 1965: *m* 1986, F/O Owen

Philip Bieleski, RNZAF, and has issue living, David Owen *b* 1989, Andrew Craig *b* 1993. —— John Francis, *b* 1947. —— Dinah Gabrielle (Crebor Cottage, Dunmere, Bodmin, Cornwall), *b* 1936: *m* 1957, Peter Maunder, who *d* 1988.
   Issue of late Rivett Arthur Guise, *b* 1902, *d* 1965: *m* 1924, Beatrice Geraldine who *d* 1979, da of late Edward Charles Rudge, of Abbey Manor, Evesham:—
Peter Rivett John (Highnam, 4 Cae Castell, Builth Wells, Powys), *b* 1928: *m* 1953, Morfydd Meredydd, da of late Lewis Morris, of St Harman, Rhayader. —— Sheila Mae (Sandpiper's, Northfield Av, Shiplake, Henley-on-Thames, Oxon RG9 3PD), *b* 1925: *m* 1952, Francis Brian Collis, who *d* 1987, and has issue living, David Brian (8 Ashcroft Close, Caversham Heights, Reading, Berks RG4 7NU), *b* 1954: *m* 1978, Kerry Alison Elizabeth, da of Derek Alfred Preece, of Little Oak, Chiltern Rd, Peppard Common, Henley-on-Thames, and has issue living, Oliver Thomas Richard Rivett *b* 1985, Elizabeth Louisa Mae *b* 1982, — Simon Christopher (10 Borderside, Yateley, Hants), *b* 1957: *m* 1983, Jane Constance Hutchins, da of Trevor Thomas Farmiloe, of 4 Longridge Close, Reading, Berks, and has issue living, Max Christopher *b* 1985.

        Granddaughter of late Francis Edward Guise (ante):—
   Issue of late John Wright Guise, *b* 1855, *d* 1916: *m* 1st, 1884, Helen Edith, who *d* 1885, da of His Honour Judge Sumner, of Hempsted Court, Gloucester; 2ndly, 1888, Charlotte, who *d* 1931, da of Edwin Crawshay:—
(By 2nd *m*) Lesa Frances, *b* 1893: *m* 1920, Capt Kingsmill Foster Manley Power, MC, Gloucestershire Regt Reserve, who *d* 1963, and has issue living, Manley Anselm, *b* 1920, — Charlotte Lesa, *b* 1922.

        Granddaughter of late Rev Vernon Lane Guise, son of late Rev Vernon George Guise, 4th son of 3rd baronet:—
   Issue of late Maj Vernon Robert Guise, OBE, MC, *b* 1885, *d* 1939: *m* 1919, Nadine Alice, who *d* 1977, da of late Andrew Charles Armstrong (Armstrong, Bt, *cr* 1841, colls):—
Veronica Louise, *b* 1921: *m* 1946, Alan Falconer, FRCS, Surg-Lieut-Com RN, and has issue living, John Hedley, *b* 1951, — Alastair, *b* 1955, — Jennifer Anne, *b* 1947, — Catherine Scott, *b* 1949. *Residence* – 71 Alexander Park Road, Muswell Hill, N10.
   In 1262 Nicholas de Gyse (having *m* a near relative of Sir John de Burgh, el son of Hubert, Earl of Kent) received in right of his wife the manor and lordship of Elmore in Gloucestershire. Sir Anselm de Gyse, son of Nicholas, received (temp 1274) a confirmation of this manor by a further grant (still in possession of the family), and assumed the de Burgh arms, differenced by a canton. His descendant, Christopher Guise, el son of William Guise, of Elmore (Sheriff of Gloucestershire 1647), was *cr* a Baronet 1661, which Baronetcy became ext at the death of the 5th baronet in April 1783; but eight months after, in Dec 1783, his cousin and heir male, John Guise (of the younger branch), of Highnam Court, Gloucester, great-grandson of Henry Guise, a younger son of William Guise, of Elmore (ante), yr brother of 1st Baronet of 1st creation, was also *cr* a Baronet. The 2nd baronet (of the 2nd creation) sat as MP for Gloucestershire. Gen Sir John Guise, 3rd Bt, GCB, was granted supporters to descend to heirs male of the body on succession to the baronetcy 1863, and the 4th and 5th Baronets were High Sheriffs of Gloucestershire.

GULL (UK) 1872, of Brook Street

Sir RUPERT WILLIAM CAMERON GULL, 5th *Baronet*; *b* 14 July 1954; *s* his father *Sir* MICHAEL SWINNERTON CAMERON, 1989; *ed* Diocesan Coll, Cape Town, and Cape Town Univ; *m* 1980, Gillian Lee, da of Robert Howard Gordon MacFarlaine, and has issue.

Arms – Azure, a serpent nowed or between three seagulls proper; a canton ermine, thereon an ostrich feather argent, quilled or, enfiled by the coronet which encircles the plume of the Prince of Wales, gold. **Crests** – 1st, a lion passant guardant or, supporting with his dexter forepaw an escutcheon azure, thereon an ostrich feather argent, quilled or, enfiled with a coronet as in the canton; 2nd, two arms embowed, vested azure, cuffs argent, the hands proper holding a torch or fired proper.
Residence – Harcourt Rd, Claremont, Cape Town, S Africa.

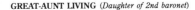

Without God labour is in vain

DAUGHTERS LIVING

Victoria Yvonne, *b* 1984. —— Katie Alexandra, *b* 1986. —— Olivia, *b* 1993.

SISTER LIVING

Katherine Dona Mary, *b* 1951: *m* 19—, — and has issue living.

AUNT LIVING (*Daughter of 3rd baronet*)

Pamela Dona Anne, *b* 1922: *m* 1946, Col Alistair James Strang Martin, CBE, Queen's Own Highlanders (ret), who *d* 1992, of Cleve House, Crooksbury, Farnham, Surrey, and has issue living, Christopher Thomas, *b* 1948, — Michael Richard Alistair, *b* 1953.

GREAT-UNCLE LIVING (*Son of 2nd baronet*)

JOHN EVELYN, MC, *b* 26 March 1914; 1939-45 War, Capt Coldstream Guards (despatches, MC): *m* 1957, Margaret Colquhoun, da of late Capel Berger of Hatfield, Herts, and has issue living, Angus William John, *b* 1963: *m* 1988, Jacqueline Mary, da of Gerald Edgar Ford, — and two adopted children, Mark Capel James, *b* 1962: *m* 1993, Lene Tang Rasmussen, of Aarhus, Denmark, — Lucinda Jane Evelyn, *b* 1961: *m* 1983, Doko Gorov, of Macedonia, and has issue living. *Residence* – Trowley Hill Farm, Flamstead, nr St Albans, Herts AL3 8DZ.

GREAT-AUNT LIVING (*Daughter of 2nd baronet*)

Rosemary Violet, *b* 1912: *m* 1954, Maj R. S. Schreiber who *d* 1978, late Coldm Gds. *Residence* – Campsea Ashe House, Woodbridge, Suffolk.

WIDOW LIVING OF FOURTH BARONET

MARGARETHA CATHERINA JOHANNA (*Dowager Lady Gull*), da of late Charles Henry Adrian Pentz, of Cape Town: *m* 19—, as his 2nd wife, Sir Michael Swinnerton Cameron Gull, 4th Bt, who *d* 1989. *Residence* – Wedgeport, Bertha Av, Newlands, Cape Town, S Africa.

This baronetcy was conferred on William Withey Gull, MD, an eminent Physician (subsequently Physician in Ordinary to HM Queen Victoria), in recognition of services rendered to HRH Albert Edward, Prince of Wales, during his severe illness in the winter of 1871; and HM Queen Victoria also, in 1872, granted the canton as an augmentation to the arms. The 2nd baronet, Sir (William) Cameron, sat as MP for Devonshire N-W Div (LU) 1895-1900.

GUNNING (GB) 1778, of Eltham, Kent

He rules alone with impartial sway

Sir CHARLES THEODORE GUNNING, 9th *Baronet*; *b* 19 June 1935; *s* his father, *Sir* ROBERT CHARLES GUNNING, 1989; *ed* Canadian Mil Coll, RNEC (Plymouth), and Tech Univ of Nova Scotia; BEng, CEng, AIMIMechE, AMIMarE; late Lt Cdr RCN; senior consultant, Eyretechnics Ltd (Ottawa); Vice-Chm RCS Nat Council in Canada since 1980: *m* 1st, 1969 (*m diss* 1982), Sarah, da of Col Patrick Arthur Eaton, of 121 Hadlow Rd, Tonbridge, Kent; 2ndly, 1989, Linda, da of Theodore Kachmar, of Montreal, and has issue by 1st *m*.

Arms – Gules, on a fesse erminois between three doves argent, as many crosses formée per pale gules and azure. **Crest** – A dove holding in its dexter claw a caduceus proper.
Residence – 2940 McCarthy Rd, Ottawa, Ontario K1V 8K6, Canada.

DAUGHTER LIVING (By 1st marriage)

Caroline Anne, *b* 1971.

BROTHERS LIVING

JOHN ROBERT (Box 1683, Peace River, Alberta, Canada), *b* 17 Sept 1944: *m* 1969, Alina Tylicki, and has issue living, Derek John Robert, *b* 1972, — Kevin Philip, *b* 1976, — Lori-Ann, *b* 1969. —— Joseph Jeremy (PO Box 2409, Peace River, Alberta, Canada) *b* 1946: *m* 1968, June Smith, and has issue living, Diana Elizabeth, *b* 1968, — Theressa Kathleen, *b* 1971, — Michelle Wendy, *b* 1973. —— David Laurence (16031, 123 St, Edmonton, Alberta T5X 2WZ, Canada), *b* 1948: *m* 1978, Claudette Dubois, and has issue living, Leslie Anita, *b* 1978, — Kristina Jaclyn, *b* 1980. —— Henry Michael (37 Mearns Drive, Stonehaven, Aberdeenshire), *b* 1949: *m* 1970, Rita Bruneau, and has issue living, Holly Michelle, *b* 1970, — Melanie Dawn, *b* 1975. —— Bernard Christopher (47 Helene Av, Dartmouth, Nova Scotia B2X 1G5, Canada), *b* 1951; Land Surveyor: *m* 1979, Elizabeth McLaughlin. —— George Peter (Box 6626, Peace River, Alberta T8S 1S4, Canada), *b* 1953; apiarist: *m* 1974, Pauline Maud Karpiak, and has issue living, George Bryce, *b* 1975, — Angela Marion, *b* 1977. —— Anthony Andrew Simon, *b* 1955.

SISTERS LIVING

Iseult Sara, *b* 1936: *m* 1970 (*m diss* 1977), Klaus Krey (Box 1241, Peace River, Alberta TOH 2XO, Canada), and has issue living, Andrew Lee, *b* 1974, — Suzanne Nicole, *b* 1972. —— Elaine Beatrice, *b* 1939: *m* 1958, Arnold Nelson Jones (Box 772, High Prairie, Alberta, Canada), and has issue living, Michael Robert, *b* 1959, — Charles Mark, *b* 1960, — George Marion, *b* 1961, — Bruce Gordon, *b* 1963: *m* 1984, Kathleen Margaret Barnes , — Christopher John Peter, *b* 1971, — Kathryn Ann, *b* 1967.

DAUGHTER LIVING OF SEVENTH BARONET

Essex Vere: *m* 1919, Basil Gerald Brooke, formerly Lieut 17th Lancers, who *d* 1969 (*see* Brooke, Bt, colls, *cr* 1903). *Residence* – 23 Halsey St, SW3.

WIDOW LIVING OF EIGHTH BARONET

HELEN NANCY (*Ann, Lady Gunning*) (Box 6602, Peace River, Alberta T8S 1S4, Canada), da of late Vice Adm Sir Theodore John Hallett, KBE, CB: *m* 1934, *Sir* ROBERT CHARLES GUNNING 8th Bt, who *d* 1989.

COLLATERAL BRANCHES LIVING

Granddaughter of late Col George Hamilton Gunning, DSO, uncle of 8th baronet:—
Issue of late Major Jack Hamilton Gunning, Indian Army, *b* 1907, *d* 1956: *m* 1st, 1938, Judith Clowes, who *d* 1942, da of late Capt Norton Clowes Castle, Roy Irish Regt; 2ndly, 1951, Kathleen Irene, who *d* 1993, da of P. W. A. Wilson, of Shirley, Surrey:—
(By 1st *m*) Cherry Hamilton (9 Linkfield, East Molesey, Surrey KT8 9SD), *b* 1939: *m* 1962, John Benjamin Lionel Underwood, Maj (ret) King's Own Roy Border Regt, and has issue living, Michael John Benjamin, *b* 1966, — Catherine Louise, *b* 1964: *m* 1992, Mark George Beatty, and has issue living, Benjamin George *b* 1994, — Jennifer Elizabeth, *b* 1967.

Granddaughters of late Brig-Gen Orlando George Gunning, CMG, DSO (infra):—
Issue of late Sir (Orlando) Peter Gunning, CMG, *b* 1908, *d* 1964: *m* 1940, Patricia Mary (42 Upper Cheyne Row, SW3), da of late Capt Dermot O'Connor, MC:—
Susan Mary, *b* 1944. —— Diana Rosemary *b* 1947: *m* 1971, Patrick Durnford, of Stoney Down, Corfe Mullen, Dorset, and has issue living, Richard Peter Henry, *b* 1974, — James Edward, *b* 1976, — Nicholas John, *b* 1980, — Clare Susannah, *b* 1978.

Grandchildren of late Col John Campbell Gunning, son of late Maj John Gunning, 6th son of 2nd baronet:—

Issue of late Brig-Gen Orlando George Gunning, CMG, DSO, Indian Army, b 1867, ka 1917: m 1902, Margaret Cecilia, who d 1951, da of late Clinton George Dawkins:—

Elizabeth Margaret Mary (North Barn House, Lower Froyle, Alton, Hants), b 1905: m 1934, Rupert Macnaghten Cecil Thursfield, who d 1979.

Issue of late Capt Henry Ross Gunning, b 1879, d 1951: m 1st, 1904, Charlotte Henrietta, who d 1908, da of late Anthony Harley Bacon; 2ndly, 1914, Violet Gwendoline, who d 1973, da of late Robert Cubitt:—

(By 2nd m) Richard Ross, b 1928: m 1951, Hilda, da of John Ronald Staniforth, and has issue living, Christopher John Ross, b 1955 and has issue living, Jennifer Christina, b 1976, — Timothy Robin, b 1959 and has issue living, Brodie Adam, b 1982, — Heather Jean, b 1954. Residence – 58-901 Kentwood Lane, Victoria, BC, Canada. ——— (By 1st m) Henrietta Marion (212-250, 36th Av E, Vancouver, BC, Canada), b 1905. ——— Evelyn Briliana (Flat 4, 7 Burlington Place, Eastbourne, E Sussex BN21 4AS), b 1907.

The 1st baronet was successively Minister Plenipotentiary at the Courts of Berlin and St Petersburg and the 2nd baronet was successively MP for Wigan (1800-1802), Hastings (1802-6), and East Grinstead (1812-18). Sir Robert, 3rd Bt, sat as MP for Northampton 1830-31, and was High Sheriff of Northamptonshire 1841-2, and Sir Henry, 4th Bt, was successively R of Knockyn, Incumbent of Horton, and R of Wigan, and Rural Dean. The 7th baronet, Brig-Gen Sir Charles Vere Gunning, CB, CMG, served in S Africa 1900-02 and during European War 1914-18 (despatches twice).

GUNSTON (UK) 1938, of Wickwar, co Gloucester

Sir JOHN WELLESLEY GUNSTON, 3rd Baronet; b 25 July 1962; s his father, Sir RICHARD WELLESLEY, 1991; ed Harrow, and RMA Sandhurst: m 1990, Rosalind Gordon, yst da of Edward Gordon Eliott, of Bower's Mill House, nr Guildford, Surrey, and has issue.

Arms – Not exemplified at time of going to press.
Residence – 8 Leathwaite Rd, SW11 1XQ.

SON LIVING

RICHARD ST GEORGE, b 3 July 1992.

HALF-SISTER LIVING (daughter of 2nd baronet and 1st wife, Elizabeth Mary, eldest da of Sir Arthur Colegate, MP)

Caroline Jane, b 1950: m 1971, Jonathan Robert Felton Peel, and has issue living, Edmund Robert Felton, b 1979, — Victoria Mary, b 1972, — Lucy Caroline, b 1975. Residence – —

MOTHER LIVING

JOAN ELIZABETH MARIE, only da of late Reginald Forde, of Inanda, Johannesburg, S Africa, and formerly wife of H. B. Coldicott: m 1959 (m diss 19—), as his 2nd wife, Sir Richard Wellesley Gunston, 2nd Bt, who d 1991. Residence – —.

WIDOWS LIVING OF FIRST AND SECOND BARONETS

EVELYN BLIGH (GARDENIA), OBE (Gardenia, Lady Gunston), da of Howard Bligh St George (see St George, Bt, colls); OBE 1944: m 1917, Sir Derrick Wellesley Gunston, 1st Bt, MC, who d 1985. Residence – 55 Onslow Square, SW7 3LR.

VERONICA ELIZABETH (Veronica, Lady Gunston), da of Maj — Haynes, and widow of Capt Vivian Graham Loyd: m 1976, as his 3rd wife, Sir Richard Wellesley Gunston, 2nd Bt, who d 1991. Residence – The Arboretum, Tidebrook, Wadhurst, E Sussex TN5 6NY.

The 1st baronet, Sir Derrick Wellesley Gunston, MC, yr son of Maj Bernard Hamilton Gunston (see D Wellington, colls, 1953 Edn), Bernard Hamilton Gunston (see D Wellington, colls, 1953 Edn), was MP for Thornbury Div of Glos 1924-45, served as Parliamentary Priv Sec to Min of Health 1926-29, to Chancellor of the Exchequer 1931-36, and to Jt Under-Sec of State for War 1940-42, and was a Member of Parliamentary Mission to Newfoundland 1943.

GUNTER 1901, of Wetherby Grange, Collingham, West Riding of Yorkshire (Extinct 1980)

Lt-Cdr Sir RONALD VERNON GUNTER, RNVR, 3rd and last Baronet; d 1980.

DAUGHTERS LIVING OF THIRD BARONET

(By 1st m) Hazel Ursula Anne, b 1927: m 1948, Kjell Christian Andresen, and has issue living, Peter Christian Gunter, b 1952, — Hazel Anne Christine Gunter, b 1955. Residence – Endsleigh, Crossway, Walton-on-Thames, Surrey. ——— Jane Hilda Clara, b 1929: m 1950, Harry Ian Lee-Duncan and has had issue, Linda-Jane Gunter (8 Willow Walk, Cambridge CB1 1LA), b 1952, — Diana Charlotte Gunter, b 1954, d 1988, — Alexandra Karen Gunter, b 1959.

GUTHRIE (UK) 1936, of Brent Eleigh Hall, co Suffolk

Sir MALCOLM CONNOP GUTHRIE, 3rd *Baronet*; *b* 16 Dec 1942; *s* his father, *Sir* GILES CONNOP MCEACHARN, OBE, DSC, 1979; *ed* Millfield: *m* 1967, Victoria, da of late Douglas Willcock, and has issue.

ᴀrms – Per chevron argent and azure, in chief two eagles displayed of the second, and in base a lymphad with oars and sails furled of the first, pennons flying gules. Crest – A cubit arm in armour proper, charged with two crosses patée fitchée in pale azure, holding in the hand proper a grenade sable, fired also proper.
Residence – Brent Eleigh, Belbroughton, Stourbridge, Worcs DY9 0DW.

SON LIVING

GILES MALCOLM WELCOME, *b* 16 Oct 1972; *ed* Shrewsbury.

DAUGHTER LIVING

Islay Mary Welcome, *b* 1968.

AUNT LIVING (*Daughter of 1st baronet*)

Diana Mary, *b* 1919.

WIDOW LIVING OF SECOND BARONET

RHONA (*Rhona, Lady Guthrie*) (Les Vaux, Rozel, St Martin, Jersey JE3 6AJ), only da of late Frederic Stileman of Bombay: *m* 1939, Sir Giles Connop McEacharn Guthrie, OBE, DSC, 2nd Bt, who *d* 1979.

COLLATERAL BRANCH LIVING

Issue of late Alastair Peter Guthrie, 3rd but yst surv son of 2nd Bt, *b* 1944, *d* 1986: *m* 1966, Elizabeth (Stanley Mill, Chippenham, Wilts), yr da of late Valentin Schaposchnikoff:—
Alexander Valentine Connop, *b* 1966. —— Barnaby Giles, *b* 1969.

The 1st Baronet, Sir Connop Thirlwall Robert Guthrie, KBE, was a financier and a director of public companies. In 1914-18 War he was Capt Grenadier Guards (wounded), a Special Representative in USA of Min of Shipping 1916-19, and a Member of USA Govt Shipping Control Cttee 1918-19. In 1939-45 he was Head of Security Div of British Security Co-ordination in W Hemisphere 1941-5, and an Hon Air Commodore Auxiliary Air Force. The 2nd baronet, Sir Giles Connop McEacharn Guthrie, OBE, DSC, served in 1939-45 War in Fleet Air Arm as fighter and test pilot (Lt-Cdr RNVR 1943); Man Dir of Brown Shipley & Co Ltd, Dir of Prudential Assurance Co Ltd, Chm and Ch Exec of BOAC, Dir of BEA and Chm of Air Transport Insurance Ltd.

Gwynne-Evans, see Evans.

Hagart-Alexander, see Alexander.

Haggerston, see Constable-Maxwell-Scott, Bt (cr 1642).

HALL (NS) 1687, of Dunglass, Haddingtonshire

Sir DOUGLAS BASIL HALL, KCMG, 14th *Baronet*; *b* 1 Feb 1909; *s* his brother, *Sir* NEVILLE REYNOLDS, 1978; *ed* Radley, and Keble Coll, Oxford (MA); JP of Devon, and a Member of Police Authority for Devon and Cornwall 1971-79; entered Overseas Civil Ser as a Cadet, N Rhodesia 1930; Dist Officer 1932-50; Sen Dist Officer 1950-53, Provincial Commr 1953, Admin Sec 1955-56, Sec for Native Affairs 1956, and Gov and C-in-C of Somaliland Protectorate 1959-60; CMG 1958, KCMG 1959: *m* 1933, Rachel Marion, who *d* 1990, da of late Maj Ernest Gartside-Tippinge, RA, and has issue.

Arms – Azure, a chevron argent between three cranes' heads erased at the necks or, and on an inescutcheon or charged of a lion rampant gules within a double tressure flory counterflory of the last. **Crest** – A stork sitting on a mount in a watching posture proper.
Residence – Barnford, Ringmore, nr Kingsbridge, Devon TQ7 4HL.

SON LIVING

JOHN DOUGLAS HOSTE (Brook Mill, Buckfastleigh, S Devon TQ11 0HL), *b* 7 Jan 1945; *ed* Dover Coll, Gonville and Caius Coll, Camb (BA), and Southampton Univ (Cert Ed); Vice Principal (Academic) Dartington Coll of Art: *m* 1972, Angela Margaret, da of George Keys, of 2 Barnsfield Lane, Buckfastleigh, S Devon, and has issue living, Thomas James, *b* 10 Dec 1975, — Bernard Neville, *b* 1979.

DAUGHTERS LIVING

Marion, *b* 1940; *ed* Trin Coll, Dublin (MA): *m* 1965, John Francis Fuller-Sessions, MA, of Orchard Farm, Parwich, nr Ashbourne, Derbys DE6 1QB, and has issue living, Nicholas Francis Blair, *b* 1974, — Ruth, *b* 1967, — Sara, *b* 1969. —— Ruth, *b* 1942: *m* 1963, Anthony Bernard Cragg (PO Box 60, Umhlanga Rocks, Natal, S Africa 4320), and has issue living, Stephen Browning, *b* 1966, — Christopher Douglas, *b* 1968, — Timothy Hugh, *b* 1970, — Ann Louise, *b* 1965: *m* 1992, Christopher Charles Peter Latham, and has issue living, Alfred Michael, *b* 1992, — Emily Rachel, *b* 1993.

DAUGHTERS LIVING OF TWELFTH BARONET

Mary Jane Rosamond, *b* 1922; 1939-45 as 3rd Officer WRNS: *m* 1946, Mark Peter Whitlock, solicitor, of The Old Parsonage, Houghton St Giles, Walsingham, Norfolk, and has issue living, John Mark, *b* 1955, — Paul Mark, *b* 1957, — Martin Mark, *b* 1959, — Mary Louise, *b* 1947, — Jane Frances Mary, *b* 1949. —— Elizabeth Katharine Marion, *b* 1925; *ed* Edinburgh Univ (BSc); MRCVS: *m* 1949, Oliphant Fairburn Jackson, PhD, MRCVS, who *d* 1991, of Little Stagenhoe, Horningtoft, Dereham, Norfolk NR20 5ED, and has issue living, James Ellis, *b* 1959, — Anthony Oliphant, *b* 1961, — Rosemary Frances, *b* 1955. —— Teresa Madeleine, *b* 1930: *m* 1952, Herbert Norman Constantine, of Laskill, Hawnby, York, and has issue living, Robert Francis, *b* 1953, — Nigel Loudon, *b* 1954, — Neville Egerton, *b* 1959: *m* 1990, Karen, only da of Mrs J. Tushingham, of Bamber Bridge, Lancs, — Serena Mary, *b* 1963: *m* 19—, Stephen M. Rainbow, 2nd son of W/Cdr E. Rainbow, of Thorp ARch, Yorks, and has issue living, Emily Laura Francesca *b* 1992.

WIDOW LIVING OF THIRTEENTH BARONET

DOROTHY MAUD (*Dorothy, Lady Hall*) (Ash Cottage, Ash, Dartmouth, S Devon), da of late William Lawrence Jones: *m* 1957, Sir Neville Reynolds Hall, 13th baronet, who *d* 1978.

Sir James Hall, 4th baronet, MP for St Michael's, was President of the Royal Society of Edinburgh. Sir Martin Julian Hall, OBE, 10th baronet, was Director of Food Section, Min of Munitions during 1914-19 War, and Ch Reconstruction Officer for Scotland, Min of Labour.

HALL (UK) 1919, of Burton Park, Sussex

Sir John Bernard Hall, 3rd *Baronet; b* 20 March 1932; *s* his father, *Lieut-Col Sir* Douglas Montgomery Bernard, DSO, 1962; *ed* Eton, and Trin Coll, Oxford (MA); Lt R Fus (RARO); Lord of Manor of Barlavington; Chm The Nikko Bank (UK) plc; Liveryman and Member of Court of Assistants, Clothworkers' Co; Memb St Alban's Diocesan Synod and Diocesan Finance Board: *m* 1957, Delia Mary, da of late Lt-Col James Archibald Innes, DSO (*see* V Downe, colls, 1985 Edn), and has issue.

Arms – Vert, on a fesse or, between in chief a cross-crosslet fitchée between two talbots' heads erased argent collared and ringed gules, and in base a like talbot's head, three escallops sable. **Crest** – A talbot's head erased sable, ears argent, gorged with a chaplet or, garnished with roses gules, between two cross-crosslets fitchée or.
Residences – Penrose House, Patmore Heath, Albury, Ware, Herts SG11 2LT; Inver House, Lochinver, Lairg, Sutherland IV27 4LJ.

SON LIVING

David Bernard *b* 12 May 1961; *ed* Eton, and York Univ. *Residence* – Rose Cottage, Holly Lane, Haughton, Stafford ST18 9JS.

In Deo Fides

Trust in God

DAUGHTERS LIVING

Caroline Evelyn, *b* 1959; *ed* Cobham Hall, and Durham Univ. —— Julia Nancy, *b* 1965; *ed* Cobham Hall, and Edinburgh Univ.

HALF-SISTER LIVING

Pamela Mary, *b* 1916: *m* 1st, 1936 (*m diss* 1944), Richard Haliburton Bentley; 2ndly, 1944 (*m diss* 1948), Ivan Lorn Buchanan; 3rdly, 1949, Norman Percy Hackforth. *Residence* – Honeysuckle Cottage, Wittersham, Kent.

MOTHER LIVING

Nancie Walton, only da of late John Edward Mellor, CB, JP, DL: *m* 1st, 1925 (*m diss* 1950), as his 2nd wife, Lt-Col Sir Douglas Montgomery Bernard Hall, DSO, 2nd Bt; 2ndly, 1962, Col Peter James Bradford, DSO, MC, TD, who *d* 1992. *Residences* – Long Crumples, Alton, Hants; Tumore Lodge, Lairg, Sutherland.

The 1st baronet, Sir Douglas Bernard Hall (son of late Bernard Hall, JP, first Mayor of City of Liverpool, of Villa Mariposa, Cannes, France), sat as MP for Isle of Wight (*C*) Jan 1910 to Oct 1922 and was High Sheriff of Sussex 1907.

HALL (UK) 1923, of Grafham, co Surrey

Sir (Frederick) John (Frank) Hall, 3rd *Baronet; b* 14 Aug 1931; *s* his father, *Sir* Frederick Henry, 1949; *ed* Bryanston; Partner, KPMG Peat Marwick 1987-93; Dir Thomson McLintock Associates 1976-87; founded KPMG Career Consultancy Services 1983, ret 1993; Sr Manager McLintock Mann & Whinney Murray 1969-76, The Nestlé Co Ltd 1965-69; Personnel Manager Johnson Wax Ltd 1963-65, Personnel Officer The Nestlé Co Ltd 1959-63, Personnel Manager Universal Pattern & Precision Engrg Co Ltd 1955-59; Dir Roffey Park Institute 1978-90 (Chm 1985-87, Vice-Chm 1983-85): *m* 1st, 1956 (*m diss* 1960), Felicity Anne, da of late Edward Rivers-Fletcher, of Norwich; 2ndly, 1961 (*m diss* 1967), Patricia Ann, da of late Douglas Atkinson, of Greystead, Longlands Rd, Carlisle; 3rdly, 1967, re-married his 1st wife, Felicity Anne (ante), and has issue by 2nd and 3rd *m*.

Arms – Sable, a cross moline between in the first and fourth quarters a talbot's head erased and in the second and third a chaplet of oak or. **Crest** – A demi-griffin sable holding between the claws a portcullis or.
Residence – Carradale, 29 Embercourt Rd, Thames Ditton, Surrey, KT7 OLH.

DAUGHTERS LIVING (By 2nd marriage)

Nicola Jane, *b* 1962. —— Samantha Mary, *b* 1965.

(By 3rd marriage)

Antonia Anne, *b* 1970. —— Victoria Joy, *b* 1973.

BROTHER LIVING

David Christopher, *b* 30 Dec 1937: *m* 1st, 1962 (*m diss* 1987), Irene, da of William Duncan, of 2 Tollohill Pl, Kincorth, Aberdeen; 2ndly, 19—, Annie Madelaine Renée Olivier, adopted da of late Bottemanne Raould, of Thieusies-Lez Soignies (Mons), Belgium, and has issue living (by 1st *m*), John Christopher, *b* 22 May 1965, — Olwen Evelyn, *b* 1967. *Residence* – 22 Buckstone Row, Edinburgh EH10 6TP.

SISTER LIVING

Olwen Mary Primrose, *b* 1928: *m* 1st, 1958 (*m diss* 1977), Carlyle Herbert Peter Gardner (*see* B Blyth, 1944 Edn), who *d* 1992; 2ndly, 1977, James Alexander Macrae, and has issue living (by 1st *m*), Alan Frederick Peter (PO Box 95044, 546 Swanson Rd, Swanson, Auckland 8, NZ), *b* 1952: *m* 1st, 1972 (*m diss* 1993), Pamela Susan Wheal; 2ndly, 1994, Christine Penelope Metcalf, and has issue living (by 1st *m*), Geoffrey Alan Peter *b* 1973, Nicola Susan *b* 1975, — Marcus Hillier Clive, *b* 1958, — Crispin John Stuart Hyde, *b* 1961, — Jonathan Carlyle Heiko, *b* 1963, — Jason Peter Alan, *b* 1965, — Matthew Reginald Saul, *b* 1968, — Merrily Mary Susan, *b* 1955: *m* 1986, Anthony Willis, — Josephine Juliet, *b* 1956: *m* 1978 (*m diss* 1993), Jonathan Peter Matich, — Susannah Mary Ann, *b* 1962. *Residence* – 3 Nandina Place, Kaiapoi, N Canterbury, NZ.

The 1st baronet, Sir Frederick Hall, KBE, DSO, Chm and Managing Director of Mercantile Marine Finance Corporation Ltd, and a Member of Lloyd's and the Baltic Exchange, sat as MP for Dulwich Div of Camberwell (*C*) 1910-32.

HALSEY (UK) 1920, of Gaddesden, co Hertford

The spoken word cannot be recalled

Rev Sir JOHN WALTER BROOKE HALSEY (*Rev Brother John Halsey*), 4th *Baronet*; *b* 26 Dec 1933; *s* his father, *Capt Sir* THOMAS EDGAR, DSO, RN, 1970; *ed* Eton and Magdalene Coll, Camb (BA).

𝕬rms – Argent, on a pile sable three griffins' heads erased of the field. 𝕮rest – A dexter cubit arm proper, habited gules, the cuff argent, holding a griffin's claw erased or.
Residence – The Fraternity, 23 Manse Rd, Roslin, Midlothian EH25 9LF.

SISTER LIVING

Margaret Anne, *b* 1938: *m* 1961, John Farnon, of Old Bell House, Market Lavington, Devizes, and has issue living, Jennifer Anne, *b* 1962, — Nicola Jane, *b* 1964, — Alison Sarah, *b* 1966.

AUNTS LIVING (*Daughters of 2nd baronet*)

Agatha: *m* 1942 (*m diss* 1976) Alan Edmondson Bainbridge, and has issue living, Thomas Howard, *b* 1943: *m* 1977, Isabel Frances Collins, — Andrew Halsey, *b* 1944: *m* 1973, Helen Brown, and has issue living, Alexander James *b* 19—, Elizabeth Anne *b* 19—, — David James Macalpine, *b* 1950: *m* 1974, Judith Roslyn Manley, and has issue living, Fiona *b* 1979, Megan *b* 19—, — Patricia Mary, *b* 1946: *m* 1976, John Bruce McBride, — Jean Vivien, *b* 1955. —— Evelyn Cecilia: *m* 1944, Brig Frederick Manus De Butts, CMG, OBE, DL, late SCLI, of Church Cottage, Hoggeston, Buckingham, and has issue living, David Frederick, *b* 1950: *m* 1977, Barbara Elizabeth Scott Hooper, and has issue living, Richard Frederick *b* 1978, Michael McCrea *b* 1980, Lucy Katherine *b* 1983, — Caroline Mary, *b* 1952: *m* 1974, Anthony Hugh Bond, and has issue living, Jonathan James Hugh *b* 1977, Rupert Charles *b* 1980, Victoria Jane *b* 1984.

COLLATERAL BRANCHES LIVING

Issue of late Lt-Cdr William Edmund Halsey, RN, yr son of 2nd baronet, *b* 1903, *d* 1986: *m* 1931, Barbara Dorothea, who *d* 1993, da of late Charles Lindsay Orr Ewing, MP (*see* Orr Ewing, Bt, colls):—
Bridget, *b* 1934: *m* 1958, Edward Alfred Heycock, elder surv son of Morris Sadler Heycock, MC, of Bardennoch, Moniaive, Thornhill, Dumfriesshire DG3 4HZ and has issue living, Susan Mary, *b* 1959: *m* 19—, William Kennedy McConnel (*see* Montagu-Pollock, Bt, colls), — Caroline Bridget, *b* 1961, — Jennifer Lucy, *b* 1966.

Grandsons of late Rev Canon Frederick Halsey (infra):—
Issue of late Lt-Col Guy Marsden Halsey, TD, JP, *b* 1908, *d* 1990: *m* 1939, Juliet Mary Gough (Whitehouse Farm, Gaddesden Row, Hemel Hempstead, Herts HP2 6HG), da of late Capt Robert Wemyss Muir Arbuthnot, MC (*see* Arbuthnot, Bt, colls):—
NICHOLAS GUY, TD (The Golden Parsonage, Gaddesden Row, Hemel Hempstead, Herts HP2 6HG; *Club* – Brooks's), *b* 14 June 1948; *ed* Eton, and RAC Cirencester; Maj RGJ(V); High Sheriff Herts 1995; FRICS: *m* 1976, Viola Georgina Juliet, da of Maj George Thorne, MC, DL, ERD (*see* B Peel), of Blounts Farm, Sonning Common, Reading, Berks, and has issue living, Guy Francis Johnston, *b* 1981. —— Robert Frederick, *b* 1950; *ed* Eton, and RAC Cirencester; FCA: *m* 1976, Elizabeth Virginia, da of John Holman, and has issue living, Daniel John, *b* 1978, — Samuel Treve *b* 1983.

Issue of late Rev Canon Frederick Halsey, 3rd son of 1st baronet, *b* 1870, *d* 1952: *m* 1901, Audrey Katharine, who *d* 1969, da of late Lt-Col William Marsden, of Cedar Court, Farnham:—
Katharine Audrey (7 Chestnut Close, Potten End, Berkhamsted, Herts). —— Barbara (Old House Cottage, Combe, Oxon): *m* 1961, John Parr Curgenven, who *d* 1982, el son of late Sir Arthur Joseph Curgenven.

Issue of late Adm Sir Lionel Halsey, GCMG, GCVO, KCIE, CB, 4th son of 1st baronet, *b* 1872, *d* 1949: *m* 1905, Morwenna, who *d* 1959, da of Major Bevil Granville, of Wellesbourne Hall, Warwick:—
Joan, *b* 1910; is a JP for Herts: *m* 1933, George Lockhart Wood, who *d* 1959, and has issue living, John Lockhart (The Hoo, Gt Gaddesden, Hemel Hempstead), *b* 1935: *m* 1963, Rosemary Sonia Despard, da of Richard Graham Hensley Hopkins, and has issue living, George Edmund Richard, *b* 1966, Kirstin Rebecca *b* 1968, — Lionel David (Manor Farm, Milcombe, Banbury, Oxon), *b* 1938; Lt-Col Welsh Gds (ret); Extra Equerry to HRH the Duke of Edinburgh 1965-67: *m* 1960, Belinda Mary, da of late Gilbert Graham Balfour (*see* Halsey, Bt, 1990 Edn), and has issue living, James Lionel Norman *b* 1963, Sarah Morwenna *b* 1961, Alexandra Louise *b* 1965, — Richard George (Markham House, Badminton, Avon), *b* 1939: *m* 1963, Penelope Gay, da of Lt-Col John Bertie Harris Daniel, MBE, MC, and has issue living, Andrew John *b* 1966: *m* 1991, Rachel Claire Morris (and has issue living, Angus Richard *b* 1993, Elinor Claire *b* 1991), Emma Ruth *b* 1965, — Edmund Michael (The Old Rectory, Holwell, Hitchin, Herts), *b* 1943: *m* 1971, Elizabeth Anne, da of Sqd-Ldr Robert Roland Patrick Fisher, RAF (ret) and has issue living, Sarah Georgina *b* 1974, Ann Louise *b* 1977, — Ruth Mary, *b* 1945: *m* 1973, James Henry Wood Ritchie, of Drissaig House, Lochavich, by Taynuilt, Argyll, and has issue living, Fiona Mary *b* 1975, Margaret Jean *b* 1976. *Residence* – The Old Schoolhouse, Whipsnade, Dunstable, Beds. —— Ruth, *b* 1915. *Residence* – Parsonage Piece, Whipsnade, Dunstable, Beds.

This family is descended from John Halsey of Great Gaddesden, Herts, who was living 1512. The 1st Baronet Rt Hon Sir (Thomas) Frederick Halsey (son of Thomas Plumer Halsey, MP), sat as MP for Herts (C) 1874-85, and for W Herts 1885-1906 and d 1927.

HAMBLING (UK) 1924, of Yoxford, co Suffolk

Discern and decide

Sir (HERBERT) HUGH HAMBLING, 3rd *Baronet*, *b* 3 Aug 1919; *s* his father, *Sir* (HERBERT) GUY (MUSGRAVE), 1966; *ed* Eton; late Flt-Lt RAF; formerly in BOAC, Montreal; 1939-45 War: *m* 1st, 1950, Anne Page, who *d* 1990, da of late Judge Hugo Edmund Oswald, of Seattle, USA; 2ndly, 1991, Helen Seymour, elder da of Donald Mackinnon, of Marida Yallock, Victoria, Australia, and widow of David Maitland Gavin, of Clabon Mews, SW3, and has issue by 1st *m*.

𝕬rms – Argent, a sword erect sable between two flaunches azure, each charged with a hank of cotton of the field. Crest – A falcon supporting with the dexter claw a distaff proper, and charged on the body with a bezant.
Seat – Rookery Park, Yoxford, Suffolk. *Address* – 1219 Evergreen Point Rd, Bellevue, Washington 98004, USA; Royal Brunei Airlines, c/o The Boeing Co, Box 3707, Seattle, Washington 98124, USA.

SON LIVING *(By 1st marriage)*

(HERBERT) PETER HUGH, *b* 6 Sept 1953; *ed* Univ of Washington (BSc); Co-founder and Ch Operating Officer Digital Control (Inc), WA: *m* 1st, 1982 (*m diss* 1989), Jan Elizabeth, da of Stanton Frederick, Jr, of Seattle, Washington; 2ndly, 1991, Lorayn Louise, da of Frank Joseph Koson, and has issue living (by 2nd *m*), Colin Hugh, *b* 1991, — Austin Peter, *b* 1993. *Residence* – 2108 92nd Avenue NE, Bellevue, WA 98004, USA.

SISTERS LIVING

Margherita, *b* 1912: *m* 1937, Fl-Lt Maurice Hare, who *d* 1993, yst son of Maj-Gen Sir Steuart Welwood Hare, KCMG, CB, and has issue living, David Steuart (23 Vale Road, Claygate, Esher, Surrey), *b* 1942: *m* 1st, 1969 (*m diss* 1983), Julie, da of Walter Pierre Courtauld; 2ndly, 1986, Pippa, only da of R.I. McDonald, and has issue living (by 1st *m*), Lucas Welwood Bruno *b* 1971, Samuel James *b* 1974, Fergus Lincoln *b* 1977, (by 2nd *m*) Poppy Helen *b* 1988, — Robin Gordon (Fordley Hall, Middleton, Saxmundham, Suffolk), *b* 1944: *m* 1st, 1973 (*m diss* 1987), Caroline Mary, da of Edward Felix Mason, and formerly wife of William Oscar Watson; 2ndly, 1989, Margaret Julia, da of Leo William Ritchie, and previously wife of (i) Mark Leigh Scorer, and (ii) John Stewart Bassett, and has issue living (by 1st *m*), Reuben Edward Hare *b* 1975, Rachel Veronica *b* 1978, — Philippa, *b* 1938: *m* 1st, 1959 (*m diss* 1965), Timothy Peckover Burrill; 2ndly, 1967, Simon Pierre Courtauld, of Inglewood Lodge, Kintbury, Newbury, Berks, and has issue living (by 1st *m*), Kim Guy Augustine *b* 1973, Leila Alice *b* 1975. *Residence* – The Cottage, Rookery Park, Yoxford, Suffolk. —— Mollie Gordon *b* 1915: *m* 1958, Robert Geoffrey Smith, of Beveriche Farm, Yoxford, Suffolk.

The 1st baronet, Sir (Henry) Herbert Hambling, son of Lt-Col William James Hambling, JP, of Dunstable, Bedford, was Dep Chm of Barclays Bank (Limited), of Barclays Bank (France) (Limited), Barclays Bank (Dominion, Colonial and Overseas), and of Barclays Bank SAI, first Gov Director of Imperial Airways Ltd, 1924-30 (formed as a result of report presented by Hambling Committee of which he was Chm), and a Director of North British and Mercantile Insurance Co, and of Ocean Marine Insurance Co (Limited); Financial Member of Min of Munitions during European War 1914-19 (Knt): *m* 1st, 1882, Thirza, who *d* 1891, da of William George Twigg, solicitor, of Dublin; 2ndly, 1893, Isabella Mary, who *d* 1916, da of Frederick Brown, of Clapham; *d* 1932.

HAMILTON (NS) 1646, of Silvertonhill, Lanarkshire

Sir (ROBERT CHARLES) RICHARD CARADOC HAMILTON, 9th *Baronet*; *b* 8 Sept 1911; *s* his father, *Major Sir* ROBERT CARADOC, 1959; *ed* Charterhouse, and St Peter's Coll, Oxford: *m* 1952, Elizabeth Vidal, da of late Sir William Pell Barton, KCIE, CSI, and has issue.

Arms – Gules, a gillie flower stemmed and leaved proper between three cinquefoils ermine, all within a bordure or. **Crest** – A horse's head and neck couped argent, maned or.
Residence – The Old Rectory, Walton, Warwick CV35 9HX.

SON LIVING

ANDREW CARADOC, *b* 23 Sept 1953; *ed* Charterhouse, and St Peter's Coll, Oxford (MA): *m* 1984, Anthea Jane, da of late Frank Huntingford, of Hindhead, Surrey, and has issue living, Alice, *b* 1986, — Harriet, *b* 1989, — Imogen Rose, *b* 1993.

DAUGHTERS LIVING

Susanna Eve, *b* 1956: *m* 1990, Richard Andrew Freeman, yr son of late Harold Freeman, of Piddinghoe, E Sussex, and has issue living, Gabriella Eve Hamilton, *b* 1993. —— Sophia Louisa, *b* 1964. —— Penelope Katherine, *b* 1966: *m* 1989, Trevor Wells, son of William Wells, of Brighton.

BROTHER LIVING

Oliver Anson, *b* 1916: *m* 1957, Barbara Mary, da of Frank Willcox, of Perranporth, Cornwall. *Residence* – 10 Buddle Close, Tavistock, Devon PL19 0EG.

COLLATERAL BRANCHES LIVING

Grandsons of late Frank Hamilton (infra):—
Issue of late Ian Frank Howden Hamilton, *b* 1916, *d* 1982: *m* 1950, Zelma (Rooftops, St Dunstan's Terrace, Canterbury, Kent CT2 8AX), da of Laurence Theodore Snyman:—
Paul Howden (The Red House, New St, St Dunstan's, Canterbury, Kent CT2 8AU), *b* 1951: *m* 1980, Elizabeth Anne Harrison, and has issue living, Alexandra Isabel, *b* 1983, — Annabelle Kate, *b* 1985. —— Mark Howden (11 Eden Rd, Claremont 7700, Cape, S Africa), *b* 1955: *m* 1983, Sally Anne Macklin, and has issue living, Guy Howden, *b* 1991. —— Warwick Howden (PO Box 444, Jukskei, 2153 Transvaal, S Africa), *b* 1959: *m* 1990, Jacqueline, da of Frederick Arthur Smith, of Lyon House, Lynsted, Kent.

Issue of late Frank Hamilton, 2nd son of 7th baronet, *b* 1878, *d* 1934: *m* 1913, Mary Elizabeth, who *d* 1961, da of late John Williams Batterham, MB, FRCS, of St Leonards-on-Sea:—
Joan Mary Hamilton, *b* 1915: *m* 1941, Stanley Abbott Silson, and has issue living, Ian Frank, *b* 1943: *m* 1976 (*m diss* 19—), Barbara Thompson, — Raymond Robert Hamilton, *b* 1946, — Simon Hatchard, *b* 1957: *m* 1982, Sophia Stallbom, — Mary Elizabeth Joy, *b* 1952: *m* 1983, David Anthony Rocke, FRCP (UK), FFA (SA), of 12 Pearson Rd, Everton 3610, Natal, S Africa. *Residence* – 15 Fairydene Village, 18 Stapleton Rd, Sarnia 3610, S Africa.

Granddaughter of late Frederic Howden Faulconer Hamilton (infra):—
Issue of late Howden McMinn Hamilton, *b* 1900, *d* 1988: *m* 1935, Patricia Campbell (42 Fieldway, Wavertree Garden Suburb, Liverpool L15 7LU), only child of Matthew Currie, of Ayr:—
Gloria Constance Barbara, *b* 1937: *m* 1956, Edward Watson, and has issue living, Andrew Charles Howden, *b* 1958.

Grandchildren of late Howden Anson Philip Hamilton, el son of Capt Frederick William Hamilton, 3rd son of 5th baronet:—
Issue of late Frederic Howden Faulconer Hamilton, *b* 1877, *d* 1959: *m* 1st, 1899, Jessie Jean, who *d* 1929, elder da of late W. McMinn; 2ndly, 1930, Beatrice Agnes, who *d* 1955, only da of late Samuel Banfield of Exeter:—
(By 1st *m*) Howden McMinn (35 Belgrave Rd, Aigbarth, Liverpool 17) *b* 1900: *m* 1935, Patricia Campbell, only child of Matthew Currie, of Ayr, and has issue living, Gloria Constance Barbara, *b* 1937: *m* 1956, Edward Watson, and has issue living, Andrew Charles Howden *b* 1958. —— Frederic William Seymour (42995 Adams Rd, RR1 Sardis, BC VOX 170, Canada) *b* 1906: *m* 1930, Florence Maud, who *d* 1982, da of George John Saby, of Cambridgeshire, and has issue living, Kathleen Anita, *b* 1931, — Barbara Joanne, *b* 1933: *m* 1955, Oscar Mitchell Taylor, of Delta, BC, Canada, and has issue living, Keith Donald *b* 1958: *m* 1979, Penny Dawn Millar (and has issue living, Allan Keith *b* 1981, Carl Brian *b* 1984, Stephanie Anne Mary *b* 1987), Colleen Susan *b* 1956: *m* 1978, Vincent James Lee, of Perth, Australia (and has issue living, Dennis James *b* 1981, Vanessa Joanne *b* 1983, Deborah Janette *b* 1987). —— Constance, *b* 1912: *m* 1941, Richard Haugh, of Screel, Fishers Brae, Coldingham, Berwicks, and has issue living, Howden Hamilton, *b* 1950: *m* 1977, Amanda, yst da of Stanley Bragg, of Gilderson, Leeds, and has issue living, Helen Kirsty *b* 1978, Shona Ann *b* 1980, — Robert Seymour (twin), *b* 1950: *m* 1974, Marion Henderson Cunningham, only da of Friedrich Lenz, of Schönlanke, Niekosken, and of Livingstone, W Lothian, and has issue living, Julia Lenz *b* 1978.
Issue of late Capt Henry Rudston STUART-HAMILTON, Gordon Highlanders (who assumed by deed poll 1920, the additional surname of Stuart), *b* 1883, *d* 1962: *m* 1920, Mabel Mary, who *d* 1968, el da of late Rev Edmund Milnes Ellerbeck:—
Donald Maclaren (The Shooting Greens, Potarch, Banchory AB31 4BL), *b* 1926; *ed* Harrow, and King's Coll, Camb (MA); Capt The Black Watch (TA); MIMSM: *m* 1956, Jill, MSAOT, yr da of late Lt-Col David Guy Porteous, OBE, JP, of St Cyrus, Angus, and has issue living, Clova Claire Ducarol, *b* 1959: *m* 1988, Michael Andrew Stinton, of 92 Walton St, Oxford OX2 6EB, — Alison Fenella, *b* 1967.

Granddaughter of late Lieut-Col Henry Charles Hamilton, son of late Henry Charles Hamilton, CSI, 4th son of 5th baronet:—
Issue of late Charles Norman Maclean Hamilton, *b* 1885, *d* 1957: *m* 1926, Molly Eileen, who *d* 1986, da of late D. Crowe, MB, of Melfield, Blackrock, co Dublin:—
Anne Maclean, *b* 1927. *Residence* – 24 Oakleigh Court, Station Rd West, Oxted, Surrey RH8 9EY.
This is the nearest branch of the Ducal House next to the great family of Abercorn, descending from Alexander Hamilton of Silvertonhill, brother of 1st Lord Hamilton. Sir Robert Hamilton, 1st Bt, a steady loyalist, was a favourite of Charles I; his

patent of baronetcy was not, however, recorded in the General Register owing to the then confusion and distraction of the country.

HAMILTON, First Creation (GB) 1776, of Marlborough House, Hampshire Second Creation (UK) 1819, of Trebinshun House, Brecknockshire

Virtue is the only nobility
Sola nobilitas virtus

Sir EDWARD SYDNEY HAMILTON, 7th *Baronet* of 1st, and 5th *Baronet* of 2nd creation; *b* 14 April 1925; *s* his father, *Sir* (THOMAS) SYDNEY PERCEVAL, 1966; *ed* Canford; late RE.

Arms – Quarterly: 1st and 4th, gules, three cinquefoils pierced ermine, 2nd and 3rd, argent, a lymphad with her sails furled sable. **Crest** – Out of a ducal coronet or, an oak-tree proper fructed of the first and penetrated transversely in the main stem by a frame-saw proper, the frame also of the first, and the blade inscribed with the word "Through."
Residence – The Cottage, East Lavant, W Sussex P018 0AL.
Capt Sir John Hamilton, RN, 1st Bt of Trebinshun, grandson of William Hamilton (one of the five "Kentish Petitioners" in 1701), brother of 6th Earl of Abercorn, distinguished himself at the Siege of Quebec 1775. Adm Sir Edward Joseph Hamilton, younger son of 1st Bt (*cr* 1776) was *cr* a Bt of Marlborugh House, Hants, 1819. Sir Edward Archibald Hamilton, 2nd Bt (*cr* 1819), *s* in 1892 as 4th Bt (*cr* 1776).

HAMILTON (UK) 1937, of Ilford, co Essex (extinct 1992)

Sir PATRICK GEORGE HAMILTON, 2nd and last *Baronet*.

WIDOW LIVING OF SECOND BARONET

WINIFRED MARY (PIX), CBE, MA (*Lady Hamilton*), only da of late Hammond Beaconsfield Jenkins, of Maddings, Hadstock, and formerly wife of Prof John Richard Nicholas Stone, CBE: *m* 1941, Sir Patrick George Hamilton, 2nd Bt, who *d* 1992.
Residences – Flat 7, 39 Hyde Park Gate, SW7 5DS; 21 Madingley Rd, Cambridge CB3 0EG.

Hamilton-Dalrymple, see Dalrymple.

STIRLING-HAMILTON (NS) 1673, of Preston, Haddingtonshire

For my country

Sir MALCOLM WILLIAM BRUCE STIRLING-HAMILTON, 14th *Baronet*; *b* 6 Aug 1979; *s* his father, *Sir* BRUCE, 1989.

Arms – Gules, three cinquefoils within a bordure argent. **Crest** – An armed man from the middle brandishing a sword aloft proper.
Residence – Afton Lodge, Mossblown, By Ayr, Ayrshire KA6 5AS.

SISTERS LIVING

Georgina Claire, *b* 1970. —— Iona Stephanie, *b* 1985.

AUNTS LIVING (*daughters of 12th baronet*)

Joanna Eileen, *b* 1930: *m* 1955, Lt-Col Ian Kroyer MacKinnon, Queen's Own Highlanders (Seaforth and Camerons). —— Eila Mary, *b* 1939: *m* 1st, 1959, Lt Timothy Martin Woodford, RN, who *d* 1966 (*see* Crofton, Bt, *cr* 1801, colls; 1976 Edn); 2ndly, 1967, George Rudolf Wratislaw Walker, MA, and has issue living, (by 1st *m*) Charlotte Amanda, *b* 1960: *m* 1981, Capt Charles Rodney Style, RN (*see* Style, Bt, colls). — Amanda Caroline, *b* 1962, — (by 2nd *m*) Harriet Nicola, *b* 1970, — Emily Mary, *b* 1972.

WIDOW LIVING OF THIRTEEENTH BARONET

STEPHANIE (*Lady Stirling-Hamilton*), el da of William Campbell, LRCP, LRCS, of Cozac, 32 Monument Rd, Alloway, Ayr: *m* 1968, Sir Bruce Stirling-Hamilton, 13th Bt, who *d* 1989. *Residence* – .

COLLATERAL BRANCHES LIVING

Grandson of late Hubert Hamilton, 2nd son of 9th baronet:—
Issue of late William Stirling Hamilton, *b* 1869, *d* 1958: *m* 1898, Kathleen, who *d* 1961, da of late George Robert Elsmie, CSI:—

ROBERT WILLIAM (Haskers, Westleton, Suffolk), *b* 26 Nov 1905; *ed* Winchester, and Magdalen Coll, Oxford; FBA 1960: *m* 1935, Eileen Hetty, el da of late Francis Goldworth Lowick, and has issue living, *Rev* Andrew Robert (16 Cranston Close, Reigate, Surrey), *b* 1937; *ed* New Coll, Oxford (MA); FCA: *m* 1972, Josephine Mary, da of Reginald Sargant, — William Alexander Hubert (c/o National Westminster Bank, 62 Victoria St, SW1P 1RX), *b* 1941; *ed* Trin Coll, Camb (MA): *m* 1966, Cecilia Louise Somerville, da of late Maj Charles Erling Bernard Catt (Somerville, Bt, colls, ext), and has issue living, Alexander James Erling *b* 1967, Anna Cecilia Louise *b* 1969, — Thomas, *b* 1952; *ed* Magdalen Coll, Oxford (BA): *m* 1st, 1978, Cornelia, da of Willy Brüllmann, of Zuben Switzerland; 2ndly, 1991, Sally Lisa, da of late Donald Charles McArthur, and has issue living (by 2nd *m*), Robert Louis *b* 1993, — Penelope Frances, *b* 1936: *m* 1st, 1960 (*m* annulled 1985), Maj Robert Alan Mountcastle Seeger, MC, RM (ret); 2ndly, 1989, Lt-Col Brereton Robert Fairclough, MC, TD, S Lancs Regt (ret), of Garden Cottage, Aldersey Park, Handley, Chester CH3 9ED, and has issue living (by 1st *m*), Frances Clare *b* 1965: *m* 1994, Avard Warren Kaleoaloha Pereira, Katharine Anne *b* 1966, — Katharine Jane Patricia *b* 1955; *ed* Camberwell Art Coll: *m* 1987, Bernard Francis Purcell, and has issue living, George Alexander *b* 1992, Stephanie Jane *b* 1990.

    Grandchildren of late Lt-Col William Gavin Hamilton (infra):—
    Issue of late Capt John William Stirling Hamilton, MC, *b* 1919, *d* 1959: *m* 1945, Kathleen Dorothea, da of John Alexander Thomson, MBE, of Tordarroch, Helensburgh:—
Alastair Colin Stirling (Tillyfourie Farm, Monymusk, Aberdeenshire), *b* 1954: *m* 1979, Miranda Louise, da of Jeffrey Watson Boughey, of Whitehills Farm, Monymusk, and has issue living, Rory Colin Stirling, *b* 1980, — James Alexander, *b* 1982, — Thomas Daniel, *b* 1986. —— Alison Lesley, *b* 1947: *m* 1970, Nicholas Parsons, of Polmaily House Hotel, Drumnadrochit, Inverness-shire, and has issue living, Alexander, *b* 19—, — Claudia, *b* 19—. —— Daphne Helen, *b* 1950: *m* 1980, Michael Murray, of Kilmahumaig, Crinan, Argyll, and has issue living, William, *b* 19—, — Nina, *b* 19—.

    Grandchildren of late Thomas Hamilton, MD, FRCS, 3rd son of 9th baronet:—
    Issue of late Lieut-Col William Gavin Hamilton, *b* 1874, *d* 1937: *m* 1st, 1908, Louise, who *d* 1914, da of late Alison Cunningham, of Peterborough; 2ndly, 1916, Helen, who *d* 1950, da of late Dugald Stewart Macphee, of Glasgow:—
(By 2nd *m*) Alastair Gavin, DSC (Dunmar, Tighnabroaich, Argyll PA21 2EA), *b* 1922; Lt Cdr RN (ret); 1939-45 War (DSC): *m* 1956, Gillian Bomford, and has had issue, Jock, *b* 1960, — Gail, *b* 1958: *m* 1986, Patrick J. Dempsey, and *d* 1993, leaving issue, Harry John *b* 1991, Katherine Phoebe *b* 1988, — Katharine, *b* 1964: *m* 1989, R. Martin Pender, and has issue living, Patrick Iago *b* 1992. —— Margaret Audrey, *b* 1918; is 2nd Officer WRNS; 1939-45 War: *m* 1946, Charles Ian Turcan, of Oxey Barn, Woodside, Lymington, Hants, and has issue living, Gavin Charles, *b* 1948, — Alan Ronald Hamilton, *b* 1952: *m* 1985, Gillian Hart, and has issue living, Mathew *b* 1987, Sarah *b* 1989, — Lydia Helen, *b* 1950: *m* 1978, Nicholas Hampton Oldham Clough, of 159 Maldon Rd, Colchester, Essex, and has issue living, Anthony Oldham, *b* 1984, — David James, *b* 1988, — Charlotte Emma, *b* 1981.
This family descends from Sir John Hamilton of Fingalton, yr brother of Sir David Hamilton of Cadzow (*dc* 1392) ancestor of Duke of Hamilton. Sir William Hamilton, 1st Bt, was *cr* a Baronet with remainder to his heirs male whatsoever. On the death of Sir Robert, 2nd Bt 1701, the baronetcy passed to his kinsman Sir Robert of Airdrie, 5th in descent from John who was killed at Flodden 1513, yr brother of Robert of Preston, ancestor of 1st Bt, but the baronetcy was not re-assumed until 1834 by Sir William *de jure*, 9th Bt, who had been served heir male to the 2nd Br 1816. He was Prof of Logic and Metaphysics at Edinburgh Univ. Gen Sir William, CB, 10th Bt assumed by deed poll, in 1889, the additional surname of Stirling, his grandmother Elizabeth being a da of William Stirling of Drumpellier, whose son established in 1818 representation of the family of Stirling of Cadder.

HAMMICK (UK) 1834, of Cavendish Square, London

To be praised by one already praised

Sir STEPHEN GEORGE HAMMICK, 5th *Baronet b* 27 Dec 1926; *s* his father, *Sir* GEORGE FREDERICK, 1964; *ed* Stowe, and RAC Cirencester; High Sheriff of Dorset (1981), DL 1989: *m* 1953, Gillian Elizabeth, yr da of late Maj Pierre Elliot Inchbald, MC (*see* Bingham, Bt, 1985 Edn), and has issue.

𝔞rms – Paly of four or and vert, a bordure ermine charged with seven hurts, on a chief azure a lion passant argent. ℭrest - A demi-lion per pale or and vert holding an escarbuncle gold.
Residence – Badgers, Wraxall, Dorchester, Dorset DT2 0HN.

SONS LIVING

PAUL ST VINCENT (Butterfly Cottage, Lower Wraxall, Dorchester, Dorset), *b* 1 Jan 1955; *ed* Sherborne: *m* 1984, Judith Mary, da of Ralph Ernest Reynolds, of Lorien, Grange Rd, Wareham, Dorset. —— Jeremy Charles, *b* 1956.

DAUGHTER LIVING

Wendy Jane, *b* 1960: *m* 1990, Bob Koster, of Albrecht Thaerlaan 47, 3571EE Utrecht, Holland, son of late Jacob Koster, and has issue living, a son, *b* 1991, — a da, *b* 1992.

COLLATERAL BRANCHES LIVING

    Issue of late Rear-Adm Alexander Robert Hammick, brother of 4th baronet *b* 1887, *d* 1969: *m* 1918, Nancy, who *d* 1964, el da of D. Ross-Johnson:—
Anne Felicity (The Old House, Lodsworth, Sussex), *b* 1919.

    Issue of late Capt Stephen Frederick Hammick (Oxfordshire and Bucks LI) only son of 3rd baronet, *b* 1871, *d* of wounds received in action 1916: *m* 1906, Muriel Katharine, who *d* 1924, da of Capt Andrew Hamilton Russell, formerly 58th Regt of The Heath House, Petersfield, Hants:—
Penelope Katherine, MB, BS (46 Castle Rd, Salisbury), *b* 1910.

    Grandchildren of late Stephen Hammick, 3rd son of 2nd baronet:—
    Issue of late Maj St Vincent Frederick Hammick, *b* 1886, *d* 1976: *m* 1919, Annie Caroline Massingberd, who *d* 1978, da of late Aubone Aldrich Pyke, of The Hermitage, Netley Abbey:—

Stephen Aubone, DSC, b 1922; Cdr RN; 1939-45 War (DSC, despatches twice): m 1943, Mary Elizabeth, da of John Laurence Westmacott (see Hamilton-Spencer-Smith, Bt, colls, 1980 Edn), and has issue living, Stephen Timothy John, b 1946: m 1969, Raymonde, da of Maj Eugene I. J. Carson, of S Africa, and has issue living, Bryone Catherine Annie b 1978, — Susan Patricia, b 1945: m 1973, Henry James Craven Smith, of Tettenhall, Wolverhampton, and has issue living, Henry Stapleton b 1975, Jane Rachel Anne b 1977. —— Mary Désirée Massingberd, b 1930: m 1953, Colin Edward Foster, and has issue living, Michael Colin, b 1954, — Christopher John, b 1956, — Caroline Antonia, b 1957. —— Adrianne Elaine Patricia, b 1937: m 1964, Vincent George Jarvis Ball, and has issue living, Anthony St Vincent, b 1965, — Stephen Jarvis, b 1967, — David Jonathan, b 1971.

Granddaughters of late Maj St Vincent Frederick Hammick (ante):—
Issue of late Lt-Cdr Aubone St Vincent Hammick, RN, b 1925, d 1992: m 1948, Cynthia Florence Katharine (444 Uthank Rd, Norwich), da of William George Shiell (see B Airedale, 1972-73 Edn):—
Marion, b 1949: m 1967, Ian Donald Pickett, FCII, of 57 Salisbury Av, St Albans, Herts, and has issue living, Melissa Juliette, b 1967, — Eleanor Theresa, b (twin) 1967. —— Imogen Katherine, b 1952: m 1st, 1972, John Blandford; 2ndly, 1977, David Megginson, and has issue living (by 2nd m), Edward b 1985, Katherine Rose b 1980. —— Miranda Jane, b 1958: BA; has issue living (by Jonathan Parkinson), Martha Louise b 1993.

Grandchildren of late Sir Murray Hammick, KCSI, CIE, 7th son of 2nd baronet:—
Issue of late Maj Henry Alexander Hammick, OBE, MC, b 1890, d 1968: m 1919, Mabel Emily (May), who d 1990, da of Sir Philip Edward Pilditch, MP, 1st Bt:—
Henry Edgar Murray (9 Newenham Rd, Lymington, Hants), b 1919; late Lt RNVR: 1939-45 War: m 1949, Eleanor Macleod, da of Cdr Patrick Bruce Lawder, RN, and has issue living, Elizabeth Helen Macleod, b 1951: m 1992, Mark William Scott, and has issue living, Chloë Eleanor b 1992, — Anne Olivia Mary, b 1953. —— †Charles Cyril Willmott b 1927; late Maj Gren Guards: m 1st, 1953 (m diss 1959), Mary Rose, only da of late Col Walter Hugh Crichton, CIE; 2ndly, 1961, Georgina (writer, Georgina Heyman), da of late Maj-Gen George Douglas Gordon Heyman, CB, CBE; 3rdly, 1984, Carol Elspeth (Higher Waterston Farm, Puddletown, Dorchester, Dorset DT2 7SW), da of late Brig Richard Montagu Villiers, DSO (see E Clarendon, colls), and formerly wife of Gerald Charles Mordaunt (see Mordaunt, Bt, colls), and d 1990, leaving issue (by 1st m), Piers St Vincent Charles, b 1954, — Charlotte Emily Dorothea, b 1955: m 1985 (m diss 1987), Michael P. Dennis, and has issue living, Oliver Charles Frederick b 1986, — (by 2nd m) Thomas Henry Heyman St Vincent, b 1963, — Katherine Emily Amanda, b 1965, — Rose Sophia, b 1970. —— Alexander Philip (The Priory, Woodbury, Exeter), b 1928: m 1954, Pamela Mary, da of C. Prosper-Liston, of Penang, and has issue living, Murray Philip St Leger, b 1957; late Capt 14th/20th King's Hussars: m 1984, Alexandra-Carolin, yr da of C. H. Preuss, of Buckholz, Hamburg, and has issue living, Alexander Charles Frederick Prosper Love b 1988, Philip Henry Murray St Vincent Love b 1990, Catherine Edwardina Pamela Mary Love b 1993, — Melinda Mary, b 1955: m 1981, Richard Guy Hilliard, only son of late R. G. Hilliard, and has issue living, Alexandra Cary b 1985, Georgina Mary b 1988, — Victoria Rosanne, b 1958: m 1982, Capt John Gale, and has issue living, Emily Caroline b 1984, Amanda Catherine b 1987, — Nicola May, b 1961: m 1989, Anthony Alexander de Nouaille Rudge, elder son of Anthony Rudge, of Church Farm, Churchover, Warwicks, and has issue living, Alexander William Edward Findlay de Nouaille b 1992, Serena Mary Kate Felizarda b 1991. —— Anthea Elizabeth Eve, b 1922: m 1949, Dennis John Dale Shepherd, and has issue living, Justin Philip William, b 1952, — Miranda Dorothy Emila, b 1950, — Zoë Alexandra Denise, b 1956, — Isobel Anthea, b 1956, — Melissa May, b 1966.
Sir Stephen Love Hammick, FRCS, 1st baronet (el son of Stephen Hammick, Alderman of Plymouth), was an eminent surgeon and physician, and 1st Surg of RN Hospital, Plymouth. The 3rd baronet, Sir St Vincent Alexander Hammick, served in New Zealand War 1864-5 (medal, and specially mentioned).

Hamond-Græme, see Græme.

HANHAM (E) 1667, of Wimborne, Dorsetshire

To be, rather than to seem

Sir MICHAEL WILLIAM HANHAM, DFC, 12th *Baronet*, b 31 Oct 1922; only son of Patrick John Hanham, yst son of Col Phelips Brooke Hanham, brother of 9th baronet; s his kinsman, *Sir* HENRY PHELIPS, 1973; *ed* Winchester; 1939-45 War as Fl-Lt RAFVR (DFC): m 1954, Margaret Jane, only da of late Wing-Cdr Harold Thomas, RAF, of Marine Court, St Leonards-on-Sea, and has issue.

Arms – Quarterly, or and gules, on a bend sable three crosses paté fitchée of the first. *Crest* – A griffin's head erased, beaked sable.
Residence – Deans Court, Wimborne, Dorset BH21 1EE.

SON LIVING

WILLIAM JOHN EDWARD, b 4 Sept 1957; ed Winchester, and The Courtauld Inst of Art (BA): m 1982 (m diss 1986), Elizabeth Ann, yr da of Paul Keyworth, of Farnham, Surrey. *Residence* – 77 Tavistock Rd, W11 1AR.

DAUGHTER LIVING

Victoria Jane, b 1955: m 1987, David L. Gross, son of Dr Joseph Gross, of Chippaqua, New York, and has issue living, Hugo Augustus William, b 1989, — Dulcie Harriet Jane, b 1992.
Sir John Alexander Hanham, 9th baronet, and his son Sir John Ludlow Hanham, 10th baronet, were Apparitors-Gen of Province and Diocese of Canterbury.

HANMER (GB) 1774, of Hanmer, Flintshire

Keep fast honour

Sir JOHN WYNDHAM EDWARD HANMER, 8th *Baronet*; *b* 27 Sept 1928; *s* his father, *Lt-Col Sir* (GRIFFIN WYNDHAM) EDWARD, 1977; *ed* Eton; Capt (ret) R Dagoons; a JP for Clwyd, High Sheriff 1977, and DL 1978: *m* 1954, Audrey Melissa, el da of late Maj Arthur Christopher John Congreve, of Westering, Yeoman's Lane, Newtown, Newbury, Berks, and has issue.

Arms – Argent, two lions passant guardant azure. **Crest** – On a chapeau azure turned up ermine a lion sejeant guardant argent.
Residence – The Mere House, Hanmer, Whitchurch, Shropshire SY13 3DG.

SONS LIVING

(WYNDHAM RICHARD) GUY, *b* 27 Nov 1955; *ed* Wellington Coll; late Blues and Royals: *m* 1986, Elizabeth A., yr da of Neil Taylor, of Frampton-on-Severn, Glos, and has issue living, Thomas Wyndham William, *b* 10 May 1989, — George Hugh Richard, *b* 1992, — Alicia Marina, *b* 1994. *Residence* – The Stables, Bettisfield Park, Whitchurch, Shropshire SY13 2JZ. —— Edward Hugh, *b* 1957; *ed* Wellington Coll; Capt late Blues and Royals.

SISTERS LIVING

Joan Essex, *b* 1922. —— Pamela Aileen (*Lady Wilson*), *b* 1923: *m* 1947, Capt Sir Thomas Douglas Wilson, 4th Bt, MC, who *d* 1984. *Residence* – Lillingstone Lovell Manor, Bucks. —— Evelyn Mary, *b* 1926.

COLLATERAL BRANCHES LIVING

Grandchildren of late John Hanmer, 2nd son of Rev Henry Hanmer, brother of 3rd and 4th baronets:—
Issue of late Group Capt Henry Ivan Hanmer, DFC, RAF, *b* 1893, *d* 1984: *m* 1st, 1937, Margaret Florence Mary, who *d* 1947, only da of late Rev Henry Kennth Warrand, of Westhorpe Hall, Southwell, Notts; 2ndly, 1954, Lady Frances Jane Cole (1 Church Way, Grendon, Northampton), da of 5th Earl of Enniskillen:—
(By 1st *m*) John Henry Warrand (Stubbins Farm, Stubbins Lane, Southwell, Notts), *b* 1938; Capt 17th/21st Lancers (ret); High Sheriff of Notts (1981): *m* 1964 (*m diss* 1989), Penelope Clare, da of Sir Denis Le Marchant, 5th Bt, and has issue living, Thomas Stephen, *b* 1971, — Isabel Jane, *b* 1965, — Harriet Mary, *b* 1969. —— William Richard, *b* 1945: *m* 1976, Maria Paula Vianna, of Sao Paulo, Brazil, and has issue living, Daniel Henry Vianna, *b* 1981, — Alexander Richard Vianna, *b* 1983. —— Flora Elizabeth, *b* 1939: *m* 1967, Frederick John Sasse, of Hendy, Afonwen, Mold, Clwyd, and has issue living, Stephen John, *b* 1968, — Matthew Alexander, *b* 1974, — David Edward Jeremy, *b* 1979, — Selina Margaret, *b* 1970. —— (By 2nd *m*) †Thomas Edward Trevor, *b* 1956; *d* 1980.
Issue of late William Francis Busby Hanmer, *b* 1899, *d* 1980: *m* 1st, 1927, Margaret, who *d* 1967, da of Archibald Cameron Norman, of The Rookery, Bromley Common (Wake Bt, colls); 2ndly, 19—, Bethia Ann, da of late Joseph Condy, of Umtali:—
(By 1st *m*) John Anthony (Mutare, Zimbabwe), *b* 1928: *m* 1952 (*m diss* 1973), Margaret May, da of I. G. Morrison, of Cape Town; 2ndly, 1973, Dale Berenice, da of late J. A. Dickinson, of Johannesburg, S Africa, and has issue living (by 1st *m*), Quentin William, *b* 1952: *m* 1976, Colleen, da of J. Campbell-Morrison, of Umtali, — Andrew Ian, *b* 1958, — Deborah Anne, *b* 1954: *m* 1974, Muller Maas, of Umtali, — (by 2nd *m*), Julia Mary, *b* 1976. —— Richard Norman Montagu (Edmonton, Alberta, Canada), *b* 1937; BSc, Cape Town, AMSAIMechE, PEng, MEIC: *m* 1st, 1963, Joyce Catherine, who *d* 1973, da of late Ernest Philpot, of Beckenham, Kent; 2ndly, 1974, Mrs Myrna Dorothy Tanner, da of late A. G. Plumb, of Bulawayo, and has issue living (by 1st *m*), Anthony David, *b* 1967, — Gillian Margaret, *b* 1964: *m* 1985, Way Choy, and has issue living, Jessica Joyce *b* 1987, Vanessa Mei Lei *b* 1992. —— Phoebe Margaret, *b* 1931; Community of St Mary the Virgin, Wantage, Berks. —— Janet Virginia, *b* 1932: *m* 1971, Charles George Davis Sutherland, of 92 Glenmount Rd, Buderim, Qld 4556, Australia, and has issue living, George Francis Hanmer, *b* 1972; *ed* Queensland Univ (BEng). —— Catherine Yvonne, *b* 1936: *m* 1958, Keith Allen, of Old Presthayes, Eccliffe, Gillingham, Dorset SP8 5RE, and has issue living, John Hanmer, *b* 1958: *m* 1984, Jane Louise Ward-Lee, of Greenfield Hall, Laleham, Middx, and has issue living, Hayley Claire *b* 1986, Olivia Catherine *b* 1988, — Charles William, *b* 1960: *m* 1985, Helen Frances Jones, of Holt, Clwyd, and has issue living, Joanna Rachel *b* 1988, Catherine Rebecca *b* 1992, — Stephen Guy, *b* 1963: *m* 1988, Giselle Victoria Margaret Becker, of Shepperton, Middx, and has issue living, Guy Robert *b* 1990, Georgia Giselle *b* 1993, — Caroline Elizabeth *b* 1965: *m* 1991, Craig James Allan, PhD, of Winnipeg, Manitoba, Canada, and has issue living, Genevieve Catherine Armande *b* 1994.

Grandchildren of late Rev Hugh Hanmer, 6th son of Rev Henry Hanmer (ante):—
Issue of late Robert Hugh Hanmer, OBE, MC, *b* 1895, *d* 1971: *m* 1922, Mary Helen, who *d* 1945, da of late Nathaniel Spens:—
Hugh Niel (Fontevrault, Letcombe Regis, Wantage, Oxon OX12 9JP), *b* 1926: *m* 1953, Diana, da of Robert Hurst, of Lustleigh, Devon, and has issue living, Robert David (15c Brussels Rd, SW11 2AF), *b* 1957: *m* 1989, Isabel, da of John de Meur, of Sydney, NSW, and has issue living, Daisy *b* 1994, — Lucia Caroline (Dr) (155, 2502LT, The Hague, Holland), *b* 1956.
Issue of late Lt-Col Arthur Richard Hanmer, MBE, TD, *b* 1899, *d* 1976: *m* 1929, Violet Millicent, who *d* 1968, da of late Maj William John Corbett-Winder, of Vaynor Park, Berriew, Powys:—
John Richard Lyon (Honeysuckle Cottage, E Hendred, Wantage, Oxon), *b* 1940: *m* 1979, Gillian Mary, yr da of George Herbert Smith, of Aldfield Farm, East Hendred, Wantage, Oxon. —— Sara Elizabeth, *b* 1938: *m* 1973, Charles Henry Wroughton Michell, of 10 Wandon Rd, SW6 2JF (*see* Carden, Bt, *cr* 1887, 1976 Edn), and has issue living, Samuel Richard Alfred, *b* 1979; *ed* Eton.
Issue of late Brig John Michael Hanmer, DSO, OBE, *b* 1907, *d* 1977: *m* 1934, Esther (Tarrant Monkton Cottage, Blandford, Dorset), da of Reginald Black, DL, JP, of Prees Hall, Whitchurch, Shropshire:—
Michael David Adam (The Old Granary, Gt Wilbraham, Cambridge) *b* 1935; *ed* Stowe and Clare Coll, Camb (BA): *m* 1964, Judy Carol, yr da of Cecil Jack Fairchild, of Tunbridge Wells, and has issue living, Clare Lucinda, *b* 1965; *ed* Clare Coll, Camb (BA), — Julia Caroline, *b* 1968; *ed* Brasenose Coll, Oxford (BA). —— Rev Canon Richard John (52 The Close, Norwich), *b* 1938; *ed* Winchester, and Peterhouse, Camb (MA): *m* 1972, Sheila, da of Robert King, of Tettenhall, Wolverhampton, and has issue living, Jonathan James, *b* 1974, — Adam Robert, *b* 1976, — Frances Rachel, *b* 1982.

Grandsons of late Brig John Michael Hanmer, DSO, OBE (ante):—
Issue of late Henry Hanmer, *b* 1943, *d* 1989: *m* 1972, Cristina Beatriz (who *m* 2ndly, 1991, José Oliveri-Biagiani, of Av Gral Santander 1782, Apt 202, Carrasco, Montevideo, Uruguay), da of Prof Hector D'Elia, of 21 de Setiembre 3122, Montevideo, Uruguay:—

Edward John, b 1974. ——— Stephen Patrick, b 1975.

Granddaughter of late George Hanmer, only son of late Humphrey Hanmer, 3rd son of late Rev John
Hanmer, 3rd son of 2nd baronet:—
Issue of late Humphrey George Hanmer, b 1886, d 1927: m 1st 1914 (m diss 1924), Beatrice Winnifred, da of late
George Sumpter, of Oamaru, New Zealand; 2ndly, 1925, Muriel Emma, who d 1985, da of George Henry Bostock,
of Staunton Springs, W Australia:—
(By 2nd m) Elizabeth Muriel, b 1929: m 1951, Arthur Cecil John Coates, who d 1958, and has issue living, David John (8
Weldon Way, City Beach, 6015 Perth, W Australia), b 1953: m 1983, Julie Howard, and has issue living, Christopher Michael
b 1985, Ellen Margaret b 1987, — Anne Muriel, b 1955. Residence – 53 Duncan Street, Wanganui, New Zealand.

Grandsons of late Thomas Hanmer, son of late William Hanmer, 6th son of 2nd baronet:—
Issue of late Thomas William Hanmer, b 1868, d 1950: m 1911, Ivy Mira Frances, who d 1965, only da of late
Charles John Dodd, of The Belfry, Uckfield, Sussex:—
Patrick William Talgai (Framfield, Broadgait, Gullane, E Lothian) b 1915; Capt RN (ret); former Sec The Hon Co of
Edinburgh Golfers, Muirfield (Hon Life Member): m 1992, Mrs Sadie Rydings, of Broombrough, Wirral. ——— Nicholas
Brian, MBE (Westholme West, Cumberland St, Woodbridge, Suffolk), b 1921; Maj (ret) R Sussex Regt; formerly Sen Dist
Commr, Colonial Ser; MBE (Civil) 1960: m 1st, 1944, Felicity Mary, who d 1969, only da of Frank William Sly, of Bruton;
2ndly, 1970, Betty May, da of Harry Smith, of Sudbury Hill, and has issue living (by 1st m), David Nicholas Frank (Buckland, Slapton, Kingsbridge, Devon), b 1944; Maj Parachute Regt (ret): m 1st, 1968 (m diss 1977), Susan, da of George
Inveriarity, DFC, of Brighton; 2ndly, 1978, Sarah, da of Dr Roger Blackney, of Kirkham, Babbacombe, Torquay, Devon, and
has had issue (by 1st m), †Guy David b 1971; d 1989, Emma Jane b 1969, a da b 1973, — Oliver William, b 1955: m 1st,
1977 (m diss 1989), Christine Ann, da of Jeffrey Benjamin Woodin, of North Walsham, Norfolk; 2ndly, 1994, Melinda Lee, da
of Colin Zweck, of Henty, NSW, and has issue living (by 1st m), Gavin Edward b 1982, Claire Louise b 1980, — Jill
Elizabeth (c/o ANZ Bank, Coolum Beach, Qld, Australia), b 1951: m 1st, 1978 (m diss 1981), Iain Murray; 2ndly, 1981,
Christopher Kenneth Peachey, only son of late Kenneth Cavalier Peachey, of Sydney, Australia. ——— Denys Beryl (4621
Pipe Line Rd, Vic, BC, Canada), b 1917: m 1st, 1939 (m diss 1942), Maj Charles Harry Campbell, Indian Army, who d 1944;
2ndly, 1943, Maj Peter Michael Harry Dalzell McLaughlin, CD, Canadian Army (ret) and Maj Indian Army (ret), who d 1971,
and has issue living (by 2nd m), Kevin Michael Dalzell (3567 Ravine Way, Vic, BC V8X 4Z1, Canada), b 1949: m 1969,
Bonnie Shirley Davies, and has issue living, Dalzell Michael Talgai b 1969, Maya Denys Shirley b 1972: m 1991, John Russell
Battiste Carter (and has issue living, Rebecca b 1992, Cheyenne Jessica Frances b 1994), Kara Bonnie Shawne b 1980, Dana
Michelle Tami b 1982, — Shawn Denys Dalzell, b 1955, — Maureen Daphne Hanmer, b 1944: m 1967, David Walter Carter,
of 866 Latoria Rd, Vic, BC, Canada, and has issue living, Blair Alexander b 1974. Elektra Arlene b 1980, — Meira Petricia, b
1951; assumed surname of Hanmer until remarriage: m 1st, 1970 (m diss 1984), Gary Wayne Tennent; 2ndly, 1987, Logan
Eric Mathison, of 4807 Townsend Drive, Vic, BC, Canada, and has issue living (by 1st m), Leah Michelle b 1975, Stephanie
Annette b 1977.

Grandson of late Lt-Col Lambert Alfred Graham Hanmer, DSO, IA, elder son of late Rear-Adm John
Graham Job Hanmer (infra):—
Issue of late Lt-Col Richard Graham Hanmer, b 1906, d 1986: m 1939, Helen (Forbury Farm, Kimbolton,
Leominster, Herefordshire), yst da of late Dr A.W. Campbell, of Sydney, NSW, Australia:—
David Graham (Yew Tree Cottage, Kimbolton, Leominster, Herefordshire; Cavalry Club), b 1940; ed Wellington Coll; late
Capt R Dragoons: m 1st, 1968 (m diss 1984), Susan Evelyn, da of Brig I.M. Christie; 2ndly, 1988, Bo White, and has issue
living (by 1st m), Piers Christie Graham, b 1971, — Eugenie Claire, b 1973.

Grandchildren of late Rear-Adm John Graham Job Hanmer, son of late Capt Job Thomas Syer Hanmer,
RN, son of late Capt Job Hanmer, RN, 2nd son of 1st baronet:—
Issue of late Thomas Walden Hanmer, b 1875, d 1949: m 1903, Ida, who d 1961, 2nd da of A. Whitby Simpson, of
Armidale, NS Wales:—
John Walden, ED, b 1915; is a JP; 1939-45 War with 6th Australian Div (pow); Greek Medal 1979: m 1949, Jean Eileen
Davies, el da of Arthur Archibald Sterling Nixon, of Claremont, Oaklands, NS Wales, and has issue living, Ruth Madeleine, b
1950, — Jean Anne, b 1955, — Patricia Margaret, b 1957. Residence – Claremont, Oaklands, nr Corowa, NS Wales. Clubs –
Royal Sydney Golf, and Imperial Service (Sydney). ——— Helen Walden (20 Bertha Rd, Cremorne, Sydney, NSW. Clubs –
Royal Sydney Golf, and Queen's), b 1903: m 1958, Ernest Charles Stumm, who d 1974.

This family is of considerable antiquity in Flintshire. Sir John de Hanmer, of Hanmer, was Constable of Carnarvon Castle
temp Edward I. His great-grandson, Sir Jenkin Hanmer, joined Owen Glendower in his rebellion against Henry IV, and was
killed at the battle of Shrewsbury in 1403. The 1st baronet (cr 1774), Sir Walden, MP for Sunbury in two Parliaments, was
15th in descent from Sir John de Hanmer. The 3rd baronet sat as MP for Shrewsbury (L) 1832-37, for Hull 1841-47, and for
Flint 1847-72, when he was created Baron Hanmer; he died sp in 1881, when the Peerage became extinct, and the Baronetcy
reverted to his brother. The 6th Baronet was High Sheriff of Flintshire 1902. There was an earlier Baronetcy (cr 1620) in
the Hanmer family, which became ext in 1746.

HANSON (UK) 1887, of Bryanston Square, co Middlesex

By the fear of God and assiduity

Sir ANTHONY (LESLIE OSWALD) DOMINIC SEAN HANSON, 4th *Baronet*; *b* 27 Nov 1934; *s* his half-brother, *Sir* RICHARD LESLIE REGINALD, 1951, *ed* Gordonstoun, and Exeter Univ (B Ed); late RNVR: *m* 1964, Denise Jane, da of Richard S. Rolph, BEM, of Stoke-sub-Hamdon, and has issue.

Arms – Or, a chevron counter compony gules and argent, cotised of the second, between three martlets sable; in the centre chief point a crescent also of the second. **Crest** – On a fasces fessewise or, a martlet rising sable.
Residence – Woodland Cottage, Woodland, Ashburton, Devon.

DAUGHTER LIVING

Charlotte, *b* 1971.

COLLATERAL BRANCH LIVING

Issue of late Sir Francis Stanhope Hanson, 2nd son of 1st baronet, *b* 1868, *d* 1910: *m* 1897, Pearl Norcott, who *d* 1960; (she *m* 2ndly, 1926, Maj Henry Noel Winter, late Roy Fusiliers, who *d* 1952), da of late Charles Albert Winter, JP, of 33 Hyde Park Sq, W:—

Violet Gwendoline Pearl, *b* 1899: *m* 1st 1919 (*m diss* 1923), William Bullivant; 2ndly, 1924 (*m diss* 1944), Capt Donald Selfe Leonard Gregson, formerly Indian Cav; 3rdly, 1946 (*m diss* 1949), John Roland Adams, QC. *Residence* – Little Gubbions, Great Leighs, Chelmsford, Essex.

The 1st baronet, Sir Reginald, was Lord Mayor of London 1886-7, and sat as MP for City of London (*C*) 1891-1900.

HANSON (UK) 1918, of Fowey, Cornwall

SEMPER PARARE.

To be ready always

Sir (CHARLES) JOHN HANSON, 3rd *Baronet*; *b* 28 Feb 1919; *s* his father, *Sir* CHARLES EDWIN BOURNE, 1958; *ed* Eton, and Clare Coll, Camb: late Capt Duke of Cornwall's LI: *m* 1st 1944 (*m diss* 1968), Patricia Helen, only child of late Adm Sir (Eric James) Patrick Brind, GBE, KCB; 2ndly, 1968, Violet Helen, da of late Charles Ormonde Trew, and formerly wife of late Capt Philip Cecil Landon Yorke, OBE, RN (*see* E Hardwicke, colls), and has issue by 1st *m*.

Arms – Argent, three lions rampant in chevron between as many mascles azure. **Crest** – A lion rampant azure, holding in the dexter forepaw an antler or, and resting the sinister paw upon two mascles fesseways and interlaced of the last.
Residence – Gunn House, Shelfanger, nr Diss, Norfolk IP22 2DP.

SON LIVING (By 1st marriage)

CHARLES RUPERT PATRICK (125 Ditchling Rd, Brighton, E Sussex), *b* 25 June 1945: *m* 1977, Wanda, da of Don Arturo Larrain, of Santiago, Chile, and has issue living, Alexis Charles, *b* 25 March 1978.

DAUGHTER LIVING (By 1st marriage)

Bridget Clare, *b* 1948: *m* 1969, Michael Grahame Cloete Graham-Cloete, and has issue living, James Montrose Stuart, *b* 1975, — Hermione Clare, *b* 1977.

SISTER LIVING

Violet Alice Rosalind (Mount Pleasant, Tellisford, nr Bath), *b* 1909: *m* 1930 (*m diss* 1970), Capt Robert Godmond Poole, RN (ret), and has had issue, Scilla Rosalind, *b* 1935: *m* 1964 (*m diss* 1982), Anthony Francis Raikes, and *d* 1992, leaving issue, Simon Anthony (63 St Peter's St, N1 8JR) *b* 1965: *m* 1989, Hon Tamsin Margaret Jay, da of Hon Peter Jay, and of Baroness Jay of Paddington (Life Baroness), Vanessa Rosalind *b* 1972, — Serena Mary, *b* 1944.

The 1st baronet, Sir Charles Augustin Hanson (a partner in the firm of Coates, Son & Co, stockbrokers, of 99 Gresham Street, EC), was Lord Mayor of London 1917-18, and sat as MP for S-E, or Bodmin, Div of Cornwall (*U*) 1916-22. The 2nd baronet, Sir Charles Edwin Bourne Hanson, was a partner in the firm of Coates, Son & Co, stockbrokers, of 99 Gresham Street, EC2, Major Duke of Wellington's Regt, and High Sheriff of Cornwall 1939.

HARDY (UK) 1876, of Dunstall Hall, co Stafford

Armed with faith bold

Sir RUPERT JOHN HARDY, 4th *Baronet*; *b* 24 Oct 1902; *s* his father, *Sir* BERTRAM, 1953; *ed* Eton, and Trin Hall, Camb (BA 1925); Lieut-Col (ret) The Life Guards: *m* 1930, Hon Diana Joan Allsopp, da of 3rd Baron Hindlip, and has issue.

Arms – Argent, on a bend invected plain cotised gules, three catherine wheels or; on a chief of the second as many leopards' faces of the third. **Crest** – A dexter arm embowed in armour proper, garnished or, entwined by a branch of oak vert, charged with two catherine wheels, the one above, the other below the elbow gules, the hand grasping a dragon's head erased proper.
Residence – Gullivers Lodge, Guilsborough, Northampton NN6 8RB. *Club* – Turf.

SON LIVING

RICHARD CHARLES CHANDOS (Springfield House, Gillingham, Dorset SP8 5RD), *b* 6 Feb 1945; *ed* Eton: *m* 1972, Venetia Wingfield, da of Simon Wingfield Digby, MP, of Haydon Gate, Sherborne, and has issue living, Arabella Venetia Jane, *b* 1976, — Jacquetta Anne, *b* 1977, — Georgina Charlotte, *b* 1982, — Henrietta Alicia Diana, *b* 1986.

DAUGHTER LIVING

Rosemary Diana (Redmoor Lodge, Guilsborough Rd, W Haddon, Northants NN6 7AD), *b* 1931: *m* 1953 (*m diss* 1972), Robert David Black (later Sir Robert David Black, 3rd Bt), and has had issue (*see* Black, Bt).

COLLATERAL BRANCHES LIVING

Issue of late Lt-Col Hugh Bertram Hardy, yr son of Sir Bertram Hardy, 3rd Bt, *b* 1907, *d* 1988: *m* 1933, Joan Stella Gwendolyn (Box 148, Limuru, Kenya), da of Charles Hammond Dracott, and formerly wife of James Alexander Guthrie:—
Audrey Elizabeth Una, *b* 1936: *m* 1965, Charles Frederick Backhouse (c/o Bank of Montreal, Calgary, Alberta, Canada), and has issue living, David Hugh, *b* 1971, — Isabelle Joan, *b* 1969.

Grandchildren of late Rt Hon Laurence Hardy (infra):—
Issue of late Maj Arthur Evelyn Hardy, *b* 1893, *d* 1986: *m* 1918, Nancy Marion, who *d* 1983, da of late Horace George Devas, formerly of Nizels, Hildenborough, Kent (*see* E Cawdor, colls, 1924 Edn):—
Gerald Alan, *b* 1926: *m* 1953, Carolyn, da of late Maj-Gen Arthur Charles Tarver Evanson, CB, MC, and has issue living, Sarah, *b* 1957: *m* 1972, William John Hurley, of Pedlinge Farm, Hythe, Kent, and has issue living, Kathryn Jane *b* 1985, Susannah Evelyn *b* 1988, Lucinda Barbara *b* 1990, — Jane, *b* 1958. *Residence* – Sandling Park, Hythe, Kent. —— Ruth, *b* 1919; a JP for Kent: *m* 1940, Col Charles Reginald Tuff, Buffs, DL (ret), and has issue living, Timothy Charles, *b* 1947, — Geoffrey, *b* 1954, — Prunella Primrose, *b* 1942. *Residence* – Hogs Green, Sandling, Hythe, Kent.

Issue of late Rt Hon Laurence Hardy, 4th son of 1st baronet, *b* 1854, *d* 1933: *m* 1886, Evelyn Emily, who *d* 1911, da of John Gathorne Wood, of Thedden Grange, Alton:—
Maurice John, MBE, *b* 1902; *ed* Eton, and Ch Ch, Oxford; 1939-45 War as Major RE; MBE (Mil) 1946: *m* 1926, Rosalie Kathleen, who *d* 1979, da of late Brig-Gen Tyrell Other William Champion de Crespigny (Champion de Crespigny, Bt, ext), and has issue living, Jane (Fox Hollow, Sandhurst Lane, Rolvenden, nr Cranbrook, Kent), *b* 1931: *m* 1955, Peter Leonard Eckersley, who *d* 1988, and has issue living, Peter David Charles *b* 1957: *m* 1987, Juliet Emma Margaret, da of Derek Graham Blundell Knight of Little Dane, Biddenden, Ashford, Kent (and has issue living, Peter Maurice Percival *b* 1989, Cliantha Florence Beatrice *b* 1991, Evangeline Violet Margaret *b* 1993), Clare Arabella *b* 1960: *m* 1981, David Richard Stapylton Fairbank (*see* V Chetwynd, colls) (and has issue living, Thomas David Peter *b* 1984, Arabella Clare Mary *b* 1987), Suzanne Jane *b* 1962: *m* 1982, Charles Roderick Roberts. *Residence* – Peasmarsh Place, nr Rye, E Sussex.
Sir John, 1st baronet, sat as MP for Midhurst (C) 1859, for Dartmouth 1860-68, and for S Warwickshire 1868-74. Sir Bertram, 3rd baronet was High Sheriff of Staffordshire 1925.

HARE (UK) 1818, of Stow Hall, Norfolk

Non viderised esse

Not to seem, but to be

Sir PHILIP LEIGH HARE, 6th *Baronet*; *b* 13 Oct 1922; son of late Edward Philip Leigh Hare, youngest son of 2nd baronet; *s* his kinsman, *Sir* THOMAS, 1993; *ed* privately: *m* 1950, Anne Lisle, 2nd da of Maj Geoffrey Nicholson, CBE, MC (E Annesley, colls), and has issue.

Arms – Gules two bars or, a chief indented of the last. **Crest** – A demi-lion rampant argent, gorged with a ducal coronet or.
Residence – The Nettings, Hook Norton, Banbury, Oxon OX15 5NP.

SON LIVING

NICHOLAS PATRICK (Old Manor Farm, Culkerton, nr Tetbury, Glos GL8 8SS), *b* 27 Aug 1955; *ed* Bryanston: *m* 1982, Caroline Keith, da of Terence Playfair Keith Allan, of Elsted Green, nr Midhurst, W Sussex, and has issue living, Thomas, *b* 7 Aug 1986, — Robert *b* 1987.

DAUGHTER LIVING

Louisa Kathleen, *b* (twin) 1955: *m* 1981, Benson Whittle, of Utah, USA, and has issue living, Charlotte, *b* 1981.

HALF-SISTER LIVING

Elizabeth Mildred Leigh (4 Old Museum Court, Haslemere, Surrey GU27 2JR), *b* 1915.

DAUGHTER LIVING OF THIRD BARONET

Joan Muriel Leigh (The Patch, Green Lane, Ilsington, nr Newton Abbot, S Devon TQ13 9RB), *b* 1905.

DAUGHTERS LIVING OF FOURTH BARONET

(By 1st wife, Doreen Pleasance Anna, eldest da of late Maj Sir Richard Ludwig Bagge, DSO)

Jean Bridget (11 Lady Jane Court, Cavendish Av, Cambridge), *b* 1929: *m* 1st, 1949 (*m diss* 1957), Nigel E. Beard; 2ndly, 1957 (*m diss* 1971), Richard John Wallis, son of late Leonard John Wallis, of Merton Park, SW19, and has issue living, (by 1st *m*) Jeremy Nigel Thomas, *b* 1953, — Laraine Susan, *b* 1950, — (by 2nd *m*) Robin John, *b* 1961.

(By 2nd wife, Natalie Alexandria Elizabeth Julia, only child of late Capt Baron Oscar Gerard de Langué)

Angela Florence Natalie, *b* 1948: *m* 1971, Terence Ronald Duke, and has issue living, Simon, *b* 1976, — Penelope Jane Deirdre, *b* 1974. —— Lorna Lillianne Katrina, *b* 1957: *m* 1975, Michael Page, and has issue living, David, *b* 1976, — Jonathan, *b* 1980, — Andrew, *b* 1981, — Thomas, *b* 1982.

(By 3rd wife, Barbara Mary Theodora (Ann), infra)

Mary Ann, *b* 1961: *m* 1993, Anthony Jacklin.

DAUGHTERS LIVING OF FIFTH BARONET

Lucy Rose, *b* 1962. —— Elizabeth Florence, *b* 1964: *m* 1992, William Nicholas Esse, son of late David Charles Scott Esse, of Horsley, Glos, and has issue living, Barnaby Samuel Hare, *b* 1993.

WIDOWS LIVING OF FOURTH AND FIFTH BARONETS

BARBARA MARY THEODORA (ANN) (*Ann, Lady Hare*) (Stow Bardolph, King's Kynn, Norfolk), yst da of late Joseph Arthur Walton: *m* 1960, as his 3rd wife, Maj Sir Ralph Leigh Hare, 4th Bt, who *d* 1976.
Lady ROSE AMANDA BLIGH (*Lady Rose Hare*) (Stow Bardolph, King's Lynn, Norfolk PE34 3HU), 2nd da of 9th Earl of Darnley: *m* 1961, Sir Thomas Hare, 5th Bt, who *d* 1993.
Sir Nicholas Hare, twice Speaker of the House of Commons and sometime Master of the Rolls (a Commissioner to execute the Office of Lord Chancellor and Keeper of the Great Seal 1555), purchased Stow Bardolph in 1553. His great-great-great-nephew Ralph Hare (son of Sir John Hare, Knt) was *cr* 1st Baronet of Stow Bardolph in 1641. Mary, second da of his son Sir Thomas Hare, 2nd Bt (*cr* 1641), and sister and eventual co-heiress of the 5th Bt (at whose death in 1764 the Baronetcy became ext), married Thomas Leigh, of London, son of Edward Leigh, of Iver, Bucks (will proved 1689) and in common descent with the Stoneleigh Abbey family, from the Leighs of Cheshire. Her grandson, Thomas Leigh, who succeeded to Stow Bardolph (son of Thomas Leigh, of Iver, Bucks), served with distinction in the American war, assumed in 1791 by Act of Parliament the surname of Hare in lieu of his patronymic of Leigh, and was *cr* a Baronet in 1818, becoming Sir Thomas Hare, 1st Bt. The 2nd baronet was Capt 2nd Life Guards, while the 3rd was Lieut 2nd Life Guards, and High Sheriff of Norfolk 1906.

HARFORD (UK) 1934, of Falcondale, co Cardigan

Inter· ulrumque·tene·

Hold between the two

Sir (JOHN) TIMOTHY HARFORD, 3rd *Baronet*; *b* 6 July 1932; *s* his father, Lt-Col *Sir* GEORGE ARTHUR, OBE, 1967; *ed* Harrow, Worcester Coll, Oxford, and Harvard Business Sch: *m* 1962, Carolyn Jane, only da of late Brig Guy John de Wette Mullens, OBE, of North House, Weyhill, Andover, and has issue.

Arms – Sable, two bendlets argent between three cross-crosslets fitchée in pale of the last. **Crest** – In front of flames issuant therefrom a phœnix proper, two cross-crosslets fitchée in saltire argent.
Residence – South House, South Littleton, Evesham, Worcs.

SONS LIVING

MARK JOHN, *b* 6 Aug 1964. —— Simon Guy, *b* 1966.

DAUGHTER LIVING

Clare Elisabeth, *b* 1963: *m* 1989, Nicholas Clatworthy, yr son of late Peter Clatworthy, of Bayswater, and has issue living, Guy Peter, *b* 1992.

BROTHER LIVING

Piers Scandrett (Church Farm, Great Somerford, Chippenham, Wilts), *b* 1937; *ed* Eton, and Worcester Coll, Oxford: *m* 1st, 1961 (*m diss* 1972), Hyacinthe Cecilia, da of Lt-Col Nigel Walter Hoare, OBE, TD (*see* Portal, Bt, colls); 2ndly, 1975, Patricia Jane, da of Air Commodore Patrick Burnett, and has issue living (by 1st *m*), Henry Scandrett, *b* 1963, — Charlotte Anstice, *b* 1965, — (by 2nd *m*) William Patrick, *b* 1976.

SISTER LIVING

Robina Elspeth, *b* 1934: *m* 1956, Jeremy Christopher Glyn, who *d* 1984, and has issue (*see* B Wolverton, colls). *Residence* – Upton Farm House, Upton, Andover, Hants.
The 1st baronet, Major Sir John Charles Harford (son of late John Battersby Harford, of Falcondale, co Cardigan, and of Blaise Castle, Henbury, Bristol) was created a baronet June 1934, and *d* July 1934.

HARINGTON (E) 1611, of Ridlington, Rutland

NODO·FIRMO·

With a firm knot

Sir NICHOLAS JOHN HARINGTON, 14th *Baronet*; *b* 14 May 1942; *s* his uncle, *Sir* RICHARD DUNDAS, 1981; *ed* Eton, and Ch Ch, Oxford (MA).

Arms – Sable, a fret argent. **Crest** – A lion's head erased or, langued and collared gules, buckled of the first.
Residences – 99 Clarendon Rd, W11 4JG; Ring'o Bells, Whitbourne, Worcester WR6 5RT.

BROTHER LIVING

DAVID RICHARD (7 Vale Grove, W3 7QP), *b* 25 June 1944; *ed* Westminster, and Ch Ch, Oxford: *m* 1983, Deborah Jane, eldest da of Maurice William Catesby, MC, of Long Compton, Warwicks, and has issue living, John Catesby, *b* 7 Jan 1984, — Christopher, *b* 1986.

SISTER LIVING

Susan Alexandra, *b* 1948: *m* 1977, Anis Nacrour, of 38 rue du Roseau, 78610 Le Perray-en-Yvelines, France, and has issue living, Aurélien-Antoine John Mourad, *b* 1985, — Alexandre Philippe, *b* 1988.

COLLATERAL BRANCHES LIVING

Grandchildren of late Rev Charles Harington, 2nd son of 11th baronet:—
Issue of late Sir Charles Robert Harington, KBE, *b* 1897, *d* 1972: *m* 1923, Jessie McCririe, who *d* 1975, da of Rev James Craig, of The Manse, Kirkpatrick-Durham, Kirkcudbright:—
Michael (16 Coval Gdns, East Sheen, SW14), *b* 1924; *ed* Trin Hall, Camb (MA), and Univ Coll Hosp Medical Sch; MB, BChir, FRCP: *m* 1958, Marta Rosenfeld, and has issue living, Robert Michael, *b* 1963; *ed* Trin Coll, Oxford (DPhil): *m* 1988, Pamela, da of P. Nadash, of Columbia, Maryland, USA, — Amanda, *b* 1967; *ed* St Paul's Girls' Sch, and St John's Coll, Camb; Bar Inner Temple 1989. —— Alison Mary, *b* 1927; MB, BChir: *m* 1952, Derek Raymond Bangham, MB, BS, FRCP, of 4 Crown Close, Highwood Hill, NW7, and has issue living, Charles Richard Mark, *b* 1955; BM, BCH, MRCP, PhD, MRCPath: *m* 1990, Jocelyne Marie Ragody Hughes, PhD, and has issue living, George Richard Derek *b* 1991, Madeleine Edith *b* 1993, — Humphrey Bernard, *b* 1957: *m* 1980, Elizabeth Mary Stafford Baker, and has issue living, Charles Stafford *b* 1987, Guy Nicholas *b* 1992, Olivia Charlotte *b* 1989, — Celia Elizabeth, *b* 1954; MB, ChB, DRCOG, — Jessica Frances, *b* 1961: *m* 1990, John Graham Lawrence. —— Margaret Jane (43 Upton Lovell, Warminster, Wilts), *b* 1931.

Issue of late His Honour Judge Edward Harington, 3rd son of 11th baronet, *b* 1863, *d* 1937: *m* 1906, Louisa Muriel, who *d* 1963, only da of late Herbert C. Erskine Vernon:—

(Edward Henry) Vernon (16 Lower Mill St, Ludlow, Shropshire), *b* 1907; *ed* Eton; Bar Inner Temple 1930; was Private Sec to Lord Chancellor and Dep Sergeant-at-Arms in House of Lords 1934-40; Austrian Control Commn Legal Div, and Assist Sec of Commns to Lord Chancellor 1945, a Dept Judge Advocate 1946, and Assist Judge Advocate Gen 1955; Dep Chm Herefordshire Quarter Sessions 1969-72; a Recorder of Crown Court 1972-75; Chm of Hereford Worcester, Warwicks, and W Midlands Agric Wages Cttee 1976-81; District Councillor of Malvern Hills District Council since 1979; a Gold Staff Officer at Coronation of King George VI; 1939-45 War as Maj Coldm Gds: *m* 1st, 1937 (*m diss* 1949), Mary Elizabeth, da of late Louis Edwin William Egerton (M Hertford, colls); 2ndly, 1950, Mary Johanna Jean, JP, da of late Lt-Col Ralph George Snead Cox, MC, and has issue living (by 1st *m*), Victoria Jane, *b* 1941: *m* 1973, Sidney Morgan Whitteridge, VRD, MRCS, LRPC, of Inverlael Lodge, Loch Broom, by Ullapool, Ross-shire, and has issue living, Ashley Edward John *b* 1976, Mary Ruth *b* 1974, — (by 2nd *m*) (Marie) Louisa, *b* 1951: *m* 1979, Robin Pagan Taylor, of The Pulpits, Little Hereford, Shropshire SY4 4AU, and has issue living, William Vernon *b* 1980, Philip Edward *b* 1984, — Susan Anne J, *b* 1953: *m* 1984, David Robert Geoffrey Scott, of Upper Hamnish Farm, Leominster, Herefords, yr son of late Cdr Geoffrey Thomas Archibald Scott, RN, and has issue living, Edwina Alexandra *b* 1985, Sophie Amelia *b* 1987. —— Kenneth Douglas Evelyn Herbert, *b* 1911; *ed* Stowe Sch; Bar Inner Temple 1952; Hon Attaché, British Legation, Stockholm 1930-32; a JP and Acting Dep Chm of Quarter Sessions in Greater London 1966-67, a Metropolitan Magistrate 1967-84; 1939-45 War, Maj Coldm Gds: *m* 1st, 1939, Lady Cecilia Bowes-Lyon, who *d* 1947, da of 15th Earl of Strathmore; 2ndly, 1950, Maureen Helen, who *d* 1992, da of late Brig-Gen Sir Robert (Chaine Alexander) McCalmont, KCVO, CBE, DSO, and has issue living (by 2nd *m*), Michael Kenneth (32 Hitherfield Rd, SW16), *b* 1951; *ed* Eton and Ch Ch, Oxford; Bar Inner Temple 1974: *m* 1984, Deirdre Christine Kehoe, and has issue living, Robert John Michael *b* 1988, Charlotte Mary Ann *b* 1985, Caroline Lucy Christine *b* 1991, — Jonathan Edward McCalmont, *b* 1955; *ed* Eton; 2nd Lt Coldm Gds: *m* 1st, 1983 (*m diss* 1986), Lucinda Margaret, only da of Maj William Lloyd (John) Baxendale (*see* E Fortescue); 2ndly, 1989, Susan Antonia, yst da of Anthony Walter Fenwick, of Eaton Grange, Eaton, nr Grantham, Lincs, and has issue living (by 2nd *m*), Antonia Lucy Diana *b* 1991, Katherine Rose Caroline *b* 1994. *Residence* – Orchard End, Upper Oddington, Moreton in Marsh, Glos. *Club* – Cavalry and Guards'.

Grandchildren of late Brig-Gen John Harington, CB, CMG, DSO (infra):—
  Issue of late Maj John Temple Harington, DSO, MBE, *b* 1909, *d* 1983: *m* 1946, Catherine (Strathrusdale Lodge, Ardross, Alness, Ross and Cromarty), da of late Lt-Col Donald Cameron, of Fordon, The Nile, Tasmania:—
Richard Donald John (Wester Baldoon, Ardross, Alness, Ross and Cromarty), *b* 1948; *ed* Winchester, and Hertford Coll, Oxford: *m* 1974, Jane Pickin, da of Peter Wellburn Bayliss, of Burcher Court, Titley, Kington, Herefordshire, and has issue living, Alastair Peter John, *b* 1983, — Lucy Aline, *b* 1979, — Miranda Jane, *b* 1980. —— Serena Catherine Lucy, *b* 1947: *m* 1971, Julian G. Barrow, of 33 Tite St, SW3, and has issue living, Cecilia Margaret, *b* 1975, — Eugenie Catherine, *b* 1977. —— Cecilia Aline, *b* 1953: *m* 1994, Jacques Richard, of 60 rue Doudeauville, 75018 Paris, France.

Issue of late Brig-Gen John Harington, CB, CMG, DSO, 5th son of 11th baronet, *b* 1873, *d* 1943: *m* 1908, Lady Frances Aline Temple-Gore-Langton who *d* 1952, da of 4th Earl Temple, of Stow:—
Aline Lucy (*Hon Mrs Walter Keppel*), *b* 1918: *m* 1941, Lt-Com Hon Walter Arnold Crispian Keppel, DSC, RN (*see* E Albemarle). *Residence* – Barton House, Meonstoke, Hants.

Granddaughter of late Arthur Champernowne, son of Henry Champernowne, el son of Arthur Champernowne (infra):—
  Issue of late Arthur Melville Champernowne, *b* 1871, *d* 1946: *m* 1907, Helen Iris, who *d* 1950, el da of Lieut-Col Herbert John Ouchterlony Walker, late RA, formerly of Leeford, Budleigh Salterton:—
Katharine Iris (Parnham's Farm, Melbury Abbas, Shaftesbury, Dorset), *b* 1912: *m* 1949, Wing-Cdr Adrian Henry Paull, AFC, who *d* 1965, and has issue living, Angela Iris Constance, *b* 1951.

Grandson of late Rev Richard Champernowne, son of late Arthur Champernowne (who assumed the surname and arms of Champernowne 1774), son of late Rev Richard Harington, 2nd son of 6th baronet:—
  Issue of late Francis Gawayne Champernowne, *b* 1866, *d* 1921: *m* 1911, Isabel Mary, who *d* 1969, da of late George Burvill Rashleigh, Bar-at-law, of Riseley, Horton-Kirby, Dartford and 5 Stone Buildings, Lincoln's Inn, WC (E Darnley):—
David Gawen, *b* 1912; *ed* Winchester, and King's Coll, Camb (Fellow 1937-48); a Fellow of Trin Coll, Camb; Prof of Statistics, Oxford Univ 1948-59; Prof of Economics & Statistics, Camb Univ 1970-78: *m* 1948, Wilhelmina Barbara Maria, da of late Petrus Ludovicus Dullaert, of Zutphen, Holland, and has issue living, Arthur Francis, *b* 1949, — Richard Peter, *b* 1953: *m* 1986, Jackie, da of Bill Wills, of Petersfield, Hants. *Residence* – 25 Worts Causeway, Cambridge, CB1 4RJ.

John, son of Robert de Haverington, of Haverington (now Harington), Cumberland, was one of the barons summoned to Parliament by Edward II. His lineal descendant, Sir John Harington of Exton, co Rutland, brother of the 1st baronet, and tutor to the Princess Elizabeth, daughter of James I, was created Baron Harington, which title became extinct on the death of the 2nd baron. Sir James, 3rd baronet, one of the Judges commissioned (but who refused to sit) to try Charles I, was, by an Act of 13 Car II, nevertheless excepted at the Restoration out of the general acts of indemnity, and with Lord Monson, Sir Henry Fieldings, and others subjected to personal degradation from his honours and rendered personally incapable of bearing arms or title of dignity (but the penalty did not forfeit the honours or attaint the blood). Sir Richard, 11th Bt, was a Metropolitan Police Magistrate 1871-2, and a Judge of County Courts 1872-1905. Sir Richard, 12th Bt, was a Puisne Judge of High Court, Calcutta 1899-1913.

STAFFORD-KING-HARMAN (UK) 1914, of Rockingham, co Roscommon (Extinct 1987)

Lt-Col Sir CECIL WILLIAM FRANCIS STAFFORD-KING-HARMAN, 2nd and last *Baronet.*

DAUGHTER LIVING OF SECOND BARONET

Cicely Joan, *b* 1918: *m* 1943, Capt George Heffernan Dennehy, late Irish Guards, who *d* 1990, 2nd son of late George Heffernan Dennehy, of Ballymanus, Stradbally, Queen's Co, and has issue living, Rosemary Anne *b* 1944: *m* 1964, Charles Ralph Nicolas Tindal, of Ballyloughan, Bruckless, co Donegal, eldest son of G/Capt Nicolas Henry Joseph Tindal, RAF (ret), of Ballyloughan, and has issue living, Nicolas Henry Charles *b* 1965, Richard Mark *b* 1968, Matthew Thomas *b* 1973, Katherine Mary *b* 1966 Emma Caroline *b* 1970, Victoria Jacqueline Frances *b* 1971, Lucy Josephine *b* 1977, — Sarah Elizabeth, *b* 1949: *m* 1970 (*m diss* 1990), Don Leopoldo de Bolivar Torres, of Seville, and has issue living, Isabel *b* 1970, Alexandra Rose *b* 1974, — Mary Katharine, *b* 1951: *m* 1st, 1977 (*m diss* 1984), David Starkie; 2ndly, 1984 (*m diss* 1993), Joseph Jenkins, of Grove City, Pennsylvania, USA, and has issue living, (by 1st *m*) Lauryn Hannah *b* 1978, (by 2nd *m*) Cayli Sunrise *b* 1984, Orion *b* 1985, — Caroline Jean, *b* 1954: *m* 1975 (*m diss* 1979), Stuart Anthony Reed; 2ndly, 1982, Heribert Ernst Schiansky, of Kailasa, Ministerley, Shrewsbury, Shropshire, and has issue living (by 2nd husband), Jethro *b* 1983, Holly *b* 1980, Frances *b* 1990. *Residence* – 19 Archery Fields, Odiham, Hants.

COLLATERAL BRANCH LIVING

Issue of late Capt Edward Charles Stafford-King-Harman, Irish Guards, el son of 1st baronet, *b* 1891, *ka* 1914, having assumed by Roy licence 1900 the additional surname of King-Harman: *m* 1914, Olive (who *m* 2ndly, 1921, Wilfred Stuart Atherstone Hales Pakenham Mahon (*d* 1980), and *d* 1981), only da of late Capt Henry Pakenham Mahon (*see* E Longford, colls):—

Lettice Mary (*posthumous*), *b* 1915: *m* 1st, 1935 (*m diss* 1971), Col Robert Humphrey Lomer, MBE, Gren Gds, who *d* 1990; 2ndly, 1975, Maj George Henry Errington, MC, late 10th Hussars, who *d* 1989, and has issue living (by 1st *m*), Caroline Mary, *b* 1937: *m* 1st, 1957 (*m diss* 1964), Maj Patrick Haselden Wood, late 11th Hussars; 2ndly, 1964, Maj Neil Gordon Ramsay, Scots Gds, of St Anns, Alyth, Perthshire, and has issue living (by 2nd *m*), Melanie Mary *b* 1966: *m* 1990, John J. M. St John, yst son of Lt-Col Charles A. R. L. St John, of Glebe Manor, Havant, Hants, and an adopted da, Victoria Anne *b* 1968, — Lavinia Rohays (184 Latymer Court, Hammersmith Rd, W6 7JQ), *b* 1939: *m* 1968 (*m diss* 1973), Cdr Harry James Startin, RN.

Harmood-Banner, see Banner.

HARMSWORTH (UK) 1922, of Freshwater Grove, Parish of Shipley, co Sussex

Bene · qui · sedulo

He who acts diligently acts well

Sir HILDEBRAND HAROLD HARMSWORTH, 3rd *Baronet; b* 5 June 1931; *s* his father *Sir* HILDEBRAND ALFRED BERESFORD, 1977; *ed* Harrow and Trin Coll, Dublin: *m* 1960, Gillian Andrea, only da of William John Lewis, of Tetbury, Glos, and has issue.

Arms – Azure, two rolls of paper in saltire or, banded in the centre gules, between four bees volant of the second. **Crest** – Issuant out of a coronet composed of three roses set upon a rim or, a cubit arm erect, the hand grasping a roll of paper fessewise proper.
Residence – Ewlyn Villa, 42 Leckhampton Rd, Cheltenham GL53 0BB.

SON LIVING

HILDEBRAND ESMOND MILES, *b* 1 Sept 1964; *ed* Dean Close Sch, and Crewe and Alsager Coll: *m* 1988, Ruth Denise, da of Dennis Miles, of Cheltenham, and has issue living, Alice Katherine Elspeth, *b* 1990, — Grace Hester Elaine, *b* 1991.

DAUGHTERS LIVING

Claire Elen Mary, *b* 1961. —— Kirsten Elizabeth Ashley, *b* 1963.

SISTER LIVING

Ingeborg Kathleen Elen, *b* 1926: *m* 1951, Capt Thomas James Johnson, RA, who *d* 1963, and has issue living, Ingeborg Caroline Kathleen Elen, *b* 1952, — Melissa Eugenie Ingeborg Thomasine, *b* 1954, — Atalanta Kathleen Ingeborg Elen, *b* 1962: *m* 1989, Raymond Clive Wright. *Residence* – Chiffley Grange, Staplefield, Sussex.

WIDOW LIVING OF SECOND BARONET

ELEN (*Elen, Lady Harmsworth*) (Aucassin, Le Vallon, St Clair, Le Lavandou, France), da of Nicolaj Billenstein, of Randers, Denmark: *m* 1925, Sir Hildebrand Alfred Beresford Harmsworth, 2nd Bt, who *d* 1977.

COLLATERAL BRANCH LIVING

Issue of late (Chamberlain) Michael Hildebrand Harmsworth, 3rd son of 1st baronet, *b* 1903, *d* 1955: *m* 1st, 1931, Barbara Irene, who *d* 1941, da of Henry Savile Dean; 2ndly, 1945, Lucette Charlotte, only da of Jean Riché, of Paris:—
(By 2nd *m*) John Hildebrand, *b* 1949. —— Charles Hildebrand, *b* 1951. —— (By 1st *m*) Josephine Angela, *b* 1932. —— Melanie Barbara, *b* 1934.

Sir Hildebrand Harmsworth, 1st Bt (son of late Alfred Harmsworth, Bar-at-law), was a younger brother of the 1st Viscount Northcliffe (ext), and the 1st Viscount Rothermere; edited *New Liberal Review* 1901-4, and was sometime Proprietor of *The Globe*.

HARRIS (UK) 1932, of Bethnal Green, co London

Sir JACK (WOLFRED) ASHFORD HARRIS, 2nd *Baronet, b* 23 July 1906; *s* his father, *Rt Hon Sir* PERCY ALFRED HARRIS, 1952; *ed* Shrewsbury, and Trin Hall, Camb (BA 19—); sometime Pres of Wellington Chamber of Commerce; European War 1939-45 with New Zealand Forces: *m* 1933, Patricia, da of Arthur P. Penman, of Wahroonga, near Sydney, NS Wales, and has issue.
Residence – Te Rama, Waikanae, near Wellington, New Zealand. *Clubs* – Royal Automobile, Wellington (New Zealand).

SONS LIVING

CHRISTOPHER JOHN ASHFORD, *b* 26 Aug 1934: *m* 1957, Anna, da of F. de Malmanche, of Auckland, New Zealand, and has issue living, Andrew Frederick Ashford, *b* 1958, — Charlotte Anna, *b* 1960, — Phoebe Jane Ashford, *b* 1963. *Residence* – 21 Anne St, Wadestown, Wellington, NZ. —— Paul Percy Ashford (28 Middlehead Rd, Mosman, NSW, Australia), *b* 1945: *m* 1969, Gail, da of late Arthur Stewart, of Manchester, and has issue living, Mark Percy, *b* 1970, Nicholas, *b* 1978, Samuel *b* 1980, Sophie, *b* 1973.

DAUGHTER LIVING

Margaret, *b* 1939.

BROTHER LIVING

Thomas Nicholas Robinson, *b* 1908; *ed* King's Sch, Burton, and Trin Hall, Camb; is Lieut RNVR: *m* 1942, Lucille, only child of D. H. Jonas, and has issue living, Antony Guy David Bloxham, *b* 1943.

The 1st baronet, Rt Hon Sir Percy Alfred Harris (son of Wolf Harris, of 197 Queen's Gate, SW), was MP for S (or Harborough) Div of Leicestershire 1916-18, and for S-W Div of Bethnal Green 1922-45, and was Ch Liberal Whip 1935-45.

HARRIS (UK) 1953, of Chepping Wycombe, Bucks

Sir ANTHONY TRAVERS KYRLE HARRIS, 2nd *Baronet*: *b* 18 March 1918; *s* his father, *Marshal of the RAF Sir* ARTHUR TRAVERS, GCB, OBE, AFC, 1984; *ed* Oundle; World War II 1939-45 with Queen Victoria's Rifles and Wilts Regt; Auxiliary Units 1941; ADC to GOC-in-C Eastern Command 1944.

ᴬrms – Azure a chevron ermine between in chief two hedgehogs and in base an eagle displayed or. Crest – Issuant from an astral crown or a mount vert thereon a hedgehog gold.
Residence – 33 Cheyne Court, Flood St, SW3 5TR.

SISTERS LIVING

Marigold Patricia (Beechdale House, W Anstey, S Molton, N Devon), *b* 1920: *m* 1946, Robert William Armitage, TD, who *d* 1978, and has issue living, Rupert Dudley (71 York Mansions, Prince of Wales Drive, SW11 4BW), *b* 1947, *ed* Eton: *m* 1976, Venetia, da of Anthony Greville-Bell, of 20 Sumner Place, SW7, and has issue living, Edward James *b* 1979, Katherine Rose *b* 1981, — Peter James (151 North End House, Fitzjames Av, W14 0RT), *b* 1950; *ed* Eton, and Camb Univ: *m* 1974, Flavia, da of Mark Phillips. —— Rosemary Jeanne, *b* 1923.

HALF-SISTER LIVING

Jacqueline Jill (*Hon Mrs Nicholas Assheton*), *b* 1939: *m* 1960, Hon Nicholas Assheton, and has issue (*see* B Clitheroe). *Residence* – 15 Hammersmith Terr, W6 9TS.

The 1st baronet, Marshal of the RAF Sir Arthur Travers Harris, GCB, OBE, AFC, 1914-18 War with 1st Rhodesian Regt, RFC and RAF in S-W Africa, France, India, Mesopotamia and Middle East (despatches); 1939-45 War (despatches), was Air Officer Cmdg-in-Chief, Bomber Command 1942-45; received Freedom of Honiton 1945, of Chepping Wycombe 1946, and City of London 1978; Hon LLD Liverpool 1946, and was awarded many foreign orders.

HARRISON (UK) 1922, of Eaglescliffe, co Durham

While I breathe, I hope

Sir (ROBERT) COLIN HARRISON, 4th *Baronet*; *b* 25 May 1938; *s* his brother, *Sir* (JOHN) WYNDHAM, 1955; *ed* Radley, and St John's Coll, Camb: *m* 1963, Maureen Marie, da of late E. Leonard Chiverton, and has issue.

Arms – Per chevron azure and or, in chief two demi-lions rampant of the second and in base a lymphad sable. **Crest** – Upon a fernbrake a falcon rising proper, belled and charged upon the sinister wing with a fleur-de-lis or. *Residence* – Stearsby Hall, Stearsby, York Y06 4SA.

SON LIVING

JOHN WYNDHAM FOWLER, *b* 14 Dec 1972.

DAUGHTERS LIVING

Rachel Deborah, *b* 1966: *m* 1991, Alistair G. Waddell, elder son of W. Waddell, of Lochgreen Cottage, Troon, Ayrshire. *Residence* – Hong Kong. —— Claire Grace, *b* 1974.

SISTER LIVING

Judith May *b* 1935: *m* 1962, Paul Standing, and has issue living, Christopher Hugh, *b* 1965, —— Jane Kathleen, *b* 1963.

The 1st baronet, Sir John Harrison (son of John Harrison, of Stockton-on-Tees), was Mayor of Stockton 1903, 1906, 1916, 1917, and 1918.

HARRISON (UK) 1961, of Bugbrooke, co Northampton

Sir MICHAEL JAMES HARWOOD HARRISON, 2nd *Baronet*; *b* 28 March 1936; *s* his father, *Sir* (JAMES) HARWOOD, 1980; *ed* Rugby; JP 1993; a Member of Lloyd's, and of Council of Sail Training Assocn, Vice-Pres of Assocn of Combined Youth Clubs; a Liveryman of Mercer's Co (Master 1986-87), and a Freeman of City of London; Chm Berrite Ltd: *m* 1967, (Rosamund) Louise, da of late Edward Buxton Clive, of Swanmore Lodge, Swanmore, Southampton, and has issue.
Residence – 35 Paulton's Sq, SW3. *Clubs* – MCC, Boodle's, Royal Harwich Yacht.

SONS LIVING

EDWIN MICHAEL HARWOOD, *b* 29 May 1981. —— Tristan John, *b* 1986.

DAUGHTERS LIVING

(Auriol) Davina, *b* 1968. —— Priscilla Caroline, *b* 1971.

SISTER LIVING

Joanna Kathleen *b* 1939: *m* 1966, William Ashton Sanders, of Nine Chimney House, Balsham, Cambridge CB1 6ES, and has issue living, James William Ashton, *b* 1968.
The 1st baronet, Sir (James) Harwood Harrison, TD, MP (son of Rev Ernest Wivelsfield Harrison, of Bugbrooke, Northampton), was Brevet-Col 4th Suffolk Regt (TA); Assist Govt Whip 1954-56, Lord Commr of the Treasury 1956-59, Comptroller of HM Household 1959-61, Chm Select Sub Cttee on Defence and Overseas Affairs 1971-79; also MP (C) for Eye Div of Suffolk 1951-79.

CRADOCK-HARTOPP (GB) 1796, of Freathby, Leicestershire

Sir JOHN EDMUND CRADOCK-HARTOPP, TD, 9th *Baronet*, son of late Francis Gerald Cradock-Hartopp, son of late Col Edmund Charles Cradock-Hartopp, 2nd son of 3rd baronet; *b* 8 April 1912; *s* his kinsman, *Sir* GEORGE FRANCIS FLEETWOOD, 1949; *ed* Uppingham; European War 1939-45 as Major RE (despatches twice): *m* 1953, Prudence, 2nd da of Sir Frederick William Leith-Ross, GCMG, KCB, and has issue.

Arms – Quarterly: 1st and 4th, sable, a chevron argent between three otters passant argent, *Hartopp*; 2nd and 3rd, per saltire gules and argent crusily, three boars' heads two and one, couped counterchanged, *Cradock*. **Crest** – Out of a ducal coronet or a pelican argent vulning herself proper, *Hartopp*.
Residence – The Cottage, 27 Wool Rd, Wimbledon Common, SW20 0HN. *Clubs* – East India, Devonshire, Sports, Public Schools, Royal and Ancient, and MCC.

DAUGHTERS LIVING

Melinda Anne, *b* 1954: *m* 1984, Murray Lewis, only son of late Rev Raymond Lewis, of E Dean, E Sussex, and has issue living, Jonathan Murray, *b* 1988, — Katherine, *b* 1990. —— Nicola Jane, *b* 1957. —— Joanna Elizabeth, *b* 1960: *m* 1985, Michael Victor Charter, 2nd son of Victor Noël Charter, of Chelmsford, Essex.

SISTER LIVING

Gwendoline Mary, *b* 1909: *m* 1938, Group Capt John Stanton Fleming Morrison, DFC, RAFVR, who *d* 1961, and has issue living, Elizabeth Mary, *b* 1942. *Residence* – The Lea, Dogmersfield, Basingstoke, Hants.

COLLATERAL BRANCH LIVING

Grandchildren of late Col Edmund Charles Cradock-Hartopp, younger son of 3rd baronet:—
Issue of late Major Louis Montague Cradock-Hartopp, *b* 1884, *d* 1957: *m* 1916, Marjorie Somerville, who *d* 1971, only da of James Falshaw Watson, MICE, MIME, formerly of Park House, Codsall Wood, Staffs;—
KENNETH ALSTON, MBE, DSC (Keepers, Yeovilton, Yeovil, Som BA22 8EX), *b* 26 Feb 1918; Lt-Com (ret) RN; an Assoc Member of Institute of Management; American Legion of Merit; MBE (Mil) 1946: *m* 1942, Gwendolyn Amy Lilian, da of late Capt Victor Crowther Upton, and has issue living, Christina, *b* 1948: *m* 1977, Thomas Montagu Hickman, of 60 Acre Lane, SW2, and has issue (*see* Hickman, Bt, colls). —— Virginia Anne, *b* 1922: *m* 1952, Michael Henry Tindall Carter, and has issue living, Christopher Henry James, *b* 1953: *m* 1980, Jane Anne Hardie, and has issue living, Sophie Louise *b* 1987, —— Geraldine Anne, *b* 1956: *m* 1st, 1985, Bruce Gordon Scott Coles; 2ndly 1994, William Sam Fletcher, of Pulvertoft Hall, Gedney, Lincs, and has issue living (by 1st *m*), Alexander Henry Rufus Scott *b* 1987, James Edward Rupert Scott *b* 1989, —— Paula Margaret, *b* 1962. *Residence* – Tydd Manor, Wisbech, Cambridgeshire.

Edward Hartopp, MP for Leicestershire, was created a baronet 1619, and the baronetcy became extinct 1762, on the death, without male issue, of Sir John, 4th baronet, whose granddaughter and heiress, Anne Hurlock, married 1777, Edmund Bunney, of The Newark, Leicester, who assumed the surnames of Cradock-Hartopp, and was created a baronet 1796. Sir Charles William Everard Cradock-Hartopp, 6th Bt, was a 1st Sec in Diplo Ser.

HARTWELL (UK) 1805, of Dale Hall, Essex

Sorte suâ contentus
Contented with his lot

Sir (FRANCIS) ANTHONY CHARLES PETER HARTWELL, 6th *Baronet*; *b* 1 June 1940; *s* his father, *Sir* BRODRICK WILLIAM CHARLES ELWIN, 1993; *ed* Thames Nautical Training Coll, HMS *Worcester*; Cadet RNR, Cadet P & OSN Co, Navigation Officer; Univ of Southampton (Sch of Navigation), Master Mariner 1971; Merchant Navy 1958-75; MRIN, MNI, MCIT; Port Management, Marine Surveyor and Consultant: *m* 1968 (*m diss* 1989), Barbara Phyllis Rae, da of late Henry Rae Green, of Sydney, NSW, Aust, and has issue.

Arms – Sable, a buck's head cabossed argent, attired or, between the attires a cross patée-fitchée of the last; in chief a lion passant guardant per pale of the second and third; on a canton ermine two bars per pale azure and gules. **Crest** – On a mount vert within seven pales or, the second and fifth charged with a spear-head argent imbrued proper, a hart lodged argent, the dexter foot on a well of the last, and in the mouth a sprig of oak vert.
Residence – Trevean, Highlands Rd, Barton-on-Sea, Hampshire BH25 7BL.

SON LIVING

TIMOTHY PETER MICHAEL CHARLES, *b* 8 July 1970; *ed* Allhallows Sch, and Nene Univ, Northampton.

MOTHER LIVING

Marie Josephine, da of late Simon Peter Mullins: *m* 1937 (*m diss* 1950), as his 1st wife, Sir Brodrick William Charles Elwin Hartwell, 5th Bt, who *d* 1993.

WIDOW LIVING OF FIFTH BARONET

MARY MAUDE, MBE (*Lady Hartwell, MBE*), da of J. W. Church, of Bedford: *m* 1951, as his 2nd wife, Sir Brodrick William Charles Elwin Hartwell, 5th Bt, who *d* 1993. *Residence* – 50 High St, Lavendon, Olney, Bucks MK46 1HA.

COLLATERAL BRANCHES LIVING

Grandchildren of late Sydney Charles Elphinstone Hartwell, 3rd son of 2nd baronet:—
Issue of late Maj-Gen John Redmond Hartwell, CB, DSO, *b* 1887, *d* 1970: *m* 1st, 1911 (*m diss* 1921), Nina Oliver, da of late Gen George Francis William St John, CB; 2ndly, 1929, Hazel Hay Liston, who *d* 1945, da of late Sir John Benton, KCIE; 3rdly, 1946, Edith Elizabeth (4A De Walden Court, Eastbourne), da of late F. W. Frosdyke:—
(By 1st *m*) Diana Marion, *b* 1912: *m* 1st, 1934, Lt-Col Sidney Clive Blaber, RA, who was *ka* Belgium 1944; 2ndly, 1951, Stephen Terrell, OBE, TD, QC, of Tanyard Cottage, Ninfield, Battle, Sussex, and has issue living (by 1st *m*), Marcus, *b* 1942, —— Carol Ann, *b* 1940: *m* 1973, Charles Bruce Nairn (*see* Nairn, Bt), —— (by 2nd *m*) Peter, *b* 1951, — Paul, *b* 1953. —— (By 2nd *m*) Barry Benton, *b* 1933; Cdr RN: *m* 1st, 1956 (*m diss* 1968) Lois Maureen, yst da of Eric C. Bratt, of Bexhill, Sussex; 2ndly, 1970, Elizabeth Linley, yst da of Linley Underwood, of Linden House, Countesthorpe, Leics, and has issue living (by 1st *m*), Karen Fiona, *b* 1961, —— (by 2nd *m*), Jonathan Barry, *b* 1975, —— Charlotte Linley, *b* 1973.

Issue of late Frederick Edward Hartwell, youngest son of 2nd baronet, *b* 1857, *d* 19—: *m* 1881, Susan Mary Ann, da of William Green, of Wannamboor, Victoria, Australia:—
Frederick Sydney, *b* 1886. —— Broderick William, *b* 1889. —— John Malcolm, *b* 1903. —— George Rollen, *b* 1905. —— Ada Wilhelmina, *b* 1887. —— Frances Mary Ann, *b* 1895. —— Julia Sarah, *b* 1901. —— May Alicia, *b* 1908.

Capt Humphrey Hartwell received grants of land in co Limerick and Kings co 1666. The 1st baronet Adm Sir Francis John Hartwell, was Col Deptford and Woolwich Volunteers, and Director of Greenwich Hospital.

HARTY (UK) 1831, of Prospect House, Roebuck, Dublin (Extinct 1939)

Sir LIONEL LOCKINGTON HARTY, 4th and last *Baronet.*

DAUGHTER LIVING OF FOURTH BARONET

Eileen Rhoda. *Residence* – Belrobin, Newtown Park Avenue, Blackrock, Dublin.

HARVEY (UK) 1933, of Threadneedle Street, City of London

(*Sir*) CHARLES RICHARD MUSGRAVE HARVEY, 3rd *Baronet*; 7 April 1937; *s* his father, *Sir* RICHARD MUSGRAVE, 1978, but does not usé title; *ed* Marlborough, and Pembroke Coll, Camb: *m* 1967, Celia Vivien, da of George Henry Hodson, and has issue.

SON LIVING

PAUL RICHARD, *b* 2 June 1971.

DAUGHTER LIVING

Tamara Catherine, *b* 1977.

SISTER LIVING

Joanna Musgrave, *b* 1934: *m* 1958, Angus Donald Macintyre, Fellow of Magdalen Coll, Oxford, of Achaglachgach, by Tarbert, Argyll, and 8 Linton Rd, Oxford, and has issue living, Benedict Richard Pierce, *b* 1963: *m* 1993, Katherine Muir, — Magnus William Lachlan, *b* 1971, — Katherine Cressida Eve, *b* 1962.

AUNTS LIVING (*daughters of 1st baronet*)

Ruth Musgrave (945 Arlington Av, Berkeley, Calif), *b* 1902: *m* 1930 (*m diss* 1953), George MacGowan Harper, and has issue living, Jane Alison, *b* 1932: *m* 1959, Lt-Col Justus Michael Molitor Lenschau, US Army, who *d* 1993, and has issue living, James Gabriel Molitor, *b* 1961: *m* 1989, Angelina Renee, da of Mrs Shirley Huddleston Royer, of Memphis, Tenn, USA (and has issue living, Alexandra *b* 1993), Katherine Jane *b* 1964. —— Eleanor Paget Musgrave, *b* 1905: *m* 1930, Edward Kent Haliburton Karslake (Darell, Bt, colls), who *d* 1988, and has issue living, Antony Edward Kent (Nymet St George House, George Nympton, S Molton, Devon), *b* 1932; Brig late Royal Green Jackets: *m* 1956, June Pauline, el da of Henry William Harris Eastwood, and has issue living, John Burgess (27 Ingersoll Rd, W12) *b* 1956: *m* 1983, Naomi Celia, eldest da of Rt Hon Timothy Hugh Francis Raison, MP (Cunard, Bt, colls), of Hillbreak, Brill, Bucks (and has issue living, Samuel Kent *b* 1990, Eleanor Veldes *b* 1985, Clare Laura, *b* 1988), William Edward Kent (109 Hopton Rd, SW16) *b* 1963: *m* 1989, Sarah Ann, da of William G. Hynard, of Violets Lane, Furneux Pelham, Buntingford, Herts (and has issue living, Emma Kate *b* 1992), Caroline Sarah *b* 1960: *m* 1989, Luis Talavera Corona, son of late Agustin Talavera Becerril, of Mexico City (and has issue living, Thomas *b* 1990, Alexander *b* 1992), Henrietta Sarah *b* 1965: *m* 1993, James B. Forsyth, son of James Forsyth, of Bamburgh, Northumberland, — Sophia Susan (14 Duke St, S Molton, N Devon), *b* 1935: *m* 1964 (*m diss* 1983), Donald Watkins Brown, and has issue living, Stephen Scott *b* 1969, Geoffrey Mark *b* 1972, Bridget Joan *b* 1967, — Mary Leonora, *b* 1944: *m* 1966, Andrew Nicholas Dakin Goodhart, of 35 Mount Park Rd, W5, and has issue living, Gavin John *b* 1976, Rachel Mary *b* 1970, Catherine Jervis Ruth *b* 1973. *Residence* – 13 Duke St, South Molton, N Devon.
The 1st baronet, Sir Ernest Musgrave Harvey, KBE (son of late Rev Charles Musgrave Harvey, V of Hillingdon, Middlesex, and Preb of St Paul's) was a Director and Dep Gov of Bank of England.

Harvie-Watt, see Watt.

Havelock-Allan, see Allan.

HAWKEY (UK) 1945, of Woodford, co Essex (Extinct 1975)

Sir ROGER PRYCE HAWKEY, 2nd and last *Baronet.*

DAUGHTER LIVING OF SECOND BARONET

Sarah Elizabeth, *b* 1934: *m* 1960, William de Vallières Frith, Chevalier de l'Ordre du Merite Agricole (1968), Chevalier de L'Ordre National du Mérite (1976), and Chevalier de la Légion d'Honneur (1992), of Lizards Leap, Warwick, Bermuda, and has issue living, William Roger, *b* 1963, — Benjamin James, *b* 1964, — Carter Andrew, *b* 1970.

HAWKINS (GB) 1778, of Kelston, Somersetshire

PRO·DEO·ET·REGE

For God and the king

Sir HOWARD CÆSAR HAWKINS, 8th *Baronet*; *b* 17 Nov 1956; *s* his father, *Sir* HUMPHRY VILLIERS CAESAR, 1993; *ed* Hilton Coll, S Africa; S African Air Force 1975.

Arms – Argent, on a saltire engrailed sable a quatrefoil between four fleurs-de-lis or. **Crest** – On a mount vert a hind lodged or, the dexter forefoot resting on a gunstone.
Residence –

BROTHER LIVING

RICHARD CAESAR, *b* 29 Dec 1958; *ed* —. *Residence* – .

SISTERS LIVING

Carol Lee, *b* 1953. —— Kathryn Anne, *b* 1954. —— Helena Julia, *b* 1963.

AUNT LIVING (*daughter of 6th baronet*)

Joy Blanche, *b* 1921: *m* 1st, 1944, John Stobart Longworthy; 2ndly, 1977, James Sloane Hume Maxwell, of 35 Ferguson Rd, Illovo, Sandton 2196, S Africa, and has issue living (by 1st *m*), Humphrey John, *b* 1945: *m* 1975, Lynne Edward. —— Veronica Anne, *b* 1951.

WIDOWS LIVING OF SIXTH AND SEVENTH BARONETS

(MARJORIE) BLANCHE (*Blanche, Lady Hawkins*), da of Arthur Edward Hampden-Smithers, of Springs, Transvaal: *m* 1920, Sir Villiers Geoffrey Caesar Hawkins, 6th Bt, who *d* 1955. *Residence* – 187 Lynnwood Road, Brooklyn, Pretoria, Transvaal, S Africa.
ANITA (*Lady Hawkins*), da of Charles H. Funkey, of Michigan, USA: *m* 1952, Sir Humphry Villiers Caesar Hawkins, 7th Bt, who *d* 1993. *Residence* – 41 Hume Rd, Dunkeld, Johannesburg, S Africa.

COLLATERAL BRANCHES LIVING

Grandchildren of late Arthur Cæsar Hawkins, 7th son of 3rd baronet:—
Issue of late Percy Cæsar Hawkins, *b* 1863, *d* 19—: *m* 18—, Catherine Ripkin, who *d* 1937:—
Rupert Cæsar, *b* 1901. —— Oscar Cæsar, *b* 1908: *m* 19—, Zella Bunn, and has issue living, John Michael Cæsar, *b* 19—, —— Patrick Cæsar, *b* 19—. —— Percy Cæsar, *b* 1910. —— Julia Louisa, *b* 19—. —— Kathleen Laura, *b* 19—. —— Cecelia Margaret, *b* 19—. —— Adeline Daisy, *b* 19—.
Issue of late Cyril Cæsar Hawkins, *b* 1878, *d* 1955: *m* 1909, Lulu, who *d* 1955, da of W. H. E. During:—
Marie, *b* 1910. *Residence* – Johannesburg, S Africa.

Grandchildren of late Reginald Hawkins, 2nd son of late Rev Henry Annesley Hawkins (*infra*):—
Issue of late Lieut-Col Eustace Fellowes Sinclair Hawkins, DSO, OBE, RASC, *b* 1881, *d* 1954: *m* 1908, Patience, da of Capt J. Henderson, late 12th Lancers:—
Patrick Reginald Cæsar, *b* 1918. —— Honour Marie Marguerite, *b* 1913.

Grandchildren of late Rev Henry Annesley Hawkins, yr son of the Rev Charles Hawkins, eldest son of Serjeant-Surgeon Charles Hawkins 4th son of 1st baronet:—
Issue of late Arthur Cockburn Hawkins, *b* 1852, *d* 19—: *m* 1883, Agnes, da of H. Carmichael:—
Henry Cecil Carmichael, *b* 1884: *m* 1907, Winnifred, da of John Robinson, and has issue living, Cecil Arthur Robinson, *b* 1908, — Harold Percy, *b* 1909, —— Winnifred Agnes Ruth, *b* 1910. —— Arthur Charles, *b* 1885. —— Reginald Cæsar, *b* 1890. —— Agnes Isabel, *b* 1889. —— Frances Kathleen, *b* 1892.

Granddaughter of late Cdr Caesar Hugh Hawkins, RN, elder son of late Rev Charles James Hawkins, elder son of late Rev Charles James Hawkins (*ante*):—
Issue of late Caesar Hugh George Wills Hawkins, *b* (*posthumous*) 1889, *d* 1947: *m* 1st, 1914 (*m diss* 1926), Margaret Edith, who *d* 1980, da of late James Shaw Robertson, of The Vache, Chalfont St Giles; 2ndly, 1930, Diodata (who *d* 1991, having *m* 2ndly, 1948 (*m diss* 1956), Archibald Laurence Lyall, who *d* 1964, and 3rdly, 19—, Marco Lucic-Roki, of Venice), da of late Count Bernhard Caboga, of Dubrovnik, Ragusa:—
(By 1st *m*) Margaret Elizabeth Anne, *b* 1917: *m* 1st, 1940, Lieut Hilliard Baxley Wilson, USNR, who *d* 1961; 2ndly, 1967, James Rowland Lowe, who *d* 1969, and *d* 1986, leaving issue (by 1st *m*), Penelope Jane, *b* 1944: *m* 1st, 1972 (*m diss* 19—), Michael McClure; 2ndly, 19—, Charles Giorgi. *Residence* – 947 Green St, San Francisco, Calif 94133, USA.

Granddaughter of late Cæsar Hugh George Wills Hawkins (*ante*):—
Issue of late Lieut Cæsar Charles Hawkins, DSC, RN, *b* 1915, *d* on active ser 1940: *m* 1937, Mary Redwood Vachell (who *m* 2ndly, 1945, Desmond John Dudley Torrens, MBE, MB, late Lieut-Col RAMC, and *d* 1962), da of Edmund Hann:—
Alice Penelope, *b* 1938: *m* 1961, Robin Audley Clinton Vivian, B92 Res Amiral, Marina Baie des Anges 06270, Villeneuve-Loubet, France (*see* B Vivian, colls).

Granddaughter of late Edward Caesar Hawkins, son of late Caesar Richard Hawkins, son of late Rev Edward Hawkins, DD, el son of late Rev Edward Hawkins, 5th son of 1st baronet:—
Issue of late Cdr Richard Pennell Caesar Hawkins, RN, *b* 1899, *d* 1990: *m* 1st, 1929 (*m diss* 1952), Enid Helen, who *d* 1983, da of Rev John Warren Corbould-Warren, Rector of Caistor with Markshall; 2ndly, 1964, Mary Constance Emily (Shelton Hall, Long Stratton, Norfolk), da of Rev Frank Percy Law, Rector of Shelton, Norfolk:—
(By 1st *m*), Diana Elizabeth, *b* 1930: *m* 1953, Anthony Pott.

Grandson of late Rev Robert Hawkins, 4th son of late Rev Edward Hawkins (*ante*):—
Issue of late Col Herbert Pennell Hawkins, CBE, *b* 1859, *d* 1940: *m* 1910, Hester Vera, who *d* 1972, da of Fleetwood Rynd, formerly of Mount Armstrong, co Kildare:—
Gerald Francis Cæsar (Newton Orchard, Pound Lane, Whitestone, Exeter EX4 2LJ), *b* 1912; *ed* Eton, and Oxford Univ (BM and BCh), MRCS England and LRCP London; 1939-45 War as Maj RAMC: *m* 1940, Patricia Enid Lambart, da of Maj

Alexander George Lambart Sladen, MC, of Crabtree Furlong, Haddenham, Bucks, and has issue living, Julia Margaret, *b* 1946: *m* 1971, Ilgvars Spruntulis, of 26 Homefield Rd, Heavitree, Exeter, Devon, and has issue living, Ben *b* 1979, Liza Mia *b* 1975.
The 1st baronet, Sir Cæsar Hawkins (son of late Cæsar Hawkins), was Serjeant-Surg to George II and George III.

HAWLEY (GB) 1795, of Leybourne Grange, Kent

Sir HENRY NICHOLAS HAWLEY, 8th *Baronet*; *b* 26 Nov 1939; *s* his father, *Maj* Sir DAVID HENRY, 1988 (but does not use title); *ed* Stowe.

Arms – Vert, a saltire engrailed or. **Crest** – A dexter arm in armour proper, garnished or, holding in the hand a spear in bend sinister, point downwards, also proper.
Residence – No Man's Friend, New York, Lincoln LN4 4YE.

SISTERS LIVING

Margaret Serena, *b* 1946. *Residence* – 49 Watling Cres, Handbridge, Chester CH4 7HD. —— Penelope Marion, *b* 1948: *m* 1971, Richard M. Mansell-Jones. *Residence* – 19 Astell St, SW3 3RT.

WIDOW LIVING OF SEVENTH BARONET

HERMIONE (*Lady Hawley*), da of late Col Lancelot Mare Gregson, OBE (*see* E Lichfield, 1973-74 Edn): *m* 1938, Maj Sir David Henry Hawley, 7th Bt, KRRC, who *d* 1988. *Residence* – Tanglewood, 36 Louth Rd, Horncastle, Lincs.

HAWORTH (UK) 1911, of Dunham Massey, co Chester

Sir PHILIP HAWORTH, 3rd *Baronet*; *b* 17 Jan 1927; *s* his father, *Sir* (ARTHUR) GEOFFREY, 1987; *ed* Dauntseys, and Reading Univ (BSc 1948): *m* 1951, Joan Helen, da of late Stanley Percival Clark, of Ipswich, and has issue.

Arms – Azure, on a bend between two stags' heads couped or, as many garbs gules. **Crest** – Issuant out of grass proper a stag's head gules arme and collared with a chain or.
Residence – Free Green Farm, Over Peover, Knutsford, Cheshire WA16 9QX.

SONS LIVING

CHRISTOPHER, *b* 6 Nov 1951; *ed* Rugby, and Reading Univ (BSc); ARICS. *Residence* – 11 Mossbury Rd, SW11 2PA. —— Mark, *b* 1956; *ed* Rugby. —— Simon Nicholas, *b* 1961; *ed* Rugby, and Reading Univ. —— Adam Ewart, *b* 1964; *ed* Rugby, and Magdalene Coll, Camb.

DAUGHTER LIVING

Penelope Jane, *b* 1953; *ed* Sheffield Univ.

BROTHER LIVING

Jeremy Geoffrey, *b* 1931; *ed* Dauntseys, and New Coll, Oxford. *Residence* – The Bog Farm, Minsterley, Shropshire.

SISTERS LIVING

Jennefer, *b* 1928: *m* 1952, Herbert Hilton Minnis, and has issue living, Sterling Herbert, *b* 1953, — Russell Harold, *b* 1954, — Quentin Geoffrey, *b* 1963, — Royan Alexander, *b* 1974, — Jedda Alison, *b* 1957, — Sonya Jennefer, *b* 1960. *Address* – PO Box 1720, Nassau, Bahamas. —— Alison, *b* 1934: *m* 1958, Richard Crosfield Godlee, of The Grange, Clay Lane, Handforth, Wilmslow, Ches, and has issue living, Deborah Claire, *b* 1961, — Sarah Haworth, *b* 1965.
The 1st baronet, Sir Arthur Adlington Haworth (son of late Abraham Haworth, JP, of Bowdon, Cheshire), sat as MP for S Div of Manchester (*L*) 1906-12, and was a Junior Lord of the Treasury Feb to March 1912.

HAY (NS) 1635, of Smithfield, and Haystoun, Peeblesshire (Dormant 1966)

Sir BACHE MCEVERS ATHOLE HAY, 11th *Baronet*; *d* 1966, and at time of going to press no name appears on the Official Roll of Baronets in respect of this title.

COLLATERAL BRANCHES LIVING

Issue of late Capt Robert Athole Hay, elder brother of 11th baronet, *b* 1890, *d* 1939: *m* 1914, Margaret, who *d* 1928, da of late Richard Heywood Heywood Jones, of Badsworth Hall, York:—

Sarah Dorothea, *b* 1924: *m* 1946, David Rimington Tetley, of Brawby Park, Malton, N Yorks, and has issue living, Christopher Michael (Manor Farm, Little Habton, N Yorks), *b* 1948; *ed* Harrow; Capt 16th/5th Lancers: *m* 1972, Camilla Ann Molyneux Linton, da of late Maj-Gen Gerald Patrick Linton Weston, CB, CBE, DSO, of N Warnborough, Hants, and has issue living, Hugo Donald *b* 1975, Robin David *b* 1977, Charlotte Rose *b* 1979, Fiona Myfanwy *b* 1982, — Catherine Jane (49 Acacia Gdns, Bathpool, Taunton, Somerset), *b* 1950: *m* 1973 (*m diss* 1982), James Kimber McGavin, and has issue living, Joseph Sule Eric *b* 1974, Emma Simone *b* 1976, and further issue (by Francis Deas), Briar Dawn Annu *b* 1979.

Descendants of John, 3rd Lord Hay of Yester, great-great-uncle of 1st baronet, of whom the Marquess of Tweeddale is the presumed heir to the baronetcy.

The 1st baronet was an Esquire of the body of James VI. With his patent of baronetcy he received 16,000 acres of land in Nova Scotia. The 3rd baronet inherited only the title, which on his death, in 1683, became dormant. In 1762 James Hay, MD, claimed and assumed the baronetcy, was served heir to his great-great-grandfather, John Hay of Kingsmeadows — a younger brother of the grandfather of the 1st baronet — by a jury assembled at Perth 1805, and subsequently, in 1806, matriculated arms as a baronet in the Lyon Office.

HAY (NS) 1663, of Park, Wigtownshire

Sir JOHN ERROLL AUDLEY HAY OF PARK, 11th *Baronet*; *b* 3 Dec 1935; *s* his father, *Sir* ARTHUR THOMAS ERROLL, ISO, 1993; *ed* Gordonstoun, and St Andrew's Univ (MA honours 1960).

Arms – Argent, three escutcheons gules and in chief an ox-yoke fesseways proper.
Address – c/o National Westminster Bank, Fitzroy Square, London W1P 6DX.

WIDOW LIVING OF TENTH BARONET

ROSEMARY EVELYN ANNE (*Lady Hay of Park*), da of late Vice Adm Aubrey Lambert, and formerly wife of Nigel de Glanville Waymouth: *m* 1943, as his 2nd wife, Sir Arthur Thomas Erroll Hay of Park, 10th Bt, ISO, who *d* 1993. *Address* – c/o Lloyds Bank, Farnham, Surrey GU9 7HT.

COLLATERAL BRANCH LIVING

Issue of late Arthur George Beresford Hay, 3rd son of 8th baronet, *b* 1878, *d* 1949: *m* 1913, Louise Emily May, who *d* 1939, da of late Lieut-Col Henry Robert Carden, DL, of Fishmoyne, Tipperary:—

Evelyn Alice Carden, *b* 1914: *m* 1945, Charles John Barton, late Palestine Police, and has issue living, Mary Hay, *b* 1948.

The present baronet is senior male representative of Sir Gilbert Hay, of Dronlaw, 2nd son of Sir Thomas Hay, of Erroll, Constable of Scotland. By the marriage of Sir John Hay, 7th Bt of Park, with Sarah Beresford Cossins (da of John Cossins by Hon Elizabeth Susannah Thicknesse Tuchet, da of 19th Baron Audley), his descendants are in remainder to the Barony of Audley.

HAY (NS) 1703, of Alderston

Spare Nought

Sir RONALD FREDERICK HAMILTON HAY, 12th *Baronet*; *b* 1941; *s* his father, *Sir* RONALD NELSON, 1988: *m* 1978, Kathleen, da of John Thake, and has issue.

Arms – Quarterly: 1st and 4th, azure, three fraises, *Fraser*; 2nd and 3rd, gules, three bars ermine, *Gifford of Yester*; over all, upon an escutcheon of pretence argent three escutcheons gules, in the centre a key fesseways wards downwards sable, *Hay*. Crest – A goat's head erased, argent, armed or.
Residence – Aspendale, Victoria 3195, Australia.

SONS LIVING

ALEXANDER JAMES, *b* 1979. —— Anthony Ronald, *b* 1984.

DAUGHTER LIVING

Sarah Jane, *b* 1981.

SISTER LIVING

Pamela Rosemary, *b* 1945: *m* 1972, Michael Edward Finnegan, and has issue living, Mark Andrew, *b* 1977, — Jodie Dawn, *b* 1980.

AUNTS LIVING

Lucy, b 1901. —— Thelma Violet, b 1914: m 1938, Frank Coulton, and has issue living. *Residence* – Unit 38, Gleneaon, 207 Forest Way, Belrose, NSW 2085, Australia.

WIDOW LIVING OF ELEVENTH BARONET

RITA (*Rita, Lady Hay*), da of John Munyard: m 1940, Sir Ronald Nelson Hay, 11th Bt, who d 1988. *Residence* – 17 Murrumbeena Crescent, Murrumbeena, Victoria 3163, Australia.

COLLATERAL BRANCHES LIVING

Issue of late Howard Augustus Hay, 4th son of 6th baronet, b 1828, d 1884: m 1853, Sarah, who d 1902, da of Henry Harris, of Bitterne, Southampton:—
Douglas Hector, b 1869: m 1896, Amy Margaret, da of Alexander Jansen, formerly of Ridgway, Ontario, Canada, and has issue living, Douglas Howard Jerome, b 1898, — Thelma Arline, b 1903. —— Jane Sophia Louisa: m 1902, William Watts, and has issue living, Ernest Hay, b 1904.

Grandchildren of late James Shaw Hay (infra):—
Issue of late Conran Ker Hay, b 1882, d 1958: m 1908, Grace, who d 1960, da of Thomas B. Horsfield, of Manchester:—
Alexander Horsfield (Westtown School, Westtown, Pa, USA 19395), b 1912; MA; a Sch Teacher: m 1st, 1939, Bernice Louise, who d 1968, da of Walter C. Woodward, of Richmond, Indiana, USA; 2ndly, 1969, Agnes Marshall, da of George Ferguson Finnie, of Glasgow, and has issue living (by 1st m), Conran Alexander, b 1946, — Arminal Elizabeth, b 1943. —— Gordon Conran (689 Westmount Hill's Drive, London, Ont, Canada), b 1919, MEd, Prof Emeritus: m 1943, Elizabeth Jean, da of Edward Henry Stevenson, of Renfrew, Ont, Canada, and has issue living, Stuart Gordon, b 1946; MSc: m 1975, Christiane Morisset, of St Michel, Quebec, and has issue living, Gregoire Alexander b 1976, — Alexander Edward, b 1949; PhD: m 1984, Jocelyne Hellou, of Montreal, and has issue living, Philip Conran b 1988, Natasha Bronwen b 1986, — Elizabeth Grace, b 1951; BA: m 1985, Mark Fried, of Swampscott, Mass, USA, and has issue living, Ben Angus b 1988, Sochi Bess b 1985, — Jean Anne, b 1957; BMus: m 1989, Ignatius Solis, of Mexico City, and has issue living, Carlos Andreas b 1990.
Issue of late Thomas Corlett Hay, VD, b 1883, d 1952: m 1930, Muriel, da of the Rev Charles Harry Dant, R of Babcary, Taunton:—
Pamela Jane, b 1931: m 1956, John G. Ewing, and has issue living, James Johanathan, b 1965, — Masindi Jane, b 1958, — Katherine Winifred Anne, b 1963. —— Bettine Muriel, b 1932; a SRN: m 1962, René Bouganon, of Johannesburg.

Granddaughter of late Alexander Murray Hay, el son of late Capt John Hay, half-brother of 5th baronet:—
Issue of late James Shaw Hay, b 1850, d 1908: m 1st, 1880, Charlotte Anne, da of William Corlett, of Ramsey, Isle of Man; 2ndly, 1889, Arminal Walmsley, da of James Scotson, of Liverpool:—
(By 2nd m) Muriel Scotston, b 1891: m 1921, Georges Louis Bard.

Grandchildren of late Loraine Macdonald Hay (infra):—
Issue of late Sydney Bertram Macdonald Hay, b 1918, d 1981: m 1945, Joan Reis:—
Phillip Michael Macdonald, b 1946. —— Roger Macdonald, b 1948. —— Aubrey Andrew Macdonald, b 1949. —— Edmund Macdonald, b 1954. —— Anthony Macdonald, b 1956. —— Ann Maureen, b 1951. —— Kathleen, b 1953.

Grandchildren of late Loraine Geddes Hay, 3rd son of late Lt-Col Thomas Pasley Hay, 3rd son of late Capt John Hay (ante):—
Issue of late Loraine Macdonald Hay, b 1883, d 1961: m 1917, Mequeline Eugenie Hamel-Smith, who d 1978:—
Denise Rita, b 1920: m 1st, 1940, Rudolph Armine Moze, who d 1944; 2ndly, 1948, Roberto Pelgo Lopez; 3rdly, 1954, Rupert Loraine Hay (infra), and has issue living, (by 1st m) Patricia Angela, b 1941: m 1970, Senator Conrad O'Brien, and has issue living, Jason Errol b 1973, Sharon Mary b 1971. —— Mary Mildred, b 1924: m 1948, Aldred Mitchell, and has issue living, Alfred Bernard, b 1950, — William Joseph, b 1958, — Bernadette Mary, b 1949: m 1969, Michael David Diaz, and has issue living, Pamela Bernadette b 1970, — Denise Mequeline, b 1951: m 19—, John A. C. Forster, and has issue living, Andrew Donald b 1969, — Nanette Celine, b 1954, — Susan Marie, b 1955, — Sidney Debra, b 1959.
Issue of late James Carrington Hay, b 1888, d 1961: m 1921, Maria Cynthia Fifi, who d 1956:—
Rupert Loraine (Alderston, Smart St, St Augustine, Trinidad), b 1924: m 1954, Denise Rita (ante), da of late Loraine Macdonald Hay. —— Ranald Louis, b 1925; ed St Francis Xavier Univ (BSc), and McGill Univ (BEng), PEng Ont: m 1955, Lorraine Marianné, da of late Frederick John Fecteau, of Toronto, and has issue living, Ranald Joseph, b 1956, — Dominic Louis, b 1958, — Cynthia Maria, b 1959, — Genevieve Anne, b 1960, — Marianne Noel, b 1962, — Laurie Elizabeth, b 1965. —— Donald Joseph (Smart St, St Augustine, Trinidad), b 1927: m 1955, Lola Sue Martin, and has issue living, Donald Roger Paul, b 1956; ed Kent State Univ, Ohio, USA (BSc Architecture), and Wisconsin Univ, Milwaukee (Masters in Architecture and Urban Planning): m 1982, Maureen Ellen Baker, of Cleveland, Ohio, — Bruce Victor Joseph, b 1959; ed W Indies Univ, Trinidad (BSc Eng), — Christopher Michael Charles, b 1967, — Paula Emily Rebecca, b 1966.

Grandchildren of late Maj-Gen Woulfe Hay, son of late Lieut-Col Thomas Pasley Hay (ante):—
Issue of late Alexander Hay, b 1872, d 1923: m 1909, Kathleen, da of late Gordon Styles Hare, of Croydon:—
James Woulfe, b 1910: m 1933, Edith Mary, da of Arthur Henry Myrton, of Johannesburg, S Africa, and has issue living, Bertha Lillian, b 1934. —— Hilda Rose, b 1937. —— William Henry Ker, b 1912: m 1938, Violet Mary, da of late Harold Mortimer, of Manchester, and has issue living, Lynette Florence, b 1939, — Evadne Felicity, b 1943, — Merilyn Wendy, b 1951. *Residence* – Summer Place, 4 Sunbird St, Elspark, Elsburg, Transvaal, S Africa.

Descendants of late Thomas Hay (Lord Huntingdon, a Scottish Lord of Session), grandfather of 5th baronet:—

Grandchildren of late William Montgomery Hay, son of late Capt Henry Hird Hay, 5th Dragoon Guards, great-grandson of late Thomas Hay (ante):—
Issue of late Vincent Henry Hay, b 1889, d 1949: m 1915, Edicel Bassett, who d 1959:—
Wayne W., b 1918: m 1942, Harriet Johnson, and has issue living, Michael William, b 1943, — Robert Wayne, b 1950, — Ronald Patrick, b 1957, — Barbara Ann, b 1945, — Becky Ann, b 1948, — Jacqueline Marie, b 1953, — Catherine Marie, b 1960. —— Helen Francis, b 1922: m 1946, Richard Connell, and has issue living, Thomas Richard, b 1949, — Timothy Peter Joseph, b 1959, — Mary Theresa Louise, b 1947, — Mary Catherine, b 1952, — Mary Anita, b 1954, — Mary Jennifer, b 1956, — Mary Elizabeth, b 1958.

Granddaughter of late Capt Henry Hird Hay, 5th Dragoon Guards (ante):—
Issue of late Vincent Henry Fulford Hay, b 1868, d 1936: m 1905, Olive Ellen, da of Thomas John Richards, of Liskeard, Cornwall:—

Majorie Letitia, *b* 1907: *m* 1937, Frederick Guy Darvall, banker, and has issue living, Diana Hay, *b* 1938. *Address* – c/o National Bank of Australasia Ltd, Jandowaae, Queensland.

This family, anciently seated at Huntingdon, E Lothian, and at Mordington and Thornydykes Berwickshire, is descended in direct line from the old House of Lockerwort and Yester, whose progenitor was William de Haya (cup bearer to Malcolm IV and William the Lion), who *d* 1170. Sir John Hay, 1st baronet (el son of Thomas Hay, of Alderston, E Lothian (lineally descended from Sir Edmond Hay, of Linplum (*v* 1429-49), younger brother of Sir David Hay, of Yester (*v* 1475), ancestor of the Marquesses of Tweeddale)), was *cr* a Baronet with remainder to heirs male forever. The 8th Baronet, Sir William Henry, a housepainter by trade, *d* in Australia in 1927, and was *s* by his brother, Sir Edward Hamilton, who *d* 1936, without proving his succession or using the title.

DALRYMPLE-HAY (GB) 1798, of Park Place, Wigtownshire

Sir JAMES BRIAN DALRYMPLE-HAY, 6th *Baronet*, son of late Lieut-Col Brian George Rowland Dalrymple-Hay, son of late George Houston Dalrymple-Hay, son of late Col George James Dalrymple-Hay, 2nd son of 2nd baronet; *b* 19 Jan 1928; *s* his kinsman, *Sir* CHARLES JOHN *CVO*, 1952; *ed* Blundell's; sometime Lieut RM: *m* 1958, Helen Sylvia, da of late Stephen Herbert Card, of Reigate, Surrey, and has issue.

Arms – Quarterly: 1st and 4th, or, on a saltire azure nine lozenges of the field, all within a bordure gules; 2nd and 3rd, argent, three escutcheons gules in chief on ox yoke lying fess-ways proper. **Crests** – 1st, a rock per pale azure and or; 2nd, between two piles or issuant from the torse a falcon proper, charged on the breast with an escutcheon gules. **Supporters** – Two volunteers belonging to the Corps of Wigton in their uniforms of the year 1800 all proper.
Residence – The Red House, Church St, Warnham, Horsham, W Sussex RH12 3QW.

DAUGHTERS LIVING

Fiona Louise, *b* 1963: *m* 1993, Richard M. Norcross, only son of Donald Norcross, of Churchdown, Glos. —— Charlotte Ann, *b* 1966. —— Lucie Helen, *b* 1969.

BROTHERS LIVING

JOHN HUGH (Little Meadow, Forty Green Rd, Knotty Green, Beaconsfield, Bucks HP9 1XL), *b* 16 Dec 1929; *ed* Blundell's Sch; sometime Capt R Scots Fusiliers: *m* 1962, Jennifer Phyllis Roberta, da of late Brig Robert Johnston, CBE, and has issue living, Malcolm John Robert, *b* 1966. —— Ronald George Inglis (Glenluce, Lee's Gully Rd, Tetoro RD4, Waiuku, Auckland, NZ), *b* 1933; *ed* Blundell's Sch: *m* 1973, Anne Valerie, da of Bernard James Dawson, and has issue living, Russell James *b* 1977.

HALF-BROTHER LIVING

Christopher Hamish (Klein Constantia, PO Box 160, Letsitele, 0885, N Transvaal), *b* 1941: *m* 1968, Margaret Linda Smith, and has issue living, Hamish Ian, *b* 1971, — Amanda Jane *b* 1975.

COLLATERAL BRANCHES LIVING

Granddaughter of late Col George Houston Dalrymple-Hay, 5th and yst son of late Col George James Darlymple-Hay, 2nd son of 2nd baronet:—
Issue of late Lt-Col Hugh Brereton Dalrymple-Hay, DSO, IA, *b* 1900, *d* 1987: *m* 1939, Gwendyth Margaret (who *m* 2ndly, 1994, — Blake, of 1a Moorfield Rd, Woodbridge, Suffolk), da of late Lt-Col Norman L. Callard:—
Janet Margaret, *b* 1941: *m* 1963 (*m diss* 1986), Anthony David Stericker, only son of J. A. Stericker and has issue living, Johanna Margaret, *b* 1966, — Sophia Harriett, *b* 1968, — Lucinda Jean, *b* 1969. *Residence* – Brownings, Pytches Rd, Woodbridge, Suffolk.

Granddaughter of late Lt-Col Stair Francis Barton Dalrymple-Hay, yst son of late Col George James Dalrymple-Hay (ante):—
Issue of late Com Christopher Montague Vernon Francis Dalrymple-Hay, DSC, RN, *b* 1896; *d* on active ser 1944: *m* 1st, 1919 (*m diss* 1929), Mary Teresa, who *d* 1977, yr twin da of late Lt-Col Edward Henry Joseph Mostyn (Mostyn, Bt, colls); 2ndly, 1929, Helen Violet, da of H. K. Grierson, formerly of Castle Douglas:—
(By 1st *m*) Mary Cecily Edith Teresa, *b* 1920: *m* 1947, John Walter Ferlex Lloyd-Johnes.

Granddaughter of late Houston Stewart Dalrymple-Hay, 3rd son of 2nd baronet:—
Issue of late James Stewart Dalrymple-Hay, *b* 1860, *d* 1931: *m* 1886, Emily, da of William Irving:—
Mary Grace (Glenluce, Woy Woy, NSW), *b* 1888.

Grandchildren of late Richard Tycho Dalrymple Hay (infra):—
Issue of late Charles Stewart Dalrymple-Hay, MC, *b* 1891, *d* 1972: *m* 1922, Barbara (22 Amaroo Pl, Yass, NSW), da of late Warwick Chambers, of Sydney, NSW:—
John Warwick (Glen Luce, Free Selectors Rd, RMB 337A Fox Ground, NSW 2534) *b* 1928; author and lecturer: *m* 1953, Barbara Deidre, da of M. Moir, of Canberra, and has issue living, Heather Nan, *b* 1954, — Ann Louise, *b* 1956. —— Ann, *b* 1924; 1939-45 War with WRANS: *m* 1947, David Thompson, stockbroker, of 41 Bundabah Av, St Ives, Sydney, NSW.

Grandchildren of late Houston Stewart Dalrymple-Hay (ante):—
Issue of late Claude Thomas Hugh Vans Dalrymple-Hay, *b* 1865, *d* 1953: *m* 1898 (*m diss* 1921), Belle, who *d* 1967, da of Frank Wheelhouse:—

Houston Francis Wilfred, *b* 1907; an Assoc of Australian Soc of Accountants: *m* 1st, 1938 (*m diss* 1943), Marie Hawke; 2ndly, 1967, Olive May, da of late John Jacob Worner. *Residence* – 5/55 King Street, Wollstonecraft, NSW 2065, Australia. —— Isobel Ellen Ruby (Unit 2, Retirement Village Laurieton, NSW 2443) *b* 1904: *m* 1924, Arthur John Peverley Hall, LLB, who *d* 1975 and has issue living, Isobel Wendy Anne, *b* 1928.

Issue of late Houston Stewart Dalrymple-Hay, *b* 1871, *d* 1956: *m* 1906, Daisy Annie, who *d* 1928, da of David Davis, of Christchurch, New Zealand:—

Houston Stewart, *b* 1909; formerly Capt 2nd Australian Imperial Force: *m* 19—, Peggy Fitzmaurice, who *d* 1982, da of Argyle Charles Charleston Loftus, of Brighton, Victoria, and has issue living, Charles Stewart, *b* 1949. —— Helene Fitzmaurice, *b* 1951: *m* 1975, Christopher James Bell, of 181 Rymans Rd, Eltham North, Vic 3095, and has issue living, Simon Christopher *b* 1981, James Stewart *b* 1983. *Residence* – 96 Raglan Street, Mosman, NS Wales. —— Barbara (4 Howell Av, Lane Cove, Sydney, NS Wales), *b* 1938, Charles John Newhill Leleu, OBE, formerly Roy Australian Air Force, who *d* 1961, and has issue living, John Stewart Newhill, *b* 1939, — Antonia Blanche Newhill, *b* 1945: *m* 1971, Melchor Puig Scribani, of Caracas, Venezuela, now of 38 Lady St, Mt Colan, NSW, and has issue living, Damian Antonio *b* 1972, Natalia Daniela *b* 1975. —— Nancy Stair, *b* 1915: *m* 1940, Frank Lawrence Fletcher, and has issue living, James Lawrence, *b* 1941, — Susan Stair, *b* 1945: *m* 1970, Peter Brian Barton Pollock, of 26 Ryeburn Av, E Hawthorn, Victoria, NSW, and has issue living, Peter James *b* 1972, Simon Stewart *b* 1974, Robert Lawrence *b* 1978. — Josephine Daisy, *b* 1948: *m* 1972, Timothy Martin Harpur, of 22 Suffolk Av, Collaroy, NSW, and has issue living, Richard Sydney Frank *b* 1978, Sophie Irene *b* 1974, Elizabeth Nancy (twin) *b* 1974. *Residence* – 6 Beauty Point Rd, Beauty Point, NSW. —— Elizabeth Mary, *b* 1921: *m* 1947, Roy Charles Cooper, CBE, and has issue living, Peter Charles *b* 1951: *m* 1984, Catherine Black, and has issue living, Elizabeth Marie *b* 1985, Zoe Catherine *b* 1987, — Donald Stewart, *b* 1957: *m* 1987, Heather-Mary, — Sally Victoria, *b* 1948: *m* 1969, John Neale Sturrock, and has issue living, Angus John *b* 1973, Kate Elizabeth *b* 1975. *Residence* – Unit 12, Coronation Towers, 24 Dunmore Terr, Auchenflower, Qld 4066, Australia.

The 1st baronet, Col Sir John Dalrymple, of Dunragit, Wigtownshire, married the daughter of Sir Thomas Hay, 3rd Bt, of Park, on inheriting whose estates in 1794 he assumed by Roy licence the name of Hay. The 3rd baronet, Adm Rt Hon Sir John Charles, sat as MP for Wakefield (C) 1862-65, for Stamford 1866-80, and for Wigton Burghs 1880-85. The 5th baronet, Sir Charles John Dalrymple-Hay, CVO, was a Clerk in Foreign Office 1887-95, and in Privy Council Office 1895-1928.

HEAD (UK) 1838, of Rochester, Kent

Sir FRANCIS DAVID SOMERVILLE HEAD, 5th *Baronet*; *b* 17 Oct 1916; *s* his father, *Sir* ROBERT POLLOCK SOMERVILLE 1924; *ed* Eton, and Peterhouse, Camb (BA 1937); Major (ret) Queen's Own Cameron Highlanders; 1939-45 War: *m* 1st, 1950 (*m diss* 1965), Susan Patricia, da of late Arthur Douglas Ramsay, OBE (*see* Ramsay, Bt, *cr* 1806, colls); 2ndly, 1967, Penelope Marion Acheson, da of late Wilfrid Archibald Alexander (*see* Hagart-Alexander, Bt) and has issue by 1st *m*.

Arms – Argent, a chevron ermines between three unicorns, heads couped sable. **Crest** – A unicorn's head, couped ermine.
Residence – 63 Chantry View Rd, Guildford, Surrey GU1 3XU. *Club* – Naval and Military.

SON LIVING (By 1st marriage)

RICHARD DOUGLAS SOMERVILLE, *b* 16 Jan 1951; *ed* Eton, Magdalene Coll, Camb (BA), and Bristol Poly (BA): *m* 1991, Edwina, da of late Edward Mansell, of Underwood, Notts.

DAUGHTER LIVING (By 1st marriage)

Diana Mary Frances, *b* 1954; BA: *m* 1983, Michael Robert Parkin, only son of F. R. Parkin, of Pittenween, Fife, and has issue living, Zuleika Florence Rosa, *b* 1988.

BROTHER LIVING

John Kenelm Somerville, *b* 1918; *ed* Wellington Coll, and at Oriel Coll, Oxford (MA); BEd Calgary; 1939-45 War, with RAMC and Intelligence Corps: *m* 1942, Lilah Doreen Prittie Wingfield, da of late Lt-Col Samuel James Chatterton Prittie Perry, FRCS (V Powerscourt, colls), and has issue living, Patrick John Somerville (1406-20, Avenue N, Lethbridge, Alberta, T1H 4W3, Canada), *b* 1943: *m* 1971 (*m diss* 1986), Karen Carla, da of Emanuel Karl Schaufele, of Schuler, Alberta, Canada, and has issue living, Kathleen Patricia *b* 1974, Sheila Nadine *b* 1979, — David Charles Somerville (2627-49 A Street, Edmonton, Alberta T6L 3X2), *b* 1949: *m* 1978, Constance Faye, da of Clifford Schowalter, of Edmonton, Alberta, and has issue living, Phillip Arthur Somerville *b* 1983, Graeme Douglas Somerville *b* 1986, Alana Christine *b* 1991, — Sarah Grace Edith, *b* 1947: *m* 1972, Ronald James Zezulka, of 331 Queensland Rd SE, Calgary T2J 3S4, Alberta, Canada, and has issue living, Michael John Jaroslav *b* 1977, — Angela Lilah Mary (twin) *b* 1949: *m* 1973, Joseph Andrew Panter, of Box 242, Clyde, Alberta T0G 0PO, Canada, and has issue living, David James *b* 1974, Jennifer Anne *b* 1979. *Residence* – 123 First St NW, Medicine Hat, Alberta T1A 6H2, Canada.

SISTER LIVING

Angela Grace Mary *b* 1922: *m* 1941, Henry Paddison Granlund, DSC, who *d* 1993. late Lt RNVR, and has issue living, Hew Richard Paddison (7 Bell Hill Ridge, Petersfield, Hants GU32 2DZ), *b* 1943; BA, CDipAF; Lt-Cdr RN: *m* 1977, Gillian Hazel, da of Rev Canon J. J. Cresswell, of Eastleach, Turville, Glos, and has issue living, Charles Richard Alexander *b* 1979, Angus Gordon Howard *b* 1981, — Karen Mary, *b* 1945: *m* 1981, Jeremy Patrick New, of 3 Bythorn St, SW9, — Margaret Jane, *b* 1950: *m* 1st, 1973 (*m diss* 1977), Anthony Hewett-Hicks; 2ndly, 1988, Christopher Ian Peters, of 1 Dunkirk Bank, Amberley, Stroud, Glos GL5 5AX, and has issue living, George Duncan *b* 1990. *Residence* – Little Weekhayne, Southleigh, Colyton, Devon EX13 6JA.

COLLATERAL BRANCH LIVING

Granddaughters of George Burges Digby Head, yr son of 3rd baronet:—
Issue of late Com Robert Digby Head, DSC, RN, *b* 1917, *d* 1956: *m* 1946, Lorraine, ARRC (Balgay, Dewlands Way, Verwood, Dorset BH21 6JN), who *m* 2ndly, 1967 (*m diss* 1973), William Gerard Fallon, da of late Townley Walter Dowding, of Dolphin Sq, SW1:—

Pauline Anne (Brick Cottage, Gorsely, Ross-on-Wye, Herefords), *b* 1948: *m* 19—, Graham d'Arcy. ——— Linda Mary, *b* 1951: *m* 1st, 1971 (*m diss* 1976), Paul Richard Wilder; 2ndly, 1978 (*m diss* 1980), Stephen Robert Whitby; 3rdly, 1982, Michael Benjamin Bobak, of 11 Berkeley Pl, Wimbledon, SW19 4NN and has issue living (by 1st *m*), Robert James, *b* 1972, — (by 3rd *m*) Danielle Anne, *b* 1982.

The 1st baronet, Right Hon Sir Francis Bond Head, KCH, PC (grandson of Moses Mendes, of Old Buckenham, Norfolk, and London, who *m* Anna Gabriella, 2nd da and co-heir of Rev Sir Francis Head, 4th Bt, of The Hermitage, Kent (*ext*), and whose surname her heirs of the body were authorised to assume by Roy licence 1770), was Lieut-Gov of Upper Canada 1835-38.

CHADWYCK-HEALEY (UK) 1919, of Wyphurst, Cranleigh, co Surrey, and New Place, Luccombe, Somerset.

Believe in me

Sir CHARLES EDWARD CHADWYCK-HEALEY, 5th *Baronet*; *b* 13 May 1940; *s* his father, *Lt-Col Sir* CHARLES ARTHUR, OBE, TD, 1986; *ed* Eton, and Trin Coll, Oxford (MA 1968): *m* 1967, Angela Mary, eldest da of late John Metson, of Brook End, Little Dunmow, Essex, and has issue.

Arms – 1st and 4th gules, four fusils engrailed and conjoined in bend, ermine between two lilies leaved and slipped proper, *Healey*; 2nd and 3rd gules, an anchor cabled within an orle argent, charged with eight martlets of the field (*Chadwyck*). **Crest** – 1st, in front of four fusils engrailed and conjoined fessewise ermine a lily as in the arms, *Healey*; 2nd, a talbot's head gules, charged on the neck with an escutcheon argent, thereon a martlet as in the arms, *Chadwyck*.
Residence – Manor Farm, Bassingbourn, Cambs SG8 5NX.

SON LIVING

EDWARD ALEXANDER, *b* 2 June 1972.

DAUGHTERS LIVING

Catherine, *b* 1970. ——— Faith, *b* 1977.

BROTHERS LIVING

Nicholas Gerald (39 Fairlawn Av, W4 5EF), *b* 1946; *ed* Eton: *m* 1978, Alison Jill, only da of Dr. N. Stevens, of Morris House, Fishmarket St, Thaxted, Essex, and has issue living, Gerald Norton, *b* 1979, — Cherry Kathleen, *b* 1980. ——— Peregrine James (Vern Leaze, Calne, Wilts), *b* 1950; *ed* Eton: *m* 1973, Julia Mary, el da of Sir Richard James Boughey, 10th Bt, and has issue living, Oliver Peregrine, *b* 1982, — Alice Rachel, *b* 1977, — Rose Henrietta, *b* 1980.

SISTERS LIVING

Philippa Harriet (16 Cabul Rd, SW11), *b* 1943: *m* 1974 (*m diss* 1987), Jeremy Michael Lubbock (*see* B Avebury, colls). ——— Serena Margaret, *b* 1948: *m* 1971, Jeremy D. Nickson, of Mount Pleasant House, Great Shefford, Newbury, Berks, and has issue living, George Howard, *b* 1977, — Francesca Verena, *b* 1975, — Theresa Viola, *b* 1980.

AUNT LIVING (*daughter of 2nd baronet*)

Rosa Mary Philippa, *b* 1907: *m* 1933, Cyril George Holland-Martin, JP, who *d* 1983, and has issue living, Timothy David (Overbury, Tewkesbury, Glos), *b* 1936; *ed* Eton; late 2nd Lt 12th R Lancers: *m* 1977 (*m diss* 1988), Caroline Mary, only da of late Thomas Francis Blackwell, of Langham Hall, Bury St Edmunds, — Robert George (18 Tite St, SW3), *b* 1939; *ed* Eton: *m* 1976, Dominique, da of Maurice Pierre Gabriel Fromaget, of Paris, and has issue living, Emily Marie Charlotte *b* 1978, Tamara Sophie *b* 1980, — Faith Mary, *b* 1949: *m* 1972, Capt Anthony Hallett, RN, of 26 Nassau Rd, SW13 9QE, and has issue living, James Anthony *b* 1976, Edward George *b* 1978, Thomas Alexander Pitfield *b* 1981. *Residence* – Whitcombe, Overbury, Tewkesbury, Glos.

WIDOW LIVING OF FOURTH BARONET

VIOLA (*Viola, Lady Chadwyck-Healey*), da of late Cecil Lubbock (*see* B Avebury, colls): *m* 1939, Lt-Col Sir Charles Arthur Chadwyck-Healey, 4th Bt, OBE, TD, who *d* 1986. *Residence* – 38 Castle Court, River Park, Marlborough, Wilts SN8 1NH.

COLLATERAL BRANCH LIVING

Issue of late Oliver Nowell Chadwyck-Healey, 3rd son of 1st baronet, *b* 1886, *d* 1960: *m* 1916, Gwendoline Mary, who *d* 1979, da of Major Hugh Charrington, of Hill Cottage, Taplow, Bucks:—

John Hugh, *b* 1922; *ed* Eton; formerly Capt Rifle Brig; N Africa, and Italy 1943-5 (wounded). *Residence* – 9d Thistle Grove, SW10 9RR. ——— Patience Mary, *b* 1917; late Junior Com ATS: *m* 1946, Lieut-Col Peter St George Hereward Maxwell, MC, Highland LI and has issue living, Philip Hugh, *b* 1947, — Ian Peter, *b* 1949, — Gillian Mary, *b* 1954, — Penelope Frances, *b* 1956. *Residence* – Pettistree Grange, Woodbridge, Suffolk.

The 1st baronet, Sir Charles Edward Heley Chadwyck Chadwyck-Healey, KCB, KC, Hon Capt RNR, was Chm Admiralty Vol Committee 1903-14, commanded a Hospital Ship during European War 1915-18, and was *cr* a baronet for valuable service on Admiralty Transport Arbitration Board. The 2nd baronet Sir Gerald Edward Chadwyck-Healey, CBE, was Director of Materials and Priority, Admiralty 1918.

HEATHCOTE (GB) 1733, of Hursley, Hampshire
(Name pronounced "Hethcut")

Et Dieu mon appui
And God my help

Sir MICHAEL PERRYMAN HEATHCOTE, 11th *Baronet, b* 7 Aug 1927; *s* his father, *Sir* LEONARD VYVYAN, 1963; *ed* Winchester, and Clare Coll, Camb; late 2nd Lieut 9th Lancers; in remainder to the Earldom of Macclesfield: *m* 1956, Victoria, el da of Com James Edward Rickards Wilford, RD, RNR, of Ackland Cottage, Shirley Holms, Lymington, Hants, and has issue.

Arms – Ermine, three pomels each charged with a cross or. **Crest** – On a mural crown azure, a pomey .charged with a cross or between two wings displayed ermine. **Second Motto** – "Deus prosperat justos" (*God prospers the just*).
Residence – Warborne Farm, Boldre, Lymington, Hants SO41 5QD.

SONS LIVING

TIMOTHY GILBERT, *b* 25 May 1957. —— George Benjamin, *b* 1965.

DAUGHTER LIVING

(Harriet) Louise, *b* 1962: *m* 1982, Richard J. Rouse, of Sea Cottage, Westfield Rd, Lymington, Hants only son of Lt-Cdr P. J. Rouse, RN (ret), of Tarnaut House, Tiptoe, Hants.

SISTER LIVING

Pamela Mary, *b* 1923: *m* 1945, (John) Gilbert Jones, of Walnut Tree Cottage, Harkstead, Ipswich, Suffolk, and has issue living, Richard Edmund, MBE, *b* 1947 (c/o Glasgow Univ, Glasgow): *m* 1987, Euphemia Photos, and has issue living, Alexander Xenophon *b* 1988, Michael Andronicus *b* 1991, Simon Maximian *b* 1993, —— Rosemary Anne, *b* 1948: *m* 1975, T. J. Aston, and has issue living, Emma *b* 1979.

COLLATERAL BRANCHES LIVING (*All male line in special remainder to Earldom of Macclesfield*)

Granddaughter of late Rev Gilbert Vyvyan Heathcote, father of 9th and 10th baronets:—
Issue of late William Charles Perceval Heathcote, *b* 1867, *d* 1937: *m* 1921, Ruth, who *d* 1950, da of late Arthur Malcolm Heathcote (infra):—
Anne, *b* 1923: *m* 1945, Baron Diederic W. van Lynden, Ambassador Netherlands Foreign Ser of Lange Voorhout, 48 The Hague, and has issue living, Jan Willem Alexander, *b* 1948, — Carel Diederic Aernout, *b* 1954, — Carola, *b* 1947: *m* 1969, Jonkheer A. G. Beelaerts van Blokland.

Grandchildren of late Reginald St Alban Heathcote, DM, FRCP, yst son of late Rev Gilbert Vyvyan Heathcote (ante):—
Issue of late Anthony Giles Salvin Heathcote, CD, *b* 1919, *d* 1970: *m* 1953, Kathleen Joan (276 McKee Av, Willow-dale, Ont, Canada), only da of H. Dawson, of Burton-on-Trent, Staffs:—
William Reginald Salvin, *b* 1955. —— Andrew Henry Salvin *b* 1962. —— Jean Viola, *b* 1954. —— Catherine Dawson, *b* 1959. —— Ann Elisabeth, *b* 1960. —— Ruth Margaret, *b* 1963.

Grandson of late James Shirley Heathcote, eldest son of late Arthur Malcolm Heathcote, 6th son of 5th baronet:—
Issue of late Martin Shirley Heathcote, *b* 1914, *d* 1992: *m* 1948, Mary Gertrude, da of Dr H. H. Nowland, of Sydney, NSW:—
Richard Desmond (Warrawong, Tambar Springs, NSW), *b* 1950: *m* 1973, Carmel, da of William Montgomery, of Ganalgang, Trangie, NSW, and has had issue, James Martin, *b* 1974, — Samuel William, *b* 1978, — Benjamin Richard, *b* 1990, — Sophie Louise, *b* 1976, — Amy Patricia, *b* 1982; *d* 1984. —— Pamela Shirley, *b* 1949: *m* 1971, Gasper Rey i de Grief. —— Ann Margaret, *b* 1956.

Grandchildren of late Capt Arthur Cleveland Heathcote, RN, son of late Adm Edmund Heathcote, son of late Rev Samuel Heathcote, 3rd son of 3rd baronet:—
Issue of late Maj Eustace Cleveland Heathcote, RM, *b* 1895, *d* 1976: *m* 1926, Marie Macmurrough Teresa, who *d* 1977, da of late J. J. Kavanagh:—
Michael Edmund (Hursley Cottage, Dockenfield, nr Farnham, Surrey), *b* 1931; Capt RM (ret): *m* 1959, Jean, el da of D. J. V. Hamilton-Miller, of Shrewsbury House, Ditton Hill, Surrey, and has issue living, Kathryn Gay, *b* 1961: *m* 1987, Christopher David McDonald Cann, son of G. D. T. Cann, of Cardiff, — Georgina Anne (twin), *b* 1961: *m* 1986, (Alfred Joseph Gerard Robert) Alain Rey, of Beau-Bassin, Mauritius, son of Jacques Robert Rey, of Beau-Bassin, Mauritius, and has issue living, Olivier Michael Robert *b* 1987, — Jenny Louise, *b* 1964. —— Valerie, *b* 1929; late 2nd Officer WRNS.

Granddaughter of late Charles Heathcote (*b* 1833), 5th son of William Lovell Heathcote, el son of Adm Sir Henry Heathcote, 4th son of 3rd baronet:—
Issue of late Frederick Lovell Heathcote, *b* 1875, *d* 1968: *m* 1901, Mimmie Ethel Ziervogel, who *d* 1938:—
Joan, *b* 1910: *m* 1938, Maurice E. Wilmot, who *d* 1986, of Home for the Aged, Alexandria, 6185, S Africa, and has issue living, Chester George, *b* 1948, — Felicity Mary, *b* 1940: *m* 1964, John St Laurence Beaufort, and has issue living, Sandra *b* 1966.

Grandchildren of late Frederick Lovell Heathcote (ante):—
Issue of late Geoffrey Charles Heathcote, *b* 1906, *d* 1988: *m* 1939, Megan Edith Pugh-Jones (Crestwood, PO Newton Park, Port Elizabeth, S Africa):—
Charles William (Crestwood, PO Newton Park, Port Elizabeth, S Africa), *b* 1942: *m* 1967, Hester Cornelia de Lange, and has issue living, Charles Geoffrey, *b* 1981, — Karen Sarah, *b* 1968, — Lucille Megan, *b* 1970, — Dianne May, *b* 1972, — Marian Louise, *b* 1976. —— Warwick Geoffrey, *b* 1946: *m* 1969, Helena Louisa Marais, and has issue living, Geoffrey Charles Lovell, *b* 1973, — Elizabeth Anne, *b* 1970, — Caroline Louise, *b* 1987. —— Geoffrey Lovel, *b* 1951: *m* 1975, Laura Glen HUGHES (*née* Anderson), and has issue living, Olivia Megan, *b* 1980, — Carmen Joy, *b* 1982. —— Eleanor May, *b* 1948: *m* 1968, Lysle Horace Wilmot, and has issue living, Mark Lysle, *b* 1969, — David Geoffrey, *b* 1972, — Suzanne Megan, *b* 1969, — Michelle May, *b* 1978.

Issue of late Albert Ziervogel Heathcote, *b* 1909, *d* 1977: *m* 1943, Doreen Oke Thomas (Glenfield, PO Box 7071, Newton Park, Port Elizabeth, S Africa):—
Frederick Malcolm (PO Box 7071, Port Elizabeth, S Africa), *b* 1944: *m* 1972, Elenor Fourie, and has issue living, Frederick Henry, *b* 1973, — Llewellyn Malcolm, *b* 1975. —— Albert Dennisson (PO Box 252, Humansdorp, S Africa), *b* 1946: *m* 1969, Elizabeth Stoutjesdyk, and has issue living, Yvonne Sharon, *b* 1970, — Carol Lisé, *b* 1973, — Lynne Denise, *b* 1976, — Hellen Delia, *b* 1980. —— Richard John (PO Box 252, Humansdorp, S Africa), *b* 1948: *m* 1969, Finette van Gend, and has issue living, Charmaine Sunette, *b* 1969, — Richelle Doreen, *b* 1970, — Teresé Finette, *b* 1975, — Jacqueline Melodé, *b* 1978. —— Hilary Oke, *b* 1950: *m* 1975 (*m diss* 1979), Wiliam Kirkman Allen, and has issue living, Wilfred Gavin, *b* 1976.

Grandchildren of late Charles William Heathcote (infra):—
Issue of late Frederick Lennox, Heathcote, *b* 1903, *d* 1969: *m* 1932, Mildred Walkenshaw Shaw, who *d* 1974:—
Leon Geoffrey (PO Box 998, Gweru, Zimbabwe), *b* 1934: *m* 1957, Gillian Jean Lawson, and has issue living, Frederick Garth (PO Box 809, Gweru, Zimbabwe), *b* 1958, — Mark Andrew, *b* 1962, — Jean Pamela, *b* 1960: *m* 1980, Glendyn Stephen Delamere Thompson (PO Box 633, Gweru, Zimbabwe), and has issue living, Bruce Glen *b* 1988, Shay Jean *b* 1983, Donna Caron *b* 1985. —— Roy (5 Farthing Hill, Po Borrowdale, Harare, Zimbabwe), *b* 1938: *m* 1965, Gillian Helen Dalling, and has issue living, Paul Roy, *b* 1972, — Amanda Kim, *b* 1968. —— Frederick Noel, *b* 1945: *m* 1967, Catherine Caryln Barry, and has issue living, Clive Noel (PO Marondera, Zimbabwe), *b* 1968, — Wayne Douglas, *b* 1972, — Kelly, *b* 1980. —— Stella Lenore, *b* 1933: *m* 1950, Bruce John Humpage, of 3 Canary Close, Avondale, Harare, Zimbabwe, and has issue living, Denise Marie, *b* 1953: *m* 1971, John Sealy, and has issue living, Gail *b* 1971, Leigh-Anne *b* 1974, — Carol Gail, *b* 1955: *m* 1974, Neville Thompson. —— Colleen, *b* 1936: *m* 1954, Errol Dennis Roberts (PO Box 598, Gweru, Zimbabwe), and has issue living, Cheryl Gail, *b* 1955: *m* 1979, Stephan William Cloete, and has issue living, Barry James *b* 1980, Ashley *b* 1983, — Melody Gaynor, *b* 1957: *m* 1984, Roland Francis Woods, and has issue living, Craig Dennis *b* 1988, Wendy Frances *b* 1986, — Fiona Gaylin, *b* 1958: *m* 1981, Bryan Matthew Rabie, and has issue living, Robert Matthew *b* 1985, Tracey-Lee *b* 1982, — Beverley Colleen, *b* 1959: *m* 1978, Anthony Kreft, and has issue living, Sean Anthony *b* 1982, Nicolette Colleen, *b* 1980. —— Cleone, *b* 1942: *m* 1963, Rodney E. M. Roberts, of Gweru, Zimbabwe, and has issue living, Shane Gavin, *b* 1965, — Felicity Ann, *b* 1967.

Grandchildren of late Charles Heathcote (*b* 1833) (ante):—
Issue of late Charles William Heathcote, *b* 1877, *d* 1918: *m* 1st, 19—, Sophie Kichner, who *d* 1910; 2ndly, 1911, Nellie van Heerden, who *d* 1918:—
(By 1st *m*) Millicent Pearl, *b* 1908: *m* 1937, Harry Dale, and has issue living, Margaret Ann *b* 1939: *m* 1st, 1960 (*m diss* 1962), Peter Reynecke; 2ndly, 1963, Michael Herbert Smit, and has issue living (by 1st *m*) Millicent Sharon *b* 1961, (by 2nd *m*) Steve Carl *b* 1967, Irene Tessa *b* 1965, Fiona Ann *b* 1969. —— (By 2nd *m*) Kathleen Mary, *b* 1912: *m* 1933, Rev Martin Luther Janse van Rensburg, and has issue living, Luther Calvyn *b* 1935: *m* 1959, Anne Elizabeth Nieuwoudt, and has issue living, Johanna Maria *b* 1960, — Marleen, *b* 1938: *m* 1960, Johannes Daniel Nieuwoudt, of Hoopstad, Orange Free State, S Africa. —— Emma Ida May, *b* 1915: *m* 1937, Jacobus Wessel Janses van Rensburg, and has issue living, Jacobus Hendrikus, *b* 1938, — Martin Luther, *b* 1946, — Jacobus Wessel, *b* 1949, — Kathleen Mary, *b* 1943, — Alida Jacoba, *b* 1949. *Residence* – Hertzogville, Orange Free State, S Africa.
Issue of late Fitzroy Hamilton Heathcote, *b* 1881, *d* 1938: *m* 1903, Edith Beamish, who *d* 1947:—
Grace Sybil Beamish, *b* 1904: *m* 1930, Norman Sharwood, of 5 Brickmakerskloof, Port Elizabeth, S Africa, and has issue living, Norma Dorothy, *b* 1931: *m* 1954, Tristan McGibbon Maynier, c/o Standard Bank, Queenstown, S Africa, and has issue living, Derek *b* 1959, Nicolette *b* 1956: *m* 1980, Matthew Haxton Millar Guiney (and has issue living, Jacquelyn Martha *b* 1981, Gillian Norma *b* 1983). —— Ida Beamish, *b* 1906: *m* 1932, William Leslie Lyddon Farrant, c/o Box 375, Pretoria, S Africa, and has issue living, Leslie Heathcote, *b* 1935: *m* 1961, Antoinette du Toit, — David Heathcote (c/o Box 375, Pretoria, S Africa), *b* 1937. —— Winifred Beamish, *b* 1917: *m* 1st, 1935, John Rennie, who was *ka* 1942; 2ndly, 1944, Patrick Dairmid Dolan, who *d* 1981; 3rdly, 1994, John Radforth Mountjoy, of 48 Douglas Av, Craighall, 2196 Johannesburg, S Africa, and has issue living (by 1st *m*), Myrle Allison, *b* 1938: *m* 1963, Paul de Vere Noake, of 49 Douglas Av, Craighall, Johannesburg, S Africa, and has issue living, John de Vere *b* 1964, Susan *b* 1966, — (by 2nd *m*) Elizabeth Ann, *b* 1945: *m* 1965, Alan Tucker, of 9 Government Rd, Beauty Point, 2088 Mosman, Sydney, NSW, Australia, and has issue living, Robert Kidger *b* 1967, James Kidger *b* 1969, George Kidger *b* 1971, Ian Kidger *b* 1973.
Issue of late Cecil Heathcote, *b* 1883, *d* 1918: *m* 1911, Engela Starr, who *d* 1941 (having *m* 2ndly, 1930, Maurice Meek, formerly of PO Willoughby's Siding, Zimbabwe), el da of Ambrose George Campbell Shaw:—
Cecil Starr, *b* 1912: *m* 1935, Norah Edith, da of Walter James, and has issue living, Janet Mary, *b* 1949: *m* 1976, John Marshall, of E London, S Africa, and has issue living, Andrew Keith *b* 1983, Pamela Susan *b* 1979. —— Ambrose Carl Starr (Village House, PO Esigodini, Zimbabwe), *b* 1915: *m* 1940, Dorothy, yr da of W. B. Richards, of Fort Victoria, Zimbabwe, and has issue living, David Starr (6 Ada Attwell Rd, Ilanda, Bulawayo, Zimbabwe), *b* 1952, — Sylvia Starr, *b* 1956: *m* 1979, Michael Basil Gibbons, of 39 Stanley Rd, Irene 1675, S Africa, and has issue living, Richard Michael *b* 1985, Lara Kathryn *b* 1983. —— Mary Lesley Starr, *b* 1913: *m* 1937, Harry Edward Smith. *Residence* - Stanhope Farm, Somabula, Zimbabwe.
Issue of late Albert Jerrold Heathcote, *b* 1887, *d* 1964: *m* 1st, 1914 (*m diss* 19—), Dorothy Twycross; 2ndly, 1945, Mrs Muriel Korsten, who *d* 1961, and has issue:—
(By 1st *m*) William Jerrold, *b* 1915: *m* 1959, Johanna Hofmeyr. —— John Albert, *b* 1916; formerly Sergt, Union Defence Force, S Africa: *m* 1944, Mrs Rosemary Hilda Beresford Carter, da of Oswald Beresford Lonsdale, and has issue living, Charles John Beresford, *b* 1948: *m* 1978, Anna Krystyna, da of Jerzy Rafal Cywinski, — Phyllis May Beresford, *b* 1945: *m* 1968, Lawrence A. Green, — Rosemary Alice Beresford, *b* 1953. —— George Twycross (Stutterheim, E Cape, S Africa), *b* 1918: *m* 1943, Elizabeth Mary Allport, and has issue living, Michael John, *b* 1954, — Dorothy Ann, *b* 1955.

Grandchildren of Cecil Starr Heathcote (ante):—
Issue of late Maj Cecil Walter Heathcote, *b* 1936, *d* 1984: *m* 1st, 1955, Sylvia Ann Boyd Varty, who *d* 1959; 2ndly, 1961 (*m diss* 1978), Jennifer Gaie Brinsley; 3rdly, 1981, Hendrika Albertha Roos (née Kotze) (Northcliff, Johannesburg, S Africa):—
(By 1st *m*) Susan Norah, *b* 1958: *m* 1980, Terrence André Mangnall, of Harare, Zimbabwe, and has issue living, Mark John, *b* 1982, — Paul Ian, *b* 1985. —— (By 2nd *m*) Debbie Gaie, *b* 1962: *m* 1983, Lionel Victor Moore, of 19 Walter Hill Av, Eastlea, Harare, Zimbabwe, and has issue living, Rory Victor, *b* 1984, — Kerry Gaie, *b* 1986. —— Carol Jean, *b* 1964: *m* 1983, Graham Peter Rattey, of Mafikeng, Bophuthatswana, and has issue living, Kai Mark, *b* 1985. —— Linda Heidi, *b* 1971.

Grandchildren of late William Lovell Heathcote (ante):—
Issue of late Henry Heathcote (yst son), *b* 18—, *d* 1893: *m* 18—, Lætitia Murray (she *m* 2ndly, 19—, Rev F. Stewart):—
Henry Gage, *b* 1877. —— Clifford, *b* 18—. —— Mary, *b* 18—: *m* 18—, Clem Will. —— Alice Eleanor, *b* 1886: *m* 1905, Arthur James Ford, Div Sec Boy Scouts' Asso, and has issue living, John Lovell Heathcote, *b* 1906, — Frank Stewart Heathcote, *b* 1915, — Arthur Dymond Heathcote, *b* 1920, — Muriel, *b* 1908, — Evelyn (twin), *b* 1908. —— Ine, *b* 18—.

Grandchildren of late Lieut George Gage Heathcote, RN, son of late Adm Sir Henry Heathcote (ante):—
Issue of late Gage Charles Heathcote, *b* 1842, *d* 1895: *m* 1879, Hermina Aletta Fourie, da of A. Van Wych:—
Edward Munro, *b* 1882. —— Aletta Caterina, *b* 1879: *m* 1898, Gerhadus Jacobus Van de Nerve. —— Emily, *b* 1887: *m* 1902, Ernest Alfred Hornby. —— Hermina Aletta, *b* 1889: *m* 1905, William George August.
Issue of late William Heathcote, Lieut SA Cavaliers, *b* 1884, *d* 1961: *m* 19—, Helena Cathrina Faure, who *d* 1985:—

William Charles (Box 439, Keetmanshoop, SW Africa), b 1929: m 1955, Connie Danie van Niekerk, and has had issue, William, b 1958: m 19—, Annemarie van Zyl, and has issue living, Elizmarie b 1988, — Conrad, b 1960 d 1985, — Raymond, b 1964. —— Maria Wilhelmina, b 1919: m 1940, Norman Charles Venables, of Lushington Park, PO Kidds Beach, East London, S Africa, and has issue living, Keith Norman, b 1942: m 1965, Yvonne Valerie Flugel, and has issue living, Bevan Keith b 1972, Sandra Lee b 1966: m 1991, John James Ward (and has issue living, Jay Cameron b 1989, Ryan b 1992), Terri-Ann b 1969, — Peter Kevin, b 1956: m 1978, Janet Edith Ewers, and has issue living, Wesly b 1981, Dal b 1983, — Bernadette, b 1945: m 1966, Johan Martinus Els, and has issue living, Hank b 1969, Dominique b 1968. —— Thora, b 1922: m 19—, William Herbert van Schoor (PO Box 2013, Johannesburg, S Africa), and has issue living, Denise Thora, b 1944: m 1965, Alva Felix Walter Oldknow, of 39 The Willows, 4th Av, Florida, Transvaal, — Marlene Diedré, b 1948: m 1969, Lukas Matthee Auó. —— Maureen Cathrine, b 1937: m 1961, Petrus Jacobus Alwyn van der Merwe, and has issue living, Petrus, b 1962, — Rudolph, b 1965, — Marina, b 1966.

Granddaughters of late Gage Charles Heathcote (ante):—
Issue of late Thomas Munro Heathcote, b 1848, d 1890: m 1879, Augusta Euphine, da of late E. Philipps:—
Emma Katherine, b 1882. —— Marian, b 1885.

Granddaughter of late Rev Gilbert Heathcote, son of late Capt Gilbert Heathcote, 5th son of 3rd baronet:—
Issue of late Frederick Arthur Heathcote, b 1851, d 1925: m 1887, Evelyn Constance, who d 1938, da of late Frederick Elin, of Hazlemount, Ryde, Isle of Wight:—
Gertrude Evelyn Atherley, b 1893: m 1920, Richard Picton Rosser, MB, ChB, and has issue living, John Gilbert Heathcote, b 1922, — Charles, b 1929.

Granddaughters of late Thomas Jenkyns Heathcote, el son of late Rev Thomas Heathcote, son of late Samuel Heathcote, 4th son of 2nd baronet:—
Issue of late Rev Wyndham Selfe Heathcote, b 1862; d 19—: m 1888, Agnes, who d 1934, da of Rev James Macdonall:—
Catherine Moultrie Maud (Los Angeles, USA), b 1891: m 19—.
Issue of late George Wadham Bruce Heathcote, OBE, b 1868, d 1944: m 1895, Mary, da of Mark Bate:—
Grace Mary, b 1896: m 1923, Thomas B. Randall.

Granddaughter of late John Cuthbert Heathcote, son of late Rev Samuel John Heathcote, 2nd son of late Rev Thomas Heathcote (ante):—
Issue of late Lt-Col John Robert Campbell Heathcote, b 1879: d 1947: m 1st, 1898 (m diss 1920), Margaret McClellan; 2ndly, 1920, Mary Gertrude, da of late Oscar Brandt:—
(By 1st m) Evelyn Marie, b 1899.

The 1st baronet, Sir William, MP for Southampton and Buckingham, m Elizabeth, only da of the 1st Earl of Macclesfield (Lord Chancellor), to whose peerages Sir William's heir is in remainder. The 3rd baronet was MP for Hampshire; the 4th baronet, also MP (C) for Hants, assumed the additional surname of Freeman. The 5th baronet, Rt Hon Sir William, DCL, sat as MP for Hampshire (C) 1826-32, for N Hampshire 1837-49, and for Oxford University 1854-68. The 9th baronet, Rt Rev Sir Francis, DD, was Bishop of New Westminster, British Columbia, 1941-50.

HEATHCOTE (GB) 1733, of London

Sir GILBERT SIMON HEATHCOTE, CBE, 9th *Baronet*, only son of Lt-Col Robert Evelyn Manners Heathcote, DSO, R Scots and later RA, only son of Capt Robert Heathcote, only son of Capt George Augustus Frederick Heathcote, LG, el son of Robert Heathcote, 3rd son of baronet, b 21 Sept 1913; s his kinsman, (GILBERT) JAMES HEATHCOTE-DRUMMOND-WILLOUGHBY, 3rd and last Earl of Ancaster and 8th Baronet, 1983; ed Eton; Brig (ret) RA; CRA 50th Div 1960-62, Ch of Staff, Middle East Command 1962-64, and Brig RA Scottish Command 1964-66; 1939-45 War in N-W Europe; MBE (Mil) 1945, CBE (Mil) 1964: m 1st, 1939 (m diss 1984), Patricia Margaret, da of Brig James Travers Leslie, MC; 2ndly, 1984, Ann, da of W/Cdr J. A. Hatton, and widow of Brig James Frederick Charles Mellor, DSO, OBE, and has issue by 1st m.

Arms – Ermine, three pomeys, each charged with a cross or. Crest – On a mural crown azure, a pomey as in the arms, between two wings displayed ermine.
Property — Manton, Oakham, Leics. Residence – The Coach House, Tillington, Petworth, W Sussex GU28 0RA. Clubs – Garrick, Army and Navy.

SON LIVING (By 1st marriage)

MARK SIMON ROBERT, OBE, b 1 March 1941; ed Eton, and Magdalene Coll, Camb (BA); P & O Orient Lines, Foreign and Commonwealth Office, BP Co plc; OBE (Civil) 1988: m 1975, Susan, da of late Lt-Col George Ashley, The Cameronians (Scottish Rifles), of Rosamundford, Aylesbeare, Devon, and has issue living, Alastair Robert, b 18 Aug 1977, — Nicholas Alexander, b 1979. Address – c/o Upton Dean, Upton, nr Andover, Hants.

DAUGHTER LIVING (By 1st marriage)

Joanna, b 1947.

SISTER LIVING

Evelyn Suzanne Valhalla, b 1917: m 1st, 1938 (m diss 1952), Henry Lester Louis Morriss, who d 1963; 2ndly, 1952, Robert John Colling, who d 1981, and has issue living (by 1st m), Hugo Henry, b 1939; ed Downside, and Univ Coll, Oxford: m

1967, Marie Diston, da of David Scull, of Philadelphia, USA, — Amanda Mary, *b* 1942: *m* 1965, Cosimo Prantera, and has issue living, Sophie *b* 1965, Costanza *b* 1967.

HALF-SISTER LIVING

Diana Nesta (Somerby House Farm, Somerby, Leics), *b* 1923: *m* 1953, Michael James Mellows, who *d* 1974, and has issue living, Anna Caroline, *b* 1954: *m* 1982, Edward Henry Garnier, and has issue (*see* B Walsingham), — Julia Dominica, *b* 1956: *m* 1992, William John Newlands Moore, — Antonia Philippa, *b* 1960.

COLLATERAL BRANCHES LIVING

Grandson of late Rev Thomas Heathcote, 2nd son of late Robert Heathcote, 3rd son of 3rd baronet:—
Issue of late William Lionel Heathcote, *b* 1874, *d* 1961: *m* 1919, Alice Mabel, who *d* 1972, da of late Rev John Dand Todd, R of Newton Folkingham:—
Gilbert Michael, *b* 1924: *m* 1953, Dorothy, da of H. W. Pratchett, and has issue living, Jane Michele, *b* 1954: *m* 1980, Russell Curtis, eldest son of A. Curtis, of New Malden, Surrey, — Amanda Joy, *b* 1959: *m* 1984, Graham Denny Girling, of 55 Radnor Rd, Harrow, Middx, yr son of D. Girling, of Kingsbury, NW9, — and an adopted da, Annabel Dorothy, *b* 1967. *Residence* – Janda Cote, 8 Armand Close, Nascot Wood, Watford, Herts.

Grandsons of late John Moyer Heathcote, el son of late John Heathcote, MP (*b* 1834), son of late John Moyer Heathcote, grandson of 2nd baronet:—
Issue of late Arthur Ridley Heathcote, *b* 1877; *d* 1951: *m* 1909, Margaret Georgina, who *d* 1944, only surviving da of late Horace Broke, of Gladwyns, Essex:—
John Horace Broke, *b* 1910; *ed* Eton, and Trin Coll, Camb (BA 1932): *m* 1949, Dorelle Geraldine, da of late Lt-Col Gerald Dominic Rice, DSO, of Fermoy, co Cork, and has issue living, Miranda Lydia, *b* 1950: *m* 1973, Guy Anthony Belcher, of 6 Connaught Sq, W2, son of Anthony George Belcher, of Chiddingfold, Surrey, and has issue living, Tara *b* 1977, — Venetia Catherine, *b* 1951: *m* 1982, Nicholas Annesley Marler Thompson, of Maxgate, George Rd, Kingston-upon-Thames, el son of Sir Richard Hilton Marler Thompson, 1st Bt, and has issue (*see* Thompson, Bt, *cr* 1963). *Residence* – Maxgate, George Rd, Kingston-upon-Thames, Surrey KT2 7NR. ——— Norman Richard, *b* 1914; *ed* Eton, and Trin Coll, Camb: *m* 1946, Margaret Enid, da of Alan Keith Burnett, of Durban, S Africa, and has issue living, Richard John, *b* 1951, — Katherine Louise, *b* 1952, — Diana Elizabeth (twin), *b* 1952. *Address* – c/o Rhodesia House, 429 Strand, WC2.
Sir GILBERT HEATHCOTE, KB, MP in four Parliaments, Lord Mayor of London 1711 and one of the originators of the Bank of England; *cr* a Baronet 1733; *d* 1733; *s* by his son *Sir* JOHN, 2nd Bt; was MP for Grantham 1715-22, and for Bodmin 1733-4; *d* 1759; *s* by his son *Sir* GILBERT, 3rd Bt, MP for Shaftesbury; *d* 1785; *s* by his son *Sir* GILBERT, 4th Bt; was MP for Lincolnshire 1796-1802 and 1806, and for Rutland (*L*) 1812-41; *d* 1851; *s* by his son *Sir* GILBERT JOHN, 5th Bt, *b* 16 Jan 1795; sat as MP for Boston (*L*) 1820-31. Lincolnshire South 1832-41 and Rutland 1841-6: was Lord-Lieut of Lincolnshire: *cr Baron Aveland* (peerage of UK) 1856: *m* 1827, Hon Clementina Elizabeth, in her own right Baroness Willoughby de Eresby, da of 19th Baron Willoughby de Eresby; *d* 1867; *s* by his son GILBERT HENRY, 2nd Baron and 6th Baronet, who *s* as 24th Baron Willoughby de Eresby 1888, and was *cr Earl of Ancaster* (Peerage of UK) 1892. On the death in 1983 of his grandson, (GILBERT) JAMES, 3rd Earl of Ancaster, 4th Baron Aveland, 26th Baron Willoughby de Eresby and 8th Baronet (of London), the first two peerages became extinct, the Barony of Willoughby de Eresby passed to his daughter (see that title), and the Baronetcy to his kinsman, *Brig Sir* (GILBERT) SIMON HEATHCOTE, CBE, descendant of Robert Heathcote, 3rd son of 3rd Baronet.

HENNIKER-HEATON (UK) 1912, of Mundarrah Towers, Sydney, Australia

There is light in letters

Sir YVO ROBERT HENNIKER-HEATON, 4th *Baronet*; *b* 24 April 1954; *s* his father, *Wing-Cdr Sir* (JOHN VICTOR) PEREGRINE, 1971; memb NW Leics Dist Cncl; MIIA: *m* 1978, Freda, da of Brian Jones, of The Hollies, Broughton Astley, Leics, and has issue.

Arms – Argent on a bend sable three bulls, heads couped of the first, over all on an escutcheon of pretence, quarterly of six; 1st, vert, three escutcheons argent, each charged with a bordure engrailed or, *Burrell*; 2nd, argent, three battering rams fessways in pale proper headed and garnished azure, *Bertie*; 3rd, or, fretty azure, *Willoughby*; 4th, vert, three eagles displayed fessways or, *Owen Gwynedd*; 5th, gyronny of eight or and sable, *Campbell*; 6th, per pale sable and gules, on a cross between four fleurs-de-lys argent, five pheons azure, *Banks*. **Crest** – Out of a crest coronet gules, a bull's head argent.
Residence – 7 Brendon Way, Ashby de la Zouch, Leics LE6 5EW.

SON LIVING

ALASTAIR JOHN, *b* 1990.

DAUGHTER LIVING

Julia Sermonda, *b* 1987.

SISTER LIVING

Priscilla Margaret, *b* 1949: *m* 1976, Iain James Saddler Mann, and has issue living, Alison Catriona, *b* 1977, — Jessamy Roberta, *b* 1980.

HALF SISTERS LIVING

Jacqueline (c/o Hoare & Co, 16 Waterloo Pl, SW17), *b* 1931: *m* 1959, Michael Ferris, and has issue, Rory, *b* 1959, — Michaela Jacqueline, *b* 1961: *m* 19—, Jorge de Villanova-Rattazzi. ——— Anthea Jennifer, *b* 1934.

WIDOW LIVING OF THIRD BARONET

MARGARET PATRICIA (*Margaret, Lady Henniker Heaton*), da of late Lt Percy Wright, Canadian Mounted Rifles: *m* 1948, as his 2nd wife, Wing-Cdr Sir (John Victor) Peregrine Henniker Heaton, 3rd Bt, who *d* 1971.

COLLATERAL BRANCHES LIVING

Issue of late Maj Clement Algernon Charles Henniker-Heaton, yst son of 2nd Bt, *b* 1909, *d* 1983: *m* 1940, Marjorie (Clevemede, Goring-on-Thames, Reading), da of William E. Speight, of Bournemouth:—
John Lindsey (Northwoods House, Northwoods, Winterbourne, Bristol BS17 1RS), *b* 1946; *ed* Wellington, and Emmanuel Coll, Camb (MA): *m* 1970, Elisabeth Gladwell, and has issue living, Anthony James, *b* 1974, — Robert Piers, *b* 1978. —— Charles Peter (Old Orchard, Crown East Lane, Lower Broadheath, Worcs WR2 62H), *b* 1956; *ed* Eton: *m* 1989, Julia A., da of Derek Johnson, of Much Hadham, Herts, and has issue living, Alexander James Peter, *b* 1992, — Toby Anthony, *b* 1994. —— Hilary Rose, *b* 1948: *m* 1976, Edward Holloway, and has issue living, Nicholas Henniker, *b* 1977, — William David, *b* 1980, — Rachel Sermonda, *b* 1983, — Charlotte Anne (twin), *b* 1983.

Issue of late Sir Herbert Henniker Heaton, KCMG, 3rd son of 1st baronet, *b* 1880, *d* 1961: *m* 1st, 1909, Susan Angèle Phœbe, who *d* 1922, da of late Lindsey Talbot-Crosbie of Ardfert Abbey, Ardfert, co Kerry; 2ndly, 1926, (Helena) Iris, who *d* 1927, da of late Sir Henry Edward McCallum, GCMG; 3rdly, 1947, Gladys Meta, who *d* 1962, da of late Col Claud Francis, and widow of Col George Going, S Staffordshire Regt:—
(By 1st *m*) Dermot Wynne, *b* 1922: *m* 1956, Joan Townsend, and has issue living, Colin Edward Richard, *b* 1956, — Keith Patrick, *b* 1962. —— (By 2nd *m*) Christopher Robin, *b* 1927; late Nigerian Civil Ser: *m* 1st, 1952 (*m diss* 1967), Elizabeth da of H. Curtis, MD, of Bermuda; 2ndly, 1967, Estelle Patricia, who *d* 1986, da of Samuel John Newing, of Cheshunt, Herts, and *d* 1990, leaving issue, (by 1st *m*) Elizabeth Anne, *b* 1954: *m* 1974, Anthony James Walter, and has issue living, Aaron James *b* 1976, Rebecca Elizabeth *b* 1980. —— (By 1st *m*) Rose Phoebe Anne (Beaufort House, Beaufort, co Kerry), *b* 1914: *m* 1945, Maj Norman Keith Cameron, Coldm Gds, who *d* 1971, and has had issue, Alastair, *b* 1951, *d* 1989 in the Falkland Is, — Donald, *b* 1953, — Jane, *b* 1950, — Susan, *b* 1956. —— Priscilla Angèle Moira (Gable Cottage, Biddestone, Chippenham, Wilts), *b* 1916: *m* 1940, Walter Theodore Ballantyne, who *d* 1971, and has issue living, Priscilla Sarah Anne, *b* 1943: *m* 1968, Sven Gahlin, and has issue living, Adam Hugo *b* 1972, Lucia Karin *b* 1970.

Issue of late Capt Arthur Henniker-Heaton, RN, 4th son of 1st baronet, *b* 1883, *d* 1965: *m* 1913, Vera Isabel, who *d* 1965, da of late Hamilton Atherley:—
Michael Hamilton Henniker, *b* 1914: 1939-45 War as Maj R. Signals: *m* 1st, 1937; 2ndly, 1956, Brenda (MILLER), da of Morrison Davies; 3rdly, 1957, Elizabeth Catherine, FLA, da of Maurice Budgett.

Grandchildren of late Capt Arthur Henniker-Heaton, RN (ante):—
Issue of late Lt-Cdr Robin James Henniker-Heaton, RNVR, *b* 1915, *d* 1985: *m* 1st, 1951, Sylvia Elizabeth, yr da of Julian Charles Grumbar, MBE; 2ndly, 1958, Barbara (28 Eastbourne, Willingdon, Sussex), da of William Newman Ayres:—
(By 2nd *m*) Anthony, *b* 1958. —— Sally, *b* 1961.
The 1st baronet, Sir John Henniker Heaton, introduced a motion in House of Commons (1886) for Universal Ocean Penny Postage, and was instrumental in carrying a large number of postal reforms, and especially in reducing Postal Rates to India and Australia 1890, and Penny Postage to America 1908; carried Imperial Postage Resolution 1898, and sat as MP for Canterbury (C) 1885 to 1910. The 2nd baronet, Sir John, assumed the surname of Henniker Heaton.

Henderson-Stewart, see Stewart.

HENNIKER (UK) 1813, of Newton Hall, Essex

Sir ADRIAN CHANDOS HENNIKER, 9th *Baronet*; *b* 18 Oct 1946; *s* his father, *Sir* MARK CHANDOS AUBERON, CBE, DSO, MC, 1991; *ed* Marlborough: *m* 1971, Ann, da of Stuart Britton, of Malvern House, Fairwater Rd, Llandaff, Cardiff, and has issue.

Arms – Or, on a chevron gules between two crescents in chief, and in base an escallop azure, three estoiles argent. **Crest** – An escallop or, charged with an estoile gules.
Residence – Llwyndu Court, Abergavenny, Gwent.

DEUS
MAJOR COLUMNA
God is the greatest support

DAUGHTERS LIVING

Victoria Louise, *b* 1976. —— Holly Georgina, *b* (twin) 1976.

SISTER LIVING

Fiona Jane, *b* 1951: *m* 1977, Peter Jan Milewski, M Chir, FRCS, of Dorney Wood, Llawhaden, Pembrokeshire, and has issue living, Andrew Mark Jan, *b* 1982, — Henry Bish Chandos, *b* 1984, — Lucy Kathleen Amina, *b* 1984, — Anna Denys Olive, *b* 1987.

AUNT LIVING (*sister of 8th baronet*)

Alison Margaret, *b* 1909. *Residence* – 117 Thoroughfare, Woodbridge, Suffolk.

DAUGHTERS LIVING OF SIXTH BARONET

Beryl Inger HENNIKER-HUGHAN, *b* 1904. *Residence* – Marchdyke, Dalry, Kirkcudbrightshire. —— Alison Frances HENNIKER-HUGHAN (Wilbury House, 52 Wilbury Rd, Hove, Sussex BN3 3PS), *b* 1910: *m* 1936 (*m diss* 1947), John Gladstone (E Shrewsbury, colls).

KATHLEEN DENYS (*Dowager Lady Henniker*), da of late John Anderson, of Pilgrim's Way, Farnham, Surrey: *m* 1945, Sir Mark Chandos Auberon Henniker, 8th Bt, CBE, DSO, MC, who *d* 1991. *Residence* – 27 Western Rd, Abergavenny, Gwent NP7 7AB.

COLLATERAL BRANCH LIVING

Grandson of late Rev Robert Henniker, 3rd son of late Aldborough Brydges John Henniker, 3rd son of 1st baronet:—

Issue of late Col Alan Major Henniker, CBE, RE, *b* 1870, *d* 1949: *m* 1902, Blanche Marie, who *d* 1961, da of late James Gadsden, of Lannion, Brittany:—

RICHARD FREDERICK, *b* 10th June 1906; *ed* Camb Univ (MA); a FRIBA; 1939-45 War as Maj RE: *m* 1938, Daphne Irene, da of late Capt C. J. Maxwell. *Residence* – Haddon Fields, Membury, Axminster, Devon.

The Hon Sir Brydges Trecothick Henniker, 1st baronet, was yst son of 1st Baron Henniker, he sat as MP for Kildare in the last Irish Parliament, the 4th baronet was Private Sec to Local Govt Board 1877-80, and Registrar-Gen of Births, Deaths, and Marriages 1880-1900. The 6th baronet, Adm Sir Arthur John Henniker-Hughan, CB, assumed the additional surname of Hughan 1896, and served during European War 1914-16 with Grand Fleet (1914-15 star); was Adm Sup-Devonport Dockyard 1916-19, and sat as MP for Galloway (*U*) 1924-5. The 7th baronet, Lieut-Col Sir Robert John Aldborough Henniker, MC, served in European War 1914-18 (MC), and in European War 1940-45.

HENRY (UK) 1923, of Cahore, co Londonderry

Sir JAMES HOLMES HENRY, CMG, MC, TD, 2nd *Baronet*; *b* 22 Sept 1911; *s* his father, *Rt Hon Sir* DENIS STANISLAUS, 1925; *ed* Mount St Mary's Coll, Chesterfield, at Downside Sch, and Univ Coll, London (BA); Bar Inner Temple 1934; appointed Crown Counsel, Tanganyika 1946, Legal Draftsman 1949, Solicitor-Gen 1952, and Attorney-Gen Cyprus 1956, QC, Tanganyika 1953, and Cyprus 1957; a Member of Foreign Compensation Commn 1960-83 (Chm 1977-83); 1939-45 War in Middle East and Italy as Capt London Irish Rifles (R Ulster Rifles) (wounded MC); CMG 1960: *m* 1st, 1941 (*m diss* 1948), Susan Mary, da of Arthur G. Blackwell; 2ndly, 1949, Christina Hilary, da of Sir Hugh Oliver Holmes, KBE, CMG, MC, QC, and widow of Lt-Cdr Christopher Hayward Wells, RN (*see* Wells, Bt, *cr* 1944, colls), and has issue by 2nd *m*.

Residence – Kandy Lodge, 18 Ormond Av, Hampton-on-Thames, Middlesex TW12 2RU. *Club* – Travellers', Royal Commonwealth Society.

DAUGHTERS LIVING (By 2nd marriage)

Teresa Violet, *b* (Nov) 1949: *m* 1982, Gordon Stewart, of 7 Vanbrugh Fields, Blackheath, SE3, and has issue living, Edmund James, *b* 1985, — Roland Valentine *b* 1988. —— Christina Mary, *b* 1951: *m* 1979, Peter William Irving Ingram, and has issue (*see* Ingram, Bt, colls). —— Rosemary Jane, *b* 1955: *m* 1990, Peter Winckley, son of John Winckley, of E. Aberthaw, S Glam.

SISTERS LIVING

Denise Olive, MB, BS, MRCS, LRCP (7 Morley Rd, Farnham, Surrey). —— Alice Ellen, BSc: *m* 1946, Alan Newton, who *d* 19—, of 3 Oakdene, 64 Bourne Way, Hayes, Bromley, Kent BK2 7HA. —— Lorna Mary (7 Morley Rd, Farnham, Surrey).

COLLATERAL BRANCH LIVING

Issue of late Denis Valentine Henry, yr son of 1st baronet, *b* 1917, *d* 1983: *m* 1956, Elisabeth (307 Revidge Rd, Blackburn, Lancs BB1 8DF), da of Rowland Walker:—

PATRICK DENIS, *b* 20 Dec 1957. *Residence* – 2 Oakwood Place, Leeds LS8 2JD. —— Jessica Ellen, *b* 1960: *m* 1988, Ian Beech, of 1 Park Av, Bridgwater, Som TA6 7EE. —— Martha Olive, *b* 1961.

The 1st baronet, Rt Hon Sir Denis Stanislaus Henry, LLD, sat as MP for S Div of Londonderry co (*CoU*) 1916-21, and was Solicitor-Gen for Ireland 1918-19, Attorney-Gen 1919-21, and Lord Ch Justice of N Ireland 1921-5.

BUCHAN-HEPBURN (UK) 1815, of Smeaton Hepburn, Haddingtonshire
(Name pronounced "Bukkan-Hebburn")

To restore an ancient house

Sir (JOHN) ALASTAIR TRANT KIDD BUCHAN-HEPBURN OF SMEATON HEPBURN, 7th *Baronet; b* 27 June 1931; son of late John Trant Buchan-Hepburn, son of late Capt John Buchan-Hepburn, eldest son of John Buchan of Clune, co Fife, 2nd son of 2nd Bt; *s* his kinsman (3rd cousin), *Sir* NINIAN BUCHAN ARCHIBALD JOHN, 1992; *ed* Charterhouse, and St Andrews Univ; Capt (ret) late 1st King's Dragoon Gds; attached Household Cav 1953, attached Swiss Cav 1954, was ADC to GOC Malaya 1955-57; Member Inst of Brewing, and Member Baronets' Trust: *m* 1957, Georgina Elizabeth, SRN, late Lieut QARANC, only da of late Oswald Morris Turner, MC, of Armathwaite, Cumberland, and has issue.

Arms – Quarterly: 1st and 4th, gules, on a chevron argent a rose between two lions rampant of the first, *Hepburn;* 2nd, argent, three lions, heads erased gules, *Buchan;* 3rd, argent an anchor in bend azure, on a chief of the last three cranes or, *Beck.* **Crests** – 1st, a horse argent, furnished gules, tied to a yew tree proper, over it the motto "Keep tryst", 2nd, the sun in the dexter chief with a sunflower in full blow open to it proper, over it the motto "Non inferiora secutus" (*Not having followed mean pursuits*). **Supporters** – *Dexter,* a lion, gules; *sinister,* a heron with an eel in its beak proper.
Residence – Chagford, 60 Argyle St, St Andrews, Fife KY16 9BU. *Club* – Royal and Ancient.

SON LIVING

(JOHN) CHRISTOPHER ALASTAIR (Chagford, 60 Argyle St, St Andrews, Fife KY16 9BU; 11 School Rd, Twyford, Winchester, Hants S021 1QQ), *b* 9 March 1963; *ed* Cheltenham Coll, and Portsmouth Univ (BA, DipArch); Principal Officer Tenant Services Unit, Dundee District Council since 1994: *m* 1990, Andrea, da of Kenneth Frederick Unwin, of Elmview, Ryarsh, Kent, and has issue living, (John) James Christopher Thomas, *b* 1 Dec 1992.

DAUGHTERS LIVING

Caroline Georgina, *b* 1958; *ed* Gray's Sch of Art, Aberdeen (BA): *m* 1987, Andrew William Pollard Thomson, of Greendams Farmhouse, Drumoak, Kincardineshire AB31 3HQ, son of Dr William Pow Thomson, of Edinburgh, and has issue living, Hamish Andrew Buchan, *b* 1993. —— Sarah Elizabeth, *b* 1960; *ed* Univ Coll of N Wales, Bangor (BA): *m* 1988, David Arthur Cox, of Kettins House, Kettins, Blairgowrie, Perthshire PH13 9JL, only son of late Arthur Maurice Cox, and has issue living, Nicholas David Maurice, *b* 1990, — Frederick Alastair, *b* 1992. —— Louise Mary, *b* 1966; *ed* Dollar Acad: *m* 1989, (Alexander) David Stewart Kinnear, of New Easter Delfour, Alvie Estate, Kincraig, by Kingussie, Inverness-shire PH21 1ND, only son of late Alexander Norman Stewart Kinnear, of Druimore, Findhorn, Morayshire.

SISTER LIVING

Elizabeth Agnes Joyce, *b* 1933; *ed* St Leonard's Sch, St Andrews, and St Andrews Univ (MB and ChB 1956): *m* 1957, James Archibald Scott, CB, LVO, FRSE, of 38 Queen's Cres, Edinburgh EH9 2BA, and has issue living, Thomas James Buchan, *b* 1962, — Robert Alastair Howie, *b* 1964, — Hector Michael Hepburn, *b* 1969, — Rachel Elizabeth Frances, *b* 1960.

SISTER LIVING OF SIXTH BARONET

Primrose Eda, *b* 1917; European war 1939-45 in First Aid Nursing Yeo: *m* 1949, Major Ulick Edmund Burke Roche, S Wales Borderers (*see* B Fermoy, colls), who *d* 1990. *Residence* – Ynysfor, Penrhyndeudraeth, Gwynedd Ll48 6BJ.

WIDOW LIVING OF SIXTH BARONET

(MARY) ANGELA (*Dowager Lady Buchan-Hepburn*), da of late Thomas Ian Scott, of Balfunning, Balfron, Stirlingshire, formerly wife of John Miller Richard, and widow of Jack Walch Lyne: *m* 1991, as his 2nd wife, Sir Ninian Buchan Archibald John Buchan-Hepburn of Smeaton Hepburn, 6th Bt, who *d* 1992. *Residence* – Kailzie, by Peebles, Tweeddale EH45 9HT.

This family descends from the Buchans, lairds of Auchmacoy, Aberdeenshire, who claim descent from the Celtic Mormaers and Earls of Buchan. The 13th laird was recognised in 1792 as Chief of the name of Buchan. The lands of Alexander were erected into a barony 1598. His 2nd son, George, was ancestor of John Buchan of Letham, East Lothian, whose 1st wife, Elizabeth (*d* 1742) was sister and heir of George Hepburn of Smeaton Hepburn, East Lothian. Their son and heir George in 1764 *s* his maternal uncle as heir of line of Hepburn of Smeaton Hepburn and to that barony, and was recognized in the name and arms of Buchan-Hepburn. He was Advocate 1763, Judge of Admiralty Court 1790-1 and Baron of the Exchequer, Scotland 1800-14. On retirement he was *cr* a Baronet in 1815.

The Hepburns of Smeaton Hepburn descended from Adam 3rd son of Sir Patrick Hepburn of Waughton and Luffness to whom his father granted these lands in 1538. The Hepburns of Waughton descended from Sir Patrick of Waughton, uncle of Sir Patrick Hepburn of Hailes, who was *cr* Lord Hailes 1452/3. The 2nd Lord Hailes was in 1482 *cr* Earl of Bothwell, but both dignities were forfeited 1567 on attainder of James 4th Earl (and 1st Duke of Orkney), 3rd husband of Mary, Queen of Scots. He *d* without legitimate issue 1578.

Herne (Buckworth-Herne-Soame), see Soame.

Heron (Heron-Maxwell), see Maxwell.

Hervey-Bathurst, see Bathurst.

HEWETT (UK) 1813, of Nether Seale, Leicestershire

Seek nothing beyond your sphere

Sir PETER JOHN SMITHSON HEWETT, MM, 6th *Baronet*; *b* 27 June 1931; *s* his father, *Sir* JOHN GEORGE, MC, 1990; *ed* Bradfield Coll, and Jesus Coll, Camb (BA); Bar Gray's Inn 1954: *m* 1958, Jennifer Ann Cooper, only child of late Emrys Thomas Jones, OBE, of Nairobi, Kenya, and has issue.

Arms – Gules, on a chevron embattled argent, between three owls of the second, each crowned with an eastern coronet or, as many bombs fired proper. **Crest** – Out of a mural crown or, the stump of an oak-tree with branches, thereon a hawk proper gorged with an eastern coronet, belled gold. **Supporters** – *Dexter*, a tiger proper gorged with an eastern crown or; *sinister*, a buffalo charged on the shoulder with a trefoil slipped, all proper.
Address – PO Box 15669, Nairobi, Kenya.

SONS LIVING

RICHARD MARK JOHN, *b* 15 Nov 1958; *ed* Bradfield, and Jesus Coll, Camb (BSc). *Residence* – 188 Lovibonds Av, Orpington, Kent BR6 8EN. —— David Patrick John, *b* 1968; *ed* Bradfield, Reading Univ (BSc), and St Hugh's Coll, Oxford (MSc). *Address* – PO Box 190, Eldoret, Kenya.

DAUGHTER LIVING

Joanna Yuilleen, *b* 1960: *m* 1993, Patrick Fitzgerald Blundell, elder son of Maj Alan F. Blundell, of Gooseberry Hill, W Australia. *Residence* – 7 Sandover Rd, Darlington, W Australia.

BROTHER LIVING

Richard Harald, *b* 1933; *ed* Gordonstoun: *m* 1959, Bridget Elizabeth Anne, only da of late Alistair John Kirkman Finlay, and has had issue, Anthony John Finlay, *b* 1962; *d* 1982, — Julia Caroline, *b* 1960: *m* 1984, Michael Hyde-Duder, of Box 24460, Nairobi, Kenya, and has issue living, James Hyde *b* 1986, Siana Nicole *b* 1985. *Residence* – PO Box 15033, Nairobi, Kenya.

COLLATERAL BRANCHES LIVING

Issue of late George Nele Hewett, yst son of 4th baronet, *b* 1901, *d* 1972: *m* 1931, Margaret Skaife (Vitré, Coldash, Newbury), da of G. T. Denis de Vitré:—
Denis Nele, *b* 1932; Lt RN (ret). *Address* – PO Box 246 Keri Keri, Bay of Islands, NZ. —— Jeremy Patrick Nele (78: 6616 Alii Drive, Kailua Kona, 96740 Hawaii), *b* 1935: *m* 1963, Norma Shirley Garnett Smith, and has issue living, Geoffrey Alexander, *b* 1966, — Harald Randall Marsh, *b* 1969, — Kari Denise, *b* 1964.

Grandchildren of late Capt Charles William Hewett, RN, 2nd son of late Frank William Hewett (infra):—
Issue of late Brig William George Hewett, OBE, MC, *b* 1894, *d* 1973: *m* 1st, 1922 (*m diss* 1931), Louise Susan, da of late Francis R. Wolfe; 2ndly, 1932, Beatrice, who *d* 1961, da of late Lt-Col James Francis Donegan, CB:—
(By 1st *m*) Richard William (78 Walton St, SW3), *b* 1923; Maj RA (ret); Malaya 1953 (despatches); Chm and Man Dir The Readers Digest UK; Dir International Operations Readers Digest USA since 1986: *m* 1954, Rosemary, yr da of Basil Cridland, MC, TD, of Fernhurst, Sussex, and has issue living, Vanessa Annabel, *b* 1957, — Virginia Carolyn Rose, *b* 1960: *m* 1985, Dominic Marius Dennis Anthony Wheatley, of 64 Orbain Rd, SW6 7JY, elder son of Dennis Anthony Marius Thomas Wheatley, of Ridgway Gdns, Wimbledon, SW19, and has issue living, a son *b* 1991, Charlotte Rose *b* 1989. —— (By 2nd *m*) Sarah Margaret Arianwen, *b* 1942.
Issue of late Capt George Stuart Hewett, CBE, Roy Indian Navy, *b* 1863, *d* 1937: *m* 1899, Maude Mary Brind, who *d* 1958, da of Surg-Gen Henry Kendall, formerly Army Med Depart:—
Neale Brind Stuart (9 Egmont Rd, Ngongotaha, NZ), *b* 1906; Cdr (ret) Roy Indian Navy Reserve; a JP of NZ: *m* 1930, Thecla Edana, who *d* 1993, yst da of A. J. Davis, and has issue living, Neale John Patrick (PO Box 357 Seven Hills, NSW 2147, Australia), BEM, *b* 1931; *ed* Ampleforth; ACA; Kenya 1953 (BEM): *m* 1960 (*m* annulled 198—), Felicity Anne, da of late B. H. Kerby, and has issue living, Matthew Patrick George *b* 1969, Merri Bernard Neale *b* 1961, Felicity Sheena *b* 1963, Anita Noreen *b* 1967, — George Andrew Kendall, *b* 1942: *m* 1967, Sharon Rose, yst da of W. Souster, of Takapuna, Auckland, NZ, and has issue living, Jason Conrad Neale *b* 1969, Brind Nicholas Andrew *b* 1974, — Jeanne Marie Thecla, *b* 1933: *m* 1955, Alan Dever, of Glenbrook Station, c/o Putorino PO, Hawkes Bay, NZ, and Tiromaunga, Puketapu Po, Hawkes Bay, NZ, and has issue living, Neale Alan Kendall *b* 1958, Alan Guy *b* 1961, Wendy Janet Thecla *b* 1956, Penelope Jeanne *b* 1959, Catherine Adelaide *b* 1967.
Gen Right Hon Sir George GCB, 1st baronet, was Col 61st Regt, and C-in-C of the Forces in India, in Ireland. The 2nd baronet, a Col in the Army, was a distinguished Officer in Peninsular War.

HEWITT (UK) 1921, of Barnsley, West Riding, co Yorshire

Sir NICHOLAS CHARLES JOSEPH HEWITT, 3rd *Baronet*; *b* 12 Nov 1947; *s* his father *Maj Sir* JOSEPH, 1973: *m* 1969, Pamela Margaret, only da of Geoffrey J. M. Hunt, TD, of Broadacres, Scalby, Scarborough, and has issue.

Arms – Sable, a chevron in chief three owls or. **Crest** – Upon the battlements of a tower argent an owl proper.
Residence – Colswayn House, Huttons Ambo, York YO6 7HJ.

SONS LIVING

CHARLES EDWARD JAMES, *b* 15 Nov 1970. —— Michael Joseph, *b* 1973.

DAUGHTER LIVING

Victoria Alexandra Margaret, *b* 1978.

BROTHER LIVING

Timothy George, *b* 1950.

SISTER LIVING

Semper cadem

Always the same

Elizabeth Margaret, *b* 1945.

WIDOW LIVING OF SECOND BARONET

MARGUERITE (*Marguerite, Lady Hewitt*) (Lebberston Hall, nr Scarborough), da of Charles Burgess, of Deepdene, Filey: *m* 1940, Maj Sir Joseph Hewitt, 2nd Bt, who *d* 1973.

HEYGATE (UK) 1831, of Southend, Essex
(Name pronounced "Haygate")

Sir RICHARD JOHN GAGE HEYGATE, 6th *Baronet*; *b* 30 Jan 1940; *s* his brother, *Sir* GEORGE LLOYD, 1991; *ed* Repton, and Balliol Coll, Oxford: *m* 1st, 1968 (*m diss* 1972), Carol Rosemary, da of late Cdr Richard Michell, RN, of Leith House, Amberley, Surrey; 2ndly, 1974 (*m diss* 1988), Jong-Ja Hyun, da of In Suk, of Seoul; 3rdly, 1988, Susan Fiona, da of late Robert Buckley, of Cobblers Cottage, Peasmarsh, E Sussex, and has issue by 2nd and 3rd *m*.

Arms – Gules, two bars argent, on a bend or, a torteau between two leopards' faces azure. **Crest** – A wolf's head erased gules.
Residence – 29 Rossetti Gdns Mansions, Flood St, SW3 5QX.

SONS LIVING (*by 3rd marriage*)

FREDERICK CARYSFORT GAGE, *b* 28 June 1988. —— Robert George Liam, *b* 1991.

Boulogne et Cadiz

Boulogne and Cadiz

DAUGHTER LIVING (*by 2nd marriage*)

Eun-Hee Isobella Gage, *b* 1977.

DAUGHTERS LIVING OF FIFTH BARONET

Joanna, *b* 1977. —— Catherine, *b* (twin) 1977.

MOTHER LIVING

Gwyneth Eliot, da of late John Eliot Howard Lloyd: *m* 1936 (*m diss* 1947), has his 2nd wife, Sir John Edward Nourse Heygate, 4th Bt, who *d* 1976. *Residence* – 29 Rossetti Gdns Mansions, Flood St, SW3 5QX.

WIDOW LIVING OF FIFTH BARONET

HILDEGARD MATHILDE (*Dowager Lady Heygate*), da of August Anton Kleinjohann, of Wildstrasse 69, Duisburg, Germany: *m* 1960, Sir George Lloyd Heygate, 5th Bt, who *d* 1991. *Residence* – Willow Grange, Wissett, Halesworth, Suffolk.

COLLATERAL BRANCHES LIVING

Granddaughters of late Maj William Howley Beaumont Heygate, son of late William Unwin Heygate, 2nd son of 1st baronet:—
Issue of late Lieut-Col Gerald Heygate, DSO, RFA, *b* 1882, *d* 1954: *m* 1916, Cynthia, who *d* 1963, da of C. Darley, of Thorne:—

Katherine Raymonde Anne (c/o National Westminster Bank, 185 Sloane St, SW1), *b* 1917: *m* 1940 (*m diss* 1953), Capt John Bayley Middleton Horner, Irish Guards, and has issue living, Sarah Elizabeth Raymonde Anne, *b* 1942: *m* 1962, Virgil Pomfret, of 25 Sispara Gdns, SW18, and has issue living, Virgil Alexander *b* 1966, Emma Louise *b* 1965. ——— Felicity Cynthia June, *b* 1926: *m* 1950, Lt-Cdr Charles Owen, DSC, RN (ret), of Flat 31, 15 Portman Sq, W1, and has issue living, Rupert Charles (91 Cambridge St, SW1) *b* 1956: *m* 1988, Astrid Bigbie, and has issue living, Charles William *b* 1990, Henry Beaumont *b* 1991, — Caroline Angela, *b* 1954: *m* 1983, James Richard Dunsmuir Knox, of Martnaham Lodge, by Ayr, Ayrshire, and has issue living, Bryce William Dunsmuir *b* 1992, Constance Felicity Rose *b* (twin) 1992.

Issue of late Maj Lionel Clement Heygate, *b* 1893, *d* 1947: *m* 1st, 1918, Janet Leigh, who *d* 1923, only da of late Richard Jeston Ogle, of Christchurch, NZ; 2ndly, 1935 (*m diss* 1943), Yvonne Sylvia, da of late W. F. Tyler—
(By 1st *m*) Diana Juliet Beaumont (61 Campana Rd, SW6 4AT), *b* 1920: *m* 1946, Lt-Col John Francis Rush, RASC, who *d* 1992, and has issue living, Charles Burlison OGLE-RUSH, *b* 1947; *ed* Uppingham; assumed by deed poll 1968 the surname of Ogle-Rush: *m* 1977, Melanie Elizabeth Roche, da of Austin Hasslacher, of Bowler's Farm, Dockenfield, Farnham, Surrey, and has issue living, Michael Pellew Roche *b* 1980, Sophie Elizabeth *b* 1982, — Diana Louise OGLE-RUSH, *b* 1949; assumed by deed poll 19— the surname of Ogle-Rush in lieu of Bailey: *m* 1972 (*m diss* 1977), Michael Bailey. ——— (By 2nd *m*) Marilyn Jennifer, *b* 1938: *m* 1966, John Brigg Charles Fountaine, of Moor Farm, Great Bircham, King's Lynn, Norfolk PE31 6QP, yr son of Adm Charles Andrew Fountaine, CB, of Narford Hall, King's Lynn, Norfolk, and has issue living, Alexandra Juliet Catherine, *b* 1973, — Auriole Diana Eleanor, *b* 1975.

Granddaughters of late Major Edward Nicholas Heygate, 3rd son of 1st baronet:—
Issue of late Capt Richard Lionel Heygate, *b* 1859, *d* 1926: *m* 1895, Eleanor Mary Gwenllian, who *d* 1958, da of late Edward James Evans:—
Mary Ursula, *b* 1896: *m* 1930, Capt Eustace King-King, formerly Queen's R Regt, who *d* 1975, and has issue living, Edward Michael, *b* 1931; *ed* Stowe. *Residence* - . ——— Gladys Henrietta, *b* 1898: *m* 1st, 1924, Major Brereton Rigby, who *d* 1931; 2ndly, 1934, Richard Thomas, and has issue living, (by 1st *m*) Richard Arthur, *b* 1926: *m* 1950, Margaret Stocker, and has issue living, Janice Anita *b* 1951, Yvonne Linda *b* 1953, — Walter Oswald, *b* 1931, — (by 2nd *m*) Harold Mostyn, *b* 1936: *m* 1960, Kathleen Ada Hughes, and has issue living, Richard Edward *b* 1963, Roger Harold *b* 1970, Elizabeth Mary *b* 1960. *Residence* – Buckland, Docklow, Leominster, Hereford.
The 1st baronet was Lord Mayor of London 1822, City Chamberlain 1843-4, and MP for Sudbury in two Parliaments. Thomas Heygate, of Hayes, was Provost Marshal General under the Earl of Essex at the capture of Cadiz; his father held the same position in the Army, and was present before St Quintin; he was afterwards Provost Marshal in Scotland. Nicholas Heygate, the celebrated collector of curious books and writings, was of this family. Sir Frederick, 2nd baronet, was MP for co Londonderry (C) 1859-74, and the 3rd baronet, Sir Frederick Gage, was Parliamentary Under-Sec to Lord-Lieut of Ireland 1887-8. Sir John, 4th baronet, was a journalist and novelist, his first wife, Hon Evelyn Gardner, was formerly wife of Evelyn Waugh, the celebrated author.

HEYWOOD (UK) 1838, of Claremont, Lancashire

Alte volo
I fly high

Sir PETER HEYWOOD, 6th *Baronet*; *b* 10 Dec 1947; *s* his father, Sir OLIVER KERR, 1992; *ed* Bryanston, and Keble Coll, Oxford (BA 1969): *m* 1970, Jacqueline Anne, da of Sir Robert Frederick Hunt, CBE, of Maple House, Withington, Glos, and has issue.

Arms – Argent, three torteaux in bend between two bendlets gules; on a canton of the last a cross-patée or. **Crest** – On a mount vert the trunk of a tree with two branches sprouting therefrom and entwined with ivy, thereon a falcon wings displayed all proper.
Residence – 64 Newbridge Rd, Weston, Bath, Avon BA1 3LA.

DAUGHTERS LIVING

Vanessa Jane, *b* 1975. ——— Annabel Sarah, *b* 1976.

BROTHERS LIVING

MICHAEL (Kings Acre, Leys Rd, Tostock, Bury St Edmunds, Suffolk), *b* (twin) 10 Dec 1947; *ed* Bryanston, and Keble Coll, Oxford (BA 1969): *m* 1972, Carolyn Awdry, da of late Ian Joseph Greig, and has issue living, Daniel Oliver, *b* 1979, Katie May, *b* 1977. ——— James Philip, *b* 1951; *ed* Bryanston: *m* 1978, Alizen, da of Reginald Merryweather, FRCS, of Painswick, Glos, and has issue living, Jack Theyre, *b* 1981, — Barnabas Timothy, *b* 1985, — Lucy, *b* 1979.

AUNT LIVING (*sister of 5th baronet*)

Joan Margaret, *b* 1919: *m* 1950, John Marsden Preston, of Boxhanger Cottage, Box, Stroud, Glos, and has issue living, Nicolas, *b* 1952; *ed* Lyceé Français, London.

WIDOW LIVING OF FIFTH BARONET

DENISE (*Dowager Lady Heywood*), yr da of late Jocelyn William Godefroi, MVO, and formerly wife of Hon David Montague de Burgh Kenworthy (later 11th Baron Strabolgi): *m* 1947, Sir Oliver Kerr Heywood, 5th Bt, who *d* 1992. *Residence* – Rose Cottage, Elcombe, Stroud, Glos.

COLLATERAL BRANCHES LIVING

Granddaughters of late Lt-Col Gerald Graham Percival Heywood, TD, yst son of 2nd baronet:—
Issue of late Graham Scudamore Percival Heywood, *b* 1903, *d* 1985: *m* 1937, Valerie, who *d* 1992, da of Lt-Col Railton Wyatt, of Locks Heath, Hants:—
Susan Mary, *b* 1938: *m* 1961, John Michael Knight, of Oakwood, Itchen Abbas, Winchester, Hants, SO21 1AX, and has issue living, Timothy John, *b* 1963: *m* 1991, Lynda Marie, da of Keith Seymour, of Bradford, Yorks, — Nicola Susan, *b* 1962: *m* 1989, Glenn Allan Royall, of Ulladulla, NSW, Australia, and has issue living, Lachlan Allan *b* 1992, Charlotte Louise *b* 1991, — Deborah Ann, *b* 1965, — Bridget Julia, *b* 1970. ——— Veronica Anne, *b* 1942.

Grandchildren of late Henry Arthur Heywood, son of late Rev Henry Robinson Heywood (*infra*):—

Issue of late Geoffrey Henry Heywood, CBE, b 1903, d 1986: m 1931, Magdeleine Jeanne Georgette Marie, who d 1987, yr da of late Jean Herpin, of Paris:—
Claude Geoffrey (1626 Verling Av, Saanichton, BC V8M 1W8, Canada), b 1933; ed Repton, and Gonville and Caius Coll, Camb (MA); late Lt RA; HM Overseas Civil Service, Kenya 1957-62; Dep Min of Labour, Prov of BC: m 1960, Anne Helen, da of Theron Wilding-Davies, of Fayre Ways Stud Farm, Dorstone, Herefordshire, and has issue living, James Claude, b 1962, — Peter Geoffrey, b 1965: m 1989, Heather Joan, elder da of Barry Gill, of Brentwood Bay, BC, — Sarah Anne, b 1963: m 1991, Colin Derek Ewart, elder son of Hampton Ewart, of co Armagh. —— Claire Margaret, b 1938: m 1st, 1961 (m diss 1968), Mark Hugh Learoyd Piercy; 2ndly, 1973, Alexander Campbell Newton Ferguson, of Bernisdale, Hook Heath, Woking, Surrey GU22 0LE, and has issue living (by 1st m), Giles Hugh Scott, b 1966: m 1994, Camilla Anne, eldest da of Giles Sim, of Littles Farmhouse, Shalford Green, Braintree, Essex, — Emma Magdeleine, b 1963: m 1989, Edward Vincent Knox, of Godalming, Surrey.
Issue of late Rev Charles Richard Heywood, b 1908, d 1979: m 1939, Alice Ruth (5 Stoney Furlong Rd, Baslow, Bakewell, Derbys), da of Dr W. Henry Dobie, of Chester:—
Richard Henry Norman (11 Birch Drive, Brantham, Manningtree, Essex), b 1946; ed Workshop Coll; formerly Sec Gen Jaycees Internat; MIMS, MICFM: m 1971 (m diss 1987), Melody Dawn, el da of Col J. A. H. Nicholson, of Quinton, Bamford, Sheffield, and has issue living, Tamsin Melody, b 1975, — Nicola Dawn, b 1977. —— Margaret Anne, b 1950.

Grandchildren of late Charles Christopher Heywood, MB, MRCS, MRCP, 4th son of late Rev Henry Robinson Heywood (infra):—
Issue of late Very Rev Hugh Christopher Lempriere Heywood, b 1896, d 1987: m 1920, Margaret Marion, who d 1982, da of late Herbert Vizard, of Whitepost House, Redhill, Surrey:—
Peter (2 Dalemoor Gdns, Aspley Park Drive, Nottingham NG8 3EB), b 1922; ed Haileybury, and Gonville and Caius Coll, Camb (MA); FCP; formerly Capt Oxford and Bucks LI; Headmaster of William Sharp Comprehensive Sch, Nottingham 1968-87. —— Ann Rosemary, b 1930: m 1954, Thomas Strachan James, of The Mill House, 32 Mill Lane, Linton, Cambridge CB1 6JY, and has issue living, Christopher William, b 1955, — Timothy Robert, b 1956, — Pamela Susan, b 1961.
Issue of late Alan Lempriere Heywood, b 1899, d 1960: m 1925, Constance, who d 1988, da of Mrs Frederick Swales, of Simla:—
Denys Guy Lempriere (Deddington Manor, Deddington, Oxford), b 1926; ed Denstone and Caius Coll, Camb; Gp Capt RAF; commanded No 94 (F) Sqdn, and No 617 Sqdn (Dambusters) (ret); Bursar Tudor Hall Sch, Banbury 1977-88: m 1957, Elizabeth Ann, da of late J. Jeffrey Baker, of Windyridge, Altwood, Rd, Maidenhead, and has issue living, Robin Guy, b 1958: m 1984, Mitchiko, da of John Cole, of Deddington, — Simon John, b 1966: m 1992, Alison, da of Garry Cook, of Adderbury, Oxon, — Annabel Jane, b 1961, — Carol Elizabeth, b 1962: m 1992, Charles Skinner, of Winchester. —— Adrian Christopher Lempriere (c/o The Willows, Sandown Park, Tunbridge Wells, Kent), b 1928; ed Denstone, and Selwyn Coll, Camb (MA); formerly 2nd Lt RA: m 1962, Patricia Mollie Gardner, da of Guy Goulden, of 16 Grange Rd, Eastbourne, and has issue living, Christopher Lempriere, b 1962: m 1991, Lisa Mary Buckley, of Oldham, Lancs, — Guy Lempriere, b 1965: m 1993, Tracy Jane McCormack,of Melbourne, Australia.
Issue of late Basil Lempriere Heywood, b 1903, d 1989: m 1930, Phyllis Miriam (6 Pheasant Field, Hale, Liverpool L24 5SD), da of late John Orchard, Bar-at-Law, of Haigh Moor, Topsham, Exeter:—
John Basil Sumner (6 Pheasant Field, Hale, Liverpool L24 5SD), b 1933; CEng, MIEE. —— Christopher Richard (Rozel, Ditchling Rd, Haywards Heath, W Sussex RH17 7RF), b 1949: m 1971, Susan Rosa, da of Thomas William Howarth, of Tynwald, The Moorings, Preston Brook, Runcorn, Cheshire, and has issue living, Christopher David, b 1979, — Nicola Jane, b 1974. —— Diana Ruth, b 1937: m 1st, 1963, Michael John Evans, who d 1988; 2ndly, 1991, Brian Victor Woodcock, of 14 Pheasant Field, Hale, Liverpool L24 5SD, and has issue living (by 1st m), Andrew Michael (58 Duckworth Grove, Longbarn, Warrington, Cheshire), b 1964; ed Girton Coll, Camb (BA): m 1993, Sheelagh Marie Jones, — Christopher Philip, b 1966, — Jennifer Lesley, b 1968.

Grandchildren of late Rt Rev Bernard Oliver Francis Heywood, DD (infra):—
Issue of late Michael Henry Lempriere Heywood, b 1900, d 1990: m 1941, Marjorie (The Hollies, Barningham, Richmond, Yorks), da of C. B. Wood, of High Green, Sheffield:—
Charles Michael Lempriere, b 1942: m 1963, Robina Anne Pattison, and has issue living, Benjamin Michael Lempriere, b 1971, — Lucy Catherine Adamson, b 1977. —— Peter Bernard Martin, b 1946. —— David Mark, b 1947. —— Margaret Adamson, b 1944.
Issue of late Oliver Martin Heywood, b 1904, d 1982: m 1946, Eileen Maud (Virginia Cottage, Church Rd, Rotherfield, E Sussex), da of late Dr Martin Liebert, of Beckenham, Kent:—
Timothy David Lempriere (PO Box 25335, Abu Dhabi, United Emirates), b 1948; ed Haileybury: m 1st, 1972 (m diss 1986), Kathleen Ellen, da of J. L. Waldman, of Caracas; 2ndly, 1986, Jane, da of late Julian Sherrard, of Tunbridge Wells, Kent, and has issue living (by 1st m), Benjamin Michael, b 1973, — (by 2nd m) Sophie Henrietta, b 1986, — Jessica Jane, b 1989, — Joanna Clare, b (twin)1989. —— Jonathan Martin (Scripp, Foxhunt Green, Waldron, E Sussex), b (twin) 1948; ed Haileybury: m 1982, Elizabeth Mary, da of Thomas Wilks, of Laggan, Isle of Islay, Argyll, and has issue living, Thomas Martin, b 1985, — Emma Caroline, b 1983, — Kate Elizabeth Bridget, b 1993.

Grandchildren of late Rev Henry Robinson Heywood, 5th son of 1st baronet:—
Issue of late Rt Rev Bernard Oliver Francis Heywood, DD, sometime Lord Bishop of Ely, b 1871, d 1960: m 1895, Marion Maude, who d 1957, 2nd da of late Capt Percy Reid Lempriere:—
Charles Bernard Mark (21 St Andrew's Drive, Charmouth, Dorset), b 1906; ed Haileybury, and at Emmanuel Coll, Camb (MA); late Capt Oxford and Bucks LI: m 1941, Julia Veronica, who d 1977, da of late John Denis Cronin, of Cork. —— Francis Melville (30 The Bayle, Folkestone, Kent), b 1908; ed Haileybury, and Gonville and Caius Coll, Camb (MA); an Assist Master at Haileybury 1931-35; Fellow of Trinity Hall, Camb 1935-39; Master of Marlborough Coll 1939-52, and Warden of Lord Mayor Treloar Coll, Froyle, Hants 1952-69: m 1937, Dorothea Kathleen, who d 1983, da of Sir Basil Edgar Mayhew, KBE, and has had issue, †Simon Paget, b 1945; ed Marlborough, New Coll, Oxford (BA, DPhil), and Harvard Univ (Kennedy Memorial Scholar 1967): m 1967 (m diss 1972), Sheila Madeleine, only da of Sir Frank Stannard Gibbs, KBE, CMG and d 1984, — Susan Frances (9 Residence des Canadiens, Puys, 76370 Neuville les Dieppe, Seine Maritime, France), b 1939: m 1965 (m diss 1984), Jean Marc Duquesne, and has issue living, Marc Dominic b 1966, Benjamin Piers b 1969, Sebastian Paul b 1972, — Janion Lempriere (Bruce Rd RD5, Te Awamutu, NZ) b 1947; BSc London; MB, BS, MRCS, LRCP: m 1972, Robert John LeQuesne, MB, BS, MRCS, LRCP, and has issue living, Nicholas Robert Paget b 1981, Katherine Amy b 1977, Rebecca Janion b 1978.
The 1st baronet, an eminent banker of Manchester, led the Reform Agitation in Lancashire, and sat as MP for that county in the Parliament preceding the passing of the Reform Bill of 1832. His yst brother, James Heywood, FRS, who d 1897, sat as MP for North Lancashire (L) in the Parliaments of 1847 and 1852. The 2nd baronet was High Sheriff of Lancashire 1851. The 3rd baronet was High Sheriff of Derbyshire 1899. The 4th baronet, Lieut-Col Sir (Graham) Percival, CB, DSO, TD, TA (ret), served in European War 1914-18 (DSO).

HICKMAN (UK) 1903, of Wightwick, Tettenhall, Staffordshire

By fire and sword

IGNE ET FERRO

Sir (RICHARD) GLENN HICKMAN, 4th *Baronet; b* 12 April 1949; *s* his father, *Sir* (ALFRED) HOWARD WHITBY, 1979; *ed* Eton: *m* 1981, Heather Mary Elizabeth, da of Dr James Moffett, of Westlecot Manor, Swindon, Wilts, and has issue.

Arms – Party per saltire sable and or, two leopards' faces jessant-de-lis in pale and as many fleur-de-lis in fesse, all counterchanged. Crest – A Phœnix issuing out of flames, transfixed through the mouth by a tilting-spear palewise proper, each wing charged with two annulets erect and interlaced or.
Residence – Grains Farm, Lower Blunsdon, nr Swindon, Wilts SN2 4DF. *Club* – Turf.

SONS LIVING

CHARLES PATRICK ALFRED, *b* 5 May 1983. —— Edward William George, *b* 1990.

DAUGHTER LIVING

Elizabeth Margaret Ruth, *b* 1985.

UNCLE LIVING (*son of 2nd baronet*)

Patrick Nelson (Hale Park, Fordingbridge, Hants; 65 Onslow Gdns, SW7; *Club* – White's), *b* 1921; F/L RAFVR (ret); a Freeman of City of London, and a Livery-man of Fishmongers' Co: *m* 1st, 1944 (*m diss* 1950), Leontine Mariette (Marylena), da of Capt James Allan Dyson Perrins, MC and bar, JP, late Welsh Guards; 2ndly, 1953 (Margaret) Gail, da of Col Cassell Ryan St Aubyn, 60th Rifles of 34 Rue de la Faisanderie, Paris XVI, and has issue living, (by 1st *m*) (Patrick) Rupert COTTRELL (Newbold House, Clipston, Market Harborough, Leics; *Clubs* – Boodle's, R Yacht Sqdn, Beefsteak, Jockey Club Rooms), *b* 1945; assumed by deed poll 1953 the surname of Cottrell in lieu of his patronymic; *ed* Gordonstoun: *m* 1st, 1968 (*m diss* 1989), Claire, el da of Lt-Col J. G. Round, OBE, JP, DL; 2ndly, 1989, Anne, only da of late Arthur Ralph Holbrook, of Mahon House, Cropwell Butler, Notts, and has issue living (by 1st *m*), Nicholas Rupert Round *b* 1970, Jessica Victoria *b* 1974, —— Rozanna Mariette, *b* 1946; assumed by deed poll 1953 the surname of Cottrell in lieu of her patronymic: *m* 1969, Michael John Hardy Hammond, and has issue living, James David Hardy *b* 1972, Matthew Charles Perrins *b* 1975, —— (by 2nd *m*) (Patrick) Sloan, *b* 1955: *m* 1993, Candida R. d'Ombrain, da of Dr Roderick William Grant, of Alderholt Park, Fordingbridge (*see* By Ardilaun, colls, 1944 Edn), —— Vivien Anne, *b* 1957: *m* 1983, Edmund B. MacDonald, jr, of 263 28th Av, San Francisco 94121, California, USA, son of Edmund B. MacDonald, of San Francisco, and has issue living, Angus Nelson *b* 1987, Fiona *b* 1990.

WIDOW LIVING OF SECOND BARONET

NANCY BERYL (*Beryl, Lady Hickman*), da of late Capt Trevor George Morse-Evans, JP, Barrister-at-law (Inner Temple), MA (Cantab), MFH: *m* 1940, as his 2nd wife, Sir Alfred Edward Hickman, 2nd baronet, who *d* 1947. *Residence* – Holmbush House, Faygate, nr Horsham, W Sussex.

WIDOW LIVING OF THIRD BARONET

MARGARET DORIS (*Margaret, Lady Hickman*) (Leaper Cottage, Letchmore Heath, Herts), only da of Leonard Kempson, of Potters Bar, Middlesex, and formerly wife of Denis Thatcher (later Sir Denis Thatcher, 1st Bt): *m* 1948, Sir (Alfred) Howard Whitby Hickman, 3rd baronet, who *d* 1979.

COLLATERAL BRANCHES LIVING

Granddaughters of late Alfred William Hickman, el son of 1st baronet:—
Issue of late Lieut-Col Arthur Hickman, *b* 1891, *d* 1959; *m* 1914, Dorothy Gwendolen, RRC, who *d* 1957, da of late Edward Charles Rudge, JP, DL, of Abbey Manor, Evesham:—
Christine Gwen, TD, *b* 1920; late Major WRAC (TA). —— Pamela Jill, *b* 1921; formerly Subaltern ATS. *Residence* – 308A Barkham Rd, Wokingham, Berks.

Grandchildren of late Brig-Gen Thomas Edgecombe Hickman, CB, DSO, 4th son of 1st baronet:—
Issue of late Capt Thomas Alfred Kenneth Hickman, *b* 1912; *ka* 1940: *m* 1936, Leila Philippa, of Holme Cottage, Church St, Nunnington, York YO6 5US (who *m* 2ndly, 1945, Major Eric Inman Scott, MC, who *d* 1967), el da of Lt-Col Montagu Martindale Parry-Jones, MC (*d* 1969), Roy Fusiliers (Borrowes, Bt):—
Thomas Montagu (60 Acre Lane, SW2), *b* 1940; *ed* Eton; Major (ret) The Life Gds: *m* 1st, 1967 (*m diss* 1974), Lieselotte Brandstetter, of Vienna; 2ndly, 1977, Christina, da of Lt-Cdr Kenneth Alston Cradock-Hartopp, MBE, DSC, RN (ret) (*see* Cradock-Hartopp, Bt, colls), and has issue living (by 1st *m*), Thomas Michael, *b* 1972, —— Lucinda Ann, *b* 1970: *m* 1991, Anthony Kenneth Noel Terry, eldest son of Peter Noel Leetham Terry, of Cherry Hill, Brandsby, York, —— (by 2nd *m*), Alexander Kenneth, *b* 1980, —— Louise Amy, *b* 1978. —— Mary Elizabeth, *b* 1937: *m* 1st, 1962 (*m diss* 1975), Timothy Haworth, son of late Maj Philip Knight Haworth, MC, of Filey, N Yorks; 2ndly, 1975, Richard Malise Graham, of Cedar Hill, Roscrea, co Tipperary, and has issue living (by 2nd *m*), Lileth Rosamund Anne, *b* 1975, —— Ruth Leila Margaret, *b* 1977.

Grandchildren of late Maj Charles Edward Hickman, *b* 1890, *d* 1963: 5th son of 1st baronet:—
Issue of late Edward Hickman, *b* 1890, *d* 1963: *m* 1st, 1915, Edith Barbara, who *d* 1915, da of late Frank Spencer, JP, of Egerton, Harrow-on-the-Hill; 2ndly, 1921, Dorothy, who *d* 1966, da of late W. Deans Forster, of Ponteland, Newcastle-upon-Tyne:—
(By 2nd *m*) David Michael Roy (Tower House, West Castle St, Bridgnorth, Shropshire), *b* 1930: *m* 1st, 1959 (*m diss* 1967), Eileen Elizabeth, yr da of late Brian Robert Boyd, of Belfast; 2ndly, 1978, Valerie Beatrice, el da of Frank Victor Collins, of Wolverhampton, and has issue living (by 1st *m*), Charles John, *b* 1960, —— Timothy Robert (Ilex Trees, Mickleham, Surrey), *b* 1964: *m* 1990, Vanessa Caroline, eldest da of Lt-Col R. A. Latchford, of Düsseldorf, Germany, and has issue living, Camilla Beatrice *b* 1990, —— Peter Richard (twin), *b* 1964. —— Catherine Elaine, *b* 1926: *m* 1st, 1949, Giles Reid Walker, who *d* 1951 (*see* Walker-Okeover, Bt, colls); 2ndly, 1955, Patrick Campbell Hall, of Cae Grugog, Trearddur Bay, Holyhead, Anglesey LL65 2UD, and has issue living (by 1st *m*) (*see* Walker-Okeover, Bt, colls), —— (by 2nd *m*) Andrew Campbell, *b* 1957.

Issue of late Wilfred Haden Hickman, *b* 1892, *d* 1973: *m* 1915, Kathleen Mary Stuart, who *d* 1978, da of Edward Noel Nason, MD, of Nuneaton:—

Wilfred Ian Edward (Clifton Manor, Clifton upon Dunsmore, Rugby), *b* 1916; JP for Warwicks: *m* 1940, Muriel Claire, da of late William Horsnall, of Nuneaton, Warwicks. —— Denis Stewart, MC (28 Kingham Rd, Churchill, Oxford OX7 6NE), *b* 1918; late Capt RASC; 1939-45 War in Italy (MC, 1939-41 Africa and Italy stars, prisoner): *m* 1st, 1947 (*m diss* 1964), Peggy Barbara (MCALPINE), who *d* 19—, da of late John Ernest Sanders, of Gresford; 2ndly, 1965, Jean, da of A. Urwin, of Tynemouth, and has issue living, (by 2nd *m*) Tara Jane, *b* 1966, — Rona Stuart, *b* 1967, — Anya Lucy, *b* 1969. —— Christopher Wolf Arden (Barnhill, Naunton, Stow-on-the-Wold, Glos), *b* 1925; 1939-45 War with RASC: *m* 1949, Daphne Esther, da of John Alec Clift, and has issue living, Rachael, *b* 1951: *m* 1979, Peter Austin, of Ludbridge Mill, East Hendred, Wantage, Oxfordshire OX12 8LN, and has issue living, William Michael *b* 1980, James Peter *b* 1983, Claire Poppy Rosina *b* 1986, — Rosemary, *b* 1953, — Gillian, *b* 1955, — Joanna, *b* 1964. —— Rona Kathleen, *b* 1921; 1939-45 War with WRNS: *m* 1943, Reginald Alfred Reardon Smith, and has issue living, Christopher John Harry Reardon (139 Learg St, Coolum, Queensland, Australia) *b* 1946: *m* 1967, Frances Barnes, and has issue living, David Harry Reardon *b* 1978, Paula Maria *b* 1967, Tina Georgina *b* 1971, — William Jeremy Reardon (Winnipeg, Manitoba, Canada), *b* 1949: *m* 1st, 19— (*m diss* 19—), Margaret Harrap; 2ndly, 19—, Judith —, — Anthea Kathleen, *b* 1944: *m* 1st, 1967 (*m diss* 19—), Michael Monks; 2ndly, 19—, Richard Holborow, of Tetbury, Glos, and has issue living (by 1st *m*), Emma Kathrine *b* 1969, — Janice Caroline, *b* 1953: *m* 1979, Antony Collins, and has issue living, Timothy Gerald *b* 1980, Sarah Jocelyn *b* 1983.

Grandchildren of late Victor Emanuel Hickman, 6th son of 1st baronet:—

Issue of late Cdr Geoffrey Victor Hickman, DSC, RN, *b* 1890, *d* 1975: *m* 1st, 1914, Josephine Helen, who *d* 1933, da of Lt-Col Walter Reginald Fox, formerly RA; 2ndly, Gwendoline Dorothy Miell:—

(By 1st *m*) Hugh Geoffrey, *b* 1916; 1939-45 War as Lt S Staffs, Regt. —— Geraldyne Rosemary Margaret, *b* 1917: *m* 1946, Richard Wiltshire, of 4 Claverdon Close, Solihull, and has issue living, Hugh Richard, *b* 1947: *m* 1970, Barbara Gwenyth Price, and has issue.

Issue of late John Owen Hickman, 7th son of 1st baronet, *b* 1870, *d* 1949: *m* 1903, Nancy Viola, who *d* 1963, da of Harry Barlow:—

Michael Ranulf (The Acorn, Bovingdon, Herts), *b* 1922; *ed* Wellington Coll, and Trin Hall, Camb; Bar Middle Temple 1949; formerly Fl-Lt RAFVR; appointed a Circuit Court Judge 1974: *m* 1943, Diana, da of Col D. C. H. Richardson, 10th Hussars, and has issue living, Peter Derek, *b* 1951: *m* 1974, (Hilary) Clare, da of Don Sadler, of Gwelo, Zimbabwe, and has issue living, Richard Ranulf *b* 1977, Adam Derek *b* 1980, — Susan Marilyn, *b* 1948: *m* 1972, Aris Alexander Pierre Zarpanely, of 2 Old Dock Close, Kew Green, Surrey, and has issue living, Petros Alexander *b* 1975, Rene Diana *b* 1977. —— Angela Mary, *b* 1924: *m* 1st, 1943, Charles Gordon Richards, who was *ka* 1943; 2ndly, 1948, William Freshwater, who *d* 1989, and has issue living (by 2nd *m*), Michael David Latimer, *b* 1950, — Martin Walter James, *b* 1958, — Jane Elizabeth Mary, *b* 1948, — Christine Ellen Nancy, *b* 1962. *Residence* – Chaiya, Ball Hill, Newbury, Berks.

Grandchildren of late John Owen Hickman (ante):—

Issue of late John Barlow Hickman, *b* 1904, *d* 1932: *m* 1925, Joan (9 Hakeburn Rd, Cirencester, Glos), da of late Kyrle Chatfield Hankinson, of Eden Mount, Tunbridge Wells:—

John Kyrle, CMG (Ivy Bank, Oare, nr Marlborough), *b* 1927; *ed* Tonbridge, and Trin Hall, Camb (BA), Diplo Ser CMG 1977: *m* 1956, Jennifer, da of Reginald Kendall Love, and has issue living, Matthew John Kyrle, *b* 1964: *m* 1994, Andrea F., da of late D. J. P. Hudson, and of Sra Adriana Kimber, of Santiago, Chile, — Andrew Giles Lovell, *b* 1966, — Catherine Lucy, *b* 1960: *m* 1987, Tom Owen Edmunds, of The Coach House, Tal-y-Coed Court, nr Monmouth, Gwent NP5 4HR, son of David Owen Edmunds. —— Richard Malim (The Malt Shovel, Vigo, Burcot, Bromsgrove, Worcs), *b* 1930; *ed* Tonbridge, and Pembroke Coll, Camb (BA); *m* 1962, Judy Penelope Sylvia, da of Brig Charles Douglas Armstrong, CBE, DSO, MC, and has issue living, Marcus Sebastian Charles, *b* 1963, — Jonathan Edward Barlow, *b* 1964. —— Dinah (Trehu, Pulla Cross, Truro, Cornwall), *b* 1929: *m* 1953, John Frederick Saunders, and has issue living, Richard Neville, *b* 1955, — Joanna Elizabeth, *b* 1958.

The 1st baronet, Sir Alfred Hickman, Chm of Alfred Hickman (Limited), sat as MP for Wolverhampton (*C*) 1885-6, and 1892-1906.

HILL (I) 1779 of Brook Hall, Londonderry

Attempt not, or accomplish

Sir JOHN ALFRED ROWLEY HILL, 11th *Baronet*; *b* 1940; *s* his half-brother, *Sir* RICHARD GEORGE ROWLEY, MBE, 1992; *ed* —: *m* 19, — —, da of —, of —.

Arms – Sable, a chevron erminois between three leopards' faces argent. **Crest** – A talbot's head couped sable, guttés d'eau, collared gules, studded and ringed or.
Residence – Western Australia.

SISTER LIVING

Margaret Anne Rowley, *b* 1942. *Residence* – —.

DAUGHTERS LIVING OF TENTH BARONET

Charlotte Mary Rowley, *b* 1976. —— Georgina Emma Rowley, *b* 1977.

WIDOWS LIVING OF EIGHTH AND NINTH BARONETS

EDITH MURIEL (*Edith, Lady Hill*), da of W— O— Thomas, of Oakhurst, Liverpool, and Bryn Glas, Mold, N Wales: *m* 1919, Sir (George) Cyril Rowley Hill, 8th Bt, who *dsp* 1980. *Residence* – Oakfield, Havord Road, Gwernymynydd, Mold, N Wales.
JESSIE ANNE (*Jessie, Lady Hill*), da of — Roberts, of —, Leics: *m* 1939, as his 2nd wife, Sir George Alfred Rowley Hill, 9th Bt, who *d* 1985. *Residence* – 6 Harris Close, The Granthames, Lambourn, Berks.

COLLATERAL BRANCHES LIVING

Grandchildren of late Rowley John Hill (infra), son of Marcus Hill, el son of Capt Rowley John Hill, 2nd son of Rev John Beresford Hill, 2nd son of 1st baronet:—
　　　Issue of late Leslie Thomas Hill, *b* 1897, *d* 1958: *m* 1920, Irene Howlett:—
Joan Maria *b* 1925: *m* 1945, Leslie Bailey, and has issue living, Kenneth Leslie, *b* 1946, — Cheryl Larraine, *b* 1948. —— Dorothy Irene, *b* 1928: *m* 1947, Herbert Alfred Morley, and has issue living, Christopher John, *b* 1950, — Carol Anne, *b* 1948.
　　　Issue of late Claude Adam James Hill, *b* 1901, *d* 1991: *m* 1928, Ruby Alice (8 Lancaster Rd, Mooroolbank, Vic, Aust), da of Robert Mallett:—
ALLAN CLAUDE JAMES (18/20 Havelock St, Lawrence, NSW 2460, Aust), *b* 1936: *m* 1970 (*m diss* 1978), Rachel ST JUST, da of Geoffrey Filsell, and has issue living, Marcus Adam James, *b* 1974, — Sonya Rachel Anne, *b* 1972. —— Joyce Patricia, *b* 1933: *m* 1951, Geoffrey Paul, of 8 Lancaster Rd, Mooroolbank, Vic, Aust, and has issue living, Allan Geoffrey, *b* 1952, — Cheryl Therese, *b* 1955: *m* 1987, Andrew Rhodes, of 112 Chirnside St, West Footscray, Vic, Aust, and has issue living, Gene Paul *b* 1987.
　　　Issue of late Marcus George Hill, *b* 1904, *d* 1993: *m* 1929, Lydia May Liddle:—
†George Frederick, *b* 1930: *m* 1951, Jean Craggel, and *d* 1991, having had issue, Anthony Rowland, *b* 1961, — Debra, *b* 1964, — Sallyanne, *b* 1966; *d* 1989. —— Kevin Leslie (49 Fraser St, Sunshine, Vic 3020), *b* 1935: *m* 1959, Wendy Chandler, and has issue living, Mark, *b* 1961: *m* 1986, Caryn Geddes, and has issue living, Joshua Mark *b* 1992, — Paul, *b* 1964: *m* 1989, Tina-Jane Pinchen. —— Patricia Miriam, *b* 1932: *m* 1954, Rolf Ludviksen, of 26 Poole St, Deer Park, Vic 3023, and has issue living, John Kenneth (75 Tarella Drive, Kealba, Vic 3021), *b* 1955: *m* 19—, Tracey Ruth, da of John McLoone, and has issue living, Michael John *b* 1991, — Brett, *b* 1972, — Leanne Michelle (16 Locke St, Essendon, Vic 3040), *b* 1959: *m* 1977 (*m diss* 1983), Allan Borg, and has issue living, Melinda Amy *b* 1979. —— Dawn Anne, *b* 1939: *m* 1963, John Justin, of 7 Bellair Av, Glenroy, Vic 3046, and has issue living, Kenneth, *b* 1964, — Darren, *b* 1966, — Glen *b* 1971.
　　　Issue of late Cyril Edward Hill, *b* 1908, *d* 1988: *m* 1931, Mary Elizabeth (Unit 16/2, High Field Rd, Canterbury, Vic 3126, Aust), da of Francis Tinker:—
James Rowland Edward (Lot 7, 9 Arnold St, Kilsyth, Melbourne, Vic, Aust), *b* 1943: *m* 1969, Lynette Jean, da of — Berry, and has issue living, Jason James, *b* 1972, — Christophe Eric, *b* 1974. —— Janice Ann, *b* 1940: *m* 1962, Ronald Arthur Haynes, of 39 Sandy St, Nunawading, Vic 3131, Aust, and has issue living, Diane Mary, *b* 1964, — Michelle Lucy, *b* 1966, — Joanne Lisa, *b* 1969: *m* 1990, Carl Gittins, of 4/34 Oak St, Seymour, Vic 3660, Aust, — Belinda Jane, *b* 1975. —— Elizabeth Dianna, *b* 1945: *m* 1967, Constantine Politis, of 16 Russell Av, Mooroolbank, Vic, Aust, and has issue living, Andrew Edward, *b* 1973, — Jeannette Ann, *b* 1969, — Debra Lee, *b* 1971.

　　　Grandchildren of late Marcus Hill (ante):—
　　　Issue of late Rowley John Hill, *b* 1873, *d* 1960: *m* 1896, Anne Elizabeth Morrow, who *d* 1912:—
Albert John, *b* 1912: *m* 1935, Annie Melba, da of Edgar William Johnstone.
　　　Issue of late James Henry Sale Hill, *b* 1885, *d* 1954: *m* 1910, Ethyl May Woodbury, who *d* 1967, of Wangaratta, Victoria:—
Roy Ernest (Rau St, Albury, NSW, Australia), *b* 1914: *m* 1935, Phyllis Jean Allen, of Ringwood, Victoria, and has issue living, Lorres Ann, *b* 1938: *m* 19—, Robert E. Johnson, of Launceston, Tasmania, and has issue living, Antony *b* 1964, David *b* 1970, — Catherine Elizabeth, *b* 1966. —— James Herbert (Rau St, Albury, NSW), *b* 1912: *m* 1936, Charlotte Ethel Bastion. —— Olive May, *b* 1915: *m* 1933, Allan Klinberg.
　　　Issue of late Philip Ernest Hill, *b* 1887, *d* 1960: *m* 1913, Hilda Maria Ambrosina Cooper, who *d* 1966:—
Clem Ernest, *b* 1913. —— Stanley George (27 Summerhill Av, E Malvern, Melbourne 3145, Vic, Aust), *b* 1935: *m* 1964, Patricia Ann McLellan, and has issue living, Philip William Adrian, *b* 1966, — Paul Timothy, *b* 1968, — Michael John, *b* 1975, — Catherine Elizabeth, *b* 1979. —— Philis May, *b* 1917: *m* 1938, George Lewis Robinson, of 49 Hardy Av, Wagga Wagga, NSW, and has issue living, Helen, *b* 1940: *m* 1960, —, — Shirley, *b* 1942: *m* 1962 —, — Dawn, *b* 1950, — Maree, *b* 1956. —— Thelma Rose, *b* 19—: *m* 19—, Ronald Charles Wheeler, and has issue living, Garry, *b* 19—, — Robert, *b* 19—, — Janet, *b* 19—.

　　　Grandchildren of late Marcus Henry Sale Hill (infra):—
　　　Issue of late Wilfred Henry Hill, *b* 1906, *d* 1972: *m* 1936, Thelma Mattingly:—

Robert Maxwell, *b* 1938: *m* 1962, Wendy Cross, and has issue living, Christopher, *b* 19—, — Robyn, *b* 1962, — Julie, *b* 1965. —— Lesley Robin Gael, *b* 1949: *m* 1966, Gavan McEntee, and has issue living, Gavan Chayne, *b* 1966, — Brett Owen, *b* 1968, — Stephen Robert, *b* 1969. —— Dawn Adeline, *b* 1937: *m* 1963, Raymond Wilkins, and has issue living Lionel David, *b* 1964, — Deborah Margery, *b* 1967, — Dionne Beryl, *b* 1970.

Issue of late Henry George Hill, *b* 1909, *d* 1988: *m* 1940, Eileen Webb (Port Chalmers, Otago, NZ):—
Harold Alexander, *b* 1941: *m* 1st, 19— (*m diss* 19—), Fay Ogarman; 2ndly, 19— (*m diss* 19—), Cynthia Joan Letherland. —— Francis John, *b* (twin) 1941: *m* 1963, Margaret —, and has issue living, David John, *b* 1963: *m* 1986, Joanne —, and has issue living, Cheryl Maree *b* 1987, — Brett Christopher, *b* 1966, — Yvonne Clare, *b* 1970. —— Owen Patrick, *b* 1943. —— Mervyn George, *b* 1945: *m* 1967, Janet Murgatroyd, and has issue living, Aaron Mervyn, *b* 1967, — Adrian Bevan, *b* 1974, — Leanne Marie, *b* 1968, — Deborah Anne, *b* 1970. —— Michael David, *b* 19—: *m* 1974, Robyn —, and has issue living, Allan Paul, *b* 1981, — Jocelyn, *b* 1979. —— Sharon Joy, *b* 1947: *m* 1966, David Dick, and has issue living, Steven Kidmond, *b* 1968, — Tracey Joy, *b* 1969. —— Angela Fay, *b* 19—: *m* 1975, Ian Page, and has issue living, Steven, *b* 1979, — Anita, *b* 1981. —— Eileen Christine, *b* 19—: has issue living, Tania Marie, *b* 1974.

Grandchildren of late George Henry Hill, 3rd son of Capt Rowley John Hill (ante):—
Issue of late Marcus Henry Sale Hill, *b* 1870, *d* 1946: *m* 1903, Emma Frances, da of Henry Kenton, of Lower Harbour, Port Chalmers, New Zealand:—
Edward Albert, *b* 1911: *m* 1935, Jessie Margaret McWilliam, who *d* 19—, da of Robert Wilson, of Whakatane, NZ, and has issue living, Edward Wilson Sale, *b* 1936, — Robert George, *b* 1940, — Leonard James, *b* 1943, — Marwyn Albert, *b* 1955, — Margaret Elizabeth, *b* 1938. —— Russell Sale (33 Dunton Rd, Welcome Bay, Tauranga, NZ), *b* 1913: *m* 1945, Pearl Iris, da of Lewis Septimus Civil, of Pukekohe, NZ, and has issue living, Marie June, *b* 1946: *m* 1968, David Ivor Jones, of Manawahe, Bay of Plenty, NZ, and has issue living, Glenn David *b* 1969, Justine Joanne *b* 1971, — Carolyn Lesley, *b* 1947: *m* 1982, Gerry McGillicuddy (B Eng), of Mongonui, Northland, NZ. —— †Ernie Parker *b* 1916: *m* 1946, Jessie May Court (Deborah Bay, Port Chalmers, NZ), of Waimate, S Canterbury, NZ, and *d* 1992, leaving issue, Malcolm Ross, *b* 1947: *m* 19— (*m diss* 19—), Clare McAlley, and has issue living Sarah-Jane Frances *b* 1978, Rebecca Ailsa *b* 1981, — Donald Graeme, *b* 1962, — Janice Audrey, *b* 1950: *m* 1st, 1970 (*m diss* 19—), Lindsay Wilson; 2ndly, 1974, Neville Billington, and has issue living, (by 1st *m*) Jocelyn Anne *b* 1971, Deborah Kaye *b* 1973, (by 2nd *m*) Philip John *b* 1975, Craig Neville *b* 1978, — Nellie May, *b* 1952: *m* 1976 (*m diss* 19—), Stephen Rayston, and has issue living, Michael Alexander *b* 1979, — Barbara Ann, *b* 1959: has issue living, Kelly Marie *b* 1978. —— Thelma Alice (9 Islington St, Te Aroka, N Island, NZ), *b* 1920: *m* 1940, Walter James McLay, who *d* 1986, and has issue living, Ernest James, *b* 1941: *m* 1961, Sylvia May Rolf, and has issue living, Stephen James *b* 1962: *m* 1984, Linda Quigley (and has issue living, Christopher James *b* 1988), Kenneth Stuart *b* 1963: *m* 1987, Sarah Ash, Peter Ernest *b* 1967, Donna Ann *b* 1964, — Douglas Stuart, *b* 1942: *m* 1969, Carol Jean Grice, and has issue living, Jason Stuart Marshall *b* 1971, Scott Douglas *b* (twin) 1971, Katrina Maree *b* 1969, — Alastair David, *b* 1946: *m* 1980 Bronwen Roger, and has issue living, Joanne Beth *b* 1981, Heather Ruth *b* 1983, Rebecca Lois *b* 1986, — Trevor Sale, *b* 1947: *m* 1982, Carol Cunningham, — Norman Walter, *b* 1951: *m* 1982, Sandra Grubber, and has issue living, Bradley Walter *b* 1984, Jonathan David *b* 1986, — Ian Murray, *b* 1956: *m* 1984, Fiona Mary Lowery, and has issue living, James Murray *b* 1987, — Sheryl Joy, *b* 1949: *m* 19—, Hugh Kay Sueistrup, and has issue living, Shawn Kay *b* 1971, Darrell Boyes *b* 1974, Kassandra Joy *b* 1972. —— Myra Edith, *b* 1922: *m* 1945, Bruce Bannermann, who *d* 1991, of 10 Wigan St, Gore, Southland, NZ, and has issue living, Kevin Bruce (50 Caulfield St, Ranfurly, NZ), *b* 1947: *m* 1976, Cheryl McLeod, and has issue living, Dwayne Marcus *b* 1983, Natalie Ann *b* 1981, — Andrew Henry, *b* 1950: *m* 1973 (*m diss* 1994), Shirley Newlove, and has issue living, Brendon Peter *b* 1974, Shane Bruce *b* 1976, Jenny Marie *b* 1979, — Neville William, *b* 1955, — Nola Mae, *b* 1946: *m* 1967, Norman Russell Anderson, of Ashley Downs, Clinton, S Otago, NZ and has issue living, Ernest Keith, *b* 1973 James Bannerman *b* 1976, Diane Marie *b* 1969, Glenys Mae *b* 1970, — Marion Frances, *b* 1949: *m* 1st, 1967, Ian Ross Lamberth, who *d* 1985; 2ndly, 1985, Gerald Delahunt, and has issue living (by 1st *m*), Steven Ross *b* 1968, Warrenn George *b* 1974, Susan Margaret *b* 1970: *m* 1993, Geoffrey Townsend, and has issue living, Kylie Renée KENNY *b* 1987, Damian Jay KENNY *b* 1988, a da *b* 1994, — Loraine Joy, *b* 1972: *m* 1st, 1972 (*m diss* 19—), Peter Donaldson; 2ndly, 1992, Phillip Wright, and has issue living, Aaron Mark *b* 1973, Joanne Robyn *b* 1972, Philippa Marie Wright *b* 1988, — Denise Myra, *b* 1960: *m* 1982, Claude Gemmell, and has issue living, Bruce *b* 1982, Shaun Jason *b* 1989, Sasha Rose *b* 1984, Regan Dallas *b* 1987, Hami Jade *b* 1991. —— Dorothy Loraine, *b* 1924: *m* 1956 (*m diss* 19—), James Barclay, and has issue living, Bruce Lindsay, *b* 1957: *m* 1977, Pauline Joy Adams, of Palmerston N, NZ, and has issue living, Patrick Allan *b* 1978, Kevin Philip *b* 1981, — Christopher Warren, *b* 1958, — Sandra Kaye, *b* 1961: *m* 1979, Stewart James Wallis, of Camden, NSW, and has issue living, Joleen Lisa Wallis *b* 1979, Logan James *b* 1981.

Grandsons living of late Marcus Henry Sale Hill (ante):—
Issue of late Leonard Graham Hill (twin), *b* 1911, *ka* 1942: *m* 1935, Christina Agnes Allan Wilson, of Section 3, Awakaponga, RD Whakatane, New Zealand:—
Graham Robert Marcus (Corner of Pakeha and Mar Sts, Matata, Bay of Plenty, NZ), *b* 1936: *m* 1958, Shirley Whan, of Sydney, Australia, and has issue living, Michael Peter John, *b* (Jan) 1960, — Leonard Graham, *b* (Dec) 1960, — Warren Stephan, *b* 1962, — Stanley Norman, *b* 1963, — Deborah Joy, *b* 1964. —— Allan Henry (3 Windsor Rise, Whakatane, NZ), *b* 1938: *m* 1959, Raewyn Alice Smith, of Whakatane, New Zealand, and has issue living, Douglas Allan, *b* 1960: *m* 1986, Linda Duncum, of Rotorua, NZ, — Gordon France, *b* 1962: *m* 1990, Deborah D. Hunter, of Rotorua, NZ, and has issue living, Rory Nathan *b* 1991, Krystal Moira *b* 1984, — Rowley Wilson, *b* 1964: *m* 1993, Sharon Naylor, of Warwick, Qld, — Murray Richard, *b* 1967: *m* 1991, Leah Longdon, of Rotorua, NZ.

Grandchildren of late George Henry Hill (ante):—
Issue of late George Rowley Sale Hill, *b* 1874, *d* 1936: *m* 1899, Elizabeth Attfield, who *d* 1941:—
Three sons. —— Five daughters.
Issue of late Louis Hill, *b* 1878, *d* 19—: *m* 19—, Elizabeth Walker, who *d* 19—:—
Two sons and a daughter.
Issue of late Percy Graham Hill, *b* 1883, *d* 1953: *m* 1905, Mary Ellen Wilson:—
George Arthur Graham, *b* 1905: *m* 1931, Kathleen Geary, and has issue living, David Graham, *b* 1931, — Donald Percival, *b* 1937, — Russell George, *b* 1942, — Douglas John, *b* 1943, — Valerie May, *b* 1946. —— Percival Thomas, *b* 1913: *m* 1939, Maude Monk. —— Helen Caroline (7 Menzies Court, Wyndham, Southland, NZ), *b* 1910: *m* 1927, William Robert Lewis, who *d* 1981. and has issue living, William Leonard (Wallacetown, Southland, New Zealand), *b* 1932: *m* 1956, Jeanette McGregor, and has issue living, Bruce David *b* 1958: *m* 1985 Anne Marie Glendening (and has issue living, Scott William *b* 1988), Donald Percival *b* 1959: *m* 1981, Nicola Ann Dennison (and has issue living, Bradley Donald *b* 1984), Rodney William *b* 1961: *m* 1987, Heather Woods, Susan Gaye *b* 1960: *m* 1984, George Paul Hastings, — Mary Catherine, *b* 1928: *m* 1952, Maxwell Maurice Murphy, of 49 Peel St, Westport, New Zealand, and has issue living, Brian William *b* 1955: *m* 1981, Kathryn Margaret Peick, of Westport, NZ (and has issue living, Thomas Brian *b* 1988, Jacinta Kathryn *b* 1985, Emma Grace *b* 1992), Anthony Maxwell *b* 1958: *m* 1981, Marcia Dianne Tipping (and has issue living, Samuel Maurice *b* 1982, Andrew William *b* 1984, James Anthony *b* 1992, Rebekah May *b* 1988), Patrick Thomas *b* 1961: *m* 1988, Cathy Ann Talbot (and has issue living, Cody Allan *b* 1993, Teagan Rae *b* 1990), Helen Margaret *b* 1954: *m* 1973, Anthony John Robertson, (and has issue living, Blair Anthony *b* 1979, Glen Francis *b* 1981, Mia Catherine *b* 1985), Gloria Mary *b* 1957: *m* 1983, Bernard John Hutchinson (and has issue living, Hannah Louise *b* 1992), Kathleen Ann *b* 1963: *m* 1986, Andrew Robin Hobern (and has issue living, Michael *b* 1994, Clare Alyce *b* 1992), Julie Maureen *b* 1964, — Vera Joy, *b* 1930: *m* 1954, John J. Walsh, of Menzies Ferry No. 1 RD, Edendale, Southland, NZ, and has had issue, Angela Mary *b* 1956: *m* 1979, Russell Caldwell (and has issue living, Hayden James *b* 1983, Kieran John *b* 1985, Ryan Gerrad *b* 1987, Nadia Lauren *b* 1981, Olivia Leah *b* 1989), Jillian Caroline *b* 1960, *d* 1986, Maree Jane *b* 1962: *m* 1983, Maurice John Crawford, of Waghorn's Rd, RD Waharoa, Matamata, New Zealand (and has issue living, Matthew John *b* 1984, Krystal Jillian *b* 1987), Leanne Ruth *b* 1966: *m* 1987,

Ross McLeod (and has had issue, Daniel Ross *b* and *d* 1984), Denise Louise *b* 1968, — Lorna Ellen, *b* 1939: *m* 1958, John Desmond Wright, of 49 Tees St, Oamaru, NZ, and has issue living, Darrell John (106A Eden St, Oamaru, NZ) *b* 1959: *m* 1982, Carol Margaret Blair (and has issue living, Christopher John *b* 1988, Michelle Leigh *b* 1987), Graham Norman *b* 1960, Paul Robert *b* 1961, — Dawn Margaret, *b* 1942: *m* 1961, Stuart Gray, of 61 Forth St, Mataura, Southland, NZ, and has issue living, David Andrew *b* 1962, Julie Margaret Irene *b* 1964: *m* 1986, Nigel John Blackler (and has issue living, Holly Margaret *b* 1988), — Sonia Carol, *b* 1947: *m* 1965, Alexander George Kelly, of 476 Racecourse, Invercargill, Southland, NZ, and has issue living, Allan Peter *b* 1966, Katrina May *b* 1969.

The 1st baronet, Sir Hugh Hill (son of late Rowley Hill, MP), was MP for Londonderry. The 2nd baronet, a Privy Councillor, sat as MP for city and co of Derry 1795-1830; he was successively Clerk of the Irish House of Commons, Vice-Treasurer of Ireland, Governor of the Island of St Vincent, and Governor of Trinidad. The 4th baronet, Major Sir John Hill, served throughout the Indian Mutiny with Bengal Light Cav. The first ancestor of this family, originally of Buckinghamshire, was Treasurer of Ireland under Oliver Cromwell.

HILL (UK) 1916, of Bradford

Sir JAMES FREDERICK HILL, 4th *Baronet*; *b* 5 Dec 1943; *s* his father, *Sir* JAMES, 1976; *ed* Wrekin Coll, and Bradford Univ: *m* 1966, Sandra Elizabeth, da of late J. C Ingram, of Summerfield, S Parade, Ilkley, W Yorks, and has issue.

Arms – Or, on a fesse between three leopards' faces sable, as many roses leaved and seeded proper. **Crest** – Upon a rock charged with two roses as in the arms a merino ram statant proper.
Residence – Roseville, Moor Lane, Menston, Ilkley, W Yorks LS29 6AP.

SON LIVING

JAMES LAURENCE INGRAM, *b* 22 Sept 1973.

DAUGHTERS LIVING

Juliet Clare, *b* 1969: *m* 1989, James Christopher Kaberry, elder son of Hon Sir Christopher Donald Kaberry, 2nd Bt, and has issue (*see* B Kaberry). —— Georgina Margaret, *b* 1971. —— Josephine Valerie, *b* 1973.

SISTERS LIVING

Attempt not, or else accomplish

Anita Joan, *b* 1931: *m* 1953, Michael John Riley, who *d* 1988, and has issue living, Peter James Wynne, *b* 1956, — Christopher John, *b* 1960, — Wendy Jeanne, *b* 1954. —— Ellen Barbara, *b* 1936: *m* 1960, Edward Norman Robson, of Braeside, Trebetherick, Wadebridge, Cornwall, and has issue living, Susan Joy, *b* 1960, — Jacqueline Ann, *b* 1963, — Penelope Jane, *b* 1967. —— Florence Margaret (twin) (Windsor Mews, Windsor Rd, Vincent, E London, S Africa), *b* 1943: *m* 1965 (*m diss* 19—), Terence John Coombs, and has issue living, Tessa Annette, *b* 1965, — Linda Margaret, *b* 1967, — Tracey Elizabeth, *b* 1973.

WIDOW LIVING OF THIRD BARONET

MARJORY, JP (*Marjory, Lady Hill*) (Brea House, Trebetherick, Wadebridge, Cornwall), da of late Frank Croft, of Brocka, Lindale, Grange-over-Sands: *m* 1930, Sir James Hill, 3rd Bt, who *d* 1976.

COLLATERAL BRANCH LIVING

Issue of late Arthur James Hill, el son of 1st baronet, *b* 1876, *d* 1935: *m* 1898, Eleanor Beatrice Hindle, who *d* 1975, da of late Thomas Duxbury, FCS, AMICE, of Temple Moyle, Darwen:—
Noeline Etrenne (*Lady Aarvold*), *b* 1909: *m* 1934, His Honour Judge (Sir Carl Douglas) Aarvold, OBE, TD, DL, JP, Recorder of London (ret), who *d* 1991, and has issue living, Christopher Olaf, *b* 1943: *m* 1981, Sandi Gazzard, and has issue living, Tobias Carl *b* 1981, Dominic Ralph Ole *b* 1983, Camilla Louise *b* 1984, — James Hillary, *b* 1946: *m* 1976, Dr Jillian Stanley Jones, and has issue living, Daniel Alexander *b* 1977, Thomas William *b* 1982, Eleanor Pippin *b* 1980, — John Merriman, *b* 1947: *m* 1976, Elizabeth Rumball, of Johannesburg, S Africa, and has issue living, Robert John Douglas *b* 1978, Angus David Merriman *b* 1981, Douglas Henry Eric *b* 1984. *Residence* – Coach House, Crabtree Lane, Westhumble, Dorking.

The 1st baronet, Sir James Hill (son of late William Hill, of Harden, Bingley, Yorkshire), was head of the firm of Sir James Hill & Sons, wool merchants (which he founded in 1890), and sat as MP for Central Div of Bradford (*L*) 1916-18.

HILL (UK) 1919, of Green Place, Stockbridge, co Southampton (Extinct 1944)

Lieut-Col Sir NORMAN GRAY HILL, MC, 2nd and last *Baronet*; *ka* 1944.

DAUGHTER LIVING OF FIRST BARONET

Rosalind Mary Theodosia; MA and BLitt Oxford; Prof Emerita of History, London Univ; FRHistS; FSA. *Residence* – 7 Loom Lane, Radlett, Herts.

ERSKINE-HILL (UK) 1945, of Quothquhan, co Lanark

Sir (ALEXANDER) ROGER ERSKINE-HILL, 3rd *Baronet*; *b* 15 Aug 1949; *s* his father, *Sir* ROBERT, 1989; *ed* Eton, and Aberdeen Univ (LLB): *m* 1984, Sarah Anne Sydenham, elder da of late Dr Richard John Sydenham Clarke, and has issue.

Arms – Quarterly: 1st grand quarter, azure, a hill argent, charged with two pens, points downwards in saltire, quills or, feathers sable, in chief the sun in his splendour, *Hill*, 2nd grand quarter, counterquarterd, 1st and 4th, argent, on a pale sable, a cross-crosslet fitches or, *Erskine of Shielfield*; 2nd, azure, a bend between two cross-crosslets fitchees or, *Mar*, 3rd, or, on a bend azure three mascles of the field, and in the sinister chief a round buckle of the second, *Haliburton*; all within a bordure per pale azure and sable, a canton or charged with a fleur-de-lys of the second, for difference; 3rd grand quarter, counterquartered, 1st argent, on a mount in base a lion rampant vert, on a chief of the second a crescent between two mullets or, *Halcro*; 2nd, or a fesse chequy azure and argent, a border gules charged with eight round buckles of the first, *Stewart of Barscube*; 3rd, or, on a bend gules, three buckles of the first, *Bonkyll* of that ilk; 4th, argent a heart purpure ensigned with an imperial crown proper, on a chief gules, three pallets or, *Keith of Galston*; 4th grand quarter, argent, a lion rampant, azure, armed and langued gules, on a chief of the second, an elephant's head, cabossed of the first, tusked or, accompanied by two lymphads of the first under full sail proper, *Galloway*. **Crest** – 1st, a stag's head couped proper, attired sable, 2nd, a dexter arm from the elbow, couped proper, the hand grasping a cross-crosslet fitchee or.

SON LIVING

ROBERT BENJAMIN, *b* 6 Aug 1986.

DAUGHTER LIVING

Kirsty Rose, *b* 1985.

BROTHER LIVING

Henry James, *b* 1953; *ed* Eton: *m* 1979, Gwen Carolyn, da of Ian Russell Chalmers.

SISTERS LIVING

Carola Marion, *b* 1943: *m* 1st, 1963 (*m diss* 1978), (Richard) David Christopher Brooke (*see* Brooke Bt, *cr* 1662); 2ndly, 1981, as his 3rd wife, Robin Andrew Stormonth Darling, of Balvarran, Enochdhu, Blairgowrie, Perthshire PH10 7PA. —— Alison, *b* 1945: *m* 1966, John Selby North Lewis, of Walwick Hall, Humshaugh, Hexham, Northumberland, and has issue living, Selby James, *b* 1968, — Harriet Alison, *b* 1970, — Rebecca Elspeth, *b* 1975, — Hannah Margaret, *b* 1979.

AUNT LIVING (*daughter of 1st baronet*)

Jean Halcro, *b* 1928: *m* 1st, 1950, Derek John Seth-Smith, who *d* 1964; 2ndly, 1972, George Henry Smith-Wright, and has issue living (by 1st *m*), Frederick Alexander, *b* 1963: *m* 1992, Kathryn R., eldest da of Comdt Barry O'Sullivan, of Naas, co Kildare, and has issue living, Jack Alexander *b* 1994, — Kay Christian, *b* 1951: *m* 1981, Charles W. King, of 12 Hambalt Rd, SW4, yr son of Col C. W. King, of Cutham Hill House, Bagenden, Cirencester, Glos, and has issue living, Henry Charles James *b* 1983, Laura Christian *b* (twin) 1983, Alice Jane *b* 1987, — Rosemary Jean, *b* 1954: *m* 1977, Maj Peter F. S. Gwatkin, Welsh Gds, of 66 Greenhill Rd, Moseley, Birmingham, son of late John Stapleton Gwatkin, and has issue living, Frederick John Stapleton *b* 1983, Amy Jean Stapleton *b* 1980, Martha Elspeth *b* 1986, Hannah Rosemary Theophila Stapleton *b* 1990, — (Mary) Jane, *b* 1957: *m* 1984, William Lee Rothery, son of George W. Rothery, of The High Street, Odiham, Hants, and has issue living, Charles Alexander *b* 1987, Arthur George *b* 1992, Rosemary Anne *b* 1985. *Residence* – 34 Moore St, SW3.

WIDOW LIVING OF SECOND BARONET

CHRISTINE ALISON (*Dowager Lady Erskine-Hill*); ARCM 1970; only da of late Capt Henry James Johnstone, RN, of Alva (*see* Johnstone, Bt, colls): *m* 1942, Sir Robert Erskine-Hill, 2nd Bt, who *d* 1989. *Residence* – Hareleigh House, Libberton, Carnwarth, Lanarkshire ML11 8LX.

COLLATERAL BRANCH LIVING

Issue of late John Colville Erskine-Hill, DSC, VRD, yr son of 1st baronet, *b* 1921, *d* 1984: *m* 1959, Myra Elizabeth (South Lodge, Forest Row, Sussex), da of late Cdr Richard Homewood, RN:—
Mark Colville, *b* 1960: *m* 1992, Lucy Diana Elspeth, da of D. B. Hulme, of Reigate, Surrey, and has issue living, Alice, *b* 1993. *Residence* - The White House, Walking Bottom, Peaslake, nr Guildford, Surrey. —— David John, *b* 1962.

The 1st baronet, Sir Alexander Galloway Erskine-Hill, KC (son of Robert Alexander Hill) was a Director of London & NE Railway and sat as MP for N Div of Edinburgh (*U*) 1935-45. Sir Robert, 2nd Bt, was Chm The Life Assocn of Scotland Ltd 1960-85, and ptnr Chiene & Tait, CA, Edinburgh 1946-80.

Hill-Wood, see Wood.

HOARE (I) 1784, of Annabella, Cork

The hour approaches

Sir TIMOTHY EDWARD CHARLES HOARE, 8th *Baronet*; *b* 11 Nov 1934; *s* his father, *Maj Sir* EDWARD O'BRYEN, 1969; *ed* Radley, Worcester Coll, Oxford (MA), and London Univ (MA); Dir Careerplan Ltd since 1970, Dir New Metals & Chemicals since 1966, Dir World Vision UK since 1983, Memb General Synod since 1970, Crown Appointments Commn 1987-92, Church and State Commn 1970; sometime 60th Rifles (Nat Service Commn): *m* 1969, Felicity Anne, da of late Peter Boddington, JP, of Stratford-upon-Avon, and has issue.

Arms – Sable, a double-headed eagle displayed within a bordure engrailed argent. **Crest** – A deer's head and neck proper, erased argent.
Residence – 10 Belitha Villas, Barnsbury, N1 1PD.

SON LIVING

CHARLES JAMES, *b* 15 March 1971.

DAUGHTERS LIVING

Louisa Hope, *b* 1972. —— Kate Annabella, *b* (twin) 1972.

SISTER LIVING

Catherine Mary, *b* 1937: *m* 1963, David James Clark, and has issue living, David Noah, *b* 1966, — Ezra David, *b* 1968, — Abel David, *b* 1971, — Hester Catherine, *b* 1973.

WIDOW LIVING OF SEVENTH BARONET

NINA MARY (*Nina, Lady Hoare*) (61 Flask Walk, NW3), da of late Charles Nugent Hope-Wallace, MBE (*see* M Linlithgow, colls): *m* 1932, Maj Sir Edward O'Bryen Hoare, 7th Bt, who *d* 1969.

COLLATERAL BRANCHES LIVING

Grandchildren of late John Hoare (infra):—
Issue of late James O'Bryen Hoare, *b* 1910, *d* 1967: *m* (Jan) 1941, Helen Dorey Hardie, who *d* 1991:—
Richard James O'Bryen (242 Hurstmere Rd, Takapuna, Auckland, NZ), *b* 1947: *m* 1971, Sally Ann, da of John Cornwell, of Northcote Auckland, NZ, and has issue living, David O'Bryen, *b* 1974, — Matthew James, *b* 1976, — Rosemary Jane, *b* 1978. —— Stewart John (27 Morvern Rd, Mt Eden, Auckland, NZ), *b* 1949: *m* 1976, Marcelle, da of Elie Bitoun, of Fez, Morocco, and has issue living, Andrew James *b* 1982. —— Janet O'Bryen, *b* (Nov) 1941: *m* 1965, William Frank Richardson, of 45 St Leonard's Rd, Mt Eden, Auckland 4, NZ, and has issue living, Michael George, *b* 1970, — Diana Helen, *b* 1967.
Issue of late John Leslie Hoare, *b* 1919, *d* 1991: *m* 1945, Maxine Heaslip:—
Susan Elizabeth, *b* 1946: *m* 1970, Michael Clifford Quinnell, of Closeburn, Brisbane, Qld, and has issue living, Mark Alexander, *b* 1976. —— Jane Victoria, *b* 1950: *m* 1977, Marion Lester Woods, of Salt Lake City, Utah, USA, and has issue living, Clare Marcello, *b* 1980, — Caroline Elizabeth, *b* 1983, — Hannah Victoria, *b* 1987.

Granddaughters of late Rev James O'Bryen Dott Richard Hoare, el son of Joseph James Parish Hoare, 3rd son of 3rd baronet:—
Issue of late John Hoare, *b* 1874, *d* 1954: *m* 1904, Margaret Jane Leversedge, who *d* 1959:—
Joan Mary, *b* 1905: *m* 1931, Harry Albert Cameron, who *d* 1983, and has issue living, John Bruce (63 Greentrees Av, Brookfield, Qld), *b* 1933: *m* 1961, Jennifer Dines Mackay, and has issue living, Christine Louise *b* 1962: *m* 1987, Geoffrey Douglas Crozier, of 5 Maroa Close, Chapel Hill, Qld (and has issue living, James Allen *b* 1992, Louise Jane *b* 1990), Fiona Judith *b* 1963: *m* 1992, David Hubert Finney, of 38 Beaconsfield Terrace, Gordon Park, Qld (and has issue living, Kate Elizabeth *b* 1994), Belinda Anne *b* 1965, — Margaret Anne, *b* 1932: *m* 19—, Grahame Iliff Barry, of 361 Warners Bay Rd, Charlestown, NSW, and has issue living, David Bruce (23 Bilba Cresent, Marylands, NSW) *b* 1955: *m* 1985, Gillian C. Howie (and has issue living, Dean Cameron *b* 1987, Lisa Danielle *b* 1988), Richard John (19 Broulla St, Baulkham Hills, NSW) *b* 1961: *m* 1992, Julie Maguire, Helen Margaret *b* 1957: *m* 1980, Matthew Gooden, of 147 Castle Hill Rd, Castle Hill, NSW (and has issue living, Alexander Matthew *b* 1981, Daniel Benedict *b* 1983, Dominic Thomas *b* 1988, Jerome Patrick *b* 1990, Cecily Rita *b* 1986, Prudence Jane *b* 1992), — Diana Molly, *b* 1943: *m* 1st 19— (*m diss* 1981), Kevin Patrick Shone; 2ndly, 1982, Jules Le Lievre, of Old West Coast Rd, Christchurch, NZ, and has issue living (by 1st *m*) Robert *b* 1970, Michael *b* 1976, Jonathan *b* 1976. *Residence* – 63 Greentrees Av, Brookfield, Qld. —— Margaret Alice, *b* 1912: *m* 1943, Jack Steane Comport, who *d* 1961, and has issue living, Stephen (15 The Grange, E Malvern, Vic), *b* 1944: *m* 1st, 1966 (*m diss* 1972), Mary Boyd Thomson; 2ndly, 1973, Gillian Elizabeth Sinton, and has issue living (by 2nd *m*), David John *b* 1980, Michael Douglas *b* 1982. *Residence* – 28 Latimer St, Holland Park, Qld. —— Molly Gertrude, *b* 1913: *m* 1942, Patrick Shine, who *d* 1985, and has issue living, John (2 Mayfield Av, Woolwich, NSW), *b* 1946 (Prof): *m* 1969, Kathleen Mary Morgan, and has issue living, Michael Patrick *b* 1972, Rebecca Kathleen *b* 1970, — Richard (30 Farnell St, Boronia Park, NSW), *b* 1950: *m* 1978, Terri Sue Griffith, of Penn, USA, and has issue living, James Macquarie *b* 1982, Benjamin Griffith *b* 1984, — Judith Mary (62 Hamilton St, Lane Cove, NSW), *b* 1948: *m* 1971, Joseph Ohana, of Beersheba, Israel, and has issue living, David Patrick Yaniv *b* 1978, Yael Simma *b* 1973. *Residence* – 59 Sofala Av, Lane Cove, NSW.
Issue of late Denys Hoare, *b* 1876, *d* 1958: *m* 1906, Frances York, who *d* 1959:—
Norah Frances O'Bryen, *b* 1907: *m* 1940, John Edward Buxton, who *d* 1981, and has issue living, Joanna Elizabeth, *b* 1941: *m* 1964, Maj Christopher Timothy Rawdon Leefe, of West Farm House, Harriotts, Lane, Ashtead, Surrey, and has issue living, Mark Rawdon *b* 1966, Thomas Rawdon *b* 1968, — Frances Jane *b* 1944: *m* 1967, John Edward Holford, of Kings Cottage, Elmdon, Saffron Walden, and has issue living, Rebecca Jane *b* 1968, Melanie Sarah *b* 1970, Elizabeth Alice *b* 1975, — Annabel Mary, *b* 1948: *m* 1971, Michael Bonhote Rodney Foster, of Tadworth Cottage, Tadworth St, Tadworth, Surrey, and has issue living, James Edward Bonhote *b* 1982, Lucy Annabel Henrietta *b* 1974, Harriet Mary Emma *b* 1976. *Residence* – 20 Bartholomew Court, South Bank, Dorking, Surrey.

Granddaughter of late Cyril Bertie Edward Hoare, son of late Edward Senior Hoare, 7th son of late Joseph James Parish Hoare (ante):—
Issue of late Wing-Com Bertie Rex O'Bryen Hoare, DSO, DFC, *b* 1912, *d* 1947: *m* 1945, Lucy, who *d* 1970, da of Richard Nimmo Watson, of Harrogate:—

Rosemary Verity O'Bryen (*posthumous*), *b* 1947: *m* 19—, Nicholas Russell (Box 14357, Nairobi, Kenya), and has issue living, Samantha O'Bryen, *b* 1980.

Grandson of late Edward Hoare, son of late Rev Thomas Hoare, 3rd son of 2nd baronet:—
Issue of late William Wallis Hoare, MD, FRCS, LRCP, *b* 1871, *d* 19—: *m* 1903, Kathleen Mary Bolton, of Ascot, Brisbane, Queensland:—
Edward Bryan, *b* 1905.

Granddaughters of late Edward Wallis Hoare, FRCVS (infra):—
Issue of late Edward William Wallis Hoare, *b* 1902, *d* 1966: *m* 1936, Elizabeth, who *d* 1977, da of late Angus Baillie, of Glasgow:—
Elizabeth McLean (Redcliffe, 1a Sinclair Drive, Helensburgh, Dunbartonshire G84 9BB), *b* 1937. —— Barbara, *b* 1948: *m* 1st, 1979 (*m diss* 1984), Geoffrey Goddin; 2ndly, 1987, Paul Green, of 10 Ranelagh Drive North, Grassendale, Liverpool L19 9DS, and has issue living, (by 1st *m*) Alastair William, *b* 1979.

Granddaughter of late Capt William Jesse Hoare, son of late Rev Thomas Hoare (ante):—
Issue of late Edward Wallis Hoare, FRCVS, *b* 1863, *d* 1920: *m* 1899, Emily, who *d* 1961, da of late Henry Lindsay Helen, of Dublin:—
Viola Cecilia, *b* 1913: *m* 1939, Richard Roberts Gorsuch, and has issue living, Diarmind Roberts, *b* 1941: *m* 1970, Jane, el da of Arthur Stanley Peacock of Vancouver, — Terence Richard, *b* 1947: *m* 1969, Patricia, da of Arthur Stanley Peacock, of Vancouver, — Deirdre Cecilia, *b* 1943: *m* 1970, Michel le Bell, — Maeve Emily, *b* 1946: *m* 1972, Keith Harrison, of Ch Ch, NZ. *Residence* – 6811, 236th St, RR6, Langley, BC, Canada.
The 1st baronet, Sir Joseph, MP for Askeaton in the Irish House of Commons, was many years Advising Counsel at Dublin Castle. It has been represented that he lived in *three centuries* — viz, from 25 Dec 1699, to 24 Dec 1801. Recent researches, however, show that he was born on 25 Dec 1707, and died on 24 Dec 1801. At the age of 93 he attended in his place in Parliament to vote against the Union. Sir Edward, the 2nd baronet, sat as MP for Carlow 1769-76.

HOARE (GB) 1786, of Barn Elms, Surrey

Sir PETER RICHARD DAVID HOARE, 8th *Baronet*, *b* 22 March 1932; *s* his father, *Sir* PETER WILLIAM, 1973; *ed* Eton: *m* 1st, 1961 (*m diss* 1967), Jane, only da of late Daniel Orme, of Bulleigh Barton, Ipplepen, S Devon; 2ndly, 1978 (*m diss* 1982), Katrin Alexa, da of late Erwin Bernstiel, and formerly wife of Sir Michael Robin Adderley Hodson, Bt; 3rdly, 1983, Angela Francesca de la Sierra, yr da of late Fidel Fernando Ayarza, of Santiago, Chile.

Arms – Sable, an eagle displayed with two heads argent, charged on the breast with an ermine spot, a bordure engrailed of the second. **Crest** – An eagle's head and neck erased argent charged with an ermine spot.
Address – c/o Hoare & Co, 37 Fleet St, EC4.

BROTHER LIVING

In ardua
For arduous undertakings

DAVID JOHN (Luscombe Castle, Dawlish, S Devon), *b* 8 Oct 1935; *ed* Eton: *m* 1st, 1965, Mary Vanessa, yst da of Peter Cardew, of Westhanger, Cleeve, Bristol; 2ndly, 1984, Virginia Victoria Labes, da of Michael Menzies, of Long Island, NY, and has issue living (by 1st *m*), Simon Merrick, *b* 1967.

COLLATERAL BRANCHES LIVING

Granddaughter of late Peter Merrik Hoare, grandfather of 7th baronet:—
Issue of late Lennox Merrik Noel Colt Hoare, *b* 1871, *d* 1924: *m* 1895, Evelyn Augusta, who *d* 1952, da of late Thomas Gerard, of Claughton, near Birkenhead, Cheshire:—
Alda Evelyn, *b* 1905: *m* 1929, Brig Henry Anthony Lampen Shewell, OBE, late RE, who *d* 1974, and has issue living, John Michael Henry (The Lindens, Hutton Rd, Ash Vale, Aldershot, Hants GU12 5EY), *b* 1931; Maj ACC (ret): *m* 1959, Alison Averil Jones, and has issue living, Christopher John Henry *b* 1961, Anthony Martin Edward *b* 1962, — Alda Mary *b* 1933: *m* 1962, John Charles Allday Mousley, of Norleigh House, Widecombe-in-the-Moor, Newton Abbot, Devon TQ13 7TF, and has issue living, Peter John Hunter *b* 1963: *m* 1991, Jacqueline Frances Shelbourne, Claire Alda Louisa *b* 1964: *m* 1987, Maj Neil Guy Trepess Polley, Kings Royal Hussars, of Grantsfield, Kimbolton, Herefordshire, and has issue living, Lucy Alda Elspeth *b* 1991, Alicia Charlotte Oenone *b* 1994. *Residence* – Bramble Down, Denbury, Devon.

Grandchildren of late Charles Arthur Richard Hoare, son of late Peter Richard Hoare (*b* 1803), son of Peter Richard Hoare, 5th son of 1st baronet:—
Issue of late Wilfrid Arthur Richard Hoare, *b* 1876, *d* 1971: *m* 1915, Helen Adria, da of late Col Harry Hepenstall Rose Heath, CB:—
Richard Michael St George, *b* 1918: *m* 1947, Gladys Margaret Tysack, and has issue living, Richard Charles, *b* 1947: *m* 19—, Helen, da of —, and has issue living, Michael John *b* 19—, — Nigel, *b* 1949, — John Michael, *b* 1950. —— Jacquetta Adria Margaret (Sorley Farm, Kingsbridge, S Devon), *b* 1916: *m* 1st, 1940 (*m diss* 1946), Terence Stafford, Lt RAPC; 2ndly, 1946, Dudley Fisher, who *d* 19—, and has issue living, (by 1st *m*) Rebecca, *b* 19—: *m* 19—, —, and has issue living, Bridget *b* 19—, — (by 2nd *m*) Noel Hugh, *b* 1949, — Philipa Jacquetta (twin), *b* 1949, — Heather Sophia, *b* 1953.
Issue of late Reginald Arthur Hoare, *b* 1878, *ka* 1918: *m* 1909, Una Mildred, who *d* 1951, da of Thomas C. Williams, of Wellington, New Zealand:—
Reginald Merrick (Blue Cottage, Lower Froyle, nr Alton, Hants) *b* 1918: *m* 1st, 1950, Barbara Jean, who *d* 1984, da of Francis John Buckland (B Melchett); 2ndly, 1984, Meriel Karen, da of late Michael Gold, and has issue living (by 1st *m*), Charles Mark (58 Whellock Rd, Chiswick, W4), *b* 1961: *m* 1984, Morag White, — Paul Reginald Richard, *b* 1963, — Diana Charlotte, *b* 1956: *m* 1978, William Taunton, of 27 Longburton, nr Sherborne, Dorset, and has issue living, Mathew William *b* 1984, Rebecca Charlotte *b* 1982, — Clare Githa, *b* 1958. —— Anne Temple, Githa (Old Larkhayes, Dalwood, Axminster, Devon), *b* 1916: *m* 1945, Vere Justin Tweedie MC, son of late Adm Sir Hugh Justin Tweedie, KCB, and has issue living, Simon Vere, *b* 1954, — Sarah Patricia, *b* 1947: *m* 1968, Edward Charles Townsend, — Amanda Jane, *b* 1948.
Issue of late Ralph Francis Hoare, *b* 1881, *d* 1956: *m* 1906, Katherine Hallen, who *d* 1969, da of R. J. Sumner Drinkwater, of Northbrook, Orillia, Ontario, Canada:—

Eric Reginald, b 1918: m 1949, Rosemary Brodie Hallowell, da of Francis Vickerman Lumb, and has issue living, Geoffrey Charles Brodie, b 1953, — Richard Sumner Anthony, b 1955, — Wendy Pamela Brodie, b 1961: m 1989, Gerald Timothy Griffin, son of James Griffin, of Edmonton, Alberta. Residence – Salus House, West Sechelt, BC, Canada. —— Peter Richard (204 Park St, Orillia, Ontario, Canada), b 1920: m 1960, Beverley Jean, da of Arthur Frederick Hessel, and has issue living, Barbara Lynne, b 1965: m 1992, James Arthur Orell, son of Arthur F. Orell, of Toronto, — Deborah Katherine Jean, b 1969. —— Margaret Katherine Dorothy (Apt 103-S, 412 Muskoka Rd, Orillia, Ontario L3V 6M5, Canada), b 1907: m 1938, William Stephens Gill, who d 1951, and has issue living, Peter William (Edgewood Farm, RR2, Orilla, Ontario, Canada), b 1939: m 1967, Angela Patricia, da of Ernest D. Gillezeau, of St Vincent, WI, and has issue living, Jeremy David Hallen b 1968, Nicholas Anton Stephens b 1971, — Ralph John David (42 Andrea Cres, Orillia, Ontario L3V 6W5, Canada), b 1947: m 1976, Marlene Elsie, da of Hugh Doyle, of Orillia, Ontario, and has issue living, Trevor William Hugh b 1981, Ryan David b 1984, — Margaret Natalie Katherine, b 1944: m 1965, Bruce Teague Budd, of 10534 26th Av, Edmonton, Alberta T6J 4B9, Canada, son of Luther H. Budd, of Montreal, Quebec, and has issue living, Teague William Garth b 1971, Donicka Anne Evelyn b 1966, Tehranna Margaret Katherine b 1969. —— Natalie Kathleen Grove, b 1915. Residence – Apt 412, 55 Broadway Av, Toronto, Canada.

The 1st baronet's father was Lord Mayor of London 1745. Sir Henry Ainslie Hoare, 5th Bt, was MP for Windsor (L) 1865-6 and for Chelsea 1868-74.

HOARE (UK) 1962, of Fleet Street, City of London (Extinct 1986)

Sir FREDERICK ALFRED HOARE, 1st and last Baronet.

DAUGHTERS LIVING OF FIRST BARONET (by 1st marriage)

Mary Rose, b 1944. —— Marinella, b 1952: m 1988, Jeremy Alfred Franks, son of Jack Franks, of 71 Portland Pl, W1, and has issue living, Alexei, b 1988, — a da, b 1989. Residence – 100 Eaton Pl, SW1.

HOBART (UK) 1914, of Langdown, co Southampton
(Name pronounced "Hub'bert")

The giver makes the gift valuable

Sir JOHN VERE HOBART, 4th Baronet; b 9 April 1945; s his father Lieut-Cdr Sir ROBERT HAMPDEN, 1988; is hp to Earldom of Buckinghamshire: m 1980, Kate, only da of late George Henry Iddles, of Cowes, I of Wight, and has issue.

Arms – Quarterly, 1st, sable, an estoile of six rays or between two flaunches ermine, Hobart; 2nd, argent, a saltire gules between four eagles displayed azure, Hampden; 3rd, argent, three battering-rams fessewise in pale proper, armed and garnished azure, Bertie; 4th, quarterly, gules and or, in the first quarter a mullet argent, Vere. Crest – A bull statant per pale sable and gules bezanté, in his nose a ring or.
Residence – Shore End, Queen's Rd, Cowes, Isle of Wight.

SONS LIVING

GEORGE HAMPDEN, b 10 June 1982. —— James Henry Miles, b 1986.

BROTHERS LIVING

Robert Henry (12 Brunswick Gdns, W8), b 1948; ed Harrow: m 1976, Una-Mary Diana, da of late Archibald Henry Parker (see E Macclesfield, colls), and has issue living, Sophie Camilla, b 1978, — Jessica, b 1980. —— Anthony Hampden, b 1956: m 1985, Katherine Anne, 3rd da of Robert Noel Willis Fleming, of Acorn House, St Helens, Isle of Wight, and has issue living, Charles Hampden, b 1986.

SISTER LIVING

Penelope Diana, b 1954: m 1979, Robert Maunsell Hunter-Jones, son of Michael Hunter-Jones, of Burmington House, Shipston-on-Stour, Warwicks.

WIDOW LIVING OF THIRD BARONET

CAROLINE FLEUR (Dowager Lady Hobart), yr da of late Col Henry Monckton Vatcher, MC, of Valeran, St Brelade's, Jersey, widow of 11th Duke of Leeds, and formerly wife of Peter Hendrick Peregrine Hoos (see B Brownlow): m 1975, as his 2nd wife, Lt-Cdr Sir Robert Hampden Hobart, 3rd Bt, who d 1988. Residence – The Boat House, Cowes, I of Wight.

The 1st baronet, Sir Robert Henry Hobart, KCVO, CB (el son of late Very Rev Hon Henry Lewis Hobart, DD, Dean of Windsor and Wolverhampton) (E Buckinghamshire, colls), was Private Sec to Sec of State for War, Postmaster-Gen, Ch Sec for Ireland, and Sec of State for India 1863-74 and 1889-95, and to four Secs for Scotland 1886-7 and 1892-5, Sec for Coronation of King Edward VII 1902, Gold Staff Officer at Coronation of King George 1911, MP for Hampshire, New Forest Div (L) Jan 1906 to Jan 1910, and Official Verderer of the New Forest 1907-27. The 2nd baronet, Sir (Claud) Vere Cavendish Hobart, DSO, OBE, was Major Grenadier Guards, and Lieut-Col Hampshire Regt, and was Gold Staff Officer at Coronations of King Edward VII and King George V.

HOBHOUSE (UK) 1812, of Broughton-Gifford, Bradford-on-Avon, and of Monkton Farleigh, Wiltshire

The hope of a better life

SIR CHARLES JOHN SPINNEY HOBHOUSE, 7th *Baronet; b* 27 Oct 1962; *s* his father, *Sir* CHARLES CHISHOLM, TD, 1991; *ed* Eton: *m* 1993, Katrina, da of late Maj-Gen Sir Denzil Macarthur-Onslow, CBE, DSO, ED (*see* E Onslow, colls).

Arms – Per pale azure and gules, three crescents, two and one, argent, issuing therefrom as many estoiles irradiated or. **Crest** – Out of a mural crown per pale azure and gules, a crescent and estoile as in the arms.
Residence – The Manor, Monkton Farleigh, Bradford-on-Avon, Wilts BA15 2QE.

UNCLE LIVING (*son of 5th baronet*)

JOHN SPENCER, AFC, *b* 15 Nov 1910; *ed* Eton, and — Coll, Oxford; formerly Squadron Leader RAF: *m* 1940, Mary, who *d* 1991, yr da of late Llewelyn Roberts, MD, of Porthcawl. *Residence* – Farleigh Court, Farleigh, Hungerford, nr Bath, Avon.

AUNT LIVING (*daughter of 5th baronet*)

Audrey, *b* 1912: *m* 1934 (*m diss* 1952), Maj-Gen Cecil Llewellyn Firbank, CB, CBE, DSO, late Somerset LI, who *d* 1985, and has issue living, Simon Christopher, *b* 1937: *m* 1962 (*m diss* 1988), Caroline Anne, only da of Lt-Col J. T. C. Howard, of East Pennard, Shepton Mallet, Som, and has issue two sons and one da. *Residence* – Old Mill, Bourton, Gillingham, Dorset.

WIDOW LIVING OF SIXTH BARONET

ELSPETH JEAN (*Dowager Lady Hobhouse*), yr da of late Thomas George Spinney, of Mazagan, Morocco: *m* 1959, as his 2nd wife, Sir Charles Chisholm Hobhouse, 6th Bt, TD, who *d* 1991. *Residence* – South Wing, The Manor, Monkton Farleigh, Bradford-on-Avon, Wilts BA15 2QE.

COLLATERAL BRANCHES LIVING

Issue of late Benjamin Arthur Hobhouse, 3rd son of 5th baronet, *b* 1914, *d* 1970: *m* 1942, Valerie Cuthbertson, who *d* 1990, da of late Dr John Cuthbertson Walker, of Barnwell, Troon, Ayrshire;—
John Cam (13/11 College Lane, Gibraltar), *b* 1947: *m* 1971 (*m diss* 1982), Mary Angela Deakins, da of Arthur George Newton, and has issue living, a da, *b* 19—, — a da, *b* 19—. —— Carol Ann, *b* 1943: *m* 1964, George Rogers, of 35 Sunnyhill Rd, Salisbury, Wilts, and has issue living, Bruce Andrew, *b* 1967.

Issue of late Maj Hugh Cam Hobhouse, 4th and yst son of 5th baronet, *b* 1917, *d* 1987: *m* 1st, 1939 (*m diss* 1947), Diana, yr da of Philip George; 2ndly, 1949 (*m diss* 1965), Aline Rosemary, formerly wife of Lt-Col David Theodor Dobie, DSO, and only da of Lt-Col David Walter Hunter Blair (*see* Hunter Blair, Bt, colls); 3rdly, 1965, Judy Margaret (Manor Farm, East Compton, Shepton Mallet, Som), da of late J. D. Tisdall, of Butcombe, Som:—
(By 1st *m*) Mark Cam, *b* 1940; *ed* Eton; Lieut RAC: *m* 1975, Stephanie, da of late Capt K. E. Buxton, and has issue living, Benjamin Alexander Cam, *b* 1979, — Matthew Jack *b* 1979. —— (By 2nd *m*) James Charles, *b* 1951; *ed* Millfield: *m* 1974, Sarah, da of David Sladen, and has issue living, Rebecca Sarah, *b* 1980, — Nicola, *b* 198—. —— Martin Hugh John, *b* 1955; *ed* Eton: *m* 1981, Julia Isobel, da of Dr David Andrew Young Craib, of Ruxley, Hankham, Pevensey, E Sussex, and has issue living, Hugh, *b* 19—, — Alexander, *b* 1986, — George, *b* 1991, — a da, *b* 1993. —— Julia Mary, *b* 1956: *m* 1985, Henry G. Buckmaster, son of late Richard Guy Buckmaster, of Radway, Warwicks, and has issue living, (Eleanor) Rose, *b* 1986, — Camellia Aline, *b* 1988, — Lily Henrietta, *b* 1990. —— (By 3rd *m*) Sophie Victoria, *b* 1967.

Sir Benjamin Hobhouse, 1st Bt, descended from the Hobhouses of Minehead, Somerset, was MP for Bletchingley 1797, for Grampound 1802, and for Hendon 1806-18, and Ch Sec, Board of Control, India 1801-03, and 1806-07. Rt Hon Sir John Cam Hobhouse, 2nd baronet, created Baron Broughton 1851, was one of the poet Byron's most intimate friends. He was MP for Westminster 1820-33, for Nottingham 1838-47, and Harwich 1849-51; Secretary for War 1832-3, Secretary for Ireland 1833, Chief Commissioner of Woods and Forests 1834, President of the Board of Control 1835-41 and 1846-51, and author of several important works. He died 1869, when the barony became extinct, and the baronetcy passed to his nephew, Sir Charles Parry Hobhouse. The 4th baronet, Rt Hon Sir Charles Edward Henry Hobhouse, TD, sat as MP for Wilts, E or Devizes Div (*L*) 1892-95, and for Bristol, E Div 1900-1918, and was Church Estate Commr 1906-7. Under-Sec of State for India 1907-8, Financial Sec to Treasury 1908-11, Chancellor of Duchy of Lancaster 1911-14, and Postmaster-Gen 1914-15.

HODGE (UK) 1921, of Chipstead, co Kent

Sir JOHN ROWLAND HODGE, MBE, 2nd *Baronet, b* 1 May 1913; *s* his father, Sir ROWLAND FREDERIC WILLIAM, 1950; *ed* Wrekin Coll; formerly Lieut-Com RNVR; formerly Lieut Oxfordshire and Bucks LI; European War 1939-40 (MBE); MBE (Mil) 1940: *m* 1st, 1936 (*m diss* 1939), Peggy Ann, only da of Sydney Raymond Kent; 2ndly, 1939 (*m diss* 1961) Joan, only da of late Sydney Foster Wilson; 3rdly, 1962 (*m diss* 1967), Jeanne Wood Anderson, da of late Cdr W. E. Buchanan, of Edinburgh; 4thly, 1967, Vivienne, da of Alfred Knightley, of Norwood, and has issue by 2nd and 4th *m*.

Arms – Sable, an eagle wings addorsed and inverted or between three crescents argent. **Crest** – An eagle as in the arms supporting with the dexter claw an increscent argent and looking at the rays of the sun issuant from clouds proper. *Residence* – Sutherland Drive, Gunton Park, Lowestoft, Suffolk NR32 4LP. *Clubs* – Naval, British Racing Drivers, Royal Malta Yacht.

SON LIVING (*By 4th marriage*)

ANDREW ROWLAND, *b* 3 Dec 1968.

DAUGHTERS LIVING (*By 2nd marriage*)

Wendy Madeline, *b* 1941: *m* 1st, 1962 (*m diss* 1971), Michael Dennis Whiting; 2ndly, 1973, John Edward Aitken Kidd, of 3 Hereford Mews, W2 5AN, and of Old House, Ewhurst Green, Surrey (*see* B Beaverbrook, 1985 Edn), and has issue living (by 1st *m*), Nicholas D'Arcy, *b* 1962, — Deborah Joanna, *b* 1964, —

Glory the reward of virtue

(by 2nd *m*) Jack Edward, *b* 1973, — Jemma Madeleine, *b* 1974, — Jodie Elizabeth, *b* 1978. ——— Sally Joan (6601 East Hummingbird Lane, Scottsdale, Arizona, USA), *b* 1943. ——— Vicki Alexandra (Calais, Enterprise, Barbados), *b* 1946: *m* 1969, George Ian Alexander Heath.

(*By 4th marriage*)

Louise Vivienne, *b* 1970.

SISTER LIVING

Vivien Rosemary, *b* 1911: *m* 1st, 1930, St John Henry Legh Clowes (B Clanmorris); 2ndly, 1941, Hugh Gordon Murton-Neale, and has issue living, (by 1st *m*) Timothy Legh, *b* 1932, — Susan Carol, *b* 1935. *Residence* – The Old Tannery, Smallhythe Rd, Tenterden, Kent.

COLLATERAL BRANCH LIVING

Issue of late Peter Rowland Hodge, yr son of 1st baronet, *b* 1915, *d* 1982: *m* 1st, 1940 (*m diss* 1945), Mia, da of late Capt Sir (Albert) Noel Campbell Macklin, of Fairmile, Cobham, Surrey; 2ndly, 1951, Margaret Norma (Clifford Lodge, High St, Hurstpierpoint, Sussex BN6 9PX), da of Harold Plow, of Broadway, Barnton, Cheshire:—
(By 2nd *m*) Jacqueline Jane (Copyhold Cottage, Loch Lane, Partridge Green, Horsham, W Sussex RH13 8EF), *b* 1954: *m* 1991, Richard A. D. Jesse, and has issue living, Lawrence Rowland, *b* 1992. ——— Bridgitte Michele, *b* 1956: *m* 1989, Patrick L. Field.
The 1st baronet, Sir Rowland Frederic William Hodge (son of John Rowland Hodge), was a Shipbuilder and Chm of Eltringhams, Ltd of Quay-on-Tyne, Northumberland.

HODSON (I) 1787, of Holybrooke House, Wicklow

Peace and love

Sir MICHAEL ROBIN ADDERLEY HODSON, 6th *Baronet*; *b* 5 March 1932; *s* his father, *Maj Sir* EDMOND ADAIR, DSO, 1972; *ed* Eton; Capt (ret) Scots Gds: *m* 1st, 1963 (*m diss* 1978), Katrin Alexa, da of late Erwin Bernstiel, of St Andrew's House, St Andrew's Major, Dinas Powis, Glam; 2ndly, 1978, Catherine, da of John Henry Seymour, of Wimpole St, W1, and formerly wife of Ralph Denne, and has issue by 1st *m*.

Arms – Sable, a chevron between three martlet, or. Crest – A dove close azure, beaked and membered or, holding in her beak an olive-branch proper.
Residence – The White House, Awbridge, Romsey, Hants S051 0HF.

DAUGHTERS LIVING *(By 1st marriage)*

Tania Elizabeth, *b* 1965. —— Alexa Adderley, *b* 1966: *m* 1990, Christopher Michael Chambers, of 12 Tynemouth St, SW6, son of W. M. Chambers, of Chipping Camden, Glos, and has issue living, Lara Adderley, *b* 1992, — Gemma Marlis, *b* 1994. —— Jane Katrina, *b* 1970.

BROTHER LIVING

PATRICK RICHARD (Shipton Slade Farm, Woodstock, Oxford OX7 1QQ) *b* 27 Nov 1934; *ed* Eton; Capt (ret) Rifle Bde; *m* 1961, June, only da of late Herbert Michael Shepherd-Cross, of The Old Rectory, Brandsby, Yorks, and has issue living, Mark Adair (52 Orbain Rd, SW6), *b* 1964: *m* 1991, Kathleen (Kate) Mary Florence, only da of late William Rippon Bissill (*see* B Nunburnholme), — James Patrick, *b* 1966: *m* 1993, Fiona Marion, 2nd da of Michael Herbert Johnson-Ferguson (*see* Johnson-Ferguson, Bt), — Rupert Edward, *b* 1972.

UNCLE LIVING

Cecil George (Crocnaran House, Kingstown, Moyard, co Galway), *b* 1900: *m* 1934, Betty Estelle, da of late Capt Arthur Jewel North, MC, of Vale Mascal, Bexley, Kent.

COLLATERAL BRANCH LIVING

Granddaughters of late Richard Edmond Hodson, 3rd son of 3rd baronet:—
Issue of late Gilbert Stanley Hodson, *b* 1895, *d* 1972: *m* 1948, Felicity Margaretta (Luska, Puckane, Nenagh, co Tipperary), yr da of late Lt-Col Hon Claud Patrick Brabazon, OBE (*see* E Meath, colls):—
Kathleen Margaret, *b* 1949: *m* 1980, Charles Gerald Dalby, and has issue (*see* Smiley, Bt). *Residence* – Dalbie House, Castle Donington, Derbys DE14 2PP. —— Marion Felicity, *b* 1951: *m* 1989, Bruce Swanhuyser, of White Salmon, Washington, USA, and has issue living, Robin Adair, *b* 1990, — Emma Paige, *b* 1993.
Sir Robert Hodson, 1st baronet, was descended in direct line from the Rev John Hodson, who belonged to a family long settled at Houghton, Staffordshire, and who assisted in the escape of King Charles I from Oxford in 1646. After the Restoration, Dr Hodson was successively Dean of Clogher and Bishop of Elphin; he *d* 1686.

HOGG (UK) 1846, of Upper Grosvenor Street, co Middlesex

Glory gives strength

Maj Sir ARTHUR RAMSAY HOGG, MBE, 7th *Baronet; b* 24 Oct 1896, son of Ernest Charles Hogg, son of Charles Swinton Hogg, 2nd son of 1st baronet; *s* his cousin, *Sir* KENNETH WEIR, OBE, 1985; *ed* Sherborne, and Ch Ch, Oxford (BA 1921, MA 1929); European War 1914-18 as Capt Roy W Kent Regt (twice wounded), European War 1940-45 as Major, Gen List; MBE (Mil) 1945: *m* 1924, Mary Aileen Hester Lee, who *d* 1980, da of Philip Herbert Lee Evans, of Coolhurst, Manor Rd, Bournemouth, and has issue.

Arms – Argent, three boars' heads erased azure, langued gules, between two flaunches of the second, each charged with a crescent of the field. **Crest** – Out of an eastern crown argent, an oak-tree fructed proper, and pendent therefrom an escutcheon azure charged with a dexter arm embowed in armour, the hand grasping an arrow in bend sinister, the point downwards also proper.
Residence – 27 Elgin Rd, Bournemouth, Dorset BH3 7DH.

SONS LIVING

MICHAEL DAVID (19 Woodlands Rd, Barnes, SW13 0JZ), *b* 19 Aug 1925; *ed* Sherborne, and Ch Ch, Oxford (BA 1950, MA 1953); European War 1943-45 as Capt Grenadier Guards: *m* 1956, Elizabeth Anne Therese, eldest da of late Sir Terence Edmond Patrick Falkiner, 8th Bt, and has issue living, Piers Michael James (13 South Ealing Rd, W5 4QT), *b* 25 April 1957: *m* 1982, Vivien, yr da of Dr Philip Holman, of 3 Atwood Av, Kew, Surrey, and has issue living, James Edward *b* 11 Sept 1985, Sarah Alice *b* 1988, — Adam Charles, *b* 1958: *m* 1987, Alison Pauline, da of Nicholas Selby, of 45 Gwendolen Av, Putney, SW15, and has issue living, Daniel Richard *b* 1988, Madeleine Victoria *b* 1989, — Oliver John, *b* 1961. —— Mark Arthur Philip (Hithe End Cottage, Tanner's Lane, Eynsham, Witney, Oxon OX8 1HJ), *b* 1928; *ed* Sherborne, and Ch Ch, Oxford (BA 1949, BSc 1950, MA 1953): *m* 1st, 1955 (*m diss* 1977), Jennifer Mary, da of late Michael Farrer Spurrell, of Greenhayes, Reigate, Surrey; 2ndly, 1977, Jane Margaret, da of late Rev Alan James Sutherland Symon, and formerly wife of David R. Lawrence, and has issue living (by 1st *m*), Stephen Mark, *b* 1960: *m* 1986, Deborah, er da of Cyril Skipworth, of 42 Charnock View Rd, Sheffield S12 3HJ, and has issue living, Charlotte Katherine *b* 1988, — Philippa Mary, *b* 1956: *m* 1979, Jeremy James Leon, 2nd son of late Arthur Jesse Douglas Leon, of 87 Three Bridges Rd, Crawley, Sussex, and has issue living, Frances Clare *b* 1983 Nicola Robyn *b* 1987, — Sally Elizabeth, *b* 1958: *m* 1985, Simon Hamling, — Nicola Frances, *b* 1962. —— Simon Charles (Meadow Cottage, Church St, Beckley, Oxford OX3 9UT), *b* 1936.

DAUGHTER LIVING

Anthea Aileen, *b* (twin) 1936: *m* 1957, Ian Stewart Gordon Carmichael, of The Old Manse of Loth, by Helmsdale, Sutherland, son of late Col D.R. Gordon Carmichael, of Powntley Copse, nr Alton, Hants, and has had issue, Donald Malcolm, *b* 1961; *d* 1984, — Alison Fiona, *b* 1958: *m* 1982, Nigel J. Llewelyn-Price, son of G.F. Price, — Victoria Anthea, *b* 1966: *m* 1989, Giles E. Gordon Brown, elder son of B. R. Cooper, and has issue living, Emily Megan *b* 1991.

COLLATERAL BRANCHES LIVING

Grandchildren of late Quintin Hogg, 7th son of 1st baronet:—
Issue of late Rt Hon Sir Douglas McGarel Hogg (*Viscount Hailsham*), *b* 1872; *cr Viscount Hailsham* 1929 (*see* B Hailsham of St Marylebone).

Issue of late Sir Malcolm Nicholson Hogg, *b* 1883, *d* 1948: *m* 1910, Lorna, who *m* 2ndly Com N. B. Deare (dec), and *d* 1978, da of late Sir Frank Clement Offley Beaman, sometime a Puisne Judge of High Court of Judicature, Bombay:—
Sir John Nicholson, TD (The Red House, Botley Rd, Shedfield, Southampton; Brooks's Club) *b* 1912; *ed* Eton, and Balliol Coll, Oxford; Dep Chm of Williams & Glyn's plc, 1970-83, and of Gallaher, Ltd 1964-78, Chm of Banque Francaise de Credit International Ltd 1972-83, and a Dir of Prudential Corpn plc 1964-85, The R Bank of Scotland Group plc 1965-82, and Honeywell, Ltd 1972-80; Sheriff of co London 1960, a Fellow of Eton 1951-70, and Chm of Abu Dhabi Investment Board 1967-75; Chm Export Guarantees Advisory Council 1962-67, and a Member of Commonwealth War Graves Commn 1958-64; 1939-45 War as Maj KRRC ((TA) in Greece, Crete, W Desert, N Africa and NW Europe): *m* 1948, Barbara Elisabeth, da of Capt Arden Franklyn, of New Place, Shedfield, Hants, and widow of Brig Viscount Garmoyle, DSO, late Rifle Bde, el son of 4th Earl Cairns, and has issue living, Malcolm David Nicholson (Lanterns, Mapledurham, Basingstoke RG25 2LU), *b* 1949: *m* 1975, Mary Clare, only da of late Maj Richard Francis Preedy, RE, and has issue living, Richard John Nicholson *b* 1982, Lucy Mary Arden *b* 1977, Alice Emily Geraldine *b* 1979, — Susan Elisabeth, *b* 1954: *m* 1980, Jeremy A. J. F. Burnett Rae, of The Ponts Cottage, S Moreton, Didcot, Oxon OX11 9AG, and has issue living, Henry Oliver *b* 1985, Charles Frederick *b* 1986, Emma Louise *b* 1983. —— Vivien Yzabel Suzanne Nicholson (23 Christchurch Rd, SW14), *b* 1915: *m* 1st, 1939 (*m diss* 1946), Cdr Henry Morland, R Indian Navy; 2ndly, 1947 (*m diss* 1954), John R. Caldwell; 3rdly, 1955, Thomas Melmoth Walters, who *d* 1974, and has issue living (by 1st *m*), Michael Henry, *b* 1941, — Miles Quintin (6 Hereford Sq, SW7; Travellers' Club), *b* 1943; *ed* Radley, and Lincoln Coll, Oxford; late Man Dir The First Boston Corpn; writer: *m* 1972, Guislaine, da of Guy Vincent Chastenet de la Maisoneuve, and has issue living, Catherine Natasha *b* 1973, Georgia Susanna *b* 1976.

The 1st baronet, Rt Hon Sir James Weir Hogg, Registrar of the Supreme Court of Judicature and Vice-Admiralty Court, Calcutta 1815-33, was twice elected Chm of E India Co and sat as MP for Beverley (*C*) 1834-47 and for Honiton 1847-57. The 2nd baronet, Sir James Macnaghten, KCB, was Chm of Metropolitan Board of Works 1870-89, and was MP for Bath (*C*) 1865-8, for Truro 1871-85, and for Middlesex, Hornsey Div, 1885-7, when he was *cr Baron Magheramorne*, having in 1877 assumed the additional surname of McGarel. The Barony of Magheramorne became ext in 1957 on the death of 4th Baron and 5th baronet.

LINDSAY-HOGG (UK) 1905, of Rotherfield Hall, Rotherfield, Sussex

Sir EDWARD WILLIAM LINDSAY-HOGG, 4th *Baronet*; *b* 23 May 1910; *s* his nephew, Sir WILLIAM LINDSAY, 1987; *ed* Eton: *m* 1st, 1936 (*m diss* 1946), Geraldine Mary (the actress and producer Geraldine Fitzgerald), da of late Edward Martin Fitzgerald, of Greystones, co Wicklow; 2ndly, 1957, Kathleen Mary, widow of Capt Maurice Cadill, MC, and da of James Cooney, of Carrick-on-Suir, co Tipperary, and has issue by 1st *m*.

Arms – Per pale indented vert and azure, on a bend or three boars' heads couped sable. **Crest** – Issuant out of a mural crown argent a boar's head erect sable holding in the mouth a sprig of oak fructed proper.
Residence –

SON LIVING (By 1st marriage)

MICHAEL EDWARD, *b* 5 May 1940; film dir: *m* 1967 (*m diss* 1971), Lucy Mary, only da of Donald Davies, of Enniskerry, co Wicklow. *Residence* - 9 Fitzwilliam Place, Dublin 2.

DAUGHTER LIVING OF THIRD BARONET

Sarah Frances, *b* 1961: *m* 1982, Simon John Gatliff, and has had issue, George Auben, *b* 1990; *d* 1991, — John William, *b* 1994, — Rosie Frances, *b* 1988. *Residence* - 1267 Ocean View Blvd, Pacific Grove, Calif 93950, USA.

WIDOW LIVING OF THIRD BARONET

MARIE TERESA (*Marie, Lady Lindsay-Hogg*), da of late John Foster, of St Helen's, Lancs: *m* 1987, as his 2nd wife, Sir William Lindsay-Hogg, 3rd Bt, who *d* 1987.

The 1st baronet, Sir Lindsay Hogg, assumed by Roy licence 1906, the additional surname of Lindsay, and sat as MP for S, or Eastbourne, Div of Sussex (*C*) Oct 1900 to Jan 1906.

HOLCROFT (UK) 1921, of Eaton Mascott, Berrington, co Salop

Constant and faithful

Sir PETER GEORGE CULCHETH HOLCROFT, 3rd *Baronet*; *b* 29 April 1931; *s* his father, Sir REGINALD CULCHETH HOLCROFT, TD, 1978; High Sheriff Shropshire 1969-70, JP 1976: *m* 1956 (*m diss* 1987), Rosemary Rachel, da of late Capt George Nevill Deas, 8th Hussars (M Anglesey, colls), and has issue living.

Arms – Argent, a cross engrailed between in the 1st and 4th quarters an eagle wings elevated sable, preying upon an infant proper, swaddled gules, banded or. **Crest** – Upon a log lopped proper, a raven sable holding, in the dexter paw a sword erect, also proper.
Residence – Berrington House, Berrington, Shrewsbury.

SONS LIVING

CHARLES ANTHONY CULCHETH, *b* 22 Oct 1959: *m* 1986, Mrs Elizabeth Carter, yr da of late John Raper, of Four Crosses, Powys, and has issue living, Toby David Culcheth, *b* 5 Feb 1990, — Samara Elisabeth, *b* 1988. —— Thomas Marcus Culcheth, *b* 1967. —— Alexander James Culcheth, *b* 1969.

DAUGHTER LIVING

Tania Melanie, *b* 1961.

BROTHER LIVING

Michael William Culcheth (Wrentnall House, Pulverbatch, Shrewsbury, Shropshire SY5 8ED), *b* 1935; *ed* Radley; Lt-Cdr RN (ret): *m* 1968 (*m diss* 1978), Amanda Victoria, da of Wing-Cdr Ian Roy Cardew Macpherson, DFC, AFC, of Winterbourne Abbas, Dorset.

SISTERS LIVING

Ann Cherida, *b* 1929: *m* 1952, John Dewé Neville Lake (*see* Walsham, Bt, colls). —— Mary Virginia, *b* 1939: *m* 1960, Maj William Kemp Trotter, 11th Hussars, and has issue living, James William Dale *b* 1964: *m* 19—, Nicola, eldest da of Vivian Mahaffy, and has issue living, Hebe Florence *b* 1994, — Henry Edward Dale, *b* 1966, — Philip George Dale, *b* 1969, — Victoria Mary, *b* 1962: *m* 1989, Capt Nicholas J. Thomas, The Queen's Own Hussars, son of Maj T. J. Thomas, of Hey House, Heytesbury, Wilts. *Residence* - The Deanery, Staindrop, co Durham.

COLLATERAL BRANCH LIVING

Issue of late John Culcheth Holcroft, Lieut 3rd Co London Yeo, 3rd son of 1st baronet, *b* 1905, *ka* 1941: *m* 1932, Beatrice Mathewson, who *d* 1985, da of late George F. Feathers:—
Timothy Gilbert Culcheth (Northbrook, Bentley, Hants), *b* 1934; *ed* Radley; Capt (ret) 11th Hussars; JP: *m* 1st, 1958, Joanna Eve, who *d* 1983, da of Adm Sir Stuart Sumner Bonham-Carter, KCB, CVO, DSO; 2ndly, 1982, Charmian Joy, formerly wife

of (i) Frederick James Meynell (*see* E Halifax, colls), and (ii) James Richard Nicholson (*see* Nicholson, Bt, *cr* 1912), and only da of late Maj Harcourt Michael Scudamore Gold, MC, of W Stratton House, Winchester, Hants (*see* Trent, By), and has issue living (by 1st *m*), Alexandra Jane, *b* 1962: *m* 1986, Andrew Fion Bethune Norman, only child of Alexander Vesey Bethune Norman, CBE, Master of the Armouries, HM Tower of London, and has issue living, Natasha *b* 1992, — Caroline Joanna, *b* 1966: *m* 1993, Charles J. D. Todhunter, only son of Michael John Benjamin Todhunter, of The Old Rectory, Farnborough, nr Wantage, Oxon. —— Tania, *b* 19—: *m* 1956, Mark Richard Geoffrey Cory-Wright, of Tilhill House, Tilford, Surrey, and Burnham Market, King's Lynn, Norfolk, and has issue (*see* Cory-Wright, Bt).

The 1st baronet, Sir George Harry Holcroft (son of late William Holcroft, JP, of Prescot House, Stourbridge), was Chm of Littleton Collieries (Limited), High Sheriff of Staffordshire 1913-14, and rendered notable sers to Birmingham Univ.

HOLDEN (UK) 1893, of Oakwoth House, Keighley, Yorkshire

Sir EDWARD HOLDEN, 6th *Baronet*; *b* 8 Oct 1916; *s* his father, *Sir* ISAAC HOLDEN, 1962; *ed* Leys Sch, Christ's Coll Camb, and St Thomas's Hosp; MRCS England and LRCP London 1942; DA England 1945, Fellow of Faculty of Anæsthetists 1958: *m* 1942, Frances Joan, el da of John Spark, JP, of Ludlow, Stockton-on-Tees.

Arms – Or, a chief azure, over all a bend nebulée between two roses gules. **Crest** – Issuant from a chaplet of oak vert, an eagle's head erased or, gorged with a collar gemel azure.
Residence – Moorstones, Ruebury Lane, Osmotherly, Northallerton, N Yorks DL6 3BG.

BROTHER LIVING

PAUL, *b* 3 March 1923: *m* 1950, Vivien Mary, yst da of late Hedley Broxholme Oldham, of Allesley, Coventry, and has issue living, Michael Peter (1 Greenways, Pembroke Rd, Woking, Surrey GU22 7D4), *b* 1956, — Judith Margaret (15 Clayton Rd, Prestwich, Manchester), *b* 1952: *m* 1st 1974 (*m diss* 1979), Robert Forrest; 2ndly, 19—, Tumelty, — Susan Diana, *b* 1953: *m* 19—, Aked. *Residence* – Glenside, Rowhills, Heath End, Farnham, Surrey GU9 9AU.

SISTERS LIVING

Ruth, *b* 1915. —— Helen, *b* 1918: *m* 1947, William Herbert Chapman, MB, ChB, of 6 Jennifer Way, Rossmoyne, W Aust 6155, and has issue living, Andrew, *b* 1948, — Richard Holden, *b* 1953, — Bridget, *b* 1950: *m* 1971, Peter Herbert Stone, — Anne, *b* 1957. —— Janet, *b* 1920: *m* 1946, Capt George Richmond Aagaard Welsh, RAOC, of 12 Bylands, White Rose Lane, Woking, Surrey, and has issue living, Geoffrey Peter, *b* 1948, — Raymond Michael, *b* 1949, — Malcolm Nigel, *b* 1950.

COLLATERAL BRANCH LIVING

Grandchildren of late Peter Wood Holden, 2nd son of Edward Holden, 2nd son of 1st baronet:—
Issue of late Duncan Holden, *b* 1907, *d* 1985: *m* 1930, Helen (Te Mara, Miller Rd, Havelock North, NZ), da of Kinross White, of Hawkes Bay, NZ:—
Peter Ritson (Forest Gate, Onga Onga, Hawkes Bay, NZ), *b* 1933: *m* 1958, Juliet, da of Keith de Castro, of Christchurch, NZ, and has issue living, Duncan Dudley *b* 1963, Matthew Keith *b* 1967, Deborah Elizabeth *b* 1959, Caroline Jane *b* 1961, — Diana Margaret, *b* 1930: *m* 1955, John Morris Williams, of Kaiaua, Tolaga Bay, NZ, and has issue living, Michael *b* 1956, — Philip *b* 1960, — Fiona *b* 1958, — Jennifer *b* 1961.

The 1st baronet, Sir Isaac Holden (son of Isaac Holden, of Gunends, Alston, Cumberland), was senior partner in the firm of Isaac Holden and Sons, Wool combers, of Alston Works, Bradford, and sat as MP for Knaresborough (L) 1865-68, for Yorkshire, W Riding, N Div 1882-85, and for Yorkshire, W Riding, N Part, Keighley Div 1885-95. The 2nd baronet, Sir Angus Holden sat as MP for Bradford, E Div (L) 1885-86, and for Yorkshire, E Riding, Buckrose Div, 1892-1900, and was *cr Baron Holden*, of Alston, co Cumberland (peerage of United Kingdom) 1908. In 1951, on the death of the 3rd Baron Holden, the peerage became ext, but the baronetcy passed to his cousin, Sir Isaac Holden (nephew of 1st Baron Holden), who succeeded as 5th baronet.

HOLDEN (UK) 1919, of The Firs, Leigh, co Lancaster

I owe all things to God

Sir JOHN DAVID HOLDEN, 4th *Baronet*, only son of late David George Holden, el son of 3rd baronet; *b* 16 Dec 1967; *s* his grandfather, *Sir* GEORGE, 1976: *m* 1987, Suzanne Cummings, of York, and has issue.

Arms – Sable, on a pale ermine between two chevrons or a covered cup of the last. **Crest** – In front of a rising sun in its splendour or, a moorcock sable, jelloped and wattled gules.
Residence – 13 Sterne Av, Tang Hall, York YO3 0TF.

DAUGHTER LIVING

—, *b* 19—.

UNCLE LIVING (*son of 3rd baronet*)

BRIAN PETER JOHN, *b* 12 April 1944: *m* 1984, Bernardette Anne Lopez, da of George Gerard O'Malley, of Manchester.

AUNTS LIVING (*daughters of 3rd baronet*)

Patricia Margaret Anne, *b* 1942; *m* 1963, David Coates Mitchell, of Lynden Royd, 60 Scott Lane West, Riddlesden, Keighley, Yorks, and has issue living, Kieron (14 Moorthorpe Av, Bradford Moore, Bradford, W Yorks), *b* 1970: *m* 1991, —, and has issue living, James Declan *b* 1992, Kyle Patrick *b* 1993, — Deborah, *b* 1964: *m* 1989, David John Petty, of 45 Airedale Rd, Undercliffe, Bradford, W Yorks. —— Deirdre Rosemary, *b* 1949: *m* 1969, David Marsh, of 23 Impstone Rd, Pamber Heath, Basingstoke, and has issue living, Andrew David, *b* 1974, — Christopher George, *b* 1986, — Nicola Catherine *b* 1972.

GREAT-UNCLE LIVING (*son of 2nd baronet*)

James Temple (22 Lambs Rd, Thornton, Blackpool, Lancs), *b* 1922: *m* 1st, 1948 (*m diss* 1956), Olive, da of Henry Thompson Kirby; 2ndly, 1957, Golda Bracey, da of Clifford Shirley, and has issue living (by 1st *m*), Peter James, *b* 1954, — Jacqueline Peta, *b* 1950 — (by 2nd *m*), Carl Temple, *b* 1963; LLB: *m* 1992, Caroline Anne, da of Stanley Gould, of Llanferres.

GREAT-AUNT LIVING (*daughter of 2nd baronet*)

Margaret, *b* 1916: *m* 1942, Maj E. R. Webster, R Corps of Signals, of Green Banks, Beechwood Lane, Culcheth, nr Warrington, Cheshire, and has issue living, Pamela Pixie Anne (Glen House, Upper Rochestown, Co Cork), *b* 1946: *m* 1970, Timothy Joseph Cahill, FRCS, who *d* 1988, and has issue living, Timothy Joseph *b* 1977, Bryan Anthony Ernest *b* 1979, Jeremy James *b* 1981, Joanne Amanda *b* 1971, Rachael Louise *b* 1972, — Carol Yvonne Margaret, *b* 1949: *m* 1973, Kenneth G. Wilcock, and has issue living, Ian Michael *b* 1977, James Richard *b* 1982, Jennifer Louise *b* 1975.

MOTHER LIVING

Nancy (Woodhouse Grange, Sutton-in-Derwent, York), da of H. W. D. Marwood, of Bodnor House, Whenby, York: *m* 1964, David George Holden (ante), who *d* 1971, el son of 3rd baronet.

COLLATERAL BRANCHES LIVING

Issue of late Christopher William Holden, 2nd son of 3rd baronet, *b* 1940, *d* 1968: *m* 1965, June (who *m* 2ndly, 1970, Barry Hargreaves Beaumont, of Manor Farm, Wyton, Hull), da of Stephen Carrington:—
Sara, *b* (*posthumous*) 1968.

Issue of late John Holden, 2nd son of 2nd baronet, *b* 1918, *d* 1985: *m* 1940, Margaret Lois, who *d* 1985, da of Ivan Sharpe, of Southport:—
Robin John (Tall Trees, Barry Rise, Bowdon, Altrincham, Cheshire), *b* 1943; *ed* Oundle; FCA; Pres Manchester Soc of Chartered Accountants 1984; Hon Treas Manchester Chamber of Commerce and Industry since 1983: *m* 1964, Margaret Susan, da of G. I. Rushton, of Birkdale, and has issue living, Richard Ingham, *b* 1966, — Jonathan Robin, *b* 1969. —— Anthony Ivan (6 Ravenscourt Square, W6 0TW), *b* 1947; *ed* Oundle, and Merton Coll, Oxford (MA); biographer: *m* 1971 (*m diss* 1988), Amanda Juliet, MA, LGSM, LRAM, ARCM, da of Sir Harold Brian Seymour Warren, MRCS, LRCP, of 94 Oakley St, SW3, and has issue living, Samuel Ivan, *b* 1975, — Joseph Anthony, *b* 1977, — Benjamin John, *b* 1979.

Issue of late Arthur Holden, 4th son of 1st baronet, *b* 1897, *d* 1993: *m* 1st, 1920, Laura, who *d* 1949, da of H. Williams; 2ndly, 1949, Dorothy (Agincourt, Woodlands Av, Rustington, Sussex), da of Nathan Seddon, of Eccles:—
(By 1st *m*) Arthur John (Eagerly Bank, Andrew Lane, Bolton, Lancs), *b* 1921: *m* 1949, Ethel Hall, of Bolton, Lancs.

Grandchildren of late Arthur Holden, 4th son of 1st baronet (ante):—
Issue of late Henry David Holden, *b* 1922, *d* 1980: *m* 1947, Marjorie (Anglezarke, Belmont Rd, Penn, Wolverhampton), da of T. A. Brown, of Astley Bridge, Bolton:—
David Lawrence (27 Richmond Drive, Tinacre Grange, Perton), *b* 1948: *m* 1971, Sharon Joyce, da of A. C. W. Mobbs, of Perton, and has issue living, Robert Arthur, *b* 1972, — Emma Jane, *b* 1974. —— Andrew Charles (Cote Leasowe, Heath House Lane, Codsall, Wolverhampton), *b* 1949: *m* 1972, Susan, da of J. W. Dicken, of Bilston. —— William John (Knights Close, Penkridge, Staffs), *b* 1953: *m* 1975, Patricia Joan, da of R. C. Knight, of Wolverhampton. —— Madeline Julie, *b* 1967: *m* 1989, David Raymond Haynes, of 5 Ayrton Close, Perton, Wolverhampton, and has issue living, Lauren Victoria, *b* 1991.

Issue of late John Holden, 5th and yst son of 1st baronet, *b* 1900, *d* 1977: *m* 1925, Rita, da of H. Walton, of Reedley, Burnley:—
Derek John (5 Greystoke Court, 29 Albemarle Rd, Beckenham, Kent BR3 2HL), *b* 1927: *m* 1951, Patricia Kathleen, da of F. Mansfield, of Heaton Moor, and has issue living, Richard John, *b* 1960: *m* 1982, Atie, da of G. Nieuwenhuis, of Durban N, S Africa, — Elizabeth Anne, *b* 1955. —— Norman Michael (7 Trafford Av, Westville, Durban, S Africa), *b* 1928: *m* 1957, Enid N, da of M. Smith, of Adelaide, S Aust, and has issue living, Christopher Derek, *b* 1959, — Peter James, *b* 1960.

—— Gillian Nancy, *b* 1935: *m* 1964, Dennis George Edwin Cox, of Highlands, Berden, Bishop's Stortford, and has issue living, Gordon Michael, *b* 1967, —— Julia Alison, *b* 1965.

Sir John Henry Holden, 1st Bt (son of John Holden), was twice Mayor of Leigh, Lancashire. The 2nd baronet, Sir George, was also twice Mayor of Leigh.

HOLDER (UK) 1898, of Pitmaston, Moseley, Worcestershire

Sir (JOHN) HENRY HOLDER, 4th *Baronet*; *b* 12 March 1928; *s* his father, *Sir* JOHN ERIC DUNCAN, 1986; *ed* Eton, and Birmingham Univ (Dip in Malting and Brewing): *m* 1960, Catharine Harrison, who *d* 1994, yr da of late Leonard Baker, of Stone Lane, Kinver, nr Stourbridge, Worcs, and has issue.

Arms – Per pale indented or and gules three chevronels ermine, in chief two trefoils slipped and countercharged. **Crest** – On the battlements of a tower per pale or and argent, charged with a cross gules, a lion sejant per pale indented azure and of the third supporting with the dexter paw an anchor argent.
Residence – 47 St Paul's Rd North, West Walton Highway, Wisbech, Cambs PE14 7DN.

SONS LIVING

NIGEL JOHN CHARLES, *b* 6 May 1962; *ed* Wisbech Gram Sch, and The Isle Coll, Wisbech.
—— Hugo Richard, *b* (twin) 1962: *m* 1991, Barbara, only da of Walter Plenk, of Sperberstrasse 42, 81827 Munich, Germany, and has issue living, Alexander John, *b* 1993.

Nisi Dominus frustra

It is in vain without the Lord

b 1993.

DAUGHTER LIVING

Bridget Georgina, *b* 1964: *m* 1991, Christopher L. T. Davis, only son of L. F. Davis, of Burrough Green, Newmarket, Suffolk, and has issue living, Thomas Henry Frederick,

SISTERS LIVING

Anthea Josephine, *b* 1930: *m* 1961, Peter Wilbraham Swayne, of The Old Ground, Whitmore Lane, Halse, Taunton, Somerset TA4 3AH, yr son of Philip Coney Swayne, of Higher Down, Over Stowey, Somerset. —— Meryl Evelyn, *b* 1936.

AUNT LIVING (*daughter of 2nd baronet*)

Nancy Lilian (Flat 4, 16 Elm Park Gdns, SW10), *b* 1907.

MOTHER LIVING

Evelyn Josephine, elder da of late William James Fletcher Blain, of Tybroughton Hall, Whitchurch, Shropshire: *m* 1927 (*m diss* 1948), as his 1st wife, Sir John Eric Duncan Holder, 3rd Bt, who *d* 1986. *Residence* – The Tudor House, Charlynch, Bridgwater, Somerset.

WIDOW LIVING OF THIRD BARONET

MARJORIE EMILY (*Marjorie, Lady Holder*), da of late Frank Reynolds Markham, of Cape Town and of London: *m* 1971, as his 2nd wife, Sir John Eric Duncan Holder, 3rd Bt (MA Oxon), who *d* 1986. *Residence* – Clare Park, Crondall, Farnham, Surrey GU10 5DT.

COLLATERAL BRANCHES LIVING

Granddaughters of late Alfred Ernest Holder (infra):—
Issue of late Lt-Col Charles Frederic Chavasse Holder, RA, *b* 1910, *d* 1989: *m* 1951, Margaret (Balsam House, Wincanton, Som BA9 9HT), yst da of A. E. Wrigley, of Gaines, Whitbourne, Worcs:—
Lucy Margaret, *b* 1953: *m* 1987, David B. Badham-Thornhill, of Holton House, Wincanton, Som, son of Maj D. G. B. Badham-Thornhill, of Cheltenham, and has had issue, Thomas Charles George, *b* 1989, — Edward David, *b* 1993, — Ruth, *b* and *d* 1991, — Helen, *b* (twin) 1991. —— Judith Mary, *b* 1954.

Issue of late Alfred Ernest Holder, 3rd son of 1st baronet, *b* 1879, *d* 1963: *m* 1909, Gwendoline Louisa Ryland, who *d* 1976, da of late Sir Thomas Chavasse, MD, of The Linthurst Hill, Barnt Green, Worcs:—
Gwendoline Mary Chavasse, *b* 1913: *m* 1943, Lawry Knight, of 59 Victoria Rd, Topsham, Exeter, and has issue living, William, *b* 1945, — Caroline, *b* 1944. —— Phyllis Margaret Chavasse, *b* 1918: *m* 1st, 1956 (*m diss* 1967), as his 2nd wife, William Raymond John Evelyn Whateley, now Balfour (*see* Page-Wood, Bt, colls); 2ndly, 1967, Lt-Col Matthew Wakefield Drury Evelyn Wood (*see* Page-Wood, Bt, colls).

HOLDERNESS (UK) 1920, of Tadworth, co Surrey

Sir RICHARD WILLIAM HOLDERNESS, 3rd *Baronet*; *b* 30 Nov 1927; *s* his father, *Sir* ERNEST WILLIAM ELSMIE, CBE, 1968; *ed* Corpus Christi Coll, Oxford (MA): *m* 1953, Pamela, da of late Eric Chapman, CBE, of Drovers, White Lane, Guildford, Surrey, and has issue.
Residence – Bramfold Court, Nutbourne Rd, nr Pulborough, W. Sussex RH20 2HA.

SONS LIVING

MARTIN WILLIAM, b 24 May 1957: m 1984, Elizabeth D., da of Dr D. Thornton, of 54 Deramore Park, S Belfast, and has issue living, Matthew William Thornton, b 23 May 1990, — Tessa Elizabeth Mary, b 1992. —— Andrew James, b 1962: m 1989, Charlotte E. M., elder da of Michael Broadbent, of Shrewton, Wilts, and has issue living, Henrietta Emily Alice, b 1993.

DAUGHTER LIVING

Jane Carleton, b 1955: m 1976, Richard David Bruce Pailthorpe, BSc, of The Chase, Charlton, Chichester, W Sussex, and has issue living, Nicholas Richard Bruce, b 1980, — Victoria Emma Carleton, b 1983.

SISTER LIVING

Margaret Carleton, b 1929; MB, ChB Edinburgh 1954; FFARCS: m 1965, William Frederick Walter Southwood, MD, MCh, FRCS, of 1 Aldwick Av, Bognor Regis, W Sussex, and has issue living, Robert William, b 1966, — John Carleton, b 1967.
The 1st baronet, Sir Thomas William Holderness, GCB, KCSI (son of late John William Holderness, of Liverpool), was sometime Permanent Under-Sec of State for India.

HOLLAND (UK) 1917, of Westwell Manor, co Oxford

Faire Devoir en bonne-esperance

To do (one's) duty in good hope

Sir GUY HOPE HOLLAND, 3rd *Baronet*; b 19 July 1918; s his brother, Sir JIM SOTHERN, TD, 1981; ed privately, and Ch Ch, Oxford; late Capt Roy Scots Greys; m 1945, Joan Marianne, only surv child of late Capt Herbert Edmund Street, 20th Hussars, and has issue.

Arms – Azure, a lion rampant guardant within an orle, surrounded by four mullets and as many fleur-de-lis alternately all argent. **Crest** – A fox séjant gules, collared argent, supporting with the dexter forepaw an anchor or.
Residence – Sheepbridge Barn, nr Eastleach, Cirencester, Glos GL7 3PS. *Clubs* – Boodle's, Pratt's.

DAUGHTERS LIVING

Davina Huntly, b 1946: m 1981, Guy Timothy Geoffrey Conant, DL, of Bulwick Park, Corby, Northants, 2nd son of late Sir Roger Conant, 1st Bt, CVO, and has issue (*see* Conant, Bt). —— Georgiana, b 1951: m 1979, Nicholas Antony Norman Stuart Robertson, of The Old Rectory, Thorpe Malsor, Kettering, Northants, son of Antony Stuart Robertson, CBE, and has issue living, Ralph Edmund Sothern Stuart, b 1982, — Guy Sothern Antony, b 1985.

DAUGHTERS LIVING OF SECOND BARONET

Jennifer Lisabeth Gwynllyn, b 1940. —— Claerwen Belinda, b 1942.

WIDOW LIVING OF SECOND BARONET

ELISABETH HILDA MARGARET (*Elisabeth, Lady Holland*) (Dderw, Rhayader Powys), only child of Thomas Francis Vaughan Prickard, CVO, CA, FRICS, of Dderw, Rhayader, Powys: m 1937, Sir Jim Sothern Holland, 2nd Bt, who d 1981.
The 1st baronet, Sir (Alfred Reginald) Sothern (1876-1948) (son of late Benjamin Herbert Holland, Colonial Civil Ser, Registrar of Deeds for Cape Colony), was HM Trade Commr, S Africa 1908-14, Director-Gen of Inspection of Munitions 1916, Chm, Central Mining and Investment Corporation Ltd 1924-31, and 1941-5, and Rhodes Trustee 1932-48; High Sheriff Oxon 1943.

HOLLINS (UK) 1907, of Greyfriars, Broughton, co Palatine of Lancaster (Extinct 1963)

Sir FRANK HUBERT HOLLINS, 3rd and last *Baronet*.

COLLATERAL BRANCHES LIVING

Issue of late Philip Leslie Hollins, 3rd son of 1st baronet, b 1878, d 1933: m 1919, Doris Mary, who d 1969, da of Charles Arthur Abraham (Parker, Bt cr 1681):—
Anne, b 1923: m 1st, 1947 (m diss 1951), Brig Percy de Courcy Jones, King's Shropshire LI; 2ndly, 1953, Peter Robert Gibson, of 15 Warren Hill Rd, Woodbridge, Suffolk, and has issue living, (by 1st m) Nigel Anthony de Courcy, b 1948: m 1982, Jane Wilson, of Ulverston, Lancs, — (by 2nd m) Christopher Robert, b 1956: m 1980, Margaret Ruth, da of John Anthony Salt, — Philip James, b 1959: m 1984, Linda, da of John Todd, of Ipswich, Suffolk, — Julia Elizabeth, b 1954: m 1982, Dr John Stanger, son of Dr Robin Stanger, of Burlesdon, Hants.

Issue of late John Chard Humphrey Lancelot Hollins, 4th son of 1st baronet, b 1890, d 1938: m 1914, Ruth, who d 1977, da of late John Keil Tullis, of Glasgow:—
Ruth Jean (Gelston, Dawson Lane, Whittle le Woods, Chorley, Lancs), b 1928.

HOLT (UK) 1916, of Cheetham, co Palatine of Lancaster (Extinct 1968)

Sir EDWARD HOLT, 2nd and last *Baronet*.

WIDOW LIVING OF SECOND BARONET

MARGARET (*Lady Holt*), da of T. S. Lupton, formerly of Runswick, Cheadle Hulme, Ches: *m* 1931, Sir Edward Holt, 2nd Bt, who *d* 1968, when the title became ext.

HOME (NS) 1671, of Blackadder, co Berwick
(Name pronounced "Hume")

Look to the end

Sir WILLIAM DUNDAS HOME, 14th *Baronet*; son of late John Home, elder son of 13th baronet; *b* 19 Feb 1968; *s* his grandfather, *Sir* DAVID GEORGE, 1992; *ed* Cranbrook Sch, Sydney.

Arms – Quarterly; 1st, azure on a chevron argent three roses gules, *Blackadder*; 2nd, vert, a lion rampant argent langued and armed gules, *Home*; 3rd, argent, three popinjays, vert beaked and limbed gules, *Pepdie*; 4th, argent, a cross engrailed azure, *Sinclair*. **Crest** – An adder sable in pale, holding in its mouth a rose gules, leaved and stalked vert. **Supporters** – *Dexter*, an otter; *sinister*, a falcon, both proper.
Residence – 32 Parsley Rd, Vaucluse, NSW 2030, Australia. *Club* - Royal Sydney Golf.

SISTER LIVING

Georgina Helen, *b* 1969.

UNCLE LIVING (*son of 13th baronet*)

PATRICK, *b* 4 July 1941; *ed* Harrow: *m* 1984, Catherine Mary, yr da of James McLaren Henderson, of Spittalrigg, Haddington, E Lothian, and has living, David McLaren, *b* 6 March 1993, — Janet, *b* 1986. *Residence* – Winterfield, North Berwick, E Lothian EH39 4LY. *Clubs* – Royal and Ancient, The Hon Co of Edinburgh Golfers.

AUNT LIVING (*daughter of 13th baronet*)

Hermione (*Lady Malcolm*), *b* 1934; *ed* Lady Margaret Hall, Oxford (BA); a JP for Inner London 1971-84: *m* 1959, Sir David Peter Michael Malcolm, 11th Bt, of Whiteholm, Gullane, E Lothian EH31 2BD.

MOTHER LIVING

Nancy Helen (*Lady Gorton*), elder da of Harry Greenlaw Elliott, of Perth, W Australia, and widow of Cdr Ian Macgregor, RAN: *m* 2ndly, 1966, John Home, who *d* 1988, elder son of Sir David George Home, 13th Bt; 3rdly, 1993, Rt Hon Sir John Grey Gorton, GCMG, AC, CH. *Residence* – 32 Parsley Rd, Vaucluse, NSW 2030, Australia.

The Homes of Blackadder descend from John, 4th son of Sir David Home of Wedderburn, who fell at Flodden 1513, whose sons present there were known as the "Seven Spears of Wedderburn." John Home of East Blackadder *m* 1518, Beatrix, el da and co-parcener of Robert Blackadder of that Ilk. On the failure of descendants of her yr sister who *m* Robert Home, another of the "the Spears," the whole barony passed to this family. The Homes of Wedderburn descend from Sir David Home (living 1453), yr son of Sir Thomas Home of that Ilk, ancestor of the Earls of Home. Sir John Home, 5th in descent from John of Easter Blackadder, was *cr* a baronet with remainder to heirs male of his body. Sir George Home, 7th baronet, was Vice-Adm of the Blue. The 10th baronet in 1878 assumed the additional surname of Speirs.

Home-Purves-Hume-Campbell, see Campbell.

HONYWOOD (E) 1660, of Evington, Kent

Every good thing is from above

Sir FILMER COURTENAY WILLIAM HONYWOOD, 11th *Baronet*: *b* 20 May 1930; *s* his father, *Col Sir* WILLIAM WYNNE, MC, 1982; *ed* Downside, RMA Sandhurst, and RAC Cirencester (MRAC Diploma); FRICS; late 3rd Carabiniers (Prince of Wales' Dragoon Gds); Assist Surveyor Min of Agric Fisheries and Food, Maidstone 1966-73, Surveyor Cockermouth, Cumbria 1973-74, Sr Lands Officer SE Region Central Electricity Generating Board 1974-78, Regional Surveyor and Valuer 1978-88, Agricultural Compensation and Restoration Consultant to UK Nirex Ltd 1988-89; Company Secretary Honywood Business Consultancy Services Ltd: *m* 1956, Elizabeth Margaret Mary Cynthia, 2nd da of late Sir Alastair George Lionel Joseph Miller, 6th Bt (*cr* 1788), and has issue.

𝕬rms – Argent, a chevron between three hawks' heads erased azure beaked or.
𝕮rest – A wolf's head couped ermine.
Residence – Greenway Forstal Farmhouse, Hollingbourne, Maidstone, Kent ME17 1QA.

SONS LIVING

RUPERT ANTHONY PAGAN (185 Primrose Lane, Shirley Oaks Village, Croydon CR0 8YQ), *b* 2 March 1957. —— Simon Joseph, *b* 1958; BA, MRTPI.

DAUGHTERS LIVING

Mary Caroline, *b* 1961; SRN, SCM. —— Judith Mary Frances, *b* 1964.

SISTERS LIVING

Rosamund Iseulte Mary, *b* 1924; 1939-45 War with WRNS: *m* 1947, Paul Anthony Prior, late Lt RNVR, and has issue living, Jacqueline Mary, *b* 1950; *ed* Sussex Univ (BSc), London (PhD): *m* 1972, Timothy Charles Feline, PhD, and has issue living, William James *b* 1979, David Charles *b* 1981, Eleanor Ruth *b* 1983, — Helen Catherine, *b* 1953; SRN, SRCN: *m* 1976, Aribert Wolframm, and has issue living, Thomas *b* 1980, Martin Hawtayne *b* 1982, Yvonne Bianca *b* 1978, — Sarah Jane, *b* 1956: *m* 1975, Leslie Howe, — Emma Charlotte Claudia, *b* 1962; NNEB. *Residence* – Rochegude, 30430 Barjac, France. —— Zaidée Maud Elsie, *b* 1926; SRN, SCM, Edinburgh: *m* 1954, Lt-Cdr Douglas Inglefield Haywood, RN, and has issue living, Richard Douglas, *b* 1964; BA: *m* 1986, Malika Dukali, and has issue living, Karima Frances *b* 1986, Aisha Zaidée *b* 1992, — Elizabeth Zaidée, *b* 1955; BSc, PhD, — Katherine Mary, *b* 1962; SRN: *m* 1989, Derek Moore, — Patricia Anne, *b* 1967; DCRR. *Residence* – Downgate Cottage, N Petherwin, Launceston, Cornwall PL15 8LR.

COLLATERAL BRANCH LIVING

Grandchildren of late Guy Honywood, 8th son of 7th baronet:—
Issue of late Thomas Guy Honywood, *b* 1903, *d* 1968: *m* 1st, 19—, —; 2ndly, 1931, Anne Gertrude Molloy (64 McMaster St, Invercargill, NZ):—
(By 1st *m*) Guy Thorpe (15 Kelvin St, Oamaru, NZ), *b* 19—: *m* 19—, Adriane —. —— (By 2nd *m*) Barry (Box 50 PO, Castle Hill, NSW 2154, Australia), *b* 1932: *m* 19—, Anne —, and has issue living, Michael, *b* 19—, — Matthew, *b* 19—. —— Bernadette Margaret, *b* 1936: *m* 1960, Nepia Tauri Maniapoto, RNZA Regt Korean War, of 44 Wharenui Rd, Rotorua, NZ, and has issue living, Maru John, *b* 1967; BMS, — Moana Maree, *b* 1961; LLB: *m* 19—, William Wakatere Jackson, of 44 Tamaki Av, Otahuhu, Auckland, NZ, and has issue living, Kimiora Hikurangi Elijah *b* 1990, — Katarina Mae, *b* 1962: *m* 19—, Warren Ruru Morgan, of 290 Old Taupo Rd, Rotorua, NZ, and has issue living, Nepia Thomas *b* 1986, Katarina Aroha *b* 1991, — Niki Ann, *b* 1964, — Keri Lee, *b* 1965: *m* 19—, David Cheer, of 141 Tavistock Rd, Waipukurau, NZ, — Lisa Aroha, *b* 1969; BEd.

The 1st baronet was Sir Edward Honywood (son of late Sir John Honywood, High Sheriff of Kent 1607-9). Sir John Honywood, 4th baronet, was MP for Steyning 1784-5 and 1788-90, for Canterbury 1790-1802, and for Honiton 1802-6. Sir John William Honywood, 8th baronet, was an Alderman of Kent County Council.

HOOD (UK) 1922, of Wimbledon, co Surrey

Sir HAROLD JOSEPH HOOD, TD, 2nd *Baronet*; *b* 23 Jan 1916; *s* his father, *Sir* JOSEPH, 1931; *ed* Downside; is Lieut RA (TA); a Dir of Catholic Herald Ltd; appointed Editor of *The Catholic Who's Who* 1952; a Knt of St Gregory the Great (Knt Cdr 1978), and Knt of Magistral Grace, Sovereign Mil Order of Malta 1986: *m* 1946, Hon Ferelith Rosemary Florence Kenworthy, da of 10th Baron Strabolgi, and has issue.

Arms – Argent, on a mount vert an oak tree fructed proper, a chief sable, thereon a bow stringed also proper. **Crest** – A demi-stag proper resting the sinister foot on a fret or.
Residence – 31 Avenue Road, St John's Wood, NW8 6BS. *Clubs* – MCC, RAC.

SONS LIVING

JOHN JOSEPH HAROLD, *b* 27 Aug 1952. —— Basil Gervase Francis Gerard, *b* 1955.

DAUGHTERS LIVING

Josepha Ferelith Emma Margaret-Mary, *b* 1953: *m* 1981, Ian Murray, eldest son of Sir Donald Murray, KCVO, CMG, late HM Amb to Sweden, and has issue living, Andrew Duncan Culverwell, *b* 1985, — Alasdair Angus Culverwell, *b* 1987, — Kirstie Iona Culverwell, *b* 1990. —— Margaret Marie Elizabeth Felicia, *b* 1965: *m* 1990, Michael Gresslin, son of Heinz Gresslin, of Badenweiler, Germany.

COLLATERAL BRANCH LIVING

Issue of late Robin Adrian Hood, yst son of 1st baronet, *b* 1924, *d* 1993: *m* 1949, Miriam Teresa, who *d* 1991, yr da of late Don Humberto Blanco-Fombona:—
Simon Joseph Paul Blanco (12 Parliament Mews, Thames Bank, Mortlake, SW14), *b* 1951: *m* 1st, 1979 (*m diss* 1989), Josette Elian, only da of Jean Baumgartner, of Montchoisi 55, Lausanne, Switzerland; 2ndly, 1990 (*m diss* 1991), Judith M., only da of D. W. Prickett, of Kingston Hill, Surrey, and has issue living (by 1st *m*), Victoria Alexandra, *b* 1984. —— Martin Joseph Blanco, *b* 1953; *ed* Downside. —— Bernadette Marie Blanco, *b* (twin) 1953. —— Anne-Marie Elena Kathleen Blanco, *b* 1957: *m* 1979, Nicholas Edward True, CBE, of 114 Palewell Park, SW14 8JH, son of late Edward T. True, of W Bridgford, and has issue living, James Alexios Edward, *b* 1981, — Thomas-Leo Richard, *b* 1984, — Sophia Miriam Marie-Louise Blanco, *b* 1992.
The 1st baronet, Sir Joseph Hood, a solicitor, sometime a Dep Chm British American Tobacco Co Ltd, sat as MP for Wimbledon (*U*) 1918-24, and was Mayor of Wimbledon 1930-31.

FULLER-ACLAND-HOOD (UK) 1806 of Hartington, co Derby, and 1809, of St Audries, co Somerset (Extinct 1990)

Sir (ALEXANDER) WILLIAM FULLER-ACLAND-HOOD, 8th Baronet of Hartington and 6th Baronet of St Audries; last *Baronet*.

DAUGHTER LIVING OF EIGHTH (AND SIXTH) BARONET

Elisabeth Anne (11216 Jumper Mesa Rd, SR1, Box 38 D6, Littlerock, Cal, 93543, USA), *b* 1931: *m* 1st, 1952 (*m diss* 1960), Richard C. Pferdner, who *d* 1989; 2ndly, 1968, Wallace G. Henry, who *d* 1972, and has issue living (by 1st *m*) Richard Charles, *b* 1959: *m* 19—, Lisa —, — Kathleen Marie, *b* 1957: *m* 19—, Robert Sacks, and has issue living, Joshua *b* 19—, Allison E. *b* 19—, — (by 2nd *m*), Eric William, *b* 1969.

HOOPER (UK) 1962, of Tenterden, co Kent (Extinct 1987)

Sir ANTHONY ROBIN MAURICE HOOPER, 2nd and last *Baronet*.

DAUGHTERS LIVING OF FIRST BARONET (*by 1st marriage*)

Bobyl Jane, *b* 1924: *m* 1945, Lt-Cdr Bernard Vann, MBE, DSC, RN, of Woodlands, Kemble Wick, Cirencester, Glos GL7 6EQ, and has issue living, Michael, *b* 1946, — James, *b* 1949.

(*by 2nd marriage*)

Emma Charlotte HOOPER, *b* 1949: *m* 1st, 1968 (*m diss* 1973), Razek Mamarbachi; 2ndly, 1979, Babar Khan Mumtaz, and has issue living (by 2nd *m*), Chungaiz, *b* 1980, — Aruna, *b* 1982.

HOPE (NS) 1628, of Craighall, co Fife

But hope is unbroken

Sir JOHN CARL ALEXANDER HOPE, 18th *Baronet*; *b* 10 June 1939; *s* his father, *Group-Capt Sir* ARCHIBALD PHILIP, OBE, DFC, AE, 1987; *ed* Eton: *m* 1968, Merle Pringle, da of late Robert Douglas, of Southside, Holbrook, Ipswich, and has issue.

𝔄rms – Azure, a chevron or between three bezants. 𝔠rest – A broken terrestrial globe surmounted by a rainbow issuing out of a cloud at each end all proper. 𝔖upporters – Two female figures representing Hope in vestments vert, on their heads garlands of flowers, each resting her exterior hand on an anchor all proper.
Residence – 9 Westleigh Av, SW15 6RF.

SON LIVING

ALEXANDER ARCHIBALD DOUGLAS, *b* 16 March 1969; *ed* Eton.

DAUGHTER LIVING

Natasha Anne, *b* 1971.

BROTHER LIVING

Charles Archibald, *b* 1945; *ed* Eton, Balliol Coll, Oxford (BA), London Univ (MA) and — Coll Camb (MA); lecturer at Warburg Inst: *m* 1977, Jennifer Katharine, da of John Hadley, of Godmanchester, Huntingdon, and has issue living, Thomas, *b* 1978.

AUNT LIVING (*daughter of 16th Baronet*)

Katharine Anne (The Colt House, Chieveley, Newbury, Berks RG16 8XB), *b* 1916: *m* 1st, 1939, Fl-Lt Carl Raymond Davis, DFC, AAF, who was *ka* during Battle of Britain 1940; 2ndly, 1945, Maj Eric George Ewart Rayner, RA, who *d* 1978, and has issue living (by 1st *m*), Carl Michael (Marymead Cottage, Chieveley, Newbury, Berks RG16 8UX), *b* 1940: *m* 1st, 1963 (*m diss* 1987), Carolyn Rachel, da of John White, of Cushat Wood, Potten End, Berkhamsted; 2ndly, 1987, Carolyn Jane, da of late Earnest Smith Hall, of Solihull, Warwickshire, and has issue living, (by 1st *m*) Carl Robert *b* 1971, Helen Rachel *b* 1966, Julie Theresa, *b* 1968, — (by 2nd *m*) Gillian Mary, *b* 1948: *m* 1986, Peter Alan Cardiff, of 29 Stokenchurch St, Fulham, SW6 3TS.

COLLATERAL BRANCHES LIVING

Issue of late Lt-Col Hugh Alexander Hope, OBE, MC, KRRC, yst son of 16th baronet, *b* 1914, *d* 1982: *m* 1949, Cynthia Evelyn (7 High St, Sherston, Wilts SN16 0LQ), da of late Lt-Col Algernon Corbert Turnor, MC, RHG (B Londesborough):—
Andrew Hugh, *b* 1951; *ed* Quantock Sch, Over Stowey, Somerset: *m* 1982 (*m diss* 1992), Rosanna Jane, da of Gilbert Ian Noel Johnstone, of Cross Cottage, Brixton Deverill, Warminster, Wilts, and has issue living, Oliver Hugh, *b* 1989, — Clara Harriet, *b* 1986.

Granddaughter of late Capt Graham Archibald Hope, eldest son of late Archibald Godfrey Hope, 2nd son of late Maj-Gen Archibald Hugh Hope, son of late Hugh Hope, 4th son of 9th baronet:—
Issue of late Sqdn-Ldr Nigel Hope, *b* 1907, *d* on active ser 1939: *m* 1936, Evelyn Di (who *m* 2ndly, 1950, William Bryant), yr da of late Harry Arnaud Watson, of Emsworth, Hants:—
Alison (*posthumous*), *b* 1940.

Grandson of late Major Richard Berwick Hope, 3rd son of late Archibald Godfrey Hope (ante):—
Issue of late Alexander Erskine Hope, Lieut Bedfordshire and Herts Regt, *b* 1917, *ka* 1944: *m* 1941, Lilias Mary Phyllis (who *m* 2ndly, 1948, Lt-Col Gerard Francis Kirkpatrick Daly, RE), da of late Rev William Herbert Austwick:—
Alexander David Austwick (*posthumous*), *b* 1945; *ed* Bloxham; actor.

Granddaughter of late Major Cecil Arthur Hope, 2nd son of late James Hope, WS, *b* 1818, 4th son of late John Hope, MD, FRS, grandson of late Sir Archibald Hope (Lord Rankeillour of the Court of Session), 2nd son of 2nd baronet:—
Issue of late Lieut-Col Arthur Clement Hope, MBE, *b* 1891, *d* 1961: *m* 1933, Elizabeth Hale, da of Frederick W. Wallace, of Redjacket, Washington, USA:—
Jean Elizabeth, *b* 1937: *m* 1960, Sergio Pizzicaria.

Grandchildren of late Edward William Hope, OBE, MD, DSc (infra):—
Issue of late John Edward Bowring Hope, *b* 1901, *d* 1957: *m* 1927, Catherine, who *d* 1979, da of Robert Stephen Hubbersty, MD, of Avenue House, Sunderland:—
Michael Stephen Edward (Apt 503 Brentwood Park, Portugal Cove Rd, St Johns, Newfoundland, Canada A1B 4H9), *b* 1928; late 2nd Lieut RHG: *m* 1st, 1957, Edith Rosemary Byrne, who *d* 1962, da of late Mrs Margaret Roberts, of Bexhill-on-Sea; 2ndly, 1964, Catherine Emily, da of late Frederick Bradshaw, and widow of William Kenneth Latham, of Newfoundland, and has issue living, (by 1st *m*) Nigel John Charles *b* 1959: *m* 1983, Janet, da of Reginald Gordon Warner, of 78 Crestway, Roehampton, SW15, — Michelle Catherine Margaret, *b* 1958: *m* 1981, Nicholas Charles Devereux, of 9 Poplar Rise, Little Aston, W Midlands, and has issue living, Christopher Charles *b* 1981, Jennifer Sarah *b* 1985, — (by 2nd *m*) Catherine Charlotte, *b* 1964: *m* 1988, David John Fell, of 55 Vale Close, Harpendon, Herts, and has issue living, James Michael *b* 1990, Thomas Charles *b* 1993, — Louise Joan, *b* 1969. —— Christopher John (1 Port Hill Drive, Shrewsbury), *b* 1931; late 2nd Lt King's Shropshire LI: *m* 1956, Louise Alicia, da of late Joseph Hall, of St John's, Newfoundland, and has issue living, Peter John, *b* 1959: *m* 1989, Terry-Ann, da of Dennis Polkey, of Devon, and has issue living, Katherine Jane *b* 1990, — Susan Louise, *b* 1960. —— Catherine Eve, *b* 1941: *m* 1963, Alastair John Padraic Hardie, of Westfield House Farm, Thropton, Northumberland, and has issue living, Timothy John Alexander, *b* 1979, — Jane Catherine Sheelagh, *b* 1964, — Lucy Anne, *b* 1967, — Catherine Mary, *b* 1980.

Granddaughters of Robert Wallis Hope, el son of late Col Robert Hope, *b* 1763, son of Capt Robert Hope, grandson of Sir Archibald Hope (ante):—

Issue of late Edward William Hope, OBE, MD, DSc, *b* 1856, *d* 1950: *m* 1899, Charlotte Rennie, who *d* 1962, da of John Bowring, of Liverpool:—
Marjory Mary, *b* 1901: *m* 1940, Francis Stephen Hubbersty, of 34 The Grove, Marton, Middlesbrough. —— Elsa Rennie (51 Caldy Rd, W Kirby, Wirral, Merseyside, L48 2HF), *b* 1905: *m* 1925, Lionel Bishop Ridley, who *d* 1965.

Granddaughter of late Col John Urmson Hope, DSO (*infra*):—
Issue of late Lt-Col John Patrick Molesworth Hope, *b* 1913, *d* 1975: *m* 1938 (*m diss* 1947) (Margaret) Clare Aida, da of Lionel Julian Walford, of Middleton Stoney, Bicester, Oxon:—
Virginia Anne (4 Phillimore Gdns Close, W8), *b* 1942.

Grandchildren of late Maj-Gen John Edward Hope, el son of Col John Isaac Hope, yr son of Col Robert Hope (*b* 1763) (*ante*):—
Issue of late Col John Urmson Hope, DSO, *b* 1881, *d* 1967: *m* 1907, Christine Jessie Shelton (181 Lauderdale Mansions, Lauderdale Rd, Maida Vale, W9), da of Augustus Shelton Hooper, JP, of Hong Kong:—
Christine Mary Shelton (32 Moberly Rd, Salisbury), *b* 1909: *m* 1st, 1929 (*m diss* 1934), Capt Frank Wilson Houghton, RA; 2ndly, 1938, Maj-Gen Harry Pratt Sparks, CBE, MC, who *d* 1965, and has issue living, (by 2nd *m*) Charles Pratt, *b* 1941: *m* 1967, Brigitte Marie-Louise Marcelle Jeanneau, and has issue living, William Xavier Pratt *b* 1972, Marie-Ann Ruth *b* 1970, — Jane, *b* 1939: *m* 1964, Eric Hugh Legat, and has issue living, Patricia Jane *b* 1965, Vanessa Sarah *b* 1967, Joanna Mary *b* 1971.
Issue of late Rev George Archibald Hope, *b* 1882, *d* 1950: *m* 1929, Edith Margaret Aston (35 Kent Rd, Southsea), da of late Martin Aston Key, OBE, MD:—
Robert Frank Molesworth Hope, *b* 1934; *ed* Marlborough, and New Coll, Oxford (BA 1957): *m* 1957, Jacqueline Pierrette Regine, da of Paul Marcel Albert Forer, of 9 Rue de Lille, Marseilles, France, and has issue living, Frank George Aston, *b* 1959, — Patrick James Mailhe, *b* 1960. *Residence* – 35 Kent Rd, Southsea. —— Charles Aston, *b* 1940; *ed* Marlborough and Emmanuel Coll, Camb (BA); Solicitor 1968: *m* 1967, Kathryn Elizabeth, da of Capt Wilfred Williams, Merchant Navy (ret), and has issue living, Philip Aston, *b* 1968, — Nicholas Astley, *b* 1970. —— Elizabeth, *b* 1937: *m* 1966, Rev John Nigel Rowe, MA, BD. —— Clare Urmson, *b* 1943.

Descendants of late Sir Charles Hope, KT (son of late John Hope, son of late Sir James Hope, KB, 6th baronet of 1st baronet), who was *cr Earl of Hopetoun*, 1703 (*see* M Linlithgow).

John Hope, of the High St, Edinburgh, Burgess of that City, alias Petit John, Trumpeter at the Court of King James IV, left issue three sons, the eldest of whom, Henry Hope, Burgess and Guildbrother of Edinburgh, was father of the 1st baronet, Sir Thomas, Lord Advocate of Scotland. He had fourteen children, two of whom were upon the Bench when he pleaded as Lord Advocate; from this circumstance, it is imagined, arises the privilege which that officer of the Crown enjoys of pleading with his head covered, it having been considered derogatory for a father to uncover before his sons. In 1643 he was appointed Commissioner to the General Assembly of the Church of Scotland, a dignity which was not again enjoyed by any commoner for nearly three centuries. The 11th baronet was MP for Midlothian (C) 1845-53. Sir John Augustus, OBE, 16th baronet, was MP for Midlothian (Edinburghshire) (C) Sept 1912 to Nov 1918, and for N Div of Midlothian and Peeblesshire, Dec 1918 to Oct 1922. Gp Capt Sir Archibald Hope, 17th Bt, played a distinguished role in the aviation world, served European War 1939-45 (despatches twice, DFC, OBE).

Hope-Dunbar, see Dunbar.

HORLICK (UK) 1914, of Cowley Manor, co Gloucester

By labour and knowledge

Sir JOHN JAMES MACDONALD HORLICK, **5th** *Baronet*, *b* 9 April 1922; *s* his father, *Lt-Col Sir* JAMES NOCKELLS, OBE, MC, 1972; *ed* Eton; late Capt Coldm Gds; Dep Chm of Horlicks Ltd, 1968-72; CStJ: *m* 1948, June, da of late Douglas Cory-Wright, CBE (*see* Cory-Wright, Bt), and has issue.

Arms – Argent, a lion rampant and on a chief gules between two bulls' heads cabossed a garb of barley or. **Crest** – In front of a garb of barley or a lion's head erased gules.
Residences – Tournaig, Poolewe, Achnasheen, Ross-shire; Howbery Lane Cottage, Nettlebed, Henley-on-Thames, Oxon; 43 Montpelier Sq, SW7.

SON LIVING

JAMES CUNLIFFE WILLIAM, *b* 19 Nov 1956; *ed* Eton; 2nd Lt Coldm Gds Res 1979: *m* 1985, Fiona Rosalie, eldest da of Andrew Mclaren, of Alcester, Warwicks, and Mrs Harry Digby, and has issue living, Alexander, *b* 8 April 1987, — Jack Orlando, *b* 1989, — Hugo Roland, *b* 1991. *Residence* – Braelangwell House, Balblair, Dingwall, Ross-shire IV7 8LQ.

DAUGHTERS LIVING

Harriet Anne, *b* 1950; BA London: *m* 1970, Antony Lansdowne Granville, of Tachbrook House, Stourton, nr Shipston-on-Stour, Warwicks, and has issue (*see* Rose, Bt *cr* 1872). —— Araminta, *b* 1953; MCSP: *m* 1975, Edward Rory Carson, of Perseverance Cottage, Harpsden, Henley-on-Thames, Oxon, only son of Hon Edward Carson (*see* Carson, By), and has issue living, Toby Edward, *b* 1977, — Jonathan Henry, *b* 1979, — Oliver James, *b* 1982, — Bartholomew John, *b* 1988.

SISTER LIVING

Ursula Priscilla Marie Gabrielle, *b* 1916: *m* 1st, 1936 (*m diss* 1940), Capt Stafford Vaughan Stepney Howard, Coldstream Guards (Reserve) (*see* D Norfolk, colls); 2ndly, 1940, Lt-Col John Frederick Herron Weaver, 1st King's Dragoon Gds (ret), and has had issue (by 1st *m*) (*see* D Norfolk, colls), — (by 2nd *m*), Martin John Herron, *b* 1941; *ed* Eton: *m* 1965, Virginia

Frances, elder da of Edward Segal, of New York City, USA, and was *k* in a motor accident 1971, leaving issue, Jesse Martin Herron *b* 1970. — Christopher Giles Herron, *b* 1946; *ed* Eton: *m* 1974, Rosamund Betty, yst da of Lionel Geoffrey Mayhew, and has issue living, Frederick Giles Herron *b* 1977, Jonathan Martin Herron *b* 1986, Flora Xaviere Herron *b* 1975, Johanna Kate Herron *b* 1983. *Residences* – Greywalls, Gullane, E Lothian; 47 Glebe Pl, SW3 5JE.

DAUGHTERS LIVING OF THIRD BARONET

Natasha (Apt 16, Gaucin, Malaga, Spain), *b* 1935. —— Anna (17 The Little Boltons, SW10), *b* 1938: *m* 1st, 1960 (*m diss* 1971), Peter Gammon; 2ndly, 1973, Tim Fraser Wright, and has issue living (by 1st *m*), Anthony John, *b* 1965, — Tania Jane, *b* 1962.

DAUGHTERS LIVING OF SECOND BARONET

Roma Ernestine (*Roma, Countess of Dartmouth*) (15B Bedford Towers, Brighton), *b* 1903: *m* 1923, 8th Earl of Dartmouth, who *d* 1962. —— Elizabeth Ann (Betsan) (Conch, Kate St, Alexandra Headland, Sunshine Coast, Qld), *b* 1914: *m* 1933, John Balfour Symington Coats, and has issue living, Callum (Mail Service 591, Stewart's Rd, Wolvi via Gympie, Queensland 4570) *b* 1939: *m* 1st, 1967 (*m diss* 1981), Emily Jane Archer; 2ndly, 1985, Muriel Florence Wattinne, and has issue living, (by 1st *m*) Angus Orlando *b* 1968, Guy Oliver Balfour *b* 1972, — Christopher David (5156 NE 5th St, Seattle, Wa 98105, USA), *b* 1943: *m* 1966, Margaret Helen Van Etten, and has issue living, James John *b* 1978, Mercedes Jane *b* 1970, — Ian Forester Mungo (Forest Glen Sound, Forest Glen, Buderim, Queensland 4556, Australia), *b* 1953: *m* 1986, Anna Birrell, — Mary Manuela, *b* 1937: *m* 1959, Francis Skorka, of Essendon Rd, Anstead, Brisbane, Qld 4070, and has issue living, Lester Carl *b* 1963: *m* 1987, Tracey Anne Symons, of Redcliffe, Qld (and has issue living, Kelly Ann *b* 1992), Darius Brian Christopher *b* 1970, Catherine Benita *b* 1966: *m* 1984, Lennard Thomas Walbank, of Nundah, Qld (and has issue living, Thomas Shane Ronald *b* 1991, Katie Louise *b* 1993), Meri-Anne Kaye *b* 1976.

Sir James Horlick, 1st Bt, son of James Horlick of Ruardean, Glos was Lord of Manor of Cowley, Glos, High Sheriff of Glos 1902, and Chm and Pres of Horlicks Ltd.

HORNBY (UK) 1899, of Brookhouse, St Michael, Blackburn, County Palatine of Lancaster
(Extinct 1971)

Sir HENRY RUSSELL HORNBY, 2nd and last *Baronet*.

DAUGHTER LIVING OF SECOND BARONET

Jean Margaret (Cranford, Worlington, Mildenhall, Suffolk IP28 8RX), *b* 1915: *m* 1946, Maj-Gen Lionel Charles Manners-Smith, CBE, who *d* 1975, and has issue living, Maurice Charles Hornby (42 Edgar Rd, Winchester, Hants SO23 9TN), *b* 1948; Col late Royal Green Jackets: *m* 1974, Elizabeth, yst da of Maj-Gen Allan Elton Younger, DSO, OBE, of The Manor House, Twyford, Winchester, Hants SO21 1RH.

DAUGHTER LIVING OF FIRST BARONET

Annette Mary (Flat 25, 5 Elm Park Gdns, SW10 9QQ), *b* 1905.

HORNE (UK) 1929, of Shackleford, Surrey

Fronti Nulla Fides

Sir (ALAN) GRAY ANTONY HORNE, 3rd *Baronet*; *b* 11 July 1948; *s* his grandfather, Lt-Col Sir ALAN EDGAR, MC, 1984: *m* 1980, Cecile Rose, da of Jacques Desplanche, of 5 rue de Cheverny, Romorantin, France.

Arms – Gules, a fret vair between two boars passant one in chief and one in base or. **Crest** – A dexter arm vested gules, cuffed or, holding in the hand proper a hunting horn, and charged on the sleeve with a fret gold.
Residence – Château du Basty, Thenon, Dordogne, France.

HALF-AUNT LIVING

Edith Margery Jay, *b* 1916; European War 1939-45 as Junior Com ATS: *m* 1944, Maj Thomas Fiddian Reddaway, who *d* 1967, and has issue living, Edgar James Fiddian, *b* 1945; *ed* Oundle, and Westfield Coll, Univ of London, — William Thomas, *b* 1948; *ed* Oundle, and Bedford Coll, Univ of London, — Henry Sills, *b* 1950; *ed* Oundle, and Bedford Coll, Univ of London, — Richard Alan, *b* 1952; *ed* Oundle and Oriel Coll, Oxford, — Michael Jay, *b* 1956; *ed* Oundle, and Balliol Coll, Oxford, — Susan Mary, *b* 1949; *ed* St Mary's, Calne, and Queen Elizabeth Coll, Univ of London. *Residence* – Saltingsgarth, Brancaster, Norfolk.

The 1st baronet, Sir (William) Edgar Horne (el son of late Edgar Horne, of Witley, Surrey), was Chm of Prudential Assurance Co, and MP for Surrey, Guildford Div (*U*) 1910-22. Sir Alan Edgar Horne, 2nd Bt, MC, served in World War I 1914-19 in France and Balkans (despatches four times, MC and French Croix de Guerre), and in World War II in Middle East as Lt-Col Roy Pioneer Corps.

Horsbrugh-Porter, see Porter.

HORSFALL (UK) 1909, of Hayfield, Glusburn, West Riding of Yorkshire

By industry and honour

Sir JOHN MUSGRAVE HORSFALL, MC, TD, 3rd *Baronet*; *b* 26 Aug 1915; *s* his father *Sir* (JOHN) DONALD, 1975; *ed* Uppingham; late Maj Duke of Wellington's (W Riding) Regt; Underwriter at Lloyd's; formerly a Dir of Hayfield Textiles Ltd, and of Worsted Spinners Fedn, Ltd (Pres 1962-64), and of Skipton Building Soc; a JP for N Yorks County; Burma 1939-45 (MC): *m* 1940, Cassandra Nora Bernardine, da of late George Wright, of Brinkworth Hall, Elvington, York, and has issue.

Arms – Gules, in chief two horses' heads couped argent bridled azure, and in base a rose of the second, barbed and seeded proper. **Crest** – A horse's head couped ermine, issuing from a chaplet of roses gules.
Residence – Greenfield House, Embsay, Skipton, N Yorks.

SONS LIVING

EDWARD JOHN WRIGHT (Long Thatch, Uffington, Faringdon, Oxon SN7 7RP), *b* 17 Dec 1940; *ed* Uppingham: *m* 1965, Rosemary, da of Frank N. King, of East Morton, Keighley, and has issue living, David Edward, *b* 1966, — Robert Ian, *b* 1968, — James Christopher, *b* 1971. —— Donald James Linton (25 Stirling Rd, Edinburgh, EH5 3JA), *b* 1942; *ed* Uppingham and Jesus Coll, Camb (MA): *m* 1965, Angela Mary, da of Henry Firth, of Ilkley, and has issue living, Peter Linton (assumed additional christian name of John by deed poll 1982), *b* 1970, — Richard Michael (assumed additional christian name of Henry by deed poll 1989), *b* 1973, — Elizabeth Jane, *b* 1968.

DAUGHTER LIVING

Henrietta Nora, *b* 1947: *m* 1987, Arthur Eubank, of Millstone Moor, Cockermouth, Cumbria.

BROTHERS LIVING

Donald Fawcett, TD (Fairleigh, Draughton, Skipton, N Yorks), *b* (twin) 1915; *ed* Uppingham, and King's Coll, Camb (MA); formerly Capt Duke of Wellington's (W Riding) Regt; is an Underwriter at Lloyd's: *m* 1947, Jeanne Elizabeth, da of Col F. Longden Smith, of Woodlands, Skipton, and has issue living, Michael Fawcett (Waulkmill, Strachan, Banchory, Kincardineshire AB3 3NS), *b* 1948: *m* 1979, Elizabeth Anne, da of Isaac Pickthall, of Barrow in Furness, and has issue living, Timothy Michael *b* 1981, Luke Benjamin *b* 1982, Donald Isaac *b* 1985, — Peter John, *b* 1953: *m* 1978, Lesley Jane, da of Robert Hardy, of Lothersdale, N Yorks, and has issue living, James Robert *b* 1983, Louise Rachael *b* 1981, — Patricia Jane, *b* 1950: *m* 1974, Thomas Andrew Hoyle, and has issue living, Katie Jane *b* 1977, Harriet Louise *b* 1979, — Susan Elizabeth, *b* 1955, — Sara Louise, *b* 1966. —— Patrick David (Poole House, Arkholme, Carnforth, Lancs), *b* 1921; *ed* Uppingham; is an Underwriter at Lloyds; formerly Capt Duke of Wellington's (W Riding) Regt: *m* 1947, June, da of Capt S. H. Clough, of Bailey Cottage, Skipton-in-Craven, and has had issue, Christopher David (Overslade, Sedgwick, Kendal), *b* 1948: *m* 1970 (*m diss* 1988), Sally, da of Frank S. Greenwood, of Ingleton, and has issue living, Jonathan David *b* 1973, Philip Edward *b* 1975, Robert John *b* 1981, — Carol Anne, *b* 1951: *m* 1975, Anthony Raymond Collinson, of The Coach House, Capernwray, Carnforth, Lancs LA6 1AL, and *d* 1991, leaving issue, John Horsfall *b* 1980, Poppy Henrietta *b* 1983.

The 1st baronet, Sir John Cousin, Chm of W Riding of Yorkshire County Council, was a worsted spinner and banker, and provided Glusburn Technical Institute.

HORT (GB) 1767, of Castle Strange, Middlesex

WELL·WIN·WELL·WEAR

Sir JAMES FENTON HORT, 8th *Baronet; b* 6 Sept 1926; *s* his father, Sir FENTON GEORGE, 1960; *ed* Marlborough, and at Trin Coll, Camb (BA, MB, BChir): *m* 1951, Joan, da of late Edward Peat, of Swallownest, Sheffield, and has issue.

Arms – Azure, a cross or between in the first and fourth quarters a rose argent, barbed and seeded proper. **Crest** – An eagle reguardant, wings expanded, holding in the beak a chaplet of laurel all proper.
Residence – Poundgate Lodge, Uckfield Rd, Crowborough, Sussex.

SONS LIVING

ANDREW EDWIN FENTON, *b* 15 Nov 1954: *m* 15 Nov 1986, Mary, da of Jack Whibley, of Spalding, Lincs, and has issue living, James, *b* 1989, — Jennifer *b* 1987. —— Timothy George, *b* 1960.

DAUGHTERS LIVING

Jane Antonia, *b* 1958. —— Diana Rachel, *b* 1962.

BROTHERS LIVING

Richard Patrick Arthur, *b* 1931; *ed* Harrow, and at Trin Coll, Camb (MA 1959): *m* 1956, Agnete Mannheimer, and has issue living, Nicholas Patrick Fenton, *b* 1962, — Rebecca Maria, *b* 1957, — Elsa Katinka, *b* 1960. *Address* – Kungstensg 59 4tr, S11329, Stockholm, Sweden. —— Robert William Lucas, *b* 1936; *ed* Marlborough, and at Trin Coll, Camb (MA); *m* 1973, Eleanor Mary Coburn. *Residence* – Meentashesk, Glencolumcille, co Donegal.

SISTERS LIVING

Elizabeth (36 Berkeley Vale Park, Berkeley, Glos GL13 9TG), *b* 1925: *m* 1951, Sqdn Ldr Eric George Holmes, MBE, RAF, who *d* 1975, and has issue living, Helen Margaret, *b* 1952, — Georgina Slaney, *b* 1954. —— Barbara Anne, *b* 1929: *m* 1961, George Bruce Sackville Berkeley, and has issue living, Martin Sackville Hamilton, *b* 1964, — Emma Louise Diana, *b* 1962, — Sara Jane Arabella, *b* 1966.

COLLATERAL BRANCHES LIVING

Issue of late Maj Aylmer Victor Dyson Hort, MBE, TD, yr son of 6th baronet, *b* 1897, *d* 1981: *m* 1927, Lois Mary, da of late Col Clifford Phillips, VD, TD, DL, of Coolgreany, Malpas, Newport, Monmouth:—
John Aylmer Laybourne (239 Bramcote Lane, Wollaton, Nottingham), *b* 1931; *ed* Marlborough, and Trin Coll, Camb (MA): *m* 1958, Leela, da of R. G. Senan, of 123 Anson Rd, Penang, and has issue, Peter Senan Aylmer, *b* 1958, — Michael John Laybourne, *b* 1960, — Patrick Marcus Govind, *b* 1971. —— Daphne Lois (36 Alanthus Close, Lee Green, SE12 8RE), *b* 1930; *ed* Lady Margaret Hall, Oxford (MA). —— Frances Mary, *b* 1937: *m* 1963, John Cameron Simpson, MB, FFARCS, of 38 Kidbrooke Gdns, Blackheath, SE3, and has issue living, James Aylmer, *b* 1964, — David Cameron, *b* 1966.

Issue of late Rev Francis Fitzgerald Hort, brother of 6th baronet, *b* 1868, *d* 1942: *m* 1912, Margaret Charis, who *d* 1972, da of late Rev Joseph Henry Gray, Fellow of Queens' Coll, Camb:—
Margaret Frances, *b* 1913; *ed* Girton Coll, Camb (MA): *m* 1952, John Hunter Terry, who *d* 1976, and has issue living, Stephen John Anthony, *b* 1955, — Rosemary Frances, *b* 1953. *Residence* – 11 Bandon Rd, Girton, Cambridge.
The 1st baronet was Consul-General at Lisbon, the 2nd baronet sat as MP for Kildare 1831-2; the 3rd baronet, a Lieut-Gen in the Army, served with distinction throughout the Crimean war 1854-5, and the 6th baronet, Sir Arthur Fenton, was 33 years a Master at Harrow School.

HOSKYNS (E) 1676, of Harewood, Herefordshire

VINCULA·DA·LINGUÆ·VEL·TIBI·LINGUA·DABIT

Bind the tongue or the tongue will
bind thee

Sir BENEDICT LEIGH HOSKYNS, 16th *Baronet*; *b* 27 May 1928; *s* his brother, *Sir* JOHN CHEVALLIER, 1956; *ed* Haileybury, and at Corpus Christi Coll, Camb (MB and BChir 1952); Gen Practitioner (ret) Capt RAMC (ret): *m* 1953, Ann, da of Harry Wilkinson, and has issue.

Arms – Per pale azure and gules, a chevron between three lions rampant or.
Crest – A lion's head erased or, with flames of fire out of his mouth proper, ducally crowned of the first.
Residence – Russell House, Wherry Corner, High St, Manningtree, Essex CO11 1AJ.

SONS LIVING

EDWYN WREN, *b* 4 Feb 1956; Senior Chorister, King's Coll, Camb 1969; *ed* Nottingham Univ (MB, BS); MRCP (1984); Consultant Paediatrician, Leicester Gen & Leicester Royal Infirmary since 1993 *m* 1981, Jane, da of John Sellers, and has issue living Robin Chevallier, *b* 5 July 1989, — Lucy Mary, *b* 1993.
—— John Chandos, *b* 1961; *ed* Gonville and Caius Coll, Camb (BA), and Middlesex Hosp.

DAUGHTERS LIVING

Janet Mary, *b* 1954; *ed* York Univ (BA, CertEd); ARCM; Sr Lecturer, Music in Educn, Univ of Central England, Birmingham: *m* 1982, Christopher Harris.
—— Sarah Leigh, *b* 1959; *ed* Birmingham Univ (Vice-Chancellor's Prize, BA); LGSM (MusTh), ARCM 1981; Dir Music Therapy, Guildhall Sch of Music: *m* 1989, Julian Peter C. Raphael, son of Ven Timothy John Raphael, Archdeacon of Middlesex, and has issue living, Dorothy Clare, *b* 1990.

BROTHER LIVING

Anthony Hungerford (25 Hamilton Gdns, NW8), *b* 1932; *ed* Marlborough; formerly Lt Roy Fusiliers; Korea 1952: *m* 1958, Hon Katharine Margaret Kaldor, el da of late Baron Kaldor (Life Baron), and has issue living, Nicholas Clement, *b* 1967, — Jane Frances, *b* 1962, — Teresa Mary, *b* 1963.

SISTER LIVING

Catherine Mary Trym, *b* 1935: *m* 1967, Sol Picciotto, and has issue living, Anna Rachel, *b* 1968.

COLLATERAL BRANCHES LIVING

Grandchildren of late Rear-Adm Peyton Hoskyns, CMG, MVO, 5th son of 9th baronet:—
Issue of late Major Oswald Peyton Latham Hoskyns, *b* 1883, *d* 1922: *m* 1913, Evelyn Mary, who *d* 1965, da of Joseph Herbert Blacklock, formerly of Overthorpe House, Banbury:—
Rev John Algernon Peyton (Riverknoll, Hoarwithy, Hereford HR2 6QF) *b* 1920; *ed* Pembroke Coll, Camb (MA); formerly Maj R Signals; *m* 1st, 1944, Ann Veronica, who *d* 1968, da of C. Harrison, of King's Worthy, Winchester; 2ndly, 1970, Andrea Evelyn, who *d* 1991, da of late Adm Sir Henry Bertram Pelly, KCVO, CB (*see* Pelly, Bt, colls), and has issue living (by 1st *m*), Oswald Christopher Peyton (2 Churchgate House High St, Hambledon, Hants P07 6RS), *b* 1954; Police Sergeant, Hants Constabulary: *m* 1990, Julie Anne, da of Gordon Geddes, of 22 Garden Close, Watton, Thetford, Norfolk, and has issue living, Benedict Mungo Peyton *b* 1990, Fergus *b* 1991, — Rachel Susan, *b* 1946: *m* 1969, S/Ldr Robert Andrew Lund, RAF, of 16 Margerison Rd, Ben Rhydding, Ilkley, W Yorks LS29 8QU, and has issue living, Mark Edward *b* 1973, Suzanne Elizabeth *b* 1977, — Jane Elizabeth Carol, *b* 1947: *m* 1972, Rodney Alexander Sinclair, of 41A Onslow Av, Auckland, NZ, and has issue living, James Lawrence *b* 1980, Charlotte Ann Hoskyns *b* 1973, Amy Elizabeth *b* 1976, Sarah Jane *b* 1977, — Juliet Ann, *b* 1951: *m* 1973, Ian Richard Doswell, MRIPHH, of The Post Office, Shapwick, Blandford Forum, Dorset DT11 9JT, and has issue living, Ewan Rufus *b* 1978, Gwendoline Natasha *b* 1976.
Issue living of late Cdr John Walter Hoskyns, RN, *b* 1892, *d* 1980: *m* 1917, Magdalen Rose Wyndham, who *d* 1991, da of late Peter Hawker, of Longparish House, Hants:—
Hungerford Robert Leo (16 Chatham Park, Cleveland Walk, Bath, Avon BA2 6JR), *b* 1921; *ed* Charterhouse, and Fitzwilliam House Camb (MA), Cert Ed (London); late Lt Rifle Bde. —— Rosemary Eleanor Peyton (50 Greenway Lane, Bath), *b* 1919; BA (Open Univ): *m* 1949, Maj Geoffrey Nelson Stanton, KOYLI, who *d* 1978, and has issue living, David John Nelson, *b* 1958: *m* 1988, Catharine Mary Crick, — Juliet Rose Brailsford, *b* 1952, — Sarah Dorothy Macduff, *b* 1955: *m* 1980, Martin Gordon Walters, of Cambridge, and has issue living, three children. —— Zara Stephanie Jardine (c/o Lloyds Bank plc, Cox's & King's Branch, 6 Pall Mall, SW1), *b* 1929; F/O, WRAF (Reserve).

Grandchildren of late Ven Benedict George Hoskyns, 6th son of 9th baronet:—
Issue of late Lieut-Col Chandos Benedict Arden Hoskyns, *b* 1895, *d* of wounds received in action 1940: *m* 1920, Joyce, who *d* 1979, da of Austin Taylor, of 30 Eccleston Square, SW:—
Sir John Leigh Austin Hungerford (c/o Child & Co, 1 Fleet St, EC4Y 1BD), *b* 1927; formerly Capt Rifle Brig; Head of Prime Minister's Policy Unit 1979-82; Dir-Gen, Inst of Directors 1984-89; *cr* Kt Bach 1982: *m* 1956, Miranda, only da of Tom Mott and has issue living, Barnaby Chandos Tom (214 Broomwood Rd, SW11), *b* 1959: *m* 1990, Victoria S., da of Conrad Sandler, of 22 Warwick Av, W9, and has issue living, Jake Austin Thomas *b* 1990, Fred Daniel Rufus *b* 1992, — Benedict John Hungerford, *b* 1963: *m* 1993, Sally, yr da of C. Hodges, of Dunton, Norfolk, — Benedicta Tamasine Maria, *b* 1961. —— David Chandos Benedict (The Oast House, Wittersham, Kent) *b* 1929: *m* 1958, Sheelagh Marion, da of Hon Sir Patrick Redmond Joseph Barry, and has adopted children, Simon Chandos, *b* 1965, — Jessica Marion, *b* 1967: *m* 1989, Iain Macdonald Johnston, elder son of late Alan Johnston, of Wickambrook, Suffolk, and has issue living, Archie *b* 19—, Flora Marion *b* 1992. —— Benedicta Lucia, *b* 1922: *m* 1955 (*m diss* 1989), Richard E. Vernon, actor, and has issue living, Thomas Richard Adam, *b* 1958, — Sarah Benedicta, *b* 1956.

Grandsons of John Hoskyns (1836-1926), eldest son of Edwyn Bennet Hoskyns (1804-1848), eldest son of John Hoskyns, MD, of Dublin, 4th son of 6th baronet:—
Issue of late William John Hoskyns, *b* 1871, *d* 1948: *m* 1900, Caroline Borer:—
John D. (1804 Kenmore, Grosse Pointe Woods, MI 48236, USA), *b* 1902: *m* 1935, Therese Stascuk, and has had issue, one son (*dec*). —— Marian (3627 Millay, Troy, MI 48083, USA), *b* 1916: *m* 1935, Howard Shirkey, and has issue living, Howard, *b* 1942, — Suzanne, *b* 1936, — Joanne, *b* 1938, — Julianne, *b* 1945, — Christine, *b* 1950.
Issue of late Louis Charles Hoskyns, *b* 1878, *d* 1955: *m* 1930, Irene Beck (neé Pease), who *d* 1981:—

Louis C. (Lan Yair Country Club, Box 18161, Spartanburg, S Carolina, USA), *b* 1930: *m* 1952 (*m diss* 1982), Joan Vandermale, and has issue living, Louis C, *b* 1964, — Mary Jo (3175 C-8 Summit Sq Drive, Oakton, Virginia 22124, USA), *b* 1952, — Lynn Ann (22 Colleton Drive, Charleston, S Carolina 29407, USA), *b* 1953: *m* 1973 (*m diss* 1975), Stephen Michael Sentell, and has issue living, Colleen Elizabeth *b* 1974, — Suzanne Arrian (103 Larkspur Lane, Spartanburg, S Carolina 29301, USA), *b* 1960: *m* 1988, Mitchell Paul Peterson. — Gordon William (1599 14th Av, Boca Raton, Fla 33486, USA), *b* 1933: *m* 1st, 1963 (*m diss* 1974), Mary Lou Foit; 2ndly, 1976, Leah Besch Easton.
     Issue of late James Patrick Hoskyns, *b* 1887, *d* 1953: *m* 1st, 1908, Lena Lusk, who *d* 1934; 2ndly, 19—, Jane Doty:— (By 1st *m*) Alice, *b* 1909: *m* 19—, Martin Frankhouse, and has issue living, Jerrold, *b* 1931. — Helen, *b* 1912: *m* 19—, Russell Wright, and has issue living, John, *b* 19—, — Janice, *b* 19—. — (By 2nd *m*) James L. (31493 Mound Rd, Warren, MI 48092, USA), *b* 19— (*m diss* 19—), Judith McCausland, and has issue living, James T. (11386 Farthing, Sterling Heights, MI 48078, USA), *b* 1957, — Gail E., *b* 1958.

          Grandson of late Chandos Hungerford Hoskyns (1838-1929) (infra):—
     Issue of late Edwin Allen Hoskyns, *b* 1871, *d* 1960: *m* 1907, Margaret Barton, who *d* 1942:—
Chandos Allen (923N 33W Av, Tulsa, Oklahoma 74127, USA), *b* 1911: *m* 1945, Mildred McPherson.

          Grandchildren of late Edwyn Bennet Hoskyns (1804-1848) (ante):—
     Issue of late Chandos Hungerford Hoskyns, *b* 1838, *d* 1929: *m* 1st, 18—, Catherine, da of Ira Morris Allen, MD; 2ndly, 18—, Mary; 3rdly, ca 1901, Mary Anne, who *d* 1954, da of William Hipkiss:—
(By 3rd *m*) Wesley Lucien (19 Linwood Av, Buffalo, NY 14202, USA), *b* 1903: *m* 1st, 1930 (*m diss* 19—), Marjorie Louise, who *d* 1981, da of George Joseph Fix; 2ndly, 19— (*m diss* 19—), Alice Blythe; 3rdly, 19— (*m diss* 19—), Catherine Akester, and has issue living (by 1st *m*), Wesley Francis (12 Chesham Way, Fairport, NY 14450, USA), *b* 1932: *m* 1958, Caroline Frances Davis, of Idaho, and has issue living, William Anthony *b* 1962: *m* 1986, Susan Patricia Bramhill (and has issue living, Spencer John Chandos *b* 1991, Alexandra Allyce Caroline *b* 1989), Robert Nicholas *b* (twin) 1962: *m* 1985, Nancy Paige Sailors (and has issue living, Wesley Sailors *b* 1987, Cooper Davis (a son) *b* 1988, Brick Carlos *b* 1993), Diane Carole *b* 1960: *m* 1982, Kevin Noble Faulkner (and has issue living, Jonathan Noble *b* 1985, Lisa Marie *b* 1983, Caroline Elizabeth *b* 1992), Nancy Renee *b* 1971: *m* 1992, Thomas Christian Nienstedt, — Joyce Louise, *b* 1933: *m* 1952, Kenneth Lawrence Cooper, and has issue living, Steven Alfonse *b* 1953, Donald Kenneth *b* 1956, Kenneth Lawrence *b* 1958, Michael Joseph *b* 1961: *m* 1991, Cheryl Ann Marquart (and has issue living, Dylan Michael *b* 1993), Thomas William *b* 1964. — Chandos (Mike) (508 Cayuga Creek Rd, Alden, NY 14004, USA), *b* 1906: *m* 1942, Eleanor Hoskins, and has issue living, Clayton Chandos (303 Broadway, Darien Center, NY 14040, USA), *b* 1949: *m* 1974, Barbara Sobolewski, and has issue living, Sarah Ann *b* 1981, Laura Elizabeth *b* 1985, — Loren Russell (509 Cayuga Creek Rd, Alden, NY 14004, USA), *b* 1951: *m* 1983, Barbara Holtenhoff, and has issue living, Michael Chandos *b* 1983, Caitlyn Elizabeth *b* 1986, — Nancy Elizabeth, *b* 1952: *m* 1970, Michael Paul Noody, and has issue living, Brian Michael *b* 1971, Kevin Paul *b* 1973. — Lucy Caroline, *b* 1911: *m* 1942, Willard Wakeman English.

          Grandsons of late Chandos Hungerford Hoskyns (1838-1929) (ante):—
     Issue of late William James Hoskyns, *b* 1908, *d* 1983: *m* 1st, 1934 (*m diss* 1953), Jean Louise McMullen, who *d* 1988; 2ndly, 1959, Margaret Norman:—
(By 1st *m*) William Roy (4819 W Desert Hills Drive, Glendale, Arizona 85304, USA), *b* 1936: *m* 1956, Marilyn Jane Miller, and has issue living, Donald James (10030 N 49th Lane, Glendale, Arizona 85302, USA), *b* 1960: *m* 1st, 1980 (*m diss* 1987), Rika Rundall; 2ndly, 1989, Tamra Garcia, and has issue living (by 1st *m*), Chelsea *b* 1982, Alyssa *b* 1984, (by 2nd *m*) Elayna *b* 1993, — Robert John (adopted son), *b* 1964, — Brenda Jeanne, *b* 1957: *m* 1st, 1975 (*m diss* 1991), Rodney Abbott; 2ndly, 1992, Wade Beauchaine, and has issue living (by 1st *m*), Justin *b* 1986, Stacie Joy *b* 1976, Tina Winifred *b* 1981. — Leslie Laing (6119 Pine Wood Rd, Oakland, Calif 94611, USA), *b* 1941: *m* 1970 (*m diss* 1974), Stephanie Irene Muth.

          Grandson of John Hoskyns (*b* 1827), 4th son of John Hoskyns, MD (ante):—
     Issue of late John Hoskyns, *b* 1872, *d* 1963: *m* 1911, Florence May, who *d* 1966, da of Alfred Taylor, of Sydney, NSW:—
Chandos John (29 Woodcroft Av, St Georges, Adelaide, S Australia), *b* 1915: *m* 1938, Harriet Anderson, da of Andrew Anderson Sundquist, of NSW, and has issue living, Max (6 Cumulus Place, Willeton, W Australia 6155), *b* 1940: *m* 1964, Lottie Jolliffe, of Manilla, NSW, and has issue living, Wayne Gregory *b* 1967, Lena Gay *b* 1965: *m* 1985, John Kraima, Mandy Jane *b* 1969, — Craig (Warners Rd, Upper Hermitage, Houghton, S Australia 5131), *b* 1944: *m* 1962, Beverley Joan Westbrook, of Loxton, S Australia, and has issue living, Joanne Kaye, *b* 1962: *m* 1982, Joseph Anthony Mamone (and has issue living, Rachel *b* 1982, Rebecca *b* 1985), Sharon Julie *b* 1965: *m* 1987, Martin Leigh Goldsworthy, of Loxton, S Australia (and has issue living, Benjamin Nathan *b* 1990), Natalie Ruth *b* 1970, — Paul (20 Morland Av, Stoneyfell, S Australia 5066), *b* 1945: *m* 1969, Deirdre Margaret Saunders, of Adelaide, and has issue living, Andrew John *b* 1970, Elizabeth Anne *b* 1972, Sarah Louise *b* 1974.

          Grandchildren of late James Hoskyns-Abrahall, 2nd son of late Rev John Charles James Hoskyns-Abrahall, el son of late Rev John Hoskyns-Abrahall (*b* 1773), el son of late Rev John Hoskyns-Abrahall, son of late Rev John Hoskyns-Abrahall (who assumed the additional surname and arms of Abrahall), yst son of 2nd baronet:—
     Issue of late Major John Hoskyns Hoskyns-Abrahall, *b* 1864, *d* 1924: *m* 1900, Frances Elizabeth, who *d* 1941, da of late J. H. Vessey, of Halton Manor, Spilsby, Lincolnshire:—
Dorothea Frances, *b* 1916: *m* 1st, 1942 (*m diss* 1962), Charles Robert Gardiner; 2ndly, 1962, Lt-Cdr Alliston Temple Clough Hazledine, RNR, of 61 Regents Park, Exeter EX1 2NZ, and has issue living (by 1st *m*), Christopher Charles (5 Clipped Hedge, Hatfield Heath, Bishops Stortford, Herts CM22 7EG), *b* 1942: *m* 1st, 1967, Janet Marie Lack; 2ndly, 1986, Brenda Hebb, and has issue living, (by 1st *m*) Rebekah Jane *b* 1968: *m* 1991, Gerald Cooper (and has issue living, Joseph *b* 1993), Alice Mary *b* 1972, (by 2nd *m*) Claire Christine *b* 1986, — Peter Patrick Fairfax (177 Avenue Louise, 1050 Brussels, Belgium), *b* 1948: *m* 1974, Nicole Adrienne Marie Stalleart, and has issue living, Miles Dexter *b* 1988, — Catherine Juliet, *b* 1944: *m* 1970, Richard Stephen George Sale, Barrister, of Cambridge House, Longwater Lane, Finchampstead, Berks RG11 4NR, and has issue living, George William Alexander *b* 1972, Mary Margaret *b* 1971: *m* 1993, Philip Richards, of 95 Morden Hill, SW13 7NP, — Juliet Anne *b* 1974, Jessica May Victoria *b* 1977, Fenella Grace Dorothea *b* 1983, Emily Caroline *b* 1985, — Victoria, *b* 1947: *m* 1972, Derrick William Swain, of 8 Cinnamon Row, Plantation Wharf, SW11 3TW, and has issue living, Andrew Charles *b* 1972, Christy-Anne *b* 1974, Naomi Frances *b* 1980.
     Issue of late Major Christopher Henry Hoskyns-Abrahall, *b* 1871, *ka* 1915: *m* 1895, Alice Maude Mary, da of — Allen:—
†James, MM, *b* 1897; European War 1914-19 with Australian Forces (wounded, MM): *m* 1923, Minnie Elizabeth Holland, who *d* 1990, of Coolup, WA, and *d* 1967, leaving issue, Christopher Leslie (27 Norman St, Innaloo, W Australia 6018), *b* 1925: *m* 1947, Phyllis Mae Sansome, of Gosnells, WA, and has issue living, Terrence Ross *b* 1954: *m* 1978, Beverley Ann Keeley, of Harvey, WA (and has issue living, Shaun Ross *b* 1981, Adam James *b* 1984), Brian Leslie *b* 1956: *m* 1984, Kerry Nelson, of Balga, WA (and has issue living, Joshua Andrew *b* 1985), Kathleen Elizabeth *b* 1950: *m* 1st, 1970, John Leslie Brewer, of Claremont, WA; 2ndly, 1978, Alan Ronald Dawson, of Carine, WA (and has issue living (by 1st *m*), Michael John *b* 1972, Shelly Anne *b* 1970, (by 2nd *m*) Philip Gregory *b* 1979), Lynette Jean *b* 1953: *m* 1973, Kevin Malcolm Langman, of Dargaville, NZ (now of Port Hedland, WA) (and has issue living, Daniel Graham *b* 1976, Sandra Alice *b* 1978), — Ernest John, *b* 1926: *m* 1948, Margaret Winscom, of Katanning, WA, and has issue living, Ian John *b* 1948, Douglas Frank *b* 1950, Gregory Alan *b* 1955, Mary Pauline *b* 1954, — Colin James, *b* 1927, — Ellen Maude, *b* 1923: *m* 1946, Leslie Charles

Limbrick, of Fremantle, WA, and has issue living, Raymond George *b* 1948, Keith Leslie *b* 1950, Kevin Colin *b* 1951, Philip John *b* 1954, — Beatrice Angela, *b* 1930: *m* 1952, Hamilton McCormick, of Gingin, WA, and has issue living, Gary Thomas *b* 1953, Jeffrey David *b* 1954.

Grandchildren of late Bennet Hoskyns-Abrahall, CBE, el son of late Theophilus Bennet Hoskyns-Abrahall, 2nd son of late Rev John Hoskyns-Abrahall (*b* 1773) (ante):—
   Issue of Rt Rev Anthony Leigh Egerton Hoskyns-Abrahall, Bishop Suffragan of Lancaster, *b* 1903; *d* 1982: *m* 1937, Margaret Ada, who *d* 1986, da of late F. G. Storey, Bar-at-law, of Sunderland, and sister of late Lord Buckton (ext):—
John Benedict Leigh (Earby Hall, Newsham, Richmond, N Yorks), *b* 1939; *ed* St John's Sch, Leatherhead, and RAC Cirencester; FRICS: *m* 1970, Mary Delamain, da of late Lt-Col Mansel Jackson, DSO and bar, MC, and has issue living, Bennet Mansel Leigh (140 Stephendale Rd, SW6), *b* 1971; *ed* Eton, and Durham Univ (BA), — John Harry Wren, *b* 1975; *ed* Radley, — Edward Anthony Egerton, *b* 1977; *ed* Eton. —— Anthony David Wren (20 Grange Rd, Barnes SW13 9RE), *b* 1943; Lt RN (ret): *m* 1965, Phyllis Penrose, yr da of late Rear-Adm William Penrose Mark-Wardlaw, DSO, and has issue living, Mark Egerton Wren, *b* 1966, — Sarah Katherine Phyllis, *b* 1971. —— Janet Elizabeth Rosemary, *b* 1938: *m* 1962, Nicholas George Hurry, of 3 Kitson Rd, SW13, and has issue living, Fiona Elizabeth, *b* 1963, — Victoria Mary, *b* 1967.
   Issue of late (Andrew) John Chandos Hoskyns-Abrahall, *b* 1905; *d* 1978: *m* 1935, Awdey Lorraine, BEM, who *d* 1992, da of Sir Norman Alexander Leslie, KBE:—
John Hungerford Leslie (RD3, Box 3951, Reading, Pa 19606, USA), *b* 1945: *m* 1973, Winifred Scherrer, of Calif, USA, and has issue living, Alexander Philip, *b* 1978, — Megan Selina, *b* 1976. —— Harriet Hoskyns-Abrahall (1025 Lindbergh Drive, Atlanta, Georgia 30324, USA), *b* 1939; legally resumed her maiden name 1989: *m* 1965 (*m diss* 1981), Edward Brendan Lynch, WS, and has issue living, Bahama Leslie Chandos, *b* 1977. —— Lucinda, *b* 1940: *m* 1972, Graham de Putron Tardif, of Cranbrook, Kent, and has issue living, Benjamin Charles de Putron, *b* 1972, — Kate Amanda de Putron, *b* 1975, — Lucy Mia de Putron, *b* 1981. —— Amanda (Cedarwood Lane, Carrboro, N Carolina 27510, USA), *b* 1940 (twin): *m* 1972 (*m diss* 1985), Burton K. Fox, and has issue living, Joshua Maxwell, *b* 1976, — Gemma Lorraine, *b* 1979.

Grandchildren of late Chandos William Hoskyns-Abrahall, MRCS, 2nd son of late Theophilus Bennet Hoskyns-Abrahall (ante):—
   Issue of late Sir (Theo) Chandos Hoskyns-Abrahall, CMG, *b* 1896, *d* 1975: *m* 1st, 1925 (*m diss* 1944), Clare Constance Maria, who *d* 1990, da of Lt-Col Richard Frederick Drury, CBE, 2ndly, 1944, Lois Jennet, da of late Rev Canon Hugh Lambert Ogle, Canon of Ripon:—
(By 1st *m*) Robin Chandos (Woodlands House, Cupid Green, Herts HP2 7BA), *b* 1928; *ed* Haileybury; formerly Lieut R W African Frontier Force; Dir Subsidiary Co of Unilever: *m* 1st, 1950 (*m diss* 1962), Petronella Elisabeth, da of John E. Cantlon, of co Carlow; 2ndly, 1962, Margaret Angela, da of Frank Keggins, of Knowle, Warwicks, and has issue living (by 1st *m*), Scarlett, *b* 1952: *m* 1984, John Punthöller, of Amsterdam (now of Rottingdean, E Sussex), and has issue living, Theo Alexander *b* 1990, — Gail, *b* 1955: *m* 1979, Stephen Brendell, of 1 Nash Cottage, Fownhope, Hereford, and has issue living, Dominic *b* 1980, Rebecca *b* 1984, — (by 2nd *m*), Charles Chandos *b* 1964; *ed* Haileybury.

Grandchildren of late Sir (Theo) Chandos Hoskyns-Abrahall, CMG (ante):—
   Issue of late Follett Peter Hoskyns-Abrahall (actor, as Mark Follett), *b* 1934, *d* 1983: *m* 1960, Carole (Hill Farm, Tendring, Essex), da of Edwin Alexander Marks, of Chigwell, Essex:—
Edwin Follett Eden, *b* 1965; *ed* The Leys Sch. —— Emma Clare Elizabeth, *b* 1963.
The 1st baronet, Sir Bennet, MP for Herefordshire, was son of Serjeant John Hoskyns MP, whose courageous and patriotic eloquence in the House of Commons, *temp* James I, against the encroachments of the Stuart dynasty upon the liberty of Parliament and the people, occasioned his confinement in the Tower, — hence the motto since borne by his descendants. Sir John, 2nd baronet, one of the founders of the Royal Society, succeeded his friend Sir Christopher Wren as President thereof, and received the honour of knighthood. Sir Hungerford, 4th baronet, a distinguished soldier throughout Marlborough's campaigns, was MP for Hereford. The 9th baronet, Rev Sir John Leigh, was R of Aston Tyrrold and Hon Canon of Ch Ch, Oxford. The 12th baronet, Rt Rev Sir Edwyn Hoskyns, DD, Bishop of Burnley (Suffragan for Diocese of Manchester) 1901-4, and Lord Bishop of Southwell 1904-25. The 13th baronet, Rev Sir Edwyn Clement, MC, DD, Chap to Bishop of Derby, Pres, Fellow, Dean and, Librarian of Corpus Christi Coll, Camb, and Hon Canon of Derby Cathedral. The 14th baronet, Sir Chandos Wren, F/O RAF VR, was *k* on flying operations over Norway 1945.

HOULDSWORTH (UK) 1887, of Reddish, Manchester, co Lancaster, and Coodham, Symington, Ayrshire
(Name pronounced "Hoaldsworth")

To be bent, not to be broken

Sir RICHARD THOMAS REGINALD HOULDSWORTH, 5th *Baronet*; *b* 2 Aug 1947; *s* his father, *Lt-Col Sir* REGINALD DOUGLAS HENRY, OBE, TD, 1989; *ed* Bredon Sch, Tewkesbury: *m* 1st, 1970 (*m diss* 1979), Jane, only da of Alistair Orr, of Sydehead, Beith, Ayrshire; 2ndly, 1992, Ann Catherine, eldest da of late Capt Jean Jacques Tremayne, MN, of Sway, Hants, and has issue by 1st and 2nd *m*.

Arms – Ermine, the trunk of a tree in bend raguly eradicated at the base proper, between three foxes' heads erased gules. Crest – A stag's head erased gules, attired and collared or, the attires banded with a hank of cotton argent. *Residence* – Kirkbride, Glenburn, Crosshill, Maybole, Ayrshire.

SONS LIVING *(By 1st marriage)*

SIMON RICHARD HENRY *b* 6 Oct 1971. —— Nicolas Peter George, *b* 1975.

(By 2nd marriage)

Matthew James, *b* 1992.

SISTERS LIVING

Myrtle Janet Mary, *b* 1935; *m* 1959, Philip Nicholas Charles Howard, of 47 Ladbroke Grove, W11 3AR, and has issue living, John Henry Nicholas, *b* 1961, — James Reginald Mark, *b* 1976, — Juliette Margaret, *b* 1960: *m* 1988, Justin Henry Francis Whiteley, yr son of Peter John Henry Whiteley (*see* Guilford, E). —— Rosemary Margaret, *b* 1939: *m* 1962 (*m diss* 1990), (William) John Tevenar Usher, and has issue (*see* Usher, Bt colls).

UNCLE LIVING *(son of 3rd Baronet)*

Walter William Whitmore, TD, *b* 1906; Major (ret) Sherwood Foresters, served 1939-45 War (despatches): *m* 1945, Hazell Marcella, da of late J. P. Shepherd, of Barbados, and has issue living, Charles William Shepherd (The Old Vicarage, Somerford Keynes, Cirencester, Glos), *b* 1946: *m* 1971, Jacqueline, only da of Paul Smith, of Biddestone, Wilts, and has issue living, Zoë Anne *b* 1974, Joanna Clare *b* 1976, — Hazell Mary Fiona, *b* 1954. *Residence* – The Fold, Sheep St, Stow-on-the-Wold, Glos. *Club* – Caledonian.

WIDOW LIVING OF FOURTH BARONET

MARGARET MAY (*Dowager Lady Houldsworth*), da of late Cecil Emilius Laurie (*see* Laurie, Bt colls): *m* 1934, Lt-Col Sir Reginald Douglas Henry Houldsworth, 4th Bt, OBE, TD, who *d* 1989. *Residence* – Glenburn, Crosshill, Maybole, Ayrshire.

The 1st baronet, Sir William Henry Houldsworth, sat as MP for Manchester (C) 1883-5, and for N-W Div of Manchester 1885-1906. The 3rd baronet, Sir William Thomas Reginald, Houldsworth, CBE, TD, was Hon Col Ayrshire Yeo (Lieut-Col Comdg 1923).

HOULDSWORTH (UK) 1956, of Heckmondwike, West Riding of Yorkshire (Extinct 1990)

Sir (HAROLD) BASIL HOULDSWORTH, 2nd and last *Baronet*.

DAUGHTER LIVING OF SECOND AND LAST BARONET

(Sarah) Belinda Clifford, *b* 1949.

WIDOW LIVING OF SECOND BARONET

NORAH CLIFFORD (*Lady Houldsworth*), da of Arthur Halmshaw, of Heckmondwike, York: *m* 1946, Sir (Harold) Basil Houldsworth, 2nd and last Bt, who *d* 1990.

Houstoun-Boswall, see Boswall.

HOWARD (UK) 1955, of Great Rissington, co Gloucester

Sir (Hamilton) Edward de Coucey Howard, GBE, 2nd *Baronet*; *b* 29 Oct 1915; *s* his father *Sir* (Harold Walter) Seymour 1967; *ed* Radley, and Worcester Coll, Oxford; Hon DSc, London; Lord Mayor of London 1971-72; HM Lieut for City of London; an Alderman of City of London; Chm of the firm of Charles Stanley & Co Ltd, Stockbroker; a Liveryman of Gardeners' Co (Master 1961-62); 1939-45 War as F/O RAF (despatches); GBE (Civil) 1972: *m* 1943, Elizabeth Howarth, da of late Maj Percy H. Ludlow, and has issue.

Arms – Azure, two wings conjoined in lure and in chief as many cross-crosslets fitchée or, a chief of the last thereon between two leaves of the india rubber tree proper a pale vert charged with a bezant. **Crest** – A toucan holding in the dexter claw and feeding on an apple slipped and leaved all proper.
Residence – Courtlands, Bishops Walk, Shirley Hills, Surrey CR0 5BA. *Clubs* – City Livery, City of London.

SONS LIVING

David Howarth Seymour (25 Luke St, EC2), *b* 29 Dec 1945; *ed* Radley, and Worcester Coll, Oxford (MA); an Alderman of the City of London; Man Dir Charles Stanley & Co Ltd, Stockbroker, and Liveryman of Gardeners' Co (Master 1990-91): *m* 1968, Valerie Picton, only da of late Derek Weatherly Crosse, of Chase House, Callis Court Rd, Broadstairs, and has issue living, Robert Picton Seymour, *b* 28 Jan 1971, — James Picton Seymour, *b* 1979, — Caroline Picton Seymour, *b* 1970, — Victoria Picton Seymour, *b* 1975. —— John Ludlow Seymour, *b* 1948; *ed* Grenville Coll, Devon: *m* 1983, Virginia Margaret, only da of Richard J. Purkis, of Shirley, Surrey, and has issue living, Rupert, *b* 1988, — Emily, *b* 1990, — Harriet Elizabeth, *b* 1993.

COLLATERAL BRANCH LIVING

Issue of late David Seymour de Coucey Howard, yr son of 1st baronet, *b* 1919, *d* 1954: *m* 1942 (*m diss* 1949), Jean McMurdo, da of late Thomas McMurdo Heywood:—
Jennifer Anne de Coucey, *b* 1945.

Hudson-Kinahan, see Kinahan.

HUGHES (GB) 1773, of East Bergholt, Suffolk

Sir David Collingwood Hughes, 14th *Baronet*; *b* 29 Dec 1936; *s* his father, *Sir* Richard Edgar 1970; *ed* Oundle and Magdalene Coll, Camb (MA): *m* 1964, Rosemary Ann, only da of late Rev John Pain, and has had issue.

Arms – Quarterly, 1st azure, a lion rampant or, *Hughes*; 2nd gules, a lion rampant reguardant or, *Elistan Glodrydd*; 3rd, azure, three crowns in pale or, *Beli Mawr*, 4th, per bend sinister ermine and ermines, a lion rampant or, *Tudor Trevor*, 5th, or, a lion rampant reguardant sable, *Gwaeth Voyd*; 6th, per pale azure and sable, three fleur-de-lis or, *Ynyr, King of Gwent*; 7th, sable, a chevron between three goats' heads erased or, *Ithel Velyn*; 8th, azure, a lion cowed passant guardant or, *Llewellyn Aur Dorchog*.
Residence – The Berristead, Wilburton, Ely, Cambs.

SONS LIVING AND DECEASED

Thomas Collingwood, *b* 16 Feb 1966. —— Timothy John Pell, *b* 1968. —— Benjamin Richard, *b* 1969. —— Anthony George David, *b* 1972; *d* in a road accident 1991.

SISTER LIVING

Elizabeth Barbara, *b* 1933: *m* 1964, Paul Ronald Scott Lever, of Leftwich Heyes, Davenham, Northwich, Cheshire, and has issue living, Christopher Mark, *b* 1965: *m* 1989, Susan Elizabeth Mullin, and has issue living, James Richard *b* 1993, — Alison Clare, *b* 1967, — Catherine Elizabeth, *b* 1969.

UNCLE LIVING

Charles Collingwood, *b* 1907; 1939-45 War as Capt RA: *m* 1937, Sheila Dorothea, da of late Col Walter Henry Patrick Law, DSO (Brooke, Bt, *cr* 1919), and has issue living, Peter Collingwood (Larch House, 543 Limpsfield Rd, Warlingham, Surrey, CR3 9DX), *b* 1943; *ed* Oundle, and at Pomfret Sch, Conn, USA: *m* 1965, Susan Elizabeth Ann Cubitt, and has issue living, Natasha Sarah *b* 1967: *m* 19—, Richard Gray (and has issue living, Francesca *b* 1994), Kate *b* 1970, Victoria *b* 1972. *Residence* – 6 Renson Close, Hessett, Bury St Edmunds, Suffolk.

AUNT LIVING

Rosemary Sybil (The Granary, Weatherhill Farm, Icklingham, Bury St Edmunds, Suffolk), *b* 1909: *m* 1937, Col George William Browning, OBE, Welsh Gds, who *d* 1981, and has issue living, John Montague George (Weatherhill Farm, Icklingham, Bury St Edmunds) *b* 1944: *m* 1970, Mary-Grace Feachem, and has issue living, Christopher George John *b* 1972, Timothy Robert *b* 1974, — Mary Joan, BEM, *b* 1938; BEM (1992): *m* 1962, Rev Andrew Alexander Macintosh, BD, Dean of St John's College, Cambridge, and has issue living, George Alexander John *b* 1967; Welsh Gds, Thomas Andrew Charles *b* 1974, Rachel Alison Mary *b* 1964, — Frances Evangeline, *b* 1941: *m* 1964, Col John Granville Beaumont Rigby, OBE, R Regt Fus (ret), and has issue living, Peter Alexander Beaumont *b* 1965, Simon William Granville *b* 1967. *Residence* – Penn Cottage, Corton, Warminster, Wilts.

DAUGHTER LIVING OF TWELFTH BARONET

Diana Margaret (*Dowager Lady Mowbray*), *b* 1905: *m* 1927, Sir George Robert Mowbray, 5th Bt, KBE, who *d* 1969. *Residence* – Starvehill House, Mortimer, Berks.

WIDOW LIVING OF THIRTEENTH BARONET

JESSICA (*Jessica, Lady Hughes*) (Holmwood, 30 Fowlers Rd, Salisbury SP1 2QU), da of late B. C. Broomhall, FRCS: *m* 1967, as his 2nd wife, Sir Richard Edgar Hughes, 13th baronet, who *d* 1970.

COLLATERAL BRANCHES LIVING

Issue of late Cdr Alfred Marcus Hughes, OBE, RN, brother of 13th baronet, *b* 1900, *d* 19—: *m* 1934, Hope Frances, who *d* 19—, da of late Arthur George Pritchard;—
Pamela Mary, *b* 1939: *m* 1965, Col Colin Humphrey Cowley Howgill, ret, of 1204 Wiesman Court, Wolf Trap Green, Great Falls, Va 226649, USA, and has issue living, Michael Colin, *b* 1968, — David Charles, *b* 1970, — Susan Rosemary, *b* 1967.

Grandchildren of late Arthur Hughes, eldest son of late Arthur Hughes (*b* 1836), 3rd son of William Hughes, Barrister-at-law, 4th son (2nd by 2nd *m*) of 3rd baronet:—
Issue of late Richard Arthur Warren Hughes, OBE, *b* 1900, *d* 1976: *m* (Jan) 1932, Frances Catharine Ruth, who *d* 1985, da of late Gardner Sebastian Bazley (*see* Bazley, Bt):—
Rev Robert Elyston-Glodrydd (Clogwyn Melyn, Talsarnau, Gwynedd LL47 6TP), *b* 1932; *ed* Trin Coll, Oxford (MA); M Litt, Birmingham Univ: *m* 1960, Sheila Basketts, and has issue living, Claire Frances Rosemary, *b* 1961, — Rachel Catherine, *b* 1964, —— Owain Gardner Collingwood, *b* 1943. —— Penelope, *b* 1934; *ed* Somerville Coll, Oxford (MA): *m* 1958, Robin Paul Minney, and has issue living, Thomas, *b* 1960, — Hugo Benjamin Paulus, *b* 1962, — James, *b* 1963, — Richard, *b* 1967. —— Lleky Susannah, *b* 1936: *m* 19—, Stavros J. Papastavrou, MA, decd, and has issue living, Vassili Alexander Dimitri, *b* 1960. —— Catherine Phyllida, *b* 1940: *m* 1960, Colin Michael Wells, of 39 Charles St, Ottawa, Canada, and has issue living, Christopher William Llewellyn, *b* 1961, — Dominic Richard Alexander, *b* 1963.

Granddaughter of late Capt John William St John Hughes, 5th son of 8th baronet:—
Issue of late Major Frederick St John Hughes, MVO, OBE, *b* 1866, *d* 1956: *m* 1908, Mabel, who *d* 1965, da of late David Evans, of Ffrwdgrech, Breconshire:—
April Mary (Ivy Cottage, Sprayton, Crediton, Devon), *b* 1913: *m* 1939, Gp Capt Hugh Smeddle, DFC, and has had issue, Robert Adam Hughes, *b* 1948: *m* 1st, 1972 (*m diss* 1982), Sarah Anne, da of Maj Ernest Howarth, MBE (*see* E Meath); 2ndly, 1988, Daryl Anne, da of Maj R. E. Brookes, of West Hill Farm, Okehampton, and has issue living, (by 1st *m*) William Robert *b* 1976, Vanessa Mary *b* 1974, (by 2nd *m*) Samuel Edward *b* 1988, Lucy Susan *b* 1990, — Susan Ostara Mary, *b* 1947, *d* in a motor acc 1967, while on a Durham Univ expdn to India.

Grandchildren of late Arthur Hughes (*b* 1836) (ante):—
Issue of late Alfred Collingwood Hughes, *b* 1864, *d* 1915: *m* 1897, Ada Mary, who *d* 1940, da of Edmond Drage:—
Stanley Collingwood, *b* 1903. —— Jack Collingwood, *b* (twin) 1903. —— Harry Leonard Collingwood, *b* 1906: *m* 19—, Pamela Phillips, and has issue living, a son, *b* 1943.
Issue of late Robert Hughes, *b* 1870, *d* 1929: *m* 1900, Ella Fanny, who *d* 1953, da of Frederick Boldero:—
Robert Bernard (Calle Buen Aire, 26 3rd Piso B, Villa Carlos, Minorca, Spain), *b* 1906. —— Margaret Rosemary (Residencia de Anlians, Mahon, Minorca, Spain), *b* 1909: *m* 1938 (*m diss* 1976), John Hannaford; 2ndly, 1979, William Woodward, who *d* 1991.

This ancient family, according to the College of Arms, is descended from Elistan Glodrydh, Earl of Hereford (*b* 933). The 1st baronet, Capt Sir Richard Hughes, RN, when Commissioner of Portsmouth Dockyard (1773), entertained George III. Sir Richard, the 2nd baronet, Adm of the Red, was second in command under Lord Howe at the relief of Gibralter; he also captured the "Solitaire," and gained victory against the French off Barbados 1782. The 10th baronet Sir (Alfred) Collingwood Hughes, served during European War 1914-18, as Major 4th Vol Batn Suffolk Regt (despatches), and was High Sheriff of Suffolk 1923-4.

Hughes-Hunter, see Hunter.

HULSE (GB) 1739, of Lincoln's Inn Fields

Sir (HAMILTON) WESTROW HULSE, 9th *Baronet*; *b* 20 June 1909; *s* his father, *Sir* HAMILTON (JOHN), 1931; *ed* Eton, and at Ch Ch, Oxford; Bar Inner Temple 1932; formerly Wing-Com RAF Vol Reserve; European War 1939-45 (despatches): *m* 1st (Jan) 1932 (*m diss* 1937), Philippa Mabel, da of late A. J. Taylor, of Strensham Court, Worcestershire; 2ndly, 1938, Ambrosine Nellie Orr, who *d* 1940, only da of late Capt H. S. Orr Wilson, R. H. A., of Dunardagh, Blackrock, co Dublin; 3rdly, 1945 (*m diss* 1954), Dorothy, who *d* 1991, only da of late William Durran, of 80 Church Street, W, and widow of James Anderson McKay Hamilton; 4thly, 1954, Lucy Elizabeth Smitheyt, da of Col George Redesdale Brooker Spain, CMG, TD, FSA, and has issue by 1st *m*.

Arms – Per fesse argent and ermine, three piles, one issuing from the chief, between the others reversed, sable. **Crest** – A buck's head couped proper attired or, charged on the neck with a place surmounted by two bezants; between the attires a sun of the last.
Residence – Breamore, Hants. *Clubs* – Carlton, Leander.

SONS LIVING *(By 1st marriage)*

EDWARD JEREMY WESTROW, *b* 22 Nov 1932; *ed* Eton; late Capt Scots Gds; High Sheriff Hants 1978; DL Hampshire 1989: *m* 1957, Verity Ann, da of William Pilkington, of Ivywell, Routes des Issues, St John, Jersey, and has issue living, (Edward) Michael Westrow, *b* 1959: *m* 1986, Doone A., da of Iain Brotherton, of London, and Mrs Pamela Brotherton, of Earlswood House, Pitton, Salisbury, Wilts, and has issue living, Edward Westrow *b* 4 March 1993, Venetia *b* 1987, Roseanne *b* 1989, Natasha *b* 1990, — Camilla Ann, *b* 1962: *m* 1991, Luca C. Corona, of San Marco 3832, Venice, Italy, son of Giuseppe Corona, of 17 via Mozart, Milan, and has issue living, Alexander Tenzin *b* 1991. *Residence* – Breamore House, nr Fordingbridge, Hants SP6 2DF. ⸺ Richard Arthur Samuel (The Old Chapel, Netton, Salisbury SP4 6AW), *b* 1936; *ed* Eton; late 2nd Lt Scots Gds: *m* 1963, Caroline Susan Joan, da of Lt-Col Sir George David Elliott Tapps Gervis Meyrick, 6th Bt, MC, and has issue living, George Richard,

To be rather than to seem

b 1967, — Frances Caroline, *b* 1968.

This family descends from the Hulses of Norbury, Cheshire, and has common origin with the Holles Earls of Clare, of whom the 4th and last Earl was *cr* Duke of Newcastle (*cr* 1694, ext 1711), when his Holles estates were devised to his nephew, Thomas Pelham who was *cr* Duke of Newcastle 1715. The 1st baronet was Physician to Queen Anne, and to Kings George I and George II.

HULTON (UK) 1905, of Hulton Park, Parish of Deane, and co Palatine of Lancaster (Extinct 1993)

Sir GEOFFREY ALAN HULTON, 4th and last *Baronet*.

SISTER LIVING OF FOURTH BARONET

Barbara Joan, *b* 1921; formerly Junior Com ATS: *m* 1945, Capt John Edward Vincent Butterfield, Duke of Wellington's Regt, only son of late Lt-Col Edward Butterfield, DSO, of Bexhill-on-Sea, Sussex, and has issue living, Hugh Alan John, *b* 1946; *ed* Wellington, — Neil Roger, *b* 1949; *ed* Wellington, — Gillian Diana, *b* 1955. *Residence* – Bridge House, Church Lane, Bishops Sutton, Alresford, Hants SO24 0AE.

WIDOW LIVING OF FOURTH BARONET

MARY PATRICIA (*Lady Hulton*), eldest da of Patrick Arnold de Vere Reynolds, of Ashfort, Alexandra Rd, Farnborough, Hants: *m* 1945, Sir Geoffrey Alan Hulton, 4th Bt, JP, DL, who *d* 1993. *Residence* – The Cottage, Hulton Park, Over Hulton, Bolton BL5 1BE.

Hume-Campbell, see Campbell.

Hume-Williams, see Williams.

Hunter Blair, see Blair.

Huntington-Whiteley, see Whiteley.

HUTCHISON (UK) 1923, of Hardiston, co Kinross (Extinct 1972)

Sir ERIC ALEXANDER OGILVY HUTCHISON, 2nd and last *Baronet.*

DAUGHTERS LIVING OF SECOND BARONET (*By 1st marriage*)

Morna, *b* 1925: *m* 1947, Desmond Berry, and has issue living, Bruce Graham, *b* 1948, — Michael John, *b* 1950, — Patricia Fayrer, *b* 1949, — Morna Lilian, *b* 1952, — Marian Loraine (twin), *b* 1952. —— Sheila, *b* 1926: *m* 1956 (*m diss* 1985), Eric Alexander Masterton Wood, MB, ChB, MRCP, MRCPE, DPM, and has issue living, Jonathan Paul Masterton, *b* 1958, — Christopher Malcolm Fayrer, *b* 1962, — Alastair Graham Spens, *b* 1964, — Jeremy Douglas, *b* 1966. —— Patricia, *b* 1928: *m* 1st, 1950 (*m diss* 1954), Julian St Leger (*see* B Bagot, colls, 1990 Edn); 2ndly, 1955, Michael Cain, FRIBA, and has issue living, (by 1st *m*), Harriet Claire, *b* 1951, — (by 2nd *m*) Sebastian, *b* 1957, — Marius, *b* 1958, — Benedict, *b* 1960. *Residence* – 3 Rosemont Rd, Richmond, Surrey.

(*By 2nd marriage*)

Jane Moir Ogilvy, *b* 1958.

HUTCHISON (UK) 1939, of Thurle, Streatley, co Berks

Sir PETER HUTCHISON, 2nd *Baronet*; *b* 27 Sept 1907; *s* his father, *Sir* ROBERT, MD, FRCP, 1960; *ed* Marlborough, and at Lincoln Coll, Oxford (MA); admitted a Solicitor 1933; Dep Clerk of the Peace and of the County Council, E Suffolk 1947-71, and Clerk of the Peace and County Solicitor 1971-72: *m* 1949, Mary-Grace, da of late Very Rev Algernon Giles Seymour (*see* Culme-Seymour, Bt, colls), and has issue. *Residence* – Melton Mead, nr Woodbridge, Suffolk.

SONS LIVING

ROBERT (Lower Rd, Grundisburgh, Suffolk), *b* 25 May 1954; *ed* Marlborough: *m* 1987, Anne Margaret, elder da of Sir (Godfrey) Michael David Thomas, 11th Bt (*cr* 1694), and has issue living, Hugo Thomas Alexander, *b* 16 April 1988, — Guy Piers Giles, *b* 1990. —— Mark Seymour, *b* 1960.

DAUGHTERS LIVING

Elspeth, *b* 1950: *m* 1975, John Richard Feneran Bryers, of Highwood Cottage, Kilnwick, Driffield, Yorks, YO25 9JF, and has issue living, Henry Peter Newman, *b* 1977, — George Richard Timothy, *b* 1983, — Charlotte Emily, *b* 1979. —— Alison Margaret, *b* 1951: *m* 1990, Peter Brendon Wintgens, elder son of Leonard Wintgens, of Reigate, Surrey.

BROTHER LIVING

Michael Duncan, *b* 1912; *ed* Eton, and Magdalen Coll, Oxford: *m* 1945, Margery Betty Martin, and has issue living, Paul Michael, *b* 1959, — Sara Laetitia, *b* 1949, — Margaret Ann, *b* 1953.

SISTER LIVING

Ann Felicity, *b* 1917; JP of Surrey: *m* 1945, Geoffrey Martin Greenwood, who *d* 1994, and has issue living, John Gerald, *b* 1946, — Alan Graham, *b* 1948, — Charles Duncan, *b* 1954, — Victoria Jean, *b* 1950. *Residence* – Saxons, Frensham, Farnham, Surrey.

The 1st baronet, Sir Robert Hutchison, MC, CM (son of Robert Hutchison, of Carlowrie, Kirkliston) was Pres of Roy So of Med 1934-6, and of Roy Coll of Physicians 1938-41.

HUTCHISON (UK) 1956, of Rossie, co Perth

Sir PETER CRAFT HUTCHISON, CBE, 2nd *Baronet*; *b* 5 June 1935; *s* his father, *Sir* JAMES RILEY HOLT, DSO, TD, 1979; *ed* Eton, and Magdalene Coll, Camb (BA); Lt late R Scots Greys; Chm of Hutchison & Craft Ltd, insurance brothers, Glasgow, and sometime Chm Board of Trustees Royal Botanical Gardens, Edinburgh; Vice-Chm British Waterways Board, and Board Memb Scottish National Heritage since 1994; CBE (Civil) 1992; *m* 1966, Virginia, da of late John Millar Colville, of Gribloch, Kippen, Stirlingshire, and has issue.

Arms – Argent, an arrow fessways vert, feathered gules and barbed or, between two lymphads vert, sails furled gules, in chief, and a parachute azure, stringed vert and ringed or, in base; in dexter chief the canton of a Baronet of the United Kingdom.
Crest – A parachute as in the arms, the ring transversed of an arrow fessways also as in the arms.
Residences – Milton House, Milton, by Dumbarton, G82 2TU; 32 Moore St, SW3. *Club* – Cavalry and Guards', Western (Glasgow).

SON LIVING

JAMES COLVILLE, *b* 7 Oct 1967.

Imbert-Terry, see Terry.

INGILBY (UK) 1866, of Ripley Castle, Yorkshire.

My right

Sir THOMAS COLVIN WILLIAM INGILBY, 6th *Baronet*; *b* 17 July 1955; *s* his father *Maj Sir* JOSLAN WILLIAM VIVIAN, 1974; *ed* Eton, and Royal Agric Coll, Cirencester; ARICS 1982; CAAV 1983: *m* 1984, Emma Clare Roebuck, da of Maj Richard R. Thompson, of Whinfield, Strensall, York, and has issue.

Arms – Sable, an estoile argent within a bordure engrailed gobony or and gules.
Crest – A boar's head couped and erect argent, tusked or, in the mouth an estoile of the last.
Seat – Ripley Castle, Harrogate, N Yorkshire HG3 3AY.

SONS LIVING

JAMES WILLIAM FRANCIS, *b* 15 June 1985. —— Joslan Richard Ryland, *b* 1986. —— Jack Henry Thomas, *b* 1990.

DAUGHTER LIVING

Eleanor Jane Pamela, *b* 1989.

SISTERS LIVING

Caroline Diana Colvin, *b* 1949: *m* 1986, David Francis Wakefield, eldest son of late F.H. Wakefield, of Ogston Hall, Higham, Derbyshire. —— Katherine Benita Colvin, *b* 1951: *m* 1974, Richard Denis Kingsmill Wallace, and has issue living, Sally Diana, *b* 1981.

WIDOW LIVING OF FIFTH BARONET

DIANA (*Diana, Lady Ingilby*) (Ripley Castle, Harrogate, Yorks), da of late Brig-Gen Sir George Lethbridge Colvin, CB, CMG, DSO: *m* 1948, Maj Sir Joslan William Vivian Ingilby, 5th Bt, who *d* 1974.

COLLATERAL BRANCH LIVING

Issue of late Lt-Col John Uchtred Macdowall Ingilby, OBE, brother of 4th baronet, *b* 1874, *d* 1948: *m* 1904, Marjorie Cecily, MBE, who *d* 1957, el da of late William Robert Phelips, of Montacute House, Stoke-under-Ham:—
Joan Alicia, *b* 1911. *Residence* – Coleshouse, Askrigg, Leyburn, Yorks DL8 3HH.

This family, of great antiquity, has been seated at Ripley Castle since *temp* Edward III, and has three times received the honour of a baronetcy. Sir William Ingilby, of Ripley, was created a baronet in 1642, which baronetcy became ext in 1772, on the death of his gt-grandson, Sir John Ingilby, 4th Bt. In 1781, John Ingilby, natural son of the 4th Bt, who inherited his estates was *cr* a baronet. This title became ext in 1854 on the death of his son, Sir William Amcotts-Ingilby, 2nd Bt (who also inherited, by special remainder in 1805, the baronetcy conferred in 1796 upon his maternal grandfather, Sir Wharton Amcotts). Sir Henry John Ingilby, of Ripley, 1st Bt of the third creation in 1866 was eldest son of the Rev Henry Ingilby, brother of the 1st Bt of the second creation (1781) and succeeded by devise to the family estates.

Inglefield-Watson, see Watson.

INGLIS (NS) 1703, of Glencorse, Midlothian (formerly Mackenzie of Gairloch, Ross-shire)
(Name pronounced "Ingles")

Sir RODERICK JOHN INGLIS OF GLENCORSE, 10th *Baronet*; *b* 25 Jan 1936; *s* his father, Sir MAXWELL IAN HECTOR, 1974; *ed* Winchester and Edinburgh Univ (MB, ChB): *m* 1st, 1960 (*m diss* 1975), Rachel Evelyn, da of Lt-Col N. M. Morris, of Dowdstown, Ardee, co Louth; 2ndly, 1975 (*m diss* 1977), Geraldine, yr da of R. H. Kirk, of Thaxted, Essex; 3rdly, 1986, Marilyn, da of A.L. Irwin, of Glasgow, and has issue by 1st, 2nd and 3rd *m*.

Arms – Azure, a lion rampant argent, armed and langued gules, on a chief of the second three mullets sable. **Crest** – A demi-lion as in the arms, holding in his dexter fore-paw a mullet argent.
Residence – 18 Cordwalles Rd, Pietermaritzburg, Natal, S Africa 3201. *Club* – Country, Pietermaritzburg.

SONS LIVING *(By 1st marriage)*

IAN RICHARD, *b* 1965. —— Alexander Colin, *b* (twin) 1965.

(By 3rd marriage)

Harry Mackenzie, *b* 1987.

DAUGHTERS LIVING *(By 1st marriage)*

Amanda Fiona, *b* 1963.

(By 2nd marriage)

Harriet, *b* 1977.

COLLATERAL BRANCHES LIVING

Grandchildren of late Lt-Col Harry Maxwell Mackenzie, RA, grandson of 4th baronet:—
Issue of late Engineer-Com Harry Ponsonby MACKENZIE, RN (ret), *b* 1877, *d* 1948: *m* 1915, Gladys Dalziel, who *d* 1966, yr da of late William Weatherly, of Woolongoon, Mortlake, Victoria, Australia:—
Alastair John, *b* 1922; formerly Lt Roy Austn Naval VR; 1939-45 War (despatches twice): *m* 1955, Isabel Anne, da of late Capt Andrew Kelt, RAMC, of Pickdick, Brede, Sussex, and has issue living, Roderick John Andrew, *b* 1962, —— Kythé Jane, *b* 1956: *m* 1978 (*m diss* 1982), Francis Gurry, —— Iona Margaret, *b* 1957, —— Mairi Anne, *b* 1959, —— Margaret Isabel Alexandra, *b* 1970. *Residence* – Hillside, Ararat, Vic, Aust. —— Kenneth William, *b* 1928: *m* 1962, Jennifer Margaret, only da of late Col Patrick Hyde, OBE, and has issue living, Caroline Margaret, *b* 1963, —— Elizabeth Georgina, *b* 1965, —— Fiona Jennifer, *b* 1970. *Residence* – Trawalla, Vic, Aust.
Issue of late Colin Rae MACKENZIE, *b* 1887, *d* 1973: *m* 1913, Nora Constance, da of late Herbert Guernsey, of Victoria, BC, Canada:—
Margaret Elaine (Grianach, Lettock, N Kessoch, Inverness-shire), *b* 1914: *m* 1st, 1937 (*m diss* 1958), Gerald Ashby Wodehouse Garland, who *d* 1965; 2ndly, 1958, C. R. Cuthbert (*dec*), and has issue living, (by 1st *m*) Angela Robin, *b* 1938, —— Jennifer Sara, *b* 1942: *m* 1965, Edward John Roberts, and has issue living, Benjamin Alexander *b* 1966, Nicholas Justin *b* 1967, William Wayland *b* 1970. —— Nora Kythé, *b* 1917; 1939-45 War as Section Officer WRCAF: *m* 1944, Capt Victor Browne, RCN, of 9 Seagate, 10110 3rd St, Sidney, BC V8L 3B3, Canada, and has issue living, Colin Victor Alleyne, *b* 1946, —— Susan Kythé, *b* 1949. —— Christine Ponsonby, *b* 1928: *m* 1953 (*m diss* 19——), Adrian C. Boehme, and has issue living, Justin Christian, *b* 1959, —— Nicholas Christian, *b* 1962, —— Anna Kythé, *b* 1958.

Grandchildren of late Marjory Kythé (Lady Stirling of Fairburn), only da of 7th baronet:—
Issue of late Marjory Charlotte Mackenzie of Gairloch (*s* to the baronial estate of Gairloch on the death of her uncle, Sir Hector David Mackenzie, 8th Bt), and, with her husband, was recognized in the surname of Mackenzie of Gairloch by decree of Lyon Court 1959, *b* 1920, *d* 1988: *m* 1941, Brig William Alexander Mackenzie of Gairloch (formerly Stevenson), DSO, OBE, late Queen's Own Cameron Highrs, who *d* 1982:—
John Alexander MACKENZIE OF GAIRLOCH (Conan House, Conan Bridge, Ross-shire; c/o Glyn Mills & Co, Holt's Branch, Kirkland House, Whitehall, SW1), *b* 1944; late 2nd Lieut Queen's Own Highrs: *m* 1969, Marian, da of late Col E. Seabourne Williams. —— Andrew James, *b* 1949. —— James, *b* 1957. —— Alexandra Mary, *b* 1941: *m* 1962, Andrew Gray-Muir, of Sundial, Gilmerton, Edinburgh 9, and has issue living, William John, *b* 1966, —— Elizabeth Kythé, *b* 1963. —— Sara Marjory, *b* 1945: *m* 1967, James MacAlpine Gregor Grant, of Roskill House, Munlochy, Ross-shire (*see* Arbuthnot, Bt, *cr* 1823, colls, 1909 Edn), and has issue living, Annabel Elizabeth, *b* 1968, —— Clare Marjory, *b* 1970, —— Lucy Sara, *b* 1975.
Kenneth Mackenzie, created a Baronet of Nova Scotia 1703, was son of Alexander Mackenzie, 7th of Gairloch, and sat as MP for Ross-shire 1702. Sir Kenneth John Mackenzie, 7th Bt, was King's and Lord Treasurer's Remembrancer for Scotland 1900-21, and a Scottish Ecclesiastical Commr 1925-9. On the death in 1958 of the 8th baronet, Sir Hector Mackenzie, MC, Lord-Lt of Ross-shire, the baronial estate of Gairloch, held from 1476, devolved on his niece, Marjory Charlotte Stirling, Mrs Stevenson, as Mrs Mackenzie, 15th of Gairloch, whilst the baronetcy passed to the heir male as Sir Maxwell Ian Hector Inglis of Glencorse, 9th Bt, under this name and designation, pursuant to the entail of the Rt Hon John Inglis, Lord Glencorse, Lord Justice-General of Scotland. Sir Maxwell was son of Hector Ian Maxwell Mackenzie-Inglis of Glencorse (who both assumed 1929 the additional surname of Inglis of Glencorse), son of Lt-Col Harry Maxwell Mackenzie, RA, son of John Mackenzie, 4th son of 4th Bt. In 1958 Sir Maxwell was recognized by decree of Lyon Court in the surname of Inglis of Glencorse. He was in Political Ser Gold Coast 1928-37, and Lord Lt of Midlothian 1964-72.

INGRAM (UK) 1893, of Swineshead Abbey, Lincolnshire.

In hoc signo vinces

Under this sign you

shall conquer

Sir JAMES HERBERT CHARLES INGRAM, 4th *Baronet; b* 6 May 1966; *s* his grandfather, *Major Sir* HERBERT, 1980; *ed* Eton, and Cardiff Univ.

Arms – Quarterly, argent and or, gutée de poix, on a fesse invected gules four escallops of the second. **Crest** – On a rock proper, issuant from a wreath of cinquefoils or, a griffin's head erased quarterly gules and argent, charged on the neck with an escallop countercharged.
Residence – 8 Lochaline St, W6 9SH.

HALF-BROTHER LIVING

NICHOLAS DAVID, *b* 12 June 1975.

SISTER LIVING

Frances Jane, *b* 1964.

HALF-SISTER LIVING

Caroline Robin, *b* 1979.

AUNTS LIVING (*Daughters of 3rd baronet*)

Marion Judith, *b* 1937: *m* 1969, Graham H. Harvey-Evers, of Domaine de la Rose, 06650 Opio, France, AM and has issue living, Charles James, *b* 1970, — David Edward, *b* 1971. —— Vivian Helen, *b* (twin) 1937: *m* 1963, Oliver Turnbull, of Cleabarrow, Windermere, Cumbria (*see* E Stamford, 1990 Edn), and has issue living, Harry Jonathan Peveril, *b* 1971, — Jane Lucy, *b* 1965: *m* 1991, Charles Waddington, and has issue living, Toby George *b* 1993, — Clare Catherine, *b* 1966: *m* 1990, Edward Barham, and has issue living, Emily Catherine *b* 1993, — Sarah Mary, *b* 1968. —— Anne Carolyn, *b* 1952: *m* 1974, Alan C. Weston Peck, of Hurst Lodge, nr Twyford, Berks, and has issue living, Alexander Robin, *b* 1981, — Frances Miranda, *b* 1978.

GREAT UNCLE LIVING (*Son of 2nd baronet*)

Michael Warren, OBE, *b* 1917; *ed* Winchester, and Balliol Coll, Oxford (BA 1945); a JP and DL for Glos, Maj late Gren Gds; OBE (Civil) 1986: *m* 1944, Auriol Blanche, el da of late Lt-Gen Sir Arthur Francis Smith, KCB, KBE, DSO, MC (*see* E Kintore, colls), and has issue living, Andrew David Michael (30 King Henry's Rd, NW3 3RP), *b* 1945: *m* 1969, Carole Letitia, da of Maj John David Summers, of Marsh Cottage, Old Romney, Romney Marsh, Kent, and has issue living, Matthew William Michael *b* 1971, Toby David Warren *b* 1972, — Susan Elizabeth, *b* 1947: *m* 1969, John Humphrey Colquhoun, of Brooke House, Frocester, Stonehouse, Glos, and has issue living, Mark Humphrey *b* 1973, James Arthur *b* 1975, Auriol Emma *b* 1982, — Nicola Mary, *b* 1951; JP Cornwall: *m* 1970, Paul Archer Tyler, CBE, MP, and has issue living, Dominick Michael Archer *b* 1975, Sophie Grace Auriol *b* 1972, — Auriol Jacqueline, *b* 1957. *Residence* – The Manor House, S Cerney, Cirencester.

WIDOW LIVING OF SON OF THIRD BARONET

Sallie Willoughby (South Acre, Streatley, Berks), da of late Frank Hilary Minoprio, of Hessle Well House, Heswell, Cheshire: *m* 1973, as his 2nd wife, (Herbert) Robin Ingram (only son of 3rd baronet), who *d* 1979.

MOTHER LIVING

Shiela (8 Pitt St, W8), only da of Charles Peczenik, of 7 Grosvenor Sq, W1: *m* 1st, 1963 (*m diss* 1971), as his 1st wife, (Herbert) Robin Ingram (only son of 3rd baronet), who *d* 1979; 2ndly, 1972 (*m diss* 1985), Count Fritz Dietlof von der Schulenburg.

COLLATERAL BRANCHES LIVING

Issue of late Sir Bruce Stirling Ingram, OBE, MC, son of 1st baronet, *b* 1877, *d* 1963: *m* 1st, 1904, Amy, who *d* 1947, da of John Foy, of 16 Bolton Gdns, SW5; 2ndly, 1947, Lily, who *d* 1962, da of Sydney Grundy:—
(By 1st *m*) Averil Stirling, *b* 1905: *m* 1945, Capt Jean Prost, who *d* 19—, of 81 rue de La Pompe, Paris XVI, France.

Grandchildren of late Collingwood Ingram (*infra*):—
Issue of late Ivor Laing Ingram, *b* 1907, *d* 1990: *m* 1936, Winifred (27 West Knowe, Bidston Rd, Birkenhead), da of late William Battle Waterhouse, of Wallasey, Cheshire:—
John Anthony (Wardle Old Hall, Wardle, Nantwich, Cheshire), *b* 1941: *m* 1963, Jacqueline Ann, da of William Alexander Lockley Cook, of Gotley, Westerham, Kent, and has issue living, Christopher William Ivor Lockley, *b* 1965, — Louis Anthony Lockley, *b* 1968. —— Jill Susan Rosemary, *b* 1948: *m* 1969, Clyde Dennis Gordon Coltart, of Browfield, Dale End Rd, Barnston, Wirral, Cheshire, and has issue living, Rupert Gordon, *b* 1971, — Amanda Jane, *b* 1973.
Issue of late Mervyn Jeffrey Ingram, MB, BCh, MRCS, LRCP, *b* 1909, *d* 1993: *m* 1936, Joan Doreen (Pynes Farmhouse, Pitney, Langport, Som), da of late Engr Capt Arthur Philip Leslie Dupen, RN:—
Collingwood William Malcolm (37 Poplar Grove, W11), *b* 1939: *m* 1976, Susan Anne, da of Dudley Love, of Solihull, and has issue living, William Mervyn, *b* 1980, — Rosalind Annabel, *b* 1978. —— Priscilla Jane, *b* 1937: *m* 1963, Dudley Allen Doust, of Westbrook House, West Bradley, Glastonbury, Som, and has issue living, Hannah Victoria, *b* 1963: *m* 1990, Sean Michael Gresham Barrington, of The Old College Arms, Stour Row, Dorset, — Elinor Jane, *b* 1966. —— Charlotte Certhia, *b* 1944: *b* 1944: *m* 1964 (*m diss* 1993), Charles St Vigor Fox, and has issue (*see* E—Ewing, Bt, cr 1886, colls).
Issue of late Maj William Alastair Ingram, RA, *b* 1913, *d* 1975: *m* 1947, Daphne Anne, ARRC (8 St James Villas, Winchester), el da of late Reginald Bramley Van Wart, OBE, of Llwyngwril, Merionethshire:—
Peter William Irving, *b* 1950; *ed* Winchester, and Univ of Kent (BA 1977): *m* 1979, Christina Mary, 2nd da of Sir James Holmes Henry, 2nd Bt, CMG, MC, TD, and has issue living, Sarah Christina, *b* 1980, — Corinna Alice, *b* 1983. —— Heather Anne, *b* 1948: *m* 1969, Michael Paget Bowyer, of Lockerley Water House, Lockerley, Romsey, Hants, and has issue living, James William Paget, *b* 1974, — Caroline Sarah, *b* 1972.

Issue of late Collingwood Ingram, yst son of 1st baronet, *b* 1880, *d* 1981: *m* 1906, Florence Maude, who *d* 1980, only child of Henry Rudolph Laing, of 5 Cadogan Gdns, SW3:—

Certhia Mary (Springhill Oast, Iden Green, Benenden, Cranbrook, Kent), *b* 1917: *m* 1940, Charles Gerald Harden, who *d* 1983, and has issue living, Alastair Geoffrey, *b* 1943: *m* 1982, Evelyn Maguire, and has issue living, Niall Charles Brendan *b* 1983, Alastair Francis *b* 1984, Marina Catherine *b* 1990, — Richard Charles (New Lindsey, Spring Lane, Burwash, Etchingham, E Sussex), *b* 1946: *m* 1976, Elizabeth Catherine Lacy, el da of Evelyn Charles Lacy Hulbert-Powell (*see* B St Levan), and has issue living, Charles John *b* 1981, Annabel Mary *b* 1977, Rosemary Juliet *b* 1979, — Veryan Penelope, *b* 1941: *m* 1964, Ernest Pollard, of Springhill Farm, Benenden, Kent, and has issue living, John Collingwood *b* 1968, Tessa Mary *b* 1966, — Frances Mary, *b* 1956: *m* 1980, Paul Stryker Meier, of Bouldon Mill, Craven Arms, Shropshire.

The 1st baronet, Sir William James Ingram, sometime Managing Director of the *Illustrated London News*, sat as MP for Boston (L) 1874-80, 1885-6, and 1892-5.

INNES (NS) 1628, of Balvenie, Bannffshire.
(Name pronounced "Innis")

Let it be done without blemish

SINE CRIMINE FIAT

Sir PETER ALEXANDER BEROWALD INNES OF BALVENIE, 17th *Baronet*; *b* 6 Jan 1937; *s* his father, *Lt-Col Sir* (RONALD GORDON) BEROWALD, OBE, 1988; *ed* Prince of Wales Sch, Nairobi, and Bristol Univ (BSc); FICE: *m* 1959, Julia Mary, yr da of late Alfred Stoyell Levesley, MSc, FRSC, of Burlington Rd, Bristol, and has issue.

Arms – Argent, three mullets in chief azure. **Crest** – A dexter arm, armed and couped at the elbow, holding a broadsword in pale proper. **Supporters** – Two greyhounds argent. *Seat* – Balvenie Castle, Banffshire. *Residence* – The Wheel House, Nation's Hill, Kings Worthy, Winchester, Hants S023 7QY.

SONS LIVING

(ALEXANDER) GUY BEROWALD (Storkgate House, Baydon Rd, Lambourn, Berks), *b* 4 May 1960; *ed* Queen Mary's Coll, Basingstoke: *m* 1986, Sara-Jane, da of late Dennis Busher, of Moraira, Spain. — Alastair John Peter, *b* 1965; *ed* Newcastle Univ (BSc).

DAUGHTER LIVING

Fiona Julie, *b* 1963.

BROTHER LIVING

George Guy Alfred, *b* 1941; *ed* Massey Univ, NZ (Dip Agric). *Address* – PO Box 1069, Esperance, W Australia.

SISTER LIVING

Catherine Eythan, *b* 1940: *m* 1st, 1962 (*m diss* 1970), Mark Grant Oliver; 2ndly, 1974, Hugh Leslie Sanderson, who *d* 1985; 3rdly, 1993, Donald Campbell Dawson, and has issue living (by 1st *m*), Karen Elizabeth, *b* 1965. — Alison Mary, *b* 1967. *Residence* – Lesmurdie House, Lesmurdie, W Australia.

UNCLE LIVING (*brother of 16th baronet*)

William Alexander Disney, *b* 1910; *ed* Marlborough; Lt-Col (ret) Gordon Highlanders; Vice-Lieut for Banffshire 1971-87; served 1939-45 War: *m* 1939, Mary Alison, only da of late Francis Burnett-Stuart, of Howe Green, Hertford, and has issue living, Michael Alexander (St Mary's Farm, Cupar, Fife KY15 4NF), *b* 1954; *ed* Glenalmond, and Durham Univ (BA), Dip Hort Kew; and has issue living (by Carolyn Ann Scott), Rosanna Mary Scott INNES *b* 1988, — Jonathan Berowald (33 Croft Rd, Thame, Oxon OX9 3JF), *b* 1955; *ed* Glenalmond, St Andrew's Univ (MA), and Reading Univ (MSc): *m* 1986, Jane Angela, da of Lt-Col John Dalton Stephenson, of Cefn Parc, Brecon. *Residence* – Heath Cottage, Aberlour, Banffshire AB3 9QD.

AUNT LIVING (*sister of 16th baronet*)

Elizabeth Katherine Mary (Hill Cottage, Fressingfield, Eye, Suffolk), *b* 1918: *m* 1st, 1943 (*m diss* 1948), Maj James Robertson-McIsaac; 2ndly, 1948, Col Eric Dighton Mackenzie, CMG, CVO, DSO, who *d* 1972, and has issue living, (by 2nd *m*) (*see* Mackenzie, Bt, *cr* 1890).

WIDOW LIVING OF SIXTEENTH BARONET

ELIZABETH CHRISTIAN (*Christian, Lady Innes*), el da of late Lt-Col Charles Henry Watson, DSO: *m* 1961, as his 2nd wife, Lt-Col Sir (Ronald Gordon) Berowald Innes of Balvenie, 16th Bt, OBE, who *d* 1988. *Residence* – The Loom House, Aultgowrie, Muir of Ord, Ross-shire IV6 7XA.

COLLATERAL BRANCHES LIVING

Granddaughter of late Alexander Innes, *b* 1846, son of late Alexander Innes, *b* 1812, el son of William Innes, son of Alexander Innes of Breda and Cowie, 2nd son of John Innes of Edingight, grandfather of 9th baronet:—

Issue of late Col Sydney Armitage Innes, DSO, The Black Watch, *b* 1879, *d* 1960: *m* 1903, Constance Edith, who *d* 1957, da of late Samuel Blain:—

Sylvia, *b* 1909: *m* 1944, Maj-Gen Frank McLean Richardson, CB, DSO, OBE, RAMC, and has issue living, Hugh Alexander, *b* 1946: *m* 1981, Zaleha Pawan, of Kuala Lumpur, and has issue living, Christopher Johan Roland *b* 1984, Noelle *b* 1988, — Alastair Neil, *b* 1953: *m* 1980, Mariane Angela, da of John Curry, of co Mayo, and has issue living, Simon Alexander *b* 1988, Saoirse Joanna *b* 1981, — Jennifer Jane, *b* 1944. *Residence* – 4B Barnton Av West, Edinburgh.

Grandsons of late Sydney Armitage Innes, DSO (ante):—

Issue of late Lt-Col Berowald Alfred Innes, The Black Watch, *b* 1904, *d* 1981: *m* 1931, Betty Ida (Viewlands House, 25 Viewlands Rd, Perth, Perthshire), da of late Alastair Campbell Sandeman, of Fonab, Pitlochry, Perthshire:—

Colin Berowald (Saltoun Hill, E Saltoun, Pencaitland, E Lothian EH34 5DZ), *b* 1936; *ed* Wellington; Maj late The Black Watch: *m* 1971, Clovannis Jane, da of late Lt-Col Charles Frederick Cathcart, DSO (*see* E Cathcart, colls), and has had issue, †Andrew Berowald, *b* 1963; *d* 1991, — Katherine Candida, *b* 1967: *m* 1994, Charles Ernest Peppiatt, yr son of Brian Peppiatt, of Ford, Bucks, — Emily Jane, *b* 1969. —— Malcolm Alastair (132 Wakehurst Rd, SW11 6BS; 10 Regent Terrace, Edinburgh), *b* 1939; *ed* Wellington, and Trin Hall, Camb; late 2nd Lt Scots Gds: *m* 1976, Celia Jane Strang, LVO, el da of Jock Wykeham Strang Steel (*see* Steel, Bt), and has issue living, Robert Alexander, *b* 1980, — Fiona Bridget, *b* 1983. —— James Alexander (Newbigging Birks, Oxnam, Jedburgh TD8 6NA), *b* (twin) 1939; *ed* Gordonstoun: *m* 1969, Frances, yst da of Hugh Leggat, and has issue living, Rory Alexander, *b* 1977, — Melissa Jane, *b* 1972.

Grandchildren of late Lt-Col Francis Newell Innes of Learney, son of Col Thomas Innes of Learney, CVO, LLD, 2nd son of William Innes, son of Alexander Innes of Breda and Cowie, 2nd son of John Innes of Edingight, 7th in descent from Robert Innes of Innermarkie (infra):—

Issue of late Sir Thomas Innes of Learney, GCVO, LLD, FSA (Scot), Lord Lyon King of Arms 1945-69, *b* 1893, *d* 1971: *m* 1928, Lady Lucy Buchan (The Laigh Riggs, Torphins, Aberdeenshire), da of 18th Earl of Caithness:—

Thomas Innes of Learney (Learney, Torphins, Aberdeenshire, AB3 4NB; Roy Northern and University Club, Aberdeen); *b* 1930; *ed* Edinburgh Acad, and Edinburgh Univ (BSc Agric); late R Signals; OStJ; Pres of Deeside Field Club 1971-76: *m* 1958, Rosemary Elizabeth, yr da of late Brig Cecil Vivian Staveley Jackson, CIE, CBE, of Burnside, Aboyne, Aberdeenshire, and has issue living, Maureen Cecilia, *b* 1962: *m* 1985, Duncan John Cullen Grant, yst son of late Sir Francis Cullen Grant, 12th Bt, and has issue (*see* Grant, Bt, *cr* 1688). —— Berowald Fortescue, FSA (Scot) (Inverisla, Rothiemay, Huntly, Aberdeenshire), *b* 1931; *ed* Melville Coll. —— Sir Malcolm Rognvald of Edingight, KCVO, FSA (Scot), WS (35 Inverleith Row, Edinburgh; New (Edinburgh) and Puffin's Clubs), *b* 1938; *ed* Edinburgh Acad, and Edinburgh Univ (MA, LLB); CVO 1981, KCVO 1990; KStJ; Falkland Pursuivant Extraor 1957-58, Carrick Pursuivant 1958-72, Marchmont Herald 1972-81, and Lord Lyon King of Arms and Sec of the Order of the Thistle since 1981; Lyon Clerk and Keeper of the Records, Lyon Court 1966-81; a Member of Queen's Body Guard for Scotland (Royal Company of Archers): *m* 1963, Joan, only da of Thomas D. Hay, CA, and has issue living, John Berowald (Edingight, Keith, Banffshire; 8 Eton Terrace, Edinburgh), *b* 1965; *ed* Edinburgh Acad, Heriot Watt Univ (BSc), and RMA Sandhurst; Lieut The Gordon Highlanders, — Colin William of Kinnairdy (Kinnairdy Castle, Bridge of Marnoch, Banffshire), *b* 1967; *ed* Edinburgh Acad, and Aberdeen Univ (LLB, LLM): *m* 1993, Joanna, only da of David Judge, of Birchwood, Herefordshire, — Michael Thomas of Crommey (Crommey Castle, Aberchirder, Banffshire), *b* 1970; *ed* Edinburgh Acad, St Andrews Univ (MA), and Chester Law Sch. —— Sybil Marjorie (56 Darnell Rd, Edinburgh), *b* 1934.

Descendants of late Major James Innes of Thrumster, great-grandson of James Innes of Thursater, 5th in descent from William Innes of Thursater, yst son of Robert Innes, 2nd of Innermarkie and great-great-uncle of 1st Baronet:—

Grandchildren of late Lt-Gen James John McLeod Innes, VC, CB, only son of James Innes, 5th son of Major James Innes of Thrumster (ante):—

Issue of late Hugh McLeod Innes, *b* 1862, *d* 1944: *m* 1894, Margaret, who *d* 1948, da of James Bird:—

Christina McLeod (Wilton Cottage, Jordans, Bucks), *b* 1902: *m* 1925, Frank Vigor Morley, PhD, who *d* 1980, and has had issue, John Donald Innes (40 Hillside Close, Chalfont St Peter, Bucks), *b* 1926; *ed* New Coll, Oxford (MA): *m* 1962, Alice Millicent, da of J. T. Flook, and widow of George Boast, — Hugh Oliver, *b* 1928; FRCO, ARCM; *d* 1987, — Susanna Loveday, *b* 1932: *m* 1956, John Guthrie Smithson, of Corner Cottage, Jordans, Bucks, and has issue living, Michael John *b* 1957; BSc: *m* 1982, Emilia, da of Klimos Shaylou, of Nicosia, Cyprus (and has issue living, Sophie Marina *b* 1984), Robert Hugh *b* 1963; BSc, Deborah Mary *b* 1959: *m* 1981, Richard Zealey, of Chalfont St Peter, Bucks (and has issue living, David John *b* 1983, Phillip James *b* 1989, Christina May *b* 1986), — Christina Margaret Peregrine (37 Wolverton Rd, Newport Pagnell, Bucks), *b* 1940; *ed* The Open Univ (BA).

Grandchildren of late Arthur Donald Innes, yr son of late Lt-Gen James John McLeod Innes, VC, CB (ante):—

Issue of late Neil McLeod Innes, *b* 1903, *d* 1989: *m* 1931, Nancy Audrey, who *d* 1987, da of James Temple Stephens, of Melbourne, Australia:—

Roderick Temple McLeod (Rose Cottage, Upper Swanmore, Hants SO32 2QQ), *b* 1938: *ed* Marlborough; Lt Cdr RN (ret); FRICS: *m* 1962, Diana Selkirk, da of late Eric S. Drew, and has issue living, James McLeod, *b* 1966; *ed* Milton Abbey; ARICS, — Charles McLeod, *b* 1969; *ed* Sherborne, and Reading Univ (BSc): *m* 1994, Nathalie, da of Giles Sharp, of Tanworth-in-Arden, Warwicks. — Catherine McLeod, *b* 1934: *m* 1954, Guy Francis Symondson, of Heathfield House, Windlesham, Surrey, and has issue living, Bevil Charles, *b* 1955: *m* 1985, Lucy Elizabeth, da of Douglas Hardinge Anderson (*see* E Halsbury), and has issue living, Robert Michael *b* 1986, Foy Rohais *b* 1987, Minnette Elizabeth *b* 1989, — Robin Francis, *b* 1957: *m* 1986, Alison Gaddie, and has issue living, Angus John *b* 1988, Alexandra Mary Catherine *b* 1989, — Alastair James Guy, *b* 1958: *m* 1985 (*m diss* 1993), Mrs Rosemary Hardingham (*née* Cole). —— Fiona McLeod, *b* 1939: *m* 1st, 1960, Simon Noel Chick, who *d* 1982; 2ndly, 1986, Barry Gray Brookes (PO Box 49, Yarram, Vic 3971, Australia), and has issue living (by 1st *m*), Theresa Nicola, *b* 1960: *m* 1987, Maj Jeremy Russell, RGJ, of Manor Farm, Compton Valence, Dorchester, Dorset DT2 9ES, and has issue living, Edward Simon Chick, *b* 1993, Alice Elizabeth Newton *b* 1991, Camilla Louise Newton *b* (twin) 1993, — Philippa Helen, *b* 1963: *m* 1986, Hugo James, of Gardener's Cottage, Hampton, Dorchester, Dorset DT2 9DZ, and has issue living, Grace Daisy *b* 1992, Flora Emily *b* (twin) 1992, — Sarah Rebecca (Thrae, Compton Valence, Dorchester, Dorset DT2 9ER), *b* 1967.

Grandchildren of late Ven George Archibald Clunes Innes, Archdeacon of Hamilton, Vic, Aust, son of late Maj Archibald Clunes Innes, 3rd Buffs, 6th son of Maj James Innes of Thrumster (ante):—

Issue of late George Archibald Clunes Innes, *b* 1870, *d* 19—: *m* 1900, Agnes Mary Gowthorpe, who *d* 1937:—

Charles McLeod, *b* 1902: *m* 1931, Elspeth Anne, da of Charles Bilbe, of Dululu, N Qld, and has issue living, Lorraine, *b* 1932, — Ian, *b* 1933, — Colin, *b* 1935, — Alan, *b* 1947, — Patty, *b* 1935, — Mary, *b* 1938, — Jillian, *b* 1941. —— Enid Emily, *b* 1904: *m* 19—, Donald James Mackay, and has issue living, Shirley, *b* 1931.

Descendants of Captain Peter Innes, 79th Foot, 3rd son of William Innes in Olliclate, and younger brother of Major James Innes of Thrumster (ante):—

Granddaughters of late Peter Innes, son of late Robert Innes of Hayfield in Olrig, only son of Capt Peter Innes, 79th Foot (ante):—

Issue of late Lt-Col Robert Innes, *b* 1891, *d* 1963: *m* 1913, Charlotte Lloyd Heming, who *d* 1972:—
Frances Mary, *b* 1918: *m* 1946, James Thomas, who *d* 1965. —— Margaret Joan, *b* 1925: *m* 1952, Douglas Comrie, and has issue living, Laurie Douglas, *b* 1954: *m* 1979, Maria Claire Allard, — Michael Raoul, *b* 1962, — Charlotte Ann, *b* 1953: *m* 1980, T. Jeffrey Davidson, and has issue living, John Douglas *b* 1983, Jessica Jane *b* 1982, — Mary Jane, *b* 1963.

Descendants of John Innes of Coxton, grandson of Patrick Innes of the Keam of Duffus, great-great-great-uncle of 1st baronet (*see* that title).

The limitations of this baronetcy are to heirs male whatsoever, as contained in the "signature," or warrant for the patent and *heredibus masculis quibuscunque* in the latter, on record in Lyon Court, and on the death of the 8th baronet in 1817, John Innes, of Edingight (having been served heir male general to his predecessor in the title on 12 Jan 1818), assumed the baronetcy as 9th Bt, and as heir male of John Innes of Edingight, great-great-uncle of the 1st baronet. The 12th baronet was Vice-Lieut for Banffshire.

INNES (NS) 1686, of Coxton, co Moray.

Sir DAVID CHARLES KENNETH GORDON INNES OF COXTON, 12th *Baronet*; *b* 17 April 1940; *s* his father, *Sir* CHARLES KENNETH GORDON, 1990; *ed* Haileybury, and London Univ (BScEng); AGGI: *m* 1969, Marjorie Alison, da of Ernest Walter Parker, and has issue.

Arms – Argent, three mullets within a bordure embattled azure, in dexter canton argent a saltire azure surmounted of an inescutcheon or charged with a lion rampant within a double tressure flory counterflory gules (for his Baronetcy of Nova Scotia). **Crest** – A dexter arm in armour, the hand naked holding a skean in pale, both proper, issuing from an embattled tower argent masoned sable, port gules.
Residence – 28 Wadham Close, Shepperton, Middx TW17 9HT.

SON LIVING

ALASTAIR CHARLES DEVERELL, *b* 17 Sept 1970; *ed* Haileybury, and Southampton Univ.

DAUGHTER LIVING

Dione Elizabeth Colquhoun, *b* 1974.

SISTER LIVING

Daphne Margaret Colquhoun, *b* 1948: *m* 1971, Nigel Geoffrey Wolseley Haig, of Sparkfield House, High St, Newnham on Severn, Glos, and has issue living, Jonathan Peter Wolseley, *b* 1975, — Katharine Jane Innes, *b* 1976.

AUNT LIVING (*Daughter of de jure 10th baronet*)

Eleanor Joan, *b* 1913: *m* 1938, Trevor Walter Mimpriss, MB, MS, FRCS, and has issue living, Timothy John (Wern Bach, Tal-y-Bont, Bangor, Gwynedd), *b* 1940; MA, MB, BChir, Camb; FFARCS: *m* 1964, Wendy Anne, da of Donald Pryce, and has issue living, Robert Charles *b* 1971, Rosemary Jill *b* 1965, Hilary Anne *b* 1967, — John Graham (Orchard Close, The Downs, Givons Grove, Leatherhead, Surrey), *b* 1944: *m* 1966, Lorraine, da of Donald Lovell, and has issue living, Graham Donald *b* 1968, James Christopher *b* 1970, — Jill Alison, *b* 1942: *m* 1966, Lt-Cdr David Richard Monro Gregory, RN, of 32 Midmar Gdns, Edinburgh, son of Vice-Adm Sir (George) David (Archibald) Gregory, KBE, CB, DSO, and has issue living, Peter James *b* 1967, Caroline Joan *b* 1969, Nicola Helen *b* 1972. *Residence* – 4 Midmar Avenue, Edinburgh EH10 6BS.

COLLATERAL BRANCHES LIVING

Grandchildren (by 1st *m*) of late Edward George Innes (*b* 1854), son of Edward Innes (*b* 1827), next brother of *de jure* 9th baronet:—
Issue of late Edward David Ballantyne Innes, *b* 1884, *d* 1967: *m* 1st, 1906, Ethel Agnes Isobel, who *d* 1929, da of Charles Lucas; 2ndly, 1933, Viney Isobel, da of Patrick Keogh, of Gawlis, NWC, Tasmania:—
(By 1st *m*) John Holdsworth, *b* 1915: *m* 1960, — . —— Robert Maxwell, *b* 1917: *m* 19—, Jean Marshal, and has issue living, Barbara Ann, *b* 1944, — Margaret Diane, *b* 1946. —— Gwendolen Eleanor (6 Randall St, Sandy Bay, Hobart, Tasmania), *b* 1906. —— Marjory Betty, *b* 1913: *m* 1939, James Benjamin Greer. —— (By 2nd *m*) George Berowald, *b* 1938. —— Jean Elizabeth, *b* 1934. —— Pauline Margaret, *b* 1939.
Issue of Vivian Oswald Innes, *b* 1888, *d* 1971: *m* 1912, Teresa, da of Matthew Fitzpatrick:—
Gordon Vivian, *b* 1922: *m* 1951, Rhonda Helen, da of Denis Direen, of Lymington, Hants. —— Cecil Alfred, *b* 1923. —— Leila Anne (Glen Fern, Port Cygnet, Tasmania), *b* 1913: *m* 19—, F. Dillon.
Issue of late Eric Edward Innes, *b* 1891: *m* 1st, 1917, Winifred Shelma, who *d* 1921, da of Edward Charles O'Brien; 2ndly, 1925, Doris Cecilia, da of Brian Kilmartin:—
(By 1st *m*) Edward George (Linga Longa, Port Cygnet, Tasmania), *b* 1919: *m* 1942, Ruth Minnie, da of Ralph Norris, and has issue living, Nigel David, *b* 1944, — Christopher Wayne, *b* 1948.
Issue of late Athol Rupert Innes, *b* 1893, *d* 1973: *m* 1922, Kathleen (Kia Ora Mail Box, Lymington Rd, Cygnet, 7112, Tasmania), da of Edward Crease:—
William James, *b* 1924: *m* 1st, 1950, Avis Lorraine, da of Victor Eugene Yelland; 2ndly, 1967, Claire Adelaide, da of R. A. Batty, of Adelaide, SA, and has issue living, (by 1st *m*) Wendy Anne, *b* 1951, — Josephine Lilian, *b* 1953, — (by 2nd *m*) Bronwyn Heather, *b* 1971. —— Sheila Jean, *b* 1927: *m* 1957, James Florance Turnour, of 58 Union St, E Brighton, Vict, Aust, and has issue living, Keppel John, *b* 1959, — Quentin David, *b* 1962, — Louise Marguerite, *b* 1958.

Grandchildren of late Edward Innes (*b* 1827), next brother of *de jure* 9th baronet:—
Issue of late Edward George Innes, *b* 1854, *d* 1904: *m* 1st, 1880, Jane, who *d* 1884, da of Philip Ballantyne; 2ndly, 1886, Marjory, who *d* 1946, da of Jacob Christie:—
(By 2nd *m*) Adrian Arthur (48 Bayfield St, Bellerive, Tasmania), *b* 1900: *m* 1927, Daisy, da of Francis Calvert Smith, and has issue living, Roy Edward (Clifton Beach Rd, Sandford, Tasmania), *b* (Dec) 1927: *m* 1963, Shirley Esther, da of Victor Richardson Clements, and has issue living, Shane Edward *b* 1969, Kim Nyree *b* 1972, — George Calvert (1 Lanena St, Bellerive, Tasmania), *b* 1932: *m* 1965, Chou Seng, da of Thar Yu Mok, and has issue living, Andrew Gary *b* 1969, Trevor Craig *b* 1971. —— Ismay Anne, *b* 1898. *Residence* –

Issue of late William Innes, *b* 1859, *d* 1928: *m* 1887, Adelina Bianca Alexandrina, who *d* 1946, da of William Allsopp:—

Francis Allsopp, *b* 1888; Lieut-Com RNR; European War 1914-18 (Croix de Guerre with palms): *m* 1926, Marjorie Rolleston, da of William Tucker Pyke, and has issue living, Berowald Francis, *b* 1928, — William, *b* 1935. *Residence* – 61 Seaview Street, Balgowlah, Sydney, NS Wales. —— William Edward Allsopp, *b* 1893: *m* 1923, Lyla Alta, da of Frederick Charles Thomson-Brown, of Launceston, Tasmania, and has issue living, Desmond Erick, *b* 1926, — Patricia Joan, *b* 1925. —— Arthur Berowald, *b* 1899: *m* 1926, Irene Eva Eastman, and has issue living, Graeme Alastair, *b* 1932, — Darren Arthur, *b* 1936, — Janet Lucille, *b* 1930, — Sandra Ann, *b* 1938. —— Gordon Tulloh, *b* 1904: *m* 1931, Brienetta Grace, da of Leonard Harold O'Brien. —— Clothilde, *b* 1897. *Residence* – Hobart, Tasmania.

Grandchildren of late George Innes, yst brother of *de jure* 9th Bt, and of Edward Innes (*b* 1827) (ante):—
Issue of late George Peacock Innes, *b* 1863, *d* 1936: *m* 1893, Susanna Robina, da of Robert Mills:—
George Donald, *b* 1905; is Municipal Engineer at Miniwa: *m* 1932, Florence Elizabeth Younger. —— Myrtle Robina, *b* 1894. —— Elizabeth Stuart, *b* 1898; Emergency Ambulance Corps 1939-44. *Residence* – 56 Shirley Road, Wollstonecroft, Sydney, NS Wales.

Granddaughters of late Edward Henry Innes, Fleet Paymaster RN, son of Rev Dr James Innes, uncle of *de jure* 9th Bt:—
Issue of late Lt-Col George William Holt Innes, MBE, *b* 1900, *d* 1983: *m* 1931, Alexandra, who *d* 1977, da of Dunbar Marshall, of Natchez, Mississippi, USA:—
Vivien Holt, *b* 1932: *m* 1959, John Kennedy Wagstaff, of 52 Salmons Lane, Whyteleafe, Surrey CR3 0AN, and has issue living, Clarissa Christine, *b* 1960: *m* 1983, Phillip John Dann, of 1b Claremont Rd, Highgate, N6 5DR, and has issue living, Isabelle Alexandra *b* 1990, Eleanor Louise *b* 1993, — Martine Charis, *b* 1962: *m* 1st, 1986 (*m diss* 1990), Stephen Patrick Cotton; 2ndly, 1991, Lawrence Michael Biddle, of Flat 26 Sussex Mansions, 83 Old Brompton Rd, SW7 3LB, and has issue living (by 2nd *m*), Thomas Lawrence *b* 1993, Alexandra Grace *b* 1991, — Vanessa Jacynth, *b* 1971. —— Valerie Evelyn (16 Newark Rd, S Croydon, Surrey CR2 6HQ), *b* 1935: *m* 1958 (*m diss* 1978), Mervyn Russell Chute, and has issue living, Nigel Anthony, *b* 1960, — Rosalind Alexandra, *b* 1962.

This baronetcy was conferred on Sir Alexander Innes, of Coxton, MP for Moray (with remainder to heirs male whatsoever). The Coxton family is a yr branch of Innes of Balvenie, *cr* Bt 1628, descending from Patrick, in the Keam of Duffus, 5th son of Walter Innes of Innermarkie (*d ca* 1499). Sir Alexander Innes' direct line became ext with his gt-grandson, Sir David, 5th Bt, who *d* 1803. The baronetcy descended to Sir Alexander, gt-grandson of John, 1st of Inaltrie, yr brother of 1st Bt. On the death in 1886 of Sir George, 8th Bt, succession reverted to (Sir) Charles Innes, FRIBA, *de jure* 9th Bt, son of Edward Innes (*b* 1792) and 6th in descent from John, 3rd son of John Innes, 2nd of Coxton, and gt-uncle of 1st Bt. Sir Charles Kenneth Gordon, grandson of (Sir) Charles, was placed on the Roll of Baronets in 1973, as 11th Baronet of Coxton.

ISHAM (E) 1627, of Lamport, Northamptonshire.
(Name pronounced "Eye-shum")

I show, I sham not

Sir IAN VERE GYLES ISHAM, 13th *Baronet*, el son of late Lt-Col Vere Arthur Richard Isham, MC, el son of Arthur Charles Isham, only son of Rev Arthur Isham, yr son of Rev Henry Charles Isham, 5th son of 7th baronet; *b* 17 July 1923; *s* his kinsman, *Sir* GYLES, 1976; *ed* Eton, and Worcester Coll, Oxford; NW Europe 1944, BAOR 1945-47 as Capt Co of London Yeo; patron of one living.

𝕬rms – Gules, a fesse wavy and in chief three piles also wavy, points meeting in fesse argent. 𝕮rest – A demi-swan, wings displayed argent, beaked sable. 𝕸ottoes – "Ostendo non Ostento", and "On things transitory resteth no glory." *Residence* – 40 Turnpike Link, Croydon, Surrey, CR0 5NX. *Club* – Overseas.

BROTHER LIVING

NORMAN MURRAY CRAWFORD, OBE (5 Langton Way, Park Hill, Croydon, Surrey); *b* 28 Jan, 1930; *ed* Stowe, and Univ of Cape Town; BArch (Distn); RIBA; OBE (Civil) 1988: *m* 1956, Joan, da of late Leonard James Genet, of Umtali, Zimbabwe, and has issue living, Richard Leonard Vere (8 Fitzwilliam Rd, SW4 0DN), *b* 1958: *m* 1990, Julia Claire Mary, da of David Frost Pilkington, of 66 Granville Park West, Aughton, nr Ormskirk, Lancs, and has issue living, Angus David Vere *b* 26 Oct 1992, — Vere Murray Gyles (Hill Pasture, Broxted, Dunmow, Essex CM6 2B2), *b* 1960: *m* 1991, Lynne Janette, da of late Howard Warren Armishaw, of Alberta, Canada, and has issue living, Maximilliano Vere *b* 1991, Oscar Howard Vere *b* 1993, — Elizabeth Angela *b* 1957: *m* 1980, Richard Nigel Brayshaw.

The Isham family took their name from the village of Isham in Northamptonshire, where they were found holding land under William I. A cadet branch of the family was established at Pytchley in the 13th century, from whom the present family descend. Robert Isham of Pytchley was Escheator of Northamptonshire under Henry VI, and Solicitor to Elizabeth, Queen of Edward IV. Gyles Isham was MP for Peterborough twice in the reign of Queen Mary I. His younger brother, John, a prosperous Mercer, established himself at Lamport in 1560, and his grandson Sir John, High Sheriff of Northamptonshire, was created a baronet in 1627, having previously been knighted by James I. His son, Sir Justinian, a staunch Royalist, suffered severely for his loyalty, but became MP for Northamptonshire on the Restoration. Sir Justinian, the 4th baronet, MP for Northants, upon the landing of the Prince of Orange appeared in arms against James II at Nottingham. The 5th and 6th baronets were also MPs for Northamptonshire. Sir Gyles Isham, 12th Bt, FSA, was High Sheriff of Northants in 1958 and a Trustee of the National Portrait Gallery 1964-76.

ISHERWOOD (UK) 1921, of Raggleswood, Chislehurst, Kent (Extinct 1946)

Sir WILLIAM ISHERWOOD, 2nd and last *Baronet*.

DAUGHTERS LIVING OF SECOND BARONET

Annette Marie, *b* 1934: *m* 1956, J. D. Smyth, of 27 Bath Rd, Emsworth, Hants. —— Diane Joan, *b* 1936: *m* 1957, F. B. Green. *Residence* – Hever Gdns, Bickley, Kent.

WIDOW LIVING OF SECOND BARONET

IRENE JEANNE, da of C. Pittolo: *m* 1932, Sir William Isherwood, 2nd Bt, who *d* 1946, when the title became ext; 2ndly, 1947, David Stevenson Watt. *Residence* – 17 Henty Gdns, Chichester, W Sussex.

JACKSON (UK) 1815, of Arlsey, Bedfordshire

Sir ROBERT JACKSON, 7th *Baronet*, only son of late Maj Francis Gorham Jackson, RE, 2nd son of 4th Baronet; *b* 16 March 1910; *s* his cousin, Sir JOHN MONTRESOR, 1980; *ed* St George's Coll: *m* 1943, Maria Esther, da of Leon P. Casamayou, of Montevideo, Uruguay, and has had issue.

Arms – Argent, on a fesse between a goat's head couped in chief and a ship in full sail in base proper, a greyhound courant between two pheons or, within a bordure of the second charged with eight bezants. **Crest** – A goat's head couped argent guttée de sang, armed and bearded or, gorged with a collar gules charged with three bezants, from the collar a line reflexed of the third, the rings gold.
Residence – Santiago de Chile 1243, Montevideo, Uruguay.

DAUGHTERS LIVING AND DECEASED

Victoria Maria, *b* 1945; *d* 19—. —— Bertha Mary, *b* 1949.

DAUGHTER LIVING OF FIFTH BARONET

Bernice Evelyn Abrey, *b* 1917: *m* 1st, 1940, Wing-Com Patrick Edward Geoffrey Gunnell Connolly, RAF; 2ndly, 1954, Frederick John Ralph, and has issue living, (by 1st *m*) Richard Edward Geoffrey Gunnell, *b* 1942, — Penelope Ann, *b* 1941: *m* 1970, W. J. R. Govett, of 62 Glebe Place, SW3 5JB. *Residence* – Hawkswood, Stevens Crouch, Battle, Sussex.

COLLATERAL BRANCHES LIVING

Grandchildren of late Welby Charles Jackson, 2nd son of John Jackson, 2nd son of 1st baronet:—
Issue of late John Keith Jackson, *b* 1872, *d* 1957: *m* 1914, Anna Maria Bertha, who *d* 1953, da of —Arnold, of Freeling, South Australia:—
KEITH ARNOLD, *b* 24 April 1921: *m* 1950, Pauline Mona, da of B. P. Climo, of Wellington, New Zealand, and has issue living, Neil Keith, *b* 12 May 1952: *m* 1973, Sandra Whitehead, and has issue living, Stephen Keith *b* 27 Sept 1973, Paul Alan *b* 1976, — Colin Paul, *b* 1954: *m* 1976, Shirley Hair, — Bruce John *b* 1957, — Kenneth Grant, *b* 1961, — Claire Alison, *b* (twin) 1954: *m* 1979, Graham John Close, and has issue living, Jason John *b* 1980, Tyrell Dan *b* 1983. *Residence* – 6 Coast Rd, Wainuiomata, Lower Hutt, NZ. —— Noela Grace, *b* 1916: *m* 1945, Arthur Lambourn, of 16 Beaumont Av, Lower Hutt, NZ, and has issue living, Graham John *b* 1946: *m* 1968, Ngaire Johnson, and has issue living, Clynton Arthur *b* 1970, Suesan Barbara *b* 1968.
Issue of late William Alfred Jackson, *b* 1878, *d* 1965: *m* 1904, Emily, who *d* 1952, da of John Hale, formerly of Westport, NZ:—
Grace Irene, *b* 1906: *m* 1937, Stephen Frederick Louis Cooper, of Gladstone, Wairarapa, NZ, and has issue living, Stephen Jackson, *b* 1952. —— Elizabeth, *b* 1911: *m* 1937, Arthur David McKay, of 62B Essex St, Masterton, Wairarapa, NZ, and has issue living, Arthur Thomas, *b* 1937: *m* 1960, Jocelyn Celia Goodwin, and has issue living, David William, *b* 1961, Iain Thomas *b* 1967, Shona Margaret *b* 1963, — Rex David, *b* 1953: *m* 1975, Beverley Ann O'Dea, and has issue living, Andrew Thomas *b* 1985, Natasha Louise *b* 1982, Kate Amanda *b* 1990, — Colleen Mary, *b* 1941: *m* 1963, Philip Cotter, and has issue living, Kathryn Mary *b* 1964, Tania Elizabeth *b* 1965, Maria Louise *b* 1967, Julia Jane *b* 1971, — Marie Elizabeth, *b* 1943: *m* 1974, Maurice Doran, and has issue living, James Gerard *b* 1976, Richard John *b* 1979.
Issue of late Sidney Leybourne Jackson, *b* 1886, *d* 1974: *m* 1915, Daphne, who *d* 1948, da of William Halse, of Wellington, NZ:—
Peggy Elinor, *b* 1917: *m* 1941, Archibald Douglas Wallace, who *d* 1986, of 80a Te Mata Rd, Havelock North, Hawkes Bay, NZ, and has issue living, James Leybourne (Sundrum Woodbury, RD 21, Geraldine, NZ); LLB; *b* 1946: *m* 1973, Evelyn Wilder, 2nd da of Sir (Hugh) John Dyke Acland, KBE, of Mount Peel, Canterbury, NZ (*see* Acland, Bt, *cr* 1678, colls), and has issue living, James Ormond, *b* 1974, Antonia Acland, *b* 1977, Henrietta Harper *b* 1979, — Simon John Lewis (87 Clyde St, Island Bay, Wellington, NZ), *b* 1949: *m* 1st, 1978 (*m diss* 19—), Anne Braithwaite; 2ndly, 19—, Susan Patterson, and has living (by 2nd *m*), George *b* 1988, Henry *b* 1992, — Judith Margaret, *b* 1943: *m* 1964, Col Thomas Arthur Aldridge, of 48 Omahu Rd, Remuera, Auckland, NZ, and has issue living, Michael Douglas Arthur, *b* 1966, Patrick Leybourne Thomas *b* 1970, Louise Elizabeth *b* 1965.

Grandchildren of late Gordon Francis Welby Jackson, 4th and yst son of late Welby Charles Jackson (ante):—
Issue of late John Richard Jackson, *b* 1924, *d* 1987: *m* 1947, Leslie Kay, da of James McKay Heise, of Raetihi, NZ:—
Peter, *b* 1951: *m* 1991, Guadalupe Rosales, and has issue living, Igor, *b* 1991. —— John Terence (59 Glen Rd, Kelburn, Wellington 5, NZ), *b* 1956: *m* 1989, Toni, da of Ernest Cornish Cosgrove, of Wellington, NZ, and has issue living, Timothy Richard *b* 1989, — Lillian Jane, *b* 1991. —— James, *b* 1964; has issue living (by Désirée Marie Jones), Hayden Jesse Jones JACKSON, *b* 1991, — Mitchell Lee Jones JACKSON, *b* 1993. —— Margaret Gail, *b* 1949: *m* 1968 (*m diss* 1994), Wong Teck

Sing, of Melbourne, Victoria, Australia, and has issue living, Geoffrey Peter Dow, *b* 1968, — Conrad Dow, *b* 1972, — Vera Dow, *b* 1971. ———— Kathleen, *b* 1954.

    Descendants (if any) of late Hugh Whiteman Jackson (3rd son of John Jackson — ante), *b* 1842, *d* 1929: *m* 1869 Charlotte, who *d* 1929, da of A. W. Hayward, of Wellington New Zealand, and had issue, sons and das.

    Grandchildren of late Murray James Hamilton Jackson, 4th son of John Jackson (ante):—
    Issue of late William John Jackson, *b* 1895, *d* 1980: *m* 1924, Ella, da of Robert Guppy:—
Alan Hamilton (8 Hunter Place, New Plymouth, NZ), *b* 1924: *m* 1949, Lynn, da of late Arthur Prichard Lindsay, of 106 Spring St, Tauranga, NZ, and has issue living, William Lindsay, *b* 1956, — Murray Grant, *b* 1959, — Anne Agnes, *b* 1953. ———— Robert John, *b* 1939: *m* 1962, Ruth Wynitta Lamb, and has issue living, Stephen John, *b* 1965, — Andrew Phillip, *b* 1969, — Brenden James, *b* 1970, — Pauline Ruth, *b* 1963: *m* 1989, Craig Robert Whiting. ———— Esme Ruth, *b* 1925. ———— Ella Marion, *b* 1927: *m* 1950, Cecil Edmund Rawhiti Smith, of 20 Bracken Av, Epsom, Auckland 3, NZ, and has issue living, Cecil David, *b* 1951, — Bruce Edmund, *b* 1953, — Peter Raymond, *b* 1954, — Paul Barry, *b* 1959, — Rodney John, *b* 1964, — Margaret Ann, *b* 1957, — Beverley Joy, *b* 1962. ———— Evelyn Isabel, *b* 1931: *m* 1956, Ashley Gordon Howan, of 7 Hunter Place, New Plymouth, NZ, and has issue living, Lance, *b* 1959, — Philip, *b* 19—, — Cherry, *b* 1957.
    Issue of late Murray Spearink Jackson, *b* (twin) 1895, *d* 197-: *m* 1921, Mary (McLeod's Bay, Whangarei, NZ), da of William Robinson:—
David Murray James, *b* 1921; Salvation Army Offr: *m* 1950, Olive, da of Reginald Frederick Wilde, of Yeovil, Som, and has issue living, Paul Murray *b* 1951, — Verna Elizabeth, *b* 1954. ———— Edmund Robinson (Apotic Rd, RD5, Hikurangi, Whangarei, NZ), *b* 1923; sheep farmer: *m* 1st, 1945, Viola Thelma, who *d* 1966, da of late Hans Ries, of Pohokura, NZ; 2ndly, 1968, Nancy Elizabeth Pyle, and has issue living, (by 1st *m*) Peter Edmund, *b* 1948, — Geoffrey Kendal, *b* 1952, — Raewyn Ada, *b* 1947: *m* 1968, Alan Cole, of Kaitaia, NZ, and has issue living, Ruth *b* 1969, — Linda Mary, *b* 1954, — (by 2nd *m*) Russell Joseph, *b* 1970. ———— Harold Stuart, *b* 1926: *m* 1961, Eleni, da of Savvas Michalis, of Dhymes, Limmasol, Cyprus, and has issue living, Andros Vassilis, *b* 1962, — Nikos Manolis, *b* 1963. ———— Graham George, *b* 1935; MA, MD; lecturer in anthropology, Auckland Univ.

    Granddaughter of late Judge Elphinstone Jackson, el son of Judge Welby Brown Jackson, 3rd son of 1st baronet:—
    Issue of late Mountstuart Hungerford Jackson, *b* 1860, *d* 1925: *m* 1886, Ethel Beatrice who *d* 1954, da of David Cowrie, a Member of Viceroy of India's Council:—
Dorothy Hungerford, *b* 1890: *m* 1922, Col Spence Daer Reid, late RAMC, who *d* 1954, and has issue living, Peter Daer, CB (The Border House, Cholderton, nr Salisbury, Wilts), *b* 1925; Maj-Gen (ret); CB 1981: *m* 1956, Olive Jean Courtenay, da of W Courtenay Snook, of River Cottage, Yeolmbridge, Cornwall, and has issue living, Duncan Andrew Daer *b* 1959, — Ian Daer (1 Cedar Cres, Woy Woy, NSW), *b* 1927; *ed* Edinburgh Univ (MB and ChB 1950): *m* 1956, Olive Jean Courtenay, da of W Courtenay Snook, of River Cottage, Yeolmbridge, Cornwall, and has issue living, Hamish Ian Daer *b* 1957, Angus Courtenay Daer *b* 1962, Heather Susan Daer *b* 1959, — Joan Pamela Daer, *b* 1924: *m* 1956, Martin Vlaanderen, of Eigen Haard, Piccadilly Rd, Crafters 5152 S Aust, and has issue living, Martin Richard *b* 1957, Robert Laurens *b* 1964, Rosemarie Anne *b* 1958, Fiona Veronica *b* 1960.

    Grandchildren of late Mountstuart Hungerford Jackson (ante):—
    Issue of late Cecil Hungerford Jackson, *b* 1887, *d* 1978: *m* 1916, Marian Blanche, who *d* 1971, da of late Cdr Francis S. Wheeler, RN:—
Audrey Madeline Hungerford, *b* 1920: *m* 1944, Robert Douglas Howe, MBE, SQA, ICS, of The Manor House, Martock, Som, and has issue living, Peter Mountstuart (41 Drax Av, Wimbledon, SW19), *b* 1948: *m* 1983, Anne-Marie Boys, and has issue living, Michael Mountstuart *b* 1984, — Veronica Joan, *b* 1946: *m* 1968, James William Goodford, of The Old Rectory, Chilton Cantelo, Yeovil, Som, and has issue living, Andrew Christopher John *b* 1970, Richard Michael James *b* 1972, Simon Charles Jasper *b* 1979, Georgina Helen Jane *b* 1975.
    Issue of late Col Laurence Hungerford Jackson, IA, *b* 1889, *d* 1985: *m* 1919, Freda Isabella Mary, who *d* 1978, da of Col Edmund Henry Dalgety, CB:—
Peter Hungerford (Hadstock Hall, Hadstock, Cambridge), *b* 1925; is Maj RE (ret): *m* 1953, Joyce Thomasina, da of Lt-Col V.H. Wells-Cole, late KOYLI, and has issue living, Amelia Mary Hungerford (*Hon Mrs James R. V. Brandon*), *b* 1955: *m* 1991, Hon James Roderick Vivian Brandon, eldest son of Baron Brandon of Oakbrook (Life Baron), — Catherine Ann Hungerford, *b* 1957.

    Grandchildren of late Maj-Gen George D'Aguilar Jackson, 4th son of Judge Welby Brown Jackson (ante):—
    Issue of late Harold Frederick D'Aguilar Jackson, *b* 1877, *d* 1942: *m* 1903, Anna Lillian, widow of Count von Stadie, of Kœnigsberg, Germany:—
William Douglas D'Aguilar, *b* 1904; *ed* California Institute of Technology, and at S California Univ; is Col US Army, and Ch of Research and Development Div, Office of QMG, US Army; has Legion of Merit with Oak Leaf Cluster: *m* 1933, Margaret Williams, and has issue living, Margaret Anne, *b* 1938, — Susan, *b* 1940. ———— Hyacinthe Lilian D'Aguilar, *b* 1908; *ed* S California Univ: *m* 1933, John Machell Procter, who *d* 1941.

The 1st baronet, an East Indian Co Director, sat as MP for Dover, and the 3rd baronet was murdered at Lucknow in 1857 during the Indian Mutiny.

JACKSON (UK) 1869, of The Manor House, Birkenhead

Boldly, faithfully, successfully

Sir (WILLIAM) THOMAS JACKSON, 8th *Baronet*; *b* 12 Oct 1927; *s* his father, *Sir* WILLIAM, 1985; *ed* Mill Hill, and RAC Cirencester: *m* 1951, Gilian Malise, elder da of late Col John William Stobart, MBE, of Farlam Ghyll, Brampton, Cumbria, and has issue.

Arms – Azure, a fesse between two goat's heads couped in chief and a fleur-de-lis in base argent, two flaunches of the last. **Crest** – On a ragged staff fessewise sable, a goat's head couped argent, semée of trefoils vert.
Residence – Fell End, Mungrisdale, Penrith, Cumbria CA11 0XR.

SONS LIVING

(WILLIAM) ROLAND CEDRIC (Summer Hill, 14 Glebe Rd, Welwyn, Herts AL6 9PB), *b* 9 Jan 1954; *ed* Wycliffe Coll, St Peter's Coll, Oxford (MA), and Exeter Coll, Oxford (DPhil): *m* 1977, Nicola Mary, MA, DPhil, yr da of Prof Peter Reginald Davis, MB, BS, PhD, FRCS, of Polvean, St Mawes, Cornwall, and has issue living, Adam William Roland, *b* 19 May 1982, — James Anthony Foljambe, *b* 1984, — Oliver Thomas Peter, *b* 1990. —— Piers Anthony (26 Astral Av, The Drive, Hipperholme, Brighouse, W Yorks HX3 8NN), *b* 1955; *ed* Keswick Sch, and Derwent Coll, York (BA): *m* 1980, Anne-Marie, elder da of late Patrick Quigg, of Norfolk Dr, Belfast, and has issue living, Carl Patrick Thomas, *b* 1981, — Luke Dominic Gregory, *b* 1985, — Ben Philip Joseph, *b* 1988. —— Jolyon Thomas, *b* 1957; *ed* Keswick Sch, and RMA Sandhurst; Lt-Col RGJ: *m* 1986, Serena A., elder da of David Howell, of Albert Bridge Rd, SW11, and has issue living, Thomas Sebastian Esme, *b* 1993, — Alicia Sophie, *b* 1989.

SISTER LIVING

Ankaret Tarn, *b* 1934: *m* 1955, Maj Timothy Richard Riley, DL, The Rifle Bde, of Burbank House, Blencow, Penrith, Cumbria, and has issue living, Nicola Ankaret Katherine, *b* 1959, — Antonia Elizabeth Tarn, *b* 1962: *m* 1992, Michael Reid, of 7 New Cottages, Snailwell, Newmarket, Suffolk, and has issue living, Jennifer Tarn *b* 1993.

DAUGHTERS LIVING OF SIXTH BARONET

Angela Mary Mather (Sansome's Farm House, Ellen's Green, Rudgwick, Sussex), *b* 1925: *m* 1947, Francis Ambrose More O'Ferrall, who *d* 1976, and has issue living, Susan Angela (*Baroness Beaverbrook*), *b* 1948: *m* 1974, 3rd Baron Beaverbrook, — Theresa Mary (*Hon Mrs Wentworth P. I. Beaumont*), *b* 1950: *m* 1975, Hon Wentworth Peter Ismay Beaumont, el son of 3rd Viscount Allendale, — Emma Rose, *b* 1956. —— Elizabeth Georgiana Mather (*Viscountess Cowdray*), *b* 1926: *m* 1953, as his 2nd wife, 3rd Viscount Cowdray. —— Sarah Gillian Mather (36 Cambridge Rd, SW11), *b* 1929: *m* 1955, Henry Lester Louis Morriss, who *d* 1963, and has had issue, James Nicholas, *b* 1958; *d* 1993, in Thailand, — Annabel Ruth (*Lady Fairfax of Cameron*), *b* 1957: *m* 1982, 14th Lord Fairfax of Cameron, — Henrietta Sarah, *b* 1961: *m* 1988, James W. Petit, and has issue living, William *b* 19—, Eliza Mary Lara *b* 1991.

WIDOW LIVING OF SEVENTH BARONET

INA (*Ina, Lady Jackson*), da of James Leonard Joyce, FRCS: *m* 1966, as his 2nd wife, Sir William Jackson, 7th Bt, who *d* 1985. *Residence* – 8 West View, Gelt Rd, Brampton, Cumbria, CA8 1QC.

COLLATERAL BRANCHES LIVING

Issue of late Capt Henry Mather-Jackson, 9th Lancers, el son of 3rd baronet, *b* 1894, *d* 1928: *m* 1920, Florence, who *d* 1980, da of late Granville W. Garth, of New York:—
Rosemary, *b* 1924: *m* 1949, Stanley Joe Legouix, and has issue living, Geoffrey John Henry, *b* 1954, — Susan Yvette, *b* 1950. *Residence* – 2 Orchard Green, Chilton Foliat, Hungerford, Berks.

Grandson of late Rt Hon Frederick Huth JACKSON (infra):—
Issue of late Frederick Huth Jackson, *b* 1896, *d* 1966: *m* 1st, 1920 (*m diss* 1929), Helen, da of late Prof Sir Paul Vinogradoff, LLD; 2ndly, 1940, Frederica Frances, who *d* 1975, da of Duncan Tucker, of Burnham-on-Sea:—
(By 1st *m*) Patrick Huth, *b* 1922.

Granddaughters of late Lt-Col Henry Humphrey Jackson, OBE, MC, TD (infra):—
Issue of late Lt-Col Thomas Geoffrey Henry Jackson, R Green Jackets, *b* 1926, *d* 1979: *m* 1957, Judith Margaret (who *m* 2ndly, 1981, Colin MacPherson), da of Capt Henry Mangles Denham, CMG, RN:—
Catherine Margaret, *b* 1958: *m* 1983, Howard William Arthur Palmer, son of W. A. Palmer, of Bussock Wood, Newbury, Berks, and has issue living, Thomas Howard, *b* 1988, — Laura Margaret, *b* 1984, — Emily Rose, *b* 1986, — Harriet Bridget *b* 1991. —— Victoria Georgina, *b* 1960: *m* 1987, David Mark Stewart, and has issue (*see* E Galloway, colls). —— Louise Sarah, *b* 1966. —— Joanna Henrietta, *b* (twin) 1966.

Grandchildren of late Brig-Gen Geoffrey Meinertzhagen JACKSON, TD (infra):—
Issue of late Lt-Col Henry Humphrey Jackson, OBE, MC, TD, *b* 1895, *d* 1969: *m* 1924, Georgina, who *d* 1974, da of H. Howard Middleditch, JP, of Tamworth House, Duffield:—
John Guy Carmichael (Copse Hill, Osmaston, Ashbourne, Derbys DE6 1LU), *b* 1931; *ed* Harrow; JP and DL Derbys: *m* 1973, Flora Mary Margaret, da of Lt-Col William Herbert Olivier, TD, DL, and has issue living, Georgina Mary, *b* 1974, — Ann Margaret, *b* 1976. —— Ann Georgina Laird, *b* 1928: *m* 1952, Maj Colville Graham Wemyss, Rifle Bde, of West Lodge, Upham, Southampton SO31 1JP, son of late Gen Sir Henry Colville Barclay Wemyss, KCB, KBE, DSO, MC, and has issue living, Henry Graham, *b* 1956; *ed* Wellington Coll: *m* 1984, Diana Bridget, da of R. K. Selby, of Halsemere, Surrey, and has issue living, Nicholas Henry, *b* 1988, Eleanor Rose *b* 1986, — Alice Caroline, *b* 1953: *m* 1986, Stephen Walter Hubert Lacey, son of late David Lacey, of Highgate, London, and has issue living, William David *b* 1990, Alice Megan *b* 1987.
Issue of late Capt Guy Rolf Jackson, MC, *b* 1896, *d* 1966: *m* 1937, Shelagh (St Andrews, Higham, Derby), da of late A. Ignatius Tolhurst, of Gravesend:—
Geoffrey Laird (Plas Newydd, Llanfair DC, Ruthin, Clwyd LL15 2EP), *b* 1940; *ed* Ampleforth, and RAC, Cirencester: *m* 1963, Ruth Clare, JP, da of D. F. N. Campion, of Okirai, Wanganui, NZ, and has issue living, Jonathan Guy Campion, *b* 1964: *m* 1990, Mary Rose M., only da of late Col Peter Arkwright, OBE, — Charles Desmond Bertram, *b* 1965, — Rupert James

Humphrey, *b* 1968, — William David Geoffrey, *b* 1970. —— Robert Humphrey (14 Dewhurst Rd, W14 0ET), *b* 1943; *ed* Ampleforth, and Brasenose Coll, Oxford: *m* 1971, Margaret Letitia, da of James Matthew Barrie, of Polruan, Cornwall, and has issue living, Guy Nicholas Barrie, *b* 1975, — David Geoffrey Barrie, *b* 1978. —— Jane Mary, *b* 1938.

     Granddaughters of late Thomas Hughes Jackson (*b* 1834), 3rd son of 1st baronet:—
     Issue of late Rt Hon Frederick Huth JACKSON, *b* 1863, *d* 1921: *m* 1895, Clara Annabel Caroline, who *d* 1944, da of late Rt Hon Sir Mountstuart Elphinstone Grant-Duff, GCSI, CIE, FRS, of 11 Chelsea Embankment, SW, and Lexden Park, Colchester:—
Anne Marie Huth (*Hon Mrs Christopher E. Fremantle*), *b* 1909; *ed* Cheltenham Ladies' Coll, and Lady Margaret Hall, Oxford (MA); *m* 1930, Hon Christopher Evelyn Fremantle (*see* B Cottesloe). *Residence* – 252 East 78th St, New York 10021, USA.
     Issue of late Brig-Gen Geoffrey Meinertzhagen JACKSON, TD, *b* 1869, *d* 1946: *m* 1893, Jessie Cowper Coles, who *d* 1945, da of late Henry Hyndman Laird, of Birkenhead:—
(Elizabeth) Bridget Huth (Mount Hall, Llanfair Caereinion, Powys) *b* 1909; formerly Controller ATS.
     Issue of late Thomas Hughes JACKSON, *b* 1872, *d* 1926: *m* 1910, Eileen, who *d* 1980, da of late Edward Devery, of Gisborne, New Zealand:—
Hermine Catherine, *b* 1911: *m* 1939, George Henry Lloyd Davies, and has issue living, Thomas Hughes Lloyd (20 Foster Cres, Belmont, Lower Hutt, NZ), *b* 1942: *m* 1966 (*m diss* 1986), Anne Mary, da of N. J. McHugh, of Lower Hutt, NZ, and has issue living, Guy William Lloyd, *b* 1972, Caroline Jane Lloyd *b* 1975, — David William Lloyd, VRD, *b* 1947: Lt RNZNVR: *m* 1970, Alison Margaret, da of Prof D. A. Kidd, of Christchurch, NZ, and has issue living, Huw Alexander *b* 1982, Bronwen Sara Lloyd *b* 1973, Megan Kate Lloyd, *b* 1975, Edwina Mair *b* 1978, — Susan Hermine Lloyd (1 St Andrews Grove, Lower Hutt, NZ), *b* 1948: *m* 1974, Wilhelmus Julicher, of Swalmen, Netherlands, and has issue living, Justin Peter Lloyd *b* 1979, Nikki Catherine Lloyd *b* 1977. *Residence* – 1 St Andrews Grove, Lower Hutt, NZ. —— Barbara Eileen Marian, *b* 1918: *m* 1947, Lt Thomas Joseph Bourke RNZNVR, who *d* 1987, and has issue living, Gerard Thomas Hughes (Ratanui, 92 Waterloo Rd, Lower Hutt, NZ), *b* 1948: *m* 1974, Joy Patricia, da of R. H. Matthews, JP, of Otoka, Waipukurau, Hawkes Bay, NZ, and has issue living, James Thomas Henry *b* 1976, Amanda Joy *b* 1978, Hannah Kathryn *b* 1980, — John Patrick, *b* 1955. *Residence* – 99 Waterloo Rd, Lower Hutt, NZ.

Sir William Jackson, 1st Bt, son of Peter Jackson of Warrington, Surg, by his wife, Sarah, only da of Henry Mather of Warrington, was MP (*L*), Newcastle-under-Lyne 1847-65 and N Derbys 1865-68. The 3rd baronet, Lord Lieut of Mon, assumed in 1886 the additional surname of Mather.

JACKSON (UK) 1902, of Stansted House, Stansted, Essex.

Aut mors aut victoria

Either death or victory

Sir MICHAEL ROLAND JACKSON, 5th *Baronet*; *b* 20 April 1919; *s* his father, *Sir* (WALTER DAVID) RUSSELL, 1956; *ed* Stowe, and Clare Coll, Camb (MA); formerly Fl Lt RAFVR Chartered Engineer (MIEE, FIQA) (ret): *m* 1st, 1942 (*m diss* 1969), (Hilda) Margaret, da of late Cecil George Herbert Richardson, CBE; 2ndly, 1969, Hazel Mary, da of late Ernest Harold Edwards, and has issue by 1st *m*.

𝖆rms – Ermine, on a pile azure, between two fountains proper, a sheldrake or. 𝕮rest – On a fountain proper a sheldrake or.
Residence – Jolliffe's House, Stour Row, Shaftesbury, Dorset SP7 0QW.

SON LIVING (By 1st marriage)

THOMAS ST FELIX, *b* 27 Sept 1946, *ed* Stowe, and Southampton Univ (BA Hons); Man Dir Billington Jackson Advertising Ltd: *m* 1980, Georgina Victoria, da of George Harold Malcolm Scatliff, of Springlands Farm, Wineham, Sussex, and has issue, Lucy Harriet *b* 1982, — Charlotte Dare, *b* 1986. *Residence* – 70 Marryat Rd, Wimbledon SW19 5BN.

DAUGHTER LIVING (By 1st marriage)

Sally Ann, *b* 1944.

DAUGHTER LIVING OF SECOND BARONET

Nancy Amelia, *b* 1924: *m* 1948, Michael John Bowman-Vaughan, and has issue living, Michael Thomas, *b* 1959, — Annabel Leslie, *b* 1949, — Juliet Euphrosyne, *b* 1951, — Venetia Mary, *b* 1954. *Residence* – 9 Cope Place, W8.

DAUGHTERS LIVING OF THIRD BARONET

Dawn Nesta (Farthing Cottage, Gun Hill, Heathfield, Sussex), *b* 1909. —— Joyce Katherine (The Dower House, Headbourne Worthy, Winchester SO23 7JG), *b* 1910: *m* 1937 (*m diss* 1954), Lt-Col John Ralph Walker, and has had issue, Gay, *b* 1941, *d* 1986. —— Meryl Julian (6 Manor Gate, St John's Av, Putney, SW15), *b* (twin) 1910: *m* 1939, Herbert Sharpe Currie, who *d* 1964, and has issue living, Julian David Sharpe, *b* 1944, — Caroline Joyce, *b* 1941. —— Daphne Myddelton (Garden Hill Cottage, Steep, Petersfield, Hants), *b* 1914: *m* 1st, 1939, Sqdn Ldr Frederick U. Hollins, AFC, RAFVR, who was *ka* 1942; 2ndly, 1948, Maj Malcolm Comrie Gray, Worcestershire Regt, and has issue living, (by 1st *m*) Sarah Daphne, *b* 1941, — (by 2nd *m*) Fiona Catherine, *b* 1949.

The 1st baronet, Sir Thomas, was Chm and Director (sometime Ch Manager) of Hong Kong and Shanghai Bank, Hong Kong. The 2nd baronet, Brig-Gen Thomas Dare Jackson, DSO, MVO, late King's Own Roy Regt, was Assist Mil Sec to Gov of Gibraltar 1910-14, and served in S African War 1901-2 and European War 1914-17.

JACKSON (UK)1913, of Eagle House, Wimbledon, Surrey

Sir NICHOLAS FANE ST GEORGE JACKSON, 3rd *Baronet*; *b* 4 Sept 1934; *s* his father, *Sir* HUGH NICHOLAS, 1979; *ed* Radley, Wadham Coll, Oxford, and Royal Academy of Music; Organist, Composer and Harpsichordist; Member of Court of Drapers' Co (Junior Warden 1985, Warden 1993); Dir Concertante of London, St David's Cathedral Bach Festival, and Santes Creus Festival, Spain; Organist at St Anne's Ch, Soho 1963-71, and St James's Piccadilly 1971-74, St Lawrence Jewry-next-Guildhall 1974-77 and of St David's Cathedral 1977-84; annual tours of Spain 1979-89; Recitals and Broadcasts in Berlin 1967, Recitals in Paris 1972, and 1975, and USA 1975-88, etc: *m* 1st, 1961 (*m diss* 1968), Jennifer Ann, da of F. A. Squire, of 8 Marylebone St, W1; 2ndly, 1972, Nadia Françoise Genevieve, da of Georges Michard, Director de la Maison de la Culture, St Etienne, 42, France, and has issue by 2nd *m*.

Arms – Argent, a greyhound courant ermines, between three eagles' heads erased sable. **Crest** – A demi-horse argent, guttée de sang, maned and hoofed sable.
Residence – 42 Hereford Rd, W2 5AT. *Club* – Bath.

SON LIVING *(By 2nd marriage)*

THOMAS GRAHAM ST GEORGE, *b* 5 Oct 1980.

SISTER LIVING

Louise Loftus, *b* 1946.

WIDOW LIVING OF SECOND BARONET

VIOLET MARGUERITE LOFTUS (*Violet, Lady Jackson*) (38 Oakley St, SW3), da of late Loftus St George (*see* St George, Bt, colls): *m* 1931, Sir Hugh Nicholas Jackson, 2nd Bt, who *d* 1979.
Sir Thomas Graham Jackson, RA, 1st Bt was an architect who designed many churches, private houses, and scholastic and public buildings in Oxford and Cambridge and elsewhere, and was author of many books on architecture.

Mather-Jackson, see Jackson, Bt, cr 1869.

JAFFRAY (UK) 1892, of Skilts, Studley, Warwickshire

Sir WILLIAM OTHO JAFFRAY, 5th *Baronet*; *b* 1 Nov 1951; *s* his father, *Col Sir* WILLIAM EDMUND, TD, 1953; *ed* Eton: *m* 1981, Cynthia Ross (*née* Corrington), da of Mrs William M. Geering, of Montreal, Quebec, Canada, and has issue.

Arms – Argent, three pallets sable on a fesse cotised gules, four mullets or. **Crest** – On a mound in front of two palm branches in orle vert, a mullet as in the arms.
Residence – The Manor House, Priors Dean, Petersfield, Hants GU32 1BP.

SONS LIVING

NICHOLAS GORDON ALEXANDER, *b* 18 Oct 1982. —— Jack Henry William, *b* 1987. —— William Lawrence Paget, *b* 1990.

Post nublia Phoebus
After clouds sunshine

DAUGHTER LIVING

Alexandra Marina Ross, *b* 1984.

WIDOW LIVING OF FOURTH BARONET

ANNE (*Anne, Lady Jaffray*), only da of late Capt John Otho Paget, MC, of Thorpe Satchville Hall, nr Melton Mowbray, and formerly wife of late Sir John Godfrey Worsley-Taylor, 3rd Bt, a Member of Hants Co Council 1964-80: *m* 1950, as his second wife, Col Sir William Edmund Jaffray, TD, DL, 4th Bt, who *d* 1953. *Residence* – Flat A9, Sloane Avenue Mansions, Sloane Av, SW3 3JF.

The 1st baronet, Sir John, founded the Jaffray Chronic Hospital, Birmingham, and was many years connected with the *Birmingham Daily Post*. The 3rd baronet, Sir John Jaffray (Lt Worcestershire Yeo), was *ka* 1916. The 4th baronet, Sir William Edmund Jaffray, TD, was Col (ret) late Comdg Warwickshire Yeo and a JP and DL for Warwickshire.

JAMES (UK) 1823, of Dublin (Extinct 1979)

Sir FULLARTON JAMES, CBE, 6th and last *Baronet*.

COLLATERAL BRANCH LIVING

Granddaughters of late Charles Pierce Rowley James, 2nd son of Charles Henry James, 4th son of 1st baronet:—
Issue of late Rowley Kingston James, *b* 1901, *d* 1938: *m* 1926, Vera Léontine, who *d* 1983, da of Arnold Fatio Bideleux:—
Elizabeth Virginia, *b* 1928: *m* 1953, William John Hindmoor Youdale, of St Martin, Mougins, France, 06, and has had issue, James Robert, *b* 1954: *m* 1982, Alicia, da of Julian Vasquez, of Glendale, California, USA, — Peter William, *b* 1958, — Frederick Michael, *b* 1969, — Angela Jane, *b* 1956; *(dec)*. ——— Sheila Margaret, *b* 1931: *m* 1955, Nigel Henry Whitfeld, of 50 Parkstone Av, Parkstone, Dorset, and has issue living, Nicholas Rowley, *b* 1958, — Toby Martin, *b* 1959, — Lisa Gabrielle, *b* 1966. ——— Patricia Mary *b* 1933.
This family came originally from Somersetshire. Thomas, — whose father, Capt Thomas James, undertook, by the command of Charles I, a voyage to discover the north-west passage, — sold his estates in Somersetshire, went to Ireland, as an officer in Cromwell's army at the time of the Rebellion, and eventually settled in King's County. The 1st baronet, Sir John Kingston, KB, was Lord Mayor of Dublin 1821-2 and 1840-41, and the 2nd baronet, as el son of a baronet, received knighthood 1854. The 6th baronet, Sir Fullarton, CBE, Ch Constable of Radnorshire and Northumberland, *d* 1955, when the baronetcy became Dormant. The last heir Mr Gerard Bowes Kingston James *d* 1979.

Jamsetjee Jejeebhoy, see Jejeebhoy.

JARDINE (NS) 1672, of Applegirth, Dumfriesshire

Beware; I am present!

Sir ALEXANDER MAULE JARDINE OF APPLEGIRTH, 12th *Baronet*; *b* 24 Aug 1947; *s* his father, *Col Sir* WILLIAM EDWARD, OBE, TD, 1986; 23rd Chief of Clan Jardine; *ed* Gordonstoun; a Member of Queen's Body Guard for Scotland (Royal Company of Archers): *m* 1982, Mary Beatrice, only da of late Hon John Michael Inigo Cross (*see* V Cross), and has issue.

Arms – Argent, a saltire and chief gules, the last charged with three mullets of the field pierced of the second. **Crest** – A spur-rowel of six points argent. **Supporters** – *Dexter*, a horse at liberty proper; *sinister*, a man in armour having a scimitar at his side proper.
Residence – Ash House, Thwaites, Millom, Cumbria LA18 5HY.

SONS LIVING

WILLIAM MURRAY, yr of Applegirth, *b* 4 July 1984. ——— John Alexander Cross, *b* 1991.

DAUGHTERS LIVING

Kirsty Sybil, *b* 1986. ——— Jean Maule, *b* 1988.

BROTHER LIVING

William (Driftway Cottage, Dullingham Ley, Newmarket, Suffolk), *b* 1952; *ed* Sedbergh.

AUNT LIVING (*Daughter of 10th baronet*)

Christian Maule: *m* 1940, Lieut-Col Charles Patrick Anderson, Argyll and Sutherland Highlanders, and has issue living, Charles Adair (Ravensheugh, Selkirk), *b* 1946: *m* 1973, Patiénce, da of Joseph Crewdson Howard, and has issue living, Lewis Adair *b* 1978, Ralph Oliver *b* 1985, Alice Selby *b* 1976, — Roderick William (Blantyre, Lenox, Mass, USA), *b* 1950: *m* 1983, Evelyne Corbier, — Andrena Christian, *b* 1943: *m* 1969, Col Alastair Scott-Elliot, Argyll & Sutherland Highrs, of Shorelands, Kippen, Stirlingshire, and has issue living, Robin James *b* 1970, Simon Charles *b* 1972, — Araminta Patricia, *b* (twin) 1950: *m* 1985, Peter John Hall, of 35 Elk Point, Durango, Col, USA. *Residence* – Ulva Ferry, I of Mull, Argyllshire.

WIDOW LIVING OF ELEVENTH BARONET

ANN GRAHAM MAITLAND (*Ann, Lady Jardine of Applegirth*), da of late Lt-Col Claud Archibald Scott Maitland, Gordon Highlanders, of Dundrennan and Cumstoun, Stewartry of Kirkcudbright: *m* 1944, Sir William Edward Jardine of Applegirth, 11th Bt, OBE, TD, who *d* 1986. *Residence* – Little Dyke, Dalton, Lockerbie, Dumfriesshire.

COLLATERAL BRANCHES LIVING

Granddaughter of late Rev Charles John Jardine (*infra*):—
Issue of late Edward William Ratcliff Jardine, *b* 1872; *d* 19—: *m* 1910, May Janet, da of Capt J. Hubby, of El Toro, California, USA:—
Dorothea Twining, *b* 1911. *Residence* –

Issue of late Rev Charles John Jardine, 3rd son of 7th baronet, *b* 1839, *d* 1917, *m* 1870, Martha, who *d* 1918, el da of late Edward Twining, MRCS, of Walthamstow:—

Peter St John, b 1879: m 1919, Monica Maud, da of Capt Leonard Head, E Lancashire Regt, and has issue living, Piers Leonard, b 1921. —— Margaret Dorcas Mary: m 1901, Frank Fullerton Dyas, and has issue living, Maxwell Wing, b 1902.

Grandchildren of late Frank Lascelles Jardine, el son of Capt John Jardine, 4th son of 6th baronet:—
Issue of late Bertie Bootle Arthur Lascelles Jardine, b 1884, d 1973: m 1919, Bessie Duffy, who d 1966:—
Marie Dempster Lascelles, b 1920: m 19—. —— Elizabeth Margaret Lascelles, b 1927: m 19—, Ronald Williamson, of 22 Mainsail St, Marlin Waters, Gold Coast, Qld, Aust 4223, and has issue living.

Granddaughter of late Capt John Jardine (ante):—
Issue of late Frank Lascelles Jardine, b 1841, d 1919: m 1873, Sana Solia, who d 1923, niece of Malietoa, King of Samoa:—
Elizabeth Hamilton Sana Lascelles (18 Gotha St, Cleveland, Brisbane, Qld, Aust 4163), b 1895: m 1919, Maj Charles Richard Sheldon, who was k (together with his only son, Cholmondeley Charles Lennox) as a Japanese Prisoner of War 1942, and has issue living, Betty Pamela, b 1920: m 1942, Thomas Ivy, of c/o 18 Gotha St, Cleveland, Qld 4163, and has issue living.
Issue of late John Robert Jardine, b 1847, d 1911: m 1883, Elizabeth Catherine, 2nd da of Hon Thomas Lodge Murray-Prior, of Maroon, Logan River, Queensland, MLC and sometime Postmaster-Gen of Queensland:—
Francis Alexander Lascelles, b 1893; 1914-18 war (wounded): m 1924, Madge Dorothy Blackman, of Brisbane, and has issue living, Murray Hugh Lascelles, b 1925: m 1950, Alma Glenise Byrne, and has issue living, Jan Frances Lascelles b 1952, Mary Elizabeth Lascelles b 1958.
Sir Alexander Jardine was cr a baronet of Nova Scotia with remainder to his heirs male whatsoever. This line are Chiefs of the Clan Jardine.

JARDINE (UK) 1916, of Godalming, co Surrey

Sir ANDREW COLIN DOUGLAS JARDINE, 5th Baronet; b 30 Nov 1955; s his father, Brig Sir IAN LIDDELL, OBE, MC, 1982; ed Charterhouse; late RGJ; Henderson Administration Group plc 1981-92, Dir Gartmore Investment Trust Management Trust Ltd 1992-93, Member Securities Inst; Member Queen's Body Guard for Scotland (Royal Company of Archers).

Arms – Gules, a saltire argent charged in the centre point with a lotus flower proper, on a chief of the second six mullets of the first. Crest – A mullet of six points pierced gules, between two palm branches proper.
Residence – 99 Addison Rd, W14 8DD.

Beware, I am here

BROTHER LIVING

MICHAEL IAN CHRISTOPHER, b 4 Oct 1958; ed Charterhouse: m 1982, (Maria) Milky Pineda, and has issue living, Oliver Michael Ian, b 20 Feb 1983, — Adrian Douglas Francis, b 1986. Residence – 12 Graham Av, Ealing, W13 9TQ.

SISTERS LIVING

Harriet Ann, b 1949: m 1972, Anthony Malcolm Douglas Palmer, RGJ, and has issue living, Edward Anthony Douglas, b 1975, — Henry Arthur Douglas, b 1982, — Alice Georgina, b 1976. —— Jean Margaret, b 1951: m 1984 (m diss 198-), (James) Andrew Gardiner Baird, elder son of Sir James Richard Gardiner Baird, 10th Bt, MC, and has issue (see Baird, Bt, cr 1695).

AUNTS LIVING (Daughters of 3rd baronet)

Elizabeth, b 1921: m 1946, John Edward Sharpley, BM, BCh, and has had issue, Mark Alastair, b 1947, — Oliver John, b 1949, — Sarah Marily, b 1952; d 1992. Residence – Field House, Fulbrook, near Burford, Oxon. —— Gillian Fiona, b 1930: m 1954, Ian Grant MacKenzie, MD, FRCS, who d 1986, and has issue living, Alistair Grant, b 1955, — Angus Colin, b 1957, — Andrew Kenneth, b 1958. Residence – Nether Kingshill, Kingswells, Aberdeenshire.

WIDOW LIVING OF FOURTH BARONET

PRISCILLA DAPHNE (Lady Jardine), da of Douglas Middleton Parnham Scott-Phillips, of Halkshill, Largs, Ayrshire: m 1948, Brig Sir Ian Liddell Jardine, 4th Bt, OBE, MC, who d 1982. Residence – Teal House, Cheriton, Alresford, Hants SO24 0PW.

COLLATERAL BRANCHES LIVING

Issue of late Lionel Westropp Jardine, CIE, 3rd son of 1st baronet, b 1895, d 1980: m 1922, Marjorie Mildred (6 Victoria Rd, W8 5RD), only da of Maj Richard John Woods, OBE:—
John Alexander, b 1939; ed Charterhouse: m 1971, Catherine Marie, da of André Trentesaux, of Lille, France, and has issue living, Emily, b 1979, — Alice, b 1980. —— Barbara Ann, b 1925: m 1964, Neville John Cooper, of 6 Victoria Rd, W8 5RD, and has issue living, Susan Ann, b 1964, — Henrietta Jane, b 1967. —— Jean Alison, b 1928: m 1949, Frederick Disney Rivers Currie, and has issue (see Currie Bt, colls).

Issue of late Rev Canon Kenneth William Seymour Jardine, 4th son of 1st baronet, b 1899, d 1960: m 1926, Katharine Frances, who d 1932, da of W. Cranswick Noad, formerly of Mount Tabor House, Perth:—
Rev David Eric Cranswick (The Rectory, Enham Alamein, Andover, Hants SP11 6HU), b 1930; ed Corpus Christi Coll, Oxford (MA, Dip Th 1954); R Christ Church, Smannell with St George, Enham Alamein, Andover since 1989: m 1955, Elsie Vera Susan Shanks, and has issue living, Charles Kenneth Herbert, b 1960: m 1988, Jacqueline Hannah, and has issue living, Ruari John b 1994, Catriona Louise b 1992, — Katharine Shelagh Margaret, b 1957: m 1984, Angus G. Grandfield, and has issue living, Colin Douglas Hugh b 1988, Alexander David George, b 1992, Francis Gregory Charles b 1994, Ruth Katriona b 1986, — Rachel Heather Agnes, b 1965.
The 1st baronet, Sir John Jardine, KCIE, LLD, JP, was a Puisne Judge of Bombay High Court 1885-97, and sat as MP for Roxburghshire (L) 1906-18. The 3rd baronet, Maj-Gen Sir Colin Arthur Jardine, CB, DSO, MC, DL, late RA, was Dep Gov of Gibraltar, a Member of House of Laity, Church Assembly, Mil Sec to Com-in-Ch, British Expeditionary Force 1939-40, and

Director of Army Welfare 1943. The 4th baronet, Brig Sir Ian Liddell Jardine, OBE, MC, Coldm Gds, was ADC to HM 1976-78.

BUCHANAN-JARDINE (UK) 1885, of Castle Milk, co Dumfries.

Beware; I am present!

The lion's anger is noble

Sir (ANDREW) RUPERT JOHN BUCHANAN-JARDINE, MC, 4th *Baronet*, *b* 2 Feb 1923; *s* his father, *Capt Sir* JOHN WILLIAM, 1969; *ed* Harrow, and RAC Cirencester; Maj RHG; DL of Nithsdale and Annandale and Eskdale: *m* 1950 (*m diss* 1975), Jane Fiona, da of Sir Archibald Charles Edmonstone, 6th Bt, and has issue.

Arms – Quarterly 1st and 4th per pale argent and or a saltire gules, on a chief engrailed of the third three mullets of the first, *Jardine*; 2nd, or, a lion rampant gules with a double tressure flory counter-flory, sable, *Buchanan*; 3rd, sable, a chevron, between three bears' heads argent, muzzled gules, *Leny*. **Crests** – 1st, a spur rowel of six points gules, *Jardine*; 2nd, a sword erect in pale proper, hilted and pommelled or.
Seat – Castle Milk, Lockerbie, Dumfries-shire. *Residence* – Dixons, Lockerbie, Dumfries-shire. *Club* – MCC.

SON LIVING

JOHN CHRISTOPHER RUPERT (Castle Milk, Lockerbie, Dumfries-shire), *b* 20 March 1952; *ed* Harrow, and RAC Cirencester: *m* 1975, Pandora Lavinia, yr da of Peter Murray Lee, and has issue living, a son, *b* 28 July 1994, — Tessa Mary, *b* 1979, — Katie Luella, *b* 1980, — Lorna Jane, *b* 1984, — Juliet Marina, *b* 1986, — Alice Fiona, *b* 1988.

DAUGHTER LIVING

Diana Gwendolyn Jean (27 Pier House, Cheyne Walk, SW3), *b* 1955.

HALF-BROTHER LIVING

(Charles) James (27 Queens Gate Place Mews, SW7; Turf, New (Edinburgh), White's, and R Hong Kong Jockey Clubs), *b* 1946; *ed* Stowe, and Trin Coll, Camb; ARIBA: *m* 1967 (*m diss* 1978), Lady Susan Ankaret Howard, da of 11th Earl of Carlisle; 2ndly, 1978, Irmgard Margarethe, da of Maj Rudolf Bormann, and has issue living, (by 1st *m*) Flora Jane, *b* 1971, — (by 2nd *m*) Claire Isabel, *b* 1980, — Olivia Rose, *b* 1982.

HALF-SISTER LIVING

Caroline Anne, *b* 1952.

WIDOW LIVING OF THIRD BARONET

PRUDENCE AUDREY (*Prudence, Lady Buchanan-Jardine*) (Moulin de la Mourachonne, 06370 Mouans Sartoux, France, AM), da of William Haggie, of Knayton, Thirsk, Yorks: *m* 1944, as his 2nd wife, Capt Sir John William Buchanan-Jardine, 3rd Bt, who *d* 1969.

The 1st baronet, Sir Robert Jardine, the 2nd baronet, Sir Robert William Buchanan Jardine, and the 3rd baronet, Sir John William Buchanan-Jardine, were successively head of the firm of Jardine, Matheson and Co, merchants in China. The 1st baronet also sat at MP for Ashburton (*L*) 1865-8, for Dumfries Burghs 1868-74, and Dumfriesshire 1880-92. The 3rd baronet assumed the additional surname of Buchanan since his grandmother, Margaret Seton, wife of the 1st baronet, was da of John Buchanan Hamilton of Leny, Perthshire, and sister and heir of John Hamilton-Buchanan, Ch of Clan Buchanan.

JARVIS (UK) 1922, of Hascombe Court, co Surrey (Extinct 1965)

Sir (ARNOLD) ADRIAN JARVIS, 2nd and last *Baronet*.

DAUGHTER LIVING OF FIRST BARONET

Brenda Beryl (*Lady Williams*), *b* 1907; a JP for Denbighshire: *m* 1932, Sir Francis John Watkin Williams, 8th Bt, QC, JP, of Llys, Middle Lane, Denbigh.

DUNNINGTON-JEFFERSON (UK) 1958, of Thorganby Hall East Riding of Yorkshire

Sir MERVYN STEWART DUNNINGTON-JEFFERSON, 2nd *Baronet*; *b* 5 Aug 1943; *s* his father *Lt-Col Sir* JOHN ALEXANDER, DSO, 1979; *ed* Eton: *m* 1971, Caroline Anna, only da of late John Bayley, of Hillam Hall, Monk Fryston, Yorks, and has issue.

Arms – Quarterly: 1st and 4th, gules, a griphon sejant wings addorsed argent, a bordure engrailed of the last charged with eight pellets, *Jefferson*; 2nd and 3rd, paly of six argent and azure, on a chief gules a bezant between to annulets or, *Dunnington*. **Crests** – 1st griphon as in the arms gorged with a collar gemel, azure in the beak a lily slipped proper, *Jefferson*; 2nd, a horse current argent gorged with a collar gules charged with a bezant between two annulets or, *Dunnington*.
Residence – 7 Bolingbroke Grove, SW11 6ES. *Clubs* – MCC, and Queen's.

SON LIVING

JOHN ALEXANDER, *b* 23 March 1980.

DAUGHTERS LIVING

A CRUCE SALUS

Salvation by the Cross

Annabelle Mary, *b* 1973. —— Emma Elizabeth, *b* 1978.

SISTER LIVING

Rosemary Nicolette, *b* 1941.

WIDOW LIVING OF FIRST BARONET

(FRANCES) ISOBEL (*Isobel, Lady Dunnington-Jefferson*) (Rectory Cottage, Escrick, York Y04 6LE), da of Col Herbert Anderson Cape, DSO, of Thorganby, York: *m* 1938, Lt-Col Sir John Alexander Dunnington-Jefferson, DSO, 1st Bt, who *d* 1979.

JEHANGIR (UK) 1908, of Bombay

Sir HIRJI JEHANGIR, 3rd *Baronet*, *b* 1 Nov 1915: *s* his father, *Sir* COWASJEE, GBE, KCIE, 1962; *ed* St Xavier's Sch, Bombay, and Magdalene Coll, Camb; Chm of Jehangir Art Gallery, Bombay, Pres Parsi Public Sch Soc, Chm Cowasji Jehangir Charitable Trust: *m* 1952, Jinoo, elder da of late Kakushroo H. Cama, and has issue.

Arms – Azure, a sun in splendour within an orle of mullets, or, on a canton argent a rose gules slipped proper in bend surmounting a lotus flower in a bend sinister also proper. **Crest** – Upon a mount a column, thereon flames of fire all proper.
Residences – Readymoney House, 49 Nepean Sea Rd, Bombay, 400 036; 24 Kensington Court Gdns, Kensington Court Place, W8. *Clubs* – Royal Over-Seas League, Willingdon (Bombay).

SONS LIVING

JEHANGIR, *b* 23 Nov 1953: *m* 1988, Jasmine, da of Beji Billimoria, and has issue living, Cowasji (a son), *b* 28 March 1990. —— Ardeshir, *b* 1956.

SISTER LIVING

Sylla, *b* 1914: *m* 1946, Richard Holmes, of 24 Kensington Court Gdns, W8.

By special Act of Legislative Council of India 1911 (dissolved 1964), all future holders of the title were to relinquish their own names and assume those of the 1st baronet. The 1st baronet, Sir Cowasjee Jehangir (who assumed the name of Cowasjee Jehangir in lieu of Jehangir Cowasjee), was nephew and adopted son and heir of late Sir Cowasjee Jehangir, CSI, a leader of the Parsee Community, a great Philanthropist, and Industrialist, and a lineal descendant of Hirji Jehangir Readymoney, who resided in Bombay in 1717, and was the Banker to East India Company. Sir Cowasjee Jehangir, GBE, KCIE, 2nd Bt, was Member of Bombay Corporation 1902-21, and Chm 1914-15, a MEC Bombay 1921-26, and a MLA Delhi 1932-47.

JEJEEBHOY (UK) 1857, of Bombay

Sir JAMSETJEE JEJEEBHOY, 7th *Baronet*, el son of late Rustamjee Jamsetjee Jejeebhoy, nephew of 4th Baronet: *b* 19 April 1913; *s* his kinsman, *Sir* Jamsetjee, 1968, when he assumed the name of Jamsetjee Jejeebhoy, in lieu of Maneckjee Rustamjee Jejeebhoy; *ed* Bombay Univ (BA): *m* 1943, Shirin, da of late Jehangir Hormusjee Cama, and has issue.

𝕬rms – Azure, a sun rising above a representation of "the Ghauts" (mountains near Bombay) in base, and in chief two bees volant, all proper. 𝕮rest – A mount vert, thereon a peacock (close) amidst wheat, and in the beak an ear of wheat all proper.
Residence – Beaulieu, 95 Worli Seaface, Bombay 25.

SON LIVING

Rustomjee, *b* 16 Nov 1957; *ed* Bombay Univ; B Com, LLM: *m* 1984, Delara, da of Jal N. Bhaisa, and has issue living, Jehangir, *b* 20 Jan 1986.

DAUGHTER LIVING

Ayesha, *b* 1952.

DAUGHTERS LIVING OF SIXTH BARONET

Shireen (Sett Minar, Pedder Road, Bombay 26, India) *b* 1952, Deanna, *b* 1953. —— Geeta, *b* 1955.

DAUGHTER LIVING OF FIFTH BARONET

Aimai, *b* 1918: *m* 1942, Nozer Ereach D. Pandole, who *d* 1983. *Residence* – Silverene, 63 Worli Sea Face, Bombay, India.

COLLATERAL BRANCH LIVING

Granddaughter of late Jamsetjee Cursetjee Jamsetjee Jejeebhoy, brother of 4th baronet, *b* 1860, *d* 1916: *m* 1882, Awabai Sharpurjee Dhunjeebhoy, who *d* 1926:—
Issue of late Cursetjee Jejeebhoy, *b* 1897, *d* 1982: *m* 1937, Mary Feroze Jehangir:—
Pirojbai, *b* 1938: *m* 1988, Burjor Sohrabji Cooper, of Darbhanga Mansion, Carmichael Rd, Bombay 26.
The 1st baronet, Sir Jamsetjee, Knt, a wealthy Parsee merchant, was renowned for his benevolence, charity, munificence, and loyalty, a reputation that was also earned by his son, the 2nd baronet. In 1860 a special Act of the Legislative Council of India was passed, with the sanction of HM Queen Victoria, by which all future holders of the title are to relinquish their own names and assume that of the 1st baronet. The 3rd baronet was MLC of Bombay. The 4th baronet was Sheriff of Bombay 1900. The 5th baronet was Dep Pres of Indian Legislative Assembly 1921-31. The 6th baronet was an Industrialist and Banker.

JENKINSON (E) 1661, of Walcot, Oxfordshire, and Hawkesbury, Gloucestershire

I obey, I do not serve

Sir JOHN BANKS JENKINSON, 14th *Baronet*; *b* 16 Feb 1945; *s* his father, *Sir* ANTHONY BANKS, 1989; *ed* Eton, and Univ of Miami: *m* 1979, Josephine Mary, da of late Samuel William Marshall-Andrew, and has issue.

𝕬rms – Azure, on a fesse wavy argent, a cross-patée gules, in chief two estoiles or. 𝕮rest – A sea-horse assurgent, or maned azure, supporting a cross-patée as in the arms.
Seat – Hawkesbury, Badminton, Avon. *Residence* – Hawkesbury Home Farm, Badminton, Avon.

SON LIVING

GEORGE ANTHONY SAMUEL BANKS, *b* 8 Nov 1980.

DAUGHTER LIVING

Samantha Emma, *b* 1983.

SISTERS LIVING

Jennifer Ann, *b* 1947: *m* 1976, Robert Waddington, son of late George Waddington, of Lytham, Lancs, and has issue living, Thomas Anthony, *b* 1977, — Guy George, *b* 1979. *Residence* – The Old Vicarage, Upper Minety, Malmesbury, Wilts SN16 9PY. —— Emily Frances Joan, *b* 1953: *m* 19—, Miguel Malgaret, of Fort Lauderdale, Florida, USA, and has issue living, Christopher, *b* 1977.

WIDOW LIVING OF THIRTEENTH BARONET

FRANCES (*Frances, Lady Jenkinson*), da of Harry Stremmel, of New York, USA: *m* 1943, Sir Anthony Banks Jenkinson, 13th Bt, who *d* 1989. *Residence* – 491 South Church St, Grand Cayman, BWI.

COLLATERAL BRANCH LIVING

Grandchildren of Lt-Col George Seymour Charles Jenkinson, DSO, son of late John Henry Jenkinson, brother of 11th baronet:—
Issue of late Capt Robert Charles Horace Jenkinson, *b* 1900, *d* 1970: *m* 1st, 1925 (*m diss* 1936), Hon Barbara Vernon Harcourt, OBE, who *d* 1961; 2ndly, 1938, Gwyneth, da of A. Llewellyn Matthews:—
(By 1st *m*) Julian Charles Lewis (Folly Faunts House, Goldhanger, Maldon, Essex), *b* 1926; *ed* Eton: *m* 1953, Diana Catherine, only da of late Maj George Henry William Baird (*see* Baird, Bt, *cr* 1809, colls), and has issue living, Dermot Julian, *b* 1954: *m* 1979, Miranda Jane, el da of John Maxwell Menzies, of Kames, Berwickshire (*see* Dawson Bt *cr* 1920), and has issue living, Oliver John Banks *b* 1984, Emily Lavinia *b* 1981, — Karen Barbara, *b* 1957: *m* 1981, Capt Robert Sturdee Mason, WG, — Laura Louise Diana, *b* 1966. —— Clare Barbara, *b* 1933: *m* 1955, William McCully, of Leitrim Farm, Loughries, Newtownards, co Down, and has issue living, Patrick William, *b* 1965, — Lucinda Barbara, *b* 1962. —— (By 2nd *m*) Frances Caroline (Sycamore House, Swanton Novers, nr Melton Constable, Norfolk NR24 2RB), *b* 1942.

The 1st, 2nd, 3rd, 4th and 5th baronets were successively Members of Parliament for Oxfordshire; the 7th baronet, celebrated statesman, was created Earl of Liverpool, and his son, the 8th baronet and 2nd earl, was for many years Prime Minister of England. The peerage became extinct on the death of the 3rd earl, when the baronetcy devolved upon his cousin, Sir Charles, 10th Bt, MP for Dover, who was nephew of the 1st Earl of Liverpool. Sir George, 11th Bt, sat as MP for Wiltshire, N (*C*) 1868-80.

JENKS (UK) 1932, of Cheape, in the City of London

Sir (MAURICE ARTHUR) BRIAN JENKS, 3rd *Baronet*; *b* 28 Oct 1933; *s* his father, *Sir* RICHARD ATHERLEY, 1993; *ed* Charterhouse: *m* 1962, Susan Lois, eldest da of (Frank) Leslie Allen, of Glenside, Star Lane, Hooley, Coulsdon, Surrey, and has issue.

Arms – Per fesse indented sable and argent, on a pile or a boar's head, and in base two boars' heads all couped sable; on a chief ermine a representation of the sword and mace of the City of London in saltire proper. **Crest** – A sinister arm embowed vested sable, cuffed argent, grasping in the hand a sword in bend proper, pommel and hilt or, enfiled with a ducal coronet gold.
Residence – Warren House, Savernake, Marlborough, Wilts SN8 3BQ.

DECVS·RECTE·PETO

I seek honour honourably

DAUGHTER LIVING

Marjorie Emma, *b* 1964.

ADOPTED SON LIVING

Timothy Charles, *b* 1967.

BROTHER LIVING

RICHARD JOHN PETER (26 Ilchester Place, W14), *b* 28 June 1936; *ed* Charterhouse; late 5th Royal Inniskilling Dragoon Guards; FCA: *m* 1963, Juniper Li-Yung, eldest da of late Tan Sri Y. C. Foo, of 18 Golf Club Rd, Ipoh, Malaysia, and has issue living, Richard Albert Benedict, *b* 1965; *ed* Eton, and New Coll Oxford, — Melissa Kate Rosalind, *b* 1967, — Serena Anne Louise, *b* 1970.

WIDOWS LIVING OF FIRST AND SECOND BARONETS

CONSTANCE EDITH (*Constance, Lady Jenks*), da of William Richard Currie, of Eden Park, Beckenham, Kent: *m* 1939, as his 2nd wife, Sir Maurice Jenks, 1st Bt, who *d* 1946. *Address* – c/o Bennett, Welch & Co, Bank Chambers, Weston Hill, Upper Norwood, SE19 1TY.
MARJORIE SUZANNE ARLETTE (*Dowager Lady Jenks*), da of Sir Arthur Philip du Cros, 1st Bt: *m* 1932, Sir Richard Atherley Jenks, 2nd Bt, who *d* 1993. *Residence* – 42 Sussex Sq, W2 2SR.

COLLATERAL BRANCH LIVING

Issue of late Cdr Robert Fergus Jenks, DSC, RN, yr son of 1st baronet, *b* 1909, *d* 1982: *m* 1st, 1933 (*m diss* 1938), Joyce Wynne, only da of A. E. Booth, of Hendon; 2ndly, 1939, Molly Estelle (No 7 The Cloisters, South St, Wells, Som BA5 1SA), 3rd da of Lt Cdr Albert Edward Griffiths, RN (ret), of Parkstone, Dorset, and formerly wife of Fl Lt John F. Dales, RAF:—
(By 2nd *m*) Robert Philip (Menmar, Moll de Llevant 303, Mahon, Menorca, Spain), *b* 1948; *ed* in Rhodesia, and HMS Worcester; Yacht Broker: *m* 1st, 1968 (*m diss* 1983), Susan, only da of John B. Campbell, of Henley-on-Thames, Oxon; 2ndly, 1990, Tracy Jane, only da of Colin V. Hives, of Stone Farm, Hailey, Ipsden, Oxon. —— Sally Elizabeth, *b* 1945: *m* 1968 (*m diss* 19——), John Norman Anderson Wylie, only son of late Lieut John Norman Anderson, USN, and Mrs Joan Wylie, and adopted son of Amos K. Wylie, of New York, and has issue living, Peter, *b* 1978, — Sarah, *b* 1974.

The 1st baronet, Sir Maurice Jenks (son of Robert Isaac Jenks, of Clapham, SW), was an Alderman of City of London (Sheriff 1930-31, and Lord Mayor 1931-32).

JEPHCOTT (UK) 1962, of East Portlemouth, co Devon.

SIR (JOHN) ANTHONY JEPHCOTT, 2nd *Baronet*; *b* 21 May 1924; *s* his father, *Sir* HARRY, 1978; *ed* Aldenham, St John's Coll, Oxford, and LSE (BCom); Hon FFA, RACS 1990, Hon FANZCA 1992; 1939-45 War with REME, later RAEC; formerly Manufacturer of Anaesthesia Equipment; Man Dir Penlon Ltd 1952-73, and of Pen Medic Ltd, NZ, 1973-78: *m* 1st, 1949 (*m diss* 1978), Sylvia Mary, da of Thorsten F. Relling, of Wellington, NZ; 2ndly, 1978, Josephine Agnes, da of Philip Sheridan, of Perth, W Aust, and has issue by 1st *m*.

Arms – Azure two chevronels between in chief a mortar and pestle between two escallops or and in base an open book proper edged and clasped or. **Crest** – A dove supporting with dexter claw a rod of Æsculapius proper the serpent vert. **Motto** – Scientia Salutem Feramus.
Address – 26 Sage Rd, Kohimarama, Auckland 5, NZ.

DAUGHTERS LIVING (By 1st marriage)

Helen Mary (13A Tullis Close, Sutton Courtenay, Abingdon, Oxon), *b* 1953: *m* 1977 (*m diss* 1989), David Asbury, and has issue living, Richard Andrew James, *b* 1982, — Alexander Philip Ralph, *b* 1984, — Anna Ruth, *b* 1980. —— Caroline Ruth, *b* 1955: *m* 1979, Nigel Clark Flower, of Hill Farm House, Brinton, Melton Constable, Norfolk, and has issue living, Hugo Gregory, *b* 1985, — Felix James, *b* 1988, — Harriet Christina, *b* 1990.

BROTHER LIVING

NEIL WELBOURN (Thalassa, E Portlemouth, Salcombe, S Devon TQ8 8PU), *b* 3 June 1929; *ed* Aldenham, and Emmanuel Coll, Camb (MA): *m* 1st, 1951, Mary Denise, who *d* 1977, da of Arthur Muddiman, of Abbots Mead, W Clandon, Surrey; 2ndly, 1978, Mary Florence, da of late James John Daly, and has issue living (by 1st *m*), David Welbourn, *b* 1952, — Mark Lanwer, *b* 1957: *m* 1983, Lysa Ann, da of Francis John Rigden, of 50 Cliff Garden, Telescombe Cliff, Sussex, and has issue living, Richard Lanwer *b* 1989, — Penelope Mary, *b* 1955.

The first baronet was Hon Pres and Chm Glaxo Group Ltd; also Pres Assocn of British Chemical Manufacturers 1952-55, Pres of Roy Institute of Chemistry 1953-55, and Chm of Council for Scientific and Industrial Research 1956-61, and of Sch of Pharmacy, Univ of London, 1948-69; also Gov LSE 1952-68, and of N London Collegiate Sch 1957-*ca* 1976.

JERVIS-WHITE-JERVIS (I) 1797, of Bally-Ellis, Wexford (Extinct 1947)

Sir HENRY FELIX JERVIS-WHITE-JERVIS, 5th and last *Baronet*.

COLLATERAL BRANCH LIVING

Issue of late Herbert Jervis-White-Jervis, brother of 4th baronet, *b* 1858, *d* 1934: *m* 1893, Beatrice Georgiana, who *d* 1939, da of late Col Sir Samuel Brise Ruggles-Brise, KCB (Bowyer-Smijth, Bt):—
Beatrice *b* 1898; *ed* Newnham Coll, Camb (BA 1919, MA 1920), and London Univ (MB and BS 1925); MRCS England and LRCP London 1924: *m* 1937, Erst Ellis, who *d* 1952. *Address* – c/o Mr A. H. P. Hope, Red Towers, Melton, Woodbridge.

CLARKE-JERVOISE (UK) 1813, of Idsworth Park, Hampshire (Extinct 1933)

Sir DUDLEY ALAN LESTOCK CLARKE-JERVOISE, 7th and last *Baronet*.

DAUGHTER LIVING OF SEVENTH BARONET

Gladys Agnes, *b* 1909: *m* 1936, Kenneth Southam, MRCS, LRCP, and has issue living, Gilian Margaret, *b* 1938, — Bridget Anne, *b* 1940; *m* 1966, Henry Charles Frank Wickham-Smith, RD, of 8 Wellswood Gdns, Rowlands Castle, Hants, and has issue living, Simon James Southam *b* 1968; BA. *Residence* – 78 Bowes Hill, Rowlands Castle, Hants.

JESSEL (UK) 1883, of Ladham House, Goudhurst, co Kent

Sir CHARLES JOHN JESSEL, 3rd *Baronet*; *b* 29 Dec 1924; *s* his father, Sir GEORGE, MC, 1977; *ed* Eton, and Balliol Coll, Oxford; 1939-45 War as Lieut 15/19th Hussars (despatches); JP (Kent) 1960-78: *m* 1st, 1956, Shirley Cornelia, who *d* 1977, da of John Waters, of Northampton; 2ndly, 1979 (*m diss* 1983), Gwendoline Mary, da of late Laurence Devereux, OBE, and widow of Charles Langer, and has issue by 1st *m*.

Arms – Azure, a fesse raguly ermine, between three eagles' heads erased argent, in the centre chief point a torch erect fired proper. **Crest** – A torch fessewise fired proper, surmounted by an eagle volant argent, holding in the beak a pearl of the last.
Residence – South Hill Farm, Hastingleigh, Ashford, Kent TN25 5HL. **Club** – Cavalry and Guards'.

SONS LIVING *(By 1st marriage)*

GEORGE ELPHINSTONE, *b* 15 Dec 1957; *ed* Milton Abbey, and RAC Cirencester: *m* 1988 (*m diss* 1993), Rose Amelia, yr da of James Coutts-Smith, of Wallington, Herts. *Residence* – Stoakes Cottage, Hastingleigh, Ashford, Kent TN25 5HG. *Clubs* – Cavalry and Guards', Farmers'. —— Alastair John (Satins Hill Farmhouse, Sissinghurst, Kent TN17 2AH), *b* 1959; *ed* Stowe: *m* 1988, Gail Alexandra, only da of Gordon Partridge, of The Barbican, EC2, and has issue living, Thomas George William, *b* 1990, — Camilla Alice Louise, *b* 1991.

DAUGHTER LIVING *(By 1st marriage)*

(Cornelia) Sarah, *b* 1963.

WIDOW LIVING OF SECOND BARONET

(JOAN) BETTY (*Betty, Lady Jessel*) (Ladham House, Goudhurst, Kent), da of late Dr David Ewart, OBE, MD, FRCS, of Chichester, and formerly wife of 2nd Baron Russell of Liverpool: *m* 2ndly, 1948, as his 2nd wife, Sir George Jessel, MC, 2nd Bt, who *d* 1977.

COLLATERAL BRANCH LIVING

Grandchildren of late Sir Richard Hugh Jessel (infra):—
Issue of late David Charles George Jessel, *b* 1924, *d* 1985: *m* 1st, 1950 (*m diss* 1978), Hon Amelia Grace FitzRoy, da of 2nd Viscount Daventry; 2ndly, 1980, Matilda McCormick, of Kentucky, USA (22 Cambridge Rd, SW11):—
(By 1st *m*) Richard James, *b* 1954; *ed* Eton: *m* 1982, Harriot Josephine, da of late Wilfred J. (Mike) St Pierre Bunbury, and has issue living, David Hugh Joseph, *b* 1986, — George FitzRoy, *b* 1990, — Edwina Mary Grace, *b* 1984. *Residence* – 9 Cresswell Gdns, SW3. —— Davina Jane, *b* 1952: *m* 1st, 1970 (*m diss* 1976), Hon Richard Tyrell-Kenyon, who *d* 1982 (*see* B Kenyon); 2ndly, 1977 (*m diss* 1984), James Remington-Hobbs; 3rdly, 1988, Charles Richard Markham Phillips, and has issue living (by 1st *m*: *see* B Kenyon), — (by 2nd *m*), Max Hugh, *b* 1979, — (by 3rd *m*) Richard David Markham, *b* 1988, — David Charles, *b* 1991. *Residence* – 33 Ursula St, SW11 3DW.

Issue of late Sir Richard Hugh Jessel, yr son of 1st baronet, *b* 1896, *d* 1979: *m* 1st, 1923, Margaret Ella, who *d* 1953, 2nd da of Sir George James Graham Lewis, 2nd Bt; 2ndly, 1954, Daphne, who *d* 1971, da of late William Buckley Gladstone, and widow of Maj Thirlwall Philipson, MC, Life Gds; 3rdly, 1972, Diana Mary (who *m* 4thly, 1981, Col J. C. Cockburn, DSO, MBE, Argyll and Sutherland Highers (ret)), yr da of Maj William Edward Gatacre, of de Wiersse, Vorden, Holland, widow of Col George Richard Trotter, R Scots Greys, and formerly wife of James Edward Michael Clark-Hall:—
(By 1st *m*) Robin Richard (12 Crooms Hill Grove, Greenwich SE10 8HB. *Club* – Garrick), *b* 1930; *ed* Eton, and at Balliol Coll, Oxford (BA); Bar Lincoln's Inn 1953: *m* 1957, Audrey Gertrude, el da of late Alexander Newman Howard, and has issue living, Simon Dana, *b* 1958: *m* 1986, Christina Julia, yst da of Dennis Reeves, of Parkstone, Dorset, and has issue living, Ella *b* 1988, — Alexander Robin, *b* 1961, — Michael Richard, *b* 1965, — Virginia Penelope, *b* 1967. —— Edith Marie, *b* 1926; *ed* St Hilda's Coll, Oxford (MA): *m* 1947, William Joseph Straker-Smith, late Capt Coldm Gds, who *d* 1987, of Carham, Cornhill-on-Tweed, Northumberland, and has issue living, Peter Dalrymple (Wark Common Farm, Cornhill-on-Tweed, Northumberland TD12 4RR), *b* 1951; *ed* Eton, and Pembroke Coll, Camb (BA): *m* 1981, Susan Steuart, and has issue living, Henry Falkland *b* 1982, Willa *b* 1984, — Richard David (8 Rossetti Gardens Mansions, Flood St, SW3), *b* 1959; *ed* Harrow, — Tessa Diana, *b* 1949: *m* 1969, John Robert Robson, of Melbourne Stud, Ayot Green, Welwyn, Herts, and has issue living, James *b* 1973, Claire *b* 1972.

The 1st baronet, Charles James (High Sheriff of Kent 1903), was el son of late Rt Hon Sir George Jessel, PC, Master of the Rolls and one of the most eminent Judges of his time. The 2nd son, Herbert Merton, was *cr* a Baronet 1917 and Baron Jessel 1924.

JOHNSON (GB) 1755, of New York, in North America

Deo Regique debeo

I owe all to God and the King

Not even difficulties frighten me

— Charlotte Sophia Carol, *b* 1956.

Sir PETER COLPOYS PALEY JOHNSON, 7th *Baronet*, *b* 26 March 1930; *s* his father, *Lt-Col Sir* JOHN PALEY, MBE, 1975; *ed* Wellington Coll; late Capt RA; Dir of Nautical Publishing Co Ltd 1971-81; author of *Ocean Racing and Offshore Yachts, Guinness Book of Yachting Facts and Feats*, etc: *m* 1st, 1956 (*m diss* 1972), Clare, da of late Dr Nigel Patrick Bruce, BM, BCh (*see* Bruce, Bt, *cr* 1804, colls); 2ndly, 1973, Caroline Elisabeth, twin da of late Wing-Cdr Sir (Eric) John Hodsoll, CB, and has issue by 1st and 2nd *m*.

Arms – Argent, two lions counter-rampant supporting a dexter hand gules, in chief three estoiles of the last, and in base a salmon naiant in water proper. **Crest** – An arm gules, encircled with a ducal coronet or, the hand grasping a sword proper, pommel and hilt gold. *Residence* – Dene End, Buckland Dene, Lymington, Hants SO41 9DT. *Clubs* – Royal Ocean Racing, Royal Yacht Squadron.

SONS LIVING

(By 1st *m*) COLPOYS GUY, *b* 13 Nov 1965; *ed* Winchester, and King's Coll, London (BA); FRGS: *m* 1990, Marie Louise Carmel, da of John Holroyd, of Guildford, Surrey, and has issue living, Colpoys William, *b* 28 Dec 1993. *Residence* – 21 Elthiron Rd, SW6 4BN. *Club* – Royal Ocean Racing. ⸻ (By 2nd *m*) Nicholas Frederick, *b* 1977.

DAUGHTERS LIVING (By 1st marriage)

Marina Grace, *b* 1960. ⸻ Alison Fiona, *b* 1961.

SISTER LIVING

Wanda Helene Paley (1a Cobb's Well, Fowey, Cornwall PL23 1BP), *b* 1933: *m* 1955 (*m diss* 1977), Paul Weychan, and has issue living, Paul Corydon, *b* 1960,

HALF-SISTER LIVING

Issue of late Lt-Col Sir John Paley Johnson, 6th Bt, MBE, by his 2nd wife, Jasmine Lydia, Announcer-Hostess, Directorate of Television BBC, who *d* 1991 (having *m* 2ndly, 1948 (*m diss* 1953), Frank Hugh Shirley Fox; 3rdly, 1954, Howard Marshall, who *d* 1974), da of late Lt-Col Hon Noel Gervase Bligh, DSO, yr son of 8th Earl of Darnley:—
Sarah Jack Paley (Church Lane Cottage, Wylye, Warminster, Wilts BA12 0Q2), *b* 1942: *m* 1st, 1963 (*m diss* 1970), Ezra Mager, of New York City; 2ndly, 1972 (*m diss* 1983), Nels Royden Johnson, and has issue living, (by 1st *m*) Dickon Porter, *b* 1969, ⸻ Emma Rachel, *b* 1964, ⸻ (by 2nd *m*) Daniel Alexander, *b* 1972.

UNCLE LIVING

Peter Warren, DSO, OBE, DFC, AFC, *b* 1908; late Group-Capt RAF and Civil Air Attaché, British Embassy, Bonn; 1939-45 War (despatches, DFC, AFC, DSO); DSO 1945. OBE (Civil) 1954: *m* 1st, 1934 (*m diss* 1961), Joan Agnes, who *d* 1972, da of late Capt Percy Richard Hare, TD (*see* E Listowel, colls); 2ndly, 1961, Margaret Anne, who *d* 1987, da of Capt Guy Wychelo Bower, DSC, RN (ret), of Rose Cottage, Fordwich, Kent, and has issue living, (by 1st *m*) Hugo Robert Warren, *b* 1939: *m* 1963, Sally Allen, of Boston, Mass, USA, and has issue living, Claudia Agnes *b* 1964, ⸻ Virginia, *b* 1936: *m* 1961 (*m diss* 1983), Marchese Umberto Valdambrini-Accoramboni, and has issue living, Robert *b* 1963, Richard Warren *b* 1965, Julia Louise *b* 1971. *Residence* – 23 Albury Park, Albury, Guildford, Surrey GU5 9BB. *Club* – MCC.

COLLATERAL BRANCHES LIVING

Granddaughters of late Major Frederick Colpoys Ormsby Johnson, 2nd son of late Vice-Adm John Ormsby Johnson (infra):—
Issue of late Brigadier Guy Allen Colpoys Ormsby Johnson, CBE, MC, *b* 1886, *d* 1957: *m* 1911, Mary Isabella, who *d* 1977, da of late Col Benjamin Geale Humfrey (E Ranfurly, colls):—
Emily Mary Ormsby (Wood Cottage, Tobermory, Isle-of-Mull, Argyll), *b* 1912: *m* 1st, 1934, Group-Capt Edward Stephen Dru Drury, RAF, who *d* 1948; 2ndly, 1951, Maj Miles Garrick, who *d* 1978, and has issue living, (by 1st *m*) Stephen Guy Dru, MBE, *b* 1939; Group-Capt RAF; MBE (Mil) 19—, ⸻ Michael Humfrey Dru, MBE, *b* 1942; Lt-Col LI; MBE (Mil) 1977. ⸻ Eileen Ormsby, *b* 1918: *m* 1945, Finlay George Mackintosh, MB, ChB, of Dunsfold, Moor Rd, Bramhope, Leeds, and has issue living, Alan Finlay, *b* 1948, ⸻ Fiona Mary, *b* 1945, ⸻ Diana Barbara, *b* 1952.

Grandchildren of late Vice-Adm John Ormsby Johnson, son of late Col Charles Christopher Johnson, 7th son of 2nd baronet:—
Issue of late Capt Alexander Adair Johnson, FRCVS, *b* 1873, *d* 1927: *m* 1894, Emma Jane, who *d* 1940, da of —:—
Ralph Harold Ormsby, *b* 1897; late New Zealand Mounted Rifles; 1914-18 War: *m* 1923, and has issue living, Alexander Ormsby, *b* 1929. *Residence* – 90 McFadden's Road, St Albans, Christchurch, New Zealand. ⸻ John Ormsby, *b* 1909: *m* 1936, ⸻ *Address* – Corner of Guys Rd and Factory Rd, Janefield, Mosgiel, Dunedin, New Zealand. ⸻ Gertrude, *b* 1895: *m* 1928, James Augustus Williamson. *Residence* – 66 Wiggins St, Sumner, Christchurch, New Zealand. ⸻ Sybil Renira, *b* 1909: *m* 19—, ⸻ Derret. ⸻ Phyllis Ormsby, *b* 1917: *m* 19—, ⸻ Savage. *Residence* –

Grandson of late Capt Edward Colpoys Johnson, son of late Col Charles Christopher Johnson (ante):—
Issue of late Hubert Colpoys Johnson, *b* 1878, *d* 1925: *m* 1916, Mary Anne, da of Thomas Philip Howe, formerly of Newport Pagnell, Bucks:—
Graham Christopher Colpoys, *b* 1917: *m* 1951, Joan Winifred Mary, who *d* 1958, da of John Bernard Colbeck, of Wakefield, Yorkshire, and has issue living, Anne Winifred Mary, *b* 1952.

The 1st baronet, Gen Sir William Johnson, of an ancient family in Ireland named Macshane, went in early life to America, and conducted the expedition to Crown Point, and gained the battles of Crown Point and Niagara, for which services he was created a baronet, and received £5,000 from the Government, and also large grants of land in the Province of New York, then part of the British dominions. He settled on the Mohawk river, and brought the Senecas—one of the revolted tribes, and inveterate enemies of the English—to a treaty in 1764. He was sole representative of Indian affairs for the northern parts of America for George II, and Col of the six united nations, their allies and dependants. Sir John, the 2nd baronet, was also Superintendant-Gen of Indian Affairs in North America. He remained loyal to the Crown at the outbreak of the American Revolution, and raised two battalions of Roy New York Regt which he commanded. He was largely responsible for loyalist settlement in Canada. Sir William Johnson built Johnson Hall in 1764 three miles from Fort Johnson. This is now a fully restored NY State Historic Site, at Johnstown, NY, USA.

JOHNSON (UK) 1818, of Bath

Thou hast conquered, and we live

Never unready

Sir PATRICK ELIOT JOHNSON, 8th *Baronet*; *b* 1955; *s* his father, *Sir* ROBIN ELIOT, 1989; *ed* —.

Arms – Per pale sable and azure, on a saltire argent between three towers or, fired proper, one in chief and two in fesse, and two tilting spears saltirewise in base of the second, five cocks of the first. **Crest** – A tower argent, on the battlements a cock proper. **Supporters** – *Dexter*, a grenadier habited and accoutred, arms ordered proper; *sinister*, a light infantry man habited and accoutred, arms trailed proper, supporting with his exterior hand a flagstaff also proper, therefrom flowing a banner gules, inscribed "New Ross" in letters of gold. *Residence* –

SISTERS LIVING

Judith Marguerite, *b* 1956. —— Heather Mary, *b* 1959.

DAUGHTERS LIVING OF FIFTH BARONET

Barbara Patty (20 Claremont Rd, Twickenham, Middx), *b* 1918: *m* 1942, Charles Frederick Roetter, who *d* 1977, and has issue living, Martyn Frederick Alexander Gurney, *b* 1944; *ed* St Paul's (Foundation Scholar), and Brasenose Coll, Oxford (Scholar); Research Fellow, Univ Coll, Oxford: *m* 1976, Joyce Stevens, and has issue living, Alexander Charles *b* 1978, Nicolas Martyn *b* 1980, Natasha Chantal *b* 1983, — Christine Frances Ada, *b* 1946: *m* 1971, Stephen A. Rhodes, and has issue living, Molly Jane *b* 1975, Colette Lindsay *b* 1977. —— Monica Lena, *b* 1921: *m* 1st, 1941 (*m diss* 1952), Marshall Douglas Clare; 2ndly, 1957, Dr Florencio Enrique Escardo of Juncal 1335-1C, Buenos Aires, Argentina, and has issue living, (by 1st *m*) Michael Charles Allen, *b* 1945: *m* 1st, 1969 (*m diss* 1974), Dianae, da of Bruce Hamilton Wardrope, of 758 Waterford Av, Winnipeg, Manitoba, Canada; 2ndly, 1980, Fay Margaret Foster, and has issue living (by 2nd *m*), Brendan Marshall Foster *b* 1982, — Marcia Dorothy, *b* 1943: *m* 1965, Michael Bennie, who *d* 1974, and has issue living, Christopher Michael *b* 1966, Claire Julia *b* 1969, — (by 2nd *m*) Florencio Julian, *b* 1958: *m* 1981, Irene Matyas, — Monica Carmen, *b* 1960: *m* 1982, Fernando Garcia-Pullés, and has issue living, Josefina Maria *b* 1984, — Pilar, *b* 1963.

MOTHER LIVING OF SEVENTH BARONET

Molly, da of late James Payn, of Harding, Natal: *m* 1925, Maj Percy Eliot Johnson, who *d* 1962. *Residence* – —

WIDOW LIVING OF SEVENTH BARONET

Barbara Alfreda, da of late Alfred T. Brown, of Germiston, Transvaal: *m* 1st, 1954, Sir Robin Eliot Johnson, 7th Bt, who *d* 1989; 2ndly, 19—, — . *Residence* – —Australia.

COLLATERAL BRANCHES LIVING

Granddaughter of late Maj Arthur Cyril Beaumont Johnson, son of Gen Sir Charles Cooper Johnson, GCB, 6th son of 2nd baronet:—
Issue of late Lt-Col Charles Robert Johnson, *b* 1902, *d* (of wounds received in action) 1941: *m* 1935, Mrs Eileen Agnes Johnson, who *d* 1976, da of late G. C. Mothersill, of Bedford:—
Diana Evelyn, *b* 1935.

Granddaughter of late Maj-Gen Alured Clarke Johnson, CB, 8th son of 2nd baronet:—
Issue of late Lt-Col Gilbert Ward Johnson, *b* 1866, *d* 1924: *m* 1923, Marion, da of C. H. Truslove, of Sale, Cheshire:—
Patricia Danino, *b* (*posthumous*) 1924.

Grandson of late Col Archibald Acheson Johnson, 9th son of 2nd baronet:—
Issue of late Lt-Col Allen Edwin Johnson, DSO, *b* 1878, *d* 1972: *m* 1913, Phoebe Dora Wynn, who *d* 1961, da of late Maj Alfred Elias:—
Allen Antony Wynn (Pond Cottage, Potten End, Berkhamsted, Herts), *b* 1916; *ed* Charterhouse, and St John's Coll, Oxford; formerly RA: *m* 1939, Helen Janet Margaret, only da of W. A. Annett, of Greystoke, Berkhamsted, and has issue living, Mark Allen William Wynn (12 Routh Rd, SW18), *b* 1946; *ed* Berkhamsted Sch (Foundation Scholar), and St John's Coll, Oxford: *m* 1969, Caroline Jane, only da of C. R. E. Bowles of London, and has issue living, Alexander Mark Wynn, *b* 1970, Melissa Caroline *b* 1973, Lydia Jane *b* 1980, — Christopher Wynn, *b* 1948; *ed* E Anglia Univ.
The 1st baronet, Sir Henry, GCB, son of Allen Johnson of Kilternan, co Dublin, and yr brother of Sir John Johnson-Walsh, 1st Bt, of Ballykilcavan, (ext 1953), was Col of the 5th Regt and Governor of Ross Castle. The 2nd baronet, Sir Henry Allen, was a distinguished military officer in the Peninsular War. The 3rd baronet, Sir Henry Franks Frederic, was Col Comdg Forces in Jamaica, Windward and Leeward Islands. The 4th baronet, Sir Henry Allen William, CB, was Brig-Gen late KOYLI.

Johnson-Ferguson, see Ferguson.

Johnson-Walsh, see Walsh.

JOHNSTON (NS) 1626, of Caskieben, Aberdeenshire

Live that you may live hereafter

Sir THOMAS ALEXANDER JOHNSTON, 14th *Baronet*; *b* 1 Feb 1956; *s* his father, Sir THOMAS ALEXANDER, 1984.

Arms – Quarterly: 1st and 4th, argent, a saltire sable, on a chief gules, three cushions or, *Johnston*; 2nd and 3rd, azure, on a bend or between three harts' heads erased argent, attired of the second, as many cross-crosslets fitchée of the second, *Mar* and *Garioch of Caskieben*, composed together on one coat. **Crest** – A Phœnix in flames proper. **Supporters** – Two naked Indians proper, wreathed about the head and middle with laurel vert.
Residence – .

SISTERS LIVING

Helen Du Bois, *b* 1944: *m* 1969, Phillip Thomas Sargent, of 857 Rim Crest Drive, West Lake Village, Cal 91361, USA, and has issue living, John Harrison, *b* 1972, — Bradford Gage, *b* 1976, — Lydia Gaillard, *b* 1981. —— Leslie Sheldon, *b* 1951: *m* 1972, David Charles Krempa, and has issue living, David Alexander, *b* 1984, — Mary Helen, *b* 1978, — Melissa Leslie, *b* 1980.

AUNT LIVING (*Daughter of 12th Baronet*)

Dianne, *b* 1926: *m* 1948, Samuel H. Andrews III, and has issue living, Samuel Henry, *b* 1949, — Bruce Sheldon, *b* 1950, — John Norville, *b* 1960, — Mark Alexander, *b* 1961, — Paula Burke, *b* 1952, — Lucia Dianne Andrews, *b* 1958. *Residence* – Citronelle, Alabama, USA.

WIDOW LIVING OF THIRTEENTH BARONET

HELEN TORREY, da of Benjamin Franklin Du Bois: *m* 1st, 1941, Sir Thomas Alexander Johnston, 13th Bt, who *d* 1984; 2ndly, 1989, Dr Charles Trewartha Lenton, Jr.

COLLATERAL BRANCHES LIVING

Issue of late William Norville Johnston, 2nd son of 11th baronet, *b* 1894, *d* 1959: *m* 1921, Catherine, da of Thomas Murray, of Mobile, Alabama, USA:—

WILLIAM NORVILLE, *b* 1922: *m* 1952, Kathrine Pauline, da of Herbert Sigfred Solberg, of Mobile, and has issue living, William Norville *b* 1955, — Stephen Gregory, *b* 1958, — Paul Brady, *b* 1959, — Kathryn Mary *b* 1953. —— Claude Edward, *b* 1930: *m* 1960, Lucy, da of Bernard Teague Mahorner, of Mobile, and has issue living, Edward Ryan *b* 1961, — Bernard Mathias, *b* 1965, — Mary Teague, *b* 1960, — Laura Jean, *b* 1964, — Courtney Anne, *b* 1971, — Elizabeth Leigh, *b* (twin) 1971. —— Marion, *b* 1924: *m* 1955, Thomas Ross Johnson, of 7 Dogwood Circle, Spring Hill Station, Mobile, Alabama, USA, and has issue living, Thomas Ross III, *b* 1957, — Margaret Murray, *b* 1956: *m* 1986, Edward Luckett King, son of Dr Robert King, of Spring Hill, Alabama, — Elizabeth Barry, *b* 1961. —— Helen Jean, *b* 1926: *m* 1955, William Earle Bidez, of Birmingham, Alabama, USA, and has issue living, William Earle, *b* 1957, — Jeanne Marie, *b* 1956, — Erin Anne, *b* (twin) 1957, — Catherine Leary, *b* 1961.

Issue of late Frederick Rukard Johnston, 3rd son of 11th baronet, *b* 1897, *d* 1962: *m* 1925, Grace (decd), da of John A. McRae, of Clio, Alabama, USA:—

Joyce Rukard, *b* 1951: *m* 1951, Wallace Abney Burgess, US Navy (ret), of 1007 Whitestone Lane, Houston, Texas, USA, and has issue living, Douglas Abney, *b* 1956, — Patricia Olivia, *b* 1952, — Suzanne McRae, *b* 1954, — Joyce Johnston, *b* 1957, — Carolyn Norville, *b* 1962.

Sir George Johnston (son of John Johnston, of Caskieben, Aberdeenshire), Sheriff of Aberdeen, was created a baronet of Nova Scotia 1626 with remainder to his heirs male whatsoever. Sir Thomas Alexander Johnston, 12th Bt, was Ch of Hydro-Power Branch, Dist Office, Mobile, Alabama.

JOHNSTONE (NS) 1700, of Westerhall, Dumfriesshire

Sir FREDERIC ALLAN GEORGE JOHNSTONE, 10th *Baronet*: *b* 23 Feb 1906; *s* his father, *Sir* GEORGE FREDERIC THOMAS TANKERVILLE, 1952; *ed* Imperial Ser Coll: *m* 1st, 1933 (*m diss* 1941), Gladys Hands; 2ndly, 1946, Doris, da of late W. L. Shortridge, of Blackheath, SE, and has issue by 2nd *m*.

Arms – Not matriculated at Lyon Office at time of going to press.

SONS LIVING (*By 2nd marriage*)

(GEORGE) RICHARD DOUGLAS, *b* 21 Aug 1948; *ed* Magdalen Coll Oxford: *m* 1976, Gwyneth, da of Arthur Bailey, of Hastings, and has issue living, Frederic Robert Arthur, *b* 18 Nov 1981, — Caroline *b* 1983. —— Ian Allan, *b* 1954.

COLLATERAL BRANCHES LIVING

Grandchildren of late Major James Henry L'Estrange Johnstone, MVO, son of James Johnstone, eldest son of James Raymond Johnstone, only son of John Johnstone, MP, 5th son of 3rd baronet:—

Issue of late Capt Henry James Johnstone, RN, *b* 1895, *d* 1947: *m* 1923, Alison, who *d* 1984, da of late T. W. McIntyre, of Sorn Castle, Ayrshire:—

Sir (John) Raymond, CBE (Wards, Gartocharn, Dunbartonshire G83 8SB), *b* 1929; *ed* Eton, and Trin Coll, Camb; Managing Dir of Murray Johnstone & Co Ltd, Glasgow; Chm Forestry Commn since 1989: *m* 1979, Susan Sara, only da of late Capt Christopher Gerald Gore (*see* E Eglinton, 1990 Edn), formerly wife of late Basil Reginald Vincent Ziani de Ferranti, and widow of Peter Quixano Henriques; *cr* CBE (Civil) 1988, and Ktd 1993. —— Christine Alison (*Dowager Lady Erskine-Hill*), *b* 1924: *m* 1942, Sir Robert Erskine-Hill, 2nd Bt, who *d* 1989. *Residence* – Quothquhan Lodge, Biggar, Lanarkshire.

Issue of late Andrew Wauchope Johnstone, *b* 1903, *d* 1980: *m* 1932, Eleanor Blanche Helen Margaretta Vere-Laurie (PO Box 44, Hudson, PQ, Canada JOP 1J0), da of Lt-Col George Brenton Laurie, RIR (*see* V Massereene, colls):—

James Andrew Francis (35 Front St South, Unit 209, Mississauga, Ont, Canada L5H 2I6), *b* 1939; *ed* Eton, and Mil Coll, Canada: *m* 1st, 1963 (*m diss* 1978), Helen Christina, el da of late Ivan F. Wade, of 4 Pointe Claire, PQ, Canada; 2ndly, 1982, Carole, widow of Norman Burke, of Westmount, Quebec, and has issue living (by 1st *m*), Sheila Christine, *b* 1964, — Anne Laurie, *b* 1965, — Jennifer Frances, *b* 1968: *m* 1994, Donald Scott, of Port Moody, BC, Canada, — Kathleen Helen, *b* 1970. —— Gillian Margaret (Springfield House, Aldringham, Leiston, Suffolk, IP16 4PZ), *b* 1935: *m* 1957 (*m diss* 1985), Rev Edmund Selwyn Haviland, and has issue living, Andrew Mark James, *b* 1965, — Margaret Vivienne, *b* 1958, — Angela Helen, *b* 1960, — Jane Eleanor, *b* 1963. —— Jacqueline Veronica (10 O'Connor's Rd, Beacon Hill, NSW, Australia), *b* 1936: *m* 1st, 1966 (*m diss* 1975), Thomas Patrick Fitzgerald, of Sydney, NSW; 2ndly, 1977 (*m diss* 1980), Mark Anthony Salfus, and has issue living, (by 1st *m*) John Wauchope, *b* 1967, — (by 2nd *m*) Damien Anthony James, *b* 1978.

Grandchildren of late Maj FitzRoy Augustus Beauclerk Johnstone (infra):—
Issue of late FitzRoy Montague Veitch Johnstone, *b* 1922, *d* 1979: *m* 1956, Dora (Cornaa Mill, Maughold, IoM), da of late Alexander Lofthouse:—

FitzRoy Jonathan, *b* 1957; *ed* Stowe; Dir Jones Lang Wootton, Sydney, Australia: *m* 1989, Jane Alexandra, da of Peter Crothers, of Mildura, Australia. —— Judith Helen, *b* 1959: *m* 1984, John Stewart Morton, and has issue living, Alexander James, *b* 1985, — Thomas Oliver, *b* 1988, — Stewart John, *b* 1989, — William Roy, *b* 1991. —— Jennifer Alison, *b* 1962: *m* 1990, Patrick Douglas Gerard Hodson, and has issue living, James Roy Namani, *b* 1994, — Hannah Rachel, *b* 1992.

Grandson of late Lieut-Com Somerset James SOMERSET-JOHNSTONE, RN (infra):—
Issue of late Major FitzRoy Augustus Beauclerk Johnstone, *b* 1878, *d* 1931: *m* 1915, Alida Helen, who *d* 1968, da of late Andrew Veitch:—

James Veitch (Rose Lea, The Close, Llanfairfechan, Gwynedd, N Wales), *b* 1924; *ed* Lancing; Sub-Lieut RNVR 1943-45: *m* 1950, Nancy Hayes, da of late Henry Atkinson, and has issue living, Ian James FitzRoy (Glasfryn, Valley Rd, Llanfairfechan, Gwynedd), *b* 1952; *ed* St Paul's, and Aston Univ; Ptnr Real Car Co: *m* 1989, Rosalynde Patricia, eldest da of Michael John Mills, and has issue living, Callum James *b* 1988, — Peter Montague Veitch (34 Bell Rd, Bottisham, Cambs), *b* 1956; *ed* Holland Park; Conservationist: *m* 1990, Fiona Catherine, yr da of Lt-Cmdr C. A. J. French, RN (ret), and has issue living, Jamie Peter *b* 1994.

Grandsons of late Gen Montague Cholmeley Johnstone, 3rd son of late James Raymond Johnstone (ante):—
Issue of late Lt-Cdr Somerset James SOMERSET-JOHNSTONE, *b* 1864, *d* 1942, having assumed by deed poll 1900 the additional surname of Somerset: *m* 1st, 1877, Elizabeth Ann, who *d* 1886, da of William Jackson Johnson, of Hootton, Cheshire; 2ndly, 1887 (*m diss* in America 1900), Isabel Ann, who *d* 1934, da of Joseph Charles Mappin, formerly of 38 Harrington Gardens, SW; 3rdly, 1900 (*m diss* 1910), Louisa Hodder, who *d* 1914:—

(By 2nd *m*) James Montague Cholmely, *b* 1889; *ed* Bedford Sch; a Master Mariner; late Lieut RNR; sometime in Australian Navy; European War 1914-17, present at surrender of German New Guinea Sept 1914, and at destruction of the *Emden* Nov 1914: *m* 1917, Alice Maud, da of Frederick Witham, and has issue living, Fitzroy Somerset, *b* 1927; European War 1943-5 as Radio Officer in Merchant Navy: *m* 1952, Francesca Hodson, da of Edward Wareing, of 20 Craven Gardens, Wimbledon, SW, and has issue living, Peter James *b* 1955, Susan Frances *b* 1953, — Mauriel Sydney, *b* 1918, — Audrey Philippa, *b* 1923, — June Octavia, *b* 1932. —— Malcolm Bruce SOMERSET, *b* 1893; *ed* Sherborne; European War 1914-18 on Staff 2nd Army Head Quarters for defence of Sussex, Capt Reserve of Cav attached Army Remount Ser, and Comdg 49th Remount Squadron in Salonika (despatches); assumed by deed poll 1932, the surname of Somerset only.

Grandchildren of late Col Montague George Johnstone, DSO, 2nd son of late Gen Montague Cholmeley Johnstone (ante):—
Issue of late Major Montague Joseph Charles Somerset Johnstone, late RSG, *b* 1882, *d* 1953: *m* 1st, 1900, Victoria Louise, who *d* 1916, da of late James Stewart, of Glasgow; 2ndly, 1916 (*m diss* 1928), Mary Marion Spottiswood, who *d* 1949, da of late George Bayley, of Manuel, Stirlingshire; 3rdly, 1928, Margaret, da of late Sir John Foster Fraser:—

(By 2nd *m*) Roy Henry Montague, MBE, *b* 1919; *ed* Eton, and Magdalene Coll, Camb; 1939-45 War as Maj 60th Rifles, on Staff, War Office, and in France and Germany (despatches, MBE); MBE (Mil) 1945; a Member of London Stock Exchange 1956-74; Trustee St Clement Danes Holborn Estate Charity: *m* 1st, 1939 (*m diss* 1960), Barbara Marjorie, who *d* 1990, da of late Maj Felix Walter Warre, OBE, MC, of Wytherston, Powerstock, Dorset; 2ndly, 1961, Mme Françoise Terlinden, and has issue living, (by 1st *m*) Roland Richard Montague (Poorton Hill, Powerstock, Bridport, Dorset), *b* 1941; *ed* Eton; late Lt 60th Rifles; Solicitor 1967; Partner, Slaughter & May 1973-91: *m* 1968, Sara Outram Boileau, da of late Lt-Col John Garway Outram Whitehead, MC, of 10 Blackfriars St, Canterbury, and has issue living, Andrew Henry Montague, *b* 1969; *ed* Eton, — William Arthur Montague, *b* 1973; *ed* Clayesmore, — Mark Montague (42 Howards Wood Drive, Gerrards Cross, Bucks), *b* 1944; *ed* Eton; late Lt Queen's R Rifles (TA): *m* 1971, Rosalind Margaret, da of late Donald Macphee, DSC, FRICS, of Tylers Green, Bucks, and has issue living, Kerry Montague *b* 1972, Amanda Lee Montague *b* 1974, — Torquil James Montague, *b* 1953; *ed* Eton; CA 1977; merchant banker: *m* 1988, Irena Katharin Buller, da of Maj Ivor Roger Harding Curtis, VRD, RMR, of Wareham, Dorset, and has issue living, Joshua James *b* 1991, Alice Victoria *b* 1993, — Fiona Montague, *b* 1946: *m* 1977, David Wilkins, of 75 Kenley Rd, Kingston-on-Thames, Surrey, and has issue living, Peter Jonathan *b* 1978, Helen Sarah *b* 1981, — (by 2nd *m*) Carol Peter Montague *b* 1961. *Residence* – 16 Leonard Court, Edwardes Sq, Kensington, W8. *Club* – Pratt's. —— (By 1st *m*) Désirée Barbara Montague, *b* 1908. —— Eileen Agnes Montague, *b* 1909: *m* 1931 (*m diss* 19—), Raymond Horwood Hazell, and has issue living, Charles Jonathan, *b* 1938, — Louise, *b* 1933, — Anastasia, *b* 1936. —— Rosemary Maud Montague, *b* 1913: *m* 1936 (*m diss* 19—), Nicholas Desborough Burnell. —— (By 2nd *m*) Gloria Montague (Rashwood, Droitwich, Worcs), *b* 1918. —— (By 3rd *m*) Alastair Montague, *b* 1928.

Granddaughters of late Gen Montague Cholmeley Johnstone (ante):—
Issue of late Lieut-Col Francis Fawkes Johnstone, *b* 1849, *d* 1919: *m* 1st, 1878 (*m diss* 1886), Henrietta Jane, da of James Sullivan; 2ndly, 1887, Harriet Lavinia, who *d* 1910, da of late Richard Sargent and widow of Capt Charles Francis Gregg, of 7th Hussars and 6th Inniskilling Dragoons:—

(By 1st *m*) Mary Louisa Leonora: *m* 1897, Percy Kitchin. —— Frances Geraldine Jane.

Granddaughters of late Lt-Col Francis Fawkes Johnstone (ante):—
Issue of late Major Charles Campbell Gosling Johnstone, *b* 1889, *d* 1942: *m* 1st, 1912 (*m diss* 1927), Laura Mary, da of late Lt-Col Willoughby B. Hemans, RA; 2ndly, 1928, Nina, da of late Col Valentine de Sventorgetsky, Russian Imperial Guard:—

(By 1st *m*) Violet Mary St Clair, *b* 1914. —— Jean Hermione, *b* 1922.

Granddaughters of late John Heywood Johnstone, MP, son of late Rev George Dempster Johnstone, 4th son of late James Raymond Johnstone (ante):—

Issue of late George Horace Johnstone, OBE, DL, *b* 1882, *d* 1960: *m* 1910, Alison, who *d* 1978, da of the Ven Stamford Raffles Raffles-Flint (Archdeacon of Cornwall, and Canon of Truro), of Nansawsan, Ladock, Cornwall:— Elizabeth Alison, *b* 1911. —— Rachel Mary, *b* 1916: *m* 1st, 1934 (*m diss* 1944), Robert Washbourne Money; 2ndly, 1946 (*m diss* 1949), James Henderson; 3rdly, 1957, Jack Spenceley-Collins, and has issue living, (by 1st *m*) Stuart Washbourne, MBE, *b* 1935; Maj SCLI; MBE (Mil) 1964, — Robert Graham Ernlie Washbourne *b* 1936. —— Jennifer Ruth (*Lady Galsworthy*), *b* 1921: *m* 1942, Sir John Edgar Galsworthy, KCVO, CMG, HM Foreign Ser (ret), who *d* 1992, and has issue living, Arthur Michael Johnstone (Trewithen, Grampound Rd, nr Truro, Cornwall TR2 4DD), *b* 1944; DL Cornwall: *m* 1st, 1972, Charlotte Helena Prudence, who *d* 1989, da of Lt-Col Stuart Maxwell Roberts, Alderman of the City of London; 2ndly, 1991, Sarah Christian, da of Cmdr the Rev Peter Durnford, RN (ret), and has issue living (by 1st *m*), Stamford Timothy John *b* 1976, Olivia Victoria Jane *b* 1974, Susannah Catherine Rose *b* 1979, — Alison Merryn, *b* 1947, — Bridget, *b* 1952, — Amanda Elizabeth, *b* 1959. *Address* – Lanzeague, St Just-in-Roseland, Cornwall.

Descendants of late Richard Johnstone (el son of late Col John Johnstone, 2nd son of 2nd baronet), who was *cr* a *Baronet* 1797 (with special remainder to the male issue of his brother, Charles John) (*see* B Derwent).

Descendants of late Charles John Johnstone (2nd son of late Col John Johnstone (ante)), (*see* B Derwent). This family descend from Matthew Johnstone of Pettinain (later called Westraw), Lanarkshire, said to have been a yr son of Sir Adam Johnstone of that Ilk (*d* 1454), ancestor of the Marquesses of Annandale (dormant 1792). Sir John Johnstone of Westershall, 8th in descent from Matthew was *cr* a Baronet with remainder to his heirs male. He represented Dumfries in the Scottish Parliament, and voted for the Union. Sir William, 5th Bt, assumed the surname of Pulteney on marriage to Frances Pulteney, heir to her cousin the Earl of Bath, and died without male issue 1805; his only child Henrietta Laura, was created Countess of Bath, and died without issue 1808. The 6th baronet, Sir John Lowther, MP for Weymouth 1810-11, twice declined a peerage offered to him by Spencer Perceval.

JONES (UK) 1919, of Treeton, West Riding of Yorkshire

Sir SIMON WARLEY FREDERICK BENTON JONES, 4th *Baronet*; *b* 11 Sept 1941; *s* his father, *Sir* PETER FAWCETT BENTON, OBE, 1972; *ed* Eton, and Trin Coll, Camb (MA); JP for Lincs; High Sheriff of Lincs 1977-78: *m* 1966, Margaret Fiona, da of David Rutherford Dickson, of Barrow Lodge, Bury St Edmunds, and has issue.

Arms – Per chevron argent and sable, in chief two dragons heads erased gules, and in base two crosses patée fitchée in saltire or. **Crest** – A demi gryphon gules, grasping a miner's pickaxe, head downwards in pale or.
Seat – Irnham Hall, nr Grantham, Lincs.

SONS LIVING

JAMES PETER MARTIN, *b* 1 Jan 1973. —— David William Anthony, *b* 1975. —— Alastair Frederick Malcolm *b* 1981.

DAUGHTERS LIVING

Fiona Charlotte, *b* 1967. —— Fleur Alexandra, *b* 1970.

SISTER LIVING

Jill Benton (*Hon Lady McAlpine*), *b* 1937: *m* 1959, Hon Sir William Hepburn McAlpine, 6th Bt, of Fawley Hill, Fawley Green, Henley-on-Thames.

AUNTS LIVING (*Daughters of 2nd baronet*)

Pamela Benton (St Heliers Hotel, Clifton Gdns, Folkestone, Kent CT20 2ET), *b* 1908: *m* 1930 (*m diss* 1948), Percival John Parker Stephenson, who *d* 1973 (*see* Stephenson, Bt, colls). —— Rachael Mary Benton, *b* 1918: *m* 1941, George Ronald Murray Kydd, and has issue living, Ian Murray, *b* 1945: *m* 1972, Elizabeth, da of Richard Blackburn, and has issue living, Benjamin Murray *b* 1972, Joel Murray *b* 1975, — Donald Hamish, *b* 1947: *m* 1970, Christine, da of Owen Gough, and has issue living, Lorraine Grace *b* 1971, Samantha Melanie Jane *b* 1973. *Residence* – 23 Chapel St, Grassington, Skipton, N Yorks BD23 5BE.

GREAT-AUNT LIVING (*Daughter of 1st baronet*)

Katharine Mary, *b* 1904: *m* 1933, Lt-Col William Herbert Olivier, TD, JP, DL, LLD, who *d* 1992, and has issue living, Jasper William Dacres, *b* 1938: *m* 1973, Virginia Whitaker, — James Stephen, *b* 1944; Lt-Col RHG: *m* 1968, Sally Anne Simonds, — Flora Mary Margaret, *b* 1936: *m* 1973, John Guy Carmichael Jackson, — Julie Katharine, *b* 1941: *m* 1966, Patrick Julian Dawnay (*see* V Downe, colls). *Residence* – Ashford Hall, Bakewell, Derbyshire, DE5 1QA.

COLLATERAL BRANCH LIVING

Issue of late Capt Charles Frederick Ward Jones, yr son of 1st baronet, *b* 1884, *d* 1971: *m* 1921, Dorothy, who *d* 1962, only da of R. H. Allen, of Hemingfield, Worksop, Notts:— David Robert Ward, *b* 1925; *ed* Repton; Capt RHG (Reserve): *m* 1954, Sally, da of Col H. Cantan, of Bridport, Dorset, and has issue living, Emma, *b* 1956, — Kathryn, *b* 1960, — Harriet, *b* 1963. —— Anne Ward, *b* 1922: *m* 1950, Charles Douglas Pain, of The Priory Farmhouse, S Leverton, nr Retford, Notts, and has issue living, Michael Ward Eames, *b* 1957: *m* 1986, Christina Elisabeth Ljungström. —— Beth Ward, *b* 1924: *m* 1950, Michael William Ollyver Antill, of Woodhouse Hill, Holbeck, Worksop, Notts, and has issue living, Timothy William, *b* 1954, — Sarah Penelope, *b* 1952. Sir Frederick John Jones, 1st Bt, was Pres Mining Assocn of Gt Britain, Chm, S Yorks Coal Trade Assocn, and Miners' Conciliation Board.

LAWRENCE-JONES (UK) 1831, of Cranmer Hall, Norfolk

Marte et arte
By war and art

Sir CHRISTOPHER LAWRENCE-JONES, 6th *Baronet, b* 19 Jan 1940; *s* his uncle, *Sir* LAWRENCE EVELYN, MC, TD, 1969; *ed* Sherborne, and Gonville and Caius Coll, Camb (MA, MB, BChir); DIH, FRCP, FFOM; formerly Ch MO ICI Group, Millbank, SW1; past Chm Medichem, and past Pres section of Occ Med Royal Soc of Medicine; formerly Memb Management Cttee, British Occ Health Research Foundation, and formerly Memb of Board, Faculty of Occ Med RCP; Lord of Manor of Fakenham, Norfolk: *m* 1967, Gail, da of late Cecil Arthur Pittar, FRACS, of Auckland, NZ, and has issue.

Arms – Azure, on a fesse or, three grenades fired proper; in chief a castle, and over it the word "Netherlands" in letters of gold; in base a lion couchant argent, gorged with a ribbon gules fimbriated azure, therefrom suspended a representation of the gold medal presented to the 1st baronet for his services at Badajoz. **Crest** – In front of a castle a lion couchant argent gorged with a wreath of laurel, and pendent therefrom an escutcheon gules charged with a representation of the Badajoz medal as in the arms. *Club* – Royal Cruising.

SONS LIVING

MARK CHRISTOPHER, *b* 28 Dec 1968. —— John Alexander, *b* 1971.

DAUGHTERS LIVING OF FIFTH BARONET

Nancy Lawrence, *b* 1913: *m* 1941, David Vivian Morse, FRCS, who *d* 1993, of The Old Vicarage, Doddington, Wooler, Northumberland, and has issue living, Jonathan Patrick, *b* 1942; *ed* Eton, and Balliol Coll, Oxford, — Oliver James, *b* 1949, — Annabel Harriet, *b* 1944: *m* 1972, Alexander Urquhart, and has issue, two das. —— Vivien Lawrence, *b* 1923: *m* 1942, Simon Anthony Roland Asquith, who *d* 1973 (*see* E Oxford and Asquith, colls). *Residence* – 44 Gilpin Av, East Sheen, SW14 8QY. —— Lavinia Lawrence, *b* 1925: *m* 1980, Frank Monaco. *Residence* – 28 Radnor Walk, SW3.

This family was settled at Sunny Hill, Carmarthenshire for several generations. David Jones moved to Norfolk in the 17th century. Maj-Gen Sir John Jones, 1st Bt, was a distinguished officer in RE, serving in the Peninsular War. He *m* 1816, Catherine, da of Effingham Lawrence, of Long Island, NY. Sir Lawrence Jones, 2nd Bt, was murdered at Macri, in Turkey, 1845. Sir Lawrence Jones, MC, 5th Bt, was author of "Victorian Boyhood", "Edwardian Youth" and "Georgian Afternoon".

PRICHARD-JONES (UK) 1910, of Bron Menai, Dwyran, Llangeinwen, Anglesey

Sir JOHN PRICHARD-JONES, 2nd *Baronet; b* 20 Jan 1913; *s* his father, *Sir* JOHN, 1917; *ed* Eton, and Ch Ch, Oxford (BA honours 1934, MA); Bar Gray's Inn 1936; Capt late The Queen's Bays: *m* 1st, 1937 (*m diss* 1950), Heather Vivian Mary, da of Sir Walter Richard Nugent, 4th Bt, *cr* 1831 (of Donore); 2ndly, (Feb) 1959, Helen Marie Thérèse, da of late J. F. Liddy, Dental Surg, of 20 Lawrence St, Drogheda, and has issue by 1st and 2nd *m*.

Arms – Gules, a lymphad in full sail or, on a chief of the second, two escutcheons of the first. **Crest** – A demi-lion gules, resting the sinister paw on a boar's head erased or.
Residence – Allenswood House, Lucan, co Dublin.

SON LIVING *(By 1st marriage)*

DAVID JOHN WALTER, *b* 14 March 1943; *ed* Ampleforth, and Ch Ch, Oxford (BA Hons).

DAUGHTER LIVING *(By 2nd marriage)*

Susan Marie *b* (Nov) 1959.

COLLATERAL BRANCH LIVING

Issue of late Capt Richard William Prichard-Jones, yr son of 1st baronet, *b* 1914, *d* 1986: *m* 1943, Margaret Woodburn (Sally) (The Forge, Whittlesford, Cambs), da of Sqdn-Ldr Ronald Herbert Wingfield Davidson, of 605 Hood House, Dolphin Sq, SW1:—

Richard Stephen, *b* 1952; *ed* Bryanston. —— Marie Anne, *b* 1948.

Sir John, JP, DL, LLD, 1st Bt, sometime head of the firm of Dickins and Jones (Limited), of 226-244 Regent Street, W, founded and endowed the Prichard-Jones Institute and Cottage Homes, Newborough, Anglesey, and donated the Prichard-Jones Hall of Univ Coll of N Wales, of which he was Senior Vice-Pres; he assumed by deed poll (registered at the College of Arms) 1917 the surname of Prichard-Jones.

PRYCE-JONES (UK) 1918, of Dolerw, co Montgomery (Extinct 1963)

Sir Pryce Victor Pryce-Jones, 2nd and last *Baronet*.

WIDOW LIVING OF SECOND BARONET

Syra Roantree (*Lady Pryce-Jones*) (The Manor Cottage, Great Ryburgh, Norfolk), only da of late Francis O'Shiel, of Omagh, co Tyrone: *m* 1938, Capt Sir Pryce Victor Pryce-Jones, 2nd Bt, who *d* 1963, when the title became ext.

JOSEPH (UK) 1942, of Stoke-on-Trent, co Stafford (Extinct 1951)

Sir Francis L'Estrange Joseph, KBE, 1st and last *Baronet*.

DAUGHTERS LIVING OF FIRST BARONET

Rosamund Mary, *b* 1919; resumed by deed poll 1962 her former surname of Birley: *m* 1st, 1942 (*m diss* 1956), Maj Peter Rouse Addison Birley, 17th/21st Lancers; 2ndly, 1956, Christopher Bevis Sanford; 3rdly, 1968, Daniel Vincent O'Donovan, Barrister, who *d* 1977, and has issue living, (by 1st *m*) David Peter Francis (56 Huron Rd, SW17), *b* 1943; *ed* Harrow, and Ch Ch, Oxford: *m* 1985, (Carole) Jan, da of late Dr John Foxton, of Brigg, Lincs, and has issue living, Sam David John *b* 1986, George Charles Foxton *b* 1989, Frederick Peter Francis *b* 1989, — (by 2nd *m*), Francis L'Estrange, *b* 1957. —— Cynthia Violet Maud, *b* 1921: *m* 1946, Col Peter Stanley Walter Dean, R Anglian Regt (ret), of Foresters, Tostock, Bury St Edmunds, Suffolk.

KABERRY (UK) 1960, of Adel cum Eccup, City of Leeds

Hon Sir Christopher Donald Kaberry, 2nd *Baronet*; *b* 14 March 1943; *s* his father, Donald, Baron Kaberry of Adel, TD (Life Baron) in his baronetcy, 1991; *ed* Repton; FCA 1967: *m* 1967, Gaenor Elizabeth Vowe, yr da of Cecil Vowe Peake, MBE, of Redbourn, Herts, and has issue.

Arms – Per fesse argent and azure and a pile reversed counterchanged three double-warded, keys wards upwards also azure each enfiled by a chaplet of holly proper and of roses argent barbed and seeded also proper. **Crest** – On a wreath of sable and azure a weeping willow tree proper pendent from the trunk thereof by a ring a fleece or.
Residence – The Croft, Rookery Lane, Wymondham, Leics LE14 2AU.

SONS LIVING

James Christopher, *b* 1 April 1970; *ed* Oakham: *m* 1989, Juliet Clare, eldest da of Sir James Frederick Hill, 4th Bt (*cr* 1916), and has issue living, Jonathan James Alexander, *b* 12 May 1989, — Oliver George Henry, *b* 1991. —— Angus George, *b* 1972.

DAUGHTER LIVING

Claire Elizabeth, *b* 1974.

BROTHERS LIVING

Hon Andrew Murdoch Scott, *b* 1946; *ed* Repton, and E Anglia Univ (BA); FCA 1972. *Residence* – Thorpe Arch Hall, Boston Spa, W Yorks.

Hon Simon Edmund John, *b* 1948; *ed* Repton; admitted Solicitor 1974. *Residence* – Adel Willows, Otley Rd, Leeds 16.

The 1st baronet, Donald Kaberry, TD, son of Abraham Kaberry, of Leeds, was admitted Solicitor 1930, Dep Lord Mayor of Leeds 1946-47, Parl Sec Board of Trade April to Oct 1955, Member of Mr Speaker's Panel of Chairmen 1974-83, etc; MP for NW Div of Leeds (C) 1950-83, DL W Yorks 1976; 1939-45 War as Col 63rd Medium Regt, Dunkirk and NW Europe RA (despatches twice); *cr* Baron *Kaberry of Adel*, of Adel, City of Leeds (Life Baron) 1983; *d* 1991.

KAYE (UK) 1923, of Huddersfield, co York

Spectemur agendo

Let us be judged by our actions

Sir DAVID ALEXANDER GORDON KAYE, 4th *Baronet*; *b* 26 July 1919; *s* his brother, *Sir* STEPHEN HENRY GORDON, 1983; *ed* Stowe, and Camb Univ (BA); MRCS Eng and LRCP London 1943: *m* 1st, 1942 (*m diss* 1950), Elizabeth Rosemary, only da of Capt Malcolm Hurtley, of Baynards Manor, Horsham, Sussex; 2ndly, 1955, Adelle Frances, da of Denis Lionel Thomas, of Brisbane, Qld, and has issue by 2nd *m*.

Arms – Or, a bend cotised invected between two escutcheons sable each charged with a rose argent, barbed and seeded proper. **Crest** – Upon a staff raguly fessewise or a goldfinch proper, holding in the beak a rose argent, barbed, seeded, leaved and slipped proper.
Residence – 594 Lower Bowen Terrace, New Farm, Brisbane 4005, Qld, Australia.

SONS LIVING *(By 2nd marriage)*

PAUL HENRY GORDON, *b* 19 Feb 1958: *m* 1984, Sally Ann Louise, da of—. —— John Egidio Gordon, *b* 1967.

DAUGHTERS LIVING *(By 2nd marriage)*

Yvonne Marie, *b* 1956. —— Denise Anne, *b* 1960. —— Alaine Freda, *b* 1962. —— Marita Margaret, *b* 1970.

COLLATERAL BRANCH LIVING

Issue of late Brian Joseph Gordon Kaye, brother of 4th Bt (ante), *b* 1920, *d* 19—: *m* 1947, Anne, only da of Frederick Henry Grisewood, OBE, of Hewshotts, Liphook, Hants:—
Angus Frederick Gordon, *b* 1962.

The 1st baronet, Sir Joseph Henry, was Senior Director of Kaye and Stewart (Limited), of Huddersfield, and a Director of London, Midland and Scottish Railway Co, and of Lloyds Bank (Limited).

LISTER-KAYE (UK) 1812, of Grange, Yorkshire

Keep your own kin kind

Sir JOHN PHILIP LISTER LISTER-KAYE, 8th Baronet; *b* 8 May 1946; *s* his father, Sir JOHN CHRISTOPHER LISTER, 1982; *ed* Allhallows Sch; lecturer, writer and broadcaster on Conservation of Nature and the Environment; founder dir of Scottish Conservation Charity, The Aigas Trust, 1979; Exec Dir Aigas Field Centre Ltd since 1980; Member Internat Cttee World Wilderness Foundation since 1984, Chm Scottish Advisory Cttee RSPB 1986-92; Nature Conservancy Council 1989-91; NW Regional Chm Nature Conservancy Council for Scotland 1992; NW Regional Chm Scottish Natural Heritage since 1992; author of *The White Island* (1972), *Seal Cull* (1979), *The Seeing Eye* (1980) and *One For Sorrow* (1994): *m* 1st, 1972 (*m diss* 1988), Sorrel Deirdre (later Lady Sorrel), el da of Count Henry Noel Bentinck (later 11th Earl of Portland); 2ndly, 1989, Lucinda Anne, JP for Ross-shire, eldest da of Robin Law, of Withersfield, Suffolk, and formerly wife of Hon Evan Michael Ronald Baillie (*see* B Burton), and has issue by 1st and 2nd *m*.

Arms – Quarterly, 1st and 4th, argent, two bendlets sable, *Kaye*; 2nd and 3rd, ermine on a fesse sable three mullets or, the whole within a bordure wavy azure, *Lister*. **Crests** – 1st, a goldfinch proper, charged on the breast with a rose gules; 2nd, a buck's head proper, erased wavy or, attired sable, and in the mouth a bird-bolt bendwise of the third, flighted argent.
Residence – Aigas House, Beauly, Inverness-shire IV4 7AD. *Clubs* – Caledonian, Farmers'.

SON LIVING *(By 1st marriage)*

JOHN WARWICK NOEL LISTER, *b* 10 Dec 1974.

DAUGHTERS LIVING *(By 1st marriage)*

Amelia Helen, *b* 1976. —— Melanie Jenifer, *b* (twin) 1976.

(by 2nd marriage)

Hermione Anne Lucinda Lorne, *b* 1990.

SISTER LIVING

Mary Eugenia Helen, *b* 1944: *m* 1970 (*m diss* 1994), Nigel Carrel, of Ganarew Farm, Ganarew, Monmouth, Gwent, and has issue living, Christopher-James, *b* 1971, — Gareth Nigel Andrew, *b* 1974, — Huw Stephen, *b* 1981, — Lucinda Helen Jane, *b* 1977.

AUNT LIVING (*Daughter of 6th baronet*)

Rosamond Eugenia Mary, *b* 1912: *m* 1945, Maj Edward Osmond Thornhill Simpson, who *d* 1992, and has issue living, Mark Thornhill, *b* 1951, — Sarah Thornhill, *b* 1946, — Julia Thornhill, *b* 1947. *Residence* – 7275, Balaclava St, Vancouver V6N 1M7, BC, Canada.

COLLATERAL BRANCHES LIVING

Grandchildren of late Arthur Lister-Kaye (*infra*):—
Issue of late John Arthur Lister-Kaye, *b* 1895, *d* 1974: *m* 1923, Emily Alice, da of James Henry Cooper, of Hayling Island:—
Warwick Arthur, *b* 1929. —— Stella Maud, *b* 1924: *m* 1943, William John Stewart Boyd, of Vic, BC, Canada.

Issue of late Arthur Lister-Kaye, brother of 6th baronet, *b* 1876, *d* 1943: *m* 1st, 1895, Lottie Emmeline, da of John Woodward; 2ndly, 1900, Gertrude, who *d* 1945, da of J. Hall, formerly of Gore House, New Milton, Hants:—
(By 1st *m*) Helen, *b* 1896. —— (By 2nd *m*) Arthur Lister, *b* 1903.

Sir John Kaye, of Woodsome, Almondbury, Yorks, Col of Horse in the service of Charles I, was created a baronet in 1642. He later raised 700 men to fight for the King but suffered heavily at the Battle of Naseby 1645. His title and estates were forfeit as a result of his loyalty to the Crown, but he survived the Restoration in 1660, paying £50 to Parliament for the redemption of his estates. The 4th Bt, Sir John, MP for York 1734-40 and Lord Mayor of York 1737, was responsible for the restoration of Micklegate Bar, which bears his arms. He was also a known Jacobite sympathizer and harbored Jacobite rebels after the Battle of Culloden. This baronetcy became extinct on the death of the 6th Bt in 1809, but in 1812 Sir John Lister-Kaye, natural son and testamentary heir of the 5th Bt received a Baronetcy. The 3rd Bt, Sir John Pepys Lister-Kaye, was a Groom-in-Waiting to King Edward VII 1908-10.

KEANE (UK) 1801, of Cappoquin, co Waterford

The stroked cat is meek

Sir RICHARD MICHAEL KEANE, 6th *Baronet*; *b* 29 Jan 1909; *s* his father, *Lt-Col Sir* JOHN, DSO, 1956; *ed* Sherborne, and Ch Ch Oxford: *m* 1939, Olivia Dorothy, da of Oliver Hawkshaw, TD, of Chisenbury Priory, Wilts, and has issue.

Arms – Gules, three salmon naiant in pale argent. **Crest** – A cat-a-mountain sejant proper, in his dexter paw a staff displaying a banner.
Residence – Cappoquin House, co Waterford.

SONS LIVING

JOHN CHARLES, *b* 16 Sept 1941; *ed* Eton, and Ch Ch, Oxford: *m* 1977, Corinne, da of Jean Everard de Harzir, of Waroux, Alleur, Belgium, and has issue living, Christopher, *b* 1981, — Gregory, *b* 1982, — Amelia, *b* 1987. —— David Richard, *b* 1950; *ed* Eton, and Balliol Coll, Oxford: *m* 1973, Julia, da of Henry Bowring, of The Old Orchard, Bembridge, Isle of Wight, and has issue living, Henry, *b* 1982, — Jessica, *b* 1978, — Rosanna Emily, *b* 1980, — Camilla, *b* 1985.

DAUGHTER LIVING

Vivien Eleanor, *b* 1940: *m* 1961, Simon Pleydell-Bouverie (*see* E Radnor, colls). *Residence* – The Castle House, Deddington, Oxon.

SISTERS LIVING

Adelaide Mary, *b* 1907: *m* 1933, Cecil Denis Pegge, of Carrigeen, Cappoquin, co Waterford, and has issue living, a son, *b* 1937. —— Sheila, *b* 1911: *m* 1935, Christopher Edward Knight, and has issue living, Michael John, *b* 1939; *ed* Eton, and New Coll, Oxford: *m* 1970, Caroline Francesca, el da of Alexander Kendal Humphrey Fletcher, and has issue living, Julian Francis *b* 1971, Cassandra Louise *b* 1972, Claudia Helen *b* 1977, — Jonathan Christopher, *b* 1943; *ed* Eton, and Architectural Association: *m* 1977, Hilary Anne Durnford, and has issue living, Oliver James *b* 1977, Imogen Laura *b* 1979, — Martin David, *b* 1946, *ed* Eton, and Trin Coll, Dublin: *m* 1971, Eleanor Clare, da of James Malcolm Harrison, and has had issue, Edward Martin *b* 1976, Tamsin Jane *b* 1974, Hermione Clare *b* 1982, *d* 1985, Sophie Clare *b* 1988, — Susan Jane, *b* 1937. *Residence* – Quarry House, East St, Turners Hill, W Sussex RH10 4PU. —— Madeline Lucy; *b* 1914: *m* 1938, Donald Godfrey Emerson, CBE, of Meads House, Leighterton, Tetbury, Glos, GL8 8UW, and has issue living, James Seymour, *b* 1941; *ed* Marlborough, and Trin Coll, Dublin: *m* 1st, 1964 (*m diss* 1971), Bridget Eileen Mary, da of Lt-Col Wyndham Marsden Knatchbull (*see* B Brabourne, colls); 2ndly, 1971, Jennifer Ruth Clement, and has issue living, (by 1st *m*) Suzanne Mary *b* 1964, Gillian Lucy *b* 1966, (by 2nd *m*) Richard Donald *b* 1971, Sarah Louise *b* 1974, — Judith Lucy, *b* 1943: *m* 1967, Michael Maurice Fletcher Watson, and has issue living, — Carol Georgena, *b* 1944: *m* 1971, Robert Lorne Hyndham, of Ottawa, Canada, and has issue living, — Mary Eleanor, *b* 1953.

COLLATERAL BRANCHES LIVING

Issue of late Capt George Michael Keane, RN, 2nd son of 4th baronet, *b* 1875, *d* 1957: *m* 1909, Violet, who *d* 1974, da of late Theodore McKenna, of 22 Portland Place, W1:—
Ann Patricia, *b* 1910: *m* 1934, Christopher Leslie Thompson, Group Capt, RAF (ret), and has issue living, Christopher Mark, *b* 1935, — Jonathan Michael Adrian, *b* 1938: *m* 1970, Barbara Anne, da of F. Scrowcroft, — Andrew Theodore, *b* 1941. *Residence* – Coldenhale, Eastham, Tenbury Wells, Worcs.

Granddaughters of late Lieut-Col Richard Henry Keane, CBE (*infra*):—
Issue of late Robert Lumley Keane, *b* 1910, *d* 1946: *m* 1938, Mary Nesta (Dysert, Ardmore, co Waterford), da of late Walter C. Skrine, of Ballyrankin House, Ferns, co Wexford:—

Adele Sara, *b* 1940: *m* 1972, George Pyne Phipps, of Kilcor Castle, Castle Lyons, co Cork. —— Virginia, *b* 1945: *m* 1969, Kevin Brownlow, film historian, of 7 Manor Mansions, Belsize Park Gdns, NW3, and has issue living, a da, *b* 1984.

The 1st baronet was successively MP for Bangor and Youghal, the 2nd baronet sat as MP for Waterford (*L*) 1832-5, and the 3rd baronet was High Sheriff for co Waterford in 1856 and the 4th baronet in 1881. Sir John Keane, 5th Bt was a Senator of Irish Free State for 26 years a Councillor of State, Republic of Ireland, Gov of Bank of Ireland, and High Sheriff of co Waterford in 1911.

KELLETT (UK) 1801, of Lota, Cork

Sir STANLEY CHARLES KELLETT, 7th *Baronet*; *b* 5 March 1940; *s* his father, *Sir* STANLEY EVERARD KELLETT, 1983; *m* 1st, 1962 (*m diss* 1968), Lorraine May, da of F. Winspear; 2ndly, 1968 (*m diss* 1974), Margaret Ann, da of James W. Bofinger; 3rdly, 1982, Catherine Lorna, da of W. J. C. Orr, and has issue by 3rd *m*.

Arms – Quarterly: 1st and 4th, argent, on a mount vert a boar passant sable, armed, bristled, and chained or *Kellett*; 2nd and 3rd, argent, a cross gules, in the first quarter a fleur-de-lis of the second, *Haddock*. **Crest** – An armed arm proper, holding a truncheon or.
Residence – 58 Glad Gunson Drive, Eleebana, NSW 2280.

DAUGHTER LIVING (By 3rd marriage)

Leah Catherine Elizabeth, *b* 1983.

SISTER LIVING

Margaret Joy, *b* 1942: *m* 1963, Percival William Horton, AASA(S), of 506 Great Western Highway, Faulconbridge, NSW 2776, and has issue living, Phillip William, *b* 1967, — Colin Stanley, *b* 1969, — Deborah Jane, *b* 1964: *m* 1983, Andrew Philip Howe.

UNCLE LIVING (Brother of 6th baronet)

Feret ad astra virtus
Virtue will bear you to the
skies

CHARLES REX (9 Ashfield Place, Glen Alpine, NSW 2560, Australia), *b* 1916: *m* 1940, Florence Helen Bellamy, who *d*'1984, and has issue living, Maxwell Rex (4 Daisy St, Roselands, NSW 2195, Australia), *b* 1947; FCPA: *m* 1968, Jennifer, da of N. Maher, and has issue living, Jane Maxine *b* 1974, — Peter Charles (9 Ashfield Place, Glen Alpine, NSW 2560, Australia), *b* 1949: *m* 1973, Jennifer, da of K. Pike, of W Aust, and has issue living, Renee Helen *b* 1977, Lauren Ann *b* 1979, — Marilyn Helen, *b* 1942: *m* 1966 Bruce Malcolm Morgan, of Lot 39, Kent Rd, Picton 2571, NSW, and has issue living, Gavin Charles *b* 1974, Karen Lee *b* 1969: *m* 1990, Ian William Spedding, of 52 Castlereagh St, Tahmoor, NSW 2573, Australia, Joanne Lynne *b* 1971: *m* 1991, Jason Kenneth Watson, of 52 Castlereagh St, Tahmoor, NSW 2573, Australia. —— Ray Weaver (10 Cutler Rd, Engadine, NSW 2233, Australia), *b* 1916: *m* 1940, Daisy Miriam Payne, and has issue living, Rev John Raymond (153 Brooks St, Bar Beach, Newcastle 2300, NSW), *b* 1942; *ed* Univ of NSW (BSc), and Melbourne Coll of Divinity (BD): *m* 1st, 1965 (*m diss* 1982), Sandra, da of N. Holman; 2ndly, 1982, Rita Marjorie, da of G. Wiggins, and has issue living, (by 1st *m*) David John *b* 1973, Michelle Ruth *b* 1971, — Bruce Lawrence (121 Washington Dr, Bonnet Bay, NSW 2226, Australia), *b* 1945: *m* 1969, Susan, da of J. Butler, and has issue living, Bronwyn Jane *b* 1973, Jacqueline Ruth *b* 1975, — Graham Edward (23 Taft Place, Bonnet Bay, NSW, 2226), *b* 1948; BSc: *m* 1970, Leonie, da of R. Adams, and has issue living, Joshua Morgan *b* 1977, Skye Emma *b* 1975.

WIDOW LIVING OF FIFTH BARONET

IDA MARY GRACE WEAVER (*Ida, Lady Kellett*): *m* 1952, Sir Henry de Castres Kellett, 5th Bt, who *d* 1966.

WIDOW LIVING OF SIXTH BARONET

AUDREY MARGARET PHILLIPS (*Audrey, Lady Kellett*) (33 Caroma Av, Kyeemagh, NSW): *m* 1938, Sir Stanley Everard Kellett, 6th Bt, who *d* 1983.

COLLATERAL BRANCH LIVING

Issue of late William Augustus Kellett, 3rd son of 3rd baronet, *b* 1889, *d* 1952: *m* 1919, Janet Victoria, who *d* 1936, da of Andrew Peart:—
William Andrew Henry (32 Panoramic Grove, Glen Waverley, Victoria, Australia), *b* 1920; AASA: *m* 1945, Florence, da of late Leslie James Williamson, of Koornang Rd, Carnegie, Victoria, and has issue living, James Andrew (53 Sevenoaks Rd, Burwood East, Vic 3151, Australia), *b* 1952: *m* 1st, 1974 (*m diss* 1987), Kveta, da of Karel Prochazka, of Johannesburg, S Africa; 2ndly, 1993, Dianne, da of John Goddard, of Glen Waverley, Vic, Australia, and has issue living (by 1st *m*), Tamara *b* 1977, — Anne Louise, *b* 1947: *m* 1968 (*m diss* 1994), Robert James Fitzpatrick, and has issue living, David James *b* 1972, Scott Andrew *b* 1973, Sarah Louise *b* 1978, — Christine Elizabeth, *b* 1950: *m* 1970 (*m diss* 1980), John Adrian Bailey, and has issue living, Justin Daniel *b* 1973, Jacqueline Marie *b* 1971.

This baronetcy was created with special remainder to the heirs male of Richard Kellett, of Lota, co Cork, the father of the 1st baronet. On the death of the 2nd baronet, Sir William, in 1886 the title passed (in accordance with the special remainder) to the descendants of the yr brother (Henry de Castres Kellett, *b* 1776) of the 1st baronet, whose third son was Henry de Castres Kellett, father of Sir Henry de Castres Kellett, 3rd Bt (for 40 years a Councillor of Kew, Melbourne). He did not assume the title until 1906. Sir Henry de Castres Kellett, 4th Bt, *d* 25 July 1966. His only son Sir Henry de Castres Kellett, 5th Bt, *d* 6 Aug 1966.

KEMP (E) 1642, of Gissing, Norfolk (Extinct 1936)

Sir KENNETH HAGAR KEMP, CBE, 12th and last *Baronet.*

COLLATERAL BRANCH LIVING

Issue of late Capt Robert Hamilton Kemp, only son of 12th baronet, *b* 1877, *d* 1933: *m* 1908, Violet Mary, da of late Capt R. C. Dalrymple Stewart-Muirhead, Roy Horse Guards:—
Margaret Violet Nancy (43 Coniston Court, Holland Rd, Hove, E Sussex), *b* 1910: *m* 1932, Henry Richard Hurrell, who *d* 1973. —— Peggy Isabelle, *b* 1914: *m* 1939, Major Richard Harold Arnaud Painter, Essex Regt, of 2 Aylesbury, York Ave, Hove, E Sussex, and has issue living, Richard Hamilton, *b* 1947: *m* 1979, Patricia Leslie Hook, and has issue living, Mark Richard *b* 1986, — Kathleen Leslie *b* 1984, — Gillian Mary, *b* 1943: *m* 1972, Daniel J. De Groote, and has issue living, Neal *b* 1973, Jason *b* 1976.

KENNARD (UK) 1891, of Fernhill, co Southampton

Sir GEORGE ARNOLD FORD KENNARD, 3rd *Baronet*; *b* 27 April 1915; *s* his brother, *Sir* LAURENCE URY CHARLES, 1967; *ed* Eton; Lt-Col (ret) late Comdg 4th Queen's Own Hussars; 1939-45 War (despatches twice, prisoner): *m* 1st, 1940 (*m diss* 1958), Cecilia Violet Cokayne, only da of Maj Cecil John Cokayne Maunsell, JP (E Munster, colls); 2ndly, 1958 (*m diss* 1974), Mrs Molly Jesse Rudd Miskin, yr da of late Hugh Wyllie, of Fishbourne, Sussex; 3rdly, 1985, Nicola CAREW, only da of late Capt Peter Gawen Carew (*see* Carew, Bt, colls), and formerly wife of Charles Louis Breitmeyer; 4thly, 1992, Georgina, da of Sir Harold Augustus Wernher, 3rd Bt, GCVO, TD, and widow of Lt-Col Harold Pedro Joseph Phillips, and has issue by 1st *m.*

At spes non fracta
But hope is not broken

Arms – Per chevron gules and azure, a chevron engrailed argent between in chief two keys, wards downwards, or, and in base a sword erect proper, pommel and hilt or. **Crest** – A dexter cubit arm erect in armour proper, charged with a buckle gules, the hand grasping a key in bend or, and a broken sword in bend sinister proper. **Residence** – 13 Burton Court, Franklin's Row, SE3 4TA. **Club** – Cavalry and Guards'.

DAUGHTER LIVING *(By 1st marriage)*

Zandra, *b* 1941: *m* 1962, Maj John Middleton Neilson Powell, Queen's R Irish Hussars (Catsley Farmhouse, Corscombe, Dorchester, Dorset), and has issue living, Edward Coleridge Cokayne, *b* 1964, — Louise Cecilia Middleton, *b* 1966.
Queen Victoria signified her intention of bestowing a Baronetcy upon Coleridge John Kennard but he having died before the patent was gazetted, the dignity was conferred on his grandson Coleridge Arthur FitzRoy Kennard, only child of late Hugh Coleridge Downing Kennard.

KENNAWAY (GB) 1791, of Hyderabad, East Indies

Sir JOHN LAWRENCE KENNAWAY, 5th *Baronet*; *b* 7 Sept 1933; *s* his father, *Sir* JOHN, 1956; *ed* Harrow, and Trin Coll, Camb; patron of one living: *m* 1961, Christina Veronica Urszenyi, MB, ChB, and has issue.

Arms – Argent, a fesse azure between two eagles displayed in chief gules, and in base, through an annulet of the third, a slip of olive and another of palm in saltire proper. **Crest** – An eagle rising proper, from the beak an escutcheon pendent azure, charged with the sun in splendour also proper. **Seat** – Escot, Ottery St Mary, Devon EX11 1LU.

SON LIVING

JOHN MICHAEL, *b* 17 Feb 1962; *ed* King Edward's Sch Bath, and Hampshire Coll of Agric: *m* 1988, Lucy Frances, yr da of Dr Jeremy Houlton Bradshaw-Smith, of Ottery St Mary, Devon, and has issue living, Olivia Ursula, *b* 1993.

DAUGHTERS LIVING

Julia Frances, *b* 1965. —— Irma Annabelle, *b* 1968.

BROTHER LIVING

Richard Noel (19 MacMillan Av, Christchurch, NZ) *b* 1935; *ed* Eton (King's Scholar) and King's Coll, Camb (Scholar); Sen lecturer in Political Science.

SISTER LIVING

I shall ascend

Mary Joyce, *b* 1940. *Residence* – 16 Sunny Hill, New Lane, Ottery St Mary, Devon.

COLLATERAL BRANCHES LIVING

Granddaughters of late Rev Richard Arthur Kennaway, 4th son of 2nd baronet:—
Issue of late Mark John Kennaway, *b* 1880, *d* 1960: *m* 1920, Dorothy, who *d* 1958, da of late Edward Hick, formerly of Chartridge, Chesham:—
Anne, *b* 1922: *m* 1946, Gerald Wardlaw Scott, who *d* 1988, of Corner Cottage, Fletching, Uckfield, E Sussex, and has issue living, Philip Wardlaw, *b* 1950: *m* 1977, Julia Margaret Newnham (*née* Newbery), and has issue living, Oliver Wardlaw *b* 1978, — Deborah, *b* 1948: *m* 1973 (*m diss* 1980), Torbjorn Stene, and has issue living, Rebecca *b* 1973. —— Mary Elizabeth, *b* 1924: *m* 1948, Bernard Stratton Davis, OBE, who *d* 1983, Malayan Civil Ser, of PO Box 269, Girne, Mersin 10, Turkey, and has issue living, Mark John Stratton, *b* 1952: *m* 1980, Valerie Rainsbury, and has issue living, John Charles Stratton *b* 1981, William Adam *b* 1985, Catherine *b* (twin) 1981, — Sarah Elizabeth, *b* 1951; has issue living (by John Wyllie), Jack WYLLIE-DAVIS *b* 1985, Joel WYLLIE-DAVIS *b* 1987, — Maroulla Judith, *b* 1954: *m* 1979, Jeremy Peter Haile, and has issue living, Scott Matthew *b* 1983, Peter *b* 1988, Sarah *b* 1982, Emily Rebecca *b* 1985. —— Philippa Jane, *b* 1927: *m* 1962, Alexander Keith Boyle, of 4 White Point Rd, Whitby, N Yorks YO21 3JR, and has issue living, David Kennaway, *b* 1964: *m* 1987, Armida Asunta Eslava, — Michael Kennaway, *b* 1967: —— Kirsteen Susan, *b* 1965: *m* 1989, Herbert Van Courtlandt Bailey, and has issue (*see* B Glanusk, colls). —— Susan Helen, *b* 1928: *m* 1966, His Honour Judge John Reginald Whitley, of Kingsrod, Kingsley Green, Haslemere, Surrey, and has issue living, Elizabeth Rose, *b* 1967.

Grandson of late Rev Charles Lewis Kennaway, grandson of 1st baronet:—
Issue of late Charles Roger Kennaway, *b* 1880, *d* 1914: *m* 1907, Margaret Evelyn, who *d* 1917, da of Rev Robert Bagot Chester Everard (B Bagot, colls):—
Roger Charles Lewis, *b* 1910; *ed* Harrow; Capt late Oxfordshire and Bucks LI (Supplementary Reserve): *m* 1st, 1936 (*m diss* 1947), Alethea Winifrede, da of late F. N. Lloyd; 2ndly, 1947, Pamela Lavender, da of Lt-Cdr T. C. M. Bellairs, RN, and widow of Group-Capt Patrick Bruce Bine Ogilvie, DSO, DFC (Renshaw, Bt, colls), and has issue living, (by 1st *m*) Roger Ian (32 Rylett Crescent, W12 9RL), *b* 1938; FRICS: *m* 1964, Gabrielle Mary Anna, da of late Lt-Col D. I. C. Tennant, of Bosham, Sussex, and has issue living, Charles Lewis *b* 1966, Hugh Edward *b* 1969, Anthony Francis *b* 1973, — (by 2nd *m*) Rose Margaret Ruth, *b* 1949: *m* 1970 (*m diss* 1993), Quintin Gerald Wyvern Batt, and has issue living, Camilla Louise *b* 1973. *Residence* – Tremoor Combe, St Breward, Cornwall.

The 1st baronet, Sir John, in 1788 was appointed Resident at the Court of the Nizam, with whom, on the breaking out of the war with Tippoo Sultan, he concluded treaties of peace between the allied powers and Tippoo, who ceded half his dominions and paid £3,300,000 to the Allies. The 3rd baronet, the Rt Hon Sir John Henry, PC, CB, sat as MP for Devonshire (C) 1870-85, and for Honiton Div of Devonshire 1885-1910.

KENNEDY (UK) 1836, of Johnstown Kennedy, co Dublin

I adhere to virtue

Sir MICHAEL EDWARD KENNEDY, 8th *Baronet*; *b* 12 April 1956; *s* his father, *Lt-Col Sir* (GEORGE) RONALD DERRICK, OBE, RA, 1988; *ed* Rotherfield Hall, Sussex; *m* 1984, Helen Christine Jennifer, da of Patrick Lancelot Rae, of Nine Acres, Halstead, Kent, and has issue.

Arms – Sable, on a fesse between three esquires' helmets argent, a fox courant proper. **Crest** – A dexter arm embowed in armour, the hand grasping an oak-branch all proper.
Seat – Johnstown Kennedy, Rathcoole, Co Dublin. *Residence* – 48 Telston Lane, Otford, Kent TN14 5LA.

SON LIVING

GEORGE MATTHEW RAE, *b* 9 Dec 1993.

DAUGHTERS LIVING

Constance, *b* 1984. —— Josephine, *b* 1986.

SISTER LIVING

Carolyn Phyllis, *b* 1950: *m* 1979, Jan Gerard Willemszoon Blaauw, of Hong Kong, and has issue living, Keir Alexander Kennedy, *b* 1982, — Patrick Jan Kennedy, *b* (twin) 1982. *Residence* – 7 Beverly Court, 2D Shui Fai Terrace, Stubbs Rd, Hong Kong.

UNCLE LIVING (son of 6th baronet)

Mark Gordon, *b* 1932; *ed* Clifton. *Residence* – Flat 4, Kennet Court, St John's Rd, Newbury, Berks.

AUNT LIVING (daughter of 6th baronet)

Julia Maureen Patricia, *b* 1934: *m* 1961, George Hector Miller, of Middle Chantry, Carter's Lane, Wickham Bishops, Essex, and has issue living, Rupert Leslie Derrick, *b* 1965: *m* 1986, Yvette Marie Gabrielle Brewster, and has issue living, Sian Louise Georgina *b* 1988, Sophie Jane Yasmin *b* 1990, Natasha Leslie *b* 1993, — Katrina Phyllis Evelyn, *b* 1962: *m* 1993, Ian Roy Cooke, — Rachel Susan, *b* 1964: *m* 1992, Stuart Michael Banning, — Grania Sarah, *b* 1968.

WIDOW LIVING OF SEVENTH BARONET

NOELLE MONA (*Noelle, Lady Kennedy*), da of Charles Henry Green, of Hunworth, Melton, Constable, Norfolk: *m* 1949, Lt-Col Sir (George) Ronald Derrick Kennedy, 7th Bt, OBE, RA, who *d* 1988. *Residence* – Harraton Square, Church Lane, Exning, Suffolk CB8 7HF.

COLLATERAL BRANCHES LIVING

Granddaughter of late Capt Francis Kennedy, 4th son of 1st baronet:—
Issue of late John Arthur Kennedy, *b* 1858, *d* 1913: *m* 1881, Evelyn Maude, who *d* 1921, da of late H. G. Bromilow, of Southport:—
Olive Eileen, *b* 1889.

Grandchildren of late Edward Robert Kennedy (infra):—
Issue of late Robert Kennedy, *b* 1911, *d* 1990: *m* 1935, Catherine Frances (Loughananna House, Kilbehenny, co Limerick), da of late Maj Robert Gregory, MC, of Coole Park, co Galway:—
Robert Edward (Creighton Park, Dandaragan, WA, Australia), *b* 1940: *m* 1969, Sandra Joan, da of S. A. Giles, of Yericoin, W Australia, and has issue living, Edward Robert, *b* 1980, — Jane Catherine, *b* 1972, — Megan Anne, *b* 1974. —— Benjamin James, *b* 1942: *m* 1980, Margaret Lorna, da of George Clark, of Portsoy, Banff, and has issue living, Graham John Clark, *b* 1982, — Heather Catherine, *b* 1983, — Julia Susan, *b* 1985. —— Susan, *b* 1936: *m* 1970 (*m diss* 19—), Wing-Cdr Ian Traill Sutherland, RAAF. —— Margaret Jane, *b* 1937: *m* 1964, Col David Andrew Robert Murray Brown, late The Queen's Royal Irish Hussars (c/o Midland Bank, Lichfield, Staffs), and has issue living, Robin David, *b* 1964, — Belinda Jane, *b* 1966.

Grandchildren of late Robert Kennedy, 5th son of 1st baronet:—
Issue of late Edward Robert Kennedy, *b* 1860, *d* 1925: *m* 1905, Beryl Doris, who *d* 1988, aged 101, da of E. Lumsdaine, of Sydney, NS Wales:—
Percy William, *b* 1914: *m* 1936, Joan, da of Sydney Cooper, and has issue living, William Roger, *b* 1940: *m* 1966, Vivienne Gloria, da of James O'Shea, and has issue living, John Edward *b* 1967, Darby James *b* 1971, *d* 1993, — Richard August, *b* 1943, — Rosemary Ann Caroline, *b* 1937: *m* 1957, Allan Ross, of Irishtown, Rathfreigh, Tara, co Meath, — Evelyn Geraldine Margaret, *b* 1942, — Judith Patricia Wilhelmena, *b* 1953. *Residence* – Weston Park, Leixlip, co Dublin. —— Maeve: *m* 1932, George John Robinson, who *d* 1958, and has issue living, John Edward Bernard, *b* 1933, — George William Richard (Stepaside, The Curragh, co Kildare), *b* 1934: *m* 1964, Susan, da of late Maj Cyril Hall, of Gilltown, Kilcullen, co Kildare, and has issue living, Emma Jane Anna *b* 1965, Lara Camilla Patricia *b* 1969, — Bryan Patrick Valentine, *b* 1940, — Mary Rose, *b* 1936: *m* 1961, Seamus Hayes, — Doris Teresa, *b* 1943: *m* 19—, T. O'Hanlon. *Residence* – Phepotstown, Kilcock, co Meath. —— Grania Geraldine: *m* 1947 (*m diss* 1956), Capt Edward de Lérisson Cazenove, late Coldm Gds, and has issue living, Patrick Ralph de Lérisson, *b* 1947, Nicola Louise, *b* 1949: *m* 1st, 1976 (*m diss* 1983), Sir (Brian) Charles Pennefather Warren, 9th Bt; 2ndly 1994, as his 2nd wife, Charles St Vigor Fox (*see* Orr-Ewing, Bt, colls), of Langham House, Gillingham, Dorset. *Residence* – Synone Stud, Cashel, co Tipperary.

Grandchildren of Adm Francis William Kennedy, CB, son of late Robert Kennedy (ante):—
Issue of late Capt Francis Henry Kennedy, RN, *b* 1900; *d* 1981: *m* 1931, Magdalen Frances, who *d* 1976, da of late George FitzAdam-Ormiston, of Pockeridge Park, Wilts:—
Robert Francis (37 Chiddingstone St, SW6), *b* 1935: *m* 1976, Sally Mary, da of A. B. Antram of Keyes Wells, Petworth, and has issue living, Andrew Francis, *b* 1980. —— John Ormiston (20 Greville Park Rd, Ashtead, Surrey), *b* 1938; *ed* Stowe, and Queen's Coll, Camb (MA): *m* 1969, Margaret Mary, el da of H. G. N. Lee, of Holmwood Lodge, Frome, Som, and has issue living, Christopher Patrick, *b* 1971, Annabel Margaret, *b* 1973. —— Bridget Magdalen, *b* 1942: *m* 1974, Alexander Lindsay, of Balgedie House, Easter Balgedie, by Kinross KY13 7HQ, and has issue living, Philip John, *b* 1975.
Sir John Kennedy, 1st Bt, was great-grandson of Darby O'Kennedy, of Ballikeiroge Castle, co Waterford.

KIMBER (UK) 1904, of Lansdowne Lodge, Wandsworth, co London

You may break, but you shall not bend me

Sir CHARLES DIXON KIMBER, 3rd *Baronet*; *b* 7 Jan 1912; *s* his father, Sir HENRY DIXON, 1950; *ed* Eton, and Balliol Coll, Oxford (BA 1933); Dip Social Anthropology 1948: *m* 1st, 1933 (*m diss* 1950), Ursula, who *d* 1981, da of late Ernest Roy Bird, MP; 2ndly, 1950 (*m diss* 1965), Margaret only da of late Francis John Bonham, of 13 Dudley Rd, Wimbledon, SW, and has issue by 1st and 2nd *m*.

𝕬rms – Argent, a torteau between three choughs proper, on a chief engrailed gules, three estoiles of the first. 𝕮rest – A bull's head cabossed sable horned argent, between the horns an estoile or.
Residence – 2 Duxford, Hinton Waldrist, Faringdon, Oxon.

SONS LIVING *(By 1st marriage)*

TIMOTHY ROY HENRY (Newton Hall, nr Carnforth, Lancs LA6 2NZ), *b* 3 June 1936; *ed* Eton: *m* 1st, 1960 (*m diss* 1974), Antonia Kathleen Brenda, da of Sir Francis John Watkin Williams, 8th Bt, QC, (*cr* 1798); 2ndly, 1979, Susan Hare, da of late J. K. Brooks, and widow of Richard Coulthurst North, of Newton Hall, nr Carnforth, Lancs, and has issue living (by 1st *m*), Rupert Edward Watkin, *b* 1962, — Hugo Charles, *b* 1964. —— Nicholas John, *b* 1937; *ed* Eton. —— Robert (New Bois, Windsor Lane, Little Kingshill, Gt Missenden, Bucks HP16 0DP), *b* 1941; *ed* Eton: *m* 1964, Carolyn Evelyn Garth, da of Frederick Griffiths-Jones, of West Barn, Little Missenden, Bucks, and has issue living, Jane Guthrie, *b* 1967: *m* 1989, Mark Charles Etheridge, and has issue living, Charles Robert Guthrie *b* 1994, — Amanda Ann, *b* 1970.

DAUGHTER LIVING *(By 2nd marriage)*

Rhys Catherine (4F Victoria Works, Graham St, Birmingham B1 3PE), *b* 1951; Dip in Landscape Architecture (Glos), ALI: *m* 1977, Michael Fox, RIBA, who *d* 1993.

SISTER LIVING

Audrey Patricia (Old Teemstones, Grove Rd, Beacon Hill, Hindhead, Surrey), *b* 1913: *m* 19—, Harold James Stocks, who *d* 1963.

HALF-SISTER LIVING

Ella Florence Irene, *b* 1903.

COLLATERAL BRANCHES LIVING

Grandchildren of late Percy Dixon Kimber, 3rd son of 1st baronet:—
Issue of late Guy Mackenzie Kimber, *b* 1899, *d* 1985: *m* 1926, Ellen Elizabeth Margaret, who *d* 1977, da of late Rev J. Jardine-Lockhart, of Paignton, Devon:—
David Percy (Maritzdaal, Dargle, Natal), *b* 1930: *m* 1953, Elizabeth Mary Paterson, da of Tom Paterson Owens, CBE, of Weybridge, Surrey, and has issue living, Richard Guy, *b* 1956, — Christopher David, *b* 1961: *m* 1988, Shelley Bennett, — Jeannet Elizabeth, *b* 1954: *m* 1976, Jean-Henri Coppez, and has issue living, Henri Jean-Patric *b* 1978, Jean-Marc Guy *b* 1980, — Georgina Louise, *b* 1957: *m* 1985, Roland Zittera. —— Michael Jardine (Selsley, Dargle, Natal), *b* 1932: *m* 1957, Mary Elizabeth, da of late J. A. Dales, of Pietermaritzburg, Natal, and has issue living, James Michael, *b* 1958, — Guy Barrington, *b* 1962, — Kathryn Mary, *b* 1966.

Grandchildren of late Walter Dixon Kimber, 4th son of 1st baronet:—
Issue of late Eric Dixon Kimber, *b* 1898, *d* 1956: *m* 1926, Gwendolen Isa Dow, who *d* 1980, da of late Lawrence C. French, of High Trees, Godalming, Surrey:—
Anthony Dixon (Greytown, Natal), *b* 1927: *m* 1957, Joan Lilian Patterson, and has issue living, Brett Dixon, *b* 1960, — Erica-Jane, *b* 1959: *m* 1988, Paul Richard Benham, — Carolyn Suzanne, *b* 1963. —— Roger Dixon, *b* 1929: *m* 1957, Sandra, da of late Leslie Guy Gold, MC, of Sussex House, 35 Sussex Place, W2, and has issue living, Richard Orlando Dixon, *b* 1957: *m* 1984, Nicola Anne, da of Christopher Andrew Balck-Foote, of Stockcross, Berks, and has issue living, Henry Dixon Balck *b* 1988, Alexander Hudson Balck *b* 1993, Jessica Poppy Balck *b* 1985, — Eric Guy Piers, *b* 1961, — Catherine Miranda, *b* 1959: has issue living, Jaime Rose Muir *b* 1988. *Residence* – Higher Menchine Down, Black Dog, Crediton, Devon. —— Winifred Margaret (10 Nelson St, Woollahra, Sydney, NSW, Australia), *b* 1930: *m* 1959, Lawrence Kevin Tonkin, MB BS, who *d* 1993, and has issue living, Lawrence Eric, *b* 1963, — Shauna Kerry, *b* 1960: *m* 19—, Frank Curreti, and has issue living, Edwardo *b* 1989, Isobella *b* 1992.
Issue of late Allan Dixon Kimber, *b* 1903, *d* 1987: *m* 1st, 1939 (*m diss* 1959), Daphne Mary, da of Richard Guy Chaloner Ogle, of Natal; 2ndly, 1964, Sylvia Margaret, da of late Garnet Edwin Driver, solicitor, of Natal:—
(By 1st *m*) Daphne Jane, *b* 1940: *m* 1st, 1964 (*m diss* 1966), John Campbell, of Natal; 2ndly, 1968 (*m diss* 1973), Peter Glen Cox, and has issue living (by 1st *m*), Paula Catherine, *b* 1965, — (by 2nd *m*) Glen Alexander Marc, *b* 1969, — Michael Piers, *b* 1970, — Joshua Richard Alan, *b* 1971. —— Susan Mary, *b* 1942: *m* 1963 (*m diss* 1974), George Desmond Fairfoot, and has issue living, Samuel Christian, *b* 1964, — Thomas Jason, *b* 1968, — Matthew Adam, *b* 1969. —— Nancy Florence, *b* 1946: *m* 1974, Henry Clive Bowring, of Park Farm House, Bodiam, Sussex, and has issue living, Guy Allan Clive, *b* 1975, — Hugh Rennie, *b* 1977.
The 1st baronet, Sir Henry, founded the legal firm of Kimber and Ellis, and sat as the first MP for Wandsworth (C) 1885-1913. The 2nd baronet, Sir Henry Dixon, was Ch Commoner, City of London 1919, and Senior Partner in the legal firm of Kimber, Williams, Sweetland & Stinson.

KING (UK) 1815, of Charlestown, Roscommon

Sir WAYNE ALEXANDER KING, 8th *Baronet*; *b* 2 Feb 1962; *s* his father, *Sir* PETER ALEXANDER, 1973; *ed* Sir Roger Mawood's Sch, Sandwich, Kent, and Algonquin Coll, Ottawa: *m* 1984, Laura Ellen, da of Donald James Lea, of Almonte, Ontario, and has issue.

Arms – Sable, a lion rampant double queued or. **Crest** – An escallop gules.
Residence – 146 High St, Almonte, Ontario K0A 1A0, Canada.

Spes tutissima coelis
Our safest hope is in Heaven

SON LIVING

PETER RICHARD DONALD, *b* 4 May 1988.

SISTER LIVING

Dorothy Jane *b* 1964.

WIDOW LIVING OF SEVENTH BARONET

JEAN MARGARET, da of Christopher Thomas Cavell, of Deal: *m* 1st, 1957, Sir Peter Alexander King, 7th Bt, who *d* 1973; 2ndly, 1978, Rev Richard Graham Mackenzie.

KING (UK) 1888, of Campsie, Stirlingshire

Honour is the reward of industry

HONOS·INDUSTRIÆ·PRÆMIUM

Sir JOHN CHRISTOPHER KING, 4th *Baronet*; *b* 31 March 1933; *s* his father, *Sir* JAMES GRANVILLE LE NEVE, TD, 1989; *ed* Eton; Sub-Lt RNVR, 1 Lt Berks Yeo TA: *m* 1st, 1958 (*m diss* 1972), Patricia Monica, only da of late Lieut-Col Kingsley Osbern Nugent Foster, DSO, OBE; 2ndly, 1984, Mrs (Aline) Jane Holley, el da of late Col Douglas Alexander Brett, GC, OBE, MC, and has issue by 1st *m*.

Arms – Azure, on a fesse argent between a lion's head erased or in chief, and two billets of the third in base, three round-buckles of the field. Crest – A redbreast proper.
Residence – Stillwater, Box 218 Mathews Courthouse, Va 23109, USA.

SON LIVING *(By 1st marriage)*

JAMES HENRY RUPERT, *b* 24 May 1961; *ed* Eton.

DAUGHTER LIVING *(By 1st marriage)*

Melanie Avril, *b* 1963: *m* 1989, Jeremy Legge, and has issue living, Hamish, *b* 1991, — Charles, *b* 1992.

SISTERS LIVING

Susan Penelope, *b* 1929: *m* 1957, Christopher Marsden-Smedley, yr son of late Basil Furtvoye Marsden-Smedley, OBE, and has issue living, Timothy Charles, *b* 1959, — Philip John, *b* 1961, — Catherine Penelope, *b* 1964: *m* 1992, Christopher D. Miller, yr son of Maj David Miller, of Pyrford, Surrey. *Residence* – Church Farm, Burrington, nr Bristol, Avon. —— Diana Bridget, *b* 1935: *m* 1957, Francis Hoare (*see* E Coventry, 1955 Edn), and has issue living, James Alexander, *b* 1959, — Edward Eustace, *b* 1961, — Richard Francis, *b* 1967, — Arabella Peggy Marian, *b* 1968. *Residence* – Loubcroy Lodge, Lairg, Sutherland.

WIDOW LIVING OF THIRD BARONET

PENELOPE CHARLOTTE (*Dowager Lady King*), da of late Capt Edmund Moore Cooper Cooper-Key, CB, MVO, RN (*see* Wigram, Bt, colls, 1973-74 Edn): *m* 1928, Sir James Granville Le Neve King, 3rd Bt, TD, who *d* 1989. *Residence* – Sutton Manor, Sutton Scotney, Winchester, Hants.

COLLATERAL BRANCH LIVING

Issue of late John Alastair King, *b* 1905, *d* 1991, 2nd son of 2nd baronet: *m* 1st, 1929 (*m diss* 1939), Veronica Mary, who *d* 1967, only da of late Col Bertram Abel Smith, DSO, MC; 2ndly, 1939 (*m diss* 1956), Ruby Enid, yr da of late Henry George Atkinson-Clark; 3rdly, 1957, Pierina (Downs Farmhouse, Baunton, Cirencester, Glos), da of — Holt, of —:—
(By 1st *m*) Rhona Lavinia, *b* 1932. —— (By 2nd *m*), Elisabeth Jane, *b* 1941. —— (By 3rd *m*), Sarah Rosemary, *b* 1959.
Sir James King, 1st Bt (son of John King, of Campsie, co Stirling, a merchant of Glasgow), was Lord Provost of Glasgow 1886-89. He received Queen Victoria on her visit to Glasgow in 1888.

King (Stafford-King-Harman), see Harman.

DUCKWORTH-KING (GB) 1792, of Bellevue, Kent (Extinct 1972)

Sir JOHN RICHARD DUCKWORTH-KING, 7th and last *Baronet*.

DAUGHTERS LIVING OF SIXTH BARONET

Anne Eva Katharine *b* 1915: *m* 1940 Christopher Willoughby Jardine, CB, who *d* 1982, and has issue living, Theresa Barbara Lettice (31 Great Tattenhams, Epsom Downs, Banstead, Surrey KT18 SRF), *b* 1942: *m* 1st, 1961 (*m diss* 1973), Anthony Harold Hazell; 2ndly, 1979, Reginald Alfred William Jones, and has issue living, (by 1st *m*), James Christopher *b* 1962, Deborah Anne *b* 1963, — Victoria Agnes, *b* 1945: *m* 1968, Peter Nicholas Christian Bordewich, of Rock Hill, Wolverley, Kidderminster, Worcs, and has issue living, Luke George Batchelor *b* 1974, Magnus James Roness *b* 1975, Camilla Anne *b* (twin) 1975, — Cassandra Caroline Mary, *b* 1954: *m* 1988, William John Jeremy Chubb, of 4 Grove Lane, SE5, son of John Chubb, CMG, of Beckley, E Sussex, and has issue living, Oliver Octavius *b* 1989, Elizabeth Anne *b* 1992, Dido Mary Francesca *b* 1994. *Residence* – 8 St Loo Court, Flood St, SW3. —— Caroline Agnes (2 Erskine Rd, NW3 3AJ), *b* 1916.

WIDOW LIVING OF SEVENTH BARONET

ALICE PATRICIA (*Lady Duckworth-King*) (47 Avenue de Hassan 11, Tangier, Morocco), da of Thomas Rutledge, of Fugar House, Ravensworth, co Durham; *m* 1943, as his 2nd wife, Sir John Richard Duckworth-King, 7th Bt, who *d* 1972, when the title became ext.

KINLOCH (NS) 1686, of Gilmerton, East Lothian

I aspire higher

Sir DAVID KINLOCH, 13th *Baronet*; *b* 5 Aug 1951; *s* his father, *Maj Sir* ALEXANDER DAVENPORT, 1982; *ed* Gordonstoun: *m* 1st, 1976 (*m diss* 1986), Susan, da of Arthur Middlewood, of North Side Farm, Kilham; 2ndly, 1987, Maureen, da of Robert Carswell, and has issue living by 1st and 2nd *m*.

Arms – Azure, a boar's head erased between three mascles or. **Crest** – An eagle rising proper.
Seat – Gilmerton House, North Berwick, East Lothian.

SONS LIVING *(By 1st marriage)*

ALEXANDER, *b* 31 May 1978.

(by 2nd marriage)

Christopher Robert, *b* 1988. —— Matthew Carswell, *b* 1990.

DAUGHTER LIVING *(By 1st marriage)*

Alice, *b* 1976.

HALF-BROTHER LIVING *(Son of 12th baronet by 3rd m)*

James Alexander, *b* 1967.

SISTERS LIVING *(Daughters of 12th baronet by 2nd wife, Hilda Anna, who d 1986, da of Thomas Walker, of Edinburgh)*

Victoria, *b* 1947: *m* 1981, Martin Teale, of 99 White Lion Rd, Amersham, Bucks. —— Harriet, *b* 1949: *m* 1st, 1967 (*m diss* 1973), Colin John Weddell; 2ndly, 1988, Ian Napier Thomson, of The Kennels, W Saltoun, by Pencaitland, E Lothian, and has issue living (by 1st *m*), Jennifer Katherine Graham, *b* 1968. —— Ann (twin with her brother David), *b* 1951: *m* 1984, George Kenneth Banks, and has issue living, Justin Christopher, *b* 1985.

HALF-SISTERS LIVING *(Daughters of 12th baronet by 1st wife, Alexandra, da of Frederick Y. Dalziel, of New York, USA)*

Emily Lucy (*Hon Mrs Hugh Astor*), *b* 1930: *m* 1950, Hon Hugh Waldorf Astor (*see* B Astor of Hever). *Residences* – Folly Farm, Sulhamstead, Berks; 79 Ashley Gdns, Thirleby Rd, SW1P 1HG. —— Jean Alexandra (5 Cadogan Sq, SW1), *b* 1934.

WIDOW LIVING OF TWELFTH BARONET

ANN MAUD (*Ann, Lady Kinloch*), da of late Group-Capt Frank Leslie White, of London: *m* 1965, as his 3rd wife, Maj Sir Alexander Davenport Kinloch, 12th Bt, who *d* 1982. *Residence* – Greenacre, 87 Hepburn Gdns, St Andrews, Fife KY16 9LT.

COLLATERAL BRANCHES LIVING

Issue of late Francis Kinloch, 3rd son of 10th baronet, *b* 1863, *d* 1916: *m* 1896, Marion Eva, da of late Charles Nairne Marshall, of Curriehill, New Zealand:—
Lucy Margaret, *b* 1899.

Granddaughter of late Charles Henry Alexander Frederick Camillo Everard John James Rocheid, great-grandson of Alexander Kinloch (who assumed the surname of Rocheid), 4th son of 3rd baronet:—
Issue of late Colin William Hilmar Otto Rocheid, *b* 1881, *d* 1954: *m* 1st, 1911, Elizabeth, who *d* 1935, da of late Ernst von Schröder; 2ndly, 1942, Catherine Jung, who *d* 1959:—
(By 1st *m*) Elisabeth Marie Olga Harriet Ernestine, *b* 1912: *m* 1936, Capt Joachim von Sametzki, who *d* 1946. *Residence* – .

The 1st baronet, Sir Francis Kinloch (son of Andrew Kinloch, merchant of Rochelle), was Lord Provost of Edinburgh. The 10th baronet, Capt Sir Alexander Kinloch, Grenadier Guards, served in Crimea 1854-5. The 11th baronet, Brig-Gen Sir David Alexander Kinloch, CB, MVO, served with Grenadier Guards in S Africa 1899-1902, and in European War 1914-19.

KINLOCH (UK) 1873, of Kinloch, co Perth

Not degenerate

Sir DAVID OLIPHANT KINLOCH, 5th *Baronet*; *b* 15 Jan 1942; *s* his father, *Sir* JOHN, 1992; *ed* Charterhouse; CA: *m* 1st, 1968 (*m diss* 1979), Susan Minette, yst da of late Maj-Gen Robert Elliott Urquhart, CB, DSO; 2ndly, 1983, Sabine, only da of Philippe de Loes, of 5 Rampe de Cologny, 1223 Cologny, Geneva, Switzerland, and has issue by 1st and 2nd *m*.

𝔄rms – Quarterly; 1st, grand quarter azure, a boar's head erased between three mascles or, a crescent of the second in chief for difference, *Kinloch*; 2nd, grand quarter gules, a chevron embattled between three crescents argent, *Oliphant*; 3rd, grand quarter parted per fesse argent and sable, a chevron between three cinquefoils counter-changed, *Balneavis*; 4th grand quarter counter-quartered; 1st, gules, a broken spear and a standard saltireways argent, the last charged with a cross of the field and fringed or; 2nd, azure, a cat salient argent; 3rd, argent, on a saltire sable nine mascles of the first within a bordure azure; 4th, or, three bars wavy gules, each charged with an escallop of the field, all *Smyth*. ℭrest – A young eagle perched, looking up to the sun in his splendour all proper.
Residences – House of Aldie, Fossoway, Kinross, Kinross-shire KY13 7QH; 29 Walpole St, SW3 4QS.

SON LIVING *(By 2nd marriage)*

ALEXANDER PETER, *b* 30 June 1986.

DAUGHTERS LIVING *(By 1st marriage)*

Katherine Cecilia, *b* 1972. —— Emily Nicole, *b* 1974. —— Nicola Marjorie, *b* 1976.

(by 2nd marriage)

Sophie, *b* 1994.

SISTERS LIVING

Susan Cecilia, *b* 1935: *m* 1960, Malcolm Henry Rogers, of 11 Warrender Court, North Berwick, E Lothian EH39 4RR, and has issue living, John Andrew, *b* 1965. —— Wendy Diana, *b* 1962. —— Diana Evelyne, *b* 1940: *m* 1960, William Stewart Addis, of Coldharbour, Warninglid, by Haywards Heath, Sussex RH17 5SN, son of Sir William Addis, KBE, CMG, and has issue living, William Dickon, *b* 1962, —— Sarah Diana, *b* 1963, —— Madelaine Rosemary, *b* 1968.

AUNT LIVING *(daughter of 3rd baronet)*

Barbara Cecilia, *b* 1913: *m* 1937, Charles Gairdner Dalrymple Tennant, Maj late RASC, who *d* 1991, and has issue living, Thomas Peregrine, *b* 1939; Lt RN (ret): *m* 1972, Finella Susan, da of Geoffrey Hooper, and has issue living, Edward Charles *b* 1978, Emma Clare *b* 1975, —— Edward Kinloch, *b* 1943, —— Tanera Cecilia, *b* 1940: *m* 1962, Michael Charles Averdieck, of Glebe House, Catworth, Huntingdon, Cambs, and has issue living, William John *b* 1963, Charles Edward *b* 1965, James Ulric *b* (twin) 1965: *m* 1993, Anne Geddes, —— Victoria Margaret, *b* 1950: *m* 1976, Peter Mackenzie Duke, of Oldtown of Carnaveron, Muir of Foulis, Alford, Aberdeenshire, and has issue living, Robert Mackenzie *b* 1980, Kirstie Mary *b* 1982.
Residence – Cruivie, Rosemount, Blairgowrie, Perths.

WIDOW LIVING OF FOURTH BARONET

DORIS ELLALINE (*Dowager Lady Kinloch*), el da of late Charles Joseph Head, of 24 Imber Close, Esher, Surrey: *m* 1934, Sir John Kinloch, 4th Bt, who *d* 1992. *Residence* – Aldie Cottage, Kinross, Kinross-shire KY13 7QH.

COLLATERAL BRANCH LIVING

Issue of late James Kinloch, 2nd son of 2nd baronet, *b* 1884, *d* 1950: *m* 1909, Julia Madeline, who *d* 1962, da of late George W. Boase, of Broughty Ferry:—
Colin David (26 Curtis Rd, Ashdell Park, Alton, Hants GU34 2SD), *b* 1918; a Chartered Engineer: *m* 1945, Gertrude Lilian Mary, da of E. R. Bollom, and has issue living, Nigel George, *b* 1951: *m* 1976, Elizabeth Anne, da of Geoffrey Browning, of Winchester, and has had issue, David Geoffrey Ian *b* 1982, James Colin George *b* 1986 *d* 1987, Andrew Malcolm Robert *b* 1989, Jennifer Mary Ruth *b* 1984, Catherine Brenda Anne *b* 1988, —— Bridget Eleanor Mary, *b* 1948: *m* 1974, Christopher James Biggs, of 16 Nuneham Sq, Abingdon, Oxon OX14 1EH, and has issue living, Patrick Mark James *b* 1980, Alison Samantha Mary *b* 1978, Deborah Katharine Louise *b* 1981, Sarah Elizabeth Helen *b* 1982. —— Sheila Maysie, *b* 1910: *m* 1938, Brig Arthur Catchmay Tyler, CBE, MC, DL, Mil Knt of Windsor, late Welch Regt, and has issue living, Richard Hugh (Sheldon House, Monyash, Derbys), *b* 1939; Capt late R Regt of Wales: *m* 1st, 1963 (*m diss* 1981), Suzan Gaynor, da of Lt-Col Sam Griffith, OBE; 2ndly, 1982, Beverley Gayle, da of late Arthur Rodgers, OBE, of Kuwait, and has issue living (by 1st *m*), Christopher Charles Griffith, *b* 1965, Nicholas Hugh Griffin *b* 1966, (by 2nd *m*) Caroline Mary *b* 1984, Eleanor Jane *b* 1992, —— Andrew James, *b* 1950: *m* 1971, Judith Margaret, da of Alan Gale, —— John Philip, *b* 1951: *m* 1973, Valerie Eileen, da of R. L. Luckin, and has issue living, Christopher Philip *b* 1978, —— Mary Joyce, *b* 1941: *m* 1966, Bruce George Draper, of 25 Odenwald Rd, Eaglemont, Vic 3084, Aust, and has issue living, Jeremy Charles Bruce *b* 1971, Nicholas James *b* 1973, Catherine Louise *b* 1969. *Residence* – 17 Fosters Way, Bude, Cornwall EX23 8HF. —— Elspeth (Halliwell Nursing Home, Kingswood Rd, Tunbridge Wells, Kent TN2 4UN), *b* 1912: *m* 1938, Lt-Cdr Malcolm David Wanklyn, VC, DSO (two Bars), RN, who was *ka* 1942, and has issue living, Ian David Kinloch (Ashwick House, Chelmarsh, Bridgnorth, Salop), *b* 1939, Lt-Cdr RN: *m* 1971, Penelope, el da of Capt Charles Wickham Malins, DSO, DSC, RN, and has issue living, Alastair David *b* 1973, Oliver Charles *b* 1975, Catriona Louise *b* 1977.
The lands of Kinloch of that Ilk were situated at Collessie, the head of Rossie Loch, Fifeshire, of which family charters date from 1210, but were sold in the 16th century. David Kinloch, physician and traveller, a descendant of this line, acquired lands in Perthshire which were erected into the Barony of Kinloch temp James VI. His grandson, Sir David Kinloch of that Ilk was created a baronet 1685, it is said to have been with remainder to his heirs male whatsoever though no record exists in the Great Seal Register, Sir James Kinloch, 3rd Bt, took part in the 1745 rising, was tried and condemned to death, and the baronetcy became forfeited, but having escaped to France he was subsequently pardoned. His son William, who dsp, sold Kinloch to his kinsman, Capt George Oliphant Kinloch (grandson of James, yr brother of 1st baronet), whose son George Kinloch of Kinloch fled to France as an outlaw 1819 for advocating reform, but in 1832 was elected the first MP for Dundee. His son, Sir George Kinloch, was the 1st Bt of the present creation.

KIRKPATRICK (NS) 1685, of Closeburn, Dumfriesshire

Sir IVONE ELLIOTT KIRKPATRICK, 11th *Baronet*; *b* 1 Oct 1942; *s* his father, *Sir* JAMES ALEXANDER, 1954; *ed* Wellington Coll, and St Mark's Coll Univ Adelaide.

Arms – Argent, a saltire and chief azure, the last charged with three cushions or. **Crest** – A hand holding a dagger in pale, distilling drops of blood. **Supporters** – Two talbot hounds argent. *Address* – 82 Stanenborough St, Adelaide 5066, S Australia.

BROTHER LIVING

ROBIN ALEXANDER, *b* 19 March 1944; *ed* Wellington Coll.

MOTHER LIVING

Ellen Gertrude, only da of Capt Robert Perceval Elliott, late RNR, of Ismailia: *m* 1st, 1941 (*m diss* 1953), Sir James Alexander Kirkpatrick, 10th Bt, who *d* 1954; 2ndly, 1955, John Ogilvie Corbin, MB, BS, FRCS.

COLLATERAL BRANCHES LIVING

Granddaughters of late Charles William Sharpe Kirkpatrick, 4th son of 6th baronet:—
Issue of late Thomas Stripling Kirkpatrick, *b* 1867, *d* 1937: *m* 1903, Amy Louisa, who *d* 1962, da of Walter Norris:—
Grace Amy May, *b* 1905: *m* 1926, William Henry Williams, and has issue living, Derek Henry (44 Ammersham Av, Paddonhurst, Bulawayo, Zimbabwe), *b* 1929: *m* 1953, Kathleen Elizabeth Knipe, and has issue living, Peter Duncan *b* 1956, Paul Arnold *b* 1957, Margaret Ann *b* 1959, — Olive Amy, *b* 1932: *m* 1954, John Faulding Sissison, of 16 Willow Way, Pinelands, Cape Province, S Africa, and has issue living, Michael Faulding *b* 1959, Noel Faulding *b* 1961, — Janet Ann *b* 1943: *m* 1960, Roger Stewart Johnson, and has issue living, Susan Barbara *b* 1960, Shirley Catherine *b* 1961.

Grandchildren of late Thomas Frederick Kirkpatrick (infra):—
Issue of late Leslie Maurice Kenneth Kirkpatrick, *b* 1925, *d* 1962: *m* 1948, Rose Lillian May, da of late Frederick George Walker:—
David Christopher (7 Fulbourne Close, Luton, Beds LU4 9PW), *b* 1950: *m* 1973, Betty Margaret, da of Leslie Augustus Radford, and has issue living, Victoria Alice, *b* 1981, — Joanna Louise, *b* 1985. —— Paul Anthony, *b* 1953. —— Stephen Robert *b* 1960: *m* 1983, Jill, da of Ernest Albert Flewin. —— Maureen Ann *b* 1952.

Grandchildren of late Charles Bartram Kirkpatrick (*b* 1873) (infra):—
Issue of late Thomas Frederick Kirkpatrick, *b* 1894, *ka* 1940: *m* 1920, Mabel who *d* 1971, da of late John James Childs:—
Beryl, *b* 1920: *m* 1941, Stanley R Fairbrass, and has issue living, Alan, *b* 1942, — Brian Malcolm, *b* 1944, — Melvyn Denis, *b* 1948, — Geoffrey, *b* 1950, — Keith Anthony, *b* 1958.
Issue of late Charles Bartram Kirkpatrick, *b* 1899, *d* 1936: *m* 1921, Lillian (who *m* 2ndly, 1950, George Albert May, of 63 The Fairway, Bickley, Bromley Kent), da of Samuel Charles Podd:—
Charles Bartram, *b* 1922: *m* 1944, Winifred Rosa, da of George Gaffney, and has issue living, Charles Bartram (49 Norheads Lane, Biggin Hill, Kent) *b* 1945: *m* 1967, Angela Mary, da of Sidney Ernest MacClaren Dooley, and has issue living, Paul Charles *b* 1972. —— Residence – 16 Foyle Drive, South Ockendon, Essex. —— Donald (Closeburn, 4 Wilderness Rd, Hurstpierpoint, Sussex), *b* 1934: *m* 1964, Janet Olive, da of late Walter Young, and has issue living, Kay, *b* 1965, — Linda, *b* 1967. —— Edna Florence, *b* 1924: *m* 1946, Henry Crook, of Old Scoresdown, Lynton, Devon EX35 6LJ, and has issue living, John David, *b* 1951, — Hilary June, *b* 1955. —— Lilian, *b* 1926: *m* 1945, Sydney Thew, and has issue living, Sydney Charles, *b* 1946, — Colin James, *b* 1947, — Robert John, *b* 1948, — Donald Patrick, *b* 1950, — Michael Allan, *b* 1952. *Residence* –
Issue of late James Arthur Kirkpatrick, *b* 1902, *d* 1935: *m* 1929, Ruby, da of Charles Heat, of Brixton, SW:—
Barbara, *b* 1931. *Residence* –

Grandson of Charles William Sharpe Kirkpatrick (ante):—
Issue of late Charles Bartram Kirkpatrick, *b* 1873, *d* 1944: *m* 1893, Helena Sarah Riches, who *d* 1936, da of William Minns, of Peckham, SE:—
Sydney Frank, *b* 1912; late Flying Officer RAF Vol Reserve; 1939-45 War as Flight-Sergeant RAF (Belgian Croix de Guerre with palm): *m* 1943, Margaret Elizabeth Cowell, and has issue living, Valerie, *b* 1946; BA, — Sandra Kirkpatrick, *b* 1953: *m* 1974, Stephen Gent, of 32 Thompson Rd, Brighton, Sussex.

Grandson of late Robert Herries Kirkpatrick, 5th son of 6th baronet:—
Issue of Wallace Herries Kirkpatrick, *b* 1886, *d* 1967: *m* 1920, Lilian Ivy, who *d* 1976, da of late Walter Oughton Hill:—
Wallace Bruce (Duke's Lodge, Alresford Rd, Winchester), *b* 1921; late Lt N Staffs Regt: *m* 1946, Irene Sylvia, who *d* 1990, da of late Harold Victor Colls, and has issue living, Scott Herries (The Arches, Broughton, Hants), *b* 1947: *m* 1970, Sandra Jean, da of Leonard Arthur Charles Hall, and has issue living, Gavin James *b* 1972, Charles Stuart *b* 1981, Victoria Jane *b* 1974, — Gavin Bruce (Croft Cottage, Lower Moors Rd, Colden Common, nr Twyford, Hants), *b* 1951: *m* 1st, 1973 (*m diss* 1987), Linda, da of William Prosser, of Llandrindod Wells; 2ndly, 1994, Susan Mary, da of Walter Marr, of Winchester, and has issue living (by 1st *m*), James William Bruce *b* 1976, Emily Elizabeth *b* 1979.

Grandchildren of late Maj-Gen Charles Kirkpatrick, CB, CBE (infra):—
Issue of late Air Vice-Marshal Herbert James Kirkpatrick, CB, CBE, DFC, *b* 1910, *d* 1977: *m* 1937, Pamela Evelyn Darvill (Gretton Court, Girton, nr Cambridge), da of late Lt-Col H. D. Watson, Indian Army:—
Roger Hugh (3 Cambridge Rd, E Twickenham, Middx), *b* 1939: *m* 1965, Julia Margaret, da of late John W. Mortimore, of Broadstone, Dorset, and has issue living, Amanda Dorothy, *b* 1974, — Christabel Pamela, *b* 1977. —— John Edward (Petworth St, Cambridge), *b* 1944: *m* 1964, Johanna Elizabeth, da of late Patrick Johnston, of Guildford, Surrey, and has issue living, Jeremy Mark, *b* 1964, — Julian Gwinell, *b* 1966, — Dustin John, *b* 1971. —— Christopher Charles (9 Atlas Mews, Islington, N7), *b* 1948: *m* 1984, Kathleen Anne, formerly wife of John Walsh, and da of late Thomas Christopher Purcell, of co Kilkenny, and has issue living, James Charles John, *b* 1981. —— Elizabeth Susan, *b* 1942: *m* 1966, Fl-Lt Kenneth A. D. Evans, RAF, of 60 Carlyle Rd, Cambridge, and has issue living, Nicholas Christopher, *b* 1966, — Rebecca Kate, *b* 1968. —— Grizelda Jean, *b* (twin) 1948: *m* 1st, 1967, Hugh John Allen; 2ndly, 1974, Alan Graham Stuck, of 62 High St, Hampton, Middx, and has issue living (by 1st *m*), Jonathan Spencer, *b* 1968.

Granddaughters of late Dep Surg-Gen James Kirkpatrick, MC, son of late Roger Kirkpatrick (*b* 1779), 2nd son of 4th baronet:—
Issue of late Maj-Gen Charles Kirkpatrick, CB, CBE, *b* 1879, *d* 1955: *m* 1909, Elsie Isobel, who *d* 1970, da of late Herbert John Hamilton Fasson, ICS:—
Hilda May (Ashdean, Whiteparish, Salisbury), *b* 1920: *m* 1st, 1940, Maj James Michael Jourdier, E Surrey Regt; 2ndly, 1954, David Arthur Yellowlees; 3rdly, Brian Butler, and has issue living, (by 1st *m*) Anthony Maxwell Kirkpatrick (The Shrubbery House, Stanford Bridge, Worcester), *b* 1946: *m* 1974, Cecilia Maye, da of Lt-Col R. A. Conner, of Maldon, Essex, and has issue living, Peter Gilbert Kirkpatrick *b* 1983, Sophie Maye *b* 1975, Jessica Isobel *b* 1977, Louise Caroline *b* 1980, — Avril Patricia, *b* 1947: *m* 1969, John Hamish Carysfort Loch, of Monksford Cottage, St Boswells, Roxburghshire, and has issue living, Rupert John Carysfort *b* 1970, Rosalind Cecilia Carysfort *b* 1972.

Grandchildren of late Dep Surg-Gen James Kirkpatrick, MD (ante):—
Issue of late James Ivone Kirkpatrick, CA, *b* 1866, *d* 1918: *m* 1905, Elizabeth Margaret, who *d* 1959, da of David Thomson, of Edinburgh:—
Ivone (46 Nightingale Av, Greenfields, East London 5201, S Africa), *b* 1907; *ed* Edinburgh Acad, and Edinburgh Univ; WS 1933; 1939-45 War as Group-Capt AuxAF: *m* 1936, Ruth, da of late W. R. Peterson, of East London, S Africa, and has issue living, Ivone William (3 Kepersol St, Ferndale 2196, Johannesburg, S Africa), *b* 1944; a Co Dir: *m* 1st, 1967 (*m diss* 1983), Velia Elizabeth Mignon, da of John Hartdegan, of Parys, Orange Free State; 2ndly, 19—, Lyn—, and has issue living (by 1st *m*), Sean Roger *b* 1968, Anne Margaret *b* 1971.
The 1st baronet, Sir Thomas Kirkpatrick was created a baronet with remainder to heirs male whatsoever. He built the mansion of Closeburn, which was burnt to the ground through the carelessness of drunken servants on 29 August 1748, and all the portraits, plate, etc, with most of the family papers, were consumed. Two boxes of papers dating back to the 16th century were deposited in Register House, Edinburgh in 1952. HIM the Empress Eugénie, wife of HIM Napoleon III, Emperor of the French, was descended from the Kirkpatricks, Barons of Closeburn. Her great-grandfather was William Kirkpatrick, of Conheath, and her lineage traces back through the Conheath and Kirkmichael branches of the family to Alexander Kirkpatrick, of Kirkmichael, who was yr brother of Sir Thomas Kirkpatrick (who *d* 1502), ancestor of the 1st baronet. Sir James Alexander Kirkpatrick, 10th Bt, was Flight-Lieut RAF Vol Reserve and Assist Game Warden, Kenya.

KLEINWORT (UK) 1909, of Bolnore, Cuckfield, Sussex

Nil sine labore

Nothing without labour

Sir RICHARD DRAKE KLEINWORT, 4th *Baronet*; *b* 4 Nov 1960; *s* his father Sir KENNETH DRAKE, 1994; *ed* Stowe, and Exeter Univ (BA): *m* 1989, Lucinda, da of William Shand Kydd, of Horton Hall, Horton, Bucks, and has issue.

Arms – Or, a lion rampant sable, on a chief of the last three oak trees eradicated proper. **Crest** – On a mount vert, three leaves of clover proper. *Residence* – Heaselands, Haywards Heath, W Sussex RH16 4SA.

SON LIVING

RUFUS DRAKE, *b* 16 Aug 1994.

HALF-BROTHERS LIVING

ALEXANDER HAMILTON, *b* 1975. —— Michael Drake, *b* 1977.

SISTER LIVING

Marina Rose, *b* 1962.

HALF-SISTER LIVING

Selina Helen Louisa, *b* 1981.

AUNT LIVING (*sister of 3rd baronet*)

Gillian Mawdsley, *b* 1937: *m* 1957, Michael Raymond Warren, JP, and has issue living, Charles Raymond, *b* 1963: *m* 1993, Sarah Elizabeth, da of Richard Lionel Mather, — Davina Mary, *b* 1958: *m* 1979, Rev Peter Elliot Irwin-Clark, of The Vicarage, Wordsworth Rd, Shirley, Southampton SO15 5LX, and has issue living, Benjamin John *b* 1983, Jessamy Claire *b* 1987, — Susanna Rachel, *b* 1975. *Residence* – Banks Farm, Barcombe, Lewes, Sussex.

WIDOW LIVING OF SECOND BARONET

YVONNE (*Yvonne Lady Kleinwort*), da of late John Bloch: *m* 1938, Sir Alexander Santiago Kleinwort, 2nd Bt, who *d* 1983.

WIDOW LIVING OF THIRD BARONET

MADELEINE HAMILTON (*Madeleine, Lady Kleinwort*), eldest da of Ralph Taylor, of Larrea 1152, Buenos Aires, Argentina: *m* 1973, as his 2nd wife, Sir Kenneth Drake Kleinwort, 3rd Bt, who *d* 1994. *Residence* – La Massellaz, 1126 Vaux-sur-Morges, Switzerland.

COLLATERAL BRANCH LIVING

Issue of late Sir Cyril Hugh Kleinwort, 5th son of 1st baronet, *b* 1905, *d* 1980: *m* 1933, Elisabeth Kathleen (Eyford House, Upper Slaughter, Cheltenham, Glos), da of Francis Forde, of Newbury, Berks:—
Serena Elizabeth, *b* 1936: *m* 1960, David Alfred Acland (*see* Acland, Bt, *cr* 1890, colls). —— Charlotte, *b* 1938: *m* 1st, 1965, (Richard) Lawrence Baillieu; 2ndly, 1972, (Nevile) Martin Gwynne (*see* Morrison-Bell, Bt (ext)); 3rdly, 1980, Alan Cyril Heber-Percy (*see* D Northumberland, colls), and has issue living (by 1st *m*), Richard, *b* 19—, — J— A— Serena, *b* 1968, — (by 2nd *m*) (*see* Morrison-Bell, Bt (ext)). —— Susanna, *b* 1942: *m* 1962, David Alphy Edward Raymond Peake, of Sezincote, Moreton-in-Marsh, Glos, son of late Sir Harald Peake (*see* V Ingleby).
Sir Alexander Drake Kleinwort, 1st Bt (son of late Alexander Frederic Henry Kleinwort), was a Banker and Partner in the firm of Kleinwort, Sons & Co, of 20 Fenchurch Street, EC3; Sir Kenneth Drake, 3rd baronet: *m* 1st, 1959, Lady Davina Rose Pepys, who *d* 1973, da of 7th Earl of Cottenham.

KNILL (UK) 1893, of The Grove, Blackheath, Kent

Sir JOHN KENELM STUART KNILL, 4th *Baronet*, *b* 8 April 1913; *s* his father, Sir JOHN STUART, 1973; *ed* Downside; Lt RNVR; 1939-45 War: *m* 1951, Violette Maud Florence Martin, who *d* 1983, da of Leonard Martin Barnes, of Durban, S Africa, and has issue.

Arms – Gules, semée of crosses botonnée fitchée a lion rampant, all or, on a chief of the last a fasces fessewise, head to the dexter proper. **Crest** – A demi-lion or, holding in the dexter paw a cross botonnée fitchée azure, and supporting with the sinister a fasces in bend proper.
Residence – Canal Cottage, Bathampton, Avon BA2 6TW.

Nil desperandum
Never despairing

SONS LIVING

THOMAS JOHN PUGIN BARTHOLOMEW, *b* 23 Aug 1952: *m* 1977, Kathleen Muszynski.
—— Jenkyn Martin Benedict Stuart, *b* 1954.

HALF-BROTHERS LIVING

Gyles Braoze Hamish Stanislas Stuart, *b* 1945: *m* and has issue, two da.
—— Rognvald Gabriel Nigel Alistair Stuart, *b* 1946: *m* and has issue, one da.

HALF-SISTER LIVING

Gloriana Leonora Dorothea Marie, *b* 1937: *m* 1959, CPO William Charles Morehead, RN (ret), of 33 Brompton Walk, Darlington, co Durham DL3 8RT, son of William Morehead, of Blaston, nr Market Harborough, Leics, and has issue living, Simon William (30 Ennerdale Terrace, Low Westwood, Tyne and Wear), *b* 1961: *m* 198—, Stephanie, —— Sarah Maria Evelyn, *b* 1960: *m* 1983, Peter McDonnell, of 9 Canonbie Rd, Forest Hill, SE23 3AW.
Sir Stuart Knill, 1st Bt, was head of the firm of John Knill and Co, wharfingers, and Lord Mayor of London 1892-3. Sir (John) Stuart Knill, 2nd Bt, was Lord Mayor of London 1909-10.

KNOTT (UK) 1917, of Close House, Heddon-on-the-Wall, Northumberland (Extinct 1949)

Sir (THOMAS) GARBUTT KNOTT, 2nd and last *Baronet*.

WIDOW LIVING OF FIRST BARONET

Elizabeth, da of late Col V. C. Gauntlett, of St Helier, Jersey: *m* 1st, 1932, as his second wife, Sir James Knott, 1st Bt, who *d* 1934; 2ndly, 1943, Com Edward Owen Obbard, DSC, GM, RN, who *d* 1951. *Residence* – Samares Manor, Jersey.

KNOWLES (GB) 1765, of Lovell Hill, Berkshire

Sir CHARLES FRANCIS KNOWLES, 7th *Baronet*; *b* 20 Dec 1951; *s* his father, Sir FRANCIS GERALD WILLIAM, FRS, 1974; Dip Arch, RIBA, FRSA, Oxford School of Architecture, Architect: *m* 1979, Amanda Louise Margaret, da of Lance Lee Bromley, MA, M Chir, FRCS, of 26 Molyneux St, W1, and has issue.

Arms – Azure, a naval crown between four crosses crosslet in cross, all within a cross resarcelly disjoined between as many crosses crosslet all or. **Crest** – An elephant statant argent, supporting with the trunk an anchor or.
Residence – Wyndham Croft, Turners Hill, W Sussex RH10 4PS.

SONS LIVING

(CHARLES) WILLIAM FREDERICK LANCE, *b* 27 August 1985. —— Edward Francis Annandale Bromley, *b* 1989.

SISTERS LIVING

Averina Constance Frances, *b* 1950: *m* 1969, Martin Dacre Northmore-Ball, FRCS, Orthopaedic Surg, of Higher Grange, Ellesmere, Shropshire SY12 9DH, and has issue living, Lawrence Henry Arthur Knowles, *b* 1986, —— Letitia Emily Ruth, *b* 1976. —— Emma Irene Anne, *b* (twin) 1951: *m* 1976, Michael Henry Geddes Ablitt of 14 Westland Rd, Faringdon, Oxon, and has issue living, Zoë Christiana, *b* 1979, —— Helen Angela Emma, *b* 1981, —— Sophie Hannah Rachel, *b* 1985, —— Tessa Catherine Ruth, *b* 1988. —— Christiana Joan Elizabeth Ruth, *b* 1956: *m* 1979, Giles Adrian Ivo Payne, of 210 Marlborough Rd, Oxford, only son of Ivo Payne (infra), and has issue living, Charlotte Liberty Ruth, *b* 1987.

Semper · paratus
Always ready

WIDOW LIVING OF SIXTH BARONET

RUTH, da of late Rev Arthur Brooke-Smith, and widow of P/O Richard Guy Hulse, RAF: *m* 2ndly, 1948, Sir Francis Gerald William Knowles, FRS, 6th Bt, who *d* 1974; 3rdly, 1979, Ivo Payne, of West Ridge, Manton Down Rd, Marlborough, Wilts (ante).

COLLATERAL BRANCH LIVING

Issue of late Robert Cosby Knowles, 5th son of 4th baronet, b 1888, d 1972: m 1929, Phyllis Eve, who d 1992, da of late Rev Canon Ward Thomas, of Lorne, Vic, Aust:—
Peter Cosby (Namarva, Winton, Qld, Aust), b 1930: m 1st, 1957 (m diss 1977), Gloria, da of H. Oaten; 2ndly, 1977, Jane Winifred, da of B. Cooper, of Kenmore, Brisbane, and has issue living, (by 1st m) Richard Cosby, b 1969, — Sandra, b 1969, — Kerry, b 1964, — Judith Anne, b 1967, — (by 2nd m) Imogen Winifred, b 1988. —— Michael Cosby (21 Bonview Rd, Malvern, Vic, Aust), b 1936; M Com Qld; PhD Edinburgh; Sr lecturer, Monash Univ, Aust: m 1965, Ann, da of G. R. Mountain, MA, AM, of Malvern, Vic, Aust, and has issue living, Stephen Francis, b 1970, — Fiona Mary, b 1972.
This family is descended from Charles Knollys, titular 4th Earl of Banbury temp James II. The 1st baronet, Sir Charles, Adm of the White, and Rear-Adm of Great Britain, a distinguished naval commander, was Governor of Louisburg, Cape Breton, 1745-6, and of Jamaica 1752-6, and in 1770 was appointed, by the Empress Catherine II of Russia, Chief President of HIM's Admiralty, with a seat in the Russian Council. Adm Sir Charles Henry, GCB, 2nd Bt, distinguished himself in his profession, and commanded the "Goliath" in the memorable battle of Capt St Vincent, 14th Feb 1797, when the Spanish fleet was defeated. The 3rd baronet, Sir Francis Charles, FRS, was a mathematician who gained the Telford Prize and was elected FRS in 1830. Vice-Adm Sir Charles G. F. Knowles, 4th Bt, served in Burma War 1852-3, commanded Niger Expedition 1864, and was thanked by Admiralty for services on Coast of Cuba during insurrection of 1870-71, and for quelling in 1880 insurrection in Danish Island of Santa Cruz, and by Colonial Office for services on Newfoundland Fisheries when in command of the "Lapwing" 1872. The 5th baronet, Sir Francis Howe Seymour Knowles, was Physical Anthropologist to Geographical Survey, Canada, and a prehistorian of note. The 6th baronet, Sir Francis Gerald William, MA, DPhil, DSc, FRS, was a distinguished pioneering research biologist and author. He was Head of Biology Dept, Marlborough College, 1938-58, Reader and Prof of Comparative Endocrinology, 1967, at Birmingham Univ, and Prof of Anatomy and Head of Dept of Anatomy, Kings Coll, London Univ, 1967-74.

LACON (UK) 1818, of Great Yarmouth, Norfolk.

Sir EDMUND VERE LACON, 8th *Baronet*; b 3 May 1936; s his father *Sir* GEORGE VERE FRANCIS, 1980; *ed* Woodbridge Sch: *m* 1963, Gillian, only da of Jack Henry Middleditch, of Wrentham, and has issue.

Arms – Quarterly, per fesse indented erminois and azure, in the 2nd quarter a wolf's head erased or. Crest – On a mount vert a falcon proper, belled or, collared and charged on the breast with a cross flory gules.
Residence – Milbrook, Holton St Peter, Halesworth, Suffolk IP19 8PN.

Probity is true honour

SON LIVING

EDMUND RICHARD VERE, b 2 Oct 1967.

DAUGHTER LIVING

Anna Kathryn, b 1965.

BROTHER LIVING

George Julius (Larcomb Farmhouse, Diptford, Totnes, S Devon TQ9 7PD), b 1938; ed Duncan Hall Sch: m 1968, Elizabeth Rodger, only da of Archibald Kelly, of Sheffield, and has issue living, Sarah Elizabeth, b 1970, — Emma Blanche, b 1973.

DAUGHTER LIVING OF FIFTH BARONET

Dorothy Beecroft, b (posthumous) 1912: m 1st, 1932 (m diss 1946), Robert Desmond Ropner (Knt 1959), who d 1977 (see Ropner, Bt, cr 1904, colls); 2ndly 1946, Capt D. B. M. Curtis, and has issue living, (by 1st m) (see Ropner, Bt, cr 1904, colls), — (by 2nd m) Amanda Murray, b 1948.

WIDOW LIVING OF SEVENTH BARONET

KATHLYN IRIS (Kathlyn, Lady Lacon) (7 South Green, Southwold, Suffolk), da of late Edward Pilbrow, of 1 Carlyle Square, SW3, and formerly wife of Charles Marriott Morrell: m 1957, as his 2nd wife, Sir George Vere Francis Lacon, 7th Bt, who d 1980.

COLLATERAL BRANCHES LIVING

Grandson of late Thomas Beecroft Ussher Lacon, 2nd son of 3rd baronet:—
Issue of late Henry Reginald Dunbar Lacon, b 1884, d 1960: m 1912, Hilda Mary, who d 1965, da of late William Bruce Slayter, MD, FRCS, of Halifax, Nova Scotia:—
Reginald William Beecroft, DSC (Denman Island, Vancouver, BC, Canada), b 1913; Cdr RN (ret); 1939-45 War (despatches four times, DSC, and Bar): m 1st, 1948 (m diss 1976), Joan Denyer Briscoe (DUNOLLY), da of late Albert J. George; 2ndly, 1976, Beatrice, da of late G. H. V. Burroughs, of Calgary, Alberta, and widow of Myles A. Ellissen, MC, and has had two adopted children, George Christopher Jocelyn, b 1955, d 1973, — Victoria, b 1952: m 19—, Richard H. St M. Kemmis Betty, The Queen's Own Hussars, eldest son of Lt. Col Peter Kemmis Betty, of Hampton Hill House, Swanmore, Hants.

Granddaughter of late Capt Henry Sidney Hammet Lacon, 3rd son of 3rd baronet:—
Issue of late Gordon Massy Lacon, b 1886, d 1918: m 1909, Phyllis, who d 1963 (having m 2ndly, 1920, John Alan Clutton-Brock, of Oakfield, Weybridge, who d 1925, and 3rdly, 1926, Charles Geoffrey Keith Hulbert, who d 1963), da of His Honour late Judge Robert Woodfall, Judge of County Court Circuit No 44, of Nutfield, Weybridge:—
Pamela Abbott, b 1912: m 1st, 1936 (m diss 1946), John Edward Hodgson; 2ndly, 1949, Wing-Cdr Philip S. Gage, RAF (ret), of Green Cottage, Kington Langley, Chippenham, Wilts SN15 5NP, and has issue living, (by 1st m) Robert John (2 St Hilda's Rd, SW13 9JQ), b 1937: m 1st, 1963 (m diss 1971), Caroline Joan Eve Kingdon; 2ndly, 1976, Hon Jean Margaret Brand, da of 5th Viscount Hampden, and has issue living, (by 1st m) Jonathan Charles b 1968, Sarah Jane b 1965, (by 2nd m) Thomas Edward b 1981, — Penelope Jane, b 1939: m 1st, 1964 (m diss 1967), John Harmon Clary; 2ndly, 1976 (m diss 1985), David

Gavin Clark; 3rdly, 1988, William Love, of 3 Swallow St, Turners Hill, Crawley, W Sussex and has issue living, (by 1st *m*) James Alistair *b* 1965: *m* 1987, Lara Jayne Pope.

The present baronet is in direct descent from Edmund Lacon, who settled in Yorkshire early in the seventeeth century, belonging to a yr branch of the very ancient family of Lacon settled in Shropshire *temp* Edward III. Sir Edmund Lacon was created a baronet in 1818 and *d* 1839. The 2nd baronet, Sir Edmund Knowles Lacon, was High Sheriff of Norfolk. The 3rd baronet was MP for Great Yarmouth (*C*) 1852-7, and 1859-68, and for Norfolk N 1868-88. The 5th baronet was Capt 12th Lancers, and served in S African War 1899-1901 (Queen's medal with 3 clasps, King's medal with 2 clasps). The 6th baronet, Sir George Haworth Ussher Lacon, DSO served in S Africa 1901, and during European War 1914-19 as Lieut-Col Roy Warwickshire Regt (DSO).

LACY (UK) 1921, of Ampton, co Suffolk.

Sir HUGH MAURICE PIERCE LACY, 3rd *Baronet*; *b* 3 Sept 1943; *s* his father, *Sir* MAURICE JOHN PIERCE, 1965; *ed* Aiglon Coll, Switzerland: *m* 1968, Deanna, da of Howard Bailey, of Stourbridge.

Arms – Gyronny or and gules, on a bend sable a Lacy knot between two martlets of the first. **Crest** – An eagle rising or, gorged with a collar gemelle gules and resting the dexter claw on a Lacy knot sable. *Residence* –

BROTHER LIVING

PATRICK BRYAN FINUCANE (11 Tudor Gdns, Barnes, SW13), *b* 18 April 1948; *ed* Downside: *m* 1971, Phyllis Victoria, da of Edgar P. H. James, of 6 Berkeley Rd, Barnes, SW13, and has issue living, Finian James Pierce, *b* 24 Sept 1972, — Alexandra Victoria, *b* 1977.

SISTER LIVING

Jeanne Clare, *b* 1942: *m* 1st, 1965 (*m diss* 1973), David Leslie Morgan; 2ndly, 1976, Andrew Findlay, of Trochelhill, Fochabers, nr Elgin, Morayshire IV32 7LN, and has issue living, (by 1st *m*) Dominic Maurice David, *b* 1969, — Miranda Jean, *b* 1967, — (by 2nd *m*) John Andrew Pierce, *b* 1977.

HALF-SISTER LIVING

Honours are enhanced by deserts

Susan Mary (Holtye House, Cowden, Edenbridge, Kent), *b* 1936: *m* 1961, Michael John Gemmell, who *d* 1988, and has issue living, Andrew James, *b* 1969, — Catriona Sarah, *b* 1963: *m* 1989, Peter Ion Wright, of 56 Taybridge Rd, Battersea, SW11 5PT, and has issue living, Harry Michael Ion *b* 1993, Edwina Primrose *b* 1991, — Lucy Charlotte, *b* 1964.

The 1st baronet, Sir Pierce Thomas Lacy (2nd son (by 2nd *m*) of John Pierce Lacy, of Oak Mount, Edgbaston, Birmingham) was Chm of Birmingham Stock Exchange, and Founder of British Trusts Asso and of British Shareholders' Trust.

LAKE (GB) 1711, of Edmonton, Middlesex.

Sir (ATWELL) GRAHAM LAKE, 10th *Baronet*; *b* 6 Oct 1923; *s* his father, *Capt* SIR ATWELL HENRY, CB, OBE, RN, 1972; *ed* Eton; Sr Tech Adviser MOD; ret 1983; Gilbert and Ellice Mil Forces 1944-45; Colonial Admin Ser 1945-55 (Sec to Govt of Tonga 1950-53); British High Commn New Delhi 1966-68; FCO 1969-72: *m* 1983, Mrs Katharine Margaret Lister, da of late D. W. Last.

Arms – Quarterly: 1st, (coat of augmentation) gules, a dexter arm embowed in armour, issuing from sinister side of the shield, holding in the hand a sword erect, all proper, thereto affixed a banner argent charged with a cross between sixteen escutcheons gules, on the centre of the cross a lion of England; 2nd, sable, a bend, between six crosslets fitchée, argent; 3rd, quarterly, argent and sable, on a bend gules, three mullets argent; 4th argent, a chevron between three boars' heads couped sable. **Crest** – 1st, a cavalier in a fighting posture, his scarf gules, his left arm hanging down as wounded and useless, holding the bridle in his teeth, his face, sword, armour, and horse embrued, all proper; 2nd, a horse's head argent, charged with a fesse, cottised gules. *Address* – Magdalen Laver Hall, Chipping Ongar, Essex.

Un Dieu, un roy, un cœur
One God, one king, one
heart

BROTHER LIVING

EDWARD GEOFFREY (High Acre, Cowgill, Dent, Cumbria), *b* 17 July 1928; *ed* Eton: *m* 1965, Judith Ann, da of John Fox, and has issue living, Mark Winter, *b* 1968, — Sophie Louise, *b* 1971.

COLLATERAL BRANCHES LIVING

Issue of late Willoughby Alfred Lake, 2nd son of 9th baronet, *b* 1925, *d* 1986: *m* 1952, Elizabeth Elsie Faith (Ashleigh, Much Hadham, Herts), da of Sir Rupert Turner Havelock Clarke, 2nd Bt:—
Susan Kathleen, *b* 1961. —— Catherine Jane, *b* 1962.

Grandsons of late Winter Atwell Edward Lake, son of late Capt Andrew Winter Lake, 5th son of 4th baronet:—

Issue of late Lieut-Col Ernest Atwell Winter Lake, CBE, Indian Army (ret), *b* 1886, *d* 1945: *m* 1924, Phyllis Marjorie, da of J. G. Silcock, formerly ICS:—

John Winter Atwell, *b* 1925: *m* 1955, Elsie, da of R. Milburn, of Long Marton, Westmorland. —— Winter Philip Edward, *b* 1930: *m* 1956, Vera, da of A. G. Liddell, of Durham.

Sir Edward Lake, Chancellor of the Diocese of Lincoln, and Advocate-General in Ireland, was, for his loyalty and services to Charles I, granted by that monarch the coat of augmentation now borne by the family, and the exceptional privilege of nominating a person to be created a baronet. He did not, however, avail himself of this privilege, and, in consequence, a baronetcy was in 1711 conferred on his great-nephew and heir, Bibye Lake, Sub-Governor of the African Co.

LAKIN (UK) 1909, of The Cliff, Borough of Warwick.

One God, one king, one heart

Sir MICHAEL LAKIN, 4th *Baronet*; *b* 28 Oct 1934; *s* his father, *Sir* HENRY, 1979; *ed* Stowe: *m* 1st, 1956 (*m diss* 1963), Margaret, da of Robert Wallace, of Mount Norris, co Armagh; 2ndly, 1965, Felicity, da of Anthony Denis Murphy, of Londiani, Kenya, and has issue by 2nd *m*.

Arms – Quarterly: indented argent and azure, in the 1st and 4th quarters a pellet charged with a lion's head erased of the first. **Crest** – A dexter cubit arm vested sable cuffed azure, the hand grasping a plasterer's trowel proper. *Address* – c/o Little Sherwood Hill, Tunley, nr Cirencester, Glos.

SON LIVING *(By 2nd marriage)*

RICHARD ANTHONY, *b* 26 Nov 1968.

DAUGHTER LIVING *(By 2nd marriage)*

Mary Jane, *b* 1966: *m* 1992, Charles Adrian Clark, of Lowesmoor Farm, Cherrington, Tetbury, Glos GL8 8SP, son of late Walter Clark, and has issue living, Emma Louise, *b* 1993.

AUNT LIVING *(Daughter of 2nd baronet)*

Cynthia, *b* 1907. *Residence* – Sherwood Hill, Tunley, Cirencester.

COLLATERAL BRANCHES LIVING

Grandson of late Henry Gilbert Lakin, 2nd son of 1st baronet:—

Issue of late Lt-Col John Lakin, TD, *b* 1910, *d* 1989: *m* 1939, Hon (Helena) Daphne Pearson (Hammerwood House, Iping, Midhurst, Sussex GU29 0PF), da of 2nd Viscount Cowdray:—

Michael Simon, *b* 1955: *m* 1st, 1977 (*m diss* 1987), Mireille Farjon; 2ndly, 1987, Amanda Ann, only da of James Thomas Durrant Shaw, TD, of Scottow Hall, Norfolk (*see* Durrant, Bt, 1960 Edn), and has issue living (by 1st *m*), Benjamin John, *b* 1981, — (by 2nd *m*) Johnathan James, *b* 1989, — Piers Thomas, *b* 1991, — (by 1st *m*) Laura Daphne, *b* 1984.

Issue of late Edward Lyon Lakin, 3rd son of 1st baronet, *b* 1879, *d* 1922: *m* 1912, Dorothy Barklie, who *d* 1969, da of Col Barklie Cairns McCalmont, CB (B Kingsale):—

Richard Barklie, DSO, DSC, *b* 1914; *ed* RNC Dartmouth; is Lt-Cdr RN (ret); 1939-45 War (despatches, DSO, DSC and Bar, USA Legion of Merit); DSO 1943: *m* 1st, 1936, Pamela Mary Helen, who *d* 1981, da of late Group Capt Philip Jackson-Taylor, RAF; 2ndly, 1987, Pansy Myra Edith, da of late Col Algernon Lothian Bonham Carter, DSO, of Buriton, Petersfield, Hants, and widow of Cdr Jo Allan Phillips, RN, and has issue living (by 1st *m*), Robin Lyon (19 Windarra Cres, Wahroonga, NSW 2076, Aust), *b* 1938; *ed* Eton: *m* 1964, Gillian Claire, da of Peter Baily, of South Farm, Gt Whittington, Northumberland, and has issue living, Jessica Honor Katherine *b* 1966, Nicola Anne Pamela *b* 1970, — Mark Philip (20 Kelso Place, W8 5QG), *b* 1941; *ed* Eton: *m* 1988, Christina Lisa Josephine, da of late Patrick Dolan (USA Legion of Merit), of Much Hadham, Herts, and widow of Peter Gordon Shiach, of Ardgilzean, Elgin, Morayshire, and has issue living, Patrick Barklie *b* 1989, Henry Lyon *b* 1991, Molly Kathleen *b* 1993, — Julian Barklie (Juniper Cottage, Farringdon, Hants GU34 3DT), *b* 1948; *ed* Eton: *m* 1973, Penelope Jane, da of John Almond, of Burghclere, Berks, and has issue living, Olivia Mary *b* 1978, Arabella Louise *b* 1980, — Amanda Joy (Rosemary House, Northleach, Glos GL54 3HJ), *b* 1947: *m* 1981 (*m diss* 1990), Christopher Euan Philip Charles Courtney, — Caroline Madeline, *b* 1953: *m* 1984, Richard Frederick Wallis, of 23 Crabtree Lane, SW6 6LP, yr son of late Charles Wallis, of Bryanston Square, W1, and has issue living, Jack Charles Lyon *b* 1990, Daisy Pamela *b* 1987, — Serena Pamela, *b* (twin) 1953: *m* 1986, Giles Selwyn Robinson, of Henley on Thames, Oxon, eldest son of Donald Edgar Robinson, of Perthshire, and has issue living, Harry Edgar Selwyn *b* 1989, Molly Pamela *b* 1992. *Residence* – Seaview House, Seaview, Isle of Wight PO34 5ET.

Issue of late Major Michael Lawrence Lakin, DSO, MC, 11th Hussars, 4th son of 1st baronet, *b* 1881, *d* 1960: *m* 1914, Kathleen, who *d* 1930, da of late Lord Maurice FitzGerald (D Leinster, colls):—

Maurice Victor, MC, *b* 1919; *ed* Eton; late Capt 17th/21st Lancers; European War 1940-44, in N Africa (wounded, MC): *m* 1st, 1951 (*m diss* 1956), Huguette Paule Clemence, da of Robert Cauvin, of Paris; 2ndly, 1959 (*m diss* 1971), Silvanni, da of Ngot-Vong, of Pnom Penh, Cambodia, and has issue living, (by 2nd *m*) Michael, *b* 1960. — Richard, *b* 1964: *m* 1990, Claire, da of Roland Coutant, of Vinon sur Verdon, Var, France, and has issue living, Alexandre *b* 1992, Camille *b* 1991. *Residence* – Cabrol, Flayosc, Var, France.

Sir Michael Henry Lakin, 1st Bt (son of Henry Lakin, of Malvern), was Mayor of Warwick, Vice-Chm of County Council for Warwickshire, and High Sheriff of that County.

LAMBERT (GB) 1711, of London.

By pursuing one attains

Sir PETER JOHN BIDDULPH LAMBERT, 10th *Baronet*, only son of late John Hugh Lambert, elder son of Hugh Biddulph Lambert, only son of Rev William Henry Lambert, 6th son of 5th baronet; *b* 5th April 1952; *s* his cousin, Sir GREVILLE FOLEY 1988; *ed* Upper Canada Coll, Toronto, Trent Univ, Peterborough (BSc), and Univ of Manitoba, Winnipeg (MA): *m* 1989, Leslie Anne, da of Richard Welkos Lyne.

Arms – Argent, on a mount an oak-tree vert, and a greyhound courant gules. **Crest** – Out of a ducal coronet or three ostrich feathers, the dexter feather gules, the centre argent, and the sinister azure. **Residence** – 483 Spadina Rd, Toronto, Ontario M5P 2W6, Canada.

DAUGHTER LIVING

Maeve Edith Jean, *b* 1992.

UNCLE LIVING (*son of late Hugh Biddulph Lambert, ante*)

ROBERT WILLIAM, *b* 6 June 1911; sometime in Merchant Navy: *m* 1948, Margaret Daphne Harvey. *Residence* – Route 1, Box 717, Elgin, Texas 78621, USA.

AUNTS LIVING (*daughters of late Hugh Biddulph Lambert, ante*)

Nina Joan *b* 1916: *m* 1st, 1941 (*m diss* 1948), Guy Duncan Tucker; 2ndly, 1951, Eric Harold Dehn, and has issue living (by 1st *m*), Michael Duncan Hugh (1 Trelawney Rd, Bristol 6), *b* 1942: *m* 1970, Stephanie West, and has issue living, Rebecca *b* 1971, Zoë *b* 1974, — (by 2nd *m*) Jacqueline Tessa, *b* 1952: *m* 1980, Robert Baxter, of 83b Albion Drive, E8, — Nicola Louisa, *b* 1954: *m* 1981, Dominique Bonnard, of 18 rue Gabrielle de Bourbon, 79100 Thouars, France, and has issue living, Camille André Jean *b* 1984, Thomas Michel Eric *b* 1987. *Residence* – 5 Trelawney Rd, Bristol 6. —— Julia Margaret, *b* 1920; 1939-45 War in WAAF. *Residence* – Priory Cottage, Heythrop Rd, Chipping Norton, Oxon OX7 5TA.

DAUGHTERS LIVING OF NINTH BARONET

(Isabel) Pamela, *b* 1933: *m* 1979, Denys Leonard Taaffe, of Trevalor, 6 St Matthew's Hill, Wadebridge, Cornwall PL27 6DX. —— (Roma) Ann, *b* 1934: *m* 1956, Gp Capt Colin John Phillips, RAF (ret), of SeeNeedles, Keyhaven, Lymington, Hants SO41 0TJ, and has issue living, David Jonathan, *b* 1958: *m* 1992, Joanne Susan Shore, and has issue living, Matthew James *b* 1993, — Adrian Greville, *b* 1959: *m* 1982, Patricia Lyons, and has issue living, Sarah May *b* 1991, Elizabeth Louise *b* 1993, — Carolyn Ann, *b* 1962: *m* 1986, Stuart Brown, and has issue living, Samuel Jonathan *b* 1993, Charlotte Ann *b* 1989, Rebecca Emily *b* 1991. —— Carole Joy (16 High House Drive, Inkberrow, Worcs WR7 4EG), *b* 1940: *m* 1st, 1960 (*m diss* 1963), Raymond Bennett; 2ndly, 1968 (*m diss* 1987), Nicholas Jason Hill; 3rdly 1991, Colin Geoffrey Russell, and has issue living, (by 2nd *m*) Jason Stirling, *b* 1970, — Michelle Jane, *b* 1973.

DAUGHTER LIVING OF EIGHTH BARONET

Eileen Grey, *b* 1922: *m* 1st, 1942 (*m diss* 1946), 11th Earl of Harrington; 2ndly, 1947, John Phillip Bissill, MC, who *d* 1988, and has issue living, (by 1st *m*) (see E Harrington), — (by 2nd *m*) Alexandra Diana, *b* 1950: *m* 1979, Peter Brinton Williams, of The Home Farm, Enville, nr Stourbridge, and has issue living, Harry John *b* 1981, George Edward *b* 1985, Jane Charlotte *b* 1982. *Residence* – Enville Hall, Stourbridge, Worcs.

WIDOW LIVING OF NINTH BARONET

(EDITH) ROMA (*Roma, Lady Lambert*), da of Richard Batson: *m* 1932, Sir Greville Foley Lambert, 9th Bt, FCA, who *d* 1988. *Residence* – Flat 5, Henleydale, Stratford Rd, Shirley, Solihull, Warwicks.

COLLATERAL BRANCHES LIVING

Grandson of late Mortan Lambert, son of Alan Lambert, son of Francis John Lambert, 3rd son of 4th baronet :—
Issue of late Montague Victor Lambert, *b* 1904; *d* 1979: *m* 1st, 1931, Ena Sylvia Victoria, who *d* 1944, da of late George Grossmith; 2ndly, 1948, Janis Mary, who *d* 1984, da of late Capt Wilfrid Brittain Squirl-Dawson, of Higham, Suffolk:—
(By 2nd *m*) Charles Geoffrey Mortan, *b* 1956.

Grandson of late Jasper Lambert, son of late Alan Lambert (ante):—
Issue of late Alan Forsyth Lambert, *b* 1901, *d* 19—: *m* 1935, Olive Edith, who *d* 1990, da of late Frederick Long:—
Philip Jasper (1 Burwood Close, Ringley Park Rd, Reigate, Surrey), *b* 1936.

Sir John Lambert, 1st Bt, of the Isle of Rhé, France, settled in England as a merchant, and was one of the Directors of the South Sea Co. In 1710 he supplied the Treasury with money, and for this service was created a baronet. The 7th baronet, Sir Henry Foley, assumed by Roy licence, 1905, for himself and issue, the surname of Grey in lieu of his patronymic, and the arms of Grey quarterly with those of Lambert, and was High Sheriff of Worcestershire 1901.

LANE (UK) 1913, of Cavendish Square, St Marylebone. (Extinct 1972).

Sir WILLIAM ARBUTHNOT LANE, CBE, 2nd and last *Baronet*.

DAUGHTER LIVING OF SECOND BARONET

Susan Charlotte Arbuthnot, *b* 1938: *m* 1964, John Nicolas Bowker, and has issue living, Mark James Arbuthnot Lane, *b* 1967, — Katy Louise, *b* 1968.

LANGHAM (E) 1660, of Cottesbrooke, Northampton.

Nor suffers them to be savage

Sir JAMES MICHAEL LANGHAM, TD, 15th *Baronet*; *b* 24 May 1932; *s* his father, *Sir* JOHN CHARLES PATRICK, 1972; *ed* Rossall; Capt N Irish Horse: *m* 1959, Marion Audrey Eleanor, da of Oswald Barratt, of Tanzania, and has issue.

Arms – Argent, three bears' heads erased sable, muzzled or. **Crest** – A bear's head as in the arms.
Residence – Claranagh, Tempo, Enniskillen, co Fermanagh.

SONS LIVING

JOHN STEPHEN, *b* 14 Dec 1960: *m* 1991, Sarah Jane, da of late John Denis Verschoyle-Greene, of Bushfield House, Cashedermot, co Kildare, and of Mrs John Alexander, of Milford House, co Carlow. *Residence* – Tempo Manor, Tempo, Enniskillen, co Fermanagh. —— Rupert William (27 Broadley Street, NW8 8BN), *b* 1963: *m* 1989, Karen, da of M. Soderberg, of Runcorn, Cheshire.

DAUGHTER LIVING

Lucinda Jane, *b* 1966.

The 1st baronet, Sir John, was knighted by Charles II at The Hague, being one of a deputation from the city of London to wait on HM in Holland. When Sheriff of London in 1642, he, with several other gentlemen, was imprisoned for refusing to publish "An Act for the exheridation of the Royal line, the abolishment of Monarchy in the Kingdom, and the setting up of a Commonwealth". Sir John, 6th Bt, left £6,000 to the Corporation of London to found a society for the relief of poor soldiers, sailors and their wives. Sir (Herbert) Charles Arthur, 13th Bt, was High Sheriff of co Fermanagh 1930.

LANGMAN (UK) 1906, of Eaton Square, City of Westminster (Extinct 1985).

Sir JOHN LYELL LANGMAN, 3rd and last *Baronet*.

DAUGHTERS LIVING OF THIRD BARONET

Josephine Frances, *b* 1938. —— Judith Ann Camilla, *b* 1949: *m* 1972, Ian K. Gibson.

DAUGHTERS LIVING OF SECOND BARONET

Mary Eleanor, *b* 1908. —— (Nora) Elizabeth Ferrar, *b* 1919: *m* 1955, John Archibald Montgomery, and has issue living, Archibald John, *b* 1957, — James Lyell, *b* 1961, — Katherine Elizabeth, *b* 1956. *Residence* – North Cadbury Court, Somerset.

WIDOW LIVING OF THIRD BARONET

IRIS PAMELA GASKELL (*Lady Langman*), only da of Capt Spencer Kennard, formerly of Purslow Hall, Craven Arms, Shropshire: *m* 1936, Sir John Lyell Langman, 3rd Bt, who *d* 1985. *Residence* – The Goslings, Gooseacre Lane, Cirencester, Glos.

LANGRISHE (I) 1777, of Knocktopher Abbey, Kilkenny.

Sir HERCULES RALPH HUME LANGRISHE, 7th *Baronet*; *b* 17 May 1927; *s* his father, *Capt Sir* TERENCE HUME, 1973; *ed* Eton; late Lt 9th Lancers: *m* 1955, Hon Grania Sybil Enid Wingfield, only da of 9th Viscount Power-scourt, and has issue.

Arms – Quarterly, or and sable, four covered cups counterchanged. **Crest** – A lion rampant per fesse or and sable.
Residence – Arlonstown, Dunsany, co Meath. *Club* – Kildare Street and University.

Medio tutissimus ibis
You will walk safest in a
middle path

SON LIVING

JAMES HERCULES (Derrypatrick, Drumree, co Meath), *b* 3 March 1957: *m* 1985, Gemma Mary Philomena, eldest da of Patrick O'Daly, of Ferndale, Kiltale, Dunsany, co Meath, and has issue living, Richard James Hercules, *b* 8 April 1988, — Victoria Anna Jean, *b* 1986.

DAUGHTERS LIVING

Miranda Grania, *b* 1959: *m* 1984, Christopher John Markes, of Old Kilcarty, Dunsany, co Meath, eldest son of late John Edward Markes, of Recess, co Galway, and has issue living, Alice Olivia, *b* 1987, — Louisa Meriel, *b* 1990. —— Georgina Emma, *b* 1961: *m* 1989, Dr S. Ross Wallace, son of Dr John Wallace, of Clare, S Australia, and has issue living, Oliver William, *b* 1993. —— Atalanta Sue, *b* 1963: *m* 1992, J. Arthur R. Pollock, elder son of John David George Pollock, of Mountainstown, Navan, co Meath (*see* Barrington, Bt, 1947 Edn).

BROTHER LIVING

Patrick Nicholas, TD (The Manor House, Sellindge, Ashford, Kent), *b* 1932; *ed* Eton; late Maj Leicestershire and Derbyshire Yeo (TA) and a Member of Lloyd's: *m* 1957, Penelope Jill, only child of the late Lt-Cdr Kenneth Horley, RN, and has issue living, Caroline, *b* 1958: *m* 1984, Patrick J. Drury, and has issue living, Leonie Marianne *b* 1983, Rosalind Elizabeth *b* 1985, — Marianne Stuart, *b* 1961: *m* 1988, Nicholas Di Biasio, and has issue living, Adam *b* 1987, Jamie *b* 1990, George *b* 1993.

COLLATERAL BRANCHES LIVING

Issue of late Robert Gore Langrishe, yst son of 6th baronet, *b* 1936; *d* 1982: *m* 1966, (Eleanor) Barbara Muriel (who *m* 3rdly, 1983, Hugh Curran), da of late Reginald Arthur Lygon (*see* E Beauchamp, colls), and formerly wife of William James Cavendish-Bentinck (D Portland, colls), who *d* 1966:—
Robin Stuart, *b* 1967.

Grandson of late Henry Hoadly Langrishe, eldest son of late Richard Langrishe, 5th son of 3rd baronet:—
Issue of late Lt-Col Roger Patrick Hercules Langrishe, *b* 1905, *d* 1969: *m* 1949, Doris May, who *d* 1988, da of late Thomas Sidney Bott, of 16 Beech Rd, Oxford:—
James Hoadly (11 Heath Lawns, Catisfield, Fareham, Hants), *b* 1951; *ed* King's Sch, Canterbury; Lt-Cdr RN: *m* 1979, Ann Helen, da of late Robert Arthur Jutson, of Bushey, Herts, and has issue living, Katherine Jane, *b* 1980, — Claire Jennifer, *b* 1982.

Grandchildren of late Richard Langrishe, 5th son of 3rd baronet:—
Issue of late Lieut-Col John du Plessis Langrishe, DSO, RAMC, *b* 1883, *d* 1947: *m* 1914, Helen Dorothy, who *d* 1981, da of late Philip George Collins:—
Philip John Duppa (Birches, Pembroke Rd, Woking, Surrey), *b* 1917: *ed* Cheltenham, and Pembroke Coll, Camb (BA 1938); formerly Capt RA: 1939-45 War (prisoner, escaped): *m* 1st, 1948 (*m diss* 1963), Phyllis Edwina, da of C. V. Vanbergen, of Bassett, Hildenborough, Kent; 2ndly, 1963, Isabel Angus, yr da of Sir (Alexander) Knox Helm, GBE, KCMG, of The Old Rectory, Tewin, Herts, and has issue living, (by 1st *m*) Charles William John (Greystones, 27 Hawkhirst Rd, Kenley, Surrey CR2 5DN), *b* 1949: *m* 1973, Philippa Anne, da of John Jenkins, and has issue living, Philip Charles Nicholas *b* 1976, Emma Charlotte *b* 1978, Nicola Anne *b* 1980, — Patrick du Plessis (Weston Manor, Weston, Honiton, Devon), *b* 1952: *ed* Exeter Univ (LLB 1973); solicitor: *m* 1972, Lynda Audrey, da of Stanley Edward Bellman, and has issue living, Thomas du Plessis *b* 1980, Catherine Mary *b* 1976, Tamsin Clare Audrey *b* 1978, Frances Anne *b* 1983, Clare Madeleine *b* 1986, Marie Anna *b* 1992. —— Hugh Richard (8 Nyth Gwennol, Saundersfoot, Dyfed SA69 9PW) *b* 1923: *ed* Cheltenham; formerly Lt (A)RNVR (Air Arm): *m* 1955, Pamela Mary, da of late William E. Downes, of Bourton Hall, Much Wenlock, Shropshire, and has issue living, John William, *b* 1959; *ed* Wrekin Coll, and Southampton Univ (BSc), — Jane Dorothy, *b* 1956: *m* 1985, Charles John Miller, MICE, of 34 Gilmais, Bookham, Leatherhead, Surrey KT23 4RP, son of late C. H. Miller, and has issue living, Philip James *b* 1990, Hollie Claire *b* 1988. —— Dorothy Pratt (3 Palace Gate, Odiham, Hants), *b* 1921: *m* 1st, 1946 (*m diss* 1972), Clifford Anthony Weston, formerly Capt RA; 2ndly, 1974, Robert Lonsdale Fell, DFC, RAFVR, who *d* 1985, and has issue living (by 1st *m*), Richard Anthony, *b* 1947, — Christopher Nigel, *b* 1949, — Douglas Neil, *b* 1951.

Grandsons of late Lt-Col Richard Bellingham Langrishe, 3rd son of late Richard Langrishe (ante):—
Issue of late Lt-Col Richard Courtenay Gibson Langrishe, *b* 1912, *d* 1983: *m* 1940, Jean Gertrude Abercrombie, who *m* 2ndly, 1984, S/Ldr Michael Edward Townsend, RAF, da of late George Dingwall Thomson, MRCS:—
Richard Dingwall (The Moorings, Upper Clatford, Andover, Hants SP11 7QL), *b* 1941; *ed* Cheltenham, and RMCS Shrivenham (BSc Eng); Maj (Ret): *m* 1964, Angela Walmsley Marett, el da of David Walmsley Marett Tims, of Crookham Village, Hants, and has issue living, Belinda Jane Marett, *b* 1967, — Rebecca Kate, *b* 1970. —— Nicholas du Plessis (Castle View, Carew, Tenby, Dyfed), *b* 1942: *ed* Cheltenham: *m* 1966, Anna Victoria Airy, only da of S/Ldr Michael Edward Townsend, RAF, (ante), and has issue living, Oonagh Richarda du Plessis, *b* 1972.

This family is descended from Sir Nicholas Langrish, Kt, who was seized of the Manor of Langrish, Hants, AD 1273. The Irish branch is descended from Rafe, or Ralph (of Borden), 3rd son of Nicholas Langrishe, of Langrishe. Ralph Langrishe of Borden died between 1542-59; the 3rd in descent from him was Major Hercules Langrishe, Carver in Ordinary to Queen Henrietta Maria, who prevented the arrest of the "Five Members" by Charles I, and the 7th was the 1st baronet, Sir Hercules, who sat for forty years as MP for Knocktopher in the Irish Parliament. He was a Privy Councillor, and foremost in his advocacy for repealing the severe laws enacted against Roman Catholics.

LARCOM (UK) 1868.

Sir (CHARLES) CHRISTOPHER ROYDE LARCOM, 5th *Baronet*; *b* 11 Sept 1926; *s* his father *Sir* PHILIP, 1967; *ed* Radley, and Clare Coll, Camb (MA); a FCA: *m* 1956, Barbara Elizabeth, da of Balfour Bowen, and has issue.

Arms – Argent, on a mount a hawthorn bush proper, and in chief an eagle displayed gules. **Crest** – On a cap of maintenance azure turned up ermine a martlet sable, with a fleur-de-lis in its beak or.
Residence – 4 Village Cay Marina, PO Box 145, Road Town, Tortola, British Virgin Islands. *Club* – Bath.

Le Roy, la Loy
The King, the Law

DAUGHTERS LIVING

Mary Elizabeth, *b* 1957: *m* 1983, Joseph William Arnold. —— Jane Catherine, *b* 1958: *m* 1988, Andrew J. Edyvean, of Grey Cottage, 48 Far St, Wymeswold, Leics, son of L. A. Edyvean, of Urchfont, Wilts, and has issue living, Charlotte Louise, *b* 1994. —— Julia Dorothy, *b* 1961: *m* 1982, John Dyer, and has issue living, Benjamin Charles, *b* 1985, Sophie Claire, *b* 1984. —— Anna Balfour, *b* 1962.

SISTER LIVING

Monica Rosemary Georgina, *b* 1921: *m* 1942, William Eric Walrond, of 7 Old House Close, Church Rd, Wimbledon, SW19, and has issue living, Patricia Mary, *b* 1943, —— Anne Carol, *b* 1947, — Christine Diana, *b* 1953.

The 1st baronet, Maj-Gen Rt Hon Sir Thomas Aiskew Larcom, KCB, PC (son of late Capt Joseph Larcom), served in RE, and was subsequently Under-Sec of State for Ireland. The 2nd baronet, Lieut-Col Sir Charles Larcom served in NZ War 1863-4. The 3rd baronet, Major Sir Thomas Perceval Larcom, DSO, served with RA during European War 1914-18.

LATHAM (UK) 1919, of Crow Clump, Walton-upon-Thames, co Surrey.

Sir RICHARD THOMAS PAUL LATHAM, 3rd *Baronet*: *b* 15 April 1934; *s* his father, *Sir* (HERBERT) PAUL, 1955; *ed* Eton, and Trin Coll, Camb (BA 1957, MA 1962): *m* 1958, (Marie-Louise) Patricia, da of late Frederick Hooper Russell, of Vancouver, British Columbia, and has issue.

Arms – Gules, an eagle displayed or, between two bezants in fesse, on a chief of the second a cross moline sable between two roses of the field. **Crest** – An eagle, wings elevated, inverted and addorsed or, resting the dexter claw on a torteaux and charged on the wing with a cross as in the arms.
Residence – 2125 Birnam Wood Drive, Santa Barbara, California 93108, USA.

DAUGHTERS LIVING

Nicola Patricia, *b* 1959: *m* 1986, Colin David Jones, of Vancouver, BC, Canada. —— Alison Kathleen, *b* 1965.

The 1st baronet, Sir Thomas Paul Latham, was many years Joint Managing Director, and sometime Dep Chm of Courtaulds, Ltd, also rendered sers to Min of Pensions during European War 1914-19. The 2nd baronet, Sir (Herbert) Paul Latham was a Co Councillor for London, E Lewisham Div 1928-34, and sat as MP for Scarborough and Whitby Div of N Riding of Yorkshire (C) 1931-41.

By fortune and labour

DICK-LAUDER (NS) 1690, of Fountainhall, Haddingtonshire.

Prudence is the guardian of the tower.

Dwell as if about to depart

Sir PIERS ROBERT DICK-LAUDER, 13th *Baronet*; *b* 3 Oct 1947; *s* his father, *Maj Sir* GEORGE ANDREW, 1981.

Arms – Gules, a griffin salient within a bordure argent. **Crest** – A tower with portcullis down, the head and shoulders of a sentinel appearing above the battlements in a watching posture proper. **Supporters** – Two lions rampant argent.
Residence – 91 Womerah Av, Rush Cutters Bay, Sydney, Australia.

BROTHER LIVING

MARK ANDREW, *b* 3 May 1951: *m* 1970 (*m diss* 1982), Jeanne, da of — Mullineaux, of Bolton, Lancs, and has issue living, Martin, *b* 1976. *Residence* – 3 Sunnymead Terrace, Totnes, Devon.

SISTERS LIVING

Georgina Jane, *b* 1949: *m* 1973, her cousin, Nicholas Ernest Kerr-Smiley, and has issue (*see* Smiley, Bt, colls). —— Selina Rose, *b* 1955: *m* 1978, Piers Henry Chandler, son of D. C. B. Chandler, of Sutton Coldfield, Warwicks, and has issue living, a son, *b* 1988.

WIDOW LIVING OF TWELFTH BARONET

HESTER MARGUERITE (*Lady Dick-Lauder*), da of late Lt-Col George Cecil Minett Sorell-Cameron, CBE (B Tollemache): *m* 1945, Maj Sir George Andrew Dick-Lauder, 12th Bt, who *d* 1981. *Residence* – 17 Vine Court Rd, Sevenoaks, Kent TN13 3UU.
    This family is of Norman origin, De Lavedre being mentioned among the barons who accompanied Malcolm Canmore into Scotland. Sir Robert de Law-edre, a companion in arms of Sir William Wallace, was several times Ambassador to England from Robert I. William Lauder was Bishop of Glasgow and Chancellor of Scotland 1423, and his brother was Bishop of Dunkeld. Many of the family attained knightly honours. The 2nd baronet was a Senator of the College of Justice, with the courtesy title of Lord Fountainhall; and the 5th baronet, who assumed the additional surname of Dick, married his cousin, Isabel, heiress of William Dick, of Grange, who was in direct descent from the Royal House of Plantagenet. Sir John North Dalrymple Dick-Lauder, 11th Bt, was Lt-Col Indian Army.

LAURIE (UK) 1834, of Bedford Square, Middlesex.

Virtue is always flourishing

Sir ROBERT BAYLEY EMILIUS LAURIE, 7th *Baronet*; *b* 8 March 1931: *s* his father, *Maj-Gen Sir* JOHN EMILIUS, CBE, DSO, 1983; *ed* Eton: *m* 1968, Laurelie Meriol Winifrida, da of late Sir Reginald Lawrence William Williams, MBE, ED, 7th Bt (*cr* 1798) and has issue.

Arms – Sable, a cup argent with a chaplet between two laurel branches, all issuing out of the same, vert. **Crest** – Two laurel branches in saltire proper.
Residence – The Old Rectory, Little Tey, Colchester, Essex C06 1JA.

DAUGHTERS LIVING

Clare Meriol, *b* 1974. —— Serena Catherine, *b* 1976.

SISTERS LIVING

Rosemary Evelyn Anne, *b* 1924: *m* 1949, Cdr Robin Henry Ramsay Moodie, RN (ret), and has issue living, John Ramsay, *b* 1955: *m* 1989, Caroline Mary Hughes, and has issue living, Sam Ramsay *b* 1991, Iona Vive *b* 1993, — Edward Robin, *b* 1956: *m* 1993, Patricia Fitzgerald. *Residence* – Hill House, Penton Mewsey, Andover Hants. —— Marian Clare (*Baroness Laing of Dunphail*), *b* 1927: *m* 1950, Baron Laing of Dunphail (Life Baron).
    Residence – High Meadows, Windsor Road, Gerrards Cross, Bucks SL9 8ST.

COLLATERAL BRANCHES LIVING

Issue of late Cecil Emilius Laurie, 3rd son of 3rd baronet, *b* 1862, *d* 1919: *m* 1900, Helen Janet Douglas, who *d* 1919, da of late Lieut Robert Douglas Campbell, RN (B Blythswood, colls):—
Cassandra Gladys, *b* 1905. —— Margaret May (*Dowager Lady Houldsworth*), *b* 1908: *m* 1934, Lt-Col Sir Reginald Douglas Henry Houldsworth, 4th Bt, *cr* 1887, OBE, TD, who *d* 1989. *Residence* – Kirkbride, Maybole, Ayrshire. —— Christina Eve, *b* 1912: *m* 1938, Kenneth Murray McCall, who *d* 1987, and has issue living, David James, *b* 1941: *m* 1971, Evelyn Lucy, da of late Thomas McCosh, of Pitcon, Dalry, Ayrshire, and has issue living, Philippa, *b* 1973, Sarah Christina, *b* 1978, Emma Elizabeth *b* 1982, — William Kenneth, *b* 1944: *m* 1971, Hon Gillian Patricia Denman, da of 5th Baron Denman, and has issue living, Hamish Spencer Murray *b* 1972, Robert Andrew Calum *b* 1981, Fiona Jane *b* 1975, — Patricia Helen, *b* 1942: *m* 1970, Timothy Morgan Hughes, of Fanvile Head Farm, Hook Norton, Oxon, and has issue living, Charles Edward Kenneth *b* 1971, Davina Jane *b* 1973, Iona Caroline *b* 1978, — Joan, *b* 1948: *m* 1969, Capt John James Dean Barrow, of Camp Farm, Farmington, Northleach, Glos, and has issue living, Richard Raymond *b* 1971, Georgina Rachael *b* 1975. *Residence* – Barbuie, Moniaive, Dumfriesshire. —— Elizabeth Janet, *b* 1915: *m* 1st, 1947 (*m diss* 1960), Francis Mar-

shall; 2ndly, 1960, Francis Dudley Rose, who *d* 1968, and has issue living, (by 1st *m*) Julian Emilius Harold, *b* 1950, — Janet Philippa Ann, *b* 1949.

Grandchildren of late Cecil Emilius Laurie (ante):—
Issue of late Ronald Edward Laurie, *b* 1911, *d* 1952: *m* 1941, Rosemary Lilian Fullerton, of 23 Southlands, Hexham, Northumberland:—
ANDREW RONALD EMILIUS (7 St Oswalds Rd, Hexham, Northumberland), *b* 20 Oct 1944: *m* 1970, Sarah Anne, el da of C. D. Patterson, of Hexham, and has issue living, John Christopher Emilius, *b* 1971, — Michael James Edward, *b* 1973. —— Rosemary Helen, *b* 1942: *m* 1966, David McMullan, of 2 Lostock Av, Poynton, Cheshire, SK12 1DR, and has issue living, Andrew David Sean, *b* 1970.

Grandchildren of late Kennett BAYLEY, son of late Rev Kennett Champain Bayley, 2nd son of 1st baronet:—
Issue of late Kennett Champain BAYLEY, *b* 1873, *d* 1935: *m* 1902, Norah Kathleen, who *d* 1963, only da of late Capt Henry William Roberts, formerly 98th Regt, of Hollingside, Durham:—
John Maurice, DSC, *b* 1905; *ed* Rugby; Cdr (ret) RN: *m* 1935, Mary Boyd, da of F. M. Osborn, of Sheffield, and has issue living, *Rev* Michael John (27 Meadow Bank Av, Sheffield, S7 1PB), *b* 1936: *ed* Rugby, and Corpus Christi Coll, Camb (MA); PhD Sheffield: *m* 1963, Fleur, da of J. Jones, of Calverley, and has issue living, Robin Kennett *b* 1966, Andrew John *b* 1968, Jill Ruth *b* 1964: *m* 1987, Hugh Bowden, son of Rev Dr J. S. Bowden, of Highgate, Emma Susan *b* 1970, — Kennett Ian, *b* 1941; *ed* Bradfield; Capt 1st R Green Jackets: *m* 1955, Helen Julia, da of P. D. Benjafield, of Shalford, Surrey, and has issue living, Benjamin George Robson *b* 1967, Sarah Mary Helen *b* 1969, — Peter Charles, *b* 1943; *ed* Durham: *m* 1980, Catherine Anne, da of Dr J. Dunclee, of Saskatoon, Canada, and has issue living, Ellen Elizabeth *b* 1984. *Residence* – Hillside, Barningham, nr Richmond, N Yorks.
Issue of late Col Arthur George BAYLEY, CBE, DSO, *b* 1878, *d* 1949: *m* 1923, Katharine Mary Frederica, who *d* 1952, da of late Brig-Gen Francis Alexander Fortescue, CB, CMG (E Fortescue, colls):—
Elizabeth Frances Mary Louise (26B Elm Park Rd, SW3), *b* 1924: *m* 1st, 1947 (*m diss* 1953), John David Nicholas Retallack, late Maj Welsh Gds; 2ndly, 1953, Francis Trelawny Williams, who *d* 1977 (Salusbury-Trelawny, Bt); 3rdly, 1983, James Andrew Moffett, Lt-Cdr USNR (ret), and has issue living, (by 2nd *m*) Trelawny Michael, *b* 1957: *m* 1994, Olivia Rosemary, da of late Cmdr Axel Mortensen, of Oxton, Notts.

The 1st baronet, Right Hon Sir John Bayley, was for many years a Judge of the Queen's Bench, and subsequently a Baron of the Exchequer. Rev Sir John Robert Laurie Emilius Bayley, 3rd Bt, assumed by Roy licence 1887 the surname and arms of Laurie of Maxwelton, in lieu of his patronymic. The 4th baronet, Col Sir Claude Villiers Emilius Laurie, CB, DSO, served in S Africa 1900-1902 (despatches, DSO).

LAWES (UK) 1882, of Rothamsted, co Hertford.

Pour la Foi.
For the faith.

Sir (JOHN) MICHAEL BENNET LAWES, 5th *Baronet*; *b* 24 Oct 1932; *s* his father, *Sir* JOHN CLAUDE BENNET, 1979; *ed* Elizabeth Coll, Guernsey.

Arms – Quarterly: 1st and 4th argent, three bendlets gules on a chief sable, a barrulet dancetteé or; 2nd and 3rd or, two flaunches azure, on a chief nebuly of the second three estoiles or. **Crest** – 1st, a Saracen's head affrontée, and couped below the shoulders proper, wreathed about the temples, and tied in a bow or and gules; 2nd, on a mount vert the trunk of a tree fessewise eradicated and sprouting to the dexter, surmounted by an ermine passant proper.
Address – c/o Barclays Bank, Lymington, Hants.

HALF-SISTER LIVING

Janet Caroline, *b* 1940: *m* 1964, John Christopher Berney-Ficklin, and has issue living, Todd Alexander, *b* 1975, — Karen Lawes, *b* 1973.

WIDOW LIVING OF FOURTH BARONET

NAOMI CONSTANCE HELEN (*Lady Lawes*) da of Lancelot Wykeham Badnall: *m* 1938, as his 2nd wife, Sir John Claude Bennet Lawes, 4th Bt, who *d* 1979.

The 1st baronet, Sir John Bennet Lawes, DSc, FRS, achieved considerable fame as a practical experimental agricultural chemist. He was grandson of Thomas Lawes, who inherited Rothamsted from his maternal uncle John Bennet. Rothamsted was inherited by the last named from his cousin Thomas Wittewronge in 1763, as the maternal grandson of James Wittewronge of Rothamsted, Recorder of St Albans.

LAWRENCE (UK) 1858, of Lucknow.

Sir JOHN WALDEMAR LAWRENCE, OBE, 6th *Baronet*; *b* 27 May 1907; *s* his brother, *Sir* HENRY EUSTACE WALDEMAR, 1967; *ed* Eton, and New Coll, Oxford (MA); editor of *Frontier*; late Press Attaché at Moscow; Chm of GB-USSR Assoc; Pres of Keston Institute; Officer of Order of Orange Nassau of the Netherlands; OBE (Civil) 1945: *m* 1st, 1948, Mrs Jacynth Donaldson-Hudson, who *d* 1987, da of late Rev Francis George Ellerton; 2ndly, 1988, Mrs Audrey Viola Woodiwiss, widow of John Woodiwiss.

Arms – Ermine, on a cross raguly gules an eastern crown or; on a chief azure two swords in saltire proper, pommels and hilts gold, between as many leopards' heads argent. **Crest** – Out of an eastern crown or, a cubit arm entwined by a wreath of laurel and holding a dagger all proper.
Residence – 24 St Leonards Terr, SW3 4QG.

BROTHER LIVING

Never give in

GEORGE ALEXANDER WALDEMAR, *b* 22 Sept 1910; *ed* Eton, and Trin Coll Camb: *m* 1949, Olga, da of Peter Schilovsky, and has issue living, Henry Peter, *b* 2 April 1952: *m* 1979, Penelope Maureen Nunan, and has issue living, Christopher Cosmo *b* 1979, Isabelle Olga Jane *b* 1984, — Natalie Honoria, *b* 1951: *m* 1980, Mehrdad Shokoohy, — Catherine Letitia, *b* 1953: *m* 1976, Stephen James Paul Todd, and has issue living, Peter James *b* 1982, Helen Anna *b* 1979. *Residence* – Brockham End, Bath, Avon BA1 9BZ.

Sir Alexander Hutchinson Lawrence, 1st Bt, was *cr* a Baronet with remainder to his issue male, failing which to his yr brother, and was accidentally killed, 27 Aug 1864, by the falling of a bridge on the Tibet road, India. He was el son of the illustrious Sir Henry Montgomery Lawrence, KCB, who fell in defence of Lucknow in 1857.

LAWRENCE (UK) 1867, of Ealing Park, Middlesex.

Sir WILLIAM FETTIPLACE LAWRENCE, 5th *Baronet*; *b* 23 Aug 1954; *s* his father, *Maj Sir* WILLIAM, 1986; *ed* King Edward VI Sch, Stratford upon Avon.

Arms – Ermine, a cross raguly gules, in the first and fourth quarters a serpent nowed proper. **Crest** – A griffin's head couped argent, in front thereof a serpent nowed proper.
Residence – The Knoll, Walcote, near Alcester, Warwickshire B49 6LZ.

SISTERS LIVING

Lavinia Margaret, *b* 1947: *m* 1971, Julian Conway Seymour, of Waterdale House, E Knoyle, Salisbury, Wilts, and has issue (*see* M Hertford, colls). —— Carolyn Mary (Hookers Place, Bentworth, Alton, Hants GU34 5RB), *b* 1949: *m* 1972 (*m diss* 1990), Nicholas Peter Evelyn, and has issue living, Rupert Peter, *b* 1973, — James Nicholas, *b* 1976.

WIDOW LIVING OF FOURTH BARONET

PAMELA MARY (*Lady Lawrence*), yr da of James Edgar Gordon, of Beechbank, Bromborough, Wirral, Cheshire: *m* 1945, as his 2nd wife, Maj Sir William Lawrence, 4th Bt, who *d* 1986. *Residence* – The Knoll, Walcote, nr Alcester, Warwicks.

By mind and work

COLLATERAL BRANCH LIVING

Issue of late Aubrey Trevor Lawrence, MBE, KC, 2nd son of 2nd baronet, *b* 1875, *d* 1930: *m* 1901, Constance Emily Fanning, who *d* 1957, da of late Joseph McGaw, of Mickleham Downs, Dorking, and Kooba, NS Wales:—
Peter Stafford Hayden (Simeons, Little Milton, Oxford), *b* 1913; *ed* Eton, and Ch Ch, Oxford (MA); Assist Master at Eton Coll 1936-77 (House Master 1951-68); 1939-45 War as Lt-Cdr RNVR, Radar Officer (despatches): *m* 1940, Helena Frances, da of late Hon George William Lyttelton (*see* V Cobham, colls), and has issue living, Aubrey Lyttelton Simon, *b* 1942; *ed* Eton, and Ch Ch, Oxford (MA 1985): *m* 1984, Danielle de Froidmont, and has issue living, Thomas Lyttelton de Froidmont *b* 1985, — Robin Peter Charles, *b* 1950; *ed* Millfield, — Pamela Jane, *b* 1945; *ed* North Foreland Lodge, and Univ Coll, London (BA, 1970, PGCE 1978): *m* 1981, Stuart Wooler, and has issue living, Harry Peter Lawrence *b* 1988, Alice Honor Lawrence *b* 1982, — Anthea Mary, *b* 1947; *ed* North Foreland Lodge, and London Univ (BEd): *m* 1980, Clinton Cavers, — Jemima Rachel, *b* 1956; *ed* Wycombe Abbey, and Royal Northern Coll of Music (GMus): *m* 1978, Joseph Severs Taylor, and has issue living, Oscar George *b* 1987, Rowan Joseph *b* 1988, Bryn Hugh *b* 1990, Ivy Rosanna *b* 1985, — Susanna Lucy, *b* 1958; *ed* Lord Williams's Sch, Thame, and Leeds Univ (MB ChB 1981).

The 1st baronet, a distinguished surgeon, was a FRS, a Corresponding Member of Institute of France, a Member of the principal scientific socs of Europe and America, twice President of the College of Surgeons, and for many years Sergeant-Surgeon to HM Queen Victoria. The 2nd baronet, Sir Trevor, sat as MP for Mid Surrey 1875-85 and for S-E Div of Surrey 1885-92, and was 28 years Pres of Roy Horticultural So and 12 years Treasurer of St Bartholomew's Hospital.

LAWRENCE (UK) 1906, of Sloane Gardens, Chelsea.

Sir DAVID ROLAND WALTER LAWRENCE, 3rd *Baronet*; *b* 8 May 1929; *s* his father, *Lt-Col Sir* (PERCY) ROLAND (BRADFORD), MC, 1950; *ed* Radley, and RMC; sometime Capt Coldstream Guards: *m* 1955, Audrey, da of Brigadier Desmond Young, MC, and formerly wife of 11th Duke of Leeds.

Arms – Ermine, an escarbuncle or, surmounted by a lotus flower proper, on a chief arched gules a dragon passant or. **Crest** – A cubit arm, vested gules, cuffed ermine, holding in the hand a plane leaf proper, and charged on the sleeve with a trefoil slipped or. **Supporters** – On either side a heron holding in the beak a sprig of plane fructed proper.
Residence – 28 High Town Rd, Maidenhead, Berks SL6 1PB.

BROTHER LIVING

CLIVE WYNDHAM (Woodside, Frant, nr Tunbridge Wells, Kent TN3 9HW), *b* 6 Oct 1939; *ed* Gordonstoun; late Lt Coldm Gds: *m* 1966, Sophia Annabel Stuart, da of Ian Hervey Stuart Black, of Dumbarnie Cottage, Bridge of Earn, Perthshire, and has issue living, James Wyndham Stuart, *b* 1970, — Simon Roland Stuart, *b* 1973, — Hugo Hervey Stuart, *b* 1975.

SISTERS LIVING

Jean Jacqueline, *b* 1926: *m* 1950, Harold Channing Quitman, and has issue living, Jeremy Roland Channing, *b* 1953, — Annabel Susan Maude, *b* 1951. *Residence* – Rookley Farmhouse, Upper Somborne, Stockbridge, Hants. ——— Susan Louise, *b* 1944: *m* 1965, Norman Gardner, of Montreal, and has issue living, Suzanne Vanessa *b* 1965, — Amanda Sarah, *b* 1968.

COLLATERAL BRANCH LIVING

Issue of late Capt (Henry Walter) Neville Lawrence, 2nd son of 1st baronet, *b* 1891, *d* 1959: *m* 1933, Sarah, who *d* 1947, da of Nicholas Murray Butler, of New York, USA:—

Walter Nicholas Murray, *b* 1935: *m* 1961, Sally Louise, da of Lt-Col A. B. O'Dwyer, and has issue living, Sarah Louise, *b* 1962: *m* 1986, Andrew Crawley, who *d* 1988, and has issue living, Charles Murray *b* 1987, Jessica Mary *b* 1988, — Catherine Jane, *b* 1964: *m* 1992, Rupert Elliott. *Residence* – Grey Walls, Hook Heath, Woking.

The 1st baronet, Sir Walter Roper Lawrence, GCIE, GCVO, CB (son of George Lawrence, JP, of Trevella, Llangwm, Monmouthshire), was Private Sec to Viceroy of India 1898-1903, Ch of Staff for visit of TRH the Prince and Princess of Wales to India 1905-6, and a member of Council of India 1907-9. The 2nd baronet, Sir (Percy) Roland (Bradford) Lawrence, MC, was Lt-Col Coldstream Guards.

Lawrence-Jones, see Jones.

LAWSON (UK) 1900, of Weetwood Grange, Headingley-cum-Burley, West Riding of Yorkshire.

Arise, and shine forth

Sir JOHN CHARLES ARTHUR DIGBY LAWSON, DSO, MC, 3rd *Baronet*; *b* 24 Oct 1912; *s* his father, *Maj Sir* DIGBY, TD, 1959; *ed* Stowe, and RMC; Chm of Fairbairn Lawson, Ltd and subsidiary cos 1968-79; a Member of Council Univ of Leeds 1972-79; 2nd Lt 11th Hus (PAO) 1933; served in Palestine 1936 (despatches); seconded Transjordan Frontier Force 1939-40; Western Desert 1940-43 (wounded, despatches thrice); T/Lt-Col 1943 as Gen Montgomery's apptd advisor on Armoured reconnaissance to Gen Patton in N Africa 1943 (wounded); US Marine Staff Course, Quantico, Virginia 1944; Personal Liaison Offr to Gen Montgomery at 21st Army GP, N France 1944; Cmdg Inns of Court Regt 1944-46; ret 1947; Col 11th Hus (PAO) 1965-69, and on their amalgamation with 10th Hus (PWO), Col R Hus 1969-72; MC 1940; DSO 1943; US Legion of Merit 1943: *m* 1st, 1945 (*m diss* 1950), Rose, who *d* 1972, da of late David Cecil Bingham, Lt Coldm Gds (E Lucan, colls), and widow of William M. L. Fiske, P/O RAF, who *d* (of wounds received in action in Battle of Britain) 1940, previously wife of 7th Earl of Warwick; 2ndly, 1954, Tresilla Anne Eleanor, who *d* 1985, da of late Maj Eric Buller Leyborne Popham, MC, and formerly wife of John Garland de Pret Roose, and has issue by 2nd *m*.

Arms – Per chevron argent and or, a chevron invected sable, plain cotised vert, between two martlets in chief of the third and a trefoil slipped in base of the fourth. **Crest** – Between two arms embowed, proper the hands holding a sun in splendour a trefoil, as in the arms the whole surmounted by a rainbow also proper.
Residence – Hillmore Cottage, Bishops Hull Rd, Taunton, Som TA1 5ER. *Club* – Cavalry and Guards'.

SON LIVING *(By 2nd marriage)*

CHARLES JOHN PATRICK, *b* 19 May 1959; *ed* Harrow, Univ of Leeds, and RAC, Cirencester (Dip Est Mng); ARICS; Dir Jackson Stops and Staff Consortium, Exeter: *m* 1987, Lady Caroline Lowther, 3rd da of 7th Earl of Lonsdale, and has issue living, Jack William Tremayne, *b* 6 Dec 1989. — Thomas Charles Lancelot, *b* 1992. — Tess, *b* 1988. *Residence* – Heckwood, Sampford Spiney, Yelverton, Devon PL20 6L9.

BROTHER LIVING

Patrick William, *b* 1914: *m* 1939, Jean Mary, da of late Col Sydney Ernest Smith, CBE, of Stuckeridge, Oakford, Devon, and has issue living, Nicholas Patrick David (Morestead, Windlesham Rd, Chobham, Surrey); *b* 1940: *m* 1st, 1962 (*m diss* 1970), Anne Sommerville de Laval Harvie; 2ndly, 1971, Jill, da of Clifford Wendover Beeson, and formerly wife of Duncan M. Atkinson and has issue living, (by 1st *m*) Julian Alexander Nicholas *b* 1963, Rebecca de Laval *b* 1965, — (by 2nd *m*) Rupert Christopher David *b* 1972, — Timothy James (Bourn Lodge, Bourn, Cambs CB3 7SX; MCC and Farmers), *b* 1942; FRICS: *m* 1965 Elizabeth White, and has issue living, Mark James *b* 1968, Simon Alexander *b* 1970, Peter John *b* 1974, — Michael Shaun (Great House Farm, Lynwick St, Rudgwick, Sussex), *b* 1945: *m* 1970, Jane Hamilton, and has issue living, James Patrick *b* 1972 Richard Shaun, *b* 1973, Henry John, *b* 1978. *Residences* – St Mary's House, Langford, nr Bristol; 57 Cheval Pl, SW7.

HALF-BROTHERS LIVING

Arthur Simon Albert (Tithe Barn, Crowcombe, nr Taunton, Somerset), *b* 1925; is Lt-Col N Somerset Yeo; formerly Lieut 11th Hussars: *m* 1st, 1953 (*m diss* 1961), Virginia Elizabeth Grace, da of late Maj William Steel Huddleston, RHA; 2ndly, 1961 (*m diss* 1986), Alison Deirdre, el da of Lt-Col Ian Balmain; 3rdly, 1987, Magdalen Cecilia, widow of John Eric Staniland, and elder da of late Lt-Col Francis Michael Benedict Carey Boylan, MBE, of Collierstown House, Bellewstown, Drogheda, co Meath, and has issue living (by 1st *m*), Piers James, *b* 1957; Capt Royal Hussars (PWO): *m* 1985, Belinda, eldest da of R. Garnham, of Bethersden, Kent, and has issue living, Bertram Digby Alexander *b* 1991, Arabella Harriet *b* 1987, Phoebe Elizabeth Grace *b* 1989, — (by 2nd *m*), Frances Lisa Victoria, *b* 1962, — Louise Christian, *b* 1963: *m* 1992, Michael Gatcombe, — Clare Alison, *b* 1968: *m* 1989, David Burnett, and has issue living, Aaron *b* 1991, Rebecca *b* 1990. —— Simon Digby (Manor Farm House, Barton Hartshorn, nr Buckingham, Bucks MK18 4JX), *b* 1945; *ed* Sherborne, London Univ (BA), and Oxford Univ (MLitt, DPhil): *m* 1972, Georgina Mary, da of Sqdn Ldr J. C. G. Sarll, DFC, and has issue living, Thomas Digby, *b* 1975, — Daisy Alexandra Ruth, *b* 1983.

SISTER LIVING

Daphne Olive, *b* 1910: *m* 1936, Maj Richard Edwin Fearing Cely Trevilian, TD, DL, and has issue living, John Maurice Richard, *b* 1948: *m* 1971, Penelope, yst da of Raymond Hodgson, of Craig, Balmaclellan, Kirkcudbrightshire, and has issue living, Thomas Richard John *b* 1976, Alice Mary *b* 1974, — Jane Mary, *b* 1938: *m* 1960, Adam Stanislaus Kwiatkowski, and has issue living, Damian Michael Richard *b* 1965, Sophia Helena *b* 1963: *m* 1984, Nicholas James Prestige, stepson of late Maj John Prestige, — Susanna Rose, *b* 1939: *m* 1st, 1962 (*m diss* 1970), Jeremy Gwynne Pilcher; 2ndly, 1972, Ewan Iain MacLeod Hilleary, of 197 Pottle St, Horningsham, Wilts, and has issue living (by 1st *m*), Jonathan Swaine *b* 1965, Katharine Alexandra *b* 1963: *m* 1991, Charles Rupert Hunter, son of late Brig (Henry) Michael Allan Hunter, CVO, DSO, MBE *(see* Vy Plumer, 1968 Edn) (and has issue living, Sam Alexander *b* 1992), Charlotte Serena *b* (twin) 1963: *m* 1992, James Paul Gilfred Studholme, yr son of Sir Paul Henry William Studholme, 2nd Bt, (by 2nd *m*) Angus Ewan MacLeod *b* 1977, — Teresa Melliscent, *b* 1946: *m* 1971, Edward Anthony Dawson, and has issue living, Edward Finch *b* 1971, Hannah Dinah *b* 1974. *Residence* – Midelney Manor, Langport, Somerset.

The influential Co of Lawson's of Leeds, textile machinery manufacturers, was founded by Samuel Lawson in 1812. His grandson, the 1st baronet, Sir Arthur Tredgold Lawson, was Chm of Fairbairn, Lawson, Combe-Barbour Ltd, a Director of Great Eastern Railway, Vice-Chm Yorkshire Conservative Newspaper Co, Dir *Yorkshire Post*, and a Chevalier of the Legion of Honour. The 2nd baronet, Major Sir Digby Lawson, TD, was Chm of Fairbairn, Lawson, Combe-Barbour, Ltd, of Leeds and Belfast, and of Urquhart Lindsay & Robertson Orchar, Ltd, of Dundee.

HOWARD-LAWSON (UK) 1841, of Brough Hall, Yorkshire.

Sir JOHN PHILIP HOWARD-LAWSON, 6th *Baronet*; *b* 6 June 1934; *s* his father, Sir WILLIAM HOWARD LAWSON, 1990; *ed* Ampleforth; assumed by Royal Licence 1962 the surname and arms of Howard, and subsequently resumed his patronymic in addition to the surname of Howard 1992: *m* 1960, Jean Veronica, only da of late Col John Evelyn Marsh, DSO, OBE, and has issue.

Arms – Gules on a bend between six cross crosslets fitchee argent an escutcheon or charged with a demi lion rampant pierced through the mouth with an arrow within a double tressure flory counterflory of the first in chief a mullet for difference and (for distinction) a cross botonny gules. **Crest** – On a chapeau gules turned up ermine a lion statant guardant the tail extended or ducally gorged argent charged on the shoulder with a mullet for difference and (for distinction) on the body with a cross botonny gules.
Seat – Corby Castle, Carlisle, Cumbria.

SONS LIVING

PHILIP WILLIAM HOWARD, *b* 28 June 1961; *ed* Ampleforth: *m* 1st, 1988 (*m diss* 1992), Cara Margaret, only da of Hon Martin Michael Dominick Browne *(see* B Oranmore and Browne); 2ndly, 1993, Isobel Anne Oldridge, elder da of late Christopher George James Oldridge de la Hey, and of Mrs Peter Vivian Lloyd Verney, of Skiveralls House, Chalford Hill, Glos. —— Thomas John, *b* 1963; *ed* Ampleforth.

DAUGHTER LIVING

Julia Frances Veronica, *b* 1964.

BROTHERS LIVING

Hugh William LAWSON (Croftlands, Heads Nook, Carlisle), *b* 1936; *ed* Ampleforth: *m* 1961, Margaret Ann, elder da of late Maj Richard Gubbins Mounsey Heysham, of Castletown, Carlisle, and has issue living, Simon David, *b* 1962; *ed* Ampleforth: *m* 1989, Lucy Rose, da of James Morrish, of Ham Farm, Wellington, Somerset, — Philippa Joan, *b* 1963: *m* 1993, Philip A. J. Leech, elder son of Jeremy Leech, of Hovingham, York, — Pollyanne Lucy, *b* 1970. —— (Arthur) Mark LAWSON (Brough House, Alves, by Forres, Moray), *b* 1940; *ed* Ampleforth: *m* 1968, Rosemary Veronica, da of Samuel Parkington Vickery, of Ardwell, Newland, Glasgow, and has issue living, Henry Benedict, *b* 1970; *ed* Ampleforth, — Charlotte Niamh, *b* 1975.

SISTER LIVING

Mary Frances, *b* 1947: *m* 1969, Julian Rupert Smithers, of Haversham Grange, Haversham, nr Milton Keynes, Bucks, and has issue living, William Rupert John, *b* 1973; *ed* —, — Louisa Jane, *b* 1971.

DAUGHTERS LIVING OF FOURTH BARONET

Valerie Anne, *b* 1936: *m* 1960, Benjamin Worthington (*see* E Aylesford, 1940 Edn), who *d* 1984, and has issue living, Greville Thomas, *b* 1963; *ed* Ampleforth, — Ursula, *b* 1962: *m* 1988, Capt (Archibald) Edward (Charles) Edmonstone, eldest son of Sir Archibald Bruce Charles Edmonstone, 7th Bt, — Lucy, *b* 1967. *Residence* – Wood House, Brough Park, N Yorks. —— Alethea Jill Clare, *b* 1939. *Residence* – The Stallion Box, High Green, Catterick Village, N Yorks.
Sir William, 1st Bt, was son of John Wright, of Kelvedon, by Elizabeth, yr da of Sir John Lawson, 5th Bt (*cr* 1665), of Brough Hall, whose surname he assumed. Sir Henry Joseph Lawson, 3rd Bt, *m* 1899, Ursula Mary, who *d* 1960, only child and heir of Philip John Canning Howard, of Corby Castle, Cumberland, descended from Col Sir Francis Howard, of Corby Castle, son of Lord William Howard, 3rd son of 4th Duke of Norfolk, and yr brother of Sir Philip Howard, ancestor of the Earls of Carlisle.

Lawson-Tancred, see Tancred.

LEA (UK) 1892, of The Larches, Kidderminster, Worcestershire, and Sea Grove, Dawlish, Devon

Semper fidelis
Always faithful

Sir THOMAS WILLIAM LEA, *5th Baronet*; *b* 6 Sept 1973; *s* his father, *Sir* (THOMAS) JULIAN, 1990; *ed* Uppingham.

Arms – Or, a fesse indented gules, between in chief two lions passant of the second, in base a rock, thereon a beaver proper, spotted ermine, holding in the mouth a sprig of willow slipped vert. **Crest** – In front of a mount vert, thereon a demi-heraldic antelope argent, supporting a bird bolt erect or, three pheons fessewise sable.

BROTHERS LIVING

ALEXANDER JULIAN, *b* 28 Oct 1978; *ed* Oakham. —— Oliver David Pell, *b* 1983.

SISTERS LIVING AND DECEASED

Rebecca Barbara, *b* 1972. —— Henrietta Katherine, *b* 1976; *d* 1989.

AUNTS LIVING (*Daughters of 3rd baronet*)

Rosemary, *b* 1927. *Residence* – 1245 Park Av, New York, NY, USA. —— Philippa Margaret, *b* 1929: *m* 1960, Orlando Michael Philip Kenyon-Slaney (*see* B Kenyon, cols). *Residence* – Bachelors Cottage, High Halden, Ashford, Kent. —— Lavinia Ann, *b* 1932: *m* 1960, Andrew Bethell Marsden-Smedley (*see* B Westbury, cols, 1985 Edn), and has issue living, Robert Andrew, *b* 1962, — William Bethell, *b* 1964: *m* 1991, Alexandra G. B., elder da of John Kirkland, of Lochbie, Duddenhoe End, Saffron Walden, Essex. *Residence* – The Glebe House, Bayton, nr Kidderminster, Worcs.

WIDOWS LIVING OF THIRD AND FOURTH BARONETS

DIANA SILVA (*Diana, Lady Lea*), only da of James Howard Thompson, MIME, of Coton Hall, Bridgnorth, Shropshire, and formerly wife of Capt Guy William Bannar-Martin, IA: *m* 1950, as his 2nd wife, Sir Thomas Claude Harris Lea, 3rd Bt, who *d* 1985. *Residence* – Harp House, Lower Broad St, Ludlow, Shropshire.
GERRY VALERIE (*Lady Lea*), only da of late Capt Gibson Clarence Fahnestock, USAF: *m* 1970, Sir (Thomas) Julian Lea, 4th Bt, who *d* 1990. *Residence* – Mallaby House, Queens Lane, Chevington, Bury St Edmunds, Suffolk IP29 5RF.

COLLATERAL BRANCHES LIVING

Issue of late Wing Cdr Robert Francis Gore Lea, OBE, 2nd son of 2nd baronet, *b* 1906, *d* 1994: *m* 1st, 1939, Valerie Josephine, who *d* 1948, da of Lieut Sir James Henry Domville, RN, 5th Bt; 2ndly, 1956, Susan (Le Clos du Chemin, St Peter, Jersey, CI), da of late John Greenwood, of The Priory of Lady St Mary, Wareham, Dorset:—
(By 2nd *m*) Francis Rupert Chad (Duxford Mill, Cambridgeshire), *b* 1957; *ed* Eton: *m* 1987, Hon Susan Kinnaird, da of 13th Lord Kinnaird. —— (By 1st *m*) Annabel Ophelia Clare, *b* 1945: *m* 1973, Simon Ricketts, of 69 Fentiman Road, SW8 1LH, and has issue living, Theo, *b* 1975, — Catriona, *b* 1977.

Issue of late John Sydney Birch Lea, 3rd son of 2nd baronet, *b* 1911, *d* 1984: *m* 1954, Elisabeth Edith Maunsell (Kemerton House, Crowle, Worcs), da of Lt-Col Philip Victor Willingham Gell, of Hopton Hall, Wirksworth, Derbyshire:—
Richard John Philip, *b* 1957: *m* 1990, Jane Hopkins. —— Sarah Caroline Aileen, *b* 1956: *m* 1st, 1986, Robin Greenshields (later Davenport Greenshields), of Davenport House, Worfield, Shropshire; 2ndly, 1991, Peter William Richard Sankey (*see* Milburn, Bt), of Cranmere, Worfield, nr Bridgnorth, Shropshire WV15 5LP, and has issue living (by 1st *m*), William John Peter, *b* 1989, — (by 2nd *m*) (*see* Milburn, Bt).

Grandson of late Rev Percy Harris Lea, yr son of 1st baronet:—
Issue of late George Francis Percivale Lea, *b* 1901, *d* 1987: *m* 1934, Maria, who *d* 1987, da of Wilhelm Schultz, of Vienna, and of Bratislava, Czechoslovakia:—
Francis William Peter, *b* 1944; *ed* Hill Sch, Pottstown, PA, USA, and Brown Univ, RI, USA; FCA; *m* 1977, Audrey Christine, da of Maurice Davison, of Cuckfield, Sussex. *Residence* – 34 Radnor Rd, Weybridge, Surrey KT13 8JU.

William Butcher: *m* 1792, Elizabeth, da of Francis Lea, of Kidderminster. Their son, George Butcher Lea, assumed by Roy Licence 1834, the surname of Lea. His son, Sir Thomas Lea, of the Larches, Kidderminster, MP for Kidderminster, co Donegal and S Londonderry, was *cr* a Baronet 1892.

LECHMERE (UK) 1818, of The Rhydd, Worcestershire
(Name pronounced "Letchmere")

Sir BERWICK HUNGERFORD LECHMERE, 6th *Baronet*; *b* 21 Sept 1917; *s* his father, *Capt Sir* RONALD BERWICK HUNGERFORD, 1965; *ed* Charterhouse, and Magdalene Coll, Camb; FRICS; JP and DL; High Sheriff of Worcs 1962; Vice-Lieut for co Hereford and Worcester 1977; CStJ: *m* 1st, 1952 (*m diss* 1954), Susan Adele Mary, only child of Cdr George Henry Maunsell-Smyth, RN; 2ndly, 1954, Norah Garrett, el da of late Col Christopher Garrett Elkington, DSO, DL, of The Moat House, Cutnall Green, Worcs.

𝕬rms – Gules, a fesse, and in chief two pelicans vulning themselves or. 𝕮rest – A pelican as in the arms.
Residence – Church End House, Hanley Castle, Worcester WR8 0BL.

SISTER LIVING

Joan Penelope Alice, *b* 1919.

Christ in the pelican

COLLATERAL BRANCH LIVING

Issue of late Anthony Hungerford Lechmere, 3rd son of 3rd baronet, *b* 1868, *d* 1954: *m* 1920, Cicely Mary, who *d* 1964, da of late Rev Charles Bridges, R of Bredenbury, Herefordshire, and widow of William George Lupton, of The Green, Bromyard, Herefordshire:—
REGINALD ANTHONY HUNGERFORD (Primeswell, Evendine Lane, Colwall, nr Malvern, Worcs), *b* 24 Dec 1920; *ed* Charterhouse, and Trin Hall, Camb; formerly Capt 5th Roy Inniskilling Dragoon Guards: *m* 1956, Anne Jennifer, da of late A. C. Dind, of Orbe, Switzerland, and has issue living, Nicholas Anthony Hungerford (82 Stapleton Rd, SW17 8DX), *b* 24 April 1960: *m* 1991, Caroline Jane, yr da of Lt-Col Gerald Patrick Gahan, of Tisbury, Wilts, and has issue living, Frederick Patrick Hungerford *b* 9 Dec 1992, — Adam Francis, *b* 1962, — Mark Edmund Dind, *b* 1966, — Jennifer Sarah, *b* 1959.

This family obtained lands at Hanley, Worcestershire, in the eleventh century, which have been in the family ever since. Sir Nicholas Lechmere, of Severn End, MP for Bewdley, was a Baron of the Exchequer temp William III. His grandson, Nicholas, sometime Solicitor and Attorney-General, Chancellor of the Duchy of Lancaster, was created Baron Lechmere of Evesham 1721. The 3rd baronet sat as MP for Tewkesbury (C) 1866-68, for Worcestershire W 1876-85, for Worcestershire W, or Bewdley Div 1885-92, and for Worcestershire S or Evesham Div 1892-94.

LEEDS (UK) 1812, of Croxton Park, Cambridgeshire

Sir CHRISTOPHER ANTHONY LEEDS, 8th *Baronet*; *b* 31 Aug 1935; only child of late Maj Geoffrey Hugh Anthony Leeds, yr brother of 6th Bt; *s* his cousin, *Sir* GEORGE GRAHAM MORTIMER, 1983; *ed* King's Sch, Bruton, Lond Univ (BScEcon), and Univ of S California (MA): *m* 1974 (*m diss* 1980), Elaine Joyce, da of late Sq Ldr Cornelius Harold Albert Mullins.

Arms – Argent, a fesse gules between three eagles displayed sable, within a bordure wavy of the second. **Crest** – A staff raguly vert, thereon a cock gules wings expanded, combed, wattled, beaked, and legged or, debruised by a bendlet wavy sinister ermine. *Address* – University of Nancy II, 23 Blvd Albert 1er, BP 33-97, 54015 Nancy, France. *Residence* – 7 Rue de Turique, 54000 Nancy, France. *Club* – Lansdowne.

Vigilate!

Watch ye!

DAUGHTERS LIVING AND DECEASED OF SEVENTH BARONET

Miranda Noel Winnaretta, *b* 1956: *m* 1981, Maxim Alexander Mackay-James, of Higher Wynford House, Wynford Eagle, Dorchester, Dorset DT2 0ET, yr son of Lt-Cdr P. M. Mackay-James, of La Rochelle, Lake Alfred, Florida, USA. —— Anthea Jane, *b* 1958, *d* in Indonesia 1989. —— Harriet Annabelle, *b* 1962: *m* 1983, Maj Richard John Carrow, RGJ, only son of David Carrow, of Little Hill, Hartley Wintney, Hants, and has issue living, Anthony, *b* 19—, — Hugh David, *b* 1991, — Rozel Anthea, *b* (twin) 1991.

DAUGHTER LIVING OF SIXTH BARONET

Rhodanthe Winnaretta, *b* 1929: *m* 1st, 1952, Ronald David Hutton, MC, late Capt RE, who *d* 1984; 2ndly, 1991, Cmdr Gerald M. B. Selous, OBE, VRD, JP, and has issue living (by 1st *m*), Matthew Charles Arthur (Broom Farm, Chedgrave, Norwich RN14 6BQ), *b* 1953; *ed* Eton, and Ch Ch, Oxford (MA); Solicitor and Tax Consultant: *m* 1984, Anne Elizabeth Caroline, elder da of Leslie Leppard, of Axminster, Devon, and has issue living, David Thomas Charles *b* 1988, Victoria Emily Louise *b* 1986, Alexandra Charlotte Kate *b* 1990, — Deborah Helen, *b* 1955; *ed* Benenden, and York Univ; journalist: *m* 1984, Charles David Sandys Stebbings, of 40 Belitha Villas, N1, son of late David Stebbings, of Wapping Pierhead, E1, and has issue living, Archie David *b* 1987, Romilly Paris (da) *b* 1989, Eleanor Clemency *b* 1993, — (Cecilia) Paris, *b* 1955; *ed* Bedgebury Park; schoolteacher: *m* 1982, Nigel Quarles Back, FCA, of 4 Christchurch Rd, Norwich NR2 2AD, and has issue living, Charles *b* 1986, Emma *b* 1984, Katherine *b* 1988, — Louisa Winn (74 Ledbury Rd, W11), *b* 1957; *ed* Benenden, Bristol Univ and AA; architect: *m* 1991, Matthias Sauerbruch. *Residence* – Langley Grange, Langley, Norwich, Norfolk, NR14 6BL.

COLLATERAL BRANCHES LIVING

Grandchildren of late Henry Leeds, 2nd son of 2nd baronet:—
Issue of late Very Rev Joseph Edward Henry Leeds, BD, *b* 1857, *d* 1907: *m* 1881 (*m diss* 1891), Elizabeth Massey, da of late Richard Quin, JP, of Firgrove House, Innishannon, co Cork:—
Marion Adelaide Lucy, *b* 1882. —— Lilian Anna Marian, *b* 1884: *m* 1907, H. Davison.
Issue of late Edward Adderley Oglander Leeds, *b* 1869, *d* 1923: *m* 1895, a da of R. F. Vevers, of Hereford:—
Vera Mary, *b* 1898.
Issue of late Charles George Stretton Leeds, MD, *b* 1875; *d* 1909: *m* (March) 1905, Louisa Christian (who *d* 1960, having *m* 2ndly, 1921, Archibald Clark, of Ferryden, Montrose, who *d* 1936, and 3rdly, 1940, John McLinden, of Glasgow, who *d* 1960), only da of late James Barker Duncan, WS, of 6 Hill Street, Edinburgh:—
Lilian Margaret, *b* 1908; Diploma of Art, Edinburgh Coll of Art 1929.

Grandchildren of late William Henry Montagu Leeds, eldest son of late Capt William Montagu Leeds, 3rd son of 2nd baronet:—
Issue of late Aubrey Leeds, *b* 1903, *d* 1992: *m* 1933, Barbara, who *d* 1994, only child of J. Travis, of Lightcliffe, Yorks:—
ANTONY HILDYARD *b* 15 Dec 1937: *m* 1966 (*m diss* 1973), Elizabeth Helen Cornell, of Toronto. —— Sally Gillian *b* 1936: *m* 1961, John A. Nation, BSc, PhD, and has issue living, Philip David Oliver, *b* 1962, — Robert James Anthony, *b* 1964. —— Sharman, *b* 1953.

Grandchildren of late Charles Frederick Augustus Leeds (infra):—
Issue of late Charles Hildyard Denham Leeds, *b* 1902, *d* 1975: *m* 1940, Merran Elizabeth (Box 927, Claresholm, Alberta T0L 0T0, Canada), da of late J. H. Drew, of Kitscoty, Alberta, Canada:—
John Charles Hildyard (408 Ranch Estates Bay, NW, Calgary, Alberta, T3G 1T6 Canada), *b* 1941; BSc, Civil Eng: *m* 1965, Eileen Rose, da of late Joseph F. Shalka, of Fort Kent, Alberta, and has issue living, Michael John Hildyard, *b* 1975, — Diane Katherine, *b* 1967: *m* 1992, Rodney Orr, — Brenda Merran, *b* 1971. —— Charles Eric Montagu (Box 927, Claresholm, Alberta T0L 0T0, Canada), *b* 1945: *m* 1971, Patricia Marlene, da of Irwin E. Brown, of Stavely, Alberta, and has issue living, Montagu Charles, *b* 1975, — Shayne Irwin, *b* 1977, — Cameron Wesley, *b* 1981. —— James Douglas Logie (Box 42, Claresholm, Alberta T0L 0T0, Canada), *b* 1948: *m* 1972, Irene Mary, da of J. R. Hughes, of Longview, Alberta, and has issue living, Anthony Hildyard, *b* 1975, — Christopher James, *b* (twin) 1975, — Mark Douglas, *b* 1983, — Paula Marie, *b* 1978. —— Helen Merran, *b* 1951; BSc Pharmacy.
Issue of late Eric Edward Leeds, *b* 1907, *d* 1994: *m* 1934, Freda Foster:—
Jacqueline May, *b* 1935: *m* 1955, Robert Radleigh Hugh Tatham, and has issue living, Roderick Hugh, *b* 1958, — Catherine Ann, *b* 1956, — Carolyn Jill, *b* 1960, — Susan Margaret, *b* 1963.

Granddaughter of late Capt William Montagu Leeds, 3rd son of 2nd baronet:—
Issue of late Charles Frederick Augustus Leeds, *b* 1868, *d* 1951: *m* 1902, Mildred Katharine Mary, who *d* 1938, da of late Denham Robinson, of St Hilda's, Hampton Wick:—
Marjorie Mary Mildred (Box 401, Claresholm, Alberta, Canada), *b* 1904: *m* 1935, Henry Sharples, who *d* 1972, and has issue living, Mildred Joanne, *b* 1939: *m* 1962, Anthony Perlich, of Box 1057, Lethbridge, Alberta, T1J 4A2, Canada, and has issue living, David Anthony *b* 1969, Jeanine Marie *b* 1971, Nancy Joan *b* 1978, — Carol Barbara, *b* 1940: *m* 1st, 1960 (*m diss* 1973), Donald Charles Stewart; 2ndly, 1973, Terence Willard Henker, of Box 202, Claresholm, Alberta T0L 0T0, Canada, and has issue living (by 1st *m*), Donald Charles Henry *b* 1964: *m* 1994, Whitney Camille Conrad, Barbara Joan *b* 1962: *m* 1990, Paulin Larochelle (and has issue living, Geoffrey Donald *b* 1993), Patricia Marjorie *b* 1967: — Kathleen Marjorie, *b* 1943: *m* 1966, Kenneth Eugene Tratch, of 2217 27th St South, Lethbridge, Alberta, T1K 2T1, Canada, and has issue living, Robert Kenneth *b* 1971, Carole Anne, *b* 1967: *m* 1986, Vaughn Sterenberg, Karen Kathleen *b* 1968: *m* 1994, Dennis Hoffman, — Judith Susan, *b* 1945: *m* 1966, Helmut Charles Meckelborg, of RR 8-22-16, Lethbridge, Alberta, T1J 4P4, Canada, and has issue living, Douglas Charles *b* 1969, James Joseph *b* 1970, Susan Kathleen *b* 1967: *m* 1st, 1989 (*m diss* 1993), Brian

Ostrander; 2ndly, 1994, Jason Lynn Taylor, of Calgary (and has issue living (by 1st *m*), Robyn Johanna *b* 1991, Lauren Alberta *b* 1994).

Granddaughter of late George Leeds, 3rd son of 1st baronet:—
Issue of late Rev William Howard Leeds, *b* 1853, *d* 1893: *m* 1886, Ethel Beatrice, who *d* 1937, el da of Charles H. Perkins, of the Admiralty:—
Gabriel Frances (Pythouse, Tisbury, Wilts), *b* 1889.

Granddaughters of late Edward Montagu Leeds, 5th son of 1st baronet:—
Issue of late Edward Ernest Leeds, *b* 1859, *d* 1919: *m* 1884, Emma Seddon, who *d* 1939, da of late S. Seddon Wal-bank, MD, of Duluth, Minnesota, USA:—
Jessie Louisa, *b* 1886: *m* 19—, Fitzgerald Moore. —— Kate Frances, *b* 1887: *m* 19— Philip Seddon Mellor.
Issue of late Lieut-Col Thomas Louis Leeds, CMG, DSO, *b* 1869, *d* 1926: *m* 1904, Clara Guion, who *d* 1940, da of Lieut-Col Henry S. Kilbourne, US Army:—
Sylvia Guion, *b* 1914: *m* 1943, Douglas Campbell Ward-Campbell, of 37 Church Square Mansions, Harrogate, Yorks, and has issue living, Iain Gordon Leeds (12 Rossett Green Lane, Harrogate, Yorks), *b* 1944; *ed* Marlborough, and Trin Coll, Camb (MA); FCA: *m* 1966, Christine Mary, da of Dr Bernard Clive Nicholson, of Harrogate, and has issue living, Robert Iain Nicol *b* 1969: *m* 1993, Diane Jennifer Martin, Gordon James *b* 1970, David Leeds *b* 1975, Andrew Douglas Clive *b* 1979, John Alexander *b* 1981, Mary Sylvia Frances *b* 1973, —— Nicholas Carlton Guion (256 Waterloo St N, Cambridge, Ontario, Canada), *b* 1947; *ed* Marlborough: *m* 1973, Dorothee Anastasia, only da of Wasyl Pikula, of Cambridge, Ontario, Canada, and has issue living, Belinda Maria Sylvia *b* 1977, Kimberley Meghann Leeds *b* 1979.
Sir George William Leeds, 1st Bt, of Croxton Park, Cambs, was Equerry to the Duke of Sussex. The manor of Croxton was purchased by an ancestor of this family about 1568.

LEES (UK) 1804, of Blackrock, Dublin

I have accomplished

EXEGI

AN HONEST MAN'S THE NOBLEST WORK OF GOD

Sir THOMAS HARCOURT IVOR LEES, 8th *Baronet*; *b* 6 Nov 1941; *s* his father, Sir CHARLES ARCHIBALD EDWARD IVOR, 1963; no information concerning this baronet has been received since 1970.

Arms – Azure, a fesse checky argent and sable, between six cross-crosslets fitchée, three in the chief and three in the nombril points or, and three billets, two in the honour and one in the base, points of the second. **Crest** – A dexter hand couped above the wrist and erect proper, grasping a crescent or.

DAUGHTER LIVING OF FIFTH BARONET

Mary Helen, *b* 1928: *m* 1949, David Stuart Hahn, and has issue living, Stuart Arthur, *b* 1949. —— Harold Daniel, *b* 1953. *Address* – 3 Valsayn Av, Valsayn Park, Curepe, Trinidad.

COLLATERAL BRANCHES LIVING

Issue of late Edwin Leslie Lees, 4th son of 4th baronet, *b* 1866, *d* 1937: *m* 1900, Annie, who *d* 1961, da of Jabez Charlton, of Southall, Middlesex:—
Geraldine Barbara Elizabeth, *b* 1910. —— Josephine Edwina Agnes, *b* 1917: *m* 1940, Edmund Ross Spencer, who *d* 1942.

Issue of late Capt Cecil Harcourt Folder Lees, 6th son of 4th baronet, *b* 1873, *d* 1921: *m* 1st, 19—, Nellie Hayes, who *d* 1903; 2ndly, 1905, Frances Louisa Wegg, who *d* 1913; 3rd, 1917, Jeannie King, who *d* 1967, da of George Paterson, of Edinburgh:—
(By 1st *m*) Constance Lilian (307 Bulwer St, Pietermartitzburg, S Africa), *b* 1900: *m* 1920, Ernest Wilson, who *d* 1963, and has issue living, Douglas Ernest, *b* 1921, —— Leslie Erroll, *b* 1924, —— Cynthia Esther, *b* 1927: *m* 1st, 1949 (*m diss* 1954), Howard Raymond Comins; 2ndly, 1959, Raymond Allison, and has issue living, (by 2nd *m*) Lee Constance *b* 1962, Wendy Edith *b* (twin) 1962. —— (By 2nd *m*) Esmé Frances (PO Box 1849, Durban, S Africa), *b* 1910: *m* 1938 (*m diss* 1946), George Franklin James, and has issue living, Veronica Anne, *b* 1939: *m* 1963, James Anthony Gordon, and has issue living, Michael James Lockhart, *b* 1965, Melissa Anne Helga *b* 1967, Nicola Barbara Janetta *b* 1969, Gillian Sarah Esme *b* 1972.

Grandchildren of late John Cathcart Lees, son of Cathcart Lees, MD, son of 2nd son of 1st baronet:—
Issue of late John Rutherfoord D'OLIER-LEES, *b* 1887, *d* 1972: *m* 1923, Margery, who *d* 1975, da of Thomas H. Scott, of Sunderland:—
JOHN CATHCART (The Cottage, Southampton Rd, Ringwood, Hants BH24 1JD; Naval and Military Club), *b* 12 Nov 1927; formerly Lt 2nd Bn Border Regt and SAS Regt (Artists Rifles) TA: *m* 1957, Wendy Garrold, yr da of late Brian Garrold Groom, of Craig Elm, Eskbank, nr Edinburgh, and has issue living, Trevor John Cathcart, *b* 1961: *m* 1992, Susan Ciabrello, —— James Scott Lewis, *b* 1963. —— Edmund Campbell (Lapley Farmhouse, Coaley, Dursley, Glos), *b* 1929; FCA: *m* 1960, Hilary Vernon, da of John Harbord, of Englewick, Englefield Green, Surrey, and has issue living, Robert Arthur Campbell, *b* 1963, —— Caroline Margery, *b* 1961: *m* 1990, Richard James Dean, and has issue living, Edward James *b* 1992, —— Deborah Helen, *b* 1962. —— Elizabeth, *b* 1925: *m* 1956, Geoffrey John Martin, of Flagstones, Brattlewood, Sevenoaks, Kent TN13 1QS, and has issue living, Timothy John Hoit, *b* 1958: *m* Merryn Blacklock, and has issue living, Thomas Geoffrey Hoit *b* 1986, Lisa Adele *b* 1984, Catherine Lee *b* 1989, —— Robin Geoffrey, *b* 1959. —— Helen Campbell (15c Whittingstall Rd, Parsons Green, SW6), *b* 1926.

Grandchildren of late John Rutherfoord D'OLIER-LEES (ante):—
Issue of late Thomas Rutherfoord D'OLIER-LEES, *b* 1931, *d* 1984: *m* 1960, Anne Elizabeth (Old Post Office, Oving, nr Chichester, Sussex), da of William Simpson Dalgetty, MB, ChB, of 1 Polwarth Terr, Edinburgh 11:—
Guy Rutherfoord, *b* 1962. —— Mark Angus, *b* 1964. —— Catherine Anne, *b* 1966. —— Julia Elizabeth, *b* 1968.

Grandchildren of late Edward Lees, 2nd son of William Eden Lees, 5th son of 1st baronet:—
Issue of late Harcourt Lees, *b* 1843, *d* 1939: *m* 1867, Mary Masey, who *d* 1914, da of Joseph Burke, formerly of The Lodge, Templemore:—
Harcourt Edward, *b* 1884: *m* 1961, Eileen, widow of Edward Byron de Lacy. *Residence* – Flat 25, Brunswick Manor, Bangor, co Down. —— Ethel Sophia Harriet Western.

Granddaughter of late Thomas Orde Hastings Lees, only son of late Rev John Lees, el son of late Thomas Orde Lees, 6th son of 1st baronet:—
Issue of late Lt-Col Thomas Orde Hans Lees, OBE, AFC, *b* 1877; *d* 1958: *m* 1st, 1902, Rhoda Isabel, who *d* 1930, da of late P. Musgrave, and widow of R. Lovat Fraser; 2ndly, 1932, Ellaline Hisako:—
(By 2nd *m*) Zoe Orde Eloise, *b* 1936.
Sir John Lees, 1st Bt, son of Adam Lees of Cumnock, Ayrshire, distinguished himself with the British troops in Germany under the Marquess of Granby. He was afterwards successively Usher of the Black Rod, Secretary of War, and Secretary to the Post Office in Ireland.

LEES (UK) 1897, of South Lytchett Manor, Lytchett Minster, Dorset

Without haste, without rest

Sir THOMAS EDWARD LEES, 4th *Baronet*; *b* 31 Jan 1925; *s* his father, *Col Sir* JOHN VICTOR ELLIOTT, DSO, MC, 1955; *ed* Eton, and Magdalene Coll, Camb; is a JP for Dorset (High Sheriff 1960); European War 1943-5 as Aircraftsman RAF (wounded): *m* 1949, Faith Justin, only da of George Gaston Jessiman, OBE, of Swaynes Living, Great Durnford, Wilts, and has issue.

𝔄rms – Per chevron dovetail argent and gules, in chief two millrinds sable, and in base an owl of the first. 𝔠rest – On a millrind fessewise sable an owl argent.
Residence – Post Green, Lytchett Minster, Dorset.

SON LIVING

CHRISTOPHER JAMES (Post Green Farm, Lytchett Minster, Poole, Dorset), *b* 4 Nov 1952; *ed* Eton, and Edin Univ (BSc 1976); Royal Wessex Yeo: *m* 1st, 1977 (*m diss* 1988), Jennifer, da of John Wyllie, of Newton Stewart, Wigtownshire; 2ndly, 1989, Clare, da of Austen Young, FRCS, of Sheffield and Ynyslas, and has issue living (by 2nd *m*), John, *b* 1992, — Gabriel (da), *b* 1990, — Rosamund, *b* 1994.

DAUGHTERS LIVING

Sarah Margaret, *b* 1951: *m* 1979, John Marcus Omond, and has issue living, Marcus James Mucha, *b* 1979, — Andrew Simon Mucha *b* 1981, — Tamsin, *b* 1984. —— Bridget Selina, *b* 1954: *m* 1976, Martin Christopher Green, of Kitchermans, Huntick Rd, Lytchett Minster, Dorset, and has issue living, Thomas Andrew, *b* 1978, — Alice Hannah, *b* 1981. —— Elizabeth Jane, *b* 1957.

SISTERS LIVING

Katharine Margaret, *b* 1918: *m* 1944, Gerald Henry Rawlinson, who *d* 1975, and has issue living, Carol Margaret *b* 1945: *m* 1st, 1967 (*m diss* 1969), Robert Simmons; 2ndly, 1973, Edward Welstead, of Rayland Manor, Lustleigh, Devon, and has issue living, (by 1st *m*) Rebecca Margaret *b* 1968, (by 2nd *m*) Alexander *b* 1978. —— Rosamund Elizabeth, *b* 1921: *m* 1943, Prof Dominick Conway, MD, FRCP, DCH, who *d* 1989, and has issue living, James Robin, *b* 1945, — Oliver Patrick, *b* 1951, — Bryony May, *b* 1946, — Dawn Madeline, *b* 1948, — Alison Elizabeth, *b* 1949, — Diana Rosemary, *b* 1956, — Florentia Anne, *b* 1959, — Emily Rosamund, *b* 1960. *Residence* – 720 Lonsdale Rd, Manor Park, Ottawa, Canada. —— (Benita) Anne, *b* 1923: *m* 1949, Lt-Col John Anthony Sandbach Barkworth, 3rd Carabiniers, of 1 Sackville St, Winterborne Kingston, Dorset, and has issue living, Anthony Julian Sandbach, *b* 1955: *m* 1985, Catherine, da of Bruce Barnard, of New Zealand, — Primrose Madeline, *b* 1951, — Clare Helena, *b* 1953. —— Jane Madeline (Jarvis, Lytchett Minster, Dorset), *b* 1926: *m* 1st, 1946 (*m diss* 1962), Sq Ldr Simon Hugh Kevill-Davies, RAF (*dec*); 2ndly, 1966 (*m diss* 1971), Michael Vaughan Brian, DSc, and has issue living, (by 1st *m*) Hugh John *b* 1948, — Sheila Anne, *b* 1950: *m* 1979, Patric Morissey, — Benita Jane *b* 1954: *m* 1985, Thomas Francis Coningham Denny, yr son of Sir Anthony Coningham de Waltham Denny, 8th Bt.

COLLATERAL BRANCH LIVING

Granddaughters of late Capt Bernard Percy Turnbull Lees, MC (infra):—
Issue of late Michael Lees, late Capt The Queen's Own Dorset Yeo and SOE, author *The Rape of Serbia* (1990), *b* 1921, *d* 1992: *m* 1944, Gwendolen (Portman Place, Blandford Forum, Dorset), elder da of late (Edgar) Stanley Johnson, of Meadowside, Twickenham:—
Christine Mary, *b* 1946; Bar Inner Temple 1967: *m* 1966, Antonio de Padua Jose Maria Bueno, QC, of 7 Pitt St, W8, and has issue living, Nicola Anna Christina, *b* 1967, — Julia Catherine Mary, *b* 1972, — Emily Antonia Mercedes, *b* 1988. —— Michèle Anne, *b* 1954.

Issue of late Capt Bernard Percy Turnbull Lees, MC, 3rd son of 1st baronet, *b* 1891, *d* 1922: *m* 1919, Mary, who *d* 1980, da of late Col Philip John Joseph Radcliffe, CMG (*see* Radcliffe, Bt, colls, 1980 Edn):—
Bernadette Mary, *b* (*posthumous*) 1923; formerly 3rd Officer WRNS; Master of Applied Psychology, Clinical and Educational, Murdoch Univ, Western Australia 1981: *m* 1st, 1943, Fl-Lt Richard Osborne Curtis, RAFVR (*ka* 1944); 2ndly, 1956, Lt-Col Gordon Robin Kingston Lyon, OBE, 3rd Carabiniers, of Lot 9, Wilderness Rd, Prevelly, W Aust 6285, and has issue living (by 2nd *m*) Kim Philip, *b* 1960.
The 1st baronet, Sir Elliott Lees, DSO, sat as MP for Oldham (C) 1886-1892, and for Birkenhead 1894-1906, and served during S African War 1900-1901. The 2nd baronet, Sir Thomas Evans Keith Lees, Lieut Dorset Yeo, was *ka* 1915. The 3rd bronet, Sir John Victor Elliott Lees, DSO, MC, was Lt-Col KRRC and subsequently Col Comdg 5th Batn Dorset Regt, and was twice wounded during European War 1914-18.

LEES (UK) 1937, of Longdendale, co Chester

Sir (WILLIAM) ANTONY CLARE LEES, 3rd *Baronet*; *b* 14 June 1935; *s* his father, *Sir* WILLIAM HEREWARD CLARE, 1976; *ed* Eton, and Magdalene Coll, Camb (MA): *m* 1986, Joanna Olive Crane.

Arms – Sable, two bars argent, on a chief of the last a garb or, between two roses gules, barbed and seeded proper. **Crest** – Upon a rock proper, a lion rampant gules, supporting a flagstaff, also proper, flowing therefrom a banner sable, charged with a garb or.
Residence – Robin Hill, Yarlington, nr Wincanton, Som BA9 8DX.

SISTER LIVING

Jennifer Dorothy Clare, *b* 1932: *m* 1953, John Benn Arnold Wallinger, of Beechland Farmhouse, Newick, Sussex BN8 4RX, and has issue living, John Christopher Arnold, *b* 1956, — Timothy Hereward Arnold, *b* 1960, — Vanessa Jennifer Clare, *b* 1962.

AUNT LIVING (*Daughter of 1st baronet*)

Enid Clare, *b* 1901. *Residence* – The Cottage, Chinley, Derbyshire.

WIDOW LIVING OF SECOND BARONET

PERGE·SED·CAUT

Go on, but cautiously

DOROTHY GERTRUDE (*Dorothy, Lady Lees*) (Robin Hill, Yarlington, nr Wincanton, Som BA9 8DX), da of Francis Alexander Lauder: *m* 1930, Sir William Hereward Clare Lees, 2nd Bt, who *d* 1976.
The 1st baronet, Sir (William) Clare Lees, OBE, LLD (son of late William Lees, of Birkdale), was Chm of Bleachers' Asso, Ltd, Dep Chm of Martins Bank, and Chm of Martins Bank, Ltd (Manchester Board).

LEESE (UK) 1908, of Send Holme, Send, Surrey

Sir JOHN HENRY VERNON LEESE, 5th *Baronet*; *b* 7 Aug 1901; *s* his kinsman, *Sir* ALEXANDER WILLIAM, 1979.

Arms – Gules, a fesse embattled counterembattled between in chief two falcons belled or and in base a hand erect couped at the wrist, holding a dagger in pale proper, pommel and hilt gold. **Crest** – A falcon belled or, supporting with the dexter paw a flagstaff proper, beaded and tasselled or, therefrom flowing to the dexter a banner gules charged with a dagger inpale proper, pommel and hilt gold.
Residence –

VITA CARA CARIOR LIBERTAS

Life is dear, liberty is dearer

COLLATERAL BRANCHES LIVING

Issue of late Lt-Col Neville Leese, DSO, OBE, RASC, 3rd son of 1st baronet, *b* 1872, *d* 1948: *m* 1893, Matilda, da of J. Saunders:—
Cicely Violet: *m* 1921, Leonard Hay Mottram, and has issue living, Peter Hay, *b* 1922; 1941-45 War in RASC, — Joe Neville, *b* 1927; is Lt-Col Austn Regular Army, late RCT and Dorset Regt: *m* 1st, 1954 (*m diss* 1977), June Patricia Mary, only child of Lt-Col C. F. Garfit, IMS (ret), of Alhama Springs, 91 Altea La Vieja, Altea, Alicante, Spain; 2ndly, 1978, Moira Livingstone, only da of William Finnie, of Canberra ACT, and has issue living (by 1st *m*), Richard Neville Garfit *b* 1957, David Leonard Garfit *b* 1963, — Pamela Mary, *b* 1924. ⸺ Mary Aurelia Neville: *m* 1928, John Frederick Fawcett, and has issue living, Joan Mary, *b* 1928, — Rosemary Ann, *b* 1938. ⸺ Joyce Alice Noreen: *m* 1936, William Eric Oldnall, and has issue living, William Neville Russell, *b* 1943, — Felicity Ann Russell, *b* 1937, — Tessa Mary Russell, *b* 1939.

Issue of late Major Clive Leese, MBE, 6th son of 1st baronet, *b* 1888, *d* 1932: *m* 1916, Dorothy, who *d* 1949, da of late Alfred Dickson, of Chester:—
Cynthia Hilary, *b* 1919; Lt-Col WRAC. *Residence* – 54 Gordon Place, W8.
The 1st baronet, Sir Joseph Francis (*cr* a Knt 1895), sat as MP for Lancashire (NE) Accrington Div (*L*) 1892-1910, and was Recorder of Manchester 1893-1913. Lt-General Sir Oliver Wm Hargreaves Leese, KCB, CBE, DSO, 3rd Bt, late Coldm Gds, commanded 15 (Scottish) Div 1941, Guards Armoured Div 1941-42, 30 Corps 1942-43, and was C-in-C Allied Land forces, S-E Asia 1944-45, GOC-in-C Eastern Command 1945-46, and Lt of Tower of London 1954-57.

le FLEMING (E) 1705, of Rydal, Westmorland

Pax, copia, sapientia

Peace, plenty, wisdom

Sir QUENTIN JOHN LE FLEMING, 12th *Baronet*; *b* 27 June 1949; *s* his father, *Sir* WILLIAM KELLAND, 1988: *m* 1971, Judith Ann, da of C. J. Peck, JP, of Ashhurst, Manawatu, NZ, and has issue.

𝕬rms – Gules, a fret argent. 𝕮rest – A serpent nowed holding in its mouth a garland of olive and vine all proper.
Residence – 147 Stanford St, Ashhurst, NZ.

SON LIVING

DAVID KELLAND, *b* 12 Jan 1976. ——— Andrew John, *b* 1979.

DAUGHTER LIVING

Josephine Kay, *b* 1973.

BROTHERS LIVING

Peter Douglas, *b* 1958. ——— Murray Kelland, *b* 1960.

SISTERS LIVING

Rosemary Lynette, *b* 1951: *m* 1975, Howard Asplin, and has issue living, Steven, *b* 1977, — Blair, *b* 1979, — Neil, *b* 1982. ——— Elaine Dawn, *b* 1963: *m* 1980, John Buchanan, and has issue living, Timothy, *b* 1983, — Richard, *b* 1986. ——— Marie Louise, *b* 1955. ——— Vicki Karin, *b* 1964: *m* 1989, Roger Whitmore.

UNCLES LIVING (*sons of 10th baronet*)

Gordon Halsey (78 Ngatai St, Manaia, Taranaki, NZ), *b* 1925: *m* 1962 Lorna Marjorie, da of R. F. Trim, of Trimoana, RD Eltham, NZ, and has issue living, Mark Ronald Feltham, *b* 1965, — Roderick Gordon Hudleston, *b* 1970, — Ruth Maree, *b* 1963, — Helen Lorna, *b* 1964, — Alison Halsey, *b* 1967. ——— Lindsay Craig (31 Whakapaki st, PO Box 8, Urenui, NZ), *b* 1927: *m* 1955, Jean Irene, da of F. G. Campbell, of Patea, Taranaki, NZ, and has issue living, John Fraser, *b* 1958, — Hugh Vincent, *b* 1959, — Frances Mary, *b* 1956, — Annette Isabel, *b* 1963, — Louise Joy, *b* 1969.

WIDOW LIVING OF ELEVENTH BARONET

NOVEEN AVIS (*Noveen, Lady le Fleming*), da of C. C. Sharpe, of Rukuhia, Hamilton, NZ: *m* 1948, Sir William Kelland le Fleming, 11th Bt, who *d* 1988. *Residence* – Kopane, RD6, Palmerston North, NZ.

COLLATERAL BRANCH LIVING

Grandchildren of late Richard Thomas le Fleming, son of late William le Fleming, 2nd son of 6th baronet:—
Issue of late Richard Henry Edward le Fleming, *b* 1892, *d* 1960: *m* 1918, Mabel Gladys (of 151, Seaview Road, Westown, New Plymouth, New Zealand), da of Henry Parslow:—
Albert Edward, *b* 1923; European War 1939-45 with Roy New Zealand Air Force: *m* 1946, Eileen Ellen, da of John Moffet, and has issue living, Richard John, *b* 1953, — Judith Merle, *b* 1949. *Residence* – Dudley Road, Inglewood, Taranaki, New Zealand. ——— Noala Doris, *b* 1920: *m* 1942, Raymond Peterson, and has issue living, Janice Margaret, *b* 1945, — Fay Maralyn, *b* 1948. *Residence* – Manutake, Hawera, New Zealand.

This family claims to be descended from Sir Michael le Fleming, of Furness living in 1127. The Visitation of Westmorland 1665 carried the pedigree down to Sir Daniel Fleming of Rydal Hall, Cumberland, father of 1st baronet. The 1st baronet sat as MP for Westmorland 1696-1707, and the 2nd baronet was Bishop of Carlisle 1734-47.

LEGARD (E) 1660, of Ganton, Yorkshire

By the cross to heaven

Sir CHARLES THOMAS LEGARD, 15th *Baronet*; *b* 26 Oct 1938; *s* his father, *Sir* THOMAS DIGBY, 1984; *ed* Eton; MInstM: *m* 1st, 1962, Elizabeth, da of John M. Guthrie, of Church Meadows, Hutton Buscel, Scarborough; 2ndly, 1987, Caroline Sarah, da of late Maj Arthur Ralph Kingsley Weston, of Howlet Hall, Sleights, Whitby, Yorks, and has issue by 1st *m*.

Arms – Argent, on a bend between six mullets pierced of the field gules, a cross-patée or. **Crest** – A greyhound passant or, collared sable, studded argent. *Seat* – Scampston Hall, Malton, N Yorks.

SONS LIVING *(By 1st marriage)*

CHRISTOPHER JOHN CHARLES, *b* 19 April 1964; *ed* Eton: *m* 1986, Miranda M., da of Maj Fane Travers Gaffney, of Crossbank Hill, Hurworth, co Durham (*see* Feilden, Bt, colls). *Residence* – 177 Boundaries Rd, Balham, SW12 8HE. —— Edward Thomas, *b* 1966; Capt The Light Dragoons: *m* 1993, Lucy F., eldest da of Ivone Peter Kirkpatrick, of Donhead St Andrew, Dorset.

DAUGHTER LIVING *(By 1st marriage)*

Louise Elizabeth, *b* 1969.

BROTHERS LIVING

William Robert (Lowthorpe Lodge, Lowthorpe, Driffield, Yorks), *b* 1943; *ed* Eton, and Roy Agric Coll, Cirencester: *m* 1st, 1967, Sally Ann, da of late W. H. Craig; 2ndly, 1978, Helen, only da of R. Geoffrey Le-Pine, of Little Driffield, Yorks, and has issue living, (by 2nd *m*) Arabella Mary Elaine, *b* 1978, — Victoria Helen, *b* 1980. —— James Digby (The Deer Park, Scampston, Malton, N Yorks), *b* 1946; *ed* Eton: *m* 1969, Daphne Jane, el da of Denis West, of Belgrave Lodge, Chester, and has issue living, Thomas James St Quintin, *b* 1971; *ed* St Edward's Oxford, and RAC Cirencester, — Sophie Jane, *b* 1973.

COLLATERAL BRANCHES LIVING

Issue of late William Ernest Legard, F/O RAF, yst son of 13th baronet, *b* 1911, *ka* 1940: *m* 1939, Alice (Appleton House, Appleton-le-Street, Malton, Yorks, who *m* 2ndly, 1943, Col Basil Perry Beale, OBE, MC, DL, who *d* 1967), da of Hon George Ellis Vestey (*see* B Vestey, colls):—
Anne, *b* 1940: *m* 19—, Frank Curtis Luckow; 2ndly, 1965, Harry O'theil Seymour, and has issue living, (by 1st *m*) William Frank, *b* 1962, — Laura *b* 1963. — (by 2nd *m*) Donna Anne, *b* 1966: *m* 1992, Michael Whiteside, and has issue living, Siena Katherine Seymour *b* 1993. *Address* – PO Box 311, De Funiak Springs, Florida, USA.

Grandchildren of late Col Sir James Digby Legard, KCB, el son of late Capt James Anlaby Legard, RN, el son of late Rev William Legard, 4th son of 5th baronet:—
Issue of late Col Alfred Digby Legard, CBE, *b* 1878, *d* 1939: *m* 1902, Winifred (who *d* 1962, having *m* 2ndly, 1947, as his second wife, Maj-Gen George Henry Addison, CB, CMG, DSO, who *d* 1964), only da of late Col Sir William George Morris, KCMG, CB:—
Diana, *b* 1918: *m* 1950, John Percival Wheeler, and has issue living, Michael John, *b* 1952, — Bridget Diana, *b* 1954: *m* 1983, Michael Wood, son of Brig R. B. P. Wood, of Leverstock Green, Herts, and has issue living, Patrick Michael Olive *b* 1991, Rebecca Diana *b* 1989. *Residence* – Bockingfold, near Marden, Kent.

Granddaughters of late Lieut George Percy Legard, RN, 2nd son of late Col Sir James Digby Legard, KCB (ante):—
Issue of late Lt-Col Charles Percy Digby Legard, *b* 1906, *d* 1980: *m* 1934, Gertrude Kate, who *d* 1969, da of Arthur Thomson, late of Heathside, Wimbledon Common, SW, and Java:—
Sarah Anthea, *b* 1939: *m* 1966, Capt Malcolm James Sherwin, Queen's Own Hussars, and has issue living, Simon Patrick, *b* 1967, — Amanda Kate, *b* 1969. —— Dinah Annabel (Stearsby Hagg Farm, Stearsby, York), *b* 1941: *m* 1964 (*m diss* 1984), James Harrison Holt (*see* Reckitt, Bt, ext), and has issue living, Philip James Harrison, *b* 1965: *m* 1990, M. Jane R., eldest da of Ewan Harper, of Titchmarsh, Northampton, — Michael Vernon Charles, *b* 1966, — Elizabeth Rebecca, *b* 1969. —— Lavinia Anlaby, *b* 1944: *m* 1982, Robin George Newman (*see* E Clarendon, 1971 Edn).

Grandson of late Col Sir James Digby Legard, KCB (ante):—
Issue of late Richard Anlaby Legard, *b* 1880, *d* 1973: *m* 1929, Dorice, who *d* 1976, da of late Harold Ostler, of Hull:—
Richard Digby (Apartado 110, Garrucha, Almeria, Spain), *b* 1930: *m* 1st, 1966 (*m diss* 1975), Mrs Jean H. Dodd, of York; 2ndly, 1985, Joan Frances Hall, da of late Francis Johnson Flynn, and has issue living (by 1st *m*), James Richard Anlaby, *b* 1967; *ed* Worksop, and RMA Sandhurst.

Grandsons of late Rev Francis Digby Legard, son of late George Legard, el son of late Digby Legard, 5th son of 5th baronet :—
Issue of late Brig-Gen D'Arcy Legard, CMG, DSO, *b* 1873, *d* 1953: *m* 1908, Lady Edith Margaret Emily Mary Foljambe, who *d* 1962, da of 1st Earl of Liverpool (*cr* 1905):—
Antony Ronald, MBE, *b* 1912; *ed* Winchester, and Trin Coll, Oxford; formerly Maj RE (TA); 1939-45 War (MBE); MBE (Mil) 1940: *m* 1946, Maud, da of Clifford Schwabe, of Cuddington Grange, Northwich, Ches, and has issue living, Simon Littledale (Codd Hall, Common Lane, South Cave, Brough, N Humberside), *b* 1947: *m* 1971, Heather Temperton, and has issue living, Richard Simon *b* 1976, Helen Louise *b* 1974, — David Antony, *b* 1953, — Diana May, *b* 1950. *Residence* – Fairway, Delamere, Northwich, Ches. —— Peter Herbert, *b* 1917; *ed* Shrewsbury, and Edinburgh Univ; late Lt Lanarkshire Yeo: *m* 1959, Brenda Valerie, only da of late Lt-Col S. Kidd, TD, DL, of Haresgill, Penrith, Cumbria, and has issue living, Jonathan Antony, *b* 1961, — Edith Veronica Jane *b* 1964. *Residence* – 11 Glan Aber Park, Chester.

Grandchildren of late Rev Charles Legard, MC (infra):—
Issue of late Lt-Cdr George Hugo Digby Legard, MBE, RN, *b* 1920, *d* 1966: *m* 1944, Eve Lilian (who *m* 2ndly, 1973, Guy Alexander Hughes, of Yew Tree Plat, Winchelsea, Sussex TN36 4EN), da of late Capt Francis Howard, DSC, RN:—

Robin Hugo Charles (53 Harwood Rd, SW6), *b* 1945; *ed* Milton Abbey, and Selwyn Coll, Camb (MA). —— Joanna Frances (19 Rankeillor St, Edinburgh), *b* 1948. —— Hilary Jane, *b* 1951.

Grandson of late Digby Charles Legard, only son of late Rev Digby Charles Legard, yr son of late Digby Legard (ante):—

Issue of late Rev Charles Legard, MC, *b* 1887, *d* 1976: *m* 1918, Ethel Gertrude, who *d* 1973, da of late Rev George Strickland Marriott, R of Sigglesthorne:—

John Bruce (75 Holland Park, W11), *b* 1924; *ed* Cheltenham.

This family is of great antiquity in Yorkshire, and possessed the manor of Anlaby as early as the 12th century. The 1st baronet, Sir John, was MP for Scarborough, and an eminent royalist. Sir Charles, 11th Bt, was Chm of E Riding of Yorkshire County Council, and MP for Scarborough (C) 1874-80.

LEICESTER (I) 1671, of Timogue, Queen's co (Extinct 1968)

Sir CHARLES BYRNE WARREN LEICESTER, 9th and last *Baronet.*

DAUGHTER LIVING OF EIGHTH BARONET

(By 2nd *m*) Meriel Jeanne, *b* 1931: *m* 1956, Sidney John Winder, and has issue living, Michelle Ann, *b* 1958: *m* 19—, —, — Nicola Jane, *b* 1960, — Robyn Marte, *b* 1968. *Residence* – 1595 Amberlea Drive South, Dunedin, Florida 34698, USA.

COLLATERAL BRANCHES LIVING

Issue of late Lt-Col Byron Leicester, brother of 8th baronet, *b* 1868, *d* 1929: *m* 1895, Guendolen Margaret, who *d* 1908, da of late John Brooke, of Honley, Yorkshire:—

Meriel Guendolen, *b* 1899: *m* 1922, Col Eric Adrian Hayes-Newington, DSO, OBE, Indian Army (ret) and has issue living, Patricia Margaret (7 Old Forest Lodge, Beacon Rd, Crowborough, Sussex TW6 1VE), *b* 1924: *m* 1946 (*m diss* 1953), John Sheridan, and has issue living, Bridget Ann *b* 1948, — Erica, *b* 1928: *m* 1956, Kenneth Roland Tull, of 1170 Lake Charles Drive, Roswell, Georgia 30075, USA. —— Lesbia Evelyn Margaret, *b* 1908; assumed by deed poll 1926 the name of Margaret Leicester FLETCHER-TOOMER in lieu of Lesbia Evelyn Margaret Leicester.

Granddaughter of late Maj William Frederick Leicester, father of 9th baronet:—

Issue of late Lieut-Col George William Frederic Leicester, *b* 1895, *d* 1944: *m* 1932, Katherine Anne (who *m* 2ndly, 1945, Lt-Col A. Frankland, of The Gables, Hopton Cangeford, Ludlow), da of late Col Lawrence Chenevix Trench, CMG, DSO (*see* B Ashtown, colls):—

Elizabeth Meriel Anne, *b* 1935.

LEIGH (UK) 1918, of Altrincham, Cheshire

Sir RICHARD HENRY LEIGH, 3rd *Baronet, b* 11 Nov 1936; *s* his uncle, *Sir* JOHN, 1992; *ed* Aiglon Coll, Switzerland: *m* 1st, 1962 (*m diss* 1977), Barbro Anna Elizabeth, el da of late Stig Carl Sebastian Tham, of Sweden; 2ndly, 1977, Cherie Rosalind, el da of late Douglas Donald Dale, of La Blanchie, Cherval, France, and widow of Alan Reece, RMS.

Arms – Argent, on a cross engrailed quadrant gules, a garb or between in chief two roses of the second, barbed and seeded proper. **Crest** – A cubit arm vested gules, cuffed argent, grasping a staff in bend sinister proper, pendant therefrom a banner of the second, charged with a cross-couped of the first. *Residence* – Trythall Vean, Madron, Penzance, Cornwall TR20 8SY.

HALF-BROTHER LIVING

CHRISTOPHER JOHN (The Spinney, Wendens Ambo, Saffron Walden, Essex), *b* 6 April 1941; *ed* Radley: *m* 1963, Gillian Ismay, only da of William King Lowe, of The Bell House, Guiting Power, Glos, and has issue living, Edward John, *b* 1 April 1970; *ed* Bishop's Stortford Coll, — Caroline Nicola, *b* 1967.

HALF-SISTER LIVING

Victoria Anne, *b* 1945; *ed* St James's, Malvern: *m* 1967, Jasper Rodney Archer, of The Malt House, Stapleford, nr Salisbury, Wilts, son of Lt-Col Rodney Archer, MC, of Millfield, Haslemere, Surrey, and has issue living, Nicholas Jasper, *b* 1971, — Sophie Louise, *b* 1973.

UNCLE LIVING (son of 1st baronet)

David, BM, BCh, *b* 1921; *ed* Eton, and New Coll, Oxford (MA); CStJ: *m* 1945, Rosemary Eleanor, da of late William Henry Wyburn-Mason, of Rosemont, Clytha Park, Newport, Mon, and has issue living, Peregrine William Roger Wyburn, *b* 1955; *ed* Eton, Exeter Univ (BA), and RAC, Cirencester (DipSurv): *m* 1992, Laura Dawn, da of Col Vincent Warwick Calmady-Hamlyn, of Leawood, Bridestowe, Devon, and has issue living, Ranald Geoffrey Merlin *b* 1992, — Corinna Eleanor Elizabeth Wyburn, *b* 1951; *ed* Westonbirt: *m* 1992, Col Keith George Turner, MBE, son of late Maj Herbert George Turner. *Residence* – High Coombe, Coombe Hill, Bruton, Somerset BA10 0QA.

The 1st baronet, Sir John Leigh (son of John Leigh, JP, of Brooklands, Cheshire), was proprietor of *The Pall Mall Gazette* (before amalgamation with *Evening Standard*). In European War 1914-18 he equipped a hospital for wounded officers at

Altrincham, and founded, maintained, and was Chm of Canadian Officers' Club. He sat as MP for Clapham Div of Wands-worth (C) 1922-45.

LEIGHTON (E) 1693, of Wattlesborough, Shropshire

Dread shame

Sir MICHAEL JOHN BRYAN LEIGHTON, 11th *Baronet*; *b* 8 March 1935; *s* his father, *Col Sir* RICHARD TIHEL, TD, 1957; *ed* Stowe, and RAC Cirencester; is patron of one living: *m* 1st, 1974 (*m diss* 1980), Mrs Amber Mary Ritchie; 2ndly, 1991, Mrs Diana Mary Gamble, and has issue by 2nd *m*.

𝕬rms – Quarterly, per fesse indented or and gules. ℭrest – A wyvern with wings expanded sable.
Seat – Loton Park, Shrewsbury. *Club* – MCC.

DAUGHTER LIVING *(By 2nd marriage)*

Eleanor Angharad Diana, *b* 1992.

SISTERS LIVING

Lavinia Ann, *b* 1932: *m* 1958, Major Edward Arthur Trevor Bonnor-Maurice, Cold-stream Guards, and has issue living, Emma Mary, *b* 1959: *m* 1986, Mark William Fane, and has issue living, Harry Lachlan *b* 1992, Alice Daisy (twin) *b* 1992, — Frances Flavia, *b* 1962. *Residence* – Bodynfoel Hall, Llanfechain, Montgomeryshire. —— Judy Johanna Kathleen, *b* 1937. —— Elizabeth Linda Mary *b* 1938: *m* 1st, 1977 (*m diss* 1984), David James Treasure, Monmouthshire Regt; 2ndly, 1988, Vyvian Clover, Parachute Regt.

The Leightons derive their name from Leighton in Shropshire, where they were seated in the 12th century. They inherited, *temp* Edward IV, the estates of Wattlesborough and Loton, through the Mawddwys and the Burghs by the marriage of John Leighton with a coheiress of the last-named family. The county of Shropshire was represented in Parliament by Richard de Leighton, AD 1312-18, and has since often been represented by members of this family. Sir Edward Leighton, 2nd Bt changed the residence from the ancient castle of Wattlesborough to the house at Loton, which he greatly enlarged in 1712. Sir Baldwyn Leighton, 8th Bt, sat as MP for Shropshire S (C) 1877-85. Col Sir Richard Tihel Leighton, 10th Bt, Shropshire Yeo, was High Sheriff of Salop 1956.

FORBES-LEITH OF FYVIE (UK) 1923, of Jessfield, co Midlothian

I wait in hope

God assisting

Sir ANDREW GEORGE FORBES-LEITH OF FYVIE, 3rd *Baronet*; *b* 20 Oct 1929; *s* his father, *Sir* (ROBERT) IAN (ALGERNON), KT, MBE, 1973; *ed* Eton: *m* 1962, Jane Kate, who *d* 1969, only da of late David McCall-McCowan, of Dalwhat, Moniaive, Dumfries, and has issue.

𝕬rms – Quarterly, 1st grand quarter or, a cross-crosslet fitchée sable between three crescents in chief and as many fusils in base gules, *Leith*; 2nd grand quarter quarterly, 1st and 4th azure, on a chevron between three bears' heads couped argent, muzzled gules, a man's heart proper, between two skenes of the first, pommelled or, *Forbes of Balfing*; 2nd azure, a fesse chequy argent and of the first between three boars' heads erased or, within a bordure indented of the second, *Gordon of Badenscoth*; 3rd argent, a fir-tree growing out of a mount in base vert, surmounted of a sword in bend, supporting on its point an Imperial head erased azure, armed and langued gules, *Gregory*; crown proper, in sinister chief and dexter base a lion's 3rd grand quarter, parted per fesse azure and argent, in chief three bears' heads couped of the second, muzzled gules, and in base as many unicorns' heads erased sable, *Forbes of Ballogie*; 4th grand quarter argent, on a bend gules between two mullets in chief, and in base a hunting horn, sable, stringed of the second, three buckles or, *Burn*. ℭrest – 1st, a cross-crosslet fitchee sable *Leith*; 2nd, a bear's head and neck couped argent, muzzled azure, *Forbes*; 3rd a dexter cubit arm in armour bendways, the hand naked proper holding a cross-crosslet fitchée erect in pale gules, *Burn*.
Residences – Fyvie Castle, Fyvie, Aberdeenshire (now National Trust property); Dunachton, Kingussie, Inverness-shire. *Clubs* – Royal Northern (Aberdeen), Highland (Inverness).

SONS LIVING

GEORGE IAN DAVID, *b* 26 May 1967. —— John Charles, *b* 1969.

DAUGHTERS LIVING

Miranda Jane, *b* 1963: *m* 1990, Julian N. W. McHardy, son of Col W. G. McHardy, CVO, MBE, MC, of Woodend House, Banchory, Kincardineshire, and has issue living, Andrew William Jock, *b* 1992, — Iona Jane, *b* 1994. —— Louisa Mary, *b* 1965: *m* 1991, Thomas William Leader, yr son of Henry William Leader, of 41 Warwick Gdns, W14, and of Mrs G. H. Maingot, of Sugar House, Tobago.

SISTERS LIVING

Anne Rosdew, *b* 1932: *m* 1959, Angus Maitland Pelham Burn, of Knappach, Banchory, Kincardineshire, and has issue living, Amanda Mary, *b* 1961, — Lucy Rosdew, *b* 1963, — Emily Louise, *b* 1964, — Kate Ruth, *b* 1966. —— Mary Elizabeth, *b* 1934: *m* 1961, Maj James Gresley McGowan, 15th/19th King's Roy Hussars, of Benridge Hall, Ponteland, Northumberland (*see* Gresley, Bt, colls, 1973-74 Edn), and has issue living, Charles Gresley (Southlands Farm, Gunnerton, Hexham, Northumberland NE48 4EA), *b* 1962: *m* 1989, Deborah Ann, da of Dr Joseph Edward Gordon, of The Villa, Seaton Burn, Newcastle upon Tyne, and has issue living, Hector Joseph Gresley *b* 1991, Rosanna Mary *b* 1994, — Hugo John, *b* 1964, — Lorna, *b* 1967

Sir Charles Rosdew Forbes-Leith of Fyvie, OBE, 1st Bt, yst son of Gen Robert Burn, Col Comdt RA: *m* 1891, Hon Ethel Louise Forbes-Leith, OBE, only da of and heir of 1st Baron Leith of Fyvie (*ext*), and by edict of Lord Court 1925, assumed the surname and arms of Forbes-Leith of Fyvie, for himself, his wife and son, under terms of the will of his father-in-law; MP for Torquay (*U*) 1910-23, Col TA and Lt-Col R Dragoons; served in Hazara Expedition 1888, S African War 1900 and 1914-18 War. His el son Arthur Herbert Rosdew was was *ka* Ypres 1914; the yr son, Sir (Robert) Ian (Algernon) Forbes-Leith of Fyvie, KT, MBE, was Lord Lt of Aberdeenshire 1959-73.

Alexander Burn bought Kingston, East Lothian 1765, which was sold in 1813 by his son, John Burn, grandfather of 1st Bt. Baron Leith of Fyvie was el son of Rear-Adm John James Leith (descended from the Leiths, successively of Barnis, co Aberdeen, Edingarioc, New Leslie in the Garioch, and Leith Hall) by his wife Margaret, da and heir of Alexander Forbes of Blackford, Aberdeenshire, descended from Duncan Forbes of Corsindae, 2nd son of 2nd Lord Forbes.

Leith-Buchanan, see Buchanan.

LE MARCHANT (UK) 1841, of Chobham Place, Surrey

Sir FRANCIS ARTHUR LE MARCHANT, 6th *Baronet*; *b* 6 Oct 1939; *s* his father, Sir DENIS, 1987, *ed* Gordonstoun, and RA Schools.

Arms – Azure, a chevron or between three owls argent. **Crest** – Out of a ducal coronet an owl's leg erect or.
Seat – Hungerton Hall, Grantham, Lincolnshire. *Address* – c/o Midland Bank plc, 88 Westgate, Grantham, Lincs NG31 6LF.

SISTER LIVING

(Penelope) Clare (Colston Bassett House, Colston Bassett, Notts), *b* 1944: *m* 1964 (*m diss* 1990), Capt John Henry Warrand Hanmer, and has issue (*see* Hanmer, Bt, colls).

WIDOW LIVING OF FIFTH BARONET

Me Minerva lucet
Minerva is my light

ELIZABETH ROWENA (*Lady Le Marchant*), da of Arthur Hovenden Worth, of Hovenden House, Fleet, Lincs: *m* 1933, Sir Denis Le Marchant, 5th Bt, who *d* 1987. *Residence* – Hungerton Hall, Grantham, Lincs.

COLLATERAL BRANCHES LIVING

Granddaughters of late Alfred Gaspard Le Marchant (infra):—
Issue of late Sir Spencer Le Marchant, *b* 1931, *d* (7 Sept) 1986: *m* 1955, Lucinda Gaye (*Lady Le Marchant*) (The Saltings, Yarmouth, Isle of Wight), da of Brig Hugh Nugent Leveson-Gower, late RA (*see* D Sutherland, colls):—
Perronelle Jane, *b* 1956: *m* 1979, James Wallace Hudleston, yr son of Wilfrid Andrew Hudleston, and has issue living, Hugh Edward, *b* 1983, — Tamara Avril, *b* 1980. —— Geva Ann, *b* 1958: *m* 1991, Dr Michael McCaldin, elder son of Dr John McCaldin, of Down House, Anerley, Natal.

Issue of late Alfred Gaspard Le Marchant, yr son of 4th baronet, *b* (twin) 1906, *d* (3 March) 1986: *m* 1929, Turdis, who *d* (11 March) 1986, da of late Einar Mortensen, of Holte, Denmark:—
MICHAEL, *b* 28 July 1937; *ed* Eton: *m* 1st, 1963 (*m diss* 19—), Philippa, eldest da of late Ralph Batchelor Denby, of Tanyard, Sharpthorne, Sussex; 2ndly, 1981, Sandra Elisabeth Champion, da of — Kirby, and has issue living (by 1st *m*), Piers Alfred, *b* 1964, — Dickon John, *b* 1968, — Melissa Winifred, *b* 1965, — Antonia Ruth, *b* 1970. *Residence* – White Lodge, 15 Bathwick Hill, Bath, Avon BA2 6EW. —— Pamela, *b* 1933: *m* 1st, 1957, Henry Douglas-Pennant, who *d* 1986 (*see* B Penrhyn, colls); 2ndly, 1988, Very Rev Patrick Reynolds Mitchell, Dean of Windsor. *Residence* – The Deanery, Windsor Castle, Berks SL4 1NJ.

The father of Sir Denis Le Marchant, 1st Bt, Maj-Gen John Gaspard Le Marchant (a lineal descendant of Peter Le Marchant, President of the States, and Lieut-Governor of Guernsey in the 13th century), was killed at the battle of Salamanca, while leading the heavy brigade of cavalry. Brig-Gen Sir Edward Thomas Le Marchant, KCB, CBE, 4th Bt, was High Sheriff of Nottinghamshire 1930, Chm of Nottinghamshire TA Asso 1931-45, and Dep Chm of Quarter Sessions, Nottinghamshire 1933-45. Sir Denis Le Marchant, 5th Bt, was Capt Cheshire Yeo (Res), and Lieut Nottingham (Sherwood Rangers) Yeo, and High Sheriff of Lincolnshire 1958-59; his elder son, Peter Edward, *b* 1934, *ed* Eton, and Lincoln Coll, Oxford, *dvp*.

LENNARD (UK) 1880, of Wickham Court, co Kent (Extinct 1980)

Lt-Col Sir STEPHEN ARTHUR HALLAM FARNABY LENNARD, 3rd and last *Baronet*.

WIDOW LIVING OF THIRD BARONET

MARGARET JEAN (*Lady Lennard*) (5692 Elm St, Vancouver, BC), only da of Daniel Hockin, of Vancouver, and widow of Group Capt William Neville Cumming, OBE, DFC, RAF: *m* 1970, as his second wife, Lt-Col Sir Stephen Arthur Hallam Farnaby Lennard, 3rd Bt, who *d* 1980, when the title became ext.

BARRETT-LENNARD (UK) 1801, of Belhus, Essex

Rev Sir HUGH DACRE BARRETT-LENNARD, 6th *Baronet*; only son of late Sir Fiennes Cecil Arthur Barrett-Lennard, el son of Capt Thomas George Barrett-Lennard, grandson of John Barrett-Lennard, 2nd son of 1st baronet; *b* 27 June 1917; *s* his kinsman, *Sir* (THOMAS) RICHARD FIENNES, OBE, 1977; *ed* Radley; formerly Capt Essex Regt; 1939-45 War (despatches); a Priest of London Oratory.

Arms – Quarterly: 1st and 4th, or, on a fesse gules three fleurs-de-lis or, within a bordure wavy, *Lennard*; 2nd and 3rd, party per pale barry of four counterchanged argent and gules, *Barrett*; all within a bordure wavy sable. **Crest** – Out of a ducal coronet or an Irish wolf dog's head per fesse argent and ermine, charged with an escallop per fesse nebuly, gules and sable. (The 1st baronet also obtained from the Lyon office in Edinburgh a grant of supporters, viz.—two lions rampant or, each charged with a collar quarterly argent and gules; but the grantee's domicile being in England this grant was illegal.)
Address – The Oratory, SW7 2RP.

POUR BIEN DÉSIRER

To wish well

DAUGHTER LIVING OF FIFTH BARONET

Anne, *b* 1923: *m* 1949, Rev John Charles Pollock (*see* Pollock, Bt, *cr* 1866, colls). *Residence* – Rose Ash House, South Molton, Devon EX36 4RB.

COLLATERAL BRANCHES LIVING

Granddaughter of late Rev Dacre Barrett-Lennard, brother of 2nd baronet:—
Issue of late Dacre Barrett-Lennard, *b* 1884, *d* 1948: *m* 1915, Mabel Ella (Gable Cottage, Aldham Hadleigh, Suffolk), da of James Sage, of The Yew Tree Farm, Aldham, Suffolk:—
Viva Dacre, *b* 1923. *Residence* – Gable Cottage, Aldham Hadleigh, Suffolk.

Grandchildren of late Trenchard Goodenough Barrett-Lennard, yst son of late George Barrett-Lennard, 2nd son of John Barrett Lennard, 2nd son of 1st baronet:—
Issue of late Sqdn-Ldr Dacre Barrett-Lennard, RAF *b* 1906, *ka* 1944: *m* 1938, Una (37 The Cliff, Wellington Rd, Wallasey, Merseyside L45 2NL), da of Leo Burn, of Wallasey, Cheshire:—
Paula, *b* 1943: *m* 1969, David Ambrose Staines, of 1 Old Orchard, Hawthorne Lane, Wilmslow, Cheshire SK9 5DH, and has issue living, Dacre Ambrose, *b* 1977, — Rachel, *b* 1975.
Issue of late Roy Barrett-Lennard, *b* 1909, *d* 1979: *m* 1939, Joyce Christine Elizabeth, who *d* 1985, da of Stuart Robert Drinkwater, of Coventry:—
RICHARD FYNES (The Schoolhouse, nr Bodmin, Cornwall PL30 3PD), *b* 6 April 1941. —— Peter John (2 Farmhouse Cottage, Leatherhead Rd, Oxshott, Surrey KT22 0EZ), *b* 1942: *m* 1979, Sonja, da of Vladimir Belacic, of 23 Autuna Branka Simica, 41000 Zagreb, Yugoslavia, and has issue living, Simon James, *b* 1980. —— Penelope Anne, *b* 1948.

Grandchildren of late Edmund Thomas Dacre Barrett-Lennard (infra):—
Issue of late Geoffrey Barrett-Lennard, *b* 1908, *d* 1988: *m* 1933, Lorna Margaret, da of A. B. Lodge, of York:—
John (Annandale, Beverley, W Aust), *b* 1949: *m* 1976, Leita Catherine, da of R. A. McLean, of Beverley, W Aust, and has issue living, James Dacre, *b* 1981, — Claire, *b* 1979, — Marie, *b* 1984. —— Sarah Margaret, *b* 1936: *m* 1963, Archibald Stewart Fraser, of 17 Euston Av, Highgate, S Aust, and has issue living, John Buchanan, *b* 1966, — Geoffrey Lodge, *b* 1968, — Catherine Margaret, *b* 1971. —— Judith (17 Forrest St, Beverley 6304, W Aust), *b* 1938: *m* 1969, Robert Henry Magill, who *d* 1974, and has issue living, Peter John, *b* 1972, — David James Henry, *b* 1974, — Catherine Elizabeth, *b* 1970.
Issue of late Edmund Thomas Keith Barrett-Lennard, *b* 1911, *d* 19-: *m* 1938, Margaret (Woonderlin, Beverley, W Aust), da of A. V. Clarke, of Beverley, W Aust:—
Edmund Timothy Dacre, *b* 1941. —— Douglas John (Woonderlin, Beverley, W Aust), *b* 1944: *m* 1974, Dorothy Marianne, el da of Gordon Derwent Crosthwaite, of Glenroa, Margaret River, W Aust, and has issue living, Derwent Thomas Keith, *b* 1976. —— Richard (Milepool, Beverley, Western Australia), *b* 1950; AMF Vietnam: *m* 1975, Lorna Jean, da of Donald A. Sprigg, of Strathallen, Wagin, W Aust, and has issue living, Michael James, *b* 1978, — Jeremy, *b* 1980. —— Helen Mary (Forrest St, Beverley, Western Australia), *b* 1939: *m* 1959, —, and has issue living, Christopher James Blake, *b* 1960, — Thomas William Timothy, *b* 1966, — Catherine Jane Blake, *b* 1962.

Grandchildren of late Edmund George Barrett-Lennard, son of late Edmund Thomas Henry Barrett-Lennard, son of George Barrett-Lennard, 3rd son of 1st baronet:—
Issue of late Edmund Thomas Dacre Barrett-Lennard, *b* 1881, *d* 1945: *m* 1907, Kathleen Rosina who *d* 1939, da of Thomas D. Pettigrew:—
Anthony Leslie (84/31 Williams Rd, Nedlands, W Aust 6009), *b* 1913: *m* 1943, Ethel Barbara, da of R. F. Adams, of Sydney, NSW, and has issue living, Antony John William, *b* 1953: *m* 1981, Alison, da of P. R. Bremner, of Beverley, WA, and has issue living, Benjamin James *b* 1987, Jodie Louise *b* 1985, — Carmen Lesley, *b* 1944, — Jill Kathleen, *b* 1946: *m* 1974, Allan Wall, of 63 Webster St, Nedlands, W Aust, and has issue living, Timother Lawler *b* 1976, Carmen Belinda *b* 1978, — Sally Anne, *b* 1951: *m* 1979, George Jenkin Ellis Smith, and has issue living, Thomas William *b* 1983, Hilary Rebecca *b* 1981.
Issue of late Francis Barrett-Lennard, *b* 1882, *d* 1960: *m* 1910, Elsie Selina, who *d* 1950, da of Thomas George Walker, of Beverley, W Australia:—
Thomas Edmund (Drumclyer, Beverley, W Australia), *b* 1916; is a Farmer: *m* 1948, Lesley Vernon, da of Vernon Bland Gibson, of Perth, W Australia, and has issue living, Graham Francis, *b* 1953: *m* 1984, Dina Campbell, da of John Pike Campbell Curlewis, of Toronto, NSW, Australia, and has issue living, Edmund George *b* 1986, Marika Joan *b* 1984, — Felicity Anne, *b* 1949; BEd, Dip PE: *m* 1977, Russell John Perry, PhD, BSc, son of Alfred Trevor Perry, of Perth, Western Australia, and has issue living, Philippa Louise *b* 1982, Elizabeth Emma *b* 1985, — Jennifer Jane, *b* 1950; WATC: *m* 1975, Vernon Ashley, son of Julius Vernon Brockman, of Beach Grove, Busselton, Western Australia, and has issue living, James Julius *b* 1977, Ashley Edmund Vernon *b* 1980, — Dinah Louise, *b* 1955; WATC, BHSAI: *m* 1987, Ronald John Fleming, of Glenesk, Muchea, Western Australia. —— Launa, *b* 1911: *m* 1940, Horace Arnold Butler, of Beverley, W Australia, and has issue living, Lennard Wilfred, *b* 1944, — Frances Merrilyn, *b* 1943.
Issue of late Henry Barrett-Lennard, *b* 1884, *d* 1960: *m* 1912, Muriel Ellen, da of John Trevelyan:—
Trevor Henry (Camblebren, Gairdner River, W Australia), *b* 1922, is a Farmer; European War 1939-45, with Australian Imperial Force: *m* 1951, Audrey, yr da of Albert E. Wilhelm, of Beverley, W Australia, and has issue living, Cameron (Beaming Hill, Gairdner River, W Australia), *b* 1952: *m* 1979, Kathryn Faye, da of Colin V. Ellis, of Violet Town, Victoria, and has issue living, Dale Cameron *b* 1982, Deanna Jane *b* 1981, Krystelle Amy *b* 1985, — Brent, *b* 1957: *m* 1984, Jillian Elizabeth, da of William E. Meier, of Toocelup, Bremer Bay, W Australia, and has issue living, Clay *b* 1988, Holly Elizabeth *b* 1985, — Leonie Gaye, *b* 1954: *m* 1977, Raymond John Ward, of Bridgetown, W Australia, and has issue living, Benjamin

Trevor *b* 1978, — Belinda Anne, *b* 1963: *m* 1987, Graham John Yuill (PO Box 8, Esperance, W Australia), and has issue living, Rhys Raymond *b* 1989, Kyra Corrine *b* 1990.
  Issue of late Alexander Forrest Barrett-Lennard, *b* 1895, *d* 1941: *m* 1917, Eva May, who *d* 1973, da of Edward Berry:—
Alexander Dacre (Belhus, Box 58, Beverley, W Aust), *b* 1921; F/Sgt RAAF: *m* 1949, Dorothea Ann, da of James Davidson Weaver, of Beverley, W Aust, and has issue living, Gregory Dacre, *b* 1958: *m* 1985, Margaret Louise, da of Alan J. Croft, of City Beach, W Aust, and has issue living, Jackson Dacre *b* 1988, Alix Louise *b* 1990, Rebecca Ann *b* 1992, — Susan, *b* 1950: *m* 1st, 1971, Kenneth Charles Baston; 2ndly, 1981, Phillip James Hill, of PO Box 225, Beverley, Western Australia 6304, and has issue living, (by 1st *m*) George Derek *b* 1974, Richard Charles *b* 1976, (by 2nd *m*) Guy Phillip *b* 1982, — Meredith, *b* 1953: *m* 1973, Philip Anthony Cockerill, of Geraldton, W Aust, and has issue living, Benjamin Dacre *b* 1976, Joseph Anthony *b* 1978, Samuel Charles *b* 1980, Zachary Philip *b* 1984, — Vicki, *b* 1955. —— Peggy Amy, *b* 1918: *m* 1946, Durward Toleman, who *d* 1981, and has issue living, David Forrest, *b* 1952: *ed* Univ of Melbourne (BSc (Hons), BCom), — Michael Fiennes, *b* 1955: *m* 1985, Suzanne Joy, da of Bruce Herbert Whitaker, of Donvale, Victoria, and has issue living, Kate Suzanne *b* 1986, Penny Nicole *b* 1988. *Residence* – 208 Mahoney's Rd, Burwood East, 3151, Victoria, Aust.

      Grandchildren of George Hardey Barrett-Lennard, eldest son of late Edward Graham Barrett-Lennard,
      eldest son of late Edward Pomeroy, 5th son of 1st baronet:—
  Issue of late George Graham Barrett-Lennard, *b* 1887, *d* 1968: *m* 1911, Maud Gladys Hastings, da of G. W. Hester, of Dalgarup Park, Bridgetown, W Aust:—
Fynes (St Leonards, Kondut, W Aust), *b* 1915: *m* 1949, Florence Ray, da of W. C. Williams, of Nedlands, W Aust, and has issue living, Kingsley Ian Michael, *b* 1954, — William Ashley Dacre, *b* 1957, — Wendy Roslyn, *b* 1950: *m* 1972, Ralph Dunstan Pomery, of, and has issue living, Sharon Anne *b* 1974, Michelle Louise *b* 1977, — Helen Elizabeth, *b* 1951: *m* 1974, Kimberley John Clifton. —— Douglas Graham (The Crescent, Gingin, W Aust), *b* 1916: *m* 1943, Olive Davidson, and has issue living, David Thomas, *b* 1945 (Belhus, Upper Swan, W Aust), — Joan, *b* 1946: *m* 1970, Keith McMullan, of Caprice Rd, Geraldton, W Aust, — Kaye Julie, *b* 1959. —— Lancelot (Averley Downs, Kondut, W Aust), *b* 1918; MB and BS Adelaide: *m* 1945, Patricia Ida, da of J. Porter, of Northam, W Aust, and has issue living, Michael Scott, *b* 1949, — *Rev* Richard John Stirling (16 Bellairs Road, Kardinya, W Aust) *b* 1951: BA (Hons), MA (Oxon), PhD: *m* 1st 1973 (*m diss* 1990), Rosalind, da of late Robert Willis; 2ndly, 1990, Julie Louise, da of Leslie Gibson, and has issue living (by 1st *m*), David John *b* 1978, Jeremy Robert *b* 1981, — Simon Hugh *b* 1957, — Patricia Ruth, *b* 1947: *m* 1972, Richard Stevenson, — Kathleen Ann, *b* 1954. —— Godfrey Trevor, *b* 1926; *ed* Perth Univ, W Aust (BSc, BA and at Chicago Univ) (Dr in Psychology 1959); Prof in Psychology, Univ of Waterloo, Ont: *m* 1948, Helen, da of William Love, of 40 Harvey St, Mosman Park, W Aust, and has issue living, John Graham, *b* 1953, — Lance Godfrey, *b* 1955, — Sirri Anne, *b* 1960, — Katherine Gail, *b* (twin) 1960, — Judith Helen, *b* 1966. —— Irwin Prescott (St Leonards, Kondut, W Australia), *b* 1929; *ed* W Australia Univ (BSc Agriculture, MSc): *m* 1953, Berwine Ruth, da of Dr Leigh Cook, of Stirling Highway Claremont, W Australia, and has issue living, Edward Graham, *b* 1953, — Hugh Anthony, *b* 1955, — James Irwin, *b* 1961, — Ann Mary, *b* 1958. —— Hester, *b* 1913: *m* (Feb) 1937, Hubert Leake Shields, of Glenvar, Wongan Hills, W Aust 6603, and has issue living, Graham Michael, *b* 1946: *m* 1969, Lynette, da of John Gale, of Yelbeni, W Aust, and has issue living, Michael Graham *b* 1973, Marnie Jane *b* 1974, Kellie Anne *b* 1977, — Peter William Hubert, *b* 1950: *m* 1980, Mary Charm, da of Frederick Hamilton, of Moora, W Aust, and has issue living, William Hubert *b* 1984, Stuart Frederick *b* 1986, Philippa Robin *b* 1981, — Anthony Hubert, *b* 1955, — Robin Wendy, *b* (Dec) 1937: *m* 1961, Dr Roy Montague Green MSc (17 Piridari Rd, City Beach, W Aust) and has issue living, Julie Anne *b* 1964, Cathy Susan *b* 1965, — Waverley Hester, *b* 1939: *m* 1970, Robin Ladyman, of Katanning, W Aust, and has issue living, Lara *b* 1972, Tanya *b* 1974, — Christine Mary, *b* 1944: *m* 1967, Robert Weise, of Highbury 6313, W Aust, and has issue living, Michael William *b* 1969, Timothy *b* 1971, Anthony *b* 1973, — Elizabeth Ann, *b* 1953: *m* 1980, John Casey, of Auckland, NZ, and has issue living, Nicola Simone *b* 1985, Asha *b* 1987.
  Issue of late Trevor St Aubyn Barrett-Lennard, *b* 1889, *d* 1970: *m* 1st, 1912, Susan Mary, who *d* 1939, da of C. W. Ferguson, of Houghton, Swan, W Aust; 2ndly, 1942, Edith Mary, who *d* 1968, da of John Edward Wedge:—
(By 1st *m*) Ferguson (W Swan Rd, W Swan 6056, W Aust) *b* 1913. —— Donald (Houghton, Middle Swan, W Aust), *b* 1916: *m* 1940, his cousin, Dorothy, da of C. O. Ferguson (*see* Barrett-Lennard, Bt, colls, 1985 Edn), and has had issue, Bruce, *b* 1944, *d* 1950, — Brian, *b* 1952, — Flora, *b* 1947: *m* 1972, Lawrence Alec Smith, and has issue living, Kathryn Rachel *b* 1980. —— (By 2nd *m*) Barbara, *b* 1948: *m* 1968, Stuart William Green, of 25 Gloucester St, Victoria Park 6100, W Aust, and has issue living, Philip Edward Spencer, *b* 1968, — Julian St Aubyn, *b* 1973, — Rosemarie Catherine, *b* 1970. —— Elizabeth, *b* 1949: *m* 1968, Gregory Allan Harris, of 7 Rubida Court, Boronia 3155, Victoria, Australia, and has issue living, Trevor Allan, *b* 1968, — Daniel Raymond, *b* 1974.
  Issue of late St Aubyn Edward Barrett-Lennard, *b* 1899, *d* 1956: *m* 1933, Betty Corona, who *d* 1981, da of Edward Sidney Simpson, DSc, of Millpoint, South Perth, W Australia:—
Richard St Aubyn (Belhus Farm, Upper Swan, W Aust), *b* 1938: *m* 1965, Sandra, el da of Keith Irwin Bedford Smith, of Alfred Cove, W Aust, and has issue living, Nigel Dacre, *b* 1968, — Philip St Aubyn, *b* 1972, — Amy Wilson *b* 1966. —— John Dacre, *b* 1940: *m* 1970, Lynette Marie, el da of Robert Atkinson of W Perth, W Aust, and has issue living, Mark Robert, *b* 1970, — Timothy Stewart, *b* 1972, — Daniel Thomas John, *b* 1977, — Bethwyn Ruth, *b* 1975.

      Grandchildren of late St Aubyn Edward Barrett-Lennard (ante):—
  Issue of late George Simpson Barrett-Lennard, *b* 1934, *d* 1972: *m* 1961, Angela Clare (who *m* 2ndly, 1978, Rev Frank Bazely, of The Rectory, Yule Av, Middle Swan, W Aust 6056), da of Alfred Raymond Stevens, of W Swan, W Aust:—
David Anthony, *b* 1966: *m* 1993, Julieanne, da of Theodore Charles Fisher, of Lockridge, W Aust. —— Michael John, *b* 1972. —— Susan Fairlie, *b* 1963: *m* 1990, Phillip Stephen Hall, son of Ronald Alan Hall, of Red Hill, W Aust, and has issue living, Teresa Elisabeth, *b* 1992, — Kate Louise, *b* 1993.

      Grandchildren of late Edward Graham Barrett-Lennard (ante):—
  Issue of late Victor Dacre Barrett-Lennard, *b* 1874, *d* 1930: *m* 1906, Blanche Isabel, who *d* 1958, da of Robert Allen:—
Lucille (57 Watkins Rd, Dalkeith, W Aust), *b* 1915: *m* 1940, John Hill Chellew, who *d* 1981, and has issue living, John Alexander, *b* 1949: *m* 1974, Penny, da of Malcolm Devine, of Melrose Station, Leonora, W Aust, and has issue living, Cameron John *b* 1977, Amanda Jane *b* 1981, — William Lennard, *b* 1951: *m* 1976, Billie Keiller, and has issue living, Duncan *b* 1985, Jacqui (twin) *b* 1985, — Mary Diane, *b* 1941: *m* 1965, John Kingsley Baldock, of Wattle Grove, W Aust, and has issue living, Jeremy John *b* 1971, Catherine Jane *b* 1968, Judith Mary *b* 1971, — Margaret Anne, *b* 1947: *m* 1969, Andrew Henry Skreiner, and has issue living, Hugh Michael *b* 1976, Anna Nadine *b* 1973, — Elizabeth Jill, *b* 1953: *m* 1st, 1977, David Arthur Cannon; 2ndly, 1982, Dr Henly Harrison, and has issue living, (by 2nd *m*) Amy Elizabeth *b* 1982.

      Grandsons of late Victor Dacre Barrett-Lennard (ante):—
  Issue of late Dacre Barrett-Lennard, *b* 1906, *d* 1961: *m* 1943, Maisie, da of J. Vile, of Aubury, NSW:—
John Dacre (Mobedine, York, W Aust), *b* 1944: *m* 1972, Margaret, da of Peter Lee, of Cottesloe, W Aust, and has issue living, Dacre, *b* 1974, — Peter John, *b* 1977, — Elizabeth May, *b* 1982.
  Issue of late Ernest Stuart Barrett-Lennard, *b* 1910, *d* 1980: *m* 1939, Lorraine, da of Allen Mair, of Swanbourne, W Aust:—
Robert Allen, *b* 1941: *m* 1965, Judith Anne, da of Horace Joseph Stone, of Merredin, W Aust, and has issue living, Clare Lois, *b* 1967, — Melissa, *b* 1969. —— Sandra Lorraine, *b* 1942: *m* 1966, Geoffrey Wackett, of Quairading, W Aust, and has issue living, Andrew, *b* 1968. —— Jennifer Jill, *b* 1947.

Granddaughter of late Arthur St Aubyn Barrett-Lennard (infra):—
    Issue of late Arthur Viveash Barrett-Lennard, *b* 1910, *d* 1983: *m* 1952, Joan (Toodyay Rd, Gidgegannup, W Aust), da of Frederick Short, of Claremont, W Aust:—
Jane Margaret, *b* 1953: *m* 1973, Bernard Drag, of Cirencester, Glos, and has issue living, Timothy Viveash, *b* 1979, — Heather Rosalie, *b* 1976.

Grandchildren of late Edward Graham Barrett-Lennard (ante):—
    Issue of late Arthur St Aubyn Barrett-Lennard, *b* 1876, *d* 1953: *m* 1906, Fanny Susan, who *d* 1949, da of Samuel Henry Viveash:—
Frank St Aubyn (17 Martock Way, Karrinyup, W Aust 6018), *b* 1912: *m* 1942, Constance Rosalie, da of the Ven Archdeacon L. W. Parry, of Perth, W Aust, and has issue living, Rosalie Susan (8 Bent Street, City Beach, 6015, W Aust), *b* 1945: *m* 1st, 1966, Ian Maxwell Greenham, who *d* 1988; 2ndly, 1991, Kim Sears, and has issue living (by 1st *m*), Anthony Ian St Aubyn *b* 1970, Deborah Susan *b* 1968, — Marian Ruth, *b* 1947: *m* 1977, S/Ldr Roger Ashton Clark, RAAF, and has issue living, Paul Robert *b* 1980, Nicholas James *b* 1982, — Constance Anne, *b* 1951: *m* 1972, Neil Bates, — Jennifer Robyn, *b* 1954: *m* 1978, Bryce Edward Hayes-Thompson, of Doodlakine, W Australia, and has issue living, Owen Bryce *b* 1980, David Frank *b* 1983, Ruth Verna *b* 1985. —— Edward Guy (Nundah, Northam, W Aust; 7 Albert St, S Perth, W Aust), *b* 1919: *m* 1960, Dymity Ann, da of V. W. Shotter, of Perth, W Aust, and has issue living, Edward William, *b* 1967, — Guy St Aubyn, *b* 1969, — Lindal Dymity, *b* 1963: *m* 1988, Herbert Dennis Wessels, of Bannister Springs, Boddington, W Aust.
    Issue of late John Evelyn Barrett-Lennard, *b* 1881, *d* 1967: *m* 1911, Frances Amy, who *d* 1954, da of Edward Kay Courthope, of Perth, W Australia:—
Frances Josephine (9 Alexander Rd, Dalkeith, W Australia 6009), *b* 1913: *m* 1940, Geoffrey Howard Gwynne, who *d* 1984, and has issue living, John Howard, *b* 1946; *ed* W Aust Univ (BSc): *m* 1969, Deborah Judith, da of A. B. Walton, of Perth, W Aust, and has issue living, Christopher *b* 1976, Belinda Judith *b* 1972, Katherine Anne *b* 1969, — Geraldine Frances, *b* 1941: *m* 1967, Jens Dalhoff Jorgensen, of Aalborg, Denmark, and has issue living, Michael Dalhoff *b* 1971, Frances Dalhoff *b* 1968: *m* 1990, Scott Leary, Pia Dalhoff *b* 1982, — Angela Madeline, *b* 1953. —— Judith (Unit 23, 31 Williams Rd, Nedlands, W Australia), *b* 1914: *m* 1941, Ashburton Hall Clark, who *d* 1975, and has issue living, John Jeremy, *b* 1941: *m* 1969, Geraldine Lesley, da of L. J. Locke, of Perth, W Aust, and has issue living, Anthony Phillip *b* 1974, Catherine Rosanne, *b* 1971, — Frances Louise, *b* 1946: *m* 1941, Trevor William Tyson, of 101 Townshend Rd, Subiaco, W Aust, and has issue living, Dale Lee *b* 1982. —— Anne (Kerralong, Arthur River, 6315, W Aust), *b* 1916: *m* 1946, Edward Alexander Glyn Watkins, who *d* 1985, and has issue living, Jonathan George Glyn, *b* 1948: *m* 1986, Rhonda Evelyn, da of Thomas Benton, and has issue living, Isaac Thomas Edward *b* 1987, — Daniel Glyn, *b* 1955: *m* 1986, Frances Anne, da of Eugene Patrick O'Callaghan, of Perth, W Aust, and has issue living, Chauncy Patrick *b* 1990, Hamish Eugene *b* 1993, Bridget Glyn *b* 1987, — Miranda Glyn, *b* 1952: *m* 1977, Andrew Forte, and has issue living, Woodrow Andrew *b* 1983, Georgina Amy *b* 1979. —— Prudence, *b* 1918: *m* 1946, Frank Ernest Heymanson, of 13 Vix St, Nedlands, W Aust, and has issue living, John Simon, *b* 1953: *m* 1st, 1975, Jane Carruthers; 2ndly, 1990, Concetta Caratazzolo, and has issue living (by 1st *m*), Jonathan Simon *b* 1980, Kate Louise *b* 1977 (by 2nd *m*) Antonina *b* 1994, — Janet Louise, *b* 1947: *m* 1976, Patrick John Nodwell, and has issue living, Joanne Helen *b* 1977, Emma Louise *b* 1979, Shelly Prudence *b* 1983, — Jennifer Anne, *b* 1950: *m* 19—, Jack McAdam, and has issue living, Samson Roscoe *b* 1976, Luke *b* 1986.

Grandchildren (by 1st *m*) of late William Barrett-Lennard (infra):—
    Issue of late Walter James Barrett-Lennard, *b* 1883, *d* 1954: *m* 1904, Mary, who *d* 1967, da of late James Lawther, of Russell, Manitoba:—
Walter James (5991 Selkirk St, Vancouver, BC, Canada), *b* 1914: *m* 1947, Beatrice Elizabeth, da of Dr C. T. Crowdy, of Montreal, Canada, and has issue living, James Thomas, *b* 1956, — Elizabeth Jane, *b* 1949, — Deborah Dacre, *b* 1949, — Naomi Barbara, *b* 1952. —— Margaret, *b* 1911: *m* 1936, Col Donald Spankie, OBE, Canadian Inf. *Residence* –
    Issue of late Hardinge Barrett-Lennard, *b* 1890, *d* 1959: *m* 1st, 1922, Annie, da of Harry Wyles, of Victoria, BC; 2ndly, 1930, Leontine Leffler, who *d* 1975, of New York City:—
(By 2nd *m*) Joan, *b* 1933: *m* 1955, Roy Hubbard, of 196-15, 89th Av, Hollis, NY 11423, USA. —— Mildred, *b* 1935: *m* 1957, Eli Friedman, of 1049 E 17th St, Brooklyn, NY 11230, USA.

Grandchildren of late Walter James Barrett-Lennard, 8th son of 1st baronet:—
    Issue of late William Barrett-Lennard, *b* 1857, *d* 19-: *m* 1st, 1880, Margaret, who *d* 1890, da of Capt Boswell, of Peterborough, Ontario; 2ndly, 1892, Laura Sophia, who *d* 1910, da of Thomas Garnier Johnson, of The Oaklands, Biuscarth, Manitoba, Canada:—
(By 2nd *m*) William Louis, MC, *b* 1893; formerly Lt Canadian Inf; European War 1915-18 (wounded, MC): *m* 1920, Agnes Mildred, da of late Nathanial Dowsett, of Lethbridge, Alberta, Canada. —— Charles, *b* 1895; European War 1914-18 with Canadian Inf, and in RAF: *m* 19-, Florence Sylvia Shafer, of Vancouver, British Columbia. —— Mabel Sophia: *m* 1918, Brigadier Arthur Harry Langham Godfrey, DSO, MC, Australian Mil Forces, who was *ka* 1942, and has issue living, John Elliott, *b* 1919; is in Australian Mil Forces: *m* 19-, Patricia, only da of Air Commodore Owen (Washington) de Putron, CBE, — Edward Arthur, *b* 1921, — Charles Lovett, *b* 1924, — Mildred Isabel, *b* 1922. *Residence* –

Grandchildren of late Lt-Col John Barrett-Lennard, CBE, 3rd son of Walter James Barrett-Lennard, 8th son of 1st baronet:—
    Issue of late Rev Dacre Fiennes Barrett-Lennard, *b* 1888, *d* 1975: *m* 1st, 1910, Charlotte Dorothy Evelyn, who *d* 1937, da of late Rev Henry Chichele Hart Bampton (E Albemarle, colls); 2ndly, 1940, Irene Phyllis, who *d* 1986, da of Mark Moss, of Rook Hall, Cressing:—
(By 1st *m*) Richard Dacre (13 Collingham Rd, SW5), *b* 1921. —— Michael Henry (12 Chisholm Court, St Peters Road, W6), *b* 1923. —— John Fiennes (97 St Michael's Av, Guildford, Surrey), *b* 1926: *m* 1984, Monica Anne, da of late Henry John Wood. —— Rachel Margaret (26 Grange Av, New Duston, Northampton NN5 6SR), *b* 1928: *m* 1950, Maurice Harry Dickenson, who *d* 1993, and has issue living, Trevor David, *b* 1955. —— (By 2nd *m*) Philip Francis Dacre (Six Mile House, Acle Rd, Great Yarmouth, Norfolk NR30 1TH), *b* 1947: *m* 1986, Josephine Albertina Elizabeth, da of late Joseph Albert Colchester.

Grandchildren of late Villiers Barrett-Lennard (infra):—
    Issue of late Richard Barrett-Lennard, *b* 1892, *d* 1967: *m* 1917, Kathleen, who *d* 1988, da of Alfred Blake, of Duxmere, Ross-on-Wye:—
Robert Villiers, *b* 1924. —— June Rosemary (85 Compton Place, Carpenders Park, Herts), *b* 1922.

Granddaughter of Walter James Barrett-Lennard (ante):—
    Issue of late Villiers Barrett-Lennard, *b* 1865, *d* 1903: *m* 1885, Laura, who *d* 1954, da of late George Clement, of Nottingham:—
Dorothy Mabel, *b* 1890: *m* 1914, John Hugh Cecil Murray; 2ndly, 1931, Percival Robert Hopkins, who *d* 1956, and has issue living, (by 1st *m*) John Keith Lennard, *b* 1916: *m* 1939, Evelyn Dawn, da of late Col E. V. Anderson, and has issue living, Evelyn Anne *b* 1944. *Residence* – .
The 1st baronet, Sir Thomas, of Belhus, Essex (natural son and testamentary heir of Thomas Barrett-Lennard, 17th Lord Dacre), was MP for S Essex, and the 2nd, Sir Thomas, was High Sheriff of co Monaghan 1868.

LEON (UK) 1911, of Bletchley Park, Bletchley, Buckinghamshire

Sir JOHN RONALD LEON, 4th *Baronet*; *b* 16 Aug 1934; *s* his father, *Sir* RONALD GEORGE, 1964; *ed* Eton, Millfield, and Byam Shaw Sch of Art; late 2nd Lt King's Roy Rifle Corps; actor (as John Standing) *m* 1st, 1961 (*m diss* 1972), Jill, da of Jack Melford, actor; 2ndly, 1984, Sarah Kate, da of Bryan John Forbes, the film dir, and has issue by 1st and 2nd *m*.

Arms – Gules: two sunflowers erect, slipped, leaved, and eradicated or, seeded sable. **Crest** – Issuant out of a mural crown or, a demi-lion gules supporting between the paws a sunflower erect, slipped and leaved gold, seeded sable. *Residence* – 10632 Ashton Av, Westwood, Los Angeles, California, USA.

SON LIVING *(By 1st marriage)*

ALEXANDER JOHN, *b* 3 May 1965; *ed* Bryanston.

(by 2nd marriage)

Archie, *b* 1986.

DAUGHTERS LIVING *(By 2nd marriage)*

India, *b* 1985. —— Octavia, *b* 1989.

BROTHER LIVING

Timothy Michael George (26 Benbow Rd, W6; Fermor House, Somerton, Oxon), *b* 1938; *ed* Stowe; late Sub-Lt RNVR: *m* 1969, Suzanne, da of Col H. Kinnear, JP, late KOYLI.

COLLATERAL BRANCH LIVING

Grandson of late Reginald Herbert Leon, 2nd son of 1st baronet:—
Issue of late Richard Neville Leon, *b* 1909, *d* 1981: *m* 1941, Margery Frances, who *d* 1991, only da of Sir William Henry Robinson, KCMG, CBE:—
David Richard, *b* 1946: *m* 1970, Maria Amelia da Conceicao, only da of Domingos Jacinto, of Lisbon, and has issue living, Daniel James, *b* 1976, — Jennifer Rachel, *b* 1972. *Residence* – Benton Cottage, Peters Green, Bodiam, E Sussex TN32 5UN.
The 1st baronet, Sir Herbert Samuel Leon (High Sheriff of Bucks 1909), sat as MP for Bucks N, or Buckingham, Div (*L*) 1891-5. Sir Ronald George Leon, 3rd Bt, *b* 1902, Memb London Stock Exchange: *m* 1st, 1924, Rosemary Armstrong; 2ndly, 1932 (*m diss* 1945), Dorothy Katherine (Kay Hammond, the actress, who *d* 1980, having *m* 2ndly, 1946, Sir John Selby Clements, CBE, actor and dir, who *d* 1988), da of Sir Guy Standing, KBE; 3rdly, 1947, Alice Mary Holt.

LESLIE (NS) 1625, of Wardis and Findrassie, Morayshire (Dormant 1967)

Sir (HENRY JOHN) LINDORES LESLIE, 9th *Baronet*, *d* 1967, and at the time of going to press no name appears on the Official Roll of Baronets in respect of this title.

DAUGHTER LIVING OF NINTH BARONET

Elizabeth Jean (*Lady Hyde Parker*) *b* 1952: *m* 1972, Sir Richard William Hyde Parker, 12th Bt, of Melford Hall, Long Melford, Suffolk, and has issue (*see* Parker, Bt, cr 1681).

DAUGHTER LIVING OF EIGHTH BARONET

Nancy Jean, *b* 1923: *m* 1946, Col (William Henry) Gerard Leigh, CVO, CBE, Life Gds, and has issue living, John Norman Gerard (The Old Rectory, Doynton, Bristol), *b* 1949; *ed* Eton: *m* 1977, Lavinia Sheila, da of Leopold (Leo) Richard Seymour (*see* M Hertford, colls) and has issue living, Louisa Helen *b* 1980, Emily Rose *b* 1982, Laura Katherine *b* 1984, — David William Philip (16 Ormeley Rd, SW12 9QE), *b* 1958: *m* 1990, Julie S., eldest da of H. A. Rall, of Forrest Town, Johannesburg, S Africa, and has issue living, James Henry *b* 1991, Jessica Rose *b* 1993, — Carolyn Jane Gerard, *b* 1947: *m* 1977, as his 2nd wife, Charles Edward Riou Benson, of 7 Trevor Sq, SW7, and has issue living, Honor May *b* 1980, — Camilla Madelaine Gerard *b* 1952: *m* 1979, as his 2nd wife, Hugh Leopold Seymour, elder son of Leopold (Leo) Richard Seymour, and has issue (*see* M Hertford, colls). *Residences* – 15 Eaton Mansions, Cliveden Place, SW1; Hayes, East Woodhay, Newbury, Berks RG15 0AN.

WIDOW LIVING OF NINTH BARONET

COLETTE KATHLEEN (RUSSEL-WALLING), (*Lady Leslie*) (Otten Hall, Belchamp Otten, Sudbury, Suffolk), da of late Dr George Theodore Cregan, MC, Croix de Guerre, of 57 Sloane St, SW1: *m* 1950, Capt Sir (Henry John) Lindores Leslie, 9th Bt, who *d* 1967.

COLLATERAL BRANCHES LIVING

Grandchildren of late John Leslie, el son of late Thomas Leslie, 3rd son of 4th baronet:—
Issue of late Frank Harvey Leslie, *b* 1874, *d* 1965: *m* 1st, 1915, Amelia Caroline, who *d* 1918, da of Alexander Russon; 2ndly, 1918, Agnes Maude, who *d* 1948, da of Frank Spooner:—
(By 1st *m*) (PERCY) THEODORE, *b* 19 Nov 1915; presumed heir to Baronetcy.

(In remainder)

Descendants of George Leslie of Crichie, uncle of 1st baronet (*see* Leslie, Bt, *cr* 1876).
This family is descended from the ancient family of Leslie of Balquhain, who are also ancestors of the Counts Leslie of the
Holy Roman Empire. The lands of Balquhain in 1340 were erected into a barony by Charter from David II. Sir Andrew
Leslie, 3rd Baron of Balquhain, was Master of the Horse in the Royal Army at Harlaw, 1411. Sir John Leslie, 1st Bt of
Wardis was created a Baronet in 1625 with remainder to his heirs male whatsoever. On the death of the 2nd baronet the
baronetcy reverted to his uncle, William, 2nd son of John Leslie, of Wardis, father of the 1st baronet, but he declined to
assume the title as the Wardis estates did not accompany it. His four sons, all died without issue. The baronetcy remained
dormant for many years, until it was assumed (without service of heirship) by John Leslie, who was 4th in descent from
Norman, next brother of 3rd Bt. The Baronets of Glaslough, co Monaghan *cr* (UK) 1876, are therefore in remainder.

LESLIE (UK) 1876, of Glaslough, co Monaghan

GRIP FAST

Sir JOHN NORMAN IDE LESLIE, 4th *Baronet*; *b* 6 Dec 1916; *s* his father,
Sir (JOHN RANDOLPH) SHANE, 1971; *ed* Downside, and Magdalene
Coll, Camb (BA); Capt Irish Gds, Knt of Honour and Devotion
Sovereign Mil order of Malta, and Knt Cdr Order of St Gregory the
Great; 1939-45 War (prisoner).

Arms – Quarterly, 1st and 4th argent, on a bend azure between two holly leaves
vert, three buckles or; 2nd and 3rd or, a lion rampant gules, debruised by a
ribbon sable. **Crest** – A griffin's head erased gules.
Residence – Glaslough, co Moneghan. *Clubs* – Travellers', Circolo della Caccia
(Rome).

BROTHER LIVING

DESMOND PETER ARTHUR (Castle Leslie, Glaslough, co Monaghan), *b* 29 June
1921; *ed* Ampleforth, and Trin Coll, Dublin; Composer, Author, Film Producer,
and Discologist; late Fl Sgt Pilot RAF: *m* 1st, 1945, Agnes, only da of Rudolph
Bernauer, of Budapest, Hungary; 2ndly, 1970, Helen Jennifer, da of late Lt-Col
E. I. E. Strong, of Tor House, Wiveliscombe, Som, and has issue living (by 1st
m), Shaun Rudolph Christopher, *b* 1947, — Christopher Mark, *b* 1952: *m* 1982,
Cliona Manahan, and has issue living, Luke Daniel *b* 1987, Leah *b* 1992, —
Antonia Kelvey, *b* 1963, — (by 2nd *m*) Samantha Helen, *b* 1966, — Camilla
Patricia, *b* 1968.

COLLATERAL BRANCHES LIVING

Issue of late William Seymour Leslie, 3rd son of 2nd baronet,
b 1889, *d* 1979: *m* 1929, Gwenyth Rawdon (Castle Leslie
(West), Glaslough, co Monaghan), da of Rawdon Roden:—
Jennifer Constance, *b* 1930. *Residence* – Castle Leslie (West), Glaslough, co Monaghan.

Issue of late Capt Lionel Alister David Leslie, sculptor, author and explorer, 4th and yst son of 2nd
baronet, *b* 1900, *d* 1987: *m* 1942, Barbara Yvonne, da of Edwin Alexander Enever:—
Leonie Deirdrie Elise, *b* 1944: *ed* Trin Coll, Dublin (BA 1967): *m* 1975, Luiz Monteiro de Barros, of Rio de Janeiro, and has
issue living, Leo Alexander, *b* 1976, — Jaime Norman Jerome, *b* 1977. *Residence* – 38 Bloemfontein Av, W12 4BL.

John Leslie, DD, Bishop of the Isles, Scotland, translated to Raphoe, Ireland 1633, and Clogher 1661, was the first of this
family to possess Castle Leslie or Glaslough. He was son of George Leslie of Crichie, 2nd son of Walter Leslie of Wardis
(*see* E Rothes) and uncle of 1st Bt (*cr* NS 1625), to which baronetcy his line is in remainder. Sir John Leslie, 1st baronet,
sometime Capt 1st Life, was MP for co Monaghan and a noted painter. The 2nd baronet, Sir John, CBE, was Lt Grenadier
Guards and Lt-Col Roy Irish Fusiliers, and served in Egypt 1882, in S Africa 1900, and in 1914-18 War (CBE). Sir John, who
was the last Lord Lieut and Custos Rotulorum co Monaghan, *m* 1884, Leonie Blanche, da of Leonard Jerome, of New York
(grandfather of Sir Winston Churchill). The 3rd baronet was the writer Sir (John Randolph) Shane Leslie, and his da, Anita
Leslie, was also a distinguished writer.

LETHBRIDGE (UK) 1804, of Westaway House, and Winkley Court, Somerset

TRUTH

SPES · MEA · IN · DEO

My hope is in God

Sir THOMAS PERIAM HECTOR NOEL LETHBRIDGE, 7th *Baronet*; *b* 17 July 1950; *s* his father, *Sir* HECTOR WROTH, 1978; *ed* Milton Abbey, and RAC Cirencester: *m* 1976, Susan Elizabeth, el da of Lyle Rocke, of Maryland, USA, and has issue.

Arms – Argent, over water proper, a bridge of five arches embattled gules, and over the centre arch a turret, in chief an eagle displayed sable charged on the breast with a bezant. Crest – From a bridge embattled of one arch gules a demi-eagle displayed sable, wings erminois charged on the breast with a leopard's face or. Motto over Crest – "*Truth*".
Residence – Honeymead, Simonsbath, Minehead, Som. *Clubs* – Farmers', Turf.

SONS LIVING

JOHN FRANCIS BUCKLER NOEL, *b* 10 March 1977. —— Edward Christopher Wroth, *b* 1978. —— Alexander Ralph Periam, *b* 1982. —— Henry Charles Hesketh, *b* 1984.

DAUGHTERS LIVING

Georgina Rose Alianore, *b* 1980. —— Rachel Elizabeth Mary, *b* 1986.

SISTER LIVING

Mary Jacintha, *b* 1948: *m* 1974, Brig Richard J. Heywood, OBE, Coldm Gds, of Manor Farm Stables, Ingoldisthorpe, King's Lynn, Norfolk, and has issue living, Richard Anthony, *b* 1977, — Anna Rose, *b* 1975.

WIDOW LIVING OF SIXTH BARONET

EVELYN DIANA (*Baroness Nugent*) da of late Lt-Col Francis Arthur Gerard Noel, OBE (*see* E Gainsborough, colls), and widow of Maj John Vivian Bailey, Roy Scots Fus: *m* 2ndly, 1946, Sir Hector Wroth Lethbridge, 6th Bt, who *d* 1978; 3rdly, 1979, as his 3rd wife, David James Douglas Nugent, Baron Nugent (*see* E Westmeath, colls), who *d* 1988.

COLLATERAL BRANCHES LIVING

Issue of late Hugh Francis Hesketh Lethbridge, 4th son of 4th baronet, *b* 1867, *d* 1935: *m* 1912, Edith Maude, da of Thomas Mellor Robinson, of Metford, Natal:—
Hugh Mytton Fitzwarine, *b* 1913: *m* 1945, Elsie Murray, da of late Very Rev Dean Bartlet, of Aberdeen, and has issue living, Hugh George, *b* 1948, — Jennifer Murray, *b* 1946. —— Wroth Thomas Hesketh Bourchier, *b* 1914. —— Delphine Edith Conyers Bourchier, *b* 1922.

Grandchildren of late John Acland Musgrave Lethbridge (infra):—
Issue of late Duncan John Leghe Lethbridge, *b* 1898, *d* 1962: *m* 1922, Phyllis Muriel (ANDERSON), who *d* 1971, da of T. Stanley Chappell, of Chadshunt, Warwicks:—
June Florence, *b* 1926: *m* 1944, Mario A. Fog, of 217A Lucy Creek Drive, Beaufort, S Carolina 29902, USA, and has issue living, Duncan Lethbridge, *b* 1948: *m* 1989, Sarah McLane, — Stephen Chase, *b* 1952: *m* 1979, Wendy Merritt Dixon, and has issue living, Merritt Lawrence *b* 1981, Courtnay Andrews *b* 1984. —— Ann, *b* 1930: *m* 1951, Graham Lusk Platt, of 40 Walnut Tree Lane, Cold Spring Harbor, Long Island, New York 11724, USA, and has issue living, Graham Leghe, *b* 1959; has issue living, Jeremy Redding Knox *b* 1983, — Gordon Lethbridge, *b* 1962: *m* 1993, Mary M. Walsh, — Christina May, *b* 1956: *m* 19—, Michael J. Nelson, and has issue living, Adrien Leghe *b* 1979, Lindsay Ann *b* 1981, Louisa May *b* 1985, Sandi Grey *b* 1989.
Issue of late Harold Reginald Lethbridge, *b* 1901, *d* 1972: *m* 1942, Shirley Ivy Grace (LIDSTONE), da of William Mascall, of Cambridgeshire:—
Duncan Stuart (St Francis Bay, S Africa), *b* 1943: *m* 1969, Catherine Jean Beveridge, da of late John Sneddon, of Kinross, Scotland, and has issue living, Duncan Reginald John, *b* 1973, — Claire Cecilia, *b* 1975. —— Reginald Martin Peter, *b* 1946. —— Richard Christopher Noel, *b* 1949; *d* 1968.

Issue of late John Acland Musgrave Lethbridge, 5th son of 4th baronet, *b* 1869, *d* 1934: *m* 1894, Florence Martin, who *d* 1931, da of Sidney Wood Cooper, of New York, USA:—
Annie Gwendoline, *b* 1896: *m* 1st, 1916, Capt Guy Clavering Wetherall, formerly RASC; 2ndly, 1945, Capt Thorold Murray Smith, MC, and has issue living, (by 1st *m*) Robert Guy, *b* 1917, — Peter Martin, *b* 1919.

Grandchildren (by 3rd *m*) of late Capt Walter Miguel Lethbridge, MC (infra):—
Issue of late Walter Miguel Lethbridge, *b* 1923, *d* 1991: *m* 1st, 1949 (*m diss* 1968), Nora, da of Eduardo Barrios; 2ndly, 1957 (*m diss* 1982), Jill Margaret, da of late Robert Gibson Nethery, MRCS, LRCP, of 5 St Patrick's Court, Bath; 3rdly, 1982, Silvely (Calle Pedroza, Residencias Miami, Piso 6 Apt 20, La Florida, Caracas 1030, Venezuela), da of late Viktor Kalve Grandin, of Riga, Latvia:—
(By 1st *m*) Walter Alexander (100 rue St Honoré, 75001 Paris, France), *b* 1950: *m* 1st, 1971 (*m diss* 1988), Elsie, da of Guy Derozieres-Le comte, of Lille, France; 2ndly, 1988, Patricia Douglas, and has issue living, (by 1st *m*) Alexis Guillaume, *b* 1971, — Chloé, *b* 1980. —— (By 2nd *m*) Arabella Margaret, *b* 1962: *m* 1986, Charles Edward Budgett, 18 Mythern Meadow, Bradford-on-Avon, Wilts, son of Rev Preb Anthony Thomas Budgett, of Wellington, Som, and has issue living, Holly Katharine, *b* 1989, — Vanessa Margaret, *b* 1992.
Issue of late Rodney Thomas Lethbridge, *b* 1925, *d* 1978: *m* 1st, 1942 (*m diss* 1944), Sara, da of R. Miranda; 2ndly, 1949 (*m diss* 1955), Fedora, da of Ernesto Moya; 3rdly, 1956, Marcelle Goulet:—
(By 2nd *m*) Doris Elizabeth, *b* 1950. —— (By 3rd *m*) Rodney Thomas, *b* 1957. —— Michael Walter, *b* 1964. —— Suzanne Carmen, *b* 1962.

Grandchildren of late Capt Walter Alexander Charles Lethbridge (infra):—
Issue of late Walter Miguel Lethbridge, MC, *b* 1886, *d* 1964: *m* 1st (Jan) 1907 (*m diss* 19—), Anna Agnes, da of V. Gunter; 2ndly, 1913 (*m diss* 19—), Catherine Matilda, da of F. M. Marsh; 3rdly, 1919, Carmela, who *d* 1980, da of Miguel I. Aguilera:—

(By 1st *m*), Frances Rose, *b* (Nov) 1907. —— (By 3rd *m*) Douglas Nelson (84th St, No 240-Apt Z, Surfside 33141, Miami Beach, Fla, USA), *b* 1933: *m* 1st, 1954 (*m diss* 196-), Margaret, da of George Isnor; 2ndly, —; 3rdly, —; 4thly, —; 5thly, —; 6thly, 19— (*m diss* 19—), Maria Cecilia Urrutia, of Columbia; 7thly, —; 8thly, — and has issue living, (by 1st *m*) Michael, *b* 1955, — Maureen, *b* 1956, — (by later *m*) 2 children. —— Carmen Rosa, *b* 1927: *m* 1st, 1950 (*m diss* 19—), Luis F. Pineiro; 2ndly, 19—, — Menendes, of Lodlam Point, 6880 SW 44th St, Apt 204, Fla 33155, USA, and has issue living (by 1st *m*) Luis Felipe, *b* 1952, — Rose Marie, *b* 1959, — Katherine, *b* 1968.

Grandson of late Walter Buckler Lethbridge, 6th son of 3rd baronet:—
Issue (by 1st *m*) of late Capt Walter Alexander Charles Lethbridge, *b* 1865, *d* 1931: *m* 1st, 1885 (*m diss* in USA), Rosa Maria, da of Miguel del Monte, of Havana; 2ndly, 1902 (*m diss* 1922), Blanche, da of John Bingham, a Judge of the High Court, New York; 3rdly, 1922, Marie José Léona, yst da of late Josef Léon Mondron, of The Château des Hamendes, Charleroi, Belgium:—
John George Jules, *b* 1888; formerly in US Navy, and Fl Lt RAF; 1914-18 War: *m* 1917, Dorothy Josephine, da of Le Roy M. Taylor, of Washington, USA, and has issue living, John George, *b* 1917. — Robert Mortimer, *b* 1921.

Grandson of late Ambrose Yarburgh Lethbridge, el son of late Charles Lethbridge, el son of late Rev Thomas Prowse Lethbridge, 3rd son of 2nd baronet:—
Issue of late Thomas Charles Lethbridge, *b* 1901, *d* 1971: *m* 1st, 1924 (*m diss* 1943), Sylvia Frances, who *d* 1973, only child of Rev Arthur Gordon Robertson (Canon of Salisbury Cathedral), of Rowdens, Netherhampton, Salisbury; 2ndly, 1944, Mina Elizabeth, only da of Rev Matthew Graham Leadbitter, of The Rectory, Moretonhampstead, Devon:—
(By 1st *m*) Christopher John (South Farmhouse, Upton Lovell, Warminster, Wilts), *b* 1925; *ed* Wellington Coll, and St John's Coll, Camb.

Sir John Lethbridge, 1st Bt, was the only son of John Lethbridge, of Westaway House, Pilton, and *m* Dorothea, el da and co-heir of William Buckler, of Boreham, Wilts. The 2nd baronet, Sir Thomas Buckler, Lethbridge, sat as MP for Somersetshire 1806-12 and 1820-30.

LETT (UK) 1941, of Walmer, co Kent (Extinct 1964)

Sir HUGH LETT, KCVO, CBE, DCL, ScD, MB, FRCS, 1st and last *Baronet*.

DAUGHTERS LIVING OF FIRST BARONET

Sheila Buckston, *b* 1910: *m* 1946, Maj Gordon Appleford Lett, DSO, who *d* 1989, and has issue living, Hugh Brian Gordon, *b* 1949; Bar Inner Temple 1972: *m* 1979, Angela Susan Jaques, and has issue living, Julian Peter Hugh *b* 1984, Robin Jonathan Hugh *b* 1986, Toby Alexander Hugh *b* 1992, Stephanie Rachel Buckston *b* 1988, — Valerie Buckston, *b* 1947; LRAM. —— Joan Buckston, *b* 1918: *m* 1941, Hugh William Cochrane Bailie, MB, FRCS (Edin), late Capt RAMC, who *d* 1980, and has issue living, Hugh Richard Molyneux (Honeymead, 64 Raglan Road, Reigate, Surrey RH2 0HP), *b* 1950; FRICS, FRVA: *m* 1975, Susan Jane Rees, and has issue living, Hugh Alistair Cochrane *b* 1981, Catherine Anne *b* 1978, — Lyndon Lett, *b* 1942; MB, BCh, DO: *m* 1974, Richard Austen Bloxham, MB, BS, MRCP, of 7 Langston Av, Palmerston North, North Island, NZ, and has issue living, David Andrew *b* 1975, Helen Jane *b* 1977, Megan Louise *b* 1979, — Fiona Buckston, *b* 1944; MB BCh, FRCS (Edinburgh): *m* 1990, Michael Taylor, of 12 Chartwell Grove, Mapperley Plains, Nottingham NG3 5RD. *Residence* – 2A Orchard Drive, Tonbridge, Kent.

LEVER (UK) 1911, of Hans Crescent, Chelsea

By courage and faith

Sir (TRESHAM) CHRISTOPHER ARTHUR LINDSAY LEVER, 3rd *Baronet*, *b* 9 Jan 1932; *s* his father, *Sir* TRESHAM JOSEPH PHILIP, FRSL, 1975; *ed* Eton, and Trin Coll, Camb (MA); commn'd 17th/21st Lancers 1950; naturalist and author; FLS: *m* 1st, 1970 (*m diss* 1974), Susan Mary, da of late John Armytage Nicholson, of Enniscoe, Crossmolina, co Mayo, and Milestown, Dunboyne, co Meath; 2ndly, 1975, Linda Weightman McDowell, da of late James Jepson Goulden, of Tennessee, USA.

Arms – Quarterly 1st and 4th, tierce in pairle sable, gules and azure, three bear's heads one and two erased, muzzled or; 2nd and 3rd argent, a chevron invected ermines between two keys erect the wards to the dexter in chief sable, and an Esquire's helmet in base proper. **Crest** – 1st, in front of a rising moon proper, a cormorant sable; 2nd, a dexter arm embowed in armour, the hand proper holding a key in bend sinister, the wards upwards sable, and encircled above the elbow with a chaplet or roses argent, leaved vert.
Residence – Newell House, Winkfield, Berks SL4 4SE. *Club* – Boodle's.

WIDOW LIVING OF SECOND BARONET

(CLODAGH) PAMELA (*Pamela, Lady Lever*) (Lessudden, St Boswells, Roxburghshire), only child of late Lt-Col Hon Malcolm Bowes-Lyon, CBE (*see* E Strathmore, colls), and formerly wife of the late Lord Malcolm Avondale Douglas-Hamilton, OBE, DFC (D Hamilton): *m* 1962, as his 2nd wife, Sir Tresham Joseph Philip Lever, FRSL, 2nd Bt, who *d* 1975.

Sir Arthur, 1st Bt, a JP for Essex, was a yr brother of Sir Maurice Levy, 1st Bt (*cr* 1913), of Great Glen House, co Leicester, and son of late Joseph Levy, of Leicester; he was a member of Roy Commn on Coast Erosion, and sat as MP for Harwich (*L*) 1906-10, and Hackney, Central (NL) 1922-23; assumed by deed poll 1896 and by Roy licence 1911 the additional surname of Lever; Sir Tresham Joseph Philip, 2nd Bt, was author of various historical works including *The Life and Times of Sir Robert Peel*, *The House of Pitt*, and *The Herberts of Wilton*.

LEVINGE (I) 1704, of High Park, Westmeath

No footsteps backwards

Sir RICHARD GEORGE ROBIN LEVINGE, 12th *Baronet*; *b* 18 Dec 1946; *s* his father, Major *Sir* RICHARD VERE HENRY, MBE, TD, 1984; *m* 1st, 1969 (*m diss* 1978), Hilary Jane, da of Dr Derek Mark, of Wingfield, Bray, co Wicklow; 2ndly, 1978, Donna Maria Isabella d'Ardia Caracciolo, yr da of HE late Prince Ferdinando d'Ardia Caracciolo dei Principi di Cursi, of Haddington Rd, Dublin 4, and has issue by 1st and 2nd *m*.

Arms – Vert, a chevron or, three escallops argent in chief. **Crest** – An escallop argent, within a garland proper.
Residences – Clohamon House, Bunclody, co Wexford, Republic of Ireland.

SONS LIVING *(By 1st marriage)*

RICHARD MARK, *b* 1970.

(By 2nd marriage)

Robin Edward, *b* 1978.

DAUGHTER LIVING *(By 2nd marriage)*

Melissa Louise, *b* 1980.

BROTHER LIVING

Michael James, *b* 1948. *Residence* – 2 Vicarage Crescent, Hatfield Peverel, Chelmsford, Essex.

SISTERS LIVING

Elizabeth Anne, *b* 1937: *m* 1957, Walter Wright Lee, Jr, only son of Walter Wright Lee, of 145 East 35th St, New York. —— Susan Maureen, *b* 1944: *m* 1965, Douglas P.W. Wright, yr son of late Rev E.H. Wright. —— Mary Irene, *b* 1952: *m* 1976, Charles Philip Cooper, of Markree Castle, Collooney, co Sligo, yst son of late Lt-Cmdr Edward Francis Patrick Cooper, of Markree Castle, co Sligo.

MOTHER LIVING

BARBARA MARY, 2nd da of George Jardine Kidston, CMG, of Hazelbury Manor, Box, Wilts: *m* 1935 (*m diss* 1976), as his 1st wife, Sir Richard Vere Henry Levinge, 11th Bt, MBE, TD, who *d* 1984. *Residence* – Garden House, Markree Castle, Collooney, co Sligo.

WIDOW LIVING OF ELEVENTH BARONET

JANE ROSEMARY (*Jane, Lady Levinge*), da of John Thomas Stacey, of East Dereham, Norfolk, and formerly wife of Dennis Millward: *m* 1976, as his 2nd wife, Sir Richard Vere Henry Levinge, 11th Bt, MBE, TD, who *d* 1984. *Residence* – Abbey Lodge, Rectory Lane, Itchen Abbas, Hants.

COLLATERAL BRANCHES LIVING

Grandchildren of late Maj Thomas Vere Levinge (infra):—
Issue of late William James Levinge, *b* 1929, *d* 1987: *m* 1954, Heather Mary Johnson (41 Bridge Rd, Welwyn Garden City, Herts), of Brackley, Northants:—
Nicholas Vere, *b* 1955: *m* 1983, Kathryn Bampton, and has issue living, Thomas John, *b* 1986. —— Edward James, *b* 1957: *m* 1984, Sandra Ann Dunne, and has issue living, Andrew William, *b* 1992, — Joanna Louise, *b* 1990. —— Sarah Jennifer Louise, *b* 1961.

Issue of late Major Thomas Vere Levinge, 2nd son of 9th baronet, *b* 1880, *d* 1949: *m* 1928, Dorothy, who *d* 1977, da of J. Ingman, of Northampton:—
Thomas Gerald, *b* 1934: *m* 19—, Stella Field, and has issue living, a son, *b* 1964.

Issue of late Bernard George Levinge, 5th son of 9th baronet, *b* 1887, *d* 1953: *m* 1912, Stella Parsons:—
Reginald Noel (9 Dent St, Penrith, NSW), *b* 1927: *m* 1950, Pearl Kathleen, da of late Walter Wright Armstrong, and has issue living, Geoffrey Paul, *b* 1952: *m* 1970, Sandra, da of A. Kiggins, and has issue living, Mark Andrew *b* 1974, Kerry Ann *b* 1971, Tracy Maree *b* 1980, — Maureen Ann, *b* 1956: *m* 1978, Christopher Fehon, of 1B Minna St, Burwood, NSW 2134, and has issue living, Luke *b* 1985, Rebecca *b* 1982, Emma *b* (twin) 1985, — Sharon Maree, *b* 1963: *m* 1983, Christopher Carl, and has issue living, Michael James *b* 1985, Adrian Noel *b* 1986, Amanda Lee *b* 1984.

Issue of late Major George Edward Levinge, brother of 9th baronet, *b* 1862, *d* 1926: *m* 1895, Elizabeth Louisa, da of John Wiley, of Brisbane, Queensland:—
George Onslow, *b* 1896. —— William John, *b* 1903.

Granddaughter of late Harry Corbyn Levinge, eldest son of 6th baronet:—
Issue of late Sir Edward Vere Levinge, KCIE, CSI, *b* 1867, *d* 1954: *m* 1900, Alys Adèle, who *d* 1952, da of Maj-Gen Charles Frederic Thomas:—
Vera Alys, *b* 1911: *m* 1938, Count (Michael) Karl von Althann, who *d* 1978, and has issue living, *Count* (Michael) Robert, *b* 1939, — *Count* (Michael) Alexander, *b* 1940: *m* 1978, Maria Kammerlander, and has issue living, *Count* Wenzel *b* 1979, *Count* Quintin *b* 1982, *Countess* Clementine *b* 1980, — *Count* (Michael) Victor, *b* 1944: *m* 1972, Maria de la Natividad del Valle, of Haverford, Pa, USA, and has issue living, *Count* Charles *b* 1980, — *Countess* Caroline *b* 1980, — *Countess* Maria Olga, *b* 1941: *m* 1975, Count Ferdinand von Coreth zu Coredo, and has issue living, *Countess* Julie *b* 1976, *Countess* Isabelle *b* 1978, — *Countess* Maria Christina *b* 1942: *m* 1966, Don José Manuel de Ruiz Gonzalez, who *d* 1980, and has issue living, José Carlos *b* 1967, Alejandro Miguel *b* 1970, Veronica *b* 1974, — *Countess* Maria Therese Margarethe, *b* 1949: *m* 1983, François-

Charles Pictet, Swiss Amb to the Court of St James's (Swiss Embassy, 21 Bryanston Sq, W1). *Residence* – A3435, Zwentendorf a d Donau, Lower Austria.

Grandchildren of late Richard William Chaworth Levinge, eldest son of Charles William Levinge (infra):—
Issue of late Capt Richard Hugh Levinge, b 1879, d 1926: m 1914, Jennie Moncrieth Howitt, who d 1977, only da of late George Bell McCreedy, of Belfast, and S Africa:—
Mary Frances Jenoyr (21 Ridgeway Rd, Headington, Oxford) b 1918; SRN; Nursing Officer, Churchill Hosp, Oxford.
Issue of late Frederick Rufane Levinge, b 1890, d 1981: m 1929, Rona Elizabeth, who d 1971, da of late Richard M. Hawker, of Bungaree, Clare, S Aust:—
Frederick Charles Richard (Messamurray, Box 20, Naracoorte, S Aust 5271), b 1939: m 1969, Tessa Mary, only da of R. W. Barton, of Gisborne, NZ, and has issue living, Charles Richard Wynne, b 1973, — Georgina Rona, b 1971.

Grandson living of late Capt Richard Hugh Levinge (ante):—
Issue of late Rev (Evelyn) Hugh Jenoyr Levinge, RN, b 1915, d 1981: m 1955, Sheila Joy, who d 1992, da of S. L. R. Etherton, LLB, BSc, of Detroit, USA:—
Richard St John (Broadway, 8 Hall Road, Leckhampton, Cheltenham, Glos GL53 0HE), b 1956: m 1979, Mary Juliet, da of Radnor Outhwaite, of Cale Green, Stockport, and has issue living, Daniel Richard, b 1983, — Victoria Louise, b 1984.

Grandchildren of late Surg-Maj Edward Levinge, 2nd son of late Charles William Levinge, only son of late Richard Hugh Levinge, 4th son of 4th baronet:—
Issue of late Edward Vere Bryce Levinge, b 1889, d 1922: m 1916, his cousin, Ethel Violet, who d 1924, da of late George Cardwell Porter, MD, of Castleacre, Norfolk (see Levinge, Bt, 1924 Edn):—
Bryce Leonard, b 1922; is a Farmer. —— Avice Ethel Mary: m 1st, 1944, Ward Shepard, who d 1953; 2ndly, 1953, George Alfred Robinson, and has issue living, (by 1st m) Carol Jean, b 1946, — (by 2nd m) Bryce Levinge, b 1954, — Guy Herrick, b 1957. Address – PO Box 275, Falls Church, Virginia, USA.

Granddaughters of late Robert Degennes Levinge, 4th son of late Marcus Anthony Levinge, only son of late Mark Anthony Levinge, 5th son of 4th baronet:—
Issue of late Walter Hodson Levinge, b 1894, d 1982: m 1945, Marion Blanche, who d 1974, da of Rev Francis Cockle, Rector of Aasleagh, Leenane, co Galway:—
Hester Sylvia, b 1947: m 1970, Trevor David Scott, of Mount Venus House, Woodtown Rd, Rathfarnham, co Dublin. —— Daphne Elaine Sybil, b 1950; PhD: m 1979, Jonathan Joseph Shackleton, of Beech Park, Clonsilla, co Dublin, and has issue living, David Levinge, b 1981, — Jane Hester, b 1984, — Hannah Lydia, b 1987. —— Marion Alison Patricia, b 1951: m 1981, Charles Gillard Couper, of Creaghduff, Athlone, co Meath, and has issue living, Alister Milne, b 1984, — Sally Marion, b 1981.
The 1st baronet, Right Hon Sir Richard Levinge, was Lord Chief Justice of the Common Pleas in Ireland and the 7th baronet, Sir Richard George Augustus, sat as MP for co Westmeath (L) 1857-65. The 10th baronet, Sir Richard William, Lieut 1st Life Guards, was ka Oct 1914.

LEVY (UK) 1913, of Humberstone Hall, co Leicester
(Name pronounced "Levvy")

By courage and faith

Sir EWART JOSEPH MAURICE LEVY, 2nd *Baronet*; b 10 May 1897; s his father, Sir MAURICE, 1933; ed Harrow; High Sheriff of Leics 1937-38; JP for Leicester 1934; 1940-45 War with 21st Army Group as Lt-Col Roy Pioneer Corps (despatches): m 1932, Hylda Muriel, who d 1970, el da of late Sir Albert Levy, of Devonshire House, W1, and has issue.

Arms – Argent, a chevron inverted ermines between two keys erect, the wards to the dexter, in chief sable, and an Esquire's helmet in base proper. **Crest** – A dexter arm embowed in armour, the hand holding a key in bend sinister the wards upwards sable, and encircled above the elbow with a chaplet of roses argent, leaved vert.
Residence – Welland House, Weston-by-Welland, Market Harborough, Leics.
Club – Reform.

DAUGHTER LIVING

Caroline Anne Patricia, b 1933: m 1st, 1965 (m diss 1971), George Robert Paterson Coles; 2ndly, 1971, Terence John McInnes Skinner, of John O'Gaunt House, Melton Mowbray, Leics.

SISTER LIVING

Alix Cordelia (11 Beech Grove House, Beech Grove, Harrogate, Yorks), b 1894.
The 1st baronet, Sir Maurice Levy, sat as MP for Mid, or Loughborough, Div of Leicestershire (L) 1900-18, and was a JP and DL for Leicestershire (High Sheriff 1926), and knighted 1907.

LEWIS (UK) 1902, of Portland Place, Marylebone, co London, and The Danish Pavilion, Overstrand, Norfolk (Extinct 1945)

Lieut-Com Sir GEORGE JAMES ERNEST LEWIS, OBE, RNVR, 3rd and last *Baronet*; (*ka* 1945).

DAUGHTER LIVING OF SECOND BARONET

Elizabeth Bertha, *b* 1897: *m* 1928 (*m diss* 1938), George Wansbrough, and has issue living, Joseph, *b* 1934, — Miriam Beatriz, *b* 1932. *Residence* – Broughton Poggs, Lechlade, Gloucestershire.

ORR-LEWIS (UK) 1920, of Whitewebbs Park, Enfield, co Middlesex (Extinct 1980)

Sir (JOHN) DUNCAN ORR-LEWIS, 2nd and last *Baronet*; *d* 1980.

DAUGHTER LIVING OF SECOND BARONET

Marie Ardyn, *b* 1922: *m* 1942, Affleck Macpherson and has issue living, Alastair Duncan, *b* 1960, — Marjorie Gay, *b* 1946. *Residence* –

LEWTHWAITE (UK) 1927, of Broadgate, Parish of Thwaites, co Cumberland

Virtue reaching towards heaven

Sir RAINALD GILFRID LEWTHWAITE, 4th *Baronet*, CVO, OBE, MC; *b* 21 July 1913; *s* his brother, *Sir* WILLIAM ANTHONY, 1993; *ed* Rugby, and Trin Coll Camb (BA 1934); Brig late Scots Gds; Mil Attche 1964, and Defence Attache at British Embassy, Paris, 1965-68; 1939-45 War in Middle East (MC), France, Holland, Germany and Italy; OBE (Civil) 1974, CVO 1975: *m* 1936, Margaret Elizabeth, MBE, who *d* 1990, da of Harry Edmonds, of New York, USA, and has had issue.

𝕬rms – Ermine, a cross flory azure, fretty or. 𝕮rest – A garb or, bound by a serpent nowed proper, holding in the mouth a cross-crosslet fitchée gules.
Residences – Earls Cottage, 14 Earls Walk, W8 6LP; Broadgate, Millom, Cumbria LA18 5JZ.

SONS LIVING AND DECEASED

DAVID RAINALD (49 Ranelagh Grove, SW1W 8PB), *b* 26 March 1940; *ed* Rugby, and Trin Coll Camb (BA 1960): *m* 1969, Diana Helena, twin da of late William Robert Tomkinson, TD (*see* Blane, Bt (ext)), and has issue living, Emma Victoria, *b* 1971, — Mary-Claire, *b* 1972. —— †John Valentine, *b* 1944; *ed* Eton, and Harvard: *m* 1967, Elizabeth Georgiana (Carters Barn, Latton, Cricklade, Wilts), da of Richard John Bramble Mildmay-White (*see* By Mildmay of Flete, 1990 Edn), and *d* 1990, leaving issue, Alice Georgiana, *b* 1969, — Martha Grace, *b* 1970.

DAUGHTERS LIVING AND DECEASED

Margaret Sylvia, *b* 1937. —— Mary Rose, *b* 1946; *d* 1949.

DAUGHTER LIVING OF THIRD BARONET

Catherine Jane, *b* 1954: *m* 1986, William Tobias Hall, 2nd son of S. J. Hall, of Stratfield Turgis, Hants, and has issue living, Francesca, *b* 1990, — Sophie, *b* (twin)1990.

WIDOW LIVING OF THIRD BARONET

LOIS MAIRI (*Lady Lewthwaite*), only child of late Capt Struan Robertson Kerr-Clark (*see* E Drogheda, 1966 Edn): *m* 1936, Sir William Anthony Lewthwaite, 3rd Bt, who *d* 1993. *Address* – c/o 73 Dovehouse Street, SW3 6JZ.
Sir William Lewthwaite, 1st Bt (Vice-Lieut of Cumberland 1921-2 and 1923-4, and Dep Chm of Quarter Sessions) was Chm Conservative Asso of Egremont Div of Cumberland 1904-24 (many years Treasurer).

LEY (UK) 1905, of Epperstone Manor, Epperstone, co Nottingham
(Name pronounced "Lee")

Maj Sir FRANCIS DOUGLAS LEY, MBE, TD, 4th *Baronet*; *b* 5 April 1907; *s* his brother, Sir GERALD GORDON, TD, 1980; *ed* Eton, and Magdalene Coll, Camb; is Maj Derbyshire Yeo, RAC (TA Reserve), and a JP and DL; High Sheriff of Derbys 1956; MBE (Civil) 1961: *m* 1931, Violet Geraldine, who *d* 1991, el da of late Maj James Gerald Thewlis Johnson, DSO (Alleyne, Bt), and has issue.

Arms – Argent, six lozenges conjoined in bend between two broken tilting spears gules. **Crest** – In front of a cubit arm in armour a hand grasping a broken tilting spear, four lozenges conjoined fesseways gules.
Residence – Pond House, Shirley, Brailsford, Derby DE6 3AS.

POST·MORTEM·SPERO·VITAM

I hope for life after death

SON LIVING

IAN FRANCIS (Fauld Hall, Tutbury, Staffs; Whites Club), *b* 12 June 1934; *ed* Eton; late 2nd Lieut 10th Royal Hus; High Sheriff of Derbyshire 1985: *m* 1957, Caroline Margaret, el da of late Maj George Henry Errington, MC, of Zimbabwe, and has issue living, Christopher Ian, *b* 2 Dec 1962, — Virginia Mary, *b* 1960: *m* 1988, Samuel C. Thomasson, eldest son of Christopher Thomasson, of Boothby Graffoe, Lincs, and has issue living, Jack James *b* 1990, Laurie Francis *b* 1992.

DAUGHTER LIVING

Susan Alison, *b* 1937: *m* 1960, Charles Edward Weatherby, of Mixbury Lodge Farm, Brackley, Northants, and has issue living, Camilla Jane, *b* 1963: *m* 1993, William J. H. Hiley, of 9 Worfield St, SW11 4RB, son of Peter Hiley, of Steep, Hants (*see* M Linlithgow, colls), — Fiona Mary, *b* 1965: *m* 1990, Paul R. Webber, son of John Webber, of Cropredy, Oxon.

SISTER LIVING

Mary Rhoda (Nesley Down, Westonbirt, Tetbury, Glos), *b* 1906: *m* 1944, Maj Geoffrey Charles Bishop, 9th Lancers, who *d* 1970.

DAUGHTERS LIVING OF THIRD BARONET (*By 1st marriage*)

Elizabeth Bridget Rhoda, *b* 1937: *m* 1965, Roger Humphrey Boissier, of Easton House, The Pastures, Repton, Derby DE6 6GG, and has issue living, Rupert John *b* 1967, — Clare Louise, *b* 1968. —— Annabel Alison, *b* 1939: *m* 1960, David Eric Cramer Stapleton, of Armathwaite Place, Armathwaite, Carlisle, and has issue living, Serena Jane Clare, *b* 1961: *m* 1990, David Hugo Martyn Williams-Ellis, son of late John Williams-Ellis, of Carregfelen, Porthmadog, N Wales, and has had issue, Hugo John George *b* 1992, Emily Rose *b* and *d* 1991, Phoebe Constance Mary *b* 1994, — Charlotte Jessica Louise, *b* 1963: *m* 1987, Bertrand Maurice Van Houtte de la Chaise, of 30 rue Montmartre, 75001 Paris, France, son of Jacques Van Houtte de la Chaise, of Deauville, France, and has issue living, Edward Henri Cramer *b* 1991, Alexandra Constance Marie *b* 1989, — Victoria Lucy Annabel, *b* 1974. —— Lara Alexandra Mary-Rose, *b* 1974. —— Caroline Sheila (*Countess of Lonsdale*), *b* 1943: *m* 1975, as his 4th wife, 7th Earl of Lonsdale, and has issue (*see* E Lonsdale).
Sir Francis Ley, 1st Bt, Gov, Director, and Founder of Ley's Works in Derby, was High Sheriff of Notts 1905.

NAYLOR-LEYLAND (UK) 1895, of Hyde Park House, Albert Gate, co London

Sir PHILIP VYVIAN NAYLOR-LEYLAND, 4th *Baronet*; *b* 9 Aug 1953; *s* his father, Sir VIVYAN EDWARD, 1987; *ed* Eton, RMA Sandhurst, NY Univ Business Sch, and RAC Cirencester; Lieut LG; MFH: *m* 1980, Lady Isabella Lambton, yst da of Antony Claud Frederick Lambton (6th Earl of Durham until he disclaimed his title 1970), and has issue.

Arms – Quarterly, 1st and 4th, ermine, on a fesse engrailed sable, between nine ears of barley, three, three, and three vert, banded or in chief, and three like ears in base, a lion passant of the last between two escallops argent and for distinction a canton gules, *Leyland*; 2nd and 3rd, per pale or and argent, a pale sable fretty of the first between two lions rampant of the third, and for distinction a canton gules, *Naylor*. **Crest** – 1st, A mount vert, thereon an escallop argent, surmounted by a demi-eagle erminois, wings endorsed azure, bezantée, in the mouth three ears of barley vert, and charged for distinction with a cross-crosslet gules, *Leyland*; 2nd, a lion passant sable, charged on the body with two saltires or, resting the dexter forepaw upon a shield, charged with the arms of Naylor, and charged further for distinction with a cross-crosslet also or, *Naylor*.
Residences – Nantclwyd Hall, Ruthin, N Wales; The Ferry House, Milton Park, Peterborough, Cambs PE6 7AB.

FIDUS·ET·AUDAX

Faithful and bold

SONS LIVING

THOMAS PHILIP, *b* 22 Jan 1982. —— George Antony, *b* 1989. —— Edward Claud, *b* 1993.

DAUGHTER LIVING

Violet Mary, b 1983.

HALF-SISTERS LIVING (*Daughter of 3rd Baronet by 2nd wife, Noreen Starr, da of late W/Cdr Peter Anker-Simmons, DFC, RAF; see Bailey, Bt*)

Cleone Mary Veronica, b 1968.

(by 3rd wife)

Virginia, b 1983. —— Jessica Pamela, b 1987.

UNCLE LIVING (*Son of 2nd Baronet*)

Michael Montagu George, MC, b 1926; formerly Capt The Life Guards: m 1953, Jacqueline Marie Françoise, yr da of Maj Ides Floor, DSO, MBE, of Lullenden, East Grinstead, Sussex, and has issue living, David George Edward, b 1955; Lt LG: m 1978, Jane Lucinda, el da of Lt-Col John Monsell Christian, MC, KRRC, of Clifferdine House, Rencomb, Glos, and has issue living, John b 1984, Frederick George b 1987, Victoria b 1982, — Joanna Rosemary Jane, b 1961: m 1st, 1985 (m diss 1989), Nigel James Norman, elder son of Sir Mark Annesley Norman, 3rd Bt; 2ndly, 1989, Philip S. O. Lambert, of 8 Soudan Road, SW11, yr son of Capt Richard Lambert, of Garthgwynion, Machynlleth, Wales, and has issue living (by 2nd m), Jack b 1990, Laura b 1992. *Residence* – The Red House, Lacock, Chippenham, Wiltshire SN15 2LB.

AUNT LIVING (*Daughter of 2nd Baronet*)

Veronica Rosemary, b 1932: m 1955 (m diss 1975), Peter Cyril Alexander Munster (*see* E Dudley, colls, 1980 Edn), and has issue living, Alexander Paul, b 1961, — Sarah Hélène, b 1957, — Marina Claire, b 1960. *Residence* – 3 Queens Gate Place Mews, SW7 5BG.

MOTHER LIVING

Hon Elizabeth Anne Marie Gabrielle Fitzalan Howard (*Hon Lady Hastings*), yr da of 2nd Viscount Fitzalan of Derwent (*ext* 1962): m 1st, 1952 (m diss 1960), as his 1st wife, Sir Vivyan Edward Naylor-Leyland, 3rd Bt, who d 1987; 2ndly, 1975, Sir Stephen Lewis Edmonstone Hastings, MC. *Residence* – 12A Ennismore Gdns, SW7.

WIDOW LIVING OF THIRD BARONET

JAMEINA FLORA (*Jameina, Lady Naylor-Leyland*), da of James Freeman Reid: m 1980, as his 3rd wife, Sir Vivyan Edward Naylor-Leyland, 3rd Bt, who d 1987. *Residence* – Le Neuf Chemin, St Saviours, Guernsey, CI.

COLLATERAL BRANCH LIVING

Issue of late (Alick) David Yorke Naylor-Leyland, LVO, late Lieut Gren Guards, yst son of 2nd baronet, b 1926, d 1991: m 1st, 1953 (m diss 1962), Diana Elizabeth Lea (who m 2ndly, 1962, 7th Earl of Wilton), da of Roy Galway, of St Ronans, Winkfield Row, Berks; 2ndly, 1962 (m diss 1969), Dita Douglas (AMORY), da of J. Gordon Douglas, Jr, of Prince's Neck, Newport, Rhode Island, USA; 3rdly, 1973, Carolyn S. Neilson, who d 1989:—
(By 1st m) Michael Alexander Robert, b 1956: m 1st, 1984 (m diss 19—), Lucy C., da of Henry Potts, of Eglingham Hall, Alnwick, Northumberland; 2ndly, 1990, HRH Princess Tania Saskia Viktoria-Luise of Hanover, only child of HRH late Prince Welf Ernst August Andreas Philipp Georg Wilhelm Ludwig Berthold of Hanover (*see* ROYAL FAMILY), and has issue living, (by 2nd m) Jake John, b 1993. *Residence* – 10 Wallgrave Rd, SW5 0RL. —— Amanda Jane, b 1954: m 1977 (m diss 1982), Thomas Skiffington. *Residence* – Phantom Cottage, Chippenham, Ely, Cambs. —— (By 2nd m) Nicholas Edward, b 1962. —— (By 3rd m) Edward Frederick, b 1975.
The 1st baronet, Sir Herbert Scarisbrick, was MP for Colchester (C) 1892-95, and for Lancashire (S-W), Southport Div (L) 1898-9. The 2nd baronet, Sir Albert Edward Herbert, was Sheriff of Denbighshire 1921, and was sometime an Hon Attaché, British Legation, Berne, and British Embassy, Paris.

LIGHTON (I) 1791, of Merville, Dublin

Sir THOMAS HAMILTON LIGHTON, 9th *Baronet*; b 4 Nov 1954; s his father, *Sir* CHRISTOPHER ROBERT, MBE, 1993; *ed* Eton: m 1990, Belinda Jean, elder da of John Fergusson, of Barnhillies, Castle Douglas, Kirkcudbrightshire, and has issue.

Arms – Barry of eight argent and vert, over all a lion rampant crowned with an eastern crown or, armed and langued azure, a canton of Ireland. **Crest** – A lion's head erased crowned with an eastern crown or, langued azure.

SONS LIVING

JAMES CHRISTOPHER HAMILTON, b 20 Oct 1992. —— Harry John Hamilton, b (twin) 1992. —— A son, b 1994.

DAUGHTER LIVING

Fortitudine et prudentia

By fortitude and prudence

Celina Hamilton, b 1991.

HALF-SISTERS LIVING

Bridget Mary, b 1927: m 1949, Brig Anthony Onslow Lawrence Lithgow, MC, late Black Watch (RHR) (E Onslow, colls), who d 1988, and has issue living, Nigel Christopher Douglas, b 1950, — Sarah Vivienne Hamilton, b 1952, — Grania Claire Bridget, b 1953. —— Virginia Hamilton, b 1929.

WIDOW LIVING OF EIGHT BARONET

EVE (*Eve, Lady Lighton*), only da of Rear Adm Alexander Livingston Penrose Mark-Wardlaw, of Loseberry, Claygate, Surrey, and widow of Maj Henry Stopford Chetwode Ram, RE: *m* 1985, as his 3rd wife, Sir Christopher Robert Lighton, 8th Bt, MBE, who *d* 1993.

Sir Thomas Lighton, 1st Bt, son of John Lighton of Raspberry Hill, co Derry, was a Dublin banker, High Sheriff of Co Dublin 1790 and co Tyrone 1801, and MP for Tuam 1790-97, and Carlingford 1798-1800. At the time of his death his firm was known as Lighton, Needham & Shaw. The last named partner, Robert Shaw, was also created a baronet.

LINDSAY (UK) 1962, of Dowhill, co Kinross

Sir RONALD ALEXANDER LINDSAY OF DOWHILL, 2nd *Baronet*; *b* 6 Dec 1933; *s* his father, *Sir* MARTIN ALEXANDER, CBE, DSO, 1981; *ed* Eton, and Worcester Coll, Oxford (MA); Lt Gren Gds 1952-54; FCII (1964); Dir Oxford Members Agency Ltd since 1989; a Member of Queen's Body Guard for Scotland (R Co of Archers); Vice-chm Anglo-Spanish Soc (Encomienda de la Orden de Isabel la Católica 1988); Chm Standing Council of the Baronetage: *m* 1968, Nicoletta, yr da of late Capt Edgar Storich, Royal Italian Navy (ret), and has issue.

Arms – Gules, a fess chequy argent and azure, between a mullet of the second in chief and the base barry undy or and of the third; in a dexter canton argent a sinister hand couped apaume erect of the first. **Crest** – A castle triple-towered proper, port gules, tower-caps argent. **Supporters** – Two doves proper, gorged of collars chequy argent and azure.
Residence – 104 Edith Rd, W14 9AP.

SONS LIVING

JAMES MARTIN EVELYN, *b* 11 Oct 1968. —— Hugo Edgar, *b* 1970. —— Robin Ronald Edward, *b* 1972.

DAUGHTER LIVING

Lucia Linda, *b* 1974.

BROTHER LIVING

Oliver John Martin, CBE (Brookwood House, Brookwood, Surrey), *b* 1938; Col Gren Gds (ret); Dir Treloar Trust; a Member of Queen's Body Guard for Scotland (R Co of Archers); FRHistS, MICFM; author of *The Lasting Honour - The Fall of Hong Kong 1941* (1978) and *At The Going Down of the Sun - Hong Kong and South East Asia 1941-45* (1981), editor of *A Guards General: The Memoirs of Sir Allan Adair* (1986); CBE (Mil) 1993: *m* 1964, Lady Clare Rohais Antonia Elizabeth Giffard, yr da of 3rd Earl of Halsbury, and has issue living, Mark Oliver GIFFARD-LINDSAY, *b* 1968, —— Victoria Louise Elizabeth Clare, *b* 1967: *m* 1988, Gregory F. M. T. Wheatley, 2nd son of Anthony Wheatley, —— Fiona Emily Margaret, *b* 1972.

SISTER LIVING

Jacynth Rosemary (*Lady Mark Fitzalan Howard*), *b* 1934: *m* 1961, Lord Mark Fitzalan Howard, and has issue (*see* D Norfolk). *Residence* – 13 Campden Hill Sq, W8 7LB.

MOTHER LIVING

Joyce Emily (*Joyce, Lady Lindsay*) (40 Ladbroke Rd, W11 3PH), da of late Maj Hon Robert Hamilton Lindsay (*see* E Crawford, colls): *m* 1932 (*m diss* 1967), Sir Martin Alexander Lindsay, 1st Bt, CBE, DSO, who *d* 1981.

Sir Martin Alexander Lindsay, the 1st baronet, was 22nd in descent from Sir William Lindsay of Rossie, 1st of Dowhill (*b* 1350), uncle of 1st Earl of Crawford. The estate was sold by James, 13th Laird, and his son Martin in the 18th century. The coat of arms of Adam, 5th of Dowhill (*d* 1544) is shown in the armorial of Sir David Lindsay of the Mount, Lyon King of Arms. Adam had a crown charter of confirmation of "his barony of Crambeth called Dowhill" in 1541. Earlier such charters are in 1353 by David II, in 1397 by Robert III and in 1447 by James II. The 1st baronet, Sir Martin, was the first MP for Solihull, from 1945 to 1964. He led the longest self-supporting sledge journey of 1,050 miles across Greenland in 1934 (*see* Guinness Book of Records). In 1944/45 he commanded the 1st Battalion The Gordon Highlanders in 16 operations in North-West Europe. This battalion led the Siegfried Line breakthrough, not far from where in 1814 Sir Martin's great-grandfather Col Martin Lindsay, CB, led the bayonet charge which broke through the French defences at Merxem when commanding the 78th Regiment (The Seaforths). Sir Martin's books include *Sledge* (1934), *So Few Got Through* (1945), and *The Baronetage* (1977).

Lindsay-Hogg, see Hogg.

Lister-Kaye, see Kaye.

Liston Foulis, see Foulis.

LITHGOW (UK) 1925, of Ormsary, co Argyll

By sea and land

Sir WILLIAM JAMES LITHGOW, 2nd *Baronet*; *b* 10 May 1934; *s* his father, *Sir* JAMES LITHGOW, GBE, CB, MC, TD, 1952; *ed* Winchester; Hon LLD Strathclyde 1979; CEng, FRINA, CBIM, FRSA, Fellow Scottish Council, Member of Queen's Body Guard for Scotland (Royal Company of Archers) 1964; DL Renfrewshire 1970; Chm of Lithgows Ltd 1959-1984 and since 1988, Dir since 1956; Chm Scott Lithgow Drydocks Ltd 1967-78; Vice-Chm Scott Lithgow Ltd 1968-78; Chmn Western Ferries (Argyll) Ltd 1972-85; Chmn Hunterston Development Co Ltd since 1987, Dir since 1981; Chm Campbeltown Shipyard Ltd 1970-85, Dir since 1985; Chm Landcatch 1981-85, Dir since 1985; Shipbuilding Employer's Federation 1961-62; Dir Bank of Scotland 1962-86; Dir Lithgows Pty Ltd since 1972; Member, British Committee Det Norske Veritas 1966-92; Exec Cttee Scottish Council for Development and Industry 1969-85; Greenock Dist Hosp Bd 1961-66; Gen Bd Nat Physical Lab 1963-66; Hon Pres Students Assoc and Member Court of Univ of Strathclyde 1964-69; Clyde Port Authority 1969-71; Scottish Regional Council of CBI 1969-76; W. Central Scotland Plan Steering Cttee 1970-74; National Ports Council 1971-78; Scottish Milk Marketing Board 1979-83; Chm Iona Cathedral Management Bd 1979-83; Winston Churchill Memorial Trust Council 1979-83: *m* 1st, 1964, Valerie Helen, who *d* 1964, da of late Denis Herbert Scott, CBE, of Farley Grange, Westerham, Kent; 2ndly, 1967, Mary Claire, da of Col Frank Moutray Hill, CBE, of East Knoyle, Salisbury, Wilts, and has issue by 2nd *m*.

Arms – Per chevron sable and argent three estoiles in chief of the second, and in base in a seaundy azure and of the second a galley, sails furled of the first, flagged gules. Crest – An otter on a rock proper.
Seat – Ormsary, by Lochgilphead, Argyllshire.

SONS LIVING *(By 2nd marriage)*

JAMES FRANK, *b* 13 June 1970. —— John Alexander, *b* 1974.

DAUGHTER LIVING *(By 2nd marriage)*

Katrina Margaret, *b* 1968.

SISTERS LIVING

Margaret Helen, *b* 1928: *m* 1951, Geoffrey Robert Rickman, and has issue living, Stephen Lithgow, *b* 1952, — Robert James, *b* 1957, — Andrew George, *b* 1960, — Catherine Margaret, *b* 1953. *Residence* – Sullington Old Rectory, Storrington, Pulborough, W Sussex. —— Ann Barlow, MBE, *b* 1931: *m* 1952, William Simon Wilson, and has issue living, Mark Lithgow, *b* 1960, — Sarah Rosalind, *b* 1953, — Judith Clare, *b* 1957. *Residence* – Ballochmorrie House, Barrhill, by Girvan, Ayrshire.

The 1st baronet, Sir James Lithgow, GBE, CB, MC, TD, DL, JP, LLD (son of late W. T. Lithgow, of Drums, Renfrewshire), was a Shipbuilder of Port Glasgow, a Member of Board of Admiralty 1940-46, Vice-Lieut for Renfrewshire, Hon Col TA, and first Freeman of Burgh of Port Glasgow.

LLEWELLYN (UK) 1922, of Bwllfa, Aberdare, co Glamorgan

Character is destiny

Sir HENRY (HARRY) MORTON LLEWELLYN, CBE, 3rd *Baronet; b* 18 July 1911; *s* his brother, *Sir* RHYS, 1978; *ed* Oundle, and Trin Coll, Camb (MA); DL for Mon, and a JP 1953-67; High Sheriff of Mon 1966; Chm C. L. Clay and Co (coal importers) 1936-46, Chm Whitbread Wales Ltd 1958-72, Member Wales Tourist Board 1968-74, Chm Sports Council for Wales 1971-81; Dir Chepstow Racecourse; Vice-Chm of Civic Trust for Wales, Chm Wales Bd Nat Building Soc, and formerly Chm Eagle Star Assurance Co (Wales Board); a Member of Nat Hunt Cttee 1946, Jockey Club since 1969, and Council of World Wildlife Fund since 1986; Chm of British Show Jumping Assoc 1972-76; Pres British Equestrian Fedn 1976-80 and of the Roy Welsh Agricultural Soc 1984; joined Warwicks Yeo 1939 and Staff Coll Haifa 1942, GSO II OPS 8th Army Oct 1942, GSOI (Operational Liaison) 21st Army Group 1944; 1939-45 War in Iraq, Syria, Western Desert, N Africa, Sicily, Italy, and NW Europe (despatches twice, OBE, US Legion of Merit); has Roy Humane Soc's Medal: show jumping Olympic Gold Medallist, Helsinki 1952, and Olympic Bronze Medallist, London 1948; OBE (Mil) 1945, CBE (Civil) 1953, Knt 1977: *m* 1944, Hon Christine Saumarez, da of 5th Baron de Saumarez, and has issue.

Arms – Per chevron or and gules, in chief a lion passant and in base three chevronels all counterchanged. **Crest** – A demi-dragon holding in the mouth a dexter hand couped proper.
Residence – Ty'r Nant, Llanarth, Raglan, Gwent. *Clubs* – Cavalry and Guards', Jockey, Shikar.

SONS LIVING

DAVID ST VINCENT (27 Hill St, W1), *b* 2 April 1946; *ed* Eton: *m* 1980 (*m diss* 1987), Vanessa Mary Theresa, yr da of Lt-Cdr Theodore Bernard Peregrine Hubbard, RN (*see* D Norfolk), and has issue living, Olivia Anna Christina, *b* 1980, — Arabella Dominica, *b* 1983. ——— Roderic (Roddy) Victor (Yew Tree House, Westbury, nr Brackley, Northants NN13 5JR), *b* 1947; *ed* Shrewsbury; landscape gardener, journalist, broadcaster, and author: *m* 1981, Tatiana Manora Caroline, da of late Paul Soskin, film producer, and has issue living, Alexandra Manora Tatiana, *b* 1982, — Natasha Anna Christina, *b* 1984, — Rose-Anna Alice, *b* 1987.

DAUGHTER LIVING

Anna Christina, *b* 1956: *m* 1987, Christopher Charles Elletson, of 5A Egerton Terrace, SW3 2BX, son of late C. E. Elletson, of Douglas, IoM.

BROTHER LIVING

(William Herbert) Rhidian, MC, *b* 1919; *ed* Eton; Maj late Welsh Gds; DL of Cardiganshire, High Sheriff 1967-68; Member Cardiganshire Co Council 1961-70, Member of Cardiganshire Agric Exec Cttee, and Traffic Commr, S Wales; and a Member of Court of Govs, Nat Library of Wales 1967-68, and Univ of Wales 1968-70; 1939-45 War in France, N Africa, Italy and Greece (despatches, MC): *m* 1943, Lady Honor Morvyth Malet Vaughan, da of 7th Earl of Lisburne, and has issue living, Trefor Wilmot (Hill Farm House, Ipsden, Oxon), *b* 1947: *m* 1973, Heather Mary, da of Richard Lucas, of The Lydiate, Heswall, and has issue living, Catrin Sarah Malet *b* 1981, Elinor Victoria Sian *b* 1985, — Cordelia, *b* 1949: *m* 1969, Angus Lamont, of Beech House, Chiddingfold, Surrey, and has issue living, Douglas Ross *b* 1973, Camilla Rose *b* 1971, — Gaynor Malet, *b* 1952: *m* 1977, Edward James Sutcliffe Garrett, of 146 New Kings Rd, SW6, and has issue living, Nicholas Edward Sutcliffe *b* 1982, Lucinda Felicity *b* 1979, Melissa Kinvara *b* 1987. *Residence* – 4 St Omer Rd, Guildford, Surrey GU1 2DB.

SISTERS LIVING

Margaret Elaine (*Lady Anderson*), *b* 1913: *m* 1935, Sir Donald Forsyth Anderson, who *d* 1973, son of late Sir Alan Garrett Anderson, GBE, and has issue living, Gillian Elizabeth (21 Carlotta Rd, Sydney, NSW), *b* 1936: *m* 1966 (*m diss* 19—), William Peter Grant Davies, — Jennifer Forsyth, *b* 1937: *m* 1965, Anthony David Loehnis, CMG, of Haughton House, Churchill, Oxon (*see* E Harrowby, colls), — Lindsay Garrett, *b* 1942; JP for Droxford, Hants: *m* 1962, Robert Trench Fox, of Cheriton House, nr Winchester, — Susan Elaine (*Countess of Darnley*), *b* 1945: a JP for Havant, Hants: *m* 1965, 11th Earl of Darnley, of Netherwood Manor, Tenbury Wells, Worcs. *Residence* – 9 Hamilton House, Vicarage Gate, W8 4HL. ——— Elizabeth Aileen Maud, *b* 1914; formerly Wing Officer WAAF; 1939-45 War: *m* 1946, Lt-Col David Mathew Caradoc Prichard, Roy Welch Fusiliers, who *d* 1986, and has issue living, Robert David Caradoc, *b* 1947, — Colin Hubert Llewellyn (Lodge Farm, Barcombe, Lewes, E Sussex), *b* 1949: *m* 1977, Jane Helen, da of Paul Chamberlain, of Groombridge, E Sussex, and has issue living, Claire Helen *b* 1982, Eleanor Jane *b* 1984, Lydia Diana *b* 1988, — William de Burgh (Gobion Manor, Abergavenny, Gwent), *b* 1953; Capt Welsh Guards: *m* 1983, Judith Elizabeth Thorneycroft, da of late Richard Thorneycroft Salt, of The Old Farm, Over Whitacre, Warwicks, and has issue living, Thomas David Caradoc *b* 1990, Georgina Lydia *b* 1986, Olivia Charlotte *b* 1988. *Residence* – Gobion Manor, Abergavenny, Gwent. ——— Magdalene Clare, *b* 1922: *m* 1948, Alexander Wyndham Hume Stewart-Moore, DL, of Moyarget Farm, 98 Moyarget Rd, Ballycastle, co Antrim, and has issue living, Christopher Wyndham Hume (71 Milson Rd, W14 0LH), *b* 1949: *m* 1981, Penelope Sarah, yr da of Edward Foster James, CMG, OBE (*see* B Poltimore, colls), and has issue living, Henry Wyndham Hume *b* 1983, Eliza Caroline Clare *b* 1987, — Michael David, *b* 1950: *m* 1981, Susan Jane, el da of John Alan Lionel Kinnaird, of Capeldale, Killinchy, co Down, and has issue living, Thomas John *b* 1983, Edward Alexander *b* 1986, Sally Frances *b* 1990, — (James) Anthony, *b* 1953: *m* 1982, Guion, yr da of late Edward Fifield, of Greensboro, N Carolina, USA, and has issue living, James Alexander *b* 1987, Gillian *b* 1989, — Gillian Clare, *b* 1956: *m* 1987, Donald Murray Keith, of The Manor House, Carleton Green, Yorks, son of Donald Keith, FRCOG, and has issue living, Frederick Donald David *b* 1993, Emily Margaret *b* 1989.

COLLATERAL BRANCH LIVING

Issue of late Sir David Treharne Llewellyn, 3rd son of 1st baronet, *b* 1916, *d* 1992: *m* 1950, Joan Anne, OBE, formerly Squadron Officer WAAF, Head of War Cabinet Cipher Office (The Well House, Yattendon, Berks), da of late Robert Henry Williams, of Bonvilston House, Bonvilston, nr Cardiff:—

Robert Crofts Williams (5 Drakefield Rd, SW17 8RT), *b* 1952; *ed* Eton; ACII; Dir Bain Clarkson Ltd 1986-87; Dir Jardine Insurance Brokers International Ltd 1987-93: *m* 1st, 1975, Susan Constance, who *d* 1980, el da of Hubert Miller-Stirling, of Cape Town, S Africa; 2ndly, 1981 (*m diss* 1989), Lucinda Roberte, only da of Alexander Clement Gilmour (*see* B Gilmour of Craigmillar); 3rdly, 1989, Sarah Dominica, da of Maj Gavin Anderson, of Swallow Cottage, Little Cressingham, Norfolk, and of late Mrs Michael Giles (*see* B Kilmaine, 1990 Edn), and has issue living (by 2nd *m*), Dominic Robin Crofts, *b* 1984, — Zara Marie-Louise, *b* 1986. —— David Rhidian, *b* 1957: *m* 1984, Mrs Susan Edwards, elder da of late Edward Edmiston, Headmaster Papplewick Sch Ascot. —— Emma Victoria, *b* 1951: *m* 1974, Bruce H. Dinwiddy, c/o Foreign and Commonwealth Office, SW1A 2AH, and has issue living, Thomas Rhidian, *b* 1979. —— Celia Rose, *b* 1976.

The 1st baronet, Sir David Richard Llewellyn (son of late Rees Llewellyn, JP, of Bwllfa House, near Aberdare), was Chm of Welsh Associated Collieries, Ltd, Lysaght Iron & Steel, Ltd, and other Cos, and Pres of Cardiff Univ Coll.

LLEWELLYN (UK) 1959, of Baglan, co Glamorgan

Gwell angau na chywilydd

Sir MICHAEL ROWLAND GODFREY LLEWELLYN, 2nd *Baronet*; *b* 15 June 1921; *s* his father, Col *Sir* (ROBERT) GODFREY, CB, CBE, MC, TD, 1986; *ed* Harrow; late Capt Gren Gds: World War II Italy 1943-44; a JP and DL for W Glamorgan, High Sheriff 1980, Vice Lord Lieut 1986, and Lord Lieut since 1987: *m* 1st, 1946 (*m diss* 1951), Bronwen Mary, da of Sir (Owen) Watkin Williams-Wynn, 8th Bt; 2ndly, 1956, Janet Prudence, yst da of Lt-Col Charles Thomas Edmondes, JP, DL, of Ewenny Priory, Bridgend, Glamorgan, and has issue by 2nd *m*.

Arms – Per fesse embattled azure and or a javelin erect between two boars' heads erased in chief, and like a boars' head erased between two javelins in base all counter charged. **Crest** – Upon a rock proper a boar's head erased or in front of three Javelins, one in pale and two in saltire, also proper.
Residence – Glebe House, Penmaen, nr Swansea, W Glamorgan SA3 2HH.

DAUGHTERS LIVING *(By 2nd marriage)*

Sarah Janet, *b* 1958. —— Carolyn Frances, *b* 1959. —— Lucy Mary, *b* 1963.

SISTER LIVING

Wenllian Kennard, *b* 1923: *m* 1949, Maj Wyndham Jermyn Hacket Pain, JP, DL, late Gren Gds, High Sheriff of Surrey 1988-89, of Dixton Lodge, Hadnock, Monmouth, Gwent NP5 3NQ, elder son of Col Michell Hacket Pain, of Upper Lostiford, Wonersh, nr Guildford, Surrey, and has issue living, Nicholas Wyndham Llewellyn, *b* 1953; *ed* Harrow, and RMA; served Gren Gds 1972-76 (despatches, Ulster 1974), — Simon Michell, *b* 1956; *ed* Harrow: *m* 1993, Vicky Robyn, elder da of N. C. Myers, of Cambridge, NZ.

The 1st Baronet, Col Sir (Robert) Godfrey Llewellyn, CB, CBE, MC, TD, JP, DL, was son of Robert William Llewellyn, JP, DL, of Cwrt Colman, Bridgend, and Baglan Hall, Briton Ferry, Glamorgan. He was High Sheriff of Glamorgan 1947 and of Monmouthshire 1963, Pres Nat Union of Conservative and Unionist Assocns 1962, and Chm of Organizing Cttee for VIth British Empire and Commonwealth Games 1958, and was knighted in 1953.

DILLWYN-VENABLES-LLEWELYN (UK) 1890, of Penllergaer, Llangyfelach and Ynis-y-gerwn, Cadoxton juxta Neath, Glamorganshire
(Name pronounced "Dilwin-Venables-Hlooellin")

Dread shame

Sir John Michael Dillwyn-Venables-Llewelyn, 4th *Baronet*; *b* 12 Aug, 1938; *s* his father, *Brig Sir* (Charles) Michael, MVO, 1976; *ed* Eton, and Magdalene Coll, Camb: *m* 1963 (*m diss* 1972), Nina, da of late Lt J. S. Hallam, KRRC; 2ndly, 1975, Nina Gay Richardson Oliver, and has issue by 1st *m*.

Arms – Quarterly: 1st and 4th, argent, gutée de poix, three chevronels gules, in base a lamb passant proper, *Llewelyn*; 2nd, azure, two bars each cotised between five mullets, three in chief and two in base all argent, and for difference a cross-crosslet or, *Venables*; 3rd gules, on a chevron nebulée argent, five trefoils slipped of the first, *Dillwyn*; on an escutcheon of pretence the Arms of *Venables* without distinctions. **Crests** – 1st, on a trunk of a tree fessewise eradicated and sprouting to the dexter, a lamb passant proper, bearing a banner gules charged with three chevronels argent, *Llewelyn*; 2nd, a wyvern wings expanded gules, each wing charged with a fesse argent, issuant from a weir basket proper, the dexter claw resting on a mullet azure, charged for difference as in the arms, *Venables*; 3rd, in front of a stag's head couped proper three trefoils slipped vert, *Dillwyn*.
Residence – Llysdinam, Newbridge-on-Wye, Llandrindod Wells, Powys LD1 6NB.

DAUGHTERS LIVING *(By 1st marriage)*

Georgina Katherine, *b* 1964: *m* 1989, Antony H. Mead, 2nd son of Humphrey Mead, of Moyaux, Normandy. —— Emma Susan, *b* 1967.

SISTER LIVING

Mary Julia, *b* 1936: *m* 1971, Michael B. Elster, of Gwarcae, Llanddew, Brecon, Powys, and has issue living, Jake, *b* 1972, —— Caitlin, *b* 1974.

WIDOW LIVING OF THIRD BARONET

Lady Delia Mary (*Lady Delia Dillwyn-Venables-Llewelyn*), (Llysdinam, Newbridge-on-Wye, Llandrindod Wells, Powys LD1 6NB), da of late Capt Michael Hugh Hicks-Beach, MP, Viscount Quenington (*see* E St Aldwyn); raised to the rank of an Earl's da 1920: *m* 1934, Brig Sir (Charles) Michael Dillwyn-Venables-Llewelyn, MVO, 3rd Bt, who *d* 1976.

The 1st baronet, Sir John Talbot Dillwyn-Llewelyn (son of late John Dillwyn-Llewelyn, FRS, of Penllergaer, co Glamorgan), was Mayor of Swansea 1890, and sat as MP there (C) July 1895 to Oct 1900. The 2nd baronet, Col Sir Charles Leyshon Dillwyn-Venables-Llewelyn, CB, was High Sheriff of Radnorshire 1924, and Lord Lieut 1929-49, and sat as MP for Radnorshire (C) Jan to Nov 1910. The 3rd baronet, Sir (Charles) Michael Dillwyn-Venables Llewelyn, MVO, was Lord Lieut of Radnorshire 1949-74, and Vice-Lieut of Powys 1974-76.

LLOYD (UK) 1960, of Rhu, co Dunbarton

Sir RICHARD ERNEST BUTLER LLOYD, 2nd *Baronet*; *b* 6 Dec 1928; *s* his father, *Maj Sir* (ERNEST) GUY RICHARD, DSO, 1987; *ed* Wellington, and Hertford Coll, Oxford (MA); commn'd The Black Watch 1948; ADC to GOC Malaya 1948-49; banker, Dir Glyn Mills and Co 1964-70, Chief Executive Williams and Glyn's Bank 1970-78, successively Dep Chm, Chief Executive, Chm and Dep Chm Hill Samuel Bank Ltd since 1978, Chm Vickers since 1992, and dir of other public companies; Gov Ditchley Foundation, Hon Treasurer British Heart Foundation; Member Ind Dev Advisory Board 1972-76, NEDC 1973-77, Overseas Projects Board 1981-85, and Advisor Board Royal Coll of Defence Studies since 1987: *m* 1955, Jennifer Susan Margaret, elder da of late Brig Ereld Boteler Wingfield Cardiff, CB, CBE, of Easton Court, nr Ludlow, Shropshire, and has issue.

Arms – Per bend, sable and gules, a lion rampant regardant argent, goutté of the second, surmounted of a fess or, charged with a barrulet dancette azure, a bordure invected of the fourth. **Crest** – A demi-lion argent goutté and langued gules, holding in bend forward two spears sable points upwards or.
Residence – Sundridge Pl, Sundridge, Sevenoaks, Kent TN14 6DD.

SONS LIVING

(RICHARD) TIMOTHY BUTLER (Fieldings, School Rd, Little Horkesley, Colchester, Essex), *b* 12 April 1956; *ed* Wellington, and RAC Cirencester: *m* 1989, Wilhelmina S. M., yr da of G. H. A. Schut, of Amstelveen, The Netherlands, and has issue living, Daphne, *b* 1993. —— Simon Wingfield Butler, *b* 1958; *ed* Eton, and Hertford Coll, Oxford (BA): *m* 1984, Catherine Rosemary Chanter, and has issue living, Christopher Timothy Butler, *b* 1986, — Jeremy Richard Butler, *b* 1988, — Jessica, *b* 1991. —— Henry Butler, *b* 1965; *ed* Eton, and Bristol Univ (BSc): *m* 1992, Joanna M., elder da of James Gourlay Freeland, of Grenna House, Chilson, Oxon.

SISTERS LIVING

Margaret Kynaston, *b* 1920: *m* 1948, Percy Bruce Southmayd Fowler, DM, FRCP, late Maj RAMC, and has issue living, Michael Bruce, *b* 1951; *ed* Harrow; MB, MRCP, FACC: *m* 1st, 1978, Dr Linda Jane Fenney; 2ndly, 1992, Sherry Farr, and has issue living (by 1st *m*), Jack *b* 1981, Katherine Jane *b* 1980, Emily Louise *b* (twin) 1981, — Guy Richard John, *b* 1961; *ed* Harrow; MB, BS, — Susanne Jane, FRCGP; *b* 1949: *m* 1970, Richard Antony Savage, FRCGP, and has issue living, Thomas Michael *b* 1978, Samuel Richard *b* 1984, Emma Louise *b* 1981, — Amanda Jill, *b* 1952; MRCP: *m* 1979, Andrew Duncan Platts, FRCS (Edin), FRCS (Lond), FRCP, and has issue living, Nicholas James *b* 1982, Helen Jane *b* 1981, Catherine Frances *b* 1987. *Residence* – Shirley Holms, Gerrards Cross, Bucks SL9 8JH. —— Elizabeth Hunt (*Lady Denny*), *b* 1924: *m* 1949, Sir Alistair Maurice Archibald Denny, 3rd Bt (*cr* 1913), and has issue. *Residence* – Crombie Cottage, Abercrombie, Anstruther, Fife KY10 2DE.

The 1st baronet, Maj Sir (Ernest) Guy Richard Lloyd, of Rhu Cottage, Carrick Castle, Lochgoilhead, Argyll (*see* Green-Price, Bt, 1961 Edn), served in European War 1914-18 (despatches, DSO), and European War 1939-40 with Royal Warwickshire Regt in France; sat as MP for Renfrewshire, E Div (*U*) 1940-59; ktd 1953; DL Dunbartonshire 1953-87.

SINCLAIR-LOCKHART (NS) 1636, of Murkle, co Caithness, and Stevenson, co Haddington

Corda serrata fero
I bear a locked heart

Sir SIMON JOHN EDWARD FRANCIS SINCLAIR-LOCKHART, 15th *Baronet*; *b* 22 July 1941; *s* his father, *Sir* MUIR EDWARD, 1985: *m* 1973, Felicity Edith, only da of late Ivan Lachlan Campbell Stewart, of Havelock North, New Zealand, and has issue.

Arms – Quarterly: 1st and 4th, argent, a man's heart proper within a fetter-lock sable, on a chief azure three boar's heads erased argent all within a bordure, ermine, charged with three crosses patee gules; 2nd and 3rd, argent, on a saltire engrailed gules, four bezants. **Crest** – A boar's head erased argent.
Address – 13 Franklin Terr, Havelock North, Hawkes Bay, New Zealand.

SONS LIVING

ROBERT MUIR, *b* 12 Sept 1973. —— James Lachlan, *b* (twin) 1973.

DAUGHTER LIVING

Fiona Mary, *b* 1979.

SISTER LIVING

Sara Ann May (Camnethan, RD7, Feilding, New Zealand), *b* 1942; has resumed the surname of Sinclair-Lockhart: *m* 1968 (*m diss* 19—), Nicholas Welcome Willcock.

WIDOW LIVING OF FOURTEENTH BARONET

(OLGA) ANN (*Ann, Lady Sinclair-Lockhart*), da of late Claude Victor White Parsons, of Hawkes Bay, New Zealand: *m* 1940, Sir Muir Edward Sinclair-Lockhart, 14th Bt, who *d* 1985. *Residence* – Camnethan, RD7, Feilding, New Zealand.

COLLATERAL BRANCH LIVING

Issue of late Bruce Sinclair-Lockhart, LLM, yst son of 11th baronet, *b* 1910, *d* 1965: *m* 1940 (*m diss* 1949),
Joan Marian Belle Quilliam, of New Plymouth, NZ:—
Sally Elisabeth, *b* 1942: *m* 1964, Stuart William Veitch, c/o Private Bag, Waimata, Gisborne, NZ, and has issue living, Guy
Bruce, *b* 1966, — William Ronald *b* 1968, — Michael Richard, *b* 1970, — Katie Jane, *b* 1973.

Sir John Sinclair (son of George Sinclair of Edinburgh) was created a baronet of Nova Scotia with remainder to heirs male
whatsoever. Sir Robert, 3rd Bt was a Privy Councillor and a Baron of the Exchequer. Sir John Sinclair, 4th Bt: *m* 1698,
Martha, da and eventually heir of Sir John Lockhart of Castlehill, a Lord of Session (Lord Castlehill). Sir John Gordon
Sinclair, 8th Bt, a distinguished Admiral, served sixty-three years in the Royal Navy. On the death of his son Sir Robert
Charles Sinclair, 9th Bt in 1899 the baronetcy passed to a descendant of James Sinclair, yr son of the 5th baronet, who on
inheriting Castlehill 1764, assumed the surname of Lockhhart. The 10th baronet Maj-Gen Sir Græme A. Lockhart, CB (who
served during Persian and Indian Mutiny Campaigns) assumed the additional surname of Sinclair. Sir Robert Duncan
Sinclair-Lockhart, 11th Bt, was son of late George Duncan Lockhart (whose grandfather assumed the surname of Lockhart
in lieu of his patronymic), a descendant of late James Lockhart Sinclair, 2nd son of 5th baronet. The 12th baronet, Sir
Graeme Sinclair-Lockhart, sometime 2nd Lieut Scottish Horse (Scouts), served 1914-18 and 1939-45 Wars, and in the Russo-
Finnish War. He was *s* by his brother, Sir John, 13th Bt, Maj RA, District Commr Kenya, Colonial Serv.

LOCOCK (UK) 1857, of Speldhurst, Kent (Extinct 1965)

Sir CHARLES BIRD LOCOCK, 3rd and last *Baronet.*

DAUGHTER LIVING OF THIRD BARONET

Vera Frances, *b* 1920: *m* 1st, 1939, Capt Philip McDonald Bottome, RASC; 2ndly, 1946, Cyril Stevens: *m* 3rdly, 1972 (*m diss*
1978), Malcolm Paul Holman, and has issue living, (by 2nd *m*) Anthony Charles, *b* 1948: *m* 1st, 1972 (*m diss* 1979), Sally
Jean Boyns; 2ndly, 1979, Carolyn Ann Mason, and has issue living, (by 2nd *m*) Robin William *b* 1979, — Nigel Derek, *b*
1951: *m* 1972 (*m diss* 1975), Susan Hilary Saunders, and has issue living, Michelle Jane, *b* 1972 — (by 1st *m*) Patricia Anne,
b 1941: *m* 1st, 1960 (*m diss* 1966), Raymond Bey-Leveld; 2ndly, 1987, Roger Alan Geddes, and has issue living, (by 1st *m*)
Kevin Wayne, *b* 1961: *m* 1987, Sharon Amoedo, Barry Gordon, *b* 1963, — (by 2nd *m*) Anita Janet Christine, *b* 1956: *m* 1980,
Michael Vaughan Johnson, and has issue living, James Michael *b* 1989, Kate Louise *b* 1987.

COLLATERAL BRANCHES LIVING

Issue of late Charles Bardolf Locock, son of 3rd baronet, *b* 1905, *d* 1961: *m* 1950, Frances Daphne, who *d*
1974, eldest da of late Cdr Ralph Hicks, RN, of Pyrford, Surrey:—
Frances Anne, *b* 1951: *m* 1986, Quentin Turton Cross, and has issue living, Alexander Orlando, *b* 1989. *Residence* – Two
Ways, Madeira Rd, W Byfleet, Surrey.

Granddaughter of late Rev Alfred Henry Locock, 2nd son of 1st baronet:—
Issue of late Charles Dealtry Locock, *b* 1862, *d* 1946: *m* 1889, Ida Gertrude, who *d* 1962, da of late Col Herbert
Locock, 5th son of 1st baronet:—
Elsa, *b* 1891. *Residence* –

Granddaughter of late Col Herbert Locock, CB, RE, 5th son of 1st baronet:—
Issue of late Sir Guy Harold Locock, CMG, *b* 1883, *d* 1958: *m* 1906, Esther Mary Eleanor, who *d* 1955, only child of
William James Reade:—
Rosemary Esther, *b* 1907: *m* 1938, John Wyndham Stanton, and has issue living, Richard Holbrow, *b* 1940: *m* 1974, Janet
Vanessa Watson, and has issue living, William Holbrow *b* 1979, Charles Robert Dymock *b* 1982, — Anthony Guy, *b* 1943: *m*
1970, Julia Mary Osborn-King, and has issue living, Henry John Arthur *b* 1975, Olivia Esther Victoria *b* 1977, Sophie Susan
Emily *b* 198-, Arabella Mary Lucy *b* 1983, — Susan Mary, *b* 1947: *m* 1970, Dr Martin Fraser, and has issue living, Ian
Anthony Charles *b* 1971, Rosemary Susan *b* 1974.

LODER (UK) 1887, of Whittlebury, Northamptonshire, and of High Beeches, Slaugham, Sussex

A sound conscience is a wall of brass

Sir GILES ROLLS LODER, 3rd *Baronet*, son of late Capt Robert Egerton Loder, son of 2nd baronet, who was *ka* 1917; *b* 10 Nov 1914; *s* his grandfather, *Sir* EDMUND GILES, 1920; *ed* Eton, and Trin Coll, Camb (MA); formerly Lieut 98th (Surrey and Sussex Yeo) Field Brig RA (TA); High Sheriff of Sussex 1948; a DL for W Sussex and a JP for Sussex: *m* 1939, Marie Violet Pamela (an OStJ) only da of late Bertram Hanmer Bunbury Symons-Jeune, of Runnymede House, Old Windsor, and has issue.

Arms – Azure, on a fesse between two escallops or, three bucks' heads cabossed proper. **Crest** – Between two escallops or, a bucks head cabossed and pierced with an arrow bendwise point to the sinister proper.
Residence – Ockenden House, Cuckfield, Sussex RH17 5LD. *Club* – Royal Yacht Squadron.

SONS LIVING

EDMUND JEUNE (Eyrefield Lodge, The Curragh, co Kildare), *b* 26 June, 1941; *ed* Eton; FCA: *m* 1st, 1966 (*m diss* 1971), Penelope Jane, da of Ivo Forde; 2ndly, 1992, Susan Warren, da of V. W. Warren Pearl, of Lindfield, Sussex, and has issue living (by 1st *m*), Gillian Marie, *b* 1968: *m* 1992, James D. P. Morgan, son of David Morgan, of Northchapel, Sussex. ——— Robert Reginald (Leonardslee Gardens, Horsham, Sussex), *b* 1943; *ed* Eton, and Trin Coll, Camb (BA): *m* 1967, Quenelda Jane, da of Sir John Ledward Royden, 4th Bt, and has issue living, Christopher Giles, *b* 1968, — Peter Thomas, *b* 1972, — Catherine Marie Violet, *b* 1970, — Mary Charlotte, *b* (twin) 1972.

COLLATERAL BRANCHES LIVING

Grandchildren of late Wilfred Hans Loder, 2nd son of 1st baronet:—

Issue of late Hubert Sydney Loder, *b* 1888; *d* 1982: *m* 1918 (*m diss* 1944), Brenda, who *d* 1981, da of Charles McNeill:—

Simon John (Clapton Court, Crewkerne, Som TA18 8PT; White's and Pratt's Clubs), *b* 1932; *ed* Eton; late Capt Gren Gds: *m* 1st, 1962 (*m diss* 1978), Kathleen Alexandra, el da of Richard Evelyn Fleming, MC, TD (*see* B Wyfold); 2ndly, 1979, Penelope Anne Mary, da of Sir Charles Marcus Mander, 3rd Bt, and formerly wife of Michael Rollo Hoare, and has issue living, (by 1st *m*) David Richard, *b* 1964: *m* 1990, Cressida, da of Ian Landless, of Duns Tew, Oxon, — Alexander Hugh, *b* 1965, — John Alistair, *b* 1968, — (by 2nd *m*) James Robert, *b* 1981. ——— Jean Mary (Dam Farm House, Brailsford, Derby), *b* 1919: *m* 1939, Stephen Dane Player, who *d* 1979, and has issue living, Peter Dane (Whatton Manor, Whatton in the Vale, Notts), *b* 1941: *m* 1970, Catherine Esther, eldest da of Col Gerald Vigors de Courcy O'Grady (The O'Grady), MC, of Kilballyowen, Bruff, co Limerick, and formerly wife of Rupert Hugh Stobart, and has issue living, Edward Dane *b* 1973, Alice Mary *b* 1971, — James Stephen (Bradley Park South, Brailsford, Derby), *b* 1945: *m* 1968, Philippa Headley, da of Frank Headley Richardson, and has issue living, Andrew Headley *b* 1970, Duncan James *b* 1972, — Nicholas Charles William, *b* 1948, *d* 1969, — Karen Jean, *b* 1940: *m* 1963, Dermot Kelly, of The Coach House, Dowdeswell, Cheltenham, Glos GL5 J44, and has issue living, Patrick Dermot Stephen *b* 1968, Doone *b* 1963, Anna *b* 1966. ——— Gillian, *b* 1925: *m* 1952, John Johnston Kirkpatrick, FLAS, FRICS, MBH, of Horn Park, Beaminster, Dorset, and Church Hill, Newcastle, co Down, N Ireland, and has issue living, Christopher James (Compton Graze, Little Compton, Moreton-in-Marsh, Glos GL56 ORT), *b* 1953: *m* 1978, Annabel Susan, da of Frederick McLean Hayward, of Gosebury Hall Farm, Nonnington, Kent, and has issue living Lucy Diana *b* 1984, Sophie Clare *b* 1986, Chloe Laura *b* 1991, — Nicholas Yvone John, *b* 1959: *m* 1990, Hon Joanna Norrie FitzRoy Newdegate, only da of 3rd Viscount Daventry, and has issue living, a son *b* 1992, a da *b* 1994, — Francis Hugh (52 Walham Grove, SW6 1QR), *b* 1962: *m* 1990, Miranda J., eldest da of David Fitzwilliam-Lay, of Bloxham, Savernake Forest, Wilts, and has issue living, George Hugh *b* 1992, Henry James *b* 1993, — Robin Kenneth Anthony, *b* 1969, — Rose Cecilia, *b* 1955: *m* 1977, James Adair Wigan, and has issue (*see* Wigan, Bt, colls), — Sara Gillian, *b* 1956: *m* 1983, Preston Martin Charles Rabl, of Winterbourne Manor, Newbury, Berks RG16 8AU, and has issue living, Francesca Sara *b* 1984, Sophia Rose *b* 1986, Georgina Moira *b* 1988.

Issue of late Gerald Walter Erskine Loder, 5th son of 1st baronet, who was *cr Baron Wakehurst* 1934 (see that title).

MORRISON-LOW (UK) 1908, of Kilmaron, co Fife

Perils delight me. Prudence excels

Sir JAMES RICHARD MORRISON-LOW, 3rd *Baronet*: *b* 3 Aug 1925; *s* his father, *Sir* WALTER JOHN, 1955; DL of Fife: *m* 1953, Anne Rawson, da of late Air Commodore Robert Gordon, CB, CBE, DSO, and has issue.

Arms – Quarterly, 1st and 4th argent, two wolves counterpassant sable, armed and langued gules, on a chief of the last three fleurs-de-lis of the first, *Low*; 2nd and 3rd per chevron or and ermine three saracens' heads couped at the neck proper, turbaned vert, *Morrison*. **Crest** – 1st, and eagle's head between two thistles slipped proper, *Low*; 2nd, a saracen's head proper, turbaned vert, *Morrison*.
Seat – Kilmaron, near Cupar, Fife KY15 4NE.

SON LIVING

RICHARD WALTER, *b* 4 Aug 1959.

DAUGHTERS LIVING

Alison Dorothy, *b* 1955. —— Jean Elspeth, *b* 1957. —— Susan Elizabeth, *b* 1963: *m* 1989, Graham William Latham, of No 1 Meadow Cottages, Church St, Sturminster Marshall, Dorset BH21 4BU, eldest son of K. O. E. Latham, of Poole, Dorset.

BROTHER LIVING

(Colin) John (Route 1, Box 302, Easton, Maryland 21601, USA), *b* 1928: *m* 1st, 1953, Susan Désirée MacDougal, who *d* 1977, da of P. C. M. Watson, of George, S Africa; 2ndly, 1980, Mrs Anne de Clerk, and has issue living, (by 1st *m*) Katherine Dorothy, *b* 1955: *m* 1978, Peter Jarman, of Stirling, Australia, —— Corinna Helen, *b* 1959: *m* 1984 (*m diss* 1989), Mark Brettel, son of Ray Brettel, of Teulada, Alicante, Spain.

WIDOW LIVING OF SECOND BARONET

(HENRIETTA) WILHELMINA MARY (*Dowager Lady Morrison-Low*), da of late Maj Robert Walter Purvis, of Gilmerton, Fife (Gilmour, Bt, cr 1897): *m* 1948, as his second wife, Sir Walter John Morrison-Low, 2nd baronet, who *d* 1955. *Residence* – Kingsbarns House, 6 The Square, Kingsbarn, nr Andrews, Fife.
Sir James Low, Knt, 1st Bt, el son of William Low, of Kirriemuir, by Janet, his wife, da of Alexander Morrison, of Kirriemuir, was Lord Provost of Dundee 1893-6. Sir Walter John Morrison-Low, 2nd Bt, assumed by deed poll (enrolled at College of Arms) 1924, the additional surname of Morrison.

LOWE (UK) 1918, of Edgbaston, City of Birmingham

Sir THOMAS WILLIAM GORDON LOWE, 4th *Baronet*; *b* 14 August 1963; *s* his father, *Sir* FRANCIS REGINALD GORDON, 1986; Bar-at-law; *ed* Stowe, LSE London Univ (LLB), and Jesus Coll, Camb (LLM).

Arms – Erminois, on a bend engrailed cottised plain azure between two Stafford knots sable, three wolves' heads erased or. **Crest** – A demi-gryphon erminois, resting the sinister paw on a Stafford knot sable.
Residence – 8 Seymour Walk, SW10.

BROTHER LIVING

CHRISTOPHER FRANCIS, *b* 25 Dec 1964. *Residence* – Lake Constance, W Germany.

MOTHER LIVING

Francesca Cornelia, da of Siegfried Steinkopf, of Berlin: *m* 1961 (*m diss* 1971), as his 1st wife, Sir Francis Reginald Gordon Lowe, 3rd Bt, who *d* 1986. *Residence* –

WIDOW LIVING OF SECOND BARONET

HELEN SUZANNE (*Helen, Lady Lowe*), da of late Sandys Stuart Macaskie, solicitor: *m* 1971, as his 2nd wife, Sir Francis Reginald Gordon Lowe, 3rd Bt, who *d* 1986. *Residence* – Pelham House, 9 Bath Road, Cowes, Isle of Wight PO31 7QN.

I hope for better things

COLLATERAL BRANCHES LIVING

Issue of late Arthur Holden Lowe, 2nd son of 1st baronet, *b* 1886, *d* 1924, Evelyn, who *d* 1949, da of Alfred Philpot, of Bexhill-on-Sea:—
John Evelyn, *b* 1928; MA, FSA; author: *m* 1st, 1956 (*m diss* 1981), Susan Helen Sanderson; 2ndly, 1989, Yukiko Nomura, and has issue living (by 1st *m*), Mark John, *b* 1957, — Dominic Simon, *b* 1961, — Judith Anne, *b* 1962. *Residence* – Paillole-Basse, Cours, 47360 Praysass, France. —— Jill Rosemary, *b* 1937: *m* 1957, Peter Gibbons, of 170 Cambridge St, SW1, and has issue living, Nicholas Arthur, *b* 1960, — Caroline Evelyn, *b* 1958, — Lucinda Mary, *b* 1961, — Julia Anne, *b* 1963, — Mary Jane, *b* 1967.

Issue of late Wing Cdr John Claude Malcolm Lowe, yst son of 1st baronet, *b* 1888, *d* 1970: *m* 1912, Winifred Olsson, who *d* 1968:—

Anthony John (Unicorn Cottage, Wallcrouch, Wadhurst, Sussex), *b* 1913: *m* 1948, Mrs Rosemary Beatrice Richards, elder da of late Capt A.H. Hollins, and has issue living, Charles *b* 1949, — Nicholas (twin), *b* 1949: *m* 1974, Rosemary Jane, da of Maurice Henry Frank Charman, and has issue living, Elizabeth Jane *b* 1980, Katherine Louise *b* 1981, — Timothy, *b* 1953, — Joanna, *b* 1958. —— Elizabeth Sydney, *b* 1928: *m* 1957, Edward C. Richardson, of 540 Banbury Rd, Oxford, and has issue living, Henry Edward Carleton, *b* 1961, — Conan Sacheverell Carleton, *b* 1963, — Emma, *b* 1958, — Sophie, *b* 1959.

Issue of late Dorothy Mary Lowe, da of 1st baronet, *b* 1893, *d* 1969: *m* 1916 (*m diss* 1934), Maj Robert Harley Egerton Bennett MC, Som LI:—

Peter Egerton BENNETT, *b* 1917; *ed* Malvern Coll, and RADA; Actor and Dir: *m* 1971, Sheila, da of late Rev William Bramwell-Jones, and *d* 1989. *Residence* – 39 Bedford Gdns, W8 7EF.

The 1st baronet, Rt Hon Sir Francis William Lowe, DL, was sometime a partner in the legal firm of Lowe and Jolly, and sat as MP for Birmingham, Edgbaston Div (*C*) 1898 to 1929.

LOWSON (UK) 1951, of Westlaws, co Perth

Sir IAN PATRICK LOWSON, 2nd *Baronet; b* 4 Sept 1944; *s* his father, *Sir* DENYS COLQUHOUN FLOWERDEW, 1975; *ed* Eton, and Duke Univ, USA; an OStJ: *m* 1979, Mrs Tanya Theresa H. Du Boulay, only da of Raymond F. A. Judge.

Arms – Quarterly; 1st and 4th per saltire argent and azure, in chief a sealion sejant and in base a fleur-de-lys sable, in each flank a garb or, *Lowson*; 2nd per chevron argent and pean a chevronel invected on the upper side between two sealions segant sable in chief and another in base of the first, *Flowerdew*; 3rd erminois, three catherine-wheels two and one sable within a bordure engrailed azure, over all a chief gules thereon a hill with lines of defence all proper, in dexer chief a mullet argent, *Scott*. **Crest** – 1st a garb or; 2nd a demi-man habited azure, garnished gules wreathed about the temples argent and sable holding in the right hand a sprig of two roses, one of the second, the other of the third, stalked and leaved proper.
Residence – 23 Flood Street, SW3 5ST. *Clubs* – Boodle's, Pilgrims, Brook (NY).

SON LIVING

HENRY WILLIAM, *b* 10 Nov 1980.

DAUGHTER LIVING

Katherine Louisa Patricia, *b* 1983.

SISTERS LIVING

Gay Ann (*Countess of Kinnoull*), *b* 1938: *m* 1961, 15th Earl of Kinnoull (15 Carlyle Sq, SW3 6EX; Pier Hse, Seaview, I of Wight). —— Melanie Fiona Louisa, *b* 1940: *m* 1964, Charles Archibald Adam Black, of 1 Astell St, SW3 (D Roxburghe), and has issue living, Adam Sebastian, *b* 1965, — Holly Patricia Louisa, *b* 1968.

WIDOW LIVING OF FIRST BARONET

Hon ANN PATRICIA MACPHERSON (*Hon Lady Lowson*) (Oratory Cottage, 33 Ennismore Gdns Mews, SW7 1HZ), da of 1st Baron Strathcarron; an OStJ: *m* 1936, Sir Denys Colquhoun Flowerdew Lowson, 1st Bt, who *d* 1975.

Sir Denys Colquhoun Flowerdew Lowson, 1st Bt, son of James Gray Flowerdew Lowson JP, PhD, of Balthayock, Perthshire, was Lord Mayor of London 1950-51 (Festival of Britain year).

LOWTHER (UK) 1824, of Swillington, Yorkshire

Sir CHARLES DOUGLAS LOWTHER, 6th *Baronet*, *b* 22 Jan 1946; *s* his father, *Lt-Col Sir* WILLIAM GUY, OBE, 1982; *ed* Winchester; Col, commanded Queen's R Irish Hus 1986-89: *m* 1st, 1969 (*m diss* 1975), Melanie Pensée FitzHerbert, da of late Roderick Christopher Musgrave; 2ndly, 1975, Florence Rose, yst da of late Col Alexander James Henry Cramsie, OBE, of O'Harabrook, Ballymoney, co Antrim, and has issue by 2nd *m*.

Arms – Or, six annulets sable, a crescent for difference. **Crest** – A dragon passant argent.
Seat – Erbistock Hall, nr Wrexham, Clwyd LL13 0DE.

The magistrate shows the man

SON LIVING *(By 2nd marriage)*

PATRICK WILLIAM, *b* 15 July, 1977.

DAUGHTER LIVING *(By 2nd marriage)*

Alice Rose, *b* 1979.

SISTER LIVING

Grizelda Leonora, *b* 1948: *m* 1968, Capt Timothy Michael Bell, Scots Gds, and has issue living, Matthew Guy, *b* 1974, — Katherine Leonora, *b* 1971.

AUNT LIVING *(Daughter of 4th baronet)*

Doreen Margaret, *b* 1910. *Residence* – 3 Mill Court, Overton, near Wrexham.

WIDOW LIVING OF FOURTH BARONET

RUTH KYNASTON (*Dowager Lady Lowther*), da of Charles Francis Kynaston Mainwaring (Rankin, Bt, *cr* 1898): *m* 1936, as his second wife, Lieut-Col Sir Charles Bingham Lowther, CB, DSO, 4th baronet, who *d* 1949. *Residence* – Lightwood, Lightwood Green, Overton, Wrexham.

WIDOW LIVING OF FIFTH BARONET

GRANIA SUZANNE (*Grania, Lady Lowther*), yst da of late Maj Archibald James Hamilton Douglas-Campbell, OBE, of Blythswood House, Renfrew (By Clarina, ext); OStJ: *m* 1939, Lt-Col Sir William Guy Lowther, OBE, 5th Bt, who *d* 1982. *Residence* – Cefyndd Farm, Erbistock, Wrexham.

COLLATERAL BRANCHES LIVING

Grandchildren of late Col John George Lowther, CBE, DSO, MC, TD (infra):—
Issue of late Capt George Hugh Lowther, *b* 1912, *d* 1976: *m* 1938, Sheila Rachel Isabel, who *d* 1980, da of late Maj Phipps Foster:—
James, *b* 1947; *ed* Eton: *m* 1987, Karen H., da of James Wallace, of Boston, Mass, USA, and has issue living, James William Dolfin, *b* 1991, — Natasha Jane, *b* 1988, — a da, *b* 1994. *Residence* – Holdenby House, Northampton. —— Sheila Ann, *b* 1943: *m* 1964, John Byng Oswald Carleton Paget, of 40 Gloucester Walk, W8, and has issue living, James Nicholas, *b* 1966, — William Byng, *b* 1968, — Rory Edward, *b* 1971.

Issue of late Col John George Lowther, CBE, DSO, MC, TD, brother of 4th baronet, *b* 1885, *d* 1977: *m* 1911, Hon Lilah Charlotte Sarah White, who *d* 1976, da of 3rd Baron Annaly:—
John Luke, CBE (Guilsborough Court, Northampton), *b* 1923; Capt late KRRC; CBE (Civil) 1983; Lord Lieut Northants since 1984: *m* 1952, Jennifer Jane, el da of late John Henry Bevan, CB, MC (E Lucan), and has issue living, Hugh William (Nortoft Grange, Guilsborough, Northants NN6 8QB), *b* 1956: *m* 1985, Hon Amanda Ursula Georgina Vivian, elder da of 4th Baron Swansea, and has had issue, Bertie *b* and *d* 1989, Flora Miriam *b* 1988, Georgia *b* 1991, Lucia *b* 1994, — Sarah Charlotte Margaret, *b* 1954: *m* 1977, Henry Merton Henderson, 2nd son of John Ronald Henderson, CVO, OBE, of West Woodhay House, Newbury, and has issue living, Harry Oliver *b* 1979, Katie Sarah *b* 1981, — Lavinia Mary, *b* 1958: *m* 1983, Julian Edward Tomkins, of 10 Guildford Rd, SW8 2BX, son of Sir Edward Emile Tomkins, GCMG, CVO, of Winslow Hall, Winslow, Bucks, and has issue living, Benjamin Henry *b* 1988, Geordie Edward *b* 1991. —— Bridget Elizabeth, *b* 1921: *m* 1947, Robert Alister Henderson (*see* Clerke, Bt, 1980 Edn), and has had issue, Robert David Charles (Battle House, Goring-on-Thames, Oxon), *b* 1948: *m* 1975, Odette Anne, da of late Lloyd Llewellyn Andersson, of Parktown, Johannesburg, and has issue living, Camilla Elizabeth *b* 1977, Laura Catherine *b* 1979, Celia Anne *b* 1982, — James, *b* 1955: *m* 1978, Susan Clare Evelyn (who *m* 2ndly, 19—, Charles Dingwall), da of David Cuthbert Tudway Quilter (*see* Quilter, Bt, colls), and *d* 1991, leaving issue, Sophie Elizabeth *b* 1979, Emily Anne *b* 1981, Alice Beatrice *b* 1985, — Emma Mary, *b* 1950: *m* 1st, 1971 (*m diss* 1978), Hugh Leopold Seymour (*see* M Hertford, colls); 2ndly, 1979, J. L. David Aschan; 3rdly, 1982, Paul Anthony Irby, of Swaites Farm, Echinswell, Newbury, Berks, and has issue living, (by 2nd *m*), Clare Louise *b* 1979, Eliza Beatrice *b* 1981, (by 3rd *m*) (*see* B Boston).

The 1st baronet, many years, MP for Cumberland, was brother to William, 1st Earl of Lonsdale, and the 2nd baronet was successively MP for Cockermouth, Wigton, and York. The 4th baronet, Lieut-Col Sir Charles Bingham, CB, DSO, was Lieut-Col Northants Yeo and High Sheriff of Northants 1926.

LUCAS (UK) 1887, of Ashtead Park, Surrey, and of Lowestoft, co Suffolk

Sir THOMAS EDWARD LUCAS, 5th *Baronet*, son of late Ralph John Scott Lucas, 2nd son of Maj Ernest Murray Lucas, 3rd son of 1st baronet; *b* 16 Sept 1930; *s* his cousin, Maj Sir JOSCELYN MORTON, KBE, MC 1980; *ed* Wellington Coll, and Trin Hall, Camb (MA): *m* 1st, 1958, Charmian Margaret, who *d* 1970, only da of late Col James Stanley Powell, of Drayton Court, SW10; 2ndly, 1980, Mrs Ann J. Graham Moore, and has issue by 1st *m*.

𝕬rms – Per bend argent and gules, a bend dovetailed between six annulets, all counterchanged, 𝕮rest – Issuant from a wreath of oak or a dragons head, wings addorsed gules, semée of annulets argent.
Address – Shermans Hall, Dedham, Essex C07 6DE.
Club – Athenaeum.

SON LIVING *(By 1st marriage)*

SPES · ET · FIDES

Hope and faith

STEPHEN RALPH JAMES, *b* 11 Dec 1963; *ed* Wellington Coll, and Edinburgh Univ (BCom).

BROTHER LIVING

Patrick Timson, VRD and bar (The Hollies, Court Green Heights, Hook Heath, Woking, Surrey; Royal Naval Club), *b* 1933; *ed* Wellington Coll; Maj (RMR): *m* 1958, Anne, da of Jack Westcott, of Yeovil, Som, and has issue living, Simon James Timson, *b* 1960; *ed* Wellington Coll, and City Univ, London (BSc), — Julian Patrick, *b* 1962; *ed* Wellington Coll, and Univ Coll, Cardiff (BSc).

COLLATERAL BRANCHES LIVING

Grandchildren of late Rev Francis Granville Lewis Lucas, 4th son of 1st baronet:—
Issue of late Brig Hubert Francis Lucas, CBE, *b* 1897, *d* 1990: *m* 1921, Evelyn Irene Sophie Phipps, who *d* 1993, da of late Brig-Gen Edmund John Phipps Hornby, VC, CB, CMG:—
Diana Joan, *b* 1931: *m* 1954, Capt John Brian St Vincent Hawkins, Dorset Regt (ret), of Acres Cut, 4 Lime Close, Dorchester, Dorset, and has issue living, Rowena Fay (Brownston House, School Lane, Harby, Leics), *b* 1955: *m* 1986, Lt Cdr David Lawrence Barrow, who *d* 1989, — Wendy Susan, *b* 1957: *m* 1988, Robert Leonard Creed, of 166 Hatton Rd, Bedfont, Middx, and has issue living, Martin Geoffrey Hubert HAWKINS-CREED *b* 1989, 'Richard David Francis HAWKINS-CREED *b* 1991.
Issue of late Maj Arthur John Lucas, *b* 1903, *d* 1986: *m* 1930, Margaret Ruth, who *d* 1989, da of late Col Joseph Francis Noel Baxendale, CB, TD (Heathcoat, Bt):—
James Granville (Yew Tree Cottage, Port Navas, Falmouth, Cornwall), *b* 1932; *ed* Harrow; Lt Cdr RN (ret): *m* 1st, 1957 (*m diss* 1973), Suzanne Molly, da of Edward Fitzroy Talbot-Ponsonby (*see* E Shrewsbury, colls); 2ndly, 1973, Ann Marie Mason, and has issue living (by 1st *m*), Jonathan Delight, *b* 1964, — Charles Granville *b* (twin) 1964, — (by 2nd *m*) Serena Kate, *b* 1977. —— Jennifer, *b* 1936: *m* 1972, Hugh Cecil Toomer, of 5 Eccleston Sq, SW1.

Grandchildren of late Maj Evelyn Penn Lucas, MC, yst son of 1st baronet:—
Issue of late Capt Timothy Stovin Lucas, MC, TD, *b* 1916; *d* 1981: *m* 1942, Joanna Repington (Sharow Hall, Ripon, N Yorks), only child of Charles Bernard Mathews, of Lob's Wood, Ilkley, Yorks:—
Charles Evelyn Penn (Sharow Hall, Ripon, N Yorks), *b* 1943; *ed* Eton: *m* 1967 (*m diss* 1989), Antoinette Maria, only da of late Baron Henri von Westenholz, of Blakesware, Much Hadham, Herts, and has issue living, Piers Timothy Everard, *b* 1970, — Harry Rudolph Penn, *b* 1976, — Nina Antoinette, *b* 1971. —— Charlotte Theresa Stovin (Weavers, Fewcott, nr Bicester, Oxon), *b* 1945: *m* 1966 (*m diss* 1971), Christopher Frank Stuart Irwin, and has issue living, Alexander Christian Stovin, *b* 1970, — Sophia Georgette Kate, *b* 1968.

Lucas (Munro-Lucas-Tooth), see Tooth.

RAMSAY-FAIRFAX-LUCY (UK) 1836, of The Holmes, Roxburghshire

Sir EDMUND JOHN WILLIAM HUGH RAMSAY-FAIRFAX-LUCY, 6th *Baronet*; *b* 4 May 1945; *s* his father, *Maj Sir* BRIAN FULKE, 1974; *ed* Eton; Dip RA Schs: *m* 1st, 1974 (*m diss* 19—), Sylvia, da of Graeme Ogden, of The Old Manor, Rudge, Somerset; 2ndly, 1986 (*m diss* 1989), Lady Lucinda Lambton, eldest da of Antony Claud Lambton (6th Earl of Durham until he disclaimed his title 1970).

Arms – 1st and 4th grand-quarters, gules, 1st semée of cross crosslets, three lucies haurient argent, a canton of the last, *Lucy*; 2nd and 3rd grand quarters, quarterly 1st and 4th argent, three bars gemel sable surmounted by a lion rampant gules, armed and langued azure, *Fairfax*; 2nd, *per pale argent and or, an eagle displayed sable, armed, beaked and membered gules, Ramsay*; 3rd counter-quartered, 1st and 4th azure, a branch of palm between three fleurs-de-lis or, 2nd and 3rd gules, three annulets or, stoned azure, in the centre of three counter-quarters a crescent or for difference, *Montgomerie*. **Crests** – 1st, out of a ducal coronet gules a boar's head argent guttée de poix, between two wings sable: billettée or charged on the neck, with a cross-crosslet sable, *Lucy*; 2nd, a lion passant guardant proper, *Fairfax*. **Mottoes** – *Dexter*, By truthe and diligence, *Lucy*; *sinister*, Fare fac, *Fairfax*.
Seat – Charlecote Park, Warwick.

SISTER LIVING

(Mary Caroline Alys) Emma, *b* 1946: *m* 1st, 1967, James Empson Scott, MA, MB, BCh, FRCS; 2ndly, 1982, as his 2nd wife, James Louis Lambe (*see* Corbet, Bt, 1990 Edn), and has issue living, (by 1st *m*) Sophie Katherina Rosie, *b* 1970, — Charlotte Christina Bianca, *b* 1974.

COLLATERAL BRANCHES LIVING

Issue of late Capt Ewen Aymer Robert Ramsay-Fairfax-Lucy, yst son of 3rd baronet, *b* 1899, *d* 1969: *m* 1930, Margaret Westall, who *d* 1994, da of Sir John Westall King, 2nd Bt (*cr* 1888):—
DUNCAN CAMERON (The Malt House, Charlecote, Warwick CV35 9EW), *b* 18 Sept 1932; *ed* Eton; FCA: *m* 1964, Janet Barclay, da of P. A. B. Niven, of Malt Cottage, Charlecote, Warwick, and has issue living, Spencer Angus, *b* 1966, — Anna Margaret Barclay, *b* 1969. —— Robin Spencer, *b* 1937. —— Jennifer Frances, *b* 1935: *m* 1962, Dr (Ronald) Ian Talbot Cromartie, CMG, who *d* 1987, and has issue living, Alan Duncan Talbot, *b* 1964, — David Francis Ian, *b* 1970, — Selina Margaret Lucy, *b* 1967. —— Christina Alison, *b* 1943: *m* 1964, John Anthony Chandley Pugh, FCA, and has issue living, Jonathan Chandley, *b* 1966, — Rosanna Lucy, *b* 1968, — Martha Elizabeth, *b* 1971.

Issue of late Com William George Astell RAMSAY-FAIRFAX, CMG, DSO, RN, 3rd son of 2nd baronet, *b* 1876, *d* 1946: *m* 1909, Lilian Kate, who *d* 1957, da of late Henry Rich, of Abbey Lodge, Malmesbury:—
Victor George Hargrave, DSC, *b* 1912; Lt-Cdr (ret) RN; 1939-45 War (despatches, DSC): *m* 1939, Christian Geraldine Mary, who *d* 1967, only child of late Lt-Col Frederick Arthur Irby (B Boston, colls), and has issue living, Victor Ferdinand Desmond, *b* 1944, — Pepita Christian, *b* 1942. *Residence* – 73 High St, Lavenham, Suffolk, CO10 9PT. *Club* – Army and Navy.

This family claims descent from the same stock as Lord Fairfax of Cameron. Vice-Adm Sir William George Fairfax, a distinguished naval officer, was made a Knight Banneret for bravery displayed by him at the battle of Camperdown, and in consideration of his services a baronetcy was conferred upon his only surviving son, Col Sir Henry Fairfax, who *m* 1830 (as his 1st wife) Archibald Montgomerie, da and eventually heir of Thomas Williamson (afterwards Williamson-Ramsay), by Elizabeth, da and co-heir of Robert Ramsay of Camno and Arthurstown, Forfar. The 2nd baronet, Col Sir William George Herbert Taylor, assumed the additional surname and arms of Ramsay 1876, and the 3rd baronet, Sir Henry William, CB, assumed by Royal Licence the additional surname of Lucy 1892, and Cameron 1921, having *m* 1892, Ada Christina, da and heir of Henry Spencer Lucy, of Charlecote, Warwickshire.

LUSHINGTON (GB) 1791, of South Hill Park, Berkshire

Sir JOHN RICHARD CASTLEMAN LUSHINGTON, 8th *Baronet*; *b* 28 Aug 1938; *s* his father, *Sir* HENRY EDMUND CASTLEMAN, 1988; *ed* Oundle; Partner MaST (Management and Skills Training): *m* 1966, Bridget Gillian Margaret, only da of late Col John Foster Longfield, of Knockbeg, Saunton, N. Devon, and has issue.

𝕬rms – Or, on a fesse wavy between three lions' heads erased vert, as many ermine spots or. 𝕮rest – A lion's head erased vert, charged on the erasure with three ermine spots or, ducally gorged argent.
Residence – The Glebe House, Henham, Bishops Stortford, Herts.

SONS LIVING

RICHARD DOUGLAS LONGFIELD, *b* 29 March 1968; BA; Fl Lt RAF. —— Greville Edmund Longfield, *b* 1969; BA. —— Thomas Robert Longfield, *b* 1975.

SISTERS LIVING

Fides nudaque veritas

Faith and naked truth

Caroline Elizabeth, *b* 1942: *m* 1964, Patrick Donald Bloss, FCA, of Dene House, The Green, Shamley Green, Guildford, Surrey GU5 0UA, and has issue living, James Patrick, *b* 1972, — Diana Elizabeth, *b* 1967, — Victoria Caroline *b* 1970. —— Penelope Daphne, *b* 1945: *m* 1967, Ronald Gulliver, LLB, FCA, of The Old Chapel, New Mill, Eversley, Hants, and has issue living, Christopher Ronald, *b* 1974, — Patricia Jean, *b* 1976.

UNCLE LIVING *(son of 6th baronet by 1st marriage)*

Algernon Herbert Greville (15 Flinders Parade, Barwon Heads, Victoria 3227, Australia), *b* 1910; S-W Pacific 1944-45 as Capt Australian Imperial Force (despatches): *m* 1st, 1948, Mary Elizabeth Gweneth, who *d* 1959, da of C. J. Dunbar, of Dunbarton, Bairnsdale, Victoria, Australia; 2ndly, 1961, Marjory Lorrainé Breheny, da of C. W. Le Plastrier, of Woodend, Victoria, Australia.

HALF-UNCLE LIVING *(son of 6th baronet by 2nd marriage)*

Patrick Hay Castleman (56 Suzanne Av, Morphett Vale, S Aust 5162) *b* 1931; late RAF: *m* 1957, Ann Marie, el da of Ferdinand Mohr, of 37 Neutorstrasse, Mainz, Germany, and has issue living, Kurt, *b* 1958: *m* 1985, Susane Annette, da of Lionel Burton, of 14 Lochness Av, Adelaide, and has issue living, Joshua Hay Castleman *b* 1991, Grace Alexandra *b* 1992, — Werner, *b* 1960: *m* 1985, Sylvia Angelika, da of Sigismund Krause, of 81 O'Sullivan Beach Rd, Morphett-Vale, and has issue living, Sean Matthew *b* 1987, Alexander James *b* 1992 Tarryn Rebecca *b* 1986, — Horst, *b* 1966, — Elke Christine, *b* 1964: *m* 1992, Robert Melten, yst son of Nicholas Melten.

HALF-AUNT LIVING *(daughter of 6th baronet by 2nd marriage)*

Pamela Anne, *b* 1929: *m* 1952, Peter Lindsay Jones, of 19 Aberdare Av, Drayton, Cosham, Portsmouth, PO6 2AT, and has issue living, Alistair, *b* 1953: *m* 1st, 1975 (*m diss* 1986), Heather McKennes; 2ndly, 1993, Shaari Horowitz, — Laurence, *b* 1959, — Martin Edward, *b* 1964, — Margaret Amanda, *b* 1955: *m* 1976, Michael Joseph Reilly, of Denver, USA, and has issue living, Patrick Joseph *b* 1977, Dennis John *b* 1979, — Rosemary Anne, *b* 1957: *m* 1989, Nicholas John Pullen, and has issue living, Adam James *b* 1990, Rebecca Louise *b* 1992, — Sarah Louise, *b* 1966.

WIDOW LIVING OF SEVENTH BARONET

PAMELA ELIZABETH DAPHNE (*Pamela, Lady Lushington*), elder da of late Maj Archer Richard Hunter, of The White Cottage, Rectory Rd, Wokingham, Berks: *m* 1937, Sir Henry Edmund Castleman Lushington, 7th Bt, who *d* 1988. *Residence* – Gramerci, Eversley Centre, Hants RG27 0NB.

COLLATERAL BRANCH LIVING

Grandson of late Sydney George Lushington, 2nd son of late Edward Harbord Lushington, eldest son of late Rt Hon Stephen Lushington, MP, 2nd son of 1st baronet:—
Issue of late Lt-Col Franklin Lushington, *b* 1892, *d* 1964: *m* 1st, 1916 (*m diss* 1948), (Mary Marjorie) Bridget, who *d* 1977, da of Ernest Howard; 2ndly, 1949, Eleanora, who *d* 1964, da of Niels Illeris, of Bagsvaerd, Denmark:—
(By 1st *m*) Stephen (9 High Wickham, Hastings, Sussex), *b* 1917; *ed* Eton, and New Coll, Oxford; late RA: *m* 1st, 1941 (*m diss* 1951), Maureen, da of Maj John Pook; 2ndly, 1951 (*m diss* 1972), Sonia, da of Harry Ratoff; 3rdly, 1972, Beatrice, da of Irvan O'Connell, of Winchester, Va, USA, and widow of Theodore Roethke, and has issue living, (by 1st *m*) Mark, *b* 1942: *m* 1966, Cora, da of Sidney Kaplan, of Northampton, Mass, USA, and has issue living, Jacob *b* 1968, — (by 2nd *m*) Catherine Rachel, *b* 1953: *m* 1975, Richard Marc Greenblatt.

This family was settled in E Kent from the 14th century. Sir Stephen Lushington, 1st Bt, of South Hill Park, Berks (grandson of Stephen Lushington of Sittingbourne, who purchased the Manor of Rodmersham) was Chm of Hon East India Co 1790.

LYLE (UK) 1929, of Glendelvine, co Perth

Sir GAVIN ARCHIBALD LYLE, 3rd *Baronet*, son of late Capt Ian Archibald de Hoghton Lyle, Black Watch, el son of 2nd baronet; *b* 14 Oct 1941; *s* his grandfather, *Col Sir* ARCHIBALD MOIR PARK, MC, 1946; *ed* Eton: *m* 1967 (*m diss* 1985), Susan, only da of John Vaughan Cooper, and has issue.

Arms – Gules, fretty or surmounted of a gallery, oars in saltire, sails furled sable, flagged gules, the sails charged with a crescent of the second for difference. **Crest** – A cock or crested gules.
Residence – Glendelvine, Caputh, Perthshire, PH1 4JN.

SONS LIVING

IAN ABRAM, *b* 25 Sept 1968. —— Jake Archibald, *b* 1969. —— Matthew Alexander, *b* 1974. —— Joshua, *b* 1979. —— Samuel, *b* 1981.

DAUGHTER LIVING

Rachel, *b* 1971.

SISTER LIVING

Lorna, *b* 1939: *m* 1st, 1959, Timothy Cyprian George Thomas Elwes (*see* B Rennell, 1973-74 Edn); 2ndly, 1979, Walter Ronald Alexander, and has issue living, (by 1st *m*) Ian Anthony Archibald de Hoghton Cary (Jubilee House, 13 Jubilee Place, SW3), *b* 1961: *m* 1990, Deborah J., elder da of David Winckles, of Bovey Tracey, Devon, — Gavin Esmond Cary, *b* 1962, — Amanda Dorothy Cary, *b* 1964: *m* 1992, Matthew D. Austin, only son of John Austin, of Arden House, Warwicks, — Lydia Elinor Cary *b* (twin), 1964.

UNCLE LIVING (*Son of 2nd baronet*)

Archibald Michael, *b* 1919; *ed* Eton, and Trin Coll, Oxford; Lt-Col (ret) Scottish Horse, and late Maj Black Watch; Vice Lord Lieut and a JP for Perthshire, and a Member Queen's Body Guard for Scotland (Roy Co of Archers); *m* 1942, Hon Elizabeth Sinclair, who *d* 1994, yr da of 1st Viscount Thurso, and has three das, Veronica, *b* 1943: *m* 1967, Magnus Duncan Linklater, of 5 Drummond Place, Edinburgh EH3 6PH, and has issue living, Alexander Ragnar *b* 1968, Saul Archibald Robert *b* 1970, Freya Elizabeth Erica *b* 1975, — Janet, *b* 1944: *m* 1975, Richard Cooper, and has issue living, Daisy *b* 1983, Hester *b* 1985, Matilda *b* 1988, — Sarah Caroline, *b* 1963. *Residence* – Riemore Lodge, Dunkeld, Perths.

AUNT LIVING (*Daughter of 2nd baronet*)

Dorothea, *b* 1914, *m* 1937 (*m diss* 1962), Rear-Adm Viscount Kelburn, CB, DSC (subsequently 9th Earl of Glasgow), who *d* 1984. *Residences* – Marwell House, Owlesbury, nr Winchester, and Albany, Piccadilly, W1.

MOTHER LIVING

Hon Lydia Yarde-Buller, da of 3rd Baron Churston: *m* 1st, 1938, Capt Ian Archibald de Hoghton Lyle, Black Watch (ante), who was *ka* 1942; 2ndly, 1947 (*m diss* 1960), 13th Duke of Bedford. *Residence* – Little Ribsden, Windlesham, Bagshot, Surrey.

Sir Alexander Park Lyle, 1st Bt, was a shipowner, and gt-grandson of Abram Lyle, of Greenock, who founded the firm of Abram Lyle & Sons in 1796 (previously MacDonald & Lyle). The 1st Lord Lyle of Westbourne was a nephew of the 1st Bt.

Lynch-Blosse, see Blosse.

Lynch-Robinson, see Robinson.

McALPINE (UK) 1918, of Knott Park, co Surrey

Hon Sir WILLIAM HEPBURN McALPINE, 6th *Baronet*; *b* 12 Jan 1936; *s* his father, (ROBERT) EDWIN, Baron McAlpine of Moffat (Life Baron) in his Baronetcy 1990; *ed* Charterhouse; a Dir Sir Robert McAlpine Ltd: *m* 1959, Jill Benton, only da of late Lt-Col Sir Peter Fawcett Benton Jones, 3rd Bt, OBE, and has issue.

Arms – Per chevron vert and or, two chevronels one in chief argent the other in base azure. **Crest** – A cubit arm grasping a chaplet of pine fructed all proper. *Residence* – Fawley Hill, Fawley Green, Henley-on-Thames, Oxon RG9 6JA.

SON LIVING

ANDREW WILLIAM, *b* 22 Nov 1960; *ed* Stowe: *m* 1991, (Caroline) Claire, yr da of Frederick A. Hodgson, of Sheffield, Yorks, and has issue living, Frederick William Edwin, *b* 25 Aug 1993.

DAUGHTER LIVING

Lucinda Mary Jane, *b* 1964.

BROTHERS LIVING

Hon Robert Alistair (*Baron McAlpine of West Green*), *b* 1942; *cr* Baron McAlpine of West Green (Life Baron) 1983 (see that title).
Hon David Malcolm, *b* 1946; *ed* Stowe; Dir Sir Robert McAlpine Ltd: *m* 1971 (*m diss* 1993), Jennifer Anne, da of Eric Hodges, and has issue living, Robert Edward Thomas William, *b* 1978, — Katherine Alexandra Donnison, *b* 1972, — Elizabeth Louise, *b* 1973.

SISTER LIVING

Hon Patricia Garnett, *b* 1932: *m* 1950, Hon Robin Sandbach Borwick, Lieut The Life Guards (ret), of Neptune House, Newells Lane, Bosham, Sussex PO18 8PS, son of 3rd Baron Borwick.

DAUGHTER LIVING OF SECOND BARONET

Zelie Agnes Elise Conde (Woodgates Cottage, Ford Manor, Dormansland, Lingfield, Surrey), *b* 1910: *m* 1934, Surg-Cdr Wilfred Treize Rougier Chapman, VD, RNVR, MRCS, LRCP, who *d* 1981, and has issue living, Zeralda Lillias, *b* 1939: *m* 1st, 1962 (*m diss* 1970), Trevor Adrian Soutry; 2ndly, 1977, Alphonse Michaele Micallef, MD, of Lower Stonehurst Farm, E Grinstead, Sussex, and has issue living (by 1st *m*), Giles Robert Adrian *b* 1964: *m* 1994, Mrs Anne Yolande Tranter Broadbent, da of — Cartright, Lucinda Caroline *b* 1969, — Nonie Elizabeth, *b* 1942, — Penelope Margaret, *b* 1944: *m* 1966, David Ronald Adam, of Lower Sandhill House, Halland, nr Uckfield, Sussex, and has issue living, Angus Ronald *b* 1969, Gavin David *b* 1976, Annabelle Jane *b* 1968: *m* 1993, Maj Charles Andrew Stuart, Katherine Lucy *b* 1972.

COLLATERAL BRANCHES LIVING

Grandchildren of late William McAlpine, 2nd son of 1st baronet:—
Issue of late Malcolm Donnison McAlpine, *b* 1909; *d* 1982: *m* 1939, Diana Mary (Little Burton, Burton Lazars, Melton Mowbray, Leics), da of Sidney Bruce Askew, of Nutfield, Surrey:—
Ian Malcolm, *b* 1942; *ed* Oundle, and Clare Coll, Camb (MA): *m* 1967, Caroline Mary, da of William Henry Ward, of Wisbech, Cambs, and has two adopted children, Julian Angus Ian, *b* 1970, — Susannah Melanie, *b* 1972. *Residence* – Peatling Hall, Peatling Parva, Leics. —— Bruce Andrew, *b* 1947; *ed* Oundle, and Clare Coll, Camb: *m* 1st, 1974 (*m diss* 1992), Ingrid Christliebe, da of Alfred Reynolds Schlosshauer, of Neckarhausen, Germany; 2ndly, 1993, Marina Ernestine Hirschberg, da of late Hubert, Baron von Breisky, of Salzburg, Austria. *Residence* – 43 Elm Park Gardens, SW10 9PA. —— Susan Mary, *b* 1945: *m* 1968, Leonard Maxwell Robert Harvey, of Lyneham House, Yealmpton, nr Plymouth, Devon, and has issue living, Damon, *b* 1971.

Granddaughter of late Sir (Thomas) Malcolm McAlpine, KBE (*infra*):—
Adopted da of late Sir Robin McAlpine, CBE, *b* 1906; assumed by deed poll 1939 the christian name of Robin in lieu of Robert; *d* 1993: *m* 1st, 1939, Nora Constance, who *d* 1966, yr da of F. H. Perse, formerly of Rochester, Kent; 2ndly, 1970, Mrs Philippa Janet Nicolson, who *d* 1987, da of Sir (Eustace) Gervais Tennyson d'Eyncourt, 2nd Bt, and formerly wife of Nigel Edward Nicolson, MBE (*see* B Carnock, colls):—
Carolyn Peta, *b* 1944: *m* 1965, Nigel Robert Elwes, and has issue living, Andrew Julian Robert, *b* 1969; *ed* Eton, and Edinburgh Univ, — Serena Clare, *b* 1967, — Melisa, *b* 1973. *Residence* – Aylesfield, Alton, Hants GU34 4BY.

Issue of late Sir (Thomas) Malcolm McAlpine, KBE, 3rd son of 1st baronet, *b* 1877, *d* 1967: *m* 1903, Maud, who *d* 1969, da of James Gibson Dees:—
Malcolm Hugh Dees (Highfields, Withyham, Hartfield, E Sussex TN7 4DB), *b* 1917; late Lt-Col RE; a Dir of Sir Robert McAlpine Ltd: *m* 1944, Sheila Margaret, el da of late Maj F. Raeburn Price, of Fordyce, N Foreland, Thanet, and has issue living, Adrian Neil Raeburn (14 Caroline Terr, SW1W 8JS), *b* 1944; Dir Sir Robert McAlpine Ltd; a Gov Milton Abbey Sch since 1987: *m* 1983, Angela Mary, yr da of Dr George Hickie, of Mill House, Ashton Keynes, Wilts, and has issue living, Angus Neil Adrian *b* 1993, Antonia Louise Philippa *b* 1984, Olivia Alice Gemma *b* 1986, — Cullum (Cold Ashton Manor, Chippenham, Wilts SN14 8JU), *b* 1947; assumed the forename of Cullum in lieu of Malcolm Robert by deed poll 1963; Dir Sir Robert McAlpine Ltd: *m* 1973, Amanda, yr da of Robert Lamdin, of Horsted Keynes, Sussex, and has issue living, Robert Harry *b* 1975, Gavin Malcolm *b* 1976, Hector George *b* 1980, Douglas James *b* 1983, — Hamish (79 Wardour St, W1V 3TH), *b* 1954. —— Kenneth (The Priory, Lamberhurst, Kent), *b* 1920; late F/O RAFVR; High Sheriff of Kent 1973-74, DL of Kent; Gov St Bartholomew's Hosp 1972-74, Gov and Dep-Chm Eastbourne Coll 1968-84; FRAeS: *m* 1955, Patricia Mary, da of late Capt Francis William Hugh Jeans, CVO, RN, and has issue living, Richard Hugh, *b* 1958: *m* 1991, Linda Elizabeth, only da of late William Leighton Wee, of San Francisco, USA, and has issue living, Thomas Leighton *b* 1992, — James Thomas Hemery, *b* 1960.

Grandchildren of late Sir Alfred (David) McAlpine, 4th son of 1st baronet:—
Issue of late Alfred James McAlpine, *b* 1908, *d* 1991: *m* 1st, 1931 (*m diss* 1940), Peggy Barbara, eldest da of late John Ernest Sanders, of Gresford, Denbighshire; 2ndly, 1940 (*m diss* 1951), Mary Kinder, da of Frank Musgrave

Read; 3rdly, 1951 (*m diss* 1959), Mrs Rosemary Lavery, who *d* 1983, da of late Maj Charles Hugh Gregory-Hood (*see* V Hood, colls, 1980 edn); 4thly, 1959 (*m diss* 1979), Eleanor Margaret Rangel, da of late John Nicholson Wallace, of Lisbon; 5thly, 1979, Cynthia Greenaway (Gerwyn Hall, Marchwiel, nr Wrexham, Denbighshire; The Towers, Llanarmon, Dyffryn Ceiriog, Denbighshire), da of Harry Whitney:—

(By 1st *m*) Robert James (Tilston Lodge, Tilston Fearnall, Tarporley, Cheshire), *b* 1932; *ed* Harrow; a Dir Sir Alfred McAlpine & Son Ltd: *m* 1st, 1956 (*m diss* 19—), Jane, who *d* 1992, eldest da of James Anton, of Tudor House, Rumsley, nr Bridgnorth, Shropshire; 2ndly, 1981, Mrs Angela J. Bell, only da of late Maj E. W. Langford-Brooke, of Cheshire, and has issue living (by 1st *m*), Euan James, *b* 1958: *m* 1983, Fiona Elizabeth, eldest da of Charles Aylmer Eade, of Uppington House, Telford, Shropshire, and has issue living, Tom *b* 1991, Flora *b* 1989, Rosie *b* 1993, — Christopher William, *b* 1965: *m* 1991, Sarah Louise, da of Anthony Rundell, of Clapham, SW, — Sara Jane (*Hon Mrs Robin Cayzer*), *b* 1961: *m* 1982, Hon (Herbert) Robin Cayzer, eldest son of 2nd Baron Rotherwick, — (by 2nd *m*) Emma Antonia, *b* 1982. —— Alfred William, *b* 1935; *ed* Harrow; *d* as the result of a road accident 1962, *unm*. —— (By 2nd *m*) Valerie Ann, *b* 1942: *m* 1st, 1962 (*m diss* 1966), Julian Noyes; 2ndly, 1967, Peter Shaw, of Barley End, Aldbury, Tring, Herts, and has issue living (by 1st *m*), William, *b* 1963, — (by 2nd *m*) Samantha Margaret, *b* 1969, — Joanna Mary, *b* 1972. —— (By 3rd *m*) Sally Dorothy (49 Campden Hill Rd, W8 7DY), *b* 1952: *m* 1975 (*m diss* 1990), as his 3rd wife, (Bernard) Godfrey Argent, and has issue living, Jenna Charlotte, *b* 1980.

Issue of late Granville Ramage McAlpine, 5th son of 1st baronet, *b* 1883; *d* 1928: *m* 1922, Beatrice Mary Donald, who *d* 1936:—

Maureen Agnes, *b* 1925: *m* 1949, Frederick Stanley Thornton, MBE, who *d* 1994, and has issue living, David Malcolm, *b* 1950: *m* 1973, Stephanie Patricia Mills, and has issue living, Simon Edward *b* 1983, — Andrew William (Willow Orchard, Frating Rd, Gt Bromley, Colchester, Essex C07 7JW), *b* 1953: *m* 1981, Jacqueline Mary Deane, and has issue living, James Ashley *b* 1984, Tobias William *b* 1987. *Residence* – Conifers, 1 St Clare Drive, Colchester, Essex C03 3TA.

Issue of late (Archibald) Douglas McAlpine, MD, FRCP, 6th son of 1st baronet, *b* 1890, *d* 1981: *m* 1st, 1917, Elizabeth Meg Sidebottom, who *d* 1941; 2ndly, 1945, Diana Christina Dunscombe, who *d* 1981, da of late Bertram Plummer:—

(By 1st *m*) (Robert Douglas) Christopher, CMG (Longtree House, Cutwell, Tetbury, Glos GL8 8EB), *b* 1919; *ed* Winchester, and New Coll, Oxford (MA); Foreign Office 1946-47, Assist Private Sec to Sec of State 1947-49, Control Commn for Germany as 2nd and later 1st Sec 1949-52; Foreign Office 1952-54, British Embassy, Lima 1954-56, and Moscow 1956-59, Foreign Office 1959-62, Dep Consul-Gen, New York 1962-65, and Counsellor, British Embassy, Mexico City 1965-68; a Dir of Baring Bros & Co Ltd 1969-79, Dir Clarkson (Holdings) plc 1980-87; 1939-45 War as Lt-Cdr RNVR (Fleet Air Arm) (CMG 1967): *m* 1943, Helen Margery Frances, da of late Capt Astley Cannan, and has issue living, David Douglas Christopher (64 Gloucester Rd, Kew, Richmond, Surrey), *b* 1949; *ed* Winchester, and E Anglia Univ: *m* 1973, Susan Mary, da of Richard John Boileau Walker, and has issue living, Thomas David *b* 1977, Laura Esme *b* 1980, Martha Rose *b* 1983, Jessica Mary Sucharita *b* 1986, — Robert John (12 Elizabeth Gardens, Meysey Hampton, Glos GL7 5LP), *b* 1953: *m* 1987, Sheila Maureen, da of E. J. Arseneault, of Winnipeg, Manitoba, Canada, and has issue living, Sophia Madeleine *b* 1993, — Sarah Margaret, *b* 1946: *m* 1971, Timothy George Holloway, of Glebe House, Lamer Lane, Wheathampstead, St Albans, Herts AL4 8RH, and has issue living, Benjamin Richard *b* 1973, Katharine Helen *b* 1975. —— Florence Mary, *b* 1922; formerly 3rd Officer WRNS: *m* 1952, Peter Alexander MacDonell, who *d* 1986, of Rose Court, Fortrose, Ross-shire, and has issue living, Charlotte Anne, *b* 1954: *m* 1979, Peter Maltin, and has issue living, Charles Alexander *b* 1992, Zoe Alexandra *b* 1987, — Maria Christian, *b* 1959; has issue living, Molly Isolde *b* 1992. —— (By 2nd *m*) Alastair Bertram (Flat 5, 65 Cadogan Gdns, SW1), *b* 1945: *m* 1968 (*m diss* 1973), Ann, da of Maj Bernard Winchester.

The 1st baronet Sir Robert McAlpine, JP (son of Robert McAlpine of Newarthill, Lanarks), founded the firm of Sir Robert McAlpine & Sons, civil engineering and building contractors, and *d* 3 Nov 1934. He was *cr* a *Baronet* (UK) of Knott Park, co Surrey 1918. The 5th baronet, Sir (Robert) Edwin McAlpine, ptnr Sir Robert McAlpine & Sons Ltd, was *cr* Knt 1963, *s* his brother in his baronetcy 1983, and was *cr Baron McAlpine of Moffat*, of Medmenham, co Bucks (Life Baron) 1979.

MACARA (UK) 1911, of Ardmore, St Anne-on-the-Sea, co Lancaster

By wisdom not by might

Sir HUGH KENNETH MACARA, 4th *Baronet*; *b* 17 Jan 1913; *s* his brother, *Sir* (CHARLES) DOUGLAS, 1982.

ⁿrms – Ermine, an oak tree eradicated in bend dexter, surmounted by a sword proper, hilted and pommelled or, in bend sinister, supporting on its point an Imperial Crown of the second, on a chief of the third, a spider sable between two thistles also proper. Crest – A stag reguardant lodged in front of an oak tree proper.
Residence –

SISTER LIVING

Aileen Lillah, *b* 1908.

DAUGHTERS LIVING OF THIRD BARONET

Pamela Alison, *b* 1927: *m* 1954, John Gordon Raymond Romer, and has issue living, Charles John, *b* 1958, — Gordon Clive, *b* 1960, — Gillian Avril, *b* 1955, — Susan Claire, *b* 1970. *Residence* – 22 Cranston Grove, Gatley, Ches. —— Quenilda Jennifer, *b* 1929: *m* 1954, Peter Graham Dobson, and has had issue, Trevor William, *b* 1957, — John Keith, *b* 1963, *d* 1982, — Susan Jane, *b* 1954, — Valerie, *b* 1956, — Kay Elizabeth, *b* 1960. *Residence* – 7 Clyst Valley Rd, Clyst, St Mary, Exeter.
The 1st baronet, Sir Charles Wright Macara (son of Rev William Macara, Min of Free Church, Strathmiglo, Fife), was Chm of Henry Bannerman & Sons, Ltd.

MACARTNEY (I) 1799, of Lish, Armagh

Sir JOHN BARRINGTON MACARTNEY, 6th *Baronet*, el son of late John Barrington Macartney, 3rd son of 3rd baronet; *b* 1917; *s* his uncle, *Sir* ALEXANDER MILLER, 1960; is a retired Dairy Farmer: *m* 1944, Amy Isobel Reinke, who *d* 1978, and has issue.

ⁿrms – Or, a stag trippant, within a bordure gules. Crest – A hand holding a slip of a rose tree with three roses thereon all proper.
Residence – 37 Meadow St, N Mackay, Queensland 4740.

SON LIVING

JOHN RALPH (PO Box 589, Queanbeyan, NSW 2620, Australia), *b* 1945; Petty Officer RAN (ret); served in Malaya 1964-65 and Vietnam 1968-69; Teacher at Bruce Coll of Technical and F Education 1979-82; Head of Dept since 1982: *m* 1966, Suzanne Marie Fowler, of Nowra, NSW, and has issue living, Donna Maree, *b* 1968, — Karina Lee, *b* 1971, — Katharine Ann, *b* 1974, — Anita Louise, *b* 1979.

SISTERS LIVING

Evelyn Catherine, *b* 1911: *m* 1931, Albert Edward Ellwood, of 23 Milne Lane, W Mackay, Qld 4740, and has issue living, Alan John (4740 Gargett via Mackay, Qld), *b* 1935: *m* 1963, Hester da of H. Lewis, of Mackay, Qld, and has issue living, Derek John *b* 1968, Charmaine Mary *b* 1964, Dianne Lucy *b* 1966, — Edward Graham (5 Piccadilly St, Geebung 4734, Aust 2611), *b* 1945: *m* 19—, Helen Mary, da of Thomas Chadwick of Dalby, Qld, and has issue living Damian Ralf *b* 1974, — Audrey Philomene, *b* 1932: *m* 1952, Noel Nathaniel Perry, of Matcham, Gracemere, via Rockhampton, Qld 4702, and has issue living, Gregory John *b* 1957, Shane Nathaniel *b* 1971, Christine Anne *b* 1953, Janette Patricia *b* 1955, Judith Marie *b* 1956, Kathleen Ellen *b* 1959, — Marie

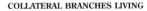

It stimulates, but it adorns

STIMULAT SED ORNAT

Claire, *b* 1934: *m* 1956, Franciscao Antonius Brieffres, of 4740 Kuhabul, via Mackay, Qld, and has issue living, Frank John *b* 1957, Peter Eugene *b* 1961, Anthony John *b* 1964, Lynette *b* 1958, Trudy Bernadette *b* 1959, Melita Maree *b* 1963, Yvonne *b* 1966. —— Constance (Mail Service 656, Mackay, Queensland 4740, Australia), *b* 1912: *m* 1939, Stanley Dan Desbois, who *d* 1983, and has issue living, Kevin, *b* 1941: *m* 1966, Janet Elizabeth Gordon, of Mackay, Qld, and has issue living, Sean Kevin *b* 1975, Michelle Maree *b* 1968, Andrea Jane *b* 1969, — Clive John, *b* 1948: *m* 1973, Bernadette Mary Murphy, and has issue living, Timothy John *b* 1976, Graham Stanley *b* 1983, Sharon Ann *b* 1978, Jennifer Mary *b* 1981.

COLLATERAL BRANCHES LIVING

Issue of late Herbert Charles Macartney, 4th son of 3rd baronet, *b* 1876, *d* 1953: *m* 1913, Frances, da of Mountiford Tooker, of Yeppoon, Queensland:—
Patricia Catherine, *b* 1917: *m* 1941, Leslie John Campbell, of Inverness, Calliope, Gladstone, Qld, and has issue living, Alan Leslie John Macartney, *b* 1952, — Diana Ruby, *b* 1942, — Rosemary Frances, *b* 1945, — Ailsa Catherine, *b* 1947. —— Frances Evelyn, *b* 1924: *m* 1953, John Smith. *Residence* – Brisbane, Qld.

Issue of late David Edwin Macartney, 6th son of 3rd baronet, *b* 1880, *d* 1957: *m* 1st, 1912, Flora Gordon, who *d* 1914, da of E. K. Ogg, of Rockhampton, Queensland; 2ndly, 1920, Ella Margaret McCulloch, who *d* 1978, da of Daniel Craig, of Longreach, Qld:—
(By 2nd *m*) Alexander Macdonald (11 Chermside Drive, Warwick, Qld 4370, Australia), *b* 1921; formerly Flight-Lt RAAF: *m* 1959, Penelope Ann, da of C. B. Freeman, of Brisbane, Qld, and has issue living, John Alexander (Crane Rd, Castle Hill, NSW 2154), *b* 1961; Fl Lieut RAAF: *m* 1986, Robyn Mary, da of E.M. Norling, of Wellington, NZ, — Deborah Ann, *b* 1962: *m* 1985 (*m diss* 1994), — , and has issue living, Arianna Ella *b* 1990, — David Edwin, *b* 1924; formerly in R Austn Navy: *m* 1948, Elizabeth Lillias, da of L. Ewert, of Rotorua, NZ, and has issue living, David Edwin, *b* 1951, — Anthony Craig, *b* 1956,

— Diane Ewert, *b* 1952: *m* 1977, David John McBryde, and has issue, James David *b* 1983, Fiona Diane *b* 1981. —— John Craig (PO Box 1, Mount Nebo, Qld 4520) *b* 1927; formerly in AIF: *m* 1951, Betty Katrine, da of Dr Leckie, of Ingham, Qld, and has issue living, — Belinda Lee, *b* 1952. —— Wallace Herbert (49 Nevin St, Aspley, Brisbane, Qld 4034), *b* 1929: *m* 1973, Judith Anne, da of A. K. Addison, of Brisbane, and has issue living, Robyn Judith, *b* 1976. —— Margaret Miller, *b* 1923: *m* 1949, Capt David Henry Hopton, formerly Ansett Airlines, of PO Box 242, Edge Hill, N Qld 4870, and has issue living, John Macartney, *b* 1950: *m* 1980, Diane Rita Cavanagh, — Peter Coulter, *b* 1955: *m* 1980, Christine Ann Cosgriffe, and has issue living, James Duncan *b* 1988, Stephanie Lee *b* 1984, Angela Margaret *b* 1986, — Jason Craig, *b* 1956: *m* 1983, Julie Ann McLaren, and has issue living, Toby John *b* 1985, Fraser McLaren *b* 1987, Joshua Craig *b* 1989 . —— Catherine Ella, *b* 1926: *m* 1962, Donald Grayling, RN, of 13 Cliff Av, Winston Hills, Sydney, NSW 1253, and has issue living, Donald David, *b* 1968, — Fiona Ella, *b* 1964.

Issue of late Victor Alan Macartney, yst son of 3rd baronet, *b* 1887, *d* 1969: *m* 1915, Elsie Maria, da of late Robert McKie, of Brisbane:—
Harold Kenneth, *b* 1919; Singapore 1941 with AIF (prisoner): *m* 1951, Beatrice, da of Henry Apsley Carlyle Lowe, of Burling, Terrigall, NSW, and has issue living, William John, *b* 1959, — Diana Eileen, *b* 1955. —— Elinor Macartney, *b* 1917; late Sister Austn Army Nursing Ser; Middle East 1940-41: *m* 1942, Maj Francis Stephen Small, AIF, of Royston Park, Ourimbah, NSW, and has issue living, Roderick Cameron Macartney, *b* 1943, — Robert Francis, *b* 1949, — Rosemary Elinor, *b* 1945, — Margaret Anne (twin), *b* 1949.

Issue of late William George Macartney, 2nd son of 2nd baronet, *b* 1835, *d* 188-: *m* 1872, Bessie, da of late Robert Bayley Tyser, of Wellington, New Zealand:—
Ernest George, *b* 1880. —— Eileen Agnes. *Residence* –

Grandsons of late Edward Hussey Burgh Macartney (infra):—
Issue of late James Edward Macartney, *b* 1911, *d* 1977: *m* 1946, Margaret Casson, da of late Herbert Ernest Bennett:—
John Alexander, *b* 1947: *m* 1977, Lynette Kathleen, da of Gordon Vaughan, and has issue living, Edward John *b* 1978. —— William James, *b* 1948: *m* 1970, Sherryl, da of Wallace George Humfry, and has issue living, Benjamin Wallace, *b* 1972, — Christopher John, *b* 1973, — Jack Hussey Burgh, *b* 1981.

Grandchildren of late Edward Hardman Macartney, son of the Very Rev Hussey Burgh Macartney (first Dean of Melbourne), yr son of 1st baronet:—
Issue of late Edward Hussey Burgh Macartney, *b* 1867, *d* 1930: *m* 1st, 1904, Jane Alexandra, who *d* 1909, da of Alexander Richardson McNab; 2ndly, 1910, Constance May, who *d* 1960, da of Edward Griffith:—
(By 2nd *m*). John Hussey Burgh (7 Tutus St, Balgowlah, NSW 2093), *b* 1915; Lt-Cdr RAN (ret): *m* 1945, Geraldine, da of Eli Leach, of Darwen, Lancs, England, and has issue living, Francesca May, *b* 1948; BA, LLB, Sydney: *m* 1972, Christopher William Beale, BA, LLB Sydney, MBA Harvard, and has issue living, Julian Macartney *b* 1986, Andrew Macartney *b* 1988. —— (By 1st *m*) Jean Marion Isobel, *b* 1908: *m* 1954, William Balston, who *d* 1960. —— (By 2nd *m*) Catherine Frances, *b* 1913: *m* 1933, A. N. Magnus. —— Constance Eleanor, *b* 1922, *m* 1950, David Howley.
Issue of late Charles Perry Macartney, *b* 1880, *d* 1947: *m* 1912, Daphne Violet, who *d* 1976, da of Henry King:—
Violet Moore, *b* 1914. *Residence* – 33 Proctors Road, Dynnyrne, Hobart, Tasmania. —— Nancy Gower (43 Tramway Parade, Beaumaris, Melbourne, Vic 3193) *b* 1920: *m* 1958, Leonard J. Basterfield, who *d* 1988, and has issue living, Josephine Nancy, *b* 1960.

The 1st baronet, Sir John, MP (yr son of William Macartney of Lish, co Armagh, MP for Belfast), prior to his being created a baronet, received knighthood for his services in promoting inland navigation in Ireland.

McCONNELL (UK) 1900, of The Moat, Strandtown, Belfast

A conquerer amidst difficulties

(*Sir*) ROBERT SHEAN McCONNELL, 4th *Baronet*; *b* 23 Nov 1930; *s* his father, *Sir* ROBERT MELVILLE TERENCE, VRD, 1987, but does not use the title; *ed* Stowe, Queens' Coll, Camb (MA), and Univ of British Columbia (MSc); ARICS, FRTPI.

𝔄rms – Per pale azure and gules, to the dexter a ship in full sail proper, to the sinister an arm embowed and couped at the shoulder argent, the hand grasping a trefoil slipped or, on a chief of the fourth, three stags' heads cabossed sable. **𝔠rest** – A stag's head erased azure attired and charged on the neck with a bee volant or.

BROTHERS LIVING

JAMES ANGUS (Rory's Glen, 219 Old Holywood Rd, Holywood, co Down), *b* 18 Dec 1933; *ed* Stowe; FSVA; JP; Capt RARO: *m* 1957, Elizabeth Jillian, da of late Derek Edmund Harris, of Sydenham, Belfast, and has issue living, Terence Reade, *b* 16 Nov 1959; Maj Royal Irish Regt (ret): *m* 1987, Lorel Natalie Willetts, and has issue living, James Alexander *b* 1989, Kitty Sarah *b* 1991, — Edmund Fraser, *b* 1961, — Joanne Christina, *b* 1958: *m* 1979, Richard Sholdis, and has issue living, Robert James *b* 1984, Christopher John *b* 1989; Jennifer Elizabeth (twin) *b* 1984, Rachel Rosemary *b* 1987, — Victoria Wylie, *b* 1965, — Emma-Jane Wylie, *b* (twin) 1965, — Alison Clare, *b* 1967. —— William Donn (Laurelbrae, Saintfield Rd, Lisburn, co Antirm), *b* 1938; *ed* Stowe: *m* 1963, Daphne Elisabeth, only da of late Robert Simms, of Bangor, co Down, and has had issue, Robert Randal, *b* 1966: *m* 1993, Sarah Annaliese Kirk, — Stewart Neale, *b* 1972, — Penelope Elisabeth, *b* 1964, *d* 1970.

SISTER LIVING

Elisabeth Moyne, *b* 1935: *m* 1958, Robert Henry Cooke Ramsay (Ardreagh, Marino, Holywood, co Down), and has issue living, Richard Patrick James, *b* 1960, Magnus Robert Neale, *b* 1967, — Roslyn Moyne Elisabeth, *b* 1962.

WIDOW LIVING OF THIRD BARONET

ALICE ANN MARY (*Alice, Lady McConnell*), da of late Robert Graham Glendinning, of Lennoxvale, Belfast, and formerly wife of James Hillis, of Newgrove, Ballylesson: *m* 1967, as his 2nd wife, Sir Robert Melville Terence McConnell, 3rd Bt, VRD, who *d* 1987. *Residence* – Pigeon Hill, Island Rd, Killyleagh, co Down.

COLLATERAL BRANCH LIVING

Issue of late (Jackson) Desmond McConnell, yr son of 2nd baronet, *b* 1912, *d* 1986: *m* 1948, Honor Muriel (Little Galleons, 52 Craigdarragh Rd, Helen's Bay, Bangor, co Down BT19 1UB), da of late Robert Henry Cooke Ramsay, of Fairholme, Craigdarragh Rd, Helen's Bay, co Down, and widow of Sqdn Ldr Richard Ashton Shuttleworth, RAF:—

Rory Desmond Ramsay (Ardville, Old Quay Rd, Holywood, co Down), *b* 1957; *ed* Marlborough: *m* 1982, Karen, da of James McClean, of Bangor, co Down, and has issue living, Jamie Desmond, *b* 1984, — Hayley Elizabeth, *b* 1987, — Alexandra Jane, *b* 1991. —— Kathryn Fiona, *b* 1948: *m* 1970, Maj Anthony Randel, of Langdon, Langdon Cross, Launceston, Cornwall, and has issue living, Sophia Honor, *b* 1971.

Issue of late Alfred Edward McConnell, 2nd son of 1st baronet, *b* 1880, *d* 1963: *m* 1919, Emma (Yvonne) Dougal, who *d* 1957:—

Rt Hon Robert William Brian (Aughnahough, Lisburn, co Antrim), *b* 1922; *ed* Sedbergh, and Queen's Univ, Belfast (BA, LLB); Bar N Ireland 1948; MP for S Antrim, NI Parliament (*U*) 1951-68; Pres of Industrial Court NI 1968-88; PC N Ireland 1964: *m* 1951, Sylvia Elisabeth Joyce, da of late Samuel Agnew, of Belfast, and has issue living, Richard Alfred, *b* 1955: *m* 1988, Julie Ellis, — Samuel James, *b* 1958: *m* 1985, Christine Molly Smyth, and has issue living, Laura Elizabeth *b* 1987, Ruth Mary *b* 1990, Joanne Christine *b* 1993, — Helen Elizabeth, *b* 1964: *m* 1987, Thomas Nelson, and has issue living, Philip *b* 1989.

The first baronet, Sir Robert John McConnell (son of Joseph McConnell, of Clougher, co Antrim), was Lord Mayor of Belfast 1900, and the 2nd baronet, Sir Joseph, was MP for co Antrim at Westminster (*U*) May 1929 to Aug 1942.

McCOWAN (UK) 1934, of Dalwhat, co Dumfries

We press forward to heaven

Sir HEW CARGILL McCOWAN, 3rd *Baronet*; *b* 26 July 1930; *s* his father, Sir DAVID JAMES CARGILL, 1965.

Arms – Argent, a saltire between four anchors sable roped or. **Crest** – An eagle rising proper.
Residence –

BROTHER LIVING

DAVID WILLIAM CARGILL, *b* 28 Feb 1934: *m* and has issue living, David, *b* 1975, — a da, *b* 19—.

AUNT LIVING (*daughter of 1st Baronet*)

Margaret Elisabeth, *b* 1894: *m* 1931, Alexander Osborne Bonnar. *Residence* –

WIDOW LIVING OF SECOND BARONET

MURIEL EMMA ANNIE (*Lady McCowan*) (Auchenheglish, Alexandria, Dunbartonshire), da of William Charles Willmott, of Deal: *m* 1928, Sir David James Cargill McCowan, 2nd baronet, who *d* 1965.

The 1st Baronet, Sir David McCowan (son of Hew McCowan, of Ayr), was a Senior Partner in the firm of William Euing & Co, marine insurance brokers, of 8 Royal Exchange Buildings, Glasgow, and Hon Pres of Scottish Unionist Assocn.

McCULLAGH (UK) 1955, of Lismara, Parish of Carnmoney, co Antrim. (Extinct 1974)

Sir JOSEPH CRAWFORD McCULLAGH, 2nd and last *Baronet*.

WIDOW LIVING OF SECOND BARONET

ELIZABETH (*Lady McCullagh*), da of James Copeland: *m* 1937, Sir Joseph Crawford McCullagh, 2nd Bt, who *d* 1974, when the title became ext.

BOSVILLE MACDONALD (NS) 1625, of Sleat, Isle of Skye

By sea and land. Virtue for its own sake

Sir IAN GODFREY BOSVILLE MACDONALD OF SLEAT, 17th *Baronet* and 25th *Chief of Sleat*; *b* 18 July 1947; *s* his father, *Sir* (ALEXANDER) SOMERLED ANGUS, MC, 1958; High Sheriff Humberside 1988: *m* 1970, Juliet Fleury, only da of late Maj-Gen John Ward-Harrison, of Hazel Bush House, Malton Rd, York, and has issue.

𝔄rms – (as recorded at Lyon Office)—Quarterly, 1st and 4th grand quarters counter-quartered, 1st argent, a lion rampant gules, armed and langued azure, 2nd or, a hand in armour fessewise proper, holding a cross-crosslet fitchée gules, 3rd argent a lymphad, sails furled and oars in action sable, flagged gules, and 4th vert a salmon naiant in fesse proper, *Macdonald*; 2nd and 3rd grand quarters, argent, five lozenges conjoined in fesse gules and in chief three bears' heads erased at the neck sable, muzzled or, a canton, ermine, *Bosville*. ℭrest – 1st, a hand in armour fessewise, holding a cross-crosslet fitchée gules *Macdonald*; 2nd, a bull passant argent, armed or, issuing from a hurst of oaks, charged on the shoulder with a rose proper, *Bosville*. 𝔖upporters – Two leopards proper, collared or.
Seats – Thorpe Hall, Rudston, Driffield, E Yorks Y025 0JE; Osmigarry Lodge, Isle of Skye.

SON LIVING

SOMERLED ALEXANDER, *b* 30 Jan 1976.

DAUGHTERS LIVING

Deborah Fleury, *b* 1973. —— Isabel Mary, *b* 1983.

BROTHER LIVING

James Alexander (12 Poplar Grove, W6), *b* 1949; *ed* Ardingly.

SISTERS LIVING

Janet Elizabeth, *b* 1950: *m* 1980, John Joseph Trapp, of Swann House, Swaffham Bulbeck, Cambs CB5 0NE, elder son of late R. E. Trapp and Mrs L. Reynolds, and has issue living, Alexander John Nicolai, *b* 1984. —— Annabel Celia Dorothy, *b* 1953: *m* 1987, Clive Duncan Evans, of West Croft Farm, Rudston, Driffield, E Yorks, son of late M. R. Evans, of Swansea, and has issue living, Benedict Ian, *b* 1989, — Caitlin Mary, *b* 1993.

UNCLE LIVING (*Son of 15th baronet*)

Nigel Donald Peter CHAMBERLAYNE-MACDONALD, LVO, OBE, *b* 1927; Maj (ret) late Scots Guards; a Member of the Queen's Body Guard for Scotland (Royal Company of Archers); Equerry to HRH the Duke of Gloucester 1954-55, and again 1958-60, and Assist Private Sec to HRH the Duke of Gloucester 1958-60; Extra Equerry to HRH the Duke of Gloucester 1964-74; a Gentleman Usher to HM The Queen since 1979; High Sheriff of Hants 1974, and DL 1975; OStJ; assumed by deed poll 1958 the surname of Chamberlayne before his patronymic; Chm of Hants and I of Wight Assocn of Boys' Clubs 1967-83, a Vice-Pres 1983, and a Vice-Chm of Nat Assocn of Boys' Clubs 1969-90, Pres Coaching Club 1982-90; LVO 1960, OBE (civ) 1981: *m* 1958, Penelope Mary Alexandra, only child of late Tankerville Chamberlayne, of Cranbury Park, Hants, and has had issue, Alexander Nigel Bosville, *b* 1959: *m* 1991, Shirley Irene, da of late George Cecil Pridmore, of Swayfield, Lincs, — Thomas Somerled, *b* 1969, — Diana Mary (*Countess of Lindsay*) *b* 1961: *m* 1982,16th Earl of Lindsay, — Frances Penelope, *b* 1965, *d* 1985. *Residences* – Cranbury Park, Winchester; 17 William Mews, Lowndes Sq, SW1; Glaschoille House, Knoydart, Mallaig, Inverness-shire.

AUNTS LIVING (*Daughters of 15th baronet*)

Jean Alice, *b* 1919: *m* 1952, Lieut-Col Basil John Ringrose, DSO, TD, of Royal Oak, Morby, nr Boston, Lincs. —— Angela Daphne Rachel, *b* 1923: *m* 1957, James Michael Gardner Fell, and has issue living, Peter James, *b* 1960, — Rachel Mary, *b* 1959. *Address* – University of Pennsylvania, Philadelphia, USA.

WIDOW LIVING OF SIXTEENTH BARONET

MARY ELIZABETH (*Mary, Lady Bosville Macdonald of Sleat*), da of late Lt-Col Ralph Crawley-Boevey Gibbs: *m* 1946, Sir (Alexander) Somerled Angus Bosville Macdonald of Sleat, 16th baronet, MC, who *d* 1958. *Residence* – West Croft Farm, Rudston, Driffield, E Yorkshire.

COLLATERAL BRANCHES LIVING

Descendants of Godfrey William Wentworth Macdonald, 4th Baron Macdonald, 3rd (but el born after the English *m* of his parents) son of late Godfrey Macdonald, 3rd Baron Macdonald and 11th baronet (*see* B Macdonald).

Descendants of late Donald Macdonald 1st of Castleton, 2nd son of 1st baronet:—

Grandchildren of late Rev James Alexander Donald John Macdonald, 10th of Castleton, son of James Alexander Macdonald, 9th of Castleton, eldest son of James Macdonald, 8th of Castleton, 6th in descent from Donald Macdonald (ante):—
Issue of late Donald John Macdonald, 12th of Castleton, *b* 1897, *d* 1984: *m* 1932, Cecilie Frances Jess, who *d* 1987, da of late Ernest George Evan-Williams, of Johannesburg, S Africa, and adopted da of Maj James Alexander Macdonald, DSO, MC:—
Ranald Alexander, 13th of Castleton (12 Wren St, WC1), *b* 1937; late Cameron Highlanders: *m* 1st, 1964, Eleanor Russell; 2ndly, 1988, Lee Honeyman, and has issue living (by 1st *m*), Shona, *b* 1965, — (by 2nd *m*) Catriona Michelle, *b* 1990. —— Cecilie Ruth Faith, *b* 1933: *m* 1974, Andrew Barclay, of 109 Hyndland Rd, Glasgow, and has issue living, Carol Hope, *b*

1975. —— Catherine Stella, *b* 1941: *m* 1962, Graham Robertson Harvey, of Ferndale, Forres, Morayshire, and has issue living, David Ranald Macdonald, *b* 1965, — Dawn Caroline, *b* 1968: *m* 1991, William Andrew Hawking, of Oldfield Farm, Wilts, and has issue living, Flora Louise *b* 1994, — Louise Robertson, *b* 1969: *m* 1994, Gavin Logan Willins, of Edinburgh. —— Frances Ruth (Achnandarrach, Plockton, Ross-shire), *b* 1944: *m* 1968, Austin Bankhead, who *d* 1990, and has issue living, Jamie Macdonald, *b* 1969, — Patrick Augustine, *b* 1971, — Robin Francis, *b* 1978.

Grandsons of late Edward William Johnstone Macdonald (infra):—
Issue of late Roderick Norman Douglas Macdonald, *b* 1886, *d* 1971: *m* 1912, Eleanor Davison, of Toronto, who *d* 1969:—
Alexander Douglas, *b* 1923: *m* 1941, Gertrude Noreen Davis, of Toronto, and has issue living, Geoffrey Alex, *b* 1952, — Pamela, *b* 1948.

Granddaughter of late James Alexander Macdonald, 9th of Castleton (ante):—
Issue of late Edward William Johnstone Macdonald, *b* 1858, *d* 1931: *m* 1884, Emily Hurst, who *d* 1958:—
Marjorie Johnstone, *b* 1895: *m* 1932, Augustus Frederick Weiss, and has issue living, Marjorie Eileen, *b* 1933: *m* 1957, John Ross Crumplin, of 25 Plough Lane, Purley, Surrey, and has issue living, Timothy John Ross *b* 1958, Nicholas Macdonald *b* 1961, Russell Iain *b* 1966, — Pamela Jean, *b* 1935: *m* 1960, Dr John Cyril Oakley, and has issue living, Julian Richard *b* 1964, Karen Pamela *b* 1961, — Alison Macdonald, *b* 1939. *Residence* – 30 The Pines, St James' Rd, Purley, Sussex.

Grandsons of late Inspector-Gen Sir John Denis Macdonald, KCB, MD, FRS, 3rd son of late James Macdonald, 8th of Castleton (ante):—
Issue of late Capt John Denis Macdonald, Roy Canadian Veterinary Corps, *b* 1873, *d* 1940: *m* 1908, Minnie Gunter:—
Geoffrey John Gunter, *b* 1910: *m* 1930, Muriel Eleanor Tingle, and has issue living, Michael Douglas, *b* 1940, — Heather Margaret, *b* 1942, — Janet Elizabeth, *b* 1947. —— James Edward Somerled, *b* 1912. —— Ewen Reginald, *b* 1915: European War 1939-45 with Gordon Highlanders: *m* 19—, Elsie Glanville, and has issue living, Angus John, *b* 1943, — Alison Celia, *b* 1947.
Issue of late William Richard Macdonald, *b* 1876, *d* 1950: *m* 1st, Olive—; 2ndly, 19—, Erina Archer:—
(By 2nd *m*) Richard John, *b* 1940.

This Baronetcy was created with remainder to heirs male whatsoever and a special clause of precedency provided that it should have precedency of all former baronets (Sir Robert Gordon only excepted) "tho' their patents were of a prior date", whereby, if that clause is in force, it is now second in the order of Nova Scotia baronets. In 1776, Sir Alexander Macdonald, 9th Bt, was created *Baron Macdonald*, of Slate, co Antrim (peerage of Ireland). Godfrey Macdonald (afterwards 3rd Baron and 11th Baronet) assumed by Roy licence 1814, on inheriting the estates of Bosville of Thorpe and Gunthwaite, the surname of Bosville in lieu of his patronymic. On succession to the titles in 1824 he resumed the surname of Macdonald after that of Bosville. He died in 1832, having *m* (in an English Church) Dec 15th, 1803, Louisa Maria La Coast, da of HRH Prince William Frederick, Duke of Gloucester by Lady Almeria Carpenter, and ward of Farley Edsir. The validity of a Scottish *m* said to have taken place with the same lady in 1799 having been disputed, he was *s* in the Irish peerage by his son Godfrey William Wentworth, born after the date of the English *m*, but according to a decree of the Court of Session in June 1910, the father being domiciled in Scotland, that *m* legitimated according to the law of Scotland, Alexander William Robert Macdonald, *b* 12 Sept 1800, prior to the date of the English *m*, who had *s* to the Thorpe and Gunthwaite estates, and to whom therefore the Nova Scotia baronetcy of 1625 passed *de jure*. On entering into possession of the Bosville estates in 1832 he assumed by Roy licence the surname of Bosville in lieu of Macdonald. His grandson, Alexander Wentworth Macdonald Bosville, thus became 14th Baronet in 1910, and resumed the family surname of Macdonald after that of Bosville (recognised by Court of Lord Lyon 1910). The present baronet is heir-male and representative of Sir Donald Macdonald, 1st Bt (descended from Hugh Macdonald, first of Sleat, a son of Alexander, Lord of the Isles, Earl of Ross, by a da of Gillepatrick Roy), and representative of the family of Macdonald of Sleat, in the Island of Skye.

McEWEN (UK) 1953, of Marchmont, co Berwick, and Bardrochat, co Ayr

Dieu Premier Servi

Sir JOHN RODERICK HUGH MCEWEN, 5th *Baronet*; *b* 4 Nov 1965; *s* his brother, Sir JAMES FRANCIS LINDLEY, 1983; *ed* Ampleforth, and Univ Coll, London.

Arms – Quarterly: 1st and 4th, or, a lion rampant azure, gorged with a ducal crown proper, on a chief of the second three garbs of the field, *McEwen*; 2nd and 3rd, gules, three headless cranes argent, *Finnie*. **Crest** – The trunk of an oak tree sprouting proper.
Residence – Polwarth Crofts, Greenlaw, Duns, Berwickshire TD10 6YR.

SISTERS LIVING AND DECEASED

Mary Christian, *b* 1956. —— Catherine Veronica, *b* 1958; *d* (drowned off the coast of Africa) 1983. —— Helena Mary Elizabeth, *b* 1961. —— Isabella Gabriel Anne, *b* 1968.

DAUGHTERS LIVING OF SECOND BARONET

Margaret, *b* 1959: *m* 1980, Edward John Ivo Stourton (*see* B Mowbray, colls). —— Mary Gabriel, *b* 1963: *m* 1989, (Vincent) Patrick Byrne (*see* B Lawrence). —— Christina, *b* 1964: *m* 1992, Anthony D. L. Norton, son of David Norton, of Buckland St Mary, Somerset.

UNCLES LIVING (*Sons of 1st baronet*)

Alexander Dundas, *b* 1935; *ed* Eton; late Queen's Own Cameron Highlanders: *m* 1960, (Princess) Cecilia, da of HSH late Franz, 2nd Prince Weikersheim, and has issue living, Alexander Francis, *b* 1962: *m* 1988, Natasha Durac, elder da of Peter H. D. Marr, and has issue living, Thomas Peter Dundas *b* 1989, Archie James *b* 1992, — Hugo Gabriel, *b* 1965, — Sophia Christina, *b* 1961. *Residence* – Bardrochat, Colmonell, Ayrshire. —— John Sebastian, *b* 1942; *ed* Eton, and Trin Coll, Camb: *m* 1975, Gillian, da of D. M. Heeley, and has issue living, David, *b* 1977, — Duncan Dundas, *b* 1979. *Residence* – 74 St Augustine's Rd, NW1 9RP.

AUNT LIVING *(Daughter of 1st baronet)*

Christian Mary, OBE *(Dowager Baroness Hesketh)*, *b* 1929; High Sheriff of Northants 1981; a DL of Northants; Hon LLD (Univ of Leicester) 1982; OBE (Civil) 1983: *m* 1949, 2nd Baron Hesketh, who *d* 1955. *Residences* – Pomfret Lodge, Hulcote, Towcester, Northants; 20a Tregunter Rd, SW10.

WIDOW LIVING OF SECOND BARONET

CLARE ROSEMARY, only child of Col John William Eric Graves Sandars, OBE, TD, of Gate Burton Hall, Gainsborough, Lincs *(see* B Graves, 1959 Edn): *m* 1st, 1958, Sir James Napier Finnie McEwen, 2nd Bt, who *d* 1971; 2ndly, 1973, Kenneth Wagg, of Lower Portrack, Holywood, Dumfries-shire.

WIDOW LIVING OF THIRD BARONET

BRIGID CECILIA *(Lady McEwen of Marchmont)*, only da of James Laver, CBE: *m* 1954, Sir Robert Lindley McEwen, 3rd Bt, who *d* 1980. *Residence* – Polwarth Crofts, Duns, Berwickshire TD10 6YR.

COLLATERAL BRANCH LIVING

　　　　　Issue of late Roderick (Rory) McEwen, 3rd son of 1st Baronet, *b* 1932, *d* 1982: *m* 1958, Romana, da of late Raimund von Hofmannsthal:—
ADAM HUGO, *b* 9 Feb 1965. —— Flora Mary Alice, *b* 1959: *m* 1988, Anthony David Willard Mason, son of late John Harradine Mason, of Haddenham, Bucks. —— Samantha Mary, *b* 1960. —— Christabel Mary, *b* 1962: *m* 1983, Hon Edward Richard Lambton (styled Lord Durham since 1970), only son of Antony Claud Frederick Lambton (6th Earl of Durham until he disclaimed his title 1970), and has issue *(see* E Durham), — and further issue (by Julian Miles Holland), Mabel Ray Britannia, *b* 1990.
Sir John (Helias Finnie) McEwen, 1st Bt, was MP for Berwick and Haddington (C) 1931-45, Parliamentary Under-Sec of State for Scotland 1939-40, and a Lord Commr of the Treasury 1942-44: *m* 1923, Bridget Mary, who *d* 1971, eldest da of Rt Hon Sir Francis Oswald Lindley *(see* B Lovat, 1949 Edn); *d* 1962; *s* by his eldest son, Sir James Napier Finnie McEwen, 2nd Bt; served 1939-45 War (wounded): *m* 1958, Clare Rosemary, only child of Col William Eric Graves Sandars *(see* B Graves, 1959 Edn); *d* 1971; *s* by his brother, Sir Robert Lindley McEwen, 3rd Bt; barrister-at-law: *m* 1954, Brigid Cecilia, only da of James Laver, CBE; *d* 1980; *s* by his elder son, Sir James Francis Lindley McEwen, 4th Bt; *dunm* 1983; *s* by his brother, Sir John Roderick Hugh McEwen, 5th Bt.

McFARLAND (UK) 1914, of Aberfoyle, co Londonderry

This I'll defend

Sir JOHN TALBOT McFARLAND, 3rd *Baronet*, TD; *b* 3 Oct 1927; *s* his father, *Sir* BASIL ALEXANDER TALBOT, CBE, ERD, 1986; *ed* Marlborough, and Trin Coll, Oxford; Capt RA ret; a DL of City of co of Londonderry 1956-82; Councillor, Londonderry Corp 1955-69; High Sheriff of co Londonderry 1958, and of City of co of Londonderry 1965 and 1966; mem Londonderry Port Harbour Commrs 1965-73, NW Hosp Management Cttee 1960-73; Chm Lanes Gp of Cos, Dir Londonderry Gaslight Co Ltd 1960, and Donegal Holdings Ltd 1966; Chm Londonderry & Lough Swilly Rlwy Co 1978-81, McFarland Farms Ltd, and J.T. McFarland Holdings 1984: *m* 1957, Mary Scott, el da of late Dr William Scott Watson, of Dunmore House, Carrigans, co Donegal, and has issue.

Arms – Argent, a saltire engrailed gules, between two roses in pale and a thistle and shamrock in fesse all proper. **Crest** – A demi-savage holding in the dexter hand an antique crown all proper.
Residence – Dunmore House, Carrigans, Co Donegal. *Clubs* – Kildare and University (Dublin), Northern Counties (Londonderry).

SONS LIVING

ANTHONY BASIL SCOTT (31 Walham Grove, SW6), *b* 29 Nov 1959; *ed* Marlborough, and Trin Coll, Dublin (BA); ACA: *m* 1988, Anne Margaret, 3rd da of Thomas Kennedy Laidlaw, of Gernonstown, Slane, co Meath, and has issue living, Max Anthony, *b* 1993, — Amelia Elizabeth, *b* 1990. —— Stephen Andrew John, *b* 1968; *ed* Glenalmond, and RAC Cirencester.

DAUGHTERS LIVING

Shauna Jane, *b* 1957: *m* 1982, Andrew Louis Hamilton Gailey, MA, PhD. *Residence* – The Manor House, Eton, Berks. —— Fiona Kathleen, *b* 1963: *m* 19—, William Orme. *Residence* – Wych Cottage, High St, Waterbeach, Cambs.
The 1st baronet, Sir John, was a partner in the firm of McCrea and McFarland, engineering contractors, of Belfast and Londonderry, Chm of Mulhollands (Limited), drapers and of Brewsters (Limited), bakers, of Londonderry, Proprietor of Lough Swilly Steamship Co, and Chm of Lough Swilly Railway Co. The 2nd baronet, Sir Basil Alexander Talbot, CBE, ERD, was a Senator of N Ireland and HM Lt for the City of Londonderry.

MACGREGOR (UK) 1828, of Savile Row, Middlesex

Sir EDWIN ROBERT MACGREGOR, 7th *Baronet*; *b* 4 Dec 1931; *s* his father, *Sir* ROBERT JAMES McCONNELL, MM, 1963; *ed* Univ of British Columbia (BA Sc 1955, MA Sc 1957): *m* 1st 1952 (*m diss* 1981), Margaret Alice Jean, da of Arthur Peake, of Haney, British Columbia; 2ndly, 1982, Helen Linda Herriott, and has issue by 1st *m.*

Arms – Argent, from a mount base an oak-tree surmounted by a sword in bend proper, and in chief two eastern crowns gules, all within a bordure engrailed of the last. **Crest** – A human hand couped at the wrist and holding a dagger erect proper, pommel and hilt gold.
Address – 6136 Kirby Rd, RR3, Sooke, BC VOS INO, Canada.

SON LIVING *(By 1st marriage)*

IAN GRANT, *b* 22 Feb 1959.

DAUGHTERS LIVING *(By 1st marriage)*

Valerie Jean, *b* 1956. —— Jessie Elizabeth Marlene, *b* 1963.

BROTHER LIVING

Arthur Joseph, *b* 1933; *ed* Univ of British Columbia (MD 1958): *m* 1st, 1957, Carole Isabel, who *d* 1984, da of W. L. Valens, MD, of Victoria, British Columbia; 2ndly, 1985, Brenda Margaret Hanson, and has issue living (by 1st *m*), Ann Lorraine, *b* 1960. — Jean Louise, *b* 1962. *Residence* – 2597 Vista Bay Rd, Victoria, British Columbia.

SISTERS LIVING

Margaret Gertrude, *b* 1937: *m* 1963, Cyril George White, of 6172 Pepperell St, Halifax, Nova Scotia. —— Patricia Elizabeth, *b* 1939: *m* 1966, John Peramaki, of 981 Gloria Pl, Victoria, BC, Canada. —— Nancy Lane, *b* 1942: *m* 1972, Hubert Foulds, who *d* 1991. *Residence* – 3-1015 Moss St, Victoria, British Columbia.

COLLATERAL BRANCH LIVING

Issue of late Brig-Gen Charles Reginald Macgregor, CB, DSO, 2nd son of 3rd baronet, *b* 1847, *d* 1902: *m* 1893, Maud (who *m* 2ndly, 1903, Addison Yalden Thomson), da of A. dés Moustiers Campbell, formerly of Oakley House, Abingdon, Berks:—
Helen Maud, *b* 1894. *Address* – c/o Westminster Bank, Terminus Road, Eastbourne, Sussex.
Sir Patrick Macgregor, 1st Bt, son of James Macgregor of Bellimore, Inverness-shire, was Serjeant-Surgeon to King George IV.

MAC GREGOR OF MAC GREGOR (GB) 1795, of Lanrick, co Perth

Srioghal mo dhream
Royal is my race

Sir GREGOR MAC GREGOR OF MAC GREGOR, 6th *Baronet*; *b* 22 Dec 1925; *s* his father, *Capt Sir* MALCOLM, CB, CMG, RN, 1958; *ed* Eton; Brig late Scots Guards; ret 1980; a Member of Queen's Body Guard for Scotland (Roy Co of Archers), and 23rd Chief of Clan Gregor; Grand Master Mason of Scotland 1988: *m* 1958, Fanny, only da of Charles Hubert Archibald Butler, of Le Pavillon, Newport, Essex, and has issue.

Arms – Argent, an oak-tree eradicated and fructed in bend sinister proper, surmounted of a sword in bend azure, carrying on its point in the dexter canton an antique crown gules. **Crest** – A lion's head proper crowned with an antique crown or. **Supporters** – Dexter, a unicorn argent, crowned and horned or; sinister, a stag proper, tyned azure.
Residence – Bannatyne, Newtyle, Angus PH12 8TR. *Clubs* – Pratt's, and New (Edinburgh).

SONS LIVING

MALCOLM GREGOR CHARLES (Bannatyne, Newtyle, Angus PH12 8TR) *b* 23 March 1959, *ed* Eton; Maj Scots Guards, a Member of Queen's Body Guard for Scotland (Royal Company of Archers); FRGS: *m* 1988, Cecilia Margaret Lucy, elder da of Sir Ilay Mark Campbell, 7th Bt (*cr* 1808). —— Ninian Hubert Alexander *b* 1961.

SISTER LIVING

Anna Gylla, *b* 1929: *m* 1950, James Christopher Ellis, AADip, ARIBA, and has issue living, Giles Christopher, *b* 1951, — Conrad James, *b* 1965, — Anna Gabrielle, *b* 1953, — Katherine Gylla *b* 1957. *Residence* – Localitá Coi 11, Torri del Benaco, 37010 Verona, Italy.

E'en do and spair nocht

COLLATERAL BRANCHES LIVING

Grandson of late Alexander Ronald Mac Gregor (infra):—
Issue of late Lt-Cdr Malcolm Findanus Mac Gregor, *b* 1908, *d* 1990: *m* 1st, 1930 (*m diss* 1940), Rachel Katharine, da of Hon Eustace Scott Hamilton-Russell, OBE (*see* V Boyne); 2ndly, 1941, Mariquita Gwen Alison (Cardney, Dunkeld, Perthshire PH8 0EY), da of A.J. Webbe:—
(By 2nd *m*) Alpin Findanus (79 Stockwell Park Rd, SW9 0DB), *b* 1941: *m* 1965, Maria Christina Elisabeth, da of D. C. Brunow, OBE, of Kotka, Finland, and has issue living, Euan Alexander *b* 1972, Callùm Randal, *b* 1977, Alasdair Duncan *b* 1979.

Issue of late Maj Donnchadh Tearlach Mac Gregor, ERD, R Scots Greys, *b* 1914, *d* 1974: *m* 1st, 1944 (*m diss* 1949), Nighean, da of Col Alastair Norman Fraser, DSO, MB; 2ndly, 1954, Roxana Mary Jocelyn, who *d* 1989, da of Jocelyn Walker, of Oaklands, Isfield, Sussex:—
(By 1st *m*) Randal Alasdair (Came, Dorchester, Dorset DT2 8NU), *b* 1945, Capt R Scots Dragoon Gds: *m* 1st, 1973 (*m diss* 1977), Lynn Vanessa, da of Maj Tommy Vale, MBE, of Farthings, Kingston Broadway, Shoreham by Sea, Sussex; 2ndly, 1978, Sarah, da of Maj Nigel Martin, of Came House, Dorchester, and has issue living (by 2nd *m*) Morag Nicotina, *b* 1978, — Malvina Iona, *b* 1982. ——— (By 2nd *m*) Isabel Maryel, *b* 1956. ———— Catriona Gabrielle, *b* 1968.

Issue of late Alexander Ronald Mac Gregor, yr son of 4th baronet, *b* 1878, *d* 1960: *m* 1907, Gertrude Blanche, who *d* 1959, da of late Charles Archibald Murray (E Mansfield, colls):—
Dorviegelda Malvina (Stone Lodge, Browning Hill, Baughurst, Basingstoke), *b* 1910: *m* 1st, 1939, Sqdn-Ldr Hon (Robert Alexander) Greville Baird: RAF, who was *ka* 1943 (*see* E Kintore); 2ndly, 1947, Sqdn-Ldr Algernon Ivan Sladen, DSO, RAF, who *d* 1976 (E Dunmore), and has issue living, (by 1st *m*) (*see* E Kintore, colls), — (by 2nd *m*), Angus Murray (Glen Carron, Achnashellach, Ross-shire), *b* 1950.

The royal descent of this ancient clan can be traced to remote antiquity, Gregor Garubh, or "The Stout", having fought under King Duncan I. In the early part of the 17th century there were feuds between numerous clans, the Mac Gregors being persecuted with such fury that any person might mutilate or slay them with impunity. In this situation they continued till they were courted to join the Solemn League and Covenant, upon promises of future friendship; but they declared, "That as they *bore the crown on the point of their swords*, they would not fail to use the latter in support of the former". They are the only instance of a race being forbidden to bear their family name, which was first proscribed by James VI, owing to treachery and misrepresentation. They were restored by Charles II, 1661, to their estates, and permitted to bear their own name. In the reign of William and Mary the law of proscription was again revived, and continued in force until its repeal in 1774. The name was not, however, restored until a Royal Licence to resume it was obtained by Sir John Murray (properly Mac Gregor) 1822. Sir Malcolm, CB, CMG, 5th Bt was Capt RN and served in European War 1914-18.

McGRIGOR (UK) 1831, of Campden Hill, Middlesex

Royal is my tribe
S'rioghal mo dhream

Sir CHARLES EDWARD McGRIGOR, 5th *Baronet*; *b* 5 Oct 1922; *s* his father, *Lieut-Col Sir* CHARLES COLQUHOUN, OBE, 1946; *ed* Eton; formerly Capt Rifle Bde; Exon of Queen's Body Guard, Yeomen of the Guard 1970-85, and Member of Queen's Body Guard for Scotland (Roy Co of Archers); 1939-45 War in N Africa and Italy (despatches): *m* 1948, Mary Bettine, da of Sir Archibald Charles Edmonstone, 6th Bt, and has issue.

Arms – Argent, a fir-tree growing out of a mount in base vert surmounted by a sword point upwards in bend proper, pommel and hilt gold, in the dexter chief an eastern crown gules, on a chief azure a tower or, between the badge of the Order of the Tower and Sword on the dexter, and that of the Crescent on the sinister. **Crest** – A lion's head erased gules, crowned with an eastern coronet or.
Residences – Upper Sonachan, by Dalmally, Argyll PA33 1BJ.

SONS LIVING

JAMES ANGUS RHODERICK NEIL (Ardchonnel House, by Dalmally, Argyll PA33 1BW), *b* 19 Oct 1949; *ed* Eton: *m* 19—, Caroline F., da of late Jacques Roboh, of Paris, and has issue living, Sibylla, *b* 1988, — Sarah, *b* 1989. ——— Charles Edward, *b* 1959.

DAUGHTERS LIVING

Lorna Gwendolyn, *b* 1951. ——— Kirsty Rowena Amabel, *b* 1953; resumed her maiden name 1991 until remarriage: *m* 1st, 1979, David Norman G. Barraclough, eldest son of Geoffrey Barraclough, of Madrid; 2ndly, 1993, as his 2nd wife, Roderick John Maclaren (*see* Cs Loudoun) and has issue living (by 1st *m*), Hector, *b* 1979, — Amabel, *b* 1983, — (by 2nd *m*) (*see* Cs Loudoun).

The 1st baronet, Sir James, KCB, FRS, was for thirty-six years Director-General of the Army Medical Department, and three times Lord Rector of Marischal College, Aberdeen. A statue of him erected outside the Barracks at Chelsea was subsequently removed and re-erected at the RAMC buildings at Millbank, while there is a bust of him in Wellington College, and a stall dedicated to his memory in the Garrison Church at Portsmouth. The 3rd baronet, Sir James Roderick Duff, Capt late Rifle Brig, was many years senior partner in the late firm of Sir Charles R. McGrigor, Bart, and Co, army agents and bankers. The 4th baronet, Sir Charles Colquhoun, OBE, was Lieut-Col Rifle Brig.

MACKENZIE (NS) 1673, of Coul, Ross-shire

Purified by adversity

Sir PETER DOUGLAS MACKENZIE, 13th *Baronet*, only son of late Henry Douglas Mackenzie, elder son of Keith Douglas Mackenzie, yr son of Col Henry Douglas Mackenzie, eldest son of Rev Charles Mackenzie, 3rd son of John Mackenzie of Torridon (*d* 1820), 4th in descent from Simon Mackenzie, 2nd son of 1st baronet; *b* 23 April 1949; *s* his kinsman, *Sir* ROBERT EVELYN, 1990; *ed* —: *m* 1982, Jennifer, da of Ridley Boyce, and has issue.

Arms – Quarterly: 1st and 4th azure, a deer's head cabossed or, *Mackenzie*; 2nd and 3rd gules, a boar's head couped argent, *Chisholm*. **Crest** – A boar's head erect or between the attires of a stag fixed to a scalp sable. **Supporters** – *Dexter*, an armed Highlander in full custume proper; *sinister*, a roebuck proper. **Residence** –

DAUGHTERS LIVING

Alison Douglas, *b* 1985. —— Sarah Douglas, *b* 1988.

SISTER LIVING

Ann Douglas, *b* 1943: *m* 1975, Michael Wallace Mayne, and has issue living, Douglas Wallace, *b* 1976, — Rory Douglas, *b* 1979. *Address* – PO Box 10036, Rivonia 2128, S Africa.

AUNT LIVING (*daughter of late Keith Douglas Mackenzie, ante*)

Joan Douglas (Nashleigh Cottage, Chesham, Bucks), *b* 1909: *m* 1943, Maj Kenneth David Harris, King's Dragoon Gds, who *d* 1967, and has issue living, Peter David (13 Caroline Terrace, SW1), *b* 1949: *ed* —: *m* 1981, Anne Elizabeth, da of — Anwyl-Davies, of, — Gillian Diana, *b* 1947: *m* 1981, Raymond Wright, of Bystock House, 76 Lyford Rd, SW18, and has issue living, David William Benedict *b* 1988, Eleanor Faith Rosina *b* 1986.

WIDOW LIVING OF TWELFTH BARONET

ELIZABETH CAMPBELL (*Dowager Lady Mackenzie*), da of late Renard Pearth, of Pittsburgh, USA: *m* 1963, as his 2nd wife, Sir Robert Evelyn Mackenzie, 12th Bt, who *d* 1990. *Residence* – 18 Melton Court, Old Brompton Rd, SW7 3JQ.

COLLATERAL BRANCHES LIVING

Granddaughters of late Keith Douglas Mackenzie, yr son of Col Henry Douglas Mackenzie (ante):—
Issue of late Keith Douglas Mackenzie, *b* 1912, *b* 1984: *m* 1937, Thelma, da of — Reeders:—
Judy Douglas, *b* 1940: *m* 1962 Lt Graham Douglas Ferguson, SAAF, of 294 Albert St, 0181 Waterkloof, Pretoria, Transvaal, S Africa, and has issue living, Ian Douglas, *b* 1964, — Kim Douglas, *b* 1962: *m* 1984, David James Sharp, — Lynn Douglas, *b* 1968, — Lee-Ann Douglas, *b* 1971. —— Jenifer Mary Douglas, *b* 1994: *m* 1965, Jeremy David Garrett, of 7 Dromedaris Rd, Land en Zeezicht, Somerset West 7130, Cape Province, S Africa, and has issue living, Craig Douglas, *b* 1968, — Geoffrey Keith, *b* 1972, — Nikki Jane, *b* 1970.

Granddaughters of late Henry Augustin Ornano Mackenzie, 8th son (only son by 2nd *m*) of 7th baronet:—
Issue of late George Henry Louis Mackenzie, *b* 1872, *d* 1960: *m* 1907, Lilian Mary, who *d* 1958, el da of Richard Rodney Pope, formerly ICS:—
Mary Zeta Bingham, *b* 1909: *m* 1931, Philip Henry Burch, who *d* 1932, Lieut Indian Army, and has issue living, Deirdre Raine Mary, *b* 1932, — Phillida Mary, *b* (posthumous), 1933: *m* 1965, Aloysius John Zadnik (Box 33, Taber, Alberta, Canada), and has issue living, Philip John *b* 1967, Michael Peter *b* 1968, Elizabeth Anne *b* 1970. *Address* – c/o National & Grindlays Bank, 13 St James's Sq, SW1. —— Eira Margaret Antonia, *b* 1913: *m* 1938, Owen James Esmonde, of Cloneen, Glendalough, co Wicklow (*see* Esmonde, Bt).

Grandchildren (by 1st *m*) of late Capt Roderick Henry Turing Mackenzie (infra):—
Issue of late Maj Keith Roderick Turing Mackenzie, OBE, MC, *b* 1921, *d* 1990: *m* 1949, Barbara Kershaw (Garden Cottage, Thistle Lane, South St, St Andrews, Fife), da of late W. H. Miles, of Deal, Kent:—
MILES RODERICK TURING, *b* 18 April 1952: *m* 1983, Hiroko Sato, of Tokyo, Japan. —— Angus Keith Turing, *b* 1965. —— Sarah Jane Kershaw, *b* 1950: *m* 1975, Alan Forrest Franchi, of 9 Osborne Pl, Aberdeen. —— Susannah Mary, *b* 1957: *m* 1979, Seumas McKinnon Lorimer, of Spott Mill, Spott, E Lothian.

Grandsons of late Henry Turing Mackenzie, son of late Rt Rev Henry Mackenzie, DD (infra):—
Issue of late Capt Roderick Henry Turing Mackenzie, *b* 1891, *d* 1963: *m* 1st, 1920 (*m diss* 1932), Helen Margaret, da of late J. P. Dalzell; 2ndly, 1934, Helen Monica Bradley (14 Gybbons Rd, Rolvenden), da of late Lt-Col William Bradley Roberts, DSO:—
(By 2nd *m*) Bruce Sydenham, *b* 1935; Maj late Queen's Lancashire Regt: *m* 1963, Sheila Hope Evan, da of the Rev Aubrey Lionel Evan Hopkins, late V of Holy Trin, Folkestone, and has issue living, Kevin Roderick, *b* 1964; *ed* Lancaster Univ (BA): *m* 1992, Alexandra Mary Morton, and has issue living, Joseph Michael *b* 1994, — Neil Kenneth, *b* 1966; *ed* Nene Coll, Northampton (BA), — Tessa Claire, *b* 1970, — Kirsty Celia, *b* 1971. —— Michael Sydenham *b* 1940; *ed* Trin Coll, Dublin (BA).

Grandson of late Stanley John Mackenzie (by 1st *m*) (infra):—
Issue of late Stanley Charles William WYNN-MACKENZIE, *b* 1870, *d* 19—: *m* 1900, G Whitehouse:—
Douglas Stanley, *b* 1903.
Issue, if any, of late Kenneth Maurice WYNN-MACKENZIE, *b* 1880, *d* 19—: *m* 1917.

Grandchildren (by 2nd *m*) of late Stanley John Mackenzie, son of Rt Rev Henry Mackenzie, DD (Bishop Suffragan of Nottingham), yst son of John Mackenzie of Torridon (*d* 1820) (ante):—
Issue of late Noel Donald George Mackenzie, *b* 1899, *d* 1981: *m* 1931, Elsie Kate (Sunnydene, 27 Greensleeves Av, Broadstone, Dorset, BH18 8BJ), da of William Henry Mitchell:—
Donald William John (c/o Hongkong & Shanghai Banking Corporation, Ocean Centre, Hong Kong), *b* 1935: *m* 1969, Cheryl Patricia Elizabeth, da of Cyril Leslie Charles Allen, of Cheriton, Llyswen, Breconshire, and has issue living, Nicholas Richard John, *b* 1974, — Christopher Stuart, *b* 1977. —— Marian Audrey, *b* 1944: *m* 1966 (*m diss* 1975), Kaddour Amari, and has issue living, Nadia, *b* 1966, — Samira, *b* 1970.

Grandchildren of late Capt Kenneth Mackenzie, only son of late John Ord Mackenzie, WS, son of late Richard Mackenzie, son of late John Mackenzie of Dolphinton, son of late Kenneth Mackenzie, 2nd son of late John Mackenzie of Delvine, 3rd son of 1st baronet:—

Issue of late John Moncreiff Ord Mackenzie, WS, *b* 1911, *d* 1986: *m* 1936, Delia Alice (Dolphinton House, Dolphinton, Lanarkshire), da of Lt-Col Wyndham Damer Clark, JP, DL (E Mayo, colls):—

Richard Wyndham John, *b* 1939: *m* 1969, Diane Gracie Petters, and has issue living, Douglas John, *b* 1972, — Delia Joan, *b* 1970. —— Elizabeth Anne, *b* 1937. —— Diana Ord, *b* 1944. —— Cynthia Rose, *b* 1946: *m* 1969, Capt Colin Grant Ogilvie Hogg, KOSB, and has had issue, Vanessa Charlotte Ogilvie, *b* 1972, — Nicola Joanna Ogilvie, *b* and *d* 1974, — Sarah Jane Ogilvie, *b* 1976. —— Angela Viviane, *b* 1949.

Issue of late Kenneth Ord Mackenzie, *b* 1912, *d* 1994: *m* 1955, Penelope June (Springfield Cottage, Sherborne St John, Basingstoke), da of Neville Brace Colt (Rawlinson, Bt, colls):—

Virginia Anne, *b* 1958: *m* 1988, Hans H. von Celsing, of 77 Cambridge St, SW1V 4PS, yr son of Capt Folke von Celsing, of Stockholm, Sweden, and has issue living, Henrik Alexander Folke, *b* 1990, — Christian Frederick, *b* 1992. —— Caroline Jane, *b* 1960: *m* 1987, Hector W. H. Sants, son of John Sants, of Killin, Perthshire, and has issue living, Hector Alexander, *b* 1989, — Edward Kennett Richard, *b* 1990, — Arthur Frederick Joseph, *b* 1994.

Issue of late Col Alastair Douglas Mackenzie, CBE, *b* 1917, *d* 1989: *m* 1945, Diane, da of late Col Arthur John Henry Sloggett, CBE, DSO:—

Mark Tresloggett, *b* 1950.

Alexander Mackenzie of Coul, father of Sir Kenneth Mackenzie, 1st baronet, was a natural son of Colin Cam (one-eyed) Mackenzie, 11th of Kintail (*d* 1594) and half-brother of 1st Lord Mackenzie of Kintail (ancestor of the Earls of Seaforth) and of Sir Roderick Mackenzie of Tarbat (ancestor of the Earls of Cromartie). Sir John Mackenzie, 3rd baronet, participating in the Jacobite rising 1715, was included in the act of attainder passed against the Earl of Mar and his adherents. He died without male issue, and despite the forfeiture, the Baronetcy has been assumed since 1702, it being claimed that the attainder did not extend to collateral branches, and that the *title* as well as the estates devolved upon his brother.

Mackenzie (NS) 1703, of Gairloch, Ross-shire, see Inglis.

MACKENZIE (NS) 1703, of Scatwell, Ross-shire

I shine but do not burn

Sir RODERICK McQUHAE MACKENZIE, 12th *Baronet*; *b* 17 April 1942; *s* his father, *Capt Sir* RODERICK EDWARD FRANÇOIS McQUHAE, CBE, DSC, 1986; *ed* Sedbergh, King's Coll, Univ of London, and St George's Hosp; MB, BS, MRCP (UK), FRCP (C), DCH: *m* 1970, Nadezhda (Nadine), da of Georges Frederic Leon Schlatter, Baron von Rorbas of Buchs-K-Zurich, Switzerland, and has issue.

Arms – Quarterly, 1st, azure, a deer's head cabossed or, *Mackenzie of Scatwell*; 2nd, or, a mountain azure, inflamed gules; 3rd, gules, three legs of a man in armour proper flexed in triangle, garnished and spurred or, *Macleod of Lewis*, 4th, azure, a deer's head cabossed or within a bordure of the last charged with eight crescents of the first, *Mackenzie of Findon*. **Crest** – The sun in his splendour or. **Supporters** – *Dexter*, a savage wreathed about the head and middle with laurel and carrying with his dexter hand a club over his shoulder, all proper; *sinister*, a deer proper.

Without stain

SON LIVING

GREGORY RODERICK McQUHAE, *b* 8 May 1971.

DAUGHTER LIVING

Nina Adelaïda, *b* 1973.

SISTERS LIVING

Marie Isobel Campbell, *b* 1939: *m* 1964, Air Vice-Marshal Richard C. Allerton, CB, RAF, of Bicton Mill, Bicton, Liskeard, Cornwall, and has issue living, James Roderick Orde, *b* 1967, — Christopher Edward Orde, *b* 1970. —— Fiona Louise, *b* 1943: *m* 1969, Lt-Cdr Timothy Patrick Havers, RN, of Corner House, 153 Dalling Rd, Ravenscourt Park, W6 0ER, and has issue living, (James) Angus, *b* 1978, — Louisanna Marie, *b* 1973, — Laetitia Anastasia Sophie, *b* 1982.

AUNT LIVING (*Sister of 11th baronet*)

Phyllis Marion, *b* 1899: *m* 1922, Capt James Millar Begg, RN (ret), who *d* 1954, and has issue living, Kathleen Mary Iris, *b* 1923: *m* 1947, Brig Henry L. Broome Salmon, OBE, of The Old Rectory, Launton, Oxon OX6 0DP, and has issue living, Marion Jane Broome *b* 1949: *m* 1974, Thomas Richard Holland Sowler, TD, FTII, Solicitor, of Unthank Hall, Haltwhistle, Northumberland NE49 0HX (By Rotherham, ext) (and has issue living, Thomas Henry James Holland *b* 1982, Richard Mordaunt George Holland *b* 1989, Phyllis Elisabeth May Holland *b* 1977), Anthea Maud Broome, *b* 1953: *m* 1991, John Alexander Streeter, of The Dower House, Sizewell, nr Leiston, Suffolk.

MOTHER LIVING OF TENTH BARONET

Elizabeth Carrington (120 Church St, Clifton Forge, Virginia 24422, USA), da of late William Barbee Settle, Counsellor-at-law, of S Boston, Va, USA: *m* 1954, Kenneth Roderick Mackenzie, who *d* 1960.

The 1st baronet sat as MP for Ross-shire 1702-07, and the 5th baronet was Lord-Lieutenant of that county, and MP thereof 1822-31. This family is a collateral branch of the Mackenzies, Earls of Cromarty (title attainted 1746), and the present baronet claims he is representative, as heir male collateral, of Sir John Mackenzie of Tarbat (created a baronet of Nova Scotia by Charles I, 21 May 1628, with remainder to heirs male whatsoever, — "haeredibus masculis et talliae"). This same Sir John Mackenzie of Tarbat was the father of George, 1st Earl of Cromarty. The great-grandfather eight times removed of the present baronet was Sir Roderick Mackenzie of Tarbat and Coigeach, who was knighted in 1609 by James I of England and VI of Scotland.

MACKENZIE (UK) 1890, of Glen Muick, Aberdeenshire

This is the way to the stars

Sir (ALEXANDER GEORGE ANTHONY) ALLAN MACKENZIE, CD, 4th *Baronet d* 5 Jan 1993, since when the succession to the baronetcy has not been established.

Arms – Per pale indented azure and or, a stag's head cabossed counterchanged. **Crest** – A dexter hand grasping a sword bendwise proper.

DAUGHTERS LIVING AND DECEASED

Margaret Ann, *b* 1939: *m* 1974, Richard L. Mullin, and *dsp* 1989. —— Kathryn Heather, *b* 1946. —— Linda Alexandra, *b* 1949: *m* 1970, Brock J. Eayrs, BA, LLB, and has issue living Jennifer Alexandra, *b* 1973, — Alison Marjorie Ellen, *b* 1977, — Elizabeth Brooke Jane, *b* 1989. —— Allain Fenton, *b* 1953: *m* 1974, J. F. M. Beltgens, and has issue living, Christopher John Mackenzie, *b* 1978, — Jessica Kathryn Ann, *b* 1982.

WIDOW LIVING OF FOURTH BARONET

MARJORIE (*Lady Mackenzie*), da of A. F. McGuire, of Vancouver, BC, Canada: *m* 1937, Sir (Alexander George Anthony) Allan Mackenzie, 4th Bt, CD, who *d* 1993.

COLLATERAL BRANCH LIVING

Issue of the late Col Eric Dighton Mackenzie, CMG, CVO, DSO, yst son of 2nd Bt, *b* 1891, *d* 1972: *m* 1948, Elizabeth Kathrine Mary (Hill Cottage, Fressingfield, Eye, Suffolk IP21 5SA), da of late Capt James William Guy Innes, CBE, JP, RN, (*see* Innes, Bt, *cr* 1628), and formerly wife of Maj James Robertson-McIsaac:—

(James William) Guy (Tresowes Hill Farm, Ashton, nr Helston, Cornwall), *b* 1946; *ed* Stowe: *m* 1972 (*m diss* 1980), Paulene Patricia Simpson, and has issue living, Amanda Louise, *b* 1972, — Iona Elizabeth Rose, *b* 1978. —— Allan Walter, *b* 1952. —— Lucy Elizabeth Victoria, *b* 1949.

The 1st baronet, Sir James Thompson Mackenzie (son of George Mackenzie, of Aberdeen), was a DL for Ross-shire and Middlesex. The 3rd baronet, Sir Victor Audley Falconer, DSO, MVO, was Col Scots Guards, a Groom-in-Waiting to King George V, and an Extra Groom-in-Waiting to King Edward VIII and King George VI. He served during European War 1914-18 (DSO). The descendants of Sir Allan Mackenzie, 4th Bt, CD, are also in remainder to the barony of Berners.

MUIR MACKENZIE (UK) 1805, of Delvine, Perthshire

Straight at difficulties

Sir ALEXANDER ALWYNE BRINTON MUIR MACKENZIE, 7th *Baronet*; *b* 8 Dec 1955; *s* his father, *Capt Sir* ROBERT HENRY, 1970; *ed* Eton and Trin Coll, Camb: *m* 1984, Susan Carolyn, yst da of John David Henzell Hayter, of Adbury Court, nr Newbury, Berks, and has issue.

Arms – Quarterly: 1st and 4th, argent, on a fesse azure, three estoiles or, *Muir*; 2nd and 3rd, azure, a buck's head cabossed or, *Mackenzie*, all within a bordure nebuly quarterly gules and argent, the badge of a British baronet being placed in surtout. **Crest** – 1st, a sword and olive-branch in saltire proper; 2nd, a dexter hand grasping a dart in bend sinister proper. **First Motto** – "In utrumque paratus" (*In everything prepared*). **Second Motto** – "Recte ad ardua" (*Straight at difficulties*).
Residence – Buckshaw House, Holwell, nr Sherborne, Dorset DT9 5LD.

SON LIVING

ARCHIE ROBERT DAVID, *b* 17 Feb 1989.

DAUGHTER LIVING

Prepared for either fortune

Georgina Mary, *b* 1987.

SISTER LIVING

(Charmian) Miranda, *b* 1948: *m* 1968, Robert Dennis Smyly (*see* By of Buckland, 1980 Edn), of Sunderland Hall, Galashiels, Selkirkshire, TD1 3PG, and has issue living, Richard, *b* 1972, — Henrietta, *b* 1970.

WIDOW LIVING OF SIXTH BARONET

MARY TERESA (*Mary, Lady Muir Mackenzie*) (Flat A, 62 Pont St, SW1), da of late Dr James Mathews, and widow of John Geoffrey Turner, of Lower Old Park, Farnham, Surrey: *m* 1963, as his 2nd wife, Capt Sir Robert Henry Muir Mackenzie, 6th Bt, who *d* 1970.

The 1st baronet, Sir Alexander Muir, descended from the Muirs of Cassencarrie (a very ancient family), assumed the additional surname of Mackenzie upon succeeding to the estates of his great-uncle John Mackenzie, of Delvine, Perthshire, 3rd son of Sir Kenneth Mackenzie, 1st baronet of Coul. The 4th baronet *d* 1918, and the 5th baronet, Sir Robert Cecil, MC, Lieut Durham LI, was *ka* 1918.

MACKESON (UK) 1954, of Hythe, co Kent

Sir RUPERT HENRY MACKESON, 2nd *Baronet*, *b* 16 Nov 1941; *ed* Harrow, and Trin Coll, Dublin (MA); late Capt RHG, and Lt Buffs Regt (TA); *s* his father, *Brig Sir* HARRY RIPLEY, 1964: *m* 1968 (*m diss* 1972), Hon Camilla Margaret, da of Baron Keith of Castleacre (Life Baron) (*see* E Kintore).
Residence –

Arms – Vair four roses three and one or. **Crest** – A lion's gamb erased or supporting an escutcheon gules charged with a rose or.

SISTER LIVING

Fiona Mariella, *b* 1946: *m* 1965, Capt Hamish Leslie Gray-Cheape, late Gren Gds, JP, High Sheriff of Warwicks (1984), a DL for Warwicks since 1990, of Hill House, Walcot, Alcester, Warwicks, and has issue living, Hugo James, *b* 1968, — George Hamish, *b* 1971.

Sir Harry Ripley Mackeson, 1st baronet, son of Henry Mackeson of Littlebourne House, Littlebourne, Kent, was MP for Hythe (C) 1945-50, and for Folkstone 1950-59. He was Dep Ch Conservative Whip 1950-52, Senior Lord Commr of the Treasury 1951-52, and Sec for Overseas Trade 1952-53.

MACKWORTH (GB) 1776 of The Gnoll, Glamorganshire

Rather death than shame

Sir DAVID ARTHUR GEOFFREY MACKWORTH, 9th *Baronet*, only son of late Vice-Adm Geoffrey Mackworth, CMG, DSO, 5th son of 6th baronet; *b* 13 July 1912; *s* his uncle, *Col Sir* HARRY LLEWELLYN, CMG, DSO, 1952; *ed* Farnborough Sch, and RNC Dartmouth; Cdr (ret) RN; a Member of R Inst of Navigation; formerly Drafting Cdr RN Barracks, Devonport, and Naval Adviser to Director of Guided Weapon Research and Development, Mins of Supply: *m* 1st, 1941 (*m diss* 1971), Mary Alice (ROBINSON-SMITH), who *d* 1993, da of late Thomas Henry Grylls, of 36 Great Ormond Street, WC; 2ndly, 1973, Beryl Joan, 3rd da of late Pembroke Henry Cockayn Cross, and formerly wife of late Ernest Henry Sparkes, and has issue by 1st *m*.

ᴀrms – Per pale indented sable and ermine, on a chevron gules, five crosses-patée or. Crest – A cock proper.
Residence – 36 Wittering Rd, Hayling Island Hants P011 9SP. *Clubs* – Royal Naval (Portsmouth), Royal Ocean Racing, Royal Yacht Squadron, and Royal Naval Sailing Assocn.

SON LIVING *(By 1st marriage)*

DIGBY JOHN (Blagrove Cottage, Fox Lane, Boars Hill, Oxford OX1 5DS), *b* 2 Nov 1945; *ed* Wellington; late Lt AAAC in Malaysia and Vietnam; with BA Helicopters, Ltd: *m* 1971, Antoinette Francesca, da of Henry James McKenna, of 40 Gyllingdune Gdns, Ilford, Essex, and has issue living, Octavia, *b* 1977.

SISTERS LIVING

Betty Mabel, *b* 1911. —— Lorna Alice, *b* 1918.

COLLATERAL BRANCHES LIVING

Issue of late Capt Francis Julian Audley Mackworth, 2nd son of 6th baronet, *b* 1876, *ka* 1914: *m* 1910, Dorothy Conran, who *m* 2ndly, 1922, Charles Edward Gatehouse, and *d* 1976, da of late Arthur Hastings Lascelles, of Belmore, Narbeth, Pembroke:—
Cecily Joan (6 Rue des Coutures-St Gervais, Paris 75003), *b* 1911: *m* 1st, 1935, Leon Donckier de Donceel, who *d* 1938; 2ndly, 1956, Marquis de Chabannes la Palice, of Château du Brèvedent, Calvados, France, who *d* 1980, and has issue living, (by 1st *m*) Pascale, *b* 1936.

Issue of late Col John Dolben Mackworth, CBE, 7th son of 6th baronet, *b* 1887, *d* 1939: *m* 1913, Marianne Annette, who *d* 1968, da of H. W. Sillem, of The Pines, Horsell, Surrey:—
Josephine Ann, *b* 1914: *m* 1st, 1937, Major Patrick Owen Lyons, who *d* 1941, Indian Army Ordnance Corps; 2ndly, 1942, Lt-Col Noel James, MBE, RAOC, of Tower House, 4 Bath Rd, Cowes, I of Wight, and has issue living, (by 2nd *m*) Christopher Noel Mackworth, *b* 1946, — John Gwyn Mackworth, *b* 1951, — (by 1st *m*) Mary Annette, *b* 1939, — Bridget Carol Dolben, *b* 1940.

Grandson of late Horace Euguene Mackworth, 2nd son of 4th baronet:—
Issue of late Lt-Col Norman Walter Mackworth, MB, ChB, FRCS, IMS, *b* 1878, *d* 1950: *m* 1908, Isabel Largie, MA, who *d* 1967, da of late William Anderson:—
Norman Humphrey, PhD, MB, ChB (16232 Camellia Terr, Los Gatos, Cal 95030, USA), *b* 1917; *ed* Aberdeen Univ (MB and ChB); PhD Camb; *m* 1941, Jane Felicity, MB, BChir, PhD, yr da of late Capt Walter Hugh Charles Samuel Thring, CBE, RN, and has issue living, Alan Keith (4433 West 9th Av, Vancouver, BC, Canada V6R 2C9), *b* 1945: *m* 1969, Marian Elizabeth, da of J. V. Fry, and has issue living, Bryn Sarah *b* 1972, — Hugh Francis, *b* 1958, — Jean Clare, *b* 1942: *m* 1964, David Surry, and has issue living, Patrick David *b* 1969, Susan Alicia Mackworth *b* 1971, Kathleen Jane Mackworth *b* 1973.

Grandchildren of late Audley Mackworth, 2nd son of late Herbert Francis Mackworth, el son of late Lieut Herbert Mackworth, RN, 2nd son of 3rd baronet:—
Issue of late Air Vice-Marshal Philip Herbert Mackworth, CB, CBE, DFC, *b* 1897, *d* 1958: *m* 1921, Winifred Kathleen June, who *d* 1967, da of William Moss:—
Richard Charles Audley (27 Wellington Sq, SW3), *b* 1924; *ed* Camb Univ (MA); MSc Eng London; MIMechE; MIWE; DIC; formerly Fl-Lt RAF: *m* 1960, Rosalind Jean, da of Rev A. Walters, V of Wychbold, Worcs, and has issue living, Julia Kathleen, *b* 1968, — Victoria Alma Louise, *b* 1971. —— James Digby (The Old School House, Littleworth, Faringdon, Oxon SN7 8ED), *b* 1927; *ed* Camb Univ (MA); Maj (ret) REME; CEng, FIMechE: *m* 1st, 1952 (*m diss* 1968) Marjorie Wilding; 2ndly, 1968, Anna Marjorie Wilson Melling, who *d* 1983; 3rdly, 1984, Susan Elizabeth Parsons, and has issue living, (by 1st *m*) Charles Digby *b* 1958, Amanda Jane *b* 1956.

This family is of considerable antiquity in Shropshire and Derbyshire, and a member of it fought at Poitiers in 1356. Sir Francis Mackworth, a distinguished royalist, fought on the side of Charles I. Col Humphrey Mackworth, a man of considerable note *temp* Commonwealth, was MP for Salop, was Governor for Shrewsbury, and one of Cromwell's Council. The 1st baronet sat as MP for Cardiff, and the 2nd baronet bequeathed the Gnoll Castle estate to his widow. The 8th baronet, Col Sir Harry Llewellyn Mackworth, CMG, DSO, Roy Corps of Signals, was Ch Signal Officer, Egypt 1924-27.

MACLEAN (NS) 1631, of Dowart and Morvaren, Argyllshire

Hon Sir LACHLAN HECTOR CHARLES MACLEAN, 12th *Baronet; b* 25 Aug 1942; *s* his father, CHARLES HECTOR FITZROY, Baron Maclean, KT, GCVO, KBE, PC (Life Baron) in his baronetcy 1990; *ed* Eton; 28th Chief of Clan Maclean; Maj Scots Guards (ret); DL Argyll and Bute 1993: *m* 1966, Mary Helen, eldest da of William Gordon Gordon, of Lude, Blair Atholl, Perthshire, and has had issue.

Arms – Quarterly: 1st, argent, a rock gules; 2nd argent, a dexter hand fessewise couped gules holding a cross-crosslet fitchée in pale azure; 3rd, or, a lymphad, oars in saltire, sails furled, sable, flagged gules; 4th, argent, a salmon naiant proper, in chief two eagles' heads erased respectant gules. **Crest** – A tower embattled argent. **Supporters** – *Dexter*, a seal proper; *sinister*, an ostrich with a horseshoe in its beak proper.
Seat – Duart Castle, Isle of Mull.
Residence – Arngask House, Glenfarg, Perthshire PH2 9QA.

SONS LIVING

MALCOLM LACHLAN CHARLES, *b* 20 Oct 1972; *ed* —. —— Andrew William, *b* 1979.

DAUGHTERS LIVING AND DECEASED

Emma Mary, *b* 1967. —— Sarah Elizabeth Helen, *b* 1969, *d* 19—. —— Alexandra Caroline, *b* 1975.

SISTER LIVING

Hon Janet Elizabeth, *b* 1944: *m* 1974, Maj Nicholas Michael Lancelot Barne, Scots Guards (ret) (*see* Orr Ewing, Bt, *cr* 1886, colls, 1969 Edn), and has issue living, Alasdair Michael Fitzroy, *b* 1979, —— Hamish Nicholas Charles, *b* 1981. *Residence* – Blofield House, Blofield, Norwich, Norfolk.

WIDOW LIVING OF LIFE BARON AND ELEVENTH BARONET

JOAN ELIZABETH (*Elizabeth, Baroness Maclean*), da of late Capt Francis Thomas Mann (*see* Mann, Bt): *m* 1941, Baron Maclean, KT, GCVO, KBE, PC (Life Baron), who *d* 1990. *Residences* – Wilderness House, Hampton Court Palace, Surrey KT8 9AR; Duart Castle, Isle of Mull.

COLLATERAL BRANCH LIVING

Issue of late Capt Charles Lachlan Maclean, RN, 2nd son of 10th baronet, *b* 1874, *d* 1958: *m* 1st, 1904, Hon Philadelphia Sybil Robertson, who *d* 1945, da of late Baron Robertson, a Lord of Appeal in Ordinary; 2ndly, 1952, Christian Mary, who *d* 1983, da of the Rev M. Taggart, of Lyne, Peeblesshire, and widow of Hedley Briggs-Constable:—
(By 1st *m*) Finovola Sybil, *b* 1907: *m* 1929, Henry Norman Wilson, formerly Lt Black Watch (R Highlanders), and has issue living, Charles Jeremy, *b* 1930. —— Robert Malcolm, *b* 1935. *Residence* – Princeland, Coupar Angus, Perths.

(1) *Sir* LACHLAN Maclean of Morvern, son and heir of Hector Og Maclean of Duart; a zealous supporter of Charles I; *cr* a Bt 1631, with remainder to his heirs male whatsoever: *m* Mary, da of Roderick Macleod of Macleod; *d* 1649; *s* by his el son **(2)** *Sir* HECTOR, 2nd Bt; *b* about 1625; *d* unm, *k* fighting for Royal cause at Innerkeithing 1651; *s* by his brother **(3)** *Sir* ALLAN, 3rd Bt; *b* about 1637: *m* Giles, da of John Macleod of Macleod; *d* 1674; *s* by his only son **(4)** *Sir* JOHN, 4th Bt; present with his clan at Killiecrankie 1689 and Sheriffmuir 1715; *m* about 1704 Mary, da of Sir Aeneas Macpherson of Invereshie; *d* about 1719; *s* by his son **(5)** *Sir* HECTOR, 5th Bt; *b* about 1704; imprisoned in Tower of London 1745-47 as a Jacobite; *d* unm 1751; *s* by his kinsman **(6)** *Sir* ALLAN, 6th Bt, (gt-grandson of Donald Maclean of Brolas, half-brother of 1st Bt): *m* Una, da of Hector Maclean of Coll; *d* 1783; *s* by his kinsman **(7)** *Sir* HECTOR, 7th Bt (grandson of Hector Og, gt-uncle of 6th Bt); *d* unm 1818; *s* by his half-brother **(8)** *Sir* FITZROY JEFFREYS GRAFTON, Lt-Gen; present at capture of Martinique and Guadaloupe: *m* 1st, 1794, Elizabeth, who *d* 1832, da of Charles Kidd, and widow of John Bishop of Barbados; 2ndly, 1838, Frances, who *d* 1843, da of Rev Henry Watkins, and widow of Henry Campion; *d* 1847; *s* by his el son **(9)** *Sir* CHARLES FITZROY, 9th Bt; *b* 1798; Col: *m* 1831, Emily Eleanor, who *d* 1838, da of Rev Canon Hon Jacob Marsham, DD (E Romney); *d* 1883; *s* by his son **(10)** *Sir* FITZROY DONALD, KCB, 10th Bt, *b* 1835; Ch of Clan Maclean; recovered Duart Castle 1910; Comdg 13 H; Crimean War; *m* 1872, Constance Marianne, who *d* 1920, da of George Holland Ackers, of Moreton Hall, Ches; *d* 1936; *s* by his grandson, **(11)** *Sir* CHARLES HECTOR FITZROY, 11th Bt, KT, GCVO, KBE, PC, *b* 1916; Lord Lieut Argyll and Bute, Chief Scout of the Commonwealth, Lord Chamberlain of the Household, Lord High Commr to Gen Assembly of Church of Scotland, a Permanent Lord in Waiting and Chief Steward of Hampton Court Palace, Chllr Royal Victorian Order (Royal Victorian Chain), author of children's books; *cr Baron Maclean*, of Duart and Morvern, co Argyll (Life Baron) 1971: *m* 1941, Joan Elizabeth, da of late Capt Francis Thomas Mann (*see* Mann, Bt); *d* 1990; *s* by his son **(12)** *Sir* LACHLAN HECTOR CHARLES, 12th Bt.

MACLEAN (UK) 1957, of DUNCONNEL, co Argyll

Sir FITZROY HEW MACLEAN OF DUNCONNEL, KT, CBE, 1st *Baronet*, 15th Hereditary Keeper and Captain of Dunconnel in the Isles of the Sea, son of late Maj Charles Wilberforce Maclean, DSO, OBE; *b* 11 March 1911; *ed* Eton and King's Coll, Camb (MA, Hon LLD, Glasgow and Dundee); appointed 3rd Sec Diplo Ser 1933, and 2nd Sec 1938; served in Paris and Moscow; was Parliamentary Under-Sec of State for War and Financial Sec to War Office 1954-57; author of "Eastern Approaches" and other works; 1939-45 War with Queen's Own Cameron Highlanders and 1st SAS Regt; Brig Comdg British Mission to Yugoslav Partisans 1943-45 (CBE, French Croix de Guerre, Order of Kutusov of Russia, Yugoslav Partisan Star); Hon Col 23 SAS 1984-88; MP for Lancaster (*C*) Oct 1941 to Oct 1959, and for Bute and N Ayrshire Oct 1959 to Feb 1974; CBE (Mil) 1944, KT 1993: *m* 1946, Hon Veronica Nell Fraser, da of 14th Lord Lovat, and widow of Lt Alan Phipps, RN (*see* M Normanby, colls), and has issue.

Arms – Quarterly, 1st, argent, a lion rampant gules, armed and langued azure; 2nd, azure, a castle triple towered argent, masoned sable, windows, portcullis and flags gules; 3rd, or, a dexter hand couped fessways gules, holding a cross crosslet fitchée azure; 4th, or, a galley, sails furled, oars in saltire sable, flagged gules, in a sea in base vert a salmon argent; at the centre point a portcullis sable for difference. Above the shield, from which is pendent from its proper riband the Badge of a Baronet of the United Kingdom, and behind which are placed in saltire a key wards outwards or and a rod gules garnished or, being insignia for his office of Hereditary Keeper and Captain of Dunconnel Castle, is placed his chapeau gules furred ermine (as feudal baron of Strachur). **Crest** – A lochaber axe in pale between a branch of laurel and a branch of cypress in open chaplet all proper.
Residence – Strachur House, Argyll. *Clubs* – White's, Pratt's, New (Edinburgh).

SONS LIVING

CHARLES EDWARD, yr of Dunconnel *b* 31 Oct 1946; *ed* Eton and New Coll, Oxford: *m* 1986, Deborah, da of Lawrence Young, of Chicago, and has issue living, Margaret Augusta, *b* 1986, — Katharine Alexandra, *b* 1988, — Charlotte Olivia, *b* 1991.
—— (Alexander) James (Flat 4, 49 Drayton Gardens, SW10), *b* 1949; *ed* Eton: *m* 1st, 1983 (*m diss* 1989), Sarah, el da of Hugh Janson, of Barn House, Aldbourne, Wilts; 2ndly, 1993, Sarah C., da of Nicolas Thompson, of Ennismore Gdns, SW7.
Maj Charles Wilberforce Maclean, DSO, OBE, father of the 1st baronet, was 4th son of Lt-Col Allan Henry Maclean, RHA, grandson of Lt-Col Alexander Maclean, 13th Chief of Ardgour, Argyll. His ancestor, Donald, yr son of Lachlan Bronnach, 7th of Duart (*see* Maclean Bt, *cr* 1631) slew MacMaster of Ardgour and appropriated his lands, about 1432, obtaining a grant thereof from Alexander, 3rd Lord of the Isles. This was confirmed by James IV in 1494.

MacLEOD (UK) 1924, of Fuinary, Morven, co Argyll

Hon Sir JOHN MAXWELL NORMAN MacLEOD, 5th *Baronet*; *b* 23 Feb 1952; *s* his father, Very Rev GEORGE FIELDEN, Baron MacLeod of Fuinary, MC, DD (Life Baron), in his baronetcy 1991; *ed* Gordonstoun.

Arms – Azure, a castle triple-towered argent, masoned sable, windows and protcullis gules, on a chief of the second an open book proper, leaved of the fourth. **Crest** – A bull's head cabossed sable, horned or, between two keys wards uppermost of the last.
Residence – Fuinary Manse, Loch Aline, Morven, Argyll.

BROTHER LIVING

Hon NEIL DAVID, *b* 25 Dec 1959; *ed* —. *Residence* – —.

SISTER LIVING

Hon Eva Mary Ellen, *b* 1950. *Residence* – .
The 1st baronet, Sir John Mackintosh MacLeod (son of Very Rev Norman MacLeod, DD, of Barony Church, Glasgow, and Dean of the Order of the Thistle), sat as MP for Central Div of Glasgow (*Co U*) 1915-18, and for Kelvingrove 1918-22. The 2nd baronet, Sir John Mackintosh Norman, was Unicorn Pursuivant of Arms 1925-29, and Rothesay Herald 1929-39. The 3rd baronet, Capt Sir Ian Francis Norman, Intelligence Corps, *d* on active ser during European War 1944. The 4th baronet, Very Rev Sir George Fielden, MC, DD, was Leader of Iona Community 1938-67, Moderator of Gen Assembly of Church of Scotland 1956-57, and Chaplain to HM in Scotland 1956-65; *cr Baron MacLeod of Fuinary*, of Fuinary in Morven, co Argyll (Life Baron) 1967: *m* 1948, Lorna Helen Janet, who *d* 1984, da of Rev Donald MacLeod of Balvonie, of Inshes, Inverness, and *d* 1991.

McLEOD (UK) 1925, of The Fairfields, Cobham, Surrey
(Name pronounced "McLoud")

HOLD · FAST

Sir CHARLES HENRY McLEOD*, 3rd *Baronet*; *b* 7 Nov 1924; *s* his
father, *Sir* MURDOCH CAMPBELL, 1950; *ed* Winchester: *m* 1957,
(Anne) Gillian, who *d* 1978, yr da of Henry Russell Bowlby (V
Combermere, colls), and has issue.

Arms – Ermine, on a pile azure between two lotus flowers in base or a castle
triple-towered argent, masoned sable, windows and porch gules. **Crest** – In front
of two flags in saltire gules, staves proper, a bull's head caboshed also gules.
Residence – Coombe Green Cottage, Lea, Malmesbury, Wilts SN16 9PF.

Murus aheneus esto

Be thou a brazen wall

SON LIVING

JAMES RODERICK CHARLES, *b* 26 Sept 1960: *m* 1990, Helen M., elder da of Capt
George T. Cooper, OBE, RN, of Lilliput, Poole, Dorset.

DAUGHTERS LIVING

Belinda Ann, *b* 1957: *m* 19—, Shaker. —— Nicola, *b* 1958: *m* 1st, 1981 (*m diss*
1985), Nigel Iorwerth Stodart Parry, elder son of John Stanley Hammond Parry,
of Staplegordon, Seale, Surrey; 2ndly, 19—, — Duffain; 3rdly, 1990, John
Spencer Warwick Bampfylde, of 56 Ames St, Paekakariki, Wellington, NZ, yst
son of Hon David Cecil Warwick Bampfylde (*see* B Poltimore).
The 1st baronet, Sir Charles Campbell McLeod (son of the Rev Norman
McLeod, of N Uist), was Chm of National Bank of India, Ltd, and of Imperial
Tea Co, Ltd.
*His el brother Roderick Campbell McLeod, *b* 1921; Lieut Scots Guards; *ka* at
Salerno 1943.

McLINTOCK (UK) 1934, of Sanquhar, co Dumfries

By virtue and labour

Virtute · et · Labore

Sir MICHAEL WILLIAM McLINTOCK, 4th *Baronet*; *b* 13 Aug 1958; *s* his
father, *Sir* WILLIAM TRAVEN, 1987.

Arms – Azure, a book expanded or, leaved gules, over all a writing pen
palewise proper. **Crest** – A lion passant or, holding in his dexter paw a thistle
slipped proper.

BROTHERS LIVING

ANDREW THOMSON, *b* 2 Dec 1960. —— Kevin Robert, *b* 1963.

UNCLE LIVING (son of 2nd baronet)

Peter Thomson, *b* 1933; *ed* Harrow: *m* 1st, 1954 (*m diss* 1977), Fiona, yst da of
Gen Sir Philip Christian, 4th Bt, GBE, CB, DSO, MC; 2ndly, 1986, Patricia-
Anne, da of —, and has issue living (by 1st *m*), Traven Thomson Christison, *b*
1957; *ed* Edinburgh Acad: *m* 1984, —, and has issue living, Sarah *b* 1987, —
Morar, *b* 1955: *m* 1986, David Honeyman, and has issue living, Ailsa *b* 1986.
Residence – Springfield, Penicuik, Midlothian.

GREAT-AUNT LIVING (daughter of 1st baronet)

Mary Lyons, *b* 1912: *m* 1st, 1937, Capt Malcolm George Lillingston, King's Drag
Gds, who was *ka* 1941; 2ndly, 1947, Maj Robert Bradford Myles, MC, late Royal
Inniskilling Fus, who *d* 1981, and has issue living (by 1st *m*), Mark Campbell, *b*
1938; *ed* Eton, and Magdalene Coll, Camb, — Diane Margaret, *b* 1941: *m* 1963,
Robin Andrew Paterson, CA, of Lees Court, Matfield, Tonbridge, Kent, and has
issue living, Jamie John Lillingston LILLINGSTON-PATERSON *b* 1967; *ed* Eton;
assumed addl surname of Lillingston 1987, Joanna Mary Lillingston *b* 1965: *m*
1990, Michael Richard John Bell, yst son of Lt-Cdr Peter Bell, of Yeabridge Close, S Petherton, Som, and has issue living,
Hollie Mary Ann *b* 1993, Camilla Margaret Lucy *b* (twin) 1993, — (by 2nd *m*) Nicholas Robert William Bradford, *b* 1954; *ed*
Eton, — Sarah Louise Bradford, *b* 1950: *m* 1982, Michael James Corbett Robinson, of 8 Gorst Rd, SW11 6JE, and has issue
living, Jonathon Myles *b* 1986, Cara Myles *b* 1984, — Penelope Jean Bradford, *b* 1952: *m* 1979, Dr Anthony Pitt Lipscomb.
Residence – Coach House, Lees Court, Matfield, Tonbridge, Kent.

WIDOW LIVING OF THIRD BARONET

Mrs (MURIEL) HEATHER HOMFRAY NEWMAN (*Lady McLintock*), da of late Philip Dennis Homfray-Davies: *m* 1974, as his 2nd
wife, Sir William Traven McLintock, 3rd Bt, who *d* 1987. *Residence* –

MOTHER LIVING

Andrée, da of Richard Lonsdale-Hands, of 6 Av Edouard Dapples, Lausanne: *m* 1952 (*m diss* 19—), as his 1st wife, Sir
William Traven McLintock, 3rd Bt, who *d* 1987. *Residence* –
The 1st baronet, Sir William McLintock, GBE, CVO (son of Thomson McLintock), was senior partner in the firm of
Thomson McLintock & Co, chartered accountants, of 33 King William Street, EC4, and Glasgow.

MACLURE (UK) 1898, of The Home, Whalley Range, near Manchester, co Palatine of Lancaster

Paratus sum
I am ready

Sir JOHN ROBERT SPENCER MACLURE, 4th *Baronet*; *b* 25 March 1934; *s* his father Lt-Col *Sir* JOHN WILLIAM SPENCER, OBE, 1980; *ed* Winchester; Headmaster of Croftinloan Sch, Pitlochry since 1978: *m* 1964, Jane Monica, da of late Rt Rev Thomas Joseph Savage, Bishop of Zululand and Swaziland, and has issue.

Arms – Argent, on a chevron engrailed azure between in chief two roses and in base a quatrefoil gules, a martlet between two escallops of the field. **Crest** – An eagle's head erased argent between four roses gules, stalked and leaved on each side proper. *Residences* – Croftmhor, Pitlochry, Perthshire PH16 5JR; Wild Goose Cottage, Gooseham, Morwenstow, Bude, N Cornwall EX23 9PG. *Club* – Royal and Ancient Golf; MCC.

SONS LIVING

JOHN MARK, *b* 27 Aug 1965; *ed* Winchester. *Residence* – Chesham Lodge, Rossway Park, Berkhamsted, Herts HP4 3UB. —— Thomas Stephen, *b* 1967. —— Graham Spencer, *b* 1970. —— Stephen Patrick Ian, *b* 1974.

BROTHER LIVING

Patrick Stanley Winton King (Flat 2, 25 Christchurch Rd, Winchester, Hants SO23 9SU; *Clubs* – Oriental, Royal Greenjackets, MCC), *b* 1939; *ed* Winchester; consultant.

SISTER LIVING

Elspeth Rosemary, *b* 1930; SRN: *m* 1955, Maj-Gen Michael Matthews, CB, DL, who *d* 1993, and has issue living, Graeme Michael Ian (110 Newland, Witney Oxon), *b* 1959: *m* 1987, Sophie L. K., yr da of Ralph Denne, of Henley-on-Thames, and of Lady Hodson, of Romsey, and has issue living, Benjamin Michael David *b* 1989, Oscar William *b* 1991, Mungo George *b* 1993, — James Binding, *b* 1966: *m* 1990, Jennifer J. Harper-Hill, — Nichola Jane, *b* 1957, — Elspeth Julie, *b* 1963. *Residence* – Salthouse Cottage, Widemouth Bay, Bude, Cornwall.

UNCLE LIVING (*Son of 2nd baronet*)

Edward Stanley Winton, *b* 1909; Lt-Com (ret) RN: *m* 1938, Jeanette Kathleen, who *d* 1969, da of late Anton Bakker, of Sydney, Aust, and has issue living, Caroline Eleanor Kathleen (Abeelstraat 154, 3329 A H Dordrecht, Netherlands), *b* 1939; *ed* London Univ (BA): *m* 1964 (*m diss* 1989), Gerard Jozef van Tienen, and has issue living, Robbert Rudolf *b* 1967, Richard Mark *b* 1970, — Margaret Elizabeth Anne, *b* 1941: *m* 1969, Raymond D. Hibberd, of 24 Warfield Av, Waterlooville, Hants, and 4 rue de la Liberation, Plerguer, Brittany, France, and has issue living, Simon Philip *b* 1972, Nicholas Adam *b* 1975, — Yvonne Irene Valerie, *b* 1943: *m* 1st, 1964 (*m diss* 1972), Albert Brian Challinor; 2ndly, 1972, Brian Henry Thompson, RN, of 35 George V Av, Westbrook, Margate, Kent, and has issue living (by 1st *m*), Ian Grant *b* 1965, Susan Jane *b* 1967 (by 2nd *m*) Fiona Kate *b* 1973, Alexandra Louise *b* 1975, Caroline Elizabeth *b* 1978. *Residence* – Flat No 1, Hinton House, Jubilee Rd, Waterlooville, Hants PO7 7QX.

AUNT LIVING (*Daughter of 2nd baronet*)

Edith Mary Ursula, *b* 1916: *m* 1939, Louis Gordon Oliphant Hutchison, sometime F/O RAFVR, who *d* 1959, and has issue living, Alexander Gordon Oliphant (Batworthy Mill, Batworthy, nr Chagford, Devon), *b* 1943: *m* 1967, Jennifer Marilyn, da of Alun Blackwell, and has issue living, Alexander Valentine Oliphant *b* 1968, William Lawrence Oliphant *b* 1969, James Hardy Oliphant *b* 1973, — Susan Ruth Oliphant (Les Bourges, Salles 47150, Monflanquin, France), *b* 1940: *m* 1st, 1959, John Chislett, who *d* 1962: 2ndly, 1962 (*m diss* 1975), Jonathan Frederick Macnaught Ruddick; 3rdly, 1976, Colin Costello-Jones, and has issue living, (by 1st *m*) Miles Gordon *b* 1960: *m* 1986, Elizabeth Robinson (and has issue living, Hannah Georgina *b* 1986), (by 2nd *m*) Francis Louis *b* 1962, Simon William *b* 1964, Charlotte Nina *b* 1966, Romany Lara *b* 1974, (by 3rd *m*) Benjamin Llewelyn *b* 1981, Harriet *b* 1984, — Philippa Anne Oliphant *b* 1946: *m* 1st, 1963 (*m diss* 1970), Donald Stuart Oldham; 2ndly, 1972, Patrick John Bugg, and has issue living, (by 1st *m*) Tamsin *b* 1963: *m* 1985, Jonathan Seymour (and has issue living, Alice *b* 1986), Jessica *b* 1966: *m* 1988, James Eager (and has issue living, Amy *b* 1989), (by 2nd *m*) Fletcher Charlie *b* 1973. *Residence* – Ramon, Salles 47150, Monflanquin, France.

The 1st baronet was Hon Sec to Cotton Famine Relief Fund 1862-65, and MP for Stretford 1886-1901.

McMAHON (UK) 1817
(Name pronounced "McMahn")

Sir BRIAN PATRICK McMAHON, 8th *Baronet*; *b* 9th June 1942; *s* his father, Sir (WILLIAM) PATRICK 1977; *ed* Wellington Coll, Wednesbury Tech Coll (BSc 1964) AIM (1965): *m* 1981, Kathleen Joan, da of late William Hopwood.

Arms – Per saltire or and ermine, a lion passant azure between two lions passant-reguardant gules. **Crest** – An arm embowed in armour, holding a sword wavy, all proper, surmounted of a portcullis gules, chained or. **Supporters** – On either side a private of the 10th Foot habited and accoutred, and holding in the exterior hand a musket proper.
Residence – 157B Wokingham Rd, Reading, Berks RG6 1LP.

BROTHER LIVING

Thus we defend ourselves and our sacred rights

SHAUN DESMOND (Dendron, 21 Old Vineyard Rd, Constantia, Cape, S Africa), *b* 29 Oct 1945; *ed* Wellington Coll: *m* 1st, 1971, Antonia Noel, da of Antony James Adie, of Rowington, Warwicks; 2ndly, 1985, Jill Rosamund, yr da of Dr Jack Cherry, of 44 Park Rd, Abingdon, Oxon, and has issue living, (by 2nd *m*) Patrick John Westropp, *b* 7 Feb 1988. —— Charles Beresford, *b* 1989.

The 1st baronet, Right Hon Sir John McMahon, was a Privy Councillor for Ireland and Private Secretary and Keeper of the Privy Purse to George IV. His next brother was also created a baronet (*cr* 1815, ext 1926). The 1st baronet of this creation was succeeded under a limitation in the patent by his second brother, Gen Sir Thomas, GCB, Col of 10th Foot, and Com-in-Chief of the Forces at Bombay.

MACNAGHTEN (UK) 1836, of Bushmills House, co Antrim

Sir PATRICK ALEXANDER MACNAGHTEN, 11th *Baronet*, *b* 24 Jan 1927; *s* his father *Sir* ANTONY, 1972; *ed* Eton and Trin Coll, Camb: *m* 1955, Marianne, da of Dr Erich Schaefer, of Cambridge, and has issue.

Arms – Quarterly: 1st and 4th argent a dexter hand fessways proper holding a cross-crosslet fitchée azure; 2nd and 3rd argent, a tower gules. **Crest** – A tower embattled gules. **Supporters** – Two roebucks proper.
Residence – Dundarave, Bushmills, co Antrim BT57 8ST.

SONS LIVING

MALCOLM FRANCIS, *b* 21 Sept 1956. —— Edward Alexander, *b* 1958. —— David Charles, *b* 1962.

BROTHERS LIVING

Antony Martin (Ballyvester House, Donaghadee, co Down), *b* 1930; *ed* Eton, and Trin Coll, Camb: *m* 1959, Catherine Frances, da of Rev Charles ffolliott Young, and has issue living, Philip Martin, *b* 1965, — Antony Charles, *b* 1971, — Ruth Helen, *b* 1964: *m* 1992, Dr Jonathan Holbrook, — Imogen Alice, *b* 1970. —— Charles Edmund (The Croft, Church St, Seal, nr Sevenoaks, Kent), *b* 1937; *ed* Eton, and Trin Coll, Camb: *m* 1976, Mary Jane, da of John W. Saunders, of West Hartford, Connecticut, USA, and has issue living, Alexander, *b* 1977, — Mary Joanna, *b* 1979.

SISTER LIVING

Diana Mary, *b* 1929: *m* 1951, Myles Richard Eckersley, and has issue living, Alison, *b* 1954, — Fiona Jane, *b* 1955. *Residence* – Elm View, Lockerley, nr Romsey, Hants.

AUNTS LIVING

Mary Frances (8 Redwoods, Alton Rd, Roehampton, SW15), *b* 1903: *m* 1931, Laszlo Péri who *d* 1965, and has had issue, William, *b* 1936, — Matthew, *b* 1942: *d* ca 1960, — Anne, *b* 1931. —— Anne Catherine (23 Wymondley Rd, Hitchen, Herts), *b* 1908: *m* 1st 1936, James Ernest Skilbeck, who *d* 1947; 2ndly, 1947, Arnold Richardson Ashby, who *d* 1994, and has issue living, (by 1st *m*) John, *b* 1942, — Catherine, *b* 1947.

WIDOW LIVING OF TENTH BARONET

MAGDALENE (*Magdalene, Lady Macnaghten*) (Dundarave, Bushmills, co Antrim), el da of late Edmund Fisher: *m* 1926, Sir Antony Macnaghten, 10th Bt, who *d* 1972.

COLLATERAL BRANCHES LIVING

Granddaughter of late Alfred Hill Macnaghten, 6th son of Francis Macnaghten, 3rd son of 1st baronet:—
Issue of late Lieut-Col Balfour Macnaghten, DSO, 12th Roy Lancers, *b* 1875, *d* 1945: *m* 1902, Hilda, who *d* 1958, da of W. G. Lardner, of 11 Fourth Avenue, Hove, Sussex:—
Daphne, *b* 1914: *m* 1940, Lieut-Col Richard Percival Hawksley Burbury, Duke of Cornwall, LI, who *d* of wounds received in action in Normandy. *Residence* – Portesbery Woods, Camberley, Surrey.

Granddaughter of late Elliot Macnaghten (*b* 1837), son of late Elliot Macnaghten (*b* 1807), 4th son of 1st baronet:—
Issue of late Russell Elliot Macnaghten, *b* 1860, *d* 1918: *m* 1891, Mary, da of late Frederick Berry, of Churchdown, Gloucestershire:—
Kathleen Edith, *b* 1903: *m* 1934, Edward C. R. Cardinall, of Skaha Lake, Penticton, BC, Canada, and has issue living, Edward Russell, *b* 1936, — Sandra Margaret, *b* 1934, — Chloe Joan (twin), *b* 1936.

Grandchildren of late Col William Hay Macnaghten, CB, son of late Elliot Macnaghten (ante):—
Issue of late Brig-Gen Ernest Brander Macnaghten, CMG, DSO, *b* 1872, *d* 1948: *m* 1906, Yvonne Marie, who *d* 1950, da of late Surg-Lieut-Col J. S. Forrester, Roy Horse Guards:—
James Steuart, *b* 1914; *ed* Eton and Ch Ch, Oxford (MA); Maj RA (ret) and Maj RA (TA Reserve); 1939-45 War. —— Joan Yvonne Marie, *b* 1911. *Residence* – Gorse Cottage, Eversley Cross, Basingstoke, Hants. —— Awdry Clarisse (twin), *b* 1914: *m* 1936, Brig Anthony Donald Macdonald Teacher, CBE, DL, who *d* 1969, and has issue living, Anthony James Moreton (Hadlow Place, nr Tonbridge, Kent TN11 0BW), *b* 1937; *ed* Wellington Coll, and Ch Ch, Oxford (MA): *m* 1969, Rosemary Chloë, High Sheriff of Kent 1994, da of late Maj Sir Henry Joseph d'Avigdor-Goldsmid, 2nd Bt, DSO, MC, TD, and has issue living, Harry Donald Macdonald *b* 1970; *ed* Eton, and Ch Ch, Oxford (BA), (Laura) Poppy *b* 1973; *ed* Wycombe Abbey, and LMH Oxford, Petra Rose *b* 1980, Sarah Cordelia *b* 1983, — Hugh Macdonald, *b* 1943: *m* 1977, Rosemary, only da of Sir David John Hatherley Page Wood, 7th Bt, and has issue living, James Henry MacDonald *b* 1979. —— Renée Gavrelle, *b* 1918: *m* 1st, 1938, Lt-Cdr Alexander Arthur Wyndham Baker, RN, who *d* 1969; 2ndly, 1971, William Henry Guilland Stenson, and has issue living (by 1st *m*), Mark Alexander (The Old School, Fyfield, Abingdon, Oxon), *b* 1940; *ed* Ch Ch, Oxford (MA): *m* 1964, Meriel, da of Capt Edward Hugh Frederick Chetwynd-Talbot, MBE (*see* E Shrewsbury, colls), and has issue living, Alexander Duncan *b* 1968, Miranda Gavrelle *b* 1970, — Gavin Jeremy, *b* 1944: *m* 1971, Joanna Gwendoline, da of Gp Capt G. B. Bell, RAF.
Issue of late Leslie Hay Macnaghten, *b* 1875, *d* 1950: *m* 1906, Hilda Mary Ethelind who *d* 1973, da of late Rev Jocelyn Barnes, V of St Breage, Cornwall:—
Geoffrey Leslie, *b* 1909; 1939-45 War as Fl-Lt RAFVR; late Imp Cancer Research Fund: *m* 1937, Hilary Marriott, who *d* 1989, da of late T. A. Marriott Castle, and has issue living, Jennifer Rosemary, *b* 1939: *m* 1968, David Guthrie Mattinson, of 14 Rectory Gardens, Broadwater, Worthing, W Sussex BN14 7TE, and has issue living, John *b* 1974, Michelle *b* 1966, — Sarah Lynne, *b* 1954. —— Douglas Melville (Derriford House, Pinewood Hill, Fleet, Hants GU13 9AW), *b* 1911; *ed* Wellington Coll; late Spicers Internat Ltd, of Reed House, 82 Piccadilly, W1; 1939-45 War in N Africa and Italy as Maj RASC (Africa star, Italy star, 1939-45 star): *m* 1946, Thecla Isabel, who *d* 1987, twin da of late John Mundell Reid, of Greenock, and has issue living, Lorraine Thecla Ethelind, *b* 1947: *m* 1982, Alastair Ford-Young, and has issue living, Jeremy David *b* 1984, Nicholas James *b* 1985, — Camilla Dawn (The Cottage, Holmwood Place, Ide Hill Rd, Four Elms, Edenbridge, Kent TN8 6NT), *b* 1950: *m* 1971 (*m diss* 1979), Timothy William Whittle; has issue living, Anastasia Isabella *b* 1993.

Grandchildren of late Leslie Hay Macnaghten (ante):—
Issue of late Lieut Cyril Jocelyn Gillichrist Macnaghten, RNVR, *b* 1907, *ka* 1943: *m* 1932, Mary Evelyne, who *d* 1954, da of late G. E. Mullens, of Teddington, Australia:—
Alexander Michael Gillichrist (Jabiru Jetty, 12 Kiap Road, Yunderup Canals, W Australia 6208), *b* 1940; *ed* Wellington Coll, and at Roy Agricultural Coll, Cirencester; a Member of Commonwealth Inst of Valuers: *m* 1st, 1971 (*m diss* 1975), Vanessa, da of Duncan Charles Beresford-Ord, of Beverley Lodge, Mill Point Rd, S Perth, Aust; 2ndly, 1983, Vanessa Keran, 2nd da of late David Pay, of Palma, 1 Brock Terr, Grange, St Peter Port, Guernsey, CI. —— Angela Kay, *b* 1935: *m* 1960, John Woodward, of High House, Scopwick, Lincs LN4 3PA, and has issue living, Andrew St John, *b* 1965, — Sarah Mary, *b* 1963.

Grandsons of late Sir Henry Pelham Wentworth Macnaghten (infra):—
Issue of late Capt Angus David Henry Macnaghten, *b* 1923, *d* 1988: *m* 1952, Sally, who *d* 1991, only child of late Edward Watts, of Ashfields, Great Canfield, Essex:—
David Edmund, *b* 1954; *ed* Stowe. —— Stuart Ben (72 Carthew Rd, W6 0DX), *b* 1957: *m* 1st, 1988, Joanna Crittall; 2ndly, 1993, Mrs Emma Monaghan (née Majdalany), and has issue living (by 1st *m*), Ben Henry, *b* 1989. —— Patrick Henry, *b* 1959: *m* 19—, Pamela J., yr da of S/Ldr K. J. White, of Skellingthorpe, Lincs.

Grandson of late Rev Henry Alexander Macnaghten, 5th son of late Elliot Macnaghten (*b* 1807) (ante):—
Issue of late Sir Henry Pelham Wentworth Macnaghten, *b* 1880, *d* 1949: *m* 1919, Frances Alice, who *d* 1969, da of Very Rev James Cropper, R of Penshurst, Kent:—
Robin Donnelly (Prospect House, Tisbury, Wilts SP3 6QQ), *b* 1927; *ed* Eton (KS), and King's Coll, Camb; Headmaster of Sherborne Sch 1974-88: *m* 1961, Petronella Anne, da of Lt-Col A. T. T. Card, of The Old Vicarage, Holt, Wimborne, Dorset, and has three adopted children, Alexander Hugh, *b* 1965: *m* 1994, Gillian, da of Ronald Law, of Dundee, — James Donnelly, *b* 1969, — Frances Bridget, *b* 1967: *m* 1990, Trevor William Jolley, of 3 Emmington, N Thame, Oxon, yr son of Rev Arthur Jolley, of Boston, Lincs, and has issue living, Hannah *b* 1992, Laura *b* 1994.

Adoptive granddaughter of late Capt Angus Charles Rowley Steuart Macnaghten, Lieut Black Watch (Royal Highlanders), only son of late Sir Steuart Macnaghten, 6th son of late baronet:—
Adopted da of late Maj Angus Derek Iain Jacques Macnaghten, *b* 1914, *d* 1992: *m* 1957, Daphne, who *d* 1984, only da of late Horace Nettleship Soper, of 15 Stanley Crescent, W11:—
Fiona, *b* 1962: *m* 1990, Martin K. Asquith, only son of late E. Asquith, of Blewbury, Oxon, and has issue living, Eleanor Daphne, *b* 1993.

The family of Macnaghten is of great antiquity in the Western Highlands. In 1267, Alexander III granted to Gillichrist Macnaghten and his heirs the custody of the castle and island of Fraocheilean, on condition that he should rebuild it, and keep it fit for the reception of the king whenever he should visit it. His great-grandson Duncan, was one of the band that accompanied James Douglas in his attempt to deposit the heart of Robert Bruce at Jerusalem. The 1st baronet, Sir Francis, a Judge of the Supreme Court of Madras 1809-15, and of Calcutta 1815-25, assumed the additional surname and arms of Workman by Roy licence 1809. The 4th baronet, Rt Hon Sir Edward, GCB, GCMG, was MP for co Antrim (*C*) 1880-85, and for Antrim co, N Div 1885-87 when he became a Lord of Appeal in Ordinary, with title of *Baron Macnaghten* (Life Peerage). The 6th baronet, Sir Edward Henry Macnaghten, Lieut Black Watch (Royal Highlanders), was *ka* July 1916, and his yr brother, Sir Arthur Douglas Macnaghten, 7th baronet, Lieut Rifle Brig, was also *ka* Sept 1916.

Macpherson-Grant, see Grant.

MACREADY (UK) 1923, of Cheltenham, co Gloucester

Sir NEVIL JOHN WILFRID MACREADY, CBE, 3rd *Baronet*; *b* 7 Sept 1921; *s* his father, *Lieut-Gen Sir* GORDON NEVIL, KBE, CB, CMG, DSO, MC, 1956; *ed* Cheltenham and St John's Coll, Oxford (MA); Man Dir of Mobil Oil Co, Ltd 1975-85; Chm Crafts Council 1984-91; Chm Horseracing Advisory Council 1986-93; Dep Chm British Horseracing Bd since 1993; 1939-45 War as Capt RA (despatches); CBE (Civil) 1982: *m* 1949, Mary, only da of late Sir (John) Donald Balfour Fergusson, GCB, and has issue.

Arms – Argent, on a chevron azure between three leopard's faces gules, two swords, the points in saltire proper, pommels and hilts or. **Crest** – On a wreath of the colours, in front of two swords points upwards in saltire proper, pommels and hilts or, a cubit arm also proper, grasping a snake vert.
Residence – The White House, Odiham, Hants RG25 1LG. *Clubs* – Boodles, Jockey (Paris).

SON LIVING

CHARLES NEVIL, *b* 19 May 1955: *m* 1981, Lorraine, da of Brian McAdam, of Connah's Quay, Deeside, Clwyd, and has issue living, James Nevil *b* 26 Nov 1982, — Laura Mary, *b* 1984.

DAUGHTERS LIVING

Caroline Elisabeth, *b* 1950: *m* 1978, Clive F Tucker, of Whitewold House, Woldingham, Surrey, and has issue living, two das. — Sarah Diana Mary, *b* 1953. — Anna Louise, *b* 1963.
The 1st baronet, Gen Rt Hon Sir (Cecil Frederick) Nevil Macready, GCMG, KCB (son of William Charles Macready, actor), served in Egyptian Expedition 1882, S Africa 1899-1902, and European War 1914-18 as AG (KCMG, GCMG), and was Commr of Metropolitan Police 1918-20, and Com-in-Ch of Troops, Ireland 1920-22. The 2nd baronet, Lieut-Gen Sir Gordon Nevil Macready, KBE, CB, CMG, DSO, MC, was Col Comdt RE Assist Ch of Imperial Gen Staff, War Office 1940-2, Ch of British Army Staff, Washington, USA 1942-6, Regional Commr, Hanover 1946-7, British Chm of Bipartite Economic Control Office in Germany 1947-8, Regional Commr, N Rhine-Westphalia 1948-9, and Economic Advisor to United Kingdom High Commr 1949-51.

MACTAGGART (UK) 1938, of King's Park, City of Glasgow

Sir JOHN AULD MACTAGGART, 4th *Baronet*; *b* 21 Jan 1951; *s* his father, *Sir* IAN AULD, 1987; *ed* Shrewsbury, and Trin Coll, Camb (MA): *m* 1st, 1977, Patricia, yst da of late Maj Harry Alastair Gordon, MC (*see* E Wavell); 2ndly, 1991, Caroline, yst da of Eric Charles Williams, of Fair Acre, 20 Meadway, Esher, Surrey, and has issue by 2nd *m*.

Arms – Argent, on a bend sable between two owls proper, three escallop shells or. **Crest** – A tower proper masoned sable, windows and port gules.
Residences – Ardmore House, Ardtalla Estate, Islay, Argyll; 55 St James's St, SW1A 1LA.

SON LIVING (By 2nd marriage)

JACK AULD, *b* 11 Sept 1993.

DAUGHTER LIVING (By 2nd marriage)

Kinvara May, *b* 1992.

BROTHER LIVING

Philip Auld, *b* 1956: *m* 1978, Frances, only da of late Christy George Peters, of New York, USA.

SISTERS LIVING

Jane Lindsay MACTAGGART, *b* 1949; has resumed the surname of Mactaggart: *m* 1974 (*m diss* 1978), Keith Douglas Henry Baines. *Residence* – Ardilisry, Southdown, Wanborough, nr Swindon, Wilts SN4 0DB. — Fiona Margaret, *b* 1953. *Residence* – 61 Taybridge Rd, SW11 5PX.

UNCLES LIVING (*sons of 2nd Baronet*)

Neil Auld, *b* 1925; *ed* Massachusetts Institute of Technology, Cambridge, Massachusetts (BS 1952); formerly Capt RE: *m* 1953, Sheila, who *d* 1990, da of Hon Herbert A. McKinney, of Nassau, Bahamas, and has issue living, Neil Auld, *b* 1959, — Andrew Auld, *b* 1962, — Ann Elizabeth, *b* 1955, — Robin (da), *b* 1957, — Tara, *b* 1960. *Address* – PO Box N1593, Nassau, Bahamas. — Alastair Auld (Sandy), *b* 1928; *ed* Harvard Univ (BA, MBA); late Lieut (P) RCNR: *m* 1959, Cecile Macy, da of Josiah M. Erickson, of Greenwich, Conn, USA, and has issue living, Alastair Auld, *b* 1966, — Mara Macy, *b* 1963, — Fiona Osborn, *b* 1964. *Address* – PO Box 3160, Edmonton, Alberta, Canada.
The 1st baronet, Sir John Auld Mactaggart (son of late Neil Mactaggart of Glasgow), was a Housing Expert, and Chm of Western Heritable Investment Co, Ltd, of Glasgow, London, and Canada. He presented King's Park to City of Glasgow. The

2nd baronet, Sir John (Jack Auld) Mactaggart was for many years Managing Dir of Mactaggart & Mickel Ltd, builders and estate developers, of Glasgow and Edinburgh. Sir Ian Mactaggart, 3rd Bt, was chm Soc for Individual Freedom and chm of Western Heritable Investment Co Ltd.

MacTaggart-Stewart, see Stewart.

MADDEN (UK) 1919, of Kells, co Kilkenny

FORTIOR·QUI·SE·VINCIT

*He is stronger who
conquers himself*

Sir CHARLES EDWARD MADDEN, GCB, 2nd *Baronet*: *b* 15 June 1906; *s* his father, *Adm of the Fleet, Sir* CHARLES EDWARD, GCB, OM, GCVO, KCMG, DCL, LLD, 1935; Adm (ret): Ch of Naval Staff, New Zealand 1953-5, Dep Ch of Naval Personnel 1955-7, Flag Officer, Malta 1957-9, Flag Officer, Flotillas, Home Fleet 1959-60, C-in-C Plymouth 1960-63, and C-in-C Home Fleet, and C-in-C E Atlantic Command (NATO) 1963-65; Chm Roy Nat Mission to Deep Sea Fishermen 1971-81, Trustee National Maritime Museum 1968 (Chm 1972-77), and Vice-Chm Sail Training Assocn 1968-70; Vice-Lieut of Greater London 1969-81; 1939-45 War (despatches twice); *cr* CB (Mil) 1955, KCB (Mil) 1961, GCB (Mil) 1965: *m* 1942, Olive, who *d* 1989, da of late George Winchester Robins, of Caldy, Cheshire and has issue.

Arms – Sable, a falcon with his wings expanded, preying on a mallard all argent, on a chief ermine out of a naval crown between two cross-crosslets gules, from a staff in bend a flag of St George, all proper. **Crest** – On a ducal coronet or a falcon rising argent, holding in his beak a cross-crosslet fitchée gules.
Residence – 21 Eldon Road, W8 5PT.

DAUGHTER LIVING

Roseann, *b* 1945: *m* 1972, John Richard Beddington, 3 Pine Forest Rd, Toronto, Ontario M4N 3E6, Canada, and has issue living, James Edward, *b* 1973, — David Paul Madden, *b* 1975.

SISTERS LIVING

Joan, *b* 1912: *m* 1939, Lt-Col Henry Morison Vere Nicoll, DSO, OBE, late RA, of North Field, Manton, Oakham, Rutland, and has issue living, Graham Morison (The Cottage, Church Lane, Somerby, nr Melton Mowbray, Leics), *b* 1940; *ed* Eastbourne Coll; Capt Welsh Gds: *m* 1st, 1965 (*m diss* 1976), Lucinda Marjorie, yr da of Capt Timothy John Gurney, of The White House, nr Buntingford, Herts (*see* de Bathe, Bt, ext); 2ndly, 1972, Jane, da of Maj Thomas Edward Dealtry Kidd, MBE, RCA (*see* B Beaverbrook, 1985 Edn); 3rdly, 1980, Mrs Jacquelyn Alexander (*née* Bray), and has issue living (by 1st *m*), Simon Morison *b* 1968, (by 3rd *m*) Harry Michael *b* 1983, — Kenneth Charles (52 Bassett Rd, W10), *b* 1942; *ed* Marlborough: *m* 1968, Veronica Gillian, da of C. P. Payne, of Cape Town, and has issue living, Alastair Charles *b* 1973, Sara Jane *b* 1971, Georgina Clare *b* 1981, — Adrian Michael (Freynestown Stud, Dunlavin, co Wicklow), *b* 1949; *ed* Marlborough: *m* 1976, Meriel Jane, da of late Capt James McCarthy, of Navan, co Meath, and has issue living, James Henry *b* 1981, Annabel Jane *b* 1979, — Neville Henry (6119 Andrus Rd, Boulder, Colorado 80301, USA), *b* 1954; *ed* Marlborough: *m* 1984, Carrie Virginia, only da of Dr W. Robert Wentz, of 4301 David St, Durham, N Carolina, and has issue living, Alexander Robert *b* 1986, John Morison *b* 1988, Sabrina Fiennes *b* 1993. ——— Hope (120 Northumberland Court, Northumberland Rd, Leamington Spa, Warwickshire CV2 6HN), *b* 1914: *m* 1939 (*m diss* 1947), Maj John Henry Beardmore Batten, Royal Fus, and has issue living, Patrick John Beardmore, *b* 1941; *ed* Ampleforth: *m* 1965 (*m diss* 1978), Diana Lyn, da of H. L. Brooke, and has issue living, Annabell Jane Beardmore *b* 1965, Katherine Nicola Beardmore *b* 1968, Sally Elizabeth Beardmore *b* 1970. ———— Mary Elizabeth (25 Eldon Rd, W8), *b* 1920: *m* 1st, 1939 (*m diss* 1952), Raymond Guy Vere Nicoll, MC, who *d* 1981; 2ndly, 1952 (*m diss* 1956), Maj Desmond Richard FitzGerald, late Irish Gds; 3rdly, 1969, Cdr Charles Raymond Barrett, RN, who *d* 1970, and has issue living (by 1st *m*) Mark Raymond (24 Eldon Rd, W8), *b* 1942; *ed* Eton: *m* 1968, Virginia Anne, da of late Maj J Christopher Vernon Miller, of Blackwell Grange, Shipton-on-Stour, and has issue living James *b* 1971, Edward *b* (twin) 1971, Claire *b* 1970, Tamara Ann, *b* 1978, — Nigel Edward (The Chantry, Upper Chute, Wilts), *b* 1947; *ed* Eton: *m* 1st, 1969, (Corinna) Jane, da of late John Goring, CBE, TD (*see* Goring, Bt); 2ndly, 1991, Catharine Euphan, formerly wife of Hon John Edward Malet Vaughan (*see* E Lisburne), and only da of J. P. Waterer, of Coombe Bissett, Salisbury, and has issue living, (by 1st *m*) Adam Nigel *b* 1972, Rory Raymond *b* 1978, Zoe Gabrielle *b* 1971, Corinna Mary *b* 1980, (by 2nd *m*) Frederick John *b* 1993.

COLLATERAL BRANCH LIVING

Issue of late Lt-Col John Wilmot Madden, MC, RA, yr son of 1st baronet, *b* 1916, *d* 1990: *m* 1941, Beatrice Catherine, JP, who *d* 1989, only da of William Arthur Sievwright, WS, of Moncrieff House, St Andrews, Fife:—
PETER JOHN (Kaymito Cottage, San Carlos Heights, Quiot Pardo, Cebu City, Cebu, Philippines), *b* 10 Sept 1942; *ed* Bundell's, and RMA Sandhurst; late Capt RA: *m* 1993, Mrs Vellie Laput Co, da of Cirilo Laput, and widow of Roberto Co. ——— Charles Jonathan (Gasper Lodge, Pen Selwood, Wincanton, Somerset BA9 8LX), *b* 1949; BSc, MTech, MBA: *m* 1980, Kirsteen Victoria, da of John Ronald Noble, of Wayside, St Andrews, Fife, and has issue living, Samuel Charles John, *b* 1984, — Sophie Emma, *b* 1982. ——— Susan Kate, *b* 1946: *m* 1970, Richard Leoline Jenkins, LVO, TD, late Capt 1st The Queen's Dragoon Gds, of Delbridge House, Wendy, Royston, Herts SG8 0HJ, and has issue living, Sarah Alexandra, *b* 1972, — Caroline Louise, *b* 1973.
The 1st baronet, Adm of the Fleet Sir Charles Edward Madden, GCB, OM, GCVO, KCMG, DCL, LLD (son of Capt J. W. Madden, 4th Regt), served in Egyptian War 1882, and in European War 1914-19 as Ch of Staff and 2nd in Command of Grand Fleet (thanked by Parliament, *cr* a Baronet, granted £10,000), and was Com-in-Ch of Home and Atlantic Fleets 1919-22 and First Sea Lord of the Admiralty and Ch of Naval Staff 1927-30.

MADGE (UK) 1919, of St Margaret's Bay, co Kent (Extinct 1962)

Sir FRANK WILLIAM MADGE, 2nd and last *Baronet*.

DAUGHTERS LIVING OF SECOND BARONET

Pauline, *b* 1928: *m* 1951, Capt Peter Jack Shaw, CBE, RN, and has had issue, Christopher John, *b* 1957, *d* 1992: *m* 1983, Olive Victoria Whales, — Carol Anne, *b* 1952: *m* 1975, Lt Cmdr Michael William Livett, RN, and has had issue living, Ian Michael *b* 1979, Peta Jane *b* 1977. *Residence* – Woodside, Rogate, Petersfield, Hants GU31 5DJ. —— Doreen (West Wold House, Prestbury, Cheltenham), *b* 1931: *m* 1954 (*m diss* 1970), Hubert Mark Thursfield, and has had three adopted children, Dominic Simon, *b* 1960: *m* 1985 (*m diss* 1988), Briony Daniell, — Susanna Katherine, *b* 1960, *d* 1989: *m* 1988, André Jacques Ernest Simon, — Sophia Belinda Rachael, *b* 1964. —— June *b* (twin) 1931: *m* 1963, Peter John Ball, MB, BChir, of 11 Nevill Park, Tunbridge Wells TN4 8NN, and has issue living, Martin Hugh, *b* 1964, — Angela Wendy, *b* 1965: *m* 19—, Lawrence Barolsky, and has issue living, Jenna *b* 1993, — Louise Clare, *b* 1968: *m* 19—, Ewout Van Manen, — Juliet Amanda, *b* 1970. —— Gillian, *b* 1937: *m* 1972, Richard William Honner, and has issue living, Emma Sophie *b* 1973; has issue living (by Paul Caples), Sophie Katherine Honner *b* 1992, Josephine Kate *b* 1974.

MAGNUS (UK) 1917, of Tangley Hill, Wonersh, co Surrey.

By faith and work.

Sir LAURENCE HENRY PHILIP MAGNUS, 3rd *Baronet*, *b* 24 Sept 1955; *s* his uncle, *Sir* PHILIP MONTEFIORE MAGNUS-ALLCROFT, CBE, 1988; *ed* Eton, and Ch Ch Oxford (MA); Exec Dir Samuel Montagu & Co Ltd since 1988: *m* 1983, Jocelyn Mary, eldest da of Robert Henry Foster Stanton, and has issue.

Arms – Bendy of six gules and vert, on a fesse or an open book proper between two martlets sable. **Crest** – A magnolia tree flowered proper.
Residence – Flat 8, 44 Lower Sloane St, SW1W 8BP.

SONS LIVING

THOMAS HENRY PHILIP, *b* 30 Sept 1985. —— Edmund Robert Hilary, *b* 1991.

DAUGHTER LIVING

Iona Alexandra, *b* 1988.

SISTER LIVING

Caroline Anne (23 Frithville Gdns, W12 7JG), *b* 1951; *ed* Benenden.

AUNTS LIVING (*sisters of 2nd baronet*)

Jessie Dora: *m* 1935, David Hugh Sandell, MD, FRCS, of 44 Burton Court, Chelsea, SW3, and has issue living, Robert Laurie (56 Dale St, Chiswick, W4 2BZ) *b* 1938; *ed* Eton, and Ch Ch, Oxford: *m* 1969 (*m diss* 1991), Stephanie Getz, and has issue living, Adam Jonathan William *b* 1972, Alexandra Jessica Laurie *b* 1975, — Jenifer Celia Emily, *b* 1936; Bar Lincoln's Inn 1958; LSE: *m* 1962, Nicholas Bridges-Adams, Recorder of Crown Court, of Fornham Cottage, Fornham St Martin, Bury St Edmunds, Suffolk. —— Ruth Emily: *m* 1946, as his 2nd wife, Denzil Charles Sebag-Montefiore, of 129 Rivermead Court, Ranelagh Gdns, SW6 3SD, and has issue living, Charles Adam Laurie (21 Hazlewell Rd, SW15 6LT; *Clubs* – Brooks's, Beefsteak) *b* 1949: *ed* Eton, and St Andrew's Univ; *m* 1979, Pamela Mary Diana, yr da of late Archibald Tennant (*see* Glenconner, B, colls), and has issue living, Archibald Edward Charles *b* 1987, Elizabeth Anne *b* 1982, Laura Rose *b* 1984, — Mary Pamela, *b* 1951; Bar Middle Temple 1974: *m* 1973, David Murray Davidson, son of Col Robert St Clair Davidson, of The Manor House, Upham, Hants, and has issue living, Denzil Jonathan Robert *b* 1975, Susanna Mary *b* 1978, Felicity Dora *b* 1982.

MOTHER LIVING

Rosemary Vera Anne, eldest da of late George Henry Masefield, of 88 Chelsea Park Gdns, SW3, and widow of Quentin Berkeley Hurst: *m* 1950, Lt-Col Hilary Barrow Magnus, TD, QC, who *d* 1987, yr son of Laurie Magnus, elder son of Sir Philip Magnus, 1st Bt. *Residence* – Cragmore House, Wye, Kent TN25 5BJ.

The 1st baronet, Sir Philip Magnus, a pioneer of technical education, sat as MP for London Univ (*U*) 1906-22; *s* by his grandson, Sir Philip Montefiore Magnus-Allcroft, CBE, FRSL, FRHistS, biographer and historian, author of *Kitchener* (1950), *Gladstone* (1954), *King Edward The Seventh* (1964), etc; assumed by deed poll 1951 the additional surname of Allcroft.

MAHON (UK) 1819, of Castlegar, co Galway
(Name pronounced "Mahn")

Sir WILLIAM WALTER MAHON, 7th *Baronet*; *b* 4 Dec 1940; *s* his father, *Sir* GEORGE EDWARD JOHN, 1987; *ed* Eton; a member of HM Bodyguard of The Honourable Corps of Gentleman at Arms 1993: *m* 1968, Rosemary Jane, yr da of late Lt-Col Michael Ernest Melvill, OBE, of The Long House, W Linton, Peeblesshire, and has issue.

Arms – Per fesse sable and argent, an ostrich countercharged, in the beak a horseshoe or. Crest – A dexter arm embowed in armour in the hand grasping a sword wavy all proper.
Address – c/o Guinness Mahon and Co Ltd Private Bank, 9 Idol Lane, EC3 5AW.

Moniti meliora
sequamur
*Having been warned
let us follow better
things*

SON LIVING

JAMES WILLIAM, *b* 29 Oct 1976.

DAUGHTERS LIVING

Annabel Jane, *b* 1970. ——— Lucy Caroline, *b* 1972.

BROTHER LIVING

Timothy Gilbert, *b* 1947; *ed* Crookham Court, Newbury: *m* 1971, Penelope Telfer, elder da of Maj Thomas B McDowell, of St Thomas, Rathfarnham, co Dublin, and has issue living, Rupert Thomas George, *b* 1974, — Myles Francis, *b* 1980, — Antonia Margaret, *b* 1976. *Residence* – 7 Sunbury Gdns, Dartry, Dublin 6.

SISTER LIVING

Jane Evelyn, *b* 1944: *m* 1967 (*m diss* 1978), Peter Alec Charles Moore, and has issue living, Alannah Katharine, *b* 1969. *Residence* – 12 Althorp Rd, SW17.

HALF-SISTER LIVING

Sarah Caroline, *b* 1959. *Residence* – 133 Westbridge Rd, SW11.

UNCLE LIVING (*son of 5th baronet*)

Luke Bryan Arthur DILLON-MAHON, *b* 1917; *ed* Eton, and Trin Coll Camb (BA); assumed by deed poll 1966, the surname of Dillon-Mahon: *m* 1949, Audrey Doreen da of late Ernest John Vipond, MBE, MC, and has issue living, Robert John George, *b* 1954: *m* 1983, Caroline Mary, yst da of late Hon John Forbes (*see* E Granard), and formerly wife of Dominick Charles Hamilton, and has issue living, Luke John *b* 1984, — Susan, *b* 1950: *m* 1978, George Wilmer Hatfeild Gossip, of Tullanisk, Birr, co Offaly, and has issue living, William Luke George Hatfeild *b* 1983. *Residence* – Tullanisk, Birr, co Offaly.

WIDOW LIVING OF SIXTH BARONET

SUZANNE (*Suzanne, Lady Mahon*), da of late Thomas Donnellan, of Pirbright, Surrey: *m* 1958, as his 2nd wife, Sir George Edward John Mahon, 6th Bt, who *d* 1987. *Residence* – 16 St James's Terr, Winchester, Hants SO22 4PP.

COLLATERAL BRANCHES LIVING

Issue of late John FitzGerald Mahon, 4th son of 4th baronet, *b* 1858, *d* 1942: *m* 1898, Lady Alice Evelyn Browne, who *d* 1970, da of 5th Marquess of Sligo:—
Sir (John) Denis, CBE, *b* 1910; *ed* Eton, and Ch Ch, Oxford (MA); Hon DLitt Newcastle 1969, Oxford 1994; Art Historian and FBA, a Trustee of National Gallery 1957-64, and 1966-73, medal for Benemeriti della Cultura, Italy 1957, and Accademico d'Onore, Clementine Acad of Bologna 1964, and Serena Medal for Italian Studies, British Academy 1972; CBE (Civil) 1967, Knt 1986. *Residence* – 33 Cadogan Sq, SW1X OHU.

Issue of late Edward Mahon, 6th son of 4th baronet, *b* 1862, *d* 1937: *m* 1911, Lilette Caroline Julia, da of late James K. Rebbeck, of Victoria, British Columbia:—
Bryan Edward (2003, 82nd Av SE, Mercer Island, Washington 98040, USA), *b* 1913: *m* 1960, Marolyn Miriam, da of late C. Laverne Smith, MD, of Seattle, Wash, USA, and has issue living, Ross Mackenzie, *b* 1961, — Lilette Elizabeth, *b* 1963.
Sir Ross Mahon 1st Bt, MP for Granard and Ennis, was el son of Ross Mahon of Castlegar (*d* 1788), whose grandfather Capt Bryan Mahon of Castlegar, served in Earl of Clanricarde's Regt of Inf, James II's Army at Battle of the Boyne 1690.

MAINWARING (UK) 1804, of Over Peover, Cheshire (Extinct 1934)
(Name pronounced "Mannaring")

Sir HARRY STAPLETON MAINWARING, 5th and last *Baronet*.

DAUGHTER LIVING OF FIFTH BARONET

Zara Sophie Kathleen Mary, *b* 1917: *m* 1st, 1940 (*m diss* 1949), Capt Hon (Alexander) Ronald George Strutt, Coldm Gds, afterwards 4th Baron Belper; 2ndly, 1949, Peter Victor Ferdinand Cazalet, JP, DL, Welsh Gds (Heron-Maxwell, Bt), who *d* 1973, and has issue living (by 1st *m*) (*see* B Belper), — (by 2nd *m*) Victor Anthony (13 Vicarage Gdns, W8 4AH), *b* 1951: *m* 1976, (Mary) Isabel Dorothy, da of late Hon George William ffolkes Dawnay (*see* V Downe, colls), and has issue living,

Edward Peter *b* 1981, Catherine Rosemary *b* 1979, Clare Elizabeth *b* 1983, — Anthony Peter, *b* 1953. *Residence* – 26 Wilton Row, SW1.

MAITLAND (UK) 1818, of Clifton, Midlothian

By counsel and courage

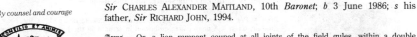

Sir CHARLES ALEXANDER MAITLAND, 10th *Baronet*; *b* 3 June 1986; *s* his father, Sir RICHARD JOHN, 1994.

Arms – Or, a lion rampant couped at all joints of the field gules, within a double tressure flory counterflory azure. **Crest** – A lion sejant, affrontée gules, ducally crowned or, and holding in his dexter paw a drawn sword proper, pommelled and hilted gold, and in the sinister a fleur-de-lis azure.
Residence – Burnside, Forfar, Angus.

SISTER LIVING

Alice Emma, *b* 1983.

UNCLE LIVING (*Son of 8th baronet*)

ROBERT RAMSAY, *b* 14 July 1956: *m* 1984, (Georgina) Claire, yst da of John Drysdale, of Kilrie, Kirkcaldy, Fife, and has issue living, Harry Robert, *b* 1986, — John Richard, *b* 1992, — Cara Claire, *b* 1989, — Anna Victoria, *b* 1991. *Residence* – Dowalty, Crathes, Banchory, Kincardineshire.

AUNT LIVING (*Daughter of 8th baronet*)

Jane Fiona, *b* 1963: *m* 1988, Hugo Peter Haig, son of Anthony Haig, of Scaniport, Inverness, and has issue living, Christopher Edward (Kit), *b* 1993, — Archie-Anne Rose, *b* 1992.

GREAT UNCLES LIVING (*Sons of 7th baronet*)

John Ramsay, *b* 1924; formerly Sqdn-Ldr RAF: *m* 1st, 1952 (*m diss* 19—), Nan Margaret, da of late Brig Charles Bannatyne Findlay, CBE, MC; 2ndly, 1968, Kathleen Mary, da of late Vivian Charles Desmond, and has issue living (by 1st *m*), David Ramsay, *b* 1954, — James, *b* 1957: *m* 1987, Sarah Elizabeth, only da of Malcolm Selwyn Shaw, — Jean Findlay, *b* 1959, — (by 2nd *m*), Keith John, *b* 1969. —— James, *b* 1927: *m* 1959, Mavis Ann, el da of H. J. Kennaway, of Keithock, Brechin, Angus, and has issue living, Alexander Henry, *b* 1964, — Amanda Helen, *b* 1960: *m* 1994, Maj David Limb, yst son of Roy Limb, of Hadley Wood, Herts, — Fiona Ann, *b* (twin) 1960. *Residence* – Clathic, Crieff, Perthshire.

GREAT AUNT LIVING (*Daughter of 7th baronet*)

Helen Florence, *b* 1923: *m* 1952, Col Thomas David Lloyd-Jones, OBE (Reswallie, Forfar, Angus), and has issue living, John Ramsay, *b* 1954: *m* 1982, Henrietta Cicely, only da of Henry Gabriel Richards Pickthorn (*see* Pickthorn, Bt), and has issue living, Alexander *b* 1986, Lucy *b* 1989, Celia *b* 1992, — Peter Neil, *b* 1956: *m* 1989, Victoria Rees, and has issue living, Frederick *b* 1990, George *b* 1991, — Caroline Margaret, *b* 1961: *m* 1987, Marc Villiers Townsend, son of Reginald Townsend, of Rugby.

DAUGHTER LIVING OF SIXTH BARONET

Petronilla Kathleen Florence, *b* 1916: *m* 1951, Malcolm Park, OBE, who *d* 1963, and has issue living, Malcolm John Maitland, *b* 1955: *m* 1982, Nicola Anne Jackson, and has issue living, David Malcolm *b* (twin) 1986, Emma Caroline *b* 1984, Marianne Beatrice *b* 1986. *Residence* – Stour Hill, Sturminster Newton, Dorset DT10 1ED.

WIDOWS LIVING OF EIGHTH AND NINTH BARONETS

LAVENDER MARY JEX (*Lavender, Lady Maitland*) (Burnside, Forfar, Angus), yst da of late Francis William Jex Jackson, of Kirkbuddo, Forfar: *m* 1951, Maj Sir Alexander Keith Maitland, 8th Bt, who *d* 1963.
CARINE C. A. (*Lady Maitland*) (Burnside, Forfar, Angus), elder da of J. St G. Coldwell, of Somerton, Oxford: *m* 1981, Sir Richard John Maitland, 9th Bt, who *d* 1994.

COLLATERAL BRANCHES LIVING

Grandchildren of late George Keith Maitland, yr son of George Ramsay Maitland, WS, 2nd son of Alexander Maitland, advocate at Scottish bar, eldest son of 2nd baronet:—
Issue of late Angus Charles Marjoribanks Maitland, *b* 1887, *d* 1986: *m* 1923, Mary Brigid, who *d* 1946, da of Thomas O'Callaghan, of Claremorris, co Mayo:—
Rev Keith Marjoribanks, *b* 1925; a priest at Downside Abbey. —— Natalie Mary (15 Bellevue, Clifton, Bristol BS8 1DB), *b* 1924: *m* 1980, Joseph Bibbing, who *d* 1989. —— Joan Mary, *b* 1928: *m* 1952, Noel Martin Fisher, DSC, of 37A Lyncombe Hill, Bath BAZ 4PQ, and has issue living, Dominic Mayne, *b* 1953, — Andrew Martin, *b* 1954, — Aidan Hugh, *b* 1959, — Paul Gregory, *b* 1960, — Mary Brigid, *b* 1956, — Catharine Mary, *b* 1957, — Lucy Elizabeth, *b* 1963, — Anna Claire, *b* 1964, — Jane Frances, *b* 1965. —— Angela Helena Mary, *b* 1933: *m* 1959, Raymond Geoffrey Daniel, of the Willow, Willows Vale, Frome, Somerset, and has issue living, Charles Martin, *b* 1961, — Francis Keith, *b* 1965, — Brigid Mary, *b* 1959, — Helen Margaret, *b* 1963.

Grandchildren of late Lieut-Col Reginald Charles Frederick Maitland, DSO, only son of late Maj Reginald Paynter Maitland, grandson of Gen Frederick Maitland, 4th son of 1st baronet:—
Issue of late Alastair Reginald Maitland, *b* 1915, *d* 1990: *m* 1947, Mary (Gables, Linden Chase, Uckfield, Sussex), da of late Campbell Mansbridge:—
Iain David Paynter, *b* 1954. —— Andrew Reginald Campbell, *b* 1963. —— Penelope Mary, *b* 1948. —— Carolyn Judith, *b* 1951.
Issue of late Maj Geoffrey Ernald Maitland, *b* 1918, *d* 1992: *m* 1st, 1945 (*m diss* 1967), Diana Joy, da of Maj James Pridham, RA; 2ndly, 1971 (*m diss* 1980), Mrs Eleanor Williamson, da of James Salter:—

(By 1st *m*) Alastair Charles Frederick, *b* 1958. —— Diana Jane, *b* 1945: *m* 1967, Michael J. Brooke, of Woods Farm, Burrow Hill, Chobham, Surrey GU24 8BY, and has issue living, Mark, *b* 1969, — James, *b* 1971, — Christopher, *b* 1983, — Katie, *b* 1976. —— Patricia Anne, *b* 1947: *m* 1st, 1977 (*m diss* ca 1981-82), Robert Campbell; 2ndly 1991, Richard Law, and has issue living (by 1st *m*) Julian, *b* 1980, — (by 2nd *m*) David, *b* 1992. —— Susan Mary, *b* 1952: *m* 1991, Patrick Blackwell, of PO Box 438, Woollahra, NSW 2025, Aust. —— (Sarah Gillian) Gabrielle, *b* 1954: *m* 1987, David Hylton Briggs, of 34 Cadogan Place, SW1X 9RX, eldest son of W/Cdr G. H. Briggs, of The Farmhouse, Strettington, Sussex, and has issue living, Thomas, *b* 1990, — Lucy *b* 1992. —— (By 2nd *m*) Alexander James, *b* 1971.

The 1st baronet, Gen Hon Sir Alexander Maitland, Col of the 49th Foot, was 5th son of the 6th Earl of Lauderdale; the 2nd baronet assumed the additional surname of Gibson, and the 3rd baronet, Sir Alexander Charles Maitland, assumed the additional surname of Ramsay before those of Gibson and Maitland. The 7th baronet, Sir George Ramsay Maitland, DSO, was Lt-Col 14th Jat Lancers and a Member of Queen's Body Guard for Scotland (Roy Co of Archers).

RAMSAY-STEEL-MAITLAND (UK) 1917, of Sauchie, co Stirling (Extinct 1965)

Sir KEITH RICHARD FELIX RAMSAY-STEEL-MAITLAND, 3rd and last *Baronet.*

DAUGHTER LIVING OF SECOND BARONET

Gay, *b* 1929: *m* 1949, Lt-Com Roger Martin Stafford, RN (ret), who *d* 1990. *Residence* – Sauchiburn House, Stirling.

WIDOW LIVING OF SECOND BARONET

MATILDA BRENDA (*Lady Ramsay-Steel-Maitland*), da of late Thomas Doughty, of Coalbrookdale: *m* 1942, as his 2nd wife, Sir (Arthur) James (Drummond) Ramsay-Steel-Maitland, 2nd baronet, who *d* 1960. *Residence* – Castle Gogar, Edinburgh 12.

MAKINS (UK) 1903, of Rotherfield Court, Henley-on-Thames, co Oxford

In lumine luce. *Shine thou in the light*

Sir PAUL VIVIAN MAKINS, 4th *Baronet*; *b* 12 Nov 1913; *s* his brother, *Lt-Col Sir* WILLIAM VIVIAN, 1969; *ed* Eton, and Trin Coll, Camb (MA); Maj (ret) Welsh Guards; Knt of Magistral Grace of Order of Malta; 1939-45 War: *m* 1945, Maisie, who *d* 1986, da of Maj Oswald Henry Pedley, of Gibraltar, and widow of Maj Cecil Leander John Bowen.

𝕬rms – Argent, on a fesse embattled counter embattled gules, between in chief two falcons proper belled or, and in base a lion's face of the second, an annulet or between two bezants. 𝕮rest – A dexter arm embowed in armour proper encircled by an annulet or and holding a flag staff, therefrom flowing a banner argent charged with a lion's face gules.
Address – Casas Cortijo 135, Sotogrande, Provincia de Cadiz, Spain.

DAUGHTERS LIVING OF THIRD BARONET

Carolyn Diana Mary, *b* 1933: *m* 1956, LeRoy Tuttle Morgan, and has issue living, Diana Vivian, *b* 1958. — Teresa Adelaide, *b* 1959, — Eleanora Carroll, *b* 1961, — Cecilia Hay, *b* 1964, — Maria Abell (twin) *b* 1964, — Olivia Dudley, *b* 1972. *Residence* – Alodialea Farm, 25214 Peachtree Rd, Clarksburg, Md 20871-9101, USA. —— Penelope Anne (*Baroness Harvey of Tasburgh*), *b* 1935: *m* 1957, 2nd Baron Harvey of Tasburgh. *Residence* – Crownick Woods, Restronguet, Mylor, Falmouth, Cornwall.

SISTER LIVING

Elisabeth Mary Savile, *b* 1904.

The 1st baronet, Sir William Thomas, sat as MP for S Essex 1874-85, SE Essex 1885-86, and Walthamstow, 1886-92. 1st Baron Sherfield (*cr* 1964) is a grandson of Henry Thomas Makins, Bar-at-law, yr brother of 1st baronet.

MALCOLM (NS) 1665, of Balbedie and Innertiel, co Fife

Ardua tendo
Attempt difficult things

Dei dono sum quod sum
By the grace of God I
am what I am

Sir DAVID PETER MICHAEL MALCOLM, 11th *Baronet, b* 7 July 1919; *s* his father, *Maj Sir* MICHAEL ALBERT JAMES, 1976; *ed* Eton, and Magdalene Coll, Camb (BA); CA; a Member of Royal Company of Archers (Queen's Body Guard for Scotland); late Maj Scots Gds; 1939-45 War; Staff Capt 1944, and a GSO 1945: *m* 1959, Hermione, el da of Sir David George Home, 13th Bt, and has issue.

Arms – Or a saltire azure between four stags' heads couped gules, a bordure indented of the third. **Crest** – A pyramid encircled by a laurel wreath proper.
Residence – Whiteholm, Whim Rd, Gullane, E Lothian EH31 2BD. *Clubs* – Pratt's, New (Edinburgh).

DAUGHTER LIVING

Fiona Alice Jane, *b* 1962: *m* 1992, Oliver George Stephenson (*see* Stephenson, Bt, colls).

SISTERS LIVING

Margaret Jane Venetia, *b* 1923; formerly 3rd Officer WRNS: *m* 1945, Christopher Robert Vesey Holt, CVO, VRD, and has issue living, Nicholas James Vesey, *b* 1947, — Ianthe Evelyn Vesey, *b* 1950: *m* 1975, Rodney Charles Hudson, and has issue living, Julian Charles *b* 1979, Felicity Jane *b* 1983. *Residence* – Westbury Manor, W Meon, Petersfield, Hants. —— Morar Catherine Beryl, *b* 1929: *m* 1959, as his 2nd wife, Oswald Whitwell Ainscough, late Maj King's (Liverpool) Regt, of Abbots Brow, Kirkby Lonsdale, Lancs.

WIDOW LIVING OF TENTH BARONET

KATHLEEN (*Kathleen, Lady Malcolm*) (Flat 1, 11 Onslow Sq, SW7), da of late Cdr George Jonathan Gawthorne, RN, and formerly wife of James Melvin: *m* 1947, as his 2nd wife, Maj Sir Michael Albert James Malcolm, 10th Bt, who *d* 1976.

COLLATERAL BRANCHES LIVING

Issue of late Major Alexander Ernest William Malcolm, TD, RA (TA), yr son of 9th baronet, *b* 1900, *d* 1959: *m* 1st, 1925, Olive Leah, da of Walter Scott, of Sydney, NS Wales; 2ndly, 1941, Mrs Sybil Mary Grenfell (who *m* 3rdly, 1963, Aubrey Vernon), da of late Hugh Peacock, of Greatford Hall, Stamford:—
Alexandra Mary, *b* 1943: *m* 1964, Simon Ward, actor, of 22 Antrim Mansions, NW3, and has issue living, Sophie Anna, *b* 1965; actress: *m* 1988, Paul Hobson, son of late George Hobson, — Claudia Thomasine, *b* 1969.

Grandchildren of late Major Charles Edward Malcolm, brother of 9th baronet:—
Issue of late Arthur William Alexander Malcolm, CVO, *b* 1903, *d* 1989: *m* 1928, Hester Mary who *d* 1992, da of Samuel Furneaux Mann, of Victoria, Australia:—
JAMES WILLIAM THOMAS ALEXANDER (Thatchers Barn, Worplesdon, Surrey GU3 3RD; *Clubs* – MCC, Royal St George's Golf), *b* 15 May 1930; *ed* Eton, and RMA; late Col Welsh Guards; cmnd'd Welsh Guards 1972-76; Appeals Dir, British Heart Foundation 1976-89; High Sheriff of Surrey 1991-92: *m* 1955, Gillian Heather, da of Elton Humpherus, of Kennards, Leigh, Kent, and has issue living, Alexander James Elton, *b* 30 Aug 1956; Major Welsh Guards: *m* 1982, Virginia Elizabeth, da of Capt Alfred Coxon, RN, and has issue living, Edward Alexander Humpherus *b* 1984, Thomas William *b* 1990, Camilla Petronell *b* 1987, — Robin William, *b* 1958, — Julia Mary, *b* 1960: *m* 1984, Julian Neville Guy Spurling, son of Jeremy Michael Lovett Spurling, and has issue living, Jonathan Henry William *b* 1987, Frederic James Lovett *b* 1989, Harry Alexander *b* 1992, — Annabel Heather, *b* 1967: *m* 1993, Capt Patrick C D Toyne Sewell, son of Maj-Gen Timothy Toyne Sewell. —— Ian William Ruthven (76 Adelaide St, Woollahra, Sydney, NSW 2025, Australia), *b* 1933; *ed* Eton, and Magdalene Coll, Camb: *m* 1963, Mrs Christie Moss, only da of John Bramley, of Bloemfontein, S Africa, and has issue living, Robert van Riet, *b* 1965: *m* 1993, Susan, da of T. H. Cass, of Ruislip, Middlx, — William David, *b* 1967, — John Alexander, *b* 1968.

John Malcolm, of Balbedie, Lochore, and Innertiel, *b* 1611, was appointed Chamberlain of Fife 1641, and Member of Scottish Parliament 1650; he *d* 1692, having *m* Margaret, who *d* 1698, aged 72, da of Sir Michael Arnot, of that Ilk, and had six sons, of whom John, the el, was created a Baronet of Nova Scotia 1665, while the third son, Alexander, became a Senator of the College of Justice with the title of Lord Lochore 1687, and Lord Justice-Clerk and a Privy Councillor 1688; James fourth son, fought at Killicrankie and was attainted. The 1st baronet was succeeded by his el son John, 2nd baronet, who was followed in the Baronetcy by his third son, Michael, served heir as 3rd baronet in 1784. The 4th baronet was James (Lieut-Gov of Sheerness), who had been served heir-general to his father, Robert Malcolm, of Grange, 2nd son of 1st baronet, in 1795. At the death of Sir James, Lieut-Gov of Sheerness, in 1805, the dignity passed to John, 8th child of Michael Malcolm, 3rd son of 1st baronet, at whose decease, in 1816, his el son, Michael, was served heir to his father, and in 1828 his son, John, as 7th baronet. In 1886 Sir James, son of James Malcolm, 2nd son of 5th baronet, was served heir to his cousin, as 8th baronet. At his death in 1901 the Baronetcy passed to his kinsman, Sir James William Malcolm, 9th Bt, who in 1897 had recorded the pedigree in the Lyon Office. The 10th baronet, Maj Sir Michael Albert James Malcolm, Scots Gds was a Member of Standing Council of The Baronetage 1954-76.

MALET (GB) 1791, of Wilbury, Wiltshire
(Name pronounced "Mallet")

My strength is from on high

Sir HARRY DOUGLAS ST LO MALET, 9th *Baronet*; *b* 26 Oct 1936; *s* his father, *Col Sir* EDWARD WILLIAM ST LO, OBE, 1990; *ed* Downside, and Trin Coll, Oxford (BA); late Lt Queen's Royal Irish Hussars; JP: *m* 1967, Julia Gresley, da of Charles Harper, of 54 Irvine St, Peppermint Grove, Perth W Australia, and has issue.

ℨrms – Azure, three escallops or. ℭre𝔰t – Out of a ducal coronet or, an heraldic tiger's head issuant ermine.
Address – Wrestwood, RMB 184, Boyup Brook, WA 6244, Australia.

SON LIVING

CHARLES EDWARD ST LO, *b* 30 Aug 1970; *ed* Blundell's; commd'd Queen's Royal Irish Hussars 1990.

SISTERS LIVING

Mary Jane St Lo, *b* 1938; has Nat Diploma of Design, and Oxford Univ Certificate of Fine Art: *m* 1970, Robert Pickering, of 101 North Rd, Bassendean, Perth, W Aust, and has issue living, Samuel Thomas Carrigton St Lo, *b* 1970, — William Benedict St Lo, *b* 1972. —— Micaela Elizabeth Benedicta *b* 1939; has Oxford Univ Certificate of Fine Art: *m* 1963, Maj-Gen Edwin Beckett, CB, MBE, Prince of Wales' Own Regt, and has issue living, Simon Turlo, *b* 1965, — Alexander Crispin, *b* 1979, — Thomas James, *b* 1980, — Diana Vola, *b* 1964.

AUNT LIVING *(Daughter of 7th baronet)*

Helen Agnes St Lo, *b* 1911: *m* 1934, Alan Douglas Stoddart, and has issue living, Alan Malet, *b* 1936: *m* 1961, Sally Noryl Harknes, and has issue living, Mark Alan *b* 1962, Benjamin Noryl *b* 1966, Emma Jane *b* 1964, Charlotte Helen *b* 1967, — Robert Douglas, *b* 1939: *m* 1967, Barbara Palmer, and has issue living, Timothy Robin *b* 1972, Rachel Louise *b* 1970, — Murray Laurence, *b* 1942: *m* 1970, Caroline Anne Windham, and has issue living, Craig Bowring *b* 1972, Duncan Laurence *b* 1974, — Gareth Bowring (Leadburn House, Leadburn, West Linton, Peeblesshire EH46 7BE), *b* 1947: *m* 1975, Lorna Christine Allan, yst da of Richard Oliver MacMahon Williams, MBE, MC, WS (*see* Rose, Bt, *cr* 1874, colls), and has had issue, Douglas Oliver Bowring *b* 1988, Sophie Helen *b* 1978, Katherine Anne *b* 1980, Camilla May *b* 1982, Alice *b* and *d* 1986, Clementine Rose *b* 1990, — Mary Lynette St Lo, *b* 1946: *m* 1968, Magnus Charles Mowat, of New Park House, Whitegate, nr Northwich, Cheshire, and has issue living, Charles Patrick Magnus *b* 1969, Alexander John *b* 1970, Hugh Laurence *b* 1973. *Residence* – Middle Halsway, Crowcombe, Taunton, Som. TA4 4BA.

COLLATERAL BRANCHES LIVING

Grandchildren of late Major Guilbert Edward Wyndham Malet, el son of Rev William Wyndham Malet, 3rd son of 1st baronet:—
Issue of late Lieut-Col Alexander Wyndham Malet, Indian Army, MVO, *b* 1886, *d* 1956: *m* 1921, Kathleen Betty, who *d* 1993, da of Brig-Gen Alexander Cadell, Indian Army:—
Richard Wyndham (Hollybush, Sevenhampton, Cheltenham, Glos GL54 5SL), *b* 1923; late Capt Indian Army; Far East 1941-47; MBIM; in management of tea estates, India and Africa 1947-60; Management Advisory Officer, Rural Development Commission: *m* 1956, Judith Winifred Ferguson, yst da of D. McEwen, of Kirkby Lonsdale, and has had issue, Claire Alexandra, *b* 1965: *m* 1993, Simon Hale, — Sarah Agnes, *b* 1969; *d* 1985 (Sarah Malet Trust Regd Charity No 299769R established in her memory). —— Sylvia Mary Fanshaw, ARCM, LRAM, *b* 1925: *m* 1948, John William Theodore Tapp, and has issue living, Nicholas Charles Theodore, *b* 1952, — Caroline Linda, *b* 1956. *Residence* – Southborough House, Ashcombe Av, Surbiton, Surrey. —— Kathleen Mary, ARCM, LRAM, *b* 1934.
Issue of late Edward Barnabas Wyndham Malet, *b* 1894, *d* 1961: *m* 1st, 1921 (*m diss* 1950), Esther Grace Macdonald, who *d* 1969, da of Rev Gilbert Lyon (formerly V of Cloford, Frome), of Wican Croft, Bishopsteignton, Teignmouth, Devon; 2ndly, 1950, Aileen Nina Mary, who *d* 1981, el da of F. W. Cumming, of Parklands, Bradninch, Devon:—
(By 1st *m*) Michael Edward Guilbert (Knockwood House, Nether Wallop, Stockbridge, Hants), *b* 1922; Maj RA (ret): *m* 1953, Judith Rowley, el da of E. Rowley Lewis, of Battledown, Cheltenham, and has issue living, Mark Wyndham (45 Hartismere Rd, SW6), *b* 1956: *m* 1984, Lilyan, da of Capt M. N. Herrera, of Caracas, Venezuela, and has issue living, Barnabas Wyndham *b* 1986, Alexandra Sophie *b* 1988, — James Edward Barnabas, *b* 1964, — Mary Pepita, *b* 1954: *m* 1977, Michael O'Kelly Webber, and has issue living, Thomas Edward O'Kelly *b* 1984, Jessica Grace *b* 1982. —— Wendy (4 Church View, Bourton, Gillingham, Dorset), *b* 1926.

Grandchildren of late Major Harold Wyndham Malet, son of late Col Harold Esdaile Malet, son of late Rev William Wyndham Malet (ante):—
Issue of late Capt John Wyndham, *b* 1910, *ka* 1940: *m* 1937, June Rosalind (who *d* 1991, having *m* 2ndly, 1943, Capt Wladyslaw Galica, who *d* 1951), da of late Capt John Broadley Harrison Broadley, of Welton House, Brough, E Yorkshire:—
Greville John Wyndham, OBE (The Walled House, Hatherop, Cirencester, Glos), *b* 1939; *ed* Harrow; Lt-Col R Hussars: *m* 1972 (*m diss* 1993), Hon Margaret Cherry Wigram, el da of 2nd Baron Wigram, and has issue living, Charles Neville Wyndham, *b* 1976, — Henrietta Margaret June, *b* 1978. —— (Leola) Dawn Wyndham *b* 1938: *m* 1961, Capt John David Graham Nicholson, RHA, son of Gen Sir Cameron Gordon Graham Nicholson, GCB, KBE, DSO, MC, and has issue living, John Andrew Graham, *b* 1964, — Edward Wyndham Graham, *b* 1966, — Davina June, *b* 1962. *Address* – c/o Lloyds Bank, 6 Pall Mall, SW1.

Grandchildren of late Allan Arthur Grenville Malet, son of late Lieut-Col George Grenville Malet, 4th son of 1st baronet:—
Issue of late Col George Edward Grenville Malet, OBE, late RAOC, *b* 1898, *d* 1952: *m* 1st, 1922 (*m diss* 1938), Gwendolen Iliffe (who *m* 2ndly, 1938, Rear-Adm Ernest William Leir, DSO, and *d* 1980), da of Brig-Gen James Aubrey Gibbon, CMG; 2ndly, 1939, Margaret Bell Wright, resumed her former married name of Malet by deed poll (Flat 8, 21 Shrudlands Rd, Berkhamsted, Herts), who *m* 2ndly, 1967, Patrick Walsh, JP, who *d* 1980:—

(By 1st *m*) (Baldwin) Hugh Grenville (The Vyne, Blue Anchor, nr Minehead, Som TA24 6JX), *b* 1928; *ed* Wellington Coll, and King's Coll, Camb (MA); PhD (Salford); Sudan Political Ser 1950-56; author; Pres W S Village History Soc; Lecturer in Local History, Salford Univ since 1973: *m* 1959, Kathleen Patricia, who *d* 1983, da of Arthur Morris, of Whitby, Cheshire, and has issue living, Durand David Grenville, *b* 1965; *ed* St Chad's Coll, Durham; Barrister-at-law, — Jane Phoebe Grenville, *b* 1962. —— Barbara Madeline Anne, *b* 1924; JP for Somerset: *m* 1947, Edward Hugh Michael Counsell, CBE, HM Diplomatic Service (ret), of The Monks House, Montacute, Somerset, and has issue living, John Aubrey Malet, *b* 1949, — Christopher Anthony Malet, *b* 1952, — Hugh Michael Malet, *b* 1962. ——(By 2nd *m*) Michael Ian Grenville (Riverside, Station Rd, Tisbury, Wilts), *b* 1939; *ed* Berkhamsted, and St Andrews Univ (MA); PhD (LSE London): *m* 1st, 1964 (*m diss* 1980), Alison Little; 2ndly, 1980, Jennifer Jones, and has issue living, (by 1st *m*) Iain Martin, *b* 1964, — Saffron Margaret, *b* 1968, — Jonquil May, *b* 1970, — (by 2nd *m*) Emily Helen, *b* 1980. —— Zenobia Margaret Grenville, *b* 1942; *ed* St Anne's Coll, Oxford: *m* 1967, Michael Venner, of Libra, Loders, nr Bridport, Dorset, and has issue living, Miriam Anna, *b* 1969, — Katriona Jeanne, *b* 1979.

Grandchildren of late Cdr Herbert Rivers Malet, late RNVR, yr son of late Arthur Malet, 5th son of 1st baronet:—
Henry Guy Rivers Malet, *b* 1894, *d* 19—: *m* 1st, 1917, (*m diss* 19—), Olga Muriel, da of James Balfour, of Paignton, Devon; 2ndly, 19—, Tessa West:—
Vyvyan Arthur Rivers, *b* 1927. —— Olga Diana Valentine Rivers, *b* 1925: *m* 1951, F. A. Heilingbrunner. —— Patience Violet Rivers, *b* 1930: *m* 1954 (*m diss* 19—), Leslie G. Walton.

William Malet, founder of this family in England, was a companion of William the Conqueror at Hastings, and probably (according to Sir Anthony Wagner) the only one from whom a male line descent to the present day can be traced. His son, Robert Malet, of Eye, was the first Lord Chamberlain of England, and William Malet, of Curry Mallet, was a Magna Carta Baron. A branch was settled at Enmore, Somerset from the twelfth century to 1681. Sir Baldwin Malet, of St Audries and Poyntington, Somerset, ancestor of this branch, descended from Sir Baldwin Malet, Solicitor Gen to Henry VIII, yr son of Thomas Malet, of Enmore (*d* 1502). A Baronetcy for services during the civil war was conferred by Charles II, on Sir Thomas Malet, of Poyntington, who *d* before the patent passed under the great seal. He was one of the Judges sent to the Tower by Cromwell, from the Court at Maidstone, for refusing to grant a summons against a clergyman who would not give up using the Book of Common Prayer. Sir Charles Warre Malet, was *cr* a Bt, for diplomatic services in India. The 2nd Bt, Sir Alexander, KCB, was Min to the German Confederation 1852-66. The 4th Bt, Rt Hon Sir Edward, GCB, GCMG, PC, was Min to Belgium 1883-84, and Ambassador to Germany 1884-95. The 7th Bt, Lt-Col Sir Harry Charles Malet, DSO, OBE, served in S Africa 1899-1902, and 1914-18 War.

Mallaby-Deeley, see Deeley.

MALLINSON (UK) 1935, of Walthamstow, co Essex

·INDE·QUERCUS·

Thence the oak

Sir WILLIAM JOHN MALLINSON, 4th *Baronet*; *b* 8 Oct 1942; *s* his father, *Sir* (WILLIAM) PAUL, 1989; *ed* Charterhouse: *m* 1968 (*m diss* 1978), Rosalind Angela, da of Rollo Hoare, of The Dower House, Dogmersfield, Hants, and has issue.

Arms – Ermine, three pallets gules, in chief two crescents or, and in base an acorn leaved and slipped proper. Crest – A cubit arm, the hand grasping a stock of a tree, snagged and eradicated proper.
Residence – The Watch House, Bembridge, Isle of Wight PO35 5NQ.

SON LIVING

WILLIAM JAMES, *b* 22 April 1970.

DAUGHTER LIVING

Kate Sophia, *b* 1972.

SISTER LIVING (*daughter of 3rd baronet by 1st marriage*)

Angela Mary, *b* 1941; MRCS (Eng); LRCP (London); DPM: *m* 1964, Edward Tuppin Scrase, BA, MB, BChir, FFA, RCS, of Prospect Farm, Llanidloes, Powys, and has issue living, Ivan, *b* 1968, — Aeron Michael, *b* 1980, — Hannah, *b* 1967.

WIDOW LIVING OF THIRD BARONET

MARGARET COOPER, BA, MB, BS (*Lady Mallinson*), da of late S A Bowden, of Barnstaple, N Devon, and formerly wife of late Surg-Lieut R. H. Gorrill, RNVR: *m* 1968, as his 2nd wife, Sir (William) Paul Mallinson, 3rd Bt, who *d* 1989. *Residences* – 25 Wimpole St, W1M 7AD.

COLLATERAL BRANCHES LIVING

Issue of late Stanley Tucker Mallinson, 2nd son of 1st baronet, *b* 1884, *d* 1955: *m* 1919, Dora Selina, who *d* 1960, da of late William B. Burridge, of Boscombe, Hants:—
Anthony William, *b* 1923; *ed* Marlborough, and at Gonville and Caius Coll, Camb (BA and Exhibitioner 1948, LLM 1949); admitted a Solicitor (honours) 1951; formerly Major RA: *m* 1955, Heather Mary, da of late Thomas Arthur Mansfield Gardiner. *Residence* – 15 Douro Place, W8 5PH.

Issue of late Col Sir Stuart Sydney Mallinson, CBE, DSO, MC, JP, DL, 3rd son of 1st baronet, *b* 1888; *d* 1981: *m* 1916, Marjorie Gray, CBE, who *d* 1969, da of late Rev Alfred Soothill, Headmaster of Ashville Coll, Harrogate:—
Justin Stuart (Bredy Farm, Burton Bradstock, Bridport, Dorset DT6 4ND), *b* 1923; *ed* Marlborough, and Jesus Coll, Camb; sometime Capt Gren Gds: *m* 1944, Juliana Beatrice, only da of late Samuel Martin, of St Helens, I of Wight, and has issue

living, John Michael Stuart (Black Down Cottage, Hemyock, Cullompton, Devon EX15 3RJ), *b* 1945; *ed* Marlborough Coll, and Reading Univ (BSc Agric): *m* 1968, Elizabeth Margaret, BSc, da of John Cloke, MRCVS, of Walsall, Staffs, and has issue living, Jonathan Justin Stuart *b* 1971, Elspeth May Stuart *b* 1974, Jane Marjorie *b* 1979, — Jennifer Jane Stuart, *b* 1949: *m* 1971, Lt-Cdr Nicholas Graham Talbot Harris, RN, and has issue living, Charles Justin Talbot *b* 1983, Antonia Diana Stuart *b* 1975, Francesca Louise Talbot *b* 1979. —— Terence Stuart (28 Albion St, W2 2AX), *b* 1929; *ed* Marlborough, and Jesus Coll, Camb (MA): *m* 1955, Anne Mary Butler, JP, Lord Mayor of Westminster 1986-87, da of late D. Butler Wilson, MC, of Burlington Lodge Alderley Edge, Cheshire, and has issue living, Lawrence Stuart (65 St Michael's St, W2 1QR), *b* 1957, *ed* Marlborough, and Jesus Coll, Camb (MA): *m* 1990, Angela Marie Christine, da of Henry Sulivan, of Weybridge, Surrey and has issue living, Barnaby Henry Stuart *b* 1993, — Michael David Stuart (16 Elvaston Pl, SW7 5QF), *b* 1959; *ed* Marlborough, and Fitzwilliam Coll, Camb (MA), Dip Arch, RIBA: *m* 1987, Helen P. M. (head of Coll of Architecture & Design, Univ of N London), eldest da of Alan Powell, of Cheltenham, Glos, and has issue living, Rosanna Marjorie Bernice *b* 1989, — Roland Arthur Stuart, *b* 1966; BSc, — Sheila Mary Anne, *b* 1961; BA: *m* 1988, Nicholas Spencer Charrington, eldest son of Maj Gerald Anthony Charrington, of Layer Marney Tower, Colchester, Essex CO5 9US, and has issue living, Alice Calmeyer *b* 1990, Hannah Mary *b* 1991, — Grace Elizabeth, *b* 1993.

Grandchildren (by 2nd *m*) of late Maj Lancelot Victor Mallinson, MC, yst son of 1st baronet:—
Issue of late Alastair Mallinson, *b* 1932, *d* 1986: *m* 1955, Rosemary (Rue des Saulniers, 44420 Mesquer, France), da of late Charles Cecil Harvey:—
Guy, *b* 1958. —— Alexandre, *b* 1964. —— Florence, *b* 1962.

The 1st baronet, Sir William Mallinson (son of late John Mallinson, of Forest Gate, E7) was a JP for Essex (Chm of Beacontree Bench). The 2nd baronet, Sir William James, was High Sheriff of Surrey 1933, a DL for the County of Surrey, and JP (Croydon Bench). The 3rd baronet, Sir (William) Paul, was a medical practitioner, Surg Lt Cmdr RNVR, and held the Family Order of Brunei.

MANDER (UK) 1911, of The Mount, Tettenhall, co Stafford

Live well

Sir CHARLES MARCUS MANDER, 3rd *Baronet*; *b* 22 Sept 1921; *s* his father, *Sir* CHARLES ARTHUR, 1951; *ed* Eton, and Trin Coll, Camb; late Capt Coldstream Guards; Chm Arlington Securities Ltd, of St James's 1983, Chm London & Cambridge Investments Ltd; High Sheriff of Staffs 1962-3; European War 1939-45 a Capt Coldstream Guards in Egypt, Italy, and N-W Europe: *m* 1945, Maria Dolores Beatrice, da of late Alfred Edmund Brödermann, of Gross Fontenay, Hamburg, Germany, and has issue.

ᴀrms – Gules, on a pile invected erminois, three annulets interlaced, two and one of the field. Crest – A demi-lion couped ermine holding in the paws two annulets interlaced fessewise gules, between two buffalo horns of the last.
Residence – Little Barrow, Moreton-in-Marsh, Glos GL56 9DW.

SONS LIVING

(CHARLES) NICHOLAS (Owlpen Manor, Uley, Glos GL11 5BZ) *b* 23 March 1950; *ed* Downside, and Trin Coll, Camb (MA); co-founder of Mander Portman Woodward (private tutors) of Kensington, 1973; dir of publishing and land companies in UK and Spain; Member of Lloyd's: *m* 1972, Karin Margareta, da of late Gustav Arne Norin, of Stockholm, Sweden, and has issue living, (Charles) Marcus Septimus Gustav, *b* 26 July 1975; *ed* Eton, — Benedict Edward Arthur, *b* 1977, — Hugo Richard Theodore, *b* 1981, — Fabian Edmund Quintin, *b* 1987, — Sarra Mary, *b* 1973; *ed* St Mary's, Ascot. —— Francis Peter Edward (Heath Barn, Donnington, nr Moreton-in-Marsh, Glos GL56 OXU; 140 Park Lane, W1Y 3AA), *b* 1952; *ed* Downside, Grenoble Univ, and RAC Cirencester; Commercial pilot, founded Mandair Promotions 1983, and Francis Mander Photography 1990; Member of Lloyds: *m* 1990, Georgina Jane, elder da of Cmdr Edward Theodore Thring, RN, of Rapsgate Park, Cirencester, Glos, and has issue living, Luke Edward Charles, *b* 1994.

DAUGHTER LIVING

Penelope Anne Mary, *b* 1946: *m* 1st, 1965 (*m diss* 1978), Michael Rollo Hoare; 2ndly, 1979, Capt Simon John Loder, Gren Gds, of Clapton Court, Crewkerne, Som TA18 8PT, and has issue living, (by 1st *m*) Venetia Elizabeth, *b* 1965, — Fiona Mary, *b* 1969, — (by 2nd *m*) (*see* Loder, Bt, colls).

SISTERS LIVING

Ann Marietta Patience, *b* 1914; JP for Glos, and Fellow King's Coll, London: *m* 1939, Hugh Patrick Stirling, of Witney House, Leafield, Oxford, and has two adopted children, Nicholas Charles (Dipton Cottage, Corbridge, Northumberland), *b* 1947; *ed* Eton; 16th/5th Queen's Royal Lancers; FRCA; MFH: *m* 1975, Elizabeth Emma, da of Brig V. W. Barlow, DSO, OBE, and has issue living, William Nelson *b* 1979, Frances *b* 1980, Patience *b* 1983, Alexandra Emma *b* 1989, — Charlotte Amelia, *b* 1950; *ed* Cranborne Chase, and Bristol Univ (BA): *m* 1973, Paul Francis Sandilands, of Falcutt House, Helmdon, Northants, and has issue living, Frederick James *b* 1982, Marietta Minette *b* 1980. —— Carinthia Jill, *b* 1920; formerly in WRNS: *m* 1st 1944, James Ramsden, who *d* 1956; 2ndly, 1964, Lt-Cdr James de Votier Grosvenor Wallis, RN (ret), of Le Friquet, Bailiff's Cross Rd, St Andrews, Guernsey, and has issue living (by 1st *m*), James Tobit, *b* 1948; *ed* Sheffield Univ (BA): *m* 1st, 1973 (*m diss* 1983), Linda, da of Walter Critchlow, of St Bruno, PQ, Canada; 2ndly, 1985, Ann Miller-Williams, and has issue living, (by 1st *m*) Sarah Jill *b* 1977, (by 2nd *m*) Edward Henry James *b* 1988, Sian Amelia *b* 1986, Daisy Katherine *b* 1990, — Charles Riordan, *b* 1949: *m* 1974, Elizabeth Mary, only da of Stewart Kilpatrick, of Fogdens Barn, Bury, Sussex.

COLLATERAL BRANCHES LIVING

Granddaughter of late Gerald Poynton Mander, FSA (infra):—
Issue of late Philip FitzGerald Mander, *b* 1915, *d* 1972: *m* 1942, Priscilla Patricia, BA (The Folley, Stableford, Bridgnorth, Shropshire), da of late Lt-Col Edmund de Warrenne Waller, MC, Indian Army:—

Rev Philippa Hazel Jeanetta, *b* 1944; *ed* Cheltenham Ladies' Coll, Exeter Univ (BA), and Queen's Theological Coll; ordained deacon 1988, priest 1994: *m* 1965, John Patrick Thorneycroft, MA, of Kemberton Hall, Shifnal, Salop, and has issue living, Hugh Martin Sumner, *b* 1967, — Martin Philip, *b* 1977, — Veryan Ruth, *b* 1971, — Naomi Priscilla, *b* 1975.

Granddaughter of late Philip FitzGerald Mander (ante):—
Issue of late (Patrick) Oliver Mander, *b* 1951, *d* 1982: *m* 1978, Gabrielle Patricia (120 Old Brompton Rd, SW7), only da of late Geoffrey Terence Weaver:—
Hannah Rachel, *b* 1982.

Issue of late Gerald Poynton Mander, FSA, yr son of 1st baronet, *b* 1885, *d* 1951: *m* 1913, Nancy Steward, who *d* 1960, da of late Lieut-Col R. H. Hargreaves, JP, DL, of Knightley Grange, Staffordshire:—
Catherine Daphne, *b* 1914. —— Hilary Nancy, *b* 1924: *m* 1st, 1946 (*m diss* 1981), William Reginald Purslow, who *d* 1991; 2ndly, 1985, Anthony Michél Jarrey, and has issue living (by 1st *m*), Ian Gerald Steward, *b* 1949: *m* 1st, 1971 (*m diss* 1982), Sally Anne, only da of Gordon Matthews, of Milton House, Shipton-under-Wychwood, Oxon; 2ndly, 1988, Susan Kathryn, da of Capt Colin McKeand Little, RN (ret), of Queen Camel, Som. *Residence* – Stayt's Farm, Church Westcote, nr Kingham, Oxford OX7 6SF.
The 1st baronet, Sir Charles Tertius Mander (Chm of Mander Bros Limited, of Wolverhampton), was High Sheriff of Staffordshire 1903, and Mayor of Wolverhampton 1892-6 (Hon Freeman 1897). The 2nd baronet, Sir Charles Arthur Mander, was High Sheriff for Staffordshire 1926, and Mayor of Wolverhampton, 1932 and 1936 (Hon Freeman 1946).

MANN (UK) 1905, of Thelveton Hall, Thelveton, Norfolk

Statesman

Sir RUPERT EDWARD MANN, 3rd *Baronet*, el son of Edward Charles Mann, DSO, MC, only son of Maj William Edgar Mann, DSO, 2nd son of 1st Bt; *b* 11 Nov 1946; *s* his gt uncle, *Sir* (EDWARD) JOHN, 1971; *ed* Malvern: *m* 1974, Mary Rose, da of Geoffrey Butler, of Cheveley Cottage, Stetchworth, Newmarket, Suffolk, and has issue.

Arms – Argent, a chevron sable, between in chief two crosses moline, and in base an annulet gules. Crest – A demi-man in armour proper, the helmet adorned with four feathers argent, holding in his dexter hand a cross moline as in the arms.
Seat – Billingford Hall, Diss, Norfolk.

SONS LIVING

ALEXANDER RUPERT, *b* 6 April 1978. —— William Edward, *b* 1980.

BROTHER LIVING

Andrew William, *b* 1947, *ed* Malvern.

AUNTS LIVING

Ann Sara (Westcott Barton Lodge, Middle Barton, Chipping Norton, Oxon), *b* 1916; 1939-45 as Junior Cdr ATS (despatches): *m* 1950, Charles John Cunningham, MA, FRIBA, who *d* 1994, and has issue living, Alexander Kenneth, *b* 1956: *m* 1980, Frances, da of His Honour Judge John da Cunha, of Mobberley, Cheshire, and has issue living, Maximilian Edward *b* 1986, Ivo Alexander James *b* 1991, Camilla Lucy *b* 1988, — Edward James, *b* 1962: *m* 1990, Melissa Ann, da of Daryl H. Foster, of Perth, W Aust, and has issue living, James Alexander *b* 1992, — Sara Mary, *b* 1952, — Clare Margaret, *b* 1953: *m* 1983, Edward Gold, son of Dr S. C. Gold, MD, FRCP, and has issue living, Christopher Charles *b* 1984, Simon Piers *b* 1988. —— Penelope Jane (Hoe Hall, Dereham, Norfolk), *b* 1924; a JP of Norfolk: *m* 1950, Michael Telfair Keith, who *d* 1966, and has issue living, James Edward, *b* 1960: *m* 1987, Victoria Rosemary, da of Roy E. Cook, of Cawood, N Yorks, and has issue living, Edward Michael *b* 1991, Rosanna Victoria *b* 1989, Alicia Rose Juliet *b* 1993, — Rosemary Ann, *b* 1951: *m* 1983, Michael Charles Fetherston-Dilke, of Maxstoke Castle, Warwicks, son of Capt Charles Beaumont Fetherston-Dilke, RN, and has issue living, George Michael *b* 1985, Edward Charles *b* 1986, Sarah *b* 1989, — Priscilla Mary, *b* 1953: *m* 1979, Fergus Hew Grant Laing, of Craggan, Grantown-on-Spey, Moray, and has issue (*see* E Stair, colls).

MOTHER LIVING

Pamela Margaret, only da of late Maj Frank Haultain Hornsby, RFA (B Belper): *m* 1945, Edward Charles Mann, DSO, MC, who *d* 1959 (ante).

COLLATERAL BRANCH LIVING

Issue of late Capt Francis Thomas Mann, 3rd son of 1st Bt, *b* 1888, *d* 1964: *m* 1916, Enid Agnes, who *d* 1976, da of late George A. Tilney:—
(Francis) George, CBE, DSO, MC (Great Farmhouse, West Woodhay, Newbury, Berks RG15 0BL), *b* 1917; *ed* Eton, and Pembroke Coll, Camb; formerly Maj Scots Guards (Supplementary Reserve); 1939-45 War in N Africa and Italy (wounded, MC, DSO); DSO 1945, CBE (Civil) 1983: *m* 1949, Margaret Hildegarde, el da of late W. Marshall Clark, of Johannesburg, S Africa, and has issue living, Simon Francis, *b* 1952; *ed* Eton, and RMA Sandhurst; Capt Scots Guards 1971-81 and 1991-92: *m* 1977 (*m diss* 1986), Jennifer, da of David Barham, of Hole Park, Rolvenden, and has issue living, Peter George *b* 1980, Jack *b* 1982, Sophie *b* 1985, — Richard William (Goosedown Farm, Dolton, Winkleigh, Devon), *b* 1953: *m* 1983, Selina Rose Thoroton, only da of late Maj Robert Christopher Thoroton Hildyard, MC, RA, of Plaister Pitts, Scrayingham, Yorks, and has issue living, Edgar *b* 1985, Perdita *b* 1986, — Edward John (101 Studdridge St, SW6 3TD), *b* 1961: *m* 1986, D. Clare de C., da of Archie A. de C. Hunter, of Southcombe Farm House, Thorncombe, Chard, Dorset, and has issue living, a son *b* 1989, Georgia *b* 1991, — Sarah Margaret, *b* 1960: *m* 1989, Hugh Grootenhuis, son of Peter Grootenhuis. —— John Pelham, MC (290 Weed St, New Canaan, Conn 06840, USA), *b* 1919; *ed* Eton, and Pembroke Coll, Camb; formerly Maj Scots Guards; 1939-45 War (MC): *m* 1st, 1942 (*m diss* 1975), Ann Marguerite, only da of late Col John Grahame Brockbank, CMG, DSO, of The Manor House, Steeple Langford, Salisbury; 2ndly, 1976, Isabel, da of Dr Alton Ochsner, of New Orleans, USA, and has

issue living, (by 1st *m*) James John Francis (Bricklayers Farm, West Woodhay, Newbury, Berks RG15 OBP), *b* 1946: *m* 1976 (*m diss* 1994), Effie Sarah Anne, da of late Norman Hepple, RA, of 10 Sheen Common, Richmond, Surrey, and has issue living, Thomas James *b* 1979, Frederick John *b* 1986, Rachel Poppy Jillian *b* 1977, — Charles Edward Lionel, *b* 1948: *m* 1980, Jane, da of Thomas Elliott, of Sale, Cheshire, and has issue living, Charlotte Joanna *b* 1981, — Celia Marguerite (*Baroness Norrie*), *b* 1943: *m* 1964, 2nd Baron Norrie. —— Joan Elizabeth (*Elizabeth, Baroness Maclean*), *b* 1923: *m* 1941, Baron Maclean (Life Baron), who *d* 1990. —— Margaret Enid, *b* 1924; formerly in WRNS: *m* 1951, Maj Seaton Patrick Hayes Simonds, MC, RHA (ret), of Manor Farm, Syde, Cheltenham, and has issue living, Peter Hayes, *b* 1966: *m* 1990, Karen, da of Daniel Smith, of Wellesly, Barnstaple, — Susan Enid, *b* 1954: *m* 1978 (*m diss* 1983), Timothy D. E. Rees, — Anne Margaret, *b* 1958: *m* 1989, John Treadwell, son of Lt-Col G. W. Treadwell, OBE, and has issue living, Edward *b* 1991, Louisa *b* 1993, — Nicola Mary, *b* 1968, — Catherine Elizabeth, *b* 1970.
The 1st baronet, Sir Edward Mann (son of Thomas Mann, of Thelveton Hall, Scole, and Roseneath House, Winchmore Hill, N), was Chm of Mann, Crossman & Paulin, Ltd, of Brandon's Putney Brewery, Ltd.

MANSEL (E) 1622, of Muddlescombe, Carmarthenshire

What he wishes,

he wishes fervently

Sir PHILIP MANSEL, 15th *Baronet*; *b* 3 March 1943; *s* his father, *Sir* JOHN PHILIP FERDINAND, 1947; *ed* Grosvenor Coll, Carlisle, and Carlisle Gram Sch: *m* 1968, Margaret, only da of Arthur Docker, of Hainings Gate, Moorhouse, Carlisle.

🛡**rms** – Argent, a chevron between three maunches sable. **Crest** – A cap of maintenance gules, turned up ermine, enflamed on the top proper.
Seat – Maesycrugiau Manor, Maesycrugiau, Carmarthenshire.

SONS LIVING

JOHN PHILIP, *b* 19 April 1982. —— Richard James, *b* 1990.

DAUGHTER LIVING

Nicol, *b* 1978.

AUNTS LIVING (*Daughters of 13th baronet*)

Margaretta Cecil, *b* 1913: *m* 1940, Lt-Cdr Ralph Leonard West, RN (ret), and has issue living, Richard Mansel, *b* 1946, — Christopher Leonard, *b* 1951, — Aileen Margaretta, *b* 1941. —— Juliet, *b* 1917: *m* 1939, Group Capt Richard Eric Burns, CBE, DFC, and has issue living, Richard Harcourt, *b* 1943, — Christine Georgina, *b* 1941, — Gillian, *b* 1948. *Residence* – Corner Cottage, Ashby Lane, Bitteswell, Lutterworth, Leics.

WIDOW LIVING OF FOURTEENTH BARONET

HANNAH, da of Ben Rees, of Cwmhuplyn, Pencader: *m* 1st, 1940, Sir John Philip Ferdinand Mansel, 14th baronet, who *d* 1947; 2ndly, 1949, — Harrison. *Residence* – Hall Flatt, Scaleby, Carlisle.

COLLATERAL BRANCHES LIVING

Issue of late Regnier Ranulf Dabridgecourt Mansel (son of 13th baronet), *b* 1919, *d* 1984: *m* 1941, Mary Germaine (Taliaris, Maesycrugiau, Carmarthenshire), da of W/Cdr W. St J. Littlewood, OBE, of Braemar, Stanmore, Middlesex:—
Anthony Ranulf, *b* 1946: Capt RCT (V); AInstBM: *m* 19—, Joan Evans, of Neath, and has issue living, Richard Mark, *b* 1973, — Robert Courtney, *b* 1976. —— Robert Edward, *b* 1948: Capt RAMC (V); MB, BS Lond; FRCS Eng, LRCP Lond: *m* 1st, 19—, Ingrid Powell; 2ndly, 1987, Elizabeth C. Skone, niece of the Bishop of Tonbridge, and has issue living (by 1st *m*), Joanna Margaret, *b* 1971, — Juliet Claire, *b* 1977, — (by 2nd *m*), Rhys Edward Regnier, *b* 1989, — Courtenay Robert John, *b* 1994, — Charlotte Elizabeth, *b* 1988. —— Roderick Rhys, *b* 1959. —— Isabel Theresa, *b* 1949. —— Frances, *b* 1952.

Grandson of late Rev Canon John Colvile Morton Mansel-Pleydell, 2nd son of late John Clavell Mansel-Pleydell, eldest son of Col John Mansel, CB, 3rd son of 9th baronet:—
Issue of late Ralph Morton Mansel-Pleydell, *b* 1895, *d* 1932: *m* 1920, Countess Margurite Marie, who *d* 1968, da of Count Aymard d'Ursel:—
Philip Morton (2 Lower Clenston, Blandford, Dorset DT11 0NY), *b* 1922; *ed* Ampleforth Coll; Lt-Cdr RN (ret); 1939-45 War: *m* 1961, Dagmar Rosalie, da of late Theodore Louis Bowring, CMG, OBE, and has issue living, John Bowring Morton, *b* 1963, — Rosanna Vivien, *b* 1965: *m* 1990, Werner van Zuylen, of Le Pavillon, Chateau de et à, 4601 Argenteau, Belgium, eldest son of Baron Edouard van Zuylen, of Argenteau, Belgium, and has issue living, Edmond Marc Dominic *b* 1992, Charles *b* 1994.

Grandsons of late Ralph Morton Mansel-Pleydell (ante):—
Issue of late David Gabriel Morton Mansel-Pleydell, DFC, *b* 1923, *d* 1973: *m* 1963, Elisabeth Susan (42 Bloomfield Terr, SW1; Barneston Manor, Steeple, Dorset), da of John McVean Luard, of Court St, Nayland, Suffolk:—
Toby Edmond Luard Morton, *b* 1964. —— Harry Rupert Delalynde Morton, *b* 1966. —— Thomas Oliver Clavell Morton, *b* 1969. —— Charles David Luttrell Morton (*posthumous*), *b* 1973.

Grandchildren of late Col John Delalynde Mansel, eldest son of George Pleydell Mansel, 2nd son of Col John Mansel, CB, 3rd son of 9th baronet:—
Issue of late Maj Rhys Clavell Mansel, *b* 1891, *d* 1969: *m* 1st, 1916, Sylvia Nina, who *d* 1944, da of Sir Guy Theophilus Campbell, 3rd Bt; 2ndly, 1944 (*m* annulled 1946), Mrs Margaret Georgina Walker, da of late Dr H. F. G. Noyes; 3rdly, 1947, Archie Anne, who *d* 1986, da of Hugh Montgomery Cairnes, of Fox Hall, Raheny, co Dublin:—
(By 1st *m*) John Clavell (Smedmore, Wareham, Dorset BH20 5PG), *b* 1917; *ed* Eton, and Ch Ch, Oxford (MA); Maj (ret) Rifle Bde; JP and DL for Dorset; High Sheriff of Dorset 1968; 1939-45 War: *m* 1945, Damaris Joan, da of late Hyde Hyde-Thomson, of 36 Victoria Rd, W8, and has had issue, Richard John Clavell, *b* 1949; *d* 1993, — Philip Robert Rhys, *b* 1951;

writer, — Lavinia Sylvia MANSEL, *b* 1946; resumed her maiden name 1991: *m* 1968 (*m diss* 1991), Alexander Quentin Jones, and has issue living, Alexander Daniel Mansel *b* 1978, Benjamin Robin Clavell *b* 1980, Owen Toby Rhys *b* 1984. —— Elizabeth Madeline Nina (17 St Martins Lane, Wareham, Dorset), *b* 1919: *m* 1961 (*m diss* 1966), Sir Malby Sturges Crofton, 5th Bt (*cr* 1838). —— Felicité Mary Adeline (29 Ruttan Bay, Winnipeg, Manitoba, Canada R3T 0H5), *b* 1924: *m* 1952 (*m diss* 1978), Peter Warner, and has issue living, William Francis, *b* 1957, — Susanna Elizabeth Juliet, *b* 1953: *m* 19—, Harold Polsky, and has issue living, Elizabeth *b* 19— (and has issue living, Alura Rachelle Poschner BOLDUC POLSKY *b* 19—), — Ianthe Sylvia, *b* 1954, — Sarah Adeline WARNER, *b* 1959; continues to use her maiden name: *m* 1993, Thomas Peter Kobar, of 274 1st St East (Box 4194), The Pas, Manitoba R9A 1R2, Canada, — Charlotte Anne, *b* 1965, — Oenone Jane, *b* 1966. —— Pamela Sylvia, *b* 1926: *m* 1953, Nicholas Cole McClintock, CBE, KStJ, late Snr Resident, Northern Nigeria, of Lower Westport, Wareham, Dorset BH20 4PR, and has issue living, Alexander Edward Franklin (Frank) (Baranco da Estrada, 7665 Santa Clara a Velha, Baixo Alentejo, Portugal), *b* 1959; *ed* Eton: *m* 1986, Julia (Lulu) Adeline, yr da of Thomas Henry Luckock, of Flint House, Barkway, Royston, Herts, and has issue living, Archie *b* 1988, Araby Tessa *b* 1989, Alexandra Adeline *b* 1992, — Michael Leopold Elphinstone (6 Westport Rd, Wareham, Dorset BH20 5PR), *b* 1960; *ed* Milton Abbey: *m* 1991, Mrs Anne K. Lee, da of R. T. Greenwood, of Shipley, W Yorks, — Sylvia Araby Jane, *b* 1954: *m* 1979, Malcolm Wright, of Cricket Green Cottage, Ewhurst Green, Cranleigh, Surrey GU6 7RR, and has issue living, Pamela Melesina Marion *b* 1981, Katherine Elizabeth Jane *b* 1984, — Elizabeth Melesina, *b* 1962: *m* 1992, Anthony F. Loring, of 83 Tunis Rd, W12 7EY, son of late Brig Walter Loring, CBE, of Slingsby, Yorks, and has issue living, Frances Claudia *b* 1993. —— (By 3rd *m*) Hugh Clavell (Thornmoor House, South Middlebere, nr Wareham, Dorset BH20 5DY), *b* 1948; *ed* Eton: *m* 1st, 1973, Jennifer Ann, yr da of Brian Ashford-Russell, of 1 Cheyne Walk, SW3, and The Lindens, Alresford, Hants; 2ndly, 1984, Diana Theresa Violet, yst da of late Lt-Col Conyers Stephen Scrope, MC (*see* D Sutherland, 1980 Edn), and has issue living (by 2nd *m*), Rhys Clavell, *b* 1987, — Isabella Maria, *b* 1985.

Granddaughters of late Algernon Lascelles Mansel (infra):—
Issue of late John William Morton Mansel, TD, *b* 1909, *d* 1974: *m* 1952, Gillian Valerie (Kingsmoor Cottage, Salford, Chipping Norton, Oxon OX7 5YN) (who *m* 2ndly, 1977, John M. S. Barnard, who *d* 1979), el da of late Douglas Harold Whinney, of South Moreton Manor, Didcot, Berks:—
Isita Susan, *b* 1954: *m* 1st, 1978 (*m diss* 198-), J. Peter Raffe; 2ndly, 1988, Roy Thomas Pickering, of Nailsworth, Netting Close, Hook Norton, Oxon, and has issue living (by 1st *m*), Jonathan Luke, *b* 1980, — Sally Jane Isita, *b* 1979. —— Philippa Clare, *b* 1955.

Grandson of late Capt Arthur Edmund Mansel, yst son of late Col John Mansel, CB (3rd son of 9th baronet):—
Issue of late Algernon Lascelles Mansel, *b* 1868, *d* 1942: *m* 1906, Isita Rodger, who *d* 1948, da of late William Wilson, formerly of 52 Prince's Gate, SW:—
Edmund Clavell, OBE, MC (Chestnuts, Bishop Wilton, York YO4 1RU), *b* 1915; *ed* Winchester, and RMA Woolwich; Lt-Col (ret) RA; 1939-45 War (despatches, MC); OBE (Mil) 1960: *m* 1954, Ann, da of late Capt Claud Anthony Merriman, RN, of Newton House, Longparish, Hants, and has issue living, Timothy Mervyn Charles, *b* 1961; *ed* Winchester, and Bristol Univ (BSc), — Catherine Gillian, *b* 1956: *m* 1979, Rupert Michael Walter James Dilnott-Cooper, of 23 Glenmore Rd, NW3 4BX, and has issue living, Edward Kenneth Timothy *b* 1989, William Rupert Mansel *b* 1993.

Sir Francis Mansel, 1st Bt (*cr* 1622) was a yr brother of Sir Thomas Mansel, of Margam Abbey, Glam, who was *cr* a baronet 1611. The latter's gt-grandson, Sir Thomas, 5th Bt, was *cr* Lord Mansel of Margam, in 1712, *ext* 1750. On the death of Sir John William Bell Mansel, 11th Bt (*cr* 1622), in 1883, his kinsman Richard, *b* 1850 (son of Maj Courtenay Mansel, formerly Phillips) son of Richard Phillips, formerly Mansel, yr son of 9th Bt, who *m* in Scotland, in or about 1838, Eliza, da of Rev John Sidney (a decree in Court of Session, Edinburgh, pronounced validity of this *m* in Scotland 1906). He *m* the same lady in St Paul's, Liverpool 1847, assumed the baronetcy as 12th Bt; he *d* 1892, having *m* 1st, 1878, Maud Margaretta Bowen, who *d* 1885, da of John Jones, of Maes-y-Crugiau Hall, co Carmarthen, and 2ndly, 1891, Ada Alice Lea, who *d* 1916. He was followed by his son (by 1st *m*), Courtenay Cecil Mansel (de facto 13th Bt), who in 1903, discontinued using the title, when, with his assent, it was taken up as 12th baronet, by his uncle (Sir) Edward Berkeley Mansel, *b* 1839 el son of Maj Courtenay Mansel (ante). He *dsp* 1908, when the title was resumed by his nephew Sir Courtenay Cecil Mansel (ante), as 13th Bt.

MAPPIN (UK) 1886, of Thornbury, co York (Extinct 1975)

Sir FRANK CROSSLEY MAPPIN, 6th and last *Baronet*.

DAUGHTERS LIVING OF SIXTH BARONET

Ivy Marjorie, *b* 1914: *m* 1941, Air Commodore Theodore Jasper MacLean de Lange, CBE, DFC; RNZAF (ret) of Kohanga, Otaramarae, RD4, Rotorua, NZ. —— Ethel Thorpe *b* 1917: *m* 1944, George Fenwick, MD. *Residence* – 157 Arney Rd, Auckland 5, NZ.

SISTER LIVING OF FOURTH BARONET

Molly Violet, *b* 1907: *m* 1st, 1928 (*m diss* 1930), Francis Ferdinand Maurice Cook (afterwards 4th Bt); 2ndly 1930 (*m diss* 19—), Maj W. St. J. Macarthey; 3rdly, 19—, N. Walker.

MARKHAM (UK) 1911, of Beachborough Park, Newington, Kent

Tenacious of purpose

Sir CHARLES JOHN MARKHAM, 3rd *Baronet*; *b* 2 July 1924; *s* his father, Sir CHARLES, 1952; *ed* Eton; is Lieut 11th Hussars; was Vice-Chm, Nairobi Co Council 1953-55, and a MLC, Kenya 1955-60; appointed Pres, Roy Agricultural Soc of Kenya 1958; European War 1943-45 (despatches); KStJ 1973: *m* 1949, Valerie, only da of Lt-Col E. Barry-Johnston, of Kenya, and has issue.

Arms – Azure, on a pale argent, three lozenges, palewise sable, issuant from a chief engrailed or, a demi-lion gules. **Crest** – A winged lion guardant or, the head surrounded by a halo gules and resting the dexter forepaw on a lozenge sable.
Address – PO Box 42263, Nairobi, Kenya. *Clubs* – MCC, and Muthaiga (Kenya).

SONS LIVING

(ARTHUR) DAVID (PO Box 42263, Nairobi, Kenya), *b* 6 Dec 1950: *m* 1977, Carolyn L., yr da of Capt Mungo Park, of Carraig, Breac, Baily, co Dublin, and has issue living, Tanya Valerie Helen, *b* 1979, — Joanna Mary Hilda, *b* 1981.
—— Richard Barry, *b* 1954: *m* 1985, Ann C., yst da of Ian Malcolm-Smith, of Mombasa, and Mrs Yvonne Malcolm-Smith, of Canterbury, Kent, and has issue living, Nicholas Charles, *b* 1987, — Matthew James, *b* 1990.

DAUGHTER LIVING

Elizabeth-Anne, *b* 1958: *m* 1983, Peter J. Bateman, of PO Box 610, Francistown, Botswana, elder son of Col A. J. Bateman, of Baulking, Oxon, and has issue living, Jessica Elisabeth, *b* 1987.

HALF-BROTHER LIVING

John (c/o Williams & Glyn's Bank, 9 Pall Mall, SW1), *b* 1933; *ed* Gordonstoun; is Maj RA: *m* 1st, 1961 (*m diss* 1987), Yvonne, da of Neil-Buchanan; 2ndly, 1987, Elizabeth, da of late Von Langnau, and has issue living (by 1st *m*), Toby John, *b* 1966: *m* 1994, Natasha, da of Walter Brunn, — Annalise Elizabeth, *b* 1963: *m* 1986, Anthony Cowley.

SISTER LIVING

Mary, *b* 1921: *m* 1st, 1946 (*m diss* 19—) Senator Joseph Dana Roberts; 2ndly, 1977, James Austin Hughes, who *d* 19—.

WIDOW LIVING OF SECOND BARONET

(FREDERICA) BETTY CORNWALLIS (CRAWFORD) (*Betty, Lady Markham*), da of late Hon Christian Edward Cornwallis Eliot, OBE (*see* E St Germans, colls): *m* 1942, as his 3rd wife, Sir Charles Markham, 2nd baronet, who *d* 1952. *Address* – PO Box 583, Mbabane, Swaziland.

COLLATERAL BRANCHES LIVING

Granddaughters (by 1st *m*) of late Mansfield Markham, 2nd son of 1st baronet, *b* 1905, *d* 1971: *m* 1st, 1927 (*m diss* 1942), Mrs Beryl Purves (the aviatrix, Beryl Markham), who *d* 1987, da of Charles B. Clutterbuck, of Kenya; 2ndly, 1944, Mary Ellen, who *d* 1987, da of late Capt A. Adley, of Calcutta:—
Issue of late Gervase Markham, *b* 1929, *d* in a motor accident 1971: *m* 1952, Viviane, who *d* 1987, da of Joseph Bruiltet, of Les Hesperides, St Germain en Laye 78100, France:—
Fleur, *b* 1953. —— Valerie-Carol, *b* 1955: *m* 1982, Daniel Rollet, of 27 rue Garibaldi, Lyon 69006, France, son of Georges Rollet, of Lyons, and *d* 1988.

Issue of late Arthur Markham, 3rd son of 1st baronet, *b* 1911, *d* 1943: *m* 1936, Althea (who *m* 2ndly, 1946, William John Martin Begg, who *d* 1986), da of late Warren David Heinly, of Los Angeles, USA:—
Michael Arthur (Southerly, Smith's Parish, Bermuda), *b* (*posthumous*) 1944; *ed* Trin Coll Sch, Canada, Menlo Coll, Cal (BS, BA), and Florida Atlantic Univ; Chm of the Pedry Mine: *m* 1976, Geke, da of D. De Jager, of Holland, and has issue living, Moshe Arthur, *b* 1977, — John Lloyd, *b* 1979, — Hanna Althea Marion, *b* 1981, — Julia Grace, *b* 1990, — Joy Elizabeth, *b* 1992.

The 1st baronet, Sir Arthur Basil Markham (son of Charles Markham, JP, of Tapton House, Derbyshire), was a Director of the Tredegar Iron and Coal Co, and Founder of Doncaster Amalgamated Collieries; and sat as MP for Mansfield Div of Notts (*L*) 1900-1916.

MARLING (UK) 1882, of Stanley Park and Sedbury Park, co Gloucester

Sir CHARLES WILLIAM SOMERSET MARLING, 5th *Baronet*; *b* 2 June 1951; *s* his father, *Lt-Col Sir* JOHN STANLEY VINCENT, OBE, 1977; *ed* Harrow: *m* 1979, Judi P., adopted da of Thomas W. Futrille, of Sunningdale, Berks, and has issue.

Arms – Argent, three bars gules each charged with five bezants; in chief a lion passant gules. **Crest** – In front of a tower argent three bezants; the tower capped with a cupola, thereon a flag-staff proper from which flows a pennant gules.
Residence – Woodcray Manor Farm, Wokingham, Berks RG11 3HG. *Clubs* – White's, Chelsea Arts.

DAUGHTERS LIVING

Georgina Katharine *b* 1982. —— Aimy Frances, *b* 1984. —— Laura Beatrice, *b* 1990.

SISTERS LIVING

Miranda Mary, *b* 1941: *m* 1966, Anthony John Cordle, late Capt Coldm Gds, of 23 Durand Gdns, SW9, and has issue living, Lucia Georgina Diana, *b* 1968, —— Jessica Grace Rosanne, *b* 1972. —— Harriet Anne, *b* 1944. —— Virginia Frances, *b* 1946; *m* 1978, Colin Bowie, of Dragon's Lair, Moor Lane, Wincanton, Som BA9 9EJ, and has issue living, John Adrian Charles *b* 1977, —— Geoffrey David *b* 1979.

We are a prey to none

The 1st baronet sat as MP for Gloucestershire West (*L*) 1868-74 and for Stroud 1875-80. The 2nd baronet was High Sheriff of Gloucestershire 1888. The 3rd baronet, Col Sir Percival Scrope Marling, VC, CB, served in S Africa 1881, in Egypt 1882, with Suakim Expedition 1884 (VC), with Nile Expedition 1884-5, in S Africa 1899-1902 (CB) and during European War 1914-15.

MARR (UK) 1919, of Sunderland, co Palatine of Durham

(*Sir*) LESLIE LYNN MARR, 2nd *Baronet*, son of late John Lynn Marr, OBE, el son of 1st Baronet; *b* 14 Aug 1922; *s* his grandfather, *Sir* JAMES, CBE, 1932, but does not use title; *ed* Shrewsbury, and Pembroke Coll, Camb (MA); late Fl Lt RAF: *m* 1st, 1948 (*m diss* 1956), Dinora Delores Mendelson; 2ndly, 1962, Lynn Heneage, and has issue by 2nd *m*.

Arms – Azure, the mast and sail of a ship, pennon flying, within eight estoiles in orle or. **Crest** – A bell charged with a fouled anchor proper.

DAUGHTERS LIVING (*By 2nd marriage*)

Joanne Lesley, *b* 1963. —— Rebecca Lynn, *b* 1966.

COLLATERAL BRANCHES LIVING

Grandchildren of late William Bell Marr, yr son of 1st baronet:—
Issue of late Allan James Marr, CBE, *b* 1907, *d* 1989: *m* 1936, Joan de Wolf, who *d* 19—, da of John Ranken, of Sunderland:—
JAMES ALLAN (2 Peppermines, Brancepeth, Durham DH7 8ED), *b* 17 May 1939; *ed* Oundle, and Newcastle Univ: *m* 1964, Jennifer, yr da of late John William Edmund Gill, of Ellerslie, Bishop Auckland, and has issue living, Allan James William, *b* 8 Oct 1965; *ed* Strathallan: *m* 1988, Dawn, da of George Ridley, of —, and has issue living, Liam James Allan *b* 1991, —— Roderick John, *b* 1971, —— Lucy Joan, *b* 1968. —— Jennifer Wendy, *b* 1936: *m* 1960, Nicholas Warren Willink, of Greenhills, Crook, Kendal, 2nd son of Derek Edward Willink, JP, of Mirefoot, Burnside, Kendal, and has issue living, Patrick John, *b* 1964, ——

Labour conquers all things

Amanda Frances, *b* 1961: *m* 19—, John Peter Trickett, of Fortshot Farm, nr Leeds, and has issue living, Robin James *b* 1988, Alastair (twin) *b* 1988, —— Susan Joan, *b* 1963: *m* 1992, Ian Charles Michael Harrison, of Great Dunmow. —— Gillian Mary, *b* 1941: *m* 1974, Richard Tatton Wedderburn Hewetson, and has issue living, Richard Allan Webster, *b* 1975, —— Edward Anthony, *b* 1976.

Issue of late Norman Carse Marr, *b* 1910, *d* 1980: *m* 1935, Flora McDonald, who *d* 1985, da of Kenneth McDonald Cameron, of West Hartlepool:—
Jeremy Norman (4430 Piccadilly, W Vancouver, BC, Canada), *b* 1940: *m* 1968, Gillian Yvonne, only da of late P. J. Hugo, of Johannesburg, S Africa, and has issue living, Kyle Jeremy, *b* 1974, —— Jordan Hugo, *b* 1977. —— Dair Norman, *b* 1941: *m* 1964, Douglas Ian Henry Henderson, and has issue living, Stuart Philip, *b* 1968, —— Karen Frances, *b* 1966, —— Avril Louise, *b* 1971. —— Alexandra Norman, *b* 1944: *m* 1975, Ian Nicol.

Issue of late Arthur Lynn Marr, *b* 1914, *d* 1991: *m* 1941, May Victoria (12 King John's Court, Ponteland, Newcastle-upon-Tyne NE20 9AR), da of Harry Bernard Bradshaw, of St Ouen, Jersey:—
Bernard Lynn (Deneholme, Acomb Drive, Wylam, Northumberland), *b* 1943; *ed* Oundle: *m* 1968, Judith, da of late Ronald Henry Richards, of Durcroft, Wood Lane, Astwood Bank, Worcs, and has issue living, Katherine Lynn, *b* 1972, —— Jane Victoria, *b* 1974, —— Helen Judith, *b* 1979. —— Mary Singleton, *b* 1946: *m* 1972, Christopher Broom-Smith, of Auchenskeoch Lodge, Dalbeattie, Kirkcudbrightshire DG5 4PG. —— Victoria Lynn, *b* 1951: *m* 1976 (*m diss* 19—), Henry Jeremy Meadows, and has issue living, Carl Jeremy, *b* 1980, — James Arthur Henry, *b* 1983, — Joanna Lynn, *b* 1977.

The 1st baronet, Sir James Marr, CBE, was a shipbuilder, Chm of Sir James Laing & Sons, Ltd, of Sunderland, of Sunderland Forge & Engineering Co, Ltd, of T. W. Greenwell & Co, Ltd, of Sunderland and of Joseph I. Thompson & Sons Ltd, of Sunderland and a Member of Lloyd's Registry of Shipping.

SMITH-MARRIOTT (GB) 1774, of Sydling St Nicholas, Dorset

Sir HUGH CAVENDISH SMITH-MARRIOTT, 11th *Baronet, b* 22 March 1925; *s* his father, *Sir* RALPH GEORGE CAVENDISH, 1987; *ed* Bristol Cathedral Sch: *m* 1953, Pauline Anne, who *d* 1985, only da of Frank Fawcett Holt, of Abbotsway, Bristol, and has issue.

𝖆𝖗𝖒𝖘 – Quarterly: 1st and 4th, barry of six, or and sable, in chief two escallops gules, *Marriott;* 2nd and 3rd, sable, a fesse erminois cotised or, between three martlets of the last , each charged with an ermine spot, *Smith.* 𝕮𝖗𝖊𝖘𝖙 – 1st, a mount vert, thereon a talbot passant sable, guttée de larmes, collared and line reflexed over the back or; 2nd, a greyhound sejant gules, collared and a line reflexed over the back or, charged on the shoulder with a mascle argent.
Residence – 26 Shipley Rd, Westbury-on-Trym, Bristol BS9 3HS.

DAUGHTER LIVING

Semper fidelis
Always faithful

Julie Anne, *b* 1958: *m* 1978, David Anthony Graveney, and has issue living, Adam Hugh Francis, *b* 1982, — Charlotte Pauline, *b* 1986. *Residence* – 6 Southover Close, Westbury-on-Trym, Bristol.

BROTHER LIVING

PETER FRANCIS, *b* 14 Feb 1927; *ed* Bristol Cathedral Sch: *m* 1961, Jean Graham Martin, only da of James Sorley Ritchie, of Harare, Zimbabwe, and has issue living, Martin Ralph, *b* 1962, — Neil Hugh, *b* 1964, — Ian Peter, *b* 1967, — Mark Nicholas, *b* 1974, — Paul Graham, *b* (twin) 1974. *Residence* – 88 Maidenhall, Highnam, nr Gloucester.

SISTER LIVING

Doris Mary, *b* 1929: *m* 1957, Alexander Stewart MacCaig, 11 Shipley Rd, Westbury-on-Trym, Bristol, and has issue living, Helen Mary, *b* 1958: *m* 1985, John Michael Burton, and has issue living, Thomas Michael *b* 1989, Andrew Jack *b* 1992, Kathryn Anne *b* 1986, — Susan Jane, *b* 1961: *m* 1988, Dr David Richardson, and has issue living, Polly Francesca *b* 1991, Maisie Jane *b* 1994, — Anne Elizabeth, *b* 1964.

DAUGHTER LIVING OF EIGHTH BARONET *(By 2nd marriage)*

Rosemary Kathleen, *b* 1916: *m* 1944, Henry Everett, who *d* 1965 (E Galloway, colls), and has issue living, William Marriott (Roughfield Farm, Hurst Green, Sussex TN19 7QY), *b* 1946; ARICS: *m* 1976, Caroline Dawn Colley, and has issue living, George Henry Arthur *b* 1978, Cecelia Hermione Rosemary *b* 1985, — Barbara Rosemary, *b* 1948: *m* 1st, 1968, Timothy James Gerard Dyas; 2ndly, 1972, John Derek Hall; 3rdly, 1980, John Lawrence Crowell, of 22 All Farthing Lane, SW18, — Helen Rosalind, *b* 1954: *m* 1984, Jonathan David Patrick Barnes, of 7 Priory Walk, SW10.

WIDOW LIVING OF TENTH BARONET

BARBARA MARY *(Dowager Lady Smith-Marriott),* da of G. C. Brown, ACA, and widow of Lt J. A. Cantlay, DLI: *m* 1966, as his 3rd wife, Sir Ralph George Cavendish Smith-Marriott, 10th Bt, who *d* 1987. *Residence* – 28A Westover Rd, Westbury-on-Trym, Bristol.

COLLATERAL BRANCHES LIVING

    Grandchildren of late Reginald Bosworth Smith, 2nd son of Reginald Southwell Smith, 5th son of 2nd baronet:—
    Issue of late Gerard Hugh Bosworth Smith, *b* 1868, *d* 1940: *m* 1893, Olive Yates:—
Reginald Claude, *b* 1899: *m* 1929, Evelyn Whittington, of Panama City, Florida, USA, and has issue living, Reginald Claude, *b* 1930, — Wayne Edward, *b* 1932, — Evelyn Joan, *b* 1935, — Geraldine, *b* 1942. —— Ellinor Joan, *b* 1896. —— Vera Bosworth, *b* 1904: *m* 1st, 1921 (*m diss* 1923), Manuel M. Paula; 2ndly, 1925, David Joseph Keene. —— Bertha Bosworth, *b* 1908: *m* 1926, Roy Bronson.
    Issue of late Reginald Montagu Bosworth Smith, CBE, *b* 1872, *d* 1944: *m* 1st, 1905 Agnes Val, who *d* 1915, da of G. Val Davies; 2ndly, 1916, Kate Evelyn, who *d* 1975, da of late Frederick Charles Pardoe Radclyffe, of Birmingham:—
(By 2nd *m*) Reginald Bosworth, LLB, *b* 1917; BA and LLB, 1938; is a Solicitor; Middle East 1942-45 as Trooper 6th S African Armoured Div: *m* 1965, Helen Margaret, da of late Ernest R. Stidworthy, of East London, S Africa. *Address* – PO Box 577, East London, S Africa. —— Alan Bosworth, *b* 1919; is a CA (S Africa), and a FSAA; Middle East 1940-45 as Gunner S African Artillery: *m* 1949, Helen, da of John Mackenzie, of Johannesburg, and has issue living, Michael John Bosworth (30 Esmereld Rd, St Francis Bay, S Africa), *b* 1951; BA, BCom, CA S Africa: *m* 1st, 1982 (*m diss* 1985), Colleen May Hauptfleisch; 2ndly, 1985, Elizabeth Ann Ringstead, and has issue (by 2nd *m*), Matthew Edward *b* 1988, — Pamela Anne, *b* 1953; BA: *m* 1973, Keith Oliver Butler-Wheelhouse, of Cromwell House, 48 Park Drive, Port Elizabeth, S Africa, and has issue living, Duncan *b* 1981, Andrew *b* 1985. *Address* – 4 Christopherson Rd, Dunkeld, Johannesburg, S Africa. —— (By 1st *m*) Daphne Evangeline Bosworth, *b* 1909: *m* 1932, John Awdry Cottrell, OBE, Dir of African Education, Zambia 1948-58, and has issue living, Christopher Bosworth (Transvaal Museum, PO Box 413, Pretoria 0001, S Africa), *b* 1934; *ed* Rhodes Univ, S Africa (BSc), and at Queens' Coll, Camb (PhD); Junior Research Fellow, Churchill Coll 1960-61; Prof of Zoology Univ of Zimbabwe 1980-86; Head Curator of Lepidoptera, Transvaal Museum since 1986: *m* 1962, Meriol Lesley, da of Col Millard, of Taunton, and has issue living, John Gray *b* 1964, Christopher Noel *b* 1966, — Richard Gray (PO Box 2536, Johannesburg, S Africa), *b* 1935; is a Chartered Accountant, and Partner in Cooper & Lybrand, Johannesburg: *m* 1971, Moya Ann, da of George R. English, of Rochford, Essex, and has issue living, Edward Christopher *b* 1974, Peter Richard *b* 1975, — Gilbert Reginald James (Management Consultant, The Corporate Consulting Group (Pty) Ltd, 604 Boland Bank Building, Lower Burg St, Cape Town, S Africa), *b* 1944; *ed* Queen's Coll, Camb (BA), and Columbia Univ, New York (MBA): *m* 1971, Phoebe Madelaire, da of Dr Tage Madelaire Nielsen, of New London, Conn, USA, and has issue living, Ariel Daphne *b* 1974, Miranda Claire *b* 1977. *Address* – Red Cross Home, 302 Main Rd, Walmer 6070, Port Elizabeth, Cape Prov, S Africa. —— Ursula Gwendolin Bosworth (21 2nd Av, Linden, Johannesburg 2195, S Africa), *b* 1911: *m* 1st, 1934 (*m diss* 1947), Arnold Lingen Watson, solicitor; 2ndly, 1947, William Patrick Temple Scott, who *d* 1971, and has issue living (by 1st *m*),

Toni Elaine (21 2nd Av, Linden, Johannesburg 2195, S Africa), b 1936: m 1957, Maj Jeremy Alexander Keble White Frere, 1st R Anglian Regt, of 21 Second Av, Linden, Johannesburg 2195, S Africa, and has issue living, Martin Adrian b 1958; ed Witwatersrand Univ (BSc): m 1987, Anabel, da of Patrick Warren-Gash, of Worthing Sussex.

    Issue of late Bertrand Nigel Bosworth Smith, b 1873, d 1947: m 1912 (m diss 1932), Mary Constance, who d 1961, da of late David Inche-Bett, of New Hall, Forfarshire:—

Mary Nigella, b 1913: m 1946 (m diss 1960), Peter de Lande Long, FRICS, FLAS, and has issue living, Ian Bartholomew (c/o ESA, Darmstadt, W Germany), b 1949; ed Winchester and York Univ (MA): m 1970, Marjorie, da of Dr Hamilton, of Dublin, — Jonathan (Moore Stephens, Leidersdorf, NY, USA), b 1951; ed Winchester and London Univ; ACA: m 1978, Marianne Skuzinski, — Peter Graeme, b 1952; ed Winchester and Trin Coll, Camb; MICE. ——— Janet Wickham, b 1918: m 1939, Claude Scott Nicol, CBE, TD, MD, FRCP, late Col RAMC (V), and has issue living, Alasdair Gordon b 1944: m 1974, Julie Mayston Collings, of Essendon, Melbourne, Aust, and has issue living, Stuart b 1977, — Judy, b 1943: m 1966, John Diggory de Bourbel Rochfort, of White Ways, Headley, Newbury, and has issue living, Christopher Michael b 1969, Jeremy b 1971, James b 1974, — Melany, b 1946: m 1973, Piers Hayward Hughes, of 43 Priory Rd, Kew, Richmond, Surrey, and has issue living, Robert b 1976, Katherine Melany b 1974. Residence – 40 Ferncroft Av, Hampstead, NW3.

    Issue of late Mervyn Henry Bosworth Smith, b 1878, d 1950: m 1st, 1914 (m diss 1919), Sophie, da of John Warmington, of Ninnes, Lelant, Cornwall; 2ndly, 1920 (m diss 1926), Mary Annette Morcum, of Johannesburg, S Africa; 3rdly, 1927, Sarah Aletta, da of H. W. Fourie, of Johannesburg, S Africa:—

(By 2nd m) †Anthony Mervyn Bosworth, b 1925: m 1951, Jean Rosemary, el da of A. Peerman, of Erin Stables, Sandown, Johannesburg, S Africa, and d 1992, leaving issue, Mervyn Nigel Bosworth, b 1957; ed Univ of Natal (BSc) (Civil Engineering) 1981: m 1984, Maryna Elizabeth van Niekerk, and has issue living, Sadie Elizabeth b 1987, Jessica Danielle b 1989, — Gwen Bridget, b 1953: m 1981, Ian Watson, of Tarry-a-While, 33 Buckingham Rd, Kloof, Natal, and has issue living, Cameron Nicholas b 1983, Oliver Hylton b 1986. Residence – Blesbok Ridge, PO Box 132, Nottingham Road, Natal 3280, S Africa.

    Issue of late Nevil Digby Bosworth Smith, CB, b 1886, d 1964: m 1913, Gladys, who d 1965, da of late John Francis Wood, of Uffculme, Devon:—

Richard Nevil BOSWORTH-SMITH (7 Hillside Rd, Northwood, Middlesex), b 1926; ed Harrow, and Balliol Coll, Oxford (MA); assumed the additional surname of Bosworth 1969: m 1960, Anne, el da of late John Ree, of Pinner, Middx, and has issue living, Nevil John Bosworth, b 1961, — Mary Margaret Bosworth b 1964.

      Grandsons of late Capt Hugh Francis Wyldbore WYLDBORE-SMITH, RN, eldest son of late Rev Francis Alfred Smith, eldest son of late Rev Francis Smith, 6th son of 2nd baronet—

    Issue of late Lt-Cdr Hugh Deane WYLDBORE-SMITH, RN, b 1907, who was ka 1941: m 1937, Rachel Caroline Lucy (The White House, Husborne Crawley, Beds), el da of late Rev Edward Yarde Orlebar, of Crawley Park, Beds:—

Nicolas Hugh WYLDBORE-SMITH (The Courtiers, Clifton Hampden, Abingdon, Oxon), b 1938; ed Wellington, and St James, Maryland, USA: m 1964, Gillian Mary, da of late Leslie Carman, of Fareham, Hants, and has issue living, Alexander Hugh Nicolas, b 1969, — James William, b 1971.

    Issue of late John Henry Wyldbore-Smith, b 1916; d 1982: m 1939, Robina, who d 1993, da of late Capt Francis Welsford Ward, of Bosloe, Cornwall:—

William Francis WYLDBORE-SMITH (Bremhill Manor, Calne, Wilts; Brooks's Club), b 1948; ed Marlborough: m 1974, Mrs Prisca Faith Jenney, yr da of Rev Peter Nourse, of Leominster, Herefordshire, and has issue living, Philippa, b 1977. ——— Robina Ann, b 1943: m 1977, (Richard Robert) Bindon Plowman, and has issue living, Andrew John Napier, b 1979, — Felicity Frances Robina, b 1980. ——— Susan Elizabeth, b 1950.

      Grandsons of late Rev Francis Alfred Smith, eldest son of late Rev Francis Smith, 6th son of 2nd baronet:—

    Issue of late Rev William Reginald Wyldbore Smith, b 1874, d 1943: m 1905, Dorothy, who d 1969, da of late George Green, of Watford Field House, Watford:—

†(Reginald) Anthony Wyldbore, b 1909: m 1933, Honor Christine Dyott, who d 1984, da of late George Wilmot, of Coleshill, Warwicks, and d 1987, leaving issue, Michael Anthony Wyldbore WYLDBORE-SMITH (Moat Cottage, Berkswell, W Midlands CV7 7BX), b 1944; ed Cheltenham; assumed by deed poll 1969 the additional surname of Wyldbore: m 1967, Sheila Margaret, da of E.C.H. Organ, of Kenilworth, and has issue living, Sarah b 1969, Nicola b 1971, Claire b 1977. ——— Sir Francis Brian Wyldbore WYLDBORE-SMITH, CB, DSO, OBE (Grantham House, Grantham, Lincs; Naval and Military and Buck's Clubs), b 1913; ed Wellington, and RMA, Woolwich; assumed by deed poll 1966, the additional surname of Wyldbore; Maj-Gen, late RHA and 15th/19th KR Hussars (Comdg 1953-56, Col since 1970); Ch to Staff to C-in-C, Far East 1963-65; GOC 44th Inf Div and Home Cos Dist, and Dep Constable of Dover Castle 1965-68; ret 1968; 1939-45 War in Middle East, Italy and NW Europe (MBE, DSO, OBE); MBE (Mil) 1943, DSO 1944, OBE (Mil) 1945, CB (Mil) 1965; cr Knt 1980: m 1944, Hon Molly Angela Cayzer, da of 1st Baron Rotherwick, and has issue living, Brian Robin, b 1957, — Carolyn Molly, b 1944: m 1968, Harry O. Ditson, and has issue living, Sam Lennie b 1984, Lucy Rebecca b 1975, Melissa Martha b 1978, — Angela Maureen, b 1947: m 1975, Barrie Giffard-Taylor, of Barnbridge Farm, East Tytherton, Chippenham, Wilts, and has issue living, James William b 1982, Jemima Alice b 1977, Emily Victoria b 1979, — Penelope Ann, b 1948: m 1973, James E. Herdman, only son of late John Patrick Herdman, of Carricklee House, co Tyrone, and has issue living, Emerson John b 1979, Katherine Louise b 1977, — Nicola Jane, b 1952.

      Grandchildren of late Rev Heathcote Smith, son of Maj Edward Heathcote Smith, 7th son of 2nd baronet:—

    Issue of late Sir Clifford Edward Heathcote-Smith, KBE, CMG, b 1883, d 1963: m 1909, Elaine, who d 1967, da of late John J. Spiegethal de Fonton, of Cannes:—

Clifford Bertram Bruce HEATHCOTE-SMITH, CBE (4 Britts Farm Rd, Buxted, E Sussex), b 1912; ed Malvern, and at Pembroke Coll, Camb; late HM Diplo Ser; acting Senior Clerk, House of Commons; CBE (Civil) 1963: m 1940, Thelma Joyce Engström, and has issue living, Charles Clifford Ralph, b 1949, — Max Christopher, b 1950: m 1982, Drusilla Mary Derrick. ——— Elaine Mary Elizabeth, b 1914: m 1936, Rear Adm Roger Stanley Wellby, CB, DSO, DL, of Oakengrove, Hastoe, Tring, Herts HP23 6LY, and has issue living, Anthony William b 1969, Kate d'Esterre b 1968, — Christopher Mark, b 1943; ed Ch Ch, Oxford: m 1982, Barbara, da of Frank Elston, of Liverpool, and has issue living, Peter Nicholas Elston b 1986, Jack William Heathcote b 1988, — Peter Martin Heathcote, b 1946; ed Ch Ch, Oxford: m 1988, Helen Matson.

The 1st baronet, Sir John Smith (son of late Henry Smith, of New Windsor, Berks), was High Sheriff of Dorset 1772. The 4th baronet, Sir William Marriott, assumed, by sign manual 1811, the additional surname and arms of Marriott, and the 5th was High Sheriff of Dorset 1873.

MARSDEN (UK) 1924, of Grimsby, co Lincoln

Thanks to God

Sir NIGEL JOHN DENTON MARSDEN, 3rd *Baronet*; *b* 26 May 1940; *s* his father, *Sir* JOHN DENTON, 1985; *ed* Ampleforth: *m* 1961, Diana Jean, elder da of Air Marshal Sir Patrick Hunter Dunn, KBE, CB, DFC, and has issue.

𝕬rms – Sable, a fesse dancettée ermine, in chief two fleur-de-lis argent and in base a ship sailing to the sinister proper. 𝕮rest – In front of a unicorn's head erased sable charged with two barrulets gules as many roses argent, barbed and seeded proper.
Residence – 1 Grimsby Rd, Waltham, Grimsby, South Humberside DN37 0PS.

DAUGHTER LIVING

Lucinda Ann, *b* 1962. —— Rose Amanda, *b* 1964. —— Annabel Juliet, *b* 1968.

BROTHER LIVING

SIMON NEVILLE LLEWELYN (The Presbytery, Hainton, Lincoln LN3 6LR), *b* 1 Dec 1948; *ed* Ampleforth and Sorbonne, Paris: *m* 1st, 1970 (*m diss* 1978), Catherine Thérèsa, yr da of late Brig James Charles Windsor-Lewis, DSO, MC (*see* B Burnham, 1969 Edn); 2ndly, 1984, Caroline, yst da of John Stanton, of Houghton St Giles, Walsingham, Norfolk, and has issue living (by 2nd *m*), Tadgh Orlando Denton, *b* 25 Dec 1990, — Skye Atalanta, *b* 1988.

SISTERS LIVING

Vanessa Ann (The Bothy, Tullichettle, Comrie, Perthshire), *b* 1941: *m* 1968 (*m diss* 19—), Francis John Whitehead, son of Maj Thomas B. Whitehead, of Chisbury Farm, nr Marlborough, Wilts, and has issue living, Mark John Bovil, *b* 1975. —— Caroline Jane, *b* 1946: *m* 1970, Richard Thomas Widdowson Noton, of Bockingham Hall, Copford, Colchester, Essex CO6 1DR, and has issue living, Charles Richard Marsden, *b* 1975, — Henrietta Caroline Marsden, *b* 1979.

AUNT LIVING (*Daughter of 1st baronet*)

Agnes Isabelle, *b* 1920: *m* 1941, Capt Frederick William Tackaberry Storey, RASC, only son of Rev John William Storey, of Staplegrove Rectory, Taunton, and has issue living, Michael William Tackaberry, *b* 1942; *ed* Sherborne, — Jonathan William Tackaberry *b* 1948; *ed* Sherborne, — Alastair William Tackaberry, *b* 1949, — Jane Patricia, *b* 1951, — Penelope Caroline, *b* 1953, — Sally Anne, *b* 1957. *Residence* – Baymead Cottage, 2 Baymead Lane, North Pemberton, nr Bridgwater, Somerset.

WIDOW LIVING OF SECOND BARONET

HOPE (*Hope, Lady Marsden*), yr da of late G. E. Llewelyn, of Bryngawr, Aberkenfig, Glamorgan: *m* 1939, Sir John Denton Marsden, 2nd Bt, who *d* 1985. *Residence* – Wold Cottage, Greetham, nr Horncastle, Lincs.

The 1st baronet, Sir John Denton Marsden (son of William Dent Marsden, of Aldmondbury, Huddersfield), was Principal of Consolidated Fisheries Ltd, of Grimsby, Swansea and Lowestoft.

Mather-Jackson, see Jackson.

MATHESON (UK) 1882, of Lochalsh, co Ross

FAC ET SPERA

O'CHIAN

Do and hope

Sir FERGUS JOHN MATHESON OF MATHESON, 7th *Baronet*; Ch of Clan Matheson; *b* 22 Feb 1927; *s* his brother, *Maj Sir* TORQUHIL ALEXANDER, 1993; *ed* Eton; Maj Coldm Gds 1945-64; a Member of HM's Body Guard of the Hon Corps of Gentlemen at Arms since 1979, Standard Bearer since 1993: *m* 1952, Hon Jean Elizabeth Mary Willoughby, JP, yr da of 11th Baron Middleton, KG, MC, and has issue.

Arms – Gyronny of eight sable and gules, a lion rampant or, armed and langued azure, overall on a canton argent a dexter hand appaumée gules. **Crest** – Issuant from an antique crown or a hand brandishing a scimitar fessways all proper. **Supporters** – Two brown bears proper, each gorged with an antique crown or.
Residence – The Old Rectory, Hedenham, Bungay, Suffolk NR35 2LD.
Club – Army and Navy.

SON LIVING

ALEXANDER FERGUS, YR OF MATHESON, *b* 26 Aug 1954; *ed* Eton, and Durham Univ; Maj Coldm Gds; temporary Equerry to HM The Queen 1982-84; Chief of Staff British Forces Belize 1992-94: *m* 1983, Katharine Davina Mary, only da of (William Richard) Michael Oswald, CVO (*see* M Exeter), and has issue living, Andrew William Fergus, *b* 12 March 1985, — Archie James Torquhil, *b* 1987, — Louisa Alexandra Matilda, *b* 1989.

DAUGHTERS LIVING

Elizabeth Angela Matilda, *b* 1953: *m* 1978, Martin Claude Thompson, of The Old Rectory, Little Bytham, Lincs, elder son of late Maj E. C. O. Thompson, and has issue living, Charles Guy Martin, *b* 1981, — Mara Angela Matilda, *b* 1979, — Siana Camilla Elizabeth, *b* 1989. —— Fiona Jean Lucia, *b* 1962: *m* 1986, Andrew Thomas Kendall, of 49 Lansdowne Gdns, SW8, elder son of John Kendall, of Danybryn, Vaynor, Merthyr Tydfil, Glam, and has issue living, Edmund Andrew Fergus, *b* 1991, — Lucia Amelia Fiona, *b* 1988.

DAUGHTERS LIVING OF SIXTH BARONET

Eleanor Mary Francesca, *b* 1955. —— Isobel Sophia, *b* 1957: *m* 1986, William George Craven, of 16 Allotment Lane, Castor, Peterborough, Cambs PE5 7AS, 2nd son of John Craven, MRCVS, and has issue living, Frances Elizabeth, *b* 1987, — Emily Flora, *b* 1989.

WIDOW LIVING OF SIXTH BARONET

SERENA MARY FRANCESCA (*Serena, Lady Matheson of Matheson*), only child of late Lt-Col Sir (James) Michael Peto, 2nd Bt (*cr* 1927): *m* 1954, Sir Torquhil Alexander Matheson of Matheson, 6th Bt, DL, who *d* 1993. *Residence* – Trees Farm, Standerwick, Frome, Somerset BA11 2PT.

Mathesons occupied the lands of Lochalsh from the 13th century. Their chief being one of those arrested and executed at Inverness in 1427, the estates were granted to Celestine of The Isles, whose granddaughter, Margaret, conveyed the half to her husband Macdonell of Glengarry. John Matheson, who in 1728 married, as his second wife, Margaret Mackenzie, a descendant of this marriage, acquired Attadale in 1730. Their great-grandson and heir male, Alexander Matheson, a partner in Jardine Matheson, and Matheson & Co, having in 1851, purchased Lochalsh, was created a baronet under that designation in 1882. He sat as MP for Inverness District (*L*) 1847-68, and for Ross and Cromarty 1868-84. Sir Alexander Perceval Matheson, 3rd Bt, was a Senator of Commonwealth of Australia. Gen Sir Torquhil George Matheson, KCB, CMG, 5th Bt, commanded 3rd Coldstream Guards, 46th Inf Bde, 20th Light, 4th and Guards Divs, 1914-18, Waziristan Field Force 1920-24, and was GOC in C W Command, India, 1931-35. He also commanded a company of the 2nd Batn Ross-shire HG 1940-42, covering S W Ross-shire. Maj Sir Torquhil Alexander Matheson of Matheson, 6th Bt, *s* his kinsman, Col Bertram Matheson of Matheson, MC, as Ch of Clan Matheson by tanistry 1975; Member HM's Body Guard of Hon Corps of Gentlemen-at-Arms, Clerk of the Cheque and Adjutant.

MATHIAS (UK) 1917, of Vaendre Hall, St Mellons, co Monmouth (Extinct 1991)

Sir RICHARD HUGHES MATHIAS, 2nd *Baronet*; *d* 4 Jan 1991.

DAUGHTERS LIVING OF SECOND BARONET

Anna Patricia (35 Ifield Rd, SW10), *b* 1938: *m* 1962 (*m diss* 1971), Lt-Cdr Eric Clive Hastings, RN, and has issue living, Nichola Jane, *b* 1964. —— Virginia Turton, *b* 1942.

MAXWELL (NS) 1681, of Monreith, Wigtownshire

I renew my strength

Sir MICHAEL EUSTACE GEORGE MAXWELL, 9th *Baronet*; *b* 28 Aug 1943; *s* his uncle, *Capt Sir* AYMER, 1987; *ed* Eton, and London Univ; ARICS.

Arms – Argent, an eagle with two heads displayed sable, beaked and membered gules; on the breast an escutcheon of the first, charged with a saltire of the second, surcharged in the centre with a hurcheon (hedgehog), or, all within a bordure gules. **Crest** – An eagle rising proper.
Seat – Monreith House, Port William, Newton Stewart DG8 9LB, Wigtownshire. *Residences* – Laundry House, Farming Woods, Brigstock, Northants NN14 3JA; 56 Queensmill Rd, SW6 6JS.

SISTER LIVING

Diana Mary, *b* 1942; has issue living (by Patrick Helmore), Katharine Diana, *b* 1984, — Charlotte Jessica, *b* (twin) 1984. *Residence* – 15 Cupar Rd, SW11.

MOTHER LIVING

Dorothy Vivien, elder da of late Capt George Ernest Bellville, JP, of Fermyn Woods Hall, Northants: *m* 1940 (*m diss* 1949), Maj Eustace Maxwell, Argyll & Sutherland Highrs, yr brother of 8th Bt, who *d* 1971. *Residence* – Fermyn Woods Hall, Brigstock, Northants.

COLLATERAL BRANCH LIVING

Descendants, if any, of Alexander Charles Maxwell, yr son of Maj Hamilton Maxwell, BSc (*d* 1829), 3rd son of 4th baronet, who left issue four sons.

The Maxwells of Monreith derive from Sir Edward Maxwell of Tinwald, co Dumfries, yr son of 1st Lord Maxwell (*cr* 1440) ancestor of the Earls of Nithsdale (*see* L Herries). The Maxwells of Tinwald became ext in early 18th century. Herbert Maxwell, yr brother of Edward Maxwell of Tinwald, *m* 1541, Margaret Maxwell, heir of Monreith. Fourth in descent from whom was the 1st baronet, Sir William. The 7th baronet, Rt Hon Sir Herbert, KT, PC, LLD, DCL, FRS, was Lord-Lieut of Wigtownshire 1903-35, MP for Wigtownshire (*C*) 1880-1906, and a Lord of the Treasury 1886-92.

Maxwell (Constable-Maxwell-Scott), see Scott.

HERON-MAXWELL, (NS) 1683, of Springkell, Dumfriesshire

May it flourish again

Sir NIGEL MELLOR HERON-MAXWELL, 10th *Baronet*; *b* 30 Jan 1944; *s* his father, *Sir* PATRICK IVOR, 1982; *ed* Milton Abbey: *m* 1972, Mary Elizabeth Angela, only da of William Ewing, of co Donegal, and has issue.

Arms – Quarterly: 1st and 4th, argent, on a saltire sable, an annulet or, stoned azure; in base, a crescent of the second; all within a bordure gules charged with eight bezants, *Maxwell*, 2nd and 3rd, gules, on a bend argent a rose between two lions passant gules, *Heron*. **Crest** – A dexter hand proper holding an eagle's neck erased with two heads sable. **Supporters** – Two eagles close-reguardant sable.
Residence – 105 Codicote Rd, Welwyn, Herts AL6 9TY.

SON LIVING

DAVID MELLOR, *b* 22 May 1975.

DAUGHTER LIVING

Claire Louise, *b* 1977.

BROTHERS LIVING

Colin Mellor, *b* 1952; *ed* Down House: *m* 1976, Angela, only da of Sabin Nistor, of Petrosani, Rumania, and has issue living, Kirsten Diana, *b* 1982, — Hayley Claudia, *b* 1983. —— Paul Mellor, *b* 1957; *ed* Knights Templar.

AUNT LIVING (*Daughter of 8th baronet*)

Rachel Mary, *b* 1922: *m* 1947, Roy Martin Macnab, D Litt et Phil, FRSA, and has issue living, Simon Martin, *b* 1955, — Celia Mary, *b* 1949: *m* 1988 (*m diss* 1993), Brian John Weller. *Address* – 9/86 Elm Park Gdns, SW10 9PD.

WIDOW LIVING OF NINTH BARONET

DOROTHY GERALDINE EMMA (*Geraldine, Lady Heron-Maxwell*) (9 Cowslip Hill, Letchworth, Herts), yr da of late Claud Paget Mellor: *m* 1942, Sir Patrick Ivor Heron-Maxwell, 9th Bt, who *d* 1982.

COLLATERAL BRANCH LIVING

Granddaughter of late Capt John Heron Maxwell-Heron, el son of late Rev Michael Heron Maxwell-Heron, 4th son of 4th baronet:—
Issue of late Capt Basil Charles Montagu Maxwell-Heron, *b* 1878, *ka* 1916: *m* 1905, Mary, who *d* 1957, da of late Garrett O'Byrne:—
Rita Steuart Mary *b* 1905: *m* 1927, Antony William Hamilton Nelson, Pilot-Officer RAF and has issue living, John Edward Arthur Hamilton, *b* 1935, — Patricia Anne, *b* 1930: *m* 19—, P. L. Braine, — Sheila Steuart Mary, *b* 1932: *m* 19—, J. C. Horrocks. *Residence* – 7, Sutton Court, Chiswick, W4.

This baronet is head in the male line of Maxwells of Pollock, and Chief of the Clydesdale Maxwells. The 4th baronet, Sir John, assumed the additional surname and arms of Heron, having *m* 1802, Mary, da and heir of Patrick Heron of Heron in Kirouchtree. Sir John 7th baronet, was Capt 15th Hussars, and a Member of HM's Body Guard for Scotland (Roy Co of Archers).

STIRLING-MAXWELL (NS) 1682 and (NS) 1707, of Pollock, Renfrewshire (Dormant 1956)

Sir JOHN MAXWELL STIRLING-MAXWELL, KT, 10th *Baronet, d* 30 May 1956.

DAUGHTER LIVING OF TENTH BARONET

Anne, *b* 1906: *m* 1930, John Moreton-Macdonald (now Maxwell Macdonald) (*see* E Ducie, colls), and has issue living, JOHN RONALD (Gortinanane House, Tayinloan, Argyll PA29 6XG) *b* 22 May 1936; eventual heir to the baronetcy under the terms of the 1707 remainder; *ed* Winchester: *m* 1964, Eleanor Ruth, da of T. B. Laird, and has issue living, John Ranald *b* 1965, Angus *b* 1967, Victoria Anne *b* 1971, — Donald, *b* 1938 (*see* E Ducie, colls). *Residence* – Gortinanane House, Tayinloan, Argyll PA29 6XG.

COLLATERAL BRANCHES LIVING (*Males and Females in remainder*)

Grandchildren of late Brig-Gen Archibald Stirling of Keir (infra):—
Issue of late Lt-Col William Joseph Stirling of Keir, *b* 1911; *d* 1983: *m* 1940, Susan Rachael, who *d* 1983, da of Lt-Col Hon Noel Gervase Bligh, DSO (E Darnley):—
Archibald Hugh STIRLING OF KEIR (Ochtertyre, Stirling FK9 4UN), *b* 1941; *ed* Ampleforth: *m* 1st, 1964 (*m diss* 1977), Charmian Rachel, yr da of Lord George Francis John Montagu-Douglas-Scott (*see* D Buccleuch); 2ndly, 1982 (*m diss* 1993), Enid Diana Elizabeth (later Dame Diana Rigg, DBE), da of late Louis Rigg, and formerly wife of Menachem Gueffen, and has issue living (by 1st *m*), William Rory Alexander, *b* 1965, — Ludovic David, *b* 1967, — (by 2nd *m*) Rachael Atlanta, *b* 1977. —— John Alexander, *b* 1948: *m* 1st, 1971, Mrs Susan Burton, only da of Edmund Black, of Johannesburg; 2ndly, 1985, Olivia Louise, da of Maj Patrick Waller, and has issue living (by 2nd *m*), Joseph Patrick William, *b* 1985, — Hugh David Archibald, *b* 1993, — Christabel Georgia, *b* 1987. —— Hannah Ann (*Viscountess Cranborne*), *b* 1944: *m* 1970, Robert Michael James, Viscount Cranborne, el son of 6th Marquess of Salisbury. —— Magdalen, *b* 1945: *m* 1969, Patrick Petit, and has issue living, Benjamin, *b* 19—.

Issue of late Brig-Gen Archibald STIRLING OF KEIR, 2nd son of 9th baronet *b* 1867, *d* 1931: *m* 1910, Hon Margaret Fraser, OBE, who *d* 1973, da of 13th Lord Lovat:—
Margaret Elizabeth Mary (*Countess of Dalhousie*), *b* 1914; is a CStJ: *m* 1940, 16th Earl of Dalhousie. *Residence* – Brechin Castle, Brechin, Angus.

This family is of the oldest branch of the Maxwells, Earls of Nithsdale. Sir John Maxwell of Pollok distinguished himself at an early age in chivalry, especially at the celebrated battle of Otterburn, or Chevy Chase (1388), where he captured Sir Ralph Percy, son of the Earl of Northumberland, and brother of the renowned "Hotspur". The Baronetcy was first conferred in 1682 upon John Maxwell of Pollok (son of Sir George Maxwell), with remainder to heirs of the body, but a further patent was issued in 1707 extending remainder to heirs of entail in his lands and estates. The 9th baronet, Sir William Stirling-Maxwell, who as heir of entail succeeded under the special limitation, was MP for Perthshire (*C*) 1852-68 and 1874-8, and received as a Commoner the exceptional honour of being created a KT. Sir John Maxwell Stirling-Maxwell was MP for Coll Div of Glasgow (*C*) 1895-1906 and was also created a KT.

MEDLYCOTT (UK) 1808, of Ven House, Somerset

He that sows in tears shall reap

in joy

Sir MERVYN TREGONWELL MEDLYCOTT, 9th *Baronet*, son of late Thomas Anthony Hutchings Medlycott, 2nd son of 7th baronet; *b* 20 Feb 1947; *s* his uncle, Sir (JAMES) CHRISTOPHER, 1986; Fellow Soc of Genealogists; Memb AGRA; Pres (formerly Founder and Hon Sec 1975-77, Chm 1977-84, and Vice-Pres 1984-86), Somerset & Dorset Family History Soc.

Arms – Quarterly, per fesse indented gules and azure, three lions rampant, two and one, argent. **Crest** – Out of a mural crown gules a demi-eagle with wings elevated or.
Residence – The Manor House, Sandford Orcas, Sherborne, Dorset DT9 4SB.

SISTERS LIVING

Julia Elizabeth, *b* 1939: *m* 1965 (*m diss* 1986), Michael John Bazeley Smith, and has issue living, Timothy John Medlycott, *b* 1966, — Philip Anthony Medlycott, *b* 1971, — Catherine Frances Sarah, *b* 1968. *Residence* – Edmondsham House, Edmondsham, Cranborne, Wimborne, Dorset BH21 5RE. —— Philadelphia Jane, *b* 1941: *m* 1967, Rupert Oliver, and has issue living, Kim, *b* 1970, — Philadelphia Jo, *b* 1972. *Residence* – The Residence, Kenchester, Hereford HR4 7QJ. —— Sarah Nell, *b* 1944: *m* 1971, Kenneth Dale Ritchey, and has issue living, Jonathan Dale, *b* 1975, — Emily Jane, *b* 1977. *Address* – 112 Wright Rd, Beckley, W Virginia 25801, USA.

MOTHER LIVING

Cecilia Mary, da of late Maj Cecil Harold Eden, of Tregonwell Lodge, Cranborne, Dorset: *m* 1938, Thomas Anthony Hutchings Medlycott, who *d* 1970, 2nd son of 7th baronet. *Residence* – Cowleaze, Edmondsham, Wimborne, Dorset BH21 5RE.

This family descends from James Medlycott, of Ven House, Milborne Port, Som, Master in Chancery, and MP for Milborne Port 1710-22. His son Thomas, of Ven House, *d* 1763 without surviving issue, and settled his estates on his maternal nephew, Thomas Hutchings, who accordingly adopted the name and arms of Medlycott. His son, Sir William Coles Medlycott, 1st Bt, was MP for Milborne Port 1790-91.

MELLOR (UK) 1924, of Culmhead, Somerset (Extinct 1990)

Sir JOHN FRANCIS MELLOR, 3rd *Baronet*; *d* 8 Nov 1990.

WIDOW LIVING OF THIRD BARONET

ALIX MARIE (*Lady Mellor*), da of late Charles François Villaret, of London W1: *m* 1948, Sir John Francis Mellor, 3rd Bt, who *d* 1990. *Residence* – Birchlea, Lone Oak, Redehall Rd, Smallfield, Horley, Surrey.

STUART-MENTETH (UK) 1838, of Closeburn, Dumfriesshire, and Mansfield, Ayrshire

Whilst I live I hope

Sub sole nihil

Nothing under the sun

Sir JAMES WALLACE STUART-MENTETH, 6th *Baronet*; *b* 13 Nov 1922; *s* his father, Sir WILLIAM FREDERICK, 1952; *ed* Fettes Coll, St Andrews Univ, and Trin Coll, Oxford (MA); sometime Lieut Scots Guards; European War 1939-44 in N Africa and Italy (wounded): *m* 1949, (Dorothy) Patricia, da of late Frank Grieves Warburton, of Thorrington, Stirling, and has issue.

Arms – Quarterly: 1st and 4th, or, a bend chequy argent and sables 2nd and 3rd, azure, three buckles or; the whole within a bordure gules. **Crest** – A lymphad sable.
Residence – Nutwood, Auchencairn, Castle Douglas, Kirkcudbrightshire DG7 1QZ.

SONS LIVING

CHARLES GREAVES (Hillend House, Dalry, Ayrshire KA24 5JR), *b* 25 Nov 1950; *ed* Trin Coll, Oxford: *m* 1976, Nicola Mary Jane, da of Vincent Charles Raleigh St Lawrence, of 102 Exeter St, Salisbury, and has issue living Alice Clare, *b* 1977, — Celia Jane, *b* 1978, — Sarah Harriet, *b* 1982. —— (William) Jeremy, *b* 1953: *m* 19—, Rosalind, eldest da of J. Lane, of Ruislip, Middlesex, and has issue living, James William, *b* 1987, — Lucy Ann, *b* 1985.

BROTHER LIVING

Charles Granville (Woodchester House, Woodchester, Glos, RAC), *b* 1928: *ed* Oxford Univ (BA); late 2nd Lt Scots Guards; Underwriting Member of Lloyd's: *m* 1963, Priscilla Helen, el da of late Thomas Newman, of Widdicombe House, Kingsbridge, Devon (*see* Newman, Bt, *cr* 1836), and has issue living, James William Francis, *b* 1965, — Alexander Granville, *b* 1971, — Alice Caroline, *b* 1969.

SISTER LIVING

Ludivina Frances, *b* 1927: *m* 1947, Capt William Sawbridge How, Hon Artillery Co, who *d* 1990, and has issue living, Stuart Sawbridge, *b* 1950, — Anthony Edward, *b* 1951, — Helen Frances, *b* 1955.

COLLATERAL BRANCHES LIVING

Grandchildren of late Walter Erskine Stuart-Menteth (infra):—
Issue of late Maj Walter Granville Stuart-Menteth, *b* 1906, *d* 1970: *m* 1st, 1937 (*m diss* 1950), Marianne Marguerite, who *d* 1975, da of Jules Cuenod, of La Tour de Peilz, Switzerland; 2ndly, 1957, Edith Pauline, da of James Harold Wadsworth:—
(By 1st *m*) Charles Henry, *b* 1938; *ed* Rugby. —— James Sleigh, *b* 1940: *m* 1968, Barbara Richardson. —— Marie Octavia, *b* 1939.

Issue of late Walter Erskine Stuart-Menteth, 4th son of 4th baronet, *b* 1877, *d* 1956: *m* 1905, Violet Grace, who *d* 1970, yst da Henry Lafone, formerly of 59 Onslow Sq, SW:—
Henry Alexander, DSC (16 Inverleith Terr, Edinburgh 3), *b* 1912; Cdr RN; 1939-45 War despatches, DSC: *m* 1952, Penelope, only da of Digby Giles, of Toorak, Melbourne, Aust, and has issue living, Andrew Alexander (18 Marion St, Brighton, Melbourne, Vic 3186, Australia), *b* 1954: *m* 1988, Pamela, da of Capt J. C. Chapman, of Melbourne, Australia, and has issue living, James Alexander *b* 1989, Lucy Linda *b* 1990, — Walter Henry, *b* 1957, — Harriet Lucy, *b* 1959: *m* 1991, James H. Brennan, 2nd son of Lt-Col M. W. Brennan, of Painswick, Glos, and has issue living, Thomas Michael *b* 1992. —— Lucy Violet, *b* 1911: *m* 1942, Maj Donald Brain, Princess Patricia's Canadian LI, who was *ka* 1943, and has issue living, Donald Rowan, *b* 1943; *ed* Fettes. *Residence* – Crossways, Godstone, Surrey.
This family is lineally descended in the male line from Walter (third son of Walter, Lord High Steward of Scotland), who *m* 1258 the Countess of Menteth, and thus acquired that earldom. He left two sons, who both assumed the surname of Menteth, viz, Alexander, 6th Earl of Menteth, and Sir John Menteth, Lord of Arran, etc, who *m* Elyne, daughter of Gratney, Earl of Mar, and whose granddaughter, Janet Keith, *m* Robert, 1st Lord Erskine, and thus the Erskines acquired the earldom of Mar. Sir John Menteth of Ruskie (who *d* before 1333), from whom the Stuart-Menteths trace their descent, was a yr brother of Alexander, 6th Earl of Menteth. This Earldom was forfeited on the execution of Murdoch Stewart, Duke of Albany in 1425. The father of the 1st baronet, Rev James Stuart-Menteath, assumed by sign-manual, in 1770 the additional surname of Stuart "for himself and his posterity." The 2nd baronet resumed the ancient name of Menteth, but his two yst brothers retained the name of Menteath. Sir James, 3rd baronet, became a naturalized American.

METCALFE (UK) 1802, of Chilton, Berkshire (Extinct 1979)

Sir THEOPHILUS JOHN METCALFE, 8th and last *Baronet*.

SISTER LIVING OF EIGHTH BARONET

Peggy Theophila, LVO, OBE, *b* 1920; ret from FCO 1980; 1939-45 War as Senior Com ATS (MBE); MBE (Mil) 1945, OBE (Civ) 1974, LVO 1980. *Residence* – Scribbins, Benenden, Kent.

MEYER (UK) 1910, of Shortgrove, Newport, Essex

RAST · ICH · ROST · ICH

Rest not rust not

Sir ANTHONY JOHN CHARLES MEYER, MP, 3rd *Baronet*; *b* 27 Oct 1920; *s* his father, *Sir* FRANK CECIL, 1935; *ed* Eton, and New Coll, Oxford; is a Trustee of Shakespeare National Memorial Theatre; European War 1941-45 as Lieut Scots Guards (wounded); entered HM's Foreign Ser 1947; 1st Sec Paris 1956, Moscow 1957, and at Foreign Office 1958-62; PPS to Ch Sec of the Treasury (Mr Maurice Macmillan, MP) 1970-72, and to Sec of State for Employment (Rt Hon Maurice Macmillan, MP) 1972-74; Chm, Franco-British Parl Relations Cttee; MP for Eton and Slough (*C*) 1964-66, for W Flintshire 1970-83, and for Clwyd N W 1983-92; Policy Dir European Movement since 1992; Publications, "A European Technological Community 1966", "Stand Up and Be Counted" 1990, "A Federal Europe: Why Not" 1992, Founder and Dir of "Solon" 1969; Offr of Légion d'honneur 1983: *m* 1941, Barbadee Violet, only child of late A. Charles Knight, JP, FSA, of Lincoln's Inn, WC, and Herne Place, Sunningdale, Berks, and has issue.

𝕬rms – Sable, a key wards downwards or between four bezants. 𝕮rest – A cock sable, armed, combed, and wattled or, holding in the dexter claw a key as in the arms.
Residence – 9 Cottage Place, Brompton Sq, SW3 2BE. *Club* – Beefsteak.

SON LIVING

(ANTHONY) ASHLEY FRANK, *b* 23 Aug 1944; *ed* Eton: *m* 1966 (*m diss* 1979), Susan Mathilda, da of Charles Freestone, and has issue living, Sophie Mathilda Barbadee, *b* 1972.

DAUGHTERS LIVING

Carolyn-Clare Barbadee (7 Cottage Place, Brompton Sq, SW3), *b* 1943: *m* 1965 (*m diss* 1988), Charles Francis Sands, and has issue living, Robert Charles, *b* 1970, — David Francis, *b* 1974. ⸻ Tessa Violet, *b* 1955: *m* 1977, David Peter Murdoch, of 3 Luxemburg Gdns, W6, and has issue living, Iona Dorothy, *b* 1984, — Frances Evelyn *b* 1986, — Sienna Rose Adèle, *b* 1992. ⸻ Sally Minette, *b* 1961: *m* 1989, Marcus John Vergette, of Coombe Farm, Highampton, Beaworthy, Devon, only son of Nicholas Vergette.

The 1st baronet, Sir Carl Ferdinand Meyer, was a Director of National Bank of Egypt, and the 2nd baronet, Sir Frank Cecil, sat as MP for Great Yarmouth (*C*) 1924-9.

MEYRICK (UK) 1880, of Bush, Pembrokeshire
(Name pronounced "Merrick")

Without God, without anything;

God and enough

Sir DAVID JOHN CHARLTON MEYRICK, 4th *Baronet*; *b* 2 Dec 1926; *s* his father, *Col Sir* THOMAS FREDERICK, TD, DL, JP, 1983; *ed* Eton, and Trin Hall Camb (MA); formerly a Chartered Surveyor and a Land Agent: *m* 1962, Penelope Anne, el da of late Cdr John Bertram Aubrey Marsden-Smedley, RN (*see* B Westbury, colls, 1985 Edn), and has issue.

Arms – Quarterly; 1st and 4th, sable, on a chevron argent between three staves raguly or, inflamed proper, a fleur-de-lys gules between two Cornish choughs respectant also proper, *Meyrick*; 2nd and 3rd, or, a lion rampant gules, a sinister quarter quarterly 1st and 4th, gules, ten besants, three, two, and one, 2nd and 3rd argent on a mount vert, a lion passant guardant or, *Charlton*. **Crests** – 1st, a tower argent, having on its top a mount vert, and thereon a Cornish chough proper, and holding in the dexter claw a fleur-de-lys gules, *Meyrick*; 2nd, out of an eastern coronet or, a leopard's head, issuant gules, *Charlton*.
Seat – Gumfreston, Tenby, Dyfed, Wales. *Residence* – Bush House, Gumfreston, Tenby, Pembrokeshire SA70 8RA

SONS LIVING

TIMOTHY THOMAS CHARLTON, *b* 5 Nov 1963; *ed* Eton, and Bristol Univ. ⸻ Simon Edward, *b* 1965; *ed* Shrewsbury, and RAC Cirencester: *m* 1989, Jennifer Amanda, yr da of J. B. Irvine, of Thornton, Fife. ⸻ Christopher John, *b* 1967; *ed* Eton, and Trin Hall Camb.

BROTHERS LIVING

Frederick Rowland, *b* 1928; *ed* Eton, and RMA Sandhurst; Maj (ret) 15th/19th King's Roy Hussars: *m* 1985 (*m diss* 1993), Patricia Anne Busswell-Dewitte, eldest da of late Dennis William Busswell, KRRC, of Lisbon. *Residence* – 49 Harbour Villa, Goodwick, Fishguard, Dyfed. ⸻ Richard Eric, *b* 1936; *ed* Monkton Combe, and RAC Cirencester; a Chartered Surveyor: *m* 1962, Catherine Ann, el da of late Col Vivian Joseph French Popham, S Wales Borderers, of Begelly, Kilgetty, Pembs. *Residence* – Lower Helland, Bodmin, Cornwall.

HALF-BROTHER LIVING

John Herbert, *b* 1952; *ed* Abbotsholme: *m* 1982, Sandra Dawn, only da of L. V. Blackman, of Lewes, E Sussex, and has issue living, Matthew Thomas, *b* 1986, — Alistair Charles, *b* 1988. *Residence* – 63 Dawson Drive, Trimley St Mary, Ipswich.

SISTERS LIVING

Mary Joan, *b* 1930: *m* 1954, Ian Marshall Lang, and has issue living, Patrick John, *b* 1957, — Edward Nicholas, *b* 1959: *m* 1989, Louise Costin, — Ivy Frances, *b* 1960: *m* 1992, David P. C. Tennick, of Pretoria, S Africa. *Residence* – Whitewick Farm, Stogursey, Som. ⸻ Susan Ethel, *b* 1932: *m* 1954, Roland Owen-George, of Hillside, Garway, Herefs HR2 8RL. ⸻ Penelope Ann, *b* 1939: *m* 1966, Michael McGarvie, of 19 Styles Hill, Frome, Som, and has issue living, Emma Louise, *b* 1969, — Victoria Grace, *b* 1971, — Alice Katherine *b* 1974.

AUNTS LIVING (*Daughters of 2nd Baronet*)

Rachel Eva, *b* 1905: *m* 1929, Laurence Lithgow, who *d* 1972, and has issue living, James Frederick, *b* 1933, — Esther Mary, *b* 1930: *m* 19—, — Nicholson, — Ruth, *b* 1934. ⸻ Violet (*Baroness Merthyr*), *b* 1908; is a Serving Sister of Order of St John of Jerusalem: *m* 1932, 3rd Baron Merthyr, who *d* 1977. *Residence* – Churchton, Saundersfoot, Pembrokeshire.

COLLATERAL BRANCH LIVING

Issue of late Walter Thomas Meyrick, 5th son of 1st baronet, *b* 1882, *d* 1953: *m* 1st, 1914 (*m diss* 1935), Mabel Violet Blanche, da of late Col Arthur Hill Sandys Montgomery, Rifle Brig, and widow of Percy Downes; 2ndly, 1935, Mary Jocelyn (Sawmill Close, Sharperton, Morpeth), da of Sir James Ernest Thorold, 14th Bt:—

(By 2nd *m*) Walter James Charlton, *b* 1936; *ed* Eton: *m* 1965, Gillian, yr da of late W. Macduff Urquhart, of Edinburgh, and has issue living, St John James Charlton, *b* 1969, — William Andrew Charlton, *b* 1976, — Louisa Mary Charlton, *b* 1966, — Sophia Rachel Charlton, *b* (twin) 1966. ⸻ Michael Alan Charlton, *b* 1937. ⸻ Christopher Thomas Charlton, *b* 1946: *m* 1975, Caroline Mary (who *m* 2ndly, 1985, Julian Richard Freeland, of Green Close, Combe, Oxon OX7 2N5, yst son of Maj P. K. Freeland, of Ipplepen, Devon), elder da of Iain Hugh Webster, of Forest Row, Sussex, and *d* 1979. ⸻ Mary Rhoda Charlton, *b* 1944: *m* 1971, Colin A. Matheson, and has issue living, Nicholas Simon, *b* 1973, — Patrick William Christopher, *b* 1979, — Camilla Karen, *b* 1976.

The 1st baronet, Col Sir Thomas Charlton Meyrick, KCB, DL, JP (son of St John Chivarton Charlton, DL, JP, of Apley

Castle, Salop), was MP for Pembroke Dist (*C*) 1868-74, and assumed 1858, by Roy licence the surname of Meyrick, his maternal grandfather being Thomas Meyrick of Bush, Pembrokeshire, descended from the Meyricks of Bodorgan, Anglesey.

TAPPS GERVIS MEYRICK (GB) 1791, of Hinton Admiral, Hampshire
(Name pronounced "Tapps Gervis Merrick")

Heb dhu, heb dhim, dhu
a digon
Without God, without anything;
God and enough

Sir GEORGE CHRISTOPHER CADAFAEL TAPPS GERVIS MEYRICK, 7th *Baronet*; *b* 10 March 1941; *s* his father *Lt-Col Sir* GEORGE DAVID ELIOTT, MC, 1988: *ed* Eton, and Trin Coll, Camb; patron of two livings; *m* 1968, Jean Louise, yst da of late Lord William Walter Montagu Douglas Scott, MC (*see* D Buccleuch, colls), and has issue.

Arms – Quarterly: 1st and 4th, sable, on a chevron argent between three bands erect raguly or, inflamed proper, a fleur-de-lis gules between two Cornish choughs respecting each other proper, *Meyrick*; 2nd, argent, six ostrich feathers, three, two, and one, sable in the centre point a pellet, *Gervis*; 2nd and 3rd, azure, on a fesse or, between three rhinoceroses argent, as many escallops gules, *Tapps*. **Crest** – 1st, a tower argent, thereon upon a mount vert a Cornish chough holding in the dexter claw a fleur-de-lis; 2nd, a mount vert, thereon three ostrich feathers, one in pale and two in saltire sable, banded by a wreath of oak or; 3rd, a greyhound couchant per pale argent and sable charged on the body with two escallops fessewise countercharged. **Seats** – Hinton Admiral, nr Christchurch, Dorset; Bodorgan, Anglesey.

SON LIVING

GEORGE WILLIAM OWEN, *b* 1970. —— Charles Valentine Llewelyn, *b* 1972.

DAUGHTER LIVING

Suzannah Daisy, *b* 1978.

SISTER LIVING

Caroline Susan Joan, *b* 1942: *m* 1963, Richard Arthur Samuel Hulse, of 23 Seymour Walk, SW10, yr son of Wing-Cdr Sir (Hamilton) Westrow Hulse, 9th Bt.

AUNT LIVING (*daughter of 5th baronet*)

Susan Hermione, *b* 1919: *m* 1945, Peter John Green, MC, and has issue living, Christopher, *b* 1946. *Residence* – Minstead Manor, Minstead, Lyndhurst, Hants.

WIDOW LIVING OF SIXTH BARONET

ANN (*Dowager Lady Tapps Gervis Meyrick*), da of late Clive Miller, of Melbourne, Australia: *m* 1940, Lt-Col Sir George David Eliott Tapps Gervis Meyrick, 6th Bt, MC, who *d* 1988. *Residence* – Waterditch House, Bransgore, Christchurch, Dorset.

COLLATERAL BRANCH LIVING

Grandchildren of late Capt Richard Owen Tapps Gervis Meyrick, yr son of 4th baronet:—
Issue of late Capt Richard Anthony Tapps Gervis Meyrick, *b* 1920, *d* 1964: *m* 1949, Alexandra Adèle (Zandra) (Sheafhayne Manor, Yarcombe, Honiton, Devon) (who *m* 2ndly, 1967, Antony Rising Baxter), da of Brig Rupert John Brett, DSO, of Langsmeade House, Milton Common, Oxon:—
James David, *b* 1950: *m* 1988, Nicola Jane, da of H. M. Williams, of White House, Llantilio Crossenny, Abergavenny, Gwent. —— Sarah Jacintha Barbara, *b* 1952: *m* 1989, Walter John Dowe Taylor.

The 2nd baronet, Sir George William Tapps, MP for Christchurch 1832-6, assumed in 1835 the additional surname of Gervis, while the 3rd baronet assumed in 1876 by Roy licence the further additional surname of Meyrick. The 4th baronet, Sir George Augustus Eliott Tapps Gervis Meyrick, was High Sheriff of Hants 1900. The 5th baronet, Sir George Llewelyn Tapps Gervis Meyrick, Major (ret) 7th Hussars, was High Sheriff of Anglesey 1939.

Meysey-Thompson, see Thompson.

MIDDLETON (E) 1662, of Belsay Castle, Northumberland

Sir LAWRENCE MONCK MIDDLETON, 10th *Baronet*; *b* 23 Oct 1912; *s* his brother, *Sir* STEPHEN HUGH 1993; *ed* Eton; BSc Forestry, Edinburgh 1939: *m* 1984, Mrs Primrose Westcombe, da of Lawrence Haynes Adams, of Shrubland House, Soham, Cambs.

𝔄rms – Quarterly gules and or, in the 1st quarter a cross flory argent. 𝔆rest – A wild man proper, bearing in his arms an oak tree eradicated bendways or. *Address* – Estate Office, Belsay Castle, Newcastle-upon-Tyne NE20 0DY.

COLLATERAL BRANCH LIVING

Grandchildren of late Henry Nicholas Middleton, brother of 7th baronet:—
Issue of late Lambert William Middleton, *b* 1877, *d* 1941: *m* 1922, Lady Sybil Grey, OBE, who *d* 1966, da of 4th Earl Grey:—
HENRY LAMBERT (Enbrook House, Ball Hill, nr Newbury, Berks RG15 0NU), *b* 26 Aug 1923; *ed* Eton, and New Coll, Oxford: *m* 1964 (*m diss* 1978), Susan Jenifer, da of William Arthur Fearnley-Whittingstall, TD, QC, of The Old Manor House, Melbourn, Cambs, and widow of Hon Rodney Mathias Berry, TD (*see* V Camrose), and has issue living, Laura Sybil Rose, *b* 1969. —— Mary Sybil, *b* 1925: *m* 1948, Capt John Brooke Boyd, KOSB, of Whiterigg, Melrose, Roxburghshire TD6 9HE, and has issue living, Simon John (34 Kimberley Rd, Cambridge), *b* 1949; *ed* Eton, and New Coll Oxford: *m* 1979, Julia Mary Seiber, — James Lambert (Rue Rotselaerlaan 13, 3180 Tervuren, Belgium), *b* 1952; *ed* Eton, — Caroline Elizabeth *b* (twin), 1952, — Diana Mary, *b* 1955: *m* 1990, Neil Braithwaite, of Aydon Grange, Corbridge, Northumberland.

Sir William Middleton, 1st baronet, of Belsay Castle, Northumberland (*d* 1690), descended from Sir John Middleton who acquired large estates temp Richard II on *m* to Christian eventual co-heir of John de Stryvelyn, who was summoned to parliament from 1363 to 1371 and who re-acquired Belsay Castle. The 6th baronet, Sir Charles, in compliance with the testamentary injunction of his maternal grandfather, Lawrence Monck, of Caenby, Lincolnshire, changed his name, in 1799, by Roy sign-manual, from Middleton to Monck; and the 7th baronet, and his brother, Henry Nicholas, in 1876, resumed the original surname of Middleton.

MILBANK (UK) 1882, of Well, co York, and of Hart, co Durham

Sir ANTHONY FREDERICK MILBANK, 5th *Baronet*, *b* 16 Aug 1939; *s* his father, *Maj Sir* MARK VANE, KCVO, MC, 1984; *ed* Eton; Chm Moorland Assocn; CLA Executive; RSPB Council: *m* 1970, Belinda Beatrice, yr da of Brig Adrian Clements Gore, DSO (*see* Gore, Bt, colls), and has issue.

𝔄rms – Gules, a saltire argent, gutte de poix between two lions heads couped in pale, and as many roses in fesse of the second. 𝔆rest – A lion's head couped argent, gutte de poix, charged with a pale gules, thereon three roses, also argent. *Seat* – Barningham Park, Richmond, N Yorks DL11 7DW.

SONS LIVING

EDWARD MARK SOMERSET, *b* 9 April 1973. —— Toby Adrian Jameson, *b* 1977.

DAUGHTER LIVING

Alexina Victoria, *b* 1971.

BROTHER LIVING

(Arthur) John (The Old Laundry House, Smeeth, Ashford, Kent, TN25 6ST), *b* 1940; *ed* Gordonstoun: *m* 1969, Rosalind Eleanor Lucy, da of G. E. L. Townshend, of Pretoria, S Africa, and has issue living, Robert Andrew, *b* 1972, — Lucy Verena, *b* 1970.

UNCLE LIVING (*son of 3rd baronet*)

Denis William Powlett, TD, *b* 1912; *ed* Radley; is Maj RA (TA): *m* 1934, Doreen Frances, who *d* 1991, da of Sir Richard Pierce Butler, OBE, 11th Bt (*cr* 1628), and has issue living, Mark Richard (Chirume Ranch (Box 767), Marondera, Zimbabwe), *b* 1937: *m* 1st, 1966 (*m diss* 1989), Frances Elizabeth, da of Richard V. Holme; 2ndly, 1993, Mrs Nicola Mary Sclater, da of late Antony Cropper, of Tolson Hall, Kendal, Cumbria, and has issue living (by 1st *m*), Robert Frederick *b* 1968, Henry Mark Thomas *b* 1970, Jack Patrick *b* 1979, — Penelope Ann (Box 628, Umtentweni 4235, S Africa), *b* 1935: *m* 1st, 1955, Capt John Frederick de Vere Shaw, Kenya Regt, who *d* 1960 (*see* Shaw, Bt, *cr* 1821, colls); 2ndly, 1970, Hougham Robert Mills, and has issue living (by 1st *m*) (*see* Shaw, Bt, *cr* 1821), — Susan Fiona, *b* 1942: *m* 1963, Antony Roger Pelly, of Little Limber Grange, Limber, nr Grimsby, Lincs, and has issue (*see* Pelly, Bt). *Residence* – Southbrook, Galphay, Ripon, N Yorks.

WIDOW LIVING OF FOURTH BARONET

Hon VERENA AILEEN MAXWELL (*Hon Lady Milbank*), da of 11th Baron Farnham, and widow of Charles Lambart Crawley (Crawley-Boevey, Bt): *m* 1938, as his 2nd wife, Maj Sir Mark Vane Milbank, 4th Bt, KCVO, MC, who *d* 1984. *Residence* – Barningham Park, Richmond, N Yorks.

COLLATERAL BRANCH LIVING

Issue of late Maj John Gerald Frederick Milbank, 2nd son of 3rd Bt, *b* 1909, *d* 1991: *m* 1938, Louisa Harriet, who *d* 1974, only da of late Edward Beaumont Cotton Curtis, of Caynham Cottage, Ludlow, Shropshire (Curtis, Bt):—

David John (Gayles Fields, Dalton, Richmond, Yorks), *b* 1940; *ed* Gordonstoun: *m* 1971, Clarissa Mary, da of Capt S. L. Bigge, of Langdale, Melsonby, Yorks, and has issue living, James John, *b* 1974, — Nicholas Charles, *b* 1975. —— Charles Gerald (34 ave de Montmorency, 60500 Chantilly, France), *b* 1942; *ed* Eton; a racehorse trainer: *m* 1973, Mrs Wendy Wright, da of late E. N. Johnson, of Newton Firs, Newton, by Frodsham, Cheshire, and has issue living, Philip Augustus, *b* 1974, — Camilla, *b* 1975, — Sophie Kathleen, *b* 1977.

The 1st baronet, Sir Frederick Acclom Milbank, 2nd son of late Mark Milbank of Thorpe-Perrow, was MP for M Riding of York 1865-85, and for York, N Riding, Richmond Div 1885-6. The 2nd baronet, Sir Powlett Charles John, sat as MP for Radnorshire (C) 1895-1900. The 4th baronet, Sir Mark Vane, KCVO, MC, was Master of HM Household and Extra Equerry to HM 1954-67.

Milborne-Swinnerton-Pilkington, see Pilkington.

MILBURN (UK) 1905, of Guyzance, Parish of Shilbottle, Northumberland

Sir ANTHONY RUPERT MILBURN, 5th *Baronet*; *b* 17 April 1947, elder son of late Maj Rupert Leonard Eversley Milburn, yr son of 3rd baronet; *s* his uncle, Sir JOHN NIGEL, 1985; *ed* Eton, and RAC, Cirencester; ARICS, MRAC: *m* 1977, Olivia Shirley, yst da of Capt Thomas Noel Catlow, CBE, RN, of Rose Cottage, Tunstall, by Carnforth, Lancs, and has issue.

Arms – Per fesse or and gules, a pale counterchanged between two bears' heads erased in chief sable, muzzled of the first, and as many bear's heads also erased and muzzled in base or. **Crest** – In front of a bear's head erased sable, muzzled or, four mascles interlaced fesseways of the last. **Badge** – On a millrind sable, an escallop shell argent.
Seat – Guyzance Hall, Acklington, Northumberland.

DUM · SPIRO · SPERO

While I breathe I hope

SONS LIVING

PATRICK THOMAS, *b* 4 Dec 1980. —— (Edward) Jake, *b* 1987.

DAUGHTER LIVING

Lucy Camilla Anne, *b* 1982.

BROTHER LIVING

Michael Richard, *b* 1950; *ed* Eton.

SISTERS LIVING

Caroline Anne (*Lady Renwick*), *b* 1945: *m* 1966, Sir Richard Eustace Renwick, 4th Bt, of Whalton House, Whalton, Morpeth, Northumberland. —— Diana Rosemary (34 Salcott Rd, SW11), *b* 1949: *m* 1970 (*m diss* 1980), Richard Murrough Wilson, and has issue living, Nicholas Rupert Gerald, *b* 1974.

AUNTS LIVING (*Daughters of 3rd baronet*)

Darea Joan, *b* 1923: *m* 1950, Maj George Harold Michael Sankey, late Staffs Yeo, of Shackerley Hall, Albrighton, Wolverhampton, Staffs, eldest son of late Col Harold Bantock Sankey, CBE, MC, TD, DL, of Whiston Hall, Albrighton, and has issue living, Christopher Michael David, *b* 1952; *ed* Shrewsbury, — Peter William Richard (Cranmere Worfield, Bridgnorth, Shropshire WV15 5LP), *b* 1953; *ed* Shrewsbury: *m* 1991, Mrs Sarah Caroline Aileen Davenport Greenshields, only da of late John Sydney Birch Lea (*see* Lea, Bt, colls), and has issue living, Georgina Elisabeth Joan *b* 1992, — Nicola Mary Joan, *b* 1955, — Virginia Karen Margaret, *b* 1957. —— Susan Anne (*Lady Farr*), *b* 1937: *m* 1960, Sir John Arnold Farr, MP, of 11 Vincent Sq, SW1, and Shortwood House, Lamport, Northants, elder surv son of late Capt John Farr, JP, of Worksop Manor, Notts, and has issue living, Jonathan, *b* 1962, — George Nelson, *b* 1967: *m* 1992, Jane F., da of C. R. Lachlan, of Melbourne, and of Mrs David Gape, of Caxton, Cambs, and has issue living, Harriet Philippa Joan *b* 1994.

WIDOW LIVING OF FOURTH BARONET

DOROTHY JOAN (*Dorothy, Lady Milburn*), eldest da of Leslie Butcher, of Dunholme, Lincs: *m* 1940, Sir John Nigel Milburn, 4th Bt, who *d* 1985. *Residence* – Brainshaugh, Acklington, Morpeth, Northumberland.

COLLATERAL BRANCHES LIVING

Issue of late John Davison Milburn, 3rd son of 1st baronet, *b* 1886, *d* 1972: *m* 1922, Grace Emily, who *d* 1934, only da of late Stuart MacRae, of Conchra, Ross-shire:—

Angela Mary (Highcliff, Little Switzerland, Douglas, Isle of Man), *b* 1925. —— Sybil Pauline (Highcliffe, Little Switzerland, Douglas, Isle of Man), *b* 1926.

Issue of late Capt Archibald William Milburn, 4th son of 1st baronet, *b* 1887, *d* 1965: *m* 1931, Eleanor Lilias (Victora), who *d* 1983, da of Maj Nevill Arthur Charles de Hirzel Tufnell, of Langleys, Chelmsford:—

Mark Anthony William (Apart 164, Arrecife de Lanzarote, Canary Islands), *b* 1932; *ed* Eton, le Rosey, and RMA; PhD, FLS, FSA; late Maj Special Air Ser (TA) and late Lt R Scots Greys: *m* 1968 (*m diss* 1976), Angela Margaret Cromwell, da of late Lt Col Geoffrey Stephen Carmac Weigall, and formerly wife of David Francis Brougham Maitland Edye, and has issue living, Francis Shahid, *b* 1969; *ed* Millfield; BSc. —— Sarah Caroline Georgiana (Langleys, Gt Waltham, Chelmsford, Essex CM3 1AH), *b* 1935: *m* 1956, David Robert Micklem, son of late Cdr Sir (Edward) Robert Micklem, CBE, RN, and has issue living, Alexander David Robert, *b* 1965: *m* 1990, Jennifer Jane, elder da of Dr Maurice Healy, and has issue living, Oliver David *b* 1991, Henry James *b* 1993, — Lucy Victoria Cornelia, *b* 1958: *m* 1984, Peter John Bradford Gibson, and has issue living, Archibald John Peter *b* 1991, Olivia Emily Victoria *b* 1987, Alice Emma Louise *b* 1989, — Anna Caroline, *b* 1960: *m* 1987, Jonathan James Grew, and has issue living, James Edward *b* 1988, Jeremy Charles *b* 1993, Louisa Sarah *b* 1990.

This family is descended from Thomas Milburn, of Broomhope in Birtley, North Tynedale (*d* 1705). The 1st baronet, Sir John Davison Milburn, was High Sheriff for Northumberland 1905. The 3rd baronet, Sir Leonard John Milburn, was High Sheriff of that co 1928. The mother of Sir Anthony Rupert Milburn, 5th Bt, was Anne Mary (*d* 1991), da of late Maj Austin Scott Murray, MC, of Heckfield Place, Basingstoke (*see* B Mowbray, colls). This lady, being with her cousin Mary sole co-heir to the family of Scott Murray of Danesfield and Hambledon, co Bucks, was granted by Lord Lyon the arms of *Murray of Philiphaugh* with a difference 14 Dec 1955, and of *Scott of Trabourn* with a difference 29 Aug 1966.

ST JOHN-MILDMAY (GB) 1772, of Farley, co Southampton (Dormant 1955)
(Name pronounced "Sinjun-Mildmay")

Rev Sir (AUBREY) NEVILLE ST JOHN-MILDMAY, 10th *Baronet*, *d* in 1955. His only surviving son, Verus Arundell Maunder St John-Mildmay, *dsp* in 1965, without having claimed the baronetcy, and at the time of going to press no name appears on the Official Roll of Baronets in respect of this title.

COLLATERAL BRANCH LIVING

Grandsons of late John Walter Paulet St John-Mildmay, son of late Arthur George St John-Mildmay, son of late Edward St John-Mildmay, 8th son of 3rd baronet:—
Issue of late Michael Paulet St John-Mildmay, *b* 1901, *d* 1993; presumed heir to the baronetcy from 1965: *m* 1933, Joan Elizabeth, who *d* 1977, da of late Brig-Gen Hugh Roderick Stockley, CIE, of Alkerton Grange, Eastington, Glos:—
Walter John Hugh (Hollam House, Dulverton, Som), *b* 3 Sept 1935; *ed* Wycliffe Coll, Emmanuel Coll, Cambridge (BA), Hammersmith Coll of Art and Building, and RAC, Cirencester; the presumed heir to the baronetcy. —— Michael Hugh Paulet (Drakestone House, Stinchcombe, Dursley, Glos), *b* 28 Sept 1937; *ed* Wycliffe Coll, and Emmanuel Coll, Cambridge (BA 1961): *m* 1965, Mrs Crystal Margaret Ludlow, and has issue living, Henry Walter, *b* 1971, — Oliver James, *b* 1973, — Emilia Alice Joan, *b* 1977.

MILES (UK) 1859, of Leigh Court, Somersetshire

Labora sicut bonus miles
Work like a good soldier

Sir WILLIAM NAPIER MAURICE MILES, 6th *Baronet*; *b* 19 Oct 1913; *s* his father *Lt-Col Sir* CHARLES WILLIAM, OBE, 1966; *ed* Stowe, and Jesus Coll, Camb: *m* 1946, Pamela, da of late Capt Michael Dillon, and has issue.

Arms – Azure, a chevron paly of six ermine and or between three lozenges argent, each charged with a fleur-de-lis sable. **Crest** – Upon a rock a dexter arm embowed in armour the hand grasping an anchor entwined by a cable proper. *Residence* – Old Rectory House, Walton-in-Gordano, Clevedon, Avon BS21 7AW.

SON LIVING

PHILIP JOHN, *b* 10 Aug 1953.

DAUGHTERS LIVING

Catherine Anne Elizabeth, *b* 1947: *m* 1974, Peter Charles Beloe, of Madam's End Farm, Hardwicke, Gloucester and has issue living, William Alexander Peter, *b* 1977. —— Phoebe Caroline, *b* 1983. —— Lorraine, *b* 1950: *m* 1972, Martin Hugh Sessions-Hodge, of Cross Tree Farm, Walton-in-Gordano, Clevedon, Avon, and has issue living, James Anthony, *b* 1975, — Henry George Patrick, *b* 1977, — Abigail Theodora, *b* 1980.

BROTHER LIVING

Charles William Noel, *b* 1915: *m* 1940, Jacqueline (Dickie), da of Robert Cross, and has issue living, Phinola Jane, *b* 1943. *Residence* – Wheelers, Hound Green, Mattingley, Basingstoke, Hants.

COLLATERAL BRANCH LIVING

Issue of late Capt William Henry Miles, yr son of 4th baronet, *b* 1888; *d* 1975: *m* 1912, Lilian, who *d* 1972, da of Hon Sir Hartley Williams, of 93 Cadogan Gdns, SW:—
Lilian Mary (64 Bishops Mansions, Bishops Park Rd, SW6), *b* 1914: *m* 1939, Alan Grant Maby, who *d* 1965. —— Pamela (Ossington House, Newark), *b* 1916; *m* 1st, 1947, Lt-Col William Maxwell Evelyn Denison, JP, DL, who *d* 1972; 2ndly, 1974, Prof Daniel Goedhuis, Netherlands Embassy, and has issue living, (by 1st *m*) Georgina Jane, *b* 1948.

This family, from Ledbury, Herefordshire, became merchants of Bristol in the 18th century. Philip John Miles of Leigh

Court, Som, was Mayor of Bristol 1780, and MP for Westbury, Corfe Castle and Bristol. His son, Sir William, 1st Bt, was MP for Chippenham, Romney, and E Somerset (*C*). Sir Philip John William, 2nd Bt, was MP for E Somerset (*C*) 1878-85.

MILLAIS (UK) 1885, of Palace Gate, Kensington, co Middlesex, and of St Ouen, Jersey
(Name pronounced "Millay")

Ars longa, vita brevis

Art endureth, life is short

Sir Geoffroy Richard Everett Millais, 6th *Baronet*; *b* 27 Dec 1941; *s* his father, *Sir* Ralph Regnault, 1992; *ed* Marlborough.

Arms – Per bend sinister or and azure, an estoile of eight points between three fleurs-de-lys, two in fesse and one in base, all counter-changed. **Crest** – In front of a dexter hand gauntleted and couped gules an estoile of eight points or. *Residence* – D19 Sloane Avenue Mansions, Sloane Av, SW3 3JH.

SISTER LIVING

Caroline Mary Felicity, *b* 1940: *m* 1963, David Anthony Campbell-Jones, only son of late Mervyn Campbell-Jones, and has issue living, Henry David Mervyn, *b* 1972; *ed* Radley, — Serena Caroline Mary, *b* 1969; *ed* Royal Naval Sch, Haslemere.

UNCLE LIVING (son of 4th baronet)

Edward Gray St Helier, *b* 15 March 1918; *ed* Radley; late Capt Anti-Aircraft Regt RA: *m* 1947, Rosemary Barbara, yr da of late Brig-Gen Frederick George Lucas, CB, CSI, CIE, DSO, 5th Royal Gurkha Rifles, and has issue living, Andrew Michael, *b* 13 April 1948; *ed* Clayesmore, — John Frederick, *b* 1949; *ed* Radley, — Peter William, *b* 1951; *ed* Radley, — David Gray, *b* 1959; *ed* Monkton Combe: *m* 1993, Susanna M., da of late Dr Patrick Maybin and of Dr Maureen Maybin, of Ballylesson, co Down, — Fiona, *b* 1960. *Residence* – Crosswater Farm, Churt, Surrey.

MOTHER LIVING

Felicity Caroline Mary Ward (*Felicity, Lady Millais*), da of late Brig-Gen William Ward Warner, CMG, by his wife, Hon Clarice May, da of 2nd Baron Borwick: *m* 1st, 1932 (*m diss* 1938), Maj John Peyton Robinson, 8th Hussars; 2ndly, 1939 (*m diss* 1947), as his 1st wife, Sir Ralph Regnault Millais, 5th Bt, who *d* 1992.

WIDOW LIVING OF FIFTH BARONET

Babette Irene (*Lady Millais*), yr da of late Maj-Gen Harold Francis Salt, CB, CMG, DSO (*see* Salt, Bt, *cr* 1899, colls), widow of Maj John de Grey Tatham Warter, MC, and formerly wife of Victor William Henry Sefton-Smith: *m* 3rdly, 1975, as his 3rd wife, Sir Ralph Regnault Millais, 5th Bt, who *d* 1992. *Residence* – Elizabeth Court, 47 Milmans St, SW10 0DA.

COLLATERAL BRANCH LIVING

Issue of late John Guille Millais, 4th son of 1st baronet, *b* 1865, *d* 1931: *m* 1894, Fanny Margaret, who *d* 1960, da of late Philip George Skipwith, of Hundleby, Lincolnshire:—
(Hesketh) Raoul le Jarderay, *b* 1901; Capt (ret) late Scots Guards: *m* 1st, 1926, Elinor Clare, who *d* 1953, da of late Allan Ronald Macdonell, of Montreal; 2ndly, 1949, Mrs Katharine Edith Prior-Palmer, who *d* 1985, da of late Frank Bibby, CBE, of Hardwick Grange, Shrewsbury, and has issue living, (by 1st *m*) John Ronald Raoul Lees-Millais (Rockley Manor, Marlborough), *b* 1927; assumed the additional surname of Lees: *m* 1952, Lavinia Charlotte, da of late Capt Geoffrey William Martin Lees, of Falcutt House, Brackley, Northants, and has issue living, David John Geoffroy *b* 1953: *m* 1980, Jane V. H., el da of Kenneth J. Forder, of Steeple Close, Church Gate, SW6 (and has issue living, a son *b* 1982, a da *b* 1987, a da *b* 1991), Colin Everett (Whittlebury Park, nr Towcester, Northants) *b* 1957: *m* 1991, Frances Maria Loftus, only da of Humphry Stuart Loftus Tottenham, of Minchens, Bramley, Hants (*see* Archdale, Bt, 1972-73 Edn) (and has issue living, Sophie Frances Margery *b* 1994), Patrick James *b* 1958: *m* 1987, Fiona Astrid, yst da of late Maj John Edward Joicey, MC (and has issue, Marcus John *b* 1989, Rory *b* 1990), Joanna Clare *b* 1954: *m* 1981, Thomas Hornby Graham Cooper, of East Markham Hall, Newark, Notts, son of late Brig Thomas Cooper, of Bottom Farm, Eaton, Grantham, Lincs (and has issue living, Alexander Thomas *b* 1986, Louisa Clare *b* 1989, Emma Lavinia *b* 1985), Fiona Katherine *b* 1964, — Hugh Geoffroy (The Stables, Kirtlington Park, Oxon), *b* 1929: *m* 1957, Suzy Falconnet, and has issue living, Ian *b* 1958, Joshua *b* 1961, Tara Romaney *b* 1967, — (by 2nd *m*), Hesketh Merlin, *b* 1950; *ed* Milton Abbey; Capt R Hussars (PWO): *m* 1981, Amanda W., da of James Fletcher, of 8 Avonmore Mansions, Avonmore Rd, W14 (and has issue living, Raoul Edward *b* 1981, Iona Effie *b* 1983, Katherine Alice *b* 1986). *Residence* – Westcote Manor, Kingham, Oxon.
The 1st baronet, Sir John Everett Millais (son of John William Millais, of Jersey), was an eminent painter and Pres of Roy Acad.

MILLER (E) 1705, of Chichester, Sussex

Sir JOHN HOLMES MILLER, 11th *Baronet*, *b* 1925; *s* his father, *Sir* ERNEST HENRY JOHN, 1960: *m* 1950, Jocelyn Edwards, of Wairoa, New Zealand, and has issue.

𝕬rms – Argent, a fesse wavy azure, between three wolve's heads erased gules. 𝕮rest – A wolf's head erased gules charged on the neck with a fesse azure. *Residence* – 60 Tamatea Rd, Taupo, NZ.

DAUGHTERS LIVING

Roslyn Mary, *b* 1955. ——— Diana Jocelyn, *b* 1958: *m* 19—, Murray John Telford, of Paraparaumu, NZ.

BROTHER LIVING

HARRY (53 Koha Rd, Taupo, NZ), *b* 15 Jan 1927: *m* 1954, Gwynedd Margaret, da of R. P. Sherriff, of St Anthony, Paraparaumu, NZ, and has issue living, Anthony Thomas (261 Kohimarama Rd, Auckland 5, NZ), *b* 4 May 1955: *m* 1990, Barbara Battersby, and has issue living, three children, — Sara Margaret, *b* 1957: *m* 1986, Garth Laing, and has issue living, Maggie Eleanor, *b* 1992, — Judith Christine, *b* 1960.

SISTERS LIVING

Hilary, *b* 1921: *m* 1945, John Alexander Nisbet, of 10 Weka Rd, Taupo, NZ, and has issue living. ——— Norah Jessie, *b* 1923: *m* 1949, Roy Galloway Gardiner, of 68A Wakeman St, Pahiatua, NZ, and has issue living.

COLLATERAL BRANCHES LIVING

Issue of late Charles Holmes Miller, yr son of 9th baronet, *b* 1905, *d* 1984: *m* 1st, 1936, Hester Amelia, who *d* 1974, da of E. J. Wilde; 2ndly, 1975, Pauline Rochfort (2/26 Clyde Rd, Napier, NZ):—
(By 1st *m*) Patrick Holmes, *b* 1941. ——— Paul Greville, *b* 1943. ——— Monica Jane, *b* 1938. ——— Elizabeth Hope, *b* 1940.

Grandchildren of late Hon Sir Henry John Miller (first elected Speaker of NZ Legislative Council), 2nd son of 6th baronet:—
Issue of late William Nicholson Miller, *b* 1868, *d* 1950: *m* 1906, Edith Mary, da of J. C. Forsyth:—
William Maxwell (74 Haldane St, Beaumaris, Victoria 3193, Australia), *b* 1913; MICE Aust, Chartered Civil Engr (ret): *m* 1938, Marjory, da of late L. M. Bell, MICE, and has issue living, Leonard Maxwell (6/126 Albert St, E Melbourne 3002, Australia), *b* 1948; BCEng, MICE Aust, Chartered Civil Engr: *m* 1975, Ruth Annette Vile, and has issue living, Daniel James *b* 1976, Katherine Rachel *b* (twin) 1976, Rebecca Sarah *b* 1977, — Diana Marjory, *b* 1940; BA, Dip Arch: *m* 1963, Jeremy David Pope, LLB, and has issue living, Adam Quentin *b* 1969, Samuel William *b* 1974, Jemima Mary *b* 1971, — Mary Nicholson, *b* 1947; MBA, BA, Dip Soc Studies: *m* 1976, Yoram Zamir, of New York, and has issue living, Talor Miller *b* 1981, — Robyn Elizabeth, *b* 1951; BA, Dip Ed: *m* 1973, Geoffrey Collis, Dip Ed, and has issue living, Matthew William *b* 1980, Jacqueline Louise *b* 1983. ——— Margaret May (Waiapu House, Havelock North, NZ), *b* 1907: *m* 1937, Edward Ernest Zohrab, who *d* 1970, and has issue living, Margaret Ann, *b* 1938: *m* 1964, Jerome Glazebrook Whyte, of Clive, Hawkes Bay, NZ, and has issue living, — Jenny Elizabeth, *b* 1940: *m* 1964, John Mundell Ewart, of 33 Portland Rd, Remuera, Auckland, NZ, and has issue living, — Patricia Joan, *b* 1947: *m* 1970, Bryan Gifford Moore, of Wharemoa, Otoroa, Kaeo, Northland, NZ, and has issue living.
Issue of late Lieut-Col George Ralph Miller, DSO, *b* 1874, *d* 1948: *m* 1916, Violet Mary, who *d* 1981, da of late W. H. Teschemaker, of Kauro Hill, Otago, New Zealand:—
Cecil Ralph, TD (70 Ballabrooie Way, Douglas, Isle of Man), *b* 1917; Maj Parachute Regt ret: *m* 1981, Marie, da of Stephen Sumner, and widow of Maj Robert Thomas Williamson, The Cameronaians (ret), of Edinburgh. ——— Anthony John (Shadwell Cottage, High Hurstwood, Uckfield, E Sussex TN22 4AB), *b* 1920: *m* 1952, Sheila Doreen, da of Lt-Col L. Harvey, of Clare Glen, High Hurstwood, Sussex, and widow of Sqdn-Ldr M. Savage, and has issue living, Richard Charles Cecil, *b* 1956: *m* 1984, Eileen Joy, da of E. R. Odey, of Norfolk, and has issue living, Mark George Ralph *b* 1987, Matthew Anthony Edward *b* 1989, — Timothy John, *b* 1957, — Jennifer Anne, *b* 1952: *m* 1st, 1976, Peter Antony Twist, who *d* 1979; 2ndly, 1988, Warren Sullivan, of Sydney, NSW, Australia, and has issue living, (by 2nd *m*) Luke Anthony *b* 1989, Françoise Alice *b* (twin) 1989.
Sir Thomas Miller, 1st Bt, was son of Mark Miller, Alderman of Chichester, and was several times Mayor of that city. The 1st, 2nd, and 3rd baronets each represented Chichester in Parliament, and the 5th baronet sat as MP for Portsmouth.

MILLER (GB) 1788, of Glenlee, Kirkcudbrightshire

Sir STEPHEN WILLIAM MACDONALD MILLER OF GLENLEE, 8th *Baronet*, MB, BS, FRCS, MRCGP; *b* 20 June 1953; *s* his father, *Sir* (FREDERICK WILLIAM) MACDONALD, 1991; *ed* Rugby, and St Bart's Hosp: *m* 1st, 1978, Mary Carolyn, who *d* 1989, only da of Gwynedd Bulkeley Owens, of 2 Westfield Av, Oakes, Huddersfield; 2ndly, 1990, Caroline Mary Clark, da of Leslie A— E— Chasemore, of Shebbear, Devon, and widow of Harold Frederick Clark, and has issue by 1st *m*.

Arms – Argent, a cross moline azure, in chief a lozenge between two mullets of the second and in base a bar wavy vert. **Crest** – A human hand couped at the wrist; the third and fourth fingers folded in the hand proper. **Supporters** – Two roebucks proper.
Residence – The Lawn, Shebbear, Beaworthy, Devon EX21 5RU.

SON LIVING *(By 1st marriage)*

JAMES STEPHEN MACDONALD, *b* 25 July 1981.

DAUGHTER LIVING *(By 1st marriage)*

Katherine Helen, *b* 1983.

SISTER LIVING

Alison Hilary, *b* 1951: *m* 1976, John Glover Freeman, of Holly Farm, Bergh Apton, Norwich, and has issue living, William Griffin Henry, *b* 1981, — Thomas Michael Percy, *b* 1984.

HALF-UNCLES LIVING *(Sons of 6th baronet by his 3rd wife, Cynthia Rosemary, who d 1991, da of Frederick Edward Huish)*

Graham Frederick Alastair (Coral Gables, Florida, USA), *b* (Sept) 1938; *ed* Pangbourne: *m* 1968, Gaynor, who *d* 1988, da of Tudor Whitcombe, of Cardiff, S Wales, and has issue living, Alastair, *b* 1971; B Eng, — Penelope, *b* 1969; *ed* Univ of Wales, Cardiff (BSc). —— George Edward John, *b* 1946: *m* 1970, Merrill, da of T. G. Morris, and has issue living, Christopher Carl Edward, *b* 1980, — Stephanie Claire, *b* 1971; *ed* Univ of Wales, Swansea (BSc).

HALF-AUNTS LIVING

(Daughters of 6th baronet by his 2nd wife, Margaret May, da of Frederick Shotter)

Pamela Ann Mary, *b* 1928: *m* 1950, John Ward Randolph Nicholson, of Crag View Farm, North Rigton, nr Huby, Yorks, and has issue living, Mark John Anthony, *b* 1952, — Martin Euan Thomas, *b* 1955, — Moray John Fergus, *b* 1962, — Myles Ian Vaughan, *b* 1964, — Magnus Francis Benedict, *b* 1966, — Mungo Patrick Lee, *b* 1969, — Annette Mary Ward, *b* 1951, — Philippa Mary Randolph, *b* 1954, — Iona Frances Marianne, *b* 1957, — Alexandra Mary Elizabeth, *b* 1959. —— Elizabeth Margaret Mary Cynthia (*Lady Honywood*), *b* 1931: *m* 1956, Sir Filmer Courtenay William Honywood, 11th Bt, FRICS, of Greenway Forstal Farmhouse, Hollingbourne, Maidstone.

(Daughter of 6th baronet by his 3rd wife)

Teresa Rosemary Ann, *b* 1939: *m* 1961 (*m diss* 1976), Grenfell King, and has issue living, Julian Grenfell, *b* 1972.

WIDOW LIVING OF SEVENTH BARONET

(MARION JANE) AUDREY (*Audrey, Lady Miller of Glenlee*), only da of late Richard Spencer Pettit: *m* 1947, Sir (Frederick William) Macdonald Miller of Glenlee, 7th Bt, who *d* 1991. *Residence* – Ivy Grange Farm, Westhall, Halesworth, Suffolk IP19 8RN.

The 1st baronet, Sir Thomas (*d* 1789), son of William Miller, WS, and grandson of Matthew Miller of Glenlee, Kirkcudbright, was Lord President of the Court of Session in Scotland, with the title of Lord Barskimming. Sir William, the 2nd baronet (*d* 1846), was a Lord of Session with the title of Lord Glenlee.

MILLS (UK) 1921, of Ebbw Vale, co Monmouth

Sir PETER FREDERICK LEIGHTON MILLS, 3rd *Baronet*: *b* 9 July 1924; *s* his father, *Sir* (FREDERICK LEIGHTON) VICTOR, MC, 1955; *ed* Eastbourne Coll, and Natal Univ (BSc Agriculture 1952); formerly in Rhodesia Civil Ser; late Lieut Roy Gurkha Rifles; European War 1943-5: *m* 1954, Pauline Mary, da of L. R. Allen, of Calverton, Nottinghamshire, and has issue.

Arms – Sable, three millrinds in pale or between two swords erect proper, pommels and hilts of the second. **Crest** – A peewit's head, the neck encircled by a serpent nowed, both proper.
Address – PO Box A474, Avondale, Harare, Zimbabwe.

SON LIVING

MICHAEL VICTOR LEIGHTON, *b* 30 Aug 1957: *m* 1981, Susan —.

The first baronet, Sir Frederick Mills (son of late Leighton Mills, of Sunderland) was Chm of Ebbw Vale Steel and Iron Co, Ltd, Sheriff for Monmouthshire 1912, and MP for E Div of Leyton (*C*) 1931-45. The second baronet, Major Sir (Frederick Leighton) Victor Mills, MC, RA (Reserve) was Director of Public Works, Sierra Leone 1939-42 and of Uganda 1942-7, and served during European War 1914-18 (MC).

MILMAN (GB) 1800, of Levaton-in-Woodland, Devonshire

Lieut-Col Sir DEREK MILMAN, MC, 9th *Baronet*; *b* 23 June 1918; *s* his brother, *Sir* DERMOT LIONEL KENNEDY, 1990; *ed* Bedford Sch; Lt-Col (ret) 3rd E Anglian Regt; 1939-45 War with 5th Indian Div in Middle East (MC): *m* 1942, Christine, da of Alfred Whitehouse, of Sutton Coldfield, and has issue.

Arms – Azure, a serpent nowed or, between three sinister gauntlets open, two in chief and one in base argent. **Crest** – A hart lodged, per pale ermine and erminois attired and unguled or, charged on the body with two hurts fesseways.
Residence – Forge Cottage, Wilby Rd, Stradbroke, Suffolk IP21 5JN.

SONS LIVING

DAVID PATRICK (71 Camden Rd, Sevenoaks, Kent), *b* 24 Aug 1945; *ed* —, and London Univ (BEd, MA): *m* 1969, Christina, da of John William Hunt, of Leigh on Sea, Essex, and has issue living, Thomas Hart, *b* 1976, — Katharine Jane, *b* 1975. ⸺ Terence Martin (98 New Dover Rd, Canterbury, Kent), *b* 1947; *ed* Bedford School, and London Univ: *m* 1976, Sandra Wendy Elizabeth, da of Frederick Garrett, of Canterbury, Kent, and has issue living, William Frederick, *b* 1984, — Alexandra Elizabeth, *b* 1979.

DAUGHTER LIVING OF EIGHTH BARONET

Celina Anne MILMAN (4147 Burkehill Pl, W Vancouver, BC V7V 3M8, Canada), *b* 1945: *m* 1968 (*m diss* 1980), John Springett Appleby, and has issue living, Tristan Dermot Springett, *b* 1968, — Tremayne Robert, *b* 1974.

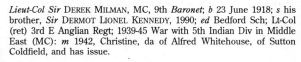

God with us, who against us?

WIDOW LIVING OF EIGHTH BARONET

MURIEL (*Dowager Lady Milman*), only da of John Edward Scott Taylor, of King's Lynn, Norfolk: *m* 1941, Maj Sir Dermot Lionel Kennedy Milman, 8th Bt, who *d* 1990. *Residence* – 7 Old Westhall Close, Warlingham, Surrey.

COLLATERAL BRANCHES LIVING

Issue of late Lt-Col Malcolm Douglas Milman, RA, 2nd son of 7th baronet, *b* 1915, *d* 1987: *m* 1940 (*m diss* 1949), Sheila Maud, da of Albert Maurice Dudeney:—
Felicity Ann, *b* 1941: *m* 1965, Peter Robin Flockton, of RR#1 Apple Hill, Ontario KOC 1BO, Canada, and has issue living, Phyllida Fiona, *b* 1969: *m* 1994, Michael Gerald Gillissie, of Ottawa, Canada, — Vanessa, *b* 1971. ⸺ Penelope Fiona, *b* 1943: *m* 1964, Anthony Stuart Darroch, of Witham-on-the-Hill, Lincs, and has issue living, Ian George, *b* 1965, — James Anthony, *b* 1967.

Grandchildren of late Stephen Walter Milman, 4th son of 4th baronet:—
Issue of late Gerald Stephen Milman, *b* 1908, *d* 1987: *m* 1944, Noreen (El Venado, Casilla de Correo 27, La Cumbre, Sierras de Cordoba, Argentina), da of Thomas Johnston Elliot:—
Ian Stephen, *b* 1946: *m* 1978, Gloria Wassermann. ⸺ Stephanie Rosalind, *b* 1949: *m* 1975, Robert Albert Christopher Lovell, and has issue living, Andrew Christopher, *b* 1979, — Mark Stephen, *b* 1982. ⸺ Angela Caroline, *b* 1952: *m* 1974, Peter Scott Kirkwood, and *d* 1991, in an aeroplane accident, leaving issue, Catriona Alexandra, *b* 1979, — Melanie Jane, *b* 1980, — Caroline Louise, *b* 1989. ⸺ Geraldine Stella, *b* 1956: *m* 1988, Marcelo di Tomasi, and has issue living, Stephen George, *b* 1992, — Patrick Gerald, *b* 1993.

Issue of late Com Henry Augustus Milman, OBE, RN, 5th son of 4th baronet, *b* 1882, *d* 1952: *m* 1912, Genevieve IRVING MILMAN, who *d* 1984, da of John Irving, of Victoria, BC:—
John Alexander Ralph, OBE, *b* (Nov) 1912; *ed* Haileybury; Major (ret) Highland L I and Mil Attaché, Budapest; Mohamand Campaign 1934; Mil Attaché, Budapest, 1953-55; 1939-45 War as acting Lt-Col in Middle East, Burma, and Italy (wounded,

despatches, OBE); OBE (Mil) 1943: *m* 1943, Daphne Mary, da of Alexander Andrew Bisset, and has issue living, John Andrew Francis Pretyman, *b* 1945, — Anne Isabel Jane, *b* 1943.

Issue of late Major Hugh Milman, OBE, yst son of 4th baronet, *b* 1884, *d* 1959: *m* 1914, Marjorie, only da of late Malcolm McCullock Paterson, MICE, formerly of the Croft, Pannal, Harrogate:—
Stephanie Grace, *b* 1915. —— Diana Constance, *b* 1920: *m* 1942, Capt John Michael Merry, RA, and has issue living, Bruce, *b* 1944, — David, *b* 1945, — Tessa, *b* 1947, — Miranda, *b* 1950, — Dilys, *b* 1956. *Residence* – Tunnel Cottage, Knapp Lane, Ledbury, Herefordshire HR8 1JD.

Granddaughters of late Humphrey Radcliffe Milman, son of late Walter Charles Gordon Milman (infra):—
Issue of late John Walter Francis Milman, *b* 1928, *d* 1984: *m* 1955, Jean Margaret, who *d* 1984, da of G. C. Till, of Gunard, I of Wight:—
Pamela Rosemary, *b* 1961. —— Laura Frances, *b* 1965.

Issue of late Walter Charles Gordon Milman, 3rd son of 3rd baronet, *b* 1853, *d* 1907: *m* 1886, Edie Helen Blythe, who *d* 1955, da of John Alexander Radcliffe, formerly of Ordsal, Cobham, Surrey:—
Isabel Joan, *b* 1898: *m* 1922, Maj William M. Martineau, MC, RASC, who *d* 1983, and has issue living, Josephine Helen, *b* 1923: *m* 1959, John Van Valkenburg. *Residence* – 5555 Dover Rd, Richmond, BC V7C 4K6, Canada.

Granddaughters of late Lt-Col Everard Stepney Milman, 6th son of Lt-Gen Francis Miles Milman, 2nd son of 1st baronet:—
Issue of late Lt-Col Octavius Rodney Everard Milman, DSO, *b* 1882, *d* 1971: *m* 1911, Mary Freya, who *d* 1979, el da of late Rev William Edward Haigh, Hon Canon of Bristol:—
Joanna Woolstone (Little Orchard, Bracken Rd, Seaford, Sussex), *b* 1912: *m* 1939, Maj Denys Paul Bulkeley, RA, who *d* 1981, and has issue living, Richard Milman (Lane End, 9 St Botolph's Lane, Orton Longueville, Peterborough), *b* 1940: *m* 1967, Elizabeth Mahoney, and has issue living, Thomas William *b* 1971, Joanna Louise (twin) *b* 1971. —— Patricia Freya, *b* 1920: *m* 1942, Lionel Noel Woolf, of 7B Bedford Towers, Cavendish Place, King's Rd, Brighton BN1 2JG, and has issue living, Inigo Rodney Milman, *b* 1946: *m* 1970, Susan Rebecca Davis, and has issue living, Bethia Fearne Milman *b* 1974, — Christopher Patrick Milman, *b* 1947: *m* 1969, Linda Johnston, and has issue living, Simon Justin *b* 1970, Jonathan Marcus *b* 1973, — Nicholas David Milman *b* 1953: *m* 1973, Ann Elizabeth March, and has issue living, Benjamin Douglas *b* 1978.
Sir Francis Milman, 1st Bt of Levaton in Woodland, Devon, was Pres of Roy Coll of Physicians 1811-13, and Physician to King George III. Sir William Ernest Milman, MM, 6th Bt *d* (Aug), 1962, and his brother and successor, Brig-Gen Sir Lionel Charles Patrick Milman, CMG, 7th Bt *d* (Nov) 1962.

Milne-Watson, see Watson.

MILNER (GB) 1717, of Nun Appleton Hall, Yorkshire

Sir (GEORGE EDWARD) MORDAUNT MILNER, 9th *Baronet*, el son of late Brig-Gen George Francis Milner, CMG, DSO, 2nd son of late Henry Beilby William Milner, 2nd son of 4th baronet: *b* 7 Feb 1911; *s* his kinsman, Sir WILLIAM FREDERICK VICTOR MORDAUNT, 1960; *ed* Oundle; was Stipendiary Steward of Jockey Club of S Africa 1954-9; Steward of Cape Turf Club 1960-76; Steward of Jockey Club of S Africa 1977-80; Mem of Council of Thoroughbred Breeders Assoc 1975-82; author of *Inspired Information, Vaulting Ambition, The Last Furlong, Thoroughbred Breeding*, and *The Godolphin Arabian*; European War 1939-45 as Capt RA: *m* 1st, 1935, Barbara Audrey, who *d* 1951, da of Henry Noel Belsham, of Hunstanton, Norfolk; 2ndly, 1953, Katherine Moodie Bissett, da of late D. H. Hoey, of Dunfermline, Fifeshire, and has issue by 1st *m*.

Arms – Per pale or and sable, a chevron between three horses' bits counterchanged.
Crest – A horse's head couped sable, maned and bridled or between a pair of wings gold.
Residence – Oude Natte, Valleij, Klapmuts, Cape Province, S Africa. *Club* – Rand (Johannesburg).

Addit frena feris
He puts bridles on the brutal

SONS LIVING *(By 1st marriage)*

TIMOTHY WILLIAM LYCETT, *b* 11 Oct 1936. —— Charles Mordaunt (PO Box 41, Klapmuts, Cape, S Africa), *b* 1944: *m* 1965, Lady Charlene Mary Olivia French, el da of 3rd Earl of Ypres, and has issue living, Marcus Charles Mordaunt, *b* 1968, — Patrick Edward French Mordaunt, *b* 1969, — Alexander George French Mordaunt, *b* 1981.

DAUGHTER LIVING *(By 1st marriage)*

Georgina Madeleine Mary, *b* 1939: *m* 1961, Arthur Henry Bertram Grattan-Bellew (see Grattan-Bellew, Bt). *Residence* – Hole Farm, Gt Waldingfield, Sudbury, Suffolk.
The 1st baronet, MP for York City, was Grand Master of the Freemasons in England. The 2nd baronet was Receiver-General of Excise, the 3rd baronet sat as MP for York City 1790-1811, the 5th baronet sat as MP therefor 1848-57, and the 7th baronet, Rt Hon Sir Frederick George Milner, GCVO, PC, sat as MP therefor 1883-5 and for Nottinghamshire, Bassetlaw Div 1890-1906.

Milnes-Coates, see Coates.

MOIR (UK) 1916, of Whitehanger, Fernhurst, co Sussex

Sir ERNEST IAN ROYDS MOIR, 3rd *Baronet*; *b* 9 June 1925; *s* his father, *Sir* ARROL, 1957; *ed* Rugby, and Gonville and Caius Coll Camb (BA 1949); European War 1943-45 with RE: *m* 1954, Margaret Hanham, da of George Eric Carter, of Cranbrook, Netheroyd Hill, Huddersfield, and has issue.

𝕬rms – Argent, a span of a bridge ernarched, embattled, and in perspective, checky or and azure, between three Moors' heads coupled sable, each banded of the second and third, and distilling three drops of blood proper. 𝕮rest – Upon a span of a bridge as in the arms a Moor's head affrontée couped at the shoulders sable, banded or and azure, collared checky of the same. *Residence* – Three Gates, 174 Coombe Lane West, Kingston-upon-Thames, Surrey KT2 7DE.

SONS LIVING

CHRISTOPHER ERNEST (77 Dora Rd, Wimbledon, SW19 7JT), *b* 22 May 1955; *ed* King's Coll Sch, Wimbledon: *m* 1983, Vanessa, yr da of Victor Alfred Crosby, of 109 Poplar Rd South, Merton Park, SW19, and formerly wife of Joseph William Kirtikar, and has issue living, Oliver Royds, *b* 1984, — Alexander Victor, *b* (twin) 1984. —— Timothy James, *b* 1959. —— Nicholas Ian, *b* 1961.

SISTER LIVING

By virtue, not otherwise

Joy Yvonne, *b* 1927: *m* 1st, 1948 (*m diss* 1954) Lieut Sir Baldwin Patrick Walker, RN, 4th Bt (*cr* 1856); 2ndly, 1954 (*m diss* 19—), Michael Haggerty, and has issue living, (by 2nd *m*) John Wyeth, *b* 1957, — Susan Bret, *b* 1955, — Gillian Ruth *b* 1958. *Residence* – 14 St Peter's St, Rochester, Kent.

The 1st baronet, Sir Ernest William Moir, was head of the firm of Ernest William Moir & Co Ltd, engineers, which he founded, and a Director of S Pearson & Son Ltd, contracting engineers. The 2nd baronet, Sir Arrol Moir, was Vice-Pres of Institute of Patentees.

Molesworth-St Aubyn, see St Aubyn.

MOLONY (UK) 1925, of the City of Dublin

(*Sir*) (THOMAS) DESMOND MOLONY, 3rd *Baronet*, does not appear on the Official Roll of the Baronetage, *b* 13 March 1937; *s* his father, *Sir* HUGH FRANCIS, 1976, but does not use title; *ed* Ampleforth, and Trin Coll, Dublin; late P/O RAF: *m* 1962, Doris, da of late E. W. Foley, of Cork, and has issue.

𝕬rms – Gules, six arrows in saltire between two bows erect to dexter and sinister or, a chief ermine. 𝕮rest – A dexter arm embowed in armour proper charged with a fleur-de-lys gules, the hand in a gauntlet holding a sword of the first. *Residence* – 4/39 Gipps St, Toowoomba, Queensland, Australia.

DAUGHTERS LIVING

Jennifer Mary, *b* 1963. —— Grace Ann, *b* 1964. —— Daphne Julia Rose, *b* 1965. —— Lynda Jacqueline Clare, *b* 1967.

COLLATERAL BRANCH LIVING

In God and not in my bow will I hope

Grandchildren of Rt Hon Sir Thomas Francis Molony, 2nd son of 1st baronet:—
Issue of late Sir Joseph Molony, KCVO, QC, Judge of Courts of Appeal of Jersey and Guernsey, *b* 1907, *d* 1978: *m* 1936, Carmen Mary (who *m* 2ndly, 1989, Reginald A. Slay, of 3 Lyefield Court, Emmer Green, Reading RG4 8AP), only da of late Frankland Dent, PhD, MSc:—
PETER JOHN (Rock House, Great Elm, Frome, Som BA11 3NY), *b* 17 Aug 1937; *ed* Downside, and Trin Coll, Camb (MA); FCA: *m* 1964, Elizabeth Mary, el da of Henry Clervaux Chaytor, of Cambridge, and has issue living, (James) Sebastian, *b* 1965, — (John) Benjamin, *b* 1966, — (Simon) Benedict, *b* 1972, — (Thomas) Francis, *b* 1975, — (Carmen) Jane, *b* 1967. —— John Fernando (30 St Ann's Lane, Godmanchester, Cambs PE18 8JE), *b* 1949; *ed* Downside and Trin Coll Camb: *m* 1985, Caroline Christine, yst da of Brig Wilfred Ponsonby, OBE, of West Burton, N Yorkshire, and has issue living, Nicola Carmen, *b* 1986, — Catherine Elizabeth, *b* 1988. —— Mary Carmen, *b* 1939: *m* 1963, Martin Noble Wells, of 34 Beeleigh Rd, Maldon, Essex CM9 7QH, and has issue living, Nicholas Thomas Clinton, *b* 1964, — Adrian Francis, *b* 1966, — Jonathan Patrick, *b* 1968, — Joanna

Kate, *b* 1971. ——— Angela Carmen, *b* 1942: *m* 1967, Philip Vincent, of Taverners, Woodeaton, Oxford OX3 9TH, and has issue living, Patrick Henry Morse, *b* 1970, — Bruno Charles, *b* 1979, — Antonia Louise, *b* 1968, — Katherine Eleanor, *b* 1974.

The 1st Baronet, Rt Hon Sir Thomas Francis Molony (son of James Molony, of Harcourt Street, Dublin), was appointed HM's 2nd Serjeant-at-Law, Ireland 1911, Solicitor-Gen for Ireland 1912, and Attorney-Gen for Ireland 1913, and was Judge of High Court of Justice in Ireland (King's Bench Div) 1913-15, a Lord Justice of Appeal 1915-18, and Lord Ch Justice of Ireland 1918-24.

MONCREIFFE OF THAT ILK (NS) 1685, of Moncreiffe, Perthshire.

Sir (RUPERT) IAIN KAY MONCREIFFE OF THAT ILK, 11th *Baronet*, CVO, QC, 24th Chief of the Name and Arms of Moncreiffe, *d* 1985 and was *s* by his elder son, the 24th Earl of Erroll (*see that title*).

DAUGHTER LIVING OF NINTH BARONET

Katharine Elisabeth MONCREIFFE OF MONCREIFFE, *b* 1920; 24th feudal Baroness of Moncreiffe; 1939-45 War with WRNS at Station X, Bletchley. *Seat* – Moncreiffe, Perthshire. *Club* – Kennel.

WIDOW LIVING OF ELEVENTH BARONET

HERMIONE PATRICIA (*Lady Moncreiffe of that Ilk*), da of late Lt-Col Walter Douglas Faulkner, MC, Irish Gds (*see* D Buccleuch, colls): *m* 1966, as his 2nd wife, Sir (Rupert) Iain Kay Moncreiffe of that Ilk, 11th Bt, CVO, QC, who *d* 1985. *Residence* – 24 Gordon Place, W8 4JE.

This family derives its surname from the hill of Moncreiffe, which has been in their possession since before surnames were first adopted in Scotland. "Moncreiffe" is the Old Gaelic place-name *Monadh Craoibhe* (the Hill of the Sacred Bough), and on its summit stood the dry-stone stronghold of the Pictish Kings; while the Moncreiffe arms indicate them to have probably been cadets of the same branch of the ancient royal stock as the lairds of Dundas (*see* M Zetland). Sir Mathew of Moncreiffe was confirmed in the lands by royal charter in 1248; and Malcolm Moncreiffe, 6th of that Ilk, had a new charter of the free Barony of Moncreiffe in 1455. Sir Thomas Moncreiffe, 14th of that Ilk, who was *cr* a Baronet with remainder to heirs male whatsoever in 1685, was 4th in descent from Hew Moncreiffe, 2nd son of John Moncreiffe, 8th of that Ilk (*d* 1496). The el son, Sir John Moncreiffe, 9th of that Ilk (*k* at Flodden 1513) was great-grandfather of Sir John Moncreiffe, 12th of that Ilk, who was *cr* a Baronet 1626. His son Sir John Moncreiffe of that Ilk, 2nd Bt, being childless, the Baronetcy (*cr* 1626) passed eventually to the line of his uncle Archibald Moncreiff, Heritable Prior of Elcho (*see* B Moncreiff); but in 1667 the Crown confirmed a family arrangement whereby Sir John made over the feudal Barony of Moncreiffe to his kinsman Thomas Moncreiffe, who thus succeeded him as Chief and became 14th of that Ilk and was later *cr* 1st Bt (1685). The 11th baronet, Sir (Rupert) Iain Kay Moncreiffe of that Ilk, CVO, QC, a distinguished genealogist and writer on heraldic and genealogical subjects, was successively Kintyre Pursuivant and Albany Herald.

Montagu-Pollock, see Pollock.

Montague-Barlow, see Barlow.

MONTGOMERY (UK) 1801, of Stanhope, Peeblesshire

Sir (BASIL HENRY) DAVID MONTGOMERY, 9th *Baronet*, only son of late Lt-Col Henry Keith Purvis-Russell Montgomery, OBE; *b* 20 March 1931; *s* his uncle, *Sir* BASIL RUSSELL PURVIS-RUSSELL-HAMILTON-MONTGOMERY, 1964; *ed* Eton; a JP and DL of Kinross-shire: *m* 1956, Delia, da of late Adm Sir (John) Peter Lorne Reid, GCB, CVO (*see* Reid, Bt, *cr* 1897, colls), and has issue.

Arms – Quarterly, 1st and 4th azure, three fleurs-de-lis or; 2nd and 3rd gules, three annulets or, stones azure, over all, dividing the quarters, a cross wavy of the second, charged with three cinquefoils, in fesse ermine. Crest – A Dexter Hand holding a sword indented on the back like a saw proper. *Residence* – Kinross House, Kinross KY13 7ET.

SON LIVING

JAMES DAVID KEITH, *b* 13 June 1957; *ed* Eton, and Univ of Exeter; late Capt The Black Watch: *m* 1983, Elizabeth Lynette, eldest da of Lyndon Evans, of Tyla Morris Farm, Pentyrch, Mid-Glamorgan, and has issue living, Edward Henry James, *b* 1986, — Iona Rosanna, *b* 1988. *Residence* – 70 Hillier Rd, SW11.

DAUGHTERS LIVING

Caroline Jean, *b* 1959: *m* 1983, Nicholas J. K. Liddle, eldest son of Alan Liddle, of 38 Hurlingham Rd, SW6, and has issue living, Alexander Allan Kessel, *b* 198-, — Lucy Delia, *b* 198-, — Harriet Susan, *b* 1991. —— Davina Lucy, *b* 1961: *m* 198-, Humphrey Martin Butler, eldest son of Geoffrey Butler, of Cheveney Cottage, Stetchworth, Newmarket, and has issue living, Bertie James, *b* 1991, — Hector Charles, *b* 1993. —— Iona Margaret, *b* 1972. —— Laura Elizabeth, *b* 1974.

SISTER LIVING

Veronica Mary Anthea, *b* 1935.

DAUGHTER LIVING OF EIGHTH BARONET

Sheila, *b* 1923; 1941-45 War with New Zealand WAAF (Radar): *m* 1st, 1945 (*m diss* 1959), John Martin Griffith; 2ndly, 1967, Desmond Edward Widgery, who *d* 1989, and has issue living (by 1st *m*), Andrea Suzanne, *b* 1946: *m* 1975, Alexander Palmarczuk, — Gael Virginia, *b* 1949: *m* 1982, Sqdn Ldr Gordon Graham, RAF, who *d* 1990 (*k* on mil ser). *Residence* – Warroch, Newstead, RD, Hamilton, NZ.

MOTHER LIVING

Cynthia Louisa Winifred (Kinross House, Kinross), da of John Allan Maconochie Welwood, of Kirknewton, Midlothian, and Garvock, Fife (E Perth, colls): *m* 1930, Lt-Col Henry Keith Purvis-Russell-Montgomery, OBE, who *d* 1954.

COLLATERAL BRANCHES LIVING

Grandchildren of late Herbert Elphinstone Montgomery, yr son of Capt Thomas Henry Montgomery, yst son of 2nd baronet:—
Issue of late Brig Arthur Herbert Montgomery, OBE, TD, FICA, late RA, *b* 1902, *d* 1978: *m* 1939, Féodora Kathleen Alice (13 Belvedere AV, Wimbledon, SW19), da of late Henry Bligh Forde:—
James Henry Anson (Wellow Mead, Sherfield English, Romsey, Hants), *b* 1945: *m* 1st, 1972 (*m diss* 1977), Carolyn Winifred Finlay; 2ndly, 1984, Julia Rosamund (actress Fiona Richmond), da of late Rev John Harrison, of Cornwall, and has issue living (by 2nd *m*), Tara Féodora, *b* 1984. —— Rachel Janet, *b* 1940: *m* 1972, Max Monsarrat, of Le Tournier, Latouille-Lentillac, St Céré, Lot 46.400, France. —— Sylvia Mary (*Baroness Crathorne*), *b* 1942: *m* 1970, 2nd Baron Crathorne.

Granddaughters of late William Montgomery, son of late Robert Montgomery, 4th son of 1st baronet:—
Issue of late Robert Hamilton Montgomery, *b* 1863, *d* 1943: *m* 1898, Evelyn Mary, who *d* 1951, da of late Rev Frederick Vernon, V of Shawbury, near Shrewsbury:—
Dorothy Vernon, *b* 1909: *m* 1952, William Smoot Rust, and has issue living, William Montgomery, *b* 1952. *Residence* – Magbie Hill, Warrenton, Virginia, USA.
Issue of late Rev Colin Francis Montgomery, *b* 1867, *d* 1906: *m* 1894, Evelyn, who *d* 1948, da of late Henry Webb, of Worcester:—
Evelyn Ruth (2 Beauvale Close, Ottery St Mary, Devon), *b* 1902: *m* 1926, Ven Richard Hamilton Babington, formerly Archdeacon of Exeter, who *d* 1984, and has issue living, Richard Andrew, *b* 1927, — Gervase Hamilton, *b* 1930, — Susan Mary, *b* 1933, — Felicity Ruth, *b* 1939.

Grandchildren of late Robert Hamilton Montgomery (ante):—
Issue of late Ian Stuart Montgomery, *b* 1900, *d* 1984: *m* 1942, Neva, da of late Ogden Minton, of Greenwich, Connecticut, USA:—
Brian Stuart, *b* 1952: *m* 1976, Patty —, of Warrenton, Va, USA. —— Ann Vernon, *b* 1945: *m* 1967, James R. Egan, of 167 Samoset Drive, Hanover, Mass, USA, and has issue living, Cheryl Ann, *b* 1970, — Mischell, *b* 1974. —— Sheila Minton, *b* 1949: *m* 1972, Mervin J. Marles, of New York, USA, and has issue living, Merv John, *b* 1978, — Ian Stuart, *b* (twin) 1978.
Issue of late Adm Alan Robert Montgomery, US Navy, *b* 1905, *d* 1964: *m* 1st, 1928 (*m diss* 1940), Josephine Marie, da of late Edward J. Straine, of Philadelphia; 2ndly, 1941, Mary Helen, da of George E. Kohlhaas, of San Bernadino, California, USA:—
(By 1st *m*) Robert Edward, *b* 1932. —— Doris Marie, *b* 1929.

Grandson of late Rev Colin Francis Montgomery (ante):—
Issue of late Squadron Leader Robert Maxwell Montgomery, RAF, *b* 1897, *d* 1977: *m* 1st, 1924 (*m diss* 1936), Eleanor Pierce Adams, who *d* 1957; 2ndly, 1936, Audrey Winifred, who *d* 1980, only da of C. Field, of The Hazels, Worplesdon, Surrey:—
Andrew John (Farthingham House, Farthingham Lane, Ewhurst, Surrey), *b* 1937: *m* 1965, Maureen Patricia, da of M. J. Roberts, of Morden, Surrey, and has issue living, Robert Maxwell, *b* 1968, — Michael Andrew, *b* 1971.

This is a younger branch of the Montgomeries, Earls of Eglinton, descended from Robert Montgomerie of Giffen, yr brother of the 1st Lord Montgomerie. William, 5th in line from Robert, acquired the lordship of Magbiehill, Ayrshire. The 1st baronet, Sir James Montgomery, MP for Peebles 1768-76, was Chief Baron of the Exchequer in Scotland 1775-81. His elder brother, William of Magbiehill, was also created a baronet, but his title became extinct 1831. Sir James, the 2nd baronet, was Lord Advocate of Scotland 1804-06, and represented Peebles for nearly thirty years. The 3rd baronet, Sir Graham (Lord-Lt of Kinross-shire), sat as MP for Peeblesshire 1852-68, and for Selkirkshire and Peeblesshire (C) 1868-80, and was a Junior Lord of the Treasury 1866-68. The 7th baronet, Sir Henry James, was Lord-Lt for Kinross-shire, and assumed 1907 for himself and issue the additional surname of Purvis-Russell (having *m* 1882 Mary Maud, MBE, da of T. Purvis-Russell of Warroch, Kinross-shire), and in 1933 the further surname of Hamilton for himself only. His son, Sir Basil Russell Purvis-Russell-Hamilton-Montgomery, 8th baronet, was recognized in that name by decree of Lord Lyon 1948.

Montgomery Cuninghame, see Cuninghame.

MOON (UK) 1855, of Portman Square, Middlesex

Sir PETER WILFRED GILES GRAHAM MOON, 5th *Baronet*; *b* 24 Oct 1942; *s* his father, *Sir* (ARTHUR) WILFRED GRAHAM, 1954; *ed* Lancing; Man Dir Harkel Development Corp Ltd, and Chm Irans Continental Corp Ltd: *m* 1st, 1967 (*m diss* 1992), Mrs Sarah Gillian Chater, da of late Lt-Col Michael Carson Lyndon Smith, MC, MB, BS (*see* Smith, Bt, colls, *cr* 1897); 2ndly, 1993, Mrs Terry Lynn de Vries, da of W. Coetzee, of Brackenfell, Cape Town, S Africa, and has issue by 1st *m*.

Arms – Argent, an eagle displayed gules, charged on the breast with two swords in saltire proper; on a chief nebuly azure, a fasces erect or, between two crescents argent. **Crest** – A crescent argent, in front of a fasces in bend or, surmounting a sword in bend sinister proper.
Residence – Holdfast House, Holdfast, nr Upton-on-Severn, Worcs WR8 0RA.
Clubs – Royal Cork Yacht, Master Mariners (Cape Town).

Keep an even mind

SONS LIVING *(By 1st marriage)*

RUPERT FRANCIS WILFRED GRAHAM, *b* 29 April 1968; *ed* Marlborough, and Exeter Univ. —— Thomas Edward Bradshaw Graham, *b* 1972; *ed* Dean Close, Cheltenham.

COLLATERAL BRANCHES LIVING

Grandchildren of late Rev Cecil Graham Moon (infra):—
Issue of late Lt-Col Edward Horace Graham Moon, 15th/19th Hussars, *b* 1904, *d* 1990: *m* 1931, Cynthia Rosamond, who *d* 1989, da of L. Avery:—
John Jeremy Edward Graham, MBE (Thrintoft House, Thrintoft, Northallerton, N Yorks), *b* 1932; *ed* Sherborne; Maj 15th/19th Hussars (ret); Lt-Col Army Legal Corps; MBE 1985: *m* 1st, 1958 (*m diss* 1964), Jane Mary, da of T. J. Cundy, of Brant Broughton, Lincs; 2ndly, 1966, Dorrit, el da of Gert Andersson, of Gongehusevej 174, Copenhagen, Denmark, and has issue living (by 1st *m*), Francis Edward Graham, *b* 1962: *m* 1986, Lorraine, eldest da of Michael Willoughby, of Hinton Waldrist, Oxon, and has issue living, Camilla Sarah Jane *b* 1992, — Caroline Rachel Graham, *b* 1960: *m* 1987, Charles Nicholas Frank, of Costock Grange Stud, Costock, nr Loughborough, Leics LE12 6XE, son of Charles Frank, of Standlake, Oxon, and has issue living, Georgina Rachel *b* 1990, Elizabeth Jane *b* 1992. —— (by 2nd *m*), Christian Graham, *b* 1967, — Thomas Edward Graham, *b* 1969. —— Camilla Mary Graham, *b* 1939: *m* 1972, Clinton Bourdon, and has issue living, Jeremy Edward Currier, *b* 1979, — Timothy Francis Avery, *b* 1981.

Issue of late Rev Cecil Graham Moon, yst son of 2nd baronet, *b* 1867, *d* 1948: *m* 1898, Mary Andalusia, who *d* 1970, da of John Barnard Hankey:—
John Cecil Graham, *b* 1919; *ed* Eton; Maj (ret) 15th/19th Hussars: *m* 1952, Susan Mary Milburn, yr da of late Edward Reed, of Ghyllheugh, Longhorsley, Northumberland, and has issue living, Belinda Mary Graham, *b* 1954: *m* 1977, Marek William Kwiatkowski (*see* E Dartmouth), — Amanda Jane Graham, *b* 1958: *m* 1985, Thomas G. Bowring, eldest son of Geoffrey Bowring, of Halton Park, Lancaster, and has issue living, a da *b* 1991, — Philippa Ann Graham, *b* 1959. *Residence* – Springfield Mews, Corbridge, Northumberland.

The 1st baronet, Sir Francis Graham Moon, an eminent fine-art publisher, and Lord Mayor of London 1854-5, was created a baronet during his Mayoralty in recognition of the visit of the Emperor Napoleon III and the Empress of the French to the Guildhall, April 1855. Sir (Arthur) Wilfred Graham Moon, the 4th baronet, was ADC to Gov of Fiji 1929-31.

MOON (UK) 1887, of Copsewood, Stoke, co Warwick

Vincit omnia veritas

Truth conquers all

things

Sir ROGER MOON, 6th *Baronet, b* 17 Nov 1914; *s* his brother *Sir* EDWARD, MC, 1988; *ed* Sedbergh; served with Johore Volunteer Engineers in Malaya and Singapore; prisoner-of-war in Thailand 1942-45: *m* 1950, Meg, yr da of late Arthur Mainwaring Maxwell, DSO, MC, of Moss Vale, NSW, Australia, and grand-da of Maj-Gen Sir William Throsby Bridges, KCB, CMG, founder of the Australian Imperial Forces, and has issue.

Arms – Argent, an eagle displayed gules; two flaunches of the last, each charged with a fleur-de-lis of the field, on a chief of the second three crescents of the first. **Crest** – A fleur-de-lis argent in front of a demi-eagle displayed gules, charged on the breast with an escutcheon of the first bearing a crescent also gules.
Residence – The Barn House, Wykey, Ruyton-XI-Towns, Shropshire SY4 1JA.

DAUGHTERS LIVING

Sarah Corinna, *b* 1951. —— Gillian Adèle, *b* 1954: *m* 1986, William Andrew Johnston, yr son of late Brian Johnston, CBE, and has issue living, Harry Edward Duff, *b* 1987, — Emily Rose, *b* 1988, — Georgia Grace, *b* 1990. —— Patricia Isolda, *b* 1955: *m* 1982, Peter W. A. Hogg, of House 6, Pacific View, 22 Cape Rd, Hong Hom Kok, Hong Kong, only son of late Lt-Col A. G. Hogg, OBE, of Ibthorpe House, Hurstbourne Tarrant, Hants, and has issue living, Anthony Oliver Richard, *b* 1985, — Camilla Adèle, *b* 1983, — Arabella Louisa Daphne, *b* 1987.

BROTHER LIVING

HUMPHREY (22 Brewitt Rd, Estcourt, Natal, Rep of S Africa), *b* 9 Oct 1919: *m* 1st, 1955 (*m diss* 1964), Diana Marion, da of late F. Basil Hobson, of The Homestead, Freshwater Bay, Isle of Wight; 2ndly, 1964, Elizabeth Anne Drummond, who *d* 1994, da of late George Archibald Drummond Angus, and widow of Henry James Butler, of Lusaka, and has issue living (by 1st *m*), Susan Caroline, *b* 1957, — Vicki Georgina, *b* 1960, — (by 2nd *m*) Jennifer Claire, *b* 1966.

SISTERS LIVING

Ursula, *b* 1912: *m* 1945, Peter Henry Joscelyne, who *d* 1958, and has had issue, Hugh Anthony, *b* 1947; *d* 1990, — Nigel Townshend, *b* 1949. —— Mary, *b* 1913. —— Gwynneth Elinor, *b* 1916.

DAUGHTER LIVING OF THIRD BARONET

Lila Colleen, *b* 1931: *m* 1953, George Garroway Little, who *d* 1992, and has issue living, Gregory Robert, *b* 1959, — Sharon Colleen, *b* 1961. *Residence* – 4132 Balkan St, Vancouver 10, BC.

WIDOW LIVING OF FIFTH BARONET

MARY (*Mary, Lady Moon*), only child of late Capt Benjamin Conolly: *m* 1947, Sir Edward Moon, 5th Bt, MC, who *d* 1988. *Residence* – Heath House, Crickheath, Oswestry, Shropshire SY10 8BN.

COLLATERAL BRANCHES LIVING

Granddaughters of late Sir Ernest Moon, KCB, KC yst son of 1st baronet:—
Issue of late Arthur Moon, MC, QC, *b* 1882, *d* 1961: *m* 1912, Marjorie Isabel, who *d* 1966, da of Charles Lancelot Andrewes Skinner, formerly 4th Hussars (E Bessborough):—
Penelope Kathleen, *b* 1924: *m* 1950, (Count) Thomas Andreas Constantine Lubienski, of 93 Thorpe Rd, Peterborough, and has issue living, Andrew, *b* 1952: *m* 1990, Louise King, — Henry Roger, *b* 1960: *m* 1991, Petra Limberg, and has issue living, Jonathon *b* 1991, Matthew Gloag, of 3/33 Royal Terrace, Edinburgh, and has issue living, Emma, *b* 1972, — Sorcha Ann, *b* 1974. —— Sarah, *b* 1956: *m* 1989, Peter Cutts, of 36 Calbourne Rd, SW12, and has issue living, Richard Adam Moon, *b* 1991,, — Alexander Charles Famin, *b* 1992.

Sir Richard Moon, 1st baronet (son of Richard Moon, a Liverpool merchant) was Chm of London of London and North-Western Railway Co 1861-91.

MOORE (UK) 1919, of Hancox, Whatlington, Sussex

I strive against adversity

(*Sir*) NORMAN WINFRID MOORE, 3rd *Baronet* (has established his claim but does not use the title); *b* 24 Feb 1923; *s* his father, *Sir* ALAN HILARY 1959; *ed* Eton, and Trin Coll, Camb (BA 1943); PhD Bristol 1954; sometime Lieut RA; Senior Prin Scientific Officer, Nature Conservancy 1965-83, and Visiting Prof, Wye Coll, Univ of Lond 1979-83; Chm Farming and Wildlife Advisory Group since 1983; European War 1942-45 (wounded, prisoner): *m* 1950, Janet, PhD, only da of Paul Singer, and has issue.

Arms – Argent on a fesse between two garbs azure, three mullets or (also on an inescutcheon the arms of *Burrows*; azure between three fleurs de lys erminois a sword in pale point upwards proper, pommel and hilt or). **Crest** – In front of a Moor's head proper, a garb, barwise or.
Residence – Farm House, Swavesey, Cambridge.

SON LIVING

PETER ALAN CUTLACK, *b* 21 Sept 1951; *ed* Eton and Trin Coll, Camb BA (1973), DPhil (Oxon) 1980: *m* 1989, Pamela Edwardes, and has issue living, Paul Edwardes, *b* 1990. —— Esther Edwardes, *b* 1993.

DAUGHTERS LIVING

Caroline Mary Phyllis, *b* 1953; Barrister-at-Law: *m* 1982, Richard Anthony Cohen, and has issue living, Toby Benedict, *b* 1983, — Guy Peter Gillachrist, *b* 1988, — Mary Beatrix, *b* 1986. —— Helena Meriel, *b* 1957: *m* 1986, David Alexander, and has issue living, Rose Maribel, *b* 1990, — Catherine Janet (twin), *b* 1990, — Harriet Alannah, *b* 1994.

BROTHER LIVING

Richard Gillachrist, *b* 1931; *ed* Trin Coll, Camb (BA); Pres of Union Soc, Camb 1955; formerly on editorial staff of *News Chronicle*, Sec Gen of Liberal International, and Private Sec to Leader of Liberal Party; Political Sec to Federation of Liberal and Democratic Parties of the European Community: *m* 1955, Ann Hilary, only da of late Wing-Cdr Charles Cleaver Miles, MC, RAF, and has issue living, Charles Hilary, *b* 1956; Editor of *The Sunday Telegraph* since 1992: *m* 1981, Caroline Mary, elder da of Ralph Lambert Baxter, and has issue living, William *b* 1990, Katharine *b* (twin) 1990, — Rowan William Gillachrist, *b* 1961: *m* 1991, Elizabeth Triep, — Charlotte Sydney, *b* 1959: *m* 1987, Mark V. E. Smith, of Hancox, Whatlington, Battle, Sussex, and has issue living, George *b* 1990, Samuel *b* 1991. *Residence* – 17 rue des Cultes, Brussels 1000, Belgium.

SISTERS LIVING

Hilary Mary, *b* 1927. —— Meriel Edith Milicent, *b* 1936: *m* 1961, Rt Rev John Keith Oliver, Bishop of Hereford, of the Palace, Herefore, and has issue living, Thomas Hilary, *b* 1964, — Henry Caspar William, *b* 1968, — Mary Philomena, *b* 1971. Sir Norman Moore, MD, LLD, FRCP, 1st Bt (only son of Robert Ross Rowan Moore, Bar-at-law, of Broughton, Lancashire), was Emeritus Lecturer on Principles and Practice of Med at St Bartholomew's Hospital, and Pres of Roy Coll of Physicians 1918-21.

MOORE (UK) 1923, of Colchester, Essex (Extinct 1992)

Sir EDWARD STANTON MOORE, OBE, 2nd and last *Baronet*.

SISTERS LIVING OF SECOND BARONET

Doris Vera, *b* 1907: *m* 1939, Patrick Seeton of 31 York Av, Scottsville, Pietermaritzburg, Natal, and has issue living, John, *b* 1940, — David, *b* 1943: *m* 1964, Jeann Griffioen, and has issue living, Jacqueline Doris, *b* 1965. —— Audrey Evelyn *b* 1908: *m* 1937 (*m diss* 1946), Maj Ernest Pattison Shanks, who *d* 1994, and has issue living, Oliver Edward Pattison, *b* 1939: *m* 1965, Amanda Nina, da of Cdr James Andrew Stewart-Moore, RN, of Ballydivity, co Antrim. *Residence* – Fairlight, Beaconsfield Rd, Chelwood Gate, Sussex.

WIDOW LIVING OF SECOND BARONET

MARGARET (*Lady Moore*), elder da of late T. J. Scott-Cotterell, of Hoshigaura, Chipstead Valley, Surrey: *m* 1946, Sir Edward Stanton Moore, 2nd Bt, OBE, who *d* 1992.

COLLATERAL BRANCHES LIVING

Issue of late Brig Eric Edward James Moore, DSO, Col R Inniskilling Fus, 3rd son of 1st baronet, *b* 1894, *d* 1979: *m* 1928 (*m diss* 1948), Gertrude, who *d* 1972, da of Frank Fellows Vanderhoef, of New York:—
Mary Elizabeth Deirdre, *b* 1937: *m* 1965, David Tudor Evans, of Homeland, Bunbury Heath, Tarporley, Cheshire, and has issue living, Peter Edward Gwilym, *b* 1967, — Juliet Mary Enid, *b* 1969.

Issue of late Wing-Cdr Ronald George Moore, 4th son of 1st baronet, *b* 1903, *d* 1981: *m* 1st, 1928, Barbara Kathleen, da of Charles Elwes, 2ndly, 1942, Angela Mary, da of Paul Cammiade:—
(By 1st *m*) Anne Cecilia, *b* 1929: *m* 1954, John Hetherington, and has issue living, Christopher, *b* 1955, — Cary, *b* 1957, — Philip, *b* 1958, — Simon Charles, *b* 1965.
The 1st baronet, Sir Edward Cecil Moore, senior partner in the firm of Edward Moore and Sons, chartered accountants, of 4 Chiswell St, EC1, was Sheriff of London, 1914-15, and Lord Mayor 1922-23.

MOORE (UK) 1932, of Moore Lodge, co Antrim

The brave may fail but cannot yield

Sir WILLIAM ROGER CLOTWORTHY MOORE, TD, 3rd *Baronet*; *b* 17 May 1927; *s* his father, *Sir* WILLIAM SAMSON, DL, JP, 1978; *ed* Marlborough, and RMC; Lt R Inniskilling Fus 1945; 1950-63 Maj N Irish Horse; High Sheriff co Antrim 1964; Chm of board of Visitors HM Prisons in N Ireland 1971; BBC Broadcaster 1963-66; UK Gov Internat Platform Assoc, USA 1980: *m* 1954, Gillian, da of John Brown, of co Antrim, and has issue.

Arms – Azure, on a chief indented or, a spur sable between two mullets pierced gules. Crest – Out of a ducal crest coronet or, a blackamoor's head, face to dexter proper, wreathed about the temples argent and sable.
Club – Boodle's.

SON LIVING

RICHARD WILLIAM, *b* 8 May 1955; *ed* Portora; Lieut R Scots 1974.

DAUGHTER LIVING

Belinda Jane, *b* 1956: *m* 1978, Timothy James Bryce Duncan, of Castlehill, Kirkmahoe, Dumfries, yst son of late Sir Arthur Bryce Duncan.

COLLATERAL BRANCH LIVING

Issue of late Capt Joseph Roger Moore, 2nd son of 1st baronet, *b* 1895, *d* 1951: *m* 1920, Florence Amy, who *d* 1948, da of Lt-Col John Patrick, DL, of Dunminning, co Antrim:—
Jean Florence Helen, *b* 1923: *m* 1949, Robert Andrew Young, and has issue living, Timothy David, *b* 1950: *m* 1979, Sarah Elizabeth Armorel Leng, — Alexandra Louise, *b* 1952: *m* 1984, John Crawford Cone. *Residence* – Falcon Cottage, South Warnborough, Basingstoke, Hants.
The 1st baronet, the Rt Hon Sir William Moore, PC (el son of late William Moore, MD, JP, of Moore Lodge, Ballymoney, co Antrim), was Parliamentary Private Sec to Ce Sec for Ireland (Rt Hon G. Wyndham, MP) 1902-4, Senior Crown Prosecutor, Belfast 1915-17, and Treasurer, King's Inns, Dublin 1918-20; became a Judge of High Court of Justice (King's Bench Div) 1917, a Lord Justice of Appeal for N Ireland 1921, and Lord Ch Justice of N Ireland 1925; retired 1937; sat as MP for N Antrim Div of Antrim co (C) 1899-1906, and for N Armagh Div Armagh co Nov 1906-17.

MOORE (UK) 1956, of Kyleburn, co Ayr (Ext 1971)

Sir THOMAS (CECIL RUSSELL) MOORE, CBE, 1st and last *Baronet*.

WIDOW LIVING OF FIRST BARONET

PENELOPE (*Lady Moore*) (Bogside House, Monkton, Ayrshire), da of late Lt-Col Samuel Gurney Sheppard, DSO, and widow of Robert Lawrence Angus, DL, of Ladykirk, Monkton, Ayrshire: *m* 1950, as his 2nd wife, Sir Thomas (Cecil Russell) Moore, CBE, 1st Bt, who *d* 1971, when the title became ext.

MORDAUNT (E) 1611, of Massingham Parva, Norfolk
(Name pronounced "Mordant")

Ferro comite
The sword my companion

Sir RICHARD NIGEL CHARLES MORDAUNT, 14th *Baronet*; *b* 12 May 1940; *s* his father, *Sir* NIGEL JOHN, MBE, 1979; *ed* Wellington Coll: *m* 1964, Myriam, da of — Atchia, of — and has issue.

Arms – Argent, a chevron between three estoiles sable. Crest – A Saracen's head full faced proper, wreathed round the temples argent and sable.
Residence – 1/11 Motherwell St, South Yarra, Melbourne, Vic 3141, Australia.

SON LIVING

KIM JOHN, *b* 1966.

DAUGHTER LIVING

Michele, *b* 1965.

BROTHERS LIVING

David Arthur John, *b* 1942: *m* 1969, Elizabeth Aske, da of William Edgel Luke, and has issue living, Katherine Elizabeth Aske, *b* 1970, — Alexandra Caroline Aske, *b* 1972.
—— Peter Anthony Charles (9 Napier Av, SW6), *b* 1946: *m* 1972, Angela Mary, da of Ralph Arthur Hubbard (*see* B Addington, colls), and formerly wife of (Luke Edward) Timothy Hue Williams, and has issue living, Alastair Nigel Charles, *b* 1974, — Anna Rose, *b* 1981.

SISTER LIVING

Tessa Anne, *b* 1947: *m* 1974, David Anthony Nutting, and has issue (*see* Nutting, Bt).

AUNT LIVING (*Sister of 13th baronet*)

Cynthia Violet, *b* 1918.

COLLATERAL BRANCHES LIVING

Grandchildren of late Gerald John Mordaunt (infra):—
Issue of late Eustace John Mordaunt, *b* 1901, *d* 1988: *m* 1934, Anne Frances, who *d* 1976, only da of late Alastair Gilmour:—
David John, *b* 1937; *ed* Wellington Coll; Royal Northumberland Fus 1955-57; Assist Master Wellington Coll 1963-86, and Housemaster 1968-79: *m* 1990, Catharine Hilary, da of John Mayne, CB, of Westminster, SW1. *Residence* – Torbreck Lodge, Essich, by Inverness IV1 2DJ. —— Gerald Charles, *b* 1939; *ed* Wellington Coll: *m* 1965 (*m diss* 1981), Carol Elspeth, da of late Brig Richard Montagu Villiers, DSO (*see* E Clarendon, colls), and has issue living, James Richard John, *b* 1967, —— Christopher Charles, *b* 1969, —— Tanya Alexandra, *b* 1974, —— Harriet Georgia, *b* 1980. *Residence* – 55 Melody Rd, SW18. —— Angela Mary, *b* 1934: *m* 1955, David Neil Carr, of Yarlet Hall, nr Stafford, and has issue living, Philip Donald Mordaunt, *b* 1959, —— Sally Jane, *b* 1956: *m* 1st, 1977 (*m diss* 1987), Anthony Mitchell; 2ndly, 1989, Andrew Simms, and has issue living, (by 1st *m*) Andrew David *b* 1982, —— Judith Anne, *b* 1961: *m* 1983, Patrick Dickinson.

Issue of late Gerald John Mordaunt, brother of 12th baronet, *b* 1873, *d* 1959: *m* 1900, Grace Adeline, who *d* 1965, yst da of late Col E. C. Impey, of 33 Holywell, Oxford:—
Robin Charles, *b* 1909; *ed* Wellington Coll, and Univ Coll, Oxford: *m* 1940, Brita, da of C. Thoren, of Stockholm, Sweden, and has issue living, Timothy John (60 Karina Terrace, Palmerston North, NZ), *b* 1949: *m* 1976, Heather Gowing, and has issue living, Guy John *b* 1977, Anthony Charles *b* 1979, Samuel John *b* 1986, Rebecca Jean *b* 1982, —— Kristina Birgitta, *b* 1946: *m* 1967, Christopher McVeigh (17 Repton St, Christchurch, NZ), and has issue living, Brita *b* 1970, Carlotta *b* 1971, Anna *b* 1974, Juliet *b* 1978. *Residence* – 9 Ocean View Terrace, Sumner, nr Christchurch, NZ.

Grandchildren of late Harry Mordaunt, 4th son of late John Mordaunt, 17th Lancers, son of Rev Charles Mordaunt, 2nd son of 6th baronet:—
Issue of late Christopher John Mordaunt, *b* 1879, *d* 1954: *m* 1st, 1907, Helena Charlotte, da of Capt R. N. Young, RHA; 2ndly, 1916, Mary Patricia, who *d* 1975, da of Lt-Col J. C. Cautley, Roy W Kent Regt:—
(By 1st *m*) Richard John, VRD, *b* 1908; *ed* Woodbridge Sch; Lt-Cdr RNR, European War 1939-45: *m* 1st, 1930, Nancy, who *d* 1986, da of late Major T. C. Toler, DL, of Swettenham Hall, nr Congleton, Ches; 2ndly, 1988, Sarah Anne, da of late W/Cdr E. Seymour Williams, and has issue living (by 1st *m*), (Thomas) Christopher John (Brawby Lodge, Brawby, Malton, N Yorks), *b* 1934; is a Capt 9th Queen's Roy Lancers: *m* 1959, Belinda Madeline, da of Thomas Cecil Gouldsmith (*see* Laurie Bt, colls, 1961 Edn), of Coneysthorpe, Malton, Yorks, and has issue living, (Sarah) Camilla *b* 1961: *m* 1985, William Richard Ashton Shuttleworth, of Brook House, Stanton Lacy, Ludlow, Shropshire (*see* V Cross, 1990 Edn) (and has issue living, Tom William Ashton *b* 1990, Alexandra Sophie Ashton *b* 1987), Sophie Jane *b* 1967, —— Rosemary Jane, *b* 1931: *m* 1957, Lyndon Bolton, of Arrat's Mill, by Brechin, Angus, and has issue living, Lyndon *b* 1958, Timothy William *b* 1963, —— Nicola Anna Mary, *b* 1944. *Residence* – Dodington Manor, Chipping Sodbury, Avon. —— (By 2nd *m*) Stephen Clare (Horseshoe House, 51 Sydney Blds, Bath, BA2 6DB), *b* 1925; Master Mariner, Capt P & O SN Co (ret): *m* 1950, Joan, da of late Louis Henry Poppleton, of Nightingale Villa, Batheaston, and has issue living, Guy Roger, *b* 1952; *ed* Grenville Coll, Bideford: *m* 1980, Deborah Anne, yst da of B. A. G. Norton, and has issue living, Simon Richard Stephen *b* 1988, Sally Jane *b* 1985, —— Ann Patricia, *b* 1956: *m* 1978, John Quartly, and has issue living, Amy *b* 1979, Ruth *b* 1981, Emma *b* 1982. —— Katherine Patricia (Wyke Croft, 36 Brandy Hole Lane, Chichester, Sussex), *b* 1918: *m* 1950, David Isard, who *d* 1980, and has issue living, John David, *b* 1951; *ed* Cranleigh, and Leicester Univ.

Osbert le Mordaunt, a Norman knight, was possessed of Radwell, in Bedfordshire, by the gift of his brother, who had it of William I for his services, and for the services of his father, in the conquest of England. The 1st baronet, Sir l'Estrange Mordaunt, distinguished himself in the wars of the Low Countries, *temp* Elizabeth I Sir Charles, the 3rd baronet, has his estates sequested for his loyalty to Charles I. The 5th, 6th, 7th, 9th, and 10th baronets each represented Warwickshire in Parliament, while the 7th baronet was also a Groom of the Bedchamber.

HUGHES-MORGAN (UK) 1925, of Penally, co Pembroke

Without God, without anything

Judge Sir DAVID JOHN HUGHES-MORGAN, CB, CBE, 3rd *Baronet; b* 11 Oct 1925; *s* his father, *Sir* JOHN VERNON, 1969; *ed* RN Coll, Dartmouth; Sub-Lt RN (ret); Maj-Gen Army Legal Corps (ret 1984); 1939-45 War; a Recorder (1983); a Circuit Judge on South-eastern Circuit since 1986; MBE (Mil) 1959, CBE (Mil) 1973, CB (Mil) 1983: *m* 1959, Isabel Jean Blacklock Gellatly Milne, da of John Milne Lindsay, of Annan, Dumfriesshire, and has issue.

𝕬rms – Quarterly, 1st and 4th, a griffin segreant sable, over all a chevron of the second charged with a mullet between two fleur-de-lis of the first, *Morgan;* 2nd and 3rd, sable, a lion rampant guardant between two fleur-de-lis in fesse or; on a chief engrailed of the second, two Cornish choughs proper, *Hughes.* 𝕮rest – 1st, in front of a reindeer's head erased or, collared and chained sable, a fleur-de-lis between two mullets also sable, *Morgan;* 2nd, in front of a demi-lion rampant guardant argent, charged on the shoulder with a fleur-de-lis sable, two swords saltireways proper, pommels and hilts or, *Hughes.*
Address – c/o National Westminster Bank, 143 High St, Bromley, Kent BR1 1JL.

SONS LIVING

(IAN) PARRY DAVID (34 Elliott Rd, W4 1PE), *b* 22 Feb 1960: *m* 1992, Julia K., elder da of R. J. S. Ward, of Amersham, Bucks. —— Jonathan Michael Vernon, *b* 1962. —— Mark Richard Milne, *b* 1964: *m* 1988, Sophia Frances, yst da of Graham Rogers, of Hungerford House, Fordingbridge, Hants, and has issue living, Daniel, *b* 1988, — Theo, *b* 1990, — Felix, *b* 1992.

COLLATERAL BRANCHES LIVING

Issue of late Capt (Thomas Parry) Michael JONES-PARRY, S Wales Borderers, 2nd son of 2nd Bt, *b* 1928; *d* 1982; assumed by deed poll 1961 the surname of Jones-Parry in lieu of his patronymic: *m* 1952, Gillian (White Hart Cottage, Westbrook, Boxford, Newbury, Berks), yr da of Reginald Carter Stern, of Arden, Weybridge, Surrey:—
David Anthony, *b* 1954; *ed* Wellington: *m* 1983, Jacqueline Rowland-Rouse, and has issue living, Thomas Edward, *b* 1986, — Matthew Nicholas, *b* 1991, — Gemma, *b* 1987. —— Caroline Anne: *m* 1975, Baron Hugues M. F. d'Achon, of Paris, 3rd son of Baron Antoine d'Achon. —— Sarah Margaret, *b* 1961.

Issue of late Sq-Ldr David James Hughes-Morgan, RAF, yr son of 1st baronet, *b* 1903, *d* 1967: *m* 1935, Evelyn, who *d* 1965, da of John Windsor-Richards, of Plas, Caerleon, Mon:—
Elizabeth Dolores, *b* 1936: *m* 1960, John Brill, MA, of Rookhurst, Coast Hill Lane, Westcott, nr Dorking, Surrey, and has issue living, Timothy John, *b* 1965, — Jonathon Richard, *b* 1966, — Edward James, *b* 1969.
The 1st baronet, Sir David Hughes-Morgan (son of late David Morgan, of Henllys, Llandovery), was Chm of *Western Mail,* and High Sheriff of Breconshire 1898-9. He assumed by deed poll (enrolled in College of Arms) 1925 the additional surname of Hughes.

MORRIS (UK) 1806, of Clasemont, Glamorganshire

By the shield of faith

Sir ROBERT BYNG MORRIS, 10th *Baronet,* son of Percy Byng Morris, son of Cdr Frederick Morris, 3rd son of 2nd baronet; *b* 25 Feb 1913; *s* his kinsman, *Sir* CEDRIC LOCKWOOD, 1982: *m* 1947, Christine Kathleen, da of Archibald Field, of Toddington, Glos, and has issue.

𝕬rms – Sable, on a saltire engrailed ermine a bezant, charged with a cross couped gules. 𝕮rest – A lion rampant or, charged on the shoulder with a cross couped gules, within a chain in the form of an arch or.
Residence – Norton Creek Stables, RR5 Norton Creek Rd, St Chrysostome, Quebec, Canada.

SON LIVING

ALLAN LINDSAY, *b* 27 Nov 1961: *m* 1986, Cheronne Denise, eldest da of Dale Whitford, of Par, Cornwall, and has issue living, Chelsea Alana, *b* 1992.

DAUGHTERS LIVING

Geraldine Ann, *b* 1948: *m* 1st, 1969 (*m diss* 1981), Gilbert Baxter, Jr; 2ndly, 1984, Thomas Millard of Vancouver, BC, and has issue living, (by 1st *m*) Jennifer Carly, *b* 1950: *m* 1972 (*m diss* 19—), Andrew Jamieson. —— Roberta Crystal, *b* 1965; Jr Dressage Canadian Champion 1983.

WIDOW LIVING OF SEVENTH BARONET

OLIVE IRENE (*Olive, Lady Morris*), da of William Davies, of Swansea: *m* 1938, Sir Herbert Edward Morris, 7th baronet, who *d* Aug 1947.

COLLATERAL BRANCHES LIVING

Issue of late Frank Hall BYNG-MORRIS, brother of 8th baronet, *b* 1869, *d* 1954 (having assumed by deed poll

1927 the additional surname of Byng): *m* 1913, Irene Catherine, who *d* 1968, da of Lt-Col Rogers-Harrison, of Kenilworth, Pittville Lawn, Cheltenham:—
Daphne Veronica, *b* 1914: *m* 1942, Norman Halfhead, who *d* 1988, and has issue living, Christopher Norman, *b* 1946: *m* 1984, Francesca Waterhouse, and has issue living, Michael Christopher *b* 1986, Lucy Christina *b* 1985. *Residence –*

Issue of late Col John Morris, 2nd son of 3rd baronet, *b* 1850, *d* 1916: *m* 1881, Jessie who *d* 1941, da of William Fowler:—
Jessie Harriet Amy Blanch: *m* 1923, Capt Bertram Wellingtonn Parker, late Queen's Own Roy W Kent Regt. *Residence –* The Firs, Chelston, Torquay.
This family descends from Robert Morris of Bishops Castle and Cleobury, Salop, whose grandson, Sir John Morris of Clasemont, was created a baronet in 1806. The 9th Baronet, Sir Cedric, was a noted painter and horticulturalist.

Morrison-Bell, see Bell.

Morrison-Low, see Low.

Mosley, (GB) 1781, of Ancoats, Lancashire, and of Rolleston, Staffordshire (see B Ravensdale).

EDWARDS-MOSS (UK) 1868, of Roby Hall, Lancashire

(*Sir*) DAVID JOHN EDWARDS-MOSS, 5th *Baronet*, *b* 2 Feb 1955; *s* his father, Sir JOHN HERBERT THEODORE, 1988, but at the time of going to press, his name does not appear on the Roll of the Baronetage, nor does he use the title; *ed* Cranleigh.

Arms – 1st and 4th, quarterly, ermine and erminois a cross-patée azure between six billets, three in chief and three in base gules, *Moss*; 2nd and 3rd, argent a lion rampant-guardant sable on a chief dancetté of the last two eagles displayed of the first, a canton or, *Edwards*. **Crest** – 1st, issuant from the battlements of a tower or, charged with a rose gules slipped vert, a griffin's head ermine, charged on the neck with a cross-pattée azure; 2nd, a rock proper, therefrom rising a dove argent (charged on the breast, for distinction, with a cross-crosslet gules), holding in the beak an olive branch and surmounted by a rainbow also proper.
Residence –

En la rase je fleurie
I flourish in the rose

BROTHERS LIVING

PETER MICHAEL, *b* 26 Sept 1957: *m* 1988, Jenifer Cadisch, and has issue living, John Herbert Theodore, *b* 1992. —— Paul Richard, *b* 1960. —— Christopher James, *b* 1963. —— Jonathan Francis William, *b* 1967.

SISTER LIVING

Penelope Anne, *b* 1956: *m* 1988, Michael Geoffrey Jennings, and has issue living, Johnnie Sam, *b* 1991. —— Kathrine Sarah, *b* 1989.

AUNT LIVING (*sister of 4th baronet*)

Rosemary Ethel Amy, *b* 1917. *Residence –* 3 Church Av, Henley-on-Thames, Oxon RG9 2BY.

WIDOW LIVING OF FOURTH BARONET

JANE REBIE (*Lady Edwards-Moss*), da of Carteret John Kempson: *m* 1951, Sir John Herbert Theodore Edwards-Moss, 4th Bt, who *d* 1988. *Residence –* Ruffold Farm, Cranleigh, Surrey.

COLLATERAL BRANCH LIVING

Grandchildren of late Maj John Edwards-Moss, RGA, 2nd son of 2nd baronet:—
Issue of Capt Thomas Richard Edwards-Moss, *b* 1921, *d* 1974: *m* 1st, 1943 (*m diss* 1952), Bridget Doreen, da of late Maj Hon Richard Coke (*see* E Leicester, colls); 2ndly, 1953, Monica Hughes (4 Marlborough Buildings, Bow St, Langport, Som TA10 9PH), da of late Maj H. G. Wilkinson, BSc, Burma Ser (ret):—
(By 1st *m*) John Richard, *b* 1947; *ed* Eton: *m* 1976, Penelope, only da of Michael Horne, of Bath Villas, Mill Hill, Newmarket, Suffolk, and has issue living, Thomas Michael, *b* 1980. — Rose Bridget, *b* 1981, — Letitia Patience, *b* 1983. *Residence –* Glebe Farm House, E Leake, Loughborough, Leics LE12 6LE. —— (By 2nd *m*) Stella Lucy, *b* 1958.
Sir Thomas Edwards-Moss, 1st baronet, assumed, by Roy licence, 1851, the additional surname and arms of Edwards, having *m* 1847, Amy Charlotte, da and heir of Richard Edwards of Roby Hall, Lancs.

MOSTYN (E) 1670, of Talacre, Flintshire
(Name pronounced "Mostin")

Life by the death of the lion

My help is from the Lord

Sir WILLIAM BASIL JOHN MOSTYN, 15th *Baronet*; *b* 15 Oct 1975; *s* his father, Sir JEREMY JOHN ANTHONY, 1988.

Arms – Per bend sinister ermine, and ermines, a lion rampant or. **Crest** – On a mount vert a lion as in the arms.
Residence – The Coach House, Church Lane, Lower Heyford, Oxon.

SISTERS LIVING

Casimira Anita Maria, *b* 1964. —— Rachel Johanna Maria, *b* 1967.

UNCLE LIVING (*son of 13th baronet*)

TREVOR ALEXANDER RICHARD (39B Elgin Crescent, W11 2JD), *b* 23 May 1946: *m* 1986 (*m diss* 1988), Elizabeth, da of Peter Dax.

AUNTS LIVING (*daughters of 13th baronet*)

Sara Ann, *b* 1932: *m* 1957, Ranjit Banerji, of 7 London Place, Oxford OX4 1BD, and has issue living, Bijoya, *b* 1957: *m* 1983, Ian Chisholm, of 10 Molescroft Park, Beverley, Humberside HU17 7EA, and has issue living, Rory *b* 1989, Anna *b* 1987, — Sabita, *b* 1961: *m* 1989, Arild Bergh, of 87 Lytton Rd, Oxford OX4 3NY, and has issue living, Maia *b* 1994, — Juthika, *b* 1963: *m* 1987, David Nicholas Slaughter, of Penny Cottage, London Rd, Henfield, W Sussex BN5 9JJ. —— Joanna Mary Patricia, *b* 1939: *m* 1960, Hugh Edward Sarne Griffith, of La Mariscala 315, San Isidro, Lima 27, Peru, and has issue living, Hugh Pyers Sarne (5 St Dunstan's Rd, W6), *b* 1962, — Isolde Gemma Sarne, *b* 1961: *m* 1988, Ian Aitken Georgeson, of Flat 3, 355 Argyle St, Glasgow G2 8LT, — Bronwen Anita, *b* 1963, — Samantha Joanna, *b* 1967, — Phoebe Abigail, *b* 1976.

GREAT AUNT LIVING (*sister of 13th baronet*)

Hermione Mary Josephine (13 Oving Rd, Whitchurch, nr Aylesbury, Bucks), *b* 1906: *m* 1942, Joseph Mostyn, Col Polish Army, who *d* 1969 (naturalized a British subject 1949, when he abandoned by deed poll his surname of Tuzinkiewicz), and has issue living, Richard Jan Joseph (Old Manor Farm, Broughton, Aylesbury, Bucks), *b* 1942: *m* 1966, Annette Christian Garrick, and has issue living, Suki Hermione *b* 1968, Melissa Bernadette *b* 1970, Chloe Mary *b* 1975, — Paul (Mill Hook Farm, Granborough, Buckingham), *b* 1945: *m* 1971, Elizabeth Catherine Bernadette, da of Peter Northcote Lunn, CMG, OBE (V Gormanston), and has issue living, Toby Joseph *b* 1975, Theresa Antoinette *b* 1973, Olivia Mary *b* 1977, — Simon Edward Basil (Kings Court, Talley, Dyfed), *b* 1947: *m* 1973, Alison Mary Bridget, da of Capt J. Thomas, RN, and has issue living, Samuel John Savage *b* 1975, Freddy Joseph George *b* 1980, Harry Edward Llewelyn *b* 1987, Polly Elizabeth Hermione *b* 1973, Meg Joan Elizabeth *b* 1983, — Wanda Hermione Krystyna (twin), *b* 1942: *m* 1964, Capt Terence Percyvall Hart Dyke (*see* Dyke, Bt, colls).

WIDOW LIVING OF FOURTEENTH BARONET

CRISTINA BEATRICE MARIA (*Lady Mostyn*), da of Marchese Pier Paolo Vladimiro Orengo, of Turin, Italy: *m* 1963, Sir Jeremy John Anthony Mostyn, 14th Bt, who *d* 1988. *Residence* – The Coach House, Church Lane, Lower Heyford, Oxon.

COLLATERAL BRANCHES LIVING

Grandchildren of late Lieut-Col Edward Henry Joseph Mostyn, only son of late Capt Edward Henry Mostyn, 2nd son of 7th baronet:—
   Issue of late Capt Joseph Edward Hubert Mostyn, TD, *b* 1888, *d* 1960: *m* 1920, Gertrude Clare, da of late John Hutchinson:—
Edward John, TD, *b* 1922; *ed* Ampleforth; is Capt RA (TA), and a Qualified Asso of Land Agents' So; Hon Research Fellow Reading Univ; formerly Flight-Lieut RAF; European War 1941-45 (despatches): *m* 1945, Dorothy Brady, and has had issue, Francis Edward Terence, *b* 1946, — Stephen John, *b* 1949, — Sara Juliet, *b* 1955; *d* 19——. *Residence* – Rosemary Cottage, Chapel Row, Bucklebury, Berks RG7 6P3.
   Issue of late Maj Joseph Cecil Mary Mostyn, MC, *b* 1891, *d* 1971: *m* 1924, Joan Wake, who *d* 1975, da of Guy Shorrock:—
Jerome John Joseph (c/o Lloyds Bank plc, 4 Dean Stanley St, SW1P 3HU), *b* 1933; *ed* Downside: *m* 1st, 1956 (*m diss* 1971), Mary Anna Bridget Ghislaine, da of Ronald F. Medlicott; 2ndly, 1972, Ana Julia Novoa, who *d* 1980; 3rdly, 1988, Rosemary Joy Hamilton, widow of (Alan) Ross McWhirter, and da of Leslie C. H. Grice, and has issue living (by 1st *m*), Nicholas Anthony Joseph Ghislain (10 Regents Park Terr, NW1 7EE), *b* 1957, — Mark Francis Joseph Ghislain (49 Wandsworth Bridge Rd, SW6 2TB), *b* 1959, — Giles Patrick Joseph Ghislain, *b* 1967, — Joanna Charlotte Mary Ghislaine, *b* 1963, — (by 2nd *m*) Philip Anthony Julio Jerome, *b* 1978, — Anna Teresa Joan, *b* 1973. —— Philomena Cecilia Mary (8 Upper Brook St, Oswestry, Shropshire SY11 2TB), *b* 1926: *m* 1949, Hugh Dudley Symon, MA, MRCS, FRCP, who *d* 1980, and has issue living, Andrew Nicholas Dudley, *b* 1950, — Neil Antony *b* 1953: *m* 1981, Victoria Allison Edwards, — Pyers Hugh, *b* 1957; BSc Univ of Wales: *m* 1986, Patricia Mary Roberts. —— Charmian Mary (c/o Nat Westminster Bank, 39 The Borough, Farnham, Surrey GU9 7NR) *b* 1938: *m* 1966, Guy Hipsley Cooper, who *d* as the result of an accident 1986, and has issue living, Tarquin Rupert Christopher Mostyn, *b* 1975, — Sophy Maria, *b* 1968, — Jonquil Kate, *b* 1971, — Alice Teresa Mostyn, *b* 1972.
   Issue of late Joseph Philip David Mostyn, *b* 1894, *d* 1929: *m* (Jan) 1928, Mary Catherine (who *m* 2ndly, 1931, Brigadier Desmond Seymour Keenan), da of Richard Cecil Moss:—
Sir (Joseph) David (Frederick), KCB, CBE (c/o Lloyds Bank, Broad St, Lyme Regis, Dorset), *b* (Nov) 1928; Gen late R Green Jackets; GOC Berlin 1980-83, Military Sec 1983-86, Adjt Gen, Min of Defence 1986-88, Col Cmdt Light division 1983-86, Army Legal Corps 1983-88; MBE (Mil) 1962, Despatches Brunei 1963, CBE (Mil) 1974, KCB (Mil) 1988; Kt of the sovereign Mil Order of Malta (1974): *m* 1952, Diana Patricia, da of late Brig Bertrand Cecil Owens Sheridan, MC, and has issue living, Philip Joseph, *b* 1955; Lt-Col—: *m* 1985, Helen Catharine Stewart, da of late Maj George Stewart Nickerson, of Cour, by Campbeltown, Argyll, and has issue living, Isobel Mary *b* 1987, Alice Mary *b* 1989, Rosanna Mary *b* 1990, Clare *b* 1993, — (David) Mark (Joseph), *b* 1960: *m* 1989, Jane Carolyn, da of J. W. Rhodes, of Melbourne, Australia, and has issue living, Joshua Marcus Joseph *b* 1991, William Joseph, *b* 1992, — Rupert Joseph Sheridan, *b* 1961, — Matthew Anthony, *b* 1971, — Celia Mary, *b* 1953, — Katherine Mary, *b* 1973.

Descendants of late Charles Browne-Mostyn, el son of late Charles Browne-Mostyn (infra) who became 6th *Baron Vaux of Harrowden* on the termination of the abeyance in his favour 1838 (see that title).

Grandchildren of late Charles Browne-Mostyn, 2nd son of 5th Bt:—
Issue of late Henry Browne-Mostyn, *b* 1867, *d* 1946: *m* 1901, Virginia who *d* 1953, da of Thomas J. McLain, USA Consul, Bahamas:—
Thomas Mervyn *b* 1904: *m* 1948, Ella Aurora, da of late Gustav Larson, and *d* 1988. —— Ruth Mary, *b* 1902: *m* 1931, Hughes Adams Shank, who *d* 1968, and *d* 1988, leaving David Hughes, *b* 1941: *m* 1966, Elaine Christina Furst, and has issue living, Michael Aaron *b* 1969, Jacob Adams *b* 1981, — Margaret Elizabeth, *b* 1936: *m* 1958, James Patrick Jarboe, MD, of Rosecroft, St Mary's City, Maryland, USA, and has issue living, Thomas Hughes *b* 1969, Karen Elizabeth *b* 1959, Barbara Gail *b* 1960, Mary Kathleen *b* 1965, Jessica Rose *b* 1972.
Issue of late Francis Llewellyn Mostyn (twin), *b* 1873 *d* 1959: *m* 1901, Sarah Thornton, who *d* 1925:—
Charles Francis Llewellyn, *b* 1904: *m* 1933, Marion McKay, and has issue living, Francis Llewellyn, *b* 1935: *m* 1958, Yvonne Brown, and has issue living, Douglas William Francis *b* 1959, Donald Mayne *b* 1960, — Trevor Angus *b* 1946, — Gwendolyn Grace, *b* 1937: *m* 1958, Leonard Alexander Gynlai, and has issue living, Edward Llewellyn Alexander *b* 1959, Sarah Theresa Marion *b* 1960. *Residence* – Woolford Station, S Alberta, Canada.
Issue of late Capt George William Mostyn, *b* 1874, *d* 1939: *m* 1897, Isabel Almond:—
Vaux Almond, *b* 1906; late Maj Australian Imperial Force: *m* 1st, 1934, Mavis Jean Marshall, who *d* 1958; 2ndly, 1964, Monica Lewsey Jackson, who *d* 1985. *Residence* – 17 Frederick St, Glengowrie, S Australia.
Issue of late Iltyd Edward Mostyn, *b* 1881, *d* 1958: *m* 1901, Lily Humphry, who *d* 1984:—
Charles Gerard, *b* 1910: *m* 1936, Ruth Winona, who *d* 1988, da of William Brown, and has issue living, Trevor Iltyd (380 Hidhurst Pl, W Vancouver, BC V7S 1K1, Canada), *b* 1940: *m* 1979, Sarah Katherine Ford. *Residence* – 305-8840 No 1 Rd, Richmond, BC V7C 4C1, Canada. —— Gwendolyn Mary, *b* 1905: *m* 1939, Charles Allen Higginson, and has issue living, Brenda Lynne, *b* 1940: *m* 1963, Kirby Michael O' Donaughy, DDS, Box 276, Rossland, BC, Canada, and has issue living, Denise Margaret *b* 1964, Theresa Lynne *b* 1967, Kelly Corinne *b* 1969, — Kathleen Mary, *b* 1942: *m* 1962, Lorne Richard Simpson, of 5900, Unsworth Rd, Sardis, BC, Canada, and has issue living, Thomas Allen *b* 1967, Barbara Kathleen *b* 1964. *Residence* – 45687 Spadina Av, Chilliwack, BC V2P 1T8, Canada.

Grandsons of late Iltyd Edward Mostyn (ante):—
Issue of late Iltyd Humphry Mostyn, *b* 1907, *d* 1982: *m* 1934, Joan Athol, who *d* 1989, da of Charles J. Radwell:—
(David) Pyers, *b* 1938: *m* 1963, Susan Wallace Johnson, and has issue living, Richard Pyers (39 Oak St, Whitehorse, Yukon, Canada), *b* 1963: *m* 1990, Shona Sugrue, and has issue living, Richard Thomas *b* 1994, — David Wallace, *b* 1967, — Peter Llewellyn, *b* 1968. *Residence* – 19 Parson's Ridge, Kanata, Ontario, Canada K2L 2MI. —— Richard Clive, *b* 1945: *m* 1986, Ursula Anna Schmiing. *Residence* – 1979 W 36th Av, Vancouver, BC V6M 1K7, Canada.
This is one of the numerous Welsh families who trace their descent in the male line from Tudor Trevor, who was the ruler of Hereford early in the tenth century. Richard ap Howell, a lineal descent from the above, was seated at Mostyn, *temp* Henry VII, and his son Thomas, who assumed the name of Mostyn, is an ancestor in female line of Baron Mostyn. Thomas Mostyn's yr brother, Pyers Mostyn, of Talacre, was gt grandfather of Sir Edward, 1st baronet.

MOTT (UK) 1930, of Ditchling, co Sussex

Bold in dangers

Sir JOHN HARMAR MOTT, 3rd *Baronet*, *b* 21 July 1922; *s* his father, *Sir* ADRIAN SPEAR, 1964; *ed* Radley, and New Coll, Oxford (MA, BM, BCh); and Middx Hospital; MRCGP; 1939-45 War as F/O RAF: *m* 1950, Elizabeth, da of late Hugh Carson, FRCS, of Selly Oak, Birmingham, and has issue.

Arms – Sable, four crescents in cross the horns turned inwards, argent. **Crest** – An estoile of eight points argent encircled by an annulet or.
Residence – Staniford, Brookside, Kingsley, Cheshire WA6 8BG.

SON LIVING

DAVID HUGH, *b* 1 May 1952; *ed* Shrewsbury, Sussex Univ (BSC), Birkbeck Coll Lond Univ (MSc), and Queen Mary Coll, Lond Univ (PhD): *m* 1980, Amanda Jane, only da of Lt-Cdr D. W. P. Fryer, RN (ret), of 20 Westover Rd, Fleet, Hants, and has issue living, Matthew David, *b* 1982, — Jonathan William, *b* 1984.

DAUGHTERS LIVING

Jennifer, *b* 1954: *m* 1977, Robert Alexander Buckey, and has issue living, Mark Robert, *b* 1981, — James John *b* 1983. —— Alison Mary, *b* 1958; *ed* Southampton Univ (BM); MRCP; has issue living, Jack Lewis Mott Kinnersley, *b* 1993.

SISTERS LIVING

Anne Lawrence (Kerensa, 3 Chute Lane, Gorran Haven, St Austell, Cornwall), *b* 1915; *ed* St Anne's Coll, Oxford (MA): *m* 1st, 1939, Anthony Dockray Phillips, DSO, DFC, RAF, who was *ka* 1944; 2ndly, 1946 (*m diss* 1961), Wilfred Robert Peasley, DFC, RAF; 3rdly, 1983, David John Hodges, and has issue living, (by 1st *m*) Anthony Adrian (Teddington House, Warminister, Wilts), *b* 1942; *ed* Shrewsbury, and Merton Coll, Oxford: *m* 1970, Lucinda Aris, and has two adopted children, Anthony Julian *b* 1980, Katherine Mary *b* 1979, — (by 2nd *m*) Patricia Mary Anne, *b* 1947: *m* 1968, Peter James Crowe, of Tregarth, 28 Chute Lane, Gorran Haven, St Austell, Cornwall PL26 6NU, and has issue living, Tasman Peter *b* 1968, James Alywyn *b* 1971, Matthew Tristan George *b* 1973, Elena Catherine *b* 1977, — Julia Jane (Lowenek, Tregony, Truro, Cornwall), *b* 1950: *m* 1969 (*m diss* 1988), Alan Nigel Clark, and has issue living, Alexander Edward *b* 1977, Dominic *b* 1979, Justin *b* 1982, — Lydia Elizabeth, *b* 1953: *m* 1973 (*m diss* 1988), David Charles Whetter, and has issue living, Timothy Andrew *b* 1978, Thomas Charles *b* 1985, Donna Marie *b* 1980. —— Monica Mary, *b* 1919: *m* 1st, 1948 (*m diss* 1978), Robert Milne Sellar; 2ndly, 1978, John Linfield, of Jasmine House, Bruton Rd, Evercreech, Shepton Mallet, Somerset BA4 6HY, and has issue living (by 1st *m*), Robert John, *b* 1950, — Mary Milne, *b* 1949: *m* 1970, Robin Edward Austin Webb, of Hill House, Holcombe, nr Bath BA3 5EF, and has issue living, William Austin *b* 1972, Robert *b* 1975, George *b* 1978, Rachael Frances *b* 1971, Julia *b* 1984.

COLLATERAL BRANCH LIVING

Issue of late Mark Dobell Mott, yr son of 1st baronet, *b* 1892, *d* 1975: *m* 1st, 1916 (*m diss* 1936), Mary Coryndon, da of late James Henry Greathead; 2ndly, 1936, Martha Lewis, da of Arthur Willis, of Witton Gilbert, co Durham:—

(By 2nd *m*) Peter Lewis, *b* 1944; *ed* Manchester Univ (BA) and Calif Univ (MA). —— Diana Dobell, *b* 1947.

The 1st baronet, Sir Basil Mott, CB, FRS (son of Frederick Thompson Mott of Birstall Hill, near Leicester), was a Consulting Civil Engineer and a Past Pres of Institution of Civil Engineers.

MOUNT (UK) 1921, of Wasing Place, Reading, Berks

Prudently and constantly

(*Sir*) (WILLIAM ROBERT) FERDINAND MOUNT, 3rd *Baronet*; *b* 2 July 1939; *s* his uncle, *Sir* William Malcolm, 1993, but does not use the title: *ed* Eton, Vienna Univ, and Ch Ch Oxford (MA); Editor Times Literary Supplement since 1990: *m* 1968, Julia Margaret, twin da of Archibald Julian Lucas (B Grenfell), and has issue.

Arms – Or, on a mount vert a lion rampant azure, ducally crowned or, between in chief two roses gules, barbed and seeded proper. **Crest** – Upon a mount vert a fox salient proper, supporting a ragged staff erect sable.
Residence – 17 Ripplevale Grove, N1 1HS.

SONS LIVING

WILLIAM ROBERT HORATIO, *b* 12 May 1969; *ed* Westminster, and Magdalen Coll Oxford. —— Henry Francis, *b* 1971; *ed* Westminster, and Magdalen Coll Oxford.

DAUGHTER LIVING

Mary Julia, *b* 1972; *ed* Westminster, and Worcester Coll, Oxford.

SISTER LIVING

Frances Leone, *b* 1941. *Residence* – 1 Steps Farm, Polstead, Colchester, Essex.

DAUGHTERS LIVING OF SECOND BARONET

Cecilia Mary (*Lady Dugdale*), *b* 1931: *m* 1967, Sir William Stratford Dugdale, CBE, MC, 2nd Bt, of Merevale Hall, Atherstone, Warwickshire, and Blyth Hall, Coleshill, Birmingham. —— Mary Fleur, *b* 1934: *m* 1962, Ian Donald Cameron, of The Old Rectory, Peasemore, Newbury, and has issue living, (Allan) Alexander, *b* 1963: *m* 1990, Sarah Louise, 2nd da of (William) George Fearnley-Whittingstall, of Springhill, Eastington, Glos, and of Mrs Douglas Montagu Douglas Scott, of Half-ord, Warwicks, and has issue living, Imogen Clare *b* 1992, — David William Donald, *b* 1966, — Tania Rachel, *b* 1965, — Clare Louise, *b* 1971. —— Viola Clare, *b* 1938: *m* 1960, Dr John Robert Blyth Currie, and has issue living, Thomas Mark, *b* 1966, — Mary Teresa, *b* 1962, — Anna Magdalen, *b* 1964.

WIDOW LIVING OF SECOND BARONET

ELIZABETH NANCE, JP (*Lady Mount*), da of Owen John Llewellyn, formerly of The Thatched House, Moulsford, Berks: *m* 1929, Sir William Malcolm Mount, 2nd Bt, who *d* 1993. *Residence* – Wasing Place, near Reading, Berks RG6 4NG.

COLLATERAL BRANCH LIVING

Issue of late George Richard Mount, 3rd and yst son of 1st baronet, *b* 1911, *d* 1991: *m* 1936, (Patricia) Elizabeth, who *d* 19—, da of late John Anthony Baring, of New York:—

(Serena) Georganne, *b* 1941: *m* 1969, Claude Royston Johnson, of 26 Devonshire Place, W1, son of Capt (S) Royston Henry Johnson, CBE, RN, of Old Barn House, Wootton, Boars Hill, Oxford.

The 1st baronet, Sir William Arthur Mount, CBE (son of late William George Mount of Wasing Place, Berks), was MP for S, or Newbury, Div of Berkshire (C) Oct 1900 to Jan 1906, and Jan 1910 to March 1918, and for Berks, Newbury Div, Dec 1918 to May 1922. Parliamentary Private Sec to successive Chancellors of the Exchequer (Rt Hon Sir Michael Hicks-Beach, Bt, MP, and Rt Hon C. T. Ritchie, MP) 1900-1902, and Civil Member of British Claims Commn in France 1916-17.

MOUNTAIN (UK) 1922, of Oare Manor, co Somerset, and Brendon, co Devon

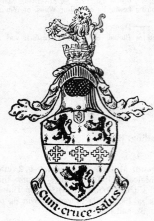

Safety with the Cross

Sir DENIS MORTIMER MOUNTAIN, 3rd *Baronet*; *b* 2 June 1929; *s* his father, *Sir* BRIAN EDWARD STANLEY, 1977; *ed* Eton; late Lt Royal Horse Gds; Pres Eagle Star Holdings 1958-93, Chm and Man Dir of Eagle Star Insurance Co Ltd 1974-85; Dir Rank Organisation plc 1968-94, Bank of Nova Scotia since 1978, Allied London Properties since 1986: *m* 1958, (Hélène) Fleur Mary Kirwan, da of John William Kirwan-Taylor, of Chemin de Carvalho 3, 1009 Pully, Switzerland, and has issue.

Arms – Ermine, on a fesse azure between three lions rampant guardant sable, each holding between the forepaws an escallop gules, three cross-crosslets argent. **Crest** – Issuant from the battlements of a tower proper, a demi-lion guardant argent, holding between the paws an escallop gules.
Residences – The Manor, Morestead, Winchester, Hants S021 1LZ; 12 Queens Elm Sq, Old Church St, SW3 6ED. *Clubs* – Nat Sporting, Blues and Royals.

SONS LIVING

EDWARD BRIAN STANFORD, *b* 19 March 1961; late Maj The Blues and Royals: *m* 1987, Charlotte Sarah Jesson, da of His Honour Judge (Henry) Pownall, and has issue living, Thomas Denis Edward, *b* 14 Aug 1989, — Harry Brian Pownall, *b* 1991, — Camilla, *b* 1993. —— William Denis Charles, *b* 1966: *m* 1994, Emma V. G., da of Cmdr Patrick Mitchell, of Chorleywood, Herts.

DAUGHTER LIVING

Georgina Lily Fleur, *b* 1959: *m* 1986, Nigel Charles Blake Macpherson, only son of Ian Macpherson, of The Old Hall, Blofield, Norwich, Norfolk, and has issue living, Charles Edward Ian, *b* 1989, — Lara Alexandra Fleur, *b* 1991, — Katie Victoria Lily, *b* 1994.

BROTHER LIVING

Nicholas Brian Edward (17 Hollywood Road, SW10), *b* 1936; *ed* Eton, and St Catherine's Coll, Camb; formerly Lt R Horse Gds: *m* 1965, Penelope, yr da of late M. H. Shearme, of 15 Astell St, SW3, and has issue living, Henry Nicholas *b* 1967, — Nathalie Frances, *b* 1970.

SISTER LIVING

Fleur Caroline, *b* 1933: *m* 1955, Dane Peter Douetil, of Busbridge Lakes House, Godalming, Surrey, and has issue living, Dane Jonathan, *b* 1960, — Guy William, *b* 1963, — William Walton, *b* 1966, — Nicola Fleur, *b* 1957; *d* 19—.

WIDOW LIVING OF SECOND BARONET

DORIS ELSIE (*Doris, Lady Mountain*) (75 Eaton Sq, SW1), el da of late Eric Charles Edward Lamb, of 2 Queen St, Mayfair, W1: *m* 1926, Sir Brian Edward Stanley Mountain, 2nd Bt, who *d* 1977.
The 1st baronet, Sir Edward Mortimer Mountain (son of late Henry Stanford Mortimer Mountain), was Chm of Eagle Star Insurance Co, Ltd. The 2nd baronet, Sir Brian Edward Stanley Mountain was Pres of Eagle Star Insurance 1974-77, and Chm 1948-73.

MOWAT (UK) 1932, of Cleckheaton, West Riding of Yorkshire (Extinct 1968)

Sir ALFRED LAW MOWAT, DSO, OBE, MC, JP, DL, 2nd and last *Baronet*.

DAUGHTER LIVING OF SECOND BARONET

Joan Mary Louise (*Lady Shaw*), *b* 1923: *m* 1951, Sir Michael Norman Shaw, DL, JP (who was *cr* a Life Baron 1994), and has issue living, Charles Michael Mowat, *b* 1952: *m* 1979, Sarah, da of late Dr — Bremner, and has issue living, Roland Charles *b* 1984, Jeremy Bremner (twin) *b* 1984, Lucy Kathleen *b* 1986, — James William, *b* 1955, — Jonathan David, *b* 1957: *m* 1985, Gillian Susan, yr da of Rollo Belsham, of Lower Swell, Stow-on-the-Wold, Glos. *Residence* – Duxbury Hall, Liversedge, Yorkshire.

DAUGHTER LIVING OF FIRST BARONET

Lucy Marcia. *Residence* – The Grange, Cleckheaton, Yorkshire.

MOWBRAY (UK) 1880, of Warennes Wood, Berkshire

Suo stat robore virtus

*Virtue stands in its own
strength*

Sir JOHN ROBERT MOWBRAY, 6th *Baronet*; *b* 1 March 1932; *s* his father, *Sir* GEORGE ROBERT, KBE, 1969; *ed* Eton, and New Coll, Oxford; DL Suffolk 1993: *m* 1957, Lavinia Mary, da of Lt-Col Francis Edgar Hugonin, OBE, JP, RA (Walker, Bt, *cr* 1868), and has issue.

Arms – Quarterly, 1st and 4th gules, a lion rampant ermine; two flaunches or, each charged with three billets in pale azure, *Mowbray*; 2nd and 3rd per pale azure and sable a chevron embattled, between in chief two roses, and in base a cross pattée or, *Cornish.* **Crests** – 1st, an oak tree or, pendent from the tree an escutcheon gules charged with a lion's head erased argent; 2nd, a Cornish chough between two branches of laurel proper. **Second Motto** – "Deus pascit corvos" (*God feedeth the ravens*), *Cornish.*
Residence – The Hill House, Duffs Hill, Glemsford, Suffolk CO10 7PP.

DAUGHTERS LIVING

Mary Clare, *b* 1959: *m* 1984, James Duncan Delevingne, son of late E. N. Delevingne, and has issue living, Benjamin James, *b* 1984, — Oliver Guy, *b* 1988. —— Teresa Jane, *b* 1961. —— Katherine Diana, *b* 1965: *m* 1993, David Norman Chastel de Boinville, son of Gerard Nicolas Pyemont Chastel de Boinville, MC, TD, of Walkern Hall, Herts.

SISTERS LIVING

Carolyn Mary, *b* 1930: *m* 1952, Stamford Robert Francis Vanderstegen-Drake, and has issue living, John Peter, *b* 1955: *m* 1986, Charlotte Susannah, da of Brian Gunn, of Quarry Close, Winscombe, Avon, and has issue living, John William *b* 1988, — Mark Stamford, *b* 1959: *m* 1986, Susan, da of Cmdr Alan Dickie, of Bowdown House, Rodborough Common, Stroud, — Clare Rosdew, *b* 1953: *m* 1st, 1978 (*m diss* 1984), (William) Gerald Cheyne (*see* Cheyne, Bt, colls); 2ndly, 1984, Christopher J. B. Bromfield, of The Old Coaching House, Lacock, Chippenham, Wilts, eldest son of late Dr F. B. Bromfield, of The Blue House, Rodborough Common, Stroud, Glos, and has issue living (by 1st *m*) (*see* Cheyne, Bt, colls), (by 2nd *m*), George Frank *b* 1985, Alice Mary *b* 1987. *Residence* – The Old Tannery, Ecchinswell, Newbury. —— Elizabeth Rose, *b* 1936: *m* 1964, Capt Patrick Hector Raymond Glennie, RN (The Old Mill House, Clanfield, Portsmouth, Hants), and has issue living, Christopher Arthur John, *b* 1966: *m* 1991, Christina Marie, da of Cyril Steiner, of Stevensville, Michigan, USA, — Alexander Patrick, *b* 1970, — Sarah Frances, *b* 1965.

WIDOW LIVING OF FIFTH BARONET

DIANA MARGARET (*Dowager Lady Mowbray*) (Starvehill House, Mortimer, Berks), da of late Sir Robert Heywood Hughes, 12th Bt (*cr* 1773): *m* 1927, Sir George Robert Mowbray, 5th Bt, KBE, who *d* 1969.

The Rt Hon Sir John Robert Mowbray, 1st baronet, el son of Robert Stirling Cornish, of Exeter, assumed by Roy licence 1847 the surname of Mowbray in lieu of his patronymic, his wife, Elizabeth Gray, being da and heir of George Isaac Mowbray of Bishopswearmouth, co Durham, and Mortimer, Berks. He sat as MP for Durham City (*C*) 1853-68 and for Oxford Univ 1868-99, and was Judge Advocate-Gen and Judge Marshal 1858-59 and 1866-68, and "Father of the House of Commons" 1898-99. The 2nd baronet, Sir Robert Gray Cornish, sat as MP for Lancashire, SE, Preswich Div (*C*) 1886-95, and for Brixton Div of Lambeth 1900-06.

MUIR (UK) 1892, of Deanston, Perthshire

*I am not broken by
hardships*

Sir RICHARD JAMES KAY MUIR, 4th *Baronet*; *b* 25 May 1939; *s* his father *Sir* JOHN (HARLING) MUIR, 1994: *m* 1st, 1965 (*m diss* 1974), Susan Elizabeth, da of George A. Gardener, of Calcutta and Leamington Spa; 2ndly, 1975, Lady Linda Mary Cole, da of 6th Earl of Enniskillen, and has issue by 1st and 2nd *m*.

Arms – Per chevron argent and or, on a chevron cotised azure, a redbreast proper between two mullets of the first, in chief as many fleurs de lis on the third. **Crest** – A Saracen's head couped, wreathed with laurel proper, charged on the neck with a mullet azure.
Residence – Park House, Blair Drummond, Perthshire.

DAUGHTERS LIVING (By 1st marriage)

Louisa Jane, *b* 1967. —— Catherine Elizabeth, *b* 1968.

(by 2nd marriage)

Daisy Mary, *b* 1977. —— Anna Charlotte, *b* 1979.

BROTHERS LIVING

IAN CHARLES (Well Cottage, Poulner, Ringwood, Hants), *b* 16 Sept 1940: *m* 1967, Fiona Barbara Elspeth, da of Maj Stuart Mackenzie, of Rose Cottage, Charlton All Saints, Salisbury, and has issue living, Sophie Amanda Nöel, *b* 1969, — Lisa Jane Fiona, *b* 1973, — Juliet Sara Kirstie, *b* 1978. —— Andrew Hugh John (Itchen Lodge, Itchen Abbas, Winchester, Hants), *b* 1943: *m* 1st, 1969 (*m diss* 1993), Primrose Jean Onslow, da of Robert B. How of St Andrews, Fife (*see* E Onslow, colls); 2ndly, 1993, Ann Mary, da of — Corbally, and formerly wife of — Jenkins, and has issue living (by 1st *m*), Philip John Frederick, *b* 1974, — Alexandra Juliet, *b* 1971. —— James Francis (Underhill, Muthill Perthshire), *b* 1948: *m* 1975, Griselda C, da of Sir Anthony Nathaniel Stainton, KCB, QC, and has issue living, John Alexander Hector, *b* 1976, — William Anthony Nathaniel, *b* 1979. —— Robert William, *b* 1950.

SISTERS LIVING

Fiona Mary, *b* 1938: *m* 1968, Walter Goetz, of 19 Alexander Place, SW7, and 86 Rue de Bac, Paris, and has issue living, Sebastian, *b* 1970, — Dominic, *b* 1971. —— Margaret Elizabeth (*Lady Aird*), *b* 1946: *m* 1968, Sir (George) John Aird, 4th Bt, of Grange Farm, Evenlode, Moreton-in-Marsh, Glos, and has issue (*see* Aird, Bt).

AUNT LIVING

Margaret Vivian, *b* 1912: *m* 1938, Eric Gerald Hayes, who *d* 1959, and has issue living, David Richard MUIR OF KNOCK (Pityoulish, Aviemore, Inverness-shire), *b* 1939: *m* 1968, Hon Sarah Maclay, da of 2nd Baron Maclay, — Helen Jane (*Hon Mrs Robert Younger*), *b* 1941: *m* 1971, Hon Robert Edward Gilmour Younger (*see* V Younger of Leckie). *Residence* – Craigdhu, Barbreck, Lochgilphead, Argyll.

WIDOW LIVING OF THIRD BARONET

ELIZABETH MARY (*Dowager Lady Muir*), el da of late Frederick James Dundas (*see* M Zetland, colls): *m* 1936, Sir John (Harling) Muir, 3rd Bt, who *d* 1994. *Residence* – Bankhead, Blair Drummond, Perthsire.

COLLATERAL BRANCHES LIVING

Grandchildren of late James Finlay Muir, 2nd son of 1st baronet:—
    Issue of late Lt-Cdr Gerald Robin Muir, OBE, RN *b* 1917, *d* 1991: *m* 1st, 1940, Doreen Margaret, who *d* 1982, yr da of late Charles Wanford Watney, of Quay Cottage, Weare Giffard, Devon; 2ndly, 1983, Margaret Claire, da of late Llewellyn Arthur Hugh-Jones, OBE (*see* B Auckland, colls, 1980 Edn), and widow of (i) Philip Dalton Worthington, MBE, and (ii) Lt-Cdr Thomas Mervyn Smith Dorrien Smith, of Tresco Abbey, Isles of Scilly:—
(By 1st *m*) Hugh James Robin (PO Box 521, Malanda, N Queensland 4885, Australia), *b* 1944: *m* 1969, Maureen Yearsly, and has issue living, Andrew James, *b* 1970, — Jeremy Kim, *b* 1973. —— Nicholas John (Dunduff, Braco Castle Farm, by Dunblane, Perthshire), *b* 1953: *m* 1st, 1975, Janet Mary Bain, who *d* 1978, da of Sir Colin Moffat Bain Campbell, MC, 8th Bt; 2ndly, 1980, Angela Cramp, and has issue living (by 2nd *m*), David Stuart, *b* 1981. —— Sarah Nadějda WILLIAMS (Blaenau Dwr Farm, Froncysyllte, Llangollen, Clwyd), *b* 1940; has assumed the surname of Williams: *m* 1965 (*m diss* 1982), Alexos Katsikides, of Athens, and has had issue, Simion, *b* 1966; *d* 1987, — Maria, *b* 1967; *d* 1976. —— Anne Catriona, *b* 1943: *m* 1970, Maj John Philip Ogilvy Gibb, of Glenisla House, Blairgowrie, Perthshire PH11 8QL, and has issue living, Alastair John Richard, *b* 1972, — Nicholas James Harry, *b* 1975, — Catriona Mary, *b* 1971. —— Jean Charlotte, *b* 1946: *m* 1970, Lieut Alexander Michael Gregory, RN, of Duncryne House, Gartocharn, by Alexandria, Dumbartonshire, and has issue living, Charlotte Clare, *b* 1971, — Katherine Jane, *b* 1973, — Helen Veronica, *b* 1979, — Sarah Rachel, *b* 1982. —— Diana Rachel, *b* 1949: *m* 1985, James Lonergan, of Graigue Little, New Inn, Cashel, co Tipperary, and has issue living, James Robin, *b* 1986, — Rosanna Rachel, *b* 1988, — Clare Charlotte, *b* 1989.

    Issue of late John Buchanan Muir, 3rd son of 1st baronet, *b* 1876, *d* 1956: *m* 1911, Agnes Heather Gardiner, who *d* 1961, da of late John Gardiner Muir, of 2 Grosvenor Cres, SW.
Diana Heather, *b* 1915: *m* 1950, John Anthony Francis Binny, and has issue living, Anne Heather, *b* 1951: *m* 1st, 1979 (*m diss* 1982), David Child, 2ndly, 1983, Jonathan Guy Chambers, of Kiftsgate Court, Campden, Glos, and has issue living, (by 2nd *m*), Robert Edward *b* 1983, Patrick William Jack *b* 1987, Clare Heather *b* 1983, — (Katherine) Emma, *b* 1953: *m* 1976, Philip Austin George Mackenzie, and has issue (*see* D Grafton). *Residence* – Kiftsgate Court, Campden, Gloucestershire. —— Bettine Clara (Hidcote Vale, Campden, Glos), *b* 1917.

    Issue of late Matthew William Muir, yst son of 1st baronet, *b* 1878, *d* 1922: *m* 1912, Clara Gardiner (who *d* 1952, having *m* 2ndly, 1925, Major David Johnstone Mitchell, MC, who *d* 1954, late King's Roy Rifle Corps), yst da of John Gardiner Muir:—
Gillian Rachel, *b* 1914: *m* 1940, Evan Morgan Williams, and has issue living, Ian Muir, *b* 1942, — Hugh Frederick, *b* 1943. *Residence* – Ballyvolane Stud, Bruff, co Limerick, Ireland.
The 1st baronet, Sir John Muir was Lord Provost of Glasgow 1889-92. The 2nd baronet, Sir (Alexander) Kay Muir, was High Sheriff of co Waterford 1929.

Muir Mackenzie, see Mackenzie.

MUNRO (NS) 1634, of Foulis-Obsdale, Ross-shire

Sir IAN TALBOT MUNRO, 15th *Baronet*; *b* 38 Dec 1929; *s* his 1st cousin once removed, *Sir* ARTHUR HERMAN, 1972; *ed* Bradfield Coll.

𝕬rms – Or, an eagle's head erased gules, langued azure, a label of three points of the second charged with three lions' heads erased argent, and in dexter chief a canton of a Baronet of Nova Scotia. 𝕮rest – An eagle displayed proper, charged across his breast and wings with a label of three points gules charged with three lion's heads erased argent. *Residence* – 22 rue d'Occitanie, 11120 Ginestas, Aude, France.

UNCLE LIVING

MALCOLM (Whitegates, Rock, Wadebridge, Cornwall PL27 6JZ), *b* 24 Feb 1901; FAIA: *m* 1931, Constance, da of William Carter, and has issue living, Mary Lee, *b* 1935: *m* 1955, David Rex Denny, of Pool Park, St Tudy, Bodmin, Cornwall, and has issue living, Sally Louise *b* 1961: *m* 1989, Robert Gerald Leeds Scovell, of 7 Lena Drive, Groby, Leicester, Felicia Mary *b* 1965: *m* 1987, Richard Michael Latham Jones, of Merryfield Cottage, Rock, Cornwall (and has issue living, William David Studley *b* 1994, Lucy Mary Studley *b* 1992).

DAUGHTERS LIVING OF FOURTEENTH BARONET

Audrey Muriel, *b* 1924: *m* 1946, Donald Ernest Fifield, of Greystones, Malling Rd, Teston, Maidstone, and has issue living, Richard Donald, *b* 1947. —— Betty Millicent, *b* 1926: *m* 1950, Brian Leslie Wright, of 8 Conisboro Av, Caversham, Reading, and has issue living, Gail Louise, *b* 1951, — Linda Ann, *b* 1953.

DAUGHTERS LIVING OF THIRTEENTH BARONET

Beatrice Maud (3 Field Close, E Molesey, Surrey), *b* 1891: *m* 1919, William Lidyard Bligh, who *d* 1978, and has issue living, Beatrice Olive Joan, *b* 1920: *m* 1944, Kenneth Sidney Hansford, of Ashcombe, 11a Links Rd, Ashtead, Surrey, and has issue living, Anthony Nicholas, *b* 1950: *m* 1981, Gillian Barbara Crouch (and has issue living, Caroline Victoria *b* 1983), Colin Gordon *b* 1956, — Molly Dora, *b* 1925: *m* 1953, Philip George Bunker, of 7 Crummock Close, Bramcote, Nottingham, and has issue living, Timothy John *b* 1956, Nicholas Philip *b* 1958. —— Florence Elizabeth (Hollywood, Cal, USA), *b* 1897: *m* 1st, 1918, Robert Cameron, of Glasgow, who *d* 1928; 2ndly, 1932 (*m diss* 1963), Leonard Frederick Burnett; 3rdly, 1964, Jack Maddock, and has issue living (by 1st *m*) Donald Marsh, *b* 1922: *m* 1943, Caroline Cunningham, of Liverpool, and has issue living, Keith *b* 1945, Ian *b* 1947, Craig *b* 1951, Michelle *b* 1949, Zhan *b* 1953, — (by 2nd *m*) Roy Beech, *b* 1932, — Zhan Jacqueline, *b* 1935, — Sonia Christine, *b* 1936: *m* 1954, Joseph le Parc, of New York, USA. —— Grace, *b* 1908: *m* 1931, William Price, of 119 Crystal Palace Rd, E. Dulwich, SE22, and has issue living, Jean, *b* 19—, — Sylvia, *b* 19—, — Barbara, *b* 19—. —— Minnie Isabel, *b* 1914: *m* 1935, M. Ernest Price, and has issue living, Ernest Talbot, *b* 1939: *m* 1965, Patricia, da of Albert Edward Green, — Jacqueline, *b* 1935: *m* 1957, George James Fox, and has issue living, Dawn Leslie *b* 1959.

STEPMOTHER LIVING

Simone (24 Bramcote, York Rd, Weybridge, Surrey), da of late Louis Jean Bareau, and widow of Rudolph Lancaster Fisk: *m* 1950, as his 2nd wife, Robert Hector Munro, who *d* 1965.

COLLATERAL BRANCHES LIVING

Issue of late Percy Munro, brother of 12th and 13th baronets, *b* 1870, *d* 1953: *m* 1909, Annie Louise, who *d* 1963, da of William Henderson Pearson, of Kennington SE:—
Hector George Hamilton (18 Davigdor Rd, Hove), *b* 1912: *m* 1947 (*m diss* 1975), Clare Amelia Emily, da of late Herbert Pitcher, and has issue living, Desirée Yvonne, *b* 1944: *m* 1962, Othman Merichan, of 32, Jalan Maktob, Kuala Lumpur, Malaysia, — Wendy Amelia, *b* 1945: *m* 1961, Ray Williams, 12 Ellen Place, Hove. —— Irene Louisa (70 Larbert Rd, Streatham, SW6), *b* 1915: *m* 1940, William Archer Lawrence, and has issue living, Michael, *b* 1943, — Iain, *b* 1944.

Issue of late Arnold Harry Munro, brother of 12th and 13th baronets, *b* 1871, *d* 1968: *m* 1st, 1895, Matilda Ethel, da of Samuel Long; 2ndly, 1909, Hilda Marion, who *d* 1961, da of William Smith, of Nunhead, SE15:—
(By 1st *m*) Margory Ethel, *b* 1897. —— (By 2nd *m*) Kenneth Arnold William (3 Courtrai Rd, Honor Oak Park, SE23), *b* 1910: *m* 1935, Olive Freda, da of Francis Broome, of Nunhead, SE15, and has issue living, Ian Kenneth (Foulis, Gold Cup Lane, Ascot, Berks SL5 8NP), *b* 1940, — Christine Freda, *b* 1944: *m* 1971, Capt K. Bridle, of Timbers, Barclay Park, Aboyne ABE SJP, and has issue living, Christopher *b* 1972, Andrew *b* 1975. —— Roland Alec Wilfred (Maycroft, 223 Crookston Rd, Eltham Park, SE9 1YE), *b* 1911: *m* 1937, Queenie May Munro, da of E. Johnson, of Nunhead, SE15, and has issue living, Godfrey Roland (184 Greenvale Rd, Eltham Park, SE9 1PQ), *b* 1938: *m* 1985, Julie Pamela Munro, da of R. Gosling, of N Cheam, Surrey, and has issue living, Rupert Roland *b* 1987, Lawrence Godfrey *b* 1990, Victoria Ella May *b* 1993, — Yvonne May, *b* 1943: *m* 1967, Kenneth B. Parkes, and has issue living, Alexander James *b* 1977.

Issue of late Eva Marion Munro, da of 11th Baronet, *b* 1881 *d* 1976: *m* 1904, Lt-Col Cecil Claud Hugh Orby Gascoigne, DSO, who *d* 1929:—
Patrick MUNRO OF FOULIS, TD (Foulis Castle, Evanton, Ross-shire; MCC), *b* 1912; *ed* Imperial Ser Coll and RMC; Capt late Seaforth Highlanders; DL of Ross and Cromarty (Vice-Lt 1969); 1939-45 War (Prisoner); assumed by decree of Lyon Court 1937 the surname and arms of Munro of Foulis and recognised as Chief of Clan Munro: *m* 1946, Eleanor Mary, da of late Capt Hon William Joseph French (*see* B de Freyne), and has issue living, Hector William, *b* 1950: *m* 1974, Sarah Margaret Katharine, da of late Henry George Austen de l'Etang Herbert Duckworth (*see* B Chatfield), and has issue living, Finnian George *b* 1975, Isabella Katharine *b* 1978, Aline Angela *b* 1981, — Harry Robert Gascoigne, *b* 1954: *m* 1976, Lynda, da of Cecil Cranton, of Nova Scotia, Canada, and has issue living, Eva Marian *b* 1983, Fiona *b* 1986, Monica Bernice *b* 1988, — John Alexander Seymour, *b* 1959: *m* 1979, Silvia Charlotte Maria, 4th da of Knud Johan Ludvig, Count von Holstein-

Ledreborg, of Ledreborg, Denmark, by his wife HRH Princess Marie Gabrielle of Luxembourg, and has issue living, Alexander b 1985, Tatiana Angela Marie b 1983, — Charlotte Eva (Keirhill, Balfron, by Glasgow G63 OLG), b 1947: m 1st, 1975, John William Betts Donaldson, who d 1985, son of late Norman Fraser Graham Donaldson, of Ballindalloch, Balfron, Stirlingshire; 2ndly, 1992, Col Robin Chester Vaughan Hunt, son of late Gen Sir Peter Mervyn Hunt, GCB, DSO, OBE, and has issue living (by 1st m), William Betts b 1980, Robert John b 1983, Joanna Eva b 1977. —— Robert Clifton (2 Hampton Place Edinburgh EH12 5JA), b 1915: Maj late Seaforth Highlanders: m 1st, 1940 (m diss 1954), Sylvia Rapozo; 2ndly, 1954, Margaret, da of late N. E. Douglas Menzies, of Newtownairds, Dumfries, and has issue living (by 1st m), Robert Hugh, b 1941, — Caroline Orby, b 1946: m 1st, 1968, Michael Robarts; 2ndly, 1973, Andrew Gordon-Duff, and has issue living (by 2nd m) (see Baird, Bt, cr 1809), — (by 2nd m), Matilda Anne, b 1955: m 1979, Michael Charles Bevan, of Sothenbury Farm, Scaynes Hill, Haywards Heath, W Sussex RH17 7PE, only son of late Maj T. H. Bevan, of Miltown Grange, co Louth, and has issue living, Conor Thomas Hector b 1983, Georgina Kathleen b 1991. —— †Cecil Alastair Hector, b 1916; ed Imperial Ser Coll; m 1947, Jean Muller, who d 1959, and d 1993, leaving issue, Michael Neil Clifton (Grove Cottage, Aberlady, E Lothian EH32 0RB), b 1949: m 1975, Anna Jennifer, el da of John Milne, of Nether Clifton, Southwick, Dumfries, and has issue living, James Neil Crispin b 1979, Peter John Hector b 1987, Gemma Eva Pamela b 1981, — Patrick Edward Cecil b 1950; Lt-Col Scots Gds: m 1979, Penny J., el da of late Maj Alastair K. MacGeorge, of The Glebe House, Cockpen, Bonnyrigg, Midlothian, and has issue living, Cecily b 1991. —— Marion Erica, b 1906: m 1934, Brig George Des Champs Chamier, OBE, KOYLI, who d 1987, son of late Sir Edward Maynard Des Champs Chamier, KCSI, KCIE, and has issue living, Anthony Edward Des Champs (Achandunie House, Ardross, Ross and Cromarty), b 1935: m 1962, Anne-Carole Dalling, and has issue living, Daniel William Des Champs b 1964, Amy Louise Des Champs b 1962, — George Washington Des Champs, b 1947: m 1974, Janet Michele St Clair, — Antoinette Des Champs, b 1938: m 1973, Angus Buchan Gordon, FRCS, and has issue living, James Buchan b 1974, Madeleine Claire b 1976, — Georgiana Des Champs, b 1949: m 1979, Adrian Gruzman, and has issue living, Angus Michael b 1982, Alice Freyer b 1980, Amelia Anastasia b 1989. —— Joan Orby, b 1910: m 1st, 1937, Alastair Gordon-Ingram, Colonial Police; 2ndly, 1947, His Honour Harold William Paton, DSC, who d 1986, and has issue living, (by 1st m) Donald Alexander, b 1938, — (by 2nd m) Mary Joanne Letitia, b 1948.

The 1st baronet, Col Hector Munro of Foulis, Ross-shire, was created a baronet of Nova Scotia with remainder to heirs male whatsoever. On the death of his son, Sir Hector Munro in 1651, the title reverted to Sir Robert Munro, 3rd baronet (grandson of George, uncle of 1st baronet). The 6th baronet, Sir Robert Munro MP, fought at Fontenoy, and was killed at the battle of Falkirk 1746. Sir Charles Munro, 9th baronet (4th cousin of his predecessor) was distinguished in the Peninsular War, and commanded a Div of Colombian Army under Bolivar.

MUNRO (UK) 1825, of Lindertis, Forfarshire

Sir ALASDAIR THOMAS IAN MUNRO OF LINDERTIS, 6th Baronet; b 6 July 1927; s his father, Sir (THOMAS) TORQUIL ALPHONSO, 1985; ed Landon Sch, USA, Georgetown Univ, Washington, DC, Pennsylvania Univ, and IMEDE, Lausanne, Switzerland: m 1954, Marguerite Lillian, da of late Franklin R. Loy, of Dayton, Ohio, USA, and has issue.

𝕬rms – Or, and eagle's head erased gules, encircled by a branch of laurel on the dexter and of oak on the sinister side both proper; on a chief argent the representation of an Indian hill-fort, and beneath in letters of gold the word "Badamy"; on a canton gules, a representation of a gold medal presented by the East India Co the the 1st baronet for his services in Seringapatam in 1790. 𝕮rest – An eagle close proper, having a representation of the medal above mentioned pendent from its neck by a ribbon, the dexter claw resting upon an escutcheon gules, charged with a representation of an Indian hill-fort, and beneath in letters or gold, the world "Badamy" as in the arms, and in the beak a sprig of club moss.
Residence – River Ridge, Box 940, Waitsfield, Vermont 05673, USA.

SON LIVING

KEITH GORDON, b 3 May 1959; ed Cardigan Mount Sch, Kimball Union Acad, and Univ of New Hampshire: m 1989, Jada Louise, da of Adrian Elwell, of Waitsfield, Vermont, and has issue living, Zachary Adrian, b 1992.

DAUGHTER LIVING

Karen Fiona, b 1956: m 1980 (m diss 1988), Robert David Macmichael, Jr, of New London, New Hampshire, son of Robert David Macmichael, of New London, New Hampshire, and has issue living, Josh Munro, b 1981, — Blake Thomas Ian, b 1984.

HALF-BROTHER LIVING

James Kenneth Torquil, b 1941; ed Bradfield: m 1970 (m diss 19—), Camilla Ann, yr da of late Cdr J. Nigel Ball, DSC, RN, and has issue living, Iona Katharine, b 1973, — Flavia Isla, b 1975, — Camilla Morna, b 1977.

HALF-SISTER LIVING

Fiona Margaret (Hon Mrs Nicholas H.E. Hopkinson), b 1937: m 1957, Hon Nicholas Henry Eno Hopkinson, who d 1991, only son of 1st Baron Colyton. Residence – Drumleys, Lindertis, Kirriemuir, Angus DD8 5NU.

COLLATERAL BRANCHES LIVING

Grandchildren of late Ian Charles Ronald Walker-Munro (infra):—
Issue of late Thomas Ian Michael Walker-Munro, *b* 1922, *d* 1965: *m* 1947, Hon Marjorie Amy Biddulph, da of 3rd Baron Biddulph:—
Thomas Malcolm, *b* 1948. —— Sarah Amy, *b* 1950: *m* 1973, Brig Melville Stewart Jameson, CBE, R Scots Dragoon Gds, and has issue living, Melville Harry Stewart, *b* 1977, — Michael Andrew Stewart, *b* 1980.
Issue of late Patrick Angus Walker-Munro, *b* 1924, *d* 1993: *m* 1950, Mary Barnett, who *d* 1980, da of late R. Y. Phillips:—
Ian David Torquil (404 Galston Rd, Galston 2159, NSW, Australia), *b* 1951: *m* 1982, Mrs Suellan Lough, of Sydney, Australia, and has issue living, Brenton Neil Patrick, *b* 1985, — Alaisdair John Torquil, *b* 1988, — Catherine, *b* 1983. —— (Charles Michael) Angus (34 Forest End, Fleet, Hants GU13 9XE), *b* 1953: *m* 1981 (*m diss* 19—), Christine Margaret, da of Albert Arthur Humphrey, of 29 Marley Av, Bexleyheath, Kent, and has issue living, Peter Michael Angus, *b* 1985.

Grandchildren of late Lieut-Com Edward Lionel Walker-Munro, RN, 2nd son of 3rd baronet:—
Issue of late Ian Charles Ronald Walker-Munro *b* 1889, *d* 1952: *m* 1919, Morna Violet, who *d* 1988, da of Sir Hugh Thomas Munro, 4th Bt:—
Lionel Malcolm (64 Bourne St, SW1), *b* 1929. —— (Roderick) Hugh (Kinnettles House, Forfar, Angus), *b* (twin) 1929: *m* 1st, 1964, Irene, who *d* 1976, da of late Roderick Watt Edgar; 2ndly, 1993, Brenda, da of late Donald Wheelton, and has issue living (by 1st *m*) 1965: *m* 1993, Susan, da of Keith Howman, of Ashmere, Shepperton, Middx, — Geordie Roderick Hamish, *b* 1968: *m* 1993, Lorraine Rose, only da of Patrick Orchard, of Carandain, Perthshire.
This family descends from John Munro, 1st of Miltown, yr son of Hugh Munro, 9th of Foulis. The 1st baronet, Maj-Gen Sir Thomas, KCB, was Governor of Madras 1820-27.

Munro-Lucas-Tooth, see Tooth.

MUNTZ (UK) 1902, of Clifton-on-Dunsmore, Warwickshire (Extinct 1940)

Sir GERARD PHILIP GRAVES MUNTZ, RN, 3rd and last *Baronet*; *ka* 1940.

DAUGHTER LIVING OF SECOND BARONET (*By 2nd marriage*)

Désirée Violet, TD, *b* 1916: *m* 1940, Capt Alfred John Spencer Hancock, King's Roy Rifle Corps, and has issue living, Gerard Spencer MOLYNEUX (Bodcott Farm, Moccas, Hereford), *b* 1948, assumed the surname of Molyneux by deed poll 1968, — Antonia *b* 1946: *m* 1st, 1977 (*m diss* 198—), Martin Whitfield; 2ndly, 1985 (*m diss* 1991), Philip Holbourn, and has issue living (by 1st *m*), John Robert *b* 1978, Simon Peter *b* 1981. *Residence* – Broad Close, Coates, Cirencester.

MURRAY (NS) 1628, of Blackbarony, Peeblesshire

Fear God

Sir NIGEL ANDREW DIGBY MURRAY OF BLACKBARONY, 15th *Baronet*, *b* 15 Aug 1944; *s* his father *Sir* ALAN JOHN DIGBY, 1978; *ed* St Paul's Sch, Argentina, Salesian Agric Tech Sch, Argentina, and Roy Agric Coll, Cirencester: *m* 1980, Diana Margaret, yr da of Robert Campbell Bray, of Sarmiento 1443, (2624) Arias, Prov de Córdoba, Argentina, and has issue.

Arms – Or, a fetterlock azure, on a chief of the last three mullets argent. **Crest** – A dexter hand holding a scroll proper.
Residence – Establecimiento Tinamú, CC 115, 2624 Arias (Prov de Córdoba), Argentina.

SON LIVING

ALEXANDER NIGEL ROBERT, *b* 1 July 1981.

DAUGHTERS LIVING

Rachel Elisabeth Vanda Digby, *b* 1982. —— Evelyn Caroline Digby, *b* 1987.

BROTHERS LIVING

Kenelm Gerald Digby (Crofts, Woodside Rd, Chiddingfold, Surrey), *b* 1946; *ed* St Paul's Sch, Argentina, and Birmingham Univ (BSc electronics): *m* 1973, Jolandë St Clare Byrne, only child of Mrs Francis Mellor, of Nottingham, and has issue living, Alan James Digby, *b* 1980, — Olivia Lucile Caroline Digby, *b* 1977. —— Peter Francis Digby, *b* 1947; *ed* St Paul's Sch Argentina, Shuttleworth, Agric Coll (NDA), and Bangor Univ (BSc Agric Econ). —— Denis Jermyn Digby (The Farmyard, Upper Llandwrog, Fron, Gwynedd), *b* 1949; *ed* St Paul's Sch Argentina, and Bangor Univ (BSc Forestry): *m* 1980, Christiane Baars, who *d* 1993, and has issue living, David Christopher, *b* 1981, — Lawrence Stephan, *b* 1986, — Teresa Mabel, *b* 1983.

AUNT LIVING

Eileen Charmion Digby, b 1910: m 1930, David Hinchcliff-Mathew, who d 1974, and has issue living, Murray Alan, b 1933: m 1958, Marilyn Nazabal Chapman, da of Don Evaristo Nazabal, of Rufino, Argentina, and has issue living, David b 19—, Andrew b 19—, Marjory Charlotte b 1959, Carol b 1961, Rose Ann b 19—, Alexandra b 19—, — John Gervase, b 1947: m 1984, Susan Penelope, da of Donald Maxwell Jack, and has issue living, Daniel b 1985, Vanessa b 1987. *Residence* – Estancia Los Flamencos, Sancti Spiritu, Prov Sta Fé, Argentina.

WIDOW LIVING FOURTEENTH BARONET

MABEL ELISABETH (*Mabel, Lady Murray of Blackbarony*), 2nd da of late Arthur Bernard Schiele, of Arias, Argentina: m 1943, Sir Alan John Digby Murray of Blackbarony, 14th baronet, who d 1978.

COLLATERAL BRANCHES LIVING

Grandson of late Col Kenelm Digby Murray, DSO, 4th son of 10th baronet:—
Issue of late Lieut-Col Archibald Digby Murray, DSO, RA, b 1878, d 1949: m 1905, Rosamund, who d 1980, da of late Thomas Davey, of Bannerleigh, Leigh Woods, Bristol:—
Archibald John, b 1907; is Lt-Col Black Watch (ret); 1939-45 War: m 1st, 1935, Nancy, who d 1974, da of Philip George, of Barrow Gurney, Som; 2ndly, 1977, Phyllis Walker, da of late Surg Rear-Adm David Walker Hewitt, CB, CMG, MD, BCh, FRCS, and widow of Surg Capt P. G. Burgess, MVO, RN, and has issue living, (by 1st m), John Archibald Digby (Churchill Court, Churchill, Avon BS19 5QW), b 1941; ed Harrow; JP: m 1975, Janet, da of Adam Johnstone, OBE, of Temple Wood, Caple Surrey, and has issue living, Angus John Digby b 1976, Nicola Rosamund b 1979, Alice b 1982, — Gillian Claire, b 1946: m 1978, Roger Philip Latham. *Residence* – Woodford, Dartmouth, Devon TQ6 9PA.

Grandchildren of late Lt-Col Archibald Digby Murray, DSO, RA (ante):—
Issue of late Maj Ian Digby Murray, b 1912, d 1974: m 1944, Pamela, who d 1988, only da of Claud Parbury, of De-whurst, Wadhurst, Sussex:—
Julian Charles Digby, b 1949: m 1974, Gillian Frazer. —— Petrina Rosamund, b 1947: m 1970, Manuel Moran, of Madrid, and has issue living, Mark, b 1977, — Sophia, b 1976, — Ania, b (twin) 1977. —— Charlotte Davey, b 1954: m 1977, Grahame Royds Gordon Nicholson, and has issue living, Ian Royds Gordon, b 1981, — Rupert Grahame Murray, b 1983, — Sabrina Pamela, b 1989.

Grandson of late Col Kenelm Digby Murray, DSO (ante):—
Issue of late Col Kenelm Digby Bold Murray, CB, DSO, b 1879, d 1947: m 1911, Gwendolen, who d 1979, da of late Thomas Andrew de Wolf, of Sydney, NS Wales:—
Andrew Digby, b 1916; Lieut-Col (retired) RA: m 1947, Joan (ROBERTS), da of Major A. Nelson Allen, of Leigh, Surrey, and has issue living, Anna Teresa, b 1947.

Grandchildren of late Lieut-Gen Sir James Wolfe Murray, KCB, son of late James Wolfe Murray (b 1814), son of late James Wolfe Murray (Hon Lord Cringletie), great-grandson of late Alexander Murray, 4th son of 2nd baronet:—
Issue of late Capt George Wolfe Murray, b 1876, d 1955: m 1910, Katherine, who d 1955, da of late Rev Thomas Jones, R of Llanbedr, Crickhowell:—
Thomas Wolfe, b 1913; ed St Bees, and Faraday Hse (Diploma): m 1946, Violet May, da of late Alexander Scott, of Vancouver, British Columbia, and has issue living, Alexander James Wolfe, b 1949; ed Perth High Sch, and Univ of British Columbia (BA), — Robin Wolfe, b 1951; ed Perth Academy, and St Andrews Univ (BSc (Hons), PhD), — Patricia Ann Wolfe, b 1947, — Susan May Wolfe, b 1958. *Residence* – Hycroft, Hatton Road, Kinnoull, Perth. —— Katherine Jean Wolfe, b 1911: m 1958, James Gordon Fyfe, TD, WS, DL. *Residence* – Meldonfoot, Peebles. —— Miriam Arabella Elizabeth Wolfe, b 1916: m 1950, Albert Victor Baker, and has issue living, Victor George, b 1954: m 1975, Christine Mary Hollis, — Katherine, b 1951. *Residence* – Inglenook, Winsor Lane, Winsor, Southampton.

Grandchildren of late Cdr Philip Charles Knightly Wolfe Murray (infra):—
Issue of late Lt-Col Robert Alexander Wolfe Murray, DSO, MC, b 1889, d 1973: m 1923, Isobel Mary, who d 1970, da of late Edward Armistead Baxter, of Kincaldum, Forfarshire:—
James Wolfe (House of Daviot, Daviot, Inverness-shire), b 1931; ed Harrow; Capt (ret) Queen's Own Highlanders; a Member of Queen's Body Guard for Scotland (Royal Company of Archers): m 1st, 1961 (m diss 1969), Baroness Catherina Ingrid Madelaine, da of late Baron Eugene Fredrik Christer Con Stedingk, of Ullaberg, Stjärnhov, Sweden, 2ndly, 1976, Sally Ann, only da of Eric Gordon Bean, of Burnside, Struy, Inverness-shire, and has issue living (by 1st m), Chanette Pauline Catharina, b 1964, — Tatjana Thesy Isma, b 1965, — (by 2nd m), James Wolfe, b 1978. —— Sibil Pauline Wolfe, b 1924: m 1951, Lt-Col Frank Derek Carson, OBE, Queen's Own Highlanders, of 8 Kingsburgh Rd, Murrayfield, Edinburgh, and has issue living, Philip Derek Murray, b 1955: m 1993, Alison Marguerite, da of Cdr Graham Creedy, LVO, RN, — Rachel Isma Ann, b 1957: m 1st, 1979 (m diss 1984), Capt Christopher Glyn-Jones; 2ndly, 1987, Timothy Horrox, and has issue living, (by 1st m) Caroline Mary b 1980, Alexandra Pauline b 1982, (by 2nd m) Charlotte Julia b 1988, Olivia Julia b 1990, — Iona Fair-lie Edith, b 1959.

Grandchildren of late Cdr Philip Charles Knightly Wolfe Murray, son of James Wolfe Murray (b 1814) (ante):—
Issue of late Lt-Col David Knightley Wolfe Murray, b 1897, d 1970: m 1920, Ivry Cordelia, who d 1984, da of Montagu Townsend, of 8 North Pallant, Chichester:—
Christopher Michael Wolfe (Easter Slap, Dirleton, E Lothian), b 1929; ed Oundle; Capt Gordon Highlanders (ret): m 1st, 1955 (m diss 1980), Jacqueline, da of Col Sir John Turnbull Usher, OBE, 4th Bt; 2ndly, 1980, Alison Isabel Rowe, da of late James Boyd, TD, DL, of Carradale, Helensburgh, and has issue living, (by 1st m) Dorinda Mary, b 1957: m 1984, Murray Ross Maclean Hancock, of 280 Amess St, N Carlton, Melbourne, Australia, and has issue living, Sam Fergus b 1991, Benjamin Rory b 1993, — Erica Jacqueline, b 1959: m 1986, Malcolm Brinkworth, of The Malt House, St Mary Bourne, Hants, and has issue living, Alexander b 1989, Christopher Rory b 1993, Faye Tamsin b 1988, — Serena Jean, b 1964: m 1989, Justin J. B. Varcoe, of The Long Barn, Par, Cornwall, elder son of Beaumont Varcoe, of Nanscawen, Par, Cornwall. —— Ivri Patricia, b 1922: m 1951, Charles Mailert Wormser, of 65 East 96th St, New York 10028, USA, and has issue living, Andrew Charles, b 1953, — Nina Carolyn, b 1955.

Grandchildren of late Brig-Gen Arthur Wolfe Murray, CB, son of James Wolfe Murray (b 1814) (ante):—
Issue of late Lt-Col Malcolm Victor Alexander Wolfe Murray, The Black Watch, b 1908, d 1985: m 1st, 1935, Lady Grizel Mary Boyle, who d (at sea as result of enemy action) 1942, eldest da of 8th Earl of Glasgow; 2ndly, 1947, Zofia, who d 1968, da of M. Jacza Chamiec, of Warsaw, Poland:—
(By 1st m) James Archibald Wolfe (13 Howards Lane, SW15), b 1936; ed Eton, and Worcester Coll, Oxford; Group Regional Dir S America of United Distillers: m 1st, 1963 (m diss 1976), Hon Diana Lucy Douglas-Home, da of Baron Home of the Hirsel (Life Baron); 2ndly, 1978, Amanda Felicity, elder da of late Anthony Street, and has issue living, (by 1st m) Rory

James Wolfe (57 Broughton Rd, SW6), *b* 1965: *m* 1987, Marion J., da of late Dr Phillip Arthur Zorab, of Golden Hill, Chepstow, and has issue living, Harry *b* 1990, Flora Jessica *b* 1992, — Fiona Grizel Wolfe, *b* 1964: *m* 1991, Andrew M. Shufflebotham, son of David Shufflebotham, of Mijas, Spain, and has issue living, Molly Rita *b* 1994, — Clare Elizabeth Wolfe, *b* 1969, — (by 2nd *m*) Andrew Alexander Wolfe, *b* 1978. ———Angus Malcolm Wolfe, *b* 1937: *m* 1961, Stephanie Vivian, da of late Maj Hadden Royden Todd, and has issue living, Kim Alexander Wolfe, *b* 1962, — Rupert Hamish Wolfe, *b* 1963, — Gavin Scott Wolfe, *b* 1966, — Magnus Wolfe, *b* 1968. ——— (By 2nd *m*) Teresa Mary Wolfe, *b* 1950.

Descendants of late Sir Gideon Murray, 3rd son of late Andrew Murray, uncle of 1st baronet, of who the el son was *cr* Lord Elibank (*see* L Elibank).

Descendants of late William Murray, yst son of late Andrew Murray, uncle of 1st baronet, whose son, late William Murray was created a baronet in 1630 (*see* Murray, Bt, *cr* 1630).

Sir Archibald Murray, 1st baronet, a first cousin of 1st Lord Elibank, was created a baronet with remainder to his heirs male whatsoever.

MURRAY (NS) 1630, of Dunerne, Fifeshire

Sir ROWLAND WILLIAM MURRAY, 15th *Baronet*, *b* 22 Sept 1947; *s* his father, *Sir* ROWLAND WILLIAM PATRICK MURRAY, 1994; *ed* Georgia State Univ; Pres Southern Furniture Galleries; Vice-Pres Ball-Stalker Inc: *m* 1970, Nancy Diane, da of George C. Newberry, of Orlando, Florida, and has issue.

Arms – Not matriculated at Lyon Office.
Residence – 4364 E Brookhaven Drive, Atlanta, Georgia 30319, USA.

SON LIVING

ROWLAND WILLIAM (IV), *b* 31 July 1979.

DAUGHTER LIVING

Ryan McCabe, *b* 1974.

BROTHERS LIVING

Edward George (635 Creekwood Crossing, East Rowswell, Georgia 30076, USA), *b* 1951; marketing and merchandising consultant, D.C. & Co: *m* 1975, Glenda Sharon, da of John Foutes, and has issue living, Michael Betton, *b* 1971. ———Robert Michael (6819 Brewster Court, Columbus, Georgia 31904, USA), *b* 1953; *ed* Young Harris Coll, Georgia, Columbus Coll, Georgia (BS), and Troy State Univ (MBA); Lt-Col US Army: *m* 1981, Vickie, da of Helen Kent, of Augusta, Georgia, and has issue living, Robert Michael, *b* 1985, — Ashley Kathren, *b* 1989. ———Christopher Joseph (11 Plumosa Drive, Cassellberry, Florida, USA), *b* 1957: *m* 1984, Kimberly Ann, da of James Johnson, and has issue living, Nicholas Christopher, *b* 1986, — Jessica Kirsten, *b* 1988.

SISTERS LIVING

Helen Brooke, *b* 1945: *m* 1st, 19—, Clinton S. Ferguson; 2ndly, 1980, Capt Ronald Grant Reppert, US Army, of 1322 Andover Rd, Richmond, Va 23229, USA, and has issue living, (by 1st *m*) Clinton S., *b* 1970, — Julia H., *b* 1971, — (by 2nd *m*) Stephen Harris, *b* 1984. ———Patricia Marie, *b* 1949: *m* 1977, Edward Scoloro, of 3303 Decatur Av, Tampa, Florida, USA, and has issue living, Anthony Edward *b* 1985, — Nina Murray, *b* 1988.

GREAT AUNT LIVING (*Daughter of 12th baronet*)

Laura Magdalen Irving, *b* 1887: *m* 1907, Gerald Alexander Marlowe-King, and has issue living, Alexander William (83 Hillcrest Rd, Mt Vernon, NY 10552, USA), *b* 1910; Assist Treas of Dry Dock Savings Bank, New York: *m* 1935, Helen Laurette McMahon, and has issue living, William Alexander *b* 1937; *ed* Iona Coll, New Rochelle, NY; (BA): *m* 1967, Geraldine Tierney, Junellen Mary, *b* 1940: *m* 1960, Denis Robert Sullivan (and has issue living, Steven Alexander *b* 1961, Dennis Robert *b* 1962, Kevin William *b* 1964), — George Robert (2800, N Holliston, Ataldena, Cal 91001, USA), *b* 1911: *m* 1937, Ruth Sheets, and has issue living, Gerald John *b* 1937: *m* 1967, Roxanne Pettigrew, Georgette Alexandria *b* 1939: *m* 1956, Louis Griffiths (and has issue living, Stephen John *b* 1959, John Wayne *b* 1960), — Kenneth Gandy (187 Fern St, Fairfield, Conn, USA), *b* 1912: *m* 1937, Blanche Connelly, and has issue living, Kenneth Gary *b* 1939: *m* 1959, Sherrin O'Toole (and has issue living, Kenneth Michael *b* 1960), John William *b* 1942; *ed* Conn Univ; (BA); late Capt USAF: *m* 1965, Patricia Ann O'Connell (and has issue living, John Patrick *b* 1965, Kenneth Scott *b* 1968), — Donald Murray *b* 1915.

WIDOW LIVING OF THIRTEENTH BARONET

RUBY (*Ruby, Lady Murray*) da of S Hearn, of Helmdon, Northants: *m* 1938, as his second wife, Lieut-Col Sir Edward Robert Murray, 13th Bt, DSO, who *d* 1958.

WIDOW LIVING OF FOURTEENTH BARONET

SARAH JAYNE WIKLE (*Sarah, Lady Murray*), da of Walter W. LaFevre: *m* 1991, as his second wife, Sir Rowland William Patrick Murray, 14th Bt, who *d* 1994. *Residence* – 2820 Peachtree Rd NE, Apt No 1312, Atlanta, Georgia 30305, USA.

COLLATERAL BRANCHES LIVING

Issue of late Robert Lithgow Murray, 3rd son of 12th baronet, *b* 1881, *d* 1942: *m* 1908, Harriet Pope:—
Vernon Robert William (314 S Circle Dr, Boynton Beach, Florida, USA), *b* 1909: *m* 1934, Elizabeth Camberne Kirkwood, and has issue living, Vernon Kirkwood, *b* 1945: *m* 1966, Linda Tischler, and has issue living, Christine Lynn *b* 1966, — Harriet Elizabeth, *b* 1937; *ed* State Univ, New York (MS): *m* 1958, Dale Aldrich Edwards of 2 Plane Tree Lane, Dix Hills, NY, USA, and has issue living, Daniel Vernon *b* 1962, Susan Dale *b* 1959, Carolyn Kirkwood *b* 1968, — Phyllis Vernon, *b* 1939: *m* 1st, 1957 (*m diss* 1978), Adrian Cecil Stanley; 2ndly, 1981, Roy Awbrey, of 704 Abbey Arch, Virginia Beach, Va, USA, and has issue living (by 1st *m*), Kenneth William *b* 1960, Edward Murray *b* 1966, Janet Elizabeth *b* 1958, Alice Camberne Stanley *b*

1970. —— Robert Atholl, *b* 1914: *m* 1935, Mary Ellen Guinan, and has issue living, Robert Atholl, *b* 1937, — James Ivor, *b* 1947, — Diane, *b* 1942.

Grandchildren of late Robert Lithgow Murray (ante):—
Issue of late James Edward Murray, *b* 1911, *d* 1963: *m* 1934, Dorothy Elizabeth Holley (38-38, 217th St, Bayside, NY, USA):—
Donald MacLean, *b* 1945; *ed* Mass Inst of Technology. —— Elizabeth Anne, *b* 1938: *m* 1957, Louis H. Cabrol, of Route de Maraussan, Beziers, Herault, France, and has issue living, Jean Louis, *b* 1964, — Jacques, *b* 1970, — Marie Theresé, *b* 1958. —— Danielle, *b* 1960, — Alice, *b* 1961, — Helene, *b* 1963. —— Susan Eleanora, *b* 1939: *m* 1st, 1958 (*m diss* 1982), James A. Kowalski; 2ndly, 1984, Francis Roland, of 726 Dartmouth Av, Silver Spring, Md, USA, and has issue living, (by 1st *m*) Glenn R, *b* 1960, — Gary W, *b* 1962, — James Edward, *b* 1964, — Melissa Jill, *b* 1969.

Issue of late William Gerard Pulteney Murray, 4th son of 12th baronet, *b* 1891, *d* 1953: *m* 1919, Frances Swarts:—
Allan Gerald, *b* 1928: *m* 19—, Penny Phillips, and has issue living, William *b* 19—, — June Ann, *b* 19—, — Gail, *b* 19—.
The 7th baronet, a distinguished military officer during the first American war, was subsequently Secretary at War. He married in 1794 Right Hon Henrietta (in her own right) Countess of Bath, and assumed the surname of Pulteney but died without issue.

MURRAY (NS) 1673, of Ochtertyre, Perthshire

Sir PATRICK IAN KEITH MURRAY OF OCHTERTYRE, 12th *Baronet*; *b* 22 March 1965; *s* his father, *Sir* WILLIAM PATRICK KEITH, 1977; *ed* Christ Coll, Brecon, and London Academy of Music and Dramatic Art.

Arms – Azure, three mullets argent, in the centre a cross of the second surmounted on a saltire gules both couped, **Crest** – olive-branch proper. *Residence* – 12 Burgos Grove, Greenwich, SE10 8LL.

GREAT AUNT LIVING

Bethia Ioné (1 Hillpark Av, Edinburgh 4), *b* 1911: *m* 1939 (*m diss* 1966), Paul Nicholas Robert Harding Edgar, who *d* 1989, and has issue living, John George Keith (10 Ormidale Terrace, Edinburgh EH12 6EQ), *b* 1949: *m* 1976, Jennifer Kyles, and has issue living, Caroline Julia *b* 1982, Louisa Clare *b* 1985, Georgina Liska (twin) *b* 1985, — Amanda Elizabeth, *b* 1944: *m* 1st, 1968, John Murray Byers, who *d* 1985; 2ndly, 19—, Capt George Hogg, of 12 Glencairn Cres, Edinburgh EH12 5BS, and has issue living (by 1st *m*), James Paul Edward Murray *b* 1973, Katharine Lucy Victoria *b* 1971, — Susan Nicola, *b* 1945: *m* 1968, (Ian) Douglas Lowe, of Dalkeith Home Farm, Dalkeith, Midlothian, and has issue living, Cecilia Jean *b* 1973.

MOTHER LIVING

Susan Elizabeth, da of Stacey Jones, of Sheephouse, Hay-on-Wye, Powys: *m* 1st, 1963 (*m diss* 1973), as his 1st wife, Sir William Patrick Keith Murray, 11th Bt; 2ndly, 1976, James Carr Hudson, PhD, of Flat 6, 16 Harcourt Terr, SW10, and Old Ffordfawr, Hay-on-Wye, Herefordshire.

WIDOW LIVING OF ELEVENTH BARONET

Deirdra (folk singer, as Dee Dee Woods), da of Norman Wood, of Crail, Fife: *m* 1975, Sir William Patrick Keith Murray of Ochtertyre, 11th Bt, who *d* 1977.

COLLATERAL BRANCHES LIVING

Grandchildren of late Archibald Lamont Keith-Murray, 10th son of 7th baronet:—
Issue of late David KEITH-MURRAY, *b* 1900, *d* 1968: *m* 1932, Nancy May (126 Mount Baker Cres, Salt Spring Island, BC V8K 2J7), da of late Henri Gautschi, of Vancouver, BC:—
PETER (895 Brentwood Heights, Brentwood Bay, BC, Canada V8M 1A8), *b* 12 July 1935; Maj Canadian Forces (ret): *m* 1960, Judith Anne, da of late William Andrew Tinsley, of Sarnia, Ont, and has issue living, (David) Andrew, *b* 7 Dec 1965, — Leslie Anne, *b* 1961: *m* 1989, Paul Joseph Lascelle. —— (David) Mark (525 Baylis Rd, Qualicum Beach, BC V9K 2G2, Canada), *b* 1939: *m* 1960 (*m diss* 1984), Hazel, da of late Amos Pineau, of Prince Edward Is, and has issue living, David Wayne, *b* 1961, — Christopher Mark, *b* 1964. —— Marnie KEITH-MURRAY, *b* 1937; resumed her maiden name 1978: *m* 1958 (*m diss* 1979), Douglas Tufts, of Madoc, Ont, and has issue living, Paul Anthony *b* 1960, — Colin Douglas, *b* 1964, — Andrea Dee, *b* 1959.

Grandchildren of late Henry Dundas Murray, 5th son of 6th baronet:—
Issue of late William Tullibardine Murray, *b* 1863, *d* 1923: *m* 1886, May Elisabeth Margaret, da of late James Bell, MD, of Kaipara, New Zealand:—
Henry Lamont, *b* 1891. —— Yolande, *b* 1887. *Residence* – New Zealand.

Grandson of late George Joseph Murray, grandson of late Alexander Murray, son of Patrick Murray, 2nd son of 2nd baronet:—
Issue of late Capt Alexander Penrose Murray, *b* 1863, *d* 1926: *m* 1st, 1891, Nina, who *d* 1894, da of Col Alexander Solovtsoff; 2ndly, 1895, Ethel Chorley, da of late Maj-Gen Arthur Hill:—
(By 2nd *m*) Charles, *b* 1895. *Residence* –

Granddaughters of late Mackenzie Murray, son of late John Murray, great-grandson of late Mungo Murray, yst son of 1st baronet:—

Issue of late Edward Mackenzie Murray-Buchanan, *b* 1874, *d* 1956 (having assumed the additional surname of Buchanan on succeeding to the estate of Leny 1919): *m* 1913, Jean Isabella Shaw, who *d* 1952, da of James Carmichael, of Arthurstone, Meigle, Perthshire:—

Euphemia Cecilia, *b* 1915: *m* 1st, 1940, Maj Francis William Clark, of Ulva, who was *ka* 1944; 2ndly, 1956, Lieut-Col John Hay Young, DSO, MC, who *d* 1979, and has issue living (by 1st *m*) Francis Malcolm, *b* 1942: *m* 1971, Georgina Jane, da of late Maj S. J. Swinton Lee, Seaforth Higlanders, and has issue living, John Francis *b* 1971, Michael James *b* 1972, Fiona Janet *b* 1980. *Residence* – West Lodge, 3a Glen Rd, Bridge of Allan, Stirlingshire. —— Phoebe Aeonie, *b* 1922: *m* 1952, John Craufuird Roger Inglis, and has issue living, Richard David (4 Marine Rd, Gullane, E Lothian), *b* 1953: *m* 1980, Pauline Goldie, and has issue living, Crawford *b* 1986, Zoe *b* 1982, Charlotte *b* 1984, —— John Edward (2 Redcliffe Mews, SW10 9JU), *b* 1961: *m* 1991, Marina B., da of Roger Hall Lloyd, of Kensington, W8, —— Jean Helen, *b* 1955: *m* 1980, Christopher Smith, of 1 Wester Coates Terr, Edinburgh, and has issue living, Jeremy Gordon *b* 1983, Camilla Helen *b* 1985, —— Fiona Ann, *b* 1957: *m* 1993, Mark A. Ramsay, —— Sheena Mary, *b* 1960: *m* 1986, Michael Crerar, of 19 Gordon Rd, Edinburgh, and has issue living, Gordon *b* 1993, Katherine *b* 1991, —— Susan Patricia, *b* 1964. *Residence* – Inglisfield, Gifford, E Lothian.

The 1st baronet, Sir William Murray, a cadet of Tullibardine (*see* D Atholl), was created a baronet with remainder to his heirs male whatsoever. The 6th baronet, *Sir* Patrick Murray, sat as MP for Edinburgh (City) 1806-12, and was afterwards Baron of Court of Exchequer in Scotland. The 7th Baronet, Sir William Murray, on his marriage in 1833, to Helen Margaret Oliphant, only child of Sir Alexander Keith of Dunnottar, Knt Marischal of Scotland, assumed the name of Keith before that of Murray, which name was used by all his descendants, until the succession of the 10th Baronet, who reverted to Murray.

MUSGRAVE (E) 1611, of Hartley Castle, Westmorland

Without changing

Sir CHRISTOPHER PATRICK CHARLES MUSGRAVE, 15th *Baronet*; *b* 14 April, 1949; *s* his father, *Sir* CHARLES, 1970; patron of one living: *m* 1978 (*m diss* 1992), Megan, da of Walter Inman, of Hull, and has issue.

Arms – Azure, six annulets or, three, two, and one. **Crest** – Two arms embowed in armour proper, the hands grasping an annulet or.
Address – Watermill House, Beach Rd, Weybourne, Holt, Norfolk NR25 7SR.

DAUGHTERS LIVING

Helena, *b* 1981. —— Antonia, *b* 1987.

BROTHER LIVING

JULIAN NIGEL CHARDIN, *b* 8 Dec 1951; *ed* S Wymondham Coll, and Queen Mary Coll London (BSc): *m* 1975, Gulshanbanu Buddrudin, and has issue living, Anar (a da), *b* 1980, —— Ruth, *b* 1983.

MOTHER LIVING

Olive Louise Avril, only da of Patrick Cringle, of Holme-on-Sea, Hunstanton: *m* 1st, 1948 (*m diss* 1961), Sir Charles Musgrave, 14th Bt, who *d* 1970; 2ndly, 1961, Peter Charles Nelson, of Tans End, Wells-on-Sea, Norfolk.

This family was originally settled at Musgrave in Westmorland. Thomas Musgrave, *temp* Edward III, was summoned by writ and sat as peer of the realm for twenty-three years. Sir Philip, 2nd baronet, a distinguished Royalist, sat as MP for Westmorland 1640-42: after the battle of Worcester, he attended King Charles II of France, in Holland and Scotland, whence he retired to the Isle of Man, which he bravely defended under the Countess of Derby. For his great Services a Warrant creating him Baron Musgrave of Hartley Castle was issued, but he did not take out the patent. The 5th baronet, MP for Carlisle, was Clerk to the Privy Council, and the 6th baronet sat as MP for co Westmorland. Sir Philip, 8th baronet, was MP for Carlisle, and Sir Richard, 11th baronet, sat as MP for E Cumberland and was Lord-Lieut of Westmorland.

MUSGRAVE (I) 1782, of Tourin, Waterford

Sir RICHARD JAMES MUSGRAVE, 7th *Baronet*; *b* 10 Feb 1922; *s* his father, *Sir* CHRISTOPHR NORMAN, OBE, 1956; *ed* Stowe; Capt late Indian Army: *m* 1958, Maria, da of late Col Mario Cambanis, of Athens, Greece, and has issue.

Arms – Azure, six annulets, or, three, two, and one. **Crest** – Two arms in proper, gauntleted and supporting an annulet or.
Residences – Knightsbrook, Trim, co Meath; Komito, Syros, Greece.

SONS LIVING

CHRISTOPHER JOHN SHANE, *b* 23 Oct 1959; *ed* Cheltenham. —— Michael Shane, *b* 1968: *ed* Cheltenham.

DAUGHTERS LIVING

Olivia Mirabel, *b* 1958. —— Anastasia Maria, *b* 1961: *m* 1980, Robert Michael Wilson-Wright (*see* Yate, By, ext), and has issue living, Michael Almroth, *b* 1983, — Sophie Margaret, *b* 1980. —— Charlotte Elizabeth, *b* 1963: *m* 1989, James Hanly, and has issue living, Jack Alexander, *b* 1991. —— Alexandra Victoria, *b* 1965.

SISTER LIVING

Elizabeth Anne, *b* 1931: *m* 1955 (*m diss* 1980), Thomas Aydon Bates, and has issue living, Giles Langley, *b* 1963; *ed* Ampleforth, — Benedict Loftus, *b* 1964; *ed* Ampleforth: *m* 1993, Alison Kilner, and has issue living, Dominic Michael *b* 1990, William Thomas *b* 1992, a son *b* 1994, — Annabelle Carol Elizabeth, *b* 1955: *m* 1980 (*m diss* 1991), Samuel Rodd Morshead, yr son of late Maj Christopher Morshead, of Bellewstown House, co Meath, and has issue living, Charles Christopher Thomas *b* 1981, Samuel Harry *b* 1983, — Belinda Ann, *b* 1957: *m* 1st, 1981, David W. Pulford, yr son of late Rev Walter William Pulford; 2ndly, 1985, Robin David Erskine, of 33 Shakespeare Rd, W7 1LT, and has issue (by 2nd *m*) (*see* E Mar and Kellie, colls), — Corrinne Lucy, *b* 1958: *m* 1st, 1976 (*m diss* 1982), Athanasios Komninos; 2ndly, 1982, Fawzard Saffari Shooshterri, and has issue living, (by 2nd *m*) Sebastian Thomas Dariush *b* 1985,

Without changing

Francesca Elizabeth *b* 1988, — Teresa Astrid, *b* 1959: *m* 1981, Nicholas C. H. Somerville, only son of late Maj A. J. Somerville, of Bury St Edmunds, Suffolk, and has issue living, Fedora Isabella Charlotte *b* 1989. *Residence* – Pagos 85, Syros, Greece.

COLLATERAL BRANCHES LIVING

Issue of late Maj Francis Edward Musgrave, brother of 6th baronet, *b* 1894, *d* 1975: *m* 1919, Kathleen Ethel, who *d* 1966, da of late Lt-Col Charles William Grey, Durham Ll:—
Patricia Kathleen, *b* 1921: *m* 1946, David Michael Bay, of 11 E Common, Harpenden, Herts and has issue living, Nicholas Michael (1 New Cottages, Bendish, Hitchin, Herts), *b* 1948: *m* 1975, Jane Lilly, — Anthony David, *b* 1951. —— Shelagh Monica, *b* 1927: *m* 1956, Michael R. P. Boyd-Moss, and has issue living, Robin James, *b* 1959, — Nicola Margaret, *b* 1958.

Issue of late Robert Musgrave, uncle of 6th baronet, *b* 1870, *d* 1940: *m* 1905, Amy Lindsay, who *d* 1939, da of Brig-Surg F. Lindsay Dickson, of Vancouver, British Columbia:—
Robert John, *b* 1905: *m* 1934, Marjorie Winnifred Chinneck, who *d* 1973, and has issue living, Jean Marjorie Frances, *b* 1935, — Daphne Edith Amy, *b* 1936.

Grandchildren of late Robert Musgrave (ante):—
Issue of late Edward Lindsay Musgrave, *b* 1907, *d* 1985: *m* 1949 Judith Bradfield Stevens:—
Anthony Richard, *b* 1955: *m* 1984, Celia Lydia Mary Lane, and has issue living, Alexander Anthony John, *b* 1991. —— Robert Lindsay, *b* 1958; has issue living (by Theresa Mary Killoran), Patrick James MUSGRAVE, *b* 1994. —— Susan Patricia, *b* 1951: *m* 1st, 19—, — Nelson; 2ndly, 1986, Stephen Douglas Reid, of PO Box 2421, Sidney, BC, Canada V8L 3Y3, and has issue living (by 1st *m*), Charlotte Amelia Musgrave, *b* 1989, — (by 2nd *m*) Sophie Alexandra Musgrave, *b* 1989. —— Mary Kathleen, *b* 1961: *m* 1982, William Arthur Broughton, and has issue living, Christopher William, *b* 1984, — Marcus Edward, *b* 1990, — Jennifer Kathleen, *b* 1987.
This Baronetcy was conferred on Richard Musgrave, MP, el son of Christopher Musgrave, of Tourin, co Waterford, with special remainder to his yr brothers, under which remainder the 2nd baronet, Sir Christopher, succeeded. The 3rd baronet sat as MP for co Waterford, and the 4th baronet was Lord-Lieut and Custos Rotulorum of co Waterford.

MUSPRATT (UK) 1922, of Merseyside, City of Liverpool (Extinct 1934)

Sir MAX MUSPRATT, 1st and last *Baronet*.

DAUGHTERS LIVING OF FIRST BARONET

Frances Kate; *b* 1898: *m* 1923, Howard Raymond John Feeney, who *d* 1977, and has issue living, Max Howard, *b* 1928; *ed* Stonyhurst, — Patrick Dalrymple, *b* 1931, — June Mary, *b* 1925, — Jasmine Ann, *b* 1936. —— Vanda May, *b* 1901: *m* 1926, George Frederick Killwick, and has issue living, Georgette, *b* 1926. *Residence* – Whispers, 12 Hill Brow, Hove, Sussex.

MYNORS (UK) 1964, of Treago, co Hereford

Sir RICHARD BASKERVILLE MYNORS, 2nd *Baronet*, *b* 5 May 1947; *s* his father, *Sir* HUMPHREY CHARLES BASKERVILLE, 1989; *ed* Marlborough, and Corpus Christi Coll, Camb; musician; Assistant Dir of Music, King's Sch, Macclesfield 1970-73; Dir of Music, Wolverhampton Gram Sch 1973-81, Merchant Taylors' Sch 1981-88, Belmont Abbey Sch, Hereford 1988-89: *m* 1970, Fiona Bridget, da of late Rt Rev George Edmund Reindorp, DD, sometime Bishop of Salisbury, and has issue.

ᄀᆞrms – Sable, an eagle displayed or, beaked and membered gules, on a chief azure, bordured argent, a chevron between two crescents in chief and rose in base of the last.
Residence – Treago, St Weonards, Hereford HR2 8QB.

DAUGHTERS LIVING

Alexandra Fiona, *b* 1975. —— Frances Veronica, *b* 1978. —— Victoria Jane, *b* 1983.

SISTERS LIVING

Elizabeth Baskerville, *b* 1940: *m* 1962, Jeremy Longmore Russell, of Batch Cottage, Almeley, Hereford HR3 6PT, and has issue living, Thomas Lancelot, *b* 1965, — Jennifer Frances, *b* 1969. —— Catherine Baskerville, *b* 1944: *m* 1966, Christopher Mordaunt Richards, 4 St Ronan's Av, Redland, Bristol BS6 6EP, and has issue living, Benedict William Mordaunt, *b* 1972, — Sophia Janet, *b* 1969, — Clare Eleanor, *b* 1974. —— Philippa Baskerville, *b* 1950: *m* 1977, Rev Alan Duce, of 2 Temple Gdns, Lincoln, and has issue living, Patrick Richard, *b* 1984, — Eleanor Rachel, *b* 1979, — Catherine Veronica, *b* 1981. —— Jane Margery Baskerville, *b* 1952: *m* 1974, Nicholas Kersteman King, of 12 Whiteford Rd, Mannameads, Plymouth PL3 5LX, and has issue living, Hugh Samuel, *b* 1982, — Theresa Jane, *b* 1977, — Jennifer Vivien, *b* 1980.
The first baronet, Sir Humphrey Charles Baskerville Mynors, was a Dir of the Bank of England 1949-54, and Dep Gov 1954-64.

NAIRN (UK) 1904, of Rankeilour, Collessie, and Dysart House, Dysart, Fifeshire

Sir MICHAEL NAIRN, 4th *Baronet*; *b* 1 July 1938; *s* his father, *Sir* (MICHAEL) GEORGE, TD, 1984; *ed* Eton, and INSEAD: *m* 1st, 1972, Diana Gordon, who *d* 1982, eldest da of F. Leonard Bligh, of Pejar Park, Woodhouselee, NSW, Australia; 2ndly, 1986, Mrs Sally Jane Straker, yr da of Maj William P.S. Hastings, of Brandy Well, Eglingham, Alnwick, Northumberland, and formerly wife of Maj Ivan Charles Straker, and has issue by 1st *m*.

ᄀᆞrms – Per fesse argent and sable, on a chaplet four escallops, all counterchanged. Crest – Three thistles conjoined in stalk entwined with two roses all slipped proper.
Address – PO Box 55, Dundee DD1 9JJ.

SON LIVING *(By 1st marriage)*

MICHAEL ANDREW, *b* 2 Nov 1973. —— Alexander Gordon, *b* 1975.

DAUGHTER LIVING *(By 1st marriage)*

Emma Helen Beatrice, *b* 1980.

BROTHER LIVING

Charles Bruce, *b* 1942; *ed* Eton, and McGill Univ, Montreal (BA): *m* 1973, Carol Ann, da of late Lt-Col Sidney Clive Blaber (*see* Hartwell, Bt, colls), and has issue living, Amy, *b* 1985.

AUNT LIVING *(Daughter of 2nd baronet)*

Elizabeth Barbara, *b* 1915: *m* 1st, 1938 (*m diss* 1947), Maj Alexander Oliphant Hutchison, Fife and Forfar Yeo; 2ndly, 1948 (*m diss* 1958), Leon Robert de Notto; 3rdly, 1961, (John) Michael Wentworth, of Gainsborough House, Odiham, Hants, and has issue living, (by 1st *m*) Roderick Alexander Oliphant (Strathairly, Upper Largo, Fife), *b* 1943: *m* 1970, Gillian Boddy of Lochaillort, Inverness-shire, — Edward Anthony Oliphant (19 Dover Park Drive, Roehampton, SW15 5BT), *b* 1946: *m* 1971, Polly Matilda Saunders, of Yew Tree Cottage, Droxford, Hants, and has issue living, Jeremy George Oliphant *b* 1979, Daisy Frances Alexandra *b* 1977, — Caroline Victoria Oliphant, *b* 1941: *m* 1st, 1963 (*m diss* 1970), George Charles Caswell Cornelius; 2ndly, 1973, (Robert) Michael Marshall, MP, of Old Inn House, Slindon, Arundel, Sussex, and has issue living, (by 1st *m*) Deborah Caswell Oliphant *b* 1965, Katherine Caswell Oliphant *b* 1967.

WIDOW LIVING OF THIRD BARONET

HELEN LOUISE (*Helen, Lady Nairn*), yr da of late Maj Ernest James Webster Bruce, MC, RFA, of Melbourne, Australia: *m* 1936, Sir (Michael) George Nairn, 3rd Bt, TD, who *d* 1984. *Residence* – Wester-Pitcarmick, Bridge of Cally, Blairgowrie, Perthshire PH10 7NW.

COLLATERAL BRANCH LIVING

Issue of late Sir Robert SPENCER-NAIRN, Bt, TD (2nd son of 1st baronet), who was *cr a Baronet* 1933.
See Spencer-Nairn, Bt.
The 1st baronet, Sir Michael Barker, was Chairman of Michael Nairn and Co (Limited), linoleum manufacturers, of Kirkcaldy, and of Nairn Linoleum Co, of Kearny, USA.

SPENCER-NAIRN (UK) 1933, of Monimail, co Fife

Sir ROBERT ARNOLD SPENCER-NAIRN, 3rd *Baronet*; *b* 11 Oct 1933; *s* his father, Lt-Col *Sir* DOUGLAS LESLIE SPENCER, TD, 1970; *ed* Eton, and Trin Hall, Camb; late Lt SG: *m* 1963, Joanna Elizabeth, da of late Lt-Cdr George Stevenson Salt, RN (*see* Salt, Bt, *cr* 1899, colls), and has issue.

Arms – Per fesse argent and sable, on a chaplet four escallops, all counter-changed; in the chief point a crescent of the second for difference. **Crest** – A terrestrial sphere with semi-meridian and stand proper.
Residence – Barham, Cupar, Fife.

SONS LIVING

JAMES ROBERT, *b* 7 Dec 1966. —— Andrew George, *b* 1969.

DAUGHTER LIVING

Katharine Elizabeth, *b* 1964.

BROTHER LIVING

John Chaloner (3960 West 13th Av, Vancouver BC, Canada), *b* 1938; *ed* Eton; late 2nd Lt R Dragoons: *m* 1st, 1966 (*m diss* 1970), Barbara Lynn, da of Murray Kamichik, of Montreal, Canada; 2ndly, 1971, Lucie, da of late Pierre Belanger, Canada, and has issue living (by 2nd *m*), John Henderson, *b* 1973, —— Kim Sheilagh, *b* 1975, —— Tara Lucie, *b* 1977.

HALF-BROTHER LIVING

(Christopher) Frank (Culligran, Struy, Beauly, Inverness-shire), *b* 1949; *ed* Eton, and Magdalene Coll, Camb; FCA; MBA Cape Town: *m* 1975, Juliet Constance, da of Oswald Frank Baker Baker of Eskhill, Forfar, Angus (E Perth, colls), and has issue living, Douglas Frederick, *b* 1986, —— Philippa Lucy, *b* 1980, —— Jenny Anne Helen, *b* 1983.

SISTERS LIVING

Mary Elizabeth, *b* 1931: *m* 1953, Maj Andrew Beatty Houstoun, OBE, MC, DL, late R Dragoons, and has issue living, William Robert (Cairnhall, Lintrathen, Kirriemuir, Angus), *b* 1954; *ed* Harrow, and Edinburgh Univ: *m* 1981, Sarah Molly, da of Col Charles Sievewright, CB, MC, DL, of Talland House, South Cerney, Cirencester, Glos, and has issue living, Camilla Mary *b* 1983, Rosemary Sarah *b* 1984, —— David Waldron (Glenkilrie, Blacklunans, Blairgowrie, Perthshire), *b* 1957; *ed* Harrow: *m* 1989, Morag Lynne, da of John Davidson, of Forter, Glenisla, Perthshire, and has issue living, Andrew James *b* 1990, Claire Kathryn *b* 1992, —— Alexander Michael (Kerbet House, Kinnettles, by Forfar, Angus DD8 1TQ), *b* 1958; *ed* Harrow: *m* 1988, Margaret Susan, da of Duncan Kerr, of Kingennie, Angus, and has issue living, Michael Paterson *b* 1990, Robert Duncan *b* 1992, —— Andrew Neil, *b* 1961; *ed* Harrow, and RAC Cirencester. *Residence* – Lintrathen Lodge, Kirriemuir, Angus.

HALF-SISTER LIVING

Teresa Leslie, *b* 1952: *m* 1975, John Mungo Ingleby, of Malling Farm, Port of Menteith, Stirling, and has issue living, Mungo Henry *b* 1981, —— (John) Frederick, *b* 1988, —— Kim Louise, *b* 1978, —— Rosie, *b* 1990.

UNCLES LIVING (*Sons of 1st baronet*)

Michael Alastair Spencer, TD, *b* 1909; *ed* Trin Hall, Camb (MA); JP; formerly Major Fife and Forfar Yeo (TA): *m* 1935, Ursula Helen, da of late Howson Foulger Devitt (*see* Devitt, Bt, *cr* 1916, colls), and has issue living, Angus (La Fontaine, Rue du Pont, St John, Jersey), *b* 1947: *m* 1968, Christina Janet, da of late Col Hugh Gillies, and has issue living, Michael Angus *b* 1975, Fiona Louise *b* 1974, —— Sarah Ursula, *b* 1937: *m* 1967, John Scoular, of Tonderghie, Whithorn, Wigtownshire, and has issue living, Alastair John Greenshields *b* 1972, Anys Helen *b* 1978, —— Catriona Jane, *b* 1945: *m* 1st, 1969 (*m diss* 1980), Paul Hosegood Kirton, elder son of late Robert James Kirton, CBE; 2ndly, 1986, George Edward Derrington Tremlett, of River House, The Green, Elstead, Godalming, Surrey GU8 6DA, son of late Laurence Edward Paul Tremlett, and has issue living (by 1st *m*), Ian Nigel *b* 1970, Clare Helen *b* 1972, Lena Harriett *b* 1974, Mary Rose *b* (twin) 1974. *Residence* – Baltilly House, Ceres, Fife KY15 5QG. —— Robert Frank, *b* 1910; *ed* Trin Hall, Camb (BA 1932, MA 1936); sometime Capt The Black Watch (TA): *m* 1st, 1936 (*m diss* 1949), Caroline Isabel, da of H. A. Chadwick, of Calgary, Canada; 2ndly, 1954, Mary Anna, da of Walter E. Hettman, of San Francisco, California, and has issue living, (by 1st *m*) Isabel Susan *b* 1937: *m* 1966, Brig Nicholas John Ridley, OBE, Queen's Own Highlanders (Christison, Bt), and has had issue, Nicholas Charles Philip Christ-ison *b* 1973, Alexia Kathleen *b* 1967, *d* 1992, Susanna Mary *b* 1969, —— (by 2nd *m*) Martha Ann, *b* 1955: *m* 1984, Seth M. Milliken II, and has issue living, Eliza Clark *b* 1987, —— Charlotte Emily, *b* 1957: *m* 1989, Duncan MacGuigan, —— Elspeth Margaret, *b* 1958: *m* 1981 (*m diss* 1988), Edgar W. Swift, and has issue living, Clinton Spencer *b* 19—, —— Margaret Cynthia, *b* 1965. *Residence* – Castle Carey, St Peter Port, Guernsey.

AUNTS LIVING *(Daughters of 1st baronet)*

Kathleen Matilda, MBE, *b* 1913: *m* 1st, 1938 (*m diss* 1948), Maj Ronald Richards, TA; 2ndly, 1948, William Webb, who *d* 1991, and has issue living, (by 2nd *m*) William Spencer, *b* 1948, — Alan Gordon, *b* 1951, — Michael Charles, *b* 1952. *Residence* – Mendlesham Manor, Stowmarket, Suffolk. ⸺ Helen Clare, *b* 1917: *m* 1st, 1939, Maj John Henry Courthope Powell, Fife and Forfar Yeo (TA), who was *ka* 1944; 2ndly, 1945, John William Gardner Hume, who *d* 1976, and has issue living, (by 1st *m*) Elizabeth Clare, *b* 1942: *m* 1965, Rev Canon Colin T. Scott Dempster, of Old Faskally House, Killiecrankie, Pitlochry, Perthshire, and has issue living, Robert Andrew *b* 1967, Harry Colin *b* 1985, Clare Ann *b* 1969, — Margaret Ann, *b* 1944: *m* 1966, Stephen James Lindsay, and has issue living, Richard Stephen *b* 1969, Charles Ludovic *b* 1974, Andrew James Ronald *b* 1977, Jane Margaret *b* 1966, — (by 2nd *m*) Mary *b* 1947: *m* 1971, John FitzGerald, of The Old Rectory, Rodmarton, Cirencester, Glos, and has issue living, John William Broun *b* 1973, Edward James Broun *b* 1975, Katherine Mary *b* 1979, Louisa Clare *b* 1984. *Residence* – Damside, Auchterarder, Perthshire. ⸺ Adela Margaret (*Baroness Colnbrook*), *b* 1924: *m* 1944, Baron Colnbrook, KCMG, PC (Life Baron)

The 1st baronet, Maj Sir Robert Spencer-Nairn, TD (2nd son of Sir Michael Barker Nairn 1st Bt, of Rankeilour, Springfield, Fife), by Emily Frances, da of Alfred Rimington Spencer, was Major Fife and Forfar Yeo. In 1928 he adopted the surname of Spencer-Nairn.

NAIRNE (UK) 1917, of Kirkcudbright (Extinct 1945)

Sir (JOHN) GORDON NAIRNE, 1st and last *Baronet*.

DAUGHTER LIVING OF FIRST BARONET

Sybil Isabel Mary Macartney, *b* 1896: *m* 1918 (*m diss* 1949), Lieut-Col Basil Laing Clay, OBE, Queen's Own Roy W Kent Regt. *Residence* – Miswell Orchard, Tring, Herts.

NALL (UK) 1954, of Hoveringham, co Nottingham

Sir MICHAEL JOSEPH NALL, 2nd *Baronet*; *b* 6 Oct 1921; *s* his father *Col Sir* JOSEPH, DSO, TD, 1958; *ed* Wellington Coll; Lt-Cdr RN (ret); DL Notts 1970, High Sheriff 1971-72, and Vice Lord-Lieut 1989-91; Pres of Nottingham Chamber of Commerce and Industry 1972-74; 1939-45 War: *m* 1951, Angela Loveday Hanbury, da of Air Ch Marshal Sir (William) Alec Coryton, KCB, KBE, MVO, DFC, and has issue.

Arms – Per chevron barry of six gules and or and of the first, in chief two stag's heads caboshed proper and in base a lion rampant guardant of the second. Crest – Within a leathern garter buckled gules, a bee or.
Residence – Hoveringham Hall, Nottingham, NG14 7JR.

SONS LIVING

EDWARD WILLIAM JOSEPH, *b* 24 Oct 1952; *ed* Eton; late Maj 13th/18th Royal Hussars (QMO) Light Dragoons. ⸺ Alexander Michael (Lime Kiln House, Ticknall, Derbyshire DE7 1JF), *b* 1956; *ed* Eton; late Capt 2nd RGJ: *m* 1982, Caroline Jane, yr da of Anthony L. à'C. Robinson (*see* B Heytesbury, 1990 Edn), and has issue living, William Alexander Coryton, *b* 1985, — Katharine Caroline, *b* 1986.

BROTHER LIVING

William George Joseph, *b* 1926; *ed* Wellington Coll; European War 1944-45 as Lieut 13th/18th Royal Hussars (QMO): *m* 1961, Jennifer Jane, el da of L. Aylwin Richardson, FRCS, of Minstead, Hants, and has issue living, Charles William Joseph, *b* 1965; *ed* Rugby; BA, ACA, — Richard George Aylwin, *b* 1966; *ed* Rugby; BA, DipM: *m* 1993, Sarah Helen, el da of B. J. Wood, of Ablington, Glos, — Olivia Jane Caroline, *b* 1970. *Residence* – Farm House, Wellow, Newark on Trent, Notts NG22 0EA.

SISTERS LIVING

Elizabeth Josephine, TD, *b* 1920; a JP of Notts; 1939-45 War with ATS. *Residence* – Hall Close, Hoveringham, Notts NG14 7JR. ⸺ Rosemary Alice Anne, *b* 1923; 1939-45 War, Army Remount Depot, Melton Mowbray 1939-41, Admiralty Ops Sigs 1942-45: *m* 1947, Peter Bingham Inchbald, Capt RA (*see* Bingham, Bt, ext, 1985 Edn), and has issue living, Peter Joseph Nicholas, *b* 1951, — Guy William Benjamin, *b* 1952: *m* 1981, Hazel Brenda, yst da of E. Trant, of Esk Bank, Dalkeith, Midlothian, and has issue living, Robin Peter Guy *b* 1991, Joanne Elizabeth *b* 1982, Jenny Anne *b* 1984. *Residence* – Holdfast Manor, Upton-on-Severn, Worcs. ⸺ Diana Christian Isabella, *b* 1924; 1939-45 War with Mobile Red Cross attached RN: *m* 1950, Col Sidney John Watson, MBE, late RE (B Dulverton), of Ballingarrane, Clonmel, co Tipperary, and has issue living, John Wilfred, *b* 1952; *ed* Eton and RAC Cirencester; ARICS; 1978 World three-day-event Championship (Silver Medal): *m* 1977, Julia Morrish, and has issue living, Samuel James *b* 1980, Suzannah Irene *b* 1980, Rosalind Sara *b* 1982, — Elizabeth Sandra, *b* 1953; SRN: *m* 1975, Richard Vincent Craik-White, and has issue living, James Richard *b* 1977, Henry William *b* 1979.

The 1st baronet, Col Sir Joseph Nall, DSO, TD (el son of Joseph Nall, of Hoveringham and Broom Cottage, High Legh, Cheshire) was a Director of several Transport and Industrial undertakings; ktd 1924, a DL for Lancashire and Notts (High Sheriff 1952-3), Pres of Institute of Transport 1925-26, and MP for Hulme Div of Manchester (*U*) 1918-29, and 1931-45. He served in European War 1914-18 (wounded, despatches, DSO).

NAPIER (NS) 1627, of Merchistoun

Faith preserved renders prosperous;
Look well; Without stain

Sir JOHN ARCHIBALD LENNOX NAPIER OF MERCHISTOUN, 14th *Baronet*; *b* 6 Dec 1946; *s* his father, *Sir* WILLIAM ARCHIBALD, 1990; *ed* St Stithians, and Witwatersrand Univ, Johannesburg; MSc (Eng), PhD: *m* 1969, Erica, da of late Kurt Kingsfield, of Johannesburg, and has issue.

Arms – Quarterly, 1st and 4th argent, on a saltire engrailed between four roses gules, the roses barbed vert, five mullets of the field, *Napier of Merchistoun*; 2nd, azure, a lion rampant argent, crowned or, *MacDowall of Garthland*; 3rd argent, a fess azure voided of the field, between three demi-lions crowned gules, *Milliken of that Ilk*. **Crests** – *Dexter*, on a chapeau gules furred ermine, *for the feudal Barony of Merchistoun*; an arm grasping an eagle's leg proper, talons expanded gules, *Napier of Merchistoun; Sinister*, A demi-lion rampant gules, holding in his dexter forepaw a dagger or, *Milliken of Culcreuch*. **Supporters** – Two eagles with their wings closed proper.
Residence – Merchiston Croft, PO Box 65177, Benmore, 2010, S Africa.

SON LIVING

HUGH ROBERT LENNOX, *b* 1 Aug 1977.

DAUGHTER LIVING

Natalie Ann, *b* 1973.

WIDOW LIVING OF THIRTEENTH BARONET

KATHLEEN MABEL (*Dowager Lady Napier of Merchistoun*), da of late Reginald Greaves, of Tafelberg, Cape Province: *m* 1942, Sir William Archibald Napier of Merchistoun, 13th Bt, who *d* 1990. *Residence* – Merchistoun Croft, P.O. Box 65177, Benmore 2010, S Africa.

COLLATERAL BRANCHES LIVING

Granddaughters of late William Edward Stirling Napier (infra):—
Issue of late Lt-Col William Edward Stirling Napier, MC, TD, *b* 1893, *d* 1983: *m* 1919, Audrey, who *d* 1986, da of late William Houlding, of Liverpool, and Arcachon, France:—
Elizabeth June Houlding (Greylag, Merilbah Rd, Bowral, NSW 2576, Australia), *b* 1920: *m* 1947, Lt-Col Gerald Patrick Gardner-Brown, RA (ret), who *d* 1994, and has had issue, Elspeth Susan, *b* 1948, — Vivien Patricia, *b* 1951, *d* 1987: *m* 1974, John Grant Pagan, only son of Brig Sir John Ernest Pagan, CMG, MBE, TD, FRGS, and has issue living, Jonathan Edward *b* 1981, Peter Napier *b* 1983. —— Lavinia, *b* 1924: *m* 1947, Capt C. Czarkowski-Golijeivski, 14th Polish Lancers. —— Elspeth Mary, *b* 1933: *m* 1957, Denbigh Hamilton Harding, of Halcyon, Shootersway Lane, Berkhamsted, Herts, and has issue living, Caroline, *b* 1958, — Fiona, *b* 1960, — Unity, *b* 1962.

Issue of late William Edward Stirling Napier, 3rd son of 9th baronet, *b* 1858, *d* 1900: *m* 1884, Jane Catherine, who *d* 1945, da of late W. M. Reid:—
Aleck Douglas, *b* 1894; formerly Lt RASC: *m* 1927, Dorris Mary Clara, da of late Victor Hide Hill, and has issue living, Alexander Colin, *b* 1930, — John Stirling, *b* 1935.
This family is a branch of the Earls of Levenax or Lennox (title extinct), and is said to have taken its name from a saying by Alexander III (of Scotland), after battle, that Lennox had *na peer* (no equal). Sir William, the 8th baronet, was served heir male general to Archibald, 3rd Baron Napier, 1817, and afterwards assumed the baronetcy—one of the oldest in Scotland—which had remained dormant for 134 years. Sir Alexander Lennox Milliken Napier, 11th Bt, Capt Grenadier Guards, was ADC to Gov-Gen and Com-in-Ch of Australia (Earl of Dudley) 1910-12; he served in S Africa 1902, and in European War 1914-17 (twice wounded).

NAPIER (UK) 1867, of Merrion Square, Dublin

Sir CHARLES JOSEPH NAPIER, 6th *Baronet*; *b* 15 April 1973; *s* his father, *Sir* ROBERT (ROBIN) SURTEES, 1994.

Arms – Argent, on a saltire engrailed between four roses gules, five escallops or. **Crest** – A dexter cubit arm erect proper, charged with a rose gules, the hand grasping a crescent argent.
Residence – Upper Chilland House, Martyr Worthy, Winchester, Hants SO21 1EB.

UNCLE LIVING *(son of 4th baronet)*

JOHN LENNOX (86 Ennerdale Rd, Kew, Richmond, Surrey; City of London, MCC), *b* 25 Jan 1934; *ed* Eton: *m* 1967, Cecily, da of late Arthur Mortimer, of Malta, and has issue living, James Alexander, *b* 1969; *ed* Oundle, — Jessica, *b* 1971.

WIDOW LIVING OF FOURTH BARONET

ISABEL MURIEL (*Isabel, Lady Napier*), 2nd da of late Maj Henry Siward Balliol Surtees, JP, DL, of Redworth Hall, co Durham: *m* 1931, Sir Joseph William Lennox Napier, 4th Bt, OBE, who *d* 1986. *Residence* – 17 Cheyne Gdns, SW3 5QT

WIDOW LIVING OF FIFTH BARONET

JENNIFER BERYL (*Lady Napier*), da of late Herbert Warwick Daw, of Flint Walls, Henley-on-Thames, and formerly wife of Mark R. Palmer, of Houston, Texas: *m* 1971, Sir Robert (Robin) Surtees Napier, 5th Bt, who *d* 1994. *Residence* – Upper Chilland House, Martyr Worthy, Winchester, Hants SO21 1EB.

Without blemish

COLLATERAL BRANCH LIVING

Issue of late Maj Charles MacNaughten Napier, 2nd son of 3rd baronet, *b* 1896, *d* 1967: *m* 1923 (*m diss* 1939), Dorothy Constance, who *d* 1960, da of late Col Reginald Hawkins Hall Dempster, DSO, of Dunnichen and Auchterforfar:—
Lennox Alexander Hawkins, CB, OBE, MC (c/o Barclay's Bank, Monmouth, Gwent), *b* 1928; Maj-Gen late RRW (ret); DL Gwent, High Sheriff 1988; Chm Central Transport Consultative Cttee, Inspector Public Inquiries, and Memb British Transport Police Cttee; OStJ; MBE (Mil) 1965, OBE (Mil) 1970, CB (Mil) 1983: *m* 1959, Jennifer Dawn, da of B Wilson, and has issue living, Philip Martin Lennox, *b* 1964; Capt RRW: *m* 1990, Philippa N., elder da of James Rawson, of Chaigley, Clitheroe, Lancs, and has issue living, Phoebe Henrietta *b* 1992, Louisa Rodier *b* 1994, — Joanna Dawn, *b* 1962: *m* 1987, Lt-Col Robert Hanbury Tenison Aitken, Royal Regt of Wales, of Manor Farm House, Urchfont, nr Devizes, Wilts, only son of Capt Harry Kerr Aitken, MC, Argyll and Sutherland Highrs, — Sally Vanessa, *b* 1967. —— Audrey Lennox, *b* 1926: *m* 1958, Lt Col Henry Christian Ewart Harding, MC, of Furzey Lodge, Beaulieu, Hants, and has issue living, William George Charles, *b* 1964, — Sarah Constance Hope, *b* 1961: *m* 1992, Oliver Dacres Wise, el son of Derek Wise, of Barcombe, Sussex, and has issue living, Henry Gerard Dacres *b* 1993, — Susan Jane Napier, *b* 1966.

This family claim descent from a branch of the family of Sir Robert Napier, Bt, of Luton Hoo (*cr* 1611) which established itself in Ireland about 1700 and from which the 1st baronet, Sir Joseph Napier, of Merrion Square, descended.
The 1st baronet, Sir Joseph, PC, DCL, LLD, sat as MP for Dublin University (C) 1848-57 and was Lord Chancellor of Ireland 1858-9, a member of the Judicial Committee of the Privy Council 1868-81, First Lord Commissioner for Custody of Great Seal in Ireland 1874, and Vice-Chancellor of Dublin University 1867-80. The 3rd baronet, Lieut-Col Sir William Lennox, was *ka* in the Dardanelles 1915, when serving as Major with 4th Batn S Wales Borderers. The 5th baronet, Sir Robert (Robin) Surtees, assumed the forename of Surtees in lieu of those of Aubone Siward.

Naylor-Leyland, see Leyland.

NEAVE (GB) 1795, of Dagnam Park, Essex

Sir PAUL ARUNDELL NEAVE, 7th *Baronet*; *b* 13 Dec 1948; *s* his father, Sir ARUNDELL THOMAS CLIFTON, 1992; *ed* Eton; stockbroker: *m* 1976, Coralie Jane Louise, eld da of Sir Robert George Caldwell Kinahan, ERD, of Castle Upton, Templepatrick, co Antrim, and has issue.

𝕬rms – Argent, on a cross sable five fleurs-de-lis or. 𝕮rest – Out of a ducal coronet gold a lily, stalked and leaved vert, flowered and seeded or.
Residence – Queen's House, Monk Sherborne, Hants RG26 5HH. *Club* – Boodle's.

Those things only are becoming which are honourable

SOLA·PROBA·QUÆ·HONESTA

SONS LIVING

FREDERICK PAUL KINAHAN, *b* 25 Jan 1981. —— Julian Robin Kinahan, *b* 1983.

BROTHER LIVING

Robert Joshua (Greatham Moor, Liss, Hants), *b* 1951; *ed* Eton.

SISTERS LIVING

Dilys Richenda, *b* 1947: *m* 1968, Timothy Hayward Hobson, of Harvard Farm, Halstock, Yeovil, Som BA22 9SZ, and has issue living, Jake Timothy, *b* 1971, — Barnaby John, *b* 1974, — Samuel Jeffrey, *b* 1979, — Richenda Eveline, *b* 1969. —— Serena Mary, *b* 1955.

UNCLE LIVING (*son of 5th baronet*)

Kenelm Digby (Saunders Farm, Camden Hill, Sissinghurst, Kent TN17 2AR), *b* 1921; *ed* Harrow; Capt (ret) Welsh Gds; N-W Europe 1944-45 (wounded): *m* 1st, 1949, Venetia, only child of late Harold Digby Neave (gt-grandson of William Augustus Neave, 4th son of 2nd Bt), and late Mrs Johnson; 2ndly, 1970, Marian Rosamond, da of late Gerald Hartley Lees, and has issue living (by 1st *m*), Nicola Venetia, *b* 1956: *m* 1976, Robert Reagan, of Cowley Close, Cheltenham, Glos, and has issue living, Paul *b* 1979, Jonathan *b* 1984, Louise *b* 1982, — Dorinda Mary, *b* 1958: *m* 1985, Barry Shell, of Quebec St, Vancouver, BC, Canada, and has issue living, Samuel *b* 1987, Davina *b* 1991.

AUNT LIVING (*daughter of 5th baronet*)

Dorina Mary Eileen (Wren House, 32 Vicarage St, Warminster, Wilts), *b* 1911: *m* 1936, Brig Frederick Gillespie Austin Parsons, CBE, late Royal Northumberland Fus, who *d* 1992, and has had issue, Anthony Frederick Arundell, MBE, *b* 1937; *ed* Wellington Coll; Lt-Col RRF (Mil) 1976: *m* 1965, Jane (26 Mark Ash, Warminster, Wilts), da of John Llewellin, of Solomons, Long Compton Warwicks, and *d* of wounds received on active service in N Ireland 1982, leaving issue, Charles *b* 1965, James *b* 1971, — Robert Gillespie (Chapel House, Church Path, Purton, nr Swindon, Wilts), *b* 1942; *ed* Wellington Coll; Capt 1st RRF (ret): *m* 1st, 1969 (*m diss* 1976), Anne Penelope Stanton, da of Maj Joseph Prestwich, of Highland Farm, Ossington, Notts; 2ndly, 1983 (*m diss* 1986), Nicola, da of Patrick Dyas, OBE, of Broadbridge Heath, Sussex, and has issue living (by 1st *m*), Rollo Crispin Gillespie *b* 1971, Eugénie Sophia Gillespie *b* 1972.

COLLATERAL BRANCHES LIVING

Grandchildren of late Sheffield Airey Neave, CMG, OBE (*infra*):—
Issue of late Lt-Col Airey Middleton Sheffield Neave, DSO, OBE, MC, TD, MP, *b* 1916, *d* 1979: *m* 1942, Diana Josceline Barbara (*cr Baroness Airey of Abingdon*, 1979), who *d* 1992, da of Thomas Arthur Walter Giffard, MBE, of Chillington Hall, Wolverhampton (Trollope Bt):—
Hon (Richard) Patrick Sheffield (16 Maze Rd, Kew, Richmond, Surrey), *b* 1947; *ed* Eton, and City of London Poly: *m* 1980, Elizabeth Mary Catherine, yr da of late Cuthbert Edward Alphonso Riddell, of Hermeston Hall, Worksop, Notts, and has issue living, James Riddell Airey, *b* 1983, — Thomas Edward Riddell Airey, *b* 1985, — Matthew Robert Riddell Airey, *b* 1993. —— *Hon* William Robert Sheffield (20 Kirkstall Rd, SW2), *b* 1953; *ed* Eton: *m* 1986, Joanna Mary Stuart, 2nd da of James Stuart Paton, of The Old Vicarage, Gt Hockham, Norfolk, and has issue living, Richard Digby Stuart, *b* 1987, — Sebastian Airey Stuart, *b* 1989. —— *Hon* Marigold Elizabeth Cassandra, *b* 1944: *m* 1968, William Richard Broughton Webb, DL, of Barbers, Martley, Worcs, and has issue living, Edward Alexander Broughton, *b* 1970, — Katherine Angela Mary, *b* 1970.

Grandchildren of late Sheffield Henry Morier Neave, el son of Sheffield Neave, 3rd son of 2nd baronet (*infra*):—
Issue of late Sheffield Airey Neave, CMG, OBE, *b* 1879, *d* 1961: *m* 1st, 1915, Dorothy, who *d* 1943, da of late Lt-Col Arthur Thomson Middleton, JP, 13th Hussars, of Ayshe Court, Horsham, Sussex; 2ndly, 1946, Mary Irene, who *d* 1993, da of Henry Hodges, of Broadway Hall, Churchstoke, Montgomery:—
(By 1st *m*) Digby John Sheffield (1 Rue Champflour, 78160 Marly-le-Roi, France), *b* 1928; *ed* Eton, and at Merton Coll, Oxford: *m* 1st, 1958, Ulla, who *d* 1963, da of A. B. Schmidt, of Gilleleje, Denmark; 2ndly, 1966, Christiane, da of E. J. Corty, of L'Etang-la-Ville, France, and has issue living, (by 1st *m*) Victoria Janet (*Hon Mrs Hugh N. T. Fairfax*), *b* 1959: *m* 1984, Hon Hugh Nigel Thomas Fairfax, 2nd son of 13th Lord Fairfax of Cameron, — Philippa *b* 1960, — (by 2nd *m*), Lionel Digby Sheffield, *b* 1966: *m* 1992, Hon Victoria Alice, 2nd da of Baron McAlpine of West Green (Life Baron). —— Rosamund Malua, *b* 1921: *m* 1939, Capt Edward Noble Sheppard, Essex Yeo, of The Old Dairy, Consent Lane, Bildeston, Suffolk.
Issue of late Lt-Col Richard Neave, *b* 1881, *d* 1962: *m* 1912, Helen Elizabeth Mary, who *d* 1976, da of late Robert Miller:—
Robert Morier Sheffield, MC, MRCVS (Layer Breton Lodge, Colchester, Essex), *b* 1917, *ed* London Univ; is Major 13th/18th Hussars (Supplementary Reserve); European War 1939-44 (wounded, MC): *m* 1952, Philippa Elizabeth, only da of late Lt-Col (Vincent) Basil Ramsden, DSO, MC (V St Davids, colls), and has issue living, Julia Helen, *b* 1953: *m* 1976, Charles David Walker, of Westport, Conn, USA, and has issue living, Bennett Neave *b* 1984, Megan Philippa *b* 1980, Lydia Joy *b* 1982, — Lucinda (Lucy) Philippa, *b* 1954: *m* 1983, Michael Philip Muller, of Tithe Farmhouse, Hitcham Lane, Burnham, Bucks SL1 7DP, elder son of Dr Walter Muller, of Cheltenham, and has issue living, Thomas Robert *b* 1992, Katharine Elise *b* 1985, Jessica Philippa *b* 1986, Rebecca Madeleine *b* 1989, — Harriet Elise Bunty, *b* 1957. —— Julius Arthur Sheffield, CBE (Mill Green Park, Ingatestone, Essex), *b* 1919; *ed* Sherborne; Maj (ret), 13th/18th Hussars (Reserve); JP and DL for Essex; OStJ 1988; 1939-45 War (despatches); MBE (Mil) 1945, CBE (Civil) 1978: *m* 1951, Helen Margery, da of late Lt-Col Percy Morland Acton-Adams, DSO, of Clarence Reserve, Kaikoura, NZ, and has issue living, (Helen) Penelope, *b* 1952: *m* 1981, Michael Wilson, and has issue living, Esme Beatrice *b* 1983, Julia Rose *b* 1985, — (Joan) Miranda Mary, *b* 1954: *m* 1979, (George) Anthony John Bowles, of Holmhead, Corsock, Castle Douglas, Kirkcudbrightshire DG7 3DT, and has issue (*see*

Barwick, Bt, colls), — Venetia Beatrice, b 1958: m 1982, William Lebus, yr son of Oliver Lebus, of 25 Victoria Rd, W8, and has issue living, Frederick Oliver b 1985, Henry William b 1991, Tomasina Olivia b 1987. —— Beatrice Honoria Sheffield (Garden Cottage, Drinkstone Park, Bury St Edmunds, Suff), b 1916: m 1952, Eustace Blewitt Robinson, who d 1992, and has had issue, Eleanor Mary, b 1953, d 1992: m 1977, Julian Richard Edwards, and has issue living, Alexander Julian b 1981, James Blewitt b 1984.

Grandchildren of late Edward Strangways Neave son of late Sheffield Neave, 3rd son of 2nd baronet (ante):—
Issue of late Edward Arthur Neave, b 1883, d 1960: m 1916, Evelyn Margaret, who d 1966, da of George Augustus Lamb (British Guiana Police), of Rye, Sussex:—
Digby Seymour, b 1921; is a FRICS; Senior Partner Messrs Neave, Tinworth and Nuan, Chartered Quantity Surveyors; 1939-45 War as Lieut RA in N-W Europe: m 1948, Chrystel, authoress, only da of Prof Poul P. Outzen-Boisen, Knt of Dannebrog, OBE, of Rungsted Kyst, Denmark.
Issue of late Guy Morier Neave, b 1886, d 1950: m 1925, Dorothy, who d 1961, da of late J. E. Ponsonby-Steele:—
June Violet, b 1928: m 1956 Bryan Francis Blake, of 115 Meadvale Rd, Ealing, W5, and has issue living, Stephen Guy, b 1958, — Judith Clare, b 1960: m 1987, Bernard Carl Greatbatch, of First Tower, St Helier, Jersey, CI, and has issue living, Toby William b 1990, Robin Stephen b 1991, Chloë Ruth b 1988. —— Rose Ann, b 1930: m 1955, Robert Arthur Jackman, of 6 Overwood Drive, King's Park, Glasgow, S4, and has issue living, Scott Robert, b 1963: m 1991, Eileen Jane, da of Robert Trail, of Paisley, Renfrewshire, — Lindsey Ann b 1961: m 1984, Stuart Allan Horton, Sgt RAF, and has issue living, Sarah Ann b 1985, Michelle Ashley b 1989, Philippa Abigail b 1990.

Grandchildren of late Rev William Alexander Neave, el son of late William Augustus Neave, 4th son of 2nd baronet:—
Issue of late Lionel Digby Neave, MRCS, LRCP, b 1873, d 1951: m 1909, Winifred, who d 1956, da of Michael Burke:—
Nelson Digby (Flat 3, 32 Fitzwilliam St, Kew, Victoria 3101, Australia), b 1914; 1939-45 War as F/Lt RAFVR: m 1936, Betty Ross, of Liverpool, and has issue living, Marilyn Kathryn, b 1938: m 1st, 1958 (m diss 1974), Samuel Shub, MRACP, of Victoria, Australia; 2ndly, 1983, Dr Anthony Challinor, BSc, PhD (Camb), FGS, of 29 Hestercombe Av, SW6 5LL, and Le Bosc, Sauveterre, 82110 Lamzerte, Tarn et Garonne, France, and has issue living (by 1st m), Martin David Neave (Flat 1, 24 Gardyne St, Bronte, Sydney, Australia) b 1959: m 1991, Helen Bongiorno, Caroline Leanne b 1960: m 1987, James Ford, 166 Ormond Rd, Elwood, Melbourne, Australia (and has issue living, Charles James b 1988, Oliver b 1990), Melissa Louise b 1965. —— John Alexander (17 Netheredge Drive, Knaresborough, N Yorks, HG5 9DA), b 1919: m 1946, Jacqueline, only child of F. Ranger, of Holyhead, Anglesey, and has issue living, David John b 1954: m 1976, Jacqueline Irene, da of Peter Flack, of Haughley, Suffolk, — Judith Marion, b 1948: m 1969, James Brame, of Highwood, Topcliffe, N Yorks, and has issue living, James Kenneth b 1969, Danielle 1980, Kimberley 1982, — Margaret Alison, b 1950: m 1st, 1969, (m diss 1981), Jean-Claude Estripeau; 2ndly, 1983, Alan Parnham of 17 Western Rd, Lancing, Sussex, and has issue living by 1st m, Natalie Isabelle b 1970, Tamsin Jane b 1976, — Catherine Mary, b 1951: m 1971, Hartwig Waldemar Nicolaus of 5 Rose Rd, Rochester 14624, NY, USA, and has issue living, Heidi Marie b 1971. —— Geoffrey Lionel (Flat 1, 1 Marmara Dr, Elsternwick, Vic 3185, Australia), b 1920; ed Ascham Coll, and County High Sch, Clacton-on-Sea; 1939-45 War with Roy Hampshire Regt in Italy and Greece: m 1964, Freda Mary Walmsley, da of late G. H. Hobson, of Lincoln. —— Mary Winifred, b 1913: m 1933, Rev Dennis Victor Wright, AKC, who d 1982, and has issue living, Stephen John Neave, b 1934; ed Brentwood Sch, and at Co High Sch, Buckhurst Hill, Essex: m 1960, Jennifer Anne, SRN, da of Arthur John Carter, of Chingford, Essex, and has issue living, Christopher Jonathan Neave b 1961, Nigel Robin Neave b 1962, Samantha Jane b 1966, — Rev Martin Neave (The New Rectory, Church Rd, Baginton, Coventry CV8 3AR), b 1937; ed King's Coll, London (AKC 1st class honours 1961); Bishop of Coventry's Officer for Social Responsibility, — Ruth Mary, b 1943; SRN; Certificate in Ed. Residence – 6 Willoughby Rd, Banbury, Oxon.

Grandchildren of late Francis Digby Spencer Neave, 2nd son of late William Augustus Neave (ante):—
Issue of late Francis Digby Neave, b 1874, d 1943: m 1910, Ethelberta, who d 1970, da of late Edward Washbourn, of St Albans, Christchurch, New Zealand:
John Digby (32 James St, Glenfield, Auckland, NZ), b 1916; formerly Ch Instructor at Canterbury Aero Club: m 1939, Martha Dorothy, who d 1985, da of late R. F. Francis, of St Albans, Christchurch, NZ, and has issue living, Richard Francis, b 1941: m 1962, Patricia Lorraine McGuire, and has issue living, Roger John Francis b 1962, Deborah Michelle b 1965, Amanda Gaye b 1969, — Barbara Alice, b 1940: m 1962, Ramon Juan Saunders, of 54 Holland Av, Hillcrest, Auckland 10, NZ, and has issue living, David John b 1968, James Richard Neave b 1972, Rachael Louise b 1974, — Eleanor Elizabeth, b 1943: m 1964, Bruce Peter Anderson, and has issue living, Thomas Digby b 1970, Philip Richard b 1972. —— Henry Washbourn, b 1918: m 1st, 1945 (m diss 1949), Doreen Melba, da of late J. W. Wright Spreydon; 2ndly, 1953, Sheila Duncan, da of R. H. Bennetts, of Christchurch, NZ, and has issue living, (by 2nd m) Alistair Dudley Digby (1351, Whangaparaoa Rd, Hibiscus Coast, NZ), b 1956: m 1978, Lorraine Mary, da of J. Irvine, of Auckland, NZ, — Richard Henry Digby (71 Deepdale St, Burnside, Christchurch 5, NZ), b 1960, — Diana Sheila, b 1954: m 1979, Brett Michael Russell, of Christchurch, NZ. Residence – 10 Lynmouth Av, Karori, Wellington, NZ. —— Arthur Kenelm b 1924: m 1st, 1951, Fendalton, Christchurch, NZ, Elizabeth Marie (DOYLE), who d 1983, da of late George Brady; 2ndly, 1984 (m diss 1993), Winifred Emma Bates, da of Roy Stiggants. Residence – Ceduna, S Aust. —— Elizabeth Marjorie, b 1911: m 1941, Grgo Franicevic, who d 1981, of 5 Tui St, Fendalton, Christchurch, NZ, and has issue living, Vincent Peter Ivan (5 Tui St, Fendalton, Christchurch, NZ), b 1942: m 1963 (m diss 1972), Maritza Ann Frances Glucina, — Edward John Grgo, b 1946: m 1967 (m diss 1986), Margaret Anne Blay, and has issue living, Lisa Marie b 1967, Anita Margaret b 1969, Terry b 1974, — Paul Francis Anton, b 1949: m 1983, Shona Lorna Mitchell, and has issue living, Scott Anton b 1989, Kim Marie b 1991, — Lois Ethel (74 Point Rd, Monaco, Nelson), b 1944: m 1st, 1966 (m diss 1988), Geoffrey Herbert Heath; 2ndly, 1990, Robert Basil Thombs Colley, and has issue living (by 1st m), Michael Geoffrey, b 1969, Thomas James, b 1970, Katrina Louise, b 1973, — Mara Elizabeth, b 1948: m 1978, Peter Charles Abrams, and has issue living, Anna Mara b 1979, Sarah Katherine Louise, b 1981.

Granddaughters of late Lt-Col Everard Strangways Neave, 3rd son of late William Augustus Neave (ante):—
Issue of late Everard Reginald Neave, b 1877, d 1951 (having assumed in 1910 the additional surname of Hay before his patronymic): m 1910, Amy Charlotte Paterson Balfour Hay of Leys and Randerston, who d 1971, da of late Peter Hay-Paterson:—
Beatrice Rosemary, b 1911; is a SRN: m 1939, Capt Colin Napier Christie, Black Watch, and has issue living, Mary Helen, b 1941: m 1970, James Beaton Marshall, of Ormlie, Bankend Rd, Bridge of Weir, Renfrewshire, — Anna Margaret, b 1943: m 1970, Derek O'Shea, of 49 Woodfield Cres, Ealing, W5, and has issue living, Catherine Janet b 1972, Linda Margaret b 1975. —— Diana Hope, b 1918 late WRNS: m 1st, 1940, David James Reoch Ritchie, P/O RAFVR, who was ka 1943; 2ndly, 1950, Ryszard Habdank-Kolaczkowski, late Lt RA and Polish AF, of 280 Easy St, 515 Mountain View, Cal 94043, USA, and has issue living, (by 2nd m) Anita Marya Star b 1951: m 1976, Piotr Daniel Moncarz, of 3255, Emerson St, Palo Alto, Cal 94306, USA and has issue living, Sylvana Marya, b 1981. —— Griselda Nancy, b 1920; formerly Subaltern ATS: m 1943, Henry Feliks Jascoll (formerly Jaszczolt), late Polish Army, of 28 Ravensbourne Gdns, Ealing, W13, and has issue living, Dominic Peter Hay (HAY OF LEYS (21 Warrenside Close, Blackburn, Lancs, BB1 9PE), b 1945; recognised in the surname of Hay of Leys by decree of Lord Lyon 1986, — John Henry David (2633 Hazelwood Rd, Lancaster, PA 17601, USA), b 1949; ed London Sch of Econs, London Univ (MScEcon): m 1974, Dorothy (Dorie) Ann, da of Homer K. Luttringer, and has issue living, Jennifer Elizabeth b 1983.

Grandchildren of late Arundell Francis Robert Irvine Neave, (infra):—
Issue of late Lt-Cdr Arundell Richard Yorke Irvine Neave, DSC, RN, *b* 1915, *d* 1977: *m* 1941, Barbara Marie (Puffins, 10 High St, Lee-on-Solent, Hants), only da of late Frederick Charles Evelyn Liardet, of Beech Park, Newton Abbot:—
Guy Richard Irvine, *b* (Dec) 1941; *ed* King's Sch, Worcester, and Queen Mary's Coll, London (PhD); research member of Inst D'Education, Fondation Européenne de la Culture, Université Dauphine, Paris. —— Penelope Gay (Puffins, 10 High St, Lee-on-Solent, Hants), *b* 1945: *m* 1966 (*m diss* 1977), Duncan Edward McBarnet, and has issue living, Justin Guy, *b* 1970, —— Alasdair Mathew, *b* 1972.

Granddaughter of late Richard Irvine Neave, el son of late George Peters Neave, son of late Richard Neave, 3rd son of 1st baronet:—
Issue of late Arundell Francis Robert Irvine Neave, *b* 1874, *d* 1918: *m* 1902, Mona Lewis, who *d* 1958:—
Muriel Catherine, *b* 1907: *m* 1928, Graham Thorpe, of Westfield, Calpe Av, Lyndhurst, Hants.

Granddaughter of late Cecil Howard Neave; elder son of George Howard Neave, yr son of George Peters Neave (ante):—
Issue of late Geoffrey Howard Neave, *b* 1917, *d* 1983: *m* 1946, (Mary) Therese Jeanette (21 Cornell Av, Rumford, Rhode Is, USA), da of late Joseph Adelard Voyer:—
Bernadette Blanche Dolores, *b* 1947: *m* 1968, Arvid Charles Nelson, late US Marines, and has issue living, Michael Shawn, *b* 1969, —— Robert David, *b* 1973.

The Neave family lived at Tivetshall, Norfolk, temp Henry IV. Sir William Le Neve, Clarenceux King of Arms 1660, belonged to a younger branch. Sir Richard Neave, of Dagnam Park, Essex, 1st Bt, was Governor of the Bank of England 1780.

NELSON (UK) 1912, of Acton Park, Acton, of Denbigh

Sir JAMIE CHARLES VERNON HOPE NELSON, 4th *Baronet*; *b* 23 Oct 1949; *s* his father, *Sir* WILLIAM VERNON HOPE, OBE, 1991; *ed* Redrice: *m* 1983, Maralynn Pyatt, da of late Albert Pyatt Hedge, of Audenshaw, Lincs, and has issue.

𝕬rms – Quarterly, 1st and 4th gules, on a fesse between three daggers points downwards or, two sinister hands couped of the field; 2nd and 3rd argent, a pile engrailed ermines between two lions' heads erased in base gules, langued azure, a chief vair all within a bordure vert. 𝕮rests – 1st, in front of a sun rising or, a sinister arm embowed in armour proper, the hand grasping a dagger point downwards as in the arms; 2nd, issuant from clouds proper charged with three mullets azure, a globe fracted at the top under a rainbow with clouds at each end proper.
Residence – 39 Montacute Rd, Tintinhull, Yeovil, Somerset BA22 8QD.

Per se confidens
Confident in oneself

SON LIVING

Liam Chester, *b* 1982.

BROTHERS LIVING

DOMINIC WILLIAM MICHAEL (Barretts Mill, Corton Denham, Sherborne, Dorset), *b* 13 March 1957; *ed* St Edward's, Malta: *m* 1981, Sarah, el da of late John Neil Hylton Jolliffe (*see* B Hylton, colls), and has issue living, Barnaby John, *b* 1982, —— Thomas Dudley, *b* 1984, —— George Marcus, *b* 1986. —— Declan Hugh Plantagenet, *b* 1968.

SISTERS LIVING

Deirdre Elizabeth Ann (Bently Cottage, Cuckfield, Sussex), *b* 1947: *m* 1st, 1980 (*m* annulled 1985), Martin Thomas; 2ndly, Dr John Dillow Macguire, of Bently Cottage, 12 The Highlands, Cuckfield, W Sussex RH17 5HL, and has issue living (by 1st *m*), Peter, *b* 1981. —— Cary Georgina (2 Court Barton, Crewkerne, Somerset), *b* 1952. —— Sophie Lucia, *b* 1971.

WIDOW LIVING OF THIRD BARONET

Hon ELIZABETH ANN BEVIL CARY (*Hon Lady Nelson*), da of 14th Viscount Falkland: *m* 1945, Sir William Vernon Hope Nelson, 3rd Bt, OBE, who *d* 1991. *Residence* – The Old Post House, Chiselborough, Somerset.

Sir William, 1st Bt (son of James Nelson, of Cooldrinagh, Ireland), was Chm of the Nelson Line (Liverpool) (Limited), and of the Nelson Steam Navigation Co.

NEPEAN (UK) 1802, of Bothenhampton, Dorsetshire
(Name pronounced "Nepeen")

Sir EVAN YORKE NEPEAN, 6th *Baronet*; *b* 23 Nov 1909; *s* his father, *Major Sir* CHARLES EVAN MOLYNEUX YORKE, 1953; *ed* Winchester, and Downing Coll Cambridge (BA 1931, MA 1947); Lt-Col (ret) R Corps of Signals; Mohmand Operations 1936 (medal with clasp); 1939-45 War in Middle East and Western Desert (Africa Star with clasp): *m* 1940, (Georgiana) Cicely, da of late Maj N. E. G. Willoughby, Middlesex Regt, and has issue.

Arms – Gules, a fesse wavy erminois between three mullets argent. **Crest** – On a mount vert a goat passant sable, charged on the side with two ermine spots in fesse or, collared and horned gold.
Residence – Goldens, Teffont, Salisbury, Wilts SP3 5RP.

Respice
Look back

DAUGHTERS LIVING

Susan Cicely, *b* 1941: *m* 1961, James Martin Norman Aylmer Hall, of 1 Partridge Down, Olivers Battery, Winchester, and has issue living, Richard John Nepean Aylmer, *b* 1964: *m* 1988, Tracy-Jane Boal, — Patrick Robert Aylmer, *b* 1966, — Katherine Mary Aylmer, *b* 1963: *m* 1986, Russell Wheeldon, and has issue living, Christopher Andrew *b* 1989, — Carole Margaret Aylmer, *b* 1967. —— Judith Sarah, *b* 1946: *m* 1993, Edgar Noel Goldthorp, of Black Sheep House, Healey, nr Masham, Ripon, N Yorks HG4 4LH. —— Gillian Helen, *b* 1950: *m* 1982, Paul Stevens, of 36 Wessington Park, Calne, Wilts, and has issue living, David Yorke, *b* 1986, — Jonathan Edward, *b* 1988.

COLLATERAL BRANCHES LIVING

Granddaughter of late Col Herbert Augustus Tierney Nepean, son of late Rev Evan Nepean, 4th son of 1st baronet:—
Issue of late Brigadier Herbert Evan Charles Bayley Nepean, CB, CSI, CMG, Indian Army, *b* 1865, *d* 1951: *m* 1st, 1892, Alice Maud, who *d* 1950, da of late Surg-Maj Hamilton Ross, of Ballinacrae House, Ballymoney, co Antrim; 2ndly, 1950, Muriel, da of late Rev R Butler Faulkner, of Oak Park House, Dawlish, Devon:—
(By 1st *m*) Clare Agnes Betty, *b* 1905. *Residence* – Summercourt, Shute Hill, Teignmouth, Devon TQ14 0DB.

Granddaughters of late Cdr St Vincent Nepean, MVO, RN, 4th son of Col Herbert Augustus Tierney Nepean (ante):—
Issue of late Leonard Percyval St Vincent Nepean, *b* 1879, *d* 1932: *m* 1909, Ellen Mary, who *d* 1957, da of late Matthew Edwards, of St Petersburg:—
Anne Camilla Catharine, *b* 1910: *m* 1st, 1932 (*m diss* 1947), Alfred Lingley Bennett; 2ndly, 1948, John Herbert McQuade, who *d* 1980, and has issue living, (by 1st *m*) Gordon Lingley Nepean (Portree, 109 Guildford Rd, Bagshot, Surrey), *b* 1936: *m* 1st, 1958 (*m diss* 1972), Faith Merritt, who *d* 1988; 2ndly, 1979, Christine Stephanie Barbara Maria Whipps, and has issue living, (by 1st *m*) Lingley Graham Nepean *b* 1959: *m* 1989, Fiona, da of — Eccleston (and has issue living, Harry Lingley Nepean *b* 1992), Robert *b* 1966: *m* 1993, Valerie Anderson, Sally Jacqueline *b* 1957: *m* 1980 (*m diss* 1991), Duncan Edward Sibbald (and has issue living, Kieran *b* 1982, Kimberley *b* 1981), Angela *b* 1961: *m* 1984, Ian Bowerman (and has issue living, Andrew *b* 1991, Amy Samantha *b* 1989), (by 2nd *m*) Christian *b* 1980, — Roger Lingley Nepean, *b* 1937: *m* 1966, Diana Jacqueline Westcob, and has issue living, Nicola *b* 1967: *m* 1991, Simon Bush, Tamsin *b* 1970, Justine *b* 1978. *Residence* – Calle Nuñes de Arce 4-1 Interior, 35005 Las Palmas, Gran Canaria, Canary Islands, Spain.
This family came from St Just, Cornwall. Right Hon Sir Evan Nepean, 1st Bt, was MP for Queensborough and Bridport, Sec of the Admiralty, Chief Sec for Ireland, and Gov of Bombay.

NEVILLE (UK) 1927, of Sloley, co Norfolk (Extinct 1994)

Sir RICHARD LIONEL JOHN BAINES NEVILLE, 3rd *Baronet*; *b* 15 July 1921; *s* his half-brother, *Lt-Col Sir* (JAMES) EDMUND HENDERSON, MC, 1982; *ed* Eton, and at Trin Coll, Camb (MA); served in World War II as Capt Oxf & Bucks Lt Infty, and Royal W AFrican Frontier Force, Burma Campaign 1944-45; Master of Bowyers' Co 1972-74; patron of one living. Sir Richard Neville *d* 2 Aug 1994, when the title became *extinct*.

Arms – Quarterly, 1st & 4th Gules, a bend sinister ermine surmounted of a bend argent, thereon three annulets sable, 2nd & 3rd Sable a chevron invected vair between three lions rampant or each holding between its paws an escutcheon argent charged with an eagle's head erased azure. **Crest** – An eagle displayed sable, on the breast and on each wing an escutcheon or, charged with a lion's head erased also sable.
Residence – Sloley Hall, Norwich, NR12 8HA.

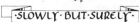
·SLOWLY·BUT·SURELY·

DAUGHTERS LIVING OF SECOND BARONET

Rosalind Angela Mary, *b* 1933: *m* 1954, Philip Murray Gorton, of The Emplins, Gamlingay, Sandy, Beds, and has issue living, Simon Neville (Home Farm, Sloley, Norwich), *b* 1957: *m* 1985, Ann, da of Peter Donald Hull and has issue living, Peter Neville *b* 1986, Emma Jane *b* 1987, — Mark Philip (The House, Broons Green, Dymock, Glos), *b* 1960: *m* 1st, 1982 (*m diss* 1990), Elizabeth Jane, da of Brian David Carter; 2ndly, 1990, Deborah, da of Harry Cook, and has issue living (by 2nd *m*), Alice Muriel *b* 1990, — David Colin, *b* 1962, — Elizabeth Clare, *b* 1958: *m* 1983, Quenton Hayton Hill, of Golder Cottage, Sloley, Norwich, and has issue living, James David *b* 1988, Hannah Christine *b* 1986.

—— Jane Shirley (Cubitt Cottage, Sloley, Norfolk), *b* 1934: *m* 1st, 1963 (*m diss* 1977), Vivian Vincent Esch; 2ndly, 1977 (*m diss* 1985), Patrick Thomas Foulkes, and has issue living (by 1st *m*), Nicholas Charles, *b* 1966, —— Rupert Vivian Neville, *b* 1967.

WIDOW LIVING OF SECOND BARONET

BETTY (*Lady Neville*) (61 Yarmouth Rd, N Walsham, Norfolk), da of George Legerton Cowell, and formerly wife of Peter Thornton Cowell: *m* 1981, as his 2nd wife, Lt-Col Sir James Edmund Henderson Neville, 2nd Bt, who *d* 1982.
The 1st baronet, Sir Reginald James Neville Neville, was son of James Sewell Neville (1827-1912), Bar-at-law, of Sloley Hall, Norfolk, sometime Judge of the High Court of Calcutta who assumed by R Licence the name and arms of Neville 1885 in lieu of White as a grandson of John White and his wife Mary (*d* 1833) da and co heir of Ralph Neville, of Barton under Needwood, Staffs. He sat as MP for Wigan (*C*) 1910-18, and for E Norfolk 1924-29, and was Recorder of Bury St Edmunds 1905-43.

NEWMAN (UK) 1836, of Mamhead, Devonshire

Sir GEOFFREY ROBERT NEWMAN, 6th *Baronet*; *b* 2 June 1947; *s* his father, *Sir* RALPH ALURED, 1968; *ed* Kelly Coll; late Lieut Gren Gds: *m* 1980, Mary Elizabeth, yr da of late Col Sir Martin St John Valentine Gibbs, KCVO, CB, DSO, TD (*see* Fowler, Bt ext, 1966 Edn), and has issue.

Arms – Azure, three demi-lions rampant argent, semée of cross-crosslets, langued gules. **Crest** – A lion rampant per chevron azure gutté-de-l'eau and argent gutté-de-sang.
Residence – Blackpool House, Dartmouth, S Devon TQ6 0RG.

SON LIVING

ROBERT MELVIL, *b* 4 Oct 1985.

DAUGHTERS LIVING

Frances Joyce, *b* 1983. —— Elsie Laura, *b* 1987. —— Louisa Bridget, *b* 1990.

BROTHER LIVING

Richard Claude, *b* 1951: *m* 1992, Louise Dorothy Catherine, only child of late Gordon Alexander Egerton Ruck (*see* B Braybrooke).

SISTERS LIVING

Zabian Carlotta Annette Alfreda, *b* 1948. —— Louisa Ann (Blackpool House, Dartmouth, S Devon TQ6 0RG), *b* 1955: *m* 1977 (*m diss* 1982), Andrew William Kingsley Thomas, and has issue living, William Lydston, *b* 1983, —— Rachael Elizabeth Ann, *b* 1987.

WIDOW LIVING OF FIFTH BARONET

Hon ANN ROSEMARY HOPE (*Hon Lady Newman*), (Blackpool House, Dartmouth, S Devon), da of late Capt the Hon Claude Hope-Morley (*see* B Hollenden colls): *m* 1946, Sir Ralph Alured Newman, 5th Bt, who *d* 1968.

COLLATERAL BRANCHES LIVING

Grandchildren of late Robert Lydston Newman, el son of Thomas Holdsworth Newman, 3rd son of 1st baronet:—
Issue of late Capt Thomas Newman, *b* 1906, *d* 1980; Capt Grenadier Guards; MA Ch Ch, Oxford; FRSA: *m* 1938, Helen, who *d* 1972, da of Sir (Charles) Alban Young, KCMG, MVO, 9th Bt (*cr* 1769):—
Peter Thomas Lydston (The Manor House, Coryton, Okehampton, Devon), *b* 1944; *ed* Eton, and Ch Ch, Oxford (MA); FCA: *m* 1981, Catherine Jane, da of Alistair James Lilburn, of Coull, Aboyne, Aberdeenshire (*see* Reid, Bt, cr 1922, 1980 Edn), and has issue living, Rupert Thomas Lydston, *b* 1984, —— William Alistair, *b* 1988, —— Harriet Joan, *b* 1986. —— Priscilla Helen, *b* 1939: *m* 1963, Charles Granville Stuart-Menteth, of Woodchester House, Woodchester, Glos (*see* Stuart-Menteth, Bt), and has issue (*see* Stuart-Menteth, Bt). —— Elizabeth Clare, *b* 1941: *m* 1964, (Robert Myles) Randal MacDonnell, of 17 Malbrook Rd, SW15, and has issue living, Julian Sorley Randal, *b* 1967: *m* 1992, Sophia Helen, da of David Reed, of Bath, and has issue living, Amity Catherine *b* 1993, —— Natasha Clare, *b* 1965, —— Louisa Helen, *b* 1971.

Grandchildren of late Alured Newman, 4th son of 1st baronet:—
Issue of late Maj Edward Devon Newman, *b* 1885, *d* 1977: *m* 1st, 1909 (*m diss* 1926), Violet Ethel, da of late Rev Morgan Kirby; 2ndly, 1926, Hilda, who *d* 1970, da of Leonard Norman Barrow, JP, of Normanton Hall, Southwell, Notts:—
(By 1st *m*) Edward John Alured (PO Box 1216, Pinetown, Natal 3600, S Africa), *b* 1915; *ed* Radley: *m* 1st, 1947 (*m diss* 1958), Katherine Dolores, formerly wife of Stephen Townsend, and da of Frank Bazette, of Newbury, Berks; 2ndly, 1964, Winifred Betty, formerly wife of Eric Paull, and da of Charles Rowe, of Wellington, NZ, and has issue living, (by 1st *m*) Priscilla Elizabeth (Maestro Perez Cabrero 62A, 08021 Barcelona, Spain), *b* 1949: *m* 1969 (*m diss* 1989), Eugene de Pau, and has issue living, Gregory, *b* 1972. —— Myra Beatrice, *b* 1914: *m* 1946, Lt-Col William Bagnall, OBE, who *d* 1984, of Upper Brook House, Marchington, Uttoxeter, Staffs, and has issue living, William Edward Hampshire (2 Brook House, New Pond Rd, Compton, nr Guildford, Surrey), *b* 1947: *m* 1969, Bridget, da of Kenneth Charles Pearce, and has issue living, William Richard *b* 1978, Jessica Jane *b* 1976, —— Felicity Jane, *b* 1951: *m* 1977, Nicholas John Sutton Mills, of Bank House Farm, Hyde Lea, Stafford.
The 1st baronet, Sir Robert William Newman (son of Thomas Newman, of Dartmouth) sat as MP for Exeter, and was High Sheriff of Devon 1827. The 2nd baronet, Capt Sir Robert Lydston, Grenadier Guards, was *ka* 1854. The 3rd baronet, Sir Lydston, was High Sheriff of Devon, 1871. The 4th baronet, Sir Robert Hunt Stapylton Dudley Lydston, sat as MP for Exeter (*U* latterly *Ind*) 1918-31 and was *cr Baron Mamhead*, of Exeter, co Devon 1931.

NEWMAN (UK) 1912, of Cecil Lodge, Newmarket, co Cambridge

By hard work and with honour

Sir FRANCIS HUGH CECIL NEWMAN, 4th *Baronet*; *b* 12 June 1963; *s* his father, *Sir* GERARD ROBERT HENRY SIGISMUND, 1987; *ed* Eton, and Pennsylvania Univ, USA: *m* 1990, Katharine M., yr da of (Cecil Ralph) Timothy Edwards, of Grendon Court, Upton Bishop, Herefords, and has issue.

𝔄rms – Argent, an ostrich proper, on a chief azure, a lozenge of the field between two bezants. 𝔆rest – Out of an antique coronet or, a springbok's head proper.
Residences – Burloes, Royston, Herts SG8 9NE; 40 Cadogan Place, SW1.

SON LIVING

THOMAS RALPH GERARD, *b* 7 Jan 1993.

DAUGHTER LIVING

Lily May Violet, *b* 1994.

BROTHERS LIVING

Geoffrey John, *b* 1966; *ed* Eton, and Bristol Univ. —— Christopher George *b* 1969; *ed* Eton, and Napier Univ, Edinburgh.

SISTER LIVING

Susanna Philippa Helen, *b* 1962: *m* 1985, Julian Eldon Gorst, eldest son of John Michael Gorst, MP, and has issue living, Henry Eldon Geoffrey, *b* 1991, — Rose Philippa Tatiana, *b* 1990. *Residence* – Oxcombe Manor, Horncastle, Lincs.

UNCLE LIVING (*son of 2nd baronet*)

John Francis (Compton Park, Compton Chamberlayne, Salisbury, Wilts SP3 5DE), *b* 1930; *ed* Eton; late Lt Roy Horse Gds; Dir Blick plc, Galloway Group Ltd, and other Cos: *m* 1963, Caroline Henrietta, yr da of Lt-Col Angus John Campbell Rose, of Dunira Garden House, Comrie, Perthshire, and has issue living, Anthony John Cecil, *b* 1966; *ed* Harrow, and RAC Cirencester, — Henrietta Mary Alison (*Countess of Caledon*), *b* 1964: *m* 1989, as his 2nd wife, 7th Earl of Caledon, — Sarahjane Caroline, *b* 1968; *ed* Bristol Univ.

AUNTS LIVING (*daughters of 2nd baronet*)

Annabel Cecilia Mary, *b* 1922: *m* 1947, Maj Peter Merton Beckwith-Smith, who *d* 1984, and has issue living, James Merton, *b* 1948; *ed* Tabley House, Knutsford, — Anne Honor Mary, LVO, *b* 1951; appointed Lady in Waiting to HRH The Princess of Wales 1981; LVO 1990. *Residence* – Bishopstone House, Salisbury, Wilts SP5 4AS. —— Lynette Johanna Violet (1 Sloane Court East, SW3), *b* (twin) 1927. —— Rosalind Cynthia (Chestnut Brow, Church Rd, Bramshott, Liphook, Hants), *b* 1936: *m* 1969, Francis Albert John Watson, who *d* 1973, and has issue living, Jeremy John Albert, *b* 1970, — Joanna Clare Elizabeth, *b* 1972.

WIDOW LIVING OF THIRD BARONET

CAROLINE PHILIPPA (*Caroline, Lady Newman*), da of late Brig Alfred Geoffrey Neville, CBE, MC (*see* B Braybrooke, colls): *m* 1960, Sir Gerard Robert Henry Sigismund Newman, 3rd Bt, who *d* 1987. *Residence* – Burloes, Royston, Herts; 1 Sloane Court East, SW3.

COLLATERAL BRANCH LIVING

Issue of late Guy Arthur Newman, son of 1st baronet, *b* 1904, *d* 1982: *m* 1930, Hon Jean Sybil Loch (Stanners Hill Manor, Chobham, Surrey), da of 2nd Baron Loch:—
Mary Ella, *b* 1931: *m* 1954, Lt Col William Richard Edgedale, The Life Guards, of 34 Edna St, SW11, and has issue living, James William, *b* 1963: *m* 1993, Sarah Louise Jenkinson, — Mirabel Jean Elaine, *b* 1955, — Emma Margaret, *b* 1956: *m* 1983, Orlando dos Santos, of 55 Rowena Crescent. SW11, and has issue living, Frederick Andrew William *b* 1986, Ella Clementine *b* 1989, Charlotte Maria Elizabeth *b* 1993, — Sarah Jane, *b* 1965. —— Diana Margaret Anna (23 Glebe Place, SW3), *b* 1934.
—— Ann Elizabeth, *b* 1937: *m* 1965, Richard James Randal MacDonnell, of Ivy Lodge, Churchill, Avon, and has issue living, Simon Guy Randal, *b* 1968, — Crispin Paul Geoffrey Randal, *b* 1974, — Tania Alice, *b* 1966.
Sir Sigmund NEUMANN, 1st Bt (son of Gustav Neumann, of Fuerth, Bavaria), was partner in the firms of S Neumann and Co, merchants, of Salisbury House, EC, and Neumann, Luebeck and Co, bankers. Sir Cecil Gustavus Jacques Newman, 2nd Bt, who was High Sheriff of Herts 1939, and Pres of National Asso Fishery Board 1946-51, assumed by Roy licence 1936 the surname of Newman in lieu of Neumann.

NEWSON (UK) 1921, of Framlingham, co Suffolk (Extinct 1950)

Sir PERCY WILSON NEWSON, 1st and last *Baronet*.

DAUGHTER LIVING OF FIRST BARONET

Audrey Joan (*Audrey, Lady Twisleton-Wykeham-Fiennes*), *b* 1912: *m* 1931, Lieut-Col Sir Ranulph Twisleton-Wykeham-Fiennes, 2nd Bt, DSO, R Scots Greys, who *d* of wounds received in action 1943. *Residence* – Robins, Lodsworth, Petworth, Sussex.

Newson-Smith, see Smith.

NEWTON (UK) 1900, of The Wood, Sydenham Hill, Lewisham, Kent, and Kottingham House, Burton-on-Trent, co Stafford

Faveat fortuna
May fortune favour

Sir (HARRY) MICHAEL REX NEWTON, 3rd *Baronet; b* 7 Feb 1923; *s* his father, *Sir* HARRY KOTTINGHAM, OBE, 1951; *ed* Eastbourne Coll; late Lieut King's Roy Rifle Corps; Past Master The Girdlers' Co; 1939-45 War in N Africa and Middle East (wounded): *m* 1958, Pauline Jane, only da of Richard John Frederick Howgill, CBE, of Branscombe, Sullington Warren, Storrington, Sussex and has issue.

Arms – Azure, two bones in saltire between as many roses argent, on a chief or, a lotus flower slipped proper. **Crest** – Out of the battlements of a tower an arm erect, the hand grasping a sword in bend sinister proper suspended therefrom a flag argent charged with a sword erect between two branches of oak proper.
Residence – Cliff House, Old Lyme Rd, Charmouth, Dorset DT6 6BW. *Club* – R Ocean Racing.

SON LIVING

Rev GEORGE PETER HOWGILL, *b* 26 March 1962; *ed* Sherborne, and Pembroke Coll, Camb (MA); Curate of St Thomas's, Blackpool since 1993: *m* 1988, Jane L., twin da of John Rymer, and has issue living, Sarah Rebecca, *b* 1991, — Kate Evangeline, *b* 1992. *Residence* – 8 Collingwood Av, Blackpool, FY3 8BZ.

ADOPTED DAUGHTERS LIVING

Lucinda Jane, *b* 1964. —— Julia Kate, *b* 1967: *m* 1994, Daryn K. Hufton-Rees, only son of Kenneth Rees, of Manchester. —— Jennifer Anne, *b* (twin) 1967.

BROTHER LIVING

Rev Canon Christopher Wynne, *b* 1925; *ed* Eastbourne Coll, and Trin Hall, Camb (MA); formerly Urban Dean of Milton Keynes: *m* 1950, Margaret, da of John Ormerod, of Accrington, and has issue living, Jeremy John, *b* 1952, — Peter Michael, *b* 1953. *Residence* – 24 Slade Court, Watling St, Radlett, Herts.

The 1st baronet, Sir Alfred James Newton, Chm of Harrods (Limited), was Lord Mayor of London 1899-1900, when he founded City of London Imperial Vol during S African War (Baronetcy conferred); also an Hon Freeman of Scarborough and Londonderry, and sixteen years Gov of the Hon the Irish So. The 2nd baronet, Sir Harry Kottingham Newton, OBE, was Vice-Chm of Harrods (Limited), and was MP for N-E Div of Essex (U) 1910-18, and for Harwich Div thereof 1918-22.

NEWTON (UK) 1924, of Beckenham, co Kent

Faveat-fortuna
May fortune favour

Sir KENNETH GARNAR NEWTON, OBE, TD, 3rd *Baronet, b* 4 June 1918; *s* his father, *Sir* EDGAR HENRY, 1971; *ed* Wellington; Master of Leathersellers' Co 1977-78, Master of Feltmakers' Co 1983-84; Gen Commr for Income Tax 1961; Pres British Leather Fedn 1968-69; Pres Internat Council of Tanners 1972-78; Chm Garnar Booth plc 1972-87; chm Govs Colfe's Sch 1982-; Lt-Col RASC (TA); 1939-45 War; MBE (Mil) 1944, OBE (Civil) 1969: *m* 1st, 1944, Margaret Isabel, who *d* 1979, da of Rev Dr George Blair, of Dundee; 2ndly, 1980, Pamela Sidney, widow of F. T. K. Wilson, and has issue by 1st *m*.

Arms – Argent, on a chevron between three eagles displayed azure, as many garbs or. **Crest** – A bear's head couped argent, muzzled gules, charged on the neck with three crescents interlaced azure.
Residence – Wildways, High Broom Lane, Crowborough, E Sussex TN6 3SP.

SONS LIVING (By 1st marriage)

JOHN GARNAR (North House, Wyboston, Beds), *b* 10 July 1945; *ed* Reed's Sch, Cobham: *m* 1972, Jacynth Anne Kay Miller, and has issue living, Timothy Garnar, *b* 4 Sept 1973, — Alistair Blair, *b* (twin) 1973, — Andrew Robert, *b* 1975. —— Peter Blair (Park House, Souldern, nr Bicester, Oxon), *b* 1950; *ed* Wellington: *m* 1983, Fiona S., only da of W.Q. FitzGerald, of Penny Broom, Burnham Market, Norfolk, and has issue living, Alex Blair, *b* 1988, — Rory James, *b* 1990.

WIDOW LIVING OF SECOND BARONET

ALICE MARY (*Alice, Lady Newton*) (14 Castle Hill View, Sidford, Sidmouth, Devon), da of late Henry Barber, of Surbiton, and widow of Glyn Rosser: *m* 1968, as his 2nd wife, Sir Edgar Henry Newton, 2nd Bt, who *d* 1971.

COLLATERAL BRANCH LIVING

Issue of late Sidney Arthur Newton, 2nd son of 1st baronet, *b* 1901, *d* 1978: *m* 1933, Oonagh, who *d* 1990, da of late John Fleming, of Dublin:—
Hedley John (Moat Farm House, Kettle Green, Much Hadham, Herts), *b* 1936; *ed* Charterhouse, and Trinity Hall, Camb (MA, LLB); solicitor 1960; a Liveryman of Vintners' Co: *m* 1964, Virginia, da of James Archibald Baiss, and has issue living, Marcus James, *b* 1966, — Charles Benedict, *b* 1968, — Caspar John, *b* 1971. —— Shane (*Baroness Gisborough*), *b* 1934: *m* 1960, 3rd Baron Gisborough, of Gisborough House, Guisborough, Cleveland. —— Gaidagh, *b* 1947: *m* 1968, James Martin Strong, of West Bradley, Templeton, Tiverton, Devon.
The 1st baronet, Sir Louis Arthur Newton (son of late Reuben Newton, of Macclesfield), was a Surveyor, and an Alderman and Lieut of City of London (Senior Sheriff 1916-17, Lord Mayor 1923-4), a County Councillor for London 1931-4, High Sheriff of Kent 1940-41, and sometime Hon Col 56th (1st London) Div Train RASC.

NICHOLSON (UK) 1912, of Harrington Gardens, Royal Borough of Kensington

Sir CHARLES CHRISTIAN NICHOLSON, 3rd *Baronet*; *b* 15 Dec 1941; *s* his father, *Sir* JOHN NORRIS, KBE, CIE, 1993; *ed* Ampleforth, and Magdalen Coll, Oxford: *m* 1975, Martha Rodman, da of Col Stuart Warren Don, and widow of Niall Hamilton Anstruther-Gough-Calthorpe (*see* Anstruther-Gough-Calthorpe, Bt).

Arms – Per pale nebuly azure and gules two bars argent guttée de poix, in chief two suns in splendour proper. **Crest** – A lion's head couped sable guttée d'eau before a sun in splendour proper.
Residence – Turners Green Farm, Elvetham, Hartley Wintney, Hants RG27 8BE.
Clubs – Brooks's, Pratt's, Royal Yacht Squadron.

BROTHER LIVING

JAMES RICHARD LOTHIAN, *b* 24 Oct 1947; *ed* Ampleforth, and Churchill Coll, Camb: *m* 1st, 1974 (*m diss* 1980), Charmian Joy, da of Maj Harcourt Michael Scudamore Gold, MC (*see* By of Trent); 2ndly, 1980, Sarah Hazel, da of Richard Alan Budgett, of Kirtlington, Oxford, and has issue living (by 2nd *m*), Edward, *b* 1983, — Lara, *b* 1986. *Residence* – The Stableyard, Kirtlington Park, Oxford.

SISTERS LIVING

Quietate et Confidentia

Tessa Mary, *b* 1944: *m* 1967, Piers Anthony Constantine Howard Phipps, of Trerose Manor, Mawnan, Falmouth, Cornwall, only son of late Sqdn Ldr Francis Constantine Phipps. —— Mary Louise Petronella, *b* 1950: *m* 1973, Adam Trevor Kelly Smail, of Spring Hill, Compton Abdale, Glos, son of Lt-Col Adam Trevor Smail, DSO, of Edgeworth Manor, Stroud, Glos.
The 1st baronet, Sir Charles Norris Nicholson, sat as MP for Doncaster Div of S Part of W Riding of Yorkshire (*L*) 1906-18.
The 2nd baronet, Sir John Norris Nicholson, KBE, CIE, was Chm Ocean Steamship Co 1957-71 and of Martin's Bank 1962-64, Vice Lord-Lieut of Isle of Wight 1974-80 and Lord-Lieut 1980-86.

NICHOLSON (UK) 1958, of Winterbourne, Royal co of Berks (Extinct 1991)

Sir GODFREY NICHOLSON, 1st and last *Baronet*, *d* 14 July 1991.

DAUGHTERS LIVING OF FIRST BARONET

Rose Helen (*Lady Luce*), *b* 1937: *m* 1961, Rt Hon Sir Richard Napier Luce, of Dragons Farmhouse, Cowfold, Horsham, Sussex, son of late Sir William Henry Tucker Luce, GBE, KCMG, and has issue living, Alexander Richard, *b* 1964, — Edward Godfrey, *b* 1968. —— Laura Violet (*Lady Montgomery Cuninghame*), *b* 1939: *m* 1964, Sir John Christopher Foggo Montgomery Cuninghame, 12th Bt, of The Old Rectory, Brightwalton, Newbury, Berks and has issue (*see* Cuninghame, Bt). —— Emma Harriet, MP (*Miss Emma Nicholson*), *b* 1941; MP for Devon West and Torridge (*C*) since 1987: *m* 1987, Sir Michael Harris Caine, son of late Sir Sydney Caine, KCMG. —— Harriet Mary, *b* 1946: *m* 1969, Charles Hamilton Flower (D Abercorn, colls) (c/o William's & Glyn's Bank, 67 Lombard St, EC3), and has issue living, Katharine Mary, *b* 1972, — Sarah Constance, *b* 1976.

NICOLSON (NS) 1629, of that Ilk, and of Lasswade, Midlothian (Dormant 1961)

Sir HAROLD STANLEY NICOLSON, 14th *Baronet*, *d* 1961, and at the time of going to press no name appears on the official Roll of Baronets in respect of this title.

COLLATERAL BRANCH LIVING

Issue of late Lionel Rutherford Nicolson, WS, 3rd son of 12th baronet, *b* 1887, *d* 1957: *m* 1932, Kathleen Mary (Little Gables, Street End Lane, Broad Oak, Heathfield, Sussex), da of late Henry Gane Moon:—
Anne, *b* 1939: *m* 1963, Miles Hansen, of Bletchinglye Farm, Bletchinglye Lane, Rotherfield, Sussex, and has issue living, Piers James, *b* 1966, — Clare Louise, *b* 1969.

John Nicolson of that Ilk and Lasswade, Midlothian, was *cr* a baronet 1629 with remainder to his heirs male whatsoever, with a grant of land in Nova Scotia. On the death of Sir James, 7th Bt, 1743, the baronetcy became dormant. Arthur, *de jure* 8th Bt (*d* 1793) was a great-grandson of James, Bishop of Dunkeld, next brother of 1st Bt. In 1826, Sir Arthur, *de jure* 10th Bt, grandson of Arthur, was served heir male of 7th Bt. The Baronetcy again became dormant on the death of the 14th Bt in 1961.

NIGHTINGALE (E) 1628, of Newport Pond, Essex

Sir CHARLES MANNERS GAMALIEL NIGHTINGALE, 17th *Baronet*; *b* 21 Feb 1947; *s* his father, Sir CHARLES ATHELSTAN, 1977; *ed* St Paul's Sch; BA (Open Univ) 1990; Sr Exec Officer, Dept of Health.

For king and country

𝕬rms – Per pale ermine and gules, a rose countercharged. 𝕮rest – An ibex sejant argent, tufted, armed, and maned or.
Residence – 16 Unity Grove, Harrogate, N Yorks HG1 2AQ.

SISTERS LIVING

Nadine Mary Rosalie (54 Willow Close, Quintrell Downs, Newquay, Cornwall TR8 4NQ), *b* 1938: *m* 1st, 1959 (*m diss* 1972), Peter Maurice Edmunds; 2ndly, 1972, Derek Frederick Curtis, and has issue living, (by 1st *m*) Thomas Charles, *b* 1961, — David Michael, *b* 1963, — Jeremy John, *b* 1964, — Jane Elizabeth, *b* 1965, — (by 2nd *m*) James *b* 1972. —— Clothilde Muriel Frances, *b* 1939: *m* 1964, Derek Edward Glenister, of 2 Albany Close, Ickenham, Middx, and has issue living, Frances Mary, *b* 1966, — Clare Julia, *b* 1968.

WIDOW LIVING OF SIXTEENTH BARONET

NADINE (*Lady Nightingale*) (12 Jacob's Pool, Okehampton, Devon EX20 1LJ), da of late (Charles) Arthur Diggens: *m* 1932, Sir Charles Athelstan Nightingale, 16th Bt, who *d* 1977.

COLLATERAL BRANCHES LIVING

Grandchildren of late Lacy Gamaliel Nightingale, KC, son of late Percy Nightingale, el son of late Thomas Henry Nightingale, RN, 2nd son of 11th baronet:—
Issue of late Manners Percy Nightingale, MRCS, LRCP, *b* 1908, *d* 1974: *m* 1936, Mary Ursula, who *d* 1983, da of late Rev George Saunders Gilbert, of Groombridge, Sussex:—
EDWARD LACY GEORGE (Kneesworth, Lynton, N Devon), *b* 11 May 1938; *ed* Exeter Sch; Master Mariner. —— Jane Elizabeth, *b* 1940.
Issue of late Neville Gascoyne Nightingale, *b* 1911, *d* 1989: *m* 1946, Nancy Esther (56 Shelfanger Rd, Diss, Norfolk), da of late Godfrey James Whistler, of Ross-on-Wye, Hereford:—
Thomas Lacy Manners, *b* 1947: *m* 1993, Lois Allison, only da of late Rev Thomas Oswald Welch Glass, of Roydon, Norfolk. *Residence* – 102 Denmark St, Diss, Norfolk.

Granddaughter of late Percy Nightingale, el son of late Thomas Henry Nightingale, RN (ante):—
Issue of late Maj-Gen Manners Ralph Wilmott Nightingale, CB, CMG, CIE, DSO, *b* 1871, *d* 1956: *m* 1st, 1907, Anna, who *d* 1924, da of Arthur George Forestier-Walker, formerly ICS; 2ndly, 1930, Violet Marion, who *d* late Lt-Col H. M. E. Brunker, The Cameronians, and widow of Capt C. A. G. Cunningham, N Staffordshire Regt:—
(By 1st *m*) Tessa Frances Moyra, *b* 1908: *m* 1930, Brig Harold Gordon Fowler, OBE, Indian Army (ret), and has issue living, Patricia Jacqueline, *b* 1931, — Veronica Jane, *b* 1935, — Tessa Pauline, *b* 1938. *Residence* – 20 Trafalgar Court, Farnham, Surrey.

Grandsons of late Maj-Gen Manners Ralph Wilmott Nightingale, CB, CMG, CIE, DSO (ante):—
Issue of late Lt-Col George Manners Nightingale, MC, *b* 1913, *d* 1992: *m* 1946, Mrs Alison Cornwallis Sutton (Wits End, Grayshott Rd, Headley Down, Hants), da of late Col James Cameron, RE, and formerly wife of Stanley William Vernon Sutton:—
Christopher George Manners, *b* 1949; *ed* Kelly Coll, and RMA Sandhurst; Capt Staffordshire Regt: *m* 1st, 1971, Marie-Claudette, da of Marc Roger Tenermont; 2ndly, 1978, Anna Sorina, da of Christian Niels Fischer, and has issue living (by 2nd *m*), Edward George Manners, *b* 1985. —— Jeremy John Charles, *b* 1952; *ed* Wellington Coll.

Granddaughters of late James Edward Nightingale, 2nd son of Thomas Henry Nightingale, RN (ante):—
Issue of late Ernest Albert Nightingale, *b* 1867, *d* 1945: *m* 1893, Sarah Annette Thorntone, who *d* 1947, da of late John Austen:—
Irene Mary (Imperani Park, Ficksburg, S Africa), *b* 1899: *m* 1926, Norman Owen Halse, who *d* 1966, and has issue living, Norma Rene, *b* 1927, — Varney Marren, *b* 1934, — Rosemary Joy, *b* 1943.
Issue of late Thomas Cecil Parry Nightingale, *b* 1885; *d* 1950: *m* 1911, Anita Adendorff:—
Joy Thelma *b* 1913: *m* 1936, Cornie Hugo Liesching, and has issue living, Frederick Jabris, *b* 1937, — Cornie, *b* 1940, — Anita Lorraine, *b* 1945, — Margaret, *b* 1947.

Grandchildren of late Claud Robert Nightingale, MC, son of late Frederick Charles Nightingale, son of late Geoffrey Nightingale, 7th son of 10th baronet:—
Issue of late Christopher Carnac Nightingale, *b* 1913, *d* 1970: *m* 1941, Muriel de Lissa (39 Gander Hill, Haywards Heath, Sussex), da of late F. D. Philips, of Leatherhead:—
Nicholas John, *b* 1942: *m* 1968, Susan Kay, da of Philip Lyth, of Park Hill, Southwell, Notts and has issue living, Thomas James, *b* 1977, — Rebecca Jane, *b* 1972, — Elizabeth Jane, *b* 1976. —— Anne Christine, *b* 1944: *m* 1972, Kenneth Ian Murchison, of 21 Calvert Av, Killara, NSW 2071, Aust, and has issue living, Scott Timothy, *b* 1973, — Hamish Charles, *b* 1977, — Emma Georgina, *b* 1974. —— Patricia Ruth, *b* 1950: *m* 1979, Ian Christie of 131 Mount View Rd, N4, and has issue living, Edward Nightingale, *b* 1987, — Beatrice Nightingale, *b* 1980, Laura Nightingale, *b* 1982, — Isabel Nightingale, *b* 1985.
Issue of late Robert Forbes Nightingale, *b* 1917, *d* 1993: *m* 1st, 1940 (*m diss* 1956), Lesley Phyllis, da of late S. Kenneth West; 2ndly, 1956, Dora, who *d* 1992, da of George Henry Kirkpatrick:—

(By 1st *m*) Peter Robert (Meadowbank, The Avenue, Godalming, Surrey), *b* 1947: *m* 1968, Joan Anne, da of late J. A. Kerr, and has issue living, James Peter, *b* 1974, — Andrea Jane, *b* 1969, — Helen Mary, *b* 1971. —— Richard John (Blackdown Cottage, Denbigh Rd, Haslemere, Surrey), *b* 1948: *m* 1971, Frances Catherine, da of late C. B. Green, and has issue living, Catherine, *b* 1972.

Sir Thomas Nightingale, 1st Bt, of Newport Pond, Essex, was High Sheriff of Essex 1627. On the death in 1722 of Sir Robert, 4th Bt, a Dir of Hon East India Co, his estates devolved on his cousin, Robert Gascoyne. The baronetcy should have passed to Edward Nightingale, of Kneesworth, Cambs, son of Geoffrey, yr son of 1st Bt, but succession was not established until Sir Edward Nightingale recorded his pedigree and established his right to the title as 10th baronet in 1797.

NIXON (UK) 1906, of Roebuck Grove, Milltown, co Dublin, and Merrion Square, City of Dublin

Always ready

Rev Sir KENNETH MICHAEL JOHN BASIL NIXON, SJ, 4th *Baronet*, 2nd son of late Maj Sir Christopher William Nixon, 2nd Baronet; *b* 22 Feb 1919; *s* his brother, *Maj Sir* CHRISTOPHER JOHN LOUIS JOSEPH, 1978; *ed* Beaumont Coll, and Heythrop Coll, Oxford; a Roman Catholic Priest and Member of the Society of Jesus.

𝖆rms – Azure, on a chevron engrailed between three frets couped or, as many trefoils vert, on a chief indented of the second, a cat passant between two fleams of the field. 𝕮rest – A leopard rampant azure bezantee, holding in the dexter paw a fleam or.
Address – St George's Coll, PB 7727, Causeway, Zimbabwe.

DAUGHTERS LIVING OF THIRD BARONET

Anne Louise Catherine, *b* 1954; MB, BSc, MRCP, MRC (Path): *m* 1980, Jonathan Anthony Miller, MB, BCh, MRCP, and has issue living, David Christopher, *b* 1988, — Nicholas Jonathan, *b* 1989. —— Mary Joan Teresa, *b* 1957; MCSP, SRP: *m* 1988, Eric Olivier Léchere, and has issue living, Jeremy, *b* 1989, — Samuel, *b* 1992. —— Sally Veronica Rose, *b* 1961; BDS, FDS (RCS): *m* 1989, Andrew Kenneth Robson, MB, BS, FRCS, eldest son of Dr Angus Robson, of Princes Risborough, Bucks, and has issue living, Lucy Dorothy, *b* 1990, — Rosie Esme, *b* 1992.

BROTHER LIVING

CECIL DOMINIC HENRY JOSEPH, MC, (Salt Winds, Torridge Rd, Appledore, N Devon), *b* 5 Feb 1920; *ed* Beaumont Coll; Major Roy Ulster Rifles: *m* 1953, Brenda, da of late Samuel Lycett Lewis, and widow of Maj M. F. McWhor, and has issue living, Simon Michael Christopher *b* 1954, — Michael David Hugh, *b* 1957, — Kenneth Philip Guy, *b* 1959, — Susan Penelope, *b* 1955.

WIDOW LIVING OF THIRD BARONET

JOAN LUCILLE MARY (*Lady Nixon*) (c/o Lloyds Bank, St George's Rd, Wimbledon, SW19), only da of Robert Felix Mervyn Brown, of Rangoon, Burma: *m* 1949, Maj Sir Christopher John Louis Joseph Nixon, MC, 3rd Bt, who *d* 1978.

The Rt Hon Sir Christopher John Nixon, PC, MD, LLD, 1st Bt, was an eminent physician, Vice-Chancellor of National Univ of Ireland, and Pres of Veterinary Coll of Ireland. The 2nd Bt, Major Sir Christopher William Nixon, DSO, RA (ret), served during European War 1914-18 (DSO). The 3rd baronet was a Maj in R Ulster Rifles and served in Burma (MC) and Palestine in WW II, and in Korea 1950-51 (wounded, despatches).

NOBLE (UK) 1902, of Ardmore and Ardardan Noble, Cardross, co Dumbarton

By virtue and valour

Sir DAVID BRUNEL NOBLE, 6th *Baronet; b* 25 Dec 1961; *s* his father, Sir MARC BRUNEL, CBE, 1991; *ed* Eton: *m* 1987 (*m diss* 1993), Virginia Ann, yr da of late Roderick Lancaster Wetherall, MBE, of Platt Oast, St Mary's Platt, Kent, and has issue.

𝕬rms – Argent, three bay leaves slipped proper. 𝕮rest – A dexter hand couped, holding a dagger all proper. 𝕾upporters – Two wild men, wreathed and cinctured with bay leaves, each supporting with the exterior hand a holly tree eradicated, and resting the exterior foot on the roots thereof, all proper (These were granted to descend hereditarily.)
Residence – Deerleap House, Knockholt, Sevenoaks, Kent, TN14 7NP.

SONS LIVING

RODERICK LANCASTER BRUNEL, *b* 8 Dec 1988. —— Alexander David, *b* 1990.

BROTHER LIVING

Charles Richard Austin, *b* 1963; *ed* Harrow.   *Residence* – Deerleap House, Knockholt, Sevenoaks, Kent TN14 7NP.

SISTER LIVING

Anna Margaret, *b* 1957: *m* 1984, John Edward Llewellyn Porter, who *d* 1987, son of late Stephen Porter, and has issue living, George Edward, *b* 1986. *Residence* – Deerleap House, Knockholt, Sevenoaks, Kent TN14 7NP.

UNCLE LIVING (*son of 4th baronet*)

Peter Saxton Fitzjames, CBE (Flax Cottage, Ham Common, Richmond, Surrey TW10 7JB), *b* 1929; *ed* Eton, and Magdalene Coll Camb; CBE (Civil) 1977: *m* 1st, 1954 (*m diss* 1966), Elizabeth Emmeline, da of late Launcelot William Gregory Eccles, CMG, MC; 2ndly, 1966 (*m diss* 1980), Helena Margaret, da of late Thomas Essery Rose-Richards, and previously wife of David Anthony Harries; 3rdly, 1980, Penelope Margaret, da of late Leslie Landeau, and has issue living, (by 1st *m*) Simon Peter Saxton Fanshaw, *b* 1958, — (by 2nd *m*) James Essery Brunel, *b* 1968.

AUNT LIVING (*daughter of 4th baronet*)

Lilias Mulgrave, *b* 1931: *m* 1951, Capt Robin John Sheepshanks, CBE, DL, late King's Dragoon Guards (V Chelmsford), and has issue living, David Richard, *b* 1952, — Richard John, *b* 1955, — Andrew Charles, *b* 1960, — Christopher James, *b* 1964. *Residence* – The Rookery, Eyke, Woodbridge, Suffolk.

DAUGHTER LIVING OF SECOND BARONET

Veronica Margaret (*Veronica, Baroness Gainford*), *b* 1900: *m* 1921, 2nd Baron Gainford, who *d* 1971. *Residence* – Taigh na Seanamhair, Tayvallich, Lochgilpehead, Argyll.

WIDOW LIVING OF FIFTH BARONET

JENNIFER LORNA (JANE) (*Dowager Lady Noble*), da of late John Mein Austin, of Flinthill, W Haddon, Northants: *m* 1956, Sir Marc Brunel Noble, 5th Bt, CBE, who *d* 1991. *Residence* – Deerleap House, Knockholt, Sevenoaks, Kent TN14 7NP.

COLLATERAL BRANCHES LIVING

Issue of late Sir John Henry Brunel Noble (3rd son of 1st baronet), who was *cr* a *Baronet* 1923:—
See Noble, Bt, *cr* 1923.

Grandson of late Philip Ernest Noble, 4th son of 1st baronet:—
Issue of late Maj Horace Westcott Noble, *b* 1899, *d* 1980: *m* 1st, 1929 (*m diss* 1934), Joan Marion, only child of H. R. Miller, of 65 East 55th St, New York, USA; 2ndly, 1946, Mrs Edna Louise Malone, da of late Charles Johnson, of Chicago, USA:—
(By 1st *m*) Philip Ralph, *b* 1930; *ed* Eton.

The 1st baronet, Sir Andrew Noble, the well-known expert on explosives, joined the firm of Sir W. G. Armstrong & Co in 1860, and eventually became Chm; he was a Member of the first Committee of Explosives until dissolved in 1880, and High Sheriff of Northumberland 1896. The 4th baronet, Sir Humphrey Brunel Noble, MBE, MC, was High Sheriff of Northumberland 1956.

NOBLE (UK) 1923, of Ardkinglas, co Argyll

Sir IAIN ANDREW NOBLE, OBE, 3rd *Baronet*: *b* 8 Sept 1935; *s* his father, *Sir* ANDREW NAPIER, KCMG, 1987; *ed* Eton, and Univ Coll, Oxford (MA); Scottish Council (Development and Industry) Edinburgh 1964-69; Joint Founder and Man Dir Noble Grossart Ltd 1969-72; Joint Founder and Chm Seaforth Maritime Ltd 1972-77; Chm Noble and Co Ltd, Merchant Bankers, of Edinburgh, since 1980; Dir Adam & Co plc, Bankers, of Edinburgh, 1983-93; Dir New Scotland Insurance Gp plc, of Glasgow, since 1986; Dir Premium Investment Trust plc since 1993; Proprietor Fearann Eilean Iarmain and Barony of MacDonald, Isle of Skye since 1972, Chm Pràban Ltd (whisky proprietors) of Eilean Iarmain since 1977; a founding trustee Coll of Sabhal Mor Ostaig 1974-84; Memb Edinburgh Univ Court 1970-73; Dep Chm Traverse Theatre Club, Edinburgh 1966-69; Trustee Nat Museums of Scotland 1987-91; Chm Scots Australian Council; Pres Saltire Soc: *m* 1990, Lucilla Charlotte James, da of late Col Hector Andrew Courtney Mackenzie of Dalmore, OBE, MC, TD, JP, DL.

Arms – Per pale Argent and Vert three bay leaves counterchanged, and on a canton Argent a sinister hand couped apaumé Gules for his Baronetcy. Above the Shield from which is pendent the proper badge of a Baronet of the United Kingdom is placed an Helm befitting his degree with a Mantling Vert doubled Argent, and on a Wreath of the Liveries is set for. **Crest** – A bay tree Vert, trunk Sable, ensigned with an estoile Argent and in an Escrol over the same this Motto "Mairidh an Duilleag".
Residence – An Lamraig, Eilean Iarmain, Isle of Skye IV43 8QR. *Club* – New (Edinburgh).

BROTHER LIVING

TIMOTHY PETER *b* 21 Dec 1943; *ed* Eton, and Univ Coll, Oxford (MA); Bar Gray's Inn 1969; INSEAD, Fontainebleau (MBA) 1970; Exec Dir Lyle Shipping plc, Glasgow, 1976-1984 and Noble & Co Ltd, Merchant Bankers, of Edinburgh, since 1984; Dir Waverley Mining Finance plc since 1988, Premium Underwriting plc since 1993, and The British Ski Federation Ltd since 1993; Chm Business Archives Council of Scotland since 1987: *m* 1976, Elizabeth Mary, da of late Alexander Wallace Aitken, and has issue living, Lorne Andrew Wallace, *b* 1980, — Andrew Iain Brunel, *b* 1984, — Sasha Heidi Elizabeth, *b* 1978. *Residence* – Ardnahane, Barnton Avenue, Edinburgh EH4 6JJ. *Club* – New (Edinburgh).

SISTER LIVING

Laila Ilona, *b* 1937: *m* 1958, Kenneth Magnus Spence, who *d* 1989, son of late Col Patrick Magnus Spence, MC, and has issue living, Magnus Andrew, *b* 1959, — Patrick Matthew, *b* 1967, — Melanie Jane, *b* 1961. *Residence* – 60 Ellerby St, SW6 6EZ.

AUNT LIVING *(daughter of 1st baronet)*

Anastasia Mary Elizabeth (The Square, Ardkinglas, Cairndow, Argyll), *b* 1911.

WIDOW LIVING OF SECOND BARONET

SIGRID (*Sigrid, Lady Noble*), 2nd da of Johan Michelet, Norwegian Diplo Ser: *m* 1934, Sir Andrew Napier Noble, 2nd Bt, KCMG, who *d* 1987. *Residence* – 11 Cedar House, Marloes Rd, W8 5LA.

COLLATERAL BRANCHES LIVING

Issue of late John Samuel Brunel Noble, 2nd son of 1st baronet; *b* 1909, *d* 1972: *m* 1934, Elizabeth Virginia, who *d* 1983, da of late William Louis Lucas (Goldsmid, Bt, ext):—
Simon John (Ardkinglas, Cairndow, Argyll; Boodle's, New Club (Edinburgh)) *b* 1936; *ed* Eton, and Oxford Univ; Chm Wine Imports Edinburgh Ltd and Loch Fyne Oysters Ltd; Dir of Noble and Co Ltd, and Edinburgh Tapestry Co Ltd. —— Sarah, *b* 1935: *m* 1957, Peter Whitton Sumsion, of Bachie Barn House, Cairndow, Argyll, and 42 Dudley Dr, Glasgow, and has issue living, David, *b* 1958, — Daniel, *b* 1967, — Virginia, *b* 1960, — Lucy, *b* 1963. —— Christina Campbell, *b* 1942: *m* 1980, Kranti Singh, who *d* 1992, of 66 Hungerford Rd, N7 9LP, and has issue living, Rahul John, *b* 1976, — Tara Anastasia, *b* 1977.

Issue of late Rt Hon Michael Antony Cristobal Noble (Baron Glenkinglas), yst son of 1st baronet, *b* 1913, *d* 1984: *m* 1940, Anne (*Baroness Glenkinglas*) (Strone, Cairndow, Argyll), da of late Sir Neville Arthur Pearson, 2nd Bt, of Dunstan's (ext):—
See Glenkinglas, By.

The 1st baronet, Sir John Henry Brunel Noble (3rd son of Sir Andrew Noble, CB, 1st Bt, of Ardmore (*cr* 1902)), awarded the Order of the Sacred Treasure of Japan, was a Director of London and N-E Railway and many other Cos.

(Edinburgh).

Norie-Miller, see Miller.

NORMAN (UK) 1915, of Honeyhanger, Parish of Shottermill, co Surrey

Live but do not forget

Sir MARK ANNESLEY NORMAN, 3rd *Baronet*, DL; *b* 8 Feb 1927; *s* his father, *Air-Commodore Sir* (HENRY) NIGEL ST VALERY, CBE, 1943: *ed* Winchester, and RMA; Lieut Coldstream Guards 1945-47 and Flying Officer, No 601 Squadron, R Aux AF (GD Pilot 1953-56); High Sheriff of Oxfordshire 1983-84; DL Oxfordshire (1985); Gazetted Air Commodore, R Aux AF, and appointed Hon Air Commodore No 4624 (County of Oxford) Movements Sqdn, R Aux AF 1983: *m* 1953, Joanna Camilla, da of Lt-Col Ian James Kilgour (*see* Forestier-Walker, Bt, colls, 1985 Edn), and has issue.

Arms – Sable, a thunderbolt, and in chief two crosses patée pierced with the eight symbols of Fhohe or the Pa-qua and charged with a rounder containing the eastern symbol known as Tae Keigh' all or. **Crest** – Upon mount vert a spear erect, transfixing a Saracen's head, all proper. **Supporters** – On either side a Norseman proper.
Residence – Wilcote Manor, Wilcote, Chipping Norton, Oxon, OX7 3EB.
Clubs – White's, MCC, Pratt's, Royal Air Force, Royal Southern Yacht, SWSYC.

SONS LIVING

NIGEL JAMES, *b* 5 Feb 1956; late Maj 13th/18th Royal Hussars (QMO), Sultan of Oman's Armoured Regt; Dir Morgan Grenfell International Funds Management Ltd: *m* 1st, 1985 (*m diss* 1989), Joanna Rosemary Jane, da of Michael Montagu George Naylor-Leyland, MC, of Church Farm, Coates, Cirencester, Glos (*see* Naylor-Leyland, Bt); 2ndly, 1994, Mrs Juliet Clare Louise Marriott, da of Richard Lloyd Baxendale, of Aston Park House, Aston Rowant, Oxon. *Clubs* – White's, Annabels.

—— (Antony) Rory, *b* 1963.

DAUGHTER LIVING

Lucinda Fay, *b* 1965: *m* 1988, Stanislas Richard Marie Aubertin, son of Christian Aubertin, of Neuilly-sur-Seine, France, and has issue living, a son, *b* 1991, — a son, *b* 1994.

BROTHERS LIVING

(Nigel) Desmond, CBE, *b* 1929; CBE (Civil) 1971: *m* 1st, 1956 (*m diss* 1965), Barbara Anne, only da of late Capt Mark Fogg Elliot, DSO, RN; 2ndly, 1965, Mrs Boel Elisabeth Holmsen, only da of late Gösta Suenson, of Malmo, Sweden, and has issue living, (by 1st *m*) Henry Mark Desmond, *b* 1957, — Alexander Robert, *b* 1959, — (by 2nd *m*) Roderick Peregrine, *b* 1966, — Roland, *b* 1971, — Lisa Jemima, *b* 1969. —— Torquil Patrick Alexander (24 Avenue Rd, NW8), *b* 1933: *m* 1961, Elizabeth Anne, da of Alexander Victor Edward Paulet Montagu (10th Earl of Sandwich until he disclaimed his title 1964), and has issue living, Alexander Jesse, *b* 1962, — Casey William, *b* 1963, — Caspar Joe, *b* 1966, — Lucy Patricia, *b* 1964, — Amy Jean Mary, *b* 1969.

UNCLES LIVING (*Sons of 1st baronet*)

Willoughby Rollo (28 Ranelagh House, Elyston Place, SW3; The Grange, South Hating, Petersfield, Hants), *b* 1909; *ed* Eton, and Magdalen Coll, Oxford; Maj Gren Gds; Chm The Boots Co, Ltd 1961-72 (Vice-Chm 1954-61); Vice Chm of English China Clays, Ltd 1968-81, a Dir of Guardian Royal Exchange Assurance, Ltd, of Nat Westminster Bank (Chm of Eastern Region) and Sheepbridge Engineering, Ltd, and an Underwriting Member of Lloyd's; High Sheriff of Leicestershire 1960-61: *m* 1st, 1934 (*m diss* 1973), Hon Barbara Jaqueline Boot, da of 2nd Baron Trent; 2ndly, 1973, Anna Caroline, da of late William Greville Worthington (E Aylesford), and formerly wife of Oliver Patrick Miller Haskard, and has issue living, (by 1st *m*) Jeremy Nicholas, *b* 1935: *m* 1980, Mrs Danuska Maria Weeks, da of late Mr Grajewski, of Wroclaw, Poland, — Sarah Jessica, *b* 1940: *m* 1st, 1960 (*m diss* 1967), Peter Egerton-Warburton (*see* Grey-Egerton, Bt, colls); 2ndly, 1967, Peter David Rickett, and has issue living, (by 1st *m*) (*see* Grey-Egerton Bt, colls), (by 2nd *m*) Nicola Barbara *b* 1970, Lucinda Frances *b* 1971, — Tessa Roselle, *b* 1944: *m* 1968, George Maurie Pope, late Capt Coldm Gds, and has issue living, Edward *b* 1970, Emily *b* 1972, Arabella *b* 1975. —— Antony Charles Wynyard, OBE, *b* 1912; *ed* Eton, and Magdalen Coll, Oxford; Wing-Cdr AAF (Reserve); 1939-45 War (despatches, OBE); OBE (Mil) 1945: *m* 1937, Anne, only da of John Watson Hughes, of Pontruffyd, Trefnant, Denbighshire. *Residences* – Lausanne Palace, Lausanne, Switzerland; Château de la Garoupe, Antibes, France, AM.

The 1st baronet, Rt Hon Sir Henry Norman, PC (son of late Henry Norman), was MP for S Div of Wolverhampton (*L*) 1900-1910, and for Blackburn 1910-23. The 2nd baronet, Air Commodore Sir (Henry) Nigel St Valery, CBE, Auxiliary Air Force (Reserve), was *ka* 1943.

NORTH (UK) 1920, of Southwell, co Nottingham

With courage and fidelity

Sir (WILLIAM) JONATHAN FREDERICK NORTH, 2nd *Baronet*, son of late Hon John Montagu William North (*see* E Guilford); *b* 6 Feb 1931; *s* his maternal grandfather, *Sir* WILLIAM NORTON HICKING, 1947; *ed* Marlborough Coll: *m* 1956, Sara Virginia, da of late Air Ch Marshal Sir (James) Donald Innes Hardman, GBE, KCB, DFC, and has issue.

𝕬rms – Quarterly, 1st and 4th azure, a lion passant or, three fleurs-de-lis argent, *North*; 2nd and 3rd, argent, semée of lozenges vert, a bordure, gules, *Hicking*. 𝕮rest – A dragon's head erased sable, ducally gorged and chained or. *Residence* – Frogmore, Weston-under-Penyard, Herefordshire HR9 5TQ.

SON LIVING

JEREMY WILLIAM FRANCIS, *b* 5 May 1960, *ed* Marlborough: *m* 1986, Lucy A., da of G. A. van der Meulen, of Tunbridge Wells, Kent, and has issue living, Jocelyn Montagu Dudley, *b* 23 March 1989, — Francis Augustus Roderick, *b* 1990, — Polly Antonia, *b* 1992.

DAUGHTERS LIVING

Charlotte Amelia, *b* 1958: *m* 1989, Matthew Dufton Tester, yst son of late Maurice Tester, of Long Barn House, Cowfold, Sussex. — Harriet Cordelia Henrietta, *b* 1963: *m* 1984, (Seymour) Thomas Thistlethwayte, son of Seymour Thistlethwayte, of Sheet Mill House, Petersfield, Hants, and has issue living, Oliver Seymour, *b* 1990, — Daisy Alexandra, *b* 1988, — Cecily Alice, *b* 1992.

SISTER LIVING

Georgiana Mary, *b* 1928: *m* 1960, Esmond Unwin Butler, CM, CVO, who *d* 1989, and has issue living, Mark William, *b* 1961, — Clare Martine, *b* 1963. *Residence* – 149 Rideau Terr, Ottawa, Ontario, Canada.

The 1st baronet, Sir William Norton Hicking (son of late George Hicking, of Nottingham), sometime Chm of Nottingham and Notts Banking Co, and High Sheriff of Notts 1913-14, was *cr* a Baronet in 1917 with the usual limitation to heirs male of the body, but in 1920 a further creation was granted failing heirs male of the body of the grantee, with special remainder to the first and every other son of Mabel Doris Willoughby (el da of 1st Bt), and the heirs of their bodies and with like remainder to the male issue of any yr das of the 1st Bt. On the death of the 1st Bt in 1947 the Baronetcy of 1917 became ext and that of 1920 passed to the son of his yr da, Muriel Norton, formerly wife of the Hon John Montagu William North, 2nd son of 8th Earl of Guilford.

Norton-Griffiths, see Griffiths.

NUGENT (I) 1795, of Ballinlough, co Westmeath

Decrevi
I have decreed

Sir JOHN EDWIN LAVALLIN NUGENT, 7th *Baronet*, and 4th Count of the Austrian Empire; *b* 16 March 1933; *s* his father, *Sir* HUGH CHARLES, 1983; *ed* Eton; late Lieut Irish Gds; High Sheriff of Berks 1981; JP Berks: *m* 1959, Penelope Anne, elder da of late Brig Richard Nigel Hanbury, CBE, TD, and has issue.

𝕬rms – Ermine, two bars gules. 𝕮rest – A cockatrice vert. *Seat* – Ballinlough Castle, Clonmellon, co Westmeath.

SON LIVING

NICHOLAS MYLES JOHN, *b* 17 Feb 1967; *ed* Eton.

DAUGHTER LIVING

Grania Clare, *b* 1969.

BROTHER LIVING

David Hugh Lavallin (Clobemon Hall, Ferns, Enniscorthy, co Wexford; Ross Castle, Mount Nugent, co Cavan; 25 Eaton Place, SW1. *Club* – Cavalry and Guards'), *b* 1935; *ed* Eton; late Lt Irish Gds; Knt of Sovereign Mil Order of Malta, and Kt Cmdr of Order of Holy Sepulchre of Jerusalem with Star Grand Officer, and Lord of Castletown Delvin, co Westmeath: *m* 1st, 1960 (*m diss* 1990), Lady Elizabeth Maria Guinness, da of late Maj Arthur Onslow Edward, Viscount Elveden, el son of 2nd Earl of Iveagh; 2ndly, 1991, Djong-Zha, only da of In-Suk Hyun, of Seoul, Korea, and formerly wife of Sir Richard Heygate, 6th Bt, and has issue living (by 1st *m*), Charles Rupert, *b* 1962: *m* 1989, Louise V., yr da of Timothy Nixon, of The Old Vicarage, Pampisford, Cambridge, — Hugo John, *b* 1963: *m* 1989, Louise, yr da of Thomas Elliot Rutherford, of Park Daill, Hawick, Scotland, and has issue living, Isaac Sean *b* 1992, — Rory David Neeld Lavallin, *b* 1971, — Sheelin Rose, *b* 1967.

WIDOW LIVING OF SIXTH BARONET

MARGARET MARY LAVALLIN (*Margaret, Lady Nugent*), da of late Rev Herbert Lavallin Puxley, of The White House, Chaddle-worth, Newbury, Berks (Neeld, Bt): *m* 1931, Sir Hugh Charles Nugent, 6th Bt, who *d* 1983. *Residence* – Cronk Ghennie House, Bowring Rd, Ramsey, IoM.

COLLATERAL BRANCH LIVING

Grandchildren of late Charles James Nugent (infra):—
Issue of James Andrew William Nugent, *b* 1909, *d* 1965: *m* 1936, Dardanella, who *d* 1983, da of David Webber, of Wairoa, NZ:—
Trevor Charles, *b* 1940. —— Brian David, *b* 1942. —— Rayna Joy, *b* 1941.
Issue of Frederick Nugent, *b* 1914, *d* 1983: *m* 1939, Rita Kara (Mahia, Hawke's Bay, NZ), da of T. Carrol of Wairoa, NZ:—
Mark, *b* 1950. —— Valentine, *b* 1952. —— Pearl, *b* 1940. —— Brenda, *b* 1941. —— Diana, *b* 1954. —— Dixie, *b* 1957.
Issue of Charles Joseph Nugent, *b* 1918, *d* 1980: *m* 19—, Kathleen, da of Edgar Jenkinson of Gisborne, NZ:—
Peter James, *b* 1947. —— Graham, *b* 1953. —— Kenneth John, *b* 1955. —— Margaret Anne, *b* 1950. —— Raewyn Gay, *b* 1961.

Grandchildren of late James O'Reilly Nugent, 4th son of 3rd baronet:—
Issue of late Charles James Nugent, *b* 1881, *d* 1961: *m* 1907, Anne, who *d* 1961, da of William King, formerly of Napier, New Zealand:—
Patrick Hulme, *b* 1912: *m* 1940, Mary McFalls Quin, of Glasgow, who *d* 198—, and has issue living, Barry Hulme Joseph, *b* 1946, — Darryl Charles, *b* 1952, — Lynette Ann, *b* 1940, — Janice Patricia, *b* 1944. —— †Richard King, *b* 1923: *m* 1947, Doreen Mabel, da of Townsend May, of New Plymouth, New Zealand, and *d* 1993, leaving issue, Sandra May, *b* 1947, — Karen Louise, *b* 1952, — Anne Marie Eva, *b* 1954. —— Hubert Thomas Michael, *b* 1925: *m* 19—, Ngaire, da of George Able, of Wairoa, New Zealand, and has issue living, Alan Grant, *b* 1949, — Glenis Joy, *b* 1950. —— Florence Maud, *b* 1916: *m* 19—, Norman Jones, and has issue living, Howard Gilbert, *b* 1939: *m* 1963, Kathleen Elizabeth Sherridan, — Warren Charles, *b* 1942, — Michael O'Reilly, *b* 1947. *Residence* – Frasertown Rd, Wairoa, Hawke's Bay, New Zealand. —— Marie Tepaea Diana (3/10 Geddis Av, Maraenui, Napier, NZ), *b* 1921: *m* 1938, Moat Mervyn Hoggard, who *d* 1982, and has issue living, Shona Faye, *b* 1939: *m* 1960 (*m diss* 197—), Colin Thomas William Bailey, and has issue living, Andrea Jane *b* 1960: *m* 1991, David Paul Burton (and has issue living, Rea Louise *b* 1993), Grant Colin *b* 1962: *m* 1991, Lynda Gwenith O'Brien (and has issue living, Laura Jayne *b* 1993, Lisa Marie *b* 1969). —— Anne Barbara, *b* 1927: *m* 1951, Roy Alexander Andrew Ross, and has issue living, Judith Ann, *b* 1953: *m* 1976, Robert Chadwick Smith (c/o Lakeland Marine Ltd, Rauhato, Taupo, PO Box 827, NZ), and has issue living, Haylee Ann *b* 1980, Renee Adrienne *b* 1982, — Deborah Irene, *b* 1956: *m* 19— and has issue. —— Sharon Barbara, *b* 1959: *m* 19—, and has issue. —— Angela Leslie, *b* 1961: *m* 19—, and has issue.
Issue of late Walter Lonergan O'Reilly Nugent, *b* 1884, *d* 1949: *m* 1911, Amelia Bateup, who *d* 1966:—
Joan Florence, *b* 1917: *m* 1940, Donald Evelyn Fenner, and has issue living, Janet Nugent, *b* 1946: *m* 1971, Michael Cansdale, and has issue living, Andrew Richard *b* 1976, Penelope Alice *b* 1972. *Residence* – 24 The Boulevard, Pevensey Bay, E Sussex BN24 6SB. —— Gwennyth Eileen Mary, *b* 1928: *m* 1949, Alfred Stokes, of 25 Victoria Rd, Mayfield, Sussex, and has issue living, Patrick John, *b* 1954: *m* 1979, Jenny Garsad, and has issue living, William Conrad *b* 1980, — Sally Ann, *b* 1950: *m* 1970, Graham White, and has issue living, Sarah Jayne *b* 1974, — Jennifer Mary, *b* 1952: *m* 1972, Malcolm Palmer, and has issue living, Aaron James *b* 1975, Paul Malcolm *b* 1978, Michelle Louise *b* 1982, — Teresa Jill, *b* 1962.
Issue of late Wilfrid Basil Nugent, *b* 1885, *d* 1976: *m* 1916, Alice Isobel, da of late Theodore Manson West:—
Diana Mary Hampshire, *b* 1918.

The original surname of this Family was O'Reilly (a very ancient Irish sept). Sir Hugh O'Reilly, 1st Bt, assumed by Royal Licence 1812 the surname of Nugent on the death without issue of his maternal uncle, John Nugent of Tulloughan, Gov of Tortola and the Virgin Islands, el son of Andrew Nugent, of Dysart, co Westmeath, and Lady Catherine Nugent, yr da of Thomas, 4th Earl of Westmeath. His brother was the Austrian Field Marshal Count Andrew O'Reilly (*cr* Count of the Holy Roman Empire 1797), and their sister was created Baroness Talbot of Malahide. The 3rd baronet, Sir John Nugent, was Chamberlain to the Emperor of Austria and was created a Count of the Austrian Empire.

NUGENT (UK) 1806, of Waddesdon, Berkshire

I have decreed

Sir ROBIN GEORGE COLBORNE NUGENT, 5th *Baronet, b* 11 July 1925; *s* his father, *Capt Sir* (GEORGE) GUY BULWER, 1970; *ed* Eton; ARIBA; Lt Gren Gds 1943-48; Italy 1944-45: *m* 1st, 1947 (*m diss* 1967), Ursula Mary, da of late Lt-Gen Sir Herbert Fothergill Cooke, KCB, KBE, CSI, DSO; 2ndly, 1967, Victoria Anna Irmgard, da of late Dr Peter Cartellieri, and has issue by 1st *m.*

𝔄rms – Ermine, two bars within a bordure engrailed gules, on a canton of the last a dagger erect proper, pommel and hilt or. 𝔠rest – A cockatrice vert, gorged with a plain collar or, pendent therefrom an escutcheon gules, charged with a dagger erect as in the arms. 𝔖upporters – Two cockatrices vert, wings endorsed, collared or, pendent therefrom a shield gules, charged with a dagger as in the arms.

SONS LIVING *(By 1st marriage)*

CHRISTOPHER GEORGE RIDLEY, *b* 5 Oct 1949; *ed* Eton and East Anglia Univ: *m* 1985, Jacqueline Vagba, and has issue living, Terence, *b* 1 March 1986, — Rufus, *b* 1987, — Benjamin, *b* 1991. —— Patrick Guy, *b* 1959.

DAUGHTER LIVING *(By 1st marriage)*

Philippa Mary, *b* 1951.

BROTHER LIVING

Jeremy Charles Clare, *b* 1936: *m* 1960, Joy, da of A. H. Waterson, and has issue living, Nigel Howard Clare, *b* 1963, — Julian Guy Bulwer, *b* 1965, — Fiona Clare, *b* 1967.

SISTER LIVING

Dinah, *b* 1922; 1942-45 War in WRNS: *m* 1950, Capt John William Huyshe Bennett, DSC, RN, of Farleigh Plain, Hinton Charterhouse, Bath, and has issue living, Timothy Nugent Huyshe, *b* 1951, — Nicholas John William, *b* 1957.

The 1st baronet, Sir George Nugent GCB, DCL, was a Field Marshal in the Army.

NUGENT (UK) 1831, of Cloncoskoran, Waterford (Extinct 1929)

Sir JOHN NUGENT, 3rd and last *Baronet.*

COLLATERAL BRANCH LIVING

Issue (by 2nd *m*) of late Lt-Cdr Gilbert Richard de la Poer Nugent, RN, el son of 3rd baronet, *b* 1884, *d* 1927: *m* 1st, 1904, Marjorie, who *d* 1910, yr da of late Capt Charles Smith, of Goderiche, Sydney, N S Wales; 2ndly, 1922, Lucinda Elinor (who *d* 1954, having *m* 3rdly, 1933, Lieut-Col O. T. O'Kelly Webber, late RE and Roy Corps of Signals), da of C. C. Colley, and formerly wife of late Edward George Hemmerde, KC:—

†Mary, *b* 1924: *m* 1947, Capt Anthony Raymond Wynter-Bee, RA (ret), of Beldam Bridge Farm, Chobham, Surrey (who *m* 2ndly, 1980, Elizabeth Anne, da of late Adm Sir Richard Symonds-Tayler, KBE), and *d* 1976, leaving issue, Lucinda Mary, *b* 1951: *m* 1975, Peter Michael Day, and has issue living, James Peter Anthony *b* 1985, Catherine Mary *b* 1980, Louise Ruth *b* 1983, — Elizabeth Joan, *b* 1953: *m* 1976, Lt-Col Maxwell Pearse Gandell, The Parachute Regt, and has issue living, Andrew William Pearse *b* 1981, Mary Sarah Lillian *b* 1984, Alice Elizabeth Kerr *b* 1988, — Rosamund Eve, *b* 1959: — Daphne Ann, *b* 1962: *m* 1986, Paul Mark Dillon-Robinson, and has issue living, Edward John *b* 1993, Rebecca Mary *b* 1991.

NUGENT (UK) 1831, of Donore, Westmeath

I have decreed

Sir PETER WALTER JAMES NUGENT, 5th *Baronet*; *b* 26 Jan 1920; *s* his father, *Sir* WALTER RICHARD, 1955; *ed* Downside; European War 1940-45 as Major Hampshire Regt: *m* 1947, Anne Judith, only da of Major Robert Smyth, of Gaybrook, Mullingar, co Westmeath, and has issue.

Arms – Ermine, two bars gules; in dexter chief a martlet azure for difference.
Crest – A wyvern vert on the breast a martlet or.
Residence – Blackhall Stud, Clane, co Kildare.

SONS LIVING

WALTER RICHARD MIDDLETON, *b* 15 Nov 1947. —— Andrew Robert, *b* 1951.

DAUGHTERS LIVING

Fiona Georgina, *b* 1949. —— Laura Anne, *b* 1954.

SISTERS LIVING

Heather Vivian Mary, *b* 1917: *m* 1937 (*m diss* 1950), Sir John Prichard-Jones, 2nd Bt. *Residences* – Moyvore, Mullingar, co Westmeath; 30 Claylands Rd, SW8 1NZ. —— Gloria Aileen, *b* 1925: *m* 1946, Michael Meade Carvill, Capt Irish Guard's Reserve.

James Nugent, of Donore, was created a baronet 1768, but on the death of his brother, who succeeded by special remainder, the title became extinct. The Donore estate passed to their nephew, Thomas Fitzgerald, RN, who assumed, without Roy licence, the name of Nugent, and his son was created a baronet. Sir Walter Richard Nugent, 4th Bt, was High Sheriff of co Westmeath 1922-3, a Director and Dep Gov of Bank of Ireland, and Chm of Great Southern Railways of Ireland. He sat as MP for S Westmeath Div of co Westmeath (N) 1907-18, and was a Senator of Irish Free State 1928-39.

NUTTALL (UK) 1922, of Chasefield, Parish of Bowdon, co Chester

Either do not attempt, or complete

Sir NICHOLAS KEITH LILLINGTON NUTTALL, 3rd *Baronet*; *b* 21 Sept 1933; *s* his father, Lieut-Col *Sir* (EDMUND) KEITH, 1941; *ed* Eton and RMA; Maj (ret) R Horse Gds: *m* 1st, 1960 (*m diss* 1971), Rosemary Caroline, el da of Christopher York, DL, of Long Marston Manor, York (Milner Bt); 2ndly, 1971 (*m diss* 1975), Julia Jill Beresford, da of late Col Thomas Cromwell Williamson, DSO, of Beaumont Hall, Thorpe-le-Soken, Essex, and formerly wife of Darel Sausmarez Carey; 3rdly, 1975 (*m diss* 1983), Miranda Elizabeth Louise, da of Richard St John Quarry, and formerly wife of late Peter Richard Henry Sellers, CBE, the actor; 4thly, 1983, Eugenie Marie Alicia, eldest da of William Thomas McWeeney, and has issue by 1st, 3rd and 4th *m*.

Arms – Or, on a pile sable between in base two roses gules barbed and seeded proper, a shacklebolt of the field. Crest – A Dalmatian hound sejant proper, collared and chained and resting the forefoot on a shacklebolt sejant.
Address – PO Box N7776, Nassau, Bahamas. *Club* – White's.

SONS LIVING *(By 1st marriage)*

HARRY, *b* 2 Jan 1963. *Residence* – 5 Redcliffe Sq, SW10 9LA.

(By 4th marriage)

Nicholas Alexander David, *b* 1985.

DAUGHTERS LIVING *(By 1st marriage)*

Tamara, *b* 1967.

(By 3rd marriage)

Gytha Miranda, *b* 1975. —— Amber Louise, *b* 1976. —— Olympia Jubilee, *b* 1977.

COLLATERAL BRANCH LIVING

Issue of late Clive Nuttall, 3rd son of 1st baronet, *b* 1906, *d* 1936: *m* 1931, Eileen Daphne Elizabeth, da of late Lt-Col Horatio Douglas Russell, DSO:—
Clive Patrick, *b* 1933.

The 1st baronet, Sir Edmund, was head of the firm of Nuttall and Co, civil engineering contractors, of Trafford Park, Manchester. The 2nd baronet, Lieut-Col Sir (Edmund) Keith, was *ka* 1941.

NUTTING (UK) 1902, of St Helens, Booterstown, co Dublin

Death rather than disgrace

Rt Hon Sir (HAROLD) ANTHONY NUTTING, 3rd *Baronet*; *b* 11 Jan 1920; *s* his father, *Lt-Col Sir* HAROLD STANSMORE, 1972; *ed* Eton, and Trin Coll, Camb; Leics Yeo 1939-40 (invalided), Foreign Ser in France, Spain and Italy 1940-45; Chm of Young Conservative & Unionist Movement 1946-47, Vice-Chm of Nat Union of Conservative Assocns 1949-50, and Chm 1950-51, and Chm of Conservative Overseas Bureau, and of Nat Exec Cttee of Conservative Party 1951-52, Joint Parl Under-Sec of State for Foreign Affairs 1951-54, and Min of State for Foreign Affairs, Leader of UK Delegation to UN Assembly, and UK Repres on Disarmament Comm 1954-56; MP for Melton Div of Leics (C) 1945-56; Special Writer for New York Herald Tribune 1957-58 and author of "I Saw for Myself" 1958, "Disarmament" 1959, "Europe Will Not Wait" 1960, "Lawrence of Arabia" 1961, "The Arabs" 1964, "Gordon, Martyr and Misfit" 1966, "No End of a Lesson, The Story of Suez" 1967, "Scramble for Africa" 1970, "Nasser" 1972; PC 1954: *m* 1st, 1941 (*m diss* 1959), Gillian Leonora, da of late Capt Edward Jolliffe Strutt (*see* B Rayleigh, colls); 2ndly, 1961, Anne Gunning, who *d* 1990, da of late Arnold Barthrop Parker, of Cuckfield, Sussex; 3rdly, 1991, Margarita, da of late Carlos Sanchez, of Havana, Cuba and has issue living by 1st *m*.

Arms – Chevrony of six gules and vert three gryphons segreant or, on a chief of the last as many nut branches slipped proper. **Crest** – A demi gryphon segreant enclosed between two nut branches proper.
Seat – Achentoul, Kinbrace, Sutherland. *Residence* – 7 Ashchurch Park Villas, W12.

SONS LIVING (By 1st marriage)

JOHN GRENFELL (Chicheley Hall, Newport Pagnall, Bucks MK16 9JJ; Albany, Piccadilly, W1), *b* 28 Aug 1942; *ed* Eton, and McGill Univ, Canada (BA); Bar Middle Temple 1968; elected to Senate of Inns of Court and Bar 1975; Chm of the Young Bar 1978; Treasury Council at Central Criminal Ct since 1981; Trustee Nat Heritage Memorial Fund since 1991: *m* 1973, Diane, da of John Rutherford Blundell, of Havant, Hants, adopted da of Capt Duncan Kirk, and widow of 2nd Earl Beatty, and has issue living, James Edward Sebastian, *b* 12 Jan 1977, — Victoria Emily, *b* 1975. — David Anthony (Newhouse, Terling, Chelmsford, Essex), *b* 1944; *ed* Eton, and Trin Coll, Camb (BA): *m* 1974, Tessa Anne, da of Lt-Col Sir Nigel John Mordaunt, 13th Bt, MBE, and has issue living, Belinda, *b* 1975, — Serena, *b* 1977, — Alexandra, *b* 1979.

DAUGHTER LIVING (By 1st marriage)

Zara Nina, *b* 1947: *m* 1966 (*m diss* 1970), Martin Guy Stephenson (V Hawarden, colls), and has issue living, Katya, *b* 1967.

COLLATERAL BRANCH LIVING

Issue of late Capt Arthur Ronald Stansmore Nutting, OBE, MC, 3rd son of 1st baronet, *b* 1888, *d* 1964: *m* 1st, 1912 (*m diss* 1932), Edith Allen, who *d* 1953, da of Walter Brooks; 2ndly, 1932, Patricia Elizabeth (Stable Cottage, North Breache, Ewhurst, Surrey), da of Henry R. Jameson, of Drumleck, Howth, co Dublin:—

(By 2nd *m*) Peter Robert (North Breache Manor, Ewhurst, Surrey; 103 More Close, St Paul's Court, W14), *b* 1935; *ed* Eton; Late Irish Guards; past Chairman of Edward & John Burke, Ltd; J P (Inner Lond); Financial Consultant and Dir of Companies: *m* 1965, Cecilia Hester Louise Constance, el da of Cosmo Rex Ivor Russell (*see* B Ampthill, colls), and has issue living, William Frederick, *b* 1968, — Rupert Edward, *b* 1971, — Amanda Charlotte, *b* 1966: *m* 1991, James Edward Thornton, eldest son of Michael Thornton, of Ringwood, Hants. — Nicholas Ronald (Yard Farm, Ewhurst, Surrey), *b* 1937; *ed* Eton: *m* 1st, 1962, Caroline Elsie Houghton, da of Brig F. W. Houghton Beckford, RA, of Vancouver, BC; 2ndly, 1977, Annette Moira, da of Percy Charles Briscoe, and has issue living (by 1st *m*), (Ann) Olivia, *b* 1963: *m* 1991, Rupert Hew Williams Barrington, (*see* Barrington, Bt, colls), — Sarah Caroline, *b* 1965: *m* 1991, Sean Eugene John Martin McDonald, elder son of John McDonald, of Ballyholland, Newry, co Down.

The 1st baronet, Sir John Gardiner Nutting, DL, was Chm of E and J Burke, Ltd, a JP and DL, and High Sheriff of co Dublin 1895-6.

OAKELEY (GB) 1790, of Shrewsbury

I fear not, but am cautious

Sir JOHN DIGBY ATHOLL OAKELEY, 8th *Baronet*; *b* 27 Nov 1932; *s* his father, *Sir* (EDWARD) ATHOLL, 1987; *ed* privately; holder of 24 World, European and National sailing titles, author of several books on sailing; Man Dir Miller and Whitworth, Freedom Yachts, Dehler Yachts UK: *m* 1958, Maureen Frances, da of late John Cox, of Hamble, Hants, and has issue.

ᴬrms – Argent, on a fesse between three crescents gules as many fleurs-de-lis or. Crest – A dexter arm, embowed in armour proper charged with two fleurs-de-lis or, each in a crescent gules, in the hand a scimitar proper hilt or.
Residence – 10 Bursledon Heights, Long Lane, Bursledon, Hants.

SON LIVING

ROBERT JOHN ATHOLL, *b* 13 Aug 1963: *m* 1989, Catherine Amanda, da of late William Knowles, FRCS, and has issue living, Olivia Kate, *b* 1993.

DAUGHTER LIVING

Marina Anne, *b* 1961; *ed* Southampton Univ (LLM, BA): *m* 19—, Capt Robert E. Gordon, son of late Frank Gordon, and of Mrs Pamela Davies, of Vancouver, BC, and has issue living, Conrad James, *b* 1991, — Rebecca Elise, *b* 1993.

HALF-SISTER LIVING *(daughter of 7th baronet by 4th marriage)*

Lorna Olivia Athole, *b* 1961; RGN: *m* 1987, Julian Roe, and has issue living, one son and one da. *Residence* – 6 Birbeck Way, Futtenham, Norwich NR12 7LG.

UNCLE LIVING *(brother of 7th baronet)*

Rowland Henry, *b* 1909; *ed* Clifton Coll, and at New Coll, Oxford (BA 1930); in Malayan Civil Ser 1931-58, Commonwealth Relations Office 1959-65, and Diplo Ser 1966-69: *m* 1940, Diana Margaret, da of late John Arthur Hayward, MD, FRCS, and has issue living, Christopher Rowland (175 Short St, Stoneville PO, W Aust 6081), *b* 1941; *ed* Winchester, Trin Coll, Dublin (BA), and Univ of W Aust (MBA): *m* 1973, Margaret, da of late Gilbert Carson, of Merredin, W Aust, and has issue living, Andrew Gilbert *b* 1974, Timothy Christopher *b* 1976, Paul David *b* 1978, Caroline Rachel *b* 1981, — Henry Francis (77 Copers Cope Rd, Beckenham, Kent BR3 1NR), *b* (twin) 1941; *ed* Clifton, and St Thomas's Hosp (MB BS); FRCP (London), MRCPsych, FLS; Consultant Psychiatrist St Thomas's Hosp, SE1: *m* 1968 (*m diss* 1988), Penelope Susan, LRCP, MRCS, da of Wilfred Barlow, BM, BCh, of 3 Albert Court, Kensington Gore, SW7, and has issue living, Matthew Thomas *b* 1968, Edward James *b* 1970, Rachel Mary *b* 1973, — Rosamond Margaret, *b* 1946; *ed* Walthamstow Hall, and Sheffield Univ: *m* 1969, Henry David Warriner (Broadmoor Farm, Little Wolford, Shipston-on-Stour, Warwicks), and has issue living, Michael Francis *b* 1970, Timothy David *b* 1974, Sarah Caroline *b* 1971, — Auriol Mary, *b* 1947; *ed* Walthamstow Hall, Roy Ballet Sch, and Bishop Otter Coll: *m* 1977, Peter Nicolas Chisholm, of Headmaster's House, Yehudi Menuhin School, Cobham, Surrey KT11 3QQ. *Residence* – Gowerbank, Littleworth, Chipping Campden, Glos GL55 6BB.

AUNTS LIVING *(sisters of 7th baronet)*

Rosemary, *b* 1903; *ed* Headington Sch, Oxford, and Evendine Court, Colwall: *m* 1940, Mervyn Cecil ffranck Sheppard, CMG, MBE, Malayan Civil Ser, and has issue living, Lavender Frances, *b* 1941: *m* 1st, 1962 (*m diss* 1981), Richard Giles Saker, Lt RN (ret); 2ndly, 1987, Francis John Buckland, of Tandlaw Steading, Hawick, Roxburghshire TD9 7NY (*see* E Lichfield, colls, 1990 Edn), and has issue living (by 1st *m*), Iain Richard Mark *b* 1962; *ed* Radley; 1st The Queen's Dragoon Gds: *m* 1992, Kate, da of Ian Macdonald, of Higher Hill Farm, Butleigh, Som, Robin David Mervyn *b* 1963; *ed* Radley, Emma-Rose Everilde *b* 1968; *ed* Wychwood Sch, Oxford, and Eastbourne Coll: *m* 1988 (*m diss* 1994), Joseph Jasiewicz (and has issue living, Charles Alexander Francis Beaumont *b* 1992), Zoë Arabella Helena *b* 1970; *ed* Oxford High Sch, and Durham Univ (BA). *Residence* – Linden House, West Wittering, nr Chichester, Sussex P020 8QF. —— Mary, *b* 1913; *ed* St Hilda's Coll, Oxford (MA); Head Mistress of Craighead Diocesan Sch, Timaru, NZ 1940-55; Head Mistress of St Felix Sch, Southwold, Suffolk 1958-78. *Residence* – 8 Newland Close, Eynsham, Oxon OX8 1LE.

WIDOW LIVING OF SEVENTH BARONET

SHIRLEY (*Shirley, Lady Oakeley*) (Nomad, Lynton, Devon), da of Herbert W. Church, of 2 Northwood Rd, Tonbridge, Kent: *m* 1960, as his 4th wife, Sir (Edward) Atholl Oakeley, 7th Bt, who *d* 1987.

This family was long settled at Oakeley, Bishop's Castle, Shropshire, and Sir Charles Oakeley, 1st Bt, was Governor of Madras 1790-94. Sir Charles Richard Andrew Oakeley, 6th Bt, was Joint Managing Director of the firm of Oakeley Vaughan & Co Ltd, insurance brokers. Sir (Edward) Atholl Oakeley, 7th Bt, was European Heavy-weight Wrestling Champion 1932.

OAKES (UK) 1939, of Nassau, Bahama Islands

Sir CHRISTOPHER OAKES, 3rd *Baronet*; *b* 10 July 1949; *s* his father, *Sir* SYDNEY, 1966: *m* 1978, Julie Dawn, da of Donovan Cowan, of Canada, and has issue.

Arms – Or on a fesse sable between in chief an acorn slipped and leaved and in base a maple leaf proper, three maple leaves of the field. Crest – Issuant from a chaplet of roses gules a demi-lion rampant or, grasping in the dexter paw an acorn slipped and leaved proper.
Address – Site 15, Comp 18 RR7, Vernon, BC, Canada V1T 7Z3.

SON LIVING

VICTOR, *b* 6 March 1983.

DAUGHTER LIVING

Greta Anna Eunice, *b* 1979.

SISTERS LIVING

Through difficulties

Felicity, *b* 1952: *m* 1987, Steven Stuart Simpson. —— Virginia Viveca, *b* 1954: *m* 1982, Gavin Andrew McKinney, son of J. Andrew McKinney, and has issue living, Morgan Gavin, *b* 1983, — Sydney Analia (a da), *b* 1987. *Address* – PO Box 556330, Nassau, Bahamas.

UNCLE LIVING (*Son of 1st baronet*)

Harry Philip (PO Box N222, Nassau, Bahamas), *b* 1932: *m* 1958, Christiane, only da of Rudolf Botsch, of Hamburg, Germany, and has issue living, Harry Newell, *b* 1958, — Philip Gale, *b* 1961, — Michael Lewis, *b* 1966, — Bianca Eunice, *b* 1963.

AUNT LIVING (*Daughter of 1st baronet*)

Nancy VON HOYNINGEN-HUENE (PO Box N3229, 28 Queen St, Nassau, Bahamas, and Marsella 44, Mexico 6, DF Mexico), *b* 1925; resumed by deed poll in the Bahamas 1975 the surname of von Hoyningen-Huene: *m* 1st, 1942 (*m* annulled 1949), Alfred de Marigny; 2ndly, 1952 (*m* diss 1956), Baron Ernst-Lyssardt von Hoyningen-Huene; 3rdly, 1962, Patrick Claude Henry Tritton, and has issue living, (by 2nd *m*) *Baron* Alexander George Lyssardt, *b* 1955.

The 1st baronet, Sir Harry Oakes (son of William Pitt Oakes, of Sangerville, Maine, USA), was a Member of Legislative Council of Bahamas.

OAKSHOTT (UK) 1959, of Bebington, co Palatine of Chester

Hon Sir ANTHONY HENDRIE OAKSHOTT, 2nd *Baronet*; *b* 10 Oct 1929; *s* his father, HENDRIE DUDLEY, *Baron Oakshott* (Life Peer) and 1st Baronet, 1975; *ed* Rugby: *m* 1965 (*m* diss 1981), Valerie Anne Doreen, who *d* 1988, da of Jack Vlasto, of 2 Denbigh House, Hans Place, SW1, and formerly wife of (1) Donald John Ross, and (2) Michael de Pret-Roose.

Arms – Per chevron azure and gules in chief two arrows in saltire between as many branches of oak slipped and fructed or an in base a bear passant argent. Crest – In front of a mount vert thereon an oak tree proper fructed gold the main-stem transfixed by two arrows in fesse points to the dexter also proper a bow fessewise or.
Residence – Farmcote, Bledington, Oxfordshire. *Club* – White's.

BROTHER LIVING

Hon MICHAEL ARTHUR JOHN (Isle Tower, Holywood, Dumfries DG2 0RW), *b* 12 April 1932; *ed* Rugby: *m* 1st, 1957, Christina Rose Methuen, who *d* 1985, da of late Thomas Banks, of Solai, Kenya; 2ndly, 1988, Mrs Helen Clare JONES, da of late Edward Ravell, of Woodhall Spa, Lincs, and has issue living (by 1st *m*), Thomas Hendrie, *b* 1959, — Charles Michael (Fares Stables Ltd, Newsells Park, Barkway, Royston, Herts), *b* 1961: *m* 1989, Anne C., da of William Stapleton, of Newry, co Down, and has issue living, Roseanne *b* 1990, Alice *b* 1993. —— Angus Withington, *b* 1965.

Sir Hendrie Dudley Oakshott, MBE, 2nd son of Arthur John Oakshott of Merle Dene, Bidsdon, Cheshire, was a Lord Commr of HM Treasury 1952-55, Comptroller of HM Household 1955-57, Treasurer 1957-59, and PPS to Sec of State for Foreign Affairs 1959-60, and to Chancellor of Exchequer 1961-62; MP for Bebington (*C*) 1950-64; *cr* a Baronet 1959, and Baron Oakshott, of Bebington, co Palatine of Chester (Life Baron) 1964.

O'BRIEN (UK) 1849, of Merrion Square, Dublin, and Boris-in-Ossory, Queen's County

The strong hand uppermost

Sir TIMOTHY JOHN O'BRIEN, 7th *Baronet*; *b* 6 July 1958; *s* his grand-father, *Sir* DAVID EDMOND, 1982; *ed* Millfield.

Arms – Argent, three lions passant-guardant per pale gules and azure, armed or, all within a bordure vert. **Crest** – From a castle argent in flames, a naked arm embowed, the hand grasping a sword, all proper.
Residence –

BROTHER LIVING

JAMES PATRICK ARLAND, *b* 22 Dec 1964; *ed* Millfield.

SISTERS LIVING

Doone Victoria, *b* 1959. —— Melanie Frances Ann, *b* 1961.

AUNT LIVING (*Daughter of 6th baronet*)

Audrey Mary, *b* 1935: *m* 1963, Conrad Andrew Roman Dobrzynski, of Brand Hall, Norton in Hales, Market Drayton, Shropshire TF9 3PT, and has issue living, Sophia Catherine *b* 1966, — Emma Natasha, *b* 1972.

DAUGHTER LIVING OF FIFTH BARONET

Mary Clare (43 Finstock Rd, W10), *b* 1943: *m* 1st, 1961 (*m diss* 1976), John Peter James Hare; 2ndly, 1990, Frederick Edward Pearson, and has issue living (by 1st *m*), David John Brent (68 Dalgarno Gdns, W10), *b* 1963, — Kerry-Jane, *b* 1966: *m* 1989, Stephen Henry Martin, of Bay Tree Cottage, Farmington, nr Northleach, Glos GL56 3DN, son of R. Martin.

DAUGHTERS LIVING OF FOURTH BARONET

Patricia Mary Gabrielle (45 Burntwood Grange Rd, Wandsworth Common, SW18 3JY): *m* 1955 (*m diss* 1961), Walter William Burgoyne Chalwin, and has issue living, Simon William Burgoyne (77 Hendham Rd, Wandsworth, SW17 7DH), *b* 1956: *m* 1983, Teresa Mary Young, — Nicola Clare, *b* 1957: *m* 1st, 1978 (*m diss* 1981), Nicholas George Mark Seymour (*see* M Hertford colls); 2ndly, 1981, Richard Eric Champion Jones, of 37 Lower Camden, Chislehurst, Kent. —— Sheelagh Tessa Ursula: *m* 1954, Caird Wentworth Gordon Wilson, son of late Lt-Gen Sir Gordon Wilson, KCSI, CB, CBE, MC, and has issue living, Robert Caird, *b* 1955: *m* 1993, Diana Rosemary, da of David Lethbridge, of Hawkes Bay, NZ, and has issue living, Rebecca Frances *b* 1994, — Alexander Hugh Gordon, *b* 1957: *m* 1982, Susan Katharine, da of Capt H. R. C. Young, RN (ret), and has issue living, Philip Hugh Caird *b* 1984, Angus Robert Gordon *b* 1992, Miranda Frances Katharine *b* 1986. *Residence* – Church Farm House, Melbury Abbas, Shaftesbury, Dorset SP7 0EA. —— Shaunagh Gundrede: *m* 1972, John Nares Addinsell, who *d* 1991. *Residence* – The Old Hall, Brilley, Whitney-on-Wye, Hereford.

MOTHER LIVING

Sheila Winifred, only da of Sir Charles Arland Maitland Freake, 4th Bt (ext): *m* 1957, John David O'Brien, el son of 6th Bt, who *d* 1980.

COLLATERAL BRANCH LIVING

Issue of late Gerald Patrick O'Brien, yr son of 6th Bt, *b* 1930, *d* 1979: *m* 1960, Frances Huband de Savoie (30 Applegarth Rd, W14), yst da of Col William Thornton Huband Gregg, DSO, OBE, of Ballyknockane House, Clonmel, co Tipperary:—
Lyndall Jane, *b* 1961. —— Lucy Frances, *b* 1964. —— Rachel Shirin, *b* 1965. —— Deborah Susan, *b* 1969.

This family claims to represent the powerful house of O'Brien Ara, of the line of Thomond. Sir Timothy O'Brien, son of Timothy O'Brien of co Tipperary, 1st Bt, MP for Cashel (*L*) 1846-59, was a merchant of Dublin who took a leading part in the reform of its Corporation and contributed largely to the redemption of the Municipal property. He was Lord Mayor of Dublin 1844 and again 1849, being specially elected to receive Her Majesty on her first visiting Ireland, on which occasion he was created a baronet. Sir Patrick, 2nd Bt, sat as MP for King's co (*L*) 1852-85. Sir Timothy Carew, 3rd Bt, was a DL and JP of co Cork, and served in 1914-18 War as Capt R Irish Fusiliers, and as Maj Remount Ser (despatches).

O'CONNELL (UK) 1869, of Lakeview, Killarney, co Kerry, and of Ballybeggan, Tralee, co Kerry

Reason and strength

Sir MAURICE JAMES DONAGH MacCARTHY O'CONNELL, 7th *Baronet*; *b* 10 June 1958; *s* his father, *Sir* MORGAN DONAL CONAIL, 1989; *ed* Ampleforth: *m* 1993, Francesca Susan, only da of Clive Raleigh, of Hong Kong.

Arms – Per fesse argent and vert, a stag trippant proper between three trefoils slipped counterchanged. **Crest** – A stag's head erased argent, charged with trefoil slipped vert (Ulster Office 1667).
Residence – Lakeview House, Killarney, Co Kerry.

BROTHER LIVING

JOHN MORGAN ROSS MacCARTHY, *b* 17 April 1960; *ed* Ampleforth, Regents Park Coll, Oxford (MA), and Guildhall Sch of Music (AGSM).

SISTERS LIVING

Frances Mary Margaret MacCarthy, *b* 1954: *m* 1986, Roy W. Telling, of Turnpike Cottage, London Rd, Blewbury, nr Didcot, Oxon, only son of late W. Telling, of Wolverhampton, and has issue living, Ross Morgan William, *b* 1989. —— Susan Jane Anne, *b* 1956: *m* 1993, Julian R. Glasgow, yr son of Dr James Glasgow, of Rockland St Mary, Norwich. —— Katherine Lucila Jean, *b* 1964. —— Claire Helen Pauline, *b* 1969.

AUNT LIVING (*Daughter of 5th baronet*)

Joan Mary Lucilla Margaret, *b* 1926; formerly 3rd Officer WRNS: *m* 1953, Lieut-Com John Allen Victor Hickley, RN (ret), of Birchdale, RD10, Waimate, S Canterbury, NZ, and has issue living, Martin Maurice Victor, *b* 1957: *m* 1984, Robyn Myrie, eldest da of Douglas Williams Jenkins, of Mosgiel, NZ, and has issue living, Cameron Douglas Victor *b* 1988, Patrick Joseph Victor *b* 1991, Joanna Louise *b* 1985, — Grania Margaret Leslie, *b* 1959.

WIDOW LIVING OF SIXTH BARONET

ELIZABETH (*Elizabeth, Lady O'Connell*), only child of late Maj John MacCarthy-O'Leary, of Lavenders, West Malling, Kent: *m* 1953, Sir Morgan Donal Conail O'Connel, 6th Bt, who *d* 1989. *Residence* – Lakeview House, Killarney, co Kerry.

COLLATERAL BRANCH LIVING

Issue of late Basil Morgan O'Connell, KPM, yst son of 4th baronet, *b* 1900, *d* 1971: *m* 1st, 1935, Lucila, who *d* 1953, da of Maj Henry Hugh Peter Deasy, of Cnoc Na Faire, Carrigahorig, Eire; 2ndly, 1962, Georgia Bard Shearer (Box 131, Solebury, Pa 18963, USA), widow of Mortimer Haldeman O'Connor:—
(By 1st *m*) Maurice Hugh Ricardo Ross (12 Rostrevor Rd, Dublin 6), *b* 1936; *ed* Ampleforth, Peterhouse, Camb (MA) and Trin Coll, Dublin (MEd, HDip Ed); NUI (Dip Cat) a Member of Dublin City Council 1967-74; Seanad Eireann 1981-83, Nat Exec, Fine Gael Party; Replacement Candidate, European Parl Elections, Dublin 1984: *m* 1961, Ann, el da of Hugh Gillespie, of the Old Rectory, Kiltegan, Baltinglass, co Wicklow, and has issue living, Carlos Donal John, *b* 1963; Irish Junior Decathlon Champion, — Morgan Basil Peter, *b* 1965, — Maurice William Hugh Rickard, *b* 1966, — Ross Paul Francis, *b* 1968, — Lucila Marie Valdemara Georgia, *b* 1962, — Sarah Emily, *b* 1973. —— Seamus Morgan Basil Ross, *b* 1941; *ed* Ampleforth, and Trin Coll, Dublin (BA).

The 1st baronet was the yst and last surviving brother of Daniel O'Connell, QC, MP, of Darrinane Abbey, Senior Representative of the ancient Irish sept of O'Connell, and nephew of Lieut-Gen Count Daniel O'Connell of the French Service by whose efforts the officers of the disbanded French Irish Brig enrolled in the Service of King George III in 1794.

OGILVY (NS) 1626, of Inverquharity, Forfarshire

I despise earthly dangers

Sir FRANCIS GILBERT ARTHUR OGILVY, 14th *Baronet*; *b* 22 April 1969; *s* his father, *Sir* DAVID JOHN WILFRID, 1992; *ed* Glenalmond, and RAC Cirencester.

Arms – Quarterly: 1st and 4th, argent, a lion passant-guardant gules, gorged with an open crown, and crowned with a close imperial one or, *Ogilvy*; 2nd and 3rd, argent, an eagle displayed sable, beaked and membered gules, *Ramsay of Auchterhouse*. **Crest** – A demi-lion gules. **Supporters** – Two wild men wreathed about the head and temples with leaves, trampling upon serpents, and holding branches in their exterior hands all proper.
Seat – Winton House, Pencaitland, East Lothian.
Residence – Winton Cottage, Pencaitland, East Lothian EH34 5AT.

AUNTS LIVING *(Sisters of 13th baronet)*

Katharine Olivia Mary, *b* 1916: *m* 1947, William Packe, of Low Wood, Winthorpe, Newark, Notts, son of Charles James Melville Packe, of Rothley, Leics, and has issue living, Thomas Gilbert (East Philipstoun Farmhouse, Linlithgow, W Lothian EH49 7RY), *b* 1948; *ed* Gordonstoun, and RAC Cirencester: *m* 1994, Sally Margaret, yr da of late Maj John Basil Ready, — Andrew James (The Steward's House, Bledington, Oxford OX7 6UZ), *b* 1951; *ed* Radley, and RAC Cirencester: *m* 1981, Aloÿse Anne, only da of Christopher James Morrell Blackie, and has issue living, Frederick Christopher William *b* 1987, Olivia Aloÿse Hester *b* 1984. —— Hester Mary, *b* 1921; *ed* Edinburgh Univ (MA), and Oxford Univ (BA): *m* 1951, David Scott of Glenaros, of Glenaros, Aros, Isle of Mull, elder son of late Sir Basil Scott, former Chief Justice of Bombay, and has issue living, Colum Basil, *b* 1954; *ed* Stowe, and RAC Cirencester: *m* 1992, Sarah Louise, yr da of Michael Charles Watson Credland, and has issue living, Angus Michael David *b* 1993, — Margaret Isobel, *b* 1952: *m* 1991, Brian Simons, and has issue living, Jamie Mark *b* 1987, Samuel Isaac Michael *b* 1992, — Christian Mary Gertrude, *b* 1955: *m* 1984, Anthony Latham, son of Leslie Latham, and has issue living, Andrew David *b* 1987, Brendan Michael *b* 1994, Helen *b* 1986, Mairi Isobel *b* 1992, — Helen Olivia Katharine, *b* 1958: *m* 19—, Alistair Danter, son of John Danter, and has issue living, Fiona Marie Josée *b* 1993.

WIDOW LIVING OF THIRTEENTH BARONET

PENELOPE MARY URSULA (*Lady Ogilvy*), only da of late Capt Arthur Lafone Frank Hills, OBE, of White Court, Penshurst Station, Kent: *m* 1966, Sir David John Wilfrid Ogilvy, 13th Bt, who *d* 1992. *Residence* – Winton Cottage, Pencaitland, East Lothian EH34 5AT.

COLLATERAL BRANCHES LIVING

Issue of late Capt Frederick Charles Ashley Ogilvy, RN, 3rd son of 10th baronet, *b* 1866, *d* 1909: *m* 1904, Gertrude Lilian (who *d* 1971, having *m* 2ndly, 1913, 9th Earl of Elgin and Kincardine, who *d* 1917; 3rdly, 1923, Lt-Col John Alexander Stirling of Kippendavie, DSO, MC, who *d* 1957), da of late Cdr William Sherbrooke, formerly RN, of Oxton Hall, Southwell, Notts:—
Ann Howard, *b* 1905: *m* 1932, John Gurney, JP, el son of late Sir Eustace Gurney, and has had issue, Priscilla Ann, *b* 1937: *m* 1958, W. Gregory F. Meath Baker, of Hasfield Court, Gloucester, and has issue living, (William John) Clovis *b* 1959; *ed* Eton, and Oxford Univ: *m* 1985, Elizabeth Diana, eldest da of Charles Woodham-Smith, of Earls Court, SW5 (and has issue living, Boadicea Louisa Ann *b* 1988, Agnes Charlotte Gertrude *b* 1990, Constance Daffodil Bohemia *b* 1992), (Samuel) Justin (Francis) *b* 1961; *ed* Eton, and Edinburgh Sch of Art: *m* 1989, Eliza Rose Robertson, yst da of Air Vice Marshal Geoffrey Cairns, CBE, AFC, of Powells, Kenn, Devon (and has had issue, Samuel Romulus *b* and *d* 1992, Hannibal Eustace Pilate *b* 1993) Hugh Lysander Luke *b* 1964; *ed* Eton, Joshua Ralph *b* 1965; *ed* Eton, and Courtauld Inst, — Jean Elizabeth (*Lady Mayhew*), *b* 1939: *m* 1963, Rt Hon Sir Patrick Barnabas Burke Mayhew, QC, MP (HM Attorney Gen since 1987), of Twysden, Kilndown, nr Cranbrook, Kent, and has issue living, James Barnabas Burke *b* 1964, Henry Edmund Burke *b* 1965, Tristram Thomas Burke *b* 1968, Jerome Patrick Burke *b* 1970, — Elizabeth Olivia, *b* 1943: *m* 1968, Timothy Arnold Neil Bristol, of The Chantry, Ely, Cambs, and has issue living, Benjamin Timothy Fitzroy *b* 1972, Samuel Frederick John *b* 1983, Arabella Fredericka Ann *b* 1970, — Elizabeth Rachel *b* 1946; *d* 1982, — Ruth Christian *b* 1948: *m* 1970, Maj George Clive Forestier-Walker, Coldm Gds, of Mulberry House, Heather Drive, Sunningdale, Berks (*see* Forestier-Walker, Bt, colls). *Residence* – Walsingham Abbey, Norfolk.

Issue of late Lt Cmdr John Augustine Ogilvy, RN, brother of 13th baronet and yr son of late Gilbert Francis Molyneux Ogilvy, JP, yst son of 10th baronet, *b* 1915, *d* 1993: *m* 1942, Margaret Vivienne Lyndall (Old North Manse, E Linton, E Lothian), eldest da of late Col William Thornton Huband Gregg, DSO, OBE, late Royal Irish Fus, of Ballynockane House, co Tipperary:—
†Angus William, *b* 1945; *ed* Eton, and Stirling Univ (BA Hons): *m* 1st, 1968 (*m diss* 1980), Sally, da of Michael Long; 2ndly, 1980, Helen (6 Queen's Rd, King Park, Stirling FK8 2QY), da of John Dudley Massingham, CMG, of Pershore, Worcs, and *d* 1989, leaving issue, (by 1st *m*) ANDREW JOHN, *b* 23 April 1972, — Robert Iain Michael, *b* 1974, — (by 2nd *m*) James Angus John, *b* 1982, — Thomas Alasdair William, *b* 1984. — Diana Lyndall, *b* 1946.

Grandchildren of late Walter Tulliedeph Ogilvy (*b* 1852) (*infra*):—
Issue of late Angus Edward Ogilvy, *b* 1880, *d* 1928: *m* 1910, Margaret, who *d* 1956, da of Lieut-Col Sir James Frederick Stuart-Menteth, 4th Bt, of Rownhams Mount, near Southampton:—
†Walter Tulliedeph, *b* 1911: *m* 1st, 1947, Christina Alexandra Sutherland, who *d* 1949, da of A. Polson, of Spinningdale, Sutherland; 2ndly, 1950, Audrey Kingsley, da of A. G. Weeks, of Limpsfield, Surrey, and *d* 1987, leaving issue, (by 2nd *m*) Fiona Audrey, *b* 1952: *m* 1974 (*m diss* 1980), Christopher Cook, and has issue living, Nicola Jane *b* 1975, Claire Annabel *b* 1977, — Susan Margaret, *b* 1955: *m* 1974 (*m diss* 1978), John Pelly. *Residence* – Rosemary Cottage, Buxted, Sussex.
Issue of late Brigadier David Ogilvy, CIE, DSO, OBE, *b* 1881, *d* 1949: *m* 1906, Vere Grace, da of late Sir Henry Fawcett, KCMG, Ch Justice of the Levant:—
Vere Edith OGILVY, *b* 1912; resumed by deed poll 1955 the surname of Ogilvy: *m* 1932, Lt-Col Charles Herbert Harberton Eales, MC, Indian Cav, who *d* 1941, and has issue living, John David OGILVY, *b* 1934; assumed by deed poll 1955 the surname of Ogilvy in lieu of his patronymic; *ed* Wellington Coll; Lt-Cdr RN (ret): *m* 1958, Felicity Neilson, da of late Maj Hugh Jack Melville, of Wendover, Bucks, and has issue living, David Guy Francis Melville *b* 1960, Alasdair James Eales (Battlehurst, Kirdford, W Sussex) *b* 1961: *m* 1989, Fleur S. C., da of Ian Vergin Brooke, of The Quell, Blackdown, W Sussex (and has issue living, Flora Alexandra Claire *b* 1992), — Mary Ann Vere, *b* 1935: *m* 1st, 1957 (*m diss* 1973), Charles Pepler Norton; 2ndly, 1980, Capt James Quintin Penn Curzon (*see* E Howe, colls), who *d* 1985; 3rdly, 1987, as his 2nd wife, Maj John David Makgill-Crichton-Maitland (*see* E Lauderdale, colls), and has issue living, (by 1st *m*) Anthony Charles Pepler *b*

1958: *m* 19—, S. C. Jane, only da of Dr Keith Haward Bywater, of Haward House, Old Road, Ruddington, Notts (and has issue living, Edward James Pepler *b* 1987), Julian Alexander Pepler *b* 1959, Marina Caroline Vere *b* 1961: *m* 1985, Capt James Farquhar Robin Campbell, late The Queen's Own Highlanders (*see* E Cawdor, colls), Josephine Sarah Vere *b* 1964.
 Issue of late Walter Tulliedeph Ogilvy, *b* 1883, *d* 1912: *m* 1910, Nora, who *d* 1958, da of Rev Canon Thomas Hewan Archdale, JP, formerly V of Tanfield, Tantobie, co Durham, and Rural Dean:—
Mary Archdale, *b* 1910: *m* 1933, Bryan Stuart Potter, and has issue living, David Stuart, *b* 1934; *ed* Gordonstoun, and Witwatersrand Univ, S Africa (BScEng): *m* 1961, Dorothy Anne, da of H. Longden, of S Hawke, Woldingham, Surrey, and has issue living, Andrew Tulliedeph *b* 1963, James Henry Stuart *b* 1964, Charles David Ogilvy *b* 1967, Helen Ruth *b* 1969, — Timothy Stuart, *b* 1938: *m* 1963, Joan Louise, da of F. St Leger Wills, and has issue living, Julian Frederick Stuart *b* 1964, Thomas George Stuart *b* 1969, Sophie Elizabeth *b* 1966, — Tulliedeph Ogilvy Stuart, *b* 1942: *m* 1st, 19—; 2ndly, 19—; 2ndly, 19—, Jill, da of F. Muddiman, and has issue living, Rachel Margaret *b* 1976, Miriam Nora Louise *b* 1978, — Charles Stuart, *b* 1946: *m* 1970, Maeve Elfrida, da of D. Band, and has issue living, Douglas Luke Charles *b* 1978, Josephine Isabelle *b* 1981, — Roderick Alexander Stuart, *b* 1953: *m* 1976, Rosemary Jane, da of P. Mallett, and has issue living, Randolph Bryan Stuart *b* 1976, Christopher Paul Stuart *b* 1981, — Valerie Stuart, *b* 1936: *m* 1972, Anthony Greville Drew. *Address* – Box 26 Bergvlei, Transvaal 2012, S Africa.
 Issue of late Lieut-Col Gilbert Mark Haworth Ogilvy, King's Own Scottish Borderers, *b* 1887, *d* on active ser 1945: *m* 1915, Mildred Scott, who *d* 1925:—
Mildred Cecil, *b* 1916: *m* 1944, Lieut Thomas Duerdin-Dutton, RNVR.

  Granddaughter of late David Ogilvy, son of late Alexander Ogilvy, 6th son of 5th baronet:—
 Issue of late Walter Tulliedeph Ogilvy, *b* 1852, *d* 1927: *m* 1st, 1878, Eleanor May Edith Lumley, who *d* 1902, da of late Edward Lumley Haworth, 28th Regt; 2ndly, 1903, Winifred, who *d* 1909, da of Rev Henry Edward Maskew; 3rdly, 1910, Christina, who *d* 1956, da of Col Bannatyne Macleod, formerly Bombay Artillery:—
(By 2nd *m*) Earna, *b* (twin) 1909: *m* 1931, W. J. Forrester, who *d* 1975, and has issue living, David Alton (18 Shasta Rd, Lesmurdie, W Aust), *b* 1932; *ed* Camb Univ (MA, LLM, ACIS); Barrister: *m* 1959, Fay Garner, who *d* 1979, and has issue living, Richard Alton *b* 1961, Susan May *b* 1965, — Thelma *b* 1934: *m* 1960, Neil Pearson, of Box BE46, Belvedere, Harare, Zimbabwe, and has issue living, Lesley Dawn *b* 1961, Janette Nancy *b* 1962. *Residence* – c/o 18 Shasta Rd, Lesmurdie, W Aust.
 Issue of late Angus Ogilvy, *b* 1855, *d* 1928: *m* 1886, Rose Serena, who *d* 1923, da of late Abercromby Dick, WS, and Bar-at-law:—
Abercromby Graham, *b* 1889; *ed* Marlborough; Lt-Col (ret) Indian Army; Mohmand Expedition 1915, Afghanistan 1919, Waziristan 1920: *m* 1923, Sibyl Mary Abbott Green, of East Donyland Hall, Colchester.

Sir John Ogilvy was created a Baronet with remainder to heirs male whatsoever. The 2nd baronet was MP for Angus 1665-78. The 5th baronet sold the estate of Inverquharity, which had been in the family for fourteen generations. Sir John, 9th Bt, sat as MP for Dundee (*L*) 1857-74. The 11th baronet Sir Gilchrist Nevill, Lieut Scots Guards, was killed in action during European War Oct 1914.

Ogilvy-Wedderburn, see Wedderburn.

OHLSON (UK) 1920, of Scarborough, North Riding of co of Yorkshire

Sir BRIAN ERIC CHRISTOPHER OHLSON, 3rd *Baronet*; *b* 27 July 1936; *s* his father, Sir ERIC JAMES, 1983; *ed* Harrow, and RMA; late Lieut Coldstream Gds; money broker (ret).

Arms – Argent, in waves of the sea a steamer proper, on a chief azure three fir trees eradicated also proper. **Crest** – In front of a sun in splendour proper, a motor wheel sable.
Residence – 1 Courtfield Gdns, SW5 0PA. *Clubs* – Hurlingham, MCC, and Cavalry and Guards'.

BROTHER LIVING

PETER MICHAEL, *b* 18 May 1939; *ed* Harrow, and Trin Coll, Camb (BA): *m* 1968, Sarah, only da of Maj-Gen Thomas Brodie, CB, CBE, DSO. *Residence* – 33 The Avenue, Kew, Surrey TW9 2AL.

SISTER LIVING

Christine Rose, *b* 1950.

Do to others as thyself

WIDOW LIVING OF SECOND BARONET

MARJORIE JOAN (*Lady Ohlson*), 2nd da of late Charles Henry Roosmale-Cocq, of Dorking, Surrey: *m* 1935, Sir Eric James Ohlson, 2nd Bt, who *d* 1983. *Residence* – Half Penny House, 287 Petersham Rd, Richmond, Surrey.

COLLATERAL BRANCH LIVING

 Issue of late Gerald Thomas Ohlson, 2nd son of 1st baronet, *b* 1917, *d* 1971: *m* 1943, Marjorie Beryl, da of Trevor Davies:—
Christopher Mark, *b* 1944.

The first baronet, Sir Erik Olof Ohlson (who had been knighted in 1915), son of Anders Ohlson, of Fellingsbro, Sweden, was a shipowner, a coal and coke exporter, and a timber importer, of Hull.

WALKER-OKEOVER (UK) 1886, of Gateacre Grange, co Lancaster, and Osmaston Manor, co Derby

Sir PETER RALPH LEOPOLD WALKER-OKEOVER, 4th *Baronet*; *b* 22 July 1947; *s* his father, *Lt-Col Sir* IAN PETER ANDREW MONRO, DSO, TD, 1982; *ed* Eton, and RMA Sandhurst; Capt Blues and Royals; DL Staffs 1992; patron of one living: *m* 1972 (*m diss* 1991), Catherine Mary Maule, el da of Col George Patrick Maule Ramsay (*see* Dalhousie, colls), and has issue.

Arms – Quarterly, 1st and 4th, ermine, on a chief gules three bezants, *Okeover*; 2nd and 3rd or, three pallets gules surmounted of a saltire argent charged with a stag's head erased proper on a chief azure a garb between two stars of six points of the first, *Walker*. Crests – 1st, an oak tree eradicated proper fructed or mantled gules doubled argent; 2nd, out of a ducal coronet or a dragon ermine armed azure langued gules, mantled gules doubled argent, both *Okeover*; 3rd, a cornucopia proper, *Walker*.
Seats – Okeover Hall, Ashbourne, Derbyshire; House of Glenmuick, Ballater, Aberdeenshire.

SONS LIVING

ANDREW PETER MONRO, *b* 22 May 1978. —— (Patrick) Ralph, *b* 1982.

DAUGHTER LIVING

Georgina Elizabeth, *b* 1976.

SISTERS LIVING

Elizabeth Anne, *b* 1940: *m* 1969, Lt-Cdr Timothy William Clowes, RN (ret), and has issue living, Catriona Helen, *b* 1971, — Sophie Fiona, *b* 1974. —— Jane Katharine, *b* 1942.

WIDOW LIVING OF THIRD BARONET

DOROTHY ELIZABETH (*Elizabeth, Lady Walker-Okeover*) (Park Cottage, Osmaston, Ashbourne, Derbyshire DE6 1LT), da of late Josceline Reginald Heber Percy (*see* D Northumberland, colls): *m* 1938, Lt-Col Sir Ian Peter Andrew Monro Walker-Okeover, 3rd Bt, DSO, TD, who *d* 1982.

COLLATERAL BRANCHES LIVING

Granddaughter of late Col John Reid WALKER, TD, 2nd son of 1st baronet:—
Issue of late Capt Codrington Gwynne Reid Walker, *b* 1895, *d* 1963: *m* 1921, Gwendoline Phyllis, who *d* 1974, da of late James Munro Walker (infra):—
Jean, *b* 1922; WRNS 1942-45: *m* 1949, Nicholas Knoop, BSc(Eng), FICE, of Ville ès Normans, Trinity, Jersey, CI, and has issue living, Alexander Jonathan, *b* 1951: *m* 1988, Sal Magundi, — Sandra, *b* 1950: *m* 1973, Jean-Paul Vonrospach, of 11 Rue des Etats, 54000 Nancy, France, and has issue living, Alexander Kerry *b* 1982, Melany Claire *b* 1980.

Granddaughter of Capt Codrington Gwynne Reid WALKER (ante):—
Issue of late Giles Reid Walker, *b* 1925, *d* 1951: *m* 1949, Catherine Elaine (who *m* 2ndly, 1955, Patrick Campbell Hall, of Cae Grugog, Trearddur Bay, Holyhead, Anglesey), da of late Maj Charles Edward Hickman (*see* Hickman, Bt, colls):—
Gilean Phyllis (*posthumous*), *b* 1951.

The 1st baronet, Sir Andrew Barclay Walker (son of Peter Walker, of Auchinflower, near Ballantrae, co Ayr, and Warrington, co Lancaster), was Mayor of Liverpool 1873-4, and 1876-7 and High Sheriff of Lancashire 1886, and made many munificent gifts to the City of Liverpool. The 2nd baronet, Lt-Col Sir Peter Carlaw Walker, TD: *m* 1899, Ethel Blanche, sister and co-heir of Haughton Ealdred Okeover, MVO, of Okeover, Staffs, descended from Orme de Okeover living 1138. The 3rd baronet, Sir Ian Peter Andrew Monro Walker-Okeover, assumed by Roy Licence 1956 the additional surname of Okeover after his patronymic, and the Arms of Okeover quarterly with those of Walker.

O'LOGHLEN (UK) 1838, of Drumconora, Ennis

The anchor of safety

(Name pronounced "O'lochlen")

Sir COLMAN MICHAEL O'LOGHLEN, LLB, 6th *Baronet*, son of late Henry Ross O'Loghlen, 6th son of 3rd baronet; *b* 6 April 1916; *s* his uncle, Sir CHARLES HUGH ROSS, 1951; *ed* Xavier Coll, Melbourne, and Melbourne Univ; is a Stipendiary Magistrate, Lae, Territory of New Guinea, and late Capt Australian Imperial Force; was Acting Judge of Supreme Court of Territory of Papua and New Guinea May to Aug 1957: *m* 1939, Margaret, da of Francis O'Halloran, of Melbourne, Australia, and has issue.

Arms – Gules, a man in armour in the act of shooting an arrow from a longbow towards the sinister, all proper. Crest – On a ducal coronet or, an anchor erect entwined with a cable, all proper.
Residence – Ellengrove, Queensland 4077, Australia.

SONS LIVING

MICHAEL, *b* 21 May 1945. —— Bryan, *b* 1946. —— Ross, *b* 1948. —— Hugh, *b* 1952.

DAUGHTERS LIVING

Margaret, *b* 1940. —— Janet, *b* 1942.

SISTERS LIVING

Ella Allison: *m* 1944, John Cardiff O'Connell, Flying Officer Roy Australian Air Force, and has issue living, Ross John *b* 1945. —— Doreen Sinclair.

AUNTS LIVING (*Daughters of 3rd baronet*)

Ella Maude: *m* 1922, George Herbert Williams, who *d* 1957, son of late Hon Sir Hartley Williams. —— Frances Mary; a nun. —— Clare Mary.

MOTHER LIVING

Doris Irene, da of late Percival Horne, RA: *m* 1912, Henry Ross O'Loghlen (ante), who *d* 1944. *Residence* – Melbourne, Australia.

COLLATERAL BRANCHES LIVING

Issue of late Bryan James O'Loghlen, 4th son of 3rd baronet, *b* 1875, *d* 1920: *m* 1909, Violet Elizabeth Amelia, who *d* 1951, da of late Daniel Grant, of Bendigo, Australia:—
Elizabeth: *m* 1944, Fl-Lt Ian Cutler, RAAF, of 50 Madeline St, Burwood, Melbourne, Aust, and has issue living, Elizabeth Ann, *b* 1945, — Felicity Margaret, *b* 1948.

Granddaughter of late Henry Ross O'Loghlen, 6th son of 3rd baronet:—
Issue of late Ross Bryan O'Loghlen, Flying Officer Roy Australian Air Force, *b* 1914, presumed *d* (as a prisoner in Japanese hands) 1944: *m* 1941, Phyllis, da of George Nason, of Horsham, Victoria, Australia:—
Susan Anne, *b* 1943.

The 1st baronet, Right Hon Sir Michael, a distinguished lawyer, was MP for Dungarvan (L) 1835-6, a Baron of the Exchequer in Ireland 1836-7, and Master of the Rolls there 1837-42. He was the first Roman Catholic who, since the Revolution of 1688, was raised to a judicial office either in England or Ireland. The 2nd baronet was a Privy Councillor, and MP for co Clare (L) 1863-77. The 3rd baronet was Attorney-Gen of Victoria (Australia) 1878-81, Premier thereof 1881-3, and again Attorney-Gen 1893-4, and sat as MP for co Clare (HR) 1877-9. The 4th baronet was HM's Lieut for co Clare.

ONSLOW (GB) 1797, of Althain, Lancashire

Forward with caution

Sir JOHN ROGER WILMOT ONSLOW, 8th *Baronet*; *b* 21 July 1932; *s* his father, *Sir* RICHARD WILMOT, TD, 1963; *ed* Cheltenham: *m* 1st, 1955 (*m diss* 1973), Catherine Zoia, da of Henry Atherton Greenway, of The Manor, Compton Abdale, nr Cheltenham; 2ndly, 1976, Susan Fay, 2nd da of E. M. Hughes, of Frankston, Vic, Aust, and has issue by 1st *m*.

Arms – Argent, a fesse gules between six Cornish choughs proper. *Crest* – An eagle sable preying upon a partridge or. *Second Motto* – 'Semper fidelis' (*Always faithful*).
Address – c/o Barclays Bank, Fowey, Cornwall. *Club* – Nautico (Majorca).

SON LIVING (*By 1st marriage*)

RICHARD PAUL ATHERTON, *b* 16 Sept 1958.

DAUGHTER LIVING (*By 1st marriage*)

Joanna Elizabeth, *b* 1956.

SISTERS LIVING

Tessa Elizabeth, *b* 1930: *m* 1st, 1953 (*m diss* 1964), John Leonard Hargrave; 2ndly, 1969, John Vernon Mossman, and has issue living (by 1st *m*), Belinda Anne Constance, *b* 1955, — Jane, *b* 1956. —— Jill Angela, *b* 1941: *m* 1962, Patrick E. Lavin, of Casilla 14220, Santiago 15, Chile, and has issue living, Sean Paul, *b* 1967, — Christopher Patrick, *b* 1970, — Cecily Ann, *b* 1965. —— Sally Constance, *b* 1946.

AUNT LIVING (*Daughter of 6th baronet*)

Ursula Joan, *b* 1916: *m* 1948, John Archibald Harris and has issue living, Robert James Onslow, *b* 1952, — Geoffrey Archibald Onslow, *b* 1954, — Richard Charles Onslow, *b* 1958. *Residence* – 20 Ridgeway Rd, Salisbury, Wilts.

COLLATERAL BRANCHES LIVING

Issue of late John Vernon Onslow, yr son of 6th baronet, *b* 1919, *d* 1985; *m* 1946, Anne Broun (Luckington Manor Stables, Luckington, Chippenham, Wilt), da of Gavin Hutchison:—
Charlotte Anne Mildred, *b* 1947: *m* 1974, Charles E. Wilkinson, of The Coach House, Sutton Benger, Chippenham, Wilts, and has issue living, James Maurice, *b* 1975, — John Charles, *b* 1977, — Anne Nora, *b* 1980. —— Victoria Joy Nora, *b* 1950: *m* 1972, (Lionel) Jeffrey Lippiatt, of Manor Farm, Alderton, Chippenham, Wilts, and has issue living, Miranda Kate, *b* 1978, — Emma Suzanna, *b* 1982.

Grandchildren of late Rev Matthew Richard Septimus Onslow, 4th son of 4th baronet:—
Issue of late Capt Richard Francis John Onslow, MVO, DSC, RN, *b* 1896, *ka* 1942: *m* 1st, 1920, Sylvia Rachel, who *d* 1933, da of Rev Alfred Edward Green-Price, V of Norton, Radnorshire (Green-Price, Bt); 2ndly, 1939, Jessie Violet Betty (CStJ) (who *d* 1993, having *m* 2ndly, 1951 (*m diss* 1956), Major Arthur Christopher John Congreve, who *d* 1992), da of late Brig-Gen Reynold Alexander Gillam, CMG, DSO:—
(By 1st *m*) Anthea Mary, *b* 1925; formerly in WRNS: *m* 1947, Lt-Col Edward Courtenay Phillips, MC, JP, DL, 60th Rifles, of Chase House, Monnington-on-Wye, Herefordshire, and has issue living, Sarah Angela Josephine, *b* 1948: *m* 1968, Robert Anthony Corbett, of Newchurch Farm, Kinnersley, Hereford, and has issue living, Benjamin *b* 1969, Tom *b* 1971, Hannah *b* 1977, — Harriet Anne Jennifer, *b* 1953: *m* 1977, Maj Peter Edward Cheney, MBE, WG (ret), and has issue living, Joss Edward *b* 1990, Melita Clare *b* 1982, Theodora May *b* 1983, Lettice Rose *b* 1986.
Issue of late Herbert Frank Onslow, *b* 1899, *d* 1970: *m* 1934, Hon Lena Barbara Joan Ogilvie-Grant, who *d* 1981, da of 4th Baron Strathspey:—
Roger Cranley Seafield (7 Links View, Baunton Lane, Cirencester, Glos), *b* 1934; *ed* Christ's Hosp: *m* 1959, Eileen Margaret, da of late J. A. J. Barnard, of The Borough, Crondall, Hants, and has issue living, Susan Helen, *b* 1965: *m* 1990, Philip Tattersall, — Clare Louise, *b* 1967: *m* 1988, Alan Robert Smith, and has issue living, Holly Iris *b* 1988.

Granddaughters of late Capt Richard Francis John Onslow, MVO, DSC, RN (ante):—
Issue of late Capt Richard Thomas Onslow, RM, *b* 1922: *m* 1947, Gillian Doriel (Westend House, Hambledon, Hants P07 6TB), el da of Edward Clemson, of Gaston House, E Bergholt, Suffolk:—
(Sylvia) Jane, *b* 1951. —— Geraldine Victoria, *b* 1954: *m* 1987, Nicholas Mark Keith, of 16 St John's Hill Grove, SW11 2RG, son of late J. R. Keith, and has issue living, William Richard, *b* 1977, — Hebe, *b* 1990.

Granddaughter of late Brig-Gen Cranley Charlton Onslow, CB, CMG, CBE, DSO (infra):—
Issue of late Lt-Cdr Denzil Richard Cranley Onslow, RNR, *b* 1909, *d* 1973: *m* 1940, Bernadine, who *d* 1976, da of David Blackburn:—
Judith Marylyn, *b* 1946: *m* 1970, George Sheffield Kinnear, of 3 Abbots Way, Hartford, Northwich, Ches, and has issue living, James Onslow Glyn, *b* 1986, — Amanda Jane, *b* 1971, — Felicity Esther Helen, *b* 1975.

Granddaughters of late Hamilton Cranley Onslow, el son of late Thomas Onslow, 3rd son of 2nd baronet:—
Issue of late Brig-Gen Cranley Charlton Onslow, CB, CMG, CBE, DSO, *b* 1869, *d* 1940: *m* 1904, Sydney Alice Hastings, who *d* 1962, da of late Surg-Gen Sir Benjamin Franklin, KCIE:—
Margaret Vivien, *b* 1918: *m* 1943, Johnston McDowell, of The Old Quaker House, Milverton, Som, and has issue living, Hugh Geoffrey, *b* 1947, — Brian Johnstone, *b* 1954, — Jane Maureen, *b* 1944, — Fiona Margaret, *b* 1961. —— Jocelyn Anne Sydney (Avenue House, Chapel Yard, South St, Castle Cary, Som), *b* 1922: *m* 1953, Cdr Leonard Charles Sutton Sheppard, OBE, RN (ret), who *d* 1992.

Granddaughter of late Col Gerald Charles Penrice Onslow, 2nd son of late Lt-Col Arthur Walton Onslow (infra):—
Issue of late Lieut-Com Arthur Gerald Onslow, DSC, RN, *b* 1885, *ka* at Battle of Jutland 1916: *m* 1912, Elsie Hindle

(who *d* 1976, having *m* 2ndly, 1918, Adm Sir Henry Daniel Pridham-Wippell, KCB, CVO, who *d* 1952), da of late J. Hinde-Crouch, of Palmeira Av, Hove, Sussex:—

Diana Rosemary, *b* 1915: *m* 1938, Patrick Longstaff, formerly Capt 5th Roy Inniskilling Dragoon Guards, and has issue living, Nigel Anthony Onslow, *b* 1942: *m* 1966, Jean Anne McCormick and has issue living, Julia Rosemary *b* 1968. *Residence* – Thatchings, Fairwarp, Sussex.

     Granddaughter of late Lt-Col Arthur Walton Onslow, 4th son of 2nd baronet:—
     Issue of late Lieut-Col Richard Cranley Onslow, Indian Army, *b* 1857, *d* 1934: *m* 1883, Edith Margaretta, who *d* 1934, da of Francis Beer:—

Alice Mary (Fairfield Hotel, Aliwal Rd, Wynberg, Cape Town, S Africa): *m* 1914, Capt Francis Richard Savage, formerly Cheshire Regt, who *d* 1960, and has issue living, Gerald Onslow, *b* 1916; Maj late Queen's Roy Regt.

This family is descended from Lieut-Gen Richard Onslow, nephew of 1st Baron Onslow, and uncle of the 1st Earl of Onslow, and is in special remainder to the Barony of Onslow (*see* E Onslow, colls). The 1st baronet, Admiral Sir Richard Onslow, GCB, and General of Marines, was second in command at Camperdown, and was created a baronet for distinguished services at that battle.

OPPENHEIMER (UK) 1921, of Stoke Poges, co Bucks

In adversity undismayed

Sir MICHAEL BERNARD GRENVILLE OPPENHEIMER, 3rd *Baronet*; *b* 27 May 1924; *s* his father, *Sir* MICHAEL, 1933; *ed* Charterhouse, and Ch Ch, Oxford (MA 1952, B Litt 1955); late Lieut S African Artillery: *m* 1947, (Laetitia) Helen, BPhil, MA, DD, da of Lieut-Col Sir Hugh Vere Huntley Duff Munro-Lucas-Tooth, 1st Bt (*cr* 1920), and has issue.

𝕬rms – Azure, two swords in saltire proper, pommeled and hilted or, between two lions passant of the last. 𝕮rest – A demi-koodoo proper, resting the sinister hoof on a rose gules, barbed and seeded proper.
Residence – L'Aiguillon, Rue des Cotils, Grouville, Jersey JE3 9AP. *Clubs* – Kimberley (S Africa), Victoria (Jersey).

DAUGHTERS LIVING

Henrietta Laetitia Grenville, *b* 1954: *m* 1978, Adam Lawrence Scott, and has issue living, Patrick Aaron, *b* 1986, — Eleanor Rose, *b* 1989. —— Matilda Magdalen Grenville, *b* 1956: *m* 1978, Neil G. A. King, and has issue living, Dorothy Xanthe, *b* 1987, — Hannah Magdalen, *b* 1988, — Elsa Mary, *b* 1990, — Lily Alexandra, *b* 1993. —— Xanthe Jennifer Grenville (*Hon Mrs Ivo A. R. Mosley*), *b* 1958: *m* 1977, Hon Ivo Adam Rex Mosley, and has issue (*see* B Ravensdale).

AUNT LIVING (*Daughter of 1st baronet*)

Madeleine Hilda (*Baroness Devlin*), *b* 1909; formerly a JP for Wilts: *m* 1932, Baron Devlin, a Lord of Appeal in Ordinary (Life Baron), who *d* 1992. *Residence* – West Wick House, Pewsey, Wilts.

     Sir Bernard Oppenheimer, 1st Bt (son of Edward Oppenheimer), was Chm of S African Diamond Corporation, Ltd, and the New Vaal River Diamond and Exploration Co. In 1917 he inaugurated diamond-cutting factories for Discharged and Disabled Soldiers.

CAMPBELL-ORDE (GB) 1790, of Morpeth, Northumberland

Gentle and Strong

Sir JOHN ALEXANDER CAMPBELL-ORDE, 6th *Baronet*; *b* 11 May 1943; *s* his father, *Maj Sir* SIMON ARTHUR, TD, 1969; *ed* Gordonstoun: *m* 1973 (*m diss* 1988), Lacy Rals, only da of T. Grady Gallant, of Nashville, Tennessee, USA, and has issue.

Arms – 1st and 4th sable, three salmon hauriant per pale argent and or, *Orde*; 2nd and 3rd, gyronny of eight or and sable within a bordure componée ermine and vert, in the centre a crescent of the last for difference, *Campbell*. **Crests** – 1st, an elk's head erased or, gorged with a collar invected sable; 2nd, a dexter hand proper, holding a spur or, strap also proper.
Address – PO Box 22974, Nashville, Tennessee 37202, USA.

SON LIVING

JOHN SIMON ARTHUR, *b* 15 Aug 1981.

DAUGHTERS LIVING

Alexandra Louise, *b* 1974. —— Alice Theodora, *b* 1976. —— Octavia Maie, *b* 1978.

BROTHER LIVING

Peter Humphrey, *b* 1946; *ed* Gordonstoun: *m* 1st, 1976 (*m diss* 1992), Mrs Perdita Bennett, da of Alexander Peter Fordham Watt, and formerly wife of Richard Bennett, 2ndly, 1992, Penelope Jane Armstrong, da of late Mark Alexander Wynter-Blyth, MA, Prin The Rajkumar Coll, Rajkot, India.

SISTER LIVING

Caroline Jane, *b* 1940; *ed* N Foreland Lodge, and the Sorbonne: *m* 1967, Christopher John Davies, MA, of Westgate House, Dedham, Colchester, Essex CO7 6HJ, and has issue living, John Humphrey Stewart, *b* 1969, —— Simon William Gardner, *b* 1970; BA (Cantab), —— Caroline Celia Hyde, *b* 1973.

AUNT LIVING (Daughter of 4th baronet)

Alice Maie (Grianin House, Glenfinnan, Inverness-shire), *b* 1897: *m* 1917, Rev James Humphrey Copner Macfarlane-Barrow, formerly V of Inverary Argyllshire, who *d* 1943, and has had issue, Seumas Donnchadh MACFARLANE *b* 1922; renounced surname of Barrow 1956, Beatrice Harriet (99 Gregory St, Geralaton 6530, W Aust), da of Capt Christopher St Barbe Shields, and *d* 1981, leaving issue living, James Peter Raymund *b* 1957, Simon Ruairidh *b* 1958, Christopher Donnchadh Diarmad *b* 1959, Ian Andrew *b* 1963, Rosamund Lucy Alice *b* 1961, Julia Maie Louise *b* 1967, —— Padruig Francis (Quaintways, Killiney Hill Rd, Killiney, co Dublin) *b* 1929: *m* 1967, Ann Maria Coen, of co Galway, and has issue living, Sine Mary *b* 1968, Ailse Brighde *b* 1970, Dearbhail Anna *b* 1971, —— Ian Tearlach MACFARLANE (Glenfinnan House, Glenfinnan, Inverness-shire), *b* 1931; renounced the surname of Barrow 1977: *m* 1966, Isobel Nicholas Alexander, of Edinburgh, and has issue living, Duncan James *b* 1969, Ian Robert *b* 1970, Jane Isabella *b* 1967, —— Calum Seumas (Craig Lodge, Dalmally, Argyll), *b* 1932: *m* 1962, Mary Ann, da of Maj Gabriel Thomas Grisewood, of Invereinie, Farr, Inverness, and has issue living, Magnus Calum *b* 1968, Ruth Magdalene *b* 1963, and three adopted sons: Seamus Magnus *b* 1965, Fergus Paul *b* 1967, Mark Christpher Murray *b* 1973, —— Maie Bridget (Bohuntine, Roy Bridge, Inverness-shire), *b* 1926: *m* 1962, Donald Joseph MacDonald, who *d* 1967, and has issue living, Donald Hamish *b* 1962, Alastair Ninian *b* 1964, Eilidh Mairi *b* 1965, Catherine Margaret *b* 1966.

WIDOW LIVING OF FIFTH BARONET

ELEANOR HYDE (*Eleanor, Lady Campbell-Orde*) (Westgate House, Dedham, Colchester, Essex, CO7 6HJ), da of late Col Humphrey Watts, OBE, TD, of Haslington Hall, Ches: *m* 1938, Maj Sir Simon Arthur Campbell-Orde, TD, 5th Bt, who *d* 1969.

COLLATERAL BRANCHES LIVING

Granddaughter of late Colin Ridley Campbell-Orde, 2nd son of 3rd baronet:—
Issue of late Bernard Arthur Campbell-Orde, *b* 1901, *d* 1974: *m* 1st, 1939 (*m diss* 1955), Pamela, who *d* 1979, da of late Brig-Gen John Cecil Wray, CB, CMG, CVO, TD, and formerly wife of Col Robert Hugh Arthur Lucas; 2ndly, 1955, Nancy Mabyn Bradley (Old Farm, Trebetherick, Wadebridge, Cornwall), da of Maj Thomas Langdon Trethewy, DCLI:—
Jennifer Mary, *b* 1940: *m* 1st, 1959 (*m diss* 1971), Robin Alfred Clive Salmon, Merchant Navy; 2ndly, 1977, Reuben Harry Gunn, of 39 Whitworth Close, Gosport, Hants, and has issue living (by 1st *m*), Timothy John, *b* 1960, —— Robert Bernard, *b* 1961, —— Belinda Jane, *b* 1964, —— (by 2nd *m*) Sarah Louise, *b* 1978.

Issue of late Henry Campbell Campbell-Orde, yst son of 3rd baronet, *b* 1877, *d* 1954: *m* 1st, 1901, Marie Elizabeth, who *d* 1913, da of John S. Barr, of Newcastle-on-Tyne; 2ndly, 1927, Ruth, who *d* 1985, da of late Robert Thomas, of Penarth, S Wales:—
(By 2nd *m*) Alexander Powlett (Willow Cottage, Newbridge Green, Upton-on-Severn, Worcs), *b* 1928; Petty Officer (Radar Electrical Artificer) RN (ret). —— Colin Robert (Cruachan, Kingweston Rd, Charlton Mackrell, Somerton, Som TA11 6AH), *b* 1935; CEng, MIMechE, MFRAeS: *m* 1959, Audrey Isobel, da of Raymond S. Griffiths, of Brentford, Middx, and has issue living, Andrew Colin (53 Finch Close, Shepton Mallet, Som), *b* 1969; *ed* Millfield: *m* 1991, Susan, da of Brian Parsons, and formerly wife of Peter Hill, and has issue living, Joseph Harry *b* 1993, —— Tamzin Ruth, *b* 1960: *m* 1985, Dennis David James Elliott, of 60 Grove Av, Yeovil, Som, and has issue living, Adam David Stewart *b* 1986, Christopher James Robert *b* 1988, Daniel David James *b* 1991, —— Sarah Elizabeth, *b* 1965: *m* 1993, David Montague Road, of Hurst Farm, Woodborough Sands, Pewsey, Wilts. —— Morwenna (Westwinds, Parkwall Rd, Llandedeyrn, Cardiff), *b* 1929; SRN: *m* 1951 (*m diss* 19—), George Ernest Turner, and has issue living, Ian George, *b* 1965, —— Tracey Christine, *b* 1958, —— Alison Meryl, *b* 1961: *m* 1984, Stephen Kingdon.

The 1st baronet, Adm Sir John Orde, Adm of the White, and, finally, Vice-Adm of the Red, Governor of Dominica 1783-93, was yr brother of the 1st Baron Bolton. The 3rd baronet assumed by Roy licence 1880 the additional surname of Campbell, his mother having been Eliza, el da and co-heir of Peter Campbell of Kilmory, Argyll, descended from Campbell of Auchinbreck (*see* Campbell Bt, *cr* 1668).

Orr Ewing, see Ewing.

Orr-Lewis, see Lewis.

OSBORN (E) 1662, of Chicksands, Bedfordshire

Sir RICHARD HENRY DANVERS OSBORN, 9th *Baronet*; *b* 12 Aug 1958; *s* his father, *Sir* DANVERS LIONEL ROUSE, 1983; *ed* Eton; Christie's 1979-83, Colnaghi 1984-86, Fine Art Consultant; Assoc Dir Paul Mitchell Ltd.

Arms – Argent, a bend between two lions rampant sable. **Crest** – A lion's head argent ducally crowned or.
Residence – 25 Queen's Gdns, W2 3BD.

SISTER LIVING

Sarah, *b* 1950: *m* 1989, Christopher Gwyn Saunders-Davies, of The Thatched Cottage, Greatbridge, Romsey, Hants S051 0HB, son of late A. O. Saunders-Davies, of The Island, Romsey, Hants.

COLLATERAL BRANCH LIVING

Quantum in rebus inane
*How much vanity there
is in human affairs*

Grandson of late Lieut-Col Danvers Henry Osborn, 5th son of 5th baronet:—
Issue of late Danvers Osborn, *b* 1864, *d* 1929: *m* 1906, Inez, who *d* 1953, 2nd da of Henry Smith, of Victoria, British Columbia:—
WILLIAM DANVERS, *b* 4 June 1909; assumed the names of William Danvers in lieu of his Christian names of George Schomberg by deed poll (registered in Supreme Court of British Columbia) 1936: *m* 1939, Jean Burns, da of R. B. Hutchinson, of Vancouver, British Columbia, and has issue living, Cheryl Elizabeth, *b* 1945. *Residence* – 2676 Seaview Road, Victoria, British Columbia.

The 1st baronet, Sir John Osborne, was son of Sir Peter Osborne, Governor of Guernsey, grandson of Peter Osborne, who purchased Chicksands Priory in 1576, and was Treasurer's Remembrancer to Henry VIII, Keeper of the Privy Purse to Edward VI and Commr of Ecclesiastical Affairs to Queen Elizabeth I. He was Treasurer's Remembrancer 1674-98 and received his Baronetcy in recognition of all the family had suffered in the cause of Charles I. Sir Danvers, 3rd baronet, was son of John Osborne (el son of 2nd baronet), who altered the spelling of his name to Osborn to avoid confusion with the family of the Duke of Leeds. He was Governor of New York before the War of Independence. Sir George, 4th Bt, commanded Scots Gds 1779 and was a Gen in the Army, MP for Bedford, and Groom of the Bedchamber to George III. Sir John, 5th Bt, was for many years an MP, and was a Lord Commr of the Admiralty. Sir Peter Osborne's da Dorothy *m* Sir William Temple, to whom she wrote the famous love letters.

OSBORNE (I) 1629, of Ballintaylor, co Tipperary

Sir PETER GEORGE OSBORNE, 17th *Baronet*; *b* 29 June 1943; *s* his father, *Lieut-Col Sir* GEORGE FRANCIS, MC, 1960; *ed* Wellington Coll, and Ch Ch, Oxford: *m* 1968, Felicity, da of late Grantley Loxton-Peacock, of 13 Eaton Place, SW1, and has issue.

Arms – Gules, on a fesse cotised or two fountains, over all a bend argent. **Crest** – A sea-lion holding a trident.
Residence – 21 St Petersburg Pl, W2 4LA.

SONS LIVING

GEORGE GIDEON OLIVER, *b* 23 May 1971; assumed the additional forename of George by deed poll 1988. —— Benedict George, *b* 1973. —— Adam Peter, *b* 1976. —— Theo Grantley, *b* 1985.

BROTHER LIVING

Pax in bello
Peace in war

James Francis (Port Lympne, Lympne, Hythe, Kent CT21 4PD), *b* 1946: *m* 1971, Felicity Jane, only da of Peter Boutwood, of Holmes Farm, W Wittering, Sussex, and has three sons, Toby James Robert, *b* 1977 (adopted), — George Dominic Peter, *b* (twin) 1977 (adopted), — Harry Lucas, *b* 1988.

SISTERS LIVING

Jennifer Jane, *b* 1939. ——— Caroline Mary, *b* 1941.

COLLATERAL BRANCH LIVING

Issue of late Edward Osborne, only brother of 15th baronet, *b* 1861, *d* 1939: *m* 1895, Phyllis Eliza, who *d* 1966, da of late George Whitley, of Fairholme, Weybridge:—
†Stanley Patrick, *b* 1904; *ed* Felsted, and at Univ Coll, N Wales (BSc); AFRAeS: *m* 1st, 1931, Muriel Harvey, BA, who *d* 1967, da of Llewellyn Harvey Matthews, of Shrewsbury; 2ndly, 1969, Mary Enid Lyon (Ordesa, Harpswood Lane, Saltwood, Hythe), of Goole, Yorks, and *d* 1989, leaving issue (by 1st *m*), Anthony Trevor (22 St Peter's Way, Edgmond, Shropshire), *b* 1934; *ed* Felsted, and Emmanuel Coll, Camb (MA); CEng, MICE: *m* 1958, Beryl Anne Shadbolt, of Cambridge, and has issue living, Marcus Duncan Fitzwilliam *b* 1967, Catherine Frances *b* 1961, Nicola Clare *b* 1963, ——— Edward Peter (Fairview Cottage, West Down, Ilfracombe, Devon), *b* 1938; *ed* Felsted, and Peterhouse, Camb (BA): *m* 1961, Marjorie, da of William Newton, of Fleetwood, Lancs, and has issue living, John Philip *b* 1963, Judith Carol *b* 1962, Janet Elizabeth *b* 1964. ——— Nora Gladys (Fieldend, 22 Harpswood Lane, Hythe, Kent), *b* 1906.

The 2nd and 7th baronets each represented the co of Waterford in Parliament. The 8th baronet was a Privy Councillor in Ireland, and sat as MP for Carysfort. The 9th baronet was MP for Carysfort and Sheriff of Waterford 1795. The 11th baronet was MP for Carysfort and subsequently for Enniskillen. Sir George Francis Osborne, MC, 16th baronet was Lieut-Col Roy Sussex Regt.

Osborne-Gibbes, see Gibbes.

OUTRAM (UK) 1858
(Name pronounced "Ootram")

I know not how to change my faith

Sir ALAN JAMES OUTRAM, 5th *Baronet*, son of late James Ian Outram, son of late Rev Arthur Outram, 3rd son of 2nd baronet; *b* 15 May 1937; *s* his great-uncle, Sir FRANCIS DAVIDSON, OBE, 1945; *ed* Marlborough, and St Edmund Hall, Oxford (MA); Under Master, Harrow Sch; Lt-Col TAVR: *m* 1976, Victoria Jean, da of late George Dickson Paton, of Bexhill-on-Sea, E Sussex, and has issue.

Arms – Or, on a chevron embattled, between three crosses flory gules, five escallops of the first. **Crest** – Out of an eastern crown a demi-lion or, gorged with a wreath of laurel proper, holding between the paws a cross-flory gules. **Supporters** – On either side a royal Bengal tiger guardant proper, gorged with a wreath of laurel vert and on the hand an eastern crown or.
Residence – 57 High St, Harrow-on-the-Hill, HA1 3HT, Middx.

SON LIVING

DOUGLAS BENJAMIN JAMES, *b* 15 March 1979.

DAUGHTER LIVING

Alison Catharine, *b* 1977.

SISTER LIVING

Margaret Evelyn, *b* 1935: *m* 1st, 1956, Richard Coverley Champion; 2ndly, 1985, Peter Denby Gilbert, of 47 Hollis Way, Southwick, Trowbridge, Wilts BA14 9PH, and has had issue (by 1st *m*), Anthony Richard Coverley, *b* 1964, — Jean Margaret, *b* 1958: *m* 1989, Martin Galloway Booth, and has issue living, Christopher Albert Galloway *b* 1990, Edward Martin Galloway *b* 1992, — Jennifer Fleur, *b* 1960: *m* 1983, David Reginald Higgins, and has issue living, Stephen Richard *b* 1988, Katherine Joanna *b* 1990, — Joanna Esmé, *b* 1963: *m* 1984, Michael William Gooden, and *d* 1986.

COLLATERAL BRANCHES LIVING

Grandchildren of late Rev William Outram, yst son of 2nd baronet:—
Issue of late Rev Francis Henry Outram, *b* 1907, *d* 1946, Eileen Grace (The Annexe, Haining House, Taylor's Lane, Bosham, Chichester, Sussex), da of late Rev L. A. McClintock Newbery:—
John Douglas (Haining House, Taylor's Lane, Bosham, Chichester), *b* 1947; *ed* Marlborough, Liverpool Univ (BEng), and Birmingham Univ (MSc); Man Dir Outram Research Ltd: *m* 1970, Valerie Ann, da of Geoffrey Wilson, of Whitley Bay, and has issue living, Nicholas Francis, *b* 1973, — Philip Maxwell, *b* 1976, — Rachel Helen, *b* 1978, — Katy Ann, *b* 1981. ——— Margaret Eleanor, *b* 1949: *m* 1975, Peter Francis Charters, of Withybed, Duck St, W Lavington, nr Devizes, Wilts SN10 4LG, and has issue living, Richard Francis *b* 1977, — Simon James, *b* 1979, — Robin Andrew, *b* 1982.
Issue of late James Richard Outram, *b* 1911, *d* 1986: *m* 1939, Lucy Dora (Richardson House, Englefield Green, Surrey TW20 OJY), yst da of late Jacob Andreas Frerichs, of Johannesburg, S Africa:—
Francis William (76 Sloane, St, SW1), *b* 1946; *ed* Scarborough Coll. ——— Richard Graham (43 Richmond Place, Bath BA1 4QA), *b* (twin) 1946; *ed* Marlborough. ——— Keith Alastair, *b* 1947; *ed* Scarborough Coll. ——— Nicola Elspeth (55 Southford Rd, Dartmouth, Devon TQ6 9QT), *b* 1940: *m* 1962, David Alistair Kingsley Cooper, who *d* 1988, son of late Thomas Esmond Kingsley Cooper, MA, and has issue living, James Alexander, *b* 1969; *ed* King's Sch, Worcs, and Exeter Univ, — Jennifer Mary, *b* 1967: *m* 1994, Malcolm Bernard Yallop, of The Old School House, School Lane, Kedington, Suffolk.

OWEN (UK) 1813, of Orielton, Pembrokeshire

Honesty is the best policy

Sir HUGH BERNARD PILKINGTON OWEN, 5th *Baronet*; *b* 28 March 1915; *s* his father, *Capt Sir* JOHN ARTHUR, 1973; *ed* Chillon Coll, Switzerland.

Arms – Gules, a chevron or, between three lions rampant or.
Residence – 63 Dudsbury Rd, Ferndown, Dorset.

BROTHER LIVING

JOHN WILLIAM (12 Elizabeth Av, St Brelade, Jersey), *b* 7 June 1917; *ed* Charterhouse; late Capt 4th/7th Roy Dragoon Gds: *m* 1963, Gwenllian Mary, MBE, Wing Officer WRAF, el da of late E. B. Phillips, of Barry, Glam.

John Lord, MP for the Pembroke Burghs, and Lord-Lieut of Pembrokeshire, assumed the name of Owen on inheriting the estates of Sir Hugh Owen, 6th Bt (*cr* 1641). Sir Arthur Owen, MP, 3rd Bt of the first creation, is stated to have given the deciding vote for a Bill containing provisions for ensuring the Protestant succession to the British Throne, after riding in unprecedented haste from Wales for that purpose. Sir Arthur Owen's grandda, Corbetta, was mother of the Sir John Owen, *cr* a baronet 1813. The 2nd baronet sat as MP for Pembroke Dist (*L*) 1826-38 and 1861-68: he *m* 1st, 1825, Angelina, who *d* 1844, sister of 1st Lord Tredegar; 2ndly, 1845, Henrietta, who *d* 1894, da of Hon Edward Rodney, RN, son of the famous Adm, 1st Lord Rodney. The baronetcy of the first creation (1641) became ext at the death in 1851 of Sir William Owen-Barlow, 8th baronet. The 3rd baronet of this creation, Sir Hugh Charles, served at siege of Montevideo 1845-46, and in Kaffir War 1846-47 (medal).

CUNLIFFE-OWEN (UK) 1920, of Bray, co Berks

Honesty is the best policy

Sir HUGO DUDLEY CUNLIFFE-OWEN, 3rd *Baronet*; *b* 16 May 1966; *s* his father, *Sir* DUDLEY HERBERT, RN, 1983; *ed* King William's Coll, Isle of Man.

Arms – Quarterly, 1st and 4th, sable, a lion rampant between three crosses couped within a bordure, all or, *Owen*; 2nd and 3rd, sable, three conies courant in pale with two flaunches argent, *Cunliffe*. **Crests** – 1st, a lion rampant sable charged with three crosses couped in pale or, *Owen*; 2nd, a greyhound sejant argent, collared sable, in front of a flag-staff proper, flowing therefrom a banner also charged with a cross gules.
Residence –

SISTER LIVING (*Daughter of 2nd baronet by 3rd marriage*)

Sophie Jean, *b* 1965.

HALF-SISTER LIVING (*Daughter of 2nd baronet by 2nd marriage*)

Juliana Diana, *b* 1957: *m* 1980, Stephen Markeson, and has issue living, Oliver James, *b* 1984, — Lucy Juliana, *b* 1982.

AUNTS LIVING (*Daughters of 1st baronet*)

Philippa Helen, *b* 1926: *m* 1st, 1945 (*m diss* 1952), Denis Macduff Burke; 2ndly, 1952 (*m diss* 1963), Archie Alistair Baring; 3rdly, 1966, Peter William Thorn Warren, who *d* 1973; 4thly, 1979, Gilbert Hugh Sandbach Toller, and has issue living, (by 1st *m*) David Macduff *b* 1948, — Alexandra Yvette, *b* 1946, — (by 2nd *m*) Adrian Allistair, *b* 1957, — Sarah Elizabeth, *b* 1954. —— Diana Elizabeth (Queens Lodge, Beldam Bridge Rd, Chobham, Surrey), *b* 1928: *m* 1st, 1947 (*m diss* 1955), William Gavin Buchanan; 2ndly, 1964 (*m diss* 1967), Cdr Richard O'Brien, RN; 3rdly, 1967 (*m diss* 1991), Antony Hanbury, and has issue living, (by 1st *m*) Gray Hugo, *b* 1948, — Diana Victoria, *b* 1951.

WIDOW LIVING OF SECOND BARONET

JEAN (*Lady Cunliffe-Owen*), only da of late Surg-Cdr A. N. Forsyth, RN: *m* 1964, as his 3rd wife, Sir Dudley Herbert Cunliffe-Owen, 2nd Bt, RN, who *d* 1983.

This family descends from Joseph Owen of Crookes Moor, Shelfield, who *m* 1746, Sarah, da and co-heir of Samuel Skargell, by Elizabeth da of John Cunliffe. The 1st baronet, Sir Hugo Cunliffe-Owen (son of Sir (Francis) Philip Cunliffe-Owen, KCB, KCMG, CIE, great-grandson of Joseph Owen), was Pres of British-American Tobacco Co.

Page-Wood, see Wood.

PAGET (UK) 1871, of Harewood Place, Middlesex

Sir JULIAN TOLVER PAGET, CVO, 4th *Baronet*, son of late Gen Sir Bernard Charles Tolver Paget, GCB, DSO, MC, 3rd son of Rt Rev Francis Paget, DD, 2nd son of 1st baronet; *b* 11 July 1921; *s* his 1st cousin once removed, *Sir* JAMES FRANCIS, 1972; *ed* Radley, and Ch Ch, Oxford (MA); Lt-Col Coldm Gds; 1939-45 War; a Gentleman Usher to HM 1971-91; CVO (1984): *m* 1954, Diana Frances, da of late Frederick Spencer Herbert Farmer, of Vicars Hill Lodge, Lymington, Hants, and has issue.

Arms – Sable; on a cross engrailed, between in the 1st and 4th quarters an eagle displayed and in the 2nd and 3rd a heraldic tiger passant argent, an escallop of the first. Crest – A heraldic tiger passant argent, gorged with a collar and charged with two escallops sable.
Residence – 4 Trevor St, SW7 1DU. *Clubs* – Cavalry and Guards', Flyfishers'.

Labor ipse voluptas
Worth itself is pleasure

SON LIVING

HENRY JAMES (21 Stokenchurch St, SW6 3TS), *b* 2 Feb 1959; *ed* Radley: *m* 1993, Mrs Margarete E. Varvill, da of late Halfdan Lynner, and has issue living, Bernard Halfdan, *b* 4 July 1994.

DAUGHTER LIVING

Olivia Jane, *b* 1957: *m* 1992, Nigel J. Cox, son of Basil Cox.

COLLATERAL BRANCH LIVING

Granddaughters of late Rt Rev Francis Paget, DD, Lord Bishop of Oxford, 2nd son of 1st baronet:—
Issue of late Lt-Col Humphrey Paget, MC, *b* 1891, *d* 1985: *m* 1918, Elizabeth Caroline, who *d* 1970, da of Sir Lewis Tonna Dibdin:—
Elizabeth Frideswide, *b* 1921; 1939-45 War in ATS: *m* 1950, Lt-Col John Darwin Maling, DSO, MC, RA, of 10 Warbler Grove, Waikanae, NZ, and has issue living, Thomas Anthony Darwin, *b* 1951, — Sarah Geraldine, *b* 1952, — Elizabeth Anne, *b* (twin) 1952, — Joanna Katherine, *b* 1956. —— Jean Marianne, *b* 1924; 1939-45 War in WAAF: *m* 1966, Robert Ian Cheyne Macpherson, of 1 Waitara Rd, St Heliers, Auckland, NZ. —— Helen Rosemary, *b* 1929: *m* 1966, George Albert Longman, of 2 Doatshayne Close, Musbury, Axminster, Devon EX13 6BQ.

Sir James Paget, 1st Bt, son of Samuel Paget of Great Yarmouth, was Sergeant-Surg to Queen Victoria and Surg to King Edward VII when Prince of Wales. Sir John Rahere, 2nd Bt, was a KC.

PAGET (UK) 1886, of Cranmore Hall, co Somerset

Sir RICHARD HERBERT PAGET, 4th *Baronet*; *b* 17 Feb 1957; *s* his father, *Sir* JOHN STARR, 1992; *ed* Eton: *m* 1985, Richenda Rachel, da of Rev Preb John Theodore Cameron Bucke Collins (*see* B Hazlerigg, 1990 Edn), and has issue.

Arms – Sable, on a cross invected argent, between four eagles displayed ermine, an eagle displayed between four lions passant of the first. Crest – A demi-heraldic tiger sable, maned, tufted, and gorged with a collar vallary argent, and holding in its mouth an eagle's leg erased at the thigh or.
Residence – Burridge Heath Farm, Little Bedwyn, Marlborough, Wilts SN8 3JR.

DICIENDO·Y·HACIENDO
Saying and doing

DAUGHTERS LIVING

Emma Rachel, *b* 1986. —— (Richenda) Elizabeth, *b* 1988. —— Camilla Mary, *b* 1991.

BROTHER LIVING

DAVID VERNON JOHN, *b* 26 March 1959; *ed* Eton, and Trinity Coll, Cambridge: *m* 1990, Cluny Patricia Maxine, da of late Cmdr Duncan Macpherson, of Gaskmore, Laggan, Scotland, and Radbroke Hall, Shrewsbury, and has issue living, Alexander Lachlan John, *b* 14 June 1994. — Antonia, *b* 1992. *Residence* – Lodge Cottage, Groton, Boxford, Sudbury, Suffolk.

SISTERS LIVING

Patricia Mary, *b* 1945: *m* 1975, Philip John Anthony Hawkes, of 60 rue de Varenne, 75007 Paris, and Château de Missery, 21210 Saulieu, France, and has issue living, Lucy Mary, *b* 1980. —— Rosemary Muriel, *b* 1948: *m* 1971, Christopher Ralph William Richard Inge, of Westmead, Bleadney, nr Wells, Som BA5 1PF, and has issue living, Alexia Diana Nancy, *b* 1977, Olivia Dorothy Jane, *b* 1980. —— Elizabeth Frances, *b* 1950, Lady-in-Waiting to HRH The Princess Margaret, Countess of Snowdon since 1979: *m* 1st, 1981 (*m diss* 1985), Dr Angus A. D. Blair; 2ndly, 1989, Maj-Gen Charles Gerard Courtenay Vyvyan, CBE, RGJ (*see* Vyvyan, Bt, colls). —— Davina Jane, *b* 1951: *m* 1972, Rev (James) Adrian Hunter Pollard, and has issue living, (Etienne) James Hunter, *b* 1979, — Benjamin David Hunter, *b* 1979. —— Susan Glynne, *b* 1960: *m* 1988, Maj Simon Thornhill, SG, of 55 Larkhill Rise, SW4, yr son of late Thomas Thornhill, of Buzzards Bay, Mass, USA, and has issue living, Catherine Starr, *b* 1991, — Fiona Surtees, *b* 1993.

AUNT LIVING (*Daughter of 2nd baronet*)

Sylvia Mary, OBE (*Lady Chancellor*) (Rosey Cottage, Shellingford, nr Faringdon, Oxon SN7 7QA), *b* 1901; OBE (Civil) 1976: *m* 1926, Sir Christopher John Chancellor, CMG, who *d* 1989, son of Lt-Col Sir John Robert Chancellor, GCMG, GCVO, GBE, DSO, and has issue living, John Paget (Crown House, Caxton, Cambs), *b* 1927: *m* 1959 (*m diss* 1968), Hon (Mary) Alice Joliffe, da of 4th Baron Hylton, and has issue living, (John) Edward Horner *b* 1962, Isabel Rose *b* 1959: *m* 1982, John Joseph Boothby (*see* Boothby, Bt, colls), Katharine Sylvia Anthony *b* 1961: *m* 1989, William Woodard Self, son of Prof Peter Self, of Canberra Australia (and has issue living, Alexis *b* 1990), Anna Theodora *b* 1965, — Alexander Surtees (1 Souldern Rd, W14), *b* 1940: *m* 1964, Susanna Elizabeth, only da of late Martin Ridley Debenham (*see* Debenham, Bt, colls), and has issue living, Elizabeth Beatrice *b* 1964: *m* 1990, Alexander Evelyn Michael Waugh, and has issue (*see* E Onslow), Cecilia Mary *b* 1966, — Teresa, *b* 1933: *m* 1st, 1963 (*m diss* 1977), Edward Victor Gatacre; 2ndly, 1982, John Campbell Wells, of la Scarsdale Villas, W8 6PT, and Chapel Farm, E Chiltington, E Sussex BN7 3BA, and has issue living (by 1st *m*), Thomas Jerome *b* 1954: *m* 1990, Elsebeth, da of Jorgen Tholstrup, (and has issue living, Jack Victor *b* 1992), William *b* 1956: *m* 1994, Catherine Lucy Emily, da of Sir Nigel Edward Seely, 5th Bt, (Alice) Amelia *b* 1960, Maria Teresa *b* 1964, Cecily *b* 1967, Dorothy (Dolly) Perpetua *b* 1971, — Susanna Maria, *b* 1935: *m* 1958, Nicholas John Johnston, of Shellingford House, Faringdon, Oxon, and has issue living, Clara Mary *b* 1960: *m* 1987 (Edward) Percy Keswick Weatherall, elder son of Capt Anthony Weatherall, of Cowhill Tower, Dumfries (and has issue living, Bertram Edward Johnson *b* 1989, Stella Nony *b* 1991, a da *b* 1994), Lily Silvia *b* 1962: *m* 1991, Daniel Stevens, son of Dr Dominic John Charles Stevens, of Bolton, Rose Pamela Muriel *b* 1963, Silvy Margaret *b* 1968: *m* 1993, Benjamin J. K. Weatherall, yr son of Capt Anthony Weatherall (ante).

WIDOW LIVING OF THIRD BARONET

NANCY MARY (*Dowager Lady Paget*), da of late Lt-Col Francis Woodbine Parish, DSO, MC: *m* 1944, Sir John Starr Paget, 3rd Bt, who *d* 1992. *Residence* – Haygrass House, Taunton, Somerset TA3 7BS.

Rev John Paget, R of Pointington, Somerset, for 54 years until his death 1745, purchased that manor and sold his lands at Daventry. His son, Rev Thomas Paget, held the same living 1745 until his death 1783. By the marriage of his son Richard to Mary, el da and eventually heir of James Moore, Cranmore Hall, Somerset, passed to this family. Their great grandson, Rt Hon Sir Richard Horner Paget, 1st baronet was many years Chm of Somerset Quarter Sessions and County Council, and sat as MP for E Somerset (*C*) 1865-68, for Mid Somerset 1868-85, and for Wells Div of Somersetshire 1885-95.

PALMER (E) 1660, of Carlton, Northamptonshire

May the success be equal to the labour

Sir GEOFFREY CHRISTOPHER JOHN PALMER, 12th *Baronet*; *b* 30 June 1936; *s* his father *Lieut-Col Sir* GEOFFREY FREDERICK NEILL, 1951; *ed* Eton; is patron of two livings: *m* 1957, Clarissa Mary, el da of Stephen Francis Villiers-Smith (*see* B Northbourne, colls, 1980 Edn), and has issue.

𝔸rms – Sable, a chevron or, between three crescents argent. 𝔸rest – A wyvern, wings addorsed or, armed and langued gules.
Seat – Carlton Curlieu Hall, Leicestershire.

DAUGHTERS LIVING

Sophia Mary, *b* 1959: *m* 1987, Michael H. W. Neal, of Legsheath, nr E Grinstead, Sussex, only son of (Harry) Morton Neal, CBE, of Great Sarratt Hall, Sarratt, Herts, and has issue living, Harry Morton Geoffrey, *b* 1988, — Jemima Mary, *b* 1991. —— Celina Lucinda, *b* 1961: *m* 1986, William Alexander Mavourn Francklin, of The Oak House, Hinxton, Cambs, yr son of Cmdr (Mavourn Baldwin) Philip Francklin, DSC, of Gonalston Hall, Notts, and has issue living, Henry Alexander John, *b* 1988, — Clementine, *b* 1990, — Daisy, *b* 1993. —— Isabella Anne, *b* 1962: *m* 1993, David W. R. Harrington, son of Ronald Harrington, of Shatwell Cottage, Yarlington, Som, and has issue living, Lavinia Juliet, *b* 1994. —— Rosanna Jane, *b* 1967: *m* 1993, Edward J. G. Peel, son of John Peel, of Dudgrove, Fairford, Glos.

BROTHER LIVING

JEREMY CHARLES (Manor House, Stoke Abbott, Beaminster, Dorset DT8 3JT; 6 Furber St, W6), *b* 16 May 1939; *ed* Eton, and Univ of Tours: *m* 1968, Antonia, yr da of late Astley Dutton, and has issue living, Drew Herrick, *b* 1974, — Tom Jeremy, *b* 1977.

COLLATERAL BRANCHES LIVING

Grandchildren of late Major Herrick Augustus Palmer, son of late Rev Henry Palmer, 3rd son of 5th baronet:—
    Issue of late Frederick Charles Palmer, *b* 1866, *d* 1930: *m* 1897, Eleanor Annie, who *d* 1942, da of late Henry Wilson Sharpin, FRCS, of 34 Sillwood Road, Brighton:—
Dorothy Esther, *b* 1898.
    Issue of late Lieut-Col Robert Henry Palmer, DSO, *b* 1868, *d* 1947: *m* 1909, Margaret Finch, who *d* 1955, el da of late Gerard Finch Dawson:—
Robert Henry Charles, *b* 1916; *ed* Clifton, and Wadham Coll, Oxford (Organ Scholar, MA, BMus); Organist, St Mary's, Oak Bay, Victoria, BC 1961-83; Conductor of Choir, Univ of Victoria 1965-69; formerly Music Master, Westminster Abbey Choir Sch, and an ARCM; 1939-45 War with RAF. —— Mary Margaret Elizabeth, *b* 1914: *m* 1944, Genille Hilton Jordayne Cave Browne-Cave, PhD (*see* Cave Browne-Cave, Bt, colls). *Residence* – 3480 Simpson St, Apt 901, Montreal, Quebec H3G 2N7, Canada.

The 1st baronet, Sir Geoffrey, sat as MP for Stamford in the Long Parliament, and was subsequently one of the Commissioners at the Treaty of Uxbridge, Attorney-General to Charles II, and Chief Justice of Chester. The 3rd, 4th, and 5th baronets successively represented Leicestershire in Parliament.

PALMER (GB) 1791, of Wanlip Hall, Leicestershire

Sir JOHN EDWARD SOMERSET PALMER, 8th *Baronet*; *b* 27 Oct 1926; *s* his father, Sir JOHN ARCHDALE, 1963; *ed* Canford, Pembroke Coll, Camb (BA 1951, MA 1957), and Durham Univ (MSc Agric Eng 1953); late Lt, RA; Colonial Agricultural Ser, N Nigeria 1953-62, R. A. Lister & Co, Dursley 1962-63, and at Overseas Liaison Unit, National Institute of Agricultural Engineering, Silsoe, Beds 1964-68; a consultant, Dir W. S. Atkins Agriculture 1979-87: *m* 1956, Dione Catharine, da of late Charles Duncan Skinner, and has issue.

Arms – Argent, on two bars sable three trefoils slipped of the first, in chief a greyhound courant of the second, collared or. Crest – On a mount vert a greyhound sejant sable, gorged with a collar or, rimmed gules, and charged on the shoulder with a trefoil slipped argent. *Seat* – Newland, nr Coleford, Glos. *Residence* – Gayton House, Gayton, Northants NN7 3EZ.

SON LIVING

ROBERT JOHN HUDSON (38 Marney Rd, SW11 5EP; Royal Ocean Racing Club), *b* 20 Dec 1960; *ed* St Edward's Sch, Oxford, Grey Coll, Univ of Durham (BA), and Cambridge Univ (BA): *m* 1990, Lucinda Margaret, da of Michael Barker, of 14 Harley Gdns, SW10, and has issue living, Charles Henry Somerset, *b* 12 Oct 1992.

DAUGHTER LIVING

Harriet Alyson Ducarel, *b* 1959: *m* 1987, Andrew Lorne Campbell Byatt, son of Sir Hugh Campbell Byatt, KCVO, CMG, of Leargnahension, by Tarbert, Argyll.

BROTHER LIVING

Robert Archdale (Dorhall Farm, Chaddesley Corbett, nr Kidderminster, Worcs DY10 4QQ), *b* 1930; *ed* Canford, and St Andrews Univ (MA 1951); late 2nd Lt RA; HM Overseas Civil Ser, Uganda 1955-62; Sr Assist Sec Univ of Birmingham 1962-89: *m* 1963, Rosalie Margaret, da of Keith Newell, of Wentworth, Neston, Ches, and has issue living, Philip David Archdale, *b* 1969, — Jeremy Frederick Mathews, *b* 1972, — Catherine Ducarel, *b* 1963: *m* 1991, Stephen William Milgrew Piggin, son of Desmond Piggin, of Auckland, NZ, — Sarah Rosalie, *b* 1965: *m* 1992, Peter Mark Creber, son of David Creber, of Saltash, Cornwall, and has issue living, Thomas Jack *b* 1994.

The 1st baronet, Sir Charles Grave Hudson, was a Director of the South Sea Co, and High Sheriff of Leicestershire 1780. Sir Charles Thomas, 2nd baronet, assumed the surname of Palmer, by Royal sign-manual, 1813, on succeeding to the estates of his maternal grandfather, Henry Palmer, of Wanlip.

PALMER (UK) 1886, of Grinkle Park, co York, and of Newcastle-upon-Tyne

May the success be equal to the labour

Sir (CHARLES) MARK PALMER, 5th *Baronet, b (posthumous)* 21 Nov 1941; *s* his father, *Major Sir* ANTHONY FREDERICK MARK, 1941; *ed* Eton; was a Page of Honour to HM 1956-59: *m* 1976, Hon Catherine Elizabeth Tennant, yr da of 2nd Baron Glenconner, and has issue.

Arms – Sable, on a chevron between three crescents in chief and a lion passant in base argent, two tilting spears chevronwise proper. Crest – In front of a tilting spear erect proper a wyvern or, resting the dexter foot on a crescent argent. *Residences* – Mill Hill Farm, Sherborne, Glos; 15 Bramerton St, SW3.

SON LIVING

ARTHUR MORRIS, *b* 9 March 1981.

DAUGHTER LIVING

Iris Henriette, *b* 1977.

SISTER LIVING

Antonia Mary (*Lady Christopher J. Thynne*), *b* 1940: *m* 1968, Lord Christopher John Thynne, of Britmore House, Donhead St Andrew, nr Shaftesbury, Dorset SP7 9EB (*see* M Bath).

AUNTS LIVING

Diana Mabel, *b* 1917: *m* 1939, Squadron-Leader Vivian William Huntington, JP, who *d* 1989, and has issue living, Nicholas Charles, *b* 1940, — Anthony Patrick, *b* 1942, — Peter William, *b* 1945: *m* 1983 (*m diss* 1994), Philippa Carolyn, elder da of Sir Archibald Bruce Charles Edmonstone, 7th Bt, and has issue living, Thomas William *b* 1988, Louise Mary *b* 1986, — Richard Ian, *b* 1946. *Residence* – Bonawe House, Taynault, Argyll. —— Angela, *b* 1921; sometime in WRNS: *m* 1948, Lt-Col John Turnbull, MC, 11th Hussars, who *d* 1986, and has issue living, Richard, *b* 1951: *m* 1978, Sally, da of — McKeen, and has issue living, Robert *b* 1980, James *b* 1982, — Michael, *b* 1953, — Anna, *b* 1950. *Residence* – Well Cottage, Lingen, Bucknall, Salop.

WIDOW LIVING OF FOURTH BARONET

Henriette Alice, DCVO (*Lady Abel Smith*), da of late Cdr Francis Charles Cadogan, RN (*see* E Cadogan, colls); a JP; appointed a Lady-in-Waiting to HM the Queen when HRH Princess Elizabeth 1949, a Woman of the Bedchamber to HM the Queen 1952-53, an Extra Woman of the Bedchamber 1953-73, since when again a Woman of the Bedchamber to HM the Queen; CVO 1964, DCVO 1977: *m* 1st, 1939, Maj Sir Antony Frederick Mark Palmer, 4th baronet, who was *ka* 1941; 2ndly, 1953, Brig Sir Alexander Abel Smith, KCVO, TD, JP (D Somerset, colls), who *d* 1980. *Residence* – The Garden House, Quenington, Cirencester, Glos.

COLLATERAL BRANCHES LIVING

Grandaughters of Capt Lionel Hugo Palmer (infra):—
Issue of late Charles Lionel Palmer, *b* 1909, *d* 1987: *m* 1937, Karoline (LRAM) (52 Patika Av, Weston, Ontario M9N 2E9, Canada), da of late Maj Carl Gach, of Vienna:—
Diana Lillian (7811 Yonge St, Apt 1110, Thornhill, Ontario L3T 4S3, Canada), *b* 1939. —— Marjorie Tessa, *b* 1950: *m* 1978, Dennis Tallevi, of 1234 April Drive, Mississauga, Ontario L5J 3J7, Canada.

Issue of late Capt Lionel Hugo Palmer, 6th son of 1st baronet, *b* 1870, *d* 1914: *m* 1st, 1894, Ida Brae, who *d* 1905, da of Wilberforce Wilson (formerly Surveyor-Gen of Hong Kong); 2ndly, 1906, Blanche, who *d* 1965, only da of Walter Balmford, of York:—
(By 2nd *m*) Marjorie Blanche, *b* 1907; is a Member of Imperial So of Teachers of Dancing; late Junior Com ATS: *m* 1939, Philip Ashford Klitz, who *d* 1942. *Residence* – 27 Abbey House, Cirencester, Glos GL7 2QU.

Issue of late Godfrey Mark Palmer, 7th son of 1st baronet, *b* 1878, *d* 1933: *m* 1906, Eleonora Mary, who *d* 1965, da of late Alexander Geddes, of Blairmore, Aberdeenshire:—
Mark, TD, *b* 1917; *ed* Eton and abroad; European War 1939-45 as Major 2nd Batn Princess Louise's Kensington Regt (TA) (American Bronze Star): *m* 1939, Rosemary Aileen, da of late Edward Welton, and has issue living, Ferelith Alison (*Hon Mrs James Drummond*), *b* 1946: *m* 1st, 1971 (*m diss* 1984), Ashley Gordon Down; 2ndly, 1988, Hon James Reginald Drummond (*see* E Perth), and has issue living (by 1st *m*), John Mark Palmer, *b* 1979, Selina Eleanor *b* 1975. *Residence* – Stanners Hill House, Chobham, Woking, Surrey. —— Myrtle Frances (East Cottage, Oswaldkirk, York YO6 5XZ), *b* 1912; resumed the surname of Palmer in lieu of Robinson by deed poll 1944: *m* 1st, 1940 (*m diss* 1944), Fl-Lt Guy Robinson, RAF; 2ndly, 1948 (*m diss* 1962), Horace Barker; 3rdly, 1967, Edward Walsh Tetley, and has issue living (by 2nd *m*), Rachel Kay, *b* 1950: *m* 1974, Christopher Rodney Wilson, of 8 Foskett Rd, SW6, and has issue living, Mark Christopher *b* 1984, Serena Annabel *b* 1980.

The 1st baronet, Sir Charles Mark, was a coal-owner and founder of the town of Jarrow, of which he was the first Mayor 1875, and was MP for N Durham (*L*) 1874, and from 1874 to 1885, and for Jarrow Div of co Durham 1885 to 1907. The 4th baronet, Major Sir Anthony Frederick Mark, RA, was *ka* 1941.

Palmer (Fuller-Palmer-Acland), see Acland.

PARKER (E) 1681, of Melford Hall, Suffolk

Sir RICHARD WILLIAM HYDE PARKER, 12th *Baronet*; *b* 5 April 1937; *s* his father, *Sir* WILLIAM STEPHEN HYDE, 1951; *ed* Millfield, and Roy Agricultural Coll, Cirencester: *m* 1972 (Elizabeth) Jean, da of late Sir (Henry John) Lindores Leslie, 9th Bt (*cr* 1625), and has issue.

Arms – Quarterly: 1st and 4th, sable, a buck's head cabossed, between two flaunches argent, *Parker*; 2nd and 3rd azure, a chevron between three lozenges or, *Hyde*. Crest – A dexter arm erect, vested azure, slashed and cuffed argent, holding in the hand proper an attire of a stag gules.
Seat – Melford Hall, Long Melford, Suffolk.

SON LIVING

WILLIAM JOHN HYDE, *b* 10 June 1983.

DAUGHTERS LIVING

Beata Hyde, *b* 1973. —— Margaret Hyde *b* (twin), 1973. —— Lucy Hyde, *b* 1975.

SISTER LIVING

Elisabeth Mary Hyde (*Baroness Camoys*), *b* 1939: *m* 1966, 7th Baron Camoys, of Stonor Park, Henley on Thames, Oxon, and has issue (*see* B Camoys).

WIDOW LIVING OF ELEVENTH BARONET

Ulla Ditlef, da of late Professor C. Ditlef Nielsen, DPh, of Copenhagen, Denmark: *m* 1st, 1931, Sir William Stephen Hyde Parker, 11th baronet, who *d* 1951; 2ndly, 1954, Frederick William Hammond, who *d* 1967. *Residence* – Melford Hall, Long Melford, Suffolk.

COLLATERAL BRANCHES LIVING

Issue of late Laurence Hyde Parker, 5th son of 9th baronet, *b* 1870, *d* 1950: *m* 1906, Ada Letitia Moor, who *d* 1968, el da of late Joseph Alphonsus Horsford, MRCS, of Long Melford, Suffolk:—

Laurence Edmond Hyde, *b* 1912; late Fl Lt RAFVR; 1939-45 War: *m* 1953, Margarethe Van Thörne, and has issue living, Anthony Laurence Hyde, *b* 1958: *m* 1986, Bridget Charlotte, yst da of late Arthur Stearns, of Ranworth House, Harleston, Norfolk, and has issue living, Thomas Frederick Laurence Hyde *b* 1989, Sophie Antonia Hyde *b* 1992, — Michael Edmond Hyde, *b* 1961, — Jane Katarina Hyde, *b* 1954: *m* 1977, J. Skybak. *Residence* – Smeetham Hall, Bulmer, Sudbury, Suffolk. —— Mary Hyde, MBE, *b* 1908; 1939-45 War as Squadron Officer, WAAF, (despatches); MBE (Civil) 1977. *Residence* – Smeetham Hall, Bulmer, Sudbury, Suffolk.

Granddaughters of Capt John Barnardiston Hyde Parker, 7th son of 9th baronet:—
Issue of late Edmond Francis Hyde Parker, *b* 1912, *d* 1966: *m* 1946, Naomi (Huish Farm, Huish Episcopi, Langport, Somerset), da of late Dr. D. Carmichael Thomas, of Langport, Som:—
Auriol Katharine Hyde, *b* 1950: *m* 1974, Maj Meyrick David Griffith-Jones, 13th/18th R Hussars (Queen Mary's Own) (ret), of King's Stag House, King's Stag, Sturminster Newton, Dorset, and has had issue, Edmond Laugharne Hyde, *b* 1979, — Jocelyn Hyde Laugharne *b* 1980, *d* 1988, — Piers Laugharne Hyde *b* 1989, — Eluned Hyde Laugharne (twin), *b* 1989. —— Sophia Naomi Lucy Hyde, *b* 1952: *m* 1970, Glynn Mark Alexander Gray-Read, of The Forge, Gotton, Cheddon Fitzpaine, Taunton, Somerset, and has issue living, Oliver Mark Forrester, *b* 1980, — Julian Frederick Thomas, *b* 1982. —— Harriet Ann Hyde, *b* 1953: *m* 1983, Alexander John Maxwell Findlater, of 8 Freegrove Rd, N7, only son of Herbert Maxwell Findlater, of The Glebe Cottage, Bucklebury, Reading, Berks, and has issue living, Frederica Harriet Maxwell, *b* 1986, — Leonora Frances Maxwell, *b* 1988.

Grandchildren of late Harry Richard Hyde Parker, yst son of Maj-Gen John Boteler Parker, son of Adm Sir Hyde Parker, 2nd son of 5th baronet:—
Issue of late Reginald John Parker, *b* 1894, *d* 1957: *m* 1927, Violet Jackson:—
(Reginald Harry) Richard Hyde (6 Manor Close, Ickleford, Hitchin, Herts), *b* 1931: *m* 1st, 1957 (*m diss* 1961), Dorothy Margaret Stanley; 2ndly, 1962, Anne Bulmer, and has had issue (by 2nd *m*), Simon Richard Hyde, *b* 1985, *d* 1985, — Emma Jayne Hyde, *b* 1962. —— Eve Frances Hyde, *b* 1932; is a SRN: *m* 1968, William Leavey. *Residence* – 4 Salcombe Drive, Earley, Reading.
Issue of late Edward Hyde Parker, *b* 1899, *d* 19—: *m* 1928, Ethel, who *d* 19—, da of Henry Mortimore:—
Alan Hyde, *b* 1933; *ed* Hertford, and Birmingham Univ (BSc). —— David Hugh Hyde (16 May Tree Av, Garden Village, Hull), *b* 1934: *m* 1959, Brenda, da of Henry McIntosh, BEM, and has issue living, Rosemary Hyde, *b* 1960, — Anne Hyde, *b* 1962.

The 1st baronet, Sir Hugh, was an Alderman of London. The 2nd baronet, Sir Henry, *m* Margaret, da and heir of Alexander Hyde, Bishop of Salisbury, 1st cousin of 1st Earl of Clarendon, Lord Chancellor. The 5th baronet, Adm Sir Hyde, commanded in the action of St Lucia 1780, and in the memorable action with the Dutch on the Dogger Bank 1781. In 1782 he was nominated to the chief command of the British Fleet in the East Indies. He sailed from England in the 'Cato,' which vessel never having been heard of after leaving Rio de Janeiro, is supposed to have been lost with all hands. Other members of this family have also been distinguished both in the Navy and the Army.

PARKER (UK) 1844, of Shenstone Lodge, Staffordshire

Sir (WILLIAM) PETER BRIAN PARKER, 5th *Baronet*; *b* 30 Nov 1950; *s* his father, *Sir* (WILLIAM) ALAN, 1990; *ed* Eton; FCA; ptnr Stephenson Nuttall & Co, Newark: *m* 1976, Patricia Ann, da of R. and Dorothy Evelyn Filtness, of Lea Cottage, Beckingham, Lincoln, and has issue.

𝕬rms – Gules, a chevron or between three leopards' faces or. 𝕮rest – A leopard's head erased, affrontée, ducally gorged or.
Residence – Apricot Hall, Sutton-cum-Beckingham, Lincoln, LN5 0RE.

SON LIVING

JOHN MALCOLM, *b* 14 May 1980.

DAUGHTER LIVING

Sub libertate qui etem
Under liberty rest

Lucy Emma, *b* 1977.

SISTER LIVING

Lindy Ruth, *b* 1947; *ed* Durham Univ (BA): *m* 1969, Prof Robert Samuel Moore, PhD, of Bennachie, Carmel Rd, Holywell, Clwyd CH8 6DD, and has issue living, David Kenneth, *b* 1974, — Heloise Catherine, *b* 1976.

AUNT LIVING (*Daughter of 3rd baronet*)

(Ruth Kathleen) Betty, *b* 1920; 1939-45 War with First Aid Nursing Yeo: *m* 1947, Richard Arthur Cole-Hamilton (*see* E Enniskillen, colls), who *d* 1992. *Residence* – Hawthorn Villa, 386 Ferry Rd, Edinburgh EH5 3QG.

WIDOW LIVING OF FOURTH BARONET

SHEELAGH MARY (*Sheelagh, Lady Parker*), only da of late Dr Sinclair Stevenson, of Beech Lawn, Fareham, Hants: *m* 1946, Sir (William) Alan Parker, 4th Bt, who *d* 1990. *Residence* – Apricot Hall, Sutton-cum-Beckingham, Lincoln LN5 0RE.

COLLATERAL BRANCHES LIVING

Issue of late John Douglas Parker, 2nd son of 3rd baronet, *b* 1924; *d* 1980: *m* 1958, Iris Anne, who *d* 1959, yst da of late Cdr G. A. Titterton, RN, of 4 Clarence House, Granville Rd, Eastbourne:—
Timothy John, *b* 1959.

Granddaughter of late Col William Frederick Parker, elder son of Adm George Parker, 2nd son of 1st baronet:—

Issue of late Capt William Mackworth Parker, Rifle Brig (Prince Consort's Own), *b* 1886, *ka* 1915: *m* 1912, Lillian Ursula, an OStJ who *d* 1966 (having *m* 2ndly, 1921, Vice-Adm Everard John Hardman-Jones, CB, OBE, who *d* 1962), da of late Col Sir Arthur Pendarves Vivian, KCB (B Swansea, colls):—
Letitia Margaret (Delamore, Cornwood, Ivybridge, Devon), *b* 1914: *m* 1942, Dennis Seaver Dollard, who *d* 1983, and has issue living, Anthony Brian Christopher, *b* 1949, — Gavin James Dominic, *b* 1950.

Issue of late Cyril George Parker, *b* 1890; *d* 1968: *m* 1st, 1921, Beatrice, who *d* 1928, da of W. Harris; 2ndly, 1934, Margaret May, da of John Holmes Graham, and widow of Wallace Bruce MagDougall:—
(By 1st *m*) Laurence Frederick Cyril, *b* 1922: *m* 1951, Dorothy May, da of R. S. Kent, and has issue living, Allen Kent, *b* 1954, — Beatrice Anne, *b* 1952, — Donna Gail, *b* 1956, — Nancy Kay, *b* 1958.

Grandchildren of late Mackworth Praed Parker (infra):—
Issue of late Capt Gerard Parker, *b* 1896, *d* 1976: *m* 1st, 1921, Dorothy, who *d* 1954, da of late Lt-Col Francis Marwood Hext; 2ndly, 1958, Jill Lettice Mary, el da of R. W. K. Nott:—
(By 2nd *m*) Gerard Mackworth, *b* 1958. —— Julius Praed, *b* 1959. —— Susan Mary, *b* 1961.

Granddaughter of late Adm George Parker (ante):—
Issue of late Mackworth Praed Parker, *b* 1865, *d* 1926: *m* 1893, Sybil Edith, who *d* 1934, da of late Lieut-Col John Arthur Thomas Garratt, JP:—
Sybil Muriel, *b* 1895: *m* 1921, Maj Montagu Irvine Gedoin Jenkins, DSO, who *d* 1948, and *d* 1978, leaving issue living, Vivien Naomi, *b* 1930.

The 1st baronet, grandson of the Right Hon Sir Thomas Parker (of Park Hall, Staffordshire, Lord Chief Baron of the Exchequer), commanded in the Tagus during the war between Dom Pedro and Dom Miguel; he was a Lord of the Admiralty in 1834 and 1835-41, principal naval ADC to HM Queen Victoria. Commander-in-Chief during Chinese war 1841-2, in Mediterranean 1845-52, and at Devonport 1854-57, and sometime Senior Admiral of the Fleet. Thomas Parker, father of 1st Earl of Macclesfield, was a yr son of George Parker, of Park Hall (*d* 1675).

PARKYNS (E) 1681, of Bunney Park, Nottinghamshire (Dormant 1926)

(Although the existence of an heir is probable, since the death of the 6th Baronet in 1926 a right to the Baronetcy has not yet been officially established).

DAUGHTER LIVING OF SIXTH BARONET

Sylvia Dorothy, *b* 1887: *m* 1912 (*m diss* 1931), Allan Gilbert Cram, and has issue living, Thomas, *b* 191—, — a da, *b* 19—.

COLLATERAL BRANCHES LIVING

Grandchildren of late Edwin Garling Territt Parkyns (infra):—
Issue of late Garling Alfred Parkyns, *b* 1913, *d* 1984: *m* 1935, Lucy Frances Laycock (Lot 3, 50 Bent St, Tuncurry, NSW, Australia):—
Garling Alfred (Lot 72, Sprimont St, Canterbury Estate, Bald Hills, Queensland 4036, Australia), *b* 1936: *m* 19—, and has issue living, Alan, *b* 19—, — Geoffrey, *b* 19—. —— Frances Ann, *b* 1938. —— Yvonne, *b* 1943. —— Janette, *b* 1945. —— Marie, *b* 1948.

Grandchildren of late Francis Charles Parkyns, son of Edward Territt Parkyns, son of Capt Levett Broadley Parkyns (*b* 1779), grandson of George Parkyns, brother of 3rd baronet:—
Issue of late Edwin Garling Territt Parkyns, *b* 1890, *d* 1975: *m* 1912, Emily Alice, who *d* 1974, da of late George Walter Wood, JP, of Mill Rd, Liverpool, NSW:—
Kenneth George (2 Rose St, Liverpool, NSW 2170), *b* 1917: *m* 1945, Patricia May Robins, and has issue living, Robert Carswell, *b* 1946, — Lindsay Hampton, *b* 1948. —— Clifford Edwin Frederick (26 Rose St, Liverpool, NSW 2170, Australia), *b* 1926: *m* 1950, Shirley Dawn Hornby, and has issue living, Gregory Edwin, *b* 1952: *m* 1979, Mary Richards, and has issue living, Ryan *b* 1979, Guy *b* 1991, Clayton *b* 1984, — Vicki Anne, *b* 1962: *m* 1985, Christopher Andrew Livingstone, and has issue living, Jayde *b* 1987, Emily *b* 1991, Kyrstal *b* 1992. —— Gladys Lorraine (4 Rose St, Liverpool, NSW 2170), *b* 1915: *m* 1936 (*m diss* 19—), Kenneth Leonard Weston-Brown, and has issue living, Brian, *b* 1936: *m* 1956, Margaret Calpin, and has issue living, Deborah *b* 1958: *m* 1987, Dennis Low, and has issue living, Briana *b* 1989, Lian 1991, Megan *b* 1965: *m* 1984, David Spencer, and has issue living, Joshua *b* 1985, Elizabeth *b* 1990, — Kenneth Weston, *b* 1938: *m* 1959, Hazel Cheesman, and has issue living, Andrew *b* 1964: *m* 1991, Rosemary Christopher, Craig *b* 1973, Murray *b* 1975, Justine *b* 1968: *m* 1990, Jason Thelander, and has issue living, Georgia *b* 1991, — Peter Weston (Lot 1, Lake Rd, Elrington, NSW 2325, Australia), *b* 1946: *m* 1966, Joy Clark, and has issue living, Ian *b* 1974, Glen *b* 1976, Ryan *b* 1984, Emily *b* 1979, Sara *b* 1981, — Wendy Lorraine, *b* 1940: *m* 1960, Bruce McGowan, and has issue living, Robert *b* 1962: *m* 19—, Dianne Allison, and has issue living, Christopher *b* 1993, Sharon *b* 1960: *m* 19—, Peter Hellyer, and has issue living, Mark *b* 1990, Nicole *b* 1988. —— Enid Dorothy, *b* 1922: *m* 1947, Donald Douglas Floyd, of 14 Rose St, Liverpool, NSW, Australia, and *d* 1991, leaving issue living, Douglas Stewart, *b* 1948: *m* 1970, Christine Holland, and has issue living, Bradley *b* 1981, Michele *b* 1972, Kylie *b* 1974, Renee *b* 1979, — Robyn Lorraine, *b* 1950: *m* 1972, Robert Perrim, of 18 Gardenia Av, Emu Plains, NSW, and has issue living, Brett *b* 1974, Stuart *b* 1980, Amanda *b* 1976, Narelle *b* 1978.

Grandsons of late Edward Territt Parkyns (ante):—
Issue of late Edwin Downing Parkyns *b* 1865, *d* 19—: *m* 1896, Cassilla Cole, who *d* 1955:—
Henry Jones, *b* 1896. —— Edwin Arnold Allan, *b* 1898.
Issue of late Henry Garling Parkyns, *b* 1867, *d* 1938: *m* 1907, Mary McClifty, who *d* 1944:—
Daniel George, *b* 1916: *m* 1942, Evelyn Mary Cook.

PASLEY (GB) 1794, of Craig, Dumfriesshire
(Name pronounced "Paisley")

*Fighting for my king
and country*

Sir (JOHN) MALCOLM SABINE PASLEY, 5th *Baronet*; *b* 5 April 1926; *s* his father, *Sir* RODNEY MARSHALL SABINE, 1982; *ed* Sherborne, and Trin Coll, Oxford (MA); Emeritus Fellow of Magdalen Coll, Oxford, FBA: *m* 1965, Virginia Killigrew, da of Peter Lothian Killigrew Wait, of Kew, Surrey, and has issue.

Arms – Azure, on a chevron argent between two roses in chief of the last, and an anchor in base or, three thistles slipped proper. **Crest** – Out of a naval coronet gold, a sinister arm in armour proper, grasping in the hand a staff thereon a flag argent, charged with a cross couped gules, and on a canton azure a human leg erect, couped above the knee or.
Residence – 25 Lathbury Rd, Oxford.

SONS LIVING

ROBERT KILLIGREW SABINE, *b* 23 Oct 1965. —— Humphrey Sabine, *b* 1967.

COLLATERAL BRANCHES LIVING

Grandsons of late William Sabine Pasley (infra):—
Issue of late Eric Kinnersley Sabine Pasley, *b* 1900, *d* 1975: *m* 1st, 1928, Thelma, who *d* 1948, da of late John Power, of Auckland, NZ; 2ndly, 1949, his cousin, Rona Norma Sabine, who *d* 1978, da of late Russell Sabine Pasley (infra):—
(By 1st *m*) Thomas Sabine (141 Moana Av, Nelson, NZ), *b* 1929; a Member of Real Estate Inst NZ: *m* 1958, Helen Aroha, da of Justin Beauchamp Foster-Barham, of Nelson, NZ, and has had issue, Malcolm Sabine, *b* 1960, — Alastair Sabine, *b* 1963: *m* 1993, Elizabeth, da of William Rackley, of Nelson, — Hamish Sabine *b* 1964; *k* in an accident 1982. —— Warren Sabine (3 Butler St, Opawa, Christchurch, NZ), *b* 1931: *m* 1955 (*m diss* 1980), Margaret Mae, el da of John Douglas McIntosh, of Dunedin, NZ, and has issue living, Jonathan Douglas Sabine, *b* 1961, — Joanne Tui Sabine, *b* 1959. —— John Clinton Sabine (116 Queen St, Northcote, Auckland, NZ), *b* 1936: *m* 1960, Monica Therese, da of Patrick Reilly, of Christchurch, NZ, and has issue living, Matthew Patrick, *b* 1961: *m* 1984, Julie, da of Roderick Langridge, of Auckland, and has issue living, Thomas Michael *b* 1988, — Paul Joseph Eric, *b* 1962: *m* 1991, Amanda, da of John Fear, of Auckland, and has issue living, Emma Rose *b* 1994, — John Nicholas, *b* 1963, — Thomas Anthony, *b* 1966: *m* 1988, Jane, da of Sean Walsh, of Auckland, and has issue living, Andrew Sean Sabine *b* 1990, Alexandra Hannah Sabine *b* 1992, — Clare Monica, *b* 1968.

Granddaughters of late Rodney Stewart Lyons Sabine Pasley, 2nd son of 2nd baronet:—
Issue of late Montagu Thomas Sabine Pasley, *b* 1869, *d* 1947: *m* 1900, Agnes Jane, who *d* 1965, da of late John Innes, of Invercargill, NZ:—
Nancy Sabine, *b* 1907: *m* 1932, Robert Paterson Barr. *Residence* – 1360 Burnaby Street, Vancouver, British Columbia.
Issue of late William Sabine Pasley, *b* 1870, *d* 1938: *m* 1900, Florence Annie Heloise, who *d* 1959, da of late W. H. Kinnersley:—
Dorothy Madelene Sabine, *b* 1906: *m* 1939, Victor Patrick Coghlan, who *d* 1986. *Residence* – 8 Victoria Rd, Nelson, NZ.

Grandchildren of late Russell Sabine Pasley, yst son of late Rodney Stewart Lyons Sabine Pasley (ante):—
Issue of late Maitland Sabine Pasley, *b* 1914, *d* 1972: *m* 1943, Nancy Molyneux (56 Severn St, Islands Bay, Wellington, NZ), da of John Phillips, of Te Puke, NZ:—
Philip Sabine (Bamfords Rd, R.D.1 Lyttelton, Christchurch, NZ), *b* 1945: *m* 1969, Colleen Monica, el da of Daniel Doyle, of Ch Ch, NZ, and has issue living, Stuart Sabine, *b* 1974, — Andrea Sabine, *b* 1972, — Vanessa Sabine, *b* 1977. —— Russell Sabine, *b* 1947. —— Christine Sabine, *b* 1950: *m* 1972, Robert John Lang.

Grandchildren of late Capt Montagu Wynyard Sabine Pasley, RA (infra):—
Issue of late Maj-Gen Joseph Montagu Sabine Pasley, CB, CBE, MVO, *b* 1898, *d* 1978: *m* 1st, 1926 (*m diss* 1948), Christina Joan, da of John Darby, of Hillmorton House, nr Rugby; 2ndly, 1950, Dorothy Beatrice, da of W. J. Fance, of Parkstone, Dorset, and widow of F/Lt C. W. Parsons:—
(By 1st *m*) Anne Sabine, *b* 1929: *m* 1st, 1951 (*m diss* 1977), Maj John G. Melsom; 2ndly, 1978, Brig Guy Reginald Rowbotham, CBE, of Nobles House, 18 Station Rd, Petersfield, Hants GU32 3ES, and has issue living (by 1st *m*) Andrew John (South House, Ham, nr Marlborough, Wilts), *b* 1953; *ed* Uppingham: *m* 1980, Melanie Claire, da of Maj James Derek Kenyon-Hague, MC, of South House, Ham, Marlborough, Wilts (*see* Thompson, Bt, cr 1806), and has had issue, Harry George *b* 1984, Andrew Jack *b* 1987 *d* 1988, Edwina Lily *b* 1989, Cecily Kate *b* 1992. —— (By 2nd *m*) Malcolm Peter Sabine, *b* 1956; *ed* Marlborough.

Granddaughter of late Maj Maitland Warren Bouverie Sabine Pasley, 3rd son of 2nd baronet:—
Issue of late Capt Montagu Wynyard Sabine Pasley, RA, *b* 1863, *d* 1944: *m* 1891, Grace Lilian, who *d* 1919, da of late Capt J. H. H. St John:—
Lillian Katherine Sabine, *b* 1895: *m* 1919, Alexander Louis Courtenay Lumsden, who *d* 1959, and has issue living, Alexander Sabine Courtenay (The White House, Deptford, nr Warminster, Wilts), *b* 1921; 1939-34 War as Fl-Lt RAFVR: *m* 1st, 1943, Elisabeth Jean, da of Group-Capt B. P. H. de Roeper, AFC, RAF; 2ndly, 1951, Elisabeth Vrena, da of late Sqdn-Ldr W. R. Adkins; 3rdly, 1969, Elizabeth Moncrieff, da of late Lt-Col Alexander Robert Cheale, TD, of Tunbridge Wells, and formerly wife of Colin W. Morley, and has issue living, (by 2nd *m*) Peter Alexander Courtenay, *b* 1961, (by 1st *m*) Julia Frances Sabine *b* 1945, (by 2nd *m*) Penelope Elisabeth Courtenay *b* 1956.

Grandchildren of late Capt Hamilton Sabine Pasley, 5th son of 2nd baronet:—
Issue of late Richard Sydney Sabine Pasley, *b* 1862, *d* 1911: *m* 1897, Mary Victoria, who *d* 1942, da of Sir Henry Dalrymple Des Vœux, 5th Bt:—
Audrey Christina Sabine, *b* 1905. *Residence* – Wistaria Cottage, Maresfield, Sussex.
Issue of late Charles Malcolm Sabine Pasley, *b* 1864, *d* 1907: *m* 1903, Berthe, who *d* 1964, da of late Comte de Rilly:—
Charles Hamilton Sabine (55 Ewan St, Margate 4019, Qld, Aust), *b* 1906; Roy Australian Air Force (ret); 1939-45 War (despatches): *m* 1933, Marjorie May Heales, and has issue living, Helen Sabine, *b* 1934.

Granddaughter of late Richard Sydney Sabine Pasley (ante):—

Issue of late Arthur Dalrymple Sabine Pasley, *b* 1903, *d* 1980: *m* 1st, 1943, Doris, who *d* 1950, da of Herbert Rastell; 2ndly, 1950, Hilda Mary, da of William H. Gardner:—
(By 2nd *m*) Victoria Mary Sabine, *b* 1952: *m* 1975, Fernando Antonio Palacios, of Santiago, Chile.

The 1st baronet, Adm Sir Thomas Pasley, was created a baronet, with remainder to the issue male of his daughters successively, and in 1808 was succeeded by his grandson, Thomas Sabine, who assumed by Roy licence the surname of Pasley, 1809.

Paston-Bedingfeld, see Bedingfeld.

Pauncefort-Duncombe, see Duncombe.

PEARSON (UK) 1916, of St Dunstan's, co London (Extinct 1982)

Sir Neville Arthur Pearson, 2nd and last *Baronet*.

DAUGHTERS LIVING OF SECOND BARONET (*By 1st marriage*)

Anne (*Baroness Glenkinglas*), *b* 1923: *m* 1940, Baron Glenkinglas (Life Baron), of Strone, Cairndow, Argyll, who *d* 1984.

(*By 2nd marriage*)

Sally, *b* 1929: *m* 1961 (*m diss* 1986), (Timothy Sydney) Robert Hardy, CBE, actor, and writer, and has issue living, Emma Jocelyn Cressida Myfanwy, *b* 1963: *m* 1989, Hamish A. Bullough, son of Alaisdhair Bullough, and has issue living, Alice Miranda *b* 1991, — Justine Elinor Eldrydd, *b* 1966. *Residence* – Upper Bolney House, Upper Bolney, Henley on Thames.

PEARSON (UK) 1964, of Gressingham, co Palatine of Lancaster

Sir (Francis) Nicholas Fraser Pearson, 2nd *Baronet*; *b* 28 Aug 1943; *s* his father, *Sir* Francis Fenwick, MBE, 1991; *ed* Radley; Capt 3rd Bn Rifle bde 1961-60; ADC to C-in-C Far East 1969; company dir: *m* 1978, Henrietta, da of Cdr Henry Pasley-Tyler, of Coton Manor, Guilsborough, Northants.
Address – c/o Natwest Bank, Kirkby Lonsdale, Cumbria. *Club* – Carlton.

SISTER LIVING

Susan Alison Mary, *b* 1941: *m* 1961, Peter Sharp, of Linden Hall, Borwick, Carnforth, Lancs, and has had issue, James Edward, *b* 1967, — Harriet Nicola, *b* 1962, — Joanna Katharine Rose, *b* 1963, *d* 1989.

WIDOW LIVING OF FIRST BARONET

Katharine Mary (*Katharine, Lady Pearson*), da of Rev David Denholm Fraser, of Sprouston, Kelso, Roxburghshire: *m* 1938, Sir Francis Fenwick Pearson, 1st Bt, MBE, who *d* 1991. *Residence* – The Old Vicarage, Burton in Lonsdale, Carnforth, Lancs.

The 1st baronet, Sir Francis Fenwick Pearson, MBE, son of Frank Pearson, of Kirkby Lonsdale, Westmorland, was ADC to Viceroy of India 1934-36, Under Sec Indian Political Dept 1942-45, and Ch Min Maipur State 1945-47, MP (C) for Clitheroe Div of Lancs 1959-70, PPS to Rt Hon Alec Douglas-Home 1963-64, and Chm Central Lancs New Town Development Corpn 1971.

PEASE (UK) 1882, of Hutton Lowcross and Pinchinthorpe, co York

Sir (ALFRED) VINCENT PEASE, 4th *Baronet; b* 2 April 1926; *s* his half-brother, *Sir* EDWARD, 1963, *ed* Bootham Sch, York.

Arms – Per fesse azure and gules, a fesse nebuly ermine between two lambs passant in chief argent, and in base upon a mount proper a dove rising argent, holding in the beak a pea stalk, the blossom and pods proper. **Crest** – Upon the capital of an Ionic column a dove rising, holding in the beak a pea stalk as in the arms.
Residence – 149 Aldenham Rd, Guisborough, Cleveland TS14 8LB.

BROTHER LIVING

JOSEPH GURNEY, *b* 16 Nov 1927; *ed* Bootham Sch, York; was a Member of Guisborough Urban District Council 1950-53; Pres NW Regional Liberal Party 1970 and 1971: *m* 1953, Shelagh Munro, da of Cyril G. Bulman, of Great Langdale, Ambleside, Westmorland, and has issue living, Charles Edward Gurney, *b* 1955, — Jane Elizabeth Gurney, *b* 1957: *m* 1990, Colin Charles Bright, elder son of William C. J. Bright, of Southsea, Hants. *Residence* – Oak Tree House, Woodhall, Askrigg, Leyburn, N Yorks DL8 3LB.

SISTER LIVING

Anne Phillida, *b* 1923; formerly in WRNS: *m* 1946, Major Edward Mark Chetwynd-Stapylton, King's Roy Rifle Corps (*see* V Chetwynd, colls). *Residence* – 110 Western Rd, Lewes, E Sussex BN7 1RR.

Peace and hope

COLLATERAL BRANCHES LIVING

Issue of late Capt Christopher York Pease, Yeo, younger son of 2nd baronet, *b* 1886; *ka* 1918: *m* 1910, Margaret Philippa, who *d* 1959, da of late Walter Johnson, JP (Bell, Bt, *cr* 1885):—
Rachel Hebe Philippa, *b* 1911: *m* 1940, Richard Selby Smith, Lieut-Com, RNVR, and Prof Emeritus of Educ Tasmania Univ, and has issue living, Christopher Selby (56 Rotherwood St, Richmond, Victoria 3121), *b* 1942; DPhil Oxon; Visiting Prof, Monash Univ: *m* 1967, Joy Miriam, da of Thomas McGeehan, of Myrtleford, Vic, Aust, and has issue living, David Selby *b* 1969, Hugh Thomas *b* 1975, — Peter Selby (1 Hill St, Blackburn, Vic 3101, Aust), *b* 1948; BCE: *m* 1971, da of John Holroyd, of Rosanna, Vic, Aust, and has issue living, Andrew Selby *b* 1976, Anne Jane *b* 1974, Robyn Clare *b* 1980. *Residence* – Derwent Waters Residential Club, Cadbury Rd, Claremont, Tasmania 7011.

Issue of late Rt Hon Joseph Albert Pease (2nd son of 1st baronet), who was *cr Baron Gainford* 1916 (see that title).

PEASE (UK) 1920, of Hummersknott, Borough of Darlington, co Durham

Sir RICHARD THORN PEASE, 3rd *Baronet, b* 20 May 1922; *s* his father, *Sir* RICHARD Arthur, 1969; *ed* Eton; late Capt 60th Rifles: *m* 1956, Anne, da of late Lt-Col Reginald Francis Heyworth, 1st R Dragoons (*see* By Tweedmouth), and formerly wife of Fl Lt David Henry Lewis Wigan, RAFVR, and has issue.

Arms – Per fesse azure and gules, a fesse nebuly ermine between two lambs passant in chief argent, and in base upon a mount proper a dove rising argent, holding in the beak a pea stalk, the blossom and pods proper. **Crest** – Upon the capital of an Ionic column a dove rising, holding in the beak a pea stalk as in the arms.
Residence – Hindley House, Stocksfield-on-Tyne, Northumberland.

SON LIVING

RICHARD PETER, *b* 4 Sept 1958.

DAUGHTERS LIVING

Carolyn Thorn, *b* 1957: *m* 1981, John Silvester Varley, only son of Philip Varley, of Garden House, Barford Hill, Warwicks, and has issue living, Emma Thorn Anne, *b* 1989. —— Nichola, *b* 1961: *m* 1991, R. Crispin Odey, only son of Richard Odey, of The Kennels, Hotham, York.

Peace and hope

BROTHER LIVING

Derrick Allix, *b* 1927: *m* 1951, Hon Rosemary Portman, da of 5th Viscount Portman, and has issue living, Jonathan Edward, *b* 1952: *m* 1979, Mary, da of Francis Moore Dutton, of Tushingham Hall, Whitchurch, Shropshire, and has issue living, Catherine Annie *b* 1982, Victoria Margaret *b* 1983, Alice Rosie *b* 1991, — Christopher Berkeley, *b* 1958: *m* 1989, Mariana, elder da of Robert Scrymsoure Steuart Fothringham, of Pourie-Fothringham and Murthly (*see* E Gainsborough, colls, 1985 Edn), and has issue living, Edward Robert *b* 1991, Dorothea Elizabeth *b* 1992, Sybilla Mary *b* 1994, — Arthur David *b* 1961: *m* 1994, Lucilla K.H., da of late T.H. Regis, of Wheathampstead, Herts, — Rosalind Jeannette, *b* 1954: *m* 1974, Evan Robert (Joss) Hanbury, of Burley-on-the-Hill, Oakham, Rutland (*see* Birkin, Bt, 1976 Edn), and has issue living, James Robert *b* 1979, William Edward *b* 1983, Susanna Rosemary *b* 1977. *Residences* – 2 Britten St, Chelsea, SW3; Upper Woodcott, Whitchurch, Hants.

SISTER LIVING

Aline Thorn, *b* 1919: *m* 1st, 1940, Patrick Claude Hannay, Flying Officer Aux Air Force, who was *ka* 1940; 2ndly, 1941 (*m diss* 1954), 3rd Earl of Inchcape; 3rdly, 1955 (*m diss* 1968), Thomas Chambers Windsor Roe, who *d* 1988, and has issue living (by 2nd *m*) (*see* E Inchcape), — (by 3rd *m*) Patrick Rupert Windsor (21 Avenue de la Poste, 1009 Pully, Vaud, Switzerland), *b* 1960, — Oriel Melanie Thorn (Rue Caroline 10, 1003 Lausanne, Vaud, Switzerland), *b* 1956. *Residence* – 63 Chemin des Osches, 1009 Pully, Switzerland.

The 1st baronet, Sir Arthur Francis Pease, son of late Arthur Pease, MP, brother of 1st Bt (*cr* 1882 ante), was 2nd Civil Lord of the Admiralty, Jan 1918 to March 1919, and High Sheriff for co Durham 1920.

PECHELL (GB) 1797, of Paglesham, Essex (Extinct 1984)
(Name pronounced "Peechell")

Sir RONALD HORACE PECHELL, 9th and last *Baronet*.

SISTER LIVING OF NINTH BARONET

Pauline Ruth Margaret, *b* 1923: *m* 1941, Rear-Adm Edmund Nicholas Poland (ret), CB, CBE, of Langlawhill, Broughton, Biggar, Lanarkshire, ML12 6HL, and has issue living, Raymond Anthony, *b* 1942; *ed* King's Coll, Taunton, and Imp Coll, London Univ (MSc): *m* 1974, Lucy Sayers, — Roger Hugh, *b* 1949; *ed* King's Coll, Taunton, and Leeds Univ (BSc): *m* 1973, Elisabeth Gutleiben, of Bad Aibling, Bavaria, and has issue living, Eva Ruth Elisabeth *b* 1978, — Andrew Quentin, *b* 1960, — Celia Frances, *b* 1947: *m* 1st, 1969 (*m diss* 1974), John Neil Gardener Govan; 2ndly, 1975 (*m diss* 1977), Richard Rohan-Irwin; 3rdly, 1978, Alfred Wolff, and has issue living (by 2nd *m*), Tracey Elizabeth *b* 1975.

WIDOW LIVING OF EIGHTH BARONET

DORIS MARGERY (*Doris, Lady Pechell*) (25 Marchwood, 8 Manor Rd, Bournemouth), da of late T. Drewitt Lobb, of Kent, and formerly wife of Lt-Col Arthur Thomas Begg Green: *m* 1971, as his 2nd wife, Sir Paul Pechell, 8th Bt, MC, who *d* 1972.

PEEK (UK) 1874, of Rousdon, Devon

Sir FRANCIS HENRY GRENVILLE PEEK, 4th *Baronet*; *b* 16 Sept 1915; *s* his father, *Sir* WILFRID, DSO, 1927; *ed* Eton, and Trin Coll, Camb; ADC to Gov of Bahama Islands 1938-39; 1939-45 War as Lt Irish Guards (despatches): *m* 1st, 1942 (*m diss* 1949), Ruby Joy Ann, who *d* 1968, da of Capt Gordon Duff, late RGA, and widow of Sir Charles Thomas Hewitt Mappin, 4th Bt; 2ndly, 1949 (*m diss* 1967), Marilyn, da of Dr Norman Kerr, of Eleuthera, Bahamas; 3rdly, 1967, Mrs Caroline Kirkwood, da of Sir Robert Lucien Morrison Kirkwood.

Arms – Azure, an estoile argent; in chief three crescents of the last. **Crest** – Two hazel nuts, slipped proper.
Residence – Villa du Parc, 8 Avenue Jean de Noailles, Cannes 06400, France.
Club – White's.

The Master comes

COLLATERAL BRANCH LIVING

Issue of late Capt Roger Grenville Peek, 9th Lancers, 2nd son of 2nd baronet, *b* 1888, *k* on duty in Ireland 1921: *m* 1919, Hon Joan Penelope Sclater-Booth, who *d* 1976, da of 2nd Baron Basing:—
WILLIAM GRENVILLE, *b* 15 Dec 1919; *ed* Eton; Capt late 9th Lancers; 1939-45 War (despatches): *m* 1950, Lucy Jane, da of late Maj Edward Dorrien-Smith, of Weir Point, Restronguet, Falmouth, and has issue living, Richard Grenville, *b* 1955, — Jane Elizabeth, *b* 1952, — Mary Susannah, *b* 1957, — Katherine Julia, *b* 1960. *Residence* – Weekemoor, Loddiswell, Kingsbridge, Devon TQ7 4DY.

Sir Henry William Peek, 1st baronet, sat as MP for Mid Surrey (*C*) 1868-84. The 3rd baronet, Sir Wilfrid, was High Sheriff of Devon 1912, and served in Mesopotamia 1916-19 on Staff, despatches, DSO.

BERESFORD-PEIRSE (UK) 1814, of Bagnall, Waterford

Sir HENRY GRANT DE LA POER BERESFORD-PEIRSE, 6th *Baronet*; *b* 7 Feb 1933; *s* his father, *Sir* HENRY CAMPBELL DE LA POER, CB, 1972; *ed* Eton and Ontario Agric Coll; late Lt Scots Gds: *m* 1966, Jadranka, da of Ivan Njers, of Zagreb, Croatia, and has issue.

Arms – Quarterly, 1sts and 4th, azure, a ducal coronet between three cross-crosslets fitchée or, *Peirse*; 2nd and 3rd, argent, semée of cross-crosslets fitchée, three fleur-de-lis sable, within a bordure wavy ermines, *Beresford*. **Crest** – 1st, a cross-crosslet fitchée or, ensigned by a mural crown gules, *Peirse*, 2nd, out of a naval crown or, a dragon's head per fesse wavy azure and gules, the lower part of the neck transfixed by a broken tilting spear in bend sinister, in the mouth the remaining part of spear in the bend, the point upwards or, *Beresford*. **Mottoes** – Nil Nisi Cruce (*Beresford*); Non Sine Pulvere Palma (*Peirse*).
Seat – Bedall Manor, Bedale, Yorks. *Residence* – 34 Cadogan Sq, SW1.

SONS LIVING

HENRY NJERS DE LA POER, *b* 25 March 1969. ——— John, *b* 1973.

Nil nisi cruce
Depend only on the cross

ADOPTIVE SISTER (*adopted da of 5th baronet*)

Mary Spiers, *b* 1947; is a SSStJ: *m* 1971, Andrew Frank Gilmour, of Pratis House, Leven, Fife KY8 5NX, yr son of Col Sir John Edward Gilmour, 3rd Bt, DSO, TD, and has issue (*see* Gilmour, Bt, *cr* 1897).

WIDOW LIVING OF FIFTH BARONET

MARGARET (*Margaret, Lady Beresford-Peirse*) (Bedall Manor, Bedale, Yorks), da of Frank Morison Seafield Grant, of Knockie, Whitebridge, Inverness-shire: *m* 1932, Sir Henry Campbell de la Poer Beresford-Peirse, 5th Bt, CB, who *d* 1972.

COLLATERAL BRANCHES LIVING

Issue of late Rev Peter de la Poer Beresford-Peirse, yr son of 4th baronet, *b* 1907, *d* 1984: *m* 1940, Muriel (Stable Flat, Danby Hill, Northallerton, N Yorks), da of late Joseph Griffiths, of Barry, S Wales:—
Hugh de la Poer (18 Southway, Carshalton Beeches, Surrey), *b* 1941: *m* 1963, Carolyn Ann Elizabeth, elder da of late Hubert George Frederick Barker, and has issue living, Julian de la Poer, *b* 1966: *m* 1994, Tracy Gates, — Claire Elizabeth, *b* 1969. ——— *Rev* Mark de la Poer (21 Crimple Meadows, Pannal, Harrogate, N Yorks), *b* 1945; *ed* Richmond Sch, Magdalen Coll, Oxford, and Coll of St Mark and St John, Chelsea: *m* 1976, Margaret Joan Arnott, and has had issue, Duncan de la Poer, *b* and *d* 1980, — Rachel Helen, *b* 1977, — Sophia Rosemary, *b* 1981. ——— Mary, *b* 1948. ——— Ruth, *b* (twin) 1948: *m* 1976, Hugh Charles Wrigley, of Danby Hill, Danby Wiske, Northallerton, N Yorks, and has issue living, Elspeth Rosemary, *b* 1977, — Camilla Mary, *b* 1980.

Granddaughters of late Rev Richard Windham de la Poer Beresford-Peirse (infra):—
Issue of late Group Capt Francis Campbell de la Poer Beresford-Peirse, RAF, *b* 1911, *d* 1986: *m* 1st, 1936 (*m diss* 1957), Lady Katharine Lillian Edgcumbe, da of 6th Earl of Mount Edgcumbe; 2ndly, 1958, Kathleen Graham, da of late Charles Machattie:—
(By 1st *m*) Susan Katherine, *b* 1940: *m* 1972, John Miles Bird, and has issue living, Tiffany, *b* 1973. ——— Philippa Jane, *b* 1944: *m* 1970, Nigel Hope.

Issue of late Rev Richard Windham de la Poer Beresford-Peirse, 2nd son of 3rd baronet, *b* 1876, *d* 1952: *m* 1st, 1910, Lady Lilian Katharine Campbell, who *d* 1918, da of 3rd Earl Cawdor; 2ndly, 1924, Katherine Mabel Helen, who *d* 1974, da of William James Yorke-Scarlett, of Fyfield House, Andover (V Valentia, colls):—
Sybil Adelaide, OBE (6 Queensdale Walk, W11 4QQ), *b* 1912; OBE (Civil) 1990; LRAM. ——— Barbara, *b* 1915: *m* 1942, Barry Martin Baker, of 6 Gloucester Mews, W2, and has issue living, Janet Bridget, *b* 1943, — Katherine Elizabeth, *b* 1946. ——— Lilian Bridget, *b* 1918: *m* 1945, Godfrey John Mapplebeck, OBE, who *d* 1991, and has issue living, Anthony Peirse, *b* 1946, — Althea Rosamund Louise, *b* 1951, — Selina Bridget Lucy, *b* 1960.

Grandchildren of late Rev Windham de la Poer Beresford-Peirse, Hon Canon of Ripon, 6th and yst son of Henry William de la Poer Beresford-Peirse, 2nd son of 1st baronet:—
Issue of late Capt Arthur Cecil Proctor de la Poer Beresford-Peirse, MBE, *b* 1890, *d* 1970: *m* 1916, Gertrude Anne Ormonde, who *d* 1974, da of late Maj Henry Wallis Prior-Wandesforde, BA, of Kirklington Hall, Yorks:—
Michael Wandesforde de la Poer (Padgepool House, Wooler, Northumberland NE71 6BD), *b* 1917; *ed* Lancing Coll; a farmer (ret): *m* 1944, Joyce Franklin, da of Phillip Hope Percival, of Potha Machakos, Kenya, and has issue living, Judith Anne Vivian, *b* 1948: *m* 1980, James Stephen Bingham Kennedy, of Dunlossit Estate, Ballygrant, Isle of Islay, Argyll PA45 7QL, and has issue living, Thomas James Peirse *b* 1984, Clare Louise *b* 1982, — Susan Alice Prior, *b* 1950: *m* 1st, 1975 (*m diss* 1982), Phillip Hamilton Newman; 2ndly, 1983, Richard William Margesson, of 27 Bridge Rd, Welwyn Garden City, Herts AL8 6UG (*see* Hagart-Alexander, Bt, 1985 Edn), and has issue living (by 2nd *m*), Lucy Emma Alexander *b* 1986. ——— *Rev* Robert Henry Windham de la Poer, OBE (30 Burt St, Albany 6330, W Aust), *b* 1922; *ed* Eton; late Flt LtRAF; Dist Officer, British N Borneo, ret 1964; OBE (Civil) 1963: *m* 1st, 1943, Margaret, who *d* 1972, da of late Edward Giles, of 72 Rue Kitchener, Alexandria, Egypt; 2ndly, 1974, Dorothy Maud, da of Percy Donald Beard, of Mel, Vic, and has issue living (by 1st *m*), Ian Arthur de la Poer (11 Asling St, Brighton, Victoria 3186, Aust), *b* 1944; *ed* Sherborne; Lt-Col RA: *m* 1968, Catherine, widow of Capt J. A. Fleming, RA, and has issue living, Giles Windham de la Poer *b* 1969, Angus Arthur de la Poer *b* 1971, Digby John de la Poer *b* 1975, — Patricia Margaret, *b* 1950: *m* 1972, Richard Stuart Callander, of Adelaide, S Aust, and has issue living, Ian Stuart *b* 1974, Fiona Margaret *b* 1978. ——— Anne Ethel Mary, *b* 1919; late Junior Cdr ATS: *m* 1942, Col Peter Anthony Lowe, late RA, of Tamerton, Upton Lovell, Warminster, Wilts, and has issue living, David Michael Peirse, *b* 1944; *ed* Sherborne; Lt-Col RA: *m* 1968, Catherine, widow of Capt J. A. Fleming, RA, and has issue living, Peter David *b* 1969. — Michael Peter, *b* 1949; *ed* Sherborne and Pa Univ, USA: *m* 1st, 1971 (*m diss* 1984), Rorie, da of G. K. Waters, of Waymart, Pa, USA; 2ndly, 1984, Sheila Zaha, of Bensalem, Pa, USA, — Elizabeth Anne, *b* 1948: *m* 1970, Richard George Goodman, and has issue living, Thomas Richard *b* 1978, James Anthony (twin) *b* 1978.

Grandchildren of late John Peirse de la Poer Beresford, el son of Rev John George Beresford (infra):—
Issue of late Capt George Wilfred Bruce de la Poer Beresford, *b* 1888, *d* 1931: *m* 1920, Louise Barbara (who *m* 2ndly, 19—, Ralph Jones Coles, who *d* 1969), da of Jacob Frederick Beck:—

John George, *b* 1923: *m* 1947, Edith Joan, da of Henry Thomas John Mellaby, and has issue living, John Henry, *b* 1948: *m* 1971, Meredith Jean, da of Murray Victor Jones, — Peter Bruce, *b* 1950: *m* 1972, Julianne La Far, da of Julian La Far Smith, — Diane Louise, *b* 1949: *m* 1972, Glen Churchill, — Cynthia Joan, *b* 1952. —— James Francis (London, Ontario), *b* 1925: *m* 19—. —— Mary Isabel, *b* 1921, Robert Campbell Moreland, and has issue living, George Alexander, *b* 1947: *m* 1969, Marilyn Christine, da of William Reginald Lower, — David Beresford, *b* 1951: *m* 1973, Leslie Michelle, da of George Franklin Bowles.

Grandchildren of late Rev John George Beresford, 3rd son of 1st baronet:—
Issue of late Rev Henry William De la Poer Beresford, *b* 1862, *d* 1932: *m* 1916, Constance Grace, who *d* 1961, da of James McLaurin, JP, of Verulam, Natal:—
Rev Canon Alfred De la Poer (Braehead House, Auburn Rd, Kenilworth, 7700 Cape, S Africa), *b* 1919; 1939-45 War in RN; Hon Canon St John's Cathedral, Umtata.
Issue of late Rev Walter Vevers de la Poer Beresford, *b* 1864, *d* 1908: *m* 1902, Eleanor Mary, who *d* 1944, da of W. R. Staveley, of Harrogate, Yorkshire:—
†Charles Denman de la Poer, *b* 1906: *m* 1950, Pamela Croot (10 Queens Rd, Bandford Forum, Dorset DT11 7JX), da of late Rev Frank Stone, MC, and *d* 1990, leaving issue, Marcus John de la Poer (23 Temple St, Oxford), *b* 1954; *ed* Clifton, and Balliol Coll, Oxford (BA), — Julia Caroline (27 Beckhampton Rd, Bath), *b* 1951: *m* 1979, Simon Mark Amos, who *d* 1987, son of E. Amos, of Blunham, Beds, and has issue living, Rosemary Cecilia *b* 1984. —— Marcus Walter de la Poer, *b* (*posthumous*) 1909; *ed* Clifton, and Merton Coll, Oxford (BMus, MA): *m* 1942, Patricia Muriel, who *d* 1992, da of late C. Reginald Fox, of Plymouth, and has issue living, Charles Richard de la Poer (Barn Hall, The Rideaway, Hemingford Abbots, Cambs PE18 9AG), *b* 1943; *ed* Clifton, Gonville and Caius Coll, Camb (MA), and London Univ (PhD): *m* 1967, Tessa, da of late H. William Dean, of Cambridge, and has issue living, John Charles de la Poer *b* 1973, Fiona Carolyn *b* 1969, — *Rev* Peter Marcus de la Poer (St George's Vicarage, St John's Av, Hillmorton Paddox, Rugby, Warwicks), *b* 1949; *ed* Cranmer Hall, Durham Univ: *m* 1979, Charlotte Frances Hester, elder da of late Rev John Grenfell McClintock, MC, and has issue living, Helen Caroline *b* 1981, Elizabeth Joy *b* 1985. *Residence* – 34 Hillmorton Rd, Rugby CV22 5AA.

The 1st baronet, Adm Sir John Poo Beresford, KCB, GCH, MP (Knight of the Tower and Sword), natural son of 1st Marquess of Waterford, and brother of Viscount Beresford (ext), sat as MP for Coleraine 1809-12 and 1814-23, for Berwick-on-Tweed 1823-26, for Northallerton 1826-32, again for Coleraine 1832-33, and for Chatham 1835-37. The 3rd Bt, Sir Henry, was Chm of N Riding of Yorkshire County Council. The 4th baronet, Major Sir Henry Bernard de la Poer, DSO, was Under-Treasurer, Middle Temple for 17 years, and served in S Africa 1900-01 as Major Imperial Yeo (DSO). The 5th Bt, Sir Henry Campbell de la Poer, CB, was Dir-Gen Forestry Commn 1962-68.

PELLY (UK) 1840, of Upton, Essex

God guiding, nothing hurts

Sir RICHARD JOHN PELLY, 7th *Baronet*; *b* 10 April 1951; *s* his uncle, Sir JOHN ALWYNE, 1993; *ed* Wellington Coll, and Wadham Coll, Oxford (BA); ACA: *m* 1983, Clare Gemma, da of late Harry Wilfred Dove, of Winchester, Hants, and has issue.

Arms – Or, on a bend engrailed azure, between two trefoils slipped vert, three martlets argent. **Crest** – Issuant from a crown vallery or, charged on the rim with three hurts, an elephant's head argent. *Residence* – The Manor House, Preshaw, Upham, Southampton SO32 1HP.

SONS LIVING

ANTHONY, *b* 30 Oct 1984. —— James Richard, *b* 1986. —— Harry Philip, *b* 1988.

SISTER LIVING

Jane Carol, *b* 1949; BA: *m* 1974, Charles Scott Bowring, PhD, son of late Frederick Bowring, of Tunbridge Wells, and has issue living, Thomas Scott, *b* 1975, — Rosemary Carol, *b* 1977.

DAUGHTER LIVING OF SIXTH BARONET (*by 2nd m to Elsie May (Hazel), who d 1987, da of late Louis Thomas Dechow*)

Margaret Elizabeth Rosanne, *b* 1952.

UNCLE LIVING (*son of 5th baronet*)

Frederick Michael (West Lodge, Preshaw, Upham, Hants), *b* 1926: *m* 1952, Jill Elizabeth, el da of late Col William Patrick Stewart Curtis, OBE (*see* Curtis, Bt, colls), and has had issue, Patrick Michael (West End Hotel, Roseangle, Dundee), *b* 1954: *m* 1980, June, da of late W. G. Edgar, and has issue living, Louise Mary *b* 1986, Charlotte Elizabeth *b* 1991, — †Alwyne Nicholas, *b* 1955; BSA Police; *d* 1987, in Harare, Zimbabwe, — Frederick Peter Douglas (BP 478, Abidjan, Côte d'Ivoire), *b* 1959: *m* 1987, Evelyne, yst da of Maurice Souilhe, of Paris, and has issue living, Curtis Vincent *b* 1987, Alwyne Nicolas *b* 1988, Adderley Charlotte *b* 1991.

AUNT LIVING (*daughter of 5th baronet*)

Carol Patricia Benita, *b* 1928: *m* 1947, Lieut Cmdr Thomas Michael Blake, RN, who *d* 1984, and has issue living, Caroline Patricia, *b* 1949: *m* 1976, John Henry Edmund Lushington, and has issue living, Katherine Elizabeth *b* 1979, Phillipa Alice *b* 1981, — Juliet, *b* 1950: *m* 1972, Howard Neil Fairman, and has issue living, Lutia Charlotte *b* 1974, Georgina *b* 1976, — Annabel, *b* 1953: *m* 1974, Richard Huxley Cowen, and has issue living, Emma *b* 1976, Victoria *b* 1977, Charlotte Annabel *b* 1982. *Residence* – Lippen Wood Farm, West Meon, Hampshire.

MOTHER LIVING

Mary Elizabeth, da of late John Luscome, of N Huish, Devon: *m* 1948, Richard Heywood Pelly, 2nd son of 5th baronet, who *d* 1988. *Residence* – Loup House, Lyme Rd, Axminster, Devon.

WIDOW LIVING OF SIXTH BARONET

(AVA) BARBARA ANN (*Barbara, Lady Pelly*), only da of late Brig Keith Frederick William Dunn, CBE: *m* 1st, 1945 (*m diss* 1950), as his 1st wife, Sir John Alwyne Pelly, 6th Bt; 2ndly, 1951 (*m diss* 1964), Maj David Michael de Lérisson Cazenove; 3rdly, 1990, as his 3rd wife, her 1st husband, Sir John Alwyne Pelly, 6th Bt, who *d* 1993. *Residence* – 9 Brook St, Bishop's Waltham, Hants SO3 1AX.

COLLATERAL BRANCHES LIVING

Branch from 4th Baronet

Issue of late Philip Vincent Pelly, yr son of 4th baronet, *b* 1898, *d* 1991: *m* 1932, Pamela Mary, who *d* 1970, only child of Sir Frederick Henry Arthur Des Voeux, 7th Bt (ext 1944):—
Brian Raymond, *b* 1935; *ed* Lancing: *m* 1962, Dinah, er da of Rev Gerald Alfred Hutchison, of Littleton Drew Rectory, Chippenham, Wilts, and has issue living, Ivan Raymond, *b* 1963, — Oliver Harding, *b* 1966, — Annabel Marguerite Pamela, *b* 1970. —— Antony Roger (Little Limber Grange, Limber, nr Grimsby, S Humberside), *b* 1937; *ed* Lancing; BSc, FRICS, late RHA: *m* 1963, Susan Fiona, yr da of Maj Denis William Powlett Milbank, TD (*see* Milbank, Bt), and has issue living, (Helen) Fiona, *b* 1964: *m* 1989, Nicholas J. Chapman, of 32a Wingford Rd, SW2, only son of J. A. Chapman, of Little Blair, Hill Head, Hants, and has issue living, Fredrick Nicholas Anthony *b* 1992, — Anna Maria Alice, *b* 1967: *m* 1988, Nicholas Mark Ryman Richards, of 8 Despard Rd, N19, er son of Nigel Richards, of 37 Evelyn Rd, Richmond, Surrey. —— Roland Des Voeux (Limes Court, Stanstead, Essex), *b* 1943; *ed* Cheltenham; solicitor 1967: *m* 1968, Diana, da of Capt James FitzGibbon, RN (ret), of Thames, NZ, and has issue living, Richard Philip, *b* 1971, — Claire Mary, *b* 1982. —— Philip Harold (Purples Farm, Bardfield Saling, nr Braintree, Essex), *b* 1948; BA; DipEd; admitted a solicitor 1977: *m* 1970, (Margaret) Helen, da of late Canon Daniel Ernest John Anthony, of Sherston, Wilts, and has issue living, Thomas Philip Anthony, *b* 1980, — Katherine Louisa, *b* 1977. —— Pamela Margaret Evelyn, *b* 1933: *m* 1957, Maurice John Greening, of Ladyfield, Acton Turville, Badminton, Glos, only child of John Greening, of Purton, Wilts, and has issue living, Harold John, *b* 1958, — James Timothy, *b* 1960, — Maurice Vincent, *b* 1964, — Mary Jacqueline, *b* 1962. —— Clare Richenda, *b* 1940: *m* 1963, Henry Hartley, and *d* 1987, leaving issue, Mark William, *b* 1964, — Madeline Mary, *b* 1967.

Branch from 2nd son of 1st Baronet

Grandchildren of late Rev Douglas Raymond Pelly, DSO (infra):—
Issue of late Air Ch Marshal Sir Claude Bernard Raymond Pelly, GBE, KCB, MC, *b* 1902, *d* 1972: *m* 1930, Margaret Ogilvie, who *d* 1990, da of late E. J. Spencer, of Hove:—
Rev Raymond Blake (12 Kio Crescent, Hataitai, Wellington, NZ), *b* 1938; *ed* Rugby, and Worcester Coll, Oxford: *m* 1st, 1964, Joanna Bickmore, yr da of John Anthony Clarke, of Home Orchard, Street, Som; 2ndly, 1990, Barbara Helen, elder da of Alan Craig, and has had issue (by 1st *m*), Aidan John Raymond, *b* 1970, — Gail, *b* and *d* 1965, — Monica, *b* 1966, — Catherine Hilda, *b* 1967; *ed* Dartington; *d* 1984. —— David Claude Raymond (Dairy Farmhouse, Coltishall, Norwich, Norfolk NR12 7AH), *b* 1941; *ed* Rugby: *m* 1974, Philippa Margaret, only da of Anthony Peter Bowman, of Hitchin, Herts, and has issue living, Tessa Patricia, *b* 1977, — Lorna Jane, *b* 1979. —— Jane Elizabeth, *b* 1931: *m* 1960, John I. Guest, of 760 Eden Pl, W Vancouver, BC, Canada, and has issue living, John William *b* 1961, — Margaret Elizabeth *b* 1960, — Maire Frances, *b* 1963.
Issue of late Rear-Adm Peter Douglas Herbert Raymond Pelly, CB, DSO, *b* 1904, *d* 1980: *m* 1932, Gwenllian Violet, who *d* 1987, da of late Capt Hon George Henry Edwardes, MC (*see* B Kensington, colls):—
Sara Ann, *b* 1937: *m* 1968, Peter Low, of Darsham House, nr Saxmundham, Suffolk, and has issue living, Tobias Blake, *b* 1969, — Nathaniel Peter, *b* 1971. —— Richenda, *b* 1939: *m* 1959, Col Douglas Alexander Nigel Capel Miers, Queen's Own Highlanders (East Farmhouse, Wylye, Warminster, Wilts), and has issue living, Lucian Douglas Ronald Capel, *b* 1962, — Mary Ann Capel, *b* 1961, — Victoria Jane Capel, *b* 1964, — Henrietta Alice Capel, *b* 1966. —— (Margaret) Clare, *b* 1942: *m* 1963, Timothy Lawrence Ireland, of Eatons Farm, Ashurst, nr Steyning, W, Sussex, and has issue living, Mark Peter Lawrence, *b* 1965, — Blake Timothy Lawrence, *b* 1972, — Nicola Gwenllian, *b* 1966, — Gemma Mary Clare, *b* 1974.
Issue of late Blake Raymond Pelly, *b* 1907, *d* 1990: *m* 1938, Mary Pamela Laidley (3 Vaucluse Rd, Sydney, NSW 2030), da of Vincent Laidley Dowling:—
Andrew Douglas Blake (8 Johnston Crescent, Lane Cove, Sydney, NSW), *b* 1939; Television Producer and Dir 1964-87: *m* 1st, 1961 (*m diss* 1978), Gaye Delyss, da of Gordon Clempson Evans, of Chatswood, NSW; 2ndly 1983, Maria Rita, da of Frank Van Ierland, of The Netherlands, and has issue living, (by 1st *m*) Fiona Elizabeth, *b* 1964, — Vanessa Pamela, *b* 1967, — (by 2nd *m*) Richard Francis Blake, *b* 1984. —— Michael Francis Blake (56 Crescent Rd, Hamilton, Brisbane, Qld), *b* 1947: *m* 1983, Nora Danaher, and has issue living, Martine Pamela, *b* 1984, — Simone Veronica, *b* 1986. —— Angela Mary Blake, *b* 1942: *m* 1965, Cdr John Spencer Compton, RAN (ret) (248 La Perouse St, Red Hill, ACT) and has issue living, James Gregory Spencer *b* 1967, — Blake John Raynor *b* 1970, — Henry Charles Grenville *b* 1977.

Granddaughter of late Rev Canon Raymond Percy Pelly, yr son of late Raymond Pelly, 2nd son of 1st baronet:—
Issue of late Rev Douglas Raymond Pelly, DSO, *b* 1865, *d* 1943: *m* 1898, Verena Noëlie, who *d* 1952, da of late Rev George W. Herbert, V of St Peter's, Vauxhall, SE:—
Stella Elizabeth Mary, *b* 1908: *m* 1934, William Richard Gowers, CBE, DCL, of Winterwell, Aston Tirrold, nr Didcot, Oxon, only son of late Sir Ernest Arthur Gowers, GCB, GBE, and has issue living, William Patrick, *b* 1936; PhD: *m* 1961, Caroline Molesworth, yr da of Dr Timothy Maurice, OBE, of 10 Kingsbury St, Marlborough, and has issue living, William Timothy *b* 1963, Rebecca *b* 1965, Katherine *b* 1970, — Ann Elizabeth Mary, *b* 1938; BEd, PhD: *m* 1963, Prof Roger Dennis Scott, DPhil, of 16 Cambridge St, Redhill, Brisbane, Aust, and has issue living, Richard Andrew *b* 1964; Midshipman RAN, Alexander Patrick *b* 1967.

Granddaughters of late Rev Canon Raymond Percy Pelly, yr son of late Raymond Pelly, 2nd son of 1st baronet:—
Issue of late Brig-Gen Raymond Theodore Pelly, CB, CMG, DSO, late Loyal Regt, and a Mil Knight of Windsor, *b* 1881, *d* 1952: *m* 1910, Moriet Elsie Maxwell, who *d* 1965, da of late Maj-Gen Arthur Gethin Creagh, CB (Wolseley, Bt, *cr* 1744, colls):—
Pamela Moriet, *b* 1911: *m* 1st, 1935, Frank Rough, who *d* 1966; 2ndly, 1968, John Moore Lorimer, who *d* 1982; 3rdly, 1993, Donald Pearson Paton, DFC, MA, of 5 Earls Manor Court, Winterbourne Earls, Salisbury, Wilts SP4 6EJ, and has issue living, (by 1st *m*) Caroline, *b* 1940: *m* 1963, John Ralph Lawrenson, of The Old Rectory, Great Waldingfield, Sudbury, Suffolk, and has issue living, Frank Ralph *b* 1967, Sophie Patricia *b* 1968. —— Patricia Carlota, *b* 1915: *m* 1948, Alan H. Maccoy, DSC, RNVR, of The Coach House, Church Rd, Shillingstone, Blandford Forum, Dorset DT11 0SL, and has an adopted son and da, Paul John Raymond, *b* 1958: *m* 1986 (*m diss* 1993), Leigh Thelma Sessions, — Catherine Richenda, *b* 1959: *m* 1981, David Peter Pickering of Bermuda, and has issue living, Samantha Clare *b* 1990.

Branch from 3rd son of 1st Baronet

Grandchildren of late Charles Brent Neville Pelly, el son of Rev Charles Henry Pelly, el son of Charles Pelly, MCS, 3rd son of 1st baronet:—
Issue of late Cdr Charles Sinclair Pelly, RN, *b* 1902, *d* 1967: *m* 1928, Caroline Mary, who *d* 1992, da of Charles Samuel Facey, MB, of Chickerell, Weymouth:—
Charles Patrick (St Mary's Lodge, Chitterne, Wilts), *b* 1935: *m* 1966, Avis Olga, da of W. H. T. Woon, and has issue living, Nigel William Sinclair, *b* 1968, — Stephen Grenville, *b* 1970, — Simon Charles Tregoning, *b* 1973. —— William Rupert Brent (Upper Langridge Farm, Lansdown, Bath), *b* 1943: *m* 1967, Judith Rowena, da of Prof Norman Henry Gibbs, DPh (*see* E Leven and Melville, colls), and has issue living, Benjamin Rupert William, *b* 1972, — Joel Peter Sinclair, *b* 1980, — Zinnia Joanne, *b* 1970, — Tabitha Louise, *b* 1978. —— Jane *b* 1931: *m* 1957, Capt Kenneth Mills, RN, The Elms, Chickerell, Weymouth, Dorset, and has issue living, Charles Richard, *b* 1958, — Patrick George, *b* 1963, — Cecilia Jane, *b* 1959.
Issue of late Major Henry Patrick Neville Pelly, *b* 1912, *ka* in Assam 1945: *m* 1939, Marion Veronica, who *d* 1992, el da of Maj Harry Sanderson of Galashiels, Roxburghshire:—
George Michael Harvey (3407 Little Brant Drive, Fort McClellan, Alabama 36205, USA), *b* 1944; Maj RA: *m* 1979, Diana, el da of Maj D. Montgomery, of Wotton, Surrey, and has issue living, Henry David Patrick, *b* 1983, — Grace Catherine, *b* 1981, — Rachel Caroline, *b* (twin) 1983. —— Sarah Rutherford, *b* 1941: *m* 1966, Jonathan Coldstream Lawley, of 56 Nightingale Lane, SW12, and has issue living, Thomas Henry, *b* 1973, — Juliet Rosemary, *b* 1969, — Katherine Jane, *b* 1970.

Grandchildren of late Maj William Francis Henry Pelly, 2nd son of Rev Charles Henry Pelly (ante):—
Issue of late Capt Charles Nigel Pelly, OBE, *b* 1908, *d* 1966: *m* 1934, Betty Joan (39 Branksome Court, Canford Cliffs, Dorset), da of Lt-Col Leo Webster Cole, OBE, of Cairo:—
Christopher Patrick Cavendish (57 Corbière Av, Parkstone, Poole, Dorset), *b* 1939; MA: *m* 1969, Brenda Amy Grosvenor, da of Alfred Mutlow Grosvenor Herd (M Bute, colls), and has issue living, Nigel Christopher Grosvenor, *b* 1973, — Amanda Rachel, *b* 1970. —— Marcus Nigel (20 Moss Paul Close, S Duncraig, W Aust 6023), *b* 1941; R Hong Kong Police: *m* 1971, Peggy Jane, da of Robert A. Wright, of Vic, BC, Canada; 2ndly, 1978, Barbara, da of S. Mason, of Harare, Zimbabwe, and has issue living, Nicholas Jonathan, *b* 1984, — Andrew Jonathan, *b* 1984. —— Sally Joan, *b* 1944: *m* 1967, Paul Edmond de Rham, of The Lawns, 17 Moorlands Rd, West Moors, Wimborne, Dorset, and has issue living, Marc Edmond, *b* 1970, — Joanna Claire, *b* 1968, — Lucy Caroline, *b* 1976, — Sophie Charlotte, *b* 1979.

Grandchildren of late Richard Stewart Pelly, 2nd son of Charles Pelly, MCS (ante):—
Issue of late Henry Conway Dobbs Pelly, *b* 1878, *d* 1908: *m* 1903, Brenda, who *d* 1935, da of W. D. Horsley, MCS:—
Stuart Horsley, *b* 19—. —— Ralph Horsley, *b* 1907; BC Civil Ser: *m* 1928, Jacobina Benson, da of G. N. Landscrown, of Aberdeen, and has issue living, Bruce Conway, *b* 1933; RCN 1950-55, served Korean War: *m* 1962, Lucille Odette, da of Rev Ernest Amex, of Grande Ligne Mission, Quebec City, and has issue, Scott *b* 1965, Susanne Lucille *b* 1963, — Brian George, *b* 1938: *m* 1958, Bernice Lorraine, da of E. E. Cave, Sgt RCMP, of Vancouver, BC, and has issue living, Michael George, *b* 1961, Steven Todd, *b* 1963, Lisa Lorraine, *b* 1964, Michele Kim, *b* 1966, — Patricia Landscrown, *b* 1929: *m* 19—, George E. Belsham, and has issue. —— Conway Horsley, *b* 19—.

Grandchildren of late Edward Pelly, 3rd son of Charles Pelly, MCS (ante):—
Issue of late Edward Raymond Pelly, *b* 1890, *d* 1963: *m* 1st, 1918, Frances Muriel, who *d* 1943, da of late Rev Alfred Shidrick, V of Milton-under-Wychwood, Oxon; 2ndly, 1944, Dorothy Jean Edna (8 Carlton House, 1251 Lawrence Av, Kelowna, British Columbia V17 6M5), el da of late J. M. Dadson, of Winnipeg, Canada:—
(By 2nd *m*) John Edward (2576 Bendale Rd, N Vancouver, BC, Canada), *b* 1947: *m* 1975, Patricia, 2nd da of Jack F. Cogger, of Surrey, and has issue living, Tod Cogger, *b* 1978, — Edward Reid, *b* 1979. —— Mary Ann, *b* 1945: *m* 1967, Douglas Alva Snowsell, of Casilla 312V, Correro 21, Santiago, Chile, and has issue living, Brandon James *b* 1969, — Colin David, *b* 1970.

Granddaughter of late Rear-Adm Francis Raymond Pelly, 4th son of Charles Pelly, MCS (ante):—
Issue of late Lt-Col Hutcheson Raymond Pelly, IA, *b* 1887, *d* 1979: *m* 1913, Kathleen Mary, who *d* 1984, da of Edward Clifford-Walsh, of St Aidens, Arklow, co Wicklow:—
Dorothy Mary Fleurette (77 Archway St, Barnes, SW13 0AN), *b* 1921; 1939-45 War (despatches).

Branch from 4th son of 1st Baronet

Grandchildren of late Albert Edgar Champion Pelly, el son of late Albert Champion Pelly, el son of Albert Pelly (*b* 1813), 4th son of 1st baronet:—
Issue of late John Pelly, *b* 1905, *d* 1981: *m* 1st, 1931, Bertha, who *d* 1935, da of John William Selwin Taylor, of Alfreton, Derby; 2ndly, 1942, Hilda May, who *d* 1977, elder da of Thomas Brewer Barrow, of Bedminster, Bristol:—
(By 2nd *m*) Derek John (Jakob-Schmid-Str 19, 85221 Dachau, Germany), *b* 1946: *m* 1985, (*m diss* 1993), Elvira Maria Lute.
Issue of late Noel Henry Pelly, *b* 1906, *d* 1974: *m* 1932, Marjorie, da of late Frank Harold Hinton, of Forest Hill, SE:—
Raymond Frank (27 Harrington Villas, Brighton BN1 6RG), *b* 1940: *m* 1964, Janet, da of late Alexander Head, of 6 Long Lodge Drive, Walton-on-Thames; 2ndly, 1994, Pauline Ruth Rowlands, da of late William Dey, of Ripon, N Yorks, and has issue living, Nicole Louise, *b* 1966; has issue living, Grace *b* 1991, — Lisette Suzanne, *b* 1969.
Issue of late Edgar Frank Pelly, *b* 1919, *d* 1954: *m* 1941, Dulcie Vera Manning, who *m* 2ndly, 1959, Dennis Smith, of 4 Probyn Close, Frenchay, Bristol:—
Dorinda May, *b* 1945: *m* 1965, John Scoltock, of 7 Oakdale Av, Downend, Bristol, and has issue living, Simon John, *b* 1969, — Amanda Louise, *b* 1968. —— Julia Ruth, *b* 1947: *m* 1966, Terry Gilborson, of 89 Gorse Hill, Fishponds, Bristol, and has issue living, Mark Julian, *b* 1966, — Sarah Lewise, *b* 1969.

Granddaughters of late Russell George Pelly, son of late William Henry Pelly, 2nd son of Albert Pelly (*b* 1813) (ante):—
Issue of late Russell Steele Pelly, *b* 1910, *d* 1993: *m* 1945, Agnes Mysie (32 Verena Terr, Perth PH2 0BZ), da of late F. H. Macpherson, solicitor of Ayr:—
Frances Elsie, ARSA, *b* 1947. —— Lindsay Grace, *b* 1950: *m* 1976, John Warrender Gow, and has issue living, David Russell, *b* 1979, — Hazel Joan, *b* 1977, — Morven Elizabeth, *b* 1983. —— Mysie Ann, *b* 1953: *m* 1981, Robert Ferguson, and has issue living, Ruaraidh, *b* 1989, — Shuna Margaret, *b* 1985.
Issue of late Anthony Roger Pelly, *b* 1915, *d* 1972: *m* 1st, 1947, (*m diss* 1965), Joan, da of late Gp Capt Martin William Flack, CBE, MB; 2ndly, 1968, Mrs Eileen Cleveland (73 Warrington Cres, Maida Vale, W9), da of late Joseph Prior:—
(By 1st *m*) Sarah Jane, *b* 1949.

Granddaughter of late Capt John Henry Pelly, RN, 3rd son of late Albert Pelly (*b* 1813) (ante):—
Issue of late Charles Thorne Pelly, *b* 1890, *d* 1966: *m* 1922, Lilian May, who *d* 1976, da of late Rear-Adm John William Ham, CB:—

Pauline Elizabeth, *b* 1927: *m* 1st, 1948, Peter Anthony Welsford; 2ndly, 1961, Aveling Jocelyn Pickard, of 17 The Leys, Esher Rd, Walton-on-Thames, Surrey KT12 4LP, and has issue living (by 1st *m*) Paul Simon, *b* 1953, — Penelope Ann, *b* 1949: *m* 1975, Stuart Hall, and has issue living, Simon Leslie *b* 1983, Oliver Charles *b* 1986.

Branch from 5th son of 1st Baronet

Grandson of late John Gurney Richard Pelly, eldest son of late Capt Richard Wilson Pelly, RN, 5th son of 1st baronet:—
Issue of late Vivian Gurney Pelly, *b* 1881, *d* 1949: *m* 1st, 1907, Dorothy Penrose, who *d* 1972, el da of William Henry Sewell, formerly of Epping Place, Epping; 2ndly, 1946, Hilda Victoria Cole:—
(By 1st *m*) Douglas Gurney, *b* 1910; formerly Lt Maritime RA; High Sheriff of Essex 1962: *m* 1935, Monica, da of late Lt-Col Arthur Wignall Tate, DSO (*see* Tate, Bt, colls), and has issue living, John Gurney (Spring Hill, E Malling, Kent), *b* 1938: *m* 1973, Vanda Joan, da of Col Hubert Mortimer Allfrey, MC, TD (E Romney, colls), and has issue living, Sam Gurney *b* 1974, James Rupert *b* 1976, Guy Wignall *b* 1982, — William Henry (The Old Rectory, Sherrington, Warminster, Wilts), *b* 1946: *m* 1975, Anne, yr da of Francis Byrne, and has issue living, Henry Francis *b* 1978, Rupert Alexander *b* 1980, — Claire Rose *b* 1943: *m* 1st, 1966 (*m diss* 1981), 17th Earl of Pembroke and Montgomery; 2ndly, 1984, Stuart Wyndham Murray Threipland, of Homington Farm, Homington, Salisbury, Wilts. *Residence* – Swaynes Hall, Widdington, nr Newport, Essex.

Grandchildren of late Rev Canon Richard Arnold Pelly (infra):—
Issue of the Rev Canon Richard Lawrence Pelly, *b* 1886, *d* 1976: *m* 1927, Rosa Salome, MB (20 Middle St, Salisbury, Wilts), da of late Rt Rev John Wordsworth, DD, 93rd Lord Bishop of Salisbury (Williams, Bt, *cr* 1915):—
Richard Christopher Wordsworth (Stonyroad, Audishaw Lane, Boylestone, Derbys DE6 5AE), *b* 1938; *ed* Marlborough, and Clare Coll, Camb (BA): *m* 1962, Ruth Elinor, da of Philip Askey, of Weaverham, Ches, and has issue living, Richard Hugh, *b* 1964, — David John, *b* 1972, — Katherine Jane, *b* 1966: *m* 1991, Jasper John Pleydell-Bouverie, yr son of Hon Reuben Pleydell-Bouverie (*see* E Radnor). — Hugh John Wordsworth (Wake House, Ebbesbourne Wake, Salisbury, Wilts SP5 5JL), *b* 1945; *ed* Marlborough; MB, BS, DCH: *m* 1972, Jane Mary Fergusson, and has issue living, Tom Fergus, *b* 1975, — Matthew David, *b* 1977, — Adam, *b* 1979, — Christopher Hugh, *b* 1982, — Claire Alexandra, *b* 1990. —— Elizabeth Mary, *b* 1929: *m* 1952, Wyndham M. Jordan, MA, BM, BCh, DRCOG, of 81A Beccles Rd, Bungay, Suffolk NR35 1HU, and has issue living, Christopher Wyndham (Highbury, Love Lane, Shaw, Newbury, Berks RG13 2DY), *b* 1956; BSc: *m* 1979, Gillian Smith, and has issue living, Anthony *b* 1989, Zalha *b* 1987, — Rosalind Cicely, *b* 1955; MA: *m* 1986, Robert Tatam, of 21 Sheredan Rd, Highams Park, E4 9RW, and has issue living, Luke *b* 1989, — Diana Salome, *b* 1959; BA: *m* 1983, Timothy Benge-Abbott, of 7 Southland Close, Colchester, Essex CO4 4QH, and has issue living, Daniel *b* 1986, Joel *b* 1989, — Alison Faith, *b* 1961; MB, BS, DRCOG, DCH, MRCGP: *m* 1983, Timothy Clarke, BSc, PhD, of 19 Rye St, Bishop's Stortford, Herts. —— Rosa Jane, *b* 1931. —— Juliet Rachel, *b* 1933: *m* 1964, William Gibbins Webb, of 17 Church Rd, Laverstock, Salisbury, Wilts SP1 1QX, and has issue living, Rachel Sally, *b* 1965, — Rhoda Jane, *b* 1966: *m* 1989, Andrew Thomas Agerbak, of 78 William St, Oxford OX3 0ER. —— Robina Catherine, *b* 1935: *m* 1958 (*m diss* 1986), Timothy Sherwood Hattersley, MB, BChir, of 3 Mill Race, Salisbury, and has issue living, Andrew Tym, *b* 1958; MB, BChir, MRCP: *m* 1986, Katharine Dick, and has issue living, Ruth *b* 1991, Rosie *b* 1993, — William John, *b* 1960; BSc, — Richard Wordsworth, *b* 1964; MB, BS: *m* 1991, Susan Herbert.

Grandchildren of late Rev Canon Richard Arnold Pelly, 2nd son of Capt Richard Wilson Pelly, RN (ante):—
Issue of late Francis Brian Pelly, AFC, *b* 1889, *d* 1984: *m* 1913, (Edith) Beatrice, who *d* 1984, da of late Rev William James Packe, V of Feering, Kelvedon:—
†Michael Brian, *b* 1915; *ed* Bryanston; CEng: *m* 1946, Mary Margaret (The Mill House, Feltham Lane, Frome, Som BA11 5NB), da of late Herbert Southerden Burn, CBE, and *d* 1994, leaving issue, Roger Brian (39 Parkhill Av, Dyce, Aberdeen), *b* 1950; *ed* Bryanston, Southampton Univ and Birmingham Univ (MSc), MIOSH: *m* 1st, 1980 (*m diss* 1986), Monica Giovanna Deorsola; 2ndly, 1987, Kiki Joyce McFarlane, — David Arnold (56 Honeybrook Rd, SW12), *b* 1954; *ed* Bryanston, York Univ and Bradford Univ (BTech): *m* 1989, Deborah Susan Mattison, and has issue living, Henry Theodore *b* 1992, — Nicola Susan (3255 Cedar Av, Westmount, Montreal, Quebec, Canada), *b* 1948; *ed* Sherborne Sch for Girls and Sidcot Sch: *m* 1972 (*m diss* 1977), Peter Charles Jeffery; has issue (by Harry Parnass), Talia Shane *b* 1984. —— Peter Richard (Green Farm, Bovingdon Green, Bovingdon, Herts HP3 0LF), *b* 1916; *ed* Bryanston; CEng: *m* 1945, Kathleen Irene, da of late S. W. Moorhouse, of Guildford, and has issue living, Lynda Ann, *b* 1947: *m* 1980, Edward Macalister-Smith, of 9 Whittox Lane, Frome, Somerset BA11 3BY, and has issue living, Sam Henry *b* 1982, Mathilda Rose *b* 1983, — Kathleen Georgina, *b* 1951: *m* 1975, E. V. Caldwell, of Moses Plat Farm, Speen, Aylesbury, Bucks. —— Margaret Beatrice (Rosebay Cottage, 15 Langham Place, Rode, Bath, Avon BA3 6PL), *b* 1921: *m* 1st, 1943 (*m diss* 1959), Theodore Sanger; 2ndly, 1969, Jovan Ulic, of Belgrade, and has issue living (by 1st *m*), Melody, *b* 1947: *m* 1970, Peter Wright, and has issue living, Megan Jenett *b* 1973, Alice Rosamund *b* 1979, Madelene Rose *b* 1980, — Katrina Scarlett, *b* 1952: *m* 1977, Michael Power, and has issue living, Katherine *b* 1978, Molly *b* 1980, Ellen *b* 1983.
Issue of late Capt Arthur Roland Pelly, *b* 1895, *d* 1966: *m* 1920, Phyllis Elsie, who *d* 1974, da of late Alexander Duff Henderson, of Hampstead, NW:—
John Gordon (Anceford House, Stockton-on-Teme, Worcs WR6 6UX), *b* 1923; *ed* Marlborough; Lt RNVR; 1939-45 War (despatches): *m* 1947, Patricia Maureen, da of late Maj Hugh Clarence Fuller, of Arran Lodge, Crossabeg, co Wexford, and has issue living, John Henry Patrick Fuller (Cleave House, Fordcombe, Kent TN3 0RJ), *b* 1953; *ed* Marlborough: *m* 1980, Susan Elizabeth, da of Michael A. Briggs, of Harts, Penshurst, Kent, and has issue living, Freddie John Fuller *b* 1986, Clare Elizabeth *b* 1984, Serena Rose *b* 1989, — Priscilla Jane, *b* 1949: *m* 1972, David Dalziel Mundell, of Nelgai, Condamine, Qld, and has issue living, John Dalziel *b* 1977, Andrew Hugh Dalziel *b* 1979, Sarah Richenda *b* 1973, Lucinda Clare *b* 1975, — Caroline Anne, *b* 1950: *m* 1973, Michael Eliot Howard, of Green Farm, Sankyns Green, Worcester, and has issue living, Nicholas Henry *b* 1979, Harry Eliot *b* 1982, Joanna Clare *b* 1977. —— Derek Roland (The Bowling Green, The Downs, Great Dunmow, Essex), *b* 1929; *ed* Marlborough and Trin Coll, Camb (MA): *m* 1953, Susan, da of John Malcolm Roberts, of 4 Macartney House, Chesterfield Walk, Greenwich, SE10, and has issue living, Samuel Roland *b* 1960, — Rosemary Jane *b* 1955: *m* 1988, Mark C. Campbell, son of D. M. Campbell, of Colesbourne, Glos, and has issue living, Alexander Leo *b* 1990, Euan Henderson *b* 1992, — Catherine Susan, *b* 1958: *m* 1982, Simon A. W. Osborn, only son of Col M. A. C. Osborn, of Shaftesbury, Dorset, and has issue living, George Ashby Arthur *b* 1990, Cicely Mai Elsie *b* 1986, Anna Catherine Pelly *b* 1988. —— Mary Duff, *b* 1921: *m* 1945, George T. B. Stevens, solicitor, of Barn Corner, All Cannings, Devizes, Wilts, and has issue living, Charles Bridges, *b* 1946; *ed* Cheltenham Coll: *m* 1972, Jeanette MacDonald, da of late Walter Moore, of Barbados, and has issue living, Edward George Bridges *b* 1976, — David George, *b* 1951; *ed* Cheltenham Coll, and St Bartholomew's Hosp (BSc, MB, BS): *m* 1976, Philippa Mary, da of Charles Richard Pemberton Steer, of Llandevaud, Gwent, and has issue living, Hugh Richard *b* 1979, Alec Charles *b* 1982, — Lucia Mary, *b* 1956: *m* 1981, Philip Charles Dinkel, RIBA, son of Prof Michael Dinkel, of Bussage, Glos, and has issue living, Henry Michael George *b* 1988, Charlotte Mary *b* 1986. —— Janet Elizabeth (83 Bainton Rd, Oxford OX2 7AG), *b* 1926: *m* 1953 (*m diss* 1981), Michael L. Fenwick, PhD, and has issue living, Alison Jane, *b* 1955, — Anne Richenda, *b* 1957, — Juliet Nicola, *b* 1959: *m* 1992, Derwin Nazarino, of 4305 SW 100th St, Seattle, USA.

Grandchildren of late Capt Richard Wilson Pelly, RN (ante):—
Issue of late Adm Sir Henry Bertram Pelly, KCVO, CB, *b* 1867, *d* 1942: *m* 1904, Lilian Katharine Hawkshaw, who *d* 1966, da of Sir William Vincent, 12th Bt (*cr* 1620, ext):—
Douglas Charles Vincent (4 Shapley Hill, Winchfield, Hants, RG27 8BU), *b* 1908; Com RN (ret); 1939-45 War (despatches): *m* 1938, Catherine Loraine, da of Edwyn Conran, of Hurlingham, Buenos Aires, and has issue living, Douglas Edwyn Vincent

(10 Freelands Rd, Cobham, Surrey KT11 2ND), *b* 1951: *m* 1974, Susan Margaret, da of George Hards, of Cobham, Surrey, and has issue living, Matthew James *b* 1984, Jessica *b* 1975, Samantha *b* 1976, — Anne Loraine, *b* 1939: *m* 1966, Lachlan Nicholas Ferrar Forbes, of Culhuinich, Glass, Huntly, Aberdeenshire AB54 4YA, and has issue living, Lachlan Pelly Ferrar *b* 1970, Angus Maxwell Pelly *b* 1971, — Gillian Esmé, *b* 1942: *m* 1983, Timothy C. Caffell, of 54 Tartar Rd, Cobham, Surrey, 2nd son of E. W. Caffell, of Cobham, Surrey, and has issue living, Anna Margaret Juliet *b* 1985, — Catherine Elizabeth, *b* 1948: *m* 1973, Simon Maxwell, and has issue living, Daniel *b* 1976, Oliver *b* 1977, Dominic *b* 1981. —— Adrian Vincent, LVO (Coombeside, E Meon, Petersfield, Hants GU32 1PB), *b* 1919; late Lt RNVR; HM's Land Steward at Windsor 1951-71; a JP; *cr* MVO 1962, LVO 1971: *m* 1975, Margaret Esterel, el da of Roger Lambert, of Cuckseys Farm, Bletchingley, Surrey. —— Esterel Alice Muriel, OBE, *b* 1906; OBE (Civil) 1953: *m* 1928, Brig Philip Reginald Antrobus, CBE, MC, DL, who *d* 1986, son of late Sir Reginald Lawrence Antrobus, KCMG, CB. *Residence* – 33 Castle Gardens, Swan St, Petersfield, Hants GU32 3AG.

Grandchildren of late Edmund Nevill Richard Pelly, 3rd son of late Capt Richard Wilson Pelly, RN (ante):—
Issue of late Capt John Noel Pelly, CBE, RN, *b* 1888, *d* on active ser 1945: *m* 1924, Rosalind, who *d* 1957, da of late R. G. Gatehouse, of Abbot's Grange, Bebington, Cheshire:—
John Stewart Gatehouse, *b* 1930: *m* 1960, Helen Josephine, da of Denys Heaton Hirst, of 46 Lightridge Rd, Fixby, Huddersfield, and has issue living, Jennifer Œnone, *b* 1965, — Catherine Allison, *b* 1967, — Helen Rosalind, *b* 1969, — Isobel Serena, *b* 1973. *Residence* – Great Wilsey Farm, Haverhill, Suffolk. —— Rosemary Œnone, *b* 1927: *m* 1956, Gordon Nelmes, who *d* 1992, and has issue living, John Pelly, *b* 1957: *m* 1988, Fiona Jane, da of Robert Nalder, of Underriver, Kent, and has issue living, Flora Mary *b* 1991, Emma Rosemary *b* 1993, — Godfrey Edward, *b* 1959, — Edmund Gordon, *b* 1965, — Rosalind Jane, *b* 1962: *m* 1986, Charles Richard Maurice Bishop, and has issue living, Thomas Richard Chilton *b* 1993, Rosanna Emily Margaret *b* 1990 *Residence* – Gardner's Farm, Hatfield Peverel, nr Chelmsford, Essex.
Issue of late Lt-Col (Edmund) Godfrey Pelly, DSO, MC, *b* 1889, *d* on active ser 1939: *m* 1919, Isabel Amy, who *d* 1988, da of late Robert Henry Fowler, of 5 Park Square West, NW:—
Robert Hubert (Victoria House, Pierce Lane, Fulbourn, Cambridge CB1 5DL), *b* 1923; *ed* Shrewsbury, and Trin Coll, Camb (BA 1950); 1939-45 War as Capt Lothians and Border Yeo (despatches): *m* 1951, Eirolys Elizabeth, da of late Maj le Gendre George William Horton-Fawkes, OBE, of Farnley Hall, Otley, Yorks, and has issue living, Richard Fowler, *b* 1955: *m* 1983, Michelle Colette, yr da of Dr Henri Bouteille, of St Etienne, France, and has issue living, Isabelle *b* 1986, Victoria Sarah *b* 1988, Mathilde *b* 1990, — Robert Simon Horton (47 Isis St, SW18 3QL), *b* 1960: *m* 1989, Rachel M., yst da of Peter Hamilton-Ely, of Fovant, Wilts, and has issue living, Camilla *b* 1993, — Serena Louise, *b* 1953: *m* 1974, Stephen John Richards, and has issue living, Thomas Linton *b* 1980, Clare Lucy *b* 1979. —— Antoinette Joan, *b* 1920: *m* 1942, Capt Kenneth W. Macleod, who *d* 1983, and has issue living, Neil Godfrey, *b* 1947: *m* 1973, Sheila Anne, da of Crawford Tyler, of St Marys, Ont, Canada, and has issue living, Steven Kenneth *b* 1975, Jeffrey *b* 1985, Amy *b* 1978, Diana *b* 1981, — Allison Ann, *b* 1946: *m* 1st, 1968, Robert Hellett, of Kimbolton, who *d* 1970; 2ndly, 1975, Geoffrey Hugh Fellows, of 4 Brockhall Rd, Flore, Northants, and has issue living, (by 1st *m*) Robert Henry *b* 1970, — Flora Margaret, *b* 1952: *m* 1976, Graham Gilbert, of 4 Moor Cottages, nr Wellingboro', Northants, and has issue living, Kris Graham *b* 1978, Rory Neil *b* 1980.

Grandchildren of late Herbert Cecil Pelly, 4th son of late Capt Richard Wilson Pelly, RN (ante):—
Issue of late Humphrey Richard Pelly, *b* 1886, *d* 1955: *m* 1916, Barbara Vidal, who *d* 1965, da of Frederick Scrutton, of Woolpits, Nutfield, Surrey:—
Juliet (Cobblers Cottage, Bishop Monkton, Harrogate, N Yorks), *b* 1920: *m* 1946, George Ian Bray, MBE, who *d* 1985, and has issue living, Rose Elizabeth *b* 1950, — Annabel Lucy, *b* (twin) 1950.
Issue of late Capt Gilbert Cecil Pelly, RN, *b* 1892, *d* 1961: *m* 1921, Constance Margery, who *d* 1952, da of late F. E. Tweenbrook Glazebrook, of Manila:—
David Cecil, *b* 1922; Lt-Cdr RN (ret); 1939-45 War (despatches, French Croix de Guerre); yr brother of Trinity House: *m* 1950, Angela Mary, da of late Capt Wilfrid Pearse Gandell, CBE, RN (ret), and has issue living, Richard Cecil, *b* 1951: *ed* Marlborough, and Selwyn Coll, Camb (MA, MSc, CEng, MI MechE); Capt RN: *m* 1974, Fleur Veronica, only da of late John Desmond Proctor, of North View, High Trees Rd, Reigate, Surrey, and has issue living, Jonathan Henry *b* 1988, Cécile *b* 1977, Victoria Clare *b* 1982, — Nicholas John, *b* 1953: *ed* Marlborough, Birmingham Univ (BSc), and London Business Sch (MSc): *m* 1st, 1977 (*m diss* 1987), Elaine Margaret, el da of George G. Illingworth, of Dalmore, West Park Rd, Cupar, Fife; 2ndly, 1990, Sally, da of late Jack Odell, of Topeka, Kansas, USA, and has issue living (by 1st *m*), Alistair George *b* 1981, Catriona Marie *b* 1983, (by 2nd *m*) James David *b* 1992, — Patrick David (18 Badshot Park, Badshot Lea, Farnham, Surrey GU9 9JZ), *b* 1955; *ed* Marlborough, and Manchester Univ (BSc): *m* 1985, Margaret Julie, da of Scott Gray, of Coal Aston, Sheffield, and has issue living, Ralph Jonathan *b* 1986, Christopher Scott *b* 1988, — Gilbert Ralph *b* 1966; *ed* Marlborough; Capt RM, — Alexandra Helen, *b* 1961; *ed* Midhurst Gram Sch, and Birmingham Univ (BSocSc): *m* 1988, Ian Mark McLaren Pearson, eldest son of Malcolm J. S. Pearson, of Granary Cottage, Coningsby Lane, Fifield, Berks SL6 2PF, and has issue living, Hamish James McLaren *b* 1993 *Residence* – Walden, Marley Common, Haslemere, Surrey GU27 3PU. —— John Kenneth (Cedar Croft, Rural Route 5, Bolton, Ont, Canada, L7E 5S1), *b* 1923; Lt (ret) RN: *m* 1946, Joan Campbell, only da of late J. C. Fraser, of Cedar Ridge, Scarborough, Ont, Canada, and has issue living, David Fraser, *b* 1948; BSc (RMC), Lt-Cdr (ret), Canadian Armed Forces; FRGS, FRCGS: *m* 1st, 1970 (*m diss* 1974), Sara Lynn, da of late Alan Nicholson, of Charlottetown, Prince Edward Island, Canada, 2ndly, 19—, Laurie, da of Joseph McGinnis, of New Jersey, USA, — Brian Gordon (41 Underhill Crescent, Aurora, Ontario, Canada L4G 5S3), *b* 1954; BMath (Waterloo Univ); ASA, ACAS: *m* 1978, Lynn Dorothy, el da of Russell Henry Pearson, of Manitoulin Island, Ontario, and has issue living, Kyle Russell John *b* 1984, Heather Kathryn *b* 1981, Colleen Leslie *b* 1986, — Elizabeth Gail, *b* 1951: *m* 1975, John David Henry, of 127 Parkview Av, Willowdale, Ontario, Canada M2N 3Y4, and has issue living, Kimberly Beth *b* 1981, Robyn Lynn *b* 1984, Laura Louise *b* 1986. —— Peter Jeremy (Under Westwood, Upper Swainswick, Bath BA1 8BZ), *b* 1930: *m* 1953, Dorothy Joan (Joanna), da of Capt Thomas William Robert Hill, RA (see B Dick-Cunyngham, Bt (ext), 1980 Edn), and adopted da of late Christopher Ransom, of Monk's Wall, Otterton, Budleigh Salterton, and has issue living, Anthony John, *b* 1956: *m* 1983, Jane Chisholm, only da of Noel Hair, of Wylam, Northumberland, and has issue living, Stephen Nicholas James *b* 1985, David Samuel Henry *b* 1988, Joanna Elizabeth Chisholm *b* (twin) 1988, — Lyndsay Madeleine, *b* 1954: *m* 1980, Peter St L. Kyrke-Smith, son of B. H. S. Kyrke-Smith, of Penbedw, Nannerch, Clwyd, and has issue living, George Henry *b* 1991, Laura Elizabeth *b* 1983, Hanne Sarah *b* 1985, Rebecca Lucy *b* 1987, — Elizabeth Joanna Clare, *b* 1958: *m* 1990, Anthony John Fielding, of Slaley Bridge, Northumberland, and has issue living, Leo Anthony *b* 1993, Molly Alexandra *b* 1992, — Nicolette Jane, *b* 1960, — Ann Catherine, *b* 1964.
Issue of late Sir Kenneth Raymond Pelly, MC, *b* 1893, *d* 1973: *m* 1919, Elspeth Norna, who *d* 1978, da of late Robert Campbell Grant, of Hale Edge, S Nuffield:—
Andrew Desmond, DFC (Halings, Balcombe, Haywards Heath, Sussex), *b* 1923; formerly F/Lt RAF: *m* 1945, Nancye Jean, da of Lt-Col Eric Tillyer Tatham (*see* B Digby, colls), and has issue living, Ian Raymond, *b* 1949: *m* 1974 (*m diss* 1993), Alana Murray, of Brisbane, Aust, — Angela Pauline (133 Georgia, Pointe Claire, Quebec, Canada), *b* 1947: *m* 1970 (*m diss* 1987), Douglas Frederick Wentzel, and has issue living, Kristian Douglas Andrew *b* 1979, Karla Juli-Anne *b* 1973, Alexandra Korin *b* 1975, — Christine Mary, *b* 1952: *m* 1972, Timothy Cross, Col RAOC, and has issue living, Alexander Leigh *b* 1974, Stephen David *b* 1990, Gemma Charlotte *b* 1977, — Fiona Elizabeth *b* 1955. —— Ursula Elspeth (New Barn, Colgate, Sussex), *b* 1921; formerly WRNS: *m* 1945, Lt Robert George Malloch Brown, SANF(V), who *d* 1967, and has issue living, George Mark, *b* 1953: *m* 1989, Patricia Anne Cronam, and has issue living, Maddison Jane *b* 1991, Isabel Anne *b* 1994.

Grandchildren of late Capt Richard Wilson Pelly, RN (ante):—
Issue of late Alfred Digby Pelly, *b* 1862, *d* 1940: *m* 1899, Evelyn Sophia, who *d* 1970, da of late Rev Edward John Harford (Bridges, Bt):—

Richard Edward, b 1905: m 1941, Diana Marthe Desgrand Mitchell, who d 1991, and has issue living, Louise Sophia PELLY (500 Avenue Rd, Apt 1407, Toronto, Ont, Canada M4V 2J6), b 1943; ed Concordia Univ, Montreal (BA 1973), McGill Univ, Montreal (LLB 1976, BCL 1977), and Harvard Univ (LLM 1978); Bar Quebec 1979, and Onnt 1990; QC 1991; joined Stikeman, Elliott 1980, ptnr since 1985; joined Gowing, Strathy & Henderson 1994; Commemorative Medal for 125th Confedn of Anniversary of Canada 1992; has resumed the surname of Pelly: m 1967 (m diss 1971), Donald MacTaggart; has issue living, Alexandra Caroline Diana PELLY b 1985, — Harriet Elizabeth Annabel (70 Third Av, Ottawa, Ont, Canada K1S 2J8), b 1948; ed McGill Univ, Montreal (BAPsych 1977, MSW 1985); resumed the surname of Pelly until re-marriage: m 1st, 1984 (m diss 1988), Francis Rohland Stark; 2ndly, 1991, Gerald Graham. Residence – West End, Coggeshall, Essex. —— Violet Evelyn, b 1900: m 1923, the 10th Marquis de Ruvigny, who d 1941, and has issue living, Michael Francis Wriothesley Meredith Tom Bridges, b 1927; s his father as 11th Marquis de Ruvigny (cr France 1652): m 1956, Patricia Kirkpatrick, el da of late C. Kirkpatrick Pile, of Barbados, and has issue living, Count Rupert Francis James Henry (70 Hotham Rd, Putney, SW15) b 1959; ptnr Price Waterhouse since 1992: m 1987, Kumudini Nelun, yst da of Dr C. S. Ratnatunga, of Woodside Park, London, Rachel Anne b 1956: m 1976, Philip Alan Rubery, of Westcourt Houst, The Chase, Oxshott, Surrey, (and has issue living, Henry Philip Michael Nicholas b 1984, Georgina Rachel Eugenie b 1983). Residence – 3 Langside Av, Roehampton, SW15.

Branch from 8th son of 1st Baronet

Granddaughter of late Leonard Pelly, yr son of late Percy Leonard Pelly, 8th son of 1st baronet:—
Issue of late Eric Percy Leonard Pelly, b 1894, d 1978: m 1924, Helen Marjorie, who d 1968, da of late Edmund Richmond Wade, of Boston, USA:—
Rosamund Ann, b 1950: m 1950, Elliott Merriam Viney, DSO, MBE, TD, FSA, of Cross Farmhouse, Quainton, Aylesbury, Bucks HP22 4AR, and has issue living, Diana Susan, b 1952: m 1979, Hugh Scrimgeour, of 1 Teignmouth Rd, NW2, son of Robin Scrimgeour, of Lockeridge, Marlborough, and has issue living, Daniel b 1981, Alexander b 1984, Sophie Rebecca b 1988, — Amanda Louise, b 1954: m 1983, Tom Deakin, of 9 Hazlebury Rd, SW6, and has issue living, Jack Elliott b 1987, Charley b 1989.

The Pellys were settled in Dorset from the early 14th century, continuing with John Pelly of the co of Dorset, living 1419, William Pelly, gentleman, of Sturminster Marshall, living 1431/32, John Pelly, Kt (ca 1430-1510), William, of Sturminster Newton, living 1539, and John of Okeford Fitzpaine living 1539/69. In 1581 Thomas Pelly m Mary, da of Robert Nicles, Mayor of Poole, the family continuing in that town, as merchants, and ship owners with William (1593-1659) Overseer of the Poor 1622, William (1620-91) and John (1644-1720) Younger Brother of Trinity House. His son, Capt John Pelly (1683-1762) Elder Brother of Trinity House married, 2ndly, Grisella, da of Capt Thomas Collet, HEICS, of Barking, Essex. His son (by his 1st wife, Martha Lapthorne), was Capt John Pelly, HEICS, of Upton (1711-1762), Younger Brother of Trinity House, who m Elizabeth, da of Henry Hinde, of Aveley. Their son, Henry Hinde Pelly (1744-1818) inherited the Upton and Aveley estates. He was Capt HEICS, Elder Brother of Trinity House and High Sheriff of Essex in 1780; m Sally, da of Capt John Blake, HEICS, of Watcombe, Hants. Their eldest son, John Henry Pelly (1777-1852), of Upton, was created 1st baronet in 1840. He was Gov of the Bank of England, Gov of Hudson's Bay Co and Deputy Master of Trinity House. He was s by his eldest son, Sir John Henry (1809-64), 2nd Bt, who was s by his eldest son, Sir Henry Carstairs (1844-77), 3rd Bt, who was s by his half-brother, Sir Harold (1863-1950), 4th Bt, who was s by his eldest son, Sir Harold Alwyne (1893-1981), 5th Bt, who was s by his eldest son, Sir John Alwyne (1918-1993), 6th Bt.

Pennington-Ramsden, see Ramsden.

PERKS (UK) 1908, of Wykham Park, Neithrop, co Oxford (Extinct 1979)

Sir (ROBERT) MALCOLM MEWBURN PERKS, 2nd and last Baronet.

DAUGHTERS LIVING OF SECOND BARONET

Rosemary (Grove House, Selling, nr Faversham, Kent), b 1919; sometime Section Officer WAAF: m 1942, Lieut-Col Frederick Onslow Alexander Godwyn Bennett, who d 1993, and has issue living, James Malcolm, b 1949, — Elaine Roselle, b 1945, — Louise Rosemary, b 1946, — Claire Rosamund, b 1951, — Francesca Rosalind, b 1959. —— Felicia Dorothy (The Barn, King Steps, Brecon, Powys), b 1921: m 1st, 1940 (m diss 1958), Robert Lyle; 2ndly, 1959 (m diss 1986), Ruggero Galletta, and has issue living, (by 1st m) Hugh Robert, b 1941, — Philip Dominic, b 1949, — Felix Gregory, b 1953, — Thelma Cristina Elizabeth, b 1944, — Miranda Maria, b 1946, — (by 2nd m) Flavio Raul Turiddu, b 1960, — Giuseppina Graziana Eva Francesca, b 1959.

PERRING (UK) 1963, of Frensham Manor, Surrey

PROUD·TO·SERVE

Sir RALPH EDGAR PERRING, 1st *Baronet*, son of late Col Sir John Ernest Perring; *b* 23 March 1905; *ed* Univ Coll Sch; Chm Perring Furnishings Ltd 1948-81, and John Perring, Ltd; a Lieut for City of London, JP Co London, a Gov Christ's Hosp, St Bartholomew's Hosp, and Imperial Coll of Science and Technology, Vice-Pres of Roy Bridewell Hosp, Pres of Langbourn Ward Club, and a KStJ; Master of Tin Plate Workers' Co 1944-45, a Member of Court of Common Council, City of London 1948-51, an Alderman 1951-75, Chmn of Spitalfields Market Cttee 1951-52, a Member of London Co Council 1952-55, Sheriff of London 1958-59, and Lord Mayor of London 1962-63; Chm of Cttee for Exports to Canada 1967-69, Vice-Chm 1964-67; a Dir of Confedn Life Insurance Co of Canada since 1968; a Knight Cdr of Order of George I of Greece, a Cdr of Valour of Cameroons, a Grand Officer of Order of Leopold of Belgium Order of Homayoun of Iran, Grand Cross of Merit of Republic of Germany; 1939-45 War as Lt RA (TA); Knt 1960: *m* 1928, (Ethel) Mary, who *d* 1991, da of Henry T. Johnson, of Putney, SW, and has issue.

Arms – Argent, on a pile barry wavy of eight azure and of the field, between two walnut trees eradicated proper, a lion rampant gules. **Crest** – Upon the trunk of a walnut tree, fessewise with two branches sprouting therefrom proper a sword erect or.
Residence – 15 Burghley House, Somerset Rd, Wimbledon SW19 5JB.

SONS LIVING

JOHN RAYMOND, TD (21 Somerset Rd, Parkside, Wimbledon, SW19), *b* 7 July 1931; *ed* Stowe: *m* 1961, Ella Christine, da of late Maj Anthony George Pelham (*see* E Chichester, colls), and has issue living, John Simon Pelham, *b* 1962, — Mark Ralph Pelham, *b* 1965, — Emma Mary, *b* 1963: *m* 1994, Christian Philip Heyman, son of Hans Heyman, of Dorking, Surrey, — Anna Margaret, *b* 1968: *m* 1992, Edward Pery Standish (*see* B Byron). —— Michael Arthur (Chateau Waltermitty, Eynesse, 33220 Ste-Foy-la-Grande, France), *b* 1937; *ed* Stowe, and Trin Coll, Camb (MA, MB, BChir): *m* 1961 (*m diss* 1988), Elizabeth, da of late Air Commodore Eric Delano Barnes, CB, AFC, and has issue living, Nicholas David Delano, *b* 1963, — Michael Charles Delano, *b* 1965, — Thomas Edward Delano, *b* 1971, — Ralph Andrew Delano, *b* 1973.

COLLATERAL BRANCH LIVING

Issue of late Richard Eric Perring, 2nd son of 1st baronet, *b* 1933, *d* 1971: *m* 1964, Faith (43 Hertford Av, E Sheen, SW14) (who *m* 2ndly, 1974 (*m diss* 1982), William John Stainton Clutterbuck, and resumed her former surname of Perring by deed poll, 1983), da of late Sir Peter (Arthur Percival Hay) Aitken:—
Christopher James, *b* 1965. —— Antony William, *b* 1967. —— Graham Michael, *b* 1970.

PERROTT (UK) 1911, with precedence from 1 July, 1716 (Extinct 1922)

Sir HERBERT CHARLES PERROTT, CH, CB (6th of GB 1716 creation according to Roll of Baronets), 1st (of UK 1911 creation), and last *Baronet*.

DAUGHTER LIVING OF SIXTH (GB) AND FIRST (UK) BARONET

Helena Ruth (*Helena, Viscountess Maitland*), *b* 1912; is an OStJ: *m* 1936, Viscount Maitland, who was *ka* 1943, only son of 15th Earl of Lauderdale. *Residences* – Park House, Makerston, Kelso, Roxburghshire TD5 7PA; Flat E, 34 Cadogan Sq, SW1X 0JL.

PETIT (UK) 1890, of Petit Hall, Island of Bombay

Consequitur quodcunque
petit
*He obtains whatever he
seeks*

Sir DINSHAW MANOCKJEE PETIT, 4th Baronet, *b* 13 Aug 1934; *s* his father, Sir DINSHAW MANOCKJEE, 1983, and changed his name from Naswanji Dinshaw Petit to Dinshaw Manockjee Petit; *ed* Prince of Wales Indian Military Coll, and Malvern Coll; Pres N.M. Petit Charities, of Sir D.M. Petit Charities, of F.D. Petit Sanatorium, of Persian Zoroastrian Amelioration Fund, of Petit Girls' Orphanage, of D.M. Petit Gymnasium, and of J.N. Petit Inst of Native Gen Dispensary; Trustee of Soc for Prevention of Cruelty to Animals and mem of Man Cttee of B.D. Petit Parsi Gen Hosp: *m* 1st, 1964 (*m diss* 1985), Nirmala MODY, da of Maj Gen Nanavati, of Bombay; 2ndly, 1986, Elizabeth Maria Tinkelenberg, and has issue by 1st *m*.

Arms – Azure, on a chevron argent, between three urns of the last, therefrom issuant flames proper, as many bees volant, also proper. **Crest** – A ship under sail at sea, in front thereof an anchor fessewise, all proper.
Residence – Petit Hall, Nepean Sea Rd, Bombay.

SONS LIVING *(By 1st marriage)*

JEHANGIR, *b* 21 Jan 1965. —— Framjee, *b* 1968.

SISTER LIVING

Dina, *b* 1931: *m* 1961, Yves Jean Robert Louis Morange, and has issue living, Shireen Isabelle, *b* 1962, —— Ann Dina, *b* 1965.

COLLATERAL BRANCHES LIVING

Grandchildren of late Cowasjee Dinshaw Petit, el son of 1st baronet:—
Issue of late Pestonjee Cowasjee Petit, *b* 1866, *d* 1932: *m* 1894, Perzojbai Cowasjee Parukh:—
Hirabai (Hill Side, Nepean Sea Rd, Bombay), *b* 1898.
Issue of late Hormasjee Cowasjee Petit, *b* 1868, *d* 1939: *m* 1891, Perozbai Sorabjee Patuck:—
Cowasjee (35 New Kantwady Rd, Bandra, Bombay, 50), *b* 1893: *m* 1919, Nawajbai Pherozyshaw Dadyburjor, and has issue living, Sorabjee *b* 1921: *m* 1946, Cleta Mathias, and has issue living, Marius *b* 1948, Stephen *b* 1950, Cory Ann *b* 1951, Sean *b* 1953, Gavin *b* 1960, Jenne Lou *b* 1955, — Sheila, *b* 1926: *m* 1953, Julian Bartlett, and has issue living, Darius *b* 1955, Zarir *b* 1958, Pheroza *b* 1959. —— Dinshawjee, *b* 1903: *m* 1940, Milthibai D. Poocha, and has issue living, Freny, *b* 1941, — Homa, *b* 1945. —— Mithibai, *b* 1892. *Residence* – Ram Mansion, Nepean Sea Rd, Bombay, India.

Grandchildren of late Bomanjee Dinshaw Petit (infra):—
Issue of late Dhunjibhoy Bomanji Petit, *b* 1881, *d* 1957: *m* 1900, Humabai, who *d* 1949, el da of Jalbhoy Ardeshir Sett:—
Manockjee, *b* 1900: *m* 1927, Perin Maneckji Vacha. *Residence* – Sett Minar, Peddar Road, Bombay. —— Ruttonbai, *b* 1906: *m* 1st, 1934 (*m diss* 19—), Karl J. Khandalawala; 2ndly, Lama Anagarika Govinda. —— Kuverbai, *b* 1908: BA 19—, LLB 19—: *m* 1939, Rustom F. Vakharia, and has issue living, Shirinbai, *b* 1940, — Roshan, *b* 1943.
This baronetcy was granted with remainder to (i) Framjee Dinshaw Petit, 2nd son of the 1st baronet (Sir Dinshaw Manockjee Petit, a merchant and millowner of Bombay, who had served as Sheriff of Bombay and been Knighted 1887), and the heirs male of his body lawfully begotten, and (ii) the heirs male of the body of the 1st baronet. By special Act of the Legislative Council of India, all holders of the title relinquish their own name on succession and assume those of the 1st baronet.

PETO (UK) 1855, of Somerleyton Hall, Suffolk

Ad finem fidelis
Faithful to the end

Sir HENRY GEORGE MORTON PETO, 4th *Baronet*, *b* 29 April 1920; *s* his father, Sir (HENRY) FRANCIS MORTON, 1978; *ed* Sherborne, and Corpus Christi Coll, Camb: *m* 1947, Frances Jacqueline, JP, da of late Ralph Haldane Evers, of Milan, and has issue.

Arms – Per pale indented or and gules barry of six, two annulets in fesse, all counterchanged. **Crest** – On a rock proper a sinister wing or, thereon three annulets gules.
Residence – Stream House, Selborne, Alton, Hants GU34 3LE.

SONS LIVING

FRANCIS MICHAEL MORTON (Cowdenknowes Mains, Earlston, Berwickshire TD4 6AA), *b* 1949: *m* 1974, Felicity Margaret, da of late Lt-Col John Alan Burns, of Fairfield, Cole Rd, Bruton, Som (*see* Hope-Dunbar, Bt, colls), and has issue living, David James Morton, *b* 25 Aug 1978, — George Francis John, *b* 1980. —— Robert Henry Haldane (117 East Sheen Av, SW14 8AX), *b* 1950: *m* 1975, Susan, only da of William Judge, of 25 Model Cottages, East Sheen, SW14, and has issue living, Thomas William Morton, *b* 1977, — Edward Henry Haldane, *b* 1979.

BROTHER LIVING

William Neill (Hansford House, Umberleigh, N Devon EX37 9ES), *b* 1922; *ed* Sherborne: *m* 1st, 1943 (*m diss* 1962), Jacqueline Mary Valentine, who *d* 1971, da of late Gurth Edelsten, of Eastmore, PO Flora, Marquard, OFR; 2ndly, 1962, Ann Bernal, only da of late Lt-Col Theodore Thompson Laville, of Little Garth, Sampford Peverell, nr Tiverton, Devon, and has issue living (by 1st *m*), James Francis Morton (Glan Cerrig, Llanfaglan, Caernarfon, Gwynedd LL54 5RS), *b* 1944: *m* 1st, 1969, Daphne, who *d* 1981, yr da of Thomas Henry Kennedy, of Blackwood, Auldgirth, Dumfries; 2ndly, 1987, Dorothy, yr da of Maurice Wilson, of Cooper House, Selside, Kendal, and has issue living, (by 1st *m*) Mark Edward *b* 1971, Alexander

George *b* 1979, Rebecca Jane *b* 1975, — William Gurth (Anwoth House, Gatehouse-of-Fleet, Castle Douglas, Kirkcudbrightshire DG7 2EF), *b* 1949; *ed* Wellington, and RMA Sandhurst; late Maj 13th/18th R Hussars: *m* 1976, Alice Caroline, da of late Dermot Holdsworth Harling Turner, of Kildalloig, Campbeltown, Argyll, and has issue living, Roland Harry Morton *b* 1982, Alice Jane *b* 1979.

HALF-BROTHER LIVING

Raymond John (Ridgeway House, Child Okeford, Dorset DT11 8QY), *b* 1950; *ed* Ampleforth, and Brunel Univ: *m* 1986, Monica Marie, da of Thomas Barlow, of Chapeltown, Yorks.

COLLATERAL BRANCHES LIVING

Grandchildren of late William Herbert Peto, 3rd son of 1st baronet:—
Issue of late Major Ralph Harding Peto, *b* 1877, *d* 1945: *m* 1st, 1909 (*m diss* 1923), Frances Ruby Vera, who *d* 1951, da of late Lieut-Col Walter James Lindsay (E Crawford, colls); 2ndly, 1937, Mechtilde Christiane, who *d* 1958, da of late Count Maximilian von Arco-Zinneberg, and widow of H. S. H. Karl Max, 6th Prince Lichnowsky, GCVO, sometime German Ambassador in London:—
(By 1st *m*) Maud Rosemary Peto (c/o Coutts Bank, Duncannon Branch, 440 Strand, WC2), *b* 1916; resumed by deed poll 1961 the surname of Peto: *m* 1934 (*m diss* 1958), Viscount Hinchingbrooke (later 10th Earl of Sandwich, until he disclaimed his titles 1964).
Issue of late Sir Geoffrey Kelsall Peto, KBE, *b* 1878, *d* 1956: *m* 1st, 1903, Pauline, who *d* 1950, da of late William Quirin, of Boston, USA, and widow of Lieut-Col R. Cokayne-Frith, 15th Hussars; 2ndly, 1951, Edna Frances, who *d* 1977, da of late Edward B. Hilton, of Paris, and New York, and widow of Capt Sir Denzil Cope, 14th Bt:—
(By 1st *m*) Anthony (c/o Coutts & Co, 440 Strand, WC2), *b* 1907; *ed* Eton: *m* 1936, Baroness Barbara, da of Baron Hermann Wrangel, of Genarp, Sweden, and has issue living, Ursula, *b* 1938: *m* 1960, Richard Alan Opperman.

Issue living of late Basil Edward Peto (7th son of 1st baronet), who was *cr* a *Baronet* 1927:—
See Peto, Bt, *cr* 1927.

Sir Samuel Morton Peto, 1st Bt, MP for Norwich (*L*) 1847-55, and subsequently for Finsbury and Bristol, was the el son of William Peto, of Cookham, Berks.

PETO (UK) 1927, of Barnstaple, co Devon

Faithful to the end

Sir MICHAEL HENRY BASIL PETO, 4th *Baronet*; *b* 6 April 1938; *s* his father, *Brig Sir* CHRISTOPHER HENRY MAXWELL, DSO, 1980; *ed* Eton, and Ch Ch, Oxford (MA); Bar Inner Temple 1960; Member of Stock Exchange 1963: *m* 1st, 1963 (*m diss* 1970), Sarah Susan, yst da of Maj Sir Dennis Frederick Bankes Stucley, 5th Bt; 2ndly, 1971, Lucinda Mary, da of Sir Charles Douglas Blackett, 9th Bt, and formerly wife of Ewan Iain Macleod Hilleary, and has issue living by 1st and 2nd *m*.

Arms – Barry or and gules per pale indented counterchanged in chief a boar's head erased proper and in base two annulets counterchanged. **Crest** – On a rock proper a sinister wing or, thereon three annulets gules.
Residence – Lower Church Cottage, Cliddesden, Basingstoke, Hants. *Club* – Pratt's.

SONS LIVING *(By 1st marriage)*

HENRY CHRISTOPHER MORTON BAMPFYLDE, *b* 8 April 1967; *ed* Eton. *Residence* – Court Hall, North Molton, Devon EX36 3HP.

(By 2nd marriage)

Hugh David, *b* 1974. —— Charles Michael, *b* 1977.

DAUGHTERS LIVING *(By 1st marriage)*

Emma Rose, *b* 1965: *m* 1994, Harry N. Matovu, yr son of late Leonard Matovu, of Vienna. —— Marina Sarah, *b* 1968.

BROTHER LIVING

Nicholas John (Grey Walls, Chadlington, Oxon; White's and Pratt's Clubs), *b* 1939; *ed* Eton, and RMA Sandhurst; Capt 9th/12th Lancers, ADC (to Gen Norman Wheeler) BAOR 1964: *m* 1st, 1969 (*m diss* 1978), Anne Colquhoun, el da of late John Tysen, New York; 2ndly, 1979 (*m diss* 1989), Lucinda Hilary, da of late Owen George Endicott Roberts, and formerly wife of Demetri P. Marchessini; 3rdly, 1991, Mrs Zoë Westropp, da of Charles Douglas Neville Walker, of 58 rue Singer, Paris, and formerly wife of Anthony Henry (Harry) Westropp, and has issue living (by 1st *m*), Alexander Tysen, *b* 1973.

SISTER LIVING

Elizabeth Mary, *b* 1936: *m* 1958, Ronald Philip Murphy, of Shippool House, Innishannon, co Cork, and has issue living, Charles Christopher Ronald, *b* 1959, — Richard Norbert, *b* 1961.

DAUGHTER LIVING OF SECOND BARONET

Serena Mary Francesa (*Serena, Lady Matheson of Matheson*), *b* 1928: *m* 1954, Maj Sir Torquhil Alexander Matheson of Matheson, 6th Bt, who *d* 1993. *Residence* – Trees Farm, Standerwick, Frome, Somerset BA11 2PP.

COLLATERAL BRANCH LIVING

Issue of late Major (Basil Arthur) John Peto, King's Dragoon Guards, 3rd son of 1st baronet, *b* 1900, *d* 1954: *m* 1934, Patricia Geraldine (66 Whitelands House, Cheltenham Terr, SW3) (who *m* 2ndly, 1955, Lt-Col Hugh Granville Leveson Dudley Ryder, TD (*see* E Harrowby, colls)), da of late Gerald Macleay Browne, OBE:—

Jonathan Basil Morton (Bealings House, Woodbridge, Suffolk; Pratt's Club), *b* 1942; *ed* Eton; Coldm Gds 1962-66; ADC to Gov of Qld 1963-66: *m* 1969, Hon Selina Lilian Hughes-Young, da of 1st Baron St Helens, and has issue living, Amyas John, *b* 1969, — Harold Patrick Basil, *b* 1974, — Daisy Elizabeth, *b* 1971, — Augusta Mary, *b* 1977, — Violet Selina, *b* 1984.
—— Virginia Anne (Raswell Cottage, Loxhill, Godalming, Surrey), *b* 1935: *m* 1955 (*m diss* 1981), Gerard Wyndham Morgan-Grenville (*see* Ly Kinloss), and has issue. —— Joanna Dava, *b* 1938: *m* 1957, Capt Charles St John Graham Moncrieff, Scots Gds (*see* V Bolingbroke, colls, 1985 Edn), and has issue living, Alexander Charles Graham, *b* 1967, — Charlotte Henrietta, *b* 1959: *m* 1987, Benjamin Heath, yr son of William Heath, of Guildford, Surrey, and has issue living, Rory William *b* 1988, Pollyanna Rose *b* 1992, — Miranda Caroline (*Hon Mrs Mark F. R. Baring*), *b* 1961: *m* 1983, Hon Mark Francis Robert Baring, el son of 7th Baron Ashburton, and has issue (*see* B Ashburton), — Rosanna Claire, *b* 1965. *Residence* – Easter Elcho, Rhynd, Perthshire. —— Sarah Christian Pandora (*Lady Bathurst*), *b* 1940: *m* 1959, Adm Sir David Benjamin Bathurst, GCB (*see* E Bathurst, colls).

The 1st baronet, Sir Basil Edward Peto (7th son of Sir Samuel Morton Peto, 1st Bt (*cr* 1855)), was MP for E or Devizes Div of Wilts (C) 1910-18 and for Barnstaple Div of Devon 1922-3, and 1924-35. Lt-Col Sir J. Michael Peto, 2nd Bt, Coldm Gds, served in World War I 1915-18 (despatches), and in World War II 1939-45.

PETRIE (UK) 1918, of Carrowcarden, Castleconnor, Barony of Tireragh, co Sligo

Trust, but observe

Sir PETER CHARLES PETRIE, CMG, 5th *Baronet*; *b* 7 March 1932; *s* his half-brother, *Lt-Col Sir* (CHARLES) RICHARD BORTHWICK, 1988; *ed* Westminster, and Ch Ch Oxford (MA); HM Diplomatic Service, 2nd Sec UK Del NATO Paris 1958, 1st Sec New Delhi 1961, Chargé d'Affaires Kathmandu 1963, 1st Sec UK Mission to UN, New York 1969, Counsellor Bonn 1973; Head of European Integration Dept, FCO 1976, Minister Paris 1979-85, HM Amb to Belgium 1985-89, since when Adviser to Governor of Bank of England; late 2nd Lieut Gren Gds; CMG (1980): *m* 1958, Countess Lydwine Maria Fortunata, da of Count Charles Alphonse v Oberndorff, of The Hague and Paris, and has issue.

Arms – Azure, on a bend between a stag's head couped and three cross cross-lets fitchée argent, as many escallops gules. **Crest** – A demi-eagle displayed proper gazing at a sun or.
Residences – 16A Cambridge St, SW1V 4QH; 40 rue Lauriston, Paris 16e; Hameau du Jardin, Lestre, 50310 Montebourg, Normandy.

SONS LIVING

CHARLES JAMES, *b* 16 Sept 1959; *ed* American Coll, Paris (BA), INSEAD, Fontainebleau; 2nd Lieut 67th French Inf Regt; chief senior consultant Coopers and Lybrand 1987-90, UN Emergency Unit Sudan 1990-92, UN Operation Somalia 1992-94: *m* 1981, France, da of Comte Bernard de Hauteclocque, of Chateau d'Etrejust, Picardie, and has had issue, Arthur Cecil, *b* 15 Feb 1987, — Oliver Bernard, *b* 1989, — Victor François, *b* 1992, — Cecilia Marie Bernard, *b* and *d* 1985. —— Wilfrid John, *b* 1965; *ed* Ecole St Jean de Passy, Lycée Louis Le Grand, and Ecole Polytechnique: *m* 1989, Fabienne, da of Louis Lacaille, of 3 Blvd Flandrin, 75116 Paris.

DAUGHTER LIVING

Leticia Jacqueline Fortunata Cecilia, *b* 1961: *m* 1989, Pierre-André de Chalendaer, and has issue living, François, *b* 1990, — Jacques, *b* 1992.

DAUGHTER LIVING OF SECOND BARONET

Violet Haddon, *b* 1913: *m* 1st, (Jan) 1937, Charles Edward Wilson Sleigh; 2ndly, 1950, William Dalziel Mungall Allison, who *d* 1957, and has issue living (by 1st *m*) Thomas Edward (The Gardens Cottage, E Saltoun, nr Pencaitland, E Lothian EH34 5DS), *b* 1939: *m* 1965, Daphne Mary Walker, da of Dr Charles Boness-Jones, of Bengal, India, and has issue living, David Edward *b* 1969, Charles Timothy Fisher *b* 1971, Patricia Mary *b* 1967, — Rosemary Anne, *b* (Dec) 1937: *m* 1st, 1956 (*m diss* 1975), Walter Ronald Alexander; 2ndly, 1982, His Honour Judge (George Leon Severyn) Dobry, CBE, of 40 Chester Row, SW1, and has issue living (by 1st *m*), Walter *b* 1957, Charles Edward *b* 1963, Rosalind *b* 1959, Caroline *b* 1961, — (by 2nd *m*) Robert William Mungall (The Cottage, Saltoun Home Farm, E Saltoun, nr Pencaitland, E Lothian EH34 5DT), *b* 1951: *m* 1982, Pamela Louise, da of William Dougal Taylor. *Residence* – 6 Camus Park, Edinburgh EH10 6RY.

WIDOW LIVING OF FOURTH BARONET

JESSIE ARIANA BORTHWICK (*Dowager Lady Petrie*), da of late Cdr Patrick Straton Campbell, JP, RN, of Westleton, Saxmundham, Suffolk: *m* 1962, Lt-Col Sir (Charles) Richard Borthwick Petrie, 4th Bt, TD, who *d* 1988.

Sir Charles Petrie, 1st baronet (son of Alexander Petrie, of Carrowcarden, Enniscrone, co Sligo, grandson of Peter Petrie, of Newburgh, Fife, and great grandson of George Petrie, of Port Leithen, Aberdeen), was Lord Mayor of Liverpool 1901-2, and Leader of Conservative Party. His son, Sir Charles Petrie, 3rd baronet, CBE, the eminent historian and author, was Knt Order of Civil Merit (Spain), Com of Orders of Crown of Italy, of George I of Greece, and of Isabella the Catholic of Spain, and Pres of Mil History Soc of Ireland.

PEYTON (GB) 1776, of Doddington, Cambridgeshire (Extinct 1962)

Sir ALGERNON THOMAS PEYTON, 7th and last *Baronet*.

DAUGHTERS LIVING OF SEVENTH BARONET

Delia, *b* 1916: *m* 1943, Major Benjamin George Barnett, MBE, TD, Oxfordshire Yeo (ret); High Sheriff of Oxon 1969; and has issue living, David John Wheate, *b* 1946: *m* 1971, Annabel Mary, da of Peter Owen of Mixbury, Northants, and has issue living, James Peter Wheate *b* 1973, Toby Luke *b* 1981, Hermione, *b* 1975, — Charles Henry, *b* 1948: *m* 1978, Georgina Ross, da of David Coventry Greig, of Muirhead of Balgray, Irving, Ayrshire, and has issue living, John Robert *b* 1983, Flora Anne *b* 1979, — Rosemary Dorothea, *b* 1953. *Residence* – The Stud House, Great Purston, Brackley, Northants NN13 5PL. —— Elisabeth Rosamund, *b* 1919: *m* 1943, Capt John Nigel Bingham, Coldstream Guards (*see* E Lucan, colls). *Residence* – Stone House, Brimpton, Reading.

Philipson-Stow, see Stow.

FOLEY-PHILIPPS (UK) 1887, of Picton Castle, co Pembroke (Extinct 1962)

Sir RICHARD FOLEY FOLEY-PHILIPPS, 4th and last *Baronet*.

DAUGHTER LIVING OF SECOND BARONET

Sheila Victoria Katrin (*Baroness of Dunsany*), *b* 1912; is DStJ: *m* 1st, 1932, Major John Frederick Foley, Baron de Rutzen, Welsh Guards, who was *ka* in Italy 1944, having in 1918 received Roy licence (for himself and the heirs male of his body on succession) to use the title within the British Dominions; 2ndly, 1947, as his 2nd wife, 19th Baron of Dunsany, and has issue living (by 2nd *m*) (*see* B Dunsany). *Residence* – Dunsany Castle, co Meath.

PHILLIPS (UK) 1912, of Tylney Hall, Rotherwick, co Southampton

Sir ROBIN FRANCIS PHILLIPS, 3rd *Baronet*; *b* 29 July 1940; *s* his father, Capt Sir LIONEL FRANCIS, 1944; *ed* Aiglon Coll, Switzerland.

Arms – Or, on a pile azure, between two greyhounds courant in base sable, a lion rampant of the first, guttée-des poix. **Crest** – A demi-lion azure, charged on the shoulder with two annulets interlaced paleways or, between as many nuggets of gold.
Residence – 12 Manson Mews, SW7.

AUNT LIVING

Mary Pamela, *b* 1919: *m* 1943, Arthur Owen Hunt, and has issue living, Clive Anthony, *b* 1944: *m* 1980, Philippa Jane Samuel, and has issue living, William Edward *b* 1987, Annabel Carolyn Philippa *b* 1984, — David Charles, *b* 1947: *m* 1974, Julia Vivian Bennett, and has issue living, Peter Lionel *b* 1981, Gemma Helen *b* 1976, Vanessa Caroline *b* 1979, — Paula Caroline, *b* 1950. *Residence* – Moat Manor, Kingston Blount, Oxford OX9 4RZ.

WIDOW LIVING OF SECOND BARONET

CAMILLA MARY, da of late Capt Hugh Algernon Parker (*see* E Macclesfield, colls): *m* 1st, 1939, Capt Sir Lionel Francis Phillips, 2nd Bt, who was *ka* in Italy 1944; 2ndly, 1950, John George Pisani, who *d* 1982, of 21 Chancellor House, 17 Hyde Park Gate, SW7 5DQ.

The 1st baronet, Sir Lionel Phillips (son of late Philip Saunders Phillips, merchant of London), was a partner in the late firm of Wernher, Beit & Co, of 1 London Wall Buildings, EC; sometime Chm Central Mining & Investment Corporation Ltd, and Rand Mines Ltd; Hon Col 10th S African Inf and 1st S African Field Ambulance; one of the leaders of the Transvaal Reform Movement 1896, resulting in Jameson Raid (sentenced to death by Judge Gregorovski, sentence commuted to fine of £25,000); a MLA, S Africa 1910-15; prominently associated with Transvaal gold-mining industry, and five times Pres of Transvaal Chamber of Mines. The 2nd baronet, Capt Sir Lionel Francis, RA (TA), was *ka* in Italy 1944.

Truth conquers

FAUDEL-PHILLIPS (UK) 1897, of Grosvenor Gardens, St George, Hanover Square, co London, and Queen's Gardens, West Brighton, co Sussex (Extinct 1941)

Sir LIONEL LAWSON FAUDEL FAUDEL-PHILLIPS, 3rd and last *Baronet*.

DAUGHTER LIVING OF THIRD BARONET

Helen Bridget (*Countess of Kilmorey*), *b* 1918; resumed her former style 1990: *m* 1st, 1941, 5th Earl of Kilmorey, who *d* 1977; 2ndly, 1978 (*m diss* 1990), Harold William Elliott. *Residence* – 8 The Dormers, Highworth, Swindon, Wilts.

PICKTHORN (UK) 1959, of Orford, co Suffolk

Sir CHARLES WILLIAM RICHARDS PICKTHORN, 2nd *Baronet*; *b* 3 March 1927; *s* his father, *Rt Hon Sir* KENNETH WILLIAM MURRAY, 1975; *ed* Eton, and Corpus Christi Coll, Camb; Bar Middle Temple 1952: *m* 1951, Helen Antonia, only da of late Sir James Gow Mann, KCVO, and has issue.
Residences – Manor House, Nunney, nr Frome, Som; 3 Hobury St, SW10.

SON LIVING

JAMES FRANCIS, *b* 18 Feb 1955; *ed* Eton. *Residence* – 45 Ringmer Av, SW6 5LP.

DAUGHTERS LIVING

Caroline, *b* 1958. —— Frances, *b* 1960: *m* 1982, Crispin Bernard Noël Kelly (*see* D Norfolk).

BROTHER LIVING

Henry Gabriel Richards, *b* 1928; *ed* Eton, and Trin Coll, Camb: *m* 1955, Mary, da of Cecil James Juxon Talbot Barton, CMG, OBE, and has issue living, John, *b* 1957, — Andrew, *b* 1961, — Thomas David Alexander, *b* 1967: *m* 1993, Nicola, da of His Honour Judge (John Declan) Sheerin, of Rougham, Suffolk, — Henrietta Cicely, *b* 1959: *m* 1982, John Ramsay Lloyd-Jones (*see* Maitland, Bt). *Residence* – 54 Chelsea Park Gdns, SW3.

SISTER LIVING

Catherine Ann Monica, *b* 1925: *m* 1950, Neil Atkinson Iliff, CBE, who *d* 1973, and has issue living, Charles, *b* 1952; *ed* Eton and Trin Coll, Camb: *m* 1989, Monica, da of Jerome Dessain, — Catherine, *b* 1955: *m* 1989, Andrew Saul, — Elizabeth, *b* 1957, — Mary, *b* 1958, — Georgina, *b* 1963. *Residences* – 32 Chipstead St, SW6 3SS; Rosehill, Orford, Woodbridge, Suffolk.

Rt Hon Sir Kenneth William Murray Pickthorn, 1st Bt, was MP for Camb Univ (*C*) 1935-50, and Carlton, Notts 1950-66. He was Parl Sec, Min of Education 1951-54.

PIERS (I) 1661, of Tristernagh Abbey, Westmeath

Sir CHARLES ROBERT FITZMAURICE PIERS, 10th *Baronet*, *b* 30 Aug 1903; his father *Sir* CHARLES PIGOTT, 1945; Lt-Cdr (ret) RCNVR; formerly Manager of Midland Doherty Ltd, of Duncan, BC, Canada: *m* 1936, Ann Blanche Scott, who *d* 1975, only da of late Capt Thomas Ferguson, Roy Highlanders, and has had issue.

Arms – Azure, three lions passant-guardant in fesse, between two double cotises argent. **Crest** – An arm embowed vested azure, charged with three plates and cuffed argent the hand holding a broken flagstaff, the flat azure, on a chief argent three torteaux.
Address – PO Box 748, Duncan, BC, Canada V9L 3Y1.

Noble is the lion's anger

SON LIVING

JAMES DESMOND, *b* 24 July 1947: *m* 1975, Sandra Mae Dixon, and has issue living, Stephen James, *b* 1979, — Christine Sarah, *b* 1976.

DAUGHTER DECEASED

Sarah Constance, *b* 1942: *m* 1970, Michael C. Weld, and *d* 1988, leaving issue, Diana Kristen, *b* 1971, — Andrea Jane, *b* 1974.

COLLATERAL BRANCHES LIVING

Granddaughter of late Henry Piers, 2nd son of late Rev Octavius Piers, 5th son of 5th baronet:—
Issue of late Lieut-Col Henry Octavius Piers, RA, *b* 1856, *d* 1945: *m* 1886, Lise, who *d* 1937, da of Dep Surg-Gen Johnston Ferguson:—
Gwendolen Mary (Redcliff Court Hotel, Cyprus Rd, Exmouth), *b* 1889.

Grandsons of late Lt-Col William Barrington Piers, el son of late Col Thomas Tristram Piers, 5th son of late Rev Octavius Piers (ante):—
Issue of late William Price Barrington Piers, *b* 1905, *d* 1974: *m* 1935, Ursula Mary Bence, who *d* 1993, da of Rev George Alfred Charles Smith-Cranmoor, R of Baldock, Herts:—
Anthony Tristram Barrington (Withy Cottage, Wrantage, Taunton, Som TA3 6DJ), *b* 1939; Maj 1st Devonshire and Dorset Regt (ret): *m* 1st, 1964 (*m diss* 1981), Susan Jacqueline Dawn, only da of Lt-Col H. T. Bayldon, MC, of Las Palmas, Canary Islands; 2ndly, 1981, Mrs Mary Gertrude Eveleen Croft, da of D.H. Baker, of Farnham, Surrey, and has issue living (by 1st *m*), Christopher William Barrington, *b* 1973, — Ann-Marie Barrington, *b* 1965: *m* 1988, Kevin Crampton, and has issue living, Connor Sebastian *b* 1990, Rory Leto *b* 1992, — Bridget Dawn Barrington, *b* 1967: *m* 1993, Anton Matthews. —— Brian

William Barrington (7 Ross St, Toowoomba, Queensland 4350, Australia), *b* 1941: *m* 1970, Stephanie Ellen Elizabeth, da of late Capt Attoe, of London, and has issue living, Robert Courtney Barrington, *b* 1973, — Samantha Barrington, *b* 1971.
——— Charles Barrington (95 Belladona Rd, Roodekranz Ext 7, Roodepoort 1725, Transvaal, S Africa), *b* 1943: Lt-Col (ret) Rhodesian African Rifles: *m* 1980, Judy Melanie Pamela, da of P. D. Fuller, of Shurugwi, Zimbabwe, and has issue living, Niall Barrington, *b* 1984.

Granddaughters of late Col Thomas Tristram Piers (ante):—
Issue of late Rev Samuel Octavius Piers, *b* 1869, *d* 1940: *m* 1901, Mabel Marion, who *d* 1951, da of G. Smith, of Ipswich:—
†Charles Stuart Tristram, *b* 1920; Sub-Lt, RN; served 1939-45 War; *d* as a result of enemy action 1941. ——— Violet Marion, *b* 1905: *m* 1st, 1931, Louis Brown, who *d* 1934; 2ndly, 1939, George Paul, and has issue living, (by 2nd *m*) Jacqueline Evelyn, *b* 1940. ——— Evelyn Helena, *b* 1909: *m* 1st, 1938, George Damer, Lt RCA, who was *ka* in Italy 1944; 2ndly, 1972, Robert Owen Fowler, AMIEE, of Liverpool, Nova Scotia, and has issue living (by 1st *m*), George Terence Stuart (Hazelbank, 14 Beech Rd, Reigate, Surrey), *b* 1940; BSc: *m* 1964, Michèle Mary Godwin Prouten, and has issue living, Justin Dawson *b* 1967, Miranda Jane *b* 1968, Annabel Katie Louise *b* 1974. ——— Ruth Pauline, *b* 1925: *m* 1946, Thomas Eric Hazeldine, AMICE, and has issue living, Keith Trevor, *b* 1947; BEng, MBA: *m* 1970, Ethel Mae Fraser, and has issue living, Julia Lee *b* 1975, Amy Katherine *b* 1977, Laura Mae *b* 1979, — Piers Martyn, *b* 1957: *m* 1st, 1984, Iva MacKenzie, who *d* 1992; 2ndly, 1994, Wendy Wyer, and has issue living (by 1st *m*), Tia Lee-Anne *b* 1984, Dana Christine *b* 1986, (by 2nd *m*) Heidi Lee Grace *b* 1994, — Carol Anne, *b* 1948: *m* 1970, James E. Dewar, and has issue living, Brydone Michael *b* 1980, Jennifer Laura *b* 1975, Kimberly Margaret *b* 1978, — Sally Jane, *b* 1949: *m* 1971, Dr Arnie Chestnut, and has issue living, Matthew Robert *b* 1979, Heidi Anne *b* 1974, Shannon Gail *b* 1977, — Gail Melissa, *b* 1955: *m* 1980, William Moffatt, of 6620 Jubilee Rd, Halifax, Nova Scotia B3H 2H4, Canada, and has issue living, Jonathan Eric Douglas *b* 1991, Luke Stuart *b* 1994, Rachel Alexandra Hazeldine *b* 1990. *Residence* – Blueberry Shores, Liverpool, Nova Scotia B0T 1K0, Canada.

Grandchildren of late Walter Barrington Piers (infra):—
Issue of late Grahame Barrington Piers, *b* 1913, *d* 1980: *m* 1950, Shirley O'Brien (Suite 310, 404, E 80th Av, Vancouver, BC, Canada):—
Richard Barrington, *b* 1953.
Issue of late Cecil Edwin Piers, *b* 1914, *d* 1987: *m* 1941, Ethel Sheppard (PO Box 301, Montrose, BC, Canada V0G 1P0):—
Kenneth Barrington (Schelf Straat No 1, 3295TK S'Gravendeel, Holland), *b* 1943: *m* 1966, Maartje Wolf. ——— Penelope Ann, *b* 1946: *m* 1972, Brian Denton, of 2134 Graham Av, Prince Rupert, BC V8J 1C8, Canada, and has issue living, Trevor Piers, *b* 1975, — Laura Lynn, *b* 1973.

Grandchildren of late Shute Barrington Piers (infra):—
Issue of late Walter Barrington Piers, *b* 1890, *d* 1964: *m* 1913, Mary Cecilia Onn, who *d* 1983:—
Harry Gordon (309-3901 32nd Av, Vernon, BC, Canada), *b* 1920; formerly Warrant Officer, RCAF; Inspector of Customs and Immigration (ret): *m* 1st, 1946, Sally Chisholm; 2ndly, 1970, Helen Street, and has issue living (by 1st *m*), James Walker, *b* 1947.
Issue of late Grahame Sedway Piers, *b* 1892, *d* 1970: *m* 1917, Dorothy Mary, who *d* 1971, da of G. D. Heather:—
Heather, *b* 1918: *m* 1945, Anthony Freeman, FCA, of Fernhill Cottage, Ide Hill, Sevenoaks and has issue living, Michael Edmund Piers, *b* 1946, — Anthony Piers, *b* 1956, — Chloe Anne, *b* 1949, — Amanda Jane, *b* 1953.

Granddaughters of late Capt Shute Barrington Piers, RN, 6th son of late Rev Octavius Piers (ante):—
Issue of late Shute Barrington Piers, *b* 1864, *d* 1947: *m* 1888, Gertrude, who *d* 1938, da of Charles Henry Nottingham:—
Gladys Nottngham, *b* 1893: *m* 1920, W. Serle, who *d* 1940, and has issue living, Patrick Philip Oswald, *b* 1921; Sqdn Ldr RAF (ret): *m* 1st, 1940, Sheila Foster, of Bexhill-on-Sea; 2ndly, 1965, Nicole Lecoq, and has issue living (by 2nd *m*) Roy Anthony Michael *b* 1941; Inspector, Metropolitan Police: *m* 1964, Elizabeth Mary, da of —, (and has issue living, Paul *b* 1966, Keith *b* 1968, Fiona *b* 1965), John Patrick David *b* 1944; Capt RAOC, Peter Norman James, *b* 1949; RAF (by 2nd *m*) Robert Barrington *b* 1966.
Issue of late Henry Handyside Bruce Piers, *b* 1865, *d* 1935: *m* 1902, Eva Gertrude, who *d* 1962, da of G. B. Pennell:—
Mary Eva Patricia, *b* 1905: *m* 1939, Arthur Mather Grundy, who *d* 1940, and has issue living, John Martin, *b* 1940; Col R Regt of Wales (ret): *m* 1974, Sheila Mary Evans, and has issue living, James David Piers *b* 1976, Anna Charlotte *b* 1980. *Residence* – 7 Long Alley, St Helens Churchyard, Abingdon, Oxon OX14 5EJ. ——— Margaret Marion, *b* 1906: *m* 1938, Rt Rev Leslie Stibbard, Assist Bishop of Newcastle, NSW (ret), 62 Kemp St, Hamilton, 2303, NSW, and has issue living, David Piers (Roughit, via Singleton, 2330, NSW), *b* 1943: *m* 1966, Janet Pauline, da of late Dale Harrison, of Lawrence, NSW, and has issue living, Dermot Harrison *b* 1969, Samantha Marion *b* 1968, Fenella Joanne *b* 1973, — Stephen Patrick (145A Everton St, Hamilton, NSW 2303), *b* 1947: *m* 1974, Jillian Margaret, da of Bruce Robert McGavin, of New Lambton, NSW, and has issue living, Sophie Anne *b* 1989, — Ruth, *b* 1940: *m* 1963, Noël Bernard McFayden, of 38 Janet St, Merewether, NSW, and has issue living, David James *b* 1964; RAN, Michael Stuart *b* 1969, Lisa Jane *b* 1965, — Miriam Anne, *b* 1950: *m* 1969, George David Swan, of 16 Raymond St, Speers Point, NSW, and has issue living, Fiona Louise *b* 1969, Jennifer Anne *b* 1972. ——— Helen Alice, *b* 1914: *m* 1944, Rev John Lionel Mortimer, who *d* 1983, of Foxlease, Maiden Bradley, Warminster, Wilts, and has issue living, *Rev* Lawrence George, *b* 1945; Communications Officer, Diocese of Coventry: *m* 1st, 1973, Catriona Lane, who *d* 1982; 2ndly, 1992, Rosemary Bartlett, and has issue living (by 1st *m*), John Lawrence *b* 1978, Rebecca Magdalena Helen *b* 1974, Rosamund Clare *b* 1976, — Michael Piers, *b* 1946: *m* 1985, Ann, da of James Jenkinson, of Aldershot, and has issue living, Benjamin *b* 1987, Emily *b* 1985, — Christopher Hugh, *b* 1949.

Grandchildren of late Henry Handyside Bruce Piers (ante):—
Issue of late Maj Eustace Pennell Piers, *b* 1910; *d* 1979: *m* 1941, Jean Mavis (Gable End, Castle Cary, Somerset BA7 7AR), da of John Edward Ralph, of Streatham Hill, SW:—
William James Shute Barrington, *b* 1948; *ed* Millfield, and Brunel Univ; BTech, MIMech E: *m* 1978, Janet Anne, da of late Kenneth Arthur Fream, of Bristol, and has had issue, Adam Ralph Barrington, *b* 1980, — Oliver Henry, *b* 1982, *d* 1984, — Thomas Michael, *b* 1985, — Sarah Elizabeth, *b* 1987. *Residence* – 101 Aylesbury Rd, Aston Clinton, Bucks HP22 5AJ. ——— Angela Mary, *b* 1942: *m* 1965, Peter Kiero Watson, of 66 Finches Gdns, Lindfield, Sussex RH16 2PB, and has had issue, James Kiero *b* 1966, — Thomas Piers Kiero, *b* 1969, *d* 1970, — Edward Piers Kiero, *b* 1970. ——— Clare Rosamund Pennell (twin), *b* 1948: *m* 1984, Peter William Dodd, of 4 Russell Rd, W14.

This baronet is descended from William Piers, son of Henry Piers, of Piers Hall, Yorks, who is said at one time to have saved the Princess Elizabeth from the fury of her sister, Queen Mary, by conveying her privately away. After that princess ascended the throne, he was sent by Her Majesty to Ireland, and received a grant of the abbey of Tristernagh, in Westmeath. He was afterward appointed Governor of Carrickfergus and Seneschal of the county of Antrim, and in 1565 obtained the reward of 1,000 marks for bringing in the head of the rebel Shane O'Neil. The 9th baronet, Sir Charles Pigott, was Major (ret) Canadian Mil and served in S Africa 1900-1901, and in European War 1914-19.

PIGOT (GB) 1764, of Patshull, Staffordshire

Always ready

Sir GEORGE HUGH PIGOT, 8th *Baronet, b* 28 Nov 1946; *s* his father *Maj-Gen Sir* ROBERT ANTHONY, CB, OBE, 1986; *ed* Stowe: *m* 1st, 1967 (*m diss* 1973), Judith Sandeman, elder da of late Maj John Hele Sandeman-Allen, RA (*see* E Woolton, 1985 Edn); 2ndly, 1980 (*m diss* 1993), Lucinda Jane, yr da of Donald Charles Spandler, of Chiddingfold, Surrey, and has issue by 1st and 2nd *m.*

𝔄rms – Ermine, three lozenges conjoined in fesse sable. ℭrest – A Wolf's head erased argent.
Residence – Comfrey Cottage, Padworth, Berks RG7 4JX.

SON LIVING *(By 2nd marriage)*

GEORGE DOUGLAS HUGH, *b* 17 Sept 1982. —— Robert Edward Richard, *b* 1984.

DAUGHTER LIVING *(By 1st marriage)*

Melanie Barbara, *b* 1969.

HALF-BROTHER LIVING

Robert James, *b* 1971; *ed* Eton.

SISTER LIVING

Louise, *b* 1943: *m* 1966, Peter Mellor, of Brinksway House, Shottermill, nr Haslemere, Surrey son of A. R. Mellor, of Lamb Cottage, Newtown, IoW, and has issue living, Nicola, *b* 1970, — Suzanna, *b* 1975, — Katherine, *b* 1979.

HALF-SISTER LIVING

Sarah Sophia, *b* 1975.

DAUGHTERS LIVING OF SIXTH BARONET

Margaret, *b* 1914: *m* 1st, 1940, Maj Donald Ian Molteno, Black Watch, who was *ka* 1944; 2ndly, 1949, (Edward) John Macdonald Dent, of Manor Farm, Broughton, Stockbridge, Hants, and has issue living, (by 1st *m*) Susan Ferelith, *b* 1941, Gillian, *b* 1942. —— Jean (twin), *b* 1914: *m* 1944, Capt A. Murray Robertson, Black Watch, of The Lowes, Dunkeld, Perths, and has issue living, Alastair John, *b* 1946. —— Diana Gillian, *b* 1918.

WIDOW LIVING OF SEVENTH BARONET

SARAH ANNE (*Sarah, Lady Pigot*), eldest da of late David Richard Colville (*see* V Colville, colls): *m* 1968, as his 2nd wife, Sir Robert Anthony Pigot, CB, OBE, RM, who *d* 1986. *Residence* – Wray House, Bembridge, IoW.

The 1st baronet, Sir George Pigot (Governor of Madras 1755-63 and 1775-7, and MP for Wallingford 1765-8 and subsequently for Bridgnorth), was created a Baronet with special remainder to his brothers Robert and Hugh; in 1765 he became Baron Pigot, which title expired on his death 1777. He bequeathed the celebrated Pigot diamond, valued by skilful lapidaries at £30,000, to his brothers, Gen Sir Robert, the 2nd baronet, and Adm Hugh Pigot, and his sister, Margaret Fisher; it was subsequently disposed of under an Act of Parliament 1800, by way of lottery, for £23,998 16s. The 4th baronet sat as MP for Bridgnorth (C) 1832-53. The 7th baronet, Sir Robert Pigot, CB, OBE, was Maj-Gen RM, Dep Standing Group NATO, Rep with N Atlantic Council, Paris, and Ch of Staff RM.

PIGOTT (UK) 1808, of Knapton, Queen's County

Sir (BERKELEY) HENRY SEBASTIAN PIGOTT, 5th Baronet; *b* 24 June 1925; *s* his father, *Maj Sir* BERKELEY, 1982; *ed* Ampleforth; European War 1944-45 with RM: *m* 1954, Jean Olive, only da of late John Williams Balls, of Holly Lodge, Surlingham, Norfolk, and has issue.

Arms – Ermine, three lozenges in fesse sable, a crescent for difference. **Crest** – A wolf's head erased proper, collared or.
Residence – Brook Farm, Shobley, Ringwood, Hants.

SONS LIVING

DAVID JOHN BERKELEY (91 Bellemoor Rd, Upper Shirley, Southampton S01 2QW), *b* 16 Aug 1955; *ed* Moor Park, Ludlow, and Hurn Court, Bournemouth: *m* 1st, 1981 (*m diss* 1984), Alison Fletcher; 2ndly, 1986, Julie, da of Eric Gordon Wiffen, of 28 Fitzroy Close, Bassett, Southampton, and has issue living (by 2nd *m*), Christabel Maria, *b* 1989.
—— Antony Charles Philip, *b* 1960.

DAUGHTER LIVING

Sarah Jane Mary, *b* 1964.

SISTERS LIVING

Here and elsewhere

Mary Stephanie, *b* 1920: *m* 1st, 1951, Peter Friedrich Sika; 2ndly, 1959, Com Walter Higham, RN, and has issue living, (by 2nd *m*), Stephen Walter, *b* 1960. *Residence* – 12 Dragon St, Petersfield, Hants.
—— Mary Veronica, *b* 1922: *m* 1944, Stefan Wysogota-Kwasniewski, and has issue living, Casimir Stefan, *b* 1946: *m* 1973, Laura Clements, and has issue living, Alexandra Christabel *b* 1980, — Sabina Orietta, *b* 1945: *m* 1st, 1964, Derek Johnstone Brooke; 2ndly, 1968, Andrew Holt, and has issue living, (by 1st *m*) Gregory Damien Amadeus *b* 1965, (by 2nd *m*) Trystan *b* 1969, Thor *b* 1973, Luke *b* 1977. *Residence* – Martyr's Way, Walsingham, Norfolk.

The 1st baronet, Sir George, was son of Major-Gen Thomas Pigott, MP, of Knapton, Queen's Co, and Sir Charles, 3rd Bt, served in the Crimea.

PILDITCH (UK) 1929, of Bartropps, Weybridge, co Surrey

Sir RICHARD EDWARD PILDITCH, 4th *Baronet*; *b* 8 Sept 1926; *s* his brother, *Sir* PHILIP JOHN FREDERICK, 1954: *ed* Charterhouse: European War 1944-45 with RN, in India and Ceylon: *m* 1950, Pauline Elizabeth Smith, and has issue.

Arms – Per chevron invected sable and or, two ancient galleys in chief, and in base an eagle displayed all counter changed. **Crest** – A bear sejant proper, muzzled and gorged with a chain or, pendent therefrom an escutcheon sable charged with an eagle displayed gold.
Residence – 4 Fisherman's Bank, Mudeford, Christchurch, Dorset.

SON LIVING

JOHN RICHARD, *b* 24 Sept 1955.

DAUGHTER LIVING

Fiona, *b* 1951: *m* 1982, Patrick John Payne, son of Austin Ralph Payne.

DAUGHTERS LIVING OF THIRD BARONET

Frances Jean, *b* 1952: *m* 1978, George Phillips Yeats, son of George Yeats, and has issue living, Frederick Xavier, *b* 1983. —— Felicity Mary, *b* (*posthumous*) 1954: *m* 1975, Richard Austin, of Buttergate Barn, Sykes' Fold, Leeming, Oxenhope, nr Keighley, W Yorks BD22 9SH, son of Herbert Wilfred Charles Austin, and has issue living, Nicholas Charles, *b* 1982, — Charlotte Susannah Frances, *b* 1985.

HALF-SISTER LIVING

Rosalind Phyllis Muriel, *b* 1946: *m* 1969, Allan Owen-Taylor.

WIDOW LIVING OF THIRD BARONET

PHYLLIS JEAN, el da of Maj Dudley Cautley Stewart Smith, MBE, of Weybridge, Surrey: *m* 1st, 1948, Sir (Philip John) Frederick Pilditch, 3rd Bt, who *d* 1954; 2ndly, 1977, David Smith. *Residence* – 2 St Mary's Mews, Ludlow, Shropshire SY8 1DZ.

COLLATERAL BRANCH LIVING

Issue of late Maj Edgar Lewis Pilditch, TD, yr son of 1st baronet, *b* 1901, *d* 1986: *m* 1936, Anne (4 St James Close, Ruscombe, Twyford, Reading, Berks), da of Richard Llewellyn Weeks, of Broomhaugh House, Riding Mill, Northumberland, and formerly wife of — Goodchild:—
Simon Andrew Llewellyn, MRAC (c/o Nat Westminster Bank Ltd, 64 Bayswater Rd, W2), *b* 1938; *ed* Eton, McGill Univ, Montreal (BA), and RAC Cirencester; Company Dir: *m* 1969 (*m diss* 19—), Ute, da of late Siegfried Johannes Mayr, of Kitzbühel, Tyrol, and has issue living, Olivia Margaret, *b* 1970.

The 1st baronet, Sir Philip Edward Pilditch (son of late Philip John Pilditch, of Plymouth), sat as MP for Spelthorne Div of Middlesex (*U*) 1918-31.

PILE (UK) 1900, of Kenilworth House, Rathgar, co Dublin

Sine labe nota
*Known without
dishonour*

Sir FREDERICK DEVEREUX PILE, MC, 3rd *Baronet*; *b* 10 Dec 1915; *s* his father, *Gen Sir* FREDERICK ALFRED, GCB, DSO, MC, 1976; *ed* Weymouth Coll, and RMC Sandhurst; Col late R Tank Regt; British Joint Sers Mission Washington, DC 1957-60; Comdt RAC Driving and Maintenance Sch 1960-62; 1939-45 War (MC): *m* 1st, 1940, Pamela, who *d* 1983, el da of late Philip Henstock, of Newbury, Berks; 2ndly, 1984, Mrs V. Josephine A. Culverwell, previously wife of late Gerald D. Culverwell, and has issue by 1st *m*.

Arms – Azure, three piles argent, on a chief ermine, a castle with two towers proper between two harps or, stringed of the second. **Crest** – on a ducal coronet or, charged with a cross-botonée azure, a pelican with wings addorsed and inverted proper. *Residence* – Beadles, Cowbeech, E Sussex. *Club* – MCC.

DAUGHTERS LIVING (*By 1st marriage*)

Fiona Devereux, *b* 1941: *m* 1976, Mark William Towse. —— Vanessa Anne, *b* 1951: *m* 1972, Rory Gilchrist Graham Mackean, of 4 Colyton Rd, SE22, and has issue living, Thomas, *b* 1985, — Charlotte, *b* 1979, — Virginia, *b* 1980.

COLLATERAL BRANCHES LIVING

Issue of late Major Walter Devereux Pile, yr son of 1st baronet, *b* 1887, *d* 1959: *m* 1921, Margaret Lucy, MBE, who *d* 1989, el da of Thomas Irvine Bonner, MA, MB, CM, formerly of 22 Ivy Road, Shipley, Yorkshire:—
Anne Devereux, *b* 1932: *m* 1961, David Evan Daniel, of The White House, 56 Lark Lane, Liverpool L16 8YA.

Issue of late Sir John Devereux Pile, yr son of 2nd baronet, *b* 1918; *d* 1982: *m* 1946, Katharine Mary (Munstead, Godalming, Surrey GU8 4AR), da of late Austin George Shafe:—
ANTHONY JOHN DEVEREUX (The Manor House, Pitsford, Northampton NN6 9AZ), *b* 7 June 1947; *ed* Durham Sch; Maj LI (ret): *m* 1977, Jenny Clare, da of Peter H. Youngman, of Fenn St, Westleton, Suffolk, and has issue living, Thomas Charles Devereux, *b* 6 April 1978, — Hugh James Devereux, *b* 1980, — Harriet Rose Devereux, *b* 1983. —— Timothy Simon Devereux (1 Beech Park Drive, Barnt Green, Birmingham B45 8LZ), *b* 1953; *ed* Haileybury, and Durham Univ (BA): *m* 1977, Jean Patricia Lynne Thomas, and has issue living, Jonathan Matthew Devereux, *b* 1981, — Christopher James Devereux, *b* 1984, — Victoria Jane Devereux, *b* 1987, — Rebecca Claire Devereux, *b* 1991. —— Jennifer Jane Devereux, *b* 1950: *m* 1973, Huw J. Alban Davies, DM, FRCP, of Troutbeck, Otford, Sevenoaks, Kent TN14 5PH, and has issue living, Henry Christopher, *b* 1975, — Hester Margaret, *b* 1977, — Katharine Clare, *b* (twin) 1977. —— Sarah Katharine Devereux (61A Linden Gdns, W4 2EW), *b* 1960; BA: *m* 1st, 1987, C. Richard J. Bate; 2ndly, 1994, David Alan Jones, of 56 Iffley Rd, W6 9PA.

The 1st baronet, Sir Thomas Devereux Pile, was High Sheriff of Dublin 1898, and Lord Mayor 1900.

MILBORNE-SWINNERTON-PILKINGTON (NS) 1635, of Stanley, Yorkshire

Now thus, now thus

Sir THOMAS HENRY MILBORNE-SWINNERTON-PILKINGTON, 14th *Baronet*; *b* 10 March 1934; *s* his father, *Sir* ARTHUR WILLIAM, MC, 1952; *ed* Eton; formerly in Roy Scots Greys; Chm of Thomas and James Harrison Ltd 1980, Charente Steamship Co Ltd 1977: *m* 1961, Susan, da of Norman Stewart Rushton Adamson, of Durban, S Africa, and has issue.

Arms – Quarterly: 1st and 4th, argent, a cross flory, voided gules, *Pilkington*; 2nd, argent, a cross formé fleuretté sable, surmounted by a bend engrailed gules, *Swinnerton*; 3rd, per pale, argent and gules, a cross patonce between, in the sinister chief and dexter base two leopards' faces counter-changed, *Milborne*. **Crests** – 1st, on a mount vert a boar passant argent, charged with a cross formé fleuretté sable; 2nd, a mower with his scythe proper, habited per pale argent, and sable; 3rd, a demi-lion per fesse argent and gules, holding between the paws a leopard's face of the first.
Residence – King's Walden Bury, Hitchin, Herts. *Club* – White's.

SON LIVING

RICHARD ARTHUR, *b* 4 Sept 1964; *ed* Eton, and RAC Cirencester: *m* 1994, Katya T., da of Terence J. Clemence, of Wilton Crescent, SW1.

DAUGHTERS LIVING

Sarah Elizabeth, *b* 1962: *m* 1993, James B. Anderson, son of Ian Anderson, of La Goulée, France. —— Joanna, *b* 1967.

SISTERS LIVING

Sonia Margery, *b* 1937: *m* 1st, 1965, Anthony Dominic Dyke Rogers, who *d* 1984; 2ndly, 1990, Ib Jorgensen, of Airlie, Lucan, co Dublin, and has issue living (by 1st *m*), John Dyke Darby, *b* 1968, — Anthony Patrick, *b* 1971. —— Carole Mary (Brainge, Putley, Ledbury, Herefordshire), *b* 1942: *m* 1962, James Bowes Daly, who *d* 1989 (B McGowan), and has issue living, Dermot Christopher, *b* 1964, — Henry Duncan James, *b* 1966. —— Moira Elizabeth, *b* 1943: *m* 1969, Benjamin Hanbury, of Green Man House, Cowlinge, Newmarket, and has issue living, Emma Jane, *b* 1970, — Amanda Aline, *b* 1973.

MOTHER LIVING OF FOURTEENTH BARONET

ELIZABETH MARY, da of Major John Fenwick Harrison (B Burnham): *m* 1st, 1931 (*m diss* 1950), Maj Sir Arthur William Milborne-Swinnerton-Pilkington, 13th Bt, MC, who *d* 1952; 2ndly, 1950, Maj Patrick Henry Anthony Burke, Gren Guards, who *d* 1964. *Residence* – The Old Rectory, Beauparc, Navan, co Meath.

COLLATERAL BRANCH LIVING

Issue of late Ulick O'Connor Milborne-Swinnerton-Pilkington, 2nd son of 12th baronet, *b* 1903; *d* 1979: *m* 1951, Angela Mary Purcell (who *m* 2ndly, 1981, Cdr Edward Alfred Eborall, RNVR, FIEE, of Tally Ho House, Castletownshend, co Cork), da of late Gerald de Purcell Cotter (*see* Cotter, Bt, colls):—
Lionel Ulick (62 Manor Court, Knocknacarra, Salthill, Galway), *b* 1956; *ed* Univ Coll, Cork (MA), and Toronto Univ (PhD): *m* 1990, Elizabeth Susan, PhD, da of Col Hugh Tilley, of Ottawa, Canada, and has issue living, Colin Patrick, *b* 1993. —— Michael Gerald, *b* 1959; *ed* Trin Coll, Dublin (BSc).

This family descends from Robert Pilkington, of Sowerby, Yorks, 3rd son of Sir John Pilkington, of Pilkington, Lancs (*d* 1421). Sir Arthur Pilkington, of Stanley, nr Wakefield, received a Baronetcy of Nova Scotia, probably with remainder to heirs male whatsoever (the patent was not entered in the Geat Seal Register of Scotland), and a grant of 6,000 acres in Nova Scotia. Sir William Pilkington, 8th Bt (*d* 1850): *m* Mary, da and co-heir of Thomas Swinnerton, of Butterton Hall, Staffs, by Mary, da and heir of Charles Milborne, of Wonastow, Monmouth. His yst son, Sir Lionel Pilkington, 11th Bt, took by Roy Licence 1856 the surnames of Milborne-Swinnerton but subsequently resumed the final name of Pilkington. The 13th baronet, Sir Arthur William Milborne-Swinnerton Pilkington, MC, was Major 16th/5th Lancers.

PINSENT (UK) 1938, of Selly Hill, City of Birmingham

Sir CHRISTOPHER ROY PINSENT, 3rd Baronet; *b* 2 Aug 1922; *s* his father *Sir* ROY, 1978; *ed* Winchester; taught at Camberwell Sch of Art 1962-86; 1939-45 War as Leading Aircraftman RAF: *m* 1951, Susan Mary, da of John Norton Scorer, of Fotheringhay, and has issue.

Arms – Argent a saltire flory vert, between four chaffinches proper. **Crest** – Upon a fleur-de-lis couped vert, two chaffinches addorsed proper.
Residence – The Chestnuts, Castle Hill, Guildford.

SON LIVING

THOMAS BENJAMIN ROY, *b* 21 July 1967.

DAUGHTERS LIVING

Laura Candace, *b* 1954: *m* 1978, Timothy Bartel Smit, son of Jan Adrianus Bartel Smit, of Arnhem, Holland, and has issue living, Jeremy Alexander Bartel, *b* 1980, — Samuel Christopher, *b* 1984, — Laura Marian, *b* 1982. —— Joanna Mary, *b* 1957: *m* 1991, James David Simpson, son of John Leonard Simpson, of Woodlands Farm, Barwick-in-Elmet, Yorks, and has issue living, Ella Bennett, *b* 1993.

BROTHER LIVING

Michael Roy (61 Wellington Rd, Birmingham), *b* 1927; *ed* Marlborough; admitted a solicitor 1952; 1939-45 War as Lt R Signals: *m* 1952 (*m diss* 19—), Stella Marie, da of late Basil Priestman, of Birmingham, and has issue living, William Ross, *b* 1955, — Nicola Jane, *b* 1957, — Tonya Mary, *b* 1959: *m* 1986, William James Wood, yr son of late Sir Frank Wood, KBE, CB, and has issue living, Richard Foucard *b* 1989.

SISTER LIVING

Rosemary, *b* 1930; *ed* Edgbaston High Sch: *m* 1960, Keiden John Knapp Barrow, of Hazelhope, Stalisfield, Faversham, Kent ME13 0HY, and has issue living, Clive Andrew Knapp, *b* 1962: *m* 1991, Lynne Catherine, da of Roy Thornton Marsden, of Taupo, NZ, and has issue living, Alexandra Catherine *b* 1991, — Clare, *b* 1964: *m* 1987, Alastair Michael Gordon, son of late Alexander Nigel Gordon.

COLLATERAL BRANCHES LIVING

Grandchildren of late Com Clive Pinsent, RN (infra):—
Issue of late Lt-Cdr Andrew Clive Macpherson Pinsent, RN, *b* 1922, *d* 1982: *m* 1945, Gloria Poppy Marie, who *d* 1979, da of late Capt (Cecil) Herbert Tollemache:—
Anthony Andrew Macpherson (4 North Pallant, Chichester, W Sussex), *b* 1946; *ed* Radley: *m* 1969, Clare Natalie, da of Victor Reynolds, of Estremoz, Portugal, and has issue living, Charles Victor R., *b* 1973, — Amelia Clare, *b* 1976. —— David Tollemache, *b* 1948; *ed* Radley: *m* 1976, Susie, da of Mrs J. Chandler, of Mosman, NSW, and has issue living, Rollo Tollemache, *b* 1978, — Hugo G., *b* 1980. —— Susan Catherine, *b* 1953: *m* 1976, Kerry John Pfeiffer, and has issue living, Olivia K., *b* 19—.
Issue of late Lt-Cdr James Macpherson Pinsent, RN, *b* 1925, *d* 1983: *m* 1st, 1956 (*m diss* 1972), Daphne Miranda, da of Capt Kenneth Lanyon Harkness, CBE, DSC, RN (ret); 2ndly, 1976, Eleanor Mary Penrose (Audrey) (13 Felden St, SW6), da of late Dr Victor Penrose Robinson, MA, BM, BCL:—
(By 1st *m*) Oliver Clive (17 Wellwood Court, Upper Richmond Rd, Putney SW13 6JM), *b* 1964: *m* 1989, Catherine C., da of R. C. Bennett, of Putney. —— Camilla Louise, *b* 1962: *m* 1983, Capt Mark P. Colacicchi, 13th/18th R Hus (QMO), of Ariel Cottage, Graffham, nr Petworth, W Sussex, eldest son of late Count Paul Colacicchi, of 9 St Dionis Rd, SW6, and has issue living, James Paul, *b* 1985, — Rory Adam, *b* 1986, — Sophie Antonia, *b* 1989.

Issue of late Com Clive Pinsent, RN (ret), 2nd son of 1st baronet, *b* 1886, *d* 1948: *m* 1921, Kathleen Jane, who *d* 1974, da of late George Macpherson, DL, JP, of The Lloyd House, Wolverhampton:—
Rev Ewen Macpherson, *b* 1930: formerly Lt RN: *m* 1962, Jean Grizel, da of late Maj-Gen Neil McMicking, CB, CBE, DSO, MC, and has issue living, Matthew Clive *b* 1970, — Katherine Jane *b* 1963: *m* 1991, Thomas W. Tyson, twin son of D. Tyson, of Dorf House, Widdington, Essex, — Emma Charlotte, *b* 1964. *Residence* – The Cross House, Child Okeford, Blandford, Dorset.

Issue of late Col John Ryland Pinsent, CBE, DSO, 3rd son of 1st baronet, *b* 1888, *d* 1957: *m* 1915, Kathleen May, who *d* 1969, da of late Col E. G. Boyce:—
John Laurance, *b* 1916; admitted a solicitor 1946; is a farmer; European War 1939-45 as Major RA: *m* 1940, Margaret Molyneux, el da of late R. Vernon Favell, and has issue living, John Edward, *b* 1950, — Margaret Anne, *b* 1941: *m* 1964, Rev John Lawrence Simpson, of The Vicarage, Curry Rivel, Somerset, and has issue living, Benjamin John Lawrence *b* 1970, Joanna Mary *b* 1965, Jessamie Anne, *b* 1968, — Mary, *b* 1943: *m* 1964, Denis Theodore Archdale, of Roseworthy Barton, Camborne, Cornwall, and has issue living, Nicholas Henry *b* 1966, Audley Mervyn *b* 1969, Rachael Mary *b* 1968, — Jennifer, *b* 1944: *m* 1969, Capt Christopher Louis Wreford-Brown, DSO, RN, and has issue living, Paul Christopher *b* 1972, Julia Anne *b* 1970, Amanda Jane *b* 1976, — Elizabeth Jane *b* 1948. *Residence* – Higher Ludbrook, Ermington, S Devon. —— Richard Alan, *b* 1931: *m* 1954, Mary Matruh, da of Group-Capt John Benjamin Graham, OBE, MC, AFC, and has issue living, Dinah, *b* 1955, — Susan Melanie *b* 1964.

The 1st baronet, Sir Richard Alfred Pinsent (son of late Richard Steele Pinsent), was Pres of Law So 1918-19.

PLATT (UK) 1958, of Rusholme, City of Manchester

Sir (Frank) Lindsey Platt, 2nd *Baronet, b* 16 Jan 1919; *s* his father, *Sir* Harry, MD, MS, FRCS, 1986; *ed* Stowe, Magdalen Coll, Oxford, and The Sorbonne; Bar Inner Temple 1954; 1939-45 War and Maj Intelligence Corps: *m* 1951, Johanna Magdalena Elisabeth, da of late Friedrich Wilhelm Laenger, of Westphalia.

Arms – Azure in base a lyre-bird tail displayed proper and in chief a portcullis chained between two dexter gloves or. **Crest** – A falcon close proper grasping with the dexter claw a surgeon's scalpel blade upward and inward or.
Residence – 3 Sherwood Av, Fallowfield, Manchester 14.

SISTERS LIVING

Honor Mary Munro, *b* 1917: *m* 1939, Cedric Harald Flurscheim, of 20 Moore St, SW3, and has issue living, Jacqueline Mary, *b* 1940: *m* 1964 (*m diss* 1992), John Philip Simms, of 82 Greenwich South St, Greenwich, SE10, and has issue living, Benjamin John *b* 1965, — Elizabeth Sally Lindsey (138 Lee Av, Toronto, Ontario M4E 2P3), *b* 1943: *m* 1970 (*m diss* 1988), Michael Pelzer. —— Rosemary Elizabeth (76 Peppercombe Rd, Eastbourne, E Sussex BN20 8JN), *b* 1921: *m* 1948, Trevor Lewis Midgley, who *d* 1978, and has issue living, Jonathan David, *b* 1950: *m* 1983, Julia Margaret Chinnery, and has issue living, James Alexander Lewis *b* 1986, — Amanda Jane Elizabeth, *b* 1953: *m* 1979, Jerome Peter Duncanson, and has issue living, Peter Robin *b* 1994, Sophie Elizabeth *b* 1984. —— Sara Margaret Helen, *b* 1927: *m* 1952, Capt Lawrence Hugh Williams, RM (*see* Williams, Bt, *cr* 1798). *Residence* – Old Parciau, Marianglas, Anglesey. —— Diana Primrose Rowley, *b* 1932: *m* 1955, Robin Gwynne Jennings, of 134 Rosendale Rd, Dulwich, SE21 8LG (Wake, Bt, *cr* 1621, colls), and has issue living, Nicholas David de Burgh, *b* 1959, — Robin Hereward, *b* 1963, — Charles Rupert, *b* 1968, — Sarah Primrose, *b* 1961: *m* 1990, Anthony Hook, and has issue living, Megan Elizabeth April *b* 1993.

Sir Harry Platt, 1st B, MD, MS, FRCS, was Consultant Adviser in Orthopaedics, Min of Health, 1940-63, Prof of Medicine Manchester Univ 1945-65, and Pres R Coll of Surgs of England 1954-57.

PLATT (UK) 1959, of Grindleford, co Derby

Hon Sir Peter Platt, 2nd *Baronet; b* 6 July 1924; *s* his father Robert Baron Platt (Life Baron) in his Baronetcy, 1978, *ed* Abbotsholme Sch, and Magdalen Coll, Oxford (BMus, BLitt, MA, FGSM); Prof of Music, Sydney Univ, Aust; 1939-45 War with RNVR (despatches): *m* 1948, Jean Halliday, da of Dr Charles Philip Brentnall, and has issue.

Arms – Or fretty sable plate on a pale gules a rod of aesculapius gold. **Crest** – In front of a demi plate a nightingale in full song proper.
Residence – 1 Ellison Pl, Pymble, NSW 2073, Aust.

SON LIVING

Martin Philip (25 Manchester St, Dunedin, NZ), *b* 9 March 1952: *m* 1971, Frances Corinne Moanna, da of Trevor Samuel Conley, and has issue living, Philip Stephen, *b* 17 Oct 1972, — Timothy Martin, *b* 1980, — Suzanne, *b* 1971, — Rachael, *b* 1976.

DAUGHTERS LIVING

Margaret, *b* 1949: *m* 1969 (*m diss* 1978), Anthony Pratt Kaye. —— Katherine, *b* 1956: *m* 1988, Alexander Hendrik Vincent Beasley, son of Robert Beasley, of Auckland, NZ.

SISTERS LIVING

Hon Joan Elizabeth, *b* 1927: *m* 1952, John Bunting Allen, of Maxstoke House, 2 Highfield Road, Hazel Grove, Stockport, Cheshire, and has issue living, Jonathan Robert, *b* 1953, — Paul Bunting, *b* 1956, — Mark Benedict, *b* 1965. —— *Hon* Helen Margaret, *b* 1933: *m* 1954, Cecil Henry Stowasser, of 1/9 Park Rd, Nedlands, W Aust, and has issue living, Peter, *b* 1955, — Robert, *b* 1956, — Michael, *b* 1960.

WIDOW LIVING OF LIFE BARON AND FIRST BARONET

Sylvia Jean, ARCM (*Sylvia, Lady Platt*) (53 Heathside, Hinchley Wood, Esher, Surrey), da of late Sidney Charles Caveley, and formerly wife of John Alfred Haggard: *m* 1974, as his 2nd wife, Baron Platt (Life Baron), 1st Bt, who *d* 1978, when the peerage became ext.

Robert Platt, MSc, MD, FRCP, son of William Platt, schoolmaster, of London and Grindleford, Derbys; was Editor of *Quarterly Journal of Medicine* 1948-55, Pres of Roy Coll of Physicians, London 1957-62, and Chm of Clinical Research Board, Med Research Council 1964-67; 1939-45 War as Brig RAMC; was *cr* a baronet 1959 and *Baron Platt*, of Grindleford, co Derby (Life Baron) 1967.

POLE (E) 1628, of Shute House, Devonshire

Sir (JOHN) RICHARD WALTER REGINALD CAREW POLE, 13th *Baronet*; *b* 2 Dec 1938; *s* his father, *Sir* JOHN GAWEN CAREW, DSO, TD, 1993; *ed* Eton, and Royal Agric Coll, Cirencester; late Lt Coldm Gds; a Liveryman of Fishmongers' Co, elected to Court 1993; a Co Councillor for Cornwall 1973-93, High Sheriff 1980, and DL 1988; Devon and Cornwall Cttee, Nat Trust 1978-83; Min of Agriculture's Regional Advisory Cttee 1970-80; Gov Seale Hayne Agric Coll 1979-89, and Plymouth Coll since 1985; part-time Dir SW Electricity Bd 1981-90; Devon and Cornwall Police Authority 1973-89 (Chm 1985-87); Pres R Cornwall Show 1981; Member SW Regional Cttee W of England Building Soc 1989-91; Dir Theatre Royal Plymouth since 1985; Pres Surf Life Saving Assocn of Great Britain 1975-86; Countryside Commissioner since 1991; Trustee of National Heritage Memorial Fund since 1991, and Tate Gallery since 1993: *m* 1st, 1966 (*m diss* 1973), Hon Victoria Marion Ann Lever, da of 3rd Viscount Leverhulme, KG, TD;

Pollet virtus
Virtue is powerful

2ndly, 1984, Mary, LVO, da of late Lt-Col Ronald Dawnay (*see* V Downe, colls), and has issue living by 2nd *m*.

Arms – Azure, semée of fleurs-de-lis or, a lion rampant argent.
Seat – Antony House, Torpoint, Cornwall PL11 2QA. *Clubs* – Pratt's.

SONS LIVING (*By 2nd marriage*)

TREMAYNE JOHN CAREW, *b* 22 Feb 1974; *ed* Eton. —— John Alexander George Carew, *b* 1975; *ed* Eton; a Page of Honour to HM Queen Elizabeth The Queen Mother 1990-92.

SISTERS LIVING

Elizabeth Mary, *b* 1929: *m* 1953, David Cuthbert Tudway Quilter, DL (*see* Quilter, Bt). *Residence* – Milton Lodge, Wells, Somerset. —— Caroline Anne (*Hon Mrs Paul Asquith*), *b* 1933: *m* 1963, as his 2nd wife, Hon Paul Asquith, who *d* 1984 (*see* E Oxford and Asquith, colls). *Residence* – 41 Quarrendon St, SW6.

WIDOW LIVING OF TWELFTH BARONET

JOAN SHIRLEY (*Joan, Lady Carew Pole*), da of late Rear Adm Charles Maurice Blackman, DSO, and widow of (i) Maj Jocelyn Arthur Persse, Rifle Bde, and (ii) Lt-Col Francis Edgar Fulford, of Great Fulford, Dunsford, Exeter: *m* 1979, as his 2nd wife, Sir John Gawen Carew Pole, 12th Bt, DSO, TD, who *d* 1993. *Residence* – Horson House, Torpoint, Cornwall.

COLLATERAL BRANCHES LIVING

Issue of late Maj Patrick William Butler POLE-CAREW, brother of 12th baronet, *b* 1913, *d* 1971: *m* 1st, 1939 (*m diss* 1950), Sonia, who *d* 1976, da of Sir (William Eley) Cuthbert Quilter, 2nd Bt; 2ndly, 1950, Mary Patience (Clashaphouca, Clogheen, co Tipperary) da of late Maj Richard Ernest Gilchrist Phillips, and formerly wife of Ronald Ewan Cameron:—
(By 1st *m*) Rosemary, *b* 1940.

Grandchildren of late Charles Edward Pole-Carew, uncle of 12th baronet:—
Issue of late Maj Gerald Ayshford Pole-Carew, *b* 1887, *d* 1969: *m* 1915, Eileen Flora Lismore, who *d* 1989, da of late Surg-Maj George Henry Kenneth MacDonald O'Callaghan, CMG:—
Charles Oliver (Flat B, 1 Royal Cres, W11 4SL), *b* 1923; *ed* Claysmore. —— Christopher Gerald (Shute Barton, Shute, Devon), *b* 1931; *ed* RNC Dartmouth; formerly Lt RN; High Sheriff of Notts 1979-80: *m* 1954, Gillian, only da of Clive Burton, of Addo, Cape Province, S Africa, and has issue living, (Gerald Anthony) Peregrine (Trowle, Donhead St Mary, Shaftesbury, Dorset SP7 9DP), *b* 1957; *ed* Radley, and RMA Sandhurst: *m* 1st, 1984, Claudia A., only da of David Wolfers, of Barnes, London; 2ndly, 1991, Georgina E. M., da of Charles Harris, of Longonot Farm, Naivasha, Kenya, and has issue living (by 2nd *m*), Tatiana Cecily Alice *b* 1993, — Delia Elizabeth, *b* 1955: *m* 1981, Charles Benedict de Broca Madden, yst son of Dr James George Madden, of the Glebe House, Tollesbury, Essex, and has issue living, James Antony Grellan *b* 1982, Edward Christopher Otha *b* 1984, Thomas Mark Ambrose *b* 1988, — Camilla Janet, *b* 1962: *m* 1982, Dominic John Earle Welby, yr son of Sir (Richard) Bruno Gregory Welby, 7th Bt, and has issue (*see* Welby, Bt). —— Geraldine Frances Flora, *b* 1917. —— Eileen Loveday (83 Gowan Av, SW6 6RQ), *b* 1930: *m* 1955 (*m diss* 1964), Brian Arnold Miller.

Grandchildren of late Reginald Charles Somers Pole, eldest son of late Reginald Carolus Pole (*infra*):—
Issue of late Reginald Edward Morice de la Pole, *b* 1893, *d* 1948: *m* 1924, Dorothy Ethel Christine (Bentleys, 4 Ellice Rd, Oxted, Surrey), da of late Charles William Searle, JP, of Larchwood, Sunninghill, Ascot, Berks:—
Pauline Marjorie Doreen, *b* 1925: *m* 1951, Squadron-Leader Frederick John Crewe, RAF (ret), and has issue living, Roderic Guy Pole, *b* 1952: *m* 1987, Tina Norris, — Alastair Frederick, *b* 1954: *m* 1978, Elaine Ruth Blackburn, and has issue living, Sam Richard *b* 1978, Joseph Paul *b* 1982, — Felicity Jane, *b* 1953: *m* 1978 (*m diss* 1983), Paul Antoni Coleburt, — Virginia Rosemarie Pauline, *b* 1955: *m* 1984, Derek Alan Lawrence. *Address* – c/o National Westminster Bank, Bromley, Kent. —— Rosemary Ethel Greason, *b* 1927: *m* 1957, Patrick Eric Edward Walsh, of 18 Denewood Rd, West Moors, Wimborne, Dorset, and has issue living, Guy Patrick (66 North St, Crewkerne, Somerset), *b* 1957: *m* 1982, Rachel Gough, — Penelope Jane, *b* 1958, — Jill Christine, *b* 1960, — Kim Elizabeth, *b* 1962. —— Lucille Dorothy Carew, *b* 1938: *m* 1969, Stuart Malcolm Forbes Keir, of Brook Cottage, Tanhouse Rd, Oxted, Surrey, and has issue living, James Alexander, *b* 1976.
Issue of late Lionel Robert Glanville Pole, *b* 1902, *d* 1965: *m* 1924 (*m diss* 19—), Gertrude Gregory:—
Reginald Robert, *b* 1925: *m* 1953, Sylvia Patricia Sullivan, and has issue living, a son *b* 19—, — Susan Carole, *b* 1954, — a da, *b* 19—.
Issue of late Percival Arthur Carew Pole, *b* 1904, *d* 1965: *m* 1934, Irene Clare French, who *d* 1975:—
Geoffrey Arthur (3 Mill Pond Rd, Windlesham, Surrey), *b* 1935: *m* 1961, Patricia, da of W Sweetman, of Birmingham, and has issue living, Julia, *b* 1963, — Diana (twin), *b* 1963, — Susan Caroline, *b* 1964. —— Roger Charles, *b* 1939: *m* 1959, Joyce, only da of W Powell, of Worcester Park, Surrey, and has issue living, Mark Nicholas Charles, *b* 1961, — John Damian, *b* 1967, — Carey Thérèse, *b* 1959, — Joanne Sarah, *b* 1963. —— Jennifer Clare, *b* 1937: *m* 1961, Dudley Hasting Wheeler, of Friars Pardon, Hurworth-on-Tess, co Durham, and has issue living, Clare Frances, *b* 1963, — Alison Mary, *b* 1966.

Grandchildren of late Reginald Carolus Pole, 2nd son of Rev Edward Pole (*b* 1805), 2nd son of Rev Edward Pole, DD, 3rd son of Reginald Pole, son of Rev Carolus Pole, 3rd son of 3rd baronet:—
  Issue of late Percival Edward Pole, *b* 1867, *d* 1952: *m* 1905, Margaret Edith, who *d* 1941, da of late John Leith, JP, of Aberdeen:—
John Edward Carolus, *b* 1906: *m* 1942, Joan Alexandrina Lamont, da of late Robert Mitchell, of Aberdeen.
  Issue of late Albert Edward Pole, *b* 1875, *d* 1940: *m* 1907, Sophia Buckingham, who *d* 1955, el da of late Edward Alexander Buckingham Hay, of Alaington, Dalkeith Avenue, Dumbreck, Glasgow:—
Edward Alexander, *b* 1911: *m* 1940, Sheila Ferguson, da of James Welsh of 580 Tollcross Road, Tollcross, Glasgow.
—— Reginald Carew, *b* 1914: *m* 1939, Mary MacKinnon, da of R. P. Don, of 46 Walnut Crescent, Possilpark, Glasgow, and has issue living, Reginald Carew, *b* 1942, — Isobel Buchannan Colquhoun, *b* 1947. —— Annie Laing Hay, *b* 1908.
  Issue of late Courtenay Alexander Pole, *b* 1888, *d* 1967: *m* 1917, Janet Watson, who *d* 1955, da of late James Deans, of Highbury Park, Mount Florida, Glasgow:—
Reginald Alexander Carolus (Ardfern, 12b Cawdor St, Nairn), *b* 1920; Lt (Ex Sp) RNVR 1939-45, Clyde Div RNR 1946-65, late Lt-Cdr VRD, RNR; founder Member RNVR Club Scotland (S V Carrick), Glasgow: *m* 1959, Dorothy Betty Wallace, da of late David Green Roddick, of 47 Moraine Dr, Glasgow.

    Grandson of late Courtenay Alexander Pole (ante):—
  Issue of late Courtenay Deans Carew Pole, *b* 1925, *d* 19—: *m* 1951, Aileen Munro, da of John M. Crawford:—
Alan John Carew, *b* 1958.

    Granddaughter of late John Pole, 5th son of Rev Edward Pole (ante):—
  Issue of late Herbert Edward Pole, *b* 1882, *d* 1965: *m* 1930, Ena Marsh (Glenloch, Rowley Drive, nr Cranleigh, Surrey):—
Millicent Rosemary, *b* 1933: *m* 1958, Peter Cox, of Petamille, 3 Park Way, Gt Bookham, Surrey, and has issue living, Gawen Peter, *b* 1967, — Emma Louise, *b* 1964.

The 1st baronet was MP for Devonshire, the 2nd Baronet represented Honiton in Parliament, and the 3rd and 5th baronets each sat as MP for co Devon. The 6th baronet assumed in 1790 the surname of De-la-Pole, which his successor discontinued, and the 8th baronet assumed in 1838 the surname of Reeve-de-la-Pole, and afterwards discontinued it. The 10th Baronet resumed the surname of de la Pole 1895. Sir Frederick Arundell de la Pole, 11th baronet, was High Sheriff of Devon 1917.

POLE (GB) 1791, of Wolverton, Hampshire

Sir PETER VAN NOTTEN POLE, 5th *Baronet*, son of late Arthur Chandos Pole, grandson of late Gen Edward Pole, 4th son of 2nd Baronet; *b* 6 Nov 1921; *s* his kinsman, *Sir* CECIL PERY VAN-NOTTEN-POLE, 1948; FASA; ACIS; accountant; 1939-45 War as Flight-Sgt R Aust AF: *m* 1949, Jean Emily, da of late C. D. Stone, of Borden, W Aust, and has issue.

Arms – Argent, a chevron between three crescents gules, a mullet for difference. **Crest** – A falcon rising proper, a mullet for difference. **Supporters** – On either side a lion reguardant proper (the Supporters of HSH William, Landgrave of Hesse-Cassel), debruised by a pale of three tinctures, the first half per pale gules and argent, the second half azure (originally conferred on the 1st Baronet by the Landgrave and confirmed by Roy Warrant of 1794 to the Baronet and his successors).
Residence – 130/60 Kalinda Drive, City Beach, W Australia 6015.

SON LIVING

PETER JOHN CHANDOS (41 Webster St, Nedlands 6009, W Australia), *b* 27 April 1952: *m* 1973, Suzanne Norah, da of Harold Raymond Hughes, of 81 Archdeacon St, Nedlands, W Aust 6009, and has issue living, Michael Van Notten, *b* 12 May 1980, — Andrew Van Notten, *b* 1986, — Naomi Suzanne, *b* 1983.

DAUGHTER LIVING

Anne, *b* 1957: *m* 1982, Martin Paul Carr, of 17 Kurrajong Place, Greenwood, W Australia 6024.

SISTERS LIVING

Marjorie van Notten, *b* 1923. *Residence* – 83/60 Kalinda Drive, City Beach, W Australia 6015.

COLLATERAL BRANCH LIVING

    Granddaughter of late Capt Edward Albert Pole, son of late Gen Edward Pole, 4th son of 2nd baronet:—
  Issue of late Edward Alexander Chandos Pole, *b* 1867, *d* 1945: *m* 1st, 1910, Gertrude Magdalene, who *d* 1933, da of Herbert Emms; 2ndly, 1935, Mrs Evelyn Catherine Remington, da of Capt E. C. Smith, of Clacton:—
(By 1st *m*) Esmé Katherine, *b* 1911: *m* 1935, Raphe Willoughby Humphrey, who *d* 1962, and has had issue, Ralph Gordon Chandos, *b* 1936, — Michael Sacheverell Willougbhy, *b* 1939; *d* 1984. *Residence* – 130 Newton Rd, Newton, Swansea, W Glamorgan.

This is a branch of the ancient Derbyshire family of Pole, many members of which have distinguished themselves in the field, notably German Pole, who commanded in Ireland, and served against the Armada. They were also descended in the female line from a sister of Sir John Chandos, KG, chief commander at Crecy and Poitiers. Millicent, daughter of Charles Pole, of Holcroft, married Charles Van-Notten, a London merchant, son of Charles Van-Notten (a descendant of Henry Van-Notten, ennobled 1499 by the Emperor Maximilian I, and whose only son Charles received from Charles V the titles of Lord of Ath and Vander-Notten, and Chatelaine of Alost), a merchant of Amsterdam and London. He assumed the surname of Pole, and was created a baronet with remainder to the heirs male of his body, failing which to those of his daughter

Susannah. Susannah *m* 1802 Isaac Minet, but her male line is understood to have become ext with the death of her son without male issue. The 3rd baronet assumed in 1853, by Roy licence, the additional and original paternal name of Van-Notten. On his death in 1948, the baronetcy reverted to the line of Gen Edward Pole, Col 12th Lancers, 4th son of 2nd Bt.

POLLEN (GB) 1795, of Redenham, Hampshire

Sir JOHN MICHAEL HUNGERFORD POLLEN, 7th *Baronet*, only son of late Lieut-Com John Francis Hungerford Pollen, RN, el son of late Capt Francis Gabriel Hungerford Pollen, CBE, RN, 4th son of late John Hungerford Pollen, yr brother of 3rd baronet; *b* 6 April 1919; *s* his kinsman, *Sir* JOHN LANCELOT HUNGERFORD, 1959; *ed* Downside, and Merton Coll, Oxford; is Capt RA: *m* 1st, 1941 (*m diss* 1956), Angela Mary Oriana, who *d* 1990, da of late Maj Felix John Russi, MC, 5th Roy Inniskilling Dragoon Guards; 2ndly, 1957, Mrs Diana Alice Jubb, da of late A. E. Timbrell, and has issue by 1st *m*.

Arms – Azure, on a bend cotissed or, five escallops vert between six lozenges argent, each charged with an escallop sable. **Crest** – A pelican per pale or and azure, vulning herself, and feeding her young proper, charged on the wings elevated with a lozenge, as in the arms.
Residence – Rodbourne, Malmesbury, Wilts.

SON LIVING *(By 1st marriage)*

RICHARD JOHN HUNGERFORD, *b* 3 Nov 1946; *ed* Worth: *m* 1971, Christianne Mary, da of Sir (William) Godfrey Agnew, KCVO, CB, and has had issue, William Richard Hungerford, *b* 28 June 1976, — Jonathan Charles, *b* 1979, — Andrew Francis, *b* 1982, — Alexander Christian, *b* 1986, — Joseph Anthony, *b* and *d* 1991, — Isabel Mary Ruth, *b* 1975, — Alice Charlotte Mary, *b* 1984, — Beatrice Veronica Mary, *b* 1992. *Residence* – Dunsfold Ryse, Chiddingfold, Surrey GU8 4YA.

DAUGHTER LIVING *(By 1st marriage)*

Jane Oriana Mary, *b* 1942: *m* 1962, Roger Tilney Grafftey-Smith, of Monks Farmhouse, Sherborne, Cheltenham, Glos GL54 3DR, son of late Sir Laurence Barton Grafftey-Smith, KCMG, KBE, and has issue living, Simon Laurence (150 Bennerley Rd, SW11), *b* 1968; *ed* Winchester, and Exeter Univ; Guiness Mahon & Co Ltd since 1989, — Max Anthony, *b* 1974, — Selina Dora, *b* 1971.

SISTER LIVING

Susan Mary, *b* 1917. *Residence* – By Scarlett's Wood, Hare Hatch, Twyford, Berks.

COLLATERAL BRANCHES LIVING

Issue of late Sir Walter Michael Hungerford Pollen, MC, uncle of 7th baronet, *b* 1894, *d* 1968: *m* 1925, Rosalind Frances (Norton Hall, Mickleton, Glos) da of late Robert Benson, of Buckhurst, Withyham, Sussex, and 16 South St, Park Lane, W1:—
Peregrine Michael Hungerford (Norton Hall, Mickleton, Glos; 6 Redan St, W14; Balranald House, N Uist), *b* 1931; *ed* Eton, and Ch Ch Oxford: *m* 1958, Patricia Helen, da of late Lt-Col Gerald Barry, MC (*see* Barry, Bt, colls), and has issue living, (Peregrine) Marcus Hungerford, *b* 1964; *ed* Eton, — Susannah Hungerford, *b* 1959, — Arabella Rosalind Hungerford, *b* 1961; *ed* St Swithun's, Winchester, and Queen's Coll London; designer: *m* 1985, Giacomo Dante Algranti, son of Gilberto Algranti, of via Crivelli 20, Milan, and has issue living, Jesse Gilberto *b* 1986, Samuel Peregrine *b* 1989. —— Pandora Mary Hungerford (Argyll House, Cirencester, Glos), *b* 1928; LRCP & S Ireland; formerly Prin, Hatherop Castle Sch, Coln-St-Aldwyn, Glos: *m* 1949, Charles Edward Moorhead, who *d* 1953, and has issue living, Rosalind Catherine, *b* 1950: *m* 19—, Dermot Gleeson, and has issue living, Patrick Charles Thomas *b* 1984, Catherine Mary *b* 1981, — Annabel Mai, *b* 1951: *m* 19—, Hjalmar Schiøtz, of Norway, and has issue living, Tanja Katrine *b* 1976, Marianne *b* 1981, Nina *b* 1985.

Grandchildren of late Arthur Joseph Lawrence Pollen (infra):—
Issue of late Francis Anthony Baring Pollen, *b* 1926, *d* 1987: *m* 1950, Marie Thérèse (*Viscountess Sidmouth*) (who *m* 2ndly, 1993, as his 2nd wife, 7th Viscount Sidmouth), da of His Honour late Sir Joseph (Alfred) Sheridan:—
John Stephen Hungerford, *b* 1959: *m* 1988, Jacqueline Ann, yr da of Brian H. Caro, of The Old Rectory, Wittersham, Kent, and has issue living, Francis Arthur Hungerford, *b* 1989, — Anthony Oswald Lawrence, *b* 1992. —— Clare (*Viscountess Asquith*), *b* 1951: *m* 1978, Raymond Benedict Bartholomew Michael, Viscount Asquith, elder son of 2nd Earl of Oxford and Asquith, KCMG, and has issue. *Residence* – The Manor House, Mells, Frome, Somerset. —— Katharine, *b* 1954: *m* 1979, Richard Pflaum, and has issue living, Dominic Richard, *b* 1985, — Julia, *b* 1982, — Thea Mary, *b* 1990. —— Roseanna, *b* 1956: *m* 1984, Ferdinand Carabott-Tortell, and has issue living, Arthur John Rupert *b* 1986, — Juno Clare Emily, *b* 1989. —— (Mary) Louise, *b* 1969.

Grandchildren of late Arthur Joseph Hungerford Pollen, son of John Hungerford Pollen, next brother of 3rd baronet:—
Issue of late Arthur Joseph Lawrence Pollen, *b* 1899, *d* 1968: *m* 1926, Hon Daphne Baring, who *d* 1986, da of 3rd Baron Revelstoke:—
Patrick Laprimaudaye (USA), *b* 1928: *m* 1963, Nell, yst da of late John Murphy, of Sweetmount House, New Ross, co Wexford, and has issue living, Patrick Benedict Peter, *b* 1965, — Laurence Joseph, *b* 1968, — Ciaran, *b* 1966, — Christopher, *b* 1972, — Patricia, *b* 1970. —— Cecilia Mary, *b* 1930: *m* 1952, Christopher Robert Hull, of Claremont House, Wimbledon, SW19, and has issue living, Rupert Teilo David, *b* 1959, — Caspar William, *b* 1960, — Thomas Richard, *b* 1964, — Simon Paul Timothy, *b* 1966, — Lucy Bridget, *b* 1955, — Barbara Margaret, *b* 1957. —— Lucy Margaret, *b* 1932: *m* 1955, Philip Vincent Belloc Jebb, of Beenham Hatch, Bucklebury, Berks RG7 6NR, and has issue living, Matthew Hilary, *b* 1958: *m* 1987, Serena Emma Rose, elder da of Hon Richard Morgan Oliver Stanley, and has issue (*see* B Stanley of Alderley), — Louis Bernard, *b* 1959, — Magdalen Marianne Francesca, *b* 1956, — Christian Agnes Valentine, *b* 1961. —— Mary Rose Catherine, *b* 1940: *m* 1967, Hugo Laurence Joseph Brunner, of 26 Norham Rd, Oxford (*see* Brunner, Bt). —— Margaret Mary Clare, *b* 1943: *m* 1966, Patrick Hyde Kelly, of 23 Charleville Rd, Rathmines, Dublin, and has issue living, Arthur Edmund Campion, *b* 1971, — James Patrick Simeon, *b* 1980, — Beatrice Maeve, *b* 1968.

Grandson of late John Hungerford Pollen (ante):—
Issue of late Arthur Joseph Hungerford Pollen, *b* 1866, *d* 1937: *m* 1898, Maud Beatrice, who *d* 1962, da of late Sir Joseph Lawrence, of Oaklands, Kenley, Surrey:—
John Anthony Lawrence, *b* 1900: *m* 1931, Bridget Gertrude, who *d* 1956, da of late Maj Cuthbert Leigh Blundell-Hollinshead-Blundell (Astley, Bt), and has issue living, Anne Bridget, *b* 1934. *Residence* – Lime Tree House, Upper Strand St, Sandwich, Kent. *Club* – Brooks's.

Grandchildren of late Lt-Col Stephen Hungerford Pollen, CMG son of late John Hungerford Pollen (ante):—
Issue of late Lt-Col Stephen Derek Hungerford Pollen, MBE, *b* 1908; *d* 1969: *m* 1944, Marion Leigh Howard, who *d* 1990, da of late Capt Thomas Storie Dixson:—
Anthony Stephen Hungerford, *b* 1946; *ed* Eton, and RMA Sandhurst; *d* 1974. —— Helen Leigh, *b* 1948. —— Margaret Anne, *b* 1952.

Grandchildren of late John Hungerford Pollen (ante):—
Issue of late Lieut-Col Clement Hungerford Pollen, *b* 1869, *d* 1934: *m* 1912, Mabel Brenda who *d* 1964, da of late Alan Southey Dumbleton of Victoria, British Columbia:—
Hubert Clement Hungerford (3 Dinorben Av, Fleet, Hants GU13 9SG), *b* 1913; *ed* Downside; late Indian Army: *m* 1954, Quita, da of late A. Edward Baker, of Salop, and Fiji. —— Cynthia Brenda, *b* 1914: *m* 1943, Lt Ronald Malcolm Marshall, RN (ret), who *d* 1981, and has issue living, Robin Michael Hungerford, *b* 1943, — Bernard Mark Sebastian, *b* 1945, — John Henry Hubert, *b* 1948, — Clement Wilfrid Ronald Pollen, *b* 1951, — Rosemary Winefride Brenda, *b* 1950. *Residence* – 7 Mount Terrace, Taunton.

This family came originally from Lincs. Edward Pollen became London Merchant temp James I and *d* 1636. His son, grandson and great-grandson, all named John, were MPs for Andover. The last named, father of Sir John, 1st baronet, was one of the Judges of Wales and *d* 1776.

POLLOCK (UK) 1866, of Hatton, Middlesex

Boldly and strenuously

Sir GEORGE FREDERICK POLLOCK, 5th *Baronet*; *b* 13 Aug 1928; *s* his father, *Sir* (FREDERICK) JOHN 1963; *ed* Eton, and Trin Coll, Camb (MA); solicitor 1956; late 17th/21st Lancers; Hon Fellow of Roy Photographic Soc, Pres (1978); FBIPP; FRSA; former Chm of London Salon of Photography, and of Photenrop (UK) Cttee: *m* 1951, Doreen Mumford, da of late Norman Ernest Keown Nash, CMG, and has issue.

Arms – Quarterly, 1st and 4th azure, three fleurs-de-lis within a bordure engrailed or, in dexter chief point on a canton ermine a portcullis of the second, *Pollock of Balgray*; 2nd and 3rd vert, a saltire or, between three bugles in fess and in base argent, garnished gules, within a bordure engrailed, dexter chequy of the second and first, sinister of the second, the whole within a bordure ermine for difference, *Pollock of that Ilk*. **Crest** – A boar passant, quartered or and vert, pierced through the sinister shoulder with an arrow proper. **Supporters** – Two talbots sable, each gorged with a collar or and pendent therefrom a portcullis of the last.
Residence – 83 Minster Way, Bathwick, Bath, Avon BA2 6RL. 3QH. *Club* – Downhill Only.

SON LIVING

DAVID FREDERICK, *b* 13 April 1959: *m* 1985, Helena R, only da of late LJ. Tompsett, OBE, of Tadworth, Surrey, and has issue living, Anna-Lisa Frances, *b* 1989 *Residence* – Camelot Cottage, 43 Chequers Lane, Walton-on-the-Hill, Tadworth, Surrey KT20 7SF.

DAUGHTERS LIVING

Charlotte Anne, *b* 1952. —— Catherine Frances Jill, *b* 1955.

COLLATERAL BRANCHES LIVING

Grandchildren of late Archibald Gordon Pollock, yr son of Robert John Pollock, 3rd son of 1st baronet:—
Issue of late Hamilton Rivers Pollock, *b* 1884, *d* 1940: *m* 1912, Eveline Morton, who *d* 1940, da of Thomas Bell, of Newcastle-on-Tyne:—
Martin Rivers, *b* 1914; *ed* Winchester, and Trin Coll, Camb (BA and Senior Scholar 1936); *m* 1941, Jean Ilsley, el da of Frank Ilsley Paradise, and has issue living, Julian Rivers, *b* 1942, — Jonathan Ilsley, *b* 1948: *m* 1980, Susan, da of Dr Tom Pollock, — Jessamy, *b* 1941, — Lisa Jane, *b* 1944. —— Marian Eveline, *b* 1918. —— Margaret Gordon, *b* 1921: *m* 1943, Boris Kidel, and has issue living, Audrey, *b* 1943, — Mark Rivers, *b* 1947. *Residences* – 7/10 Wohllebengasse, Vienna, Austria; La Garde, Freinet, Var, France.

Granddaughter of late Col Ralph Charles Geoffrey Pollock, el son of Harry Frederick Pollock, el son of George Frederick Pollock (infra):—
Issue of late Maj (Ralph) John Hamilton Pollock, RA, *b* 1921, *d* 1980: *m* 1st, 1948 (*m diss* 1955), Patricia Clarice Marion, da of Capt Arthur Thompson, late Northants Regt; 2ndly, 1957 (*m diss* 1968), Elizabeth Ormond, da of late Charles Mills Maclean, of Savannah, Georgia, USA, and formerly wife of Robert Martin; 3rdly, 1968, Lady Zinnia Rosemary (who *m* 5thly, 1982, Jamie H. Judd, of Stewkley Grange, Leighton Buzzard, Beds), da of 4th Earl of Londesborough, and formerly wife of (1) Peter Comins, (2) John David Leslie Melville, who *d* 1984 (*see* E Leven and Melville, colls, 1980 Edn), (3) Maj Hugh Cantlie:—
(By 1st *m*) Sally Anne St George, *b* 1952.

Granddaughters of late William Rivers Pollock, MD, MRCS, FRCP, 4th son of late George Frederick Pollock (infra):—

Issue of late Humphrey Rivers Pollock, MRCS, LRCP, *b* 1889, *d* 1964: *m* 1920, Eleanor Violet, who *d* 1973, da of late Willoughby Aston Littledale (Thursby, Bt):—

Mary Rivers, *b* 1921; MCSP: *m* 1st, 1960, Charles Tristan D'Oyly, MBE, who *d* 1981; 2ndly, 1990, Philip R. R. Coad, MC, who *d* 1993. *Residence* – 129 Swan Court, SW3. —— Joan Littledale, *b* 1924; *ed* Oxford Univ (MA): *m* 1948, Francis Alexander de Hamel, MD, of 25 Howard St, Macandrew Bay, Dunedin, NZ, and has issue living, Michael Alexander, *b* 1949; *ed* Otago Univ (MA); MRSP: *m* 1982, Alison Patricia Holcroft, of Nelson, NZ, and has an adopted son, Stephen Wai Lam *b* 1984, — Christopher Francis Rivers, *b* 1950; *ed* Otago Univ (BA), and New Coll, Oxford (D Phil); FSA; Dir Sotheby's: *m* 1st, 1978 (*m diss* 1989): Christine Leslie Carmody, of Nelson, NZ; 2ndly, 1993, Mette Tang, da of Axel Tang Svendsen, of Copenhagen, and formerly wife of David Melville Bromby Simpson, and has issue living (by 1st *m*), Alexander John Pudsay *b* 1981, Edwin Willoughby Rivers *b* 1984, — Geoffrey William, *b* 1953: *m* 1981, Philippa Sarah, da of Dr Max Nash, of Remuera, NZ, and has issue living, Adam Culyer Nash *b* 1983, Jane Sarah Nash *b* 1985, — Richard John Bruno, *b* 1960; *ed* Canterbury Univ (MSc): *m* 1987, Philippa Lynne White, MD, of Blenheim, NZ, and has issue living, Roy William *b* 1991, James Michael *b* 1993, — Quentin David Humphrey, *b* 1963; *ed* Otago Univ (LLB): *m* 1991, Judith Anne Clark, of Christchurch, NZ, and has issue living, Stephanie Jane Littledale *b* 1992.

Issue of late Rt Hon Sir Ernest Murray Pollock, KBE (5th son of late George Frederick Pollock (infra)), who was *cr Viscount Hanworth* 1936 (see that title).

Granddaughter of late George Frederick Pollock, 4th son of 1st baronet:—
Issue of late Rt Rev Bertram Pollock, KCVO, DD, Lord Bishop of Norwich 1910-42, *b* 1863; *d* 1943: *m* 1928, Joan Florence Helena, who *d* 1986, da of late Rev Algernon Charles Dudley Ryder (*see* E Harrowby, colls):—
Mary Rosalind Frances Felicia, *b* 1931.

Grandchildren of late Hon Sir Charles Edward Pollock, 5th son of 1st baronet:—
Issue of late George Hume Pollock, *b* 1870, *d* 1924: *m* 1900, Margaret Agnata, who *d* 1954, da of Sir Richard Harington, 11th Bt:—
Agnata Cecilia, *b* 1907. *Residence* – Quendon Cottage, Quendon, nr Saffron Walden, Essex. —— Margaret Georgina, *b* 1913; *m* 1948, Richard Tresillian Gabb, MB, BCh, who *d* 1986. *Residence* – Beverley House, Stansted Mountfitchet, Essex CM24 8AE.

Issue of late Robert Pollock, *b* 1874, *d* 1957: *m* (Jan) 1914, Ethel Mary Purefoy, who *d* 1970, da of James Crofts Powell, of 13 Chester St, Grosvenor Pl, SW:—
Martin James, *b* (Dec) 1914; *ed* Charterhouse, and Trin Coll, Camb (BA 1936); admitted a solicitor 1946; is Lieut RNVR: *m* 1942, Pamela Valentine, da of late Valentine Leslie Douglas Uzielli, and has issue living, Robert Valentine, *b* 1957, — Carolyn Alice, *b* 1944: *m* 1st 1967 (*m diss* 1971), Michael Bernard Thorold, Scots Gds (*see* Thorold, Bt, colls); 2ndly, 1976, Anthony Edward Henson, of Elm Tree House, Tillers Green, Dymock, Glos, and has issue (by 1st *m*) (*see* Thorold, Bt, colls), — Rosalind Janet, *b* 1948; SEN: *m* 1975, John Edward Fawkes, of Kenyons, W Horsley, Surrey, and has issue living, Mark Alexander *b* 1977, Juliette Elizabeth *b* 1982. *Residence* – West Crosside, Knowstone, S Molton, N Devon. —— *Rev* John Charles, *b* 1923; *ed* Charterhouse, and Trin Coll, Camb (BA 1946, MA 1948); formerly Capt Coldm Gds: *m* 1949, Anne, da of Sir Thomas Richard Fiennes Barrett-Lennard, 5th Bt, OBE. *Residence* – Rose Ash House, S Molton, Devon EX36 4RB. —— Honor Purefoy, *b* 1916: *m* 1939, James Frederick Priestley, MC, and has issue living, Hugh Michael (52 Stanford Rd, W8), *b* 1942; *ed* Winchester and Worcester Coll, Oxford: *m* 1968, Caroline Clarissa Duncan, only da of Brig John Hume Prendergast, DSO, MC, and has issue living, Alexandra Mary Duncan *b* 1971, Susannah Caroline Louise *b* 1974, — Richard James, *b* 1947: *m* 1980, Iona Rosalind, da of Maj Ion Melville Calvocoressi, MBE, MC, of Court Lodge, Westerham, Kent (*see* M Ailsa, colls), and has issue living, Laura Katherine *b* 1982, Rosanna Victoria *b* 1985, Isabel Louise *b* 1988, — Sarah Veronica (Ovington Park, Alresford, Hants), *b* 1944: *m* 1st, 1967, Brian David Bond, who *d* 1981; 2ndly, 1990, Robert George Thorne, and has issue living (by 1st *m*), Michael Alan Shaw *b* 1968, Edward Brian Shaw *b* 1970, Annabel Clare *b* 1971, Marina Alice *b* 1976. *Residence* – Upton Manor, Andover, Hants SP11 0JR.

Granddaughter of late George Hume Pollock (ante):—
Issue of late Com Charles Harington Pollock, DSC, RN, *b* 1906; *d* 1983: *m* 1938, Patricia Aileen Domville, who *d* 1957, da of late Herbert Payne Heming, of Victoria, BC, Canada, and widow of Capt H. Leicester Leverin, RCE:—
Ann Patricia, *b* 1939: *m* 1961, Maj Richard Cecil Wallace, RCT, of Kemps, Hill Green, Clavering, Saffron Walden, Essex, and has had issue, Charles Pollock, *b* 1963, — Oliver James Shannon, *b* 1970, *d* 1976.

Grandchildren of late Maj-Gen Sir (Frederick) Richard Pollock, KCSI, 7th son of 1st baronet:—
Issue of late Dighton Nicolas Pollock, *b* 1864, *d* 1927: *m* 1921, Hon Margaret Anna Buckmaster, who *d* 1929, da of 1st Viscount Buckmaster:—
Richard Stanley, *b* 1922. *Residence* – 20 Porchester Terrace, W2. —— John Dighton, *b* 1924.

Grandchildren of late Douglas Warren Pollock, MBE, yst son of late Sir Edward James Pollock, 9th son of 1st baronet:—
Issue of late Maj Jack Warren Pollock, RA, *b* 1913; *d* 1981: *m* 1949, Hazel (The Bridge House, Shoreham, Kent TN14 7SJ), da of late Henry Arthur Hinton, of Shrewsbury, and widow of Maj Howard Bourne, Hon Artillery Co:—
Nicholas Charles Valentine, *b* 1950; *ed* Winchester, New Coll, Oxford (MA), and Southampton Univ (MSc). —— Christopher James Douglas, *b* 1956; *ed* Winchester, and Worcester Coll, Oxford: *m* 1984, Sarah, da of David Geddes Mitchell, of Iffley, Oxford, and has issue living, Felix Alexander, *b* 1989, — Tobias Frederick, *b* 1992. —— Miranda Penelope Gillian, *b* 1952: *m* 1992, (Brian Edward) Nicholas O'Brien (*see* B Inchiquin, colls), of 83a Cromwell Rd, SW19 8LF.

The Right Hon Sir Frederick, 1st baronet, was Lord Chief Baron of the Court of Exchequer, 1844-68. He was a son of David Pollock, saddler, of Charing Cross, a descendant of David Pollock, of Balgray, Renfrewshire, *b* about 1631, great-grandson of Charles Pollock of Greenhill, yr son of David Pollock of that Ilk. David Pollock, the saddler, also had two other sons who attained great eminence, viz, Sir David Pollock, Chief Justice of Bombay, and Field Marshal Sir George Pollock, Baronet, GCB, GCSI, Constable of the Tower of London. The senior line Pollock of Pollock became ext in the 19th century. The 2nd baronet was for many years Senior Master of the Supreme Court of Judicature and Queen's Remembrancer. The 3rd baronet was a Privy Councillor, KC and Admiralty Judge of the Cinque Ports 1914-36. The 4th baronet was an Officer Legion of Honour.

MONTAGU-POLLOCK (UK) 1872, of the Khyber Pass

Boldly and strenuously

Let us be examined by our conduct

Sir GILES HAMPDEN MONTAGU-POLLOCK, 5th *Baronet*; *b* 19 Oct 1928; *s* his father, *Sir* GEORGE SEYMOUR, 1985; *ed* Eton, and de Havilland Aeronautical Tech Sch; De Havilland Enterprise 1949-56, Bristol Aeroplane Co Ltd 1956-59, Bristol Siddeley Engines Ltd 1959-61, J. Walter Thompson Co Ltd 1961-69, C. Vernon and Sons Ltd 1969-71, Acumen Marketing Group Ltd 1971-74, 119 Pall Mall Ltd 1972-78, John Stork and Partners Ltd 1980-89, Management Consultant since 1974, Associate Korn/Ferry International since 1989: *m* 1963, Caroline Veronica, yr da of late Richard Francis Russell, of 18 The Grange, Wimbledon, SW19, and has issue.

Arms – Quarterly, 1st and 4th, azure, three fleurs-de-lis within a bordure embattled or for his distinguished services in the Afghan war on a chief of the second an eastern crown gules, super-inscribed "Khyber," and on a canton ermine three cannons fesseways in pale sable *Pollock*; 2nd and 3rd, parti per pale argent and gules, a fesse lozengy counterchanged *Montagu*; in the middle chief point a cross moline, also counterchanged. **Crests** – 1st, a lion rampant guardant argent adorned with an eastern crown or, holding in his dexter paw in bend sinister an Afghan banner displayed gules, bordered or and vert, the staff broken in two, in his sinister paw a part of the broken staff in an escrol over the motto, "Affghanistan" *Pollock*; 2nd, a boar passant quarterly embattled or and vert, pierced through the sinister shoulder with an arrow proper *Pollock*; 3rd, a griffin's head couped, wings expanded or, gorged with a collar lozengy *Montagu*. **Supporters** – *Dexter*, an heraldic tiger sable, maned, tufted, and gorged with an eastern crown, and chained, chain being reflexed over the back or, and pendent from the collar an escutcheon or, charged with a bomb fired proper; *sinister*, a talbot gorged, chained, and charged as the dexter.
Residence – The White House, 7 Washington Rd, Barnes, SW13 9BG. *Club* – Inst of Directors.

SON LIVING

GUY MAXIMILIAN, *b* 27 Aug 1966; *ed* Eton, and Hatfield Poly.

DAUGHTER LIVING

Sophie Amelia, *b* 1969.

SISTER LIVING

Karen Aagot Georgina, *b* 1931: *m* 1952, Richard Eliot Hodgkin, yr son of late Brig Adrian Eliot Hodgkin, OBE, MC, and has issue living, Harry John, *b* 1961; *ed* Radley and Ealing College (LLB); Bar: *m* 1990, Karen Lesley Pearce, and has issue living, Polly Grace *b* 1992, — Edward Eliot, *b* 1963; *ed* Radley, and Jesus Coll, Oxford (BA, DPhil): *m* 1993, Karen Lesley Jones, — Georgina Elizabeth, *b* 1954: *m* 1975 (*m diss* 1979), Nicholas David Douro Hoare, and has issue living, Caspar Michael Douro *b* 1977. *Address* – c/o Drummonds Branch, The Royal Bank of Scotland, 49 Charing Cross, SW1A 2DX.

UNCLE LIVING (Son of third baronet)

John Gathorne, *b* 1911; *ed* Oundle: *m* 1943, Elizabeth Metcalf, who *d* 1989, da of late Carl Herbert Coston, of South Hadley Falls, Massachusetts, USA, who *d* 1989, and has issue living, Stephen Hull, *b* 1945: *m* 1979, Barbara Ann, da of Ralph J. Betschart, — Christopher James, *b* 1952: *m* 1980, Dianne Kristen, da of Eugene M. Spear, and has issue living, Toby William *b* 1986, Jennifer Ann *b* 1982, — Margaret Bell, *b* 1948: *m* 1972, Robert Lewis Merkow, of Hartland, Wisconsin, USA, who *d* 1989, and has issue living, Sarah Ellen *b* 1981, Carla Lauren *b* 1984. *Residence* – 4905 S Lafayette, Englewood, Colorado 80110-7012, USA.

COLLATERAL BRANCHES LIVING

Issue of late Hubert Vernon Montagu-Pollock, 2nd son of 3rd baronet, *b* 1902; *d* 1970: *m* 1945, Delia Florence Alice, who *d* 1977, da of late Herbert Snowden, and widow of Harold Edward Pearce:—
Jonathan David (Bridge Cottage, Winterbourne Stoke, Salisbury, Wilts SP3 4SW; Army and Navy and RGJ (London) Clubs), *b* 1947; *ed* Charterhouse; late 2nd Lt R Green Jackets: *m* 1979, Deirdre Clare, yr da of John Edward Binding, of Rock, N Cornwall, and has issue living, Thomas George, *b* 1983, — Archer William, *b* 1986.

Issue of late Sir William Horace Montagu-Pollock, KCMG, 3rd son of 3rd baronet, *b* 1903, *d* 1993: *m* 1st, 1933 (*m diss* 1945), (Frances Elisabeth) Prudence, who *d* 1985, da of late Sir John Fischer Williams, CBE, KC, of Lamledra, Gorran Haven, Cornwall (D Atholl, colls); 2ndly, 1948, Barbara (181 Coleherne Court, SW5 0DU), da of late Percy Hague Jowett, CBE, of 28 Drayton Gds, SW10, and formerly wife of Thomas Josceline Gaskell:—
(By 1st *m*) Hubert George Murray (Low Beckfoot, Barbon, Carnforth, Cumbria LA6 2LE), *b* 1935; *ed* Winchester; MA; PhD; Past Fellow of Trin Coll, Camb; Reader in Surface Physics, Lancaster Univ: *m* 1960, Emmerentia Johanna, yr da of J.B. de Jong Cleyndert, of Palegates Farm, Henham, Essex, and has issue living, Harriet Marthe, *b* 1961, — Catherine Juliet, *b* 1963, — Annabel Frances, *b* 1966. —— Fidelity Juliet, *b* 1940: *m* 1962, Alan Charles Barclay Dean, MB, FRCS, of Balgone House, N Berwick, E Lothian EH39 5PB, and has issue living, Marcus William Fischer, *b* 1963; RIBA, RIAS, — Juliet Augusta Carolyn, *b* 1965, — Corinna Lucy Henrietta, *b* 1967. —— (By 2nd *m*) Matthew John (28 Seymour Buildings, Seymour Place, W1), *b* 1951; *ed* Westminster, and Ch Ch, Oxford: *m* 1984, Aliaa, da of late Abdel Rahman Zayed, and has issue living, a da, *b* 1991.

Granddaughters of late Hugh Pollock (infra):—
Issue of late Hugh Wykeham David Pollock, *b* 1900, *d* 1972: *m* 1934, Barbara, who *d* 1993, da of Sir Philip Bealby Reckitt, OBE, 3rd Bt (ext):—
Bridget Wykeham (Lowlands Farm, Shrewley, Warwicks), *b* 1935: *m* 1960 (*m diss* 1977), Michael John Marshall, son of Sir Arthur Gregory George Marshall, OBE, DL, and has issue living, Robert David, *b* 1962: *m* 1992, Julia Kathleen, yr da of Timothy Patrick Hamilton-Russell (*see* B Ashbourne), — James Gregory, *b* 1964, — Belinda Louise, *b* 1960: *m* 1988, Adrian

Richard Hill, — Cressida Micael, *b* 1967. —— Ann Catherine (Coshandrochaid, Tayvallich, Argyll), *b* 1938. —— Jane (Winderwath, Penrith, Cumbria), *b* 1945.

Granddaughters of late George David Pollock, FRCS, 2nd son of 1st baronet:—
Issue of late Hugh Pollock, *b* 1859, *d* 1944: *m* 1898, Alice, who *d* 1971, da of late Cornwallis Wykeham-Martin (B Llangattock)—
Frances Alison (*Dowager Lady Anson*), *b* 1903: *m* 1923, Lt-Col Sir Edward Anson, 6th Bt, RA, who *d* 1951. *Residence* – 85 Boundstone Rd, Rowledge, Farnham, Surrey.
Issue of late Col Evelyn Pollock, CBE, RA, *b* 1861, *d* 1951: *m* 1890, Mary, who *d* 1936, da of late Henry Jefferd Tarrant, Bar-at-law:—
Jean, *b* 1914: *m* 1st, 1940, Maj Gerard Joseph McCann, RM, who was *ka* 1943; 2ndly, 1951, Group Capt Slocombe Gomez, CBE, RAF, who *d* 1972, and has issue living, (by 1st *m*) Peta Jean Madeleine, *b* 1941 — (by 2nd *m*) Nicholas David (Carretera de Boadilla del Monte, 52-7°B, Madrid 24, Spain), *b* 1952; *ed* Sherborne: *m* 1976, Felicidad Mediavilla, and has issue living, Karen Alexandra *b* 1978, Gillian *b* 1982. *Residence* – Las Gaviotas 3°-5A, Paseo San Pedro, Altea, Alicante, Spain.

Granddaughter of late Col Evelyn Pollock, CBE, RA (ante):—
Issue of late Sir Ronald Evelyn Pollock, *b* 1891, *d* 1974: *m* 1st, 1921, Margery, who *d* 1959, da of late Samuel Fitze; 2ndly, 1963, Pamela, who *d* 1989, only da of late Francis Winckworth Anstice Prideaux, OBE, and widow of Percy John Hodsoll Stent, CIE, ICS:—
(By 1st *m*) Anne Margery, *b* 1924; formerly in WRNS: *m* 1st, 1958 (*m diss* 1979), Clive Robert Basche; 2ndly, 1981, Richard Holman Parsons, Lt-Cdr RN, of Fiddlers Green, 9 Grenehurst Way, Petersfield, Hants, and has issue living (by 1st *m*), Timothy James, *b* 1961: *m* 1988, Melanie Jane Lawson, and has issue living, Charlotte Louise *b* 1990, Sophie *b* 1993, — Clare Nicola, *b* 1959: *m* 1983, Jonathan Gordon Drew, and has issue living, James Newcombe *b* 1983, Robert Edmund *b* 1986, Christopher Gordon *b* 1987.

Grandchildren of late Lt-Col Frederick George Pollock, el son of late Archibald Reid Swiney Pollock, 4th son of 1st baronet:—
Issue of late Lt-Col Harry Clement Pollock, MBE, *b* 1883, *d* 1971: *m* 1st, 1914 (*m diss* 1928), Dorothy Beatrice, da of late Sir Theodore Caro Piggott; 2ndly, 1929, Constance Ferne, who *d* 1943, da of late Alfred Russell, of Rushall, Staffs; 3rdly, 1944, Winifred Eileen (14A Queens Rd, Royston, Herts), da of late W. T. C. Macgregor, of Wick, Caithness:—
(By 1st *m*) John Basil (224A Connaught Rd, Brookwood, Woking, Surrey, GU24 0AH), *b* 1920; BSc London Eng (Metallurgy); ARSM: *m* 1949, Betty Angela, da of H. A. Lusher, of Sevenoaks, Kent, and has issue living, Christopher Robert, *b* 1954, — Anne Patricia, *b* 1951, — Sarah Gillian, *b* 1957. —— (By 3rd *m*) Martin Donald, *b* 1948; *ed* Churchill Coll, Camb (MA); PhD (Cosmology).
Issue of late Archibald Frederick Pollock, *b* 1885, *d* 1941: *m* 1922, Ada Gertrude, who *d* 1979, da of late Albert Imossi, of Gibraltar:—
David Frances (126 Grovedale Rd, Floreat Park, Perth, W Australia 6014), *b* 1928; *ed* RMA; late Major RA; Dep Executive Dir Austn Red Cross Soc (W Aust Div): *m* 1959, Diana Mary, da of Maj F. J. Andrews, of Hemingford Lodge, London Rd, Cheam, Surrey, and has issue living, James Robert, *b* 1962; *ed* Univ of W Aust (BCom), — Gillian Mary, *b* 1960: *m* 1983, David Ian Hill, of 44 Needlewood St, Kambalda, W Aust, son of Ian Hill, of Auckland, NZ. —— Mary, *b* 1924: *m* 1946, Bryan L. Epsom, late Capt Queen's Own Roy W Kent Regt, and has issue living, Hugh David, *b* 1949, — Guy Bryan, *b* 1954, — Paul Robert, *b* 1956. *Address* – c/o PO Box 40026, Nairobi, Kenya.
Issue of late William Hamilton Pollock, *b* 1887, *d* 1976: *m* 1915, Sara Amanda, who *d* 1981, da of late Jose Santos Tello, of Chile:—
†Richard Douglas (Alsacia 84, Las Condes, Santiago, Chile), *b* 1924; a Chemical Engineer, Federico Santa Maria Univ, Chile: *m* 1956, Maria Helia, da of late Ceferino Veloso, of Santiago, Chile, and *d* 1990, leaving issue, William Douglas, *b* 1957; Industrial Engr, Chile Univ: *m* 1990, Agnes Joyce, da of Richard Sharman Claude, of Viña del Mar, Chile, and has issue living, Michael Douglas *b* 1993, Agnes Marianne *b* 1990, — James Edward, *b* 1959; Electrical Engr, Chile Univ: *m* 1986 (*m diss* 1992), Macarena, da of Claudio Mas Ferret, of Santiago, Chile, and has issue living, Benjamin Edward *b* 1988, Vincent *b* 1991, Macarena Sofia *b* 1987, — Philip Andrew, *b* 1962; Industrial Engr, Chile Univ: *m* 1988, María Gabriela, da of Juan Lasnibat Aninat, of Santiago, Chile, and has issue living, Philip Anthony *b* 1990, Anne Mary *b* 1991, — Maureen Elizabeth, *b* 1960: *m* 1986, Pablo Emanuel Quiñones de León, of Santiago, Chile, and has issue living, Luis Felipe *b* 1987, Juan Pablo *b* 1989, José Antonio *b* 1992.

Granddaughter of late Archibald Reid Swiney Pollock (ante):—
Issue of late Maj-Gen John Archibald Henry Pollock, CB, *b* 1856, *d* 1949: *m* 1898, Lillian Forrester, who *d* 1954, da of J. Fortune:—
Justina Lillian (Pansy), *b* 1902: *m* 1926, Frederic Whigham McConnel, of Blair House, 8 High St, Kirkcudbright, and has issue living, James Frederic Whigham (Whitehouse, Newcastle, Monmouth, Gwent), *b* 1929: *m* 19—, Judith Marian Culpin, — John William (Lettrick, Dunscore, Dumfries-shire DG2 0UX), *b* 1931: *m* 19—, Lois Christine Lyon, and has issue living, James Archibald Robert *b* 1958: *m* 19—, Sarah Helen Walker (and has issue living, James Archibald Frederic Whigham *b* 1994), John Andrew Douglas *b* 1961, William Kennedy *b* 1962: *m* 19—, Susan Mary, da of Edward Alfred Heycock (*see* Halsey, Bt, colls) (and has issue living, Jennifer Kathryn Halsey *b* 1993), Fiona Mary *b* 1957: *m* 19—, Ian Macpherson (and has issue living, Morag Fiona *b* 1988, Katherine Anne *b* 1989).

Sir George Pollock, 1st baronet, yr brother of Rt Hon Sir Frederick Pollock, 1st baronet of Hatton (*cr* 1866) commanded the army with great distinction in the first Afghan war. He attained the rank of Field-Marshal, and was sometime Constable of the Tower. Sir Frederick, 2nd baronet, assumed by Roy licence in 1873 the additional surname of Montagu, having *m* 1861, Laura Caroline, da of Henry Seymour Montagu of Westleton Grange, Suffolk.

PONSONBY (UK) 1956, of Wootton, co Oxford

Sir ASHLEY CHARLES GIBBS PONSONBY, KCVO, MC, 2nd *Baronet; b* 21 Feb 1921; *s* his father, *Col Sir* CHARLES EDWARD, TD (*see* B de Mauley, colls) 1976; *ed* Eton, and Balliol Coll, Oxford; late Capt Coldm Gds 1939-45 War (wounded, MC, 1945); Lord Lieut of Oxfordshire since 1980; *cr* KCVO 1993; KStJ 1989: *m* 1950, Lady Martha Butler, yr da of 6th Marquess of Ormonde, and has issue.

Arms – Gules, a chevron between three combs argent. **Crest** – Out of a ducal coronet or three arrows, points downwards, one in pale and two in saltire, entwined at the intersection by a snake proper.
Residence – Woodleys, Woodstock, Oxford OX20 1HJ.

SONS LIVING

CHARLES ASHLEY (Grims Dyke Farm, Woodstock, Oxford OX20 1HJ), *b* 10 June 1951; *ed* Eton, and Ch Ch, Oxford (MA): *m* 1983, Mary Priscilla, yr da of late Maj Arthur Richard Bromley Davenport, of Knutsford, Cheshire, and has issue living, Arthur Ashley, *b* 15 Sept 1984, — Frederick Edward, *b* 1986, — Alice Elizabeth, *b* 1988. —— Rupert Spencer, *b* 1953; *ed* Eton, and Reading Univ: *m* 1985, Amanda, MBE, elder da of Michael Keith Beale Colvin, MP, of Tangley House, Andover, Hants (*see* B Cayzer), and has issue living, Emily Mary, *b* 1990, — Eleanor Rose, *b* 1993. —— Luke Arthur *b* 1957; *ed* Eton: *m* 1985, Nicola J., yr da of Gen Sir Roland Kelvin Guy, KCB, CBE, DSO, of Stourpaine, Dorset, and has issue living, Edmund (Ned) Brabazon *b* 1989, — Lucy India Clare, *b* 1991. —— John Piers, *b* 1962; *ed* Eton, and Gonville and Caius Coll, Camb: *m* 1994, Serena N., da of Robert Marshall, of Nairobi, Kenya.

SISTERS LIVING

Priscilla Dora (*Priscilla, Lady Bacon*), *b* 1913; a DL of Norfolk: *m* 1936, Lt-Col Sir Edmund Castell Bacon, KG, CBE, TD, 14th Bt, who *d* 1982. *Residence* – Orchards, Raveningham, Norwich NR14 6NS. —— Diana Mary, *b* 1916: *m* 1940, Rev Canon Mark Meynell (*see* E Halifax, colls). *Residence* – 2 Double St, Framlingham, Suffolk. —— Lavinia Rosalind (*Lady Hamilton*), *b* 1919: *m* 1947, Sir Michael Aubrey Hamilton, of Lordington House, Chichester, and has issue living, John Ashley, *b* 1948: *m* 1975, Audrey Carola, only da of Capt Nigel William Ivo Naper, of Loughcrew, Oldcastle, co Meath (V Valentia), and has issue living, Mark Emmanuel Naper *b* 1979, Robin Michael Elijah *b* 1982, Meg Rosaleen Gabriel, *b* 1977, — Caroline Mary, *b* 1950: *m* 1980, Stephen M. Codner, son of John Codner, of Breadstone House, Glos, and has issue living, Jesse Anne *b* 1981, Rose Elizabeth *b* 1983, — Susanna, *b* 1954: *m* 1982, Rufus Anthony Reade, and has issue living, Benedict *b* 1984, Hannah *b* 1988, — Jane Lavinia, *b* 1958, *m* 1984, Garth K. P. Watkins, and has issue living, Jonathan Michael *b* 1986, Simon Alexander *b* 1988. —— Juliet Barbara Anna, *b* 1923: *m* 1949, Rt Hon James Edward Ramsden, and has had issue, Thomas James Ponsonby, *b* 1950: *m* 1983, Jane Ann, yr da of late John Eustice, of Omaha, Nebraska, USA, and has issue living, James Thomas Eustice *b* 1985, Matthew John *b* 1987, William Joseph *b* 1990, Mary Juliet Eustice *b* 1984, — George Edward (The Old Rectory, Settrington, Malton, Yorks), *b* 1953: *m* 1986, Jane Slane Sloan, formerly wife of Anthony Charles Vaughan Wynn (*see* B Newborough), and elder da of Rev William Thompson, of Oxnam Manse, Jedburgh, Roxburghshire, and has issue living, Edward William *b* 1989, Laura Vida *b* 1988, Juliet Charlotte Rose *b* 1992, — Richard Ashley (10 Michael Fields, Forest Row, E Sussex RH18 5BH), *b* 1954: *m* 1978, Kristin Maria, only da of John Waldroup, of Carmel, Calif, USA, and has issue living, Thalia *b* 1985, Marika *b* 1986, Kaelyn *b* 1988, — Emma Juliet Geraldine, *b* 1957: *m* 1981, Rev John G. W. Oliver, only son of G. F. Oliver, MBE, of Mistley, Van Dieman's Lane, Bath, and has issue living, Sarah *b* 1993, — Charlotte Mary Rose, *b* 1960: *m* 1982, Mark Lawrence Cheverton, yr son of Rev David Cheverton, of Cruachan Cottage, Preston-under-Scar, Leyburn, Yorks, and was *k* with her husband in a motor accident 1991. *Residences* – Old Sleningford Hall, Ripon, Yorks; 10 Cleaver Sq, Kennington, SE11.

Sir Charles Edward Ponsonby, TD, DL, 1st Bt, grandson of 2nd Baron de Mauley, was MP for Sevenoaks (*C*) 1935-50, PPS to Sec of State for War 1940, and to Sec of State for Foreign Affairs 1941-45.

POORE (GB) 1795, of Rushall, Wiltshire

Sir HERBERT EDWARD POORE, 6th *Baronet; b* April 1930; *s* his father, *Sir* EDWARD, 1938.

Arms – Argent, a fesse azure between three mullets gules. **Crest** – A cubit arm erect vested sable, slashed argent, cuffed ermine, charged with two mullets in fesse or, grasping in the hand an arrow proper.
Residence – Curuzu Cuatia, Corrientes, Argentina.

SISTERS LIVING

Elsie Felly, *b* 1923: *m* 1947, Jorge Ball, and has issue living, Jorge Eduard, *b* 1948, — Alberto Carlos, *b* 1949, — Roberto, *b* 1954, — Susana Beatriz, *b* 1952. —— Betty Gladys, *b* 1926.

UNCLE LIVING

NASIONCENO, *b* 1900: *m* 19—, Juana Borda, who *d* 1943, and has issue living, Roger Ricardo, *b* 1930, — Roberto, *b* 1932: *m* 1964, Norma Onhaso, — Percy Nasionceno, *b* 1933, — Argentina *b* 1927, — Gloria *b* 1928, — Tady Esterlina, *b* 1938.

AUNTS LIVING

Francesca, *b* 1898. —— Rosalie, *b* 1905: *m* 1930, Juan F. Garmedia. *Residence* – Belgrano, 912 Curuzu Cuatia, Argentina.

Pauper, non in spe
Poor, but not in spirit

PRO.

REGE·LEGE· GREGE

WIDOW LIVING OF FIFTH BARONET

AMELIA (*Lady Poore*), da of Senor Santiago Guliemone, of Estancia La Blanca, Estacion Acuna, Corrientes, Argentine Republic: *m* 1922, Sir Edward Poore, 5th baronet, who *d* 1938. *Residence* – Curuzu Cuatia, Corrientes, Argentina.

COLLATERAL BRANCHES LIVING

(*In special remainder*)

Grandsons of late Capt Mark Saurin Poore (infra):—
Issue of late Robert Poore (who assumed by Roy Licence 1932 the surname of Poore-Saurin-Watts), *b* 1904, *d* 1973: *m* 1945, Rosemary Philippa (Brown Edge, W Malvern, Worcs WR14 4BJ) (who *m* 2ndly, 1974, James Richardson, MRCS, LRCP, who *d* 1986), da of Maj Richard Norman Winstanley, of Rownham's House, nr Southampton:—
†(Robert) Mark, *b* 1946; *d* 1953. —— †Edward Richard POORE, *b* 1948; *ed* Harrow, and Lausanne Univ; relinquished the additional surnames of Saurin-Watts 1983; *d* 1991, in Haifa, Israel. —— Andrew Philip POORE-SAURIN-WATTS (Barkby Close, 47 Cottenham Park Rd, Wimbledon, SW20), *b* 1951; *ed* Milton Abbey, and Lausanne Univ.

Granddaughter of late Maj Roger Alvin Poore, DSO, RWF, 3rd son of late Maj Robert Poore (infra):—
Issue of late W/Cdr Roger Dennistoun Poore, RAF, *b* 1916, *d* 1987: *m* 1949, Peta (33 Phillimore Gdns, Campden Hill, W8), widow of W/Cdr Walter Ronald Farley, DFC, and da of late William George Coast, of Finchley:—
Victoria Lorne Peta, *b* 1956: *m* 1981, (Geoffrey Robert) James Borwick, elder son of Hon Robin Sandbach Borwick, and has issue (*see* B Borwick).

Grandchildren of late Major Robert Poore, son of late Robert Montagu Poore, son of late John Montagu Poore, 2nd son of late Edward Poore, brother of 1st baronet:—
Issue of late Capt Mark Saurin Poore, *b* 1869, *d* 1931: *m* 1900, Irene, who *d* 1943 (having *m* 2ndly, 1933, Major Harry Grant Thorold, of Cranford Hall, Northants), da of late Edward Hanslope Watts, of Hanslope Park, Bucks:—
(Louisa) Florentia, *b* 1905: *m* 1932, Leslie Woods Haslett, who *d* 1992, of Apart 404, 1460 Docteur Penfield, Montreal, Canada, and has issue living, (Leslie) Mark, *b* 1933: *m* 1959, Jane Aikins, da of Robert David Mulholland, of Montreal, and has issue living, Andrew Mark *b* 1961, Thomas Leslie *b* 1962, Peter Aikins *b* 1964, Jennifer Anne *b* 1968, — Robert David, *b* 1937: *m* 1963, Lucy, da of Christopher Eberts, of Ottawa, and has issue living, Elizabeth *b* 1964, Mary Martha *b* 1966, — Richard Stuart, *b* 1940: *m* 1965, Katharine, da of Ernest Boyne, of St John, New Brunswick, and has issue living, Christopher Leslie *b* 1967, Michael *b* 1970, Robert *b* 1974, — Christian Florentia, *b* 1935: *m* 1956, David Gladwin Turnbull, of Rothesay, New Brunswick, and has issue living, Douglas Alasdair Stuart *b* 1958, Charles Laughlin *b* 1960, Douglas David *b* 1963, Christian Benita *b* 1957, — Benita Jane, *b* 1938.
Issue of late Philip Poore, *b* 1874, *d* 1937: *m* 1918, Cicely Eleanor who *d* 1978, da of Sir Edward Arthur Barry, 2nd Bt:—
Philip Barry, MC, *b* 1919; formerly Capt and temporary Major Wilts Regt; Burma 1944-5 with Gold Coast Regt (MC): *m* 1954, Jennifer Mary, da of Lieut-Col S. C. H. Worseldine, IMS (ret), of Nelson, New Zealand, and has issue living, Philip William, *b* 1956, — Anna Cicely, *b* 1954, — Sara Eleanor, *b* 1958, — Helen Jennifer, *b* 1960. *Residence* – Pakaraka, RD2 Kaikohe, Bay of Islands, New Zealand. —— Robert Roger, *b* 1924; BSc Engineering 1949: *m* 1952, Diana Marion, da of John Davis Canning, of Oakbourne, Waipukurua, New Zealand, and has issue living, Marion Rosalind, *b* 1953, — Caroline Louise, *b* 1955, — Elizabeth Julia, *b* 1957, — Judith Rosamund, *b* 1958. *Residence* – 17 Kelvin Road, Remuera, Auckland, NZ. —— Anne Benita, *b* 1922: *m* 1946, Thomas Campbell Lindesay (PO Box 164, Kerikeri, Bay of Islands, NZ), and has issue living, Philip Edward (418 Remuera Rd, Auckland, NZ), *b* 1947: *m* 1971, Barbara Lesley Hargrave, — Thomas Reginald, *b* 1953, — Clare, *b* 1950: *m* 1st, 1972 (*m diss* 19—), Rodney Burke; 2ndly, 19—, Michael Gadsby, of Flat 1, Marchwood Cres, London W5, — Erica Anne, *b* 1955.

The family descend from Philip Poore of Amesbury, Wilts (will proved 15 July 1585), whose son Philip was settled at Durrington, nearby. Though earlier genealogical proof has not been established, it is likely that this family has common ancestry with the brothers Herbert le Poer or Poor, last Bishop of Old Sarum, who *d* 1217, and Richard who succeeded him as Bishop of Salisbury, and built the Cathedral at New Sarum, which was consecrated in 1225.

PORRITT (UK) 1963, of Hampstead, co London

Hon Sir JONATHON ESPIE PORRITT, 2nd *Baronet*; *b* 6 July 1950; *s* his father, ARTHUR ESPIE, Baron Porritt, GCMG, GCVO, CBE (Life Baron) in his Baronetcy 1994; *ed* Eton, and Magdalen Coll, Oxford; Dir Friends of the Earth 1984-90: *m* 1986, Sarah, da of Malcolm Staniforth, of Malvern, Worcs, and has issue.

𝕬𝖗𝖒𝖘 – Or, a serpent in bend vert between two lions heads erased gules, on a chief of the last two swords points upwards in saltire of the first, between as many roses argent both surmounted by another gules barbed and seeded proper. 𝕮𝖗𝖊𝖘𝖙 – On a wreath or and gules, a demi heraldic antelope gules armed azure collared or; holding a torch of the last enflamed proper between two fern fronts vert.
Residence – 9 Lypiatt Terrace, Cheltenham, Glos GL50 2SX.

DAUGHTERS LIVING

Eleanor Mary, *b* 1988. —— Rebecca Elizabeth, *b* 1991.

BROTHER LIVING

Hon JEREMY CHARLES, *b* 19 Jan 1953; *ed* Eton: *m* 1980, Penny, da of J. H. Moore, of London, Ontario, Canada, and has issue living, Andrew Sebastian Alexander, *b* 1982, — Hugo James, *b* 1986. *Residence* – Château de la Chevalerie, 27680 Saint-Samson-de-la-Roque, France.

SISTER LIVING

Hon Joanna Mary, *b* 1948: *m* 1969, Simon Patrick Meredith Hardy, and has issue living, Henry Patrick, *b* 1975, — George Peter, *b* 1978. *Residence* – 23 Baronsmead Rd, SW13.

MOTHER LIVING

KATHLEEN MARY (*Baroness Porritt*), da of late Alfred Sidney Peck, of Spalding, Lincs: *m* 1946, as his 2nd wife, Baron Porritt, GCMG, GCVO, CBE (Life Baron), who *d* 1994. *Residence* – 57 Hamilton Terrace, NW8 9RG.

The 1st baronet, Brig Sir Arthur Espie Porritt, GCMG, GCVO, CBE, *b* 1900, was Surg to HM King George VI 1946-52, Sjt-Surg to HM The Queen 1952-67, and Gov-Gen of NZ 1967-72; Pres BMA 1960-61, Royal Coll of Surgs 1960-63, and Royal Soc of Medicine 1966-67; also Memb Internat Olympic Cttee (Bronze Medallist 100 metres Paris Olympics 1924); *cr Baron Porritt*, of Wanganui, NZ, and of Hampstead, Greater London (Life Baron) 1973; *d* 1994.

PORTAL (UK) 1901, of Malshanger, Church Oakley, co Southampton

Sir JONATHAN FRANCIS PORTAL, 6th *Baronet*; *b* 13 Jan 1953; *s* his father, *Sir* FRANCIS SPENCER, 1984; *ed* Marlborough, and Edin Univ: *m* 1982, Louisa Caroline eldest da of (Frederick) John Charles Gordon Hervey-Bathurst (*see* Hervey-Bathurst, Bt), and has issue.

Arms – Per Saltire azure and gules, a portal flanked by two towers argent; on a chief ermine a crescent of the first betwen two mullets of the second. **Crest** – A portal flanked by two towers argent, each charged with a fleur-de-lis azure, and a wreath of laurel in base vert.
Residence – Burley Wood, Ashe, Basingstoke, Hants RG25 3AG.

SONS LIVING

WILLIAM JONATHAN FRANCIS, *b* 1 Jan 1987. —— Robert Jonathan, *b* 1989, — John Arthur Jonathan, *b* 1993.

BROTHER LIVING

Philip Francis, *b* 1957; *ed* Radley, and Durham Univ: *m* 1989, Catherine Decker, and has issue living, Simon Joe, *b* 1988, — Louis Philip, *b* 1991. Resides in Portugal.

HALF-SISTER LIVING (*Daughter of 5th baronet by 1st wife, Rowena, who d 1948, da of Paul Selby, of Johannesburg*)

(Rowena) Jeanne, *b* 1931: *m* 1957, Richard James Livingstone Altham, of Crunnells Green House, Preston, Hitchin, Herts, and has issue living, David Richard Spencer, *b* 1959, — Robert Patrick James, *b* 1960, — Alastair John Livingstone, *b* 1963.

SISTER LIVING

Mary Jane, *b* 1955.

WIDOW LIVING OF FIFTH BARONET

JANE MARY (*Jane, Lady Portal*), DL (Hants 1991), da of late Albert Henry Williams, OBE (mil), of The Flint House, Langstone, Havant, Hants: *m* 1950, as his 2nd wife, Sir Francis Spencer Portal, 5th Bt, who *d* 1984. *Residence* – Priors Barton Cottage, Kingsgate Rd, Winchester, Hants SO23 9QF.

COLLATERAL BRANCHES LIVING

Grandson of late Brig-Gen Sir Bertram Percy Portal, KCB, DSO (infra):—
Issue of late Maj Melville Edward Bertram Portal, MBE, *b* 1900, *d* 1971: *m* 1926, Hon Cicely Winifred Goschen, who *d* 1980, da of 2nd Viscount Goschen:—
Simon George Melville (9 Kelso Place, W8; Cavalry Club), *b* 1927; late Capt 17th/21st Lancers, Palestine 1948, Korea 1950-51 (attached 8th Hussars), attached Trucial Oman Levies 1955-56; ADC to C-in-C Far East Land Forces 1958-59; a Member of London Stock Exchange 1960-65: *m* 1962 (*m diss* 1971), Gillian, yst da of late Maj James Cyril Aubrey George Dance, MP, of Moreton House, Moreton Morrell, Warwicks, and has issue living, Robert Melville, *b* 1967; actor.

Issue of late Brig-Gen Sir Bertram Percy Portal, KCB, DSO, 3rd son of 1st baronet, *b* 1866, *d* 1949: *m* 1899, Hon Margaret Louisa Littleton, who *d* 1945, da of 3rd Baron Hatherton:—
Charlotte Mary, *b* 1903: *m* 1929, Col Richard James Longfield, late RA, who *d* 1987, and has issue living, Desmond Richard Henry (Paccombe Farm House, Downton, Salisbury, Wilts SP5 3PP; *Club* – Army and Navy), *b* 1931; *ed* Wellington Coll; Brig late RA: *m* 1959, Jennifer, yr da of Clement William Robert Spencer Thomas, of Upper Honeydon, Bedford, and has issue living, James Desmond Spencer *b* 1964: *m* 1993, Rosalind S. G., 2nd da of Michael Pulvertaft, of Sunshine Beach, Qld, Australia, Melanie Louisa *b* 1961: *m* 1986, Simon Jonathan Hoare (and has issue living, Oliver George David *b* 1990, Robert Patrick James *b* 1992), Harriet Sarah *b* 1965, Charlotte Jane *b* 1970. *Residence* – Lower Silton, Gillingham, Dorset. —— Hyacinthe Eveline, *b* 1904: *m* 1929, Malcolm Arthur Æneas Mackintosh, who *d* 1966, and has issue living, Angus Malcolm (St Algar's Farm, W Woodlands, Frome, Somerset), *b* 1930: *m* 1958, Brenda Joyce, el da of Clement William Robert Spencer Thomas (ante), and has had issue, Ewan Angus *b* 1960 *d* 1977, Robert Malcolm *b* 1962, Alexander William *b* 1963, William Aeneas *b* 1973, — Anne Evelyn, *b* 1936: *m* 1986, John Harrison, of Ashford House, Madley, Hereford. *Residence* – Orchard Plot, E Chaldon, Dorset. —— Margaret Cecilia, *b* 1908: *m* 1939, Capt John Shirley Sandys Litchfield-Speer, OBE, RN, who *d* 1993 (having subsequently relinquished the surname of Speer, and used that of Litchfield only), and has issue living, Mark Shirley Portal (The Hermitage, Boxley, Maidstone, Kent) *b* 1940; Lt RN (ret): *m* 1974 (*m diss* 1978), Marcia

Osorio, and has issue living, Vasco *b* 1974, Larissa *b* 1975, — †Sophie Mary Cecilia, *b* 1942: *m* 1970, John Irvin, of 6 Lower Common South, SW15, and *d* 1992, having had issue, Luke Litchfield *b* 1973, Emilie Jane *b* 1970, Amy Hyacinthe *b* 1978, — Virginia Margaret, *b* 1945. *Residence* – Snowfield, Bearsted, Kent. —— Sophie, MBE, *b* 1910; sometime Junior Com ATS; MBE (Mil) 1947. —— Cecilia Violet, *b* 1911: *m* 1937, Lt-Col Nigel Walter Hoare, OBE, TD, who *d* 1988, and has issue living, Hyacinthe Cecilia, *b* 1938: *m* 1961 (*m diss* 1972), Piers Scandrett Harford, son of Sir George Arthur Harford, 2nd Bt, — Joanna Bridget, *b* 1940: *m* 1961, Jeremy Francis Patrick Durham-Matthews, late Capt Irish Gds, of Southington House, Overton, Basingstoke, Hants, and has issue living, John Patrick Nigel *b* 1967, Miranda Elizabeth *b* 1962: *m* 1988, Simon John Hitchman Collins, of The Elms, Tilshead, Salisbury, Wilts (and has issue living, Timothy Walter Hitchman *b* 1988, Isabel Cecilia *b* 1990, Frances Joanna *b* 1994), Lucy Mary *b* 1965: *m* 1989, Richard John Bamford, of 26 Strutton Ground, SW1P 2HR (and has issue living, Constance Amelia *b* 1991, Elizabeth Maria *b* 1993), Catherine Ann *b* 1972, — Louisa Margaret, *b* 1945: *m* 1968, Trevor John Bisset Newman, of The Holt, Ashford Hill, Newbury, Berks, and has issue living, Zachary John Bissett *b* 1972, Henrietta Louisa *b* 1975, Veronica Margaret *b* 1977. *Residence* – Southington House, Overton, Basingstoke, Hants.

The 1st baronet, Sir Wyndham Spencer Portal (7th son of late John Portal, JP, DL, of Laverstoke, Hants), was Chm of London and S-W Railway Co, and *d* 1905. The 2nd baronet, Sir William Wyndham, was Chm of Portals, Ltd and Dep Chm of London and S-W Railways. The 3rd baronet, Sir Wyndham Raymond, GCMG, DSO, MVO, was Managing Director of Portals Ltd, a Director of Great Railway Co, and Min of Works and Buildings and First Commr of Works 1942-4, and was created *Baron Portal*, of Laverstoke, co Southampton (peerage of United Kingdom) 1935, and *Viscount Portal*, of Laverstoke, co Southampton (peerage of United Kingdom 1945). He *d* 1949, when the Barony and Viscountcy became ext and the Baronetcy devolved upon his uncle, Sir Spencer John, 4th baronet, who was Pres of Trustee Savings Bank Asso, and a Dir of Portals. His only surv son, Sir Francis Spencer, 5th Bt, DL Hants 1967, and High Sheriff 1963, was Chm and later Dir of Portals Ltd 1949-68, Dir of Wiggins Teape, and Royal Exchange Assurance Co, Pres and Chm Southern Region YMCA, etc.

HORSBRUGH-PORTER (UK) 1902, of Merrion Square, City and Co of Dublin

Sir JOHN SIMON HORSBRUGH-PORTER, 4th *Baronet*; *b* 18 Dec 1938; *s* his father, Sir ANDREW MARSHALL, DSO, 1986; *ed* Winchester, and Trin Coll, Camb: *m* 1964, Lavinia Rose, 2nd da of Ralph Meredyth Turton, of Kildale Hall, Whitby (*see* V Chetwynd, colls), and has issue.

Arms – Argent, on a bend azure between in chief a portcullis, and in base two keys saltirewise sable, three bells of the field. **Crest** – On a fasces fessewise a cherub, all proper.
Residence – Bowers Croft, Coleshill, Amersham, Bucks HP7 0LS.

SON LIVING

ANDREW ALEXANDER MARSHALL, *b* 19 Jan 1971; *ed* Winchester.

DAUGHTERS LIVING

Anna Josephine, *b* 1965: *m* 1993, Nicholas J.F. McNulty, son of John McNulty, of Formby, Merseyside. —— Zoë Mary, *b* 1967: *m* 1994, Nicholas S. Curtis, only son of Andrew Curtis, of Knutsford, Cheshire.

SISTERS LIVING (*Daughters of 3rd baronet*)

Susan (*Lady Barlow*), *b* 1936: *m* 1962, Sir John Kemp Barlow, 3rd Bt, of Bulkeley Grange, Malpas, Cheshire, and has issue (*see* Barlow, Bt, *cr* 1907). —— Caroline Elaine, *b* 1940: *m* 1986, Col J. B. Henderson, of Cottage-on-the-Green, Barton-on-the-Heath, Moreton-in-Marsh, Glos GL56 0PJ.

COLLATERAL BRANCHES LIVING

Granddaughters of late Alexander Horsbrugh Porter, 2nd son of 1st baronet:—
Issue of late William Eric Horsbrugh Porter, *b* 1905, *d* 1985: *m* 1929, Monica Ruth Lisalie, who *d* 1986, da of late Capt Anthony Fitz Maude (*see* V Hawarden, colls):—
Dympna Monica, *b* 1931: *m* 1st, 1950, Patrick St John Brawn, who *d* 19—; 2ndly, 1975, Richard Jones, and has issue living, (by 1st *m*) Daniel, *b* 1954, — Michael Patrick, *b* 1958, — Anna Livia, *b* 1955, — Isabel Frances, *b* 1965. —— Phyllida, *b* 1934: *m* 1956, Donald Kenneth McAlpine, of 12 Martindale Rd, SW12, and has issue living, Louisa Ngaire, *b* 1958, — Fiona Caroline, *b* 1961.

The 1st baronet, Rt Hon Sir Andrew Marshall Porter (son of late Rev John Scott Porter), was Master of the Rolls in Ireland 1883-1906 and sat as MP for co Londonderry (*L*) Dec 1881 to Dec 1883. The 2nd baronet, Sir John Scott Porter, assumed the additional surname of Horsbrugh 1911.

POUND (UK) 1905, of Stanmore, co Middlesex

By good faith and vigilance

FIDE·ET·VIGILANTIA

Sir JOHN DAVID POUND, 5th *Baronet*; *b* 1 Nov 1946; *s* his father, *Sir* DEREK ALLEN, 1980; *ed* Burebank Sch, Aylsham, Norfolk: *m* 1st, 1968 (*m diss* 1978), Heather Frances O'Brien, only da of Harry Jackson Dean; 2ndly, 1978, Penelope Ann, el da of Grahame Rayden, and has issue by 1st and 2nd *m*.

Arms – Argent a sword erect proper surmounted of a fesse gules, thereon three mullets argent, in chief two boars' heads erased sable. **Crest** – A castle proper, charged with a shield argent, thereon a sword erect proper.
Residence – Coppice Lodge, Lythe Hill, Shrewsbury, Shropshire SY3 0BS.

SONS LIVING *(By 1st marriage)*

ROBERT JOHN, *b* 12 Feb 1973.

(By 2nd marriage)

Christopher James, *b* 1982. —— Nicholas Edward, *b* 1986.

SISTER LIVING

Diana Marilyn, *b* 1944: *m* 1966, Keble Stuart Paterson, and has issue living, Timothy Keble, *b* 1968, — Caroline Elizabeth, *b* 1971. *Residence* – Hadley House, Beche Rd, Cambridge.

WIDOW LIVING OF FOURTH BARONET

JOAN AMY (*Joan, Lady Pound*) (Corner Farmhouse, Watton Rd, Shipdham, Thetford, Norfolk IP25 7RL), da of James Woodthorpe, of Boston, Lincs: *m* 1942, Sir Derek Allen Pound, 4th Bt, who *d* 1980.

The 1st baronet, Sir John Pound, head of the firm of John Pound and Co, portmanteau manufacturers, of 81-4, Leadenhall Street, EC, was Sheriff of London 1895-6, and Lord Mayor of London 1904-5, and the 2nd baronet, Sir (John) Lulham, was an Alderman of City of London (Aldgate Ward) 1915-21. The 3rd baronet, Sir Allen Leslie, was a Solicitor and sole member of the firm of Pound & Pound, of Egham and Bracknell.

POWELL (UK) 1897, of Wimpole Street, St Marylebone, co London
(Name pronounced "Poel")

Anima in amicis una

One mind amongst

friends

Sir NICHOLAS FOLLIOTT DOUGLAS POWELL, 4th *Baronet*; *b* 17 July 1935; *s* his father *Sir* RICHARD GEORGE DOUGLAS, MC, 1980; *ed* Gordonstoun; late Lt Welsh Gds: *m* 1st, 1960 (*m diss* 1987), Daphne Jean, yr da of Maj George Henry Errington, MC, of Chadwell Hall, Essex, and Chadwell, Ruwa, Zimbabwe; 2ndly, 1987, Davina Hyacinth Berners, elder twin da of Michael Edward Ranulph Allsopp (*see* B Hindlip, colls) and has issue by 1st and 2nd *m*.

Arms – Gules, a lion rampant within a bordure engrailed or, in the dexter chief point a mullet argent within an annulet of the second. **Crest** – A lion's head erased argent, charged with a collar flory counter flory gules.
Residence – Hillside Estate, Bromley, Zimbabwe.

SONS LIVING *(By 1st marriage)*

JAMES RICHARD DOUGLAS, *b* 17 Oct 1962: *ed* Peterhouse, Zimbabwe, and RAC Cirencester: *m* 1991, Susanna Frances, eldest da of David Murray Threipland, and has issue living, Douglas James Folliott, *b* 22 Oct 1992.

(by 2nd marriage)

Benjamin Ranulph Berners, *b* 1989.. —— Oliver Michael Folliott, *b* 1990.

DAUGHTER LIVING *(By 1st marriage)*

Catherine Mary, *b* 1961: *m* 1991, Walter Ruprecht, eldest son of Joseph Ruprecht, and has issue living, Anastasia Laura, *b* 1993.

(by 2nd marriage)

Mamie Josephine Berners, *b* 1992.

SISTERS LIVING

Bryony Josephine Anne (19 Ackmar Rd, SW6 4UP), *b* 1933: *m* 1955 (*m diss* 1968), Christopher Lucas Thomasson, and has issue living, Samuel Charles, *b* 1956, — Mary Elizabeth, *b* 1958. —— Julia Mary, *b* 1943: *m* 1973, Jeremy John Twynam, of

Kitemore House, Faringdon, Oxon SN7 8HR, and has issue living, Henry Thomas Alexander, *b* 1977, — Leonora Mary Alexandra, *b* 1975.

WIDOW LIVING OF THIRD BARONET

Alice Maria, el da of Wilhelmus den Bode, of Utrecht: *m* 1st, 1980, as his second wife, Sir Richard George Douglas Powell, 3rd Bt, MC, who *d* 1980; 2ndly, 1982, Lt-Col Donald John Arthur Grant.

The 1st baronet, Sir Richard Douglas Powell, KCVO, MD, FRCP, was Physician Extraor to Queen Victoria 1887-99, and Physician-in-Ord 1899-1901, Physician Extraor to King Edward VII 1901-7, and Physician-in-Ord 1907-10, and to King George V 1910-25; also Pres of Roy Coll of Physicians 1905-10. The 3rd baronet, Sir Richard George Douglas Powell, MC, was Dir-Gen of Inst of Directors 1954-74: *m* 1st, 1933, Elizabeth Josephine, who *d* 1979, only da of late Lt-Col Osmond Robert McMullen, CMG, of Presdales Hall, Ware, Herts; 2ndly, 1980, Alice Maria, el da of Wilhelmus den Bode, of Utrecht.

POWER (UK) 1836, of Kilfane, Kilkenny (Dormant 1928)

Sir GEORGE POWER, 7th *Baronet, d* 1928, and the next heir, his cousin, GERVASE PARKER POWER, is believed to have died in America some years ago. At the time of going to press no name appears on the Official Roll of Baronets in respect of this title.

COLLATERAL BRANCH LIVING

Grandchildren of late Ambrose William Bushe Power, eldest son of Ven Ambrose Power, Archdeacon of Lismore, 4th son of 1st baronet:—
Issue of late Maj Ambrose Grattan Power, *b* 1887, *d* 1926: *m* 1908, Ada Mary, who *d* 1968, yst da of late Richard Austin Cooper Chadwick, of Ballinard, co Tipperary:—
Anthony Ambrose Grattan (19 Langley Way, Hemingford Grey, Huntingdon, Cambs, PE18 9DB), *b* 1917; *ed* Charterhouse; Maj (ret) R Anglian Regt: *m* 1961, Sarah Judith, only da of late Joseph Halford Gough, of Cookham, Berks, and has issue living, Lavinia Frances, *b* 1964, — Georgina Rachel, *b* 1966, — Amy Katherine, *b* 1968. —— Iris Frances Mary, *b* 1914: *m* 1943, as his 2nd wife, Capt Thomas Abdy Combe, Gren Gds, who *d* 1983. *Residence* – Oaks Corner, Hemingford Abbots, Huntingdon, Cambs PE18 9AP.

Sir John Power, 4th baronet, died of wounds received at Lindley during S African War 1900, and Sir Derrick, 5th baronet, died in S Africa during the same war 1902.

POWER (UK) 1841, of Roe Buck House, co Dublin (Extinct 1930)

Sir THOMAS TALBOT POWER, 6th and last *Baronet.*

DAUGHTER LIVING OF THIRD BARONET

Eileen Mareli, *b* 1880: *m* 1902, Major Durham Simpson Matthews, OBE, JP, who *d* 1950. *Residence* – 39 Hill Street, Berkeley Square, W1.

POWER (UK) 1924, of Newlands Manor, Milford, Southampton

For my country always

Sir ALASTAIR JOHN CECIL POWER, 4th *Baronet*; *b* 15 Aug 1958; *s* his father, *Sir* JOHN PATRICK MCLANNAHAN, 1984.

Arms – Or, on a bend gules between two foxes' heads erased proper three crescents of the first; on a chief of the second as many escallops argent. **Crest** – A stag's head erased proper, gorged with an antique crown and between the attires a cross patée or.
Residence –

BROTHER LIVING

ADAM PATRICK CECIL, *b* 22 March 1963.

SISTER LIVING

Belinda Jane, *b* 1960.

AUNT LIVING (*Daughter of 2nd baronet*)

Hilary Diana Cecil (*Countess of Buchan*), *b* 1930: *m* 1957, 17th Earl of Buchan, of Newnham House, Basingstoke, Hants.

GREAT UNCLE LIVING (*son of 1st baronet*)

George Frederick Cecil McLannahan, *b* 1919; *ed* Eton and in Switzerland; formerly acting Maj Welch Regt; Liaison Officer to RAF 1940; Capt late War Dept Fleet (salvage explosives); Councillor of Lymington Borough 1948-65, and a Member of Co Council Adoption Cttee 1950-65, and HM Harbour Commr 1960-65; Founder of Sea Rescue Ser, now Inshore Rescue RNLI; a Gov of Wessex Hosp Group, a Member of Territorial Cttee (Army South), and a Gov of County Council Schs in Hants; Ch Eng 1965, AFCA; Underwriting Member of Lloyd's 1977-87; assumed the additional name of McLannahan 1954; (Arms enrolled at the College of Arms 1969: **Arms** - Or on a Bend Gules between two Foxes heads erased proper three Crescents of the first on a Chief of the second as many Escallops Argent impaling those of Quarterly 1 and 4 Vair Argent and Sable in Chief two inescutcheons Gules each charged with a Cross Paty fitchy Or (*Stanton*); 2, Per pale nebuly Azure and Sable three demi Lions couped each holding between the paws a Cross crosslet fitchy Or (*Harrison*); 3, Gironny of eight Argent and Vert a Lion rampant reguardant Erminois (*Evans*). **Crest** - On a wreath of the colour a Stag's head proper gorged with an Antique Crown and between the attires a cross paty fitchy Or. **Badge** - A Sprig of Broom and a Sprig of Shamrock saltirewise proper enfiled by a Circlet Or): *m* 1st, 1940 (*m diss* 1947), Joy Mervyn, da of late Dr Geoffrey Noott, of Fern Down Hill, Ferndown, Dorset; 2ndly, 1948, (Monica) Angela Mary, who *d* 1990, da of late Lt-Com Henry Guy Stanton, RN (ret) (B Castlemaine, colls), and has issue living, (by 1st *m*) David George Cecil (Islands, Acedia, Casares, Malaga, Costa del Sol, Spain), *b* 1941; *ed* Repton: *m* 1968, Jennifer Anne, da of late Cdr Thompson, of Jersey, and has issue living, January Georgina *b* 1979, — Mervyn Peter, *b* 1944; *ed* Repton: *m* 1976, Diana Louise, da of late Graham Alexander Michael, of Wigston, Leicester, and has issue living, Henry George Alexander *b* 1978, Camilla Joy Cynthia *b* 1976, — (by 2nd *m*) Bridie Maureen McLannahan, *b* 1951: *m* 1972, Joseph Gavin Bonello, of Riverside, Westover Lane, Ringwood, Hants, and has two adopted children, Michael Gavin James Stuart *b* 1976, George Gavin Richard Matthew *b* 1977, — Sheena Patricia McLannahan, *b* 1954: *m* 1975, Capt Peter Jeremy Walton Ledger, RM (ret) of Westgate House, Western Rd, Canford Cliffs, Poole, Dorset, and has issue living, Araminta Elizabeth Walton *b* 1984, — Louisa Roxane McLannahan (83 High Town Rd, Ringwood, Hants BH21 1NS), *b* 1957: *m* 1st, 1976, Robert Derek Philip (Metropolitan Police), who was *k* 1983; 2ndly, 1987 (*m diss* 1991), Jeremy David Barrell, BSc, and has issue living, (by 1st *m*) Niesha Roxane McLannahan *b* 1983, (by 2nd *m*) Sussana Louise Roxane *b* 1988. *Residence* – 3 Burnett Rd, Christchurch, Dorset BH23 2DL. *Clubs* – Royal Yachting Assocn, RN Sailing Assocn, Keyhaven Yacht Club, Club Nautico Estepona (Spain).

GREAT AUNT LIVING (*daughter of 1st baronet*)

Lilian Hartley Cecil: *m* 1930, Paul Van Kleeck Kingston, MD, who *d* 1988, and has issue living, Peter Charles (688 Hillsdale Av, Toronto, Canada), *b* 1945: *m* 1983, Nancy Allison, da of Oscar Clark, and has issue living, Alexander *b* (twin) 1984, Christopher *b* (twin) 1984, Philip *b* 1988, — Timothy Paul, *b* 1949: *m* 1st, 1983 (*m diss* 1987), Kathleen Procopio; 2ndly, 1992, Tani Bowman, — Katharine Martha, *b* 1943: *m* 1968 (*m diss* 1993), Jack Calvin Hartje, PhD, of 6120 San José Blvd W, Jacksonville, Florida, USA, and has issue living, Neil *b* 1978, Naomi *b* 1974. *Residence* – 400 N Flagler Drive, Apt 1105, W Palm Beach, Florida 33401, USA.

MOTHER LIVING

Melanie, adopted da of Hon Richard Alastair Erskine (*see* E Buchan): *m* 1957 (*m diss* 1967), as his 1st wife, Sir John Patrick McLannahan Power, 3rd Bt, who *d* 1984.

The 1st baronet, Sir John Cecil Power (son of William Taylor Power, of Belfast, co Down, and Sheen, Surrey) sat as MP for Wimbledon (*U*) 1924-45, and was Founder of Roy Institute of International Affairs. Sir Ivan McLannahan Cecil Power, 2nd Bt, was Chm of various industrial Cos in Union of S Africa and a Co Councillor for London. Sir John Patrick McLannahan Power, 3rd Bt, was a Dir of Arthur Beale, Ltd.

PRESCOTT (UK) 1938, of Godmanchester, co Huntingdon

Sir MARK PRESCOTT, 3rd *Baronet*, son of late Maj (William Robert) Stanley Prescott, MP, yr son of 1st baronet; *b* 3 March 1948; *s* his uncle, Sir RICHARD STANLEY, 1965; *ed* Harrow.

Arms – Per chevron pean and erminois, on a chief or, a rose gules, barbed and seeded proper, between two leopards' faces sable. **Crest** – Upon the battlements of a tower proper, a leopard statant sable.
Residence – Heath House, Moulton Rd, Newmarket CB8 8DU.

AUNT LIVING (*daughter of 1st baronet*)

Louise Bernice, MBE, *b* 1903; MBE (1978): *m* 1928, Reginald Gray, of 24 St Katherine's Mews, Totnes, Devon, and has issue living, David Stanley, *b* 1931.

The 1st baronet, Col Sir William (Henry) Prescott, CBE, DL (son of John Prescott, of Blackburn), was an Alderman and Chm of Middlesex County Council, Chm of Metropolitan Water Board, and of Lee Conservancy Board, High Sheriff for Middlesex 1929, and for Cambs and Hunts 1938, and MP for N Div of Tottenham (*Co U*) 1918-22.

He conquers who endures

Prescott-Westcar, see Westcar.

PRESTON (UK) 1815, of Beeston St Lawrence, Norfolk

Sir RONALD DOUGLAS HILDEBRAND PRESTON, 7th Baronet; *b* 9 Oct 1916; *s* his father, Sir THOMAS HILDEBRAND, OBE, 1976; *ed* Westminster, Trin Coll, Camb (MA Hons), and Ecole des Sciences Politiques, Paris; 1939-45 War in Middle East and Italy (8th Army), Austria and Allied Control Commn to Bulgaria; late Maj Intelligence Corps; Reuters Correspondent in Belgrade 1948-53, Times Correspondent in Vienna and E Europe 1953-60, and in Tokyo 1960-63; Diplo Ser 1963-76: *m* 1st, 1954 (*m diss* 1971), Smilya Stefanovic, of Belgrade, Yugoslavia; 2ndly, 1972, Pauleen Jane, da of late Paul Lurcott, of Albany Cottage, Fairwarp, Sussex.

Arms – Ermine, on a chief sable three crescents or. **Crest** – A crescent or.
Clubs – Travellers', Norfolk, Tokio.

SISTER LIVING

Stella Tatiana Gertrude, *b* 1920; former opera singer and UN civil servant: *m* 1962, Eugene Hartzell, Mus Bach and Mus M (Yale Univ), of Pfarrhofgasse 13/21, Vienna III, and has issue living, Eugenie Belinda Tamara, *b* 1963, — Melanie Anne Sonia, *b* 1964.

DAUGHTERS LIVING OF FIFTH BARONET

Juliet Mary (*Hon Mrs Richard N. Manners*), *b* 1921: *m* 1945, Hon Richard Neville Manners, of Cromer Hall, Norfolk (*see* B Manners). —— Patricia Evelyn (Home Farm House, Cromer, Norfolk NR27 9JG), *b* 1923: *m* 1962, John Louis Benedict Todhunter, OBE, who *d* 1980 (B Kenyon, colls).

I hope for a brighter light

COLLATERAL BRANCHES LIVING

Grandchildren of late Col Philip Henry Hulton Preston (*infra*):—
Issue of late Lt-Col Philip Henry Herbert Hulton Preston, OBE, MC, *b* 1914, *d* 1973: *m* 1st, 1940, Katherine Janet, who *d* 1968, da of Dr B. C. Broomhall; 2ndly, 19—, Jean Mary, da of Harold Neale Turner:—
(By 1st *m*) PHILIP CHARLES HENRY HULTON, *b* 31 Aug 1946; *ed* Nautical Coll, Pangbourne: *m* 1980, Kirsi Sylvi Annikki, da of late Eino Yrjö Pullinen, of Mukkulankaju 29, F46 Lahti, Finland, and has issue living, Philip Thomas Henry Hulton, *b* 1990, — Katherine Louise Tuula, *b* 1982, — Emily Jean Charlotte, *b* 1985. —— Caroline Elizabeth, *b* 1943: *m* 1974, Paul Louis Edelin de la Praudiere, of 128 Palewell Park, SW14 8JH, and has issue living, Philip Louis, *b* 1975, — William Francis Paul, *b* 1977.

Granddaughter of late Lt-Col Henry Edward Preston, el son of Thomas Edward Preston, 2nd son of 1st baronet:—
Issue of late Col Philip Henry Hulton Preston, *b* 1879, *d* 1963: *m* 1914, Dorothy May (Acer Place, Ash, Aldershot, Hants), only da of late Brig-Gen Herbert Alexander Kaye Jennings, CIE, RA:—
Marjorie, *b* 1917: *m* 1939, Miles Pacey Cheales, of Willow Cottage, Broad St, Guildford, Surrey, and has issue living, Justina Victoria, *b* 1945, — Briony Margaret, *b* 1948, — Mary Henrietta Miles, *b* 1951: *m* 1971, Philip Alistair Barter, and has issue living, Oliver Philip Tom *b* 1975, Alexander John *b* 1975, — Alexandra Marjorie, *b* 1952: *m* 1976, Charles Thornton Hardy.

The 1st baronet, Sir Thomas, was a son of Henry Hulton, of Andover, by Elizabeth, eldest daughter of Isaac Preston of Beeston St Lawrence, whose estates he inherited, and in 1804 assumed the name and arms of Preston. The Prestons have held Beeston since 1640. According to family tradition, Jacob Preston was one of four confidants who attended Charles I during his imprisonment, and who was presented by that monarch, as a last mark of attachment, with an emerald ring still preserved in the family.

PREVOST (UK) 1805, of Belmont, Hampshire
(Name pronounced "Prev-o")

Servatum cineri
Kept for the dead

Sir CHRISTOPHER GERALD PREVOST, 6th *Baronet*; *b* 25 July 1935; *s* his father, *Sir* GEORGE JAMES AUGUSTINE, 1985; *ed* Cranleigh; late 60th Regt: *m* 1964, Dolores Nelly, only da of late Dezo Hoffmann, of 1 Crispian Close, Neasden Lane, NW10 1PW, and has issue.

Arms – Azure, a dexter arm in fesse issuing from a cloud in the sinister fesse point, the hand grasping a sword erect proper, pommel and hilt or, in chief two mullets argent. **Crest** – A demi-lion rampant azure, charged on the shoulder with a mural crown or, the sinister paw grasping a sword erect as in the arms. **Supporters** – Two grenadiers of the 16th Foot, each supporting with exterior hand a flag flying, that on the dexter flying to the sinister and inscribed "West Indies," and that on the sinister gules, to the dexter, and inscribed "Canada." **Residence** – Box 3072, Vale da Rabelho, 8200 Albufeira, Portugal.

SON LIVING

NICHOLAS MARC, *b* 13 March 1971.

DAUGHTER LIVING

Ruth Annette, *b* 1964: *m* 1986, Steven Walter Wrench, of 18 Swallowdale, Great Clacton, Essex CO15 4HA, and has issue living, Laura Annette, *b* 1988.

HALF BROTHERS LIVING (*Sons of 5th baronet by 3rd marriage*)

James William, *b* 1952, *ed* Aldenham. —— Edward Charles, *b* 1953; *ed* Aldenham.

SISTER LIVING

Felicity Jane, *b* 1936: *m* 1970, Hisham Pilus, of 192 Jalan Terasek, Bangsar, Kuala Lumpur 59100, Malaysia, and has issue living, Muhammad Yusuf, *b* 1977, — Sofia Jane, *b* 1972, — Sarah Louise, *b* 1974.

WIDOW LIVING OF FIFTH BARONET

PATRICIA BETTY (*Patricia, Lady Prevost*), da of late William Porter, of Kilburn, NW: *m* 1952, as his 3rd wife, Sir George James Augustine Prevost, 5th Bt, who *d* 1985. *Residence* – 45 Carneton Close, Quantock, Newquay, Cornwall.

COLLATERAL BRANCH LIVING

Issue of late Lieut-Col George Herbert Prevost, Indian Army, yr son of 3rd baronet, *b* 1868, *d* 1951: *m* 1901, Katharine Alice, who *d* 1911, da of W. R. Glennie, formerly of Chilbolton, Hants:—
Constance Charlotte, *b* (twin) 1911.

The 1st baronet, Lt-Gen Sir George Prevost (el son of Gen Augustine Prevost, of Geneva, who settled in England), was Col of the 60th Regt, Gov of Canada and Commander of the Forces in British North America. The Supporters were granted in 1816 by King George III to the widow of the 1st baronet in lieu of a Peerage, as Lady Prevost felt she did not have sufficient means to support the dignity.

PRICE (UK) 1815, of Trengwainton, Cornwall

Sir FRANCIS CARADOC ROSE PRICE, 7th *Baronet*, *b* 9 Sept 1950; *s* his father, *Sir* ROSE FRANCIS, 1979; *ed* Eton, Melbourne Univ (LLB), and Alberta Univ (LLM): *m* 1975, (Hon Madam Justice) Marguerite Jean, da of Roy Samuel Trussler, of Victoria, BC, and has issue.

𝕬rms – Sable, a chevron erminois between three spear-heads argent, embrued at the points proper. 𝕮rest – A dragon's head vert, erased gules, holding in the mouth a sinister hand erect couped at the wrist and dropping blood all proper. *Residence* – 9677-95 Avenue, Edmonton, Alberta, Canada, T6C 2A3. *Clubs* – Centre Club and Faculty Club (Edmonton)

All depends on God

DAUGHTERS LIVING

Adrienne Calantha Rose, *b* 1976. —— Megan Kathleen Rose, *b* 1977. —— Glynis Nicola Rose, *b* 1982.

BROTHER LIVING

NORMAN WILLIAM ROSE (73 Fawnbrake Av, SE24 0BE), *b* 17 March 1953; *ed* Eton, and Gordonstoun: *m* 1987, Charlotte Louise, da of Randolph Rex Bivar Baker, of Yelverton, Devon, and has issue living, Benjamin William Rose, *b* 16 Sept 1989, — Timothy Charles Rose, *b* 1991.

AUNTS LIVING (*Daughters of 5th baronet*)

Helen Jocelyn, *b* 1920: *m* 1950, Maj-Gen Logan Scott-Bowden, CBE, DSO, MC, of Prospect Farm, Cottesmore Lane, Ewelme, Oxon, and has issue living, Robert Logan, MBE, *b* 1955; Lt-Col Royal Scots; served NI (MBE 1992): *m* 1980, Nicola Frances, yr da of Maj H. T. K. Phillips, of Longcot, Oxon, and has issue living, Christopher William *b* 1987, Camilla Frances *b* 1984, — James Russell, *b* 1958; Maj WG: *m* 1988, Nicola Jane, yr da of Anthony J.V. Shepherd, of Park Farm, Alderley, Glos, and has issue living, Harry Russell *b* 1989, Edward Jonathan *b* 1991, Arthur James *b* 1993, — Peter William, *b* 1962, — Claire Anne, *b* 1952: *m* 1978, Charles John Maitland Wilmoth, of 3 Old House, Merriscourt, Churchill, Oxon, and has issue living, George James *b* 1980, Harriette Jocelyn *b* 1984, — Alexandra Marjorie, *b* 1960: *m* 1990, Andrew H. C. Ballingall, of Flat 3, 5 Sinclair Gdns, Shepherds Bush, W14 0AU, only son of of late H. Campbell Ballingall, of Simonstown, Cape Province, S Africa. —— Anne Charlotte (14 rue du Pont aux Choux, Paris, France), *b* 1927.

WIDOW LIVING OF SIXTH BARONET

KATHLEEN JUNE (*June, Lady Price*) (Dormer Cottage, Park Rd, Stoke Poges, Bucks), da of late Norman William Hutchinson, of Toorak, Melbourne, Australia: *m* 1949, Sir Rose Francis Price, 6th baronet, who *d* 1979.

COLLATERAL BRANCHES LIVING

Issue of late Maj William Russell Rose Price, yr son of 5th baronet, *b* 1916, *d* 1985: *m* 1st, 1945 (*m diss* 1953), Joan Ross-Hurst, of Calcutta; 2ndly, 1954, Aline Flora (10 St Ronan's Rd, Sheffield), da of David Silverman:—
(By 2nd *m*) Gillian Isobel, *b* 1959. —— Julia Jane, *b* 1962.

Grandchildren of late Capt Francis Henry Talbot Price (infra):—
Issue of late Leslie Frederick Talbot Price, *b* 1904, *d* 1972: *m* 1924, (*m diss* 1953), Hon Diana Frederica, who *d* 1979, da of late Hon Maurice Raymond Gifford, CMG (*see* B Gifford):—
Maurice Rose Talbot (96A Victoria Rd W, Pennant Hills, NSW 2120, Australia), *b* 1929: *m* 1959, Elaine, only da of C. J. Burford, of Kuala Lumpur, Malaya, and Sydney, Australia, and has issue living, Martin Paul, *b* 1961, — Michael John, *b* 1964. —— Michael Henry Charles Rose (9 McCrea Pl, Turramurra, NSW 2074, Australia), *b* 1932: *m* 1962, Lyndsay June, da of C. L. Messner, of Harpenden, Herts. —— Pamela, *b* 1925: *m* 1944, F/Lt John William Reid, DFC, RNZAF, and has issue living, Martin James, *b* 1946, — William John, *b* 1952, — Julia, *b* 1948, — Diana, *b* 1949, — Isabella Patricia, *b* 1957.

Granddaughter of late Capt Henry Talbot Price, RN, brother of 3rd baronet:—
Issue of late Capt Francis Henry Talbot Price, *b* 1872, *d* 1930: *m* 1899, Florence, only da of Frederick Hurdle:—
Olive May Talbot, *b* 1900: *m* 1924, Count St John Vivian Beaumont de Beaufort Molyneux (*cr* Holy Roman Empire 1710), who *d* 1962.

Granddaughters of late Col Thomas Caradoc Rose Price, CB, 3rd son of John Price, 4th son of 1st baronet:—
Issue of late Brig-Gen Thomas Rose Caradoc Price, CMG, DSO, *b* 1875, *d* 1949: *m* 1911, Dorothy Patience, who *d* 1969, only da of late Sir Henry William Verey:—
Mary Dorothy Rose, *b* 1918: *m* 1948, John Dugdale Holt Wiseman, MA, PhD, formerly Dep Keeper of Mineralogy, British Museum of Natural History, and has issue living, John Paul Holt (Coarsewell Farm, Ugborough, Ivybridge, Devon), *b* 1949; *ed* Shrewsbury: *m* 1989, Jane Trant, and has issue living, Catherine Jane *b* 1990. *Residence* – Hornbeam House, Waltham St Lawrence, Berks.
Issue of late Lieut-Com Vivian Franklin Lyon Rose Price, RN, *b* 1881; *d* on active ser 1915: *m* 1912, Jean Purvis Mills, who *d* 1939:—
Vivian Judith Elizabeth Rose (111A Cranmer Court, SW3), *b* 1915: *m* 1937, Col George Francis Taylor, CBE, who *d* 1979, and has issue living, Jeremy Vivian George, *b* 1940: *m* 1967, Sally, da of John Parnell, and has issue living, Gemma Vivian *b* 1971, — Sarah Jane Elizabeth, *b* 1943: *m* 1968, Thomas Peart, and has issue living, Rachel *b* 1969, Scarlett *b* 1971, — Anna-Lisa, *b* 1949.

Grandchildren of late Brig-Gen Thomas Rose Caradoc Price, CMG, DSO (ante):—
Issue of late Lt-Col Robert ROSE PRICE, DSO, OBE, Welsh Gds, *b* 1912, *d* 1988: *m* 1948, Hon Maureen Maude Tower Butler (98 Old Church St, SW3), 2nd da of 27th Baron Dunboyne:—
(Thomas Geoffrey) Timothy Rose (The Wadfield, Winchcombe, Cheltenham, Glos), *b* 1948; *ed* Eton: *m* 1975, Leila Anne Katherine, da of Sir Richard Guy Carne Rasch, 3rd Bt, and has issue living, Dominic Charles Rose, *b* 1978, — Patrick David Caradoc, *b* 1980, — Katherine Leila Sarah, *b* 1985. —— Sarah Maureen Rose, *b* 1947: *m* 1968, Michael John Burrell,

barrister-at-law, of 6 St Peter's Sq, W6, and has issue living, James Michael, b 1976, — Amanda Caroline, b 1971, — Nicola Sarah, b 1973.
Issue of late Dennistoun John Franklyn Rose Price (actor Dennis Price), b 1915, d 1973: m 1939 (m diss 1950), Joan Schofield:—
Susan Joan Rose, b 1940: m 1967, Thomas H. Mapp, of 85 Langham Rd, Teddington, Middx, and has issue living, Joel Dennis, b 1979, — Kate Miranda, b 1972. —— Tessa Alexandra Rose, b 1943: m 1965, Hugh Thomas Burnett, FCA, of 36 Wilbury Villas, Hove, E Sussex BN3 6GD, and has issue living, Rupert Thomas, b 1971, — Lucy Eleanor, b 1966: m 1990, Roger Bracken, and has issue living, Sophie Madeleine b 1992, — Emily Tamelayne, b 1968.

Grandson of late George Price, 5th son of 1st baronet:—
Issue of late Cyril Oliver Rose Price, MBE, b 1880, d 1961: m 1910, Edith Muriel, who d 1956, da of late Donald Campbell Ridout, of Toronto:—
George Donald Rose (26 Utkinton Rd, Tarporley, Ches), b 1911; ed Haileybury, and Emmanuel Coll, Camb (MA): m 1947, Dorothy Christine, da of late Major Eric Fairclough, DSO.

Grandson of late Thomas Price, 6th son of 1st baronet:—
Issue of late Arthur Henry Price, b 1850, d 1916: m 1872, Minna, da of late Samuel P. Oxley, of Valparaiso:—
Samuel Percy, b 1878: m 1st, 1906, Margaret Elinor, who d 1906, da of late James Grant, of Dunheanish, Oban; 2ndly, 1912, Anita, da of T. A. Mackay, of Concepcion, Chile, and has issue living, (by 2nd m) John Samuel, b 1921; is Pilot Officer Chilean Air Force (Reserve): m 1943, Joan Margaret, who d 1954, da of Frank Williams, of Cochabamba, Bolivia, and has issue living, Samuel John Rose b 1950, Peter Rose b 1954, Anita Margaret Rose b 1944, Sandra Joan Rose b 1947, Jennifer Rose b 1953, — Michael Patrick, b 1922; is Pilot Officer Chilean Air Force (Reserve): m 1945, Evelyn Mabel, da of late Eric Saffery, of Talcahuano, Chile, and has issue living, Anthony Samuel Patrick Rose b 1953, Thomas Eric Rose, b 1956, Heather Evelyn Rose b 1946, Marylyn Rose b 1949, Gillian Rose b 1951, — Carmen, b 1915: m 1st, 1935, Lt Oswald Marcus Cheke, DSC, RN, who was ka 1941; 2ndly, 1942 (m diss 1951), James Byrne; 3rdly, 1953, Manuel Hidalgo, and has issue living, (by 1st m) Marcus Oswald b 1936, Francis Patrick b 1940, (by 2nd m) Jacqueline b 1945, Rosanna Amber b 1949, (by 3rd m) Ana Manuela b 19—, Maria Victoria (twin) b 19—, — Pearl Rose, b 1917: m 1st, 1938, Rudolph Seyler; 2ndly, 1947, Edward George Yriberry, and has issue living, (by 1st m) Christopher Louis b 1939, (by 2nd m) Pearl Anita b 1954. Residence – 462 Casilla, Valparaiso, Chile.

Grandchildren of late Arthur Henry Price (ante):—
Issue of late Arthur Douglas Price, b 1873, d 1951: m 1st, 1901 (m diss 1922), Wilhelmine Marion, who d 1955, da of late Robert Adolphe Claude, of Valparaiso; 2ndly, 1922, Augustine Laetitia, da of Jacques Benoit:—
(By 1st m) Violet Marion Rose, b 1902: m 1926, Joaqúin Santiago Andrés Monuz Arlegui, who d 1939, and has issue living, Joaquin Santiago Federico, b 1930, — Veronica Marion, b 1927: m 1st, 1951, Alexander Edmund Gough Gubbins Browne, who d 1952; 2ndly, 1960, Alfonso Necocha Beauchemin, and has issue living (by both m). —— Beatrice Mary Rose (c/o Gordon Dadds & Co, 80 Brook St, W1), b 1904: m 19—, —, who d 19—. —— Olivia Margaret Rose, b 1910: m 1932, José-Maria Souviron, and has issue living, Alvaro Souviron Price, b 1933: m 1958, Ximena Grebe, and has issue living, Pilar Souviron b 1959, Beatrice Souviron b 1960, — Jacqueline Souviron Price, b 1936: m 1958, Luis Urrejola Dittborn, of Santiago, Chile, and has issue living, Daniel Urrejola b 1959, Sebastian Urrejola b 1961, Caroline Urrejola b 1962. —— Eveleen Mina Rose (c/o Banco de A Edwards y Cia, Valparaiso, Chile), b 1913: m 19—, (m diss 19—).

Grandchildren of late Rev Thomas Rose Price (infra):—
Issue of late Rev Thomas Neville Vreichvras Churchill Rose Price, MA, b 1911, d 1970: m 1939, Edna Mary, who d 1979, da of late Howard Edge, of Wolverhampton:—
Robin Francis Neville Rose, (Trouts Holiday Flats, South Hallsands, nr Kingsbridge, Devon), b 1945: m 1970, Alison Margaret, da of Denis Rogers, of Torcross, Devon, and has issue living, Andrew Rose, b 1975, — Sarah Rose, b 1973. —— Heather Mary Rose, b 1942: m 1st, 1965 (m diss 1976), Richard James Biddle; 2ndly, 1978, Harry Denys Barron, of Denysholme, Chilworth, Old Village, Southampton, and has issue living (by 1st m), Marc Jonathan Seymour (Long Bangan, Sarawak, Malaysia), b 1967: m 1993, Payang Tingan, — Roy Lindley Stirling, b 1969, — Paul Ashley Sheridan, b 1974, — Tiffany Lynn, b 1970.

Granddaughter of late Arthur Henry Price (ante):—
Issue of late Rev Thomas Rose Price, b 1874, d 1940: m 1901, Frances Louisa Salisbury, who d 1943, da of Frederick Churchill, MD, FRCS:—
Joy Gerrardine Salisbury Rose, b 1918: m 1939, Rupert George Pearce, and has issue living, Peter Wayne, b 1947: m 1969, Kay Teresa Harris, and has issue living, Jeremy Robert b 1974, Lisa Kelly b 1972, Anna b 1977, — Wendy Lynne, b 1941: m 1964, William Harper Ritchie, and has issue living, Peter Graham b 1966, Grant Phillip b 1970, Kathryn Margaret b 1968, — Pauline Frances, b 1944: m 1968, Donald George Foster, and has issue living, Daniel Richard b 1970, Emily Victoria b 1971, Faye Louise b 1974, — Faye Fiona, b 1949: m 1970, Wayne Allan Parkhill, and has issue living, Jesse Andrew b 1981, Charlotte Faye b 1979, — Estelle Suzanne, b 1951: m 1972, Christopher John Alleyne, and has issue living, Timothy Francis b 1984, Melissa Gerrardine b 1975, Holly Felicity b 1979. Residence – Hoon Hay Valley, Christchurch 3, NZ.

Francis Price, b about 1635, believed to be descended from Caradoc Vreichvras, Prince between the Wye and Severn, settled in Jamaica soon after its conquest in 1655. He acquired Worthy Park in St Johns 1670, and was a Member of House of Assembly and Maj of Militia. He married Elizabeth Booth, widow of Col William Rose, of Rose Hall, Jamaica. His son, Col Charles Price, was testamentary heir of his uterine brother, Thomas Rose, and inherited his Jamaica estates. His el son Charles, Speaker of House of Assembly, was cr a Bt 1768, which title became ext on the death of the 2nd Bt 1788 (also Speaker of House of Assembly). John Price, 2nd son of Col Charles Price, was grandfather of Sir Rose Price, 1st Bt of the 2nd and present creation. Sir Rose Price, 4th Bt, was k during S African War 1901.

GREEN-PRICE (UK) 1874, of Norton Manor, Radnorshire

Live to-day

Sir ROBERT JOHN GREEN-PRICE, 5th *Baronet*; *b* 22 Oct 1940; *s* his father, Capt *Sir* JOHN, 1964; *ed* Shrewsbury; Capt (ret) RCT; ADC to Gov of Bermuda 1969-72; Instructor Concord Sch of English, Tokyo 1973-76; Lecturer in English, Teikyo Univ 1976-82, and Chiba Univ of Commerce since 1982.

𝕬rms – Sable, a chevron invected argent between three escutcheons of the last, each charged with a spear-head of the first embrued proper. 𝕮rest – In front of a dragon's head erased vert, holding in the mouth a dexter hand, couped at the wrist gules, three escallops argent.
Residence – 4-A Shoto Mansions, 5-4-20 Shinden, Ichikawa-shi, Chiba-ken, 272 Japan.

SISTER LIVING

Roseanne, *b* 1943: *m* 1st, 1963, Richard Lowe, Maj Queen Elizabeth's Own Gurkha Rifles; 2ndly, 1984, Michael Hender, and has issue living, (by 1st *m*) Timothy, *b* 1963, — Deborah, *b* 1965, — Sophie Louise, *b* 1969. *Residence* – Dukes, Bradninch, nr Exeter, Devon EX5 4QN.

WIDOW LIVING OF FOURTH BARONET

JEAN CHALMERS SCOTT (*Lady Green-Price*) (Gwernaffel, Knighton, Powys), da of David Low Stark, of Arbroath: *m* 1956, as his 2nd wife, Capt Sir John Green-Price, 4th Bt, who *d* 1964.

COLLATERAL BRANCHES LIVING

Issue of late John Powell Green-Price, 5th son of 2nd baronet, *b* 1878, *d* 1927: *m* 1907, Julia Helen Ouchterlony Norman, who *d ca* 1959, da of Harold Manners-Norman:—

(POWELL) NORMAN DANSEY, *b* 22 July 1926; adopted by his uncle Sir Robert Green-Price, 3rd Bt, 1944; *ed* Shrewsbury; late Lieut WG; High Sheriff Radnorshire 1969; MFH: *m* 1963, Ann Stella, da of late Brig Harold George Howson, CBE, MC, TD, of North House, Carlton-in-Lindrick, Worksop, Notts, and has issue living, Simon Richard, *b* 10 May 1964, — Stella Rachel, *b* 1965. *Residence* – Hivron, Bleddfa, Knighton, Radnorshire LD7 1NY.

Issue of late Llewellyn James Green-Price, yst son of 2nd baronet, *b* 1881, *d* 1962: *m* 1919, Ethel Lilian, da of S. Faram, of Kepax, Worcester:—
Olive Maude, *b* 1922.

Grandchildren of late Rev Herbert Chase Green-Price (infra):—
Issue of late Lt-Col Francis Chase Green-Price, *b* 1896, *d* 1975: *m* 1934, Joan Atcherley, who *d* 1991, da of late Guy Dobell, of Crickhowell:—
John Chase, *b* 1947: *m* 1986 (*m diss* 1989), Susan Elizabeth, da of Kenneth Woodyatt, of Pixie Lane, Braunton, N Devon. *Residence* – Wendover, Croyde Bay, N Devon EX33 1NP. —— Susan Marion, *b* 1939.

Issue of late Rev Herbert Chase Green-Price, 2nd son of 1st baronet, *b* 1855, *d* 1919: *m* 1895, Susan Alice, who *d* 1951, el da of William Henry Barneby (E St Aldwyn):—
Richard Henry, *b* 1905; *ed* Radley: *m* 1931, Ruby Beatrix, da of late Robert Thomas Rowan, of Shanghai, and has issue living, Anthony Chase, *b* 1933: *m* 1980, Joyce Betty Schrieber, — Susan Anne, *b* 1943: *m* 1967, Alfred Ian Ryder. *Residence* – RD1 Te Kuiti, NZ.

Issue of late Rev Alfred Edward Green-Price, 4th son of 1st baronet, *b* 1860, *d* 1940: *m* 1893, Mary Louisa, who *d* 1922, da of late Very Rev H. Edwards, Dean of Bangor:—
Alice Monica (Nash Cottage, Fownhope, Hereford), *b* 1907: *m* 1969, Richard Vivian Glynne Williams.

The 1st baronet, Sir Richard, son of late George Green, of Knighton, assumed, by Roy licence 1874, the additional surname of Price, being heir to his maternal uncle, Richard Price of Norton Manor, Radnorshire. He sat as MP for Radnor Boroughs (*L*) 1862-9, and for Radnorshire 1880-85. Sir Robert Henry, 3rd Bt was High Sheriff of Radnorshire 1930.

RUGGE-PRICE (UK) 1804, of Spring Grove, Richmond, Surrey

VIVE · UT · VIVAS

*Live 'here) so that you may live
(thereafter)*

Sir CHARLES KEITH NAPIER RUGGE-PRICE, 9th *Baronet*; *b* 7 Aug 1936; *s* his father, *Lt-Col Sir* CHARLES JAMES NAPIER, 1966; *ed* Middleton Coll, Ireland: *m* 1965, Jacqueline Mary, yr da of Maj Pierre Paul Loranger, MC, CD, and has issue.

Arms – Quarterly, 1st and 4th, gules, a lion rampant argent, *Price*; 2nd and 3rd, sable, on a chevron invected argent, between three mullets or pierced of the field, an unicorn's head erased of the first, *Rugge*. **Crests** – 1st, a lion rampant argent, holding in the dexter paw a rose slipped proper; 2nd, a talbot passant argent, gored with a collar and pendent therefrom an escutcheon sable, thereon the head of an ibex couped, also argent.
Residence – 2 Lorne Cres, St Albert, Alberta, Canada T8N 3R2.

SONS LIVING

JAMES KEITH PETER, *b* 8 April 1967. —— Andrew Philip Richard, *b* 1970.

SISTERS LIVING

Angela Muriel Frances, *b* 1938: *m* 1970, Martyn Samuel, of 9 Farfield Close, Bovey Tracey, Devon, and has issue living, Bernard Charles, *b* 1971, — Edward Hugh, *b* 1974. —— Jane Marjorie Agnes (Tangora, 20 Sea Way, Sea Lane, Middleton-on-Sea, Sussex), *b* 1943: *m* 1965 (*m diss* 19—), Leslie C.Tankard, and has issue living, Nigel Peter Stewart, *b* 1970, — Wendy Julie Angela, *b* 1967. —— Catharine Sarah Christina, *b* 1948.

UNCLE LIVING (son of 7th baronet)

Anthony Arthur Keith, CBE (47 Draycott Place, SW3; Cavalry and Guards' Club), *b* 1914; *ed* Harrow; Col late 13/18th Hussars; OC 13/18th R Hussars 1956-58; CBE (Mil) 1967: *m* 1st, 1939 (*m diss* 1948), Joan Lisette Douglas, da of Alan Douglas Pilkington, of Dean Wood, Newbury; 2ndly, 1952, Mrs Mary Joy Campbell, da of late John Eric Horniman, and has issue living, (by 1st *m*) Anthony Jeremy (60 Lincoln Ave, Purchase, NY 10577-2302, USA), *b* 1940: *m* 1st, 1963 (*m diss* 19—), Sarah Oliva Valentine, da of Maj Tom Adam, of Denmore, Aberdeen; 2ndly, 1972, Beverly Ann Davidson, da of Lt-Col Lance Granville Davidson Brett, of Corfe, Som; 3rdly, 1981, Carolyn Anne, only da of Sir Richard Ashton Beaumont, KCMG, OBE, and formerly wife of Michael Brodrick Hicks Beach (*see* E St Aldwyn, colls), and has issue living (by 1st *m*) Andrew Christian (499 King's Rd, SW3 0TU) *b* 1964: *m* 1991, Sophie A., yr da of A. J. Hind, and of Mrs W. Hipwell, of Norwich, Barnaby Douglas *b* 1969, Matilda Candide *b* 1970, (by 2nd *m*) Edward Jason Napier *b* 1973, (by 3rd *m*) Robert Jake *b* 1982, — James Keith Alan (Stainswick Manor, Shrivenham, Swindon, Wilts), *b* 1944: *m* 1st, 1967 (*m diss* 1972) Elizabeth Mary, da of Lt-Col James Innes, of Larkenshaw, Chobham, Surrey (*see* B Westbury); 2ndly, 1976, (Mary) Alexa, da of late Arthur Patrick Usher Crookshank, and has issue living (by 1st *m*), Lucy Caroline *b* 1969, (by 2nd *m*) Samantha *b* 1979, Kinvara *b* (twin) 1979, Alice *b* 1985, — (by 2nd *m*) Juliet, *b* 1954: *m* 1979, Thomas M. S. Hughes Hallett, of 49 Eglantine Rd, SW18, and has issue living, Archie James Arthur *b* 1983, Grace Marjorie *b* 1986.

AUNTS LIVING (*Daughters of 7th baronet*)

Catharine Marjorie (*Lady Balfour*) (Bridles, Donhead St Mary, Shaftesbury, Dorset) *b* 1904: *m* 1930, Lt-Gen Sir Philip Maxwell Balfour, KBE, CB, MC, late RA, who *d* 1977. —— Lois Mary Maitland (The Old Rectory, Winterborne Anderson, Blandford, Dorset), *b* 1911: *m* 1932, Lt-Col Aylmer Lochiel Cameron, DSO, MC, late RHA, who *d* 1982, and has issue living, Ewen Duncan, OBE, *b* 1935; Brig The Black Watch (RHR): *m* 1973, Joanna Margaret, da of late Maj James Malcolm Hay of Seaton (*see* M Tweeddale, colls).

WIDOW LIVING OF EIGHTH BARONET

MAEVE MARGUERITE (*Maeve, Lady Rugge-Price*), da of Edgar Stanley de la Peña, of Hythe, Kent: *m* 1935, Lt-Col Sir Charles James Napier Rugge-Price, 8th Bt, who *d* 1966.

COLLATERAL BRANCHES LIVING

Grandchildren of Alfred Adams Price, grandson of Ralph Price, 3rd son of 1st baronet:—
Issue of late Kenneth Alexander Price, *b* 1869, *d* 19—: *m* 1904, Helen Mary, who *d* 1942, 2nd da of William Baldwin George:—
Arthur Basil, *b* 1916: *m* 1939, Ethel Frances Brindle. —— Douglas Leonard, *b* 1922: late Fl Lt RAF: *m* 1943, Hazel Irene Boyles. —— Ethel Marian, *b* 1905: *m* 1930, Kenneth Couch. —— Phyllis, *b* 1908: *m* 1941, Leslie Henry, late Canadian Army.

Grandchildren of late Petley Lloyd Augustus Price (infra):—
Issue of late Capt Augustus Robert Petley Price, *b* 1885, *d* 1945: *m* 1922, Augusta Elsy Maud, who *d* 1980, da of Gilbert Wilkes, of Ganges, British Columbia:—
Augustus Robert Kenrick, *b* 1927. —— Elsy Mary, *b* 1923: *m* 1963, Raymond Perks, and has issue living, John Robert Raymond, *b* 1965, — David Raymond, *b* 1966.

Granddaughter of late Lieut-Col Augustus Price, el son of late Richard Price, 4th son of 1st baronet:—
Issue of late Petley Lloyd Augustus Price, *b* 1856, *d* 1910: *m* 1884, Mary Cotton, who *d* 1946, da of late Com Frederick Arthur Egerton, RN (Grey-Egerton, Bt, colls):—
Elizabeth Rosina May, *b* 1886: *m* 1915, Alexander Thomas Benthall Charlesworth Lt RFC, who was *ka* 1917.

Grandchildren of late Petley Lloyd Augustus Price (ante):—
Issue of late Harold Tudor Egerton Price, *b* 1888, *d* 1965: *m* 1927, Margaret Frances, da of Edward Fotheringham Layard, of Southsea, Hants:—
John Harold Petley, *b* 1928: *m* 1953, Edith, da of late J. Lee, of Victoria, BC. —— Ruth Gladys, *b* 1930.

Granddaughter of late Major Edward Augustus Uvedale Price (infra):—

Issue of late Lt-Cdr Geoffrey Uvedale Price, RNVR, b 1885, d 1960: m 1908, Winifred Ethel, who d 1963, only da of late Edgar L. Price, of The Bays, Oakhill Rd, East Putney, SW:—
Vivienne Betty Henrietta, b 1910: m 1934, Brigadier Maurice Rapinet Mackenzie, DSO, RA, and has issue living, Michael Philip Uvedale Rapinet, b 1937; ed Downside, and Oxford Univ. Residence – Hylands Oast, Little London, Horam, E Sussex TN21 0BG.

Grandchildren of late Gen George Uvedale Price, 4th son of late Richard Price, 4th son of 1st baronet:—
Issue of late Major Edward Augustus Uvedale Price, b 1854, d 1905: m 1881, Elizabeth Henrietta, who d 1905, da of Henry J. P. Dumas, JP for Surrey:—
Kathleen Janette: m 1912, Capt Leslie Granville Waller, late Intelligence Corps, and has issue living, Margaret Evelyn Henrietta, b 1913: m 1939, Jacques Lioni, of Mr Sixlaan 3, Amstelveen, Holland, and has issue living, David Alexander b 1941, John Christopher Granville b 1945, Helen Mary b 1947. Residence – 62 Melbury Gardens, Wimbledon, SW20.
Issue of late Col Cyril Uvedale Price, CMG, b 1868, d 1956: m 1st, 1902, Ethel Maude, who d 1916, da of late Capt William Henry Ashe; 2ndly, 1919, May Edith, who d 1967, da of late Robert Lewis, of Damaraland:—
(By 2nd m) Roger Uvedale, b 1921; Burma 1942-45 as Capt Indian Army: m 1946, Angela Marcella Exton, da of Brig Wallis, Indian Army and has issue living, Myfanwy Uvedale, b 1948: m 1st, 1968 (m diss 1989), Peter John Penney; 2ndly, 1992, Michael John Payne, of South Lodge, 22 Lansdowne Rd, Angmering, W Sussex BN16 4JX, and has issue living (by 1st m), Ian Richard b 1970, Samantha Helen b 1973. Residence – Thistlegate, 51 Winkfield Row, Horndean, Hants PO8 9TL.

Grandson of late Ralph Mountague Rokeby Price, 4th son of the Rev Thomas Charles Price, el son of Thomas Price, 5th son of 1st baronet:—
Issue of late Arthur Mountague Rokeby Price, b 1892, d 1941: m 1916, Eliza, who d 1983, da of Victor Kuylen, of Stann Creek, British Honduras:—
Ralph Mountague Rokeby, CPM (4429 Kawanee Av, Metairie, La 70002, USA), b 1917; formerly Principal Assist Sec, British Honduras, CPM for Meritorious Ser; 1939-45 War Capt Caribbean Regt: m 1942, Margarita Matilda Ernestina, da of Nazario Cervantes, of Belize, British Honduras, and has had issue, Ralph Mountague Rokeby, b 1946: m 1976, Kim, da of Harold Maranto, Jr, of Louisiana, USA, and has issue living, Jared b 1978, Joshua b 1980, Andrew b 1982, Adam b 1984, Jennifer Leigh b 1977, — Arthur Richard Rokeby (41228 Eldorado Dr, Hammond, LA 70403, USA), b 1949: m 1972, Elaine Sand, and has issue living, Jason Richard b 1974, Scott Richard b 1979, — †David Francis Rokeby, b 1956, d 1986, — †Michael John Rokeby, b 1958, d 1987, — Patricia Elizabeth Rokeby, b 1943: m 1963, Marvin Robert Sabido, of 1905 Kent Av, Metairie, La 70001, USA, and has issue living, Marvin Robert b 1964, David Andrew b 1967, Christopher Ian b 1967, Steven Scott b 1975, — Alice Mae Rokeby, b 1948: m 1972, Lloyd Perrien, of 2604 N Sibley St, Metairie, La 70003, USA, and has issue living, Todd Andrew b 1973, Derek Lloyd b 1976, — Margaret Joan Rokeby, b 1952, — Carolyn Mary Rokeby, b 1962.

Grandchildren of late Arthur Mountague Rokeby Price (ante):—
Issue of late Arthur Victor Rokeby Price, b 1921, d 1964: m 1955, Bridget Ellen (510 S Archer St, Anaheim, Cal, USA), da of Micheal Austin Flynn, of Canada:—
Michael Craig, b 1959. —— Richard Arthur (twin), b 1959. —— Bridget Ellen, b 1956. —— Judith b 1958. —— Jennifer, b (twin) 1958. —— Margaret Mary, b 1961. —— Sheila Rose, b 1962. —— Elizabeth Anne, b 1964.

Grandchildren of late Thomas Plumer Price (infra):—
Issue of late Capt Thomas Ralph Plumer Price, b 1885, d 1967: m 1916, Ruth Beatrice, who d 1978, da of late Sydney Harris, of The Gables, Hagley Rd, Edgbaston:—
Richard Ralph Plumer (5310 Fairholme Rd, RR5, Victoria BC, Canada, V8X 4M6), b 1926: m 1954, Audrey Chrystal, da of late James Anderson Gray, of London, Ont, and has issue living, James Plumer, b 1957, — Norman Plumer (2236 Florence St, Victoria, BC V8R 5E8), b 1959: m 1979, Bronwyn Anne, da of Robert Fox, of Victoria, BC, and has issue living, Tristian Christina b 1980. —— Ruth Rosemary Plumer (10 Garden Mews, Warsash, Southampton SO31 9GW), b 1920: m 1946 (m diss 1953), Robert Alfred John Sindall, FO, RAF, and has issue living, David Robert Plumer b 1947: m 1978 Susan Jane Humby, — Sally Ann, b 1949: m 1st, 1969 (m diss 1975) Stephen Philip Clarke; 2ndly, 1977, Roger David Hogben, of 21 Nutwick Rd, Denvilles, Havant, Hants, and has issue living (by 1st m), Rachel Melanie b 1970, Sarah Elizabeth b 1972, — (by 2nd m) Helen Abigail b 1977.

Granddaughter of late Rev Thomas Charles Price, el son of late Thomas Price, 5th son of 1st baronet:—
Issue of late Thomas Plumer Price, b 1861, d 1930: m 1884, Elizabeth Laura Middleton, who d 1946, da of late Capt Richard George Collins (formerly 57th Regt), of Melbourne House, Cullompton:—
Phyllis Joan Plumer b 1895: m 1918, Capt Thomas Brunyée Harston, LLB, solicitor (formerly Capt Liverpool Regt), who d 1951, and has issue living, Antony Plumer Brunyée, MB, MRCOG, b 1924; Lt-Col (ret) RAMC, — Bridget Elizabeth Uvedale, b 1931.

Grandchildren of late Capt Spencer Cosby Price, 3rd son of Thomas Price (ante)—
Issue of late Spencer Edward Cosby Price, b 1873, d 19—: m 1894, his cousin, Eleanor Ann, of Mark Whatmore:—
Spencer Kendrick Sydney, b 1902. —— Nesta Joan Cosby, b 1900.

The 1st baronet, Alderman Sir Charles Price, was MP for the City of London 1802-12, and Lord Mayor thereof 1802-3. Sir Arthur James, 5th baronet, assumed in 1874, by Roy licence, the additional surname of Rugge. Lieut-Col Sir Charles Frederick Rugge-Price, 7th baronet RFA, served in S Africa 1900-1901, and in European War 1914-18.

Prichard-Jones, see Jones.

PRIMROSE (UK) 1903, of Redholme, Dumbreck, Govan, co of City of Glasgow

Fidelity and confidence

Sir JOHN URE PRIMROSE, 5th *Baronet*; *b* 28 May 1960; *s* his father, *Sir* ALASDAIR NEIL, 1986; *ed* Buenos Aires: *m* 1983 (*m diss* 1987), Marion Cecilia, da of Hans Otto Altgelt, of Buenos Aires, Argentina, and has issue.

Arms – Per fesse argent and ermines, on a fesse vert between in chief a mill rind between two cross-crosslets fitchée gules, and in base a salmon on its back argent, holding a signet ring in its mouth, three primroses slipped proper. **Crest** – A hand couped at the wrist grasping a primrose slipped proper.
Residence – Puerto Victoria, Alto Parana Misiones, Argentina.

DAUGHTERS LIVING

Christine Anne, *b* 1984. —— Jennifer Diana, *b* 1986.

BROTHER LIVING

ANDREW RICHARD, *b* 19 Jan 1966.

SISTERS LIVING

Doris Sofia, *b* 1962. —— Deborah Marina, *b* 1964.

WIDOW LIVING OF FOURTH BARONET

(ELAINE) NOREEN (*Lady Primrose*), only da of Edmund Cecil Lowndes, of Buenos Aires, Argentina: *m* 1958, Sir Alasdair Neil Primrose, 4th Bt, who *d* 1986. *Residence* – Ada Elflein 3155, 1642 San Isidro, Provincia de Buenos Aires, Argentina.

COLLATERAL BRANCH LIVING

Issue of late Hugh Dunsmuir Primrose, yr son of 2nd baronet, *b* 1909, *d* 1979: *m* 1935, Kathleen, da of late Samuel Tyler, of Long Sutton, Lincs:—
Iain Dunsmuir (Lymburghs Farm, Marnhull, Sturminster Newton, Dorset DT10 1HN), *b* 1941; *ed* King's Coll, Taunton: *m* 1971, Roberta Jeanette, da of Frederick Clapp, of Bristol, and has issue living, James Robert, *b* 1973, — Fiona Joanne, *b* 1971, — Nicola Kathryn, *b* 1976.

The 1st baronet, Sir John Ure Primrose (senior partner in the firm of William Primrose and Sons, flour millers, of Centre Street, Glasgow), was Chm of Clyde Navigation Trustee 1907-9, Lord Provost of Glasgow 1903-5, and Lord-Lieut of co of the City of Glasgow.

Prince-Smith, see Smith.

PRINGLE (NS) 1683, of Stichill, Roxburghshire

Faith crowns

Lt-Gen Sir STEUART ROBERT PRINGLE, KCB, 10th *Baronet*; *b* 21 July 1928; *s* his father, *Squadron Leader Sir* NORMAN HAMILTON, 1961; *ed* Sherborne; Hon DSc City Univ (1982); formerly Commandant Gen RM; formerly Chm and Ch Exec Chatham Historic Dockyard Trust; Pres St Loye's Coll Foundation, Exeter; KCB (Mil) 1982: *m* 1953, Jacqueline Marie, only da of Wilfrid Hubert Gladwell, of La Rocque, Jersey, and has issue.

Arms – Azure, three escallops or. **Crest** – A saltire azure within a garland of bay-leaves proper. *Residence* – 76 S Croxted Rd, Dulwich, SE21.

SONS LIVING

SIMON ROBERT (5 Hyde Vale, Greenwich, SE10 8QQ), *b* 6 Jan 1959; *ed* Worth Abbey, and Trinity Coll Oxford (BA): *m* 1992, Pamela Margaret, da of George Hunter, of Belfast, and has issue living, Siena Evangeline, *b* 1994. —— Julian Andrew James, *b* 1961.

DAUGHTERS LIVING

Shelagh Mary Frances, *b* 1954: *m* 1st, 1975, Jasper J. H. Dale; 2ndly, 19—, Gary Nicholas Newton, and has issue living, Jessica Anne, *b* 1978, — Katherine Frances, *b* 1980, — Alexa Mary Elizabeth, *b* 1983. —— Nicola Ann, *b* 1956: *m* 1981, Clive Gordon Harris, and has issue living, Robert Keith, *b* 1985, — Callum Charles, *b* 1993, — Geraldine Marie, *b* 1982.

AUNT LIVING (*Daughter of 8th baronet*)

Friendship reflects honours

Mary Elizabeth *b* 1916: *m* 1st, 1938 (*m diss* 1963), Major G. Wallace Anderson; 2ndly, 1963, Richard Anthony Mann Roberts, only son of Capt R. M. Roberts, of

The Old Manor, Ivinghoe, Leighton Buzzard, and has had issue (by 1st *m*), Veronica Bethia, *b* 1939; *d* 1976, — also an adopted son, John Louis Wallace, *b* 1950. *Residence* – 11 Parkwood Rd, Wimbledon, SW19.

COLLATERAL BRANCHES LIVING

Issue of late Ronald Steuart Pringle, 2nd son of 8th baronet, *b* 1905; *d* 1968: *m* 1938, Janet Patricia Todd, who *d* 1983, da of late Capt George Todd Pickford, RNR, of Nairobi, Kenya:—
Norman Murray, *b* 1941; FCIS, FCMA: *m* 1st, 1966, Lysbet Watkins-Pitchford; 2ndly, 1993, Patricia Nadine Millem, and has issue living (by 1st *m*), Alastair Steuart Ronald, *b* 1972, — Sian Amanda, *b* 1972. Resides in Maadi, Cairo. —— James Bruce (5 St Mary's Pl, Newbury, Berks), *b* 1943: *m* 1965, Rosemary Jean Collis, and has issue living, Andrew James Edward, *b* 1975, — Jean Frances, *b* 1967, — Marion Clare, *b* 1970, — Angela Mary, *b* 1971. —— Priscilla Frances, *b* 1944: *m* 1st, 1964 (*m diss* 1972), Anthony Mark Dorman; 2ndly, 1976 (*m diss* 1991), Derek John McIntosh, and has issue living (by 1st *m*), Louise Margaret, *b* 1965: *m* 198-, Paul John Preston, and has issue living, Leigh Mark *b* 1985, Christopher James *b* 1988, Robert Steven *b* 1990, Steven Jonathan *b* 1992, Lisa Clare *b* 1987.

Issue of late James Drummond Pringle, yst son of 8th baronet, *b* 1906, *d* 1960: *m* 1st, 1932 (*m diss* 1946), Nina Beryl, who *d* 1988, el da of P. W. Trutwein, formerly Sessions Judge, Burma; 2ndly, 1947, Mrs Pauline Cunliffe:—
(By 1st *m*) Norman Alastair (27 Lynton Green, Maidenhead), *b* 1933; *ed* Stonyhurst: *m* 1956 (*m diss* 1979), Diana Joan, da of Victor Clarke, and has issue living, Robin Alastair, *b* 1962: *m* 1984, Anne Samuel, — Susan Jane, *b* 1960: *m* 1st, 1977 (*m diss* 1980) Alan Watkins; 2ndly, 1980, Tony Bennett, and has issue living (by 2nd *m*), Nadia *b* 1980, — Dawn Anne, *b* 1965: *m* 1982, Terry Spracklen, and has issue living, Kayleigh Louise *b* 1985, — Beth Kelcei, *b* 1991, — Lydia Kimberley, *b* 1993. —— (By 2nd *m*) John, *b* 1948. —— Melanie, *b* 1955.

The Pringles of Stichill are heirs male and representatives of the Hop-Pringles of Craglatch and Newhall, co Selkirk. Sir Robert Pringle of Stichill, 1st baronet, *s* to Newhall 1667 on the extinction of the elder branch of the family.

PROBY (UK) 1952, of Elton Hall, co Huntingdon

Manus haec inimica Tyrannis

This hand is unfriendly to tyrants

Sir PETER PROBY, 2nd *Baronet*, *b* 4 Dec 1911; *s* his father, Maj *Sir* RICHARD GEORGE, MC, JP, 1979; *ed* Eton, and Trin Coll, Oxford (BA); Capt Irish Gds; Bursar of Eton 1953-71; a DL for Cambs, and Lord Lieut 1981-84; FRCS: *m* 1944, Blanche Harrison, only da of Col Henry Harrison Cripps, DSO, R Fus, and has issue.

ᴁrms – Quarterly: 1st and 4th, ermine on a fesse gules a lion passant or, *Proby*; 2nd and 3rd, argent, two bars wavy azure, on a chief of the last an estoile between two escallops or, *Allen*; Ԏrest – An ostrich's head erased proper, ducally gorged and holding in the beak a key or.
Residence – Pottle Green, Elton, Peterborough PE8 6SG.

SON LIVING

WILLIAM HENRY *b* 13 June 1949; *ed* Eton, Lincoln Coll, Oxford (MA), and Brooksby Coll of Agric; FCA; Chm HHA Taxation Comm 1986-94; Pres Historic Houses Assocn since 1993 (Dep Pres 1988-93); farmer: *m* 1974, Meredyth Anne, da of Dr Timothy David Brentnall, of Corner Cottage, Preston, nr Uppingham, Leics, and has issue living, Alexandra Meredyth Anne, *b* 1980, — Alice Katherine, *b* 1982, — Frances Rose Gwyneth, *b* 1986, — Isabella Victoria Hamilton, *b* 1991. *Residence* – Elton Hall, Elton, Peterborough PE8 6SH.

DAUGHTERS LIVING

Sarah Blanche, *b* 1945; *ed* Lady Margaret Hall, Oxford (MA, BM, BCh): *m* 1968, Peter George Mills, MA, BCh, FRCP, of 158 Tachbrook St, SW1, son of Dr George William Mills, MBE, and has issue living, James Douglas George, *b* 1972, — Robert Peter, *b* 1975, — Elizabeth Sarah Jane, *b* 1980. —— Charlotte Mary, *b* 1957; *ed* Lady Margaret Hall, Oxford (MA, MB, BS), MRCP: *m* 1984, Stephen John Hay, son of Maj John Hay, of Cheltenham, and has issue living, Matthew John Claud, *b* 1990, — Matilda Blanche, *b* 1989, — Flora Millie Rose, *b* 1994. —— Christine Elisabeth, *b* (twin) 1957: *m* 1983, Christopher T. C. Dobbs, yst son of J. A. Dobbs, of Charlton Musgrave, Som, and has issue living, Rachel Alice, *b* 1992.

SISTERS LIVING

Margaret *b* 1920; a JP for Dorset: *m* 1948, Jack Harry Harrison Cripps, of Bramble Cottage, 10 French Mill Lane, Shaftesbury, Dorset, and has issue living, Harry Richard, *b* 1949: *m* 1974, Vivien Barbara, da of Roy North, and has issue living, Elizabeth Blanche *b* 1977, Sarah Margaret *b* 1979, — Peter John, *b* 1954: *m* 1983, Hazel Anne, da of Jack Fox, — Thomas Philip (twin), *b* 1954: *m* 1979, Elizabeth Margaret, da of Oliver Sugden, and has issue living, Margaret Jane *b* 1981, — Barbara Mary, *b* 1952: *m* 1973, Giles T. R. Droop, and has issue living, Alastair Philip *b* 1980, Alison Jane *b* 1978. —— Patience (*Lady Moberly*) (twin), *b* 1923; *ed* Lady Margaret Hall, Oxford (BA, BM and BCh); MRCP: *m* 1959, Sir John Campbell Moberly, KBE, CMG, HM Diplo Ser, of The Cedars, Temple Sowerby, Penrith, and 35 Pymers' Mead, Croxted Rd, SE21 8NH, son of Sir Walter Hamilton Moberly, GBE, KCB, DSO, and has issue living, Richard John, *b* 1962: *m* 1992, Catharine J. F., da of Noel Baker, — Nicholas Hamilton, *b* 1963: *m* 1991, Margaret Fiona Clare, da of J. H. Callan, of Horley, Surrey, and has issue living, Emma Lucy Victoria *b* 1993, — Clare Elizabeth, *b* 1967.

WIDOW LIVING OF FIRST BARONET

EILEEN YVONNE (Abbey Lodge, Beverley, Harrogate, N Yorks GH3 5AX), da of Walter Edwin Ambrose Helps, of Trevarth Manor, Gwennap, Cornwall, and widow of F/Lieut Reginald Kenneth Harris, RAF: *m* 2ndly, 1972, as his 2nd wife, Maj Sir Richard George Proby, 1st Bt, MC, JP, who *d* 1979; 3rdly, 1991, Eric Holman Stirk, of Abbey Lodge, Bewerley, Harrogate, Yorks.

COLLATERAL BRANCH LIVING

Issue of late Capt Claud Proby, IG, 2nd son of 1st baronet, *b* 1917, *d* 1987: *m* 1942, Patricia Amelia (1 Chestnut Close, Gt Waldingfield, Sudbury, Suffolk), da of Lt-Cmdr Vyvyan Whitmore Pearce, RN:—
Patrick James (21 Greenacres, Gt Waldingfield, Sudbury, Suffolk), *b* 1944; *ed* Eton. —— Caroline Fiona, *b* 1943: *m* 1st, 1969 (*m diss* 1988), 6th Viscount Hampden; 2ndly, 1990, Christopher K. St J. Bird. —— Joanna Margaret, *b* 1946: *m* 1970, Edward Richard Woods, NZ Ambassador to Russia, son of Archdeacon Samuel Woods, and has issue living, James Christopher, *b* 1972, — Samuel Richard, *b* 1973. *Address* – NZ Foreign Ministry, Parliament Bldgs, Wellington, NZ. —— Jocelyn Elizabeth, *b* 1950; *m* 1993, Donald Retson, of Edmonton, Alberta, Canada, and has issue living, Serena Christine, *b* 1992.

This family is descended in the female line from William Proby, first cousin of Sir Thomas Proby, Bt, upon whose death in 1689 the baronetcy became extinct, and from the Earls of Carysfort, whose Irish Earldom and Barony, and English Barony became extinct on the death of the 5th Earl in 1909. Lady Elizabeth Emma Proby, a sister of the last Earl of Carysfort, married Rt Hon Lord Claud Hamilton, MP, brother of 1st Duke of Abercorn, and their son, Col Douglas James Hamilton, assumed by Roy licence 1904 the surname of Proby. The 1st baronet, Maj Sir Richard Proby, was Pres of Country Landowners' Assocn 1947-51.

Probyn-Jones, see Jones.

Proctor-Beauchamp, see Beauchamp.

Pryce-Jones, see Jones.

PRYKE (UK) 1926, of Wanstead, co Essex

Sir DAVID DUDLEY PRYKE, 3rd *Baronet*; *b* 16 July 1912; *s* his father, *Sir* (WILLIAM ROBERT) DUDLEY, 1959; *ed* St Lawrence Coll, Ramsgate; late Common Councilman, City of London; a Liveryman of Turners' Co, Master 1985-6: *m* 1945, Doreen Winifred, el da of late Ralph Bernard Wilkins, of Winchmore Hill, N, and has issue.

𝖆rms – Per pale or and argent, on a cross invected azure two fasces erect in pale and as many mascals in fesse all of the first. 𝖈rest – Two arms embowed, the hands proper supporting a fasces erect or, each arm charged with a mascal of the last.
Residence – 27 Wantz Haven, Princes Rd, Maldon, Essex CM9 7HA.

DAUGHTERS LIVING

Madge, *b* 1946. —— Anita, *b* 1949.

BROTHER DECEASED

†William Dudley, *b* 1914; *ed* Highgate; formerly Capt Duke of Cornwall's LI; a Liveryman of Plumbers' Co (Master 1969-70); 1939-45 War: *m* 1940, Lucy Irene (Peggy), who *d* 1984, da of late Frank Madgett, of Whetstone, N, and *d* 1994, leaving issue, CHRISTOPHER DUDLEY (69 Wendell Rd, Stamford Brook, W12 9SB), *b* 17 April 1946; *ed* Hurstpierpoint: *m* 1973 (*m diss* 1986), Angela Gay, da of Harold Noel Meek, of Holly Cottage, Crowell, nr Kingston Blount, Oxon, and has issue living, James Dudley *b* 29 Dec 1977, — Rosemary Susan (21 Eastern Rd, Fortis Green, N2), *b* 1949.

SISTER LIVING

Patricia Margaret, *b* 1919. *Residence* – 40 Temple Av, N20.

The 1st baronet, Sir William Robert Pryke (son of Richard Reeve Pryke), of Bury St Edmunds, was Chm of Pryke & Palmer, Ltd, iron and hardware merchants of 40 and 41 Upper Thames Street, EC, and Lord Mayor of London 1925-6. The 2nd baronet, Sir (William Robert) Dudley Pryke, was Chm of Pryke & Palmer, Ltd, iron and hardware merchants, of 40 and 41 Upper Thames Street, EC.

SAUNDERS-PRYSE (UK) 1866, of Gogerddan (Extinct 1962)

Sir PRYSE LOVEDEN SAUNDERS-PRYSE, 5th and last *Baronet*.

DAUGHTER LIVING OF FOURTH BARONET

Margaret Angharad Elinor, *b* 1903: *m* 1930, Godfrey S. Briggs, who *d* 1941.

Purves (Home-Purves-Hume-Campbell), see Campbell.

QUILTER (UK) 1897, of Bawdsey Manor, Bawdsey, Suffolk

Sir ANTHONY RAYMOND LEOPOLD CUTHBERT QUILTER, 4th *Baronet*; *b* 25 March 1937; *s* his father, *Sir* (JOHN) RAYMOND CUTHBERT, 1959; *ed* Harrow: *m* 1964, (Mary) Elise, el da of Col Brian Sherlock Gooch, DSO, TD, of Tannington Hall, Woodbridge (*see* Gooch, Bt, *cr* 1746, colls), and has issue.

Arms – Argent, on a bend invected gules, between three Cornish choughs proper, two cross crosslets of the first. **Crest** – In front of an arm vambraced proper, the hand grasping a battle-axe in bend sinister sable, head argent, the wrist entwined by a wreath of the third and second, a Cornish chough proper.
Seat – Sutton Hall, Woodbridge, Suffolk.

Plutôt mourir que changer

Rather die than change.

SON LIVING

GUY RAYMOND CUTHBERT, *b* 13 April 1967: *m* 1992, Jenifer J., only da of John Redvers-Cox, of Melton, Suffolk.

DAUGHTER LIVING

Juliet Elise, *b* 1965.

WIDOW LIVING OF THIRD BARONET

MARGERY MARIANNE (*Margery, Lady Quilter*) (Pettistree Hall, Sutton, Woodbridge, Suffolk), da of late Sir (James) Douglas Cooke, of Kingston House, Princes' Gate, SW7: *m* 1935, Sir (John) Raymond Cuthbert Quilter, 3rd Bt, who *d* 1959.

COLLATERAL BRANCHES LIVING

Issue of late Percy Cuthbert Quilter, 4th son of 1st baronet, *b* 1879 *d* 1947: *m* 1909, Gladys Clare Alice, who *d* 1973, da of late Charles Clement Tudway (Hervey-Bathurst, Bt):—
David Cuthbert TUDWAY QUILTER, *b* 1921; *ed* Eton; assumed by deed poll 1962 the additional surname of Tudway before his patronymic; DL Somerset (Vice Lord-Lieut since 1978): *m* 1953, Elizabeth Mary, da of Sir John Gawen Carew Pole, 12th Bt, DSO, TD, and has issue living, Simon John Cuthbert, *b* 1955, — Susan Clare Evelyn, *b* 1957: *m* 1st, 1978, James Henderson, who *d* 1991; 2ndly, 19—, Charles Dingwall, of Lasham House, Alton, Hants, and has issue living, (by 1st *m*) (*see* Lowther, Bt, *cr* 1824, colls), (by 2nd *m*) a son *b* 1993, — Lucy Anne, *b* 1961: *m* 1984, Dr Christopher D. B. Daniel, yr son of Ian Daniel, of Oaklands, Fressingfield, Eye, Suffolk, and has issue living, Jonathan David *b* 1985, Katie *b* 1987. *Residence* – Milton Lodge, Wells, Som. —— Diana Primrose, *b* 1916: *m* 1st, 1942 (*m diss* 1945), as his 2nd wife, Brig Lancelot Merivale Gibbs, CVO, DSO, MC, who *d* 1966; 2ndly, 1947, Archibald Tennant, who *d* 1955 (*see* B Glenconner, colls). *Residence* – 12 Victoria Sq, SW1.

Grandchildren of late Ronald Eustace Cuthbert Quilter (infra):—
Issue of late William Ronald Cuthbert Quilter, *b* 1937; *d* 1981: *m* 1962, Jennifer Ann (who *m* 2ndly, 1985, Reginald J.T. Hill, of Holfield Grange, Coggeshall, Essex), da of Cdr Evelyn John Tamlyn, RD, RNR (ret), of Yew Tree Farm, Pleshey, Chelmsford, Essex:—
Benjamin William Cuthbert, *b* 1963: *m* 1992, Helen Lidwina, da of Hendrik Akerboom, of Henderson, Auckland, NZ, and has issue living, Samuel William John, *b* 1993. *Residence* – Titirangi, Auckland, NZ. —— Melissa Jane, *b* 1966: *m* 1992, Dennis Embleton, son of late Dr Philip Embleton, of Aldeburgh, Suffolk, and has issue living (Dennis) Harry Faraday, *b* 1993. *Residence* – London House, Charsfield, Woodbridge, Suffolk.

Grandson of late Maj Eustace Cuthbert Quilter, OBE, 5th son of 1st baronet:—
Issue of late Ronald Eustace Cuthbert Quilter, *b* 1907, *d* 1972: *m* 1934, Doreen Mary, who *d* 1988, da of late Charles Sandbach Parker, of Fairlie House, Fairlie, Ayrshire:—
Thomas Eustace Cuthbert, *b* 1940; *ed* Eton, and Roy Coll of Music: *m* 1st, 1966 (*m diss* 1969), Joy Winifred Thérèse, da of Wing-Cdr G. F. R. Duffy, of Broadwell, Glos; 2ndly, 1992, Mary T. Griffiths.

The 1st baronet, Sir Cuthbert, was one of the Founders of the National Telephone Co (Limited), and sat as MP for S, or Sudbury, Div of Suffolk (LU) 1885-1906. The 2nd baronet, Sir (William Eley) Cuthbert, sat as MP for Suffolk, S or Sudbury Div (C) 1910-18.

RADCLIFFE (UK) 1813, of Milnesbridge House, Yorkshire

Virtue for its own sake

Sir SEBASTIAN EVERARD RADCLIFFE, 7th *Baronet*; *b* 8 June 1972; *s* his father, *Capt Sir* (JOSEPH BENEDICT) EVERARD HENRY, MC, 1975.

Arms – Argent, a bend engrailed sable charged with a crescent of the field for difference. **Crest** – A bull's head erased sable, horns argent, tipped or, gorged with a ducal coronet of the second.

HALF-SISTER LIVING

Susan Elizabeth Mary, *b* 1940.

WIDOW LIVING OF SIXTH BARONET

MARCIA HELEN (Château de Cheseaux, 1033 Vaud, Switzerland), da of Maj David Turville-Constable-Maxwell (*see* L Herries of Terregles): *m* 1st, 1968, as his 2nd wife, Sir (Joseph Benedict) Everard Henry Radcliffe, MC, 6th Bt, who *d* 1975; 2ndly, 1988, Howard Montagu Stuart Tanner.

COLLATERAL BRANCHES LIVING

Issue of late Hugh John Reginald Joseph Radcliffe, MBE, 2nd son of 5th baronet, *b* 1911, *d* 1993: *m* 1937, Marie-Therese (Mariquita) (The White House, Stoke, Andover, Hants SP11 0LU), yst da of Maj-Gen Sir Cecil Edward Pereira, KCB, CMG:—

MARK HUGH JOSEPH (The Malt House, Upton, Andover, Hants SP11 0JS; Cavalry and Guards' Club), *b* 22 April 1938; *ed* Downside: *m* 1963, Anne, da of Maj-Gen Arthur Evers Brocklehurst, CB, DSO, and has issue living, Lucinda Mary, *b* 1964, — Emily Marie Louise, *b* 1968, — Camilla Mary, *b* 1971. — Anthony Joseph (Hermitage House, Hermitage, Newbury, Berks), *b* 1942; *ed* Downside: *m* 1964, Rachel Mary, eldest da of Joseph Russell Goddard, of Harmony Hall, Barbados, and has issue living, James Russell Joseph, *b* 1965: *m* 1992, A. Louisa, yst da of Mrs Elizabeth Poyser, of South Place, Moor Park, Middlesex, and has issue living, Polly Anna *b* 19—, — Julian Everard Joseph, *b* 1967: *m* 19—, Deborah, el da of T. Key, of Compton, Berks, — Philippa, *b* 1975. — *Most Rev Fr* Timothy Peter Joseph, OP (Convento S. Sabino, Piazza P. d'Illiria 1, Aventino, 00153 Rome, Italy), *b* 1945; *ed* Downside, and St John's Coll, Oxford (MA, Hon Fellow 1993); Prior Provincial of the English Province of the Order of Preachers (The Dominicans), 1988-92, since when Master of the Order of Preachers. — Paul John Joseph (Rudges Hill, Ramsden, Oxon OX7 3AT), *b* 1949; *ed* Downside: *m* 1978, Nora H., yr da of late Sigmund Hjornevik, and has issue living, Alexander Hugh Joseph, *b* 1982, — Emma Marie Clare, *b* 1980. — Richard Joseph (14 Langham Place, W4 2QL), *b* 1954; *ed* Downside: *m* 1981, Gillian, da of Maj D.W. Mart, of Felixstowe, Suffolk, and has issue living, Harry Hugh Joseph, *b* 1985, — Lucy Elizabeth, *b* 1983. — (Teresa) Jane (97 Altenburg Gdns, SW11 1JQ), *b* 1939.

Issue of late Joseph Francis Edward Radcliffe, 2nd son of 4th baronet, *b* 1891, *d* 1940: *m* 1922, Marjorie Sophia, who *d* 1973, da of Sir Francis Charles Edward Denys-Burton, 3rd Bt (Denys, Bt):—

Elizabeth Denyse Mary, *b* 1923; 1941-45 War with WAAF: *m* 1952, Ives Bonapace, and has issue living, Charles, *b* 1953, — Mark, *b* 1955, — William, *b* 1958, — Caroline, *b* 1954, — Jane Mary, *b* 1961, — Isabelle, *b* 1964. — Louise Marie Antoinette, *b* 1928: *m* 1956, Alec Pearson Carn, of Highbury, Thornford, Sherborne, Dorset, and has issue living, Nicholas (36B Douglas Rd, N1; The Old Manse, Stansfield, Suffolk), *b* 1957; *ed* Bradfield; MA Oxon 1987: *m* 1992, Eveline, da of Louk Ochtmann, of Brussels, and has issue living, Alexander Radcliffe *b* 1993, — Jonathan, *b* 1960; *ed* Bradfield, and Reading Univ (BSc), — Vanessa Mary, *b* 1963; MRCVS Bristol 1987; PhD 1994, — Francesca Georgina, *b* 1969; *ed* Exeter Univ (BSc), — Alexandra Sophia, *b* 1972; BA London Univ 1993.

Issue of late Robert John Peter Joseph Radcliffe, 4th son of 4th baronet, *b* 1898, *d* 1974: *m* 1929, Ursula Evelyn Mary, who *d* in a house fire 1977, da of late Lt-Col Miles John Stapylton, OBE, of Myton Hall, York:—

Peter Martin Joseph, *b* 1941: *m* 1963, Pamela Ann, 2nd da of George C. Johnson, of 2 Castle Terr, Husthwaite, York. — Thomas Joseph Henry, *b* 1943. — Rosemary Anne Ursula Katherine, *b* 1930: *m* 1950, Louis Bertram Hawkswell, who *d* 1987, and has issue living, Frederick Andrew Joseph, *b* 1951; *ed* Belmont Abbey, Hereford: *m* 1974, Linda Anne Todd, and has issue living, Michael Andrew William *b* 1976, Benjamin James *b* 1977, — Martin Louis, *b* 1955; *ed* Belmont Abbey, Hereford: *m* 1976, Elsa Catherine Hall, and has issue living, Oliver Alan Louis *b* 1979, Nicholas Martin *b* 1983, — Anthony Robert, *b* 1956; *ed* Belmont Abbey, Hereford: *m* 1979, Linda Middleton, — Philip William, *b* 1958; *ed* Belmont Abbey, Hereford: *m* 1981, Jill Patricia Dorrington, and has issue living, Jon William Robert *b* 1984, Rebecca Eleanor Ann *b* 1981, — Simon, *b* 1968, — Elizabeth Ann, *b* 1960: *m* 1980, Anthony George Dorrington, and has issue, Daniel George Louis *b* 1980, Bronwen Ann *b* 1982. — Mary Elizabeth Jane (The Colt House, Easingwold, York), *b* 1939: *m* 1st, 1957, John William Courtney, who *d* 1969; 2ndly, 1985, Philip Leslie Abbott, and has issue living (by 1st *m*), Miles Stewart John, *b* 1965: *m* 1989, Tracy Anne Clarke, — Rosemary Elizabeth, *b* 1967.

Issue of late (Charles Joseph) Basil Radcliffe, 5th and yst son of 4th Bt, *b* 1900, *d* 1983: *m* 1939, (Kathleen) Norah Anne, who *d* 1994, only da of late Norman Percy, of Maloya, Colombo, Sri Lanka:—

Francis Charles Joseph (78 Millfield Rd, York), *b* 1939; *ed* Ampleforth, and Gonville and Caius Coll, Camb; Bar Gray's Inn 1962; a Recorder 1979-83: *m* 1969 (*m diss* 1982), Nicolette Hélène, el da of Eugene Randag, of Lodge Hill Farm, Butler's Cross, Aylesbury, Bucks, and has issue living, Edward Eugene Joseph, *b* 1969, — Colette Anne, *b* 1971, — Alexandra Mary, *b* 1972. — (Bryan) Anthony Joseph (24 Abbotsbury Close, W14), *b* 1941; *ed* Ampleforth; Solicitor 1963: *m* 1965, Pisana, yr da of late Conte Giuseppe Petrobelli, of Prato della Valle, Padua, Italy, and has issue living, Mark Anthony Joseph, *b* 1967, — Harry Joseph, *b* 1972, — Isabella Carolina, *b* 1974. — Kathryn Anne, *b* 1943: *m* 1965, Anthony John Tulk-Hart Bigland, of Lowgate House, Backbarrow, Ulverston, Cumbria, and has issue living, Benedict James, *b* 1972, — Emma Lucy, *b* 1967, — Sophie Kathryn, *b* 1970.

Issue of late Capt Henry Joseph Francis Radcliffe, 2nd son of 3rd baronet, *b* 1862, *d* 1928: *m* 1896, Gertrude Mary Philomena, who *d* 1955, da of late Rev John Coventry (E Coventry, colls):—

Henry Edward Joseph (Manor Cottage, Lympsham, Weston-Super-Mare), *b* 1904: *m* 1939, Ursula Mary Skeet, yr da of F. D. Workman, and has issue living, Sally Anne Ursula, *b* 1940: *m* 1966, Geoffrey P. M. Taylor, of Willow Cottage, Dundry, Bristol, and has issue living, Justin Peter *b* 1968, Juliet Clare *b* 1970, Lucinda Jane *b* 1971, Kirsty Anna *b* 1974. — Gertrude Mary Catherine, *b* 1903: *m* 1925, Philip George Bower, who *d* 1939.

This family took its name from the village of Radcliffe in Lancashire. Richard de Radclyffe, Seneschal and Minister of the Forests in Blackburnshire, accompanied Edward I in his wars in Scotland, and received from that monarch a grant of a charter of freewarren and chase in all his demesne lands of Radcliffe. Mary, da of William Radcliffe of Milnsbridge, Yorks (a descendant of William 2nd son of Richard), and sister and heir of William Radcliffe of Milnsbridge (*d* 1795): *m* Joseph Pickford of Ashton-under-Lyne, Lancs. Their son Joseph Pickford, who assumed the surname of Radcliffe in 1795, was created a baronet for distinguished public services.

RAEBURN (UK) 1923, of Helensburgh, co Dunbarton

Safe if strong

(*Sir*) MICHAEL EDWARD NORMAN RAEBURN, 4th *Baronet*; *b* 12 Nov 1954; *s* his father, *Sir* EDWARD ALFRED, 1977, but does not use title: *m* 1979, Penelope Henrietta Theodora, da of late Alfred Louis Penn, of London, and has issue.

Arms – Or, on a piece of ground in base vert a roebuck statant proper, drinking out of a burn or brook undy argent and azure running bendways, in chief an anchor sable between two roses gules, barbed and seeded of the second. **Crest** – A stag's head proper.
Residence – Little Spring Cottage, Fletching St, Mayfield, E Sussex TN20 6TN.

SONS LIVING

CHRISTOPHER EDWARD ALFRED, *b* 4 Dec 1981. —— Martin Phillip, *b* 13 Jan 1989.

DAUGHTERS LIVING

Gwendoline Mary Joan, *b* 1983. —— Janet Maria, *b* 1986. —— Victoria Beatrix Sarah Gabrielle, *b* 1992.

AUNTS LIVING (*Daughters of 2nd baronet*)

Sheila Saisie (Denecourt, Cuckmere Rd, Seaford, E Sussex), *b* 1913. —— Irene Muriel (Denecourt, Cuckmere Rd, Seaford, E Sussex), *b* 1914.

WIDOW LIVING OF THIRD BARONET

JOAN (*Lady Raeburn*) (Fourways, Turners Green, Wadhurst, E Sussex), da of late Frederick Hill, of Dartford, Kent, and Boston, Mass, USA: *m* 1950, Sir Edward Alfred Raeburn, 3rd Bt, who *d* 1977.

COLLATERAL BRANCH LIVING

Issue of late Sir Ernest Manifold Raeburn, KBE, 2nd son of 1st baronet, *b* 1878, *d* 1922: *m* 1910, Greta Mary Alison, who *d* 1975, da of late Engineer-Capt James Herbert Watson, RN:—
Sir (William) Digby Manifold, KCVO, CB, DSO, MBE (25 St Ann's Terrace, NW8 6PH; *Clubs* – Pratt's, Cavalry and Guards', Royal Yacht Squadron), *b* 1915; *ed* Winchester and Magdalene Coll, Camb (MA); Maj-Gen (ret) late Scots Gds; Comdg 2nd Bn Scots Gds 1953-55; Lt-Col Comdg Scots Gds 1958-59, Comd 1st Gds Bde Group 1960-61, Dir of Combat Development (Army) 1963-65, Ch of Staff Allied Forces N Europe 1965-68, and Ch, Army Instructor Imperial Defence Coll 1968-70; Resident Gov and Keeper of Jewel House of HM Tower of London 1971-79; 1939-45 War in Middle East, Italy and NW Europe (despatches, MBE, DSO); MBE (Mil) 1941, DSO 1945, CB (Mil) 1966, KCVO 1979: *m* 1960, Adeline Margaret, yst da of late Thomas Selwyn Pryor, MC (*see* Halsey, Bt).
The 1st baronet, Sir William Hannay Raeburn (son of late William Raeburn, of Glasgow), was head of firm of Raeburn & Verel, Ltd, and sat a MP for Dunbartonshire (*U*) 1918-23. The 2nd baronet, Sir William Norman Raeburn, CBE, was a KC.

RALLI (UK) 1912, of Park Street, City of Westminster

Sir GODFREY VICTOR RALLI, TD, 3rd *Baronet*; *b* 9 Sept 1915; *s* his father, Sir STRATI, MC, 1964; *ed* Eton; 1939-45 War, as Capt Berks Yeo RA (despatches): *m* 1st, 1937 (*m diss* 1947), Nora Margaret, only child of late Charles Forman, of Lodden Court, Spencers Wood, nr Reading; 2ndly, 1949, Jean, da of late Keith Barlow, of 3 Vicarage Gate, W8, and has issue living by 1st *m*.

Arms – Azure, a lion rampant argent semée of lozenges of the first in chief a crescent between two crosses couped of the second. **Crest** – A lion as in the arms holding between the paws a cross couped argent.
Residence – Great Walton, Eastry, Sandwich, Kent CT13 0DN. *Club* – Naval and Military.

SON LIVING (*By 1st marriage*)

Keep to the straight path

DAVID CHARLES (The Old Hall, Hardingham, Norfolk NR9 4EW), *b* 5 April 1946; *ed* Eton, and Harper Adams Agric Coll: *m* 1975, Jacqueline Cecilia, da of David Smith, and has issue living, Philip Neil David, *b* 31 March 1983, — Marina Louise, *b* 1980. *Clubs* – White's, Farmers'.

DAUGHTERS LIVING *(By 1st marriage)*

Louise, *b* 1942: *m* 1964, Ewen James Fassiefern Cameron, of The Old Vicarage, Harringworth, Corby, Northants NN17 3AF, and has issue living, James Allan Godfrey, *b* 1965, — Alistair Ewen David, *b* 1968. ——— Tessa TITTERTON, *b* 1945; adopted by her mother and her stepfather, Philip Arthur Titterton, MB, ChB, whose surname she assumed in 1952.

BROTHER LIVING

Lucas John, *b* 1920; *ed* Eton; 1939-45 War as Maj Roy Signals (despatches): *m* 1st, 1950 (*m diss* 1989), Katia, da of Constantine Droulia, of Athens, Greece; 2ndly, 1989, Mrs Jean Patricia Barrett, da of Capt Edward Morden Bennett, RN, of Wolfeton Manor, Charminster, Dorchester, and has issue living (by 1st *m*), John Strati (97 Bryanston Court, George St, W1H 7HE), *b* 1956: *m* 1986, Kathryn Martin, and has issue living, Helen Elizabeth *b* 1987, Stephanie Catherine *b* 1990, — Dora Louise, *b* 1953: *m* 1984, Nicolas Rakić, of 18 Bury Walk, SW3 6QB, and has issue living, Peter Lucas Gradimir *b* 1988, Alexander Minas Cedomir *b* (twin) 1988, Anna Katharina Lila *b* 1985. *Residence* – 14 Oxford Sq, W2 2PB.

SISTERS LIVING

Diana Myrtle (Arlington Lodge, Bibury, Glos), *b* 1918: *m* 1939, Lt-Col John Herbert (Jack) Walford, DSO, Seaforth Highlanders, who *d* 1976, and has issue living, Michael Carr (The Old House, Wolverton, Basingstoke, Hants), *b* 1943; *ed* Harrow and Royal Agric Coll, Cirencester, — (Ewan) John (203 West Prairie, Wheaton, Illinois 60187, USA), *b* 1945; *ed* Harrow, Law School (London and Guildford), and Free Univ, Amsterdam; Speelman Fellow, Wolfson Coll, Camb, 1976; PhD; Assoc Prof of Art History, Wheaton Coll, Illinois since 1981: *m* 1972, Maria, only da of late Pietro Angelo Eligio Dellù, of Milan, and has issue living Samuel Michael *b* 1973, David John *b* 1980, Deborah Maria *b* 1978, — Belinda Mary (8 St Mary Abbot's Terrace, W14), *b* 1941: *m* 1st, 1961 (*m diss* 1968) John William Hayter; 2ndly, 1986, Colin Norman McCorquodale, only son of late Maj Angus McCorquodale, and has issue living (by 1st *m*), Sarah Miranda *b* 1964: *m* 1989, Angus Sladen, of The Old House, Wolverton, Basinstoke, Hants, and has issue living, Olivia Henrietta Malvina *b* 1992, Georgina Ann Diana *b* 1994). ——— Patience Louise, *b* 1922: *m* 1944, Lt-Cdr William Edward Michael de Sivrac Dunn, RNVR (despatches), of Awliscombe House, Honiton, Devon EX14 0NP, and has issue living, Mark de Sivrac, *b* 1947, — Karen Louise, *b* 1945: *m* 1971, Alan Grieve, of Stoke Lodge, Clee Downton, Ludlow, Salop SY8 3EG, and has issue living, Thomas de Sivrac *b* 1973, Lara Louise *b* 1974.

The 1st baronet was head of the firm of Ralli Bros, East India merchants, of 25, Finsbury Circus, EC.

RAMSAY (NS) 1666, of Bamff, Perthshire (Extinct 1986)

Sir NEIS ALEXANDER RAMSAY, 12th and last *Baronet*; *d* 1986.

COLLATERAL BRANCH LIVING

Grandchildren of late William Alexander Ramsay, el son of George Gilbert Ramsay, 3rd son of 9th baronet:—
Issue of late Lt-Col George William Neil Ramsay, RA, *b* 1907, *d* 1976: *m* 1st, 1932, Maryel Hope, who *d* 1935, 2nd da of late Col Robert William Pigott Clarke-Campbell-Preston, of Ardchattan Priory, Connel, Argyllshire; 2ndly, 1937 (*m diss* 1947), Catherine Trewyn, only da of Charles Bernard Dougherty, of Ottawa, Canada; 3rdly, 1948, Muriel (80 Comares Ave, St Augustine, Florida 32084, USA), only da of late Sydney Haslett, of St Leonards-on-Sea, Sussex:—
(By 1st *m*) Maryel Susan, *b* 1935: *m* 1965, Peter Callanan Battin, of Albany, NY, USA, and has issue living, Peter Ramsay, *b* 1970, — Maia Hope, *b* 1967. ——— (By 2nd *m*) Catherine Ann, *b* 1938: *m* 1st, 1959 (*m diss* 1969), Russell Payson, of Cambridge, Mass, USA; 2ndly, 1970 (*m diss* 1973), Peter Alexander Altman, of Washington, DC, USA, and has issue living (by 1st *m*), Gilbert Russell, *b* 1962, — Katherine Ann, *b* 1964. ——— Priscilla Maud, *b* 1940:*m* 1968, Robert Taylor Adams, of Richmond, Virginia, USA, and has issue living, Priscilla Susan, *b* 1972.

RAMSAY (UK) 1806, of Balmain, Kincardineshire

Aspiro
I aspire

Sir ALEXANDER WILLIAM BURNETT RAMSAY, 7th *Baronet*; *b* 4 Aug 1938; *s* his father, *Sir* ALEXANDER BURNETT, 1965; the presumed heir to the Baronetcy of Burnett of Leys (*cr* 1626): *m* 1963, Neryl Eileen, da of J. C. Smith Thornton of Trangie, NSW, and has issue.

Arms – Argent, an eagle displayed sable, beaked and membered gules, charged on the breast with a rose of the field. **Crest** – A demi-eagle displayed sable.
Residence – Banchory, PO Box 274, Warren, NSW 2824, Australia.

SONS LIVING

ALEXANDER DAVID, *b* 20 Aug 1966: *m* 1990, Annette Plummer. ——— Ian John, *b* 1968: *m* 1993, Kerry Calvert. ——— David Burnett, *b* 1971.

SISTERS LIVING

Enid Ellice, *b* 1937: *m* 1961, Reginald Geoffrey Capel, of Calool, Manilla, NSW, and has issue living, Peter Geoffrey, *b* 1963: *m* 1992, Louise Johnston, — Dianna Enid, *b* 1965: *m* 1994, Alexander William Campbell Martin, of Jamestown, SA. ——— Patricia Thirza, *b* 1940: *m* 1965, Anthony Osborne McAlary, of Milawa, Warren, NSW, and has issue living, Anthony Alexander, *b* 1970, — Anna, *b* 1968.

AUNT LIVING *(Daughter of 5th baronet)*

Constance Agnes, *b* 1912: *m* 1938, Arthur Thomas Baldwin (Bundilla, Young, NSW, Australia), who *d* 1977, and has issue living, Ross Ramsay, *b* 1943: *m* 1971, Susan Joan, da of S. R. Oldham, of Matta Mia, Wagga Wagga, NSW, and has issue living, Angus Oldham *b* 1972, Richard Arthur *b* 1973, — Malcolm Ramsay (Brisendon Av, Collaroy, NSW, Australia), *b* 1946,

Janet Mabel, *b* 1941: *m* 1962, John Lyle Francis, of Tara, Mumbril, NSW, Australia, son of G. H. Francis, and has issue living, Hubert Thomas Lyle *b* 1967, Regina Constance *b* 1965.

COLLATERAL BRANCHES LIVING

Issue of late Herbert William Alexander Ramsay, yr son of 5th baronet, *b* 1907, *d* 1987: *m* 1936, Bessie Billingsley (29 Brae St, Inverell, NSW, Australia), yst da of Dr Wilfred Billingsley Dight, of Sydney, NSW, Australia:—
William Macalister (Girraween, Bonshaw, NSW, Australia), *b* 1939: *m* 1967, Susan Thornton, da of R T Parkinson, of Camla, Wellington, and has issue living, Timothy William, *b* 1969, — William Ross, *b* 1971, — Jennifer Susan, *b* 1962. —— Elizabeth Barton, *b* 1945: *m* 1966, Peter Angus Gough, of 8 Crane Place, Moree, NSW, Australia, and has issue living, Simon John, *b* 1972, — Phillipa Anne, *b* 1968: *m* 1989, Stephen John Smith, of 7 Myall Place, Moree, NSW, Australia, and has issue living, Nicola Elizabeth Winter *b* 1994, — Sandra Elizabeth, *b* 1969. —— Roslyn Barton, *b* 1946: *m* 1st, 1967, Geoffrey Robert Burcham; 2ndly, 1987, Keith Donald Glasson, of Kingaroy, Queensland, Australia, and has issue living, (by 1st *m*) David William, *b* 1969, — Jacqueline Judith, *b* 1971, — Georgina Elizabeth, *b* 1979.

Granchildren of late Hugh Francis Ramsay, 2nd son of 3rd baronet:—
Issue of late Hugh Entwistle Ramsay, *b* 1871, *d* 1960: *m* 1901, Elsie Lavater, who *d* 1960, da of William Cox:—
Irene Beatrice, *b* 1902: *m* 1929, Ivor George Sullivan, who *d* 1955, and has issue living, Ramsay Wakeford (4460 Cottonwood Drive, Burlington, Ontario, Canada), *b* 1933: *m* 1957, Eleanor Mary Thorpe, and has issue living, Richard Andrew Ramsay *b* 1960, Fiona Clare *b* 1962, Jennifer Mary *b* 1965, — Patricia Berenice, *b* 1934; ARCA: *m* 1961, Professor Michael Edward Mallett, DPhil, of 2 Lansdowne Circus, Leamington Spa, and has issue living, Lucien Christian Ramsay *b* 1976, Cyprian Casper Alexander *b* 1978.

Grandchildren of Hugh Entwistle Ramsay (ante):—
Issue of late Alexander Hugh Ramsay, *b* 1905, *d* 1962: *m* 1937, Ethel Charlotte, who *d* 1993, da of late Albert Upton, of Waimai, NZ:—
Patricia Marion, *b* 1945: *m* 1976, Carl Donald Tyndale Watson-Gandy, PhD, of 3 South Lodge, Stanton Fitzwarren, Swindon, Wilts SN6 7SF, and has issue living, Hugh James Ramsay, *b* 1981, — (Jane) Vere, *b* 1979. —— Eleanor Margaret, *b* 1949: *m* 1994, Serge Artemiev, of 72 Grey St, Shannon, Levin, NZ.
Issue of late John Entwistle Ramsay, *b* 1908, *ka* 1942: *m* 1937, Elizabeth Frances, da of A. H. Crichton, of Kelowna, British Columbia:—
Ian Alexander (62 Lemington Rd, Westmere, Auckland, NZ), *b* 1939: *m* 1st, 1963 (*m diss* 1988), Rosalind Sheila Tolliss, of Hildenborough, Kent; 2ndly, 1988, Lorraine Gillian Kelly, and has two sons (by 1st *m*) Norman Francis, *b* 1967, — Nicholas John, *b* 1968, — (by 2nd *m*) Alexandra Grace, *b* 1988.

Grandson of late Noel Bannerman Ramsay (infra):—
Issue of late Lieut Noel Entwistle Burnett Ramsay, RNVR, *b* 1907, *ka* 1942: *m* 1932, Phyllis Agnes (who *m* 2ndly, 1949, Lt-Col Eric T. Cuthbert, who *d* 1974, and 3rdly, 1982, Ronald George Fielder, FICS, of 7 Carlton Court, Carlton Rd, Harpenden, Herts AL5 4SY) da of Arthur H. Kilner:—
Rev Canon Alan Burnett (St Marks Vicarage, Locks Lane, Mitcham, Surrey CR4 2JX), *b* 1934; AKC: *m* 1967, Elisabeth, da of Norman Marsh, and has issue living, Christopher, *b* 1968, — Matthew John, *b* 1971, — Francis, *b* 1973, — Rachel, *b* 1969.

Grandchildren of late Lieut Noel Entwistle Burnett Ramsay, RNVR (ante):—
Issue of late Duncan Soutter Burnett Ramsay, *b* 1937, *d* 1988: *m* 1967, Carole Anne (17 Lambourn Gdns, Harpenden, Herts), da of late D. H. Briars:—
Benjamin Noel, *b* 1969. —— Daniel Bruce, *b* 1971. —— Helen Jayne, *b* 1973.

Granddaughter of late Hugh Francis Ramsay (ante):—
Issue of late Noel Bannerman Ramsay, *b* 1875, *d* 1958: *m* 1905, Edith Katharine, who *d* 1962, da of Francis Johnson, MD:—
Edith Rosemary Patricia, *b* 1915: *m* 1st, 1937, Thomas Martin Homfray Pardoe, Capt 2nd Batn Worcestershire Regt, who was *ka* Hong Kong 1941; 2ndly, 1943, Col Thomas Brian Carey, RA, who *d* 1970; 3rdly, 1975, Prof James Carl Gilbert, Univ of Hawaii, and has issue living, (by 1st *m*) Hermione Ann Felicity, — (by 2nd *m*) Shane Peter, *b* 1944, — Peter Brian Ramsay, *b* 1948. *Residences* – Rigden's Farm, Leigh, nr Reigate, Surrey; 2969 Kalakaua Av, Honolulu, Hawaii 96815, USA.

Issue of late Capt John Ramsay, 3rd son of 3rd baronet, *b* 1843, *d* 1913: *m* 1876, Florence Mary, who *d* 1936, only child of late Richard J. Hilton, of Preston House, Faversham:—
Ethel, MBE, *b* 1882; MBE (Civil) 1918: *m* 1906, Major William Thompson Armitage, formerly RA. —— Hilda, *b* 1885: *m* (Jan) 1912, Eugene Spinney, and has issue living, David John, *b* Oct 1912, — Martin Giles, *b* 1916, — Juliet Ethel, *b* 1914. —— Evelyn, *b* 1887: *m* 1909, Cuthbert Radcliffe, who *d* 1924, and has issue living, Richard, *b* 1912, — Norman, *b* 1914, — Michael, *b* 1918.

Grandsons of late Brig-Gen William Alexander Ramsay, el son of Capt Francis Ramsay, 3rd son of 2nd baronet:—
Issue of late Adm Sir Bertram Home Ramsay, KCB, KBE, MVO, *b* 1883, *ka* 1945: *m* 1929, Helen Margaret, who *d* 1993, da of Col Charles Thomson Menzies, of Kames, Greenlaw, Berwickshire:—
David Francis (74797 South Cove Drive, Indian Wells, Calif 92210, USA). *Club* – New (Edinburgh), *b* 1933; *ed* Eton, and Camb Univ (BA): *m* 1st, 1963 (*m diss* 1973), Stacey Rogers; 2ndly, 1988, Pamela –, of Calif, USA, and has issue living (by 1st *m*), Michael Stuart, *b* 1964; *ed* Stanbridge Earls, — James Alexander, *b* 1967; *ed* Eton. —— Charles Alexander (Bughtrig, Coldstream, Berwicks; Chesthill, Glenlyon, Perthshire; *Clubs* – Boodle's, Cavalry and Guards', and New (Edinburgh)), *b* 1936; *ed* Eton, and RMC; served R Scots Greys; Maj-Gen 1984 a Member of Queen's Body Guard for Scotland (Royal Company of Archers): *m* 1967, Hon Mary Margaret Hastings MacAndrew, da of 1st Baron MacAndrew, PC, TD, and has issue living, William Bertram, *b* 1969; *ed* Eton, Newcastle Univ (BA), and RMA Sandhurst; commn'd Royal Scots Dragoon Gds 1992, — Charles Burnett, *b* 1981, — Rowena Cecilia, *b* 1973, — Camilla Georgina, *b* 1976.

Grandchildren of late Robert Ramsay, son of late Capt Robert Ramsay, 3rd son of 1st baronet:—
Issue of late Marmaduke Francis Ramsay, *b* 1860, *d* 1947: *m* 1895, Alice Katherine Angelique, who *d* 1951, da of Ottiwell Charles Waterfield, formerly of Nackington House, Canterbury:—
Robert Ottiwell (Kinblethmont, Arbroath, Angus), *b* 1900: *m* 1937, Constance Aileen, da of late Major Hugh Bernard German, MC, RAMC, and has issue living, Robert David (West Mains of Kinblethmont, by Arbroath, Angus DD11 4RW), *b* 1942; *ed* Harrow, and Glasgow Univ: *m* 1966, Penelope Anne, only da of Michael Gladstone, of Great Shelford, Cambridge, and has issue living, Robert Nicholas *b* 1968; *ed* Harrow, and Reading Univ: *m* 1993, Jessica McLaren, Alexander John *b* 1969; *ed* Harrow, and Brasenose Coll, Oxford, Jonathan Charles *b* 1973; *ed* Harrow, — John Lauderdale, *b* 1945, — Sarah Margaret, *b* 1937: *m* 1st, 1962 (*m diss* 1973), Capt David John Wemyss Anstice, 10th Roy Hussars, son of Vice-Adm Sir Edmund Walter Anstice, KCB; 2ndly, 1976, as his 2nd wife, Michael John Eadon Campbell of Dunstaffnage, 21st Hereditary Capt of Dunstaffnage, who *d* 1981, of Dunstaffnage Castle, Connel, Argyllshire, and has issue living, (by 1st *m*) Robert

Christian Edmund *b* 1963, David Henry *b* 1964, James Richard *b* 1965, — Lavinia Jane, *b* 1938: *m* 1959, Patrick Robert Chalmers, who *d* 1982, and has issue living, Patrick Robert Graham *b* 1960, Virginia Jane *b* 1961, Lindsay *b* 1962, Nicola Katherine *b* 1964, — Aileen Susanna *b* 1941: *m* 1964, Colin Gibb, of Inshewan, Forfar, and has issue living, John Alexander *b* 1968, Shanestra Margaret *b* 1966.

Issue of late Robert Christian Ramsay, *b* 1861, *d* 1957: *m* 1907, Olive Zillah, who *d* 1957, da of W. W. Voss, of Penrice, Queensland:—

Alexander Robert (15 Gault Rd, Belair, S Australia 5052), *b* 1910; Cdr RNVR; 1939-45 War (DSC and Bar): *m* 1944, Helen MacGregor, da of J. M. Shaw, of Lisburn, co Antrim, and has issue living, Colin Robert (7 Edwards Bay Rd, Mosman, Sydney, Australia), *b* 1945: *m* 1968, Lyndall Clare Sundstrom, of Gatton, Qld, and has issue living, Robert Andrew *b* 1974, Susan Belinda *b* 1976, Sandra Leigh *b* 1977, — Celia Grace, *b* 1947: *m* 1st, 1966 (*m diss* 1974 in Zimbabwe), 10th Viscount Chetwynd; 2ndly, 1974, Geoffrey Burnett-Smith, of 13 Gloucester Av, Belair, S Australia, and has issue living, (by 1st *m*) (*see* V Chetwynd), (by 2nd *m*) Angus *b* 1977, — Alexandra Helen Fleur, *b* 1955: *m* 1st, 1977, Iain Lovat Fraser, who was *ka* 1978; 2ndly, 1986, Terrence John Tarlington, of 12 Leyland St, Mt Gravatt, Qld 4122, Aust. —— David Malcolm (The Woodlands, Navenby, Lincoln), *b* 1924: *m* 1948, Joan Esme, da of C. J. Murphy, and has issue living, Alan David, *b* 1951, — James Anthony, *b* 1952, — Oliver Dermot, *b* 1954, — Malcolm Robert, *b* 1956. —— Olive Joan, *b* 1916: *m* 1948, Wing-Cdr Eric Comyn Boucher, RAF, who *d* 19—, and has issue living, Angus Comyn *b* 1949, — Esther Dawn, *b* 1951, — Vanessa Jane, *b* 1954. *Residence* – The Hollies, Bredgar, Kent.

Issue of late Arthur Douglas Ramsay, OBE, *b* 1868, *d* 1952: *m* 1914, Winifred who *d* 1979, da of W. H. Turner, of Geraldton, W Aust:—

Susan Patricia (18 Cristowe Rd, SW6), *b* 1926: *m* 1st 1950 (*m diss* 1965), Maj Sir Francis David Somerville Head, 5th Bt; 2ndly, 1967 (*m diss* 1988), Henry Jagoe Shaw, FRCS, and has issue (by 1st *m*) (*see* Head, Bt).

Grandson of late Arthur Douglas Ramsay (ante):—

Issue of late Capt Michael Douglas Ramsay, Seaforth Highlanders, *b* 1918, *d* 1983: *m* 1949, Eleanor Kinsell (Lyford Cay, PO Box N7776, Nassau, Bahamas), of Florida, USA:—

Jonathan Chandler Burnett, *b* 1950: *m* 1979, Keren Jane Livingstone-Leonard, and has issue living, Alexander Douglas Burnett, *b* 1984, — Kia Nikisha Burnett, *b* 1982. *Residence* – Aerie, PO Box N52, Nassau, Bahamas.

Sir Alexander, 1st Bt (2nd son of Sir Thomas Burnett of Leys, 6th (*see* Burnett, Bt)), by his wife Catherine, sister of Sir Alexander Ramsay of Balmain, 6th and last Bt, succeeded his uncle in the Ramsay estates 1806, and assumed, by Roy licence, the surname and arms of Ramsay. Sir John Ramsay, *cr* Lord Bothwell 1485 and killed at Flodden 1513, was ancestor of Sir Gilbert Ramsay of Balmain, 1st Bt (*cr* 1625).

Ramsay-Fairfax-Lucy (Cameron-Ramsay-Fairfax-Lucy), see Lucy.

Ramsay-Steel-Maitland, see Maitland.

RAMSDEN (E) 1689, of Byram, Yorkshire

Sir JOHN CHARLES JOSSLYN RAMSDEN, 9th *Baronet*; *b* 19 Aug 1950; *s* his father, *Maj Sir* CARYL OLIVER IMBERT, CMG, CVO, 1987; *ed* Eton, and Trin Coll, Camb (MA); HM Foreign Ser: *m* 1985, (Jennifer) Jane, yr da of Rear Adm Christopher Martin Bevan, CB, of Cranborne, Dorset, and has issue.

ᴀrms – Argent on a chevron between three fleurs-de-lis sable, as many ram's heads couped at the neck argent. ᴄrest – A cubit arm in armour proper, the gauntlet holding a fleur-de-lis sable.
Address – c/o Foreign and Commonwealth Office, King Charles St, SW1.

DAUGHTERS LIVING

Isobel Lucy, *b* 1987. —— Stella Evelyn, *b* 1989.

DAUGHTERS LIVING OF SEVENTH BARONET

Phyllida Rosemary, *b* 1929: *m* 1955, Patrick Thomas Gordon-Duff-Pennington, OBE, DL (who assumed by deed poll 1955, the final surname of Pennington), and has issue living, Prunella Melissa Phyllida, *b* 1956: *m* 19—, Donald Gordon, of 9 East Rd, N Berwick, E Lothian, — Anthea, *b* 1958: *m* 1982, Timothy Charles Osborn-Jones, of 3 Norman Av, Henley-on-Thames, Oxon, son of Rev Arthur Osborn-Jones, of 24 Ainsworth Av, Ovingdean, Brighton, and has issue living, Rupert Alexander *b* 1987, Katharine Louisa *b* 1986, — Iona Arabel, *b* 1961: *m* 1988, Peter Edward Frost (who assumed the surname of Frost Pennington 1988), son of Robert C. Frost, of Balloch, Inverness-shire, and has issue living, Ewan Patrick *b* 1990, Fraser Robert *b* 1991, Isla Rose *b* 1993, — Rowena, *b* 1963: *m* 1987, (Martin) Robert Morris-Eyton, of Hallbeck, Whicham, Millom, Cumbria LA18 5LU, only son of John Reginald Morris-Eyton, of Beckside, Whicham, Millom, Cumbria, and has issue living, Patrick Geordie *b* 1993, Isobel Rosemary *b* 1989, Rebecca Melissa *b* 1991. *Residence* – Muncaster Castle, Ravenglass, Cumbria CA18 1RQ. —— Penelope Lucinda, *b* 1930: *m* 1958, Peter Anthony Neville Pennethorne Laing, of Northfields Farm House, Turweston, Brackley, Northants, and has issue living, Arabella Charlotte Lucinda, *b* 1960: *m* 1988, Toby James Foster, elder son of David Foster, of Lea Farm, Stopham, Sussex, and has issue living, Alexandra Constance Harriet *b* 1990, Prudence Charlotte Victoria *b* 1993, — Venetia Alexandra Veronica Cayetana, *b* 1961: *m* 1987, James Anthony Findlay, eldest son of

John Findlay, of Carnell, Kilmarnock, and has issue living, Christopher Anthony Genghus *b* 1991. —— Annabel (Versions Farm, Brackley, Northants), *b* 1931: *m* 1958, Col Edward Timothy Smyth-Osbourne, Coldm Gds, who *d* 1987, and has issue living, Charles William, *b* 1959: *m* 1986, Joanna Mary, elder da of Sir Hugh Guy Cubitt, CBE (*see* B Ashcombe), and has issue living, Edward John *b* 1988, William Hugh *b* 1991, Archie Alexander *b* 1994, —— Julian George (Bailiff's Cottage, Beckhampton, Marlborough, Wilts), *b* 1964: *m* 1990, Claudia A., yr da of late C. N. R. Procter, of Hemingford Rd, Cambridge, —— Michael Alexander, *b* 1967, —— Rachel Rosa, *b* 1961: *m* 1989, Robert Drysdale, yst son of late W. A. Drysdale.

SISTER LIVING OF SEVENTH BARONET

Mary Joyce (*Lady Feilden*), *b* 1907: *m* 1929, Maj-Gen Sir Randle Guy Feilden, KCVO, CB, CBE, Coldstream Guards, who *d* 1981 (*see* V Hampden, colls). *Residences* – Cot Farm, Minster Lovell, Oxford OX8 5RS; Aberardur Lodge, nr Newtonmore, Inverness-shire PH20 1BX.

WIDOW LIVING OF EIGHTH BARONET

ANNE (*Anne, Lady Ramsden*), elder da of Lt-Col Sir Charles George Wickham, KCMG, KBE, DSO, of Ashdene, Comber, co Down: *m* 1945, Maj Sir Caryl Oliver Imbert Ramsden, 8th Bt, CMG, CVO, who *d* 1987. *Residence* – Vallance Cottage, Upper Chute, nr Andover, Hants SP11 9EH.

COLLATERAL BRANCHES LIVING

Issue of late John St Maur Ramsden, el son of 6th Baronet, *b* 1902, *d* 1948: *m* 1935 (*m diss* 1948), Lady Catherine Mary Clementine Heathcote-Drummond-Willoughby, da of 2nd Earl of Ancaster (*see* Bs Willoughby de Eresby):—
(Eloise) Carola, *b* 1938: *m* 1st, 1961, George Fillmore Miller III; 2ndly, 1974, Robert E. J. Philippi, and has issue living, (by 1st *m*) Sebastian St Maur, *b* 1965; Capt The Blues and Royals: *m* 1991, Emma Caroline, da of John Harries, of Esher, Surrey, — (by 2nd *m*) James Jeremy George, *b* 1975. *Residence* – Kinlochlaggan, Inverness-shire

Grandchildren of late Capt John Charles Francis Ramsden, son of late Capt Henry James Ramsden, 3rd son of 4th baronet:—
Issue of late Lieut-Col Henry RAMSDEN-JODRELL, CMG, *b* 1871, *d* 1950 (having assumed by Roy Licence 1920 the additional surname of Jodrell) *m* 1902, Dorothy Lynch, CBE, JP, who *d* 1958, el da of late Col Sir Edward Thomas Davenant Cotton-Jodrell, KCB (V Combermere, colls):—
Frances Barbara, *b* 1905: *m* 1939, Maj John Powys Dewhurst, RA (ret). —— Mary Angela (*Lady Fielden*), *b* 1916: *m* 1940, Air Vice-Marshal Sir Edward Hedley Fielden, GCVO, CB, DFC, AFC, RAF, who *d* 1976, and has issue living, Fiona, *b* 1944: *m* 1966, Christopher Norman Hart, of Eastcourt Farm, Crudwell, Malmesbury, Wilts. *Residence* – Edenwater House, Ednam, Kelso, Roxburghshire.

Granddaughter of late Robert Henry Ramsden, son of late Robert John Ramsden, son of Robert Ramsden (*b* 1784), of Carlton Hall, Notts, son of Robert Ramsden (*b* 1753), of Carlton Hall, Notts, son of Robert Ramsden, of Osberton, Notts, 4th son of 2nd baronet:—
Issue of late Robert Charles Plumptre Ramsden, *b* 1874, *d* 1964: *m* 1934, Mary Isiline (who *m* 2ndly, 1964, David William Smith, of Wigthorpe Hill, Wigthorpe, Worksop), only da of Lt-Col W. Wetwan, of Ashley Grove, Worksop:—
Mary, *b* 1938: *m* 1960, William A. Butroid, of Wigthorpe Farm, Wigthorpe, Worksop, Notts, and has had issue, Christine Joanna, *b* 1961, — Sarah Isiline, *b* 1963, *d* 1984, — Janet Elizabeth, *b* 1965.

Grandchildren of late Robert John Ramsden, son of late Robert Ramsden (*b* 1784) (*ante*):—
Issue of late Edward Plumptre Ramsden, *b* 1848, *d* 1916: *m* 1875, Frances Elizabeth, who *d* 1941, da of William Kelly, of Blackheath, SE:—
JOHN EDWARD CECIL, *b* 5 July 1881. —— William Eustace, *b* 1882. —— Five daughters.

Grandchildren of late Algernon Feilden Ramsden, 4th son of late Robert John Ramsden (*ante*):—
Issue of late Edward Feilden Ramsden, *b* 1893, *d* 1973: *m* 1928, Rhoda Helen, who *d* 1971, da of late Ashmore Mitchell, of Edinburgh:—
Geoffrey Ashmore, *b* 1930. —— Marjorie Neish, *b* 1929: *m* 1954, Paul Hastings Tennent, of 104 Lynton Rd, Acton, W3, and has issue living, Timothy Feilden, *b* 1955, — Stephen John, *b* 1958, — Adrian Paul, *b* 1961, — Mary Frances, *b* 1963.

Granddaughter of late Robert John Ramsden (*ante*):—
Issue of late John Pemberton Ramsden, *b* 1854, *d* 1911: *m* 1883, Alice Louisa, who *d* 1924, da of late Arthur Malet (Malet, Bt, colls):—
Frances Teresa: *m* 1928, James Tisdall Davidson.

Grandchildren of late Charles Harold Lowther Ramsden (*infra*):—
Issue of late Charles Dean Ramsden, BSc, *b* 1915, *d* 1981: *m* 1940, Katherine, who *d* 1979, da of Homer F. Lightfoot:—
Charles Anthony (178 Patricia Dr, Atherton, California, USA), *b* 1943; *ed* Stanford Univ (BSc, MBA); late Lieut USNR: *m* 1969, Naomi, da of Robert F. Robinson, MD, and has issue living, Abigail Leah, *b* 1976. —— Katherine Cecile, *b* 1945: *m* 1st, 1967 (*m diss* 1971), Grant A. Mitchell, late 2nd Lieut, US Army Res; 2ndly, 1972, Michael James Gannon, of 859 Acalanes Rd, Lafayette, California 94549, USA, and has issue living, (by 2nd *m*) Geoffrey Michael, *b* 1974, — Victoria Cecile, *b* 1976.

Grandchildren of late Charles Hamilton Ramsden, son of late Rev Charles Henry Ramsden, son of late Robert Ramsden (*b* 1784), grandson of late Robert Ramsden (*b* 1708), 4th son of 2nd baronet:—
Issue of late Charles Harold Lowther Ramsden, BSc, *b* 1883, *d* 1965: *m* 1st, 1912, Cecile W., who *d* 1933, da of W. S. Childs; 2ndly, 1936, Alice Voice, who *d* 1963, widow of William R. Henderson:—
(By 1st *m*) Scott Carlton (226 Hall Drive, Orinda, Cal, USA), *b* 1923; *ed* Cal Univ (BSc); late Lt, USN Reserve: *m* 1952, Mary Alice, da of Walter Garms, and has issue living, Linda Alice, *b* 1954. —— Dorothy Childs (4720 W Continental Drive, Glendale, AZ 85308, USA), *b* 1913: *m* 1947, Paul R. Coombs, who *d* 1992, and has issue living, Walter Ramsden (3916 W Yucca Dr, Phoenix, Ariz, USA 85029), *b* 1950: *m* 1972, Joan Vivian, da of Robert Grant Comstock, and has issue living, Paul Charles *b* 1986, Michele Ramsden *b* 1979, — David Paul (3529 Newland Rd, Baltimore, Md, USA), *b* 1952: *m* 1974, Vivien Gale, da of Karnig Paternayan, and has issue living, Christopher Paternayan *b* 1983, Carolyn Paternayan *b* 1985, — Marjorie Cecile (2711 Ordway St NW, Washington, DC 20008, USA) *b* 1954. —— Helen Caroline, *b* (twin) 1923: *m* 1946, Fred Albert Wagner, of 2405 Wedgewood Way, Livermore, Cal 94550, USA, and has issue living, Fred Albert, *b* 1950, — Jay Thomas, *b* 1952, — Caroline Cecile, *b* 1948: *m* 1974, William Wesley Constable, of 8 Memory Lane, Clearlake Highlands, Calif 95422, USA, and has issue living, Remington Peter *b* 1983, Wendy Erin *b* 1979, — June Marseillette, *b* 1955: *m* 1978, David Robert Bedford, of 2185 Azalea Dr, Roswell, GA 30075, USA, and has issue living, Ryan David *b* 1981, Lauren Anne *b* 1982.

Issue of late Percival Scott Webber Ramsden, *b* 1886, *d* 1958: *m* 1910, Abigail E., who *d* 1979, da of F. E. Philbrick:—
Shirley Carolyn (Box 515, Albion, CA 95410, USA), *b* 1916: *m* 1942 (*m diss* 1948), Leslie A. Peek, and has had issue, Lynne, *b* 1943; *d* 1993. —— Marjory (1840 Tice Creek Rd, no 2235, Waterford, Walnut Creek, CA 94595, USA), *b* 1917.

Grandchildren of late Rev Charles Henry Ramsden (ante):—
Issue of late Com Francis Edward Ramsden, RN, *b* 1849, *d* 1882: *m* 1879, Emma Elizabeth, who *d* 1925, da of late Lieut-Col F. W. Birch, Indian Army:—
Francis Charles Home, *b* 1880: *m* 1927, Lilla Marguerita, da of Charles Mackenzie, and has issue living, Francis Birch, *b* 1928, — June Elizabeth Ramsden, *b* 1929. *Residence* – Wembley RR No 1, Alberta, Canada.

Grandchildren of late Arthur John Ramsden, el son of Col Arthur Charles, 3rd son of Rev William Ramsden, son of Capt George Ramsden, only son of Lt-Col Frecheville Ramsden, 6th son of 2nd baronet:—
Issue of late Major Arthur Geoffrey Francis Ramsden, DSO, RA, *b* 1887, *d* on active ser 1945: *m* 1918, Winifred, who *d* 1958, da of late S. B. Cowan, LLD:—
Geoffrey Anthony Frecheville (Tillies Farm, Forest Green, nr Dorking, Surrey), *b* 1919; LDS, RCS 19—, BDS 19—; late Capt Hampshire Regt; 1939-45 War in Middle East (despatches): *m* 1952, Pamela Barnes. —— †Peter Derek Frecheville, *b* 1922; late Lt RNVR and serving with Fleet Air Arm: *m* 1958, Barbara, who *d* 1992, da of W. S. Alexander, and *d* 1993, leaving issue, Gordon Benjamin Frecheville, *b* 1961, — Elizabeth Lee, *b* 1959, — Beverley Anne, *b* 1962. —— Justin John Frecheville (8 St Margararet's Rd, Hillcrest 3610, S Africa), *b* 1927; Group Accountant-Sec of Tozer, Kemsley & Millbourn (S Africa) (Pty), Ltd, Johannesburg: *m* 1960, Brigit Joy Barry, da of Barry Smith, of Hill Crest, Natal, and has issue living, John Henry Frecheville *b* 1963, — Timothy Geoffrey Frecheville, *b* 1965, — Paula Frances Barry, *b* 1967. —— David Bruce Frecheville (51 14th St, Parkmore 2196, S Africa), *b* 1929; late Capt RA: *m* 1958, Deirdre Mary Bouchier, and has issue living, Bruce Frecheville, *b* 1959, — Paul David Frecheville, *b* 1961, — Debra Gail, *b* 1960, — Penelope Ray, *b* 1963. —— Myra Patricia, *b* 1921: *m* 1953, Alan Rowland Lingard Escombe. —— Arminel Jill, *b* 1925: *m* 1952, Lt-Cdr Richard Thomas Leggott, MBE, RN, and has issue living, Arminel Ruth, *b* 1953, — Susan Elizabeth, *b* 1955, — Jenifer Leigh, *b* 1958. *Residence* – 56 Edwin St, Boston, Lincs.
Issue of late John Hope Frecheville Ramsden, *b* 1896, *d* 1955: *m* 1930, Hilda Marguerite Lonnen, da of late E. J. Simmons:—
Margaret Elizabeth Anne, *b* 1932: *m* 1966, Capt T. L. Browne, Int Corps, of 10 Church St, Tintinhull, Som, and has issue.

Robert Ramsden was seated at Longley Hall, *temp* Henry VIII. The 1st baronet received his baronetcy for his essential services and the distinguished zeal exhibited by him at the Revolution. The 5th baronet, Sir John William, sat as MP for Taunton (*L*) 1853-7, for Hythe 1857-9, for W Riding of York 1880-85, for Osgoldcross Div of E Part of W Riding of York 1885-6, and was Under-Sec of State for War 1857-8. Sir John Frecheville Ramsden, 6th Bt was High Sheriff of Bucks 1920. Maj Sir (Geoffrey) William Pennington-Ramsden, 7th Bt, assumed by deed poll 1925 the surname of Pennington in lieu of his patronymic, and the arms of Pennington (differenced with a canton sable) quartered with those of Ramsden, in accordance with the will of the late Lord Muncaster, and by deed poll 1958 resumed the surname of Ramsden after that of Pennington; was patron of four livings, and High Sheriff of Cumberland 1962.

RANKIN (UK) 1898, of Bryngwyn, Much Dewchurch, co Hereford

Sir IAN RANKIN, 4th *Baronet*; *b* 19 Dec 1932; *s* his uncle, Sir HUGH CHARLES RHYS, 1988; *ed* Eton, and Ch Ch, Oxford (MA), FRGS, Lieut Scots Gds (Reserve): *m* 1st, 1959 (*m diss* 1967), Alexandra, only da of late Adm Sir Laurence George Durlacher, KCB, OBE, DSC (*see* Hanson, Bt, *cr* 1887, 1968 Edn); 2ndly, 1980, June, elder da of late Capt Thomas Marsham-Townshend (*see* E Romney, colls), and formerly wife of Bryan Montagu Norman, and has issue by 1st and 2nd *m*.

Arms – Or, a cinquefoil gules, in chief a battle-axe erect between two boars' heads couped, and in base a boar's head between two battle-axes erect sable. **Crest** – In front of a cubit arm holding a battle-axe proper, three cinquefoils gules.
Residence – 63 Marlborough Pl, NW8 0PT.

SONS LIVING (By 1st marriage)

GAVIN NIALL, *b* 19 May 1962; a Page of Honour to HM The Queen 1977-79; *ed* Eton, and Buckingham Univ.

(by 2nd marriage)

Lachlan John, *b* 1980.

DAUGHTER LIVING (By 1st marriage)

Zara Sophia, *b* 1960.

BROTHER LIVING

Sir Alick Michael, *b* 1935; *ed* Eton, Lieut Scots Gds (Reserve); Kt Bach 1992: *m* 1st, 1958 (*m diss* 1976), Susan Margaret, elder da of Lt-Col Hugh Littleton Dewhurst (*see* B Forteviot, 1985 Edn); 2ndly, 1976, Suzetta, da of Patrick Nelson, of Seafield, IoM, and has issue (by 1st *m*), Rupert Mark, *b* 1962, — Clare Joanna, *b* 1961, — Annabel Louise, *b* 1964, — Juliet Rachel, *b* 1970. *Residence* – 3 Saxe Coburg Place, Edinburgh EH3 5BR.

MOTHER LIVING

Lady Jean Margaret Dalrymple, DCVO, da of 12th Earl of Stair: *m* 1931, Lt-Col (Arthur) Niall Talbot Rankin, yr son of 2nd baronet, who *d* 1965. *Residences* – House of Treshnish, Calgary, I of Mull; 3 Catherine Wheel Yard, St James's St, SW1.

WIDOW LIVING OF THIRD BARONET

ROBINA (*Robina, Lady Rankin*), FSA Scot, SRN, da of Steurt Finlay, of Comrie, Perthshire: *m* 1946, as his 2nd wife, Sir Hugh Charles Rhys Rankin, 3rd Bt, who *d* 1988. *Residence* – Bracken Cottage, Kindallochan, Pitlochry, Perthshire.

COLLATERAL BRANCH LIVING

Grandchildren of late Charles Herbert Rankin, CB, CMG, DSO, 2nd son of 1st baronet:—
Issue of late Brig William Rankin, OBE, *b* 1909, *d* 1968: *m* 1939, Pauline Sinclair (Oegrove Farm, Frampton-on-Severn, Glos GL2 7EQ), da of late Oswald Sinclair Haggie:—
Mark (5 Albany Mews, Albany Rd, SE5 0DQ), *b* 1941, late Capt 15th/19th King's R Hussars. —— Christopher John (Cefn-y-Bettws, Clyro, Hereford, and 535 E 86th St, Apt 19A, New York, NY 10028, USA), *b* 1946: *m* 1st, 1968 (*m diss* 1974), Lucinda Jane, el da of Lt-Cdr Christopher Godfrey de Lisle Bush, RN; 2ndly, 1975 (*m diss* 1989), Penelope Jane, da of Nicholas Robin Benson, of Aycote House, Rendcombe, Cirencester (D Rutland), and has issue living (by 1st *m*), Peter William, *b* 1969, — James Christopher, *b* 1972, — (by 2nd *m*), Clare Louise, *b* 1978, — Katherine Emily, *b* 1981. —— Carolyn, *b* 1943: *m* 1967, Edmund Brooke Alexander, of 59 Wooster St, New York, 10012, USA, and has issue living, Emily Sinclair, *b* 1971, — Jessica Brooke, *b* 1973. —— Jean Mary, *b* 1952: *m* 1977, Charles Anthony Letts, of The Hendom Barn, Llowes, Herefs HR3 5JK, and 9 Stanley Gdns, W11 2ND, and has had issue, Charles Alexander Frazer, *b* 1980, — Benjamin James Mark, *b* and *d* 1982, — Jeremy Finan, *b* 1984.

The 1st baronet, Sir James (Ch Steward of the City of Hereford), was High Sheriff of Hereford 1873, and sat as MP for Herefordshire, N, or Leominster, Div (C) 1880-85, 1886-1906, and 1910-12. The 2nd baronet, Lieut-Col Sir Reginald, FRHS, FRGS, Bar-at-law, was Private Sec to Sec of State for the Colonies (Rt Hon A. Lyttleton, KC, MP) 1903-4, and *Times* War Correspondent in Morocco 1908, and with Bulgarian Forces 1912; he was Lieut-Col Comdg Herefordshire Regt (TD), and second in command of W Kent Yeo; served in S Africa 1900 as trooper and Lieut Rimington's Guides (medal with three clasps); author of *A Subaltern's Letters to His Wife, With General d'Amade in Morocco* (translated into Spanish and French), *The Inner History of the Balkan War, The Royal Ordering of Gardens*, etc. Sir Hugh Rankin, 3rd Bt (*d* 1988), was a noted eccentric whose interests embraced golf (held amateur record of GB for having played on 382 courses in UK and Eire), mountain cycling (Pres Rough Stuff Cycling Accocn 1956) and comparative religion; became a Moslem (British Rep all European Moslem Congress in Geneva), and later a non-Theistic Theravda Buddhist; campaigner for 'an independent Red Republic of all Scotland, excluding Orkneys and Shetland'; Trooper 1st Royal Drag Gds 1920-22 (invalided out), 1939-45 War in India; assumed by deed poll 1932 the addl surname of Stewart, discontinued same by deed poll 1946, and assumed the forename of Hugh in lieu of his patronymic Hubert.

RASCH (UK) 1903, of Woodhill, Danbury, Essex

FAS · DUCIT

Sir RICHARD GUY CARNE RASCH, 3rd *Baronet*; el son of late Brig Guy Elland Carne Rasch, CVO, DSO, yr son of 1st baronet; *b* 10 Oct 1918; *s* his uncle, Col Sir FREDERIC CARNE, TD, 1963; *ed* Eton, and RMC, Sandhurst; Maj late Grenadier Guards; a Member of HM Body Guard of Hon Corps of Gentlemen-at-Arms 1968-88: *m* 1st, 1947 (*m diss* 1959), Anne Mary, who *d* 1989, eldest da of late Maj John Henry Dent-Brocklehurst, OBE (B Trevor); 2ndly, 1961, Fiona Mary, eldest da of Robert Douglas Shaw, of St Leonards-on-Sea, Sussex, and former wife of Humphrey John Rodham Balliol Salmon, and has issue by 1st *m*.

Arms – Quarterly; azure and gules, a cross parted and fretted or, between in the first quarter a lion rampant per bend sinister ermine and erminois; in 2nd quarter a pelican in her piety, argent; in 3rd quarter a griffin segreant of the third; and in the 4th quarter a lion rampant of the last. **Crest** – Upon a rock proper a gryphon's head azure, collared gemel or, in front thereof a leopard's face between two fleurs-de-lis of the last.
Residences – 30 Ovington Sq, SW3; The Manor House, Lower Woodford, Salisbury, Wilts. *Clubs* – Cavalry and Guards', Pratts, and White's.

SON LIVING (By 1st marriage)

SIMON ANTHONY CARNE (The White House, Manningford Bruce, nr Pewsey, Wilts), *b* 26 Feb 1948; *ed* Eton, and Royal Agric Coll Cirencester; Page of Honour to HM 1962-64: *m* 1987, Julia, elder da of Maj Michael Godwin Plantagenet Stourton (*see* B Mowbray), and has issue living, Molly Clare Anne, *b* 1990.

DAUGHTER LIVING (By 1st marriage)

Leila Anne Katherine, *b* 1952: *m* 1975, Thomas Geoffrey Timothy Rose Price, and has issue (*see* Price, Bt, colls, *cr* 1815).

BROTHER LIVING

David Alwyne Carne, *b* 1922; *ed* Eton; Maj late Grenadier Guards: *m* 1953, Lady (Elizabeth) Anne Somerset, only da of late Henry Robert Somers Fitzroy de Vere Somerset, DSO (*see* D Beaufort, colls), and has issue living, Guy Martin Carne, *b* 1959, — Jane Catherine, *b* 1955: *m* 1976 (*m diss* 1980), Michael Smedley, — Emma Caroline, *b* 1962. *Residence* – Heale Stables, Woodford, Salisbury, Wilts SP4 6NT.

The 1st baronet, Sir Frederic Carne Rasch, sat as MP for S-E Div of Essex (C) 1886-1900 and for Chelmsford Div of Essex 1900-1908.

RASHLEIGH (UK) 1831, of Prideaux, Cornwall

Sir RICHARD HARRY RASHLEIGH, 6th *Baronet*; *b* 8 July 1958; *s* his father, *Sir* HARRY EVELYN BATTIE, 1984; *ed* All Hallows' Sch, Dorset.

Arms – Sable, a cross or, between in the 1st quarter, a Cornish chough argent; in the 2nd quarter a text T, and in the 3rd and 4th a crescent all argent. *Residence* – Menabilly, Par, Cornwall PL24 2TN. *Club* – Royal Fowey Yacht.

SISTERS LIVING

Susanna Jane, *b* 1955: *m* 1984, Timothy John Peter Emerson, of Coleraine, Yelverton, Devon PL20 6BN, son of Col John Emerson, OBE, TD, DL, of Yelverton, Devon, and has issue living, Thomas Alexander, *b* 1987, — Charlotte Jane, *b* 1985. —— Frances Elisabeth (Bess), *b* 1956: *m* 1982, Jonathan Ayton Haward, of 5 Stratton Terr, Truro, Cornwall TR1 3EW, son of Dr Michael Haward, of Quethiock, Liskeard, Cornwall, and has issue living, Harry Thomas, *b* 1986, — Emma Elisabeth, *b* 1988. —— Anne Henrietta, *b* 1959: *m* 1989, Peter B. R. Argles, of Green Lane Gardens, Buckland Monachorum, Yelverton, Devon PL20 7NP, son of late Guy Kingston Argles, of Sutton Valence, Kent, and has issue living, Edward Hugh Rashleigh *b* 1992, Arthur Peter Kingston *b* 1994.

AUNTS LIVING (*Sisters of 5th baronet*)

Elizabeth, *b* 1915. —— (Mary) Vivien (Lawhyre Cottage, Fowey, Cornwall), *b* 1917: *m* 1941, Cdr Philip Kidd, RN, and has had issue, Christopher Hugh Rashleigh *b* 1949: *m* 1975, (Anne) Louise Houblon (Lower Trengale, Doublebois, nr Liskeard, Cornwall), only da of Maj Richard de Warrenne Waller, RA, of Evergreens, The Avenue, Ascot, Berks, and *d* 1994, leaving issue, George Philip Houblon *b* 1977, Toby Richard Rashleigh *b* 1979, Emily Louisa Vivien *b* 1980, — Judith Anne, *b* 1941: *m* 1966, Robin Alec Stables, of Mill House, Rilla Mill, nr Callington, Cornwall PL17 7NT, and has issue living, Timothy Hugh *b* 1969, Susanna Vivien *b* 1967, — Sarah Vivien, *b* 1943: *m* 1st, 1967 (*m diss* 1981), Angus Dormer Crichton; 2ndly, 1982, Desmond George Uniacke Bain, of Helland, nr Bodmin, Cornwall, and has issue living (by 1st *m*), Thomas *b* 1975, Camilla *b* 1969, Anne *b* 1970, — Elizabeth, *b* 1946: *m* 1st, 1967 (*m diss* 1970), John Ronald Hoskins; 2ndly, 1979 (*m diss* 1987), Robin Kemp; 3rdly, 1988, Christopher Stuart Conwy Morgan, and has issue living (by 2nd *m*), Charles Frederick *b* 1972, Henry Selby *b* 1977.

COLLATERAL BRANCH LIVING

Issue of late Peter Rashleigh, yr brother of 5th baronet, *b* 1924, *d* 1990: *m* 1949, Lola (8A Frederick St, E Gosford, NSW 2250, Australia), da of Thomas Edmonds, of NSW:—
†Edward Harry, *b* and *d* 1952. —— Margaret Anne, *b* 1950: *m* 1970, Geoffrey Carruthers, of 43 Archdall St, McGregor, Canberra 2615, ACT, Australia, and has issue living, Richard, *b* 1976, — Keryn, *b* 1973. —— Bettine Jane, *b* 1954. —— Jill Vivien, *b* 1956: *m* 1982, Max Steiger, of 171 Carrington Av, Hurstville, Sydney, NSW 2220, Australia, and has issue living, Ben, *b* 1982, — Todd, *b* 1989.

The family of Rashleigh has been seated in Cornwall since the early part of the 16th century. The 2nd baronet was MP for Cornwall E (*L*) 1874-80.

RAWLINSON (UK) 1891

Sir ANTHONY HENRY JOHN RAWLINSON, 5th *Baronet*; *b* 1 May 1936; *s* his father, *Sir* (ALFRED) FREDERICK, 1969; *ed* Millfield: *m* 1st, 1960 (*m diss* 1967), Penelope Byng, da of Rear-Adm Gambier John Byng Noel, CB (*see* E Gainsborough, colls); 2ndly, 1967 (*m diss* 1976), Pauline Strickland, da of John Holt Hardy, of Sydney, NSW; 3rdly, 1977, Helen Leone, da of Thomas Miller Kennedy, of Glasgow, and has issue by 1st, 2nd, and 3rd *m*.

Arms – Sable, three swords in pale proper, pommels and hilts or, two erect points upwards and between them the other, point downwards; on a chief embattled of the third an antique crown gules. **Crest** – Out of an antique crown or, a cubic arm erect in armour, the hand grasping a sword in bend sinister, and the wrist encircled by a laurel wreath proper. *Residence* – Heath Farm, Guist, Norfolk NR20 5PG.

SONS LIVING (*By 1st marriage*)

ALEXANDER NOEL, *b* 15 July 1964.

(*By 2nd marriage*)

Rupert Seymour, *b* 1970.

(*By 3rd marriage*)

Christopher Thomas Seymour, *b* 1981.

DAUGHTER LIVING (*By 1st marriage*)

Caroline Louise Byng, *b* 1962.

BROTHER LIVING

(Marcus) Andrew Frederick (Stody Hall, Melton Constable, Norfolk), *b* 1940; *ed* Canford: *m* 1964, Miriam Diana, el da of Richard Joice, of Mill Farm, Newton by Castle Acre, Kings Lynn, Norfolk, and has issue living, Joanna Jane, *b* 1965, — Nicola Abigail, *b* 1967, — Candida Louise, *b* 1974.

SISTER LIVING

Sarah Jane, *b* 1939: *m* 1962, Capt William Hanslip Bulwer Bulwer-Long, 9th/12th Roy Lancers, DL Norfolk 1992 (who assumed by deed poll 1963 the additional surname of Bulwer), of Heydon Hall, Heydon, Norwich, and has issue living, Edward Hanslip, *b* 1966, — Benjamin Earle, *b* 1970, — Daisy Lydia, *b* 1975.

WIDOW LIVING OF FOURTH BARONET

BESSIE FORD TAYLOR (*Bessie, Lady Rawlinson*), da of Frank Raymond Emmatt, of Harrogate: *m* 1934, Sir (Alfred) Frederick Rawlinson, 4th Bt, who *d* 1969. *Residence* – Crossways Residential Hotel, The Boulevard, Sheringham, Norfolk.
Henry Creswicke Rawlinson, GCB (son of Abraham Tyzack Rawlinson, of Chadlington, Oxford), a distinguished Orientalist, and the first decipherer of cuneiform inscriptions; MP for Reigate 1858, and for Frome (*L*) 1865-8; re-organized Shah's Army 1833-9, Political Agent at Candahar 1840-43, and a Member of Council of Sec of State for India 1858-9 and 1868-95; *cr* a *Baronet* 1891. His son, Gen Sir Henry Seymour, GCB, GCSI, GCVO, KCMG, 2nd Bt; served with Burma Expedition 1886-87, with Nile Expeditions 1897 and 1898, at battles of Atbara and Khartoum, in S Africa 1899-1902, 1914, GOC 4th Div 4th Army Corps, and 4th Army 1915-18, and as GOC in C, N Russia 1919; C in C Aldershot 1919-10, and India 1920-25; *cr Baron Rawlinson*, of Trent, co Dorset (peerage of UK) 1919; *d* 1925, when the Barony became ext, and the Baronetcy devolved upon his brother, Lt-Col Sir Alfred, CMG, CBE, DSO, 3rd Bt.

READE (E) 1661, of Barton, Berkshire

Sir KENNETH RAY READE, 13th *Baronet*; *b* 23 March 1926; yr son of LaVerne Elton Reade, 5th son of 9th baronet; *s* his cousin, *Sir* CLYDE NIXON, 1982: *m* 1944, Doreen, da of Edward Vinsant, of Ann Arbor, Michigan, USA, and has issue.

Arms – Gules, a saltire between four garbs or. **Crest** – On the stump of a tree vert, a falcon rising proper, belled and jessed or.
Residence – 1535 Pine Valley Boulevard, 110 Ann Arbor, MI 48104, USA.

DAUGHTERS LIVING

Sandra, *b* 1945: *m* 1966, Douglas Crawford, of 3479 Central, Dexter, Michigan 48130, USA, and has issue living, Michael, *b* 1966, — John, *b* 1970, — Beth, *b* 1975. —— Karen, *b* 1948: *m* 1968, James Lamb, of 8531 Jackson, Dexter, Michigan 48130, USA, and has issue living, Tammy, *b* 1970, — Jennifer, *b* 1973, — Angie, *b* 1974, — Bonnie, *b* 1975, — Jackie, *b* 1978, — Karen Ann, *b* 1980. —— Norma (P.O. Box 95, Seney, Michigan 49883, USA), *b* 1953; has issue living, Richard, *b* 1972, — William, *b* 1988, — Sara, *b* 1984.

SISTER LIVING OF TWELFTH BARONET

Hazel, *b* 1899: *m* 1919, John Neil, and has issue living, Donald George (6051 Daft St, Lansing, Ingham Co, Michigan, USA), *b* 1921. *Residence* –

COLLATERAL BRANCHES LIVING

Issue of late Elmer Compton Reade, 2nd son of 9th baronet, *b* 1877, *d* 1918: *m* 1902, Leticia Wylie:—
Laura Leticia, *b* 1908: *m* 1930, Gordon Heston. *Residence* –

Issue of late Emory Isaac Reade, 4th son of 9th baronet, *b* 1887, *d* 1939: *m* 1908, Millicent da of G. Fisk:—
Irene Norah, *b* 1911: *m* 1931, Hugh Peebles, and has issue living, Robert Bradley, *b* 1932, — David, *b* 1943, — Gloria Ann, *b* 1935. —— Eileen, *b* 1913: *m* 1935, Ronald Durrett. —— Esther, *b* 1918: *m* 1934, Lawrence Durrett. *Residence* –
The 1st baronet's paternal grandfather was knighted by Queen Elizabeth I, and a baronetcy conferred upon his uncle, John, in 1641, became extinct 1712. The 3rd baronet of the present creation sat as MP for Cricklade. Sir George Compton Reade, 9th Bt, son of John Stanhope Reade (*d* 1883) (who emigrated to Dexter Township, Washtwaw, Michigan, *ca* 1835, with his first cousin, Edwyn Bennet Hoskyns), who was a great-grandson of the 6th Bt, *d* in April 1908.

READHEAD (UK) 1922, of Westoe, Borough of South Shields, co Palatine of Durham (Extinct 1988)

(*Sir*) JAMES TEMPLEMAN READHEAD, 3rd and last *Baronet* (but did not use the title).

DAUGHTER LIVING OF THIRD BARONET

Charlotte Susan Carolynn, *b* 1947. *Residence* – Flat 18, Ladbroke Square House, 2/3 Ladbroke Sq, W11 3LX.

DAUGHTER LIVING OF SECOND BARONET

Doreen Evelyn, *b* 1916: *m* 1946, John P. Glaisyer. *Residence* – Gallowhill, Whalton, Morpeth, Northumberland.

WIDOW LIVING OF THIRD BARONET

HILDA ROSEMARY, da of G. H. Hudson, of The Manor, Hatfield, Doncaster: *m* 1946, (Sir) James Templeman Readhead, 3rd Bt (who did not use the title), who *d* 1988. *Residence* – Marlish Cottage, High St, Woodgreen, nr Fordingbridge, Hants SP6 2AU.

Reardon-Smith, see Smith.

RECKITT (UK) 1894, of Swanland Manor, North Ferriby, East Riding of York (Extinct 1944)

Sir PHILIP BEALBY RECKITT, OBE, 3rd and last *Baronet*.

DAUGHTERS OF THIRD BARONET

Barbara, *b* 1902: *m* 1934, Hugh Wykeham David Pollock, who *d* 1972, and *d* 1993, leaving issue (*see* Montagu-Pollock, Bt, colls). —— Elizabeth Kathleen (*Lady Robson*), *b* 1904: *m* 1st, 1925, Lt-Col Vernon Harrison Holt, MC, DL, JP, who *d* 1966; 2ndly, 1969, Vice-Adm Sir (William) Geoffrey (Arthur) Robson, KBE, CB, DSO, DSC, who *d* 1989, and *d* 1991, leaving issue, (by 1st *m*) James Harrison (Ravenswick, Kirkbymoorside, York YO6 6LR), *b* 1936: *m* 1st, 1964 (*m diss* 1984), Dinah Annabel, da of late Lt-Col Charles Percy Digby Legard (*see* Legard, Bt, colls); 2ndly, 1986, Mary Alison, da of Rene Thomas, of Dove Acres, Easingwold, York, and has issue living (by 1st *m*), Philip James Harrison *b* 1965: *m* 1990, M. Jane R., eldest da of Ewan Harper, of Titchmarsh, Northampton, Michael Vernon Charles *b* 1966, Elizabeth Rebecca *b* 1969, (by 2nd *m*) Thomas Harrison *b* 1986, — Annabel *b* 1944; *m* 1969, Jonathan Geoffrey Shaw, of Amat, Ardgay, Ross-shire.

REDMAYNE (UK) 1964, of Rushcliffe, co Nottingham

Hon Sir NICHOLAS JOHN REDMAYNE, 2nd *Baronet*; *b* 1 Feb 1938; *s* his father, MARTIN, Baron Redmayne, DSO, TD, PC (Life Peer), in his Baronetcy, 1983; *ed* Radley, and RMA Sandhurst: *m* 1st, 1963 (*m diss* 1976), Ann, who *d* 1985, da of Frank Birch Saunders, of The Mews, Kineton, Warwicks; 2ndly, 1978, Mrs Christine Diane Wood Hewitt, da of late Thomas Wood Fazakerley, and has issue by 1st *m*.

Arms – Gules two chevronels, between three cushions ermine tasselled or, a bordure engrailed argent. **Crest** – In front of a cushion as in the arms fessewise, a horse's head argent mane gules.
Residence – Walcote Lodge, Walcote, Lutterworth, Leics.

SON LIVING (By 1st marriage)

GILES MARTIN, *b* 1 Dec 1968.

DAUGHTER LIVING (By 1st marriage)

Camilla Jane, *b* 1966: *m* 1989, Julian Howard Trevor Beach.
Martin Redmayne, DSO, TD, PC, son of Leonard Redmayne, was Ch Govt Whip 1959-1964, MP for Rushcliffe Div of Notts (*C*) 1950-66, and was *cr* a baronet 1964, and *Baron Redmayne*, of Rushcliffe, co Notts (Life Baron) 1966.

REDWOOD (UK) 1911, of Avenue Road, St Marylebone

We have disseminated knowledge
from of old

Sir PETER BOVERTON REDWOOD, 3rd *Baronet*; *b* 1 Dec 1937; *s* his father, *Sir* THOMAS BOVERTON, 1974; *ed* Gordonstoun; late Col KOSB; Dir SERCO-IAL Ltd: *m* 1964, Gilian Waddington, only da of John Lee Waddington Wood, of Limuru, Kenya, and has issue.

Arms – Paly of six or and ermine, a lion rampant sable, on a chief azure an embattled gateway proper between two mullets of six points of the first. **Crest** – A rock, therefrom an eagle rising proper, charged on each wing with a mullet of six points, in the beak a staff raguly or.
Address – c/o National Westminster Bank, Warminster Branch, 80 Market Place, Warminster, Wilts BA12 9AW.

DAUGHTERS LIVING

Anna Kathryn, *b* 1967: *m* 1993, Capt Patrick M. Thomson, eldest son of Brig Michael Thomson, of Trouville, France. —— Colina Margaret Charlotte, *b* 1969. —— Gaynor Elizabeth, *b* 1972.

HALF-BROTHERS LIVING

ROBERT BOVERTON, *b* 24 June 1953; *ed* Truro Cathedral Sch: *m* 1978, Mary Elizabeth Wright, and has issue living, James Boverton, *b* 2 Oct 1985, —— Morwenna Anne Carlile, *b* 1982. —— Charles Boverton, *b* 1956.

HALF-SISTER LIVING

Anne Boverton, *b* 1947: *m* 1968, James Embury, and has issue living, Tristan James, *b* 1971, — Bartholomew Boverton, *b* 1972.

AUNT LIVING

Patricia Boverton, *b* 1910: *m* 1965, Harold Box, of Spring Ducks, Horton Rd, Ashley Heath, Ringwood, Hants.

WIDOW LIVING OF SECOND BARONET

URSULA (*Ursula, Lady Redwood*), da of late Rev Herbert Percy Hale: *m* 1944, as his 2nd wife, Sir Thomas Boverton Redwood, 2nd Bt, who *d* 1974.
The 1st baronet, Sir Boverton, was a well-known authority on Petroleum, and was Adviser on Petroleum to Admiralty, India Office, and Home Office.

REID (UK) 1897, of Ellon, Aberdeenshire

Nothing is hard for one who loves

Sir ALEXANDER JAMES REID, 3rd *Baronet*; *b* 6 Dec 1932; *s* his father, *Sir* EDWARD JAMES, KBE, 1972; *ed* Eton, and Magdalene Coll, Camb; Capt (ret) 3rd Bn Gordon Highlanders; Malaya 1951-53; JP and a DL of Cambridgeshire; a Dir of Cristina Securities, Ltd, Ellon Castle Estates Co Ltd, Kingston Wood Farms Ltd, and other cos; Chm of Govs, Heath Mount Sch, Hertford: *m* 1955, Michaela Ann, da of late Olaf Kier, CBE, of Cokenach, Barkway, Royston, Herts, and has issue.

Arms – Azure, a stag's head erased or, between two torches fired proper; (as an honourable augmentation) on a chief gules a lion passant guardant or, armed and langued azure (being one of the lions from the Royal arms). **Crest** – A pelican in its piety proper. **Supporters** – On either side a Royal stag or, round the neck a chain proper suspended therefrom an escutcheon azure, charged with a representation of the Imperial Crown proper.
Residence – Kingston Wood Manor, Arrington, Royston, Herts SG8 0AP. *Clubs* – Caledonian, and Farmers'.

SON LIVING

CHARLES EDWARD JAMES (Manor Court Farm, Cold Ashton, Chippenham, Wilts), *b* 24 June 1956; *ed* Rannoch, and RAC Cirencester.

DAUGHTERS LIVING

Christina, *b* 1958. —— Jennifer, *b* 1959: *m* 1986, Stephen J. Marsh-Smith, only son of David Marsh-Smith, of Penrhosfeilw, Anglesey. —— Alexandra Catherine, *b* 1965: *m* 1992, Charles A. Lloyd, only son of John Lloyd, of Tiverton, Devon.

AUNT LIVING (*Daughter of 1st baronet*)

Victoria Susan Beatrice, *b* 1908: *m* 1935, Leonard St Clair Ingrams, OBE, who *d* 1953, and has issue living, Richard Reid (Forge House, Aldworth, Reading, Berks), *b* 1937; *ed* Shrewsbury, and Univ Coll, Oxford; Ed *Private Eye* 1963-86, and *The Oldie* since 1992: *m* 1962, Mary Morgan, and has had issue (with one son dec'd), Fred V. *b* 1964: *m* 1990, Sarah Jane, da of — Lovett (and has issue living, Otis *b* 1990), Margaret (Jubby) *b* 1965: *m* 1990, David Lionel Ford (and has issue) (*see* By Brand), — Leonard Victor, OBE (Garsington Manor, Oxford), *b* 1941: *m* 1964, Rosalind Ann, el da of Antony Ross Moore,

CMG, of Tonchbridge, Brill, and has issue living, Rupert *b* 1967, Lucy *b* 1965, Elizabeth *b* 1971, Catherine *b* 1976. *Residences* – 1 Lodge Av, SW14; 43 Low Town, Collieston, Aberdeenshire.

WIDOW LIVING OF SECOND BARONET

TATIANA (*Tatiana, Lady Reid*) (16 Buckingham Terr, Edinburgh, EH4 3AD), da of late Col Alexandre Fenoult, formerly Russian Imperial Guard: *m* (Jan) 1930, Sir Edward James Reid, KBE, 2nd Bt, who *d* 1972.

COLLATERAL BRANCH LIVING

Issue of late Adm Sir John Peter Lorne Reid, GCB, CVO, yr son of 1st baronet, *b* 1903; *d* 1973: *m* 1933, Jean, who *d* 1971, da of Sir Henry Herbert Philip Dundas, MVO, 3rd Bt (*cr* 1898):—

David Lorne Dundas (Quinta das Murtas, Rua Eduardo Van-Zeller, 2710 Sintra, Portugal), *b* 1938; late Lt 15th/19th King's R Hussars: *m* 1st, 1968 (*m diss* 1979), Mrs Elizabeth Wilkinson, da of late Adam Natt; 2ndly, 1979, Tedda Ann, da of Albert Charles Webber, of Litton Cheney, Dorchester, Dorset, and formerly wife of James Sholto Arthur Douglas (*see* E Morton, colls), and has two adopted das (with 1st wife), Jacqueline May (*Countess of Northesk*), *b* 1956: *m* 1979, 14th Earl of Northesk, and has issue (*see* E Northesk), — Lorna Victoria, *b* 1972, — and issue living (by 2nd wife) Benjamin James Dundas, *b* 1983, — Leonora Emily Louise, *b* 1981. ——— Delia (*Lady Montgomery*), *b* 1935: *m* 1956, Sir (Basil Henry) David Montgomery, 9th Bt, of Kinross House, Kinross.

This Baronetcy was created on the occasion of HM Queen Victoria's Diamond Jubilee in recognition of the 1st baronet's personal services to HM, Sir James, GCVO, KCB, MD, LLD, 1st Bt, being successively Physician to Queen Victoria, to King Edward VII, and to King George V.

REID (UK) 1922, of Springburn, Co of City of Glasgow, and of Kilmaurs, co Ayr

By fortitude and labour

Sir HUGH REID, 3rd *Baronet*; *b* 27 Nov 1933; *s* his father, *Sir* DOUGLAS NEILSON, 1971; *ed* Loretto.

Arms – (as recorded at Lyon Office) Argent, a demi-eagle, wings expanded, in chief an ancient handbell between a mullet in the dexter and a cross moline in the sinister, all sable. **Crest** – A demi-eagle, wings expanded sable.
Seat – Caheronaun Park, Loughrea, co Galway.

SISTER LIVING

Joan Murray, *b* 1929: *m* 1953, John Francis Quinn, and has issue living, John Douglas, *b* 1954, — Peter Francis, *b* 1956, — James Hugh, *b* 1959, — Michael Joseph, *b* 1967, — David Paul, *b* 1969, — Kevin, *b* 1974, — Mary Teresa, *b* 1955, — Margaret Joan, *b* 1960, — Anne Bernadette, *b* 1962, — Pauline, *b* 1965. *Residence* – Caheronaun, Loughrea, co Galway.

The 1st baronet, Sir Hugh Reid, CBE, VD, LLD, MICE, DL, JP (son of James Reid of Auchterarder, JP, MICE), was Chm and Managing Director of N British Locomotive Co, Ltd.

RENALS (UK) 1895

Cavendo tutus

Safe by being cautious

Sir STANLEY RENALS, 4th *Baronet*; *b* 20 May 1923; *s* his brother, *Sir* HERBERT, 1961; *ed* City of London Freemen's Sch; late Merchant Navy: *m* 1957, Maria Dolores Rodriguez Pinto, da of late José Rodriguez Ruiz, and has issue.

Arms – Per pale gules and sable, on a fesse nebuly argent between in chief two lozenges, and in base as many fleurs-de-lis or, a fasces fessewise proper. **Crest** – On a rock a fox reguardant supporting with its dexter foot a fasces erect proper, and charged on the shoulder with a lozenge or.
Residence – 52 North Lane, Portslade, E Sussex BN4 2HG.

SON LIVING

STANLEY MICHAEL, *b* 14 Jan 1958; *ed* Falmer High Sch, and Brighton Polytechnic (BSc, CEng, MIMechE, MIMfgE); Eur Ing: *m* 1982, Jacqueline Ann, da of Roy Dennis Riley, of 26 Uplands Road, Hollingdean, Brighton, Sussex., and has issue living, Lloyd James, *b* 17 May 1985, — Frances Emma, *b* 1986.

BROTHER LIVING

Charles (South View, Bird in Eye Hill, Uckfield, Sussex), *b* 1924; *ed* City of London Freemen's Sch; with Marine Insurance Co Ltd: *m* 1965, Sheila Joyce, da of Aubrey Hugh Berry.

SISTER LIVING

Marie.

The 1st baronet, Sir Joseph Renals (son of late William Renals, of Nottingham), was a Partner in the firm of Renals & Co, merchants, and was Lord Mayor of London 1894-5.

RENSHAW (UK) 1903, of Coldharbour, Wivelsfield, Sussex

Esse quam videri
To be rather than to
seem

Sir (CHARLES) MAURICE BINE RENSHAW, 3rd Baronet; *b* 7 Oct 1912; *s* his father, *Capt Sir* (CHARLES) STEPHEN BINE, 1976; *ed* Eton; Late F/O RAF: *m* 1st 1942 (*m diss* 1947), Isabel Bassett, da of late Rev John L. T. Popkin; 2ndy, 19—, Winifred May, da of H. F. Gliddon, of Ashwater, Devon, and formerly wife of James H. T. Sheldon, and has had issue by 1st and 2nd *m*.

Arms – Per pale and per chevron or and azure, in chief two martlets, and in base a bull's head couped all counterchanged. **Crest** – In front of a griffin's head erased sable a decrescent and an increscent argent.
Residences – Tom-na-Margaidh, Balquhidder, Perthshire; Linwood, Instow, N Devon.

SONS LIVING AND DECEASED *(By 1st marriage)*

†Charles Edward Bine, *b* 1944; *d* 1954. —— JOHN DAVID, *b* 9 Oct 1945: *m* 1970 (*m diss* 1988), Jennifer, da of Group Capt F. Murray, RAF, and has issue living, Thomas, *b* 1976, — Joanna, *b* 1973, — Catherine, *b* 1978.

(By 2nd marriage)

Andrew, *b* 1947; Sqdn Ldr RAF: *m* 1977, Cherry Rose, da of Cdr John Blakeley Russell, of Sunny Ridge, Higher Slade, Ilfracombe, N Devon (*see* Chichester Bt, colls), and has issue living, Edward Chichester, *b* 1979, — Rory Andrew, *b* 1980, — Harry John, *b* 1983, — Eloise Rose, *b* 1986. —— Quintus, *b* 1952: *m* 1st, 1976 (*m diss* 1979), Heather MacGillivray, of Sydney, NSW; 2ndly, 1986, Donna Lee Helmkamp, of Michigan, USA. —— Edward, *b* 1965.

DAUGHTERS LIVING *(By 1st marriage)*

Margaret, *b* 1943: *m* 1967 (*m diss* 1988) Dr Lee Coulter Chumbley, and has issue living, Roger, *b* 1973, — Justin, *b* 1977, — Lucy, *b* 1970.

(By 2nd marriage)

Caroline, *b* 1948: *m* 1987, Richard Dumbrill, of Eperray, France. —— Janet, *b* 1950: *m* 1970 (*m diss* 1989), Dr Colin Dodd, PhD, and has issue living, Benjamin, *b* 1976, — Jennifer, *b* 1971. —— Helen, *b* 1951: *m* 1st, 1976 (*m diss* 19—), Douglas Arthur Coutts, of Lerwick; 2ndly, 19—, Ian Macdonald, of Dunvegan, Isle of Skye, and has issue living, (by 1st *m*) Andrew, *b* 1977, — (by 2nd *m*) Calum Ian Berge, *b* 1982, — Findlay Charles, *b* 1986, — Eilidh, *b* 1981, — Fiona May, *b* 1984.

SISTERS LIVING

Julia Noble Bine, *b* 1914: *m* 1940, Capt Edward William Whitfield, Indian Army, and has issue living, Michael Stephen (Plymtree, Marondera, Zimbabwe), *b* 1941; late Maj R Scots Dragoon Gds: *m* 1969, Lady Fiona Catharine Sinclair, da of late 19th Earl of Caithness, and has issue living, Edward James *b* 1971, Christine Louise *b* 1973, — Christopher George, *b* 1945: *m* 1976, Moira Everitt, and has issue living, Ivan Edward, *b* 1978, Delia Joy *b* 1980, — Wendy Martina, *b* 1942: *m* 1963, Arthur Guiffré, of Portsmouth, Rhode Island, USA, and has issue living, Christopher Paul *b* 1965, Stephen *b* 1966, Karen Elizabeth *b* 1963, — Diana Mary *b* 1952: *m* 1975, David Bridge, and has issue living, Justyn *b* 1977, Martin *b* 1979. *Address* – PO Box 3721, Marondera, Zimbabwe. —— (Caterina) Margot, *b* 1917: *m* 1945, William Robert Percy Wall, Lt A African Air Force, who *d* 1988, and has issue living, Mary Jane, *b* 1948: *m* 1969, Louis George von Bratt Reynolds, MB, ChB, of Capetown, — Jessica, *b* 1950. *Residence* – Oakleigh, Greytown, Natal.

The 1st baronet, Sir Charles Bine Renshaw (son of late Thomas Charles Renshaw, QC, of Sandrocks, Sussex), sat as MP for W Div of Renfrewshire (C) July 1892 to Jan 1906.

RENWICK (UK) 1921, of Newminster Abbey, Morpeth, Northumberland

Sir RICHARD EUSTACE RENWICK, 4th *Baronet*; *b* 13 Jan 1938; *s* his father, *Sir* EUSTACE DEUCHAR, 1973; *ed* Eton: *m* 1966, Caroline Anne, da of late Maj Rupert Leonard Eversley Milburn, of Ghyllheugh, Longhorsley, Morpeth (*see* Milburn, Bt), and has issue.

𝔄rms – Per chevron sable and argent, in chief two lymphads of the second and in base on a mount vert a horse courant of the first. 𝔠rest – In front of a lion's head erased proper, a bugle horn stringed gules.
Residence – Whalton House, Whalton, Morpeth, Northumberland NE61 3UZ.

SONS LIVING

CHARLES RICHARD, *b* 10 April 1967; Capt The Light Dragoons: *m* 1993, Mrs Jane Ann Lyles, only da of Stuart Bush, of Holly Farm, Wendling, Norfolk. —— Harry Timothy, *b* 1968. —— Rory Eustace Deuchar *b* 1975.

BROTHER LIVING

George Eustace, *b* 1947; *ed* Eton.

SISTER LIVING

Julia Diana, *b* 1935: *m* 1957 (*m diss* 1979), Jervis Joscelyn Percy, and has issue living, Corinna Josceline, *b* 1964, —— Jane Diana, *b* 1966, —— Charlotte Elizabeth, *b* 1967. *Residence* – Greenfields, Wall, Hexham, Northumberland.

WIDOW LIVING OF THIRD BARONET

DIANA MARY (*Diana, Lady Renwick*) (Whalton, Morpeth, Northumberland), da of Col Bernard Cruddas, DSO, of Middleton Hall, Morpeth: *m* 1934, Sir Eustace Deuchar Renwick, 3rd Bt, who *d* 1973.

COLLATERAL BRANCHES LIVING

Issue of late William Henry Renwick, 2nd son of 1st baronet, *b* 1880, *d* 1961: *m* 1899, Ethel Maud, who *d* 1944, da of William Ratcliffe:—
Eric Montagu, *b* 1904: *m* 1956 (*m diss* 1960), Marie Sandra, da of . —— Aubrey Forster, *b* 1912. —— Alexandra Constance, *b* 1902. —— Dorothy Forster, *b* 1905. —— Pamela Mary, *b* 1920.

Issue of late George Renwick, 3rd son of 1st baronet; *b* 1881, *d* 1937: *m* 1906, Nina, da of John Best Ferrier:—
Peter, *b* 1913. —— Peggy, *b* 1907: *m* 1931, Claude Chessher Darling, and has issue living, David, *b* 1932, — Timothy, *b* 1944, — Diana Jane, *b* 1938: *m* 1968, Peter George Cary Summers, and has issue living, Jonathan Peter *b* 1969, Caroline Cary *b* 1971.

Grandson of late Gustav Adolph Renwick, 4th son of 1st baronet:—
Issue of late Denis Adolph Renwick, *b* 1907; *d* 1983: *m* 1934, Phyllis, who *d* 1983, only da of A. B. Atkinson:—
Guy Philip (Holystone Grange, Sharperton, Morpeth, Northumberland), *b* 1936; *ed* Stowe, and Christ's Coll, Camb; late 2nd Lt R Scots: *m* 1966, (Janet) Melanie, only da of late H. James Franklin, FRIBA, of West Hepple Farmhouse, Hepple, Morpeth, Northumberland, and has issue living, Shaun Maurice, *b* 1970, — Maxwell Mark, *b* 1972.

Issue of late Septimus Renwick, MC, Scots Guards, 5th son of 1st baronet, *b* 1886, *d* 1966: *m* 1916, Margaret, who *d* 1983, da of James Turnbull:—
George Lionel (Upend, Newmarket, Suffolk), *b* 1917. —— Barbara (Upend, Newmarket, Suffolk), *b* 1922.

The 1st baronet, Sir George Renwick (son of John Nixon Renwick, of Newcastle-upon-Tyne) was a member of the firm of Fisher Renwick & Co, shipowners and brokers of Newcastle, and Managing Director of Fisher Renwick Manchester-London Steamers, Ltd; he sat as MP for Newcastle-on-Tyne (*C*) Oct 1900 to Jan 1906 and Sept 1908 to Jan 1910, and for Central Division thereof Dec 1918 to Oct 1922.

REYNOLDS (UK) 1923, of Woolton, Co Lancaster

Sir DAVID JAMES REYNOLDS, 3rd *Baronet; b* 26 Jan 1924; *s* his father, *Lieut-Col Sir* JOHN FRANCIS ROSKELL, MBE, 1956; *ed* Downside; 1942-45 War in Italy as Capt 15th/19th Hussars: *m* 1966, Charlotte Baumgartner, and has issue.

Arms – Per chevron ermine and or, in chief two lions passant gules, and in base three leopards' faces sable. **Crest** – A demi moorcock displayed proper, charged on each wing with a leopard's face or.
Residence – Blanchepierre House, Rue de la Blanchepierre, St Lawrence, Jersey.

SON LIVING

JAMES FRANCIS, *b* 10 July 1971.

DAUGHTERS LIVING

Lara Mary, *b* 1967. —— Sophie Josephine, *b* 1968.

HALF-BROTHER LIVING

John Julian, *b* 1942: *m* 1966 (*m diss* 1970), Carolyn Anne, da of Capt Hector Lorenzo Christie (*see* M Zetland).

SISTER LIVING

By persevering

Hermione Mary Elizabeth, *b* 1922: *m* 1948, Edward Raymond Courage, CBE, who *d* 1982, and has issue living, Christopher John, *b* 1962: *m* 1991, Alexandra Louise, elder da of John Charles Haynes (*see* B Vaux of Harrowden), and has issue living, Edward Francis *b* 1992. *Residences* – Edgcote, Banbury, Oxon, and 31 Abbotsbury House, Abbotsbury Rd, W8.

HALF-SISTER LIVING

Mary Merilyn, *b* 1935: *m* 1954 (*m diss* 1963), Peter Guy Henry Thorold, and has issue (*see* Thorold, Bt, colls). *Residence* – Dutch Barge Wiljan, St Mary's Church, Battersea Church Rd, SW11 3NA.

COLLATERAL BRANCH LIVING

Issue of late James Roskill Reynolds, 2nd son of 1st baronet, *b* 1904, *d* 1982: *m* 1931, Helen Mary, who *d* 1977, el da of late Charles Richard Gillow, of Leighton Hall, co Lancaster:—
Richard James Gillow (Leighton Hall, Carnforth, Lancs), *b* 1933: *ed* Ampleforth; late 2nd Lieut IG: *m* 1968, Caroline Susan, da of late Terence Kenyon, and has issue living, Katherine Elizabeth Gillow, *b* 1971, — Lucy Helen Gillow, *b* 1975. —— Simon Anthony (64 Lonsdale Rd, SW13 9JS), *b* 1939: *ed* Ampleforth: *m* 1970, Beata, el da of late Baron Siegfried von Heyl zu Herrnsheim, and has issue living, Stefan Damian, *b* 1970, — Rupert Christian, *b* 1979, — Olivia Helen, *b* 1972, — Leila Barbro, *b* 1976.

Issue of late William Francis Roskell Reynolds, 3rd son of 1st baronet, *b* 1911, *d* 1978: *m* 1934, Nancy Planche, who *d* 19—, da of Rupert Bendall:—
Nicholas Francis (Thornley House, Nether Wallop, Stockbridge, Hants SO20 8HA), *b* 1938; *ed* Downside, and Ch Ch, Oxford (MA); late 2nd Lt IG; FCA: *m* 1964, Wendy Helen Broke, twin da of late Lt Nigel Vere Broke Thurston, RN, and has issue living, Alexander, *b* 1971, — Lucy Claire Thurston, *b* 1966, — Charlotte Louise, *b* 1967. —— Juliet Mary, *b* 1936: *m* 1962, Neville Anthony Leonard Whitbread, ACA, of Lower Huxley Hall, Chester, and has issue living, James Rupert Sinanian, *b* 1970, — Victoria Mary, *b* 1963, — Alice Mary, *b* 1964, — Emilia Ann, *b* 1967.
The 1st baronet, Sir James Philip Reynolds, DSO, MP (son of Francis William Reynolds, of Hillside, Woolton, Liverpool), was senior partner of Reynolds & Gibson, cotton brokers of Liverpool, a Director of Martins Bank, Ltd, of The Royal Insurance Co (Limited), Liverpool, London and Globe Insurance Co (Limited), and Thames and Mersey Marine Insurance Co (Limited), a JP and DL, and MP for Exchange Div of Liverpool (*U*) 1929-32. The 2nd baronet, Sir John Francis Roskell Reynolds, MBE, was a partner of Reynolds & Gibson, Chm of Combined English Mills (Spinners) Ltd, and Lieut-Col Irish Guards.

RHODES (UK) 1919, of Hollingworth, co Palatine of Chester

By good ways

Sir JOHN CHRISTOPHER DOUGLAS RHODES, 4th *Baronet; b* 24 May 1946; *s* his father, *Lt-Col Sir* CHRISTOPHER GEORGE, 1964.

Arms – Azure, on a bend between two lozenges or a leopard's face gules between two holly leaves vert. Crest – Two lions' gambs erased gules supporting a lozenge charged with a holly leaf, both as in the arms. *Residence –*

BROTHER LIVING

MICHAEL PHILIP JAMES, *b* 3 April 1948: *m* 1973, Susan Elizabeth, 2nd da of Richard Patrick Roney-Dougal, of South Lodge, Norton, Shifnal, Shropshire, and has issue living, Louise, *b* 1974. *Residence –* Southdown, Blakeney, Holt, Norfolk.

SISTER LIVING

Ursula Catherine, *b* 1944: *m* 1967, Capt Peter Herbert Roberts, RA, only son of Maj Herbert Thomas Roberts, of Bexhill-on-Sea, Sussex. *Residence –* 8 Letheringsett Hill, Holt, Norfolk.

WIDOW LIVING OF THIRD BARONET

MARY FLORENCE (*Lady Rhodes*) (Purvis Lodge, Cley-next-the-Sea, Holt, Norfolk), da of late Dr Douglas Wardleworth: *m* 1943, as his 2nd wife, Lt-Col Sir Christopher George Rhodes, 3rd Bt, who *d* 1964.

COLLATERAL BRANCH LIVING

Issue of late Com Philip Wood Rhodes, RN (ret), 2nd son of 1st baronet, *b* 1894, *d* 1956: *m* 1st, 1919, Judith Beresford, who *d* 1942, da of Trevelyan Martin; 2ndly, 1944, Elspeth (181 Cranmer Court, Sloane Av, SW3), da of T. Tod, of Durban:—
(By 1st *m*) Pamela Beresford, *b* 1920: *m* 1944, Peter Coleclough, of Longlands Hall, Stonham Aspal, Stowmarket, and has had issue, Jeremy Nigel, *b* 1945, — Martin Timothy, *b* 1947; *d* 1985. —— Vivien Patricia (1 Dukes Lodge, Holland Park, W11), *b* 1927.
Sir George Rhodes, 1st Bt, was a JP for Cheshire. Lt-Col Sir John Phillips Rhodes, DSO, late RE, 2nd Bt, was Chm of Thomas Rhodes (Limited), cotton spinners and manufacturers, of Hollingworth, Cheshire, and sat as MP for Cheshire, Stalybridge and Hyde Div (*C*) 1922-23.

Rhys-Williams, see Williams.

RICH (GB) 1791, of Shirley House, Hants (Dormant 1983)

Sir ALMERIC FREDERIC CONNESS RICH, 6th *Baronet; d* 1983, and at the time of going to press no name appears on the Official Roll of Baronets in respect of this title.

COLLATERAL BRANCHES LIVING

Grandchildren of late Harold A. S. P. Rich (*b* 1865), 3rd son of Henry Osborne Ludlow Rich (*b* 1822), only son of William Osborne Ludlow Rich, 3rd son of 1st baronet:—
Issue of late Leonard H. Rich, *b* 1898, *d* 1969: *m* 19—, —:—
Gordon Leonard (*presumed heir*), *b* 1921: *m* 1942, Olive Gilks, and has issue living, Gregory, *b* 1947, — Stephen Gordon, *b* 1949. —— Joyce, *b ca* 1923. —— Shirley Osborne, *b* 1926.

Grandchildren of late Lt-Col Charles Edwin Frederick Rich, DSO, only son of late Rev John Rich, el son of late Rev John Rich (*b* 1789), 4th son of 1st baronet:—
Issue of late Cdr Charles Rodney St John Rich, RN, *b* 1900, *d* 1970: *m* 1st, 1928 (*m diss* 1936), Felicity Chesterton, da of late Sir George Thompson Hutchinson; 2ndly, 1937, Georgina Blanche (38 Onslow Gdns, SW7), only da of late Donald Francis Napier Dalrymple, of 48 Hans Place, SW1:—
(By 1st *m*) Miles Rodney (Winkton Acre, Winkton, Dorset), *b* 1931; *ed* Bradfield; MBIM; Maj RE (ret): *m* 1959, Patricia Mary, only da of late George Stuart Castle, of Stone House Farm, Frindsbury, Rochester, and has issue living, Geoffrey Stuart, *b* 1969; *ed* Canford, — Alexandra Mary, *b* 1960; BSc: *m* 1988, Nicholas David Mills, — Frances Catherine St John, *b* 1962; MEng: *m* 1984, Stephen Craig Anderson, — Philippa Clare St John, *b* 1965. —— Deirdre Frances, *b* 1934: *m* 1958, Maj James Sidney Nobbs, MBE, RE (ret), of 9 Green Lane, Ford, Salisbury, Wilts, and has issue living, Nicolas Finch, *b* 1959; Maj RTR: *m* 1985, Sara Jane Dolding, — Anthony James, *b* 1961; BSc: *m* 1992, Natalie Diane Magnaldi, — Alison Frances, *b* 1963.

Grandsons of late Edwin William Gordon Rich, el son of late William Gordon Rich, 3rd son of late Rev John Rich (*b* 1789), 4th son of 1st baronet:—
Issue of late William Gordon Rich, *b* 1897, *d* 19—: *m* 1st, 1931, Henrietta Dorothy, who *d* 1955, da of Henry Donate Tyacke, of Westmeath, Ireland; 2ndly, 1958, Rhona Elizabeth, second da of late Thomas Lyons, of Hobart, Tasmania, and widow of John Matthew Clarke:—
(By 1st *m*) Urquhart David Gordon, *b* 1934; B Agriculture; is a Solicitor. —— John Patrick Gordon, *b* 1936: *m* 19-, Jillian, da of Helyar Bishop, of Papanui, Christchurch, New Zealand, and has issue living, Nicola, *b* 1960, — Joanna, *b* 1963.

Granddaughters of late Maitland Gordon Rich, yr son of late William Gordon Rich, 3rd son of late Rev John Rich (*b* 1789), 4th son of 1st baronet:—
Issue of late Geoffrey Gordon Rich, MC *b* 1889, *d* 1975: *m* 1924, Sybil Catherine Dorothy (14 Lysaght St, Timaru, NZ), da of Maj P. H. Johnson, of Mount Torlesse Station, Springfield, Canterbury, NZ:—
Dorothy Georgiana Gordon, *b* 1927: *m* 1951, Anthony Derek Morley Pinfold, of 187 Sawyers Arms Rd, Papanui, Christchurch, NZ, and has issue living, Giles Derek, *b* 1953, — Hamish Gordon Pinfold, *b* 1972, — Mary Kathryn, *b* 1954, — Judy Cassandra, *b* 1956. ——— Penelope Rosamund, *b* 1929: *m* 1953, Frederick Gerard Ulrich, of The Rock, Cave, S Canterbury, NZ, and has issue living, Peter Herstall, *b* 1954, — Sally Rosamund, *b* 1956, — Robyn Penelope, *b* 1957, — Jan Belinda, *b* 1959. ——— Angela Maitland, *b* 1932: *m* 1957, Lennox Mounsey, Master Mariner, of 77 Bann St, Bluff, NZ, and has issue living, Gordon Lennox, *b* 1958, — Timothy John, *b* 1965, — Prudence Jane, *b* 1960, — Annabel Kay, *b* 1963.

Grandsons of late Edwin Francis Rich, son of Vice-Adm Edwin Ludlow Rich, 5th son of 1st baronet:—
Issue of late Francis Arthur Rich, *b* 1859, *d* 1938: *m* 1st, 1890, Mary Catherine, who *d* 1899, da of Gerard Spooner, formerly of Elmdon, Warwickshire; 2ndly, 1899, Henrietta, da of Gerard Spooner (ante):—
(By 2nd *m*) Ronald Philip, *b* 1900. ——— Edwin Francis, *b* 1903.

RICHARDSON (UK) 1924, of Yellow Woods, Province of Cape of Good Hope, South Africa

By courage, faith and honour

Sir ANTHONY LEWIS RICHARDSON, 3rd *Baronet*; *b* 5 Aug 1950; *s* his father, *Sir* LESLIE LEWIS, 1985; *ed* Diocesan Coll, Cape Town; Stockbroker, Rowe & Pitman, London: *m* 1985, (Honor) Gillian, da of Robert Anthony Dauney, of 5 George St, Paddington, Sydney, Australia, and has issue.

𝕬rms – Argent, an ostrich proper, on a chief sable three lions' heads erased of the field. 𝕮rest – Upon a rock a lion rampant guardant proper resting the sinister paw on a mullet, gold.
Residence – 7 Westover Rd, SW18 2RE.

SON LIVING

WILLIAM LEWIS, *b* 15 Oct 1992.

DAUGHTER LIVING

(Honor) Olivia Phoebe, *b* 1990.

BROTHER LIVING

Charles John (7 Franconia Rd, SW4 9NB); *b* 1955; *ed* Diocesan Coll, Cape Town: *m* 1987, Gigi D. M., da of late Lt-Col R. R. Morris, of Huish Farm, Sydling St Nicholas, Dorset, and has issue living, George Leslie, *b* 1991, — Jessica Kate, *b* 1988.

SISTER LIVING

Jennifer, *b* 1947: *m* 1984, Richard Michael Fearon Gold, of Windrush Farm, Stowell, Dorset, eldest son of Rev Guy Alastair Whitmore Gold, of Bridge House, Great Bealings, Woodbridge, Suffolk, and has issue living, Alexander Leslie Fearon, *b* 1985, — Edward Guy Fearon, *b* 1986.

AUNT LIVING (*Daughter of 1st baronet*)

Audrey Anne, *b* 1909: *m* 1st, 1939, John Henry Muers-Raby, who *d* 1973; 2ndly, 1983, Maj-Gen Raymond Cyril Alexander Edge, CB, MBE, and has issue living, (by 1st *m*) Nicholas Jonathan (Oakley Farmhouse, Mottisfont, Romsey, Hants), *b* 1941: *m* 1973, Victoria, da of Lt-Col Henry Christopher White Bowring, MA, FLAS, of Whelprigg, Casterton, Carnforth, Cumbria, and has issue living, Rosanna Louise *b* 1975, — Nigel Andrew (Vexford Farm, Higher Vexford, Lydeard St Lawrence, Taunton, Som), *b* 1949: *m* 1986, Fiona Jane, da of Maj Geoffrey Lloyd, and has issue living, Thomas Sebastian *b* 1987, Oliver Henry *b* 1991. *Residence* – Brook Farm, N Curry, Taunton.

WIDOW LIVING OF SECOND BARONET

JOY PATRICA (*Joy, Lady Richardson*), da of John Percival Rillstone, of Johannesburg, S Africa: *m* 1946, Sir Leslie Lewis Richardson, 2nd Bt, who *d* 1985. *Residence* – Constantia Village, Cape Town, S Africa.
The 1st baronet, Sir Lewis Richardson, CBE (son of Kaufmann Richardson), was head of the firm of L. Richardson & Co, of Port Elizabeth, London, New York, and Boston.

RICHARDSON (UK) 1929, of Weybridge, co Surrey (Extinct 1981)

Sir GEORGE WIGHAM RICHARDSON, 3rd and last *Baronet*.

DAUGHTERS LIVING OF THIRD BARONET (*By 2nd m*)

Jenifer Winifred Wigham, *b* 1945: *m* 1973, David M. Drayson, of Studmore, Brenchley, Kent, and has issue living, Timothy James, *b* 1975, — Jonathan Charles, *b* 1980, — Melanie Sarah, *b* 1976. ——— Caroline Rosa Wigham, *b* 1950. ——— Patricia Barbara Wigham, *b* 1953: *m* 1982, Alastair C. Begg, of Monks Manor, Fir Toll Lane, Mayfield, E Sussex, and has issue living, Andrew Henry Wigham, *b* 1985, — Camilla Rosemary Wigham, *b* 1984.

DAUGHTER LIVING OF FIRST BARONET

Irene Geraldine Wigham, *b* 1919: *m* 1948, Donald J. Ferguson, and has issue living, Clive Wigham, *b* 1949: *m* 1980, Camilla Anne, da of Alan Wale, of Hall Green, Minto, Hawick, Roxburghshire, and has issue living, George Wigham *b* 1983, Robert Wigham *b* 1986, — Lee Margaret, *b* 1950. *Residence* – Elworthy Farm, Greenham, Wellington, Som.

STEWART-RICHARDSON (NS) 1630, of Pencaitland, Haddingtonshire

Sir SIMON ALAISDAIR (IAN NEILE) STEWART-RICHARDSON, 17th *Baronet*; *b* 10 June 1947; *s* his father, *Sir* IAN RORIE HAY, 1969; *ed* Trin Coll, Glenalmond.

Arms – Quarterly of six: 1st and 6th, argent, on a fesse azure between a bull's head or in chief and in base a lymphad sable, a saltire of the field *Richardson*; 2nd, argent, a lion rampant azure within a bordure gules *Stewart*; 3rd, azure, three garbs or *Comyn*; 4th, argent on a bend azure three buckles or *Leslie*; 5th, gyronny of eight or and sable *Campbell*. **Crest** – A cubit arm in armour grasping a sword all proper. **Supporters** – *Dexter*, a wyvern and *sinister*, an eagle wings erect, both proper.
Residence – Lynedale, Longcross, Chertsey, Surrey, KT16 0DP.

BROTHER LIVING

Honour is gained by valour

NINIAN RORIE (Rua Nice 132, Jardim Mediterraneo, Granja Vianna, Cotia 06700, São Paulo, Brazil), *b* 20 Jan 1949; *ed* Rannoch Sch, Perthshire; industrialist, late Commercial Air Pilot: *m* 1983, Joan Kristina, da of Howard Smee, of Rio de Janeiro, Brazil, and has issue living, Edward Rorie, *b* 22 July 1988, — William Howard, *b* 1990, — Olivia Joan, *b* 1987.

SISTERS LIVING

Claudia Mavis, *b* 1946: *m* 1970, R. Anthony Wainwright, of 29 Stratford Rd, W8, and has a son and da, Guiam Edward, *b* 1985, — Sarah, *b* 1987. —— (Roslyn) Alison, *b* 1952: *m* 1984, Peter Glennerster Wear, of 33 Findon Rd, W12 9PP, and has issue living, Christopher Algernon, *b* 1988, — Jessica, *b* 1986.

WIDOW LIVING OF SIXTEENTH BARONET

AUDREY MERYL (Lynedale, Longcross, Chertsey, Surrey KT16 0DP), da of Claude Odlum, of Leinster Grove, Naas, co Kildare: *m* 1st, 1944, as his 2nd wife, Sir Ian Rorie Hay-Stewart-Richardson, 16th Bt, who *d* 1969; 2ndly, 1975, Patrick Allan Pearson Robertson, CMG.

COLLATERAL BRANCHES LIVING

Issue of late Lieut-Col Neil Graham Stewart-Richardson, DSO, 3rd son of 14th baronet; *b* 1881, *d* 1934: *m* 1924, Alexandra, who *d* 1972, da of late Peter Ralli, of 11 Hyde Park Gardens, W2:—
Peter Neil Ralli, MBE, *b* 1926; *ed* Eton; High Sheriff Norfolk 1989; Maj Coldstream Gds; Brig late Parachute Regt, Croix de Guerre 1950, MBE (Mil) 1964: *m* 1954, Patricia Ann, da of late Maj John Michael Evans Lombe, MC, RA, and has had issue, — Neil Graham John, *b* 1955; *ed* Eton; *d* 1978. —— Michael Peter Alastair (The Old Manse, Glenbuchat, Strathdon, Aberdeen AB36 8TR), *b* 1957: *m* 1982, Amanda L., only da of John Baker, of Higher Shortwood Farm, Litton, Bath, and has issue living, Rory Neil John *b* 1989, Lucy Alexandra *b* 1987, — Mary-Ann, *b* 1961: *m* 1st, 1981, (George) Dominic Mackintosh Warre, yst son of Maj John Antony Warre, MC, of Barrowden, Oakham, Leics (*see* D Devonshire, 1973-74 Edn); 2ndly, 1987, David Stewart Gemmell, of Delvine, Murthly, Perthshire PH1 4LD, son of Lt-Col Arthur Stewart Gemmell, of Ingarsby Old Hall, Leics, and has issue living, (by 2nd *m*) George Neil *b* 1988, Mary Rose *b* 1990, — Katharine Jane, *b* 1966. *Residence* – Creake Abbey, Fakenham, Norfolk NR21 9LF. —— Alastair Lucas Graham (120 Woodsford Sq, W14 8DT; 7 Kings Bench Walk, Temple, EC4) *b* 1927; *ed* Eton, and Magdalene Coll, Camb (MA); Bar Inner Temple 1952: *m* 1969, (Diana) Claire, yr da of late Brig George Streynsham Rawstorne, CBE, MC, and has issue living, James George, *b* 1971, — Hugh Neil, *b* 1977, — Sarah Alexandra, *b* 1974.

Grandchildren of late Henry Gresham Stewart-Richardson, 2nd son of 13th baronet:—
Issue of late Charles Robert Stewart-Richardson, *b* 1877, *d* 1954: *m* 1905, Edith, who *d* 1950, 2nd da of Albert Berryman, formerly of Bath:—
†Alistair De Vere (Australian, Union and Pioneers Clubs), *b* 1906; Dep Gen Manager of Bank of NSW, Sydney: *m* 1944, Joan Wilson, da of late Edward Wilson Hunt, of Lane Cove, NSW, and *d* 1983, leaving issue, Donald Bruce, *b* 1946: *m* 19—, —, and has issue living, a son *b* 19—, a da *b* 19—. —— Dudley Austin (322 Hector St, Tuart Hill, W Aust), *b* 1924: *m* 1948, Barbara Jean Clark, and has issue living Kenneth John, *b* 1950, — Peter Dudley, *b* 1953. —— Beatrice Edith, *b* 1909: *m* 1948, Clive Edwards. —— Constance, *b* 1918: *m* 1941, Harry Hatch, and has issue living, Geoffrey Neil, *b* 1943, — Brian Richard, *b* 1946, — Lorraine Elizabeth, *b* 1950. —— Sadie Mary, *b* 1921: *m* 1963, Frank Chinnock, of Mt Barker, W Aust.
Issue of late John Henry Stewart-Richardson, *b* 1879, *d* 1952: *m* 1924, Anne, who *d* 1980, da of late Thomas Jackson, of Carnforth, Lancashire:—
Ian Douglas, *b* 1925. *Residence* –

Grandchildren of late John Ramsay Stewart-Richardson, 3rd son of 13th baronet:—
Issue of late Arthur James Stewart-Richardson, *b* 1884, *d* 1950: *m* 1913, Kathleen Mary, who *d* 1964, da of late Charles Hunter, of Cambridge, New Zealand:—
Edward James (PO Box 10038, Arataki, Mt Maunganui, NZ), *b* 1915; 1939-45 War with RNZAF: *m* 1948, Heather Gladys, who *d* 1985, da of Charles Scott, of Auckland, and has issue living, John Scott (Flat 4, 7 London St, St Mary's Bay, Auckland, NZ), *b* 1950; *ed* King's Coll, Auckland, and Auckland Univ; stockbroker, — Julia, *b* 1954; *ed* St Cuthberts Sch for Girls, Auckland, and Otago Univ: *m* 1990, Christopher William Cornthwaite, and has issue living, Guy Edward *b* 1991, James William *b* 1994. *Residence* – Station Rd, RR2, Omokoroa, Tauranga, NZ. —— John Charles (1 Haworth Av, Cambridge, NZ) *b* 1925; 1939-45 War with RNZAF: *m* 1950, Edith Margaret, da of Percival McIver, of Wellington, NZ and has issue living, Ian, *b* 1954: *m* 1984, Patricia, da of Robert Searle, of Cambridge, NZ, and has issue living, Kurt Jon *b* 1984, — June, *b* 1950: *m* 1970, Allan Ross Browne, son of Ivan Browne, of Cambridge, NZ, and has issue living, Scott Michael *b* 1973, Glen Andrew *b* 1977, Aaron Paul *b* 1978. —— Kathleen Sheila, *b* 1921: *m* 1946, Derek Pocknall, of 4A Oxford St, Masterton, NZ, and has issue living, Robert, *b* 1949, — Graeme (twin), *b* 1949, — David Thomas, *b* 1953, — Susan Mary, *b* 1948, — Helen

Jean, *b* 1958.. ——— Barbara Mary, *b* 1930: *m* 1st, 1950, Harold Vosper, who *d* 1960; 2ndly, 1962, Peter G. Wilson, of 102 Burwood Rd, Matamata, NZ, and has issue living, (by 1st *m*), Frank Stewart, *b* 1951; *ed* Wanganui Collegiate: *m* 1979, Claire Jeannette, da of Lionel Montague, of Matamata, NZ, and has issue living, Kirk James *b* 1981, Lauren Jane *b* 1980, Brook Jade *b* 1986, — Richard Arthur, *b* 1953; *ed* Wanganui Collegiate, and Matamata Coll: *m* 1st, 1979, —; 2ndly, 1984, —, da of Noutsos, of Athens, Greece, and has issue living (by 2nd *m*), Nikolas *b* 1984, Sarah Elizabeth *b* 1987, — Jennifer Kaye, *b* 1955: *m* 19—, Neil Brooks, son of Keith Brooks, — (by 2nd *m*), Stewart James, *b* 1968, — Robyn Jane, *b* 1963.

Sir Robert Richardson of Pencaitland, Haddingtonshire, was created a baronet with remainder to heirs male whatsoever. On the death of the 2nd baronet 1640, the title passed to Sir James Richardson of Smeaton, grandson of Sir James, el brother of 1st baronet. This baronetcy was dormant 1821-37, when John Stewart-Richardson assumed the title on being served heir of the 12th baronet. The mother of the 13th baronet was Elizabeth, el da and co-heir of James Stewart of Urrard, Perths. The 15th baronet, Sir Edward Austin, Capt Black Watch, was *ka* 1914.

Richardson-Bunbury, see Bunbury.

RICHMOND (UK) 1929, of Hollington, co Sussex

Sir JOHN FREDERICK RICHMOND, 2nd *Baronet*; *b* 12 Aug 1924; *s* his father, *Sir* FREDERICK HENRY, 1953; *ed* Eton, and at Jesus Coll, Camb; formerly Lieut 10th Hussars (seconded Provost branch): *m* 1965, Mrs Anne Moreen Bentley, da of late Dr Robert William Paylor Hall, MC, and has issue.

Arms – Gules, on a fesse cotissed or, between two roses argent, barbed and seeded proper, a lion passant of the field. **Crest** – A demi-stag proper, charged on the shoulder with a rose as in the arms, and holding between the forelegs a rose argent, barbed, seeded, leaved, and slipped, also proper.
Residence – Shimpling Park Farm, Bury St Edmunds, Suffolk. **Club** – MCC.

DAUGHTER LIVING

Caroline Sarah, *b* 1966.

SISTER LIVING

Anne Elizabeth, *b* 1926: *m* 1958, Dudley William Reeves, and has issue living, Nicholas Mark Renny, *b* 1964, — Heather Jennifer, *b* 1962: has issue living, Myles Edward REEVES *b* 1987. *Residence* – Filgrave House, Newport Pagnell, Bucks.
The 1st baronet, Sir Frederick Henry Richmond (son of late Henry Richmond, of Marnham), was Chm of Debenhams Ltd, of 91 Wimpole Street, W1, and of Harvey Nichols and Co, Ltd.

LABOR · VINCIT
Labour conquers

RICKETTS (UK) 1828, of The Elms, Gloucestershire, and Beaumont Leys, Leicestershire

Sir ROBERT CORNWALLIS GERALD ST LEGER RICKETTS, 7th *Baronet*; *b* 8 Nov 1917; *s* his father, *Sir* CLAUDE ALBERT FREDERICK, 1937; *ed* Haileybury, and Magdalene Coll, Camb (MA); admitted a Solicitor 1949; FRSA; formerly Partner in Wellington and Clifford; 1939-45 War as Capt Devonshire Regt; Personal Assist to Ch of Staff, Gibraltar, 1942-45 and ADC to Lt-Gov of Jersey 1945-46; Hon Citizen of Mobile, Alabama, USA: *m* 1945, (Anne) Theresa, CBE, da of late Rt Hon Sir (Richard) Stafford Cripps, CH, QC (*see* B Parmoor, colls), and has issue.

Arms – On a chevron azure between three roses gules, barbed and seeded proper, two swords in chevron also proper, pommels and hilts or, their points crossing each other in saltire (that on the dexter surmounted by that of the sinister) and passing through a wreath of laurel or; on a chief of the second a naval crown between two anchors erect or. **Crest** – Out of a naval crown or, a dexter arm embowed, habited azure and charged on the sleeve with two roses argent, the hand grasping a scimitar, the arm in front of an anchor in bend sinister sable.
Residence – Forwood House, Minchinhampton, Stroud, Gloucestershire GL6 9AB.

Prend moi tel que je suis
Take me as I am

SONS LIVING

(ROBERT) TRISTRAM (47 Lancaster Av, SE27 9EL), *b* 17 April 1946; *ed* Winchester, and Magdalene Coll, Camb (MA): *m* 1969, Ann, yr da of late Eric William Charles Lewis, CB, of 31 Deena Close, Queen's Drive, W3, and has issue living, Stephen Tristram, *b* 1974, — Clare Jessica *b* 1977. ——— John Stafford (92 Thompson Av, Richmond, Surrey), *b* 1956; *ed* Winchester, and King's Coll, London: *m* 1986, Jacqueline Zifteh, and has issue living, Joseph Robert *b* 1988.

DAUGHTERS LIVING

Sarah Lilian, *b* 1947: *m* 1981, His Honour (George Frederick) Peter Mason, QC, of Lane Cottage, Amberley, Glos GL5 5AB.
—— (Isobel) Theresa, *b* 1952: *m* 1973, John Anthony Bird, and has issue living, Patrick Jack, *b* 1975, — Eileen Diana, *b* 1977.

COLLATERAL BRANCHES LIVING

Grandchildren of late Rev Richard Ernest Ricketts, son of late Com Simpson Hicks Ricketts, RN, 3rd son of 1st Baronet:—
Issue of late Rt Rev Clement Mallory Ricketts, formerly Suffragan Bishop of Dunwich, *b* 1885, *d* 1961: *m* 1920, Dorothy Frances, who *d* 1984, da of late Rt Rev George Rodney Eden, DD (*see* Eden of Winton, B, colls, 1985 Edn):—
Michael Rodney, *b* 1923 (Church Farm, Saxlingham, Holt, Norfolk); *ed* Sherborne and Trin Coll, Oxford (MA); formerly Maj KRRC; a House Master, Bradfield Coll 1950-67, Headmaster of Sutton Valence Sch 1967-80, 1939-45 War (wounded): *m* 1958, Judith Anne Caroline, el da of late Col Thomas Stanley Courtenay-Clack, TD, RA, and widow of H. J. Corry, and has issue living, Charles Michael Thomas, *b* 1960, — James Rodney Eden, *b* 1964, — Rosemary Courtenay, *b* 1958, — Katharine Elizabeth, *b* 1962. —— John Eden (World's End, Reepham, Norwich), *b* 1926; *ed* Sherborne, and Trin Coll, Oxford (MA); formerly in RM; Housemaster of School House, Worksop Coll 1959-74: *m* 1970, Isobel Claridge, da of late Charles Claridge Druce, of Flishinghurst, Cranbrook, Kent, and has issue living, Michael Tristram *b* 1971, Christopher Eden *b* 1973. —— Rosemary Ellison, *b* 1928; *ed* Cheltenham Ladies' Coll: *m* 1949, Rev Frank Richard Knight Hare, of Buxton Vicarage, Norwich, Norfolk NR9 4QR, and has issue living, Roger John SHELMERDINE-HARE, *b* 1957; assumed the additional surname of Shelmerdine by Deed Poll 1989: *m* 1981, Caroline Philippa Shelmerdine, and has issue living, Thomas Shelmerdine *b* 1985, Alicia Caroline *b* 1983, Brioni Alexandra *b* 1988, — Elizabeth, *b* 1952: *m* 1972, Richard Cane, and has issue living, Rachel Simone *b* 1974, Annabel Louise *b* 1977.
The 1st baronet, Sir Robert Tristram Ricketts, DCL, was a Vice-Admiral, and the 2nd baronet was an Admiral. The 3rd baronet in 1884 succeeded to the estates of his maternal uncle (Col Thomas R. Plumbe-Tempest), and assumed by Roy licence in that year the surname of Tempest in lieu of his patronymic.

RIDDELL (NS) 1628, of Riddell, Roxburghshire

Sir JOHN CHARLES BUCHANAN RIDDELL, CVO, 13th *Baronet*; *b* 3 Jan 1934; *s* his father, *Sir* WALTER ROBERT BUCHANAN, 1934; *ed* Eton, and Ch Ch, Oxford (BA, MA); Dep Chm IBA 1981-85; Private Sec to TRH the Prince and Princess of Wales 1985-90, a Member of the Prince's Council 1985-90; CVO 1990; DL Northumberland 1990: *m* 1969, Hon Sarah Richardson, LVO, da of Baron Richardson of Duntisbourne, KG, MBE, PC (Life Baron), of Chelsea, SW3, and has issue.

Arms – Argent, a chevron gules between three ears of rye slipped and bladed vert. **Crest** – A demi-greyhound argent. **Supporters** – Two grey-hounds argent.
Residences – Hepple, Morpeth, Northumberland; 49 Campden Hill Sq, W8.

SONS LIVING

WALTER JOHN, *b* 10 June 1974. —— Hugh Gordon, *b* 1976. —— Robert Henry, *b* 1982.

SISTERS LIVING

Jean (*Lady Pumphrey*), *b* 1920: *m* 1945, Sir John Laurence Pumphrey, KCMG, of Caistron, Thropton, Morpeth, Northumberland NE65 7LG, and has issue living, Matthew James, *b* 1946: *m* 1976, Pamela Mary Clare, da of James Wyllie Irving, and has issue living, John Wyllie Francis *b* 1979, Maximilian Oscar Edward *b* 1982, India Victoria *b* 1988, — Charles Walter Bartholomew, *b* 1948: *m* 1981, (Cynthia) Penelope Helen, only child of late David Bruce (*see* E Elgin, colls), and has issue living, Oliver James *b* 1986, David Laurence *b* 1989, Katharine Elizabeth *b* 1983, — Jonathan Henry, *b* 1954: *m* 1982, Nicola, only da of late J. A. R. N. White, of Ladbroke Rd, W8, and has issue living, Jonathan Vivian *b* 1985, Rebecca Elisabeth *b* 1986, Olivia Rachel *b* 1989, — James Laurence, *b* 1964: *m* 1991, Katherine Lucy, yr da of David Sanders, of Winchester, and has issue living, Camilla Louise *b* 1993, — Laura Mary Beatrice, *b* 1951: *m* 1983, Robert James Longair, son of Arthur Longair, of Calgary, Alberta, Canada, and has issue living, Samuel Christopher *b* 1985, Alexander Hugh *b* 1988, a da *b* 1990. —— Mary, *b* 1922: *m* 1954, Richard Laurence Ollard, of Norchard Farmhouse, Morecombelake, Bridport, Dorset DT6 6EP, and has issue living, William Richard, *b* 1957, — Edward Christopher, *b* 1959, — Elizabeth Rachel, *b* 1961. —— Anne, *b* 1924. —— Hester, *b* 1927: *m* 1956, Christopher Henry Pemberton, of Place Farmhouse, Bardwell, Bury St Edmunds, Suffolk, and has issue living, Jethro Francis *b* 1987, Sophia Rosamund *b* 1991, — (Richard) Mark (17 Melbourne Place, Cambridge), *b* 1961: *m* 1993, Mrs Olivia Mary Rokeby Nicolson, da of Antony Charles Reynardson Fane (*see* E Westmorland, colls), and formerly wife of Adam Nicolson (*see* B Carnock), — Daniel Hugh Vincent, *b* 1962, — Thomas William, *b* 1964, — Isobel Beatrice, *b* 1959: *m* 1994, David Goldblatt, 2nd son of Samuel Goldblatt, of Ra'anana, Israel.

COLLATERAL BRANCHES LIVING

Grandsons of late Major Ralph Gervase Riddell-Carre, son of late Thomas Alexander Riddell-Carre, son of late Walter Riddell-Carre, 2nd son of Thomas Riddell (*b* 1777) (*infra*):—
Issue of late Sqdn Ldr Gervase Robert Riddell-Carre, RAFVR, *b* 1906, *d* 1989: *m* 1940, Eileen Inez, who *d* 1993, only da of late John Tweedie, of Edradour, North Berwick:—
Ralph John (31 Hillway, N6 6QB), *b* 1941; *ed* Harrow: *m* 1972, Valerie Caroline Wells, only da of late W. T. W. Tickler, of White-ladies, Frinton-on-Sea, Essex, and has issue living, John Timothy, *b* 1976, — Peter Thomas, *b* 1979, — David Alexander, *b* 1978. —— Walter Gervase (13 Napier Rd, Edinburgh EH10 5AZ), *b* 1944; *ed* Harrow; CA: *m* 1975, Carolyn

Anne, eldest da of Maj A. P. P. Ricketts, of The Old Manse, Nigg, Ross-shire, and has issue living, Andrew Gervase, *b* 1979, — James Walter, *b* 1981.

Grandson of late Col Thomas William Carre Riddell, VD, son of John Carre Riddell, 3rd son of late Thomas Riddell (*b* 1777), el son of William Riddell, son of Thomas Riddell (*b* 1696), 2nd son of 4th baronet:—
Issue of late Col Consett Carre Riddell, DSO, VD, BSc, BME, MIE (Aust), *b* 1887, *d* 1953: *m* 1923, Thora, who *d* 1963, da of J. L. Menzies:—
John Walter Carre, MB, BS, *b* 1925; *ed* Melbourne Univ; *m* 1957, Margaret Louise, who *d* 1986, only da of R. W. Krohn, and has issue living, Malcolm John Carre, *b* 1960, — David Ronald Carre, *b* 1966, — Fiona Carre, *b* 1958: *m* 1989, James Posillico, of Bayville, New York, — Susan Patricia Carre, *b* 1962: *m* 1989, Michael Underwood Felton. *Residence* – 2/547 Whitehorse Rd, Surrey Hills, Vic 3127, Aust.

Grandson of late Col Edward Vansittart Dick Riddell, son of late Col Robert Vansittart Riddell (infra):—
Issue of late Major Edward Alexander Buchanan Riddell, *b* 1903, *d* 1986; *m* 1st, 1928, Mary, eldest da of Stuart Cameron, of Caulfields, Vancouver, BC, Canada; 2ndly, 1939, Mrs Irene Julia Ballance, who *d* 1961, da of late A.W.E. Bullmore, of Letchworth, Herts: 3rdly, 1962, Mrs Mary Kingzett, da of late Lt-Col John Kennington, DSO, MC, JP, DL, of Riby, Lincs:—
(By 1st m) Stuart Edward, *b* 1929: *m* 1960, Emily Spitzer, da of late Whiting N. Shepard, of Montclair, New Jersey, USA, and has issue living, Cameron Alexander, *b* 1962, — Romayne Bouvée, *b* 1964.

Granddaughter of late Col Robert Vansittart Riddell, eldest son of late Robert Riddell, great-grandson of late Walter Riddell, son of late William Riddell, 2nd son of 2nd baronet:—
Issue of late Brigadier John Balfour Riddell, DSO, *b* 1880, *d* 1960: *m* 1908, Margaret Alice, who *d* 1963, yst da of late J. W. Smith of The Rectory, Oundle:—
Elizabeth Charity (Wistaria Cottage, Cocking, Sussex), *b* 1917: *m* 1949, Alan Campbell Sinclair, who *d* 1993.

Grandsons of late Brig John Balfour Riddell, DSO (ante):—
Issue of late Lt-Col John L'Estrange Riddell, TD, *b* 1910, *d* 1984: *m* 1939, Barbara Agnes, da of late M. McC. Fairgrieve, of Edinburgh:—
Robert Balfour (c/o AIICO Insurance (Nigeria) plc, PO Box 2577, Lagos, Nigeria), *b* 1940; *ed* Edinburgh Acad; ACII: *m* 1966 (*m diss* 1984), Jean, da of late M. Allen, of London. — John Gifford (61 Belle Vue Rd, Salisbury, Wilts SP1 3YE), *b* 1942; *ed* Edinburgh Acad; Capt Merchant Navy: *m* 1966, Belinda Irene, da of late E. C. Hensler, of 20 Fisherton St, Salisbury, and has issue living, Benedict Charles John, *b* 1969: *m* 1991, Karen Anne, da of Christopher Jones, of Swanfield by Dunnet, Thurso, — Jonathan David, *b* 1973. — Archibald George Vansittart (31 Marlston Av, off Lache Lane, Chester), *b* 1954; *ed* Oundle: *m* 1982, Patricia Maria, 2nd da of late John B. Axon, of 18 Panton Rd, Chester, and has issue living, Andrew John, *b* 1986, — Alexander George, *b* (twin) 1986, and an adopted da, Kelly Jayne, *b* 1979.

Granddaughters of late William Riddell, 2nd son of late Rev Henry Riddell, 2nd son of Henry Riddell (*b* 1745), grandson of late John Riddell, 2nd son of the Rev Archibald Riddell, 3rd son of 2nd baronet:—
Issue of late John Riddell, *b* 1895, *d* 1959: *m* 1st, 1918 (*m diss* 1923), Doris Jones; 2ndly, 1925, Alys, who *d* 1982, da of John R. Savage, of Edinburgh:—
(By 1st m) Irene Yvonne, *b* 1919: *m* 1943, Richard Adamson Crow, TD, of 24 Abbey Walk, Gt Missenden, Bucks HP16 0AY, and has issue living, Richard Michael, *b* 1944: *m* 1st, 1964 (*m diss* 1974), Alexandra Drysdale Love; 2ndly, 1980, Jean Marie Westbeach, and has issue living (by 1st m), Simon Richard *b* 1969, Victoria Caroline *b* 1965: *m* 1991, Jason Bacon (and has issue living, Emily Alexandra Mathewson *b* 1994) (by 2nd m) Richard James *b* 1981, William Thomas Adamson *b* 1984, Caroline Rose *b* 1987, — Michael Anthony *b* 1948: *m* 1st, 1972 (*m diss* 1984), Penelope Laura Carter; 2ndly, 1989, Jill MacKay Ballantyne, and has issue living (by 1st m), Benjamin James *b* 1976, Rebecca Jane *b* 1974. —— (By 2nd m), Audrian, *b* 1926: *m* 1950, William Burns Hutchinson, and has issue living, Michael William (91-545 Sheraton Blvd, Burlington, Ont L7L 4B3), *b* 1961: *m* 1991, Patricia Eileen Tendam, and has issue living, Matthew Benjamin *b* 1992, — Gregory John (28 Pearl St, Leamington, Ont N8H 1J6), *b* 1962: *m* 1987, Rebecca Ann Clark, and has issue living, Andrew John *b* 1991, Ryan William *b* 1993, — Janet Louise, *b* 1954. *Residence* – 9 Lorne Av, Leamington, Ont, Canada N8H 2H6.

Grandchildren of James Riddell, yst son of Rev Henry Riddell (ante):—
Issue of late Walter Riddell, *b* 1874, *d* 1951: *m* 1917, Mary Ellinor, who *d* 1958, da of late Dr John Garbutt Hutchinson, of North Lodge, Kineton:—
John Walter Rowland, *b* 1919. —— Elizabeth Mary Ellinor, *b* 1920: *m* 1st, 1940, Lt-Col Jocelyn Arthur Garnons-Williams, S Wales Borderers, who *d* of wounds received in action in Italy 1944; 2ndly, 1945, Maj James Mirylees, Roy Corps of Signals, and has issue living, (by 1st m) Elizabeth Dawn (3 Marlborough Rd, Richmond, Surrey), *b* 1941: *m* 1st, 1965 (*m diss* 1971), David Noel Archer Braham; 2ndly, 1973, Clive Anthony John Mitchell, and has issue living, (by 1st husband) Felicity Mary Stella *b* 1964, — (by 2nd m) Fiona Nora Margaret, *b* 1945, — Clementina Mary Stewart, *b* 1953, — Jean Sheila Riddell, *b* 1956.
Issue of late Lt-Col Archibald Riddell, DSO, *b* 1882, *d* 1970: *m* 1907, Edith Mary, who *d* 1947, da of late William Lawrie, of Seleng, Assam:—
William James, MBE (Foresters, Hightown Hill, Ringwood, Hants), *b* 1909; late Maj Gen List, served in World War II; *ed* Harrow, and Clare Coll, Camb; MBE (Mil): *m* 1st, 1959, Jeannette Anne, who *d* 1972, da of late Edward Kessler, and widow of Ripley Oddie; 2ndly, 1973, Alison Frances, da of late Arthur Newton Jackson, of Wilmslow, Cheshire, and has issue living (by 2nd m), Jemma Jeannette, *b* 1976.

Grandchildren of late Lt-Col Archibald Riddell, DSO (ante):—
Issue of late Group-Capt Peter John Archibald Riddell, CBE, *b* 1914, *d* 1985: *m* 1940 (*m diss* 1968), Cynthia Mary, who *d* 1993, da of late Brooks Crompton Wood, of Bruern Abbey, Churchill, Oxford:—
Nicholas Peter (18 Myddelton Sq, EC1), *b* 1941; *ed* Harrow, and Magdalene Coll, Camb (BA); Bar Inner Temple 1964: *m* 1st, 1967 (*m diss* 1976), Felicity Jane, eldest da of D.G. Rolfe, of Kensington; 2ndly, 1976, Barbara Helen, eldest da of Peter Glucksmann, of 53 Hendon Lane, N3, and has issue living, (by 1st m) Eleanor Mary, *b* 1972, — (by 2nd m) Juliet Clare, *b* 1979, — Laura Virginia, *b* 1982. —— Catherine Mary, *b* 1944: *m* 1976, Timothy Clare O'Rorke, FRICS, of 1 St James's Gdns, W11, and has issue living, Mark Henry, *b* 1978, — David Anthony, *b* 1981.

Grandchildren of late William Law Riddell, son of Robert Riddell (*b* 1797), yst son of Henry Riddell (*b* 1745) (ante):—
Issue of late Robert Riddell, *b* 1879, *d* 1958: *m* 1908, Flora McDonald, who *d* 1961, da of Charles Samuel George Nicholson, of Duntulm, Isle of Skye:—
William Law (Oxford St, Waimate, S Canterbury, NZ), *b* 1909: *m* 1941, Jean, da of late Edwin Charles Hocking, of Dunedin, NZ, and has issue living, Robert James (40 Oriel Av, Tawa, Wellington, NZ), *b* 1942; BAgricSc NZ: *m* 1965, Marion Gwynneth, da of K. McIntosh, of Rangiora, N Canterbury, NZ, and has issue living, William Grant *b* 1973, Anna Ruth *b* 1968, Lynette Judith *b* 1970, — Eleanor Mary, *b* 1943; BA (NZ): *m* 1st, 1964 (*m diss* 1978), David John Sutherland; 2ndly, 19—, Bruce Charles Smart, of 7 Kirkdale Place, Ilam, Christchurch, New Zealand, and has issue living (by 1st m), Elliot David Law *b* 1969, Meredith Lawrie *b* 1970, Fiona Jean *b* 1967, — Helen Annette, *b* 1946; MA (NZ): *m* 1967, Roger Beach Balfour

Mee, MB, ChB, FRACS(NZ), of 11 Clark Rd, Ivanhoe, Melbourne, Victoria 3079, Australia and has issue living, Jared James Balfour *b* 1968, Nicholas Roger Alexander *b* 1970, Michaela-Jean Coates *b* 1975, Josephine Bridie Mary *b* 1982. —— Flora McDonald (39 Chapter St, Christchurch, NZ), *b* 1910: *m* 1944, John Campbell Wilson, who *d* 1964, and has issue living, Elizabeth, *b* 1946; MA (NZ). —— Charlotte Isabel, *b* 1913: *m* 1938, Ralph Alan Gibson, of Wellington, NZ, and has issue living, John Hastings, *b* 1938; BEng (NZ): *m* 1964, Barbara Dawn Shepherd, of Timara, S Canterbury, NZ, and has issue, — Margaret Flora, *b* 1940: *m* 1961, Murray Bennett, and has issue. —— Margaret Carlina, *b* 1914: *m* 1939, William Kemp Paterson, of 2 Kirrimuir St, Dunedin, NZ, and has issue living, Gaynor Margaret, *b* 1941: *m* 1969, John Lyall, of Dunedin, NZ, — Roberta Joy, *b* 1946; BSc (NZ): *m* 1968, Ian Leslie Stephenson, BSc, of Hamilton, NZ, — Isabel Janice, *b* 1950: *m* 1970, Bruce Ronald Cowan, of Dunedin, NZ. —— Joan Doreen, *b* 1927: *m* 1948, Herbert Rance Brenton, and has issue living, Mervyn Robert, *b* 1949, — Lyal James, *b* 1953, — Robyn Joan, *b* 1951. *Residence* – Geraldine, Canterbury, NZ. —— Mary Frazer (165 Weston Rd, Christchurch, NZ), *b* 1922.

Grandchildren of late Robert Riddell (*b* 1879) (ante):—
Issue of late James Riddell, *b* 1920, *d* 1972: *m* 1950, Annette Lucy (The Downs, Geraldine, S Canterbury, NZ), da of P. Forde, of 62 Darby St, Christchurch, NZ:—
Peter James, *b* 1958. —— Judith Mary, *b* 1952. —— Sally Anne, *b* 1954. —— Annette Joan, *b* 1956.
Issue of late John Buchanan Riddell, *b* 1924, *d* 1969: *m* 1948, Barbara Frances, da of F. H. Ruddenklau, of Rangatata Island, Temuka, NZ:—
Frank Buchanan, *b* 1951. —— David John, *b* 1953. —— Graham Samuel, *b* 1961. —— Gail, *b* 1949. —— Sandra Ngaire, *b* 1958.
This family is of Norman descent, and was early settled in Roxburghshire, Gervase de Ridle, or Ridel, being High Sheriff of that county in 1116. The 9th baronet was successively MP for Selkirkshire and Lanarkshire, and the 10th baronet was Recorder of Maidstone and Tenterden 1846-63, and Judge of County Courts for N Staffordshire 1859-63, and for Whitechapel 1863-79. Sir John Walter, 11th Bt, was High Sheriff of Northumberland 1897. Sir Walter Robert, 12th Bt, was Principal of Hertford College, Oxford 1922-28 and Chm U.G.C. 1930-34.

RIGBY (UK) 1929, of Long Durford, Rogate, co Sussex

I would rather die than be dishonoured

Sir (HUGH) JOHN MACBETH RIGBY, ERD, 2nd *Baronet*; *b* 1 Sept 1914; *s* his father, Sir HUGH MALLINSON, KCVO, 1944; *ed* Rugby, and Magdalene Coll, Camb; Lt-Col (ret) RCT: *m* (Jan) 1946, Mary Patricia Erskine, who *d* 1988, da of Edmund Erskine Leacock (Erskine, Bt, *cr* 1821, colls), and has issue.

Arms – Argent, on a cross flory sable a rod of Æsculapius or. **Crest** – In front of an antelope's head erased proper gorged with an antique crown or, two ostrich feathers saltirewise argent.
Residence – 5 Park Street, Macclesfield, Cheshire SK11 6SR.

SONS LIVING

ANTHONY JOHN, *b* 3 Oct 1946: *m* 1978, Mary, el da of late R. G. Oliver, of Hope Green, Adlington, Macclesfield, and has issue living, Oliver Hugh, *b* 20 Aug 1979, — Rollo Macbeth, *b* 1981, — Tom, *b* 1985, — Flora, *b* 1989. —— Hugh Macbeth, *b* 1948: *m* 1970, Kathleen Mary, da of Conrad Salber, of Rochester, NY, USA, and has issue living, Zachary John, *b* 1974, — Rachel Mary, *b* 1971. —— James Erskine, *b* 1949: *m* 1979, Victoria Mary, da of late Charles Noel Edmeston, of Rush Cottage, Gore Lane, Alderley Edge, Cheshire, and has issue living, Simon Henry Erskine, *b* 1984. —— Stephen Leacock, *b* 1952: *m* 1979, Sally Anne, da of H. E. W. (Peter) Kirby, of 20 Admiralty Rd, Felpham, W Sussex, and has issue living, William Peter, *b* 1986, — Emily Flora, *b* 1983, — Alice Olivia, *b* 1988, — Melissa Mary, *b* 1989.

BROTHER LIVING

Roger Macbeth, *b* 1922; *ed* Winchester, and Magdalene Coll, Camb; is Hon Capt Roy Armoured Corps: *m* 1957, Patricia Ann, yr da of late Capt Desmond Nevill Cooper Tufnell, DSC, RN, and has issue living, Melissa Terwick, *b* 1959: *m* 1989, Christopher Wills, and has issue living, India Macbeth *b* 1991, Iona Christie *b* 1993, — Tanya Macbeth, *b* 1961: *m* 1993, Mark Anthony Lole. *Residence* – Ansty Plum, Ansty, Salisbury, Wilts SP3 5QD.

SISTERS LIVING

Margaret Hamilton, *b* 1919: *m* 1951, Richard Kynaston Briscoe (*see* Briscoe, Bt). *Residence* – Maple House, Higher Combe Rd, Haslemere, Surrey.
The 1st baronet, Sir Hugh Mallinson Rigby, KCVO, FRCS (son of late John Rigby), was for several years Surg to HM Queen Alexandra, Serjeant-Surg to HM King George V, and Surg-in-Ord to HM King Edward VIII when Prince of Wales.

RIPLEY (UK) 1880, of Rawdon, Yorkshire

While I breathe I hope

Sir HUGH RIPLEY, 4th *Baronet*; *b* 26 May 1916; *s* his father, *Sir* HENRY WILLIAM ALFRED, 1956; *ed* Eton; late Dir of John Walker and Sons; Major (ret) King's Shropshire LI; European War 1942-5 in Tunisia and Italy (wounded, despatches twice, American Silver Star); author of *Whisky for Tea* (1991): *m* 1st, 1946 (*m diss* 1971), Dorothy Mary Dunlop, da of J. C. Bruce Jones (Dunlop Bt); 2ndly, 1972, Susan, da of W. Parker, of Keythorpe Grange, E Norton, Leicester, and has issue by 1st and 2nd *m*.

Arms – Per chevron nebuly or and vert, three lions rampant counterchanged between three cross crosslets, two in base or, and one in chief vert. **Crest** – A demi-lion reguardant vert, collared or, charged on the shoulder with a cross crosslet of the second, and holding between the paws an escutcheon argent charged with a cockerel proper.
Seat – Bedstone, Bucknell, Shropshire. *Residences* – 20 Abingdon Villas, W8 6BX; The Oak, Bedstone, Shropshire. *Club* – Boodle's.

SON LIVING *(By 1st marriage)*

WILLIAM HUGH (Dove Cottage, Bedstone, Bucknell, Shropshire), *b* 13 April 1950; *ed* Eton, and McGill Univ (BA); bookseller.

DAUGHTERS LIVING *(By 1st marriage)*

(Dorothy) Caroline, *b* 1947: *m* 1983, as his 2nd wife, Hugh John Montgomery-Massingberd, the writer, of 2/29 Clanricarde Gdns, W2, only son of John Michael Montgomery-Massingberd, of Gunby, Lincs (*see* V Hawarden, colls, 1928 Edn).

(By 2nd marriage)

Katherine, *b* 1974.

SISTER LIVING

Suzan, *b* 1919; European War 1939-45 with ATS: *m* 1951 Robert de la Garde Savery, and has issue living, Christopher Robert de la Garde, *b* 1954: *m* 1980, Margaret, yst da of Ian Archibald Slater, of Wellside, Livesey Rd, Ludlow, Shropshire, and has issue living, Alice Eugénie de la Garde *b* 1983, — Chloë Abigail de la Garde, *b* 1955: *m* 1979, Andrew John Scott Calder. *Residence* – Orchard House, Bedstone, Bucknell, Shropshire.

COLLATERAL BRANCH LIVING

Issue of late Lieut-Col Edward Robert Guy Ripley, King's Shropshire LI, el son of 3rd baronet, *b* 1911, *ka* in Normandy June 1944; *m* 1944, Sarah Stella, da of Col A. G. Pardoe, of Gravel Hill, Kington:—
Patience Ann, *b* (*posthumous*) (Dec) 1944: *m* 1963, Richard Michael Tudor Morgan, and has issue living, David Paul Edward, *b* 1964, — Timothy Michael Julian, *b* 1969, — Charlotte Sarah, *b* 1965.
Sir Henry William Ripley, 1st Bt, son of Edward Ripley of Bowling, near Bradford, was MP for Bradford (*L*) 1868-9 and 1874-80. Sir Frederick Ripley of Acacia, Rawdon, 3rd son of 1st Bt, was *cr* a baronet 1897, which became ext on death of 3rd Bt in 1954.

RITCHIE (UK) 1918, of Highlands

Sir JAMES EDWARD THOMSON RITCHIE, TD, 2nd *Baronet*; *b* 16 June 1902; *s* his father, *Sir* JAMES WILLIAM, MBE, 1937; *ed* Rugby, and The Queen's Coll, Oxford; a Dir of William Ritchie & Son (Textiles), Ltd, Patron of Ashford and Dist Caledonian Soc, a Member of Court of Assists, Merchant Taylors' Co (Master 1963-64), Hon Lt-Col late Inns of Court Regt, RAC (TA), a selected Mil Member of Kent T & AF Assocn (Member of Gen Purposes Cttee) 1953-68; Pres of Ashford Branch Roy British Legion 1951-75; a Fellow of R Soc of Arts; Jt Hon Treasurer and Chm of Finance and Gen Purposes Cttee, London Sch of Hygiene and Tropical Med, London Univ 1951-61; a Member of Finance & Gen Purposes Cttee, and a co-opted Member of Board of Management 1964-65; 1939-45 War holding various Staff and Regimental appointments (Central Mediterranean Force 1944-45): *m* 1st, 1928 (*m diss* 1936), Esme, who *d* 1939, da of late J. M. Oldham of Ormidale, Ascot; 2ndly, 1936, Rosemary, yr da of late Col Henry Sidney John Streatfeild, DSO, TD (E Lichfield), and has issue by 2nd *m*.

Arms – Argent, an anchor erect sable within a bordure ermine, on a chief of the second three lions' heads erased of the first. **Crest** – Issuant out of an antique crown or, an unicorn's head argent armed gold, charged on the neck with a torteau, thereon an anchor, also gold.
Residence – 3 Farquhar Street, Bengeo, Hertford, SG14 3BN.

Honour is acquired by virtue

DAUGHTERS LIVING *(By 2nd marriage)*

Louise Katherine, *b* 1952: *m* 1978, John Preston. —— Fiona Ruth, *b* 1953.

HALF-SISTERS LIVING

Barbara Anne Lydia Janet, *b* 1916; European War 1940-43 with ATS attached RA. *Residence* – Crackshill Cottage, Yelvertoft, near Rugby. —— Elizabeth Alice Jessie Muriel, *b* 1922: *m* 1st, 1943 (*m diss* 1954), Peter Andrew Soderling, USA Air Force; 2ndly, 1957 Robert John Ripley Blake, and has issue living, (by 1st *m*) Mark Andrew Patrick, *b* 1944.
The 1st baronet, Sir James William Ritchie, MBE, was Chm of Milners' Safe Co, and Lieut for City of London.

Rivett-Carnac, see Carnac.

ROBERTS (UK) 1809, of Glassenbury, Kent, of Brightfieldstown, co Cork and of the City of Cork

Sir GILBERT HOWLAND ROOKEHURST ROBERTS, 7th *Baronet*; *b* 31 May 1934; *s* his father, Col *Sir* THOMAS LANGDON HOWLAND, CBE, 1979; *ed* Rugby, and Gonville and Caius Coll, Camb (BA; CEng, MIMechE); served in Kenya with RE (East African GS Medal): *m* 1958, Ines Eleonore, only da of late Alfons Leo Labunski, of Danzig, and has issue.

Arms – Azure, on a chevron argent cotised or, three mullets of six points sable, pierced of the field. **Crest** – On a mount vert an eagle displayed ermine, wings argent, gorged with a chaplet of ivy proper.
Residence – 3340 Cliff Drive, Santa Barbara, Calif 93109, USA.

SON LIVING

HOWLAND LANGDON, *b* 19 Aug 1961.

DAUGHTER LIVING

Solveig Margaret, *b* 1959.

BROTHER LIVING

Walter Rookehurst (52 Warwick Sq, SW1V 2AJ), *b* 1951; *ed* King's Sch, Canterbury, and Gonville and Caius Coll, Camb (MA); admitted a Solicitor England and Wales 1978, Hong Kong 1985; Capt 4th RTR (TA): *m* 1988, Caroline Heather, da of Hugh Cocks, of Woodside Green, Essex.

ADOPTIVE SISTER LIVING

Rosamund Margaret (3 Dalby Rd, SW18), *b* 1951: *m* 1988, Steven R. Noel-Hill.

Virtue survives death

COLLATERAL BRANCH LIVING

Issue of late Capt Gilbert Howland Roberts, CBE, RD, RN, yr son of 5th baronet, *b* 1900, *d* 1986: *m* 1st, 1930 (*m diss* 1947), Marjorie, da of John Boultbee Brooks, of Blackwell Court, nr Bromsgrove, Worcs; 2ndly, 1947, Jean (Little Priors, Watcombe, Torquay, Devon), da of Edward Warren, of Yelverton, Devon:—
(By 1st *m*) Michael Gilbert, *b* 1932, formerly Lieut RM: *m* 1960 (*m diss* 1970), Felicity Roberts, da of Gordon Charles Sheppard, of Cape Town, South Africa, and has issue living, Mark Howland, *b* 1961, — John Langdon, *b* 1964, — Jennifer Leigh, *b* 1962. —— Jill Morna Boultbee, *b* 1933.

The former baronetcy of 1620 (claimed by the present holder of the 1809 creation as 14th Bt, which claim, however, has not been officially established at the Heralds' College), belonged to the old Kentish family, originally called Rookehurst and later Roobertes, and apparently became extinct on the demise in 1745 of Sir Walter, 6th Bt, who left an only daughter, Jane, who married 3rd Duke of St Albans. About 1775 the Duchess believed she had discovered the descendants of Thomas, second son of the 1st baronet, seated at Brightfieldstown, Roberts' Cove, co Cork; and the title was assumed by the then head of that family, Randal, and subsequently by his eldest son Thomas, to whom, however, a new patent of Baronetcy was passed in 1809. The ancient property of Glassenbury, Cranbrook, Kent, which had then been in the direct line for nearly seven centuries, was left by the Duchess of St Albans to the second son of this Sir Thomas, viz, Col Thomas Walton Roberts, JP (High Sheriff of Kent 1879), who *d* 1882, and devised the said property by will to his nephew, the late Major John Atkin-Roberts, JP.

ROBERTS (UK) 1909, of Milner Field, Bingley, West Riding of Yorkshire

Justly and firmly

Sir WILLIAM JAMES DENBY ROBERTS, 3rd *Baronet*; *b* 10 Aug 1936; *s* his father, *Sir* JAMES DENBY, OBE, 1973; *ed* Rugby, and Roy Agric Coll, Cirencester.

Arms – Vert, on a pile or, between two saltires in base of the last an Angora goat statant proper. **Crest** – Upon two millrinds fesseways or, an Angora goat as in the arms.
Seat – Strathallan Castle, Auchterarder, Perthshire PH3 1JZ. *Residence* – Combwell Priory, Flimwell, Wadhurst, Sussex.

SISTER LIVING

Susan Elisabeth, *b* 1934; MA Oxford: *m* 1st, 1956, Roger John Edward Liddiard, BA; 2ndly, 1974, Douglas Hills, and has issue living (by 1st *m*), Nicholas Anthony, *b* 1958, — Timothy Mark, *b* 1960, — Jonathan Miles, *b* 1962, — Rupert Alexander, *b* 1966.

AUNT LIVING

Catherine Elizabeth, *b* 1907: *m* 1928, Robert Hope Donaldson, who *d* 1964, and has issue living, Robert Bertram, *b* 1929, — William James, *b* 1934. *Residence* – 17 East Rd, W Mersea, Colchester, Essex.

COLLATERAL BRANCHES LIVING

Issue of late David Gordon Denby Roberts, yst son of 2nd baronet, *b* 1940, *d* 1971: *m* 1962, Diana Frances, (Lawhill House, Auchterarder, Perths (who *m* 2ndly), 1973, Cameron Roy Marchand Buchanan), only da of Hugh Wilson-Jones, of The White Hose, N Lopham, Diss, Norfolk:—
JAMES ELTON DENBY ROBERTS-BUCHANAN, *b* 12 July 1966. —— Gail Antoinette ROBERTS-BUCHANAN, *b* 1964.

Issue of late William Denby Roberts, 2nd son of Bertram Foster Roberts, el surv son of 1st baronet, *b* 1909, *d* 1966: *m* 1935, Helen Fyans, who *d* 1963, yr da of late Herbert Shakespeare Fenwick, of Dunedin, NZ:—
Anthony Fenwick Denby (Mossdale, Conistone-with-Kilnsey, nr Skipton, Yorks), *b* 1938; *ed* Rugby, and Univ Coll, Oxford (BA): *m* 1964, Vanessa Jean Wishart, da of Sir (James) Douglas Wishart Thomson, 2nd Bt (*cr* 1929), and has issue living, Jonathan William Denby, *b* 1966, — Nicholas David Denby, *b* 1967, — James Anthony Denby, *b* 1974. —— Peter William Denby (The Old Rectory, Whittington, via Carnforth, Lancs), *b* 1945; *ed* Rugby, and Roy Agric Coll, Cirencester: *m* 1st, 1970 (*m diss* 1977), Christine Margaret Hermione, da of late Capt Hon Anthony Gerard Hugh Bampfylde (*see* B Poltimore, colls); 2ndly, 1977 (*m diss* 1988), Grizel Elizabeth-Anne (Lulla), only da of Col Anthony Gerald Way, MC, of Kincairney, Dunkeld, Perthshire, and formerly wife of (Patrick) Joseph Scott-Plummer (*see* B Kinross), and has issue living (by 1st *m*), Emma Louise, *b* 1972, — Lucinda Ann, *b* 1973, — (by 2nd *m*), William Gerald Denby, *b* 1980. —— Ann, *b* 1936.

Issue of late Joseph Henry Nicholson Roberts, 2nd surv son of 1st baronet, *b* 1887, *d* 1946: *m* 1920, Frances Eleanor, who *d* 1983, da of G. Partington, of The Laurels, Tilehurst, Reading:—
John, *b* 1921: *m* 1st, 1949 (*m diss* 1961), Diana Emily, da of late Lawrence Norris Evans; 2ndly, 1962 (*m diss* 1972), Hon Juliana Eveline (CUNLIFFE-OWEN), da of 2nd Viscount Scarsdale; 3rdly, 1974, Maryan Gwyneth, da of Patrick Edward Aston-Talbot, and has had issue (by 1st *m*), Jane, *b* 1953: *m* 1st, 1972 (*m diss* 1977), Robin John Kershaw Roberts; 2ndly, 1978 (*m diss* 1988), Nicholas John Foster Robinson; 3rdly 1989, Robert Walter Armstrong, and has issue living, (by 2nd *m*) Max Nicholas John *b* 1984, — Sally (Hon Mrs James Bethell), *b* 1955: *m* 1st, 1979 (*m diss* 1986), Nicholas Albert Le Gallais; 2ndly, 1987, Hon James David William Bethell, 2nd son of 5th Baron Westbury, and has issue (*see* B Westbury), — (by 2nd *m*) †John James, *b* 1964, *d* 1986, — Lucinda Elizabeth, *b* 1963: *m* 1989, Pearse Bergin, and has issue living, James Michael *b* 1993, Laura Alice *b* 1991. *Residence* – L'Etoquet House, St Ouen, Jersey. —— Henry, *b* 1923: *m* 1955, Anne Dorothy, da of late John Huelin, of Cape Town, S Africa, and has issue living, Lesley Ann, *b* 1957, — Frances Mary, *b* 1963. *Residence* – La Fontaine, Trinity, Jersey.

The 1st baronet, Sir James Roberts (son of James Roberts, of Haworth, Yorkshire), was former owner of the town of Saltaire, and Chm of Sir Titus Salt, Bt, Sons & Co, Ltd, of Saltaire.

ROBERTS (UK) 1919 of Ecclesall and Queen's Tower, City of Sheffield, and West Riding of Yorkshire

Sir SAMUEL ROBERTS, 4th *Baronet*; *b* 16 April 1948; *s* his father, *Sir* PETER GEOFFREY, 1985; *ed* Harrow, and Sheffield Univ (BA); Bar Inner Temple 1972: *m* 1977, Georgina Ann, yr da of David Cory, of Bluetts, Peterston-super-Ely, S Glam, and has issue.

Arms – Sable, on a chevron couped argent, three mullets of the field, a chief dancettée or. **Crest** – Issuant out of a circlet or, a demi-lion rampant gules holding in the paws a mullet gold.
Residences – Cockley Cley Hall, Swaffham, Norfolk PE37 8AG; 6 Caversham St, SW3.

SON LIVING

SAMUEL, *b* 12 Aug 1989.

DAUGHTERS LIVING

Eleanor Judith, *b* 1979. —— Olivia, *b* 1982. —— Amelia, *b* 1985.

SISTERS LIVING

Jane, *b* 1940: *m* 1962, Claude Henri Jean-Jacques Maurin, of La Tour Villedon, 18260 Subligny, and 65 rue de Cévennes, Paris 75015, France, and has issue living, Sébastien Alexandre, *b* 1965: *m* 1994, Alison, da of Jonathan Durr, of Cape Town, SA, — Edmond Peter, *b* 1974, — Alicia, *b* 1967, — Constance, *b* (twin) 1974. —— Catherine, *b* 1943: *m* 1965, John Andrew Longworth, of 45 Ranelagh Grove, SW1, and has issue living, Stephanie Lydia, *b* 1968, — Charlotte Gay, *b* 1970, — Joanna Catherine, *b* 1973. —— Deborah, *b* 1946: *m* 1967, Peter Constantin Brun, of 60 Captain Pipers Rd, Vaucluse, Sydney, NSW 2030, Australia, and has issue living, Henry Constantin, *b* 1971, — Peter Maximilian, *b* 1974, — Julian Constantin, *b* 1981, — Rachel, *b* 1970. —— Rebecca, *b* 1955: *m* 1978, Guy Mark Vernon Whitcombe, and has issue living, Claudia Elizabeth, *b* 1984, — Madeleine Rebecca, *b* 1989.

WIDOW LIVING OF THIRD BARONET

JUDITH RANDELL (*Dowager, Lady Roberts*), da of late Randell G. Hempson: *m* 1939, Sir Peter Geoffrey Roberts, 3rd Bt, who *d* 1985. *Residence* – 7 Rembrandt Close, SW1W 8HS, and The Gate House, Cockley Cley, Swaffham, Norfolk PE37 8AG.
The 1st baronet, Rt Hon Sir Samuel Roberts, was Lord Mayor of Sheffield 1899-1900, and sat as MP for Ecclesall Div of Sheffield (C) 1901-23. The 2nd baronet, Sir Samuel Roberts, was Lord Mayor of Sheffield 1919-20, MP for Hereford Div of Herefordshire (C) 1921-9, and for Ecclesall Div of Sheffield 1929-35, and Master Cutler of Sheffield 1935-6. The 3rd baronet, Sir Peter Geoffrey Roberts, was MP for Ecclesall Div of Sheffield (C) 1945-50, and for Heeley Div of Sheffield 1950-66, Master Cutler of Sheffield 1956-57, and High Sheriff of Hallamshire 1970.

ROBINSON (E) 1660, of London

Sir JOHN JAMES MICHAEL LAUD ROBINSON, 11th *Baronet*; *b* 19 Jan 1943; *s* his grandfather, *Maj Sir* FREDERICK VILLIERS LAUD, MC, Croix de Guerre 1975; *ed* Eton, and Trin Coll, Dublin (MA); a Chartered Financial Analyst; DL of Northants since 1984; Pres British Red Cross (Northants Branch) 1982-90; Chm St Andrews Hospital Northampton 1984-94, Northampton General Hospital NHS Trust since 1994: *m* 1968, (Kathryn) Gayle Elizabeth, only child of Stuart Nelson Keyes, of Orillia, Ont, Canada, and has issue.

Arms – Quarterly: 1st and 4th, quarterly crenellée gules and or in the first quarter a lion passant-guardant or standing on a tower argent; 2nd and 3rd, vert, a buck trippant within an orle of trefoil slipped or. **Crest** – A buck trippant or, collared and lined vert, the collar charged with three trefoils slipped or.
Residence – Cranford Hall, Cranford, Kettering NN14 4AD.

SONS LIVING

MARK CHRISTOPHER MICHAEL VILLIERS, *b* 23 April 1972. —— Alexander Frederick Stuart Laud, *b* 1973.

DAUGHTER LIVING

Kathryn Anne Elizabeth, *b* 1985.

SISTER LIVING

Anne Elizabeth Villiers, *b* 1950: *m* 1975, Derek Alan Buckley, and has issue living, Samuel Michael, *b* 1978.
The 1st baronet, Sir John Robinson, nephew of Archbishop Laud, and Lord Mayor of London, was Lieut of the Tower, and did great service in promoting the coronation of Charles II. The 5th and the 6th baronets each sat as MP for Northampton.

ROBINSON (UK) 1854, of Toronto, Canada

Quickly and cautiously

Sir CHRISTOPHER PHILIPSE ROBINSON, 8th *Baronet*; son of late Christopher Robinson, QC, son of late Christopher Charles Robinson, KC, eldest son of late Christopher Robinson, KC, 3rd son of 1st baronet; *b* 10 Nov 1938; *s* his kinsman, *Sir* JOHN BEVERLEY, 1988: *m* 1962, Barbara Judith, da of Richard Duncan, of Ottawa, Canada, and has issue.

𝕬rms – Or, on a chevron between three stags trippant vert, as many cinquefoils of the field. 𝕮rest – A stag trippant vert bezantée.
Residence – 250 Thorold Rd, Ottawa, Ontario, Canada.

SONS LIVING

PETER DUNCAN, *b* 31 July 1967. —— Jonathan Richard, *b* 1969.

BROTHERS LIVING

Walter Gherardi (69 Douglas Crescent, Toronto, Ont M4W 2E6), *b* 1940; QC: *m* 1963, Alison Jean, da of Robert Stewart Fraser, of Toronto, Canada, and has issue living, Hilary Elizabeth, *b* 1967, — Alicia Isabel, *b* 1970. —— John Mowat, *b* 1942: *m* 1st, 1969 (*m diss* 1982), Joyce, da of Roy Harrod, of Orsett, Essex; 2ndly, 1988, Jane Stewart, da of Duncan K. MacTavish, QC, OBE, of Ottawa, and has issue living (by 1st *m*), Graeme Harrod, *b* 1970, — Christopher Mowat, *b* 1972.

SISTER LIVING

Neville Gherardi (31 Acacia Av, Ottawa, Ontario, Canada), *b* 1935: *m* 1956 (*m diss* 1967), Georges-Henri Carasso, of Paris, who *d* 1974, and has issue living, John Christopher, *b* 1959, — Robin, *b* 1979.

UNCLE LIVING

Hugh Lukin, *b* 1916: *m* 1st, 1941 (*m diss* 1972), Ruth Elizabeth, da of John Cotter, of Ottawa, Ont; 2ndly, 1973, Lillian Ruth, da of Jacob Milton, of Toronto, and has issue living (by 1st *m*), John Michael (Thunder Bay, Ont, Canada), *b* 1946, — David Lukin (Los Angeles, Calif, USA), *b* 1952, — Elizabeth, *b* 1955: *m* 1976, Kenneth Quinlan, of Saskatoon, Saskatchewan, Canada, and has issue living, Andrea *b* 1984. *Residence* – 401 Woburn Av, Toronto, Canada.

AUNTS LIVING

Laura Beverley, *b* 1913: *m* 1st, 1937 (*m diss* 1956), Andrew Kalitinsky; 2ndly, 1957, Adolf Kurt Placzek, and has issue living, (by 1st *m*) Sylvia (1724 Kellogg Dr, Anaheim, California 92807, USA), *b* 1945: *m* 1966 (*m diss* 1979), Roger Alan Barkley, and has issue living, Ian Andrew *b* 1970. *Residence* – . —— Wendela Isabel, *b* 1918: *m* 1957, Andrew Kalitinsky (ante), of La Jolla, California, USA.

SISTER LIVING OF SEVENTH BARONET

Constance Suzette Beverley, *b* 1914: *m* 1939 (*m diss* 1969), Edward William Sutherland, and has issue living, John Warren, *b* 1942: *m* 1962, Kathleen Croft, of Hamilton, Ontario, and has issue living, David *b* 1963, Beth *b* 1964, — Harley Peter, *b* 1948: *m* 1966, Patricia Carter, of Guelph, Ont, and has issue living, Kimberley Deanne *b* 1967, Joy Patrick *b* 1969, — David Victor, *b* 1948: *m* 1971, Jacquie Smith, of Hamilton, Ont, and has issue living, Tracey, *b* 1973, — Wendy Gayle, *b* 1940: *m* 1961, Anthony Ian Roberts, of London, Ont, and has issue living, Paul Douglas *b* 1968, Nancy Marie *b* 1962, Patricia *b* 1964, — Suzette Marion, *b* 1944: *m* 1964 (*m diss* 1969), David Teft, of Grimsby, Ontario.

COLLATERAL BRANCHES LIVING

Grandchildren of late Christopher Charles Robinson, KC (ante):—
Issue of late Peter Beverley Robinson, *b* 1915, *d* 1992: *m* 1st, 1938, Elizabeth, who *d* 1965, da of Halsey Frederick, of Mountain Lakes, New Jersey, USA; 2ndly, 1966, Nancy Carol, who *d* 1994, da of Norris Konheim, of Woodmere, NY:—
(By 1st *m*) Wendy Bouquet, *b* 1944: *m* 1965 (*m diss* 1975), Martin V. Boelitz, and has issue living, Jessica Elizabeth, *b* 1968. —— Susan Celina, *b* 1946: *m* 1st, 1966 (*m diss* 1967), Ira James Sandperl; 2ndly, 1969 (*m diss* 1981), Pierre Bain, of Comps-sur-Artuby, Var, France; 3rdly, 19—, David Peterson. —— (By 2nd *m*) Kenneth Beverley, *b* 1967. —— Alice Natalie, *b* 1969.
Issue of late (John) Beverley Robinson, *b* 1884, *d* 1954: *m* 1920, Marion (28 Foxbar Road, Toronto, 7 Canada), da of Weymouth de Lisle Schreiber, of Toronto Canada.
John Beverley, *b* 1922: *m* 1948, Constance Anne, da of James Bruce Mackinnon, of Toronto, and has issue living, Bruce Beverley, *b* 1952, — Christopher Charles, *b* 1957, — Linda de Lisle, *b* 1949, — Hilary Anne, *b* 1953. *Residence* – 194 Inglewood Drive, Toronto, Canada. —— Weymouth Hugh Beverley, *b* 1927: *m* 1956, Patricia Elizabeth, el da of Robert James Glendenning Innes, of Toronto, Canada, and has issue living, Judith Suzanne, *b* 1957, — Jennifer Leslie, *b* 1960. —— Elizabeth de Lisle, *b* 1924: *m* 1st, 1946, John Kingsford Herbert Mason, who *d* 1952; 2ndly, 1959, Capt John Littler, RCN, and has issue living, (by 1st *m*) David *b* 1950, Marion Thonia *b* 1948, Philippa *b* 1952.
Issue of late Duncan Strachan Robinson, *b* 1886, *d* 1956: *m* 1916, Emily, el da of Gordon Watson, formerly of Brandon, Manitoba:—
Duncan Gordon Strachan, *b* 1917. —— John Attrachay, *b* 1920. *Residence* – Toronto, Canada. —— Mary Emily, *b* 1917. *Residence* – Guelph, Ontario, Canada. —— Anne, *b* 1922. *Residence* – Phoenix, Arizona, USA. —— Daphne, *b* 1928. *Residence* – Toronto, Canada.

Issue of late Maj-Gen Sir Charles Walker Robinson, KCB, 4th son of 1st baronet, *b* 1836, *d* 1924: *m* 1884, Margaret Frances, who *d* 1940, da of Gen Sir Archibald Alison, GCB, 2nd Bt:—
Joan Emma Beverley, *b* 1892. —— Dorothy Margaret, *b* 1895. *Residence* – Bideford, Devon.
This family is descended from Christopher Robinson, or Cleasby, Yorkshire, who emigrated to Virginia about 1670, and was elder brother of the Rt Rev John Robinson, Ambassador to Sweden 1683-1708, Bishop of Bristol and London 1710-23, and First Plenipotentiary at the Congress of Utrecht 1713. The 1st baronet, Sir John Beverley, CB, DSL, of Oxford, having served as a Volunteer in the war of 1812 with America, was admitted to the Bar in Canada and at Lincoln's Inn, and was

subsequently (1829-62) Chief Justice of Upper Canada, and for many years member for the town of York and Speaker of the Legislative Council in the Old Province of Upper Canada. Sir John Beverley Robinson, 4th Bt, was el son of late Hon John Beverley Robinson, Lieut-Gov of Ontario 1880-87.

ROBINSON (UK) 1908, of Hawthornden, Wynberg, Cape Province, S Africa and Dudley House, City of Westminster

I have found

Sir WILFRED HENRY FREDERICK ROBINSON, 3rd *Baronet*, son of late Wilfred Henry Robinson, 3rd son of 1st baronet; *b* 24 Dec 1917; *s* his uncle, Sir JOSEPH BENJAMIN, 1954; *ed* Diocesan Coll, Rondebosch, and St John's Coll, Camb (BA 1939, MA 1944); Vice-Prin of Diocesan Coll Sch, Rondebosch; late Major Parachute Regt; Finance Offr, Soc of Genealogists 1980-92: *m* 1946, Margaret Alison Kathleen, da of late Frank Mellish, MC, of Cape Town, S Africa, and has issue.

Arms – Vert, three bezants chevronwise between two chevronels, the whole between three demi-stags couped or. **Crest** – A demi-stag or, charged with two chevronels vert, supporting with the dexter leg a flagstaff in bend sinister proper, pendant therefrom a banner bert charged with a bezant.
Residence – 24 Ennismore Gdns, SW7 1AB.

SON LIVING

PETER FRANK (9 Bingham St, N1), *b* 23 June 1949: *m* 1988, Alison Jane, eldest da of D. Bradley, of Rochester, Kent.

DAUGHTERS LIVING

Suzanne Moira, *b* 1947: *m* 1969, J. Steen Flamand, of Copenhagen, Denmark.
—— Clementine Anne Eileen, *b* 1957: *m* 1981, Jeffrey Foulser.
Sir Joseph Benjamin Robinson, 1st Bt (sometime a MLA, Mayor of Kimberley 1880, and Chm of Robinson's South Africa Banking Co, Ltd, and of many gold mines in Transvaal Colony), was yst son of late Robert John Robinson, and was nominated to a peerage in June 1922, but declined the honour. Sir Joseph Benjamin Robinson, 2nd Bt, sat in Union Parliament of S Africa 1915-19, and 1932-34.

LYNCH-ROBINSON (UK) 1920, of Foxrock, co Dublin

Faithful to the law and the king

Sir NIALL BRYAN LYNCH-ROBINSON, DSC, 3rd *Baronet*; *b* 24 Feb 1918; *s* his father, Sir CHRISTOPHER HENRY, 1958; *ed* Stowe; late Lt RNVR; Chm Leo Burnett Ltd (1970-78); 1939-45 War (DSC, Croix de Guerre): *m* 1940, Rosemary Seaton, elder da of late Capt Harold John Eller, and has issue.

Arms – Quarterly: 1st and 4th, vert, a chevron engrailed between three stags at gaze or, each charged with a fleur-de-lis azure, *Robinson*; 2nd and 3rd, azure a chevron between three trefoils and two voiders or, *Lynch*. **Crests** – 1st, Out of a crown vallery or a mount vert, thereon a stag as in the arms; 2nd, a lynx passant argent gorged with a collar gules with chain reflexed over the back or.
Residence – Flat 25, Headbourne Worthy House, Headbourne Worthy, Winchester, Hants SO23 7JG.

SON LIVING

DOMINICK CHRISTOPHER (Charnham Close, 26 Charnham St, Hungerford, Berks), *b* 30 July 1948: *m* 1973, Victoria, da of Kenneth Weir, of 37 Stokesay Rd, Sale, Manchester, and has issue living, Christopher Henry Jake, *b* 1 Oct 1977, — Anna Elizabeth Seaton, *b* 1973.
The 1st baronet, Rt Hon Sir Henry Augustus Robinson, KCB, was Vice-Pres of Local Govt Board for Ireland 1898-1920. The 2nd baronet, Sir Christopher Henry Robinson, assumed by deed poll 1947 (registered in College of Arms) the additional surname and arms of Lynch before his patronymic.

ROCHE (UK) 1838, of Carass, Limerick

Sir DAVID O'GRADY ROCHE, 5th *Baronet*; *b* 21 Sept 1947; *s* his father, *Lt-Cdr Sir* STANDISH O'GRADY, DSO, RN, 1977; *ed* Wellington Coll, and Trin Coll, Dublin; FCA; Chm Roche & Co Ltd; Cllr Lond Borough of Hammersmith & Fulham 1978-82; Worshipful Co of Saddlers: *m* 1971, Hon (Helen) Alexandra Briscoe Gully, da of 3rd Viscount Selby, and formerly wife of late Roger Moreton Frewen, and has issue.

Arms – Gules, three roaches naiant within a bordure engrailed argent. **Crest** – A rock, thereon a stork close, charged on the breast with a torteau, and holding in his dexter claw a roach all proper.
Residences – Norris Castle Farm, IoWight P032 6AZ; Bridge House, Starbotton, Skipton, N Yorks; 36 Coniger Rd, SW6 3TA. *Clubs* – Buck's, Kildare Street, University (Dublin), Royal Yacht Squadron.

DIEU · EST · MA · ROCHE

God is my rock

SON LIVING

DAVID ALEXANDER O'GRADY, *b* 28 Jan 1976.

DAUGHTER LIVING

Cecilia Evelyn Jonnë, *b* 1979.

BROTHER LIVING

Timothy O'Grady *b* 1948; *ed* St Columba's Coll, Dublin; Lt (ret) 1st Bn IG; a Freeman of City of London: *m* 1975, Lorna, da of A. T. R. Nicholson, of Ashcombe, Merstham, Surrey, and has issue living, Patrick Timothy O'Grady, *b* 1978, — Simon James O'Grady, *b* 1980. *Residence* – 40 Redstone Park, Redhill, Surrey.

WIDOW LIVING OF FOURTH BARONET

EVELYN LAURA (*Evelyn, Lady Roche*) (Monte de Cerro, Corotelo, São Bras d'Alportel, Algarve, Portugal), da of Maj William Andon, W Yorks Regt, of Jersey: *m* 1946, Lt-Cdr Sir Standish O'Grady Roche, DSO, RN, 4th Bt, who *d* 1977.
The 1st baronet, Sir David Roche, was MP for Limerick City 1832-44. Sir David Vandeleur, 2nd Bt, was Vice-Lieut of co Limerick (High Sheriff 1865), and Master of Limerick Hunt. Sir Standish Roche, 3rd Bt, was DL Carlow.

RODGERS (UK) 1964, of Groombridge, Kent

Sir (JOHN FAIRLIE) TOBIAS RODGERS, 2nd *Baronet*; *b* 2 July 1940; *s* his father, *Sir* JOHN CHARLES, 1993; *ed* Eton, and Worcester Coll, Oxford.

Arms – Azure two bars gemel dancetty argent, over all two palm branches in saltire enfiled through an ancient crown or. **Crest** – Two ravens' heads addorsed sable and gules both within a collar or pendant therefrom a rose argent barbed and seeded proper.
Residence – 34 Warwick Av, W9 2PT. *Clubs* – Brooks's, Garrick, Pratt's.

Experience is knowledge

BROTHER LIVING

(ANDREW) PIERS WINGATE, *b* 24 Oct 1944; *ed* Eton, and Merton Coll, Oxford (BA); Sec to Royal Academy of Arts (also Sec of Chantrey Bequest and British Institution Fund) 1981-; Freeman of the City of London; Member Co of Merchant Adventurers of City of York; FRSA; Chavalier de l'Ordre des Arts et des Lettres (France) 1987, Ordre National de Merite (France) 1991, Cavaliere Ufficiale Ordine al Merito della Repubblica Italiana 1992: *m* 1979, Marie-Agathe, da of late Charles-Albert Houette, Croix de Guerre, of Bléneau, France, and has issue living, Thomas, *b* 18 Dec 1979; *ed* Eton, — Augustus, *b* 1983. *Residences* – Peverell House, Bradford Peverell, Dorset; 18 Hertford St, W1.

WIDOW LIVING OF FIRST BARONET

BETSY, JP, PhD (*Lady Rodgers*), da of late Francis William Aikin-Sneath, JP, of Burleigh Court, Glos: *m* 1930, Sir John Charles Rodgers, 1st Bt, who *d* 1993. *Residence* – The Dower House, Groombridge, Kent.
The first baronet, Sir John Charles Rodgers, son of Charles Rodgers, of York, was MP (C) for Sevenoaks Div of Kent 1950-79, held several ministerial posts, and was a DL of Kent.

ROLL (UK) 1921, of The Chestnuts, Wanstead, Essex

Rev Sir JAMES WILLIAM CECIL ROLL, 4th *Baronet*; *b* 1 June 1912; *s* his father, *Sir* CECIL ERNEST, 1938; *ed* Chigwell Sch, Essex, Pembroke Coll, Oxford, and Chichester Theological Coll; V of St John the Divine, Becontree 1958-83.

Arms – Or, on a fesse indented between four billets, three in chief and one in base azure, each charged with a lion rampant, a civic wreath of the field between two bezants. **Crest** – A dexter cubit arm vested or charged with two bars wavy azure, cuffed ermine, and holding in the hand a chaplet of laurel proper.
Residence – 82 Leighcliff Rd, Leigh-on-Sea, Essex.

DAUGHTER LIVING OF SECOND BARONET

Betty Catherine, *b* 1910: *m* 1932, Charles Algernon Sharman, who *d* 1988, and has issue living, Charles James Roll, *b* 1934, — John Frederick, *b* 1936, — Patrick George, *b* 1939, — Nicholas Algernon, *b* 1945, — Briony Anna, *b* 1942. *Residence* – Front Park, 110 Thorpe Rd, Peterborough.
The 1st baronet, Sir James Roll, was Chm of Pearl Assurance Co Ltd, and Lord Mayor of London 1920-21.

ROPNER (UK) 1904, of Preston Hall, Stockton-on-Tees, Co Palatine of Durham, and Skutterskelfe Hall, Hutton Rudby, North Riding of Yorkshire

Sir ROBERT DOUGLAS ROPNER, 4th *Baronet*, *b* 1 Dec 1921; *s* his father, *Sir* (EMIL HUGO OSCAR) ROBERT, 1962; *ed* Harrow; formerly Capt RA: *m* 1943, Patricia Kathleen, da of William Edward Scofield, of West Malling, Kent, and has issue.

Arms – Per fesse indented sable and or, a pale, with three mullets pierced two and one, and as many roebucks' heads erased one and two, all counterchanged. **Crest** – In front of three tilting spears, one erect, and two in saltire, or, as many mascles interlaced fesswise of the last, thereon, a roebuck's head erased sable. *Residence* – Forest Ridge, Maresfield Park, Sussex.

SON LIVING

ROBERT CLINTON, *b* 6 Feb 1949; *ed* Harrow.

DAUGHTER LIVING

Serena Gay, *b* 1953.

SISTERS LIVING

Diana Joan, *b* 1919: *m* 1941, John Randal Elliot. —— Patricia Elizabeth, *b* 1923: *m* 1944, Lt-Col Claude MacDonald Hull, MC, and has issue living, Susan Patricia Macdonald, *b* 1948, — Fiona Elizabeth Macdonald, *b* 1950.

COLLATERAL BRANCHES LIVING

Grandchildren of Emil Hugo Oscar Robert Ropner, AMINA, 2nd son of 1st baronet:—
Issue of late Lt-Col Richard Ropner, TD, MB, ChB, RAMC, *b* 1898, *d* 1975: *m* 1928, Margaret Forbes, who *d* 1976, da of John Gilfillan Ronald, MD, of Torwood Hall, Larbet, Stirlingshire:—
Richard John Ronald, MB, ChB, *b* 1941; *ed* Harrow, and Edinburgh Univ (MB, ChB); D(Obst) RCOG; DPM; MRC Psych: *m* 1974, Janet Elizabeth, MRCP, el da of Joseph William Fox, PhD, of Marlow House, 3 Camden Park Rd, Chislehurst, Kent, and has issue living, James Richard Alexander, *b* 1977, — Victoria Elizabeth Louise, *b* 1979. —— Alison Margaret, *b* 1930: *m* 1957, Gerald Robert Savage, of The Old Quarry, Bramley, Surrey, and has issue living, Nichola Mary, *b* 1958. —— Pamela Christine, *b* 1931; *ed* Edinburgh Univ (MA): *m* 1957 (Irving) Thomas Stuttaford, MRCS, LRCP, of 8 Ipswich Rd, Norwich, Norfolk, and has issue living, Andrew Irving Ropner, *b* 1958, — Thomas Richard Ropner, *b* 1961, — Hugo John Ropner *b* 1964: *m* 19—, Joanna M., only da of late Keith Davenport, and has issue living, Oliver George Watkin *b* 1994.
Issue of late Capt (Cuthbert) Maurice Ropner, King's Own Scottish Borderers, *b* 1905, *ka* 1945: *m* 1929, Dorothea Seymour (Cestria Cottage, Whittingham, Alnwick, Northumberland), da of Rev Robert William Bell, V of Stamfordham:—
George Maurice, *b* 1934; Maj (ret) Northumberland Hussars (TA). *Residence* – Gallowshaw, Netherwitton, Morpeth, Northumberland. —— Vivien Anne, *b* 1930. —— Caroline Jane, *b* 1945.

Grandchildren of late William Ropner (*infra*):—
See Ropner Bt, *cr* 1952.
Issue of late Sir (William) Guy Ropner, *b* 1896, *d* 1971: *m* 1921, Margarita, who *d* 1973, da of Sir William Cresswell Gray, 1st Bt:—
(William Guy) David (1 Sunningdale Gdns, Stratford Rd, W8 6PX; The Lodge, Accommodation Road, Longcross, Surrey), *b* 1924; *ed* Harrow; late Capt RHA: *m* 1st, 1955, (Mildred) Malise Hare, da of late Col George Armitage, MC, TD, of Newburgh House, Coxwold, Yorks; 2ndly, 1985, Hon Charlotte Mary, da of 2nd Baron Piercy, and formerly wife of Paolo Emilio Taddei, and has issue living (by 1st *m*), Guy David Armitage (Jakemans, Berrick Salome, Wallingford, Oxon OX10 6JQ), *b* 1959: *m* 1991, Annabel Frances, elder da of Michael Odiarne Coates, of Great Shoesmiths Farm, Wadhurst, E Sussex, and has issue living, Amy Grace Coates *b* 1992, — Roderick John, *b* 1962, — Peter Gavin Malise *b* 1964, — Lucy Armitage, *b* 1957: *m* 1985, Christopher Goelet, yst son of John Goelet, of New York, and has issue living, Eloise Ropner *b* 1987, Isabelle

Guestier *b* 1989, Henrietta Zoe *b* 1992, — (by 2nd *m*) Nicholas David Piercy *b* 1986. —— Jonathan Gray (Dalesend, Patrick Brompton, Bedale, N Yorks, DL8 1JL), *b* 1931; late Lt IG: *m* 1953, Edith Avril, da of Charles Urie Peat, MC, of Wycliffe Hall, Barnard Castle, co Durham, and has issue living, (Jonathan) Mark, *b* 1954: *m* 1985, Madelyn K., only da of W. Stefanech, of San Luis Obispo, California, USA, and has issue living, James *b* 1986, Jasmine *b* 1989, — Charles Guy Corban, *b* 1959: *m* 1989, Emma J. F. E., yr da of Richard Andrews, of Courtyard House, Westow, N Yorks, and has issue living, Mary Rose Avril *b* 1991, Eugenie Annabel Pearl *b* 1993, — Paul Benedict Peat, *b* 1965: *m* 1992, Peggy A., da of Willard A. Ison, Warrant Officer USN (ret), of Salt Lake City, Utah, USA, and has issue living, Chloe *b* 1993, — Dominic Adam, *b* 1968: *m* 1991, Abigail, da of Peter de Barros Clay, of The Old Court House, The Green, Richmond-upon-Thames, Surrey, and has issue living, Inigo Thomas Robert *b* 1993, Daisy Manina Debarros *b* 1992, — Margarita Carey, *b* 1956: *m* 1979, John Dickinson, and has issue living, Tobyn Benedict *b* 1981, Amelia Sophie *b* 1983, Leila Florence *b* 1989. —— Rita Gray (13 Old Palace Lane, Richmond, Surrey), *b* 1922: *m* 1947 (*m diss* 1967), Alan Maskew Hodson, and has issue living, Alexandra Mary, *b* 1958.

Issue of late William Ropner, 3rd son of 1st baronet, *b* 1864, *d* 1947: *m* 1894, Sarah Woollacot, who *d* 1948, da of Ebenezer Cory:—

John Raymond, *b* 1903; *ed* Harrow, and Clare Coll, Camb; is a Dir of Sir R. Ropner and Co, Ltd: *m* 1928, Joan, who *d* 1993, da of late William Redhead, and has issue living, William David Jock, *b* 1939: *m* 1961 (*m diss* 1962), Elizabeth Anne Ellsworth Jones, — Jeremy Vyvyan (Firby Hall, Bedale, N Yorks; Brooks's Club): *b* 1932; *ed* Harrow, and RNC Dartmouth: *m* 1955, his cousin, Sally Talbot, da of late Maj George Talbot Willcox, MC (*see* Ropner, Bt, *cr* 1904, colls, 1985 Edn), and has issue living, Simon Jock Wilks *b* 1962, Sophia Sally *b* 1959: *m* 1991, Christopher John Mansfield, of 53 Campana Rd, SW6 4AT, son of Kenneth Mansfield, of Quarry House, Malton, N Yorks, Lisa Cleone Vivian *b* 1964: *m* 1985, Capt (Timothy) Mark Nicole, 4/7th R Dragoon Guards, son of Tom Nicole, of Slape Manor, Netherbury, Bridport, Dorset (and has issue living, Edward Tom George *b* 1990, George Charles Jeremy *b* 1993, Lucy Sophia Katherine *b* 1987), — Susan Carole, *b* 1936: *m* 1957, Maj Charles Peter Martel, of The Manor House, Gayles Richmond, Yorks, only son of late Lt-Gen Sir Giffard le Quesne Martel, KCB, KBE, DSO, MC, and has issue living, Nicholas Charles Giffard (Whitwell House, Whitwell, Richmond, N Yorks DL10 6BB) *b* 1960: *m* 1987, Sarah Jane Maxwell, only da of J. S. M. Barlow, of Minshull Hall, Nantwich, Cheshire (and has issue living, Charles *b* 1988, Hugo *b* 1993), Carole Valerie *b* 1958, Sarah Charlotte *b* 1973.

Grandchildren of late William Ropner (ante):—

Issue of late Sir Robert Desmond Ropner, *b* 1908, *d* 1977: *m* 1st, 1932 (*m diss* 1946), Dorothy Beecroft, da of Sir Edmund Lacon, 5th Bt; 2ndly, 1947, Sibyl, who *d* 1969, da of late Thomas O. Carter:—

(By 1st *m*) (Robert) Bruce Beecroft (Camp Hill, Kirklington, Bedale, Yorks) *b* 1933; Lt Welsh Gds: *m* 1960, Willow, da of James Hare, of Fieldhead, Thorner, Leeds, and has issue living, Robert James Bruce, *b* 1962: *m* 1986, Johanna Louise, yr da of Colin Strathearn Ropner Stroyan, of Teith, Doune, Perthshire (*see* Ropner, Bt, *cr* 1904, 1985 Edn), and has issue living, (Robert) Angus *b* 1988, Max *b* 1990, Poppy *b* 1993, — Nicola Molly, *b* 1965. —— Garry Lacon Jock (Ashmansworth House, Ashmansworth, Newbury, Berks), *b* 1937; late 2nd Lt, Welsh Gds: *m* 1st, 1962 (*m diss* 1973), Antonia, yr da of Maj-Gen Edward Charles Colville, CB, DSO (*see* V Colville of Culross, Colls); 2ndly, 1974, Mrs Julie Marie Swanwick, da of O. B. Aarvold; 3rdly, 1987, Mrs Marie-Louise (Sally) Raynar, da of Arthur Southcombe Brook, of Mount Dart, Totnes, Devon, previously wife of (i) late Antony Stuart Trotter, and (ii) G. K. Raynar, and has issue living (by 1st *m*), Emma Louise, *b* 1963.

Issue of late Leonard Ropner, 5th son of 1st baronet, *b* 1873, *d* 1937: *m* 1904, Georgina, who *d* 1930, da of late Murdock Mackay:—

Leonard Robert, *b* 1910: *m* 1934, Agnes Deans Bennett.

The 1st baronet, Sir (Emil Hugo Oscar) Robert Ropner (a steamship owner of West Hartlepool and a steamship builder of Stockton-on-Tees), son of Henry Ropner, of Magdeburg, sat as MP for Stockton-on-Tees (C) 1900-10.

ROPNER (UK) 1952, of Thorp Perrow, N Riding of Yorkshire

Faith and Fortitude

Sir JOHN BRUCE WOOLLACOTT ROPNER, 2nd *Baronet*; *s* his father *Sir* LEONARD, MC, TD, 1977; *b* 16 April, 1937; *ed* Eton, and St Paul's Sch, USA; High Sheriff N Yorks 1991-92: *m* 1st, 1961 (*m diss* 1970), Anne Melicent, da of late Sir Ralph Hubert Joan Delmé-Radcliffe; 2ndly, 1970 (*m diss* 1994), Auriol Veronica, yr da of late Capt Graham Lawrie Mackeson-Sandbach, of Caerllo, Llangernyw, Abergele, Denbighshire, and has issue by 1st and 2nd *m*.

Arms – Per fesse indented sable and or, a pale, with three mullets pierced two and one, and as many roebucks' heads erased one and two, all counterchanged; a crescent or for difference. **Crest** – In front of three tilting spears, one erect and two in saltire or, as many mascles interlaced fessewise of the last, thereon a roebuck's head erased sable.
Residence – Thorp Perrow, Bedale, N Yorks. **Club** – Brooks's, Northern Counties.

SON LIVING (By 2nd marriage)

HENRY JOHN WILLIAM, *b* 24 Oct 1981.

DAUGHTERS LIVING (By 1st marriage)

Jenny, *b* 1963; resumed her maiden name 1988 until remarriage: *m* 1st, 1985, William H. Bullard, son of late Gerald Bullard, of Hill Farm, Gressenhall, Norfolk; 2ndly, 1990, Graham G. D. Simpson, of 53 Canford Rd, SW11 6PB, son of Brig John Simpson, of Hants and Sydney, and has issue living, Alexander John Drysdale, *b* 1992, — Miranda Lucy Araminta, *b* 1994. —— Katherine (*Hon Mrs Henry Holland-Hibbert*), *b* 1964: *m* 1988, Hon Henry Thurstan Holland-Hibbert, elder son of 6th Viscount Knutsford, and has issue (*see* V Knutsford).

(By 2nd marriage)

Carolyn Esme, *b* 1971. —— Annabel Mariella, *b* 1974.

SISTERS LIVING

Merle Aurelia, *b* 1939: *m* 1st, 1960 (*m diss* 1968), Christopher John Spence; 2ndly, 1968, Maj Laurence Hew Williams Barrington, of Oddington Lodge, Moreton-in-Marsh (*see* Barrington, Bt colls), and has had issue, (by 1st *m*) Jeremy Mark, *b* 1963; *d* 1982, — Miranda Jane, *b* 1963: *m* 1989, Patrick Robin Barran (*see* Barran, Bt, colls), — (by 2nd *m*) (*see* Barrington Bt, colls). —— Virginia June, *b* 1941: *m* 1st, 1962 (*m diss* 1973), Anthony David Arnold William Forbes (*see* B Faringdon, colls, 1980 Edn); 2ndly, 1974, Capt John Alexander Henderson, late 14th/20th Hus, of Holly Hill, Well, Bedale, Yorks, and has issue living (by 1st *m*), Jonathan David, *b* 1964: *m* 1993, Sacha Louisa, da of Hon Robin Charles Denison-Pender (*see* B Pender), — Susanna Jane, *b* 1966: *m* 1993, William M. Amberg, yr son of Michael Amberg, of Ravenstone, Bucks.

WIDOW LIVING OF FIRST BARONET

Esme (*Esme, Lady Ropner*) (Park House, Bedale, Yorks), da of late William Bruce Robertson, of 26 Kensington Palace Gdns, W8: *m* 1932, Sir Leonard Ropner, MC, TD, who *d* 1977.

Sir Leonard Ropner, MC, TD, 1st Bt, son of William Ropner, (*see* Ropner Bt, *cr* 1904), was MP (*C*) for Sedgfield Div of co Durham, and for Barkston Ash Div of W Riding of Yorks. 1931-64, Senior partner Sir R. Ropner & Co Ltd, Shipowners, Chm of Conservative Shipping and Shipbuilding Cttee 1946-64, PPS to Sec of State for War 1924-28, and temp Chm of Cttees, House of Commons 1945-58.

ROSE (UK) 1872, of Montreal, Dominion of Canada; and 1909, of Hardwick House, Whitchurch, Oxfordshire

Sir JULIAN DAY ROSE, 5th *Baronet* of 1st, and 4th of 2nd, creation; *b* 3 March 1947; *s* his father, Sir CHARLES HENRY, 1966, in Baronetcy of Rose of Hardwick House, and *s* his kinsman, Sir FRANCIS CYRIL, 1979, in the Baronetcy of Rose of Montreal; *ed* Stanbridge Earls Sch, Romsey, and RADA; Actor and Assist Dir; co-founder of Inst for Creative Development, Antwerp; organic farmer, writer and broadcaster: *m* 1976, Elizabeth Good, da of Derrol Johnston, of Columbus, Ohio, USA, and has issue.

Arms – Or, a boar's head couped gules between three water bougets sable; on a chief of the second three maple leaves of the first. **Crest** – A harp or, stringed azure.
Residence – Hardwick House, Whitchurch, nr Reading, Oxon RG8 7RB.

I dare

SON LIVING

LAWRENCE MICHAEL, *b* 6 Oct 1986.

DAUGHTER LIVING

Miriam Margaret, *b* 1984.

SISTERS LIVING

Margaret Minna, *b* 1938: *m* 1966, John Alexander Cochrane, of Fairspear House, Leafield, Oxford, OX8 5NT, el son of Hon Sir Ralph Alexander Cochrane (*see* B Cochrane of Cults). —— Penelope Clare, *b* 1945: *m* 1975, Francis A. A. Carnwath, el son of Sir Andrew Hunter Carnwath, KCVO, and has issue living, Flora Helen, *b* 1976, — Catriona Rose, *b* 1978.

AUNTS LIVING (*Daughters of Sir Frank Stanley Rose, 2nd Bt, cr 1909*)

Amy, *b* 1911: *m* 1933, Robert Beloe, CBE, who *d* 1984, and has issue living, *Rev* Robert Francis (The Vicarage, Wicken, nr Ely, Cambs), *b* 1939: *m* 1970, Sheila Napier Millar, and has issue living, Amy Margaret *b* 1971, Christina Ruth *b* 1973, — Helen, *b* 1934: *m* 1955, Oliver Piers Stutchbury, of Gayles, Friston, E Sussex BN20 0BA, and has issue living Wycliffe Robert Trant *b* 1965, Emma Jane *b* 1955 (has issue living, Ben Joseph *b* 1978, Lucy *b* 1980), Catharine Rose *b* 1958: *m* 19—, Kevin Allen, Rosalind Amy *b* 1960: *m* 19—, Derry Robinson (and has issue living, Jessica Helen *b* 1987), — Clarissa Elizabeth *b* 1936: *m* 1963, John Eagle Higginbotham, Headmaster Leicester Gram Sch (16 Holmfield Av, Stoneygate, Leics) and has issue living, Robert Charles Trant *b* 1967, Lydia Clare *b* 1964. *Residence* – The Hill House, Queen's Rd, Richmond, Surrey. —— Helen Briar, *b* (*posthumous*) 1915: *m* 1939, Lt-Col John Granville, Oxford and Bucks LI (Halsey, Bt), who *d* 1984, and has issue living, Antony Lansdown (Tachbrook House, Stourton, nr Shipton-on-Stour, Warwicks), *b* 1945: *m* 1970, Harriet Anne, da of Sir John James Macdonald Horlick, 5th Bt, and has issue living, Edward James *b* 1972, Matilda Rose *b* 1975, — Charles, *b* 1949. *Residence* – Holly Copse, Goring Heath, nr Reading, Berks.

WIDOW LIVING OF THIRD BARONET

Hon PHOEBE MARGARET DOROTHY PHILLIMORE (*Hon Lady Rose*) (Hardwick House, Whitchurch-on-Thames, Oxon RG8 7RB), da of 2nd Baron Phillimore: *m* 1937, Sir Charles Henry Rose, 3rd Bt, (Rose Bt, *cr* 1909), who *d* 1966.

The 1st baronet, Sir Charles Day Rose, son of late Rt Hon Sir John Rose, PC, GCMG, 1st Bt (*cr* 1872, ante), sometime a partner in the American Banking firm of Morton Rose and Co, of Bartholomew Lane, EC, sat as MP for Newmarket, (*L*) 1903-10 and 1910-13. The 2nd baronet, Capt Sir Frank Stanley, 10th R Hussars, was *ka* 1914.

Rt Hon Sir William Rose, GCMG, 1st baronet, was Min of Finance, Canada 1868-69, and Receiver-Gen for Duchy of Cornwall 1883-88. He was son of William Rose of Huntingdon, Canada, who was *b* at Turiff, Aberdeenshire, of a family originally from co Nairn.

ROSE (UK) 1874, of Rayners, Buckinghamshire

Sir DAVID LANCASTER ROSE, 4th *Baronet*, son of late Ronald Paul Lancaster Rose, only son of Bateman Lancaster Rose, 5th son of 1st Baronet; *b* 17 Feb 1934; *s* his cousin, Sir PHILIP HUMPHRY VIVIAN, 1982: *m* 1965, Dorothy, da of Albert Edward Whitehead, and has issue.

Arms – Azure, a chevron invected erminois, between three water bougets in chief and one in base argent. **Crest** – A stag argent, collared, and resting the dexter fore-leg on a water bouget azure.
Residence – 20 Kingston Close, Seaford, Sussex.

SONS LIVING

PHILIP JOHN LANCASTER, *b* 1966. —— Christopher David, *b* 1968.

DAUGHTER LIVING

Probitate ac virtute

By probity and valour

Angela Mary, *b* 1967.

DAUGHTERS LIVING OF THIRD BARONET

Petica Mary, *b* 1929: *m* 1955, Judge Andrew Felix Waley, VRD, QC, and has issue living, Simon Felix, *b* 1964, — Sarah Elizabeth, *b* 1958, — Jane Felicity, *b* 1959, — Juliet Anne, *b* 1960. *Residence* – Pleasure House, East Sutton, Kent ME17 3NW. —— Susan Elizabeth Ann, *b* 1932.

SISTERS LIVING OF THIRD BARONET

Marjorie Winifred, *b* 1900: *m* 1927, Wilfred Eyre, of 835 South Garfield St, Denver, Colorado, 80209, USA, and has issue living, Richard Carmel Thomas More, *b* 1936: *m* 1965, Josepha Mary Schretlen, and has issue living, Richard Edward *b* 1966, Andrea Marjorie *b* 1967, Christina Maria *b* 1969, Judith Mary *b* 1971, — Vivian Mary Raymonde, *b* 1928: *m* 1949, John Sweeney, of 461 Race St, Denver, Colorado, USA, and has issue living, Michael Eyre *b* 1953, Timothy Andrew *b* 1957, Edward Philip *b* 1963, Mark McConnell *b* 1965, Marna Therese *b* 1950, Carol Mary *b* 1958, Kathrine Ann *b* 1960, — Elisa Virginia Mary, *b* 1932: *m* 1st, 1952 (*m diss* 19—), Charles Bennet Cobb; 2ndly, 1963, Christopher Brennan, of 22660 Pacific Coast Highway, Malibu, Cal, USA, and has issue living, (by 1st *m*) Charles Dennison, *b* 1955, Gerald Bennett *b* 1956, Marguerite Elisa *b* 1957, (by 2nd *m*) Christopher Thomas, *b* 1972, — Jane Olga Mary, *b* 1934: *m* 1960, Bruce Schuster, of 4730, South Lafayette, Englewood, Colorado, USA, and has issue living, Anthony Bruce *b* 1964, Philip Andrew *b* 1965, Christopher Paul *b* 1969, Matthew Ainsworth *b* 1972, Jane Eyre, *b* 1962. —— June Dorothy (715 Bonie Brae Blvd, Denver, Colorado, USA), *b* 1913: *m* 1938 (*m diss* 19—), Marcel Brennan, and has issue living, Christopher *b* 1939.

MOTHER LIVING

Shelagh Grant Lindsay, da of Maj Joseph Lindsey Curtis: *m* 1933 (*m diss* 1937), Ronald Paul Lancaster Rose, who *d* 1977.

COLLATERAL BRANCHES LIVING

Grandchildren of late George Alfred Sainte Croix Rose, 6th son of 1st baronet:—
Issue of late Major Ivor Sainte Croix Rose, OBE, *b* 1881, *d* 1961: *m* 1st 1907, Etta Mabel, who *d* 1918, yst da of late Com Sebastian Gassiot, RN; 2ndly, 1918 (*m diss* 1935), Nancy who *d* 1968, da of Arthur Conran Blomfield; 3rdly, 1936 (*m diss* 1951), Ruth Elldale, who *d* 1952, da of Richard White, of Nain, Labrador:—
(By 3rd *m*) George Vivian Sainte Croix (45 Woodfield Lane, Ashtead, Surrey), *b* 1939: *m* 1960, Audrey Rosamond, da of Lawrence Frederick Barrow, and has issue living, Philip Vivian Sainte Croix, *b* 1961, — Alison Charlotte, *b* 1960: *m* 1979, Adrian Christopher Rowe, of 191 Downs Barn Blvd, Milton Keynes, Bucks, and has issue living, Katherine Nancy Charlotte *b* 1991. —— (By 1st *m*) Nancy Bertha Mary Sainte Croix, *b* 1908: *m* 1934, Cdr Rupert St Aubyn Malleson, AFC, RN, who *d* 1960, son of late Maj-Gen Sir Wilfrid Malleson, KCIE, CB. —— (By 2nd *m*) Camilla Mary Sainte Croix, *b* 1919; 2nd Offr WRNS 1939-45 War: *m* 1945, Richard Oliver MacMahon Williams, OBE, MC, WS, who *d* 1981, and has issue living, Caroline Jane Sainte Croix, *b* 1947: *m* 1983, Jeremy Peter Marriage, and has issue living, Frederick Peter Oliver *b* 1986, Clare Felicity *b* 1984, Lucy Diana *b* 1989, — Nicola Valentine Blomfield, *b* 1948: *m* 1972, Brig Alistair Stuart Hastings Irwin, OBE, The Black Watch (R Highland Regt), and has issue living, George Ronald Valentine Hastings *b* 1983, Mary Rose Elizabeth *b* 1975, Laura Bridget *b* 1978, — Rosemary Anne MacMahon, *b* 1952: *m* 1973 (*m diss* 1989), Adrian Gerald Burns, and has issue living, Thomas Michael Macmahon *b* 1979, Emily Caroline *b* 1981, — Lorna Christine Allan, *b* 1954: *m* 1975, Gareth Bowring Stoddart, and has issue (see Malet Bt).
Issue of late Harcourt George Sainte Croix Rose, *b* 1883, *d* 1955: *m* 1st, 1908 (*m diss* 1920), Florence Norah, who *d* 1970, da of Arthur Elliot Deane, of Littleton House, Winchester (Hughes, Bt, *cr* 1773); 2ndly, 1920 (*m diss* 1930), Freda Victoria, who *d* 1972, da of late C. A. Keyser; 3rdly 1930, Estelle Marie, da of late Marquis of Sarzano, 8th Hussars:—
(By 1st *m*) Jean *b* 1915; European War 1939-45 with WAAF: *m* 1953, Lieut-Com Henry Francis Ormsby Hale, RN, of High View House, Langtree, Torrington, Devon, who *d* 1984.
Sir Philip Rose, 1st Bt, was Founder of the Brompton Hospital for Consumption (Hon-Sec 1841-83), and High Sheriff of Bucks 1878.

ROSE (UK) 1935, of Leith, Co of City of Edinburgh (Extinct 1976)

Sir HUGH ROSE, TD, 2nd and last *Baronet*.

DAUGHTER LIVING OF SECOND BARONET

Alison Mary (Whitfield Farm, Hawick, Roxburghshire), *b* 1936: *m* 1st, 1964 (*m diss* 1972), Ian Napier; 2ndly, 1985, John Risk Buchanan.

WIDOW LIVING OF SECOND BARONET

MARJORIE (*Lady Rose*) (Crurie, Whitfield Farm, Hawick, Roxburghshire), da of Thomas Leslie Usher, of 8 Whitehouse Terr, Edinburgh, and Hyndhope, Selkirk: *m* 1930, Maj Sir Hugh Rose, TD, 2nd Bt, who *d* 1976.

ROSS (UK) 1960, of Whetstone, Middlesex

Sir (JAMES) KEITH ROSS, RD, MS, FRCS, 2nd *Baronet*; *b* 9 May, 1927; *s* his father, *Sir* JAMES PATERSON, KCVO, 1980; *ed* St Paul's, and Middx Hosp; MB and MS London; FRCS 1956; Surg Lt-Cdr RNR; Consultant cardiac surgeon Wessex Region 1972-90: *m* 1956, Jacqueline Annella, da of late Francis William Clarke, of Banstead, Surrey, and has issue.

Arms – Per pale argent and sable a chevron between in chief lion passant and in base an anchor all counterchanged. **Crest** – A hawk rising sable between two branches of juniper leaved and fructed proper.
Residence – Moonhills Gate, Hilltop, Beaulieu, Hants SO42 7YS.

SON LIVING

ANDREW CHARLES PATERSON, *b* 18 July 1966.

DAUGHTERS LIVING

Susan Wendy, *b* 1958: *m* 1983, Nigel Timothy Wolstenholme, of The Oast House, Hoplands Farm, Kings Somborne, Stockbridge, Hants SO20 6QH, son of late J. M. Wolstenholme. —— Janet Mary, *b* 1960: *m* 1990, Timothy N. Morgan, of The Old School House, Powderham, nr Exeter, Devon, son of late N. V. Morgan, of Dibden Purlieu, Hants. —— Anne Townsend, *b* 1962: *m* 1993, Murray Anderson-Wallace, of 12 Nunhead Grove, SE15.

BROTHER LIVING

Harvey Burton, RD, MS, FRCS (Springvale, Brewery Common, Mortimer, Reading, RG7 3JE, Berks), *b* 1928; FRCS 1957: *m* 1st, 1962, Nancy Joan, da of B. C. Hilliam, of Bank Lyndhurst; 2ndly, 1988, Susan Christine, da of P. M. Blandy, of Reading, Berks, and has issue living (by 1st *m*), Edward Paterson, *b* 1963, — James Hilliam, *b* 1972, — Imogen, *b* 1970.

The first baronet, Sir James Paterson Ross, was Surg to HM 1952-64; Pres Royal College of Surgeons 1957-59; *cr KCVO* 1949.

ROTHBAND (UK) 1923, of Higher Broughton, Salford, co Palatine, of Lancaster (Extinct 1940)

Sir HENRY LESSER ROTHBAND, 1st and last *Baronet*.

GRANDDAUGHTER LIVING OF FIRST BARONET

Issue of late Percy Lionel Rothband, only son of 1st baronet, *b* 1884, *d* 1926: *m* 1918, Ellen Elizabeth Marjorie (who *d* 1956, having *m* 2ndly, 1935, Capt Wilfred Henry Furlonger, who *d* 1945), el da of William Francis Fisher, of Altrincham:—
Joan Olga Eleanor, *b* 1920: *m* 1942, Dennis Arthur Treves Atkins, who *d* 1993, and has issue living, Timothy Simon Treves, *b* 1951, — Penelope Jane, *b* 1943: *m* 1969, Peter Nicholas Geer, of 537 Eastcot Rd, W Vancouver, BC V7S 1E5, Canada, and has issue living, Noel *b* 1976, Samantha *b* 1970, Jill *b* 1973, — Marilyn Jill ATKINS, *b* 1947; has resumed her maiden name: *m* 1974 (*m diss* 1985), Johann Klein, — Priscilla Dawn, *b* 1948: *m* 1973 (*m diss* 19—), Bruce Higham, and has issue living, Alice *b* 1973. *Residence* – 21 Courtyards, Little Shelford, Cambridge CB2 5ER.

Rouse-Boughton, see Boughton.

ROWLAND (UK) 1950, of Taunton, co Somerset (Extinct 1970)

Sir WENTWORTH LOWE ROWLAND, 2nd and last *Baronet*.

DAUGHTER LIVING OF SECOND BARONET

Georgina Elizabeth Mary, *b* 1952: *m* 1977, John George Stewart Scott, of Lower Street Farmhouse, Hildenborough, Tonbridge, Kent, and has issue living, Victoria Katharine, *b* 1979, — Charlotte Elizabeth, *b* 1982.

WIDOW LIVING OF SECOND BARONET

(VIOLET MARY) ELIZABETH MACBETH (*Lady Rowland*) (4 Stonewall Park Rd, Langton Green, Tunbridge Wells, Kent), da of late A. C. Macbeth Robertson, of Dumfries: *m* 1947, Sir Wentworth Lowe Rowland, 2nd Bt, who *d* 1970.

ROWLEY (GB) 1786, of Tendring Hall, Suffolk

Sir JOSHUA FRANCIS ROWLEY, 7th *Baronet*; *b* 31 Dec 1920; *s* his father, *Col Sir* CHARLES SAMUEL, OBE, TD, 1962; *ed* Eton, and Trin Coll, Camb; formerly Capt Gren Gds; Vice-Lieut for Suffolk 1973-78, Lord-Lieut 1978-93; Patron of three livings: *m* 1959, Hon Celia Ella Vere Monckton, da of 8th Viscount Galway, and has issue.

Arms – Argent, on a band engrailed, between two Cornish choughs sable, billed and legged gules, three escallops of the field. **Crest** – A Mullet pierced or.
Residence – Holbecks, Hadleigh, Ipswich, Suffolk IP7 5PF. *Clubs* – Pratt's, Boodle's.

DAUGHTER LIVING

Susan Emily Frances, *b* 1965: *m* 1988, Robert David Holden (*see* E Powis, colls).

Ventis secundis
With favouring winds

SISTER LIVING

Alethea Susan, *b* 1922: *m* 1949, Henry Reginald Townshend, MBE, of Brook Hall, Bramfield, Suffolk, and has issue living, James Reginald, *b* 1954: *m* 1980, Olivia Mora Matthey, and has issue living, Henry Roscoe *b* 1984, Georgina Hermione *b* 1982, — Robert Charles, *b* 1956: *m* 1983, Fiona Elizabeth Mary Fraser, and has issue living, Hugh Charles *b* 1984, a son *b* 1991, Arabella Charlotte *b* 1987, — Albinia Jane, *b* 1952: *m* 1977, James Anthony Stoddart Murray, and has issue living, Susannah Albinia Frances *b* 1979, Annabel Katharine Law *b* 1981.

COLLATERAL BRANCH LIVING

Descendants of late Adm Sir Charles Rowley, GCB, GCH (4th son of Sir Joshua Rowley, 1st baronet), who was *cr* a *Baronet*, 1836.
See Rowley, Bt, *cr* 1836.
The 1st baronet, Rear-Adm Sir Joshua Rowley (son of Sir William Rowley, Adm of the Fleet), took part in the actions, of Grenada 1779, and of Martinique April and May 1780. Adm Sir Josias Rowley, GCB, nephew of 1st baronet, was created a baronet 1813, and died unmarried 1842. The 3rd baronet, Sir Joseph Ricketts Rowley, was Vice-Adm of the Blue.

ROWLEY (UK) 1836, of Hill House, Berkshire

Sir CHARLES ROBERT ROWLEY, 7th *Baronet*; *b* 15 March 1926; *s* his father, *Lt-Col Sir* WILLIAM JOSHUA, 1971; *ed* Wellington: *m* 1952, Astrid, da of late Sir Arthur Massey, CBE, MD, of 93 Bedford Gdns, W8, and has issue.

Arms – Argent, on bend engrailed between two Cornish choughs sable, three escallops of the field. **Crest** – A Mullet pierced or. **Supporters** – Two Cornish choughs proper, navally crowned or, gorged with the riband and therefrom pendent a representation of the badge of the Imperial Austrian Order of Maria Theresa also proper.
Residences – Naseby Hall, Northants; 21 Tedworth Sq, SW3.

With favouring winds

SON LIVING

RICHARD CHARLES, *b* 14 Aug 1959; *ed* Eton, and Exeter Coll, Oxford (BA): *m* 1989, (Elizabeth) Alison, da of late (Arthur) Henry Bellingham (*see* Bellingham, Bt, colls), and has issue living, Joshua Andrew, *b* 1989, — William Henry Stuart, *b* 1992. *Residence* – 15 Worfield St, SW11 4RB.

DAUGHTER LIVING

Caroline Astrid, *b* 1955: *m* 1979, Edwin Rudolph Joseph March Phillipps de Lisle, and has issue living, Alexander Edwin, *b* 1983, — Nicholas Charles, *b* 1991.

BROTHER LIVING

(Joshua) Christopher (The Hill Court, Ross-on-Wye, Herefordshire), *b* 1928.

SISTER LIVING

Avice Gwendoline, *b* 1920: *m* 1953, John Arderne Mere Latham, and has issue living, Mark Joshua Arderne, *b* 1955, — Robert William Mere, *b* 1956. *Residence* – The Forge, Cawston, Norfolk.

HALF-SISTERS LIVING

Felicity Margaret, *b* 1945: *m* 1967, (Alexander) Michael Foulds Slinger, of Slaters House, Widdington, Saffron Walden, Essex, CB11 3SN, and 34 Hornton St, W8, and has issue living, Arabella Claire Felicity, *b* 1972, — Katharine Merianna Sarah, *b* 1977. —— Prudence Elizabeth, *b* 1951: *m* 1972, Simon Geoffrey Hull, and has issue living, Thomas Gresham, *b* 1975, — Louisa Claire, *b* 1977.

WIDOW LIVING OF SIXTH BARONET

MARGARET SHEILA (*Margaret, Lady Rowley*), (The Old Stables, Widdington, Saffron Walden, Essex), da of late Harold Camp, of Stamford, Conn, USA: *m* 1940, as his 2nd wife, Sir William Joshua Rowley, 6th Bt, who *d* 1971.

COLLATERAL BRANCHES LIVING

Grandchildren of late Julius Richard Capel Molyneux Rowley, el son of late Rev Julius Henry Rowley, son of late Capt Richard Freeman Rowley, RN, 4th son of 1st baronet:—
Issue of late Capt Charles Donovan Rowley, MBE, *b* 1889, *d* 1935: *m* 1917, Hon Irene Evelyn Beatrice (who *d* 1949, having *m* 2ndly, 1941, Frank Ash, who *d* 1974, of Narborough Hall, King's Lynn, Norfolk), da of 9th Viscount Molesworth:—
John Howard (Monks' Orchard, Blakeney, Holt, Norfolk), *b* 1931; formerly Lt RA (TA): *m* 1963, Aileen Margery, da of late R. Clifford Freeman, and has issue living, Charles John Freeman, *b* 1969, — Irene Frances Elizabeth, *b* 1965. —— Nina Irene (Camphill Village, Alpha Kalbaskraal, W Cape, 7302, S Africa), *b* 1922. —— June Rose, *b* 1924: *m* 1963, Thomas Opitz, of Jim Jim, Via Darwin, Aust. —— Julia May, *b* 1934: *m* 1955, Anthony Frederick Twist, and has issue living, Andrew Charles, *b* 1958: *m* 1st, 1977, Bronwen Anne Bowden; 2ndly, 1987, Sally Michael Mangos, and has issue living (by 1st *m*), Rebecca Catherine *b* 1985, (by 2nd *m*) Samuel Wilfrid *b* 1993, — Julian Richard, *b* 1960: *m* 1981, Gillian Sandra Hooper, and has issue living, Jennifer Megan *b* 1987, Helen Victoria *b* 1989, Sarah Catherine *b* 1991, — Philip Michael, *b* 1962: *m* 1983, Elspeth Jane Barr, and has issue living, Lucy Alice *b* 1987, Emily Charlotte *b* 1989, Rosie Francesca *b* 1993, — Catherine Julia, *b* 1956, — Mai Alison (adopted da), *b* 1970. *Residence* – Clements End, Conduit Head Rd, Cambridge.

Granddaughters of late Julius Leigh Rowley (infra):—
Issue of late Robin Julius Leigh, *b* 1892, *d* 1974: *m* 1920, Edith May, who *d* 1984, da of Sidney Hugo Mumford, of Eton, Bucks:—
Thelma Jeanne, *b* 1923: *m* 1946, René Georges Lucien Paul Lefevre, of Ivydene, East Drive, Bracklesham Bay, W Sussex, and has issue living, Julian Howard Georges Alphonse, *b* 1949; *ed* Leeds Univ (BA), — Michelle Edith Germaine, *b* 1946, — Christine Rene Jeanne, *b* 1948, — Jacqueline Marguerite Frederica, *b* 1951. —— Audrey Frederica, *b* 1928: *m* 1949, Thomas Arthur Smith, of Walnut Trees, Cemetery Lane, Woodmancote, Emsworth, Hants, and has issue living, Ivan Howard Lee (Lordington Park, Lordington, Chichester, W Sussex), *b* 1952: *m* 1st, 1978, Pamela Joan, da of late Ronald Janman; 2ndly, 19—, Jessica Jane, da of David Rutland, and has issue living (by 1st *m*), James Leigh Thomas *b* 1983, Luke Robin Anthony *b* 1984, (by 2nd *m*) Harriet Jane *b* 1993, — Stephen Frederick John (Downs View, East Marden, Chichester, W Sussex), *b* 1955: *m* 1983, Shona Joyce, da of Peter McCall, and has issue living, Nicholas Edward Peter *b* 1984, Charlotte Louise *b* 1986.

Grandchildren of late Rev Julius Henry Rowley (ante):—
Issue of late Julius Leigh Rowley, *b* 1863; *d* 1943: *m* 1st, 1890, Florence, who *d* 1895, da of Harry Coe; 2ndly, 1899, Alma, da of Harry Welch:—
(By 2nd *m*) Julius Henry, *b* 1905. —— Douglas Lionel, *b* 1911. —— (By 1st *m*) Frederica Mina Mabel, *b* 1892: *m* 19—, Harvey Anderson, of PO Box 414, Posey, Calif 93260, USA, and has issue living, Bruce Milton, *b* 1922: *m*, and has issue living, Bruce Kenneth (2503 171 St SE, Bothill, Washington, USA) *b* 1945. —— (By 2nd *m*) Violet Frances, *b* 1903: *m* 19—, — Fenwick, formerly of 2159, Mission St, San Francisco, Calif, USA. —— Geraldine Winifred, *b* 1909: *m* 1932, Clarence Arthur Allendin, of Geyserville, Sonoma Co, Cal, USA. —— Hildred Vivian, *b* 1912: *m* 19—, — Wycoft. —— Alma Julia, *b* 1915.

Granddaughters of late Richard Julius Duncan Lorin Rowley (infra):—
Issue of late Frederick Duncan Lorin Rowley, *b* 1912, *d* 1968: *m* 1941, Dale (2388 East Racquet Club Rd, Palm Springs, Cal, USA), da of Joseph Antellin:—
Pamela Dale, *b* 1942. —— Loryn Lee, *b* 1946.

Granddaughter of Rev Julius Henry Rowley (ante):—
Issue of late Richard Julius Molyneux Rowley, *b* 1865, *d* 1948: *m* 1900, Idabe Sophia, who *d* 1951, da of Oscar T. Nelson, of Gothenburg, Sweden:—
Constance Frederica Julia Christina, *b* 1901: *m* 1922, Burnell Hamilton De Vos, and has issue living, Burnell Hamilton, *b* 1927, — Richard Glenn, *b* 1932.

Descendants, if any, of late Com Robert Hibbert Bartholomew Rowley, RN, 5th son of 1st baronet, *b* 1817, *d* 1860: *m* 1845, Donna Juanita di Latzona, who left issue, two sons and two das, concerning whom no details are available.
The 1st baronet, Adm Sir Charles, GCB, GCH (also Knight of Order of Maria Theresia of Austria), was 4th son of Sir Joshua Rowley, 1st Bt (creation 1786), of Tendring Hall.

ROYDEN (UK) 1905, of Frankby Hall, co Palatine, of Chester

Sir CHRISTOPHER JOHN ROYDEN, 5th *Baronet*; *b* 26 Feb 1937; *s* his father, *Sir* JOHN LEDWARD, 1976; *ed* Winchester, and Ch Ch, Oxford (MA): *m* 1961, Diana Bridget, only da of Lt-Col Joseph Henry Goodhart, MC, of Keldholme Priory, Kirkbymoorside, Yorks, and has issue.

Arms – Vert, three stags' heads erased in pale between two hunting horns in fesse or. Crest – A stag's head erased or, collared gemel vert, holding in the mouth a riband also vert, suspended therefrom a shield of the Royden arms.
Residence – Bridge House, Ablington, Bibury, nr Cirencester, Glos.

SONS LIVING

JOHN MICHAEL JOSEPH, *b* 17 March 1965; *ed* Stowe, and Reading Univ (LLB): *m* 1989, Lucilla Mary, da of John Ralph Stourton (*see* B Mowbray), and has issue living, Charlotte Alice Maude, *b* 1992. —— Richard Thomas Bland, *b* 1967.

DAUGHTER LIVING

Emma Mary Bridget, *b* 1971.

BROTHER LIVING

Thomas Cecil (Netherfield Place Farm, Battle, Sussex), *b* 1938; *ed* Winchester, Ch Ch Oxford, Univ of Maryland, LSE, Utah State Univ (MSc), and Calif State Poly Univ Pomona; Master of USA Agric; Settlement Manager, Kitale, Tanzania; Consultant Utah State Univ.

SISTERS LIVING

Catherine Anne (Wapley Cottage, Byton, nr Presteigne, Powys LD8 2HS), *b* 1945: *m* 1965 (*m diss* 1979), Christopher Synge Barton (*see* Synge, Bt, colls, 1985 Edn), and has issue living, James Edward Synge, *b* 1974, — Sarah Melissa Synge, *b* 1970. —— Quenelda Jane, *b* 1947: *m* 1967, Robert Reginald Loder, of Leonardslee Gardens, Lower Beeding, Horsham (*see* Loder, Bt).

AUNTS LIVING (*Daughters of 3rd baronet*)

Rachel Nancy, *b* 1902: *m* 1931, Lt-Col John Forbes Batten, OBE, MC, late RA, who *d* 1979, and has had issue, Rachel Ann, *b* 1932: *m* 1st, 1956 (*m diss* 1960), Peter Long; 2ndly, 1963, Leslie Ernest Sutton, MA, DPhil, FRS, Fellow of Magdalen Coll, Oxford, who *d* 1992, and *d* 1987, — Catherine Jean, *b* 1934: *m* 1955, Thomas Burtt Dowell, of 64 Berkeley Rd, Westbury Park, Bristol. *Residence* – St Luke's Nursing Home, Latimer Rd, Headington, Oxford. —— Vera Katherine, *b* (twin) 1915: *m* 1935, Charles Gavin Clark, and has issue living, David Gavin Bland, *b* 1944, — Sonia Jennifer Jane, *b* 1936: *m* 1st, 1956 (*m diss* 1965), John Cecil McGregor Cuthbert; 2ndly, 1965, Anthony James Bevan of 33 Queensferry Rd, Edinburgh, 4, — Gillian Vera, *b* 1939: *m* 1st, 1958 (*m diss* 1978), Alexander Graham Athol Turner Laing; 2ndly, 1978, Maldwin Andrew Cyril Drummond, DL JP, of Cadland House, Fawley, Southampton, and has had issue (by 1st *m*), Alexander Hubert *b* 1968, *d* 1971, Sophia Henrietta *b* 1960: *m* 1987, Charles Comninos, of 14 Butlers Wharf West, 40 Shad Thames, SE1 2YA, son of Michael Comninos, of Staithe House, Chiswick Mall, W4 (and has issue living, Alexander John *b* 1989, Marina Catherine *b* 1992), Ariane Sarah *b* 1963: *m* 1992, Edward J. Koopman, of 30 Quai d'Orléans, 75004 Paris, son of Hendrick Koopman, of St Didier au Mont d'Or, France, Laura Catherine *b* 1969, (by 2nd *m*) (*see* E Perth, colls).

WIDOW LIVING OF FOURTH BARONET

DOLORES CATHERINE (*Catherine, Lady Royden*) (Netherfield Place Farm, Battle, Sussex TN33 9PY), el da of late Cecil John Griffith Coward, of Lima, Peru: *m* 1936, Sir John Ledward Royden, 4th Bt, who *d* 1976.

COLLATERAL BRANCH LIVING

Issue of late Thomas Jerome Royden, yr son of 3rd Bt, *b* 1913, *d* 1991: *m* 1st, 1937, Catherine Mary Denton, who *d* 1970, da of late Charles Denton Toosey, of Oxton, Birkenhead; 2ndly, 1970, Lynn (201 Sweetwater Creek Dr E., Longewood, Fla 32779, USA), da of late Lloyd Aspinwall, Jr, of Mountain Lake, Lake Wales, Fla, USA:—
(By 1st *m*) Ernest Jerome (556 Forest View, Hudson, Quebec J0P 1J0, Canada), *b* 1944: *m* 1974, Suzanne Adams, and has issue living, Catherine Helene, *b* 1982. —— Anne Elizabeth Mary, *b* 1945: *m* 1967, Barry Lewis Gerken, of 37 Woodside Dr, Mass 01740, USA, and has issue living, Heather Kristin, *b* 1969, — Stefanie Rebecca, *b* 1971. —— (By 2nd *m*) Thomas, *b* 1976. —— Alexa, *b* 1972.

The 1st baronet, Sir Thomas Bland Royden, was Mayor of Liverpool 1878-9, and MP for W Toxteth Div of Liverpool (*C*) 1885-92. The 2nd baronet, Sir Thomas Royden, CH, was Chm of Cunard Steamship Co, Ltd, and a Director of Phoenix Assurance Co, Ltd, and other Cos, and sat as MP for Bootle (*Co U*) 1918-22. He was *cr Baron Royden*, of Frankby, co Chester (peerage of United Kingdom) 1944 and *d* 1950, when the Barony became ext, and the Baronetcy devolved upon his brother, Sir Ernest Bland Royden. Sir Ernest Bland Royden, 3rd Bt, was High Sheriff of Anglesey 1920.

Rugge-Price, see Price.

Ruggles-Brise, see Brise.

RUMBOLD (GB) 1779, of Wood Hall, Watton, Herts

*Praise is the excitement
of virtue*

Sir HENRY JOHN SEBASTIAN RUMBOLD, 11th *Baronet*; *b* 24 Dec 1947; *s* his father, *Sir* (HORACE) ANTHONY CLAUDE, KCMG, KCVO, CB, 1983; *ed* Eton, and William and Mary Coll, Va, USA: *m* 1978, Frances Ann, da of late Dr Albert Whitfield Hawkes, of New York City, NY, USA, and formerly wife of Julian Berry.

Arms – Or, on a chevron gules three cinquefoils of the field; a canton of the second charged with a leopard's face erminois. **Crest** – A demi-lion rampant erminois.
Residences – 19 Hollywood Rd, SW10 9HT; Hatch House, Tisbury, Wilts.

SISTERS LIVING

Serena Caroline, *b* 1939: *m* 1959, Jeremy Lancaster, of The Gables, Broadwell, Moreton-in-Marsh, Glos, and has issue living, Nicholas Horace John, *b* 1966, — Emma Charlotte, *b* 1961, — Joanna Elizabeth, *b* 1963, — Frances Mary, *b* 1968. —— Venetia Mary (Juventud Con Una Mision, Apartado Aerco 54141, Bogota 2, Colombia) *b* 1941. —— Camilla Charlotte, *b* 1943: *m* 1st, 1962 (*m diss* 1970), Hon Christopher Lionel Baliol Brett (*see* V Esher); 2ndly, 1972 (*m diss* 1983), Giles Oliver Cairnes Swayne, only son of late Sir Ronald Oliver Carless Swayne, MC, and has issue living (by 1st *m*) (*see* V Esher), — (by 2nd *m*) Orlando Benedict Carlos, *b* 1974.

AUNT LIVING (*Daughter of 9th baronet*)

Constantia Dorothy, *b* 1906: *m* 1944, Hugh William Farmar, MVO, LLD, who *d* 1987, and has issue living, (Hugh Alexander) Peregrine (Saltway House, Bibury, nr Cirencester, Glos), *b* 1945; *ed* Eton, and Keble Coll, Oxford: *m* 1973, Carole Mary Phillips, and has issue, Samuel Hugh Gregory *b* 1977, Rebecca Lucy *b* 1975, Georgina Frances *b* 1980, Charlotte Felicity *b* 1985, — Francis Edmund (1 Rectory Cottages, Sedgehill, Shaftesbury, Dorset), *b* 1948; *ed* Eton, St Martin's Coll of Art, and West of England Coll of Art: *m* 1982, Judith Madeline Povoas.
Residence – Wasing Old Rectory, Aldermaston, Berks.

WIDOW LIVING OF TENTH BARONET

PAULINE LAETITIA (*Pauline, Lady Rumbold*), da of late Hon David Francis Tennant (*see* B Glenconner, colls), and formerly wife of (1) Capt Julian Alfred Lane-Fox-Pitt-Rivers (*see* By Forster, 1980 Edn), and (2) Euan Douglas Graham (*see* D Montrose, colls): *m* 3rd, 1974, as his 2nd wife, Sir (Horace) Anthony Claude Rumbold, 10th Bt, KCMG, KCVO, CB, who *d* 1983.
Residence – Hatch Cottage, Coker's Frome, Dorchester, Dorset.

COLLATERAL BRANCHES LIVING

Issue of late Col William Edwin Rumbold, CMG, 2nd son of 8th baronet, *b* 1870, *d* 1947: *m* 1903, Elizabeth Gordon, who *d* 1948, da of late Rev J. Cameron, of Burntisland:—
Violet Elizabeth, *b* 1907: *m* 1934, Andrew Atha, who *d* 1967, and has issue living, Charles Antony, *b* 1937, — Elizabeth Amanda, *b* 1940: *m* 1967, Michael Abrahams, MBE, of Newfield, Mickley, Ripon, Yorks.

Grandchildren of late Col William Edwin Rumbold, CMG (ante):—
Issue of late Sir (Horace) Algernon Fraser Rumbold, KCMG, CIE, *b* 1906, *d* 1993: *m* 1946, Margaret Adel (Shortwoods, West Clandon, Surrey GU4 7UB), da of late Arthur Joseph Hughes, OBE, of Pages, Chigwell Row, Essex:—
Sara Josephine, *b* 1948: *m* 1969, Robert Michael Owen, QC, of 2 Beverley Rd, SW13 0LX, and has issue living, Thomas Llewellyn, *b* 1973, — Huw Algernon, *b* 1976. —— Caroline Elizabeth, *b* 1950: *m* 1981, Richard James Keevil, of Clevancy, Calne, Wilts, and has issue living, Katharine Elizabeth Adele, *b* 1982, — Cordelia Jane, *b* 1988.
Issue of late William Robert Rumbold, *b* 1912, *d* 1983: *m* 1st, 1942 (*m diss* 1952), Pamela Mary Dewe; 2ndly, 1957, Sylvia Violet, only da of Lawrence John Smith:—
(By 1st *m*) Cheryl Anne, *b* 1944: *m* 1968 (*m diss* 1979), Luca C. Dotti. *Residence* – 5 Av Calas, Geneva, Switzerland. —— (By 2nd *m*) CHARLES ANTON (Flat 1, 239 Earls Court Rd, SW5), *b* 7 Feb 1959: *m* 1987, Susan, elder da of J. M. Tucker, of Melbourne, Aust. —— Alexander Robert, *b* 1971.
Issue of late Lt-Col Alastair Gordon Rumbold, OBE, MC, *b* 1914, *d* 1992: *m* 1st, 1941 (*m diss* 1952), Tania, da of late Michael Borzakovsky; 2ndly, 1958, Auriol Cressida (4 North St, Castle Cary, Som), da of Col William Rixon Bucknall:—
(By 1st *m*) Michael Alastair, *b* 1943; *ed* Wellington: *m* 1976, Katherine Mary, da of Donal John Cagney, of Broadstairs, Kent, and has issue living, Angus Michael, *b* 1982, — Victoria Catherine, *b* 1977, — Lucinda, *b* 1979. —— (By 2nd *m*) Belinda Cressida, *b* 1962.

Granddaughter of late Thomas Henry Rumbold, 2nd son of Charles Edmund Rumbold, 5th son of 1st baronet:—
Issue of late Thomas Arthur Rumbold, *b* 1882, *d* 1972: *m* 1st, 1911, Evelyn Mary, who *d* 1954, only da of late Walter Comyn Jackson, JP; 2ndly, 1959, Elizabeth, who *d* 1973, da of late Rev T. M. B. Paterson, of Laighstone Hall, Hamilton:—
(By 1st *m*) Elizabeth Anne, MBE (*Baroness Hayter*) (Ashtead House, Ashtead, Surrey), *b* 1919; MBE (Civil) 1975: *m* 1940, 3rd Baron Hayter.

The 1st baronet, Sir Thomas, sometime MP for Melcombe Regis Dorset, and New Shoreham, Sussex, served as Aide-de-Camp to Lord Clive at Plassey (1757), was severely wounded, and was afterwards Governor of Madras. The 2nd baronet was HM's Minister at Hamburg. The 5th baronet, a Capt in the Army, was President of Nevis 1857-63, and Virgin Islands 1865-9; he was also a Col in the Ottoman Army, served with the Turkish Contingent during the Crimean war. The Rt Hon Sir Horace Rumbold, GCB, GCMG, PC, 8th Bt, was Sec of Legation at Athens 1862-4 and at Berne 1864-8, Sec of Embassy at St Petersburg 1868-71 and at Constantinople 1871-72, Min Resident and Consul-Gen in Chile 1872-78 and to Swiss Confederaton 1878-9, Envoy Extraor and Min Plen to Argentine Republic 1879-81, to Stockholm 1881-5, to Athens 1885-8, and to The Hague 1888-96, and Ambassador Extraor and Plen at Vienna 1896-1900. The 9th baronet, Rt Hon Sir Horace George Montagu, GCB, GCMG, MVO, PC, was Envoy Extraor and Min Plen to Switzerland 1916-19, and to Poland 1919-20, High Commr at Constantinople 1920-23, and Ambassador Extraor and Plen to Spain 1923-8, and Berlin 1928-33. The 10th baronet,

Sir (Horace) Anthony Claude, KCMG, KCVO, CB, was Min in Paris 1960-63, Ambassador to Thailand 1964-67, and to Austria 1967-70.

RUNCHORELAL (UK) 1913, of Shahpur, Ahmedabad, India

Sir CHINUBHAI MADHOWLAL RUNCHORELAL, 3rd *Baronet*; b 29 July 1929; s his father, Sir CHINUBHAI MADHOWLAL, 19—, whose name he then assumed in place of that of Udayan Chinubhai: m 1953, Muneera Khodadad, da of Khodadad Mancherjee Fozdar, of Bombay, and has issue. *Residence* – Shantikunj, Shahibag, Ahmedabad 380 004, India.

SON LIVING

PRASHANT, b 15 Dec 1955: m 1978, Swati Rushikesh, da of Rushikesh Janakray Mehta, of Ahmedabad, and has issue living, Abha (a da), b 1980, — Gayatri (a da), b 1981, — Roshni (a da), b 1988.

DAUGHTERS LIVING

Radhika, b 1954. —— Prasann, b 1960: m 1982, Arvind Surendra Kumar Somany, of Soma House, Ellis Bridge, Ahmedabad. —— Aradhana, b 1963.

BROTHERS LIVING

Kirtidev CHINUBHAI (Chinunath Mahader, nr Police Stadium, Shahibag, Admedabad 380 004, India), b 1932: m 1967, Meera Ratilal, da of Ratilal Tribhovandas Nanavati, of Surat, India. —— Achyut CHINUBHAI (Bālantyne Haveli, Three Gates, Ahmedabad 380 004, India), b 1941: m 1967, Uttara Vilochan, da of Vilochan Keshavlal Dhruva, of Bombay, and has issue living, Aneesh (a son), b 1969.

AUNT LIVING (*daughter of 1st baronet*)

Vasumati, b 1913: m 1937, Yashodhar Narmadashankar Mehta, Bar-at-law.
Sir Chinubhai Madhowlal Runchorelal, 1st Bt (the first Hindu Baronet to be created), was a cotton manufacturer of Ahmedaded, and a MLC; contributed largely to educational schemes in India.

RUSSELL (UK) 1812, of Swallowfield, Berkshire

Learn justice being admonished

Sir ARTHUR MERVYN RUSSELL, 8th *Baronet*, 2nd son of Sir ARTHUR EDWARD IAN MONTAGU RUSSELL, 6th Bt; b 7 Feb 1923; s his half-brother, Sir GEORGE MICHAEL, 1993.

ᴀrms – Argent, a chevron sable between three cross-crosslets fitchée azure within a bordure engrailed gules, bearing alternate bezants and escallops or. ᴄrest – A demi-lion rampant ermine, charged with a fasces proper, and bearing in his dexter paw a cross-crosslet fitchée sable.

HALF-BROTHER LIVING

CHRISTOPHER, b 22 Feb 1937; ed Charterhouse: m 1st, 1962 (m diss 1983), Ann, da of Lt-Col Clifford Donald Battersby Campling, of Syngate House, Stelling Minnis, Canterbury, Kent; 2ndly, 1983, Loveday Mary, widow of Cdr P. D. Davey, RN.

HALF-SISTER LIVING

Bettine (*Baroness Broughshane*), b 1905: m 1929, 2nd Baron Broughshane. *Residence* – 28 Fisher St, Sandwich, Kent.

DAUGHTERS LIVING OF SEVENTH BARONET

Marie Clotilde, b 1939: m 1965 (m diss 1984), Nelson Grant Mews, son of late P. Mews, of Perth, W Australia, and has issue living, Josephine Lucy, b 1974. —— Mary Christina b 1944.

WIDOWS LIVING OF SIXTH AND SEVENTH BARONETS

MARJORIE ELISABETH JOSEPHINE (*Dowager Lady Russell*) (Little Struan, Pangbourne, Berks), da of Ernest Rudman, of Foxhangers, Earley, Berks: m 1933, as his 3rd wife, Sir Arthur Edward Montagu Russell, 6th Bt, who d 1964.
JOY FRANCIS BEDFORD (*Joy, Lady Russell*), da of late W. Mitchell, of Irwin, W Australia: m 1936, Sir George Michael Russell, 7th Bt, who d 1993.

COLLATERAL BRANCHES LIVING

Grandchildren of late Major Francis Whitworth Russell, son of late Francis Whitworth Russell, 3rd son of 1st baronet:—
Issue of late Francis Whitworth Russell, *b* 1854, *d* 19—: *m* 1886, Maude Agnes, da of late Denis O'Brien, of Knockroe, Fermoy, co Cork:—
Francis Whitworth, *b* 1888. *Residence* –
Issue of late Edward Stuart Marjoribanks Harley Russell, *b* 1857, *d* 1926: *m* 1882, Mary, who *d* 1938, da of late Capt W. Phipps:—
Alice. —— Rachel. —— Kate. *Residence* –

Grandchildren of late Whitworth Russell, son of late Henry Russell, son of late Rev Whitworth Russell, 4th son of 1st baronet:—
Issue of late John Whitworth Russell, *b* 1891, *d* 1982: *m* 1915, Mary Alice, who *d* 1985, da of J. R. Anderson:—
Whitworth Athol (23 Ingleton Terr, Hamilton, NZ), *b* 1918; MB, ChB, DCP; assumed 2nd christian name of Athol by deed poll in lieu of Athelstan: *m* 1946, Marjory Ellen Ross, and has issue living, Anthony Whitworth (15 Iusoll Av, Hamilton, NZ), *b* 1951: *m* 1st, 1971 (*m diss* 1986), Catherine Sylvia Bradley; 2ndly, 1993, Catherine Patricia Felicity Orange, and has issue living (by 1st *m*), James Whitworth *b* 1979, Joanna Alice *b* 1976, Claire Jennifer *b* 1980, — Michael David, *b* 1959, — Juliet Ethne, *b* 1962: *m* 1983 (*m diss* 1990), Shaughan Bruce, and has issue living, Alexandra Ellen *b* 1987. —— Richard Hudson, *b* 1928. —— Elizabeth Alison, *b* 1934; BA: *m* 1956, David Ernest Poswillo, CBE, DDS, MD, DSc, Emeritus Prof UMDS, Guy's Hosp, Univ of London, of Ferndale, 7 Oldfield Rd, Bickley, Kent, and has issue living, Stephen David, *b* 1962: *m* 1988, Michelle Lynn Narcisse, and has issue living, Maxwell Stephen *b* 1994, — Mark Geoffrey, *b* 1964, — Deborah Jane, *b* 1958: *m* 1989, Robert William Caton, and has issue living, Lucy Harriett *b* 1994, — Mary Jill, *b* 1961: *m* 1987, Robert William Gerald Battye, and has issue living, Alexander Robert *b* 1989, Emma Alice *b* 1991.

Grandchildren of late George Cecil Russell, eldest son of late Cecil Henry Russell, son of late George Lake Russell, 5th son of 1st baronet (infra):—
Issue of late Evelyn Aylmer Cecil Russell, *b* 1891, *d* 1963: *m* 1st, 1916 (*m diss* 1923), Alice Edith, da of W. H. Wallis, of California Gully, Bendigo, Victoria, Australia; 2ndly, 1924, Irene, da of John Brodrick, JP, of Nangana, Victoria:—
(By 2nd *m*) William Henry Cecil (Strensham, Beaumont Rd, Berwick, Victoria, Australia), *b* 1927: *m* 1953, Margaret Winifred, da of Gordon Newton, of Mornington, Victoria, Australia, and has issue living, Mark Newton Cecil (Russmoore, Norbury Rd, Upper Beaconsfield, Victoria, Australia), *b* 1959: *m* 1987, Rosemary Anne, da of Alan Moore, of E Bentleigh, Victoria, Australia, and has issue living, Briony Jane *b* 1990, — Jane Elizabeth, *b* 1956: *m* 1976, Timothy Leslie Moore, 2nd son of Lt-Col Colin Moore, of East Brighton, Victoria, Australia, and has issue living, Jayce William *b* 1980, Ebby Margaret *b* 1983, — Kim Margaret, *b* 1964: *m* 1989, Mark Raymond Bloodworth, son of Raymond Bloodworth, of Rosanna, Victoria, Australia. —— Harry Arthur Cecil (Quarry Hill, 19 Belmont Av, Upwey, Victoria 3158, Australia), *b* 1931; JP: *m* 1959, Marjorie Ailsa, da of Alfred Sutton, of Hawthorn, Victoria, Australia, and has issue living, Ewen James Cecil, *b* 1967, — Sarah Anne Cecil *b* 1962, — Virginia Kate Cecil (twin), *b* 1962: *m* 1992, David Robert Edwards, son of Philip Edwards, of Hawthorn, Victoria, Australia. —— (By 1st *m*) Sadie Evelyn, *b* 1917; *ed* Melbourne Univ (BA): *m* 1940, Harold William Halls, and has issue living, Peter John, *b* 1944: *m* 1969, Marjorie, da of Rev Maurice Padman, of Snowtown, S Australia, and has issue living, Evelyn Marie *b* 1972, Joanne Michele *b* 1973, — Robin, *b* 1958: BCom LLB.
Issue of late John Hardress Cecil Russell, *b* 1896, *d* 1979: *m* 1927, Doris Marion, da of Ernest Reginald Green, of Colac, Victoria, Australia:—
John Alan Cecil (Protea Bowl, Gembrook 3782, Victoria, Australia), *b* 1928: *m* 1955, Patricia Mary Gordon, da of late Roddam Morris Douglas, of Emerald, Victoria, Australia, and has issue living, Susan Patricia, *b* 1956, — Penelope Ann, *b* 1959, — Lynette Margaret, *b* 1963, — Diane Marion, *b* 1964.
Sir Henry, 1st Bt, son of Michael Russell of Dover, was Chief Justice of Bengal. Sir Henry, 2nd Bt, was for many years Resident at the Court of Hyderabad, Sir Charles, VC, 3rd Bt, received Victoria Cross in Crimea 1854, and was MP (*C*) for Berks and Warminster. Sir George, 4th Bt, was a Judge of County Courts, Recorder of Wokingham and MP for Berks E Div (*C*).

RUSSELL (UK) 1916, of Littleworth Corner, Burnham, co Buckingham

What will be, will be

Sir CHARLES IAN RUSSELL, 3rd *Baronet*; *b* 13 March, 1918; *s* his father, *Capt Sir* ALEC Charles, MC, 1938; *ed* Beaumont Coll, and at Univ Coll, Oxford; admitted a Solicitor 1947; Consultant, formerly Snr Partner in the firm of Charles Russell & Co, of Hale Court, Lincoln's Inn, WC2; 1939-45 War as Capt RHA (despatches): *m* 1947, Rosemary, da of late Major Sir John Theodore Prestige, of Bourne Park, Bishopsbourne, Canterbury, and has issue.

Arms – Argent, a lion rampant gules, on a chief sable three escallops of the first, the whole a bordure engrailed vert. **Crest** – A goat passant argent, armed or, charged on the body fessewise with three trefoils slipped or.
Residence – Hidden House, Strand St, Sandwich, Kent CT13 9HX. *Clubs* – Garrick Army and Navy, Roy St Georges.

SON LIVING

CHARLES DOMINIC, *b* 28 May 1956; *ed* Worth Abbey: *m* 1986, Sarah Jane Murray, only da of Anthony Chandor, of Brock St, Bath, Avon, and has issue living, Charles William, *b* 8 Sept 1988. *Residence* – Stratton End, Cirencester, Glos.

DAUGHTER LIVING

Clare Harriet Faviell, *b* 1949: *m* 1974, Richard James Shepherd, of Stratton End, Cirencester, Glos, and has issue living, Edward James, *b* 1977, — Andrew Charles, *b* 1979, — Thomas Richard, *b* 1982.

COLLATERAL BRANCHES LIVING

(In special remainder)

Issue of late Gerald Cyril Russell, MC, brother of 2nd baronet, *b* 1896, *d* 1962: *m* 1923, Barbara, who *d* 1985, da of Lieut-Col Sir James Philip Reynolds, 1st Bt, DSO:—

Cyril (The Covert, Aldeburgh, Suffolk), *b* 1924: *m* 1949, (Eileen Mary) Elizabeth, da of late Major W. D. G. Batten, 3rd Gurkha Rifles, and has issue living, Gerald William, *b* 1950: *m* 1976, Tessa, da of Richard Rumsey, and has issue living, James Alexander *b* 1978, Sophie Annabel *b* 1980, Lucy Victoria *b* 1983, Kate Elisabeth *b* 1985, — Patrick James, *b* 1952: *m* 1977, Pamela Jill, da of Phillip Gordon, and has issue living, Oliver William Grant *b* 1981, Jessica Helen *b* 1984, Camilla Ellinora *b* 1987, — Nicholas Alastair, *b* 1958: *m* 1986, Heather B. L., da of Col John Burrell, of Ronay, Aldeburgh, Suffolk, and has issue living, Alastair Hamish *b* 1987. —— *Rev* John Alastair, *b* 1928; is in Holy Orders of Church of Rome. —— Colin Patrick (Hale Court, Lincolns Inn, WC2), *b* 1944: *m* 1978, Jessica Margaret, only da of Ramsay William Rainsford-Hannay, of Kirkdale, Kirkcudbright (*see* Wiseman, Bt). —— Moira, *b* 1927. —— Clodagh Mary, *b* 1933: *m* 1971, Brig David William Reid, MBE, of The Studio, Priors Hill Rd, Aldeburgh, Suffolk, son of late Sir Robert Neil Reid, KCSI, KCIE.

            Grandchildren of late Maj Denis Leslie Russell, MBE, TD (infra):—
            Issue of late (Denis) Anthony Russell, *b* 1934, *d* 1966: *m* 1961, Charlotte Mary (who *m* 2ndly, 1970, John Watcyn Lewis, of 66 Clifton Hill, NW8), yr da of late Lt-Col Sir Ian Frank Bowater, GBE, DSO, TD (*see* Bowater, Bt, *cr* 1939):—
William Anthony Bowater, *b* 1965: *m* 1989, Hilary Ann, only da of John Chaplin, of Cambridge, and has issue living, Edward John Bowater, *b* 1992. —— Amanda Charlotte, *b* 1963: *m* 1987, Charles Nicholas Yaxley, only son of John Yaxley, of Hong Kong, and has issue living, Thomas, *b* 1989.

            Issue of late Maj Denis Leslie Russell, MBE, TD, yr brother of late Gerald Cyril Russell, MC (ante), *b* 1909, *d* 1986: *m* 1932: Verena (Heather Bank, 14 Levylsdene, Merrow, Guildford, Surrey GU1 2RS), yr da of late George Henderson, of 55 Cadogen Pl, SW1, and Orchard House, Crastock, Surrey:—
David Ian (4 Westover Rd, SW18), *b* 1943; *ed* Ampleforth; a partner with Rowe & Pitman Hurst-Brown: *m* 1976, Hon Frances Marian Chant-Sempill, da of Lady Sempill. —— Sally Verena, *b* 1937: *m* 1956, William Bertram Weatherall, of Shorndown, Mursley, Bucks, son of late Lt-Col Nigel Edward Weatherall, of Caldwell House, Gilling W, Richmond, Yorks, and has issue living, Michael William (4 Hosack Rd, SW17 7QP), *b* 1958: *m* 1987, Penelope Ann, da of late Frederick Wharton Askew, of Caroline House, Redhill, Surrey, and has issue living, Edward Frederick *b* 1991, Toby William *b* 1993, — Annabel Jane, *b* 1960: *m* 1985, William George Briscoe Bevan, and has issue (*see* Brocklebank, Bt, colls), — Clare Victoria, *b* (twin) 1960: *m* 1987, James Bunten de Sales La Terrière, eldest son of Capt Ian Cameron de Sales La Terrière, of Dunalastair, Perthshire, and has issue living, Archie *b* 1990, Dominic John *b* 1993, Emma *b* 1988.

            Issue of late Lt-Col Cyril Alan Russell, yst brother of late Gerald Cyril Russell (ante), *b* 1910, *d* 1986: *m* 1st, 1937, Grace Evelyn, who *d* 1943, eldest da of William Thomas Moore, of New York, USA; 2ndly, 1944, Jean Patricia (23 Park Lane, Aldburgh, Suffolk), da of Stafford Croom Johnson, of Greenacre, Stoke Bishop, Bristol, and widow of Wing-Cdr John Ryan Cridland, AAF:—
(By 2nd *m*) Michael Alan, *b* 1947; *ed* Beaumont: *m* 1972, Penelope, yr da of Lt-Col A. R. Dawe, OBE, of Wyke Lodge, Normandy, and has issue living, Toby Alan, *b* 1974, — Michaella Katherine, *b* 1976.

            Grandchildren of late Rt Hon Francis Xavier Russell, brother of 1st Bt, *cr Baron Russell of Killowen* (Life Baron) 1929, son of Charles Russell, *cr Baron Russell of Killowen* (Life Baron) 1894:—
            Issue of late Rt Hon Charles Ritchie Russell, *cr Baron Russell of Killowen* (Life Baron) 1975, *b* 1908, *d* 1986: *m* 1st, 1933, Joan Elizabeth, who *d* 1976, only child of late James Aubrey Torrens, MD, FRCP, of 46 Wimpole St, W1; 2ndly, 1979, Elizabeth Cecilia (*Baroness Russell of Killowen*), da of AV-M William Foster Macneece Foster, CB, CBE, DSO, DFC, and widow of Judge Edward Hey Laughton-Scott, QC:—
(By 1st *m*) *Hon* Valentine Francis Xavier Michael (CP51, 1631 Moléson, Fribourg, Switzerland), *b* 1938; *ed* Beaumont, and Oriel Coll, Oxford. —— *Hon* (Francis) Damian (17 Lurline Gdns, SW11), *b* 1947; *ed* Beaumont, and Trin Coll Dublin: *m* 1994, Carole Myers, BSc, DPhil, of Hillsborough, S Yorks. —— *Hon* Julian Mary, *b* 1935; *m* 1st, 1955 (*m diss* 1974), Anthony Rodney Allfrey; 2ndly, 1975, Dr Harlan Ullman, of 1245 29th St NW, Washington DC, USA, and has issue (by 1st *m*) (*see* Fox, Bt, ext).

            Grandchildren of late Charles Russell, *cr Baron Russell of Killowen* (Life Baron) 1894 (ante):—
            Issue of late Lieut-Col Hon Bertrand Joseph Russell, DSO, *b* 1876, *d* 1960: *m* 1st, 1902, Dorothy, who *d* 1921, da of late John George Leeming; 2ndly, 1922 (*m diss* 1936), Mavis Winifred, da of late Frederick Hazell, of Frinton-on-Sea:—
(By 2nd *m*) †Michael Dudley, *b* 1923: *m* 1st, 1949 (*m diss* 1959), Jeanette Meryen, da of Major Arthur Sinclair Cannon, of Rangoon, Burma; 2ndly, 1960, Judy, yr da of Dr M. A. W. Roberts, of Dublin, and *d* 1993, leaving issue (by 1st *m*), Christopher John (19 Charles St, W1), *b* 1951; *ed* Worth: *m* 1976 (*m diss* 1981), Nicola, only da of James de Courcy Hughes, and has issue living, Dominic John *b* 1979, Lucienne Eva *b* 1977, — Julia Meryen, *b* 1954: *m* 1986, Timothy Ashworth, of Old Marsham Farm, Pett, Hastings, Sussex, and has issue living, Camilla Eileen *b* 1989, Elizabeth Annabelle *b* 1990, — (by 2nd *m*) Anna Katherine, *b* 1961, — Verena Grace, *b* 1962: *m* 1989, Andrew Bruce Weir, of 105 Trentham St, SW18 5DH, and has issue living, Oliver Michael *b* 1994, Isobelle Katherine *b* 1991. *Residence* - Meadow Court, Coombe Hill Rd, E Grinstead, W Sussex. —— (By 1st *m*) Joan (1 Stanhope Mews East, SW7), *b* 1908: *m* 1933, Charles Gordon Brand, CBE, who *d* 1966. —— Clodagh, *b* 1912: *m* 1939, Brigadier Thomas Haddon, CBE, late Border Regt, who *d* 1993, and has issue living, Paul Antony, *b* 1940; *ed* Beaumont, and Campion Hall, Oxford, — Martin Thomas, *b* 1944; *ed* Beaumont, and Worcester Coll, Oxford, — John Richard, *b* 1947; *ed* Beaumont, and Worcester Coll, Oxford. *Residence* - Mole End, Churt, Farnham, Surrey.
This Baronetcy was conferred with a special remainder (in default of heir male of the body of the grantee) to the heirs male of the body of Charles, Baron Russell of Killowen (Life Baron, *cr* 1894), father of the 1st baronet. The 1st baronet, Hon Sir Charles Russell (senior partner in the firm of Charles Russell and Co solicitors, of 37 Norfolk Street, Strand, WC), was 2nd son of late Charles, Baron Russell of Killowen (Life Baron *cr* 1894), Lord Ch Justice of England. The 2nd baronet, Sir Alec Charles Russell, MC, was Capt (retired) RA.

RUTHERFORD (UK) 1923, of Liverpool, co Palatine of Lancaster (Extinct 1942)

Sir (JOHN) HUGO RUTHERFORD, 2nd and last *Baronet*.

DAUGHTERS LIVING OF SECOND BARONET

Elspeth, *b* 1914: *m* 1939, Lieut-Col Francis William Bartlett, REME (ret), and has issue living, William John, *b* 1940, — Charles Hugo, *b* 1943, — Francis Murray, *b* 1945, — James Peter, *b* 1947, — Isabel, *b* 1951. *Residence* - 36 Laurel Drive, Willaston, S Wirral, Ches L64 1TW. —— Prudence Hero, *b* 1916: *m* 1940, John Russell Napier, DSc, MRCS, LRCP, who *d* 1987, and has issue living, John Hugo, *b* 1946, — Graham Russell, *b* 1949. *Residence* - Acharonich, Ulva Ferry, Isle of Mull PA73 6LY. —— Isabel Lavender, *b* 1925: *m* 1948, Peter Thomas Crook, and has had issue, Jeremy Peter, *b* 1954; *d* 1993, — Matthew Lancelot, *b* 1969, — Jean Isabel, *b* 1951. *Residence* - 28 Beacon Dr, W Kirby, Wirral, Merseyside.

RYAN (UK) 1919, of Hintlesham, Suffolk

Sir DEREK GERALD RYAN, 4th *Baronet*; *b* 25 March 1954; *s* his father, *Sir* DEREK GERALD, 1990; *ed* Univ of California at Berkeley (BA (Environmental Design) 1977): *m* 1986 (*m diss* 1990), Maria Teresa, da of Juan G. Rodriguez, of Lexington, Kentucky, USA.

Arms – Gules, in chief two griffins sejant respectant and combatant or, and in base a garb of rye proper. **Crest** – Upon a mount vert a griffin sejant sable, holding in the dexter claw a sword erect, and resting the sinister on a sickle or. *Address* – 4618 South Austin, St, Seattle, WA 98118, USA.

SISTERS LIVING

Anne Katherine, *b* 1951: *m* 1st, 1977 (*m diss* 1989), Edgard Puente; 2ndly, 1989, Steven Casciola. *Residence* – Villa Marjorie Apartments no 411, 1711 East Olive Way, Seattle, WA 98102, USA. —— Jenifer Hylda, *b* 1955: *m* 1985, Christopher Stirling Newall, son of Peter Newall, of Crookham Westfield Farmhouse, Cornhill on Tweed, Northumb, and has issue living, Alfred Stirling, *b* 1987, —— George Stirling, *b* 1990. *Residence* – 17 Lonsdale Sq, N1 1EN. —— Caroline Sarah, *b* 1956: *m* 1990, Jeff Chase, and has issue living, Perry *b* 1994, Monica Kristi, *b* 1991, Liza (twin) *b* 1994. *Residence* – 15 Brook Rd, Topsfield, MA 01983, USA.

MOTHER LIVING

Penelope Anne, da of late Rex Hawkings, of 139 East 94th St, New York: *m* 1947 (*m diss* 1971), as his 1st wife, Sir Derek Gerald Ryan, 3rd Bt, who *d* 1990. *Residence* – 14 Longbrook Rd, Byfield, MA 01922, USA.

WIDOW LIVING OF THIRD BARONET

KATJA (*Dowager Lady Ryan*), da of late Ernest Best, of 35 Kassel, Fuhrmannsbreite 11, Germany: *m* 1972, as his 2nd wife, Sir Derek Gerald Ryan, 3rd Bt, who *d* 1990. *Residence* – Scharfensteinstrasse 36, 6228 Eltville a Rh1, Germany.

COLLATERAL BRANCH LIVING

Issue of late Vivian Desmond Ryan, yr son of 1st baronet, *b* 1893, *d* 1950: *m* 1st, 1917, Kathleen Frances, who *d* 1945, da of late James William Helps, MICE, of Berisal, Normanton Road, S Croydon; 2ndly, 1946, Nanny, who *d* 1988, da of late Dixon Slater, of 24 Belleview, Skipton, Yorks:—
(By 1st wife) DESMOND MAURICE (S15 C8 RR4 Gower Point, Gibsons, BC, Canada V0N 1V0), *b* 1918: *m* 1942, Margaret Catherine, da of A. H. Brereton, and has issue living, Barry Desmond, *b* 1943: *m*, and has issue living, Andrew *b* 19—, — Kevin Vivian, *b* 1951: *m*, and has issue living, Martin *b* 19—, — Michael Brereton, *b* 1954: *m*, and has issue living, Aaron *b* 19—. —— Adrian James (8 Camden Studios, Camden St, NW1), *b* 1920: *m* 1st, 1941 (*m diss* 1950), Peggy Rose; 2ndly, 1952, Barbara Pitt; 3rdly, 1977, Susan Curnow, and has issue living, (by 1st *m*) Geraldine Daphne, *b* 1943, — (by 2nd *m*) Kathleen Scarlett, *b* 1954, — Vivien Frances, *b* 1957. —— Jeanette Daphne, *b* 1929. —— (By 2nd wife) John Desmond, *b* 1945: *m* 1969, Tina, da of late Arthur Percy Gregory, and has issue living, Nicola Jane, *b* 1972, — Rosalind Anne, *b* 1975. *Residence* – 11 Compton Rise, Pinner, Middx HA5 5HS.
The 1st baronet, Sir Gerald Hemmington Ryan (son of Michael Desmond Ryan, of Kildare Terr, W) was later Gen Manager and Chm of Phoenix Assurance Co.

RYCROFT (GB) 1784, of Calton, Yorkshire

Sir RICHARD NEWTON RYCROFT, 7th *Baronet*; *b* 23 Jan 1918; *s* his father, *Sir* NELSON EDWARD OLIVER, 1958; *ed* Winchester, and Ch Ch, Oxford (BA 1939); is Patron of one living; European War 1939-45 as Major on Special Work in Balkans (despatches, Knight of Order of Phoenix of Greece with swords): *m* 1947, Ann, da of late Hugh Bellingham Smith, and has issue.

Arms – Quarterly: 1st and 4th, per bend or and azure, three griffins, heads erased counterchanged; on a chief ermine, a fleur-de-lis between two roses gules, *Rycroft*; 2nd and 3rd, party per pale or and sable, a chevron between three fleurs-de-lis all counterchanged, *Nelson*. **Crest** – A griffin's head erased per bend or and azure, charged with two fleurs-de-lis counter- changed. *Residence* – Winalls Wood House, Stuckton, Fordingbridge, Hants SP6 2HG.

DAUGHTERS LIVING

Susan Marilda, *b* 1948; *ed* Trin Coll Dublin (MA): *m* 1974, Ian Martell, of Wood House, Shotley Bridge, co Durham, and has issue living, Jonathan Newton, *b* 1978, — Alice, *b* 1976. —— Sally Ann (*Viscountess FitzHarris*), *b* 1950: *m* 1969, James Carleton Harris, Viscount FitzHarris, of Greywell Hill, Greywell, Basinstoke, Hants RG25 1DB, el son of 6th Earl of Malmesbury.

UNCLE LIVING (Son of 5th baronet)

Charles Frederick, MB, BS, *b* 1914; *ed* Wellington Coll, and at Trin Coll Camb (BA; FRC Psych): *m* 1st, 1947 (*m diss* 1963), Chloe, da of late Edouard Majolier, 2ndly, 1977, Jenny, da of William Pearson, and has issue living, (by 1st *m*) Francis Edward *b* 1950; *ed* Gresham's

Sch, Holt: *m* 1975, Cherry, da of Kenneth Willmott, and has issue living, a da *b* 1977, — Alice Julia, *b* 1947; *ed* Univ of Kent (BA): *m* 1978, Ibrahim Jama, of 3 Woodside Rd, Manchester 16, and has issue, — Catherine Ann, *b* 1949: *ed* Univ of Kent (BA): *m* 1970, Christopher Piers Merriman, of Tankers' Row, S Clydach, Abergavenny, Gwent, and has issue living, Roger Christopher *b* 1975, Chloe Catherine *b* 1977. *Residence* – 2 Modbury Gdns, NW5 3QE.

AUNTS LIVING (*Daughters of 5th baronet*)

Alice Juliana Rosamond (The Paddock, 4 South Place, Lee on the Solent, Hants), *b* 1915: *m* 1st, 1938, Neil Malise Graham, who *d* 1939; 2ndly, 1943, Rev Patrick Roger Harvey, who *d* 1986, and has issue living, (by 1st *m*) Charles Edward Malise (Riccards Down House, Abbotsham, Bideford, Devon EX39 5BG), *b* 1939: *m* 1976, Lynn Marie, da of Stanley Carter, — Bruce Torquil Irving (twin) (Penhoat Luon, Guimiliau, Landivisiau, France), *b* 1939, — (by 2nd *m*) Michael Timothy John, *b* 1944; *ed* Keble Coll, Oxford (MA), and Lyons Univ, France, — Diana Lavender Mary, *b* 1946: *m* 1970, Robert Ian Fellows, and has issue living, Gregory Chad *b* 1974, Charlotte Claire *b* 1976, — Primrose Miranda Margaret, *b* 1953: *m* 1989, Michael Robert Line, and has issue living, Harriet Clare *b* 1992. —— Eleanor Mary (38 Stowe View, Tingewick, Buckingham MK18 4NY), *b* 1918; 1942-45 War in WRNS.

COLLATERAL BRANCHES LIVING

Issue of late Rev Richard Michael Rycroft, 3rd son of 5th baronet, *b* 1897, *d* 1968: *m* 1924, Evelyn Maud, who *d* 1969, da of late Francis James Driscoll, of Jersey:—
Jean Dorothea, *b* 1925; 1943-45 in WRNS: *m* 1945, Charles Spencer Goldring, of Yarmouth, Nova Scotia, and has issue living, Paul Michael (4085 Rue Berri, Montreal, Quebec, Canada), *b* 1947; *ed* St Mary's Univ (BA): *m* 1983, Ryoko Mine, and has issue living, Matthew John Wallace Yotaru Mine *b* 1985, Nathan Charles Toshiharu Mine *b* 1987, — James Philip (53 Pooler Av, Ottawa, Ontario, Canada), *b* 1948; *ed* Lond Univ (PhD): *m* 1969, Marianne Louise McLean, and has issue living, Andrew Michael Dmitri *b* 1970, Hugh Douglas Arthur *b* 1986, — Nicholas John, *b* 1954, — Hilary Adrian Jerome, *b* 1959; *ed* W Ontario Univ (Bus Ad), — Stephen Gerard, *b* 1961, — Christopher Septimus Denison (twin), *b* 1961, — Felicity Jocelyn, *b* 1965; *ed* Dalhousie Univ, Halifax (BSc). — (Mary) Elizabeth (8 Southcote Rd, N19), *b* 1935.

Issue of late Cdr Henry Richard Rycroft, OBE, DSC, RN, 4th son of 5th baronet, *b* 1911, *d* 1985: *m* 1941, Penelope Gwendoline (19 Marcuse Fields, Bosham, Chichester, Sussex), da of late Lt-Col Charles Spenser Browne Evans-Lombe, Leinster Regt, of Beer, Devon:—
RICHARD JOHN (14 Ship Rd, Burnham-on-Crouch, Essex), *b* 15 June 1946; *ed* Sherborne. —— Caroline Mary, *b* 1944; *ed* Downe House, Newbury, and Univ of Sussex (BSc): *m* 1966, Nicholas Wolryche Meyrick, of Church Farm House, Empingham, Rutland, and has issue living, Julian Timothy, *b* 1968; *ed* Univ Coll, Oxford, — Oliver Michael, *b* 1978, — Hilary Jocelyn, *b* 1970; *ed* Queen's Coll, Oxford. —— Philippa Eve, *b* 1949; *ed* Downe House, Newbury: *m* 1981, Peter Edward Jenkinson, of Fringford Cottage, Fringford, Oxon, and has issue living, Susanna Emily, *b* 1982, — Olivia Mary, *b* 1984, — Harriet Anne, *b* 1989. —— Jocelyn Penelope, *b* 1955; *ed* Wispers Sch, Haslemere: *m* 1984, Michael Piers Lawton, and has issue living, — Piers Simon George *b* 1990, Sarah Louise *b* 1988.

Granddaughters of late Maj-Gen Sir William Henry Rycroft, KCB, KCMG, 2nd son of 4th baronet:—
Issue of late Major Julian Neil Oscar Rycroft, DSO, MC, *b* 1892, *d* 1928: *m* 1920, Elizabeth Mildred Louisa, who *d* 1932, da of Sir Ralph William Anstruther, 6th Bt:—
Cynthia Margaret, *b* 1922: *m* 1949, Col Philip Dives Stenning, late RE, and has issue living, Christopher John William (58 Coniger Rd, SW6), *b* 1950; *ed* Marlborough: *m* 1981, Ruth, da of George T. C. Draper, of Swaffham, Norfolk, and has issue living, Jonathan *b* 1985, Rachel *b* 1983, — Nicholas Julian Seymour (Medstead House, Medstead, nr Alton, Hants GU34 5LY), *b* 1952; *ed* Marlborough, and Pembroke Coll, Oxford: *m* 1976, Caroline, da of late Michael Livingstone-Learmonth, MC, of Minchinhampton, Glos, and has issue living, Alexander *b* 1985, Clare *b* 1979, Emily *b* 1981, — Richard Neil (Meadcroft, Sidmouth Rd, Colyton, Devon EX13 6NP), *b* 1955; *ed* Marlborough, and Nottingham Univ: *m* 1988, Alison, da of Mrs A. E. Hooper, and has issue living, Aisha *b* 1989, Eliana Grace *b* 1990. *Address* – Sunnyside, Elie, Fife KY9 1DN. —— Evelyn Joanna Christian, *b* 1925: *m* 1953, Martin Claridge, MCh, FRCS, and has issue living, Simon Julian, *b* 1954: *m* 19—, Marit McKerchar, and has issue living, Rebecca Tatsachen *b* 1987, — Tobias James, *b* 1963, — Anna Louise, *b* 1958, — Katharine Georgina, *b* 1960. *Residence* – St Martin's House, St Martin's Av, Canterbury.

Issue of late Rev Edmund Hugh Rycroft, 3rd son of 4th baronet, *b* 1862, *d* 1932: *m* 1902, Winifred Edith, who *d* 1968, el da of late Adm of the Fleet Sir Arthur Dalrymple Fanshawe, GCB, GCVO:—
Arthur John, *b* 1905; *ed* Radley, and Corpus Christi Coll, Oxford (BA 1927). *Residence* – The Old Vicarage, Wilsford, Pewsey, Wilts.

Grandchildren of late Rev Edmund Hugh Rycroft (ante):—
Issue of late Col David Hugh Rycroft OBE, *b* 1907 *ka* 1944: *m* 1st, 1930 (*m diss* 1934), Elizabeth Edith Dilys, da of late Capt Miles Bertie Cunningham Carbery, Roy Irish Fusiliers; 2ndly, 1939, Cicely Phoebe Susanna, who *d* 1980, da of late Lt-Col Robert Bruère Otter-Barry, OBE, of Glazeley Hall, near Bridgnorth (Cs Dysart, colls, 1968 Edn):—
(By 2nd *m*) Henry David (58 Garscube Terr, Ravelston, Edinburgh EH12 6BN), *b* 1943; *ed* Radley, and St Andrews Univ (BSc); MB BS: *m* 1st, 1972 (*m diss* 1983), Nicole Elizabeth, MB, BS, da of Maurice Kenig, MD; 2ndly, 1983, Mrs Dorothea Ann Joan HEANEY, yr da of late Robert William Nicholson Evans (see Lees, Bt, *cr* 1804, colls, 1990 Edn), and has issue living (by 1st *m*), Alexander Theophilus, *b* 1975.

The 1st baronet, Rev Sir Richard Rycroft, DD, only surviving son of John Nelson, assumed the surname of Rycroft by royal sign-manual 1758. Sir Richard Nelson Rycroft, 5th Bt, and Sir Nelson Edward Oliver Rycroft, 6th Bt, were High Sheriffs of Hants 1899, and 1938, respectively.

MOLESWORTH-ST AUBYN (E) 1689, of Pencarrow, Cornwall

In se teres

Complete in itself

Sic fidem teneo

Thus I hold the faith

Sir (JOHN) ARSCOTT MOLESWORTH-ST AUBYN, MBE, 15th *Baronet*; *b* 15 Dec 1926; *s* his father, *Sir* JOHN, CBE, 1985; *ed* Eton; late Lt-Col The R Green Jackets; a JP supplementary list and a DL of Cornwall (High Sheriff 1975-76); MBE (Mil) 1963: *m* 1957, Iona Audrey Armatrude, da of late Adm Sir Francis Loftus Tottenham, KCB, CBE, and has issue.

𝔸rms – Quarterly; 1st and 4th, ermine, on a cross sable, five bezants, *St Aubyn*; 2nd and 3rd, gules, an escutcheon vair, between eight cross-crosslets in orle argent, *Molesworth*. ℭrest – A rock, thereon a Cornish chough rising, all proper. *Residence* – Pencarrow, Bodmin, Cornwall. *Club* – Army and Navy.

SONS LIVING

WILLIAM, *b* 23 Nov 1958; *ed* Harrow; late Capt The R Green Jackets: *m* 1988, Carolyn M., elder da of William H. Tozier, of Shawfield St, SW3. —— James Francis, *b* 1960; *ed* Harrow.

DAUGHTER LIVING

Emma Jane, *b* 1971.

SISTERS LIVING

Johanna Katherine (*Countess of Morley*) (Pound House, Yelverton, Devon), *b* 1929: *m* 1955, 6th Earl of Morley. —— Prudence Aline, *b* 1937: *m* 1969, Joseph Robertson Cooke-Hurle, of Long Ash, Buckland Monachorum, nr Yelverton, Devon, and has issue living, Celia Hermione, *b* 1970, — Penelope Joy, *b* 1971.

COLLATERAL BRANCHES LIVING

Issue of late Maj Hender Charles Molesworth-St Aubyn, 2nd son of 13th baronet, *b* 1901, *d* 1986: *m* 1935 (*m diss* 1946), Dulciebella Joy, da of Lt-Col John Cayzer Medlicott-Vereker (*see* V Gort, colls):—
(Caroline) Gay, *b* 1940: *m* 1963, Edward Simon Foord, of Hoyle Barn, Heyshott, Midhurst, Sussex, only son of late Brig Edward John Foord, CBE, of Vicarage Lane House, Felpham, Bognor Regis, Sussex, and has issue living, Edward Richard, *b* 1965, — Nicola Samantha, *b* 1967, — Annabel Jane, *b* 1971.

Issue of late Guy Kemyel Molesworth-St Aubyn, yst son of 13th baronet, *b* 1904, *d* 1981: *m* 1931, Catherine, JP, who *d* 1979, yst da of late Richard Tattersall Hargreaves, of Benington Park, Herts:—
Anthony William (Cobbs, Howe Street, nr Chelmsford, Essex), *b* 1936; *ed* Eton: *m* 1964, Mary Evelyn, only da of Kenneth Meiklejohn, and has issue living, Charles Hugh, *b* 1966; *ed* Eton; late Capt RGJ: *m* 1992, Zoë, da of J. J. Prow, and of Mrs F. M. Gibson, of Notts, and has issue living, Alexandra Frances *b* 1992, — Anna Victoria, *b* 1970. —— Simon Guy, *b* 1944; *ed* Eton; Maj late 60th Rifles: *m* 1977, Amanda Jane, el da of George Walker, of Knutsford, Cheshire, and has issue living, Thomas Kemyel, *b* 1981, — Cressida Juliet, *b* 1988. —— Felicity Sybil (*Hon Lady Butler*), *b* 1932: *m* 1955, Rt Hon Sir Adam Courtauld Butler, of The Old Rectory, Lighthorne, Warwick, 2nd son of late Baron Butler of Saffron Walden (Life Baron).

Grandson of late Col St Aubyn Molesworth, RA, son of late Col St Aubyn Molesworth, RE, son of late Rev John Molesworth, 2nd son of 5th baronet:—
Issue of late Major Edward Algernon Molesworth, DSO, *b* 1875, *d* 1939: *m* 1916, Ruth, da of Leslie Creery, of Lisnalurg, Shankill, co Dublin:—
St Aubyn, *b* 1917; sometime Engineer in Merchant Navy.

This family descends from Sir Walter de Molesworth, who in 1270 accompanied Edward I, when Prince Edward, to the Holy Land. The 1st baronet, Sir Hender, was Lieut-Gov of Jamaica. The 2nd baronet, MP for Bossiney, was knighted by Charles II. The 4th baronet sat as MP for Newport, Cornwall, 1734, and for Cornwall 1744-61. The 5th and 6th baronets respectively represented Cornwall 1765-75, and 1784-90. The 8th baronet, MP for East Cornwall 1832-7, for Leeds 1837-41, and for Southwark 1841-55, was Privy Councillor, and successively First Commissioner of Works, and Secretary of State for the Colonies. The 11th baronet sat as MP for Cornwall S-E, or Bodmin Div (LU) 1900-6. The 12th baronet, Rev Sir Hender, was son of late Rev Hender Molesworth (great-grandson of 5th baronet), who assumed by Roy licence 1844, the additional surname and arms of St Aubyn, his mother Catherine being da and co-heir of Sir John St Aubyn, baronet.

ST GEORGE (I) 1766, of Athlone, co Westmeath

Sir GEORGE BLIGH ST GEORGE, 9th *Baronet*; *b* 23 Sept 1908; *s* his brother, *Rev Fr Sir* DENIS HOWARD, 1989; *ed* Natal Univ (BA); 1939-45 War as Lieut Technical Sers Corps: *m* 1935, Mary Somerville, da of Francis John Sutcliffe, and has issue.

𝕬rms – Argent: a chief azure, over all a lion rampant gules, ducally crowned or, armed and langued of the second, a crescent for difference. 𝕮rest – A demi lion rampant gules, ducally crowned or, armed and langued azure.
Residence – Hatley Cottage, 28 Waterfall Garden Village, Private Bag X01, Link Hills, Natal 3652, S Africa.

Firmitas in coelo
Stability in heaven

SONS LIVING

JOHN AVENEL BLIGH, *b* 18 March 1940; *m* 1st, 1962 (*m diss* 1979), Margaret, da of John Leonard Carter, MBE, of Mayes Park House, Warnham, Sussex; 2ndly, 1981, Linda, da of Robert Perry, of 10 Dubton St, Bishoploch, Glasgow, and has issue living (by 1st *m*), Elinor Jane Bligh, *b* 1963: *m* 1990, Richard Newbold, of 4 St Leonards Rd, Claygate, Surrey, and has issue living, Cameron *b* 1991, Georgia *b* 1993, — Catherine Bligh, *b* 1966, — (by 2nd *m*) Robert Alexander Bligh, *b* 17 Aug 1983, — Benjamin Bligh, *b* 1986. *Residence* – 23 Burton St, Loughborough, Leicester LE11 2DT. —— Peter Bligh, *b* 1946; MBE (Cape Town), CA (SA); Dir County Natwest, Investment Bankers: *m* 1974, Elizabeth Meyrick, eldest da of late Alan Meyrick Williams, of Newport, Gwent, and has issue living, William Bligh, *b* 1984, — Caroline Bligh, *b* 1976, — Alice Mary Bligh, *b* 1981. *Residence* – 99 Castelnau, Barnes, SW13.

DAUGHTERS LIVING

Elizabeth Margaret Bligh, *b* 1936: *m* 1962, Peter Ivor Baikie, CA (SA), FSAA, of 21 Garrard Rd, Banstead, Surrey, and has issue living, David Peter, *b* 1963, — Derek John, *b* 1973, — Fiona Margaret, *b* 1965, — Linda Jeanne, *b* 1969. —— Catherine Mary, *b* 1937: *m* 1964, John Douglas Walker, MB, ChB, FRCOG, of 33 Fourth Av, Houghton, Johannesburg 2198, S Africa, and has issue living, John Paul Douglas, *b* 1968, — Jane Philippa Douglas, *b* 1966, — Felicity Mary Douglas, *b* 1974. —— Angela Bligh, *b* 1952; *ed* Natal Univ (BEd).

SISTER LIVING

Anne Rose, *b* 1898: *m* 1926, William Farquhar Ogilvie, who *d* 1963, and has issue living, John Alexander, *b* 1927: *m* 1954, Pamela Betty Brown, — Angus, *b* 1930: *m* 1953, Heather Wright, — Margaret, *b* 1933: *m* 1961, David George Kerby. *Residence* – 60 Jacaranda Lodge, 107 Pietermaritzburg St, Pietermaritzburg, Natal, S Africa.

COLLATERAL BRANCHES LIVING

Granddaughter of Robert James Ker St George, 2nd son of Robert St George, 3rd son of 2nd baronet:—
Issue of late Richard Christopher Bligh St George, *b* 1875, *d* 1945: *m* 1916, Alice Rosabel, who *d* 1964, el da of Lt-Col Hugh L. Donovan, of Oakhurst, S Yardley, Worcs:—
Catherine Harriet Mary Bligh (1346 Coventry Rd, Yardley, Birmingham, B25 8AN), *b* 1917.

Granddaughters of late Howard Bligh St George (infra):—
Issue of late George Baker Bligh St George, *b* 1892, *d* 1957: *m* 1917, Katharine (a Member of House of Representatives, USA Congress), da of Price Collier, of Tuxedo Park, New York, USA:—
Priscilla Avenel (Box 201 Meetetse, Wyoming 82433, USA), *b* 1919: *m* 1st, 1936 (*m diss* 1939), Angier Biddle Duke; 2ndly, 1941 (*m diss* 19-), Allan A. Ryan, and has issue living, (by 1st *m*) Angier St George Biddle (Ashburn Hall, Route 2, Kittrell, N Carolina 27544, USA), *b* 1938: *m* 1st, 1959, Jeanne S. Farmer; 2ndly, 19—, Mary Ellen, da of late Ora Cecil Haga, and has issue living (by 1st *m*), George St George *b* 1960, Benjamin Buchanan *b* 1963, — (by 2nd *m*) Katherine Delano, *b* 1943: *m* 19—, Aldrich, of Goodhap, Barrytown, New York 12507, USA.
Issue of late Col Frederick Ferris Bligh St George, CVO, *b* 1908, *d* 1970: *m* 1932, Meriel Margaret, JP, who *d* 1966, da of late Lt-Col William Scott Warley Radcliffe (E Macclesfield, colls):—
Meriel Jane Bligh St GEORGE (424 E 52 St, Apt 2A, New York, NY 10022), *b* 1933; has resumed her maiden name: *m* 1966 (*m diss* 1971), Benjamin Brandreth McAlpin. —— Elizabeth Sally Bligh, *b* 1936: *m* 1965, John Richard Alford, of Hammatethy House, St Breward, Bodmin, Cornwall, and has issue living, Charles William Bligh, *b* 1971, — Julia Meriel Bligh, *b* 1967, — Nicola Jane Bligh, *b* 1969. —— Diana Gillian Bligh (*Lady Earle*), *b* 1939: *m* 1967, Sir Hardman George Algernon Earle, 6th Bt, of Abington, Murroe, co Limerick and has issue (see Earle, Bt).

Granddaughter of late Robert St George (ante):—
Issue of late Howard Bligh St George, *b* 1857, *d* 1940: *m* 1891, Florence Evelyn, who *d* 1938, da of late George F. Baker, of 258, Madison Avenue, New York:—
Evelyn Bligh (Gardenia) (*Gardenia, Lady Gunston*), OBE, *b* 1897; Dir of Residential Nurseries, Anglo-American Relief Fund 1941-46; OBE (Civil) 1944: *m* 1917, Maj Sir Derrick Wellesley Gunston, MC, MP, 1st Bt, who *d* 1985.

Grandchildren of late George Edward St George, 3rd son of late William Oliver St George (infra):—
Issue of late Leslie George St George, *b* 1896, *d* 1968: *m* 1918, Gladys, who *d* 1941, da of Alfred McGillivray, of Ottawa:—
Leslie Richard (3 Goodwin Av, Nepean, Ont, K2E 5C4), *b* 1924: *m* 1946, Muriel Winnifred, da of John Edwards, and has issue living, Barry Edward, *b* 1949: *m* 1978, Catherine Jean, da of George P. Campbell, of Ottawa, and has issue living, Joshua Adam *b* 1980, Lauren Ashley *b* 1982, — Leslie Timothy, *b* 1961: *m* 1986, Janet Lee, da of Robert Ross Wilson, of Nepean, Ont, and has issue living, Lindsay Blair *b* 1989, Laura Leigh *b* 1991, — Gayle Mary, *b* 1953, — Beverly Ann, *b* 1954: *m* 1979, Kerry Patrick Scullion, of Ottawa, and has issue living, Timothy Patrick Pearse *b* 1983, Rory Joseph Anthony 1987. —— Robert John (1691 Lacombe Drive, Orleans, Ont K4A 2R9), *b* 1941: *m* 1968 (*m diss* 1984), Vivien Jill, da of David G. Walters, of London, England, and has issue living, Christian Robert David, *b* 1974, — Catherine Lesley, *b* 1970. —— Mary Audrey (1308-1701 Kilborn Av, Ottawa, Ont K1H 6M8), *b* 1927: *m* 1949, John Scarcella, who *d* 1989, and has issue living, Byron Michael, *b* 1949: *m* 1973, Annette, da of Lionel Aucoin, of Ottawa, and has issue living, Lisa Marie *b* 1977, — David Louis Anthony, *b* 1955, — Gordon Kenneth John *b* 1960.

Grandchildren of late William Oliver St George, 4th son of 2nd baronet:—
Issue of late Robert St George, *b* 1856, *d* 1939: *m* 1881, Elizabeth Agatha, who *d* 1935, da of Thomas Tovey, of Perth, Ontario:—

Richard Bligh, *b* 1886: *m* 1920 (*m diss* 1930), Ada Mary Barr. —— George Edgar (I) *b* 1892: *m* 1929, Ruth Mary, da of Harold Richardson, of Ottawa, and has issue living, †George Edgar (II) (1035 11 South St, Lethbridge, Alberta T1K 1P6, Canada), *b* 1929: *m* 19—, Lise Lamothe, and *d* 1992, leaving issue, Eddie *b* 19—, Richard *b* 19—, Suzanne *b* 19—, Julie *b* 19—, — Richard Bligh Harold, *b* 1935, — Michael, *b* 19—, — Tovey, *b* 19—, — Ruth Mary Madora, *b* 1931. —— Lily Madora, *b* 1882: *m* 1908, Edgar Charles Coleman, and has issue living. —— Daisy Mary Evelyn, *b* 1884: *m* 1933, Dominic F. Scanlon, who *d* 1947.

Issue of late Hercules Frank St George, *b* 1867, *d* 1938: *m* 1895, Rosaline, who *d* 1901, da of John Dunn, of Gaspé, Quebec, Canada:—
Hercules Frank, *b* 1896: *m* 1939, Marie Adeline Juliette, da of Eugene Larocque, of Ottawa.

Issue of late John Arthur St George (twin), *b* 1867, *d* 1912: *m* 1900, Lily Belle, da of John Magladry:—
William John, *b* 1907. —— Gladys Ellen, *b* 1901. —— Marjorie Ellen, *b* 1903: *m* 19—, Lawrence J. Desjardins. —— Fanny Evelyn, *b* 1905. —— Sarah Alice, *b* 1909.

Grandson of late Loftus St George (infra):—
Issue of late Clifford Fortescue Loftus St George, CBE, *b* 1894, *d* 1966: *m* 1931, Gwen Marjorie Chisholm, who *d* 1982, da of Rev William Dalton, V of Glynde, Sussex:—
John (Warren Farm, Wilmington, E Polegate, Sussex BN26 6RL), *b* 1942: *m* 1st, 1965 (*m diss* 1975), — da of —; 2ndly, 1975, Elizabeth Jane, el da of Herbert Westgate, of Shabbards, Berwick, Sussex, and has issue living (by 1st *m*), William, *b* 1967, — Lucy, *b* 1969, — Marina, *b* 1970.

Granddaughter of late James Cuffe St George, 5th son of 2nd baronet:—
Issue of late Loftus St George, *b* 1858, *d* 1952: *m* 1893, Marguerite Isabel Clifford, who *d* 1956, da of late Clifford Fortescue Borrer, of Pickwell, Cuckfield, Sussex:—
Violet Marguerite Loftus (*Violet, Lady Jackson*), *b* 1904: *m* 1931, Sir Hugh Nicholas Jackson, 2nd Bt (*cr* 1913), who *d* 1979. *Residence* – 38 Oakley St, SW3.

The 1st baronet, Sir Richard St George (second son of George St George, of Woodsgift, co Kilkenny), was MP for Athlone 1763-89. The 2nd baronet, Sir Richard Bligh, was Sec of Order of St Patrick. The 6th baronet, Sir Theophilus John, was sometime Assist Master of Supreme Court, Natal.

SALT (UK) 1869, of Saltaire, Yorkshire

What not with God helping?

Sir PATRICK MACDONNELL SALT, 7th *Baronet*; *b* 25 sept 1932; *s* his brother, *Sir* ANTHONY HOULTON, 1991; *ed* Stowe: *m* 1976, Ann Elizabeth Mary, da of late Dr Thomas Kay Maclachlan, and widow of Denys Kilham Roberts, OBE.

Arms – Azure, a chevron indented between two mullets in chief, and a demi-ostrich displayed, holding in the beak a horse-shoe in base or. **Crest** – Upon a rock, an alpaca statant, proper.
Residence – Hillwatering Farmhouse, Langham, Bury St Edmunds, Suffolk IP31 3ED.

DAUGHTERS LIVING OF SIXTH BARONET

Fenella Mary Houlton, *b* 1959. —— Rebecca Madeleine Harris, *b* 1961: *m* 1993, Alexander I.M. Kennedy, 2nd son of John Kennedy, of Kensington. —— Lucinda Mary Harriet, *b* 1964. —— Charlotte Lavinia Francis, *b* 1967: *m* 1993, Christopher James Walter Trower, 3rd son of Anthony Gosselin Trower, of Stansteadbury, Ware, Herts.

WIDOW LIVING OF SIXTH BARONET

PRUDENCE MARY DOROTHEA FRANCIS (*Prudence, Lady Salt*), yst da of late Francis Meath Baker, of Hasfield Court, Glos: *m* 1957, Sir Anthony Houlton Salt, 6th Bt, who *d* 1991. *Residence* – Dellow House, Ugley Green, Bishop's Stortford, Herts.

COLLATERAL BRANCHES LIVING

Grandchildren of late Gordon Locksley Salt; eldest son of late Titus Salt, 5th son of 1st baronet:—
Issue of late John Scarlett Alexander Salt, *b* 1905, *d* 1947: *m* 1939, Olive Mary (who *m* 2ndly, 1952, Christopher Gorton), da of William Gilbert Shapley:—
Daniel Alexander (c/o British Airways, PO Box 190104, Anchorage, Alaska 99519-0104, USA), *b* 1943: *m* 1968, Mehrchide, da of Dr A. Emami, of Teheran, and has issue living, Firoozeh Katherine, *b* 1971, — Maryam Rachel, *b* 1974. —— Nicholas John (Gwarten, Straylittle, nr Llanbrynmair, Powys SY19 7BU), *b* 1945: *m* 1971, Catherine Kimerling, da of Charles Grun, of New York, and has issue living, Aaron, *b* 1972. —— Christina Mary, *b* 1947: *m* 1976, Anthony Hart, of 61 Undercliff St, Neutral Bay, NSW 2089, Aust, son of Benjamin Hart, and has issue living, Adam John, *b* 1981.

Grandsons of late Titus Salt (ante):—
Issue of late Harold Crossley Salt, *b* 1868, *d* 1943: *m* 1906, Grace Ethel Muriel, da of late Rev Henry Madan Pratt, R of Cottesbrooke, Northamptonshire (Wilson, Bt, *cr* 1874):—
Denys Geoffrey Crossley (38 Holland Park, W11), *b* 1918; *ed* Marlborough, and St Edmund Hall, Oxford (MA): *m* 1st, 1956 (*m diss* 1963), Patricia Lee, da of late Lt-Col D. C. Pope, MC, of Red House, Sutton Montis, Somerset; 2ndly, 1989, Eva Kiesling, of Graz, Austria. —— Peter Hubert Wharton, *b* 1920; *ed* Cheltenham, and St Edmund Hall, Oxford (MA); India 1944-46 with Intelligence Corps: *m* 1951, Gillian Caryl, who *d* 1983, da of late John Hill, of Westhill, Ledbury, and has issue living, Jonathan Wharton, *b* 1953: *m* 1981, Susan Lee Jeanette, da of William McGann, of 39 Broomfield Av, Telscombe Cliffs, Brighton, and has issue living, Benjamin Wharton *b* 1982, Kate Alicia Gillian Samantha *b* 1986, — Miranda Elisabeth Caryl, *b* 1955: *m* 1980, Carteret Hunter Maunsell, of 19 Velmore Rd, Chandlers Ford, Hants, and has issue living, Mark Hugo *b* 1986, Hannah Caryl *b* 1982, Cara Alison *b* 1984. *Residence* – Jacaranda, Limpsfield, Surrey.

Sir Titus, 1st baronet, son of Daniel Salt of Bradford, sat as MP for Bradford (*L*) 1859-61.

SALT (UK) 1899, of Standon, and of Weeping Cross, co Stafford

In sale salus

Sir (THOMAS) MICHAEL JOHN SALT, 4th *Baronet*; *b* 7 Nov 1946; *s* his father, Lt-Col *Sir* THOMAS HENRY, 1965; *ed* Eton: *m* 1971, Caroline, el da of late Henry Robert John Hildyard (*see* B Kindersley, 1980 Edn).

Arms – Argent, a chevron rompu between three mullets in chief and a lion rampant in base sable. **Crest** – Three annulets interlaced sable, thereon a dove holding an olive branch proper, charged on the neck with a chevron also sable. *Residence* – Shillingstone House, Shillingstone, Dorset DT11 0QR. *Club* – Boodle's.

DAUGHTERS LIVING

Henrietta Sophia Meriel, *b* 1978. —— Alexandra Georgia May, *b* 1982.

BROTHER LIVING

ANTHONY WILLIAM DAVID, *b* 5 Feb 1950; *ed* Milton Abbey: *m* 1978, Olivia Anne, yr da of Martin Morgan Hudson, of Yokehurst Farm, S Chailey, nr Lewes, Sussex, and has issue living, Edward James Stevenson, *b* 11 June 1981, —— Henry Martin Morgan, *b* 1983.

SISTERS LIVING

Sarah Meriel, *b* 1944: *m* 1977, Malcolm David Coombs, of 10 The Close, Rickmansworth, Herts, and has issue living, Dominic Nathaniel Thomas, *b* 1986, —— Augusta Elinor Lettice, *b* 1979, —— Octavia Alexandra Elizabeth, *b* 1981. —— Jennifer Mary, *b* 1951: *m* 1977, John Joseph William Clark, of Moyston, Victoria, and has issue living, Thomas William, *b* 1979, —— Anthea Mary, *b* 1981.

WIDOW LIVING OF THIRD BARONET

MERIEL SOPHIA WILMOT (*Meriel, Lady Salt*) (Shillingstone House, Shillingstone, Dorset), da of late Capt Berkeley Cole Wilmot Williams (B Addington): *m* 1943, Sir Thomas Henry Salt, 3rd Bt, who *d* 1965.

COLLATERAL BRANCHES LIVING

Issue of late Lt-Cdr George Stevenson Salt, RN, 2nd son of 2nd baronet, *b* 1908, *d* on active service 1940: *m* 1935, Lilian Bridget (who *m* 2ndly, 1948, Capt William John Lamb, CVO, OBE, RN (ret), who *d* 1993, of Brookway, Rhinefield Rd, Brockenhurst, Hants), da of late F. S. Francis, of Champion's Farm, Pulborough, Sussex:—
James Frederick Thomas George, CB (Salterns, Lock Lane, Birdham, Chichester, W Sussex), *b* 1940; Rear Adm; cmd'd HMS *Sheffield* (sunk S Atlantic Campaign 1982); sr Naval Directing Staff at Royal Coll of Defence Studies 1988-90; ACNS (Gulf War) 1990-91; Mil Dep Defence Export Services since 1992; CB (Mil) 1991: *m* 1975, Penelope, only da of Anthony Walker, of 47 Warkton, nr Kettering, Northants, and has issue living, George William, *b* 1977, —— Charles James *b* 1979, —— Thomas Edward *b* 1983, —— John Philip, *b* 1986. —— Joanna Elizabeth (*Lady Spencer-Nairn*), *b* 1937: *m* 1963, Sir Robert Arnold Spencer-Nairn, 3rd Bt, of Barham, Cupar, Fife.

Issue of late Herbert Edward ANDERDON, 2nd son of 1st baronet, *b* 1870, *d* 1938 (having assumed by deed poll 1923, the surname of Anderdon in lieu of his patronymic): *m* 1899, Ethel Menie, who *d* 1966, da of late Henry Manisty of 169 Queen's Gate, SW7:—
Henry Manisty ANDERDON, *b* 1900; *ed* Haileybury: *m* 1929, Sybilla Marjorie, da of Lt-Col Reginald Holden Steward, OBE, and has issue living, John Nigel Steward (Nursling House, Nursling, Soton, Southampton), *b* 1931; Cdr RN (ret): *m* 1961, Mavis Marjorie, da of Lester Gibson, of Bristol, and has issue living, Alexander Philip, *b* 1963, —— Ian George Carlyle (Henlade, Taunton, Som), *b* 1936. *Residence* – Henlade, Taunton, Som.

Issue of late Rev William Manning Salt, 5th son of 1st baronet, *b* 1876, *d* 1947: *m* 1907, Mildred Nairne, who *d* 1926, da of late Col C. H. E. Graeme:—
Joan Mildred, *b* 1908; JP of Monmouth: *m* 1938, Frederick Newman Tanner. *Residence* – The Vaga, Monmouth. —— Elisabeth, *b* 1915. *Residence* – Elmbridge, Church Rd, North Newton, Bridgwater.

Issue of late Maj-Gen Harold Francis Salt, CB, CMG, DSO, yst son of 1st baronet, *b* 1879, *d* 1971: *m* 1914, Phyllis Dulce, who *d* 1965, da of late Maj E. D. Cameron, RFA:—
Primrose Phyllis, *b* 1915: *m* 1st, 1935, Maj Anthony Hope Osborne, The Queen's Bays, who was *ka* 1943; 2ndly, 1944 (*m diss* 1948), Capt Philip Quellyn Roberts, RN; 3rdly, 1962, James Mansfield Niall, of 99 Empire Circuit, Deakin, Canberra, Aust, and has issue living, (by 1st *m*) Duncan Norton Hope, *b* 1936, —— (by 2nd *m*) Paul Quellyn, *b* 1945. —— Babette Irene (*Lady Millais*), *b* 1922: *m* 1st, 1941, Maj John De Grey Tatham Warter, MC, 2nd Dragoon Gds (The Queen's Bays), who was *ka* 1942; 2ndly, 1946 (*m diss* 1972), Victor William Henry Sefton-Smith; 3rdly, 1975, as his 3rd wife, Sir Ralph Regnault Millais, 5th Bt, of Elizabeth Court, 47 Milmans St, SW10 0DA, and has issue living (by 2nd *m*) Ewan Victor William, *b* 1950, —— Susan Jane, *b* 1948: *m* 1st, 1971 (*m diss* 1976), John Henry Deen; 2ndly, 1976 (*m diss* 1987), John Leslie McClue; 3rdly, 1987, David Hyman, of 16 Mulberry Walk, SW3 6DY, and has issue (by 2nd *m*), Linsey Jane *b* 1976, Laura Leslie *b* 1977, —— Lucy Annabelle, *b* 1952: *m* 1977, Richard Hobart John de Courcy Moore, of 11 Chelsea Park Gdns, SW3 6AF, and has issue living, Francis Richard Hobart de Courcy *b* 1985, Natalie Elizabeth Victoria de Courcy *b* 1993.
The 1st baronet, Sir Thomas, a partner in the private banking firms of Stevenson, Salt and Co (Stafford Old Bank), and Bosanquet, Salt and Co (London), and Chm of Lloyds Bank, sat as MP for Stafford (*C*) 1859, 1869-80, 1881-5, and 1886-92. He was son of Thomas Salt of Standon and Weeping Cross, Staffs, whose family was settled at Rugeley in the seventeeth century. Sir Thomas Salt, 1st baronet, *m* 1861, Emma Helen Mary, da of John Lavicount Anderdon of Chislehurst, Kent, niece of Cardinal Manning.

Salusbury-Trelawny, see Trelawny.

SAMUEL (UK) 1898, of Nevern Square, St Mary Abbots, Kensington, co London

A pledge of better times

Sir JON MICHAEL GLEN SAMUEL, 5th *Baronet; b* 25 Jan 1944; *s* his father, *Sir* JOHN OLIVER CECIL, 1962; *ed* Radley, and Univ Coll, London (BSc): *m* 1st, 1966, Antoinette Sandra, da of late Capt Anthony Hewitt, RE; 2ndly, 1982, Mrs Elizabeth Ann Molinari, yst da of late Maj R. G. Curry, of Bournemouth, Dorset, and has issue by 1st *m*.

ᴀrms – Party per chevron argent and gules, two wolves' heads erased in chief sable, and in base as many squirrels sejant addorsed, each cracking a nut of the first. Crest – On a rock in front of three spears, one in pale and two in saltire proper, a wolf courant sable, pierced in the breast by an arrow argent, flighted or.
Residence – The Mill, Blackdown Park, Haslemere, Surrey GU27 3BU.

SONS LIVING *(By 1st marriage)*

ANTHONY JOHN FULTON, *b* 13 Oct 1972. —— Rupert Casper James, *b* 1974.

SISTER LIVING

Jane Lesley, *b* 1947: *m* 1966, John Henry Newman, of Gilson Court, Old Windsor, Berks SL4 2JL, and has issue living, James Michael, *b* 1969, — Timothy John Hoyt, *b* 1972.

AUNT LIVING

Eva Elizabeth, *b* 1905: *m* 1934, George Brian Stafford Cothay, who *d* 1983, and has issue living, Charlotte Ann Stafford, *b* 1936: *m* 1962, Cdr John May, MVO, RN, of Woodside, Eastergate, Chichester, and has issue living, Alexandra Louise Stafford *b* 1965. *Residence* – 20 Spinners Close, Biddenden, Ashford, Kent.

WIDOW LIVING OF FOURTH BARONET

CHARLOTTE MARY (The Old School House, W Horsley, Surrey), da of late R. H. Hoyt, of Calgary, Alberta, Canada: *m* 1st, 1942, Sir John Oliver Cecil Samuel, 4th Bt, who *d* 1962; 2ndly, 1966, Heremon James Patrick Desmond, who *d* 1971.
The 1st baronet, Hon Sir Saul, KCMG, CB, was Agent-Gen in England for NSW 1880-98.

SAMUELSON (UK) 1884, of Bodicote, Banbury, Oxfordshire

Light after darkness

Sir (BERNARD) MICHAEL FRANCIS SAMUELSON, 5th *Baronet; b* 17 Jan 1917; *s* his father, *Capt Sir* FRANCIS HENRY BERNHARD, 1981; *ed* Eton; late Lt RA; Burma 1939-45 War (despatches): *m* 1952, Janet Amy, yr da of Lt-Cdr Lawrence Garrett Elkington, of Chelsea, SW3, and has issue.

ᴀrms – Sable, three piles wavy two issuant from the chief and one from the base or, each charged with a phoenix proper. Crest – A phoenix holding in its beak a torch, and charged on each wing with a scroll.
Residence – Hollingwood, Stunts Green, Herstmonceux, E Sussex BN27 4QG.

SONS LIVING

JAMES FRANCIS (3 Manor Cottages, Buckhorn Weston, Gillingham, Dorset SP8 5HH), *b* 20 Dec 1956; *ed* Hailsham: *m* 1987, Caroline Anne Woodley, and has issue living, Miranda Alice, *b* 1990, — Naomi Harriet, *b* 1992. —— Edward Bernard, *b* 1967; *ed* Hailsham.

DAUGHTERS LIVING

Nancy Amy, *b* 1953. —— Angela Margaret, *b* 1962.

BROTHERS LIVING

Christopher Blundell (6 New Dorset St, Brighton, E Sussex), *b* 1920; *ed* Eton, and Trin Coll, Camb; 1940-45 War with Staffordshire Yeo. —— Richard (11 Heath Rd, Petersfield, Hants), *b* 1925; *ed* Eton; 1943-45 War as Lt Fleet Air Arm.

SISTER LIVING

Diana Frances (Little Lodge, Jarvis Lane, Steyning, Sussex), *b* 1922: *m* 1943, William Ord Blacklock, who *d* 1958, and has issue living, Catherine Margaret, *b* 1945: *m* 1970, Alistair Donald Mant, of Sydney, NSW, and has issue living, Eleanor Frances *b* 1972, Isabel Catherine *b* 1973, — Frances Elizabeth, *b* 1946: *m* 1st, 1970 (*m diss* 1981), Dennis Thomas Conroy; 2ndly, 1990, Allan Jarvis, of Perth, W Australia, and has issue living, (by 1st *m*), Thomas Liam *b* 1974, Joanna Mary *b* 1971, Alice Frances *b* 1973, Kate Diana May *b* 1980, — Stephanie, *b* 1952: *m* 1972, Barrie Weir, and has issue living, Adam James *b* 1976, Gemma Fay *b* 1974, Natasha Hope *b* 1977.

COLLATERAL BRANCHES LIVING

Grandchildren of late Godfrey Blundell Samuelson, 3rd son of 1st baronet:—
Issue of late Capt Bernard Godfrey Samuelson, *b* 1888, *d* 1954: *m* 1st, 1910, Hon Evelyn Amy Akers-Douglas, who *d* 1914, da of 1st Viscount Chilston; 2ndly, 1938, Patricia Christabel, da of William Wildash:—

(By 1st *m*) Peter Bernard, *b* 1912; *ed* Eton: *m* 1935 (*m diss* 1949) Wilhelmina Van Blaaderen, and has issue living, Jean Paul, *b* 1939: *m* 1962, Annette Louise, da of Hubertus Johannes Richardus Ponjee, and has issue living, Dennis John *b* 1963, Nicolas Andrew *b* 1966, Quentin Jeremy *b* 1969, Natashia Nicole *b* 1972, — Bridget, *b* 1935, — Zandra Serafina, *b* 1937.
        Issue of late Carol Hubert Francis Samuelson, *b* 1899, *d* 1984: *m* 1st, 1920, Doris, who *d* 1959, da of Capt John George Edmund Templer, formerly of Lindridge, Bishop's Teignton, Devon; 2ndly, 1961, Marjorie Hilda Donisthorpe (Strand House, Ringmore, Shaldon, Teignmouth, Devon):—
(By 1st *m*) Eleanor Caroline, *b* 1921: *m* 1946, Capt Marc Anderson Kerr, MBE, IA (ret), of Windrush, Poltimore, Exeter, Devon, and has issue living, Vyvian Frances, *b* 1947: *m* 1972, John Charles Gundry, and has issue living, Mark Alexander *b* 1983, — Fiona Charlotte Eleanor, *b* 1953: *m* 1978, Anthony Garne Fraser Peal, and has issue living, Alastair Mark Fraser *b* 1980, Nicholas Hugh Anderson *b* 1983.

        Grandchildren of late Capt Guy Weston Samuelson, 2nd son of late Godfrey Blundell Samuelson (ante):—
        Issue of late Lt-Col John Peel Weston Samuelson, MC, *b* 1917, *d* 1988: *m* 1st, 1943 (*m diss* 1951), Pamela, who *d* 1989, eldest da of late Cecil E. Winter, of Surrenden Dering, Pluckley, Kent; 2ndly, 1952, Grace Eleanor, da of late R. C. Dawson, of Ball Hill, Newbury, Berks:—
(By 1st *m*) Nigel John Esdaile (Fronwen, Alexandra Rd, Brecon, Powys), *b* 1944; Solicitor: *m* 1971, Angela Margaret, da of late Bruce Samways, of Bleadon, Weston-super-Mare, Avon, and has issue living, Alistair Paul, *b* 1976, — Robert Ernest, *b* 1979, — Diana Helen Esdaile, *b* 1973. —— Christopher Richard Leney (PO Box 472, Gibraltar), *b* 1946: *m* 1st, 1968 (*m diss* 1980), Catherine Elizabeth, da of late George M. Cooper, of Charnwood, Idutywa, S Africa; 2ndly, 1980, Diana Margaret, da of Richard Lewis, of Lahore, and has issue living (by 1st *m*), John Michael Winter, *b* 1974, — (by 2nd *m*) Nichola Robyn, *b* 1981, — Lucy Anne, *b* 1986. —— (By 2nd *m*) Robin Dawson, *b* 1953, *d* 1978. —— Eleanor Clare, *b* 1958.
        Issue of late Henry Bernard Samuelson, *b* 1919, *d* 1988: *m* 1st, 1947 (*m diss* 1949), Evelyn Patience, da of John Nairn Burt, of Ashwell House, Knaresborough, N Yorks; 2ndly, 19— (*m diss* 1961), Barbara Crossley, of Sydenham; 3rdly, 1961, Anita Jill Waring, yst da of Frederick William Guard, of Barnstaple, Devon:—
(By 3rd *m*) Francis Peel Waring (8 Burrows Close, Braunton, Devon), *b* 1961. —— Godfrey Weston Rhodes, *b* 1962. —— Kevin Guard Leney, *b* 1965. —— Clife Bernard Waring, *b* 1967. —— Henry Rhodes Hulke, *b* 1970.

        Granddaughters of late Sir Herbert Walter Samuelson, KBE, 4th son of 1st baronet:—
        Issue of late Maj Rupert Eric Herbert Samuelson, *b* 1899, *d* 1993: *m* 1930, Eileena Jane (10 Cadogan Sq, SW1), da of Arthur Reece-Jones, of Cefn-y-Parc, Barry:—
Doriel Sybil, *b* 1931: *m* 1st, 1955 (*m diss* 1972), Andrew Ridgway; 2ndly, 1972 (*m diss* 1981), Aldwin David James Hall, and has issue living (by 1st *m*), Peter Eric, *b* 1958, — Amanda Jane, *b* 1956, — Joanna Kate, *b* 1962, — Charlotte Rose, *b* 1965. —— Philippa Margaret, *b* 1934.
        The 1st baronet, Rt Hon Sir Bernhard Samuelson, FRS, founder and Chm of Sir B. Samuelson and Co (Limited) of Middlesbrough, and of Samuelson and Co (Limited) of Banbury, was Chm of Roy Commn on Technical Instruction 1881, and sat as MP for Banbury (*L*) Feb to April 1859 (when he was defeated) and 1865-85, and for N, or Banbury, Div of Oxfordshire 1885-95. He was the Pioneer of Technical Education, and sat on several Roy Commns, his baronetcy being conferred for his services in the cause of education. Sir Henry Bernard Samuelson, 2nd Bt, sat as MP for Cheltenham (*L*) 1868-74, and for Frome 1876-85.

SANDERSON (UK) 1920, of Malling Deanery, South Malling, co Sussex

Without God nothing

Sir FRANK LINTON SANDERSON, 3rd *Baronet*; *b* 21 Nov 1933; *s* his father, *Sir* (FRANK PHILIP) BRYAN, 1992; *ed* Stowe, and Salamanca Univ; RNVR 1950-65: *m* 1961, Margaret Ann (Margot), da of late John Cleveland Maxwell, of New York, USA, and has issue.

Arms – Azure, a maunch between three annulets or. **Crest** – Between two wings or a sinister arm embowed in chain-mail grasping a scimitar proper, pommelled and hilted or.
Residence – Grandturzel Farm, Burwash, E Sussex TN19 7DE.

SONS LIVING

DAVID FRANK, *b* 26 Feb 1962; *ed* Stowe, and Univ of Sussex (BA); Bar Inner Temple 1985: *m* 1990, Fiona Jane, da of Robert Bruce Ure and Mrs Barbara Michael, of Bristol. —— Michael John, *b* 1965; *ed* Stowe.

DAUGHTERS LIVING

Caroline Anne, *b* 1966. —— Nina Margaret, *b* 1968. —— Katherine Claire, *b* (twin) 1968.

BROTHER LIVING

Peter Bryan (Hole Farm, North Chailey, E Sussex BN8 4EJ), *b* 1946; *ed* Stowe, and Salamanca Univ: *m* 1970, Elizabeth Magdalena, da of John Grün, of Hove, Sussex, and has issue living, Roberta Caroline, *b* 1974.

SISTER LIVING

Merry Claire, *b* 1936: *m* 1959, David Lyle, late Capt 16th/5th R Lancers, of Yew Tree Cottage, Scaynes Hill, Sussex, and has issue living, James Robert Bryan, *b* 1961; *ed* Charterhouse, and St Edmund Hall, Oxford (BA), — Robert Giles, *b* 1964; *ed* Charterhouse, and London Sch of Economics (BA), — Edward Hugh, *b* 1970; *ed* Hurtwood House, Univ of London (BA).

AUNT LIVING (*daughter of 1st baronet*)

Pearl, *b* 1906: *m* 1st, 1928, Gerald Melville Donner (Macnaghten, Bt, colls); 2ndly, 1947, Maj Alan Sherman James, who *d* 1963, and has issue living (by 1st *m*), John Melville (Heddon Oak House, Crowcombe, Somerset; 39 Bramerton St, SW3), *b* 1930; *ed* Stowe, and RMA; Coldm Gds 1948-53 and 1956 (Suez); an Underwriting Member of Lloyd's; Man Dir Fenchurch Insurance Holdings plc 1969-74; Chm DUA Ltd 1974-90; Queen's Award for Export 1983, 1988: *m* 1952, Patricia Mary, da of late Barnet Thomas Jenkins, of Bickleigh, S Devon, and has issue living, Rupert Melville *b* 1955; *ed* Stowe, and Exeter Univ (BA); Solicitor, with Lovell, White & King 1980-82, Member of Lloyd's, Annabel Elizabeth *b* 1958; *ed* Benenden, and Exeter

Univ (BA); Member of Lloyd's, — Gillian Pearl (Clayton Minsted, Clayton, Sussex), *b* (twin) 1930: *m* 1963, Cdr Kenneth Coburn, USN, who *d* 1971, and has issue living, John Bruce *b* 1967; *ed* Tonbridge, Kimberly Gillian *b* 1965: *m* 1992, John Garth Kirkland, of 86 Central Rd, Sydney, Australia 2107, — Rosita Ann, *b* 1933: *m* 1954, Michael Beresford Burtenshaw, of Bottle Cottage, Reigate Heath, Reigate, Surrey.

WIDOW LIVING OF FIRST BARONET

JOAN (*Joan, Lady Sanderson*) (74 Greenford Gardens, Greenford, Middx), only da of late Harry Cubberley, of 4 Hill Court, Ealing, W5: *m* 1951, as his 2nd wife, Sir Frank Bernard Sanderson, 1st baronet, who *d* 1965.

COLLATERAL BRANCH LIVING

Issue of late Derek Maxwell Sanderson, yr son of 1st baronet, *b* 1914, *d* 1983: *m* 1936, Daphne (Peyrières, 82150 Montaigu de Quercy, Tarn et Garonne, France), elder da of late Frederick Ernest Bayard Elton (*see* Elton, Bt, colls):—

John Maxwell (Brook House, Tinkers Lane, Blackboys, Uckfield, East Sussex TN22 4EU), *b* 1938; *ed* Pangbourne: *m* 1962, Susan Elizabeth, WVSM, elder da of Brig Randall Thomas Kellow Pye, DSO, OBE, of Horsted Keynes, West Sussex, and has issue living, Christian Maxwell, *b* 1966; *ed* Wellington, and Univ of the West (BA Hons), Charlotte Jane, *b* 1964; *ed* Downe House. —— Richard Bryan (Finca Argaga, Valle Gran Rey, La Gomera, Canary Islands), *b* 1942; *ed* Harrow; Coldm Guards 1960-63: *m* 1964, Narima, yr da of late Louis Jonquier of Lausanne, Switzerland, and has issue living, Mark Bryan, *b* 1967, — Caspar Jason Manfred Henrique, *b* 1969. —— Christopher Derek (37 Glendavis Crescent, Toronto, Ontario ME4 16X, Canada), *b* 1948; *ed* Milton Abbey, and Dalhousie Univ (BA). —— Sally Greet, *b* 1939; *m* 1st, 1966, Lother John; 2ndly, 1988, Rev Anthony Talbot Hindley, of The Vicarage, South Malling, Lewes, E Sussex BN7 2JA, and has issue living (by 1st *m*), Rolf Peter, *b* 1967, — Dominique (da), *b* 1969.

Sir Frank Sanderson, 1st Bt, 7th son of John Sanderson of Hull, was founder of Wray, Sanderson & Co, Ltd, and an Underwriting Member of Lloyd's. He sat as MP for Darwen Div of Lancs (*U*) 1922-23, and 1924-29, for Ealing 1931-45, and for E Ealing 1945-50.

SASSOON (UK) 1909, of the City of Bombay, India (Extinct 1961)

Sir (ELLICE) VICTOR SASSOON, GBE, 3rd and last *Baronet*.

WIDOW LIVING OF THIRD BARONET

EVELYN (*Lady Sassoon*), da of William H. Barnes, of Kingsport, Tennessee, USA: *m* 1959, Sir (Ellice) Victor Sassoon, GBE, 3rd baronet, who *d* 1961, when the title became ext. *Residence* – Eves, Cable Beach, PO Box N 1706, Nassau, NP Bahamas.

Saunders-Pryse, see Pryse.

SAVORY (UK) 1890, of Brook Street, St George, Hanover Square, co London (Extinct 1961)

Sir WILLIAM BORRADAILE SAVORY, 3rd and last *Baronet*.

DAUGHTERS LIVING OF THIRD BARONET

Diana Victor, *b* 1913: *m* 1934, James Nigel Jackaman, and has issue living, Nigel Victor Charles, *b* 1939, — Elizabeth Mary, *b* 1936. *Residence* – Glebe House, Stoke Poges, Bucks SL2 4PE. —— Pamela Frances, *b* 1916: *m* 1939, Douglas Burbridge, and has issue living, Howard Harry Borradaile, *b* 1941, — Robert Anthony Carruthers, *b* 1952. *Residence* – 2 Selsey Rd, Donnington, Chichester, W Sussex P019 2SN.

SCHUSTER (UK) 1906, of Collingham Road, Royal Borough of Kensington

Sir (FELIX) JAMES MONCRIEFF SCHUSTER, OBE, TD, 3rd *Baronet*; *b* 8 Jan 1913; *s* his father *Sir* (FELIX) VICTOR, 1962; *ed* Winchester; is Col late Rifle Bde; Hon Col 5th Bn R Green Jackets, T & AVR; OBE (Mil) 1955: *m* 1937, Ragna, da of late Direktor Ole Sundo, of Copenhagen, and has issue.

Arms – Ermine, two swords in saltire, points downwards, proper, pommels and hilts, and surmounted by a lion passant or; on a chief gules, an eagle displayed argent between two human hearts or. **Crest** – On a mount vert, in front of two swords in saltire, a lion passant or, charged with two human hearts gules. *Residence* – Piltdown Cottage, Piltdown, Uckfield, E. Sussex TN22 3XB: *Club* – Bath.

DAUGHTERS LIVING

Sarah Lavinia, *b* 1941: *m* 1st, 1962 (*m diss* 1966), Theodore Phillips Burgess; 2ndly, 1972, Patrick O'Neill, and has issue living, (by 2nd husband) Sam Edward, *b* 1971, — Felix Jake, *b* 1972, — Ben Darcy, *b* 1974. —— Inger Marion Averil, *b* 1944: *m* 1967, Hugh Reginald Newcomb, of Black Swan Hall, Goudhurst, Kent, and has issue living, Toby James Moncrieff, *b* 1969, — Rupert, *b* 1971.

SISTER LIVING

Dorothy Ann Violet (Winton Barn, Alfriston, Polegate, Sussex), *b* 1921: *m* 1st, 1940, Brig Arthur Frederick Crane Nicholls, GC, Coldstream Guards, who was *ka* 1944; 2ndly, 1944, Sqdn-Ldr Archibald George Dunlop Mackenzie, RAF, and has issue living, (by 2nd *m*) Andrew Robert Archibald Dunlop, *b* 1945; *ed* Stowe: *m* 1st, 1968, Herdis Pelle; 2ndly, 19—, Sarah Anne Orme, and has issue living (by 1st *m*), Louisa *b* 1970, Sonja *b* 1972, (by 2nd *m*) Alexander Dunlop *b* 1983, Isla Clare *b* 1985, — (by 1st *m*) Jennifer Ann Crane, *b* 1943, — (by 2nd *m*) Catriona, *b* 1947: *m* 1969, Michael Dollin, and has issue living, Laura *b* 1971.

In God alone

The 1st baronet, Sir Felix (Otto) Schuster (son of late Francis Joseph Schuster, of 39 Harrington Gardens, SW), was Gov of Union of London & Smiths Bank 1895-1918, Finance Member of Council of India 1906-16, a Director of National Province Bank and Senior Partner of the firm of Schuster, Son & Co, of 90 Cannon Street, EC.

SCOTT (UK) 1806, of Great Barr, Staffordshire

Sir DOUGLAS FRANCIS SCOTT, 9th *Baronet*; *b* 26 Aug 1908; *s* his brother, *Sir* EDWARD ARTHUR DOLMAN, 1980.

Arms – Argent, on a fesse gules, cotissed azure, between three catherine-wheels sable, as many lambs passant argent. **Crest** – On a mount vert a beacon fired proper, ladder argent.

SISTERS LIVING

Florence Susan Helen, *b* 1901. —— Frances Lucy Mary, *b* 1904.

WIDOW LIVING OF EIGHTH BARONET

DOROTHY ELSIE (*Lady Scott*), da of W. H. Winchcombe, of Yorktown, S Australia: *m* 1943, Sir Edward Arthur Dolman Scott, 8th Bt, who *d* 1980.

Faithful to king and country

The 1st baronet (of Great Barr, creation April 1806) was MP for Worcester 1802-6, and his son the 2nd baronet, sat as MP for Lichfield 1831-7. The 3rd baronet of 1st, and 2nd baronet of 2nd creation, inherited at his birth the baronetcy of his maternal grandfather, Sir Hugh Bateman, of Hartington, who had, in Dec 1806, been created a baronet, with remainder (primogeniturely) to the male descendants of his daughters, Catherine Juliana (afterwards wife of Sir Edward Dolman Scott, 2nd baronet) and Amelia Anne (afterwards wife of Sir Alexander Hood, 2nd Bt of St Audries); the latter Baronetcy passed on the death of Sir Edward Dolman Scott, 6th Bt of 1st and 5th of 2nd creation in 1905 to Rt Hon Sir Alexander Fuller-Acland-Hood, PC, MP, 4th Bt of St Audries (afterwards Baron St Audries). The 7th baronet was sometime R of Teffont Ewyas.

SCOTT (UK) 1821, of Lytchett Minster, Dorsetshire (Extinct 1961)

Sir ROBERT CLAUDE SCOTT, 7th and last *Baronet*.

DAUGHTER LIVING OF SEVENTH BARONET

Hope Berthe Turner, MB, ChB, DPH, *b* 1925: *m* 1960, William Alexander Hogg, who *d* 1989, and has issue living, William Scott, *b* 1963. *Residence* – 48 Dowanside Rd, Glasgow, G12 9DW.

SCOTT (UK) 1907, of Beauclerc, Bywell St Andrews, co Northumberland

Sir (WALTER) JOHN SCOTT, 5th *Baronet*; *b* 24 Feb 1948; *s* his father, *Sir* WALTER, 1992; *ed* privately; farmer: *m* 1st, 1969 (*m diss* 1971), Lowell Patria, da of late S/Ldr Pat Vaughan Goddard, of Auckland, NZ; 2ndly, 1977, Mary Gavin, only da of Alexander Fairly Anderson, of Gartocharn, Dunbartonshire, and has issue by 1st and 2nd *m*.

Arms – Per chevron azure and or, in chief two bees volant, and in base a crescent all counterchanged. **Crest** – Between the hornes of a crescent sable a bee volant proper. *Residence* – The Flat, Dilkers Farm, Blackboys, Uckfield, Sussex.

INVITUM SEQUITUR·HONOR

Honour follows though unsought for

SON LIVING *(By 2nd marriage)*

WALTER SAMUEL, *b* 6 Dec 1984.

DAUGHTERS LIVING *(By 1st marriage)*

Rebecca, *b* 1970.

(by 2nd m)

Diana Helen Rose *b* 1977.

WIDOW LIVING OF FOURTH BARONET

ANNA-LOUISE (*Dowager Lady Scott*), da of late Aubrey Derwent Healing, of Lewes, Sussex: *m* 1991, as his 2nd wife, Sir Walter Scott, 4th Bt, who *d* 1992. *Residence* – The Flat, Dickers Farm, Blackboys, Uckfield, Sussex.

COLLATERAL BRANCHES LIVING

Grandchildren of late Mason Thompson Scott, 4th son of 1st baronet:—
Issue of late William Walter Brough Scott, *b* 1902, *d* 1980: *m* 1st, 1925 (*m diss* 1937), Bridget Margaret, da of late Charles Leigh Clay, of Wyndcliffe Court, Chepstow; 2ndly, 1937, Pamela, who *d* 1992, da of late Sir Charles William Fielding, KBE (*see* E Denbigh, colls, 1990 Edn):—
(By 2nd *m*) Charles Martin Fielding (Mawley Farm House, Quenington, Cirenceser, Glos GL2 5BW), *b* 1945; late Lt, 1st R Dragoons: *m* 1970, Jill, da of late Wing-Cdr Marcus Mowbray Hutchinson, AFC, AAF, and has issue living, Camilla Jane, *b* 1971. —— Maxine Ling Elizabeth, *b* 1939: *m* 1st, 1966 (*m diss* 1975), Manuel Diaz Camacho; 2ndly, 1975, Edward Martin Anthony Northey, of Kingston Common Farm, Kingston Lisle, Wantage, Oxon, and has issue living, (by 1st *m*) Roderigo Manuel, *b* 1967, — Carolina del Roccio, *b* 1969, — (by 2nd *m*) Andrew Edward William, *b* 1978, — Lucinda Elizabeth, *b* 1976.

Grandchildren of late Charles Thomas Scott, 5th son of 1st baronet:—
Issue of late Capt Mason Hogarth Scott, RN, *b* 1900, *d* 1971: *m* 1924, Hon Irene Florence Seely, who *d* 1976, da of 1st Baron Mottistone:—
Mason Charles, *b* 1930; late Capt Scots Gds: *m* 1953, Judith Allison Dalgleish, and has issue living, Mason Stapleton, *b* 1955, — Adam, *b* 1963: *m* 1991, Louise Sinclair Maddocks, and has issue living, Rory Sinclair *b* 1992, Laura Sinclair *b* 1993, — Emma, *b* 1957. —— John Brough, *b* 1942: *m* 1973, Susan, da of R. G. MacInnes, of Meadow House, Ewhurst, Surrey, and has issue living, Charles Ronald Brough, *b* 1976, — James Seely, *b* 1979, — Sophie Diana, *b* 1974, — Tessa Irene, *b* 1984. —— Jane Emily (*Lady Gow*), *b* 1925: *m* 1946, Gen Sir James Michael Gow, GCB, late Scots Gds, of 18 Ann St, Edinburgh, and has issue living, Roderick Charles (49 Grahampton Lane, Greenwich, CT 06830, USA), *b* 1947; late Capt Scots Gds: *m* 1977, Anne Bayart, and has issue living, Andrew Jonathan *b* 1978, Neil James *b* 1981, — Susan Jane, *b* 1949: *m* 1969, Lt-Col Malcolm Ross, CVO, OBE, late Scots Gds, of Netherhall, Bridge of Dee, Castle Douglas, Kirkcudbrightshire, and has issue living, Hector Walter James *b* 1983, Tabitha Alice *b* 1970, Flora Jane Josephine *b* 1974, — Anna Katharine, *b* 1952: *m* 1977 (*m diss* 1991), Charles Hunter, and has issue living, Timothy Michael *b* 1981, Patrick James Simon *b* 1984, Sophie Irene *b* 1977, — Belinda Catriona, *b* 1958: *m* 1987, Julius M. Drake, of 21 Creighton Rd, NW6 6EE, eldest son of Michael Drake, of 37 Rundall Cres, NW3, and has issue living, Katherine Molly Myrtle *b* 1992, — Clunie Fiona Mary, *b* 1949: *m* 1990, Samuel Cornelius Dominic Phipps and has issue (*see* M Normanby, colls). —— (Irene) Jill, *b* 1928: *m* 1951, John Gore Phillimore, CMG, of Brooklyn House, Kingsclere, Newbury, Berks, and has issue living, John Francis, *b* 1952, — Hugh Richards, *b* 1959, — Louisa Mary, *b* 1954: *m* 1975, John C. R. Paravicini, — Penelope Jane (Polly), *b* 1956: *m* 1987, John Vidal, of 40 Redcliffe Rd, SW10 9NJ, elder son of late Roland Espeut Vidal, of Oswestry, Shropshire. —— Janet Sylvia, *b* 1941: *m* 1963, Simon John Chamberlayne, of Oakham, Little Compton, Glos, and has issue living, Edward Charles, *b* 1966: *m* 1990, Zoë E., da of — Cursham, of —, — Sarah Caroline, *b* 1964, — Laura, *b* 1972. —— Jennifer Teresa, *b* 1945: *m* 1967, Alexander Patrick Scott, of 23 Caroline Terr, SW1, and has issue living, Emily Mary, *b* 1968, — Catherine Charlotte, *b* 1970.
The 1st baronet, Sir Walter Scott, JP, son of late Samuel Scott, of Holm Cultram, Cumberland; was Chm of Walter Scott (Limited), of Walter Scott and Middleton (Limited), and of Walter Scott Publishing Co (Limited).

SCOTT (UK) 1909, of Yews, Undermilbeck, Westmorland

Sir OLIVER CHRISTOPHER ANDERSON SCOTT, MD, 3rd *Baronet; b* 6 Nov 1922; *s* his father, *Sir* SAMUEL HASLAM, 1960; *ed* Charterhouse, and King's Coll, Camb (MA); Dir of Research Unit in Radiobiology, British Empire Cancer Campaign; Mount Vernon Hosp 1966-69; Consultant, Inst of Cancer Research 1974-82; Radiobiologist, St Thomas's Hosp London 1982-88; High Sheriff of Westmorland 1966: *m* 1951, Phoebe Anne, elder da of late Desmond O'Neill Tolhurst, of The Gateways, Chelsea, SW, and has issue.

Arms – (as granted 1570 to Jean Schotte, infra)—Azure a greyhound courant argent, collared gules, and attached by a line of the second to a sphere in chief or. **Crest** – A sphere or, encircled by four feathers erect, severally argent, azure, gold, and gules.
Seat – Yews, Undermilbeck, Windermere, Westmorland. *Residence* – 31 Kensington Square, W8 5HH. *Club* – Brooks's.

SON LIVING

CHRISTOPHER JAMES ANDERSON, *b* 16 Jan 1955; *ed* Bryanston, Trinity Coll, Camb, and INSEAD: *m* 1988, Emma Jane, only da of Michael John Boxhall, of Chichester, Sussex, and has issue living, Edward James Saim, *b* 25 Oct 1990, — Charles James Michael, *b* 1994, — Oenone Katharine Jennifer, *b* 1992.

DAUGHTERS LIVING

Hermione Mary, *b* 1952: *m* 1978, Dr Miles Richard Stanford, yr son of K.J. Stanford, of Langton Matravers, Dorset, and has issue living, Emma, *b* 1984, — Harriet, *b* 1986, — Olivia, *b* 1989. —— Camilla Nancy, *b* 1956: *m* 1990, David Bruce Withington, yr son of James Withington, of Competa, nr Malaga, Spain, and has issue living, Oliver, *b* 1991, — Samuel Peter, *b* 1993.

HALF-SISTER LIVING

Anne Katharine Sibella, RIBA, *b* 1912: *m* 1944, Jocelyn Wiseman Fagan Morton, who *d* 1987, son of late Sir James Morton, LLD, and has issue living, Eleanor Katharine Mary, *b* 1948: *m* 1977, Ali Resa Afsari, and has issue living, Anna Rose *b* 1979, — Frances Anne Marylee, *b* 1950: *m* 1972, Benjamin Charles Ruck Keene, and has issue living, Alexander Charles Edward *b* 1976, Dominic Nicholas John *b* 1982, Hermione Katharine Mary *b* 1978, — Beatrice Emily Margareta, *b* 1952: *m* 1980, Reginald Henry L. R. Norton, and has issue living, Thomas Henry Jocelyn *b* 1981, Natalia Beatrice Adelaide *b* 1985, — Lucia Katharine Fagan, *b* 1954: *m* 1975, Andrew Francis King, and has issue living, Robert Jocelyn Morton *b* 1985, Rosalind Frances *b* 1981, Carmel Katharine *b* 1983, Frances Sibella *b* 1987. *Residence* – 13 Acacia Gdns, NW8 6AH.

COLLATERAL BRANCH LIVING

Issue of late Francis Clayton Scott, yr son of 1st baronet, *b* 1881, *d* 1980: *m* 1911, Gwendolen Frieda Martha, who *d* 1973, da of George Jäger, of Lingdale, Birkenhead, Cheshire:—
Peter Francis, CBE (58 Cumberland St, SW1), *b* 1917; *ed* Oriel Coll, Oxford (BA 1939); formerly Capt KRRC (Supplementary Reserve); CBE 1982: *m* 1953, Prudence Mary, da of Capt Grenville Milligan, RN, and has issue living, Francis Alexander, *b* 1959, — Charlotte Rose, *b* 1954, — Madeleine Mary, *b* 1957, — Rebecca Anne, *b* 1960. —— Joan Frieda, BM, BCh (21B Inverleith Place, Edinburgh EH3 5QD), *b* 1912: *m* 1949 (*m diss* 1959), John Trevelyan, CBE (*see* Trevelyan, Bt, *cr* 1662, colls).
Sir James William Scott, 1st Bt (head of several manufacturing and mercantile firms in Lancashire, founded by John Haslam of Larkhill 1771-1820), was 12th in descent (as registered at the Heralds' Coll) from Emricus Scotus, Seneschal of the co of Solms 1484, grandfather of Jean Schotte, historian of the family, ennobled by Charles III of Lorraine. The name is now spelt Scott in accordance with its original signification, the family being descended from Scottish settlers in Franconia, a branch of whom became settled in England early in the 19th century. Sir Samuel Haslam Scott, 2nd Bt, was High Sheriff of Westmorland 1926.

SCOTT (UK) 1913, of Witley, Surrey.

Sir ANTHONY PERCY SCOTT, 3rd *Baronet*; *b* 1 May 1937; *s* his father, *Col Sir* DOUGLAS WINCHESTER, 1984; *ed* Harrow, and Ch Ch, Oxford; Bar Inner Temple 1960: *m* 1962, Caroline Teresa Anne, elder da of (William Charles) Edward Bacon, of Hill House, Mobberley, Cheshire, and has issue.

Arms – Argent, pellety, in base a lymphad sable, pennons flying to the dexter gules, in chief two crescents azure. **Crest** – An ancient cannon, firing to the dexter proper.
Residence – 1 Groveside Court, Albion Wharf, Lombard Rd, SW11 3RQ.

SONS LIVING

HENRY DOUGLAS EDWARD, *b* 26 March 1964; *ed* Harrow: *m* 1993, Carole Ruth, elder da of Derek Maddick, and of Mrs E. Roberts, of Auckland, NZ. *Residence* – 59 Church Path, Chiswick, W4 5BH. —— *Rev* Simon James, *b* 1965; *ed* Harrow, Ch Ch, Oxford, and Wycliffe Hall, Oxford; ordained 1991.

DAUGHTER LIVING

Miranda Claire, *b* 1967.

BROTHER LIVING

Alastair John Douglas *b* 1940; *ed* Harrow, and McGill Univ, Canada: *m* 1965, Virginia Mary, da of late John Gaynor, of Fairfield, Pyrford Wood, Surrey, and has issue living, William Douglas, *b* 1966, — Sarah Victoria, *b* 1969, — Penelope Mary, *b* 1974.

SISTER LIVING

Diana Jean, *b* 1934: *m* 1956, John Peter Fraser-Mackenzie, and has issue living, Robert Douglas, *b* 1959, — Elizabeth Henrietta, *b* 1958: *m* 1988, Count Thomas Ahlefeldt-Laurvig-Lehn, of Neilstrup Hovedgaard, 5762 Vester-Skerninge, Denmark, — Georgina Ann, *b* 1963: *m* 1989, Capt Charles P. H. Knaggs, of 23 Caterham Close, Pirbright, Surrey GU24 0JA, son of George H. Knaggs, of The Nook, Hales, Shropshire, — Catherine Beatrice (*Lady Calum Graham*), *b* 1966: *m* 1991, Lord Calum Ian Graham, yst son of 7th Duke of Montrose. *Residence* – Lone Cow Estate, PO Box 22, Mutorashanga, Zimbabwe.
The 1st baronet, Adm Sir Percy Moreton Scott, KCB, KCVO, LLD, served during Ashantee War 1873-4, in Expedition up the Congo against pirates 1875, in Egyptian War 1882, in S Africa 1899-1900 as Comdt of Durban, when he devised special mounting for the Naval Gun used for defence and relief of Ladysmith, and in China 1900; invented night signalling apparatus used in RN; in command of Gunnery Sch, and a Naval ADC to HM 1903-5, Inspector of Naval Target Practice 1905-7, and in command of First Cruiser Squadron 1907-8, and of Second Cruiser Squadron 1908-9 (Comdg in S African Federation Convention); appointed or Special Ser at the Admiralty 1914; took charge of Gunnery Defences of London 1915-16.

SCOTT (UK) 1962, of Rotherfield Park, Alton, Hants

Sir JAMES JERVOISE SCOTT, 3rd *Baronet*; *b* 12 Oct 1952; *s* his father, *Sir* JAMES WALTER, 1993; *ed* Eton, and Trin Coll, Camb; Editor of *Big Farm Weekly* 1984-88: *m* 1982, Mrs Judy Evelyn Lyndon-Skeggs, da of Brian Sadler Leigh Trafford (*see* B Taylor of Hadfield), of Tismans, Rudgwick, W Sussex, and has issue.

Arms – Per pale indented argent and sable a saltire counterchanged. **Crest** – Out of a circlet of pales or, a cubit arm erect habited gules cuffed ermine, the hand proper holding a paper scroll argent.
Residence – Rotherfield Park, Alton, Hants GU34 3QL.

SON LIVING

ARTHUR JERVOISE TRAFFORD, *b* 2 Feb 1984.

DAUGHTER LIVING

Alexandra Lilian, *b* 1986.

BROTHERS LIVING

Charles Clive, *b* 1954; *ed* Eton, and Trin Coll, Camb: *m* 1979, Caroline Frances, da of Hugh Grahame Jago, of Old Cottage, Campfield Pl, Leith Hill, Dorking, Surrey, and has issue living, Eleanor Gabriel, *b* 1981, — Rose Loveday, *b* 1983, — Alice Olivia, *b* 1987. *Residence* – Manor Farm, Colemore, Alton, Hants GU34 3RX. —— Alexander Archibald, *b* 1960; *ed* Eton: *m* 1986, Julia Mary Mackenzie, eldest da of Patrick William Mackenzie Dean, of E Mere, Lincs, and has issue living, Daniel Fitzroy, *b* 1987, — Rupert Patrick, *b* 1992, — Emily Rosanna, *b* 1990. *Residence* – Glebe House, Cheveley, Newmarket, Suffolk CB8 9DG.

SISTER LIVING

Susannah Maria, *b* 1963: *m* 1990, Capt James Richard Kelly, Scots Guards, only son of John Kelly, of Barnes, SW, and has issue living, Archibald Clive, *b* 1992, — George Claude, *b* 1993. *Residence* – Ardovie House, by Brechin, Angus DD9 6ST.

Samuel Arthur (Thatched Cottage, East Tisted, Alton, Hants), *b* 1926; *ed* Eton, and RMC Sandhurst; Lt 7th Queen's Own Hussars, late Capt 4th Royal Hampshire Regt (TA); Korea with 8th Hussars 1950-51: *m* 1952, Juliet Modwena, elder da of Samuel Ranulph Allsopp, CBE (*see* B Hindlip, colls), and has issue living, Henry Samuel Jervoise, *b* 1955; *ed* Eton, and RMAS; Major The Life Guards: *m* 1979, Joanna Sarah, da of James Brownlow, of The Old Rectory, Kelling, Holt, Norfolk, and has issue living, Geoffrey James Ranulph *b* 1980, Rory Samuel Jervoise *b* 1982.

WIDOW LIVING OF SECOND BARONET

ANNE CONSTANTIA (*Dowager Lady Scott*), eldest da of Late Lt-Col Clive Grantham Austin, DL, of Roundwood, Micheldever, Hants (*see* E Scarbrough, 1980 Edn): *m* 1951, Sir James Walter Scott, 2nd Bt, who *d* 1993. *Residence* – The Knapp, Colemore, Alton, Hants GU34 3RX.

COLLATERAL BRANCH LIVING

Issue of late Maj Richard Jervoise Scott, TD, yst son of 1st baronet, *b* 1929, *d* 1974: *m* 1955 (*m diss* 1972), Julia Maud, who *d* 1974, yr da of Sir Henry Robert Kincaid Floyd, 5th Bt, CB, CBE:—
Victoria Kathleen, *b* 1956: *m* 1977, Charles Herbert Parker, and has issue living, Thomas Richard, *b* 1982, — Samuel George, *b* 1984, — Emma Louise, *b* 1987. — Camilla Julia (*Lady Michael Cecil*), *b* 1958: *m* 1986, Lord Michael Hugh Cecil, yst son of 6th Marquess of Salisbury, and has issue (*see* M Salisbury). *Address* – PO Box 49428, Nairobi, Kenya.

This family descends from John Scott of Hatfield Regis, Essex, 4th son of William Scott, lord of the manor of Stapleford Tawney, Essex, who *d* 1491. Rotherfield Park, Hants, was purchased in 1808 from the 14th Marquess of Winchester by James Scott of Hammersmith, 8th in descent from John. His grandson, Archibald Edward Scott, of Rotherfield Park was father of Sir Jervoise Bolitho Scott, 1st Bt, High Sheriff of Hants 1936, and a Co Councillor 1932-65, and Official Verderer of New Forest 1950-64. Sir James Walter Scott, 2nd baronet, was Lord Lieut Hants 1982-93.

MAXWELL SCOTT (E) 1642, of Haggerston, Northumberland

Sir DOMINIC JAMES MAXWELL SCOTT, 14th *Baronet*; *b* 22 July 1968; *s* his father, Sir MICHAEL FERGUS CONSTABLE, 1989; *ed* Eton, and Sussex Univ.

Arms – Quarterly, grand-quartered; 1st grand-quarter; or, two mullets in chief and a crescent in base azure, within an orle or the second and charged at the middle chief point with a crescent sable (*Scott*); 2nd grand-quarter; azure on a bend cotised argent three billets sable (*Haggerston of Haggerston*); 3rd grand-quarter; quarterly; 1st and 4th quarters argent an eagle displayed with two heads sable, beaked and membered gules, surmounted on an escutcheon of the first charged with a saltire of the second and surcharged in the centre with an hurcheon or (*Maxwell, E of Nithsdale*); 2nd quarter counter quartered (i) and (iv) argent a saltire sable, in chief a label of three points gules (*Maxwell*); (ii) and (iii) argent three hurcheons sable (*Herries of Terregles*) 3rd quarter, quarterly, gules vair a bend or (*Constable of Everingham*); 4th grand-quarter, or on a bend azure three mascles of the first in the sinister chief point a buckle of the second (*Haliburton*). **Crest** – 1st, a nymph richly attired holding in her dexter hand the sun and in her sinister the moon all proper (*Scott*); 2nd a lion passant argent (*Haggerston of Haggerston*).
Residence – 130 Ritherdon Rd, SW17.

BROTHER LIVING

MATTHEW JOSEPH, *b* 27 Aug 1976.

SISTER LIVING

Annabel Jane, *b* 1973.

DAUGHTER LIVING OF TENTH BARONET

Ursula Edith de Marie (2 Swan Lane Close, Burford, Oxon), *b* 1910: *m* 1939, Richard Grenville Harrison, JP, who *d* 1969, and has issue living, Louis Bevill Grenville (Weaver's Cottage, Clapton Rd, Bourton-on-the-Water, Cheltenham, Glos), *b* 1940: *m* 1975, Katherine Sarah Picken, and has issue living, Charles Richard Grenville *b* 1980, — Elizabeth Rosemary, *b* 1943: *m* 1972, Guy Martin Aldersey Taylor, of Hilton of Duncrievie, Glenfarg, Perthshire PH2 9PD, and has issue living, James Edward Aldersey *b* 1978, Emma Mary Ursula *b* 1981.

DAUGHTERS LIVING OF ELEVENTH BARONET

Belinda Ann de Marie (*Lady Haggerston Gadsden*), *b* 1933: *m* 1955, Sir Peter Drury HAGGERSTON GADSDEN, GBE, AC, FEng (who assumed by Royal Licence 1973 the additional surname of Haggerston), of Harelaw House, Chathill, Northumberland NE67 5HE, and has issue living, Juliet Mary Haggerston, *b* 1956: *m* 1978, Nigel John Cartwright, and has issue living, Nicholas John Haggerston Gadsden *b* 1980, James Alexander Haggerston Gadsden *b* 1982, Charles Peter Haggerston Gadsden *b* 1989, Georgina Mary Haggerston Gadsden *b* 1984, — Caroline Mabel, *b* 1957: *m* 1983, Capt Graham C. Simpson, RA, of The Home Farm, Ellingham, Chathill, Northumberland NE67 5HG, and has issue living, Matthew Caveen Drury *b* 1985, Oliver Peter Carnaby *b* 1989, Amelia Ann de Marie *b* 1987, Belinda Rose de Marie *b* 1991, — Clare Louise, *b* 1960: *m* 1985, Iain C. H. McWhirter, elder son of late A. Ross McWhirter, of The Old Rectory, Little Blakenham, Ipswich, Suffolk, and has issue living, (Alexander) Ross *b* 1988, Annabelle Louise *b* 1986, Lucy Belinda *b* 1990, Camilla Rosemary *b* 1991, Charlotte Elizabeth *b* 1993, — Elizabeth Ann, *b* 1962. —— Jennifer Veronica Louise de Marie, *b* 1938: *m* 1959 (*m diss* 19—), Anthony Lambert Forward, and has issue living, Hugh Carnaby, *b* 1959: *m* 1988 (*m diss* 19—), Veronique Cavallier, — Andrew Lambert, *b* 1964. —— Phyllida Angela de Marie, *b* 1945: *m* 1967, Antony Roland Richard Woosnam Mills, of Mother Ivy Cottage, Trevose Head, Padstow, Cornwall PL28 8SL.

WIDOWS LIVING OF TWELFTH AND THIRTEENTH BARONETS

JOAN ADELENE (*Lady Haggerston*), da of late William Blythe-Perrett, of Ludgershall, Wilts: *m* 1956, Sir Ralph (Raphael) Stanley de Marie Haggerston, 12th Bt, who *d* 1972. *Residence* – 62 Longston Park, Beadnell, Chathill, Northumberland NE67 5BP.

DEIRDRE MOIRA (*Lady Maxwell Scott*), da of late Alexandra McKechnie: *m* 1963, Sir Michael Fergus Constable Maxwell Scott, 13th Bt, who *d* 1989. *Residences* – 10 Evelyn Mansions, Carlisle Place, SW1; Dennett Cottage, Bembridge, Isle of Wight.

COLLATERAL BRANCHES LIVING

Issue of late Ian Malcolm Maxwell Scott, brother of 13th baronet, *b* 1927, *d* 1993: *m* 1958, Susan Mary (12 Kelmscott Rd, SW11), yr da of Sir Andrew Edmund James Clark, 3rd Bt, MBE, MC, QC (*cr* 1883):— Malcolm Fergus, *b* 1960; *m* 1990 (*m diss* 1993), Tanya, yr da of William Church. —— Simon Magnus, *b* 1962: *m* 1986, Gaynor, yst da of Daniel Jones, and has issue living, Hector George, *b* 1986, — Amelia Elizabeth, *b* 1989. —— Andrew Nicholas Hugh, *b* 1966. —— Lucy Ann, *b* 1958. —— Sarah Secunda, *b* 1959. —— Catherine Monica Jane, *b* (twin) 1966. (For other collateral branches *see* L Herries of Terregles, colls).

Sir Thomas Haggerston, who commanded a regt in Charles I's army, was *cr* a Bt in 1642. On the death in 1972 of Sir Ralph (Raphael) Stanley de Marie Haggerston, who had *s* as 12th Bt in 1971, the line from Sir Thomas, 4th Bt became ext, and the title reverted to that of the 2nd son of the 3rd Bt, William Haggerston-Constable (who in 1746 inherited Everingham Park, Yorks, from his great uncle, Sir Marmaduke Francis Constable, 4th Bt, and thereupon assumed the additional name of Constable). He *m* 1758 (Lady) Winifred, da of Robert Maxwell, titular 6th Earl of Nithsdale, when he assumed by Roy Licence the surname of Constable-Maxwell. Their grandson William *s* as 10th Lord Herries of Terregles. This peer's el son Marmaduke, 11th Lord Herries, *d* 1908 without male issue (*see* L Herries), and his 3rd son Joseph assumed by Roy Licence the surname of Constable-Maxwell-Scott, on *m* 1874 to Monica, da of J. Robert Hope Scott, of Abbotsford (by his wife Charlotte Lockhart, grandda and heiress of Sir Walter Scott, 1st Bt, the eminent writer). Joseph's el son, Sir Walter Joseph was *cr* a Bt in 1932 (which became ext on his death without male issue 1954), and his 3rd son Adm Malcolm Joseph Raphael, DSO, was father of the 13th Bt.

CONSTABLE-MAXWELL-SCOTT (UK) 1932, of Abbotsford, Melrose, co Roxburgh (Extinct 1954)

Maj-Gen Sir WALTER JOSEPH CONSTABLE-MAXWELL-SCOTT, CB, DSO, 1st and last *Baronet*.

DAUGHTERS LIVING OF FIRST BARONET (*By 1st m*)

Patricia Mary MAXWELL-SCOTT, OBE, *b* 1921: re-assumed by deed poll 1951 her maiden surname of Maxwell-Scott; formerly Subaltern ATS; OBE (Civil) 1972: *m* 1944, Capt Sir Harold Hugh Christian Boulton, 4th Bt (*cr* 1905). *Residence* – Abbotsford, Melrose, Scotland. —— *Dame* Jean Mary Monica, DCVO, *b* 1923; *ed* Convent des Oiseaux, Westgate-on-Sea; a Lady-in-Waiting to HRH Princess Alice, Duchess of Gloucester since 1959; 1939-45 War as VAD; CVO 1969, DCVO 1984. *Residence* – Abbotsford, Melrose, Scotland; New Cavendish Club.

SEALE (UK) 1838, of Mount Boone, Devonshire

In heaven salvation

Sir JOHN HENRY SEALE, 5th *Baronet*; *b* 3 March 1921; *s* his father, *Sir* JOHN CARTERET HYDE, 1964; *ed* Eton, and Ch Ch, Oxford; Capt late RA; patron of one living; RIBA and Senior lectr at Plymouth Sch of Architecture: *m* 1953, Ray Josephine, da of late R. G. Charters, MC, of Christchurch, New Zealand, and has issue.

Arms – Or, two barrulets azure between three wolves heads erased sable, in the fesse point a mural crown gules. **Crest** – Out of a crown vallery or a wolf's head argent, the neck encircled with a wreath of oak vert. *Residence* – Slade, near Kingsbridge, Devon TQ7 4BL.

SON LIVING

JOHN ROBERT CHARTERS, *b* 17 Aug 1954.

DAUGHTER LIVING

Elizabeth Margaret Anne, *b* 1956.

BROTHER LIVING

Richard Styleman (Conduit Rise, Conduit Head Rd, Cambridge), *b* 1924; *ed* Eton, and Pembroke Coll, Camb: *m* 1963, Elizabeth Vazeille, da of late T. B. Bright, of Silverdale, Lancs, and has issue living, William Thomas Carteret, *b* 1964, — Margaret Rachel Vazeille, *b* 1966: *m* 1991, Paul Atputhakumar Jebarajasingam Supramaniam, of London and Singapore, and has issue living, James Timothy Bright Aiyathuraisingam *b* 1993.

SISTER LIVING

Mary Paulina, *b* 1920: *m* 1945, Col George Robert Melville Harvey More, MC, RE, who *d* 1991, and has issue living, Robert Harvey, *b* 1946: *m* 1989, Claire, da of Cdr H. Harwood, RN, of Rowde, Wilts, and has issue living, Caspar George Harvey *b* 1992, Harriet Caroline Eaton *b* 1990, — Henry Sanctuary (1436 Miramonte Av, Los Altos, Calif 94022, USA), *b* 1948: *m* 1977, Adelle Anne, da of late Harold Mackenzie Smith, of Sacramento, Calif, and has issue living, Paul Henry *b* 1979, Stephen Henry *b* 1981, Susannah Mary *b* 1993, — John William (188 Rue Pelleport, 75020 Paris), *b* 1953: *m* 1987, Martine, da of Jacques Wolf, of Paris, and has issue living, Noëlie Joanna *b* 1991, — Sarah Frances, *b* 1952. *Residence* – Bazzleways, Milborne Port, Sherborne, Dorset.

COLLATERAL BRANCHES LIVING

Issue of late Maj Henry Dendy Seale, yr son of 3rd baronet, *b* 1882, *d* 1974: *m* 1914, Lora May, who *d* 1974, da of late Cecil Hurst Bisshopp, of Fernlea, Oban, Argyllshire:—
Mary Désirée, *b* 1915: *m* 1st, 1946, Stanley James Meyers, who *d* 1974; 2ndly, 1978, Charles Eastman Adams, who *d* 198-; 3rdly, 198-, George Hutchison, of 601 Monkland Av, Montreal, Prov Quebec, Canada H4B 1J2, and has issue living (by 1st *m*), Linda May, *b* 1948: *m* 1973 (*m diss* 1981), Robert Donald Giroux, and has issue living, Sean Robert *b* 1975, Scot Donald *b* 1977.

Grandchildren of Frederick Hayne Seale (infra), 2nd son of late George Thomas Seale, yr son of late Rev Edward Taylor Seale, 3rd son of 1st baronet:—
Issue of late Richard Wentworth Seale, *b* 1904, *d* 1972: *m* 1927, Edith Hazel, who *d* 1990, da of William Brown Birch:—
Richard Laurie (32 Kincardine Crescent, Floreat Park, W Australia 6014), *b* 1930: *m* 1956, Paula Cathleen, da of late Hans Carl Bruechle, and has issue living, Richard Beaumont, *b* 1966, — Stacey Jennifer, *b* 1958, — Leanda Jane, *b* 1960, — Petrina Louise, *b* 1962.
Issue of late Gordon Frederick Seale, *b* 1906, *d* 1985: *m* 1936, Eva Vera (37 Marlow St, Wembley, W Australia), da of Charles Adams:—
Elizabeth Lenore, *b* 1939: *m* 1961, Horace Charles Kennedy, and has issue living, Shane Brett, *b* 1967, — Natalie Lisa, *b* 1965. —— Carolyn Margaret, *b* 1943.
Issue of late Walter Douglas Seale, *b* 1907, *d* 1989: *m* 1st, 1935 (*m diss* 1967), Mons Carruthers, da of Sidney Herbert Reidy-Crofts; 2ndly, 1974, Barbara Topping, who *d* 1993:—
(By 1st *m*) John Digby, *b* 1937: *m* 1st, 1960 (*m diss* 1973), Roslyn Edith, da of David Englander; 2ndly, 1980, Ann, da of James Thomas Collingwood Mullner. —— Felicity Jane, *b* 1939: *m* 1st, 1961, Evan Owen; 2ndly, 1987, Sidney Donald Bradshaw, of 156 Hensman Rd, Subiaco 6008, W Aust, and has issue living (by 1st *m*), Simon Llewellyn, *b* 1963, — Sarah Alexander, *b* 1967, — Sophia Jane, *b* 1971.
Issue of late Allan Dudley Seale, *b* 1911, *d* 1989: *m* 1947, Ilma Ruth (25 Fortune St, S Perth, W Australia 6151), da of Edward John Barrett:—
Phillip Gregory, *b* 1948: *m* 1st, 1978 (*m diss* 1981), Cheryl Davis; 2ndly, 1991, Adele Sharam. —— Brian Wentworth (23 Lofoten Way, Ferndale 6155, W Australia), *b* 1950: *m* 1970, Cheryl Lynne, da of Stanley Raey Gibb, and has issue living, Paul Langdon Wentworth, *b* 1973, — Belynda Ruth, *b* 1971, — Rebekah Michaela Alyse, *b* 1976. —— Marlene Ruth, *b* 1952: *m* 1974, Lance Rattigan, of 13 Roseberry Av, S Perth, W Australia, and has issue living, Jeremy Lance, *b* 1977, — Timothy Neal, *b* 1979, — Andrew Stephen, *b* 1982.

Issue of late Frederick Hayne Seale (ante), *b* 1878, *d* 1931: *m* 1903, Ethel Lenore, who *d* 1959, da of Joseph Nathan:—
Grace Mildred, *b* 1909: *m* 1946, Vice Adm Brian Betham Schofield, CB, CBE, who *d* 1984, and has issue living, Elizabeth Virginia, *b* 1948, — Rosemary Victoria, *b* 1950: *m* 1982, Stephen Mark Willis, of 48 Westbourne Park Rd, W2 1PH, and has issue living, Anthony Brian *b* 1987, Alexandra Rose *b* 1985, Olivia Grace *b* 1990. *Residence* – Holme, Lower Shiplake, Henley-on-Thames, Oxon RG9 3JS.

This family can trace its descent from John Seale of St Brelade, Jersey, who was *b* about 1512. According to Payne's Armorial of Jersey, the earliest reference is to Robert Seale, or Scelle, a "gens de bien" of St Brelade 1292, and other Scelles of St Brelade are mentioned in the Rolls of the Assizes 1309. John Seale Constable of St Brelade 1644-51, a yr son of John Seale Constable 1615-21 was great-grandfather of John who purchased Mount Boone, Dartmouth, about 1720. His grandson, the 1st baronet, Sir John Henry Seale, sat as MP for Dartmouth (*L*) 1832-44. The 2nd baronet, Sir Henry Paul Seale, was sixteen times Mayor of Dartmouth.

SEBRIGHT (E) 1626, of Besford, Worcestershire

To preserve equanimity

Sir PETER GILES VIVIAN SEBRIGHT, 15th *Baronet*; *b* 2 Aug 1953; *s* his father, *Sir* HUGO GILES EDMUND, 1985; is patron of one living: *m* 1st, 1977 (*m diss* 19—), Regina Maria, da of Francis Steven Clarebrough, of Melbourne, Australia; 2ndly, 1987, Madeleine, and has issue by 1st and 2nd *m*.

Arms – Argent, three cinquefoils sable. **Crest** – A tiger sejant argent, maned and crowned or. **Badges** – A garb of oats or band azure inscribed with the motto "Pro Rege".
Residence – 6 Finchley Rd, Auckland Park, Johannesburg 2092, S Africa.

SONS LIVING (By 1st marriage)

RUFUS HUGO GILES, *b* 31 July 1978.

(by 2nd marriage)

Dashiell, *b* 1987.

MOTHER LIVING

Deirdre Ann, da of late Maj Vivian Lionel Slingsby Bethell (*see* B Westbury, colls): *m* 1st, 1952 (*m diss* 1964), Sir Hugo Giles Edmund Sebright, 14th Bt, who *d* 1985; 2ndly, 1965, Anthony Melbourne-Hart, who *d* 1988. *Residence* – South Harton, Lustleigh, Newton Albot, Devon.

WIDOW LIVING OF FOURTEENTH BARONET

VICTORIA ROSAMOND (*Dowager Lady Sebright*), da of Capt Richard Taylor White, DSO, RN (ret) (*see* White, Bt, *cr* 1802), and formerly wife of David Ashton Ashton-Bostock: *m* 1984, as his 3rd wife, Sir Hugo Giles Edmund Sebright, 14th Bt, who *d* 1985. *Residence* – BP3, Clarensac 30870, France.

The 1st baronet, Sir Edward Sebright, was High Sheriff of Worcestershire *temp* Charles I. He was a warm royalist, and paid £1,109 composition for his estate to the sequestrators. Sir Thomas Saunders, the 4th baronet, was MP for Hertford 1715-36. The 7th baronet also sat as MP for Hertford, Lt-Col Sir Edgar Sebright, 11th Bt, was Equerry to HRH Princess Mary Adelaide (Duchess of Teck) 1882-92 and Extra Equerry 1892. Sir Giles Sebright, CBE, 13th Bt, was Lt-Col late Comdg Herts Regt (TA), and temporary Equerry to HM King George VI when Duke of York 1922-23.

SEELY (UK) 1896, of Sherwood Lodge, Arnold, Notts, and Brook House, Brook, Isle of Wight

NIGEL EDWARD SEELY, 5th *Baronet*, *b* 28 July 1923; *s* his father, *Maj Sir* VICTOR BASIL JOHN, 1980; *ed* Stowe: *m* 1st, 1949, Loraine, only da of late Wilfred W. Lindley-Travis, of Gatehead, Fulstone, Yorks; 2ndly, 1984, Trudi, da of Sydney Pacter, of Tunbridge Wells, and has issue by 1st *m*.

Arms – Azure, three ears of wheat banded or between two marlets in pale, and as many wreaths of roses in fesse argent. **Crest** – In front of three ears of wheat banded or, the trunk of a tree fessewise eradicated and sprouting to the dexter proper. *Residence* – 3 Craven Hill Mews, W2. *Clubs* – Buck's, Royal Solent.

DAUGHTERS LIVING *(By 1st marriage)*

Charlotte Alexandra Mary, *b* 1954: *m* 1st, 1980 (*m diss* 19—), Paul Arthur Schwartz, of 1199 Park Av, New York, USA; 2ndly, 1988, Allen Lawrence Levy, and has issue living (by 2nd *m*), Emily Rose, *b* 1989. —— Catherine Lucy Emily, *b* 1957: *m* 1994, William Gacatre, son of Edward Victor Gacatre, of de Wiersse, Gelderland, Holland (*see* Paget, Bt, *cr* 1886). —— Henrietta Louise, *b* 1962.

HALF-BROTHER LIVING *(Son of 4th baronet by his 3rd wife, Mary Frances Margaret, da of late William Ronald Collins)*

VICTOR RONALD (Church Farm, Siddington, Cirencester, Glos GL6 6EZ; *Clubs* – Army & Navy), *b* 1 Aug 1941; *ed* Eton, RMA Sandhurst and the Army Staff Coll, Camberley; Maj R Hus (PWO), served on secondment to the Sultan of Oman's Armed Forces 1970-71: *m* 1972, Annette Bruce, da of late Lt-Col J. A. D. McEwen, of Salperton House, Salperton, Cheltenham, and has issue living, William Victor Conway, *b* 16 Sept 1983, — Natasha Wilhelmina Annette, *b* 1979.

HALF-SISTERS LIVING *(Daughter of 4th baronet by his 2nd wife, Hon Patience Kemp, da of 1st Baron Rochdale)*

Victoria (Bridgewater, Spy Lane, Loxwood, W Sussex RH14 0SS), *b* 1933: *m* 1954 (*m diss* 1975), (Francis Arthur) Michael Bray, DSC, and has issue living, Charles Michael Francis (61 Fentiman Rd, SW8 1LH), *b* 1957: *m* 1992, Elspeth J., yr da of Alastair Moncrieff, of Old Bosham, Sussex, and has issue living, Alastair Charles Michael *b* 1993, — Mariana Victoria Magdalen, *b* 1956: *m* 1985, Maj Richard C.B. Sampson, The Life Guards, of Manor House, Calton, Stoke on Trent, Staffs ST10 3JX, son of Maj Richard C. Sampson, of Norwich, Norfolk, and has issue living, George Edward Richard *b* 1986, Charles Michael Henry *b* 1988, Hugo Miles Evelyn *b* 1991, — Amelia Mary, *b* 1962: *m* 1985, Andrew James Randolph Macpherson, elder son of Colin Macpherson, of Martyr Worthy, Hants, and has issue living, Matilda Mary *b* 1987, Cluny Amelia *b* 1991, Ottilie Elizabeth *b* 1993.

(Daughter of 4th baronet by 3rd wife, Mary Frances Margaret, da of late William Ronald Collins)

Alexandra Mary Hilda, *b* 1938: *m* 1966, Henry Charles Seymour, yr son of late Lt-Col Sir Reginald Henry Seymour, KCVO (*see* M Hertford, colls).

MOTHER LIVING

Sybil Helen (*Baroness Paget of Northampton*), yst da of late Sills Clifford Gibbons, of Scaynes Hill, Sussex, and widow of Sir John Bridger Shiffner, 6th Bt: *m* 2ndly, 1922 (*m diss* 1931), as his 1st wife, Maj Sir Victor Basil John Seely, 4th Bt, who *d* 1980; *m* 3rdly, 1931, Baron Paget of Northampton, QC (Life Baron), who *d* 1990.

COLLATERAL BRANCHES LIVING

Issue of late Sqdn-Ldr Nigel Richard William Seely, AuxAF (Reserve), 4th son of 2nd baronet, *b* 1902; *d* on active ser 1943: *m* 1937, Isabella Elinor Margarete (who *d* 1957, having *m* 2ndly, 1949, Edward Bromley-Davenport, who *d* 1990), da of Eugene von Rieben:—
Charles John Howell (La Bosnière, Cussay, France), *b* 1937. —— Hilton Nigel Matthew (45 Sterndale Rd, Brook Green, W14 0HT), *b* 1940: *m* 1st, 1971, Leonie Mary Taylor; 2ndly, 1993, Denise M., da of Thomas Muckle, of Rothbury, Northumberland, and has issue living (by 1st *m*), Charles Hilton, *b* 1972, — Dominic Edward *b* 1975, — (by 2nd *m*) Max Anthony Philip, *b* 1993. —— Elinor Ivy, *b* 1941: *m* 1st, 1968, Maj Martin Vyvyan Carleton-Smith, Irish Gds; 2ndly, 1990, Ian V. Fletcher, of Johannesburg, and has issue living (by 1st *m*), Robin Francis Popham, *b* 1972, — Camilla Alison, *b* 1969. —— Isabella Frances, *b* (twin) 1941: *m* 1st, 1961 (*m diss* 1966), Simon James Scrimgeour; 2ndly, 1966, Anthony Piers Covill, of 97 Arthur Rd, SW19, and has issue living, (by 1st *m*) Lucilla Jane, *b* 1963, — (by 2nd *m*) Piers Anthony Charles, *b* 1967, — Joseph William Edward, *b* 1969.

Grandsons of late Lt-Col Frank Evelyn Seely (infra):—
Issue of late Lt-Col (Frank) James (Wriothesley) Seely, MFH, *b* 1901, *d* 1956: *m* 1925, Vera Lilian, who *d* 1970, da of late Col Charles Wilfrid Birkin, CMG (*see* Birkin, Bt):—
†Michael James, *b* 1926: *m* 1st, 1952 (*m diss* 1966), Barbara Patricia Callaghan; 2ndly, 1966, Patricia Ann Auchterlonie, who *d* 1990; 3rdly, 1993, Irene Heath, and *d* 1993, leaving issue, (by 2nd *m*) Rachel (Rosie), *b* 1967. *Residence* – Ramsdale Farm, Oxton Lane, Arnold, Notts. —— Timothy Ward (Ramsdale Farm, Oxton Lane, Arnold, Notts NG5 8PU), *b* 1935; *ed* Eton; an actor: *m* 1960 (*m diss* 19—), Anne Henrietta Maria St Paul, formerly wife of James Dugdale Burridge, and only da of Horace George St Paul Butler, of High Humbledon, Wooler, Northumberland, and has issue living, Hugo Michael David St Paul (Bickerton Grange, Tom Cat Lane, Wetherby, Yorks LS22 5ES), *b* 1961: *m* 1991, J. Caroline, elder da of Dr. A. Milner, of Islip, Oxon, and has issue living, India Grace St Paul *b* 1992. —— James Richard Francis (Ringers Farm, Terling, Chelmsford, Essex CM3 2BX), *b* 1940: *m* (Jan) 1960, Wendy Mary Hutchinson, and has issue living, Christian James Russell, *b* (Dec) 1960, — Jonathan Sebastian, *b* 1962.

Issue of late Lt-Col William Evelyn Seely, b 1902, ka 1942: m 1927, Irene Lavender (who d 1977, having m 2ndly, 1943, as his 2nd wife, Maj-Gen Sir Miles William Arthur Peel Graham, KBE, CB, MC, who d 1976 (E Peel, colls)), da of Richard Francklin (V St Vincent):—
Richard Evelyn (33 Upper Park Rd, NW3), b 1928; ed Eton; Bar Gray's Inn, 1961; JP: m 1960, Helga, da of Wilhelm Schnarr, of Mainz, Germany, and has issue living, Philip Frank Evelyn, b 1963; ed Harrow, — Robert William Henry, b 1966; ed Harrow. —— Charles William (Rendham Barnes, Saxmundham, Suffolk), b 1935: m 1958, Morvyth, da of late George Arthur St George, of 4 Dyke Road Pl, Brighton, 5, and has issue living, Amy Jane Lavender b 1969, — Camilla Rose, b 1972, — Joanna Matilda, b 1974.

Issue of late Lt-Col Frank Evelyn Seely, 3rd son of 1st baronet, b 1864, d 1928: m 1st, 1899, Leila Elizma, who d 1903, da of Rev Henry Charles Russell, of Wollaton, Notts (D Bedford, colls); 2ndly, 1907, Gertrude Fanny, OBE, JP, who d 1967, da of Henry Edward Thornton, JP, of The Wymeshead, Kegworth, Derby:—
(By 1st m) Leila Emily (Leila, Viscountess Hampden), b 1900: m 1923, 4th Viscount Hampden, who d 1965. Residence – Mill Court, Alton, Hants.

Issue of late Maj-Gen Rt Hon John Edward Bernard Seely, CB, CMG, DSO (4th son of 1st baronet), who was cr Baron Mottistone 1933 (see that title).
The 1st Bt, Sir Charles, sat as MP for Nottingham (L) 1869-74, and 1880-85, and for W Nottingham 1885-86, and again for Nottingham (LU) 1892-95. The 2nd Bt, Sir Charles Hilton, was MP for Lincoln (LU) 1895-1906, and for Mansfield (Co L) 1916-18. the 3rd Bt, Sir Hugh Michael, was cr Baron Sherwood 1941; he d 1970, when the peerage became ext.

Selby-Bigge, see Bigge.

SETON (NS) 1663, of Abercorn, Linlithgowshire

Sir IAIN BRUCE SETON, 13th Baronet, b 27 Aug 1942; s his father, Sir CHRISTOPHER BRUCE, 1988, ed Colchester, and Chadacre Agric Inst: m 1963, Margaret Ann, only da of Walter Charles Faulkner, of Barlee Rd, W Australia, and has issue.

Arms – Quarterly: 1st and 4th, or, three crescents within a double tressure flory, counterflory gules, Seton; 2nd and 3rd, argent, three in escutcheons gules, Hay. Crest – A boar's head couped or, armed and langued azure. Supporters – Two greyhounds proper. Address – Belavista, PO Box 253, Bridgetown 6255, W Australia.

SON LIVING

LAURENCE BRUCE, b 1 July 1968: m 1990, Rachel, Z da of Jeffery Woods, of Bridgetown, W Australia.

DAUGHTER LIVING

Amanda Jane, b 1971.

BROTHER LIVING

Michael Charles, b 1944; ed Colchester Tech Coll: m 1973, Vida Millicent, da of late Sidney Clarence Smith, of Boxted, Essex, and has issue living, Philip Charles, b 1975, — Helen Mary, b 1978. Residence – Fingringhoe, Colchester, Essex.

SISTERS LIVING

Sarah Ann, b (twin) 1944: m 1st, 1968 (m diss 1970), Thomas Charles Usher; 2ndly, 1974 (m diss 1988), Ferdinand Winston Good. Address – Box 443, Belton, Missouri 64012, USA. —— Joanna Mary, b 1946: m 1983, Peter Gillespie, and has issue living, Giles Peter Seton, b 1986. Residence – Vicarage Farm, Halliford Rd, Sunbury on Thames, Middx.

AUNT LIVING (sister of 12th baronet)

Violet Beechie, b 1917: m 1937, Wilfred Barnard, of Harvest House, Felixstowe, Suffolk, and has had issue, Christopher John, b 1938; ed Stamford Sch; served with 46 Sqdn RASC (LCT) 1961-64, Borneo 1963-64, as Capt LCT Agebadia: m 1966, Diana Eileen, only da of Peter James Wise, of 62 Shaftesbury Av, Southampton, and has issue living, David Charles b 1972, Charlotte Diana b 1967, Joanna Suzanne b 1968, — David Seton, b 1942; ed Stamford Sch; k by lightning in S Africa 1971, — Jane Mary, b 1944, — Jean Suzanne, b 1946.

DAUGHTER LIVING OF TENTH BARONET

Egidia Hay, b 1928: m 1st, 1948 (m diss 1949), her cousin, Andrew George Seton Arnot, who d 1988 (see Seton, Bt, cr 1663, 1980 Edn); 2ndly, 1953, Norman Haynes, and has issue living (by 2nd m), Hamish (40 Jessica Rd, SW18), b 1956: m 1982, Carmella Milne-Buckley, — Alasdair, b 1960: m 1993, Jane Elizabeth Bridgman. Residence – 2 Old Palace Terrace, Richmond, Surrey.

DAUGHTER LIVING OF ELEVENTH BARONET (By 2nd marriage)

Lydia Antoinette Gordon, b 1941: m 1st, 1966 (m diss 1981), Peter Stanley Spratt; 2ndly, 1982, Norman Victor Vine, of 21B Ailsa Rd, St Margarets, Twickenham, Middx, and has issue living (by 2nd m), Antony Patrick Seton, b 1982.

WIDOW LIVING OF TENTH BARONET

JULIA, OBE, VMH (*Julia, Lady Seton*) (122 Swan Court, Chelsea Manor St, SW3), da of late Frank Clements; OBE (Civil) 1989: *m* 1962, as his 3rd wife, Sir Alexander Hay Seton, 10th baronet, who *d* 1963.

WIDOW LIVING OF TWELFTH BARONET

JOYCE VIVIEN (*Joyce, Lady Seton*), eldest da of late Oliver George Barnard, of Lockington House, Stowmarket, Suffolk: *m* 1939, Sir Christopher Bruce Seton, 12th Bt, who *d* 1988. *Residence* – Flat 1B, Papillon House, Balkerne Gdns, Colchester, Essex CO1 1PR.

COLLATERAL BRANCH LIVING

Issue (by 2nd *m*) of late Major Henry James Seton, *b* 1854, *d* 1920: *m* 1st, 1888, Elizabeth, who *d* 1897, da of late Henry James Byron (B Byron, colls); 2ndly, 1899, Marie Bowles (who *d* 1928, having *m* 2ndly, 1922, Sir Charles George Walpole, who *d* 1926 (E Orford, colls)), da of late Percy Hale Wallace:—
Marie (8b Albert Place, W8), *b* 1910; author of *Sergei M Eisenstein, A Biography, Portrait of a Director: Satyajit Ray,* and *Paul Robeson*: *m* 1942 (*m diss* 1958), Donald Louis Hesson.

Sir Walter Seton of Abercorn, 1st Bt, was *cr* a Bt with remainder to heirs male whatsoever. The present baronet is the direct male representative of Sir Alexander Seton, who *m* Elizabeth, sister and heir of John Gordon of Gordon. She in 1408 (in conjunction with her husband) received a charter of the land of Gordon. Sir Alexander was held to have been *cr* a Lord of Parliament as Lord Gordon in or before 1429. Their son Alexander, 1st Earl of Huntly, was father (by his 1st wife, Egidia Hay) of Sir Alexander Seton, ancestor of this family, and (by his 2nd wife Elizabeth Crichton) of George Seton, late Gordon, on whom he obtained a charter to settle the Earldom. In 1923 Sir Bruce Gordon Seton, 9th Bt, CB, petitioned the Crown to admit his succession and declare his right to the title of Lord Gordon in the peerage of Scotland (*cr* in or before 1429). After a lengthy hearing the Committee for Privileges of the House of Lords, while admitting that he was heir male to Sir Alexander Seton, Dominus de Gordon (subsequently created Earl of Huntly)—eldest son of Sir Alexander—could not recognize that the evidence submitted by the petitioner established the creation and existence of the dignity. Col Sir Bruce Gordon Seton, 9th Bt, CB, in 1929 unsuccessfully claimed this Lordship before the Committee for Privileges of the House of Lords. Sir Alexander Hay Seton, 10th Bt, was Carrick Pursuivant of Arms 1935-9.

SETON (NS) 1683, of Pitmedden, Aberdeenshire

I sustain the standard with my blood

This is the sure reward of labor

Sir JAMES CHRISTALL SETON, 12th *Baronet*; son of late Christall Dougal Seton, son of late Charles Seton, 5th son of 7th baronet; *b* 21 Jan 1913; *s* his kinsman, Sir ROBERT JAMES, 1993; sometime Corporal US Army: *m* 1939, Evelyn, da of Ray Hafer.

Arms – Quarterly: 1st and 4th, or, three crescents, and in the centre a man's heart distilling blood, the whole within a double tressure flory counter-flory gules, *Seton*; 2nd and 3rd, argent, a demi-otter sable, crowned or issuing out of a bar wavy of the second, *Meldrum*. **Crest** – A demi-man in military habit holding the banner of Scotland. **Supporters** – *Dexter*, a greyhound proper, collared gules; *sinister*, an otter sable.
Residence – Otterben-Lebanon, 585 North State, Route 741, Lebanon, Ohio 45036-9551, USA.

MOTHER LIVING OF ELEVENTH BARONET

Alice Ida, CBE, da of late Percy C. Hodge, Cape Civil Ser; Group Officer (ret) WRAF; CBE (Mil) 1949: *m* 1923 (*m diss* 1950), Sir John Hastings Seton, 10th Bt, who *d* 1956. *Residence* – Collin House, 108 Ridgway, Wimbledon, SW19 4RD.

COLLATERAL BRANCHES LIVING

Issue of late Charles Wallace Seton, brother of 12th baronet, *b* 1915, *d* 1975: *m* 1943, Joyce (798 Dinner St, Palm Bay, Florida 32905, USA), da of Stephen F. Perdunn:—
CHARLES WALLACE (7008 Santa Rosa Parkway, Fort Pierce, Florida 34951, USA), *b* 25 Aug 1948: *m* 1974, Rebecca, da of Robert Lowery. —— Bruce Anthony (5473 St Andrews Drive, Salisbury, Maryland 21801, USA), *b* 29 April 1957: *m* 19—, Paula, da of Emmett Harper. —— Judith Allen, *b* 1944. —— Marsha Ann, *b* 1947: *m* 1981 (*m diss* 1984), Glen Duffy, and has issue living, Steven Seton, *b* 1968. —— Terri Michele, *b* 1958: *m* 1984, William Dick (7418 Zimmerman Av, Apt 2, Delair, NJ 08110, USA) son of William Dick Sr, and has issue living, David, *b* 1985, — Thomas, *b* 1987, — Desire Michelle, *b* 1983.

Issue of late Robert Benjamin Seton, brother of 12th baronet, *b* 1917, *d* 1993: *m* 1940, Martha Mae, who *d* 1974, da of Fred Minich:—
Karen Louise, *b* 1941; BSc (Ed) Ohio Univ: *m* 1963, Michael Conrad, of 878 Viewland, Rochester Hills, Michigan 48309, USA, and has issue living, Dennis Michael, *b* 1964: *m* 1993, Bridgett, da of John George Heal III. —— Dorothy Jean, *b* 1947.

James Seton 1st of Pitmedden (gt grandfather of the 1st baronet) was 5th son of William Seton of Meldrum who descended from William Seton, 2nd son of Sir Alexander Seton of that ilk who *m* Elizabeth, heir of the Gordons. The 1st baronet, Sir Alexander, sat as MP for Aberdeenshire, and was subsequently a Lord of Justiciary, with the title of Lord Pitmedden. The 2nd baronet was MP for Aberdeenshire and one of the Commissioners appointed to treat about the union of England and Scotland. Sir James Lumsden Seton, 8th Bt, was Capt 102nd Regt, and received 2nd class of Order of Iron Cross of Germany for saving life in the field during Franco-Prussian War 1870.

CULME-SEYMOUR (UK) 1809, of Highmount,co Limerick, and Friery Park, Devonshire
(Name pronounced "Cullum-Seamer")

·FOY·POUR·DEVOIR·

Faith for duty

Sir MICHAEL CULME-SEYMOUR, 5th *Baronet*; *b* 26 April 1909; *s* his father, *Vice-Adm Sir* MICHAEL, KCB, MVO, 1925; Cdr RN (ret 1947); *s* to the Rockingham estate upon the death of his great-uncle, Rev Wentworth Watson (*see* E Sondes, 1925 Edn), 1925, which he subsequently devised upon his nephew, Cdr L. M. M. Saunders Watson 1967 (infra); RN 1926, ADC to Gov-Gen of Canada 1934-36, served 1939-45 War, Atlantic, N Africa, Normandy, and Far East (despatches); served Imperial Defence Coll 1946-47 (ret); CC North-ants 1948-55, JP 1949, DL 1958-71, High Sheriff 1966; Farmer and Landowner (Bledisloe Gold Medal 1972); active Member Contemporary Art Soc: *m* 1948, Lady (Mary) Faith (NESBITT), who *d* 1983, elder da of 9th Earl of Sandwich, and formerly wife of late Philip Booth Nesbitt, and has had issue (two sons who *d* in infancy), and has adopted his stepda.

Arms – Azure, a pair of wings conjoined in pale and surmounted of a naval crown or; on a canton argent an anchor sable. **Crest** – On a naval crown or, two brands in saltire inflamed at the ends proper, thereon an eagle rising, also proper, looking at the sun or. **Supporters** – *Dexter*, A sailor in the Royal Navy; *sinister*, a soldier of the Royal Marines holding in his exterior hand a rifle, the butt resting upon the ground, all proper. **Motto** – Foy pour devoir.

Residence – Wytherston, Powerstock, Bridport, Dorset DT6 3TQ. *Club* – Brooks's.

ADOPTED STEPDAUGHTER LIVING

(Caroline) Gemma, *b* 1939: *m* 1964 (*m diss* 1976), Andrew H. Best, and has issue living, Matthew Thomas, *b* 1966, — Anna Josephine, *b* 1965. *Residence* – The Studio, 14 Priory Av, W4.

COLLATERAL BRANCHES LIVING

Issue of late Elizabeth Culme-Seymour, only da of 4th Bt, *b* 1904, *d* 1963: *m* 1933, Capt Leslie Swain Saunders, DSO, RN (ret), who *d* 1988, of South Lodge, Rockingham Castle, Market Harborough, Leics:—
Leslie Michael MacDonald SAUNDERS WATSON, CBE (Rockingham Castle, Market Harborough, Leics; Brooks's Club), *b* 1934; assumed by deed poll 1971 the surname of Saunders Watson; *ed* Eton; Chm The British Library 1990-93; Cdr RN (ret); High Sheriff of Northants 1978; CBE (Civil) 1993; DL Northants 1979: Hon DLitt, Warwick Univ: *m* 1958, Georgina Elizabeth Laetitia, da of Adm Sir William Wellclose Davis, GCB, DSO (*see* M Normanby, 1985 Edn), and has issue living, James Michael Ross, *b* 1961: *m* 1990, Elizabeth, da of Dr Christopher Brown, — David William Wentworth, *b* 1968, — Fiona Jane Liebe, *b* 1965. —— Alasdair James Hew (17 The Little Boltons, SW10), *b* 1938; *ed* Eton: *m* 1974, Joanna Christina, da of Col John Offley Crewe-Read, OBE (*see* By Robins), and formerly wife of Capt John Anthony Frank Morton, late RHA, and has issue living, Thomas Alasdair, *b* 1978, — Alice Elizabeth, *b* 1975. —— Iain Ogilvy Swain (10 Brunswick Gdns, W8), *b* 1947; *ed* Radley: *m* 1976, Roberta Ann Phoenix, of Laguna Beach, California, USA, and has issue living, Christina Ann Swain, *b* 1983. —— Elizabeth Christina, *b* 1941: *m* 1963, William Lawrence Banks, of 13 Abercorn Pl, NW8, and Ridgebourne, King-ton, Herefordshire, and has issue living, Richard Michael, *b* 1965: *m* 1992, Chloë Berenice Josephine Macaskie, — Edward Joseph, *b* 1967.

Granddaughter of late John Wentworth Culme-Seymour, (infra):—
Issue of late John Dennis Culme-Seymour, *b* 1923, *d* 1982: *m* 1957, (Elizabeth) Jane, who *d* 1989, da of Lt-Col Kenneth Mackessack, of Ardgye, Elgin (Craik, Bt ext):—
Caroline, *b* 1959.

Issue of late John Wentworth Culme-Seymour, 2nd son of 3rd baronet, *b* 1876, *d* 1962: *m* 1918, Evelyn Mary, who *d* 1977, da of late C. A. Smith-Ryland, of Barford, Warwick:—
Jane, *b* 1925: *m* 1959, Com John Hocken Joughin, DSC, RN, who *d* 1986. *Residence* – Flat 2, 11 St Fimbarrus Rd, Fowey, Cornwall, PL23 1JJ.

Grandchildren of late Capt George Culme-Seymour (infra):—
Issue of late Maj Mark Charles Culme-Seymour, *b* 1910, *d* 1990: *m* 1st, 1935 (*m diss* 1938), Babette, only child of late David Llewelyn Patric-Jones; 2ndly, 1941 (*m diss* 1949), Princesse Hélène Marie de la Trémoïlle, 3rd da of Prince Louis Charles Marie, 12th Duc de Thouars, Prince and 11th Duc de la Trémoïlle, Premier Duc de France, 12th Prince de Tarente, and 15th Prince de Talmond, and formerly wife of Sir (William) Campbell Mitchell-Cotts, 2nd Bt; 3rdly, 1956 (*m diss* 1967), Patricia June, da of late Charles Reid-Graham, and widow of Geoffrey Edward Ansell; 4thly, 1973, Mary Darrall, only da of late Leander Armistead Riely, of Oklahoma City, USA, and widow of Philip Kidd:—
(By 3rd *m*) MICHAEL PATRICK (6 St Andrews Rd, Henley on Thames, Oxfordshire), *b* 28 April 1962: *m* 1986, Karin Fleig, and has issue living, Michael, *b* 1986, — Julian, *b* 1988. —— Miranda, *b* 1959: *m* 1990, Jonathan Fuller, of Hollywood, Los Angeles, USA. —— Sarah Louise, *b* 1961: *m* 1990, Laurence Stewart Treloar, of 30 Canoon Rd, S Turramurra, NSW 2074, Australia, and has issue living, Alice Patricia, *b* 1991.

Issue of late Capt George Culme-Seymour, 3rd son of 3rd baronet, *b* 1878, who was *ka* 1915: *m* 1909, Janet Beatrix (who *d* 1943, having *m* 2ndly, 1918, Rev Geoffrey Harold Woolley, VC, MC, Chap to Forces, Chap at Harrow Sch, formerly Capt London Regt (TA)), da of late Charles Lindsay Orr Ewing, MP (Ewing, Bt colls):—
Angela Mary, *b* 1912: *m* 1st, 1934 (*m diss* 1938) John George Spencer Churchill, who *d* 1992 (*see* D Marlborough, colls); 2ndly, 1938 (*m diss* 1942), 3rd Baron Kinross, who *d* 1976; 3rdly, 1948 (*m diss* 19-), Count René de Chatellus; 4thly, 1977, Mehmet Ali Bulent Rauf, who *d* 1987. *Residence* – 90 Vicarage Court, Vicarage Gate, W8 4HQ.

Issue of late Major Henry Hobart Culme-Seymour, 3rd son of 2nd baronet, *b* 1847, *d* 1920: *m* 1878, Kate, who *d* 1931, da of William Charles Lucy:—
Violet Katharine Maria, *b* 1891: *m* 1926, Charles de la Cour Le Maistre, CBE, who *d* 1953.

Granddaughters of late Cdr Evelyn Culme-Seymour, RN (infra):—
Issue of late Lt-Cdr Gerald Henry Hobart Culme-Seymour, RN, *b* 1914, *d* 1973: *m* 1st, 1939, Constance Helen, who *d* 1959, da of late Alfred Rendell Street (Dashwood, Bt, *cr* 1684); 2ndly, 1960, Patricia Mary (Sturdys, Wood Broughton, Cartmel, Cumbria LA11 6SJ), el da of Edward Pearson Hewetson, JP, of 15 Glebelands, Brampton, Oxon, and formerly wife of 3rd Viscount Cross:—
(By 1st *m*) Victoria, *b* 1940: *m* 1963, M. Haeri, and has issue living, David, *b* 1967, — Mina *b* 1964, — Sophia Helen, *b* 1978. —— Anne Evelyn, *b* 1941: *m* 1st, 1961 (*m diss* 1970), John L. M. Denham; 2ndly, 1972, (David) Michael (Richard Cecil) Allen, of Kidmore House, Kidmore End, Oxon, and has issue living (by 1st *m*), James Henry Seymour, *b* 1964, — Alexandra Sophia, *b* 1966 — (by 2nd *m*), Louisa Chelsea, *b* 1975. —— Catherine, *b* 1945: *m* 1972, Christopher James Munro Hartley, and has issue living, Melissa Charlotte Victoria, *b* 1974, — Victoria Elizabeth Anne, *b* 1978. —— Alexandra, *b* 1953: *m* 1975, Simon Webb, and has issue living, Rowland Henry, *b* 1978, — Clementine Laura, *b* 1982. —— (By 2nd *m*) Caroline Eve, *b* 1961.

Granddaughter of late Maj Henry Hobart Culme-Seymour (ante):—
Issue of late Cdr Evelyn Culme-Seymour, RN, *b* 1881, *d* 1970: *m* 1908, Laura Maude Amy, who *d* 1958, da of late Sir Steuart Macnaghten (Macnaghten, Bt colls):—
Patience Ann (17 Child's St, SW5 9RY), *b* 1912: *m* 1939 (*m diss* 1951), Lt-Cdr David Robert Fremantle, RNVR, who *d* 1989, and has issue (*see* B Cottesloe, colls).

Grandchildren of late Rev Richard Seymour (*b* 1877) (infra):—
Issue of late Com John Richard Arthur Seymour, OBE, DSC, RN, *b* 1905, *d* 1957: *m* 1941, Helen Augusta (who *d* 1988), having *m* 2ndly, 1973, John Edward Francis Rawlins, who *d* 1991, da of late Lt-Col Richard Edmund Corydon Luxmoore-Ball, DSO, DCM, Welsh Guards:—
Richard Paul (Sunnybrook Cottage, Lyatts Hill, Hardington Mandeville, Yeovil, Som BA22 9NR), *b* 1943: Cdr RN; AFC: *m* 1971, Valerie Ann, da of P. L. Foulsham, and has issue living, Alexander John, *b* 1974, — Mark Richard, *b* 1980. —— Anthony John, *b* 1946.
Issue of late Michael Ernest Seymour, *b* 1906, *d* 1973: *m* 1931, Gwendoline Arran, who *d* 1993, da of William Stuart Gore (*see* E Arran, colls):—
Eleanor, *b* 1932: *m* 1953, John Ferrari, of 57 McArthur St, Guildford 2161, NSW, Australia, and has issue living, Timothy John (45 Tenth Av, Oyster, Bay 2225, NSW, Australia) *b* 1954: *m* 1980, Christine Elizabeth Hanson, and has issue living, Jillian Elizabeth *b* 1984, Emma Elise *b* 1988, — Michele Jane, *b* 1958: *m* 1979, Ronald Arthur Adam, of 6 Arthur Street, Blacktown 2148, NSW, Australia, and has issue living, Mathew James *b* 1985.

Granddaughter of late Ven Albert Eden Seymour, son of late Rev Richard Seymour, 5th son of 1st baronet:—
Issue of late Rev Richard Seymour, *b* 1877, *d* 1958: *m* 1903, Annie Louisa Mary, who *d* 1909, da of late W. E. Arthur, JP, formerly of Marwood Hill, Barnstaple, Devon:—
Ruth Mary (18 Wilder Park, Horne Rd, Ilfracombe, Devon EX34 8HH), *b* 1909: *m* 1939 (*m diss* 1949), Wilfrid Harold Gillard, and has issue living, John Michael Patrick, *b* 1940.

Grandsons of late Edward Albert Seymour, MB (infra):—
Issue of late Edward Richard Fortescue Seymour, *b* 1915; *d* 1981: *m* 1943, Margaret Eileen (48 Military Rd, Rye, Sussex TN31 7NY), da of late Maj Grantham Dodd, TD, RAMC:—
Edward Grantham (4 Rue du Pont, L-5355 Oetrange, Luxembourg GD), *b* 1945: *m* 1969, Philippa Rosalie Jane, da of Geoffrey Mollet, of Henley-on-Thames, and has issue living, Edward Hugo, *b* 1979, — Guinevere Jane, *b* 1974, — Susanna Rosalie, *b* 1977, — Augustina Maria, *b* 1981. —— Charles Adrian (3 Stocklands Close, Cuckfield, Sussex), *b* 1947: *m* 1970, Sylvia Ellen, da of late A. Kimber, of Hurstpierpoint, Sussex, and has issue living, Brendan Charles, *b* 1980, — Richard Edward, *b* 1982. —— (Michael) Shaughan (4 Chelsham Rd, Clapham, SW4 6NP), *b* 1949: *m* 1975, Jane Constance Madeleine, da of late James Lytton, and has issue living, Toby James Edward, *b* 1982, — Zoë Jane, *b* 1978, — Lucy Margaret, *b* 1980. —— Gervais Richard Hugh (179 Oundle Rd, Woodston, Peterborough PE2 9QZ), *b* 1952: *m* 1st, 1973 (*m diss* 1984), Ann Shirley Trowbridge; 2ndly, 1984, Victoria Louise, da of Robert Brewer, of Newborough, Cambs, and has issue living (by 1st *m*), Rebecca Ann, *b* 1980, — (by 2nd *m*) Thomas Christopher Gervais, *b* 1984, — Ellena Victoria, *b* 1986, — and two adopted das, Joanna Claire Marie, *b* 1978, — Michaella Jayne, *b* 1980. —— James Quentin (Shephards Arms, Coates, nr Cirencester, Glos GL7 6JY), *b* 1953: *m* 1979, Rosemary Yvonne, da of Lt-Cdr Peter Hampson Wailes, RN (ret), of Thetford, Norfolk, and has issue living, Michael James, *b* 1980, — Alice Victoria, *b* 1982.

Granddaughters of late Ven Albert Eden Seymour (ante):—
Issue of late Edward Albert Seymour, MB, *b* 1884, *d* 1946: *m* 1914, Gwendolen Emily, da of late Rev William Birch Gascoigne, formerly R of Wood Eaton, Oxfordshire:—
Hester Mary, *b* 1917; SRN (ret). —— Joyce Eleanor, *b* 1918. *Residence* – 52 Lombard Court, Old Portsmouth, Hants PO1 2HU.
Issue of late Very Rev Algernon Giles Seymour, *b* 1886, *d* 1933: *m* 1921, Ida Grace, who *d* 1971, da of late Vice-Adm Robert Frederick Hammick (*see* Hammick, Bt):—
Mary Grace (*Lady Hutchison*), *b* 1924: *m* 1949, Sir Peter Hutchison, 2nd Bt. *Residence* – Melton Mead, nr Woodbridge, Suffolk.

Grandsons of late Very Rev Algernon Giles Seymour (ante):—
Issue of late Cdr Timothy Maurice Barnabas Seymour, RN, *b* 1932, *d* 1975: *m* 1954, Monica (5 Tarleton Gardens, SE23), da of late Rt Rev Wilfred Arthur Westall, Bishop of Crediton:—
Michael Nicholas, *b* 1960. —— Charles Richard, *b* 1963: *m* 1992, Deborah Miller.

The 1st baronet, Adm Sir Michael Seymour, KCB, when in command of the "Amethyst" frigate on the night of 10 Nov 1808, fell in with the French frigate "La Thetis" off L'Orient, which, after a gallant resistance, was captured. This action, for gallantry, skill, and courage, has scarcely been equalled. George III signified his approbation by presenting him with a gold medal, and Lloyd's Patriotic Fund voted him 100 guineas. The 2nd baronet assumed by Roy licence in 1842 the additional surname of Culme to perpetuate the name of his first wife, which would otherwise have become extinct. The 3rd baronet, Adm Sir Michael, GCB, GCVO, served during Crimean War 1854-55, and commanded Pacific Station 1885-7, the Channel Squadron 1890-92, and the Mediterranean Fleet 1893-6, and was Com-in-Ch at Portsmouth 1897-1900, Principal Naval ADC* to HM Queen Victoria 1899-1901, and to HM King Edward VII: Vice-Adm of Great Britain and Ireland, and Lieut of Admiralty thereof 1901-20. He married Mary Georgiana, da of Hon Richard Watson of Rockingham Castle (son of 2nd Baron Sondes). This estate was inherited by the 5th Bt in 1925. The 4th baronet, Vice-Adm Sir Michael Culme-Seymour, KCB, MVO, who commanded HMS *Centurion* at battle of Jutland 1916, was Director of Mobilizations 1914-18, Comdg British Ægean Squadron 1918-19, British Naval Forces in Black Sea, Sea of Marmara, and Caspian Sea 1919-20, 2nd in command Mediterranean 1920-23, Com-in-Ch N America and W Indies 1923-4, and Second Sea Lord of the Admiralty and Ch of Naval Personnel 1924-5.

*In which capacity Adm Sir Michael was in charge of the transportation of the Queen's body from Osbourne to Windsor Castle. When the procession reached the steep hill within the castle walls, the horses pulling the gun-carriage slipped on the icy ground, and bolted, breaking the traces, whereupon the gun carriage bearing the Queen's coffin threatened to run back into the procession. The Admiral ordered the naval contingent to take up the traces by hand, which was done with great efficiency, and a serious disaster was averted. In recognition of this, the Admiral was granted supporters to his arms by Royal Licence 1913, in perpetuity.

SHAKERLEY (UK) 1838, of Somerford Park, Cheshire

Sir GEOFFREY ADAM SHAKERLEY, 6th *Baronet*; *b* 9 Dec 1932; *s* his father, *Maj Sir* CYRIL HOLLAND, 1970; *ed* Harrow and Trin Coll, Oxford; late 2nd Lt KRRC dir of Photographic Records Ltd since 1970; *m* 1st, 1962, Virginia Elizabeth, who *d* 1968, el da of W. E. Maskell, of Little Down, Bury, Sussex; 2ndly, 1972, Lady Elizabeth Georgiana Anson, da of late Thomas William Arnold, Viscount Anson (*see* E Lichfield), and has issue by 1st and 2nd *m*.

Arms – Argent, a chevron between three hillocks vert. **Crest** – A hare rampant sable supporting a garb or.
Residence – 57 Artesian Rd, W2 5DB.

SONS LIVING *(By 1st marriage)*

NICHOLAS SIMON ADAM, *b* 20 Dec 1963. —— Peter Jonathan, *b* 1966.

DAUGHTER LIVING *(By 2nd marriage)*

Fiona Elizabeth Fenella, *b* 1973.

BROTHER LIVING

Charles Frederick Eardley (Cudworth Manor, Newdigate, Surrey RH5 5BH), *b* 1934; *ed* Harrow, and Ch Ch, Oxford: *m* 1962, Lucy Carolyn, el da of Francis St G. Fisher, of Cragg, Cockermouth, Cumbria, and has issue living, Eleanor Jane, *b* 1963, — Victoria Lee, *b* 1965: *m* 1990, Maj Charles William Nepean Crewdson, 9th/12th Royal Lancers (Prince of Wales's), son of John Crewdson, of Winster House, Winster, Windermere, Westmorland, — Philippa Patricia Alice, *b* 1970.

SISTER LIVING

Jane Eve, *b* 1930: *m* 1963, David William Phillips, of The Old Rectory, Stedham, Midhurst, Sussex, and has issue living, Katherine Elizabeth, *b* 1966: *m* 1992, Leonard J. Wadstein, of Cannes, France.

COLLATERAL BRANCHES LIVING

Grandchildren of late Major Ernest Alfred SHAKERLEY-HOWELL (infra):—
Issue of late Col Peter Francis Shakerley, OBE, *b* 1906, *d* 1994: *m* 1943, Alison May, who *d* 1992, da of late Alexander Sands, of Aberdeen:—
(Geoffrey) Clive Howell (Tredudwell Manor, Lanteglos by Fowey, Cornwall) *b* 1935; *ed* Radley, and St Edmund Hall, Oxford (BA): *m* 1965, Rosanna Ruth, da of late Thomas P. Barneby, of The Hill, Duloe, Cornwall, and has issue living, Alastair Justin Charles, *b* 1972, — Alison Clare, *b* 1970. —— (Peter) Gavin David (Pont Quay Cottage, Lanteglos-by-Fowey, Cornwall), *b* 1950; *ed* Radley, and Durham Univ (BA); Maj IG: *m* 1976, Margaret Ann, da of Bernard Hammond, of Chichester, and has issue living, Charles Alaister, *b* 1981, — Antonia Elizabeth, *b* 1983. —— Angela Madeleine (PO Box 96, Strathalbyn, S Australia 5255, Aust), *b* 1938: *m* 1st, 1958 (*m diss* 1978), William Trevor Stephens; 2ndly, 1978, Harry Dudley Phillips, who *d* 1982, and has issue living (by 1st *m*) Richard Gwyn, *b* 1961, — John Angelo, *b* 1963, — David Paul, *b* 1965, — Teresa Madeleine, *b* 1959, — and an adopted son and da, Patrick Joseph, *b* 1962, — Sandie Patricia, *b* 1966, — (by 2nd *m*) Harry Sydney, *b* 1977. —— Dawn Michelle Alison, *b* 1942: *m* 1965, Peter Joseph Knight, of 20 Hilton Rd, Lynmore, Roturua, NZ, and has issue living, Timothy William Francis, *b* 1968, — Karen Francesca, *b* 1966, — Sarah Melody Foye, *b* 1969.

Issue of late Major Ernest Alfred Shakerley-Howell, 3rd son of 2nd baronet, *b* 1866, *d* 1934: *m* 1905, Rhoda Mary Louisa, who *d* 1934, el da of late Francis Buller Howell, JP, DL, of Ethy, Lostwithiel, Cornwall (Heywood, Bt, colls):—
Denise Marian, *b* 1907: *m* 1935, James Leslie Byrne Perceval, who *d* 1945, and has had issue, Francis James (146 Matthew Flinders Dr, Cooee Bay, Rockhampton 4073, Aust), *b* 1937; *ed* James Cook Univ, N Queensland; Capt Australian Army (ret 1984); served in Vietnam 1971-72: *m* 1st, 1960 (*m diss* 1980), Judith Ann, yr da of S. F. Spinks, of Langley Burrell, Chippenham; 2ndly, 1987, Patricia Almond, and has issue living (by 1st *m*), Christiaan *b* 1968, Antoinette Mary *b* 1962, Lucinda Eleanor *b* 1963, — Anthony Ernest (7 Waverley Rd, St Albans, Herts), *b* 1938; *ed* Lincoln Coll, Oxford (BA): *m* 1965 (*m diss* 1981), Jennifer, el da of Charles Mason, of Drakes Court, Fishers Pond, Eastleigh, Hants, and has issue living, Jane Lucinda *b* 1966, Katherine *b* 1969, — John Adrian, *b* 1945, *d* 1987, — Sara Mary, *b* 1942: *m* 1982, Robert Edward Nicolas Baker, Bar-at-law, of Lucehayne, Widworthy, Honiton, Devon EX14 9JS. *Residence* – 7 Waverley Rd, St Albans, Herts. —— Kathleen Dorothy, *b* 1914: *m* 1942, Robert Arnold Hall, who *d* 1962, and has issue living, Peter Arnold (Maple Tree House, Finch Lane, Beaconsfield, Bucks), *b* 1943; *ed* Harrow; Solicitor 1969: *m* 1971, Gillian Mary Stuart, only da of John Clark, of Gillan Cove House, Gillan, Manaccan, Cornwall, and has issue living, Nicholas Robert Stuart Arnold *b* 1974, Camilla Jane Kathleen *b* 1976, Venetia Juliet Antonia *b* 1981, — Jeremy Arnold (16 Egerton Rd, Wallingford, Oxon), *b* 1949: *m* 1971 (*m diss* 1989), Julia Rosa, only child of Frank Alexander, of 12 Petworth Court, Reading, Berks, and has issue living, Laurence Alexander *b* 1977, Charlotte Louise *b* 1979, — Juliet Rosalind (Flat 6, 30 Church Lane, Merton Park, SW19 3HQ), *b* 1946: *m* 1971 (*m diss* 1987), Christopher Charles Perkins, and has issue living, Daniel Robert *b* 1977, Esther Catherine *b* 1979. *Residence* – 14 Hill Lands, Wargrave, Berks.

SHAKESPEARE (UK) 1942, of Lakenham, City of Norwich

Sir WILLIAM GEOFFREY SHAKESPEARE, 2nd *Baronet*; *b* 12 Oct 1927; *s* his father, *Sir* GEOFFREY HITHERSAY, 1980; *ed* Radley, Clare Coll, Camb (MA, MB and B Chir) and St George's Hosp; Diploma in Child Health; Hospital Practitioner, Manor House Hosp, Aylesbury, since 1972; Snowdon Working Party (Integration of Handicapped) 1974-76; Vice-Pres Nat PHAB 1977 and Vice Pres RGA since 1982; Trustee of International Globe Centre since 1991: *m* 1964, Susan Mary, da of late A. Douglas Raffel, of Colombo, Ceylon, and has issue.

Arms – Or, on a bend between in chief a portcullis and in base an anchor sable, a spear of the field. **Crest** – In front of a portcullis sable an eagle rising, grasping with the dexter claw a spear or, barbed argent.
Residence – Manor Cottage, Stoke Mandeville, Bucks. *Clubs* – MCC and Leander.

SONS LIVING

THOMAS WILLIAM, *b* 11 May 1966; *ed* Radley, and Pembroke Coll, Camb (BA 1987, MA, MPhil 1991), Lecturer in Sociology, Sunderland Univ. —— James Douglas Geoffrey, *b* 1971; *ed* Radley, and Fitzwilliam Coll, Camb (BA 1993).

WIDOW LIVING OF FIRST BARONET

ELIZABETH (*Elizabeth, Lady Shakespeare*) (Flat 6, Great Ash, Lubbock Road, Chislehurst, Kent BR7 5JZ), da of late Brig-Gen Robert William Hare, CMG, DSO, DL (*see* E Listowel, colls); Section Offr WAAF 1940-45 (despatches, Bronze Star of USA); Freeman of City of London 1974: *m* 1952, as his 2nd wife, Rt Hon Sir Geoffrey Hithersay Shakespeare, 1st Bt, who *d* 1980.

The 1st baronet, Rt Hon Sir Geoffrey Hithersay Shakespeare, PC, sat as MP for Wellingborough (*L*) 1922-23, and Norwich 1929-45; also Parliamentary and Financial Sec to Admiralty 1937-40, Parliamentary Sec to Dept of Overseas Trade April-May 1940, and Under-Sec of State for Dominion Affairs and Chm of Children's Overseas Reception Board May 1940 - March 1942.

SHARP (UK) 1920, of Heckmondwike, West Riding, co York

I strive till I overcome

Sir MILTON REGINALD SHARP, 3rd *Baronet*; *b* 21 Nov 1909; *s* his father, *Sir* MILTON, 1941; *ed* Shrewsbury, and Trin Hall, Camb; is Major RA: *m* 1st, 1935, Dorothy Mary, yr da of Bernard R. McCarrick, of Kilglass House, Ballina, Ireland; 2ndly, 1951, Marie-Louise de Vignon, of Paris.

Arms – Azure, on a fesse engrailed argent between two plates, a torteaux between two pheons gules. **Crest** – In front of a pheon sable, an eagle's head erased azure, charged with a cross-crosslet or.
Address – c/o Messrs Redfearns, Midland Bank Chambers, Heckmondwike, Yorks.

COLLATERAL BRANCHES LIVING

Issue of late Charles George Gordon Sharp, 2nd son of 1st baronet, *b* 1885, *d* 1961: *m* 19—, —, da of —, of —:—
Elizabeth, *b* 19—.

Issue of late Reginald Sharp, 3rd son of 1st baronet, *b* 1988, *d* 1969: *m* 1st, 19— (*m diss* 19—), Janet Hilda, da of — Clapham; 2ndly, 1933, Mrs Doris Eve Faulder, who *d* 1958, da of — Heath; 3rdly 19—, Marguerite Louise Eugénie (Le Jardinet, Mont Row, St Peter Port, Guernsey, CI), da of — Ondoux, of Cagnicourt, France:—
(By 2nd *m*) SAMUEL CHRISTOPHER REGINALD (2231 Bancroft Place, NW, Washington, DC 20008, USA), *b* 25 April 1936; *ed* Rugby: *m* 1st, 1958 (*m diss* 1967), Sheila A—, da of — Moodie; 2ndly, 1969, Anna M— P—, da of — Rossi, of Rome. —— Caroline Eve, *b* 1944. —— Rosemary Anne, *b* 1946.

Issue of late Herbert Sharp, 4th son of 1st baronet, *b* 189, *d* 1952: *m* 19—, —, da of —:—
John Herbert, *b* 1920; late of BBC.

Issue of late Harold (Jack) Sharp, 6th son of 1st baronet, *b* 1895, *d* 1965: *m* 19—, —, da of —Lister:—
Jack (West Bank, Burley Rd, Menston, York), *b* 1932. —— Barbara Elizabeth, *b* 1931.
Sir Milton Sheridan Sharp, 1st Bt, was Chm Bradford Dyers Asso Ltd.

SHARP (UK) 1922, of Warden Court, Maidstone, Kent

Sir ADRIAN SHARP, 4th *Baronet*; *b* 17 Sept 1951; *s* his father, *Sir* EDWARD HERBERT, 1985; *ed* Boxhill Sch, and Nat Business Coll, Cape Town; Exec Mgr Toyota Motor Co: *m* 1st, 1976 (*m diss* 1986), Hazel Patricia, only da of James Trevor Wallace, of Box 2574, Pietersburg, S Africa, and formerly wife of William Ian Barrett Bothwell; 2ndly, 1994, Denise, only da of Percy Edward Roberts, of Ironbridge, Shropshire.

Arms – Argent, on a fesse indented between two falcons' heads erased sable, three pheons or. **Crest** – Upon a mount vert a falcon rising proper, belled and resting the dexter claw upon a pheon or.
Addresses – PO Box 1485, Hillcrest 3650, S Africa; 31 Hamble Court, Broom Park, Teddington TW11 9RW.

Victory in truth

BROTHER LIVING

OWEN, *b* 19 Sept 1956; *ed* Waterford, Swaziland, and Durham Univ: *m* 1980, Caroline, da of late Jerrard Collings Van Beuge, of Durban, Natal, S Africa, and has issue living, Declan, *b* 21 July 1980, — Lyndall, *b* 1983. *Residence* – Ballito, Natal, S Africa.

SISTER LIVING

Terry, *b* 1950: *m* 1969, Ian Wilson, of La Lucia, Durban, Natal, S Africa, son of Ennis Wilson, of Ashtead, Surrey, and has issue living, Karen, *b* 1969, — Tracey, *b* 1971, — Lee, *b* 1972.

COLLATERAL BRANCH LIVING

Issue of late Wilfred James Sharp, 2nd son of 1st baronet, *b* 1880, *d* 1945: *m* 1909, Ada Frances, who *d* 1936, da of George Meek, of Beckenham:—
Edward Harold Wilfred, *b* 1910; Past Chm of Edward Sharp & Sons Ltd, Manufacturing Confectioners. *Residence* – Brymere, Norton Rd, Chart Sutton, Maidstone, Kent. —— John Rayner Edgar (The Old Mill, Sutton Valence, Maidstone), *b* 1917; *ed* Malvern, and Harvard Business Sch; Past Chm of Edward Sharp & Sons Ltd, Manufacturing Confectioners.
The 1st baronet, Sir Edward, was Founder and Chm of Edward Sharp & Sons Ltd, manufacturing confectioners of Maidstone.

SHAW (UK) 1821, of Bushy Park, Dublin

Sir ROBERT SHAW, 7th *Baronet*; *b* 31 Jan 1925; *s* his father, *Lt-Col Sir* ROBERT DE VERE, MC, 1969; *ed* Harrow, and Oklahoma (BS) and Missouri (MS) Univs; MEIC and Professional Engineer (Alberta); Lt RN (ret); 1939-45 War in NW Europe, and W Pacific: *m* 1954, Jocelyn Mary, da of late Andrew McGuffie, of Mbabane, Swaziland, and has issue.

Arms – Or, on a chevron engrailed sable, between three eagles displayed of the second, as many trefoils slipped of the first. **Crest** – A hart's head couped sable, transfixed through the neck with an arrow or, feathered argent.
Residence – 234 40th Av, Calgary, Alberta, Canada. *Club* – Alberta United Services Institute (Calgary).

DAUGHTERS LIVING

Grania, *b* 1955. —— Reinet, *b* 1960.

COLLATERAL BRANCHES LIVING

Te ipsum nosce
Know thyself

Issue of late Capt John Frederick de Vere Shaw, Kenya Regt, yr son of 6th baronet, *b* 1930, *d* 1960: *m* 1955, Penelope Ann, who *m* 2ndly, 1970, Hougham Robert Mills (PO Box 628, Umtentweni, 4235 Natal, S Africa), da of Maj Denis William Powlett Milbank (*see* Milbank, Bt):—
CHARLES DE VERE (Pigeon Farmhouse, Greenham, Newbury, Berks RG14 7SP), *b* 1 March 1957; *ed* Michaelhouse, S Africa; Maj 5th R Inniskilling Drag Gds 1975-87; businessman: *m* 1985, Sonia, elder da of Thomas Geoffrey Eden, of Dean Cottage, 23 The Street, Wrecclesham, nr Farnham, Surrey, and has issue living, Robert Jonathan de Vere, *b* 7 Aug 1988, — Alexandra Frances, *b* 1986. —— Jane Frances, *b* 1958. —— Ann Vivian, *b* 1960.

Issue of late Lieut-Col Frederick Charleton Shaw, OBE, 2nd son of 5th baronet, *b* 1895, *d* (on active service in Germany) 1945: *m* 1922, Angela (SEWALL), who *d* 1978, da of late Ricardo de Acosta:—
Mercedes Eile, *b* 1926: *m* 1956, Capt Miles Matthew Lee Hudson, 12th R Lancers, of The Priors Farm, Mattingly Green, Basingstoke, and has issue living, Mark John Frederick, *b* 1957, — Peter Charles, *b* 1960, — Richard Miles, *b* 1966, — Veronica Mary, *b* 1958.

Granddaughter of late Maj-Gen George Shaw, CB, 2nd son of 3rd baronet:—
Issue of late Frederick Shaw, *b* 1850, *d* 1928: *m* 1873, Ella Jane, da of William Willis, of USA:—

Cora Desfontaines: *m* 1909, Charles Abner Howard, LLD. *Residence* –

Grandson of late Lt-Col Wilkinson Jocelyn Shaw, 5th son of 3rd baronet:—
Issue of late Major Jocelyn Frederick de Fonblanque Shaw, *b* 1874, *d* 1936: *m* 1921, May Alberta, who *d* 1930, da of late Robert Cecil Kenward:—
Jocelyn Frederick Basil, *b* 1923; *ed* Wellington, King's Coll, London, and Miami Univ (PhD); Consulting Engineer: *m* 1964 (*m diss* 1971), Carolyn Ann, da of late Samuel Bexton Guynes, of Waco, Texas, and has issue living, Jocelyn Robert Guynes, *b* 1965, — John Frederick Darin, *b* 1967, — Edward Henry David, *b* 1969.

Granddaughter of late Charles Shaw, QC, 5th son of 1st baronet:—
Issue of late William Shaw, *b* 1857, *d* 1939: *m* 1889, Roxanna Massie, da of James Henry Bowles:—
Emily Newell, *b* 1902: *m* 1921, Charles Franklin Jenness, and has issue living, Charles Franklin, *b* 1924, — Stuart Barton, *b* 1928, — Barbara Claire, *b* 1932. *Residence* – 5621 Randall Avenue, Richmond, Virginia, USA.
The 1st baronet, Sir Robert, sat in the Irish Parliament for New Ross, and for Dublin in the Imperial Parliament 1804-26; the 3rd baronet, who was Recorder of Dublin 1828-76, and a PC of Ireland, sat as MP for Dublin (*C*) 1830-32, and for University of Dublin 1832-48.

SHAW (UK) 1908, of Wolverhampton, co Stafford (Extinct 1942)

Sir (Theodore Frederick) Charles Edward Shaw, 1st and last *Baronet*.

DAUGHTER LIVING OF FIRST BARONET

Vera Stafford, *b* 1901: *m* 1922, Charles Bradshaw Shard, formerly Lieut 14th Hussars, and has issue living, Charles William George, *b* 1927, — Johane Dawson, *b* 1925.

BEST-SHAW (E) 1665, of Eltham, Kent

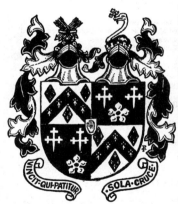

Sir John Michael Robert Best-Shaw, 10th *Baronet*, *b* 28 Sept 1924; *s* his father, *Com Sir* John James Kenward, RN, 1984; *ed* Lancing, Hertford Coll, Oxford (BA 1950, MA 1954), and Lond Univ (Cert of Ed); formerly Capt Queen's Own R West Kent Regt; R Federation of Malaya Police Force 1950-58; WW II 1942-45 (three medals); Church work 1959-71, teacher 1972-82: *m* 1960, Jane Gordon, 2nd da of Alexander Gordon Guthrie, of Hampton Court House, Farningham, Kent, and has issue.

Arms – Quarterly, 1st and 4th argent, a chevron between three fusils ermines, *Shaw*; 2nd and 3rd sable, a cinquefoil pierced, and in chief two cross-crosslets fitchée or, *Best*. Crests – 1st, six arrows interlaced, saltirewise or, tied together with belt gules, the buckle and pendant or; 2nd, issuing out of a mural crown or, a demi-ostrich argent holding in the beak a cross-crosslet fitchée or.
Residence – The Stone House, Boxley, Maidstone, Kent ME14 3DJ. *Club* – R Commonwealth Soc.

SONS LIVING

Thomas Joshua, *b* 7 March 1965; *ed* Maidstone Gram Sch, and Reading Univ (BSc 1987); Surveyor: *m* 1992, Emily Susan, da of Vivian Rubin, of Wateringbury, Kent. —— Samuel Stevenson, *b* 1971; *ed* Maidstone Gram Sch, and Exeter Coll, Oxford (BA 1992); teacher.

DAUGHTER LIVING

Lucy Ann, *b* 1961: *m* 1985 (*m diss* 1989), Terence Wentworth-Wood, and has issue living, Alexander, *b* 1985, — Christina Lily, *b* 1987.

BROTHERS LIVING

Charles John Hughes (Cornerfield House, The Hill, Charing, Ashford, Kent TN27 0LU), *b* 1928: *m* 1971, Carol Mary, 2nd da of late Joseph Martin Drew, and has issue living, Helen Mary Elizabeth, *b* 1972. —— Stephen Bosanquet (Boxley Abbey, Maidstone, Kent), *b* 1935; *ed* Ashford Sch, and Durham Univ: *m* 1964, Elizabeth Annette Freda, yst da of late Gerald Baldwin Hayward, MBE, of Athens, and has issue living, James Robert Hawley, *b* 1965: *m* 1992, Charlotte Louise, 2nd da of Nigel Ashley, of Mijas, Spain, — Hugh Edward Gerald, *b* 1975, — Louisa Margaret Aylmer *b* 1967: *m* 1988, Andrew Charles Robert Beale, son of Robert Beale, of Wellington Sq, SW3, and has issue living, Freddie James Robert *b* 1993, Roseanna Mary Elizabeth *b* 1991.

SISTERS LIVING

Mary Elisabeth Helen (Jonstone West, Egerton, Ashford, Kent TN27 9DR), *b* 1922; a JP of Kent: *m* 1st, 1943, Patrick Henry Coates, late Capt RA, who *d* 1949; 2ndly, 1968, John Melliar Adams-Beck, who *d* 1979, and has issue living, (by 1st *m*) David Carlyon (Mark's Farmhouse, Bramshaw, Lyndhurst, Hants), *b* 1944; FRICS: *m* 1970, Lavinia Jane, da of Alan O'Connor-Fenton, and has issue living, Emma Mary *b* 1973, Alice Julia *b* 1975, Georgina Ruth *b* 1980, — Simon Patrick (Rectory Farm, Raddington, Taunton, Som), *b* 1948; JP Som: *m* 1979, Katherine Jane, 2nd da of Maj Richard Hodgkinson Jessop, IA (ret), and has issue living, Thomas George Carlyon *b* 1981, Nicholas Henry Jessop *b* 1983. —— Julia Aylmer (Boxley Abbey, Maidstone, Kent), *b* 1923; 1939-45 War in WRNS. —— Hermione Theodora (Boxley Abbey, Maidstone, Kent), *b* 1926. —— Martha Mary (Boxley Abbey, Maidstone, Kent), *b* 1934.

COLLATERAL BRANCHES LIVING

Grandchildren of late Rev Robert John Shaw, son of late Rev Robert William Shaw, 5th son of 5th baronet:—

Issue of late Lewis Hugh de Visme Shaw, *b* 1865, *d* 1931: *m* 1901, Edith Mary, who *d* 1929, da of late Capt John Smyth Nelson, S Staffordshire Regt:—

Horatia Edith de Visme (Nazareth House, Queen Wilhelmina AV, Waterkloof, Pretoria 0002, S Africa), *b* 1902.

Issue of late Henry Augustus Gregory Shaw, *b* 1875, *d* 1954: *m* 1925, Eileen, who *d* 1973, el da of Charles William Howard:—

John Gregory Monson de Visme (22 Brunswick Terrace, Hove, Sussex), *b* 1930: *m* 1st, 1959 (*m diss* 1972), Helene Maud, da of Cyril Ernest Kerslake Baker, of co Down; 2ndly, 1976, Joan Phyllis, elder da of late Alfred Frank Elphick. —— Robert Henry Barnardiston de Visme (9 Cranswick Rd, Willowild, Sandton, Transvaal, S Africa), *b* 1932: *m* 1961, Valerie Ann, only da of B. R. Lobb, of Johannesburg and London, and has issue living, Philip Gregory de Visme, *b* 1970, —— Christine Ann de Visme, *b* 1965: *m* 1991, Mark John Fraser-Valentine, and has issue living, Katelyn Ann *b* 1991, Emily Jo *b* 1993. —— Eileen Ann de Visme, *b* 1928: *m* 1952, Alan Baker, and has issue living, Robert Alan, *b* 1960, —— James Paul, *b* 1963, —— Catherine Ann, *b* 1953.

Sir John, the 1st baronet, having rendered great service to Charles I during the Rebellion, and having advanced several sums of money to Charles II during that King's exile was after the Restoration appointed one of the Farmers of the Customs; Com Sir John James Kenward Best-Shaw, RN, High Sheriff of Kent, assumed by R Licence (1956) the additional surname of Best before that of Shaw and the Arms of Best quarterly with those of Shaw.

Shaw-Stewart, see Stewart.

SHEFFIELD (GB) 1755, of Normanby, Lincolnshire

Sir REGINALD ADRIAN BERKELEY SHEFFIELD, 8th *Baronet*, son of late Maj Edmund Charles Reginald Sheffield, 2nd son of 6th Bt; *s* his uncle, Sir ROBERT ARTHUR, 1977; *b* 9 May 1946; *ed* Eton; DL Humberside 1985: *m* 1st, 1969 (*m diss* 1975), Annabel Lucy Veronica, da of Timothy Angus Jones (*see* B Clifford of Chudleigh, colls, 1985, Edn); 2ndly, 1977, Victoria Penelope, da of late Ronald Clive Walker, DFC, and has issue living by 1st and 2nd *m*.

Arms – Argent, a chevron engrailed between two garbs in chief gules, and in base a sheaf of arrows proper, banded also gules. Crest – A boar's head erased at the neck or between two arrows points downwards proper.
Seat – Normanby Park, Normanby, Scunthorpe, S Humberside.

Blandly, but determinedly

SON LIVING *(By 2nd marriage)*

ROBERT CHARLES BERKELEY, *b* 1 Sept 1984.

DAUGHTERS LIVING *(By 1st marriage)*

Samantha Gwendoline, *b* 1971. —— Emily Julia, *b* 1973.

(By 2nd marriage)

Alice Daisy Victoria, *b* 1980. —— Lucy Mary, *b* 1981.

SISTERS LIVING

Serena Mary, *b* 1932. —— Fiona Mary (*Baroness Inchyra*), *b* 1939: *m* 1961, 2nd Baron Inchyra.

UNCLE LIVING *(son of 6th Baronet)*

John Vincent, CBE, *b* 1913; *ed* Eton, and Magdalene Coll, Camb (MA); is an OStJ; High Sheriff of Lincs 1944-45; CBE (civil) 1984: *m* 1st, 1936, Anne Margaret, who *d* 1969, da of Sir Lionel Lawson Faudel-Faudel-Phillips, 3rd Bt; 2ndly, 1971, France Mary Agnes, da of late Brig-Gen Goland Clarke, CMG, DSO and formerly wife of Major Ivor Crosthwaite, DSO, and has issue living (by 1st *m*), (John) Julian Lionel George (Laverstoke House, Whitchurch, Hants), *b* 1938; *ed* Eton, and Camb Univ: *m* 1961, Carolyn Alexandra, da of late Brig Sir Alexander Abel Smith, of Quenington Rectory, Cirencester, Glos (D Somerset, colls), and has issue living, John David *b* 1963, Simon Robert Alexander *b* 1964, Lionel Julian *b* 1969, Nicola Elizabeth Anne *b* 1973, — Jane Armyne, LVO (The Mill House, Sutton Courtenay, Abingdon, Oxford) *b* 1937; LVO 1993: *m* 1956 (*m diss* 1979), Jocelyn Edward Greville Stevens, CVO, and has had issue, Charles Greville Vincent *b* 1957: *m* 1980, Delphine S., da of John Dove, of Wadham House, Abbey Woods, Tromode, IoM (and has issue living, Nicholas John *b* 1988, Leonora Mary *b* 1985, Amanda Julia *b* 1992), Rupert Jocelyn Sebastian *b* 1964 *d* 1989, Pandora Anne *b* 1959: *m* 1983, Charles Hamar Delevingne, of Paddock House, Spencer Park, SW18, and has issue (*see* V Greenwood), Melinda Armyne *b* 1972, — Diana Anne, *b* 1942: *m* 1966, David Mark Norman, of Burkham House, Alton, Hants GU34 5RS, and has issue living, Jonathan Mark Ronald *b* 1972, Anna Helen *b* 1967, Isabella Julia *b* 1971, Davina Penelope *b* 1981, — Angela Margaret, *b* 1947: *m* 1966, (Anthony) Richard Brocas Burrows, of The Hall, Barham, Ipswich, and has issue living, (Edward) Brocas *b* 1975, Carey Jane *b* 1968, Joanna Molly Anne *b* 1969, (Angela) Petra *b* 1972. *Residence* – New Barn House, Laverstoke, Whitchurch, Hants.

MOTHER LIVING

Nancie Miriel Denise (Sutton Park, Sutton-in-the-Forest, York; 56 Montagu Sq, W1), da of late Edward Roland Soames, of 63 Chester Sq, SW, and widow of Lt-Cdr Glen Kidston (Astley, Bt); DL and High Sheriff Lincs: *m* 1931, Maj Edmund Charles Reginald Sheffield, 2nd son of 6th baronet, who *d* 1977.

COLLATERAL BRANCHES LIVING

Issue of late Maj George Berkeley Sheffield, 3rd son of 6th baronet, *b* 1910, *d* 1968: *m* 1st, 1935, Psyche Isabel Joan, who *d* 1945, da of late Capt Edward Altham, CB, RN; 2ndly, 1949, Hon Agnes Wilson McGowan, who *d* 1976, da of 1st Baron McGowan, and formerly wife of Maj Dermot Ralph Daly:—
(By 2nd *m*) Laura Diana, *b* 1949: *m* 1st, 1969 (*m diss* 1984), George William Pilkington; 2ndly, 1990, Paul Sednaoui, and has issue living (by 1st *m*), Harry George, *b* 1971, — Martha Mary, *b* 1972. *Residence* – Ramsden House, Ramsden, Oxon.
—— Davina Mary, *b* 1951: *m* 1981, Jonathan Derek Morley, yr son of late Brig Michael Frederick Morley, MBE, of Marlborough, Wilts, and has issue living, Thomas George Jonathan, *b* 1983, — William Frederick Duncan, *b* 1984, — Henry Quintus, *b* 1987. *Residence* – Westerdale, nr Whitby, N Yorks.

Grandsons of late Robert Stoney Oliphant-Sheffield (who assumed the additional surname of Oliphant 1901), son of Capt John Charles Sheffield, 3rd son of 4th baronet:—
Issue of late Edmund George Sheffield, *b* 1913; discontinued use of additional surname of Oliphant; *d* 1976: *m* 1939, Eva May, who *d* 1988, eldest da of Charles Blood Mulville, of Hampstead, NW3:—
John Robert (Broadfield, Southwaite, Carlisle, Cumbria CA4 0LR), *b* 1941; *ed* Harrow: *m* 1st, 1967 (*m diss* 1971), Valerie Jean, da of Capt George Ernest Towill, of St Aidans Rd, Carlisle; 2ndly, 1978, Elizabeth Helen, who *d* 1991, da of late James Turner, 3rdly, 1994, Jean Ann, da of late Charles Edward Lomas, and has issue living, (by 1st *m*) Edward John, *b* 1968, — Andrew George, *b* 1970. — Richard Charles, *b* 1944; *ed* Harrow: *m* 1st, 1966: *m* 1994, Alexandra C., da of Nicholas Butterworth, of St Leonards, Herts, (*m diss* 1972), Cheryl Mary Eleanor, only da of David Lloyd McNeil Williams, of Haling Park Rd, S Croydon, Surrey; 2ndly, 1972 (*m diss* 1982), Caroline Alison, da of Everett Ryshworth Unwin, of The Court House, Lelant, Cornwall; 3rdly, 1986, Mary Morrice, da of Charles Maclay Scott, of Ornum, 3 Camstradden Dr, Bearsden, Glasgow. — George Henry Oliphant, *b* 1948; *ed* Rannoch: *m* 1974, Christine Holdsworth.

Grandson of late Rev Frank Sheffield, 5th son of 4th baronet:—
Issue of late Rev Arthur Digby Sheffield, *b* 1897, *d* 1975: *m* 1932, Alice Katharine, who *d* 1982, da of late Donald Malcolm Scott, of 8 Chandos St, W1:—
Nigel Digby (Rookery Farm, Earl Soham, Woodbridge, Suffolk), *b* 1933; *ed* Eton and Ch Ch, Oxford (MA): *m* 1960, Helen Jane Ann Russell, el da of Lt Col Bernard Russell French, DSO, of Edgeworth, Glos, and has issue living, Timothy John Digby *b* 1966: *m* 1994, Alexandra C., da of Nicholas Butterworth, of St Leonards, Herts, — Ann Margot, *b* 1963, — Susan Margaret, *b* 1965.
The 1st baronet, Sir Charles Sheffield (originally Herbert), was an illegitimate son of John Sheffield 1st Duke of Normanby and Buckingham; he inherited the estates of his legitimate brother Edmond last Duke of Buckingham. The 6th baronet, Sir Berkeley Digby George, sat as MP for N Lindsey, or Brigg, Div of Lincolnshire (C) 1907-10 and 1922-9, and was High Sheriff of Lincolnshire 1905.

SHELLEY (E) 1611, of Michelgrove Sussex

As I find

COMME JE TROUVE

(*Sir*) John Richard Shelley, 11th *Baronet* (has established his claim but does not use the title), *b* 18 Jan 1943; *s* his grandfather, *Maj Sir* John Frederick, 1976; *ed* King's Sch, Bruton, Trin Coll, Camb (MA), (MB, BChir) and St Mary's Hosp, London Univ, DObstRCOG, MRCGP; Partner in Drs, Shelley, Doddington and Ayres, Medical Practitioners; Member Exeter Diocesan Synod 1976-79: *m* 1965, Clare, da of Claud Bicknell, OBE, ret law Commr, of Newcastle upon Tyne, and has issue.

Arms – Sable a fesse, engrailed, between three whelks or. **Crest** – A griffin's head erased, beaked argent, and ducally gorged or.
Residence – Shobrooke Park, Crediton, Devon EX17 1DG.

DAUGHTERS LIVING

Diana Elizabeth, *b* 1970: *m* 1993, John S. Moule, son of B. J. Moule, of Wellington, Shropshire. —— Helen Ruth, *b* 1972.

BROTHER LIVING

Thomas Henry, *b* 3 Feb 1945; *ed* King's Sch, Bruton, and Trin Coll, Camb (BA): *m* 1970 (*m diss* 1992), Katharine Mary Holton, and has issue living, Kirsten Rachel Irvine, *b* 1973, — Victoria Juliet, *b* 1974, — Benita Mary, *b* 1978.

UNCLE LIVING (*Son of 10th baronet*)

Philip Spencer (East Lodge, Shobrooke Park, Crediton, Devon EX17 1DG), *b* 1921; late FO RAF: *m* 1st, 1947 (*m diss* 1963), Pamela Grace, da of late Lt-Col Henry Nigel Kermack, RE; 2ndly, 1968 (*m diss* 1978), Elizabeth Philippa, da of Leonard George Edward Llewlyn, of Nairobi, and has issue living (by 1st *m*), Nigel Antony, *b* 1948: *m* 1972, Pamela Mary Inder, and has issue living, Alexandra Margaret *b* 1975, — Malcolm Frederick, *b* 1953: *m* 1974, Lynne Sharon Buckingham, — Marian Pamela, *b* 1950, — (by 2nd *m*) Nora Elizabeth, *b* 1969, — Gillian Philippa, *b* 1971.

AUNTS LIVING (*Daughters of 10th baronet*)

Mary Nora (3 Meadow Close, Westgarth Gdns, Bury St Edmunds, Suffolk IP33 3LE), *b* 1913: *m* 1940, Maj Robin Paige, MC, TD, who *d* 1969, and has issue living, Michael Robert (Ings Farm, Belchford, Horncastle, Lincs), *b* 1941: *m* 1966, Patricia Margaret Appleby, and has issue living, Nicholas Robert *b* 1972, Catherine Mary *b* 1968, Sarah Jane *b* 1970, — Timothy John (twin), *b* 1941, — Christopher David, TD (2 Mallard Close, Thorpe Hesley, Rotherham, S Yorks S61 2TW), *b* 1945; Maj RE (V): *m* 1970, Cynthia Ann Ison, and has issue living, David Hugh *b* 1976, Joanne Lesley *b* 1982. —— Frances Elizabeth, *b* 1914: *m* 1938, Rev Henry John Allen Rusbridger, who *d* 1985, of St Crispins, Brampford Speke, Exeter, and has issue living, Peter Henry James, *b* 1941: *m* 1969, Geraldine Johnston, and has issue living, Charles Peter James *b* 1971, Lucy Victoria *b* 1973, — Elizabeth Jean, *b* 1939: *m* 1963, Rev Preb Michael Bowles, of Stanmore Rectory, Middx, and has issue living,

Jeremy Michael *b* 1966, Catherine Elizabeth *b* 1964, Jennifer Susan *b* 1974, — Margaret Anne, *b* (twin) 1941: *m* 1st, 1965 (*m diss* 1976), Arthur William Frederick Sacheverel Pulford; 2ndly, 1979, Kenneth E. R. Hawkins, and has issue living (by 1st *m*), Claire *b* 1966. —— Gillian Hester (Southern Wood, Peter Tavy, Devon), *b* 1918: *m* 1949, Capt Michael William Howard, MC, Devonshire Regt, who *d* 1994 (*see* E Carlisle, colls).

MOTHER LIVING

Dorothy Irvine (Westacott, Shobrooke, Crediton, Devon), el da of late Arthur Irvine Ingram, MA, solicitor, of Bath: *m* 1940, John Shelley, who *d* 1974, el son of 10th baronet.

COLLATERAL BRANCHES LIVING

Issue of late Vice-Adm Richard BENYON, CB, CBE (assumed by deed poll 1964, and by Roy Licence 1967 (for himself and el son) the surname of Benyon in lieu of Shelley), yr son of 9th baronet; *b* 1892; *d* 1968: *m* 1929, Eve Alice (Englefield House, Reading, Berks RG7 8EL), da of late Rt Rev Lord William Rupert Ernest Cecil, DD, 65th Lord Bishop of Exeter (*see* M Salisbury, colls):—

William Richard BENYON (Englefield House, Reading), *b* 1930; Lt RN (Reg Reserve); MP for Buckingham (C) 1970-83, and Milton Keynes (C) 1983-92: *m* 1957, Elizabeth Ann, yr da of late Vice-Adm Ronald Hamilton Curzon Hallifax, CB, CBE (*see* Hughes, Bt, *cr* 1773, 1972-73 Edn), and has issue living, Richard Henry Ronald (The Lambdens, Beenham, Reading, Berks RG7 5LD), *b* 1960: *m* 1988, Emma Helen, yr da of Capt Anthony Henry Heber Villiers (*see* E Clarendon, colls), and has issue living, Harry Charles William *b* 1990, Thomas Anthony Edward *b* 1992, Frederick Richard *b* 1994, — Edward William (Hillcrest Farm, Soke Rd, Silchester, nr Reading, Berks), *b* 1962: *m* 1989, Katy E. M., yr da of Robin Crofts, of Nethercote House, Flecknoe, Warwicks, and has issue living, Charles *b* 1991, Victoria *b* 1993, — Catherine Rose Ingrid, *b* 1958: *m* 1984, Peter David Ian Haig, son of Maj Andrew Haig, of Norfolk, and has issue living, William Robin *b* 1988, Georgiana Elizabeth *b* 1989, Rachel Louisa *b* 1992, — Mary Elizabeth, *b* 1965: *m* 1990, Capt Thomas R. P. Riall, 15th/19th The King's Royal Hussars, son of Maj Patrick Riall, of Knockbawn, Kilmacanogue, co Wicklow, and has issue living, Phineas Patrick *b* 1993, Rosanna Eleanor *b* 1992, — Susannah Eve, *b* 1969. —— James Edward SHELLEY (Mays Farm House, Ramsdell, Hants), *b* 1932: *m* 1956, Judith, da of George Grubb, and has issue living, Timothy James, *b* 1966: *m* 1993, Emma Jane, eldest da of David Dinkeldein, of Whiteway Farmhouse, nr Newbury, — Philip John, *b* (twin) 1966: *m* 1994, Joanne Marie, da of Stewart England, of Ravenshead, Nottingham, — Alison Jane, *b* 1959: *m* 1990 Anthony Clavane, son of Emile Clavane, of Leeds, and has issue living, Rosa *b* 1992, — Penelope Sarah, *b* 1960. —— Andrew Thomas Rupert SHELLEY (Oakfield, Cox Green, Rudgwick, Horsham, W Sussex RH12 3DD), *b* 1933; late Maj R Green Jackets: *m* 1971, Joanna M., only da of Adm Sir (Randolph Stewart) Gresham Nicholson, KBE, CB, DSO, DSC, and has issue living, Nicholas Charles, *b* 1978, — Sarah Lucy, *b* 1974. —— David Robert SHELLEY (Church End Cottage, Kensworth, Dunstable, Beds LU6 3RA), *b* 1937: *m* 1971, Elisabeth Rhoda, yr da of late Gilbert Graham Balfour (*see* Halsey, Bt, 1990 Edn), and has issue living, Peter David, *b* 1972, — Jonathan Rupert, *b* 1974.

Grandchildren of late Spencer Shelley (*b* 1843), elder son of late Spencer Shelley (*b* 1813), 4th son of 6th baronet:—
Issue of late Spencer Shelley, *b* 1878, *d* 1941: *m* 1917, Gladys, who *d* 1947, da of E. Mulligan, of Sydney, NS Wales:—

Spencer, *b* 1920; sometime Lieut RNVR; a JP for Glos: *m* 1946, Maureen, da of Commodore Trevor Lewis Owen, OBE, RD, and has issue living, Elizabeth Grey, *b* 1948: *m* 1976, Michael D. R. Oakley, of Wyngates Farm, Mayhill, Longhope, Glos, and has issue living, James Spencer *b* 1981, Laura Elizabeth *b* 1978, — (Anna) Frances, *b* 1950: *m* 1983, Edward Osborne Cavendish, and has issue (*see* D Devonshire, colls), — Katherine Jane, *b* 1954: *m* 1981, Roger David Keyworth, of Tuatea wa, Kennedy Bay Rd, Coromandel, NZ, and has issue living, Billy Finn Shelley *b* 1988, Moana Grace Shelley *b* 1996. *Residence* – Tigh-na-Sithe, Comrie, Perthshire. —— Charles Francis, *b* 1925, sometime Sub-Lt RNVR: *m* 1951, Elizabeth Jane, who *d* 1992, only child of late Brig Sir Francis Smith Reid, CBE, and has issue living, Sarah Jane, *b* 1952, — Julia Frances, *b* 1954: *m* 1980, Charles Brereton Frater, and has issue living, George Kenneth Charles *b* 1987, Rebecca Jane *b* 1984, — Caroline Ruth, *b* 1957. *Residence* – Little Conigree, Mitcheldean, Glos. —— Frederick Norman (2 Ferguson Street, Alfred Cove, 6154, Perth, Western Australia), *b* (twin) 1925; CEng; MIMechE: *m* 1958, Ruth Mary, only da of late Rowland Colley Skitt, of Barakat, Sudan, and has issue living, Stephen Spencer (11 Peacock St, Burwood, Vic, Australia), *b* 1959: *m* 1990, Heidi Kaupert, and has issue living, James Spencer *b* 1991, Thomas Joseph *b* 1993, — Philip Norman, *b* 1960: *m* 1992, Anna Uszko, of Kew, Melbourne, Vic, — William Rowland, *b* 1964, — Anne Lucy, *b* 1963: *m* 1988, Peter James Franklin, of Perth, W Australia. —— Cynthia Kathleen, *b* 1921, sometime in WRNS: *m* 1943, Michael Richard Lloyd Hayes, DL, KStJ, CEng, FIMechE, FRINA, FIMarE, High Sheriff, Pembs, and has issue living, Sylvia Josephine Ruth (*Hon Mrs G. Andrew Lawson Johnston*), *b* 1945: *m* 1968, Hon George Andrew Lawson Johnston, of Inverernan House, Strathdon, Aberdeenshire AB3 87A (*see* B Luke), — Frances Patricia Jane, *b* 1948: *m* 1971, Julian Dyson Seddon, of The Old Vicarage, 26 Wandle Rd, Wandsworth, SW17, — Ann Wendy Felicity, *b* 1950: *m* 1972, Peter A. Cartwright, of Harfield Farm House, Curdridge, Botley, Hants, and has issue living, Thomas Aubrey *b* 1975, William Cloudesley *b* 1989, Emma Juliet *b* 1973. *Residence* – Four Ashes, Cosheston, Pembroke Dock, Dyfed, SA72 4TX.

Thomas Shelley was Lord of the Manor of Shelley, Kent, *temp* Edward I. This family can prove seven royal descents in unbroken legitimate lines from Henry III and Edward I. Michelgrove, the seat of the Shelley family for more than 300 years, was sold at the end of the 18th century, to the Duke of Norfolk, whose family later demolished it. Sir John Shelley, 9th Bt, was High Sheriff of Devon 1895. Maj Sir John Frederick Shelley, 10th Bt, was High Sheriff of Devon 1938.

SHEPPERSON (UK) 1945, of Upwood, Co Huntingdon (Extinct 1949)

Sir ERNEST WHITTOME SHEPPERSON, 1st and last *Baronet*.

DAUGHTERS LIVING OF FIRST BARONET

Rosemary Jane, *b* 1921; *ed* Newnham Coll, Camb (BA 1943): *m* 1947, Eric Arthur North Whitehead, of Merrydown Cottage, Stockland, Honiton, Devon, and has issue living, Simon Ambrose North, *b* 1952, — Margaret Loveday, *b* 1948. —— Mary Elizabeth, *b* 1927: *m* 1st, 1945, Ian Loudon Spofforth (MA Oxon), late Fl Lt RAF, who *d* 1964; 2ndly, 1968, Brig Henry Ralph Orton, of Ashbourne, Thornton Av, Warsash, Southampton, SO3 9FJ, and has issue living (by 1st *m*), Timothy Markham Shepperson, *b* 1947, — Sally Jane, *b* 1950, — Belinda Anne, *b* 1952, — Virginia Elizabeth, *b* 1956.

Sherston-Baker, see Baker.

SHIFFNER (UK) 1818, of Coombe, Sussex

Sir HENRY DAVID SHIFFNER, 8th *Baronet*; *b* 2 Feb 1930; *s* his father, *Major Sir* HENRY BURROWS, OBE, 1941; *ed* Rugby, and Trin Hall, Camb: *m* 1st, 1951 (*m diss* 1956), Dorothy, da of W. G. Jackson, of Coventry; 2ndly, 1957 (*m diss* 1970), Beryl, da of George Milburn, of Saltdean, Sussex; 3rdly, 1971, Joaquina Ramos Lopez, of Madrid, Spain, and has issue by 1st and 2nd *m*.

𝕬rms – Azure, a bend sinister, in chief two estoiles in like bend or; in base, the end and stock of an anchor gold, issuing from waves of the sea proper. 𝕮rest – An estoile or, between the rays six annulets azure.

DAUGHTERS LIVING *(By 1st marriage)*

Elizabeth Marilyn, *b* 1953. —— (By 2nd *m*) Linda Mary, *b* 1957.

WIDOW LIVING OF SIXTH BARONET

SYBIL HELEN (*Baroness Paget of Northampton*), yst da of late Sills Clifford Gibbons, of Scaynes Hill, Sussex: *m* 1st, 1918, Sir John Bridger Shiffner, 6th baronet, who was *ka* 1918; 2ndly, 1922 (*m diss* 1931), Victor Basil John Seely (later 4th Bt), who *d* 1980; 3rdly, 1931, Baron Paget of Northampton, QC (Life Baron), who *d* 1990.

COLLATERAL BRANCHES LIVING

Grandchildren of late George Bridger Shiffner, 2nd son of 4th baronet:—
Issue of late Capt George Edward Shiffner, *b* 1901, *d* 1956: *m* 1935, Kathleen Patricia, who *d* 1978, da of Lt-Col Sir Edward Boscawen Frederick, CVO, 9th Bt:—
GEORGE FREDERICK (14 Coggeshall Rd, Braintree, Essex CM7 6BY; Searles, Alderford St, Sible Hedingham, Essex), *b* 3 Aug 1936; *ed* Wellington: *m* 1961, Dorothea Helena Cynthia, da of late T. H. McLean, and has issue living, Michael George Edward, *b* 1963, — Penelope Ann Dorothy, *b* 1962. —— Susan Georgiana, *b* 1938: *m* 1st, 1963, Henry Pickup, who *d* 1975; 2ndly, 1975, Michael Scales, of Culverdown, Great Henny, Sudbury, Suffolk, and has issue living (by 2nd *m*), Timothy Michael Edward, *b* 1977.
Issue of late Capt John Scarlett Shiffner, RN, *b* 1910, *d* 1980: *m* 1940, Margaret Harriet (10 Malvern Court, Onslow Sq, SW7), da of George Tullis, of Strathenry, Leslie, Fife:—
John Robert (c/o Royal Bank of Scotland, Leslie, Fife), *b* 1941; BSc Lond CEng, FIMarE; Rear Adm RN: *m* 1969, Rosemary Anne Creyghton, da of Brig Alfred Tilly, CBE, DL, and has issue living, John Edward, *b* 1971, — Henry Charles Alexander, *b* 1975, — Caroline Mary Tilly, *b* 1973. —— Charles Tullis, *b* 1944; *ed* St Andrews Univ (MA): *m* 1978, Rosamund Mary, da of James London, of Woods Hill, W Chiltington, W Sussex, and has issue living, Robin John Landon, *b* 1982, — Katherine Landon, *b* 1979, — Elizabeth Margaret Mary, *b* 1981. —— Priscilla Mary Scarlett, *b* 1949.
The 6th baronet, Sir John Bridger Shiffner, Lieut Roy Sussex Regt, was *ka* 1918. The 7th baronet, Major Sir Henry Burrows Shiffner, OBE, RA, was *ka* 1941.

SHUCKBURGH (E) 1660, of Shuckburgh, Warwickshire

Sir RUPERT CHARLES GERALD SHUCKBURGH, 13th *Baronet*; *b* 12 Feb 1949; *s* his father, *Maj Sir* CHARLES GERALD STEWKLEY, JP, TD, 1988: *ed* Worksop Coll: *m* 1st, 1976 (*m diss* 1987), Judith, da of late William Gordon Mackaness, of Paddock Lodge, Everdon, Daventry; 2ndly, 1987, Margaret Ida, da of late William Evans, of Middleton, Derbys, and has issue by 1st *m*.

𝕬rms – Sable, a chevron between three mullets argent. 𝕮rest – A blackamoor couped at the waist proper, with a dart in his hand or.
Seat – Shuckburgh Hall, near Daventry NN11 6DT.

SONS LIVING *(By 1st marriage)*

JAMES RUPERT CHARLES, *b* 4 Jan 1978. —— Peter Gerald William, *b* 1982.

Haec manus ob patriam
This hand for my
country

SISTERS LIVING

Remony Charmian, *b* 1938: *m* 1st, 1963 (*m diss* 1978), Hugo Macdonald Price; 2ndly, 1983, Michael Taylor-Downes, and has issue living (by 1st *m*), Robin Macdonald, *b* 1970, — Justin Bryan, *b* 1973. *Residence* – The Cottage, Sherbourne, Warwick CV35 8AA. —— Amanda Maria, *b* 1946. *Residence* – The Gate House, White Colne, Colchester, Essex CO6 2PW.
This family takes its name from Shuckburgh in Warwickshire. Richard Shuckburgh, Esq, MP for the county in 1641, and father of the 1st baronet, armed all his tenants, and joined King Charles I at Edgehill, where he was knighted. After the battle of Edge Hill he retired and fortified himself on Shuckburgh Hill, where most of his tenantry were slain, and he himself was taken prisoner. After being confined in Kenilworth Castle for a considerable time, he purchased his liberty at a dear rate. His eldest son, John, was created a baronet by Charles II.

SIMEON (UK) 1815, of Grazeley, Berkshire

Neither rashly nor timidly

Sir John Edmund Barrington Simeon, 7th *Baronet*; *b* 1 March 1911; *s* his father, Sir John Walter Barrington, 1957; *ed* Eton, and Ch Ch, Oxford; Flight-Lieut (ret) RAF: *m* 1937, Anne Robina Mary, elder da of Hamilton Dean, and has issue.

Arms – Per fesse sable and or a pale counter-changed three trefoils slipped, two and one of the second, and three ermine spots one and two of the first. **Crest** – A fox passant-reguardant proper, in the mouth a trefoil slipped vert. **Supporters** – *Dexter*, a fox reguardant proper, in the mouth a trefoil slipped vert; *sinister*, a lion gules, ducally crowned or.
Residence – 987 Wavertree Rd, N Vancouver, BC V7R 1S6, Canada.

SON LIVING

Richard Edmund Barrington (20 Biggar Av, Toronto, Ontario, Canada), *b* 2 March 1943; *ed* St George's Sch, Vancouver, Univ of British Columbia (BA) and Yale (MA, PhD) Univ; Prof of Political Science and Law, Toronto Univ, subsequently Dir of Inst of Intergovernmental Relations 1976-83 and Dir of Sch of Public Admin since 1986-90; Vice-Chm Ontario Law Reform Commn since 1989: *m* 1st, 1966 (*m diss* 1989), Agnes Joan, only da of George Frederick Weld; 2ndly, 1993, Maryetta Cheney, and has issue living (by 1st *m*), Stephen George Barrington, *b* 29 Oct 1970, — Rachel Elizabeth, *b* 1973.

DAUGHTERS LIVING

Anne Emily Philippa, *b* 1938: *m* 1962, Nigel Leonard Harper Gow, of 6129 Highbury, Vancouver, BC, Canada, and has issue living, Ian Harper, *b* 1968, — Lisa Harper, *b* 1965. —— Sara Alexandra (Apt 2, 22268, 116th Ave, Maple Ridge, BC, Canada V2X 1Z5), *b* 1946: *m* 1967 (*m diss* 1994), Anthony John Williams, and has issue living, Derek John, *b* 1973, — Trevor Michael, *b* 1975, — Adria Elizabeth, *b* 1971.

COLLATERAL BRANCHES LIVING

Grandchildren of late Stephen Louis Simeon, 4th son of 3rd baronet:—
Issue of late Leonard Stephen Barrington Simeon, MC, *b* 1891, *d* 1978: *m* 1924, Ella Hazel Powys, who *d* 1980, da of late Col Powys Lane, IA, of Upper Ward, Bonchurch, I of Wight:—
Miles Powys Barrington (Daltes Farm, St Osyth, Clacton, Essex), *b* 1927: *m* 1956, Joan Mary, da of Laurence Frederick Underhay, of Clacton, Essex, and has issue living, Michael John Barrington, *b* 1957, — Robert Miles, *b* 1959: *m* 1988, Carol Ann Newcombe, and has had issue, John Robert *b* 1992, Laura Ann *b* and *d* 1988, Samantha Ann *b* 1989. —— Anne Primrose Louise (Gable End, Rickinghall, Suffolk), *b* 1925: *m* 1st, 1944 (*m diss* 1959), Louis Gustav Julian Strauss; 2ndly, 1959, Leonard Townsend, who *d* 1971; 3rdly, 1973, Gp Capt John Michael Skelton Adams, RAF (ret), CEng, FIEE, FIMechE, who *d* 1993, and has issue living (by 1st *m*), Linda Evelyn, *b* 1947: *m* 1974, Thomas Kennedy Nelson, and has issue living, Hamish Kennedy *b* 1975, Robin Simon *b* 1977, — Caroline Louise, *b* 1948: *m* 1974 (*m diss* 1981), Nicholas John de Jongh, — Diana Margaret, *b* 1955: *m* 1978 (*m diss* 1984), Peter Gilbert Marsland, and has issue living, Christopher Barrington *b* 1981.

Grandson of late Rev Geoffrey Barrington Simeon, 3rd son of Capt Charles Simeon, 75th Regt, 2nd son of 2nd baronet:—
Issue of late Geoffrey Nelthorpe Simeon, *b* 1888, *d* 1923: *m* 1919, Henrietta Mary Collingwood, who *d* 1989, da of late Rev W. Collingwood Carter, formerly V. of Shipton-under-Wychwood:—
Geoffrey John Barrington, *b* 1923; Lt-Cdr RN (ret); FRICS: *m* 1954, Elizabeth Frances Richenda, da of late Rev R. C. Rham, of Feock, Cornwall, and has issue living, Charles Richard Barrington, *b* 1958; *ed* Sherborne, — Sarah Richenda Barrington, *b* 1956, — Elizabeth Anne Barrington, *b* 1960: *m* 1987, Anthony George Harrison (11 Chilton Candover, Alresford, Hants SO24 9TX), son of late G. G. Harrison, of St Ives, Cornwall, and has issue living, George Geoffrey *b* 1988, Robert William *b* 1990. *Residence* – Maple House, Chilbolton, Stockbridge, Hants SO20 6BQ.

Granddaughter of late Lionel Barrington Simeon (*b* 1852), 4th son of Capt Charles Simeon (ante):—
Issue of late Charles John Simeon, *b* 1878, *d* 1946: *m* 1910, Elinor Yorke, who *d* 1940, da of Gen Charles King, of Milwaukee, USA:—
Elizabeth, *b* 1917: *m* 1948, Major Richard Guillemard Copleston, RE (ret). *Residence* – 34 Old Towne Rd, Cheshire, Connecticut 06410, USA.

Grandchildren of late Perceval Barrington Simeon, el son of Cornwall Simeon, 3rd son of 2nd baronet:—
Issue of late Cornwall Barrington Simeon, *b* 1889, *d* 1957: *m* 1st, 1928 (*m diss* 1947), Ellaline Margery Mary, who *d* 1966, da of late Arnold le Poer Power, of Clonmel, co Tipperary; 2ndly, 1947, Violet, MBE, who *d* 1979, only da of late Algernon Hodson, and widow of Lt-Col Neal William Douglas-Matheson, DSO, MC:—
(By 1st *m*) John Power Barrington, OBE (4 Cliff Rd, Dovercourt, Harwich, Essex CO12 3PP), *b* 1929; *ed* Beaumont Coll, and RMA Sandhurst; entered HM Dip Serv 1965, First Sec (Commercial) Colombo 1967, Bonn 1968-70, Port of Spain 1970-73 (sometime Acting High Commr), FCO 1973-75, Dep High Cmmr and Head of Post, Ibadan, Nigeria 1975-79, HM Consul Gen Berlin 1979-81 and Hamburg 1981-84 (ret); OBE (Civil) 1978: *m* 1st, 1951 (*m diss* 1955), Margareta Valborg Johanna, only da of late Erik Ahlstrom, of Norrmark, Finland; 2ndly, 1966, Norma, who *d* 1969, da of late Capt Norman Herbert Dopson; 3rdly, 1970, Carina Renate Elisabeth, da of late Michael Schüller, of Bonn, W Germany, and has issue living (by 2nd *m*), Charles John Barrington, *b* 1967; *ed* King's Sch, Canterbury. —— Ann Ella Mary, *b* 1931: *m* 1st, 1961 (*m diss* 1984), Bryan Reginald Baxter; 2ndly, 1984, Sqdn-Ldr Terence William Devey Smith, RAF (ret), of Méauduc, Beslé s. Vilaine, 44290, France, and has issue living, (by 1st *m*) Robert Bryan, *b* 1962: *m* 1988, Jacqueline, da of John Rupert Godfrey, of Monbulk, Vic, Australia, and has issue living, Jack Godfrey *b* 1989, — Timothy Reginald, *b* 1964; BA.

Granddaughter of late Cornwall Simeon, 3rd son of 2nd baronet:—
Issue of late Rev John Pole Simeon, *b* 1872, *d* 1951: *m* 1908, Dorothy, who *d* 1955, da of late Rev Sydney Benjamin Field, formerly V of Patcham:—
Joan Edith Barrington, *b* 1909: *m* 1st, 1938 (*m diss* 1945), Richard William Barnes Clarke; 2ndly, 1945, Wenzel Jaksch, who *d* 1966, and has issue living, (by 2nd *m*) George Barrington, *b* 1945: *m* 1974, Carmen Julia, da of Don Constantino Torres, of Colombia, and has issue living, David Wenzel *b* 1977, Sandra Mary *b* 1978, — Mary Dorothy Plantagenet, *b* 1947: *m* 1981, Uwe Grodd, son of Reinhold Grodd, of Stuttgart, and has issue living, Sebastian Wenzel *b* 1981. *Residence* – 62 Wiesbaden, Kohlheck, Wenzel-Jaksch St 32, Germany.

Grandchildren of late Edward Archibald Simeon, MRCS, LRCP, el son of Lt-Col Edward Simeon, 3rd son of Rear-Adm Charles Simeon, 3rd son of 1st baronet:—

Issue of late Vice-Adm Sir Charles Edward Barrington Simeon, KBE, CB, *b* 1889, *d* 1955: *m* 1918, Gladys, who *d* 1983, da of Benjamin Arkle, formerly of Spital, Cheshire:—

Hugh Michael (3 Westview Lane, S Norwark, Conn 06854, USA), *b* 1926; Cdr RN (ret): *m* 1966, Ilona Maria, da of Prof Dr Med Gustav Christian Schimert, of Munich, and has issue living, George Edward, *b* 1969, — John David, *b* 1971, — Diana Maria, *b* 1967. —— William Martin (Lot 49, Condor Drive, Nikenbah, 4655 Qld, Australia), *b* 1936; late Rifle Brig: *m* 1st, 1959 (*m diss* 1964), Doreen Mary Wren; 2ndly, 1971, Jane Naik, and has issue living (by 2nd *m*), Kathryn Mary Anne *b* 1972, Samantha Mervena *b* 1974. —— Joan Denise, *b* 1919: *m* 1947, Reginald James Pringle, MBE, late ICS, who *d* 1980, son of Sir James (Scott) Pringle, KCB, OBE, and has issue living, James Edward, *b* 1949; *ed* Camb Univ (MA, PhD); astronomer: *m* 1974, Alison May, da of Richard Leonard Sturge, of Saffron Walden, Essex, and has issue living, Edmund Richard James *b* 1980, Christopher Charles Theodore *b* 1983, — Reginald Denys, *b* 1951; *ed* Southampton Univ (BA); DPhil Oxon; FSA; historian and archaeologist, — Richard Charles, *b* 1954; *ed* York Univ (BA); MSc London Business Sch: *m* 1980, Jeanine Ghislaine, da of George Romarin, of Falisole, Belgium, — Anne Denise, *b* 1958: *m* 1986, Andrew Charles Ellis, only son of Charles Matthew Ellis, of Abbeywood, London. *Residence* – 10 Altwood Dr, Maidenhead, Berks. —— Marguerite Gladys, *b* 1922; sometime in WRNS: *m* 1946, Maj Peter Rainier Adams (ret), late RA, and Indian Army, of 3 Farmhill Rd, Waltham Abbey, Essex, EN9 1NE, and has issue living, John Rainier, *b* 1947, — Hugh Robert, *b* 1949, — Charles David, *b* 1951. —— Josephine Osyth, *b* 1932: *m* 1956, Lt-Cdr Thomas David Alexander Kennedy, RN (ret), MIMechE; CEng, and has issue living, Martin Charles, *b* 1958: *m* 1985, Suzanne Jayne, elder da of Ronald Charles Brown, of Ayr, Scotland, — Ian David, *b* 1965, — Fiona Osyth, *b* 1960: *m* 1st, 1984 (*m diss* 1988), Dominic James Shaw; 2ndly, 1989, Hugh Anstruther Rance, and has issue living (by 1st *m*), Katurah Osyth *b* 1987, (by 2nd *m*), Eleanor Yaiah Tara *b* 1990, Saskia Leah Channah *b* 1992. *Residence* – Hill House, Berecourt Rd, Pangbourne, Berks.

Grandson of late Lt-Col Edward Simeon, son of late Rear-Adm Charles Simeon (ante):—

Issue of late Herbert Richard Simeon, *b* 1865, *d* 1926: *m* 1892, Effie Dean Florence, who *d* 1938, da of Walter Moss, of Ashburton, New Zealand:—

Percival Edward Ralph (c/o Memorial Home, Gisborne, NZ), *b* 1898.

Descendants of John, Lt 54th Regt (*b* 1841) and Albert (*b* 1841), sons of Rear-Adm Charles Simeon (ante), who both left numerous issue.

Sir John Simeon, 1st baronet, MP for Reading, was senior Master of the Court of Chancery, Sir Richard Godin Simeon, 2nd baronet: *m* 1813, Louisa Edith, da and heir of Sir Fitzwilliam Barrington, 10th Bt of Barrington Hall, Essex (*cr* 1611, ext 1833).

SIMPSON (UK) 1935, of Bradley Hall, Ryton, co Palatine of Durham (Extinct 1981)

Sir (JOHN) CYRIL FINUCANE SIMPSON, 3rd and last *Baronet*.

SISTERS LIVING AND DECEASED OF THIRD BARONET

Vera, *b* 1893: *m* 1917, Richard Boys-Stones, MC, and *d* 1992, leaving issue, Claude Frank (Randle House, Corbridge, Northumberland), *b* 1920: *m* 1948, Anne Blackett, and has issue living, Richard Claude (29 Blenkarne Rd, SW11 6HZ) *b* 1954, George Francis (4 Chingford Av, Chingford, E4 6RP) *b* 1960, Sarah *b* 1951: *m* 1982, Gareth David John Goodwin, of 45a Alma Vale Rd, Clifton, Bristol BS8 2HL, — Paul Richard (Gelt Fell, Sand Lonning, Brampton, Cumbria CA8 1RA), *b* 1926: *m* 1960, Judith Ann Rutherford, and has issue living, Claire Judith *b* 1961: *m* 1985, Sqdn-Ldr Christopher Neil Philpott, of 11 Dawsons Rough, Shawbury, Shrewsbury (and has issue living, Joshua Lance *b* 1991, Samuel Christopher *b* 1993), Susan Paula *b* 1963: *m* 1991, Michael Philip Bettison, of 34 Weston Rd, Aston-on-Trent, Derby DE7 2AS, — Elise (Holly Tree Farm, Cratfield, Halesworth, Suffolk IP19 0DN), *b* 1922: *m* 1943, Capt Rudland Dallas Cairns, DSC, RN, of Hexham, Northumberland, and has issue living, Timothy Dallas (Hill Farm, Tannington, Woodbridge, Suffolk) *b* 1948: *m* 1972 (*m diss* 1987), Julia Andrea, da of George M. Sisson, of Planetrees, Wall, Hexham, Northumberland, David Rudland *b* 1981, Janet, da of James William Morley, of 1 Culloden Close, Fareham, Hants (and has issue living, Tristan David *b* 1982, Crispin Rudland *b* (twin) 1982), Fiona Alice *b* 1946: *m* 1st, 1966 (*m diss* 1982), Lt-Cdr Hon Thomas Alan Jocelyn, RN (ret), who was feared lost at sea 1991; 2ndly, 1983, Josephus Ignatius Maria Oomes, of Molletts Farm, Benhall, Saxmundham, Suffolk IP17 1JY, and has issue (by 1st *m*) (*see* E Roden), — Sonia, *b* 1924. —— Esmé, *b* 1895: *m* 1919, Walter Rupert King, and has issue living, Denis, *b* 1921, — Sheila, *b* 1922: *m* 1986, David Eeles. *Residence* – Yearle, 1 Meadway, Esher, Surrey.

Sinclair-Lockhart (cr 1636), see Lockhart.

SINCLAIR (NS) 1704, of Dunbeath, Caithness-shire

Fidelity

Sir PATRICK ROBERT RICHARD SINCLAIR, 10th *Baronet; b* 21 May 1936, son of late Alexander Robert Sinclair, brother of 8th Bt; *s* his cousin, *Sir* JOHN ROLLO NORMAN BLAIR, 1990; *ed* Winchester, and Oriel Coll, Oxford (MA); Bar Lincoln's Inn 1961; Sub Lt RNVR: *m* 1974, Susan Catherine Beresford, eldest da of Geoffrey Clive Davies, OBE, of Greenshaw, Holbrook, Ipswich, Suffolk (*see* Knowles, Bt), and has issue.

Arms – Quarterly: 1st azure, a ship at anchor, oars in saltire or, flagged gules, within a double tressure counterflory of the second; 2nd and 3rd, or, a lion rampant gules, armed and langued azure; 4th, azure, a ship under sail or, sails argent and flags gules; over all, dividing the four quarters, a cross engrailed, sable, *Sinclair;* the whole within a bordure parted per pale, the dexter side indented gules, the sinister ermine. **Crest** – A cock proper.
Address – 5 New Sq, Lincoln's Inn, WC2A 3SA.

SON LIVING

WILLIAM ROBERT FRANCIS, *b* 27 March 1979.

DAUGHTER LIVING

Helen Margaret Gwendolen, *b* 1984.

DAUGHTERS LIVING OF EIGHTH BARONET

Georgina Margaret Snowdrop SINCLAIR, *b* 1932: *m* 1955 (*m diss* 1968), John Leonard Maddocks, and has issue living, John Alexander Sinclair (202 Battersea Bridge Rd, SW11), *b* 1960, — Margaret Louise Sinclair, *b* 1962: *m* 1991, Adam Piers Scott, of Barrock House, Lyth, Caithness, and has issue living, Rory Alexander Sinclair *b* 1991, Laura Rose Sinclair *b* 1993. *Residence* – The Mount, Brewood, Staffs. —— Susan Lilian Primrose (*Countess of Swinton*), *b* 1935 (*cr* a Life Baroness, with the title of Baroness Masham of Ilton, 1970): *m* 1959, 2nd Earl of Swinton. *Residences* – Dykes Hill House, Masham, Ripon, Yorks; 46 Westminster Gdns, Marsham St, SW1P 4JG.

COLLATERAL BRANCH LIVING

Granddaughter of late Rt Hon John Sinclair, GCSI, GCIE (*cr* Baron Pentland 1909), el son of Capt George Sinclair, Bengal Army, yst son of 6th baronet:—
Issue of late Henry John, 2nd Baron Pentland, *b* 1907, *d* 1984: *m* 1941, Lucy Elisabeth Babington (*Baroness Pentland*) (4670 Independence Av, New York City, NY 10471, USA), da of late Sir Henry Babington Smith (*see* E Elgin 1944 Edn):—
Hon Mary, *b* 1942; BA Mount Holyoke, USA (1964): *m* 1976, Jon Anderson Rothenberg, of 131 East 66 St, New York, NY 10021, USA, and has issue living, Laura, *b* 19—.

This family is a younger branch of the Earls of Caithness, Sir James Sinclair of Dunbeath, 1st baronet, being a descendant of the 4th Earl. The baronetcy was *cr* with remainder to heirs male whatsoever, and on the death of the 5th baronet in 1842, it was assumed by his cousin, John Sinclair, of Barrock, as great-great-grandson of George Sinclair of Barrock, brother of William Sinclair of Dunbeath, uncle of 1st baronet, the propinquity being proved by a retour of general service 23 Dec 1842. The 7th baronet, Sir John Rose George Sinclair, DSO, was Vice-Lt for co Caithness, and served in S Africa 1900-01, and during European War 1914-18, Sir Ronald Norman John Charles Udny Sinclair, TD, DL, JP, 8th Bt, was Maj Seaforth Highlanders and Dist Resident Officer, Norderdithmarschen 1947, and British Resident Heide/Holstein 1949.

SITWELL (UK) 1808, of Renishaw, Derbyshire

Sir (SACHEVERELL) RERESBY SITWELL, 7th *Baronet*; *b* 15 April 1927; *s* his father, *Sir* SACHEVERELL, CH, 1988; *ed* Eton, and King's Coll, Camb; formerly Lieut Gren Gds, BAOR 1946-48; Advertising and PR exec 1948-60, vending machine operator 1960-70, wine merchant 1960-75; High Sheriff of Derbys 1983, Freeman of City of London 1984; a DL for Derbys since 1984, Lord of Manors of Eckington and Barlborough, Derbys, and of Whiston and Brampton-en-le-Morthen, Yorks: *m* 1952, Penelope, yr da of late Col Hon Donald Alexander Forbes, DSO, MVO (*see* E Granard, colls), and has issue.

𝔄rms – Barry of eight or and vert, three lions rampant sable. 𝔠rest – A demi-lion rampant, erased sable, holding between the paws an escutcheon per pale or and vert.
Seat – Renishaw Hall, Derbys; *Town Residence* – 4 Southwick Place, W2 2TN.

Yield not to misfortune

DAUGHTER LIVING

Alexandra Isobel Susanna Edith, *b* 1958: *m* 1991, Richard A. Hayward, elder son of Sir Jack Hayward, OBE, and has issue living, Rosaleen Catriona Sitwell, *b* 1993.

BROTHER LIVING

FRANCIS TRAJAN SACHEVERELL, *b* 17 Sept 1935; *ed* Eton; Sub-Lieut RNVR 1954-56; Royal Dutch/Shell Group 1956-66; Advertising, Public Affairs and Public Relations Consultant; Memb of Council, Lond Philharmonic Orchestra 1965-84 (Vice-Chm 1983-84), and of Byam Shaw Sch of Art 1975-91; Chm Park Lane Group 1978-91; Memb of UK Council, World Wild Fund for Nature since 1985; Chm City Liaison Group since 1988: *m* 1966, Susanna Carolyn, da of late Rt Hon Sir Ronald Hibbert Cross, KCMG, KCVO, 1st Bt, and has issue living, George Reresby Sacheverell, *b* 1967, — William Ronald Sacheverell, *b* 1969, — Henrietta Louise Vereker, *b* 1973. *Residence* – Weston Hall, Towcester, Northants NN12 8PU.

COLLATERAL BRANCH LIVING

Granddaughter of Capt Herbert Cecil FitzRoy Sitwell, son of Herbert Wellington Sitwell, son of Capt George Frederick Sitwell, 2nd son of 2nd baronet:—
Issue of late Lt-Col George FitzRoy Sitwell, US Army, *b* 1923, *d* 198-: *m* 1945 (*m diss* 1971), Elizabeth, da of Paul Freed, of Waynesboro, Virginia, USA:—
Elizabeth, *b* 1951: *m* 1969, Alfred Townsend Truitt, of Bradenton, Florida, USA, and has issue living, Anne, *b* 1972.
The Sitwells appeared early in Eckington, Derbyshire; William Cytewell, *temp* Edward III, and Roger Cytewell, *temp* Edward IV, both being holders of land there. The eventual heiress of the family, Katherine Sitwell, *m* 1727, Jonathan Hurt, and her son Francis succeeded to the Renishaw estates and assumed the name of Sitwell. The Sitwells are the only remaining representatives of the family of Reresby of Thribergh, through Mary Reresby, who in 1693 *m* William Sitwell. Sir George Reresby, 4th Bt, sat as MP for Scarborough (C) 1885-86 and 1892-95. His only da Dame Edith Louisa Sitwell, DBE, *b* 1887, *d* 1964, author, poet and critic, was Vice-Pres of R Soc of Literature 1958. His el son Sir (Francis) Osbert Sacheverell Sitwell, CH, CBE, CLitt, 5th Bt, was the poet and author; *d* 1969; his brother, Sir Sacheverell Sitwell, CH, 6th Bt, was also a noted poet and author; *d* 1988.

SKINNER (UK) 1912, of Pont Street, Borough of Chelsea

Sir THOMAS KEITH HEWITT SKINNER, 4th *Baronet*; *b* 6 Dec 1927; *s* his father *Sir* (THOMAS) GORDON, 1972; *ed* Charterhouse; Chm and Ch Exec of Reed Publishing Ltd, and a Dir of other cos: *m* 1959, Jill, da of late Cedric Ivor Tuckett, of Yardley Gables, Tonbridge, and has issue.

𝔄rms – Ermine, on a bend or, between in chief a port between two towers, flying therefrom two pennons gules to the sinister, and in base an ancient ship of the second, three maple leaves slipped vert. 𝔠rest – A griffin's head couped at the neck or, between two dragons' wings gules.
Residence – Wood Farm, Reydon, nr Southwold, Suffolk IP18 6SL.

I neither fear nor despise

SONS LIVING

(THOMAS) JAMES HEWITT, *b* 11 Sept 1962. —— Ian Ivor Hewitt, *b* 1964.

BROTHERS LIVING

Gordon Michael Hewitt (Juani Farm, PO Box 1375, Nakuru, Kenya), *b* 1930: *m* 1st, 1955 (*m diss* 1960), Josephine Dawn, da of D. S. Redman, of Bleak Hall, Biggleswade; 2ndly, 1961, Eve, da of late Vernon John Fullforth, of Whitehall Court, Whitehall, SW1; 3rdly, 1968, Jean Margaret, da of late Donald Sharp, and widow of Robin Vetch, and has issue living, (by 1st *m*) Dudley Mark Hewitt, *b* 1956, — (by 2nd *m*) Sarah Patricia, *b* 1963. —— Peter Girling Hewitt (Highway Model Farm, Downside, Cobham, Surrey), *b* 1938: *m* 1966, Jennifer, da of J. Corbett, of Perrymill, Bradley Green, nr Redditch, Worcs, and has issue living, Justin Mark Thomas, *b* 1968, — Peter Dominic Thomas, *b* 1970, — Gemma Sophia Nicola, *b* 1977.

Constance Irene, *b* 1901: *m* 1936, Claude Harry Mills, who *d* 1971. *Residence* – Pett Place, Charing, Kent.

COLLATERAL BRANCHES LIVING

Issue of late Ernest Skinner, 2nd son of 1st baronet, *b* 1880, *d* 1919: *m* 1903, Leonie Mercedes, who *d* 1964, da of late Henry William Doll, of Lancing, Sussex:—
Eva Jacqueline Leonia, *b* 1914. *Residence* – 8 Tarring Gate, St Lawrence Av, Worthing.

Issue of late John Skinner, 3rd son of 1st baronet, *b* 1882, *d* 1939: *m* 1904, Angela, da of William Dunn:—
John Reginald, *b* 1909: *m* 1949, Shirley Evelyn, da of late James Roddick, of Melbourne, Aust, and has issue living, Dawn Rosalyn, *b* 1952.

Grandchildren of late Charles Henry Skinner, yst son of 1st baronet:—
Issue of late Charles David Evelyn Skinner, *b* 1916, *d* 1987: *m* 1940, Pamela (The Pound, Yarmouth, I of Wight), da of Dr S. B. Couper, of Blaby, Leicester:—
Peter David (Elm Tree House, Kemble, Cirencester), *b* 1941; Fl Lt RAF (ret): *m* 1964, Susan Mary, da of Keith Francis Thompson, of Worcester, and has issue living, Mark David Francis, *b* 1966, — James Nicholas Peter, *b* 1982, — Sarah Lucinda, *b* 1968. —— Carol, *b* 1944: *m* 1st, 1967 (*m diss* 19—), Peter De Villiers; 2ndly, 1993, Alwyn Landman. —— Susan Pamela, *b* 1945: *m* 1965, Robert Webb.
The 1st baronet, Sir Thomas, was a Director of Canadian Pacific Railway, of Hudson's Bay Co, and of Bank of Montreal, founder of Thomas Skinner & Co (Publishers) Ltd, and founder and editor of "Stock Exchange Official Year Book" and "The Directory of Directors". Sir (Thomas) Hewitt, 2nd baronet, was Pres of Thomas Skinner & Co (Publishers) Ltd.

SKIPWITH (E) 1622, of Prestwould, Leicestershire

Without God I cannot

Sir PATRICK ALEXANDER D'ESTOTEVILLE SKIPWITH, 12th *Baronet*, son of late Grey d'Estoteville Townsend Skipwith, Flying Officer RAF Vol Reserve, el son of 11th baronet; *b* 1 Sep 1938; *s* his grandfather, *Sir* GREY HUMBERSTON D'ESTOTEVILLE, 1950; *ed* Harrow, Dublin Univ (MA), and Imperial Coll, London Univ (PhD); marine geologist in Tasmania 1966-67, Malaysia 1967-69, W Africa 1969-70, then at the Directorate Gen of Mineral Resources, Jeddah, Saudi Arabia 1970-71 and 1972-73, geological editor, Bureau de Recherches Géologiques et Minières, Jeddah, Saudi Arabia, 1973-86; Dir Imnel Publishing Ltd, London since 1987 (Man Dir 1988-89), and Dir GeoEdit, London since 1987: *m* 1st, 1964 (*m diss* 1970), Gillian Patricia, adopted da of late Charles Frederick Harwood; 2ndly, 1972, Ashkhain, da of Bedros Atikian, of Royal Cres NE, Calgary, Alberta, Canada, and has issue by 1st *m*.

Arms – Argent, three bars gules, in chief a greyhound courant sable, collared or. **Crest** – A turnstile or.
Residences – 1 rue Jean Hupeau, 45000 Orléans, France; 76 rue du Pont-aux-Moines, 45450 Donnery, France. *Clubs* – Chelsea Arts, The Arts, Zanzibar.

SON LIVING *(By 1st marriage)*

ALEXANDER SEBASTIAN GREY D'ESTOTEVILLE, *b* 9 April 1969; *ed* Harrow, and Kent Univ.

DAUGHTER LIVING *(By 1st marriage)*

Zara Alexandra Jane d'Estoteville, *b* 1967.

UNCLES LIVING *(Sons of 11th baronet)*

Egerton Grey d'Estoteville (6 Stamford Cottages, The Billings, SW10), *b* 1935; *ed* Canford; late 13th/18th Roy Hussars.
—— Peyton Stephen (c/o The Fine Art Society, plc, 148 New Bond St, W1), *b* 1939; *ed* Canford: *m* 1971, Anne, da of Capt C. E. Barren, of Seasalter, Kent, and has issue living, Grey Egerton d'Estouteville, *b* 1981, — Selina, *b* 1972, — Amber Louise, *b* 1974.

AUNT LIVING *(Daughter of 11th baronet)*

Audrey Elsie Townsend, *b* 1911: *m* 1943, Paul Antony Negretti, formerly Maj The Black Watch, and has issue living, (Antony) Simon Timothy, *b* 1945: *m* 1981, Lucinda G., yst da of late Guy Lawrence, and has issue living, Guy *b* 1983, Gipsy *b* 1989, — Annelise Audrey, *b* 1948: *m* 1975, Alexander G. M. Kemp, of Homewood Farm, Mullgowie, Qld 4341, Australia, son of J. E. Kemp, of Queensland, Australia, and has issue living, Simon James *b* 1977, Emma Bay *b* 1979. *Residence* – Thornborough Manor, Buckingham.

WIDOW LIVING OF ELEVENTH BARONET

CYNTHIA EGERTON (*Cynthia, Lady Skipwith*), da of late Egerton Leigh, of Jodrell Hall, Cheshire: *m* 1928, as his 2nd wife, Sir Grey Humberston d'Estoteville Skipwith, 11th Bt, who *d* 1950. *Residence* – Flemings, Wilton, Wilts.

COLLATERAL BRANCHES LIVING

Grandchildren of late Col Grey Townsend Skipwith, only son of Fulwar Skipwith, 3rd son of 8th Bt:—
Issue of late Lt-Col James Wemyss Skipwith, RE, *b* 1875, *d* 1950: *m* 1911, Estelle, who *d* 1961, da of late Robert Henderson, of The Wylds, Liss, Hants:—
Patrick James Townsend, *b* 1915; Lt-Col (ret) RA; Hong Kong 1941 (prisoner): *m* 1941, Beryl Daisy, da of late Arthur A. Fair, of Montree, Athlone, co Westmeath, and has issue living, Michael James Grey (Swyncombe Old School, Cookley Green, nr Nettlebed, Oxon), *b* 1951: *m* 1988, Jacqueline, da of J. Ould, of Coventry, Warwicks, — Susan Virginia, *b* 1947: *m* 1988, Christopher James Frederick Blumer (*see* E Lauderdale), — Bridget Ann, *b* 1948: *m* 1981, John Macaskill, of 12 Sheep Lane, LI, New York, NY 11560, son of late Dr John Macaskill, of Moray Place, Edinburgh, and has issue, John *b* 1984, Ben *b* 1986. *Residence* – North End, Chiddingfold, Surrey.

Grandsons of late Lt-Col James Wemyss Skipwith, RE (ante):—
Issue of late Maj John Granville Wemyss Skipwith, RA, *b* 1921, *d* 1991: *m* 1st, 1947, Margaret Lettice Mary, who *d* 1968, only da of late Col William Paget-Tomlinson, DSO, of Biggins House, Kirkby Lonsdale, Carnforth, Lancs; 2ndly, 1977, Eva Agnes (Salt Pie Cottage, Kirkby Lonsdale, Carnforth, Lancs), da of George Cooper Ingall, of Croft End, Kendal, and widow of Maj James Cameron Campbell, RE (ret):—
(By 1st *m*) Guy Paget Grey (107 Cheshire St, Market Drayton, Shropshire), *b* 1951; *ed* Shrewsbury, and Nottingham Univ: *m* 1972, Pamela, da of late Thomas N. Foster, of Edgmond, Shropshire, and has living, Thomas Grey, *b* 1979, — Robert John, *b* 1985, — Judith Lakshmi, *b* 1988. —— Philip James Henderson (Biggins Grange, Kirkby Lonsdale, Carnforth, Lancs), *b* 1957; *ed* Shrewsbury.

Grandchildren of late Col Grey Townsend Skipwith (ante):—
Issue of late Lt-Col Frederick Skipwith, *b* 1877, *d* 1964: *m* 1916, Lily Spence, who *d* 1979, da of late Lt-Col John Garvie, MD, IMS:—
Wendy Elisabeth, *b* 1927: *m* 1955, Capt Thomas Peter Robin Crane, late RASC, of Bridge Cottage, Well Lane, Midhurst, Sussex, and has issue living, Jennifer Anne, *b* 1988, David Michael Corner, of 105 Listria Park, N16, son of Freddie Corner, of Dorking, Surrey, — Caroline Virginia, *b* 1969.
Issue of late Charles Grey Yule Skipwith, *b* 1890, *d* 1967: *m* 1926, Althea Kathleen Joyce, who *d* 1973, da of late Charles Hunting, of Slaley Hall, Northumberland:—
Michael Charles (The Lotus Pottery, Stoke Gabriel, S Devon), *b* 1928: *m* 1957, Mary Elizabeth, da of R Barthram Wood, of Croft House, Kirkbymoorside, Yorks, and has issue living, Jonathan Charles d'Estoteville (The Palms, Venn Grove, Plymouth, Devon), *b* 1962; BSc: *m* 1993, Gina, da of M. P. Ferrigno, of Dournazac, France, — Joanna Lisette, *b* 1960.

Grandchildren of late Lionel Skipwith, 7th son of 8th baronet:—
Issue of late Frederick Charles Skipwith, *b* 1857, *d* 1940: *m* 1893, Mary Annie, da of G. F. Cremer, formerly of Wanganui, New Zealand:—
Gore Peyton Lewis, *b* 1894. —— Lionel Ernest, *b* 1896: *m* 1929, Eva May, da of J. Hopkins, of Auckland, New Zealand, and has issue living, Ronald Hugh, *b* 1930. *Residence* – Auckland, New Zealand.

Grandchildren of late Francis Skipwith, 4th son of late Lionel Skipwith (ante):—
Issue of late Robert Grey Skipwith, *b* 1900, *d* 1989: *m* 1937, Annemarie (7 Trust Cottages, 15 Murambi Drive, Mutare, Zimbabwe), da of late Hans Evers, of Ratzeburg, German:—
Francis Grey (Crosfields School, Shinfield, Reading, Berks), *b* 1940: *m* 1968, Jacqueline Ann, da of Charles Albert Frederick Kettley, and has issue living, Andrew William Grey, *b* 1969: *ed* Charterhouse, and Trin Coll, Camb, — Timothy Edward, *b* 1972; *ed* Charterhouse, — Barnaby James, *b* 1974; *ed* St Edward's Sch, Oxford. —— Robert Frederick (PO Box 327, Kwe Kwe, Zimbabwe), *b* 1941: *m* 1st, 1965 (*m diss* 1971), Patricia Ann Saville; 2ndly, 1971, Judith Ann, da of late Thomas Stephen Johnson, of Que Que, Zimbabwe, and has issue living (by 1st *m*), Charles Robert, *b* 1969, — (by 2nd *m*) Thomas Stephen, *b* 1975, — James Grey *b* 1976.
Issue of late Capt Lionel Peyton Skipwith, RN, *b* 1902; *d* 1978: *m* 1926, Thelma Westwood, who *d* 1988, only child of late Surg Cdr Andrian A. Forrester, of Weymouth:—
Venetia Forrester, *b* 1932: *m* 1951 (*m diss* 1991), Cdr James Michael Burnard Walkey, RN, and has issue living, Anthony Charles d'Estoteville, *b* 1955, — Justin Robert Chichester, *b* 1957.

Grandchildren of late Rev Granville Gore Skipwith (infra):—
Issue of late Philip Lionel d'Estouteville SKIPWITH-TYSER, *b* 1904, *d* 1991; assumed by Royal Licence 1958 the additional surname and arms of Tyser: *m* 1932, Elsie Barbara (Greywell House, Midlington, Droxford, Hants), da of late Col Arthur Edward Phillips, DSO, of Elm House, Winterbourne Dauntsey, nr Salisbury:—
Richard Peyton (Old House Hotel, Wickham, Hants), *b* 1937; *ed* Eton: *m* 1965, Annie Carmen Angele Marie, eldest da of André Bonnor, of Château Leyran, Villenave d'Ornon, Bordeaux, and has issue living, Julian Alexandre d'Estoteville, *b* 1972, — Anouk Barbara Hélène, *b* 1974. —— Charles Fulwar SKIPWITH (Cobbett's Restaurant, The Square, Botley, Southampton), *b* 1946; *ed* Wellington: *m* 1969, Lucy, da of late Maurice Othon, and has issue living, Naomi Barbara Marie-Françoise, *b* 1972, — Alissa Caroline Marie-Thérèse, *b* 1975, — Georgina Marie-Louise Selina, *b* 1979. —— Noel Camilla, *b* 1934: *m* 1959, Capt Anthony Charles Alston Benda, 1st The Queen's Dragoon Gds (The Old Vicarage, Crondall, Hants), son of Charles Kenneth Benda, and has issue living, Nicholas James Alston, *b* 1960, — Jonathan Charles Alston, *b* 1962, — William Philip Alson, *b* 1966.

Grandchildren of late Lionel Skipwith (ante):—
Issue of late Rev Granville Gore Skipwith, *b* 1865, *d* 1955: *m* 1899, Violet Mary, who *d* 1957, da of late George Walter Tyser, JP (Parkyns, Bt):—
Rev Osmund Humberston (16 Kingswood Court, Southcote Rd, Reading, Berks), *b* 1906; *ed* Harrow, and New Coll, Oxford (MA); sometime a Chap to Forces; formerly a Missionary; Africa and SE Asia 1941-54: *m* 1946, Philippa Katharine Jane, da of late Richard Edward Skipwith, MBE, of Ruddington, Notts, and has issue living, Peter Michael (25 The Ridgeway, Watford, Herts), *b* 1947; BSc: *m* 1970, Patricia Mary, BA, ARICS, da of David Allan, of Penrith, and has issue living, Susan Katharine, BA, *b* 1972, Rebecca *b* 1974. —— Barbara Nannette, *b* 1902: *m* 1928, Gerald William Kenyon-Slaney, OBE, who *d* 1953 (*see* B Kenyon, colls). *Residence* – 16 Smith Terrace, SW3, and Six Mount Pleasant, Tenterden, Kent.

Granddaughters of late Ernest d'Estoteville Skipwith, son of late Rev Randolph Skipwith, 10th son of 8th baronet:—
Issue of late Randolph Bruce d'Estoteville Skipwith, *b* 1880, *d* 1939: *m* 1906, Adelia L. Warnken, who *d* 1938:—
Margery Louise, *b* 1908: *m* 1936, Earle Sydney Chard, and has issue living, Carole Elizabeth: *m* 1958, Gordon Lorne Down. —— Lorraine Gladys, *b* 1909: *m* 1936, Herbert Roberts Adams, who *d* 1983, and has issue living, Donald Bruce, *b* 1942.

Grandson of late Cdr Sidmouth Stowell Skipwith, RN, yst son of 8th baronet:—
Issue of late Reginald Skipwith, *b* 1866, *d* 1931: *m* 1897, Kathleen Agatha, who *d* 1959, da of late Arthur Philip Lloyd (E Bradford, colls):—

Arthur Grey, *b* 1902; Com RN (ret): *m* 1933, Sarah Hope, da of Major Alfred James Fraser, DSO, of Woodside, Harding-stone, Northampton, and has issue living, William Grey, *b* 1938, — Sarah Jane, *b* 1943: *m* 1967, John William Finlay Robins, of Manor Farm, Longbridge Deverill, Wilts, — Rosemary Anne (twin), *b* 1943: *m* 1966, Robert Peter Richard Iliffe, of Yattendon Park, Yattendon, Berks (*see* B Iliffe, colls). *Residence* – The Old Rectory, Twyford, Hants.

This baronet claims descent from Robert d'Estoteville, Baron of Cottingham, *temp* William the Conqueror. Many of his descendants were of knightly rank, and distinguished both in war and in law, a Sir William Skipwith having been a Justice of the Queen's Bench *temp* Edward III and Richard II, and a Sir Thomas having achieved honour in the French wars was knighted by Henry V. The 1st baronet, who achieved reputation as a poet, sold the Prestwold estates in 1653. The 3rd baronet emigrated to Virginia, USA, in the middle of the 17th century. Sir Peyton Skipwith, who died in Virginia in 1805, was domiciled in England, as were his successors.

SLADE (UK) 1831, of Maunsel House, Somersetshire

Faithful and bold

Sir (JULIAN) BENJAMIN ALFRED SLADE, 7th *Baronet; b 22 May 1946; s his father, Capt Sir* MICHAEL NIAL 1962; *ed* Millfield; Dir of Shirlstar Container Transport Ltd, etc; Mem Worshipful Co of Ironmongers and Freeman of City of Lond (1979): *m* 1977 (*m diss* 1991), Pauline Carol, el da of Maj Claude Myburgh, of Inholmes Court, Hartley Wintney, Hants.

Arms – Per fesse argent and sable, a pale countercharged and three horses' heads erased two and one of the second; on a chief ermine, two bombs fired proper. **Crest** – On a mount vert, a horse's head erased sable, encircled by a chain in the form of an arch gold.
Residences – Maunsel, North Newton, Bridgwater, Somerset; 164 Ashley Gdns, Emery Hill St, SW1. *Club* – Turf.

COLLATERAL BRANCHES LIVING

Granddaughter of late Basil Alfred Slade 2nd son of 3rd baronet:—
Issue of late Lieut-Com Frederick William Patrick Slade, RNVR, *b* 1892, *d* 1928, *m* 1913, Marie, da of Edouard Perrucke:—
Mary Magdalen Althea, *b* 1914: *m* 1937, Oliver Lopez-y-Royo, son of Duke of Taurisano, and has issue living, Diego, *b* 1939, — Francis, *b* 1942, — Maria José, *b* 1937, — Isolda Dolores, *b* 1943. *Residence* –

Granddaughter of late Marcus Warre Slade, KC, 2nd son of late Rev George Fitz Slade, 11th son of 1st baronet:—
Issue of late Marcus George Savill Slade, *b* 1906, *d* 1972: *m* 1944 (*m diss* 1953), Rita Annie, da of William James Motton, of Plymouth:—
Susan Rebecca (2 Walton House, Walton St, SW3), *b* 1945; painter.

Granddaughter of late Henry Adolphus Warre Slade, 3rd and yst son of Rev George FitzClarence Slade (ante):—
Issue of late Maurice Gordon Slade, *b* 1902, *d* 1971: *m* 1934, Margaret, who *d* 1980, da of Hew Congreve Kennedy:—
Primrose, *b* 1934: *m* 1957, John Patrick Roger Heather Hayes, Lt-Col RE, of Tivoli Farms, Tivoli, NY 12583, USA, and has issue living, Phoebe, *b* 1960.

The 1st baronet, Gen Sir John, GCH, served with great distinction in the Peninsular War. The 2nd baronet was an eminent QC. Sir Alfred, 3rd baronet, who served during the Crimean War, was Receiver-Gen of Inland Revenue 1875-90.

SLEIGHT (UK) 1920, of Weelsby Hall, Clee, co Lincoln

Sir RICHARD SLEIGHT, 4th *Baronet*; *b* 27 May 1946; *s* his father, *Sir* JOHN FREDERICK, 1990: *m* 1978, Marie-Thérèse, only da of O. M. Stepan, of Bromley, Kent, and has issue.

ᴀrms – Per chevron or and sable, in chief two cross-crosslets and in base a lymphad with sail hoisted countercharged. Crest – A mast with sail hoisted argent charged with three cross-crosslets sable.
Address – c/o National Westminster Bank, 9 Hill St, Richmond, Surrey SW9 1SY.

SONS LIVING

JAMES ALEXANDER, *b* 5 Jan 1981. ⸺ Nicholas Edward *b* 1985.

WIDOW LIVING OF THIRD BARONET

JACQUELINE MARGARET (*Jacqueline, Lady Sleight*), eldest da of Maj H. R. Carter, of Brisbane, Queensland, and widow of Ronald Mundell: *m* 1942, Sir John Frederick Sleight, 3rd Bt, who *d* 1990. *Residence* – Surfers Paradise, Queensland 4217, Australia.

COLLATERAL BRANCHES LIVING

Serve all, slight none

Issue of late Maj Rowland Sleight, JP, 2nd son of 1st baronet, *b* 1877, *d* 1947: *m* 1906, Phebe Lambert, who *d* 1962, da of late Henry Smethurst, JP, of Grimsby, Lincolnshire:—
Rowland Derek Lambert, *b* 1908; *ed* Rugby: *m* 1939, Winifred, da of late Calvert Hunt of London, and has issue living, Lesley, *b* 1943: *m* 1980, Crispin de Boos, of The Bakehouse, Banham, Norfolk NR16 2HW. *Residence* – The White House, Quidenham, Norfolk NR16 2PB.

Issue of late Nelson Sleight, 3rd son of 1st baronet, *b* 1883, *d* 1939: *m* 1915, Edith Mary, who *d* 1966, da of late Christopher Dewick Charles Hunt, of Gainsborough:—
Peter, DFM, AE (Corner Cottage, Hawerby, Grimsby, S Humberside), *b* 1920; 1939-45 War as Sqdn Ldr RAF (DFM): *m* 1947, Joyce Elizabeth, el da of J. H. Dale, of The Langmore, Wold Newton, Lincolnshire, and has issue living, John Nelson (51 Park Drive, Grimsby, S Humberside), *b* 1947: *m* 1974, Susan Jennifer, da of J. C. Hewson, of Tetney, S Humberside, and has issue living, Lucy Margaret *b* 1979, Sophie Elizabeth *b* 1982, — Diana Margaret, *b* 1950: *m* 1974, James Stewart Atkinson, of Chartwell House, Messingham Lane, Scawby, Brigg, S Humberside, and has issue living, Charles William James *b* 1977, Charlotte Diana *b* 1980, Louise Joanna *b* (twin) 1980. ⸺ Violet Mary, *b* 1917: *m* 1938, Frederick Ousey Redshaw, late Lieut RNVR, who *d* 1930, and has issue living, Pamela Mary, *b* 1942: *m* 1968, George Bryan O'Toole, of Mayes Farm, Mayes Lane, Sandon, Essex, and has issue living, Laurence James *b* 1969, Howard Charles *b* 1975, Stella Elizabeth *b* 1971, Lucy Alicia *b* 1978. *Residence* – 64 Moorgate, Acomb, York.

Issue of late George Frederick Sleight, yst son of 1st baronet, *b* 1890, *d* 1954: *m* 1915, Edith Mary, who *d* 1963, da of late Edwin James Brockway, JP, of Oakham, Rutland:—
Michael Marcus, *b* 1924; *ed* privately, and Camb Univ. *Residence* – Binbrook Hall, Binbrook, Lincs LN3 6BW. ⸺ Edith Mary, *b* 1918: *m* 1947, James Davey, and has issue living, Veronica Mary, *b* 1950, — Caroline Frances, *b* 1954. *Residence* – Kelstern Hall, Louth, Lincs.
Sir George, 1st Bt, was Lord of the Manor of Kelstern, Lincolnshire. Sir Ernest, OBE, TD, 2nd Bt, was High Sheriff, DL, and JP of Lincolnshire 1946.

SMILEY (UK) 1903, of Drumalis, Larne, co Antrim, and Gallowhill, Paisley, co Renfrew

By industry, valour, and

fortitude

Lt-Col Sir JOHN PHILIP SMILEY, 4th *Baronet*; *b* 24 Feb 1934; *s* his father, *Sir* HUGH HOUSTON, 1990; *ed* Eton, and RMA Sandhurst; Lt-Col late Gren Guards; Cyprus 1958; ADC to Gov of Bermuda 1961-62; Master Grocers' Co 1992-93: *m* 1963, Davina Elizabeth, el da of late Denis Charles Griffiths, of Orlingbury Hall, nr Kettering, Northants, and has issue.

Arms – 1st and 4th, per bend azure and or, a lion rampant ermine between three pheons counterchanged, *Smiley*; 2nd and 3rd gules, on a chevron argent two mullets azure, in base a fusil of the second, *Kerr*. **Crest** – A lion's jamb erased, and holding in bend sinister a pheon shafted proper, head or. *Residence* – Cornerway House, Chobham, Surrey GU24 8SW. *Club* – Army and Navy.

SONS LIVING

CHRISTOPHER HUGH CHARLES, *b* 7 Feb 1968; *ed* Eton, and Edinburgh Univ (MA).
—— William Timothy John, *b* 1972; *ed* Eton, and Bristol Univ (BSc).

DAUGHTER LIVING

Melinda Elizabeth Eirène, *b* 1965: *m* 1991, Jonathon Mark Midelton Baker, son of John Baker, of Monmouth House, Yenston, Som, and has issue living, Archie John Midelton, *b* 1993. *Residence* – 69 Stormont Rd, SW11 5EJ.

UNCLES LIVING (*sons of 2nd baronet*)

John Claude (81 Langthorne St, SW6 6JU), *b* 1910; *ed* Eton; Hon Capt Middx Yeo (TA Reserve); 1939-42 War in Middle East: *m* 1st, 1936 (*m diss* 1942), Lady Cecilia Katherine Wellesley, who *d* 1952, da of 3rd Earl Cowley; 2ndly, 1947, Sheila Joyce (OTTER-BARRY), who *d* 1978, da of late Hon Stanhope Alfred Tollemache (*see* B Tollemache, colls, 1968 Edn), and has issue living (by 1st *m*), David Valerian (Meadwell House, Meadwell, Lifton, Devon), *b* 1938; *ed* Wellington Coll; Maj late Royal Horse Gds: *m* 1st, 1962 (*m diss* 1987), Rose-Ann, el da of Col David Greig, of Borland, Kilmarnock, Ayrshire; 2ndly, 1988, Jill Velia, widow of Lionel William (Robin) Huntington, MC, and da of late Cdr John Kershaw, DSO, and has had issue (by 1st *m*), Patrick Valerian *b* 1965; *ed* Trin Coll, Glenalmond, and Durham Univ (BA), Thomas Edward de Crespigny *b* 1967; *ed* Kiel Sch; *d* 1989, (Katherine) Cecilia *b* 1963: *m* 1990, Tom Julian Beaumont Varcoe, of 77 Winchester St, Overton, Hants, yr son of late Beaumont Varcoe, of Nanscawen, Par, Cornwall (and has issue living, Thomas Anthony Beaumont *b* 1991, Xan John Felix *b* 1992). —— David de Crespigny, LVO, OBE, MC (30 Kensington Mansions, Trebovir Rd, SW5 9TQ. *Clubs* – White's, MCC, Special Forces), *b* 1916; *ed* Nautical Coll, Pangbourne, and RMC Sandhurst; Col late Royal Horse Gds, commanded Royal Horse Gds 1952-54, Mil Attaché Stockholm 1955-58 (Knight Cdr of Order of the Sword of Sweden), and Cdr of Armed Forces of Sultan of Muscat and Oman 1958-61, and Mil Adviser to Imam of Yemen 1963-68; a Member of HM Body Guard of Corps of Gentlemen-at-Arms 1966-68; 1939-45 War with 1st Household Cav Regt in Middle East (despatches) and with Special Forces in the Balkans (MC and Bar), Far East 1945 (OBE); OBE (Mil) 1946, LVO 1952; Grand Cordon of the Order of Skanderbeg of Albania: *m* 1947, Moyra Eileen, da of late Lt-Col Lord Francis George Montagu Douglas Scott, KCMG, DSO (*see* D Buccleuch, colls), and widow of Maj Hugo Douglas Tweedie, Scots Gds, and has issue living, Xan de Crespigny (36 Rectory Grove, SW4; White's, Beefsteak, and Polish Hearth Clubs), *b* 1949; *ed* Eton and New Coll, Oxford (MA); Editor of *Africa Confidential* 1977-81; Leader writer, *The Times* 1982-83; Foreign Specialist, *The Economist* 1983-86; Moscow Correspondent, *The Daily Telegraph* 1986-89, and Washington Correspondent *The Sunday Telegraph* 1990-92, since when Political Editor *The Economist*: *m* 1983, Hon Jane Lyon-Dalberg-Acton, yst da of 3rd Baron Acton, and formerly wife of late Charles Thomas Pugh, and has issue living, Ben Richard Philip de Crespigny *b* 1983, Adam David Emerich *b* 1988, — Philip David (1-68 Songbuk-dong, Seoul, Korea), *b* 1951; *ed* Eton, and St Andrews Univ (MA); Solomon Islands Govt 1974-80, Hong Kong Govt 1980-85; W. I. Carr (Far East) 1985-90, since when Man Dir Jardine Fleming Securities.

AUNT LIVING (*Daughter of 2nd baronet*)

Patricia Margaret (3 The Lilypool, Melbourne, Derbys), *b* 1907: *m* 1st, 1931, Rupert Douglas Tollemache, who *d* 1933 (B Tollemache, colls); 2ndly, 1941, Col Charles Dalby, CBE, KRRC, who *d* 1981, and has issue living (by 2nd *m*), Charles Gerald (Castle Donington, Leics) *b* 1942; *ed* Eton; Arch Assocn Dip; ARIBA: *m* 1980, Kathleen Margaret, el da of late Stanley Hodson, of Luska, Puckane, Nenagh, co Tipperary (*see* Hodson, Bt, colls), and has issue living, Edward Charles Gerald *b* 1982, Lucy Margaretta Hyacinthe *b* 1981, — Patrick Claude John (7 Tite St, SW3; White's Club), *b* 1948; *ed* Rugby; late Royal Green Jackets; partner Cazenove & Co, Stockbrokers.

WIDOW LIVING OF THIRD BARONET

NANCY ELIZABETH LOUISE HARDY (*Nancy, Lady Smiley*), elder da of late Ernest Walter Hardy Beaton (and sister of late Sir Cecil Beaton, CBE, the photographer and designer): *m* 1933, Sir Hugh Houston Smiley, 3rd Bt, JP, DL, who *d* 1990. *Residence* – Ivalls, Bentworth, Alton, Hants GU34 5JU.

COLLATERAL BRANCHES LIVING

Issue of late Major Peter Kerr KERR-SMILEY, 2nd son of 1st baronet, *b* 1879, *d* 1943 (having assumed in 1905 the additional surname of Kerr): *m* 1905, Maud, who *d* 1962, da of Ernest L. Simpson, of New York:—
Elizabeth Maud, *b* 1907: *m* 1936, Christopher Edward Clive Hussey, CBE, who *d* 1970 (E Powis, colls). *Residence* – Scotney Castle, Lamberhurst, Kent.

Grandsons of late Maj Peter Kerr-Smiley (ante):—
Issue of late Lt-Col Cyril Hugh Kerr-Smiley, TD, *b* 1906, *d* 1980: *m* 1933, Agnes, who *d* 1986, el da of late Lt-Col George Cecil Minett Sorel Cameron, CBE (*see* B Tollemache, colls):—
Peter Simon (Towranna Farm, Huntingfield, Suffolk; Naval and Military Club), *b* 1934; *ed* Ampleforth, and RMA Sandhurst; Lt-Col Queen's Own Highlanders (Seaforth and Camerons), Arabian Peninsula 1956-57, ADC to Gov of Malta 1959-61, Queen's Messenger since 1984: *m* 1960 (*m diss* 1981), Jennifer Guise, only da of late Lt-Col Thomas Guise Tucker, MC, and has issue living, Mark Alexander (15 Granard Rd, SW12), *b* 1961; *ed* Ampleforth: *m* 1988, Manuela Marie, da of S. M. Raquez, of 205 Av Brugmann, Brussels, and has issue living, Frederick Hugh *b* 1992, Isabella Louise *b* 1990, — Robert

Justin, *b* 1965; *ed* Ampleforth, and Newcastle Univ (BA), — Emma Caroline Hyde, *b* 1963: *m* 1994, Euan D. Nicolson, yr son of late Timothy Nicolson, of Kintbury, Berks, and of Mrs Nicholas Embiricos, of Kirdford, Sussex. —— Hector Robert (Elms Hall, Colne Engaine, Essex; Boodle's Club), *b* 1937; *ed* Ampleforth; Lt Queen's Own Highlanders (Seaforth and Camerons) (TA Reserve): *m* 1962, Eleanor Jill, da of Cdr Peter Wadlow, RN (ret), and has issue living, Simon Alastair Hugh, *b* 1964; *ed* Gordonstoun: *m* 1992, Nony Mary Louise, da of Sir Richard John Uniacke Barrow, 6th Bt, — Christopher Peter Nicholas, *b* 1967; *ed* Eton, — Charlotte Elizabeth, *b* 1963: *m* 1990, Christopher Hugh Courtney Smith, son of Sir Robert Courtney Smith, CBE, and has issue living, George Hector Courtney *b* 1993. —— Nicholas Ernest, *b* 1940; *ed* Ampleforth, and Kalgoorlie Sch of Mines (MAusIMM): *m* 1973, Georgina Jane, el da of Maj Sir George Andrew Dick-Lauder, 12th Bt, and has issue living, Samantha Fiona Marguerite, *b* 1976.

Grandchildren of late Hubert Stewart Smiley, 3rd son of 1st baronet:—
Issue of late Maj (Charles) Michael Smiley, CVO, JP, *b* 1910, *d* 1991: *m* 1939, Lavinia, who *d* 1991, da of late Capt Hon (Bernard) Clive Pearson (*see* V Cowdray, colls):—
James Robin Clive (50 Martin Rd, Centennial Park, Sydney 2021, NSW, Aust), *b* 1947; *ed* Gordonstoun: *m* 1981, Jane Suzanne, da of late James Gorrie, of 24 Lynwood Av, Killara, NSW, and has issue living, Alexander Orlando Charles, *b* 1981, — Thomas Robin James, *b* 1983. —— Andrew Michael, *b* 1952; *ed* Eton; Gren Gds: *m* 1975, (Sarah) Caroline, da of late Lt-Col C. C. Coade, and has issue living, Charlotte Sarah, *b* 1983, — Sarah Miranda, *b* 1986. —— Miranda Daphne Jane (5 Cottesmore Gdns, W8 5PR), *b* 1940: *m* 1963 (*m diss* 1984), 3rd Earl of Iveagh, and has issue (*see* E Iveagh).
The 1st baronet, Sir Hugh Houston Smiley (1841-1909), was Principal Proprietor of the *Northern Whig*. The 2nd baronet, Major Sir John Smiley (1876-1930), 6th Dragoon Guards, served during S African War 1900-1902, and European War 1914-18. The 3rd baronet, Sir Hugh Smiley (1905-90), Gren Guards, served in European War 1939-45, and was High Sheriff for Hants (1959), and Vice Ld-Lieut (1973-82).

SMITH (UK) 1809, of Eardiston, Worcestershire

Sir CHRISTOPHER SYDNEY WINWOOD SMITH, 5th *Baronet*; *b* 20 Sept 1906; *s* his father, *Sir* WILLIAM SYDNEY WINWOOD, 1953: *m* 1932, Phyllis Berenice, yst da of late Thomas Robert O'Grady, of Waterford, Ireland, and Grafton, NSW, and has issue.

Arms – Sable, a cross flory or, on a chief engrailed ermine, a demi-lion issuant between two cross-crosslets gules. **Crest** – A greyhound couchant, sable, collared and line reflexed over the back or, the body charged with a cross-crosslet of the last, the dexter paw resting upon a cross flory as in the arms. *Residence* – Junction Road, via Grafton, NSW 2460, Australia.

SONS LIVING

ROBERT CHRISTOPHER SYDNEY WINWOOD, *b* 1939: *m* 1971, Roslyn Nellie, eldest da of late James Keith McKensie, of Sydney, NSW, and has issue living, Craig Robert Winwood *b* 1974, — Robyn Louise Winwood, *b* 1978. *Residence* – 13 Siren St, Port Maquarie, NSW. —— Hugh William Standish Winwood, *b* 1942: *m* 1966, Clare Philomena, eldest da of late Leslie Arthur Stinson, of Sydney, NSW, and has issue living, Christopher Hugh Winwood, *b* 1966, — Gregory Robert Winwood, *b* 1971, — Catherine Anne Winwood, *b* 1969, — Julie Stella Winwood, *b* 1973. *Residence* – 15 Jordan St, Fairfield, NSW 2169. —— Terence John Winwood, *b* 1945: *m* 1967, Helen June, da of late Donald W. McLeod, of Cootamunda, NSW, and has issue living, Ian James Winwood, *b* 1969, — Richard Charles Winwood, *b* 1972, — Jaqueline Nicole Winwood, *b* 1975. —— Matthew Roy Winwood, *b* 1947: *m* 1975, Janette Leferve, eldest da of late John Truman, of Sydney, NSW, and has issue living, Michael Winwood, *b* 1977. —— David Anthony Winwood, *b* 1949: *m* 1976, Judith Chaffey, of Grafton, NSW, and has issue living, Simon Winwood, *b* 1976, — Steven Winwood, *b* 1977. —— Ronald James Thomas Winwood, *b* 1951: *m* 1976, Rhonda Jean, eldest da of late Ronald Raine, of Sydney, NSW, and has issue living, Gary Winwood, *b* 1978, — Benjamin Winwood, *b* 1981, — Megan Winwood, *b* 1984.

DAUGHTERS LIVING

Villette Mary Winwood, *b* 1935: *m* 1961, Roger Hore, and has issue living, Andrew, *b* 1962. —— Helen Eve Winwood, *b* 1936: *m* 1957, Arthur Sydney Macalpine, and has issue living, Arthur David, *b* 1959, — Ian Christopher, *b* 1961, — Alison Helen, *b* 1965, — Jillian Elizabeth, *b* 1969. —— Frances Caroline Winwood, *b* 1941: *m* 1973, Kenneth James Hebblewhite, and has issue living, Mark Kenneth, *b* 1976, — Simon James, *b* 1978, — Rebecca Frances, *b* 1978.

BROTHER LIVING

Rupert William Winwood (42 Campbell St, Toowoomba, Queensland), *b* 1908: *m* 1940, Nancia Jean Margaret, da of John Bailey Cave, of Grafton, NS Wales, and has issue living, Geoffrey Stirling Winwood, *b* 1945: *m* 1972, Stephanie Sue, el da of W. Kelly, of Tallowoods, Cabarlah, Queensland, and has issue living, Nicholas William Winwood *b* 1977, Hugh Stirling Winwood *b* 1981, — Adrian John Winwood, *b* 1955: *m* 1984, Luciana Tranquilla, da of A. Gastaldo, of Adelaide, S Australia, — Merran Joy Winwood, *b* 1942: *m* 1977, Virgil Joseph Hull, PhD, of Keyser, W Virginia, USA, and has issue living, Meredith Fleur Winwood *b* 1980.

COLLATERAL BRANCH LIVING

Grandchildren of late William Arthur Winwood Smith, yst son of 3rd baronet:—
Issue of late Instr-Cdr Christopher William Winwood Smith, RN (ret), *b* 1893, *d* 1969: *m* 1916, Alice Muriel, who *d* 1969, da of Capt W. F. Garside, of Morden, Seaford:—
Antony Winwood, DFC (2 Harcourt, 4th/Borrow St, Bulawayo, Zimbabwe), *b* 1920; 1939-45 War in RAF. —— Pauline Muriel Winwood, *b* 1918: *m* 1st, 1949, James Mayhew; 2ndly, 1977, Richard Tudor Archer, of 7 Laurel Drive, Southmoor, Abingdon, Oxon.

SMITH (UK) 1897, Stratford Place, St Marylebone, co London

Sir (THOMAS) GILBERT SMITH, 4th *Baronet*; *b* 2 July 1937: *s* his father, *Sir* THOMAS TURNER, 1961; *ed* Huntley Sch, and Nelson Coll; Exec: *m* 1962, Patricia Christine, da of David Cooper, of Paraparaumu, NZ, and has issue.

Arms – Quarterly, or and gules, a fret between three fleurs-de-lis all counterchanged. **Crest** – A fret gules, issuant therefrom a fleur-de-lis or. *Address* – PO Box 654, Masterton, New Zealand.

Dabit qui dedit
He will give who hath given

SONS LIVING

ANDREW THOMAS, *b* 17 Oct 1965. —— Alistair Blair, *b* 1969.

DAUGHTER LIVING

Janne Fiona, *b* 1963: *m* 1988, David Carl Finlayson, of Leion, NZ.

BROTHER LIVING

Denis Michael, *b* 1945: *m* 1967, Janet, da of L. Eckhoff, of Ambarwood, RD3, Drury, NZ, and has issue living, Richard Michael, *b* 1968, — Joanna Marie, *b* 1969.

SISTERS LIVING

Barbara Elizabeth, *b* 1939: *m* 1967, Selwyn Lloyd Harris, of Sanson, NZ, and has issue living, Boyd John, *b* 1968, — Peter Thomas, *b* 1970, — Quentin Patrick, *b* 1972, — Zane Gilbert, *b* 1974. —— Gillian Madelaine, *b* 1941: *m* 1978, Michael Nicholas McCarthy, JP, of Wanganui, NZ, and has issue living, Samuel Thomas O'Meara, *b* 1980, — Trinity Madeleine, *b* 1979.

AUNTS LIVING

Jean Elizabeth, *b* 1901: *m* 1929, Andrew Naismith Fergus, BSc, MB, ChB, FRCP, Glasgow, of Buffbeards, Hindhead Rd, Haslemere, Surrey, GU27 1LH, and has issue living, John Naismith, *b* 1934; *ed* Oxford Univ (MA, BM and BCh); FRCS, FRCSE: *m* 1970, Catherine Isabel Wake, MRCS, LRCP, MB, da of David Cazes, of Les Bailleuls, St Andrew's, Guernsey, CI, and has issue living, Robert David Wenley *b* 1977, Adam Andrew Wake *b* 1978, — Margaret Elizabeth, *b* 1931, — Sheena Mary, MVO, *b* 1939, — Helen Kay, *b* 1947; PhD, BSc, MSc: *m* 1974, Ingo Evers, MA, MPhil, of Coton Hall, Bridgnorth, Shropshire WV15 6ES, and has issue living, Andrew Dominic Lothar *b* 1981. —— Madeleine Lovedy (Stangate, Hurst Green, Sussex), *b* 1909.

WIDOW LIVING OF THIRD BARONET

AGNES (*Agnes, Lady Smith*), da of Bernard Page, of Wellington, NZ: *m* 1935, Sir Thomas Turner Smith, 3rd Bt, who *d* 1961. *Residence* – 118 Liverpool St, Wanganui, New Zealand.

COLLATERAL BRANCH LIVING

Issue of the Lieut-Col Michael Carson Lyndon Smith, MC, MB, BS, MRCS, LRCP, IMS, brother of 3rd baronet, *b* 1908, *d* 1961: *m* 1936, Pauline, who *d* 1988, da of Charles Rowlatt:—
Sarah Gillian (Battens Farm, Lambourn Woodlands, Newbury, Berks RG16 17TN), *b* 1937: *m* 1st, 1958 (*m diss* 1966), Maj Anthony Gibbon Chater; 2ndly, 1967 (*m diss* 1988), Sir Peter Wilfred Giles Graham Moon, 5th Bt, and has issue living, (by 1st *m*) James Michael Douglas, *b* 1959, — Giles Addison, *b* 1961, — Piers Antony Rowlatt, *b* 1963, — (by 2nd *m*) (*see* Moon, Bt, *cr* 1855). —— Elizabeth Caroline, *b* 1940: *m* 1987, Christopher Ravenscroft, and has issue living, Michael Jack, *b* 1973. —— Alexa Pauline Lovedy, *b* 1945: *m* 19—, John Davenport. —— Joanna Esmée, *b* 1948: *m* 1969, John Alexander Broom, and has issue living, Alexander Rui Tomas, *b* 1972, — Daniel John, *b* 1978, — Orlanda Maria, *b* 1974. *Residence* – Headley Grange, Bordon, Hants.
Sir Thomas Smith, KCVO, FRCS, 1st baronet was so created on the occasion of HM Queen Victoria's Diamond Jubilee in recognition of his eminence as a Surgeon; he was Surg Extraor to Queen Victoria, Hon Sergeant-Surg to King Edward VII, and a Vice-Pres of Roy Coll of Surgeons. Sir (Thomas) Rudolph Hampden Smith, CBE, FRCS, 2nd baronet, was Hon Surg Comdg Torquay Hospital for Wounded Soldiers 1914-18.

SMITH (UK) 1920, of Kidderminster, co Worcester (Extinct 1961)

Sir HERBERT SMITH, 2nd and last *Baronet*.

DAUGHTERS LIVING OF SECOND BARONET

Emily Lindsay Cherrington, *b* 1930: *m* 1958, Joseph Thwaites. —— Martha Theresa Belinda, *b* 1933: *m* 1956, Robin Houghton Stretton, and has issue living, Martin John, *b* 1959, — Bridget Claire, *b* 1957.

DAUGHTERS LIVING OF FIRST BARONET

Mabel Merci, *b* 1899. —— Dora, *b* 1901: *m* 1922 (*m diss* 1929), George Edgar Ingman.

WIDOW LIVING OF SECOND BARONET

E. M. (GRIFFIN) (*Lady Smith*): *m* 1948, as his 2nd wife, Sir Herbert Smith, 2nd Bt, who *d* 1961, when the title became ext.

SMITH (UK) 1945, of Crowmallie, co Aberdeen

Sir ROBERT HILL SMITH, 3rd *Baronet*; *b* 15 April 1958; *s* his father, *Lt-Cdr Sir* (WILLIAM) GORDON, VRD, RN, 1983; *ed* Merchant Taylors', and Aberdeen Univ: *m* 1993.

𝕬rms – Or, on the waves of the sea, a three masted ship in full sail proper flagged gules on a chief engrailed, vert, a flame of fire between two horseshoes of the first. 𝕮rest – A sea-horse argent.
Seat – Crowmallie, Pitcaple, Aberdeenshire. *Residence* – 93 Cavendish Rd, SW12 0BN.

BROTHER LIVING

CHARLES GORDON, *b* 21 April 1959; *ed* Merchant Taylors', St Andrews Univ, and Univ of Oregon.

UNCLE LIVING (*Son of 1st Baronet*)

Robert Alexander, *b* 1920; *ed* Stowe, and Trin Coll, Camb; European War 1940-45 as Lieut RNVR: *m* 1945, Marianne, da of Serge Denissieff, and widow of George Plaoutine, of Philippeville, Algeria, and has issue living, Andrew Alexander, *b* 1946, — Robert Serge, *b* 1948. *Residence* – East Crowmallie, Pitcaple, Aberdeenshire.

WIDOW LIVING OF SECOND BARONET

DIANA MAY VIOLET PEEL (*Diana, Lady Smith*), da of Warwick Goodchild, and formerly wife of George Ian Young: *m* 1958, as his 2nd wife, Lt-Cdr Sir (William) Gordon Smith, 2nd Bt, VRD, RN, who *d* 1983. *Seat* – Crowmallie, Pitcaple, Aberdeenshire. *Residence* – 15 Cadogan Court, Draycott Av, SW3.
The 1st baronet, Sir Robert (Workman) Smith, yr son of late George Smith (Chm of "City Line", Glasgow), of Glenmorag, Argyllshire, was MP for Central Div of Aberdeenshire and Kincardineshire (*C*) 1924-1945.

SMITH (UK) 1947, of Keighley, co York

Sir CHARLES BRACEWELL SMITH, 4th *Baronet*; *b* 13 Oct 1955; *s* his brother, *Sir* GUY BRACEWELL, 1983; *ed* Harrow: *m* 1977, Carol Vivien, who *d* 1994, da of Norman Hough, of Cookham, Berks.

𝕬rms – Tierce in pairle reversed argent, gules and azure; in chief, two roses counterchanged barbed and seede proper, and in base a London pride plant flowered and eradicated also proper. 𝕮rest – Upon a rock a moorcock rising, resting the dexter foot on a double convex lens, all proper.
Address – Park Lane Hotel, Piccadilly, W1.
Sir Bracewell Smith, KCVO, 1st Bt, son of Samuel Smith of Keighley, Yorks, was MP for Dulwich (*C*) 1932-45, and Lord Mayor of London 1946-47.

CUSACK-SMITH (I) 1799, of Newtown, King's County (Extinct 1970)

Sir (WILLIAM ROBERT) DERMOT JOSHUA CUSACK-SMITH, 6th and last *Baronet*.

DAUGHTERS LIVING OF SIXTH BARONET

(By 1st *m*) Berry, *b* 1937: *m* 1960, (Hugh) Jon Foulds, and has issue living, William Mark Aubrey, *b* 1963, — Hugo Charles Berry, *b* 1967. —— (By 2nd *m*) Oonagh Mary, *b* 1948: *m* 1972, John Michael Hyland, of Circular Rd, Tuam, co Galway, and has issue living, Charles Stuart, *b* 1976, — Joanna Mary, *b* 1972, — Sarita Catherine, *b* 1979.

WIDOW LIVING OF SIXTH BARONET

ADELA MARY (*Lady Cusack-Smith*) (Bermingham House, Tuam, co Galway), da of Charles Trench O'Rorke, of Bermingham House, Tuam, co Galway: *m* 1946, as his 2nd wife, Sir (William Robert) Dermot Joshua Cusack-Smith, 6th Bt, who *d* 1970, when the title became ext.

Hamilton Spencer-Smith, see Spencer-Smith.

NEWSON-SMITH (UK) 1944, of Totteridge, co Hertford

Sir John Kenneth Newson-Smith, 2nd *Baronet*; *b* 9 Jan 1911; *s* his father, *Sir* Frank (Edwin), 1971; *ed* Dover Coll, and Jesus Coll, Camb (MA); a DL City of London 1947; a Common Councilman 1945, (Dep 1961-78), one of HM Lieuts 1947; 1939-45 War as Lt RNVR: *m* 1st, 1945 (*m diss* 1971), Vera Margaret, da of late Dr Wilfred Greenhouse Altt, CVO, CBE; 2ndly, 1972, Anne, who *d* 1987, da of late Harold Burns; 3rdly, 1988, Mrs Sarah Lucretia Wimberley Ramsay, da of Robert Bicknell, and has issue by 1st *m*.

Arms – Gules, on a chevron or, between in chief two bezants, and in base a cross pattée fitchée of the second, a pellet between two crosses pattée fitchée sable. **Crest** – Issuant from a mural crown or, a goat's head argent, armed and bearded or, eared sable and charged with a sword erect gules.
Residence – 67 East St, Warminster, Wilts BA12 9BZ.

SON LIVING *(By 1st marriage)*

Peter Frank Graham, *b* 8 May 1947; *ed* Dover Coll, and Trin Coll of Music: *m* 1974, Mary-Ann, da of Cyril C. Collins, of Chestnuts, Lovells Court, Marnhull, Sturminster Newton, Dorset, and formerly wife of Anthony Owens, and has issue living, Oliver Nicholas Peter, *b* 1975, — Emma, *b* 1977.

DAUGHTERS LIVING *(By 1st marriage)*

Susan Rosemary, *b* 1946: *m* 1978, Charles Reiss, of 91 Belsize Lane, NW3, eldest son of late Dr J. C. Reiss, and has issue living, Rowan Susannah Charlotte, *b* 1978, — Holly Clare, *b* 1980, — Bryony, *b* 1986. —— Elizabeth Jane, *b* 1953: *m* 1978, Kenneth Hall, and has issue living, Katherine Louise, *b* 1979, — Rachel Helen, *b* 1980.

SISTER LIVING

Mary Sharland, *b* 1909: *m* 1935, Maj Claude Morrison, who *d* 1967, and has issue living, *Ven* John Anthony (60 Wendover Rd, Aylesbury, Bucks), *b* 1938; *ed* Haileybury, and Jesus Coll, Camb (MA; Archdeacon of Buckinghamshire): *m* 1968, Angela, da of Jonathan Bush, and has issue living Dominic *b* 1970, Nicholas *b* 1974, Philippa *b* 1972, — Michael Bruce (The White Horse, 9 Place Luxembourg, Brussels), *b* 1939; *ed* Haileybury: *m* 1st, 1960 (*m diss* 1972), Anne Margaret, da of Archibald Hew Grace, MRCS, LRCP, of Cooden, Sussex; 2ndly, 1972, Mary, da of Lt-Col William Pollock, and has issue living (by 1st *m*), Bruce Anthony *b* 1961, Clare Fiona *b* 1964, (by 2nd *m*) Samantha Lois *b* 1978, — Jennifer Mary *b* 1943: *m* 1965, Peter Robert Daniel, of 24 Crutchfield Lane, Walton-on-Thames, Surrey, and has issue living, Mark Leslie *b* 1970, Paul Gavin *b* 1974, Karen Jane *b* 1966: *m* 19—, John Walton, of 4 Laurel Place, Staple St, nr Faversham, Kent (and has issue living, Thomas *b* 19—), Tracey Emma *b* 1968: *m* 19—, Peter Lewis, of Flat 2, 99 Stanley Rd, Carshalton, Surrey. *Residence* – The Laurels, Old London Rd, Hastings, E Sussex.

COLLATERAL BRANCH LIVING

Issue of late Capt Peter Henry Newson-Smith, RA, yr son of 1st baronet, *b* 1914, *ka* in Italy 1944: *m* 1939, Gertrude Irene, da of Frederick Lester Walker, of Georgia, USA, she *m* 2ndly, 1948, Bertrand Milton Walker, of 1200 Cherokee Drive, Waycross, Georgia, USA:—

Carole Irene, *b* 1943.

Sir Frank (Edwin) Newson-Smith, 1st Bt, son of Henry Newson-Smith, DL, CA, of London, was Lord Mayor of London 1943-44.

PRINCE-SMITH (UK) 1911, of Hillbrook, Keighley, W Riding of Yorkshire

The more prepared, the more
powerful

Sir (WILLIAM) RICHARD PRINCE-SMITH, 4th *Baronet*; *b* 27 Dec 1928; *s* his father, *Sir* WILLIAM, OBE, MC, 1964; *ed* Charterhouse, and Clare Coll, Camb (MA): *m* 1st, 1955, Margaret Ann, only da of late Dr John Carter, of Goldings, Loughton, Essex; 2ndly, 1975, Ann Christina, da of Andrew Faulds, OBE, of Lee Wick Farm, St Osyth, Clacton-on-Sea, Essex, and has issue by 1st *m*.

Arms – Per chevron nebuly or guttée de sang and gules, two stags' heads cabossed in chief of the last and a rose in base argent, barbed and seeded proper. **Crest** – A dragon's head erased gules, charged with a rose as in the arms, between a stag's attired or.
Residence – 40735 Paxton Drive, Rancho Mirage, California 92270-3519, USA.

SON LIVING *(By 1st marriage)*

JAMES WILLIAM (Morton Hall, Norwich, Norfolk NR9 5JS), *b* 2 July 1959; *ed* Gresham's, and Buckingham Univ; Capt 13th/18th Royal Hussars (Queen Mary's Own) 1979-87, Yorks Sqdn Q0Y.

DAUGHTER LIVING *(By 1st marriage)*

Elizabeth Ann, *b* 1957: *m* 1987, Colin Earl.

SISTER LIVING

Eileen Marjorie Clare, *b* 1932: *m* 1959, Stephen Hattersley Smith, and has issue living, Christopher Stephen Hattersley, *b* 1963, — Jane Clare Hattersley, *b* 1961, — Vanessa Jill Hattersley, *b* 1965. *Residence* – Eastlands, 91 Pool Rd, Otley, W Yorks LS21 1DY.

The 1st baronet, Sir Prince Smith (son of late Prince Smith, of Holly House, Keighley), was a JP for W and E Ridings of Yorkshire. The 2nd baronet, Sir Prince, assumed by deed poll 1922, the additional surname of Prince.

REARDON SMITH (UK) 1920, of Appledore, co Devon

What I do I do earnestly

Sir WILLIAM REARDON REARDON SMITH, 3rd *Baronet*; *b* 12 March 1911; *s* his father *Sir* WILLIE, 1950; *ed* Blundell's Sch; is Major RA (TA): *m* 1st, 1935 (*m diss* 1954), Nesta, who *d* 1959, da of Frederick J. Phillips; 2ndly, 1954, Beryl, da of William H. Powell, and has issue by 1st and 2nd *m*.

Arms – Argent, upon a mount vert in front of an oak tree fructed proper a lion passant gules, in chief three estoiles sable. **Crest** – In front of a mast and sail of a ship proper charged with a sphinx couchant sans wings argent, an anchor fessewise sable, entwined with a scroll silver, inscribed "HMS Romulus", in letters also sable.
Residence – Rhode Farm, Romansleigh, South Molton, N Devon EX36 4JW.

SONS LIVING *(By 1st marriage)*

(WILLIAM) ANTONY JOHN (26 Merrick Square, SE1 4JB), *b* 20 June 1937; *ed* Wycliffe Coll: *m* 1962, Susan Wight, da of Henry Wight. Gibson, of Cardiff, and has issue living, William Nicolas Henry, *b* 1963, — Giles Antony James, *b* 1968, — Harry Alexander, *b* 1979, — Henrietta Nesta, *b* 1965. —— Barrie Alan, *b* 1942; *ed* Wycliffe Coll: *m* 1965, Wendy Elizabeth, da of George William. Bigglestone, of Coventry, and has issue living, Samantha Elizabeth, *b* 1966, — Louise Suzanne, *b* 1968. —— Timothy Henry Neale (Pentre Cottage, Llanwenarth, Abergavenny, Gwent), *b* 1944; *ed* Wycliffe Coll: *m* 1966, Lynda Madeleine, da of Francis Wallace Preston, of Redditch, and has issue living, Philip Timothy Edward, *b* 1969, — James Henry Charles, *b* 1971, — Edward William Neale, *b* 1977.

(By 2nd marriage)

David Joseph William, *b* 1960.

DAUGHTERS LIVING *(By 1st marriage)*

(Nesta) Suzanne, *b* 1939: *m* 1958, Francis Edward Sutherland Hayes, DL, of Llansannor House, Cowbridge, Glam, and has issue living, Patrick Neil Sutherland, *b* 1961: *m* 1988, Jacqueline, da of late John Ford, and has issue living, Samuel *b* 1993, Aimée *b* 1990, — Thira Nesta, *b* 1960: *m* 1991, John Rudd, — Elizabeth Ann, *b* 1964: *m* 1990, Ian Mellett, — Philippa Vera, *b* 1966.

(By 2nd marriage)

Deirdre Ellen, *b* 1955. —— Amanda Mary, *b* 1958. —— Penelope Ann, *b* 1962.

BROTHER LIVING

Douglas Hamlyn (West Ash Hill, Forches Cross, Newton Abbot, Devon), *b* 1928; *ed* Marlborough, and Roy Agric Coll, Cirencester: *m* 1949, Minnie Wanna, da of John Dawson, and has had two adopted sons and an adopted da, Hugh David, *b* 1957, — Jonathan Owen, *b* 1961: *m* 19—, Diane H., only da of Douglas Webb, of Blakeney, Glos, and has issue living, Oliver *b* 1993, — Jane Elizabeth, *b* 1959; *d* 1977.

SISTER LIVING

Ellen Mary, *b* 1922: *m* 1947, Dr David Kenneth Lewis Davies, and has issue living, David Christopher, *b* 1948, — Simon James, *b* 1952, — William Peter, *b* 1953, — Mark Hamlyn, *b* 1961, — Siân Elizabeth, *b* 1956. *Residence* – 54 Palace Rd, Llandaff, Cardiff.

COLLATERAL BRANCH LIVING

Issue of late Alan John Reardon Smith, 2nd son of 2nd baronet, *b* 1914, *d* 1970: *m* 1937, Winifred Maud, who *d* 1975, da of Frederick C. Williams:—

John Philip (Greenleaves, 301 Marshfield Rd, Castleton, nr Cardiff CF3 8UU), *b* 1941: *m* 1964, Josephine Mireille, da of Frederick Wilding, of Barry, Glam, and has issue living, Charles Alan, *b* 1965, — Simon John, *b* 1966, — Katharine Lisa, *b* 1971. —— Richard William Alan (18 Berthwin St, Cardiff CF1 9JP), *b* 1946: *m* 1st, 1970 (*m diss* 1990), Suzanne Ward, da of Jonathan Preece Jones, of Coychurch, Glam; 2ndly, 1990, Nicola Jane, eldest da of Christopher Denis Yapp, of Plough House, Druidstone Rd, St Mellons, S Glamorgan, and has issue living (by 1st *m*), Dylan Alan John, *b* 1972, — Zahra Elizabeth, *b* 1973, — (by 2nd *m*) Samuel William, *b* 1990.

The 1st baronet, Sir William Reardon Smith (son of Capt Thomas Reardon Smith, of Appledore, N Devon), was a Shipowner, a Coal Exporter, an an Insurance Broker. Sir Willie, 2nd baronet, assumed by deed-poll 1929 the surname of Reardon-Smith in lieu of his patronymic.

SPENCER-SMITH (UK) 1804, of Tring Park, Hertfordshire

By war and wit

Sir JOHN HAMILTON SPENCER-SMITH, 7th *Baronet*; *b* 18 March 1947; *s* his father, Sir THOMAS COSPATRIC, 1959; *ed* Milton Abbey, and Lackham Coll of Agric: *m* 1980 (*m diss* 1992), Mrs Christine Sandra Parris, da of late John Theodore Charles Osborne, of Durrington, Worthing, Sussex, and has issue.

𝔄rms – Sable, on a fesse cottised between three martlets or, as many crescents azure, 𝔠rest – A sword proper, pommel and hilt or, and a pen argent in saltire.
Residence – Hazel House Quarantine Kennels, Elsted, Midhurst, W Sussex GU29 0JT.

DAUGHTER LIVING

Jessica Kirsten, *b* 1985.

WIDOW LIVING OF SIXTH BARONET

LUCY ASHTON (*Lucy, Lady Spencer-Smith*), only da of late Thomas Ashton Ingram: *m* 1944, Sir Thomas Cospatric Hamilton Spencer-Smith, 6th Bt, who *d* 1959.

COLLATERAL BRANCHES LIVING

Grandchildren of late Lt-Col Michael Seymour Hamilton-Spencer-Smith, DSO, MC, son of late Rev Spencer Compton Hamilton-Spencer-Smith, 3rd son of late Spencer Smith, yr brother of 2nd baronet:—
Issue of late Maj Peter Compton Hamilton-Spencer-Smith, *b* 1912, *d* 1993: *m* 1950, Philippa Mary (High Down House, Hitchin, Herts SG5 3BL), yr da of late Capt Richard Ford, Rifle Brig:—
MICHAEL PHILIP, *b* 2 April 1952; *ed* Eton. —— Gerald Peter Harry, *b* 1954.

Grandchildren of late Rev Orlando Spencer SMITH, 4th son of Spencer Smith (ante):—
Issue of late Col Gerald Montagu Spencer SMITH, DSO, RA, *b* 1881, *d* 1951: *m* 1912, Iris Mary, who *d* 1967, da of late Richard Arthur Hamilton Seymour (*see* Culme-Seymour, Bt, colls, 1980 Edn):—
Judith, *b* 1917: *m* 1940, Harry Illtyd Lee, who *d* 1985, and has issue living, James Seymour (71 Sumner Place Mews, SW7), *b* 1945; a film director: *m* 1st, 1967 (*m diss* 19—), Sally Hill, da of late Edwin Hector Gordon Brookes, AFC; 2ndly, 1978, Hannah Marion Teresa, da of Patrick Joseph Lennon, and has had issue (by 1st *m*), Orlando Spencer Seymour *b* 1968, *d* 1981 (by 2nd *m*) Edward Joseph Seymour *b* 1985, Jack Illtyd Seymour *b* 1989, Grace Olivia Seymour *b* 1986, Florence Daphne Seymour *b* 1993, — Caroline Susan, *b* 1941, — Ann (60a Stanhope Gdns, SW7), *b* 1943: *m* 1963, Nicholas Hugh Carter, and has issue living, Maximilian Hugh *b* 1965, Adam James Louis *b* 1977, Emma Louise *b* 1966, Sophie Ann *b* 1969, — Lindsey Victoria, *b* 1954: *m* 1979, Angel Peter Andrews, of 6 Grosvenor Av, SW14 8BX, and has issue living, Nyah Zoe *b* 1977, — and an adopted son, Michael Gerald Harry, *b* 1957. *Residence* – Popple Hill, Graffham, Petworth, W Sussex GU28 0QF.

Issue of late Col Richard Osbaldeston SPENCER-SMITH, *b* 1885, *d* 1962: *m* 1st, 1912, Murielle Alethe Victoria, who *d* 1931, da of Leonard Guise John Wingfield-Stratford (V Powerscourt, colls); 2ndly, 1932, Christian Louisa, who *d* 1962, da of late Lt-Col H. E. Passy:—
(By 1st *m*) Drummond Mervyn (Jade Cottage, Bidford-on-Avon, Alcester, Warwicks B50 4NL), *b* 1920, *ed* Wellington; Capt (ret) R Tank Regt: *m* 1960, June Patrysha, da of Bertram George Finn, and has issue living, Christopher Rex, *b* 1962: *m* 1986, Serena Richwood, and has issue living, Naomi Kate *b* 1987, Danielle Eve *b* 1990, — Rosalind Muriel, *b* 1960: *m* 1988, Colin George Woodnutt, and has issue living, Simon Edward *b* 1989. —— (By 2nd *m*) Rosan Winifred, *b* 1934.

Grandchildren of late Col Richard Osbaldeston SPENCER-SMITH (ante):—

Issue of late Maj Roland Wingfield SPENCER-SMITH, Royal Hampshire Regt, *b* 1916, *d* 1988: *m* 1948, Helen Rosamund (Three Corners, Old Newton Rd, Kingskerswell, Newton Abbot, S Devon TQ12 5LB), da of Lt-Col James Percy Earp, OBE, MC:—

Richard Mervyn (124 Hampstead Way, NW11 7XY), *b* 1954: *m* 1989, Sotiria Dracopoulou, and has issue living, Roland Mikhail Alexander, *b* 1990. —— Jennifer Murielle, *b* 1952: *m* 1st, 1973 (*m diss* 1984), Peter Leslie Riley; 2ndly, 1990, Simon Andrew Cyprian Dunstan, and has issue living (by 2nd *m*), Ysobel Sophie Helen, *b* 1991.

The 1st baronet, Sir Drummond Smith, not having issue, the patent of baronetcy was conferred with remainder to the issue male of his niece, Augusta (daughter of his el brother, Joshua Smith), who *m* 1798 Charles Smith, MP, of Suttons, Essex, descended from Robert Smith of Ilminster, ancestor of Smith-Marriott, Bt. Sir Drummond Cospatric Hamilton-Spencer-Smith, 5th Bt, OBE, (whose father the Rev Spencer Compton Hamilton-Spencer-Smith assumed the additional names of Hamilton and Spencer 1872, having *m* Mary, da of Adm Cospatric Baillie-Hamilton, descended from 6th Earl of Haddington), was Mil Sec to Comdt of New Zealand Forces 1910-13, and a Member of Mil Inter-Allied Commn of Control 1920-24. The 7th Bt discontinued the use of the surname of Hamilton.

VASSAR-SMITH (UK) 1917, of Charlton Park, Charlton Kings, co Gloucester

Labour and truth

Sir RICHARD RATHBORNE VASSAR-SMITH, TD, 3rd *Baronet*, son of late Major Charles Martin Vassar-Smith, 3rd son of 1st baronet: *b* 24 Nov 1909; *s* his uncle, *Sir* JOHN GEORGE LAWLEY, 1942; *ed* Lancing Coll, and Pembroke Coll, Camb (BA 1931); Headmaster of St Ronans Prep Sch since 1957; 1939-45 War as Maj RA: *m* 1932, Dawn Mary, da of Sir Raymond Wybrow Woods, CBE, and has issue.

𝕬rms – Quarterly, 1st and 4th per bend embattled azure and or, in sinister chief point a cuirass with tasces attached and in the dexter base point a well-head all counterchanged, *Smith*; 2nd and 3rd, argent, an Etruscan vase gules, in chief two fusils azure, each charged with a fleur-de-lis or, *Vassar*. 𝕬rests – 1st, a dexter arm embowed in armour proper, bound above the elbow with a scarf gules and holding in the hand an arrow in bend point downwards or and a pair of pincers in fesse sable, *Smith*; 2nd, an Etruscan vase gules between two branches of oak fructed proper, *Vassar*.
Residence – Orchard House, Hawkhurst, Kent. *Clubs* – Hawks (Camb); Rye Golf.

SON LIVING

JOHN RATHBORNE (St Ronans, Hawkhurst, Kent), *b* 23 July 1936; *ed* Eton: *m* 1971, Roberta Elaine, da of Wing Cdr Norman Williamson, and has issue living, Richard Rathborne, *b* 29 Dec 1975, — David Rathborne *b* 1978.

DAUGHTER LIVING

Juliet Rathborne, *b* 1941.

The 1st baronet, Sir Richard (son of late Richard Tew Smith), assumed by Roy licence 1904, the additional surname of Vassar, and was Chm of Lloyds Bank (Limited).

WALKER-SMITH (UK) 1960 of Broxbourne, co Herts.

Hon Sir (JOHN) JONAH WALKER-SMITH, 2nd *Baronet*; *b* 6 Sept 1939; *s* his father, DEREK COLCLOUGH, Baron Broxbourne, TD, QC, PC (life Baron) in his baronetcy 1992; *ed* Westminster, and Ch Ch Oxford: *m* 1974, Aileen Marie, only da of late Joseph Smith, and has issue.

𝕬rms – Quarterly: 1st and 4th, per fesse or and argent a portcullis sable throughout raised to the nombril point within a bordure per fesse gules and or, charged with ten acorns counter coloured, *Smith*; 2nd and 3rd, per pale azure and gules a horse passant argent hooved and crined or, between three caltrops gold, *Walker*. 𝕬rests – 1st, out of a mural crown gules masoned or a mount vert thereon a lion statant argent holding in the dexter forepaw a sword proper pommel hilt and quillons also or, the blade environed by an oak branch fructed gold, *Smith*; 2ndly, between two ostrich feathers gules quilled or a leg in armour azure garnished gold, *Walker*.
Address – 11 Doughty St, WC1.

SON LIVING

DANIEL DEREK, *b* 26 March 1980.

DAUGHTER LIVING

Charmian Lucinda, *b* 1977.

SISTERS LIVING

Hon Deborah Susan, *b* 1941: *m* 1965, Christopher Terence Sinclair-Stevenson, publisher, of 3 South Terrace, SW7 2TB. —— *Hon* Berenice Mary, *b* 1946: *m* 1967, William Andrew Weston, of 7 Royal Arcade, Albemarle St, W1X 3HD.

WIDOW LIVING OF LIFE BARON AND FIRST BARONET

DOROTHY (*Baroness Broxbourne*), da of late Capt Louis John Walpole Etherton, of Rowlands Castle, Hants: *m* 1938, Baron Broxbourne, TD, QC, PC (Life Baron), who *d* 1992. *Residence* – 7 Kepplestone, King Edward's Parade, Eastbourne, E Sussex.

Smith-Dodsworth, see Dodsworth.

Smith-Gordon, see Gordon.

Smith-Marriott, see Marriott.

SMYTH, (UK) 1956, of Teignmouth, co Devon

Sir TIMOTHY JOHN SMYTH, 2nd *Baronet*; *b* 16 April 1953; *s* his grandfather, *Brig Rt Hon Sir* JOHN GEORGE, VC, MC, 1983; *ed* Univ of NSW, MB BS (NSW); MBA (AGSM), LLB (NSW), FRACMA: *m* 1981, Bernadette Mary, da of Leo Askew, and has issue.

Arms – Ermine, on a bend beneath two unicorns' heads erased azure, three lozenges or. **Crest** – A demi bull rampant argent, issuing from a ducal coronet or, armed and horned of the same, and gorged with a collar azure, charged with three lozenges and rimmed or.
Address – PO Box 421, New Lambton, NSW 2305, Australia.

SONS LIVING

BRENDAN JULIAN, *b* 4 Oct 1981. —— Gerard Timothy, *b* 1988.

DAUGHTERS LIVING

Kathryn Mary, *b* 1983. —— Emma Louise, *b* 1985.

BROTHERS LIVING

NEC·TIMEO·NEC·SPERNO

*I neither fear mine enemy
nor do I despise him*

Christopher Charles, *b* 1954. —— John George, *b* 1957. —— Simon Gerard, *b* 1961. —— Andrew, *b* 1964.

SISTERS LIVING

Margaret Mary, *b* 1955. —— Clare Marie, *b* 1960.

AUNT LIVING (*Daughter of 1st baronet*)

Jillian Margaret, *b* 1929: *m* 1968, David George Firth, of 98 Sussex Way, N7.

MOTHER LIVING

Philomena Mary, da of John Francis Cannon: *m* 1952, Julian Smyth, who *d* 1974, el son of 1st Bt. *Residence* – 22 Ina Gregory Court, Conder, ACT 2906, Australia.

COLLATERAL BRANCH LIVING

Issue of late Robin Smyth, yst son of 1st baronet, *b* 1926, *d* 1992: *m* 1961, Joan Harrison (4 rue Villehardouin, Paris 75003), da of late W. J. Williams, of Worthing, Sussex:—
John Julian, *b* 1961.

The 1st Bt, Rt Hon Sir John George Smyth, VC, MC, served with distinction in both World Wars and was MP for Norwood Div of Lambeth 1950-66, being *cr* PC 1962.

BOWYER-SMYTH (E) 1661, of Hill Hall, Essex

Qua pote lucet

Sir THOMAS WEYLAND BOWYER-SMYTH, 15th *Baronet*; *b* 25 June 1960; *s* his father *Capt Sir* PHILIP WEYLAND, RN, 1978: *m* 1992, Sara Louise Breinlinger.

Arms – Quarterly: 1st and 4th sable, a fesse, dancettée argent, billettée sable between three lioncels reguardant of the second, each supporting an altar or, flaming proper, *Smyth*; 2nd and 3rd, or, a bend vair, cotised gules, *Bowyer*. **Crests** – 1st, a salamander in flames proper, *Smyth*; 2nd, on a ducal coronet or, an heraldic tiger sejant argent, *Bowyer*.
Address – c/o Stour House, Fordwich, Canterbury, Kent CT2 0DA.

SISTER LIVING

Amelia, *b* 1958: *m* 1982, James Duncan Johnstone Gracie, son of Rev Anthony Johnstone Gracie, of 53 Ashford Rd, Swindon, Wilts, and has issue living, Luke, *b* 1986, — Leah, *b* 1989. *Residence* – Le Moulin de Gillebert, Montjean, 16240 Villefagnan, France.

AUNT LIVING (*Daughter of 13th baronet*)

Lily Marcia BOWYER-SMIJTH, *b* 1905.

WIDOW LIVING OF FOURTEENTH BARONET

VERONICA MARY (*Dowager Lady Bowyer-Smyth*), da of Capt C. W. Bower, DSC, RN (ret), of Fordwich, Kent: *m* 1951, as his 2nd wife, Capt Sir Philip Weyland Bowyer-Smyth, RN, who *d* 1978.

COLLATERAL BRANCHES LIVING

Grandchildren of late William Baird BOWYER-SMIJTH (declaration of legitimacy granted in Scotland 1918, but not in succession to the baronetcy), son of 11th baronet, *b* 1859, *d* 1940: *m* 18—, C. V. Sweeney, who *d* 1892:—
Issue of late William Bowyer-Smijth, *b* 1889, *d* 1937: *m* 1913, Janie Isabel Norman, of Monaro Vale, Berringan, NSW:—
†William, *b* 1915: *m* 1941, Eileen May Peterson, of Corowa, NSW, and *d* 1989, leaving issue, Ian William (16 Yattenden Crescent, Baulkham Hills, NSW 2153), *b* 1942: *m* 1964, Jennifer Shepard, and has issue living, Stuart *b* 1965 (has issue living, Fiona *b* 1987), Mark *b* 1968, — Keith Raymond (Burrows St, Albury, NSW 2640), *b* 1945: *m* 1973, Lorraine Campbell, and has issue living, Bruce *b* 1977, Louise *b* 1975. *Residence* – 619 Wyse St, Albury, NSW. —— Henry, *b* 1916. —— Edward, *b* 1930. —— Betty, *b* 1921.

Issue of David Malcolm BOWYER-SMYTH (declaration of legitimacy granted in Scotland 1918, but not in the succession to the baronetcy), 5th son of 11th baronet, *b* 1869, *d* 1930: *m* 1900 (*m diss* 1910), Miriam McCheyne, da of Maj Legh Richmond Battye:—
Basil Malcolm, *b* 1901: *m* 1924, Mabel Henrietta, da of late James Samuel Tetlock, and has issue living, Barrie Malcolm (1090 Keith Rd, W Vancouver, BC), *b* 1925: *m* 1959, Margaret, da of George Kilpatrick Morrison, and has issue living, John Barrie *b* 1962, Jane Catherine *b* 1965, Elizabeth Margaret *b* 1968, — James Brian (8366 Victoria Dr, Vancouver, BC), *b* 1929: *m* 1965, Marianne, da of Max Bruno Schwaerzler, and has issue living, Marc *b* 1967, Simone *b* 1969, — David Anthony, *b* 1931: *m* 1953 (*m diss* 1972), Lee Smith, and has issue living, David *b* 1954, Michael *b* 1956, Kathie *b* 1955, Lisa *b* 1958. —— Evangeline, *b* 1904: *m* 1928, Jack Veale, and has issue living, Robert, *b* 1929, — Douglas, *b* 1933, — Joan, *b* 1931, — Nellie, *b* 1935, — Beverley, *b* 1937.

Grandchildren of late Maj Ashe WINDHAM (*b* 1863), el son of Ashe WINDHAM (*b* 1830) (who assumed the surname of Windham in lieu of Smijth-Windham by Roy Licence 1888), 2nd son of late Capt Joseph SMIJTH-WINDHAM, of Waghen Hall, Yorks (who assumed the additional surname and arms of Windham by Roy Licence 1823), yst son of 7th baronet:—
Issue of late Sir Ralph Windham, *b* 1905, *d* 1980: Ch Justice of Tanganyika: *m* 1946, Kathleen Mary (Hook's Cottage, Kingscote, Tetbury, Glos), da of Capt Cecil Henry Fitzherbert, of Millbrook, Abbeyleix, co Leix, Eire:—
JOHN JEREMY (The Hyde, Woolhope, Herefords HR1 4RE), *b* 22 Nov 1948; *ed* Wellington Coll; Capt (ret) Irish Gds and 22 SAS Regt: *m* 1976, (Rachel) Mary, da of late Lt-Col (Walter) George Finney, TD, RA (TA) (*see* E Perth, colls), and has issue living, (Thomas) Ralph, *b* 5 Aug 1985, — Katharine Anne, *b* 1981, — Emma Georgina, *b* 1983. —— Andrew Guy (Shobdon Farm, Newton St Margaret's, Vowchurch, Herefordshire HR2 0QW), *b* 1949; *ed* Wellington Coll, and Trin Coll Camb (BA); solicitor: *m* 1976, Diana Susan, yr da of Hon Norman Dunlop Galloway Galbraith (*see* B Strathclyde), and has issue living, Rory Michael, *b* 1978, — Ruth Emily, *b* 1980, — Lydia Mary, *b* 1982, — Harriet Rachel, *b* 1984. —— Penelope Susan, *b* 1952. —— Belinda Mary Victoria, *b* 1955: *m* 1989, Mark Baxter, 2nd son of David Baxter.

Grandchildren of late Ashe Windham (*b* 1830) (ante):—
Issue of late Major Ashe WINDHAM, *b* 1863, *d* 1937: *m* 1903, Cora Ellen Sowerby, who *d* 1948, 2nd da of late Capt Henry Sowerby Middleton, Oxfordshire LI:—
Ashe *b* 1916; *ed* Radley; Maj (ret) E Yorks Regt & ADC to Gov of Assam 1938-40: *m* 1940, Iris Daphne, da of Col Edward Selby Phipson, CIE, DSO, MD, IMS (ret), and has issue living, Ashe Adrian (Rectory Lodge, The Fairland, Hingham, Norfolk), *b* 1941; late Capt RA; in Diplomatic Ser: *m* 1969, Daphne Anne, da of Maj A. A. P. C. Thomas, TD (ret), and has issue living, Philippa Mary *b* 1977, — Daniel Harry (Willow Cottage, Hackford, Wymondham, Norfolk), *b* 1948; *ed* Radley, and Magdalene Coll, Camb; late R Irish, and Muscat Regt SAF: *m* 1975, Caroline Mary, da of late Richard Pelham Warren, FRCS, of Epping, Essex, and has issue living, William *b* 1978, Alexa *b* 1980. —— Joan (74 Exeter Rd, Newmarket), *b* 1904: *m* 1st, 1959, Brig Ord Henderson Tidbury, MC, who *d* 1961; 2ndly, 1964, Maj Hugh D'Oyly Lyle, late R Welch Fus, who *d* 1977. —— Anne, MBE (Green Shutters, Long Melford, Suffolk), *b* 1906; Foreign and Dip Ser (ret); MBE (Civil) 1942. —— Mève (Wawne Cottage, Offton, nr Ipswich) *b* 1909. —— Ruth (Little Beechford, Childe Okeford, Dorset), *b* 1912: *m* 1st 1938 (*m diss* 1962), Robert Bellord, Maj IG, who *d* 1970; 2ndly, 1972, Brig John Henry Patrick Woodroffe, DSO, and has issue living (by 1st *m*), Edward James WINDHAM-BELLORD (The Cottage, Cucklington, Som), *b* 1947; *ed* Downside, and Wadham Coll, Oxford; assumed the surname of Windham-Bellord 1965: *m* 1972 (*m diss* 1976), Caroline Irene, who *d* 1979, only da of Robert Grenville Plantagenet Morgan-Grenville (*see* L Kinloss), and has issue living, James Robert Grenville, *b* 1973; *ed* Downside, and King's Coll, London, — Richard Valentine (3E Butler Towers, 5 Boyce Rd, Hong Kong), *b* 1949: *m* 1st, 1974 (*m diss* 1982), Cheung Wai Lan; 2ndly, 1982, Julieta Estina Bisco, and has issue living, (by 1st *m*) Richard Valentine (Siddha) *b* 1975, Satya *b* 1976, Subhadra *b* 1977, (by 2nd *m*) Jamuna *b* 1983, — Ellen Mary, *b* 1938, — Alice Mary, *b* 1939. —— Grace, *b* 1914: *m* 1st, 1937 (*m diss* 1956), Wilfred Gerard Sydney, 7th Baron Grand d'Hauteville; 2ndly, 19—, Dottore Galli, and has issue living, (by 1st *m*) Philip Anthony Ashe, *b* 1938: *m* 1965, Tania, only da of Gerald Cramer, of

Mies, Switzerland, and has issue living, Henry *b* 1967, Eric *b* (twin) 1967, Diane Cora *b* 1971, — Jacques Pierre, *b* 1943: *m* 1st, 1968 (*m diss* 1973), Françoise Mayer; 2ndly, 1973, Marie-Claire Chappuis, and has issue living, (by 1st *m*) Marc Serge *b* 1969; (by 2nd *m*) Muriel *b* 1977, — Elisabeth Suzanne GRAND D'HAUTEVILLE, *b* 1940: *m* 1st, 1963 (*m diss* 1973), Baron Aymon de Blonay; 2ndly, 1976 (*m diss* 1984), Serge du Buis, and has issue living, (by 1st *m*) Nicolas Aymon Pierre Henri *b* 1967, Marie-Hélène Blanche Renée *b* 1964, Sophie Caroline Elizabeth Grace *b* 1970.

Granddaughters of late Sir William Windham, CBE, 2nd son of late Ashe Windham (*b* 1830) (ante):—
Issue of late William Evan Windham, *b* 1904, *d* 1977: *m* 1st, 1932, Constance Lloyd, who *d* 1939, da of James Hope Loudon, of Olantigh, Wye, Kent; 2ndly, 1962, Dorothy Muir, da of Robert Deans Johnston, of Lenzie, Lanarkshire, and widow of Carl Raymond Davis:—
(By 1st *m*) Elizabeth Aylva, *b* 1935: *m* 1955 (*m diss* 1974), George Alfred Bakewell, and has issue living, Constance Louise *b* 1957, — Charlotte Alice, *b* 1959. —— Juliet Alexa WINDHAM HACKETT, *b* 1938; assumed the additional surname of WINDHAM 1978: *m* 1962 (*m diss* 1971), Raymond Bingham Hackett.

Grandchildren of late Lt-Col Henry Steuart WINDHAM (infra):—
Issue of late Maj James Steuart WINDHAM, *b* 1917, *d* 1989: *m* 1957, Annette de Mèstre (May Hill House, Longhope, Glos), da of William John Wilkins, FRCS:—
Mark Hastings Wriothesley, *b* 1959. —— Tobias Cosmo Russell, *b* 1962. —— Sophia Louise de Mestre, *b* 1958: *m* 1982, Bruce Robinson, and has issue living, Willoughby, *b* 1993, — Lily India, *b* 1986.

Grandchildren of late Major George Smijth-Windham, 4th son of late Capt Joseph SMIJTH-WINDHAM (ante):—
Issue of late Lt-Col Henry Steuart WINDHAM (twin), *b* 1873, *d* 1958: *m* 1915, Marjory Russell, who *d* 1971, da of late Henry McLean Dymock:—
William Ashe Dymoke (Parc Gwynne, Glasbury-on-Wye, via Hereford, Radnorshire), *b* 1926; *ed* Bedford Sch (Scholar), and Christ's Coll, Camb (Scholar) (MA); Chm, Skelmersdale Development Corpn 1979-85: *m* 1956, Alison Audrey Primrose, da of late Maj Philip Pinckney Curtis, MC (*see* Curtis, Bt, colls), and has issue living, Ashe George Russell, LVO, *b* 1957; *ed* Eton, and RMA Sandhurst; Capt IG; Temp Equerry to HM Queen Elizabeth, The Queen Mother 1980-82, and an Extra Equerry since 1993; LVO 1982, — (Charles) William Fitz-Roy, *b* 1960, — Emma Rose Dymock, *b* 1959: *m* 1991, Simon Vivian Surtees Phillpotts of 70 Lilford Rd, SE5 9HR, son of late Christopher Phillpotts, CMG, of 27 Merrick Sq. SE1, and has issue living, Archie Christopher Louis *b* 1992. —— Rachel Russell, *b* 1916: *m* 1963, Lt-Col George Kinloch Sheppard, who *d* 1963, el son of late Sir William Didsbury Sheppard, KCIE.
Issue of late Arthur Russell Smijth-Windham, *b* 1874, who *d* 1915: *m* 1901, Brenda Helen, who *d* 1947, da of late Gerald Hall:—
William Russell, CBE, DSO, *b* 1907; *ed* Wellington Coll; is Brigadier late Royal Signals, a FIEE; appointed an ADC to HM 1957; Mount Everest Expeditions 1933 and 1936: 1939-45 War in Middle East and NW Europe (despatches, DSO, CBE); DSO 1942, CBE (Mil) 1946: *m* 1934, Helen Teresa Clementi, da of late Brig Hubert Clementi Smith, DSO (Clarke-Jervoise, Bt, ext), and has issue living, Simon William (Middle Lodge, Hughenden Estate, High Wycombe, Bucks MP14 4LA), *b* 1937: *m* 1960, Wendy Myra, da of Edgar William John Albrow, and has issue living, Alistair William *b* 1966, Tanya Myra *b* 1961, — Joanna Felicity (Fairseat Farm, Chew Stoke, nr Bristol), *b* 1938: *m* 1st, 1963, Peter Anthony Lazarus, who *d* 1980; 2ndly, 1984, Alan Robert Brown, and has issue living (by 1st *m*), George William, *b* 1969, Mary Helen, *b* 1966, — Prudence Helen, *b* 1945; *ed* St Hugh's Coll, Oxford (MA); Solicitor: *m* 1967 (*m diss* 1985), John Derek Walter Murdoch, and has issue living, Thomas Duncan *b* 1970, Clarissa Helen *b* 1972, Rosamond Elsie *b* 1977, — Rachel Beatrice, *b* 1946: *m* 1970, John Santer, of 78 Enborne Rd, Newbury, Berks, and has issue living, William Robert Clive *b* 1976, Harry Joseph *b* 1978, Evelyn Margaret *b* 1973, Anne Dorothy Sarah *b* 1981. *Residence* – Estate Corner, Pitney, Langport, Som. —— Diana Elizabeth, *b* 1911: *m* 1957, E. M. W. Paul, and has issue living, Isabella Brenda Windham, *b* 1948: *m* 1972, Michael Braine Morton-Smith, and has issue. *Residence* – Maysleith, Milland, nr Liphook, Hants GU30 7JN.

Sir Thomas Smith, 1st Bt of Hill Hall, Essex, High Sheriff 1663, was grandson of George, brother of Sir Thomas Smith, of Hill Hall, Sec of State to Edward VI and Elizabeth I. His son, Sir Edward 2nd Bt, adopted the spelling of Smyth, and Sir William, 7th Bt about 1796, that of Smijth. He *m* 1779, Anne, da of John Windham-Bowyer, of Woodmansterne, Surrey, and sister and heir of Joseph Windham. Her mother, Mary, was da and heir of Joseph Windham, of Twickenham, Middlesex (afterwards Ashe), by Catherine, da and co-heir of Sir Edmund Bowyer, of Camberwell. Sir Edward, 10th Bt, assumed by Roy Licence 1839 the name and arms of Bowyer-Smijth. Sir Alfred John, 13th Bt, reverted to former spelling of surname from Bowyer-Smijth to Bowyer-Smyth.

SNADDEN (UK) 1955, of Coldoch, co Perth (Extinct 1959)

Sir WILLIAM MCNAIR SNADDEN, 1st and last *Baronet*.

DAUGHTER LIVING OF FIRST BARONET

Rosemary Adele McNair, *b* 1926: *m* 1st, 1944, Capt Charles Napier Frederick Webb, S Wales Borderers, who *d* 1945 while on active ser abroad; 2ndly, 1947, Patrick Heatley Dickson, and has had issue (by 1st *m*) James Charles Napier, *b* 1946: *m* 1974, Mary Thomas, of The Old Mill, Easingwold, Yorks, and *d* 1980, — (by 2nd *m*) Elizabeth Jane, *b* 1948: *m* 1st, 1969, Michael Alexander Ligertwood, who *d* 1982; 2ndly, 1984, John Alexander Fell, of Levenside, Haverthwaite, Cumbria, and has issue living, (by 1st *m*) Mark Murray *b* 1972, Guy Alexander *b* 1975, Andrew Patrick *b* 1979, — Deborah Rose, *b* 1953: *m* 1982 (*m diss* 1989), Nigel Everard Barnes, of Johannesburg, S Africa, and has issue living, Tugela Jane *b* 1985. *Residence* – Craighead House, Blair Drummond, by Stirling.

BUCKWORTH-HERNE-SOAME (E) 1697, of Sheen, Surrey

Sir CHARLES JOHN BUCKWORTH-HERNE-SOAME, 12th *Baronet; b* 28 May 1932; *s* his father *Sir* CHARLES BURNETT, 1977: *m* 1958, Eileen Margaret Mary, da of Leonard Minton, of Caughley, Shropshire, and has issue.

Arms – Quarterly: 1st and 4th, gules, a chevron between three mallets or, a canton argent for difference, *Soame*; 2nd and 3rd, sable, on a chevron between three cross-crosslets fitchée argent, an ermine spot, *Buckworth*. **Crests** – 1st, a lure gules, garnished and stringed argent, thereon a falcon or, beaked and legged of the second; 2nd a man's head in profile armed with a helmet, the beaver up all proper. *Residence* – Sheen Cottage, Coalbrookdale, Shropshire.

SON LIVING

RICHARD JOHN, *b* 17 Aug 1970.

SISTER LIVING

Mary, *b* 1936: *m* 1958, Keith Howard Edwards, of 27 Woodside, Coalbrookdale, Shropshire, and has issue living, Robert John Edwards, *b* 1971, — Carol Jane, *b* 1964.

Sir John Buckworth, 1st baronet, was High Sheriff of London 1704. Sir Everard, the 3rd baronet, was Assist Gentleman Usher to King George II. Sir Everard, the 5th baronet, Gentleman-Pensioner and Exon of the Guard, *temp* George III, assumed the additional surname of Herne, having *m* Anne Herne, of Haviland Hall, Norfolk. Sir Buckworth Buckworth-Herne, the 6th baronet, assumed, in 1806, the additional surname of Soame by Roy licence, in compliance with the will of Sir Peter Soame, 4th baronet (title now extinct).

SOMERVILLE (I) 1748, of Dublin (Dormant 1929)

Since the death of the 2nd Baron Athlumney (who was also 6th Baronet of this creation) in 1929, the Baronetcy has remained dormant, and at time of going to press no name appears in respect of it on the Official Roll of Baronets.

COLLATERAL BRANCHES LIVING

Descendants, if any, of late Archibald James Somerville (son of late Capt William Somerville, only son of late Major William Somerville, 2nd son of 1st baronet), *b* 1803, *d* 1871: *m* 1836, Elizabeth, da of Jason Crawford, of Ballyholly, co Cavan; he left issue, Archibald James, William, Jason, Bellingham Brookes.

Grandchildren of late Capt Bellingham Arthur Somerville, 2nd son of Tenison Alan Somerville, 5th son of Capt William Somerville (ante):—
Issue of late Lt-Col Gualter Hugh Rodger Bellingham Somerville, MC, *b* 1894, *d* 1947: *m* 1925, Heather Edith, who *d* 1994, da of late Col Cecil Norris Baker, CIE:—
Patricia May Naomi (20 Carlton Rd, Oxford OX2 7SA), *b* 1929: *m* 1st, 1951 (*m diss* 1973), Lt Michael William Richmond Nicholas, RN; 2ndly, 1974, Robert James Henderson, who *d* 1977; 3rdly, 1978, Prof Thomas David Duncan Williams, who *d* 1985, and has issue living (by 1st *m*), Patrick Richmond, *b* 1952, — Elizabeth Richmond, *b* 1954: *m* 1st, 1978 (*m diss* 1984), Capt Andrew Malcolm Wright, RE; 2ndly, 1991, Robert James Turner, of 16 St Giles, Bletchington, Oxon OX5 3BX, and has issue living (by 2nd *m*), Samuel David Richmond *b* 1993, Zoë Elizabeth Richmond *b* 1992. —— Julia Heather Margaret, *b* 1931: *m* 1958, as his 2nd wife, William Bristow Stevenson, DL, MA, High Sheriff co Londonderry 1971, Chancellor Diocese of Derry and Raphoe, and has issue living, James Roger, *b* 1963, — Henry Bristow, *b* 1970, — Diana Margaret Julia, *b* 1961. *Residence* – Knockan, Feeny, co Londonderry.
Issue of late Reginald Malcolm John Bellingham Somerville, *b* 1897, *d* 1971: *m* 1st, 1928, Maude Gwendoline Constance Violet, who *d* 1935, da of late Capt A. E. H. Moore, R Dublin Fus; 2ndly, 1936, Honor Lucretia Philippa, who *d* 1985, da of late Rev Canon Philip B. Johnson, of the Rectory, Wicklow:—
(By 1st *m*) Juanita Elizabeth Maude, *b* 1932; *ed* Hillcourt Sch, and The Ling Physical Training Coll, Dublin: *m* 1964, Peter Brumby, late Chief Pilot, E African Airways. *Residence* – The Lodge, Dargle Hill, Enniskerry, co Wicklow. —— (By 2nd *m*) William Barnard Reginald Bellingham, *b* 1937; *ed* Trin Coll, Dublin (BA); Solicitor 1967; late Admin Officer, HM Colonial Ser, Tanganyika: *m* 1968, Margery Manon, el da of George Clemenger Vincent Brittain, of Craigfoodie House, Dairsie, Fife, and has issue living, James William Reginald Bellingham, *b* 1969; *ed* Radley, and Trin Coll, Dublin (LLB), — Charles John George Bellingham, *b* 1971: *ed* Kelly Coll, — Edward Henry Tenison Bellingham, *b* 1972; *ed* Radley. *Residence* – Dargle Hill, Enniskerry, co Wicklow.

The 1st baronet, Sir James Somerville, KB, was MP for Dublin City 1729, and Lord Mayor of Dublin 1737, the 4th, Sir Marcus, was MP for co Meath 1801-3, and the 5th, Rt Hon Sir William Meredyth, PC, MP for Drogheda (*L*) 1837-52, and for Canterbury 1854-65, Under-Sec for Home Depart 1846-7, and Ch Sec for Ireland 1847-52, was *cr Baron Athlumney* (peerage of Ireland) 1863, and *Baron Meredyth* (peerage of United Kingdom) 1886, in which Baronies the Baronetcy remained merged until the death of the 2nd Baron Athlumney in 1929, when both Peerages became extinct, and the Baronetcy became dormant.

AGNEW-SOMERVILLE (UK) 1957, of Clendlry, co Wigtown.

Sir QUENTIN CHARLES SOMERVILLE AGNEW-SOMERVILLE, 2nd *Baronet*; *b* 8 March 1929; *s* his father, *Cdr Sir* PETER GARNETT AGNEW, RN, 1990; assumed by Royal Licence 1950 the additional surname of Somerville after that of Agnew, and the arms of Somerville quarterly with those of Agnew, in compliance with the will of his uncle (by marriage), 2nd and last Baron Athlumney; *ed* RNC Dartmouth: *m* 1963, Hon (Margaret Irene) April Drummond, yst da and co-heiress of 15th Baron Strange, and has issue.

Arms – Quarterly, 1st and 4th, azure three mullets or, two and one, between seven cross-crosslets fitchée, three, one, two and one argent, a canton voided of the last charged with four mullets gules and as many cross-crosslets fitchée sable (*Somerville*); 2nd and 3rd, parted per saltire argent and gules, two cinquefoils in pale and as many saltires couped in fess, all counterchanged, a bordure azure (*Agnew*). **Crests** – *Dexter*, a demi-lion rampant sable, charged on the shoulder with a cross-crosslet fitchée between two mullets argent; *sinister*, an eagle rising reguardant proper, holding in the dexter claw a sword proper hilted and pommelled or.
Residence – Mount Auldyn, Jurby Rd, Ramsey, I of Man.

SON LIVING

JAMES LOCKETT CHARLES, *b* 26 May 1970; *ed* Milton Abbey.

DAUGHTERS LIVING

Amelia Rachel, *b* 1965. —— Geraldine Margaret, *b* 1967.
Cdr Sir Peter Garnett Agnew, 1st Bt, RN, was MP for Cambourne Div of Cornwall (*C*) 1931-50, and for S Div of Worcs 1955-66; also a Trustee of Historic Churches Preservation Trust.

SOUTHBY (UK) 1937, of Burford, co Oxford

Sir JOHN RICHARD BILBE SOUTHBY, 3rd *Baronet*; *b* 2 April 1948; *s* his father, *Lt-Col Sir* (ARCHIBALD) RICHARD CHARLES, OBE, 1988; *ed* Peterhouse, Zimbabwe, and Loughborough Univ (BSc): *m* 1971, Victoria Jane, eldest da of John Wilfred Sturrock, of 88 Wrottesley Rd, Tettenhall, Wolverhampton, and has issue.

Arms – Or, a chevron between three apples gules. **Crest** – A demi lion or holding in the dexter paw an apple gules.
Residence – Lomagundi, High St, Nash, Bucks MK17 0EP.

SONS LIVING

PETER JOHN, *b* 20 Aug 1973; *ed* Oundle. —— James William, *b* 1984.

DAUGHTER LIVING

Sarah Jane, *b* 1975.

UNCLE LIVING (*son of 1st baronet*)

Patrick Henry James, *b* 1913; Lt-Cdr RN (ret): *m* 1939, Lady Anne Adeline Hope, da of 2nd Marquess of Linlithgow, and has issue living, Richard Henry Alexander (The Red House, Overbury, Tewkesbury, Glos GL20 7PB), *b* 1941; *ed* Eton, and Worcester Coll, Oxford (MA): *m* 1985, Nicola Claire Wallop, eldest da of Jonathan Janson (see E Portsmouth, colls), and has issue living, Alexander Richard Janson *b* 1987, Henrietta Elizabeth *b* 1989, — Mary Anne, *b* 1946; *ed* Benenden, and Courtauld Inst, London Univ: *m* 1975, Martin Robert Kenyon, of 70 Stockwell Park Rd, SW9, and has issue (see B Kenyon, colls). *Residence* – Robins Mill, Overbury, Tewkesbury, Glos GL20 7NT.

WIDOW LIVING OF FIRST BARONET

NOREEN VERA (*Noreen, Lady Southby*) (18 Harbour View Rd, Parkstone, Poole, Dorset BH14 0PE), da of late Bernard Compton Simm, of Ashbourne, Derbys: *m* 1962, as his 2nd wife, Cdr Sir Archibald Richard James Southby, RN, 1st Bt, who *d* 1969.

WIDOW LIVING OF SECOND BARONET

IRIS MACKAY (*Iris, Lady Southby*), da of late Lt-Col Granville Mackay Heriot, DSO, RM, and widow of Brig Ian Charles Alexander Robertson: *m* 1979, as his 4th wife, Lt-Col Sir (Archibald) Richard Charles Southby, 2nd Bt, OBE, who *d* 1988. *Residences* – Greystone House, Stone, Tenterden, Kent.
Cdr Sir Archibald Richard James Southby, RN, 1st Bt, 2nd son of Richard Southby of Hodcott and Chieveley, Berks, was MP for Epsom 1928-47, Assist Govt Whip 1931-35, and a Jnr Lord of the Treasury 1935-37; Lt-Col Sir Richard Southby, 2nd Bt, OBE, was awarded American Medal of Freedom.

SPEARMAN (UK) 1840, of Hanwell, Middlesex

Sir ALEXANDER YOUNG RICHARD MAINWARING SPEARMAN, 5th *Baronet*; *b* 3 Feb 1969; *s* his father Sir ALEXANDER BOWYER, 1977: *m* 1994, Anne Stine, da of Kaj Munch, of Hyllinge, Denmark.

Arms – Azure, on a chevron ermine between three tilting spears, argent, headed or, a red deer's head erased proper. **Crest** – A lion rampant proper, gorged with a collar gemelle or, supporting a tilting spear also proper, enfiled with a mural crown or.
Address – Zorguliet, 3 Sir George Grey St, Oranjezicht 8001, Cape, S Africa.

SISTERS LIVING

Catherine Wendy Nest, *b* 1959: *m* 1979, Jonathan Mort, and has issue living, Rebecca Claire Spearman, *b* 1994. —— Lynne Dorothy Ann, *b* 1962: *m* 1982, Gregory Lloyd, and has issue living, Nicola, *b* 1988, — Chelsea Anne, *b* 1991. —— Daphne Joan Constance Eileen, *b* 1965.

UNCLE LIVING (*Son of 3rd baronet*)

RICHARD IAN CAMPBELL, *b* 14 Aug 1926; *ed* Clayesmore Sch, and Birkbeck Coll, London (BSc special honours in Zoology, PhD, DSc); Hon Sr Lecturer Univ Coll London, FLS, FZS, Fellow of Inst of Biology, Member of Soc of Experimental Biology, and of British Ecological Soc. *Residence* – 70 Hatherley Rd, Winchester, Hants SO22 6RR.

AUNT LIVING (*Daughter of 3rd baronet*)

While I breathe I hope

Joan Dorothy Ethel (The Chilterns, 70 Hatherley Rd, Winchester, Hants, SO22 6RR), *b* 1912; 1939-45 War: *m* 1960, William Taunton Oliver, who *d* 1983.

COLLATERAL BRANCHES LIVING

Issue of late Joseph William Spearman, eldest son of 2nd baronet, *b* 1879, *dvp* 1917: *m* 1900, Evelyn Daisy Oram:—
Gwendoline Daisy Elizabeth, *b* 1911: *m* 19—, — , and *d* 1994, leaving issue, Valerie, *b* 19—: *m* 19—, Guy Godefroy, of SC1 Les Vigneaux, 41130 Chatillon sur Cher, France, and has issue.

Grandchildren of late Com Alexander Young Crawshay Mainwaring Spearman, RN, half-brother of 2nd baronet:—
Issue of late Sir Alexander Cadwallader Mainwaring Spearman, *b* 1901; *d* 1982: *m* 1st, 1928 (*m diss* 1951), Diana Violet Edith Constance, who *d* 1991, da of Col Sir Arthur Havelock James Doyle, 4th Bt; 2ndly, 1951, Diana Josephine (The Old Rectory, Sarratt, Herts; Fealar, Enochdhu, Blairgowrie, Perthshire; 32 Queen Anne's Gate, SW1), only child of Col Sir (Albert) Lambert Ward, 1st Bt, CVO, DSO, TD:—
(By 2nd *m*) Lochain Alexander, *b* 9 April 1952: *m* 1977, Pilin, da of Senor de Garrigues, and has issue living, Alexander James, *b* 27 March 1984, — Jack, *b* 1986, — a da, *b* 1980. —— John Dominic, *b* 1954: *m* 1976 (*m diss* 1978), Rebecca, da of Sir Alan Lewis Wigan, 8th Bt. —— Andrew Mark, *b* 1960: *m* 1994, Elisa, da of Rt Hon Thomas Jeremy King, CH, MP. —— James, *b* 1964. —— Zara Ann Louise, *b* 1956: *m* 1979, Iain A. Milligan.

Granddaughters of late Alexander Young Spearman, el son of 1st baronet:—
Issue of late Charles Edward Spearman, *b* 1863, *d* 1945: *m* 1901, Frances Henrietta Priaulx, who *d* 1955, da of John Aikman, MD, of Birnam, Guernsey:—
Alice Louisa Jean *b* 1903: *m* 1928, Martin William Strong, who *d* 1978, and has issue living, Richard Martin (25 Newstead Way, Wimbledon, SW19), *b* 1929: *m* 1st, 1956 (*m diss* 1969), Ann Georgina, da of late Richard P. Sargent; 2ndly, 1971, Venetia Mary, da of late Ian T. Henderson, of Crawley, Hants, and has issue living (by 1st *m*), Simon Alexander *b* 1959, — Christopher John, *b* 1932; Sqdn-Ldr RAF: *m* 1956, Brenda Mary, da of late A. Willbery, and has issue living, Michael Alexander *b* 1957, Penelope Ann *b* 1959, Helen Jean *b* 1960. — Michael Charles (2727 Windover Drive, Corona del Mar, Calif 92625, USA), *b* 1935: *m* 1st, 1963 (*m diss* 1968), Lysbeth Joanna, who *d* 1970, el da of Dr C Lanyon, of Falmouth; 2ndly, 1968, Margaret Christine, da of late Edwin V. Price, of Chester, and has issue living, (by 2nd *m*), Edward Charles *b* 1970, James Alexander *b* 1972, Christopher Edwin *b* 1977, — Patricia Anne (5 Wickfield Close, Christchurch, Dorset), *b* 1931: *m* 1957, John Barrett, who *d* 19—, and has issue living, Hazel Jean *b* 1963. *Residence* – Woodside Rd, Burton Joyce, Notts. —— Ivy Joy, *b* 1912: *m* 1939, Lt-Col Thomas Harold Barnes, TD, who *d* 1971, and has issue living, Belinda Marion, *b* 1941: *m* 1963, John Part, of 93 Howards Lane, SW15, and has issue living, Emma Josephine *b* 1967: *m* 1993, Benjamin Oliver Hugh Robson, of The Little House, Biddestone, Wilts, Tracy Belinda *b* 1970, Joanna Frances *b* 1974, — Susannah Mainwaring, *b* 1944: *m* 1966, Andrew Wilson Thomson, of Ashgate Old Forge, Fivehead, Curry Rivel, Taunton, Som. *Residence* – Beechfield Cottage, Upper High St, Castle Cary, Som. —— Anne Mainwaring, *b* 1918: *m* 1940, Santiago Perez-Walker, of Ladislao Errazuriz 2171, Santiago, Chile, and has issue living, Santiago Alexander, *b* 1941: *m* 1963, Gladys Schuler, and has issue living, Santiago Gonzalo *b* 1965, Amaya Paulina *b* 1967, Carola Francisca *b* 1972, — Patrick Charles, *b* 1945: *m* 1969, Ana Maria Bulnes, and has issue living, Sebastian *b* 1971, Moira *b* 1973, — Francis Anthony, *b* 1949: *m* 1973, Maria Soledad Ramirez, and has issue living, Loreto Victoria *b* 1974, Constanza Sol *b* 1980, Paulina Eugenia *b* 1982, — Maria Olaya Evelyn, *b* 1943: *m* 1964, Arturo Mardones, and has issue living, Diego *b* 1967, Magdalena *b* 1965, Octavia *b* 1968.

Grandchildren of late Col Horace Ralph Spearman, 3rd son of 1st baronet.
Issue of late Horace Ralph Spearman, *b* 1868, *d* 19—: *m* 1890, Louisa, da of James Parker:—
Horace Layton, *b* 1896. —— Lily Alexandrina Campbell, *b* 1892. —— Isabella Lucy, *b* 1893.
Issue of late Major Alexander Young Spearman, *b* 1872, *d* 1911: *m* 1898, Mary Cramond, da of late Edward Etches, of Litchurch Grange, Derby:—
Horace Edward James, *b* 1899; *ed* Trin Coll, Glenalmond, and Uppingham; Major late RA: *m* 1934, Mary, da of late Jon Constantinescu, of Braila, Roumania.

The family of Spearman is of considerable antiquity in Durham. John Spearman, a lawyer and antiquary, was many years Under-Sheriff of Durham, and in 1678 he purchased the manor of Thornley in that county. The 1st baronet, Right Hon Sir Alexander Young, was for a long period Comptroller-General and Secretary to the Commissioners for the Reduction of the National Debt.

SPEELMAN (E) 1686

Jonkheer Sir CORNELIS JACOB SPEELMAN, 8th *Baronet*; *b* 17 March 1917; *s* his father, *Jonkheer Sir* Cornelis Jacob, 1949; *ed* Perth Univ, W Australia (BA 1958); formerly in Education Depart of Roy Dutch Army, and a Master at Geelong Gram Sch, and Clifton Coll; Tutor, Exeter Tutorial Coll; is a British subject: *m* 1972, Julia Mona Le Besque, who *d* 1978.

John Cornelis Speelman, of Batavia, *b* 1659, *d* June 1686 before the Royal Warrant directing his creation as a *Baronet* had passed the Great Seal. By Letters Patent of 9 Sept 1686, his widow, Debora, da of John Nicolaes Kievit (Attorney Fiscal to the Admiralty of the Maes), of Rotterdam, was raised to the rank of a Baronet's widow, the same Letters Patent also creating their only son and heir Cornelis, a *Baronet*. The 6th Baronet was in Royal Dutch Navy 1870-83, and sometime Burgomaster of Harlingen. The holders of this title remained resident in the Netherlands until the 8th Baronet.

Spencer-Nairn, see Nairn.

Spencer-Smith, see Smith.

SPEYER (UK) 1906, of Grosvenor Street, St George, Hanover Square, co London (Extinct 1932)

Sir EDGAR SPEYER, 1st and last *Baronet*.

DAUGHTERS LIVING OF FIRST BARONET

Pamela, *b* 1903: *m* 1926, Count Hugo Carl Maria Moÿ de Sons, who *d* 1938. *Residence* – Bell Cottage, Bury Gate, near Pulborough, Sussex. —— Vivien Clare, *b* 1907. *Residence* – 22 Irving Pl, New York City, NY 1003, USA.

SPICER (UK) 1906, of Lancaster Gate, Borough of Paddington

In God alone my hope

Sir NICHOLAS ADRIAN ALBERT SPICER, 5th *Baronet*; *b* 28 Oct 1953; *s* his father, (*Sir*) PETER JAMES (who did not use the title), 1993; *ed* Eton, and Birmingham Univ (MB, ChB 1977); medical practitioner: *m* 1992, Patricia Carol, 2nd da of Warwick Dye, of Auckland, NZ, and has issue.

𝕬rms – Per chevron or and sable, in chief two cinquefoils and in base a tower, all counterchanged. 𝕮rest – Out of the battlements of a tower a cubit arm erect in armour proper, holding in the gauntlet an annulet or.
Residence – 6 Linton Lane, Bromyard, Herefordshire HR7 4DQ.

SON LIVING

JAMES PETER WARWICK, *b* 12 June 1993.

SISTERS LIVING

Phyllida Margaret, *b* 1950: *m* 1979, David John Worcester. —— Alison Celia, *b* 1955: *m* 1980, Giles Marshall Hallam Mills, of Brixey's Farmhouse, Sandford, Ringwood, Hants BH24 3BU. —— Susanna Juliet (Flat 3, 12 Palace Rd, SW2 3NG), *b* 1963.

AUNTS LIVING (*Daughter of 3rd baronet*)

Janet Dykes, *b* 1931. —— Margaret Grace Gillespie, *b* 1933: *m* 1960, John Arnfield Heap, CMG, PhD, of The Old House, Harston, Cambridge and has issue living, Thomas John Gillespie, *b* 1966: *m* 1992, Tammany Robin Stone, — Sarah James, *b* 1961: *m* 1991, Leonard Joseph Byatt, of 5 South Rd, W Bridgford, Notts, — Alice Margaret, *b* 1964: *m* 1988, Andrew Richard Ginger.

DAUGHTERS LIVING OF SECOND BARONET

Patricia Morrison, *b* 1911: *m* 1933, Tyrrell Francis Young, of 143 Cranmer Court, SW3 3HE, and has had issue, Michael Francis Dykes, *b* 1934; *ed* Charterhouse, and Trin Coll, Camb, — David Tyrrell, *b* 1938; *ed* Charterhouse: *m* 1965, Madeline Helen Celia, only da of Anthony Burton Capel Philips, of Heath House, Tean, Stoke-on-Trent, and has issue living, Melanie Rosamond *b* 1969, Annabel Katherine *b* 19—, Corinna Helen *b* 19—, — Rosamond Alison, *b* 1944. —— Pamela Rosamond, *b* 1914: *m* 1936, John Stuart Johnstone, of Mole Hall, Widdington, nr Saffron Walden, Essex, and has issue living, Douglas Stuart, *b* 1953; *ed* Harrow, — Caroline Rosamond, *b* 1938: *m* 1963, Paul-Louis Mascaux, and has issue living, Pascal René Stuart *b* 1965. —— Althea Dykes, *b* 1918: *m* 1st, 1939, Joseph Alwyn Francis Baxendale, Lieut Surrey and Sussex Yeo, who *d* of wounds received in action 1940; 2ndly, 1945, Capt John Wynne Bankes, 14th/20th King's Hussars, of Mynachlog, North-op, Mold, Clwyd CH7 6AF, and has had issue, (by 2nd *m*) Nigel John Eldon, *b* 1946; *ed* Eton, — Andrew Dykes Scott, *b*

1955; *ed* Eton: *m* 1984, Ariane, da of late Arthur John Goodman (*see* M Anglesey, colls), and *d* 1987, — Althea Lavinia, *b* 1949: *m* 1972, Capt Andrew Duncan Gordon, Army Air Corps, of The Steading, Blair Atholl, Perthshire. *Residence* – Myna-chlog, Northop, Flints.

WIDOW LIVING OF FOURTH BARONET

MARGARET, da of late Sir (James) Steuart Wilson, of Fenn's, Petersfield, Hants: *m* 1949, (Sir) Peter James Spicer, 4th Bt (who did not use the title), who *d* 1993. *Residence* – Salt Mill House, Fishbourne, Chichester, W Sussex PO19 3JN.

The Rt Hon Sir Albert Spicer, PC, 1st baronet, was Chm of James Spicer & Sons, Ltd (later Spicers, Ltd), paper makers, wholesale stationers, and manufacturers, of 19 New Bridge Street, EC4, and sat as MP for Monmouth Dist (*L*) 1892-1900, and for Central Div of Hackney 1906-18. He was First Lay Chm of Congregational Union of England and Wales 1893, Treasurer of London Missionary So 1885-1910, and of Mansfield Coll, Oxford 1888-1921, Chm of Govs Mill Hill Sch, and Pres of London Chamber of Commerce 1907-10.

SPROT (UK) 1918, of Garnkirk, co Lanark (Extinct 1929)

Col Sir ALEXANDER SPROT, CMG, MP, 1st and last *Baronet.*

DAUGHTER LIVING OF FIRST BARONET

Nancy Margaret: *m* 1935, Capt Chichele Keppel Bampton, RN (ret), who *d* 1974. *Residence* – Croft House, Blairlogie, Stirling.

Stafford-King-Harman, see Harman.

STAMER (UK) 1809, of Beauchamp, Dublin

By valor and strength

Sir (LOVELACE) ANTHONY STAMER, 5th *Baronet*; *b* 28 Feb 1917; *s* his father, *Lt-Col Sir* LOVELACE, 1941; *ed* Harrow, Trin Coll, Camb (MA) and Roy Agric Coll, Cirencester; an AMIMI 1963; PO RAF 1939-41, and 1st Officer Air Transport Aux 1941-45; Exec Dir of Bentley Drivers Club Ltd, 1969-73, and of Bugatti and Ferrari Owners Clubs 1973-75; Hon Treas, Ferrari Owners Club 1975-81: *m* 1st, 1948 (*m diss* 1953), Stella Huguette, da of late Paul Burnell Binnie, of Brussels; 2ndly, 1955 (*m diss* 1959), Margaret Lucy, da of late Maj T. A. Belben, Indian Army; 3rdly, 1960 (*m diss* 1968), Marjorie June, da of T. C. Noakes, of St James, Cape Province, S Africa; 4thly, 1983, Elizabeth Graham, who *d* 1992, widow of G. P. H. Smith, and da of late C. J. R. Magrath, and has issue by 1st *m*.

ᴀrms – Quarterly: 1st and 4th gules on a fesse indented argent, a lion passant azure armed and langued gules, 2nd and 3rd azure the civic cap between three castles inflamed proper. Over all a cross ermine charged with the sword of state of the City of Dublin in pale proper. ᴄrest – A stag's head erased proper, gorged with a mural crown or.
Residence – 5 Windrush Court, 175 The Hill, Burford, Oxon OX18 4RE.

SON LIVING (*By 1st marriage*)

PETER TOMLINSON, *b* 19 Nov 1951; *ed* Malvern, and Southampton Univ; late Sqdn-Ldr RAF: *m* 1979 (*m diss* 1989), Dinah Louise, da of late Thomas Selwyn Berry, and has issue living, William Peter Alexander, *b* 20 Sept 1983, — Antonia Louise, *b* 1981.

DAUGHTER LIVING (*By 1st marriage*)

Lucinda Jane, *b* 1949.

COLLATERAL BRANCHES LIVING

Grandchildren of late Rev Frederick Charles Stamer, 2nd son of 3rd baronet:—
Issue of late Hugo Frederick Barnabas Stamer, *b* 1900, *d* 1980: *m* 1925, Kathleen Florence Louise, da of J. Whittome, of Vancouver:—
James Alexander Donovan, *b* 1928: *m* 1951, Patricia Louise, da of A. J. McNeil, of Duncan, BA, and has issue living, Gregory McNeil, *b* 1956. —— Marion Joan, *b* 1926: *m* 1947, John Ernest Fox, of 1147 Williams Rd, Richmond, Vancouver, BC, and has issue living, John Patrick, *b* 1950, — Geoffrey Ernest, *b* 1951, — Kathleen Jennifer, *b* 1948, — Diane Joan, *b* (twin) 1950.

Grandchildren of late William Edward Stamer, 3rd son of 3rd baronet:—
Issue of late William Arthur John Stamer, *b* 1899, *d* 1991: *m* 1935, Helen, da of Dr Wilfred Anthony Legh Jackson, of Lavington, BC:—

William John Derek (PO Box 247, Barrière, BC, Canada, VOE IEO), *b* 1940: *m* 1st, 1961 (*m diss* 1964), Marcelle Blanche, da of David Howrie, of Vernon, BC; 2ndly, 1967, Valerie Margaret, da of Roy MacQuarrie, of Revelstoke, and has had issue (by 1st *m*), Rodney William, *b* 1961, — (by 2nd *m*) John Edward, *b* 1962: *m* 1990, Carleen Gail, da of Gordon Zerr, of Barrière, BC, and has issue living, Brittany Marie *b* 1993, — Cory Wayne, *b* 1963, — William John David, *b* 1970; *d* 1989, — Patricia Leah, *b* (twin) 1970. —— Judith Cicely, *b* 1939: *m* 1st, 1957 (*m diss* 1961), Glen Fletcher, of Lavington, BC, Canada; 2ndly, 1964, Arthur G. Jaik, of 6909 Palfrey Drive, Vernon, BC, Canada V1B 1A7, and has issue living, (by 1st *m*), Rhondda Jane, *b* 1957: *m* 1981, Christopher Oostlander, and has issue living, Adam Nickolas *b* 1983, Ryan Jeffrey *b* 1985, — (by 2nd *m*), Catherine Louise, *b* 1965: *m* 1994, Paul Chabot, and has issue living, Jennifer Rose *b* 1989, Saleena Irene, *b* 1993, — Susan Christine, *b* 1968. —— Rosemary Shane, *b* 1943: *m* 1964, Ronald Edwin Haywood, of 1191 Crestwood Drive, Kamloops, BC, Canada V2C 5G8, and has issue living, John Christopher, *b* 1968, — Alison Jane, *b* 1966: *m* 1989 (*m diss* 1994), Clayton Jay Paull.

The 1st baronet, Sir William Stamer, was Lord Mayor of Dublin 1809 and 1819, and commanded a regiment of the Dublin Yeomanry during the Irish rebellion. The Rt Rev Sir Lovelace Tomlinson Stamer, DD, 3rd Bt, was Suffragan Bishop of Shrewsbury 1888-1905.

STANIER (UK) 1917, of Peplow Hall, Hodnet, co Salop

Stronger by piety

Sir ALEXANDER BEVILLE GIBBONS STANIER, DSO, MC, 2nd *Baronet*; *b* 31 Jan 1899; *s* his father, Sir BEVILLE, MP, 1921; *ed* Eton, and RMC Sandhurst: is Brigadier (ret) late Welsh Guards (Comdg 1945-48); a JP, a DL and patron of two livings; High Sheriff of Shropshire 1951; was a co Councillor for Salop 1950-8; European War 1918 in France and Belgium (MC, two medals), European War 1939-45 in France (despatches, DSO and Bar, American Silver Star, Com Order of Leopold of Belgium with palms, Belgian Croix de Guerre with palms, Legion of Honour, France); is a CStJ; DSO 1940 (Bar 1945): *m* 1927, Dorothy Gladys, who *d* 1973, el da of late Brig-Gen Alfred Douglas Miller, CBE, DSO, of Shotover House, Wheatley, Oxon, and has issue.

Arms – Or, on a pile azure ten escallops, four, three, two and one of the first. **Crest** – In front of a griffin's head, erased proper three escallops or. *Residences* – Hill House, Shotover Park, Wheatley, Oxon OX33 1QN; Park Cottage, Ludford, Ludlow, Shropshire SY8 1PP. *Club* – Cavalry and Guards'.

SON LIVING

BEVILLE DOUGLAS (Kings Close House, Whaddon, Bucks MK17 0NG; MCC), *b* 20 April 1934; *ed* Eton; late Capt Welsh Guards; ADC to Gov-Gen of Australia 1959-60; stock exchange 1960-76, Partner of Messrs Kitcat and Aitken 1969-74, Farmer from 1976: *m* 1963, (Violet) Shelagh, el da of late Maj James Stockley Sinnott, of Tetbury, Glos, and has issue living, Alexander James Sinnott, *b* 10 April 1970, — Henrietta Claire, *b* 1965, — Lucinda Katherine, *b* 1967.

DAUGHTER LIVING

Sylvia Mary Finola, *b* 1928.

COLLATERAL BRANCH LIVING

Issue of late Philip Francis Stanier, 2nd son of 1st baronet, *b* 1901; *d* 1977: *m* 1929, Kathleen Mary, who *d* 1986, da of late Edgar Turrall, JP, of Coundon Court, Coventry, Warwicks:—
Philippa Mary, *b* 1930. *Residence* – 19 Townsend Park, Luston, Leominster, Herefords.

This family, originally spelt Stonhewer, was settled at Biddulph, Staffs, from the 16th century. Sir Beville Stanier, 1st Bt, MP for Newport, Salop (C) 1908-18, and Ludlow 1918-21 and Lord of the Manors of Peplow and High Hatton, was 2nd son of Francis Stanier of The Moor House, Biddulph, Staffs, and Peplow Hall, Salop, High Sheriff of Salop, 1894.

STAPLES (I) 1628, of Lissan, co Tyrone

Sir THOMAS STAPLES, 15th *Baronet*, eldest son of late Thomas Staples, yr son of late Maj-Gen Thomas Staples, BSC, yr brother of 10th baronet; *b* 9 Feb 1905; *s* his cousin, *Sir* JOHN RICHARD, 1989: *m* 1952, Frances Annie Irvine, who *d* 1981.

Arms – Quarterly, 1st and 4th, argent, on a fesse engrailed sable between three hurts, as many ermine spots between two dragons' heads erased or, *Staples*; 2nd and 3rd, argent, a cross ragulé gules, on a chief sable two pheons or, *Jones*. **Crest** – A demi-savage azure, girt with a belt with two rings, charged with four torteaux, and holding in his hands a large staple or.
Residence – 219, 3051 Shelbourne St, Vic, Canada V8R 6T2.

BROTHERS LIVING

GERALD JAMES ARLAND, *b* 2 Dec 1909: *m* 1951, Henrietta, da of late Arland Ussher, of Blackrock, co Dublin, and has issue living, Emily Ann, *b* 1952: *m* 1st, 1974 (*m diss* 1984), Howard George Smith; 2ndly, 1988, Kerry William John McDonald, of 33 Little Meadow, Loughton, Milton Keynes, Bucks MK5 8EH, and has issue living, (by 1st *m*) Juliet Clare *b* 1980, — Jacqueline Mary, *b* 1954: *m* 1985, Timothy Pullen, of 19 Willowdale Close, Petersfield, Hants. *Residence* – 5 Little Stodham House, Liss, Hants. ⸺ Richard Molesworth (113 Huntsbury Av, Christchurch 2, NZ), *b* 1914: *m* 1954, Marjorie Charlotte Thomas, of Christchurch, NZ.

SISTERS LIVING

Grace, *b* 1906: *m* 1932, Horace Roland Rambaut Dowd, who *d* 1975, of Main St, Lismore, co Waterford, and has issue living, Peter (The Manse, East Main St, Lismore, co Waterford), *b* 1935: *m* 1961, Constance Evelyn Hornibrook, of Lismore, and has issue living, Derek Roland James *b* 1965, Charles Thomas Staples *b* 1967, Sandra Evelyn *b* 1962: *m* 1992, Sean Willoughby, of The Mall, Lismore, co Waterford, Sharon Jean Mary *b* 1964: *m* 19—, David Fergus Warren, of New Ross, co Wexford (and has issue living, Amy *b* 1989), — Thomas Charles (Barton, Deerpark Rd, Lismore, co Waterford), *b* 1944: *m* 1963, Henrietta Elizabeth, da of Francis Sweetnam, of Ballyehob, co Cork, and has issue living, Richard William Romney *b* 1967: *m* 1992, Síle Cronin, of Killarney, co Kerry, Gillian Helen *b* 1964 (has issue living (by David William Murphy, of Lismore, co Waterford), Zach Jordan DOWD *b* 19—), Diana Joan *b* 1965: *m* 1989, Patrick Brendan Kiersey, of Kilmacthomas, co Waterford (and has issue living, Jack James *b* 1992, Max Thomas *b* 1993, Hazel Kate *b* 1989), — Christopher Romney Rambaut (Doeville Deerpark, Lismore, co Waterford), *b* 1948: *m* 1976, Una Bridget Cotter, of Tallow, co Waterford, and has issue living, Robert James *b* 1982, Justin Edward *b* 1986, Louise Sarah *b* 1979. ⸺ Elizabeth Lindsay, *b* 1911: *m* 1st, 1933, Henry Eric St George Harper, who *d* 1947; 2ndly, 1961, John Frank Harris, who *d* 1971, 3rdly, 1972, James Victor Thomas Rawlence, MBE, RN, who *d* 1993, of 42 Ridgeway, Sherborne, Dorset, and has issue living (by 1st *m*), Elizabeth Lindsay St George, *b* 1937: *m* 1961, Trevor Arthur Lant, and has issue living, Myles Arthur *b* 1963, Philippa Lindsay *b* 1969. ⸺ June Pamela (22 New St, Lismore, co Waterford), *b* 1923.

DAUGHTERS LIVING OF FOURTEENTH BARONET

Eileen Sybell, *b* 1939: *m* 1968, Timothy Geary Edward Kilpatrick, of Hale House, Churt, Surrey, and has issue living, Amanda Charlotte, *b* 1971, — Sarah Patricia, *b* 1974. ⸺ Barbara Helen, *b* 1941: *m* 1st, 1970, Alistair John Hutchinson-Russell, who *d* 1973; 2ndly, 1974, Anthony Warren England; 3rdly, 1988, Keith Burton.

DAUGHTER LIVING OF THIRTEENTH BARONET

Hazel Marion, *b* 1923: *m* 1970, Harry Holbeche Radclyffe Dolling, who *d* 1986. *Residence* – Lissan House, Cookstown, co Tyrone BT80 98W.

SISTERS LIVING OF FOURTEENTH BARONET

Alice Henrietta, *b* 1909. ⸺ Eileen Patience, *b* 1917.

WIDOW LIVING OF FOURTEENTH BARONET

SYBELLA (*Lady Staples*) (Butter Hill House, Dorking, Surrey), da of late Dr Charles Henry Wade: *m* 1933, Sir John Richard Staples, 14th Bt, who *d* 1989.

COLLATERAL BRANCHES LIVING

Granddaughters of late Maj-Gen Thomas Staples, BSC, 3rd son of Rev John Molesworth Staples, and next brother of 10th baronet:—
Issue of late Noel Richard Ponsonby Staples, *b* 1879, *d* 1958: *m* 1905, Kathleen, who *d* 1966, da of late Alexander Ross Hamilton, of Glensavage, Blackrock, co Dublin:—
Anne Veronica (RR1 Maple Bay, Duncan, BC, Canada), *b* 1910: *m* 1936, Lt-Col Richard MacNaughton Lendrum, DSO, who *d* 1976, RR1, Maple Bay, Duncan, BC, Canada, and has issue living, Richard Brian, *b* 1949: *m* 1963, Gail Jeanette Robinson, — Jillian Anne, *b* 1944: *m* 1965 Raymond Thomas Benwell. ⸺ Flora Hamilton, *b* 1912. ⸺ Kathleen (twin) *b* 1920: *m* 19— (*m diss* 1972), Alexander Clarke Wilson, of 305-1676 West 11th St, Vancouver 9, BC, Canada.

Grandchildren of late Noel Richard Ponsonby Staples (ante):—
Issue of late Richard Nathaniel Staples, *b* 1908, *d* 1975: *m* 1939, Isabel MacMillan:—
Heather Anne, *b* 1941. ⸺ Sheila Isabel, *b* 1944.
Issue of late Anthony Staples, *b* 1920, *d* 1975: *m* 1950, Margaret Eva Duffield, who *d* 1970:—
Noel Leslie, *b* 1954: *m* 1972, Dwaine Grant Van Eeuwen.
The 1st baronet, Sir Thomas Staples of Lissan, co Tyrone and Faghanvale, co Derry, High Sheriff of co Tyrone 1640, was 5th son of Alexander Staples, of Yate Court, Glos. The 9th baronet, Sir Thomas, QC, Queen's Advocate in Ireland, who *d* 1865, was a distinguished lawyer.

STAPLETON (E) 1679, of The Leeward Islands

Sir (HENRY) ALFRED STAPLETON, 10th *Baronet*, son of late Brig Francis Harry Stapleton, CMG, son of late Rev Eliot Henry Stapleton, 3rd son of 7th baronet; *b* 2 May 1913; *s* his kinsman, *Sir* MILES TALBOT, 1977; *ed* Marlborough and Ch Ch, Oxford (MA); 1939-45 War as 2nd Lt Oxfordshire and Bucks LI: *m* 1961, Rosslyne Murray, da of late Capt Harold Stanley Warren, RN, of Parkstone, Dorset.

Arms – Argent, a lion rampant sable. **Crest** – Out of a ducal coronet or, a Saracen's head affrontée proper, wreathed about the temples argent and sable. *Residence* – 7 Ridgeway, Horsecastles Lane, Sherborne, Dorset. *Clubs* – Garrick, MCC.

DAUGHTER LIVING OF NINTH BARONET *(By 2nd marriage)*

Pro magnâ chartâ
For the great charter

Susan Penelope, *b* 1937: *m* 1964, Roger Fulford-Dobson, who *d* 1986, of Shepherds, Rotherfield Greys, Henley-on-Thames, Oxon, and has issue living, Giles Roger, *b* 1965, — Jasper William, *b* 1970, — Emma Susan, *b* 1967.

The 1st baronet, Sir William Stapleton, was appointed Gov of the Leeward Islands after the Restoration. Sir Thomas Stapleton, 6th baronet, inherited 1788 the Barony of le Despencer, which passed to his grandda the Hon Mary Frances Elizabeth who *m* 1845 Evelyn Boscawen, later 6th Viscount Falmouth. The baronetcy passed to his yst son, Rev the Hon Sir Francis Jarvis Stapleton, who *d* 1874.

STARKEY (UK) 1935, of Norwood Park, Parish of Southwell, and co of Nottingham

Sir JOHN PHILIP STARKEY, 3rd Baronet; *b* 8 May 1938; *s* his father, *Lt-Col Sir* WILLIAM RANDLE, 1977; *ed* Eton, and Ch Ch Oxford (MA), Sloan Fellow London Business Sch; DL (Notts) 1981; High Sheriff 1987-88: *m* 1966, Victoria Henrietta Fleetwood, da of late Lt Col Christopher Herbert Fleetwood Fuller, TD (*see* Fuller Bt, colls) and has issue.

Arms – Argent, a bend engrailed vair between six storks sable. *Residence* – A stork argent, semée of estoiles azure.
Residence – Norwood Park, Southwell, Notts NG25 0PF.

SONS LIVING

HENRY JOHN, *b* 13 Oct 1973.

DAUGHTERS LIVING

Man proposes, God disposes

Suzannah Clare, *b* 1966: *m* 1989, Jonathan Beatson-Hird, yr son of Dr John Beatson-Hird, of Oldwell, Ashton-under-Hill, nr Evesham, Worcs, and has issue living, Hubert John, *b* 1992, — Digby George, *b* 1994. —— Elizabeth Victoria, *b* 1975. —— Katherine Alexandra, *b* 1977.

BROTHER LIVING

Michael William, *b* 1946; *ed* Eton, Newcastle Univ, Trent Business Sch, and Nottingham Univ; BSc, MBA, MInstAM (Dip), MBIM: *m* 1974, Gillian Mary, da of late E. Treflyn Roberts, of Shotton, Deeside, Clwyd, and has issue living, Edward Thomas William, *b* 1978, — Isabella Irené Marianne, *b* 1983. *Residence* – Cutlersforth Farm, Halam, nr Newark, Notts NG22 8AP.

SISTER LIVING

Caroline Myrtle, *b* 1936: *m* 1957, (Frederick) John Charles Gordon Hervey-Bathurst, only son of Sir Frederick Peter Methuen Hervey-Bathurst, 6th Bt. *Residence* – Somborne Park, nr Stockbridge, Hants.

AUNTS LIVING *(Daughters of 1st baronet)*

Helen Frances: *m* 1922, Humphrey Parker-Jervis, who *d* 1948, and has issue (*see* V St Vincent, colls). *Residence* – Brook Cottage, Uley, Dursley, Glos. —— Sylvia Augusta: *m* 1st, 1925, Capt Eustace Ruffel Drake Long, CBE, RN, who *d* 1941; 2ndly, 1951, as his 2nd wife, Reginald Evelyn Welby-Pelham, who *d* 1965 (E Yarborough, colls), and has issue living, (by 1st *m*) David Andrew, *b* 1929, — Phœbe Olivia, *b* 1926: *m* 1954, Henry Martin Shone, and has issue living, Jeremy Patrick Martin *b* 1955, Anthony Michael John *b* 1957, Patrick Douglas *b* 1959, Colin Henry Philip *b* 1964. *Residence* – Hedge End, Stonely, Huntingdon, Cambs.

The 1st baronet, Sir John Ralph (el son of late Lewis Randle Starkey, DL, JP, of Norwood Park, Notts), sat as MP for Newark (C) 1906-22, Lt-Col Sir William Randle, 2nd Bt, was High Sheriff of Notts 1954-55.

STEEL (UK) 1938, of Philiphaugh, co Selkirk

Sir (FIENNES) MICHAEL STRANG STEEL, 3rd *Baronet*; *b* 22 Feb 1943; *s* his father, Sir (FIENNES) WILLIAM STRANG, 1992; *ed* Eton; Maj (ret) 17th/21st Lancers; DL Borders Region 1990; Forestry Commr since 1988; Member Queen's Body Guard for Scotland (Royal Company of Archers): *m* 1977, Sarah Jane, el da of late J. A. S. Russell, of Mayfield, Lochmaben, Dumfriesshire, and has issue.

Arms – Argent, a bend chequy sable and ermine, between two lions' heads erased gules, on a chief azure, two billets or, a crescent of the first for difference. **Crest** – A lion's head erased gules.
Residence – Philiphaugh, Selkirk TD7 5LX.

SONS LIVING

FIENNES EDWARD, *b* 8 Nov 1978; *ed* Glenalmond. —— Sam Arthur, *b* 1983.

DAUGHTER LIVING

Tara Diana, *b* 1980.

BROTHER LIVING

Colin Brodie Strang (Threepwood, Blainslie, Galashiels, Selkirkshire TD1 2PY), *b* 1945; *ed* Eton, and RAC Cirencester; chartered surveyor; FRICS: *m* 1970, April Eileen, da of Aubrey Fairfax Studd, of Cahoo House, Regaby West, Ramsey, IoM, and has issue living, James William, *b* 1973, — Alistair Fairfax, *b* 1975, — Peter Brodie, *b* 1977.

UNCLE LIVING (son of 1st baronet)

Robert Stanley Strang, *b* 1934; *ed* Eton, and RAC Cirencester: *m* 1958, Caroline Angela Elaine, only da of late Lt-Col William Hugh Carter, of Rosslyn, Tain, Ross-shire, and has issue living, David William Strang, *b* 1961; *ed* Glenalmond, and RAC Cirencester; Chartered Surveyor: *m* 1991, Fiona Louise, yr da of Dr Richard Legge, of Edinburgh, and has issue living, Alice Charlotte Strang *b* 1993, — Richard James Strang, *b* 1963; *ed* Eton. *Residence* – Sluie, Banchory, Kincardineshire AB31 4BA.

AUNT LIVING (daughter of 1st baronet)

Grizel Mabel Strang, *b* 1921. *Residence* – Beechwood, Selkirk TD7 5LU.

COLLATERAL BRANCH LIVING

Issue of late Jock Wykeham Strang Steel, 2nd son of 1st Bt, *b* 1914, *d* 1991: *m* 1945, Lesley (Haydean, Haddington, E Lothian EH41 4HN), da of late Lt-Col Sir (John) Reginald Noble Graham, 3rd Bt, VC, OBE:—
Malcolm Graham Strang, WS (Barrowmore, Mawcarse, Kinross KY13 7SL), *b* 1946; *ed* Eton, Trin Coll, Camb (BA), and Univ of Edinburgh (LLB); solicitor; sec Standing Council of Scottish Chiefs 1973-83; memb Queen's Body Guard for Scotland (Royal Co of Archers); FRSA: *m* 1972, Margaret Philippa,. da of late William Patrick Scott, OBE, TD, DL, of Kierfiold, Stromness, Orkney, and has issue living, Patrick Reginald Strang, *b* 1975; *ed* Eton, — Laura Strang, *b* 1977. —— Celia Jane Strang, LVO, *b* 1948; Lady in Waiting to HRH The Princess Royal since 1977; LVO (1989): *m* 1976, Malcolm Alastair Innes (*see* Innes Bt (*cr* 1628), colls). —— Susan Rachel Strang (*Lady Agnew of Lochnaw*), *b* 1952: *m* 1980, Sir Crispin Hamlyn Agnew of Lochnaw, 11th Bt.
The 1st baronet, Sir Samuel Strang Steel (son of late William Strang Steel, JP, DL, of Philiphaugh, Selkirk), was Major Lothians and Border Horse, MP for Ashford Div of Kent 1918-29, Pres Scottish Unionist Assoc 1937-38 and 1942-43, Lord Lieut of Selkirkshire 1948-58, Forestry Commr, a Dir of LNER and a Dir of Bank of Scotland.

Steel (Ramsay-Steel-Maitland), see Maitland.

STEPHENSON (UK) 1936, of Hassop Hall, co Derby

Medio tutissimus ibis

Thou will go safest in the middle course

Sir HENRY UPTON STEPHENSON, TD, 3rd *Baronet*; *b* 26 Nov 1926; *s* his father, *Col Sir* HENRY FRANCIS BLAKE, OBE, TD, 1982; *ed* Eton; late Capt Yorkshire Yeo; TD 19—; a Dir of Stephenson, Blake (Holdings), Ltd, and Thos Turton & Sons Ltd: *m* 1962, Susan, da of late Maj John Ernest Clowes, of Clifton, Ashbourne, Derbys, and has issue.

Arms – Vair, on a pale between two pallets gules, three leopard's faces or, two flaunches of the second. **Crest** – A rock, thereon a falcon's head erased proper, gorged with a collar vair, pendent therefrom an escutcheon vert, charged with two arrows, saltirewise, points downwards or.
Residence – Tissington Cottage, Rowland, Bakewell, Derby DE4 1NR.

DAUGHTERS LIVING

Fiona Kathleen, *b* 1964. —— Annabel Mary, *b* 1965. —— Emma Frances, *b* 1968. —— Lucy Clare, *b* 1970.

AUNTS LIVING *(Daughters of 1st baronet)*

Helena Millicent Frances (Fennel Cottage, Ashford-in-the-Water, Bakewell, Derbyshire), *b* 1906. —— Cynthia Margaret, MBE (17 Sydney House, Woodstock Rd, W4), *b* 1910; MBE (Civil) 1948. —— Emma Letitia Gertrude, *b* 1914: *m* 1941, Philip Charles Fenner Lawton, CBE, DFC, who *d* 1993, of Fenner House, Glebe Way, Wisborough Green, W Sussex, and has issue living, Charles Henry Huntly, *b* 1946: *m* 1979, Sarah Margaret, da of Rev Christopher Hugo Lambert, of 26 Abingdon Villas, W8, and has issue living, Timothy Philip Hugo *b* 1982, Hermione Margaret Clare *b* 1984, — Philippa Rosemary, *b* 1943: *m* 1974, Lt-Cdr Michael Henry White, RN, and has issue living, Richard *b* 1978, Serena *b* 1976, Lucinda *b* 1983.

WIDOW LIVING OF SECOND BARONET

JOAN (*Joan, Lady Stephenson*) (Hassop Green, Bakewell, Derbyshire), el da of late Maj John Herbert Upton, JP, of Ingmire Hall, Sedbergh: *m* 1925, Col Sir Henry Francis Blake Stephenson, OBE, TD, 2nd Bt, who *d* 1982.

COLLATERAL BRANCHES LIVING

Issue of late William Raymond Shirecliffe Stephenson, 2nd son of 1st baronet, *b* 1898, *d* 1977: *m* 1923, Madeleine Rose, who *d* 1990, da of George Montagu Butterworth, of Westward Ho!, Devon:—
TIMOTHY HUGH, TD (Lomberdale Hall, Bakewell, Derby DE4 1LU), *b* 5 Jan 1930; *ed* Eton, and Magdalene Coll, Camb; JP for Sheffield: *m* 1959, Susan Lesley, yr da of late George Arthur Harris, of Sheffield and has issue living, Matthew Francis Timothy, *b* 1960: *m* 1984, Philippa Delphine, da of John Lincoln, of Aldersley House, Chester, and has issue living, John Lewis *b* 1986, Jessica Frances *b* 1985, — Oliver George, *b* 1962: *m* 1992, Fiona Alice Jane, da of Maj Sir David Peter Michael Malcolm, 11th Bt. —— Susan Madeleine, *b* 1924: *m* 1949, Charles Graham Murray, MBE, JP, DL, of 3 Belgrave Dr, Sheffield S10 3LQ, and has issue living, Elizabeth Susan, *b* 1951, — Jane Madeleine, *b* 1953: *m* 1983, John Ferretti, and has issue living, Matthew Robert *b* 1987, James Alexander *b* 1990, — Anne Catriona, *b* 1955: *m* 1982, Frank W. Womack, and has issue living, Alastair Edward *b* 1984, Thomas Martin *b* 1986. —— Jocelyn Frances, *b* 1926: *m* 1948, David Clement Wilson, of 363 Fulwood Rd, Sheffield, and has issue living, Christopher Michael Rockley, *b* 1957, — Olivia Frances, *b* 1952: *m* 1976 (*m diss* 1989), Christopher A. Cooke, — Sarah Margaret, *b* 1954: *m* 1982, Jaime Acosta, and has issue living, Simon *b* 1985, Nicolas *b* 1988.

Issue of late Percival John Parker Stephenson, 3rd son of 1st baronet, *b* 1900, *d* 1973: *m* 1930 (*m diss* 1948) Pamela, da of Sir Walter Benton Jones 2nd Bt:—
Jennifer Barbara, *b* 1931: *m* 1958, John Henry Thornton, DL, of Alburgh House, Alburgh, Harleston, Norfolk, and has issue living, Edward John, *b* 1963, — Robert Walter, *b* 1968, — Katherine Louise, *b* 1961: *m* 1986, Timothy James Stapleton Harris, and has issue living, Georgina Rose *b* 1991, Annabel Louise *b* 1994.

Issue of late Lt-Col Charles Eustace Kenyon Stephenson, yst son of 1st baronet, *b* 1903, *d* 1971: *m* 1930, Nancy Barbara (The Outrake, Bakewell, Derbys), da of Harry Limnell Lyon, JP, of Hillam Hall, Monk Fryston, Yorks:—
Charles Lyon, TD (The Cottage, Gt Longstone, Derbys DE45 1UA), *b* 1935; *ed* Eton; Maj Royal Yeo; Man Dir Stephenson Blake (Holdings) Ltd: *m* 1st, 1960 (*m diss* 1972), Margot Jane, da of late Tony Malcolm Tinker; 2ndly, 1974, Hon Sarah Merryweather Norrie, GGSM, da of 1st Baron Norrie, and has issue living (by 1st *m*), George Lyon, *b* 1962: *m* 1990, Lucilla, da of Jeremy Clay, of Fawley Court, nr Hereford, — Rupert Nicholas, *b* 1964, — Belinda Jane, *b* 1963. — Harriet Ann, *b* 1931: *m* 1951 (*m diss* 1973 and re-married 1976), John Bulkley Herbert Francis, and has issue living, Charles Mark, *b* 1952, — Timothy, *b* 1960, — Clare, *b* 1955, — Charlotte Ann, *b* 1963.

The 1st baronet, Sir Henry Kenyon Stephenson, DSO, VD (son of late Sir Henry Stephenson, of the Glen, Endcliffe, Sheffield), was Pro-Chancellor of Sheffield Univ, Chm of Stephenson, Blake & Co, typefounders, Lord Mayor of Sheffield 1908-09 and 1910-11, Master Cutler of Sheffield 1919-20, and High Sheriff of Derbyshire 1932. He sat as MP for Park Div of Sheffield (*L*) 1918-23, and served during European War 1914-18 (DSO).

STEWART (I) 1623, of Ramelton, co Donegal

Nothing is to be despaired of

NIL DESPERANDUM

Sir ALAN D'ARCY STEWART, 13th *Baronet*; *b* 29 Nov 1932; *s* his father, *Sir* JOCELYN HARRY, 1982; *ed* All Saints', Bathurst, NSW: *m* 1952, Patricia, da of Lawrence Turner, of Ramelton, co Donegal, and has issue.

Arms – (recorded at Lyon Office)—Or, a fesse chequy azure and argent surmounted of a bend engrailed and in chief a rose gules, all within a bordure of the third charged with three lions rampant of the fourth. **Crest** – A dexter arm erect couped at the elbow, the hand holding a heart all proper.
Residence – One Acre House, Church St, Ramelton, co Donegal.

SONS LIVING

NICHOLAS COURTNEY d'ARCY, *b* 4 Aug 1953; *ed* New Univ of Ulster (BSc, Dip Ed). —— Lindsay Stephen d'Arcy, *b* 1956: *m* 1983, Jane Maria d'Arcy, da of Albert Rossley, of The Haw House, Ray, co Donegal, and has issue living, Emma Naomi d'Arcy *b* 1983.

DAUGHTERS LIVING

Constance Patricia, *b* 1954: *m* 1978, Malcolm McMillan, and has issue living, James, *b* 1980, — Peter, *b* 1981. —— Siobhan d'Arcy, *b* 1960.

HALF-BROTHERS LIVING

Brian Jocelyn, *b* 1948. —— Terence Annesley, *b* 1949.

HALF-SISTERS LIVING

Marie Jeanette, *b* 1947. —— Katherine Benedicta, *b* 1951.

COLLATERAL BRANCHES LIVING

Issue of late Malcolm Geoffrey Stewart, 4th son of 11th baronet; *b* 1908, *d* 1974: *m* 1946, Joan Cox, who *d* 1968:—
Robin Gordon Alan (50 Parkholme Rd, E8) *b* 1948: *m* 1973, Barbara Anne, da of Wilfred Miller, of Grasscroft, Yorks, and has issue living, James Malcolm, *b* 1978, — Thomas Annesley, *b* 1979, — William Francis, *b* 1984. —— Jonathan Malcolm (36 Church St, Handsworth, Birmingham 19), *b* 1951.

Issue of late James Augustus Stewart, brother of 9th baronet, *b* 1835, *d* 1915: *m* 1884, Ann Wilhelmina Jean, who *d* 1913, el da of late William Wray, of Oak Park, co Donegal:—
Edith Frances. *Residence* – Aughnoo, St Oran's Rd, Buncrana, co Donegal.

Granddaughter of late Col Harry Hutchinson Augustus Stewart, brother of 9th baronet:—
Issue of late Walter Annesley Stewart, *b* 1883, *d* 1937: *m* 1920, Phyllis Lucie (who *d* 1981, having *m* 2ndly, 1938, Benjamin Worthy Horne, of Norfolk Cottage, Waldron, Heathfield, Sussex), da of late Edmund Larkin Horne, of 34 Bolton Gdns, SW5:—
Rosemary, *b* 1928: *m* 1950, Col John Arthur Haire, late RA, of Somerville, Woodlands Rd, Bromley, Kent, and has issue living, John Stewart (33 Radnor Walk, SW3), *b* 1957; BA, — Susan Mary, *b* 1952; BA, RAS Cert (PG): *m* 1982, Frank Peter Hinks, of The Old Vicarage, Shoreham, Sevenoaks, Kent, and has issue living, Julius James *b* 1984, Alexander John *b* 1985, Benjamin Stewart *b* 1987, — Anne Rosemary, *b* 1954; MRCGP, DRCOG, DCH, MFFP: *m* 1981, Alan Frederick Graeme Groom, FRCS, of 65 Lee Rd, Blackheath, SE3 9EN, and has issue living, William Douglas Ian *b* 1985, Frederick Thomas *b* 1990, Alice Suzanne *b* 1987.

Granddaughter of late Lorenzo Moore Stewart (infra):—
Issue of late Trevor Eugene St Quinton Stewart, *b* 1907, *d* 1980: *m* 1932, Edna Maude (Unit 4/5 Woodrow Place, Dianella, Perth, WA), da of late Richard Sherman Wood:—
Pamela Jean, *b* 1934: *m* 1962, Leon Allan Kings. *Residence* – 18 Norton Drive, Dianella, Perth, W Australia.

Grandson of late Richard Quinton Stewart, yr son of late Lorenzo Moore Stewart, uncle of 9th baronet:—
Issue of late Lorenzo Moore Stewart, *b* 1882, *d* 1926: *m* 1906, Ivy Mercilla, who *d* 1967, da of late Walter Edmund Pachaud Wordsworth, of Rampur Haut, India:—
Harold Vivian Moore, *b* 1908; CEng, MIMechE: *m* 1st, 1932 (*m diss*), Ella Marie, who *d* 1986, da of late John Tracey Falconer; 2ndly, 1956, Helen Elizabeth, da of late Archibald Ronald Robb, and has issue living (by 1st *m*), Olga Deidre Moore (52 Victoria Rd, Cowes, Isle of Wight PO31 7JJ), *b* 1936: *m* 1964 (*m diss* 1991), Gordon Edward Malone, and has issue living, Amanda Jane *b* 1966; BA London, Catherine Ellen *b* 1968; BA, PhD Oxon, — Roslyn Anne Moore, *b* 1944: *m* 1966, Alan Gray Rutherford, BSc, PhD, CChem, CEng, FRSC, FInstE, FRSA, Hon Col The Parachute Regt, of 18 Murrayfield Gdns, Edinburgh EH12 6DF, and has issue living, Simon Gray *b* 1967, Sarah Caroline *b* 1971; *ed* Merton Coll, Oxford (BA), and Edinburgh Univ, — (by 2nd *m*) Michael Ian Moore (5/274 Casuarina Drive, Nightcliffe, Darwin, NT, Australia), *b* 1958; *ed* WA Univ (BCom); Maj RACT: *m* 1988, Janelle Skehan, and has issue living, Callam Michael *b* 1994, Ellenore Anne *b* 1991, — Richard Quinton Moore, *b* 1964; *ed* Curtin Univ, WA (B(app)Sc). *Residence* – 18 Nangkita Rd, Kalamunda, Perth, W Australia 6076.

This family is of common ancestry with the Earls of Galloway and Barons Blantyre (ext 1900). The 1st baronet greatly distinguished himself as a Mil Comd in the troubles of Ireland, and was created a Privy Councillor. The 3rd baronet, Master-General of the Ordnance in Ireland, was in 1682 created Lord Stewart of Ramelton and Viscount Mountjoy. The 2nd Viscount and 4th Baronet was also Master-General of the Ordnance; and the 3rd Viscount and 5th Baronet was created Earl of Blessington, but his peerages became extinct at his death in 1769. The 6th baronet sat as MP for Charlemont 1763-97, and the 7th baronet represented in Parliament Enniskillen 1783-90 and Donegal co 1802-18.

STEWART (UK) 1803, of Athenree, Tyrone

FORWARD

Sir HUGH CHARLIE GODFRAY STEWART, 6th *Baronet*; *b* 13 April 1897; *s* his father, *Sir* GEORGE POWELL, 1945; *ed* Bradfield and RMC Sandhurst; late Maj R Inniskilling Fus; High Sheriff 1955 and DL for co Tyrone 1971; 1914-18 War in France (wounded), 1939-45 War in France, and as Assist Comdt Imperial Forces Transhipment Camp, Durban, and in Syria: *m* 1st, 1929 (*m diss* 1942), Rosemary Elinor Dorothy, da of late Maj George Peacocke, formerly Roy Inniskilling Fus; 2ndly, 1948, Diana Margaret, da of late Capt J. E. Hibbert, MC, DFC, and has issue by 1st and 2nd *m*. Major Sir Hugh Stewart *d* 31 July 1994.

Arms – Quarterly, 1st, or, a lion rampant within a double tressure flory counter-flory gules; 2nd, or, a fess chequy azure and argent, in chief a portcullis sable, *Stewart*; 3rd, argent, a saltire between four roses gules, barbed vert, *Fife*; 4th, or, a lion rampant gules, *Lennox*; the whole within a bordure compony argent and azure charged with three thistles proper. **Crest** – A unicorn's head coupled argent, armed and crined or, between two olive branches proper.
Residence – Cottesbrook, Sandy Pluck Lane, Bentham, Cheltenham GL51 5UB.

SONS LIVING (By 1st marriage)

DAVID JOHN CHRISTOPHER (8 Silver St, Wiveliscombe, Som), *b* 19 June 1935; *ed* Bradfield, and RMA Sandhurst; Capt (ret) R Inniskilling Fusiliers: *m* 1959, Bridget Anne, el da of late Patrick Wood Sim, and has issue living, Siobhan Amanda, *b* 1961, — Selina Godfray, *b* 1964, — Sophie Caroline, *b* 1966.

(By 2nd marriage)

Hugh Nicholas (Lowlands, Tibberton, Glos), *b* 1955: *m* 1976, Anna Leeke, and has issue living, Keiran Andrew Liam, *b* 1979, — Cherissma, *b* 1974, — Tamesin Kerry, *b* 1977, — Lauren, *b* 1987.

DAUGHTERS LIVING (By 1st marriage)

Elinor Godfray, *b* 1930: *m* 1953, John Macdonell, of 10 North Rd, Hythe, Kent, and has issue living, Michael John Alistair, *b* 1960, — Sarah Jane Elinor, *b* 1959.

(By 2nd marriage)

Jane Diana, *b* 1949: *m* 1973, John T. Costelloe, of Bartlow, Leckhampton, Cheltenham, Glos, and has issue living, Hugh John, *b* 1974, — Nicola, *b* 1977, — Jessica, *b* 1981.

COLLATERAL BRANCHES LIVING

Granddaughter of late Capt Hugh Stewart, 2nd son of 2nd baronet:—
Issue of late Lieut-Col Hugh Stewart, DSO, MC, MB, *b* 1881, *ka* 1918: *m* 1907, Muriel Dalzell, da of Hugh McKean, of 19 Zion Road, Rathgar, Dublin:—
Muriel Denise Evelyn, *b* 1913: *m* 1942, John Gunn Murray-Matheson, MB, ChB, and has issue living, Desmond John, *b* 1950, — Nigel Hugh, *b* 1951, — Ann Christine, *b* 1943, — Rosemary Jean Denise, *b* 1947. *Residence* – 32 Elmfield Road, Gosforth, Newcastle-upon-Tyne.

Grandchildren of late George Vesey Stewart, MBE, 3rd son of Mervyn Stewart, 2nd son of 1st baronet:—
Issue of late Mervyn Archdale Stewart, *b* 1859, *d* 1951: *m* 1881, Phœbe, who *d* 1951, da of late Robert Hornidge-Gledstanes:—
Mary Sophia Ethel: *m* 1918, Robert Rutland Turner, who *d* 1927, formerly of Tauranga, New Zealand, and has issue living, Stewart Rutland, *b* 1919: *m* 1942, Kathleen, da of W. O'Connor, of Ashburton, New Zealand, and has issue living, a son *b* 1943, — Phœbe Ethne, *b* 1923: *m* 1944, Clifford Cedric Mountier.
Issue of late George Vesey Stewart, *b* 1861, *d* 1892: *m* 1890, Cecilia Isabella, who *d* 1947, da of Thomas Anderson, formerly of Jesmond, Newcastle-upon-Tyne:—
Georgina Frances (*posthumous*): *m* 1925, Norman Lawrence Wilson, and has issue living, Lawrence Stewart, *b* 1928, — George Archdale, *b* 1930, — Kerry Robin (5 Maungarei Rd, Remuera, Auckland 5, New Zealand), *b* 1933, — Patricia Cecilia, *b* 1934.

Grandsons of late John Rowley Miller Stewart (infra):—
Issue of late Mervyn Oswald Stewart, *b* 1888, *d* 1946: *m* 1915, Ivy Mona, who *d* 19-, da of Robert Ernest Lester, of Kohukohu, Auckland, NZ:—
Mervyn Leslie Lester, *b* 1916: *m* 19-, and has issue living, Trevor Rex (Takanini, Auckland, NZ), *b* 1940. —— Donald Walton (1 Mainston Rd, Remuera, Auckland, NZ), *b* 1919: *m* 1941, Joan Eunice, yst da of late Harry John Brunsdon, of Christchurch, NZ, and has issue living, Roger Alan (106 Wheturangi Rd, Greenland, Auckland, NZ), *b* 19—; Gen Mgr for L'Oreal: *m* 19—, Linda Denise Marsden, and has issue living, Hamish *b* 19—, — Stephanie Gina *b* 19—: *m* 19—, Alistair Woodhead, Alexia *b* 19—, — Sarra-Jane *b* 19—, — Ian Murray (Hopkins Crescent, Kohimarara, Auckland, NZ), *b* 19—: *m* 19—, Jo-Anne Mills, and has issue living, Barnaby *b* 19—, — Felicity *b* 19—, — Evan Alistair, *b* 19—: *m* 19—, Avril Burberry, and has issue living, Troy Anthony *b* 19—, — Andrew *b* 19—, — Lucinda *b* 19—, — Peter Mark (Ballin St, Ellersleigh, Auckland, NZ), *b* 19—: *m* 1987, Jennifer Dowling, — Juliet Cynthia, *b* 1942: *m* 1969, Donald Rex Worrall, of 15 Awatea Rd, Parnell, Auckland, NZ, and has issue living, Allister Stewart *b* 1971, Marcus James *b* 1973, Elliot John *b* 1974, Jonathan Charles *b* 1978. —— Kenneth Archdale (70 Ray Small Drive, Papakura, NZ), *b* 1922; Sr Clerk of Works, Min of Works, Auckland: *m* 1951, Elma Pearl, da of Harold Kirtlan, of Kaitai, NZ, and has issue living, Murray Kenneth, *b* 1952: *m* 19—, Barbara Lynn, da of Hugh Douglas, of Wellington, NZ, and has issue living, Daniel Craig *b* 1978, Kristy Nicole *b* 1981, — Gael, *b* 1953: *m* 19—, David Alexander Spick, and has issue living, Mathew David *b* 1975, Allister Lee *b* 1978, — Jennifer Anne, *b* 1958: *m* 1983, Peter George Neate, and has issue living, Sam George *b* 1988, Anna-Marie *b* 1985.
Issue of late George Leslie Stewart, *b* 1893, *d* 1938: *m* 1927, Lillian Alice Ridsdale:—
Ross Ridsdale (c/o PO Box 407, Gisborne, NZ), *b* 1934: *m* 1966, Jillian Michelle, da of Robert Hamilton Bartie, of Gisborne, NZ, and has issue living, Jonathan Bruce, *b* 1969.

Grandchildren of Trevor Rowley Stewart (infra):—
Issue of late Colin Trevor Stewart, *b* 1925, *d* 1968: *m* 1948, Bessie Rebie, da of Frederick Clarke Shroff, of Tauranga, NZ:—
Gary Colin, *b* 1953. —— Peter Gregory, *b* 1958. —— Colette Marie, *b* 1950.

Grandchildren of George Vesey Stewart, MBE (ante):—
Issue of late John Rowley Miller Stewart, *b* 1862, *d* 1945: *m* 1st, 1886, Ellen Louisa, who *d* 1912, da of late Henry Furness, of Kyber Pass, Auckland, New Zealand; 2ndly, 1913, Louisa Beatrice, da of Thomas Gorst Travis, of Dunedin, NZ:—
(By 1st *m*) Trevor Rowley (149 Edgecumbe Rd, Tauranga, NZ), *b* 1896: *m* 1920, Dora, da of late Edwin Hall, of Waihi, NZ, and has issue living, Shirley Rita, *b* 1921: *m* 1st, 1945 (*m diss* 1950), William Lloyd Stevens; 2ndly, 1969, Francis Victor Parker, who *d* 1973, and has issue living (by 1st *m*), Kay Stewart, *b* 1947. —— (By 2nd *m*) Lorraine Travis, *b* 1917: *m* 1937, Alfred Shepherd Willan, of Hastings Rd, Stratford, Taranaki, NZ, and has issue living, Michael Frederick Stewart, *b* 1941, — Jock Stewart, *b* 1944, — Bruce Stewart, *b* 1946, — Pamela Stewart, *b* 1939.
Issue of late Hugh Alexander Montgomery Moore Stewart, *b* 1868, *d* 1954: *m* 1st, 1891, Susan, who *d* 1926, da of late William Tasman Clark, CE, of Hobart, Tasmania; 2ndly, 1932, Edith, el da of Joseph Cantwell, of Hawke's Bay, New Zealand:—
(By 1st *m*) James Edward Frederick Vesey Tasman, *b* 18-: *m* 19-, and has issue living, Noel Montgomery, *b* 19-. —— Gilbert Harry Ranfurly, *b* 18-. —— Christina Martina Alice, *b* 19-. —— Myrtle, *b* 19-. —— (By 2nd *m*) Coral Elizabeth, *b* 19-.

Grandchildren of late Hugh Alexander Murray Stewart, 2nd son of Hugh Alexander Montgomery Moore Stewart (ante):—
Issue of Ranfurly Henry Stewart, *b* 1899, *d* 1972: *m* 19-, Emma Frances Newman, who *d* 1967:—
William Henry Albert Harvey (Ohauiti Rd, RD3, Tauranga, NZ), *b* 1929: *m* 1951, Joan Alison, da of David Prestney, and has issue living, Brian William, *b* 1966, — Julie Frances, *b* 1953: *m* 19—, Peter Robert Gray, son of Jack Gray, of Te Puke, and has issue living, Richard Bruce *b* 1977, Jennifer Louise *b* 1975, Alison Julie *b* 1980, — Colleen Margaret, *b* 1955: *m* 19—, Philip Edward Watts, son of Thomas Watts, of Tauranga, and has issue living, Andrew Thomas *b* 1980, Ryan Philip *b* 1983, Anna Liese *b* 1987, — Janelle Beverley, *b* 1957: *m* 19—, John Anthony Arts, son of Bernhard J. Arts, of Tauranga, and has issue living, Antheny James *b* 1989, Renée Marise *b* 1982, Sarah Rochelle *b* 1983, Katie Monique *b* 1985, — Debora Joy, *b* 1959: *m* 19—, Paul Anthony Hogg, and has issue living, Adam Stewart *b* 1984. —— Trevor Ernest, *b* 1931: *m* 1955, Joan Alice, da of Andrew Stanley Fisher, and has issue living, Kevin Mark, *b* 1959; has issue living, Dion Mark *b* 1984, — Steven Wayne, *b* 1962; has issue living, Matthew Allan *b* 1986, Stacey Janna *b* 1992, — David Ernest, *b* 1968, — Philip Trevor, *b* 1972, — Maureen Anne, *b* 1957; has issue living, Philippa Joan *b* 1988, — Shona Joy, *b* 1961; has issue living, Rory Shane *b* 1988, Hayley Maree *b* 1991, — Sarah Lisa-Maree, *b* 1970. —— Valerie Elizabeth Grace, *b* 1933: *m* 19—, Patrick John Donovan, and has issue living, Bruce Charles, *b* 1955; has issue living, Gene *b* 1987, — Raymond John, *b* 1957, — Suzanne Jean, *b* 1959. —— Dawn Frances, *b* 193-: *m* 19—, Ronald Leslie Nicholson, and has issue living, Linda Dawn, *b* 19—, — Christine, *b* 19—, — Ronda, *b* 19—.

Grandchildren of late Hugh Stewart, yst son of late Mervyn Stewart, 2nd son of 1st baronet:—
Issue of late Rev Mervyn James Stewart, *b* 1871, *d* 1961: *m* 1910, Margaret Emma, who *d* 1968, da of late Frederick Jeffray Steuart, formerly of Carfin, Melbourne, Victoria, Australia:—
Hugh St Clair, MBE (Oak Cottage, Cheapside Lane, Denham, Bucks UB9 5AD; Savile Club), *b* 1910; *ed* St John's Coll, Camb (MA); 1939-45 War as Lt-Col Comdg an Army Film and Photographic Unit; MBE (Mil) 1945: *m* 1934, Frances Henley, BA, who *d* 1982, only child of late Dr Henley Frank Curl, of Wokingham, and has issue living, Andrew Mervyn (37 Park Rd, Rickmansworth, Herts WD3 1HU), *b* 1943; *ed* Rugby: *m* 1st, 1966 (*m diss* 1991), Carol-Anne, da of Stanley Burritt Featherstone, of Uitenhage, S Africa; 2ndly, 1991, Maaike, da of Dr Ir Johan Joseph Breen, of Gorinchem, Holland, and has issue living (by 1st *m*), Zoë Abbygail *b* 1971, — Michael Henley (Heathlands, Keepers Lane, Hyde Heath, Bucks HP6 5RJ), *b* 1949; *ed* Rugby, and Southampton Univ: *m* 1st, 1971, Jillian Maureen, who *d* 1980, da of Stanley Gold, of Reigate; 2ndly, 1985, Ann Frances, da of Frank Harris, of Feltham, and has issue living (by 1st *m*), Simon Mark Hugh *b* 1977, Paul Daniel *b* 1978, (by 2nd *m*) Sally Ann *b* 1985, Clare Henley June *b* 1987, Hannah Daisy *b* 1989, — Penelope Agnes, *b* 1939; *ed* Somerville Coll, Oxford (MA): *m* 1962, Hugh Macdonald Eales Forsyth, of Linden Lodge, Austen Way, Chalfont St Peter, Bucks, and has issue living, Kevin Hugh *b* 1969, Angus Edward Eales *b* 1975, — Sophie Frances *b* 1971, — Trottie (twin), *b* 1949; legally assumed the forename of Trottie in lieu of Margaret; *ed* Queenswood Sch, and Girton Coll, Camb; MD: *m* 1971, Anthony Kirwan, and has issue living, Jonathan Anthony *b* 1987, Eleanor Catherine *b* 1979, Frances Marguerite *b* 1982. —— David (2425 153rd Av SE, Bellevue, Washington 98007, USA), *b* 1912; is an Assocn-Fellow of R Aeronautical Soc: *m* 1st, 1942, Marjorie Susan Carroll, who *d* 1961, yr da of the Rev Frederick Charles Costeloe, formerly V of Staveley, Carlisle; 2ndly, 1963, Grace Edman Cunningham, of Madison, Connecticut, USA, and has had issue (by 1st *m*), Gordon Archdale (640 H, Udele Av, Berkeley, Calif 94708, USA), *b* 1944; *ed* St Columba's, and Pacific Lutheran Univ (BA): *m* 1982, Cora Docken, — †Simon Jeffray, *b* 1945: *ed* St Columba's, and Washington Univ (MBA): *m* 1968, Carolyn Sroufe, who *d* 1992, and has *d* 1993, leaving issue, Patrick Jeffray *b* 1979, Rachel Elizabeth *b* 1976, — David James (431, 109th Av SE, Bellevue, Washington 98004, USA), *b* 1952; *ed* Washington Univ (MBA): *m* 1979 (*m diss* 1994), Carole Cummins, and has issue living, Michael Cameron *b* 1985, Susan Blake *b* 1989. —— Mary Jeffray (Estone, Steeple Aston, Oxon), *b* 1913; formerly Section Officer, WAAF: *m* 1944, Dr John Edgar Furness, formerly Wing-Cdr RAF, who *d* 1974, and has issue living, Diana Ruth, *b* 1944: *m* 1973, Ronald Gardner, of Spring Vale, Steeple Aston, Oxon, and has issue living, Samantha Kim *b* 1975, Karen Louise *b* 1978, Sally Marie *b* 1984.
This family descends from Capt Andrew Stewart who accompanied Lord Ochiltree from Scotland, and settled at Gortigal, co Tyrone, about 1620. The 1st baronet, the Right Hon Sir John, Attorney-General for Ireland in 1799, drafted the Act of Union, and was successively MP for cos Down and Tyrone.

STEWART (UK) 1920 of Fingask, co Perth (Extinct 1979)

Sir BRUCE FRASER STEWART, 2nd and last *Baronet*.

DAUGHTER LIVING OF SECOND BARONET

Joy Elizabeth, *b* 1932: *m* 1955, Anthony Maxwell Deans, of Kilmarnock, Cheviot RD3, N Canterbury, NZ, and has issue living, Robert, *b* 1959: *m* 1986, Penelope Jane Russell, of Hawarden, NZ, — Ian Bruce, *b* 1960, — Joanne, *b* 1956: *m* 1986, Stephen McAtamney, of Oregon, Ruapuna RD5, Ashburton, NZ, and has issue living, Daniel *b* 1987, Anthony Joshua *b* 1988, — Nicola, *b* 1957: *m* 1983, Michael James Bowie Hobbs, of 23 Harbourview Rd, Northlands, Wellington, NZ, and has issue living, Michael *b* 1987, Emily *b* 1985, — Sarah, *b* 1962.

WIDOW LIVING OF SECOND BARONET

CONSTANCE EMILY FLORENCE (*Lady Stewart*) (Christchurch, Canterbury, NZ), da of William Samuel Gray, of 49 Grantchester St, Cambridge: *m* 1925, Sir Bruce Fraser Stewart, 2nd baronet, who *d* 1979, when the title became ext.

STEWART (UK) 1920, of Balgownie, Bearsden, co Dumbarton

Sir JOHN SIMON WATSON STEWART, 6th *Baronet*; *b* 5 July 1955; *s* his father, *Sir* JOHN KEITH WATSON, 1990; *ed* Uppingham, and Charing Cross Medical Sch; MD, FRCP, FRCR: *m* 1978, Catherine Stewart, da of Henry Gordon Bond, of Heyeswood House, Shiplake, Oxon, and has issue.

Arms – (as recorded at Lyon Office)—Or, a fesse checky azure and argent between in chief a Roman Charioteer driving a chariot with two horses, and in base a demi-figure of St Kentigern habited, bearing a crozier in his left hand, his right hand raised in benediction, all proper. **Crest** – A dexter hand couped at the wrist holding a sword erect in pale proper hilted and pommelled or. *Residence* – 52 Grosvenor Rd, WR 4EG.

SON LIVING

JOHN HAMISH WATSON, *b* 12 Dec 1983.

DAUGHTER LIVING

Anna Rebecca Watson, *b* 1987.

BROTHER LIVING

James Watson, *b* 1960; *ed* Winchester, Durham Univ, and RMA Sandhurst: *m* 1987, Judy Anne, da of late John George Bamford, of Uttoxeter, Staffs, and has issue living, Thomas Murdoch Watson, *b* 1992, — Emma Victoria Watson, *b* 1990, — Alice Georgina Watson, *b* 1993. *Residence* – The Old Rectory, Melchbourne, Beds MK44 1BQ.

SISTER LIVING

Caroline Felicity Watson, *b* 1958; *ed* Lycée Française de Londres: *m* 1982, Neil Barry Solomons, FRCS (Ed), son of Dr Arthur Solomons, of Port Elizabeth, S Africa, and has issue living, Lucy, *b* 1983, — Kate, *b* 1985.

WIDOW LIVING OF FOURTH BARONET

AVRIL VERONICA, FRSA, Hon FBID, Hon MASC (*Avril, Lady Watson Stewart*), only da of late Andrew Adamson Gibb, of Glasgow; artist, calligrapher and lecturer: *m* 1980, as his 2nd wife, Sir James Watson Stewart, 4th Bt, who *d* 1988. *Residence* – Undercliff Court, Wemyss Bay, Renfrewshire PA18 6AL. *Clubs* – Royal Scottish Automobile; Royal Gourock Yacht.

WIDOW LIVING OF FIFTH BARONET

MARY ELIZABETH (*Mary, Lady Stewart*), elder da of late John Francis Moxon, of Horton Hall, Leek, Staffs: *m* 1954, Sir John Keith Watson Stewart, 5th Bt, who *d* 1990. *Residence* – Flat 55, Hans Rd, SW3 1RN.

COLLATERAL BRANCH LIVING

Issue of late Fl Lt Malcolm Gilbert Watson Stewart, DFC, yst son of 1st baronet, *b* 1898, *d* 1971: *m* 1923, Evelyn Maud, da of late John A. Stewart, of Glasgow:—
John Allan (Tepic 80 Col Roma, Mexico DF, Mexico), *b* 1928: *m* 1959, Maria del Rufugio Vargas, of Mexico City, and has issue living, John Eric, *b* 1960. —— Edith Mary Hedley, *b* 1924: *m* 1948, Francis Lockhart McCall, of 5 Clyde Park Redland, Bristol, and has issue living, Peter Lockhart, *b* 1949, — Charles Michael Lockhart, *b* 1956, — Aline Mary, *b* 1950, — Sara Elizabeth, *b* 1954, — Louise Evelyn, *b* 1963.
Sir James Watson Stewart, 1st Bt (a Chartered Accountant), was a Member of Glasgow Corporation 1904-20, and Lord Provost of Glasgow and Lord-Lieut of Co of City of Glasgow 1917-20.

STEWART (UK) 1937, of Stewartby, co Bedford

Sir RONALD COMPTON STEWART, 2nd *Baronet*; *b* 14 Aug 1903; *s* his father, *Sir* (PERCY) MALCOLM, OBE, 1951; *ed* Rugby, and Jesus Coll, Camb: *m* 1936, Cynthia Alexandra, OBE, JP, who *d* 1987, da of late Harold Farmiloe.

Arms – Or, a fesse chequy azure and argent between a portcullis with its chains in chief and in base a lymphad sails furled, oars in action sable, flagged gules. Crest – A lymphad as in the arms.
Residence – Maulden Grange, Maulden, Bedfordshire.

HALF-SISTER LIVING

Yvonne Elizabeth Diana, *b* 1915; *ed* Somerville Coll, Oxford (BA 1937, MA 1950): *m* 1948, Thomas Doggett Savory, who *d* 1988, and has issue living, Thomas Stewart, *b* 1949: *m* 1975, Susan Elizabeth Allen, and has issue living, Elizabeth Susan *b* 1986, — Malcolm Doggett, *b* 1950: *m* 1975, Julia Mary Dring, and has issue living, Edward James Doggett *b* 1980, Hannah Caroline *b* 1977, Jessica Mary Alice *b* 1987. *Residence* – Kings Head Cottage, Cley next the Sea, Norfolk.

Sir (Percy) Malcolm Stewart, OBE, 1st Bt (2nd son of late Sir Halley Stewart), was High Sheriff of Bedfordshire 1941, and Pres of Associated Portland Cement Manufacturers, Ltd, of London Brick Co, Ltd, and of other Cos.

STEWART (UK) 1960, of Strathgarry, co Perth

Sir ALASTAIR ROBIN STEWART, 3rd *Baronet*; *b* 26 Sept 1925; *s* his brother, *Sir* DAVID BRODRIBB, TD, 1992; *ed* Marlborough; Man Dir (ret) of Stewart and Harvey Ltd; Lieut Royal Glos Hussars: *m* 1953, Patricia Helen, MBE, BA, ARIBA, da of late John Alfred Merrett, of Pondhead Farm, Forest Green, Surrey, and has issue.

Arms – Quarterly, 1st and 4th; of, a fess chequy azure and argent, *Stewart*; 2nd and 3rd; argent, a galley sable, sails furled, oars in action proper, flagged gules, *Lorne*; the whole within a bordure per pale dexter vert, sinister argent, charged with three roses gules barbed and seeded vert. Crest – A unicorn's head couped argent and armed and crined or. Badges – On escutcheon at centre of quarters.
Residence – Walter's Cottage, Little Baddow, Chelmsford, Essex CM3 4TQ.

SON LIVING

JOHN KENNETH ALEXANDER, *b* 15 Dec 1961; *ed* Marlborough, and Pembroke Coll, Camb (BA).

DAUGHTERS LIVING

Judith Patricia, *b* 1954; *ed* St Felix, Chelmsford County High Sch, and Bristol Polytechnic. —— Lucy Janetta, *b* 1956; *ed* St Felix, Chelmsford County High Sch, and Newcastle Polytechnic (BA). —— Catherine Helen, *b* 1958; *ed* St Felix, Marlborough Coll, and Trin Hall, Camb (BA).

SISTERS LIVING

Janetta Kenric (1 The Ridings, Links Rd, Ashtead, Surrey), *b* 1918; *ed* Lady Margaret Hall, Oxford (BA 1942). —— Leslie Mary (No 3 Collingwood-Blue Water Rd, Beacon Way, East London, S Africa), *b* 1921; *ed* Malvern Girls' Coll: *m* 1942, John Berger, MRCVS, who *d* 1982, son of Harry August Emil Berger, of Bickley, Kent, and has issue living, David Kenneth, *b* 1964, — Jennifer, *b* 1944; *ed* Aberdeen Univ (BSc), and Berkeley Univ, Cal, USA (MSc), — Vere, *b* 1946; *ed* Aberdeen Univ (BA), and Sussex Univ, — Elizabeth, *b* 1948; *ed* Nottingham Univ (BSc); MSc Nairobi: *m* 1972 Peter Moore, and has issue living, Kathleen Lesley *b* 1980, Carissa *b* 1981.

WIDOW LIVING OF SECOND BARONET

BARBARA DYKES (*Dowager Lady Stewart*), da of late Harry Dykes Lloyd, of Hull, and widow of Donald Ian Stewart, MC: *m* 1963, Sir David Brodribb Stewart, 2nd Bt, TD, who *d* 1992. *Residence* – Sasella, 5 Niklausen, Horn, Switzerland.
This family descends from the Rev Duncan Stewart, 1st of Strathgarry, son of Donald, 4th son of Alan Stewart, 3rd of Appin. Sir Kenneth Dugald Stewart, 1st Bt, yst son of Hinton Daniell Stewart, 6th of Strathgarry, was Chm of Lancs Cotton Corporation 1928-32, and of Trustee Savings Banks Assocn, 1946-65.

HENDERSON-STEWART (UK) 1957, of Callumshill, co Perth

Sir DAVID JAMES HENDERSON-STEWART OF CALLUMSHILL, 2nd *Baronet*; *b* 3rd July 1941; *s* his father, *Sir* JAMES, MP, 1961; *ed* Eton, and Trin Coll, Oxford: *m* 1972, Anne, da of Count Serge de Pahlen, and has issue.
Residence – 90 Oxford Gdns, W10.

SONS LIVING

DAVID, *b* 2 Feb 1973. ——— Nicolas, *b* 1974. ——— André, *b* 1976.

DAUGHTER LIVING

Nathalie, *b* 1981.

SISTER LIVING

Annabel Henderson-STEWART, *b* 1943; has resumed surname of Stewart: *m* 1966, Andrew Alastair Borthwick, and has issue living, Selena Margaret, *b* 1967, — Emilie Anna, *b* 1970.

WIDOW LIVING OF FIRST BARONET

ANNA MARGARET, da of Sir Bernard Eyre Greenwell, MBE, 2nd Bt: *m* 1st, 1940, Sir James Henderson-Stewart, MP, 1st baronet, who *d* 1961; 2ndly, 1965, Geoffrey Walford Wilks, CBE, TD, of 64 Cadogan Sq, SW1, who *d* 1987.
Sir James Henderson-Stewart, MP, 1st Bt (son of late Matthew Deas Stewart), sat as MP for E Div of Fife (LU) 1933-61, and was Joint Parliamentary Under-Sec of State for Scotland 1952-57. He was officially recognised in the surname of Henderson-Stewart and the designation of Callumshill by warrant of Lord Lyon 1957.

MacTAGGART STEWART (UK) 1892, of Southwick, Stewartry of Kirkcudbright, and Blairderry, Wigtownshire. (Extinct 1948)

Sir EDWARD ORDE MACTAGGART STEWART, 2nd and last *Baronet.*

DAUGHTER LIVING OF SECOND BARONET

Faith Agnes Dervorguilla *b* 1926: *m* 1949, Henry John Brewis, MP (*see* Walker, Bt, *cr* 1868, colls, 1990 Edn), who *d* 1989, and has issue living, Francis Roger MacTaggart (Ardwell House, Ardwell, by Stranraer, Wigtownshire DG9 9LY), *b* 1950: *m* 1981, Marion Teresa, da of late Robert Anderson, — (Ralph Michael) Rodney (17 Woodthorpe Rd, Putney SW15 6UQ), *b* 1951: *m* 1979, Valerie Anne, da of late Alexander Simpson Gerard, of Glasgow, and has issue living, Katharine *b* 1981, Mairi *b* 1983, — Christopher Mark John (10 Beresford Park, Sunderland, Tyne and Wear SR2 7JU), *b* 1956: *m* 1982, Aileen Teresa, da of David Rowland, of Newcastle-upon-Tyne, and has issue living, David John *b* 1988, Catherine Flora *b* 1985, — Sylvia Katharine Moira, *b* 1952: *m* 1st, 1978, Timothy Harrison, who *d* 1981, son of late Wesley Harrison, of Taunton; 2ndly, 1985, Murray Michael Thomas Lloyd Watson, son of Alexander Watson, of Trull, Taunton, Devon, and has issue living, (by 1st *m*) Wesley John *b* 1979, Abigail Katharine *b* 1981, (by 2nd *m*) Alexander Guy Timothy *b* 1989, Alice *b* 1987. *Residence* – Ardwell House, Ardwell, by Stranraer, Wigtownshire DG9 9LY.

SHAW-STEWART (NS) 1667, of Greenock and Blackhall, Renfrewshire

I hope for better things

Maj *Sir* HOUSTON MARK SHAW-STEWART, MC, 11th *Baronet, b* 24 April 1931; *s* his brother, *Sir* EUAN GUY, 1980; *ed* Eton; Maj Ayrshire Yeo; late 2nd Lt R Ulster Rifles, Korea 1950-51 (MC 1950): *m* 1982, Lucinda Victoria, yr da of Alexander K. H. Fletcher, of the Old Vicarage, Wighill, Tadcaster, N Yorks, and has issue.

Arms – Quarterly: 1st and 4th, or, a fesse chequy azure, over all a lion rampant gules, *Stewart of Blackhall*; 2nd and 3rd, azure, three covered cups or *Shaw of Greenock*. **Crests** – 1st, a lion's head erased gules, armed and langued azure, *Stewart of Blackhall*; 2nd, holding a club over his shoulder proper, a demi-savage wreathed about the head and middle with a laurel vert, *Shaw of Greenock.* **Supporters** – *Dexter*, a lion rampant gules, armed and langued azure, gorged with a collar checky argent and azure; *sinister*, a savage, holding a club over his shoulder all proper, wreathed round the middle with laurel leaves vert.
Seat – Ardgowan, Inverkip, Renfrewshire

SON LIVING

LUDOVIC HOUSTON, *b* 12 Nov 1986.

DAUGHTERS LIVING OF TENTH BARONET (*By 1st marriage to Mary Louise, da of late Lt-Col Geoffrey Reginald Devereux Shaw*)

Fiona Mary Onyx, *b* 1954: *m* 1981, Guy Nicholas John Jewers, son of Maj J.S. Jewers, RM (ret), of Home Farm, Swalcliffe, Oxon.

(*By 2nd marriage*)

Claudia Mary, *b* 1963.

FORMER WIFE LIVING OF TENTH BARONET

Victoria Anne (*Victoria, Lady Shaw-Stewart*), yr da of W. Fryer, of 8 Springfield Av, SW10: *m* 1962 (*m diss* 1969), as his 2nd wife, Sir Euan Guy Shaw-Stewart, 10th Bt, who *d* 1980. *Residence* – 42 Sheridan Rd, Merton Park, SW19.

COLLATERAL BRANCHES LIVING

Issue of late Rev Charles Robert Shaw-Stewart, 2nd son of 7th baronet, b 1856, d 1932: m 1890, Ida Fannie
Caroline, who d 1940, da of H. W. Alfken:—
Una Mary, b 1890: m 1916, Walter Rupert Reynell, MD, FRCP, who d 1948, and has issue living, Peter Carew, b 1917, —
Anthony Charles, b 1930, — Joan Katharine, b 1918, — Anne Lenore, b 1923.

Grandchildren of late Michael Patrick Stewart, son of late John Erskine Douglas Stewart, son of late Adm
of the Fleet Sir Houston Stewart, GCB, 2nd son of 5th baronet:—
Issue of late George Archdale Stewart, b 1893, d 1959: m 1921, Myrtle, who d 1971, da of John Wheeler, of Auck-
land, NZ:—
Lois Frances, b 1925. *Residence* – Unit 4, No 8 Bowling Av, Epsom, Auckland, NZ.
Issue of late Donald Erskine Stewart, b 1905, d 1985: m 1936, Ailsa Violet Annie, who d 1970, da of John Forbes, of
Auckland, NZ:—
Donald Michael (699 Mt Eden Rd, Mt Eden, Auckland, NZ), b 1944: m 1970 (m diss 1979), Jill Mary Smith, and has issue
living, Bradley James, b 1970, — Jonathan Paul, b 1973, — Joanne Clare, b 1975.

Grandsons of late Maj-Gen John Heron Maxwell Shaw-Stewart, son of late John Shaw-Stewart, 3rd son of
5th baronet:—
Issue of late Col Basil Heron Shaw-Stewart, CMG, DSO, b 1877, d 1939: m 1916, Vera, who d 1993, da of W. H.
Caldwell, of Morar, Inverness-shire:—
Michael (Linthill, Melrose, Roxburghshire), b 1925: m 1951, Grizel Margaret Lighton, da of late Maj Alexander Caldwells
Stewart, MC (Lighton, Bt), and has issue living, Archibald John (Drummore, Doune, Perthshire), b 1953: m 1983, Judy Ann,
el da of Maj Robert Courage, CVO, MBE, of Greenlanes, Windlesham, Surrey, and has issue living, James Robert Houston b
1986, Mary Ann b 1987, Phoebe Kate b 1990, — Robert Hugh, b 1960, — Helen Katharine, b 1959. ——John William
Archibald, b 1929: m 1955, Vora June Douglas, da of Charles Whistler Mackintosh (see D Hamilton and Brandon, 1985 Edn),
and has issue living, David Hugh (Hailes, Haddington, E Lothian), b 1956: m 1984, Linda Mary Catherine, elder da of late
Terence Malin Dare Sorby, CBE, of the Old Vicarage, Markbeech, Edinbridge, Kent, and has issue living, Lachlan Hugo
Terence b 1988, Guy Philip b 1990, Alexandra Linda Yora b 1986, — Patrick Douglas, b 1958, — Alexander Malcolm, b 1960,
— Mairi Hermione Margaret, b 1962. *Residence* – Traigh House, Arisaig, Inverness-shire.

Granddaughter of late George Steuart, son of Lt-Gen George Mackenzie Steuart, great-grandson of Walter
Steuart, 3rd son of 1st baronet:—
Issue of late Capt James McAlpine Steuart, b 1868, d 1946: m 1921, Mary, who d 1981, da of late John Edward
Compton-Bracebridge, of Atherstone Hall, Warwickshire:—
Mary Veronica GOLDBERG-STEUART, b 1926; assumed the addl surname of Steuart by deed 1981: m 1950, Donald Arthur Gold-
berg, who d 1988, of Street Ashton House, Stretton under Foss, Rugby.
The present baronet is in direct male descent from Sir John Stewart, natural son of Robert III, King of Scotland, to whom
was granted the family seat of Ardgowan. Sir Michael Stewart, 3rd Bt, m 1738, Helen, sister and co-heir of Sir John Houston
of that Ilk, 4th Bt. Her mother, Margaret, was da of Sir John Shaw, of Greenock, 2nd Bt. Sir John Shaw-Stewart, 4th Bt in
1752, on the death of his great-uncle, Sir John Shaw of Greenock, 3rd and last Bt, inherited the entailed estate of Greenock
and assumed the additional surname of Shaw. Sir Euan Guy Shaw-Stewart, 10th Bt, b 1928: m 1st, 1953 (m diss 1956), Mary
Louise, da of late Lt-Col Geoffrey Reginald Devereux Shaw (see Durrant, Bt, 1960 Edn) (she m 2ndly, 1957), Patrick James
Lysaght (see B Lisle), and 3rdly, 1987, David Blackwell; Sir Euan m 2ndly, 1962 (m diss 1969), Victoria Anne, yr da of W.
Fryer, of 8 Springfield Av, SW10, and d 1980.

Stewart-Clark, see Clark.

Stewart-Rankin, see Rankin.

Stewart-Richardson, see Richardson.

STIRLING (NS) 1666, of Glorat, Stirlingshire (Dormant 1949)

Sir GEORGE MURRAY HOME STIRLING OF GLORAT, CBE, DSO, 9th *Baronet*, d 1949, and at time of going to
press no name appears on the Official Roll of Baronets in respect of this title.

DAUGHTERS LIVING OF NINTH BARONET

Jean Margaret, b 1908: m 1939, Maj Frederick Graham Sheppard Graham, Argyll and Sutherland Highlanders, who d 1990.
Residence – Rednock House, Port of Menteith, Perths. ——Marjorie Marigold Anne, b 1920: m 1943, Edward Alan Langley,
Lt RAMC, who d 1982, and has issue living, David Stirling (Glorat, Milton of Campsie, Stirlingshire), b 1945. — George
Arthur Stirling (Little Baldoran, Milton of Campsie, Stirlingshire), b 1948, — John Charles Mark (5 Fettes Row, Edinburgh),
b 1950: m 1981 (m diss 1993), Christina Maria Cavedon. *Residence* – Little Baldoran, Milton of Campsie, Stirlingshire.

COLLATERAL BRANCH LIVING

Grandson of late Charles Stirling, son of late Robert Dundas Stirling, 5th son of 5th Bt:—
Issue of late Robert Wilson Stirling, b 1890, d 1970: m 1920, Hazel (7814 Swails St Acton, Indiana, 46259, USA), da
of John Heidenreich:—

John Charles (2225, Lawrence Av, Indianapolis, Indiana, 46227, USA), *b* 1922; probable heir to Baronetcy: *m* 1944, Evelyn Essig, and has issue living, John Charles (10838, Wonderland Drive, Indianapolis, Indiana, 46239, USA), *b* 1948: *m* 1966, Valborg-Nelson, and has issue living, Jeffery Dundas *b* 1969, April Cheryl *b* 1967, — Sherry Lynn (2405, Greentree, Indianapolis, Indiana 46227, USA), *b* 1951.

Stirling-Hamilton, see Hamilton.

Stirling-Maxwell, see Maxwell.

STOCKDALE (UK) 1960, of Hoddington, co Southampton

Sir THOMAS MINSHULL STOCKDALE, 2nd *Baronet*; *b* 7 Jan 1940; *s* his father, *Sir* EDMUND VILLIERS MINSHULL, 1989; *ed* Eton, and Worcester Coll, Oxford (MA): *m* 1965, Jacqueline, da of Ha-Van-Vuong, of 293 Phan, Thanh-Gian, Saigon, and has issue.

Arms – Ermine on a bend sable between two escallops gules three pheons argent. **Crest** – Issuant from a crown or a griffin's head gules.
Residence – Manor Farm, Weston Patrick, Basingstoke, Hants RG25 2NT. *Club* – Turf.

SON LIVING

JOHN MINSHULL, *b* 13 Dec 1967.

DAUGHTER LIVING

Charlotte Fermor, *b* 1970.

BROTHER LIVING

Frederick Minshull (Thorpe Tilney Hall, Lincoln; 51 Marlborough Crescent, W4), *b* 1947; *ed* Eton, and Jesus Coll, Camb (MA): *m* 1st, 1970 (*m diss* 1989), Joanna Lennox, yr da of Capt Roger Edward Harvey, JP, DL, Scots Gds, of Parliament Piece, Ramsbury, Wilts (*see* Mainwaring, Bt, ext, 1990 Edn); 2ndly, 1992, Adele Elizabeth Lavinia, da of Lincoln Mason, of Swinton, Manchester, and has issue living (by 1st *m*), Harry Tevis Minshull, *b* 1973, — Alexander Breckenridge Minshull, *b* 1975, — Valentine Frederick Minshull, *b* 1981, — (by 2nd *m*) Charles Lincoln Minshull, *b* 1994.

WIDOW LIVING OF FIRST BARONET

Hon LOUISE FERMOR-HESKETH (*Hon Lady Stockdale*), da of 1st Baron Hesketh: *m* 1937, Sir Edmund Villiers Minshull Stockdale, 1st Bt, who *d* 1989. *Residence* – Hoddington House, Upton Grey, Basingstoke RG25 2RU.
Sir Edmund Stockdale, 1st Bt, son of late Maj Henry Minshull Stockdale, JP, of Mears Hall, Northants, was Dep Prin Bank of England 1941-45, Alderman 1948-63, Lord Mayor of London 1959-60, and one of HM Lieuts of City of London.

STOCKENSTRÖM (UK) 1840, of Maasström, Cape of Good Hoope (Extinct 1957)

Sir ANDERS JOHAN STOCKENSTRÖM, 4th and last *Baronet*.

DAUGHTER LIVING OF FOURTH BARONET

Andrée Mabel, *b* 1939: *m* 1960, James Norman Pringle Gardiner. *Residence* – 22 Fraser St, Hunters Home, Knysna, S Africa.

STOKES (UK) 1889, of Lensfield Cottage, St Paul, Cambridge (Extinct 1916)

Sir ARTHUR ROMNEY STOKES, 2nd and last *Baronet*.

DAUGHTER LIVING OF SECOND BARONET

Mary Muriel, *b* 1899. *Address* – c/o Barclays Bank, White River 1240, Transvaal, South Africa.

STONHOUSE First Creation (E) 1628; Second Creation (E) 1670, of Radley, Berkshire.

Rev Sir MICHAEL PHILIP STONHOUSE, 19th *Baronet*; *b* 4 Sept 1948; *s* his father, *Sir* PHILIP ALLAN, 1993; *ed* Medicine Hat Coll, Univ of Alberta (BA), Wycliffe Coll (MDiv); deacon 1977, priest 1978 (Diocese of Calgary, Canada); assist Curate, St Peter's Calgary 1977-80; Rector and Incumbent, Parkland Parish 1980-87, St Mark's, Innisfail and St Matthew's, Bowden 1987-92, since when of St James, Saskatoon, Saskatchewan: *m* 1977, Colleen Eleanor, da of late James Albert Councill, of Toronto, Ontario, Canada, and has issue.

𝕬rms – Argent, on a fesse sable between three hawks volant azure, a leopard's face between two mullets or. 𝕮rest – A talbot's head couped argent, collared sable, lined and catching a dove volant of the first.
Residence – 3413 Balfour St, Saskatoon, Saskatchewan, Canada S7H 3Z3.

SONS LIVING

ALLAN JAMES, *b* 20 March 1981. —— David Michael, *b* 1983. —— Philip, *b* 1987.

BROTHER LIVING

Let us seek sublimer objects

Timothy Allan, *b* 1950; BA, Dip Ed: *m* 1976, Marija, da of George Baros, of Edmonton, Alberta, and has issue living, Matthew Paul, *b* 1980, — Benjamin Judah, *b* 1983.

AUNT LIVING *(Daughter of 17th baronet)*

Margaret Eleanor, *b* 1924: *m* 1953, Lt Cdr William Mansfield La Nauze, CD, RCN, of 403 Frederick St, Midland, Ontario, Canada L4R 3P5, and has issue living, Patricia Joan, *b* 1954: *m* 1980, Paul Williams.

WIDOW LIVING OF EIGHTEENTH BARONET

WINIFRED EMILY *(Dowager Lady Stonhouse)*, eldest da of John M. Shield, of Lethbridge, Alberta, Canada: *m* 1946, Sir Philip Allan Stonhouse, 18th Bt, who *d* 1993. *Residence* – 521, 12 St SW, Medicine Hat, Alberta, Canada.

Sir George, the 3rd baronet, was fined £1,460 for his loyalty to Charles 1. In 1670 he obtained a new patent granted to himself, with the old precedency and with a special remainder to his second son, John, and his heirs male, intending thereby to exclude his first son. The el son, however, on his father's decease, claimed and enjoyed the baronetcy created by the original patent, so that there were two baronetcies in the family till, on the death (without issue) of Sir John, 6th baronet under the old creation, they became united in Sir John, 3rd baronet of the new. The 11th baronet, having been for twenty years Physician to the Northampton Infirmary, took Holy Orders, and subsequently became an eminent preacher.

STOREY (UK) 1960, of Settrington, co York

Hon Sir RICHARD STOREY, 2nd *Baronet*; *b 23 Jan 1937; s his father,* SAMUEL, Baron Buckton (Life Baron) in his Baronetcy, 1978; *ed* Winchester, and Trin Coll, Camb (BA LLB); High Sheriff N Yorks 1992; Bar Inner Temple 1962; Chm Portsmouth & Sunderland Newspapers plc since 1973; Vice-Pres Newspaper Soc (Member of Council since 1980), Press Council 1980-86; Member of Nat Council and Executive of the County of Landowners Assoc 1980-84 (Chm of Yorks Executive 1974-76); Member CBI Employment Policy Cttee 1984-88; Council Member of INCA-FIEJ Research Assoc 1983-88; Chm Hillier Arboretum Mgmt Cttee since 1989, Dir The Fleming Enterprise Investment Trust plc since 1989, Reuters Holdings plc 1986-92, The Press Assocn Ltd since 1986 (Chm since 1991); served on Yorkshire and Humberside CBI Regional Council 1974-76: *m* 1961, Virginia Anne, da of late Sir Kenelm Henry Ernest Cayley, 10th Bt, and has issue.

𝕬rms – Per fesse argent and sable a pale counter charged three storks also sable. 𝕮rest – In front of an escallop or a stork's head erased sable gorged with a mural crown gold.
Residences – Settrington House, Malton, Yorks; 7 Douro Place, W8.

SON LIVING

KENELM, *b* 4 Jan 1963; *ed* Winchester, and George Washington Univ, Washington DC (BBA).

DAUGHTERS LIVING

Elisabeth, *b* 1964: *m* 1988, Rowland Bruce Ranald Critchley, elder son of Col I. R. Critchley, of Altina, by Crieff, Perthshire, and has issue living, Fergus Ranald, *b* 1990, — Douglas Bruce, *b* 1994, — Lucilla, *b* (twin) 1990. —— Melissa, *b* 1968: *m* 1992, Christopher Nigel Paul Stourton (*see* B Mowbray, colls), of 37 Patience Rd, SW11.

SISTER LIVING

Hon Jacquetta, *b* 1930: *m* 1956, Francis Cator, of The Old House, Ranworth, Norfolk, and 12 Warwick Sq Mews, SW1, and has issue living, Charles Francis, *b* 1959: *m* 1987, Jane, widow of William J. Russell, and da of Robert Culverwell, of Luckington, Wilts, and has issue living, Samuel Charles *b* 1992, Rosanna *b* 1988, Jessica Clare *b* 1989, — Mark, *b* 1960: *m* 1991, Hon Isabel Alicia Claire Crossley, eldest da of 3rd Baron Somerleyton, and has issue living, Benjamin Hugo *b* 1988, Lara Louise *b* 1992, — Harry, *b* 1964: *m* 1992, Kathleen Jean, da of Capt Alan Mackay, of Port Macquarrie, Australia, and has issue living, Frederick Francis *b* 1993, — Elisabeth Anne, *b* 1957: *m* 1982, Rupert Thomas Newton Thistlethwayte, and has issue (*see* E Portsmouth, colls).

Samuel Storey, Life Baron and 1st Baronet, el son of late Frederick George Storey, JP, was Chm, of Ways and Means 1965-66, Pres of Portsmouth and Sunderland Newspapers, and MP for Sunderland (*C*) 1931-45, and for Stretford 1950-66; *cr a* Baronet (UK) 1960, and *Baron Buckton*, of Settrington, in E Riding, Co York (Life Baron) 1966.

STOTT (UK) 1920, of Stanton, co Gloucester

He aims at high things

Sir ADRIAN GEORGE ELLINGHAM STOTT, 4th *Baronet*, *b* 7 Oct 1948; *s* his father, *Sir* PHILIP SIDNEY, 1979; *ed* Univ of British Columbia (BSc, MSc) and Univ of Waterloo, Ontario (MMaths); Dir of Planning rural region of BC 1974-77; Town planning consultant 1977-80; Real estate portfolio manager 1980-86, Man Dir Marketing Co since 1987; MCIP.

Arms – Gules, three pallets or, each charged with as many pellets, on a chief of the second a heart between two battle-axes of the first. **Crest** – Upon a chaplet of roses fessewise gules a martlet sable.
Address – RR3, Site 320, C65 Parksville, BC, Canada V0R ZS0.

BROTHER LIVING

VYVYAN PHILIP (7 Dumbarton Drive, Kenmore, Queensland, 4069 Australia), *b* 5 Aug 1952.

UNCLES LIVING (*Sons of 2nd baronet*)

Christopher George Swailes, *b* 1924; *ed* Malvern; MRAC; European War 1939-45 in RAF Vol Reserve: *m* 1st, 1953 (*m diss* 19—), Winifred Marshall (MOSSFORD), da of William Don; 2ndly, 19—, Anne, da of — McMahon, of Lisdoonvarna, co Clare, and has issue living, (by 1st *m*) Sarah Caroline, *b* 1956, — (by 2nd *m*) Christopher John McMahon, *b* 19—. —— Derek Nicholson (29 Birngana Av, Sandy Bay, Tas, 7005 Aust), *b* 1928; *ed* Malvern; is a MIEE: *m* 1993, Eileen Bridget, da of Dr D. G. Wilde, of Epsom, Surrey.

WIDOW LIVING OF THIRD BARONET

CICELY FLORENCE (*Lady Stott*), only da of Bertram Ellingham, of Ely House, Hertford, and widow of Vincent Charles William Trowbridge, Pilot Officer Roy Canadian Air Force: *m* 1947, Sir Philip Sidney Stott, 3rd Bt, who *d* 1979. *Address* – RR3, Site 320, C65 Parksville, BC, Canada V0R ZS0.

The 1st baronet, Sir Philip Sidney Stott (son of late Abraham Henthorne Stott, of Oldham), was an architect, JP for Gloucestershire, and High Sheriff of Gloucestershire 1925. The 2nd baronet, Sir George Edward Stott, was a registered Architect, and High Sheriff of Gloucestershire 1947. The 3rd baronet, Sir Philip Sidney Stott, was a registered architect and a composer.

PHILIPSON-STOW (UK) 1907, of Cape Town, Colony of Cape of Good Hope, and Blackdown House, Lodsworth, co Sussex

Fide non fraude

By faith, not by fraud

Sir CHRISTOPHER PHILIPSON-STOW, 5th *Baronet*; *b* 13 Sept 1920; *s* his cousin, *Maj Sir* EDMOND CECIL, 1982; *ed* Winchester; late Fl Lt RAFVR: *m* 1952, Elizabeth Nairn, da of late James Dixon Trees, of Toronto, and widow of Maj Frederick George McLaren, 48th Highrs, of Canada, and has issue living.

Arms – Quarterly, 1st and 4th vert, on a cross nebulée between four leopards' faces or, a rose gules, *Stow*; 2nd and 3rd gules two chevronelles between three boars' heads couped ermine, *Philipson*. **Crest** – 1st issuant from an antique crown or, charged with a rose gules, a leopard's face gold between two wings vert, *Stow*; 2nd, issuant from a mural crown or, charged with a rose gules, a plume of five ostrich feathers alternately argent and gules, *Philipson*.
Residence – RR2, Port Carling, Ontario, Canada POB 1JO.

SONS LIVING

ROBERT MATTHEW (32 John St, Thornhill, Ontario, Canada L3T 1X8), *b* 29 Aug 1953; *ed* Thornhill Secondary Sch, and Univ of Waterloo, Ont (BASc, PEng). —— Rowland Frederic, *b* 1954; *ed* Thornhill Secondary Sch, and Univ of Waterloo (BASc, PEng): *m* 1979, Mary Susan, da of William J. N. Stroud, of Thornhill, Ont, and has issue living, Christopher William, *b* 1983, —— Kimberly Susan, *b* 1981.

COLLATERAL BRANCH LIVING

Issue of late Maj Guyon Philipson Philipson-Stow, 6th and yst son of 1st baronet, *b* 1898, *d* 1983: *m* 1925, Alice Mary, who *d* 1989 only da of R. Hilton Fagge:—
Robert Nicholas (Priors Court, Long Green, Glos; White's Club), *b* 1937; *ed* Winchester; late Lt RHG: *m* 1963, Nicolette Leila, el da of Hon Philip Leyland Kindersley (*see* B Kindersley), and has issue living, Robert Rowland, *b* 1970, —— Edward Miles, *b* 1972, —— Georgina Mary, *b* 1976. —— Helen Rosemary, *b* 1934.
Sir Frederick Samuel Philipson Stow, 1st baronet, assumed by Roy licence 1891, the additional surname and arms of Philipson, being 4th in descent from George Stow of Sutton in Ashfield, Notts, who *m* 1767, Elizabeth, da and eventual heir of John Wilberfoss, by Elizabeth, el da and eventual heir of Richard Philipson, of Beverley.

STRACEY (UK) 1818, of Rackheath, Norfolk

Sir JOHN SIMON STRACEY, 9th *Baronet*, only son of late Capt Algernon Augustus Henry Stracey, 2nd son of 6th Bt; *b* 30 Nov 1938; *s* his cousin, *Sir* MICHAEL GEORGE MOTLEY, 1971; *ed* Wellington Coll, and McGill Univ: *m* 1968, Martha Maria, da of late Johann Egger, of Innsbrück, and has issue.

Arms – Ermine, on a cross engrailed between four eagles displayed gules five cinquefoils or. **Crest** – A lion rampant erminois, ducally crowned gules supporting a cross patée-fitchée of the last.
Residence – 14 Britts Farm Rd, Buxted, E. Sussex TN22 4LZ.

DAUGHTERS LIVING

Daniela, *b* 1968. —— Nadja, *b* 1973.

SISTER LIVING

Ramona Beryl, *b* 1930: *m* 1959, Theodore Frederic Darvas, Flat 1, 5 St George's Terrace, NW1 8XH, and has issue living, Jane Caroline, *b* 1963, —— Anna Judith, *b* 1966.

SISTER LIVING OF EIGHTH BARONET

Margaret Rosalind Linley, *b* 1907: *m* 1959, Peter Edward Clement Harris, who *d* 1976, son of late Sir Austin Edward Harris, KBE. *Residence* – 189 Cranmer Court, Sloane Av, SW3.

HALF-SISTER LIVING OF EIGHTH BARONET

Dereen Elizabeth Paulette, *b* 1937: *m* 1965, James Douglas Bartlett, of Paddocks Farm, Cranbrook, Kent, and has issue living, Christopher James Edward Douglas, *b* 1966, —— Peter Sean Charles, *b* 1969, —— Richard Gerald Patrick, *b* 1971.

COLLATERAL BRANCHES LIVING

Grandchildren of late Gilbert Hardinge Stracey, 5th son of 5th baronet:—
Issue of late Lt-Col Ernest Henry Denne Stracey, *b* 1871, *d* 1948: *m* 1907, Faith Dorothy Beatrice Mounteney, who *d* 1965, da of late Henry Downes Popham:—
HENRY MOUNTENEY, *b* 24 April 1920: *m* 1st, 1943, Susanna, da of Adair Tracey; 2ndly, 1950, Lysbeth, da of Charles Ashford; 3rdly, 1961, Jeltje, yst da of Scholte de Boer, of Oppenhuizen, Friesland, Holland, and has issue living, (by 1st *m*) Amarilla, *b* 1943, —— (by 2nd *m*), Rupert, *b* 1951, —— Miranda Hinemoa, *b* 1955. *Residence* – White Barn, Walberswick, Suffolk. —— Noel

Margaret Jephson (Durham House, Balsham, Cambs), *b* 1908: *m* 1933, Maj Charles Robert Purdon Coote, who *d* 1954 (*see* Coote, Bt, *cr* 1621, colls).

Granddaughters of late Hardinge Robert Stracey, 3rd son of 4th baronet:—
    Issue of late Lt-Col Hardinge Richard Stracey, *b* 1840, *d* 1924: *m* 1883, Mary Henrietta Rennel, who *d* 1944, da of late Adm Frederick Byng Montresor:—
Constance Mary, *b* 18—. —— Elizabeth Julia, *b* 18—: *m* 1909, Charles Henry Garner Richardson and has issue living, Richard Hearle, *b* 1914, — Peter Tremayne, *b* 1916, — Elizabeth Barbara, *b* 1911, — José Antonia Doreen, *b* 1921. —— Ruth: *m* 1930, J. Wilfred Wickes, consulting engineer, of Durban, Natal, and has issue living, a da, *b* 1931. —— Margaret Diana, *b* 1896.

Grandson of late Lt-Cdr Eustace William Clitherow STRACEY-CLITHEROW (infra):—
    Issue of late Cdr Christopher Bryan STRACEY CLITHEROW, DSC, RN, *b* 1903, *d* 1977: *m* 1928, Maida Daughne Laurel (The Mill Cottage, Frogmore, East Meon, Petersfield, GU32 1QH), da of late Capt Hon Francis Almeric Butler (*see* E Lanesborough, colls):—
Dominic Peter (3 St Aubyn St, Devonport, Auckland 9, NZ), *b* 1939; *ed* Harrow and London Univ (BSc); C Eng; Lt Cdr RN (ret); employed by NZ navy: *m* 1971, Penelope Bronwen, da of L. Griffiths, of Henley-in-Arden, and has issue living, Henry Dominic, *b* 1979, — Simon Andrew, *b* (twin) 1979, — Charlotte Emma, *b* 1972, — Virginia Louise, *b* (twin) 1972.

Granddaughter of late Rev William James STRACEY-CLITHEROW (who assumed by Roy licence 1900, the additional surname and arms of Clitherow), son of late John Stracey, 5th son of 1st baronet:—
    Issue of late Lieut-Com Eustace William Clitherow STRACEY- CLITHEROW, *b* 1864, *d* 1930: *m* 1900, Frances Evelyn Veronica, who *d* 1962, da of late John Birkbeck Evelyn Stansfeld, sometime Capt 3rd Btn Duke of Wellington's (W Riding Regt):—
Mary Barbara (2 Sheldon Av, Broadway, Worcs), *b* 1909: *m* 1938, Francis Stanton Blake, who *d* 1947.

Sir Edward Stracey, 1st baronet, was the el surviving son of Sir John Stracey, Knt, Chief Judge of the Sheriffs' Court, and Recorder of London in 1746. The 5th baronet sat as MP for Norfolk East (C) 1855-7, for Yarmouth 1859-65, and for Norwich 1868-9. Sir Edward Paulet Stracey, 7th baronet, was appointed High Sheriff of Norfolk 1928.

STRACHEY (UK) 1801, of Sutton Court, Somerset

(*Sir*) CHARLES STRACHEY, 6th *Baronet*, son of late Rt Hon Evelyn John St Loe Strachey, MP; *b* 20 June 1934; *s* his 1st cousin once removed EDWARD, 2nd Baron Strachie, 1973 (but does not use title); *ed* Westminster Sch, and Magdalen Coll, Oxford: *m* 1973, Janet Megan, da of Alexander Miller, of Earls Barton, Northants, and has issue.

Arms – Quarterly: 1st and 4th argent, a cross between four eagles displayed gules, *Strachey*; 2nd and 3rd or, three crescents, two and one, sable; on a canton of the last a ducal crown, or, *Hodges*. Crest – An eagle displayed gules, charged on the breast with a cross-crosslet fitchée argent.
Address – 30 Gibson Sq, N1.

The circumstances may Change, but not the mind

DAUGHTER LIVING

Jane Alice, *b* 1975.

SISTER LIVING

Elizabeth (18 Southdean Gdns, SW19 6NU), *b* 1936: *m* 1958, Hamid al Qadhi, who *d* 1986, and has issue living, Mohammed Jemil, *b* 1959, — Samia, *b* 1964, — and an adopted da, Hannah, *b* 1962.

COLLATERAL BRANCHES LIVING

Grandchildren of late Ralph Strachey, 2nd son of late Lt-Gen Sir Richard Strachey, GCSI, FRS, LLD (infra):—
    Issue of late Richard Philip Farquhar Strachey, *b* 1902, *d* 1976: *m* 1st, 1927 (*m diss* 1940), Frances Esme, da of Charles John Rudd; 2ndly, 1943, Mrs Simonette Mary Reynolds Woods (25 Park Town, Oxford), da of Charles Foster Atchison, of Cliff Cottage, Bonchurch, Isle of Wight, and formerly wife of S. John Woods:—
(By 1st *m*) Philippa HAWTIN (La Casita Vieja, Pt da El Collado, 03729 Lliber, Alicante, Spain), *b* 1927; assumed the surname of Hawtin by deed poll 1961. —— Victoria (9 Dolforgan Court, Louisa Terrace, Exmouth, Devon EX8 2AQ), *b* 1929; assumed the surname of Hunter by deed poll 1951 (and has issue, Matthew HUNTER, *b* 1951): *m* 1952, Mark Graham Holloway, and has further issue, Sam HOLLOWAY, *b* 1953: *m* 1983, Elizabeth Anne Cotterill, and has issue living, Laura Esme *b* 1985, Rachael Emma *b* 1987, — Sophy, *b* 1955; has issue living (by John David Weaver), Frederick Mark Richard WEAVER *b* 1987, Victoria Lilian WEAVER *b* 1985, — Sarah Louise, *b* 1957; has issue living (by Jonathan Peter White), Matthew William WHITE *b* 1993, Katie May WHITE *b* 1992.
    Issue of late John Ralph Severs Strachey, *b* 1905, *d* 1983: *m* 1st, 1933 (*m diss* 1942), Isobel Bertha, who *d* 1987, da of Ronald Leslie; 2ndly, 1944, Rosemary, da of Douglas Mavor:—
(By 2nd *m*) HENRY LEOFRIC BENVENUTO, *b* 17 April 1947: *m* 1st, 1971 (*m diss* 1982), Julie Margaret Hutchens; 2ndly, 1983, Susan Christine, da of John Ernest Skinner, of Manor Cottage, 41 Court Lane, Cosham, Hants. *Address* – c/o Middleton & Upsall, Solicitors, 39 Silver St, Warminster, Wilts BA12 8PP.

Granddaughters of late Lt-Gen Sir Richard Strachey, GCSI, FRS, LLD, 3rd son of Edward Strachey (infra):—
    Issue of late Ralph Strachey, *b* 1868, *d* 1923: *m* 1901, Margaret Winifred, who *d* 1972, da of late Albert Severs:—
Ursula Margaret, *b* 1911: *m* 1939, Cyril Charles Wentzel, Bar-at-Law. *Residence* – 1 Grange Lodge, The Grange, SW19 4PR.
    Issue of late Oliver Strachey, CBE, *b* 1874; *d* 1960: *m* 1st, 1901 (*m diss* 1908), Ruby Julia, da of late Julius Mayer; 2ndly, 1911, Rachel Conn, who *d* 1940, da of late Benjamin Francis Costelloe:—
(By 2nd *m*) Barbara, *b* 1912: *m* 1st, 1934 (*m diss* 1937), Olav Hultin; 2ndly, 1937, Wolf Halpern, Leading Aircraftman, RAFVR, who *d* on active ser 1943, and has issue living, (by 1st *m*), Roger Olavson, *b* 1934. *Residence* – 15 Richmond Rd, Oxford.

Grandchildren (if any) of late William Strachey, son of late George Strachey, 6th son of late Edward Strachey, 2nd son of 1st baronet:—
Issue (if any) of late Reginald Strachey, *b* 1905, *d* 1973 (NY, USA).

The Strachie family was settled at Saffron Walden, Essex, until the 16th century. John Strachey, *b* 1634, inherited Sutton Court, Som, from his mother Elizabeth Cross: *m* 1662, Jane, da and co-heir of George Hodges, of Wedmore, Somerset, Their great-grandson, Sir Henry Strachey, of Sutton Court, MP 1770-1810, was Sec to Lord Clive 1764, and Commn for Restoring Peace to America 1774, an Under-Sec of State 1782, and Master of the Household 1794. He was *cr* a *Baronet* 1801. His great-grandson, Sir Edward, PC, 4th Bt, Treasurer of the Household 1905-10, Paymaster-Gen. 1912-15, and MP for S Som (*L*) 1892-1911, was *cr Baron Strachie*, of Sutton Court, Somerset, 1911. This Barony became ext on the death of his son Edward, 2nd Baron and 5th Bt in 1973, when the baronetcy reverted to Sir Charles, 6th Bt, grandson of John St Loe Strachey, yr brother of 1st baron.

Strickland-Constable, see Constable

Strang Steel, see Steel

STRONGE (UK) 1803, of Tynan, co Armagh

A way is to be attempted

Sir JAMES ANSELAN MAXWELL STRONGE, 10th *Baronet*; son of late Maxwell Du Pre James Stronge; *b* 17 July 1946; *s* his 2nd cousin, Capt Sir JAMES MATTHEW*, 1981; *ed* Privately.

Arms – Argent, a chevron wavy sable between three lozenges azure, in the centre chief point an estoile gules. **Crests** – 1st an eagle with two heads displayed sable, beaked and legged azure, langued gules; 2ndly, a cluster of wine grapes proper. **Second Motto** – Dulce quod utile (*That is sweet which is useful*).
Residence – Shannagh Camp Hill Community, Kilkeel, co Down.

SISTER LIVING

Helen Mary, *b* 1948: *m* 1971, Philip Rodney Allen-Morgan, of Manor South, Bishopstone, E Sussex BN25 2VD, and has issue living, William Frederick Stronge, *b* 1975, — Allanah Mary, *b* 1974, — Laura Myfanwy, *b* 1978.

DAUGHTERS LIVING OF EIGHTH BARONET

Daphne Marian, *b* 1922: late WRNS: *m* 1954, Thomas John Anthony Kingan, late Irish Guards, and has issue living, James Anthony John, *b* 1957. *Residence* – Glenganagh, Bangor, co Down. —— Evelyn Elizabeth, *b* 1925; late WRNS: *m* 1960, Brig Charles Harold Arthur Olivier, CBE, who *d* 1992. *Residence* – Rosemary Cottage, Amport, Andover.

*By decision of House of Lords 10 Sept 1941, approved by HM King George VI, which provides that where two persons have died in circumstances rendering it uncertain as to which of them survived the other, such deaths should be presumed to have occurred in order of seniority.

Sir James Matthew, DCL, 2nd baronet, was a Gentleman of the Privy Chamber, and Sir James Matthew, 3rd baronet, sat as MP for Armagh (*C*) 1864-74. The 7th baronet, Sir Charles, Sir Charles Edmond Sinclair, was HM Lieut for co Londonderry. The 8th baronet, Rt Hon Sir (Charles) Norman Lockhart, MC, was Lord Lieut for co Armagh 1939-81, Member of House of Commons, N Ireland (*U*) 1938-69 (Speaker 1945-69), and was murdered by terrorists at his residence, Tynan Abbey, co Armagh, 1981. His son, the 9th baronet, Capt Sir James Matthew MP Mid-Armagh (*U*), NI Parl 1969-72, MP for NI Assembly (Armagh) 1973-74, was murdered with his father.

STUART (E) 1660, of Hartley Mauduit, Hampshire.

Avito viret honore

*He flourishes by
ancestral honors*

Sir PHILLIP LUTTRELL STUART, 9th *Baronet* (but his name does not, at time of going to press, appear on the official Roll of Baronets), son of late Luttrell Hamilton Stuart, brother of 8th baronet; *b* 7 Sept 1937; *s* his uncle, Sir HOULTON JOHN, 1959; late F/O RCAF: *m* 1st, 1962 (*m diss* 1968), Marlete Rose, da of Otto Muth, of 1172, Pembina Highway, Winnipeg, Manitoba, Canada; 2ndly, 1969, Beverley Claire Pieri, and has issue by 1st and 2nd *m*.

Arms – Or, a fesse checky azure and argent, an inescutcheon argent charged with the lion of Scotland debruised with a bendlet raguly or. **Crest** – A roebuck statant argent, ducally gorged gules.
Residence – 5777 Dumfries St N, Vancouver, BC, Canada V5P 3A7.

SON LIVING *(By 2nd marriage)*

GEOFFREY PHILLIP, *b* 5 July 1973. *Residence* – 3 Windermere Bay, Winnipeg, Manitoba, Canada R3T 1B1.

DAUGHTERS LIVING *(By 1st marriage)*

Cynthia Louise, *b* 1963. *Residence* – 42 Arthur St N, Guelph, Ontario, Canada N1E 4T8.

(By 2nd marriage)

Brenda Claire, *b* 1969. *Residence* – 3 Windermere Bay, Winnipeg, Manitoba, Canada R3T 1B1.

COLLATERAL BRANCH LIVING

Grandchildren of late Major Arthur John Stuart, RM, 3rd son of 5th baronet:—
Issue of late Arthur Kennedy Stuart, *b* 1859, *d* 19—: *m* 1892, Luise Franziska, da of Carl Joseph Pfeifer, of Freiburg-in-Baden, Germany:—
Arthur Ernest, *b* 1896. —— Charles Edwin, *b* 1897.

The 1st baronet, Sir Nicholas Stuart (son of Simeon Stuart, of Hartley Mauduit), and the 2nd baronet, Sir Simeon, each held the office of a Chamberlain of the Exchequer. The 2nd and 3rd baronets successively sat as MP for Hampshire. In 1829, on the death of his grandfather, the last Earl of Carhampton, the 5th baronet was offered a fresh patent by George IV, which however, he did not accept. The 7th Baronet, Sir Simeon Henry Lechmere, was City Marshal of London 1893-9. The present baronet is representative of the Earldom of Carhampton (*ext*) and the Barony of Waltham (*ext*).

Stuart-Menteth, see Menteth.

Stuart Taylor, see Taylor (cr 1917).

STUCLEY (UK) 1859, of Affeton Castle, Devonshire
(Name pronounced "Stukeley")

Softly but boldly

Sir HUGH GEORGE COPLESTONE BAMPFYLDE STUCLEY, 6th *Baronet; b* 8 Jan 1945; *s* his father, *Maj Sir* DENNIS FREDERIC BANKES, 1983; *ed* Milton Abbey, and RAC Cirencester; late Lieut RHG: *m* 1969, Angela Caroline, el da of Richard Toller, of Orchard House, Kingston Lisle, Wantage, Berks, and has issue.

Arms – Quarterly: 1st and 4th, azure, three pears or, *Stucley;* 2nd and 3rd, per fesse embattled argent and sable, three bucks attires, each fixed to the scalp, counterchanged, *Buck.* **Crest** – Between a buck's attires as in the arms sable, a lion rampant or, the sinister paw holding a battleaxe resting on the shoulder proper.
Residence – Affeton Castle, Worlington Crediton, Devon.

SONS LIVING

GEORGE DENNIS, *b* 26 Dec 1970. —— Peter Richard, *b* 1972.

DAUGHTERS LIVING

Charlotte Catherine, *b* 1975. —— Lucinda Sarah, *b* 1977.

SISTERS LIVING

Margaret Cynthia, *b* 1934: *m* 1953, Gerald Arthur Hohler (V Gort), and has issue living, Thomas Edward, *b* 1958, — Henrietta Margaret Cynthia, *b* 1955: *m* 1994, Charles Richard Seymour (*see* M Hertford, colls), — Lucinda Jane Astell, *b* 1960: *m* 1982, Richard Clephane Compton (*see* M Northampton, colls). *Residence* – Trent Manor, Sherborne, Dorset. —— Rosemary Anne (*Viscountess Boyne*), *b* 1936: *m* 1956, 10th Viscount Boyne. *Residence* – Burwarton, Bridgnorth, Salop. —— Christine Elizabeth (*Baroness Cobbold*), *b* 1940: *m* 1961, 2nd Baron Cobbold. *Residences* – Knebworth House, Knebworth, Herts; 2d Park Place Villas, W2. —— Sarah Susan, *b* 1942: *m* 1st, 1963 (*m diss* 1970), Michael Henry Basil Peto (later Sir Michael Peto, 4th Bt); 2ndly, 1971, Charles Worthington, and has issue living (by 1st *m*) (*see* Peto, Bt, cr 1927), — (by 2nd *m*) Anna, *b* 1972. *Residence* – Court Hall, N Molton, N Devon.

UNCLE LIVING (*Son of 4th baronet*)

Bernard Thomas Fane, *b* 1918.

AUNT LIVING (*Daughter of 4th baronet*)

Priscilla (143 Bowerhinton, Martock, Som), *b* 1911: *m* 1936 (*m diss* 1956), Count Andrzej Zygmunt Zamoyski, who *d* 1964, and has issue living, *Count* Zygmunt Ignacy Stukeley, *b* 1937, *ed* Stowe, and Ch Ch, Oxford; — *Countess* Betka Marya (136 Hurlingham Rd, SW6), *b* 1948; *ed* Cranborne Chase, and Lady Margaret Hall, Oxford; journalist: *m* 1988 (*m diss* 1993), Benjamin Hargreaves.

WIDOW LIVING OF FIFTH BARONET

Hon SHEILA MARGARET WARWICK BAMPFYLDE (*Hon Lady Stucley*), da of 4th Baron Poltimore: *m* 1932, Maj Sir Dennis Frederic Bankes Stucley, 5th Bt, who *d* 1983. *Residence* – Hartland Abbey, N Devon.
The Stucley family (which has possessed Affeton Castle for over 600 years) came from Stukeley, Huntingdonshire, and were Sheriffs of that county, *temp* John. Sir George, 1st baronet, assumed by Roy licence, 1858, the surname of Stucley in lieu of his patronymic of Buck as lineal representative of that ancient family, and was MP for Barnstaple (*C*) 1855-9 and 1865-8. Maj Dennis F. B. Stucley, 5th Bt, was a DL and High Sheriff of Devon; Chm Regional Advisory Cttee, Forestry Comm SW 1958-75, of Timber Growers' Organisation 1966-69, and of Exmoor Nat Park (Devon) Cttee 1968-74; Master Hartland Harriers 1932-35, N Eggesford Foxhounds 1936-38, and jt Master Dulverton West Foxhounds 1952-54.

STUDD (UK) 1929, of Netheravon, Wilts

Nous·tenons·le droit

Sir EDWARD FAIRFAX STUDD, 4th *Baronet*; *b* 3 May 1929; *s* his brother, *Sir* (ROBERT) KYNASTON, 1977; *ed* Winchester; formerly Dir of Inchcape plc, Dir of Dr Graham's Homes, Chm Gray Dawes Travel, and Member of Court of Assistants of Merchant Taylors' Co (Master 1987-88 and 1993-94); late Lt Coldm Gds; Malaya: *m* 1960, Prudence Janet, da of late Alastair Douglas Fyfe, OBE, of Grey Court, Riding Mill, Northumberland, and has issue.

Arms – Gules, lion rampant between three crescents argent, on a chief masoned two tilting spears in saltire, all proper. **Crest** – Out of a mural crown two arms embowed in armour, the hands in gauntlets holding two tilting spears saltirewise, all proper.
Residence – Kingsbury House, Kingsbury Episcopi, Martock, Som TA12 6AU.
Clubs – Boodle's, and Pratt's.

SONS LIVING

PHILIP ALASTAIR FAIRFAX, *b* 27 Oct 1961: *m* 1987, Georgina A. G., da of Sir Roger Albert Gartside Neville, VRD, of Possingworth Manor, Blackboys, nr Uckfield, E Sussex, and has issue living, Kynaston Roger Fairfax, *b* 31 Dec 1993, — Imogen Mary Henrietta, *b* 1991. —— Christopher Andrew Eric, *b* 1968.

DAUGHTER LIVING

Alexandra Mary, *b* 1965.

BROTHER LIVING

Rev John Eric (Albion Lodge, Halterworth Lane, Romsey, Hants), *b* 1934; *ed* Winchester, and Clare Coll, Camb (MA): *m* 1969, Nea Mildred, yr da of late Gordon Penn Kennett, of 35 Kireep Rd, Balwyn, Vic, Aust.

SISTER LIVING

Elizabeth Stephana, *b* 1924: *m* 1954, Victor Erwin Spindel, and has issue living, Daniel Jonas Arthur, *b* 1962. *Residence* – 12 Canonbury Grove, N1.

DAUGHTERS LIVING OF THIRD BARONET

Sara Alexandra, *b* 1959. —— Jane Anastasia, *b* 1961: *m* 1988, Christopher John Hall, elder son of Sir Peter Hall, KBE, of S Chailey, Sussex, and of Leslie Caron, actress, of Rue de Bellechasse, Paris, and has issue living, Frederick Amery Kynaston, *b* 1989, — Benjamin Charles Edward, *b* 1992. —— Anne Elizabeth, *b* 1964.

WIDOW LIVING OF THIRD BARONET

ANASTASIA (*Anastasia, Lady Studd*) (Manor Farm, Rockbourne, Fordingbridge, Hants), da of late Lt-Col Harold Boscawen Leveson-Gower (*see* D Sutherland, colls): *m* 1958, *Sir* (Robert) Kynaston Studd, 3rd Bt, who *d* 1977.

COLLATERAL BRANCH LIVING

Issue of late Bernard Cyril Studd, yst son of 1st baronet, *b* 1892, *d* 1962: *m* 1925, Caryl Theodora, who *d* 1977, el da of Brig-Gen Charles de Winton, CMG:—

Diana Caryl, *b* 1928: *m* 1st, 1954 (*m diss* 1976), Anthony Ross Pope; 2ndly, 1976, Anthony Carroll Cavalier, who *d* 1986, of 1213 Shady Av, Pittsburgh, Pa, USA, and has issue living (by 1st *m*), David Bernard Anthony Edward Beauchamp, *b* 1961: *m* 1991, Janice Ann Woolheater, and has issue living, Nicholas Anthony *b* 1993, — Simon Charles Kynaston Beauchamp, *b* 1964: *m* 1989, Felicia Anna Maria Campano, and has issue living, Desirae Jeanene *b* 1993, — Sara Caryl Beauchamp, *b* 1955: *m* 1978, Colin Weston Patrick Chase, of Meadow Cottage, Wineham, nr Henfield, Sussex, and has issue living, David Weston *b* 1982, Kathryn Diana *b* 1986, — Caroline Diana Beauchamp, *b* 1957: *m* 1988, Michael Joseph Mackenzie Thorne, of 94 Ross St, Cambridge, and has issue living, Joseph William Ross *b* 1992, Pia Sophie Elizabeth *b* 1991. —— Joanell Vera, *b* 1933: *m* 1959, Lt-Col Robert Henville Chappell, OBE, late Queen's Regt, of Southdown House, Westbury Rd, Warminster, Wilts BA12 0AP, and has issue living, Gavin Bernard (Brook House, 27 Newport Mews, Portway, Warminster, Wilts), *b* 1963: *m* 1988, Jessica Lynn Holm, — Kathryn Joanell, *b* 1966: *m* 1992, Capt Simon William David Butt, Capt RRW, son of Lt-Col William Butt, of Cirencester, Glos.

The 1st baronet, Sir (John Edward) Kynaston Studd (son of Edward Studd, of Tidworth House, Wilts, and 2 Hyde Park Gardens, W), was Pres and Chm of Polytechnic, and an Alderman of City of London (Sheriff 1922-3, and Lord Mayor 1928-9).

STUDHOLME (UK) 1956, of Perridge, co Devon

Sir HENRY WILLIAM STUDHOLME, 3rd *Baronet*; *b* 31 Jan 1958; *s* his father, Sir PAUL HENRY WILLIAM, 1990; *ed* Eton, and Trin Hall, Camb (MA); ACA, ATII: *m* 1988, (Sarah) Lucy Rosita Deans-Chrystall, only da of Richard S. Deans, of Christchurch, NZ, and has issue.

Arms – Vert, a horse statant argent, caparisoned or, on a chief of the second three mullets of six points pierced gules. Crest – A horse's head argent, bridled, and charged on the neck with a spur or.
Residence – Halscombe Farm, Ide, nr Exeter, Devon EX2 9TQ. *Clubs* – Brooks's, MCC.

SONS LIVING

JOSHUA HENRY PAUL, *b* 2 Feb 1992.
Jacob William Richard, *b* 1993.

DAUGHTER LIVING

Lorna Jane, *b* 1990.

BROTHER LIVING

James Paul Gilfred, *b* 1960; *ed* Eton, and Reading Univ (BSc): *m* 1992, Charlotte Serena, twin da of Jeremy Gwynne Pilcher, of Seymour Walk, SW10 (*see* Lawson, Bt, *cr* 1900).

SISTER LIVING

Anna Katherine, *b* 1965; *ed* St Mary's, Calne, and York Univ (BSc): *m* 1992, Duncan M. Watts, yr son of T. C. Watts, of Rottingdean, E Sussex.

UNCLE LIVING (*son of 1st baronet*)

Joseph Gilfred, *b* 1936; *ed* Eton, and Magdalen Coll, Oxford (MA); late 2nd Lt 60th Rifles; Chm and MD Editions Alecto Group since 1963: *m* 1959, Rachel, yr da of late Capt Sir William Albemarle Fellowes, KCVO (*see* V Hampden, colls), and has issue living, Andrew Gilfred, *b* 1962; *ed* Univ of E Anglia (BA): *m* 1988, Joanna, yr da of Eric D Thompson, of Shamley Green, Surrey, and has had issue, Edward William Gilfred *b* and *d* 1992, Cosmo Edward Gilfred *b* 1993, — Henry Alexander, *b* 1967; *ed* Magdalen Coll, Oxford (BA), — Hugo William Robert, *b* 1968; *ed* Bristol Univ (BSc). *Residence* – The Court House, Lower Woodford, Salisbury, Wilts SP4 6NQ.

AUNT LIVING (*Daughter of 1st baronet*)

Henrietta Mary, *b* 1931: *m* 1953, Major Thomas Edward St Aubyn, 60th Rifles, CVO (*see* B St Levan colls). *Residence* – Dairy House Farm, Ashford Hill, Newbury, Berks RG15 8BL.

WIDOW LIVING OF FIRST BARONET

JUDITH JOAN MARY (*Judith, Lady Studholme*), da of late Henry William Whitbread, of Norton Bavant Manor, Wilts: *m* 1929, Maj Sir Henry Gray Studholme, 1st Bt, CVO, who *d* 1987. *Residence* – 30 Abbey Mews, Amesbury Abbey, Amesbury, Wilts SP4 7EX.
Maj Sir Henry Studholme, 1st Bt, CVO, was DL for Devon 1969, MP (*C*) for Tavistock 1942-66, Conservative Whip 1945-56, Joint Hon Treas of Conservative Party 1956-62 and Vice-Chamberlain to HM Household 1951-56.

STURDEE (UK) 1916, of the Falkland Islands (Extinct 1970)

Rear-Adm Sir LIONEL ARTHUR DOVETON STURDEE, CBE, 2nd and last *Baronet*.

DAUGHTER LIVING OF SECOND BARONET

Elizabeth Mary Doveton (*Lady Ashmore*), *b* 1919; 1939-45 War as 2nd Officer WRNS: *m* 1942, Adm of the Fleet Sir Edward Beckwith Ashmore, GCB, DSC, and has issue living, Thomas Sturdee, *b* 1955, — Susan Alexandra (*Lady Sykes*), *b* 1943: *m* 1966, Sir (Francis) John Badcock Sykes, 10th Bt (*cr* 1781), of Kingsbury Croft, Kingsbury St, Marlborough, Wilts, and has issue.

STYLE (E) 1627, of Wateringbury, Kent

Sir WILLIAM FREDERICK STYLE, 13th *Baronet; b* 13 May 1945; *s* his father, *Sir* WILLIAM MONTAGUE, 1981: *m* 1st, 1968 (*m diss* 1971), Wendy Gay, da of Gene Wittenberger, of Hartford, Wisconsin 53066, USA; 2ndly, 1986, Linnea Lorna, da of Donn Erickson, of Sussex, Wisconsin 53089, USA, and has issue by 1st and 2nd *m*.

Arms – Sable, a fesse or fretty of the field between three fleurs-de-lis gold, all within a bordure of the second. **Crest** – A wolf's head couped sable, collared or, the lower part of the neck fretty of the last.
Residence – 2430 N, 3rd Lane, Oconomowoc, Wisconsin 53066, USA.

DAUGHTERS LIVING *(By 1st marriage)*

Shannon Gay, *b* 1969. —— Erin Kay, *b* 1972.

(by 2nd marriage)

McKenna Ashleigh, *b* 1987. —— McKayla, *b* 1990.

BROTHER LIVING

FREDERICK MONTAGUE (N5866 Rockland Beach, Hilbert, WI 54129, USA), *b* 5 Nov 1947: *m* 1971 (*m diss* 1988), Sharon, da of William H. Kurz, of Menomonee Falls, Wisconsin, USA, and has issue living, Jennifer K., *b* 1977, — Christina S., *b* 1979.

AUNT LIVING *(Daughter of 11th baronet by 1st marriage)*

Helen, *b* 1913: *m* 19—, Gilbert L. Schiltz, of 943 Jacinto West Indies Bay, Venice, Florida, USA, and has issue living, Susan, *b* 19—: *m* 19—, Dennis Grosse, — Mary Lou, *b* 19—: *m* 19—, Michael Duell.

WIDOW LIVING OF TWELFTH BARONET

LA VERNE (*La Verne, Lady Style*), da of late Theron M. Comstock, of Palm Springs, California, USA: *m* 1941, Sir William Montague Style, 12th baronet, who *d* 1981. *Residence* – 334B Riverview Drive, Delafield, Wisconsin 53018, USA.

COLLATERAL BRANCHES LIVING

Issue of late Henry Albert Glenmore Style, 3rd son of 9th baronet, *b* 1862, *d* 1916: *m* 1886, Annie Lydia, da of Samuel Fletcher Goldsmith:—
Glenmore Rodney, *b* 1887: *m* 1913, Mary Margaret Tobin, and has issue living, Rodney Henry, *b* 1914: *m* 1st, 1940, — ; 2ndly, 1943, Kathleen Quillan, who *d* 1952; 3rdly, 1959, Loretta Goodyear, and has issue living, (by 2nd *m*) Mary Kathryn *b* 1947, — Gerald Eugene, *b* 1922: *m* 1945, Marguerite Keogan, and has issue living, James Robert *b* 1948, Anne Marie *b* 1952, — William Hugh, *b* 1924: *m* 1956, Mary Ann Farrell, and has issue living, Robert George *b* 1959, William Edward *b* 1961, Susan Marie *b* 1957, — Charles Albert, *b* 1926: *m* 1950, Delores Jaqua, and has issue living, Gregory Charles *b* 1950, Gary Kevin *b* 1952, — Jerome Everet, *b* 1932: *m* 1955, Margaret Ryan, and has issue living, Kathleen Michelle *b* 1956, Maureen Anne *b* 1956, — Barbara Jo *b* 1959, — Vincent Joseph, *b* 1934: *m* 1956, Jane Sizer, and has issue living, Steven Joseph *b* 1959, — Nona Marie *b* 1962, — Margaret Clare, *b* 1918; is a Franciscan Nun, — Mary Crescent *b* 1923: *m* 1944, Maurice Finney, — Elizabeth Ann, *b* 1928: *m* 1955, Gene Sullivan, and has issue living, Joseph Donald *b* 1956, Thomas Michael *b* 1958, — Catherine Theresa, *b* 1929: *m* 1951, Robert E. Olson, and has issue living, Mark Joseph *b* 1953, Stephen George *b* 1954, Jonathan *b* 1955, Eric James, *b* 1961, Julie Ann *b* 1952, Jennifer (twin) *b* 1955, Mary Beth *b* 1957, Lisa Marie *b* 1959, Ellen Christine *b* 1962. —— Rosanna Lydia, *b* 1891. —— Brenda Helen, *b* 1897. —— Viola, *b* 1897: *m* 1921, Merton Crandall Dayton.

Issue of late Brig-Gen Rodney Charles Style, 4th son of 9th baronet, *b* 1863, *d* 1957: *m* 1911, Hélène Pauline, who *d* 1975, da of late Herman Greverus Kleinwort, of 45 Belgrave Square, SW1, and Wierton Pl, Maidstone:—
Sir Godfrey William, CBE, DSC, *b* 1915; *ed* Eton; Lt-Cdr RN; an Underwriting Member of Lloyd's; served in HM Yacht "Victoria and Albert" 1938; Flag Lt to Com-in-Ch Home Fleet 1939-41; a Member of the Nat Advisory Council on Employment of Disabled People 1944-74 (Chm of Council 1964-74), of Advisory Panel to Disabled Living Foundation since 1965, and of Nat Star Centre for Youth, Cheltenham, Advisory Panel since 1966, and Council since 1970; a Gov Sir Oswald Stoll Foundation 1975-84, and of Queen Elizabeth's Foundation for the Disabled since 1975; a Member of Disablement Advisory Cttee, Maidstone, 1945-64 and Chm of Sheltered Employment Cttee of Nat Advisory Council 1954-64; 1939-45 War (despatches twice, DSC, invalided); CBE (Civil) 1960, Knt 1973: *m* 1st, 1942 (*m diss* 1951), Jill Elizabeth, da of late George Bellis Caruth, of Drumard Cottage, Ballymena, co Antrim; 2ndly, 1951, Sigrid Elisabeth, who *d* 1985, da of late Per Stellan Carlberg, of Jönköping, Sweden; 3rdly, 1986, Valerie Beauclerk, widow of Duncan McClure, and da of late Lt-Com Cecil Hulton-Sams, RN (*see* V Hawarden, colls, 1976 Edn), and has issue living (by 1st *m*) Montague William (27 rue des Romains, 68480 Bettlach, France), *b* 1943; *ed* Eton; Diplome de l'Académie des Hautes Etudes Commerciales, Paris; MBA, INSEAD: *m* 1970, Susan Jennifer, yr da of Peter Wrightson, OBE (*see* Wrightson, Bt), and has issue living, Oliver Rodney *b* 1976, Sophie Elizabeth *b* 1974, — Helen Anne, *b* 1946: *m* 1971, Lt-Col Charles Frederick Byng Stephens, Welsh Gds, and has issue living, Alexandra Claire *b* 1973, Georgina Kate *b* 1976. — Marieka Louise, *b* 1947: *m* 1969, Charles John Hamilton Fisher, of 119 Hurlingham Rd, SW6 3NJ, and has issue living, Hugo Hamilton *b* 1970, Louise Hamilton *b* 1973, — (by 2nd *m*) Charles Rodney (Wood Cottage, Cornwood, Ivybridge, Devon), *b* 1954; *ed* Eton, and Camb Univ; Capt RN: *m* 1981, Charlotte Amanda, el da of late Lt Timothy Martin Woodford, RN (Stirling-Hamilton, Bt), and has issue living, Amanda Clare *b* 1981, Annabel Daisy *b* 1983, Elizabeth Sigrid *b* 1990. *Residence* – 30 Carlyle Court, Chelsea Harbour, SW10 0UQ. *Club* – Naval and Military. —— Rodney Gerald, *b* 1920; *ed* Eton; Col RRF (OC 1st Bn RNF 1962-65); Comdt RMSM, Kneller Hall 1973-75; 1939-45 War with Coldm Gds; Licentiate of Brit Inst of Professional Photography: *m* 1st, 1944 (*m diss* 1952), Melloney, da of late Maj-Gen Sir (Sandford) John Palairet Scobell, KBE, CB, CMG, DSO; 2ndly, 1952, Barbara, da of late John A. Hill, of 102 Pond St, Natick, Massachusetts, USA, and has issue living (by 2nd *m*), William Bryant (c/o RHQ Coldstream Gds, Wellington Barracks, Birdcage Walk, SW1), *b* 1954: Maj Coldm Gds: *m* 1977, Celia Maria, yr da of Hon Robert Latham Baillieu, MBE, TD (*see* B Baillieu), and has issue living, Edward Rodney *b* 1980, Robert William *b* 1982, Jennifer Hélène *b* 1988, — Rodney Hill (Greenacre, Steeple Aston, Oxon OX5 3RT), *b* 1956; ACA, ATII: *m* 1982, Georgina Eve, yr da

of John Kinloch Kerr of Abbotrule (*see* M Lothian, colls), and has issue living, George Oliver *b* 1985, Hugo Gerald *b* (twin) 1985, Elizabeth Daisy *b* 1989, — John Glenmore, *b* 1957: *m* 1988, Concepción, only da of José Muñoz Sainz, of Corral de Calatrava, Ciudad Real, Spain, — Caroline Mary, *b* 1964: *m* 1988, Adam Francis Southwell. *Residence* – Fairmount, Sands Rd, Seale, Farnham, Surrey GU10 1LW. —— Rosamond Marguerite, *b* 1912: *m* 1st, 1934, Rear-Adm John Harvey Forbes Crombie, CB, DSO, who *d* 1972; 2ndly, 1980, Antony William Allen, and has issue living, (by 1st *m*) James Rodney Forbes, *b* 1935; Capt late Queen's Own Highlanders: *m* 1961 (*m diss* 1977), Lee Adrienne Chavet, — Rosanna Mary, *b* 1937: *m* 1964, Maj Malcolm Kenneth Shennan, late R Scots Greys, of The Old Rectory, Closworth, nr Yeovil, Som, and has issue living, Mark Douglas *b* 1970, Melissa *b* 1967, — Annabel Jean, *b* 1944: *m* 1964, Simon Gerard Younger, of Baro, Haddington, East Lothian, and has issue living, James Henry *b* 1965, Mary-Claire *b* 1967, Eugenie *b* 1968, Sophie Rosamond *b* 1973, — Julia Rosamond, *b* 1947, John Henry Trotter, of Chennelkirk House, Oxon, nr Lauder, Berwickshire. *Residence* – The Garden House, Mordington, Berwick-on-Tweed, Northumberland. —— Mary Dorothy, *b* 1918: *m* 1939, Neil Arthur Campbell, TD, of Chennell Park, Tenterden, Kent, and has issue living, Alistair Neil, *b* 1941: *m* 1970 (*m diss* 1975), Jane, da of Michael Gatehouse, — Jeremy George, *b* 1948: *m* 1973, Penelope Hudson, and has issue living, Toby George Mungo *b* 1975, Angus Neil Morgan *b* 1977, Camilla Mary *b* 1981, — Gerald Angus (Oxenbridge Cottage, Readers Lane, Iden, E Sussex), *b* 1951: *m* 1976, Dorian Isobel, da of Maj Anthony Peter Howorth Greenly (*see* Gibson, Bt, *cr* 1926), and has issue living, George Richard Angus *b* 1979, Henry Neil Edward *b* 1980, — Joanna Mary, *b* 1946: *m* 1972, Philip Thompson, and has issue living, James Courtney *b* 1974, Charles Neil *b* 1976.

Grandchildren of late Maj George Montague Style (infra):—
Issue of late Oliver George Style, *b* 1897, *d* 1973: *m* 1923, Guinevere, who *d* 1975, da of late Rev Walter Matthew Parker (Molesworth St Aubyn Bt, colls):—
George Michael Oliver, *b* 1927: *m* 1951, Mary Jeans, and has issue living, Elizabeth Mary, *b* 1952, — Sarah Jane, *b* 1955, — Caroline Ann, *b* 1956. —— Patricia Nora, *b* 1924: *m* 1946 (*m diss* 1970), Gp Capt Deryck Hugo Cross, RAF (ret), and has issue living, Robert Humphrey Hugo, *b* 1951, — Alison Guinevere Hugo, *b* 1947: *m* 1972, Gerald Bunyan, and has issue living, Kathleen Jill *b* 1973, — Frances Jane Hugo, *b* 1949: *m* 1969, Richard Charles Mortimore.

Grandchildren of late Albert Frederick Style, yst son of late Capt William Style, RN, 2nd son of late Rev Robert Style, 2nd son of 4th baronet:—
Issue of late Charles Humphrey Style, *b* 1877, *d* 1936: *m* 1899, Anne Maud Harriet, who *d* 1942, da of late Gen Sir Hugh Henry Gough, VC, GCB:—
Humphrey Bloomfield, *b* 1902; *ed* Marlborough, and Pembroke Coll, Camb: *m* 1935, Anita Dolores, who *d* 19—, da of Charles Brunson, of Antofagasta, Chile, and has issue living, Charles Humphrey, *b* 1945: *m* 1971, Elizabeth Ann Hoskin, of London, Ont, Canada, — Ursula Anne, *b* 1936: *m* 1959, William Swaisland Carter, of Toronto, Canada, and has issue living, William Alarik *b* 1963, Roberta Jean *b* 1960, Jacqueline Anne *b* 1966, Adrienne Julia *b* 1971, — Ingrid Priscilla, *b* 1939: *m* 1960, Henry Evan Cockshutt Schulman, and has issue living, Charles Eric *b* 1965, Frances Yvonne *b* 1961, Audrey Alexis *b* 1963, — Diana Maria, *b* 1941: *m* 1965, Robert Tweedy, of 7 Royal Oak, Don Mills, Toronto, Canada, and has issue living, Laura Anne *b* 1968, Lisa Diana *b* 1973.

Grandchildren of late Charles Humphrey Style (ante):—
Issue of late Hubert Anthony Style, *b* 1910, *d* 1992: *m* 1942, Enid Margaret (Broomscroft Cottage, 144 Canon Lane, Wateringbury, nr Maidstone, Kent ME18 5PQ), only da of Leonard Frederick Leonard, of Reigate, Surrey:—
John Richard (c/o Jardine Fleming Investment Management Ltd, 47th Floor Jardine House, Hong Kong), *b* 1943; *ed* Marlborough, and Coll of Law; Solicitor 1970: *m* 1990, Caroline A.M., only da of Anthony Sparrow, of Abinger Hammer, Surrey, and has issue living, Alexander Nicholas Hubert, *b* 1991, — Toby James Anthony, *b* 1994. —— (Robert) Nicholas Humphrey (11th 16th Av, Rivonia, Sandton, Transvaal, S Africa), *b* 1949; *ed* Marlborough: *m* 1982, Mrs Diana Schoeller, da of J. Leal, of Johannesburg, and has issue living, Jonathan Rupert Anthony, *b* 1982, — Freddy, *b* 1984, — Sophy, *b* (twin) 1984.
Issue of late Capt Robert Henry Style, Yeo, *b* 1881, *d* 1945: *m* 1905, Grace Winnifred, who *d* 1977, da of John Bazley-White (E Rothes):—
David Leslie, *b* 1913; *ed* Radley; European War 1939-45 as Able Seaman RN. *Residence* – Hampton Court, Isle of Man. —— Gabrielle Ursula, *b* 1911: *m* 1936, Capt Richard Taylor White, DSO, RN (ret), and has issue (*see* White, Bt, *cr* 1802). *Residence* – Tilts House, Boughton Monchelsea, Maidstone, Kent.
This family, originally seated in Suffolk, is descended from William Style, of Ipswich, father of Sir John Style Alderman of London, grandfather of Sir Humphrey Style Knt, one of the Esquires to the Body of Henry VIII, and grandfather of Sir Thomas, 1st baronet.

SULLIVAN (UK) 1804, of Thames Ditton, Surrey

(Sir) RICHARD ARTHUR SULLIVAN, 9th *Baronet; b* 9 Aug, 1931; *s* his father, *Sir* RICHARD BENJAMIN MAGNIAC, 1977, but does not use his title; *ed* Univ Cape Town (BSc), and at Massachusetts Inst of Technology (SM); MICE, PE, MASCE; Man of operations, Woodward Clyde Oceaneering: *m* 1962, Elenor Mary, el da of Kenneth Merson Thorpe, of 7 Jacqueshill Crescent, Somerset West, Cape Prov, S Africa, and has issue.

Arms – Per fesse, the base per pale; in the chief or, a dexter hand couped at the wrist grasping a sword erect gules, the blade entwined by a serpent proper, between two lions rampant respecting each other of the second; the dexter base vert, charged with a buck trippant or, on the sinister base per pale argent and sable, a boar passant counterchanged. **Crest** – On a ducal coronet or, a robin holding in the beak a sprig of laurel proper.
Residence –

What we gain by conquest we secure
by clemency

SON LIVING

CHARLES MERSON, *b* 15 Dec 1962; *ed* — Coll, Camb (BA).

DAUGHTERS LIVING

Katherine Ann, *b* 1963. ——— Sarah Elizabeth, *b* 1965. ——— Margaret Mary, *b* 1969.

BROTHER LIVING

Michael Francis (95 Harley St, W1), *b* 1936; *ed* Camb Univ (MA, MB, BCh), FRCS (Eng): *m* 1st, 1957 (*m diss* 1978), Inger, only da of Arne Mathieson, of Oslo, Norway; 2ndly, Caroline Mary, el da of Maj Christopher John Griffin, of Hall Farmhouse, Oxborough, Norfolk, and has issue living, (by 1st *m*) Richard Alexander Dermot (48 Fairlawn Grove, W4), *b* 1961; *ed* Reading Univ (BA): *m* 1993, Julia Elizabeth, eldest da of Peter Graham Macdonald-Smith, of Bloxworth, Dorset, — Vivienne Nicola, *b* 1965, — (by 2nd *m*) Emma Lucy Mary, *b* 1980.

COLLATERAL BRANCH LIVING

Issue of late Valentine Arthur Sullivan, 2nd son of Capt Richard Sullivan, RN, 2nd son of 7th baronet, *b* 1907, *d* 1965: *m* 1937, Mollie Maureen Madge, who *d* 1985, da of late W. N. Craig, of Sale, Cheshire:—
Peter Craig Valentine (601 Blouberg Heights, Blounergstrand 7441, Cape), *b* 1941. ——— Elizabeth Bridget Patricia (601 Blouberg Heights, Blounergstrand 7441, Cape, S Africa), *b* 1947.
The 6th baronet, Adm Sir Francis William Sullivan, KCB, CMG, was an ADC to Queen Victoria 1877-8. The 7th baronet, Rev Sir Frederick, was 20 years R of Southrepps.

SULLIVAN (UK) 1881, of Garryduff, co Cork (Extinct 1937)

Sir WILLIAM SULLIVAN, 3rd and last *Baronet*.

DAUGHTER LIVING OF THIRD BARONET *(By 1st marriage)*

Kathleen Mary: *m* 1914, Wilmot Humphrey Clifford Lloyd, who *d* 1948, and has issue living, Desmond Humphrey Clifford, *b* 1917; *ed* Trin Coll, Dublin (BA 19-); European War 1942-5 with London Irish Rifles, — Wilmot Anthony Clifford, *b* 1928; is Fl-Lt RAF, — Nedda Cecil Clifford: *m* 19-, James Davis.

SUMMERS (UK) 1952, of Shotton, co Flint (Extinct 1993)

(Sir) FELIX ROLAND BRATTAN SUMMERS, 2nd and last *Baronet*.

DAUGHTER LIVING OF SECOND BARONET

Micheline, *b* 1947: *m* 1970, Mark Dudley Langridge, of Shepherds Down, 3 The Ridgeway, Friston, Eastbourne, E Sussex.

DAUGHTERS LIVING OF FIRST BARONET *(by 1st marriage)*

Anne Griselda (Plas-yn-Gerddi, Lloc, Holywell, Clwyd), *b* 1916: *m* 1953, Maj Alan Edward Curtis Lake, TD, who *d* 1980.

(by 2nd marriage)

Judith Margaret, *b* 1932: *m* 1958, Gordon Elliott, of Low Abbey, Bay Horse, Lancaster, and has issue living, Geoffrey Ian, *b* 1960, — Martin Anthony, *b* 1963, — Catherine Elizabeth, *b* 1961, — Lucy Helen, *b* 1966. ——— Carolyn Elizabeth, *b* 1936: *m* 1958, Robin Hilary Beaumont Malim, of Croose Farm, Woolhope, Hereford, and has issue living, Peter Beaumont, *b* 1963, — Karen Elizabeth, *b* 1960, — Sophie Hilary, *b* 1968.

WIDOW LIVING OF SECOND BARONET

ANNA MARIE LOUISE (2 Royston Close, Friston, Eastbourne, E Sussex BN20 0EY), da of late Gustave Demaegd, of Brussels: *m* 1945, (Sir) Felix Roland Brattan Summers, 2nd Bt (who did not use the title), who *d* 1993.

SUTHERLAND (UK) 1921, of Dunstanburgh Castle, Embleton, co Northumberland

Without fear

(*Sir*) JOHN BREWER SUTHERLAND, 3rd *Baronet b* 19 Oct 1931; *s* his father, *Sir* (BENJAMIN) IVAN, 1980, but does not use title; *ed* Sedbergh, and St Catharine's Coll, Camb: *m* 1st, 1958, Alice Muireall, JP, who *d* 1984, da of late William Stamford Henderson, of Usan, Makerstoun, Kelso, Roxburghshire; 2ndly, 1988, (Ailsa) Heather, da of late David Alexander Gray, of Langley Mill, Lanchester, co Durham, and has issue by 1st *m*.

Arms – Gules, a chevron flory-counterflory between in chief three mullets and in base a lymphad all or. **Crest** – Upon the trunk of a tree a cat salient proper. *Residence* – Ross, Belford, Northumberland.

SONS LIVING (*By 1st marriage*)

PETER WILLIAM, *b* 18 May 1963: *m* 1988, Suzanna Mary, da of R. Michael Gledson, of Newlands Mill Lane, Little Shrewley, Warwick, and has issue living, Kate Alice, *b* 1993. *Residence* – Swarland East House Farm, Swarland, Felton, Morpeth, Northumberland. —— Christopher John, *b* 1965. —— Robert Brewer, *b* 1970.

DAUGHTER LIVING

Susan Muireall, *b* 1960: *m* 1992, Alastair Peter Jollans, of Southfield House, Painswick, Glos, and has issue living, Daniel John Peter, *b* 1994.

BROTHER LIVING

(David) Michael (Northfield, Lowick, Northumberland), *b* 1940; *ed* Sedbergh, and St Catharine's Coll, Camb: *m* 1966, Caroline Mary, da of late Robert Simon Hogan, of Blackrock, co Dublin, and has issue living, Julia Ruth, *b* 1967, — Serena Louise, *b* 1971, — Polly Anne, *b* 1975.

HALF-BROTHERS LIVING

William, *b* 1945; *ed* Leys Sch, Cambridge, and St Catharine's Coll, Camb: *m* 1966, Sarah Lucy, da of Dr Cecil Gilbert, of Benton, Newcastle upon Tyne, and has issue living, Mark Rupert, *b* 1967, — Dylan Paul, *b* 1970, — Hal, *b* 1988, — Ceri Jane, *b* 1968, — Amy Gael, *b* 1969. —— Owen, *b* 1947; *ed* The Leys Sch, Cambridge, and St Catharine's Coll, Camb: *m* 1971, Margaret Ann, da of Daniel Herbert Williams, of Rainhill, Liverpool, and has issue living, Jonathan Ben, *b* 1976, — Victoria Jane, *b* 1974. —— Ben (USA), *b* 1949; *ed* The Leys Sch, Cambridge, and Essex Univ: *m* 1986, Bonna Howell, and has issue living, Lesley Ann, *b* 1986.

UNCLE LIVING (*Son of 1st baronet*)

Robert Gordon (Piper's Hill, Castle Terrace, Berwick-upon-Tweed), *b* 1908: *m* 1st, 1934 (*m diss* 1958), Helen Wallace, da of late Edward Farish, of Wigton, Cumberland; 2ndly, 1958 Emily, da of late Lavinia Hayes, of Hanwell, Middlesex, and has issue living, (by 1st *m*) Arthur Ian *b* 1936, — David Wallace, *b* 1938.

WIDOW LIVING OF SECOND BARONET

MARGARET, JP (*Margaret, Lady Sutherland*) (The Smithy, Embleton, Northumberland), da of Albert Owen, of Fairways, Chalfont St Giles, Bucks: *m* 1944, as his 2nd wife, Sir (Benjamin) Ivan Sutherland, 2nd Bt, who *d* 1980.

COLLATERAL BRANCH LIVING

Issue of late Arthur Munro Sutherland, el son of 1st baronet, *b* 1894, *d* 1941: *m* 1921, Nina Marguerite Crawshay, da of late Arthur Skelton Wimble, of Whitley Bay, Northumberland, and St Helier, Jersey:—
Nina Marguerite Munro, *b* 1923: *m* 1949, James Keith W. Slater, who *d* 1968, and has issue living, Gail Munro, *b* 1950, — Kim Munro, *b* 1952, — Bill Munro, *b* 1953, — Peter Munro, *b* 1956. *Residence* – The Mill Cottage, Eglingham, Alnwick, Northumberland. —— Ann Munro, *b* 1928.
The 1st baronet, Sir Arthur Munro Sutherland, KBE (son of B. J. Sutherland of Newcastle-on-Tyne), Chm of Newcastle Commercial Exchange; was Lord Mayor of Newcastle-on-Tyne 1918-19, Pres of Chamber of Shipping of the United Kingdom 1930, and High Sheriff of Northumberland 1943.

Sutherland-Dunbar (Duff-Sutherland-Dunbar), see Dunbar.

GRANT-SUTTIE (NS) 1702, of Balgone, Haddingtonshire

Sir (GEORGE) PHILIP GRANT-SUTTIE, 8th *Baronet*; son of late Major George Donald Grant-Suttie, son of late Capt Francis Grant-Suttie, RN, 2nd son of 5th baronet; *b* 20 Dec 1938; *s* his kinsman, *Sir* GEORGE, 1947; *ed* Sussex Composite High School, New Brunswick, and at McGill Univ: *m* 1962 (*m diss* 1969), Elspeth Mary, el da of late Maj-Gen Robert Elliott Urquhart, CB, DSO, and has issue.

Arms – Quarterly: 1st and 4th, barry wavy of six azure and or; on a chief of the last, a lion rampant naissant with two tails vert, armed and langued gules, *Suttie*; 2nd and 3rd, or a chevron checky gules and of the first, between three hunting-horns sable, garnished of the second, all within a bordure of the same, *Semple*. **Crest** – A ship under full sail proper.
Residence – The Granary, Sheriff Hall, N Berwick, East Lothian EH39 5BP.

Nothing hazard, nothing have

SON LIVING

JAMES EDWARD, *b* 29 May 1965: *m* 1989, Emma Jane, yr da of Peter Craig, of Innerwick, East Lothian. *Residence* – Sheriff Hall Farm, N Berwick, E Lothian.

SISTER LIVING

Ann, *b* 1940: *m* 1st, 1958, —; 2ndly, 1967, Marinus Jan Luitwieler, of 56 Sunhurst Pl, SE Calgary, Alberta, Canada T2X 1W6, and has issue living (by 1st *m*), Susan Ann McGEE GRANT-SUTTIE (63121 2604 Kensington Rd NW, Calgary AB, Canada T2N 4S5), *b* 1960; has issue living, Nicole Noël Ann OLSON *b* 1984, — (by 2nd *m*) Rinus Jon, *b* 1968, — Melissa Ann *b* 1970.

MOTHER LIVING

Marjorie NEVILLE, da of Capt C. E. Carter, RN of Stephenville, Newfoundland: *m* 1st, 1937, as his 2nd wife, Major George Donald Grant-Suttie (ante), who *d* 1940; 2ndly, 1944, Paul Underhill, Lt, US Army.

COLLATERAL BRANCH LIVING

Grandson of late Robert Grant-Suttie, 4th son of 5th baronet:—
Issue of late Col Hubert Francis Grant-Suttie, CBE, DSO, MC, *b* 1884, *d* 1973: *m* 1920, Torfrida Alianore, who *d* 1971, da of Sir Wroth Periam Christopher Lethbridge, 5th Bt:—
(Robert) Ian (17 Mountain Av, Woodstock, Vermont 05091, USA), *b* 1926; *ed* Wellington Coll, Sorbonne, and New Coll, Oxford; late Lt Black Watch: *m* 1951, Juliet Carmen, yr da of late Lt-Col Nigel Eustace Philip Sutton (*see* Sutton, Bt, colls), and has issue living, Francis AEneas, *b* 1957: *m* 1983, Carolyn Forrest, da of Maj-Gen Robert Ginsburgh, of Chevy Chase, Maryland, USA, and has issue living, Ian Hamilton *b* 1991, Katherine Myers *b* 1988, — James Archibald, *b* 1964, — Atalanta Theresa, *b* 1955, — Roxana Idonea, *b* 1961: *m* 1986, Ogden Mills Reid, of 2810 Tramway Circle NE, Albuquerque, New Mexico 87122, USA, son of Ogden Rogers Reid, of Purchase, New York, and has issue living, Lindsay Sutton *b* 1990, Ashley Louise *b* 1993.
The 2nd and 4th baronets successively represented Haddingtonshire in Parliament, and the 4th baronet assumed the additional surname of Grant on succeeding to the estates of his aunt, Janet Grant, Countess of Hyndford.

SUTTON (GB) 1772, of Norwood Park, Nottinghamshire

Sir RICHARD LEXINGTON SUTTON, 9th *Baronet*; *b* 27 April 1937; *s* his father, Sir ROBERT LEXINGTON, 1981; *ed* Stowe: *m* 1959, Fiamma, only da of Giuseppe Marzio Ferrari, of Via S Giacomo 28, Rome, and has issue.

Arms – Quarterly: 1st and 4th argent, a canton sable, *Sutton*; 2nd and 3rd, argent, a cross flory azure, *Lexington*. **Crest** – A wolf's head erased gules.
Residence – Moor Hill, Langham, Gillingham, Dorset.

SON LIVING

DAVID ROBERT, *b* 26 Feb 1960; *ed* Milton Abbey: *m* 1992, Annette, only da of B. David, of Aller, Langport, Somerset, and has issue living, Charlotte Emily, *b* 1994.

DAUGHTER LIVING

Caroline Victoria, *b* 1965: *m* 1989, Alexander C. Gibbs, son of C. E. Gibbs, of Bourton, Dorset, and has issue living, Charles Toby, *b* 1991, — Robert Alexander, *b* 1993.

Always ready

BROTHER LIVING

James Anthony (Marsh Cottate, Penselwood, Nr Wincanton, Som), *b* 1940; *ed* Stowe: *m* 1964, Dale, only da of Capt Antony Stevens, of Windrush Mill, Windrush, Burford, Oxford, and has issue living, Tristan Anthony, *b* 1966, — Chloe Emma, *b* 1968.

WIDOW LIVING OF EIGHTH BARONET

DAPHNE GWLADYS (*Daphne, Lady Sutton*) (Clinger Farm, Wincanton, Som), only da of Maj Arnold Charles Gover, MC, of Pilton: *m* 1936, Sir Robert Lexington Sutton, 8th Bt, who *d* 1981.

COLLATERAL BRANCHES LIVING

Grandchildren of late Thomas Alexander Sutton (infra):—
Issue of late John Alexander Sutton, *b* 1915; *d* 1981: *m* 1950, (Violet) Deirdre (Badbury Wick House, Chiseldon, Wilts), el da of late James Sheringham Shepherd, of Kilbrack, Doneraile, co Cork:—
Charles Alexander, *b* 1950; *ed* Millfield: *m* 1979, Susan Nita, yr da of Brian Richard Notton, of The Old Malthouse, Wanborough, Wilts. —— Grania Jane, *b* 1952: *m* 1985, (Robert) Nicholas Bovill Whitehead, of Badbury Wick Farmhouse, Chiseldon, nr Swindon, Wilts, eldest son of T. B. Whitehead, of Chisbury, nr Marlborough, Wilts, and has issue living, Hugh Alexander Bovill, *b* 1989, — Thomas James Bovill, *b* 1989 (twin), — Eleanor Amanda Deirdre, *b* 1987.

Granddaughter of late Alexander George Sutton, 3rd son of 4th baronet:—
Issue of late Thomas Alexander Sutton, *b* 1888, *d* 1945: *m* 1913, Gwendoline, da of Thomas Forsyth-Forrest, formerly of The Querns, Cirencester:—
Margaret Pamela (*Pamela, Lady Bunbury*), *b* 1919: *m* 1940, Sir (John) William Napier Bunbury, 12th Bt, who *d* 1985. *Residence* – 9 Lee Rd, Aldeburgh, Suffolk.

Granddaughter of late Lt-Col Francis Henry Sutton, MC, 11th Hussars (PAO), only son of late Maj Francis Richard Hugh Seymour Sutton, only surv son of late Capt Francis Sutton, RHG, 3rd son of 2nd baronet:—
Issue of late Lt-Col Richard David Sutton, 11th Hussars (PAO), *b* 1923, *d* 1965: *m* 1965, Sally Christine (Evergreen Cottage, Cherington, Tetbury, Glos GL8 8SH), da of late J. D. Graeme Reid, of Gruivie, Wormit, Fife:—
Frances Elizabeth (*posthumous*) *b* 1966.

Grandchildren of late Gilbert William Sutton, 3rd son of late Rev Augustus Sutton, 5th son of 2nd baronet:—
Issue of late Cdr John Gilbert Sutton, DSC, *b* 1892; *d* 1982: *m* 1st, 1918, Eva Maud, who *d* 1919, only child of Thomas Cook, of Hobland, Bradwell, Great Yarmouth; 2ndly, 1920 (*m diss* 1940), Ida Margaret, da of Charles Halls; 3rdly 1940 (*m diss* 1950), Katherine, who *d* 1977, da of Charles Balfour-Kinnear, WS (Montgomery, Bt); 4thly 1950, Violet (Manor House, Portesham, nr Weymouth, Dorset), da of late Herbert James Godwin, OBE, of Greatham, Petersfield, Hants:—
(By 2nd *m*) Richard John Beverley (Foxfield, Ansty, Dorchester, Dorset DT2 7PJ), *b* 1922; Lt-Cdr RN; *ed* Imp Service Coll, Windsor: *m* 1949, Ann Stella, da of late Brig Charles Hall Woodhouse, OBE, MC, and has issue living, Richard Charles, *b* 1955; Maj 4th/7th R Drag Gds: *m* 1985, Jane Elizabeth, only da of Lt-Cdr John Alan Bird, RN, of The Cottage, Nottington Lane, Nottington, Weymouth, Dorset, and has issue living, Hugo George Richard *b* 1990, Sophie Georgina Elizabeth *b* 1988, — Amanda Clare, *b* 1952: *m* 1973, Robert Stephen MacKenzie, Queens R Irish Hussars. —— Felicity Ruth (Home Cottage, Puddletown, Dorchester, Dorset DT2 8TL), *b* 1926: *m* 1951, Maj Denis Cary Atkinson, 4th/7th Royal Dragoon Gds, who *d* 1985, and has issue living, Timothy Charles Garnet, *b* 1960, — Tessa Margaret, *b* 1952: *m* 1977, Maj Michael John Herbert Malyon, Roy Hus, of Lower Wyke Farm, St Mary Bourne, Andover, Hants SP11 6AW, and has issue living, Giles William Herbert *b* 1989, Mary Louise *b* 1980, Isobel Alice *b* 1982. —— (By 3rd *m*), Henry Richard, *b* 1945. —— Judith, *b* 1942: *m* 1961, Michael William Cox, and has issue living, Anthony William, *b* 1961, — Nicholas Michael, *b* 1963.

Granddaughters of late Rowland Sutton (infra):—
Issue of late Lawrence Seymour Sutton, *b* 1905, *d* 1967: *m* 1st, 1936, Muriel Geraldine, who *d* 1940, da of Maj L. A. Sherrard; 2ndly, 1942, Martha Joyce (Cefn-y-dre, Fishguard, Dyfed), da of W. L. Williams, of Cefn-y-dre, Pembrokeshire:—
(By 1st *m*) Rosemary Margaret, *b* 1937: *m* 1962 (*m diss* 1974), Jack A. Eden, and has issue living, Sally Jane, *b* 1963, — Susan Rosemary, *b* 1964. —— Molly, *b* 1940: *m* 1966, Graham J. Waterman, and has issue living, Matthew Charles, *b* 1967, — Julian Rupert, *b* 1969, — Charlotte Lucy, *b* 1973.

Granddaughter of late Rev Augustus Sutton (ante):—
Issue of late Rowland Sutton, *b* 1859, *d* 1927: *m* 1889, Augusta Margaret, who *d* 1924, da of late Rev Edmund Thomas Daubeney, R of Swaffham, Norfolk:—
Dorothy Charlotte Mary, *b* 1893: *m* 1917, John Selwyn Browning.

Grandchildren of late Maj-Gen Hugh Clement Sutton, CB, CMG (infra):—
Issue of late Lt-Col Nigel Eustace Philip Sutton, *b* 1896, *d* 1956: *m* 1st 1921, Stella Clementina, who *d* 1945, da of late Montague Whittingham Price, of 67 Eaton Place, SW (E Clarendon, colls); 2ndly, 1951, Elisabeth Clothilde Hedwige (Mrs Zita Gielgud), da of late Zoltan Gruszer, of Budapest, Hungary:—
(By 1st *m*) John Hugh Torquil, *b* 1923; *ed* Eton, and Ch Ch, Oxford; Major (retired) Coldstream Guards: *m* 1952, Carola Mariette, da of late Ulick Otway Vortigern Lloyd-Verney, OBE (*see* Verney, Bt, *cr* 1818, colls), and has issue living, Hugh Nigel John (25 Crieff Rd, SW18), *b* 1954: *m* 1987, Miranda F., only da of John Goldsmid, of Copyhold Farm, Goring Heath, Oxfordshire, and has issue living, Emma Frances Juliet *b* 1989, Olivia Henrietta Jonquille *b* 1991, Rebecca Virginia Jonquille *b* 1991, — Mark Richard, *b* 1956: *m* 1985, Rose, yst da of Samuel Carr, of Paultons Square, Chelsea, and has issue living, Thomas Samuel *b* 1991, Phoebe Esmé *b* 1988, — Catherine Stella Louise, *b* 1959. *Residence* – Bayfield Brecks, Holt, Norfolk. —— Juliet Carmen, *b* 1930: *m* 1951, Robert Ian Grant-Suttie, of Mountain Av, Woodstock, Vermont 05091, USA (*see* Grant-Suttie, Bt, colls).

Granddaughter of late Henry George Sutton, 6th son of 2nd baronet:—
Issue of late Maj-Gen Hugh Clement Sutton, CB, CMG, *b* 1867, *d* 1928 : *m* 1st, 1891, Mabel Ida, who *d* 1896, da of Sir Campbell Munro, 3rd Bt (*cr* 1825); 2ndly, 1898, Hon Alexandra Mary Elizabeth Wood, who *d* 1965, el da of 2nd Viscount Halifax (E Halifax):—
(By 2nd *m*) Elizabeth Mary, *b* 1910: *m* 1st, 1931 (*m diss* 1936), (Ronald) Mark Cunliffe Turner (knighted 1946, and *d* 1980); 2ndly, 1936 (*m diss* 1976), John Tindall-Lister, son of Col late Sir William Tindall Lister, KCMG, KCVO, MD, FRCS, and has issue living, (by 2nd *m*) Francis Hugh William Bernard, *b* 1937, — Charles John Alexander, *b* 1945, — Sarah Janet Consuelo, *b* 1947. *Residence* – Luccas Farm, Powerstock, Bridport, Dorset.

Grandchildren of late Major Robert Nassau Sutton Nelthorpe, OBE, el son of late Rev Robert Sutton, el son of late Capt Robert Nassau Sutton, 3rd son of 1st baronet:—
Issue of late Col Oliver Sutton Nelthorpe, CBE, DSO, MC, *b* 1888, *d* 1963: *m* 1914, Marjorie Elspeth Constable, who *d* 1976, da of Charles Constable Curtis (E Onslow, colls):—
Roger SUTTON NELTHORPE, MBE, TD (Scawby Hall, Brigg, Lincs), *b* 1918; *ed* Eton; late Lt-Col Nottinghamshire (Sherwood Rangers) Yeo, and a JP and DL (High Sheriff of Lincs 1970); Palestine and Middle East 1939-44, NW Europe 1944-45 (MBE); MBE (Mil) 1945. —— †John Richard SUTTON NELTHORPE, *b* 1923; *ed* Eton; is Lt RNVR: *m* 1946, Mary Elizabeth (High Barn, Welton, Lincs), only da of T. C. Brown, of The Cottage, Scawby, Lincs, and *d* 1994, leaving issue Anthony Julian, *b* 1948: *m* 1973, Margaret, yst da of R. F. Schumacher, of Upton, Didcot, Berks, and has issue living, Thomas Max *b* 1977, Clare Lydia *b* 1979. —— Ann, *b* 1919.
Issue of late Griffith Sutton Nelthorpe, *b* 1892, *d* 1947: *m* 1922, Constance Adine Maud, who *d* 1923, da of late Allan Harvey Drummond (E Perth, colls):—

Jan William, *b* 1923; is Warrant Officer RAF.

Grandson of late Richard Coningsby Sutton (infra):—
Issue of late Col Francis Richard Heywood Sutton, MC, TD, *b* 1905, *d* 1970: *m* 1st, 1929 (*m diss* 1937), Barbara
Jean, da of A. D. Tait; 2ndly, 1939 (*m diss* 1958), Vera Kathleen, da of W. J. Waldock; 3rdly, 1960, Mrs Audrey
Theodosia Madeleine Davies, who *d* 1974, da of Lancelot Squarey (E Gosford):—
(By 2nd *m*) Richard Oliver, AFC; late Lieut RN; *b* 1940; *ed* Eton: *m* 1967, Helene, da of Ministro Carlo de Franchis, of
Rome, and has issue living, Francesco Charles, *b* 1967.

Granddaughter of late Francis Richard Sutton, 3rd son of late Rev Robert Sutton (ante):—
Issue of late Richard Coningsby Sutton, *b* 1882, *d* 1905: *m* 1904, Katharine Helen, who *d* 1925, da of late Francis
Foljambe Anderson, of Lea, Lincoln (Anderson, Bt):—
Olina Margaret, *b* (*posthumous*) 1906: *m* 1934, Maj Donald Hammick Gawne, late KOR Regt, and has issue living, Robert
Atholl, *b* 1936: *m* 1966, Kae Fraser, and has issue living, Kelly Robert *b* 1970, Kevin Donald *b* 1971, — John Francis, *b* 1930:
m 1964, Hilary Ann Medforth, and has issue living, Nicola Caroline *b* 1967, Amanda Louise *b* 1971. *Residence* –

Granddaughter of late Herbert Arthur Sutton, 5th son of late Capt Frederick Sutton (infra):—
Issue of late Roland Manners Verney Sutton, *b* 1895, *d* 1957: *m* 1927, Dora, who *d* 1984, da of Elijah Whitehurst,
formerly of Overdale, Brinnington, Stockport:—
Ursula Constance, *b* 1929: *m* 1963, Norman Yearsley, of Windbrow, 307 Cromwell Lane, Burton Green, Kenilworth, and has
issue living, Jonathan Manners, *b* 1968.

Grandchildren of late Maj Charles Lexington Manners Sutton, MBE (by 1st *m*) (infra):—
Issue of late John Charles Ludlow Manners Sutton, *b* 1921, *d* 1992: *m* 1st, 1946, Daphne Agnes, who *d* 1961, only
da of William Francis Wormald, JP; 2ndly, 1962, Gillian (Willerby Lodge, Staxton, Scarborough, N Yorks), da of
Edwin Stanley Harris, of Newcastle-upon-Tyne:—
(By 1st *m*) Richard Manners, *b* 1947: *m* 1st, 1972 (*m diss* 1979), Mary de Witt, da of Charles Diebold, of Buffalo, New York;
2ndly, 1979, Penelope Jane, da of Anthony Gray Quinlan, of Scarborough, N Yorks, and has issue living (by 2nd *m*), William
Lexington Manners, *b* 1980, — Thomas Anthony Manners, *b* 1982. —— William Reginald Manners, *b* 1949: *m* 1982, Janet
Risa, da of Benjamin Chubac, of New Jersey, USA, and has issue living, Emily Anne, *b* 1983, — Lydia Beth, *b* 1985, —
Oliver Ludlow Manners, *b* 1950: *m* 1980, Virginia Sarah, da of Paul Lipscombe Marriott, of Welshpool, and has issue living,
Philip Ludlow Manners, *b* 1984, — Anna Lucy, *b* 1983. —— (By 2nd *m*) Virginia Anne, *b* 1964: *m* 1989, Sebastian J. T.
Foster, of Harrogate, son of Lt Cdr J. R. Foster, RN (ret), of Godalming, Surrey, and Mrs N. Ward, of Cleckheaton, W
Yorks.

Granddaughter of late Rev Charles Nassau Sutton, yst son of late Capt Frederick Sutton, 3rd son of late
Capt Robert Nassau Sutton (ante):—
Issue of late Maj Charles Lexington Manners Sutton, MBE, *b* 1891, *d* 1962: *m* 1st, 1917 (*m diss* 1932), Amabel
Anne, da of Major Ludlow Coape Ludlow, of Beech Green, Withyham, Sussex; 2ndly, 1932, Gladys Louise
(RICHARDSON), who *d* 19—, da of Percy Gubb:—
(By 1st *m*) John Charles Ludlow Manners (Willerby Lodge, Staxton, Scarborough, N Yorks), *b* 1921: *m* 1st, 1946, Daphne
Agnes, who *d* 1961, only da of William Francis Wormald, JP; 2ndly, 1962, Gillian, da of Edwin Stanley Harris, of Newcastle-
upon-Tyne, and has issue living, (by 1st *m*) Richard Manners, *b* 1947: *m* 1st, 1972 (*m diss* 1979), Mary de Witt, da of
Charles Diebold, of Buffalo, New York; 2ndly, 1979, Penelope Jane, da of Anthony Gray Quinlan, of Scarborough, N Yorks,
and has issue living (by 2nd *m*), William Lexington Manners *b* 1980, Thomas Anthony Manners *b* 1982, — William Reginald
Manners, *b* 1949: *m* 1982, Janet Risa, da of Benjamin Chubac, of New Jersey, USA, and has issue living, Emily Anne *b* 1983,
Lydia Beth *b* 1985, — Oliver Ludlow Manners, *b* 1950: *m* 1980, Virginia Sarah, da of Paul Lipscombe Marriott, of Welshpool,
and has issue living, Philip Ludlow Manners *b* 1984, Anna Lucy *b* 1983. — (by 2nd *m*) Virginia Anne, *b* 1964. —— (By 2nd
m) Philippa Mary, *b* 1936: *m* 1st, 1956, Derek Walter Pryke; 2ndly, 1982, John Selby-Green of Pashley Farm, Ticehurst,
Wadhurst, Sussex, and has issue living, (by 1st *m*) Kelham Charles Manners, *b* 1959, — Timothy John Manners, *b* 1961, —
Flavia Anne, *b* 1957: *m* 1986, (Leslie) Andrew Jackson, of 26 Bassingham Rd, SW18 3AG, eldest son of late Ralph Jackson, of
Hopehay, Cartmel, Cumbria.

Roland de Sutton, of Sutton upon Trent, Notts: *m* Alice, da of Richard de Lexington (now spelt Laxton), and sister and co-
heir of Robert de Lexington, of Averham, Notts, which manor was inherited by their son Robert de Sutton, who *d* 1281.
William Sutton of Averham (or Aram), Notts was father of Robert, who was *cr* Baron Lexinton, of Aram 1645 (which peerage
became ext in 1723, and whose da and heiress *m* the 3rd Duke of Rutland), and Henry, grandfather of the Rt Hon Sir
Robert Sutton. The 1st baronet, Sir Richard Sutton (son of late Rt Hon Sir Robert Sutton, KB, a distinguished diplomat) sat
as MP for St Albans 1768-80, for Sandwich 1780-84, and for Boroughbridge 1784-96, and was an Under-Secretary of State
1766-72. Capt Sir Richard Vincent Sutton, MC, 1st Life Gds and Capt and Adj, Machine Gun Regt, who *s* as 6th Bt at his
birth, in April 1891, was *ka* 1918.

SWANN (UK) 1906, of Prince's Gardens, Royal Borough of Kensington

Sir MICHAEL CHRISTOPHER SWANN, TD, 4th *Baronet*; *b* 23 Sept 1941; *s* his father, Sir ANTHONY CHARLES CHRISTOPHER, CMG, OBE, 1991; *ed* Eton; late 60th Rifles; TD: *m* 1st, 1965 (*m diss* 1985), Hon Lydia Mary Hewitt, da of 8th Viscount Lifford; 2ndly, 1988, Marilyn Ann, da of Leslie Charles Tobitt, of Montevideo, Uruguay, and has issue by 1st *m*.

Arms – Azure, a swan rousant proper within an orle of lymphads, sails furled, flags flying to the dexter, or. **Crest** – Between two buffalo's horns a demi-swan wings expanded, all proper.
Residence – 100 Hurlingham Rd, SW6 3NR.

SONS LIVING

JONATHAN CHRISTOPHER, *b* 17 Nov 1966; *ed* Eton. ——— Toby Charles, *b* 1971; *ed* Stowe.

DAUGHTER LIVING

Tessa Margaret, *b* 1969; *ed* Sacred Heart, Tunbridge Wells.

WIDOW LIVING OF THIRD BARONET

JEAN MARGARET (*Dowager Lady Swann*), da of late John Herbert Niblock-Stuart, of Nairobi, Kenya: *m* 1940, Sir Anthony Charles Christopher Swann, 3rd Bt, CMG, OBE, who *d* 1991. *Residence* – 25 Hurlingham Sq, Peterborough Rd, SW6 3DZ.

COLLATERAL BRANCHES LIVING

Granddaughters of late Harold Swann, 2nd son of 1st baronet, *b* 1880, *d* 1953: *m* 1907, Dorothea Alma, who *d* 1969, da of late Henry De Courcy Agnew (Agnew, Bt, *cr* 1629, colls):—
Issue of late Charles Brian Swann, *b* 1913, *d* 1966: *m* 1st, 1939 (*m diss* 1955), Vanessa, da of Ernest William Dalrymple Tennant; 2ndly, 1955, Ann Corben, da of Cyril Alwyn Harrison:—
(By 1st *m*) Julia Vanessa, *b* 1940: *m* 1960, Blyth Metcalf Thompson, of Applecross, 150 Empire Pl, Sandhurst, Johannesburg, S Africa, and has issue living, William Rowland Blyth, *b* 1962, — Dendy Martin Blyth, *b* 1972, — Vanessa Eirene, *b* 1961, — Moya Ann, *b* 1965, — Hannah Yvonne, *b* 1967, — Sonia Suzanne, *b* 1969. ——— Karin Clarissa, *b* 1942. ——— Virginia Caroline, *b* 1948: *m* 1971, David Winkfield Hughes, of Mid Lambrook Manor, S Petherton, Yeovil, and has issue living, Thomas Percy Winkfield, *b* 1974, — Harriet Elfreda, *b* 1972.

Grandchildren of late Geoffrey Swann (infra):—
Issue of late Major Kenneth Geoffrey Swann, MC, RA, *b* 1915, *ka* 1944: *m* 1942, Delmira Marion (who *d* 1947, having *m* 2ndly, 1947, Peter Richard Hampton), da of Sir (Ferdinand) Michael Kroyer-Kielberg, KBE:—
Christopher Kenneth (Santa Barbara, Calif, USA), *b* 1942; *ed* Eton, and Internat Sch of Geneva: *m* 1968, Kathleen Harriet Brodarick, — Penelope Ann, *b* 1944.

Issue of late Geoffrey Swann, 4th son of 1st baronet; *b* 1883; *d* 1965: *m* 1911, Florence Mildred, who *d* 1964, da of John Brodie:—
Janet Elizabeth, *b* 1913; a JP for Herts: *m* 1939, Charles Gifford Bardswell, AE, late RAFVR, Kt of the Order of Dannebrog of Denmark, of The Grange, Walkern, nr Stevenage, Herts, and has issue living, Charles Nicholas, *b* 1941: *m* 1969, Sarah Josephine, el da of Sir (Thomas) Leslie Rowan, KCB, CVO, and has issue living, Charles Leslie Geoffrey *b* 1981, Catherine Jane Elizabeth *b* 1971, Alice Victoria Josephine *b* 1974, Isabella Louise Clementine *b* 1979, — Philip Geoffrey, *b* 1948: *m* 1973, Alexandra Augusta, only child of Iver Lunn, of Towersley, Oxon, and has issue living, Josephine Elizabeth *b* 1977, Sonya Caroline *b* 1979, — Veronica Elizabeth, *b* 1945: *m* 1974, Roger Gaymer Broadie (formerly Broadie-Griffith), and has issue living, Helen Elizabeth *b* 1978, Charlotte Anne *b* 1981. ——— Phyllis Mildred, *b* 1919: *m* 1946, John Charles Fegen, DSC, late RNVR, of Porta-beg, Ballykeeran, co Westmeath, and has issue living, Richard Kenneth, *b* 1947: *m* 1982, Charmian Sadgrove, and has issue living, Robin *b* 1985, Polly Lucinda *b* 1983, — Frances Lynette, *b* 1950, — Lucy Mildred, *b* 1953: *m* 1976, Simon Burdett, and has issue living, Jonathan *b* 1983, Chloe *b* 1979. ——— Kathleen Prudence, *b* 1921: *m* 1945, Allan Priestley Thompson, QSO, late Capt NZ Engineers, former Dir Gen of NZ Forest Ser, of 8 Nicholson Rd, Wellington 4, NZ, and has issue living, Michael Kenneth, *b* 1951, — Peter Geoffrey, *b* 1955, — Andrew Brodie, *b* 1958: *m* 1987, Razimah Ishmail, — Celia Margaret, *b* 1946: *m* 1970, Brian Herbert Bockett, and has issue living, David *b* 1972, Nicholas *b* 1977, Kirsten Margaret *b* 1974.
The Rt Hon Sir Charles Ernest Swann, 1st Bt (son of late Frederick Schwann, of 23 Gloucester Square, W), sat as MP for N Div of Manchester (L) 1886-1918, and assumed by Roy licence, 1913, for himself and his issue, the surname of Swann in lieu of his patronymic.

SWINBURNE, (E) 1660, of Capheaton, Northumberland (Extinct 1967)

Sir SPEARMAN CHARLES SWINBURNE, MRCS, LRCP, 10th and last *Baronet*.

DAUGHTER LIVING OF EIGHTH BARONET

Joan Mary, *b* 1906: *m* 1937, Richard Granville Browne, who assumed by deed poll 1937 the additional surname of Swinburne, and has issue living, John *b* 1937; High Sheriff of Northumberland 1978: *m* 1966, Susan, da of Anthony Comar Wilson, and has issue living, William *b* 1967, Alice *b* 1968, — Rosalind Mary, *b* 1939: *m* 1966, Francesco Parlade, of Marbella, Spain, and has issue living, Jaimie *b* 1967, Marie Anna *b* 1971, Teresa *b* 1974. *Residence* – Capheaton Hall, Newcastle upon Tyne.

Swinnerton (Milborne-Swinnerton-Pilkington), see Pilkington.

SYKES (GB) 1781, of Basildon, Berkshire

He is wise who is assiduous

Sir (FRANCIS) JOHN BADCOCK SYKES, 10th *Baronet*; *b* 7 June 1942; *s* his father, *Sir* FRANCIS GODFREY, 1990; *ed* Shrewsbury, and Worcester Coll, Oxford (MA); Solicitor 1968; partner in legal firm of Townsends, Swindon & Newbury: *m* 1966, Susan Alexandra, art history lecturer, da of Adm of the Fleet Sir Edward Beckwith Ashmore, GCB, DSC, of South Cottage, Headley Down, Hants (*see* Sturdee, Bt (ext)), and has issue.

Arms – Argent, an eagle rising between three sykes or fountains proper; on a canton gules, a caduceus of the first. **Crest** – A demi-lady of Bengal in the complete dress of that country, holding in the dexter hand a rose gules.
Residence – Kingsbury Croft, Kingsbury St, Marlborough, Wilts SN8 1HU.

SONS LIVING

FRANCIS CHARLES, *b* 18 June 1968; *ed* Malvern, and Worcester Coll, Oxford (BA). — Edward William, *b* 1970; *ed* Winchester, and Manchester Univ (BA). — Alexander Henry Ashmore, *b* 1974; *ed* Marlborough, and Newcastle Univ.

SISTER LIVING

Elizabeth Ann Bowen (19 Torriano Cottages, off Leighton Rd, NW5), *b* 1936; *ed* Howells, Denbigh, Bedford Coll, London (BSc, MSc), and Edinburgh Univ (PhD); AFBPsS, CPsychol, ScFZS; Prof and Head of Sch of Psychology, Middx Univ, and Hon Research Fell, Univ Coll, London.

UNCLES LIVING (*Brothers of 9th baronet*)

John Patrick (4/26 Cook St, Crawley, W Australia 6009), *b* 1909: *m* 1955, Patricia Cecily, who *d* 1979, da of E. P. Graham Little. — Paul Lionel (Unit 53, Retirement Village, Charlotte St, Burradoo, NSW 2576, Australia), *b* 1915: *m* 1946, Mrs Ann Stewart, of Sydney, Australia.

AUNTS LIVING (*Sisters of 9th baronet*)

Beatrice Honora (17 Holloway Drive, Pershore, Worcs), *b* 1910: *m* 1949, Cdr Frederick D'Oyly Nind, RN, who *d* 1962, son of late Frederick William Nind. — Mary Agatha (Flat 14, St Nicholas Hospital, Salisbury, Wilts), *b* 1913: *m* 1944, William Thomas Moran Gilbert, LRCPI, LRCSI, Colonial Medical Service, who *d* 1970, son of William Reilley Starkie Gilbert. — Janet Edith (Flat 18, St Nicholas Hospital, Salisbury, Wilts), *b* 1916.

WIDOW LIVING OF NINTH BARONET

ETHEL FLORENCE (*Ethel, Lady Sykes*), da of Lt-Col John Sinclair Liddell, and widow of (i) Brian G. Macartney-Filgate, and (ii) Cdr W. Graeme Ogden, DSC, RNVR (ret): *m* 1985, as his 3rd wife, Sir Francis Godfrey Sykes, 9th Bt, who *d* 1990. *Residence* – The Mews House, Linden Gdns, Bath, Avon BA1 2YB.

COLLATERAL BRANCHES LIVING

Grandchildren of late Lt-Col William Sykes (infra):—
Issue of late Brig John Henry Sykes, *b* 1896, *d* 1975: *m* 1st, 1919, Leila, who *d* 1970, da of late D. S. Macphee; 2ndly, 1971, Florence Cathleen, who *d* 1983, da of William Turner, and widow of (1) James Mackay, and (2) Sir (Stanley) Herbert Howard:—
Margery Hope, *b* 1921.
Issue of late Richard Alexander Sykes, *b* 1912, *d* 1981: *m* 1942, Freda Serita (Elmley Castle, Pershore, Worcs), da of Lewis Field:—
William David (18 Markby Close, Duxford, Cambs), *b* 1946; *ed* St Edward's Sch, Oxford: *m* 1978, Josephine Helen White, and has issue living, Archie Frederick William *b* 1984, — Chloë Alexandra, *b* 1981. — Anthony Richard John (17 Burnaby Gdns, W4), *b* 1950; *ed* St Edward's Sch, Oxford: *m* 1982, Tessa Cox, and has issue living, Thomas Neill Alexander, *b* 1984, — Amanda Marie, *b* 1986.

Granddaughter of late Rev John Heath Sykes, yst son of Rev William Sykes, 2nd son of 2nd baronet:—
Issue of late Lt-Col William Sykes, *b* 1867, *d* 1950: *m* 1896, Eleanor Mary, who *d* 1958, da of late Capt Henry Naylor:—
Alice Margery, *b* 1904: *m* 1966, Ewart Gladstone Morrison, who *d* 1985. *Residence* – Gorseway, Sea Front Rd, Hayling Is, Hants PO11 0BA.

Grandson of late Frederick Sykes, 4th son of Rev John Heath Sykes (ante):—
Issue of late Frederick Heath Cyril Sykes, *b* 1897, *d* 1959: *m* 1934, Judith Helen, who *d* 1982, da of Wyndham Henry Stubbs, of The Leasowes, Cressage, Salop:—
Harry Wyndham (PO Box 1345, Peace River, Alberta, Canada, T0H 2X0), *b* 1936: *m* 1956, Magdalena (Lena) Amelia, da of Edward Julius Schulze, of Grande Prairie, Alberta, and has issue living, Ronald Frederick, *b* 1963, — Dianne Lea, *b* 1957: *m* 1978 (*m diss* 1986), Martin Lavoie, and has issue living, Harvest Serena *b* 1979, Yarrow Lee (a da) *b* 1983, — Patricia Lynn, *b* 1960.

Granddaughters of late Rev John Heath Sykes (ante):—
Issue of late Alfred Sykes, *b* 1872, *d* 1954: *m* 1902, Scènie Marguerite Genelle, who *d* 19—:—
Marcedèsse Doyley, *b* 1904: *m* 1st, 1932, R. Alston Jones; 2ndly, 1947, Brock R. Darling, and has issue living, (by 1st m)

George Sykes, *b* 1935. —— Gwendolyn Doyley Scènie, *b* 1906: *m* 1932, George Michael Holley. *Residence* – 944 Euclid St, Santa Monica, California, USA.

Grandchildren of late Edward Ernest Sykes, 7th son of late Rev John Heath Sykes (ante):—
Issue of late Clement Edward Heath Sykes, *b* 1911, *d* 1987: *m* 1951, Isabel L. (Pt Atkinson Light Station, Beacon Lane, W Vancouver, BC, Canada), da of Robert Parry, of N Wales:—
Sean Edward Heath, *b* 1952. —— David Robert Heath, *b* 1954. —— Sheila Anne Heath, *b* 1952.

This family have held lands in England since before 1220, in which year they were described as being in possession of land previously held by them. The 1st baronet, Sir Francis, of Ackworth Park, Yorkshire, and subsequently of Basildon Park, Berks, Chief Governor of Cossimbazar, Bengal, and Resident at the Court of the Nawab of Bengal, was successively MP for Shaftesbury and Wallingford. The 2nd baronet also sat as MP for Wallingford. The 8th baronet, the Rev Sir Frederick John was V of Stoke Canon, Exeter 1936-46. The 9th baronet, Sir Francis Godfrey, was Regional Sec (Shropshire, Cheshire, Staffs) of the Country Landowners' Assocn 1956-71.

SYKES (GB) 1783, of Sledmere, Yorkshire

Sir TATTON CHRISTOPHER MARK SYKES, 8th *Baronet*; *b* 24 Dec 1943; *s* his father, *Lt-Col Sir* (MARK TATTON) RICHARD TATTON-SYKES 1978; *ed* Eton, and Univ d'Aix-Marseilles, and R Agric Coll, Cirencester.

Arms – Argent, a chevron sable between three sykes or fountains proper. **Crest** – A demi-triton issuant from flags or reeds, blowing a shell, and wreathed about the temples with like flags or reeds, all proper.
Seat – Sledmere, Driffield, Yorkshire.

BROTHERS LIVING

JEREMY JOHN, *b* 8 March 1946; *ed* Ampleforth: *m* 1982, Pamela June, only da of late Thomas Wood. —— Christopher Simon, *b* 1948; *ed* Eton: *m* 1982, Belinda Susan Mary, yr da of Frank Thomas Robertson Giles (*see* E De La Warr), and has issue living, Joseph Francis Richard, *b* 1990, Lily, *b* 1984. —— (Richard) Nicholas Bernard, *b* 1953; *ed* Ampleforth.

SISTERS LIVING

Arabella Lilian Virginia, *b* 1950: *m* 1975, Kevin Delahunty, of Scotts Farm, Stockley, Calne, Wilts, and has issue living, Damian John Richard, *b* 1976. —— Henrietta Caroline Rose, *b* 1957: *m* 1986, Nigel Kenneth Cayzer of Thriepley House, Lundie, Dundee, 2nd son of Anthony Malcolm Galliers-Pratt, CBE, and has issue (*see* Cayzer, Bt).

COLLATERAL BRANCH LIVING

Issue of late Christopher Hugh Sykes, FRSL, author, 2nd son of 6th baronet, *b* 1907, *d* 1986: *m* 1936, Camilla Georgiana, who *d* 1983, da of late Maj-Gen Sir Thomas Wentworth Russell, KBE, CMG (*see* D Bedford, colls):—
Mark Richard (Great Norman Street Farm, Ide Hill, Kent), *b* 1937; *ed* Eton, and Ch Ch, Oxford: *m* 1st, 1962 (*m diss* 1965), Helen, only da of late Dr Arthur Norman Homewood, of Melbourne, Aust; 2ndly, 1968, Valerie, da of Robert Goad, and has issue living (by 2nd *m*), Thomas, *b* 1974, — Frederick, *b* 1983, — Joshua, *b* 1988, — Lucy, *b* 1969, — Victoria, *b* (twin) 1969, — Alice, *b* 1972.

The 1st baronet, the Rev Sir Mark, was son of Richard Sykes, an eminent merchant in Hull; the 2nd baronet, Sir Christopher, sat as MP for Beverley; the third baronet, Sir Mark, was High Sheriff and MP for York 1807-20; and the 4th baronet was the well-known sportsman, Sir Tatton Sykes. Sir Tatton, 5th baronet, was High Sheriff of Yorkshire 1869. The 6th baronet, Sir Mark, was Private Sec to Ch Sec for Ireland 1904-05, MP for Central Div of Hull (*C*) 1911-18, and for Kingston-upon-Hull, Central Div Dec 1918-19, and served during 1914-18 War as Col 5th Batn Yorkshire Regt, and as Assist Sec to War Cabinet; Signatory to the Sykes-Picot Agreement 1917. The 7th baronet, Lt-Col Sir (Mark Tatton) Richard was High Sheriff of Yorks 1948, and Pres of E Riding Georgian Soc and Northern Counties Concert Soc. He adopted the surname of Tatton-Sykes by deed poll 1977.

SYKES (UK) 1921, of Kingsknowes, Galashiels, co Selkirk

Sir JOHN (CHARLES ANTHONY LE GALLAIS) SYKES, 3rd *Baronet*, el son of late Capt Stanley Edgar Sykes, Duke of Wellington's Regt, yr son of 1st baronet; *b* 19 April 1928; *s* his uncle, *Sir* (BENJAMIN) HUGH, 1974; *ed* Churchers Coll; export merchant (ret): *m* 1954 (*m diss* 1970), Aitha Isobel, yr da of Lionel Dean, of New Mill, Huddersfield.

Arms – Per chevron gules and sable, in chief two sykes (fountains) proper, and in base a fleece or. **Crest** – A cubit arm, habited in a khaki sleeve and holding in the hand a teazle slipped and leaved proper.

WIDOW LIVING OF SECOND BARONET

AUDREY WINIFRED (*Audrey, Lady Sykes*) (Kestrel Grove, Hive Rd, Bushey Heath, Herts WD2 1JQ), da of Frederick Charles Thompson, of Cricklewood, NW2: *m* 1935, Sir (Benjamin) Hugh Sykes, 2nd Bt, who *d* 1974.

COLLATERAL BRANCH LIVING

Issue of late Michael le Gallais Sykes, yr son of late Capt Stanley Edgar Sykes (ante), *b* 1932, *d* 1981: *m* 1st, 1953, Joan, only da of Cecil Groome, of 14 Highfield Rd, Nuthall, Notts; 2ndly, 1976, Jacqueline Susan, only da of Capt C. Melia:—
(By 1st *m*) DAVID MICHAEL (The Chestnuts, Middle Lane, Nether Broughton, Leics), *b* 10 June 1954: *m* 1st, 1974 (*m diss* 1987), Susan Elizabeth, 3rd da of G. W. Hall; 2ndly, 1987, Margaret Lynne, only da of John Thomas McGreavy, and has issue living (by 1st *m*), Stephen David *b* 14 Dec 1978, — (by 2nd *m*) Joanna Lauren, *b* 1986. —— Christopher Cary, *b* 1959: *m* 1st, 1978 (*m diss* 1984), Tina, da of —; 2ndly, 1989, Anne Marie, da of —, and has issue living (by 1st *m*), Lisa Tina, *b* 1979, — Kelly, *b* 1981.
The 1st baronet, Sir Charles Sykes, KBE (son of Benjamin Sykes), was a woollen manufacturer, MP for Huddersfield (*Co L*) 1918-22, and Govt Dir of Textile Prodcn 1914-18, for which he was ktd.

SYNGE (UK) 1801, of Kiltrough
(Name pronounced "Sing")

Sir ROBERT CARSON SYNGE, 8th *Baronet*, son of late Neale Hutchinson Synge, 2nd son of 6th baronet; *b* 4 May 1922; *s* his uncle, *Sir* ROBERT MILLINGTON, 1942: *m* 1944, Dorothy Jean, da of Theodore Johnson, of Cloverdale, British Columbia, and has issue.

Arms – Quarterly: 1st and 4th, azure, three millstones proper; 2nd and 3rd, argent, an eagle displayed with two heads sable, beaked and legged gules. **Crest** – Out of a ducal coronet or, an eagle's claw proper.
Residence – 19364, Fraser Valley Highway, RR4, Langley, BC, Canada.

DAUGHTERS LIVING

Donna Joan, *b* 1946: *m* 1967, Richard David Harvey. —— Wendy Marleen, *b* 1949.

SISTER LIVING

Patricia Neale, *b* 1924: *m* 1948, Emerson Edgar Barden. *Residence* – 14227, 110th Avenue, North Surrey, British Columbia.

AUNT LIVING (*Daughter of 6th baronet*)

Jessica Helen (c/o Lloyds Bank, High St, Berkhamsted, Herts), *b* 1914: *m* 1940 (*m diss* 1949), Fl-Lt Alfred Davidson Colin Cleugh Fair, RAF.

COLLATERAL BRANCHES LIVING

We sing of heavenly things

Issue of late Edward Synge, yst son of 6th baronet, *b* 1882, *d* 1966: *m* 1901, Agnes Emily, da of James Jelley:—
NEALE FRANCIS, *b* 28 Feb 1917: *m* 1939, Katherine Caroline Bowes, and has issue living, Allen James Edward, *b* 1942, — Sharon Eileen, *b* 1943. —— Molly Eileen, *b* 1908: *m* 1929, Raymond Augustus McCarthy, of 202-144, Brunswick St, Penticton, BC, Canada, and has issue living, Raymond Edward (140 Quebec St, Prince George, BC, Canada), *b* 1930: *m* 1950, Helen, da of Roy Dagg, of Prince George, BC, and has issue living, Sharon Patricia *b* 1951: *m* 1973, Gerhard Mueller (and has issue living, Marcus Raymond George *b* 1978, Christa, *b* 1974), — Stanley Norman (1075 Lamar Place, Kamloops, BC, Canada), *b* 1941: *m* 1961, Karen Maureen, da of Maurice Gregoire, of Penticton, BC, and has issue living, Gregory Douglas *b* 1967, Edward Morris *b* 1970, Judith Maureen *b* 1962.

Granddaughter of late Edward Synge (ante):—
Issue of late Edward Synge, b 1902, d 1928: m 1925, Alma (Apt 206, 1050, W 10th Av, Vancouver, BC), da of Martin Hansen:—
Marjorie Irene, b 1926: m 1946, William Thomas Kidner, of 1005, Beaumont St, N, Vancouver, BC, Canada, and has issue living, Jacquelyn Ann, b 1951, — Patricia Lynn, b 1952.

Grandson of late Major Robert Follett Synge, el son of late Rev Robert Synge, 3rd son of 1st baronet:—
Issue of late Lieut-Col Robert Follett Muter Foster Millington Synge, b 1857, d 1941: m 1884 (m diss 1900), Charlotte Granville, who d 1942, da of Maj-Gen William James Stuart, formerly RE:—
Alan Hamilton Stuart, b 1886: ed Wellington Coll; European War 1914-19 with RFC: m 1920, Alice May Bradley, of Washington, USA.

Grandchildren of late Francis Julian Synge, 2nd son of William Webb Follett Synge (infra):—
Issue of late Capt Robert Millington Synge, b 1894, d 1964: m 1922, Cristabel Etrenne, who d 1988, da of late Charles Lyon Liddell, of The Place House, Peasmarsh, Sussex (see B Ravensworth, colls):—
Allen John Millington (2 Diamond Terrace, Greenwich SE10 8QN), b 1930; ed Trin Coll, Dublin: m 1955, Olive Rachel, da of Thomas Weir, of Ballymena, co Antrim, and has issue living, Daniel Thomas Millington, b 1963, — Timothy Auchmuty, b 1968, — Frances Clare, b 1959: m 1986, Bernard Fitzgerald Clark, of Goose Cottage, 14 Fearon St, Greenwich SE10 0RS, yr son of late Richard Clark, of Dibden Purlieu, Southampton. —— Gillian Frances, b 1933: m 1952, Col George Stanley Ames, US Marine Corps, of 305 Old Pickard Rd, Concord, Mass, USA, and has issue living, Richard Millington, b 1955, ed Gordonstoun, Duke Univ, and Georgia Univ: m 1982, Laura Mahone, da of Thomas Mahone Tolleson, of Atlanta, Georgia, USA, and has issue living, Alexander Millington b 1985, Ian Mahone b 1988, Hannah Suzanne b 1987, — John Bruton, b 1960: m 1989, Donna Jean, da of Mario Chiaravelotti, of N Conway, NH, and has issue living, Evan George b 1991, Shanna Mae b 1993, — Robert Oakes b 1969; ed Gordonstoun, and Rice Univ, — Elizabeth Whiting, b 1953, ed Concord Academy, and Duke Univ: m 1984, Alan Thomas Macdonald, son of Thomas Hugh Macdonald, of Canton, Mass, USA, and has issue living, Hugh Oakes Ames b 1986, Adrian Synge b 1988.

Grandsons of late William Makepeace Thackeray Synge, yst son of William Webb Follett Synge, 4th son of late Rev Robert Synge (ante):—
Issue of late Capt William Alfred Thackeray Synge, b 1893, d 1968: m 1920, Hilda Marjorie, who d 1967, da of Ebenezer Pike, formerly of Kilcrenagh, co Cork:—
Brian Thackeray (4 Pembroke Close, Grosvenor Cres, SW1), b 1920; formerly Hon Maj Irish Gds; a Serving Brother of Order of St John of Jerusalem: m 1st, 1945 (m diss 1970), Alison Patricia, da of Brig Victor Francis Staples Hawkins, DSO, MC, late Lancashire Fusiliers; 2ndly, 1970, Mrs Pamela Columbine de Meo, and has issue living, (by 1st m) Barry Edward Thackeray (c/o 4 Pembroke Close, Grosvenor Cres, SW1), b 1949: m 1986 (m diss 1990), Moira French, da of Thomas Macdonald, of Ancrum, Roxburghshire, — Mark Millington, b 1953: m 1984, Clare Victoria, elder da of John Bulkley Herbert Francis, of Cowley, nr Cheltenham, Glos, and has issue living, Annabel b 1987, Georgina Rose b 1989, — (Norah) Melanie, b 1947: m 1st, 1969 (m diss 1976) Anthony Elliott; 2ndly, 1984, Charles Ross Birkett, of 29 Rozel Rd, Clapham Old Town, SW4 0EY, and has issue living, (by 1st m) Rupert Francis William b 1970, Francesca Elisabeth b 1972, (by 2nd m) (Charles) John Ross b 1987, Alice Emily Rose b 1984. —— John Millington (903 Drake House, Dolphin Sq, SW1V 3NW), b 1923.
The family of Synge was seated at Bridgnorth early in the 16th century, the original name of Millington having been changed to Synge. The Rt Rev Dr Samuel Hutchinson, Lord Bishop of Killala, was father of Sir James Hutchinson, 1st Bt (cr 1782, ext, 1906) who sat as MP for Jamestown in Irish Parliament. The Rev Sir Samuel Synge, 3rd Bt, grand-nephew of the 1st and 2nd baronets, s under special remainder, and assumed the additional surname and arms of Hutchinson; his 2nd brother, Robert, was cr a baronet as above. Sir Edward Synge, 3rd Bt (cr 1801), was High Sheriff of co Cork 1844.

LAWSON-TANCRED (E) 1662, of Boroughbridge, Yorkshire

Sir HENRY LAWSON-TANCRED, 10th Baronet; b 12 Feb 1924; s his father, Major Sir THOMAS SELBY, 1945; ed Stowe, and Jesus Coll, Camb; a JP of W Riding of Yorks; 1939-45 War as Flying Officer, RAFVR: m 1st, 1950, Jean Veronica, who d 1970, yst da of late Gerald Robert Foster, of Stockeld Park, Wetherby, Yorks (see Ogilvy, Bt, 1955 Edn); 2ndly, 1978, Susan Dorothy Marie-Gabrielle, 2nd da of late Sir Kenelm Henry Ernest Cayley, 10th Bt, and formerly wife of Maldwin Andrew Cyril Drummond (see E Perth, colls), and has issue by 1st m.

Arms – Argent, a chevron between three escallops gules. Crest – An olive tree fructed proper.
Residence – Aldborough Manor, Boroughbridge, Yorkshire YO5 9EP.

Aimez Dieu
Love God

SONS LIVING (By 1st marriage)

ANDREW PETER, b 18 Feb 1952; ed Eton, and Leeds Univ; Bar Middle Temple 1977. Residence – 1 Cristowe Rd, SW6 3QF. —— Rupert Thomas, b 1953; ed Gordonstoun. —— James Gilchrist Henry, b 1956; ed Trin Coll, Glenalmond. —— Gerald Nicholas, b 1961; ed Trin Coll, Glenalmond. —— Alistair David, b 1964; ed Bootham Sch, York: m 1993, Virginia C., only da of Col Joseph Hordern, OBE, of Radwinter, Essex.

DAUGHTER LIVING (By 1st marriage)

Finella Mary, b 1959: m 1991, Nicholas S. Orr, yr son of late George Alistair Orr, of Mountgreenan, Ayrshire, and has issue living, Rosamond Anne Jane, b 1993.

BROTHER LIVING

Rev Christopher, b (twin) 1924; ed Stowe, and Trin Coll, Camb; Bar Lincoln's Inn 1950; 1939-45 War as FO RAFVR: m 1951, Cerise Eyre Campbell, el da of Sir Hugh Eyre Campbell Beaver, and has issue living, Hugh Christopher, b 1955: m 1993, Emily C.A.R., da of James Macaskie, of Yarlington, Som, and has issue living, Josephine Rose b 1993, — Cerise Elinor, b

1952: *m* 1988, David Holmes, MRCVS, son of Dudley Holmes, and has issue living, Finella Harriet Rachel *b* 1991, — Olivia Eyre, *b* 1957: *m* 1986, Richard L. Bourne, Cdr RN, of Petvins Cottage, Haselbury Plucknet, Som, son of Leonard Richard Thomas Bourne, and has issue living, Simon Richard *b* 1989, — Nicholas Hugh *b* 1992. *Residence* – 3 Minterne House, Minterne Magna, Cerne Abbas, Dorset DT2 7AX.

SISTER LIVING

Pauline, *b* 1916: *m* 1937, (Frank) Douglas Nicholson, TD, who *d* 1984, and has issue living, *Sir* Paul Douglas (Quarry Hill, Brancepeth, co Durham), *b* 1938; *ed* Harrow, and Clare Coll, Camb; late Lieut Coldm Gds; Chm Vaux Group plc since 1976; High Sheriff co Durham 1980, and DL 1980; Ktd 1993: *m* 1970, Sarah, yst da of Sir Edmund Castell Bacon, KG, KBE, TD, 13th Bt, and has issue living, Lucy *b* 1972, — Nigel Frank, *b* 1940: *m* 1982, Mrs S.A. Barnes, of Durban, S Africa, — Andrew, *b* 1945: *m* 1972, Angela, da of Vice-Adm Denis Bryan Harvey Wildish, CB, and has issue living, Rosemary *b* 1975, Caroline *b* 1976, — Mark Thomas, *b* 1950, — Frank, *b* 1954: *m* 1986, Lavinia Margaret Grace, da of Nigel John Ivo Stourton, OBE (*see* B Mowbray, colls), and has issue living, Simon Douglas *b* 1989, Hugo Frank *b* 1991. *Residence* – Harbour House, Plawsworth, nr Chester-le-Street, co Durham.

COLLATERAL BRANCHES LIVING

Grandson of late Clement William Tancred, 4th son of 7th baronet:—
Issue of late Christopher Humphrey Tancred, OBE, *b* 1888, *d* 1971: *m* 1st, 1915 (*m diss* 1923), Gladys Winifred, da of late Walter Chandler; 2ndly, 1927 (*m diss* 1938), Margery Agnes, da of late Samuel Henry Slater, CMG, CIE; 3rdly, 1938 (*m diss* 1943), Priscilla Nöel Cecilia, da of John A. Barclay, of New York; 4thly, 1944, Sadika (21 Lexham Gdns, W8 5JJ), da of R. Miligui, of Cairo, Egypt:—
(By 2nd *m*) Anthony Christopher, *b* 1930; *ed* Eton.

Grandchildren of Harry George Tancred (infra):—
Issue of late Bertram Selby Tancred, *b* 1895, *d* 1965: *m* 1924, Elsa (83 Young St, New Plymouth, NZ), da of A. V. Sims:—
Rex Selby Assheton (12B Oleander Pl, Bell Block, New Plymouth, NZ), *b* 1925: *m* 1948, Shirley Edith, da of H. Box, and has issue living, Philip Rex, *b* 1952, — Linda Joanne, *b* 1954: *m* 1972, Allan John Brooking, of Carthew St, Okato, Bell Block, NZ, son of Frederick John Brooking, of New Plymouth, and has issue living, Daniel John *b* 1976, Jemma Claire *b* 1977, Talia Louise, *b* 1979, — Susan Shirley, *b* 1955: *m* 1975, Stephan Thomas Kerr (King Rd, RD6 Inglewood, NZ), son of Kelvyn Thomas Kerr, of New Plymouth, and has issue living, Alisha Maree *b* 1981, Rachel Lee, *b* 1983. —— Lyle Ashley (205 Frankley Rd, New Plymouth, NZ), *b* 1933: *m* 1959, Beverley Ethel, da of Nelson Howard Bishop, of New Plymouth, NZ, and has issue living, Stephen Ashley, *b* 1962. —— Elwyn Elsa, *b* 1927: *m* 1954, Archibald James Gamble, of 20 Cousins Av East, Foxton Beach, Wellington, NZ, and has issue living, Craig Anthony, *b* 1965.
Issue of late Cecil Mount-Stewart-Tancred, *b* 1884, *d* 19—: *m* 1907:—
Emmie, *b* 1908.

Issue of late Harry George Tancred, son of 7th baronet, *b* 1858, *d* 1945: *m* 1st, 1881, Emily Alicia de Courcy, who *d* 1907, elder da of late Major Slingsby Bell, of Purneah, India, and the Bungalow, Napier, New Zealand; 2ndly, 1908, Rosie Elphinstone, da of late Major Slingsby Bell, and widow of Henry Warren, of New Zealand:—
(By 1st *m*) Zillah Selby, *b* 1893: *m* 1915, Raymond F. M. Atkinson, and has issue living, Veronica Selby *b* 1915: *m* 1943, Gary Elmer Gorsline, of 4304 Jeffries Av, Burbank, Cal, 91505 USA, and has issue living, Victoria Elizabeth Selby *b* 1945: *m* 1963, David Wayne Maske, of 7550 Coldwater Canyon, N Hollywood, California 91605, USA, and has issue living, Michael Andrew (6489 Hope St, Simi Valley, California 93063, USA) *b* 1964, Douglas Adam (2374 Timber Lane Circle, Simi Valley, California 93063, USA) *b* 1965: *m* 1988, Jennifer Ellen Weyand (and has issue living, Kirstie Adrianna *b* 1991), Julie Michelle *b* 1970: *m* 1992, Andi Costin Gorgescu, of 12203 Magnolia Blvd, Apt 106, Valley Village, California 91607, USA (and has issue living, Christopher David *b* 1992). *Residence* – 4304 Jeffries Av, Burbank, California 91505, USA.
This family is descended from Richard Tankard, who soon after the Conquest was possessed of lands at Boroughbridge, where still remains the ancient family house. A Christopher Tancred founded a retreat for poor gentlemen at Whixley, and also scholarships at Oxford, Cambridge, and Lincoln's Inn. The 9th baronet, Major Sir Thomas Selby, Indian Army, assumed by deed poll the additional surname of Lawson 1914, having *m* 1912 Margery Elinor, el da and co-heir of Andrew Sherlock Lawson, of Aldborough Manor, Yorks. Sir John Grant Lawson, 1st Bt (*cr* 1905), was his yr brother.

TANGYE (UK) 1912, of Glendorgal, St Columb Minor, Cornwall (Extinct 1969)

Sir BASIL RICHARD GILZEAN TANGYE, 2nd and last *Baronet.*

DAUGHTER LIVING OF SECOND BARONET

Gitta Clarisse Gilzean, *b* 1928.

WIDOW LIVING OF SECOND BARONET

CLARISSE RENEE ELIZABETH (*Lady Tangye*) (4 Farquhar Rd, Edgbaston, Birmingham), only da of late Baron Victor Schosberger de Tornya, of Tura, Hungary: *m* 1924, Sir Basil Richard Gilzean Tangye, 2nd Bt, who *d* 1969, when the title became ext.

Tapps-Gervis-Meyrick, see Meyrick.

TATE (UK) 1898, of Park Hill, Streatham, co London

Thincke and thancke

Sir (HENRY) SAXON TATE, CBE, 5th *Baronet*; *b* 28 Nov 1931; *s* his father, Sir HENRY, TD, DL, 1994; *ed* Eton, and Ch Ch, Oxford; Lt Life Gds (Army Emergency Reserve); Dir Tate & Lyle plc since 1956, Chm Exec Cttee 1973-78, Man Dir 1978-80, Vice-Chm 1980-82; Chief Exec Offr Redpath Industries Ltd Canada 1965-73; Dir Tate Appointments Ltd since 1982, Chm since 1991; Dir other Cos; FIMgt 1975; CBE 1991: *m* 1st, 1953 (*m diss* 1975), Sheila Ann, who *d* 1987, eldest da of late Duncan Robertson, of Llantysilio, Llangollen (*see* Williams-Wynn, Bt, 1985 Edn); 2ndly, 1975, Virginia Joan Sturm, and has issue by 1st *m*.

Arms – Ermine, on a pale invected azure between four Cornish choughs proper two roses argent. **Crest** – A dexter arm embowed and vested azure, cuffed or, the arm charged with two roses argent, the hand grasping a pineapple erect slipped proper between two ears of wheat saltirewise all proper. *Residence* – 26 Cleaver Square, SE11 4EA. *Club* – Buck's.

SONS LIVING *(By 1st marriage)*

EDWARD NICOLAS, *b* 2 July 1966. —— Duncan Saxon, *b* 1968. —— John William, *b* 1969. —— Paul Henry, *b* (twin) 1969.

BROTHER LIVING

(William) Nicolas, *b* 1934; *ed* Eton, and Ch Ch, Oxford; Lt Gren Gds (Emergency Reserve): *m* 1960, Sarah Rose, eldest da of Lt-Col Angus John Campbell Rose, of Dunira Garden House, Comrie, Perthshire, and has had issue, Rupert Sebastian, *b* 1962, — a son, *b* and *d* 1966, — Melissa Nairne, *b* 1964, *d* 1969, — Georgina Nairne, *b* 1969. *Residence* – 58 Guildford Grove, Greenwich, SE10 8JT.

WIDOW LIVING OF FOURTH BARONET

EDNA STOKES (*Dowager Lady Tate*): *m* 1988, as his 2nd wife, Sir Henry Tate, 4th Bt, TD, DL, who *d* 1994. *Residences* – Preston Lodge, Withcote, Oakham, Leics LE15 8DP; The Cottage, Galltfaenan, Trefnant, Clwyd.

COLLATERAL BRANCHES LIVING

Grandchildren of late Alfred Herbert Tate (infra):—
Issue of late Louis William Tate, *b* 1911, *d* 1986: *m* 1934, Mary Christine (Little Sadlers, Grayswood Rd, Haslemere, Surrey), da of late R. C. Bolton, of Anstey Lane, Alton, Hants:—
Jeremy Louis (Old Quarry Rise, Hargate Hill, Glossop, Derbys), *b* 1937: *m* 1961, Rosemary Helen, da of D. Collins, of East Drive, Sawbridgeworth, Herts, and has issue living, William James Louis, *b* 1965, — Julia Rosemary, *b* 1963, — Emma Margaret Rebecca, *b* 1976.
Issue of late John Frederick Peter Tate, *b* 1923, *d* 1989: *m* 1949, Celia Judith (7 Fisherton Island, Salisbury, Wilts SP2 7TG), da of late Adrian Corbett:—
Christopher John (30 Hesper Mews, SW5 0HH), *b* 1953: *m* 1978 (*m diss* 1991), Jane, eldest da of Capt A. Bicket, of Derwas, Dolwen, Abergele, Clwyd, and has issue living, Alexander John, *b* 1984, — Daisy Virginia, *b* 1981. —— Anne Teresa, *b* 1951; FRCR: *m* 1982, Rodney Reznek, of 15 Park Avenue North, N8 7RU. —— Nicola Helen, *b* 1955: *m* 1976, Michael van der Gucht, of Plume House, Up Nately, Basingstoke, Hants RG27 9PR, and has issue living, Charles Graham *b* 1980, Benjamin Michael *b* 1985, Sarah Celia *b* 1982, Victoria Anthea *b* 1992. —— Sophia Louise, *b* 1958: *m* 1986, Capt Thomas Wright, RGJ (c/o John Swire & Sons (HK) Ltd, PO Box 1, 9P0 Hong Kong), and has issue living, Matthew Adam Christopher *b* 1989, Katharine Elizabeth, *b* 1992.

Issue of late Alfred Herbert Tate, 3rd son of 2nd baronet, *b* 1872, *d* 1930: *m* 1910, Elsie, who *d* 1957 da of late Louis William Jelf-Petit, JP:—
Francis Herbert, *b* 1913: *m* 1937, Esther Frances, da of late Sir (John) Bromhead Matthews, KC, and has issue living, David Anthony (Stone Cross House, Crowborough, E Sussex TN6 3SH), *b* 1941: *m* 1969, Jennifer, da of Mrs Evelyn MacAndrews, of Littlestone, Kent, and has issue living, Rupert David *b* 1974, Matthew Francis *b* 1976, — Caroline Frances (14 Balaclava Rd, Surbiton, Surrey KT6 5PN), *b* 1946: *m* 1st, 1973 (*m diss* 1984), Bruce Jerrit; 2ndly, 1984 (*m diss* 1991), Guy William Brisbane, and has issue living, (by 1st *m*) Benedict Sinclair *b* 1976, Giles Zachary *b* 1978, (by 2nd *m*) Tessa Jennifer *b* 1986, — Marianne Esther, *b* 1949. *Residence* – Little Wissett, Hook Heath Gdns, Woking, Surrey GU22 0QG.

Granddaughters of late Henry Tate, 6th son of 1st baronet:—
Issue of late Capt Henry Burton Tate, *b* 1883, *d* 1962: *m* 1st, 1909 (*m diss* 1925), Ida Guendolen, who *d* 1969, da of Robin H. Legge; 2ndly, 1925 (*m diss* 1944), Mavis Constance, who *d* 1947, da of Guy Weir Hogg (B Magheramorne, colls); 3rdly, 1944, Gwen, who *d* 1957, da of late Herbert Edwards, of The Old Hall, Findern, Derbys:—
(By 1st *m*) Julia Elizabeth Mary, *b* 1919: *m* 1959, Paul Georges Bernard, of 22 Rue des Réservoirs, Versailles, France.
Issue of late Lt-Col Arthur Wignall Tate, DSO, *b* 1888, *d* 1939: *m* 1910, Violet Elaine, da of F. W. Few:—
Monica, *b* 1912: *m* 1935, Douglas Gurney Pelly (*see* Pelly, Bt, colls). *Residence* – Swaynes Hall, Widdington, near Newport, Essex.

Issue of late George Booth Tate, 7th son of 1st baronet, *b* 1857, *d* 1936: *m* 1884, Edith Katherine, who *d* 1937, da of James Walker Yates, formerly of Ashton-on-Mersey, Cheshire:—
Jane Marjorie, *b* 1895: *m* 1920, Redvers Arthur Oldham, who *d* 1960, and has issue living. *Residence* – Birchwood, Sunningdale, Berks.

Granddaughters of late George Booth Tate (ante):—
Issue of late George Vernon Tate, MC, *b* 1890, *d* 1955: *m* 1922, Evelyn Victoria Anne, who *d* 1979, da of Walter Robert Chandler, and widow (1) of 25th Baron de Clifford, and (2) of Capt Arthur Boy Stock:—
Pamela Aloysia, *b* 1923: *m* 1946, Henry Forbes, son of Adm of the Fleet Sir Charles Morton Forbes, GCB, DSO, and has issue living, Timothy John (Madrid House, 88 Bromfelde Rd, SW4 6PS), *b* 1947; *ed* Stowe: *m* 1973, Rosemary Elisabeth Balliol, da of Humphrey Salmon, and has issue living, Charles Morton *b* 1975, Edward (Ned) Alexander *b* 1983, — Amanda Aloysia, *b* 1950: *m* 1973, Peter Mackelean Woodroffe, of 13 Cadogen St, SW3 2PP, and has issue living, Justin Mackelean *b* 1977, Clifford Derry *b* 1979, — Vanessa Christina, *b* 1955: *m* 19—, John Kelly, of Glenwood, 5 King Edward Rise, Ascot, Berks SL5 8JZ. *Residence* – 5 Lyne Place Manor, Bridge Lane, Virginia Water, Surrey GU25 4ED. —— Virginia Ann, *b* 1931:

m 1953, Michael Jeremy Kindersley Belmont (*see* B Kindersley, 1980 Edn), and has issue living, Piers Antony Robert, *b* 1954: *m* 1982, Sally Anne Treweeke, and has issue living, Edward Algernon Spencer *b* 1987, Oliver Jeremy Thomas *b* 1990, — Antony Vernon Spencer, *b* 1956, — Elisa Ann, *b* 1959: *m* 1986, Richard George Ford, son of Sir Edward Ford, KCB, KCVO, ERD, and has issue (*see* By Brand). *Residence* – Gaunt Mill, Standlake, Oxon.

Sir Henry Tate, 1st Bt, the sugar magnate, gave the Tate Gallery to the nation. Sir William Henry Tate, 2nd Bt, was High Sheriff of Lancashire 1907. Sir Henry Tate, 4th Bt, TD, was Co Councillor for Rutland 1958-74, a DL 1964, and High Sheriff of Rutland 1949-50.

TAYLOR (UK) 1963, of Cawthorne in the West Riding, co York (Extinct 1972)

Sir WILLIAM JOHNSON TAYLOR, CBE, 1st and last *Baronet*.

DAUGHTERS LIVING OF FIRST BARONET

Pauline Mary, *b* 1932: *m* 1963, Dr Brian Kenneth Schlotel, of 35 The Grove, Woking, Surrey GU21 6AF, and has issue living, Mary Julia Taylor, *b* 1964. — Helen Rosalind Taylor, *b* 1967. — Carol Margaret, *b* 1937: *m* 1959, Robert Nigel David Bruce, of 20 Jackson's Edge Rd, Disley, Stockport, Cheshire SK12 2JL, and has issue living, Robert Torfine William, *b* 1962, — Robert Thurstan Taylor, *b* 1965, — Robert Andrew Johnson, *b* 1967, — Katherine Isabelle Zoe, *b* (twin) 1967.

STUART TAYLOR (UK) 1917, of Kennington, co London

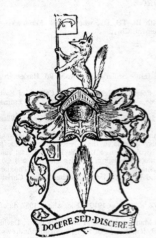

Sir NICHOLAS RICHARD STUART TAYLOR, 4th *Baronet*; *b* 14 Jan 1952; *s* his father *Sir* RICHARD LAURENCE, 1978; *ed* Bradfield; Solicitor 1977: *m* 1984, Malvena Elizabeth, BSc, MB, BS, FRCA, only da of Daniel David Charles Sullivan, of E Finchley, London, and has issue.

Arms – Per pale gules and azure a fox's brush erect or between two bezants in fesse. **Crest** – A demi-fox gules tailed or, supporting a banner also gules, charged with a seax or.
Address – 3 Horseshoe Drive, Romsey, Hants SO51 7TP.

DAUGHTERS LIVING

Virginia Caterina, *b* 1989. —— Olivia Malvena, *b* 1991.

SISTER LIVING

(Anne) Caroline, *b* 1955; *ed* St Michael's Sch, Petworth, and Grenoble Univ.

AUNT LIVING (*Daughter of 2nd baronet*)

Lesley Evelyn (17 Cambray Court, Cheltenham Glos GL50 1JU), *b* 1922; *ed* Cheltenham Ladies' Coll, and Girton Coll, Camb (MA).

WIDOW LIVING OF THIRD BARONET

IRIS MARY (*Iris, Lady Stuart Taylor*) (White Lodge, Hambrook, Chichester, Sussex PO18 8RG), da of the Rev Edwin John Gargery: *m* 1950, Sir Richard Laurence Stuart Taylor, 3rd Bt, who *d* 1978.

Sir Frederick Taylor, 1st Bt, MD, FRCP, was an eminent Consulting Physician, and Pres of R Coll of Physicians. He was *s* in 1920 by his son Sir Eric Stuart Taylor, OBE, MD, MRCP, who *d* 20 Oct 1977, having assumed the addl surname of Stuart. His son, Sir Richard Laurence Stuart Taylor, who served in World War II with RAC and R Glos Hussars, was Man Dir of Powell Duffryn Fuels Ltd. He *d* 10 Sept 1978.

WORSLEY-TAYLOR (UK) 1917, of Moreton Hall, Parish of Whalley, Co Palatine of Lancaster (Extinct 1958)

Sir FRANCIS EDWARD WORSLEY-TAYLOR, 4th and last *Baronet*.

DAUGHTER LIVING OF SECOND BARONET

Dorothea Margaret, *b* 1920. *Residence* – The Old Forge, Bashall Eaves, Clitheroe, Lancs.

DAUGHTER LIVING OF THIRD BARONET

Annette Pamela, *b* 1944. *Residence* – 57 Drayton Gdns, SW10 9RU.

TEMPLE (UK) 1876, of The Nash, Kempsey, co Worcester

Sir RICHARD ANTONY PURBECK TEMPLE, MC, 4th *Baronet*; *b* 19 Jan 1913; *s* his father, *Sir* RICHARD DURAND, DSO, 1962; *ed* Stowe, and Trin Hall, Camb; sometime Maj King's Roy Rifle Corps; European War 1939-45 (wounded, MC): *m* 1st, 1936 (*m diss* 1946), Lucy Geils, 2nd da of late Alain Joly de Lotbiniere of Montreal; 2ndly, 1950, Jean, da of late James T. Finnie, and widow of Oliver P. Croom-Johnson, and has issue by 1st and 2nd *m*.

𝕬rms – Quarterly: 1st and 4th, or, an eagle displayed sable; 2nd and 3rd, argent, two bars sable each charged with three martlets or. 𝕮rest – On a ducal coronet or, a martlet of the last.
Address – c/o The National Westminster Bank Ltd, 94 Kensington High St, W8.

Templa quam dilecta

How beloved are thy temples

SONS LIVING *(By 1st marriage)*

RICHARD (6 Clarendon Cross, W11 4AP), *b* 17 Aug 1937: *m* 1964, Emma Rose, da of late Maj-Gen Sir Robert Edward Laycock, KCMG, CB, DSO (*see* E Dudley, colls), and has issue living, Lucy Martha, *b* 1965, — Alice Frances, *b* 1967, — Daisy Louise, *b* 1971. —— Anthony St George (31 Gascony Av, NW6), *b* 1941: *m* 1986, Angelika Reda, and has issue living, Nicholas Christopher, *b* 1986.

DAUGHTER LIVING *(By 2nd marriage)*

Anne Sophia, *b* 1951: *m* 1974, Jeremy Christopher Peter Amos, of 24 Holland Park Av, W11, and has issue living, Alexander Rudolph, *b* 1978, — Benjamin Christopher, *b* 1980.

HALF-BROTHERS LIVING

Peter Paul Grenville (2 Kellerton Rd, SE13 5RD), *b* 1941: *m* 1st, 1975 (*m diss* 1980), Heather Joy, da of Duncan Alistair McKellar (*see* Cayzer, Bt), and formerly wife of Kenneth Leonard Hyman; 2ndly, 1983, Veronica Margaret, 2nd da of Geoffrey Trigg, of Southrepps, Norfolk, and has issue living (by 2nd *m*), Richard John Geoffrey, *b* 1984. —— John Anthony (Rue Niçaise 4, 1341 Ceroux-Moulty, Brussels, Belgium), *b* 1942: *m* 1967, Dominique Francine Paule Ghislaine Maire, da of Jean-Maurice Vaes, and has issue living, Jean-Marc Peter Grenville, *b* 1968, — Sophie Anne Jacqueline, *b* 1970, — Vanessa Chantal Marie, *b* 1973.

WIDOW LIVING OF THIRD BARONET

MARIE WANDA (*Marie, Lady Temple*) (38 St George's Court, Wrotham, Kent), da of late F. C. Henderson, of Bombay, India: *m* 1939, as his 2nd wife, Sir Richard Durand Temple, DSO, 3rd Bt, who *d* 1962.

This family descends from William Dicken, of Shenton, Salop, who *m* 1740, Henrietta, da and co-heir of Sir William Temple, 5th Bt of Stowe, Bucks. Their son John (grandfather of 1st baronet) assumed by Royal Licence 1796 the surname of Temple. The 1st baronet, Rt Hon Sir Richard Temple, GCSI, CIE, was Financial Member of Govt of India 1868-74, Lieut-Gov of Bengal 1874-7, Gov of Bombay 1877-80, and MP for Worcestershire S, or Evesham, Div 1885-92, and for Surrey, Kingston Div 1892-6. The 2nd baronet, Lieut-Col Sir Richard Carnac Temple, CB, CIE (Indian Army, and sometime Ch Commr Andaman and Nicobar Islands), raised and commanded Upper Burmah Vol Rifles 1887-90, raised Rangoon Naval Vol 1892, and Rangoon Vol Engineers (Submarine Miners) 1893, and was Editor and Proprietor of the *Indian Antiquary* 1884-1931. The 3rd baronet, Lt-Col Sir Richard Durand Temple served in the S African War and World War I (DSO, Croix de Guerre with palm) and was later Col cmdg 1st Army BEF, Col cmdg 27th Bn Northumberland Fus, and Col cmdg 5th Bn Worcester Regt.

Tennyson-d'Eyncourt, see d'Eyncourt.

IMBERT-TERRY (UK) 1917, of Strete Ralegh, Whimple, co Devon

Sir MICHAEL EDWARD STANLEY IMBERT-TERRY, 5th *Baronet; b* 18 April 1950; *s* his brother, *Sir* ANDREW HENRY BOUHIER, 1985; *ed* Cranleigh: *m* 1975, Frances Dorothy, da of late Peter Scott, of 25 Corfton Rd, Ealing, W5, and has issue.

ℛrms – Azure, guttée d'or three, four, three and four, on a chief of the last a bull's head caboshed between two mullets of the first. Crest – Issuant from the coronet of a French Seigneur an eagle rising proper, crowned with an Eastern crown or.
Address – c/o Lady Sackville, Knole, Sevenoaks, Kent.

SONS LIVING

BRYCHAN EDWARD, *b* 1975. —— Jack *b* 1985.

DAUGHTERS LIVING

Song, *b* 1973. —— Bryony Jean, *b* 1980.

SISTERS LIVING

Carolyn Rose (Grove Cottage, Sandy Lane, Maybury, Woking, Surrey), *b* 1947: *m* 1st, 1973 (*m diss* 1981), Peter Lauderdale Mackintosh; 2ndly, 1984, Christopher Goode, son of Brig Ernest Reginald Goode, CBE, of Milford, Surrey, and has issue living (by 1st *m*), Rory Edward Christopher, *b* 1976, — Catherine Rose, *b* 1977. —— Alison Jean, *b* 1952: *m* 1981, Julian Lorimer Sanger of The Vale House, Frostenden, Beccles, Suffolk, and has issue living, Jonathan Edward, *b* 1983, — Rachel Mary, *b* 1981.

AUNTS LIVING (*Daughters living of 2nd baronet*)

Rosanne Mildred Clothilde, *b* 1913. —— Marie Jacqueline, *b* 1923: *m* 1st, 1947 (*m diss* 1954), McRae Wyndham Greenhill; 2ndly, 1972, William Maurice Williams.

WIDOW LIVING OF THIRD BARONET

JEAN (*Baroness Sackville*), da of late Arthur Stanley Garton, of Danesfield, Marlow, Bucks; JP 1973: *m* 1st, 1944, Maj Sir Edward Henry Bouhier Imbert-Terry, MC, 3rd Bt, who *d* 1978; 2ndly, 1983, as his 3rd wife, 6th Baron Sackville. *Residence* – Knole, Sevenoaks, Kent.

The 1st baronet, Sir Henry Machu Imbert-Terry (2nd son of Henry Imbert-Terry), was Chm of Central Organization Committee of Unionist Party 1907-17. Lt-Col Sir Henry Bouhier Imbert-Terry, DSO, MC, 2nd Bt, late RA, was High Sheriff of Devon 1948.

THATCHER (UK) 1991, of Scotney, co Kent

Sir DENIS THATCHER, MBE, TD, 1st *Baronet*, son of Thomas Herbert Thatcher, of Uffington, Oxon; *b* 10 May 1915; *ed* Mill Hill; served European War 1939-45 as Maj RA (TD 1940); Dir Burmah Castrol 1970-75, Vice-Chm Attwoods plc 1983-93, Dir Quinton Hazell plc since 1968, Consultant Amec plc and CSX Corpn (US) since 1988; MBE (Mil) 1945: *m* 1st, 1942 (*m diss* 1946), Margaret Doris, only da of Leonard Kempson, of Potters Bar, Middx; 2ndly, 1951, Margaret Hilda, OM, PC (*Baroness Thatcher*) (see that title), da of late Alfred Roberts, of Grantham, Lincs, and has issue by 2nd *m*.

Arms – Gules, two chevrons or between three crosses moline argent, on a chief azure, between two fleurs-de-lys also argent, a mural crown or masoned gules. **Crest** – A demi-lion rampant or within a circlet of New Zealand ferns argent, holding between the fore-paws a pair of shears proper.
Residence – 73 Chester Sq, SW1. *Clubs* – Carlton, Buck's, E India, Pratt's.

SON LIVING *(By 2nd marriage)*

Hon MARK, *b* 15 Aug 1953; *ed* Harrow: *m* 1987, Diane, only da of T. C. Burgdorf, of Dallas, Texas, USA, and has issue living, Michael, *b* 1 Feb 1988, — Amanda Margaret, *b* 1993.

DAUGHTER LIVING *(By 2nd marriage)*

Hon Carol, *b* (twin) 1953; journalist and broadcaster.

THOMAS (E) 1694, of Wenvoe, Glamorganshire

Invincible virtue is glorious

Sir (GODFREY) MICHAEL DAVID THOMAS, 11th *Baronet*; *b* 10 Oct 1925; *s* his father, *Rt Hon Sir* GODFREY JOHN VIGNOLES, GCVO, KCB, CSI, 1968; *ed* Harrow; late Capt Rifle Bde; late Member of London Stock Exchange: *m* 1956, Margaret Greta, yr da of John Cleland, of Stormont Court, Godden Green, Sevenoaks, and has issue.

Arms – Sable, a chevron and a canton ermine. **Crest** – A demi-unicorn ermine, armed, crined, and unguled or, supporting a shield sable.
Residence – 2 Napier Av, SW6. *Clubs* – MCC; Hurlingham.

SON LIVING

DAVID JOHN GODFREY, *b* 11 June 1961.

DAUGHTERS LIVING

Anne Margaret, *b* 1957: *m* 1987, Robert Hutchison, elder son of Sir Peter Hutchison, 2nd Bt (*cr* 1939). —— Diana Elizabeth, *b* (twin) 1961: *m* 1985, Richard Allan Halford Brooks (*see* B Crawshaw, colls).

Sir John Thomas, 1st Bt, of Wenvoe, Glam (grandson of James, yr son of Edmond Thomas, of Wenvoe temp James I and Charles I) *m* 1694, Elizabeth, sister of Edmond Thomas, of Wenvoe (*d* 1677), and widow of Gen Edmund Ludlow. The baronetcy was *cr* 1694 with remainder to his brothers Edmond (who *s* 1703 as 2nd Bt) and William. Brig Sir Godfrey Vignoles Thomas, CB, CBE, DSO, 9th Bt, commanded 24th Div RA and 2nd Reserve Bde RA during 1914-18 War, was *ka* 1919. His son Rt Hon Sir Godfrey John Vignoles Thomas, GCVO, KCB, CSI, 10th Bt, was Private Sec to the Prince of Wales 1919-36, and Assist Sec when King Edward VIII, and Private Sec to the Duke of Gloucester 1937-57.

THOMAS (UK) 1918, of Garreglwyd, Anglesey

Sir (WILLIAM) MICHAEL MARSH THOMAS, 3rd *Baronet, b* 4 Dec 1930; *s* his father, *Major Sir* WILLIAM EUSTACE RHYDDLAD, MBE, 1958, *ed* Oundle: *m* 1957, Geraldine, da of Robert Drysdale, of Trearddur Bay, Anglesey, and has issue.

Arms – Per pale gules and azure, on a chevron argent between in chief a sower in the attitude of scattering seed and an eagle displayed both or, and in base a garb of the last, three fleurs-de-lis sable. **Crest** – On waves of the sea proper between two anchors sable, a ship in full sail proper.
Residence – Belan Fawr, Rhosneigr, Anglesey.

DAUGHTERS LIVING

Geraldine Dawn, *b* 1958. —— Elizabeth Penelope Kim, *b* 1959. —— Pippa-Jane, *b* 1963.

MOTHER LIVING

Enid Helena, da of Ernest Marsh, of Rawdon, Leeds: *m* 1929 (*m diss* 1946), Sir William Eustace Rhyddlad Thomas, MBE, 2nd Bt, who *d* 1957. *Residence* – Harrogate, Yorkshire.

Do right and fear nothing

WIDOW LIVING OF SECOND BARONET

PATRICIA (LARKINS) (*Patricia, Lady Thomas*): *m* 1957, as his 3rd wife, Major Sir William Eustace Rhyddlad Thomas, MBE, 2nd Bt, who *d* 1958.

COLLATERAL BRANCH LIVING

Issue of late Col Robert FREEMAN THOMAS, yr son of 1st baronet, *b* 1911, *d* 1972: *m* 1947, Marcia (who *d* 1992, having *m* 2ndly, 1955, Anthony Melville-Ross, of Lewes, Sussex, who *d* 1993), da of Maurice Sandberg:—
Sarah Anne, *b* 1948: *m* 1981, Alexander James Smith, of 3 Wallands Crescent, Lewes, E Sussex BN7 2QT, and has issue living, Luke Alastair Robert, *b* 1982.
The 1st baronet, Sir Robert John Thomas (son of late William Thomas, of Liverpool), was a Ship and Insurance Broker, and was High Sheriff of Anglesey 1912. He founded and contributed £20,000 to Welch Heroes Memorial Fund and sat as MP for Wrexham Div of Denbighshire (*Co L*) 1918-22, and for Anglesey Co (*L*) 1923-29.

THOMAS (UK) 1919, of Ynyshir, co Glamorgan

Sir WILLIAM JAMES COOPER THOMAS, TD, 2nd *Baronet; b* 7 May 1919; *s* his father, *Sir* (WILLIAM) JAMES, 1945; *ed* Harrow, and Downing Coll, Camb; Bar Inner Temple 1948; is a JP and a DL for Gwent (High Sheriff of co Monmouth 1973-74); 1939-45 War with RA: *m* 1947, Freida Dunbar, who *d* 1990, da of late F. A. Whyte, of Montcoffer, Banff, and has issue.

Arms – Argent, a bend gules, between in chief a pick sable and in base a rose of the second, barbed and seeded proper, all within a bordure also of the second. **Crest** – Upon a branch of olive fessewise an owl affrontée proper.
Seat – Tump House, Llanrothal, Monmouth, Gwent NP5 3QL.

SONS LIVING

WILLIAM MICHAEL, *b* 5 Dec 1948; *ed* Harrow, and Ch Ch, Oxford. —— Stephen Francis (4 Scraesburgh Cottages, Jedburgh, Roxburghshire), *b* 1951; *ed* Harrow, and Oriel Coll, Oxford: *m* 1986, Hon Jane Ridley, eldest da of late Baron Ridley of Liddesdale, PC (Life Baron), and has issue living, Toby James, *b* 1988, —— Humphrey William, *b* 1991.

DAUGHTER LIVING

Sara Roberta Mary *b* 1954: *m* 1988, Ian W. Jones, yr son of late G. V. Jones, of Walton-on-the-Hill, Surrey, and has issue living, Nicholas David Richard, *b* 1991, —— Katherine Louise, *b* 1989.

SISTER LIVING

Maureen Elizabeth Jane: *m* 1942, Joseph Gerald Gaskell, and has issue living, Joseph William, *b* 1947, —— Charles Peter, *b* 1950. *Residence* – Park Mount, Park Rd, Dinas Powis, S Glamorgan.
The 1st baronet, Sir (William) James Thomas (son of Thomas James Thomas), built Welsh National Med Sch at Cardiff, and was High Sheriff of Glamorganshire 1936.

THOMPSON (UK) 1806, of Hartsbourne Manor, Hertfordshire

Sir (THOMAS) LIONEL TENNYSON THOMPSON, 5th *Baronet*; *b* 19 June 1921; *s* his father, *Lt-Col Sir* THOMAS RAIKES LOVETT, MC, 1964; *ed* Eton; Bar Lincoln's Inn 1952; 1939-45 War as Flying Officer RAFVR (invalided), and subsequently as Able Seaman Roy Fleet Auxiliary (1939-45, and Aircrew (Europe) stars, Defence and Victory Medals): *m* 1955 (*m diss* 1962), Mrs Margaret van Beers, da of late Walter Herbert Browne, and has issue.

Arms – Per fesse argent and sable, a fesse counter-embattled between three falcons belled and jessed or, all within a bordure engrailed, and all counter-changed; in the chief point, also within the bordure, an anchor erect azure, cable proper. **Crest** – Out of a naval crown or, an arm in armour embowed proper, garnished gold, the hand supporting a lance erect also proper. *Address* – 16 Old Buildings, Lincoln's Inn, WC2A 3UP.

SON LIVING

THOMAS D'EYNCOURT JOHN (c/o King Sturge & Co, 7 Stratford Place, W1N 9AE), *b* 22 Dec 1956; *ed* Eton; BA, MSc; ARICS.

DAUGHTER LIVING

Sarah Catherine Elizabeth (2330 Larkin St, 5, San Francisco, CA 94109, USA), *b* 1955.

SISTER LIVING

Not by whom but in what manner

Jane Olivia Marion, *b* 1918: *m* 1st, 1938 (*m diss* 1947), David Owen Nares; 2ndly, 1948, Maj James Derek Kenyon Hague, MC, Bar-at-law, who *d* 1966, and has issue living (by 1st *m*), Caroline Harriette, *b* 1940: *m* 1961, Robert Belmont, — (by 2nd *m*) Melanie Clare, *b* 1957: *m* 1980, Andrew John Melsom (*see* Pasley, Bt, colls). *Residence* – Stud House, Chilton Foliat, Hungerford, Berks.

The 1st baronet, Vice-Adm Sir Thomas Boulden Thompson, GCB (MP for Rochester 1807-16), greatly distinguished himself, as Captain of the *Leander*, at the battle of the Nile, and afterwards in the action between *Leander* (50) and *Le Genereux* (74), and on his return to England he was knighted 1799; subsequently engaged at the battle of Copenhagen 1801, where he lost a leg; and was appointed Comptroller of the Navy 1806, being created a baronet in the last-mentioned year. Subsequently he was appointed Treasurer of Greenwich Hospital.

THOMPSON (UK) 1890, of Park Gate, Guiseley, Yorkshire

Lt-Col Sir CHRISTOPHER PEILE THOMPSON, 6th *Baronet*; *b* 21 Dec 1944; *s* his father, *Lt-Col Sir* PEILE, OBE, 1985; *ed* Marlborough; Lt-Col (ret) R Hussars (PWO); Equerry to HRH Prince Michael of Kent: *m* 1969, Anna Elizabeth, da of Maj Arthur George Callander, of Silbury House, Avebury, Marlborough, Wilts, and has issue.

Arms – Azure, a bridge of three arches embattled proper, in chief the sun in his glory between two mullets of six points pierced or in base an eagle displayed with two heads argent. **Crest** – In front of embattlements proper, a cubit arm erect, habited azure, cuffed argent, and charged with a mullet as in the arms, the hand grasping five ears of wheat or. *Address* – c/o Barclays Bank plc, PO Box No 8, 13 Library Place, St Helier, Jersey, CI. *Club* – Cavalry and Guards', Woodroffes, SMTC.

SON LIVING

Wheare vertue lys

love nevr dys

PEILE RICHARD, *b* 3 March 1975; *ed* Harrow, and Bristol Univ.

DAUGHTER LIVING

Alexandra Lucy, *b* 1973.

SISTER LIVING

Ann Mary, *b* 1939: *m* 1st, 1965 (*m diss* 1973), Arturo Cesare Pilato, son of late Gino Pilato, of Naples; 2ndly, 1973, Raymond Benjamin Cheetham, late R Hong Kong Police Force, of Hillbrook House, Dipford, Trull, Somerset, son of late Benjamin Cheetham, of Lismore, Feniton, Devon, and has issue living (by 1st *m*), Roberto Arturo Kenneth, *b* 1966; *ed* King's Coll, Taunton, and Cardiff Univ, — Leonardo Cesare, *b* 1970; *ed* King's Coll Taunton, and De Montfort Univ.

AUNT LIVING (*Daughter of 4th baronet*)

Mary Winifred, *b* 1909: *m* 1941, Hugh Kenyon, of 9 Frobisher Gdns, Boxgrove, Guildford, Surrey, son of Rev Thomas Kenyon, of Malham, Skipton, Yorks, and has issue living, Hugh Matthew, *b* 1944; *ed* Rugby, — Elizabeth Katharine, *b* 1942: *m* 1977, Francis Pasco Grenfell (*see* B Grenfell, colls).

COLLATERAL BRANCHES LIVING

Grandchildren of late Capt Gilbert Thompson, Connaught Rangers (infra):—

Issue of late Maj Christopher Smith Byrom THOMPSON ROYDS, *b* 1907; assumed by Roy licence 1936, the additional surname and arms of Royds; *d* 1967: *m* 1936, Yolande Anne (Walton House, Boston Spa, Yorks), yr da of late A. T. Hodgson, of Tatchbury Manor House, New Forest, Hants:—

Gilbert (Seymour House, Market St, Charlbury, Oxon), *b* 1939; *ed* Eton: *m* 1976, Vanessa Maxine, da of Mark Leslie Brandon (*see* V Selby). —— Matthew, *b* 1942; *ed* Eton: *m* 1969, Susan (Damaris), el da of Arthur Robert Jarrett, of Chedgrove Manor, Loddon, Norfolk. —— Timothy Christopher, *b* 1950; *ed* Stowe: *m* 1983, Anne, yr da of Gordon Shafto Hedley (*see* E Waldegrave), and has issue living, Mark Christopher, *b* 1989, — Kate, *b* 1985. —— Laura Yolanda, *b* 1947.

Grandchildren of late Reginald Thompson, 2nd son of 1st baronet:—

Issue of late Capt Gilbert Thompson, Connaught Rangers, *b* 1877, *ka* 1915: *m* 1906, Ethel Isabella, who *d* 1959, da of late Marmaduke D'Arcy Wyvill (B Rookwood):—

Laura Barbara Frances (*Lady Inglefield*), *b* 1908: *m* 1933, Sir Gilbert Samuel Inglefield, GBE, TD, who *d* 1991, and has issue living, David Gilbert Charles (The Old Rectory, Staunton-in-the-Vale, Orston, Notts), *b* 1934: *m* 1970, Jean Mary, only da of late Col Sir Alan Gomme-Duncan, MC, and has issue living, Charles Nicholas David *b* 1977, Mary Victoria *b* 1974, — (Christopher) Samuel (Bryngwyn Manor, Raglan, Gwent), *b* 1936: *m* 1971, Susan Lilias, da of Henry Turcan, of Lindores House, Newburgh, Fife, and has issue living, Edward Henry Samuel *b* 1973, Frederick Thomas Christopher, *b* 1982, Olivia Barbara Jane *b* 1972, Katherine Lilias Cecilia *b* 1977, — Elizabeth Isabel Albinia (Orchard Grange, Old Warden, Biggleswade, Beds SG18 9HB), *b* 1942: *m* 1962, Maj Christopher Wyndham Diggle, who *d* 1986, and has issue living, Robert Dominic Charles *b* 1969, Jonathan Benjamin Christopher *b* 1973, Albinia Julia *b* 1964: *m* 1988, Richard Malcolm Jannion Trustram Eve, and has issue (*see* B Silsoe), Louise Georgina *b* 1966. *Residence* – 6 Rutland House, Marloes Rd, W8 5LE. —— Naomi Isabella, *b* 1912: *m* 1935, Maj D'Arcy Armitage Dawes, late 15/19th King's R Hussars, who *d* 1967 (Armytage, Bt, colls), and has issue living, Charles Lancelot (Leacon Hall, Warehorne, Ashford, Kent), *b* 1938, Capt (ret) late 15th/19th King's R Hussars: *m* 1964, Valerie Ann, el da of Col Edward Townsend, of Fencote Hall, Northallerton, Yorks, and has issue living, Nicholas Halford *b* 1967, James Christopher *b* 1968, Isla Caroline *b* 1971, — Hermione Ann, *b* 1941: *m* 1964, John Oliver Birkbeck, of Litcham Hall, King's Lynn (*see* E Munster, 1990 Edn), and has issue living, Oliver Benjamin *b* 1973, Lucy Claire *b* 1966, Roseanna Mary *b* 1974. *Residence* – Forge Cottage, Warehorne, Ashford, Kent.

Issue of late Col Reginald Thompson, DSO, *b* 1884, *d* 1965: *m* 1st, 1922, Marjorie Olive, who *d* 1929, da of late James Arthur, of Montgomerie, Tarbolton (B Glenarthur); 2ndly, 1932, Ruth Eleanor, who *d* 1986, da of the Rev J. H. Hodgson, and widow of John C. Bradley Firth, of Blyth, Notts.

(By 1st *m*) Elizabeth Olive (Failford House, Mauchline, Ayrshire), *b* 1923: *m* 1948, Maj George Malcolm Graham, KRRC, who *d* 1980, and has issue living, James Anthony (La Hille, Fanjeaux 11270, France), *b* 1953; *ed* Sorbonne: *m* 1978 (*m diss* 1993), Hayat Lebbar, — Alexandra Mary, *b* 1949: *m* 1974, Adrian John Speir, of 12 Stratford Grove, SW15, son of late Michael Adrian Speir, of Foresters Hall, Middleton Tyas, N Yorks, and has issue living, Edward Francis *b* 1976, Harry James *b* 1979. —— Judith Mary (Day Ash, Darley, Yorkshire) *b* 1927.

Issue of late William Whitaker Thompson, 3rd son of 1st baronet, *b* 1857, *d* 1920: *m* 1889, Isabella Blanche Spencer, who *d* 1945, da of Spencer Robert Lewin, of Widford, Herts:—

Marion Jessie (20 Chapel St, Brookline, Mass 02146, USA), *b* 1890: *m* 1930, as his 2nd wife, Dows Dunham, who *d* 1984. The 1st baronet sat as MP for Bradford (*L*) 1867-8, and was Chm of the Forth Bridge and the Midland Railway Cos.

THOMPSON (UK) 1963, of Reculver, co Kent

Sir RICHARD HILTON MARLER THOMPSON, 1st *Baronet*, son of late Richard Smith Thompson; *b* 5 Oct 1912; *ed* Malvern Coll; a Co Dir; Assist Govt Whip 1952-54, Lord Commr of Treasury 1954-56, Vice Chamberlain, HM Household 1956-57, Parl Sec, Min of Health 1957-59, Parl Under-Sec of State, Commonwealth Relations Office, 1959-60, and Parl Sec, Min of Works 1960-62; a Trustee of British Museum, 1951-84; Dir of Rediffusion TV Ltd and Rediffusion Holdings 1966-83; Chm of Capital & Counties Property Co Ltd 1971-76 and Pres of British Property Federation 1976-77; Chm of British Museum Soc 1970-74 and a Member of Council, Nat Trust 1978-84; 1939-45 War as Lt-Cdr RNVR (despatches); MP Croydon W (*C*) 1950-55, and of Croydon S 1955-66 and 1970-74: *m* 1939, Anne Christabel de Vere, only da of late Philip de Vere Annesley (*see* V Valentia, colls), and has issue.

Arms – Azure a bend argent between two ship's wheels or. **Crest** – A demi figure representing a Moorish Prince proper, wreathed about the temples with a torse argent and azure, vested of a tunic paly argent and azure fringed and garnished or, at his back supported by a guige gules baldrickwise across the right dexter shoulder, a quiver azure replenished with arrows argent flighted or, from the dexter hand a martlet rising azure and in the other a bow palewise stringed gules. Inescutcheon of pretence, paly of six argent and azure, over all a hand gules, *Annesley*.
Residence – Rhodes House, Sellindge, Ashford, Kent TN25 6JA. **Clubs** – Carlton, Army and Navy.

SON LIVING

NICHOLAS ANNESLEY MARLER (Maxgate, George Rd, Kingston-upon-Thames, Surrey KT2 7NR; Carlton Club), *b* 19 March 1947; *ed* King's Sch, Canterbury, and Univ of Kent at Canterbury (BA); admitted a solicitor 1973; Mem Westminster City Council 1978-86; Dep Lord Mayor of Westminster 1983-84: *m* 1982, Venetia Catherine, yr da of John Horace Broke Heathcote, of Conington House, Peterborough, Cambs (*see* Heathcote, Bt, of London), and has issue living, Simon William, *b* 10 June 1985, — Charles Frederick, *b* 1986, — David Jonathan, *b* 1990, — Emma Louise, *b* 1991.

THOMPSON (UK) 1963, of Walton-on-the-Hill, City of Liverpool

Sir PAUL ANTHONY THOMPSON, 2nd *Baronet*; *b* 6 Oct 1939; *s* his father, *Sir* KENNETH PUGH, 1984: *m* 1971, Pauline Dorothy, da of late Robert Orrell Spencer, of Tippett House, Smithills, Bolton, Lancs, and has issue.

Arms – Per fess dancetty argent and sable of two upward and one downward points, each ending in a cross potent, three swans one in chief and two in base counterchanged. **Crest** – A demi figure affronty representing Neptune wreathed about the middle with laver proper, the mantle gules clasped and crowned with an antique crown or, supporting in the dexter hand a trident sable and in the sinister a spear proper.
Residence – 28 Dowhills Rd, Blundellsands, Liverpool.

SONS LIVING

RICHARD KENNETH SPENCER, *b* 27 Jan 1976. —— David Paul Charles, *b* 1978.

DAUGHTERS LIVING

Karena Melanie, *b* 1973. —— Nicola Robyn, *b* 1974.

SISTER LIVING

Nanne Patricia, *b* 1942: *m* 1st, 1966, T. Michael Johns; 2ndly, 1989, Neil Charles Bedford.

MEYSEY-THOMPSON (UK) 1874, of Kirby Hall, Yorkshire

Sir (HUMPHREY) SIMON MEYSEY-THOMPSON, 4th *Baronet*, son of late Guy Herbert Meysey-Thompson, grandson of 1st Baronet; *b* 31 March 1935; *s* his kinsman, *Sir* ALGAR DE CLIFFORD CHARLES, 1967.

Arms – Quarterly: 1st and 4th, per fesse argent and sable, a fesse counter-embattled between three falcons counterchanged, belled and jessed or; 2nd and 3rd, argent, a fesse between three cinquefoils sable. **Crests** – 1st, an arm embossed quarterly or and azure, guantleted proper, grasping a broken tilting spear in bend sinister or; 2nd, a dragon's head quarterly or and azure, eared gules.
Residence – 10 Church St, Woodbridge, Suffolk.

SISTER LIVING

Sarah Horatia, *b* 1944: *m* 1969, Charles William Spencer Paterson, of 14 Holland Park Avenue, W11, and has issue living, Charles Joseph Alexander, *b* 1983.

DAUGHTER LIVING OF SECOND BARONET

I wish for fair fight

See Barony of Knaresborough.
The 1st baronet, Sir Harry Stephen Meysey-Thompson, sat as MP for Whitby (L) 1859-65. The 2nd baronet, Sir Henry Meysey-Thompson, sat as MP for Knaresborough (L) April to July 1880, for N Lindsey, or Brigg, Div of Lincolnshire 1885-6, and for Handsworth Div of Staffordshire (LU) 1892-1905, and was *cr Baron Knaresborough*, of Kirby Hall, co York (peerage of United Kingdom) 1905 (ext 1929).

THOMSON (UK) 1925, of Old Nunthorpe, co York

Always faithful

Sir MARK WILFRID HOME THOMSON, 3rd *Baronet*; *b* 29 Dec 1939; *s* his father, Sir IVO WILFRID HOME, 1991; *ed* —; Lieut RN (Fleet Air Arm) 1957-65: *m* 1976, Lady Jacqueline Rosemary Margot Rufus Isaacs, only da of 3rd Marquess of Reading, and has issue.

Arms – Ermine, a lion passant guardant or, on a chief azure two keys, wards inwards of the second. **Crest** – A lion rampant or, gorged with an antique crown gules, between two roses argent barbed, seeded, leaved and slipped proper. *Residence* – 42 Glebe Place, SW3 5JE.

SONS LIVING

ALBERT MARK HOME, *b* 3 Aug 1979. —— Jake Michael Alfred, *b* 1983. —— Luke Ivo Charles, *b* (twin) 1983.

DAUGHTER LIVING

Daisy Jacqueline Carol, *b* 1977.

WIDOW LIVING OF SECOND BARONET

VIOLA MABEL (*Viola, Lady Thomson*), da of Roland Dudley, of Linkenholt Manor, Andover, Hants, and formerly wife of Keith Home Thomson, MBE: *m* 1954, as his 2nd wife, Sir Ivo Wilfrid Home Thomson, 2nd Bt, who *d* 1991.

The 1st baronet, Sir Wilfrid Forbes Home Thomson (el son of Most Rev and Rt Hon William Thomson, DD, PC, Archbishop of York), was a partner in the firm of Beckett & Co, bankers, of York.

THOMSON (UK) 1929, of Glendarroch, co Midlothian

God will provide

Sir (FREDERICK DOUGLAS) DAVID THOMSON, 3rd *Baronet*; *b* 14 Feb 1940; *s* his father, Sir (JAMES) DOUGLAS WISHART, 1972; *ed* Eton, and Univ Coll, Oxford (BA); Chm Altrust European Index Investment Trust plc since 1990; Dir Britannia Steam Ship Insurance Assocn since 1965 and Chm since 1986; Dir Cairn Energy plc since 1971; Dir Danae Investment Trust plc since 1979; Chm Jove Investment Trust since 1983; Dir Kynoch Group plc since 1990; Dir Martin Currie Pacific Trust plc since 1985; Chm Ptermazda International Capital Trust plc since 1990; Dir Through Transport Mutual Insurance Association Ltd since 1973, Chm since 1983; Mem of the Queen's Body Guard for Scotland (Royal Company of Archers): *m* 1967 (*m diss* 1994), Caroline Anne, da of Maj Timothy Stuart Lewis, R Scots Greys (*see* V Daventry), and has issue.

Arms – Argent, a stag's head cabossed gules between the attires a shakefork sable, on a chief engrailed of the second, a galley, sail furled, oars in saltire between two towers triple towered of the field. **Crest** – A dexter hand couped proper holding a cross crosslet fitchée azure. *Residence* – Glenbrook House, Balerno, Midlothian EH14 7BQ.

SONS LIVING

SIMON DOUGLAS CHARLES, *b* 16 June 1969. —— Christopher Michael David, *b* 1970.

DAUGHTER LIVING

Sarah Anne Vanessa, *b* 1974.

BROTHER LIVING

William Andrew Charles (24 Hermitage Drive, Edinburgh), *b* 1948; *ed* Gordonstoun: *m* 1976, Cecilia Bernadette Gill, and has issue living, Douglas Charles, *b* 1978, —— William Frederick *b* 1981, —— Charles David, *b* 1988, —— Julia Margaret Clare, *b* 1983.

SISTERS LIVING

Susan Evelyn Margaret, *b* 1936: *m* 1961, Capt John Michael Cavenagh, GM, and has issue living, Thomas Douglas, *b* 1966, —— Sarah Louise, *b* 1964, —— Bettina Susan Margaret, *b* 1971. *Residence* – Withcote Hall, Oakham, Rutland. —— Vanessa Jean Wishart, *b* 1942: *m* 1964, Anthony Fenwick Denby Roberts, of Mossdale, Conistone with Kilnsey, Skipton, Yorks (*see* Roberts, Bt, *cr* 1909 colls). —— Jennifer Constance Anne, *b* 1945: *m* 1989, Howard Pighills, of Conistone Fold, Conistone with Kilnsey, Skipton, N Yorks.

WIDOW LIVING OF SECOND BARONET

BETTINA (*Bettina, Lady Thomson*) (Old Caberston, Walkerburn, Peebles-shire), da of late Lt-Cdr David William Shafto Douglas, RN: *m* 1935, Sir (James) Douglas Wishart Thomson, 2nd Bt, who *d* 1972.

Sir Frederick Charles Thomson, KC, 1st Bt (son of late James Wishart Thomson, shipowner, of Glenpark, Balerno, Midlothian), sat as MP for S Div of Aberdeen (*U*) 1918-35, and was a Junior Lord of the Treasury Feb to April 1923, Solicitor-Gen for Scotland April 1923 to Jan 1924, again a Junior Lord of the Treasury Nov 1924 to Jan 1928, Vice-Chamberlain of HM's Household Jan 1928 to June 1929, and Sept to Nov 1931, and Treasurer of HM's Household Nov 1931 to April 1935. The 2nd Bt, Sir (James) Douglas Wishart Thomson sat as MP for S Aberdeen (U) 1935-46, was PPS to Minister of Shipping 1940, and Chm Ben Line Steamers Ltd 1964-70.

THOROLD (E) 1642, of Marston, Lincolnshire
(Name pronounced "Thurrald")

The stag is not a slave

Sir ANTHONY HENRY THOROLD, OBE, DSC, 15th *Baronet*; *b* 7 Sept 1903; *s* his father, *Sir* JAMES ERNEST, 1965; Capt RN (ret); a JP for Kesteven, and a Member of Kesteven Co Council 1958-74 and Leader of Lincs Co Council 1973-81; DL for Lincs, and High Sheriff 1968; Chm of Lincoln Diocesan Trust and Board of Finance 1966-71 and of Grantham HMC 1963-74; Commodore Hong Kong 1953-55, and an ADC to HM 1955-56; 1939-45 War (DSC and Bar) as Staff Officer, Operations in Force "H" and Escort Group Commander in Western Approaches, Capt 1946; OBE (Mil) 1942: *m* 1939, Jocelyn Elaine Laura, who *d* 1993, el da of late Sir Clifford Edward Heathcote-Smith, KBE, CMG (*see* Smith-Marriott, Bt, colls), and has issue.

Arms – Sable: three goats salient argent. **Crest** – A roebuck passant argent, attired or.
Seat – Syston Old Hall, Grantham, Lincs.

SON LIVING

(ANTHONY) OLIVER (8 Richmond Crescent, N1 OLZ), *b* 15 April 1945; *ed* Winchester, and Lincoln Coll, Oxford; Bar Inner Temple 1971: *m* 1977, Genevra, yst da of John L. Richardson, of Broadshaw, West Calder, Midlothian, and has issue living, Henry Lowry, *b* 6 Aug 1981, — Lydia, *b* 1985.

DAUGHTERS LIVING

Celia, *b* 1940: *m* 1962, Capt Bryan David Salwey, RN, of 5 West Hill Rd, Wandsworth, SW18 1LH, and has issue living, Roger Penruddocke, *b* 1964, — David Guy, *b* 1966, — Nicholas Anthony, *b* 1969. —— Diana Jocelyn (21 Gerrard Rd, N1 8AY), *b* 1942; MA, Edinburgh, and London; Senior Lecturer, Univ of Westminster.

SISTERS LIVING

Dorothy Aline, *b* 1908. *Residence* – 24 Bowling Green Court, Hospital Rd, Moreton-in-Marsh, Glos GL56 OBX. —— Mary Jocelyn (Sawmill Close, Sharperton, Morpeth, Northumberland), *b* 1914: *m* 1935, as his 2nd wife, Walter Thomas Meyrick, who *d* 1953 (*see* Meyrick, Bt, colls).

COLLATERAL BRANCHES LIVING

Issue of late Lt-Col Montague Thorold, yr son of 14th baronet, *b* 1906, *d* 1974: *m* 1946, Helen Moye (The Old Rectory, Stainby, Grantham, Lincs NG33 5QX), da of late Capt Barnard Stone:—
John Richard (52 Danemere St, SW15), *b* 1947; *ed* Kelly Coll, Tavistock; 2nd Lt 9/12th R Lancers; ARICS, land agent: *m* 1991, Elizabeth A., da of Lt-Col A. J. E. Cruickshank, of Coxbridge, Som, and has issue living, Guy, *b* 1992, — Alexandra, *b* (twin) 1992. —— (Rosemary) Julia (203A Castelnau, Barnes, SW13), *b* 1950.

Grandchildren of late Reginald Henry Thorold, 2nd son of late Rev Henry Baugh Thorold, el son of late Rev George Thorold, 2nd son of 9th baronet:—
Issue of late Reginald Charles Thorold, *b* 1871, *d* 1956: *m* 1906, Elizabeth McMaster, who *d* 1965, da of Nicolas Moncrieff Howitt, of Gawonga, Victoria:—
Reginald Moncrieff (21 River Rd, Camden, NSW 2570), *b* 1914: *m* 1942, Sheila Frances, who *d* 1968, da of Hugh Sinclair Mackay, of Tasmania, and has issue living, Reginald David, *b* 1945, — Elizabeth Helen, *b* 1948. —— Katharine Florence, *b* 1907. —— Elizabeth, *b* 1909. —— Bertha Edith, *b* 1911: *m* 1941, Christo Albertyn Smith, of Falmouth, Tasmania, and has issue living, Christopher John, *b* 1945, — Lillemor Elizabeth, *b* 1942. —— Margaret, *b* 1918. *Residence* – Falmouth, Tasmania.

Grandsons of late Reginald Charles Thorold (ante):—
Issue of late John Charles Nicolas Thorold, *b* 1916, *d* 1961: *m* 1948, Barbara Nicolson Arthur (Brambletye, Conara 7211, Tasmania), da of late John Nicolson Archer, of Conara, Tasmania:—
Barry John Archer, *b* 1949: *m* 1975, Joanna, only da of Keith Ian Benson, of Launceston, Tasmania, and has issue living, John Charles Nicholas, *b* 1988, — Lydia Jane, *b* 1979, — Sabina Lucy, *b* 1980, — Emma Elizabeth, *b* 1985. —— Simon Charles, *b* 1953, *d* 1970. —— Marcus Jonathan, *b* 1958.

Grandchildren of late Rev Algernon Herbert Thorold (infra):—
Issue of late Rev Michael Herbert Thorold, *b* 1904, *d* 1956: *m* 1931, Dorothy (180a Gloucester Pl, NW1), da of late George Patrick Henfrey, of The Dower House, Beckenham, Kent:—
Anthony Patrick de Buckenhold (c/o Barclays Bank, Marble Arch, W1; *Club* – Junior Army and Navy), *b* 1938; *ed* Brighton Coll, and at Sidney Sussex Coll, Camb; Maj RCT: *m* 1962, Jane Antoinette, only da of William Francis Paul Corbould of Purley, Surrey, and has issue living, Emma Jane, *b* 1963: *m* 1988, Andrew Michael Tomalin, of 7 Vale Rd North, Surbiton,

Surrey, elder son of David A. Tomalin, of Crowborough, Sussex, and has issue living, Victoria Alice *b* 1989, — Antonia Cecilia, *b* 1966. —— Ia Cecilia, *b* 1935; BA: *m* 1966, John Hamish St John McIlwaine, of 10 Cromwell Close, E Finchley, N2, and has issue living, Katherine Anne, *b* 1969.

Grandsons of late Rev Michael Herbert Thorold (ante):—
  Issue of late Michael Bernard Thorold, *b* 1942, *d* 1979: *m* 1st, 1967 (*m diss* 1971), Carolyn Alice, da of Martin James Pollock *see* Pollock, Bt, colls; 2ndly, 1971, Mary Nihan (20 Silsoe House, Park Village East, NW1 4AS), da of James Mackenzie-Mair, of Beachborough Park East, Folkestone:—
(By 1st *m*) Rupert Michael James de Buckenhold, *b* 1969. —— (By 2nd *m*) Crispin Crispian James Leofric, *b* 1973.

Grandchildren of late Rev Algernon Charles Edward Thorold, el son of Charles Thorold, 3rd son of Rev George Thorold, 2nd son of 9th baronet:—
  Issue of late Rev Algernon Herbert Thorold, *b* 1872, *d* 1931: *m* 1901, Inez Theodora, who *d* 1959, da of late Alfred Beer:—
Mary *b* 1908. *Residence* – 5 Upton House, Fore St, Hertford.
  Issue of late Arthur Charles Campbell Thorold, *b* 1873, *d* 1939: *m* 1st, 1913, Kathleen May, who *d* 1922, only da of late Frederick Jeffery; 2ndly, 1925, Jessie Isobel Marjory, who *d* 1954, da of late Francis Wellington Were, of Heidelberg, Melbourne, Australia:—
(By 1st *m*) Patrick Hayford (7 Broadbeach Blvd, Broadbeach 4218, Qld), *b* 1916: *m* 1st, 1940 (*m diss* 1949), Dorrit Wilhelmina, da of J. H. Charles, of 270 Burke Rd, Glen Iris, Melbourne, Australia; 2ndly, 1949, Naureen Margaret, only da of late William George Mason, of Armadale, Melbourne, and has issue living, (by 1st *m*) Ruth Patricia, *b* 1942: *m* 1966, Roger MacLeod Dunn, of 109 Wellington St, Kew, Melbourne, Vic, Aust, and has issue living, Lachlan Thorold MacLeod *b* 1968, Tarquin Charles MacLeod *b* 1972, Phoebe Rebecca *b* 1969, — (by 2nd *m*) Joan Michele, *b* 1952: *m* 1974, Andrew Howard Knox Wilson, of 12 Seymour Av, Armadale 3143, Vic, Aust, and has issue living, Benjamin Thorold Knox *b* 1983, Nicholas Andrew Jeffery *b* 1985, Patrick Howard Knox *b* 1989.
  Issue of late Rev Ernest Hayford Thorold, CB, CBE, DD (Chap-Gen to Forces 1931-9, and Chap to HM 1935-40), *b* 1879, *d* 1940: *m* 1913, Dorothy Frances, who *d* 1969, da of Edward Herbert, of Ludford House, Duppas Hill, Croydon:—
Rev John Robert Hayford, *b* 1916; *ed* Westminster, and at King's Coll, Camb (BA 1943, MA 1945); sometime Sub-Lieut (Sp) RNVR, and an Assist Master at Eton; is Priest of the Oratory of the Good Shepherd, and co-patron of five livings. *Residence* – St Deiniol's Library, Hawarden, Chester CH5 3DF. —— *Rev* Henry Croyland, *b* 1921; *ed* Eton, and at Ch Ch, Oxford; FSA; sometime Chap RN, and Chap to Bishop of Brechin; House Master and Chap at Lancing Coll 1949-68 and co-patron of five livings; author of *Shell Guide to Derbyshire*, *Shell Guide to Staffordshire*, *Shell Guide to County Durham*, *Shell Guide to Nottinghamshire* and joint-author of *Shell Guide to Lincolnshire*, also author of *Collins Guide to Cathedrals, Abbeys and Priories of England and Wales*, *Lincolnshire Churches Revisited* (with foreword by HRH The Prince of Wales), and *Collins Guide to the Ruined Abbeys of England, Wales and Scotland*. *Residence* – Marston Hall, Grantham.

Granddaughters of late Rev John Leofric de Buckenhold Thorold (infra):—
  Issue of late George Preston Thorold, *b* 1896, *d* 1964: *m* 1940, Madeleine Beatrice, who *d* 1988, da of A. C. De Carteret:—
Laelia Karslake, *b* 1942: *m* 1964, Julian Rodney Hartnoll, of 8 Etherden Rd, W12, and has issue living, Emma de Carteret, *b* 1965, — Jenny Moulton, *b* 1967.
  Issue of late Edward Leofric Thorold, *b* 1898, *d* 1965: *m* 1st, 1928 (*m diss* 1942), Phyllis Frances, da of A. C. Hills; 2ndly, 1942, Agnes Phyllis (St Agnes Balcombe, Sussex), da of late A. H. Johnson:—
(By 1st *m*) Brenda Frances, *b* 1929: *m* 1947, R. Hillier, of Flat 10, 19 Holland Park, W11, and has issue living, Anthony Edward, *b* 1949, — Nicholas Leofric, *b* 1952. —— (By 2nd *m*) Judith Rose, *b* 1947: *m* 1969, Michael Thorold-Palmer, of Walkleigh House, South Holmwood, Dorking, Surrey, and has issue living, Edward James, *b* 1972, — Alexandra Louise, *b* 1974.

Grandsons of late Cdr Hubert Gould William Thorold, RN, 2nd son of late Rev William Thorold, 6th son of Rev George Thorold, 2nd son of 9th baronet:—
  Issue of late Sir Guy Frederick Thorold, KCMG, *b* 1898, *d* 1970: *m* 1928, Mary Wilder, who *d* 1963, da of late Henry Mildmay Husey:—
Peter Guy Henry (25 Stanley Crescent, W11 2NA), *b* 1930; *ed* Eton, and New Coll, Oxford: *m* 1st, 1954 (*m diss* 1963), Merilyn Mary, da of Lt-Col Sir John Francis Roskell Reynolds, MBE, 2nd Bt; 2ndly, 1964, Anne, yr da of Robert Evelyn Herbert Fender, AFC, of The Manor House, Withington, Glos, and has issue living, (by 1st *m*) Marcus Guy Francis, *b* 1955: *m* 1992, Georgina C., elder da of Peter Armitage, of Tarporley, Cheshire, — Daniel Edward, *b* 1960, — Caroline Emelia, *b* 1956, — (by 2nd *m*) Nicola Anne, *b* 1965. —— Julian Hubert, *b* 1933; *ed* Eton, and New Coll, Oxford.

Grandson of late Rev William Thorold, 6th son of late Rev George Thorold (ante):—
  Issue of late Rev John Leofric de Buckenhold Thorold, *b* 1864, *d* 1940: *m* 1895, Jane Preston, who *d* 1956, da of late Preston Karslake, of White Knights, Reading:—
Charles Aubrey (99 Strawberry Vale, Twickenham, Middx), *b* 1906; *ed* Marlborough and Trin Coll, Oxford (MA, DSc): *m* 1949, Katharine Mary, da of late Rt Rev Algernon Augustus Markham, Bishop of Grantham, and has issue living, Philippa Markham, *b* 1951: *m* 1981, Nicholas Killin, MBA, of 50 Samdon St, Hamilton, NSW 2303, Australia, and has issue living, Thomas William *b* 1983, Samuel Charles *b* 1989, Emily Katharine *b* 1991, — Joanna Mary, *b* 1955; MA (Oxon), MA (Lond): *m* 1977, Paul Clifford, MA, of 14 Lakeside, Oxford, and has issue living, Sarah Katharine *b* 1981, Elizabeth Rose *b* 1984.

Grandchildren of late Algar Labouchere Thorold, son of Rt Rev Anthony Wilson Thorold DD, son of Rev Edward Thorold, 4th son of 9th baronet:—
  Issue of late Francis John Anselm Thorold, *b* 1901, *d* 1958: *m* 1932, Ann Amelia, who *d* 1979, da of late William Somers, of Wick, Somerset:—
John Christopher, *b* 1940: *m* 1966, Elizabeth Ann, da of Noe John Colborne, of Chippenham, and has issue living, Justin Algar *b* 1967. —— Catherine Ann, *b* 1933: *m* 1960 (*m diss* 1965), John Blaker (now 3rd Bt). *Residence* – Woodcote Farm, Nutley, nr Uckfield, Sussex.

Grandson of late Michael Richard Thorold, son of late Michael Wynne Thorold, son of late Rev Michael Thorold, son of late Samuel Thorold (*b* 1748), 2nd son of 8th baronet:—
  Issue of late Richard Gillbee Thorold, *b* 1859, *d* 1940: *m* 1900, Ellen Irene, who *d* 1958, da of late Edward Hogg, of The Lodge, Pinner:—
(Edward) Lionel, *b* 1905. *Residence* – Potterspury Lodge School, Towcester, Northants NN12 7LL.

The first proved ancestor of this family, Sir Richard Thorold of Selby, co York, acquired the Manor of Marston, co Lincoln by *m* (temp Edward III) to Joan, da and heir of Robert de Hough by his wife Maud da and heir of Michael de Marston. William Thorold (*d* 1569), 5th in descent from Sir Richard, purchased Cranwell, co Lincoln (demolished 1815, estates, requisitioned 1916, and sold to RAF 1920) and his son, Sir Anthony (*d* 1594) purchased Syston, Lincs. His grandson, Sir William, 1st Bt, was knighted by James I when aged 16 years. He was a Royalist and paid £4,460 to the sequestrators of his estate. Sir John Thorold, 9th Bt, built the new house of Syston 1766/75 which was enlarged by his son Sir John Hayford Thorold, 10th Bt, the book collector (*d* 1815). This house was demolished 1934 when Syston Old Hall became the seat of the Baronets. Marston Hall, the principal seat of Baronets until the 18th century, is still in the possession of this family. Three other Baronetcies of Hough-on-the-Hill (*cr* 1644), of Harmston (*cr* 1709), and of Harmston (*cr* 1740), have been conferred on this family, all of which have become extinct.

THROCKMORTON (E) 1642, of Coughton, Warwickshire

Courage is the only nobility

Sir ANTHONY JOHN BENEDICT THROCKMORTON, 12th *Baronet*; *b* 9 Feb 1916; *s* his cousin, *Sir* ROBERT GEORGE MAXWELL, 1989; *ed* Beaumont: *m* 1972, Violet Virginia, da of late Anders William Anderson.

Arms – Gules, on a chevron argent three bars gemelles sable. **Crest** – A falcon rising proper, belled and jessed or (ancient) an elephant's head. **First Motto** – Virtus sola nobilitas (*Virtue alone brings nobility*) **Second Motto** – Moribus antiquis (*With ancient manners*).
Residence – 2006 Oakes, Everett, Washington 98201, USA.

SISTER LIVING OF ELEVENTH BARONET

Ann Barbara (Spiney House, Coughton, Alcester, Warwicks), *b* 1911: *m* 1939, Ludwig Freiherr von Twickel, who *d* 1945, and has issue living, *Freiherr* Johann (John) Robert (Bethmannstrasse 7, Frankfurt/M, Germany), *b* 1940: *m* 1st, 1968 (*m diss* 1993), HSH Princess Victoria Benigna Ina Marie Cecile Friederike Luise Helene, da of HSH Prince Karl Peter Franz Andreas Biron von Curland (*see* ROYAL FAMILY); 2ndly, 1993, HSH Princess Charlotte Alexandra Marie Clothilde, da of HSH Prince Alexander Georg Maria Josef Ignatius of Croy, and formerly wife of HSH Kraft Alexander Ernst Ludwig Georg Emich, 9th Prince of Hohenlohe-Langenburg (*see* ROYAL FAMILY), and has issue living (by 1st *m*), *Freiherr* Nikolaus Maximilian *b* 1969, *Freiherr* Tassilo *b* 1976, — *Freiherr* Alexander Rudolf Ferdinand Nikolaus Zdenko (123 Warwick Way, SW1V 4HS; Tidmington Corner, Shipston-on-Stour, Warwicks CV36 5LR) *b* 1941; Lt-Col 9th/ 12th R Lancers: *m* 1973, Neville Christine, da of Garth Priestman, and has issue living, *Freiin* Angela Margaret Walburga Faith Zdenka *b* 1975; *ed* Heathfield, *Freiin* Matilda Victoria Louise Ann Zdenka *b* 1976; *ed* North Foreland Lodge.

WIDOW LIVING OF ELEVENTH BARONET

Lady ISABEL VIOLET KATHLEEN (*Lady Isabel Throckmorton*), da of 9th Duke of Rutland, and formerly wife of late Gp Capt Thomas Loel Evelyn Bulkeley Guinness, OBE: *m* 1953, as his 2nd wife, Sir Robert George Maxwell Throckmorton, 11th Bt, who *d* 1989. *Residence* – Coughton Court, Alcester, Warwickshire B49 5JA.
This baronet is descended, according to Dugdale, from John de Throckmorton, Lord of the Manor of Throckmorton *temp* Henry I. From him was descended Sir John Throckmorton, Knt, Under-Treasurer of England in the reign of Henry VI. The 1st baronet, Sir Robert Throckmorton, had his estates sequestered in the civil wars, and his house at Coughton was plundered and used as a garrison by the Parliamentary forces. The 6th baronet, Sir George Throckmorton, assumed the name of Courtenay in lieu of his patronymic in 1792, on inheriting through his mother the Courtenay estates of Molland, Devon, but he *dsp* 1826.

DOUGHTY-TICHBORNE (E) 1621, of Tichborne, Hampshire (Extinct 1968)

Sir ANTHONY JOSEPH HENRY DOUGHTY DOUGHTY-TICHBORNE, 14th and last *Baronet*.

DAUGHTERS LIVING OF FOURTEENTH BARONET

Anne Denise, *b* 1938: *m* 1959, Jonkheer John Loudon, of 26 Chelsea Sq, SW3, and has issue living, Anthony James Hugo, *b* 1966, — Arabella Miranda, *b* 1961: *m* 1994, Baron Carl-Gustaf Einar Samuel Åkerhielm, — Lisa Marie, *b* 1963: *m* 1992, Nicholas Hiley, son of Cmdr Ian Hiley. ——— Miranda Frances, *b* 1941: *m* 1961, Christopher Stephen Motley, of Chilton Grove, Atcham, nr Shrewsbury (*see* E Ranfurly, colls, 1980 Edn), and has issue living, William Michael, *b* 1962, — Mark Charles, *b* 1966, — Samantha Antonia Clare *b* 1964, — Abigail Anne Louise, *b* 1970, — Pandora Mary Denise, *b* 1971, — Denise Mary Magdalene, *b* 1949: *m* 1986, Michael Hendrie, of Down Farmhouse, Kilmeston, Hants, only son of John Hendrie, of Downs Hollow, Chipping Norton, Oxfordshire, and has issue living, Harry John, *b* 1988.

EVANS-TIPPING (UK) 1913, of Oaklands Park, Awre, co Gloucester

Sir DAVID GWYNNE EVANS-TIPPING, 5th *Baronet*; *b* 25 Nov 1943; *s* his father, *Sir* FRANCIS LORING GWYNNE-EVANS, 1993; *ed* Trin Coll, Dublin (B Agric Sci).
Residence – 11 rue Angelique-Verien, Neuilly-sur-Seine, France.

BROTHER LIVING

CHRISTOPHER EVAN EVANS-TIPPING (Symonds Farmhouse, Childrey, Wantage, Oxon OX12 9UA), *b* 1946: *m* 1974, Fenella Catherine, 2nd da of Cdr Edwin Allen Morrison, OBE, DL, of The Bury House, Odiham, Hants, and has issue living, Guy Edward Francis, *b* 1978, — Amy Clare, *b* 1976.

HALF-BROTHER AND ADOPTIVE HALF-BROTHER LIVING

Francis Tristan GWYNNE-EVANS, *b* 1960. ——— Teo Leslie GWYNNE-EVANS (adopted), *b* 1962.

SISTER LIVING

Carolyn Eve, *b* 1947: *m* 1984, Eamon Peter Toner, and has issue living, Edward Evan, *b* 1987, — Evelyn Frances, *b* 1985.

HALF-SISTERS LIVING

Melody Louise Bernadette GWYNNE-EVANS, *b* 1958. ——— Clelia Marie GWYNNE-EVANS, *b* 1965. ——— Soraya Charlotte GWYNNE-EVANS, *b* 1967.

DAUGHTERS LIVING OF THIRD BARONET (*By 1st marriage to Elspeth, da of Rt Hon Sir Godfrey Patison Collins KBE, CMG, MP*)

Sylvia Ada, *b* 1938: *m* 1967, Duncan Godfrey Stableford Smith, of 1 Almond Way, Annaty Bank, Tokai, Cape Town, S Africa, yst son of Clifford Edgar Smith, of Lynedoch, Cape Province, S Africa, and has issue living, Andrew Duncan, *b* 1973, — Philippa Silvia, *b* 1976. ——— Gwenllian Mary Hope, *b* 1939: *m* 1963, Robert Chumley Bryce Neill, of 10 Cecil Av, Melrose, Johannesburg, S Africa, elder son of R. C. Neill, of 19 Adlam Rd, Durban, S Africa, and has issue living, Robert Ian Grant, *b* 1965, — Angela Elspeth, *b* 1970, — Belinda Gwen, *b* 1973.

HALF-GREAT UNCLE LIVING (*Son of 1st baronet*)

John (c/o Barclays Bank DCO, PO Box 1004, Johannesburg, S Africa), *b* 1910.

MOTHER LIVING

Elisabeth Fforde, da of J. Fforde-Tipping, of Bellurgan Park, Dundalk, Ireland: *m* 1937 (*m diss* 1958), as his 1st wife, Sir Francis Loring Gwynne-Evans, 4th Bt, who *d* 1993.

WIDOWS LIVING OF THIRD AND FOURTH BARONETS

MONICA (*Monica, Lady Gwynne-Evans*), da of Douglas Clinch, of Durban, S Africa, and formerly wife of — Dalrymple: *m* 1946, as his 2nd wife, Sir Ian William Gwynne-Evans, 3rd Bt, who *d* 1985. *Residence* – 57 Eastwood Rd, Dunkeld, Johannesburg, S Africa.
GLORIA MARIE (*Lady Gwynne-Evans*), da of Thomas Reynolds: *m* 1958, as his 2nd wife, Sir Francis Loring Gwynne-Evans, 4th Bt, who *d* 1993. *Residence* – Chantry, Aveton Gifford, nr Kingsbridge, S Devon TQ7 4EH.

The 1st baronet, Sir William Gwynne-Evans (only son of Evan Evans, of Wain, Cardiganshire, by Mary Gwynne, widow of Charles Gwynne Pryse, of Gogerddan, Cardiganshire), received Royal Licence 1913 to continue to use the additional surname of Gwynne. Sir Evan Gwynne Gwynne-Evans, 2nd baronet, was High Sheriff of Gloucestershire 1943. Sir Francis Loring Gwynne-Evans, 4th baronet, assumed by deed poll 1943 the names of Francis Loring Gwynne Evans-Tipping in lieu of those of Francis Loring Gwynne-Evans and reverted to his patronymic by deed poll 1958. He was a professional singer under the name of Francis Loring.

TOLLEMACHE (GB) 1793, of Hanby Hall, co Lincoln

CONFIDO·CONQVIESCO

I trust and am content

Sir LYONEL HUMPHRY JOHN TOLLEMACHE, 7th *Baronet*; *b* 10 July 1931; *s* his father, Maj-Gen Sir HUMHRY THOMAS, CB, CBE, DL, 1990; *ed* Uppingham, and RAC Cirencester; Maj (ret) Coldm Gds; FRICS; JP and DL of Leics, High Sheriff 1978-79, and CC since 1985: *m* 1960, Mary Joscelyne, el da of Col William Henry Whitbread, TD, of Warren Mere, Godalming, and has issue.

Arms – Argent, a fret sable (a label of three points for difference). **Crest** – A horse's head erased gules, between two wings or pelletée (differenced as the arms).
Residence – Buckminster Park, Grantham NG33 5RU.

SONS LIVING

LYONEL THOMAS, *b* 23 Jan 1963; *ed* Stanbridge Earls. ——— Richard John, *b* 1966; *ed* Uppingham.

DAUGHTERS LIVING

Katheryne Mary, *b* 1960. ——— Henrietta Joscelyne, *b* 1970: *m* 1993, Capt David J. Chubb, The Light Dragoons, son of Cmdr Edwin Chubb, of Pennaton, S Brent, Devon.

BROTHER LIVING

Robert Hugh Thomas, *b* 1937; *ed* Uppingham, and Magdalene Coll, Camb (BA): *m* 1962, Lorraine Frances Lougheed, el da of Brig Frederick Joshua Allen, OBE, of Hambledon Cottage, Lower Bourne, Surrey, and has issue living, William Benjamin, *b* 1966; *ed* City of London Sch, and Univ Coll, London, — Rosa Frances Laila, *b* 1970. *Residence* – 27 Aubert Park, N5 1TP.

SISTERS LIVING

Priscilla Joan, *b* 1927: *m* 1952, John Chetwynd Gillett, of Gulworthy Farm, Tavistock, Devon, son of Col Sir (William) Alan Gillett, TD, DL (V Chetwynd, colls), and has issue living, Robert John Chetwynd (Rock Park, Gulworthy Farm, Tavistock, Devon), *b* 1954: *m* 1977, Clara Elizabeth, da of Gordon William Heath, PhD, of Paignton, Devon, and has issue living, Ella Clare *b* 1980, Sophie Louise *b* 1982, — Andrew William Tollemache (72 Heavitree Rd, Exeter, Devon), *b* 1958: *m* 1979, Rosemary McMahon, and has issue living, David *b* 1983, Edward *b* 1989, Esther *b* 1980, — (Diana) Mary, *b* 1953: *m* 1983, Hugh Davies, of Cherry Brook House, Tavistock, Devon, and has issue living, Peter *b* 1987, Thomas *b* (twin)1987, — Sara Jane, *b* 1962: *m* 1989, Michael Woolley, of Roundabarrow Farm, St Anne's Chapel, Cornwall, and has issue living, Daniel *b* 1991, Alice *b* 1990. —— Diana Margaret, *b* 1929: *m* 1953, Daniel Johannes Haak, of Uplands Stud, Scotland Farm, Hawkley, Liss, Hants GU33 6NH, and has issue living, Jonathan Daniel, *b* 1955: *m* 1978, Annabella Edith, da of John Wickins, of Eastergate, Chichester, and has issue living, Jochen Daniel *b* 1981, Anoushka Lara *b* 1979, Naomi Tara *b* 1985, — Roderick Johannes, *b* 1957: *m* 1980, Nicola Jane, da of Michael Cameron, MD, FRCS, FRCOG, and has issue living, Sam Michael *b* 1984, Toby Daniel *b* (twin) 1984, Charlie *b* 1985, Poppy Anna *b* 1990, — Venetia Priscilla, *b* 1959: *m* 1988, Phillip Robinson, of Southampton, and has issue living, Tristan Joshua *b* 1994, — Felicity Nora, *b* 1961: *m* 1987, Colin Rodger, of Petersfield, and has issue living, Megan Diana *b* 1988, Hannah Margaret *b* 1990, Tamsin Janna *b* 1994.

COLLATERAL BRANCHES LIVING

(*See* Cs Dysart, colls).

This baronetcy was granted to William Manners, subsequently Lord Huntingtower, el son of Louisa, Countess of Dysart, who assumed by Roy Licence the surname and arms of Talmash 1821. On his death in 1833, he was succeeded by his el son, Lionel William John Tollemache, Lord Huntingtower, who succeeded his grandmother as 8th Earl of Dysart in 1840, the baronetcy thus becoming merged in the Earldom. In 1935, on the death of the 9th Earl of Dysart, the baronetcy was released and passed to his kinsman, Sir Lyonel Felix Carteret Eugene Tollemache, who succeeded as 4th baronet.

LUCAS-TOOTH (UK) 1906, of Queen's Gate, Royal Borough of Kensington and Kameruka, co Auckland, State of New South Wales, Commonwealth of Australia (Extinct 1918)

Sir ARCHIBALD LEONARD LUCAS LUCAS-TOOTH, 2nd and last *Baronet*; Major Hon Artillery Co; *d* on active ser 1918.

DAUGHTER LIVING OF SECOND BARONET

Rosemarie Helen, *b* 1916: *m* 1st, 1936, Capt Algernon Robert Augustus Dorrien-Smith, 15th/19th King's Roy Hussars, who was *ka* 1940; 2ndly, 1945, Major Bertram William Jepson Turner, MC, Rifle Brig.

LUCAS-TOOTH (UK) 1920, of Bught, Inverness

Sir (HUGH) JOHN LUCAS-TOOTH, 2nd *Baronet*; *b* 20 Aug 1932; *s* his father, *Sir* HUGH VERE HUNTLY DUFF MUNRO-LUCAS-TOOTH, 1985; *ed* Eton, and Balliol Coll, Oxford; late Lt Scots Guards: *m* 1955, Hon Caroline Poole, eldest da of 1st Baron Poole, CBE, TD, PC, and has issue.

Arms – Quarterly, 1st and 4th gules, a demi-gryphon segreant between three feathers argent; 2nd and 3rd azure, on a bend between in chief two crescents and in base an estoile argent, three vine leaves proper. **Crests** – 1st, a gryphon segreant gules, semée of mullets, and holding in the sinister claw a feather argent; 2nd, a demi-dragon azure, holding in the paws a vine branch fructed and leaved proper.
Residences – Parsonage Farm, East Hagbourne, Didcot, Oxon OX11 9LN; 41 Lancaster Road, W14 1QJ.

Perseverantia palmam obtinebit

Perseverance will obtain the palm

DAUGHTERS LIVING

(Caroline) Maria, *b* 1956: *m* 1980, William John Hibbert, of 41 Lancaster Rd, W11, yr son of Sir Reginald Alfred Hibbert, GCMG, and has issue living, Cosima Mary, *b* 1984, — Clover Frances, *b* 1988. —— (Lucinda) Kate, *b* 1958: *m* 1980, David Mark Ackroyd, son of L. M. Ackroyd, and has issue living, Frederick William, *b* 1981, — Nancy Caroline *b* 1983, — Beatrice Alice Violet, *b* 1988. —— (Belinda) Alice, *b* 1966: *m* 1990, Aubrey Duarte Simpson-Orlebar, elder son of Michael Keith Orlebar Simpson-Orlebar, CMG, of The British Embassy, Mexico.

SISTERS LIVING

Laetitia Helen (*Lady Oppenheimer*), *b* 1926; BPhil, MA, DD: *m* 1947, Sir Michael Bernard Grenville Oppenheimer, 3rd Bt, of L'Aiguillon, Rue des Cotils, Grouville, Jersey, CI. —— Jennifer Mary, *b* 1929: *m* 1949, Maj John Desmond Henderson, Scots Guards, and has issue living, Richard, *b* 1951, — Alexander, *b* 1971, — Patricia, *b* 1950. *Residence* – Brimpton Lodge, Brimpton, Reading, Berks.

AUNT LIVING *(Sister of 1st baronet)*

Beatrice Helen Fitzhardinge, *b* 1908: *m* 1941, Lyndall Fownes Urwick, OBE, MC, of 83 Kenneth St, Longueville, N S Wales, son of late Sir Henry Urwick.

COLLATERAL BRANCH LIVING *(In special remainder)*

Issue of late Com Selwyn John Power WARRAND, RN, brother of 1st baronet, *b* 1904, *ka* 1941: *m* 1933, Frena Lingen (who *m* 2ndly, 1947, Henry Richard Charles Humphries), da of late Everard Crace, of Canberra, Aust:—

JAMES LINGEN, *b* 6 Oct 1936: *m* 1960, Juliet Rose, yr da of late T.A. Pearn, of Plymouth, Devon, and has issue living, Patrick Duncan, *b* 18 March 1962: *m* 1989, Elizabeth Margaret, yst da of Bernard Bowen, of Perth, Western Australia, — Edward Jonathon, *b* 1968: *m* 1993, Lisa Ann, eldest da of Graham Wagg, of Kentlyn, NSW, Australia, — Anna-Claire, *b* 1964: *m* 1991, Christopher George Coore, yst son of George Coore, of Canberra, ACT, and has issue living, George Thomas *b* 1993. *Residence* – Ryefields, Cobbity, NSW 2570. —— Joanna Christine, *b* 1938.

Sir Hugh Vere Huntly Duff Lucas-Tooth, 1st Bt, was the grandson of Sir Robert Lucas Lucas-Tooth, 1st Bt (*cr* 1906, ext), whose surname and arms he assumed by Roy licence 1920, and whose three sons had been killed during 1914-18 War, leaving no male issue. In default of heirs male of the body of the grantee this Baronetcy has special remainder to the other heirs male of the body of his mother, Beatrice Maude, da of 1st baronet (*cr* 1906). In 1965 Sir Hugh assumed for himself only the additional surname of Munro.

TOUCHE (UK) 1920, of Westcott, co Surrey

Be Watchful

Sir ANTHONY GEORGE TOUCHE, FCA, 3rd *Baronet*; *b* 31 Jan 1927; *s* his uncle, Sir NORMAN GEORGE, 1977; *ed* Eton; Chm Touche, Remnant and Co 1971-81; Dep Chm Nat Westminster Bank plc 1977-87 and a Dir of other financial cos: *m* 1961, Hester Christina, el da of Dr August Friedrich Werner Pleuger, of Linden Lodge, Green Rd, Birchington, Kent, and has issue.

Arms – Argent, a lion salient between a fleur-de-lis in the sinister chief and a like fleur-de-lis in the dexter base vert. **Crest** – Two fleur-de-lis gules, resting thereon a mullet of six points or.
Residence – Stane House, Ockley, Dorking, Surrey, RH5 5PQ.

SONS LIVING

WILLIAM GEORGE, *b* 26 June 1962: *m* 1987, Elizabeth Louise, yst da of Allen Bridges, of Lyford Cay, Nassau, Bahamas, and has issue living, Harry George, *b* 3 June 1992, — James Alexander, *b* 1994. —— Peter Francis, *b* 1968.

DAUGHTER LIVING

Helen Mary, *b* 1966.

SISTER LIVING

Isabel Amy, *b* 1930: *m* 1962, David Murray Arthur Reid, of The Folly, Tetbury, Glos.

DAUGHTERS LIVING OF SECOND BARONET

Penelope Maitland, *b* 1930; BSc Edinburgh 1952: *m* 1954, Joseph Edwin Mason, PhD, of Crabtree Meadow, Hope, Sheffield, and has issue living, Donald George, *b* 1955, — Brian Richard, *b* 1960, — Barbara Jane, *b* 1956. —— Brenda Margaret, *b* 1932; *ed* Newnham Coll, Camb (BA): *m* 1956 (*m diss* 19—), Ronald Edward Artus, MA, and has issue living, Colin Edward, *b* 1957, — Alan Norman, *b* 1959, — Philip Matthew, *b* 1964, — Lucy Katharine, *b* 1961.

UNCLE LIVING *(Son of 1st baronet)*

George Lawrence Capel, *b* 1903; *ed* Marlborough, and at Univ Coll, Oxford (Scholar, BA 1925); a Chartered Accountant: *m* 1st, 1928, Ursula Grace D'Oyly, who *d* 1968, da of Henry D'Oyly Bernard (D Oyly, Bt); 2ndly, 1969, Elizabeth, da of Henry Kunzer. *Residence* – Holmbush House, Ashington, Sussex.

COLLATERAL BRANCH LIVING

Issue of late Rt Hon Sir Gordon Cosmo Touche, 3rd son of 1st baronet (*b* 1895, *d* 1972), who was *cr* a baronet 1962 (see that title).

The 1st baronet, Sir George Alexander Touche (son of Anthony Murray Touche, banker, of Inverleithfield, Edinburgh), was Senior Partner in the firm of George A. Touche & Co, chartered accountants, and a Lieut for City of London (Sheriff 1915-16, and an Alderman 1915-21), and sat as MP for N Div of Islington (C) 1910-18.

TOUCHE (UK) 1962, of Dorking, co Surrey

Sir RODNEY GORDON TOUCHE, 2nd *Baronet*; *b* 5 Dec 1928; *s* his father, *Rt Hon Sir* GORDON COSMO, 1972; *ed* Marlborough, and Univ Coll Oxford: *m* 1955, Ouida Ann, el da of late Frederick Gerald MacLellan, of Moncton, New Brunswick, Canada, and has issue.

Arms – Vert, a lion rampant argent holding between the forepaws a portcullis chained or, between two fleurs-de-lis, one in sinister chief, the other in dexter base argent. **Crest** – Between two fleurs-de-lis or, a Dorking cock proper.
Residence – 2403 Westmount Pl, 1100 8th Av SW, Calgary, Alberta, T2P 3T9, Canada.

SON LIVING

ERIC MACLELLAN, *b* 22 Feb 1960: *m* 1990, Leanne Marie, da of Arthur Stringer, of Pontiex, Saskatchewan, Canada, and has issue living, Braden Stringer, *b* 1990, — Danielle Erica, *b* 1992.

DAUGHTERS LIVING

Amanda Ann *b* 1956: *m* 1978, Peter M. Bowler, and has issue living, Samuel McNamara, *b* 1987, — Sarah Jane, *b* 1983, — Anne MacLellan, *b* 1985. —— Susan Ruth, *b* 1957: *m* 1st, 1983, Pasquale Tartaglia; 2ndly, 1992, Trevor B. Arends, son of Kaj Arends, of USA, and has issue living, (by 1st *m*) Cosmo Alexander Touche, *b* 1990, — (by 2nd *m*), Sebastian Valdimar Touche, *b* 1992, — Islah Valerie Touche, *b* 1993. —— Karen Marie, *b* 1961: *m* 1986, Michael Lightstone, and has issue living, Jesse Lyon, *b* 1990, — Samantha Touche, *b* 1988, — Kate Annie, *b* 1992.

SISTER LIVING

Daphne Margaret, *b* 1927: *m* 1952, Patrick Wilfred Wells, of Snells, Great Henny, Sudbury, Suffolk, and has issue living, Derrick Gordon, *b* 1956: *m* 1984 (*m diss* 1991), Katherine Ann, yr da of Guy Simpson, of Earl Soham, Suffolk, and has issue living, George Patrick Charles *b* 1985, Elizabeth Florence *b* 1987, — William Patrick, *b* 1960: *m* 1985, Jane Elizabeth, da of John Alexander, of Ufford, Suffolk, and has issue living, Thomas Alexander *b* 1987, Robert William *b* 1990, — Jennifer Margaret, *b* 1953.
The 1st Bt, Rt Hon Sir Gordon Cosmo Touche (3rd son of 1st Bt 1920 creation), MP for Reigate (C) 1931-50, and Dorking 1950-64, was Chm of Ways and Means, House of Commons 1960-62.

Be Watchful

VIGILATE

SALUSBURY-TRELAWNY (E) 1628, of Trelawny, Cornwall
(Name pronounced "Saulsbury-Trelawny")

Deeds consonant with words

SCRIPNI CONSONA FACTA

Sir JOHN BARRY SALUSBURY-TRELAWNY, 13th *Baronet*; *b* 4 Sept 1934; *s* his father, *Sir* JOHN WILLIAM ROBIN MAURICE, 1956; *ed* HMS Worcester; Sub Lt RNVR; Dir of the Martin Walter Group Ltd 1971-74, of the Korn Ferry International Inc 1977-83, and of Goddard, Kay, Rogers Assoc since 1984 (Chairman since 1993); F Inst M 1974; JP (Kent) 1973-78: *m* 1958, Carol Knox, yr da of late C. F. K. Watson, of Saltwood, Kent, and has issue.

Arms – Quarterly: 1st and 4th, argent, a chevron sable, *Trelawny*; 2nd and 3rd, gules, a lion rampant per bend sinister argent and erminois ducally crowned between three crescents or, *Salusbury*, on a canton of the last (for *Brereton*) a bear's head erased sable, muzzled argent. **Crests** – 1st, a wolf passant proper; 2nd, a demi-lion rampant per bend sinister, as in the arms, holding in the paws a shield or charged with a bear's head sable, muzzled argent.
Residence – Beavers Hill, Rectory Lane, Saltwood, Hythe, Kent CT21 4QA. *Clubs* – Army and Navy, Buck's.

SON LIVING

JOHN WILLIAM RICHARD (278 Seabrook Rd, Hythe, Kent) *b* 30 March 1960: *m* 1st, 1980 (*m diss* 1986), Anita, yr da of Kenneth Snelgrove; 2ndly, 1987 (*m diss* 1993), Sandra Patricia, da of Joseph Thompson, of Seabrook, Hythe, Kent, and has issue living (by 1st *m*), Harry John, *b* 10 Dec 1982, — Victoria Hayley, *b* 1981, — (by 2nd *m*) Thomas Jonathon, *b* 1989.

DAUGHTERS LIVING

Jane Louise, *b* 1958: *m* 1977, Maj John R. Martin, Parachute Regt, and has issue living, James Jonathan, *b* 1982, — Emma Jane, *b* 1980. —— Amanda Sarah, *b* 1961: *m* 1980, Capt Alan M. Startin, Devonshire and Dorset Regt, and has issue living, Matthew Guy, *b* 1982, — Benjamin Marcus, *b* 1984, — Hamish William, *b* 1988, — Pollyanna Knox, *b* 1992. —— Emma Mary, *b* 1966: *m* 1988, William Ernle Hardy Vernon (*see* E Harrowby, colls).

Virtue is more noble than patrimony

VIRTUS PATRIMONIO NOBILIOR

HALF-BROTHER LIVING

William Hamelin (Ores Close Farm, Hillgrove, Wells, Som BA5 3EL), *b* 1942: *m* 1967, Meline Martha Katharina, who *d* 1969, da of late Dr Ir Cornelius P. A. Zeijlmans van Emmichoven, of The Hague.

WIDOW LIVING OF TWELFTH BARONET

ROSAMUND HELEN, da of late Arthur Reed Ropes (Adrian Ross, author and playwright): *m* 1st, 1937, as his second wife, Sir John William Robin Maurice Salusbury-Trelawny, 12th Bt, who *d* 1956; 2ndly, 1990, Christopher R. V. Bell, OBE. *Residence* – Pond Mead, 46a Lewes Rd, Ditchling, E Sussex.

COLLATERAL BRANCHES LIVING

Grandchildren of late Lt-Col James Edward Salusbury-Trelawny, OBE, 2nd son of 10th Baronet:—
Issue of late James Reginald Dorrington Salusbury-Trelawny, *b* 1908, *d* 1980; *m* 1st, 1932, Muriel Mary, who *d* 1970, da of Sir Eustace William Windham Wrixon-Becher, 4th Bt; 2ndly, 1971, Vieno Helinä (St John's Cottage, 16 The Meadows, Walberton, nr Arundel, W Sussex), yr da of late Väinö Junno, of Keni, Finland:—
(By 1st *m*), Jonathan William, OBE, *b* 1934; *ed* Charterhouse; Col Coldm Gds, OBE (Mil) 1976; *m* 1st, 1959 (*m diss* 1969), Jill Rosamonde, da of Maj-Gen Cecil Benfield Fairbanks, CB, CBE; 2ndly, 1970 (*m diss* 197—), Gillian, only child of R. J. Ratcliff, of Fossebridge House, nr Cheltenham, and has issue living (by 2nd *m*), Katherine Sophie, *b* 1972. —— Mary Letitia, *b* 1937; *m* 1966, Procter Naylor, OBE, of 17 Chapel St, Bildeston, Ipswich, and has issue living, Edward Trelawny Procter, *b* 1969, — William James, *b* 1977, — Harriet Mary, *b* 1967.

Grandchildren of late John Salusbury-Trelawny, son of late Col Harry Reginald Salusbury-Trelawny, 4th son of 8th baronet:—
Issue of late Major John Maitland Salusbury-Trelawny, MC, *b* 1892, *d* 1954: *m* 1919, Louisa Frederica, who *d* 1985, da of late Capt Guy Mainwaring, RN:—
John Guy, *b* 1919; *ed* Bradfield Coll; Capt (ret) Duke of Cornwall's LI; European War 1939-45 (wounded, prisoner): *m* 1948, Ruth Gertrude, da of late Edward Richard Marker (B Bagot, colls), and has issue living, Richard John MARKER (Combe, Honiton, Devon), *b* 1953; assumed the surname of Marker in lieu of his patronymic 1974: *m* 1978, Petronela Johana van der Mortel, of Victoria, BC, Canada, and has issue living, Karissa Ann *b* 1980, Stephanie Michelle *b* 1984, Angela Nicole *b* 1986, Joanna Petronela *b* 1988, — Peter Michael, *b* 1956, — Patrick Charles, *b* 1958, — Daphne Anne, *b* 1950, — Jill Margaret, *b* 1951. —— Philip Michael, MC (Colgare House, Lanhydrock, Bodmin, Cornwall PL30 4AE), *b* 1921; *ed* Winchester; Lt-Col (ret) The LI; N Africa and Italy 1942-45 (MC); a DL of Cornwall since 1982: *m* 1946, Jean Mary (formerly Flt Officer WAAF), who *d* 1988, only da of late Col Herbert Cecil Fraser, DSO, OBE, TD, and has issue living, Simon Jonathan (120 Earlsfield Rd, SW18. *Club* – Army and Navy), *b* 1948; *ed* Nautical Sch, Pangbourne: *m* 1st, 1974 (*m diss* 1978), Caroline Margaret, only da of Sir Nigel John Douglas Vernon, 4th Bt; 2ndly, 1978, Marian Janet, da of John MacAulay, of Poplar Hall, Ramsey, nr Harwich, Essex, and has issue living (by 2nd *m*) Edward John *b* 1979, Harry Philip *b* 1980, — Diana Jane, *b* 1947: *m* 1970, Robert Jessop Blake, of Harrington House Farm, Spilsby, Lincs, and has issue living, James Trelawny *b* 1971, Jonathan Jessop *b* 1973. —— Ann Laetitia, *b* 1924: *m* 1953, David Neil Courtenay MacWatters, and has issue living, Jonathan Courtenay *b* 1954, — Victoria Courtenay *b* 1956, — Jennifer Laetitia, *b* 1962.
This family takes its name from Trelawn or Treloen, in Cornwall. The Right Rev Sir Jonathan Trelawny, 3rd Bt, a man of great learning, was consecrated Bishop of Bristol 1685, and was one of the seven Bishops committed to the Tower by James II, which act caused a great rising among the people of Cornwall. After the Revolution, he was successively Bishop of Exeter and Winchester. Capt Sir William, RN, 6th Bt, was Governor of Jamaica. Sir William Lewis, 8th Bt, MP for East Cornwall, and Lord-Lieutenant of the county, assumed, in 1802, the additional surname of Salusbury.

TREVELYAN (E) 1662, of Nettlecombe, Somerset
(Name pronounced "Trevillian")

Sir NORMAN IRVING TREVELYAN, 10th *Baronet*, only son of late Edward Walter Trevelyan, yr son of George Edward Trevelyan, 2nd son of Rev George Trevelyan, 3rd son of Rev Walter Trevelyan, son of 4th baronet; *b* 29 Jan 1915; *s* his kinsman, Sir WILLOUGHBY JOHN, 1976, but does not appear on the Roll of the Baronetage; *m* 1951, Jennifer Mary, da of Arthur E. Riddett, of Long Orchards, Copt Hill Lane, Burgh Heath, Surrey, and has issue.

Arms – Gules, a demi-horse argent, hoofed and maned or, issuing out of water in base proper. **Crest** – Two arms counter-embowed proper, habited azure, holding in the hands a bezant.
Residence – 1041 Adella Av, Coronado, Calif 92118, USA.

SONS LIVING

EDWARD NORMAN (3180 Via Real, Carpinteria, CA 93013, USA), *b* 14 Aug 1955: *m* 1993, Debbie J. Mullin. —— George Arthur, *b* 1958.

DAUGHTER LIVING

Jane, *b* 1953: *m* 1978, David Floyd Lewis.

COLLATERAL BRANCHES LIVING

Granddaughter of late Sir Ernest John Trevelyan, DCL, yr son of Maj-Gen Henry Willoughby Trevelyan, CB, 3rd son of Ven George Trevelyan, Archdeacon of Taunton, 3rd son of 4th baronet:—

Issue of late Lt-Col Henry Trevelyan, *b* 1881, *d* 1971: *m* 1906, Josephine Marie, who *d* 1968, da of late Dr F. Antelme, of Port Louis, Mauritius:—
Mary Katharine, *b* 1926: *m* 1947, Harold Stewart Proudlock, of Heath Cottage, 16 Fields Rd, Alsager, Cheshire, and has issue living, Michael Trevelyan, *b* 1949: *m* 1976, Guyonne Christine, da of Dr W. G. Davies, of Paris, and has issue living, Eleanor Claire *b* 1977, Karen Aude *b* 1980, — David Seymour, *b* 1951, — John Stewart, *b* 1956: *m* 1988, Christina Louise, da of late G. W. Abbott, of Black Bourton, Oxon, — Susan Marie, *b* 1959: *m* 1989, Ian Nimmo.

Descendants of late Sir Charles Edward Trevelyan, KCB, son of late Ven George Trevelyan, Archdeacon of Taunton, 3rd son of 4th baronet, who was *cr a baronet* 1874:—
See Trevelyan, Bt, *cr* 1874.

Grandchildren of late Rev John Charles Trevelyan, 2nd son of Rev William Pitt Trevelyan (infra):—
Issue of late Rev Prebendary Charles William Trevelyan, MC, *b* 1887, *d* 1974: *m* 1930 Maud Dorothe, who *d* 1986, da of late Frederick Augustus Dixey, MD, FRS:—
John Francis (RD2, Te Puke, NZ), *b* 1934; *ed* Wellington Coll, and Aberdeen Univ (BSc Forestry): *m* 1958, Elizabeth Mary, da of Harvey Brockenshaw, and has issue living, Andrew John (6 Watea Rd, Mount Albert, Auckland, NZ), *b* 1961: *m* 1991, Jenny Elizabeth, da of Michael James Grainger, of Bramhall, Cheshire, — James Edward, *b* 1962; BE: *m* 1994, Vicki Kathryn, da of Anthony Wilfred Long, of Rotorua, NZ, — Fiona Catherine, *b* 1965, — Katrin Elizabeth, *b* 1966. —— *Rev* James William Irvine (The Rectory, Exeter Rd, Honiton, EX14 8AN), *b* 1937; *ed* Wellington Coll, and Selwyn Coll, Camb (MA); V of Lenham with Boughton Malherbe, Kent, 1972-78, since when R of Honiton: *m* 1969, Felicity Jane, da of Joseph Gibson and has issue living, Robert William Dixey, *b* 1970, — Lucy Catherine, *b* 1974. —— Janet Isabel, *b* 1932. —— Elizabeth Margaret, *b* 1939: *m* 1964, Robert Adrian Franklin, MA, MB (Cantab), FRCPsych, of Verno House South, Lyndhurst Rd, Christchurch, Dorset BH23 4SG, and has issue living, Nicholas Robert, *b* 1969, — Clare Elizabeth, *b* 1965, — Susan Dorothe, *b* 1967.

Granddaughter of late Rev William Pitt Trevelyan, 6th son of late Ven George Trevelyan, Archdeacon of Taunton (ante):—
Issue of late Rev George Philip Trevelyan, *b* 1858, *d* 1937: *m* 1896, Monica Evelyn Juliet, who *d* 1962, da of late Rev Sidney Philips, Hon Canon of Worcester (sometime V of Kidderminster), of The Blanquettes, Worcester:—
Urith Monica *b* 1909; *ed* Somerville Coll, Oxford (BA 1937, MA 1941): *m* 1940, Rt Rev Harry James Carpenter, 37th Bishop of Oxford, who *d* 1993, of St John's Home, St Mary's Rd, Oxford OX4 1QE, and has issue living, Humphrey William Bouverie (6 Farndon Rd, Oxford OX2 6RS) *b* 1946: *m* 1973, Mari Christina, da of Caradog Prichard, and has issue living, Clare Nia *b* 1978, Katherine Sioned *b* 1981.

Grandchildren of late Rev George Philip Trevelyan (ante):—
Issue of late John Trevelyan, CBE, *b* 1903, *d* 1986: *m* 1st, 1928 (*m diss* 1949), Kathleen Margaret, da of late Charles Pass; 2ndly, 1949 (*m diss* 1959), Joan Frieda, BM, BCh, da of Francis Clayton Scott (*see* Scott, Bt, *cr* 1909, colls); 3rdly, 1959, Jean, who *d* 1972, da of Robert Mutch; 4thly, 1974, Rosalie Evelyn, who *d* 1979, da of Joseph Lopez-Salzedo:—
(By 2nd wife) James Philip (33 Brockman Av, Dalkeith, W Aust), *b* 1948; *ed* Univ of W Aust (BEng, MEngSc); MIEAust: *m* 1971 (*m diss* 1994), Jolin, da of late Frank Edmondson, of Floreat Park, W Aust, and has issue living, Charles Francis, *b* 1974, — Nicholas James, *b* 1976, — Clare Rose, *b* 1983. —— Sarah Juliet, *b* 1950: *m* 1980, James (Jimmy) Boyle, writer and sculptor, of 5a Abbey Mount, Edinburgh, and has issue living, Suzannah Angela, *b* 1984, — Kydd, *b* 1987. —— (By 3rd *m*) Jonathan (15 The Rowans, Marchwood, Southampton SO4 4YW), *b* 1959; *ed* Bristol Univ (BSc, PhD): *m* 1980, Karen Elizabeth, da of late Kenneth Frank Ireland, and has issue living, David John, *b* 1988. —— Simon (5 Beverley Place, Springfield, Milton Keynes MK6 3LJ), *b* (twin) 1959; *ed* Birmingham Univ (BSc): *m* 1982, Isobel Catherine, da of Dr Oliver Watt, OBE, of Glasgow, and has issue living, James Oliver, *b* 1988, — Anna Joëlle, *b* 1985.
Issue of late Humphrey, Baron Trevelyan, KG, GCMG, CIE, OBE, *b* 1905, *d* 1985 (see that title).

Grandchildren of late John Spencer Trevelyan, eldest son of late Thornton Roger Trevelyan, only son of late Raleigh Trevelyan, 2nd son of Walter Trevelyan (infra):—
Issue of late John Thornton Trevelyan, *b* 1898, *d* 1970: *m* 1928, Anne Georgina, who *d* 1989, da of Prof John Dobson, Wardale, Newcastle upon Tyne:—
John Cecil Raleigh (Netherwitton Hall, Morpeth, Northumberland NE61 4NY), *b* 1933; *ed* Marlborough: *m* 1962, Jane, yr da of late Brig Roger Peake, DSO, OBE, and has issue living, John Henry Thornton, *b* 1968, — Caroline Georgina, *b* 1962, — Tessa Margaret Thornton, *b* 1966. —— Edward Calverley Thornton (Dalton House, Dalton, Northumberland), *b* 1935; *ed* Marlborough: *m* 1962, Elizabeth Anne, el da of late Geoffrey Blayney, of High Shield, Hexham, and has issue living, Julian Blackett Thornton, *b* 1963, Hugh Robert Thornton, *b* 1973, — Rosemary Joy, *b* 1965, — Amanda Fay, *b* 1967. —— Anne Margaret Thornton, *b* 1930: *m* 1953, John Humphrey Usborne, of Glan-Nant, Crickhowell, Breconshire, and has issue living, Richard Thomas, *b* 1954: *m* 198-, Henrietta E. M., 6th da of B. C. White-Spunner, of Brookes Hall, Horsington, Somerset, and has issue living, Thomas Masters *b* 1983, Alice *b* 1985, — John Edward, *b* 1956; CEng, MICE: *m* 1983, Lamorna, yr da of J. Hammond Forder, of Napier Cottage, Napier Av, SW6, and has issue living, Harriet Georgina *b* 1991. —— Joan Mary Thornton, *b* 1932: *m* 1963, George Campbell Wilkinson, TD, of The Gables, Westmancote, Tewkesbury, Glos GL20 7EU, and has issue living, Anne Margaret, *b* 1965.

Grandsons of late Capt Walter Raleigh Trevelyan, son of late Walter Raleigh Trevelyan (infra):—
Issue of late Col Walter Raleigh Fetherstonhaugh Trevelyan, Indian Army, *b* 1893, *d* 1953: *m* 1921, Olive Beatrice, who *d* 1976, (having *m* 2ndly, 1953, Col William Henry Ralston, DSO, OBE, MC, who *d* 1962), da of late Thomas Gibbons Frost, of Mollington Hall, Chester:—
Walter Raleigh, *b* 1923; *ed* Winchester; 1942-45 War as Capt Rifle Bde. *Residences* – 18 Hertford St, W1Y 7DB; St Veep, Cornwall. —— John Amyas (1 Roseacre, Tye Green, Alpheton, Suffolk CO10 9BW), *b* 1928; *ed* Winchester; sometime 2nd Lt Rifle Bde: *m* 1954, Patricia Mary, da of late Stuart Moore, and has issue living, Amyas John Stuart, *b* 1957: *m* 1988, Claire Diane, da of Harry Whittle, and has issue living, Philip John Amyas *b* 1991, Alice Margaret *b* 1989, — Oliver Willoughby, *b* 1961: *m* 1990, Louise Elizabeth, da of Alan Thompson, and has issue living, Mary Elizabeth *b* 1991, Katherine Louise *b* 1993, — Rupert Patrick, *b* 1963: *m* 1987, Sara Jane, da of Richard Glanville, and has issue living, Grace Kathryn *b* 1989, Olivia Jane *b* 1991, Anna Florence *b* 1993, — Elizabeth Virginia, *b* 1955: *m* 1984, Anthony Terrell Webb-Martin, of Bishopslea School, PO Belvedere, Harare, Zimbabwe, eldest son of J.J. Webb-Martin, of Marondera, Zimbabwe, and has issue living, Stuart John *b* 1987, Matthew Trevelyan *b* 1990.

Grandsons of late Charles Leslie Calverley Trevelyan, yr son of Walter Raleigh Trevelyan, only son of Walter Calverley Trevelyan, 3rd and yst son of Walter Trevelyan, yr son of 3rd baronet:—
Issue of late Leslie Calverley Trevelyan, *b* 1912; *d* 1982: *m* 1939, Prudence Mary, who *d* 1986, da of late Alfred S. Fawcett, of Standhills, Dore Moor, Derbyshire:—
Anthony Leslie Calverley (Three Gables, Kemerton, Glos GL20 7HR), *b* 1941; *ed* Seaford Coll: *m* 1972, Victoria, da of late Lt-Col Gordon Kenward Barker, DSO, of Bourton-on-the-Water, and has issue living, Charlotte Louise, *b* 1973, — Esm' Gwendolen, *b* 1975, — Alexandra Mary *b* 1979. —— (Amyas) Charles (Wood Stanway, nr Cheltenham, Glos; Cavalry ?

Guards' Club), *b* 1946; *ed* Harrow, and RMA; Maj R Scots Dragoon Gds (Carabiniers and Greys): *m* 1989, Angela Joan, SRN, RSCN, da of Cecil Pike, of The Wagon House, Higher Langham, Nimmer, Chard, Som, and has had issue living, Piers Calverley Charles, *b* 1990, — Prudence, *b* and *d* 1993.

The family of Trevelyan takes its name from Trevelyan in the parish of St Veep, Cornwall. The 1st baronet, Sir George, was son of George Trevelyan, who suffered greatly for his fidelity to the royal cause during the civil war. The 2nd and 4th baronets each represented Somersetshire in Parliament. Sir Walter John Trevelyan, 8th Bt, was High Sheriff of Cornwall 1906-7.

TREVELYAN (UK) 1874, of Wallington, Northumberland
(Name pronounced "Trevillian")

Sir GEORGE LOWTHIAN TREVELYAN, 4th *Baronet*; *b* 5 Nov 1906; *s* his father, *Rt Hon Sir* CHARLES PHILIPS, 1958; *ed* Sidcot Sch, and Trin Coll, Camb; craftsman in wood in the Peter Waals Workshops 1929-31, trained and taught the Alexander Technique 1931-36, Master at Gordonstoun Sch and Abinger Hill Sch 1936-41; Warden at Shropshire Adult Coll Attingham Park 1947-71; Founder, Pres and Dir Wrekin Trust 1971-92; served WWII, Capt Home Guard Training and taught at No 1 Army Coll Newbattle Abbey 1945-47: *m* 1940, Helen, da of Col John Lindsay Smith, CBE.

Arms – Gules, a demi-horse argent, hoofed and maned or, issuing out of water in base proper. Crest – Two arms counter-embowed proper, habited azure, holding in the hands a bezant.
Seat – Wallington, Cambo, Morpeth, Northumberland. *Residence* – The Barn, Hawkesbury, Badminton, Avon GL9 1BW.

ADOPTED DAUGHTER LIVING

Catriona, *b* 1944; *ed* Moreton Hall Sch, and Sussex Univ (BA): *m* 1st, 1968 (*m diss* 1984), Matthew Tomalin, son of Roger Tomalin, ARIBA, of Highgate, N6; 2ndly, 1986, Richard T. Tyson, eldest son of late Cdr A. Tyson, RN, of South Harting, W Sussex, and has had issue (by 1st *m*), Oliver Robert, *b* 1971, *d* 1990, — Jack Lindsay, *b* 1972. *Residence* – The Old Vicarage, Hawkesbury, Badminton, Avon GL9 1BW.

BROTHER LIVING

GEOFFREY WASHINGTON, *b* 4 July 1920; *ed* Oundle, and Trinity Coll, Camb (MA): *m* 1947, Gillian Isabel, da of late Alexander Wood, and has issue living, Peter John, *b* 1948, — Sandra Mary, *b* 1951: *m* 1974, David Bradley, and has issue living, Robert *b* 1980, James *b* 1982. *Residence* – Lower Silkstead, 3 Abbey Mill End, St Albans, Herts AL3 4HN.

SISTERS LIVING

Marjorie (*Lady Weaver*), *b* 1913: *m* 1941, Sir Tobias Rushton Weaver, CB, son of late Sir Lawrence Weaver, KBE, and has issue living, Lawrence Trevelyan, *b* 1948, — Kathleen, *b* 1943: *m* 1966, Nicholas John Milford Abbott, of Crouches, Church End, Great Dunmow, Essex, and has issue living, Simon Milford *b* 1971, Benjamin Tobias *b* 1973, Rachel Mary *b* 1967, Judith Caroline *b* 1969, — Caroline, *b* 1945: *m* 1986, Michael Herbert Baker, of 24 Wellington Park, Clifton, Bristol BS8 2UJ, eldest son of Henry Baker, — Rachel, *b* 1950: *m* 1974, Charles David Munn, of Hodore, Hartfield, Sussex, and has issue living, George Patrick *b* 1976, Toby Charles *b* 1984, Louise Caroline *b* 1978, Emily Claire *b* 1980. *Residence* – 14 Marston Close, NW6. —— Florence Patricia, *b* (twin) 1915: *m* 1st, 1942, Lt Frederick Philip Cheswright, RNVR, who *d* 1946; 2ndly, 1950 (*m diss* 1975), Sqdn-Ldr Reginald Joseph Jennings, MC, RAFVR, and has issue living (by 1st *m*), Hugh Weeden Nicholas (The 2 Queens, Cambo, Morpeth, Northumberland NE61 4AR), *b* 1942: *m* 1st, 1968 (*m diss* 1979), Rosemary Frances, da of late Norman Walduck, of Hatfield, Herts; 2ndly, 1980, Jean Moya, da of David William Barratt, and has issue living, (by 1st *m*) Sebastian Charles Philip *b* 1971, Rupert James Macaulay *b* 1972, — Janet Vanessa, *b* 1943: *m* 1st, 1964 (*m diss* 1985), Geoffrey Brian Parker; 2ndly, 1988, David G. Hall, and has issue living, (by 1st *m*) Philip Christopher Liam *b* 1967, Jonathan Hugh *b* 1968. *Residence* – Wallington, Cambo, Morpeth, Northumberland NE61 4AR.

COLLATERAL BRANCHES LIVING

Grandson of late Robert Calverley Trevelyan, poet and dramatist, 2nd son of 2nd baronet:—
Issue of late Julian Otto Trevelyan, *b* 1910, *d* 1988; painter: *m* 1st, 1934 (*m diss* 1950), Ursula Frances Elinor, elder da of late Bernard Richard Meirion Darwin, CBE; 2ndly, 1951, Mary (Durham Wharf, Hammersmith Terr, W6 9TS), da of late Vincent Fedden:—
(By 1st *m*) Philip Erasmus, *b* 1943; *ed* Bryanston, Dept. of Fine Art, King's Coll, Newcastle-upon-Tyne, and Royal Coll of Art: *m* 1975, Eleanor, da of late Matthew Prior, of Cambridge, and has issue living, Jack Elisha, *b* 1977, — Matthew Robert, *b* 1978, — Susannah, *b* 1987. *Residence* – Hilltop Farm, Appleton-le-Moors, Kirkbymoorside, N Yorks.

Grandchildren of late George Macaulay Trevelyan, OM, CBE, FRS, the famous historian, 3rd son of 2nd baronet:—
Issue of late Charles Humphry Trevelyan, *b* 1909, *d* 1964: *m* 1936, Mary Trumbull (Gazeley, Trumpington, Cambridge), yst da of Winchester Bennett, of Everitt St, New Haven, Conn, USA:—
Thomas Arnold (31 Orbel St, SW11 3NX), *b* 1942; *ed* Bryanston, and King's Coll, Camb (MA); MB BChir, MRCGP: *m* 1st, 1965 (*m diss* 1974), Ann, da of James Jones; 2ndly, 1974, Anita, da of Reginald Martyn Smith, of Chaddesley Corbett, Worcs, ⸱d has had issue (by 1st *m*), Harry, *b* 1968, — Emma, *b* 1966, — Selina Rose, *b* 1969, — (by 2nd *m*) Jack Humphrey, *b* 1984, — Clare, *b* 1981, — Victoria Rossanna, *b* 1986. —— George Macaulay (76a St Mark's Rd, Henley-on-Thames, ⸱944; *ed* Bryanston, Queen's Coll, Oxford, and London Sch of Econ: *m* 1st, 1967, Susan, da of Mark Pearson, of Notts; 2ndly, 19—, Valerie Elizabeth, da of Tom Preston, of School Lane, Dewsbury, W Yorks, and has issue Will Mark, *b* 1971, — Sasha France, *b* 1969, — Laura Kate, *b* 1968, — (by 2nd *m*) Thomas Trumbull, *b*

1988. —— Humphrey Bennett (74 Dartmouth Park Hill, N19), *b* (twin) 1944; *ed* Bryanston, and Trin Coll, Camb. —— Jane Winchester (188 Peckham Rye, SE22), *b* 1938: *m* 1960 (*m diss* 1984), David Armstrong, and has issue living, Richard Michael Boris, *b* 1961, — Sarah Jane, *b* 1965, — Rachel Elizabeth, *b* 1966. —— Mary Harriet, *b* 1939; MB, BS: *m* 1971, James Barton, of 96A Findhorn Place, Edinburgh.

This family is a younger branch of the Trevelyans, baronets of Nettlecombe (see colls, thereof). The 1st baronet was Gov of Madras 1859-60, and Financial member of Gov-Gen's Council at Calcutta 1862-5. The 2nd baronet, Rt Hon Sir George Otto Trevelyan, OM, DCL, LLD (a historian, and author of *The Life and Letters of Lord Macaulay*, and other works), was a Lord of the Admiralty 1869-70, Parliamentary Sec to Admiralty 1880-82, Ch Sec for Ireland 1882-4, Chancellor of Duchy of Lancaster 1884-5, and Sec for Scotland and ex-officio Keeper of the Great Seal of Scotland 1886 and 1892-5, and MP for Tynemouth (*L*) 1865-8, for the Border Burghs 1868-86 (when he was defeated), and for Bridgeton Div of Glasgow (*L*) 1887-97. The 3rd baronet, Rt Hon Sir Charles Philips Trevelyan, was Parliamentary Sec to Board of Education 1908-14, and Pres of Board of Education Jan to Nov 1924 and 1929-31, and sat as MP Elland Div of N Part of W Riding of Yorkshire (*L*) 1899-1918, and for Newcastle-upon-Tyne (*Lab*) 1922-31.

TRITTON (UK) 1905, of Bloomfield, Borough of Lambeth, co London

En Avant

Forward

Sir ANTHONY JOHN ERNEST TRITTON, 4th *Baronet*; *b* 4 March 1927; *s* his father, *Maj Sir* GEOFFREY ERNEST, CBE, 1976; *ed* Eton; Maj (ret) The Queen's Own Hussars: *m* 1957, Diana, da of late Rear-Adm St John Aldrich Micklethwait, CB, DSO (*see* Welby, Bt, colls, 1990 Edn), and has issue.

Arms – Argent, on a bend cotised gules a besant between two esquires' helmets or. **Crest** – A horse statant argent, resting the dexter forefoot upon a besant proper.
Residence – River House, Heytesbury, Warminster, Wilts BA12 0EE. *Club* – Cavalry and Guards'.

SON LIVING

JEREMY ERNEST (6 St Stephen's Terrace, SW8 1DH), *b* 6 Oct 1961.

DAUGHTER LIVING

Clarissa Mary Penelope, *b* 1959: *m* 1988, John Charles Joseph Delamere, yr son of late F. A. Delamere, of Rathgowan, Mullinger, co Westmeath, and has issue living, Hugo Fitzherbert, *b* 1989, — Camilla Sophia, *b* 1991. *Residence* – The Old Rectory, Avening, Glos GL8 8NF.

SISTER LIVING

Julia Mary, *b* 1930: *m* 1952, Richard Norman Kingzett (*see* Agnew, Bt, *cr* 1895, 1985 Edn), and has issue living, Jan Antony, *b* 1955, — Christopher Richard Colin (68 Camberwell Grove, SE5), *b* 1958: *m* 1989, Madeleine Anne, da of Theodore Peter Donahue, of North St, Litchfield, Conn, USA, and has issue living, Emily Rose Julia *b* 1990, Catherine Augusta Mary *b* 1992. *Residence* – 18 Sloane Avenue, Chelsea, SW3.

The 1st baronet, Sir (Charles) Ernest Tritton, sat as MP for Norwood Div of Lambeth (*C*) July 1892 to Jan 1906.

TROLLOPE (E) 1642, of Casewick, Lincolnshire

I hear, but am Silent

Sir ANTHONY SIMON TROLLOPE, 17th *Baronet*; *b* 31 Aug 1945; *s* his father, *Sir* ANTHONY OWEN CLAVERING, 1987; *ed* Sydney Univ (BA); breeder of Rhodesian Ridgebacks and Anglo-Arab horses: *m* 1969, Denise, da of Trevern Thompson, of N Sydney, NSW, and has issue.

Arms – Vert, three stags courant argent, attired or, within a bordure of the second. **Crest** – On a mount vert, a stag courant as in the arms, holding an oak-leaf in his mouth proper.
Residence – Churinga Lodge, 28 Midson Rd, Oakville, NSW 2765, Australia.

DAUGHTERS LIVING

Kellie Yvette, *b* 1970. —— Analese Christine, *b* 1972.

BROTHER LIVING

HUGH IRWIN (Casewick Cottage, 26 Bayswater Rd, Lindfield, NSW 2070, Australia), *b* 31 March 1947: *m* 1971, Barbara Anne, da of William Ian Jamieson, of Lawley Crescent, Pymble, NSW, and has issue living, Andrew Ian, *b* 1978, — Edwina Anne, *b* 1976, — Jennifer Kate, *b* 1980.

UNCLE LIVING (son of 15th Baronet)

Gordon Paul Clavering (Dougherty Apartments, 1 Victor St, Chatswood, NSW 2067, Australia), *b* 1918.

DAUGHTER LIVING OF THIRTEENTH BARONET

Iona Rebecca, *b* 1907: *m* 1st, 1927, Lt-Col Cleveland Mervyn Keble, OBE, Wilts Regt, who *d* 1948; 2ndly, 1953, Stephen Philp, of Welbrook, Peterchurch, Hereford, and has issue living, (by 1st *m*) Elizabeth Felicia, *b* 1928: *m* 1st, 1949 (*m diss* 1967), Lt-Col Peter Lawrence de Carteret Martin, Cheshire Regt; 2ndly, 1967, Philip Arthur Harcourt Armes, of Howard Lodge, Hurstpierpoint, Sussex, and has issue living, (by 1st *m*) David Peter de Carteret *b* 1956, Fiona Elizabeth *b* 1953: *m* 1977, Paul Jamieson Beesley, — Heather Fiona, *b* 1933: *m* 1958 (*m diss* 1964), Maj Anthony Frederick Walker, Cheshire Regt.

WIDOW LIVING OF SIXTEENTH BARONET

JOAN MARY ALEXIS (*Dowager Lady Trollope*), da of Alexis Robert Gibbes, of Balgowlah, NSW: *m* 1942, Sir Anthony Owen Clavering Trollope, 16th Bt, who *d* 1987. *Residence* – 31 Pacific Highway, Wahroonga, NSW 2076, Australia.

COLLATERAL BRANCH LIVING

Granddaughters of late Herbert Edward Trollope, only son of late Edward Hazel Trollope, son of late Rev John Trollope, son of late Rev Thomas Daniel Trollope, grandson of late Henry Trollope, 3rd son of 3rd baronet:—
Issue of late John Herbert Hazel Trollope, *b* 1908, *d* 1991: *m* 1939, Ruth, who *d* 1987, da of Frederick Warry, of Freshford, Somerset:—
Beatrice Mary, *b* 1942: *m* 1963, Peter Old, of Mountjoy's Farm, Youldon, Chilsworthy, Holsworthy, Devon, and has issue living, Andrew, *b* 1967, — Rachel, *b* 1964: *m* 1986, Mervyn William Bate, of Splatt Farm, Tresmeer, Launceston, Cornwall, and has issue living, Verity Ruth *b* 1989, Hannah Rachel *b* 1992, — Sarah, *b* 1971: *m* 1993, Wagner Rangel, Jr, of Curitiba, Brazil. —— Maureen Hazel, *b* 1945: *m* 1973, Ian Joseph Kampel, CEng, MIEE, MBIM, of 25 Holmfield Av, Iford, Bournemouth, and has issue living, Timothy Ian, *b* 1978, — Alison Jane, *b* 1975. —— Susan Bridget, *b* 1947: *m* 1969, Elemér Fejér, of 97 Goldcroft Rd, Westham, Weymouth, Dorset DT4 OEA, and has issue living, Karen Lisa, *b* 1974, — Trudy Lynne, *b* 1977.
The Rt Hon Sir John Trollope, PC, 7th Bt, MP for Lincolnshire (*C*) 1861-68, was *cr* Baron Kesteven (peerage of United Kingdom) 1868, when the Baronetcy remained merged in the Barony until the death of the 3rd Baron (*ka* 1915), when it devolved upon his cousin, Sir William Henry Trollope, 10th Bt. Sir Gordon Clavering Trollope, 15th Bt *s* Nov 1957 and *d* Oct 1958, when he was *s* by his son, Sir Anthony Owen Clavering Trollope, 16th Bt.

TROUBRIDGE (GB) 1799, of Plymouth
(Name pronounced "Troobridge")

Sir THOMAS RICHARD TROUBRIDGE, 7th *Baronet*; *b* 23 Jan 1955; *s* his father, *Lieut-Cdr Sir* PETER, RN, 1988; *ed* Eton, and Univ Coll, Durham: *m* 1984, Hon Rosemary Douglas-Pennant, yr da of 6th Baron Penrhyn, and has issue.

Arms – Or, on a bridge embattled of three arches, through which water is flowing towards the base proper, a tower of the second, thereon hoisted a broad pennant flying towards the sinister; on a canton azure, two keys in saltire, the wards upwards or. **Crest** – A dexter arm-embowed, habited azure, holding a flagstaff, thereon a flag azure charger with two keys in saltire or.
Residence – 28 Lilyville Rd, SW6 5DW. *Clubs* – Royal Automobile, Itchenor Sailing.

SONS LIVING

EDWARD PETER, *b* 10 Aug 1989. —— Nicholas Douglas St Vincent, *b* 1993.

DAUGHTER LIVING

Emily Rose, *b* 1987.

SISTERS LIVING

Amanda Marguerite, *b* 1957: *m* 1991, Timothy M. H. Payne, yst son of Anthony D. Payne, of Marnhull, Dorset. —— Camilla June, *b* 1961.

UNCLE LIVING (*brother of 6th baronet*)

Thomas (1B Gertrude St, SW10), *b* 1939: *m* 1st, 1971 (*m diss* 1977, annulment by Roman Catholic Church 1978), Baroness Marie Christine Hedwig Agnes Ida, da of late Baron Günther Hubertus von Reibnitz (*see* Royal Family, D Kent); 2ndly, 1981, Mrs Petronella Forgan (*née* von Woyrsch), formerly wife of James Russell Forgan.

AUNT LIVING (*sister of 6th baronet*)

(Elizabeth) June, *b* 1933: *m* 1956, Alan G. L. Baxter, who *d* 1988, and has issue living, Edward Thomas, *b* 1960, —— Elizabeth Anne, *b* 1958, —— Sarah Evelyn, *b* 1962, —— Mary Emma, *b* 1965, —— Louisa Jane, *b* 1969. *Residence* – 46 South St, St Andrews, Fife KY16 9JT.

WIDOW LIVING OF SIXTH BARONET

Hon VENETIA DAPHNE WEEKS (*Venetia, Hon Lady Troubridge*), da of 1st Baron Weeks: *m* 1954, Lieut-Cdr Sir Peter Troubridge, 6th Bt, RN, who *d* 1988. *Residence* – The Manor House, Elsted, Midhurst, Sussex.

COLLATERAL BRANCH LIVING

Issue of late Maj Edward St Vincent Troubridge, RM, brother of 6th baronet, *b* 1930, *d* 1992: *m* 1st, 1955 (*m diss* 1974), Jennifer Anne, da of late Edward Billing-Lewis, of Maidstone, Kent; 2ndly, 1974, Patricia Barbara (7 Liskeard Gdns, SE3), da of Maj Chevalier Hannibal Alexander Scicluna, OBE, of 29 Milner St, Sliema, Malta, and formerly wife of Cmdr P. G. Nelson, of Oslo, Norway:—
(By 1st *m*) Rodney St Vincent, *b* 1957. —— Charlotte Louise, *b* 1960. —— Emma Marguerite, *b* 1963. —— (By 2nd *m*) Amelia Clare, *b* 1974.

The 1st baronet, Adm Sir Thomas (son of late Richard Troubridge, of London), was a distinguished naval commander, and sat as MP for Yarmouth 1802-6. The 2nd baronet, Adm Sir Edward Thomas, CB, sat as MP for Sandwich 1831-47, and Col Sir Thomas, CB, 3rd Bt, greatly distinguished himself in the Crimea, where he was severely wounded. Sir Peter Troubridge, 6th Bt, was Chm of the Standing Council of the Baronetage 1981-84.

TRUSCOTT (UK) 1909, of Oakleigh, East Grinstead, Sussex

Prepared for either

IN UTRUMQUE PARATUS

GWIR·YN·ERBYN·Y·BYD

Truth against all the world

Sir GEORGE JAMES IRVING TRUSCOTT, 3rd *Baronet*; *b* 24 Oct 1929; *s* his father, *Sir* ERIC HOMEWOOD STANHAM, 1973; *ed* Sherborne: *m* 1st, 1954 (*m* annulled on his petition 1958), Irene Marion Craig Barr Brown; 2ndly, 1962, Yvonne Dora, yr da of late Frank Edward Nicholson, of Carshalton, Surrey, and has issue by 2nd *m*.

𝕬rms – Argent, three chevronels gules, between two mullets in chief of the last, pierced of the field, and a knight's helmet in base proper; a chief checky of the second and first. 𝕮rest – A fasces erect, surmounted by a palm branch slipped and an arrow saltireways, all proper.
Address – BM Quill, London WC1N 3XX.

SON LIVING

RALPH ERIC NICHOLSON, *b* 21 Feb 1966.

DAUGHTER LIVING

Ruth Emma, *b* 1967.

SISTER LIVING

Jennifer Margaret Anne, *b* 1932: *m* 1958, Lt-Cdr Edward Martyn Theodore Segar, RN (ret), of Stanton Hill, Priorsfield Rd, Godalming, Surrey GU7 2RQ, and has issue living, John Edward, *b* 1965, — Jane Margaret, *b* 1959, — Anne Mary, *b* 1962.
The 1st baronet, Sir George Wyatt Truscott (son of Sir Francis Wyatt Truscott, Lord Mayor of London 1879-80), was Chm of Brown, Knight & Truscott, Ltd, printers and stationers, of Suffolk Lane, EC, and an Alderman of City of London (Sheriff 1902-3, Lord Mayor 1908-9, Hon Freeman 1937).

TUCK (UK) 1910, of Park Crescent, St Marylebon

CUM·DEO

With God

Sir BRUCE ADOLPH REGINALD TUCK, 3rd *Baronet*: *m* 29 June 1926; *s* his father, *Major Sir* (WILLIAM) REGINALD, 1954; *ed* Canford Sch; sometime Lieut Scots Guards: *m* 1st, 1949 (*m diss* 1964), Luise, da of John C. Renfro, of Sán Angelo, Texas, USA; 2ndly, 1968, Pamela Dorothy, da of Alfred Michael Nicholson, of London, and has issue by 1st and 2nd *m*.

𝕬rms – Or, an antique lamp flaming azure, in base a hurt charged with four F's in cross of the field, on a chief of the same two hands in the act of blessing of the first. 𝕮rest – A lion sejant sable supporting with the paws an artist's palette proper, inscribed thereon the word "Thorough" sable.
Residence – Montego Bay, PO Box 274, Jamaica. *Club* – Lansdowne.

SONS LIVING *(By 1st marriage)*

RICHARD BRUCE, *b* 7 Oct 1952; *ed* Millfield. —— Christopher John, *b* 1954.

DAUGHTER LIVING *(By 2nd marriage)*

Charlotte Emily Pamela, *b* 1974.

SISTER LIVING

Moyra Grace, *b* 1920: *m* 1st, 1947, Lee David Greif, who *d* 1950; 2ndly, 1951, Major Alvin Greif, US Army Air Force, who *d* 1958; 3rdly, 1959, Nigel Digby Pemberton. *Residences* – 30 E 65th St, New York City, USA; Montego Bay, Jamaica.
Sir Adolph Tuck, 1st Bt, son of late Raphael Tuck, fine art publisher, was Chm and Managing Director of Raphael Tuck and Sons (Limited), of Raphael House, Moorfields, EC.

TUITE (I) 1622, of Sonnagh, Westmeath
(Name pronounced "Tute")

Sir CHRISTOPHER HUGH TUITE, 14th *Baronet*; *b* 3 Nov 1949; *s* his father, *Maj Sir* DENNIS GEORGE HARMSWORTH, 1981; *ed* Wellington Coll, and Liverpool Univ (BSc); PhD Bristol: *m* 1976, Deborah Anne, da of A. E. Martz, of Pittsburgh, USA, and has issue.

Arms – Quarterly, argent and gules. **Crest** – An angel vested argent, holding in the dexter hand a flaming sword proper, the sinister resting on a shield of the arms.
Residence – 100 Terry Creek Drive, Chapel Hill, NC 27514, USA.

SONS LIVING

THOMAS LIVINGSTONE, *b* 24 July 1977. —— Jonathan Christopher Hannington, *b* 1981.

BROTHERS LIVING

Jeremy Denis (Haye Farm, Haye Lane, Fingringho, Colchester, Essex), *b* 1951; *ed* Wellington Coll, and Leeds Univ (MB, FRCS): *m* 1978, Anne, da of J. Ebdon-Robinson, and has issue living, Anthony, *b* 1982, — Edward Jeremy, *b* 1984, — James Carey John, *b* 1987. —— Patrick Leslie, *b* 1954; *ed* Wellington Coll, and Leeds Univ (BSc): *m* 1992, Gillie M., da of Dr K. Martin McNicol, of Grayshott, Surrey.

WIDOW LIVING OF THIRTEENTH BARONET

MARGARET ESSIE (*Margaret, Lady Tuite*) (7 Vicarage Gdns, Grayshott, Hindhead, Surrey GU26 6NH), only da of late Col Walter Leslie Dundas, DSO: *m* 1947, Maj Sir Dennis George Harmsworth Tuite, MBE, 13th Bt, who *d* 1981.

This family, which has been settled in Ireland since 1172, is descended from Sir Richard de Tuitt who that year accompanied the Earl of Pembroke to that country. The 7th baronet was murdered at Sonnagh in 1783.

TUPPER (UK) 1888, of Armdale, Halifax, Nova Scotia

L'ESPOIR EST MA FORCE

Hope is my strength

Sir CHARLES HIBBERT TUPPER, 5th *Baronet*; *b* 4 July 1930; *s* his father, *Sir* JAMES MACDONALD, 1967: *m* 1959 (*m diss* 1975), Bernice Yvonne Quinn, and has issue.

Arms – Per fesse azure and or, on a fesse ermine between two boars passant in chief or, and a sprig of may flower slipped and leaved in base proper, three escallops gules. **Crest** – On a mount vert, a greyhound statant sable, charged on the body with two escallops or, and holding in the mouth a sprig of mayflower as in the arms.
Residence – Suite 1101, 955 Marine Drive, W Vancouver, BC, V7T 1A9.

SON LIVING

CHARLES HIBBERT, *b* 10 July 1964: *m* 1987, (Elizabeth) Ann Heaslip, and has issue living, Cara-Lyn Ann, *b* 1991. *Address* – PO Box 2064, 641 Wallace Place, Ladysmith, British Columbia, Canada VOR 2EO.

SISTER LIVING

Janet Mary, *b* 1929: *m* 1951, William John Couldwell, MD, CM, of #50-5880 Hampton Place, Vancouver, British Columbia V6T 2E9, and has issue living, William Tupper (3860 Valleylights, Pasadena, California 91107, USA), *b* 1955; BSc MDCM, PhD: has issue living, Mitchell William Galen *b* 1991, Sandrine Marie Camille *b* 1991, Genevieve Christine *b* 1993, — Susan Janice, *b* 1953; BA, BArch: *m* 1977, John Joseph McCormack, Dip Arch, MRAIC, of 4666 West 3rd Av, Vancouver, BC, Canada V6R 1N4, and has issue living, John Paget *b* 1981, Brendan William *b* 1984, Liam James Couldwell *b* 1988, — Sandra Lee (204, 3641 West 28th Av, Vancouver, BC, Canada V6S 7S3), *b* 1954; BA: *m* 1982 (*m diss* 1987), Gabor Hegedus, who *d* 1990, and has issue living, Andras Zoltan Couldwell *b* 1983.

DAUGHTER LIVING OF SECOND BARONET

Margot Stewart, *b* 1928. *Residence* – Portage Sch, Portage La Prairie, Manitoba, Canada.

DAUGHTERS LIVING OF THIRD BARONET

Janet Macdonald, *b* 1920: *m* 1944, Philip Lionel Underwood, late Capt Roy Canadian Artillery, PO Box 117, Grafton, Ont, Canada, and has issue living, Harry Charles Gordon, *b* 1951: *m* 1984, Denise Ireland, — Mary Fielding, *b* 1946: *m* 1969, Claude-Frédéric Roger Marie Ingell de Kerckhove Varent, and has issue living, Charles André Philippe *b* 1976, Derrick Tupper Daniel *b* 1978, — Nora Frances, *b* 1958: *m* 1984, Gary Jay Tenenbaum. —— Dorothy Joyce, *b* 1922: *m* 1944, Maj Edward Arunah Dunlop, OBE, GM, Queen's Own Rifles of Canada, and has issue living, Edward Arunah, *b* 1946: *m* 1976, Valerine Glen Hardacre, — Charlotte Mary Ferguson, *b* 1949. *Residence* – 6 Meredith Cres, Toronto, Canada, M4W 3B6.

COLLATERAL BRANCHES LIVING

Issue of late Maj Reginald Hibbert Tupper, QC, LLD, brother of 3rd and 4th baronets, b 1893, d 1972: m 1916, Isobel Marion Wilson, who d 1969.
Charles Gordon Hibbert (Victor), b 1918; 1939-45 War as Lt Seaforth Highlanders of Canada: m 1946, Margaret Ada, BA McGill, da of James Albert Campbell, QC, of Vancouver, and has issue living, Charles Reginald Hibbert, b 1947. —— David Wilson Hibbert, LLB, b 1921; 1939-45 War with RCAF: m 1st, 1947, Joan Margot, who d 19—, da of late Col Austin Gillies, VD, of Ottawa; 2ndly, — and has issue living, (by 1st m) Sidney Victor Hibbert, b 1948, — Charles Austin Hibbert, b 1951, — Julie Isabel, b 1953.

Grandchildren of late William Johnson Tupper, KC (Lt-Gov of Manitoba), 3rd son of 1st baronet:—
Issue of late Charles William Tupper, QC, b 1898, d 1960: m 1st, 1929, Ray Macdonald; 2ndly, 1941, Winifred Lillian Craske, who d 1956:—
(By 2nd m) Charles James (1428-75 Bamburgh Crescent, Scarborough, Ontario, Canada M1W 3W1) b 1942; BScE. —— (By 1st m) Margaret Ray, b 1931; BA, BLS: m 1956, William Macdonald Price, of 700 Cardinal, St Laurent, Quebec, Canada, and has issue living, Charles Macdonald (1354 Gatehouse Drive, Mississauga, Ontario, Canada L5H 1A5), b 1958; MD, CM: m 1983, Mary Shanahan, B Eng, and has issue living, Rae Francis b 1989, Thomas McMurray b 1990, Joseph Charles b 1992. —— Scott William (29 Cedar Circle, Dollard des Ormeaux, PQ, Canada H9B 1H7), b 1960; ARCT: m 1988, Martine Chevrier.
The name of Tupper can be traced at Bury and vicinity, W Sussex, from the 13th century. Thomas Tupper emigrated from Kent to Massachusetts in 1635. Charles Tupper, 4th in descent from him, moved to Cornwallis, Nova Scotia 1760. His grandson, Rt Hon Sir Charles Tupper, GCMG, CB, LLD, MD, 1st Bt, was fourteen consecutive times returned as MP for his native co (Cumberland, NS), and represented it for thirty-three years in the Canadian House of Commons, was Prime Min of Nova Scotia 1864-67, and was High Commr in Great Britain for Dominion of Canada 1883-87, and 1888-96, and Premier of Canada 1896.

TURING (NS) 1638, of Foveran, Aberdeenshire

Fortune aids the daring

Sir JOHN DERMOT TURING, 12th *Baronet*; b 26 Feb 1961; s his kinsman, Sir JOHN LESLIE, MC, 1987; ed Sherborne, King's Coll, Camb, and New Coll, Oxford: m 1986, Nicola Jane, da of Malcolm Douglas Simmonds, of Wimborne, Dorset, and has issue.

Arms – Argent, on a bend sable, three boars' heads or. **Crest** – A hand holding a helmet proper. **Supporters** – Two stags proper. *Residence* – 55 Shirley Av, Southampton, Hants SO15 5NH.

SONS LIVING

JOHN MALCOLM FERRIER, b 5 Sept 1988, — James Robert Edward, b 1991.

HALF-SISTERS LIVING

Inagh Jean, b 1936: m 1st, 1960 (m diss 1980), Warren Gray, solicitor; 2ndly, 1980, Herbert Aspinall, and has issue living (by 1st m), Mark Warren, b 1961, — Stephen Paul, b 1969, — Rachel Mary, b 1963: m 1990, Mark Richard Barnes, and has issue living, Thomas David b 1993, — Deborah Jean, b 1964. *Residence* – 21 Hoyles Rd, Wellington, Somerset TA21 9AH. —— Shuna, b 1940: m 19— (m diss 1983), Albert Hunt, and has issue living, Nevil, b 1970. *Residence* – 3 The High St, Small Dole, Henfield, Sussex. —— Janet Ferrier, b 1947: m 1981, Alan John Robinson, ARICS, and has issue living, Lisa Ferrier, b 1982, — Clare Elizabeth, b 1985. *Residence* – 3 The Old Cottages, Bell Lane, London Colney, Herts.

MOTHER LIVING

Beryl Mary Ada, da of Herbert Vaughan Hann: m 1960, as his 2nd wife, John Ferrier Turing, who d 1983. *Residence* – 72 Chirgwin Rd, Truro, Cornwall TR1 1TT.

WIDOW LIVING OF ELEVENTH BARONET

IRENA NINA (*Lady Turing*), da of Trevor John Tatham, of Beaconsfield, Manor Way, Lee-on-the-Solent, Hants, and widow of Capt W. W. P. Shirley-Rollison, RN: m 1975, Sir John Leslie Turing, 11th Bt, MC, who d 1987. *Residence* – 2 Northlands House, Salthill Rd, Fishbourne, Chichester, W Sussex.

COLLATERAL BRANCH LIVING

Granddaughter of late Rev John Robert Turing, brother of 7th baronet:—
Issue of late Harvey Doria Turing, b 1877, d 1950: m 1918, Violet, who d 1961, da of late Rev Harry Alsager Sheringham:—
Penelope Anne Tryon, b 1925. *Residence* – 411 Beatty House, Dolphin Sq, SW1 3PL.
Sir William Turyn attached himself to the fortunes of King David II, and shared that monarch's exile; his loyalty was however subsequently rewarded by a grant of the barony of Foveran, in Aberdeenshire, which his descendants held more than 300 years. Sir John Turing of Foveran, 1st Bt, espoused the cause of Charles I. He was taken prisoner by the Covenanters 1639 who later sacked Foveran. He fought at Battle of Worcester 1651. The right to this baronetcy was sustained by the Lyon Office in 1882 to Sir Robert Fraser Turing, 8th Bt, by a Committee of the Privy Council in 1912, and by Interlocutor of the Lord Lyon 1.

Twisleton (Twisleton-Wykeham-Fiennes), see Fiennes.

TWYSDEN (E) 1611, of East Peckham, Kent (Extinct 1970)

Sir WILLIAM ADAM DUNCAN TWYSDEN, 12th and last *Baronet.*

WIDOW LIVING OF ELEVENTH BARONET

MARY, da of late Rear Adm H. E. C. Blagrove: *m* 1st, 1945, Sir Anthony Roger Duncan Twysden, 11th Bt, who *d* 1946; 2ndly, 1949, Capt Peter Gerald Charles Dickens, DSO, MBE, DSC, RN, of Lye Green Forge, Crowborough, Sussex, who *d* 1987, el son of late Adm Sir Gerald Charles Dickens, KCVO, CB, CMG.

TYRWHITT (UK) 1919, of Terschelling, and of Oxford
(Name pronounced "Tirrit")

Sir REGINALD THOMAS NEWMAN TYRWHITT, 3rd *Baronet, b* 21 Feb 1947; *s* his father, *Adm Sir* St JOHN REGINALD JOSEPH, KCB, DSO, DSC and bar, 1961; *ed* Downside; 2nd Lieut RA 1966, Lieut 1969, RARO 1969: *m* 1st, 1972 (*m diss* 1980 and annulled 1984), Sheila Gail, da of William Alistair Crawford Nicoll, MA, LLB, of Kingsham Old Farm, Milland, Hants; 2ndly, 1984, Charlotte, only da of Capt Angus Jeremy Christopher Hildyard, DL, RA (ret) (*see* B Morris), and has issue by 2nd *m*.

ᴀrms – Gules, three tyrwhitts (lapwings) or. Crest – A woodman wreathed with oak and holding a club, all proper. Supporters – *Dexter*, a savage wreathed about the loins and head with oak proper, and holding over the shoulder in the exterior hand a club or; *sinister*, a sailor of the Royal Navy holding in the exterior hand a coil of rope proper.
Residence – 51 Whitecross St, Barton-on-Humber, S Humberside.

SON LIVING *(By 2nd marriage)*

ROBERT ST JOHN HILDYARD, *b* 15 Feb 1987.

DAUGHTER LIVING *(By 2nd marriage)*

Letitia Mary Hildyard, *b* 1988.

BROTHER LIVING

John Edward Charles, *b* 1953; MA Cantab 1975; ACA 1979: *m* 1978, Melinda Ngaire, only da of Capt Anthony Philip Towell, MC, of Long Island, New York, USA, and has issue living, St John Thomas Anthony, *b* 1980, — Oliver Edward John, *b* 1982, — Alexander William James, *b* 1984.

SISTER LIVING

Veronica Mary, *b* 1944: *m* 1979, Christopher Miles Boast, of 11 Turner St, Gawler, SA 5118, Australia, and has issue living, Charles St John, *b* 1980, — Timothy William, *b* 1982.

AUNTS LIVING *(Daughters of 1st baronet)*

Dame Mary Joan Caroline, DBE, TD, *b* 1903; Snr Controller ATS 1946-49, Brigadier WRAC 1949-50; ADC to HM 1949-51, OBE (Mil) 1946, DBE (Mil) 1949. *Residence* – 12A Tiddington Court, Tiddington, Stratford-on-Avon CV37 7AP. —— Patricia Angela Mary (Ettington Grange, Stratford-on-Avon, Warwicks, CV37 7NU), *b* 1913; late Senior Comd ATS: *m* 1945, Capt Anthony John Alfred Lacy, Suffolk Regt who *d* 1975, and has issue living, *Rev* David Anthony, *b* 1947; ordained RC Priest 1972, — John Reginald (Holly Grove, Fernbank Rd, Ascot, Berks), *b* 1948: *m* 1970, Johneen, da of Michael Whitfield, of Wellesbourne, Warwicks, and has issue living, Mark Logan Tyrwhitt *b* 1973, Michael John *b* 1981, Olivia *b* 1976, — Richard Patrick James (16 Huron Rd, SW17 8RB), *b* 1950: *m* 1973, Penelope Anne, da of Hon Simon Chelmsford Loader Maffey (*see* B Rugby), and has issue living, Timothy James *b* 1985, Laura Penelope *b* 1980, Diana Louise *b* 1984, — Anne Mary, *b* 1953.

WIDOW LIVING OF SECOND BARONET

NANCY VERONICA (*Lady Agnew*), only child of late Capt Charles Newman Gilbey, of Folkestone, Kent: *m* 1st, 1944, Adm Sir St John Reginald Joseph Tyrwhitt, KCB, DSO, DSC, 2nd Bt, who *d* 1961; 2ndly, 1965, Sir (William) Godfrey Agnew, KCVO, CB, of Pinehurst, South Ascot, Berks.
This family descends from Sir Robert Tyrwhitt, of Kettleby, Lincs, living 1322, whose ancestor was Sir Hercules Tyrwhitt, of High Trewhitt, Northumberland, 1097. This family was also seated at Cammeringham and Scotter, co Lincs. Sixteenth in descent from Sir Robert was Richard Tyrwhitt of Nantyr Hall, Denbighshire, Recorder of Chester (*d* 1836), 3rd son of John Tyrwhitt of Netherclay House, Som, and brother of Sir Thomas Tyrwhitt (later Jones), who was *cr* a Bt 1808, ancestor of Barons Berners. The 1st baronet, Adm of the Fleet Sir Reginald Yorke Tyrwhitt, GCB, DSO (son of Rev Richard St John Tyrwhitt, Rector of St Mary Magdalen, Oxford), *m* Angela Mary, da of Mathew Corbally, JP, DL, of Rathbeale Hall, co Dublin, cmd'd 1st and 3rd Flotilla and the Harwich Force 1914-18, and was Com-in-Ch China Station 1927-29, and Com-in-Ch

at the Nore 1930-33. The 2nd baronet, Adm Sir St John Reginald Joseph Tyrwhitt, KCB, DSO, DSC and bar, was Ch of Staff to Com-in-Ch Allied Forces Mediterranean 1958-9, and a Lord Commr of Admiralty, Second Sea Lord and Ch of Naval Personnel 1959-61.

USHER (UK) 1899, of Norton, Ratho, Midlothian, and of Wells, Hobkirk, Roxburghshire

With nothing base

Sir ROBERT EDWARD USHER, 6th *Baronet*; *b* 18 April 1934; *s* his brother Sir PETER LIONEL, 1990.

Arms – Gules, a saltire between four barons argent, garnished sable. **Crest** – A dexter arm couped below the elbow, vested azure, cuffed argent, holding in the hand a baton proper.
Seat – Hallrule, Hawick, Roxburghshire.

DAUGHTER LIVING OF THIRD BARONET

Jacqueline (The Garden Flat, Rosybank House, Coldstream, Berwickshire), *b* 1931: *m* 1955 (*m diss* 1980), Capt Christopher Michael Wolfe Murray, Gordon Highlanders (ret), and has issue (*see* Murray, Bt, *cr* 1628, colls).

COLLATERAL BRANCHES LIVING

Issue of late Lieut Ronald James Usher, DSC, RN, 2nd son of 2nd baronet, *b* 1892, *d* 1948: *m* 1917, Alice Margaret, who *d* 1975, el da of late Harry Lawrence Usher, of Summerfield, Dunbar:—
Hazel Jean (*Baroness Stodart of Leaston*), *b* 1918; Serving Sister Order of St John of Jerusalem 1977: *m* 1940, Baron Stodart of Leaston, PC (Life Baron), of Lorimers, N Berwick, E Lothian. —— Margaret Daphne (Little Headshaw, Ashkirk, Selkirkshire), *b* 1920: *m* 1946, William Kirkpatrick, who *d* 1967, and has issue living, Ronald James, *b* 1948, — Susan Woodrow, *b* 1949, — Margaret Anne, *b* 1953.

Granddaughter of late Lieut Ronald James Usher, DSC, RN (ante):—
Issue of late Lieut Robert Ronald Harry Usher, RN, *b* 1924, *d* 1947: *m* 1945, Jane Hall, who *m* 2ndly, 1954, James Murray Gregory-Jones, of Crossways, Victoria Sq, Penarth, Glam:—
Elizabeth Margaret, *b* 1946: *m* 1969 (*m diss* 1982), David Patrick Richards, and has issue living, Peter James, *b* 1970, — Owain David *b* 1973.

Issue of late William Dove Usher, 5th son of 2nd baronet, *b* 1904, *d* 1969: *m* 1939, Christa Elizabeth, da of Bruno von Tevenar, of Mufindi, Tanzania:—
(WILLIAM) JOHN TEVENAR (Khayalami Farm, PO Cramond, Natal, S Africa), *b* 18 April 1940; *ed* Uppingham: *m* 1962 (*m diss* 1990), Rosemary Margaret, da of Col Sir Reginald Douglas Henry Houldsworth, OBE, TD, 4th Bt (*cr* 1887), and has issue living, Andrew John (61 Waldron Rd, SW18 3TA), *b* 8 Feb 1963; *ed* Hilton Coll, S Africa: *m* 1987, Charlotte Louise Alexandra, only da of Robert Barry Eldridge, of SW10, and has issue living, Rory James Andrew *b* 11 June 1991, Callum *b* 1994, — Michael William Reginald, *b* 1967; *ed* Maritzburg Coll, — Caroline Rosemary, *b* 1966. —— Stuart Alexander, *b* 1941; *ed* Uppingham.

Issue of late Brig Thomas Clive Usher, CBE, DSO, 6th and yst son of 2nd Bt, *b* 1907; *d* 1982: *m* 1939, Valentine (Wells Stables, Hawick, Roxburghshire), da of Brig C. V. Stockwell, of Victoria, BC:—
Margaret Anne, *b* 1941: *m* 1964, Alan Harry Mactaggart, and has issue living, David Clive, *b* 1966, — William Jeremy, *b* 1970.

Issue of late Frederick Usher, 4th son of 1st baronet, *b* 1862, *d* 1909: *m* 1901, Rosie Emil (who *d* 1958, having *m* 2ndly, 1911, Colin Mackenzie Black, CVO, WS, who *d* 1943), el da of late Rev William John Knox Little, formerly V of Hoar Cross, Burton-on-Trent, and Canon and Sub-Dean, of Worcester:—
Neil John William Heriot (Culachy, Fort Augustus, Inverness-shire. Club – New), *b* 1903; *ed* Eton, and Trin Coll, Oxford; is Lieut 7th Batn King's Own Scottish Borderers; assumed on his marriage the additional surname of Murray, but has discontinued its use: *m* 1st, 1929 (*m diss* 1937), Elizabeth Evelyn, who *d* 1990, da of late Lieut-Col Frederick David Murray Baillie (4th Hussars), of Broughton and Cally, and of Ilston Grange, Leicester; 2ndly, 1938, Dorothy Margaret, da of Rev Colin William Scott-Moncrieff, and has issue living, (by 1st *m*) James Neil (Murrayton, Gatehouse of Fleet, Kirkcudbrightshire), *b* 1931; *ed* King's Sch, Canterbury: *m* 1957 (*m diss* 1977), Sara Winefred, da of late Lt-Col Laurence Richardson Younger, and has issue living, Peter James *b* 1961, Rozanne Helen *b* 1960, Diana Katherine *b* 1968.

Grandson of late Francis James Usher, 5th son of 1st baronet:—
Issue of late Francis Simeon Caverhill Usher *b* 1902, *d* 1954: *m* 1935, Jean Lindsay, who *d* 1954, da of W. E. Kitson, of Blanerne, Berwickshire:—
Francis John (Dunglass, Cockburnspath, Berwickshire TD13 5XF), *b* 1937: *m* 1967, Merilyn Haswell, only da of late William Lyle Brown, DSO, TD, MD, of White Ridge, Bamburgh, Northumberland, and has two adopted children, Simon Francis, *b* 1975, — Katharine Caverhill, *b* 1972.
Sir John Usher, 1st Bt, yst son of Andrew Usher, of Edinburgh, assisted in founding a chair of public health, Edinburgh Univ 1898, and built a public health institute 1902.

Vassar-Smith, see Smith.

VAVASOUR (UK) 1828, of Haslewood, Yorkshire

Sir GEOFFREY WILLIAM VAVASOUR, DSC, 5th *Baronet*; *b* 5 Sept 1914; *s* his father, *Capt Sir* LEONARD PIUS, 1961; Com RN (ret): *m* 1st, 1940 (*m diss* 1947), Joan Millicent Kirkland, da of Arthur John Robb; 2ndly, 1971, Marcia Christine, da of Marshall Shaw Lodge, of Batley, Yorks, and formerly wife of Maj Denis Wieler, of Feathercombe, Hambledon, Surrey, and has issue by 1st *m*.

Arms – Quarterly: 1st and 4th, or a fesse dancettée sable, in the dexter chief a cross-crosslet for difference of the second, *Vavasour*; 2nd and 3rd, sable, a bend or, between six fountains, *Stourton*. **Crests** – 1st, a cock gules charged with a fountain, *Vavasour*; 2nd, a demi-monk habited in russet, his girdle or, and wielding in his dexter hand a scourge or, thereon five knotted lashes, and in his sinister an open book or, *Stourton*.
Residence – 8 Bede House, Manor Fields, Putney, SW15. **Clubs** – Hurlingham, All England Lawn Tennis, MCC.

DAUGHTERS LIVING (By 1st marriage)

Jacqueline Mary, *b* 1941: *m* 1966, Capt Peter John Whittington (ret) 14/20th King's Hussars, of Barn's Oak, Waldron, nr Heathfield, East Sussex, and has issue living, Edward James, *b* 1977, — Anna Catherine, *b* 1974. —— Elizabeth Anne, *b* 1943: *m* 1st, 1965 (*m diss* 1968), Terence Hickman; 2ndly, 1968 (*m diss* 1988), James Monroe Woodman; 3rdly, 1989, Calvin Palme Winn, of 11109 SW 113 Place, Miami, Florida 33176, USA, and has issue living (by 2nd *m*), Elizabeth Anne, *b* 1969, — Lara, *b* 1970.

SISTERS LIVING

Elizabeth Mary, *b* 1917: *m* 1st, 1940, Lieut Michael John Priaulx Walters, RN, who *d* on active ser 1941; 2ndly, 1942, Brigadier Garth Raymond Godfrey Bird, of The Oast House, Gt Broadhurst Farm, Broad Oak, Heathfield, Sussex, and has issue living, (by 1st *m*) Simon de Lancey (Tundry House, Dogmersfield, Hants), *b* (*posthumous*) 1941: *m* 1966, Sarah, da of late Brig Thomas Gwythr Charles, and has issue living, Mark *b* 1967, Barnaby *b* 1974, Gemma *b* 1969, Abigail *b* 1976, — (by 2nd *m*) Christopher John Godfrey (78 Masbro Rd, W14), *b* 1946: *m* 1972 (*m diss* 1989), Hon Catherine Mary Dormer, yr da of 15th Baron Dormer, — Anthony Nigel Godfrey (47 Buckingham Place, Brighton, Sussex), *b* 1953, — Fiona Mary, *b* 1943: *m* 1969, Robin Alaster Nicholson, of 7 Highbury Place, N5 1QZ (*see* E Waldegrave, 1959 Edn), and has issue living, Zachary Luke *b* 1971, Solomon Rufus *b* 1974, Caspian Ned *b* 1978. —— Josephine Mary, *b* 1921; formerly 3rd Officer WRNS: *m* 1942, Rear Adm Derick Henry Fellowes Hetherington, CB, DSC, who *d* 1992, and has issue living, Mark, *b* 1950, — Virginia Mary, *b* 1947, — Teresa, *b* 1951, — Dinah Mary, *b* 1957.

COLLATERAL BRANCHES LIVING

Grandchildren of late Oswald Joseph Stanislaus Vavasour (infra):—
Issue of late Hugh Bernard Moore Vavasour, *b* 1918, *d* 1989: *m* 1950, Monique Pauline Marie Madeleine, who *d* 1982, da of Maurice Erick Beck, of St Aubin sur Scie, Seine Maritime, France:—
ERIC MICHEL JOSEPH MARMADUKE (15 Mill Lane, Earl Shilton, Leics LE9 7AW), *b* 3 Jan 1953; BSc: *m* 1976, Isabelle Baudouin Françoise Alain Cécile Cornelie Ghislaine, da of André van Hille, of 194 Tomberg, Brussels 1200, and has issue living, Joseph Ian Hugh André, *b* 1978, — Thomas Bernard André Hugh, *b* 1984, — Emilie Isabelle Marguerite Monique, *b* 1980. —— Anne Pauline Mary Draycot, *b* 1969.

Grandchildren of late Oswald Hugh Stanislaus Vavasour, uncle of 4th baronet:—
Issue of late Oswald Joseph Stanislaus Vavasour, *b* 1883, *d* 1973: *m* 1915, Mary Dorothy, who *d* 1952, da of late Bernard Moore, of The Grange, Draycott, Stoke-on-Trent:—
Dorothy Constance (Provincial House, The Rideway, Mill Hill, NW7 1EH), *b* 1916; a Sister of Charity.
Issue of late John Wilfred Leonard Vavasour, *b* 1891, *d* 1955: *m* 1940, Joyce, who *m* 2ndly, 1951, Robert William Ellett Ware (94 Riverside Rd, Albany Park, Sidcup, Kent), da of late George Frederick Mayer, of Ardleigh, Keddington Rd, Louth, Lincolnshire:—
Margaret Ann *b* 1940. —— Angela Mary, *b* 1943. —— Frances Joyce Sarah, *b* 1949.

Grandsons of late Henry Dunstan Vavasour (infra):—
Issue of late Edward Joseph Henry Vavasour, *b* 1898, *d* 1978: *m* 1927, Mary, who *d* 1975, da of late Duncan Leslie, of Perth:—
Paul (41 Serpentine Rd, Sevenoaks, Kent TN13 3XS), *b* 1929; *ed* Stonyhurst; BSc, (Lond) FICE, FIHT: *m* 1952, Pauline Mary, da of late Charles John Cable, of Sevenoaks, Kent, and has issue living, Dunstan Edward (16 Oak St, Rugby CV22 5EA), *b* 1963; *ed* Stonyhurst; MA (Oxon); MIEE: *m* 1988, Jill, da of John Edward Fellows, of Stonebroom, Derbys, and has issue living, Oliver James *b* 1991, — Catriona Mary *b* 1955; BSc (Dunelm): *m* 1992, Maj Nigel D. Wylie Carrick, 2nd King Edward VII's Own Goorkhas (The Sirmoor Rifles), elder son of Maj N. Wylie Carrick, of Duntisbourne Abbots, Cirencester, and has issue living, Lucy Elizabeth Mary *b* 1993, — Elspeth Anne, *b* 1956: *m* 1979, Paul Julian Fox, of Yeoman Oast, Manor Farm, Laddingford, Kent, and has issue living, Miles Edward *b* 1983, Oriana Mary *b* 1980, Miranda Jane *b* 1985, — Matilda Alice, *b* 1961; MA (Oxon): *m* 1988, Maj Nicholas Keith Cooper, RAMC, elder son of Basil Keith Cooper, of Croyde, Devon, and has issue living, Hugh Edward Keith *b* 1990. —— Christopher Edward (187 Glenmore Rd, Paddington, NSW 2021, Australia), *b* 1938; *ed* King's Sch, Canterbury, and Roy Agric Coll, Cirencester: *m* 1st, 1963 (*m diss* 19—), Cecilie May, da of late Cecil Dudley Morris, of Maidlands Farm, Brede, Sussex; 2ndly, 1987, Penelope Joanne, da of H. David S. Luetchford, of Noosa, Queensland, Australia, and has issue living, (by 1st *m*) Philip James Edward (282 Beaver Rd, Ashford, Kent), *b* 1964; *ed* Kelly Coll: *m* 1990, Joanna Marjorie, da of Alan George Smith, of Burwash, Sussex, and has issue living, Fenella Molly May *b* 1993, — Simon Mark Andrew (9 Wood St, Norwich, Norfolk), *b* 1966; *ed* King's Sch, Canterbury, and London Univ (MB, BS): *m* 1992, Sarah Lucy, elder da of Geoffrey Jacques, of SW7, and has issue living, Rosie Charlotte May *b* 1993, — Charles William Alexander (Magpie House, Stubbs Cross, Ashford, Kent), *b* 1971; *ed* King's Sch, Canterbury, and Oxford Brookes Univ (BA), — (by 2nd *m*) Susannah Mary-Jane, *b* 1989.
Issue of late Harold Hugh Vavasour, *b* 1902, *d* 1989: *m* 1939, Margery Constance (12 Munro St, Blenheim, NZ), da of Harold Oakley Goulter, of Blairich Station, Blenheim, NZ:—
Hugh Gerald (Hazlewood, 34 Brook St, Blenheim, NZ), *b* 1940: *m* 1966, Belinda Mary, da of Leonard Clarke, of Wellington, NZ, and has issue living, Andrew Philip Henry, *b* 1968; B Ag (Massey), — Sarah Mary Constance *b* 1967: *m* 1988, James Hadden Barr, son of Henry John Haddon Barr, of Invercargill, NZ, and has issue living, Angus Haddon Dunstan *b* 1991, Jock Henry Hugh *b* 1993, — Rachel Isolda Mary, *b* 1972, — Alice Francesca Mary *b* 1977. —— Philip Joseph (112 Karori Rd, Wellington, NZ), *b* 1943: *m* 1973, Elizabeth Robyn, da of Robert Barnett, of Bronte St, Nelson, NZ, and has issue living,

Jonathan Charles, *b* 1982, — Carolyn Elizabeth, *b* 1980. —— Nicola Mary Clare, *b* 1947: *m* 1972, Kerry Gould Louis Nolan, of Coops Rd, Kaiapoi RD, NZ, and has issue living, David, *b* 1976, — Rosamond Mary Hope, *b* 1974, — Abigail *b* 1978.
　　　Issue of late Gerard Aloysius Vavasour, *b* 1904, *d* 1983: *m* 1930, Lilian Frances (Cook St, Havelock, NZ), da of late Francis Campbell, of Blenheim, NZ:—
Michael Philip (Titania, Oberon, NSW 2787, Aust), *b* 1932: *m* 1st, 1955, Margaret Anne, who *d* 1963, da of Frederick H. B. Redward, of New Plymouth, NZ; 2ndly, 1965, Pamela Anne, da of Reginald B. Marston, of Sydney, and has issue living, (by 1st *m*) Gerard Joseph (19 Powell Drive, Queanbeyan, NSW, Australia), *b* 1956: *m* 1st, 1978 (*m diss* 1983), Colleen Bishop, of Sydney, Aust; 2ndly, 1984, Sonja Westerburg, of Queanbeyan, NSW, and has issue living, (by 1st *m*) Daniel *b* 1980, (by 2nd *m*) Alexander *b* 1990, Tamara *b* 1987, — Phillip Charles Dunstan (21 Alice Jackson Crescent, Gilmore, ACT, Aust), *b* 1960: *m* 1987, Katherine Lions, of Sydney, Aust, and has issue living, Nicola Frances *b* 1993, — Angela Margaret, *b* 1959: *m* 1979, Gary Smith, of Terrigal, NSW, and has issue living, Scott Aaron *b* 1983, Shaun Thomas *b* 1986, Jessica Leanne *b* 1989, — Rose Lillian Mary, *b* 1962, — (by 2nd *m*) Christopher Paul (4 Dart St, Oberon, NSW 2787, Aust), *b* 1966. —— Bernard John (Toi Downs, Blenheim, NZ), *b* 1933; Dip CAC: *m* 1964, Susan Ferrier, da of Bruce Colville Morton, of Wai Whiro, Takapau, and has issue living, Thomas William, *b* 1964: *m* 1992, Kris Mills, and has issue living, Kelsey May *b* 1993, — Joseph Murray, *b* 1970, — Matthew Colville, *b* 1971, — Dominic Gerard, *b* 1974, — Gerard Bruce, *b* 1977, — Maria, *b* 1966, — Katherine Mary, *b* 1968: *m* 1987, Andrew Keith Boniface, and has issue living, Karl Andrew *b* 1989, Stacey Marie *b* 1986. —— Priscilla, *b* 1936: *m* 1959, Marian Josef Adamski (Kahui Rd, RD 34, Rahotu Taranaki, NZ), and has issue living, Peter Bernard, *b* 1961, — Anthony John, *b* 1968: *m* 1988, Leanne, da of Peter Tanner, and has issue living, Haiden James *b* 1989, — Damian Joseph, *b* 1969, — Maria Ann, *b* 1963, — Frances Mary, *b* 1964, — Theresa, *b* 1966. —— Bertha Eleanor Mary, *b* 1942: *m* 1st, 1967 (*m diss* 1987), Michael John Baldwin; 2ndly, 19—, Michael Newman, of Cowslip Valley, Marlborough, NZ, and has issue living (by 1st *m*), Bruce Phillip, *b* 1970, — Anita Jane, *b* 1968, — Penelope Debra, *b* 1975. —— Colleen Mary, *b* 1943: *m* 1973, Don Alan Robertson (Craigholm Farm, McShones Rd, RD1, Richmond, Nelson, NZ), and has issue living, Gilbert Alan, *b* 1974, — James Wallace, *b* 1977, — Phillip Duncan, *b* 1981, — Colette Marie, *b* 1976, — Sophie Anne, *b* 1979.
　　　Issue of late John Louis Vavasour, *b* 1905, *d* 1987: *m* 1937, Madeleine Hope (who *m* 2ndly, 1988, her late husband's younger brother, Henry Philip Bede Vavasour) (infra), da of Ernest John Brammall, of Blenheim, NZ:—
Jeremy Dunstan Trevor (Koitaki Plantation, PO Box 133, Port Moresby, Papua New Guinea), *b* 1942: *m* 1966, Joan Reilly, da of late George Robert Moss, of Melbourne, Aust, and has issue living, Simon John, *b* 1974, — Peta, *b* 1967, — Kimble, *b* 1971. —— Anne, *b* 1938: *m* 1963, David Eric Stewart Adams, of 23 Mulara St, Alice Springs 0870, NT, Aust, and has issue living, Jacqueline Anne, *b* 1968, — Gillian Merle, *b* 1970, — Sandra Claire, *b* 1972. —— Teresa Virginia, *b* 1939: *m* 1962, Brian John Cowan, of 15 Harrier Crescent, Umhlanga Rocks 4320, Natal, S Africa, and has issue living, John Michael, *b* 1964, — Anne Juliet, *b* 1967, — Sara Jill, *b* 1971. —— Marcia Jane, *b* 1952: *m* 1979, Owen William Finger, of Mowla Bluff Station, PO Box 356, Broome 6725, W Aust.

　　　　　　　Issue of late Henry Dunstan Vavasour, uncle of 4th baronet, *b* 1850, *d* 1927: *m* 1887, Bertha Eleanor Mary, who *d* 1959, da of Thomas Peter Redwood, of Burleigh, Blenheim, New Zealand:—
Henry Philip Bede, *b* 1907: *m* 1st, 1949, Rosamond Mary, who *d* 1973, da of Daniel Riddiford, of Featherston, NZ; 2ndly, 1988, Madeleine Hope, widow of his brother John Louis Vavasour (ante), and has issue living (by 1st *m*), Peter Dunstan (The Favourite, Blenheim, NZ), *b* 1950: *m* 1978, Anna Caroline, who *d* 1985, da of David Churchill Gould, of Sunsfield, Christchurch, NZ, and has issue living, Louis Dunstan *b* 1980, Felix William *b* 1982, Claudia Annabelle *b* 1984, — Francis William Joseph, *b* 1958, — Rollo Charles Joseph (twin), *b* 1951, — Charles Edward, *b* 1954, — Mary Rosamond (twin) *b* 1954, — Aletha Thérèse, *b* 1955. *Residence* – Harford, 72 Murphy's Rd, Blenheim, NZ. —— Pearl Constantia, *b* 1895: *m* 1924, Francis Felix Reid, CBE, who *d* 1966, and has issue living, Christopher Robin (Redwood, Blenheim, NZ), *b* 1925: *m* 1958, Clare, widow of Peter Goulter, — Angela *b* 1929: *m* 1956, Richard Fawcett, of The Biggin, Bramham, Boston Spa, Yorks, and has issue living, Thomas Francis *b* 1957; *ed* Ampleforth and R Agric Coll, Cirencester, Anthony James *b* 1961; *ed* Ampleforth, Peter Edward *b* 1963; *ed* Ampleforth, Teresa Mary *b* 1958, Sarah Jane *b* 1959.

Sir Thomas Vavasour, Knt, of Hazlewood, co York, was created a baronet 1628. The title became extinct on the death of the 7th baronet 1826. The estates devolved upon his maternal cousin, the 3rd son of the 17th Baron Stourton, Hon Edward Marmaduke Joseph Stourton, who assumed the name of Vavasour, and was created a baronet (*see* B Mowbray, colls) in 1828.

Venables (Dillwyn-Venables-Llewelyn), see Llewelyn.

VERNER (UK) 1846, of Verner's Bridge, Armagh (Extinct 1975)

COLLATERAL BRANCH LIVING

　　　　　Issue of late Hubert Henry Wingfield Verner, 2nd son of 4th baronet, *b* 1868, *d* 1946: *m* 1900, Marion Henrietta, who *d* 1951, yst da of late Maj-Gen Evan Maberly, CB:—
Rose Winifred, *b* 1901. *Residence* – Little Garlands, Layer de la Haye, near Colchester.

VERNEY (UK) 1818, of Claydon House, Buckinghamshire

*One faith,
one sun*

*The promise made
to my ancestor has
been kept*

Sir RALPH BRUCE VERNEY, KBE, 5th *Baronet; b* 18 Jan 1915; *s* his father, *Sir* HARRY CALVERT WILLIAMS, DSO, 1974; *ed* Canford, and Balliol Coll, Oxford (BA); Java 1945 as Maj RA; Vice-Lt for Bucks 1965-86; High Sheriff 1957; Co Councillor of Bucks 1952-73, and Co Alderman 1961-73; Chm, Nat Cttee for England of Forestry Commn 1968-80 (Produced plan for the Chiltern Hills in 1971); Pres Country Landowners' Assocn 1961-63; Chm Nature Conservancy Council 1980-83; Member of Royal Commn on Environmental Pollution 1973-79; Trustee of Radcliffe, Ernest Cook and Chequers Trusts; KBE (Civil) 1974: *m* 1948, Mary (LRAM), da of late Percy Charles Vestey (*see* Vestey, Bt, colls), and has issue.

ᴀrms – Quarterly: 1st and 4th, azure, on a cross argent, fimbriated or, five mullets gules, *Verney*; 2nd and 3rd, paly of six erminois and pean, a bend engrailed counterchanged, *Calvert*. ᴄrests – 1st, a demi-phœnix in flames proper, charged with five mullets in cross or and looking at the rays of the sun, *Verney*; 2nd out of a mural crown argent two spears erect therefrom two pennons flowing towards the dexter, one erminois, the other pean, *Calvert*. Seat – Claydon House, Buckingham, MK18 2EX. *Residence* – Ballams, Middle Claydon, Buckingham MK18 2ET. *Club* – Cavalry and Guards'.

SON LIVING

EDMUND RALPH (Claydon House, Buckingham, MK18 2EX) (Brooks's Club), *b* 28 June 1950; *ed* Harrow, and York Univ; FRICS: *m* 1982, Daphne Primrose, da of late Col Andrew Hamilton Farquhar Fausset-Farquhar, DSO, TD, JP (*see* Macpherson-Grant, Bt, ext) and has issue living, Andrew Nicholas, *b* 9 July 1983, — Ella, *b* 1985.

DAUGHTERS LIVING

Sarah Dorothy, *b* 1953: *m* 1974, George Caird, of North End, 44 Jack Straw's Lane, Headington, Oxford OX3 0DW, and has issue living, Adam Benjamin, *b* 1977, — Oliver Ralph, *b* 1978, — Edmund George, *b* 1989, — Iona Katharine Mary, *b* 1991. —— Mary Jane, *b* 1957. —— Francesca Marjorie, *b* 1963.

BROTHERS LIVING

Rt Rev Stephen Edmund, MBE (Charity School House, Church Rd, Blewbury, Didcot, Oxon OX11 9PY), *b* 1919; *ed* Harrow, and Balliol College, Oxford (MA); late Lt and temp Capt Intelligence Corps; Canon of St George's Chapel, Windsor 1970-77; consecrated Bishop of Repton (Suffragan for Diocese of Derby) 1977; 1939-45 War in Greece and Central Mediterranean (MBE); MBE (Mil) 1945: *m* 1st, 1947, Priscilla Avice Sophie, who *d* 1974, only da of George Schwerdt, of Alresford, Hants; 2ndly, 1981, Mrs Sandra Bailey, and has issue living (by 1st *m*), Robert Francis (Lower Camelot, S Cadbury, Yeovil, Som BA22 7HA), *b* 1949; *ed* Harrow: *m* 1974, Marianne Juliet, da of Francis Henry Haine, of Box Cottage, Blockley, Glos, and has issue living, Alistair Francis *b* 1976, Nicholas Stephen *b* 1978, Christopher Felix *b* 1982, — Rachel Penelope, *b* 1952: *m* 1982, Nicholas Wheeler-Robinson, of Pigotts, North Dean, High Wycombe, Bucks HP14 4NF, and has issue living, Charles Ralph *b* 1988, Caleb John *b* 1992, Olivia Alice *b* 1989, — Helen Mary, *b* 1955: *m* 1986, Jonathan Impett, of 53 Richford St, W6, and has issue living, Thomas Gabriel *b* 1986, Lara Priscilla *b* 1989, — Katharine Priscilla, *b* 1958: *m* 1985, Michael Berman, of 19 Moreton Pl, SW1, and has issue living, Jonathan Stephen *b* 1986, Adam Michael *b* 1993, Imogen Emily *b* 1988. —— Hugh Alexander, *b* 1920; *ed* Harrow, and Oriel Coll, Oxford (BA 1946, MA 1958); sometime Lt Gren Gds; 1939-45 War (wounded): *m* 1950, Ann Mary, da of late S. E. Chesterman, of Wing, Rutland, and has had issue, †Thomas Harry, *b* 1958; *ed* Harrow; *d* 1988, as the result of a road accident, — Mark, *b* 1962; *ed* Harrow, — Jonathan *b* (twin), 1960; *ed* Harrow, — Fiona Ann, *b* 1952: *m* 1975, Mark Hope, of Sunninghill, Banchory, Kincardineshire AB31 3TR, and has issue living, Harry Alexander *b* 1988, Jonathan Mark *b* 1990, — Teresa Joan, *b* 1954: *m* 1975 (*m diss* 1980), Robin Hales, — Julia Mary, *b* 1956: *m* 1992, Iain Smith. *Residence* – The Mill, Snowshill Rd, Broadway, Worcs. —— Andrew Felix (White House, Pewsey, Wilts SN9 5DW), *b* 1921; *ed* Harrow, and Balliol Coll, Oxford; MRCS and LRCP 1948: *m* 1955, Mrs Theodosia Olive Craig, da of James W. Cropper, of Ellergreen, Kendal, and has issue living, Caspar Charles Andrew (288 Coronation Rd, Southville, Bristol BS3 1RT), *b* 1961: *m* 1986, Wilma Birnie Thomson, and has issue living, Joseph Alexander *b* 1984, George Andrew *b* 1987, Edward Jonathan *b* 1991, — Caroline Rachel, *b* 1956: *m* 1985, Guy Robert Dagul, of Britwell Lodge, Benson, Oxon OX9 6SD, son of Harvey Dagul, of St Albans, Herts, and has issue living, Samuel Matthew *b* 1990, William Arthur *b* 1993, Rose Elizabeth *b* 1988. —— *Sir* Lawrence John, TD (Central Criminal Court, Old Bailey, EC4M 7EH), *b* 1924; *ed* Harrow, and Oriel Coll, Oxford (MA); Bar Inner Temple 1952; late Lt-Col RA (TA) (R Bucks Yeo); a DL of Bucks; Dep Chm Bucks Quarter Sessions 1962-71; Dep Chm Middx Sessions 1971; a Circuit Judge 1972-90, since when Recorder of London; 1939-45 War as Capt Gren Gds and Lt Col in Roy Bucks Yeomanry TA 1947-68, hon Col of Bucks Army Cadet Force 1975-80; OStJ 1992; ktd 1993: *m* 1972, Zoë Auriel, yr da of Lt-Col Peter Goodeve Goodeve-Docker, of Kealkil, Bantry, co Cork.

SISTERS LIVING

Mary Rachel, *b* 1916: *m* 1947, Rev Geoffrey Thomas Roberts (West Flat Riding School, Grimsthorpe, Bourne, Lincs PE10 0LY), and has issue living, Gillian Marjorie, *b* 1950, — Susan Jane, *b* 1953: *m* 1982, Paul Morgan, and has issue living, Benjamin Andrew *b* 1992, Claire Susan *b* 1983, Anna Mary (twin) *b* 1983, Lucy Rachel *b* 1987. —— Catherine, *b* 1925: *m* 1947, Richard Mervyn Hare, FBA, White's Prof Emeritus of Moral Philosophy, Oxford, and has issue living, John Edmund (144 Benjamin St SE, Grand Rapids, Michigan 49506, USA), *b* 1949; *ed* Rugby, and Balliol Coll, Oxford; Prof: *m* 1976, Teresa, da of William Forsyth, of Princeton, New Jersey, USA, and has issue living, Andrew Forsyth *b* 1983, Catherine Elizabeth *b* 1980, — Bridget Rachel, *b* 1950: *m* 1976, William Toy George, Jr, of 908 E Fifth St, Bethlehem, Pa 18015, USA, and has issue living, Samuel Benton *b* 1980, Anisa Louise *b* 1982, — Amy Louise, *b* 1953: *m* 1984, Philip Gerald Knight, of 92 Hamilton Rd, Reading RG1 5RD, and has issue living, Hannah Ellin *b* 1987, — Ellin Catherine, *b* 1955: has issue living, Matt Martin *b* 19—. *Residence* – Saffron House, Ewelme, Oxon OX9 6HP.

COLLATERAL BRANCHES LIVING

Grandchildren of late Sir Harry Lloyd-Verney, GCVO, 2nd son of Col George Hope Lloyd-Verney (who assumed the additional surname of LLOYD by Roy Licence 1888), 3rd son of 2nd baronet:—
Issue of late Maj-Gen Gerald Lloyd Verney, DSO, MVO, late Irish Guards, *b* 1900, *d* 1957, having discontinued the

use of the Christian names of Harry George by deed poll 1941: *m* 1926, Hon Joyce Sybil Vivian, who *d* 1983, da of 1st Baron Bicester:—
Peter Vivian, *b* 1930; *ed* Eton, and Trin Coll, Dublin (MA); late Maj Irish Gds; an author: *m* 1st, 1959 (*m diss* 1982), Caroline Evelyn, el da of late George Anthony Harford, of Widden Hill House, Horton, Chipping Sodbury, Glos; 2ndly, 1983, Elizabeth Anne, da of Wing Cdr Harry St George Burke, RAF, of Auberies, Bulmer, Essex, and widow of Christopher George James Oldridge de la Hey, and has issue living (by 1st *m*), Harry George Vivian (The Old Forge, Ewen, Cirencester, Glos), *b* 1960: *m* 1st, 1985 (*m diss* 1989), Sarah Mary Cotterill, da of R. P. Voelcker, of Stanton St Quintin, Wilts; 2ndly, 1992, Mrs Lavinia Mary Delves Dawes, yst da of Sir Evelyn Delves Broughton, 12th Bt, and widow of Douglas D. Dawes, and has issue living (by 2nd *m*), Harriet Charity *b* 1992, — Louisa Margaret *b* 1962: *m* 1993, Matthew Jeremy Higgs, and has issue living, Florence Nettle *b* 1994, — Henrietta Nell, *b* 1965: *m* 1987, Thomas Richard William Lapage-Norris, eldest son of Capt T. E. Lapage-Norris, of Worton, Wilts. —— Bridget Mary, *b* 1926: *m* 1951, Michael Barry Sarson (Hansteads, East Hanney, Wantage, Oxon), and has issue living, Michael Vivian, *b* 1953, — David Peter, *b* 1955, Mary Anne, *b* 1959, — Jane Elizabeth, *b* 1962.

Issue of late Lt-Col Ulick Otway Vortigern Lloyd-Verney, OBE, *b* 1902, *d* 1979: *m* 1929, Esmé Louise, who *d* 1978, da of Charles Austin Smith-Ryland, of Barford Hill, Warwick:—
Harry Ulick Dennis (The Garden House, Cheriton, Alresford, Hants), *b* 1940; *ed* Eton; FCA: *m* 1976, Sarah Fane, yr da of Maj A. P. P. Ricketts, of The Old Manse, Nigg, Ross and Cromarty, and has issue living, Louisa Florence, *b* 1977, — Alice Sarah, *b* 1979, — Camilla Anne, *b* 1981. —— Anne Margaret, *b* 1930; JP Shrewsbury; DL Shropshire 1986: *m* 1951, Col John Montagu Flint, MBE, late RE, of The Dower House, Great Ness, Shrewsbury, and has issue living, Charles John Raffles (189 Camberwell Grove, SE5), *b* 1952; Barrister-at-law: *m* 1978, Diana Rosemary, el da of Maj Robert Topham, of Plasyn Grove, Ellesmere, Shrops, and has issue living, William Charles Raffles *b* 1982, Julia *b* 1984, — Michael Edward Stamford, *b* 1956: *m* 1981, Fiona, 2nd da of Prof Alasdair Steele-Bodger, of The Old Rectory, Hale, Fordingbridge, Hants, and has issue living, Alasdair Stamford *b* 1987, Oliver John Montagu *b* 1989, — Sarah Esmé, *b* 1955: *m* 1976, Maj Christopher Thomas Stanton Prestwich, 15th/19th King's R Hussars, and has issue living, Edward Joseph Stanton *b* 1985, Emma Charlotte Esmé *b* 1983, — Elizabeth Anne, *b* 1958: *m* 1983, Colin Michael Wood, and has issue living, Christopher James *b* 1987, Helen Sarah *b* 1990. —— Carola Mariette, *b* 1932: *m* 1952, Maj John Hugh Torquil Sutton, late Coldm Gds, of Bayfield Brecks, Holt, Norfolk (*see* Sutton, Bt, colls).

Grandchildren of late Frederick William Verney, 4th son of 2nd baronet:—
Issue of late Sir Ralph Verney, CB, CIE, CVO, who was *cr* a *Baronet* 1946:—
See Verney, Bt, *cr* 1946.
The 1st Bt, Gen Sir Harry Calvert, GCB, GCH, was Adjt-Gen of the Forces for 21 years. The Rt Hon Sir Harry, 2nd Bt, in 1827 assumed by Roy licence the surname of Verney in lieu of Calvert, having *s* to the Verney estates (his cousin Richard Calvert *m* the widow of Hon John Verney, el son of 1st Earl Verney). He sat as MP for Buckingham (*L*) and Bedford. The 3rd baronet, Sir Edmund Hope, Capt RN, served in Crimean War 1854-55, and Indian Mutiny 1857-58, and sat as MP for N Buckingham (*L*). The 4th Bt, Sir Harry Calvert Williams Verney, DSO, was PPS to Ch Sec for Ireland 1911-14, and Parl Sec to Board of Agric 1914; MP for Bucks (*L*) 1910-18; author of *The Verneys of Claydon* and *Florence Nightingale at Harley Street*.

VERNEY (UK) 1946, of Eaton Square, City of Westminster

One faith,
one sun

The promise made
to my ancestor has
been kept

Sir (JOHN) SEBASTIAN VERNEY, 3rd *Baronet*; *b* 30 Aug 1945; *s* his father, Sir JOHN, MC, 1993; *ed* Eton.

Arms – Quarterly: 1st and 4th, azure, on a cross argent, fimbriated or, five mullets gules, *Verney*; 2nd and 3rd, paly of six erminois and pean, a bend engrailed counterchanged, *Calvert*. **Crests** – 1st, a demi-phœnix in flames proper, charged with five mullets in cross or, and looking at the rays of the sun, *Verney*; 2nd, out of a mural crown argent two spears erect, therefrom two pennons flowing towards the dexter, one erminois, the other pean, *Calvert*.
Residences – The White House, Clare, Suffolk; 34 Gladstone St, SE1 6EY.

SISTERS LIVING

Sabrina Anne, *b* 1947. —— Juliet Rose, *b* 1949: *m* 1st, 1970 (*m diss* 19—), Michael Benjamin; 2ndly, 1979, Simon Hugh Arden Acworth, of The Old Rectory, Meonstoke, Hants, only son of Maj G. W. Acworth, MVO, of Woodeaton, Oxford, and has issue living (by 1st *m*) Thomas Michael, *b* 1971, — Julian, *b* 1973, — (by 2nd *m*) Robin, *b* 1983, — Florence Mary, *b* 1980. —— Rose Lucinda, *b* 1950: *m* 1978, Peter Zinovieff, elder son of late Maj Leo Zinovieff, and has issue living, Olga, *b* 1978, — Katarina, *b* 1981, — Iliena, *b* 1983. —— Candida Harriet, *b* 1953: *m* 1980, Timothy C. Molloy, son of Maj T. R. Molloy, MC, of Wincanton, Somerset, and has issue living, Henry, *b* 1981, — Ned, *b* 1984, — Theo, *b* 1986. —— (Alice) Angelica, *b* 1956: *m* 1984, David James Risk Kennard, yr son of late Maj Robert William Kennard, MC, TD, of Barton Farm, Guiting Power, Glos, and has issue living, Paris Timothy, *b* 1986, — Hector, *b* 1988, — Edgar Robert, *b* 1991.

AUNT LIVING (*daughter of 1st baronet*)

Joscelyne, *b* 1915: *m* 1941, Capt Andrew Thorne, late Gren Gds (B Penrhyn), who *d* 1991, and has had issue, Nicholas Andrew, *b* 1942; Capt Gren Gds: *m* 1969, Diana Lesley Kathryn (who *m* 2ndly, 1977, Ian Mitchell Thomas, of Floriston Hall, Wixoe, Sudbury, Suffolk), da of late Donald Leslie, of Horley Place, Horley, Surrey, and *d* 1976, leaving issue, Alexander Francis Andrew Nicholas *b* 1972, Camilla Claire Louise *b* 1976, — Joanna Mary, *b* 1945: *m* 1966, Maj-Gen John Peter William Friedberger, CB, CBE, of North Woolding Cottage, The Harrow Way, Whitchurch, Hants RG28 7QT, and has issue living, Richard Mark *b* 1973, Rosanna Catharine *b* 1967: *m* 1991, James Robert Perceval Armitage, son of Jeremy Armitage (and has issue living, Luke Robert *b* 1993), Lucinda Jane *b* 1970, — Carola Joscelyne, *b* 1948: *m* 1978, Nigel Howard Symington (Parsonage Farm House, Fletching, Uckfield, E Sussex), and has issue living, Lucy Elizabeth Joscelyne *b* 1980, Fiona Juliet *b* 1982, Victoria Carola *b* 1984. *Residence* – Cottage 32, Headbourne Worthy House, Winchester SO23 7JG.

WIDOW LIVING OF SECOND BARONET

(JEANIE) LUCINDA (*Lady Verney*), da of late Maj Herbert Musgrave, DSO, RE: *m* 1939, Sir John Verney, 2nd Bt, MC, who *d* 1993. *Residence* – The White House, Clare, Suffolk.

COLLATERAL BRANCH LIVING

Issue of late Lt Cdr David Verney, RN, yr son of 1st Bt, *b* 1918, *d* 1992: *m* 1948, Hon Mary Kathleen Boscawen (Trevella, St Erne, nr Truro, Cornwall), only da of 8th Viscount Falmouth:—
CHRISTOPHER RALPH EVELYN, *b* 4 Oct 1948; *ed* Eton: *m* 1976, Madeliene, da of — Lindberg, of — . ——— Margaret Mary, *b* 1950: *m* 1971, Peter Michael Bickford-Smith, of Trevarno, Helston, Cornwall, and has issue living, Michael Rupert David, *b* 1984, — Sacha Ann Mary, *b* 1975, — Charlotte Ann Bertha, *b* 1977, — Stephanie May, *b* 1989. ——— Rosemary Janette, *b* 1958: *m* 1982 (*m diss* 1991), John Kenna, yst son of Raymond Kenna, of The Pines, Foxrock, co Dublin, and has issue living, Justin, *b* 1987, — Nicholas Harry, *b* 1990, — Lamorna Daisy, *b* 1985.
The 1st baronet, Lt-Col Sir Ralph Verney, CB, CIE, CVO, Rifle Brig, son of late Frederick William Verney (yst son of Sir Harry Verney, 2nd Bt, *cr* 1818), was appointed Mil Sec to Viceroy of India, 1916-21, Sec to Speaker of House of Commons 1921-55, and an Examiner for Private Bills and Taxing Master House of Commons 1927-45: *m* 1909, Janette Cheverié Hamilton, da of Senator Hon James Thomas Walker of Sydney, Aust.

VERNON (UK) 1914, of Shotwick Park, co Chester

Vernon·semper·viret

Spring does not always flourish

Sir NIGEL JOHN DOUGLAS VERNON, 4th *Baronet*; *b* 2 May 1924; *s* his father Sir (WILLIAM) NORMAN, 1967; *ed* Charterhouse; late Lt RNVR and RNR; Dir Hogg Insurance Brokers: *m* 1947, Margaret Ellen, da of late Robert Lyle Dobell, of The Mount, Waverton, Chester, and has had issue.

Arms – Or, on a fesse azure between two cross molines in pale gules three garbs of the field. **Crest** – In front of a demi-female figure affrontée proper vested azure, around the temples an oak wreath vert, holding in the dexter hand a sickle and in the sinister two ears of wheat slipped also proper, a garb fessewise or.
Residences – Top-y-Fron Hall, Kelsterton, nr Flint, Clwyd CH6 5TF. *Clubs* – Naval, Army and Navy.

SONS LIVING AND DECEASED

JAMES WILLIAM, *b* 2 April 1949; FCA; *ed* Shrewsbury: *m* 1981, Davinia Elizabeth, elder da of late Christopher David Howard (*see* V Portman, colls), and has issue living, George William Howard, *b* 25 July 1987, — Guy Alexander Howard, *b* 1993, — Harriet Lucy Howard, *b* 1985. *Residence* – The Hall, Lygan-y-Wern, Pentre Halkyn, Clwyd. ——— John Alan, *b* 1956; *ed* Shrewsbury; *d* 1987.

DAUGHTER LIVING

Caroline Margaret, *b* 1953: *m* 1974 (*m diss* 1978), Simon Jonathan Salusbury-Trelawny (*see* Salusbury-Trelawny, Bt, colls).

SISTER LIVING

Diana Elizabeth, *b* 1922; formerly Section Officer WAAF: *m* 1st, 1943 (*m diss* 1949) (annulment Roman Catholic Church 1951), Bohuslav F. Kovarik, DFM, Czechoslovak Air Force, who *d* 1969; 2ndly, 1951, Joseph Olivier Hamelin de Grondines de Landry, of 20 Tarrant Wharf, Tarrant St, Arundel, W Sussex BN18 9NY.

COLLATERAL BRANCHES LIVING

Issue of late Humphrey Bagnall Vernon, MC, 3rd son of 2nd baronet, *b* 1895, *d* 1979: *m* 1938, Sibyl (Beechdale House, Stonecross, Exford, Somerset), yst da of late Samuel Mason Houghton, of The Marfords, Bromborough, Cheshire:—
John Humphrey (Maybank, 36 Glen Brook Rd, Priors Lee, Telford, Shropshire TF2 9QY), *b* 1940: *m* 1973, Alison Margaret, only da of William Warnock Watt, of Sheriffhales, Shrops, and has issue living, Andrew William, *b* 1981, — Nicola Jane, *b* 1978. ——— Richard Bagnall (Little Tranby, Seven Corners Lane, Beverley, N. Humberside), *b* 1944: *m* 1969, Deborah Florence, el da of Geoffrey Oswald Atyeo Briggs, MB, BCh, of The Kennels, Thoresby Park, Notts, and has issue living, Toby Richard, *b* 1971.

Grandsons of late William Allen Vernon (infra):—
Issue of late Herbert Wallace Vernon, *b* 1890, *d* 1974: *m* 1924, Gertrude, who *d* 1959, el da of Tom Jackson, JP, of Waterfoot, Heaton, Bolton:—
Bryan Tom Jackson (The Deacons, High St, Yarmouth, I of Wight), *b* 1925; *ed* Loretto; late Sub-Lt RNVR: *m* 1955, Anne Cecilia, da of late Harry S. Burgess, of Beck Hall, Thornton Dale, Yorks, and has issue living, Andrew Bryan, *b* 1955: *m* 1982, Patricia May Gorecki, and has issue living, Thomas Andrew *b* 1983, Alexandra Mary *b* 1985, — Charles Harry, *b* 1960, — Timothy William, *b* 1962: *m* 1988, Tessa Hodgson, — Belinda Anne, *b* 1957: *m* 1980 (*m diss* 1987), Timothy John Hughes-Williams, of Valbonne, Provence, France, and has issue living, Mark Alan *b* 1983, Victoria Anne *b* 1981. ——— Richard Wallace (Park Lodge, 46 Park Rd, Aldeburgh, Suffolk IP15 5EU), *b* 1927; *ed* Camb Univ (MA); late 2nd Lt RA: *m* 1955, Pamela Violet, da of late Lt-Col Alexander George William Grierson, RM (ret) (*see* Grierson, Bt, colls), and has issue living, David Grierson (77 Brodrick Rd, SW17 7DX), *b* 1956: *m* 1988, Rosemary Nicola Myer, and has issue living, William Grierson *b* 1990, Hannah Emily *b* 1992, — Simon Richard (135 Crane Drive, San Anselmo, California 94960, USA), *b* 1958: *m* 1985, Vanessa Ann Hudson, and has issue living, James Richard Alexander *b* 1988, Tobias Edward *b* 1990, Melissa Anne *b* 1992, — Sally Pamela Clare, *b* 1960: *m* 1986, Robert William Blackburn Daniell, of 8 Arminger Rd, W12 7BB, and has issue living, Thomas Christopher Hebden *b* 1988, Patrick Richard *b* 1990, Natasha Annette *b* 1993, — Joanna Caroline, *b* 1963: *m* 1986, Charles Albury George Bennett, of The Old Forge, Elmdon, nr Saffron Walden, Essex CB11 4NL, and has issue living, George Albury Richard *b* 1992.

Issue of late Reginald Thornycroft Vernon, b 1892, d 1977: m 1920, Margarita Grace, who d 1989, yr da of Joseph Constantine, of Harlsey Hall, Northallerton, Yorks:—
George Thornycroft (2539 Benvenue Av, Berkeley, Calif 94704, USA), b 1935, ed Eton, and Trin Coll, Camb. —— James Loudon (45 Egerton Cres, SW3), b 1940; ed Eton, and Trin Coll, Dublin (BA): m 1971, Elspeth Mary Stewart, da of Rev Cyril Raby Thomson, of Holy Trinity Vicarage, Southwell, Notts, and has issue living, Alexander James Constantine, b 1971, — Eliot Antony Stewart, b 1975, — Rossanna Mary Anderson, b 1976, — Tara Katharine Loudon, b 1979. —— Pamela Margaret, b 1924. —— Jean Winifred, b 1926: m 1954, John Stewart Prescot, of Fairlight House, E Grinstead, Sussex, and has issue living, Charles Stewart, b 1957, — Alastair John Vernon, b 1960, — Nigel Kenrick Grosvenor, b 1962, — Margaret Louise, b 1955. —— Margaret Elizabeth, b 1933; ed Lady Margaret Hall, Oxford (BA): m 1972, Rev Jeremy Peake (c/o British Embassy, Athens), son of late Sir Charles Brinsley Pemberton Peake.

Issue of late William Allen Vernon, 2nd son of 1st baronet, b 1860, d 1939: m 1888, Elizabeth, who d 1952, da of Herbert Marson, of Marsh House, Blyth Bridge, Staffordshire:—
Nanny Uarda Elsie, b 1901: m 1927, Prof Victor Wilkinson Dix, FRCS, who d 1992, of 8 Shandon Close, Tunbridge Wells, and has issue living.

Grandson of late William Allen Vernon (ante):—
Issue of late Sir Wilfred Douglas Vernon, b 1897, d 1973: m 1923, Nancy Elizabeth, yr da of Tom Jackson, JP, of Waterfoot, Heaton, Bolton:—
William Michael (Fyfield Manor, Fyfield, Hants), b 1926; ed Trin Coll, Camb (MA); late Lt RM; Chm of Spillers Ltd: m 1st, 1952 (m diss 19—), Rosheen Elizabeth Mary, da of late George O'Meara, of Johannesburg, S Africa; 2ndly, 1977, Jane Olivia Colston, da of late Denys Kilham-Roberts, and has issue living (by 1st m), Mark Thornycroft, b 1958: m 1986, Harriet Laura, eldest da of John Bertrand Worsley (see Clark, Bt, ext 1979), and has issue living, Jessica Rosheen b 1988, Phoebe Rose b 1991.
Sir William Vernon, 1st Baronet, was head of the firm of W Vernon and Sons, millers, of London and Liverpool. The 2nd baronet, Sir (John) Herbert Vernon, was High Sheriff of Cheshire 1926.

VESTEY (UK) 1921, of Shirley, Surrey

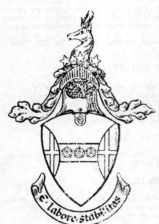

From work stability

Sir (John) Derek Vestey, 2nd *Baronet*, son of late John Joseph Vestey (b 1888, d 1932: m 1913, Dorothy Mary, who d 1918, only da of John Henry Beaver, of Gawthorpe Hall, Bingley, Yorks), el son of 1st baronet; b 4 June 1914; s his grandfather, Sir Edmund Hoyle, 1953; ed The Leys Sch, Camb; European War 1940-45 as Flight-Lieut RAF Vol Reserve: m 1938, Phyllis Irene, da of H. Brewer, of Banstead, and has issue.

Arms – Argent, on a fesse between two flaunches gules each charged with a cross throughout of the field, three roses also of the field. **Crest** – In front of a springbok's head proper three mullets argent.
Residence – Park Penthouse, 355 King's Rd, Chelsea, SW3 5ES. *Clubs* – RAC and MCC.

SON LIVING

Paul Edmund (53 Cheval Place, SW7; Manor House Farm, Bishops Sutton, Hants; *Club* – British Racing Drivers), b 15 Feb 1944; ed Radley: m 1971, Victoria Anne Scudamore, da of John Salter, of Old Ford House, Tiverton, Devon, and has issue living, Joanna Clare, b 1972, — Caroline Louise b 1975, — Georgina Jane, b 1977.

DAUGHTER LIVING

Rosamund Hope, b 1940: m 1st, 1961 (m diss 1980), Anthony Charles Brown; 2ndly, 1982, Karl Ove Arvidsson, and has issue living (by 1st m), Mark Nigel Alastair, b 1964: m 1993, Elizabeth Ann Julien, and has issue living, Vita Rosamund b 1993, — Julia Caroline, b 1962. *Residence* – Longdown Cottage, Longdown, Guildford, Surrey.

AUNT LIVING (*Daughter of 1st baronet*)

Hannah (Flat 8/9, Imperial Court, Prince Albert Rd, NW8), b 1897: m 1937, Lt-Col Eugene John O'Meara, OBE, FRCS, IMS, who d 1962.

COLLATERAL BRANCHES LIVING

Issue of late Charles Gordon Vestey, brother of 2nd baronet, b 1916, d 1986: m 1946, Monica Hope (Little Haley, Oxenhope, Keighley, Yorkshire), yr da of Arthur John Parker Heaton, of Manorlands, Oxenhope, Keighley:—
Diana Mary, b 1947: m 1st, 1968, Kenneth Cameron Simm, who d 1977; 2ndly, 1987, Thomas Mark Blackburn, of Prospect House, Bradley, Skipton, N Yorks, and has issue living, (by 1st m) Gordon Christopher Cameron, b 1970, — Holly Ann Cameron, b 1971. —— Rachel Margaret, b 1949: LRAM: m 1970, Philip Anthony Hills, BA, PhD, of The Mill House, Gt Horkesley, Colchester, Essex, and has issue living, Thomas Edmund, b 1977, — Matthew William, b 1979.

Issue of late Percy Charles Vestey, 3rd son of 1st baronet, b 1893, d 1939: m 1916, Dorothy Emmeline, who d 1976, da of late Charles David Johnson:—
Roger Edmund (11 Hyde Park Gardens, W2. *Clubs* – Cavalry, Royal Ocean Racing), b 1921; ed Harrow, and Clare Coll, Camb (BA 1946, MA 1951); late Capt Berks Yeo; European War 1940-45: m 1950, Penelope Jane, only da of late Lieut-Col Robert Arthur Little, DSO, late Australian Forces, of Melbourne, Australia, and has had issue, Charles Julian, b 1952; ed Harrow, Munich Univ and Sorbonne, Paris; d 1993, — James Patrick, b 1954; ed Harrow, and Southampton Univ; BM, MRCP: m 1981, Nicola Jane, da of late Harold Vernon Knight. —— Patricia, b 1922: m 1945, Lt William Reginald Servaes, RN (15 Bryanston Mews West, W2; South Green House, Southwold, Suffolk), and has had issue, Michael Maxwell, b 1947, d

1986, — James William, *b* 1948; *ed* Harrow: *m* 1st, 1972 (*m diss* 1975), Phoebe, da of Keith Pither Cox, of Sydney; 2ndly, 1978, Harriet, yr da of Maj Richard Neville Barclay, of Pond House, Boxted, Colchester, and has issue living (by 2nd *m*), Rebecca Mansel *b* 1981, Alice Harriet *b* 1984, — Andrew Mark, *b* 1963, — Diana Patricia, *b* 1951: *m* 1978, James Norman Hiddleston, of The Hollies, Blockley, nr Moreton-in-Marsh, Glos, and has issue living, Thomas William *b* 1981, Sarah Alexandra *b* 1979, Emma Elizabeth *b* 1986, — Elizabeth Mary, *b* 1953: *m* 1978, Timothy John Russell Fargher, of The Old Rectory, Orford, Woodbridge, Suffolk IP12 2NN, and has issue living, Matthew Philip Michael *b* 1981, Edmund James Timothy *b* 1986, Zoe Clare *b* 1979, Anna Patricia *b* 1984. ⸺ Mary (*Lady Verney*), *b* 1925; LRAM: *m* 1948, Sir Ralph Bruce Verney, KBE, 5th Bt (*cr* 1818). *Residence* – Claydon House, Bletchley, Bucks.

Issue of late Ronald Arthur Vestey, 4th son of 1st baronet, *b* 1898, *d* 1987: *m* 1923, Florence Ellen McLean, who *d* 1966, da of late Col Theodore George Luis, VD, of Broughty Ferry, Angus:—
Edmund Hoyle (Little Thurlow Hall, Haverhill, Suffolk; Iolaire Lodge, Lochinver, Sutherland. *Clubs* – Cavalry and Guards', Carlton), *b* 1932; *ed* Eton, High Sheriff Essex 1977, DL 1980, DL Suffolk 1991; late Lieut City of London Yeo; patron of five livings: *m* 1960, Anne Moubray, yr da of Gen Sir Geoffry Allen Percival Scoones, KCB, KBE, CSI, DSO, MC, and has issue living, Timothy Ronald Geoffry (Waltons, Ashdon, nr Saffron Walden, Essex), *b* 1961, — James Edmund McLean, *b* 1962, — George Moubray William (Great Thrulow Hall, Haverhill, Suffolk), *b* 1964: *m* 1989, Rachel, yr da of Patrick Osborne, of Currandooley, NSW, and has issue living, Thomas Hector Moubray *b* 1993, Ruby Constance *b* 1991, — Robin John Henry, *b* 1968: *m* 1993, Victoria Eileen Herbert, yst da of Robin Waddell, of Edinburgh, and has issue living, Georgina *b* 1994. ⸺ Florence Elizabeth Lindsay, *b* 1926: *m* 1952, Robert Lawrence Clifton-Brown (*see* Brown, Bt, colls). ⸺ Jane McLean, *b* 1928: *m* 1956, John Richard Baddeley, of Great Butts, Cousley Wood, Wadhurst, Sussex, and has had issue, Mark Christian Jon, *b* 1960: *m* 1987, Brigette Susan Alfille, and has issue living, Matthew *b* 1989, Charles David James *b* 1991, — Gary Christopher, *b* 1965; assumed the names of Gary Christopher in lieu of Edward Christopher Francis by deed poll: *m* 1989, Cecilia Barker, — Melissa Jane Elizabeth, *b* 1963, *d* 1980. ⸺ Margaret, *b* 1929: *m* 1954, James Gladstone Payne, of Ardvar, Drumbeg, via Lairg, Sutherland, and has issue living, Michael Edmund (Severals Farm, Arkesden, Saffron Walden, Essex), *b* 1959: *m* 1986, Sophie Corinne Banks, da of Jeremy John Banks Skinner, of Stocking Farm, Stocking Pelham, Buntingford, Herts, and has issue living, Fergus Edmund *b* 1990, Hector Cameron *b* 1992, Caspar James *b* 1994, — Nichola Rosemary, *b* 1955: *m* 1981, Alastair Ian McArthur, and has had issue, Matthew James *b* 1984, Harry Simon *b* 1987, Samuel George *b* 1988, Emily Clare *b* and *d* 1983, — Philippa Margaret, *b* 1963: *m* 1982, Simon Hamilton Shirley-Beavan, and has issue living, Charles Michael *b* 1984, George Ronald Benjamin *b* 1987.

Issue of late William Vestey, yst son of 1st baronet, *b* 1902, *d* 1971: *m* 1928, Ursula Frances Bowring, who *d* 1993, da of Edward H. Bowring Skimming, of Taplow House, Taplow:—
John (Orbetello, Italy; Bath and Boodles Clubs), *b* 1929: *ed* Eton: *m* 1958 (*m diss* 1977), Felicity Gay, da of Kenneth H. Crawford, of Holbrook, NSW, and has issue living, Victoria Gay, *b* 1960: *m* 1986, David Michael Russell-Hills, and has issue living, Mark William *b* 1988, Lucy Scarlett *b* 1986, — Angela Caroline, *b* 1962: *m* 1987, Paul Coleman, and has issue living, Luca John *b* 1988, — Georgina Ann, *b* 1964, — Sara Frances, *b* 1966: *m* 1991, Santiago Gaztambide, — Christina Mary, *b* 1969.

The 1st baronet, Sir Edmund Hoyle Vestey (third son of Samuel Vestey, of Liverpool), was Chm of Union International Co, and Joint Head of Blue Star Line, Ltd with his elder brother 1st Baron Vestey.

VINCENT (E) 1620, of Stoke d'Abernon, Surrey (Extinct 1941)

Rt Hon Sir EDGAR VINCENT, GCB, GCMG, FRS, 16th and last Baronet (who was *cr Baron D'Abernon* 1914, and *Viscount D'Abernon* 1926).

DAUGHTERS LIVING OF FOURTEENTH BARONET

Una Claire Margaret, *b* 1926: *m* 1950, Air Commodore Nicholas Roger Lyell Bristow, RAF, of Chidgley Cottage, Chidgley, Watchet, Som TA23 0LS, and has issue living, Robert Nicholas, *b* 1954: *m* 1982, Linda Mary Dickinson, and has issue living, Thomas Francis Edward *b* 1990, Rosemary Clare Margaret *b* 1986, — Edward Anthony (twin), *b* 1954: *m* 1983, Susan Sadaukas, — Clare Margaret, *b* 1951: *m* 1972, Colin Ian Liddell, and has issue living, Victoria Clare Margaret *b* 1981, — Jane Elizabeth, *b* 1953: *m* 1st, 1974 (*m diss* 1987), Michael Balfour Hutchings; 2ndly, 1990, William Richard Oake Holmes, and has issue living, (by 1st *m*) William Benjamin Balfour *b* 1981, Anna Clare *b* 1978, (by 2nd *m*) Katharine Alexandra *b* 1991. ⸺ Pamela Helen Frances (Combe House, Titcomb Way, Kintbury, Berks), *b* 1928: *m* 1951, Douglas R. Whittaker, who *d* 1974, and has issue living, Suzanne, *b* 1951: *m* 1973, Spencer Charles Hilton Barrett, and has issue living, Rowan Douglas Hilton *b* 1980, Seth Arthur Vincent *b* 1983, — Helen Gay, *b* 1953: *m* 1973, Timothy Philip Lyth Badgett, and has issue living, Henry Vincent *b* 1979, Katherine Joanna *b* 1981, — Judith Frances, *b* 1959: *m* 1985, Ashley Dominic Griffith, and has issue living, Rebecca Jane *b* 1989, Hannah Lucinda *b* 1991.

VINCENT (UK) 1936, of Watton, co Norfolk

Sir WILLIAM PERCY MAXWELL VINCENT, 3rd *Baronet*; *b* 1 Feb 1945; *s* his father, *Sir* LACEY ERIC, 1963; 2nd Lt Irish Gds: *m* 1976, Christine Margaret, da of Rev Edward Gibson Walton, and has issue.

Arms – Azure, a chevron between two garbs in chief and in base a castle all or. **Crest** – In front of two bird bolts points downwards saltirewise or a Labrador retriever dog, statant sable.
Residence – Whistlers, Buriton, Petersfield, Hants.

By Fortitude and Endeavour

SONS LIVING

EDWARD MARK WILLIAM, *b* 6 March 1978. —— Charles Michael Lacey, *b* 1979. —— John James Robertson, *b* 1981.

SISTER LIVING

Amanda Mildred, *b* 1942: *m* 1st, 1961, John Barry Henry Dinan, late Capt Irish Guards; 2ndly, 1984, as his 2nd wife, Gerald John Ward, of Chilton Park Farm, Hungerford, Berks (*see* E Dudley, colls), and has issue living (by 1st *m*), Mark Henry *b* 1963, — Dominic John, *b* 1966.

AUNT LIVING (*Daughter of 1st baronet*)

Christine Ena Comfort: *m* 1931, John S. Stevens.

WIDOW LIVING OF SECOND BARONET

HELEN MILICENT (*Helen, Lady Vincent*) (179 Cranmer Court, Sloane Av, SW3 3HN), yr da of late Field-Marshal Sir William Robert Robertson, 1st Bt, GCB, GCMG, GCVO, DSO (*see* B Robertson of Oakridge): *m* 1938, Sir Lacey Eric Vincent, 2nd baronet, who *d* 1963.
The 1st baronet, Sir Percy Vincent (son of Lacey Andrews Vincent, of Watton, Norfolk), was an Alderman City of London 1929-42 (Sheriff 1926-27, and Lord Mayor 1935-36).

Vœux, see Des Vœux.

VYVYAN (E) 1645, of Trelowarren, Cornwall

Sir JOHN STANLEY VYVYAN, 12th *Baronet*, only son of late Maj-Gen Ralph Ernest Vyvyan, CBE, MC, only son of late Capt Herbert Reginald Vyvyan, OBE, 2nd son of Rev Herbert Francis Vyvyan, 3rd son of Rev Vyell Francis Vyvyan, yr son of 7th Bt; *b* 20 Jan 1916; *s* his cousin *Sir* RICHARD PHILIP, 1978; *ed* Charterhouse and London Sch of Oriental Studies; 1939-45 War as Maj R Signals, in India and Arakan: *m* 1st, 1940 (*m diss* 1946), Joyce Lilia, da of late Frederick Marsh, of Kailan Mining Admin, Peking; 2ndly, 1948 (*m diss* 1958), Marie, only da of late Dr O'Shea, of Hamilton, Ont; 3rdly, 1958, Jonet Noel, eldest da of Lt-Col Alexander Hubert Barclay, DSO, MC (Mitchelson, Bt), and has had issue by 1st and 3rd *m*.

Arms – Argent, on a mount vert a lion rampant gules, armed sable. **Crest** – A horse passant furnished proper.
Residence – Trelowarren, Mawgan, Helston, Cornwall TR12 6AF. *Clubs* – Army and Navy; Royal Cornwall Yacht (Falmouth).

While we live, let us live

SON LIVING (*by 3rd marriage*)

(RALPH) FERRERS ALEXANDER, *b* 21 Aug 1960: *m* 1986, Victoria Arabella, yst da of M. B. Ogle, of Skerraton, Buckfastleigh, Devon, and has issue living, Joshua Drummond *b* 1986, — Frederick George, *b* 1987, — Rowan Arthur, *b* 1989, — Inigo Valentine, *b* 1994.

DAUGHTERS LIVING AND DECEASED (*by 1st marriage*)

Lorraine, *b* 1942; *d* 1983.

(*by 3rd marriage*)

Amanda Clare, *b* 1959: *m* 1st, 1984 (*m diss* 1988), Mark Ian Richard, Baron von Brockdorff, son of Lt-Col Baron Edward von Brockdorff, of Casa Derry, L-Ilklin, Lija, Malta; 2ndly, 1991, David John Judson, of 65 Sudbrooke Rd, SW12, and has issue living, (by 1st *m*) Alexander Mark Edward John Vyvyan, *b* 1984, — (by 2nd *m*) Josiah Barclay, *b* 1992.

HALF-SISTER LIVING

(Mary) Virginia, *b* 1934; JP: *m* 1st 1956 (*m diss* 1963), Harold Markham Mills; 2ndly, 1975 (*m diss* 1978), William Archibald Wilson; 3rdly, 1979, Douglas Frederick Redrup (Little Compton, Prior Rd, Camberley, Surrey), and has issue living (by 1st *m*), Julian Maximilian Vyvyan, *b* 1957, — Antonia Helen, *b* 1958, — Charlotte Elisabeth, *b* 1960.

STEPMOTHER LIVING

Kathleen Antonia (Limeswell Cottage, Streatley-on-Thames, Berks), only da of Haskett Farquhar Haskett-Smith, of Starcross, Devon: *m* 1930, as his 2nd wife, Maj-Gen Ralph Ernest Vyvyan, CBE, MC, who *d* 1971.

COLLATERAL BRANCHES LIVING

Grandson of late Stanhope Trefusis Vyvyan, 4th son of late Rev Herbert Francis Vyvyan, brother of 9th baronet:—
Issue of late Lester Trefusis Vyvyan, *b* 1905, *d* 1952: *m* 1934, Mary Clare Frances (2 Trenoweth, Carwinion Rd, Mawnan Smith, Falmouth, Cornwall), da of John Leeming, of Chalfont St Peter, Bucks:—
Anthony Beville (Merthen, Constantine, Falmouth, Cornwall TR11 5RU), *b* 1935; *ed* Downside: *m* 1960, Mary Winifred da of Arthur Joseph Quin-Harkin, OBE, and has issue living, Richard Trefusis, *b* 1961: *m* 1993, Claire Susan, yr da of David Williets, of Fairfield Cottage, Middleton, Warwicks, — Jonathan Vyell, *b* 1962, — Simon Courtenay, *b* 1964: *m* 1992, Jane E., elder da of Michael Lodge, of Lighthorne Rough, Lighthorne, Warwicks, and has issue living, Alexandra *b* 1993, — Charles Bevil (Riverbank House, Wharfeside Av, Threshfield, N Yorks), *b* 1965: *m* 1990, Amelia Jane, only da of G. A. Boyd, of Threshfield, N Yorks, and has issue living, George Anthony Bevil *b* 1993, Isabella Mary *b* 1991, — Paul Grenville, *b* 1969, — James Hannibal, *b* 1972, — Hugh Donnithorne, *b* 1976, — Katharine Anne, *b* 1967.

Grandchildren of late Rev Herbert Francis Vyvyan (ante):—
Issue of late Capt William Geoffrey Vyvyan, Roy Welch Fusiliers, *b* 1876, *ka* 1914: *m* 1904, Frances Mary, who *d* 1964, da of the late Edmund Salwey Ford, of Pengreep, Perranwell, Cornwall, and 17 Hyde Park Sq, W:—
James Graham (Weston House, Gresford, Wrexham, Clwyd LL12 8EN), *b* 1905; *ed* Wellington Coll and RMC; Hon Lt-Col late R Welch Fus, and DL of Denbighshire: *m* 1934, Guenilda Mary, da of late Rev Preb Arthur Harvey Thursby-Pelham, R of Upton Magna, Shrewsbury, and has issue living, Anthony Geoffrey (Villa Marguerite, 3 Avenue Fabre, 06270 Villeneuve-Loubet, France), *b* 1940; *ed* Wellington Coll, RMA, and Magdalen Coll, Oxford (MA); late Capt R Welch Fus: *m* 1970, Miranda Violet Marguerite, yr da of late Rev Robnett Walters, BD, of North Tamerton, Cornwall, and has issue living, Philip James *b* 1975, David Robnett *b* 1977, Nicholas George *b* 1980, — Cicely Mary, *b* 1936: *m* 1961, Maj Peter Leslie Rawll, late RM, of The Gables, 39 Cotswold Green, Stonehouse, Glos, and has issue living, Andrew Charles Vyvyan *b* 1963, Katherine Frances *b* 1965, — Daphne Elizabeth, *b* 1937: *m* 1965, Edward Christopher Mumford, and has issue living, Robert Vyvyan *b* 1970, Alison Clare Mary *b* 1966: *m* 1991, Timothy Robert Hazlitt Love, son of Col Stephen Love, of Brixham, S Devon, Jane Myfanwy *b* 1968. —— Opre (*Lady Maclean*), *b* 1910: *m* 1933, Vice-Adm Sir Hector Charles Donald Maclean, KBE, CB, DSC, DL (M Linlithgow, colls), of Deepdale Old Rectory, Brancaster Staithe, King's Lynn, Norfolk, and has issue living, Charles David Hector (8 Eardley Cres, SW5), *b* 1936; *ed* Wellington Coll; Capt R Scots (Lothian) Regt: *m* 1966, Judith, el da of late Donald MacLehose, of Glengair, Clynder, Dunbartonshire, and has issue living, Charles Hector *b* 1968, James Lachlan *b* 1970, — Sara, *b* 1934: *m* 1955, Maj Anthony Michael Everett, Wiltshire Regt (ret), of Enford Grange, Pewsey, Wilts, and has issue living, Simon Anthony Cunningham *b* 1956; *ed* Ampleforth, Rupert James Hector *b* 1959; *ed* Ampleforth, — Katherine Mary, *b* 1937. —— Joan Mary (*Lady Ford*) (twin), *b* 1910: *m* 1937, Sir (Richard) Brinsley Ford, CBE, FSA, and has issue living, Francis Vyvyan *b* 1941; *ed* Eton, and Ch Ch Oxford: *m* 1979, Katherine Elizabeth, da of John Owen, of Playden, Rye, Sussex, and has issue living, Arthur Richard *b* 1988, Lily Rosamund Elizabeth *b* 1980, Gloria Frances Mary *b* 1983, Sylvia Agnes Helen *b* 1985, — (Richard) Augustine, *b* 1943; *ed* Ampleforth: *m* 1978, Elizabeth, da of late Edward Frost, and has issue living, Thomas Augustine *b* 1978, Edward Brinsley *b* 1980, (Richard) Sebastian *b* 1983, Susanna Clare *b* 1986, — Marianne Adele Hermione, *b* 1937: *m* 1966 (*m diss* 1973), Patrick Martin Laver, and has issue living, Harriet Joanna Veronica *b* 1967. *Residence* – 14 Wyndham Pl, W1.

Grandchildren of late Capt (Frederick) Richard Vyvyan, *b* 1913, *d* 1991: *m* 1937 (*m diss* 1957), Barbara, da of late Montague Jones, of Hartpury, Glos:—
Charles Richard (5 Chemin de Beau-Soleil, 1206 Geneva, Switzerland), *b* 1938; *ed* Clifton, and Trin Coll, Camb (MA). —— Priscilla Mary, *b* 1941: *m* 1972, John Loraine Cherry, of Mill House, Iping, Midhurst, Sussex, and has issue living, Tarquin Loraine, *b* 1974, — Amanda Clare, *b* 1978. —— Clare, *b* 1944: *m* 1st, 1966 (*m diss* 1978), Martin Austrey Kendall; 2ndly, 1984, Richard Clarke-Hall, of Greenway Manor, Luppitt, Devon, and has issue living (by 1st *m*), Jonathan Austrey, *b* 1966, — Charles Vyvyan, *b* 1971, — Robert Bradley, *b* 1973, — (by 2nd *m*) Henrietta Vyvyan, *b* 1986.

Grandchildren of late Capt Richard Norman Vyvyan, eldest son of late Rev Thomas Grenfell Vyvyan, eldest son of late Rev Thomas Hutton Vyvyan, 3rd son of 7th baronet:—
Issue of late Capt (John) Michal Kenneth Vyvyan, *b* 1907, *d* 1991: *m* 1941 (*m diss* 1971), Elizabeth Mary, da of Hugh Gordon Lowder:—
Charles Gerard Courtenay, CBE (75 Richborne Terr, SW8), *b* 1944; *ed* Winchester, and Balliol Coll, Oxford (BA); Maj-Gen, Chief of Staff UKLF 1994, Col Comdt R Green Jackets; MBE (Mil) 1974, CBE (Mil) 1990: *m* 1989, Mrs Elizabeth Frances BLAIR, da of Sir John Starr Paget, 3rd Bt. —— George James Tawney, TD (46 Claylands Rd, SW8), *b* 1951; *ed* Eton; Barrister-at-law; late Capt R Green Jackets; Maj TA: *m* 1st, 1980 (*m diss* 1991), Diana Elizabeth Mary, da of Richard Desmond Hill, OBE, of Kingston Bagpuize, Oxon; 2ndly, 1993, Venetia Ruth Caroline, elder da of John Philip Turner, of Cheyne Walk, SW10. —— Caroline Mary Louise, *b* 1942: *m* 1963, Stephen Charles Archibald Pryor, of Brackengarth, Keasden, Clapham via Lancaster, and has issue living, Henry Charles Lister, *b* 1965, — Charles James Archibald, *b* 1971, — William Tawney Charles, *b* 1973, — Richard Charles Stephen, *b* 1976, — James Charles Edward, *b* 1979, — Rachel Elizabeth, *b* 1966.

Grandchildren of late Philip Augustus Vyvyan-Robinson, el son of Rev Philip Vyvyan-Robinson (*b* 1820), el son of Philip Vyvyan-Robinson (*b* 1777), 2nd son of Rev Richard Vyvyan, 2nd son of Richard Vyvyan, 2nd son of 3rd baronet:—
Issue of late Arthur Claude Vyvyan-Robinson, *b* 1880, *d* 1960: *m* 1923, Patricia, who *d* 1982, only child of late F. T. MacDonnell:—
Arthur Frederick, RD, *b* 1925; *ed* Nautical Coll, Pangbourne, and Pembroke Coll, Camb (MA); Lt-Cdr RNR (ret); 1939-45 War; formerly Headmaster of Royal Masonic Sch, Bushey, and Woodbridge Sch, Suffolk: *m* 1951, Patricia Jill, el da of I. W. G. Freeman, of Woking, Surrey, and has issue living, Patrick John, *b* 1955; formerly Maj R Regt Fus: *m* 1978, Rosamund Mary, el da of Maj Acton Henry Gordon Gibbon, GM, of Errington, Trillick, co Tyrone, and has issue living, Rachel Louise *b* 1981, Joanna Elizabeth *b* 1983, Tamsin Sarah *b* 1987, Henrietta Frances *b* 1989, — James Courtenay, MBE, *b* 1958; formerly Maj R Green Jackets; MBE (Mil) 1988: *m* 1988, Nicola S., da of N. Poston, of Waltham St Lawrence, Berks, and has issue living, Christopher Courtenay *b* 1994, Jessica Josselyn *b* 1990, — David Augustus, *b* 1960: *m* 1988, Charlotte, da of Oscar Husum, of Cascais, Portugal, and London, — Amanda, *b* 1953: *m* 1974, Charles Philip Metcalfe Yeoman, ARICS, el son of P. M. Yeoman, FRCS, of Monkton Combe, Bath, and has issue living, Charles William Metcalfe *b* 1978, Thomas Frederick

Metcalfe *b* 1980, Harriet Vyvyan *b* 1983. *Residence* – The Old Farmhouse, Trevone, Padstow, Cornwall PL28 8QN. —— Cecil Courtenay, *b* 1928; *ed* Charterhouse, and Jesus Coll, Camb (MA): *m* 1955, Ann Leonora Dirom, el da of V. Berwyn Jones, MRCVS, of Frocester, Glos, and has issue living, Peter Dirom Courtenay (66A Wardo Av, SW6 6RE). *Club* – Cavalry and Guards, *b* 1958; Capt HAC, — Frances Jane, *b* 1957; AGSM: *m* 1981, Michael Vincent Berrett, of 64 Warmans Close, Wantage, Oxon, only son of I.V. Berrett, of Woodford Green, Essex, and has issue living, Peter Michael Vyvyan *b* 1990, Elizabeth Tamsin Mary *b* 1985, Anna Rosamunde Dirom *b* 1987, — Katherine Armorel, *b* 1959: *m* 1986, Mark Peter Stanford, of Flat 2, 26-30 Griffiths Rd, Wimbledon SW19, eldest son of P. J. Stanford, of Dartford, Kent, and has issue living, Charlotte June *b* 1987, — Diane Elizabeth, *b* 1963; BA: *m* 1990, Ian Charles Cornock, ARICS, elder son of Maj-Gen Charles Gordon Cornock, CB, MBE, of Cranleigh, Surrey, and has issue living, Harriet Lucy *b* 1993. *Residence* – The Old House, Horsham, Martley, Worcs WR6 6PN. —— Richard, MBE, *b* 1937; *ed* Bradfield; Maj late LI; MBE (Mil) 1968: *m* 1968, Virginia Ann, da of late Lt-Col William Maitland Brewster Dunn, and has had issue, †Charles Arthur, *b* 1970, *d* 1989, — Mark William, *b* 1972; *ed* Blundell's, and Sidney Sussex Coll, Camb (BA). —— Susan Philippa, *b* 1924; 1939-45 War in WRNS: *m* 1954, John Dugmore, of 816 Ely Blvd South, Petaluma, Cal 94952, USA and has issue living, Neil Vyvyan, *b* 1957, — Geoffrey Roland, *b* 1959, — Christopher John, *b* 1965. —— Jane Theodora, *b* 1930: *m* 1955, David Kenneth Wilton Cox, and has issue living, Timothy Michael Wilton, *b* 1959, — Richard Wilton, *b* 1962, — Sarah Lamorna, *b* 1957, — Victoria Tamsin, *b* 1964. *Residence* – Preston Farm, Drewsteignton, Devon. —— Claudia Frances, *b* 1932: *m* 1957, Henry Graham Tom, and has issue living, Elizabeth Vyvyan, *b* 1959, — Juliet Vyvyan, *b* 1965. *Residence* – Lower Trewiggett, St Teath, Bodmin, Cornwall.
　　Issue of late Lt Col Francis Vyvyan-Robinson, MC, 1897, *d* 1975: *m* 1926, Aileen, da of late Dr R. H. Powers, of Southend:—
Henry Francis (PO Box 3041, Yeroskipos, Paphos, Cyprus), *b* 1928; *ed* King's Coll, Taunton; late F/O RAAF; Civil Air Pilot: *m* 1957, Susan Rosamond, da of P. A. H. Pettman, of Bournemouth, and has issue living, Hugh, *b* 1958, — Peter Francis, *b* 1963, — Sally, *b* 1960: *m* 1986, Walter Albrecht, of Ob der Mur 18, 8173 Riedt, Switzerland, and has issue living, Yannik Vyvyan *b* 1991, Michael *b* 1993, Stefanie *b* 1987, Jennifer *b* 1989, Melanie *b* (twin) 1993. —— Loveday, *b* 1930: *m* 1951, Dr Keith Maxwell Fergusson, of Cranmere, South Rd, Newton Abbot, Devon, and has issue living, Neil Vyvyan, *b* 1952, — Graham Moore, *b* 1955, — Fiona Margaret, *b* 1959, — Elizabeth Loveday, *b* 1963. —— Caroline, *b* 1934: *m* 1957, James Caruth Moore Pryde, of Arden Cottage, 19 Harefield Av, Cheam, Surrey, and has issue living, Catherine Ann, *b* 1960, — Juliet Clare, *b* 1968.

　　Grandchildren of late Hugh Norris Vyvyan, 2nd son of Rev Philip Vyvyan-Robinson (*b* 1820) (ante):—
　　Issue of late Capt Hugh Wren Vyvyan, MC, *b* 1890, *d* 1966: *m* 1st, 1917, Mary, who *d* 1930, da of Patrick Lowe, of Bridge of Allan; 2ndly, 1945, Nellie Ryan Sibson:—
(By 1st *m*) Patrick Hugh (71 Mary St, Barrie, Ontario, Canada), *b* 1918; late Sergt Royal Signals; served in World War II 1939-45 (wounded, despatches), formerly Assist Supt of Police, Federation of Malaya: *m* 1959 (*m diss* 19—), Angela, da of Viggo Christensen, of London, and has issue living, Patrick Hugh Beresford, *b* 1959. —— Beresford Haughton, *b* 1929: *m* 19—, Enid Baker, and has issue living, Geoffrey, *b* 19—, — Maryann, *b* 19—, — Wendy, *b* 19—, — Laura, *b* 19—. —— Rosemary Constance, *b* 1929 (twin): *m* 1959, Richard David Messano.

　　Grandchildren of late Capt Hugh Wren Vyvyan, MC (ante):—
　　Issue of late Capt Peter Gerald Vyvyan, RCEME, *b* 1921, *d* 1962: *m* 19—, Marjorie Thurman:—
Peter Hugh, *b* 19—. —— Rosemary Ann, *b* 19—.

　　Grandchildren of late Rev Henry Vyvyan, 3rd son of Rev Philip Vyvyan Robinson (*b* 1820) (ante):—
　　Issue of late Lt-Col Philip Henry Nugent Norris Vyvyan, OBE, MC; *b* 1881; *d* 1967: *m* 1917, Mary Caroline, who *d* 1982, da of late Rev John Stephen Flynn:—
Lalage Nugent (Well Cottage, White Chimney Row, Westbourne, Emsworth, Hants), *b* 1921: *m* 1943, John Derek Atheling Boustead, Lt R Ulster Rifles, who was *ka* in Normandy 1944, and has issue living, Lalage Tamsin Vyvyan, *b* 1943: *m* 1964, Richard Hugh Lee, Lt RE, and has issue living, James Nugent *b* 1968, Nicholas Harry Atheling *b* 1984, Angela Caroline *b* 1967.
　　Issue of late Capt Albert O'Donnel Colley Vyvyan, *b* 1884, *d* 1971: *m* 1st, 1909, Cecilia, who *d* 1949, da of W. H. Armitage, JP, of Banney Royd, Huddersfield; 2ndly, 1951, Greta Sylvia (Penhallow, The Lizard, Cornwall), da of Arthur John Dooel, of Brandeston, Suffolk:—
(By 1st *m*) Henry O'Donnel, OBE (Try-le-Bois, Greencliff, St Martin, Jersey), *b* 1910; *ed* Bradfield, and Pembroke Coll, Camb (BA); Col late REME; 1939-45 War (prisoner); OBE (Mil) 1957: *m* 1936, June, da of John Humphries, of Napier, NZ, and has issue living, Wendy (c/o Try-le-Bois, Greencliff, St Martin, Jersey), *b* 1937: *m* 1957, Lt Graham George Bell, RASC, and has issue living, Christopher Graham Vyvyan, *b* 1960, Simon Bruce O'Donnel *b* 1961, Robin Benjamin *b* 1963, Bruce St John *b* 1966, — Valerie Cecilia, *b* 1941: *m* 1st, 1966 (*m diss* 19—), David Henry La Cagnina; 2ndly, 1979, Henry Fielding Thoresby, of 12 Wexford Rd, SW12 8NH, and has issue living (by 1st *m*), Adam Vyvyan *b* 1970, Dominic Vyvyan *b* 1973.

　　Grandson of late Charles Shimmin Vyvyan (infra):—
　　Issue of late Norris Vyvyan, *b* 1900, *d* 1963: *m* 1925, Florence Elizabeth (Betty), who *d* 1967, da of the Rev W. J. Tristram, of Oldham:—
Bertram Charles Boucher, *b* 1930: *m* 1965, Jean Margaret Taylor, and has issue living, Catherine Margaret, *b* 1967.

　　Granddaughter of late Rev Philip Vyvyan-Robinson (*b* 1820) (ante):—
　　Issue of late Rev Charles Shimmin VYVYAN, *b* 1856, *d* 1930 (having discontinued the surname of Robinson 1879): *m* 1881, Rose Mary, who *d* 1950, da of late Rev John Sidney Boucher:—
Violet, *b* 1891.

　　Grandchildren of late Frederick Albert VYVYAN (who discontinued the surname of Robinson 1879), son of Rev Philip Vyvyan Robinson (*b* 1820) (ante):—
　　Issue of late Philip Vyvyan, *b* 1892, *d* 1985: *m* 1926, Mary Jacqueline, who *d* 1970, da of late John Milberne Leacock (Erskine, Bt, *cr* 1821, colls):—
Rev John Philip (Adderbury Vicarage, Banbury, Oxon; Royal Commonwealth Society), *b* 1928; *ed* Charterhouse, and New Coll, Oxford (MA 1959); a priest in the Anglican Church, Borneo 1961-64, since when Vicar of Adderbury with Milton, Oxon; late DCLI (Regular Army Reserve); Malaya 1947-48; in Overseas Service, N Borneo 1952-57; *m* 1957, Monica Yin Tsu, da of Fu Yun Fatt, of Sandakan, N Borneo, and has issue living, Richard Mark Augustine, *b* 1960, — Henry Arthur Luke, *b* 1961, — Francis Michael Hannibal, *b* 1971, — Honor Mary Anastasia, *b* 1968. —— Bernard Jeremy (37 West Hill Av, Epsom, Surrey), *b* 1930; *ed* Charterhouse, and London Univ (BScEng), FICE; late REME: *m* 1964, Constance Joan Steel, da of late Ronald Ismay Pattinson, of Stanwix, Carlisle, and has issue living, David Jeremy, *b* 1972, — Mary Louise, *b* 1965, — Juliet Penelope, *b* 1967.
　　Issue of late Edwin VYVYAN, *b* 1866, *d* 1944: *m* 1894, Florence, who *d* 1968, da of late William White, of Dublin:—
Henry Edwin, *b* 1896.
The 1st baronet, Sir Richard Vyvyan, MP, was Master of the Mint during the reign of Charles I, and followed the King to Oxford. He was one of the last six baronets created by that monarch. The 2nd and 3rd baronets each sat as MP for Cornwall, and the 8th baronet sat as MP for Cornwall (*C*) 1825-31 for Bristol 1832-7, and for Helston 1841-57. The 10th baronet, Col Sir Courtenay Bouchier Vyvyan, CB, CMG, served in S African War 1879, Matabeleland Campaign 1896, S African War 1900-1902, and European War 1914-18 (CMG).

WAECHTER (UK) 1911 of Ramsnest, Chiddingfold, Surrey (Extinct 1985)
(Title pronounced "Vechter")

Sir (HARRY LEONARD) D'ARCY WAECHTER, 2nd and last *Baronet*.

COLLATERAL BRANCH LIVING

Issue of late John d'Arcy Waechter, PhD, yr son of 1st Bt, *b* 1915, *d* 1978: *m* 1952, Caroline Dymond (46 Thames St, Sunbury-on-Thames, Middlesex), yr da of the Ven Edgar Francis Hall, Archdeacon of Totnes:—
Andrea Caroline, *b* 1953. —— Suzanne Anstice Eveline, *b* 1957.

WAKE (E) 1621, of Clevedon, Somerset

Watch and pray

Sir HEREWARD WAKE, MC, 14th *Baronet*; *b* 7 Oct 1916; *s* his father, *Maj-Gen Sir* HEREWARD, CB, CMG, DSO, 1963; *ed* Eton; Maj (ret) KRRC; Vice Lord-Lieut of Northants 1984-91; High Sheriff 1955; 1939-45 War (MC, wounded); *m* 1952, Julia Rosemary, JP, yr da of Capt Geoffrey William Martin Lees, of Falcutt House, nr Brackley, Northants, and has issue.

Arms – Or, two bars gules, in chief three torteaux. **Crest** – The Wake knot. *Residence* – The Old School House, Courteenhall, Northampton NN7 2QD. *Club* – Brooks's.

SON LIVING

HEREWARD CHARLES, *b* 22 November 1952: *m* 1977, Lady Doune Mabell Ogilvy, el da of 13th Earl of Airlie, and has had issue, John Hereward, *b* 6 Oct 1978, — Henry, *b* 1980. — Tom, *b* 1984 *d* 1985, — Laura Katherine, *b* 1986.

DAUGHTERS LIVING

Diana Julia, *b* 1955: *m* 1979, Roderick John Fleming, and has issue (*see* B Wyfold). *Residence* – The Dower House, Sarsgrove, Churchill, Oxon. —— Caroline Jane, *b* 1957: *m* 1979, Adam Richard Fleming, and has issue (*see* B Wyfold). *Address* – PO Box 4197, Rivonia 2128, Republic of S Africa. —— Sarah Jennifer, *b* 1960: *m* 1985, Rodney C.H. Morgan-Giles, son of Rear Adm Sir Morgan Charles Morgan-Giles, DSO, OBE, GM, of Upton Park, Alresford, Hants, and has issue living, August George H., *b* 1988, — Tilia Julia C., *b* 1990.

SISTERS LIVING

Margaret (*Lady Turner*), *b* 1913: *m* 1939, Sir (Ronald) Mark Cunliffe Turner, who *d* 1980, and has issue living, Christopher, *b* 1942: *m* 1964, Katrina Cameron, da of Capt Harold Keith Salvesen, of Inveralmond, Cramond, Edinburgh, — Richard Wake, *b* 1949: *m* 1985, Celia Anne, da of David Carr, of Little Brookham, Surrey, and has issue living, Imogen Sarah *b* 1993, — Roger Cunliffe *b* (twin), 1949: *m* 1974, Rosemary Jane, el da of Rt Rev Richard Fox Cartwright, DD, Bishop of Plymouth, — Catherine, *b* 1940, — Margaret, *b* 1947. *Residence* – 3 The Grove, Highgate, N6. —— Mary, *b* 1927: *m* 1947, Capt James Howard Weatherby, late 10th Hussars, and has issue living, Jeremy James, *b* 1949; *ed* Eton, — Susan (*Viscountess Ullswater*) *b* 1947: *m* 1967, 2nd Viscount Ullswater, of The Old Rectory, Docking, Kings Lynn, Norfolk. *Residence* – Cleeve House, East Knoyle, Salisbury, Wilts.

COLLATERAL BRANCHES LIVING

Issue of late Roger Wake, 2nd son of 13th baronet, *b* 1918, *d* 1988: *m* 1st, 1944 (*m diss* 1969), Olwyn Mary, da of late Col John Charles Wynne-Finch, CBE, MC (*see* E Aylesford, colls); 2ndly, 1984, Belinda Joan (Newton House, Lochmaddy, N Uist), da of Charles Patrick Crossley, and formerly wife of Timothy Michael Nicholl:—
(By 1st *m*) John, *b* 1945; *ed* Eton: *m* 1969, Isabelle, 2nd da of Comte Charles-Evrard de Dreux-Brézé, of Paris, and has issue living, Christopher, *b* 1969, — Jeremy Alistair, *b* 1974, — Charlotte, *b* 1971, — Annabelle, *b* 1986. *Residence* – L'Aumonerie, 49124 St Barthelemy d'Anjou, France. —— Charles Julian, *b* 1947; *ed* Eton, and Univ of BC, Canada: *m* 1977, Josie Abata, of Canada, and has issue living, Callum, *b* 1983, — Rowena, *b* 1978. *Residence* – 703 Linden Av, Victoria, BC, Canada V8V 4G8. —— William, *b* 1949; *ed* Eton: *m* 1986, Jehanne Deirdre Alexandra, biographer, only da of James Hamilton Williams, of Anderidan House, Curtisden Green, Kent, and has issue living, David, *b* 1991, — Catherine Mary, *b* 1986. *Residence* – 57 Macfarlane Rd, W12. —— Jane, *b* 1950: *m* 1977, (Simon) Hugh Arnold Potter, and has issue living, Simon, *b* 1982, — Emma, *b* 1978. *Residence* – Cuckoo Bush Farmhouse, Reybridge, nr Lacock, Wilts.

Issue of late Peter Wake, yst son of 13th baronet, *b* 1921, *d* 1993: *m* 1960, Marion Margaret, DL (Fairfield House, Hambleton, Hants PO7 4RY), yr da of late John Henry Bevan, CB, MC, TD, and of Lady Barbara Violet Bingham, elder da of 5th Earl of Lucan:—
Edward, *b* 1965; *ed* Eton: *m* 1991, Katherine Yvonne, only da of John Alfred Leavett-Shenley (*see* B Amherst of Hackney, colls, 1990 Edn). —— Philip Hereward, *b* 1967; *ed* Eton. —— Susan *b* 1963: *m* 1994, John Mervyn Edward Pugh, son of John Mervyn Cullwick Pugh, of Fernhill Heath, Worcs.

Grandchildren of late Col Edward St Aubyn Wake, CMG, son of late Adm Charles Wake (infra):—
Issue of late Rev Hugh Wake, *b* 1916, *d* 1993: *m* 1944, (Catherine) Marigold (32 Weavers Court, Sudbury, Suffolk), da of late Adm Sir (William) Frederic Wake-Walker, KCB, CBE (*see* Walker Bt, *cr* 1856, colls):—
Vincent Hugh (800 Grow Rd, Glasgow), *b* 1947, SRN, RSCN: *m* 1977, Ruth Mary Petersen, da of William McAulay, of Glasgow, and has issue living, Christine Grace, *b* 1978, — Rebekah Sara, *b* 1980. —— (Cedric) Philip (22 Lytton Grove, SW15), *b* 1950; MSc; MNI, Master Mariner, Lt Cdr RD RNR (ret): *m* 1978, Claire Susan Woodburn, da of William Vinten, OBE, of Suffolk, and has issue living, Marcus Philip Vinten, *b* 1990, — Charlotte Elizabeth Vinten, *b* 1982, — Suzannah

Catherine Vinten, *b* 1985, — Henrietta Claire Vinten, *b* 1992. —— Thomas Baldwin (30 Moss Gdns, Leeds), *b* 1960: *m* 1986, Valerie, da of H. Green, of Aston, Sheffield. —— Catherine Frances, *b* 1945: *m* 1st, 1966, Michael Edward Turpin, who *d* 1972; 2ndly, 1973, Vernon Charles Nott, BSc, MIAgrE, of Pelham Hall, Twinstead, Essex, and has issue living, (by 1st *m*) Edward, *b* 1969, — Sarah Jane, *b* 1967, — Rosanna Elspeth, *b* 1972, — (by 2nd *m*) Benjamin Porter, *b* 1976.

Grandson of late Maj Hugh St Aubyn Wake, MVO (infra):—
Issue of late Hugh Edward William Wake, *b* 1900, *d* 1967: *m* 1928, June Brotherton:—
Charles Hugh Edward, *b* 1930; *d* 1976, USA.

Grandchildren of late Adm Charles Wake, 2nd son of 10th baronet:—
Issue of late Major Hugh St Aubyn Wake, MVO, *b* 1870, *ka* 1914; *m* 1899, Kathleen Mary, who *d* 1938, da of Lieut-Col Edward Evans Grigg, Indian Army (formerly Commr of Kamoun):—
Kathleen Josephine (Little Garth, Forest Rd, Hale, Fordingbridge, Hants), *b* 1909: *m* 1934, Lt-Col George Douglas James McMurtrie, Somerset LI, and has issue living, Hugh Wake, *b* 1936, — Michael St Aubyn (twin), *b* 1936; Maj, 3rd Bn, Princess Patricia's Canadian LI; OMM: *m* 1958, Bridget Constantia Rubery, and has issue living, Nigel Andrew James *b* 1959, Paul Marcel *b* 1971, Marcia Kathleen *b* 1961, — Jonathan Philip James, *b* 1941: *m* 1975, Anne Kelly, and has issue living, Andrew *b* 1975, Jane *b* 1977.
Issue of late (Arthur) Leofric St Aubyn Wake, *b* 1879, *d* 1957: *m* 1911, Elma, who *d* 1971, only da of late William Edward Highett, of Melbourne, Victoria:—
Geoffrey St Aubyn, *b* 1914; is Capt Australian Imperial Force: *m* 1943, Lois Ivan-Smith, and has issue living, Carolyn Fearnley St Aubyn, *b* 1945, — Cheryl Anne, *b* 1949. *Residence* – 43 Kooyong Road, Armadale, SE3, Victoria, Australia. —— Elma Thurfrida, *b* 1912. — Diana, *b* 1913: *m* 1940, Desmond George Grace, and has issue living, Simon George, *b* 1948, — Diana Gillian, *b* 1941, — Susan Elizabeth, *b* 1943. —— Audrey, *b* 1916: *m* 1946, Angus Manning Watson. *Residence* – 43 Kooyong Rd, Armadale, SE3, Melbourne, Aust.

Grandsons of late Rev Hereward Eyre Wake, only son of late Rev Baldwin Eyre Wake, eldest son of late Rev James Hare Wake, eldest son of late Baldwin Wake, MD, elder son of late Drury Wake, 3rd son of 7th baronet:—
Issue of late Lt-Col Hereward Baldwin Lawrence Wake, *b* 1900, *d* 1983: *m* 1926, Sheila, who *d* 1991, da of late Capt Henry William Fraser Harris:—
Hereward Michael Wilfred (High Ridge, Knoll Wood, Godalming, Surrey), *b* 1927. —— Robin Eyre (Polgreen Farm, St Mawgan-in-Pydar, Cornwall TR8 4AG), *b* 1933; international ornithologist: *m* 1962, Judith Ann (Judith Wake, NDD, artist), da of Eric Hayden Barry, of West Chiltington, Sussex.
This ancient family is descended from Hugh Wac or Wake (baron by tenure of Bourne and Deeping) (*temp* King Stephen), from whom the 1st baronet was 15th in male descent. The 2nd baronet assumed the additional surname of Jones, but *d* without issue. Sir Herewald, 12th baronet, was High Sheriff of Northants 1879. Maj-Gen Sir Hereward Wake, CB, CMG, DSO, 13th baronet, was Dep Constable of Dover Castle 1929-32, and Col Comdt 1st Bn, KRRC 1938-46, and High Sheriff of Northants 1945.

WAKEFIELD (UK) 1962, of Kendal, co Westmorland

Sir (EDWARD) HUMPHRY TYRRELL WAKEFIELD, 2nd *Baronet*, *b* 11 July 1936; *s* his father, *Sir* EDWARD BIRKBECK, CIE, 1969; *ed* Gordonstoun, and Trin Coll, Camb (MA); Fellow of Pierrepont Morgan Library, USA; founder of Stately Homes Collection of Antique Furniture and Objects of Art; Exec Vice Pres of Mallett America Ltd 1970-75; Dir of Mallett and Son Antiques 1970-78, the Spoleto Festival, and the Tree of Life Foundation; Chm of Tyrell Moore Ltd, Sir Humphry Wakefield and Partners Ltd; joined NZ Everest Team on first ascent of Mount Wakefield 1991, attempted Everest 1992, member Norman Vaughan Antarctic Expedition 1993; President The Northumberland National Park Search and Rescue Team, and The Avison Trust; member of Standing Council of Baronetage, and Lord of the Manor of Chillingham; late Capt 10th R Hussars, Freeman of Kansas City, and Hon Citizen of Houston and New Orleans in USA; Hon Col in State of Louisiana; Fell of Pierrepont Morgan Library, USA: *m* 1st, 1960 (*m diss* 1964), Priscilla, el da of Oliver Robin Bagot (B Bagot, colls); 2ndly, 1966 (*m diss* 1971), Hon Elizabeth Sophia Sydney, el da of 1st Viscount De L'Isle, VC, KG, GCMG, GCVO, and formerly wife of George Silver Oliver Annesley Colthurst (*see* Colthurst, Bt); 3rdly, 1974, Hon Katherine Mary Alice Baring, da of 1st Baron Howick of Glendale, KG, GCMG, and has issue by 2nd and 3rd *m*.

Arms – Argent two barrulets sable between three owls proper. **Crest** – A bat displayed proper, charged on each wing with a crescent argent.
Seat – Chillingham Castle, Northumberland. *Clubs* – Turf, Cavalry and Guards', Harlequin Rugby Football.

SONS LIVING *(By 2nd marriage)*

MAXIMILIAN EDWARD VEREKER, *b* 22 Feb 1967; *ed* Milton Abbey, and RMA Sandhurst; 2nd Lieut Royal Hussars (PWO).

(By 3rd marriage)

John Humphry Baring, *b* 1977; *ed* Eton.

DAUGHTER LIVING *(by 3rd marriage)*

Mary Elizabeth Lalage, *b* 1975; *ed* Wycombe Abbey, and Edinburgh Univ.

BROTHER LIVING

Gerald Hugo Cropper (Bramdean House, Alresford, Hants. *Club* – White's), *b* 1938; *ed* Eton, and Trin Coll, Camb (MA) Dir of CT Bowring & Co Ltd; Pres Guy Carpenter & Co Inc, New York: *m* 1971, Victoria Rose, el da of late Maj Cecil Henry Feilden, of Bramdean House, Alresford, Hants (*see* V Hampden colls), and has issue living, Edward Cecil, *b* 1973.

WIDOW LIVING OF FIRST BARONET

CONSTANCE LALAGE (*Dowager Lady Wakefield*) (13 St Mary Abbots Terr, W14), da of late Sir John Perronet Thompson, KCSI, KCIE: *m* 1929, Sir Edward Birkbeck Wakefield, CIE, 1st Bt, who *d* 1969.

This family can trace its lineage to Roger Wakefield, of Challon Hall, Westmorland, temp Elizabeth I. Sir Edward Birkbeck Wakefield, CIE, 1st baronet (whose el brother was *cr Baron Wakefield of Kendal* 1963) was a great-grandson of Edward William Wakefield, of Birklands, Kendal, 3rd son of John Wakefield of Stricklandgate, Kendal (*d* 1829), 6th in descent from Roger; was Comptroller, HM Household 1958-60 and Treasurer, HM Household 1960-62, 1st UK Commr in Malta 1962-64 and 1st High Commr to Malta 1964-65.

WAKELEY (UK) 1952, of Liss, co Southampton

Sir JOHN CECIL NICHOLSON WAKELEY, 2nd *Baronet, b* 27 Aug 1926; *s* his father, *Sir* CECIL PEMBREY GREY, KBE, CB, 1979; *ed* Canford, and London Univ (MB and BS 1950); MRCS England; LRCP London; FRCS 1955; FACS 1973; formerly Ch Inspector, City of London Special Constabulary; former senior Consulting Surg, W Cheshire Group of Hosps, a CStJ, and a former Member of Council RCS England; former Member of Liverpool Regional Hosp Board, and of Mersey Regional Health Authority; Civil Consultant Adviser in Surgery to RAF: *m* 1954, June, da of Donald Frank Leney, of Shottermill, Haslemere, Surrey, and has issue.

𝔄rms – Argent on a chevron sable between in chief two eagles displayed azure and in base a Rod of Aesculapius proper three crescents of the field. 𝔆rest – A demi horse argent supporting between the legs a Rod of Aesculapius proper.
Residence – Mickle Lodge, Mickle Trafford, Chester.

SONS LIVING

NICHOLAS JEREMY, *b* 17 Oct 1957: *m* 1991, Sarah Ann, da of AV-M Brian Lewis Robinson, of Cheldon House, Cheldon, Devon, and has issue living, Joshua Jeremy, *b* 27 Sept 1993. —— Charles John (8 Royal York Cres, Clifton, Bristol), *b* 1959; BSc (1980), MB BS (1983), FRCS (1987), FRCSEd (1987), FRCR (1991): *m* 1984, Rachel Morag Louise, yr da of George Penrose, of Ormsby Lodge, N Ormsby, Lincs, and has issue living, Rupert William, *b* 1990, — Arthur Charles, *b* 1993.

DAUGHTER LIVING

Amanda Jane, *b* 1962; fashion designer: *m* 1st, 1985 (*m diss* 1987), Alan Louis Bresler, elder son of late Judge Max Bresler, of Memphis, Tennessee; 2ndly, 1992, Neil David Gillon, son of Norman Keith Gillon, of Perth, Western Australia. *Residence* – 13 Queens Gate Mews, SW7 5QS.

BROTHERS LIVING

Richard Michael (1 Wordsworth Mansions, Queens' Club Gardens, W14), *b* 1933; *ed* Winchester; MB and BS 1957. —— William Jeremy (Pope's Hall, Hartlip, Sittingbourne, Kent), *b* 1935; *ed* Radley; former JP for Kent: *m* 1959, Veronica, 3rd da of John Dunning Aysh, of Hardham Priory, Pulborough, Sussex, and has issue living, James Richard William, *b* 1963: *m* 19—, Gaynor Rowena, da of David Morgan, of The Hollow, Caistor Lane, Tealby, Market Rasen, Lincs, and has issue living, Alice Angharad *b* 1991, Imogen Cross *b* 1993, — Adam John Paul (Moor Street House, Seymour Rd, Rainham, Gillingham, Kent ME8 8PY), *b* 1965: *m* 1991, Melanie Henrietta, da of Michael David Brash Dingley, of Foxcote Hill, Ilmington, Warwicks, and has issue living, Lily Evelyn *b* 1993, — Miranda Elizabeth, *b* 1967: *m* 1992, John Edward Segar, son of Martin Segar, of Stanhill, Godalming, Surrey.

WAKEMAN (UK) 1828, of Perdiswell Hall, Worcestershire

Sir EDWARD OFFLEY BERTRAM WAKEMAN, 6th *Baronet*; *b* 31 July 1934; *s* his half-brother, *Sir* (OFFLEY) DAVID, 1991.

Arms – Paly wavy of six vert and argent, a saltire engrailed ermine. **Crest** – Between two palm-branches proper, a lion's head erased argent, vomiting flames, gorged with a collar engrailed and cotised vert, and charged with three ermine spots. or.

WIDOWS LIVING OF FOURTH AND FIFTH BARONETS

JOSCELINE ETHELREDA (*Josceline, Lady Wakeman*) (Radbrook Nursing Home, Shrewsbury), el da of late Maj-Gen Bertram Reveley Mitford, CB, CMG, DSO, and widow of Cdr Walter Leeke, RN (B Manners): *m* 1929, as his 2nd wife, Capt Sir Offley Wakeman, CBE, 4th baronet, who *d* 1975.

PAMELA ROSE ARABELLA (*Lady Wakeman*), da of late Lt-Col Cecil Hunter Little, DSO, MBE: *m* 1946, Sir (Offley) David Wakeman, 5th Bt, who *d* 1991. *Residence* – Peverey House, Bomere Heath, Shrewsbury, Shropshire.

Nec temere, nec timide

Neither rashly nor timidly

Sir Henry Wakeman, 1st Bt, of Perdiswell, Worcs, and Hinton Hall, Salop. Was a Member of HEICS. He was 2nd son of Thomas Wakeman, of Worcester, and *m* 2ndly, 1797, Sarah, da of heir of Richard Ward Offley of Hinton, Salop, Sir Offley, 3rd Bt, was Chm Salop Quarter Sessions 1889-1914, and Capt Sir Offley, CBE, 4th Bt, was Chm, Salop Co Council 1943-63, and a Member of LCC 1922-25.

Waley-Cohen, see Cohen.

WALKER (UK) 1856, of Oakley House, Suffolk

Sir (BALDWIN) PATRICK WALKER, 4th *Baronet*, el son of late Com Baldwin Charles Walker, only son of 3rd baronet; *b* 10 Sept 1924; *s* his grandfather, *Sir* FRANCIS ELLIOT, 1928; *ed* Gordonstoun; Lieut RN (ret); is an hereditary Pasha of Ottoman Empire: *m* 1st, 1948 (*m diss* 1954), Joy Yvonne, da of Sir Arrol Moir, 2nd Bt; 2ndly, 1954, Sandra, da of Henry Stewart; 3rdly, 1966, Rosemary Ann, da of late Henry Hollingdrake; 4thly, 1980, Vanessa Hilton, and has issue by 3rd *m*.

Arms – Gules, on a chevron between three cross-crosslets argent, an anchor sable; on a chief of the second, three stags, heads cabossed proper, a canton azure, thereon a representation of the diamond decoration of a Pasha of the Ottoman Empire, conferred on late Sir Baldwin by the Sultan for his services in Syria. **Crest** – Out of a naval crown azure, a stag's head proper, gorged with an eastern crown or.
Address – 5 Voortrekker Rd, Blanco 6531, S Africa.

SON LIVING (By 3rd marriage)

CHRISTOPHER ROBERT BALDWIN, *b* 25 Oct 1969.

DAUGHTER LIVING (By 3rd marriage)

Amanda Jane *b* 1967: *m* 1993, Michael Grant Fenner-Solomon.

BROTHER LIVING

Francis Donald Baldwin (Robin Hill, Josephine Rd, Claremont, Cape Town, Cape Province, S Africa), *b* (*posthumous*) 1927; formerly Lt KRRC: *m* 1st, 1955, Joanna, only da of Sir John Weir Russell; 2ndly, 1965, Jennifer Mary, only da of late Lt-Cdr Eric Stokoe, RN (ret), and has issue living (by 1st *m*), Caroline Lucy Marjorie, 1958, — (by 2nd *m*) Anthony Eric Charles, *b* 1966.

COLLATERAL BRANCHES LIVING

Grandchildren of late Frederic George Arthur WAKE-WALKER, yst son of 1st baronet:—
Issue of late Adm Sir (William) Frederic WAKE-WALKER, KCB, CBE, *b* 1888, *d* 1945: *m* 1916, Muriel Elsie, who *d* 1963, only da of Sir Collingwood Hughes 10th Bt (*cr* 1773):—
Christopher Baldwin HUGHES-WAKE-WALKER, *b* 1920; Capt RN (ret), has assumed the additional surname of Hughes; *ed* RNC Dartmouth; Commander RN Coll Greenwich 1959-61; Naval Attaché in Paris 1962-64; Capt Dartmouth Training Squadron 1964-66; Dir of Naval Signals 1966-68; DL Suffolk 1983, High Sherriff 1985: *m* 1944, Lady Anne Spencer (sometime 3rd Officer WRNS), only da of 7th Earl Spencer, and has issue living, David Christopher (82 Royal Hill, SE10 8RT), *b* 1947; *ed* St Andrews Univ (MA); Page of Honour to HM The Queen 1960-62; Dir Kleinwort Benson Group: *m* 1979, Jenni Rosemary, only da of Capt Patrick Vaulkhard, of Stone Cottage, Snape, Saxmundham, Suffolk, and has issue living, Frederic David *b* 1981, Nicholas John *b* 1985, — Richard Anthony, *b* 1951; *ed* St Andrews Univ (MA); Sr Regional Controller, The Central Selling Organisation: *m* 1980, Sharon Pamela, yr da of Gordon Stuart Little, of Crowborough, Sussex, and has issue living, Robert Michael *b* 1990, Kate Louise *b* 1982, Olivia Rose *b* 1984, — Michael John (22 Prairie St, Battersea, SW8 3PP), *b* 1958; *ed* RMA Sandhurst; Capt Coldstream Guards: *m* 1992, Catherine P., eldest da of B. R. Hazlitt, of Billingshurst, Sussex, — Elizabeth Sarah, *b* 1944: *m* 1970, Anthony Duckworth-Chad (High Sheriff Norfolk 1992), of Pynkney Hall, King's Lynn, Norfolk, and has issue living, James Anthony L'Etang *b* 1972, William George Christopher *b* 1975, Davina Alice *b* 1978, — Diana

Mary, *b* (twin) 1958: *m* 1980, Maj Charles Keble Macfarlane, Coldstream Guards, and has issue living, Thomas Christopher Keble *b* 1983, Georgina Cynthia *b* 1986. *Residence* – East Bergholt Lodge, Colchester, Suffolk. *Club* – Army and Navy. —— Cedric Collingwood, *b* 1923; Lt-Cdr RN (ret): *m* 1949, Iona, da of Capt J. C. Maclean, RN, and has issue living, Edward Collingwood (5 West St, Kingston, Wareham, Dorset), *b* 1952: *m* 1982, Fiona Margaret, da of Cdr Michael J. Hodgson, DSC, RN (ret), of Hill House, Turleigh, Bradford-on-Avon, Wilts, and has issue living, Thomas Collingwood *b* 1987, Eleanor May *b* 1989, — Susanna, *b* 1950: *m* 1974, Christopher Mark Dancy, MA, BM, BCh, FRCP, of 41 Berwyn Rd, Richmond, Surrey, and has issue living, Luke Henry *b* 1983, Arabella Clare *b* 1977, Martha Caroline *b* 1979, — Corinna Elizabeth, *b* 1957: *m* 1983, Francis Christopher (Fred) Carr, of 49 Moore Park Road, Fulham, SW6 2HP, son of A. E. J. Carr, of San Francisco, California, USA, and has issue living, Polly Catherine Alice *b* 1985, Matilda Rose *b* 1987. *Residence* – Terwick Wood, Rogate, Petersfield, Hants. —— Penelope Hughes (*Lady Eley*), *b* 1917: *m* 1937, Sir Geoffrey Cecil Ryves Eley, CBE, who *d* 1990, and has issue living, Piers David Christopher (35 Montague Rd, Richmond, Surrey), *b* 1941; MA, MSc: *m* 1967, Sarah Cloudesley, da of late Lt-Col David Edward Long-Price, OBE, and has issue living, Damian Edward Piers *b* 1970, Thalia Catherine *b* 1971, — Gavin Michael Geoffrey (40 Woolmead Av, NW9), *b* 1945: *m* 1st, 1974 (*m diss* 1984), Mary Belinda (Holly), el da of Maj Bruce Edward Arthur Urquhart of Craigston, Craigston Castle, Aberdeenshire, and formerly wife of Fabrizio Pratesi; 2ndly, 1994, Virginia Jo, da of Peter Williams, of 31 Parliament Hill Mansions, Lissenden Gdns, NW5, — (Susan) Ianthe, *b* 1938: *m* 1st, 1963 (*m diss* 1985), Paul Edward Cornwall-Jones; 2ndly, 1985, Peter R. del Tufo, eldest son of late Sir Vincent del Tufo, KBE, and has issue living (by 1st *m*), Imogen Annabel *b* 1967; *ed* Edinburgh Univ (MA), Theresa Hermione Chloë *b* 1971, — Chloë Sarabella, *b* 1950: *m* 1st, 1971, Richard Christian Wynne Fremantle (*see* B Cottesloe); 2ndly, 1986, Peter Blegvad, of 22 Anley Rd, W14, son of Erik Blegvad, of Wardsboro, Vermont, USA, and has issue living (by 2nd *m*), Kaye Eley *b* 1987, Alec Viggo Eley *b* 1990. *Residence* – The Change House, Gt Yeldham, Essex. —— (Catherine) Marigold, *b* 1921; sometime 3rd Officer WRNS: *m* 1944, Rev Hugh Wake, who *d* 1993, (*see* Wake Bt, colls). *Residence* – 32 Weavers Court, Sudbury, Suffolk.

The 1st baronet, Adm Sir Baldwin Wake Walker, KCB (only surviving son of late John Walker, of Whitehaven), was Comptroller of the Navy 1847-60. He served many years in the Turkish service, and was made a Pasha for his services on the coast of Syria. The 2nd baronet, Sir Baldwin Wake, CMG, CVO, was a Vice-Adm.

WALKER (UK) 1868, of Sand Hutton, co York, and of Beachampton, Bucks

Sir JAMES HERON WALKER, 5th *Baronet*; *b* 7 April 1914; *s* his father, Sir ROBERT JAMES MILO, 1930; *ed* Eton, and Magdalene Coll, Camb: *m* 1st, 1939 (*m diss* 1972), Angela Margaret, who *d* 1993, only da of late Victor Alexandre Beaufort, OBE, MC, of Steephill, Jersey; 2ndly, 1972, Sharrone Babette, el da of David Philip Read, of Clanfield, Oxon, and has issue by 1st and 2nd marriages.

Arms – Argent, on a chevron gules, between three crescents azure, as many annulets or. **Crest** – Out of a battlement argent, a dexter arm embowed in armour azure, in the hand proper a lizard vert.
Residence – Oakhill, Braddan, IoM.

How great is honesty

SONS LIVING (By 1st marriage)

VICTOR STEWART HERON (Old Cadet House, Gorey, Jersey JE3 6DS, CI), *b* 8 Oct 1942; *ed* Eton; 2nd Lt Gren Gds 1962-65, and Lt R Wilts Yeo and R Yeo 1965-73: *m* 1st, 1969 (*m diss* 1982), Caroline Louisa, yst da of late Lt-Col Frederick Edwin Barton Wignall (*see* Acland, Bt, *cr* 1678, colls, 1980 Edn); 2ndly, 1982, Svea, only da of late Capt (Ernst) Hugo Gothard Knutson Borg, and has issue living (by 1st *m*), James Frederick Heron, *b* 1970, — Andrew Robert Heron, *b* 1973, — Rosanna Celia Louisa, *b* 1979.

(By 2nd marriage)

Simon Peter, *b* 1974.

BROTHER LIVING

Peter Arthur, *b* 1918; *ed* Eton.

COLLATERAL BRANCHES LIVING

Issue of late Capt Ronald Heron Walker, 3rd son of 3rd baronet, *b* 1896, *d* 1964: *m* 1921, Noel, who *d* 1972, da of Maj Guy Edward Wentworth, of Woolley Park, Wakefield:—
Michael Anthony (Pantyffynnon, Salem, Llandeilo, Dyfed), *b* 1924: *m* 1st, 1948, Ann, who *d* 1978, da of John E. Ferguson, of Busbridge Wood, Godalming; 2ndly, 1978, Anne Lavinia, el da of Capt John Henderson, and has issue living (by 1st *m*), Caroline Margaret, *b* 1950: *m* 1969, Ian D. Doulton (The Homestead, West Green, Hartley Wintney, Hants), and has issue living, David Peter Michael *b* 1974, Jonathan Duke *b* 1980, Lucy Catherine *b* 1971, — Rosemary Ann, *b* 1954: *m* 1981, Cdr Robert Lincoln Guy, MVO, RN, — Frances Mary, *b* 1965, — (by 2nd *m*), John Michael, *b* 1979, — Andrew James, *b* (twin) 1979, — James, *b* 1984, — Ruth, *b* 1982. —— Diana Mary, *b* 1923: *m* 1969, Simon Neville Turner, who *d* 1990, of Achnash-ellach, by Strathcarron, Ross-shire, and Mertoun Glebe, St Boswells, Roxburghshire.

Issue of late Patrick Bruce Walker, MBE, 4th and yst son of 3rd baronet, *b* 1898, *d* 1988: *m* 1928, Sybil, who *d* 1986, da of Charles Byron Turner, MRCS, of Asnby-cum-Fenby, Lincs:—
Susan Anne Maud (*Hon Lady Butler*), *b* 1930: *m* 1952, Hon Sir Richard Clive Butler, of Penny Pot, Halstead, Essex, son of Baron Butler of Saffron Walden, KG, CH, PC (Life Baron), and has issue.

Grandsons of late Rev Reginald Edmund Walker (infra):—
Issue of late Rupert Alexander Seymour Walker, *b* 1910, *d* 1973: *m* 1942, Edith Mary Sutherland:—
Jack Mervyn (18 Schwantz Rd, Pembroke, Ont, Canada), *b* 1946: *m* 1968, Marjorie Aline, da of Herbert Buske, of Pembroke, Ont, and has issue living, Victoria Edith *b* 1974. —— Raymond Earle, *b* 1950.

Issue of late Rev Reginald Edmund Walker, 2nd son of 2nd baronet, *b* 1866, *d* 1945: *m* 1895, Lady Emily Mary Seymour, who *d* 1948, da of 6th Marquess of Hertford:—
Margaret Edith Mary, *b* 1901: *m* 1st, 1920, Frank Caffery; 2ndly, 1941, William Derbyshire, of 401, 1955 Ashgrove St, Victoria, BC, V8R 4N8, Canada, and has issue living, (by 1st *m*) Kathleen Ethel Mary, *b* 1934: *m* 1st, 19—, Robert Coates; 2ndly, 19—, John Jeffrey, of Burnaby 1, BC, Canada, and has issue living (by 1st *m*), Edward Francis (11 Kopper King Trailer Court, Route RR1 Whitehorse, Yukon Territory) *b* 19—: *m* 1970, Jo-Ann Shepherd (and has issue living, Jolene Mary *b* 1974), Douglas Colin Paul *b* 1953 (85 Takhina, Trailer Court, Whitehorse, Yukon Terr), Robert James *b* 1958, Kathleen Wendy Maki *b* 19—: *m* 1972, Matthew Mackie (and has issue living, Matthew Maki *b* 1974), Anita Marie *b* 1955: *m* 1973, George Polburn (and has issue living Shayne Gregory *b* 1974), Sharon Leigh *b* 1957, Phyllis Margaret *b* 1959, Debra Joan *b* 1960.

Issue of late Major Harold Maxwell Walker, 3rd son of 2nd baronet, *b* 1869, *d* 1938: *m* 1904, Marie Albreda Blanche, who *d* 1963, da of late Hon William Henry Wentworth Fitzwilliam (E Fitzwilliam, colls):—
Marya Constance, *b* 1905: *m* 1935, Reginald Dekyn Lund, who *d* 1975, and has issue living, Rosemary Diana, *b* 1937: *m* 1961, Thomas Kennedy Dalziel, of Crailing Bhan, Jedburgh, Roxburghshire, and has issue living, Ralph Kennedy *b* 1964: *m* 1988, Annette Margaret, yr da of Trevor Taylor, of Marsden, Yorks (and has issue living, Richard Ralph *b* 1991, Donald Kennedy *b* 1993), Michael Kennedy *b* 1966. —— Rachel Marie Gabrielle (Hunters Hall, Old Malton, N Yorks YO17 0HB), *b* 1913.

Issue of late Francis Henry Walker, 4th son of 2nd baronet, *b* 1870, *d* 1944: *m* 1904, Francis Mary Theresa, who *d* 1961, el da of Francis J. Palmes, formerly of Mill Mount, York:—
Evelyn Lindsay, *b* 1905: *m* 1926, Lt-Col Gerard Thomas Scofield Horton, MC, late The Queen's Bays, who *d* 1983, and has issue living, Michael Scofield (Lansdowne House, Sheep St, Shipston-on-Stour, Warwicks), *b* 1929: *m* 1965, Anne, da of Sir (Frederick) Philip Alfred William Wombwell, MBE, 6th Bt, and has issue living, James Frederick *b* 1968, Peter Michael *b* 1969, —— Patricia Lindsay (Poyntington Manor, Sherbourne, Dorset), *b* 1927: *m* 1955, Maj Tom Pickering Salisbury Woods, MBE, late RA, who *d* 1979, and has had issue, Simon Salisbury, *b* 1956, *d* 1991, Robert Gerard Salisbury *b* 1965, Caroline Lindsay *b* 1968, —— Linda Mary, *b* 1936: *m* 1956, Ronald Oakes Crowther, and has issue living, James Robert *b* 1964, Charles Gerard Oakes *b* 1967, Nicola Jane *b* 1957, Miranda *b* 1959. *Residence* – Bishops Caundle House, Sherborne, Dorset.

Issue of late Ernest Robert Walker, 5th son of 2nd baronet, *b* 1872, *d* 1942: *m* 1901, Beatrice Mary, who *d* 1938, da of Rt Hon Sir Herbert Eustace Maxwell, 7th Bt, MP (*cr* 1681):—
Silvia Mary (Aden House, 3 Annfield Rd, Inverness), *b* 1903: *m* 1924, Maj Llewellyn William Dean Wathen, 8th Hussars, who *d* 1970, and has had issue, Guy Llewellyn (Alstoe Farm, Burley, Oakham, Leics), *b* 1925; 5th R Inniskilling Dragoon Gds; Col, Defence Attaché British Embassy, Rome: *m* 1st, 1953 (*m diss* 1970), Jean Maureen, da of William Lancelot Dawes, of Malmains Manor, Pluckley, Kent; 2ndly, 1971, Hilary Margaret, adopted da of Joyce Marjorie Wigram, MB, BS (*see* Wigram, Bt, colls), and formerly wife of Stephen James Stuart Oxlade; 3rdly, 1985, Sarah Elizabeth, formerly wife of Charles Thomas Bunbury (*see* Bunbury, Bt), and da of W. D. Hancock, of Sherborne Hall, King's Lynn, Norfolk, and has issue living (by 1st *m*), Julian Peter Guy *b* 1954; Lt-Col Royal Dragoon Gds, Nigel Charles James *b* 1955; Maj 9th/12th R Lancers (POW), —— David Anthony (Torr a' Mhullaich, Dervaig, Isle of Mull), *b* 1928; *ed* Marlborough, and Roy Agricultural Coll, Cirencester: *m* 1st, 1954 (*m diss* 1974), Barbara Jean, da of late Thomas Horsburgh Gibson, of Manor Hall, Selkirk; 2ndly, 1974 (*m diss* 1981), Patricia Gilbert Ros Croasdale, da of late Charles Ros Munton, of Knutsford, Cheshire, and has issue living (by 1st *m*), Richard Llewellyn *b* 1959, Wendy Anne *b* 1956, —— Ronald James, *b* 1934; *ed* Marlborough, and Trin Coll, Dublin; late 2nd Lt 8th Hussars: *m* 1st, 1959 (*m diss* 1961), Eliza Chase Collins, of Providence, Rhode Island, USA; 2ndly, 1983, Asta Kristinsdottir, of Reykjavik, and *d* 1994, leaving issue (by 2nd wife), Seán Ronaldsson *b* 1967, Sunna Ronaldsdottir *b* 1964. —— Kathleen Elizabeth Jean (Cannons, Tibberton, Glos), *b* 1908.

Grandchildren of late Frederick James Walker, MVO, 2nd son of 1st baronet:—
Issue of late Capt Hugh Edward Walker, *b* 1865, *d* 1935: *m* 1913, Hon Marjory Winifred, who *d* 1945, da of 21st Baron Forbes:—
Rosemary Alice Champney *b* 1917: *m* 1948, Capt Hugh Shelley Le Messurier, Duke of Wellington's Regt, of Thornton Grange, Thornton Steward, Ripon, Yorks, and has issue living, Jacqueline Shelley, *b* 1949: *m* 1960, Lt Jeremy John Gaskell, The Kings' Regt, and has issue living, Victoria Jacquine *b* 1971, Joanna Louise *b* 1973, —— Susan Rosemary, *b* 1950: *m* 1977, John McDonald Green-Armytage (The Cedars, Barnes Common, SW13), and has issue living, Matthew Whitla *b* 1978, Anna Claire *b* 1981, Camilla Rose *b* 1983, Elizabeth Caroline *b* 1985. —— Marguerite Helena Mary, *b* 1919: *m* 1942, Capt Giles Grierson Tweedie (Underwood, Steilston, Dumfries), late Argyll and Sutherland Highlanders, and has issue living, Marion Veronica, *b* 1943: *m* 1978, Michael Frank Walter, and has issue living, Patrick Douglas *b* 1980, —— Jacqueline Alice, *b* 1944, —— Rosalind Mary, *b* 1947: *m* 1979, Derek Gwynn Evans, who *d* 1994, and has issue living, Mark Edward *b* 1982, Eifion Charles *b* 1983, Alison Margaret *b* 1985, Pamela Sian *b* 1988. —— Daphne Elizabeth (3 Barford St, N1 0QB), *b* 1926.

Grandsons of late Rear-Adm Charles Francis Walker, 3rd son of 1st baronet:—
Issue of late Capt Edgar Wilmer Walker, E Yorkshire Regt, *b* 1875, *ka* 1914: *m* 1906, Charlotte Rankin, who *d* 1954, having *m* 2ndly, 1919, (7th Viscount Lifford), da of Sir Robert Maule:—
Francis Robert, *b* 1910.
Issue of late Rev Philip Charles Walker, *b* 1878, *d* 1933: *m* 1916, Dorothy Ann, who *d* 1936, da of late Col Frederick Compton Howard, Rifle Brig (E Carlisle, colls):—
Anthony Charles Howard, *b* 1917; *ed* Wellington Coll: *m* 1st, 1939, Lorna (*m diss* 1946), da of H. Crabtree; 2ndly, 1952, Peggy Foster, da of John T. Hewes, of Cambridge, and has issue living, (by 2nd *m*) Timothy Heron, *b* 1954, —— Elizabeth Cavendish *b* 1956, —— Ann Cavendish *b* 1958. *Residence* – 58 Balfour Road, Blackbird Leys, Oxford. —— Philip James, *b* 1920; *ed* Uppingham Sch; formerly in RAF; European War 1939-45 in India: *m* 1951, Helen Gibson, da of Dr Milligan, late of Hessle, E Yorkshire. *Residence* – Halse Springs, Macheke, Zimbabwe.

Granddaughter of late Capt Edwyn Walker, 4th son of 1st baronet:—
Issue of late Capt Oswald Bethell Walker, 15th Hussars, *b* 1875, *ka* 1914: *m* 1910, Marcia Eugenia (who *d* 1973, having *m* 2ndly, 1920, Francois de Juge Montespieu), da of late Col John Delalynde Mansel (Mansel, Bt, colls):—
Lois Adeline, *b* 1912: *m* 1932, George Nickerson, late Coldstream Guards, who *d* 1976, and has issue living, David George Francois (4 Ladbroke Terrace, W11), *b* 1933: *m* 1957, Sarah Elizabeth da of late Col John Jewson, MC, of Mergate Hall, Norwich and has issue living, William John George *b* 1958: *m* 1989, Jayne, eldest da of Roland Pickering (and has issue living, Joshua *b* 1992), James D— Rivers *b* 1960, Camilla *b* 1965, —— Mark Oswald Julian (Boxted Lodge, Colchester), *b* 1935: *m* 1974, Elizabeth, da of F. P. Birch, and has issue living, Emma *b* 1975, Caroline *b* 1978. *Residence* – Burnt Fen, Horning, Norfolk.

Grandson of late Capt Gerald Walker, 5th son of 1st baronet:—
Issue of late Lieut-Col Bertram James Walker, CMG, DSO, *b* 1880, *d* 1947: *m* 1st, 1909 (*m diss* 1926), Josepha Margaret, who *d* 1972, da of late Sir George Donaldson, of 1 Grand Av, Hove, Sussex; 2ndly, 1940, Countess Lucie Marie Reventlow, who *d* 1984, aged 99, of Brahe Trolleborg, Denmark:—
(By 1st *m*) Anthony Gerald Bartholomew, *b* 1912; *ed* Harrow and RMC Sandhurst; Lieut-Col (ret) Somerset LI: *m* 1939, Margaret Cumberland, who *d* 1987, only da of late Col C. P. Templeton, CB, DSO, of Victoria, British Columbia, and has issue living, *Rev* Christopher James Anthony (Horseshoe Meadow Farm, Cholderton, Salisbury, Wilts SP4 0ED), *b* 1943; *ed* Harrow, and RMA Sandhurst; Lt-Col (ret) 17th/21st Lancers; Chaplain to the Forces 1987: *m* 1971, Ronwen Melody, eldest

da of late Lt-Col E. C. Barton, MC, and has issue living, Rupert Anthony Edward *b* 1972, Alice Melody Margaret *b* 1974, Lavinia Verity Rose *b* 1977, Cicily Primrose Amy *b* 1979, — Robin Charles Andrew (The Garden Flat, 30 Maida Av, W2 1ST), *b* 1944; *ed* Harrow, and McGill Univ, Montreal: *m* 1975, Selina Margaret, el da of Maj Patrick Dudley Erskine Riall, of Ballyorney House, Enniskerry, co Wicklow, and has issue living, Lucinda Margaret Riall *b* 1983, Sophie Claire *b* 1985, — Peter Gerald Edward (Binghams Farmhouse, Bower Chalke, Salisbury SP5 5BW), *b* 1948; *ed* Harrow: *m* 1980, Anne Susan Lyon, only da of late Capt N. Fellowes, and has issue living, Harry Bertram Templeton *b* 1984, Charles Peter Templeton *b* 1987, Emily Rose Cumberland *b* 1983, Amelia Anne Cumberland *b* 1989, — John Perry Donaldson (44 Cornwall Gdns, SW7 4AA), *b* 1951: *ed* Harrow; Capt 17th/21st Lancers, — Morella Cumberland, *b* 1942: *m* 1967, Robert Gwynne Cottam, of 7 Stanford Rd, W8 5PP, and has issue living, Charles Robert Edward *b* 1969, Henry Gerald Alexander *b* 1973, Rosemary Margaret Cumberland *b* 1971. *Residence* – Chattis Hill House, Stockbridge, Hants SO20 6JS.

    Grandchildren of late Arthur Walker, 8th son of 1st baronet:—
    Issue of late Edward Arthur Walker, *b* 1883, *d* 1950: *m* 1911, Frances Beatrice, who *d* 1961, da of James Davis:— Harold Edward Palmes, TD (Springwood Tower Rd North, Heswall, Ches), *b* 1917; 1939-45 War as Maj Indian Army in Burma: *m* 1951, Phyllis Nora Green, and has issue living, Michael Anthony, *b* 1951; *ed* St David's Coll, Llandudno: *m* 1983, Frances Helen Price, of Mount Isa, Qld, Aust, and has issue living, James Heron Palmes *b* 1986, Ross Francis *b* 1988, — Joan Olive Beatrix, *b* 1912: *m* 1940, Geoffrey Norman Booth, solicitor, of 77 Palm Grove, Oxton, Birkenhead, and has issue living, David Parkin, *b* 1943. —— Stella Rowena Palmes (3 Halifax Close, Wellesbourne, Warwicks), *b* 1920: *m* 1944, Cdr Harold Jack Edmund Dugdale, RNR, who *d* 1975, and has issue living, Janet Beatrice, *b* 1947: *m* 1972, Robert Lewes Sinkinson, and has issue living, Mark Luis *b* 19—, James Alexander *b* 19—, — Diana Elizabeth, *b* 1952: *m* 1989, Jan Ryszard Kacperek, and has issue living, Paul Anthony *b* 19—.

    Grandchildren of late Henry Walker (infra):—
    Issue of late Maj Henry Arthur Walker, *b* 1913, *d* 1994: *m* 1st, 1935 (*m diss* 1947), Rose Vivien, who *d* 1993, da of Raymond Robert Ulyate, of Arusha, Tanzania; 2ndly, 1948, Christine Mabel, who *d* 1973, da of Ollive Edward Hollingworth, of Step Cottage, Witchampton, Dorset; 3rdly, 1980, Patricia Blanche Neville (The Bridge House, Spetisbury, Blandford Forum, Dorset DT11 9EB), da of Ralph Neville Neville-Jones, of Broadstone Dorset, and widow of Capt C. H. Hammer, MBE, RN:—
(By 1st *m*) Robert Christopher Arthur (PO Box 584, Jwaneng, Botswana, Southern Africa), *b* 1938; *ed* King's Sch, Bruton: *m* 1964, Melody Gloriana Mignonette, yst da of late Gustavus Adolfus Carl de Friedland, of Cape Town, S Africa, and has issue living, Grant Robert James, *b* 1968; *ed* St Martin's, Johannesburg, — Juanita Marguerite Vivien *b* (Jan) 1965: *m* 1983, Ferdinando Ganchinho Carlos, of Johannesburg, and has issue living, Shane Robert Martins *b* 1984, Ivan Anibal Christopher *b* 1986, Ricardo Fernando *b* 1987, — Karine Madelaine Mignonette Tanya, *b* (Nov) 1965. —— (By 2nd *m*) Mary Woodroffe Margaret, *b* 1957: *m* 1980, John Stephen Lucas, of Wychwood, 4 Field Way, Corfe Mullen, Wimborne, Dorset BH21 3XH, and has issue living, Emma Annabel Mary, *b* 1983, — Sophie Elizabeth, *b* 1985.

    Granddaughters of late Arthur Walker (ante):—
    Issue of late Henry Walker, *b* 1885, *d* 1965: *m* 1913, Margaret, who *d* 1974, da of Robert Rowlands:— Monica Diana (5 Bon Accord, Victoria Av, Swanage, Dorset), *b* 1915: *m* 1939, Archibald Robert Octavius McMillan, OBE, who *d* 1988. —— Margaret Patricia (5 Richmond Lodge, Victoria Av, Swanage, Dorset), *b* 1919: *m* 1944 (*m diss* 1966), Eugene Larner, who *d* 1989, and has issue living, Felicity Gay (15 Gayford Rd, W12 9BJ), *b* 1945: *m* 1980 (*m diss* 1985), William McKinney, and has issue living, Clinton William Eugene *b* 1981.
    Issue of late Maj Ernest Walker *b* 1887, *d* 1970: *m* 1st, 1921, Mildred Katherine Grace, who *d* 1952, da of late Lt-Col Sir Charles Henry Brabazon Heaton-Ellis, CBE; 2ndly, 1953, Dorothy Hyacinthe, who *d* 1993, only child of late Maj Cecil William Bunbury Eames, JP, RE:—
(By 1st *m*) Peter Martin Brabazon, CBE (Drumlaggan, The Ross, Comrie, Perthshire), *b* 1922; *ed* Haileybury, and Trin Coll, Camb; Prof of Natural Hist, Edinburgh Univ: *m* 1943, Violet Wright, and has issue living, Robin John, *b* 1947, — Marian Elizabeth, *b* 1943, — Sonia Elidh, *b* 1954, — Caroline Jane Palmes, *b* 1960. —— Jonathan Mungo Palmes (Lythanger, Empshott, Hants), *b* 1929; Maj (ret) The Black Watch: *m* 1955, Diana Mary, el da of late Brig Otho William Nicholson, TD, DL (*see* E St Aldwyn 1939 Edn), and has issue living, Timothy William Mungo, *b* 1956; *ed* Millfield: *m* 1989, Julia Suzanne, eldest da of John Clifford Groves, of Lundie Castle, Edzell, Angus, and has issue living, Max John Mungo *b* 1990, — Jonathan Alexander James, *b* 1961; *ed* Millfield, — Juliette Elisabeth Charmian (*Hon Mrs William Wilson*), *b* 1958; *ed* St Mary's, Calne and Homerton Coll, Camb: *m* 1989, Hon William Edward Alexander Wilson, yr son of 2nd Baron Moran, KCMG.

    Granddaughter of late Maj Ernest Walker (ante):—
    Issue of late Lt Cdr Timothy Robin Charles Walker, RN, *b* 1925, *d* 1964: *m* 1958, Dilys, who *d* 1964, da of late Brig John Victor Dykes Radford, OBE, MC, of Clayhanger, Purse Caundle, Sherborne, Dorset:—
Sabrina Louise, *b* 1962: *m* 1983 (*m diss* 1986), Maj Roderick Alexander Ingleby-Mackenzie, Scots Gds.
Sir James Walker, 1st Bt, of Sand Hutton, Yorks, only son of James Walker of Springhead, Hull, was High Sheriff of York 1846. Sir James Robert Walker, 2nd Bt, was MP for Beverley (*C*), 1859-65.

WALKER (UK) 1906, of Pembroke House, City of Dublin

Sir HUGH RONALD WALKER, 4th *Baronet*; *b* 13 Dec 1925; *s* his father, *Maj Sir* CECIL EDWARD, DSO, MC, 1964; *ed* Wellington Coll; Member of Assoc of Supervisory and Exec Engineers; Maj (ret) RA: *m* 1971, Norna, el da of Lt-Cdr R.D. Baird, RNR (ret), of Yarford Orchards, Kingston St Mary, nr Taunton, and has issue.

Arms – Ermine, on a chevron engrailed plain cotised azure, between three hurts, each charged with a portcullis or, as many trefoils slipped of the last. **Crest** – On a Roman fasces or, banded azure, a dove of the last, holding in its beak a trefoil slipped of the first.
Address – Ballinamona Hospital, Kilmallock, co Limerick.

SONS LIVING

ROBERT CECIL, *b* 26 Sept 1974. —— Roy Edward, *b* 1977.

SISTER LIVING

Sheilagh Rosemary, *b* 1928.
The 1st baronet, Rt Hon Sir Samuel, PC, was Solicitor-Gen for Ireland 1883-5, Attorney-Gen of Ireland 1885 and 1886, Lord Chancellor of Ireland 1892-5, a Lord Justice of Appeal 1895-1905, and again Lord Chancellor 1905-11.

Walker-Okeover, see Okeover.

Walker-Smith, see Smith.

FORESTIER-WALKER (UK) 1835
(Name pronounced "Forest-tier-Walker")

Sir MICHAEL LEOLIN FORESTIER-WALKER, 6th *Baronet*; only son of Lt-Col Alan Ivor Forestier-Walker, MBE, elder son of Ivor Augustus Forestier-Walker, 5th son of 2nd Bt; *b* 24 April 1949; *s* his kinsman, *Sir* CLIVE RADZIVILL, 1983; *ed* Wellington Coll, and R Holloway Coll, London Univ (BA Hons, Cert Ed); Schoolmaster at Feltonfleet School, Cobham: *m* 1988, Elizabeth, da of Joseph Hedley, of Bellingham, Northumberland, and has issue.

Arms – Erminois, on a pile embattled azure, a mural crown charged with the word "Badajos" between two galtraps in pale or. **Crest** – On a mural crown or, encircled by a wreath of laurel vert, an ostrich proper, resting the dexter foot on a shell exploding proper. **Supporters** – *Dexter*, a lion reguardant proper, gorged with a riband gules, fimbriated azure, therefrom pendent a representation of the medal and claps presented to the 1st baronet for his services in the Peninsula; in the mouth a broken flagstaff reversed, with the eagle and French tricolored flag also proper, the latter inscribed with the word "Orthes"; *sinister*, an ostrich supporting the colours of the 50th Regt, thereon an escroll gules inscribed with the word "Vimiera" in letters of gold.

Residence – Bibury, 116 Hogshill Lane, Cobham, Surrey.

SON LIVING

JOSEPH ALAN, *b* 2 May 1992.

DAUGHTER LIVING

Chloë, *b* 1990.

SISTER LIVING

Michelle, *b* 1946: *m* 1970, Christopher K. C. Metz, of North Brook End House, Steeple Morden, Royston, Herts, and has issue living, Camilla, *b* 1977, — Rosamond, *b* 1979, — Marguerite, *b* 1984.

DAUGHTERS LIVING OF FIFTH BARONET

Lesley Jane, *b* 1951: *m* 1968, John Wheaton, of 23 Grove Rd, Rayleigh, Essex SS6 8PU, and has issue living, Joanna Lesley, *b* 1970, — Jacqueline, *b* 1971. —— Heather, *b* 1954: *m* 1972, John Gray of 28 Grove Rd, Rayleigh, Essex SS6 8PU, and has issue living, Steven John, *b* 1977, — Adam James, *b* 1981. —— Elizabeth, *b* 1958: *m* 1974, David King, of 21 Juniper Rd, Leigh-on-Sea SS9 4BQ, and has issue living, Daniel David, *b* 1975, — Kerryann, *b* 1976.

COLLATERAL BRANCHES LIVING

Granddaughter of late Radzivill Frederick Forestier-Walker, 2nd son of 2nd Baronet:—
Issue of late Radzivill Clive Forestier-Walker, *b* 1895; *d* 1973: *m* 1921, Kathleen Rose, who *d* 1975, da of late William George Tinkler, of King's Lynn, Norfolk:—
June Vivienne, *b* 1923: *m* 1954, Leonard Raymond Hayes, of Chinook, Castle Rising Rd, S Wootton, King's Lynn, Norfolk.

Grandson of late Ivor Augustus Forestier-Walker, 5th son of 2nd baronet:—
Issue of late Urbain Evelyn Forestier-Walker, *b* 1915, *d* 1974: *m* 1941, Aileen, who *d* 1976, da of Thomas Morrissey:—
Alan David, *b* 1944; *ed* Prior Park Coll, Bath; Lt-Col 7th Duke of Edinburgh's Own Gurkha Rifles: *m* 1969, Adela, da of Simon Phillip Davis, and has issue living, Robin Peter, *b* 1978, — Clare Elaine, *b* 1971, — Louise Anne *b* 1972. —— Anne Patricia, *b* 1942.

Issue of late Capt Devereux Philip Forestier-Walker, 6th son of 2nd baronet, *b* 1864, *d* 1936: *m* 1896, Isabella Constance, who *d* 1949, da of late F. G. Dalgety, of Lockerley Hall, Hants, and widow of Capt C. W. Selwyn:—
Freda Gladys (17, 31313 Livingstone Av, Cleasbrook, BC, V2S 5W6), *b* 1897: *m* 1921, William Henry Cartwright, who *d* 1962, and has issue living, Julian William Devereux, *b* 1923: *m* 1949, Margaret Elaine, da of E. Ewing, and has issue living, Elena Marr *b* 1950: *m* 1976, Donald John Rouse, Lorena Joanne *b* 1951: *m* 1972, Jacobus Antonius Ferdinand Remak (and has issue living, Jason William Johannes *b* 1976) Shelley Rae *b* 1953: *m* 1973, Terrance Glenn Pruden, Tracy Dell *b* 1961, — Barbara Mary, *b* 1922: *m* 1954, John Bannatyne McLeod, of 920 Smith Av, Coquitlam, BC. —— Honor Dorothy, *b* 1899: *m* 1934, Capt Thomas Willington Lane, late RA; MA Camb and ADC to Gov of Mauritius, who *d* 1977, and has issue living, Patrick Anthony Willington (28 High St, Manton, Marlborough, Wilts SN8 4HH), *b* 1938: *m* 1978, Dinah, da of late B. W. Righton, of Town Farm, Ebrington, Glos, and has issue living, Martin Nicholas *b* 1980, Sarah Ann *b* 1979, — Gillian, *b* 1935. *Residence* – Longdon, Bath Rd, Marlborough, Wilts.

Grandchildren of late Charles Evelyn Forestier-Walker (infra):—
Issue of late Charles Jocelyn Forestier-Walker, *b* 1912, *d* 1992: *m* 1942, Joy (Rosemary Cottage, 5 High St, Hanslope, Bucks), da of late Lt-Cdr John Robert Gill, RNR, of Christchurch, Newport, Mon:—
Charles Robert Piers (Bron Garnedd, Llanfrothen, Penrhyndeudraeth, N Wales), *b* 1950; *ed* Wellingham: *m* 1974 (*m diss* 1979), Philippa Jean White, step-da of Dr C. Bondy, and has issue living, Rowan, *b* 1977. —— Elenith Camilla, *b* 1947: *m* 1st, 1968 (*m diss* 1982), Malcolm Anthony Luker; 2ndly, 1983, James Stephen Allen, of 46 Hereford St, Cambridge CB4 3AG, and has issue living, (by 1st *m*) James Robert, *b* 1971, — Benjamin Gavin, *b* 1975, — (by 2nd *m*) Richard Arthur Llewellyn, *b* 1983, — Charles Alexander Titus, *b* 1988, — Camilla Imogen Maud, *b* 1984.

Issue of late Charles Evelyn Forestier-Walker, 9th son of 2nd baronet, *b* 1875, *d* 1931: *m* 1905, Ada Llewelyn, who *d* 1960, da of Col Robert Henry Mansel (JP and DL for Monmouthshire, formerly Major Roy Dublin Fusiliers, and Col Cmdg 2nd Vol Batn of S Wales Borderers), of Abergavenny, and Caerleon, Monmouthshire:—
(Robert Jestyn) Gwent (Barberry House, Clifford, Herefords HR3 5HF. *Club* – Brooks's) *b* 1919; *ed* Wellington Coll, an Architect (ret); 1939-45 War as Flt Lt RAF (despatches): *m* 1956, Elizabeth Ann, da of late Brig J. H. Willans, of Newton House, Sneaton, Yorks, and has issue living, Charles Aidan Gwent, *b* 1966, — (Evelyn) Rosamond, *b* 1961: *m* 1987 (*m diss* 1990), Hon Hugh Francis Kindersley, who *d* 1991, 2nd son of 3rd Baron Kindersley, — Vivien Serena Charlotte, *b* 1963: *m* 19—, G. Nicholas Tucker, son of late Maj K. O. Tucker, and has issue living, Harry Albert *b* 1994, — Daphne Miranda Clare, *b* 1964.

Grandchildren of late Lieut-Col Edmond Somerville Forestier Walker, el son of Maj-Gen George Edmond Lushington Walker, 4th son of 1st baronet:—
Issue of late Col Edmond Alec FORESTIER-WALKER, *b* 1888, *d* 1952 (having assumed by deed poll 1909, the additional surname of Forestier): *m* 1921, Eileen de Renzy, who *d* 1977, da of late Col O. H. Channer, of Brookheath, Fordingbridge, Hants:—
Edmond Annesley (Broombank, Aldeburgh, Suffolk IP15 5PQ), *b* 1922; *ed* Felsted Sch, Maj (ret) RA; 1939-45 War in N Africa and Italy (despatches); Administration Manager, Touche Ross: *m* 1st, 1944, Bridget, who *d* 1961, da of Cdr Sir Geoffrey Henry Hughes-Onslow, KBE, DSC, RN (ret) (E Onslow, colls), 2ndly, 1968, Dreenagh Denise, da of Kenneth G. Chavasse, of London, and has issue living, (by 1st *m*) George Clive (Mulberry House, Heather Drive, Sunningdale, Berks), *b* 1946; Maj Coldm Gds (ret): *m* 1970, Ruth Christian, yst da of John Gurney, of Walsingham Abbey, Norfolk (*see* Ogilvy Bt, colls), and has issue living, Camilla Christian *b* 1973, Susanna Charlotte *b* 1976, Liza Bridget *b* 1980, Mary Sarah *b* 1983, — Sally Eileen, *b* 1948: *m* 1972, Mark Andrew Muspratt-Williams, of Pastures Farm House, Caxton, Cambs CB3 8PF, and has issue living, Alexander Mark *b* 1977, Catriona Louise *b* 1975, — (by 2nd *m*) David Anthony, *b* 1972, — Annabel Dreenagh, *b* 1974. —— Claude Osborne (Babbacombe, Snape Bridge, Saxmundham, Suffolk IP17 1ST), *b* 1924; *ed* Felsted Sch; is a Co Dir: *m* 1950, Gillian Mary, da of Maj Guy Pedder, of Park House, Hoxne, nr Diss, Norfolk, and has issue living, Hugh Anthony Claude (Kencot Hill Farmhouse, Filkins, Lechlade, Glos GL7 3QY), *b* 1954; *ed* Abbotsholme; Co Dir: *m* 1976, (Elizabeth) Jane, da of Rev Christopher Birdwood, and has issue living, Edward *b* 1982, Caroline Louise *b* 1978, Rebecca Jane *b* 1980, — Melanie Diana, *b* 1956, — Katherine Susan, *b* 1960; MA (Cantab); journalist (as Katherine Forestier): *m* 1988, Zhang Zeming, of 58 Po Wah Yuen, Yung Shue Wan, Lamma Island, Hong Kong, and has issue living, Lydia Yishi *b* 1990, Laura Yiya *b* 1992.

The 1st baronet, Gen Sir George Townshend, GCB, KCTS, was a distinguished Peninsular officer, C-in-C at Fort St George, India, and Lt-Gov of Chelsea Hospital. The 2nd baronet assumed by deed poll 1893, the additional surname of Forestier.

WALLER (I) 1780, of Newport, Tipperary

Sir ROBERT WILLIAM WALLER, 9th *Baronet*; *b* 16 June 1934; *s* his father, *Sir* ROLAND EDGAR, 1958; *ed* Newark Coll of Engineering, and Fairleigh Dickinson Univ; formerly Business Manager with General Electric Co (ret 1991); a citizen of USA: *m* 1960 (*m diss* 1975), Carol Anne, da of John E. Hines, of 45 Bellevue Rd, Lynn, Mass, USA, and has issue.

Arms – Checky or and azure, on a canton gules, a lion rampant double queued of the first. **Crest** – Out of a ducal coronet a plume of five ostrich feathers, 2nd and 4th azure, 1st, 3rd and 5th argent, surmounted by an eagle's claw gules. *Residence* – 5 Lookout Terr, Lynnfield, Mass 01940, USA.

SONS LIVING

JOHN MICHAEL, *b* 14 May 1962: *m* 1986, Maria Renee Gonzalez, and has issue living, John Michael, *b* 1990, — Patrick Joseph de Warren, *b* 1992, — Jocelyn Anne, *b* 1988, — Mary Katherine, *b* 1994. *Residence* – 8632 Garfield St, Bethesda, Maryland 20817, USA. —— David Peter *b* 1963: *m* 1989, Lynn Riddle. *Residence* – 22 Mountain Av, Malden, Mass 02148, USA.

DAUGHTERS LIVING

Susan Carol, *b* 1968. —— Kathleen Ann, *b* 1970.

Honour and truth

SISTERS LIVING

Helen Mary, *b* 1924: *m* 1945, Arthur Paul Warshauer, who *d* 1990, and has issue living, Shawn Matthew, *b* 1962, — Sandra Ann, *b* 1945, — Mary Susan, *b* 1950. *Residence* – RFD 4, Box 154, Medford Farms, Goffstown, New Hampshire 03045, USA. —— Patricia Ann, *b* 1930: *m* 1st, 1949 (*m diss* 1974), Howard George Schier; 2ndly, 19—, Leonard Monroe, of 3321 19th St CT East, Bradenton, Fla 34208, USA, and has issue living (by 1st *m*), Virginia Gail, *b* 1949, — Nancy Lee, *b* 1954, — Linda Jean, *b* 1957.

COLLATERAL BRANCHES LIVING

Grandson of late Elwood Eccleston Waller, brother of 7th baronet, *b* 1876, *d* 1944: *m* 1895, Francina Claire Shaunesy, who *d* 1958:—
Issue of late Elwood Eccleston Waller, *b* 1896, *d* 1976: *m* 1921, Jane Eden, who *d* 1977:—
Elwood Eccleston (3511 Hargill Drive, Orlando, Florida 32806, USA), *b* 1922; formerly Lieut USA Air Force: *m* 1st, 1946, Marie Maupin; 2ndly, 1956, Marie Benton, and has issue living (by 1st *m*), Patrick, *b* 1949, — Susan (3019 Emerson St, Tampa, Florida 33629, USA), *b* 1947.

Descendants (if any) of Edmund Waller, brother of 6th baronet, *b* 1844, *m* 1861 and *d* 1899, leaving issue.

Descendants (if any) of Augustus Edmund Waller, *b* 1871, and Philip Percy Waller, *b* 1877, sons of Jocelyn Waller, el son of Samuel Waller, MD, brother of 4th baronet.

Grandchildren of late John Stanton Waller (infra):—
Issue of late John Clifton Waller, *b* 1903, *d* 1985: *m* 1st, 1939 (*m diss* 19—), Priscilla Frost, of Marblehead, MA, USA; 2ndly, 1953 (*m diss* 19—), Christine E. Todtschinder, of Manchester Centre, VT, USA:—
(By 1st *m*) John Clifton, Jr, *b* 1940: *m* 1st, 1964 (*m diss*), Donna Lee Smethurst, of Marblehead, MA, USA; 2ndly, 1977, Diana Casey, of Salem, MA, USA, and has issue living, (by 1st *m*) John Clifton III, *b* 1965, — Michael, *b* 1973: *m* 19—, — , and has issue living, Timothy Michael French *b* 1991 — Donna Leann, *b* 1969: *m* 19—, — , and has issue living, Shawn William Somers *b* 1989, Jeremy Michael Somers *b* 1991, — (by 2nd *m*) Darrell Hawkes, *b* 1977, — Annette Michelle, *b* 1984, — Alan Peyton Hawkes, *b* 1946: *m* 1st, 19— (*m diss*), Susan Jan Halloran, of Marblehead, MA, USA; 2ndly, 1980, Christine Renée Whalen, of Princeton, NJ, USA, and has issue living, (by 1st *m*) Todd Alan Hawkes, *b* 1968, — (by 2nd *m*) Benjamin Edward Austin Hawkes, *b* 1990. —— (by 2nd *m*) Sandra Gail, *b* 1957.

Granddaughter of late Samuel William Waller (*b* 1844), yr son of late Samuel Waller, MD (ante):—

Issue of late John Stanton Waller, *b* 1868, *d* 1921: *m* 1888, Ida Anna Finley, who *d* 1950, da of James Peyton, of Montreal, Canada:—
Margaret Patricia Eunice, *b* 1907: *m* 1928, Walter Brown Power, Jr, and has issue living, Walter Brown III, *b* 1930: *m* 1955, Sandra Sherman, and has issue living, Walter Brown IV *b* 1958, Sherman Douglas *b* 1961: *m* 1989, Christine Landry, Matthew Eli *b* 1963, Elizabeth Atwood *b* 1970, — James Peyton, *b* 1933: *m* 1965, Virginia O'Meara, and has issue living, Peyton Jay *b* 1975, Tara O'Meara *b* 1966: *m* 1991, Bradley James Gilbert, Laurel Peyton *b* 1969: *m* 1990, Michael Perry.

Grandchildren of late Edmund Henry Colclough Waller (infra):—
Issue of late Herbert Montague Waller, *b* 1907, *d* 1971: *m* 1942, Vera Germain (245 Denis St, Thunder Bay, Ont, Canada):—
Edgar Herbert (606 Tennyson Av, Oshawa, Ont L1H 3K1), *b* 1942; *ed* Lake Head Univ, Thunder Bay, Ont: *m* 1966, Sandra Yvonne Egan, and has issue living, Scott Edward, *b* 1967. —— Brian Robert (RR 1, Mapleward Rd, Kaminstiqua, Ont), *b* 1944: *m* 1965, Joan Gloria Woodgate, and has issue living, Faye Kathleen, *b* 1969, — Karen Louise, *b* 1972. —— Sharon Claire, *b* 1946: *m* 1965, Robert Bruce Nicholl, of RR 2, Devlin, Ont, and has issue living, Laura Cecile, *b* 1966, — Rhonda Jean, *b* 1968: has issue living, Robert Herbert James *b* 1989. —— Jean Patricia, *b* 1952: *m* 1972, John Charles Mayo, of RR, Thunder Bay, Ont, and has issue living, Jennifer Ann, *b* 1975.

Grandchildren of late Samuel William Waller (*b* 1844) (ante):—
Issue of late Edmund Henry Colclough Waller, *b* 1879, *d* 1970: *m* 1906, Caroline Agnes, who *d* 1967, da of late John Mann, of Grand Valley Ont:—
Arthur Edmund (48-6245 Metral Drive, Nanaimo, BC, Canada V9T 2L9), *b* 1909: *m* 1st, 1941 (*m diss* 1967), Frances, da of John Martin, of Vancouver BC; 2ndly, 1968, Mrs Alma Rickerby, da of — Taylor, and has issue living (by 1st *m*), Lynne Diane, *b* 1944. —— William Hugh, *b* 1912: *m* 1944, Alvina Koch. —— Cedric Henry (Site 32, C6, 551 Castlegar, BC, Canada V1N 3H7), *b* 1914: *m* 1939, Flora Margaret da of John George Campbell, of MacDowell, Sask, Canada, and has issue

living, Cedric Lorne (34030 Shannon Drive, Abbotsford, BC, Canada V2S 5C8), *b* 1940; *ed* BC Univ (BEd) and W Washington Univ, USA (MEd); Sch Administrator: *m* 1st, 1964 (*m diss* 1977), Doris Lorraine, da of Edward Sweetman, of Trail, BC; 2ndly, 1977, Julia Carolyn, da of George Dennison Glanville, of W Vancouver, BC, and has issue living, (by 1st *m*) Stephen Lorne *b* 1966, Richard Lawrence *b* 1968, Daniel Leonard *b* 1970 (by 2nd *m*) Jennifer Louise *b* 1980, Allison Patricia *b* 1982, — Ronald Henry (C8, Site 2, RR2 Kelowna, BC, Canada V1Y 7R1) *b* 1943; *ed* BC; Univ (BSP, MSc): *m* 1965, Gwendolyn Anne, da of William Wright, of Nelson, BC, and has issue living Michael Ronald *b* 1966, Donald William Henry *b* 1969, Christopher Bradley *b* 1970, Darren Lorne *b* 1971, Heather Diane Habiza *b* 1972. —— Thomas Geoffrey (1107 Dahl St, Prince George, BC), *b* 1916; Forestry Dept Supervisor, BC Govt (ret): *m* 1947 (*m diss* 1975), Elizabeth Margaret Esther, da of William J. Brodie, of Nelson, BC, and has issue living, Donna Elaine, *b* 1949: *m* 1971, Edward Charles Anderson, and has issue living, Nicole Dawn *b* 1974, Tara Leigh *b* 1979, — Glowena Margaret, *b* 1950: *m* 1st, 1969, Allen Lee Hutchinson; 2ndly, 1986, Leslie Alexander Cook, and has issue living (by 1st *m*), Celeste Marie *b* 1969, Michelle Jeanette *b* 1972, — Judith Darlene, *b* 1953: *m* 1st, 1973 (*m diss* 1977), Joseph Martin Walker; 2ndly, 1983, Frederick Louis Tuttosi, and has issue living (by 1st *m*), Cassandra Lee *b* 1981, (by 2nd *m*) Michael Ryne *b* 1984. —— Arnold Blair (50 Cordova Av, #302, Etobicoke, Ont M9A 4X6, Canada), *b* 1924: *ed* BC Univ (BSc); engineering consultant: *m* 1951, Janet Louise, da of William Paton Montgomery, of Montreal, and has an adopted son, Jonathan Blair, *b* 1962, — Laurie Jane, *b* 1953: *m* 1984, Christopher Benson, of 63 Anne St, Cannington, Ont LOE 1EO, and has issue living, Robin Patrick Waller *b* 1989, Mairen Rose Montgomery *b* 1992, — Elizabeth Sue, *b* 1958: *m* 1989 (*m diss* 1993), Christopher Thor Asp, of Neustadt, Ont N0G 2MO, Canada. —— Evelyn Agnes *b* 1918: *m* 1st 1937 (*m diss* 1954), James Donald Ross; 2ndly, 1961, William Wilson (1126 Gillespie Rd, RR1 Sooke, BC, Canada), and has issue living, (by 1st *m*) Shirley Norma, *b* 1938: *m* 1st, 1955 (*m diss* 1969), Allen William Wilson; 2ndly, 1980, Póvl Frederick Holm, and has issue living (by 1st *m*), Michael Allen *b* 1963, Shelley Norma *b* 1957: *m* 1983, Michael Collins. —— Beatrice Alice (Box 272, Ladysmith, BC, Canada), *b* 1922: *m* 1949, Ernest John Moretti, who *d* 1971, and has issue living, Ernest James, *b* 1950.

Grandchildren of late Hugh Jocelyn Waller (infra):—
Issue of late Hector Hugh Waller, *b* 1910, *d* 1986: *m* 1945, Mary Patricia (N Vancouver, BC, Canada), da of Ivor John Everson, of Gravesend, Kent:—
Thomas Hector (622 Shannon Crescent, N Vancouver, BC, Canada V7N 2Y9), *b* 1947: *m* 1969, Margaret Quilliam, and has issue living, Michael Hugh, *b* 1974, — Ian Denny *b* 1976. —— Sean Ivor *b* 1957. —— Mary Kathleen, *b* 1950: *m* 1972, Gerald St Laurent, of Tumbler Ridge, BC, and has issue living, Jocelyn Kathleen, *b* 1974, — Tannis Patricia Marie, *b* 1977. —— Valerie Jane, *b* 1954: *m* 19—, William Truttman; 2ndly, 1988, Pal Levitt.
Issue of late Gordon Jocelyn Waller, *b* 1912, *d* 1992: *m* 1937, Pearl Solie:—
Dennis Raymond, *b* 1938. —— Gordon Edmund, *b* 1948: *m* 1985, Dianne —, and has issue living, Mark, *b* 1996.

Issue of late Hugh Jocelyn Waller, son of late Samuel William Waller (*b* 1844) (ante), *b* 1887, *d* 1981: *m* 1909, Olive Maria, who *d* 1959, da of John Mann:—
Hugh Macartney (119 Heritage Cres, Nanaimo, BC, Canada), *b* 1922: *m* 1st, 1943, Betty Hallat; 2ndly, 1951, Florence —, and has issue living (by 2nd *m*), Kenneth Hugh, *b* 1953: *m* 1975, Anne Beswetherwick, of New Haven, Sussex, and has an adopted son, Liam Kenan Hugh *b* 1987, — Gregory Allen, *b* 1955: *m* 1980, Judith Anne Yule, and has issue living, Sean Steven *b* 1987, — Douglas William, *b* 1959: *m* 1983, Kathleen Freeman, and has issue living, Nicholas Hugh *b* 1986, Jessica Rachelle *b* 1988, — Denise Jean, *b* 1951: *m* 1973, Arthur Stanley Webb, and has issue living, Ryan Gregory *b* 1980, Jaye Scott *b* 1981, Lauren Ashley *b* 1987, — Kathleen Marie, *b* (twin) 1953: *m* 1983, Johannes Verhagen, and has issue living, Gregory William *b* 1986, Caitlin Johanna *b* 1989. —— Lilian Gladys, *b* 1911: *m* 1935, Clinton Geddes, and has issue living, Gordon, *b* 1936: *m* 1958, Judith Anne Hall, and has issue living, Clinton Douglas *b* 1965, Michael *b* 1970, Cinda Marie *b* 1959, Dayna *b* 1960. —— Olive Kathleen, *b* 1916: *m* 1941, Noel Hendry, of Vancouver, BC, Canada, and has issue living, Kenneth Noel, *b* 1944: *m* 1st, Charlotte —; 2ndly, 1987, Anne Marie —, and has issue living (by 1st *m*), a son *b* 1970, a son *b* 1971, a da *b* 19—, — Douglas, *b* 1948. —— Muriel Eleanor, *b* 1919: *m* 1941, Charles Guiguet, Curator of Birds and Mammals, Provincial Museum, Victoria, BC, of 2399 Dalhouse St, Victoria, BC, and has issue living, Mark Laurence, *b* 1950: *m* 19—, Victoria —, and has issue living, Colin *b* 19—, Michelle *b* 19—, — Joan Muriel, *b* 1942, — Patricia Lynda, *b* 1947: *m* 1969, John —, and has issue living, Matthew Guiguet *b* 1969, — Suzanne Maria, *b* 1955: *m* 198-, Bryce —, and has issue living, Tyson Bancroft *b* 1987. —— Jean Pearl, *b* 1923: *m* 1946, Laurence Cutler, and has issue living, Jerry, *b* 1947, — Ross, *b* 1952, — Gregory, *b* 1955: *m* 19—, Sherry —, and has issue living, Ryan *b* 19—, — Janet, *b* 1949: *m* 1968, Len Thony, and has issue living, Paul John *b* 1970, Corry Lynne *b* 1969, Dana Marie *b* 1973, — Debra, *b* 1957.

Grandchildren of late Robert William Waller, el son of late Robert Waller, yst brother of 4th baronet:—
Issue of late Frank Hastings Waller, *b* 1871, *d* 1953: *m* 1914, Elvie Grace, *d* as a result of enemy action 1940, da of late William Bedford, of Landour, India:—
Marjorie, *b* 1919.
Issue of late Charles Robert Waller, *b* 1877, *d* 1933: *m* 1905, Agnes Helen, da of late Francis Thorne, of Launceston, Cornwall:—
†Robert William, *b* 1910: *m* 1936, Daphne Mabel, who *d* (Oct) 1992, el da of Herbert Clifton Morton, of Pretoria, S Africa, and *d* (Aug) 1992, leaving issue, Robert David (Morville Farm, Le Hurel, St Ouen, Jersey), *b* 1939: *m* 1961, Rosalie Beryl, da of late Wilfred Easter, of Southampton, and has issue living, Hugh *b* 1965, Vanessa *b* 1963, Ursula (twin) *b* 1963: *m* 19—, Douglas A. Richardson, of Morville Farm, Le Hurel, St Ouen, Jersey, CI, — Leonard Harold (118 Cambridge Rd, King William's Town, 5600, S Africa), *b* 1953: *m* 1st, 1976, Moira, who *d* 1981, da of Frank Ferreira, of Queenstown; 2ndly, 1982, Helen Louise, da of Raymond George Hewson, of East London, and has issue living (by 1st *m*), Stephen *b* 1976, Marc *b* 1977, (by 2nd *m*), Peter *b* 1984, — Delene Ruth, *b* 1937: *m* 1961, Edgar E. Esselen, of 132 Golf Av, Club View West, Pretoria, S Africa, and has issue living, Deborah *b* 1962: *m* 1980, Gary Alan Gordon (and has issue living, Justin *b* 1984, Megan *b* 1986), Ingrid *b* 1965, — Thalia Lynnette, *b* 1943: *m* 1965, Allan Harry Griffin, of 14 Hill Cres, Amauzimtoti, Natal, and has issue living, Helen Eileen *b* 1969, Louise Daphne *b* 1971, — Daphne Jess, *b* 1945: *m* 1985, Peter Alan Anscombe, of Johannesburg, S Africa, — Heather Lynn, *b* 1949. —— Edmund John (7 Broadway, Durban, Natal), *b* 1919; 1939-45 War as Warrant Officer SAAF, in Middle East, Malta, Sicily, and Italy: *m* 1944, Alma, yst da of Edwyn Treffry-Goatley, of Durban, Natal, and has issue living, Virginia Helen, *b* 1945, — Hazel Louise, *b* 1948: *m* 1968, John Robert Lockwood, of E Yorks, England, and has issue living, Edmund Sean *b* 1973, Amanda Jane *b* 1969. —— Catherine Jocelyn (c/o Mrs S. Weir, 21 Danville Av, Virginia, Durban 4001, Natal), *b* 1906: *m* 1935, Reginald Charles Oates, and has issue living, Jillian Elizabeth, *b* 1937, — Sandra Jocelyn, *b* 1941. —— Agatha Minnie (Fountain Hill, PO Upper Tongaat, Natal 4402), *b* 1908: *m* 1933, William U. E. Cook, who *d* 1971, and has issue living, Richard Clive, *b* 1939, — Valma Jean, *b* 1935. —— Ruth, *b* 1909: *m* 1935, Richard Dennis Goble, of Beaufort, Compensation, Natal, and has issue living, Denise Joy, *b* 1938, — Sylvia Helen, *b* 1940, — Carol Ruth, *b* 1943.

Grandchildren of late Jocelyn Waller, 2nd son of late Robert Waller (ante):—
Issue of late Robert Martin Jocelyn Waller, *b* 1862, *d* 1936: *m* 1896, his cousin, Emily Mary, who *d* 1951, da of late Robert William Waller:—
Frank Martin Roden (Gerard Lodge, 7 Gerard Rd, Weston-super-Mare, Avon), *b* 1909: *m* 1948, Nora Dale, who *d* 1965, da of late Rev Cyril Edgington, of Bath, and has issue living, Robert Cyril Hardress Jocelyn, *b* 1949. —— Dorothy Minnie, *b* 1898: *m* 1919, Reginald Carp, of 12 Grange Av, Highbridge, Som, and has issue living, Thomas Walter Waller, *b* 1924, — Pamela Mary, *b* 1923.

Grandson of late William Dillon Waller, 3rd son of late Jocelyn Waller (ante):—

Issue of late Hans Jocelyn, *b* 1897, *d* 19—: *m* 1922, Mildred Vivian (2404 Hampstead, Wichita Falls, Texas 76308, USA) da of — Pennock, of Longmont, Colorado:—
Edmund Hugh (8656 W Progress Place, Littleton, Colorado 80123, USA), *b* 1929: *m* 1951, Barbara Yetter, and has issue living, Kenneth Scott, *b* 1959: *m* 1982, Karen Staley, and has issue living, Tyler Paul *b* 1989, Danielle Renée *b* 1986, — Wendy Ann, *b* 1957: *m* 1st, 1983 (*m diss* 1985), Randall J. Brunko; 2ndly, 1987, Timothy Todd, and has issue living (by 2nd *m*), Joseph Lee *b* 1988. —— Patricia Gene, *b* 1925: *m* 1948, Vern L. Klingman, and has issue living, Stephen Wesley, *b* 1957, — Nancy Rose, *b* 1955 — Candice Martha, *b* 1961.

Grandson of late Rev Alfred Jocelyn Waller (infra):—
Issue of late Hardress Jocelyn Waller, *b* 1905, *d* 1935: *m* 19—, Bessie Burrow:—
Hardress Jocelyn, *b* 1928; PhD; Neurophysiologist, Toledo Univ, Ohio: *m* 1953, Gertrude Gearhart, and has issue living, Andrew Jocelyn, *b* 1960.

Grandchildren of late Jocelyn Waller (ante):—
Issue of late Rev Alfred Jocelyn Waller, *b* 1870, *d* 1950: *m* 1903, Katherine Tarrence:—
Richard (9600 E Iliffe Av, No 281, Denver, Colorado, 80231, USA), *b* 1915: *m* 1949, Mildred Lucka, and has issue living, Sharon Rose, *b* 1951: *m* 19—, Charles Counts. —— Alice, *b* 1908: *m* 1932, Joseph C. Chiappetti, of 1113 W Azure Drive, Flagstaff, Arizona 86001, USA, and has issue living, Joanne, *b* 1935: *m* 1957, Dr Robert Wilcox, of Medford, Ore, USA, — Nancy Lou, *b* 1938: *m* 1958, Fred Marsh, of Los Alamos, N Mexico, USA.
Issue of late Harry Bernard Waller, *b* 1882, *d* 1971: *m* 1920, Anna Kruger Jorgensen, of Denmark, who *d* 1946:—
Evelyn May, *b* 1924: *m* 1949, Selwyn Barton Hoag, of 1350 Ridge Rd, Littleton, Colorado 80120, USA, and has issue living, Selwyn Barton, *b* 1950: *m* 1st, 1972, Claudia Lukas; 2ndly, 1978, Lee Lacey, and has issue living, Jason Henry *b* 1979, — Christopher Henry, *b* 1958, — Anthony Wayne, *b* 1960, — Eugenia Anne, *b* 1943: *m* 1st, 1965, Laurence V Monniger; 2ndly, 1981, Dennis Homrighausen, and has issue living, Darren Warren *b* 1983, Amanda Ann *b* 1981, — Jocelyn Deane, *b* 1955: *m* 1981, John Parker Mertens, and has issue living, Charles Parker *b* 1983.
The 1st baronet, Sir Robert Waller (son of late Samuel Waller, of Newport, Tipperary) was MP for Dundalk 1761-80, and one of the Commissioners of the Revenue. Sir Robert, 2nd Baronet, was High Sheriff for King's co in 1826.

WALLER (UK) 1815, of Braywick Lodge, Berkshire

HÆC
FRUCTUS VIRTUTIS
This is the fruit of valour

Sir JOHN STANIER WALLER, 7th *Baronet*, son of late Capt Stanier Edmund William Waller, grandson of late Rev Ernest Adolphus Waller, 2nd son of 1st baronet; *b* 27 July 1917; *s* his kinsman, *Sir* EDMUND, 1954; *ed* Weymouth Coll, and Worcester Coll, Oxford (Exhibitioner in History 1936, BA 1939); an Author and Poet and a Fellow of Roy Soc of Literature; Information Officer, Central Office of Information 1954-59; Middle East 1914-6 as Capt RASC, latterly as Press Officer: *m* 1974 (*m diss* 19—), Anne Eileen, da of Jack William Mileham, of Winterton-on-Sea, Norfolk.

𝕬rms – Sable, on a bend engrailed argent, between two bendlets *cr* three walnut-leaves of the last. 𝕮rest – On a mount vert a walnut tree proper, pendent therefrom by a ribbon gules a shield azure charged with a fleur-de-lis or.
Residence – Winchcombe, 37A Madeira Rd, Ventnor, I o Wight PO38 1QS.

SISTER LIVING

Elizabeth Mary Louisa (Winchcombe, 37B Madeira Rd, Ventnor, I o Wight PO38 1QS), *b* 1923; *ed* Oxford High Sch, and St Hilda's Coll, Oxford (Exhibitioner in History, MA BLitt); Assist Lecturer, Medieval History, Liverpool Univ, 1949-53; Baghdad 1953-58; joined HM Diplo Ser; Regional Assist Information Officer for Women's Affairs, Beirut 1961-67, Women's Affairs Officer, FCO London 1967-78, since when (self-employed) Women's Affairs Consultant.

COLLATERAL BRANCH LIVING

Issue of late Richard Alured Waller, 2nd Lieut Roy Fusiliers, yst brother of 6th baronet, *b* 1884, *d* on active ser 1917: *m* 1912, Ethel Gertrude, who *d* 1978, da of late John Tippet Drake, of Plumstead, Kent:—
Margaret Patience (The Cottage, Crawley Down, Sussex), *b* 1917: a State Registered Nurse (ret).
Sir (Jonathan) Wathen Waller, GCH, 1st Bt, of Braywick Lodge, Berks, and Pope's Villa, Twickenham, was Groom of the Bedchamber to William IV. He was son of Joshua Phipps, by Anne, da of Thomas Waller (descended from the Wallers of Groombridge Place, Speldhurst, Kent), and assumed by sign manual 1814, the surname and arms of Waller, being heir of his maternal grand-uncle James Waller of Farriers, High Wycombe.

JOHNSON-WALSH (I) 1775, of Ballykilcavan, Queen's County (Extinct 1953)

Sir HUNT HENRY ALLEN JOHNSON-WALSH, 5th and last *Baronet*.

DAUGHTER LIVING OF 5TH BARONET

Oonah Frances, *b* 1913: *m* 1937, William Frederick Kemmis, who assumed by deed poll 1945 the additional surname of Walsh before that of Kemmis (B Ashtown, colls) and *d* 1986, and has issue living, Peter William Hunt (Ballykilcavan, Stradbally, Laois), *b* 1939: *m* 1970, Ann Katherine, da of Henry Richard Langley, of Archerstown, Thurles, and has issue living, David Hunt *b* 1977, Susan Helen *b* 1972, — Michael Henry (Drumneen, Stradbally, Laois); *b* 1941: *m* 1972, Bridget Gillian, da of Donald McCall, of Heydon, Cambs, and has issue living, Francis Allen Meuric *b* 1977, Gerard Henry

Gilleathain *b* 1979, Rosetta Caitriona Bridget *b* 1973, — Olivia Anne, *b* 1943: *m* 1972, James Walter Hurton, of Marshchapel, Lincs, and has issue living, Stephen James William *b* 1973. *Residence* – Garrans, Stradbally, Laois.

WALSHAM (UK) 1831, of Knill Court, Herefordshire
(Name pronounced "Walsam")

Rest under liberty

Sir TIMOTHEY JOHN WALSHAM, 5th *Baronet*; *b* 26 April 1939; *s* his father, Rear Adm *Sir* JOHN SCARLETT WARREN, CB, OBE, 1992; *ed* Sherborne.

Arms – Quarterly: 1st and 4th per pale azure and gules, a grffin segreant wings elevated or, supporting on a tilting spear a banner flowing to the dexter argent, charged with a cross couped sable, *Garbett*; 2nd and 3rd, sable, on a cross voided or, five crosslets patée-fitchée of the last, *Walsham*. **Crest** – A demi-eagle with two heads displayed sable, having suspended from the neck, by a gold chain, an escutcheon argent, and thereon a Saracen's head erased at the neck proper, round the temples a wreath argent and azure.
Residence – Priory Cottage, Middle Coombe, Shaftesbury, Dorset.

SISTERS LIVING

Susan Elizabeth, *b* 1941: *m* 1st, 1963, Christopher James Harbour; 2ndly, 1988, Charles Michael Robertson, of Dromquinna Manor, Greenane, Blackwater Bridge P.O., nr Kenmore, co Kerry, and has issue living (by 1st *m*), Mark Christopher Bannerman, *b* 1964, — Benedict David Walsham, *b* 1967, — Matthew Alexander Walsham, *b* 1969, — Caroline Lucy Scarlett, *b* 1965. —— Jane Scarlett, *b* 1942: *m* 1963, Cdr David Colin Nairne, RN, of The Manor House, Preshaw Park, Upham, Southampton SO3 1HP, and has issue living, Charles David Scarlett, *b* 1965, — Alexander John Dalmahoy, *b* 1970, — Sarah Catriona, *b* 1964: *m* 1990, John Alexander Santos, and has issue living, Anouska Beatriz *b* 1992.

AUNT LIVING (*daughter of 3rd baronet*)

Gundreda Brydget Coytmore, *b* 1909: *m* 1931, Chichester Kennedy Crookshank, of 1 Kingsey Av, Emsworth, Hants, and has issue living, John Kennedy, *b* 1932; *ed* Repton, and RMA, Sandhurst; Capt late 5th Royal Inniskilling Dragoon Gds: *m* 1963, Phyllida Anne, yr da of Capt Ernest Charles Mylne, of Godmanstone Manor, Dorchester, and has issue living, Charles James Chichester *b* 1966, Antonia Scarlett *b* 1969, — Peter Scarlett, *b* 1935; *ed* Sherbourne: *m* 1958, Susan, da of Thomas George Watwood, of Stafford, and has issue living, Richard Chichester *b* 1962, William Thomas *b* 1965.

WIDOW LIVING OF FOURTH BARONET

SHEILA CHRISTINA (*Lady Walsham*), only da of late Cdr Bertrand Bannerman, DSO, RN (*see* Bannerman, Bt, colls): *m* 1936, Rear Adm Sir John Scarlett Warren Walsham, 4th Bt, CB, OBE, who *d* 1992. *Residence* – 19 Beckford Close, Tisbury, Wilts.

COLLATERAL BRANCH LIVING

Issue of late Percy Romilly Walsham, 2nd son of 2nd baronet, *b* 1871, *d* 1933: *m* 1899, Charlotte Cunningham Scott, who *d* 1945, da of William Wykeham Myers, MB:—
PERCY ROBERT STEWART (129 Ram Gorse, Harlow, Essex CH20 1QA) *b* 6 April 1904; *ed* —: *m* 1937, Tamara, who *d* 1981, da of — Ellis, of —, and has issue living, Gerald Percy Robert, *b* —1939; *ed* : *m* 1984, Evelyn, da of —Niebes, of —, — Diana Charlotte, *b* 1938: *m* 1959, SCM/Sgt Harley R. Linley, USAF (ret), and has issue living, Paul R— *b* 1961, Charlotte Diana *b* 1960.

The name of this family is supposed to be derived either from Walsham le Willows in Suffolk, or Walsham St Mary in Norfolk, in both of which counties, as in Cambridgeshire, the Walshams were of note, and often of knightly rank, from the end of the 11th to the beginning of the 18th century. The Walshams of Knill represent a branch that settled in Radnorshire about 400 years ago, through the marriage of John Walsham with Mary, granddaughter and heiress of Sir Jenkin Harvey of Llanvair, Knight. From this marriage lineally descended John Walsham, who *m* Barbara, granddaughter and heiress of John Knill, of Knill Court, MP for Radnor, *temp* Mary I, and was the direct ancestor of the present baronet. The 1st baronet received his baronetcy as being the eldest co-heir and representative of Gen Sir Thomas Morgan, Bt, whose title created 1660, became extinct on the death of Sir John Morgan, 4th Bt in 1767. Sir John Walsham, KCMG, 2nd Bt, was Envoy Extraor and Min Plen to China 1885-92 and to Roumania 1892-3.

WARD (UK) 1911, of Wellington, New Zealand

By courage and faith

Sir JOSEPH JAMES LAFFEY WARD, 4th *Baronet*; *b* 11 Nov 1946; *s* his father, *Sir* JOSEPH GEORGE DAVIDSON, LLM, 1970: *m* 1968, Robyn Allison, da of William Maitland Martin, of Rotorua, NZ, and has issue.

Arms – Azure, a cross moline argent between four keys wards upwards or. **Crest** – A demi-griffin azure in front of two keys in saltire wards upwards or. *Residence* – 3 Regal Place, Milford, Auckland, NZ.

SON LIVING

JOSEPH JAMES MARTIN, *b* 20 Feb 1971.

DAUGHTER LIVING

Theresa Jane, *b* 1972.

BROTHERS LIVING

Roderic Anthony (35 Coates Park Rd, Cobbitty, NSW 2570, Australia), *b* 23 April 1948: *m* 1993, Faye Mary Morrisson. —— Michael John (RD1, Wallis Rd, Ruawai, NZ), *b* 1954: *m* 1977, Alamein Sharlene Connelly, and has issue living, Christopher Davidson, *b* 1979, — Felicity Te Puawai, *b* 1980, — Joan Marie Ngaroma, *b* 1985.

SISTERS LIVING

Angela Mary (31 Vauxhall Rd, Devonport, Auckland, NZ), *b* 1945. —— Felicity Elizabeth Elinor Joan, *b* 1951: *m* 1979, Dr Graeme Warren Kidd, of 243 Bleakhouse Rd, Howick, NZ, and has issue living, Guy George Joseph, *b* 1983, — Cecille Mary, *b* 1981. —— Catherine Josephine Mina (c/o Arts Training Centre, 130 Flinder St, Victoria, Melbourne 3000, Australia), *b* 1963.

UNCLE LIVING (Son of 2nd baronet)

John Rannie (47 Webb St, Christchurch, NZ), *b* (twin) 1924; is Lt Roy New Zealand Naval VR; 1939-45 War: *m* 1948, Adrienne Lascelles, da of Herbert Hill, OBE, JP, of Christchurch, and has issue living, Jeremy John (6 Mortimer Terrace, Wellington, NZ), *b* 1957: *m* 1985, Anne Susan Lockhart, and has issue living, Oscar Joseph *b* 1989, Barnaby John Lockhart *b* 1992, — Rupert Rannie, *b* 1964: *m* 1994, Willimina Eilander, — Caroline Diana, *b* 1950: *m* 1970, Daniel Frederick von Dadelszen, of Hinerangi, RD2, Waipukurau, NZ, and has issue living, Samuel John *b* 1973, Victoria Mary *b* 1975, Lucinda Gretchen *b* 1977, — Jennifer Ann, *b* 1952: *m* 1973, Julian Simon Cowper Payton, of 64 Cole St, Masterton, NZ, and has issue living, Joseph Simon *b* 1979, Toby James *b* 1982, Anna Caroline *b* 1977.

AUNT LIVING (Daughter of 2nd baronet)

Theresa Dorothea, *b* 1916: *m* 1941, John Swaine Corry, and has issue living, David Herbert Cyril, *b* 1949, — Robert John, *b* 1953, — Angela Susan, *b* 1942: *m* 1965, Iain Anderson Ridge, of 145 London Rd, Sevenoaks, and has issue living, Angus James Anderson *b* 1966, — Rosemary Ann, *b* 1946. *Residence* – Lawn Bungalow, Bitchett Green, Sevenoaks.

COLLATERAL BRANCHES LIVING

Issue of late Cyril James Ward, 2nd son of 2nd baronet, *b* 1913, *d* 1984: *m* 1939, Janet Graham (10 Queen's Av, Christchurch, NZ) da of late Dr John Stevenson, of Fendalton, Christchurch:—
Joanna Theresa (*Lady Clifford*), *b* 1940: *m* 1968, Sir Roger Joseph Clifford, 7th Bt, and has issue (*see* Clifford, Bt). —— Celia Mary Louise, *b* 1950: *m* 1983, Richard John Craig, of PO Box 80, Te Horo, NZ, and has issue living, Holly Louise, *b* 1984, — Hannah Rose, *b* 1988.

Issue of late Gladstone William Ward, 3rd son of 1st baronet, *b* 1891, *d* 1965: *m* 1920, Sophia Polemedis, who *d* 1959, of Jerusalem:—
Myrcine, *b* 1921: *m* 1942, Dr Peter Mowbray Tripp, of 22 Clissold St, Christchurch, NZ, and has issue living, David Mowbray Ward, *b* 1949: *m* 1973, Martha McQuilkin, and has issue living, Peter James *b* 1977, Sophie Catherine *b* 1976, — John Peter, *b* 1950: *m* 1975, Amanda Moore, and has issue living, Celia Jane *b* 1980, Jessica *b* 1982, — Penelope Mary, *b* 1943: *m* 1974, Phillip Klap, and has issue living, Nicola Sophia *b* 1975, Annabelle Marie-Therese *b* 1976, — Anthia Susan, *b* 1947: *m* 1969, Richard Rollo Warburton, and *d* 1993, leaving issue, Richard John *b* 1976, Tessa Myrcine *b* 1970, Anna *b* 1972. —— Eileen Dorothea, *b* 1922: *m* 1943, Patrick Sinclair Hunter, solicitor, of Ardmore, 9 Vicarage Hill, Farnham, Surrey, and has issue living, Michael Sinclair Ward, *b* 1947: *m* 1970, Carol Rosemary Shorter, and has issue living, Piers Charles Sinclair *b* 1974, Charles Patrick Sinclair *b* 1977, Victoria Lucinda *b* 1972, — Patricia Ann, *b* 1943: *m* 1967, William Michael Hardy Spicer, and has issue living, Edward Sinclair Hardy *b* 1969, Antonia Hardy *b* 1971, Annabel Jane Hardy *b* 1974.

Issue of late Awarua Patrick Joseph George Ward, yst son of 1st baronet, *b* 1901, *d* 1961: *m* 1930, Marjorie, who *d* 19—, only da of O. M. McCormack, of Detroit, Michigan, USA:—
Patricia Marjorie, *b* 1933: *m* 1955, Duncan Cameron Bryan, who *d* 19—, and has issue living, Sheryl Cameron, *b* 1956, — Jennifer Ward, *b* 1958, — Denise *b* 1961.
The 1st baronet, the Rt Hon Sir Joseph George Ward, GCMG, VD, PC (son of William Thomas Ward, merchant), was Prime Min of New Zealand 1906-12 and 1928-30.

WARD (UK) 1914, of Wilbraham Place, Chelsea (Extinct 1973)

Sir MELVILLE WILLIS WARD, 3rd and last *Baronet*.

WIDOW LIVING OF THIRD BARONET

MARGARET MARY (*Lady Ward*), da of late Anthony Davis, of New York, USA, and widow of Capt Ralph Risley, USN: *m* 1965, as his 3rd wife, Cdr Sir Melvill Willis Ward, DSC, RN, 3rd Bt, who *d* 1973, when the title became ext.

WARD (UK) 1929, of Blyth, co Northumberland (Extinct 1956)

Sir (ALBERT) LAMBERT WARD, CVO, DSO, TD, 1st and last *Baronet*.

DAUGHTER LIVING OF FIRST BARONET

Diana Josephine (*Lady Spearman*), *b* 1921: *m* 1951, as his 2nd wife, Sir Alexander Cadwallader Mainwaring Spearman (*see* Spearman, Bt, colls), who *d* 1982. *Residences* – The Old Rectory, Sarratt, Herts; Fealer, Blairgowrie, Perthshire; 22 Queen Anne's Gate, SW1.

WARDLAW (NS) 1631, of Pitreavie, Fifeshire

Domestic virtue strengthens families

FAMILIAS·FIRMAT·PIETAS

Sir HENRY JOHN WARDLAW, 21st *Baronet*; *b* 30 Nov 1930; *s* his father, *Sir* HENRY, 1983; *ed* Melbourne Univ (MB, BS): *m* 1962, Julie-Ann, da of late Edward Patrick Kirwan, and has issue.

Arms – Quarterly: 1st and 4th, azure, three mascles or, *Wardlaw*; 2nd and 3rd, azure, three water bougets or, *Valance*. **Crest** – An estoile or.
Residence – 82 Vincent St, Sandringham, Victoria 3191, Australia.

SONS LIVING

(HENRY) JUSTIN, *b* 10 Aug 1963. —— Edward Patrick, *b* 1964. —— Simon John, *b* 1965. —— Anthony James, *b* 1968. —— Adrian Stewart, *b* 1971.

DAUGHTERS LIVING

Janet Montgomerie, *b* 1969. —— Marie Ellen, *b* 1977.

BROTHERS LIVING

Robert Murdoch (4 Connemarra St, Bexley, NSW), *b* 1940: *m* 1971, Dale Edith, da of Joseph Fetherston, and has issue lving, Dominic, *b* 1972. —— Andrew David Montgomerie; *b* 1941; *ed* Melbourne Univ (LLB): *m* 1965, Elizabeth, da of Dennis Leary, and has issue living, David, *b* 1965, — Matthew, *b* 1966, — Michael, *b* 1969, — Timothy, *b* 1964, Louise, *b* 1971. —— Gregory Wylie (15 Millicent Av, Buleen, Vic, Aust), *b* 1943: *m* 19—, and has issue living, Cameron, *b* 1970, — Alastair, *b* 1973.

SISTER LIVING

Cynthia Mary, *b* 1931; (BA, DipEd): *m* 19—, — of St Andrew's, Vic, Aust, and has issue living, Jeremy, *b* 19—, — Melanie, *b* 19—, — Abigail, *b* 19—.

COLLATERAL BRANCHES LIVING

Granddaughters of late John Walter Wardlaw (infra):—
Issue of late James Walter Wardlaw, *b* 1921, *d* 1983: *m* 1951, Carina Guenthner:—
Jane Katherine, *b* 1958: *m* 1976, Ralph Duek, of Olds, Alberta, and has issue living, Jason Brent, *b* 1981, — Lori Anne, *b* 1977, — Cheryl Lynn, *b* 1979. —— Judy Carina, *b* 1961: *m* 1982, Kenneth Randall, of Edmonton, Alberta.

Grandchildren of late Thomas Davidson Wardlaw, son of late John Wardlaw, brother of 18th baronet:—
Issue of late John Walter Wardlaw, *b* 1882, *d* 1944: *m* 1914, Iva, da of late W. W. Brigham:—
Mary Macallum, *b* 1914: *m* 1938, Safford E. Thorp, of 55 Rosemary St, New London, Conn, USA, and has had issue, Walter Wakeman, *b* 1944, *d* 1979: *m* 1967, Cynthia Anne Szegda (57 Lorenzo St, Norwich, Conn, USA), and had issue living, Walter Allen *b* 1970, Dawn Marie *b* 1968, Kristy Louise *b* 1976, — Mina Jane, *b* 1939: *m* 1st, 1956, Cofer Lee Gray, of 611 Louis Av, Ledyard, Conn, USA; 2ndly, 1983, Earl Ewers, of Milner's Mobile Home Est, Lot 20, Lynchburg, Virginia, USA, and has issue living, Safford Emory *b* 1964, Bonnie *b* 1957, *d* 1966, Ramona Lee *b* 1958: *m* 1983, Donald Jeay, of Rt 3, Box 95-A, Dillwyn, Virg, USA (and has issue), — Lorna Elizabeth, *b* 1946: *m* 1965, Lee William Coleman, of 5072C Polaris St, Eielson AFB, Alaska, USA, and has issue living, Tina Marie *b* 1966, Leah J. *b* 1969. —— Margaret Brigham, *b* 1918: *m* 1949, James Gethyn Jones, of 71 Lawrence Av West, Toronto 12, Canada, and has issue living, Richard Gethyn, *b* 1952: *m* 1981, Maureen Grierson, of Vancouver, BC, — Elizabeth Ellen, *b* 1958. —— Elizabeth Davidson (56 Jedburgh Rd, Toronto, Canada), *b* 1926.
Issue of late James Macallum Wardlaw, *b* 1884, *d* 1967: *m* 1923, Mary, who *d* 1953, da of late Robert Law:—
Thomas Davidson (72 Main St, Waterford, Ont, Canada), *b* 1924: *m* 1950, Grace Smith, and has issue living, David Macallum (316 Eunice Drive, Kingston, Ont, Canada), *b* 1952: *m* 1st, 1978 (*m diss* 1984), Jennifer Leigh, da of Wilbur Garvie, of Oaville, Ont, Canada; 2ndly, 1985, Margaret Ann, da of late Irvin Andrew Bartee, and has issue living (by 2nd *m*), Andrew Thomas *b* 1989, Alison Marie *b* 1987, and has also legally adopted his stepda, Sarah Lynn WARDLAW *b* 1980, — Robert Duncan (Box 562, Sioux Lookout, Ont, Canada), *b* 1954: *m* 1982, Rita C., da of William G. More, of Ottawa, Ont, and has issue living, James More *b* 1983, Daniel Robert MORE *b* 1989, — Craig Davidson (2681 Jerseyville Rd, Jerseyville, Ont, L0R 1R0, Canada), *b* 1956: *m* 1979, Flora Margaret, da of late Duncan Hector Allan Simpson, and has issue living, Duncan Ian Macleod *b* 1992, — Jonathan Stewart (253 Tower Crest Drive, Newmarket, Ont, Canada), *b* 1959: *m* 1988, Beth Yvonne, da of Rev John William Houstoun, of Aurora, Ontario, and has issue living, Rebecca Jillian *b* 1992. —— Robert Law (9 Oriole

Drive, Gloucester, Ont, Canada K1J 7E8), *b* 1927; BASc, MEng, PEng: *m* 1954, Felicia Jane, da of late Frank Hallett Milsum, and has issue living, Stephen James, *b* 1957, — Michael John, *b* 1960, — Anne Margaret, *b* 1958: *m* 1988, Eric Steven Teutsch, of Nepean, Ont, Canada, and has issue living, Jeffrey Stephen *b* 1989, Alexander Robert *b* 1992, — Patricia Mary, *b* 1962: *m* 1985, Peter Hermann Laurich, of Nepean, Ont, Canada, and has issue living, Jason Robert *b* 1989, Andrew Anthony *b* 1990, Bruce Patrick *b* 1993, — Laura Kathleen, *b* 1963: *m* 1993, Allan Gregory Osborne, of Ottawa, Ont, Canada. —— Janet Melville (20 Suffolk St, W, Guelph, Ont, Canada), *b* 1924.

Sir Henry Wardlaw, 1st Bt, was Chamberlain to Anne of Denmark, when Queen Consort of Scotland. He acquired Pitreavie 1606, which was erected into a Barony 1627. His baronetcy was with remainder to heirs male whatsoever, with presumably a grant of 16,000 acres in Nova Scotia, called the Barony of Wardlaw.

WARING (UK) 1935, of St Bartholomew's, City of London

Sir (ALFRED) HOLBURT WARING, 3rd *Baronet*; *b* 2 Aug 1933; *s* his father, *Sir* (ALFRED) HAROLD, 1981; *ed* Rossall: *m* 1958, Anita, da of late Valentin Medinilla, of Madrid, Spain, and has issue.

𝔞rms – Argent on a bend engrailed azure between two Rods of Aesculapius proper three crescents. 𝔠rest – A demi-wolf resting the sinister paw on a Rod of Aesculapius proper.
Residence – Earl's Croft, 30 Russell Rd, Moor Park, Northwood, Middx.

SON LIVING

MICHAEL HOLBURT, *b* 3 Jan 1964.

DAUGHTERS LIVING

Margaret Rose, *b* 1961. —— Susan Caroline, *b* 1967.

SISTERS LIVING

(Winifred) Anne, *b* 1931: *m* 1954, Michael Scott Mark, of The White House, Easingwold, nr York YO6 3AA, and has issue living, Jonathan Scott, *b* 1956, — Christopher Edward, *b* 1959. —— (Joan Catherine) Cassandra, *b* 1937: *m* 1962 (*m diss* 19—), John Barry William Holderness, of Les Varvots, St Lawrence, Jersey, and has issue living, Corinne Louisa Cassandra, *b* 1969, — Marina Isabelle Cassandra, *b* 1974.

The 1st baronet, Sir Holburt Jacob Waring, CBE, MS, FRCS (son of late Isaac Waring, of Southport, Lancashire), was sometime Dean of Faculty of Medicine, London Univ, Vice-Chancellor, London Univ, Gov of Imperial Coll of Science and Technology 1930-47, and Pres Roy Coll of Surgeons 1932-35.

WHATEVER YOU UNDERTAKE DO WELL

WARMINGTON (UK) 1908, of Pembridge Square, Royal Borough of Kensington

Sir MARSHALL GEORGE CLITHEROE WARMINGTON, 3rd *Baronet*; *b* 26 May 1910; *s* his father, *Sir* (MARSHALL) DENHAM 1935; *ed* Charterhouse; Lt-Cdr (ret) RN: *m* 1st, 1933 (*m diss* 1941), Mollie, el da of late Capt Malcolm Alfred Kennard, RN (ret), of Wonham, Bampton; 2ndly, 1942, Eileen Mary, who *d* 1969, da of late P. J. Howes; 3rdly, 1972 (*m diss* 1977), Sheila, who *d* 1988, da of late Stanley Brotherhood, JP, of Thornhaugh Hall, Peterborough, and widow of Adm Hon Sir Cyril Eustace Douglas-Pennant, KCB, CBE, DSO, DSC (*see* B Penrhyn, 1985 Edn), and has issue by 1st and 2nd marriages.

𝔞rms – Or, a lion rampant sable, charged on the shoulder with two fleurs-de-lis palewise of the first, holding between the paws a full-bottomed wig proper. 𝔠rest – An owl or, holding in the beak a penna and ink horn sable.
Residence – Swallowfield Park, Swallowfield, Reading. *Club* – MCC.

SONS LIVING (By 1st marriage)

MARSHALL DENHAM MALCOLM, *b* 5 Jan 1934.

(By 2nd marriage)

David Marshall, *b* 1944; *ed* Charterhouse: *m* 1st, 1966, Susan Mary, da of Very Rev Clifford Thomas Chapman, Dean of Exeter; 2ndly, 1981, Mrs Eileen Verdin (*née* Johnston), and has issue living (by 1st *m*), Rupert Marshall, *b* 1969, — Guy Denham, *b* 1972. —— Anthony Marshall (19 Bloom Park Rd, SW6), *b* 1946; *ed* Charterhouse; Lt, 1st Queen's Dragoon Gds: *m* 1973 (*m diss* 1987), Carolyn Patricia, who *d* 1993, el da of late J. A. H. Simonds, and has issue living, Oliver Marshall Simonds, *b* 1974; *ed* Charterhouse, — Katherine Louise, *b* 1977.

NON MIHI SED OMNIBUS

Not for myself, but for all

DAUGHTER LIVING *(By 1st marriage)*

Margaret Anne, *b* 1936; *ed* Open Univ (BA), LIMA: *m* 1962, Cdr Colin Alan (Charles) Bricknell, MBIM, RN, of Camrose, 71A High St, Hurstpierpoint, W Sussex BN6 9RE, and has issue living, Martin Charles Marshall, *b* 1963; *ed* Christ's Hosp; Capt RAMC, — Julian John, *b* 1965; *ed* Christ's Hosp, — Peter Marshall, *b* 1969; *ed* Hurstpierpoint.

SISTER LIVING

Elisabeth Barbara Marshall, *b* 1909: *m* 1st, 1933, Ian Somerled Macdonald, who *d* 1958; 2ndly, 1961, John Perfect, and has issue living, (by 1st *m*) John Marshall, *b* 1937, — Euan Ross, *b* 1940, — Elisabeth Margaret, *b* 1935, — Sheila Joy, *b* 1942. *Residence* – 18 Cryspen Court, Garland St, Bury St Edmunds, Suffolk.

COLLATERAL BRANCH LIVING

Issue of late Herbert Andrew Cromartie Warmington, 2nd son of 1st baronet; *b* 1874, *d* 1952: *m* 1st, 1904 (*m diss* 1926), Elsie, da of late John Stuart, of Stonehurst, Ardingly, Sussex; 2ndly, 1938, Helena, da of late Albert de Mersey:—

(By 1st *m*) Joan Pamela Stuart, *b* 1906: *m* 1st, 1926, Com Nigel Bellairs Deare, RN, 2ndly, 1934, Dr Vincenzo Bottari. *Residence* – Villa della Palmare, Taormina, Sicily.

The 1st baronet, Sir (Cornelius) Marshall, KC, sat as MP for W Div of Monmouthshire (*L*) 1885-95, and Sir (Marshall) Denham Warmington, 2nd Bt, was a Registrar in Bankruptcy, High Court of Justice.

WARNER (UK) 1910, of Brettenham, Suffolk

I hope

Sir (EDWARD COURTENAY) HENRY WARNER, 3rd *Baronet*; *b* 3 Aug 1922; *s* his father, *Col Sir* EDWARD COURTENAY THOMAS WARNER, DSO, MC, 1955; *ed* Eton, and Ch Ch, Oxford; sometime Lieut Scots Guards; European War 1944-45 in France (wounded): *m* 1949, Jocelyn Mary, da of Com Sir Thomas Lubbock Beevor, 6th Bt, RN, and has issue.

Arms – Per bend argent and gules two-bendlets between six roses all counterchanged. **Crest** – A Saracen's head affrontée couped at the shoulders proper, vested gules, on the head a cap chequy argent and of the second, in front thereof three roses fessewise of the third.
Residence – The Grove, Great Baddow, Essex. *Club* – Guards'.

SONS LIVING

PHILIP COURTENAY THOMAS (6 Holland Pk Mews, W11 3TG), *b* 3 April 1951; *ed* Eton: *m* 1982, Penelope Anne, yr da of late John Lack Elmer, and has issue living, Charles, *b* 30 Sept 1989, — Alexandra, *b* 1985, — Eleanor, *b* 1992. —— Richard Edward Lubbock, *b* 1952. —— Robert Henry, *b* 1957: *m* 1983, Sophie Anne Rosalie, da of Timothy Davis, of Steeple Aston, Oxon, and has issue living, Henry, *b* 19—, — George, *b* 19—, — John Robert, *b* 1994, — Rosalie, *b* 19—.

SISTERS LIVING

Anne Philippa (*Hon Mrs Henry E. Boscawen*), *b* 1927: *m* 1951, Hon Henry Edward Boscawen, Lieut RE (*see* V Falmouth). *Residence* – Garden House, High Beeches Lane, Handcross, Sussex. —— Leucha Daphne Mary, *b* 1929: *m* 1962, Mark Gerald Edward North Buxton, of Coffyns, Spreyton, Crediton, Devon (*see* Buxton, Bt, colls).

COLLATERAL BRANCH LIVING

Issue of late Capt Thomas Seymour Marius Warner, 3rd son of 1st Baronet, *b* 1903, *d* 1965: *m* 1st, 1926 (*m diss* 1929), Mrs Dorothy Russell, da of William Durran, of Caithness; 2ndly, 1929 (*m diss* 1938), Mrs Edith Dorothy Morrison, da of late Robert Bold, of Liverpool; 3rdly, 1938, Louise Cameron (Ely Cottage, Wharf Lane, Henley-on-Thames), da of late Edward M. Roberts:—

(By 3rd *m*) Courtenay Forbes (12/46 Lowndes Sq, SW1), *b* 1939; *ed* Eton; late 2nd Lt Scots Gds: *m* 1st, 1969 (*m diss* 1974), Veronica, da of Lt-Col W. M. W. Cooper, of Medlands Farm House, Hurstbourne Tarrant, Andover; 2ndly, 1974, Venetia Elizabeth, da of Maj Richard Atkinson-Turner, of Worlington, Suffolk, and has issue living (by 2nd *m*), Harry Richard Courtenay *b* 1975.

The 1st baronet, Col Sir (Thomas) Courtenay (Theydon) Warner, CB, was Lord-Lieut of Suffolk, and sat as MP for N Div of Somerset (*L*) 1892-95, and for Lichfield Div of Staffs 1896-1923. The 2nd baronet, Col Sir Edward Courtenay Thomas Warner, DSO, MC, was High Sheriff of Suffolk 1947-8, and Lieut-Col Comdg Scots Guards and Regtl Dist 1932-4.

WARREN (I) 1784, of Warren's Court, co Cork

Sir (BRIAN) CHARLES PENNEFATHER WARREN, 9th *Baronet*; *b* 4 June 1923; *s* his father, *Col Sir* THOMAS RICHARD PENNEFATHER, CBE, 1961; *ed* Wellington Coll; 1939-45 War as Lieut Irish Guards *m* 1976 (*m diss* 1983), Nicola Louise, el da of Capt Edward de Lérisson Cazenove, of Great Dalby, Leics (*see* Kennedy, Bt).

Arms – Argent, a fesse checky or and azure, between three talbots passant proper. **Crest** – A lion rampant holding a crozier proper.
Residence – The Wilderness, Castle Oliver, Kilmallock, co Limerick. *Club* – Guards'.

SISTERS LIVING

Patricia Bene Pennefather, *b* 1908: *m* 1st, 1934, William Sharman Bull, RAF, who was *ka* 1940; 2ndly, 1945, Col Frederick Wynford Dewhurst, RM, and has issue living, (by 1st *m*) Victoria *b* 1939: *m* 1957, Maj Robert Darwall, MC, RM, and has issue living, William Robert Thomas *b* 1961, Antonia Mary *b* 1958, — (by 2nd *m*) Charles Frederick, *b* 1946, — Sarah Elizabeth, *b* 1948. *Residence* – Crapstone House, Buckland Monachorum, S Devon. —— Eileen Lavinia Pennefather (Biddy), *b* 1910: *m* 1st, 1930, Group Capt Joseph Herbert Arthur Landon, DSO, OBE, RAF, who *d* 1935; 2ndly, 1950, George Joseph Spiers. *Residence* – Grange Farm, Puttenham, nr Tring, Herts.

COLLATERAL BRANCHES LIVING

Not for me, but for God and the king

Grandchildren of late Thomas Robert Warren, grandson of Thomas Warren, MP, of Monkstown, co Cork, 3rd son of 1st baronet:—
Issue of late Lt-Col William Robert Vaughton Warren, OBE, MC, RASC, *b* 1889, *d* 1981: *m* 1st, 1914 (*m diss* 1926), Marjorie May, only child of Harold Briggs, of Broadford, Chobham, Surrey; 2ndly, 1926, Violet Elsie, who *d* 1963, da of Lt-Col John Wallis Gill, JP, of Fairfield, St German's, Cornwall:—
(By 1st *m*) MICHAEL BLACKLEY (La Basse Ruol, Puget-Ville, Var, France), *b* 12 Nov 1918: *m* 1941, Marie Noelle, el da of Ernest Marcel Laffaille, OBE, hon Capt French Navy, and has issue living, Danielle Mary, *b* 1943: *m* 1967, Jean Pierre d'Adda, of 63 Av Pasteur, La Valette, Var, France, and has issue living, Sebastian Marie *b* 1973, Catherine Marie *b* 1970. —— Bridget Macree, *b* 1922: *m* 1st, 1944 (*m diss* 19—), F/O Frank Walter Ladbrook; 2ndly, 19—, Ernest William Beale, who *d* 1994, of 32 Knapton Lane, Acomb, York, and has issue living (by 1st *m*), Sara Virginia, *b* 1945: *m* 1974, David Walter Hayward, and has issue living, Peter David *b* 1978, Robin William *b* 1982, — Philippa Mary, *b* 1953: *m* 1972, John David Mead, and has issue living, Christopher John *b* 1974, Thomas William *b* 1980, — (by 2nd *m*) Andrew William, *b* 1958: *m* 1984, April Michelle Mitchell, and has issue living, Martin Andrew *b* 1987, Richard *b* 1991.

Granddaughter of late Rev Thomas Warren, 3rd son of late Thomas Warren, MP (ante):—
Issue of late Maj John Augustus Warren, *b* 1831, *d* 1907: *m* 1869, Mary Spence, da of Thomas Thimbleby, of Avenue, House, Spilsby:—
Milly Kathleen: *m* 1896, Maj Charles Henry Ashurst, late R Sussex Regt, who *d* 1966.

Granddaughters of late William Warren, 8th son of late Thomas Warren, MP (ante):—
Issue of late William Augustus Warren, *b* 18—, *d* 1923: *m* 1875, Katherine, yst da of G. Dalrymple Monteith, MD, of Wellington, New Zealand:—
Muriel Leila. —— Mildred Irene: *m* 1920, Charles H. Baker, of Flat 3, Belglen, 21 Vivian St, New Plymouth, NZ, and has issue living, Derek Charles Kuke, *b* 1921, — William Thomas Neville, *b* 1923. —— Ruby Augusta Grahæme. *Residence* – 317 Broadway, Palmerston North, NZ.

Granddaughter of late Very Rev Thomas Brisbane Warren, MA, Dean of Cork, el son of Brisbane Warren, 9th son of late Thomas Warren, MP (ante):—
Issue of late Brisbane Charles Somerville Warren, *b* 1887, *d* 1979: *m* 1922, Janey Neill (Joan), who *d* 1986, da of late T. F. M. Cartwright, of Petteridge, Brenchley, Kent:—
Elizabeth Joan Mary (Flat 2, 31 Clifton Cres, Folkestone, Kent CT20 2EN), *b* 1929.

Grandson of late Philip Somerville Warren, LRCP, LRCS, yr son of late Brisbane Warren (ante):—
Issue of late Denis Patrick SOMERVILLE WARREN, *b* 1901; *d* 1974: *m* 1946, Valerie Antonia Lloyd, da of late Frederick Lloyd Harper:—
Phillip Digby Somerville (Well Cottage, Cliffe Rd, Seaford, Sussex), *b* 1948; *ed* Columbia's Sch, St Albans: *m* 1980, Violette Khajenouri, and has issue living, Antonia Nooshin, *b* 1981, — Natasha Soussan, *b* 1982.

Grandson of late Robert Warren (*b* 1870), (infra):—
Issue of late Augustus John Warren, *b* 1909, *d* 1969: *m* 1949, Irene Joyce (The Cottage, Dunmanway, co Cork), da of late James Edwards Atkins, JP, of Brook Park, Dunmanway, co Cork:—
Rev Robert, *b* 1954; *ed* St Columba's, and Trin Coll, Dublin; ordained Priest 1979; Curate St Mary's Cathedral, Limerick, Rector, Adare, Co Limerick, 1981.

Granddaughter of late Robert Warren (*b* 1826), el son of late Rev Robert Warren (*b* 1794), el son of late Rev Robert Warren (*d* 1830), 5th son of 1st baronet:—
Issue of late Robert Warren, *b* 1870, *d* 1947: *m* 1904, Maria Frances Lumley, da of late William Lumley Perrier, of Maryborough, Douglas, co Cork:—
Gladys Irene, *b* 1908.

Grandchildren of late Maj-Gen Richard Warren, 2nd son of late Rev Robert Warren (*b* 1794), (ante):—
Issue of late Edward Albert Warren, *b* 1856, *d* 1899: *m* 1884, Emily, da of late Talbot Palmer, of Waterlooville, Hants:—
Edward Richard Lauder, *b* 1888. —— Emily Ruth, *b* 1885: *m* 1907, Patrick Hardy. *Residence* - . —— Dorothy Talbot, *b* 1887: *m* 1907, Bernard Tweedale.
Issue of late Lieut-Col Percy Bliss Warren, *b* 1864, *d* 1911: *m* 1892, Margaret Ellen, who *d* 1951, da of late William Langdon Martin, of Windsor Villas, Plymouth:—

Margaret Joan (4 Poplar Road, Burnham-on-Sea, Somerset), b 1895.

Grandchildren of late Lieut-Col Percy Bliss Warren (ante):—
Issue of late Wallis Langdon Warren, b 1900, d 1974: m 1934, Barbara, who d 1990, da of Harold Henry Durell Christian:—
Robert Nicholas Christian (Willowcroft, Thicket Grove, Newlands Drive, Maidenhead), b 1945: m 1976, Judith Catherine Harvey, and has issue living, David Nicholas Joseph b 1985, Victoria Catherine, b 1978, Rebecca Louise, b 1981, — Shirley Margaret Christian, b 1936: m 1958, Jacovas Ioannou James Koukoularides, of 261 Brownhill Rd, SE6, and has issue living, Panos John, b 1966, — Janet Sophia, b 1958, — Daphne Barbara, b 1963. ———— Jennifer Mary Christian, b 1940: m 1963, Keith Dallas Brown, of 6 Bridgenorth Rd, PO Greendale, Harare, Zimbabwe, and has issue living, Mark Dallas, b 1966: m 1993, Alison Fiona, da of Michael John Henry Beckett, of Choma, Zambia, — Anton Dallas, b 1970, — Sherrill Anne, b 1968. ———— Jocelyne Anne Christian, b 1942: m 1969, Michael Edward Younghusband, of 13 Veronica Drive, Constantia Kloof, Transvaal, S Africa, and has issue living, Sharon Leigh, b 1971, — Tracey Anne, b 1972.

Grandchildren of late Maj Geoffrey Martin Warren, son of late Lt-Col Percy Bliss Warren (ante):—
Issue of late Brian Richard Warren, b 1939, d 1987: m 1965, Angela Jean, da of late Arthur L. Yarranton, of Eardiston, Worcs:—
Oliver Martin, b 1968. ———— Emily Claire, b 1966. ———— Lucy Maud, b 1970.

Grandsons of late Vivian Brudenell Warren, 8th and yst son of Maj-Gen Augustus Edmund Warren (infra):—
Issue of late Charles Vivian Brudenell, b 1907, d 1975: m 1st, 1945, Maeve, who d 1965, da of late John Davis, of Ballina, Ireland; 2ndly, 1972, Jaqueta Maeve, who d 1979, da of Sir Arnold Henry Moore Lunn:—
(By 1st m) Robert Augustus Michael Mary (Southern Green Farm, Rushden, Buntingford, Herts), b 1948: m 1977, Jacqueline Olive Dawn Baynes, and has issue living, Dominic Charles Augustus Warren, b 1979, — Guy Andrew Francis Warren, b 1980. ———— Patrick Martin Vivian Mary (7 St Ann's Crescent, SW18 2ND), b 1951: m 1974, Frances Ann, da of Frederick Lloyd, and has issue living, Luke Lloyd, b 1975, — Duncan Charles, b 1980, — Nathan Alexander, b 1982, — Camilla Elizabeth, b 1976, — Saskia Anne, b 1982.

Granddaughters of Maj-Gen Augustus Edmund Warren, 2nd son of late Richard Benson Warren (infra):—
Issue of late Dudley Edward Warren, b 1875, d 1949: m 1913, Gundreda, da of late Col Duncan Spiller:—
Adèle Valerie, b 1928.
Issue of Vivian Brudenell Warren, b 1877, d 1973: m 1900, Lilie Barrington, who d 1937, da of Capt C. A. G. Heysham, RN:—
Vivienne Ellen, b 1912: m 1943, George Frederick Alston Shilling, of 13 Upper Wimpole St, W1.

Grandchildren of late Richard Benson Warren, Serjeant-at-law, 7th son of 1st baronet:—
Issue of late Ven Latham Coddington Warren, b 1831, d 1912: m 1st, 1855, Harriet who d 1883, da of John Henry Davidson, MD, of Edinburgh; 2ndly, 1885, Mary Georgina, who d 1911, da of late Hall Stirling:—
(By 1st m) Robert Augustus Monsell, b 1875. ———— Florence Martha Caroline. ———— (By 2nd m) Beatrice Lilian May. ———— Dorothy Edythe Mary.

Grandchildren of late Rt Hon Robert Richard Warren, LLD son of late Capt Henry Warren, 8th son of 1st baronet:—
Issue of late Henry Charles Jackson Warren, b 1852, d 1937: m 1877, Florence, who d 1944, da of late Lieut-Col Hon Robert French Handcock, 8th son of 2nd Baron Castlemaine:—
Desmond Cecil Robert, b 1895: m 1929, Violet Arabella, da of Dr F. O. Lasbrey, and has issue living, Donal, b 1930, — Jennifer Edyth Helen, b 1932, — Juliet Alice Louise, b 1938. Residence – Cherry Hill, Ballybrack, co Dublin.
This family descends from Wallis Warren who purchased in 1688 Kilbarry, co Cork, which later was renamed Warren's Court. His grandson, Sir Robert Warren, 1st Bt, was High Sheriff of co Cork 1752. Major Sir Augustus Riversdale Warren, 5th Bt, served in Crimean War and in Indian Mutiny, and was High Sheriff for co Cork in 1867. Col Sir Thomas Richard Pennefather Warren, CBE, late RASC, was Ch Constable of Bucks 1928.

WATERLOW (UK) 1873, of London

Sir CHRISTOPHER RUPERT WATERLOW, 5th Baronet, son of late (Peter) Rupert Waterlow, only son of 4th Bt; b 12 Aug 1959; s his grandfather, Sir PHILIP ALEXANDER, 1973; ed Stonyhurst; Metropolitan Police Civil Staff: m 1986, Sally-Ann, only da of Maurice Bitten, of Abbey Wood, SE2.

𝖆rms – Azure, a demi-eagle displayed, erased or, in the beak a cross-crosslet fitchee argent, on a chief of the last three wolves' heads erased sable. 𝕮rest – Upon a mount vert an oak tree in front thereof a plough, both proper. Residence – 26 Barfield Road, Bickley, Kent.

GREAT AUNT LIVING

Joyce Rosamund Amy, b (twin) 1916: m 1st, 1940 (m diss 1947), Godfrey Ian Hutchinson, Flying Officer RAF; 2ndly, 1953, David Ronald Mitchell, of Wood End Cottage, Henham, nr Bishop's Stortford, Herts, son of late Sir Frank Herbert Mitchell, KCVO, CBE, and has issue living, (by 1st m) Diana Joy (19 Priory Rd, Cambridge), b 1941: m 1962 (m diss 1984), José Perez-Gonzalez, of Torremolinos, Spain, and has had issue, Antonio Salvador b 1964: m 1986, Nichole, eldest da of Sydney Decaix, of Lewes, Sussex (and has issue living, Marco Salvador b 1990, Sebastian Raphael b 1992), Samantha Rosa b 1966: m 1989, Peter Bartram, of 39 Highfield Av, Alconbury Weston, Hunts, and d 1992, Zoë Amanda b 1975.

LABOR OMNIA VINCIT

Work conquers everything

STEPMOTHER LIVING

Ruth Margaret (*Lady Reilly*), yst da of late Edmund Cude, of Ashbrittle, Church Vale, N2: *m* 1st, 1946, Frank Davies, who *d* 1959; 2ndly, 1962, (Peter) Rupert Waterlow, who *d* 1969; 3rdly, 1969, Sir Arthur Lionel Pugh Norrington, who *d* 1982, of Grenville Manor, Haddenham, Bucks; 4thly, Sir (D'Arcy) Patrick Reilly, GCMG, OBE, of 75 Warrington Crescent, W9.

WIDOW LIVING OF FOURTH BARONET

GWENDOLINE FLORENCE ELIZABETH (*Dowager Lady Waterlow*) (11 Elmwood Av, Hawkwell, Essex), yr da of late Léon Balanché, and formerly wife of Baden Roberts Murch: *m* 1972, as his 3rd wife, Sir Philip Alexander Waterlow, 4th Bt, who *d* 1973.

COLLATERAL BRANCHES LIVING

Issue of late Anthony Edgar Russell Waterlow, 3rd son of 3rd baronet, *b* 1914, *d* 1946: *m* 1940, Barbara Winifred (16 Paultons Square, SW3), da of late Ronald Davy, of Limber Harbrough, Lincolnshire:—
NICHOLAS ANTHONY RONALD (58 Willoughby St, Kirribilli, Sydney 2061, NSW, Aust), *b* 30 Aug 1941; *ed* Harrow: *m* 1965, Rosemary, da of W. J. O'Brien, of Sydney, and has issue living, Antony William Nicholas *b* 1967, — Luke Frederick Ronald, *b* 1969, — Chloe Diana, *b* 1972.

Grandchildren of late George Sydney Waterlow, 4th son of 1st baronet:—
Issue of late Sir Sydney Philip Perigal Waterlow, KCMG, CBE, *b* 1878, *d* 1944: *m* 1st, 1902 (*m diss* 1912), Alice Isabella, who *d* 1953, da of the Right Hon Sir Frederick Pollock, 3rd Bt (*cr* 1866): 2ndly, 1913, Helen Margery, who *d* 1973, da of Gustav Eckhard, of Didsbury, Manchester:—
(By 2nd *m*) John Conrad, CMG, *b* 1916; *ed* Eton, and Trin Coll, Camb (BChir, MD, ScD; FRS); formerly Prof of Human Nutrition, London Sch of Hygiene and Tropical Med, Univ of London; FRCP; CMG 1970; FRS 1982: *m* 1939, Angela, da of late G. Wynter Gray, and has issue living, Oliver Sydney, *b* 1943, — Richard John, *b* 1945, — Sarah Jean, *b* 1941. *Residence* – Oare, Marlborough, Wilts. —— Charlotte Mary, MBE, *b* 1915; sometime an Administrative Officer, Foreign Office; Sch Teacher and Author; MBE (Civil) 1950. *Residence* – 12 Newcombe Court, Victoria Rd, Cirencester, Glos GL7 1EN.

Issue of late David Sydney Waterlow, 7th son of 1st baronet, *b* 1857, *d* 1924: *m* 1883, Edith Emma, who *d* 1932, da of late Frederick Maitland, of 18 Primrose Hill Road, NW:—
Joan Maitland, *b* 1897: *m* 1926 (*m diss* 1971) George Lambourn, and has issue living, Martin (Prospect, Cotton Hill, Starcross, Devon), *b* 1929: *m* 1st, 1951 (*m diss* 1957), Diana Godfrey; 2ndly, 1958, Jill Amanda, da of late Norman Broughton Stevenson, of Bristol, and has issue living (by 1st *m*), Nikolas *b* 1952, Tamsin *b* 1954, Charlotte Nancy *b* 1956 (by 2nd *m*) Giles Timothy *b* 1960, Hugo Gavin *b* 1963, Emma Fanny *b* 1962, — Jane, *b* 1931. *Residence* – St Andrews Home, Stick Hill, Edenbridge, Kent. —— Rosalind Maitland, *b* 1911: *m* 1936, Sheriton Clements Swan, and has issue living, David, *b* 1940, — Nicholas Clements (Brook House, Stocksfield, Northumberland) *b* 1944: *m* 1970, Susan, da of F. Wells, of Berwick-on-Tweed, and has issue living, Catharine Victoria *b* 1970, Diana Rachel *b* 1972, — Lesley Jean, *b* 1942: *m* 1964, Richard James Hamments, of Gypsy, Sandhills Meadow, Shepperton, Middx TW17 9HY. *Residence* – Milestone Cottage, Wall, Hexham, Northumberland.
Sir Sydney Hedley Waterlow, KCVO, 1st Bt, Founder and Chm of Improved Industrial Dwellings Co, Ltd, Lord Mayor of London 1872-73; MP for Maidstone 1874-80 and Gravesend 1880-85, gave Waterlow Park, Highgate to LCC in 1889. The 2nd baronet, Sir Philip Hickson Waterlow, was Chm of Waterlow and Sons, Ltd.

WATERLOW (UK) 1930, of Harrow Weald, Middlesex

I conquer through death

Sir (JAMES) GERARD WATERLOW, 4th *Baronet*; *b* 3 Sept 1939; *s* his father, Sir THOMAS GORDON, CBE, 1982; *ed* Marlborough, and Trin Coll, Camb: *m* 1965, Diana Suzanne, yr da of Sir William Thomas Skyrme, KCVO (*see* B Lyle of Westbourne), and has issue.

Arms – Argent, a lion rampant within a bordure nebuly azure, on a chief sable two shin-bones saltirewise, the dexter surmounted by the sinister or. **Crest** – A demi-lion guardant azure, in the mouth a shin-bone in bend, and holding between the paws a human skull both or.
Residence – Windmills, Hurstbourne Tarrant, Hants.

SON LIVING

THOMAS JAMES, *b* 20 March 1970.

DAUGHTER LIVING

Amanda Jane, *b* 1968: *m* 1991, Jason Patrick Howard, eldest son of Hon Patrick Greville Howard (*see* E Suffolk and Berkshire).

BROTHERS LIVING

Simon Gordon (208 Lewisburg Av, Franklin, Nashville, Tennessee, USA), *b* 1941; *ed* Marlborough, and Trin Coll Camb (MA): *m* 1971, Jane, da of late Wing Cdr Cameron Underhill, RCAF, and has issue living, Caroline Elizabeth, *b* 1973. —— John William (81 Streathbourne Rd, SW17), *b* 1945; *ed* Marlborough: *m* 1972, Camilla Dudley, da of Wing Cdr Dudley Farmer, DFC, of Rowleys, Frieth, Henley, Oxon, and has issue living, Rufus Dudley Robinson, *b* 1976, — Alec Gordon Brownrigg, *b* 1980.
Sir William Alfred Waterlow, KBE, 1st Bt, who was Man Dir of Waterlow Bros & Layton, Chm of Waterlow & Sons Ltd, and Lord Mayor of London 1929-30, was grandson of Alfred James Waterlow, el brother of Sir Sydney Hedley Waterlow, 1st Bt (*cr* 1873).

WATSON (UK) 1866, of Henrietta Street, Cavendish Square, St Marylebone, co Middlesex

Sufferings are lessons

Sir JAMES ANDREW WATSON, 5th *Baronet*; *b* 30 Dec 1937; *s* his father, *Sir* THOMAS AUBREY, 1941; *ed* Eton; Bar Inner Temple 1966: *m* 1965, Christabel Mary, el da of late Maj Kenneth Ralph Malcolm Carlisle, Rifle Brigade, of 18 York House, W8 (*see* B Aberconway, 1990 Edn), and has issue.

Arms – Azure, on a fesse dancetté between three crescents argent, as many martlets sable. **Crest** – A gryphon's head erased azure, ducally crowned or, between two branches of palm proper.
Residence – Talton House, Newbold on Stour, Stratford on Avon, Warwicks.

SONS LIVING

ROLAND VICTOR, *b* 4 March 1966. —— Alexander Bruce, *b* 1969.

DAUGHTER LIVING

Olivia Mary, *b* 1972.

AUNT LIVING (*Daughter of 3rd baronet*)

Eleanor Mary (Willow Springs, Bicester Hill, Evenley, Brackley, Northants), *b* 1914.

WIDOW LIVING OF FOURTH BARONET

ELLA MARGUERITE (*Ella, Lady Watson*), da of late Sir George Farrar, Bt (ext): *m* 1935, Sir Thomas Aubrey Watson, 4th baronet, who *d* on active ser. *Residence* – Talton Lodge, Newbold-on-Stour, Stratford-on-Avon, Warwicks.

COLLATERAL BRANCH LIVING

Issue of late John Rushworth Watson, yr son of 3rd baronet, *b* 1913, *d* 1984: *m* 1963, Amy Diana, eldest da of late Maj Harold Petit Rushton, TD, JP, of Phepson Manor, Worcs, and formerly wife of Maj Peter Wesley Dean:—
Camilla Mary, *b* 1967.
The 1st baronet, a distinguished Physician in London, was President of the Royal College of Physicians (London), the first representative of the Royal College of Physicians in Medical Council, and a Physician-in-Ordinary to HM Queen Victoria, and the 4th baronet, Sir Thomas Aubrey, Lieut Life Guards, *d* on active ser 1941.

WATSON (UK) 1912, of Sulhamstead, Sulhamstead, Abbots, Berks (Extinct 1983)

Sir NORMAN JAMES WATSON, 2nd and last *Baronet*.

WIDOW LIVING OF SECOND BARONET

BERYL (*Lady Watson*), da of Alfred Norris, widow of Sqdn-Ldr Basil Davis, RAF, and formerly wife of Sir Francis Cyril Rose, 4th and last Bt (*cr* 1872), who *d* 1979: *m* 1974, Sir Norman James Watson, 2nd Bt, who *d* 1983, when the title became ext. *Residence* – Flat 132, 55 Park Lane, W1.

WATSON (UK) 1918, of Newport, co Monmouth (Extinct 1959)

Sir GEOFFREY LEWIN WATSON, 3rd and last *Baronet*.

DAUGHTER LIVING OF THIRD BARONET

Daphne Lewin (*Hon Mrs John M. Southwell*), *b* 1907: *m* 1932, Lieut-Com Hon John Michael Southwell, RN, who was *ka* 1944 (*see* V Southwell). *Residence* – Buckclose, Longparish, Andover, Hants.

INGLEFIELD-WATSON (UK) 1895, of Earnock, Hamilton, Lanarkshire

It has flourished beyond expectation

Lt-Col Sir JOHN FORBES INGLEFIELD-WATSON, 5th *Baronet*; *b* 16 May 1926; *s* his father, *Capt Sir* DERRICK WILLIAM, 1987; *ed* Eton; Lt-Col RE (ret); Football Assoc Staff Referee Instructor since 1978.

𝕬rms – Per pale argent and or, on a mount vert an oak tree proper, the whole surmounted by two bars sable. ℭrest – The stump of an oak tree with a branch sprouting from either side, each grasped by a hand issuing from a cloud all proper. *Residence* – The Ross, Hamilton, Lanarkshire ML3 7UF.

SISTER LIVING

Sheila Margrett (14 Murrayfield Gdns, Edinburgh EH12 6DF), *b* 1931: *m* 1958, Dugald Graham-Campbell, yr of Shirvan, who *d* 1967, and has issue living, Robert John, *b* 1964: *m* 1992, Henrietta, only child of George Robert Heneage, — Sarah Alexandra *b* 1960.

MOTHER LIVING

Margrett Georgina, da of late Col Thomas Stokes George Hugh Robertson-Aikman, CB, of The Ross and Broomhilton, Lanarks: *m* 1st, 1925 (*m diss* 1939), Capt Sir Derrick William Inglefield Watson, 4th Bt, TD, who *d* 1987; 2ndly, 1945, Eric William Crawley Savill, of 12 Calverley Park, Tunbridge Wells, Kent TN1 2SH.

WIDOW LIVING OF FOURTH BARONET

THERESE (TERRY) (*Lady Inglefield-Watson*), only da of late Prof Charles Bodon, of Budapest: *m* 1946, as his 2nd wife, Capt Sir Derrick William Inglefield-Watson, 4th Bt, TD, who *d* 1987. *Residence* – Ringshill House, Wouldham, nr Rochester, Kent ME1 3RB.

COLLATERAL BRANCHES LIVING

Grandchildren of late Thomas William Watson, WS, 3rd son of 1st baronet (infra):—
Issue of late Capt Leslie Dundas Watson, *b* 1894, *d* 1975: *m* 1923, Enid Margaret (South Cottage, Dedham, Essex), da of late Col George Hay Montgomery Conran:—
SIMON CONRAN HAMILTON (51 Clapham Manor St, SW4 6DT), *b* 11 Aug 1939; *ed* Harrow: *m* 1971, Madeleine Stiles, el da of late Wagner Mahlon Dickerson, of New York City. —— Gillian Faye Lucy, *b* 1928, *d* 1990.

Issue of late Thomas William Watson, WS, 3rd son of 1st baronet, *b* 1864, *d* 1935: *m* 1891, Lucy, who *d* 1947, el da of William Henry Hamilton, of Manchester:—
Jeanette Lucy Vickers, *b* 1902: *m* 1923, Brig-Gen James Lockhead Jack, DSO, JP, who *d* 1962, and has issue living, Kenneth Hamilton Muir (Abbey Cottage, Pipewell, Northants), *b* 1931: *m* 1959, Bridget Sarah, da of Lt-Col Alan Stuart Casey, Royal Dragoons (see V Monsell), and has issue living, Richard Kenneth Hamilton *b* 1962: *m* 1992, Geraldine Jennings, Christopher James Hamilton *b* 1971, Louise Diana *b* 1964, — Angus Gavin Lockhead, *b* 1935: *m* 1960 (*m diss* 1970), Elizabeth Ann, el da of Sir John Samuel Richardson, 1st Bt (*cr* 1963) (later Baron Richardson, Life Baron), and has issue living, Charles Watson Hamilton *b* 1962: *m* 19—, —. *Residence* – The Old House, Kibworth, Leics.

Grandson of late Thomas William Watson, WS (ante):—
Issue of late Somerled Hamilton Watson, *b* 1899, *d* 1938: *m* 1925, Elma Mary, who *d* 1983, only da of late William Walker, of High Canons, Shenley, Herts:—
Julian Frank Somerled, *b* 1931; *ed* Harrow, and RAC Cirencester. *Residence* – Baythorne Park, Birdbrook, Essex. *Clubs* – Carlton, Lansdowne, Cavalry and Guards'.

Sir John Watson, 1st Bt, of Earnock, was second son of John Watson, of Bathville, Linlithgow, by his first wife. The 3rd baronet, Sir John, Lieut 16th Lancers, was *ka* 1918. Sir Derrick William Inglefield-Watson, 4th Bt, assumed by deed poll 1945 his christian name of Inglefield as an additional surname for himself and his issue.

MILNE-WATSON (UK) 1937, of Ashley, Longbredy, co Dorset

I owe all to God and country

Sir MICHAEL MILNE-WATSON, CBE, 3rd *Baronet*; *b* 16 Feb 1910; *s* his brother, *Sir* DAVID RONALD, 1982; *ed* Eton, and Balliol Coll, Oxford (MA); joined Gas Light & Coke Co, 1933, Man Dir 1933, Gov 1946-49; Chm N Thames Gas Bd 1949-64, Richard Thomas & Baldwins Ltd 1964-67, and William Press Group of Cos 1969-74; a Dep Chm British Steel Corpn 1967-69; Pres Soc of British Gas Industries 1970-71; Pres Pipelines Industries Guild 1971-72; Dir Finance for Industry 1974-80 and Dir Commercial Union Assurance Co Ltd 1968-81; Mem Council for Reading Univ 1972-80 (Pres 1975-80); Gov British United Provident Assocn 1975 (Chm 1976-81); Gov Nuffield Nursing Homes Trust 1975-80; Liveryman Grocers' Co 1947; late Sub-Lt RNVR; CBE (Civil) 1953, Knt 1969: *m* 1940, Mary Lisette, who *d* 1993, da of late Harold Carleton Bagnall, of Auckland, NZ, and has issue.

Arms – Argent, on a mount vert, an oak tree proper fructed or, over all a chevron azure charged with two mullets gold. Crest – A demi-griffin sable, gorged with an antique crown and charged on the body with two mullets palewise or.
Residences – The Stables, Oakfeld, Mortimer, Berks; 39 Cadogan Pl, SW1.

SON LIVING

ANDREW MICHAEL (22 Musgrave Cres, SW6), *b* 10 Nov 1944; *ed* Eton: *m* 1st, 1970 (*m diss* 1981), Beverley Jane Gabrielle, el da of Philip Cotton, of Majorca; 2ndly, 1983, Mrs Gisella Stafford, da of Hans Tisdall, of 105 Cheyne Walk, SW10, and has issue living, (by 1st *m*) David Alastair, *b* 1971, — Emma Victoria, *b* 1974, — (by 2nd *m*) Oliver, *b* 1985.

SISTER LIVING

Gabriel (Fox and Hounds Farm, Bolney, Sussex), *b* 1901: *m* 1929, Christian William Laurence Peel Reed, who *d* 1984, (E Peel, colls), and has issue living, Laurence Cecil (Hookhams Lurgashall, Petworth), *b* 1930; *ed* Eton and Worcester Coll, Oxford (MA): *m* 1956, Georgina, da of Thomas St John Alston, of Petworth, and has issue living, Nicholas William *b* 1958, Charles Christian Thomas *b* 1959, Andrew Laurence, *b* 1962, — Martin David (Standgates, Kirdford, Billingshurst, Sussex), *b* 1932; *ed* Eton: *m* 1957, Shirley, da of late Charles C. Naumann, of Rudgwick, Sussex, — Denys Christian (6 Wool Rd, SW20), *b* 1935; *ed* Eton: *m* 1st, 1959 (*m diss* 1972), Tessa Caroline, da of Stephen Cannon; 2ndly, 1973, Angela Frances Croft, and has issue living (by 1st *m*), Christopher Stephen *b* 1961, Jeremy Matthew *b* 1962 — (by 2nd *m*), James Christian *b* 1975.
The 1st baronet, Sir David Milne-Watson (son of late David Watson, of Edinburgh) was Gov and Managing Director of Gas Light & Coke Co, Vice-Pres of Federation of British Industries, and Hon Col The Rangers, King's Roy Rifle Corps.

HARVIE-WATT (UK) 1945, of Bathgate, co Linlithgow

Sir JAMES HARVIE-WATT, 2nd *Baronet*; *b* 25 Aug 1940; *s* his father, *Sir* GEORGE STEVEN, TD, QC, 1989; *ed* Eton, and Ch Ch Oxford (MA); FCA; Chartered Accountant; Exec Brit Electric Traction Co Ltd 1970-78; Man Dir Wembley Stadium Ltd 1973-78; Dir of Lake and Elliot Industries Ltd 1988-93; Chm of Cannons Sports and Leisure Ltd 1990-; Dir of other Cos; Member Exec Cttee of London Tourist Board 1977-80; Member The Sports Council 1980-88 (Vice-Chm 1985-88); Chm Crystal Palace National Sports Centre 1984-88; late Lt 1st Bn London Scottish Regt (TA): *m* 1966, Roseline Gladys Virginia, da of late Baron Louis de Chollet, of Le Guintzet, Fribourg, Switzerland, and has issue.

Arms – Quarterly: per fess wavy; 1st, per pale ermine and azure upon a mound in base vert, a tower proper masoned, sable roof gules, between two oak trees, also proper fructed or; 2nd, argent fretty sable, a grenade azure inflamed of nine flames, seven or and two gules; 3rd, barry wavy argent and azure, a portcullis gules; 4th, barry wavy gules and or, a dexter hand proper issuing from a manche fessways sable. Crest – A lion's gamb issuing from the torse argent, armed gules, grasping a writing quill paleways or, feathered sable.
Residence – 15 Somerset Sq, W14 8EE. *Clubs* – White's, Pratt's, Sunningdale, Queen's (Dir 1987-, Vice-Chm 1987-90, Chm 1990-93).

SON LIVING

MARK LOUIS, *b* 19 Aug 1969; *ed* Eton, and Yale Univ.

DAUGHTER LIVING

Isabelle Frances, *b* 1967; *ed* St Mary's, Ascot, and Edinburgh Univ.

BROTHER LIVING

Euan (333 East 56th St, New York City, NY, USA; Yarborough Cottage, Earlsferry, Fife KY9 1AD), *b* 1942; *ed* Eton; late 2nd Lt 1st Bn London Scottish Regt (TA); an Underwriting Member of Lloyd's; Pres Sedgwick International Marketing Services Inc: *m* 1967 (*m diss* 1979), Olivia Mason, da of William Mason Smith, of New York City, USA, and has issue living, Katrina, *b* 1968; *ed* Wycombe Abbey, Georgetown Univ, and George Washington Univ, — Jennifer, *b* 1969; *ed* Benenden, and Claremont McKenna Univ.

SISTER LIVING

Rachel, *b* 1944; *ed* Sherborne Sch for Girls, and Perugia and Edinburgh (MA) Univs: *m* 1970, Iain Gordon Fraser, WS, of 20 Lynedoch Place, Edinburgh EH3 7PY, and has issue living, Duncan, *b* 1972; *ed* Glenalmond, and St Andrews Univ, — Olivia, *b* 1974; *ed* Sherborne Girls' Sch, and Newcastle Univ.

WIDOW LIVING OF FIRST BARONET

JANE ELIZABETH (BETTIE) (*Bettie, Lady Harvie-Watt*), only da of late Paymaster-Capt Archibald Taylor, OBE, RN: *m* 1932, Sir George Steven Harvie-Watt, 1st Bt, TD, QC, who *d* 1989. *Residence* – Sea Tangle, Earlsferry, Fife, KY9 1AD.
The 1st baronet, Sir George Steven Harvie-Watt (son of James McDougal Watt of Armadale) was Parl Priv Sec to the Prime Minister (Rt Hon Winston Churchill, MP) 1941-45.

DON-WAUCHOPE (NS) 1667, of Newton

("ch" pronounced as in "Loch")

Sir ROGER HAMILTON DON-WAUCHOPE, 11th *Baronet*; *b* 16 Oct 1938; *s* his father, *Sir* PATRICK GEORGE, 1989; *ed* Hilton Coll, Natal, Durban and Pietermaritzburg Univ; a Chartered Accountant (S Africa); with Deloitte Pim Goldby: *m* 1963, Sallee, yr da of Lt-Col Harold Mill-Colman, OBE, ED, AMICE, of Durban, and has issue.

Arms – Quarterly, 1st and 4th azure, a crescent between two mullets in chief and a garb in base or (*Wauchope of Edmonstone*), 2nd, vert, on a fess argent three mascles sable (*Don of Newton Don*); 3rd, or a cross engrailed sable accompanied by an escutcheon gules in dexter chief and in sinister base a cinquefoil azure (*Rait of Edmonstone*); over all the Badge of a Baronet of Nova Scotia on an inescutcheon surmounted of an imperial crown. **Crests** – Dexter, a garb or charged of a crescent vert (*Wauchope of Edmonstone*); *sinister*, a fruit of pomegranate vert slit and seeded or (*Don of Newton Don*).
Residence – Newton, 53 Montrose Drive, Pietermaritzburg 3201, Natal, S Africa.

SONS LIVING

ANDREW CRAIG, *b* 18 May 1966; *ed* Hilton Coll, and Univ of Witwatersrand (MB, BCh): *m* 1990, Louise Sylvia, da of John Crawford Johnstone-Dougall, of Durban. —— John Hamilton, *b* 1969; *ed* Hilton Coll, and Pietermaritzburg Univ (BCom).

DAUGHTER LIVING

Georgina Anne, *b* 1970.

BROTHER LIVING

Malcolm John (P/BAG X23, Winterton 3340, Natal, S Africa), *b* 1939; *ed* Kearsney Coll, Botha's Hill, Natal: *m* 1968, Rea Marion, da of Phillip Montague Adams, of Doonside, South Coast, Natal, and has issue living, Keith John, *b* 1970, — Iain John, *b* 1975, — Jane Alice, *b* 1972, — Helen Louise, *b* 1977.

MOTHER LIVING

Ismay Lilian Ursula, da of late Sidney Richard Hodges, of Edendale, S Africa: *m* 1st, 1936 (*m diss* 1947), Sir Patrick George Don-Wauchope, 10th Bt, who *d* 1989; 2ndly, 19—, G. W. Shipman. *Address* – 16 Elgarth, St Patrick's Rd, Pietermaritzburg 3209, Natal, S Africa.

COLLATERAL BRANCHES LIVING

Grandchildren of late Rev David Maitland Wauchope, son of late Rev David Wauchope, uncle of 8th baronet:—
Issue of late Andrew Maxey Wauchope, *b* 1890, *d* 1987: *m* 1918, Mary Veronica Fisher, who *d* 1986:—
Michael Andrew Anthony (Uplands Lodge, Old Lane, Mayfield, E Sussex TN20 6AU), *b* 1925; *ed* Douai; late Lieut The Black Watch: *m* 1955, Margaret Mary Eleanor Victoria, yst da of I. S. Thomas, of Dublin, and has issue living, Piers Andrew Charles, *b* 1956; *ed* Worth; BA; Barrister; Kt of Sov Mil Order of Malta: *m* 1987, Jessica, da of Lt-Gen Sir Peter Hudson, KCB, CBE, DL, of Little Orchard, Frilsham, Newbury, Berks, and has issue living, Alasdair William *b* 1992, — Matthew Michael, *b* 1960; *ed* Douai; Kt of Sov Mil Order of Malta: *m* 19—, Elveira Ramos de Deus, and has issue living, Alice Margaret *b* 1990, — James Jonathon, *b* 1962; *ed* Winchester; LLB: *m* 19—, Helen, da of Dr W. Spiegel. —— Deirdre Veronica (5 Ventnor Villas, Hove, Sussex), *b* 1921: *m* 1964 (*m diss* 19—), Alan Henry Augustus Emery.
Issue of late Oswald Stewart Wauchope, *b* 1897, *d* 1956: *m* 1914, Dorothy Lettice White:—
James David *b* 1924: *m* 1950, Maria Sophia Zanucolli, of Florence. —— Estella Olive, *b* 1916: *m* 1943, Dr Michael West, who *d* 1946, and has issue living, Annie Jean, *b* 1922: *m* 1st, 1943 (*m diss* 1953), Leon Zuckerman; 2ndly, 1958, Zbigniew Ernest Jaworski, of 138b Golf Links, New Delhi, 110003, India, and has issue living.
Sir Alexander Don of Newton Don, Berwickshire, was *cr* a Bt with remainder to heirs male of his body. Sir William Henry Don, 7th Bt, sold Newton Don for £85,000 and became an actor. On his death in 1862 he was *s* by his kinsman, Sir John

Don-Wauchope (who resumed the surname of Don), son of Lt-Col John Wauchope, of Edmonstone, Midlothian, great-great-grandson of Patrick Don (who *m* Anne, sister and in her issue heir of Andrew Wauchope of Edmonstone), 3rd son of 1st Bt.

WEBSTER (E) 1703, of Battle Abbey, Sussex (Extinct 1923)

Sir AUGUSTUS FREDERICK WALPOLE EDWARD WEBSTER, OBE, 8th and last *Baronet.*

DAUGHTER LIVING OF EIGHTH BARONET

Lucy, *b* 1900.

COLLATERAL BRANCH LIVING

> Granddaughter of late Charles Fox Webster, son of late Col Sir Henry Vassal Webster, 2nd son of 4th baronet:—
> Issue of late Godfrey Seymour William Webster, *b* 1864, *d* 1887: *m* 1887, Ada Mary, who *d* 1947 (having *m* 2ndly, 18—, — Walker; 3rdly, 1901 (*m diss* 1906), Sir John Alexander Miller, 3rd Bt (*cr* 1874, ext), who *d* 1918; 4thly, 1908 (*m diss* 1920), Lieut-Col Maximilian John de Bathe, OBE, who *d* 1929, eldest son of Sir Henry Percival de Bathe, 4th Bt, da of Francis Henry Paget, of Birstall, Leicestershire:—
> Dorothy Muriel (*posthumous*), *b* 1888: *m* 1st, 1910 (*m diss* 1921), Lieut-Col Ian Onslow Dennistoun, MVO (formerly Grenadier Guards), who *d* 1938; 2ndly, 1928, Col N. Woevodsky (formerly Chevalier Guard). *Residence* – Castillo Cat, Roi, Palafrugell, Spain.

OGILVY-WEDDERBURN (UK) 1803, of Balindean, Perthshire

Sir ANDREW JOHN ALEXANDER OGILVY-WEDDERBURN, 7th *Baronet, b* 4 Aug 1952; *s* his father *Cdr* Sir (JOHN) PETER, 1977; *ed* Gordonstoun: *m* 1984, Gillian Meade, yr da of Richard Boyle Adderley, OBE, of Shepherds Hill, Pickering, N Yorks, and has had issue.

Arms – Not yet matriculated for present line of baronets.
Residence – Silvie, Alyth, Blairgowrie, Perthshire PH11 8NA.

SONS LIVING AND DECEASED

PETER ROBERT ALEXANDER, *b* 20 April 1987. —— Geordie Richard Andrew, *b* (twin) 1987. —— Sam, *b* 1990; *d* 1992.

DAUGHTER LIVING

Katherine, *b* 1985.

SISTERS LIVING

Henrietta Katharine, *b* 1947: *m* 1972, Sebastian P. Thewes, of Strathgarry House, Killiecrankie, Pitlochry, Perthshire PH16 5LJ, and has issue living, Robert John Peter, *b* 1974, — James Andrew, *b* 1976, — Arabella Katharine, *b* 1979, — Jemima Caroline, *b* 1981. —— Jean Aileen, *b* 1948: *m* 1983, Sam Henry Chesterton, of Buen Vino, Los Marines 21293, Prov de Huelva, Spain, yr son of Sir Oliver Sidney Chesterton, MC, and has issue living, Peter-Patrick Santiago (Jago) *b* 1984, — Charles Ernest Alfonso, *b* 1988, — Grania Laura, *b* 1986. —— Elizabeth Helen, *b* 1950.

AUNTS LIVING (*Daughters of 5th baronet*)

Janet Meta, *b* 1912; sometime Junior Com ATS: *m* 1940, Francis William Alfred Fairfax-Cholmeley, CBE, who *d* 1983, and has issue living, Caroline Ann, *b* 1941: *m* 1961, Michael John Hippisley, of Tarrie Bank, by Arbroath, Angus, and has issue living, David John *b* 1971, Fiona Jane *b* 1964, Catherine Ann *b* 1965, Lucinda Mary *b* 1969, — Mary Meta, *b* 1948: *m* 1971, Lt Mohamed Ali Dorgham Methoui, and has issue living, Halim *b* 1973, Ghazi *b* 1976. —— Elspeth Mary, *b* 1913. —— Katharine Andrea *b* 1915; is a JP: *m* 1940, George Macfarlan Sisson, OBE, and has issue living, John Edward (270 R St, Lincoln, CA 95648, USA) *b* 1943: *m* 1981, Dr Judy Pino, of California, — David George (59 Clapham Common West Side, SW4 9AT), *b* 1945: *m* 1st, 1970 (*m diss* 1993), Gillian, el da of Dr Dennis Barnes, of Mayfield, Botchergate, Carlisle; 2ndly, 1993, Deirdre Sally Angela, only da of Colin Page, of 10 Eascote Rd, Aylesbury, and has issue living (by 1st *m*), Katharine Rachel *b* 1971, Rosemary Ann *b* 1973, Suzannah Clare *b* 1975, — Alexander William (12 Mitchell Av, Jesmond, Newcastle-upon-Tyne), *b* 1949: *m* 1973, Penelope, 2nd da of Cdr Harold Turner, of The Old Rectory, Tacolneston, Norwich, and has issue living, William George *b* 1976, Alice Mary *b* 1978, Emily Rose *b* 1981, — Julia Andrea, *b* 1952: *m* 1972 (*m diss* 1987), Timothy Dallas Cairns. *Residence* – Planetrees, Wall, Hexham, Northumberland NE46 4EQ.

WIDOW LIVING OF SIXTH BARONET

ELIZABETH KATHARINE (*Dowager Lady Ogilvy-Wedderburn*) (Wester Strathgarry, Killiecrankie, Pitlochry, Perthshire PH16 5LJ), da of late John A. Cox: *m* 1946, Cdr Sir (John) Peter Ogilvy-Wedderburn, 6th Bt, who *d* 1977.

COLLATERAL BRANCHES LIVING

> Grandchildren of late Thomas Wedderburn-Ogilvy, son of late Major John Andrew Wedderburn-Ogilvy, 4th son of Peter Wedderburn Ogilvy, 2nd son of James Wedderburn Colvile (infra):—
> Issue of late Donald Stephen Wedderburn-Ogilvy, Sub-Lieut RNVR, *b* 1900, *ka* 1941: *m* 1st, 1924, Mona Alys Eustace, who *d* 1925; 2ndly 1929, Myra Carolyn Henrietta (Joy), who *d* 1990, da of late Lieut-Col Henry Montague Eustace, DSO:—

(By 1st *m*) Caryl Eustace (Pucklepeggies, 21 South Glassford St, Milngavie, Glasgow), *b* 1925; ARIBA: *m* 1953, Katharine Mary, da of William Steele, of Dundee, and has issue living, Niall, *b* 1955: *m* 1977, Elaine Isobel Margaret, el da John Coutts Meekison, and has issue living, Sarah Victoria *b* 1983, — Penelope, *b* 1959, — Verity, *b* 1965. —— (By 2nd *m*) Peter (Oak House, Froxfield, Petersfield, Hants), *b* 1931; Lt-Cdr RN (ret): *m* 1959, Philippa Sabine Burt, daughter of late Col F. A. Woods, of Winchester House, St Leonards, Sussex, and has issue living, Finella Sabine Clare, *b* 1962, — Helen Augusta Sophia, *b* 1964: *m* 1992, Angus James Lawson, of The Long Barn, Lucas Lane, Hackleton, Northants, son of Capt John Lawson, of Newton Ferrers, Devon, — Andrea Henrietta Louise, *b* 1968. —— Alys (Denton Lodge, Shute End, Wokingham, Berks), *b* 1930: *m* 1961, John Curtis Wernher Eustace, CIE, who *d* 1972, and has issue living, Catherine Helena, *b* 1962, — Cassandra Mary, *b* 1963, — Margaret Alison, *b* (twin) 1963, — Emily Anne, *b* 1967.

Grandchildren of late Major James Andrew Colvile Wedderburn-Maxwell, son of late Andrew Wedderburn-Maxwell, son of late James Wedderburn, son of James Wedderburn Colvile, 3rd son of 5th baronet, who was el son of 4th baronet of 1st creation:—
Issue of late Brig John Wedderburn-Maxwell, DSO, MC, *b* 1894, *d* 1990: *m* 1922, Hon Ann Madeline Cunliffe, who *d* 1986, da of 1st Baron Cunliffe:—
Keir, *b* 1924: *m* 1st, 1951, Ann, eldest da of Jan Brink, of Johannesburg; 2ndly, 1962, Janet, da of Oliver Hodgkin, of Rivonia, Johannesburg, and and issue living, (by 1st *m*) John, *b* 1952: *m* 1973, Barbara, only da of G.G. Bruwer, of 3 Stevenson Rd, Malindela, Bulawayo, and has issue living, James *b* 1978, a son *b* 1984, — Philip, *b* 1954: *m* 1978, Lynda Hopkins, — (by 2nd *m*) Andrew, *b* 1963, — Adrian Keir, *b* 1965, — Eloise, *b* 1967. —— John Anthony (Brewers Farm, West Tisted, Alresford, Hants SO24 OHQ), *b* 1941: *m* 1969, Priscilla Aileen Ann, da of Maj H.C. Mooney, of 37 Windermere Rd, Pietermaritzburg, Natal, S Africa, and has issue living, Andrew Franklyn, *b* 1975, — Matthew Charles, *b* 1981, — Claire Louise, *b* 1971. —— Gillian, *b* 1928; LRAM 19—; is an Asso of Guildhall Sch of Music: *m* 1954, Robert Beaumont Shepheard, son of late Percy Beaumont Shepheard, of Ewell, Surrey, and has issue living, Simon Beaumont, *b* 1957, — Janet Robina, *b* 1955, — Anne Catherine, *b* 1963, — Emma Gillian, *b* 1964. —— Robina, *b* 1932: *m* 1960, Douglas John Turner, of Huntsman's Cottage, Whistley Green, Hurst, Reading, and has issue living, Amanda Jane, *b* 1961.

Grandchildren of late Maj James Andrew Colvile Wedderburn-Maxwell (ante):—
Issue of late Henry Godfrey Wedderburn-Maxwell, MBE, *b* 1897, *d* 1970: *m* 1948, Breda O'Connor:—
Andrew Patrick, *b* 1949. —— Harry, *b* 1958. —— Dorothy, *b* 1952.

Grandchildren of late Harry George Wedderburn, 2nd son of Andrew Wedderburn-Maxwell (ante):—
Issue of late Charles Carmichael Wedderburn, *b* 1882, *d* 1951: *m* 1918, Jessie Mary, who *d* 1955, only da of late Walter Edwin Fairlie, of Bishopstone, Northwood:—
Michael Charles Fairlie, *b* 1924: *m* 1955, Mary Catherine, da of Sidney George Esbester, of Duffield, Derbyshire, and has issue living, John Michael Champion, *b* 1957, — Katherine Jane, *b* 1958, — Claire Mary, *b* 1962. *Residence* – Short Hoo, Hasketon, Woodbridge, Suffolk. *Address* – c/o American Overseas Petroleum Co, PO Box 693, Tripoli, Libya.
Issue of late Lt-Col Harry Francis Keir Wedderburn, *b* 1899, *ka* 1943: *m* 1929, Mary Sharp (Mountquhanie, Cupar, Fife KY15 4QJ), da of Lt-Col Henry Alexander Bethune (*see* Bethune, Bt. colls):—
Andrew Harry Bethune WEDDERBURN-BETHUNE (Mountquhanie, Cupar, Fife) *b* 1933; assumed 1959, the additional surname of Bethune after his patronymic; Capt The Black Watch (ret): *m* 1960, Mary Felicity Lovat Frazer, and has issue living, (Alexander) Guy, *b* 1965: *m* 19—, Lucy A., yst da of D. S. Rhodes, of Blairgowrie, Perthshire, and has issue living, Laura Rose *b* 1993, Anna Jasmine *b* (twin) 1993, — Patrick Keir, *b* 1967, — Andrew Michael Stewart, *b* 1969, — Charles Dominic, *b* 1973, — Gabrielle Mary, *b* 1962, — Frances Catriona, *b* 1964: *m* 1991, Richard Thurlow. —— Penelope Mary Bethune, *b* 1930: *m* 1949, John Piggott, and has issue living, John Wedderburn, *b* 1950, — Robin Andrew Keir Wedderburn, *b* 1957. *Residence* – Newholme, Spalding Rd, Weston Hills, Spalding, Lincs.

Granddaughter of late Capt Charles Francis Webster-Wedderburn, 2nd son of Sir James Webster-Wedderburn, grandson of Robert Wedderburn, 2nd son of 4th baronet (of 1st creation):—
Issue of late Arthur Augustus Helyar Webster-Wedderburn, *b* 1853; *d* 1919: *m* 1st, 1888, Katharine Elspeth Maude, who *d* 1907, da of late Henry Charles Hamilton, CSI (Hamilton, Bt, *cr* 1646, colls); 2ndly, 1913, Henrietta Caroline Bradley, who *d* 1946, da of late Thomas Henry Haddan, BCL Bar-at-law, and Fellow of Exeter Coll, Oxford:—
(By 1st *m*) Dorothy Hamilton, *b* 1901: *m* 1st, 1921, Capt Richard P. Hewetson, formerly RFA; 2ndly, 1934, Maj-Gen Allan Cholmondeley Arnold, CIE, CBE, MC, late Roy Fusiliers, who *d* 1962, and has issue living, (by 1st *m*) Richard Tatton Wedderburn, *b* 1924; formerly Pilot Officer RAF.

Grandchildren of late Lieut-Col John Walter Wedderburn, son of late John Wedderburn, *b* 1798, son of late John Wedderburn, son of late Thomas Wedderburn, 3rd son of 4th baronet (of 1st creation):—
Issue of late Charles David St Clair Wedderburn, OBE, *b* 1864, *d* 1931: *m* 1898, Louisa Mary, who *d* 1931, da of late Major J. E. Whaite:—
David Walter, *b* 1899; is Major RE: *m* 1925, Elizabeth, who *d* 1950, da of J. Robertson, of Perth, and has issue living, Patricia Helen Marjorie, *b* 1927: *m* 1950, Colin Henry du Plessis, and has issue living, Robin St Clair *b* 1951, Richard Geoffrey *b* 1952, — Averil Elizabeth Vernon *b* 1932.

Granddaughters of late Alexander Dundas Ogilvy Wedderburn, CBE, KC, son of late James Alexander Wedderburn, son of late John Wedderburn, *b* 1798 (ante):—
Issue of late Alexander Henry Melvill Wedderburn, CBE, *b* 1892, *d* 1968: *m* 1921, Cynthia Margaret, who *d* 1986, da of late Cecil Lubbock (*see* B Avebury, colls):—
Catherine Clarissa (The Chantry, Gt Barford, Bedford MK44 3JH), *b* 1925: *m* 1955, James Francis Robinson, TD, JP, DL, who *d* 1980, and has issue living, Adam James Nicholas, *b* 1959: *m* 1990, Katherine Adelaide Harben, and has issue living, Adelaide Harriet *b* 1991, — David Thomas, *b* 1962, — Harriet Clarissa, *b* 1957: *m* 1985, Richard Piers Bacon, of 127 John Ruskin St, SE5, son of Edward George Hedley Bacon. — Elizabeth Jane, *b* 1926: *m* 1949, Nicolas Ralph Dolignon Furse, son of Maj Sir Ralph Dolignon Furse, KCMG, DSO, and has issue living, Mark Nicolas Ralph Dolignon, *b* 1957: *m* 1981, Heather Campbell, and has issue living, Samuel Robert *b* 1982, Thomas Henry *b* 1992, Alice Jane *b* 1984, — Vanessa Jane Dolignon, *b* 1950: *m* 1987, Dr Robert S. Jackson, — Miranda Jill Dolignon, *b* 1951: *m* 1976, Carl Johnson, and has issue living, Jack Nicolas Drummond *b* 1981, Tess Jane Dolignon *b* 1986, — Corinna Margaret Dolignon, *b* 1954. —— Olivia Joan (Little White House, Church Lane, Longworth, Oxon OX13 5DX), *b* 1934: *m* 1st, 1957 (*m diss* 1972), Richard Weston Herbert; 2ndly, 1985, as his 3rd wife, Rodney Archibald Douglas-Pennant, who *d* 1993 (*see* B Penrhyn, colls), and has issue living (by 1st *m*), Catherine Alexandra, *b* 1963: *m* 1988, Richard J. Spencer, of 2 West View, Alvescot, Oxon, son of Geoffrey Spencer, of Lectoure, France, and has issue living, Henry Frederick *b* 1993.

Grandchildren of late Alexander Henry Melvill Wedderburn, CBE (ante):—
Issue of late Major David Michael Alexander Wedderburn, *b* 1922, *d* 1960: *m* 1946, Marigold Diana Sneyd, MA (who *m* 2ndly, 1960, Maj Harold Warren Freeman-Attwood, of West Flexford, Wanborough, Guildford), da of late Edward Philips, OBE, of Alsop-en-le-Dale, Derbys:—
Robert David Alexander, MA, GRSM, *b* 1948: *m* 1985, Hazel Eloisa, ARCM, da of late Rev John Humphrey Ifor-Jones, of Uppingham, Leics, and has issue living, Alister Humphrey, *b* 1987, — Susannah Kate, *b* 1990. *Residence* – 13 Rothesay Av, Richmond, Surrey TW10 5EB. —— Henry Edward Alexander (Lands Cottage, Swerford, Oxon; *Club* – Cavalry and Guards'),

b 1954; Lt Gren Gds: *m* 1984, Sarah Juliet, da of Anthony John Round, of Layer Marney, Essex, and has issue living, Polly Alexandra Round, *b* 1986, — Louisa Catherine Round, *b* 1990. —— Sarah Catherine, *b* 1952; *ed* Somerville Coll, Oxford (MA): *m* 1979, Ian Caughlin, and has issue living, Edward David, *b* 1980, — Hannah Delia, *b* 1982.

Sir John Wedderburn of Blackness, co Forfar, an advocate and Clerk of Bills, was *cr* a baronet of Nova Scotia with remainder to his heirs male for ever. On the death of Sir John, 3rd Bt in 1723, he was *s* by Sir Alexander, 4th Bt, nephew of 1st Bt. Sir John, 5th Bt, having embraced the cause of the Stuarts, served as a volunteer at the battle of Culloden, where he was taken prisoner. He was executed on Kennington Common, 1746, and his estate forfeited. His descendants, however, continued to assume the title until Sir David (7th Bt but for the attainder) PMG for Scotland, was *cr* a Baronet of UK 1803 with special remainder to the heirs male of the 4th Bt of the original creation. The 4th Bt, Sir William Wedderburn, MP for Banffshire (*L*) 1893-1903, was *s* in 1918 by his kinsman Sir John Andrew Wedderburn-Ogilvy (who assumed the surname of Ogilvy-Wedderburn 1918), 3rd in descent from James Wedderburn-Colville, yst son of 5th Bt (of first creation). His grandfather Peter Wedderburn *m* 1811, Anna, da and heir of James Ogilvy of Ruthven, co Forfar, and assumed the surname of Wedderburn-Ogilvy on the death of his father-in-law 1826.

WEDGWOOD (UK) 1942, of Etruria, co Stafford

I split asunder obstacles

Sir (HUGO) MARTIN WEDGWOOD, 3rd *Baronet*; *b* 27 Dec 1933; *s* his father, *Sir* JOHN HAMILTON, TD, 1989; *ed* Eton, and Trin Coll, Oxford (BA); Mem of Stock Exchange 1973-91, partner of Laurence, Prust & Co 1973-84, Dir of Smith New Court International Ltd 1986-91: *m* 1963, Alexandra Mary Gordon, authoress and architectural archivist at Palace of Westminster, elder da of late Judge Alfred Alexander Gordon Clark, of Berry's Croft, Westhumble, Dorking, Surrey (Lawrence, Bt *cr* 1867), and has issue.

ᶏrms – Gules, four mullets in cross and a canton argent. ℭrest – On a ducal coronet, a lion passant argent.
Residence – Pixham Mill, Pixham Lane, Dorking, Surrey.

SON LIVING

RALPH NICHOLAS, 10 Dec 1964; *ed* Westminster, Magdalen Coll, Oxford (BA), King's Coll, London (MPhil), and Cornell Univ, USA.

DAUGHTERS LIVING

Julia Mary, *b* 1966; *ed* St Theresa's, Effingham, and Sts Hilda and Bede Coll, Durham (BA). —— Frances Veronica Mary, *b* 1969; *ed* Sutton High Sch, Christ's Coll, Cambridge (BA), and Univ Coll, London.

BROTHERS LIVING

(John) Julian, *b* 1936; *ed* Stowe: *m* 1961, Sheila Mary, eldest da of late George Robert Meade, of London, and has issue living, (John) Adam, *b* 1962, — Rupert Julian, *b* 1964, — Felix Hawkshaw, *b* 1966. —— Oliver Ralph, *b* 1940; *ed* Eton.

SISTER LIVING

(Germaine) Olivia, *b* 1944: *m* 1965, David Louis Posner, who *d* 1985, son of Louis S. Posner, of New York, and has issue living, Piers Oliver, *b* 1966, — Dominic Tobias, *b* 1968.

AUNT LIVING (*Daughter of 1st baronet*)

Dame (Cicely) Veronica, OM, DBE, *b* 1910; *ed* Lady Margaret Hall, Oxford (MA); Hon LLD Glasgow 1955, Hon DLitt Sheffield, Harvard, Oxford, Keele, Sussex, and Liverpool; FBA; FRHistS; Historian; Pres of English PEN 1951-57, and English Assocn 1955-56; a Member of Royal Comm on Historical Manuscripts 1953-77; Trustee National Gallery 1962-68, 1969-76; an Officer of Order of Orange Nassau of the Netherlands; CBE (Civil) 1956, DBE (Civil) 1968, OM 1969.

WIDOW LIVING OF SECOND BARONET

PAMELA (*Pamela, Lady Wedgwood*), da of Herbert Wynn Reeves, of London, and widow of (Algernon) James Riccarton Tudor-Craig, FSA; PhD, FSA, author and art historian: *m* 1982, as his 2nd wife, Sir John Hamilton Wedgwood, 2nd Bt, TD, who *d* 1989. *Residence* – Home Farm, Leighton Bromswold, nr Huntingdon, Cambs PE18 OFL.

The 1st baronet, Brig-Gen Sir Ralph Lewis Wedgwood, CB, CMG, TD, was Ch Gen Manager of LNER 1923-39, and Chm of Railway Executive 1939-41. His el brother Josiah Clement was *cr* Baron Wedgwood 1942. Their father, Clement Francis Wedgwood, Master Potter, of Barlaston, Staffs, was great-grandson of Josiah Wedgwood, FRS, of Etruria, Staffs (*d* 1795), creator of the pottery which bears his name.

WEIGALL (UK) 1938, of Woodhall Spa, Lincoln (Extinct 1952)

Sir (WILLIAM ERNEST GEORGE) ARCHIBALD WEIGALL, KCMG, 1st and last *Baronet*.

DAUGHTER LIVING OF FIRST BARONET

Priscilla Crystal Frances Blundell: *m* 1st, 1935 (*m diss* 1943), Viscount Curzon, CBE, later 6th Earl Howe, who *d* 1984; 2ndly, 1943, as his 2nd wife, Harold Coriat, who *d* 1970, and has issue living (by 1st *m*) (*see* E Howe), — (by 2nd *m*), Christopher Archibald, *b* 1954. *Residence* - The Old School House, Farmington, Cheltenham, Glos.

WELBY (UK) 1801, of Denton Manor, Lincolnshire

Per ignem per gladium

By fire, by sword

Sir (RICHARD) BRUNO GREGORY WELBY, 7th *Baronet*; *b* 11 March 1928; *s* his father, *Sir* OLIVER CHARLES EARLE, TD, 1977; *ed* Eton and Ch Ch Oxford (BA): *m* 1952, Jane Biddulph, youngest da of late Ralph Hodder-Williams, MC, and has issue.

Arms – Sable, a fesse between three fleurs-de-lis argent. **Crest** – A cubit arm in armour issuing in bend sinister from clouds, holding a sword pommel and hilt or over flames of fire issuant from a wreath proper.
Seat – Denton Manor, Grantham, Lincs. *Residence* – 20 St Mary Abbot's Terrace, W14

SONS LIVING

CHARLES WILLIAM HODDER (Stroxton House, Grantham, Lincs), *b* 6 May 1953; *ed* Eton and RAC Cirencester; FRICS: *m* 1978, Suzanna Fiona, only da of the late Maj Ian Stuart-Routledge, of Harston Hall, Grantham, Lincs, and has issue living, Venetia Victoria, *b* 1981, — Zinnia Louisa, *b* 1985, — Isadora Barbara Pia, *b* 1993. —— Dominic John Earle, *b* 1960: *m* 1982, Camilla Janet, yr da of Christopher Gerald Pole-Carew, of Newfield Farm House, Screveton, Notts (*see* Pole, Bt, *cr* 1628, colls), and has issue living, Hector George, *b* 1993, — Maria Elizabeth, *b* 1987, — Octavia Lind, *b* 1990. —— Richard Henry Gregory, *b* 1970.

DAUGHTER LIVING

Miranda Lind, *b* 1955: *m* 1st, 1977 (*m diss* 1989), Gavin Laird-Craig; 2ndly, 1991, as his 2nd wife, Col Hugh Earle Welby-Everard, MBE, late RA (*infra*), and has issue living (by 1st *m*), Oliver John Gregory, *b* 1985, — Emma le Flay, *b* 1981.

AUNT LIVING

Joan Margaret (*Viscountess Portal of Hungerford*), *b* 1898: *m* 1919, 1st Viscount Portal of Hungerford, who *d* 1971 (*see* Bs Portal of Hungerford). *Residence* – West Ashling House, nr Chichester.

COLLATERAL BRANCHES LIVING

Grandchildren of late Edward Everard Earle WELBY-EVERARD (*infra*):—
Issue of late Capt Philip Herbert Earle Welby-Everard, OBE, DSC, RN (ret), *b* 1902, *d* 1985: *m* 1928, Lilla Anna Florence Maree Castell, JP (29 High St, Caythorpe, Grantham, Lincs), da of Magnus Spence, of Springfontein, Fig Tree, Zimbabwe:—
†Glynne Earle, *b* 1935: *m* 1963, Jan Plaisette, who *d* 1973, da of late Milton Lee Stroud, of Texas, USA, and *d* 1990, leaving issue, Ariel Edward Earle, *b* 1970, — Amanda Gay, *b* 1971, — Ariadne Melissa, *b* 1972. —— Roger Earle (Owl's House, Frieston, Caythorpe, Grantham, Lincs), *b* 1942; *ed* Eton; Lt RN (ret): *m* 1966, Isabel Anne, da of late Maj Lloyd Bucknall, and has issue living, Julian Richard Earle, *b* 1967, — Patrick Jonathan Earle, *b* 1969, — Anna Christabel, *b* 1974. —— Susan, *b* 1931: *m* 1959, George William Durrant, of Tintern, Long St, Sherborne, Dorset, and has issue living, Henry, *b* 1960, — Lucinda, *b* 1963: *m* 1987, Peter Stockley, and has issue living, Timothy Charles George *b* 1993, Laura Amber Maree *b* 1990, — Georgina, *b* 1965: *m* 1992, Miles Bodimeade.

Grandchildren of late Edward Montague Earle Welby, 4th son of 3rd baronet:—
Issue of late Edward Everard Earle WELBY-EVERARD, *b* 1870, *d* 1951, having assumed by Roy licence 1894, the additional surname and arms of Everard: *m* 1899, Gwladys Muriel Petra, who *d* 1946, da of late Rev G. W. Herbert:—
Sir Christopher Earle, KBE, CB, *b* 1909; *ed* Charterhouse and Corpus Christi Coll, Oxford (BA); Maj-Gen (ret), late R Lincs Regt; a DL for Lincs; High Sheriff 1974; Comd 264th Scottish Beach Bde (TA) 1954-57; BGS, HQ, BAOR and N Army Group 1957-59, and Ch of Staff Allied Forces, N Europe, Oslo 1959-61; GOC, Nigerian Army 1962-65; 1939-45 War (wounded, OBE); OBE (Mil) 1945, CB (Mil) 1961, KBE (Mil) 1965: *m* 1938, Sybil Juliet Wake, da of late Guy Shorrock, of Sandford Orleigh, Newton Abbot, S Devon, and has issue living, Peter Rodney Earle (Army & Navy Club), *b* 1942: *m* 1972, Jennifer Frances, twin da of Lt-Col Samuel Terence Cracroft Parsons-Smith, of Pill Heath Cottage, Andover, Hants, and has issue living, Christopher Nicholas Earle *b* 1976, Peter George Earle *b* 1982, Patricia Christabel *b* 1974, — Hugh Earle, MBE (Church Farm Cottage, Hurstbourne Tarrant, Andover, Hants), *b* 1944; Col late RA; MBE (Mil) 1984: *m* 1st, 1970, Virginia Gresley, who *d* 1989, as the result of a motor accident, da of late Maj-Gen John Edward Longworth Morris, CB, CBE, DSO, of Garden House, Burley, Hants; 2ndly, 1991, Mrs Miranda Lind Laird-Craig, only da of Sir (Richard) Bruno Gregory Welby, 7th Bt, and has issue living (by 1st *m*), Guy John Earle *b* 1979, Louisa Gresley Wake *b* 1975. *Residence* – The Manor House, Sapperton, Sleaford, Lincolnshire NG34 OTB. *Club* – Army and Navy.

Granddaughter of late Henry Earle Welby, son of late Rt Rev Thomas Earle Welby, DD, 2nd son of 2nd baronet:—
Issue of late Hugh Earle Welby, *b* 1867, *d* 1952: *m* 1908, Evelyn Borradaile, MBE, who *d* 1972, da of Adam Bell, formerly Rhodesian Civil Ser:—
Gwynyth Mary, *b* 1910: *m* 1937, Arthur Wyatt Aust, who *d* 1975, and has issue living, John Charles Wyatt, *b* 1942; Maj Rhodesian Army: *m* 1969, Pamela Drusilla Phillips, of Essexvale, Zimbabwe, and has issue living, Patrick Welby, *b* 1975, Caroline Joyce *b* 1970, Cherith Mary *b* 1972, — Elizabeth Mary, *b* 1940: *m* 1966, Brian Tozer, of Harare, Zimbabwe, and has issue living, Ian Richard *b* 1968, Nigel Stewart *b* 1970, Timothy Charles *b* 1975.

Grandchildren of late Arthur Thomas Earle Welby (*infra*):—
Issue of late Charles Earle Welby, *b* 1901, *d* 1975: *m* 1926, Lydia Elizabeth, who *d* 1984, da of Harry L. Hunt, of Madison, Wisconsin, USA:—
Arthur Earle (58 Oak Ridge Lane, Barrington, Ill 60010, USA), *b* 1927: *m* 1947, Giuliana, da of Alfredo Bruni, of Pisa, Italy, and has issue living, Allan Earle (1714 Hawkins Av, Downers Grove, Illinois 60516, USA), *b* 1958: *m* 1984, Sandra Capriotti, of Kanakee, Illinois, and has issue living, Adam Earle *b* 1988, Adriana Eda *b* 1990, — Steven Earle, *b* 1961, — Janet Rose, *b* 1955: *m* 1979, Dennis Joseph Sullivan, of 18 Davis Av, Arlington, Massachusetts 02174, USA, and has issue living, Dennis Arthur *b* 1985, Charles Orlando *b* 1990. —— Charles Earle (1357 Oxford Way, Upland, Ca 91786, USA), *b* 1935: *m* 1955, Doris Annen, of Madison, Wisc, and has issue living, Charles Earle, *b* 1959: *m* 1984, Laura Helen Wood, of Claremont, Calif, and has issue living, Megan Neville *b* 1988, — Peter Thomas Earle, *b* 1962, — Susan Kaye, *b* 1958: *m* 1982, William Scott Jones, of Zephyr Cove, Nevada, and has issue living, William Scott *b* 1986, Margaret Ashley *b* 1983, — Joanne Marie, *b* 1960: *m* 1988, Ricardo Aguilar, of Ontario, California. —— Mary Elizabeth, *b* 1931: *m* 1954, Bruce W. Ringey, of 1204 Airfield Lane, Midland, Michigan 48640, USA, and has issue living, David Bruce, *b* 1967, — Lynn Marie, *b* 1954: *m* 1977, Philip J Baker III, and has issue living, Andrew *b* 1979, Patrick *b* 1981, Laura *b* 1985, Erin *b* 1988, — Catherine Ann: *m* 1977, Mark

Willbur, and has issue living, Matthew Paul *b* 1980, Kimberly *b* 1982, Travis *b* 1988, — Karen Elizabeth, *b* 1960: *m* 1985, Roger Brandi, — Diane Lea, *b* 1963.

Granddaughters of late Rt Rev Thomas Earle Welby, DD (ante):—
Issue of late Arthur Thomas Earle Welby, *b* 1855, *d* 1908: *m* 1st, 1874, Phœbe, who *d* 1895, da of Capt de Cew; 2ndly, 1898, Maria, da of J. F. Mitchell:—
(By 2nd *m*) Muriel (Charter House, Kimbolton Road, Bedford): *m* 1921, Major Harold Godfrey St George Morgan, who *d* 1929, late RMA.
Issue of late Frederick Earle Welby, FRCSE, *b* 1858, *d* 1900: *m* 1883, Janet Anne, who *d* 1935, da of late F. Henderson, of Wick, NB:—
Edith Jessie: *m* 1st, 1920, William Adams, who *d* 19—; 2ndly, 19—. *Residence* –

Grandchildren of late Rev Arthur Earle Welby, 3rd son of 2nd baronet:—
Issue of late William Macdonald Earle Welby, *b* 1845, *d* 1885: *m* 2ndly, 1878, Jessie, da of Frederick Lucas, of Grahamstown, S Africa:—
Spencer Earle, *b* 1879. —— Glynne Earle, *b* 1881. —— Isabel Florence. —— May.
Issue of late Richard Earle Welby, *b* 1854, *d* 1932: *m* 1st, 1886, Mary Isabelle, who *d* 1892, da of late Thomas Paget, of Forton Lodge, near Lancaster; 2ndly, 1899, Alice Frances Blackburne, 3rd da of late Lieut-Col Cyril Blackburne Tew, and widow of late Vice-Adm Frederick Charles Bryan Robinson (Crofton, Bt, *cr* 1801, colls); 3rdly, 1918, Helen Mary, who *d* 1973, da of late Capt Creagh Scott:—
(By 3rd *m*) Glynne Richard Earle, *b* 1921; *ed* Camb Univ (BA 1948, MA 1957); Sqdn Ldr RAF (ret); ACIS: *m* 1st, 1945, Hilarie Elizabeth, who *d* 1957, da of H. Cecil Rowse, of St Austell, Cornwall; 2ndly, 1958, Margaret Mary, yr da of late Pius C. Brodrick, of Bolton, Lancs, and has issue living, (by 2nd *m*) Richard Edmund Charles, *b* 1961, — (by 1st *m*) Elizabeth Anne, *b* 1947, — Rosalyne Mary, *b* 1950, — Penelope Jane, *b* 1954, — (by 2nd *m*) Elizabeth Mary, *b* 1959.
The Welbys are an ancient Lincolnshire family. The first known member was Rannulf de Welleby, mil tenant of Wydo de Credun in Welby, near Grantham 1086. Sir John de Wellebi, son of Roger, gave land there to Vallis Dei Abbey in the reign of Stephen. The "Liber Niger Scaccarii," *temp* Hen II, records that Johannes de Wellebi held, in Welby, near Grantham, under Mauricius de Crun, a knight's fee and a half, "de antiquo feodo" enfeoffed before 1135. Many of them have successively sat in Parliament since 9 Henry V. The first who served as Sheriff of Lincolnshire was Roger de Welby in the 20 Richard II. The 1st, 2nd and 3rd baronets successively represented Grantham in Parliament, and the 3rd baronet assumed the additional surname of Gregory. Sir William, 4th baronet, also sat as MP for Grantham (*C*) 1857-68 and for Lincolnshire S 1868-84, and assumed by Roy licence 1876 the additional surname of Gregory. The 5th Baronet was MP for Newark Div of Notts (*C*) 1900-1906.

WELCH (UK) 1957, of Chard, co Somerset

Sir JOHN READER WELCH, 2nd *Baronet*; *b* 26 July 1933; *s* his father, *Sir* (GEORGE JAMES) CULLUM, OBE, MC, 1980; *ed* Marlborough, and Hertford Coll, Oxford (MA); late Roy Corps of Signals; admitted a Solicitor 1960; ptnr Bell Brodrick & Gray 1961-71, Wedlake Bell since 1972; Ward Clerk of Walbrook Ward (City of London) 1961-74; Registrar of Archdeaconry of London; Liveryman of Worshipful Company of Haberdashers 1955 (Court of Assistants 1973, Master 1990); Freeman of Worshipful Company of Parish Clerks 1954 (Master 1967); Chm of Cttee of Management, Lond Homes for the Elderly 1981-90; Mem of Ct of Common Council (City of Lond) 1975-86 and Chm of Planning and Communications Cttee 1981, 1982; Chm of John Fairfax (UK) Ltd 1977-90; CStJ; FRSA: *m* 1962, Margaret Kerry, da of Kenneth Douglass, of Killara, NSW, and has issue.

𝔄rms – Or on a fesse gules between six martlets azure two lions passant respectant of the first. ℭrest – An heraldic antelope's head erased or armed gules gorged with a collar composed of six pierced mullets azure chained also gules.
Residence – 28 Rivermead Court, Ranelagh Gdns, SW6 3RU. *Clubs* – City Livery; Surrey County Cricket; Hurlingham.

SON LIVING

JAMES DOUGLASS CULLUM, *b* 10 Nov 1973.

DAUGHTERS LIVING

Margaret Trudy Cullum, *b* 1965: *m* 1992, Anthony Richard Loveys Jervoise, of Rowden Manor Farm, Sampford Courtenay, Okehampton, Devon EX 20 2SJ, yr son of John Loveys Jervoise, of Herriard Park, Hants. —— Jane Olive Comrie Cullum, *b* (twin) 1965: *m* 1992, David Ross Waller, elder son of John Waller, of Alderley Edge, Cheshire.

SISTER LIVING

Rosemary Avril (6 Dunleary Court, Westcote Rd, Reading, Berks RG3 2DJ), *b* 1927: *m* 1st, 1952 (*m diss* 1963), John Osmond; 2ndly, 1963, Leighton Griffith Jones, who *d* 1983.

WIDOW LIVING OF FIRST BARONET

IRENE AVRIL (*Irene, Lady Welch*) (Walhatch, Forest Row, E Sussex RH18 5AW), da of late John Foster, OBE: *m* 1969, as his 2nd wife, Sir (George James) Cullum Welch, OBE, MC, who *d* 1980.
The 1st baronet, Sir Cullum Welch, was Lord Mayor of London 1956-57.

WELDON (I) 1723, of Dunmore, co Carlow

Bene · factum

Well done

Sir ANTHONY WILLIAM WELDON, 9th *Baronet*; *b* 11 May 1947; *s* his father, Sir THOMAS BRIAN, 1979; *ed* Sherbourne; late Lt Irish Gds; Gen Ser Medal S Arabia: *m* 1980, Amanda, da of Maj Geoffrey Edward Ford North, MC (*see* B Walsingham, colls), and formerly wife of Anthony John Wigan, and has issue.

Arms – Argent, a cinquefoil pierced gules, on a chief of the second a demi-lion issuant of the first. Crests – 1st, a demi-lion rampant argent guttée de sang; 2nd, the bust of Queen Elizabeth I (granted by Queen Elizabeth I as a special mark of favour). *Residence* – Easton Manor, Easton Royal, Pewsey, Wilts. *Club* – White's.

DAUGHTERS LIVING

Alice Louise Iona *b* 1981. —— Oonagh Leone Isobel, *b* 1983.

SISTER LIVING

Tara Louise Winifred, *b* 1943: *m* 1967, Alan Christopher Elliot, of The Old Rectory, Chilton Foliat, Hungerford, Berks, and has issue living, Dominic Ian Christopher, *b* 1975, — Sacha Louise, *b* 1968, — Larissa Mary, *b* 1970, — Natalya Isobel, *b* 1978.

WIDOW LIVING OF EIGHTH BARONET

MARIE ISOBEL (*Countess Cathcart*) (Moor Hatches, W Amesbury, Salisbury, Wilts), da of late Hon William Joseph French (*see* B de Freyne, colls): *m* 1st, 1942, Sir Thomas Brian Weldon, 8th baronet, who *d* 1979; 2ndly, 1984, as his 2nd wife, 6th Earl Cathcart.

COLLATERAL BRANCHES LIVING

Issue of late Sqdn-Ldr Terence Gordon Mackworth de Weltden Weldon, yst son of 6th baronet, *b* 1909, *d* 1970: *m* 1st, 1941 (*m diss* 1946), Suzanne Marie, da of Percy Hopkinson, of Sea Barn, Kingston Gorse, Sussex; 2ndly, 1946 (*m diss* 1969), Simonne Mireille, da of late Armand Philippon, of Aix-en-Provence, France:—
(by 2nd *m*) Oonagh Serena Elizabeth (Parc Voltina, Mas des Nigelles Bat. B, Route du Tholonet, 13100 Aix-en-Provence, France), *b* 1947; has issue living, Sarah Ilitch WELDON, *b* 1984.

Grandchildren of late Lt-Col Henry Walter Weldon, DSO (infra):—
Issue of late Brig Hamilton Edward Crosdill Weldon, CBE, RA, *b* 1910, *d* 1985: *m* 1st, 1935 (*m diss* 1946), Margaret Helen Katharine, da of Maj Frederic Passy, of Blachford, Cornwood, Devon; 2ndly, 1948, Elwyne Priscilla (3 Burnt Hill Rd, Wrecclesham, Surrey), da of Harold Richards Chaldecott, OBE, of Chantry, Leyburn, Yorks:—
(By 1st *m*) Wendy Juliet, *b* 1937: *m* 1960, Capt Ian Fothergill Grant, RN, and has issue living, Jonathan James Fothergill, *b* 1962, — Andrew William Edward Fothergill, *b* 1963: *m* 1989, Katrina Louise, da of Henry Evill, of London, — Amanda Katherine Lindley, *b* 1968. —— (By 2nd *m*) KEVIN NICHOLAS, *b* 19 April 1951: *m* 1973, Catherine Main, of Fontenay le Comte, France, and has issue living, Alexander Nicholas, *b* 1977. —— Mark Henry de Weltden, *b* 1953; Maj RHA: *m* 1980, Catherine M., yr da of late Lt-Col D. J. P. Weld, of Manor Farm, Apethorpe, Northants, and has issue living, John, *b* 1981, — Lucinda Katie, *b* 1983. —— Andrea Sari Victoria (53 Green Lane, Farnham, Surrey GU9 8QE), *b* 1948: *m* 1974 (*m diss* 1983), Richard Amyas Evetts, and has issue living, Benjamin George, *b* 1976, — Thomas Edward, *b* 1979.

Issue of late Lieut-Col Henry Walter Weldon, DSO, 5th son of 5th baronet, *b* 1878, *d* 1925: *m* 1909, Helen Louise Victoria, who *d* 1965, da of late Sir Edward Porter Cowan, of Craig-a-vad, co Down:—
Aurea Elizabeth (Southwood House, Southwood, Baltonsborough, Glastonbury, Som), *b* 1915: *m* 1942, Capt Humphrey John James Stuart, RA (B Norton), who *d* 1969, and has issue living, Julian de Weltden, *b* 1947.

Granddaughter of late Col Thomas Weldon, CIE, 5th son of 4th baronet:—
Issue of late Walter Ivan Weldon, *b* 1871, *d* 1934: *m* 1899, Edith Lucy, who *d* 1956, da of Clifton Whiting, formerly of Ashtead Grange, Surrey:—
Violet Iva, *b* 1900. *Residence* – Sentosa, 34 Summerdown Road, Eastbourne BN20 8DR.

Grandsons of late Walter Langford Weldon (infra):—
Issue of late Lt-Col Francis William Charles Weldon, MVO, MBE, MC, *b* 1913, *d* 1993: *m* 1946, Diana Geraldine (Stable Cottage, Wickwar, Glos), da of Stephen Anderson, of Straloch, by Blairgowrie, Perthshire:—
George Francis Daryl (102 Kew Green, Kew, Richmond, Surrey TW9 3AP), *b* 1946; *ed* Wellington Coll, Keble Coll, Oxford, and Carnegie-Mellon Univ, USA: *m* 1981, Jane Margaret, elder da of Maurice William George Knapman, of Orchard Close, Stoke Gabriel, Devon, and has issue living, Claire Elizabeth, *b* 1984, — Sarah Jane, *b* 1987. —— David Walter, *b* 1949; *ed* Wellington Coll: *m* 1975, Tessa Herron, and has issue living, Emilio, *b* 1982, — Sophie, *b* 1976.

Grandson of late Col Francis Weldon, 6th son of 4th baronet:—
Issue (by 2nd *m*) of late Walter Langford Weldon, *b* 1872, *d* 1922: *m* 1st, 1904, Emma Anne, who *d* 1905, da of late John Henry Tod, of 10 Courtfield Gdns, SW; 2ndly, 1910, Muriel Stewart, who *d* 1966 (having *m* 2ndly, 1924, Lt-Col William Weldon Herring-Cooper, CBE, DSO, who *d* 1953), da of William Richardson, formerly of 11 Harley House, Regent's Park, NW.
Patrick Langford Daryl, MC, *b* 1917; *ed* Wellington Coll, and Trin Coll, Camb; Maj (ret) RA; 1939-45 War with 2nd Bn Wilts Regt, Korea 1951 (despatches, MC): *m* 1955, Pamela Jane, da of Col L. B. Grant, of Burnt House, Benenden, Kent, and has issue living, Thomas Daryl, *b* 1963, — Guy Patrick *b* 1967, — Anna Grant, *b* 1958: *m* 1987, Andrew William Gadsden Reed, of 58 Strathville Rd, SW18, son of Gp Capt William Reed, of Eydon, Northants, and has issue living, Louisa Charlotte Weldon *b* 1991, — (Sarah) Kate, *b* 1960: *m* 1984, Andrew James Durham Wilkinson, of 48 Woodstock Rd, W4, son of late Geoffrey Wilkinson, and has issue living, Lucy Natasha *b* 1988, Amelia Grace *b* 1990. *Residence* – 18 Westbourne Park Rd, W2 5PH.

Grandsons of late Lt-Col Ernest Steuart Weldon, CBE, DSO, yr son of Col Francis Weldon (ante):—
Issue of late Maj Arthur Reginald Weldon, RA, *b* 1918; *d* 1982: *m* 1945, Dorothy Ann (Beanlands Park, Irthington, Carlisle), only child of William Monkhouse Pratchitt, of Crosby-on-Eden, Cumberland:—

Steuart William Pratchitt (96 Taybridge Rd, Clapham, SW11 5PS), *b* 1947; *ed* Wellington: *m* 1984, Carola Helen Victoria, elder da of John Hugh Loch, of The Market House, Aldbourne, Wilts (*see* M Hertford, colls, 1968 Edn), and has issue living, Helen Ann Freda, *b* 1986. —— Robert Arthur de Weltden, *b* 1950; *ed* Wellington: *m* 1993, Clare Frances, yr da of Richard Killingworth Hedges, of Charlton House, Shaftesbury, Dorset.

Granddaughters living of late Rev Lewen Burton Weldon, DD, 7th son of 4th baronet:—
Issue of late Lieut-Col Kenneth Charles Weldon, DSO, *b* 1877, *d* 1958: *m* 1906, Elizabeth Constance Jane, who *d* 1960, only da of late Major William Croker, Roy Inniskilling Fusiliers, of Byblox, Doneraile, co Cork:—
Elinor Constance (Grants Farm, Gallows Hill, Wareham, Dorset), *b* 1913. —— Clemence Jane (28 Leamington Rd, Charminster, Bournemouth, Hants), *b* 1915.

The patent of the 1st baronet, Sir Thomas Burdett, was conferred with remainder to the male issue of his sister Anne, wife of Walter Weldon. Col Sir Anthony A. Weldon, CVO, DSO, 6th Bt, a JP for Queen's co and co Kildare, was State Steward and Chamberlain to Lord-Lieut of Ireland and Lieut of co Kildare; *d* 1917 from the effects of shell shock.

WELLS (UK) 1944, of Felmersham, co Bedford

He who endures patiently conquers

Sir CHARLES MALTBY WELLS, TD, 2nd *Baronet*, *b* 24 July 1908; *s* his father, *Sir* (SYDNEY) RICHARD, 1956; *ed* Bedford Sch, and Pembroke Coll, Camb; is Lieut-Col RE from 1941 (acting Col 1945), served in 54 Div and 76 Div during WWII and on Bt Army Staff in Washington 1943-45: *m* 1935, Katharine Boulton, da of Frank Boteler Kenrick, of Toronto, Canada, and has issue.

Arms – Gules between two pallets a garb or bound with a ribbon azure buckled of the second pendant therefrom a hunting horn sable strings of the third between two fountains. **Crest** – A demi bear sable muzzled gules the sinister paw resting on a portcullis chained or.
Residence – 937 Mount Pleasant Rd, Toronto, Ontario M4P 2L7, Canada.

SONS LIVING

CHRISTOPHER CHARLES (6 Silverbirch Av, Toronto, Ont M4E 3K9, Canada), *b* 12 Aug 1936; *ed* McGill and Toronto (MD) Univs: *m* 1st, 1960 (*m diss* 1983), Elizabeth Florence Vaughan, da of I. F. Griffiths, of Outremont, Quebec; 2ndly, 1985, Lynda Anne, da of R. Cormack, of Toronto, and has issue living (by 1st *m*), Michael Christopher Gruffydd, *b* 1966, — Geoffrey Charles Vaughan, *b* 1970, — Felicity Elizabeth Boulton, *b* 1964, — Megan Sarah Kenrick, *b* 1969 — (by 2nd *m*), Andrew Christopher Brennan, *b* 1983. —— Anthony Richard, *b* 1947: *m* 1st, 1969 (*m diss* 1974), Frances Jane, da of Brig Gerard Boycott, of Berwick, Vic, Aust; 2ndly, 19—, Judith, da of the Rev Arthur Hamilton, and has issue living (by 1st *m*) Matthew Kenrick, *b* 1970, — (by 2nd *m*) Charles Hamilton, *b* 1978.

BROTHERS LIVING

David Franey, MC, *b* 1913; *ed* Bedford Sch; Major (ret) RA; 1939-45 War (MC): *m* 1948, Patricia Mary, da of the Rev Reginald Henry Goode, R of Houghton Conquest Bedford, and has issue living, Thomas Franey, *b* 1951. *Residence* – 43 Day's Lane, Biddenham, Bedford MU40 4AE. —— George Crichton (Abbots Lodge, Sibton, Saxmundham, Suffolk), *b* 1914; *ed* Bedford Sch, and Pembroke Coll, Camb (MB and BCh 1939); MRCP London 1946, FRCP 1959; Maj RAMC; 1939-45 War: *m* 1951, Margaret Caroline, da of late Dr Lewis Campbell Bruce. —— Oliver John, OBE, *b* 1922; *ed* Uppingham; Wing Com (ret) RAF; 1939-45 War; DL for Beds 1964; High Sheriff 1970: *m* 1949, Felicity Anne, da of Brig Maurice Edward Mascall, DSO, OBE, and has issue living, Michael Mascall, *b* 1951, — Paul Richard, *b* 1958, — Joanna Felicity, *b* 1953. *Residence* – Ickwell Grange, Biggleswade, Beds. *Club* – RAF.

SISTERS LIVING

Sydney Mary, *b* 1917: *m* 1938, Com George Edward Pollington Milburn, RN, and has issue living, Edward Barnaby Pollington, *b* 1944, — Philippa, *b* 1939, — Georgina, *b* 1940. *Residence* – Sibton, Saxmundham, Suffolk. —— Sarah Josephine (twin), *b* 1922; formerly in WRNS: *m* 1947, Michael Oliver John Gibson, MD, FRCP, and has issue living, James Michael, *b* 1950, — Timothy Wells, *b* 1952. *Residence* – The Garden House, Piddlehinton, Dorset DT2 7TE.

COLLATERAL BRANCH LIVING

Issue of late Lieut-Com Christopher Hayward Wells, RN, 2nd son of 1st baronet, *b* 1909, *ka* 1940: *m* 1937, Christina Hilary (*Lady Henry*) da of Sir Hugh Oliver Holmes, KBE, CMG, MC, QC; she *m* 2ndly, 1949, Sir James Holmes Henry, CMG, MC, TD, QC, 2nd Bt:—
John Hayward (Old Rectory, Shelton, Kimbolton, Hunts; Royal Thames Yacht Club), *b* 1938; *ed* Harrow, and Pembroke Coll, Camb; JP, High Sheriff for Beds 1989; DL for Beds 1992: *m* 1965, Heather Donriel, da of John Gordon Christie Kelly, MC, of Cape Town, and has issue living, Christopher Hayward, *b* 1966, — Richard Michael, *b* 1967, — Peter John, *b* 1970.
The 1st baronet, Sir (Sydney) Richard Wells (son of late Charles Wells, of Bedford), was Chancellor of Primrose League 1946-8, and sat as MP for Bedford Div of Bedfordshire (*U*) 1922-45.

WERNHER (UK) 1905, of Luton Hoo, Luton, Bedfordshire (Extinct 1973)

Sir HAROLD AUGUSTUS WERNHER, GCVO, TD, 3rd and last *Baronet*.

DAUGHTERS LIVING OF THIRD BARONET

Georgina (*Lady Kennard*) (13 Burton Court, Franklin's Row, SW3; Ardhuncart Lodge, Alford, Aberdeen), *b* 1919: *m* 1st, 1944, Lt-Col Harold Pedro Joseph Phillips, FRGS, who *d* 1980; 2ndly, 1992, as his 4th wife, Lt-Col Sir George Arnold Ford Kennard, 3rd Bt, and has had issue (by 1st *m*), †Nicholas Harold, *b* 1947; *ed* Eton, London Univ, and Lausanne Univ: *m* 1975, Maria Lucia (Luton Hoo, Luton, Beds), da of late Count Paul Czernin, of Schloss Hohenbrugg a.d. Raab, Fehring Stmk, Austria, and *d* 1991, leaving issue, Edward Paul Nicholas *b* 1981, Charlotte Sonia Maria *b* 1976, — Alexandra Anastasia (*Duchess of Abercorn*), *b* 1946; a Gov Harrow Sch since 1986: *m* 1966, 5th Duke of Abercorn, — Fiona Mercedes, *b* 1951: *m* 1971, James Comyn Amherst Burnett of Leys (*see* B Amherst of Hackney, colls), — Marita Georgina, *b* 1954; co-founder of The Mime Centre: *m* 1982, Randall Stafford Crawley, who was *k* in an air crash 1988 in Italy, yr son of late Aidan Merivale Crawley, MBE, of Oak Cottage, Farthinghoe, Northants (*see* Crawley-Boevey, Bt, colls, 1968 Edn), and has issue living, Aidan Harold Winston *b* 1983, Galen Randall George *b* (*posthumous*) 1988, Cosima Georgina *b* 1985, — Natalia Ayesha (*Duchess of Westminster*), *b* 1959: *m* 1978, 6th Duke of Westminster. —— Myra Alice (*Lady Butter*), CVO, *b* 1925; CVO 1992: *m* 1946, Maj Sir David Henry Butter, KCVO, MC, JP, Scots Gds, and has issue living, Charles Harold Alexander (12 Pelham Crescent, SW7), *b* 1960, — Sandra Elizabeth Zia, *b* 1948: *m* 1983, William D. Morrison, of 34 Norland Sq, W11 4PQ, yr son of Maxey N. Morrison, of Swarthmore, Penn, USA, and has issue living, Charles Nicholas *b* 1985, Sophie Natasha *b* 1987, — Marilyn Davina (*Lady Ramsay*), *b* 1950: *m* 1973, James Hubert, Lord Ramsay, of 3 Vicarage Gdns, W8, son of 16th Earl of Dalhousie, — Rohays Georgina, *b* 1952: *m* 1988, Alexander Peter Galitzine, of 48 Brunswick Gdns, W8, elder son of late Prince George Galitzine, of Eaton Sq, SW1, and has issue living, Sasha Alice Natalia *b* 1989, Nadezhda Georgina *b* 1990, — Georgina Marguerite, *b* 1956: *m* 1982, Peter Pejacsevich, of 12 Norland Sq, W11 4PX, son of Count Mark Pejacsevich, of 33 Victoria Rd, W8, and has issue living, Alexander Geza Marcus *b* 1988, Anastasia Lilla Sophie *b* 1992. *Residence* – Cluniemore, Pitlochry, Perthshire.

DAUGHTER LIVING OF SECOND BARONET

Anna Alexandra (10 Cornwall Mews South, Grenville Pl, S Kensington, SW7), *b* 1924.

PRESCOTT-WESTCAR (GB) 1794, of Theobalds Park, Hertfordshire (Extinct 1959)

Sir WILLIAM VILLIERS LEONARD PRESCOTT-WESTCAR, DSO, 7th and last *Baronet*.

DAUGHTER LIVING OF SEVENTH BARONET

Jellis, *b* 1926: *m* 19—, William Cameron.

WIDOW LIVING OF FIFTH BARONET

Elizabeth Hughes, da of William Melcer, of California, USA, and widow of Arthur Grier Fell: *m* 2ndly, 1932, Sir George Lionel Lawson Prescott, 5th Bt, who *d* 1942; 3rdly, 1953 (*m diss* 1957), Capt Peregrine Fellowes, Irish Guards, who *d* 1972.

WHEELER (UK) 1920, of Woodhouse Eaves, co Leicester

Sir JOHN HIERON WHEELER, 3rd *Baronet*; *b* 22 July 1905; *s* his brother, *Sir* ARTHUR (FREDERICK PULLMAN), 1964; *ed* Charterhouse: *m* 1929, Gwendolen Alice, da of late Alfred Ernest Oram, of Kirby Muxloe, nr Leicester, and has issue.

Arms – Sable, a chevron between in chief two talbots heads erased and in base an eagle displayed or. **Crest** – A talbot's head erased sable, eared and charged on the neck with a catherine wheel or.
Residence – 39 Morland Av, Stoneygate, Leicester LE2 2PF.

SONS LIVING

JOHN FREDERICK (Round Hill, Aldeburgh, Suffolk), *b* 3 May 1933; *ed* Bedales and Lond Sch of Printing: *m* 1963, Barbara Mary, da of late Raymond Flint, of Stoneygate, Leicester, and has issue living, John Radford, *b* 1965, — Andrew Charles, *b* 1969, — Jane Louise, *b* 1964. —— Benjamin (Benscliffe Hay Cottage, Newtown Linford, Leics), *b* 1935: *m* 1962, Brenda Ellen, da of late Arthur Goodman, of Syston, Leics, and has issue living, Miles John, *b* 1962, — Edward James, *b* 1964, — Matthew Benjamin, *b* 1966, — Rebecca Mary, *b* 1972.

SISTER LIVING

Nancie Radford. *Residence* – Holme-next-the-Sea, Norfolk.

WIDOW LIVING OF SECOND BARONET

Alice Webster (*Alice, Lady Wheeler*) (E12, Marine Gate, Marine Parade, Brighton 7, BN2 5TQ), da of late George Heath Stones: *m* 1938, Sir Arthur (Frederick Pullman) Wheeler, 2nd Bt, who *d* 1964.
The 1st baronet, Sir Arthur Wheeler (son of late Benjamin Wheeler, of Northampton) was High Sheriff of Leicestershire 1922.

Wheeler Cuffe, see Cuffe.

WHELER (E) 1660, of City of Westminster, co London

Up to the mark

Sir EDWARD WOODFORD WHELER, 14th *Baronet*; *b* 13 June 1920; *s* his father, Sir TREVOR WOOD, 1986; *ed* Radley; Capt Roy Sussex Regt 1941-47, attached Indian Army 1942-45; Overseas Audit Dept 1948-58, Kenya 1958-70: *m* 1945, Molly Ashworth, da of late Thomas Lever, late Gold Coast Civil Ser, and has issue.

Arms – Or a chevron between three leopards' faces sable. **Crest** – On a ducal coronet or, an eagle displayed gules.
Residence – 25 Cavendish Rd, Chesham, Bucks HP5 1RW.

SON LIVING

TREVOR WOODFORD (83 Middle Park, Inverurie, Aberdeenshire), *b* 11 April 1946; *ed* St Edmund's, Canterbury: *m* 1974, Rosalie Margaret, da of late Ronald Thomas Stunt, and has issue living, Edward William, *b* 14 June 1976, — Andrew Robert, *b* 1978.

DAUGHTER LIVING

Dinah Margaret, *b* 1947: *m* 1st, 1968 (*m diss* 1983), Clive Richard Knight; 2ndly, 1987, Bernard Teasdale Tomlinson, and has issue living, (by 1st *m*) Anthony Clive Wheler, *b* 1968, — Simon Mark, *b* 1972. *Residence* – 32 St Carantoc Way, Crantock, nr Newquay, Cornwall TR8 5SB.

SISTERS LIVING

Audrey Idris (34A Coombe Rd, Croyden, Surrey), *b* 1916: *m* 1940, Maj John Humphrey Wightwick, late Suffolk Regt, who *d* 1970, and has issue living, Christopher Kenneth Wheler (c/o Coutts & Co, 1 Old Park Lane, W1), *b* 1940: *m* 1st, 1966 (*m diss* 19—), Sarah Gordon Macdonald; 2ndly, 1978, Sheila Gay Morton-George and has issue living (by 1st *m*), Kathryn Jennifer *b* 1969, — Simon John Patrick Wheler, *b* 1949: *m* 1973, Annee Alfsen, of Oslo, Norway, — Nigel Martin Humphrey Wheler, *b* 1951, — Vanessa Ann Margaret Wheler, *b* 1947: *m* 1970, John Bray Needham, of Upper Whiston, Yorks, and has issue living, Gavin Timothy *b* 1971. —— Diana Edmée (The Garden House, Dewhurst, Wadhurst, Sussex), *b* 1918: *m* 1941, Leslie Francis Gordon Pritchard, MBE, TD, who *d* 1977, and has issue living, Caroline Jane, *b* 1943: *m* 1966, Dean Edward Fischer, — Susan Letitia, *b* 1947: *m* 1972, Roderic Hill, — Anne Charlotte, *b* 1948: *m* 1973, Todd Civardi, — Rachel Sarah *b* 1955: *m* 1978, Henry Mark Wyndham (*see* B Egremont).

COLLATERAL BRANCHES LIVING

Grandchildren of late Lt-Col Francis Henry Wheler, 2nd son of 10th baronet:—
    Issue of late Capt Trevor Wheler, *b* 1888, *d* 1967: *m* 1935, Enid, who *d* 1983, da of late H. R. Stokes:—
Glynne Henry Trevor, *b* 1941. —— Jane Frances Trevor, *b* 1938: *m* 1962, Kenneth Ross Thompson (Nesscroft, Box 381, PO Griffith, NSW), and has issue living, John Kenneth Glynne, *b* 1967, — Susan Jane, *b* 1963, — Jennifer Anne Frances, *b* 1965.

Granddaughters of the late Aubrey Stuart Wheler (infra):—
    Issue of late Stephen Jameson Wheler, *b* 1907, *d* 1967: *m* 1950, Annette, who *d* 1968, da of Frank Eden Smith:—
Amanda (The Flat, 8 High St, Ditchling, Sussex), *b* 1952. —— Jacqueline, *b* 1956: *m* 1987, Christopher French, of Florida, USA.

Granddaughter of late Col Charles Stuart Wheler, 3rd son of 10th baronet:—
    Issue of late Aubrey Stuart Wheler, *b* 1877, *d* 1934: *m* 1904, Blanche Christina, who *d* 1946, only da of S. W. Jameson, formerly of 28 Princes Square, Bayswater, W:—
Rosemary Blanche Jameson, *b* 1919: *m* 1948, Douglas Victor Gordon Feltham, MA, MB, BCh, and has issue living, John Leander (77 Honeywell Rd, SW11), *b* 1955; BA: *m* 1982, Michele Carla Fabian-Jones, — Hoonie Rosemary Anne FELTHAM, *b* 1950; has issue living, Leander Charles FELTHAM *b* 1979; continues to be styled by her maiden name: *m* 1986, Hugh Cecil Palmer, of Knapp House, Shenington, Banbury, Oxon OX15 6NE, and has further issue living, Gerald Hugh Feltham PALMER *b* 1987. *Residence* – 50 Michelham Gdns, Strawberry Vale, Twickenham, Middlesex.

Granddaughters of late Rev Henry Trevor Wheler, son of late Charles John Wheler, 2nd son of 7th baronet:—
    Issue of late Commodore William Alfred Wheler, *b* 1843, *d* 1933: *m* 1879, Mary Margaret, who *d* 1918, da of late William John Cumming, MRCS:—
Mary Glynne (c/o Cookhayes Guest House, Moretonhampstead, Devon), *b* 1887: *m* 1914, Rev John Augustus Kirby, who *d* 1962, and has issue living, Mary Aline Glynne, *b* 1915: *m* 1935 (*m diss* 1949), Lt-Cdr George Robert May Robertson, RN, and has issue living, Ian Antony *b* 1937, Robert Edward *b* 1939, Elizabeth Janine *b* 1946.

The 1st baronet, Sir William, was MP for Queensborough *temp* Charles II, and his wife was Laundress to the Royal Family. The 2nd baronet, Col Sir Charles, his cousin, who succeeded by a special limitation, was Governor of the Leeward Islands, MP for Cambridge University in the Long Parliament, and one of the gentlemen entrusted to carry the plate of that University to Charles II. The 9th baronet, Lieut-Col Sir Trevor, served throughout the Peninsular War, including Waterloo; and the 10th baronet, Lieut-Gen Sir Francis, CB, served in Bundlecund 1821-2, in Afghanistan 1839-40, in the Punjab 1848-9, and in Indian Mutiny 1858-9. His son, Lt-Col Sir Trevor Wheler, 11th Bt, was *b* 1828 in Lucknow, where all the wives were assembled for safety during the Indian Mutiny, while his father was on active ser.

WHICHCOTE (E) 1660, of The Inner Temple, London (Dormant or Extinct 1949)

Sir HUGH CHRISTOPHER WHICHCOTE, 10th and last *Baronet*.

DAUGHTERS LIVING OF TENTH BARONET

Isolda Sophia, *b* 1910. —— Diana Juliane, *b* 1911.

WHITAKER (UK) 1936, of Babworth, Nottinghamshire

Sir JAMES HERBERT INGHAM WHITAKER, 3rd *Baronet*; *b* 27 July 1925; *s* his father, *Maj-Gen Sir* JOHN ALBERT CHARLES, CB, CBE, 1957; *ed* Eton; High Sheriff of Notts 1969; Dep Chm of Halifax Building Soc since 1974 and Chm of London Board, and Board of Govs of Atlantic Coll; late Major Sherwood Rangers, Imperial Yeo (TA); European War 1944-45 in N-W Europe and Palestine as 2nd Lieut Coldstream Guards: *m* 1948, Mary Elizabeth Lander; former JP (Notts); da of Ernest Johnston, of Cockshut, Reigate, and widow of Capt David Urling Clark, MC, and has issue.

Arms – Per pale argent and azure a chevron embattled between three mascles counterchanged. **Crest** – A horse passant argent, gorged with a collar gemel, and resting the dexter foreleg on a mascle azure.
Seats – Babworth Hall, Retford, Notts; Auchnafree, Dunkeld, Perthshire.

Hope and faith

SON LIVING

JOHN JAMES INGHAM (The Cottage, Babworth, Retford, Notts DN22 8EW), *b* 23 Oct 1952; *ed* Eton, and Bristol Univ (BSc), FCA, AMIEE: *m* 1981, Elizabeth Jane Ravenscroft, da of L. J. R. Starke, of New Zealand, and has issue living, Harry James Ingham, *b* 1984, — Lucy Harriet Ravenscroft, *b* 1982, — Alix Catherine Hepburn, *b* 1987, — Eleanor Mary Harvie, *b* 1989.

DAUGHTER LIVING

Shervie Ann Lander, *b* 1950: *m* 1971, David William James Price, of Harrington Hall, Spilsby, Lincs, and has issue living, William James Emlyn, *b* 1973, — Hesther Jane Lander, *b* 1971.

BROTHERS LIVING

Rev David Arthur Edward (Feniton Rectory, Honiton, Devon), *b* 1927; *ed* Eton, and New Coll, Oxford; formerly Lt Coldm Gds; is a Clerk in Holy Orders: *m* 1956, Susan Mary, da of the Rev Canon Richard Hamilton Babington, of St Mary-le-Tower, Vicarage, Ipswich, and has issue living, Robert John, *b* 1957, — Michael Benjamin, *b* 1960, — Jonathan *b* 1972, — Caroline Lucy, *b* 1959, — Iona Ruth, *b* 1963. —— Benjamin Charles George (13 Elsworthy Rd, NW3), *b* 1934; *ed* Eton and New Coll, Oxford; Bar Inner Temple 1959; formerly 2nd Lt Coldm Gds; author of *The Police* 1964, *Crime and Society* 1967, editor of *A Radical Future* 1967; *Participation and Poverty* 1968, *Parks for People* 1971, *The Foundations* 1974, *Police in Society* 1979, *A Bridge of People* 1983, *The Global Connection* 1987; editor of *The Fourth World* 1972 and of *Minorities: a question of human rights* 1984; PPS to Min of Overseas Development 1966 and to Min of Housing and Local Govt 1966-67 and Parl Sec, Min of Overseas Development 1969-70; MP for Hampstead (*L*) 1966-70; Dir of Minority Rights Groups 1971-88; Dir of Gulbenkian Foundation (UK) since 1988; UK Member, UN Human Rights Sub-Commission since 1975: *m* 1964, Janet Alison, da of Alan Stewart, of Beeston, and has issue living, Daniel Peter Alan, *b* 1966, — Rasaq Andrew Ian, *b* 1972, — Quincy Rachel Suzy, *b* 1968.

The 1st baronet, Col Sir Albert Edward Whitaker, CBE, TD, (son of late Joseph Whitaker, of Hesley Hall, Notts), was a JP and DL for Notts (High Sheriff 1921) and Lord High Steward of E Retford. The 2nd baronet, Maj-Gen Sir John Albert Charles Whitaker, CB, CBE, late Coldstream Guards, was High Sheriff of Nottingham 1950, and Lord High Steward of E Retford 1952-57. He commanded Coldstream Guards 1937-39, and was Director of Mil Training 1942-45.

WHITE (UK) 1802, of Wallingwells, Nottinghamshire

Sir Thomas Astley Woollaston White, 5th *Baronet*; *b* 13 May 1904; *s* his father, *Sir* Archibald Woollaston, 1945; *ed* Wellington Coll; FRICS; a JP for Wigtown; Hon Sheriff Substitute for Wigtownshire: *m* 1935, Daphne Margaret, da of late Lt-Col Francis Remi Imbert Athill, CMG, OBE, DL, of Brinkburn, High House, Longframlington, Northumberland, and has issue.

Arms – Gules, a chevron vaire between three lions rampant or. Crest – Out of a ducal coronet argent, a demi-eagle displayed sable.
Residence – Ha Hill, Wigtown, Wigtownshire.

LOYAL · UNTO · DEATH

DAUGHTER LIVING

Bridget Juliet, *b* 1936: *m* 1962, Lt-Cdr Charles David Orr Ewing, RN (*see* Orr Ewing, Bt, colls, *cr* 1886). *Residence* – Torhousemuir, Wigtown, Wigtownshire.

BROTHER LIVING

Richard Taylor, DSO, *b* 29 Jan 1908; Capt (ret) RN; European War 1939-45 (despatches, DSO and two Bars); DSO 1940 (Bars 1941 & 1942): *m* 1936, Gabrielle Ursula, younger da of late Capt Robert Henry Style (*see* Style, Bt, colls), and has issue living, Nicholas Peter Archibald (The Stables, Canon Lane, Wateringbury, Kent), *b* 1939; *ed* Eton: *m* 1970, Susan Irene, da of G. W. B. Pollock, of Blackrock, co Dublin, and has issue living, Christopher David Nicholas *b* 1972, Simon Richard William *b* 1974, Annabelle Victoria Jocelyn *b* 1976, — Robert Leslie *b* 1945; *ed* Eton: *m* 1989, Hong Chen, — Richard Mark (60 Bessborough Place, SW1), *b* (twin) 1945; *ed* Eton: *m* 1988, Catherine Anne Isobel, only da of late Judge Karl Roy Barrington Brandon, of Fairwater, Chew Stoke, Som, — Victoria Rosamond (*Victoria, Lady Sebright*), *b* 1937: *m* 1st, 1965 (*m diss* 1983), David Ashton Ashton-Bostock; 2ndly, 1984, Sir Hugo Giles Edmund Sebright, 14th Bt, who *d* 1985, and has issue living (by 1st *m*), (Henrietta) Sophia *b* 1967: *m* 1990, Dominic Bertram Charles Tayler, son of Michael Tayler, of the Old Parsonage, Aust, nr Bristol, — Jocelyn Henrietta, *b* 1943: *m* 1966, Michael Christopher Mallock, of Cases, Greatham, Liss, Hants, and has issue living, James Rawlyn *b* 1972, Sarah Penelope *b* 1970: *m* 1992, Lieut James Edward Buck, RN, eldest son of W. A. Buck, of 10 St Michael's Rd, Stamshall, Uttoxeter, Staffs. *Residence* – Lavenders, Lavenders Rd, West Malling, Kent.

COLLATERAL BRANCHES LIVING

Issue of late Capt Archibald John Ramsay White, CBE, DSC, RN, yst son of 4th Bt, *b* 1910, *d* 1991: *m* 1949, Marguerite Elise (Stonewalls, Evenlode, Moreton in Marsh, Glos), only da of late Sir Ernest Nathaniel Bennett, JP, MP, of Cwmllecoedlog, Montgomery:—
Thomas Charles Ramsay, *b* 1952; Capt 9th/12th R Lancers (ret): *m* 1981, Mary, yr da of Edward Ross-Hime, of Orchard Cottage, 12 Chapel Street, East Malling, Maidstone, Kent, and has issue living, Charles Thomas Ramsay, *b* 1988, — Elizabeth Susannah, *b* 1983, — Clare Marguerite, *b* 1986. —— John Woollaston, *b* 1958. —— Caroline Marguerite, *b* 1950. —— Sarah Elizabeth, *b* 1960.

Grandchildren of late John White (infra):—
Issue of late George Towry White, *b* 1889, *d* 1973: *m* 1922, Evangeline, who *d* 1981, da of late John Arthur, of Feilding, NZ:—
John Woollaston (74 Broadway, Waitara, NZ), *b* 1923. —— Louis Arthur Taylor, *b* 1928: *m* 1957, Gladys Daphne, only da of John Stokes, farmer, of Kinohaku, NZ, and has issue living, Stanley George, *b* 1958, — Norman John, *b* 1959: *m* 1979, Sheryle, da of P. L. Duxfield, of Ongarue, NZ, and has issue living, Jered Colin *b* 1980, Jackie Anna *b* 1983, Camilla Amy-Anne *b* 1986, — Jeffrey Taylor, *b* 1964, — Jocelyn Amy Anne, *b* 1961, — Miriam Una, *b* 1962: *m* 1985, Robert Skinner, and has issue living, Sherilyn Rose *b* 1986, Jasmine Marie *b* 1988, — Patricia Gladys (twin), *b* 1964, — Eva Marie, *b* 1966. —— Marion Penelope, *b* 1926.

Granddaughter of late Rev Taylor White, 2nd son of 1st baronet:—
Issue of late John White, *b* 1839, *d* 1911: *m* 1876, his cousin, Louisa Caroline, who *d* 1915, da of late George Towry White, Bar-at-law:—
Joyce Alice Finderne, *b* 1897. *Residence* – 64 Ambleside Av, Telscombe Cliffs, nr Newhaven, Sussex.

(In special remainder)

Descendants (if any) of the late Lieut-Col Taylor White, brother of 1st baronet.

Sir Thomas Woollaston White, 1st baronet, who was created with remainder to his father's issue male, was 7th in descent from Thomas White, of Tuxford Manor, Notts, who *m* Anne Cecil, sister of the famous William, Lord Burghley.

WHITE (UK) 1904, of Cotham House, Bristol

Sir GEORGE STANLEY JAMES WHITE, 4th *Baronet*; *b* 4 Nov 1948; *s* his father, *Sir* GEORGE STANLEY MIDELTON, 1983; *ed* Harrow; JP, FSA: *m* 1st, 1974 (*m diss* 1979), Susan Elizabeth, da of late John Langmaid Ford; 2ndly, 1979, Elizabeth Jane, da of late Sir (William) Reginald Verdon-Smith, and formerly wife of Robert George Clinton, and has issue living by both *m*.

𝕬rms – Barry wavy of six argent and azure, over all a lymphad sable, on a chief of the second two roses of the first. 𝕮rest – Upon a mount vert a beacon fired proper, pendent therefrom a sail azure charged with a rose as in the arms.

SON LIVING *(By 2nd marriage)*

GEORGE PHILIP JAMES, *b* 1987.

DAUGHTERS LIVING *(By 1st marriage)*

Caroline Morwenna, *b* 1978.

(By 2nd marriage)

Kate Elizabeth, *b* 1983.

SISTER LIVING

Daphne Eleanor, *b* 1945: *m* 1969, Jonathan Wheeler, of 19 Glebe Place, SW3, and has issue living, Robert Frederick William George, *b* 1972; *ed* Harrow, and Bristol Univ.

WIDOW LIVING OF THIRD BARONET

DIANE ELEANOR ABDY (*Diane, Lady White*), da of late Bernard Abdy Collins, CIE, of Deccan House, Aldeburgh: *m* 1939, Sir George Stanley Midelton White, 3rd Bt, who *d* 1983. *Residence* – Acton House, Park Street, Iron Acton, nr Bristol.
The 1st baronet, Sir George White, head of the firm of George White and Co, of Bristol, was one of the pioneers of Electric Street Traction (being the first to introduce it into London, Dublin, Bristol, Middlesbrough, etc), and established the first manufactory of aeroplanes in England and introduced "Bristol" biplanes and monoplanes.

WHITE (UK) 1922, of Salle Park, Norfolk

Go forward not back

Sir JOHN WOOLMER WHITE, 4th *Baronet*; *b* 4 Feb 1947; *ed* Cheltenham Coll; *s* his father, *Sir* HEADLEY DYMOKE, 1971; *ed* Cheltenham, and RAC Cirencester: *m* 1987, Joan, da of late T. D. Borland, of Flemington, W Linton, Peeblesshire, and has issue.

𝕬rms – Quarterly, 1st and 4th, argent, a fesse chequy gules and or, over all a bend engrailed azure, an arrow point downwards of the field, *White*; 2nd and 3rd, azure, a lion rampant between four estoiles or, *Dymock*. 𝕮rest – A boar's head erased proper, pierced through the mouth with an arrow or.
Residence – Salle Park, Reepham, Norwich, Norfolk NR10 4SG.

SON LIVING

KYLE DYMOKE WILFRID, *b* 16 March 1988.

SISTERS LIVING

Morna, *b* 1944. —— Isabelle Sarah, *b* 1948.

UNCLE LIVING *(Son of 2nd baronet)*

Sir Lynton Stuart, MBE, TD, *b* 1916; *ed* Harrow, and Trin Coll, Camb (MA); DL of Hants; Member of Hants CC 1970, Vice-Chm 1976, Chm 1977-85; 2nd Lieut TA 1939; 1939-45 War in Far East (despatches, MBE); Hon Lt-Col RA, TA 1946; TARO 1948-71; MBE (Mil) 1943, Kt Bach 1985: *m* 1945, Phyllis Marie Rochfort, da of late Sir Newnham Arthur Worley, KBE, and has issue living, Anthony Douglas, *b* 1946, —— Richard Lynton, *b* 1953, —— Robert Newnham Stuart, *b* 1956: *m* 1989, Jennifer Elizabeth Anne, da of Rev Barry Hughes-Gibbs, of Pretoria, S Africa, —— Philip Dymoke (Chidden Farmhouse, Hambledon, Portsmouth, Hants), *b* 1958: *m* 1984, Fiona Elizabeth, da of James Lunn, of West Meon, Hants, and has issue living, Alexander Stuart Dymoke *b* 1986, —— Katharine Anne Rochfort, *b* 1949: *m* 1976, Christopher John Wernham, of Sydney, Aust. *Residence* – Oxenbourne House, East Meon, nr Petersfield, Hants.

AUNTS LIVING *(Daughters of 2nd baronet)*

Marguerite Isabelle (*Lady Martell*) (2 Marcuse Fields, Bosham, Chichester, W Sussex PO18 8NA), *b* 1920: *m* 1941 (*m diss* 1983), Vice Adm Sir Hugh Colenso Martell, KBE, CB, and has issue living, Richard James, *b* 1942: *m* 1966 (*m diss* 1991), Theresa Hannah Wickins, and has issue living, Jonathan James *b* 1969, Jeremy Paul *b* 1971, Emma Jane *b* 1979, —— Stuart

(Flat 26, Neville's Court, Dollis Hill Lane, NW2), *b* 1943: *m* 1st, 1968 (*m diss* 1976), Penelope Gay, da of late Christopher Hunt: *m* 2ndly, 1978, Carol, only da of Lt-Col R. H. N. Simonds, of Aldwick Bay, W Sussex (Hickman, Bt, colls), and has issue living, (by 1st *m*), Benjamin Stuart *b* 1969, Christopher Hugh Stuart *b* 1973, — Charles, *b* 1946: *m* 1968, Monica, da of Martin Gillman, of Gloucester, and has issue living, Charles Edward *b* 1971, Elizabeth *b* 1969, — Timothy Hugh, *b* 1952: *m* 1973, Elizabeth Grazyna, da of Frank Szostak, and has issue living, Marcus Timothy *b* 1977, John Robert *b* 1981, — Michael Gordon *b* (twin) 1952: *m* 1981, Fiona Jane, da of W. C. Dack, of Worthing, and has issue living, William Michael *b* 1986, Natalie Fiona *b* 1981, — Sarah Jessica, *b* 1957. —— Hélène Pauline *b* 1924; MA: *m* 1954, Lt-Col William Neville Cairns, King's Dragoon Gds (ret), who *d* 1973, and has issue living, Jeremy Dymoke Russell, *b* 1955: *m* 1984, Teresa Jane, da of Gene L. Lewis, of Rocky Mount, N Carolina, USA, — Patrick Neville, *b* 1957. *Residence* – Alderton House, New Ross, co Wexford.

WIDOW LIVING OF THIRD BARONET

ELIZABETH VICTORIA MARY (*Elizabeth, Lady White*) (Salle Park, Reepham, Norfolk), da of late Wilfrid Ingram Wrightson (*see* Wrightson, Bt, colls): *m* 1943, Sir Headley Dymoke White, 3rd Bt, who *d* 1971.

Sir Woolmer White, 1st baronet, was son of late Maj Timothy White, of Salle Park, Norfolk.

WHITE (UK) 1937, of Boulge Hall, co Suffolk

NON·SIBI·SED·ALIIS

Not for self but for others

Sir CHRISTOPHER ROBERT MEADOWS WHITE, 3rd *Baronet*; *b* 26 Aug 1940; *s* his father, *Sir* (ERIC) RICHARD MEADOWS, 1972; *ed* Bradfield Coll: *m* 1st, 1962 (*m diss* 1968), Anne Marie Ghislaine, yr da of late Maj Tom Brown, OBE, MC; 2ndly, 1968 (*m diss* 1972), Dinah Mary Sutton; 3rdly, 1976, Ingrid Carolyn, el da of Eric Jowett, of Gt Baddow, Essex.

Arms – Gules, a chevron nebuly between three boars' heads couped, two flaunches argent each charged with a cross patée of the field. **Crest** – In front of a demi tower gules, issuant therefrom, a boar's head argent, tusked and maned or, charged on the neck with a cross patée also gules, three crosses patée also argent.
Address – c/o Mrs Steinschaden-Silver, Hangersley House, Hangersley, Ringwood, Hants BH24 3JU.

AUNTS LIVING (*Daughters of 1st baronet*)

Elizabeth Margaret, *b* 1906: *m* 1941, William Elwyn Francis Evans, formerly Sqdn Ldr RAFVR, and has issue living, Charles William (Wayton House, Landulph, Saltash, Cornwall), *b* 1942; MB, BS Lond, MFOM, MPH, DTM&H; Surg-Capt RN: *m* 1975, Christina M. Cameron, and has issue living, Marion Elizabeth Victoria *b* 1976, Rachel Fiona Clare *b* 1978, Veronica Lucy Margaret *b* 1982, — Sarah Margaret, *b* 1946: *m* 1st, 1976 (*m diss* 1993), Maj Peter Hibbert; 2ndly, 1993, Edwin Steinschaden-Silver, of Hangersley House, Ringwood, Hants BH24 3JU, and has issue living (by 1st *m*), Venetia Sarah *b* 1977. *Residence* – Godshill Wood, Godshill, Fordingbridge, Hants. —— Esther Dorothy, *b* 1914; formerly 3rd Officer WRNS: *m* 1943, Lt-Cdr John Michael Chappell, RN, and has issue living, Rodney Guy Eaton (Clathy House, Crieff, Perthshire), *b* 1944; Lt RN: *m* 1971, Sarah M. Bromhead, and has issue living, Katharine Mary *b* 1972, Isobel Dorothy Denise *b* 1975, Emily Jane *b* 1980, — David Nigel, *b* 1946; Maj 9th/12th R Lancers. *Residence* – Bayfield House, Darby Green, nr Camberley, Surrey.

The 1st baronet, Sir Robert Eaton White, VD (son of late Robert Holmes White, of Boulge Hall, Suffolk), was a JP and DL for Suffolk, and Chm of E Suffolk Quarter Sessions, and Co Council, and served during European War 1914-17 as Lieut-Col Comdg 14th Batn Suffolk Regt (TF).

White (Jervis-White-Jervis), see Jervis.

DALRYMPLE-WHITE (UK) 1926, of High Mark, co Wigtown

Sir HENRY ARTHUR DALRYMPLE DALRYMPLE-WHITE, DFC, 2nd *Baronet*; *b* 5 Nov 1917; *s* his father, *Lieut-Col Sir* GODFREY DALRYMPLE, 1954; *ed* Eton, Magdalene Coll, Camb and London Univ; formerly Wing-Com RAF Vol Reserve; European War 1939-45 (DFC and Bar): *m* 1948 (*m diss* 1956), Mary, da of Capt Robert Thomas, and has issue.

Arms – Quarterly, 1st and 4th, vert a naval crown or between three roses argent, barbed and seeded proper, in centre chief an escutcheon argent charged with a representation of the gold medal presented to Adm Sir John Chambers White for his services in Egypt in the year 1801, pendant from a riband tenné, *White*; 2nd and 3rd, or, on a saltire azure between two water bougets in pale sable nine lozenges of the field, *Dalrymple*. **Crest** – 1st issuant from a coronet composed of four roses set upon a rim or a lion's head argent, *White*; 2nd, in front of a rock proper water bouget sable, *Dalrymple*.
Address – c/o Aero Club of East Africa, PO Box 40813, Nairobi, Kenya.

Virtus · sibi · munus

Virtue is worth

SON LIVING

JAN HEW, *b* 26 Nov 1950; *ed* Stowe, Huddersfield Poly, and Stirling Univ.
Sir Godfrey Dalrymple Dalrymple-White, 1st Bt (son of Gen Sir Henry Dalrymple White, KCB, who commanded 6th Inniskilling Dragoons throughout Crimean War), was Lieut-Col Grenadier Guards, served in S Africa 1900-02 and in European War 1914-18. He assumed by deed poll 1926, the additional surname of Dalrymple, and sat as MP for Southport Div of Lancashire (C) 1910-18, and for Southport 1918-23 and 1924-31.

WHITEHEAD (UK) 1889, of Highfield House, Catford Bridge, Kent.

Sir ROWLAND JOHN RATHBONE WHITEHEAD, 5th *Baronet*; *b* 24 June 1930; *s* his father *Major Sir* PHILIP HENRY RATHBONE, 1953; *ed* Radley, and Trin Hall, Camb (BA 1953); late 2nd Lieut RA; Chm of the Standing Council of the Baronetage 1984-87, Member Cttee since 1981; Chm and Trustee of Rowland Hill Benevolent Fund since 1982, Founder and Chm of The Baronets' Trust since 1984, and Gov of Appleby Gram Sch; Freeman of City of Lond and Liveryman of the Fruiterers' Co: *m* 1954, Marie-Louise, da of late Arnold Christian Gausel, of Stavanger, Norway, and has issue.

Arms – Per pale azure and sable, on a fesse invected and plain cottised or between three fleurs-de-lis of the last, a fasces erect between two eagles' heads erased proper. **Crest** – An eagle, wings expanded proper, each wing charged with a fasces erect or, supporting with the dexter claw an escutcheon of the arms.
Residences – Walnut Tree Cottage, Fyfield, Lechlade, Glos GL7 3LT; Sutton House, Chiswick Mall, W4 2PR. *Club* – Arts.

By pluck and work

VIRTUTE ET LABORE

SON LIVING

PHILIP HENRY RATHBONE, *b* 13 Oct 1957; *ed* Eton, and Bristol Univ; late Welsh Guards: *m* 1987, Emma Charlotte, da of Capt Alexander Michael Darley Milne Home, RN (ret) (*see* E Minto, colls, 1970 Edn), of Sydney, Australia. *Residence* – 8 Herbert Crescent, SW1X 0EZ. *Clubs* – Cavalry and Guards', Special Forces.

DAUGHTER LIVING

Philippa Martha Gausel (*Hon Mrs Frederick C. A. Hamilton*), *b* 1955: *m* 1st, 1976 (*m diss* 1988), Brian James Douglas Collins (*see* E Morton); 2ndly, 1991, as his 2nd wife, Frederick Carmichael Arthur, Master of Belhaven, son of 13th Lord Belhaven and Stenton, and has issue, (by 1st *m*) (*see* E Morton), — (by 2nd *m*) (*see* L Belhaven and Stenton). *Address* – c/o Coutts & Co Ltd, 15 Lombard St, EC3.

COLLATERAL BRANCHES LIVING

Issue of late Dr Peter James Palmer Whitehead, PhD, yr (twin) son of 4th baronet, *b* 1930, *d* 1992: *m* 1st, 1953 (*m diss* 1960), Monica, who *d* 1969, only da of James O'Dwyer, of Tipperary; 2ndly, 1967, Greta Maureen Caecelia (Sud-de-Villiage, 65670 Monleon Magnoac, Hautes Pyrénées, France), da of late Capt Frederick John Ransom, of Greenwich:—
(By Mrs Mavis Argwings-Kodhek (*née* Tate), who *d* 1968, of Armagh, and Kenya) Paul James (51 Lydalls Rd, Didcot, Oxon), *b* 1961: *m* 1993, Anne-Marie Mulcahy, and has issue living, Thomas Harrison, *b* 1991. —— Amanda Oonagh, *b* 1960: *m* 1987, Paul Lloyd Griffiths, of 22 Tavistock Av, Didcot, Berks, and has issue living, William Kai, *b* 1987, — Luke Aidan, *b* 1989. —— (By 2nd *m*) Peter Rathbone Palmer, *b* 1970. —— Victoria-Augusta Gordon Rathbone, *b* 1968.

Issue of late Lt-Col Gilbert Rathbone Whitehead, TD, yr son of 3rd baronet, *b* 1910, *d* 1968: *m* 1934, Adeline Joy, MA, only child of late Sydney F. Rumball, of St Leonards-on-Sea:—
Gilia Fleur (11 Fyfield Rd, Oxford), *b* 1936; MA Oxon, BSc London: *m* 1960 (*m diss* 19—), Martin Oliver Slocock, and has issue living, Oliver Rowland Benjamin, *b* 1964. — Thomas Gilbert, *b* 1969. — Eleanor Sophia (twin), *b* 1964. —— Celia Lynette, *b* 1939: *m* 1970, Edward Raphael Rowe, of 23 Portsmouth Av, Thames Ditton, Surrey KT7 0RU, and has issue living, Russell Stephen, *b* 1978. — Anthea Rosalind, *b* 1976. —— Anthea Margaret Joy, *b* 1943; MA Edinburgh: *m* 1972, John Valentine Hutchinson, of 2 The Green North, Warborough, Oxon.

Grandchildren of late Lt-Col Wilfred James Whitehead, DSO, 4th son of 1st baronet:—
Issue of late John Chase Whitehead, MBE, *b* 1913, *d* 1956: *m* 1941, Lorna Davey, who *d* 1974, da of Walter Rupert Belk:—

Carolyn, *b* 1946: *m* 1967, Patrick Geoghegan Smyth, BA, and has issue living, Dominic, *b* 1970, — Siobhan, *b* 1972, — Bridget, *b* 1974. —— Saffron Ann, *b* 1948; BSc, PhD: *m* 1st, 1974 (*m diss* 1977), Christopher Robert Butler, BSc, PhD; 2ndly, 1978, John Kenneth Davies, BSc, of 265 Burntwood Lane, SW17 0AW, and has issue living (by 2nd *m*), Thomas John, *b* 1978, — Daniel Lloyd, *b* 1980, — Lewis Robert, *b* 1983. —— Nicola Jane (265 The Parkway, Iver Heath, Bucks SL0 0RJ), *b* 1956; BSc, PhD, ARCS, DIC, CBiol, MIBiol: has issue (by Ian Stuart Thomas Fisher), Benjamin Alexander, *b* 1991, — Rebecca Emily, *b* 1990.

The 1st baronet, Sir James, was Lord Mayor of London 1888-9, and sat as MP for Leicester (*L*) 1892-4; his Baronetcy was conferred upon him "in recognition of highly valuable services during an eventful Mayoralty," in the course of which he was instrumental in settling the great Dock Strike. The 3rd baronet, Sir Rowland Edward, KC, sat as MP for Essex, S-E Div (*L*) 1906-10. Sir Philip Henry Rathbone Whitehead, 4th Bt, was Major Oxfordshire and Bucks LI, a Gov of Appleby Gram Sch, and a Trustee of Rowland Hill Benevolent Fund.

HUNTINGTON-WHITELEY (UK) 1918, of Grimley, Worcester

Sir Hugo Baldwin Huntington-Whiteley, 3rd *Baronet*; *b* 31 March 1924; *s* his father *Capt Sir* (Herbert) Maurice, RN, 1975; *ed* Eton; FCA; a DL of Worcs; High Sheriff 1971; 1939-45 War with RN (despatches); Prime Warden of Goldsmiths' Co 1989: *m* 1959, Jean Marie Ramsay, JP, DStJ, da of late Arthur Francis Ramsay Bock, and has two das.

Arms – 1st and 4th, per fesse dancette sable and gules in chief a pale or, thereon three bars of the second, in base a fleur-de-lis argent, *Whiteley*; 2nd and 3rd or, on a pale between two roses in fesse gules, barbed and seeded proper, a lion rampant between two water bougets of the first, *Huntington*. Crests – 1st, a stag's head couped argent, attired or, holding in the mouth a bell gold, *Whiteley*; 2nd, upon a mount vert a lion's head couped at the neck or, gorged with a collar vair between two roses gules, barbed, leaved and stalked proper, *Huntington*.
Residences – Ripple Hall, Tewkesbury, Glos GL20 6EY; Balleure, 71240 Etrigny, France.
Club – Brooks's.

DAUGHTERS LIVING

Sophie Elizabeth *b* 1964: *m* 1988, Dr Steven Michael Zdatny, eldest son of W. J. Zdatny, of Florida, USA, and has issue living, Samuel Oliver, *b* 1993, — Isabelle, *b* 1990. —— Charlotte Anne, *b* 1965: *m* 1993, Andrew Philip McAuliffe, ACA.

BROTHER LIVING

(John) Miles, VRD (6 Matheson Rd, W14 8SW), *b* 18 July 1929; *ed* Eton, and Trin Coll, Camb; Lt-Cdr RNR; VRD and two clasps: *m* 1960, Countess Victoria Adelheid Clementine Luise, da of late Count Friedrich Wolfgang zu Castell-Rüdenhausen (Royal Family), and has issue living, Leopold Maurice, *b* 1965, — (Alice) Louise Esther Margot, *b* 1961: *m* 1985, (Charles) Percy Sewell (*see* Williams-Wynn, Bt, 1990 Edn), and has issue living, Henry Alexander *b* 1988, Benjamin Leopold *b* 1990, — Beatrice Irene Helen Victoria, *b* 1962.

COLLATERAL BRANCH LIVING

Issue of late Eric Arthur Huntington-Whiteley, yr son of 1st baronet, *b* 1903, *d* 1972: *m* 1st, 1929 (*m diss* 1938), Enid Etta Cohn, who *d* 1983; 2ndly, 1938, Evelyn Mary, who *d* 1978, da of late Henry Munt, and formerly wife of Denis Clarke:—

(By 1st *m*) Nigel Charles (The Cottage, Charlwood, Horley, Surrey RH6 0EB), *b* 1931; *ed* Radley: *m* 1956, Gillian Margaret, da of late Jacob Franks, MRCS, LRCP, and has issue living, Charles Andrew, *b* 1957; FRICS: *m* 1981, Fiona Yvonne, da of Alan Jackson, of Mythby, Weston Turville, Aylesbury, and has issue living, Toby Charles *b* 1989, Rosie Alice *b* 1987, Florence *b* 1992, — James Alexander, *b* 1963, — Kate Elizabeth, *b* 1959: *m* 1984, Peter Charles Lowry de Montfort, elder son of Charles Henry Cliffe de Montfort, of Skibbereen, co Cork, and has issue living, Guy Alexander *b* 1987, Charles Nicholas *b* 1989, Sean Thomas *b* 1994. —— Philip Cecil (Llangattock House, Penpergwm, Abergavenny, Gwent), *b* 1933; *ed* Radley: *m* 1968, Susan Laird, da of late Maj-Gen George Warren Richards, CB, CBE, DSO, MC, and has issue living, George Adam, *b* 1971, — Camilla Mary, *b* 1970.

The 1st baronet, Sir Herbert James Huntington-Whiteley (son of late George Whiteley, of Woodlands, Blackburn, and brother of 1st Baron Marchamley), was a JP for Lancs and Worcs (High Sheriff 1913), MP for Ashton-under-Lyne (*C*) 1895-1906, and for Mid, or Droitwich Div of Worcestershire 1916-18, and assumed by Roy licence 1918, for himself and issue, the additional surname and arms of Huntington. His wife, Florence Kate, who *d* 1948, was el da of William Balle Huntington, JP, DL, of Woodlands, Darwen, Lancs. The 2nd baronet, Sir Maurice, was a naval officer who served in both World Wars and was wounded at Jutland 1916. He was High Sheriff of Worcs 1968.

WHITMORE (UK)1954, of Orsett, co Essex

Sir JOHN HENRY DOUGLAS WHITMORE, 2nd *Baronet; b* 16 Oct 1937; *s* his father, *Col Sir* FRANCIS HENRY DOUGLAS CHARLTON, KCB, CMG, DSO, TD, TED, 1962; *ed* Eton; Sports Psychologist and currently Dep Dir of Centre for International Peacebuilding: *m* 1st, 1962 (*m diss* 1969), Ella Gunilla, el da of Sven A. Hansson, of Danderyd, Sweden; 2ndly, 1977, Diana Elaine, el da of Fred A. Becchetti, of California, USA, and has issue living by 1st and 2nd *m*.

Arms – Quarterly: 1st and 4th, vert, fretty or: 2nd and 3rd, vert, fretty and a canton or charged with a cinquefoil azure pierced of the second. **Crest** – 1st, a falcon sitting on the stump of a tree with a branch springing from the dexter side all proper; 2nd, an arm couped at the elbow erect and habited or, turned up azure, holding in the hand, proper a cinquefoil of the second pierced of the first, slipped vert, all within two wings expanded gold.
Residence – Southfield, Leigh, nr Tonbridge, Kent TN11 8PJ. *Club* – British Racing Drivers.

SON LIVING *(By 2nd marriage)*

JASON, *b* 26 Jan 1983.

DAUGHTER LIVING *(By 1st marriage)*

Tina, *b* 1966.

SISTER LIVING

Anne Catherine, *b* 1933: *m* 1966, Daniel Jose Emilio O'Connell (Presidente Roca 150, Adrogué, FCGR, Buenos Aires, Argentina), and has issue living, Lucy Elizabeth, *b* 1967, — Patricia Elena, *b* 1969, — Anna Elisa, *b* 1970.

MOTHER LIVING

Ellis Christense (*Ellis, Lady Whitmore*) (a DStJ), el da of Knud Christian Johnsen, of Bergen, Norway: *m* 1931, as his second wife, Col Sir Francis Henry Douglas Charlton Whitmore, KCB, CMG, DSO, TD, TED, 1st Bt, who *d* 1962.
Sir William Whitmore of London (descended from Whitmores of Claverley, Salop) purchased the estate of Apley, Salop and *d* 1648. His son, Sir Thomas Whitmore, was created a Bt 1641. This title became ext on the death of the 2nd Bt in 1699. The present baronet descends from Richard Whitmore of Lower Slaughter, Glos, brother of 1st Bt (*cr* 1641). Capt Thomas Charles Douglas Whitmore of Orsett Hall, Essex, father of 1st Bt (*cr* 1954), sold Apley in 1867.

WIGAN (UK) 1898, of Clare Lawn, Mortlake, Surrey, and Purland Chase, Ross, Herefordshire

Sir ALAN LEWIS WIGAN, 5th *Baronet; b* 19 Nov 1913; *s* his brother *Sir* FREDERICK ADAIR, 1979; *ed* Eton, and Magdalen Coll, Oxford; former Dir of Charrington and Co (Brewers); Capt KRRC (Reserve of Officers); 1939-45 War (wounded, prisoner): *m* 1950, Robina, da of Lt-Col Sir Iain Colquhoun of Luss, 7th Bt, KT, DSO, LLD, and has issue.

Arms – Vair, on a pile or a mount in base vert, thereon a mountain ash tree proper. **Crest** – On a mount vert a mountain ash tree surmounted by a rainbow, all proper.
Residence – Badingham House, Badingham, Woodbridge, Suffolk IP13 8JP.

SON LIVING

MICHAEL IAIN (Borrobol, Kinbrace, Sutherland KW11 6UB), *b* 3 Oct 1951; *ed* Eton, and Exeter Coll, Oxford: *m* 1st, 1984 (*m diss* 1985), Frances, da of late Fl Lt Angus Barr Faucett, and Mrs Antony Reid, of Balnakilly, Kirkmichael, Perthshire; 2ndly, 1989, Julia Teresa, eldest da of John de Courcy-Ling, MEP, and has issue living (by 2nd *m*), Fergus Adam, *b* 30 April 1990, — Thomas Iain *b* 1993, — Lillias Margaret, *b* 1992.

DAUGHTER LIVING

Rebecca, *b* 1953: *m* 1st, 1976 (*m diss* 1978), John Dominic Spearman (*see* Spearman, Bt, colls); 2ndly, 1980 (*m diss* 1986), James Alwyne Compton, (*see* M Northampton, colls); 3rdly, 1991, Nicolas Pascal Camu, of 65 Finlay St, SW6 (*see* Crossley, Bt, colls).

Make use of your opportunity

COLLATERAL BRANCHES LIVING

Grandchildren of late Denis Grey Wigan (infra):—
Issue of late Maj Adair Michael Charles Wigan, Coldstream Gds Reserve of Officers, *b* 1916, *d* 1993: *m* 1939, Dawn (West Blagdon, Cranborne, Dorset), da of Charles Wilfred Gordon, of Boveridge Park, Cranborne, Salisbury:—
James Adair (Biddlesgate Farm, Cranborne, Dorset BH21 5RS; *Club* – White's), *b* 1950: *m* 1977 (*m diss* 1991), Rose Cecilia, elder da of John Johnston Kirkpatrick, FLAS, FRICS, of Horn Park, Beaminster, Dorset (*see* Loder, Bt, colls), and has issue

living, Harry Edward, *b* 1986, — Thomas Adair, *b* 1986, — Emma Charlotte, *b* 1983. —— Dominic Richard Ludlow (Rose Cottage, Martin, Fordingbridge, Hants), *b* 1951: *m* 1989, Julia, only da of late Richard Russell, of Newnham Manor, Daventry, Northants, and has issue living, Anna Jessie, *b* 1991. —— Lola Dawn, *b* 1940. —— Camilla Rose, *b* 1944.

Issue of late Denis Grey Wigan, 3rd son of 2nd baronet, *b* 1893, *d* 1958: *m* 1915, Madeline Mabel Ambrose, who *d* 1969, da of Charles Robert Whorwood Adeane, CB (B Leconfield colls):—
Elizabeth Sibell Isabel, *b* 1918: *m* 1937, Humphrey Gascoigne, who *d* 1992, of Wyndham House, Wickham Market, Suffolk, yst son of late Brig-Gen Sir (Ernest) Frederick (Orby) Gascoigne, KCVO, CMG, DSO, and has issue living, David Clive, *b* 1939; *ed* Eton; Maj RGJ Reserve of Officers: *m* 1964, Deirdre Cecil Hermione, da of Lt-Col Alec C. S. Moore, of Whites Meadow, Bicknoller, Som, and has issue living, Dominic William Wigan *b* 1965, Tobias Charles Humphrey *b* 1971, Nichola Elizabeth Blanche *b* 1968, — Martin Wyndham, *b* 1944; *ed* Eton; — Anthony Grey, *b* 1947; *ed* Gordonstoun: *m* 1970 (*m diss* 1985), Hon Olivia Clare Teresa Brett, da of 4th Viscount Esher, CBE, and has issue (*see* V Esher).
The 1st baronet, Sir Frederick Wigan, son of late John Alfred Wigan, of Clare House near Maidstone, a Director of North London Railway, and High Sheriff of cos London and Surrey 1894, *d* March 1907, and his son, Sir Frederick William, 2nd baronet, *d* in April of same year.

WIGGIN (UK) 1892, of Metchley Grange, Harborne, Staffordshire

Sir CHARLES RUPERT JOHN WIGGIN, 5th *Baronet*; *b* 2 July 1949; *s* his father, Sir JOHN HENRY, MC, 1992; *ed* Eton; Maj Gren Guards: *m* 1979, Mrs Mary Burnett-Hitchcock, only da of Brig Samuel Craven Chambers, CBE, and has issue.

Arms – Gules, three mullets of six points argent, on a chief invected or two spurs sable. **Crest** – Over a fleur-de-lis sable, a spur or between two wings erect proper, each charged with a fleur-de-lis of the first.
Address – c/o Child & Co, 1 Fleet St, EC4Y 1BD.

SON LIVING

RICHARD EDWARD JOHN, *b* 1 July 1980.

DAUGHTER LIVING

Cecilia Charlotte, *b* 1984.

BROTHER LIVING

Benjamin Henry Edward, *b* 1951; *ed* Eton, and McGill Univ, Montreal.

HALF-BROTHERS LIVING

Daniel Mark, *b* 1964; *ed* Eton. —— Jeremy James, *b* 1966; *ed* Milton Abbey.

WIDOW LIVING OF FOURTH BARONET

SARAH (*Sarah, Lady Wiggin*), da of Brig Stewart Arthur Forster, late Coldm Gds: *m* 1963, as his 2nd wife, Sir John Henry Wiggin, 4th Bt, MC, who *d* 1992. *Residence* – Honington Hall, Shipston-on-Stour, Warwickshire.

COLLATERAL BRANCHES LIVING

Grandsons of late Alfred Harold Wiggin, 4th son of 1st baronet:—
Issue of late Col Sir William Henry Wiggin, KCB, DSO, TD, DL, JP, *b* 1888, *d* 1951: *m* 1935, Elizabeth Ethelston (Betty), who *d* 1959, da of late J. Danvers Power, MVO:—
Sir Alfred William (Jerry), TD, MP (The Court, Axbridge, Som; House of Commons, SW1; *Clubs*; Beefsteak, Pratt's, and R Yacht Squadron), *b* 1937; *ed* Eton, and Trin Coll, Camb; Maj The R Yeo (ret 1978); Hon Col "A" Sqdn (Warwickshire & Worcs Yeo), The Royal Mercian & Lancastrian Yeo, TA 1992; MP for Weston-super-Mare (C) since 1969: *m* 1st, 1964 (*m diss* 1982), Rosemary Janet, only da of David L. D. Orr, of Keithley, Sandhills, Wormley, Surrey; 2ndly, 1991, Mrs Morella C. M. Bulmer (*neé* Kearton), formerly wife of James Esmond Bulmer, and has issue living (by 1st *m*), William David, *b* 1966, — Thomas Henry, *b* 1969, — Audrey Mary *b* 1974. —— Henry Walter (Brockweir Farm, nr Chepstow, Gwent NP6 7NG), *b* 1939; *ed* Eton, and Trin Coll, Camb (MA); Solicitor 1965: *m* 1st, 1962 (*m diss* 1978), Hon Julia Redmond Vaughan-Morgan, da of Baron Reigate (Life Baron): *m* 2ndly, 1978 (*m diss* 1985), Robin Margaret, da of A. Campbell B. Linwood, of Wanganui, NZ, and formerly wife of David Erskine Tolhurst; 3rdly, 1986, Mrs Diana Anstey, da of late Adm Sir Robin Leonard Francis Durnford-Slater, KCB, and formerly wife of Simon Anstey, of Toronto, Canada, and has issue living, (by 1st *m*), Lucy Redmond, *b* 1965: *m* 1990, Joel Patrick Ford, of 1401 Narrow Lane # 3, Johnson City, Tennesse 37604, USA, son of Roy B. Ford, of San Antonio, Texas, — Caroline Julia, *b* 1970, — (by 2nd *m*), Jonathan Henry, *b* 1978.
Issue of late Lt-Col Richard Arthur Wiggin, TD, *b* 1903, *d* 1977: *m* 1952, Joan Mary, who *d* 1979, only da of late Smith Whitehead, of The Croft, Nelson:—
Margaret Joan, *b* 1954: *m* 1979, Christopher John Heath, of 7 Scarsdale Villas, W8, and has had issue, William Henry Christopher, *b* 1983.

Issue of late Brig-Gen Edgar Askin Wiggin, DSO, 5th son of 1st baronet, *b* 1867, *d* 1939: *m* 1906, Emilie Margaret, who *d* 1951, da of Arthur Keen, formerly of Sandyford, Edgbaston:—
Peter Milner, *b* 1907; *ed* Eton, and RMC; Lt-Col late 11th Hussars, and a JP for Hants (late Co Councillor); 1939-45 War in Middle East and NW Europe: *m* 1933, Margaret Frances, da of late Capt Noel Christian Livingstone-Learmonth, of Cleveland House, 19 St James's Sq, SW, and has had issue, †George David Henry, *b* 1934; *ed* Eton; late Lt 11th Hussars: *m* 1958, Jennifer (who *m* 2ndly, 1993, Charles Arthur Smith-Bingham), da of late Capt Ian Stanley Akers-Douglas (*see* V Chilston, colls), and *d* 1990, leaving issue, David Peter *b* 1960; *ed* Harrow; Lieut The Royal Hussars: *m* 1991, Susan Emma, yst (twin) da of Maj Robert Philip Burrowes, of Dorrington Priory, nr Lincoln (and has issue living, George Robert *b* 1994), James George *b* 1968; *ed* Eton; 2nd Lieut The Royal Hussars, Davina Jane *b* 1962: *m* 1986, Michael Gatehouse, yr son of Capt Richard Gatehouse, DSC, RN (ret), of Easton Farm House, Newbury, Berks (and has issue living, James Richard *b* 1987, Sophie Charlotte *b* 1989), — Michael Peter (Downton Hall, Ludlow, Shropshire), *b* 1937; *ed* Eton; late Lt 11th Hussars: *m* 1962, Victoria Zara, da of late Malcolm Vaughan, of Old Westfield Farm House, Moreton Morrell, Warwicks, and has issue

living, Mark David *b* 1963 *ed* Eton: *m* 1991, Philippa A., da of David Burrows, of Tetbury, Glos (and has issue living, Tara Daisy *b* 1994), Rupert Michael *b* 1969; *ed* Wellington, Miranda Zara *b* 1965: *m* 1990, Graham J. Walsh, of 456 Taconic Rd, Greenwich, Conn 06831, USA, son of Walter Walsh, of Barrow-in-Furness, Cumbria (and has issue living, Luke Walter *b* 1992, Zara Patricia *b* (twin) 1992) Kate Victoria *b* 1972, — Sara Margaret (*Viscountess Allenby*), *b* 1942: *m* 1965, 3rd Viscount Allenby (Newnham Lodge, Newnham, Basingstoke), and has issue (*see* V Allenby). *Residence* – Chapel Cottage, Plaistow Green, Headley, Newbury. *Club* – Cavalry and Guards'.

The 1st baronet, Sir Henry Samuel, sat as MP for E Staffordshire (*L*) 1880-85, and for Staffordshire, Handworth Div (*LU*) 1885-92. Sir Henry Arthur, 2nd baronet, was High Sheriff of Staffs 1896, and Col Sir Charles Richard, 3rd baronet, was High Sheriff of Warwicks 1942.

WIGRAM (UK) 1805, of Walthamstow, Essex

Sweet is the love of one's country

Rev Canon Sir CLIFFORD WOOLMORE WIGRAM, 7th *Baronet*, son of late Robert Ainger Wigram, son of late Rev Woolmore Wigram, 5th son of Money Wigram, 2nd son of 1st baronet; *b* 24 Jan 1911; *s* his uncle, *Sir* EDGAR THOMAS AINGER, 1935; *ed* Winchester, and Trin Coll, Camb (BA 1932, MA 1936); formerly V of Marston St Lawrence, with Warkworth and Thenford, near Banbury; Non-Residentiary Canon of Peterborough Cathedral 1973-83 since when Canon Emeritus: *m* 1948, Christobel Joan, who *d* 1983, da of late William Winter Goode, of Curry Rivel, Somerset, and widow of Eric Llewellyn Marriott, CIE.

𝕬rms – Argent, on a pale gules three escallops or; over all a chevron engrailed counterchanged, and on the chief waves of the sea, thereon a ship representing an English vessel of war of the 16th century, with four masts, sails furled proper, colors flying gules. 𝕮rest – On a mount vert, a hand in armour in fesse couped at the wrist proper charged with an escallop holding a fleur-de-lis erect or. 𝕾upporters – On either side an eagle with wings elevated argent, collared gules and charged on the breast with a shamrock vert.
Residence – 2 Mold Cottages, Marston St Lawrence, Banbury, Oxon OX17 2DB.

BROTHER LIVING

EDWARD ROBERT WOOLMORE (Hilliers Lodge, St Mary Bourne, nr Andover, Hants), *b* 19 July 1913: *ed* Winchester, and Trin Coll, Camb (BA 1934), sometime Major Indian Army; formerly a Master at Westminster Sch: *m* 1944, Viva Ann, da of late Douglas Bailey, of Laughton Lodge, nr Lewes, Sussex, and has issue living, Ann Catherine, *b* 1945: *m* 1973, Fredrik Procopé, and has issue living, Robert Hjalmar *b* 1974, Christopher Cresswell *b* 1976, Harry Michael *b* 1977.

COLLATERAL BRANCHES LIVING

Branch from 2nd son of 1st Baronet:—

Grandchildren of late Rev Woolmore Wigram, 5th son of late Money Wigram (*b* 1790), 2nd son of 1st baronet:—
Issue of late Arthur Woolmore Wigram, *b* 1875, *d* 1946: *m* 1911, Avis Marion, who *d* 1972, da of late Hartley Hartley-Smith, of Upwey, Dorset:—
Peter Woolmore (Red Lodge, 22 Chiltern Hills Rd, Beaconsfield, Bucks), *b* 1913; *ed* Trin Hall, Camb (BA 1934): *m* 1st, 1936 (*m diss* 1953), Ellen Brenda, da of late William Hill, of Rockferry, Cheshire; 2ndly, 1953, Sylvia Mary, da of late Rev John Smithson Barstow, of Woolsthorpe, by Belvoir, and has issue living, (by 2nd *m*) John Woolmore, *b* 1957, — Caroline Judith *b* 1955, — Sylvia Clare, *b* 1963. —— Daphne Marion Woolmore *b* 1919.

Grandson of late Robert Wigram, 5th son of late Money Wigram (*b* 1790) (ante):—
Issue of late Robert Wigram, *b* 1874, *d* 1932: *m* 1st, 1920, Adela Mabel, who *d* 1923, da of Richard Reid, of Bramcote, Weybridge; 2ndly, 1925, Winifred Maria, who *d* 1987, da of late Capt Phipps, 24th Regt:—
(By 2nd *m*) Francis John, *b* 1926; *ed* Eton. *Residence* – Cotters Barn, Penn, Bucks.

Branch from 5th son of 1st Baronet:—

Grandchildren of late Capt Ronald Scott Jervoise Wigram, DSO, RN, son of Henry James Wigram (infra):—
Issue of late Maj Henry Frederick James Wigram, DCLI, *b* 1916, *d* (Dec) 1984: *m* 1938, (Helen) Enid, who *d* (Oct) 1984, da of F. Clyde Smith, of Netherclay House, Bishop's Hull, Somerset:—
Roger Charles Kinglake (Annesley House, Exley Lane, Halifax, W Yorks HX5 0SW), *b* 1940; *ed* Wellington Coll; Capt Light Inf (ret): *m* 1965 (*m diss* 1982), Wendy Joan, who *d* 1985, eldest da of late Brig Philip Herbert Richardson, DSO, OBE, of The Manor House, Merriott, Som; 2ndly, 1983, Christine, da of late James Kenneth Pratt, and has issue living (by 1st *m*), Giselle Rose, *b* 1966, — Susanna Nicola, *b* 1968. —— James Somerset (Hilary House, Ashburton Rd, Bovey Tracey, Devon), *b* 1950; *ed* Nautical Coll, Pangbourne: *m* 1974, Susan Jane, only da of Bryan Braithwaite-Exley, of Pant Head, Austwick, Yorks, and has issue living, Thomas Peter James, *b* 1978, — William Henry James, *b* 1981, — Tessa Vera Joyce, *b* 1988. —— Sally Kinglake, *b* 1939: *m* 1st, 1972 (*m diss* 1982), William Arthur Rose, who *d* 1987; 2ndly, 19—, —Atton, and has issue living (by 1st *m*), Alan Kindred, *b* 1972. —— (Janet) Gail, *b* 1953: *m* 1975, Timothy Wallace Kyle, Lt RN (ret), of Zirlden, 51 Broomleaf Rd, Farnham, Surrey GU9 8DQ, and has issue living, Robert Henry Remington, *b* 1986, — Laura Rachel, *b* 1977, — Thea Helen, *b* 1981.

Granddaughter of late Henry James Wigram, el son of James Richard Wigram, el son of Rt Hon Sir James Wigram, 5th son of 1st baronet:—
Issue of late Major Cyril Charles Wigram, *b* 1882, *d* 1952: *m* 1st, 1912 (*m diss* 1917), Mabel Adams; 2ndly, 1918 (*m diss* 1928), Olivia Marie, who *d* 1970, da of late Maj-Gen W. Truman, of Winterbourne, Bonchurch, I of Wight; 3rdly, 1929, Mrs Dorothy Scott, who *d* 1938; 4thly, 1946, Elizabeth, who *d* 1970, da of late Dr F. E. Sondern, of New York, and widow of J. W. New:—

(By 2nd *m*) Isolde Marianne, *b* 1919. *Residence* – Greathed Manor, Lingfield, Surrey RH7 6PA.

Branch from 6th son of 1st Baronet:—

Grandchildren of late Charles Knox Wigram (*infra*):—
Issue of late Maj James Robert Knox Wigram, *b* 1915, *d* 1984: *m* 1942, Beatrice Elizabeth, who *d* 1984, da of late Rev W. A. Sandford, of Dunstable, Beds:—
Brian Arthur Knox (1 Chevin Bank, Hazlewood Rd, Duffield, Derby DE6 4AA), *b* 1947; *ed* Wellington: *m* 1982, Glynnis Anne, da of Maurice Owens, of Kilburn, Derbyshire. —— Michele Anne, *b* 1946; BA (Hons) Reading.

Grandchildren of late William Arthur Wigram, grandson of Octavius Wigram, 6th son of 1st baronet:—
Issue of late Charles Knox Wigram, *b* 1889, *d* 1966: *m* 1st, 1914, Gladys Mary (who *d* 1955, (*m diss* 1931)), da of late Rev Robert Edward Baynes (Preb of Combe); 2ndly, 1931, Margaret Esther, who *d* 1974, da of late Capt Henry Valentine Simpson, CMG, RN (ret):—
(By 1st *m*) Valentine Knox (c/o Barclays Bank, Horsham, Sussex), *b* 1920; *ed* Haileybury; late Cpl RAF; ARICS. —— (By 2nd *m*)Susan Alice Ann, *b* 1932; *ed* London Univ (BA): *m* 1965, Colin Scorer, of 11 Stuart Grove, Teddington, Middx TW11 8RR, and has an adopted son and an adopted da, Andrew Michael, *b* 1968, — Jane Sarah, *b* 1971. —— Jennifer Jane, *b* 1935: *m* 1967, Allen Griswold (c/o First San Francisco Bank, 260 Montgomery St, San Francisco, USA).

Grandchildren (by 2nd *m*) of late Charles Knox Wigram (*ante*):—
Issue of late Patrick Knox Wigram, *b* 1937, *d* 1992: *m* 1964, Susan Mary Fyers (Peterport, Lavender Rd, Maybury, Woking, Surrey), da of Col A.R.F. Martin, of Camberley, Surrey:—
Charles Robert Knox, *b* 1968. —— Sandra Jane Fyers, *b* 1965. —— Julia Margaret Fyers, 1967.

Branch from 8th son of 1st Baronet:—

Grandchildren of late Gerrard Andrewes Wigram, 2nd son of Rt Rev Joseph Cotton Wigram, DD, Bishop of Rochester, 8th son of 1st baronet:—
Issue of late Rev Gerrard Edmund Wigram, *b* 1877, *d* 1947: *m* 1902, Maria Ismèna, who *d* 1944, 2nd da of late William Townson-Mayne:—
Francis Gerrard Mayne, *b* 1905; formerly Regional Officer, Coal Utilization Council, and an Asso Member of Institute of Fuel: *m* 1934, Helen Frances, who *d* 1990, younger da of late Dr Sidney Worthington, of Warwick, and has issue living, Gerrard Charles (Lenana, 25 Duckitt Av, Constantia 7800, S Africa), *b* 1936; FCA, and a CA, S Africa: *m* 1965, Joan Patricia, da of late James Lang, of Nairobi, and has issue living, Keith Gerrard *b* 1969, Zena Patricia Jean *b* 1966, Eileen Frances *b* 1972, — Nigel Francis (8 Heseldon Av, Rondesboch, Cape Town, S Africa), *b* 1939; CCS, BCom, MBA, PhD: *m* 1974, Lynette Monique, da of Dr Leon Stern, of Kenilworth, Cape Town, and has issue living, Andrew David *b* 1976, — Deborah Helen, *b* 1938: *m* 1961, Capt Richard Hugh Farnfield, RN, of The Rydings, Park Rd, Forest Row, Sussex RH18 5BX, and has issue living, Anthony Gilbert *b* 1963, Andrew Richard *b* 1970, Timothy Francis *b* 1971: *m* 1993, Belinda Alice Irene, da of Oliver Preston Benn (*see* Benn, *cr* 1914, colls), Helen Rosemary *b* 1965: *m* 1993, Mark Jeremy Moore-Gillon, MA, PhD, son of J. A. Moore-Gillon, of Surbiton. *Residence* – 132 Bridgewater Manor, Somerset West 7130, Cape Province, S Africa. —— Marion Rochford (Quarndon Hill, 78 The Common, Quarndon, Derbys DE6 4JY), *b* 1909: *m* 1930, William Hadden Richardson, who *d* 1968, and has issue living, James Hadden (Fern Hill, Quarndon, Derbys), *b* 1937: *m* 1961, Susan Mary, only da of J. H. K. Thomson, of Derby, and has issue living, Nicholas Hadden *b* 1963: *m* 1991, Lynn Clements (and has issue living, Katherine Jane *b* 1992, Susannah Mary *b* 1994), Timothy James Keith *b* 1970, Wendy Diana *b* 1965, — Judith Mary (Flat 4B, The Lillies, Windley, Derbys DE6 2LQ), *b* 1934: *m* 1963, John Swain Yeomans, and has issue living, Philip Hadden *b* 1964: *m* 1990, Louise Dale (and has issue living, Bethany Angela *b* 1991, Charlotte Rowena *b* 1993).

Branch from 11th son of 1st Baronet:—

Grandsons of late Rev Edmund Francis Edward Wigram, son of late Rev Frederic Edward Wigram, el son of late Edward Wigram, 11th son of 1st baronet:—
Issue of late Rev Oswald Thomas Edward Wigram, *b* 1905, *d* 1990: *m* 1935, Margaret (Scotleigh Lodge, 76 Old Exeter St, Chudleigh, Devon TQ13 0JX), da of late R.N. Barnes, of Sutton Coldfield:—
Robert Edmund (93 Investigator St, Red Hill, ACT, Australia), *b* 1936: *m* 1963, Patricia, da of L.C. Collisson, of Liverpool, NSW, and has issue living, Simon Andrew, *b* 1967: *m* 1987, Caroline Threlfall, — Christopher Anthony, *b* 1977, — Frances Elizabeth, *b* 1964, — Louise Annette, *b* 1966: *m* 1987, Anthony Fryer, and has issue living, Amy Louise *b* 1994. —— Paul Frederic (PO Box 308, Karuri, Kenya), *b* 1937; *ed* Marlborough, and Pembroke Coll, Camb (MA): *m* 1963, Christian Virginia, da of Maj H.A.R. Bucknall, MC, and has issue living, Thomas Paul Henry, *b* 1964, — Lucy Helen Gabrielle, *b* 1966, — Bronwen Serena Christian, *b* 1971. —— *Rev* Andrew Oswald (St Michael's Vicarage, Westcliff-on-Sea, Essex), *b* 1939; *ed* Marlborough; BD London: *m* 1964, Catharine, da of late Rev Canon Geoffrey Rogers, of 37 Bradford Park, Foxhill, Combe Down, Bath, and has issue living, Mark Nicholas, *b* 1967: *m* 1989, Rachel, da of Rev Guy Chapman, and has issue living, David James *b* 1991, Hannah Catharine *b* 1992, — Susanna Dora, *b* 1966, — Margaret Jane Majala, *b* 1970. —— Francis Aidan (Riggles Farm, Upottery, Honiton, Devon), *b* 1949; *ed* Marlborough, and Seale Hayne Agric Coll: *m* 1973, Christine Susan, da of late T.E. Abbey, of Tilney, Sellicks Green, Taunton, and has issue living, Timothy Francis, *b* 1974, — Richard James, *b* 1976, — Nicholas Mark, *b* 1977. —— *Rev* Ruth Margaret (7 Princes Drive, Skipton, N Yorks BD23 1HN), *b* 1941; *ed* St Michael's, Limpsfield, and Salisbury Training Coll.
Issue of late Lieut Aidan Frederic Wigram, RNVR, *b* 1907, *k* on air operations 1941: *m* 1938, Marjorie Joyce, who *d* 1963, da of late Lt-Col E. R. I. Chitty, Indian Army:—
Aidan David (High Timbers, Hartley Rd, Cranbrook, Kent, TN17 3QX), *b* 1938; *ed* Marlborough, and Univ of Wales (BSc): *m* 1968, Jeniffer Ann, da of E. N. Firmager, of Godstone, Surrey, and has issue living, Lesley Rosalind, *b* 1969.
Issue of late Edmund Hugh Lewis Wigram, MB, BCh, *b* 1911, *d* 1945: *m* 1938, Kathleen Maud (who *m* 2ndly, 1948 (*m diss* 1968)), Christopher Henry Kaye, BM, BCh (Wigram Bt, colls), yr da of late L. C. S. Hallam, of Port Arthur, Canada:—
Peter Hallam (4067 Grey Av, Montreal, PQ H4A 3N9, Canada), *b* 1939: *m* 19— (*m diss* 19—), Michelle —. —— Edmund William (Boghouse, Blagdon, Seaton Burn, Newcastle-upon-Tyne NE13 6DB), *b* 1942: *m* 1965, Diana Frances, da of Anthony Douglas Bell, MB, BS, of Sanday Is, via Kirkwall, Orkney, and has issue living, Anthony Christopher *b* 1966, — Clare Frances *b* 1969.

Grandchildren of late Rev Beresford Edward Wigram (*infra*):—
Issue of late Rev Marcus Walter Wigram, *b* 1917, *d* 1989: *m* 1941, Christina Cantrell (5 Riverway, South Cerney, Cirencester, Glos GL7 6HZ):—
Ann Margaret Joyce, *b* 1942: *m* 1964, Derek William Blandford, of 176 Watleys End Rd, Winterbourne, Bristol, and has issue living, Andrew Paul, *b* 1966, — Ian Keith, *b* 1969, — Kieron John, *b* 1971. —— Carol Frances Violet WIGRAM (8 Saxon Rd, Faversham, Kent), *b* 1946; resumed her maiden name: *m* 1976 (*m diss* 1989), Peter Guilderoy Croskin, and has issue living, Jonathan Guilderoy *b* 1978. —— Sarah Christina Agnes, *b* 1949: *m* 1970, Humphrey David Lane, of Huckstones, Cottons Lane, Ashton-under-Hill, Evesham, Worcs, and has issue living, Bridget Anna, *b* 1972, — Corinne Victoria, *b* 1974, — Kathryn Alice, *b* 1978. —— Jane Eleanor Bridget, *b* 1954: *m* 1st, 1971 (*m diss* 1986), Mark Christian Eckersley; 2ndly, 1988,

Kenneth William Augustus Robeson, of Norview, Penstowe Rd, Kilkhampton, Bude, Cornwall, and has issue living (by 1st *m*), Naomi Jane, *b* 1974, — Samantha Claire, *b* 1979.

Grandchildren of late Rev Frederic Edward Wigram (ante):—
Issue of late Rev Beresford Edward Wigram, *b* 1870, *d* 1917: *m* 1901, Jessie Violet, who *d* 1939, da of late Walter Scott of Tunbridge Wells:—
Joyce Marjorie (Swarthmore, Marsham Lane, Gerrards Cross, Bucks SL9 8HB), *b* 1905; *ed* London Univ (MB and BS 1930).
Issue of late Rev Harold Frederic Edward Wigram, *b* 1873, *d* 1946: *m* 1913, Gladys Christine, who *d* 1985 (aged 100), da of Sir Howard Warburton Elphinstone, 3rd Bt:—
Andrew Harold (17 Albury Rd, Newcastle-upon-Tyne, NE2 3PE), *b* 1919; *ed* Wellington Coll, and Trin Hall, Camb (BA); Maj RA (ret): *m* 1953, Alice Jefferson Trewhitt, who *d* 1989. —— Alexander Robert, *b* 1925; *ed* Wellington Coll, and Brasenose Coll, Oxford (MA): *m* 1958, Virginia Claire, da of late Group Capt Philip Patrick Strachan Rickard, OBE, and has issue living, Kester Jonathan, *b* 1959; *ed* Univ of Canterbury, NZ (BE Chem); C Eng, I Chem E: *m* 1983 (*m diss* 1989), Lynn, da of James Davidson, and has issue living, Elliot Simon *b* 1984, — Nicholas Simon, *b* 1960, — Luke, *b* 1977, — Sarah Christine, *b* 1963, — Aroha Kirsty, *b* 1975. *Address* - Le Bons Bay, Rural Delivery, Akaroa, Banks Peninsula, NZ. —— Gladys Veronica, *b* 1916: *m* 1st, 1938, Lt William George Player Brigstock, RNVR (*ka* 1940); 2ndly, 1943, Reginald Charles Grisedale Fennell, of The Old Vicarage, Moulsford, nr Wallingford, Oxon OX10 9JB, and has issue living (by 2nd *m*), Robert John (Kilve House, 315 Andover Rd, Newbury, Berks RG15 0WY), *b* 1944; ARICS (1970); *ed* Oundle: *m* 1975, Phoebe Joscelyn, da of Gordon Wilfred Langley-Smith, of 19 Kenilworth Av, Gloucester, and has issue living, Thomas Edward *b* 1979, Anthea Sarah *b* 1977, Megan *b* 1986, — William Richard Kenneth (22 Place Farm Way, Monks Risborough, Bucks HP17 9JH), *b* 1952; ARICS (1977); *ed* Oundle, and Birmingham Univ (BSc): *m* 1979, Sylvia Mary, da of Wilfred Fletcher, and has issue living, Margaret Ann *b* 1983. —— Rose Eleanor, *b* 1923: *m* 1954, Richard Edward Barry, of 11 Swalecliffe Rd, Tankerton, Whistable, Kent CT5 2PR, and has issue living, John Andrew (27 Estridge Close, Lowford, Bursledon, Hants SO3 8FN), *b* 1958: *m* 1982, Marion, da of late Julian Warwick, and has issue living, Alistair James *b* 1988, Elaine Christine *b* 1990, — Sylvia May, *b* 1956; BA: *m* 1976, Kim Marsh, of 127 Dene Rd, Wylam, Northumberland NE41 8EZ, and has issue living, Philip Robert *b* 1977.
Issue of late Loftus Edward Wigram, MB, *b* 1877, *d* 1963: *m* 1912, Constance Emma Letitia, who *d* 1970, da of late Rev William Gilbert Edwards, Surrogate of Oxford, and Hon Canon, formerly R of Great Haseley, Wallingford, Oxon, and Rural Dean of Cuddesdon:—
Gerald Frederic (Calverleigh Cottage, Tiverton, Devon EX16 8BB), *b* 1916; *ed* Marlborough; formerly Capt King's African Rifles: *m* 1948, Anne Christal, who *d* 1981, da of late Brig-Gen Hon Lesley James Probyn Butler, CMG, DSO (*see* B Dunboyne, colls), and has issue living, Carolyn Lesley, *b* 1950: *m* 1986, John Eastman Perry, and has issue living, Mark Andrew *b* 1987, Ben Jack *b* 1988, — Marylee Anne, *b* 1952, — Bridget Margaret, *b* 1954: *m* 1982, Jonathan Patrick Simmons, and has issue living, Michael Anthony *b* 1987, Anne Julia *b* 1985. —— Lettice Margaret, *b* 1920; *ed* Oxford Univ (BA 1942); formerly Section Officer WAAF: *m* 1951, Maj Edward Arthur Hadow, late RE, of 2 Highlands Park, Chudleigh, Devon TQ13 0JZ (M Anglesey, colls), and has issue living, John Wigram, *b* 1959: *m* 1988, Susan Frances, yr da of F.W. Naylor, of Totnes, Devon, and has issue living, George Louis *b* 1992, — Robert Edward, *b* 1968, — Rosemary Maude, *b* 1953: *m* 1st, 1974 (*m diss* 1988), David Ericson; 2ndly, 1989, Graham John White, and has issue living, (by 1st *m*) Daniel Dov *b* 1985, (by 2nd *m*) Rebecca Hadow *b* 1991, — Juliet Letitia, *b* 1955: *m* 1979, Graham Paul Herbert, and has issue living, Mark Graham *b* 1985, Emma Letitia *b* 1983, Rosanna Bethan *b* 1987, — Celia Catherine, *b* 1957: *m* 1984, Ian Cranston Shields, and has issue living, Joe *b* 1988, Kerry Mohira *b* 1985.

Granddaughter of late Rev Beresford Edward Wigram (ante):—
Issue of late Capt Winstone Beresford Wigram, *b* 1908, *d* 1988: *m* 1942, Adelaide Joyce (Dair), who *d* 1966, elder da of Rev William Aldworth Ferguson, DD:—
Erica Joyce, *b* 1943; BA Bristol: *m* 1970, Maj Ian Ferguson Sharp, RAOC, and has issue living, Jasper Henry Ferguson, *b* 1971, — Daniel William, *b* 1973. *Residence* - Slough House, Bishops Nympton, S Molton, Devon.

Granddaughters of late Loftus Edward Wigram MB (ante):—
Issue of late Michael Wigram, MRCS, LRCP, *b* 1919, *d* 1973: *m* 1945, Margaret Edith Ann (Crickerton, Buckfastleigh, S Devon), da of late W. E. Watson-Baker, of Toddington, Beds:—
Laurette, *b* 1946: *m* 1971, Brian Guest, of Wateroak, Ludgores Lane, Danbury, Chelmsford, Essex, and has issue living, William Michael, *b* 1974, — Josephine Briony, *b* 1972. —— Sarah Margaret, *b* 1949: *m* 1973, Timothy Veise, of Rectortown, Virginia, USA, and has issue living, Katherine Anne Bovington, *b* 1975, — Emily Sarah, *b* 1978. —— Jennifer Rose, *b* 1953: *m* 1974, Robert Lawson-Peebles, PhD.

Branch from 14th and yst son of 1st Baronet:—

Grandson of late Herbert Wigram, 2nd son of Rev William Pitt Wigram (infra):—
Issue of late Rt Hon Sir Clive (*Baron Wigram*) GCB, GCVO, CSI, PC *cr Baron Wigram* 1935 (see that title).

Grandchildren of late Lewis Wigram, yst son of Rev William Pitt Wigram, 14th and yst son of 1st baronet:—
Issue of late Roland Lewis Wigram, *b* 1874, *d* 1918: *m* 1907, Mildred Gladys (who *m* 2ndly, 1930, Lennox Chaplin Prendergast, and *d* 1973), el da of late Rev Canon Robert Peel Willock, R of Warmington, Banbury:—
Derek Roland (The Old Schoolhouse, The Common, Swardeston, Norwich NR14 8EB), *b* 1908; *ed* Marlborough, and Peterhouse, Camb (MA); BSc (Economics) London; House Master and Careers Master at Bryanston Sch 1936-46, and Headmaster of Monkton Combe Sch 1946-68; Chm Head Masters Conference 1963-64: *m* 1944, Catharine Mary, da of late Very Rev William Ralph Inge, KCVO, DD, and has issue living, Richard Inge (Woodlynch, Branksomewood Rd, Fleet, Hants), *b* 1944; *ed* Marlborough and R Coll of Art (MDes); Senior Partner Wigram Tivendale Associates: *m* 1971, Angela Patricia, da of Capt M. D. Rahilly, RN, of 2 Great Orchard, Upper Westwood, Bradford on Avon, and has issue living, David Roland *b* 1976, Helen Marguerite *b* 1974, — Janet Catharine Inge, *b* 1948: *m* 1975, Nicholas Charles Miller, MA, MSc, of The Old Schoolhouse, The Common, Swardeston, Norwich NR14 8EB, and has issue living, Lydia Catharine *b* 1980, Emily Joy *b* 1984. —— †Mervyn Roland, *b* 1916; *ed* Marlborough Coll, and Peterhouse, Camb (MA); HM Inspector of Schs 1959-78, and Staff Inspector 1974-78, formerly Director of Modern Languages and a Housemaster of Mill Hill Sch: *m* 1947, Beryl Margaret Morriss (27 Glasshouse Lane, Kenilworth, Warwicks CV8 2AH), and *d* 1994, leaving issue, Christopher Edward Mervyn, *b* 1954: *m* 1982, Susanne Ruth, da of Paul Johannes Schnabel, of Grossbottwar, W Germany, and has issue living, Michael Luke *b* 1986, Jessica Jade *b* 1983, Stephanie Rachel *b* 1989. — Rowena Margaret, *b* 1949: *m* 1978, Francisco Muñoz Ramirez, of Ciudad Real, Spain, — Diana Catharine, *b* 1956: *m* 1991, Paul Francis McGuire.
Issue of late Oswald Lewis Wigram, *b* 1878, *d* 1960: *m* 1914, Lucy Clare Elaine, who *d* 1962, da of the Rev Thomas Wilkinson Stephenson, V of Addingham, Penrith, and Hon Canon of Carlisle:—
Margaret Elaine, *b* 1921. *Residence* - Holme Lea, Armathwaite, Carlisle.

Grandchildren of late Oswald Lewis Wigram (ante):—
Issue of late Maj Michael Lewis Wigram, RA, *b* 1918; *d* 1983: *m* 1950, Dorothea Mary, who *d* 1964, el da of late Yorke Wood, of The Braye, Georgeham, N Devon:—
Anthony Lewis (18 Spencer Gate, St Albans, Herts), *b* 1953; *ed* St Lawrence Coll, Ramsgate: *m* 1976, Jennifer Hilary, da of Albert Thom, of 43 The Grove, Brookmans Pk, Herts, and has issue living, Robert Alexander Lewis, *b* 1981, — Michael

Anthony Yorke, *b* 1983, — David Arthur Kennedy, *b* 1986. —— Mary Elaine, *b* 1951: *m* 1977, Anthony Laurence Tucker of 50 Woodcote Rd, Caversham, Reading RG4 7BB, and has issue living, John Michael, *b* 1982, — Mark Andrew Laurence, *b* 1987, — Sarah Frances, *b* 1979.

The 1st baronet, Sir Robert Wigram, successively MP for Fowey and co Wexford, obtained eminence as a merchant; he died 1830, having had twenty-three children. The 2nd baronet, MP for Fowey, in 1832 changed, by Roy licence, his surname to FitzWygram. Lieut-Gen Sir Frederick FitzWygram, 4th Bt, sat as MP for Hampshire S. (*Q*) 1884-5, and for Hampshire S, or Fareham, Div 1885-1900, and Major Sir Frederick Loftus Francis FitzWygram, MC, 5th Bt, was taken prisoner and twice wounded during European War 1914-19 (despatches, prisoner when severely wounded; *d* from effects of captivity).

BAKER WILBRAHAM (GB) 1776, of Loventor, co Devon
(Name pronounced "Baker Wilbrum")

Rest in the haven

Sir RICHARD BAKER WILBRAHAM, 8th *Baronet*; *b* 5 Feb 1934; *s* his father, Sir RANDLE JOHN, 1980; *ed* Harrow; late Lt Welsh Guards; High Sheriff Cheshire 1991, DL 1992; Dir of J. Henry Schroder Wagg & Co Ltd 1969-89, a Trustee of Grosvenor Estate since 1981, a Gov of Harrow Sch 1982-92, and Dir Christie Hosp NHS Trust since 1990; Chm Bibby Line Group Ltd since 1992 (Dir since 1989), Dep Chm Brixton Estate plc since 1994 (Dir since 1985), Dir Majedie Investments plc since 1989; Govr Nuffield Hospitals since 1990; a Church Commissioner since 1994; Renter Bailiff, Worshipful Co of Weavers 1993-94 and Upper Bailiff 1994-95; Trustee, Dyson Perrins Museum of Worcester Porcelain since 1993; Govr The King's Sch, Macclesfield since 1986; Member of Gen Council of King Edward's Hospital Fund for London since 1986: *m* 1962, Anne Christine Peto, da of late Charles Peto Bennett, OBE, of La Haute, Fliquet, Jersey, and has issue.

Arms – Quarterly, 1st and 4th argent, three bends wavy azure, *Wilbraham*; 2nd and 3rd, per pale argent and, or on a saltire nebuly sable five escallops of the first, on a chief of the third a lion passant of the second, *Baker*. **Crests** – 1st, a wolf's head erased argent, *Wilbraham*; 2nd, a dexter arm embowed, vested azure, charged with three annulets interlaced or, cuffed argent, holding in the hand proper an arrow of the last, *Baker*.
Residence – Rode Hall, Scholar Green, Cheshire ST7 3QP.

SON LIVING

RANDLE, *b* 28 May 1963, *ed* Harrow.

DAUGHTERS LIVING

Sibella Caroline, *b* 1965: *m* 1994, Timothy Makower. —— Charlotte Cecilia Anne, *b* 1968. —— Alice Maria Elisabeth, *b* 1971.

SISTER LIVING

Letitia Ann, *b* 1931: *m* 1960, Timothy George Kirkbride, of Little Hill Farm, Buckland St Mary, nr Chard, Som TA20 3SS, and has issue living, George Edward, *b* 1967, — Harriet Ann, *b* 1964: *m* 1993, Anthony Leonard Clinton Bloomer, son of Arnold Euston Moore Bloomer (*see* B Vivian, colls).

AUNT LIVING (*Daughter of 6th baronet*)

Joyce Katharine, MBE, *b* 1902; Civilian Housing Administrator, Min of Defence 1961-72; MBE (Civil) 1959. *Residence* – Flat 2, 23 Onslow Sq, SW7 3NJ.

The 5th baronet, Sir George Barrington Baker, assumed by Royal licence 1900 the additional surname of Wilbraham, having *m* Katharine Frances, who *d* 1945, da and heir of Gen Sir Richard Wilbraham, KCB, of Rode Hall, nephew of 1st Baron Skelmersdale. The 6th baronet, Sir Philip Wilbraham Baker Wilbraham, KBE, DCL, was Sec, National Assembly of Church of England 1920-39, First Church Estates Commr 1939-54, Chancellor of Dioceses of Chester, York, Truro, Chelmsford and Durham, and Vicar-Gen of Province of York 1915-34, and of Province of Canterbury (and Dean of the Arches) 1934-55.

WILKINSON (UK) 1941, of Brook, Witley, co Surrey

Sir (DAVID) GRAHAM BROOK WILKINSON, 3rd *Baronet*; *b* 18 May 1947; *s* his father, *Sir* (LEONARD) DAVID, DSC, 1972; *ed* Millfield, and Ch Ch, Oxford; OStJ: *m* 1977, Sandra Caroline, da of Dr Richard Rossdale, and has issue.

Arms – Quarterly, argent and vair sable and or, a cross gules, in the 1st and 4th quarters a lion rampant of the fourth on a chief also of the fourth three mullets of the third. **Crest** – Issuant from a chaplet of roses argent barbed and seeded proper a demi-unicorn or.

DAUGHTERS LIVING

Louise Caroline Sylvia, *b* 1979. —— Tara Katherine Juliet, *b* 1982.

SISTER LIVING

Sylvia Davinia Gay, *b* 1948: *m* 1978, Peter Martin Gort Beaufort Grimaldi, FRCS, 16th Marquis Grimaldi, of Tyne Hall, Bembridge, IoW PO35 5NH (only son of Philip R. B. Grimaldi, 15th Marquis, who *d* 1983), and has issue living, Alicia Anne Davinia, *b* 1979, —— Carina Rose Anne, *b* 1981, —— Sophia Anne Camilla, *b* 1987.

AUNT LIVING (*Daughter of 1st baronet*)

Eileen, *b* 1916: *m* 1941, John MacNaughton Sidey, DSO, who *d* 1990, son of late John Sidey, and has issue living, Ian MacNaughton, *b* 1947: *m* 1970, Christina Willing Ashdown, and has issue living, James MacNaughton *b* 1975, Guy Xavier *b* 1979. *Residence* – 28 Hathaway Common, New Canaan, Connecticut 06840, USA.

MOTHER LIVING

Sylvia Ruby Eva Anne (*Sylvia, Lady Wilkinson*), only da of late Prof Bossley Alan Rex Gater, of Grahamstown, S Africa; DStJ: *m* 1946 (*m diss* 1967), Sir (Leonard) David Wilkinson, DSC, 2nd Bt, who *d* 1972.
Sir George Henry Wilkinson, KCVO, 1st Bt, was Lord Mayor of London 1940-41.

WILLIAMS (GB) 1798, of Bodelwyddan, Flintshire

Strong and crafty

Sir FRANCIS JOHN WATKIN WILLIAMS, QC, 8th *Baronet*; *b* 24 Jan 1905; *s* his brother, *Sir* REGINALD LAWRENCE WILLIAM, MBE, ED, 1971; Bar Middle Temple 1928, and QC 1952; served in War 1939-45, late Wing Cdr RAFVR; Recorder of Birkenhead 1950-58, and of Chester 1958-71; Recorder of Crown Court 1972-75; Chm of Anglesey 1960-71, Chm Flintshire 1961-71, and Dep Chm of Cheshire Quarter Sessions, 1952-71, Chm Medical Appeal Tribunal for N Wales Area 1954-57, Hon Member Wales and Chester Circuit 1987, and a JP for Denbighshire (High Sheriff 1957); High Sheriff of Anglesey 1963; Chancellor of Diocese of St Asaph 1966-83; Freeman of City of Chester 1960: *m* 1932, Brenda Beryl, JP, da of Sir (Joseph) John Jarvis, MP, 1st Bt, and has issue.

Arms – Argent, two foxes counter-salient in saltire the sinister surmounted of the dexter gules, a crescent for difference.
Residence – Llys, Middle Lane, Denbigh.

DAUGHTERS LIVING

Jennifer Frances Ann, *b* 1933: *m* 1st, 1954 (*m diss* 1975), Lt-Col Ivan Wise Lynch, R Green Jackets; 2ndly, 1979, Maj Basil Hugh Philips Heaton, MBE, of Rhûal, Mold, Clwyd and has issue living (by 1st *m*), Francis William Adrian (Lower Grove Cottage, Little Horwood, Bucks) *b* 1957: *m* 1982, Julia Mary Battram, and has issue living, James Lawrence Francis *b* 1983, Nicholas John Richard *b* 1985, —— William John Ivan (13 Atheldene Rd, SW18 3BN), *b* 1965: *m* 1990, Charlotte, da of John Michael Howard, of Cramond House, Pirbright, Woking, Surrey, — and an adopted da, Amanda-Jayne Charlotte, *b* 1961. —— Tessa Gillian Rosamund, MBE, *b* 1935; High Sheriff of Gwynedd 1990: *m* 1958, Michael John Stewart Preece, of Plas Llanddyfnan, Talwrn, Llangefni, Anglesey LL77 7TH, and has issue living, James Francis Stewart (33 St John's Rd, Knutsford, Cheshire WA16 0DP), *b* 1964: *m* 1990, Annabelle Katherine, eldest da of John Hartley Beckett, of Belton, Whitchurch, Shropshire, and has issue living, Daisy Angela Tessa *b* 1993, — Hugh Michael Stewart, *b* 1969, — and two das, Emily Margaret, *b* 1961: *m* 1993, Christopher Starkie Foden, of 51 Kingsley St, SW11 5LF, and has issue living, Madeline Tessa *b* 1993, —— Rosamond Alice, *b* 1963: *m* 1990, Robert James Woolf, of Rose Cottage, Great Shelford, Cambridge CI32 5EH. —— Antonia Kathleen Brenda, *b* 1939: *m* 1st, 1960 (*m diss* 1974), Timothy Roy Henry Kimber, el son of Sir Charles Dixon Kimber, 3rd Bt; 2ndly, 1974 (*m diss* 1982), Timothy George Emanuel, and has issue living, (by 1st *m*) (*see* Kimber, Bt), — (by 2nd *m*) Harry Sebastian, *b* 1975. —— Victoria Elizabeth Alice, *b* 1944: *m* 1965, Andrew Walter Loraine Paterson, of Church Stile, Town End, Radnage, Bucks, and has issue living, Harry Adrian Loraine, *b* 1968, —— Douglas Watkin Loraine *b* 1972, —— Lucinda Mona Alice, *b* 1966: *m* 1990, James Frederick, —— Jessie Brenda Antonia, *b* 1970.

HALF-BROTHER LIVING

LAWRENCE HUGH (Parciau, Marianglas, Anglesey LL73 8PH), *b* 25 Aug 1929; Capt RM (ret); High Sheriff of Anglesey 1970: *m* 1952, Sara Margaret Helen, third da of Sir Harry Platt, 1st Bt, MD, MS, FRCS, and has issue living, Emma Louise, *b* 1961; BA, ACII: *m* 1988, Radcliffe Percy Royds, of 92 Ormeley Rd, SW12, and has issue living, Harry Lawrence Percy *b* 1991, Jack Michael William *b* 1992, — Antonia Margaret, *b* 1963.

SISTER LIVING

Violet Kathleen Mary, *b* 1902: *m* 1926, Thomas Arthur Pearson, late Lieut-Cdr RNVR, who *d* 1974, and has issue living, David Arthur (Banastre Cottage, Parkgate South, Wirral, Ches), *b* 1931: *m* 1st, 1960 (*m diss* 1977), Carolyn Frances, el da of F. H. Minoprio, of Hessle Well House, Heswall, Merseyside; 2ndly, 1981, Gillian Mary, da of G. Buckley, of Badgers, Paddock Dr, Parkgate South, Wirral, Ches, and has issue living (by 1st *m*), Charles David *b* 1961: *m* 1989, Zoë Louise Hancox, Joanna Mary *b* 1963, Lucy Alexandra *b* 1968, — Thomas Martin, *b* 1933. *Residence* – Meadow Croft, Cae Mawr, Beaumaris, Anglesey.

DAUGHTERS LIVING OF SEVENTH BARONET

Laurelie Meriol Winifrida (*Lady Laurie*), *b* 1939: *m* 1968, Sir Robert Bayley Emilius Laurie, 7th Bt, and has issue (*see* Laurie, Bt). —— Juliet Elizabeth Rosamund, *b* 1942: *m* 1966, Brian Derek Price, of 52 Hazlewell Rd, Putney, SW15 6LR, and has issue living, Edmund Hugh Owain, *b* 1969, — Henry William Frederick, *b* 1973.

GRANDDAUGHTERS LIVING OF SIXTH BARONET

Issue of late Hugh Richard Grenville Williams, *b* 1927, *d* 1952: *m* 1948, Jacqueline Ferney, da of John Davison, of Livingstone, Zambia.
Jennifer Mary, *b* 1949: *m* 1st, 19—, E. Stead; 2ndly, 19—, John Manning. —— Melanie Jane, *b* 1950: *m* 19—, J. Krienke. —— Richardyne Megan, *b* 1952: *m* 19—, D. Van Emmenis.

DAUGHTER LIVING OF FIFTH BARONET

Freda Violet, *b* 1913: *m* 1st, 1937 (*m diss* 1950), Sydney Walton Hinde, who *d* 1967; 2ndly, 1959, William Vere Hodgson, of Surrey, and has had issue (by 1st *m*), Richard Courtney Buckley (Madilla Farm, Centenary, Zimbabwe), *b* 1939: *m* 1st, 1961 (*m diss* 1977), Sally Makins; 2ndly, 1978, Jeanette Kramburger, and has issue living (by 1st *m*), Stephen Ross *b* 1962: *m* 1994, Noirin Fitzpatrick, Craig Sydney *b* 1964: *m* 1989, Amanda Dalkin (and has issue living, Darren *b* 1991, Tamsan *b* 1993), Felicity Anne *b* 1967: *m* 1992, Glen Mirams (and has issue living, Shelby *b* 1993), (by 2nd *m*) Glen Richard *b* 1979, Douglas Patrick *b* 1981, Patrick Christopher *b* 1985, — Deirdre Penelope Anne, *b* 1938: *m* 1958, Basil Birkbeck Wakefield, of Piedmont, P/Bag 915, Bindura, Zimbabwe, and was killed by terrorists 1979, leaving issue, Dean Roger *b* 1960: *m* 1985, Alexandra Westwood (and has issue living, Jason *b* 1986, Tara *b* 1988), Clive Basil *b* 1964: *m* 1989, Heather Genet (and has issue living, Kendal *b* 1991, Carlton *b* 1993), Richard Owen *b* 1967, Darryl William *b* (twin) 1967: *m* 1987 (*m diss* 1989), Amanda Moeller (and has issue living, Warren *b* 1988), Deborah Odile *b* 1959: *m* 1981, Graham Taylor (and has issue living, Grant *b* 1986, Brendan *b* 1986, Keegan *b* 1989), — Patricia Rosamund *b* 1941: *m* 1961, Patrick David Hyde Smith, of 25 Belfast Rd, Emerald Hill, Zimbabwe, and has issue living, Vaughn Christopher *b* 1962: *m* 1989, Sandra Egeland (and has issue living, Ryan Patrick *b* 1992), Brent Richard *b* 1964, Natasha Jane *b* 1967, Samantha *b* 1971, — Caroline Bryer, *b* 1946: *m* 1st, 1970, Emmanuel Riez, who *d* 1971; 2ndly, 1981 (*m diss* 1992), William Rooke, and has issue living (by 2nd *m*), Amber Zuleika *b* 1987. *Residence* – Box 1914, Gaborone, Botswana.

COLLATERAL BRANCH LIVING

Granddaughter of late Major Charles Henry Bennett Williams, 5th son of 3rd baronet:—
Issue of late Col Evelyn Hugh Watkin Williams, DSO, *b* 1884, *d* 1934; *m* 1910, Florence, da of late G. A. Brett, of Ryde, Isle of Wight:—
Gwenllian Elizabeth Anne, *b* 1911: *m* 1st, 1935, Lieut Christopher Ryle Wood, RN, who assumed by deed poll 1936, the surname of Williams in lieu of his patronymic, and by Roy licence 1936, the arms of Williams, 2ndly, 1948, Campbell Sherston Smith, who assumed by deed poll 1949 the surname of Williams in lieu of his patronymic, and by Roy licence 1949 the arms of Williams, and has issue living, (by 1st *m*) Jane, *b* 1936, — Prudence, *b* 1938: *m* 1960, David Turnbull, and has issue living, Christopher Neil *b* 1962, Catherine Fiona *b* 1965.
Sir John Williams, 1st Bt, High Sheriff, Flintshire 1794-5, was grandson of John Williams, Ch Justice of Brecon, Glamorgan, and Radnor, son of John Williams, Welsh Judge, 2nd son of Sir William Williams, 1st Bt (*cr* 1688) (*see* Williams-Wynn, Bt). Sir John Williams, 2nd Bt, assumed in 1842 the additional surname of Hay, but died in 1859 without male issue.

WILLIAMS (UK) 1866, of Tregullow, Cornwall

Sir DONALD MARK WILLIAMS, 10th *Baronet*; *b* 7 Nov 1954; *s* his father, *Sir* ROBERT ERNEST, 1976; *ed* W Buckland Sch: *m* 1982, Denise, only da of Royston H. Cory, of Kashmir, Raleigh Hill, Bideford, Devon, and has had issue (Matthew, *b* and *d* 1985).

Arms – Vair, three crescents or. **Crest** – A demi-eagle azure, wings elevated sable, each charged with four bezants.
Residences – Upcott House, Barnstaple, N Devon; Kamsack, Saskatchewan, Canada.

Never despair

DAUGHTER LIVING

Hannah Louise, *b* 1987.

BROTHER LIVING

BARTON MATTHEW, *b* 21 Nov 1956.

SISTER LIVING

Phyllis June, *b* 1949.

AUNT LIVING

Leila June, *b* 1926: *m* 1st, 1952 (*m diss* 1972), Norman E. Hambley; 2ndly, 1972, Adam Casson, (141 Creighton Cres, Penticton, BC, Canada), and has issue living (by 1st *m*), Kenneth Charles Claude, *b* 1953, — Thomas Keith, *b* 1957, — Kim Lee Ann, *b* 1959.

DAUGHTERS LIVING OF SEVENTH BARONET

Eva Kathleen Victoria Daisy, *b* 1900: *m* 1935, Lt-Cdr Christopher Ernest Inman Gibbs, RNR (ret), who *d* 1947, and has issue living. —— Winifred, *b* 1901.

GREAT-AUNTS LIVING

Beatrice Lavinia *b* 1902. —— Matilda Maude, *b* 1909: *m* 1942, Robert McFadyen and has issue living, Diane Beatrice, *b* 1942.

GRANDMOTHER LIVING

Theresa Gertrude, da of R. Greafer: *m* 1922, Ernest Claude Williams, who *d* 1933. *Address* – c/o Rivercrest Lodge, Fort Saskatchewan, Alberta T0B 1P0, Canada.

WIDOW LIVING OF NINTH BARONET

RUTH MARGARET (*Ruth, Lady Williams*) (Upcott House, Barnstaple, N Devon, and Kamsack, Saskatchewan, Canada), da of Charles Edwin Butcher, of Hudson Bay: *m* 1948, Sir Robert Ernest Williams, 9th Bt, who *d* 1976.

COLLATERAL BRANCHES LIVING

Granddaughter of late Rev Leonard Alfred Williams, 4th son of 2nd baronet:—
Issue of late Lieut-Com David Cameron Williams, RN, *b* 1898, *d* 1931: *m* 1929, Violet Mary (who *m* 2ndly, 1946, Humphrey Douglas Tyringham, who *d* 1986), da of late Rev Arthur Townshend Boscawen (*see* V Falmouth, colls):—
Susan Mary, *b* 1931: *m* 1954, Maj John Michael Halford, RM (ret), and has issue living, John Wallis Williams, *b* 1955; *ed* Stanbridge Earls, — Peter David (19 Palmerston Rd, East Sheen, SW14 7QA), *b* 1957; *ed* Wellington Coll: *m* 1985, Caroline Smith, and has issue living, Edward David *b* 1988, Lucy Alexandra *b* 1991, — Julia Karenza, *b* 1961: *m* 1988, Michael Peter Mansergh, and has issue living, Annabel Karenza *b* 1990, Philippa Louise *b* 1991. *Residence* – 31 Knowle Rd, Knowle, Budleigh Salterton, Devon EX9 6AR.

Grandson of late Victor George Williams, 7th son of 2nd baronet:—
Issue of late Frederick Martyn Charles Williams, *b* 1898, *d* 1961: *m* 1935, Maud Ann (112 Kingston Row, Winnipeg, Manitoba, R2M O59), da of late Dennis Bawif, of Winnipeg, Canada:—
Martyn Dennis Victor (8-9 Ipswich Cres, Willodale, Toronto, Canada), *b* 1936; *ed* Toronto Univ (BSc Eng): *m* 1968, Beth Diane, el da of E John Koch, of Kitchener, Ont, and has issue living, Robin Lynn, *b* 1972, — Michael David, *b* 1978, — Sandra Diana, *b* 1975, — Karen Patricia, *b* 1978 (twin).

Grandchildren of late Bertram Leopold Williams (infra):—
Issue of late William Bertram Williams, *b* 1906, *d* 1960: *m* 1932, Agnes, who *d* 1968, da of John Allen, of Vancouver, BC:—
Judith Patricia, *b* 1934: *m* 1954, William Demuth McLean, of 4537 Portland St, Burnaby, BC, V5J 2P1, Canada, and has issue living, Douglas William, *b* 1958: has issue (by Patricia Kensington), Alicia Lareina *b* 1991, — Kay Elizabeth, *b* 1956: *m* 1983, Gordon Gray, and has issue living, Kristin Patricia *b* 1985, Andrea Barbara *b* 1987, — Lynn Marion, *b* 1960: *m* 1990, Paul Kirkpatrick, and has issue living, Brianne Kathleen, *b* 1979, — Colleen Kate, *b* 1981, — Leaerin Elizabeth, *b* 1982. —— Barbara Anne, *b* 1939: *m* 1959, Douglas Norman Tartaglio, of 603 1710 Radisson Dr, SE Calgary, Alberta, Canada T2A 1Z8, and has issue living, Norman William, *b* 1962: has issue living, Ryan Wayne *b* 1982, — Neil Joseph, *b* 1964: *m* 1987, Mary Kathleen, da of Walter MacNeill, — Joanne Denise, *b* 1967: *m* 1993, Peter Bukacell.
Issue of late Claude Martin Williams, *b* 1911, *d* 1977: *m* 1944, Hannah Louisa (1225 E 17th Av, Vancouver, BC, Canada V5V 1C5), da of late Capt William Massey, of Courtown Harbour, Gorey, co Wexford:—
Bertram Douglas (20571 49 A Av, Langley, BC, V3A 574), *b* 1945; Journeyman Diesel Engineer; VV Coll (JD Eng): *m* 19—, Wanda Charlotte, only da of Capt Trim, of Nanimo, BC, and has issue living, Brianne Kathleen, *b* 1979, — Colleen Kate, *b* 1981, — Leaerin Elizabeth, *b* 1982. —— William Claude (2640 Moss Av, Prince George, BC V2L 5J3), *b* 1947; BSF (BC Univ): *m* 19—, Leslie Gaye, da of Norman Steward of 4752 60 B St, Delta, BC, and has issue living, Matthew Stewart, *b* 1980, — Andrew James, *b* 1982.

Issue of late Bertram Leopold Williams, 7th son of 2nd baronet, *b* 1878, *d* 1962: *m* 1st, 1906 (*m diss*), Vera Mary, only da of Arthur Venables, JP, of Wooburn Ranche, near Vernon, British Columbia; 2ndly, 1926, Amy Muriel Douglas, yst da of late Douglas Fourdrinier, of Teddington, Middlesex:—

(By 1st *m*) Peter Robert (RR1 Big Maple, Sechelt, BC, Canada V05 380), *b* 1913.

Granddaughter of late Lieut-Col Richard Michael Williams, 2nd son of 1st baronet:—

Issue of late Capt William Phillpotts Williams, *b* 1860, *d* 1916: *m* 1901, Edith Bonella, da of the Rev James Harvey Simpson, formerly R of St Mark's, Bexhill, and Preb of Chichester:—

Elizabeth Georgiana Phillpotts, *b* 1904.

The 1st baronet, Sir William, was High Sheriff of Cornwall 1851; and the 2nd baronet, Sir Frederick Martin, sat as MP for Truro (*C*) 1865-78. The 6th baronet, Sir Burton Robert, Lieut Devonshire Regt, was *ka* 1917.

WILLIAMS (UK) 1909, of Castell Deudraeth, and Borthwen, co Merioneth

No good but God

Sir (MICHAEL) OSMOND WILLIAMS, MC, 2nd *Baronet*, son of late Capt Osmond Trahaern Deudraeth Williams, DSO, el son of 1st baronet; *b* 22 April 1914; *s* his grandfather, *Sir* (ARTHUR) OSMOND, 1927; *ed* Eton, and Freiburg Univ; Maj late R Scots Greys; a JP (1960) for Merionethshire; 1939-45 War in Middle East, Italy and N-W Europe (MC, 1944 Chevalier of Orders of Leopold II of Belgium with Palm, Belgian Croix de Guerre with Palm): *m* 1947, Benita Mary, da of late G. Henry Booker, of 3 Chesterfield House, W1, and has issue.

Arms – Argent, a chevron between in chief two mullets pierced and in base a buck trippant sable. Crest – A griffin segreant sable, holding between the fore claws a buck's head cabossed gold.
Residence – Borthwen, Minffordd, Penrhyndeudraeth, Gwynedd. *Club* – Travellers'.

DAUGHTERS LIVING

Sarah Theresa Ceridwen, *b* 1948: *m* 1981, Leo Kruidbos, otherwise Kay, of 179 lère Rue Mont Suisse, St Sauveur des Monts, Quebec J0R 1R2, Canada. —— Julia Mary Myfanwy, *b* 1952: *m* 1982, Richard Shaun O'Conor, of 31 Clarendon Road, W11.

SISTER LIVING

Elizabeth Anne (6 Denis Morgan Court, 11 Bolebrooke Rd, Bexhill-on-Sea, E Sussex TN40 1ER), *b* 1915.

The 1st baronet, Sir (Arthur) Osmond Williams, was Lord-Lieut of Merionethshire, 1909-27, and MP for Merionethshire (*L*) Oct 1900 to Jan 1910.

WILLIAMS (UK) 1915, of Bridehead, co Dorset

Nil Solidum

Sir (ROBERT) PHILIP NATHANIEL WILLIAMS, 4th *Baronet*; *b* 3 May 1950; *s* his father, *Sir* DAVID PHILIP, 1970; *ed* Marlborough, and St Andrew's Univ: *m* 1979, Catherine Margaret Godwin, da of Rev Canon Cosmo Gabriel Rivers Pouncey, of Church Walk, Little Bredy, Dorchester, Dorset, and has issue.

Arms – Argent, a greyhound between three Cornish choughs sable, beaked and membered purpure; on a bordure engrailed gules four crosses formée or between as many besants. **Crest** – A dexter arm couped, the sleeve barry of four sable and argent, charged with a cross formée per fesse counterchanged between four besants, the hand proper grasping a branch of oak vert, fructed or.
Seat – Bridehead, Little Bredy, Dorchester, Dorset DT2 9JA.

SON LIVING

DAVID ROBERT MARK *b* 31 Oct 1980.

DAUGHTERS LIVING

Sarah Catherine Anne, *b* 1982. —— Margaret Jane Louise, *b* 1984. —— Clare Elizabeth Philippa, *b* 1987.

BROTHER LIVING

(David) Michael Ralph, *b* 1955; *ed* Marlborough, and Durham Univ: *m* 1992, Charlotte P.E., only da of Capt Malcolm Syms, of Mile Path House, Woking, Surrey.

HALF-SISTER LIVING

(Mary) Venetia Honor, *b* 1939: *m* 1964, John Copson Peake, of Corscombe Court, Dorchester, Dorset.

SISTER LIVING

(Elizabeth Margaret) Ruth, *b* 1951: *m* 1975, Michael Widén, of Batsford House, St Mary Bourne, nr Andover, Hants, and has issue living, William David Alexander, *b* 1978.

AUNTS LIVING (*Daughters of 2nd baronet*)

Mary Felicity Rosa (*Lady Crawford*), *b* 1911: *m* 1939, Vice-Adm Sir William Godfrey Crawford, KBE, CB, DSC, and has issue living, Edward Philip, *b* 1940; *ed* Gordonstoun; BSA Police, Zimbabwe: *m* 1965, Rosamund Helen, da of W. Frank Wynne, of Greensyke, Ruwa, Zimbabwe, and has issue living, Alastair *b* 1974, Heather *b* 1968, Felicity *b* 1970, — David Alexander, *b* 1942; *ed* Allhallows: *m* 1968, Penelope Ann, da of Cdr C. E. J. Streatfeild, of Denhay, Broadoak, Bridport, and has issue living, David William *b* 1970, Mark Jonathan *b* 1972, Richard Henry *b* 1977, — Michael James, *b* 1951; *ed* Radley: *m* 1974, Margaret Cotton, and has issue living, Robert *b* 1982, Louise *b* 1979, — Prunella Marion Pharazyn, *b* (twin) 1942: *m* 1965, Neboysha Ranko Brashich, and has issue living, Alexander *b* 1970, Nicholas *b* 1972. *Residence* – Broadlands, Whitchurch Canonicorum, nr Bridport, Dorset. —— Jane Elizabeth Rhoda, *b* 1915: *m* 1941, Lt-Col Richard Leslie David Weber, RA, who *d* 1967, and has issue living, Jeremy, *b* 1944, — George (Scotsgrove House, nr Thame, Oxon), *b* 1946: *m* 1969, Elizabeth, el (adopted) da of Lt-Col Hon Alexander Burdett Money-Coutts, OBE (B Latymer), and has issue living, Thomas *b* 1976, Charlotte *b* 1980, — (Philippa) Emily Margaret, *b* 1950. *Residence* – The Upper Mill, Sydling St Nicholas, Dorchester, Dorset. —— (Eleanor Sarah) Joy (Old Cottage, Martinstown, Dorchester, Dorset), *b* 1927: *m* 1st, 1948 (*m diss* 1963), John Henry Fownes Luttrell, who *d* 1991; 2ndly, 1975, Peter MacGregor Coleman, who *d* 1979, and has issue living (by 1st *m*), Charlotte Rose *b* 1954: *m* 1977, Jonathan C. Yorke-Long, of Shrob Lodge, Old Stratford, Northants, and has issue living, Marcus *b* 1983, Lucy *b* 1986. —— Juliet Dorothea Chassereau *b* 1933: *m* 1956, John Douglas Young Hickman, and has issue living, (Philip) Douglas, *b* 1956: *m* 1981, Pamela Mary Hunter, and has issue living, Angela Lindsay *b* 1986, Connie Marie *b* 1988, Jennifer Lee *b* 1990, — Stephen James, *b* 1958: *m* 1988, Catherine Jean King, and has an adopted son, Alexander James *b* 1991, — Charles Nicholas, *b* 1960: *m* 1987, Gay Giselle Augustin Drescher, and has issue living, Katherine Ashley *b* 1990.

WIDOW LIVING OF THIRD BARONET

ELIZABETH MARY GARNEYS (*Elizabeth, Lady Williams*) (Stable House, Moigne Coombe, Owermoigne, Dorchester, Dorset); a DL of Dorset; High Sheriff of Dorset 1979; da of William Ralph Garneys Bond (Meysey-Thompson, Bt): *m* 1948, as his 2nd wife, Sir David Philip Williams, 3rd Bt, who *d* 1970.

COLLATERAL BRANCH LIVING

Issue of late Robert Mark Edgar Williams, 2nd son of 2nd baronet, *b* 1913, *d* 1969: *m* 1942, Juliet Susan Harriet (5 Winters Lane, Portesham, Dorchester, Dorset), da of Cdr Kenneth Berkeley Mackenzie Churchill, RN:—
Robert Norrie, *b* 1943; *ed* Radley: *m* 1971, Nesta Rosemary, da of Stewart Bell, of Stretton, Broadway, Llandrindod Wells, and has issue living, Andrew John Mark, *b* 1975, — Ann Margaret, *b* 1973. —— John Philip Mackenzie (9591 Herbert Rd, Richmond, BC, V7A 1T2, Canada), *b* 1947; *ed* Radley: *m* 1978, Louise Beverly, da of David Douglas, of Vancouver, Canada, and has issue living, Jonathan Mark, *b* 1988, — Hayley Michelle *b* 1992. —— Marcia Jane, *b* 1945: *m* 1st, 1977 (*m diss* 1979) Christopher Maples; 2ndly, 1983, Robert Machin, of Grey Cottage, Askerswell, Dorset, and has issue living (by 2nd *m*), Mark George, *b* 1984, — Sarah Ann, *b* (twin) 1984.

The 1st baronet, Col Sir Robert Williams, VD, TD (el son of late Robert Williams, of Bridehead, Dorchester), was MP for W Div of Dorset (C) 1895-1922, and sometime Hon Col 4th Batn Dorsetshire Regt. The second baronet, Sir Philip Francis Cunningham Williams, was High Sheriff of Dorset 1949.

WILLIAMS (UK) 1953, of Cilgeraint, co Caernarvon

Sir ROBIN PHILIP WILLIAMS, 2nd *Baronet*; *b* 27 May 1928; *s* his father, *Sir* HERBERT GERAINT, MP, 1954; *ed* Eton, and St John's Coll, Camb (MA); Bar Middle Temple 1954; an Insurance Broker; Member of Lloyd's; 2nd Lt (ret) RA; Vice-Chm, Fedn of Univ Conservative and Unionist Assos 1951-52, and acting Chm 1952; Chm of Bow Group 1954, and of Anti-Common Market League 1969-84; a Borough Councillor of Haringay 1968-74; Hon Sec Campaign for an Independent Britain since 1989; Lt RA 1947: *m* 1955, Wendy Adele Marguerite, only da of late Felix Joseph Alexander, of Hong Kong, and has issue.
Residence – 1 Broadlands Close, Highgate, N6 4AF.

SONS LIVING

ANTHONY GERAINT, *b* 22 Dec 1958: *m* 1990, Rachel J., elder da of Norman Jennings, of Fenny Drayton, Warwicks. *Residence* – 6 Willow Bridge Rd, N1 2LB. —— Stephen Robin Alexander, *b* 1962.

The 1st baronet, Sir Herbert Geraint Williams (son of late Thomas Williams, LLD, of Hooton, Cheshire), was MP for Reading (*U*) 1924-29, for S Div of Croydon, 1932-45, and for E Div of Croydon 1950-54, and Parliamentary Sec to Board of Trade 1928-9.

DUDLEY-WILLIAMS (UK) 1964, of City and Co of the City of Exeter

Sir ALASTAIR EDGCUMBE JAMES DUDLEY-WILLIAMS, 2nd *Baronet*; *b* 26 Nov 1943; *s* his father, *Sir* ROLF DUDLEY, 1987; *ed* Nautical Coll, Pangbourne: *m* 1972, Diana Elizabeth Jane, twin da of Robert Henry Clare Duncan, of The Wall House, High St, Haslemere, Surrey, and has issue.

Arms – Gules a chevron engrailed plain cotised between in chief two cranes respectant proper, and in base a triangular castle of three towers or. **Crest** – In front of a castle as in the arms, a wild cat rampant guardant proper.
Residence – The Manor House, Alton Pancras, Dorchester, Dorset DT2 7RW.

DAUGHTERS LIVING

Marina Elizabeth Catherine, *b* 1974. —— Lorna Caroline Rachel, *b* 1977. —— Eleanor Patricia Rosemary, *b* 1979.

BROTHER LIVING

MALCOLM PHILIP EDGCUMBE (9 Bowerdean St, SW6 3TN), *b* 10 Aug 1947; *ed* Nautical Coll Pangbourne: *m* 1973, Caroline Anne Colina, twin da of Robert Henry Clare Duncan, of The Wall House, High St, Haslemere, Surrey (ante), and has issue living, Nicholas Mark Edgcumbe, *b* 1975, — Patrick Guy Edgcumbe, *b* 1978, — Clare Helen Colina, *b* 1982.

WIDOW LIVING OF FIRST BARONET

MARGARET HELEN (*Helen, Lady Dudley-Williams*), eldest da of late Frederick Eaton Robinson, OBE, AMICE, AMIMechE, of Enfield, Middx: *m* 1940, Sir Rolf Dudley Dudley-Williams, 1st Bt, who *d* 1987. *Residence* – The Old Manse, S Petherton, Somerset TA13 5DB.

RHYS WILLIAMS (UK) 1918, of Miskin, Parish of Llantrisant, co Glamorgan

Sir (ARTHUR) GARETH LUDOVIC EMRYS RHYS WILLIAMS, 3rd *Baronet*; *b* 9 Nov 1961; *s* his father, *Sir* BRANDON MEREDITH, MP, 1988; *ed* Eton, Durham Univ, and INSEAD.

Arms – Per chevron argent and gules, in chief two cocks of the second and in base as many chevronels of the first. **Crest** – Between two fleur-de-lis argent, a goat's head couped sable, with curved horns.
Seat – Gadairwen, Groes Faen, Glamorgan. *Town Residence* – 32 Rawlings St, SW3. *Club* – Brooks's.

SISTERS LIVING

Elinor Caroline, *b* 1964. —— Miranda Pamela Cariadwen, *b* 1968.

AUNTS LIVING (*daughters of 1st baronet*)

Susan Eleanor (*Lady Glyn*), *b* 1923; Bar Inner Temple 1950; late Junior Com ATS: *m* 1946, Capt Sir Anthony Geoffrey Leo Simon Glyn, 2nd Bt (*cr* 1927), Welsh Gds; author. *Residence* – Marina Baie des Anges, Ducal Apt U-03, 06270 Villeneuve-Loubet, Alpes Maritimes, France. —— (Marion) Elspeth, *b* 1937: *m* 1981, George Chowdharay-Best, MA (Oxon), of 27 Walpole St, SW3.

WIDOW LIVING OF SECOND BARONET

CAROLINE SUSAN (*Lady Rhys Williams*), eldest da of late Ludovic Anthony Foster, of Greatham Manor, Pulborough, Sussex: *m* 1961, Sir Brandon Meredith Rhys Williams, 2nd Bt, MP, who *d* 1988. *Residences* – Gadairwen, Groes Faen, Glamorgan; 32 Rawlings St, SW3.

Col Sir Rhys Rhys Williams, DSO, QC, 1st baronet (son of late Gwilym Williams, a Judge of County Courts, of Miskin Manor, Glamorgan), Parl Sec to Min of Transport 1919, Recorder of Cardiff 1922-30, Chm of Quarter Sessions, Glamorgan, and MP for N Oxon (*L*) 1918 and for Banbury 1918-22. He assumed by deed poll 1938 the additional surname of Rhys. Sir Brandon Rhys Williams, 2nd Bt, was MP for S Kensington (*C*) March 1968 to Feb 1974, and for Kensington 1974-88, and MEP for London South East 1973-84.

Williams-Bulkeley, see Bulkeley.

Williams-Drummond, see Drummond.

Williams-Wynn, see Wynn.

WILLIAMSON (E) 1642, of East Markham, Nottinghamshire

Sir NICHOLAS (FREDERICK HEDWORTH) WILLIAMSON, 11th *Baronet*, son of late Major William Hedworth Williamson, grandson of 8th baronet; *b* 26 Oct 1937; *s* his uncle, *Sir* CHARLES HEDWORTH, 1946; *ed* Eton; late 4th/7th Roy Dragoon Guards.

Arms – Or, a chevron gules between three trefoils slipped sable. **Crest** – Out of a mural crown gules, a wyvern's head or.
Residence – Abbey Croft, Mortimer, Reading.

COLLATERAL BRANCH LIVING

Granddaughter of late Capt Cecil Hedworth J. C. L. G. Williamson, only son of late Robert Hudleston Williamson, 3rd son of 6th baronet:—
Issue of late Brig Hudleston Noel Hedworth Williamson, DSO, MC, *b* 1886, *d* 1971: *m* 1st, 1923 (*m diss* 1926), Helen Marjorie, da of Arthur Lord; 2ndly, 1926, Leila Isabel, who *d* 1983, only da of Lt-Col Robert William Peter Lodwick, of Lisheen, Camberley:—
(By 2nd *m*) Mary (*Lady Nicholas C. Gordon Lennox*), *b* 1934; an Extra Lady-in-Waiting to HRH Princess Alexandra, the Hon Lady Ogilvy, since 1990: *m* 1958, Lord Nicholas Charles Gordon Lennox, KCMG, KCVO (*see* D Richmond and Gordon).

Sir Thomas, the 1st baronet, suffered greatly for his loyalty in the civil wars, and paid £3,400 to the sequestrators for his estate. Sir Hedworth, the 7th baronet, was MP for the northern division of Durham (*L*) 1832-7, and High Sheriff of that county.

WILLINK (UK) 1957, of Dingle Bank, City of Liverpool

Sir CHARLES WILLIAM WILLINK, 2nd *Baronet*, *b* 10 Sept 1929; *s* his father *The Rt Hon Sir* HENRY URMSTON, MC, QC, 1973; *ed* Eton, and Trin Coll, Camb (MA, PhD); Housemaster, Eton Coll 1964-77: *m* 1954, Elizabeth, el da of Humfrey Andrewes, of North Grove, Highgate, N6, and has issue.

Arms – Azure, three acorns on one stem slipped or. **Crest** – Issuant from a wreath of oak leaves or, a dexter cubit arm bendwise grasping in the hand a chaplet of laurel proper.
Residence – 22 North Grove, Highgate, N6 4SL.

SON LIVING

EDWARD DANIEL, *b* 18 Feb 1957.

DAUGHTER LIVING

Penelope Jane, *b* 1959: *m* 1987, Simon John Lawrence Linnett, only son of late Prof John Linnett, of Brookside, Cambridge, and has issue living, John Lawrence Simon Albert, *b* 1993. — Henry Simon Albert, *b* 1993.

BROTHER LIVING

Stephen Henry (7 Clifton St, Plymouth PL4 9QA), *b* 1932; *ed* Eton, and Trin Coll, Oxford: *m* 1970, Mary Louise, da of Ernest R. Royston, of 52 Carslake Rd, SW, and has issue living, Henry Augustine, *b* 1971, — Annabella Mary Victoria, *b* 1975.

SISTERS LIVING

Rachel Frances: *m* 1947, Michael Kinchin Smith, son of Francis J. Kinchin Smith, of Emperor's Gate, SW7, and has issue living, Christopher Henry, *b* 1950: *m* 1974, Susan Valerie, yr da of William G. Adams, of W Wickham, Kent, and has issue living, Holly Rebecca *b* 1983, Katherine Alice *b* 1988, — *Rev* John Michael (The Rectory, Mursley, Milton Keynes, Bucks MK17 0RT), *b* 1952: *m* 1981 Caroline Anne, yr da of G. Francis Harris, of Copdock, Suffolk, and has issue living, Joseph Francis *b* 1983, Samuel John *b* 1988, David Luke *b* 1990, Eleanor Mary *b* 1985, — David Francis *b* 1954: *m* 1976 Rosalind Jane, yr da of Dr Frank Holden, of Bessacarr, Yorks, — Robert Mark, *b* 1960, — Lavinia Mary, *b* 1948: *m* 1975, John Cunningham, son of William Henry Cunningham, of Minchinhampton, Glos, and has issue living, Anna Clare *b* 1980, Ruth Elizabeth *b* 1983, Helen Mary *b* 1984, — Juliet Clare, *b* 1957: *m* 1985, Rev Malcolm James Hancock, of The Vicarage, Brassingtonn, Derby DE4 4DA, son of Isaac Hancock, of Newark, and has issue living, James Timothy Michael *b* 1989, Benjamin Andrew *b* 1991. *Residence* – The Old Bakery, Epwell, Banbury, Oxon OX15 6LA. ——— Elisabeth Mary, *m* 1951, Frank Erskine Bell, son of late Sir Ernest Albert Seymour Bell, CIE, and has issue living, Nicholas John, *b* 1953, — Catharine Elisabeth, *b* 1955: *m* 1986, Timothy Cutting, son of George Cutting, of Cambo, Northumberland, and has issue living, Daniel Christopher Frank *b* 1993. *Residence* – 14 Chaucer Rd, Cambridge CB2 2EB.

The Rt Hon Sir Henry Urmston Willink, MC, QC, son of William Edward Willink, FRIBA, of Liverpool, was MP for N Croydon (C) 1940-48, Min of Health 1943-45, Master of Magdalene Coll, Camb 1948-66, and Vice-Chancellor of Camb Univ, 1953-55, and Chancellor of Norwich and St Edmundsbury and Ipswich Dioceses 1948-55, and Dean of Arches 1955-70.

WILLS (UK) 1904, of Hazelwood, Stoke Bishop, Westbury-on-Trym, Gloucestershire, and Clapton-in-Gordano, Somerset

Sir (DAVID) SETON WILLS, 5th *Baronet*; *b* 29 Dec 1939, only son of late Maj George Seton Wills, Roy Wilts Yeo, yr son of Sir Ernest Salter Wills, 3rd Bt; *s* his uncle, *Lt-Col Sir* (ERNEST) EDWARD DE WINTON, 1983; *ed* Eton; FRICS: *m* 1968, Gillian, twin da of Albert Percival Eastoe, of Windmill Cottage, Aldbourne, Wilts, and has issue.

Arms – Gules, three suns in splendour fesswise, between two griffins passant or. **Crest** – Issuant from an annulet or, a demi-griffin gules, charged with a sun in splendour, and holding in the dexter claw a battle-axe also or.
Residences – Eastridge House, Ramsbury, nr Marlborough, Wilts; Inchrory Lodge, Glenavon Estate, Tomintoul, Banffshire.

SON LIVING

JAMES SETON, *b* 24 Nov 1970.

DAUGHTERS LIVING

Sarah Elizabeth, *b* 1969: *m* 1994, Dominic E. Pearson, son of Edward J. Pearson, of Barbican, EC2. ——— Victoria Lucy, *b* 1975. ——— Alice Louise, *b* 1980.

DAUGHTERS LIVING OF FOURTH BARONET (*By 1st marriage*)

Venetia Dawn, *b* 1927: *m* 1st, 1948 (*m diss* 1962), as his 2nd wife, Charles Robert Cecil Weld Forester (*see* B Forester); 2ndly, 1962, Alan Cripps Nind Hopkins, of Chalet Topaze, Anzere, Valais, Switzerland, and has issue living (by 1st *m*) (*see* B Forester), — (by 2nd *m*) Mark Edward Wills *b* 1963, — Peter Alan Wills (twin) *b* 1963. ——— Edwina Sylvia, *b* 1933: *m* 1st, 1952 (*m diss* 1961), Viscount Savernake (later 8th Marquess of Ailesbury); 2ndly, 1963, Maj Christopher Leslie Leo Bonn, late Welsh Gds, of La

Maison du Coin, St Ouen, Jersey, CI, and has issue living (by 1st *m*) (*see* M Ailesbury), — (by 2nd *m*) Philip Edward Leo, *b* 1964, — Camilla Georgina Alexandra, *b* 1965, — Melanie Marina Roselle, *b* 1974.

MOTHER LIVING

Lilah Mary, yst da of late Capt Percy Richard Hare (*see* E Listowel, colls): *m* 1st, 1935 (*m diss* 1946), Maj George Seton Wills (ante), who *d* 1979; 2ndly, 1946, as his 2nd wife, Col Nigel Victor Stopford Sackville, who *d* 1972 (*see* E Courtown, colls). *Residence* – The Weirs, Chilton Foliat, Hungerford, Berks.

WIDOW LIVING OF FOURTH BARONET

JULIET EVE (*Juliet, Lady Wills*), da of late Capt John Eagles Henry Graham-Clarke, JP, of Frocester Manor, Glos: *m* 1949, as his 2nd wife, Lt-Col Sir (Ernest) Edward de Winton Wills, who *d* 1983. *Residences* – Lochs Lodge, Glenlyon, Perthshire; Mount Prosperous, Hungerford, Berks.

COLLATERAL BRANCH LIVING

Issue of late Capt Arnold Stancomb Wills, yst son of 1st baronet, *b* 1877, *d* 1961: *m* 1905, Hilda Carolin, who *d* 1965, da of late Edward Lyon, of London, and New York:—
John Lycett, *b* 1910; is Maj (ret) Life Gds: *m* 1936, Hon Jean Constance Buller-Fullerton-Elphinstone, da of 16th Lord Elphinstone, and has issue living, Andrew Arnold Lyon (Middleton House, Longparish, Andover, Hants), *b* 1937; Capt (ret) Life Gds: *m* 1961, Hon Elizabeth Anne Cecil, da of 2nd Baron Rockley, and has issue living, Richard Arnold *b* 1962: *m* 1988, Netta, elder da of Lt-Col Trevor Morris, of Butlers, Donhead St Mary, Shaftesbury, Dorset (and has issue living, Anna *b* 1990, Charlotte *b* 1991), Alexander John *b* 1967: *m* 1992, Wendy A., elder da of Robin H. Leach, of Ugley Park, Ugley Green, Essex, Tessa Elizabeth *b* 1963: *m* 1993, Richard E. M. Affleck, son of Michael Affleck, of Park Farm, N Moreton, Oxon, — Susan Griselda Ann Lyon, *b* 1940: *m* 1960, Capt Charles Peregrine Albemarle Bertie, late Scots Gds (*see* E Lindsey and Abingdon, colls). *Residence* – Allanbay Park, Binfield, Berks.
The 1st baronet, Sir Edward Payson Wills, KCB (son of late Henry Overton Wills JP, of Bristol), was a Director of the Imperial Tobacco Co (Limited), and a Gov of Bristol Gen Hospital. The 2nd baronet, Sir Edward Chaning Wills (also a Director of the Imperial Tobacco Co, Limited), was High Sheriff of Devon 1915. The 3rd baronet, Sir Ernest Salter Wills, was Lord Lieut of Wilts 1930-42, and a Director of Imperial Tobacco Co.

WILLS (UK) 1923, of Blagdon, co Somerset

For our altars and our hearths

Sir JOHN VERNON WILLS, TD, 4th *Baronet*, *b* 3 July 1928; *s* his brother, Sir GEORGE PETER VERNON, 1945; *ed* Eton; a JP for Avon; a DL for Somerset 1968, and High Sheriff 1968-69 for Avon 1974; Lt-Col Comdg N Somerset and Bristol Yeo 1965-67 (Brevet Col 1967); formerly Hon Col 37th (Wessex and Welsh) Signal Regt (V); formerly Lt Coldm Gds (Reserve), Hon Capt RNR (1988); Chm of Wessex Water Authority and Member of Nat Water Council 1973-82; Chm Bristol and West Building Soc 1988-93, since when Pres, and Deputy-Chm *Bristol Evening Post* plc and Bristol United Press Ltd; Chm Bristol Waterworks Co; Pro Chancellor, Bath Univ since 1979; Hon LLD Bristol Univ 1986; Hon D Litt Univ of Bath 1993; is a KStJ: *m* 1953, Diana Veronica Cecil (Jane), only da of Douglas R. M. Baker, of The Close, Winsford, Minehead, Somerset, and has issue.

Arms – Gules, a sun in splendour between two gryphons passant in pale or. **Crest** – Issuant from an annulet or, a demi-gryphon gules, holding in the dexter claw a battle-axe gold.
Residence – Langford Court, Langford, Bristol.

SONS LIVING

DAVID JAMES VERNON, *b* 2 Jan 1955. —— Anthony John Vernon, *b* 1956: *m* 1983, Katherine A., 3rd da of Thomas Wilks, of Laggan, Bowmore, Isle of Islay. —— Rupert Charles Vernon, *b* 1959: *m* 1989, Kathryn A., 2nd da of late Gordon Board Matthews, and Mrs W. Clarke Graham, of Binixica, Menorca. —— Julian Robert Vernon, (Rickford House, Rickford, Burrington, nr Bristol) *b* 1963: *m* 1989, Fiona E. R., eldest da of T. R. Thom, of The Forge, Lower Langford, Bristol.

SISTER LIVING

Jean Mary Vernon, *b* 1925: *m* 1948, Richard Hill of Harptree Court, East Harptree, Somerset (Harford, Bt), and has issue living, Charles Peter Hill, *b* 1954: *m* 1980, Linda Elizabeth Anne, da of Alan Beresford Gordon, of Little Tumnerscourt, Godalming, Surrey, and has issue living, Matthew *b* 1989, Katie *b* 1983, Emily *b* 1986, — Angela Mary Loraine, *b* 1949, — Caryll Loraine, *b* 1951, — Sarah Loraine, *b* 1957.
The 1st baronet, Sir George Alfred Wills, was Pres of Imperial Tobacco Co of Great Britain and Ireland (Limited), and his son, Sir George Vernon Proctor Wills, 2nd Bt, was a Director of the same Company. The 3rd baronet, Sir George Peter Vernon, Lt Coldm Gds, was *ka* 1945.

WILLSHIRE (UK) 1841 (Extinct 1947)

Sir GERARD ARTHUR MAXWELL WILLSHIRE, 3rd and last *Baronet*.

DAUGHTER LIVING OF THIRD BARONET

Patricia Frederica, *b* 1925: *m* 1st, 1943 (*m diss* 1949) Greville Pollard Baylis, Lt Irish Guards; 2ndly, 1949, George Breary Girardet, and has issue living, (by 1st *m*) Greville Mark Willshire, *b* 1944, — (by 2nd *m*) Guy Maxwell, *b* 1953, — Gail Beatriz Willshire, *b* 1952.

WILMOT (GB) 1759, of Chaddesden, Derbyshire

Sir HENRY ROBERT WILMOT, 9th *Baronet*, *b* 10 April 1967; *s* his father, *Capt Sir* ROBERT ARTHUR, 1974; *ed* Eton.

Arms – Sable, on a fesse or, between three eagles' heads couped argent as many escallops gules, a canton vaire ermine and gules. **Crest** – An eagle's head couped argent gorged with a mural coronet sable, in the beak an escallop gules. *Residence* – The Garden Lodge, Chittoe, Chippenham, Wilts. SN15 2EW.

BROTHER DECEASED

Charles Sacheverel, *b* 1969; *d* 1993.

SISTER LIVING

Zoë Meriel, *b* 1971.

AUNT LIVING (*Daughter of 7th baronet*)

Pamela Ann (Chapel-on-the-Water, Ramsbury, Wilts SN8 2QE), *b* 1937: *m* 1st, 1959 (*m diss* 1967), Capt William James Stockton, late R Scots Greys; 2ndly, 1967 (*m diss* 1982), Antony Paul McCaffry, and has issue living, (by 1st *m*) Adela Louise, *b* 1961, — Henrietta Maria Caroline, *b* 1963, — (by 2nd *m*) Sophie Claire, *b* 1968.

MOTHER LIVING

Juliet Elvira (The Garden Lodge, Chittoe, Chippenham, Wilts SN15 2EW), el da of Capt Michael Neville Tufnell, CVO, DSC, RN (ret), of Curdridge Grange, Botley, Hants: *m* 1st, 1965 (*m diss* 1974), Capt Sir Robert Arthur Wilmot, 8th Bt, Scots Gds, who *d* 1974; 2ndly, 1976 (*m diss* 1980), Richard James Stanes.

COLLATERAL BRANCHES LIVING

Grandsons of the Rev Darwin Wilmot, son of late Edward Woollett Wilmot 5th son of 3rd baronet:—
Issue of late Capt Sacheverel Darwin Wilmot, RA, *b* 1885, *ka* 1918: *m* 1912, Annie Dudley, who *d* 1960, da of late Maj Gen Strover, RA:—
MARTYN SACHEVEREL, *b* 2 Sept 1914; Major (ret) RA; 1939-45 War (prisoner): *m* 1948, Mona Elizabeth, da of late S. D. M. Horner, and has issue living, Brian Sacheverel, *b* 1949: *m* 1979, Beatrice, da of Dr Ormonde George Pickard, CBE, of Dunwich, Suffolk, and has issue living, Thomas Sacheverel *b* 1980, Lucy Eleanor *b* 19—, — Robin Woollett, *b* 1950, — Anabel Sarah, *b* 1960. *Residence* – Foxlair, Fifehead St Quintin, Sturminster Newton, Dorset. —— Gordon Darwin, *b* 1918; Major (ret) Roy Scots Fusiliers: *m* 1941, Margaret Virginia Thorburn, and has issue living, Patrick Gordon, *b* 1954, — Virginia Ann, *b* 1942: *m* 1965, Jeremy Adrian Hill, MA, of Peyton Hall, Bures, Suffolk, and has issue living, Edward Justin *b* 1969, Tristram Darwin *b* 1970, Marcus Jeremy *b* 1977, — Felicity Joyce, *b* 1944: *m* 1964, Anthony P. Ziegler, MA, of Titcombs, Burford, Oxon, and has issue living, Thomas Pippin *b* 1965, Martyn Nicholas *b* 1967. *Residence* – Bruern End, Milton-under-Wychwood, Oxon OX7 6LL.

Granddaughter of late Edmund Wilmot, 7th son of 3rd baronet:—
Issue of late Rev Francis Edmund William Wilmot, *b* 1849, *d* 1911: *m* 1878, Katharine, who *d* 1939, da of late Col Thomas Coningsby Norbury Norbury, CB, of Sherridge, near Malvern (V Guillamore):—
Katharine Joyce, *b* 1888: *m* 1930, Henry Sutcliffe Crook, who *d* 1945, and has issue living, Faith Marygold, *b* 1931.
Issue of late Capt Edmund Mead Wilmot, *b* 1860, *d* 1935: *m* 1885, Agatha Georgiana, who *d* 1931, da of Francis J. Jessopp:—
Francis Hurt, *b* 1894: *m* 1935, Dorothy Fownes, el da of Harry W. Keith, MD, of Enderby, British Columbia, and has issue living, Penelope, *b* 19-. *Residence* – Vancouver, British Columbia.
The family of Wilmot settled at Sutton-upon-Soar, in Nottinghamshire, soon after the Conquest, and removed from thence into Derbyshire about the year 1539. The 1st baronet, Sir Edward Wilmot, an eminent Physician, was Physician-General to the Army, and Physician in Ordinary to George II. Col Sir Henry Wilmot, KCB, VC, 5th Bt, sat as MP for Derbyshire, S (C) 1869-85. The 6th baronet, Sir Ralph Henry Sacheverel Wilmot Capt Coldstream Guards, *d* of wounds received on active service 1918 and the 7th baronet, Maj Sir Arthur Ralph Wilmot, *d* (result of an accident whilst on active ser in Middle East) 1942. Capt Sir Robert Arthur Wilmot, 8th baronet, Scots Gds, was Equerry to HRH the Duke of Gloucester 1963-65.

WILMOT (GB) 1772, of Osmaston, Derbyshire (Extinct 1931)

Sir ROBERT RODNEY WILMOT, 6th and last *Baronet*.

DAUGHTER LIVING OF SIXTH BARONET (*By 2nd marriage*)

Kathleen Eleanor, *b* 1893: *m* 1921, Arthur Charles Melville Pym, who *d* 1956, and has issue living, Robert Marcus *b* 1922. *Residence* –

EARDLEY-WILMOT (UK) 1821, of Berkswell Hall, Warwickshire

Sir JOHN ASSHETON EARDLEY-WILMOT, LVO, DSC, RN, 5th *Baronet*; *b* 2 Jan 1917; *s* his uncle, *Maj Sir* JOHN, 1970; Cdr RN (ret); MBIM; FRSA; Monopolies Commn 1967-82; 1939-45 War (DSC); LVO 1957: *m* 1939, Diana Elizabeth, da of late Cdr Aubrey Moore, and has issue.

Arms – Quarterly, 1st, sable, a fesse or, between three eagles' heads couped argent, in the beak of each an escallop gules, *Wilmot*; 2nd, argent, on a chevron azure, three garbs or; a canton gules charged with a fret or, *Eardley*; 3rd, azure, a fesse engrailed or, between three maidens' heads proper, crined or, *Marow*; 4th, quarterly, argent and sable, a bend gules, charged with three mullets of the first. **Crests** – 1st, an eagle's head couped argent, in his beak an escallop gules; 2nd, a buck courant gules, attired and unguled or.
Residence – 41 Margravine Gdns, W6.

SON LIVING

MICHAEL JOHN ASSHETON (26 Arundel Gardens, W11), *b* 13 Jan 1941; *ed* Clifton: *m* 1st, 1971, Wendy, yr da of A. J. Wolstenholme; 2ndly, 1987, Diana Margaret, da of Robert Graham Wallis, and has issue living (by 1st *m*), Benjamin John, *b* 24 Jan 1974, — Guy Assheton, *b* 1979, — Holly Joanna, *b* 1976, — (by 2nd *m*) Poppy Clementine, *b* 1987.

DAUGHTER LIVING

Patricia Enid, *b* 1944: *m* 1966, Andrew McMeekan, of 32 Batoum Gardens, W6, and has issue living, Emily Charlotte, *b* 1974, — Isabel Heloise, *b* 1978.

BROTHER LIVING

Michael (2 Mittara Rd, Terrigal, NSW), *b* 1924: *m* 1956, Sylvia, da of Arthur Irish, of Sydney, NSW.

SISTER LIVING

Rosemary (*Hon Mrs Basil E. Feilding*) (Park Cottage, Monks Kirby, Rugby), *b* 1920: *m* 1939, Capt Hon Basil Egerton Feilding, Coldm Gds, who *d* 1970, and has issue (*see* E Denbigh).

COLLATERAL BRANCHES LIVING

Grandson of late Col Irton Eardley-Wilmot, yst son of Maj-Gen Frederick Marow Eardley-Wilmot, 2nd son of 1st baronet:—
Issue of late Capt Vere Levinge Eardley-Wilmot, *b* 1886, *d* 1965: *m* 1915, Mary Cecil, who *d* 1968, da of late H. Moffatt of Toronto:—
Hugh Irton (Forest Echo Motel, RR No 1, Norland, Ont), *b* 1925; *ed* McGill Univ (BSc).

Grandchildren of late Francis Eardley-Wilmot, 3rd son of late Rev Edward Revell Eardley-Wilmot, 3rd son of 1st baronet:—
Issue of late Rev Hubert Valentine Eardley-Wilmot, *b* 1878, *d* 1963: *m* 1908, Muriel Ivy, who *d* 1966, da of late William Lovett, of Norwich:—
Paul Revell (Woodland View, Cookham Rise, Berks), *b* 1917; *ed* St Paul's Sch: *m* 1953, Joan Violet, da of H. J. W. Shepherd, of High Wycombe, and has issue living, David Revell, *b* 1954, — Susan Mary, *b* 1957: *m* 1978, Peter William Rushton, of Clare Cottage, 40 Hale Rd, Farnham, Surrey GU9 9QH, and has issue living, Oliver William *b* 1983, Morgan David *b* 1988, Theodore Alexander *b* 1992. —— Hazel Mary, *b* 1910; *ed* Oxford Univ (BA 1931).
Issue of late Rev Canon Charles Revell Eardley-Wilmot, *b* 1880, *d* 1962: *m* 1914, Rose Meredyth, who *d* 1954, da of C. H. Bowen, of Sherbrooke, Province of Quebec, Canada:—
Robert Lloyd, *b* 1921; 1941-45 War as Sgt RCAF, attached RAF: *m* 1949, Joyce Ethel, da of Delbert Dagles, of Three Rivers, Quebec, Canada, and has issue living, David Robert, *b* 1952. —— Barbara Rose, *b* 1915; 1943-45 War as Nursing Sister RCAF attached RAF: *m* 1st, 1942, John Franklin Carr, Leading Aircraftman RCAF, who was *ka* 1942; 2ndly, 1947, Geoffrey Constable, of 36 Morewood Cres, Willowdale, Toronto, Ont, M2K 1L7, and has issue living (by 2nd *m*), Peter Geoffrey, *b* 1961, — Catherine Judith, *b* 1950, — Janet Meredyth, *b* 1953, — Susan Emily, *b* 1956. —— Cecilia Torlesse, *b* 1917; 1942-45 War as Private Canadian Women's Army Corps: *m* 1946, Eliol Albert Leyden, and has issue living, Richard Harold, *b* 1950, — Michael Peyton, *b* 1952, — Andrew Charles, *b* 1954, — Sylvia Dawn, *b* 1947, — Elizabeth Rose, *b* 1957. —— Sylvia Revell, *b* 1926: *m* 1948, Allan Adolphus Saunders, of RR2 Petitcodiac, New Brunswick, Canada, and has issue living, Nancy Peyton, *b* 1951, — Sylvia Lee, *b* 1953.
Issue of late Ernest Lancelot Eardley-Wilmot, *b* 1888; *d* 1975: *m* 1919, Margaret, da of late L. Hanlon, of Whangarei, NZ.
Philip (8 Ballaret St, Ellerslie, Auckland, NZ), *b* 1920; 1939-45 War as Flight Sgt, RNZAF: *m* 1948, Joan Hazel, da of G. R. Fox, of Auckland, NZ, and has issue living, Ronald Ernest, *b* 1953: *m* 1972, Gaylene Mildon, of Mt Wellington, Auckland, and has issue living, Matthew Ronald *b* 1973, Jamie *b* 1975, Nicholas *b* 1977, — Kay, *b* 1951: *m* 1972, William James Chapman, of Roslyn, Dunedin, NZ, and has issue living, Kirsten *b* 1974, Melanie *b* 1977. —— Eileen, *b* 1922: *m* 1943, Richard Quentin Taylor, and has issue living, Peter Raymond, *b* 1945, — Lynne Carol, *b* 1946.

Granddaughters of late Robert Eardley-Wilmot, MB, 5th son of Rev Edward Revell Eardley-Wilmot (*ante*):—
Issue of late Edward Gwynne Eardley-Wilmot, *b* 1877, *d* 1965: *m* 1904, Jane Millicent, OBE, who *d* 1964, da of Sir James William Scott, 1st Bt (*cr* 1909):—
Mary Marow, *b* 1909: *m* 1933, Capt John de Bourbel Stansfeld, MC, JP, who *d* 1975, and has issue living, John Raoul Wilmot (Dunninald, Montrose, Angus) *b* 1935; DL for Angus (1984); JP: *m* 1965, Rosalinde Rachel, da of late Desmond Gurney Buxton (*see* Buxton, Bt, colls), and has issue living, Edward John Buxton *b* 1966, Robert George Wilmot *b* 1967, Nicholas Desmond Morse *b* 1972, — Martin Raymond Eardley, *b* 1937: *m* 1990, Monica Ann Joseph, of Youngstown, Ohio.
Issue of late Lieut-Col Theodore Eardley-Wilmot, DSO, *b* 1879, *ka* 1918: *m* 1908, Mildred Clare, who *d* 1956, el da of late W. F. Reynolds, of Woodland Grange, near Leamington:—
Mildred Joan (*Baroness Cross of Chelsea*), *b* 1912: *m* 1st, 1939, Thomas Walton Davies, who *d* 1948; 2ndly, 1952, Baron Cross of Chelsea (Life Baron), who *d* 1989, and has issue living (by 1st *m*), Charles *b* 1943, — Caroline, *b* 1941, — Sophia, *b* 1946: *m* 1969, Henning Rasmussen, — (by 2nd *m*) (*see* B Cross of Chelsea). *Residence* – The Bridge House, Leintwardine, Craven Arms, Salop.

Grandson of late Maj Henry Eardley-Wilmot, 6th and yst son of Rev Edward Revell Eardley-Wilmot (ante):—

Issue of late Lambert Eardley-Wilmot, OBE, Fl Lt RAF, b 1894, d 1987: m 1930, Angela Clare Gertrude, who d 1955, 2nd da of late Col Arthur Hare Vincent, of Summerhill House, Castle Connell, co Limerick:—
Charles Vincent Burgoyne (Fir Tree House, Lower Morton, Thornbury, Bristol, Avon BS12 1LF), b 1932: m 1961, Sheila, only da of late George Frederick Broomfield, of Thornbury, Glos, and has issue living, Jane Clare, b 1962: m 1984, Geoffrey J. Sprackman, of 39 Severn Drive, Thornbury, Bristol, Avon, and has issue living, Ben Charles b 1991, Katie-Jane b 1988, — Sarah Elizabeth, b 1963: m 1990, Jeremy Northcott, of Hazel Cottage, St Tudy, Wadebridge, Cornwall, and has issue living, Emma Claire b 1993.

Grandchildren of late Gerald Stuart Eardley-Wilmot, son of late Stuart Eardley-Wilmot (infra):—
Issue of late Stuart Jeffery Eardley-Wilmot, b 1907, d 1986: m 1933, Mary, who d 1994, da of W. Y. Fleming, of Bexhill-on-Sea:—
Brian (15 Fernglen Rd S, St Heliers, Auckland, NZ), b 1939: m 1st, 1960 (m diss 1972), Margaret Robyn, da of A. Doust; 2ndly, 1980, Maureen Jean, da of George Huddlestone, of Cambridge, and has issue living (by 1st m), Stuart Allen, b 1961, — Kathryn Anne, b 1966. —— Gillian Mary, b 1935: m 1957, William H. Cook, of 346 Vesuvius Drive, Brea, California, USA, and has issue living, Victoria Mary, b 1961. —— Valerie, b 1946: m 1st, 1968 (m diss 1978), L. K. Eitzen; 2ndly, 1981, R. P. Haley, of 1160 W Farrington Drive, La Habra, California, USA.

Grandson of late Augustus Hillier Eardley-Wilmot, 6th son of 1st baronet:—
Issue of late Stuart Eardley-Wilmot, b 1847, d 1932: m 1875, Rosa Cornelia, who d 1924, da of William Johnstone, of Launceston, Tasmania:—
Parry, b 1888: m 1912, Amy, da of Percy Reynolds, of Hobartville, Richmond, NSW, and has issue living, a son, b 19—.
This family has common ancestry with the Wilmots, baronets of Osmaston (ext), and Wilmots, baronets of Chaddesden. John Eardley-Wilmot, father of 1st baronet, assumed by Roy Licence 1812 the additional surname of Eardley, as great-grandson of Elizabeth, sole heiress of Edward Eardley of Eardley, Staffs. The 1st baronet, Sir John Eardley-Wilmot, FRS, was sometime MP for North Warwickshire, and Gov of Van Diemen's Land 1843-7, and the 2nd baronet sat as MP for Warwickshire S (C) 1874-85, and was Recorder of Warwick 1852-7, and Judge of Bristol County Court 1854-63, and of Marylebone County Court 1863-71.

WILSON (UK) 1874, of Eshton Hall, co York

Loyal in everything

Brig Sir MATHEW JOHN ANTHONY WILSON, OBE, MC, 6th *Baronet*, son (by 1st m) of late Anthony Thomas Wilson, 2nd son of 4th Bt; b 2 Oct 1935; s his uncle, Sir (MATHEW) MARTIN, 1991; ed Trin Coll Sch, Ontario; formerly Exec Dir of the Wilderness Foundation (UK), and Vice-Pres of International Wilderness Leadership Foundation; Brig King's Own Yorkshire LI (ret); MC 1972, MBE (Mil) 1971 and OBE (Mil) 1979: m 1962, Janet Mary, elder da of late Edward Worsfold Mowll, JP, of Coldblow, Walmer, Kent, and has issue.

𝔄rms – Sable, a wolf rampant or, gorged with a collar gemel of the field between four mullets of six points, three in chief and one in base of the second. 𝔠rest – A demi-wolf or, gorged with a collar gemel sable, and resting the sinister paw on an escutcheon of the last, charged with a mullet as in the arms. 𝔖econd 𝔐otto – Res non verba (*Facts not words*).
Residence – Vermont, USA.

SON LIVING

MATHEW EDWARD AMCOTTS, b 13 Oct 1966; ed The King's Sch, Canterbury, and King's Coll, London Univ; Capt LI (despatches 1993); Marketing Manager, Earthwatch Europe.

DAUGHTER LIVING

Victoria Mary, b 1968; ed The King's Sch, Canterbury, and New Hall, Camb; Solicitor.

COLLATERAL BRANCHES LIVING

Issue living of late Peter Cecil Wilson, CBE, 3rd son of 4th Bt, b 1913, d 1984: m 1935 (m diss 1947), Grace Helen, da of late Arthur Ranken:—
Richard Thomas (Le Cepède, Lotissement de Clavary, 06810 Auribeau-sur-Siagne, France), b 1937: m 1964 (m diss 1974), Judith, da of Ford Jenkins, of Lowestoft, and has issue living, Alice Thomasina, b 1966, — Imogen Nancy, b 1967. —— (Edward) Philip (24 Highbury Place, N5), b 1940: m 1970, Lady Alexandra Patricia Gwendoline Jellicoe, da of 2nd Earl Jellicoe, and has issue living, Anthony Benedict, b 1980, — Patrick Peter b 1984.

Granddaughters of late Com Alec Thomas Lee Wilson (infra):—
Issue of late Lt-Col James Thomas Amcotts Wilson, JP, DL, b 1916, d 1992: m 1947, Judy Featherstone (Manor Farm, Wraxall, nr Dorchester, Dorset), da of late Maj Pierre Elliot Inchbald, MC (see Bingham, Bt, 1985 Edn):—
Carol Ann, b 1948: m 1972, David John Hugh Parry, of Broomhill, Rampisham, Dorchester, Dorset, son of late Alan Wheeler Parry, of Stoneleigh, Beaconsfield Rd, Liverpool, and has issue living, James Alan David, b 1976, — Benjamin Alec, b 1979. —— Pamela Gay, b 1951: m 1974, Edward Trevor Gwyn Lewis, of 77 Lexham Gdns, W8, son of late Rev Gwyn Lewis, and has issue living, Frances Leone, b 1975, — Kim Olivia, b 1979, — Tamsin Gwynne, b (twin) 1979. —— Vianna Jane, b 1959: m 1988, John Michael Dene, of Inpark, Cattistock, Dorchester, Dorset, son of Lt-Col John Anthony Dene, of Kilteelagh Stud, Dromineer, Nenagh, co Tipperary, and has issue living, Polly Alexandra, b 1990.

Issue of late Com Alec Thomas Lee Wilson, 3rd son of 3rd baronet, b 1883, d 1956: m 1913, Margaret (a DStJ), who d 1966, da of late Leopold Hirsch, of 10 Kensington Palace Gdns, W:—
Francis Amcotts (Garth House, Llangammarch Wells, Powys; Army and Navy Club), b 1922; 1939-45 War as Sub-Lt RNVR: m

1968, Mrs Katherine Mary Scott, da of late Robert Charles Bruce, MC (*see* E Elgin, colls), and has an adopted son and da, Robert Mathew, *b* 1970, — Jane Mary, *b* 1972.

Sir Mathew Wilson, 1st baronet, sat as MP for Clitheroe (*L*) 1847-52, for N Div of W Riding of Yorks 1874-85, and for Skipton Div of N part of W Riding of Yorks 1885-6. The 4th baronet, Lieut-Col Sir Mathew Richard Henry Wilson, CSI, DSO, 10th Hussars, served in S Africa 1899-1902 and sat as MP for S-W Div of Bethnal Green (*C*) 1914-22.

WILSON (UK) 1906, of Airdrie, New Monkland, co Lanark

Sir JAMES WILLIAM DOUGLAS WILSON, 5th *Baronet*; *b* 8 Oct 1960; *s* his father, *Capt Sir* THOMAS DOUGLAS, MC, 1984; *ed* Marlborough, and London Univ (BA): *m* 1985, Julia Margaret Louise, da of Joseph Charles Francis Mutty, of Mulberry Hall, Melbourn, nr Royston, Herts, and has issue.

Arms – Argent, a lion rampant between three mullets sable, on a chief vert a crescent of the first between two mullets pierced or. **Crest** – A demi-lion sable, charged on the body with a crescent argent between two mullets pierced or, all in pale.
Residence – Lillingstone Lovell Manor, Buckingham, MK18 5BQ.

SON LIVING

THOMAS EDWARD DOUGLAS, *b* 1990.

DAUGHTERS LIVING

Jessica Sarah, *b* 1988. —— Katrina Elizabeth, *b* 1992.

SISTERS LIVING

Sarah Ann, *b* 1950: *m* 1976, Michael J. Fleming, of Ye Olde Malting House, Greens Norton, Towcester, Northants NN12 8BE, and has issue living, Simon James, *b* 1982. —— Susan Mary, *b* 1954: *m* 1978, Robert James Nield, of 5 Belle Vue Rd, Exmouth, Devon, and has issue living, Timothy James, *b* 1979, — Michael Jonathon, *b* 1980, — Emilia Mary, *b* 1984. —— Margaret Rose, *b* 1957: *m* 1983, Jonathan Kendal James Gurney, of Mount Mill, Stratford Rd, Wicken MK19 6DG, elder son of Brian Gurney, of Handley Park, Towcester, and has issue living, Joseph Brian Thomas, *b* 1985, — Olivia Kate, *b* 1987.

AUNT LIVING (*Sister of 4th baronet*)

Aileen (16 Bramble Close, Oaklands Park, Redhill, Surrey), *b* 1915: *m* 1939, Roger Benjamin Constant, who *d* 1986, and has issue living, Roger Clive, *b* 1945; *ed* Sherborne, — Stella, *b* 1943.

DAUGHTER LIVING OF THIRD BARONET

Daphne Margaret, *b* 1922: *m* 1945, Thomas Morton Macdonald, of Coanwood Jordans, Bucks, and has had issue, Ian James, *b* 1946; *ed* Stowe, — Neil Stuart, *b* 1947; *ed* Oakham, — Alastair, *b* and *d* 1950.

WIDOW LIVING OF FOURTH BARONET

PAMELA AILEEN (*Lady Wilson*), da of Sir (Griffin Wyndham) Edward Hanmer, 7th Bt: *m* 1947, Capt Sir Thomas Douglas Wilson, 4th Bt, who *d* 1984. *Residence* – Lillingstone Lovell Manor, Buckingham, MK18 5BQ.

COLLATERAL BRANCH LIVING

Issue of late Maj John Wilson, Lanarkshire Yeo, only son of 2nd baronet, *b* 1911, *ka* 1942: *m* 1936, Zoe Jane (who *m* 2ndly 1943, Guy C. Turner, AFC, of Hay Mains, Harburn, W Calder, Midlothian), 2nd da of George Orr, of Kilduff House, East Lothian:—
Sarah Jane, *b* 1937: *m* 1959, Michael Claud Ogilvie-Thomson, WS, who *d* 1967, and has issue living, David John, *b* 1961, — Sheelagh Jane, *b* 1960. *Residence* – Hengist Hearth, 38 North Hinksey Lane, Oxford.

The 1st baronet, Sir John, was Chm of Wilsons and Clyde Coal Co (Limited), and sat as MP for Falkirk Dist (LU and *L*) 1895 to 1905.

WILSON (UK) 1920, of Carbeth, Killearn, co Stirling

Sir David Wilson, 3rd *Baronet*; *b* 30 Oct 1928; *s* his father, *Sir* John Mitchell Harvey, KCVO, 1975; *ed* Deerfield Acad, Mass, Harrow, and Oriel Coll, Oxford (MA); Bar Lincoln's Inn 1954; solicitor 1962: *m* 1955, Eva Margareta, el da of Tore Lindell, of Malmo, Sweden, and has issue.

Arms – (as recorded at Lyon Office)—Argent, a chevron gules between two mullets in chief, and in base a trefoil slipped vert. **Crest** – A demi-lion rampant gules, armed and langued azure.
Seat – Carbeth, Killearn, by Glasgow. *Residence* – Tandem House, Queen's Drive, Oxshott, Surrey KT22 0PH. *Clubs* – Lond Arts, Roy Southern Yacht, Hamble.

SONS LIVING

Thomas David (120 Balham Park Rd, SW12 8EA), *b* 6 Jan 1959; *ed* Harrow: *m* 1984, Valerie, elder da of Vivian David Davies Stogdale, of Monks Farm, Shotover, Oxon, and has issue living, Fergus, *b* 24 April 1987, — Oscar, *b* 1989.
—— Andrew (21 Av de la Marguerite, 78110 Le Vésinet, France), *b* 16 Dec 1959: *m* 1984, Penelope May, 2nd da of Brig William Turner, of The Holt, Woolton Hill, Newbury, Berks.

DAUGHTER LIVING

Annika, *b* 1961: *m* 1984, Dr David Malcolm Ratcliffe, of 63 Winchester Rd, Walton-on-Thames, Surrey KT12 2RH, son of M. Ratcliffe, of 440 Ombersley Rd, Worcester.

Always watchful

BROTHERS LIVING

John Richards (Heron's Court, Killearn, Stirlingshire), *b* 1930: *m* 1969, H. Jane, da of Maj Gilbert B. Rahr, of Huntbourne Farm, Tenterden, Kent. —— Andrew George (Little Carbeth, Killearn, by Glasgow), *b* 1933: *m* 1967, Anne-Marie Tekla, yr da of Tore Lindell, of Malmo, Sweden.
The 1st baronet, Sir David Wilson, was Convener (sometime Vice-Convener) of Stirlingshire, and a Member of Board of Agriculture for Scotland's Advisory Committee. The 2nd baronet, Sir John Mitchell Harvey Wilson, KCVO, was Keeper of The Royal Philatelic Collection 1938-69, and Pres Royal Philatelic Soc 1934-40.

Windham, see Bowyer-Smith.

WINNINGTON (GB) 1755, of Stanford Court, Worcestershire

Sir Francis Salwey William Winnington, 6th *Baronet*, son of late Francis Salwey Winnington, el son of 5th baronet, *b* 24 June 1907; *s* his grandfather, *Sir* Francis Salwey, 1931; Lieut Welsh Guards; European War 1939-40 (prisoner); is patron of three livings: *m* 1944, Anne Beryl Jane, only da of late Capt Lawrence Drury-Lowe, Scots Guards, and has issue.

Arms – Quarterly; 1st and 4th, argent, an orle between eight martlets sable, *Winnington*; 2nd and 3rd, sable, a saltire engrailed or, *Salwey*. **Crest** – A Saracen's head full-faced, couped at the shoulders proper, wreathed about the temples argent and sable.
Seat – Stanford Court, Worcester.

DAUGHTER LIVING

Charmian Anne, *b* 1945.

Gratâ sume manu

Take with a grateful hand

BROTHER LIVING

Thomas Foley Churchill, MBE, *b* 16 Aug 1910; *ed* Eton, and Balliol Coll, Oxford; is Col Grenadier Guards; MBE (Mil) 1948: *m* 1944, Lady Betty Marjorie Anson, da of 4th Earl of Lichfield, and has issue living, Anthony Edward (20 Baskerville Rd, SW18 3RW), *b* 13 May 1948: *m* 1978, Karyn, da of Francis Hubbs Kettles, and Mrs Alan Dayton, of Palm Beach, Florida, USA and has issue living, Edward Alan *b* 15 Nov 1987, Victoria Elizabeth *b* 1981, Sophia Rose *b* 1985, — Henry Thomas, *b* 1961, — Sarah Rose (*Viscountess Campden*), *b* 1951: *m* 1972, Anthony Baptist, Viscount Campden (Exton Park, Oakham, Leics LE15 8AN), el son of 5th Earl of Gainsborough, — Emma Elizabeth, *b* 1956: *m* 1981, Christopher J. Milne, of 67 Hendham Rd, SW17, and has issue living, Rupert John *b* 1986, Isabella Katherine *b* 1984, Lucinda Alice *b* 1991. *Residence* – 182 Rivermead Court, Ranelagh Gardens, SW6 3SG. *Clubs* – Pratt's, Hurlingham.

COLLATERAL BRANCHES LIVING

Granddaughters of late Capt John Taylor Winnington, son of late Capt John Taylor Winnington, 2nd son of 3rd baronet:—
Issue of late Lieut-Col John Francis Sartorius Winnington, DSO, Worcestershire Regt, *b* 1876, *d* of wounds received in action 1918: *m* 1910, Joyce Mary, who *d* 1970, da of David Marriage, of Chorley, Lancs:—

Susanne, *b* 1913: *m* 1st, 1936 (*m diss* 19-), Russell Cowell; 2ndly, 1950, John Duerdin, of Affcot Manor, Church Stretton, Salop, and has issue living (by 2nd *m*), John Patrick, *b* 1952: *m* 1986, Judy Mary Trow, of Little Stretton, and has issue living, Emma Mary *b* 1988, — Joanna Elizabeth, *b* 1950, — Frances June, *b* 1951. —— Patricia Rose, *b* 1917: *m* 1949, Robin Darell Unwin, OBE, who *d* 1991, of Longdon Hall, Tewkesbury, Glos, and has issue living, Carol John *b* 1951, — Guy Darell, *b* 1952: *m* 1984, Patricia Ann, da of Alan Derek Boydell, of Winchcombe, Glos, and has issue living, William Francis *b* 1988, Sally Victoria *b* 1986, Elizabeth Laura Dorothy *b* 1990, — Barry James, *b* 1956: *m* 1984, Susan Louise, da of George Dennis Gilbert, of Redmarley, Glos, and has issue living, Louise Rose *b* 1987, Rosanna Helen *b* 1989, Phoebe Grace *b* 1993.

Grandchildren of late Ven Edward Henry Winnington-Ingram, eldest son of Rev Edward Winnington-Ingram (*b* 1814), 2nd son of Rev Edward Winnington-Ingram (*b* 1785), 2nd son of 2nd baronet:—
Issue of late Rev Preb Edward Francis Winnington-Ingram, *b* 1883, *d* 1963: *m* 1924, Gladys Winifred (Wistan, Over Rd, Baslow, Derbys), da of John Armstrong, of Tenbury, Worcs:—
(Edward) John (Old Manor Farm, Cottisford, Brackley, Northants NN13 5SW), *b* 1926; *ed* Shrewsbury, and Keble Coll, Oxford (BA): *m* 1st, 1953, Shirley Yvoire, el da of Gerald Lamotte; 2ndly, 1973, Mrs Elizabeth Linda Few Brown, da of Geoffrey Milling, of Brading, Isle of Wight, and formerly wife of Peter Few Brown, and has issue living, (by 1st *m*) Edward Nicholas, *b* 1957, — Gerald Francis, *b* 1960: *m* 1987, Rebecca Susan, da of Terence Cocks, of Geneva, Switzerland, and has issue living, Lucy Margaret *b* 1990. —— Gladys Ann, *b* 1929: *m* 1952, Lt-Cdr Francis Nigel Oldfield Bartlett, RN (Eaton Cottage, Eaton Hill, Baslow, Bakewell, Derbys), and has issue living, Charles Nicholas Oldfield, *b* 1954, — Sarah Frances, *b* 1955, — Rachel Victoria, *b* 1957, — Joanna Elizabeth, *b* 1959.

Grandchildren of late Francis Herbert Winnington-Ingram, 2nd son of Rev Edward Winnington-Ingram (*b* 1814) (*ante*):—
Issue of late Charles William Edward Winnington-Ingram, *b* 1881, *d* 1958: *m* 1902, Maud Esther (Aylmer, Ont), da of Richard R. Jones, of Copenhagen, Ont:—
(Francis) Herbert, *b* 1906: *m* 1930, Ruth Agnes, da of Newton Newell, of Aylmer, Ont, and has issue living, Gerald Newell (PO Box 464, 58 McMurray St, Bracebridge, Ont), *b* 1935: *m* 1957, Lillian Tremblay, and has issue living, James Brian *b* 1959, Douglas Michael *b* 1964, Phyllis Anne *b* 1958, Angela Marie *b* 1969, — Charles Edward, *b* 1938: *m* Dorothy, da of —, and has issue living, one son, — Philip Herbert, *b* 1943: *m* Bea, da of —. —— Arthur Foley (RR6 Aylmer, Ont), *b* 1908: *m* 1928, Ruby Louisa, da of Edward Herries, of Luton, Ont, and has issue living, Donald Foley (RR6, Aylmer, Ont), *b* 1935: *m* 1957, Dawn Marlyn Hussar, da of the Rev Garnet Hussar Aylmer, and has issue living, Allan Foley *b* 1968, Cheryl Lynn *b* 1962. —— (Charles) Alexander, *b* 1912: *m* 1939, Doris Marjorie Buck, and has issue living, Alexander Grant, *b* 1940: *m* 1966, Carolyn Fuchsia Johnston, and has issue living, Sherri Lynn *b* 1966, and two das, — David Gary, *b* 1943: *m* 1965, Mary Ilene McClure, and has issue living, David, Deborah. —— Cecil Harold, *b* 1918: *m* 1947, Patricia Howse Green, and has issue living, William Edward, *b* 1948, — Brian Charles, *b* 1959, — Frank Barton, *b* (twin) 1959, — Beth Arlene, *b* 1952, — Beverley Irene, *b* 1953. —— Gerald, *b* 1926: *m* 1947, Edna Arletta Johnson, and has issue living, Judith Susanne, *b* 1949: *m* — Jones, and has issue living, Jennifer, — Janet Marie, *b* 1951. —— Vera Louise, *b* 1903: *m* 1928, Kenneth McGregor Hatch, who *d* 19—, and has issue living, Kenneth Herbert, *b* 1931: *m* 1953, Pamela Dianne House, and has issue living, Steven Kenneth *b* 1955: *m* 19—, Kati Mary McClung (and has issue living, Kenneth Robert *b* 1982, Gregory *b* 1984), Peter Donald *b* 1957: *m* 19—, Wendy Elizabeth Vaughan (and has issue living, Keven Donald *b* 1989), Thomas Alan *b* 1966, Nancy Laura *b* (twin) 1957: *m* 19—, Stuart William Jackson (and has issue living, Jason Blair *b* 1988), Wendy Vivian *b* 1962: *m* 1987, Edward Evans Etchells, — Donna Lucille, *b* 1928: *m* 1949, Clayton Vickers McKechnie, of Hanover, Ont, and has issue living, Stewart Douglas *b* 1952: *m* 1972, Kathleen Haskey (and has issue living, Christopher Stewart *b* 1974, Erin *b* 1979), Dean Charles *b* 1958, Janice Louise *b* 1953: *m* 1971, Edward Adrian Vanherk (and has issue living, Pamela Jenifer *b* 1971). —— Helen Patricia, *b* 1914: *m* 1938, James Arthur Ferris, who *d* 1989, and has issue living, Charles David, *b* 1942, — James Edward, *b* 1945: *m* 1968, Maureen O'Keefe, and has issue living, Jennifer Rebecca *b* 1970: *m* 19—, Richard Hartney, of Vancouver, BC (and has issue living, Kirk Russell *b* 19—, Kody James Ferris *b* 19—), Danielle Jacqueline *b* 1973, — Heather Anne, *b* 1956: *m* 1980, Rolf Larsen, of Sudbury, Ont. —— Marjorie, *b* 1920: *m* 1946, John M. Hale, and has issue living, John, *b* 19—: *m* Johanna, da of —, and has issue living, Jonathon, Jennifer, — Barbara, *b* 19—: *m* Wayne Stafford, and has issue living, Adam, Jorden. —— Audrey Lucille, *b* 1921: *m* 1948, William Ozarko, of 632 Lime Ridge Rd, RR3 Hamilton, Ont, and has had issue, John, *b* 19—, *d* 19—, — William, *b* 19—, — Catherine *b* 19—. —— Pauline, *b* 1928: *m* 1948, Edward Golibaski, and has issue living, Paul, *b* 19—, — Linda, *b* 19—.
Issue of late Herbert Arthur Winnington-Ingram, *b* 1881, *d* 1941: *m* 1912, Anna, who *d* 1924, da of Angus D. Grant, of Edmonton, Canada:—
Herbert Grant, *b* 1914: *m* 1941, Florence Beatrice Lea, and has issue living, Donald Grant, *b* 1947: *m* 1977, Ethel Langille, of Pugwash, Nova Scotia, and has issue living, Daniel Grant *b* 1979, Megan Elizabeth *b* 1981, Emily Hope *b* (twin) 1981, — Robert Craig, *b* 1953: *m* 1987, Hélène Dobrowolsky, of Whitehourse, Yukon, and has issue living, Joelle Xenia Aunalea *b* 1988, — Lea Gordon, *b* 1968: *m* 1978, Lovie Mohammed, of Toronto. —— Charles Gordon (66 Glenhaven Crescent, St Albert, Alberta T8N 1A5, Canada), *b* 1918: *m* 1st, 1944, Marion Winkler (decd); 2ndly, Joan Youngand, and has issue living (by 1st *m*), Robert Gordon, *b* 1943: *m* 1st, 19— (*m diss* 19—), Jane Bennett; 2ndly, 19—, Sharon Mills, and has issue living, (by 1st *m*) Robert Paul *b* 1966, Jill *b* 1969, (by 2nd *m*) Graham Gordon *b* 1978, Mathew James *b* 1981, Laura Sharon *b* 1982, — James Hugh, *b* 1948: *m* 1968 (*m diss* 19—), Joan Smith, — Donna Marion, *b* 1946: *m* 19—, Gerard Lemieux, and has issue living, André Gerard *b* 1971, Alène Margaret *b* 1973, Collette Marie *b* 1977. —— Marion Elizabeth, *b* 1920: *m* 1945, William Niven Duff, of 14515-84 Av, Edmonton, Alberta T5R 3X1, Canada, and has issue living, William Neil, *b* 1948: *m* 1st, 1969 (*m diss* 1971), Christine Judy Melmoth; 2ndly, 1973, Joanne Margaret Fedorow; 3rdly, 19—, Marlene Anne Hilker, and has issue living (by 1st *m*), Shae Nancy Marion *b* 1967, (by 2nd *m*), William Michael Scott *b* 1977, Brindy Veronica *b* 1981, — David Duff, *b* 1954: *m* 1976, Elizabeth Maria, da of John Van Lier, of Edmonton, and has issue living, Erin Nicole *b* 1985, Rebecca Anne *b* 1990, — Nancy Marion, *b* 1947: *m* 1969, Derek David Nash, and has issue living, Katharine Elizabeth *b* 1976, Margaret Lindsey *b* 1979. —— Anna, *b* 1924: *m* 1947, Raymond Benjamin Hager, and has issue living, Richard Raymond, *b* 1949: *m* 1982, Lesley Jane Etty, of Edmonton, — Douglas Gordon, *b* 1951: *m* Melanie Lissa Jahrig, of Ontario, and has issue living, Natalie Bree *b* 1985, — Donald Benjamin, *b* 1957: *m* Dolores Freda Patterson, of Alberta Beach, and has issue living, Jarret Benjamin *b* 1986, Jamie Donald *b* 1988. —— Laura Lillian *b* 1954: *m* 1977, Darryl Bruce Smith, of Edmonton, and has issue living, Joel Jeffrey *b* 1982, Jess Cole *b* 1981.
Issue of late John Gordon Gerald Winnington-Ingram, *b* 1889, *d* 1945: *m* 1922, Florence Mabel Byron, who *d* 1985:—
Florence Maxine, *b* 1923: *m* 1945, Alexander Harold Clark, and has issue living, David Gerald, *b* 1946: *m* 1970, Linda Jeffery, of Devon, and has issue living, Scott Jeffery *b* 1973, Cindi Jennifer *b* 1975, — Randall Gregory, *b* 1957: *m* 1988, Debora Ann Degryse, of Winnipeg, Man, and has issue living, Carly Anne *b* 1992, — Kathleen Laura, *b* 1948: *m* 1969, Robert Kenneth Chalmers, of Winnipeg, and has issue living, Laura Susan *b* 1969: *m* 1993, Cornelius Vandertop (and has issue living, Devonny Kathrine *b* 1994), Barbara Ruth, *b* 1973. —— Kathleen Hazel, *b* 1931: *m* 1956, Rev Gordon Samuel Jardine, and has issue living, Edwin James *b* 1961, — Arthur John *b* 1964, — Bonnie Jean *b* 1959: *m* 1984, Hugh Mclellan, and has issue living, Stephen Patrick *b* 1985, Kathleen Joan *b* 1987, — Donna Jean, *b* 1965, — Naomi Kathleen, *b* 1972.

Grandson of late Rev Edward Winnington-Ingram (*b* 1814) (ante):—
Issue of late George Frederick Winnington-Ingram, *b* 1859, *d* 1929: *m* 1901, Mary Beatrice, who *d* 1957, da of late John Burridge, of Charminster, Bournemouth:—
John Felix, *b* 1909.

Grandsons of late Rev Alfred Winnington-Ingram (infra):—

Issue of late Cecil Winnington-Ingram, MBE, *b* 1914, *d* 1990: *m* 1954, Maude (14 Main Rd, Biddenham, Bedford MK40 4BB), yr da of late James Bartlett Lee, of Portsmouth:—
Charles Pepys, *b* 1955. ——— (Francis) Christopher, *b* 1957.

Grandson of late Rev Edward Winnington-Ingram (*b* 1814) (ante):—
Issue of late Rev Alfred Winnington-Ingram, *b* 1861, *d* 1929: *m* 1906, Julia Margaret, who *d* 1958, da of late William Augeraud:—
Richard Sullivan, *b* 1919; Maj (ret) RE; 1939-45 War (despatches): *m* 1952, Isobel Margaret, only da of late Robin McCrae, of Kabete, Kenya, and has issue living, *Rev* David Robert (The Rectory, Offwell, Honiton, Devon EX14 9SB), *b* 1959: *m* 1990, Carol Jarvis, and has issue living, Jonathan Richard *b* 1992, — Peter Richard (4 Home Farm Cottages, Malshanger, Basingstoke, Hants RG23 7ET), *b* 1960: *m* 1989, Mrs Sarah L. J. Addie, yst da of late Archie Weir, of Edinburgh, and has issue living, Archie *b* 1993, Kitty Rose *b* 1992, — Julia Caroline, *b* 1954: *m* 1982, Peter Derek Gregson, of 15 Harling Bank, Kirkby Lonsdale, Carnforth, Lancs LA6 2DJ, 2nd son of W. D. H. Gregson, of 15 Barnton Avenue, Edinburgh, and has issue living, Heather Mary *b* 1986, Sheila Rosalind *b* 1988, — Mary Cynthia, *b* 1956: *m* 1985, Dr Edward Mark Hundert, of 8 Fuller Rd, Wellesley, MA 02181, USA, son of Irwin Hundert, of East Brunswick, New Jersey, USA, and has issue living, Carol Grace *b* 1991. *Address* – Supuko, 36 Barnton Av, Edinburgh EH4 6JL.

Grandchildren of late Gerald Constantine Winnington-Ingram, son of late Rev Edward Winnington-Ingram (ante):—
Issue of late Eric Alfred Winnington-Ingram, *b* 1902, *d* 1986: *m* 1930, Jean Emma Caroline (Charlcote, Oldlands Av, Balcombe, W Sussex), da of F. G. Hopkins, of Haddon Hill, Christchurch, Hants:—
Mariamne Jean, *b* 1933: *m* 1968, Roderick MacBeath, of The Pines, Deanland Rd, Balcombe, W Sussex. ——— Iris Hawthorne, *b* 1935: *m* 1964, John Awberry Field, of Yewtrees Farm, Balcombe, W Sussex, and has issue living, Fiona Clare, *b* 1967, — Alison Joyce, *b* 1969.

Granddaughter of late Rear-Adm Herbert Frederick Winnington-Ingram, yst son of late Rev Edward Winnington-Ingram (*b* 1785) (ante):—
Issue of late Herbert Edward Winnington-Ingram, *b* 1869, *d* 1958: *m* 1899, Agnes Maud, who *d* 1956, da of late George Bevington Foster:—
Marjorie Agnes, *b* 1901. *Residence* – Etherstone, Dorking Road, Tadworth, Surrey.
This family were lords of the manor of Winnington *temp* Edward I, and continued to reside there till the beginning of the eighteenth century. The 4th baronet was MP for Bewdley (*L*) 1832-46 and 1857-68. The present baronet is descended from Sir Francis Winnington, Knt, of Stanford Court, who was appointed in 1678 Solicitor-General to Charles II, a post which he resigned, that he might act consistently with his conscience, by supporting the Exclusion Bill. Sir Francis Salwey Winnington, 5th Bt, was High Sheriff of Worcestershire 1894.

WISEMAN (E) 1628, of Canfield Hall, Essex

Sir JOHN WILLIAM WISEMAN, 11th *Baronet*; *b* 16 March 1957; *s* his father, *Sir* WILLIAM GEORGE EDEN, CB, 1962: *m* 1980, Nancy Ann, da of Casimer Zyla, of New Britain, Conn, USA, and has issue.

Arms – Sable, a chevron ermine between three cronels argent. **Crest** – A tower or, port open argent, out of the top a demi-Moor issuant armed proper, in his right hand a dart argent, barbed or plumed or, in his left a Roman target of the last.
Residence – 395 North Road, Sudbury, Mass 01776, USA.

DAUGHTERS LIVING

Elizabeth, *b* 1983. ——— Patricia Alison, *b* 1986.

HALF-SISTERS LIVING

Margaret, *b* 1913: *m* 1936, Ramsay William Rainsford-Hannay (Maxwell, Bt, *cr* 1804 (ext)), and has issue living, David Wiseman Ramsay, *b* 1939; MA, MB, BChir, DCH: *m* 1963, Janet Gilliat, and has issue living, Mark Gilliat Rainsford *b* 1966, Neil Maxwell Rainsford *b* 1969, Stephen Rainsford Ramsay *b* 1972, — Jessica Margaret, *b* 1937: *m* 1978, Colin Russell. *Residence* – Cardoness, Gatehouse-of-Fleet, Kirkcudbrightshire DG7 2EP. ——— Rosemary, *b* 1916: *m* 1936, Lt-Col Frederick R. Hulton, RA (ret), and has issue living, Frederick William, *b* 1938: *m* 1973, Ruth Parsons, and has issue living, Mark *b* 1975, Dominic *b* (twin) 1975, — Peter Richard, *b* 1941: *m* 1969, Dorinda Stewart, and has issue living, Anna Sky *b* 1979, — Thomas Michael, *b* 1943: *m* 19—, Susan Oldman, and has issue living, Claire *b* 1975, — Rosemary Jane, *b* 1949: *m* 1970, Christopher Eliot, and has issue living, James *b* 1975, David *b* 1978, Peter *b* 1984. *Residence* – Firles, Seaford, Sussex. ——— Sheila (New York, USA), *b* 1928; is a Journalist.

Sapit qui Deo sapit
He is wise who is wise
through God

WIDOW LIVING OF TENTH BARONET

JOAN MARY (*Joan Lady Wiseman*) (32 Victoria Rd, W8), da of late Arthur Phelps, of Woodridge, Harrow, and formerly wife of Lawrence E. Lesueur: *m* 1944, as his 3rd wife, Sir William George Eden Wiseman, CB, 10th baronet, who *d* 1962.

COLLATERAL BRANCHES LIVING

Grandchildren of late Thomas Edward Wiseman (*b* 1851) (infra):—
Issue of late Thomas Edward Wiseman, *b* 1878, *d* 1959: *m* 1916, Annie, who *d* 1970, da of George William Allen:—
THOMAS ALAN, *b* 8 July 1921; *ed* Gravesend County Sch; formerly Admin Officer for Forest Products Ltd; late Staff Sergeant RAOC: *m* 1946, Hildemarie, who *d* 1991, da of Gustav Domnik, of Allenstein, E Prussia, Germany. *Residence* – 14 Havisham Rd, Chalk, Gravesend, Kent DA12 4UN.
Issue of late Frank Eldred Wiseman, *b* 1880, *d* 1938: *m* 1923, Lily Amy, who *d* 1957, da of Harry Lewis Littlewood, of Gravesend, Kent:—

†Wallis Littlewood, *b* 1924: *m* 1st, 1951, Brenda Doris, who *d* 1990, da of late Arthur Allanson, of Walmer, Port Elizabeth, S Africa; 2ndly, 1991, Margaret-Ann (PO Box 5689, Walmer 6070, Port Elizabeth, S Africa), da of late Malcolm Edward Rittenhouse, of Osgood, Indiana, USA, and *d* 1993, leaving issue (by 1st *m*), Jonathan Charles (11 Huilboom St, Randpark, Johannesburg, S Africa), *b* 1953: *m* 1980, Rita Hilda, da of L. A. Williams, of Port Elizabeth, and has issue living, Lauren Ann *b* 1983, Nicola Jane *b* 1986, — Richard Christopher (29 Catalenti Drive, Randpark Ridge - Ext 23, Randburg, S Africa), *b* 1954: *m* 1986, Dawn Lorraine, da of Patrick Hart, of Springs, S Africa, and has issue living, Christopher Phillip *b* 1987, — Barry James (19 Pamela Crescent, Walmer Downs, Port Elizabeth, S Africa), *b* 1956: *m* 1979, Brigitte, da of Hans Bülbring, of Port Elizabeth, S Africa, and has issue living, Jarrod *b* 1984, Paul Mark *b* 1986, — Margaret Alexandra, *b* 1960: *m* 1985, Peter Wilson Newton, of 19 Barrydale Rd, Miramar, Port Elizabeth, S Africa, son of Michael Newton, of Nairobi, Kenya, and has issue living, Matthew Michael *b* 1987, Bailey Louise *b* 1985.

Issue of late Frederick William Wiseman, *b* 1885, *d* 1954: *m* 1914, Charlotte Hepshibah Ward, who *d* 1966:—
John Henry Ware (258 Murray St, Rockhampton 4700, Qld), *b* 1924; 1939-45 War with R Australian Artillery in New Guinea, Bouganville and New Britain (wounded): *m* 1962, Douglas James Lung, of Bundaburg, Queensland. —— Marie Eleanor (14 Ryrie St, N Ryde, Sydney, NSW), *b* 1919: *m* 1941, Capt Stanley Thornton Shaw, RAA, who *d* 1956, and has issue living, John Alexander, *b* 1943, — Philip Thornton, *b* 1945, — Laurence Edward, *b* 1946.

Grandson of late Edward Thomas Wiseman, son of late Thomas Wiseman (*b* 1778), son of late Thomas Wiseman (*b* 1760), 2nd son of 6th baronet:—
Issue of late Thomas Edward Wiseman, *b* 1851, *d* 1918: *m* 1877, Ellen Justinia, da of George Ware:—
Louis Gerald, *b* 1881: *m* 19-, Agnes, da of —, and has issue living, Edward Thomas, *b* 19-, — Louis George, *b* 19-, — Teresa, *b* 19-, — Audrey, *b* 19-.

Granddaughter of late Edwin Wycliffe Wiseman (infra):—
Issue of late Edwin Leonard Wiseman, *b* 1897, *d* 1964: *m* 1921, Winifred May (27 Davis Av, Northfleet, Kent), da of Edward William Bassant:—
Mary, *b* 1933.

Granddaughter of late William Henry Wiseman, son of late Charles Pierce Wiseman, son of late Thomas Wiseman (*d* 1778) (ante):—
Issue of late Edwin Wycliffe Wiseman, *b* 1864, *d* 1954: *m* 1st, 1893, Rosa, who *d* 1926, da of Leonard Leonard; 2ndly, 1928, Alice Maud Mary, who *d* 1966, da of Horace Plant:—
(By 2nd *m*) Alice Rosa, *b* 1930. *Residence* – 47 Pelham Road South, Gravesend.

Grandchildren of late Pierce Wiseman, son of Charles Pierce Wiseman (ante):—
Issue of late Thomas Charles Wiseman, *b* 1873, *d* 1940: *m* 1896, Eliza, da of Charles Carpenter:—
Albert Victor, *b* 1915; is a Police Officer; formerly Flying Officer RAF: *m* 1941, Nicola, da of Leonard Foreman, and has issue living, Jonathan Thomas Charles, *b* 1946, — Simon Pierce, *b* 1949, — Elizabeth Victoria, *b* 1942. —— Gertrude Minnie, *b* 1903: *m* 1936, Thomas Jarvis, who *d* 1976, and has issue living, Michael (Glenview House, Leith Park Rd, Gravesend), *b* 1942: *m* 1972, Brenda Shaftoe, and has issue living, Alton James *b* 1976, Julia Simone *b* 1975, — Trevor (The Hollies, Byworth, Petworth, W Sussex), *b* 1946: *m* 19-, Patricia English, and has issue living, Charles Alexander *b* 1977.

Granddaughter of late Thomas Charles Wiseman (ante):—
Issue of late William Henry Wiseman, *b* 1910, *d* 1979: *m* 1937, Winifred, who *d* 1988, da of William Charles Ambrose Knight:—
Susan Marjorie, *b* 1940: *m* 1977, Ian Crowe, of 12A West End Grove, Farnham, Surrey GU9 7EG.

Grandson of late Charles John Wiseman (*b* 1862) (infra):—
Issue of late Charles John Wiseman, *b* 1904, *d* 1990: *m* 1937, Jessie (17 Holburne Gdns, Kidbrooke, SE3), da of James Arthur Laming:—
David John (East Dulwich), *b* 1939; BEd Hons; Lieut The Parachute Regt TAVR: *m* 1st, 1964 (*m diss* 1968), Susan Anne, da of Charles William Tait; 2ndly, 1977, Ann, da of Dr Henry James Walls.

Grandchildren of late Thomas Palmer Wiseman, son of late Edmund Wiseman, son of late Thomas Wiseman (*b* 1760) (ante):—
Issue of late Charles John Wiseman, *b* 1862, *d* 1936: *m* 1890, Lillie Jane, da of William Oakley:—
John Robert, *b* 1908: *m* 1931, Ethel, da of Joseph Thomas Beecham. *Residence* – Woolwich, SE18. —— Annie Elizabeth, *b* 1896: *m* 1918, Zacharia William Coles, and has issue living, Nancy Joan, *b* 1921: *m* 1944, Edward Henry Willard, of The Cock, Church St, Staines, Middx, and has issue living, Paul William, *b* 1946. —— Grace Mary, *b* 1900: *m* 1923, Walter Jefferies, and has issue living, Ronald Walter, *b* 1925, — Dennis Gordon, *b* 1927: *m* 19-, and has issue living, Beverley *b* 1952. —— Violet Mary, *b* 1903: *m* 1930, Frank Tranter, and has issue living, Jean Alma, *b* 1931.

Grandchildren of late Charles John Wiseman (*b* 1862) (ante):—
Issue of late Thomas Charles Wiseman, *b* 1897, *d* 1928: *m* 1919:—
Ronald Henry, *b* 1920; NW Europe 1944-45: *m* 1943, and has issue living, Dawn, *b* 19-. —— Constance Queenie, *b* 1921: *m* 1940. —— Betty Thomasina, *b* 1928: *m* 1946.

Granddaughter of late Charles John Wiseman (*b* 1862) (ante):—
Issue of late Alfred John Wiseman, *b* 1906, *d* 1979: *m* 1st, 1931 (*m diss* 1946), Rose Knight; 2ndly, 1946, Enid May Hurford (3 Pound Cres, Fetcham, Surrey):—
(By 2nd *m*) Linda, *b* 1949: *m* 1970, Michael Ramsay, of Athelney, 25 Scalwell Park, Seaton, S Devon.

Sir John Wiseman, great-grandfather of 1st baronet, was one of the Auditors of the Exchequer, *temp* Henry VIII, was knighted at Battle of the Spurs, and purchased Canfield Park, in Essex, *temp* Edward VI. The 1st baronet, Sir William Wiseman, was High Sheriff of Essex 1638-9. The 2nd baronet, Sir William, was High Sheriff of Essex 1659-60. The 5th baronet, Sir William, was Lieut-Col Coldstream Guards. The 7th baronet, Sir William Saltonstall, was Capt RN. The 8th baronet, Sir William Saltonstall, KCB, was Rear-Adm. The 9th baronet, Sir William, was Capt RN, and served in New Zealand War 1864-5, and Niger Expedition 1869. The 10th baronet, Lt-Col Sir William George Eden, CB, was Ch of British Intelligence Ser in USA 1917-18, and Chm of New York Cttee of Dollar Exports Board 1951-62.

WOLSELEY (E) 1628, of Wolseley, Staffordshire

HOMO·HOMINI·LUPUS

Man is as a wolf towards his
fellow man

Sir CHARLES GARNET RICHARD MARK WOLSELEY, 11th *Baronet*, son of late Capt Stephen Garnet Hubert Francis Wolseley, RA, el son of 10th baronet; *b* 16 June 1944; *s* his grandfather, *Sir* EDRIC CHARLES JOSEPH, 1954; *ed* Ampleforth; FRICS; Partner Smith Gore until 1987: *m* 1st, 1968 (*m diss* 1984), Anita Maria, el da of late Hugo J. Fried; 2ndly, 1984, Mrs Imogene E. Brown, and has issue (by 1st *m*).

Arms – Argent, a talbot passant gules. **Crest** – Out of a ducal coronet or, a wolf's head erased proper.
Seat – Wolseley Park, Rugeley, Staffs WS15 2TU.

SON LIVING *(By 1st marriage)*

STEPHEN GARNET HUGO CHARLES, *b* 2 May 1980.

DAUGHTERS LIVING *(By 1st marriage)*

Annabelle Clare Maria, *b* 1969. —— Emily Lavinia, *b* 1972. —— Lucy Margaret, *b* 1977.

SISTER LIVING

Mary Patricia Anne, *b* 1942: *m* 1973, Steuart Martin Moor, TD, FRICS, of Park Side, 4 Cliff Road, Stamford, Lincs PE9 1AH, and has issue living, Theresa Mary Geraldine, *b* 1974, — Sonya Mary Elizabeth, *b* 1976, — Caroline Stephanie Elaine, *b* 1978.

UNCLES LIVING AND DECEASED *(Sons of 10th baronet)*

Basil Charles Daniel Rudolph, *b* 1921; *ed* Ampleforth; 1939-45 War as Flight-Lt RAF: *m* 1950, Ruth Key, da of late Lt-Col William Tom Carter, OBE, of Offham, Kent, and has issue living, Anne Teresa Margaret, *b* 1951: *m* 1980, Robert Hext-Fremlin, of Southborough, Kent, and has issue living, Shelley Naomi *b* 1980, — Susanna Elizabeth Mary, *b* 1952, — Sarah Angela Clare, *b* 1954: *m* 1983, Michael George Alexander McCurrach, of Fleet, Hants, — Joanna Ruth *b* 1958. *Residence* – Moor Oak, Dymock, Glos. —— George John Carlos, *b* 1925; *ed* Ampleforth, and New Brunswick and British Columbia Univs; 1943-47 War with RAF; with BAC 1960-88 (ret). *Residence* – Rosethorpe, Finmere, Buckingham MK18 4AT. —— †Richard Edric Vincent, *b* 1928; *ed* Ampleforth, and New Brunswick Univ; sometime in Rifle Bde, and RCN: *m* 1950 (*m diss* 1969, re-*m* 1971) Alice Baltazzi, who *d* 1987, da of late Amos Tuck French, and *d* 1991, leaving issue, Stephen Richard Dulany, *b* 1954: *m* 1993, Kathleen Frances O'Ahern, — Christopher Michael Garnet, *b* 1956: *m* 1989, Cheryl M. McCormick, — Carlotta Andrea Tuck WOLSELEY-LAHCHIOUACH (313 Old Main Rd, PO Box 74, N Falmouth, Mass 02556, USA), *b* 1951: *m* 1972 (*m diss* 1982), Abdelhadi Lahchiouach, of Essaioura, Morocco, — Heather Maria Warner, *b* 1957; resumed her maiden name of WOLSELEY 1983: *m* 1975 (*m diss* 1981), James De Mello, of N Falmouth, Mass, and has issue living, Tara Maria French *b* 1976; and further issue, Brianna Maria Lindo *b* 1993.

AUNTS LIVING *(Daughters of 10th baronet)*

Frances Mary Mona Clare (Casa's Cortijo, 139, Sotogrande (Cadiz), Spain), *b* 1920; late WRNS: *m* 1953, Bernhard Wilmsen, who assumed by deed poll 1954, the additional surname of Wolseley before his patronymic and *d* 1983, and has issue living, Anthony Edric Charles (Villa Gosen, Sotogrande (Cadiz), Spain), *b* 1955; *ed* St Christopher's Sch, Letchworth, Univ of Wales, and Univ of Granada, Spain. —— Agnes Mary Ann Hilda, *b* 1923. *Residence* – Rosethorpe, Finmere, Buckingham MK18 4AT.

MOTHER LIVING

PAMELA VIOLETTE (*Pamela, Lady Wolseley*), da of late Capt F. Barry, of Old Court, Whitchurch, Ross-on-Wye; granted 1955 the style, title, place, and precedence as if her late husband had survived and succeeded to the title: *m* 1942, Capt Stephen Garnet Hubert Francis Wolseley, RA (ante), *d* of wounds received in action 1944. *Residence* – The Cottage, Wolseley Bridge, Stafford, Staffs ST17 0XR.

COLLATERAL BRANCHES LIVING

Issue of late William Ralph Joseph Wolseley, TD, JP, yr son of 9th baronet, *b* 1887, *d* 1977: *m* 1923, Ruth Gertrude, who *d* 1962, yst da of late Lt-Col Robert Halstead Hargreaves, JP, DL, of Knightley Grange, Staffordshire, and Barnside, Lancs:—
Robert William Hargreaves, *b* 1924; *ed* Canford Sch; 1939-45 War with Gren Gds and R Fus: *m* 1965, Beryl Marjorie, da of F. G. Harvey, of Norman Chapel, Aston Magna, Glos, and has issue living, Alistair Robert Hargreaves, *b* 1969, Heather Frances, *b* 1967. —— Veronica Ruth Teresa Rose, *b* 1928.

Granddaughters of late William Augustus Wolseley, MD, son of late William Bertie Wolseley, son of late Capt Henry Wolseley, 4th son of 6th baronet:—
Issue (by 2nd *m*) of late William Augustus (Daniel) Wolseley, *b* 1847, *d* 1929: *m* 1st, 1891, Harriet, who *d* 1894, da of Fraser Luckie; 2ndly, 1895, Lilian Laura, who *d* 1941, da of late Horatio Bethune Leggatt, of Worth, Sussex:—
Lilian Patricia Dysart (Flat 6, Chester Mansions, 151/153, Oakhill Rd, SW15), *b* 1908: *m* 1933 (*m diss* 1948), Alexander Mervyn Archdale, and has issue living, Dominic Edward Wolseley, *b* 1937; *ed* St Paul's Sch, and Downing Coll, Camb (MA); late RAF: *m* 1st, 1959 (*m diss* 1974), Ruth Selby, da of Charles Johnston, late US Foreign Ser; 2ndly, 1976, Donna, da of Albert Leroy Baird, of Sun City, Arizona, USA, — Anthony Quintin Wolseley, *b* 1940; *ed* Saltus Gram Sch, Bermuda.

Grandchildren of late William Wykeham Frederick Bourne, 2nd son of late Rev John Frederick Bourne, by his wife Eliza Jane, 4th da of late William Bertie Wolseley (ante):—
Issue of late James Robert Wykeham Bourne, ARICS, *b* 1885, *d* 1971: *m* 1926, Mabel, who *d* 1974, da of late William Robert Reigate:—
Norah Ann Wykeham (19 Bloomsbury Pl, Brighton), *b* 1932: *m* 1966, Colin James Outram Monro, who *d* 1983, and has issue living, John Seton, *b* 1968, — Fiona Eleanor Wykeham, *b* 1967: *m* 1989, Anthony Nathan Greenstein, and has issue living, Daniel James Sheridan *b* 1989, Eleanor Rebecca Anne *b* 1991.

Issue of late Sybil Katherine Bourne, b 1887, d 1976: m 1915, Maj Vernon Milner Montague-Smith, late W Yorks Regt, who d 1951:—
Patrick Wykeham b 1920; ed Mercers' Sch; Assist Editor of Debrett 1946-62, Editor 1962-80, Consultant Editor 1980-86; NW Europe 1944-45 as Sgt RASC: m 1974, Annabelle Christina Calvert (Brereton, 197 Park Rd, Kingston upon Thames, Surrey), da of late Noel Newton, MA, of 65 Abbotsbury Close, Kensington, W14, and d 1986.

Issue of late Phyllis Margaret Bourne, b 1895, d 1983: m 1923, Percy Raymond Cooper, who d 1972:—
Marigold Louise, b 1931: m 1955, Rev Christopher John Sutherland Gill, of Hurstleigh, Hurstwood Lane, Tunbridge Wells, and has issue living, Philip Wykeham Sutherland, b 1956; ed St Andrew's Univ: m 1992, Manuela, da of Johann Baptiste Georg Pappi, of Munich, — Timothy John Sutherland, b 1957.

Issue of late Kathleen Bourne, b 1898, d 1992: m 1917, Paul Francis Wheler Bush, who d 1961:—
Pauline Carol Wheler, b 1920: m 1942 (m diss 19—), Cyril Thomas James, and has issue living, Michael Thomas, b 1944, — Robert Steven, b 1948; late L/Cpl RE, — Kathleen Mary (Lower Wick, Dursley, Glos), b 1943: m 1967, Cdr David Heron Jennings, RN (ret), who d 1988, and has issue living, Sarah b 1968.

Descendants of late Richard Wolseley (2nd brother of 5th baronet), who was cr a Baronet 1745:—
See Wolseley, Bt, cr 1745.
This ancient Staffordshire family is descended from Siward, Lord of Wisele, fourth in descent from whom was Robert, Lord of Wolseley, temp 1281. Ralph, sixth in descent from Robert, was Fourth Baron of the Exchequer temp Edward IV. Sir Robert, 1st baronet, was a Col in Charles I's army, and suffered sequestration. Sir Charles, 2nd baronet, represented Stafford in the Parliaments of Charles I and II, and was a member of Cromwell's House of Lords. Sir William, 6th baronet, was a Gentleman of the Privy Chamber to George III.

WOLSELEY (I) 1745, of Mount Wolseley, co Carlow

HOMO·HOMINI·LUPUS

Man is as a wolf towards
his fellow man.

Sir JAMES DOUGLAS WOLSELEY, 13th *Baronet*, son of late James Douglas Wolseley, son of late Douglas St John Wolseley, only son of late Robert Warren St John Wolseley, el son of late Rev Robert Warren Wolseley, yr son of late Maj Robert Benjamin Wolseley, 6th son of late Rev William Wolseley, 3rd son of 1st baronet; b 17 Sept 1937; s his kinsman, Sir GARNET, 1991; ed Texas Christian Univ (BBA): m 1st, 1965 (m diss 1971), Patricia Lynn, da of William R. Hunter, of Mount Shasta, California, USA; 2ndly, 1984, Mary Anne, da of Thomas G. Brown, of Hilo, USA.

Arms – Argent, a talbot passant gules, a crescent for difference. **Crest** – Out of a ducal coronet, a wolf's head proper.
Residence – 4317 Clay St, Fort Worth, Texas, USA.

SISTERS LIVING OF TWELFTH BARONET

Rubina Bingham, b 1909; m 1st, 1946, Walter Leonard Openshaw, who d 1951; 2ndly, 1952, Frank Whitby, who d 1960. *Residence* – 47 Telegraph Rd, Heswall, Cheshire. —— Lalla, b 1914.

MOTHER LIVING

Olive, da of Carroll Walter Wofford: m 1935, James Douglas Wolseley, who d 1960. *Residence* – 4242 Bryant Irvin Rd #226, Fort Worth, Texas 76109, USA.

WIDOW LIVING OF TWELFTH BARONET

LILLIAN MARY (*Dowager Lady Wolseley*), da of late William Bertram Ellison, of Love Lane, Wallasey, Cheshire: m 1950, Sir Garnet Wolseley, 12th Bt, who d (Oct) 1991 *Residence* – 73 Dorothy St, Brantford, Ontario N3S 1H1, Canada.

COLLATERAL BRANCHES LIVING

Granddaughter of late William Robert Wolseley, 2nd son of Richard John Wolseley, yr son of John Wolseley, MD, 4th son of late Rev William Wolseley, 3rd son of 1st baronet:—
Issue of late Noel Cecil Wolseley, b 1889, d 1969 (naturalized as American citizen 1920): m 1913, Mae Evelyn, who d 1965, da of John J. O'Connell:—
Eileen Rita, b 1916; Dir Nursing Ser, Concord Hosp, Concord, New Hampshire, USA.

Granddaughters of late Francis Ernest Wolseley, 3rd son of late Richard John Wolseley (ante):—
Issue of late Francis Richard Wolseley, b 1875, d 1934: m 1906, Elizabeth Ellen, who d 1966, da of late John Abbott Shippey:—
Kathleen Frances Hilda, b 1908: m 1938, Hugh Wynn Jones, and has issue living, Kathleen Margaret, b 1939. —— Jacqueline Eulalie Patricia, b 1911: m 1932, John Lewis Jones, and has issue living, Jane Eulalie, b 1942, — Anne Jessie Alexandra, b 1947.

Grandchildren of late Rev Robert Warren Wolseley, yr son of late Maj Robert Benjamin Wolseley, 6th son of late Rev William Wolseley (ante):—
Issue of late Garnet Ruskin Wolseley, b 1884, d 1967: m 1937, Joan Alys, who d 1943, da of Sir Walter John Trevelyan, 8th Bt:—
JOHN WALTER (Nettlecombe, Williton, Som), b 21 April 1938; ed Westminster: m 1964 (m diss 1978), Patricia Ann Newland, and has issue living, William, b 1967, — Thomas, b 1970. —— Jane Alys TREVELYAN, b 1939; assumed surname of Trevelyan 1976: m 1963 (m diss 1976), Nicolas Alexander, architect, and d 1993, leaving issue, Julius Diccon, b 1968, — Tamsyn Trevelyan b 1966. —— Jennifer Ann Ruskin, b 1941: m 1979, Baron Roman Heinrich Gamotha, of Castello 4967, I-30122 Venezia, Italy, and d 1983, leaving issue, Tatiana Romana, b 1982.
The 1st baronet, MP for Carlow, was brother of Sir William, 5th baronet, cr 1628. Sir Capel, 9th Bt, was Vice-Consul at Archangel 1900-1909, and served during European War 1914-18 in Gallipoli, Egypt, and Palestine, also with Army of Occupation in Albania and N Russia 1919.

WOMBWELL (GB) 1778, of Wombwell, Yorkshire
(Name pronounced "Woomwell")

Sir George Philip Frederick Wombwell, 7th Baronet; *b* 21 May 1949; *s* his father, *Maj Sir* (Frederick) Philip Alfred William, MBE, 1977; *ed* Repton: *m* 1974, (Hermione) Jane, el da of Thomas S. Wrightson, of Ulshaw Grange, Middleham, Leyburn, Yorks, and has issue.

𝔄rms – Gules, a bend between six unicorns' heads couped argent. ℭrest – A unicorn's head couped argent.
Residence – Newburgh Priory, Coxwold, York YO6 4AS.

SON LIVING

Stephen Philip Henry, *b* 12 May 1977.

DAUGHTER LIVING

Sarah Georgina, *b* 1980.

SISTERS LIVING

(Elizabeth) Anne, *b* 1938: *m* 1965, Michael Scofield Horton, of Kings Lea, Kemerton, Tewkesbury, Glos (*see* Walker, Bt, *cr* 1868, colls), and has issue living, James Frederick, *b* 1968, — Peter Michael, *b* 1969. —— Hazel Maureen, *b* 1947; assumed the surname of Williamson by deed poll (1977).

COLLATERAL BRANCH LIVING

Grandson of late Arthur Charles Wombwell, only son of Charles Orby Wombwell, 4th son of 2nd baronet:—
Issue of late Major Claude Ronald Wombwell, Seaforth Highlanders, *b* 1900, *d* 1959: *m* 1936, Eva Mabel, who *d* 1988, da of late Lieut-Col Gerald Hugh Charles Madden (Macpherson-Grant, Bt):—
Gerald Arthur (40 Quarrendon St, SW6), *b* 1937; *ed* Wellington Coll: *m* 1968, Elizabeth Ann, da of John Victor Gent, of Thika, Kenya, and has issue living, Richard Brian, *b* 1973, — Camilla Susan, *b* 1970.
The 1st baronet, Sir George Wombwell, was Chairman of the East India Company, and MP for Huntingdonshire 1774-80. The 4th baronet, Sir George, served in the Crimean War, and was in the Charge at Balaclava. The 5th baronet, Sir Henry Herbert Wombwell, was Capt Roy Horse Guards.

WOMERSLEY (UK) 1945, of Grimsby, co Lincoln

Sir Peter John Walter Womersley, 2nd *Baronet*, son of late Capt John Walter Womersley, Lincolnshire Regt, yr son of 1st baronet; *b* 10 Nov 1941; *s* his grandfather, *Rt Hon Sir* Walter James, 1961; late Lt King's Own R Border Regt: *m* 1968, Janet Margaret, da of Alistair Grant, of Drayton, Norwich, and has issue.
Residence – Broomfields, Goring Rd, Steyning, Sussex, BN44 3GF.

SONS LIVING

John Gavin Grant, *b* 7 Dec 1971. —— Matthew Alastair Peter, *b* 1973.

DAUGHTERS LIVING

Margaret Frances, *b* 1969. —— Helen Kathryn, *b* 1974.

AUNT LIVING (*Daughter of 1st baronet*)

Dorothy, *b* 1911: *m* 1934, Cyril Howard Moseley, and has issue living, Walter Howard, *b* 1941, — Lavinia Anne, *b* 1938, — Philippa Clare, *b* 1944.

MOTHER LIVING

Betty, da of Cyril Williams, of Elstead, Surrey: *m* 1st, 1941, Capt John Walter Womersley, Lincolnshire Regt (ante), *ka* Italy 1944; 2ndly, 1948, Gordon Shuttlewood, who *d* 1980.
The 1st baronet, the Rt Hon Sir Walter James Womersley (son of late William Womersley, of Bradford), was MP for Grimsby (C) 1924-45, and Min of Pensions 1939-45.

WOOD (UK) 1897, of The Hermitage, Chester-le-Street, co Durham (Extinct 1946)

Sir Ian Lindsay Wood, 3rd and last *Baronet*.

SISTER LIVING OF THIRD BARONET

Heather Lindsay, *b* 1908: *m* 1932, Gilbert Keith Dunning, who *d* 1967, and has issue living, Michael Lindsay, *b* 1941.
Residence – Keeper's Cottage, Fontmell Parva, Blandford, Dorset.

WOOD (UK) 1918, of Hengrave, Suffolk (Extinct 1974)

Sir JOHN ARTHUR HAIGH WOOD, DSC, MC, 2nd and last *Baronet*.

DAUGHTER LIVING OF SECOND BARONET

Shirley Cartaret, *b* 1922: *m* 1st, 1946 (*m diss* 1964), Sqdn Ldr Ivon Arthur Frederic Donnelly; 2ndly, 1972, John Hyde Villiers, who *d* 1980, of Fort Saumarez, L'Eree, Guernsey GY7 9LR, CI, and has had issue (by 1st *m*), Miles Saumarez (Little Halnaker, nr Chichester, W Sussex PO18 0NF), *b* 1949: *m* 1981, Caroline McKay, — Marcia Anne Lavinia (resumed her maiden name of DONNELLY), *b* 1948: *m* 1967 (*m diss* 19—), Jean Gabriel Mitterand, and *d* 1984, leaving issue living, Edward *b* 1968, — Claire Leonie, *b* 1953: *m* 1st, 1975 (*m diss* 1978), Craig Francis, of Nassau; 2ndly, 1978, Richard Berlin, of 261 Hart St, Beverley Farms, MA 01915, USA, and has issue living (by 2nd *m*), Eleanor *b* 1980, Dana *b* 1981, Carina Alexandra *b* 1985.

COLLATERAL BRANCH LIVING

Issue of late Maj Edmund Walter Hanbury Wood, JP, 2nd son of 1st baronet, *b* 1898, *d* 1947: *m* 1920, Margaret, who *d* 1977, only child of late George Coles Walton:—
Rhona Gertrude Jean (6 Douro Pl, W8) *b* 1921: *m* 1948 (*m diss* 1962), Jeremy Norman Peyton-Jones, who *d* 1984 (*see* B Ebury, colls, 1980 Edn), and has issue living, Julia Caroline, *b* 1952, — Lucinda Margaret, *b* 1954: *m* 1987, R. John Guy, elder son of Edgar Guy, of Raynes Park, London.

HILL-WOOD (UK) 1921, of Moorfield, Glossop, co Derby

Every good thing is the gift of God

Sir DAVID BASIL HILL-WOOD, 3rd *Baronet*; *b* 12 Nov 1926; *s* his father, *Sir* BASIL SAMUEL HILL, 1954; *ed* Eton: *m* 1970, Jennifer Anne McKenzie Stratmann (assumed that surname by deed poll 1960), da of late Peter McKenzie Strang, and has issue.

Arms – Quarterly, 1st and 4th sable, on a bend between two roses argent, barbed and seeded or, three fleurs-de-lis gules, *Wood*; 2nd and 3rd per chevron argent and vert, in chief two acorns leaved and slipped, and in base a cross-bow bent all counterchanged, *Hill*. **Crests** – 1st, within a crown palisado or a tree proper, *Wood*; 2nd, on a mount vert a bugle horn stringed gules, *Hill*.
Residences – Dacre Farm, Farley Hill, Reading, Berks; 58 Cathcart Rd, SW10.

SONS LIVING

SAMUEL THOMAS, *b* 24 Aug 1971. —— Edward Charles, *b* 1974.

DAUGHTER LIVING

Emma Victoria, *b* 1972.

SISTER LIVING

Anne Katherine, *b* 1928.

WIDOW LIVING OF SECOND BARONET

Hon JOAN LOUISA BRAND (*Hon Lady Hill-Wood*) (Glebe Cottage, Knipton, Grantham, Lincs), el da of 3rd Viscount Hampden: *m* 1925, Sir Basil Samuel Hill Hill-Wood, 2nd baronet, who *d* 1954.

COLLATERAL BRANCHES LIVING

Issue of late Maj Denis John Charles Hill Hill-Wood, MC, 3rd son of 1st baronet, *b* 1906; *d* 1982: *m* 1932, Mary Cecilia Martin (Hunters Hill, Hartley Wintney, Hants), da of late Capt Everard Martin Smith, of Codicote Lodge, Herts:—
Peter Denis (13 Smith's Terr, SW3), *b* 1936; *ed* Eton; 2nd Lt Coldm Gds: *m* 1971, Sarah, da of Albert O'Beirne Andrews, and has issue living, Julian Peter, *b* 1974, — Charles Denis, *b* 1976, — Sarah Frances, *b* 1972. —— Angela Mary, *b* 1933: *m* 1956, Mark Eric Smith, of Ballacurn, Ballaugh, IoM, and has issue living, Matthew Eric, *b* 1960: *m* 1989 (*m diss* 1992), Hon Melanie Frances Broughton, yr da of 3rd Baron Fairhaven, and has issue living, Shamus Oliver Eric *b* 1990, — Luke Eric, *b* 1968, — Amanda Mary, *b* 1957: *m* 1984, Matthew Frewer, of Los Angeles, USA, — Lucinda Rachael, *b* 1958. —— Rachael Vivien, *b* 1940: *m* 1972, Anthony Wood, who *d* 1989, of Hunters Hill, Hartley Wintney, Hants, and has issue living, Cheska Mary, *b* 1974, — Selina Rachael, *b* 1976.

Issue of late Lt-Col Charles Kerrison Hill Hill-Wood, yst son of 1st baronet, *b* 1907, *d* (21 Sept) 1988: *m* 1936, Cecilia Katharine, who *d* (16 June) 1988, 3rd da of late Capt Everard Reginald Martin Smith, of Codicote Lodge, Herts:—
Michael Kerrison (Hill Cot, Branch Rd, Ainley Top, Huddersfield, W Yorks), *b* 1946; *ed* Milton Abbey: *m* 1st, 1970 (*m diss* 1991), Patricia Guy, of Stainland, Yorks; 2ndly, 1991, Patricia Ann Caldon, of Biggleswade, Beds, and has issue living (by 1st *m*), Steven Guy, *b* 1977, — Susan Michelle, *b* 1974. —— Ian Charles (The Bury, Barton-le-Cley, Beds), *b* 1947; *ed* Milton Abbey. —— Georgina Sarah, *b* 1940: *m* 1962, Richard Basil Holt, of 3 Caroline Place Mews, W2, and has issue living, Nicholas James, *b* 1965, — Camilla Katherine, *b* 1967, — Susanna Rachael, *b* 1969, — Caroline Lucinda, *b* 1972. —— Diana Susan, *b* 1943: *m* 1st, 1966 (*m diss* 1971), Lestock Harold George Livingstone-Learmonth; 2ndly, 1975, Ian Phillips, of 18 Campion Rd, Putney, SW15, and has issue living (by 1st *m*), Lestock Alexander Iain, *b* 1969, — (by 2nd *m*) Alastair Patrick Markham, *b* 1980, — Simon Richard Markham, *b* 1982.
The 1st baronet, Sir Samuel Hill Hill-Wood, only son of late Samuel Wood, of Moorfield, Derbyshire (whose el brother, John Hill Wood, was father of Sir John Wood, 1st Bt (*see* Wood, Bt, *cr* 1918)) assumed by Roy licence 1912 the additional surname of Hill, his grandmother having been Alice, da of John Hill, of Liverpool. He sat as MP for High Peak Div of Derbyshire (C) 1910-29.

PAGE WOOD (UK) 1837, of Hatherley House, Gloucestershire

Sir ANTHONY JOHN PAGE WOOD, 8th *Baronet; b* 6 Feb 1951; *s* his father, *Sir* DAVID JOHN HATHERLEY PAGE WOOD, 1955; *ed* Harrow.

Arms – Quarterly, argent and or, the mace of the Lord Mayor of London in pale, between an oak-tree on a mount vert fructed proper in the 1st and 4th quarters and in the 2nd and 3rd, a bull's head erased sable, charged on the neck with a bezant. **Crest** – Out of a mural crown argent, a demi-wild man, wreathed about the temples with oak fructed, in the dexter hand an oak-tree eradicated and fructed, and in the sinister a club, all proper.
Residence – 77 Dovehouse St, SW3.

SISTER LIVING

Rosemary Anne, *b* 1948: *m* 1977, Hugh Macdonald Teacher (*see* Macnaghten, Bt, colls).

UNCLE LIVING (*son of 6th baronet*)

MATTHEW PAGE, *b* 13 Aug 1924; is Capt Coldstream Guards; assumed by deed poll 1955 the additional surname of Page before his patronymic; European War 1939-45: *m* 1947, Betsann, da of Lieut-Col Francis Christesson Darby Tothill, Rifle Brig (*see* E Bandon), and has issue living, Belinda Jane, *b* 1952: *m* 1st, 1973 (*m diss* 1977), Richard John Crowder (*see* B Mowbray); 2ndly, 1985, Charles Frederick Rutford Hoste, of The Craig, Montrose, Angus, and has issue living (by 2nd *m*), James Matthew William Rutford *b* 1986, — Miranda Elizabeth, *b* 1962: *m* 1993, William B. Kendall, son of Graham Kendall, of Millow Hall, Biggleswade, Beds, and has issue living, Emily Lucy Page *b* 1994.
Residence – 31 Halsey St, SW3.

WIDOW LIVING OF SEVENTH BARONET

EVELYN HAZEL ROSEMARY (*Lady Page Wood*), da of late Capt George Ernest Bellville, of Fermyn Woods Hall, Brigstock, Northants; assumed by deed poll 1956 the additional surname of Page: *m* 1947, Sir David John Hatherley Page Wood, 7th baronet, who *d* (Nov) 1955. *Residence* – The Old Cottage, Wolverton, Basingstoke, Hants.

COLLATERAL BRANCHES LIVING

Grandson of late FM Sir (Henry) Evelyn Wood, VC, GCB, GCMG, LLD, 5th son of 2nd baronet:—
Issue of late Col Evelyn FitzGerald Michell Wood, CB, DSO, OBE, *b* 1869, *d* 1943: *m* 1st, 1893, Lilian, who *d* 1910, da of of late Charles Edward Hutton, of 63 Porchester Terrace, W; 2ndly, 1915, Alla, who *d* 1950, da of R. Morton, and widow of Hatherley Page Wood, son of late Charles Page Wood, 2nd son of 2nd baronet:—
(By 2nd *m*) Matthew Wakefield Drury Evelyn (The Orchard, Bishopsteignton, Teignmouth, Devon), *b* 1917; *ed* Brighton Coll; Lt-Col (ret) RE, late Essex Regt: *m* 1st, 1939, Marjorie, who *d* 1963, da of late Henry Thomas Longmire, of Liverpool; 2ndly, 1967, Mrs Phyllis Margaret Chavasse Whateley (infra), and has issue living, (by 1st *m*) Mark William Evelyn (27 Wood Lane, Fleet, Hants), *b* 1940: *m* 1962, Mary June, da of George Percy Miller, of Brightlingsea, and has issue living, Martin Evelyn *b* 1963, Michelle Leslie Evelyn *b* 1965.

Grandchildren (by 1st *m*) of late Lt-Col Arthur Herbert Wood (infra):—
Issue of late Evelyn (Ronald) Wood, *b* 1903, *d* 1976: *m* 1st, 1932 (*m diss* 1943), Maeve Audrey, da of late Arthur Theobald Wolfe, and widow of Emile Jacot; 2ndly, 1943, Kamal Jehangir, who *d* 1976, da of Jehangir Fardunji Dastur, of Bombay:—
(By 1st *m*) Diarmuid Evelyn (Leachin House, Tarbert, Isle of Harris, Outer Hebrides PA85 3AH), *b* 1933; *ed* Gordonstoun: *m* 1st, 1960, Beverly, BSc, who *d* 1976, da of William Richard Pearce, of La Oratava, Tenerife; 2ndly, 1977, Linda Rosemary, BA, DipEd, da of Leonard Pierpoint Petty, of Merry Meadow, Winters Lane, Redhill, Wrington, Avon, and has issue living (by 1st *m*), Damian Evelyn, *b* 1962: *m* 1991, Clare Natalie, BA, da of Richard Dallas Harington, of Hill Farm, Felsham, Suffolk, and has issue living, Benedict Damian Evelyn *b* 1993, — Thalia Evelyn, *b* 1965, — (by 2nd *m*), Duncan Fitzgerald Evelyn, *b* 1981, — Eleanor Maeve Evelyn, *b* 1984. —— (By 2nd *m*) Ananda Evelyn, *b* 1947: *m* 19—, Meena Dyal, of Bombay. —— Leela Aditi, *b* 1946: *m* 19—, Nick Dirks, of Santa Monica, USA, and has issue living, Sandhya Elina, *b* 1978.

Grandchildren of late FM Sir (Henry) Evelyn Wood, VC, GCB, GCMG, LLD (ante):—
Issue of late Lt-Col Arthur Herbert Wood, *b* 1877, *d* 1940: *m* 1st, 1900, Ethel Mary, who *d* 1923, da of late Andrew Duncan, Bar-at-law, of 71 Gloucester Place, W; 2ndly, 1923, Andrina Hunter, who *d* 1985, da of John Fernie, of Aberfeldy, Perthshire:—
(By 2nd *m*) Victor Arthur Evelyn, *b* 1927; *ed* Tonbridge; a Chartered Surveyor: *m* 1st, 1951, Olwen Mary, who *d* 1960, only da of Thomas Davies, of Studley, Warwicks; 2ndly, 1963, Matilde Francesca Rosanna, da of Girolamo Zucchelli, of Brione, Riva del Garda, Italy, and has issue living, (by 1st *m*) David Arthur Evelyn, *b* 1954, — Vaughan Thomas Evelyn, *b* 1959, — Bernice Margaret Andrina, *b* 1952, — (by 2nd *m*) Victor Vincent, *b* 1966, — Antonia Marcella Matilde *b* 1964. —— Marcella Mary, *b* 1931; *ed* New Hall Boreham, Chelmsford and London Univ (BA DipEd); Canoness Registrar of Holy Sepulchre; Headmistress of New Hall Sch, Chelmsford since 1963.

Grandchildren of late George Orme Western Wood (infra):—
Issue of late Ernest Cresswell Gaden Western Wood, MBE, *b* 1906, *d* 1984: *m* 1938, Mary Tudor (Moonie, 35 Douro Rd, Wellington Point, Queensland 4160, Australia), da of James Winnel Hill, of Goorarooman, Thallon, Queensland:—
Richard Orme Western (Moonie, 35 Douro Rd, Wellington Point, Queensland 4160, Australia), *b* 1942; *ed* Queensland Univ (BEng): *m* 1968, Jennifer Lynne, da of N.W.S. Johns, of Clayfield, Brisbane, and has issue living, Matthew Gaden Western, *b* 1969, — Gregory Orme Western, *b* 1971, — Simon James Western, *b* 1975. —— Bruce James Western (Moonie, 35 Douro Rd, Wellington Point, Queensland 4160, Australia), *b* 1951; *ed* Queensland Univ (BEng): *m* 1977, Yolande Marie-Louise, da of late Pierre Le Manach, of Morlaix, France, and has had issue, Nina Marie Western, *b* 1978, — Adeline Marie Western, *b* and *d* 1981, — Sophie Yolande Western, *b* 1981, — Nicole Alexandrina Western, *b* 1985, — Stephanie Adeline Western, *b* 1987. —— Nina Helen Western, *b* 1939. —— Rosamond Mary Western, *b* 1944; *ed* Queensland univ (Dip Speech Therapy): *m* 1972, John Franklin Verity Haselwood, and has issue living, Richard Franklin, *b* 1974, — Douglas Holmes, *b* 1976, — Louise Mary, *b* 1975.

Grandchildren of late Western Wood, *b* 1830; 3rd son of 1st baronet:—

Issue of late George Orme Western Wood, *b* 1868, *d* 1926: *m* 1904, Helen Portia, who *d* 1963, da of Adam Davidson, of Darling Downs, Queensland:—
Bernard Page Western, *b* 1908; 1939-45 War as Lt RANVR: *m* 1951, Phyllis May, da of William Henry Andrew, of 48 Shakespeare St, Mackay, Qld. *Residence* – 57 Gregory St, Mackay, Qld. —— Evelyn Hatherley Davidson, *b* 1911: *m* 1937, Ena Myer, and has issue living, Ian Hatherley Western, *b* 1942: *m* 19—, June Margaret Huch, da of Huch Redcliffe, and has issue living, Cameron Hatherley *b* 1966, Scott Norman *b* 1969, Rowena Maree *b* 1971, — David Orme Western,*b* 1946; *ed* Qld Univ (MB, BS). —— Helen Constance Western, *b* 1905: *m* 1949, Stanley Gordon. *Residence* – 29 Herries Street, Toowoomba, Queensland. —— Waveney Patricia Western, *b* 1914: *m* 1943, Capt Robert Gladstone Deacon, Australian Forces, and has issue living, Helen Page, *b* 1945.

The 1st baronet, Sir Matthew Wood, born 1767, was the son of a serge manufacturer, of Tiverton and at eleven years of age worked in his father's factory. At fourteen he was apprenticed to Mr Newton, druggist, at Exeter. After serving seven years, he became a traveller in the drug trade, and subsequently established himself in London as a chemist. He afterwards became a hop-merchant, and was chosen Alderman, served as a Sheriff, and in the year of the Peace, 1815, was elected Lord Mayor of London, to which office he was re-elected the following year. He also sat as MP for London (*L*) 1816-43. During his mayoralty he was bold and fearless. On one occasion, after a lawless mob had shot a man on Snow Hill, and were approaching the Exchange, he, with only seven others, rushed through that building, and held the rioters in check, while he arrested several of the ringleaders. He took an active part in the cause of Queen Caroline: he accompanied her through Calais and Dover, on her journey to London in 1820, and placed his house in South Audley Street at her disposal. His fortune was, after much litigation, augmented on the death of Jemmy Wood, the banker, of Gloucester, to the extent of £250,000. Among these possessions was the estate of Hatherley Court, in Gloucestershire, a fine old ivy-mantled mansion, and from its name his second son, William Page, who was Lord High Chancellor 1868-72, selected his title. Sir John Stuart Page Wood, 6th Bt, who was Com (ret) RN, *d* April 1955, and his son Sir David John Hatherley Page Wood, 7th Bt, *d* Nov 1955.

WORLEY (UK) 1928, of Ockshott, co Surrey (Extinct 1937)

Sir ARTHUR WORLEY, CBE, 1st and last *Baronet*.

DAUGHTER LIVING OF FIRST BARONET

Stella, *b* 1918: *m* 1940, Raymond Ades, TD, JP, MA, who *d* 1993, and has issue living, Timothy Raymond (94 North Rd, N6), *b* 1941; MA: *m* 1966, Josephine Dawn Tylden-Pattenson, MA, Prof of Art History, and has issue living, Thomas Joseph Edmund *b* 1971; M Phil, Henry Arthur Raymond *b* 1973, Robert Paul Timothy *b* 1981, — Anthony Edmond, *b* 1947; BSc, PhD, MSc, — Susan Jane, *b* 1943; MA, — Rosemary Sally (3 Pottery St, SE16), *b* 1951; MA. *Residence* – 37 Princes Dr, Oxshott, Surrey KT22 0UL.

WORSLEY, (UK) 1838, of Hovingham, Yorkshire

Do good to as many persons as possible

Sir (WILLIAM) MARCUS JOHN WORSLEY, 5th *Baronet*; *b* 6 April 1925; *s* his father, *Col Sir* WILLIAM ARTHINGTON, 1973; *ed* Eton, and New Coll, Oxford; a JP, DL and High Sheriff (1982) for N Yorks, HM Lord Lieut since 1987; PPS to Min of Health 1960-61, to Min without Portfolio 1962-64, and to Lord Pres of Council 1970-72; Chm Nat Trust Properties Cttee 1980-90, Dep Chm Nat Trust 1986-92; Pres of Roy Forestry Soc of Eng, Wales and N Ire 1980-82; 1939-45 War in India and W Africa with Green Howards; MP for Keighley (*C*) 1959-64, and for Chelsea (*C*) 1966-74; Second Church Estates Commr 1970-74: *m* 1955, Hon Bridget Assheton, da of 1st Baron Clitheroe, and has issue.

𝕬rms – Argent, a chief gules. 𝕮rest – A wyvern vert.
Seat – Hovingham Hall, York. *Club* – Boodle's.

SONS LIVING

WILLIAM RALPH (Wool Knoll, Hovingham, York; 93 Eaton Place, SW1. *Club* – White's), *b* 12 Sept 1956; *ed* Harrow, and RAC; late Lt QOY (TAVR), FRICS: *m* 1987, Marie-Noëlle, yr da of Bernard H. Dreesmann, of Mas de la Madone, Miramar, Alpes Maritimes, France, and has issue living, Isabella Claire, *b* 1988, — Francesca Sylvia, *b* 1992. —— Giles Arthington, *b* 1961. —— Peter Marcus, *b* 1963.

DAUGHTER LIVING

Sarah Marianne, *b* 1958: *m* 1984, Martin Stephen Robert Elwes, of 23 Baskerville Rd, SW18 3RW, elder son of late Capt Robert (Robin) Valentine Gervase Elwes, and Mrs J.H. Taylor, of The White House, Sowerby, N Yorkshire, and has issue living, James Robert, *b* 1986, — Hugo Marcus, *b* 1991, — Sophie Bridget, *b* 1988.

BROTHERS LIVING

George Oliver, TD (Bolton Hall, Wilberfoss, York, YO4 5NZ. *Club* – Boodle's), *b* 1927; *ed* Eton, and Trin Coll, Oxford (MA): *m* 1966, Penelope Suzanne Fleetwood, da of late Lt-Col Christopher Herbert Fleetwood Fuller, TD (*see* Fuller, Bt, colls), and has issue living, David Christopher, *b* 1969, — Richard Oliver Arthington, *b* 1972, — Georgina Joyce, *b* 1967, — Anne Penelope, *b* 1974. —— John Arthington (RR2 Uxbridge, Ont, Canada), *b* 1928; *ed* Eton, and Trin Coll, Oxford; Pres Morgan Trust Co of Canada: *m* 1954, Hon Carolyn Wynard Hardinge, da of 4th Viscount Hardinge, and has issue living, Henry John, *b* 1958, — Jonathan Hugh, *b* 1960, — Dickon Carol, *b* 1966, — Willa Victoria, *b* 1955, — Katharine Margot, *b* 1968.

SISTER LIVING

Katharine Lucy Mary, GCVO (*HRH the Duchess of Kent*), *b* 1933; Chancellor of Leeds Univ, 1965; appointed Controller Comdt WRAC 1967; Col-in-Ch 4th/7th Royal Dragoon Guards, Prince of Wales's Own Regt of Yorks, Army Catering Corps, and Hon Col Yorks Vol; patron of Kent Co Playing Fields Assocn, of Spastics Soc, of Cancer Relief Macmillan Fund, and of the Samaritans; GCVO 1977: *m* 8 June 1961, HRH Prince Edward George Nicholas Paul Patrick, KG, GCMG, GCVO, 2nd Duke of Kent (*see* ROYAL FAMILY). *Residences* – York House, St James's Palace, SW1.

COLLATERAL BRANCH LIVING

Issue of late Capt Edward Marcus Worsley, yr son of 3rd baronet, *b* 1891, *d* 1971: *m* 1941, Joyce Marian (Cawton Hall, Cawton, York YO6 4LW), da of late Stanley Graham Beer, of Northernhay, Bickley, Kent:—
Thomas Edward (35D Gibson Sq, N1 0RB), *b* 1947; *ed* Eton: *m* 1989, Sheila Christie, and has issue living, Nicholas Richard, *b* 1990, — Charles Robert, *b* 1993. —— Susan Marian, *b* 1942: *m* 1989, Christopher Edwin Oliver, of 46 Woodville Rd, Richmond, Surrey TW10 7QN, only son of late E. J. C. Oliver. —— Angela Joyce, *b* 1950: *m* 1973, Ian Michael Downing Strickland-Skailes, of Harston Hall, Grantham, Lincs NG32 1PS, and has issue living, Robin Edward, *b* 1977, — Lucinda Isabel, *b* 1979. —— Diana Rosalind, *b* 1953.
This family is a senior branch of the Worsleys of Worsley, Lancs. Another branch, formerly baronets of Appuldurcombe, Isle of Wight, whose title became extinct on the death of the 9th baronet in 1825, is now represented by the Earl of Yarborough.

Worsley-Taylor, see Taylor.

Worthington-Evans, see Evans.

WRAXALL (UK) 1813, of Wraxall, Somersetshire

Sir CHARLES FREDERICK LASCELLES WRAXALL, 9th *Baronet*; *b* 17 Sept 1961; *s* his father, *Sir* MORVILLE WILLIAM LASCELLES, 1978; *ed* Archbishop Tenison's Gram Sch, Croydon; a Civil Servant: *m* 1983, Lesley Linda, da of William Albert Allan, and has issue.

Arms – Lozengy erminois and azure, on a chevron gules three estoiles of eight points or. **Crest** – A buck's head cabossed and erased gules, charged on the breast with two lozenges in fesse, and between the attires an estoile or.

SON LIVING

WILLIAM NATHANIEL LASCELLES, *b* 3 April 1987.

DAUGHTER LIVING

Lucy Rosemary Lascelles, *b* 1992.

BROTHER LIVING

Peter Edward Lascelles, *b* 1967.

SISTER LIVING

Sylvia Laura, *b* 1957.

AUNT LIVING (*Daughter of 7th baronet*)

Gwendolyn Aileen, *b* 1927: *m* 1945, John Hunter, CEng, FIMechE, AFRAeS, FInstPet of Stirling, who *d* 1987, and has issue living, Kenneth Charles John (Firwood, 15 Hamfield Cl, Oxted, Surrey) *b* 1951; BSc Hons (Warwick): *m* 1976, Gillian Margaret Sutton, of Billericay, Essex, and has issue living, Martin Robert *b* 1981, Simon Richard *b* 1985, Alicia Jennifer *b* 1988, — Keith Philip (1 Tower Gdns, Bearsted, Kent), *b* 1957; BSc Hons (London Univ): *m* 1983, Louise Bernadette Maria Baede, of Amsterdam, Holland, and has issue living, Nicholas John *b* 1988, Christopher Marinus *b* 1990, Alexander Keith *b* 1993. *Residence* – 110 Devonshire Way, Shirley, Croydon, Surrey.

WIDOW LIVING OF EIGHTH BARONET

IRMGARD WILHELMINA MARIA (*Dowager Lady Wraxall*), da of late Alois Larry Schnidrig, of Zunftacker Rain 13a, Pratteln, Switzerland: *m* 1956, Sir Morville William Lascelles Wraxall, 8th baronet, who *d* 1978.
The 1st baronet, Sir Nathaniel William Wraxall, was in the Civil Service of the East India Company. The 3rd baronet, Sir Frederick, was sometime Assistant-Commissary in the Turkish Contingent and was author of several works. Sir Morville William, 6th baronet, enlisted in the Commissariat and Transport Corps, served in Nile Expedition 1884-5, and subsequently joined, in 1891, the Egyptian Coast Guard Administration.

WREY (E) 1628, of Trebitch, Cornwall

Sir GEORGE RICHARD BOURCHIER WREY, 15th *Baronet; b* 2 Oct 1948; *s* his father, *Sir* (CASTEL RICHARD) BOURCHIER, 1991; *ed* Eton: *m* 1981, Lady Caroline Janet Lindesay-Bethune, only da of 15th Earl of Lindsey, and has issue.

Arms – Sable, a fesse between three pole-axes argent, helved gules. (Quarterings: Bourchier, Plantagenet, de Bohun, etc).
Residences – 60 The Chase, SW4 0NH; Hollamoor Farm, Tawstock, Barnstaple, N Devon.

SONS LIVING

HARRY DAVID, *b* 3 Oct 1984. —— Humphrey George, *b* 1991.

DAUGHTER LIVING

Rachel Pearl, *b* 1987.

BROTHER LIVING

(Edward) Sherard Bourchier, *b* 1961; *ed* Durham Coll: *m* 1992, Hon Catherine Margaret Baring, yst da of 5th Baron Northbrook.
Residence – Pink Cottage, Tawstock, Barnstaple, N Devon.

The good time will come

AUNT LIVING (*Sister of 14th baronet*)

Diana Joan (*Hon Mrs William Rollo*), b 19—: *m* 1st, 1932 (*m diss* 1946), Jocelyn Abel Smith, who *d* 1966; 2ndly, 1946, as his 2nd wife, Hon William Hereward Charles Rollo, MC, who *d* 1962 (*see* L Rollo), and has issue living (by 1st *m*), John William, *b* 1933: *m* 1st, 1957, Ruth, da of Sir John Huggins GCMG, MC; 2ndly, 1965 (*m diss* 1974), Christine, only da of Keith Taylor, of Adelaide; 3rdly, 1975, Mary Chichester Mills, — (Bertram) Robin, *b* 1938: *m* 1st, 1961 (*m diss* 1976), Anne, yst da of Walter Kidman, of Eringa, Unley Park, Adelaide, S Aust; 2ndly, 1978 (*m diss* 1991), Kathleen Eugenie, da of George Cecil Houghton Cowell, of Elms Farm, Ashley, Newmarket, and widow of Robert Bibby Collie; 3rdly, 1993, Diana Marjorie Fielder, da of Patrick Forsell, and has issue living (by 1st *m*), William Walter *b* 1964, Rachel Muriel *b* 1969, (by 3rd *m*) Thomas Patrick *b* 1993. *Residence* – Barleythorpe, Oakham, Rutland LE15 7EQ.

DAUGHTER LIVING OF TWELFTH BARONET

Barbara Marion Celia (*Lady Strachan*): *m* 1st, 1925, Robert Darley Whelan, Flying Officer RAF, who *d* 1927; 2ndly, 1929, Sir Andrew Henry Strachan, CBE, who *d* 1976, and has issue living (by 2nd *m*), Richard Neville, *b* 1930, — Judith Meriel, *b* 1936.

WIDOW LIVING OF FOURTEENTH BARONET

SYBIL MABEL ALICE (*Sybil, Lady Wrey*), elder da of Dr George Lubke, of Durban, S Africa: *m* 1946, Sir (Castel Richard) Bourchier Wrey, 14th Bt, who *d* 1991. *Residence* – 511 Currie Rd, Durban, S Africa; Les Bellevue de Mougins, Val de Mougins, S France.

COLLATERAL BRANCHES LIVING

Grandsons of late Edward Castell Wrey, 7th son of 10th baronet:—
Issue of late Maj Christopher Bourchier Wrey, TD, *b* 1906, *d* 1976: *m* 1932 (*m diss* 1947), Ruth, only da of late Sir Harold Bowden, GBE, 2nd Bt:—
Timothy Christopher Bourchier (c/o Lloyds Bank, Berkeley Sq, W1), *b* 1937: *m* 1964, Susan, el da of William Brewer, of Troymark House, Johannesburg, S Africa, and has issue living, Marcus Valerian Bourchier, *b* 1969, — Camilla Melusine, *b* 1966. —— Benjamin Harold Bourchier (8 Somerset Sq, Addison Rd, W14 8EE), *b* 1940: *m* 1970, Anne Christine Aubrey Cherry, da of late Col Christopher Bushnell Stephenson, and has issue living, Tanya Serena, *b* 1971.

Grandsons of late Maj Reginald Charles Wrey, 8th son of 10th baronet:—
Issue of late Capt Denys Charles Bourchier Wrey, TD, *b* 1913, *d* 1991: *m* 1942, Katherine Frances Theodora (Peggy) (The Common, Smannell, Andover, Hants), da of late Rev William Francis Eliot (*see* Devitt, Bt, *cr* 1916, 1964 Edn):—
Charles Bourchier (Breach House, Compton Basset, Calne, Wilts), *b* 1949; *ed* Eton: *m* 1982, Catriona Anne, el da of Ian Wilson, and has issue living, Thomas Alexander, *b* 1983, — Edward Charles, *b* 1986, — Maximillian George Bourchier, *b* 1989. —— Mark Eliot Bourchier (The Quag, Midhurst, W Sussex GU29 0JH), *b* 1955; *ed* Harrow: *m* 1985, Loveday Elizabeth, yr da of Maj Simon Bolitho, of Trengwainton, Penzance, Cornwall, and has issue living, Alexander Mark Bourchier, *b* 1986, — Simon Sherard Bourchier, *b* 1992, — Charlotte Loveday, *b* 1989.

Granddaughters of late George Edward Bourchier Wrey, only son of late George Bourchier Wrey, son of late Edward Bourchier Wrey, 2nd son of late Rev Bourchier William Wrey, yr son of 6th baronet:—
Issue of late Cdr Edward Charles Wrey, OBE, RN, *b* 1889, *d* 1972: *m* 1914, Grace Elsie, who *d* 1940, da of late James C. Rimer, of Kelvin Grove, Newlands, Cape, S Africa:—
Elizabeth Anne, *b* 1917: *m* 1946, William Welch Flexner, of 9 Paultons St, SW3 5DP. —— Marie Jean (85 Tarrant St, Arundel, Sussex), *b* 1919: *m* 1st, 1940, David Cecil Patrick Hastings, who was *ka* Burma 1943, son of late Sir Patrick Hastings, KC; 2ndly, 1949, Michael Dowden, who *d* 1972, and has issue living, (by 1st *m*) Judith Maryanne, *b* 1941: *m* 1963, Colin Etienne Dickinson, of The Old Vicarage, Coaley, Dursley, Glos GL11 5EB, and has issue living, Anthony David Richard *b* 1965, Charlotte Lucy *b* (twin) 1965, Sophie Louise *b* 1971, — (by 2nd *m*) Edward David Michael, *b* 1950: *m* 1970, Sarah Anne Sherwin, and has issue living, Benjamin Thomas Edward *b* 1978, Emma Mary *b* 1973, Matilda Jane *b* 1975.

Granddaughter of late Rev John Wrey, yr son of late Rev Bourchier William Wrey (ante):—
Issue of late Rev Arthur Bourchier Wrey, *b* 1831, *d* 1918: *m* 1st, 1859, Helen, who *d* 1878, da of the Rev Thomas Phillpotts, Canon of Truro; 2ndly, 1881, Claudine Maud, who *d* 1904, da of late Charles Twining, KC, formerly of Halifax, NS:—
(By 2nd *m*) Mary Claudine: *m* 1st, 1913, Capt Humphrey Richard Locke Lawrence, Indian Army, *ka* 1915; 2ndly, 1928, Heathcote Dicken Statham, CBE, MusD, who *d* 1973, and has issue living (by 2nd *m*), Michael Heathcote Wrey, *b* 1929.

The family of Wrey is of considerable antiquity in Devonshire. Sir Chichester, the 3rd baronet, a faithful adherent to the royal cause, became in 1652 possessed, by marriage, of Tawstock, where the family formerly resided. His wife, Anne was 3rd da and co-heir of Edward Bourchier, Earl of Bath, and a co-heir to Barony of Fitzwarine (cr 1295). After the Restoration he was successively Colonel of the Duke of York's Regiment, Governor of Sheerness, and MP for Lostwithiel. Sir Bourchier, the 4th baronet, served under the Duke of Monmouth, and after the Restoration commanded a regiment of horse.

CORY-WRIGHT (UK) 1903, of Caen Wood Towers, Highgate, St Pancras, co London, and Hornsey, Middlesex

Sir RICHARD MICHAEL CORY-WRIGHT, 4th *Baronet*, *b* 17 Jan 1944; *s* his grandfather, *Maj Sir* GEOFFREY, 1969; *ed* Eton, and Birmingham Univ; late Lt Leics and Derbys Yeo; Patron of one living: *m* 1976, Veronica Mary, only da of James Harold Lucas Bolton, of Church Farm, Morningthorpe, Norwich, and has issue.

𝕬rms – Or, a fesse compony counter-compony azure and argent between in chief two eagles' heads erased, and in base a unicorn passant reguardant of the second. 𝕮rest – Upon a mount proper between two caltraps or a unicorn passant reguardant argent, armed, crined, and unguled, also or.
Residence – Cox's Farm, Winterbrook Lane, Wallingford, Oxon OX10 9RE.

SONS LIVING

ROLAND ANTHONY, *b* 11 March 1979. —— Jonathan James, *b* 1981. —— Felix Michael, *b* 1986.

SISTER LIVING

Juliet Susan, *b* 1942: *m* 1977, John Frederick Webster, of Beech Grove Farm House, Hethersett, Norwich, and has issue living, Robert John Julian, *b* 1983, — Charlotte Josephine, *b* 1981.

UNCLES LIVING (*Sons of 3rd baronet*)

Michael, *b* 1920; *ed* Eton; Lt RA (TA); 1939-45 War: *m* 1954, Elizabeth, OBE, DL, da of late Maj James Archibald Morrison, DSO, of Basildon Park, Berks (*see* B Trevor, 1962 Edn), widow of Capt Eric Martin Smith, MP, and previously wife of late Nigel Eric Murray Gunnis. *Residence* – Codicote Lodge, Hitchin, Herts. —— David Arthur, *b* 1925; *ed* Eton; Capt Scots Guards; 1939-45 War: *m* 1st, 1949 (*m diss* 1985), Lady Jane Katherine Douglas, da of 11th Marquess of Queensberry; 2ndly, 1985, Joy Elizabeth Jefferson, only da of late Albert Edward Dursley, of Hanham, Bristol, and has issue living, (by 1st *m*) Anthony Jonathan, *b* 1950: *m* 1988, Susana M., only da of Alfonso Torrents dels Prats, of Geneva, and London SW5, and has issue living, James Alfonso *b* 1994, Emma Mercedes *b* 1992, — Simon, *b* 1952, — Christopher James, *b* 1965. *Residence* – Quoin Cottage, Biddestone, Chippenham, Wilts SN14 7DQ. —— Mark Richard Geoffrey, *b* 1930; late 2nd Lieut 10th Roy Hussars: *m* 1956, Tania, da of late John Culcheth Holcroft (*see* Holcroft, Bt), of Northbrook, Bentley, Hants, and has issue living, Charles Alexander, *b* 1958: *m* 1988, Dorothy McNaughton, da of Samuel Watson, of Penwortham, Lancs, and has issue living, Ella Doone *b* 1991, Poppy Maud *b* 1993, — Harry William Mark, *b* 1963. *Residence* – Tilhill House, Tilford, Surrey, and Burnham Market, King's Lynn. *Clubs* – Brooks's, Pratt's.

COLLATERAL BRANCHES LIVING

Issue of late Ronald Cory-Wright, MC, 2nd son of 2nd baronet, *b* 1893, *d* 1932: *m* 1917, Geraldyn Mary, who *d* 1976, da of late Maj Henry Charles Windsor Villiers-Stuart, of Dromana, co Waterford (*see* M Bute):—
Francis Newman (Oakridge, Little Gaddesden, Berkhamsted, Herts), *b* 1925; *ed* Eton, and Merton Coll, Oxford (BA 1949, MA 1954): is Lt 15th/19th King's Roy Hussars; European War 1945 (wounded).

Issue of late Lt-Cdr Alan Cory-Wright, DSC, RN, 3rd son of 2nd baronet, *b* 1896, *d* 1964: *m* 1923, Leila Yda Cyrillia, who *d* 1982, da of Arthur Lobb, of Hatters Croft, Sawbridgeworth, Herts:—
Godfrey William (Hatfield Park, Takeley, Essex), *b* 1928; *ed* Harrow: *m* 1958, Nicole Emma, da of E. Vermeiren, of Brussels, and has issue living, Alan William (Auchessan, Crianlarich, Perthshire FK20 8QS), *b* 1965: *m* 1989, Nicki, 2nd da of Rt Rev John Richardson, Bishop of Bedford, and has issue living, Hamish Bean William *b* 1991, Jack *b* 1993, — Elizabeth Yda, *b* 1961: *m* 1989, Christopher Edward Mannion, of Ploughdenes, Bush End, Bishop's Stortford, Herts CM22 6NG, and has issue living, Zachariah Ernest Gustave (Pingu) *b* 1993, Sassi Edward Paris (a da) *b* 1990, Araminta Tanzy Ophelia *b* 1992.

Issue of late Douglas Cory-Wright, CBE, 4th and yst son of 2nd baronet, *b* 1901, *d* 1987: *m* 1924, Margaret Vivien Sarina, who *d* 1987, da of Rudolph Levy, of Birkdale, Lancs:—
June (*Lady Horlick*), *b* 1926: *m* 1948, Sir John James Macdonald Horlick, 5th Bt, and has issue (*see* Horlick, Bt). —— (Olive) Marigold, MB BS, *b* 1929: *m* 1954, David Richard Michael Curling, who *d* 1993, of The Rosary, Coleshill, Bucks (*see* Curtis, Bt, 1965 Edn), and has had issue, Richard Michael, *b* 1958, — Rosanna Virginia, *b* 1960: *m* 1990, Nicholas Guy Charles della Casa, and presumed murdered (with her husband) in N Iraq 1991, — Davina Cordelia, *b* 1964. —— Cleone Anne, *b* 1935: *m* 1956: John Wedgwood Thellusson Wood (*see* E Kimberley, colls, 1990 Edn), of Lois Weedon House, Weedon Lois, nr Towcester, Northants, and has issue living, Nicholas John Wedgwood, *b* 1961, — Amelia Jane, *b* 1959, — Rebecca Anne, *b* 1964, — Anna, *b* 1969.

Grandchildren of late Dudley Cory-Wright, yr son of 1st baronet—
Issue of late Esmond Godfrey Cory-Wright, *b* 1908, *d* 1989: *m* 1st, 1931 (*m diss* 1942), Amanda, who *d* 1981, da of E. P. Menhinick, of Treguddick, Gresham Gardens, Golders Green, NW11; 2ndly, 1949, Pepita Jane Grey (Pagewood, East Strand, West Wittering, Sussex PO20 8BA), da of Harry William Grey Bell:—
(By 1st *m*) Edward James Dudley (Roe Cottage, Piddinghoe, Newhaven, Sussex), *b* 1932; *ed* Merton Coll, Oxford: *m* 1955, Jean Olive, da of George Young, of St Albans, Herts, and has issue living, James Edward (43 Luther St, Brighton, E Sussex), *b* 1956; *ed* Univ of E Anglia (BA), PGCE: *m* 1978 (*m diss* 1993), Susan Laura, da of Sydney Bricknell, of Sutton Grove, Shrewsbury, — Nicholas John, *b* 1964: *m* 1992, Ana, da of Rodolfo Sanchez, of Madrid, — Juliet Amanda, *b* 1959: *m* 1984,

Philip Fielder, of Church House, Timsbury, Hants, and has issue living, Mark Edward *b* 1988, Victoria Frances *b* 1986. —— Amanda Menhinick, *b* 1933.

The 1st baronet, Sir Cory Francis Cory-Wright, was Chm of Wm Cory and Son (Limited), and assumed by Roy licence 1903, the additional surname of Cory. The 2nd baronet, Sir Arthur Cory-Wright, was High Sheriff for Herts 1921. The 3rd baronet, Maj Sir Geoffrey Cory-Wright, *m* 1915, Felicity, who *d* 1978, 2nd da of late Sir Herbert Beerbohm Tree, the actor-manager. His eldest son, Capt Anthony John Julian Cory-Wright, RA, *b* 1916, was *ka* 1944, at St Mauvieu, Normandy, having *m* 1940, Susan Esterel (who *d* 1993, having *m* 2ndly, 1949, Lt-Col Jocelyn Eustace Gurney, DSO, MC, of Tacolneston Hall, Norfolk, who *d* 1973), eldest da of late Capt Robert Hamond Arthur Elwes, of Congham House, Norfolk. His only son is Sir Richard Michael Cory-Wright, 4th and present baronet.

WRIGHTSON (UK) 1900, of Neasham Hall, co Durham

Sir CHARLES MARK GARMONDSWAY WRIGHTSON, 4th *Baronet*; *b* 18 Feb 1951; *s* his father, Col Sir JOHN GARMONDSWAY, TD, 1983; *ed* Eton and Queen's Coll, Camb: *m* 1975, Stella Virginia, da of late George Dean, MPS, of Garden Cottage, Middleton Tyas, N Yorks, and has issue.

Arms – Or, a fesse invected checky azure and argent between two eagles' heads erased in chief sable, and a saltire couped in base gules. **Crest** – In front of a saltire gules, a unicorn salient or.
Seat – Neasham Hall, near Darlington. *Residence* – 39 Westbourne Park Rd, W2

Veritas omnia vincit

Truth conquers all things

SONS LIVING

BARNABY THOMAS GARMONDSWAY, *b* 5 Aug 1979. —— James George, *b* 1982. —— William John, *b* 1985.

SISTERS LIVING

Penelope Linda, *b* 1940. —— Juliet Diana, *b* 1943. —— Elizabeth Ann, *b* 1946: *m* 1978, Laurent Tisné, of La Roche Abilen, St Georges du Bois, Maine et Loire, France, and has issue living, Martin, *b* 1979, — Louis, *b* 1981.

UNCLES LIVING (*Sons of 2nd baronet*)

Peter, OBE, *b* 1914, *ed* Eton; is Lieut-Col Durham LI; European War 1939-45 in France, N Africa, and Italy (OBE); OBE (Mil) 1945: *m* 1946, Pamela, da of late Lieut-Col Sir Murrough John Wilmot, KBE, and has issue living, Simon Murrough, *b* 1954: *m* 1975, Elisabeth Yvonne, da of Hubert Marcel Michelin, of Le Gressigny, 63870 Orcines, France, and has issue living, Richard Charles Peter *b* 1985, Emma Mary Rose *b* 1982, — Joanna Mary, *b* 1947: *m* 1969, Peter Jonathan Howard, of Wedds Oast, Ticehurst, Sussex, and has issue living, Benjamin Simon *b* 1975, James Edward Peter *b* 1979, Penelope Sarah *b* 1971, Alison Rebecca *b* 1972, — Susan Jennifer, *b* 1948: *m* 1970, Montague William Style, of 27 rue des Romains, 68480 Bettlach, Alsace, France, and has issue (*see* Style, Bt, colls). *Residence* – Manfield Grange, Manfield, nr Darlington.

WIDOW LIVING OF THIRD BARONET

Hon ROSEMARY MONICA DAWSON (*Hon Lady Wrightson*), da of 1st Viscount Dawson of Penn: *m* 1939, Col Sir John Garmondsway Wrightson, 3rd Bt, TD, who *d* 1983. *Residence* – Studyard House, Neasham, Darlington, co Durham.

COLLATERAL BRANCHES LIVING

Issue of late Cdr Rodney Wrightson, RN, 3rd son of 2nd baronet, *b* 1916, *d* 1992: *m* 1st, 1940, Florence Jean, who *d* 1944, elder da of late James Dunn Dunn, of Ferniecraig, Skelmorlie, Ayrshire; 2ndly, 1947, Janet Elizabeth (The Old Rectory, Codford St Peter, Warminster, Wilts), eldest da of late Brig Raymond Henry Arnold Davison Love, RA, of Overcroft, Mayford, Surrey, and formerly wife of Brig William Branfoot Wilson, OBE:—
(By 1st *m*) Jeremy Rodney (29 Lynn Close, Leigh Sinton, Malvern, Worcs WR13 5DU), *b* 1941; *ed* Eton: *m* 1970, Lindsay, da of Dr John Milroy Glen Parker, of 9 The Mount, Malton, Yorks, and has issue living, Rufus Guy, *b* 1975, — Christopher John, *b* 1985, — Amy Jean, *b* 1974. —— (By 2nd *m*) Lucinda, *b* 1948: *m* 1st, 1969, Jonathan Philip Hudson; 2ndly, 1985, John Riddell White Abbott, of Whitefield House, Wiveliscombe, Som TA4 2UW, only son of John Nesbitt White Abbott, MBE, TD, and has issue living (by 1st *m*), Henry Andrew, *b* 1972, — Emily Alice, *b* 1974.

Issue of late Wilfrid Ingram Wrightson, yst son of 1st baronet, *b* 1876, *d* 1949: *m* 1913, Victoria, who *d* 1966, da of late F. C. Winby, of 47 Portland Place, W:—
Elizabeth Victoria Mary (*Elizabeth, Lady White*) (Salle Park, Reepham, Norfolk), *b* 1914: *m* 1943, Sir Headley Dymoke White, 3rd Bt, who *d* 1971. —— Ann Winby, *b* 1917: *m* 1952, Robert le Rougetel White, BArch, ARIBA, LRAM, who *d* 1979. *Residence* – Cross Gates, Lorton, Cockermouth, Cumbria CA13 9UL.

The 1st baronet, Sir Thomas, was Chm of Head, Wrightson and Co (Limited), bridge builders, of Stockton, and sat as MP for Stockton-on-Tees (C) 1892-95, and for E Div of St Pancras July 1899 to Jan 1906.

Wrixon-Becher, see Becher.

Wykeham (Twisleton-Wykeham-Fiennes), see Fiennes.

WILLIAMS-WYNN (E) 1688, of Gray's Inn, co Middlesex

Eryr Eryrod Eryri
The Eagle of the Eagles of Snowdon

Sir (DAVID) WATKIN WILLIAMS-WYNN, 11th *Baronet*; *b* 18 Feb 1940; *s* his father, *Lt-Col Sir* (OWEN) WATKIN, CBE, 1988; *ed* Eton; late Maj 1st Royal Dragoons; OC Ches Yeo Sqdn, QOY 1971-77; Master Sir W. W. Wynn's Hounds 1971-77, Master Flint and Denbigh Hounds 1978-90, Master of own hounds (Sir W. W. Wynn's) since 1991; DL Clwyd 1966; High Sheriff Clwyd 1990: *m* 1st, 1968 (*m diss* 1981), (Harriet) Veryan Elspeth, da of late Gen Sir Norman Hastings Tailyour, KCB, DSO; 2ndly, 1983, Mrs Victoria Jane Dillon, da of late Lt-Col Ian Dudley De Ath, DSO, MBE, and formerly wife of Lt-Col R. E. Dillon, RM, and has issue by 1st and 2nd *m*.

Arms – Quarterly: 1st and 4th vert, three eagles displayed in fesse wings inverted or, *Wynn*; 2nd and 3rd gules, argent, two foxes counter-salient in saltire the sinister surmounted of the dexter gules, *Williams*. **Crest** – An eagle displayed or.
Residence – Plas-yn-Cefn, St Asaph, Clwyd LL17 0EY. *Club* – Cavalry and Guards'.

SONS LIVING *(By 1st marriage)*

CHARLES EDWARD WATKIN, *b* 1970. —— Robert Euan Watkin, *b* 1977.

(by 2nd marriage)

Nicholas Watkin, *b* 1988. —— Harry Watkin, *b* (twin) 1988.

DAUGHTERS LIVING *(by 1st marriage)*

Alexandra June, *b* 1972. —— Lucinda Jean, *b* (twin) 1972.

AUNTS LIVING *(daughters of 9th baronet)*

Joyce, *b* 1906: *m* 1929, Duncan Robertson, who *d* 1987, son of late Sir Henry Beyer Robertson, and has had issue, Sheila Ann, *b* 1929: *m* 1st, 1953 (*m diss* 1975), Henry Saxon Tate (*see* Tate, Bt); 2ndly, 1976, Humphrey Sandford, of The Isle, Shrewsbury, Shropshire, and *d* 1987, leaving issue (by 1st *m*) (*see* Tate, Bt), — Jean Margaret, *b* 1932: *m* 1956, Capt Peter Miles de Wend Greenwell, of Tregeiriog, nr Llangollen, Clywd LL20 7HU, and has had issue, Rupert Peter *b* 1959; *ed* Milton Abbey, James Robertson *b* 1963; *ed* Eton; murdered in Zimbabwe 1982, Duncan Charles de Wend *b* 1966; *ed* King's Sch, Bruton, — Bridget Jennifer (*Baroness de Clifford*), *b* 1935: *m* 1959, 27th Baron de Clifford, of Riggledown, Pennymoor, Tiverton, Devon EX16 8LR. *Residence* – Llantysilio Hall, Llangollen, N Wales. —— Margaret (*Hon Mrs Peter Hotham*), *b* 1911: *m* 1934, Maj Hon Peter Hotham, late King's Own Yorkshire LI (*see* B Hotham), who *d* 1991. *Residence* – Plas Newydd, Glascoed, Abergele, N Wales.

WIDOW LIVING OF TENTH BARONET

GABRIELLE HADEN (*Dowager Lady Williams-Wynn*), da of late Herbert Alexander Caffin, of Hazlemere, Surrey, and formerly wife of Wing Cdr W. R. A. Matheson: *m* 1968, as his 2nd wife, Lt-Col Sir (Owen) Watkin Williams-Wynn, 10th Bt, CBE, who *d* 1988. *Residence* – Eryl, Llangedwyn, Oswestry, Shropshire.

COLLATERAL BRANCHES LIVING

Grandchildren of late Charles Watkin Williams-Wynn, son of late Rt Hon Charles Watkin Williams-Wynn, 2nd son of 4th baronet:—
Issue of late Major Frederick Rowland Williams-Wynn, CB, *b* 1865, *d* 1940: *m* 1907, Beatrice Kathleen, who *d* 1913, el da of late Major Francis Cooper, RFA, of Markree Castle, Collooney, Ireland:—
John Francis WILLIAMS-WYNNE, CBE, DSO, *b* 1908; *ed* Oundle and Magdalene Coll, Camb (MA); FRAgricS; Col (ret) late RA; a JP of co Merioneth; Lord-Lieut of Merioneth 1957-74, Lieut of Gwynedd 1974-84, since when Vice Lord-Lieut; NW Frontier of India 1936-37, Burma 1943-45 (DSO); assumed by deed poll 1940 the surname of Williams-Wynne in lieu of his patronymic; Constable of Harlech Castle since 1964; DSO 1945, CBE (Civil) 1972: *m* 1938, Margaret Gwendoline Heyward, who *d* 1991, da of late Rev George Eliott Roper, and has issue living, William Robert Charles (Talybont, Tywyn, Gwynedd), *b* 1947; FRICS 1972; JP 1972: *m* 1975, Hon Veronica Frances Buxton, da of Baron Buxton of Alsa (Life Baron), and has issue living, Chloë Frances *b* 1978, Leonora Mary *b* 1980, Rose Margaret *b* 1981, — Virginia, *b* 1941; renounced her former christian names of Merion Beatrice by deed poll 1968: *m* 1st, 1964, Maj Peter Thomas Anthony Davies (who assumed the surname ABBOT-DAVIES by deed poll 1969), who *d* 1979; 2ndly, 1980, HH Sayyid Faher bin Taimur Alsaid (DPM for Security & Defence, Bait Al Falaj, 113 Muscat/Ruwi, Sultanate of Oman), and has issue living (by 1st *m*), Orion Jonathan *b* 1965, Hardwin *b* 1968, (by 2nd *m*), Latifah *b* 1981, — Jane Margaret (*Hon Mrs David Douglas-Home*), *b* 1949: *m* 1972, Hon David Alexander Cospatrick Douglas-Home, CBE, formerly Lord Dunglass (99 Dovehouse St, SW3 6JZ), only son of Baron Home of the Hirsel (Life Baron), formerly 14th Earl of Home, and has issue (*see* B Home of the Hirsel). *Residence* – Peniarth, Towyn, Merioneth. *Clubs* – Army and Navy, Pratt's. —— Annora Beatrice, *b* 1911: *m* 1st, 1935 (*m diss* 1945), Lt-Col David Sacheverell Curtis, Roy Fus (*see* Curtis, Bt, colls); 2ndly, 1945, Charles George Gordon Wainman, who *d* 1988, and has issue living (by 1st *m*) (*see* Curtis, Bt, colls), — (by 2nd *m*) Annora Mary, *b* 1946: *m* 1970, Evangelos Koemtzopoulos, of Athens, Greece, and has had issue, Nicholas *b* 1974, Mark *b* 1979, Laura *b* 1971, *d* 1978, Marina *b* 1981. *Residence* – The Tower House, Hinton St George, Som, TA17 8SS.

Descendants of late John Williams (great-grandson of John Williams, 2nd son of 1st baronet), who was *cr* a *Baronet* 1798.
See Williams, Bt, *cr* 1798.

This family descends from Cadrod Hardd, or the Handsome, a Welsh chieftain, who was Lord of Talybolion in the Isle of Anglesey about the year 1100. The 1st baronet, Sir William Williams, MP for Chester in three Parliaments, was Speaker of the House of Commons 1679-85. In 36 Car II he was tried for libel, in causing to be printed the information of Thomas Dangerfield, and although he pleaded the law and custom of Parliament, he was fined £10,000. After the Revolution, this judgement was declared illegal and against the freedom of Parliament. The 3rd baronet, Sir Watkin Williams, succeeded to the estate of Wynnstay (formerly Watstay) in 1718 under the will of Sir John Wynn, 5th Bt of Gwydir (ext), who had acquired that estate through his wife, and assumed the additional surname of Wynn. The 6th baronet sat as MP for

Denbighshire (*C*) 1841-85. The 7th baronet, Col Sir Herbert Lloyd Watkin Williams-Wynn, CB, was Hon Col Yeo, Lord-Lieut of Montgomeryshire, and a County Councillor for Denbighshire. He sat as MP for Denbighshire (*C*) May to Nov 1885. The 9th baronet, Col Sir Robert William Herbert Watkin Williams-Wynn, KCB, DSO, TD, was Lord-Lieut of Denbighshire 1928-51, and served in S Africa 1900-02, and European War 1914-18. The 10th baronet, Lt-Col Sir Watkin Williams-Wynn, CBE, was High Sheriff and Lord-Lieut of Denbighshire, and Lord-Lieut of Clwyd; served 1939-45 War (taken prisoner by Japanese and forced to work for three and a half years on the infamous Siam and Burma Rlwy); Master of Flint and Denbigh Hounds, Joint Master of Sir Watkin Williams-Wynn's Hounds (his yr son, Robert, was killed in N Ireland while serving with the 14th/20th King's Hus, 1972).

WYVILL (E) 1611, of Constable Burton, Yorkshire (Dormant 1774)

COLLATERAL BRANCHES LIVING

Granddaughter living of late William Edward Wyvill, probably *de jure* 15th Bt:—
　　Issue of late Newlon D'Arcy Wyvill, probably *de jure* 17th Bt, *b* 1895, *d* 1971: *m* 1920, Helen Lamar, da of Henry Laboin Wood:—
Willie Juanita, *b* 1923: *m* 1st, 1952 (*m diss* 1953), Walter Daniel Scheuch; 2ndly, Donald Douglas Lamond.

Grandson of late Maj Marmaduke Ibbetson Wyvill, Rifle Bde, only son of Marmaduke D'Arcy Wyvill of Constable Burton Hall and Denton Park, Yorks, el son of Marmaduke Wyvill (*d* 1896), third in descent from Edward Wyvill, 2nd son of D'Arcy Wyvill (infra), 2nd son of 4th baronet:—
　　Issue of late Marmaduke Frederic Wyvill, *b* 1912, *d* 1953: *m* 1st, 19— (*m diss* 19—), Cissy Scott; 2ndly, 1943 (*m diss* 1946), May, da of Henry Holland Bennet; 3rdly, 1947, Mrs Mary Jones, who *d* 1968, da of late Frederick Pope:—
(By 2nd *m*) Marmaduke Charles Asty (Constable Burton Hall, Leyburn, N Yorks; Brooks's Club), *b* 1945; *ed* Stowe and Roy Agric Coll, Cirencester; ARICS; Lord of Manor of Constable Burton, Leyburn, Yorks, and patron of three livings; High Sheriff of N Yorks 1986-87: *m* 1972, Margaret Ann, el da of Maj Sydney Hardcastle, RA, of Hutchins Farm, Etchingham, Sussex, and has issue living, Marmaduke D'Arcy William, *b* 1975, — Edward Paul Anthony, *b* 1977, — Frederick Charles Penrose, *b* 1983, — Katherine Marye Laura, *b* 1981.
This Baronetcy has remained dormant since the death in 1774 of Sir Marmaduke Asty Wyvill, 7th Bt. According to GEC's "Complete Baronetage", his probable heir was Marmaduke Wyvill of Anne Arundel co, Maryland, son and heir of William, who emigrated to Frederick Co, Maryland, el son of Darcy, 2nd son of 4th Bt. Marmaduke left two sons by his 1st wife, Harriet Rateby (*m* 1764) and two sons by his 2nd wife, Susanna Burgess (*m* 1775). His el son, Darcy (probably *de jure* 9th Bt) had one son Robert (probably *de jure* 10th Bt) who *dsp* about 1800. His 2nd son, Marmaduke (probably *de jure* 11th Bt) *dsp* male 1808. The succession presumably reverted to his half-brother, Walter of Calvert co, Maryland (el son of Marmaduke by his 2nd wife, and probably *de jure* 12th Bt). His son, Edward Hale (probably *de jure* 13th Bt), *b* 1812, *d c* 1894, was *s* by his son, Walter Davis (probably *de jure* 14th Bt), *b* 1834, *d* 1898. This is as far as GEC takes the line, but recent research has established that he was *s* by his only son, William Edward (probably *de jure* 15th Bt), *b* 1859, *d* 1911, who was *s* by his el son Carlisle Osborne (probably *de jure* 16th Bt), *b* 1894, *d* 1941, who was *s* by his brother Newlon D'Arcy (probably *de jure* 17th Bt), *b* 1895, *d* 1971.

YARROW (UK) 1916, of Homestead, Hindhead, Frensham, co Surrey

Sir ERIC GRANT YARROW, MBE, 3rd *Baronet, b* 23 April 1920; *s* his father, *Sir* HAROLD EDGAR, GBE, 1962; *ed* Marlborough and Glasgow Univ; a DL of Renfrewshire; Managing Dir Yarrow and Co Ltd 1958-67, Chm 1962-85, Pres 1985-87; Chm Yarrow (Shipbuilders) Ltd 1962-79; Memb Lloyd's Register of Shipping, Scottish Comm 1956-87, General Comm 1960-89; Hon Vice-Pres Roy Instn of Naval Architects since 1972; Memb of Council of Institute of Directors 1983-90; Chm of Clydesdale Bank since 1985; Pres Burma Star Assoc, Scottish Area since 1990; FRSE; Burma 1942-45, as Maj RE; MBE (Mil) 1946; OStJ: *m* 1st, 1951, Rosemary Ann, who *d* 1957, yr da of late H. T. Young, of Roehampton, SW15; 2ndly, 1959 (*m diss* 1975), Annette Elizabeth Françoise, only da of late A. J. E. Steven, of Ardgay, Ross-shire; 3rdly, 1982, Caroline Rosa Joan, da of late R. F. Masters, of Piddinghoe, Sussex, and formerly wife of Philip Botting, of Allington Farm, Offham, and has had issue by 1st and 2nd *m*.

Arms – Azure, in base on the sea proper, an ancient three-masted ship, sailing to the sinister argent, in chief two swallows volant of the last, each holding in the beak a harebell slipped also proper. Crest – Above clouds proper a swallow volant argent, holding in the beak a yarrow flower slipped also proper. *Residence* – Cloak, Kilmacolm, Renfrewshire, PA13 4SD. *Clubs* – Army and Navy, RSA.

GRANDSONS LIVING

Issue of late Richard Grant Yarrow, eldest son of Sir Eric Grant Yarrow, 3rd Bt, MBE, *b* 1953, *d* 1987: *m* 1982, Sheila Elizabeth (Craigmore Lodge, Nethy Bridge, Inverness-shire PH25 3ED), elder da of Ronald William Paul Allison, CVO, commentator, of 36 Ormond Dr, Hampton, Middx:—
Ross, *b* 1985. —— Tom, *b* 1987.

SONS LIVING *(By 2nd marriage)*

Norman Murray *b* 1960: *m* 1988, Carol Jane, elder da of Nicholas Hawkins, of Noble Tree House, Hildenborough, Kent, and has issue living, Katie Diana, *b* 1990, — Lucy Carol, *b* 1992. —— Peter Harold *b* (twin) 1960. —— David Eric, *b* 1966.

SISTERS LIVING

Eleanor Audrey (Balauchen Lodge, Milngavie, Glasgow G62 8EJ), *b* 1907: *m* 1934, Maj Harry Duncanson Boyd, MBE, TD, RA, who *d* 1964, and has issue living, Eleanor Margaret, *b* 1937: *m* 1959, Peter Murray Bruce Hutt (Strathisla, Box 33, PO Hillcrest 3650, Natal), el son of Sir (Alexander McDonald) Bruce Hutt, KBE, CMG, and has issue living, Colin Murray Bruce *b* 1960, Nigel Duncan *b* 1964, Nichola Margaret *b* 1966, — Eda Daphne, *b* 1940: *m* 1963, Christopher Roche Enslin, of 5 Bothwell Close, Tokai 7945, nr Cape Town, S Africa, and has issue living, Michael Roche *b* 1967, Ian Boyd *b* 1970, Camilla Fiona *b* 1964, — Sylvia Audrey, *b* 1944: *m* 1st, 1967 (*m diss* 1983), Alexander Baird Fergus Morton; 2ndly, 1983, David Charles Alan Norris, of Graghvar, Milngavie, Glasgow G62 8EJ, and has issue living (by 1st *m*), Peter Fergus *b* 1970, Anita Audrey *b* 1973. —— Beryl Winifred Ethne (Netherblane, Blanefield, Glasgow, G62 8EJ), *b* 1910: *m* 1st, 1932, Charles Wood Scott, who *d* 1960; 2ndly, 1969, Graeme Hardie, BEM, who *d* 1973, and has had issue (by 1st *m*), Grahame Charles Wood, *b* 1933: *m* 1962, Jean Isabel Mary Manners (10 Mosspark Av, Milngavie, Glasgow G62 8NL), and *d* 1981, leaving issue, Alan Charles Wood *b* 1966, Fiona Anne *b* 1963, Lorna Jean Ethne *b* 1965, — Avril Eleanor Yarrow, *b* 1936: *m* 1959, James Alistair Spence Meighan, of Fernbrae, Moor Rd, Strathblane, Stirlingshire G63 9EY, and has issue living, Andrew Alistair Spence *b* 1963, Marjorie Eleanor Spence *b* 1961: *m* 1984, Ranald Morton White (and has issue living, Sarah Jane *b* 1987, Alice Jennifer *b* 1990), Avril Gillian Spence *b* 1966.

HALF-SISTER LIVING

Angela Mary Rosalynde, *b* 1937: *m* 1961, David Clive Griffiths, of Wyfold Grange, Wyfold, Reading, Berks, and has issue living, David William Yarrow, *b* 1969, — Rosemary Kate, *b* 1962, — Amanda Mary, *b* 1964.

COLLATERAL BRANCH LIVING

Issue of late Norman Alfred Yarrow, 2nd son of 1st baronet, *b* 1891, *d* 1955: *m* 1915, Ada Hope (who *d* 1990, having *m* 2ndly, 1959, as his third wife, Sir Eric Stuart Taylor, OBE, MD, MRCP, 2nd Bt, who *d* 1977), da of Forrest Bertram Leeder, MRCS, LRCP, of Victoria, BC:—
Cynthia Hope (638 Transit Rd, Vict, BC, Canada V85 4Z5), *b* 1921: *m* 1st, 1944 (*m diss* 1954), Lieut Clifton Thomas Williams Hyslop, Roy Canadian Naval Vol Reserve; 2ndly, 1955 (*m diss* 19—), William F. Pinckard, and has issue living, (by 1st *m*) John David Allan, *b* 1946, — Andrew Peter, *b* 1951, — Gillian Cynthia, *b* 1949, — (by 2nd *m*) Christopher William Norman, *b* 1958, — Jonathan Mark, *b* 1960. —— Daphne Veryan, *b* 1924: *m* 1952, Lt Cdr Howard Victor Clark, RCN, of 2440 Chiltern Place, Victoria, BC, Canada V8R 3S8, and has issue living, Susan Veryan, *b* 1954, — Stephanie Jane, *b* 1958.
The 1st baronet, Sir Alfred Fernandez Yarrow (an engineer and shipbuilder), was Chm of Yarrow and Co, Ltd, shipbuilders, of Scotstoun, Glasgow, until 1922.

YOUNG (GB) 1769, of North Dean, Buckinghamshire

Sir WILLIAM NEIL YOUNG, 10th *Baronet*, son of late Capt William Elliot Young, RAMC, only son of 9th baronet; *b* 22 Jan 1941; *s* his grandfather, *Sir* (CHARLES) ALBAN, KCMG, MVO, 1944; *ed* Wellington and RMA Sandhurst; Capt 16th/5th The Queen's R Lancers (ret): *m* 1965 Christine Veronica, only da of Robert Boland Morley, of 20 Delaware Rd, W9, and Buenos Aires, and has issue.
Residence – Penchrise Peel, Hawick, Roxburghshire.

SON LIVING

WILLIAM LAWRENCE ELLIOT, *b* 26 May 1970; *ed* Eton, and Edin Univ (MA).

DAUGHTER LIVING

Catherine Clare, *b* 1967; *ed* Somerville Coll, Oxford (BA): *m* 1993, Hugh E. Powell, son of Sir Charles Powell, KCMG.

AUNT LIVING *(Daughter of 9th baronet)*

Joan Persica, *b* 1912: *m* 1936, George Rupert Raw, and has issue living, Charles Rupert, *b* 1940, — Victoria, *b* 1939, — Susan Augusta, *b* 1949.

MOTHER LIVING

Mary, da of late Rev J. Macdonald: *m* 1st, 1939, Capt William Elliot Young, RAMC (ante), *ka* 1942; 2ndly, 1945, Lieut-Col George Herbert Nash, OBE, Indian Army. *Residence* – 2 Douro Road, Cheltenham, Gloucestershire.

COLLATERAL BRANCHES LIVING

Grandsons of late Rev Henry Savill Young, son of Rev Henry Tufnell Young, 2nd son of 3rd Bt:—
Issue of late Rev Henry Brook Young, *b* 1869, *d* 1937: *m* 1920, Emmie, who *d* 1934, da of Henry Everitt, of Exning:—
William Brook Charles, *b* 1922; Sq-Ldr RAF (ret); a Civil Airline Pilot; Queen's Commendation for Valuable Ser in the Air: *m* 1949, Alma Evelyn, da of F. C. Harvey, of Reading, and has issue living, Paul Anthony Brook, *b* 1950: *m* 1st, 1975 Barbara Inkley; 2ndly, 1993, Lyn White, — Christopher Charles Brook, *b* 1953: *m* 1975, Mary Patricia Walls, — Amanda Jane Brook, *b* 1956: *m* 1st, 1975, Delwyn Dowse; 2ndly, 1982, Randal Dobbs. *Residence* - No 2 Chugg's Orchard, Cloutman's Lane, Croyde, Braunton, Devon.
Issue of late Major George Edward Savill Young, Irish Guards, *b* 1884, *d* of wounds received in action 1917: *m* 1914, Alison Jane, who *d* 1957, da of Rev Frederick John Poole, of Bishop Monkton, Ripon:—
Henry Lawrence Savill, DSO, *b* 1915; *ed* Harrow; Brig (ret) late Irish Gds; 1939-45 War (despatches, DSO); DSO 1944: *m* 1939, Noreen de Vere, da of late Thomas Brabazon Ponsonby (*see* E Bessborough, colls), and has issue living, (George Trevor) Savill (37 Lessar Av, Clapham, SW4 9HW), *b* 1941; *ed* Harrow, and Trin Coll, Dublin; late Lt Irish Gds: *m* 1983, Marion Sonia, da of Jean Paul Koch, of Rome, and has issue living, Sophie Georgiana *b* 1984, — Verona, *b* 1943: *m* 1976,

Colin Lionel Angus Fraser-Mackenzie, of Cedar House, Pilton, Somerset, and has issue living, Richard Savill Thomas *b* 1981, Peter Alexander Francis *b* 1983. *Residence* – The End House, Pilton, Somerset.

Grandchildren of late Lieut-Col Hugh Greville Young, DSO, RHA (ante):—
Issue of late Hugh Findlay Young, *b* 1919, *d* 1987: *m* 19—, Angela Elaine (15 Gloucester Rd, Coleford, Glos GL16 8BH), da of late R. G. M. Whigham:—
James Greville (Hampshire House, Hampshire Gdns, Coleford, Glos), *b* 1957: *m* 1990, Samantha, da of Lawrence Edward Sillett, of Hill Park, Stag Hill, Yorkley, Glos, and has issue living, Cecilia Angela, *b* 1990, — Matilda Judith Alice, *b* 1992. —— Giles Hugh Findlay, *b* 1964. —— Piers Jonathan, *b* 1965: *m* 19—, Julia Marie, da of Sidney Charles Barnfield, of Tewkesbury, Glos. —— Mary Rose Frederica (Oak House, The Folly, Parkend, Lydney, Glos), *b* 1958.

Granddaughter of late George Augustus Young, 4th son of 3rd baronet:—
Issue of late Harold Lawrence Young, *b* 1866, *d* 1909: *m* 1894, Beatrix Kinsey (who *m* 2ndly, 1911, George Gully), da of late William Kinsey Hayward:—
Dorothy, *b* 1903: *m* 1928, Walter Adam, MB. *Residence* – Johannesburg, S Africa.
The 1st baronet, Sir William Young (son of late William Young, MD), was Lieut-Governor of Dominica. Sir William Norris, the 5th baronet, was killed at the battle of the Alma, 1854; and his brother, Sir George John, the 6th baronet, died before Sebastopol the same year. Sir (Charles) Alban, KCMG, MVO, 9th baronet, was Envoy Extraor and Min Plen and Consul-Gen to Guatemala 1913-19, and to Yugoslavia 1919-25.

YOUNG (UK) 1813, of Formosa Place, Berkshire

BE RIGHT & PERSIST

Rt Hon Sir GEORGE SAMUEL KNATCHBULL YOUNG, MP, 6th *Baronet*; *b* 16 July 1941; *s* his father, *Sir* GEORGE PEREGRINE, CMG, 1960; *ed* Eton, and Ch Ch, Oxford (Open Exhibitioner); Fellow Univ of Surrey; a Member Lambeth Borough Council 1968-71, and GLC 1970-73; Economist, Nat Economic Development Office 1967-68; Research Fellow, Univ of Surrey 1968-69; Economic Adviser, PO Corpn 1969-74; Opposition Whip 1976-79, Chm Acton House Assocn 1972-79; Under Sec of State DHSS 1979-81, Under Sec of State for the Environment 1981-86; Comptroller HM Household 1990, since when Min for Housing, Dept of Environment; PC 1993; author of "Tourism, Blessing or Blight?"; MP for Ealing Acton (*C*) since 1974; *m* 1964, Aurelia, el da of Oscar Nemon, of Boars Hill, Oxford, and has issue.

Arms – Per fesse sable and argent: in chief two lions rampant-guardant, and in base an anchor erect with a cable, all counterchanged. Crest – A demi-unicorn couped ermine, armed, maned, and hoofed or, gorged with a naval crown azure supporting an anchor erect sable.
Residence – Formosa Place, Cookham, Berks.

SONS LIVING

GEORGE HORATIO (5 Stafford Mansions, Haarlem Rd, W14) *b* 11 Oct 1966; *ed* Windsor CFE, and Ch Ch, Oxford. —— Hugo Patrick, *b* 1970.

DAUGHTERS LIVING

Sophia Angelica, *b* 1965. —— Camilla Mary, *b* 1975.

BROTHER LIVING

Charles Evory (62 Old Rd, Oxford OX3 7LL), *b* 1943; *ed* Eton, and Ch Ch, Oxford (Open Exhibitioner): *m* 1973, Wiltrud, da of H. J. Frömbling, and has issue living, Emily Lucinde, *b* 1974, — Juliet, *b* 1975.

SISTER LIVING

Helen Mary, *b* 1947: *m* 1st, 1969 (*m diss* 1986), Digby Robert William Norton; 2ndly, 1988, Dr Tom Winnifrith, of 69 Gloucester Rd, Malmesbury, Wilts, 2nd son of Sir John Winnifrith, KCB, and has issue living (by 1st *m*), Thomas Alan Hughe, *b* 1975, — Joanna Elisabeth, *b* 1972, — Felicity Margaret, *b* 1979.

AUNTS LIVING (*Daughters of 4th baronet*)

Joan Alison, *b* 1910: *m* 1933, Robert Mathew, who *d* 1954, and has issue living, Theobald David Mathew, *b* 1942; *ed* Downside, and Balliol Coll, Oxford (MA); Windsor Herald of Arms; OStJ, — Perdita Mary, *b* 1944; BA (Sussex Univ): *m* 1965, Michael Ivar Royal Dawson, of Trafalgar House, Nelson St, Stroud, Glos, and has issue living, Daniel Cyrus *b* 1965, Robert Caspar *b* 1966, Cressida Ruth *b* 1968, Jessie Charlia *b* 1975. —— Virginia Jacomyn (*Lady Hutton*), *b* 1911: *m* 1936, Sir Noel Kilpatrick Hutton, GCB, QC, who *d* 1984, and has issue living, William Noel, *b* 1937; MA, MB, Camb; BChir; FRCP (London); inventor: *m* 1960, Doris Mary Nesfield, and has issue living, Timothy Noel *b* 1963, Duncan Neil *b* 1964, Rupert MacIntyre *b* 1971, Virginia Rozanne *b* 1961, Julia Mary *b* 1967, — Charles Edward Ilbert (The Cottage, Church Lane, Hornton, Oxon), *b* 1943: *m* 1967, Alison Victoria Featherstone, yr da of John Harvey, and has issue living, Samuel Barnaby *b* 1968, William Gabriel *b* 1970, Pegotty Alice *b* 1974, — Melissa Grace, *b* 1939: *m* 1963, James Perot, of 6 Barnes Court, 100 Garden Alley, Doylestown, PA 18901, USA, and has issue living, James Blair *b* 1965, Noelle Melissa, *b* 1963, Szerina Alice *b* 1968, — Dorothea Eacy, *b* 1948. *Residence* – 8 Wyndham Way, Oxford OX2 8DF.

COLLATERAL BRANCHES LIVING

Issue of late Courtenay Trevelyan Young, yr son of 4th baronet, *b* 1914, *d* 1974: *m* 1942, June Brinley (Browne's Lodge, 22 West St, Reigate, Surrey RH2 9BS), da of G. Brinley Richards:—

Frederick Courtenay, *b* 1948: *m* 1971, Heather Brunskell, and has issue living, Daniel Justin, *b* 1972, — Jude Aaron, *b* 1976, — Gudrun Rachael, *b* 1974. —— Jessica Catherine, *b* 1950: *m* 1976, Paul Staddon, of 7 Chepstow Rd, W2 5BP.

Issue of late Geoffrey Winthrop Young, 2nd son of 3rd baronet, *b* 1876, *d* 1958: *m* 1918, Eleanor, who *d* 1994, da of William Cecil Slingsby, formerly of Heversham, Westmorland:—
Jocelin Slingsby Winthrop, OBE (Gräfin Hildegard Str 9, 78354 Sipplingen, Germany; Alpine Club), *b* 1919; Founder and Headmaster of Anavryta Sch, Athens 1948-59, and Tutor to Crown Prince of Greece 1948-58; is a Com of Order of St George and St Constantine of Greece; 1939-45 War as Lt RNVR; OBE (Civil) 1960: *m* 1st, 1951 (*m diss* 1973), Countess Ghislaine, who *d* 1987, da of late Count Gustaf De la Gardie, of Malmö, Sweden; 2ndly, 1974, Countess Sibylle, DPhil, da of late Alexander, Count von der Schulenburg, of Duisburg, and has issue living (by 1st *m*), Mark Gustav (Holbein Str 16, 88212 Ravensburg, Germany), *b* 1952, — Geoffrey Hubert, *b* 1960; PhD; Prof of German, Univ of Waterloo, Ontario, Canada, — Sophie, *b* 1954: *m* 1985, Roger Weidlich, of Gräfin Hildegard Str, 9, 78354 Sipplingen, Germany, and has issue living, Amelie Ebba Ghislaine *b* 1989. —— Marcia Eacy Winthrop, *b* 1925: *m* 1948, Peter Newbolt, of Green Banks, Cley, Norfolk, and has issue living, Thomas Winthrop, *b* 1951, — Harry Triffitt, *b* 1953, — Barnaby Charles Slingsby, *b* 1955, — Catherine Eacy, *b* 1956.

Issue of late Rt Hon Sir Edward Hilton Young, GBE, DSO, DSC, PC, yst son of 3rd baronet, who was *cr* *Baron Kennet* 1935 (*see* that title).

Grandchildren of late Sir (William) Mackworth Young, KCSI, 3rd son of 2nd baronet:—
Issue of late Gerard Mackworth Mackworth-Young, CIE, *b* 1884, *d* 1965; assumed by deed poll 1947, the additional surname of Mackworth: *m* 1916, Natalie Lelia Margaret, who *d* 1981, da of late Rt Hon Sir Walter Francis Hely-Hutchinson, GCMG (*see* E Donoughmore, colls):—
Sir Robin (Robert Christopher Mackworth) MACKWORTH-YOUNG, GCVO (c/o Baring Bros & Co Ltd, 8 Bishopsgate, EC2; *Club* – Roxburghe), *b* 1920: *ed* Eton and King's Coll, Camb (MA); in HM's Foreign Ser 1948-55; appointed Dep Librarian, Windsor Castle 1955, and Librarian, Windsor Castle, and Assist Keeper of the Queen's Archives 1958; 1939-45 War as Sqdn-Ldr RAFVR; assumed by deed poll 1947 the additional surname of Mackworth; MVO (4th class) 1961, CVO 1968, KCVO 1975, GCVO 1985: *m* 1953, Helen Editha Rosemarie, da of W. C. R. Aue, of Menton, France, and has issue living, Charles Gerard (18 The Chase, Clapham, SW4; *Club* – Travellers'), *b* 1954; *ed* Eton and Magdalene Coll (Camb) (MA); MRCP 1980; MD 1987: *m* 1983, Lady Iona Sina Lindsay, yr da of 29th Earl of Crawford and Balcarres, and has issue living, Rose Bettina Natalie *b* 1987, Constance Ruth Sina *b* 1990. —— †Gerard William MACKWORTH-YOUNG, *b* 1926: *m* 1949, Lady Evelyn Leslie (Fisherton Mill, Fisherton de la Mere, Warminster, Wilts BA12 0PZ), da of 20th Earl of Rothes, and *d* 1984, leaving issue, Angela Clare, *b* 1951, — Susan Charlotte, *b* 1953: *m* 1987, Andrew Tribolini, of 5625 Beach Drive SW, Seattle, WA 98136, USA, son of late A. L. Tribolini, of Milwaukee, Wisconsin, — Lucinda Jane, *b* 1957: *m* 1st, 1981 (*m diss* 1984), Charles J. Lumsden; 2ndly, 1986, Oliver Matthew Sells, of 5 Paper Bldgs, Temple, EC4 7HB, son of late Sir David Perronet Sells, of Tadlow House, Royston, Herts, and has issue living (by 2nd *m*), Hugo William *b* 1988, Rosanna Mary *b* 1991, — Tessa Natalie, *b* 1959: *m* 1986, Michael G. Hardingham, of 9 Finlay St, SW6 6HE, yst son of Maj M. L. Hardingham, of E Harting, W Sussex, and has issue living, Robin Matthew *b* 1990, Luke Charles *b* 1993, Clara Louise *b* 1992. —— Honor Margaret Mackworth (Greystones, Ufton, Leamington Spa, Warwicks), *b* 1917: *m* 1938, Maj Archibald Douglas George Braithwaite, RA (ret) (Forestier-Walker, Bt, *cr* 1835; colls), who *d* 1990, and has issue living, Richard William (Tayvallich, Argyll), *b* 1944: *m* 1st, 1970 (*m diss* 1975), Claire Patricia, da of A. H. Sangster, of Kilmarnock, Ayrshire; 2ndly, 1981, Belinda Anne, da of D. F. Sheerman, of Truro, and has issue living, (by 2nd *m*) Iain Dudley *b* 1986, Shuna Anne *b* (twin) 1986, — Gerard Nicholas, *b* 1954, — Janis Mary *b* 1942: *m* 1973, James Mattinson, of Keswick, Cumbria, and has issue living, Hamish Edward *b* 1973, Sarah Jane *b* 1976, — Sarah Helen, *b* 1948. —— Lucia May Mackworth, *b* 1931: *m* 1966, Paul Mayersberg, of 5 Lowndes Court, Lowndes Sq, SW1, and has issue living, Zoltan Alexander, *b* 1969, — Natasha Catherine, *b* 1966.
Issue of late Maj Sir Hubert Winthrop Young, KCMG, DSO, *b* 1885, *d* 1950: *m* 1924, Margaret Rose Mary, who *d* 1981, da of late Col Frank Romilly Reynolds, RE:—
†Nicholas, *b* 1924; *ed* Eton, and Trin Coll, Camb: *m* 1969, Antonia Rosetta (7 Hamilton Terr, NW8 9RE), el da of late Brig Nigel Dugdale, CBE, 17th/21st Lancers (*see* Cunard, Bt, colls), and *d* 1992, leaving issue, Thomas Daniel Noah, *b* 1972, — Zoë Alexandra, *b* 1970. —— Martin Francis (Finca La Magdalena Baja, Apartado 13, 29400 Ronda, Malaga, Spain), *b* 1927; *ed* Eton, and King's Coll, Camb (MA); HM's Foreign Ser, 1948-63: *m* 1988, Catherine Carlotta, only da of late John Marshall, of Jacksonville, Florida. —— †Simon Bainbridge, *b* 1928: *m* 1954, Diana Tyndale (Martins, Whitehill, Bradford-upon-Avon), only da of late Oswald Lewis, and *d* 1984, leaving issue, James Hubert, *b* 1955, — Mark *b* 1957, *d* 1987, — Stephen, *b* 1959: *m* 1991, Margaret, da of Peter McBride, of Donegal, and has issue living, Caoimhe *b* 1993, — Emma, *b* 1961: *m* 1991, Stephen Lewis-Dale, yr son of Douglas Lewis-Dale, of Cheshire.
Issue of late Sir Mark Aitchison Young, GCMG, *b* 1886, *d* 1974: *m* 1919, Josephine Mary, who *d* 1977; a CStJ; da of late Walter C. Price:—
Sir Brian Walter Mark (Hill End, Woodhill Av, Gerrards Cross, Bucks), *b* 1922; *ed* Eton, and King's Coll, Camb (MA), Hon D Litt (Heriot Watt Univ) 1980; 1939-45 War as Lt RNVR; Headmaster of Charterhouse 1952-64; Dir of Nuffield Foundation 1964-70; Dir Gen of IBA 1970-82; Chm Christian Aid 1983-90; Memb Arts Council 1983-88; Knt 1976: *m* 1947, Fiona Marjorie, only da of late Allan Winslow Stewart, 16th Chief of Appin, and has issue living, Timothy Mark Stewart, *b* 1951; *ed* Eton, and Magdalene Coll, Camb (BA): *m* 1990, Alison M., yr da of late Geoffrey Keightley, of Wellingborough, Northants, and has issue living, Dugald Robert *b* 1992, Rowland Mark Keightley *b* 1993, — Joanna Margaret, *b* 1949; BA Durham: *m* 1974, Brig Peter Grant Peterkin, OBE, Queen's Own Highlanders, of Grange Hall, Forres, Moray, and has issue living, James Mark *b* 1977, Alexandra Mary *b* 1975. — Deborah Jane, *b* 1953: *m* 1979, Geoffrey Robert Francois Hudson (E Mar and Kellie, colls, 1963 Edn), of 26 Bolton Av, Windsor, Berks, and has issue living, Thomas Geoffrey Mark *b* 1980, Charlotte Jane *b* 1983, Sophie Emma *b* 1988. —— Denis Egerton (The Old Manse, Glenlyon, Aberfeldy, Perthshire), *b* 1926; *ed* Winchester, and King's Coll, Camb (MA); Housemaster and Head of History Dept, Strathallan Sch, Perthshire, 1952-79; Antique dealer since 1979; 1939-45 War in RNVR: *m* 1957, Judith Mary, el da of late Dr E. R. Matthews, of Nettleton, Wilts, and has issue living, Matthew Egerton, *b* 1959, — Walter Samuel Egerton *b* 1965, — Emma Faith, *b* 1960, — Cecilia Frances, *b* 1962: *m* 1982, Paul John Thompson, of London, and has issue living, Matthew Harry William, *b* 1983. —— Janet Cecilia Josephine, *b* 1930; MB and BS London; LRCP and MRCS 1955: *m* 1973, Dr R. J. Owens, of 22 Norman Rd, Hout Bay 7872, S Africa.

Grandson of late Henry Cathcart Arthur Young (infra):—
Issue of late Lieut-Com Malcolm Henry Cathcart Young, RN, *b* 1903, *ka* 1940: *m* 1930, Gwenda (who *d* 1953, having *m* 2ndly, 1946, the Rev A. Alan W. Gray), only da of late Wiliam Bromley Taylor:—
Christopher Malcolm (South Sea Farm, Kington Langley, Chippenham, Wilts), *b* 1936; *ed* Dragon Sch, Oxford, Geelong Gram Sch, Victoria, Australia, and Magdalene Coll, Camb (BA 1959, MA 1963): *m* 1960, Mary, da of late Ralph Lindsay, of Hurstmonceux, and has issue living, Richard Malcolm, *b* 1966, — Caroline Mary, *b* 1962, — Victoria Jane, *b* 1964.

Grandchildren of late Henry Young, HEICS, 3rd son of 1st baronet:—
Issue of late Henry Cathcart Arthur Young, *b* 1850, *d* 1940: *m* 1902, Florence, who *d* 1968, yst da of late Alfred Eccles, FRCS:—
Katharine Elizabth (8 Campden House, 29 Sheffield Terr, W8 7NE), *b* 1908; 1939-45 War with VAD.
Issue of late Horace Edward Broughton Young, *b* 1853, *d* 1924: *m* 1882, Ellen Elizabeth who *d* 1938, da of George Thorne, of Darcey Hey, Castle Hill, N S Wales:—
Henry Herbert, *b* 1895; European War 1916-18 as Lieut RA (severely wounded): *m* (Feb) 1920, Margaret Caroline Britania, da of late Capt James Somerville Murray, of The Sandpatch, Wentworth Fall, N S Wales, and has issue living, Andrew

Broughton, *b* (Dec) 1920, — Arnold Somerville, *b* 1923, — Horace Anthony, *b* 1925, — Robert Alexander, *b* 1927, — Janet Elizabeth *b* 1931. —— Winifred Elinor Broughton, *b* 1896: *m* 1920, David Theodore Field Nicholson, who *d* 1955, and has issue living, Peter Theodore (of 99 Copeland Rd, Beecroft, NSW), *b* 1926; *ed* Sydney Univ (BSc, BE); FIE Aust MIEE: *m* 1949, Patricia May, BSc, da of late E. T. Ohlsson, of Roseville, NSW, and has issue living, Peter Timothy James *b* 1952; BSc (Sydney Univ), Philip Theodore *b* 1954; BSc, BE (Sydney Univ); ME (Univ of NSW), Catherine Jane *b* 1955; BA (Macquarie Univ): *m* 1979, Bruce Kevin Coffee, (and has issue living, Matthew Bruce *b* 1983), Anne Elizabeth *b* 1957, Alison Patricia *b* 1961; MB, BS (Sydney Univ), — Donald Ian (c/o Forest Dept, Brisbane, Qld), *b* 1928; *ed* Sydney Univ, and Austn Forestry Sch (Diploma of Forestry and BSc Forestry 1949): *m* 1956, Grace Mary, da of Rev Harold Dennis Powley, of Africa Inland Mission, and has issue living, Graham John *b* 1957, Robert Christopher *b* 1965, Stephanie Jane *b* 1959, Joanne Christine *b* 1962, — John David *b* 1934: *m* 1974, Alice Louise, da of late Robert Kurwen Campbell, and has issue living, David Theodore Campbell *b* 1975, Frances Bryony *b* 1978, — Sheila Constance, *b* 1921: *m* 1949, John Wallace Knox, FRCS, MRCOG (ante), — Elinor Catherine, *b* 1924; *ed* Sydney Univ (MB, BS); ChB NZ, DObstRCOG Sydney; FRCOG: *m* 1950, Reginald Henry James Hamlin, OBE, MB, ChB, FRCOG (Eng), and has issue living, Richard Havelock James *b* 1953, — Alisa Mary, *b* 1931: *m* 1959, Bruce Graham Pottie, of Turrawonga, Lairas Lee, NSW, and has issue living, Dougal John *b* 1960, James Theodore Graham *b* 1961, Angus Bruce *b* 1965. *Residence* – Rosedale, Garra, NSW 2866.

Grandchildren of late Charles Ernest Young (infra):—

Issue of late Capt Henry Shedden Baring Young, MC, RA, *b* 1894, *d* 1976: *m* 1st, 1929, Eva Theodora, who *d* 1940, da of T. C. Maltby, of The Oaks, Tauranga, NZ; 2ndly, 1953, Janet Mary (20 Lamington St, Deakin, ACT 2600, Aust), only da of late Rev J. Milton Thompson, of Tonbridge, Kent:—
(By 1st *m*), James Ernest Baring (11 Upper Rosemount Rd, Nambour, Queensland 4560, Australia), *b* 1933: *m* 1st, 1959 (*m diss* 1975), Annette Florence, da of Kenneth Lane, of St Ives, NSW; 2ndly, 1976, Cheryl Beverley, da of — Price, and has issue living (by 1st *m*), Timothy James Baring *b* 1960, — Michael Henry Baring *b* 1962, — David Kenneth Baring *b* 1969, — Anthony Baring, *b* 1971. —— Dorothy Joan Baring, *b* 1930: *ed* Sydney Univ (BScAgric) and London Univ (MScAgric): *m* 1957, John Lionel Wheeler, PhD, BSc (Agric), CSIRO, of Armidale, NSW, and has issue living, Philip John Henry *b* 1961, — Ian Charles Andrew *b* 1963, — Rosemary Helen *b* 1959: *m* 1982, Andrew John Sempell, — (By 2nd *m*), Stephen Henry Baring *b* 1954: *m* 1st, 1976 (*m diss* 1989), Grace Marianne, da of Stewart Dinnen, of Launceston, Tasm; 2ndly, 1992, Nicola Helen, da of William Main, of Turramurra, NSW, and has issue living (by 1st *m*), Rachel Grace Marie *b* 1981, Clare Ruth Mary *b* 1983. —— Angela Mary Katherine, *b* 1957: *m* 1988, Dr Mark Oliver Diesendorf, of PO Box 48, O'Connor, ACT, Australia, and has issue living, Joseph James, *b* 1993.

Issue of late Charles Arthur Noel Young, AM, *b* 1899, *d* 1992: *m* 1923, Margery Bisdee Maynard, da of late Dr Maynard Pain, of Sydney and Cain:—
Charles Edward Christopher (M/S 827 Moore Park Rd, Bundaberg, Qld 4670), *b* 1926: *m* 1st, 1949, Margaret Florence, who *d* 1976, da of W. Guilford, of Killara, Sydney, NSW; 2ndly, 1986, Beverley Gaze, da of Arthur W. Edwards, of Leamington Spa, and his wife Margaret Allison (*see* Macara, Bt, colls), and has issue living, (by 1st *m*) Christopher Roderick (4 Edzell Place, Carindale, Brisbane, Qld), *b* 1950; *ed* Brisbane Anglican Gram Sch, and Univ of Queensland (B Comm, B App Sc (Applied Chem), Cert Sugar Chem); ARACI, FCIS; Company Sec of Bundaberg Sugar Co: *m* 1973, Jennifer Ann, da of J. Mackrill, of Bundaberg, Qld, and has issue living, Benjamin Roderick *b* 1982, Bianca Margaret *b* 1979, — Timothy Charles, *b* 1952; *ed* Brisbane Anglican Gram Sch, and Univ of Qld (B Bus); AASA: *m* 1979, Leonie, da of R. McDowell, of Bundaberg, Qld, and has issue living, Erin Nancy *b* 1983, Vanessa Megan *b* 1985, — *Rev* Gregory Mark, *b* 1955; *ed* Brisbane Anglican Gram Sch: *m* 1983, Michelle Suzanne, da of A. Baster, of Perth, W. Aust, and has issue living, Adam Christopher *b* 1991, Hayley Claire *b* 1985, Alyce Nicole *b* 1988, — Nicholas William, *b* 1961; *ed* N Bund High Sch: *m* 1991, Wendy Lee, da of late R. W. Basmin, of Penshurst, Sydney. —— Margery Marian (Box 181 PO, Moss Vale, NSW 2577, Australia), *b* 1924; *ed* Abbotsleigh Sch; SRN: *m* 1949 (*m diss* 1976), Norman Bruce Berry, and has issue living, Andrew Bruce (30 Shadforth St, Mosman, Sydney, NSW 2088, Australia), *b* 1950; *ed* Sydney Univ and Adelaide Univ; MB, BS, FRACP; State Dir, Emergency Neonatal Transport; Head, Dept of Neonatology, Royal Alexandra Hosp for Children, Sydney, — Simon Mark (Box 1, Bowral, NSW 1976), *b* 1956; *ed* ANU (BEc): *m* 1982, Sue, da of D. Imrie, — Hugh Jonathan (Montage, 62 Albany St, Crowsnest, NSW), *b* 1962: *m* 1992, Jennifer Green, — Susan Marian, *b* 1952; *ed* Macquarie Univ (BA): *m* 1984, William Alexander Ryan, of Abbots Court, Deerhurst, Glos, and has issue living, Alexander Cheyne *b* 1985, Phoebe Imogen Alice *b* 1987, Clare Margery Francis *b* 1989, — Philippa Jane, *b* 1954; *ed* Scegg Sch; SRN: *m* 1979, David William Learmonth Palmer, of 8 Downes Place, Hughes, Canberra, ACT, and has issue living, Angus Norman Learmonth *b* 1980, Simon David *b* 1982, Olivia Jane *b* 1984. —— Elizabeth Wendy, *b* 1927: *m* 1957, Neil James Yorkston, FRACP, FRC Psych, of 59 Blackwell, Darlington, co Durham DL3 8QT, and has issue living, Ian Charles (1 Deerness Hts, Brandon, co Durham DH7 8TQ), *b* 1960: *m* 1985, Valerie Dunford, of Edmonton, Alberta, — Catherine Judith, *b* 1958; *ed* Blackheath High Sch, Univ of Brit Columbia (BA): *m* 1985 John Christopher Allinson, of 31 Kingsmead Rd, SW2 3HV, son of James Allinson, of Bradford, and has issue living, Simon James *b* 1992, Emma Charlotte *b* 1988, — Ruth Elizabeth, *b* 1959; *ed* Blackheath High Sch, London Univ (BSc), — Ann Margery, *b* 1965; *ed* Blackheath High Sch, Univ of Brit Columbia. —— Lois Margaret, *b* 1929; *ed* Macquarie Univ; SRN: *m* 1957, Arthur Frederick Pennington, MB, BS, of 119 Kissing Point Rd, Dundas, NSW 2117, and has issue living, Jeremy Arthur, *b* 1958: *m* 198—, Denise, da of John Pountney, of Sydney, and has issue living, Jennifer Grace *b* 1989, Melanie Denis *b* 1991, — Martin Frederick, *b* 1961: *m* 1984, Heath, da of Brian Richards, of Adelaide, S Aust, and has issue living, Huon Frederick *b* 1994, Elise Patricia *b* 1988, Myanna Ellen *b* 1991, — Judith Charis, *b* 1960: *m* 1989, Malcolm Rundle, of Boronia Park, Melbourne, and has issue living, Julia Helen *b* 1993, — Mary Priscilla, *b* 1964: *m* 1986, *Rev* Richard Lane, and has issue living, Sebastian Arthur *b* 1992, Emily Cassandra *b* 1991, — Fiona Margaret, *b* 1974. —— Catherine Anne, *b* 1930. —— Philippa Lucia Charis, *b* 1937: *m* 1963, Donald Campbell Thorn, FRAIA, of 28 Rubens Grove, Canterbury, Vic, Aust, and has issue living, Christopher Ian, *b* 1964; *ed* Melbourne Univ (BCom): *m* 1990, Rosalind Heather Mills, and has issue living, Benjamin Lawrence *b* 1993, — Samuel Douglas, *b* 1967; *ed* Melbourne Univ (BEng): *m* 1990, Jane, da of Brian Willis, of Hawthorn, and has issue living, Maxwell David *b* 1992, Harrison Campbell *b* 1993, — Bronwen Margery, *b* 1965; *ed* Melbourne Univ (MB BS), FRACGP: *m* 1993, Robert Graham Wilson, of S Perth, W Aust, — Sarah Penelope Joan, *b* 1972; *ed* Monash Univ. —— Helen Rosalind (618 Windermere Av, Toronto, Ont M6S 3L8, Canada), *b* 1939; *ed* Univ of Toronto (BA, MA): *m* 1959 (*m diss* 19—), John Henry Northcote Deck, MD, FRCP (C), and has issue living, Wilbert John Northcote, *b* 1960; *ed* Upper Canada Coll, and McGill Univ (BSc, MB): *m* 1986, Carmen Leger, and has issue living, Max Antonio *b* 1991, Zoe Lise *b* 1987, Anouk *b* 1989, Emma *b* 1993, — Philip Charles, *b* 1962; *ed* Univ of Toronto (BA), — Roger Norman, *b* 1964; *ed* Upper Canada Coll, and Univ of Toronto (B Com), — Kathleen Margery, *b* 1963; *ed* Univ of Toronto (BA) and Univ of Ottawa (B Soc Sc), — Rachel Frances, *b* 1971, — Jennifer Luci Maynard, *b* 1973. —— Adrienne Penelope, *b* 1943: *m* 1976, Wilfred Galbraith, of Medway, Barolin Pony Stud, Moss Vale, NSW 2577, Australia, and has issue living, Thomas Charles *b* 1977, James Wilfred *b* 1978, Barnaby Donald *b* 1984, Annabel Christiana *b* 1980, Charina Bisdee *b* 1982. —— Carolyn Bronwen (7 Pickford Av, Eastwood, Sydney, NSW), *b* 1945: *m* 1974 (*m diss* 19—), Keith Wolfson, son of Hymie Wolfson, of Johannesburg, and has issue living, Robin Lawrence, *b* 1978, Asher David, *b* 1981, Chloe Samantha, *b* 1977.

Grandson of late Henry Young, HEICS (ante):—

Issue of late Charles Ernest Young, *b* 1855, *d* 1927: *m* 1891, Margaret Else, who *d* 1952, da of John Shedden Adam, of Ellerslie, Turramurra, Sydney, NSW:—
Ernest Stafford, *b* 1903; *ed* Sydney Univ (BE); 1939-45 War with RAAF; formerly Missionary in British N Borneo: *m* 1946, Lilian Olive, JP, da of late C. E. Mumford, of Cremorne, Sydney, NSW, and has issue living, David Hilton (63 Fairlawn Av, Turramurra, NSW 2074), *b* 1947; *ed* Sydney Univ (BEc): *m* 1972, Katherine Beatrice, da of Dr E. L. A. Rod, of Gordon, Sydney, and has issue living, Jeremy Andrew *b* 1973, Virginia Bronwyn *b* 1976, Amanda Penelope *b* 1977, — Lesley Ann, *b* 1949; *ed* Sydney Univ (BA, Dip Ed): *m* 1972, Rodney Elkington Allen, MB, BS, of 55 Kensington Rd, Bolwarra, NSW 2320,

and has issue living, Matthew James Elkington *b* 1974, Benjamin Mark Elkington *b* 1976, Andrew Stephen Elkington *b* 1979, — Rosemary Frances, *b* 1953. *Residence* – 13 Karranga Av, Killara, Sydney, NSW 2071.

Grandchildren of late Charles Ernest Young (ante):—
Issue of late Geoffrey Lawrence Young, *b* 1910, *d* 1993: *m* 1935, Irene, OAM, BSc, (33 Denman Parade, Normanhurst, NSW) da of P. W. Petter, of Swallowcliffe, Yeovil, Somerset:—
Peter Lawrence (4 Narelle Av, Pymble, NSW 2073), *b* 1935; FCILA, FCPA: *m* 1961, Jennifer Mary, da of J. M. Clift, and has issue living, Michael Lawrence *b* 1968; *ed* Sydney Univ (BE, BSc), — Judith Anne *b* 1971. —— Geoffrey Branscombe, *b* 1942. —— Susan Irene, *b* 1938; BA 1961: *m* 1966 (*m diss* 1977), William Werden Wilson, and has issue living, John Werden, *b* 1968, — Anthea, *b* 1969. —— Kathleen Patricia, *b* 1940; BSc 1961: *m* 1969, Stuart Braga, MA, M Ed Admin, FACE, of 52 Seaview St, Ashfield, NSW 2131, and has issue living, David Hugh, *b* 1970, — Christopher Stuart, *b* 1972, Andrew Geoffrey, *b* 1975. —— Jocelyn Olivia, *b* 1946: *m* 1969, Wayne Mackenzie, of 12a Felton Rd, Carlingford, NSW, and has issue living, Malcolm Geoffrey, *b* 1972, — Barbara Lorraine, *b* 1970.

Sir Samuel Young, 1st baronet, was the el son of Sir George Young, of Formosa Place, Berks, Adm of the White who served at Quebec 1759, Havana 1762, and Pondicherry 1778. Sir George Young, 3rd baronet, was a Charity Commr 1882-99, Third Charity Commr 1899-1900, 2nd Charity Commr 1900-03, and Ch Charity Commr 1903-06. Sir George Young, MVO, 4th baronet, was in Diplo Ser 1896-1914, Professor of Portuguese and Examiner in Ottoman Law in Univ of London 1919-23, and Professor of Political Science, American Univs 1929-30. Sir George Peregrine Young, CMG, 5th baronet, was Head of W Depart, Foreign Office 1950-51, HM's Min in Rome 1951-3, Assist Sec Cabinet Office 1953-5, Head of News Depart, Foreign Office 1955-56, and HBM's Min in Paris 1956-60. He *m* 1939, Elisabeth, who *d* 1957, da of Sir Hughe Montgomery Knatchbull-Hugessen, KCMG (B Brabourne, colls).

YOUNG (UK) 1821, of Bailieborough Castle, co Cavan

Sir JOHN KENYON ROE YOUNG, 6th *Baronet*, *b* 23 April 1947; *s* his father, *Sir* JOHN WILLIAM ROE, 1981; *ed* Harncourt Sch, Christchurch, Hants: *m* 1977, Frances Elise, only da of W. R. Thompson, and has issue.

𝔄rms – Argent, three piles sable, each charged with a trefoil, slipped or; on a cheif of the second three annulets of the third. ℭrest – A demi-lion rampant gules, charged on the shoulder with a trefoil slipped or, and holding in the dexter paw a sprig of three maple leaves, all proper.
Residence – Bolingey, 159 Chatham Rd, Maidstone, Kent ME14 2ND.

SON LIVING

RICHARD CHRISTOPHER ROE, *b* 14 June 1983.

DAUGHTER LIVING

Tamara Elizabeth Eve, *b* 1986.

SISTER LIVING

Eve Maureen Aldous, *b* 1949: *m* 1976 (*m diss* 1989), — Robertson.

UNCLES LIVING (*Sons of 4th baronet*)

Patrick Elliott, *b* 1917: *m* 1946, Sadie Reid, only da of Laurence Beattie, of Prestwick, Ayrshire, and has issue living, Christopher Brian Harrington, *b* 1965, — Patricia, *b* 1947, — Veronica Anne, *b* 1949, — Nancy Gay, *b* 1952. —— Michael Cyril Harrington (39 Grove Rd, Wamberal, NSW), *b* 1928: *m* 1955, Anita Patricia, who *d* 1994, only da of C. H. Duff, of Hong Kong, and has issue living, Peter Charles Harrington, *b* 1956, — Anthony Michael, *b* 1961, — Gail Louraine, *b* 1960.

The 1st baronet, Sir William, was a Director of the East India Company; and the 2nd baronet, Sir John (Gov of New S Wales 1860-67, and Gov-Gen of Canada 1868-72), was raised to the Peerage in 1870 as Baron Lisgar, but dying without issue, his peerage became extinct, and the baronetcy devolved upon his nephew, Sir William Muston Need, 3rd baronet.

YOUNG (UK) 1945, of Partick, co City of Glasgow

Sir STEPHEN STEWART TEMPLETON YOUNG, 3rd *Baronet*; *b* 24 May 1947; *s* his father, *Sir* ALASTAIR SPENCER TEMPLETON, DL, 1963; *ed* Rugby, Trin Coll, Oxford and Edinburgh Univ; Advocate (Scotland); Sheriff of Glasgow and Strathkelvin March-June 1984, since when Sheriff of North Strathclyde at Greenock: *m* 1974, Viola Margaret, da of Prof Patrick Horace Nowell-Smith (B Vernon, colls) and has issue.

Arms – Argent, on three piles issuant from a chief sable, charged with three lymphads under full sail of the 1st flagged gules, as many annulets of the 3rd. **Crest** – A lymphad or, under full sail, its sail charged of the arms, having a pennon gules with the badge of Scotland viz azure, a saltire argent, in the hoist. *Residence* – Glen Rowan, Shore Rd, Cove, Dunbartons, G84 0NU.

SONS LIVING

CHARLES ALASTAIR STEPHEN, *b* 21 July 1979. —— Alexander David, *b* 1982.

SISTER LIVING

Clare Elizabeth, *b* 1953: *m* 1975, Stephen John Beaty, of 35 Chestnut Rd, SE27 9EZ, and has issue living, Thomas Alastair Stephen, *b* 1977, — Corinne Elizabeth, *b* 1979, — Josepha Isobel, *b* 1981.

UNCLE DECEASED *(son of 1st baronet)*

†Patrick Templeton, *b* 1925; *ed* Rugby; ARIBA: *m* 1950, Jenny Loxton (3F Lansdowne Rd, W11 3AL), only da of Sir Walter Eric Bassett, KBE, MC, of Melbourne, Australia, and *d* 1992, leaving issue, Roger Spencer Masson, *b* 1954; *ed* Radley: *m* 1979, Margaret Alice Wilhelmina —. —— Jane Templeton, *b* 1952: has issue living, Gemma Lucy, *b* 1983.

AUNT LIVING *(Daughter of 1st baronet)*

Barbara Mary, *b* 1916: *m* 1939, William Echlin Hollington Grayburn, who *d* 1988, and has had issue, Jon Alastair, *b* 1943, *d* 1978: *m* 1970, Valerie Irlam, and had issue, William Alastair George *b* 1973, — Lesley Mary, *b* 1949. *Residence* – 12 Lee Rd, Aldeburgh, Suffolk.

The 1st baronet, Sir Arthur Stewart Leslie Young (son of late Daniel Henderson Lusk Young, of Glasgow), was Parliamentary Private Sec to Under-Sec of State for Scotland 1937-39, and to Sec of State for Scotland 1939-42, a Lord Commr of The Treasury 1942-44, and Vice-Chamberlain of HM's Household 1944-45; sat as MP for Partick Div of Glasgow (*U*) 1935-50.

YOUNGER (UK) 1911, of Auchen Castle, Kirkpatrick-Juxta, co Dumfries

Sir JOHN WILLIAM YOUNGER, CBE, 3rd *Baronet*; *b* 18 Nov 1920; *s* his father, *Sir* WILLIAM ROBERT, 1973; *ed* Canford and RMC Sandhurst; Maj-Gen late Coldm Gds; Dir Management and Support Intelligence 1973-76 since when C in C of St John Ambulance; 1939-45 War in Middle East (prisoner, MBE); Commr-in-Chief, St John Ambulance 1980-85; MBE (Mil) 1945, CBE (Mil) 1969; KStJ 1980: *m* 1st, 1948 (*m diss* 1952), Mrs Stella Jane Dodd, da of Rev John George Lister; 2ndly, 1953, Marcella Granito, Princess Pignatelli di Belmonte, who *d* 1989, da of late Prof Avv Roberto Scheggi; 3rdly, 1991, Mrs Anne Henrietta Maria St Paul Seely, only da of Horace George St Paul Butler, and formerly wife of (i) James Dugdale Burridge, and (ii) Timothy Ward Seely (*see* Seely, Bt, colls), and has issue (by 1st *m*).

Arms – Or, on a bend azure, between two martlets sable, three roses argent, barbed and seeded vert, on a chief gules, a crescent between two mullets of the first. **Crest** – A dexter hand holding a lance in bend proper. *Residence* – 23 Cadogan Sq, SW1X 0HU. *Club* – Boodle's, Berks Golf.

SON LIVING *(By 1st marriage)*

JULIAN WILLIAM RICHARD, *b* 10 Feb 1950; *ed* Eton, and Grinnell Univ, USA: *m* 1981, Deborah Ann Wood, and has issue living, Andrew William, *b* 14 Jan 1986. *Residence* – 6 Country Club Lane, Pelham Manor, NY 10803, USA.

DAUGHTER LIVING *(By 1st marriage)*

Quite ready

Joanna Jane, *b* 1951: *m* 1972, Timothy John Binnington, of Thakeham Place, Thakeham, nr Pulborough, W Sussex, and has issue living, Nicholas William David, *b* 1977, — Kate Louise Frances, *b* 1975.

SISTER LIVING

Margaret Elizabeth, *b* 1916: *m* 1937, John Howard Moller, late Queen's Own Cameron Highlanders, who *d* 1983, and has issue living, Christopher Pierre William Howard, *b* 1943; *ed* Charterhouse: *m* 1973, Susan Maria Scougal Burdette, da of Alban Millar Ross-Smith, of Heyshott, Sussex, and has issue living, Cassandra Maria *b* 1975, Tara Elizabeth *b* 1976, — Caroline Victoria Margaret, *b* 1939, — Maxine Faith Alexandra, *b* 1940: *m* 1966 (*m diss* 1978), Rory B. M. Nicholas. *Residence* – .
—— Diana Joan, *b* 1919: *m* 1st, 1940 (*m diss* 1947), Hon William Francis Brinsley Le Poer Trench (now 8th Earl of Clancarty); 2ndly, 1947, Dr H. Wentworth Eldredge, of Tarn House, Elm St, Norwich, Vermont, USA, Prof of Sociology, Dartmouth Coll, NH, and has issue living (by 2nd *m*), James Wentworth, *b* 1950, — Alan Wentworth, *b* 1953. *Residence* – 6161 Fieldcrest Drive, Frederick, Maryland 21701, USA.

The 1st baronet, Sir William Younger (son of late William Younger, of Auchen Castle, Moffat), was MP for S Kesteven or Stamford Division of Lincolnshire (*L*) 1895-1906, and for Peebles and Selkirk Jan to Nov 1910.

YOUNGER (UK) 1964, of Fountainbridge, co and City of Edinburgh (extinct 1992)

Sir WILLIAM McEWAN YOUNGER, DSO, DL, 1st and last *Baronet.*

DAUGHTER LIVING OF FIRST BARONET (*By 1st marriage*)

Caroline Ruth, *b* 1946: *m* 1968, Barney Platts-Mills, of 52 Novello St, SW6, 4th son of John Faithful Fortescue Platts-Mills, QC.

WIDOW LIVING OF FIRST BARONET

JUNE PECK (*Lady Younger*): *m* 1983, as his 2nd wife, Sir William McEwan Younger, DSO, DL, 1st baronet, who *d* 1992. *Residence* – 29 Moray Place, Edinburgh EH3 6DA.

PEERAGES THAT HAVE BECOME
EXTINCT, DORMANT, ABEYANT, OR DISCLAIMED

Since 1950. For Extinctions in the years 1900-50 see 1958 and earlier editions.

Peerages junior in rank will be found under the senior titles.

The family surname appears in italics (between parentheses) immediately after the title

* Peerage of United Kingdom	‖ Peerage of Scotland
† Peerage of Great Britain	§ Peerage of Ireland
‡ Peerage of England	

HEREDITARY PEERAGES EXTINCT, DORMANT or ABEYANT

* ADAMS, Baron (*Adams*) Cr 1949 Ext 1960
* AILWYN, Baron (*Fellowes*) Cr 1921 Ext 1988
* ALEXANDER OF HILLSBOROUGH, Earl (*Alexander*) Cr 1963; also *V. Alexander of Hillsborough 1950, and *B. Weston-super-Mare, 1963 Ext 1965
* ALNESS, Baron (*Munro*) Cr 1934 Ext 1955
* AMHERST, Earl (*Amherst*) Cr 1826; also *V Holmesdale, and †B Amherst Ext 1993
* AMMON, Baron (*Ammon*) Cr 1944 Ext 1960
* AMORY, Viscount (*Heathcoat-Amory*) Cr 1960 Ext 1981
* AMULREE, Baron (*Mackenzie*) Cr 1929 Ext 1983
* ANCASTER, Earl (*Heathcote-Drummond-Willoughby*) Cr 1892; also † Baron Aveland 1856 Ext 1983
* ARMSTRONG, Baron (*Watson-Armstrong*) Cr 1903 Ext 1987
* ATHLONE, Earl of (*Cambridge*) Cr 1917; also V. Trematon 1917 Ext 1957
* AVON, Earl (*Eden*) Cr 1961; also *V Eden 1961 Ext 1985.
* BADELEY, Baron (*Badeley*) Cr 1949 Ext 1951
§ BANDON, Earl of (*Bernard*) Cr 1800; also *B. Bernard 1809. §B. Bandon 1793; §V. Bandon 1795 Ext 1979
* BARNBY, Baron (*Willey*) Cr 1922 Ext 1982
§ BARRINGTON, Viscount (*Barrington*) Cr 1720; also *B Shute 1880 Dormant or Ext 1990
* BEAUCHAMP, Earl (*Lygon*) Cr 1815; also *V. Elmley 1815; *B. Beauchamp of Powyke 1806 Ext 1979
* BENNETT OF EDGBASTON, Baron (*Bennett*) Cr 1953 Ext 1957
‡ BERNERS, Baron (*Williams*) Cr 1455 Abey 1992.
* BERTIE OF THAME, Viscount (*Bertie*) Cr 1918; also *B. Bertie of Thame 1915 Ext 1954
† BERWICK, Baron (*Noel-Hill*) Cr 1784 Ext 1953
* BESSBOROUGH, Earl (*Ponsonby*) Cr 1937 Ext 1993
* BEVERIDGE, Baron (*Beveridge*) Cr 1946 Ext 1963
* BILSLAND, Baron (*Bilsland*) Cr 1950 Ext 1970
* BIRKENHEAD, Earl of (*Smith*) Cr 1922; also *V Furneaux 1922, V Birkenhead 1921, and B Birkenhead 1919 ext 1985
* BLACKFORD, Baron (*Mason*) Cr 1935 Ext 1988
* BOLSOVER, Baron (*Cavendish-Bentinck*) Cr 1880 Ext 1977
‡ BOTETOURT, Baron (*Somerset*) Cr 1305. Abey 1984
‡ BOTREAUX, Baron (*Hastings*) Cr 1368. Abey 1960
* BOYD-ORR, Baron (*Orr*) Cr 1949 Ext 1971
* BRACKEN, Viscount (*Bracken*) Cr 1952 Ext 1958
* BRAINTREE, Baron (*Crittall*) Cr 1948 Ext 1961
* BRAND, Baron (*Brand*) Cr 1946 Ext 1963
* BRECON, Baron (*Lewis*) Cr 1958 Ext 1976
* BRUCE OF MELBOURNE, Viscount (*Bruce*) Cr 1947 Ext 1967
* CAMBRIDGE, Marquess of (*Cambridge*) Cr 1917; also *E. of Eltham 1917; *V. Northallerton 1917 Ext 1981
* CAMPION, Baron (*Campion*) Cr 1950 Ext 1958
* CARISBROOKE, Marquess of (*Mountbatten*) Cr 1917; also V. Launceston, E. of Berkhamsted 1917 Ext 1960
* CECIL OF CHELWOOD, Viscount (*Gascoyne-Cecil*) Cr 1923 Ext 1958
* CHAPLIN, Viscount (*Chaplin*) Cr 1916 Ext 1981
* CHARNWOOD, Baron (*Benson*) Cr 1911 Ext 1955
* CHERWELL, Viscount (*Lindemann*) Cr 1956; also B. Cherwell 1941 Ext 1957
‡ CHESTERFIELD and †STANHOPE, Earl of (*Stanhope*) Cr 1628 and 1718, also ‡B. Stanhope of Shelford 1616 Ext 1967
* CHEYLESMORE, Baron (*Eaton*) Cr 1887 Ext 1974
* CILCENNIN, Viscount (*Thomas*) Cr 1956 Ext 1960
§ CLARINA, Baron (*Massey*) Cr 1800 Ext 1952

§ CLIFDEN, Viscount (*Agar-Robartes*) Cr 1781. Also §Baron Clifden 1776, and *Baron Robartes 1869 Ext 1974
‡ COBHAM, Baron (*Alexander*) Cr 1312-13. Abey 1951
* COHEN OF BIRKENHEAD, Baron (*Cohen*) Cr 1956 Ext 1977
* CONESFORD, Baron (*Strauss*) Cr 1955 Ext 1974
‡ CONYERS, Baron (*Pelham*) Cr 1509. Abey 1948
* COOPER OF CULROSS, Baron (*Cooper*) Cr 1954 Ext 1955
* COURTAULD-THOMSON, Baron (*Courtauld-Thomson*) Cr 1944 Ext 1954
* COURTHOPE, Baron (*Courthope*) Cr 1945 Ext 1955
* COZENS-HARDY, Baron (*Cozens-Hardy*) Cr 1914 Ext 1975
* CROOKSHANK, Viscount (*Crookshank*) Cr 1956 Ext 1961
* CUNNINGHAM OF HYNDHOPE, Viscount (*Cunningham*) Cr 1945 Ext 1963
* DARYNGTON, Baron (*Pease*) Cr 1923 Ext 1994
* DORCHESTER, Baron (*Carleton*) Cr 1899 Ext 1963
* DOUGLAS OF BARLOCH, Baron (*Douglas*) Cr 1950 Ext 1980
* DOUGLAS OF KIRTLESIDE, Baron (*Douglas*) Cr 1948 Ext 1965
* DOUGLAS OF BARLOCH, Baron (*Douglas*) Cr 1950 Ext 1980
* DOVERCOURT, Baron (*Holmes*) Cr 1954 Ext 1961
* DRUMALBYN, Baron (*Macpherson*) Cr 1963 Ext 1987
* DUFFERIN AND AVA, Marquess (*Hamilton-Temple-Blackwood*) Cr 1888; also * E of Dufferin 1871, E of Ava 1888, V Clandeboye 1871, and B Clandeboye 1850 Ext 1988
* DUGAN OF VICTORIA, Baron (*Dugan*) Cr 1949 Ext 1951
* EBBISHAM, Baron (*Blades*) Cr 1928 Ext 1991
* EGERTON OF TATTON, Baron (*Egerton*) Cr 1859 Ext 1958
* ELIBANK, Viscount (*Murray*) Cr 1911 Ext 1962
* ENNISDALE, Baron (*Lyons*) Cr 1939 Ext 1963
* ESSENDON, Baron (*Lewis*) Cr 1932 Ext 1978
* EVANS, Baron (*Evans*) Cr 1957 Ext 1963
* EVERSHED, Baron (*Evershed*) Cr 1956 Ext 1966
‖ FALCONER OF HALKERTON, Lord (*Keith*) Cr 1646 Dormant 1966
* FAIRHAVEN, Baron (*Broughton*) Cr 1929 Ext 1966
* FARRER, Baron (*Farrer*) Cr 1893 Ext 1964
‡ FAUCONBERG, Baron (*Pelham*) Cr 1283 Abey 1948
* FEVERSHAM, Earl of (*Duncombe*) Cr 1868; also *V. Helmsley 1868 Ext 1963
§ FINGALL, Earl of (*Plunkett*) Cr 1628; also §Baron Killeen 1449; * Baron Fingall 1831 Ext 1984
* FITZ ALAN OF DERWENT, Viscount (*Fitzalan-Howard*) Cr 1921 Ext 1962
† FITZWILLIAM, Earl (*Wentworth-Fitzwilliam*) Cr 1746; also §E. Fitzwilliam 1716; V Milton 1716; †Lord Fitzwilliam 1742; †B of Milton 1742; §B Fitzwilliam 1620 Ext 1979
* FLECK, Baron (*Fleck*) Cr 1961 Ext 1968
* FORSTER OF HARRABY, Baron (*Forster*) Cr 1959 Ext 1972
* FRASER OF NORTH CAPE, Baron (*Fraser*) Cr 1946 Ext 1981
* FRASER OF ALLANDER, Baron (*Fraser*) Cr 1964, disclaimed 1966 Ext 1987
‡ FURNIVALL, Baron (*Dent*) Cr 1295 Abeyant 1968
* GLENAVY, Baron (*Campbell*) Cr 1921 Ext 1984
* GLENTANAR, Baron (*Coats*) Cr 1916 Ext 1971
* GLYN, Baron (*Glyn*) Cr 1953 Ext 1960
* GODBER, Baron (*Godber*) Cr 1956 Ext 1976
* GREENE, Baron (*Greene*) Cr 1941 Ext 1952
* GREVILLE, Baron (*Greville*) Cr 1869 Ext 1987

‡ GREY DE RUTHYN, Baron (*Butler-Bowdon*)
　Cr 1324　Abey 1963
§ GUILLAMORE, Viscount (*O'Grady*)　Cr 1831; also
　§B. O'Grady 1831　Ext 1955
* HAILES, Baron (*Buchan-Hepburn*)　Cr 1957
　Ext 1974
* HAILEY, Baron (*Hailey*)　Cr 1936　Ext 1969
* HARCOURT, Viscount (*Harcourt*)　Cr 1917; also *B.
　Nuneham 1917　Ext 1979
‡ HASTINGS, Baron (*Hastings*)　Cr 1461　Abey 1960
§ HEADLEY, Baron (*Allanson-Winn*)　Cr 1797
　Ext 1994
* HENDERSON, Baron (*Henderson*)　Cr 1945
　Ext 1984
* HENEAGE, Baron (*Heneage*)　Cr 1896　Ext 1967
* HEWART, Viscount (*Hewart*)　Cr 1940; also *B.
　Hewart 1922　Ext 1964
* HEYWORTH, Baron (*Heyworth*)　Cr 1955　Ext 1974
* HILLINGDON, Baron (*Mills*)　Cr 1886　Ext 1982
* HOLDEN, Baron (*Holden*)　Cr 1908　Ext 1951
* HORE-BELISHA, Baron (*Hore-Belisha*)　Cr 1954
　Ext 1957
* HUDSON, Viscount (*Hudson*)　Cr 1952　Ext 1963
* HUNGARTON, Baron (*Crawford*)　Cr 1951
　Ext 1966
* HYNDLEY, Viscount (*Hindley*)　Cr 1948　Ext 1963
* ILKESTON, Baron (*Foster*)　Cr 1910　Ext 1952
* INMAN, Baron (*Inman*)　Cr 1946　Ext 1979
* INVERCHAPEL, Baron (*Kerr Clark Kerr*)　Cr 1946
　Ext 1951
* INVERCLYDE, Baron (*Burns*)　Cr 1897　Ext 1957
* ISMAY, Baron (*Ismay*)　Cr 1947　Ext 1965
* JACKSON, Baron (*Jackson*)　Cr 1945　Ext 1954
* JESSEL, Baron (*Jessel*)　Cr 1924　Ext 1990
* JOWITT, Earl (*Jowitt*)　Cr 1951; also *B. Jowitt
　1945, and *V. Jowitt 1947　Ext 1957
*§KENMARE, Earl of (*Browne*)　Cr 1801; also §B.
　Castlerosse and V. Kenmare 1798, §V.
　Castlerosse 1801, and *B. Kenmare 1856
　Ext 1952
§ KILLEEN, Baron (*Plunkett*)　Cr *ca* 1449　Ext 1984
* KILMUIR, Earl of (*Fyfe*)　Cr 1962; also *B. Fyfe of
　Dornock 1962, and *V. Kilmuir 1954　Ext 1967
* KINTORE, Baron (*Keith*)　Cr 1838　Ext 1966
* LAMBURY, Baron (*Lord*)　Cr 1962　Ext 1967
* LAMINGTON, Baron (*Cochrane-Baillie*)　Cr 1880
　Ext 1951
* LAWSON, Baron (*Lawson*)　Cr 1950　Ext 1965
‡ LEEDS, Duke of (*Osborne*)　Cr 1694; also ‡B.
　Osborne and ‡V. Latimer, 1673, ‡E. of Danby
　1674, ‡M. of Carmarthen 1689　Ext 1964
§ LEITRIM, Earl of (*Clements*)　Cr 1795; also B.
　Leitrim 1783, V. Leitrim 1793, and *B. Clements
　1831　Ext 1952
* LLEWELLIN, Baron (*Llewellin*)　Cr 1945　Ext 1957
* LLOYD, Baron (*Lloyd*)　Cr 1925　Ext 1985
* LOCH, Baron (*Loch*)　Cr 1895　Ext 1991
* LURGAN, Baron (*Brownlow*)　Cr 1839　Ext 1991
* LYLE OF WESTBOURNE, Baron (*Lyle*)　Cr 1945
　Ext 1976
* MABANE, Baron (*Mabane*)　Cr 1962　Ext 1969
* McCORQUODALE OF NEWTON, Baron
　(*McCorquodale*)　Cr 1955　Ext 1971
* McENTEE, Baron (*McEntee*)　Cr 1951　Ext 1953
* MAENAN, Baron (*Taylor*)　Cr 1948　Ext 1951
* MAGHERAMORNE, Baron (*McGarel-Hogg*)
　Cr 1887　Ext 1957
* MANVERS, Earl (*Pierrepont*)　Cr 1806; also †B.
　Pierrepont and V. Newark 1796　Ext 1955
* MARLEY, Baron (*Aman*)　Cr 1930　Ext 1990
* MATHERS, Baron (*Mathers*)　Cr 1952　Ext 1956
* MAUGHAM, Viscount (*Maugham*)　Cr 1939; also
　*B. Maugham 1935.　Ext 1981
* MERRIMAN, Baron (*Merriman*)　Cr 1941　Ext 1962
* MICHELHAM, Baron (*Stern*)　Cr 1905　Ext 1984
* MIDLETON, Earl (*Brodrick*)　Cr 1920; also *V.
　Dunsford 1920.　Ext 1979
* MONCKTON, Baron (*Monckton*)　Cr 1887　Ext 1971
* MONSELL, Viscount (*Eyres Monsell*)　Cr 1935
　Ext 1993
§ MOUNTMORRES, Viscount (*de Montmorency*)
　Cr 1763　Ext 1951
* MUIRSHIEL, Viscount (*Maclay*)　Cr 1963
　Ext 1992
† NEWCASTLE, Duke of (*Pelham-Clinton*)　Cr 1756
　Ext 1988
* NORMAN, Baron (*Norman*)　Cr 1944　Ext 1950
* NORMANBROOK, Baron (*Brook*)　Cr 1963
　Ext 1967
‡ NORTH, Baron (*North*)　Cr 1554.　Abey 1942
* NUFFIELD, Viscount (*Morris*)　Cr 1938; also *B.
　Nuffield 1934.　Ext 1963
* NUGENT, Baron (*Nugent*)　Cr 1960　Ext 1973
* ORMATHWAITE, Baron (*Walsh*)　Cr 1868
　Ext 1984
* PENTLAND, Baron (*Sinclair*)　Cr 1909　Ext 1984
* PERCY OF NEWCASTLE, Baron (*Percy*)　Cr 1953

　Ext 1958
* PERRY, Baron (*Perry*)　Cr 1938　Ext 1956
* PETHICK-LAWRENCE, Baron (*Pethick-Lawrence*)
　Cr 1945　Ext 1961
* PORTAL OF HUNGERFORD, Viscount (*Portal*)
　Cr 1946　Ext 1971
* PORTAL OF HUNGERFORD, Baroness (*Portal*)
　Cr 1945　Ext 1990
† PORTLAND, Duke of (*Cavendish-Bentinck*)
　Cr 1716; also †Marquess of Titchfield 1716
　Ext 1990
‡ POULETT, Earl (*Poulett*)　Cr 1706; also ‡V. Hinton
　and　‡B. Poulett of Hinton St George (may be
　dormant)　Ext 1973
* QUIBELL, Baron (*Quibell*)　Cr 1945　Ext 1962
* QUICKSWOOD, Baron (*Gascoyne-Cecil*)　Cr 1941
　Ext 1956
* RADCLIFFE, Viscount (*Radcliffe*)　Cr 1962
　Ext 1977
§ RADSTOCK, Baron (*Waldegrave*)　Cr 1800
　Ext 1953
* RAMSDEN, Baron (*Ramsden*)　Cr 1945　Ext 1955
* RANK, Baron (*Rank*)　Cr 1957　Ext 1972
* RHONDDA, Viscount (*Thomas*)　Cr 1918; also B.
　Rhondda 1918　Ext 1958
* ROBERTS, Countess (*Roberts*)　Cr 1901; also *V. St
　Pierre 1901.　Ext 1955
* ROBINS, Baron (*Robins*)　Cr 1958　Ext 1962
* ROBINSON, Baron (*Robinson*)　Cr 1947　Ext 1952
* ROMILLY, Baron (*Romilly*)　Cr 1866　Ext 1983
* RUFFSIDE, Viscount (*Brown*)　Cr 1951　Ext 1958
* RUSHOLME, Baron (*Palmer*)　Cr 1945　Ext 1977
* ST AUDRIES, Baron (*Fuller-Acland-Hood*)
　Cr 1911　Ext 1971
* ST JUST, Baron (*Grenfell*)　Cr 1935　Ext 1984
* ST LEONARDS, Baron (*Sugden*)　Cr 1852
　Ext 1985
* SALTER, Baron (*Salter*)　Cr 1953　Ext 1975
* SCHUSTER, Baron (*Schuster*)　Cr 1944　Ext 1956
* SEATON, Baron (*Colborne-Vivian*)　Cr 1839
　Ext 1955
§ SEFTON, Earl of (*Molyneux*)　Cr 1771; also V.
　Molyneux, and B. Sefton 1831　Ext 1972
† SHERBORNE, Baron (*Dutton*)　Cr 1784　Ext 1985
* SHERWOOD, Baron (*Seely*)　Cr 1941　Ext 1970
* SIMONDS, Viscount (*Simonds*)　Cr 1954; also *B.
　Simonds (Life Baron, Law Lord)　1944, * Baron
　1952　Ext 1971
* SOUTHBOROUGH, Baron (*Hopwood*)　Cr 1917
　Ext 1992
‡ STAMFORD, Earl of (*Grey*)　Cr 1628　Ext 1976;
　also ‡B. Grey of Groby 1603
‡ STANLEY, Baron (*Hastings*)　Cr 1456.　Abey 1960
* STANMORE, Baron (*Hamilton-Gordon*)　Cr 1893
　Ext 1957
* STRACHIE, Baron (*Strachey*)　Cr 1911　Ext 1973
† STRANGE, Earl (*Stewart-Murray*)　Cr 1786; also
　†B. Murray of Stanley 1786 and *B. Glenlyon
　1821　Ext 1957
*. TALBOT DE MALAHIDE, Baron (*Talbot*)　Cr 1856
　Ext 1973
§ TEIGNMOUTH, Baron (*Shore*)　Cr 1797　Ext 1981
† TEMPLETOWN, Viscount (*Upton*)　Cr 1806; also
　§B. Templetown 1776　Ext 1981
* TEMPLEWOOD, Viscount (*Hoare*)　Cr 1944
　Ext 1959
* TOVEY, Baron (*Tovey*)　Cr 1946　Ext 1971
* TREDEGAR, Baron (*Morgan*)　Cr 1859　Ext 1962
* TRENT, Baron (*Boot*)　Cr 1929　Ext 1956
* TURNOUR, Baron (*Turnour*)　Cr 1952　Ext 1962
* UVEDALE OF NORTH END, Baron (*Woodall*)
　Cr 1946　Ext 1974
* VANSITTART, Baron (*Vansittart*)　Cr 1941
　Ext 1957
* WAKEFIELD OF KENDAL, Baron (*Wakefield*)
　Cr 1963　Ext 1983
* WALERAN, Baron (*Walrond*)　Cr 1905　Ext 1966
* WAVELL, Earl (*Wavell*)　Cr 1947; also V. Wavell
　1943, and V. Keren 1947　Ext 1954
* WEBB-JOHNSON, Baron (*Webb-Johnson*)　Cr 1945
　Ext 1958
* WEEKS, Baron (*Weeks*)　Cr 1956　Ext 1960
* WHITBURGH, Baron (*Borthwick*)　Cr 1912
　Ext 1967
§ WICKLOW, Earl of (*Forward-Howard*)　Cr 1793;
　also §V. Wicklow, 1785, §B. Clonmore 1776
　Ext 1978
* WILLIAMS, Baron (*Williams*)　Cr 1948　Ext 1966
* WILLINGDON, Marquess of (*Freeman-Thomas*)
　Cr 1936; also *B. Willingdon 1910; * V.
　Willingdon 1924; *V. Ratendon 1931; *E. of
　Willingdon 1931　Ext 1979
* WILMOT OF SELMESTON, Baron (*Wilmot*)
　Cr 1950　Ext 1964
* WINDSOR, Duke of (*Windsor*)　Cr 1927　Ext 1972
* WINSTER, Baron (*Fletcher*)　Cr 1942　Ext 1961
* YPRES, Earl of (*French*)　Cr 1922　Ext 1988

LIFE PEERAGES EXTINCT

ADEANE, Baron (*Adeane*) Cr 1972 Ext 1984
AIREY OF ABINGDON, Baroness (*Airey*) Cr 1979 Ext 1992
ALEXANDER OF POTTERHILL, Baron (*Alexander*) Cr 1974 Ext 1993
ALLAN OF KILMAHEW, Baron (*Allan*) Cr 1973 Ext 1979
ALLEN OF FALLOWFIELD (*Allen*) Cr 1974 Ext 1985
ARDWICK, Baron (*Beavan*) Cr 1970 Ext 1994
ARMSTRONG OF SANDERSTEAD, Baron (*Armstrong*) Cr 1975 Ext 1980
ARWYN, Baron (*Arwyn*) Cr 1964 Ext 1978
ASHBY, Baron (*Ashby*) Cr 1973 Ext 1992
ASHDOWN, Baron (*Silverstone*) Cr 1974 Ext 1977
ASQUITH OF BISHOPSTONE, Baron (*Asquith*) Cr 1951 (Law Lord) Ext 1954
ASQUITH OF YARNBURY, Baroness (*Bonham Carter*) Cr 1964 Ext 1969
AYLESTONE, Baron (*Bowden*) Cr 1967 Ext 1994
BACON, Baroness (*Bacon*) Cr 1970 Ext 1993
BAKER, Baron (*Baker*) Cr 1977 Ext 1985
BALERNO, Baron (*Buchanan-Smith*) Cr 1963 Ext 1984
BALOGH, Baron (*Balogh*) Cr 1968 Ext 1985
BALLANTRAE, Baron (*Fergusson*) Cr 1972 Ext 1980
BANNERMAN OF KILDONAN, Baron (*Bannerman*) Cr 1967 Ext 1969
BARNETSON, Baron (*Barnetson*) Cr 1975 Ext 1981
BEECHING, Baron (*Beeching*) Cr 1965 Ext 1985
BERNSTEIN, Baron (*Bernstein*) Cr 1969 Ext 1993
BESWICK, Baron (*Beswick*) Cr 1964 Ext 1987
BISHOPSTON, Baron (*Bishop*) Cr 1981 Ext 1984
BLACK, Baron (*Black*) Cr 1968 Ext 1984
BLACKETT, Baron (*Blackett*) Cr 1969 Ext 1974
BLANCH, Baron (*Blanch*) Cr 1983 Ext 1994
BLYTON, Baron (*Blyton*) Cr 1964 Ext 1987
BOOTHBY, Baron (*Boothby*) Cr 1958 Ext 1986
BOSSOM, Baron (*Bossom*) Cr 1960 Ext 1965
BOURNE, Baron (*Bourne*) Cr 1964 Ext 1982
BOWLES, Baron (*Bowles*) Cr 1964 Ext 1970
BOYLE OF HANDSWORTH, Baron (*Boyle*) Cr 1970 Ext 1981
BRADWELL, Baron (*Driberg*) Cr 1975 Ext 1976
BRAYLEY, Baron (*Brayley*) Cr 1973 Ext 1977
BRITTEN, Baron (*Britten*) Cr 1976 Ext 1976
BROCK, Baron (*Brock*) Cr 1965 Ext 1980
BROCKWAY, Baron (*Brockway*) Cr 1964 Ext 1988
BROOKE OF CUMNOR, Baron (*Brooke*) Cr 1966 Ext 1984
BROWNE, Baron (*Brown*) Cr 1964 Ext 1985
BROXBOURNE, Baron (*Walker-Smith*) Cr 1983 Ext 1992
BRUCE-GARDYNE, Baron (*Bruce-Gardyne*) Cr 1983 Ext 1990
BUCKTON, Baron (*Storey*) Cr 1966 Ext 1978
BURNTWOOD, Baron (*Snow*) Cr 1970 Ext 1982
BURTON OF COVENTRY, Baroness (*Burton*) Cr 1962 Ext 1991
BUTLER OF SAFFRON WALDEN, Baron (*Butler*) Cr 1965 Ext 1982
BYERS, Baron (*Byers*) Cr 1964 Ext 1984
CACCIA, Baron (*Caccia*) Cr 1965 Ext 1990
CAMERON OF BALHOUSIE, Baron (*Cameron*) Cr 1983 Ext 1985
CARADON, Baron (*Foot*) Cr 1964 Ext 1990
CARRON, Baron (*Carron*) Cr 1967 Ext 1969
CASEY, Baron (*Casey*) Cr 1960 Ext 1976
CASTLE, Baron (*Castle*) Cr 1974 Ext 1979
CHAMPION, Baron (*Champion*) Cr 1962 Ext 1985
CHESHIRE, Baron (*Cheshire*) Cr 1991 Ext 1992
CHUTER-EDE, Baron (*Chuter-Ede*) Cr 1965 Ext 1965
CLARK, Baron (*Clark*) Cr 1969 Ext 1983
COHEN, Baron (*Cohen*) Cr 1951 Ext 1973
COHEN OF BRIGHTON, Baron (*Cohen*) Cr 1965 Ext 1966
COLE, Baron (*Cole*) Cr 1965 Ext 1979
CONSTANTINE, Baron (*Constantine*) Cr 1969 Ext 1971
COOPER OF STOCKTON HEATH, Baron (*Cooper*) Cr 1966 Ext 1988
COUTANCHE, Baron (*Coutanche*) Cr 1961 Ext 1973
CRAIGTON, Baron (*Browne*) Cr 1959 Ext 1993
CRAWSHAW OF AINTREE, Baron (*Crawshaw*) Cr 1985 Ext 1986
CROSS OF CHELSEA, Baron (*Cross*) Cr 1971 Ext 1989
CROWTHER, Baron (*Crowther*) Cr 1968 Ext 1972
CROWTHER-HUNT, Baron (*Crowther-Hunt*) Cr 1973 Ext 1987
DALTON, Baron (*Dalton*) Cr 1960 Ext 1962
DARLINGTON OF HILLSBOROUGH, Baron

(*Darling*) Cr 1974 Ext 1985
DAVIES OF LEEK, Baron (*Davies*) Cr 1970 Ext 1985
DAVIES OF PENRHYS, Baron (*Davies*) Cr 1974 Ext 1992
DELACOURT-SMITH, Baron (*Delacourt-Smith*) Cr 1967 Ext 1972
DELFONT, Baron (*Delfont*) Cr 1976 Ext 1994
DEVLIN, Baron (*Devlin*) Cr 1961 Ext 1992
DIPLOCK, Baron (*Diplock*) Cr 1968 Ext 1985
DONNET OF BALGAY, Baron (*Donnet*) Cr 1978 Ext 1985
DONOVAN, Baron (*Donovan*) Cr 1963 Ext 1971
DOUGLASS OF CLEVELAND, Baron (*Douglass*) Cr 1967 Ext 1978
DUNCAN SANDYS, Baron (*Duncan-Sandys*) Cr 1974 Ext 1987
EDMUND-DAVIES, Baron (*Edmund-Davies*) Cr 1974 Ext 1992
ELLIOT OF HARWOOD, Baroness (*Elliot*) Cr 1958 Ext 1994
ELWORTHY, Baron (*Elworthy*) Cr 1971 Ext 1993
EMMET OF AMBERLEY, Baroness, (*Emmet*) Cr 1964 Ext 1980
ENERGLYN, Baron (*Energlyn*) Cr 1968 Ext 1985
EVANS OF CLAUGHTON, Baron (*Evans*) Cr 1978 Ext 1992
EVANS OF HUNGERSHALL, Baron (*Evans*) Cr 1967 Ext 1982
EWART-BIGGS, Baroness (*O'Sullivan*) Cr 1981 Ext 1992
FAULKNER OF DOWNPATRICK, Baron (*Faulkner*) Cr 1977 Ext 1977
FEATHER, Baron (*Feather*) Cr 1974 Ext 1976
FERRIER, Baron (*Noel-Paton*) Cr 1958 Ext 1992
FIELDHOUSE, Baron (*Fieldhouse*) Cr 1990 Ext 1992
FISHER OF CAMDEN, Baron (*Fisher*) Cr 1974 Ext 1979
FISHER OF LAMBETH, Baron (*Fisher*) Cr 1961 Ext 1972
FISKE, Baron (*Fiske*) Cr 1967 Ext 1975
FLETCHER, Baron (*Fletcher*) Cr 1970 Ext 1990.
FLOREY, Baron (*Florey*) Cr 1965 Ext 1968
FRANCIS-WILLIAMS, Baron (*Williams*) Cr 1962 Ext 1970
FRANKS, Baron (*Franks*) Cr 1962 Ext 1992
FRASER OF LONSDALE, Baron (*Fraser*) Cr 1958 Ext 1974
FRASER OF TULLYBELTON, Baron (*Fraser*) Cr 1974 Ext 1989
FULTON, Baron (*Fulton*) Cr 1966 Cr 1986 Ext 1974
GAITSKELL, Baroness (*Gaitskell*) Cr 1963 Ext 1989
GALPERN, Baron (*Galpern*) Cr 1979 Ext 1993
GARDINER, Baron (*Gardiner*) Cr 1963 Ext 1990
GARNER, Baron (*Garner*) Cr 1969 Ext 1983
GARNSWORTHY, Baron (*Garnsworthy*) Cr 1967 Ext 1974
GEDDES OF EPSOM, Baron (*Geddes*) Cr 1958 Ext 1983
GEORGE-BROWN, Baron (*George-Brown*) Cr 1970 Ext 1985
GLENKINGLAS, Baron (*Noble*) Cr 1974 Ext 1984
GODBER OF WILLINGTON, Baron (*Godber*) Cr 1979 Ext 1980
GODDARD, Baron (*Goddard*) Cr 1944 (Law Lord), Ext 1971
GORDON-WALKER, Baron (*Gordon-Walker*) Cr 1974 Ext 1980
GORE-BOOTH, Baron (*Gore-Booth*) Cr 1969 Ext 1984
GORONWY-ROBERTS, Baron (*Roberts*) Cr 1974 Ext 1981
GRANVILLE-WEST, Baron (*West*) Cr 1958 Ext 1984
GREENWOOD OF ROSSENDALE, Baron (*Greenwood*) Cr 1970 Ext 1982
GUEST, Baron (*Guest*) Cr 1961 Ext 1984
HAIRE OF WHITEABBEY, Baron (*Haire*) Cr 1965 Ext 1966
HALE, Baron (*Hale*) Cr 1972 Ext 1985
HAMNETT, Baron (*Hamnett*) Cr 1970 Ext 1980
HART OF SOUTH LANARK, Baroness (*Hart*) Cr 1987 Ext 1991
HARVEY OF PRESTBURY, Baron (*Harvey*) Cr 1971 Ext 1994
HATCH OF LUSBY, Baron (*Hatch*) Cr 1978 Ext 1992
HAVERS, Baron (*Havers*) Cr 1987 Ext 1992
HELSBY, Baron (*Helsby*) Cr 1968 Ext 1978
HEWLETT, Baron (*Hewlett*) Cr 1972 Ext 1979
HEYCOCK, Baron (*Heycock*) Cr 1967 Ext 1990
HILL OF LUTON, Baron (*Hill*) Cr 1963 Ext 1989

HILL OF WIVENHOE, Baron (*Hill*) Cr 1967
 Ext 1969
HILTON OF UPTON, Baron (*Hilton*) Cr 1965
 Ext 1977
HINTON OF BANKSIDE, Baron (*Hinton*) Cr 1965
 Ext 1983
HIRSHFIELD, Baron (*Hirshfield*) Cr 1967 Ext 1993
HOBSON, Baron (*Hobson*) Cr 1963 (Law Lord)
 Ext 1966
HODSON, Baron (*Hodson*) Cr 1960 Ext 1984
HOLFORD, Baron (*Holford*) Cr 1965 Ext 1975
HORNSBY-SMITH, Baroness (*Hornsby-Smith*)
 Cr 1974 Ext 1985
HORSBRUGH, Baroness (*Horsbrugh*) Cr 1959
 Ext 1969
HOWARD OF HENDERSKELFE, Baron (*Howard*)
 Cr 1983 Ext 1985
HOY, Baron (*Hoy*) Cr 1970 Ext 1976
HUNT OF FAWLEY, Baron (*Hunt*) Cr 1973
 Ext 1987
HUNTER OF NEWINGTON, Baron (*Hunter*)
 Cr 1978 Ext 1994
HURD, Baron (*Hurd*) Cr 1964 Ext 1966
ILFORD, Baron (*Hutchinson*) Cr 1962 Ext 1974
IRVING OF DARTFORD, Baron (*Irving*) Cr 1979
 Ext 1989
JACKSON OF BURNLEY, Baron (*Jackson*) Cr 1967
 Ext 1970
JACKSON OF LODSWORTH, Baroness, (*Jackson*)
 Cr 1976 Ext 1981
JACOBSON, Baron (*Jacobson*) Cr 1975 Ext 1988
JAMES OF RUSHOLME, Baron (*James*) Cr 1959
 Ext 1992
JANNER, Baron (*Janner*) Cr 1970 Ext 1982
JENKINS, Baron (*Jenkins*) Cr 1959 (Law Lord)
 Ext 1969
KABERRY OF ADEL, Baron (*Kaberry*) Cr 1983
 Ext 1991
KADOORIE, Baron (*Kadoorie*) Cr 1981 Ext 1993
KAHN, Baron (*Kahn*) Cr 1965 Ext 1989
KALDOR, Baron (*Kaldor*) Cr 1974 Ext 1986
KEARTON, Baron (*Kearton*) Cr 1970 Ext 1992
KEITH OF AVONHOLM, Baron (*Keith*) Cr 1953
 Ext 1964
KILBRANDON, Baron (*Shaw*) Cr 1971 Ext 1989
KILMANY, Baron (*Anstruther-Gray*) Cr 1966
 Ext 1985
KING-HALL, Baroness (*King-Hall*) Cr 1966 Ext 1966
LANE-FOX, Baroness (*Lane-Fox*) Cr 1981 Ext 1988
LEATHERLAND, Baron (*Leatherland*) Cr 1964
 Ext 1992
LEE OF ASHERIDGE, Baroness (*Bevan*) Cr 1970
 Ext 1988
LEE OF NEWTON, Baron (*Lee*) Cr 1974 Ext 1984
LEONARD, Baron (*Leonard*) Cr 1978 Ext 1983
LEVER, Baron (*Lever*) Cr 1975 Ext 1977
LINDGREN, Baron (*Lindgren*) Cr 1961 Ext 1971
LLEWELYN-DAVIES, Baron (*Llewelyn Davies*)
 Cr 1963 Ext 1981
LLOYD OF HAMPSTEAD, Baron (*Lloyd*) Cr 1965
 Ext 1993
LYONS OF BRIGHTON, Baron (*Lyons*) Cr 1974
 Ext 1978
McALPINE OF MOFFAT, Baron (*McAlpine*)
 Cr 1976 Ext 1990
MACDERMOTT, Baron (*MacDermott*) Cr 1947
 Ext 1979
McFADZEAN OF KELVINSIDE, Baron (*McFadzean*)
 Cr 1980 Ext 1992
MACLEAN, Baron (*Maclean*) Cr 1971 Ext 1990
McLEAVY, Baron (*McLeavy*) Cr 1967 Ext 1976
MacLEOD OF FUINARY, Baron (*MacLeod*) Cr 1967
 Ext 1991
MACMILLAN, Baron (*Macmillan*) Cr 1930 (Law
 Lord) Ext 1952
MAELOR, Baron (*Jones*) Cr 1966 Ext 1984
MAIS, Baron (*Mais*) Cr 1967 Ext 1993
MARPLES, Baron (*Marples*) Cr 1974 Ext 1978
MARSHALL OF LEEDS, Baron (*Marshall*) Cr 1980
 Ext 1990
MAUDE OF STRATFORD-UPON-AVON, Baron
 (*Maude*) Cr 1983 Ext 1993
MAYBRAY-KING (*Maybray-King*) Cr 1971 Ext 1986
MILES, Baron (*Miles*) Cr 1979 Ext 1991
MITCHISON, Baron (*Mitshison*) Cr 1964 Ext 1970
MOLSON, Baron (*Molson*) Cr 1961 Ext 1991
MONSLOW, Baron (*Monslow*) Cr 1966 Ext 1966
MORRIS OF BORTH-Y-GEST, Baron (*Morris*)
 Cr 1960 Ext 1979
MORRIS OF GRASMERE, Baron (*Morris*) Cr 1967
 Ext 1990
MORRISON OF LAMBETH, Baron (*Morrison*)
 Cr 1959 Ext 1965
MORTON OF HENRYTON, Baron (*Morton*) Cr 1947
 (Law Lord) Ext 1973
MOYLE, Baron (*Moyle*) Cr 1966 Ext 1974
MURRAY OF GRAVESEND, Baron (*Murray*)

 Cr 1976 Ext 1980
NOEL-BAKER, Baron (*Noel-Baker*) Cr 1977
 Ext 1982
NORMAND, Baron (*Normand*) Cr 1947 (Law Lord)
 Ext 1962
NORTHCHURCH, Baroness (*Davidson*) Cr 1963
 Ext 1985
NUGENT OF GUILDFORD, Baron (*Nugent*)
 Cr 1966 Ext 1994
OAKSHOTT, Baron (*Oakshott*) Cr 1964 Ext 1975
OLIVIER, Baron (*Olivier*) Cr 1970 Ext 1989
O'NEILL OF THE MAINE, Baron (*O'Neill*) Cr 1970
 Ext 1990
PANNELL, Baron (*Pannell*) Cr 1974 Ext 1980
PARGITER, Baron (*Pargiter*) Cr 1966 Ext 1982
PARKER OF WADDINGTON, Baron (*Parker*)
 Cr 1958 (Law Lord) Ext 1972
PEARCE, Baron (*Pearce*) Cr 1962 (Law Lord)
 Ext 1990
PEART, Baron (*Peart*) Cr 1976 Ext 1988
PEDDIE, Baron (*Peddie*) Cr 1961 Ext 1978
PENNEY, Baron (*Penney*) Cr 1967 Ext 1991
PHILLIPS, Baroness (*Phillips*) Cr 1964 Ext 1992
PILKINGTON, Baron (*Pilkington*) Cr 1968 Ext 1983
PLANT, Baron (*Plant*) Cr 1978 Ext 1986
PLATT, Baron (*Platt*) Cr 1967 Ext 1978
PLUMMER, Baron (*Plummer*) Cr 1965 Ext 1972
PLURENDEN, Baron (*Sternberg*) Cr 1975 Ext 1978
POPPLEWELL, Baron (*Popplewell*) Cr 1966
 Ext 1977
PORRITT, Baron (*Porritt*) Cr 1973 Ext 1994
PORTER, Baron (*Porter*) Cr 1938 (Law Lord)
 Ext 1956
RAMSEY OF CANTERBURY, Baron (*Ramsey*)
 Cr 1974 Ext 1988
RAVENSDALE OF KEDLESTON, Baroness (*Curzon*)
 Cr 1958 Ext 1966
REDCLIFFE-MAUD, Baron (*Redcliffe-Maud*)
 Cr 1967 Ext 1982
REDMAYNE, Baron (*Redmayne*) Cr 1966 Ext 1983
REID, Baron (*Reid*) Cr 1948 (Law Lord) Ext 1975
REILLY, Baron (*Reilly*) Cr 1978 Ext 1990
RHODES, Baron (*Rhodes*) Cr 1964 Ext 1987
RHYL, Baron (*Birch*) Cr 1970 Ext 1981
RIDLEY OF LIDDESDALE, Baron (*Ridley*) Cr 1992
 Ext 1993
RITCHIE-CALDER, Baron (*Calder*) Cr 1966
 Ext 1982
ROBBINS, Baron (*Robbins*) Cr 1959 Ext 1984
ROBERTHALL, Baron (*Hall*) Cr 1969 Ext 1988
ROCHE, Baron (*Roche*) Cr 1935 (Law Lord)
 Ext 1956
ROSENHEIM, Baron (*Rosenheim*) Cr 1970 Ext 1972
ROWLEY, Baron (*Henderson*) Cr 1966 Ext 1968
ROYLE, Baron (*Royle*) Cr 1964 Ext 1975
RUNCORN, Baron (*Vosper*) Cr 1964 Ext 1968
RUSSELL OF KILOWEN, Baron (*Russell*) Cr 1975
 Ext 1986
SAINT BRIDES, Baron (*James*) Cr 1977 Ext 1989
SALMON, Baron (*Salmon*) Cr 1972 (Law Lord)
 Ext 1991
SAMUEL OF WYCH CROSS, Baron (*Samuel*)
 Cr 1972 Ext 1988
SEEBOHM, Baron (*Seebohm*) Cr 1972 Ext 1990
SEGAL, Baron (*Segal*) Cr 1964 Ext 1985
SELWYN-LLOYD, Baron (*Lloyd*) Cr 1976 Ext 1978
SHARP OF GRIMSDYKE, Baron (*Sharp*) Cr 1989
 Ext 1994
SHINWELL, Baron (*Shinwell*) Cr 1970 Ext 1986
SIEFF, Baron (*Sieff*) Cr 1966 Ext 1972
SILKIN OF DULWICH, Baron (*Silkin*) Cr 1985
 Ext 1988
SIMEY, Baron (*Simey*) Cr 1965 Ext 1969
SIMONDS, Baron (*see* HEREDITARY PEERAGES)
SKRIMSHIRE OF QUARTER, Baroness,
 (*Skrimshire*) Cr 1979 Ext 1979
SLATER, Baron (*Slater*) Cr 1970 Ext 1977
SNOW, Baron (*Snow*) Cr 1964 Ext 1980
SOAMES, Baron (*Soames*) Cr 1978 Ext 1987
SOMERVELL OF HARROW, Baron (*Somervell*)
 Cr 1954 (Law Lord) Ext 1960
SORENSEN, Baron (*Sorensen*) Cr 1964 Ext 1971
SPENCER-CHURCHILL, Baroness, (*Spencer-
 Churchill*) Cr 1965 Ext 1977
STEWART OF ALVECHURCH, Baroness (*Stewart*)
 Cr 1974 Ext 1984
STEWART OF FULHAM, Baron (*Stewart*) Cr 1979
 Ext 1990
STOCKS, Baroness, (*Stocks*) Cr 1966 Ext 1975
STONE, Baron (*Stone*) Cr 1976 Ext 1986
STONEHAM, Baron (*Collins*) Cr 1958 Ext 1971
STOPFORD OF FALLOWFIELD, Baron (*Stopford*)
 Cr 1958 Ext 1961
STOW HILL, Baron (*Soskice*) Cr 1966 Ext 1979
SUMMERSKILL, Baroness, (*Summerskill*) Cr 1961
 Ext 1980
SWANBOROUGH, Baroness, (*Isaacs*) Cr 1958

Ext 1971

SWANN, Baron (*Swann*) Cr 1980   Ext 1990
TANGLEY, Baron (*Herbert*) Cr 1963   Ext 1973
TAYLOR, Baron (*Taylor*) Cr 1958   Ext 1988
TAYLOR OF MANSFIELD, Baron (*Taylor*) Cr 1966
    Ext 1991
TAYSIDE, Baron (*Urquhart*) Cr 1967   Ext 1975
THOMAS, Baron (*Thomas*) Cr 1971   Ext 1980
THORNEYCROFT, Baron (*Thorneycroft*) Cr 1967
    Ext 1994
TRAFFORD, Baron (*Trafford*) Cr 1987   Ext 1989
TRANMIRE, Baron (*Turton*) Cr 1974   Ext 1994
TREVELYAN, Baron (*Trevelyan*) Cr 1968   Ext 1985
TUCKER, Baron (*Tucker*) Cr 1950   Ext 1975
TWEEDSMUIR OF BELHELVIE, Baroness,
    (*Thomson*) Cr 1970   Ext 1978
TWINING, Baron (*Twining*) Cr 1958   Ext 1967
UNDERHILL, Baron (*Underhill*) Cr 1979   Ext 1993
UPJOHN, Baron (*Upjohn*) Cr 1963 (Law Lord)
    Ext 1971
VAIZEY, Baron (*Vaizey*) Cr 1976   Ext 1984
VICKERS, Baroness (*Vickers*) Cr 1974   Ext 1994
WADE, Baron (*Wade*) Cr 1964   Ext 1988
WALSTON, Baron (*Walston*) Cr 1961   Ext 1991
WALL, Baron (*Wall*) Cr 1976   Ext 1980
WATKINS, Baron (*Watkins*) Cr 1972   Ext 1983
WELLS-PESTELL, Baron (*Wells-Pestell*) Cr 1965
    Ext 1991
WIDGERY, Baron (*Widgery*) Cr 1971   Ext 1981
WIGG, Baron (*Wigg*) Cr 1967   Ext 1983
WILLIAMS OF BARNBURGH, Baron (*Williams*)
    Cr 1961   Ext 1967
WILLIAMSON, Baron (*Williamson*) Cr 1962
    Ext 1983
WILLS, Baron (*Willis*) Cr 1963   Ext 1992
WILSON OF HIGH WRAY, Baron (*Wilson*) Cr 1976
    Ext 1980
WILSON OF RADCLIFFE, Baron (*Wilson*) Cr 1974
    Ext 1983
WINSTANLEY, Baron (*Winstanley*) Cr 1975
    Ext 1993
WINTERBOTTOM, Baron (*Winterbottom*) Cr 1965
    Ext 1992
WOLFENDEN, Baron (*Wolfenden*) Cr 1974   Ext 1985
WOOLLEY, Baron (*Woolley*) Cr 1967   Ext 1986
WOOTTON OF ABINGER, Baroness (*Wootton*)
    Cr 1958   Ext 1988
WRIGHT, Baron (*Wright*) Cr 1932 (Law Lord)
    Ext 1964
WRIGHT OF ASHTON UNDER LYNE, Baron
    (*Wright*) Cr 1968   Ext 1974
WYNNE-JONES, Baron (*Wynne-Jones*) Cr 1964
    Ext 1982
ZUCKERMAN, Baron (*Zuckerman*) Cr 1971
    Ext 1993

PEERAGES DISCLAIMED
Under the terms of the Peerage Act, 1963

* ALTRINCHAM, Barony of, (*Grigg*)
    Cr 1945   Disclaimed 1963
* ARCHIBALD, Barony of, (*Archibald*)
    Cr 1949   Disclaimed 1975
* DURHAM, Earldom of (*Lambton*) Cr Baron
    Durham 1828, Viscount Lambton and Earl of
    Durham 1833   Disclaimed 1970
* HAILSHAM, Viscountcy of, (*Hogg*) Cr Baron
    Hailsham 1928, and Viscount Hailsham
    1929   Disclaimed 1963
|| HOME, Earldom of, (*Douglas-Home*) Cr—||Lord
    Home 1473, ||(or *) Lord Home (or Hume) of
    Berwick 1604, ||Earl of Home and Lord Dunglass
    1605, and * Baron Douglas 1875   Disclaimed
    1963
* MERTHYR, Barony of (*Lewis*) Cr 1911   Disclaimed
    1977
* REITH, Barony of, (*Reith*) Cr 1940   Disclaimed
    1972
* SANDERSON OF AYOT, Barony of, (*Sanderson*)
    Cr 1960   Disclaimed 1971
‡ SANDWICH, Earldom of, (*Montagu*) Cr—Baron
    Montagu, Viscount Hinchinbrooke, and Earl of
    Sandwich 1660   Disclaimed 1964
* SILKIN, Barony of (*Silkin*) Cr 1950   Disclaimed
    1972
* STANSGATE, Viscountcy of, (*Benn*)
    Cr 1942   Disclaimed 1963

BARONETCIES THAT HAVE BECOME EXTINCT OR DORMANT

Since 1950. For Extinctions in the years 1900-50 see 1958 and earlier editions.

‡ Baronets of England (1611-1707)
† Baronets of Great Britain (1707-1800)
‖ Baronets of Nova Scotia (or Scotland) (1625-1707)
* Baronets of United Kingdom (1801 onwards)
§ Baronets of Ireland (1619-1800).

* ADAIR Cr 1838 Ext 1988
* ALISON Cr 1852 Ext 1970
* ANDERSON Cr 1920 Ext 1963
* ASTLEY Cr 1821 Ext 1994
* AYLWEN Cr 1949 Ext 1967
* BAKER Cr 1802 Ext 1959
* BANNER, HARMOOD- Cr 1924 Ext 1990
* BARBOUR Cr 1943 Ext 1951
* BARLOW, MONTAGUE- Cr 1924 Ext 1951
* BARRATT, LAYLAND- Cr 1908 Ext 1968
* BARWICK Cr 1912 Ext 1979
* BASS, Cr 1882 Ext. 1952
* BEAUCHAMP Cr 1911 Ext 1976
* BEAUCHAMP Cr 1918 Ext 1983
* BEIT Cr 1924 Ext 1994
* BELL Cr 1909 Ext 1955
* BELL, MORRISON- Cr 1923 Ext 1956
* BENN Cr 1920 Ext 1992
* BENYON Cr 1958 Ext 1959
* BIGGE, SELBY- Cr 1919 Ext 1973
* BILSLAND (*Baron Bilsland*) Cr 1907 Ext 1970
* BLADES (*Baron Ebbisham*) Cr 1922 Ext 1991
* BLAIR Cr 1945 Ext 1962
† BLAKE Cr 1772 Ext 1975
* BOLTON Cr 1927 Ext 1982
* BOOT Cr 1916 Ext 1956
* BOWMAN Cr 1961 Ext 1990
‡ †BROUGHTON, ROUSE- Cr 1641 and 1791 Ext 1963
‡ BOYNTON Cr 1618 Ext 1966
* BRAITHWAITE Cr 1954 Ext 1958
* BROCKLEHURST Cr 1903 Ext 1982
§ BROWNE (*Earl of Kenmare*) Cr 1622 Ext 1952
* BULLOCK Cr 1954 Ext 1966
‡ BURDETT Cr 1619 Ext or Dormant 1951
‖ BURNETT Cr 1626 Dormant 1959
* BURNS (*Baron Inverclyde*) Cr 1889 Ext 1957
† BURRARD Cr 1769 Ext 1965
* BUTCHER Cr 1960 Ext 1966
* BYASS Cr 1926 Ext 1976
* CAIN Cr 1920 Ext 1969
* CAINE Cr 1937 Ext 1971
* CAIRD Cr 1928 Ext 1954
* CAMERON Cr 1893 Ext 1968
* CAMPBELL (*Baron Glenavy*) Cr 1916 Ext 1984
* CAMPBELL Cr 1939 Ext 1954
‖ CAMPBELL, HOME-PURVES-HUME- Cr 1665 Ext 1960
* CARGILL Cr 1920 Ext 1954
* CHAMPNEYS, DALRYMPLE- Cr 1910 Ext 1980
* CHAMBERLAIN Cr 1828 Ext 1980
* CHARLES Cr 1928 Ext 1975
* CHILD Cr 1868 Ext 1958
* CHUBB Cr 1919 Ext 1957
* CHURCH Cr 1901 Ext 1979
* CHUTE Cr 1952 Ext 1956
* CLARK Cr 1883 Ext 1979
* COATS, GLEN- Cr 1894 Ext 1954
* COHEN Cr 1905 Ext 1968
* COLMAN Cr 1952 Ext 1966
* COOPER Cr 1905 Ext 1961
‡ COPE Cr 1611 Ext or Dormant 1972
‡ COPE Cr 1918 Ext 1966
† CORNEWALL Cr 1764 Ext 1962
* CORNWALL Cr 1918 Ext 1962
* COURTHOPE (*Baron Courthope*) Cr 1925 Ext 1955
* COWAN Cr 1921 Ext 1956
* CRAIK Cr 1926 Ext 1955
* CROSS Cr 1912 Ext 1963
* CROSS Cr 1941 Ext 1968
* CUNARD Cr 1859 Ext 1989
* CUNNINGHAM (*Viscount Cunningham of Hyndhope*) Cr 1942 Ext 1963
* CUNNINGHAM Cr 1963 Ext 1976

† CURTIS Cr 1794 Ext 1954
* DALRYMPLE Cr 1887 Ext 1971
* DALRYMPLE, ELPHINSTONE- Cr 1828 Dormant 1956
* DAVID Cr 1911 Ext 1964
* DAWSON Cr 1929 Ext 1974
* de CAPELL BROOKE Cr 1803 Ext 1968
* DE CRESPIGNY, CHAMPION- Cr 1805 Ext 1952
* DEELEY, MALLABY- Cr 1922 Ext 1963
* DENYS Cr 1813 Ext 1960
‡ DERING Cr 1527 Ext 1975
* DILLON Cr 1801 Ext 1982
* DIMSDALE Cr 1902 Ext 1978
‡ DIXIE Cr 1660 Ext 1975
* DOMVILE, POE- Cr 1912 Ext 1959
* DOMVILLE Cr 1814 Ext 1981
† DOUGLAS Cr 1786 Ext 1969
* DOUGLAS Cr 1831 Ext 1986
* DOYLE Cr 1828 Ext 1987
* DRUMMOND, WILLIAMS- Cr 1828 Ext 1976
* DUFF Cr 1911 Ext 1980
* DUFF Cr 1952 Ext 1952
* DUNCAN Cr 1905 Ext 1964
* DUNCAN Cr 1957 Ext 1974
* DUNDAS Cr 1821 Ext 1981
* DUNDAS Cr 1898 Ext 1970
* DUNN Cr 1917 Ext 1971
* DUNN Cr 1921 Ext 1976
* DUNNELL Cr 1922 Ext 1960
* ELLERMAN Cr 1905 Ext 1973
* ELLIS Cr 1932 Ext 1956
* EVANS Cr 1902 Ext 1970
* EVANS Cr 1963 Ext 1983
* EVANS, WORTHINGTON- Cr 1916 Ext 1971
* FARRER (*Baron Farrer*) Cr 1883 Ext 1964
* FINDLAY Cr 1925 Ext 1979
* FLANNERY Cr 1904 Ext 1959
* FLAVELLE Cr 1917 Ext 1985
* FOSTER Cr 1838 Ext 1960
* FOX Cr 1924 Ext 1959
* FRASER Cr 1806 Ext 1979
* FRASER Cr 1921 Ext 1992
* FRASER (*Baron Fraser of Allander*) Cr 1961 Ext 1987
* FREAKE Cr 1882 Ext 1951
* FRY Cr 1894 Ext 1987
* FRY Cr 1929 Ext 1960
* GAMMANS Cr 1956 Ext 1957
* GLYN (*Baron Glyn*) Cr 1934 Ext 1960
§ GODFREY Cr 1785 Ext 1971
* GOLDNEY Cr 1880 Ext 1974
* D'AVIGDOR-GOLDSMID Cr 1934 Ext 1987
‖ GORDON Cr 1631 Dormant 1956
† GRACE Cr 1795 Ext 1977
† GRAEME, HAMOND- Cr 1783 Ext 1969
* GRANT, MACPHERSON- Cr 1838 Ext 1983
* GRAY, ANSTRUTHER- (*Baron Kilmany*) Cr 1956 Ext 1985
* GREEN Cr 1901 Ext 1959
* GREGORY Cr 1931 Ext 1952
‡ GRESLEY Cr 1611 Ext 1976
‖ GRIERSON Cr 1685 Ext 1987
* GUNTER Cr 1901 Ext 1980
* HAMILTON Cr 1937 Ext 1992
* HAMPSON Cr 1642 Ext 1969
‡ HANSEN Cr 1921 Ext 1958
* HARMAN, STAFFORD-KING- Cr 1914 Ext 1987
* HARMSWORTH Cr 1918 Ext 1980
* HART Cr 1893 Ext 1970
* HAWKEY Cr 1945 Ext 1975
* HAY Cr 1635 Dormant 1966
‖ HEADLAM Cr 1935 Ext 1964
* HILLS Cr 1939. Ext 1955
* HINDLEY (*Viscount Hyndley*) Cr 1927 Ext 1963

BARONETCIES THAT HAVE BECOME EXTINCT, ETC

‚OARE *(Viscount Templewood)* Cr 1899 Ext 1959
[OARE Cr 1962 Ext 1986
* HOLDEN Cr 1909 Ext 1965
* HOLLINS Cr 1907 Ext 1963
* HOLT Cr 1916 Ext 1968
* HOOD (formerly BATEMAN) Cr 1806 Ext 1991
* HOOD (later FULLER-ACLAND-HOOD) Cr 1809 Ext 1990
* HOOPER Cr 1962 Ext 1987
* HOPE Cr 1932 Ext 1993
* HORNBY Cr 1899 Ext 1971
* HOULDSWORTH Cr 1956 Ext 1990
* HUGHES Cr 1942 Ext 1958
* HULTON Cr 1905 Ext 1993
* HUNTER, HUGHES- Cr 1906 Ext 1951
* HUTCHISON Cr 1928 Ext 1972
* JAFFREY Cr 1931 Ext 1953
* JAMES Cr 1823 Ext 1979
* JARDINE Cr 1919 Ext 1965
* JARVIS Cr 1922 Ext 1965
* JENNER Cr 1868 Ext 1954
* JESSEL *(Baron Jessel)* Cr 1917 Ext 1990
* JOHNSON, WEBB- *(Baron Webb-Johnson)* Cr 1945 Ext 1958
* JONES Cr 1917 Ext 1952
* JONES, PROBYN- Cr 1926 Ext 1951
* JONES, PRYCE- Cr 1918 Ext 1963
* KERR Cr 1957 Ext 1974
† KING, DUCKWORTH- Cr 1792 Ext 1972
* LAMBART Cr 1911 Ext 1986
* LANE Cr 1913 Ext 1972
* LANGMAN Cr 1906 Ext 1985
* LAURIE Cr 1942 Ext 1954
* LAWSON Cr 1831 Ext 1959
* LAWSON Cr 1905 Ext 1973
* LEE Cr 1941 Ext 1967
‡ LEICESTER Cr 1671 Ext 1968
* LENNARD Cr 1880 Ext 1980
‖ LESLIE Cr 1625 Dormant 1967
* LETT Cr 1941 Ext 1964
* LEWIS *(Baron Essendon)* Cr 1918 Ext 1978
* ORR-LEWIS Cr 1920 Ext 1980
* LOCOCK Cr 1857 Ext 1965
* LORRAINE Cr 1664 Ext 1961
* LYLE *(Baron Lyle of Westbourne)* Cr 1932 Ext 1976
* LYON *(Baron Ennisdale)* Cr 1937 Ext 1963
* McCULLAGH Cr 1935 Ext 1974
* MADGE Cr 1919 Ext 1962
* MAGNAY 1844 Ext 1960
* MAITLAND, RAMSAY-STEEL- Cr 1917 Ext 1965
* MAPPIN Cr 1886 Ext 1975
* MASON *(Baron Blackford)* Cr 1918 Ext 1988
* MATHIAS Cr 1917 Ext 1991
‖ MAXWELL, STIRLING- Cr 1682 Dormant 1956
* MELVIN Cr 1933 Ext 1952
* METCALFE Cr 1802 Ext 1979
* MIDDLEBROOK Cr 1930 Ext 1971
* MIDDLEMORE Cr 1919 Ext 1987
† MILDMAY, ST JOHN- Cr 1772 Dormant 1955
* MILLER, NORIE- Cr 1936 Ext 1973
* MILLS *(Baron Hillingdon)* Cr 1868 Ext 1982
* MITCHELL Cr 1945 Ext 1983
‡ MOLYNEUX *(Earl of Sefton)* Cr 1611 Ext 1972
* MONSON Cr 1905 Ext 1969
* MOORE Cr 1923 Ext 1992
* MOORE Cr 1956 Ext 1971
† MORGAN *(Baron Tredegar)* Cr 1792 Ext 1962
* MORRIS *(Viscount Nuffield)* Cr 1929 Ext 1963
* MOWAT Cr 1932 Ext 1968
* MURPHY Cr 1912 Ext 1963
* NEVILLE Cr 1927 Ext 1994
* NEWNES Cr 1895 Ext 1955
* NICHOLSON Cr 1859 Ext 1986
‖ NICOLSON Cr 1629 Dormant 1961
* NUGENT Cr 1961 Ext 1962

* NUGENT *(Baron Nugent of Guildford)* Cr 1960 Ext 1994
* NUSSEY Cr 1909 Ext 1971
* OCHTERLONY Cr 1823 Ext 1964
‡ OSBORNE *(Duke of Leeds)* Cr 1620 Ext 1964
§ PAUL Cr 1794 Ext 1961
* PAUL Cr 1821 Ext 1972
* PEARSON Cr 1916 Ext 1982
* PECHELL Cr 1797 Ext 1984
* PERKS Cr 1908 Ext 1979
† PEYTON Cr 1776 Ext 1962
* PHILIPPS, FOLEY- Cr 1887 Ext 1962
* POOLEY Cr 1953 Ext 1966
* PORTER Cr 1889 Ext 1974
* POYNTER Cr 1902 Ext 1968
* PRICE Cr 1953 Ext 1963
* PRYSE, SAUNDERS- Cr 1866 Ext 1962
‖ RAMSAY Cr 1666 Ext 1986
* RAMSDEN Cr 1938 Ext 1955
* RANKIN Cr 1937 Ext 1960
* REES Cr 1919 Ext 1970
† RICH Cr 1791 Dormant 1983
* RICHARDSON Cr 1929 Ext 1981
* RIPLEY Cr 1897 Ext 1954
* ROSE Cr 1935 Ext 1976
* ROSS Cr 1919 Ext 1958
* ROWLAND Cr 1950 Ext 1970
* SAMMAN Cr 1921 Ext 1960
* SASSOON Cr 1909 Ext 1961
* SAVORY Cr 1890 Ext 1961
* SCARISBRICK Cr 1855 Ext 1909
* SCOTT Cr 1821 Ext 1962
* SCOTT, CONSTABLE-MAXWELL- Cr 1932 Ext 1954
† SHORE *(Baron Teignmouth)* Cr 1792 Ext 1981
* SIMPSON Cr 1935 Ext 1981
§ SMITH, CUSACK- Cr 1799 Ext 1970
* SMITH *(Earl of Birkenhead)* Cr 1918 Ext 1985
* SMITH Cr 1920 Ext 1961
* SNADDEN Cr 1955 Ext 1959
* SPEARS Cr 1953 Ext 1974
* STANHHOPE, SCUDAMORE- *(Earl of Chesterfield)* Cr 1807 Ext 1952
* STEPHEN Cr 1891 Ext 1987
* STERN *(Baron Michelham)* Cr 1905 Ext 1984
* STEWART Cr 1881 Ext 1951
* STEWART Cr 1920 Ext 1979
* STOCKENSTROM Cr 1840 Ext 1957
* STURDEE Cr 1916 Ext 1970
‡ SWINBURNE Cr 1660 Ext 1967
* TANGYE Cr 1912 Ext 1969
* TAYLOR Cr 1963 Ext 1972
* TAYLOR, WORSLEY- Cr 1917 Ext 1958
‡ TWYSDEN Cr 1611 Ext 1970
* THOMAS Cr 1766 Ext 1972
* THOMSON Cr 1938 Ext 1953
‡ TICHBORNE, DOUGHTY- Cr 1621 Ext 1968
* VERNER Cr 1846 Ext 1975
* WALROND *(Baron Waleran)* Cr 1876 Ext 1966
* WALSH *(Baron Ormathwaite)* Cr 1804 Ext 1984
§ WALSH, JOHNSON- Cr 1775 Ext 1953
* WARD Cr 1914 Ext 1973
* WARD Cr 1929 Ext 1956
* WATSON Cr 1912 Ext 1983
* WATSON Cr 1918 Ext 1959
* WEIGALL Cr 1938 Ext 1952
* WELLS Cr 1948 Ext 1966
† WESTCAR, PRESCOTT- Cr 1794 Ext 1959
* WILLIAMS Cr 1955 Ext 1958
* WILLIAMS Cr 1935 Ext 1959
* WILLIAMS, HUME- Cr 1922 Ext 1980
‡ WILSON MARYON- Cr 1661 Ext 1978
* WINGATE Cr 1920 Ext 1978
‡ WINN *(Baron Headley)* Cr 1660 Ext 1994
† WINN *(Baron Headley)* Cr 1776 Ext 1994
* WOOD Cr 1918 Ext 1974
* YOUNGER Cr 1964 Ext 1992